578

# 1995 Working Press of the Nation™
## Volume 2

## Magazines & Internal Publications Directory

### 45th Edition

Published by National Register Publishing,
A Reed Reference Publishing Company

International Standard Book Number (Volume 1 thru 4 - set) . . 0-8352-3572-6
International Standard Book Number (Volume 1 & 2 - set) . . . 0-8352-3578-5
International Standard Book Number (Volume 2) . . . . . . . . . 0-8352-3574-2
International Standard Serial Number . . . . . . . . . . . . . . . . . 0084-1323
Library of Congress Catalog Card Number . . . . . . . . . . . . . 46-7041

Printed and bound in the United States of America.

# 1995 Working Press of the Nation™

## Volume 2
## Magazines & Internal Publications Directory
## 45th Edition

Working Press of the Nation™ Magazines & Internal Publications Directory
is compiled by

**NATIONAL REGISTER PUBLISHING**
A Reed Reference Publishing Company
121 Chanlon Road
New Providence, New Jersey 07974

| | |
|---|---|
| Mark R. Levenson | Senior Director of Marketing |
| Michael Meyer | Marketing Coordinator |
| Edward R. Blank | Director of Mailing List Sales |
| Allyn Gilhooly | Telemarketing Sales Manager |
| | |
| Judith Salk | Executive Editor |
| Edvika Popilskis | Managing Editor |
| Dawn Lombardy | Senior Editor |
| Laura Forbes | Assistant Editors |
| Zhaoxia Lian | |
| Evelyn Irvine | Senior Contributing Editors |
| Olga Neville | |
| Elizabeth Hughes | Contributing Editors |
| Vanessa Janulis | |
| Darlene Lloyd | |
| Monica Marino | |
| Jean-Marie Pierson | |
| Kristin Valli | |
| Hester Wharton | |
| Jean Kontra | Mail Processing Clerk |
| Nana Rizinashvili | Senior Systems Analysts |
| Francis So | |
| Doreen Gravesande | Production Director |
| Frank McDermott | Senior Editor, Production |
| | |
| Peter Simon | Senior Vice President Database Publishing Group |
| John Roney | Vice President, Information Systems |
| Gary Aiello | Manager, Editorial Systems |

# 1995
# *WORKING PRESS OF THE NATION*™

## VOLUME 1 - NEWSPAPER DIRECTORY

This volume contains listings of Newspapers, Feature Syndicates, News and Photo Services. Complete information is given, including circulation, frequency, wire services, material requirements, deadlines, etc. Here, in one volume, is the direct route to over 8,000 management and editorial personnel of daily and weekly newspapers in the United States. There is also an index of editorial personnel by subject, and an index of newspapers with Sunday supplements and TV supplements.

## VOLUME 2 - MAGAZINES & INTERNAL PUBLICATIONS DIRECTORY
### Now including Newsletters

This volume lists more than 5,400 magazines, including consumer, farm and agricultural, service, trade, professional, and industrial publications. Listings are grouped by subject area, so similar publications are easily referenced. There is also an alphabetical index of publications. Combined in Volume 2 are sections featuring internal publications and newsletters. These sections provide detailed information about internal and external publications of more than 2,500 companies, government agencies, clubs and other groups, as well as major newsletters published in the United States.

## VOLUME 3 - TV & RADIO DIRECTORY

This volume lists more than 13,000 TV and radio stations plus more than 5,700 local programs by subject. Detailed information includes station name, address, ownership, area population, ADI market, power, network affiliation, wire services utilized, air time, management and programming personnel, and publicity materials accepted.

## VOLUME 4 - FEATURE WRITERS, PHOTOGRAPHERS & PROFESSIONAL SPEAKERS

This volume lists more than 4,000 feature writers, photographers and professional speakers with their complete address, telephone and fax numbers, subject areas of interest, and publications accepting their work (if applicable). All categories are indexed by subject specialties.

---

Each publication individually is an excellent source of information on a specific media. As a convenience to our customers, volumes 1 & 2 are available in a special print media set or included in the complete 4-volume set.

Also available from Reed Reference Direct are mailing labels and database diskettes, customized for your use with various selects including, type of media, personnel, state selection, etc. Call Ed Blank at 800-521-8110 for details.

# TABLE OF CONTENTS

## Volume 2
### Magazines & Internal Publications Directory
### 1995 Working Press of the Nation™

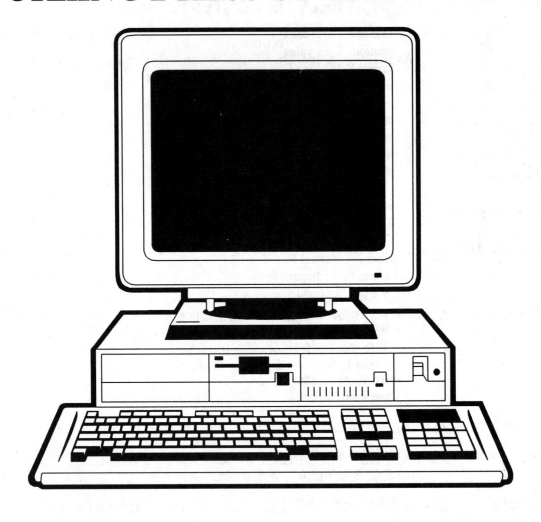

# Preface

Congratulations on your purchase of the 45th edition of *WORKING PRESS OF THE NATION*,™ the leading resource listing media information. This valuable 4-volume set is published by National Register Publishing (NRP), a Reed Reference Publishing Company, one of the world's most respected publishers of information for libraries and industry.

All information found in *WORKING PRESS OF THE NATION* is a direct result of the efforts of our in-house editorial staff. They are continually updating information in an ongoing effort to provide you with the most current data found anywhere.

- **Volume 1 - Newspaper Directory** identifies categories of this print media, including dailies and weeklies and local and national newspapers.

- **Volume 2 - Magazines & Internal Publications Directory** has added hundreds of additional titles and several new categories to make it the most comprehensive edition ever. Also included is a new section listing major newsletters.

- **Volume 3 - TV & Radio Directory** includes more than 13,000 listings of radio and television stations with detailed information on programming.

- **Volume 4 - Feature Writers, Photographers & Professional Speakers** lists in excess of 4,000 of these hard-to-find, but in great demand professionals.

In an effort to improve our products, we encourage you to contact any of our staff with recommendations or criticisms that you may have. For your convenience, you may call us TOLL FREE at 1-800-521-8110 or write to us at: *WORKING PRESS OF THE NATION*, 121 Chanlon Road, New Providence, NJ 07974. If you prefer, you may wish to fax your comments to 908-665-3560. All correspondence will be answered promptly.

Through the editorial resources available to NRP, we have increased the data collected in *WORKING PRESS OF THE NATION*. In order to expand the way *WORKING PRESS OF THE NATION* is used, we have now made our database available in IBM compatible or Macintosh formatted diskettes in either a simple label program or for use with your existing software. Customized mailing labels are also available offering various selections - all with our 100% deliverability guarantee.

We trust you will find the *1995 WORKING PRESS OF THE NATION* to be a valuable, well-organized and easy-to-use resource.

# INTRODUCTION

The Magazines & Internal Publications Directory is Volume 2 of Working Press of the Nation, a four-volume set, segmented by medium. A descriptive profile is given in the introductory pages. The Directory is designed for persons needing information for contacting media personnel or for mailing list compilation, media selection, or market analysis.

# CONTENTS

### MAGAZINES:

The information included in each listing is in-depth and comprehensive including deadline dates, publicity material requirements, editorial descriptions, reader profiles, personnel, subscription rates, plus indexes for easy cross-referencing.

The information requested from each magazine includes:

- Publication name and address
- Year established
- Publication size
- Materials accepted/included
- Printing process
- Owner name and address
- Personnel (management, editorial, and other)
- Reader profile

- Publication telephone & FAX numbers
- Publication frequency
- Subscription rates
- Freelance pay scale
- Circulation size/type
- Bureau names, addresses, and contacts
- Deadlines
- Editorial description

### NEWSLETTERS:

The information included in each listing includes:

- Publication name and address
- Year established
- Subscription rates
- Circulation size/type
- Personnel (management, editorial, and other)

- Publication telephone & FAX numbers
- Publication frequency
- Materials accepted/included
- Owner name and address
- Editorial description

### INTERNAL PUBLICATIONS:

The information requested from each internal publication sponsor includes:

- Sponsor name and address
- Publication name
- Frequency
- Publication size
- Freelance pay scale
- Editor

- Sponsor telephone number
- Publication description
- Industry affiliation
- Materials accepted
- Lead Time

The amount of information in individual listings may vary depending on the detail supplied by each publisher/sponsor.

The Directory is compiled from detailed questionnaires sent to magazine and newsletter publishers and internal publication corporate sponsors. All information is provided directly by the specific publisher/sponsor.

# ORGANIZATION

The Magazines & Internal Publications Directory contains 11 sections. The information found within each section is listed below.

## SECTION 1: Comprehensive Index of Magazine & Newsletter Subjects
- An alphabetic listing of the major subject groups used to categorize the three types of magazines and the newsletters found in the directory:
  - -Service, Trade, Professional, Industrial
  - -Farm & Agricultural
  - -Consumer
  - -Newsletter
- The group number assigned to each subject group
- Publication listings are organized by group classification within Sections 4 through 7, making this index useful in locating publications with specific subject content

## SECTION 2: Alphabetic Index of Magazine & Newsletter Titles
- A listing of all magazines and newsletters in the Directory, organized alphabetically by title
- A subject group reference indicating where the complete listing may be found

## SECTION 3: Alphabetic Cross Index of Magazine & Newsletter Subjects & Related Subject Areas
- A listing of major and related subject groups or categories, organized alphabetically by subject group, and designed to aid the user in locating publications in a given subject area and those subject groups which are related
- A cross-reference which refers the user from one major subject group to another related major subject group used in the Directory, and which also refers the user from terms not used as major subject groups to terms that are used as major subject groups

## SECTION 4: Service, Trade, Professional, Industrial Magazines
- A listing of subject groups for business publications, organized by subject group numbers ranging from 2 through 278, providing a page reference indicating where the group heading may be found within the listings
- A listing of the publications within each subject group, organized alphabetically by title

## SECTION 5: Farm & Agricultural Magazines
- A listing of subject groups for farm and agricultural publications, organized by subject group numbers ranging from 502 through 524, providing a page reference indicating where the group heading may be found within the listings
- A listing of the publications within each subject group, organized alphabetically by title

## SECTION 6: Consumer Magazines
- A listing of subject groups for consumer publications, organized by subject group numbers ranging from 602 through 674, providing a page reference indicating where the group heading may be found within the listings
- A listing of the publications within each subject group, organized alphabetically by title

## SECTION 7: Newsletters
- A listing of subject groups for newsletters, organized by subject group numbers ranging from 302 through 366, providing a page reference indicating where the group heading may be found within the listings
- A listing of the publications within each subject group, organized alphabetically by title

**SECTION 8: Index of Internal Publications by Title**
- An alphabetic listing of publications by title
- Sponsor name associated with title for easy cross referencing to main listing in Section 11

**SECTION 9: Index of Internal Publication Sponsors by Industry**
- An alphabetic listing of sponsors and their publication(s), organized by industry classification
- A table of contents providing a page reference for each industry classification

**SECTION 10: Index of Internal Publications by Subject**
- An alphabetic listing of sponsors and their publication(s), organized by editorial subject
- A table of contents providing a page reference for each editorial subject

**SECTION 11: Internal Publication Sponsors**
- A listing of the sponsors, organized alphabetically by sponsor name
- Detailed information about each sponsor's publication, as follows:
    - Sponsor name and address
    - Sponsor telephone number
    - Industry affiliation
    - Publication title
    - Frequency
    - Publication description
    - Page size requirements
    - Editorial personnel

## HOW TO USE

**MAGAZINES & NEWSLETTERS:**

The main listings which contain complete information for each publication are in Sections 4 through 7. Within each of these sections, the publications are organized by subject group.

- If you know the name of the publication, look up the title in the alphabetical index in Section 2 to find the appropriate group number under which the publication is listed.
- If you do not know the publication name, look for the subject area in the Group Index in Section 1, and refer to the publications listed in that group.
- If you do not find the subject area you need in the Group Index in Section 1, refer to the Alphabetical Cross Index in Section 3 to locate the subject you desire and the related major subject groups used in this directory.

**INTERNAL PUBLICATIONS:**

The listings and indexes are organized in order to allow easy identification of internal publications and sponsors alphabetically or by industry affiliation or editorial subject.

- Complete listings for all internal publications are found in Section 11. Since they are listed by sponsor, one must know the sponsoring organization in order to find individual publications.
- If the internal publication title is known but the sponsor is not, the alphabetical index of titles in Section 8 serves as a cross reference index to sponsor names.
- In order to identify internal publications within a certain industry, refer to Section 9.
- In order to identify internal publications within an editorial subject area, refer to Section 10.

# MAGAZINE SAMPLE ENTRY

**NATIONAL DRAGSTER** —————————————————————————— Title
2035 Financial Way ———————————————————————————— Location Address
Glendora, CA 91740
Telephone: (818) 963-7695 ————————————————————————— Telephone Number
FAX: (818) 335-6651 —————————————————————————————— Fax Number
Mailing Address: ————————————————————————————————— Mailing Address
    P.O. Box 5555
    Glendora, CA 91740
Year Established: 1960 ————————————————————————————— Year First Published
Pub. Frequency: 48/yr ————————————————————————————— Frequency of Publication
Page Size: tabloid ———————————————————————————————— Size of Publication
Subscrip. Rate: $52/yr. ————————————————————————————— Price of Publication
Publicity Materials: 06,32,33 ———————————————————————— Materials Accepted/Included
Freelance Pay: negotiable ————————————————————————————— Pay Scale to Freelancers
Print Process: web offset ———————————————————————————— Printing Process Used
Circulation: 80,000 —————————————————————————————— Number of Readers per Issue
Circulation Type: paid ——————————————————————————————— Type of Circulation

**Owner(s):**
National Hot Rod Association ———————————————————————— Ownership Name and Address
2035 Financial Way
Glendora, CA 91740
Telephone: (818) 963-7695
FAX: (818) 335-6651
Ownership %: 100 ————————————————————————————————— Percentage of Ownership

**Management:** —————————————————————————————————— Management Personnel
Neil Britt . . . . . . . . . Publisher
Sandy Wasserbeck . . Advertising Manager
Maria G. Aguilar . . . . Assistant Advertising Manager
Adriane Pierson . . . . Business Manager
Billie Petty . . . . . . . Circulation Manager
Robert Jaramillo . . . . Classified Adv. Manager
Jonie Elmslie . . . . . . Classified Adv. Manager
Linda Robertson . . . . Credit Manager
Paula Alt . . . . . . . . . Production Manager

**Editorial:** ————————————————————————————————————— Editorial Personnel
Chris Martin . . . . . . Senior Editor
Phil Burgess . . . . . . Editor
Vicky Walker . . . . . Managing Editor
Chuck Hanson . . . . . Advertising
Jill Flores . . . . . . . . Art Director
Leslie Lovett . . . . . . Photography Editor

**Desc.:** Contains race results from ———————————————————— Brief Editorial Description
championship drag racing events and
report submitted by dragstrips, and
photos on racing. Feature material
includes racer personalities, new
technical developments, publicity
material in drag racing.

**Readers:** Motorsport enthusiasts - ——————————————————— Readership Description
85% in 18-34-year-old male age group,
drivers, mechanics, high performance
industry managers & executives.

**Deadline:** ads-15 days prior to pub. date ————————————————— Editorial/Advertising Deadline(s)

# INTERNAL PUBLICATION SAMPLE ENTRY

**HARLEYSVILLE INSURANCE COMPANIES** ———————————— Internal Publication Sponsor
355 Maple Ave. ——————————————————————————— Location Address
Harleysville, Pa 19438
Telephone: (215) 256-5000 ————————————— Telephone
Fax: (215) 256-5340 ————————————————— Fax Number
Industry Affiliation: Insurance ————————————— Industry Affiliation

**Publications:** ————————————————————— Internal Publication Title(s)
*Insights for Employees*
Day Published: Bi-M. ————————————————— Frequency of Publications
Lead Times: 60 days prior to pub. Date ——————————— Lead Time for Submissions
Publicity Materials: 01,05,19,20,21 ——————————— Materials Accepted/Included
Mtls Deadline: 60-90 days prior to pub. ————————— Material Submission Deadline
Contact: Harleysville Communications
Spec. Requirements: 20 Pg.; Offset; 8-1/2 ——————— Special Requirements
    X 11
Personnel: Beth Gavis, Editor ————————————— Personnel Name(s) and Title(s)
        Randy Buckwalter, Editor
        Donald E. Diehl

*Insights for Agents*
Day Published: Q.
Lead Time: 90 Days prior to pub. Date
Publicity Materials: 01,05,19,20,21
Mtls Deadline: 90 days prior to pub. Date
Contact: Harleysville Communications
Spec. Requirements: 24 page; offset; 8-1/2
    X 11
Personnel: Linda K. Manero
        Donald E. Diehl
        Randy Buckwalter
        Frederick W. Baker

# NEWSLETTER SAMPLE ENTRY

MEDIA INDUSTRY NEWSLETTER ———————————— Title
1201 Seven Locks Rd., Ste. 300 ———————————Location Address
Potomac, Md 20854
Telephone: (301) 424-3338 ————————————Telephone Number
Fax: (301) 309-3847 ————————————————Fax Number
Year Established: 1948 —————————————Year First Published
Pub. Frequency: w —————————————————Fredquency of Publication
Page Size: standard ———————————————Size of Publication
Subscrip. Rate: $395/yr ——————————————Price of Publication
Publicity Materials: 01,10,15,28,29,30,31 —————Materials Accepted/Included
Print Process: offset ————————————————Printing Process Used
Circulation: 2,143 ————————————————Number of Readers per Issue
Circulation Type: paid ———————————————Type of Circulation

Owner(s): ——————————————————————Ownership Name and Address
Phillips Business Information, Inc.
1201 Seven Locks Rd.
Potomac, Md 20854
Telephone: (301) 424-4297
Fax: (301) 309-3847
Ownership %: 100 ————————————————Percentage of Ownership

Management: ————————————————————Management Personnel
Thomas C. Thompson  .  President
Thomas Phillips . . . . . .  Publisher
Ellen H. Stuhlmann  . . .  Publisher

Editorial: ———————————————————————Editorial Personnel
Kismet Tuksu Gould. . .  Associate Publisher
Maggie Jackman . . . . .  Marketing Editor
Lisa S. Kelley . . . . . . .  Marketing Manager
John Masterton . . . . . .  Media Group Editor
Richard Gorrio . . . . . . .  Research Reporter

Desc.: Exclusive, Inside look at media ————————Brief Editorial Description
industry with a smart snippy style.
includes coverage of circulation &
advertising trends in the media industry,
especially magazine and newspaper
publications, plus a monthly "Stock
Watch".

Readers: Publishers and other ————————————Readership Description
executives in the media industry.

## ABBREVIATIONS LIST

| | |
|---|---|
| 3/m. | 3x/month |
| 3/yr | 3x/year |
| a. | annual |
| abstr. | abstracts |
| adv. | advertising |
| aft. | afternoon |
| am | a.m. |
| AP | Associated Press |
| API | Allied Press International |
| approx. | approximately |
| Apr. | April |
| Apt. | Apartment |
| Assn. | Association |
| Asst. | Assistant |
| Aug. | August |
| Ave. | Avenue |
| bi-m. | every 2 months |
| bi-w. | every 2 weeks |
| bibl. | bibliography |
| Bldg. | Building |
| Blvd. | Boulevard |
| BUP | British United Press |
| c/o | care of |
| CanP | Canadian Press |
| CaNS | Catholic News Service |
| CiNS | City News Service |
| Cir. | Circle |
| circ. | circulation |
| CN | Capital News |
| CNS | Copley News Service |
| col. | column |
| contr. | controlled |
| CQ | Congressional Quarterly Service |
| CSM | Christian Science Monitor |
| CST | Chicago Sun Times |
| Ct. | Court |
| CT-NYT | Chicago Tribune-New York Times |
| Ctr. | Center |
| CUP | Canadian United Press |
| Cy. | County |
| d. | daily |
| Dec. | December |
| deliv. | delivery |
| Dept. | Department |
| Dir. | Director |
| DJ | Dow Jones |
| Dr. | Drive |
| E. | East |
| ea. | each |
| Ed. | Editor |
| ERR | Editorial Research Reports |
| exc. | except |
| Expy. | Expressway |
| Feb. | February |
| FIELD | Field News Service |
| Fl. | Floor |
| fortn. | fortnightly |
| Fri. | Friday |
| Ft. | Fort |
| Fwy. | Freeway |
| Gen. | General |
| GNS | Gannett News Service |
| HHS | Hearst Headline Service |
| Hwy. | Highway |
| in. | inch |
| IPN | International Photo News |
| irreg. | irregular |
| ITNA | Independent Television News Association, Inc. |
| Jan. | January |
| Jct. | Junction |
| Jul. | July |
| Jun. | June |
| KNS | Knight News Service |
| KNT | Knight News-Tribune News Service |
| KR | Knight-Ridder |
| LAT-WP | Los Angeles Times-Washington Post News Service |
| LDE | London Daily News |
| lit. | literature |

# ABBREVIATIONS LIST con't

| | |
|---|---|
| Ln. | Lane |
| LT | Times of London |
| m. | monthly |
| Mar. | March |
| MG | Manchester Guardian |
| Mgr. | Manager |
| mktg. | marketing |
| Mng. | Managing |
| MNS | Massachusetts News Service |
| mo. | month |
| Mon. | Monday |
| morn. | morning |
| Mt. | Mount |
| mult. | multiple |
| N | National News Service |
| NEA | Newspaper Enterprises Association |
| NNS | Newhouse News Service |
| No. | Number |
| Nov. | November |
| NWS | National Weather Service |
| NYT | New York Times |
| Oct. | October |
| ONS | Ottawa News Service |
| P | Pacific News Service |
| pbcty. | publicity |
| pg. | page |
| Pk. | Park |
| Pkwy. | Parkway |
| Pl. | Place |
| Plz. | Plaza |
| pm | p.m. |
| Pres. | President |
| prod. | product |
| prodn. | production |
| promo. | promotion |
| pub. | publication |
| Publ. | Publisher |
| q. | quarterly |

| | |
|---|---|
| qtr. | quarter |
| Rd. | Road |
| rec. | recording |
| rev. | review |
| R.D. | Rural Devlivery |
| Rm. | Room |
| RN | Reuters News Agency |
| Rte. | Route |
| s-a. | twice annually |
| s-m. | twice monthly |
| s-w. | twice weekly |
| S. | South |
| Sat. | Saturday |
| SC | Southern News Service |
| Sep. | September |
| SHNA | Scripps-Howard Newspaper Alliance |
| sing. | single |
| Sq. | Square |
| St. | Street |
| Sta. | Station |
| Ste. | Suite |
| Sun. | Sunday |
| Terr. | Terrace |
| Thu. | Thursday |
| Tpke. | Turnpike |
| Tue. | Tuesday |
| UPI | United Press International |
| W. | West |
| w. | weekly |
| wd. | word |
| Wed. | Wednesday |
| WIP | Washington International Report |
| wk. | week |
| WN | World News |
| WNS | Women's News Service |
| WWD | Women's Wear Daily |
| yr. | year |

# Section 1
# COMPREHENSIVE INDEX OF MAGAZINE & NEWSLETTER SUBJECTS

This index lists the major subject groups used to categorize Service, Trade, Professional, Industrial magazines, Farm and Agricultural magazines, Consumer magazines, and Newsletters included in this Directory.

Group or category numbers are assigned to each classification to aid the user in locating a particular or related subject category. Group numbers are indicated at the top of each page of the main listing sections (Sections 4,5,6 and 7) as well as at the beginning of a subject group within the listings.

In some cases the editorial content of a publication may overlap in two or more categories. Therefore, related fields should be checked through the use of the Alphabetical Cross Index, detailed in Section 3.

## FARM & AGRICULTURAL PUBLICATIONS

Listings for these classifications begin on page 5-1.

## CONSUMER PUBLICATIONS

Listings for these classifications begin on page 6-1.

## NEWSLETTERS

Listings for these classifications begin on page 7-1.

# Section 2
# ALPHABETICAL INDEX OF MAGAZINE &
# NEWSLETTER TITLES

This section lists alphabetically by publication name, magazine & newsletters published in the United States.  Group numbers are provided to assist in the location of complete listings for the publications in either section 4, 5, 6 or 7.

Group numbers for Section 4 (Service, Trade, Professional, Industrial Magazines) range from 2 through 278.

Group numbers for Section 5 (Farm and Agricultural Magazines) range from 502 through 524.

Group numbers for Section 6 (Consumer Magazines) range from 602 through 674.

Group numbers for Section 7 (Newsletters) range from 302 through 366.

## H

**J**

## K

# MAGAZINE AND NEWSLETTER TITLE INDEX

## Z

# Section 3
# ALPHABETICAL CROSS INDEX OF MAGAZINE & NEWSLETTER SUBJECTS & RELATED SUBJECT AREAS

This Alphabetical Cross Index is a cross-reference system for subject group classifications designed to facilitate the use of this Directory. The Index assists the user in locating the major subject and related subject areas where the required publications may be found.

The Alphabetical Cross Index is an Alphabetical listing of MAJOR and related subject groups or categories with corresponding group numbers for MAJOR SUBJECT GROUPS.

HOW TO USE
• Subjects printed in all capital letters, e.g., ACCOUNTING, are classifications that are used as headings in listing sections of this Directory. Those groups are also referred to as MAJOR SUBJECT GROUPS. Each MAJOR SUBJECT GROUP has a corresponding group number provided, e.g. ACCOUNTING 002.

• Subjects printed in initial capital letters, e.g. Acoustics are related classifications which are cross-referenced to a MAJOR SUBJECT GROUP. These related terms assist the user in finding the appropriate subject groups used in this Directory.

• The term "see" refers the user from a term not used as a MAJOR SUBJECT GROUP to a term which is used as a MAJOR SUBJECT GROUP.

• The term "see also" refers the user from one MAJOR SUBJECT GROUP to other related MAJOR SUBJECT GROUPS.

• Unless otherwise notified by (Consumer), (Farm) or (Newsletter) following the subject heading, all subject group references pertain to Service, Trade, Professional or Industrial magazines.

---

ACCOUNTING 002 see also BANKING 022; BUSINESS, GENERAL 038; BUSINESS - REGIONAL, STATE, METRO, LOCAL 040; FINANCE 082; BUSINESS (Consumer) 612; BUSINESS (Newsletter) 310
Acoustics see ENGINEERING, GENERAL 072
Adhesives see CHEMICAL INDUSTRIES & CHEMICAL ENGINEERING 044; INDUSTRY, GENERAL 128
ADULT (Consumer) 602
Adventure see FICTION - ADVENTURE, MYSTERY, ROMANCE, SCIENCE FICTION (Consumer) 628
ADVERTISING & MARKETING 004 see also PUBLIC RELATIONS 212; SELLING 244; BUSINESS (Newsletter) 310
Aerospace see AVIATION & AEROSPACE 018
Agriculture see GENERAL AGRICULTURE & FARMING (Farm) 510
AGRICULTURE (Newsletter) 302 see also GENERAL AGRICULTURE & FARMING (Farm) 510
Air Conditioning see CLIMATE CONTROL 050
Airline In-Flight Publications see TRAVEL (Consumer) 672
Airplanes see AVIATION & AEROSPACE 018
Airports see AVIATION & AEROSPACE 018
Alcoholic Beverages see BEVERAGES 026; BEVERAGES - REGIONAL, STATE, METRO, LOCAL 028
Alcoholism see MEDICAL & SURGICAL 158
ALMANACS (Consumer) 604
Alumni see COLLEGE & ALUMNI (Consumer) 618
Amusements see ENTERTAINMENT 074; ENTERTAINMENT (Consumer) 624
Animal Control see GOVERNMENT - MUNICIPAL, COUNTY, STATE, FEDERAL 106
ANIMALS (Newsletter) 304
Animation see ART 014
ANTIQUES & COLLECTIBLES 006; see also ART 014; AUTOMOBILES & ACCESSORIES 016; FURNITURE & UPHOLSTERY 098; HOUSEWARES & HOME FURNISHINGS 120; RETAIL TRADE 230; TOYS, CRAFTS & HOBBIES 262; ART & ANTIQUES (Consumer) 606; AUTOMOBILES & ACCESSORIES (Consumer) 608
APPAREL - MEN'S, WOMEN'S & CHILDREN'S 008 see also JEWELRY & WATCHMAKING 136; RETAIL TRADE 230; TEXTILES 258; SEWING & NEEDLEWORK (Consumer) 668; APPAREL (Newsletter) 306
APPAREL (Newsletter) 306
APPLIANCES 010 see also CLIMATE CONTROL 050;

ELECTRICAL 066; ELECTRONICS 068; FURNITURE & UPHOLSTERY 098; HOUSEWARES & HOME FURNISHINGS 120; RETAIL TRADE 230
Archery see SPORTS & SPORTING GOODS 250
ARCHITECTURE 012 see also ART 014; BUILDING & CONSTRUCTION 032; BUILDING MANAGEMENT & REAL ESTATE 034; BUILDING MATERIALS 036; CLIMATE CONTROL 050; ELECTRICAL 066; ENGINEERING, COLLEGE 070; ENGINEERING, GENERAL 072; GARDENING, LANDSCAPING & NURSERY TRADES 100; INTERIOR DESIGN & DECORATING 134; LUMBER & FORESTRY 148; HOME & GARDEN (Consumer) 640; BUILDINGS & FURNISHINGS (Newsletter) 312
ART 014 see also ANTIQUES & COLLECTIBLES 006; ARCHITECTURE 012; PRINTING & GRAPHIC ARTS 202; TOYS, CRAFTS & HOBBIES 262; ART & ANTIQUES (Consumer) 606
ART (Newsletter) 308 see also ART 014; ART & ANTIQUES (Consumer) 606
ART & ANTIQUES (Consumer) 606 see also ART 014; ANTIQUES & COLLECTIBLES 006
Asphalt see ROADS & STREETS 232; BUILDING MATERIALS 036
Association Management see BUSINESS, GENERAL 038
Astrology see OCCULT (Consumer) 654
Astronautics see AVIATION & AEROSPACE 018
Athletics see SPORTS & SPORTING GOODS 250; SPORTS (Consumer) 670; SPORTS (Newsletter) 362
AUDIO & VIDEO 015 see also RADIO & TELEVISION 220; CONSUMER ELECTRONICS (Consumer) 620; COMMUNICATIONS (Newsletter) 316
Auditoriums see GOVERNMENT - MUNICIPAL, COUNTY, STATE, FEDERAL 106; ENTERTAINMENT 074
AUTOMOBILES & ACCESSORIES 016 see also MOTORCYCLES & BICYCLES 164; PUBLIC TRANSPORTATION 214; TRAILERS & ACCESSORIES 264; TRUCKS & TRUCKING 268; AUTOMOBILES & ACCESSORIES (Consumer) 608; MOTORCYCLES (Consumer) 648; TRAVEL & TRANSPORTATION (Newsletter) 364
AUTOMOBILES & ACCESSORIES (Consumer) 608 see also MOTORCYCLES (Consumer) 648; AUTOMOBILES & ACCESSORIES 016; MOTORCYCLES & BICYCLES 164; PUBLIC TRANSPORTATION 214; TRAILERS & ACCESSORIES 264; TRUCKS & TRUCKING 268; TRAVEL

# Section 4
# SERVICE, TRADE, PROFESSIONAL, INDUSTRIAL MAGAZINES

This section contains complete listing for magazines that are work or business-related. The magazines are listed alphabetically within each subject group. Subject groups follow numerical order according to group number.

A subject listing is provided with a page reference to where each group heading may be found within the main listings.

Please refer to the Alphabetical Cross Index in Section 3 to locate related subject publications within the Service, Trade, Professional, Industrial Magazine section or related subject categories/listings in the Farm and Agricultural or Consumer Magazine or Newsletter sections.

For materials accepted/included, refer to the coded list at the bottom of each page.

## SUBJECT GROUPS INCLUDED

## Group 002-Accounting

### ACCOUNTING REVIEW, THE
21919

J. L. Kellogg Grad. School of Management
North Western University
Evanston, IL 60208-2002
Telephone: (708) 467-2650
FAX: (708) 467-1202
Year Established: 1926
Pub. Frequency: q.
Page Size: standard
Subscrip. Rate: $65/yr. members; $90/yr.
   non-members
Circulation: 18,000
Circulation Type: paid
**Owner(s):**
American Accounting Association
5717 Bessie Dr.
Sarasota, FL 34233
Telephone: (813) 921-7747
Ownership %: 100
**Management:**
Paul Gerhardt .......................Executive Director
**Editorial:**
Prof. Robert P. Magee ...........................Editor
Krishna G. Palepu ....................Associate Editor
Dan A. Simunic .......................Associate Editor
S. Mark Young ........................Associate Editor
Mark E. Zmijawski ...................Associate Editor
James R. Boatsman ..........Book Review Editor
Gail Gumauskas ...................Editorial Assistant
Laurie Rayburn ....................Production Director
**Desc.:** Carries articles written by scholars
   in the accounting and financial fields
   dealing with various aspects of
   accounting. Book reviews cover books
   on accounting and auditing, economics
   business mathematics, taxes.
**Readers:** College accounting instructors
   and professors.

### ACCOUNTING TODAY
65246

11 Penn Plz.
New York, NY 10001
Telephone: (212) 631-1594
FAX: (212) 564-9896
Year Established: 1987
Pub. Frequency: bi-w
Page Size: tabloid
Subscrip. Rate: $69/yr.
Materials: 01,02,06,15,20,21,28,29,30,32,33
Freelance Pay: $.50/wd.
Circulation: 30,000
Circulation Type: paid
**Owner(s):**
Faulkner & Gray, Inc.
11 Penn Plz.
New York, NY 10001
Telephone: (212) 631-1594
FAX: (212) 564-9896
Ownership %: 100
**Management:**
Thomas Kothman ..............................Publisher
**Editorial:**
Rick Telberg .........................................Editor
**Desc.:** Covers accounting and auditing
   standards, taxation, management,
   advisory services, and personnel.
**Readers:** Accountants in firms and
   corporations.

### CORPORATE ACCOUNTING INTERNATIONAL
66180

2970 Clairmont Rd., Ste. 800
Atlanta, GA 30329
Telephone: (404) 636-6610
FAX: (404) 636-6422
Year Established: 1989
Pub. Frequency: m.
Page Size: oversize
Subscrip. Rate: $879/10 issues
Freelance Pay: varies
Print Process: Ventura-Printer in Dublin,
   Ireland

Wire service(s): PR Wire, Businesswire
**Owner(s):**
Lafferty Publications
2970 Clairmont Rd., Ste. 800
Atlanta, GA 30329
Telephone: (404) 636-6610
Ownership %: 100
**Bureau(s):**
Lafferty Publications
IDA Tower, Pearse St.
 Dublin 2, Ireland
Contact: Niall Brady, Senior Editor

Lafferty Publications
420 Lexington Ave., Ste. 1745
New York, NY 10170
Contact: Jim Peterson
**Editorial:**
Michael Lafferty ..........................Editor in Chief
Niall Brady .................................Senior Editor
**Desc.:** The international accounting,
   reporting and auditing source.
**Readers:** CFOs and public accountants
   around the world.

### CPA CLIENT BULLETIN
68770

Harborside Financial Ctr.
201 Plz. 3
Jersey City, NJ 07311-3881
Telephone: (201) 938-3301
FAX: (201) 938-3329
Year Established: 1976
Pub. Frequency: m.
Page Size: 8 1/2″ x 11″
Subscrip. Rate: $163/yr.
Materials: 01
Circulation: 950,000
Circulation Type: controlled
**Owner(s):**
American Institute of Certified Public
   Accountants
Harborside Financial Ctr.
201 Plz. 3
Jersey City, NJ 07311-3881
Telephone: (201) 938-3301
Ownership %: 100
**Editorial:**
Anne Wagenbrenner ...............................Editor
**Desc.:** Covers the range of topics a CPA
   would discuss with small business and
   tax clients.

### CPA JOURNAL, THE
21937

530 Fifth Ave., 5th Fl.
New York, NY 10036-5101
Telephone: (212) 719-8300
FAX: (212) 719-4755
Year Established: 1927
Pub. Frequency: m.
Page Size: standard
Subscrip. Rate: $42/yr.
Materials: 01,02,05,06,10,17,25,27,28,29,
   30,32,33
Print Process: web offset
Circulation: 46,718
Circulation Type: paid
**Owner(s):**
The New York State Society of CPAs
530 Fifth Ave., 5th Fl.
New York, NY 10036-5101
Telephone: (212) 719-8300
Ownership %: 100
**Management:**
Robert L. Gray ..................................Publisher
David L. Boniface ...............Advertising Manager
Corazon Balinong .......Classified Adv. Manager
Richard M. Kapelsonn ..........................Manager
**Editorial:**
Robert L. Gray ...............................Exec. Editor
Walter M. Primoff ..................................Editor
James L. Craig, CPA ..............Managing Editor
Joanne Barry ........................Assistant Publisher
Douglas R. Carmichael ................Feature Editor
John F. Burke ..............................Feature Editor
Michael Goldstein ........................Feature Editor

Francine Medaglia ..............Production Director
Janice Johnson .............................Tax Editor
**Desc.:** Articles and monthly departments
   for professional certified public
   accountants and those in industry and
   education. Departments cover: Auditing,
   Reporting, Federal, State and Local
   Taxation, Management Services, Estate
   Planning, Administration and Computers.
**Readers:** Certified public accountants,
   controllers, CFO's, treasurers,
   attorneys.

### DISCLOSURES
68769

P.O. Box 4620
Glen Allen, VA 23058-4620
FAX: (804) 270-5311
Year Established: 1988
Pub. Frequency: m.
Circulation: 5,600
Circulation Type: paid
**Owner(s):**
Virgina Society of Certified Public
   Accountants
P.O. Box 4620
Glen Allen, VA 23058-4620
Telephone: (804) 270-5311
Ownership %: 100
**Editorial:**
Marlene A. Childs ...................................Editor
**Desc.:** Contains editorials, limited technical
   and feature articles, updates on changes
   in the accounting profession, and
   member news and benefits.

### GOVERNMENT ACCOUNTANTS JOURNAL, THE
21954

2200 Mount Vernon Ave.
Alexandria, VA 22301-1314
Telephone: (703) 684-6931
FAX: (703) 548-9367
Year Established: 1952
Pub. Frequency: q.
Page Size: standard
Subscrip. Rate: $55/yr. US; $60/yr. foreign
Circulation: 13,000
Circulation Type: paid
**Owner(s):**
Association of Government Accountants
2200 Mount Vernon Ave.
Alexandria, VA 22301-1314
Telephone: (703) 684-6931
Ownership %: 100
**Management:**
Thomas Woods ................................Publisher
**Editorial:**
Shannon Gravitte .................................Editor
**Desc.:** Authoritative discussions of
   budgeting, accounting, contract auditing
   and related financial management
   subjects as they develop in government
   and industry affected by governmental
   controls.
**Readers:** Government financial managers,
   university instructors, financial vice-
   presidents, controllers, CPAs.

### INTERNATIONAL ACCOUNTING BULLETIN
66182

2970 Clairmont Rd., Ste. 800
Atlanta, GA 30329
Telephone: (404) 636-6610
FAX: (404) 636-6422
Year Established: 1983
Pub. Frequency: 22/yr.
Page Size: oversize
Subscrip. Rate: $979/yr.
**Owner(s):**
Lafferty Publications
IDA Tower, Pearse St.
 Dublin 2, Ireland
Ownership %: 100

**Bureau(s):**
Lafferty Publications
420 Lexington Ave., Ste. 1745
New York, NY 10170
Contact: Jim Peterson, Bureau Chief
**Editorial:**
Michael Lafferty ..........................Editor in Chief
Niall Brady .............................................Editor
Lisa Jaffe ...............................................Editor
**Desc.:** To keep readers abreast of the
   most important events around the world
   that impact the public accounting
   profession.
**Readers:** Public accountants conducting
   business internationally.

### JOURNAL OF ACCOUNTANCY
21963

Harborside Financial Ctr.
201 Plz. 3
Jersey City, NJ 07311-3881
Telephone: (201) 938-3292
FAX: (201) 938-3303
Year Established: 1905
Pub. Frequency: m.
Page Size: standard
Subscrip. Rate: $50/yr.
Circulation: 320,000
Circulation Type: paid
**Owner(s):**
American Institute of Certified Public
   Accountants
1211 Avenue of the Americas
New York, NY 10036
Telephone: (212) 596-6200
Ownership %: 100
**Bureau(s):**
AICPA
1455 Pennsylvania Ave., N.W.
Washington, DC 20004
Telephone: (202) 737-6600
**Management:**
Robert P. Rainier .................................Publisher
Richard Flynn ...................Advertising Manager
Julia Esposito ...................Promotion Manager
**Editorial:**
Colleen Katz .........................................Editor
Peter Tuoky ........................Production Director
**Desc.:** Covers serious, high-level technical
   material for accountants and business
   executives on accounting auditing,
   finance, financial management,
   controllership, taxation, business and
   professional education, professional
   development and government.
   Also covers the practice of public
   accounting, management of the CPA
   office, the use of business and office
   equipment. Departments include: News
   Report, Profile, Applications in
   Accounting, For the Practicing Auditor,
   Personal Financial Planning, Recent
   EITF Actions, Technical Q's & A's,
   Management Advisory Services, Tax
   Briefs, Using Micro-computers, Profile,
   Current Reading, Practitioners Forum,
   and Official Releases.
**Readers:** Public and private accountants.

### JOURNAL OF ACCOUNTING & PUBLIC POLICY
69368

1655 Avenue of the Americas
New York, NY 10010
Telephone: (212) 989-5800
FAX: (212) 633-3990
Year Established: 1982
Pub. Frequency: q.
Subscrip. Rate: $110/yr.
**Owner(s):**
Elsevier Science Publishing Co., Inc.
1655 Avenue of the Americas
New York, NY 10010
Telephone: (212) 989-5800
Ownership %: 100

**Materials Accepted/Included:** 01-Business news 02-By-line articles 03-Fashion news 04-Food news 05-Freelance copy 06-Letters to editor 07-Real estate news 08-Sports news 09-Travel news 10-Book rev. 11-Movie rev. 12-Music rev. 13-TV rev. 14-Theater rev. 15-Coming events 16-Obituaries 17-Question & answer 18-Social announcements 19-Artwork 20-Cartoons 21-Photos 22-TV listings 23-Audio rec. 24-Video rec. 25-Books 26-Films/film clips 27-Personnel news 28-Press releases 29-New product news/photos 30-Trade lit. 31-Contracts awarded 32-Display adv. 33-Classified adv.

**Editorial:**
L.A. Gordon ..............................Editor
S.E. Loeb .................................Editor
**Desc.:** Publishes articles exploring the interaction of accounting with a wide range of disciplines including economics, public administration, political science, social psychology, policy science and the law.

69361

## JOURNAL OF ACCOUNTING RESEARCH
1101 E. 58th St.
Chicago, IL 60637
Telephone: (312) 702-7460
FAX: (312) 702-0458
Year Established: 1963
Pub. Frequency: s-a.
Subscrip. Rate: $55/yr.
Circulation: 2,800
Circulation Type: paid
**Owner(s):**
University of Chicago, Graduate School of Business
Inst. of Professional Acct.
1101 E. 58th St.
Chicago, IL 60637
Telephone: (312) 702-7460
Ownership %: 100
**Editorial:**
Katherine Schipper ..........................Editor
**Desc.:** Unpublished original research in the fields of empirical, analytic and experimental accounting.

21968

## MANAGEMENT ACCOUNTING
10 Paragon Dr.
Montvale, NJ 07645-1760
Telephone: (201) 573-9000
FAX: (201) 573-0639
Year Established: 1919
Pub. Frequency: m.
Page Size: standard
Subscrip. Rate: $125/yr.; $62.50/yr. non-profit libraries
Materials: 01,02,06,21,27,28,29,30,32,33
Print Process: web
Circulation: 100,000
Circulation Type: paid
**Owner(s):**
Institute of Management Accountants
10 Paragon Dr.
Montvale, NJ 07645
Telephone: (201) 573-9000
FAX: (201) 573-0639
Ownership %: 100
**Management:**
Gary M. Scopes ........................Publisher
I.P.C. Enterprises ..........Advertising Manager
Alice Schulmann .............Circulation Manager
Kathryn Hogan .........Public Relations Manager
**Editorial:**
Susan Jayson .......................Senior Editor
Robert F. Randall ..........................Editor
Kathy Williams ...................Managing Editor
Claire Barth .......................Computer Editor
Claire Barth ...................New Products Editor
**Desc.:** Articles and information on management, as opposed to certified public, accounting. News of the profession, monthly departments on special areas such as taxes, and management information systems, etc.
**Readers:** Financial executives, managers, controllers.

21970

## MASSACHUSETTS CPA REVIEW
105 Chauncy St.
Boston, MA 02111
Telephone: (617) 556-4000
FAX: (617) 556-4126
Year Established: 1925
Pub. Frequency: q.

Page Size: standard
Subscrip. Rate: $5 newsstand; $20/yr.
Materials: 01,02,05,06,10,15,17,21,25,28, 29,30,32
Print Process: offset
Circulation: 8,000
Circulation Type: controlled & paid
**Owner(s):**
Massachusetts Society of CPA's
105 Chauncy St.
Boston, MA 02111
Telephone: (617) 556-4000
FAX: (617) 556-4126
Ownership %: 100
**Editorial:**
Cheryl McCloud ...................Managing Editor
Alison Lewandowski ............Editorial Assistant
**Desc.:** Professional journal for CPA's in public practice, industry and education. Covers every aspect affecting the profession nationally as well as within the New England region. Most frequently reoccuring topics include accounting & auditing, computers and computer systems, taxes, business/financial planning, and education.
**Readers:** CPA's in public accounting, in industry and universities in Massachusetts and Eastern New England.
**Deadline:** story-3 mo. prior to pub. date; news-3 mo.; photo-3 mo.; ads-3 mo.

2545

## NATIONAL PUBLIC ACCOUNTANT
1010 N. Fairfax St.
Alexandria, VA 22314
Telephone: (703) 549-6400
FAX: (703) 549-2984
Pub. Frequency: m.
Page Size: standard
Subscrip. Rate: $18/yr.
Circulation: 40,000
Circulation Type: paid
**Owner(s):**
National Society Public Accountants
1010 N. Fairfax St.
Alexandria, VA 22314
Ownership %: 100
**Management:**
Stanley H. Stearman ...................Publisher
Leslie Goodwin .................Advertising Manager
Erica Whitcombe ...................General Manager
**Editorial:**
Mary Beth Loutinski ..........................Editor

68766

## NEW ACCOUNTANT
2625 W. Peterson
Chicago, IL 60659
Telephone: (312) 866-9000
FAX: (312) 866-9006
Year Established: 1985
Pub. Frequency: 8/yr.
Page Size: standard
Subscrip. Rate: $85/yr.
Circulation: 64,632
Circulation Type: controlled
**Owner(s):**
New Dubois Corp.
36 Railroad Ave.
Glen Head, NY 11545-1840
Telephone: (516) 759-3484
Ownership %: 100
**Editorial:**
Steven Polydoris ..........................Editor
**Desc.:** Covers business news with special focus on careers, issues and developments in accounting and finance.

22381

## OHIO CPA JOURNAL, THE
535 Metro Pl., S.
Dublin, OH 43017
Telephone: (614) 764-2727

Mailing Address:
P.O. Box 1810
Dublin, OH 43017
Year Established: 1941
Pub. Frequency: q.
Page Size: standard
Subscrip. Rate: $20/yr.
Freelance Pay: negotiable
Circulation: 18,000
Circulation Type: controlled
**Owner(s):**
The Ohio Society of CPA's
535 Metro Pl., S.
Dublin, OH 43017
Telephone: (614) 764-2727
Ownership %: 100
**Management:**
J. Clarke Price ...................Executive Director
James F. Rayball .............Advertising Manager
**Editorial:**
James F. Rayball ...................Managing Editor
**Desc.:** All kinds of articles that are of interest to the practicing certified public accountant, three to five thousand words. Subject matter dealing with public accounting, auditing, taxes and management services.
**Readers:** Practicing certified public accountants.

21985

## PENNSYLVANIA CPA JOURNAL
1608 Walnut St., 3rd Fl.
Philadelphia, PA 19103
Telephone: (215) 735-2635
FAX: (215) 735-3694
Year Established: 1937
Pub. Frequency: 6/yr.
Page Size: standard
Subscrip. Rate: $3/yr.
Print Process: offset
Circulation: 20,000
Circulation Type: paid
**Owner(s):**
Pennsylvania Institute of CPAs
1608 Walnut St., 3rd Fl.
Philadelphia, PA 19103
Telephone: (215) 735-2635
Ownership %: 100
**Management:**
Albert E. Trexler ...................Publisher
**Editorial:**
Bernadette S. Finnerty ............Managing Editor
Sallyann Zigenfuss ...................Advertising
Ross Wladis .............Communications Director
**Desc.:** Official publication of the state's professional society of Certified Public Accountants, The Pennsylvania Institute of CPAs. All articles used are submitted by members of the profession or members of related professions.
**Readers:** CPAs, business executives, bankers, legislators, academicians, principally throughout Pennsylvania.

22389

## PRACTICAL ACCOUNTANT, THE
11 Penn Plz., 17th Fl.
New York, NY 10001
Telephone: (212) 631-1447
FAX: (212) 967-7155
Year Established: 1968
Pub. Frequency: m.
Page Size: standard
Subscrip. Rate: $65/yr.
Circulation: 30,000
Circulation Type: paid
**Owner(s):**
Faulkner & Grey, Inc.
11 Penn Plz., 17th Fl.
New York, NY 10001
Telephone: (212) 967-7000
Ownership %: 100
**Management:**
L. Nicolas Deane ...................Vice President
L. Nicolas Deane ...................Publisher

**Editorial:**
Howard Wolosky ...................Executive Editor
**Desc.:** Feature articles are in the field of accounting, auditing, computers, practice management, and taxes. Subject matter is technical, but presentation is in a lively and readable style.
**Readers:** Accountants in public and private practice, enrolled agents and tax lawyers.

69365

## WISCONSIN CPA
180 N. Executive Dr.
Brookfield, WI 53008-1010
Telephone: (414) 785-0445
FAX: (414) 785-0838
Mailing Address:
P.O. Box 1010
Brookfield, WI 53008-1010
Year Established: 1952
Pub. Frequency: 3/yr.
Circulation: 6,900
Circulation Type: paid
**Owner(s):**
Wisconsin Institute of Certified Public Accountant
180 N. Executive Dr.
Brookfield, WI 53008
Telephone: (414) 785-0445
Ownership %: 100
**Editorial:**
Mary Jaeger ..........................Editor

## Group 004-Advertising & Marketing

21640

## ADCRAFTER, THE
1249 Washington Blvd.
Ste. 2630
Detroit, MI 48226-1852
Telephone: (313) 962-7225
FAX: (313) 962-3599
Year Established: 1905
Pub. Frequency: w.
Page Size: standard
Subscrip. Rate: $25/yr.; $35/yr. incl. roster edition; $12 roster only
Circulation: 4,800
Circulation Type: paid
**Owner(s):**
The Adcraft Club of Detroit
1249 Washington Blvd.
Ste. 2630
Detroit, MI 48226-1852
Telephone: (313) 962-7225
Ownership %: 100
**Management:**
Phil Guarascio ...................President
William A. Oswald ...................Publisher
Lee Wilson ...................Advertising Manager
**Editorial:**
Lee Wilson ..........................Editor
William Jentzen ...................Managing Editor
**Desc.:** Published by an advertising and sales association/use material pertaining to advertising or sales in general, especially with a Detroit angle. Personnel announcements pertaining to Detroit area only, and to advertising or sales people.
**Readers:** Executives in Advertising Agencies, Manufacturers And Media.

21643

## AD TRENDS
200 N. Fourth St.
Burlington, IA 52601-0001
Telephone: (319) 752-5415
Mailing Address:
P.O. Box 1
Burlington, IA 52601-0001
Year Established: 1940
Pub. Frequency: m.

**Materials Accepted/Included:** 01-Business news 02-By-line articles 03-Fashion news 04-Food news 05-Freelance copy 06-Letters to editor 07-Real estate news 08-Sports news 09-Travel news 10-Book rev. 11-Movie rev. 12-Music rev. 13-TV rev. 14-Theater rev. 15-Coming events 16-Obituaries 17-Question & answer 18-Social announcements 19-Artwork 20-Cartoons 21-Photos 22-TV listings 23-Audio rec. 24-Video rec. 25-Books 26-Films/film clips 27-Personnel news 28-Press releases 29-New product news/photos 30-Trade lit. 31-Contracts awarded 32-Display adv. 33-Classified adv.

4-3

Page Size: standard
Subscrip. Rate: $32.95-$50.30/mo.
Circulation: 120
Circulation Type: paid
**Owner(s):**
National Research Bureau
200 N. Fourth St.
Burlington, IA 52601-0001
Telephone: (319) 752-5415
Ownership %: 100
**Editorial:**
L. McNamee .............................Editor
**Desc.:** Covers all phases of newspaper
advertising and merchandising from
leading shopping centers, home centers
and food stores throughout the U.S. and
Canada as gleaned from over 100 daily
newspapers.
**Readers:** Retail store advertising, sales
promotion.

## ADVERTISING & GRAPHIC ARTS TECHNIQUES
69375
10 E. 39th St., 6th Fl.
New York, NY 10016
Telephone: (212) 889-6500
FAX: (212) 889-6504
Year Established: 1966
Pub. Frequency: m.
Subscrip. Rate: $10/yr.
Circulation: 4,600
Circulation Type: paid
**Owner(s):**
Advertising Trade Publications, Inc.
10 E. 39th St., 6th Fl.
New York, NY 10016
Telephone: (212) 889-6500
FAX: (212) 889-6504
Ownership %: 100
**Editorial:**
Dan Barron .............................Editor

## ADVERTISING-COMMUNICATIONS TIMES
21646
121 Chestnut St.
Philadelphia, PA 19106
Telephone: (215) 629-1666
FAX: (215) 923-8358
Year Established: 1977
Pub. Frequency: m.
Page Size: tabloid
Subscrip. Rate: $39/yr.; $69/2 yrs.; $95/3
yrs.; $350/lifetime
Materials: 01,02,06,10,11,13,16,17,18,25,
28,29,31,32,33
Freelance Pay: varies
Circulation: 42,000
Circulation Type: controlled
**Owner(s):**
Advertising/Communications Times, Inc.
121 Chestnut St.
Philadelphia, PA 19106
Telephone: (215) 629-1666
Ownership %: 100
**Management:**
Joseph Ball .............................President
Joseph Ball .............................Publisher
**Editorial:**
Stacey Cutler .............................Editor
Joseph Ball .............................Book Review Editor

**Desc.:** News and features covering the
local communications industry, strongly
focused on advertising developments.
Account and personnel changes, profiles
of advertising managers and companies,
spotlights on marketing programs and
promotion plans, features on interesting
people in the business. Approximately
six, by-lined articles used per issue,
remainder staff written. Much use of
news releases and publicity photos.
Departments include: Lawsuits, News
Media Notes, Delaware Valley Ad
Activity, Audio Visual, Cable, TV, Radio,
Special Events, Promotions, Printing &
Graphics, Audio-Visual Directory, Printing
Directory.
**Readers:** Company owners, upper
management, especially
marketing/advertising directors, media
representatives.
21645

## ADVERTISING AGE
220 E. 42nd St.
New York, NY 10017
Telephone: (212) 210-0169
FAX: (212) 210-0200
Year Established: 1930
Pub. Frequency: w.
Page Size: tabloid
Subscrip. Rate: $2.50/copy; $89/yr.
Materials: 01,03,04,06,07,08,09,16,21,32,33
Freelance Pay: $50-$400/article
Print Process: offset
Circulation: 90,000
Circulation Type: paid
**Owner(s):**
Crain Communications, Inc.
740 N. Rush St.
Chicago, IL 60611
Telephone: (312) 649-5200
Ownership %: 100
**Bureau(s):**
Detroit Bureau
1400 Woodbridge Ave.
Detroit, MI 48207
Telephone: (313) 446-0320
Contact: Raymond Serafin, Bureau Chief

Washington Bureau
814 National Press Bldg.
Washington, DC 20045
Telephone: (202) 662-7214
Contact: Steven W. Colford, Bureau Chief

Houston Bureau
20402 Kelliwood Lakes Ct.
Katy, TX 77450
Telephone: (713) 578-9300
FAX: (713) 578-9352
Contact: Jennifer Lawrence, Bureau Chief

Los Angeles Bureau
6500 Wilshire Blvd.
Los Angeles, CA 90048
Telephone: (213) 651-3710
Contact: Cleveland Horton, Bureau Chief

London Bureau
Cowcross Ct. 75-77
Cowcross St.
London EC1M 6BP, United Kingdom
Telephone: 44-71-608-2774
FAX: 44-71-608-1173
Contact: Laurel Wentz, European Editor

New York Bureau
220 E. 42nd St.
New York, NY 10017-5846
Telephone: (212) 210-0175
FAX: (212) 210-0200
Contact: Patricia Sloan, Bureau Chief
**Management:**
Rance Crain .............................President
Ed Erhardt .............................Publisher
John Brice .............................Advertising Manager

**Editorial:**
Steve Yahn .............................Executive Editor
Fred Danzig .............................Editor
Melanie Rigney .............................Managing Editor
John Brice .........Dir. of Custom Publishing (NY)
Larry Edwards .........Executive Editor, Features
Nancy Giges .............................International Editor
**Desc.:** Illustrated tabloid covering
worldwide news of the advertising,
marketing, publishing, electronics and
allied fields. Feature articles on people,
trends, companies. Special Reports
weekly deal with significant markets,
product categories, events.
**Readers:** Advertising, marketing,
communications professionals.
**Deadline:** story-Fri. 6:00 pm; news-Fri.
6:00 pm; photo-Tues.
69372

## ADVERTISING AGE'S CREATIVITY
220 E. 42nd St.
New York, NY 10017-5806
Telephone: (212) 210-0280
FAX: (212) 210-0200
Year Established: 1987
Pub. Frequency: m.
Page Size: tabloid
Subscrip. Rate: $29/yr.
Materials: 23,24,25,27
Circulation: 30,000
Circulation Type: controlled
**Owner(s):**
Crain Communications, Inc.
220 E. 42nd St.
New York, NY 10017-5806
Telephone: (212) 210-0100
**Management:**
John Brice .............................Associate Publisher
**Editorial:**
Anthony Vagnoni .............................Editor
**Desc.:** Covers creative developments
affecting the advertising and graphic
design field.
21679

## ADWEEK (MIDWEST EDITION)
222 Merchandise Mart Plz., Ste. 936
Chicago, IL 60654-1102
Telephone: (312) 464-0880
FAX: (312) 464-8540
Year Established: 1963
Pub. Frequency: w.
Page Size: standard
Subscrip. Rate: $95/yr.
Circulation: 16,074
Circulation Type: paid
**Owner(s):**
B.P.I. Communications, Inc.
1515 Broadway
New York, NY 10036
Telephone: (212) 536-5336
Ownership %: 100
**Management:**
Stephen Crane .............................Publisher
**Editorial:**
Scott Hume .............................Editor
Richard Brunelli .............................Associate Editor
James Kirk .............................Associate Editor
Stephen Crane .............................Sales
**Desc.:** News of advertising and marketing
in the midwest. Carries feature articles,
news.
**Readers:** Those interested in advertising
and marketing, media directors, ad
managers and others involved in the
industry.
21670

## ADWEEK (NEW ENGLAND EDITION)
100 Boylston St.
Boston, MA 02116
Telephone: (617) 482-0876
FAX: (617) 482-2921
Year Established: 1964
Pub. Frequency: w.

Page Size: standard
Subscrip. Rate: $2.50 newsstand; $99/yr.
Circulation: 9,740
Circulation Type: paid
**Owner(s):**
B.P.I. Communications, Inc.
1515 Broadway
New York, NY 10036
Telephone: (212) 536-5336
Ownership %: 100
**Management:**
Penn Tudor .............................Chairman of Board
John Babcock .............................President
Ronald Kolgraf .............................Publisher
Chris Wessel .............................Circulation Manager
**Editorial:**
Judy Warner .............................Editor
Tom Weisend .............................Associate Editor
Charles Jackson .............................Editor Emeritus
**Desc.:** A regional weekly news magazine
for the advertising-communications
business in New England.
**Readers:** Advertising managers and
agencies, PR firms, media
representatives, corporate and marketing
management.

## ADWEEK (SOUTHEAST EDITION)
21683
5 Piedmont Ctr., Ste. 507
Atlanta, GA 30305
Telephone: (404) 841-3333
FAX: (404) 841-3332
Year Established: 1980
Pub. Frequency: w.
Page Size: standard
Subscrip. Rate: $95/yr.
Circulation: 9,800
Circulation Type: paid
**Owner(s):**
B.P.I. Communications, Inc.
1515 Broadway
New York, NY 10036
Telephone: (212) 536-5336
Ownership %: 100
**Management:**
Kenneth Fander .............................President
Stephen W. Carroll, Jr. .............................Publisher
Ira Kettleman .............................Circulation Manager
**Editorial:**
Jim Osterman .............................Editor
**Desc.:** Reports on national advertising
marketing and communications news
and is edited specifically for the interests
of advertising professionals in the eight
southern states: Virginia, North Carolina,
South Carolina, Florida, Georgia,
Alabama, Mississippi and Tennessee.
Special in-depth reports and advertising
industry analyses are published
throughout the year.
**Readers:** Advertising, marketing, and sales
executives of advertising agencies and
client companies.

## ADWEEK (SOUTHWEST EDITION)
21684
2909 Cole Ave., Ste. 220
Dallas, TX 75204
Telephone: (214) 871-9550
FAX: (214) 871-9557
Year Established: 1979
Pub. Frequency: w.
Page Size: standard
Subscrip. Rate: $69/yr.
Freelance Pay: negotiable
Circulation: 8,340
Circulation Type: paid
**Owner(s):**
B.P.I. Communications, Inc.
1515 Broadway
New York, NY 10036
Telephone: (212) 536-5336
Ownership %: 100

**Materials Accepted/Included:** 01-Business news 02-By-line articles 03-Fashion news 04-Food news 05-Freelance copy 06-Letters to editor 07-Real estate news 08-Sports news 09-Travel news 10-Book rev. 11-Movie rev. 12-Music rev. 13-TV rev. 14-Theater rev. 15-Coming events 16-Obituaries 17-Question & answer 18-Social announcements 19-Artwork 20-Cartoons 21-Photos 22-TV listings 23-Audio rec. 24-Video rec. 25-Books 26-Films/film clips 27-Personnel news 28-Press releases 29-New product news/photos 30-Trade lit. 31-Contracts awarded 32-Display adv. 33-Classified adv.

**Bureau(s):**
Adweek (Houston Bureau)
P.O. Box 74
Dallas, TX 75221
Telephone: (713) 661-5496
Contact: Lisa Paikowski, Bureau Chief
**Management:**
John C. Thomas ...............Chairman of Board
J.C. Kelly ................................Publisher
Caroline Adams ..........Classified Adv. Manager
J.C. Kelly ...........................General Manager
Helen Brennan ....................Office Manager
**Editorial:**
Kathy Thacker ..............................Editor
**Desc.:** Newsweekly for advertising and
communications industries in the
Southwest.
**Readers:** Advertising & marketing
executives in the S.W. states.

59645
## ADWEEK (WESTERN EDITION)
5055 Wilshire Blvd., 7th Fl.
Los Angeles, CA 90036
Telephone: (213) 525-2270
FAX: (213) 525-2391
Year Established: 1978
Pub. Frequency: w.
Page Size: standard
Subscrip. Rate: $95/yr.
Circulation: 105,000
Circulation Type: controlled
**Owner(s):**
B.P.I. Communications, Inc.
1515 Broadway
New York, NY 10036
Telephone: (212) 536-5336
Ownership %: 100
**Editorial:**
Betsy Sharkey .............................Editor
**Readers:** Ad agencies & clients - media
departments.

21650
## ADWEEK MAGAZINE
1515 Broadway
New York, NY 10036
Telephone: (212) 536-5336
FAX: (212) 536-1416
Year Established: 1978
Pub. Frequency: w.
Page Size: standard
Subscrip. Rate: $2.50 newsstand; $95/yr.
Materials: 05,20,21
Freelance Pay: $250-$1,500/article
Circulation: 100,000
Circulation Type: paid
**Owner(s):**
B.P.I. Communications, Inc.
1515 Broadway
New York, NY 10036
Telephone: (212) 536-5336
Ownership %: 100
**Bureau(s):**
Adweek
100 Boylston, Ste. 210
Boston, MA 02116
Telephone: (617) 482-0876
Contact: Judy Warner, Editor

Adweek
3525 Piedmont Rd.
Bldg. 5, Ste. 507
Atlanta, GA 30305
Telephone: (404) 841-3333
FAX: (404) 841-3332
Contact: Jim Osterman, Editor

Adweek
936 Merchandise Mart
Chicago, IL 60654
Telephone: (312) 964-8525
Contact: Scott Hume, Editor

Adweek
2909 Cole Ave.
Dallas, TX 75204
Telephone: (214) 871-9550
Contact: Kathy Thacker, Editor

Adweek
5055 Wilshire Blvd.
Los Angeles, CA 90036
Telephone: (213) 525-2270
Contact: Shelly Garcia, Editor
**Management:**
John Babcock, Jr. ........................President
**Desc.:** Advertising and marketing news
departments include: Corridor Talk,
Calendar, Account Watch, Late News,
Media Notes, National Newswire,
Agency Profiles, Accounts in Review,
Agency Stock Watch, Informed Sources,
Agency Acquisitions, ADWEEK Critique,
Creative Solutions.
**Deadline:** story-Wed. prior to pub. date;
news-Thu.; photo-Wed.; ads-Mon.

21649
## AGRI MARKETING
11701 Borman Dr.
Ste. 100
Saint Louis, MO 63146
Telephone: (314) 569-2700
FAX: (314) 569-1083
Year Established: 1962
Pub. Frequency: m.
Page Size: standard
Subscrip. Rate: $30/yr.
Freelance Pay: $200 to $500/article
Circulation: 8,107
Circulation Type: controlled
**Owner(s):**
Doane Agriculture Services
11701 Borman Dr.
Ste. 100
Saint Louis, MO 63146
Telephone: (314) 569-2700
Ownership %: 100
**Management:**
Don Evishenko ..........................Publisher
**Editorial:**
Debbie Hartke ..............................Editor
Pam Helsing ....................Circulation Editor
**Desc.:** Covers all aspects of selling,
marketing, and communications to the
North American Farm Market.
**Readers:** Professionals selling to the farm
market managers, media, advertising
agencies.

21751
## ART DIRECTION
10 E. 39th St., 6th Fl.
New York, NY 10016
Telephone: (212) 889-6500
FAX: (212) 889-6504
Year Established: 1949
Pub. Frequency: m.
Page Size: standard
Subscrip. Rate: $29.97/yr.; $55.97/2 yrs.;
$82.49/3 yrs.
Print Process: offset
Circulation: 9,200
Circulation Type: paid
**Owner(s):**
Advertising Trade Publications, Inc.
10 E. 39th St., 6th Fl.
New York, NY 10016
Telephone: (212) 889-6500
Ownership %: 100
**Management:**
Daniel Barron ...........................Publisher
Dan Ferrerra ...................Advertising Manager
E. Ricks ....................Circulation Manager
**Editorial:**
Daniel Barron .............................Editor
Karen Jocaco ..........................Art Director
S. Lederkramer ............Production Coordinator

**Desc.:** Features, discussions, case
histories, news for the art director.
Covers art direction, commercial art,
photography. Theme must deal with
some phase of advertising art and the
creative man involved, and how good art
and design are used for effective selling.
Features are illustrated with samples
of the artist's creative work that has
been used by magazines, advertising
agencies, etc. Departments include:
News, Trade Talk, Photography,
Agencies, Production, Advertising-
Promotion, Exhibition, Book Notes,
What's Best (products, booklets, etc.);
reference section on graphic arts
production and services, films, TV
commercials.
**Readers:** Art directors, art buyers,
advertising managers, agencies & art
design studios.

65983
## BRANDWEEK
1515 Broadway
New York, NY 10036
Telephone: (212) 536-5336
FAX: (212) 536-5353
Year Established: 1985
Pub. Frequency: Mon.
Page Size: standard
Subscrip. Rate: $69/yr.
Print Process: offset web
Circulation: 26,076
Circulation Type: paid
**Owner(s):**
B.P.I. Publications
1515 Broadway
New York, NY 10036
Telephone: (212) 536-5336
Ownership %: 100
**Editorial:**
Stewart Alter ..............................Editor
John McManus ...................Editorial Director

21658
## BUSINESS MARKETING
740 N. Rush St.
Chicago, IL 60611
Telephone: (312) 649-5260
FAX: (312) 649-5462
Year Established: 1916
Pub. Frequency: m.
Page Size: standard
Subscrip. Rate: $4/copy; $44/yr.; $69/2 yr.
Circulation: 30,000
Circulation Type: controlled
**Owner(s):**
Crain Communications Inc.
740 N. Rush
Chicago, IL 60611
Telephone: (312) 649-5200
Ownership %: 100
**Bureau(s):**
Crain Communications
220 E. 42nd St.
New York, NY 10017
Telephone: (212) 210-0191
Contact: Bob Donath, Editor
**Management:**
Rance Crain .............................President
Cliff Mulcahy ...........................Publisher
**Editorial:**
Jan Jaben ................................Editor
Chuck Paustian .......................Copy Director
**Desc.:** Staff-written and contributed by-line
articles covering techniques and
strategies of industrial marketing and
communication, advertising campaign
and copy, research, sales management,
etc. Emphasis on marketing and related
activities. Covers new developments in
these areas. Uses marketing
management, advertising agency and
media.

**Readers:** Top management, marketing,
sales and advertising marketing
managers, advertising agencies,
publishers.

58771
## CABLE TV ADVERTISING
126 Clock Tower Pl.
Carmel, CA 93923
Telephone: (408) 624-1536
FAX: (408) 625-3225
Year Established: 1980
Pub. Frequency: m.
Page Size: standard
Subscrip. Rate: $550/yr.
**Owner(s):**
Paul Kagan
126 Clock Tower Pl.
Carmel, CA 93923
Telephone: (408) 624-1536
Ownership %: 100
**Management:**
Paul Kagan ............................Publisher
Judith Pinney ...................Circulation Manager

49806
## CATALOG AGE
6 River Bend Ctr.
911 Hope St.
Stamford, CT 06907
Telephone: (203) 358-9900
FAX: (203) 357-9014
Mailing Address:
P.O. Box 4949
Stamford, CT 06907-0949
Year Established: 1984
Pub. Frequency: m.
Page Size: tabloid
Subscrip. Rate: free to qualified personnel
Circulation: 12,200
Circulation Type: controlled
**Owner(s):**
Cowles Business Media
P.O. Box 4949
Stamford, CT 06907-0949
Telephone: (203) 358-9900
Ownership %: 100
**Management:**
Hershel Sarbin ..........................President
William D. Holiber .......................Publisher
**Editorial:**
Kathleen Joyce .......................Executive Editor
Laura M. Christiana .................Editorial Director
**Desc.:** Every issue provides news, and
feature coverage of various aspects of
catalog publishing and marketing:
Management, Merchandising, Creative,
Production, Printing, Direct Mail, Order
Fulfillment, Data Processing, Postal and
People. In addition, each issue has
special editorial emphasis on one of
these areas.
**Readers:** Catalog marketing executives
and suppliers.

52654
## CATALOG MARKETER, THE
522 Forest Ave.
Evanston, IL 60202-3005
Telephone: (312) 819-1890
FAX: (312) 819-0411
Year Established: 1982
Pub. Frequency: bi-w.
Page Size: standard
Subscrip. Rate: $189/yr.; $305/2 yrs.;
$405/3 yrs.
Materials: 01,05,06,29,30
**Owner(s):**
Maxwell Sroge Publishing, Inc.
522 Forest Ave.
Evanston, IL 60602
Telephone: (708) 866-1890
FAX: (708) 866-1899
Ownership %: 100
**Editorial:**
Ann Meyer ...............................Editor

---

**Materials Accepted/Included:** 01-Business news 02-By-line articles 03-Fashion news 04-Food news 05-Freelance copy 06-Letters to editor 07-Real estate news 08-Sports news 09-Travel news
10-Book rev. 11-Movie rev. 12-Music rev. 13-TV rev. 14-Theater rev. 15-Coming events 16-Obituaries 17-Question & answer 18-Social announcements 19-Artwork 20-Cartoons 21-Photos 22-TV listings
23-Audio rec. 24-Video rec. 25-Books 26-Films/film clips 27-Personnel news 28-Press releases 29-New product news/photos 30-Trade lit. 31-Contracts awarded 32-Display adv. 33-Classified adv.

4-5

**Desc.:** This is a complete and authoritative "how-to" publication on producing and mailing catalogs for effectively selling products and services to the consumer and industrial market. Team of more than 30 contributing experts from throughout U.S.

**Readers:** The subscriber base is primarily personnel in charge of various aspects of marketing, production and advertising in catalog companies in addition to individuals in advertising agencies, service bureaus and supplier companies. High degree of penetration in consumer and business to business catalog marketing operations.

## CIRCULATION 95
21651

3004 Glenview Rd.
Wilmette, IL 60091
Telephone: (708) 256-6067
FAX: (708) 441-2400
Year Established: 1962
Pub. Frequency: a.
Page Size: standard
Subscrip. Rate: $169/yr.
Materials: 32
Print Process: web offset
Circulation: 4,000
Circulation Type: controlled & paid
**Owner(s):**
Standard Rate Data Service
3004 Glenview Rd.
Wilmette, IL 60091
Telephone: (708) 256-6067
FAX: (708) 441-2400
Ownership %: 100
**Management:**
James Meyers .......................................Publisher
**Editorial:**
June Levy ...............................................Editor
**Desc.:** Annual geographic penetration of major print media; every daily and Sunday newspaper in the country.

## COUNSELOR, THE
21654

1120 Wheeler Way
Langhorne, PA 19047
Telephone: (215) 752-4200
FAX: (215) 752-9758
Year Established: 1954
Pub. Frequency: m.
Page Size: standard
Subscrip. Rate: $65/yr.
Freelance Pay: varies
Circulation: 6,000
Circulation Type: controlled
**Owner(s):**
Advertising Specialty Institute
1120 Wheeler Way
Langhorne, PA 19047
Telephone: (215) 752-4200
Ownership %: 100
**Management:**
Marvin Spike ......................................President
Marvin Spike ......................................Publisher
Mary Ellen Hudicka ..........Advertising Manager
Maria Welsh ................Circulation Manager
**Editorial:**
Catharine S. Holnick ...............................Editor
Jim Lang ......................................Art Director
**Desc.:** Covers all facets of the specialty advertising field. Departments include: Speak Up (letters to editor), Marketwise (late-breaking), Associations Directory, Rep Center, Personalities in the Profession, Kaleidoscope.
**Readers:** Management personnel of specialty advertising suppliers and distributors.

## DIRECT MARKETING
21655

224 7th St.
Garden City, NY 11530
Telephone: (516) 746-6700
FAX: (516) 294-8141
Year Established: 1938
Pub. Frequency: m.
Page Size: standard
Subscrip. Rate: $56/yr.
Freelance Pay: varies
Circulation: 23,000
Circulation Type: paid
**Owner(s):**
Hoke Communications, Inc.
224 7th St.
Garden City, NY 11530
Telephone: (516) 746-6700
**Bureau(s):**
Hoke Communications, Inc.
612 N. Michigan Ave., Ste. 606
Chicago, IL 60611
Telephone: (312) 337-0120
Contact: Joseph Rotskoff, Advertising Manager
**Management:**
Henry Hoke, Jr. ...............................Publisher
James Johnston ...............Advertising Manager
**Editorial:**
Mollie Neal .........................................Editor
Liz Gabriel ....................Administrative Assistant
**Desc.:** News, techniques and developments in the direct marketing field. By-line articles present creative techniques, campaigns, planning, case histories of successful direct mail, telemarketing, catalogs, space advertising. Uses news of new literature, suppliers, etc., plus business-to-business section in every issue.
**Readers:** Advertising, marketing and sales executives; heads of consumer and industrial companies; copywriters; fundraisers; lettershop, fulfillment, list brokers.

## FUND RAISING MANAGEMENT
22322

224 Seventh St.
Garden City, NY 11530
Telephone: (516) 746-6700
FAX: (516) 294-8141
Year Established: 1969
Pub. Frequency: m.
Page Size: standard
Subscrip. Rate: $54/yr.
Circulation: 10,000
Circulation Type: paid
**Owner(s):**
Hoke Communications, Inc.
224 Seventh St.
Garden City, NY 11530
Telephone: (516) 746-6700
Ownership %: 100
**Management:**
Henry Hoke ...............................Publisher
**Editorial:**
William Olcott ...........................Editor
Greg Gattuso ....................Associate Editor
Elaine Santoro ....................Associate Editor
**Desc.:** Each issue offers the latest in news and trends impacting fund raising, case studies and features, new products and services, lists, literature, premiums, personnel changes, campaigns, grants, tax rulings and special conference reports.
**Readers:** Fund raisers at hospitals, churches, schools and colleges, health and welfare agencies, cultural and art groups, political organizations; and fraternal and social institutions.

## HEALTHCARE ADVERTISING REVIEW
69250

1886 Colonial Village Ln.
Lancaster, PA 17605-0488
Telephone: (717) 393-1000
FAX: (717) 393-2732
Mailing Address:
P.O. Box 10488
Lancaster, PA 17605
Year Established: 1985
Pub. Frequency: bi-m.
Page Size: oversize
Subscrip. Rate: $225/yr.
Materials: 01,10,28,30,32
Circulation: 1,000
Circulation Type: paid
**Owner(s):**
Wentworth Publishing
1861 Colonial Village Ln.
Lancaster, PA 17605-0488
Telephone: (717) 393-1000
FAX: (717) 393-2732
Ownership %: 100
**Editorial:**
Sandy Bridges ...........................Editor
**Desc.:** One-of-a-kind publication that reviews consumer healthcare advertising from facilities across the U.S. The majority of the publication features print advertising, but also includes samples from outdoor, direct mail and broadcast mediums.
**Readers:** Advertising & Marketing Directors of healthcare facilities across the U.S. (titles include PR Directors, Community Relations Directors, etc.). Advertising agencies with healthcare clients. Consultants with healthcare clients.

## INCENTIVE
21657

355 Park Ave., S.
New York, NY 10010-1789
Telephone: (212) 592-6453
FAX: (212) 592-6459
Year Established: 1905
Pub. Frequency: m.
Page Size: standard
Subscrip. Rate: $48/yr.; $75/yr. foreign
Materials: 01,06,09,10,15,17,19,20,21,25,29
Freelance Pay: negotiable
Circulation: 40,000
Circulation Type: controlled
**Owner(s):**
Bill Communications, Inc.
355 Park Ave., S.
New York, NY 10010-1789
Telephone: (212) 592-6400
FAX: (212) 592-6459
Ownership %: 100
**Management:**
Richard O'Connor ...........................Publisher
Peter Edmunds ...........................Publisher
**Editorial:**
Jennifer Juergens ...........................Editor
**Desc.:** The authority on motivation in management and marketing. It reports on how companies maximize their overall performance by motivating consumers and dealers to buy, salespeople to sell, and all employees to work more effectively. It covers the motivation process from program conception and planning to implementation and evaluation. Each issue explores the measurement systems, promotion and communication techniques, and the merchandise and travel awards that form the foundation of any successful incentive campaign.
**Readers:** Leading factors, executives in all incentive-using industries.
**Deadline:** story-3 mos. prior to pub. date; ads-2 mos. prior to pub. date

## INSIDE MEDIA
68775

6 River Bend Ctr.
911 Hope St.
Stamford, CT 06907-0949
Telephone: (203) 358-9900
FAX: (203) 357-9017
Mailing Address:
P.O. Box 4949
Stamford, CT 06097-0949
Year Established: 1980
Pub. Frequency: 24/yr.
Subscrip. Rate: $49/yr.
Circulation: 31,000
Circulation Type: paid
**Owner(s):**
Cowles Business Media
6 River Bend Ctr.
911 Hope St.
Stamford, CT 06907-0949
Telephone: (203) 358-9900
Ownership %: 100
**Editorial:**
Steve Ellwanger ...........................Editor

## INTERNATIONAL ADVERTISER
65290

342 Madison Ave., Ste. 2000
New York, NY 10173-0073
Telephone: (212) 557-1133
FAX: (212) 983-0455
Year Established: 1988
Pub. Frequency: bi-m.
Page Size: standard
Subscrip. Rate: $68/yr. members; $80/yr. non-members and libraries
Materials: 02,15,25,30
Circulation: 3,600
Circulation Type: controlled & paid
**Owner(s):**
International Advertising Association
342 Madison Ave., Ste. 2000
New York, NY 10173-0073
Telephone: (212) 557-1133
FAX: (212) 983-0455
Ownership %: 100
**Editorial:**
Richard M. Corner ...................Executive Editor
Norman Vale ...........................Executive Editor
Ellen Corey ...........................Editor
**Desc.:** For IAA members in international marketing and communications.
**Readers:** Advertisers, agencies, and media worldwide.

## INTERNATIONAL PRODUCT ALERT
56245

6473 D Rte. 64
Naples, NY 14512
Telephone: (716) 374-6326
FAX: (716) 374-5217
Year Established: 1984
Pub. Frequency: s-m.
Page Size: standard
Subscrip. Rate: $600/yr.
**Owner(s):**
Marketing Intelligence Service
6473 D. Rte. 64
Naples, NY 14512
Telephone: (716) 374-6326
Ownership %: 100
**Editorial:**
Tom Vierhile ...........................Exec. Editor
Sherie Meeker-Barton ...........................Editor

**Materials Accepted/Included:** 01-Business news 02-By-line articles 03-Fashion news 04-Food news 05-Freelance copy 06-Letters to editor 07-Real estate news 08-Sports news 09-Travel news 10-Book rev. 11-Movie rev. 12-Music rev. 13-TV rev. 14-Theater rev. 15-Coming events 16-Obituaries 17-Question & answer 18-Social announcements 19-Artwork 20-Cartoons 21-Photos 22-TV listings 23-Audio rec. 24-Video rec. 25-Books 26-Films/film clips 27-Personnel news 28-Press releases 29-New product news/photos 30-Trade lit. 31-Contracts awarded 32-Display adv. 33-Classified adv.

4-6

**Desc.:** Keeping abreast of what is happening on the international scene. Many innovations have started overseas. Includes brief reports on new product introductions in 18 countries (excluding U.S. and Canada) in the consumer goods field. covering foods, beverages, non-prescription drugs, cosmetics and toiletries, pet products and miscellaneous household items. Also lists products that are extensions of existing lines and packaging changes. Recurring feature: includes photos of some of the reported products, occasional copies of advertising and brief commentaries on some of the more interesting items.

**Readers:** Marketing executives and general managers of consumer product manufacturers, advertising agencies.

## JOURNAL OF ADVERTISING
69376

University of Houston
College of Bus. Admin., Dept. of Marketing
Houston, TX 77204-6283
Telephone: (713) 743-4575
FAX: (713) 743-4572
Year Established: 1972
Pub. Frequency: q.
Page Size: standard
Subscrip. Rate: $40/yr.
Materials: 10,19,20,32
Circulation: 1,850
Circulation Type: paid
**Owner(s):**
American Academy of Advertising
**Management:**
Madeline Johnson ...............Business Manager
**Editorial:**
George M. Zinkhan .............................Editor
**Desc.:** Contributes to the development of advertising theory and its relationship to advertising practices and processes.

## JOURNAL OF ADVERTISING RESEARCH
21659

641 Lexington Ave.
New York, NY 10022
Telephone: (212) 751-5656
FAX: (212) 319-5265
Year Established: 1960
Pub. Frequency: bi-m.
Page Size: standard
Subscrip. Rate: $100/yr. US; $130/yr. foreign
Circulation: 4,800
Circulation Type: paid
**Owner(s):**
Advertising Research Foundation, Inc.
641 Lexington Ave.
New York, NY 10022
Telephone: (212) 751-5656
Ownership %: 100
**Management:**
Michael J. Naples .............................President
James H. Moore .........................Vice President
**Editorial:**
William A. Cook ..............................Editor
Kathryn Kucharski Grubb ........Managing Editor
Yvonne D. Sinakin ...................Associate Editor
Arthur J. Kover ......................Associate Editor
Kathryn Kucharski ............Production Director
Grubb
**Desc.:** Publishes papers on advertising and marketing research. Intended for practitioners and users of advertising research. Reports of findings are favored over theoretical discussion. Letters of comment and criticism are invited.
**Readers:** Research executives in agencies, advertisers, media and research organizations. Professors and students of advertising, marketing.

## JOURNAL OF CURRENT ISSUES & RESEARCH IN ADVERTISING
69386

P.O. Box 1826
Clemson, SC 29633-1826
Telephone: (803) 855-0401
FAX: (803) 654-7438
Year Established: 1978
Pub. Frequency: 2/yr.
Subscrip. Rate: $24/yr. US; $29/yr. elsewhere
Materials: 10
Print Process: offset
Circulation: 850
**Owner(s):**
CTC Press
P.O. Box 1826
Clemson, SC 29633-1826
Telephone: (803) 855-0401
Ownership %: 100
**Editorial:**
James Leigh ..............................Editor
Claude R. Martin .............................Editor

## JOURNAL OF MARKETING
21660

250 S. Wacker Dr.
Chicago, IL 60606
Telephone: (312) 648-0536
FAX: (312) 993-7540
Year Established: 1936
Pub. Frequency: q.
Page Size: standard
Subscrip. Rate: $20/yr.; $35/yr. members; $70/yr. non-members; $150/yr. corporations
Circulation: 10,000
Circulation Type: paid
**Owner(s):**
American Marketing Association
250 S. Wacker Dr.
Chicago, IL 60606
Telephone: (312) 648-0536
Ownership %: 100
**Management:**
Hope Bulger ..............................Publisher
Sally Schmitz ....................Advertising Manager
**Editorial:**
P. Rajan Varadarjian ..............................Editor
Ken Pfeifer ..............................Advertising
George Zinkhan .............Book Review Editor
**Desc.:** Articles are written for professional marketers and academics to advance the science and practice of marketing while making available new marketing discoveries, techniques, ideas, new views of old problems, new generalizations of scattered concepts. Sections include: Legal Developments in Marketing, Marketing Abstracts & Book Reviews.
**Readers:** Professional marketers, advertising specialists, business consultants, managers, and others interested in marketing in the U.S. and foreign countries.

## JOURNAL OF MARKETING RESEARCH
21661

250 S. Wacker Dr.
Chicago, IL 60606
Telephone: (312) 648-0536
FAX: (312) 993-7540
Year Established: 1964
Pub. Frequency: q.
Page Size: standard
Subscrip. Rate: $35/yr. members; $70/yr. non-members; $150/yr. corporations
Circulation: 10,000
Circulation Type: paid

**Owner(s):**
American Marketing Association
250 S. Wacker Dr.
Chicago, IL 60606
Telephone: (312) 648-0536
Ownership %: 100
**Management:**
Hope Bulger ..............................Publisher
Sally Schmitz ....................Advertising Manager
**Editorial:**
Bart Weitz ..............................Editor
Ken Pfeifer ..............................Advertising
**Desc.:** A scientific journal which publishes the best available dealing with fundamental research in marketing and in research practice.
**Readers:** Marketing research executives, analysts, research managers and planners, consultants, educators.

## MARKETING COMMUNICATIONS MAGAZINE
68772

3420 Via Oporto, No. 201
Newport Beach, CA 92663-3901
Telephone: (714) 675-4604
FAX: (714) 675-2356
Year Established: 1989
Pub. Frequency: q.
Page Size: standard
Subscrip. Rate: $7 newsstand; $22/yr.
Materials: 01,02,05,06,10,15,17,19,20,21, 23,24,25,26,27,28,29,30,31,32
Freelance Pay: $50-300/article
Print Process: offset lithography
Circulation: 15,000
Circulation Type: controlled & paid
**Owner(s):**
Meridian Media Group, Inc.
3420 Via Oporto, No. 201
Newport Beach, CA 92663-3901
Telephone: (714) 675-4604
Ownership %: 100
**Management:**
John H. Good ..............................Publisher
**Editorial:**
John H. Good ..............................Editor
Michael R. Leonard .............Director of Client Services
Diane M. Cook ..............Director of Operations
**Readers:** Executive level marketing department staff and advertising/PR agency personnel.
**Deadline:** story-1 mo. prior to pub. date; news-1 mo.; photo-1 mo.; ads-1 mo.

## MARKETING NEWS
21666

250 S. Wacker Dr., Ste. 200
Chicago, IL 60606
Telephone: (312) 993-9517
FAX: (312) 993-7540
Year Established: 1967
Pub. Frequency: bi-w. plus a. directory
Page Size: tabloid
Subscrip. Rate: $60/yr.
Materials: 02,06
Freelance Pay: negotiable
Print Process: web offset
Circulation: 30,000
Circulation Type: paid
**Owner(s):**
American Marketing Association
250 S. Wacker Dr., Ste. 200
Chicago, IL 60606
Telephone: (312) 648-0536
Ownership %: 100
**Management:**
Hope Bulger ..............................Publisher
Sally Schmitz ....................Advertising Manager
Ken Pfeifer ..............................Sales Manager
**Editorial:**
Thomas E. Caruso ..................Executive Editor
Gregg Cebrzynski ....................Managing Editor
Larry Graft ..............................Graphics Editor
Mary Love ..............................Graphics Editor

Cyndee Miller ..............................Senior Writer
**Desc.:** News articles report on American Marketing Assn. activities and on the marketing field in general. Departments include: Marketing Briefs, Viewpoint, Technology Today, Names in the News, etc.
**Readers:** Professionals in marketing management, marketing research, marketing educators, service and Ad agencies and more.

## MARKETING RESEARCH: MANAGEMENT & APPLICATIONS
67698

250 S. Wacker Dr., Ste. 200
Chicago, IL 60606
Telephone: (312) 648-0536
FAX: (312) 993-7542
Year Established: 1989
Pub. Frequency: q.
Page Size: standard
Subscrip. Rate: $47/yr. member; $70/yr. non-member
Circulation: 3,500
Circulation Type: paid
**Owner(s):**
American Marketing Association
250 S. Wacker Dr., Ste/ 200
Chicago, IL 60606
Telephone: (312) 648-0536
Ownership %: 100
**Management:**
Richard Kean ..............................Publisher
**Editorial:**
Harry O'Neill ..............................Editor
**Desc.:** Promotes a new and broader AMA definition of marketing research that stresses developing and evaluating hypotheses and theories rather than merely analyzing data.
**Readers:** For managers and practicioners of marketing research.

## MEDIA WEEK
67058

1515 Broadway
New York, NY 10036
Telephone: (212) 536-5336
FAX: (212) 536-5353
Year Established: 1970
Pub. Frequency: Mon.
Page Size: standard
Subscrip. Rate: $89/yr.
Print Process: offset web
Circulation: 18,531
Circulation Type: paid
**Owner(s):**
B.P.I. Communications, Inc.
1515 Broadway
New York, NY 10036
Telephone: (212) 764-7300
Ownership %: 100
**Management:**
John Babcock, Jr. ..............................President
Ken Marks ....................Advertising Manager
**Editorial:**
Craig Reiss ..............................Editor in Chief
William Gloede ..............Editorial Director

## MEDICAL MEETINGS
24679

63 Great Rd.
Maynard, MA 01754
Telephone: (508) 897-5552
FAX: (508) 897-6824
Year Established: 1974
Pub. Frequency: 8/yr.
Page Size: standard
Subscrip. Rate: $56/yr. US; $68/yr. Canada; $105/yr. foreign
Materials: 01,05,06,15,19,21,27,28,31,32
Freelance Pay: negotiable
Print Process: offset
Circulation: 13,647
Circulation Type: paid

**Owner(s):**
The Laux Co., Inc.
63 Great Rd.
Maynard, MA 01754
Telephone: (508) 897-5552
Ownership %: 100
**Management:**
Dean M. Laux ..............................President
Peter Huestis ..............................Publisher
Mary F. Allan ..................Business Manager
Kristin McHugh ...........Circulation Manager
**Editorial:**
Betsy Bair ..........................Editor in Chief
David Erickson ...............................Editor
**Desc.:** Provides information on the
planning of medical meetings, exhibits,
meetings management, and related
topics to association executives and
meeting planners in the fields of
medicine, dentistry, nursing, veterinary
medicine, and related healthcare
disciplines. Also served are meeting
planners in hospitals, medical schools,
private medical foundations, and
government health agencies, as well as
pharmaceutical and medical equipment
manufacturers.
**Readers:** Meeting planners and executives
of medical societies, scientific societies,
hospitals, medical schools, and
pharmaceutical and medical equipment
manufacturers.

22356
## MEETING NEWS
1515 Broadway
New York, NY 10036
Telephone: (212) 869-1300
Year Established: 1977
Pub. Frequency: m.
Page Size: tabloid
Subscrip. Rate: $9/issue; $65/yr.
Circulation: 76,000
Circulation Type: controlled
**Owner(s):**
Miller Freeman, Inc.
600 Harrison St.
San Francisco, CA 94107
Telephone: (415) 905-2200
**Management:**
Gerry Moss ...............................Publisher
**Editorial:**
Todd Englander .................Editor in Chief
Jeanne O'Brien ................Managing Editor
Kevin Marty ................Marketing Director
**Desc.:** Timely news-features on new or
expanding meeting sites and exhibit
centers; trade show developements,
current meeting planner problems and
ideas, incentive travel trends, market
research data, how-to-do-it case
histories, in-depth site analyses,
legislation transportation trends.
**Readers:** Executives and managers of
corporate offices; trade business,
professional, fraternal, medical and other
associations engaged in planning
meetings, conventions, training
programs, educational programs, or
exhibits.

22357
## MEETINGS & CONVENTIONS
500 Plaza Dr., 5th Fl.
Secaucus, NJ 07094
Telephone: (201) 902-1700
FAX: (201) 319-1796
Year Established: 1966
Pub. Frequency: m.
Page Size: standard
Subscrip. Rate: $64/yr.
Freelance Pay: $100-$1,500
Circulation: 82,000
Circulation Type: paid

**Owner(s):**
Reed Travel Group
500 Plaza Dr.
Secaucus, NJ 07094
Telephone: (201) 902-2000
Ownership %: 100
**Management:**
Mort Silverman ...........................Publisher
**Editorial:**
Lori Cioffi ...........................Editor in Chief
Jay Levin ..................................Exec. Editor
Vincent Alonzo ......................Senior Editor
Larry Letich ............................Senior Editor
Susan Crystal ........................Senior Editor
Lisa Grimaldi ........................Senior Editor
Gregg Lieberman ..................Senior Editor
Dave Higdal ..........................Senior Editor
Amalia Duarte ......................Senior Editor
David Ghitelman ..................Managing Editor
Lauren Libert-Balsamo ...............Art Director
Susanne Fritzlo ..............Assistant Art Director
Alina Dalmau ......................Assistant Editor
Craig Goldberg ...............Associate Art Director
Theresa Katunar ..................Editorial Assistant
Wendy Tiefeulbacker ..........Photography Editor
Bob Buckley ........................Production Editor
Amalia Duarte ...........Special Projects Director
**Desc.:** Articles about all types of meetings
from small company gatherings to large
conventions. Also news of new hotel
building, new convention centers,
new means of transportation, etc.
Information on meeting planning,
logistics, format, audio-visual equipment
used, etc. All feature articles are well
illustrated. Departments include Facilities
in the News, Free Literature, Letters, A-
V at Meetings, New Equipment and
Services, People. Major features
examine the issues and trends that
influence this multi-billion dollar sector,
as well as its effect on destinations and
the overall economy.
**Readers:** Association executives and
company executives. Primarily for the
meeting planner.

52693
## NON-STORE MARKETING REPORT
522 Forest Ave.
Evanston, IL 60202-3005
Telephone: (312) 819-1890
FAX: (708) 866-1899
Year Established: 1979
Pub. Frequency: bi-w.
Page Size: standard
Subscrip. Rate: $245/yr.
Materials: 01,06,30
**Owner(s):**
Maxwell Sroge Publishing, Inc.
522 Forest Ave.
Evanston, IL 60202
Telephone: (708) 866-1890
FAX: (708) 866-1899
Ownership %: 100
**Management:**
Maxwell Sroge ...........................President
**Editorial:**
Ann Meyer ..........................Editor in Chief
**Desc.:** Concise, comprehensive and
authoritative news and analysis
periodical in the area of direct
marketing. Includes detailed news
stories, special reports, financial
features, company profiles and new
technology feature. Provides the facts
behind the news along with informed
commentary.
**Readers:** Upper level management in
leading mail order and other direct
marketing companies throughout the
U.S. and several foreign countries, in
addition to consultations, marketing
professionals in related industries,
service bureaus and suppliers to these
industries.

21664
## POTENTIALS IN MARKETING
50 S. Ninth St.
Minneapolis, MN 55402
Telephone: (612) 333-0471
FAX: (612) 333-6526
Year Established: 1968
Pub. Frequency: m.
Page Size: standard
Subscrip. Rate: free to mktg. personnel;
$24/yr. US;
Freelance Pay: $50-$500/article
Circulation: 62,000
Circulation Type: free & paid
**Owner(s):**
Lakewood Publications
50 S. Ninth St.
Minneapolis, MN 55402
Telephone: (612) 333-0471
Ownership %: 100
**Management:**
Phil Newman ...............................President
Mary Hanson ..............................Publisher
Jamie Gjerdingeb ..........Advertising Manager
**Editorial:**
Catherine Eberlein ...........................Editor
Michele Mills ..................Marketing Director
**Desc.:** Contains information about
incentives, premiums, marketing
services, and incentive travel for
marketing executives.
**Readers:** Brand product managers,
directors of marketing & advertising,
marketing managers, sales promotion,
direct market, and research
professionals of the Fortune 1,000
consumer brands.

69398
## PRESENTATIONS MAGAZINE
23410 Civic Center Way, Ste. E-10
Malibu, CA 90265
Telephone: (310) 456-2283
FAX: (310) 456-8686
Year Established: 1988
Pub. Frequency: bi-m.
Page Size: standard
Subscrip. Rate: $50/yr.
Materials: 01,05,06,15,27,28,29,30,32,33
Print Process: web offset
Circulation: 70,000
Circulation Type: controlled
**Owner(s):**
Lakewood Publications
50 S. Ninth St.
Minneapolis, MN 55402
Telephone: (612) 340-4700
Ownership %: 100
**Editorial:**
Larry Tuck ......................................Editor
**Desc.:** Information for individuals
responsible for the selection of materials
needed to create and
deliver presentations.

21674
## PRODUCT ALERT
33 Academy St.
Naples, NY 14512
Telephone: (716) 374-6326
FAX: (716) 374-5217
Year Established: 1970
Pub. Frequency: Mon.
Page Size: standard
Subscrip. Rate: $600/yr.
**Owner(s):**
Marketing Intelligence Service
33 Academy St.
Naples, NY 14512
Telephone: (716) 374-6326
Ownership %: 100
**Management:**
Richard Lawrence ...........................President
**Editorial:**
Tom Vierhile ..........................Exec. Editor
Diane Beach ....................................Editor
Pat Peck ......................................... Editor

**Desc.:** Primary emphasis on new
consumer product introductions. Actively
seek items on new products, new
packaging, and marketing innovations.
Our primary orientation is consumer
products, but we will run items on
processes that could be used in making
consumer products as well. We
condense releases to important points.
No by-lines given, but inquiries
we receive will be referred to the source
of the information. Departments include:
Foods and Beverages, Non-Prescription
Drugs and Pharmaceuticals, Cosmetics
and Toiletries, Miscellaneous Household
Products, Pet Products.
**Readers:** Marketing executives and
general managers of consumer product
manufacturers, advertising agencies

21677
## SALES & MARKETING MANAGEMENT
355 Park Ave., S., 5th Fl.
New York, NY 10010-1706
Telephone: (212) 592-6200
FAX: (212) 592-6309
Year Established: 1918
Pub. Frequency: 15/yr.
Page Size: standard
Subscrip. Rate: $48/yr.
Freelance Pay: varies
Circulation: 78,000
Circulation Type: paid
**Owner(s):**
Bill Communications, Inc.
355 Park Ave. S., 5th Fl.
New York, NY 10010-1706
Telephone: (212) 592-6200
Ownership %: 100
**Management:**
Anthony Rutigliano ..........................Publisher
Joseph J. Furey ..................Business Manager
**Editorial:**
Charles Butler ..................................Editor
Charles Doherty ..........................Art Director
Marlene Scolod ..................Marketing Director
Daniel O'shea ..............................Treasurer
**Desc.:** Concentrates on the stratergies and
tactics of marketing. Carries information
on developing and managing of the
sales force. Also contains articles on
advertising, promotion, distribution,
meeting, computers, and trade shows.
**Readers:** Company executives who are in
charge of the profitable sale and
marketing of the company products and
services.

68776
## SIGN BUSINESS
P.O. Box 1416
Broomfield, CO 80020
Telephone: (303) 469-0424
FAX: (303) 469-5730
Year Established: 1986
Pub. Frequency: m.
Subscrip. Rate: $38/yr.
Circulation: 20,000
Circulation Type: paid
**Owner(s):**
National Business Media, Inc.
P.O. Box 1416
Broomfield, CO 80020
Telephone: (303) 469-0424
Ownership %: 100
**Editorial:**
Glen Richardon ...............................Editor
**Desc.:** Covers the design, production,
sales and maintenance of all types of
interior and exterior signs.

**Materials Accepted/Included:** 01-Business news 02-By-line articles 03-Fashion news 04-Food news 05-Freelance copy 06-Letters to editor 07-Real estate news 08-Sports news 09-Travel news 10-Book rev. 11-Movie rev. 12-Music rev. 13-TV rev. 14-Theater rev. 15-Coming events 16-Obituaries 17-Question & answer 18-Social announcements 19-Artwork 20-Cartoons 21-Photos 22-TV listings 23-Audio rec. 24-Video rec. 25-Books 26-Films/film clips 27-Personnel news 28-Press releases 29-New product news/photos 30-Trade lit. 31-Contracts awarded 32-Display adv. 33-Classified adv.

## SIGNCRAFT
68773

P.O. Box 06031
Fort Myers, FL 33906
Telephone: (813) 939-4644
FAX: (813) 939-0607
Year Established: 1980
Pub. Frequency: bi-m.
Page Size: standard
Subscrip. Rate: $4.95 newsstand; $25/yr.
Materials: 06,15,17,21,28,29,32,33
Print Process: web
Circulation: 20,000
Circulation Type: paid
**Owner(s):**
Signcraft Publishing Co., Inc.
P.O. Box 06031
Fort Myers, FL 33906
Telephone: (816) 939-4644
Ownership %: 100
**Editorial:**
Tom McIltrot ................................Editor
**Desc.:** Focuses on design, technique and
business management in the commerical
sign shop industry.
**Deadline:** ads-15th of 2nd mo. prior to
pub. date

## SIGNS OF THE TIMES
21682

407 Gilbert Ave.
Cincinnati, OH 45202
Telephone: (513) 421-2050
FAX: (513) 421-5144
Year Established: 1906
Pub. Frequency: 13/yr. (Buyers Guide mid-
Dec.)
Page Size: standard
Subscrip. Rate: $4/copy; $36/yr. in US;
$56/yr. in Canada
Freelance Pay: $50-$500/article
Circulation: 16,000
Circulation Type: controlled & paid
**Owner(s):**
Signs of the Times Publishing Co.
407 Gilbert Ave.
Cincinnati, OH 45202
Telephone: (513) 421-2050
Ownership %: 100
**Management:**
Dave R. Swormstedt, Jr. .....Chairman of Board
Jerry Swormstedt ................................President
Tod Swormstedt ................................Publisher
Bill Wright ................................Circulation Manager
Duane Karr ................................Office Manager

**Editorial:**
John Tymoski ................................Managing Editor
Magno Relojo ................................Art Director
Vickie Howard ................................Marketing Coordinator
Jennifer Waldeck ................................Production Coordinator
**Desc.:** Includes "state of the art" coverage
of the sign and environmental graphics
industries, with particular attention to the
people, products, techniques and events
within these industries.
**Readers:** Sign companies, sign supply
distributors, equipment and component
manufacturers, architects, and users of
signs as well as schools, libraries and
other institutions.

## SPECIALTY ADVERTISING BUSINESS
69393

3125 Skyway Cir., N.
Irving, TX 75038-3526
Telephone: (214) 252-0404
FAX: (214) 594-7224
Year Established: 1976
Pub. Frequency: m
Subscrip. Rate: $48/yr.
Circulation: 6,000

**Owner(s):**
Specialty Advertising Association
International
3125 Skyway Cir., N.
Irving, TX 75038-3526
Telephone: (214) 252-0404
Ownership %: 100
**Editorial:**
Leonard Strub ................................Editor
**Desc.:** Provides in-depth communication
with association members and others in
the specialty advertising and promotional
product industry.

## SPECIALTY ADVERTISING JOURNAL
68774

SARI Bldg.
Stuart, FL 34995
Telephone: (407) 337-2808
Mailing Address:
P.O. Box 88
Stuart, FL 34995-0088
Year Established: 1979
Pub. Frequency: m.
Page Size: tabloid
Subscrip. Rate: $79/yr.
Materials: 01,20,29,30,32,33
Print Process: web offset
Circulation: 14,000
Circulation Type: controlled & paid
**Owner(s):**
Specialty Advertising Review, Inc.
P.O. Box 88
Stuart, FL 34995-0088
Telephone: (407) 337-2808
Ownership %: 100
**Editorial:**
Weldon T. Hargrave ................................Editor
**Deadline:** ads-3rd Wed. of mo.

## ST. LOUIS ADVERTISING
21638

305 N. Broadway
St. Louis, MO 63102
Telephone: (314) 231-4185
FAX: (314) 231-4188
Year Established: 1901
Pub. Frequency: bi-m.
Page Size: standard
Subscrip. Rate: $5/yr.
Circulation: 1,000
Circulation Type: paid
**Owner(s):**
Advertising Club of Greater St. Louis
305 N. Broadway
Saint Louis, MO 63102
Telephone: (314) 231-4185
Ownership %: 100
**Management:**
Tom Koon ................................Executive Director
Jerry Maschan ................................Advertising Manager
**Editorial:**
Tom Koon ................................Editor
**Desc.:** Desires releases concerning
advertising and the graphic arts fields.
Interested in releases on marketing
studies; advertising and sales books.
Staff-written. Official publication of Ad
Club of St. Louis.
**Readers:** Advertising and graphic arts
executives in Missouri.

## SUCCESSFUL MEETINGS
21685

355 Park Ave., S.
New York, NY 10011-1706
Telephone: (212) 592-6200
Year Established: 1952
Pub. Frequency: m.
Page Size: standard
Subscrip. Rate: $48/yr. US; $65/yr. foreign
Freelance Pay: negotiable
Circulation: 77,000
Circulation Type: controlled

**Owner(s):**
Bill Communications, Inc.
633 Third Ave.
New York, NY 10017
Telephone: (212) 986-4800
Ownership %: 100
**Bureau:**
Successful Meetings
633 Third Ave.
New York, NY 10017
Telephone: (212) 986-4800
Contact: Irwin Levine, Executive Vice
President
**Management:**
Richard O'Connor ................................Publisher
**Editorial:**
Richard O'Connor ................................Exec. Editor
Martin Feldman ................................Advertising
Donald Salkaln ................................Art Department
Tom Ludlow ................................Marketing Director
**Desc.:** Company presidents, vice-
presidents, marketing executives,
promotion managers, association
executives, convention and
show managers, training directors,
exhibit managers, incentive travel
managers.
**Readers:** Planners of Meetings,
Conventions, Trade Shows and Incentive
Travel.

## TARGET MARKETING
22783

401 N. Broad St.
Philadelphia, PA 19108
Telephone: (215) 238-5300
FAX: (215) 238-5457
Year Established: 1978
Pub. Frequency: m.
Page Size: standard
Subscrip. Rate: $65/yr. US; $80/yr. foreign
Freelance Pay: $150/article
Circulation: 36,051
Circulation Type: controlled
**Owner(s):**
North American Publishing Co.
401 N. Broad St.
Philadelphia, PA 19108
Telephone: (215) 238-5300
Ownership %: 100
**Management:**
Irvin Borowsky ................................Chairman of Board
Ned Borowsky ................................President
Jo Anne Parke ................................Vice President
Andrea Nierenberg ................................Publisher
Claire Burnett ................................Circulation Manager
**Editorial:**
Dennison Hatch ................................Editor
**Desc.:** Covers all aspects of selling and
marketing through the mail and other
direct response media. For writers,
designers, catalogers, printers, list
managers and those in allied industries
for the latest news in regulations, direct
marketing techniques, equipment, and
marketing strategy.
**Readers:** Advertising and marketing
managers, circulation and fulfillment
directors, list managers, mail operations
managers, administrative managers,
mail-order companies, fund raisers,
customer service managers.

# Group 006-Antiques & Collectibles

## AMERICAN COLLECTOR'S JOURNAL, THE
59654

206 W. Fourth St.
Kewanee, IL 61443
Telephone: (309) 852-2602
Mailing Address:
P.O. Box 407
Kewanee, IL 61443
Year Established: 1963

Pub. Frequency: bi-m.
Page Size: tabloid
Subscrip. Rate: $1 newsstand; $4.25/yr.
Materials: 02,10,15,17,32,33
Freelance Pay: $20
Print Process: web offset
Circulation: 51,000
Circulation Type: paid
**Owner(s):**
American Collector's Journal Publishing
Co.
P.O. Box 407
Kewanee, IL 61443
Telephone: (309) 853-8441
Ownership %: 100
**Management:**
William Harper ................................Publisher
William Harper ................................Advertising Manager
**Editorial:**
Carol Savidge ................................Editor
**Desc.:** News and advertising of interest to
antiquers and collectors.
**Readers:** Those interested in antiques and
collectibles.
**Deadline:** story-15th of mo. prior to pub.
date; news-15th of mo. prior; ads-15th of
mo. prior

## ANTIQUES & COLLECTING MAGAZINE
53962

1006 S. Michigan Ave.
Chicago, IL 60605
Telephone: (312) 939-4767
FAX: (312) 939-0053
Year Established: 1931
Pub. Frequency: m.
Page Size: standard
Subscrip. Rate: $2.95 newsstand US;
$3.95 Canada; $24/yr. US
Materials: 01,05,06,10,32,33
Freelance Pay: $100-$200/article
Circulation: 18,000
Circulation Type: free & paid
**Owner(s):**
Dale K. Graham
1006 S. Michigan Ave.
Chicago, IL 60605
Telephone: (312) 939-4767
Ownership %: 90

Gregory K. Graham
1006 S. Michigan Ave.
Chicago, IL 60605
Telephone: (312) 939-4767
Ownership %: 10
**Readers:** Antique & limited edition
collectors, antique dealers &
associations, antique show & flea
market promoters.
**Deadline:** story-Apr. 15 prior to pub. date;
news-Apr. 15 prior; photo-Apr. 15 prior;
ads-May 1 prior to pub. date

## ANTIQUE TRADER PRICE GUIDE TO ANTIQUES & COLLECTIBLE'S
68881

100 Bryant St.
Dubuque, IA 52004-1050
Telephone: (319) 588-2073
FAX: (800) 531-0880
Mailing Address:
P.O. Box 1050-PG
Dubuque, IA 52004
Year Established: 1970
Pub. Frequency: a.
Page Size: standard
Subscrip. Rate: $13.50/yr.
Circulation: 85,000
Circulation Type: paid

**Materials Accepted/Included:** 01-Business news 02-By-line articles 03-Fashion news 04-Food news 05-Freelance copy 06-Letters to editor 07-Real estate news 08-Sports news 09-Travel news 10-Book rev. 11-Movie rev. 12-Music rev. 13-TV rev. 14-Theater rev. 15-Coming events 16-Obituaries 17-Question & answer 18-Social announcements 19-Artwork 20-Cartoons 21-Photos 22-TV listings 23-Audio rec. 24-Video rec. 25-Books 26-Films/film clips 27-Personnel news 28-Press releases 29-New product news/photos 30-Trade lit. 31-Contracts awarded 32-Display adv. 33-Classified adv.

4-9

**Owner(s):**
Antique Trader
P.O. Box 1050-PG
Dubuque, IA 52004-1050
Telephone: (319) 588-2073
Ownership %: 100
**Editorial:**
Kyle Husfloen .............................Editor
**Desc.:** Covers all categories of antiques and collectibles and their current market values.

### ANTIQUING AMERICA
68884
650 Westdale Dr.
Wichita, KS 67209
Telephone: (316) 946-0600
FAX: (316) 946-0675
Year Established: 1981
Pub. Frequency: bi-m.
Subscrip. Rate: $24/yr.
Circulation: 35,000
Circulation Type: paid
**Owner(s):**
Web Publications
650 Westdale Dr.
Wichita, KS 67209
Telephone: (316) 946-0600
Ownership %: 100
**Editorial:**
Jesse Mullins .............................Editor
**Desc.:** Covers antique market trends, trade, travel and market reports.

### GOLDMINE
58794
700 E. State St.
Iola, WI 54990
Telephone: (715) 445-2214
Year Established: 1974
Pub. Frequency: bi-w.
Page Size: tabloid
Subscrip. Rate: $2.50 newsstand; $35/yr.
Materials: 02,05,06,12,23,24,25,32,33
Freelance Pay: varies
Print Process: offset
Circulation: 30,600
Circulation Type: paid
**Owner(s):**
Krause Publications, Inc.
700 E. State St.
Iola, WI 54990
Telephone: (715) 445-2214
FAX: (715) 445-4087
Ownership %: 100
**Management:**
Greg Loescher .........................Publisher
Jim Felhofer ...............Advertising Manager
**Editorial:**
Jeff Tamarkin ...........................Editor
**Desc.:** Goldmine covers rare, out-of-print records as well as news releases, reissues, compact discs, music books and videos - anything collectible in all musical persuasions and eras from the 1940's to the 1990's. It contains articles and columns on recording artists of the past and present, discographies, and a record show calendar. Collectors buy, sell, and trade recordings in ads.
**Readers:** Primarily male, average age is 36.

### MAGAZINE ANTIQUES, THE
21729
575 Broadway
New York, NY 10012
Telephone: (212) 941-2800
FAX: (212) 941-2819
Year Established: 1922
Pub. Frequency: m.
Page Size: oversize
Subscrip. Rate: $5/copy; $38/yr.
Freelance Pay: varies
Circulation: 61,807
Circulation Type: paid

**Owner(s):**
Brant Publications, Inc.
575 Broadway
New York, NY 10012
Telephone: (212) 941-2800
Ownership %: 100
**Management:**
Sandra Brant .........................Publisher
**Editorial:**
Alfred Mayor ..................Executive Editor
Allison E. Ledes ........................Editor
Allison Ledes ...........Book Review Editor
Eleanor H. Gustafson ...........Miscellaneous
Mary Anne Hunting .............Miscellaneous
**Desc.:** The magazine deals primarily with American antiques and European antiques which have contributed to the development of an American style and tradition. It is advisable for an author to submit a query outlining his/her ideas before going ahead on an article. Most articles are of interest principally to collectors of seventeenth through nineteenth century antiques/furniture, paintings, ceramics, glass, prints, silver, textiles, etc. The material must present fresh ideas or research, be authoritative, and be written in a clear, expository style. Departments include: Current and Coming, Museum Accessions, Books About Antiques, Collectors Notes, Queries.
**Readers:** Collectors, architects, decorators, historians in field of art, antiques and preservation.

### NEW YORK ANTIQUE ALMANAC
68887
P.O. Box 335
Lawrence, NY 11559
Telephone: (516) 371-3300
FAX: (516) 371-3303
Year Established: 1975
Pub. Frequency: 10/yr.
Subscrip. Rate: $10/yr. US; $24/yr. foreign
Circulation: 61,000
Circulation Type: paid
**Owner(s):**
New York Eye Publishing Co., Inc.
P.O. Box 335
Lawrence, NY 11559
Telephone: (516) 371-3300
Ownership %: 100
**Editorial:**
Carol Nadel .............................Editor

### PRICE GUIDE
68888
100 Bryant St.
Dubuque, IA 52004-1050
Telephone: (319) 588-2073
FAX: (319) 588-2073
Mailing Address:
   P.O. Box 1050
   Dubuque, IA 52004-1050
Year Established: 1970
Pub. Frequency: bi-m.
Subscrip. Rate: $13.50/yr.
Circulation: 85,000
Circulation Type: paid
**Owner(s):**
Antique Trader
P.O. Box 1050
Dubuque, IA 52004-1050
Telephone: (319) 588-2073
Ownership %: 100
**Editorial:**
Kyle Husfloen .............................Editor

### RESTORATION MAGAZINE
57270
P.O. Box 50046
Tucson, AZ 85703-1046
Telephone: (602) 622-2201
Year Established: 1983
Pub. Frequency: q.

Page Size: standard
Subscrip. Rate: $15/yr., includes membership in ISVP
Materials: 01,05,06,08,09,10,11,13,15,16, 17,19,20,21,23,24,25,26,28,29,30,32,33
Print Process: web offset
Circulation: 15,000
Circulation Type: paid
**Owner(s):**
International Society for Vehicle Preservation
P.O. Box 50046
Tucson, AZ 85703-1046
Telephone: (602) 622-2201
Ownership %: 100
**Management:**
Elaine Jordan .................Office Manager
**Editorial:**
Walter R. Haessner .......................Editor
Bob Brown ....................Associate Editor
**Desc.:** Designed to foster the preservation and restoration of historical buildings, bridges, engines, fire equipment, tools, aircraft, industrial equipment, boats, self-propelled vehicles and related artifacts. Included are tips and techniques of restoration, product news and reporting on legislation affecting such vehicles including structures related to subject.
**Readers:** Affluent preservation oriented people, do-it-yourself restorers, collectors, and history enthusiasts.

## Group 008-Apparel-Men's, Women's & Children's

### ACCESSORIES
22973
50 Day St.
Norwalk, CT 06854
Telephone: (203) 853-6015
FAX: (203) 852-8175
Mailing Address:
   P.O. Box 5550
   Norwalk, CT 06856
Year Established: 1908
Pub. Frequency: m.
Page Size: standard
Subscrip. Rate: $4/issue; $35/yr.
Freelance Pay: $300-$700/article
Circulation: 22,000
Circulation Type: paid
**Owner(s):**
Business Journals, Inc.
50 Day St.
Norwalk, CT 06856
Telephone: (203) 853-6015
Ownership %: 100
**Management:**
G. Renfrew Brighton ...........Chairman of Board
**Editorial:**
Karen Alberg .............................Editor
Vanessa Grey ...............Managing Editor
Stuart Nifoussi .................Associate Publisher
Arthur Heilman ...............Circulation Editor
Karen Alberg ...................Miscellaneous
Phyllis Meyer ...................Miscellaneous
**Desc.:** Features cover merchandising successes, advertising, display ideas, etc. Products covered are handbags, personal leather goods, accessories, gloves, belts, jewelry. Covers news about suppliers.
**Readers:** Retailers: merchandise managers, buyers, other retail execs, accessories manufacturers, sales reps, designers.

### APPAREL INDUSTRY MAGAZINE
22682
6255 Barfield Rd.
Ste. 200
Atlanta, GA 30328-4300
Telephone: (404) 252-8831
FAX: (404) 252-4436
Year Established: 1946

Pub. Frequency: m.
Page Size: standard
Subscrip. Rate: $51/yr. Mexico & Canada; $77/yr. elsewhere; $179/yr. foreign airmail
Freelance Pay: $.20/wd.
Circulation: 18,600
Circulation Type: controlled & paid
**Owner(s):**
Shore Communications, Inc.
6255 Barfield Rd.
Ste. 200
Atlanta, GA 30328-4300
Telephone: (404) 252-8831
Ownership %: 100
**Management:**
Douglas Shore ...............Chairman of Board
Karen Schaffner ......................Publisher
**Editorial:**
Elissa McCrary .....................Senior Editor
Susan Hasty .............................Editor
Barbara Foxenburger .............Managing Editor
Karen Schaffner ...................Editorial Director
Kimberly Easley .................Editor Assistant
Jackie Loudin ...................Production Director
**Desc.:** Contributed and staff-written features covering production, distribution, marketing, design, style, trends, textiles, machinery, equipment, processes, accounting, labor relations, management, legislation.
**Readers:** Apparel manufacturers and contractors.

### APPAREL MARKETING DIGEST
68819
300 N. Washington St.
Alexandria, VA 22314
Telephone: (703) 549-8608
FAX: (703) 549-1372
Year Established: 1988
Pub. Frequency: m.
Page Size: standard
Subscrip. Rate: $120/yr.
**Owner(s):**
Wakeman-Walworth, Inc.
300 N. Washington St.
Alexandria, VA 22314
Telephone: (703) 549-8608
Ownership %: 100
**Desc.:** Alerts readers to marketing activities within the apparel industry, as well as other developments that could have impact on the marketing of apparel.

### APPAREL NEWS GROUP, THE
22684
California Mart
110 E. Ninth St., Ste. A-777
Los Angeles, CA 90795-1777
Telephone: (213) 627-3737
Year Established: 1944
Pub. Frequency: w.
Page Size: tabloid
Subscrip. Rate: $36/yr.
Materials: 03,21,27,28,29,30,32,33
Freelance Pay: varies
Circulation: 50,000
Circulation Type: controlled
**Owner(s):**
M & M Publishing Corp.
110 E. Ninth St., Ste. A-777
Los Angeles, CA 90079
Telephone: (213) 627-3737
Ownership %: 100
**Bureau(s):**
New York Apparel News
1501 Broadway, Ste. 1508
New York, NY 10036
Telephone: (212) 221-8288
Contact: Avis Cardella, Fashion Editor

Materials Accepted/Included: 01-Business news 02-By-line articles 03-Fashion news 04-Food news 05-Freelance copy 06-Letters to editor 07-Real estate news 08-Sports news 09-Travel news 10-Book rev. 11-Movie rev. 12-Music rev. 13-TV rev. 14-Theater rev. 15-Coming events 16-Obituaries 17-Question & answer 18-Social announcements 19-Artwork 20-Cartoons 21-Photos 22-TV listings 23-Audio rec. 24-Video rec. 25-Books 26-Films/film clips 27-Personnel news 28-Press releases 29-New product news/photos 30-Trade lit. 31-Contracts awarded 32-Display adv. 33-Classified adv.

**Dallas Apparel News**
2300 Stemmons Fwy., Ste. 6G44
Dallas, TX 75258
Telephone: (214) 631-6089
Contact: Kit Ring, Editor

**Chicago Apparel News**
139 Arcade 350 N. Orleans
Chicago, IL 60654
Telephone: (312) 670-2230
Contact: Ann Keeton, Editor

**Atlanta Apparel News**
250 Spring St., N.W., Ste.1W10
Atlanta, GA 30303
Telephone: (404) 688-6830
Contact: Kit Ring, Editor
**Management:**
Martin Wernicke ................................Publisher
**Editorial:**
Anne Harnagel .........................Executive Editor
Cyce Bayle ...............................Managing Editor
Bonnie McAllister ..........................Fashion Editor
Louise Damburg ..................Marketing Director
Kristi Ellis ....................................News Editor
Rick Swinger ........................................Photo
Sharon Miro ..........................................Sales
**Desc.:** News of the western states'
apparel industry on meetings, etc. Takes
own pictures of personalities.
**Readers:** Retailers, merchandise
managers, department stores, chain
stores, boutiques, manufacturers, and
designers.

**BOBBIN**                                          22269
1110 Shop Rd.
Columbia, SC 29201
Telephone: (803) 771-7500
FAX: (803) 799-1461
Mailing Address:
P.O. Box 1986
Columbia, SC 29202
Year Established: 1959
Pub. Frequency: m.
Page Size: standard
Subscrip. Rate: $48/yr.
Materials: 01,02,06,15,17,27,28,29,30,32,33
Freelance Pay: negotiable
Circulation: 9,788
Circulation Type: paid
**Owner(s):**
Blenheim Group
636 Chiswick Rd.
Columbia, SC 29202
Ownership %: 100
**Management:**
Manuel Gaetan ...................Chairman of Board
Betty Webb Moore ..................Executive Vice
President
Manuel Gaetan ................................Publisher
Jackie Ellen .........................Advertising Manager
Yvette Williams .................Circulation Manager
**Editorial:**
Susan S. Black ...................................Editor
Barbara Rose ...............................Advertising
Janyce Collins ...........................Art Director
**Desc.:** Independent monthly magazine in
the sewn products industry. Completely
devoted to all management levels.
Emphasis on production, new products,
research, personnel, and legislation
affecting sewn products. The Bobbin is
a member of the American Business
Press and Audit Bureau of Circulations.
**Readers:** Executives engaged in apparel
plants, companies and others related to
the sewn products industry.
**Deadline:** story-2 mos. prior to pub. date;
news-2 mos. prior; photo-2 mos. prior

**BODY FASHIONS/INTIMATE**           22683
**APPAREL**
7500 Old Oak Blvd.
Cleveland, OH 44130
Telephone: (216) 826-2839
FAX: (216) 891-2726
Year Established: 1913
Pub. Frequency: m.
Page Size: tabloid
Subscrip. Rate: $30/yr.; $68/yr. in Canada
& Mexico; $120/yr. foreign
Circulation: 8,010
Circulation Type: paid
**Owner(s):**
Advanstar Communications, Inc.
7500 Old Oak Blvd.
Cleveland, OH 44130
Telephone: (216) 826-2839
Ownership %: 100
**Management:**
Jill Gerson-Price ................................Publisher
Darryl Arquitte ...................Circulation Manager
**Editorial:**
Linda Harrison ..........................Editor in Chief
Lillian Hempel ...............Administrative Assistant
**Desc.:** Articles cover selling, new fashions,
news of buyers and retailers, market
news, industry news, supplier news and
trends, management of retail stores and
departments.
**Readers:** Retail executives, merchandising
managers, buyers of intimate apparel,
intimate apparel manufacturers,
purchasing agents and designers.

**CLOTHING & TEXTILES**                  69437
**RESEARCH JOURNAL**
P.O. Box 1360
Monument, CO 80132-1360
Telephone: (719) 488-3716
FAX: (716) 897-6723
Year Established: 1982
Pub. Frequency: q.
Subscrip. Rate: $45/yr.
Circulation: 1,010
Circulation Type: free & paid
**Owner(s):**
International Textile and Apparel
Association
P.O. Box 1360
Monument, CO 80132
Telephone: (719) 488-3716
**Editorial:**
Joan Laughlin ...................................Editor
**Desc.:** Presents the latest research on all
areas of clothing and textiles.
**Readers:** academic mainly

**DALLAS APPAREL NEWS**               61601
P.O. Box 586398
Dallas, TX 75258
Telephone: (214) 631-6089
Year Established: 1980
Pub. Frequency: 5/yr.
Page Size: standard
Subscrip. Rate: $36/yr.
Freelance Pay: negotiable
Circulation: 22,000
Circulation Type: controlled
**Owner(s):**
M & M Publishing Corp.
110 E. Ninth St., A-777
Los Angeles, CA 90079
Telephone: (310) 627-3737
Ownership %: 100
**Management:**
Shirley Speaker ...............................Manager
**Editorial:**
Annette Stark ...................................Editor
**Readers:** Apparel, Textile Manufacturers &
Retailers

**EARNSHAW'S INFANTS BOYS**          22671
**AND GIRLS REVIEW**
225 W. 34th St.
New York, NY 10122
Telephone: (212) 563-2742
Year Established: 1917
Pub. Frequency: m.
Page Size: standard
Subscrip. Rate: $3/issue; $24/yr.
Freelance Pay: inquiry only
Circulation: 12,000
Circulation Type: paid
**Owner(s):**
Earnshaw Publications, Inc.
225 W. 34th St.
New York, NY 10122
Telephone: (212) 563-2742
Ownership %: 100
**Bureau(s):**
Earnshaw Publications
110 E. 9th St., A-704
Los Angeles, CA 90079
Telephone: (310) 563-2742
Contact: Patricia Schumann, Advertising
Manager
**Management:**
Thomas W. Hudson, Jr. ...................President
Thomas W. Hudson, Jr. ...................Publisher
**Editorial:**
Jim Girone ...................................Editor
Vanessa Groce ....................Associate Editor
**Desc.:** Merchandising, department
management, promotion display for the
buyer of infants', children's, boys' and
girls' wear. Uses by-line features as well
as staff-written articles. Uses personals,
trade news, notes about shops.
Features on industry news, retail events
and licensing as monthly articles.
**Readers:** Infants', children's boys' and
girls' wear buyers, merchandise
personnel at discount, department and
specialty stores; resident buying offices;
licensers and licensees.

**FASHION CALENDAR**                  69450
153 E. 87th St.
New York, NY 10128
Telephone: (212) 289-0420
FAX: (212) 289-5917
Year Established: 1941
Pub. Frequency: bi-m.
Subscrip. Rate: $365/yr.
**Owner(s):**
Fashion Calendar International
153 E. 87th St.
New York, NY 10128
Telephone: (212) 289-0420
Ownership %: 100
**Desc.:** Covers national and international
fashion events and collection openings.
**Readers:** Targeted to buyers, designers,
manufacturers, retailers and the media.

**FEMME-LINES**                        22685
225 E. 36th St.
New York, NY 10016
Telephone: (212) 683-6593
Year Established: 1956
Pub. Frequency: bi-m.
Page Size: standard
Subscrip. Rate: $2 newsstand; $10/yr.
Circulation: 12,000
Circulation Type: controlled & paid
**Owner(s):**
Earl Barron Publications, Inc.
225 E. 36th St.
New York, NY 10016
Telephone: (212) 683-6593
Ownership %: 100
**Management:**
Earl Barron ...................................Publisher
S. B. Pratt ....................Advertising Manager

**Editorial:**
Earl Barron ...................................Editor
Max Menikoff ...................................Photo
**Desc.:** Feature articles emphasize trends
in products and techniques, as well as
how-to methods, all aimed to help
manufacturers produce and market
profitably and efficiently. News sections
report on developments involving
companies, materials, equipment,
organizations and personnel.
**Readers:** Executives and managers of
production, marketing, purchasing,
administration and personnel, for
manufacturers of feminine garments.

**FORMALWORDS**                        69454
401 N. Michigan Ave.
Chicago, IL 60611
FAX: (312) 321-6869
Year Established: 1987
Pub. Frequency: q.
Subscrip. Rate: free membership
Circulation: 450
**Owner(s):**
International Formalwear Association
401 N. Michigan Ave.
Chicago, IL 60611
Telephone: (312) 321-6869
Ownership %: 100
**Editorial:**
Annette Claussen ...................................Editor

**IMPRESSIONS MAGAZINE**              22331
13760 Noel Rd., Ste. 500
Dallas, TX 75240
Telephone: (800) 527-0207
FAX: (212) 302-6273
Year Established: 1977
Pub. Frequency: 15/yr.
Page Size: standard
Subscrip. Rate: $36/yr.
Freelance Pay: $150-$300/article
Circulation: 30,000
Circulation Type: paid
**Owner(s):**
Miller Freeman, Inc.
1515 Broadway
New York, NY 10036
Telephone: (212) 869-1300
Ownership %: 100
**Management:**
Darrell Denny ...................................Publisher
Irene Lopez ....................Circulation Manager
Jackie James ...................................Manager
Deborah White ..................Promotion Manager
**Editorial:**
Deborah Sexton ...................................Editor
Carl Piazza ....................Associate Publisher
Cindy Mazzola ..................Production Director
**Desc.:** Contains news articles and stories
which report on the development and
activities relating to imprintable or
imprinted sportswear and textiles.
Feature stories of people, products, and
happenings related to the industry are
welcome, subject to editor's approval.
Departments include: Letters to Editor,
Answerman, News Briefs, Shop Notes,
Selling Slants, Product Preview, Open
for Business, Business Management,
The Law, International Market Place.
**Readers:** Imprinted sportswear retailers,
textile screen printers, wholesalers and
distributors, embroiderers, department
and chain store buyers, sporting goods
retailers and other buyers allied to the
field.

**INTIMATE FASHION NEWS**            22686
309 Fifth Ave.
New York, NY 10016
Telephone: (212) 679-6677
FAX: (212) 679-6374

**Materials Accepted/Included:** 01-Business news 02-By-line articles 03-Fashion news 04-Food news 05-Freelance copy 06-Letters to editor 07-Real estate news 08-Sports news 09-Travel news 10-Book rev. 11-Movie rev. 12-Music rev. 13-TV rev. 14-Theater rev. 15-Coming events 16-Obituaries 17-Question & answer 18-Social announcements 19-Artwork 20-Cartoons 21-Photos 22-TV listings 23-Audio rec. 24-Video rec. 25-Books 26-Films/film clips 27-Personnel news 28-Press releases 29-New product news/photos 30-Trade lit. 31-Contracts awarded 32-Display adv. 33-Classified adv.

4-11

Year Established: 1895
Pub. Frequency: s-m.: 1st & 3rd Mon.
Page Size: tabloid
Subscrip. Rate: $25/yr.; $50/3 yrs.
Materials: 01,02,03,06,15,16,18,21,27,28,
  29,30,32,33
Print Process: offset
Circulation: 9,500
Circulation Type: paid
Owner(s):
Mackay Publishing Corp.
309 Fifth Ave.
New York, NY 10016
Telephone: (212) 679-6677
FAX: (212) 679-6374
Ownership %: 100
Management:
Milton J. Kristt .........................President
Milton J. Kristt .........................Publisher
Alan Szylowski .................Advertising Manager
Editorial:
Milton J. Kristt .....................Executive Editor
Desc.: Use feature stories about retailers
  showing new methods, success stories,
  etc. News stories about new shops or
  departments. No by-lines used except in
  exceptional cases. Also new product
  stories that pertain directly to industry,
  news of personnel changes. Also
  outstanding promotional stories (short)
  telling what corset, brassiere and lingerie
  manufacturers plan to do. Departments
  include: Retail News, Personnel News,
  News of the Trade, News of Suppliers,
  Obituaries, Intimate Fashions (market
  report).
Readers: Retailers, manufacturers and
  manufacturing suppliers of corsets,
  brassieres and lingerie.
Deadline: story-10 days prior to pub. date;
  news-10 days prior; photo-10 days prior;
  ads-5 days prior

22672
**JUVENILE MERCHANDISING**
370 Lexington Ave.
New York, NY 10017
Telephone: (212) 532-9290
Year Established: 1945
Pub. Frequency: m.
Page Size: standard
Subscrip. Rate: $25/yr.; $35/2 yrs.; $75/yr.
  foreign
Freelance Pay: $250/article
Circulation: 11,500
Circulation Type: controlled & paid
Owner(s):
Columbia Communications, Inc.
370 Lexington Ave.
New York, NY 10017
Telephone: (212) 532-9290
Ownership %: 100
Management:
Joseph Feldmann ......................President
Claudia DeSimone .....................Publisher
Dempsey Herlihy ..............Advertising Manager
Despina Leontarakis ..........Business Manager
Editorial:
Claudia De Simone ........................Editor
Desc.: Interested in news and features of
  interest to juvenile furniture, infants'
  wear, wheel goods, toy (and related
  lines) dealers. Includes news and
  pictures of new products in these fields,
  special displays and promotions, store
  profiles, market coverage reports of
  trade shows.
Readers: Juvenile furniture stores,
  discount stores, manufacturers and
  wholesalers, and department stores.

54051
**KIDS FASHIONS MAGAZINE**
100 Wells Ave.
Newton Center, MA 02159
Telephone: (617) 964-5100

Mailing Address:
  P.O. Box 9103
  Newton Center, MA 02159-9103
Year Established: 1976
Pub. Frequency: m.
Page Size: standard
Subscrip. Rate: $26/yr.
Freelance Pay: $150-$200/article
Circulation: 18,000
Circulation Type: controlled
Owner(s):
Larkin-Pluznick-Larkin, Inc.
100 Wells Ave.
Newton Center, MA 02159
Telephone: (617) 964-5100
Ownership %: 50
Bureau(s):
Kids Fashions Magazine
485 Seventh Ave., Ste. 1400
New York, NY 10018
Telephone: (212) 594-0880
Management:
Harold Larkin ..........................Publisher
Barbara Platt ....................Business Manager
Elayne Selig ....................Circulation Manager
Editorial:
Holly Himmelfarb ..........................Editor
Joanna Drew ...........................Art Director
Gerald Kaplow .....................Production Director
Stanley Kaye ....................Publication Director
Desc.: Written for retailers involved in the
  buying & merchandising of boys & girls
  apparel & accessories, the editorial
  focus is on fashion trends with photo
  layouts, designer interviews,
  merchandising reports, and market
  surveys.
Readers: Retailers, children's wear stores,
  boys specialty shops, department
  stores, chains & discount department
  stores. Resident buying offices,
  manufacturers, reps, distributors, media.

66325
**LA BOBINA NOTIVEST**
1110 Shop Rd.
Columbia, SC 29201
Telephone: (803) 771-7500
FAX: (803) 799-1461
Mailing Address:
  P.O. Box 1986
  Columbia, SC 29202
Year Established: 1968
Pub. Frequency: m.
Page Size: standard
Subscrip. Rate: free
Materials: 01,02,03,06,15,17,19,21,27,28,
  29,30,32,33
Freelance Pay: negotiable
Print Process: offset
Circulation: 13,000
Circulation Type: controlled
Owner(s):
Bobbin Blenheim Media Corp.
1110 Shop Rd.
Columbia, SC 29201
Telephone: (803) 771-7500
FAX: (803) 799-1461
Management:
Betty Webb ............................Publisher
Editorial:
Amy Gabriel ..............................Editor
Gabriela Wheeler .................Editorial Assistant
Desc.: Monthy mag. published in Spanish
  to apparel/sewn products mfrs. in Latin
  American Countries.
Readers: Spanish-speaking apparel/sewn
  products manufacturers.

22677
**MASCULINES**
225 E. 36th St.
New York, NY 10016
Telephone: (212) 683-6593
Year Established: 1956
Pub. Frequency: bi-m.

Page Size: standard
Subscrip. Rate: $10/yr.
Circulation: 9,000
Circulation Type: paid
Owner(s):
Earl Barron Publications, Inc.
225 E. 36th St.
New York, NY 10016
Telephone: (212) 683-6593
Ownership %: 100
Management:
Earl Barron ............................Publisher
S. B. Pratt ......................Advertising Manager
Editorial:
Earl Barron ..............................Editor
Max Menikoff ..............................Photo
Desc.: Feature articles emphasize trends
  in product development. New sections
  report on developments involving
  company personnel.
Readers: Firms and major executives of
  male garment manufacturers.

22687
**NEEDLE'S EYE, THE**
One Union Special Plz.
Huntley, IL 60142
Telephone: (708) 669-5101
Year Established: 1930
Pub. Frequency: bi-m
Page Size: standard
Subscrip. Rate: free
Materials: 01,03,09,28
Circulation: 35,000
Circulation Type: free
Owner(s):
Union Special Corp.
One Union Special Plz.
Huntley, IL 60142
Telephone: (708) 669-5101
FAX: (708) 669-3534
Ownership %: 100
Editorial:
John Caschetto ......................Executive Editor
Sharon McNelis ...........................Editor
William Creighton ...................Managing Editor
Daniel Kennedy .....................Associate Editor
Desc.: A sales promotion publication for
  Union Special Corporation
  (manufacturers of industrial sewing
  machines and automated equipment).
  The feature articles generally highlight
  the use of our machines in various types
  of sewing plants. These "plant write-
  ups" explain how a particular plant
  functions, meets production problems,
  deals with its labor force, etc. Technical
  articles are geared to aid in solving or
  easing production problems. The
  remainder of the editorial space is
  devoted to news of general interest to
  the needle trades, with the remainder
  devoted to company news, new
  machines, personnel changes, technical
  training , etc.
Readers: Sewing plant managers,
  production managers, suppliers, persons
  involved with the teaching.

61629
**NEW YORK APPAREL NEWS**
1501 Broadway, Ste. 1508
New York, NY 10018-3501
Telephone: (212) 221-8288
FAX: (212) 302-5932
Year Established: 1945
Pub. Frequency: 5/yr.
Page Size: standard
Subscrip. Rate: $36/yr.
Materials: 01,03,28,29,32,33
Circulation: 26,167
Circulation Type: paid

Owner(s):
M & M Publishing Corp.
110 E. 9th St., A-777
Los Angeles, CA 90079
Telephone: (213) 627-3737
FAX: (213) 623-5707
Ownership %: 100
Management:
Mary Rhodes ...........................Manager
Editorial:
Avis Cardella ...........................Editor
Desc.: For apparel retailers and
  manufacturers, with emphasis on the
  Northeast region.
Readers: Apparel manufacturers and
  retailers.

54048
**SPORTSTYLE**
7 W. 34th St.
New York, NY 10001
Telephone: (212) 630-4000
FAX: (212) 630-4879
Pub. Frequency: 18/yr.
Page Size: oversize
Subscrip. Rate: $35/yr.
Circulation: 27,000
Circulation Type: controlled
Owner(s):
Capital Cities/ABC, Inc.
7 W. 34th St.
New York, NY 10001
Telephone: (212) 630-4870
Ownership %: 100
Editorial:
Larry Carlat ..............................Editor

## Group 010-Appliances

54056
**ALTERNATIVE ENERGY RETAILER**
70 Edwin Ave.
Waterbury, CT 06708
Telephone: (203) 755-0158
FAX: (203) 755-3480
Mailing Address:
  P.O. Box 2180
  Waterbury, CT 06722
Year Established: 1980
Pub. Frequency: m.
Page Size: standard
Subscrip. Rate: $32/yr.
Materials: 01,02,05,06,19,20,21,28,29,30,
  32,33
Freelance Pay: $200/article
Print Process: web offset
Circulation: 14,000
Circulation Type: controlled
Owner(s):
Zackin Publications, Inc.
P.O. Box 2180
Waterbury, CT 06722
Telephone: (203) 755-0158
FAX: (203) 755-3480
Ownership %: 100
Management:
David Zackin ...........................Publisher
Linda Zackin .....................Advertising Manager
Silvia Purcaro ....................Office Manager
Henry Pacyna ...................Production Manager
Editorial:
Dave Johnston ...........................Editor
John Florian ...................Editorial Director
Brenda Bouley ....................Account Executive
Desc.: Serving the nation's retailers of
  solid fuel and gas-burning appliances
  and fireplaces with industry news and
  retail management advice.
Readers: Nation's retailers of solid fuel-
  burning appliances (wood, gas, pellet,
  coal and gas stoves, and fireplace
  products).
Deadline: story-1st of mo. 2 mos. prior to
  pub. date; news-1st of mo. 2 mos. prior;
  photo-1st of mo. 2 mos. prior; ads-1st of
  mo. 2 mos. prior

Materials Accepted/Included: 01-Business news 02-By-line articles 03-Fashion news 04-Food news 05-Freelance copy 06-Letters to editor 07-Real estate news 08-Sports news 09-Travel news 10-Book rev. 11-Movie rev. 12-Music rev. 13-TV rev. 14-Theater rev. 15-Coming events 16-Obituaries 17-Question & answer 18-Social announcements 19-Artwork 20-Cartoons 21-Photos 22-TV listings 23-Audio rec. 24-Video rec. 25-Books 26-Films/film clips 27-Personnel news 28-Press releases 29-New product news/photos 30-Trade lit. 31-Contracts awarded 32-Display adv. 33-Classified adv.

4-12

## APPLIANCE

22842

1110 Jorie Blvd., #CS9019
Oak Brook, IL 60522-9019
Telephone: (708) 990-3484
FAX: (708) 990-0078
Year Established: 1944
Pub. Frequency: m.
Page Size: standard
Subscrip. Rate: $65/yr. in US; $75/yr.
  foreign
Materials: 01,06,27,28,29,30,32,33
Print Process: web offset
Circulation: 30,600
Circulation Type: controlled & paid
**Owner(s):**
Dana Chase Publications, Inc.
Telephone: (708) 990-3484
Ownership %: 100
**Management:**
Dana Chase, Jr. ....................................President
Dana Chase, Jr. ....................................Publisher
Jim Wessel ......................Circulation Manager
Patricia Bares .........Customer Service Manager
**Editorial:**
George Shurtleff .................Production Director
**Desc.:** Covers the entire appliance
  industry. Editorial features include
  material on designs, farereparation,
  engineering, general information,
  mechanical and practical information on
  plant facilities.
**Readers:** Key management from top
  executives through supervision, including
  administrative, purchasing, engineering,
  design, sales & service and key plant
  management.
**Deadline:** news-6 wks. prior to pub. date;
  ads-1st of mo. prior to pub. date

## APPLIANCE MANUFACTURER

22843

5900 Harper Rd., Ste. 105
Solon, OH 44139
Telephone: (216) 349-3060
FAX: (216) 498-9121
Year Established: 1953
Pub. Frequency: m.
Page Size: standard
Subscrip. Rate: $8/copy; $55/yr. US;
  $125/yr. foreign
Freelance Pay: none
Circulation: 34,000
Circulation Type: controlled
**Owner(s):**
Business News Publishing
5900 Harper Rd., Ste. 105
Solon, OH 44139
Telephone: (216) 349-3060
Ownership %: 100
**Management:**
Linda M. Calkins ..................................Publisher
**Editorial:**
Norm Remich ...........................Editor in Chief
Joe Jancsurak .............................Senior Editor
Richard Babyak ......................Technical Editor
**Desc.:** Interpretively covers all areas of
  major appliance, electric housewares,
  central heating and cooling, computers,
  business and office appliances,
  commercial and institutional appliances,
  laboratory appliances, and consumer
  electronic companies' operations:
  engineering and designing appliances, in
  production, covers materials handling, all
  fabrication, metal finishing, painting and
  enameling, sub-assembly, assembly,
  packaging, shipping. Also covers
  management policies and decisions.
  Departments include: New Products,
  Bulletins, Management Update,
  Databank, Design Ideas and
  Manufacturing Ideas. Addresses the
  solutions to problems and interests of
  the Design for Manufacturing team in all
  segments of the appliance industry.

**Readers:** Administration, management,
  production & manufacturing engineers,
  design engineers, purchasing at
  consumer, commercial and
  business appliance manufacturers.

## APPLIANCE SERVICE NEWS

22844

110 W. St. Charles Rd.
Lombard, IL 60148
Telephone: (708) 932-9550
FAX: (708) 932-9552
Mailing Address:
  P.O. Box 789
  Lombard, IL 60148
Year Established: 1950
Pub. Frequency: m.
Page Size: tabloid
Subscrip. Rate: $13.50/yr. $23/2 yrs.
Materials: 01,02,06,10,15,16,23,24,25,27,
  28,29,30,32,33
Freelance Pay: $200-$300/article
Print Process: web offset
Circulation: 42,000
Circulation Type: controlled & paid
**Owner(s):**
Gamit Enterprises, Inc.
P.O. Box 789
Lombard, IL 60148
Telephone: (708) 932-9550
FAX: (708) 932-9552
Ownership %: 100
**Management:**
William Wingstedt ...............................Publisher
M.C. Wingstedt ...................Advertising Manager
F. R. Vilbar ......................Circulation Manager
**Editorial:**
William Wingstedt .......................................Editor
James J. Hodl ......................Associate Editor
Peggy Crane ...............................Miscellaneous
**Desc.:** Correspondents are on free-lance
  basis and get by-lines over special news
  or feature stories. Want news and
  features directly or indirectly related to
  electric & gas appliances, service,
  businesses in appliances, business
  dealing in servicing, maintaining and/or
  selling of coin-operated washing
  machines, etc., as well as repairmen of
  electric and gas ranges, home laundry
  equipment, sewing machines, vacuum
  cleaners, refrigerators, air conditioners,
  and smaller household appliances.
  Manufacturers (and their personnel) of
  appliances, utilities and their personnel,
  factory service stations, appliance parts
  jobbers in all categories, and
  products distributors. Occasionally make
  use of magazine style photo spread on
  good feature story. Straight news must
  have occurred within a month preceding
  publication. Do use some clippings.
**Readers:** Owners, managers &
  servicemen. Include distributors,
  equipment distributors,
  service distributors, wholesale appliance
  parts independent service organizations,
  service personnel of utilities, executives
  of appliance manufacturers.
**Deadline:** story-1st of mo. prior to pub.
  date; news-1st of mo. prior; photo-1st of
  mo. prior; ads-10th of mo. prior

## DEALERSCOPE MERCHANDISING

23164

410 Union Ave.
Framingham, MA 01701
Telephone: (508) 620-8770
FAX: (508) 620-8946
Year Established: 1986
Pub. Frequency: m.; 1st of mo.
Page Size: standard
Subscrip. Rate: $65/yr. US; $132/yr.
  foreign
Circulation: 43,000
Circulation Type: paid

**Owner(s):**
North American Publishing Co.
401 N. Broad St.
Philadelphia, PA 19108
Telephone: (215) 238-5300
Ownership %: 100
**Bureau(s):**
Dealerscope Merchandising
11965 Venice Blvd.
Los Angeles, CA 90066
Telephone: (310) 390-3333
Contact: Linda Gvora-Jaffe, Associate
  Publisher

Dealerscope Merchandising
201 E. Ogden Ave.
Hinsdale, IL 60521
Telephone: (708) 325-9555
Contact: Andy Miller; Bill Powell, Publisher

Dealerscope Merchandising
322 Eighth Ave.
New York, NY 10001
Telephone: (212) 620-7330
Contact: Liz Badglato, Manager
**Management:**
Bernard Schneyer ...............................President
**Editorial:**
Judy Bocklage ...........................Senior Editor
Richard Sherwin ......................Managing Editor
**Desc.:** Interested in all news material
  pertaining to the marketing of
  appliances/consumer electronics on
  a national and regional basis. Items on
  personnel changes and news events.
  Departments include: People, New
  Products, Audio, Video, Computers,
  Video Games, Home Office, Sell-Thru
  Video.
**Readers:** Appliance/TV dealers,
  manufacturers, mass merchandisers,
  catalog showrooms and department
  stores.

## GLOBAL APPLIANCE REPORT

68856

20 N. Wacker Dr.
Chicago, IL 60606
Telephone: (312) 984-5800
FAX: (312) 984-5823
Year Established: 1990
Pub. Frequency: m.
Subscrip. Rate: $250/yr. members;
  $350/yr. non-members
**Owner(s):**
Association of Home Appliance
  Manufacturers
20 N. Wacker Dr.
Chicago, IL 60606
Telephone: (312) 984-5800
Ownership %: 100
**Editorial:**
Craig Schulz .........................................Editor
**Desc.:** International news affecting the
  home appliance industry.

## NARDA NEWS

24588

10 E. 22nd St.
Ste. 310
Lombard, IL 60148-4915
Telephone: (708) 953-8950
FAX: (312) 953-8957
Year Established: 1943
Pub. Frequency: m.
Page Size: standard
Subscrip. Rate: $65/yr. non-members;
  $89/yr. foreign
Circulation: 5,000
Circulation Type: controlled & paid
**Owner(s):**
North American Retail Dealers Assn.
10 E. 22nd St.
Ste. 310
Lombard, IL 60148-4915
Telephone: (708) 953-8950
Ownership %: 100

**Editorial:**
Russ Gager .......................................Editor

## RETAILER & MARKETING NEWS

23093

3111 Cole Ave. at Bowen
Dallas, TX 75204
Telephone: (214) 871-2930
Mailing Address:
  P.O. Box 191105
  Dallas, TX 75219
Year Established: 1961
Pub. Frequency: m.
Page Size: tabloid
Subscrip. Rate: $12/yr.; $36/3 yrs.
Materials: 01,02,06,10,15,16,17,18,19,20,
  21,27,28,29,30,32,33
Print Process: web offset
Circulation: 8,000
Circulation Type: controlled
**Owner(s):**
Ramnvest, Inc.
3111 Cole Ave. at Bowen
Dallas, TX 75204
Telephone: (214) 871-2930
Ownership %: 100
**Management:**
Michael J. Anderson ...........................President
Michael J. Anderson ...........................Publisher
Deborah McWhorter .......Circulation Manager
**Editorial:**
Michael J. Anderson ...............................Editor
Cyndi Anderson .......................Managing Editor
Sheryl Bishop .......................Associate Editor
**Desc.:** A regional business report for
  furniture, appliance and television and
  consumer electronics dealers. All
  marketing and business news of interest
  reported to dealers in the northern half
  of state of Texas. Departments include:
  Dealerfax, memo from the Texas
  Electronics Association, Hot List,
  Consumer Electronics Section, Furniture
  fax.
**Readers:** Dealers and retailers in
  consumer electronics furniture and
  appliances.
**Deadline:** story-20th prior to pub. date;
  news-20th; photo-20th; ads-20th

## RETAILING NEWS

23174

14962 Bear Valley Rd., Ste. 288
Victoville, CA 92392
Telephone: (619) 241-2514
FAX: (619) 241-3595
Year Established: 1971
Pub. Frequency: m.
Page Size: standard
Subscrip. Rate: $25/yr.
Freelance Pay: varies
Print Process: offset
Circulation: 12,500
Circulation Type: controlled
**Owner(s):**
Retailing News
14962 Bear Valley Rd., Ste. 28
Victorville, CA 92392
Telephone: (619) 241-2514
FAX: (619) 241-3595
Ownership %: 100
**Management:**
Martin Barsky .........................................Owner
Martin Barsky ..................Chairman of Board
Martin Barsky .....................................President
Martin Barsky .....................................Publisher
**Desc.:** Covers appliances, audio, consumer
  electronics, video TV retail dealers, and
  computer dealers. Spot news coverage
  of local market and in-depth coverage of
  industry trends, new products, business
  conditions, and retail activities. Articles
  on companies and products in home
  appliance and consumer electronics.
  Use photos.

**Readers:** Retail stores in home appliances, audio, video, computers, jewelry stores, housewares, and consumer electronics products; manufacturers, buying groups and distributors.

69552

## RETAIL OBSERVER
1442 Sierra Creek Way
San Jose, CA 95132
Telephone: (408) 272-8974
FAX: (408) 272-3344
Year Established: 1990
Pub. Frequency: m.
Page Size: standard
Subscrip. Rate: $5/yr.
Materials: 01,15,27,28,29,32,33
Print Process: web
Circulation: 4,888
Circulation Type: free
Owner(s):
Retail Observer
1442 Sierra Creek Way
San Jose, CA 95132
Telephone: (408) 272-8974
FAX: (408) 272-3344
Ownership %: 100
Management:
Charles H. Edmonds ...........................Publisher
Lee Boucher ......................Associate Publisher
**Desc.:** Covers the retailing of appliances, electronics and kitchen and bath items.

68896

## ROUND BOBBIN
P.O. Box 338
Hilliard, OH 00006
Telephone: (614) 870-7211
FAX: (614) 870-0004
Year Established: 1965
Pub. Frequency: m.
Page Size: tabloid
Subscrip. Rate: $35/yr. US; $45/yr. Canada; $95/yr. elsewhere
Materials: 01,02,03,05,06,20,27,29,30,32,33
Print Process: offset
Circulation: 1,800
Circulation Type: paid
Owner(s):
International Sewing Machine Association
P.O. Box 2188
Zanesville, OH 43702-2188
Telephone: (614) 452-4541
FAX: (614) 452-2552
Ownership %: 100
Editorial:
Duane R. Meyers .............Publications Manager
**Desc.:** Provides business, marketing and other information of relevance to sewing machine and vacuum cleaner dealers. Includes association and industry developments.
**Deadline:** story-30 days prior to pub. date; ads-30 days prior to pub. date

## Group 012-Architecture

21736

## ARCHITECTURAL RECORD
1221 Ave. of the Americas
New York, NY 10020
Year Established: 1891
Pub. Frequency: 14/yr.
Page Size: standard
Subscrip. Rate: $7 newsstand; $54/yr.
Materials: 01,02,05,06,07,21,25,28,29,30, 32,33
Print Process: web offset
Circulation: 65,535
Circulation Type: paid
Owner(s):
McGraw-Hill, Inc.
1221 Ave. of the Americas
New York, NY 10020
Telephone: (212) 997-2593
Ownership %: 100

Management:
Roscoe C. Smith, III ...........................Publisher
Editorial:
Stephen A. Kliment .....................Editor in Chief
Charles D. Lim ...........................Senior Editor
Charles Hoyt ..............................Senior Editor
Karen Stein .........................................Editor
Carolyn DeWitt Koenig ...........Managing Editor
Clifford A. Pearson .................Associate Editor
Joan Blatterman ...............New Products Editor
James Russell .......................Technical Editor
**Desc.:** Covers residential and non-residential buildings such as office, stores, schools, hospitals, churches, industrial, recreation, apartments, motels and hotels, and single-family houses designed by architects. Uses contributed articles as well as staff-written. Sections devoted to architectural business, engineering for architecture, products, literature, news.
**Readers:** Architects and engineers in building business, design and engineering.
**Deadline:** story-120 days prior to pub. date; ads-1st of mo. prior to pub. date

21732

## ARCHITECTURE
1130 Connecticut Ave., N.W.
Washington, DC 20036
Telephone: (202) 828-0993
FAX: (202) 828-0825
Year Established: 1913
Pub. Frequency: m.
Page Size: oversize
Subscrip. Rate: $37/yr.; $55/2 yrs.
Freelance Pay: $300-$600
Circulation: 74,637
Circulation Type: controlled
Owner(s):
BPI
1515 Broadway
New York, NY 10036
Ownership %: 100
Management:
Robert Kliesch ...................................Publisher
Editorial:
Deborah Dietsch ........................Editor in Chief
Nancy Solomon ............................Senior Editor
Carmen Shirkey ....................Editorial Assistant
Heidi Landecker ...............Senior Design Editor
**Desc.:** Covers architectural design features, technical and practice issues, and general news, coming events, book reviews and letters to the editor.
**Readers:** Registered architects, architectural employees, students, engineers & homebuilders.

21737

## ARCHITECTURE MINNESOTA
275 Market St., Ste. 54
Minneapolis, MN 55405-1621
Telephone: (612) 338-6763
FAX: (612) 338-7881
Year Established: 1974
Pub. Frequency: bi-m.
Page Size: standard
Subscrip. Rate: $3.50 newsstand; $18/yr.
Materials: 02,05,06,10,19,21,32
Print Process: web
Circulation: 7,000
Circulation Type: controlled
Owner(s):
AIA Minnesota
275 Market St., Ste. 54
Minneapolis, MN 55405
Telephone: (612) 338-6763
Ownership %: 100
Management:
Peter Rand ........................................Publisher
Judith Van Dyne ...............Advertising Manager
Sarah Leslie ......................Circulation Manager
Editorial:
Eric Kudalis ..........................................Editor

**Desc.:** Stories of architectural and environmental interest. Design & creative living stories covering the upper Midwest.
**Readers:** Lay readers & design professionals interested in architecture & design related issues & topics.

68726

## ARCHITECTURE NEW JERSEY
900 Rte. 9
Woodbridge, NJ 07095
FAX: (201) 636-5681
Year Established: 1967
Pub. Frequency: bi-m.
Page Size: standard
Subscrip. Rate: $20/yr.
Circulation: 2,500
Circulation Type: paid
Owner(s):
New Jersey Society of Architects
900 Rte. 9
Woodbridge, NJ 07095
Ownership %: 100
Editorial:
Phillip S. Kennedy-Grant ..........................Editor
**Desc.:** Covers projects of current interest, news of architects, and issues in architecture.

21738

## DESIGN COST & DATA
8602 N. 40th St.
Tampa, FL 33604
Telephone: (813) 989-9300
FAX: (813) 980-3982
Year Established: 1958
Pub. Frequency: q.
Page Size: standard
Subscrip. Rate: $48/yr.; $96/2 yrs.
Materials: 01,08,09,12,20,28,29,30,31,32,33
Freelance Pay: $50-$250/article
Circulation: 13,000
Circulation Type: controlled & paid
Owner(s):
LM Rector, Ind.
8602 N. 40th St.
Tampa, FL 33604
Telephone: (813) 989-9300
Ownership %: 100
Bureau(s):
LM Rector, Inc.
P.O. Box 311
Monterey, CA 93942
Telephone: (408) 372-2050
Contact: Bob Welch
Management:
Lee Rector ........................................Publisher
Editorial:
Lee Rector ...............................Executive Editor
Greg Campbell ........................Managing Editor
Robert Rizzi ........................Marketing Director
**Desc.:** Edited for the professional business and financial influences responsible for management of design and project development. Detailed cost and data facts on completed buildings are published in a ready to file format that is used as a system for comparative design-cost evaluation and projecting cost increases to a future time and place. Other articles range from financial project management problems, research and development of systems and products, to industry news. Useful to top management responsible for total project development. A magazine format. An office guide, workbook and reference for permanent filing.

**Readers:** Architects, engineers, financial executives, specification writers, interior decorators, building developers, contractors, estimators, building consultants.
**Deadline:** ads-20th of mo., prior to ending mo. of quarter

67209

## FABRICS & ARCHITECTURE
645 Cedar 800
St. Paul, MN 55155
Telephone: (612) 222-2508
FAX: (612) 222-8215
Year Established: 1989
Pub. Frequency: 7/yr.
Page Size: standard
Subscrip. Rate: $19/yr.
Circulation: 11,000
Circulation Type: controlled & paid
Owner(s):
Industrial Fabric Association, International
345 Cedar 800
St. Paul, MN 55101
Telephone: (612) 222-2508
Ownership %: 100
Management:
Frank McGinty ...................................Publisher
Mary Hennessy ................Advertising Manager
Editorial:
Jean Cook ............................................Editor

68730

## FACILITIES PLANNING NEWS
P.O. Box 1568
Orinda, CA 64563
Telephone: (510) 254-1744
FAX: (510) 251-2744
Year Established: 1982
Pub. Frequency: m.
Page Size: oversize
Subscrip. Rate: $190/yr.
Materials: 02,25,28,29,30,31,32,33
Print Process: offset
Circulation: 8,100
Circulation Type: free & paid
Owner(s):
Tradeline, Inc.
P.O. Box 1568
Orinda, CA 94563
Telephone: (510) 254-1744
Ownership %: 100
Editorial:
Lee Ingalls ...........................................Editor
Todd Stone ........................................Ad Sales
**Desc.:** Reports on recently completed buildings in the areas of healthcare, R & D, corporate, institutional and high-tech construction.
**Readers:** FPN's readership includes facilities directors and managers in a variety of industries and institutions, including research, pharmaceutical, high tech, healthcare, biotechnology and government agencies.
**Deadline:** story-6 wks. prior to pub. date; news-6 wks. prior; photo-6 wks. prior; ads-1st of mo. prior

24644

## HOSPITALITY DESIGN
355 Park Ave., S.
New York, NY 10010
Telephone: (212) 592-6355
Year Established: 1979
Pub. Frequency: 10/yr.
Page Size: standard
Subscrip. Rate: $45/yr. US; $65/yr. Canada & Mexico; $95/yr. foreign airmail
Materials: 01,06,07,10,15,16,21,25,27,28, 29,30,31,32,33
Print Process: web offset
Circulation: 30,600
Circulation Type: controlled & paid

**Owner(s):**
Bill Communications Investors
633 Third Ave.
New York, NY 10017
Telephone: (212) 986-4800
Ownership %:  10

Boston Ventures
c/o Bill Communications
Ownership %:  10
**Management:**
Mary Jean Madigan ...........................Publisher
Michelle Finn .....................Advertising Manager
**Editorial:**
Mary Jean Madigan ....................Editor in Chief
Robert Janjigian ........................Executive Editor
John P. Radulski .........................Senior Editor
Suzanne Bauer ........................Managing Editor
John Lenaas ...............................Art Director
Michael Webb .....................Contributing Editor
**Desc.:** Relies heavily on top quality
architectural color photography. Covers
restaurants, clubs, senior living and
healthcare projects, and hotels.
Installation stories cover new, previously
unpublished projects. Departments
Include: Marketplace Product Review,
Solutions To Design Problems; Reviews
of Design Exhibitions, Design Books;
"Detail" (News); and "Spotlight"
(Profiles).
**Readers:** Designers and architects who
specify furnishings of hotels and
restaurants and hotel and restaurant
executives who make design related
decisions.
**Deadline:** news-6 wks. prior to pub. date;
ads-5 wks.

21742
**INLAND ARCHITECT**
3525 W. Peterson Ave.
Chicago, IL 60659
Telephone: (312) 866-9900
FAX: (312) 467-7051
Mailing Address:
   P.O. Box 10394
   Chicago, IL 60610
Year Established: 1883
Pub. Frequency: bi-m.
Page Size: oversize
Subscrip. Rate: $27/yr.; $48/2 yrs.; $62/3
yrs.
Freelance Pay: $.50-$400
Circulation: 8,000
Circulation Type: paid
**Owner(s):**
Real Estate News Corp.
3525 W. Peterson Ave.
Chicago, IL 60659
Telephone: (312) 866-9900
Ownership %: 100
**Management:**
Steve Polydros ......................................Publisher
**Editorial:**
Steve Klebba ..........................................Editor
**Desc.:** Regional professional journal edited
for architects, structural engineers, and
urban planners in the midwest. Articles
cover distinguished buildings, historic
buildings, profiles of individual arhitects
and firms, related legislation,
architectural philosophy and education,
interior design, building technology,
economics, city planning, demography,
and ecology. Departments
include: Letters, Developments, Books,
Travel.
**Readers:** Architects, planners, buffs.

68727
**JOURNAL OF ARCHITECTURE &**
**PLANNING RESEARCH**
117 W. Harrison Bldg., Ste.640-L221
Chicago, IL 60605
Year Established: 1984
Pub. Frequency: q.

Page Size: standard
Subscrip. Rate: $110/yr.
Materials: 32
Print Process: offset
**Owner(s):**
Locke Science Publishing Co.
117 W. Harrison Bldg.
Ste. 640-L221
Chicago, IL 60605
Ownership %: 100
**Editorial:**
A. Seidel ...............................................Editor
**Desc.:** Reports on recent research findings
and innovative practices.

22445
**M.B. NEWS**
1740 Ridge Ave.
Evanston, IL 60201
Telephone: (708) 869-2031
FAX: (708) 869-2056
Year Established: 1944
Pub. Frequency: m.
Page Size: standard
Subscrip. Rate: $45/yr.
Materials: 01,02,06,29,30,32,33
Freelance Pay: none
Print Process: offset
Circulation: 4,000
Circulation Type: free & paid
**Owner(s):**
Monument Builders of North America
1740 Ridge
Evanston, IL 60201
Telephone: (708) 869-2031
Ownership %: 100
**Management:**
Edward E. Simmons, CAE ...................Publisher
**Editorial:**
Donna Jones ...........................................Editor
**Desc.:** Geared to the interests of the
memorial industry, retail, wholesale,
manufacturing, supply, etc. Includes
technical news articles, announcements
of new products and processes, features
on the activities of persons and firms
within the industry, descriptions of the
services rendered by Monument Builders
of North America (International Trade
Association), and articles on any issue
of interest of importance to the
memorial industry. Regular features
include: Calender of State and District
Meetings. Departments include:
Calendar of State and District Meetings,
Membership Update, In Memoriam,
News, Officers' Profiles.
**Readers:** Leading memorialists (retail
monument dealers, suppliers to the
industry) located throughout the U.S.,
Canada, Great Britain, South Africa,
Australia, New Zealand, Philippines,
India.
**Deadline:** story-1 mo. prior to pub. date;
news-1 mo.; photo-1 mo.; ads-1 mo.

61247
**METAL ARCHITECTURE**
7450 Skokie Blvd.
Skokie, IL 60077
Telephone: (708) 674-2200
FAX: (708) 674-3676
Mailing Address:
   123 N. Poplar St.
   Fostoria, OH 44830
Year Established: 1985
Pub. Frequency: m.
Page Size: tabloid
Subscrip. Rate: $45/yr.; free to qualified
personnel
Materials: 01,08,10,11,12,13,20,23,24,25,
   26,28,30,32,33
Freelance Pay: negotiable
Print Process: web offset
Circulation: 31,700
Circulation Type: controlled

**Owner(s):**
John Lawrence
7450 Skokie Blvd.
Skokie, IL 60077
Telephone: (708) 674-2200
Ownership %:  50

Sam Milnark
123 Poplar St.
Fostoria, OH 44830
Telephone: (419) 435-8571
Ownership %:  50
**Management:**
John Garvey .............................Sales Manager
**Editorial:**
Bob Fittro ................................................Editor
LeAnn Baker ...........Assistant Managing Editor
**Desc.:** Serves private architectural/
engineering firms; city, county, state, or
federal engineering departments;
corporate architectural/ engineering
departments/ construction firms;
marketing/ manufacturing firms and
others allied to the field.
**Readers:** Qualified recipients are
registered architects, architectural
interns, engineers, building designers,
and construction specifiers.

21744
**NORTH CAROLINA ARCHITECT**
115 W. Morgan St.
Raleigh, NC 27601
Telephone: (919) 833-6656
FAX: (919) 833-2015
Year Established: 1954
Pub. Frequency: 5/yr.
Page Size: standard
Subscrip. Rate: $30/yr.
Circulation: 5,500
Circulation Type: controlled
**Owner(s):**
American Institute of Architects, N.C.
   Chapter
115 W. Morgan St.
Raleigh, NC 27601
Telephone: (919) 833-6656
Ownership %: 100
**Management:**
Johnny Moore ...................Advertising Manager
**Editorial:**
John Roth ...............................................Editor
**Desc.:** Projects designed by Chapter
members, related features to
architectures. Articles of public interest
relating to the architectural profession.
**Readers:** All registered architects in state,
engineers, state government officials.

21745
**PROGRESSIVE ARCHITECTURE**
600 Summer St.
Stamford, CT 06901
Telephone: (203) 348-7531
FAX: (203) 348-4023
Mailing Address:
   P.O. Box 1361
   Stamford, CT 06904
Year Established: 1920
Pub. Frequency: m.
Page Size: oversize
Subscrip. Rate: $48/yr.
Freelance Pay: $150-$200/page
Circulation: 55,931
Circulation Type: paid
**Owner(s):**
Penton Publishing, Inc.
1100 Superior Ave.
Cleveland, OH 44114
Telephone: (216) 696-7000
Ownership %: 100
**Management:**
Philip Hubbard ......................................Publisher
Mary Ann Novak .................Circulation Manager
**Editorial:**
Ziva Freiman ...................................Senior Editor
Mark A. Branch ..............................Senior Editor

Michael J. Crosbie ..........................Senior Editor
John Dixon .............................................Editor
Thomas Fisher ........................................Editor
Abby Bussel .................................Associate Editor
**Desc.:** Every subject affecting architectural
practice. This includes any information
of interest to every member of
architectural design and specification
teams/partners, principals, architects,
designers, job captains, specification
consulting engineering firms specializing
in building design. Covers construction
techniques, building products,
materials and equipment, books,
manufacturers' literature.
**Readers:** Architects, engineers, designers,
draftsmen.

68725
**REDWOOD NEWS**
405 Enfrente Dr., Ste. 200
Novato, CA 94949
Telephone: (415) 382-0662
FAX: (415) 382-8531
Year Established: 1949
Pub. Frequency: s-a.
Page Size: pocket
Subscrip. Rate: free
Print Process: offset lithography
Circulation: 28000
Circulation Type: controlled
**Owner(s):**
California Redwood Association
405 Enfrente Dr., Ste. 200
Novato, CA 94949
Telephone: (415) 382-0662
Ownership %: 100
**Editorial:**
Pamela Allsebrook ...............................Editor
**Desc.:** Shows redwood design for
architects and others in the building
trades.

24907
**TECHNOLOGY & CONSERVATION**
**OF ART, ARCHITECTURE &**
**ANTIQUITIES**
One Emerson Pl.
Boston, MA 02114
Telephone: (617) 227-8581
Year Established: 1976
Pub. Frequency: q.
Page Size: standard
Subscrip. Rate: $25/yr. US & Canada;
   $55/yr. elsewhere
Circulation: 15,500
Circulation Type: controlled
**Owner(s):**
The Technology Organization, Inc.
One Emerson Pl.
Boston, MA 02114
Telephone: (617) 227-8581
Ownership %: 100
**Management:**
S.E. Schur ............................................Publisher
S.E. Schur ........................Advertising Manager
**Editorial:**
S.E. Schur ...............................Executive Editor
**Desc.:** Covers the technical aspects of art
and architectural analysis, conservation,
preservation, restoration,
protection (environmental, security, fire
safety & lighting) and documentation,
emphasizing technical advances,
instruments, materials, & techniques.

**Materials Accepted/Included:** 01-Business news 02-By-line articles 03-Fashion news 04-Food news 05-Freelance copy 06-Letters to editor 07-Real estate news 08-Sports news 09-Travel news
10-Book rev. 11-Movie rev. 12-Music rev. 13-TV rev. 14-Theater rev. 15-Coming events 16-Obituaries 17-Question & answer 18-Social announcements 19-Artwork 20-Cartoons 21-Photos 22-TV listings
23-Audio rec. 24-Video rec. 25-Books 26-Films/film clips 27-Personnel news 28-Press releases 29-New product news/photos 30-Trade lit. 31-Contracts awarded 32-Display adv. 33-Classified adv.

4-15

**Readers:** Museum, art gallery and historic society directors and curators; government officials; conservators; scientists; architects; librarians; archivists; archeologists; cultural resource managers, building preservation specialists.

## Group 014-Art

**AIRBRUSH ACTION** 69519
1985 Swarthmore Ave.
Lakewood, NJ 08701
Telephone: (908) 364-2111
FAX: (908) 367-5908
Mailing Address:
 P.O. Box 2052
 Lakewood, NJ 08701
Year Established: 1985
Pub. Frequency: bi-m.
Subscrip. Rate: $23.70/yr.
Circulation: 45,000
Circulation Type: paid
**Owner(s):**
Airbrush Action, Inc.
1985 Swathmore Ave.
Lakewood, NJ 08701
Telephone: (908) 364-2111
Ownership %: 100
**Editorial:**
Clifford S. Stieglitz ............................Editor

**AMERICAN ARTIST** 21749
1515 Broadway
New York, NY 10036
Telephone: (212) 764-7300
FAX: (212) 536-5351
Year Established: 1937
Pub. Frequency: m.
Page Size: standard
Subscrip. Rate: $25.95/yr.
Circulation: 163,000
Circulation Type: paid
**Owner(s):**
BPI Communications
1515 Broadway
New York, NY 10036
Telephone: (212) 764-7300
Ownership %: 100
**Management:**
Don Frost ..............................Publisher
**Editorial:**
Stanley Marcus ...............Executive Editor
M. Stephen Doherty ...................Editor
Joan Masella .............Circulation Director
**Desc.:** Features cover artists, their work, materials and methods used, and problems solved. Such features should be queried, accompanied by photos of the artist's work. Also covers Art Mart (new products), Bulletin Board (announcements of competitions, scholarships, exhibitions), Nuts & Bolts (news items of interest), Quick Tips (technical ideas). Book Reviews are staff-written.

**ART BUSINESS NEWS** 21750
19 Old Kings Hwy., S.
Darien, CT 06820
Telephone: (203) 656-3402
FAX: (203) 656-1976
Mailing Address:
 P.O. Box 3837
 Stamford, CT 06905
Year Established: 1973
Pub. Frequency: m.
Page Size: tabloid
Subscrip. Rate: $5/issue; $39/yr.
Materials: 01,05,06,10,15,16,19,21,24,25, 27,28,29,30,32,33
Freelance Pay: $150/article
Circulation: 31,000
Circulation Type: controlled

**Owner(s):**
Myers Publishing Co., Inc.
P.O. Box 3837
Stamford, CT 06905
Telephone: (203) 356-1745
Ownership %: 100
**Bureau(s):**
Myers Publishing Co., Inc.
800 E. Northwest Hwy., Ste 400
Palatine, IL 60067
Telephone: (708) 358-4944
Contact: Brooks Male, Sales Manager
**Management:**
John R. Myers ..........................Publisher
**Editorial:**
Fergus Reid ...............................Editor
Sarah Seamark ...............Managing Editor
**Desc.:** A trade publication for the fine art and picture framing industries.
**Readers:** Art galleries, picture framers and related businesses.

**ART CELLAR EXCHANGE** 69525
2171 India St., Ste. H
San Diego, CA 92101
Telephone: (619) 338-0797
FAX: (619) 338-0826
Year Established: 1989
Pub. Frequency: m.
Subscrip. Rate: $25/yr.
Circulation: 50,000
Circulation Type: paid
**Owner(s):**
Token Art Corporation
2171 India St., Ste. H
San Diego, CA 92101
Telephone: (619) 338-0797
Ownership %: 100
**Editorial:**
P. B. Van Cleve ..........................Editor
**Desc.:** Provides a forum for buyers and sellers of fine art, as well as insight into the business of art.
**Readers:** For people interested in the visual art market.

**ART IN AMERICA** 21753
575 Broadway, 5th Fl.
New York, NY 10012
Telephone: (212) 941-2800
FAX: (212) 941-2885
Year Established: 1913
Pub. Frequency: 12/yr.
Page Size: standard
Subscrip. Rate: $4.95 newsstand; $39.95/yr.
Circulation: 60,023
Circulation Type: paid
**Owner(s):**
Brant Publications, Inc.
575 Broadway, 5th Fl.
New York, NY 10012
Telephone: (212) 941-2800
Ownership %: 100
**Management:**
Sandra Brant ..........................Publisher
Lee Weber ...............Advertising Manager
**Editorial:**
Elizabeth C. Baker .......................Editor
Nancy Marmer ...............Managing Editor
**Desc.:** A critical and historical art journal with considerable news content, concerned with the arts and with their relationship to the society from which they emerge. Focuses on painting and sculpture. Also covers photography, film and architecture. Examines the social and political issues that are relevant to our cultural institutions, to artists, to collectors, and to the visual arts in general.
**Readers:** Average age 41, college educated.

**ARTIST'S MAGAZINE** 69778
1507 Dana Ave.
Cincinnati, OH 45207
Telephone: (513) 531-2222
Year Established: 1984
Pub. Frequency: m.
Subscrip. Rate: $27/yr.
Materials: 05,06,17,19,20
Circulation: 424,000
**Owner(s):**
F&W Publications, Inc.
1507 Dana Ave.
Cincinnati, OH 45207
Telephone: (513) 531-2222
Ownership %: 100
**Editorial:**
Mary Magnus ...............................Editor

**ART JOURNAL 1995** 68732
275 Seventh Ave.
New York, NY 10001
Telephone: (212) 691-1051
FAX: (212) 627-2381
Year Established: 1941
Pub. Frequency: q.
Subscrip. Rate: $30/yr.
Circulation: 11,000
Circulation Type: paid
**Owner(s):**
College Art Association
275 Seventh Ave.
New York, NY 10001
Telephone: (212) 691-1051
Ownership %: 100
**Editorial:**
Virginia Wageman .......................Editor
**Desc.:** Focuses on critical and aesthetic issues in the visual arts of our times.

**BULLETIN OF THE CLEVELAND MUSEUM OF ART, THE** 21757
11150 E. Blvd.
Cleveland, OH 44106
Telephone: (216) 421-7340
Year Established: 1914
Pub. Frequency: 10/yr.
Page Size: 4 color photos/art
Subscrip. Rate: $25/yr. non-members
Circulation: 5,000
Circulation Type: paid
**Owner(s):**
Cleveland Museum of Art, The
Publications Department
11150 E. Blvd.
Cleveland, OH 44106
Telephone: (216) 421-7340
Ownership %: 100
**Editorial:**
Barbara J. Bradley ......................Editor
**Desc.:** Scholarly articles pertaining to art works in the Cleveland Museum of Art.
**Readers:** Museum members, art historians, students and patrons.

**JOURNAL OF AESTHETICS & ART CRITICISM** 68735
114 N. Murray St.
Madison, WI 53715
Telephone: (608) 262-4952
Year Established: 1941
Pub. Frequency: q.
Page Size: standard
Subscrip. Rate: $30/yr.
Circulation: 2,700
Circulation Type: paid
**Owner(s):**
Journal of Aesthetics & Art Criticism
**Editorial:**
Philip Alperson ..........................Editor
**Desc.:** Contains articles on aesthetics as related to visual arts, literature, music and theater.

**JOURNAL OF EARLY SOUTHERN DECORATIVE ARTS** 69345
P.O. Box 10310
Winston-Salem, NC 27108-0310
Telephone: (919) 721-7360
Year Established: 1975
Pub. Frequency: s-a.
Page Size: standard
Subscrip. Rate: $20/yr. institutions; $25/yr. individuals; $35/yr. foreign
Circulation: 1,500
Circulation Type: paid
**Owner(s):**
Museum of Early Southern Decorative Arts
P.O. Box 10310
Winston-Salem, NC 27108-0310
Telephone: (919) 721-7360
Ownership %: 100

**LEONARDO** 58759
55 Hayward St.
Cambridge, MA 02142
Telephone: (617) 625-8481
Pub. Frequency: bi-m.
Page Size: standard
Subscrip. Rate: $55/yr. individual
**Owner(s):**
MIT Press Journals
55 Hayward St.
Cambridge, MA 02142
Telephone: (617) 625-8481
Ownership %: 100
**Editorial:**
Dr. Roger Malina ........................Editor

**STAINED GLASS** 22408
6 S.W. Second St., Ste. 7
Lees Summit, MO 64063
Telephone: (800) 438-9581
FAX: (816) 524-9405
Year Established: 1906
Pub. Frequency: q.
Page Size: standard
Subscrip. Rate: $24/yr. US; $40/yr. foreign
Materials: 05,06,10,15,20,29,32,33
Freelance Pay: $25/page
Circulation: 6,000
Circulation Type: paid
**Owner(s):**
Stained Glass Association of America
6 S.W. Second St., Ste. 7
Lees Summit, MO 64063
Telephone: (800) 888-7422
Ownership %: 100
**Management:**
Truett George, Jr. ......................President
Katherine E. Gross .............Business Manager
**Editorial:**
Richard Hoover ..........................Editor
**Desc.:** To promote the finest development of the art of stained glass. Provides comprehensive coverage of the state of the art.
**Readers:** Artists, architects, interior designers, historians, stained glass practitioners & enthusiasts.

**SUNSHINE ARTIST** 68736
422 W. Fairbanks Ave., Ste. 300
Winter Park, FL 32789-3410
Telephone: (407) 539-3939
FAX: (407) 539-0533
Year Established: 1972
Pub. Frequency: m.
Page Size: standard
Subscrip. Rate: $3.95/copy; $24.50/yr.
Materials: 01,06,15,28,32,33
Print Process: web offset
Circulation: 15,000
Circulation Type: paid

**Materials Accepted/Included:** 01-Business news 02-By-line articles 03-Fashion news 04-Food news 05-Freelance copy 06-Letters to editor 07-Real estate news 08-Sports news 09-Travel news 10-Book rev. 11-Movie rev. 12-Music rev. 13-TV rev. 14-Theater rev. 15-Coming events 16-Obituaries 17-Question & answer 18-Social announcements 19-Artwork 20-Cartoons 21-Photos 22-TV listings 23-Audio rec. 24-Video rec. 25-Books 26-Films/film clips 27-Personnel news 28-Press releases 29-New product news/photos 30-Trade lit. 31-Contracts awarded 32-Display adv. 33-Classified adv.

4-16

**Owner(s):**
David F. Cook
Palm House Publishing, Inc.
422 W. Fairbanks Ave., Ste. 300
Winter Park, FL 32789-3410
Ownership %: 100
**Management:**
David F. Cook .........................Publisher
**Editorial:**
Kristine Petterson ...........................Editor
Jill Hamilton ...............Advertising Director
Bruce Borich ......................Art Director
**Desc.:** Listings and reviews of art shows, festivals and craft shows. Publishes ranking of 200 Best Shows and Festivals in the United States in September issue.
**Readers:** 95% exhibiting artists and craft artisans, 5% show directors/management.
**Deadline:** ads-25th of mo., 2 mos. prior to pub. date

21766
## WASHINGTON INTERNATIONAL ARTS LETTER
P.O. Box 12010
Des Moines, IA 50312
Telephone: (515) 255-5577
FAX: (515) 255-5577
Year Established: 1962
Pub. Frequency: 10/yr.
Page Size: pocket
Subscrip. Rate: $124/yr.
Circulation: 13,220
Circulation Type: paid
**Owner(s):**
Allied Business Consultants, Inc.
P.O. Box 12010
Des Moines, IA 50312
Telephone: (515) 288-5577
Ownership %: 100
**Management:**
Daniel Millsaps ..........................Founder
Nancy A. Fandel .......................Publisher
**Editorial:**
Nancy A. Fandel .............Editor in Chief
James S. Duncan ..........................Editor
Dianne L. Melton ..............Assistant Editor
Mark K. Oswald ..........Associate Publisher
**Desc.:** Relates information about financial matters in all arts, including organizations who receive grants and sources of grants both for individuals and for organizations. Lists private foundations who are active in the arts and humanities and reports on federal and state subsidies for arts and humanities projects. Reviews books in all arts fields, such as music, painting, sculpture, TV, radio, theatre. Departments include: Books and Publications, Grants, Private Foundations, Business Corporations becoming active in arts patronage.
**Readers:** Organizations and individuals in the arts, libraries and educational institutions arts departments.

## Group 015-Audio & Video

24561
## AUDIO
1633 Broadway
New York, NY 10019
Telephone: (212) 767-6301
Year Established: 1947
Pub. Frequency: m.
Page Size: standard
Subscrip. Rate: $24/yr.
Materials: 02,05,06,10,12
Freelance Pay: $.25-$1/wd.
Circulation: 150,000
Circulation Type: paid

**Owner(s):**
Hachette Filipacchi Magazines, Inc.
1633 Broadway
New York, NY 10019
Telephone: (212) 767-6000
Ownership %: 100
**Management:**
David Pecker .............................President
Tom Witschi .............................Publisher
Charles L. P. Watson .......Advertising Manager
Greg Roperti .................Business Manager
Leon Rosenfield .............Circulation Manager
**Editorial:**
Gene Pitts .......................Editor in Chief
Don B. Keele ......................Senior Editor
Kay Blumenthal ................Managing Editor
Teresa Carriero ......Associate Managing Editor
Douglas Hyde .........Associate Managing Editor
Anthony Catalano ..............Advertising Director
Cathy Cacchione ....................Art Director
Gerald McCarthy ................Assistant Editor
Michael Bieber ..................Assistant Editor
Bert Whyte ......................Associate Editor
Edward Tatnall Canby ..........Associate Editor
Kerry Tonning ................Production Director
Bob Meth ...................................Sales
Paula Mageri ...............................Sales
David Lauder .....................Senior Editor
**Desc.:** Contributed by-line articles discuss quality audio reproduction, equipment design and limitations, installation, components, etc. Emphasis is on equipment suitable for home use, and professional equipment and techniques. Departments include: Equipment Reviews, New Products, Book and Record Reviews and Opinion Columns.
**Readers:** Hi-Fi enthusiasts and recording, broadcast, and electronics engineers.

67213
## AUDIO/VIDEO INTERIORS
21700 Oxnard St., 1600
Woodland Hls, CA 91367
Telephone: (818) 593-3900
FAX: (818) 593-2274
Year Established: 1989
Pub. Frequency: m.
Page Size: standard
Subscrip. Rate: $19.95/yr.
Print Process: offset
Circulation: 57,765
Circulation Type: paid
**Owner(s):**
Avcom Publishing
21700 Oxnard St., Ste. 1600
Woodland Hls, CA 91367
Telephone: (818) 593-3900
Ownership %: 100
**Bureau(s):**
Avcom Publishing
237 Park Ave., 21st Fl.
New York, NY 10017
Telephone: (212) 551-3516
Contact: Jacqueline Flannery, Advertising Manager
**Management:**
Sarah Gammill ........Customer Service Manager
Joseph Goodman ................General Manager
**Editorial:**
Eric Gill ......................Executive Editor
Maureen Jenson ..........................Editor
Nate Scoble .......................Art Director
Carol R. Campbell ...........Group Publisher
Patty Harris ................Production Director
**Desc.:** Dedicated to illustrating style and technology in harmony. Combines sophisticated audio/video, home automation, and other technologies with interior design, architecture, art, furniture, and more.
**Readers:** 91% male, 9% female, affluent, early adapters.

24564
## AUDIOVIDEO INTERNATIONAL
275 Madison Ave., 12th Fl.
New York, NY 10016-1101
Telephone: (212) 752-3003
Year Established: 1973
Pub. Frequency: m.
Page Size: standard
Subscrip. Rate: $30/yr.
Freelance Pay: varies
Print Process: web offset
Circulation: 44,000
Circulation Type: controlled
**Owner(s):**
Dempa Publications, Inc.
275 Madison Ave., Ste. 610
New York, NY 10016
Telephone: (212) 682-3755
FAX: (212) 682-2730
Ownership %: 100
**Management:**
Ted Hirayama .............................President
Ted Hirayama ...........................Publisher
Bruce Jacobs ...................Advertising Manager
Soo Sonntag ...................Circulation Manager
Paul Iwayama ......................General Manager
**Editorial:**
Shin Kai ...........................Executive Editor
Nancy Klosek ...................Managing Editor
**Desc.:** Subjects covered in news and in in-depth feature stories include trends and developments in audio, hi-fi, TV, video, computers and home and personal electronics products. Special attention is given to new products and systems; retail success stories; how-to articles on merchandising, promotion, advertising, and store management. Also included are sales statistics, forecasts, international coverage of new developments, industry news, trade shows and company and people profiles.
**Readers:** Consumer electronic retailers and manufacturers.

66596
## AUDIO WEEK
276 Fifth Ave., Ste. 111
New York, NY 10001-4509
Telephone: (212) 686-5410
FAX: (212) 889-5097
Year Established: 1990
Pub. Frequency: w.
Page Size: standard
Subscrip. Rate: $275/yr. US.; $552/yr. foreign
**Owner(s):**
Warren Publishing
2115 Ward Ct., N.W.
Washington, DC 20037
Telephone: (202) 872-9200
Ownership %: 100
**Editorial:**
Paul Gluckman ...........................Editor
**Desc.:** Devoted to the audio industry including home hi-fi systems and components, personal portables, car audio and mobile electronics, custom installations, blank tape and CD-software.

58803
## AV VIDEO
701 Westchester Ave.
White Plains, NY 10604
Telephone: (914) 328-9157
FAX: (914) 328-9093
Year Established: 1972
Pub. Frequency: m.
Page Size: standard
Subscrip. Rate: $48/yr.; free to qualified
Materials: 01,05,06,15,27,28,29,30,32,33
Freelance Pay: $50-$250
Print Process: web offset
Circulation: 60,000
Circulation Type: free & paid

**Owner(s):**
Knowledge Industry Publications, Inc.
701 Westchester Ave.
White Plains, NY 10604
Telephone: (914) 328-9157
Ownership %: 100
**Management:**
Dean Eaker .............................Publisher
Hal Goodman ...........................Manager
**Editorial:**
Larry Henchey ..........................Editor
Andrea Lillo .................Associate Editor

24585
## JOURNAL OF THE AUDIO ENGINEERING SOCIETY
60 E. 42nd St.
Rm. 2520
New York, NY 10165
Telephone: (212) 661-2355
FAX: (212) 661-7829
Year Established: 1953
Pub. Frequency: 10/yr.
Page Size: standard
Subscrip. Rate: $125/yr.
Circulation: 10786
Circulation Type: paid
**Owner(s):**
Audio Engineering Society, Inc.
60 E. 42nd St.
Rm. 2520
New York, NY 10165
Telephone: (212) 661-2355
Ownership %: 100
**Editorial:**
Patricia M. MacDonald ...........Executive Editor
Abbie J. Cohen .....................Senior Editor
Daniel Von Recklinghausen ......................Editor
**Readers:** Professional audio engineers, educators, technicians, and students involved in design and manufacturing of audio equipment.

54024
## SOUND & VIDEO CONTRACTOR
9800 Metcalf
Overland Park, KS 66212
Telephone: (913) 341-1300
FAX: (913) 967-1898
Year Established: 1983
Pub. Frequency: m.
Page Size: standard
Subscrip. Rate: free to qualified personnel
Freelance Pay: negotiable
Circulation: 20,500
Circulation Type: controlled
**Owner(s):**
Intertec Publishing Corp.
P.O. Box 12901
Shawnee Msn, KS 66282
Telephone: (913) 341-1300
Ownership %: 100
**Bureau(s):**
Schiff & Associates
501 Santa Monica Blvd., #504
Santa Monica, CA 90401
Telephone: (310) 393-9285
Contact: Jason Perlman, Manager
**Management:**
Cameron Bishop .................Vice President
Dennis Milan ...........................Publisher
Kathryn Buckley .............Promotion Manager
**Editorial:**
Ted Uzzle ...................................Editor
**Desc.:** Serves the field of professional sound and video equipment installation in design/engineering firms, construction/installation companies and maintenance service companies.
**Readers:** Sound and video contractors, and other related industry professionals.

Materials Accepted/Included: 01-Business news 02-By-line articles 03-Fashion news 04-Food news 05-Freelance copy 06-Letters to editor 07-Real estate news 08-Sports news 09-Travel news 10-Book rev. 11-Movie rev. 12-Music rev. 13-TV rev. 14-Theater rev. 15-Coming events 16-Obituaries 17-Question & answer 18-Social announcements 19-Artwork 20-Cartoons 21-Photos 22-TV listings 23-Audio rec. 24-Video rec. 25-Books 26-Films/film clips 27-Personnel news 28-Press releases 29-New product news/photos 30-Trade lit. 31-Contracts awarded 32-Display adv. 33-Classified adv.

4-17

**VIDEOGRAPHY** 24607
2 Park Ave., Ste. 1820
New York, NY 10016
Telephone: (212) 213-3444
FAX: (212) 213-3484
Year Established: 1976
Pub. Frequency: m.
Page Size: standard
Subscrip. Rate: $30/yr.
Freelance Pay: varies
Circulation: 30,000
Circulation Type: controlled & paid
**Owner(s):**
P.S.N. Publications, Inc.
2 Park Ave., Ste. 1820
New York, NY 10016
Telephone: (212) 213-3444
Ownership %: 100
**Management:**
Paul Gallo .............................Publisher
David J. Miller .................Advertising Manager
**Editorial:**
Brian McKernan ...........................Editor
Mark Schubin .....................Technical Editor
**Desc.:** Contains news, trends and analysis
of the video industry, interviews with
specialists, editorials, guest columns, a
calendar of meetings and shows.
**Readers:** Video professionals.

**VIDEO INVESTOR** 58765
126 Clock Tower Pl.
Carmel, CA 93923
Telephone: (408) 624-1536
FAX: (408) 625-3225
Year Established: 1984
Pub. Frequency: m.
Page Size: standard
Subscrip. Rate: $525/yr.
**Owner(s):**
Paul Kagan
126 Clock Tower Pl.
Carmel, CA 93923
Telephone: (408) 624-1536
Ownership %: 100
**Management:**
Paul Kagan ..............................Publisher
Judith Pinney ...................Circulation Manager

**VIDEO STORE** 69256
7500 Old Oak Blvd.
Cleveland, OH 44130
Telephone: (714) 252-5300
FAX: (714) 252-5382
Year Established: 1979
Pub. Frequency: 50/yr.
Subscrip. Rate: $48/yr.
Circulation: 44,287
Circulation Type: paid
**Owner(s):**
Advanstar Communications, Inc.
7500 Old Oak Blvd.
Cleveland, OH 44130
Telephone: (714) 252-5300
Ownership %: 100
**Editorial:**
Mark Hennon ...............................Editor
**Desc.:** Includes proprietary market
research, aggressive management,
merchandising techniques, product
buying information, industry people and
news.
**Readers:** Video retailers involved in home
video sales.

**VIDEO SYSTEMS** 24605
9800 Metcalf
Overland Park, KS 66212-2215
Telephone: (913) 341-1300
FAX: (913) 967-1898
Year Established: 1975
Pub. Frequency: m.

Page Size: standard
Subscrip. Rate: $45/yr.; free to qualified
personnel
Freelance Pay: $125-$250
Circulation: 31,477
Circulation Type: controlled
**Owner(s):**
Intertec Publishing Corp.
9800 Metcalf
Overland Park, KS 66212-2215
Telephone: (913) 341-1300
Ownership %: 100
**Bureau(s):**
Intertec Publishing
888 Seventh Ave., 38th Fl.
New York, NY 10106
Telephone: (212) 332-0631
Contact: Ann B. Rosenberg, Manager

Intertec Publishing
Roseleigh House, New St.
Hinsdale, IL 60521
Telephone: (708) 887-0677
Contact: Nicholas McGeachin, Marketing
Director

Schiff & Associates
501 Santa Monica Blvd., 504
Santa Monica, CA 90401
Telephone: (213) 393-9285
Contact: Herb Schiff, Marketing Director

Intertec Publishing
55 E. Jackson Blvd.
Chicago, IL 60604
Telephone: (312) 435-2361
Contact: Vytas Urbanas, Marketing Director
**Management:**
R. J. Hancock ............................President
Cameron Bishop ......................Vice President
Duane N. Hefner .........................Publisher
Dee Unger ....................Advertising Manager
Evelyn Hornaday ...............Promotion Manager
**Editorial:**
Ned Soseman ..............................Editor
Tom Cook ..........................Managing Editor
Doug Coonrod ...........................Art Director
Kathy D. Mickelson .................Associate Editor
Tom Brick ........................Marketing Director
Carl Bentz .................Special Features Editor
Rick Lehtinen .....................Technical Editor
**Desc.:** Applications-oriented to keep video
and multimedia professionals up-to-date
on the latest production and
presentation techniques & technologies.
**Readers:** Video and multimedia production
professionals.

**VIDEO WEEK** 49831
276 Fifth Ave.
Ste. 1111
New York, NY 10001-4509
Telephone: (212) 686-5410
Year Established: 1980
Pub. Frequency: w.
Page Size: standard
Subscrip. Rate: $743/yr.
**Owner(s):**
Warren Publishing
2115 Ward Court, N. W.
Washington, DC 20037
Telephone: (202) 872-9200
Ownership %: 100
**Management:**
Roy W. Easley, III ........................Controller
Albert Warren ...........................Publisher
Betty Alvine ....................Circulation Manager
**Editorial:**
Dawson B. Nail .....................Executive Editor
Paul Warren .........................Senior Editor
Albert Warren ...........................Editor
David Lachenbruch ................Editorial Director
Gary Madderom ..................Marketing Director
**Desc.:** Reports latest news of program
sales and distribution for videocassettes,
discs, pay TV and allied media.

**Readers:** Executives in foregoing fields.

## Group 016-Automobiles & Accessories

**AFTERMARKET BUSINESS** 21803
7500 Old Oak Blvd.
Cleveland, OH 44130
Telephone: (216) 891-2604
FAX: (216) 891-2675
Year Established: 1936
Pub. Frequency: m.
Page Size: tabloid
Subscrip. Rate: $30/yr.
Materials: 01,02,05,06,15,19,20,21,32,33
Circulation: 22,500
Circulation Type: controlled
**Owner(s):**
Advanstar Communications, Inc.
7500 Old Oak Blvd.
Cleveland, OH 44130
Telephone: (216) 243-8100
Ownership %: 100
**Management:**
Douglas Ferguson .......................Publisher
**Editorial:**
Sandie Stambaugh-Cannon ........Editor in Chief
**Desc.:** Edited for buyers and operators in
the automotive retail supply and service
field.
**Readers:** Independent automotive
retailers, chain department managers,
buyers and executives, and home &
auto chains.
**Deadline:** story-6 wks. prior to pub. date;
news-6 wks. prior; photo-6 wks. prior;
ads-6 wks. prior

**AMERICAN CARWASH BUYER'S GUIDE** 21768
13222B Admiral Ave.
Marina Del Rey, CA 90292
Telephone: (310) 397-4217
Mailing Address:
P.O. Box 1107
Santa Monica, CA 90406
Year Established: 1968
Pub. Frequency: a.
Page Size: tabloid
Subscrip. Rate: $6/issue; $12/yr.;
$20/2yrs.
Materials: 01,06,15,17,27,28,29,30,31,32,33
Freelance Pay: varies
Print Process: web
Circulation: 2,000
Circulation Type: controlled
**Owner(s):**
Lott Publishing Co.
P.O. Box 1107
Santa Monica, CA 90406
Telephone: (310) 397-4217
Ownership %: 100
**Management:**
Davis Lott .............................President
Davis Lott .............................Publisher
**Editorial:**
Laurie Lott ..............................Editor
Laurie Lott ..............................Photo
**Readers:** Carwash owners, operators,
managers, investors, employees &
members of the manufacturing and
distributing companies who service the
industry.

**AMERICAN CLEAN CAR** 21769
500 N. Dearborn St.
Chicago, IL 60610
Telephone: (312) 337-7700
FAX: (312) 337-8654
Year Established: 1972
Pub. Frequency: bi-m.
Page Size: standard
Subscrip. Rate: $33/yr.

Circulation: 20,000
Circulation Type: controlled
**Owner(s):**
Crain Associated Enterprises, Inc.
500 N. Dearborn St.
Chicago, IL 60610
Telephone: (312) 337-7700
Ownership %: 100
**Management:**
Ed Goldstein ............................President
Ed Goldstein ............................Publisher
**Editorial:**
Larry Ebert ..............................Editor
Paul Partyka .......................Managing Editor
Jim Miller ........................Assistant Editor
**Desc.:** Articles include case histories of
successful carwash operation
management aids, merchandising ideas
& industry news.
**Readers:** Car wash owners and operators.

**AUTO & FLAT GLASS JOURNAL** 21771
303 Harvard E., Ste. 101
Seattle, WA 98102
Telephone: (206) 322-5120
Mailing Address:
P.O. Box 12099
Seattle, WA 98102
Year Established: 1953
Pub. Frequency: m.
Page Size: pocket
Subscrip. Rate: $30/yr.
Materials: 01,02,05,06,15,28,29,30,32,33
Freelance Pay: negotiable
Print Process: offset
Circulation: 5,700
Circulation Type: paid
**Owner(s):**
Grawin Publications, Inc.
P.O. Box 12099
Seattle, WA 98102
Telephone: (206) 322-5120
Ownership %: 100
**Management:**
J.P. Whinihan ...........................President
J.P. Whinihan ...........................Publisher
Sally Swendt ...................Advertising Manager
**Editorial:**
Mary Zabawa .............................Editor
**Desc.:** Contains step-by-step procedures
for installing glass in current model cars.
Features cover business, management
and administrative subjects relative to
glass shop operations. Departments
include: Letters, Tips, Bulletins, News,
Products, and Classifieds.
**Readers:** Auto glass replacement shop
owners and managers.

**AUTO & TRUCK INTERNATIONAL/AUTO Y CAMION INTERNACIONAL EN ESPANOL** 21776
25 N.W. Point Blvd., Ste. 800
Elk Grove Village, IL 60007
Telephone: (708) 427-2089
FAX: (708) 427-2013
Year Established: 1917
Pub. Frequency: 6/yr.
Page Size: standard
Subscrip. Rate: $50/yr.; $80/2 yrs.
Circulation: 51,604
Circulation Type: controlled
**Owner(s):**
Hunter Publishing, Inc.
25 N.W. Point Blvd., Ste. 800
Elk Grove Village, IL 60007
Telephone: (708) 427-9512
Ownership %: 100
**Management:**
James Pierce ............................President
Gary Hynes ....................Associate Publisher
**Editorial:**
Bill Wolfe ...............................Editor

**Materials Accepted/Included:** 01-Business news 02-By-line articles 03-Fashion news 04-Food news 05-Freelance copy 06-Letters to editor 07-Real estate news 08-Sports news 09-Travel news 10-Book rev. 11-Movie rev. 12-Music rev. 13-TV rev. 14-Theater rev. 15-Coming events 16-Obituaries 17-Question & answer 18-Social announcements 19-Artwork 20-Cartoons 21-Photos 22-TV listings 23-Audio rec. 24-Video rec. 25-Books 26-Films/film clips 27-Personnel news 28-Press releases 29-New product news/photos 30-Trade lit. 31-Contracts awarded 32-Display adv. 33-Classified adv.

**Desc.:** Trends, new equipment and techniques in the automotive service industries and "how-to-do-it" articles for the service department manager, the independent shop owner, the vehicle fleet manager and the service station manager. Published in separate editions in English & Spanish.

**Readers:** Vehicle dealers, independent service & dealers of parts, accessories & equipment, vehicle fleet operators, all outside of North America.

21804

## AUTOINC.

1901 Airport Fwy., Ste. 100
Bedford, TX 76021
Telephone: (817) 283-6205
FAX: (817) 685-0225
Mailing Address:
　P.O. Box 929
　Bedford, TX 76095
Year Established: 1952
Pub. Frequency: m.
Page Size: standard
Subscrip. Rate: $20/yr.
Materials: 05,06,15,28,29,30
Print Process: offset
Circulation: 14,500
Circulation Type: paid
**Owner(s):**
Automotive Service Association
P.O. Box 929
Bedford, TX 76095
Telephone: (817) 283-6205
Ownership %: 100
**Management:**
Tammy Luna .....................Advertising Manager
**Editorial:**
Roberto Michel ................................Editor
Trisha Baker ...........................Miscellaneous
**Desc.:** News and factual features relating to independent auto repair shop owners.
**Readers:** All types of auto repair shops including mechanical, collision and transmission repair.

21772

## AUTO LAUNDRY NEWS

370 Lexington Ave.
New York, NY 10017
Telephone: (212) 532-9290
FAX: (212) 779-8345
Year Established: 1953
Pub. Frequency: m.
Page Size: standard
Subscrip. Rate: $25/yr.
Materials: 01,02,05,06,15,20,27,28,29,30,
　31,32,33
Circulation: 18,500
Circulation Type: controlled
**Owner(s):**
Columbia Communications, Inc.
370 Lexington Ave.
New York, NY 10017
Telephone: (212) 532-9290
FAX: (212) 779-8345
Ownership %: 100
**Management:**
Joseph Feldman ...........................Publisher
Jim Kirk .........................Advertising Manager
**Editorial:**
Robert Storch ...............................Editor
**Readers:** Owners, operators and managers of vehicle equipment and supplies used in commercial car wash.

21773

## AUTO MERCHANDISING NEWS

461 Skytop Dr.
Fairfield, CT 06432
Telephone: (203) 371-4664
FAX: (203) 378-7285
Year Established: 1971
Pub. Frequency: m.

Page Size: standard
Subscrip. Rate: $48/yr.
Materials: 01,02,05,06,07,09,10,15,16,17,
　19,20,21,27,28,29,30,31,32,33
Freelance Pay: variable
Print Process: offset
Circulation: 25,467
Circulation Type: controlled
**Owner(s):**
Mortimer Communications, Inc.
461 Skytop Dr.
Fairfield, CT 06432
Telephone: (203) 371-4664
Ownership %: 100
**Management:**
Bill Mortimer, Jr. ........................President
Bill Mortimer, Jr. ........................Publisher
Richard Burns .................Advertising Manager
Jim Mellott .......................Production Manager
**Editorial:**
John Kozioz .......................Managing Editor
Gene Watkins .......................Miscellaneous
**Desc.:** Complete national and regional news of the volume auto aftermarket; how-to-stories, late reports on packaging, display, store layouts, new products. Departments include: News, Feature Stories, New Product Stories, Editorial Columns.
**Readers:** Automotive retail chains, mass-merchandiser, distributors, manufacturers and sales representatives.
**Deadline:** story-10th of the mo.; news-10th of the mo.; photo-10th of the mo.; ads-15th of the mo.

21778

## AUTOMOTIVE BOOSTER OF CALIFORNIA, THE

1037 N. Lake Ave.
Pasadena, CA 91104
Telephone: (818) 398-6848
FAX: (818) 398-6840
Year Established: 1928
Pub. Frequency: m.
Subscrip. Rate: $6/yr.
Materials: 01,06,15,16,18,20,21,23,24,25,
　27,28,29,30,31,32,33
Freelance Pay: $1.25/col. in.
Print Process: web
Circulation: 4,800
Circulation Type: controlled
**Owner(s):**
KAL Publications, Inc.
1037 N. Lake Ave.
Pasadena, CA 91104
Telephone: (818) 398-6848
FAX: (818) 398-6840
Ownership %: 100
**Management:**
Kathy Laderman ...........................Publisher
Lynne Kenworthy ..............Advertising Manager
Cathy Wacker ......................Business Manager
**Editorial:**
Kathy Laderman ..............................Editor
**Desc.:** Covering the automotive parts aftermarket including jobbers, manufacturers, representatives, warehouse-distributors, installers, and manufacturers throughout California and the west.
**Readers:** Automotive aftermarket (parts, warehouse) and members of the Automotive Booster Club.

21780

## AUTOMOTIVE COOLING JOURNAL

2767 Geryville Pke.
Pennsburg, PA 18041
Telephone: (215) 541-4500
FAX: (215) 679-4977
Mailing Address:
　P.O. Box 97
　E. Greenville, PA 18041

Year Established: 1956
Pub. Frequency: m.
Page Size: standard
Subscrip. Rate: $25/yr.
Freelance Pay: negotiable
Circulation: 10,500
Circulation Type: free
**Owner(s):**
National Automotive Radiator Service
　Assn., Inc.
P.O. Box 97
E. Greenville, PA 18041
Telephone: (215) 541-4500
Ownership %: 100
**Management:**
Glen Looper ..............................President
NARSA .................................Publisher
Wayne Juchno ....................Advertising Manager
**Editorial:**
Elvis Hoffpauir ..............................Editor
Jim Fortney ............Assistant Managing Editor
Wayne Juchno ....................New Product Editor
**Desc.:** The ACJ is the official publication of the National Automotive Radiator Service Assn. and the Mobile Air Conditioning Society and it reports news, views, trends and technological items of interest to the people within the radiator repair trade and the automotive air conditioning service industry.
**Readers:** National. Individuals who own or operate radiator repair shops and automotive air conditioning businesses and their suppliers and manufacturers.

21784

## AUTOMOTIVE FLEET

2512 Artesia Blvd.
Redondo Beach, CA 90278
Telephone: (310) 376-8788
FAX: (310) 376-9043
Year Established: 1961
Pub. Frequency: m.
Page Size: standard
Subscrip. Rate: $35/yr.
Circulation: 23,400
Circulation Type: controlled
**Owner(s):**
Bobit Publishing Co.
2512 Artesia Blvd.
Redondo Beach, CA 90278
Telephone: (310) 376-8788
Ownership %: 100
**Management:**
Ty F. Bobit ...............................President
Edward J. Bobit ...........................Publisher
Chuck Parker ...................Advertising Manager
**Editorial:**
Mike Antich ........................Executive Editor
Mark Becker ..........................Senior Editor
Edward J. Bobit .............................Editor
Cheryl Knight ....................Assistant Editor
Pam Reitmier ...................Production Director
**Desc.:** Inform vehicle fleet managers about management techniques and new developments in car and truck maintenance, which have a direct bearing on their operational, purchasing and management responsibilities. Editorial departments include: Letters, Personnel Personals, Calender of Events, Gas Prices, Late News, Fleet News, New Products, Used Car Prices at Auction, Advertisers Index, Editorial.
**Readers:** Passenger car, light and medium duty truck fleet purchasers, leasing, rental, utility and police car drivers, and taxi drivers.

21785

## AUTOMOTIVE INDUSTRIES

One Chilton Way
Radnor, PA 19089
Telephone: (215) 964-4255
FAX: (215) 964-4251
Year Established: 1895

Pub. Frequency: m.
Page Size: standard
Subscrip. Rate: $55/yr. in US; $110/yr.
　foreign
Circulation: 102,000
Circulation Type: controlled
**Owner(s):**
Capital Cities/ABC, Inc.
77 W. 66th St.
New York, NY 10023
Telephone: (212) 456-7777
Ownership %: 100
**Bureau(s):**
Automotive Industries
2600 Fisher Bldg/W. Grand Blvd
Detroit, MI 48217
Telephone: (313) 875-2090
Contact: John McElroy, Editor in Chief
**Management:**
James E. Henne ...........................Publisher
Rosemary Welding .........Advertising Manager
Donna M. Borrelli .............Business Manager
Jack Jones .......................Circulation Manager
**Editorial:**
John McElroy .....................Editor in Chief
Lindsay Brooke .....................Executive Editor
**Desc.:** Timely information source for the worldwide vehicle producing and supplying industries. It reports on and analyzes significant trends, issues, events, people, products and processes as they impact on design, engineering, manufacturing, marketing and management.
**Readers:** Directed to persons associated with the automotive industry in management, engineering, design, production/manufacturing, purchasing and other related fields.

21786

## AUTOMOTIVE MARKETING

One Chilton Way
Radnor, PA 19087
Telephone: (215) 964-4000
FAX: (215) 964-4981
Year Established: 1971
Pub. Frequency: 12/yr.
Page Size: tabloid
Subscrip. Rate: $3.50/issue; $36/yr. US
Materials: 01,15,27,28,29,30
Circulation: 40,211
Circulation Type: controlled
**Owner(s):**
Capital Cities/ABC Inc.
77 W. 66th St.
New York, NY 10023
Telephone: (212) 456-7777
Ownership %: 100
**Management:**
Sarah Frankson ...........................Publisher
Rosemary Welding ...........Advertising Manager
Donna Borrelli ....................Business Manager
**Editorial:**
John Wirebach .......................Senior Editor
Ted Arnold ..................................Editor
Karen Schweizer ..................Editorial Assistant
Ed Kaufman .......................Marketing Editor
Phil Katcher ......................Research Editor
**Desc.:** Edited for the distributors and retailers of automotive parts, accessories, chemicals and service. Emphasizes product line merchandising, training, movement and forecasts, and management of inventory, store site selection, return on investment, and computerization. Also reports trends of the industry, as well as external elements affecting the industry's growth.
**Readers:** Warehouse distributor, jobber and retail automotive store managers and buyers; manufacturers of automotive aftermarket parts, accessories, chemicals and oil and service bay equipment.

**Materials Accepted/Included:** 01-Business news 02-By-line articles 03-Fashion news 04-Food news 05-Freelance copy 06-Letters to editor 07-Real estate news 08-Sports news 09-Travel news 10-Book rev. 11-Movie rev. 12-Music rev. 13-TV rev. 14-Theater rev. 15-Coming events 16-Obituaries 17-Question & answer 18-Social announcements 19-Artwork 20-Cartoons 21-Photos 22-TV listings 23-Audio rec. 24-Video rec. 25-Books 26-Films/film clips 27-Personnel news 28-Press releases 29-New product news/photos 30-Trade lit. 31-Contracts awarded 32-Display adv. 33-Classified adv.

4-19

**AUTOMOTIVE MESSENGER, THE** [21788]
427 Chez Paree
Hazelwood, MO 63042
Telephone: (314) 831-4000
FAX: (314) 831-3610
Mailing Address:
P.O. Box 96
Hazelwood, MO 63042
Year Established: 1956
Pub. Frequency: m.
Page Size: tabloid
Subscrip. Rate: $10/yr.
Freelance Pay: free copy
Circulation: 15,000
**Owner(s):**
Hansen Publishing, Inc.
431 Chez Paree
Hazelwood, MO 63042
Telephone: (814) 831-4040
Ownership %: 100
**Editorial:**
Bill Winders .....................................Editor
**Desc.:** Covers geneeral automotive news
written by staff members. Editorial
departments include: MGDA
Communique, Photomotive, Area Trade
Talk, ASA News, Timely Profit Makers.
**Readers:** Personnel of service stations,
garages, rent dealers, trucking
companies, fleets.

**AUTOMOTIVE NEWS** [21789]
1400 Woodbridge Ave.
Detroit, MI 48207-3187
Telephone: (313) 446-6000
FAX: (313) 446-1680
Year Established: 1925
Pub. Frequency: w.
Page Size: tabloid
Subscrip. Rate: $2 newsstand; $80/yr.
Materials: 01,06,27,28
Freelance Pay: $8/col. in.
Print Process: web offset
Circulation: 77,401
Circulation Type: paid
**Owner(s):**
Crain Communications, Inc.
1400 Woodbridge
Detroit, MI 48207
Telephone: (313) 446-6000
Ownership %: 100
**Bureau(s):**
Los Angeles
6500 Wilshire Blvd.
Ste. 2300
Los Angeles, CA 90048
Telephone: (213) 651-3710
FAX: (213) 655-8157
Contact: Mark Rechtin

New York
220 E. 42nd St.
New York, NY 10017
Telephone: (212) 210-0127
FAX: (212) 210-0400
Contact: Jim Henry

Washington
814 National Press Bldg.
Washington, DC 20045
Telephone: (202) 662-7212
FAX: (202) 638-3155
Contact: Max Gates, Circulation Manager

Mid-south
104 E. Park Dr.
Ste. 315
Brentwood, TN 37027
Telephone: (615) 371-6654
FAX: (615) 371-6644
Contact: Lindsay Chappel

Europe
Justinianstrasse 22
60322 Frankfurt am
Main
Telephone: (49)69-24553-235
FAX: (49)69-5968-022
Contact: Diana Kurylko

Asia
7-1 Yurako-Cho
1-Chrome
Chiyoda-Ku Turkmeninstan
Telephone: (81)33-760-6477
FAX: (81)33-760-4592
Contact: Mary Ann Maskery
**Management:**
K.E. Crain .....................................Publisher
Tony Merpi .......................Advertising Manager
**Editorial:**
Ed Lapham .....................Executive Editor
Peter Brown .....................................Editor
K.E. Crain .....................Editorial Director
**Desc.:** News features cover automotive
engineering, manufacturing,
merchandising, servicing. Material written
on executive level/trends, new cars,
company news, promotion, advertising,
appointments, meetings, conventions.
**Readers:** Dealers, manufacturers,
suppliers, finance government.

**AUTOMOTIVE NEWS OF THE** [21790]
**PACIFIC NORTHWEST**
14789 S.E. 82nd Dr.
Clackamas, OR 97015
Telephone: (503) 656-1456
Year Established: 1919
Pub. Frequency: bi-m.
Page Size: standard
Subscrip. Rate: $10/yr.
Circulation: 4,500
Circulation Type: controlled
**Owner(s):**
Automotive News Association
14789 S.E. 82nd Dr.
Clackamas, OR 97015
Telephone: (503) 656-1456
Ownership %: 100
**Management:**
William H. Boyer .....................Publisher
**Editorial:**
William H. Boyer .....................................Editor
**Desc.:** Carries news of automotive trade,
especially that of interest to the Pacific
Northwest. All articles are staff-written,
but occasionally uses technical and
business articles written by people in the
trade. Departments include: New Car
and Truck Sales in Oregon, Washington
and Idaho, Gasoline Sales, New
Products, New Literature, Personal
Items, Column of Northwest Trade
Notes.
**Readers:** Car and truck dealers, garages,
superintendents, tire shops, recappers,
machine shop establishments, body
shops and all aftermarket parts stores
and warehouses in Oregon, Southern
Washington, and Southern Idaho.

**AUTOMOTIVE REBUILDER** [21791]
11 S. Forge St.
Akron, OH 44304
Telephone: (216) 535-6117
FAX: (216) 535-0874
Year Established: 1964
Pub. Frequency: m.
Page Size: standard
Subscrip. Rate: $43/yr. US; $87/yr. foreign
Materials: 01,06,15,28,29,30,32,33
Print Process: web offset
Circulation: 25,000
Circulation Type: controlled & paid

**Owner(s):**
Babcox Automotive Publications, Inc.
11 S. Forge St.
Akron, OH 44304
Telephone: (216) 535-6117
Ownership %: 100
**Management:**
Bill Babcox .....................................President
Becky Babcox .....................................Publisher
Cindy Ott .....................Advertising Manager
**Editorial:**
David Wooldridge .....................................Editor
**Desc.:** Covers core management topics;
technical information; news on new
products and services; pertinent
legislative issues; new market
opportunities; reports of OE
developments and the impact on
rebuilders; trade association news;
conference and show reports and
previews.
**Readers:** Owners and managers of the
leading volume rebuilding businesses in
each important industry segment:
production engine rebuilders; custom or
jobber machine shop engine rebuilders;
transmission rebuilders; and vehicle
mechanical (small parts) rebuilders,
including brake systems, fuel systems,
electrical units, water pumps, air
conditioning parts, and other small parts
rebuilders.

**AUTOMOTIVE RECYCLING** [21799]
3975 Fair Ridge Dr., Ste. 20N
Fairfax, VA 22033
Telephone: (703) 385-1001
FAX: (703) 385-1494
Year Established: 1974
Pub. Frequency: bi-m.
Page Size: standard
Subscrip. Rate: $30/yr.; $45/yr. foreign
Freelance Pay: $100/article
Circulation: 2,500
Circulation Type: controlled
**Owner(s):**
Automotive & Recyclers Association
3975 Fair Ridge Dr., Ste. 20N
Fairfax, VA 22033
Telephone: (703) 385-1001
FAX: (703) 385-1494
Ownership %: 100
**Management:**
William Steinkuller .....................Publisher
**Editorial:**
Christopher Murphy .....................................Editor
Christopher Murphy .................Communications
Manager
**Desc.:** Features articles designed to
improve the efficiency of businesses that
salvage reusable parts from auto
vehicles, a 6-8 billion industry in the U.S.
**Readers:** Recycling operations and used
parts businesses, in the U.S., Canada
and overseas.

**AUTO RENTAL NEWS** [67674]
2512 Artesia Blvd.
Redondo Beach, CA 90278-3210
Telephone: (310) 376-8788
FAX: (310) 376-9043
Year Established: 1988
Pub. Frequency: bi-m.
Page Size: standard
Subscrip. Rate: $25/yr. non-members;
$30/yr. in Canada; $38/yr. elsewhere
Print Process: web offset
Circulation: 16,500
Circulation Type: controlled

**Owner(s):**
Bobit Publishing Co.
2512 Artesia Blvd.
Redondo Beach, CA 90278-3210
Telephone: (310) 376-8788
Ownership %: 100
**Management:**
Charles Parker .....................................Publisher
**Editorial:**
Jon LeSage .....................................Editor
**Desc.:** For the car rental industry.
**Readers:** Rental dealerships.

**AUTO TRIM & RESTYLING NEWS** [21774]
6255 Barfield Rd., Ste. 200
Atlanta, GA 30328-4300
Telephone: (404) 252-8831
FAX: (404) 252-4436
Year Established: 1953
Pub. Frequency: m.
Page Size: standard
Subscrip. Rate: $30/yr. US; $51/yr.
Canada & Mexico; $82/yr. overseas
surface; $190/yr. overseas airmail
Materials: 01,02,05,06,15,24,25,27,28,29,
30,32,33
Freelance Pay: $50-$500
Circulation: 8,700
Circulation Type: paid
**Owner(s):**
National Assoc. of Auto Trim & Restyling
Shops
Ownership %: 100
**Management:**
Nat Danas .....................................Founder
Angelo Varrone .....................................President
**Editorial:**
Gary Fong .....................................Editor
Anne-Marie Fanguy .............Managing Editor
Kim Sandell .....................Art Director
Art Little .....................Associate Publisher
Randy Easton .............National Sales Manager
Nat Danas .....................Publisher Emeritus
**Desc.:** Covers the merchandising and
installation of auto seat covers,
convertible tops, auto interior upholstery
and accessories, new products
equipment and techniques, boat tops,
cushions, covers; and customizing,
which covers a package approach for
one of a kind cars, and includes striping,
body side moldings, block-out restyling
kits and windows, as well as "mock"
convertible conversion. Antique
restoration also covered. Also furniture
upholstery and aircraft refurbishing, as
well as van customizing.
**Readers:** Auto trim shops, installation
specialists, car restylists, customizers,
marine and furniture upholsterers,
manufacturers, jobbers and wholesalers,
and new car dealers.
**Deadline:** story-2 mos. prior to pub. date;
news-2 mos. prior; photo-2 mos. prior

**BATTERY MAN, THE** [25052]
100 Larchwood Dr.
Largo, FL 34640-2811
Telephone: (813) 586-1408
FAX: (813) 586-1400
Year Established: 1921
Pub. Frequency: m.
Page Size: standard
Subscrip. Rate: $20/yr.; $22/Yr. surface
mail overseas; $55/yr. airmail overseas
Materials: 01,05,06,15,19,20,21,27,28,29,
30,31,32,33
Freelance Pay: $.08/wd.
Print Process: offset
Circulation: 4,300
Circulation Type: paid

**Owner(s):**
Independent Battery Manufacturers
  Association, Inc
100 Larchwood Dr.
Largo, FL 34640
Telephone: (813) 586-1408
FAX: (813) 586-1400
Ownership %: 100
**Management:**
Suzanne Kellerman ..........Advertising Manager
**Editorial:**
Celwyn E. Hopkins .....................................Editor
Betty Rosser ......................Accounting Manager
Cathy Lees .........................Production Director
Sarah M. Bennett ..........Subscriptions Director
**Desc.:** Covers the battery industry,
  including the manufacture and sale of
  batteries, new developments and
  applications for batteries and general
  industry news. Articles and news stories
  are welcomed and used insofar as
  space permits. Credit is usually given in
  by-lines, or within article. Departments
  include: Events, Products, Meetings,
  Literature, Marketing, Government,
  Feedback.
**Readers:** Battery manufacturers & starting,
  ignition, lighting jobbing and retail
  specialists (Industry manufacturers,
  consultants, suppliers.)
**Deadline:** story-2 mos. prior to pub. date;
  news-1 mo. prior; photo-1 mo. prior; ads-
  1st of each mo.

### BODYSHOP BUSINESS
48843
11 S. Forge St.
Akron, OH 44304
Telephone: (216) 535-6117
FAX: (216) 535-0874
Year Established: 1982
Pub. Frequency: m.
Page Size: standard
Subscrip. Rate: $46/yr.
Materials: 01,06,15,27,28,29,30,32,33
Print Process: web offset
Circulation: 56,684
Circulation Type: controlled
**Owner(s):**
Babcox Publications, Inc.
11 S. Forge St.
Akron, OH 44304
Telephone: (216) 535-6117
Ownership %: 100
**Management:**
Bill Babcox ......................................President
Denise Lloyd .......................................Publisher
**Editorial:**
Greg Sharpless .........................................Editor
Patti Renner ......................Managing Editor
**Desc.:** The Babcox Magazine for the Body
  Repair Industry. Monthly articles and
  features addressing management,
  estimating, sheet metal work,
  painting procedures, equipment and
  supplies, current industry news, and
  product information.
**Readers:** Reaches each major segment of
  the industry including:
  independent/franchised shops;
  new and/or used vehicle dealers with
  body shops; fleet operators doing body
  repair; specialists in frame/structural
  repair; heavy duty truck, trailer or bus
  repair and refinishing shops; allied
  specialists shops, such as commercial
  body builder, customizing, glass,
  radiator, trim, truck painting and
  lettering, upholstery shops; auto -
  damage insurance appraisal firms;
  and wholesalers specializing in paint,
  body repair or equipment lines.

### BRAKE & FRONT END
21793
11 S. Forge St.
Akron, OH 44304
Telephone: (216) 535-6117
FAX: (216) 535-0874
Mailing Address:
  P.O. Box 1810
  Akron, OH 44309-1810
Year Established: 1931
Pub. Frequency: m.
Page Size: standard
Subscrip. Rate: $45/yr.
Circulation: 27,611
Circulation Type: controlled
**Owner(s):**
Babcox Publications, Inc.
11 S. Forge St.
Akron, OH 44304
Telephone: (216) 535-6117
Ownership %: 100
**Management:**
Tom Babcox ...................Chairman of Board
Bill Babcox .........................................President
Dan Cook ...........................................Publisher
**Editorial:**
Tim Fritz .......................................Senior Editor
Doug Kaufman .......................................Editor
Linda Ligman ..............................Art Director
Bob Leone .........................Contributing Editor
Larry Carley ..........................Technical Editor
**Desc.:** Departments Include: Tech Update,
  Industry Outlook, Reader Forum,
  Industry Review, Management Market,
  Brake Down, Product Showcase,
  Undercar Corner
**Readers:** Automotive aftermarket repair
  shops specializing in brake, front end,
  and suspension system service and
  general undercar repairs.

### CARS & PARTS
59649
911 Vandemark Rd.
Sidney, OH 45365
Telephone: (513) 498-0803
FAX: (513) 498-0808
Mailing Address:
  P.O. Box 482
  Sidney, OH 45365
Year Established: 1957
Pub. Frequency: m.
Page Size: standard
Subscrip. Rate: $2.95 newsstand; $22/yr.;
  foreign $27/yr.
Materials: 06,28,32,33
Circulation: 105,000
Circulation Type: paid
**Owner(s):**
Amos Press, Inc.
911 Vandemark Rd.
Sidney, OH 45365
Telephone: (513) 498-0803
**Management:**
Walter C. Reed ....................................Publisher
**Editorial:**
Robert Jay Stevens ................................Editor
Ken New ...........................................Art Director
Diane Thompson ...........Newsstand/Marketing
  Director
**Desc.:** Edited for the active automotive
  enthusiast. Focuses on authentic
  collector cars, the art of restoration and
  automotive history through profiles of
  selected feature cars, how-to articles
  and in-depth historical accounts of the
  auto companies and the men who ran
  them.
**Readers:** Automotive enthusiasts & car
  collectors.
**Deadline:** ads-8th of each mo.

### COLLISION
21798
P.O. Box M
Franklin, MA 02038-0822
Telephone: (508) 528-6211
Year Established: 1960
Pub. Frequency: 9/yr.
Page Size: standard
Subscrip. Rate: $28/yr.
Materials: 01,02,03,04,05,06,07,09,10,15,
  16,17,18,19,20,21,24,25,27,28,29,31,32
Freelance Pay: varies
Print Process: offset
Circulation: 15,000
Circulation Type: controlled & paid
**Owner(s):**
Kruza Kaleidoscopix, Inc.
P.O. Box 389
Franklin, MA 02038
Telephone: (508) 528-6211
Ownership %: 100
**Bureau(s):**
Chet Spink
San Jose, CA 95120

Ron Budman
Milton, PA 17847

David Ward
Dover, DE 19903

Lou Baffa
Brooklyn, NY 11222

William Mueller
Solon, IA 52333

Richard Jay
Ashland, MA 01721

Features
Newberg, OR 97132
Contact: Bob Bruce
**Management:**
J.A. Kruza .........................Advertising Manager
**Editorial:**
J.A. Kruza ...............................................Editor
Allen Johnson ...............................Art Director
John Mathes .......................Local News Editor
John Dean ........................New Product Editor
Beverly Call ..........................Research Director
Brad Sears ..............................Technical Editor
Ron Budman ..............................Technical Editor
M.V. Quinn ...............................Travel Editor
**Desc.:** News and how-to for owners,
  buyers, managers of dealerships and
  auto body repair shops and emergency
  road service serving Northeastern USA.
**Readers:** Managers and craftsmen of auto
  body, paint shops, and dealerships.
**Deadline:** story-6 wks. prior to pub. date;
  news-3 wks. prior to pub. date; ads-6
  wks. prior to pub. date

### COUNTERMAN
54033
11 S. Forge St.
Akron, OH 44304
Telephone: (216) 535-6117
FAX: (216) 535-0874
Year Established: 1983
Pub. Frequency: m.
Page Size: standard
Subscrip. Rate: $43/yr.; $87/2 yrs.
Circulation: 50,000
Circulation Type: controlled & paid
**Owner(s):**
Babcox Publications, Inc.
11 S. Forge St.
Akron, OH 44304
Telephone: (216) 535-6117
Ownership %: 100
**Management:**
Bill Babcox ......................................President
Bill Babcox ......................................Publisher
**Editorial:**
Gary Molinaro ......................................Editor

**Desc.:** Devoted to improving the
  effectiveness of professional counter
  sales personnel. Monthly topics include
  professional over-the-counter selling
  techniques; add-on sales; marketing
  trends/automotive technical changes;
  special product promotions; store
  appearance and maintenance;
  mechanical information for DIYers;
  customer relations; personal self-
  improvement (appearance and attitude);
  training clinics; general industry and
  legislative news; humor and feature
  stories.
**Readers:** Written exclusively for the men
  and women responsible for sales in the
  nation's automotive wholesale/retail
  aftermarket specifically directed the
  business interests of these jobber sales
  personnel.

### DEALER BUSINESS
21777
6633 Odessa Ave.
Van Nuys, CA 91406
Telephone: (818) 997-0644
Year Established: 1966
Pub. Frequency: m.
Page Size: standard
Subscrip. Rate: $36/yr.
Print Process: offset
Circulation: 33,501
Circulation Type: controlled
**Owner(s):**
McLean-Hunter West, Inc.
6633 Odessa Ave.
Van Nuys, CA 91406
Telephone: (818) 997-0644
Ownership %: 100
**Bureau(s):**
Auto Age Detroit Bureau
32068 Olde Franklin Dr.
Farmington, MI 48334
Telephone: (313) 932-3240
Contact: Mac Gordon, Bureau Chief

Washington Bureau
Telephone: (703) 554-2645
Contact: Robert McElwaine, Bureau Chief
**Management:**
Joseph Crown .....................................Publisher
John Cermak ....................Circulation Manager
**Editorial:**
C. D. Bohon ...............................................Editor
Mary Flowers ......................Managing Editor
Sean Olson ...................................Advertising
Wm. Smith ...................................Advertising
Andrew Unger ...................................Advertising
Rebecca Summerfield ...................Art Director
John Ott ...........................Production Director
**Desc.:** Covers all aspects of the retail
  automobile industry and is, by
  independent Readex study, the No.
  1 magazine in its field.
**Readers:** New car and truck dealers and
  their managers.

### EASTERN AFTERMARKET JOURNAL
21800
124 Cedarhurst Ave.
Cedarhurst, NY 11516
Telephone: (516) 295-3680
Mailing Address:
  P.O. Box 373
  Cedarhurst, NY 11516
Year Established: 1950
Pub. Frequency: bi-m.
Page Size: standard
Subscrip. Rate: $24/2 yrs.; $33/3 yrs.
Materials: 01,02,06,15,21,27,28,29,30,32,33
Freelance Pay: negotiable
Print Process: offset
Circulation: 9,500
Circulation Type: controlled

**Materials Accepted/Included:** 01-Business news 02-By-line articles 03-Fashion news 04-Food news 05-Freelance copy 06-Letters to editor 07-Real estate news 08-Sports news 09-Travel news 10-Book rev. 11-Movie rev. 12-Music rev. 13-TV rev. 14-Theater rev. 15-Coming events 16-Obituaries 17-Question & answer 18-Social announcements 19-Artwork 20-Cartoons 21-Photos 22-TV listings 23-Audio rec. 24-Video rec. 25-Books 26-Films/film clips 27-Personnel news 28-Press releases 29-New product news/photos 30-Trade lit. 31-Contracts awarded 32-Display adv. 33-Classified adv.

4-21

**Owner(s):**
Stan Hubsher, Inc.
P.O. Box 373
Cedarhurst, NY 11516
Telephone: (516) 295-3680
Ownership %: 100
**Management:**
Stan Hubsher ..............................Publisher
**Editorial:**
Rosanne Humes ...............Editorial Director
Ruth Williamson ...............Production Editor
**Desc.:** Covers issues of interest to Eastern
automotive jobbers, warehouse
distributors, wholesalers with the buying
function. Free lance articles should
query us first for content and location.
**Readers:** Eastern automotive warehouse
distributors & workers who have the
buying function.
**Deadline:** story-1 mo. prior to pub. date;
news-1 mo. prior; photo-1 mo. prior; ads-
up to closing date

**FLEET EXECUTIVE**  21821
120 Wood Ave., Ste. 615
Iselin, NJ 08830
Telephone: (908) 494-8100
FAX: (908) 494-6789
Year Established: 1957
Pub. Frequency: m.
Page Size: 4 color photos/art
Subscrip. Rate: $48/yr.
Freelance Pay: flat page rate
Circulation: 4,000
Circulation Type: paid
**Owner(s):**
National Association of Fleet
Administrators, Inc.
Telephone: (201) 494-8100
Ownership %: 100
**Management:**
David Lefever ......................Executive Director
**Editorial:**
John Feinstein ...............................Editor
John Feinstein ....................Publication Director
**Desc.:** Publishes feature articles, news
stories relating to operation of
automotive fleets used in the conduct of
business by corporations and
government agencies. Special
departments on maintenance safety and
association chapter activities.
**Readers:** NAFA members and affiliates
are responsible for the operation of
more than 2.7 million passenger cars
and light duty trucks and mini vans;
circulation restricted to members,
affiliates, advertisers and potential
advertisers.

**FLEET FINANCIALS**  67678
2512 Artesia Blvd.
Redondo Beach, CA 90278-3210
Telephone: (310) 376-8788
FAX: (310) 376-9043
Year Established: 1987
Pub. Frequency: 3/yr.
Page Size: standard
Subscrip. Rate: $28/yr.
Circulation: 16,000
Circulation Type: controlled
**Owner(s):**
Bobit Publishing Co.
2512 Artesia Blvd.
Redondo Beach, CA 90278-3210
Telephone: (310) 376-8788
Ownership %: 100
**Management:**
Charles Parker ..................Advertising Manager
**Editorial:**
Ed Bobit ...................................Editor
**Desc.:** For top executives at companies
having car fleets.

**IMPORT CAR**  48842
11 S. Forge St.
Akron, OH 44304
Telephone: (216) 535-6117
FAX: (216) 535-0874
Year Established: 1979
Pub. Frequency: m.
Page Size: standard
Subscrip. Rate: $44/yr.
Materials: 01,06,15,28,29,30,32,33
Print Process: web offset
Circulation: 30,173
Circulation Type: controlled
**Owner(s):**
Babcox Publications, Inc.
11 S. Forge St.
Akron, OH 44304
Telephone: (216) 535-6117
Ownership %: 100
**Management:**
Bill Babcox ...........................President
Brad Glazer ...........................Publisher
Cindy Ott ............................Production Manager
**Editorial:**
Mary DellaValle .......................Editor
Janine Young ....................Managing Editor
**Desc.:** Reports on marketing trends,
technical and industry news, new
products/services and legislative issues.
Other articles provide
handbook/directory materials, technical
news and commentary and market
research. Regular columns include: Data
Bank, Sourcing: Products, Sourcing:
Literature and Perspectives.
**Readers:** Import auto franchise dealers;
import auto parts and supply
jobber/dealers; import auto repair and
service specialists; import auto parts
and supplies warehouse distributors,
expeditors, and feeders.

**JET FUEL INTELLIGENCE**  69168
575 Broadway, 4th Fl.
New York, NY 10012-3230
Telephone: (212) 941-5500
FAX: (212) 941-5508
Year Established: 1991
Pub. Frequency: w.
Subscrip. Rate: $1975/yr.
**Owner(s):**
Petroleum & Energy Intelligence Weekly,
Inc.
575 Broadway, 4th Fl.
New York, NY 10012-3230
Telephone: (212) 941-5500
Ownership %: 100
**Editorial:**
Christina Haus ...............................Editor
**Desc.:** Follows developments in the
international aviation fuels trade,
including airport by airport jet fuel and
spot cargo pricing, regional trends, and
other factors influencing the market.

**LIMOUSINE & CHAUFFEUR**  67675
2512 Artesia Blvd.
Redondo Beach, CA 90278-3210
Telephone: (310) 376-8788
FAX: (310) 798-4598
Year Established: 1983
Pub. Frequency: 9/yr.
Page Size: standard
Subscrip. Rate: $28/yr. non-members;
$38/yr. in Canada; $50/yr. elsewhere
Materials: 06,27,28,30,32,33
Print Process: web offset
Circulation: 12,000
Circulation Type: paid

**Owner(s):**
Bobit Publishing Co.
2512 Artesia Blvd.
Redondo Beach, CA 90278-3210
Telephone: (310) 376-8788
Ownership %: 100
**Management:**
Sara Eastwood ...........................Publisher
**Editorial:**
Donna Englander .......................Editor
**Desc.:** Serves the information needs of the
limousine service industry.

**LOCATOR, THE**  21829
521 Whittier
Whiting, IA 51063
Telephone: (712) 458-2213
FAX: (712) 458-2687
Mailing Address:
P.O. Box 286
Whiting, IA 51063
Year Established: 1957
Pub. Frequency: m.
Page Size: standard
Subscrip. Rate: $69/yr.
Circulation: 69,000
Circulation Type: controlled
**Owner(s):**
John Holmes Publishing
Ownership %: 100
**Bureau(s):**
The Locator
521 Whittier
Whiting, IA 51063
Telephone: (712) 458-2213
Contact: Charis Lloyd, Executive Vice
President
**Management:**
John Holmes ...........................Publisher
**Editorial:**
Charis Lloyd ...............................Miscellaneous
**Desc.:** Used auto and truck parts
magazine covering 50 states, Canada,
and Mexico.
**Readers:** Dismantlers & Body Shops.
Garages, Insurance Companies. Also,
Hobbyists & Rebuilders.

**MIDWEST AUTOMOTIVE &**  21810
**AUTOBODY NEWS**
2900 W. Peterson Ave.
Chicago, IL 60659
Telephone: (312) 764-1640
Year Established: 1928
Pub. Frequency: q.
Page Size: standard
Subscrip. Rate: $10/yr.
Circulation: 11,780
Circulation Type: controlled
**Owner(s):**
Automotive Publishing Co.
2900 W. Peterson Ave.
Chicago, IL 60659
Telephone: (312) 764-1640
Ownership %: 100
**Bureau(s):**
Automotive Publishing Co.
30312 Grande Vista
Laguna Niguel , CA 92677
Telephone: (714) 495-0238
**Management:**
Automotive Publishing Co. ..................Publisher
C. L. Anderson ..................Advertising Manager
**Editorial:**
Warren Daemicke .......................Editor
Dale W. Daemicke ...............Managing Editor
**Desc.:** Subjects of general automotive
interest using publicity material relating
to new or unique items in the
automotive field.
**Readers:** Service station operators, garage
owners, ignition shops, jobbers, auto
parts, body shops, auto dealers, truck
fleet owners and towing firms.

**MIDWESTERN STATE SALVAGE**  69158
**GUIDE**
3700 Decker
Moore, OK 73160
Telephone: (405) 787-0795
FAX: (405) 787-0795
Year Established: 1968
Pub. Frequency: m.
Page Size: tabloid
Subscrip. Rate: $12/yr.
Materials: 32
Print Process: web
Circulation: 44,000
Circulation Type: free
**Owner(s):**
Midwestern Salvage Guide Magazine, Inc.
3700 Decker
Moore, OK 73160
Telephone: (405) 787-0795
FAX: (405) 793-4044
Ownership %: 100
**Editorial:**
Louanne Duckworth ......................Editor
**Readers:** Bodyshop workers, adjusters,
and auto salvagers.
**Deadline:** ads-20th of each mo.

**MMCA NEWS**  65725
501 N. Sanders
Helena, MT 59601
Telephone: (406) 442-6600
Mailing Address:
P.O. Box 1714
Helena, MT 59624
Year Established: 1949
Pub. Frequency: m.
Page Size: standard
Subscrip. Rate: $12.50/yr.
Freelance Pay: negotiable
Circulation: 850
Circulation Type: controlled
**Owner(s):**
Montana Motor Carriers Association, Inc.
P.O. Box 1714
Helena, MT 59624
Telephone: (406) 442-6600
Ownership %: 100
**Editorial:**
B.G. Havdahl ...............................Director
**Desc.:** Covers all phases of motor carrier
industry.
**Readers:** Motor carrier executives,
employees, city officials & municipal
employees.

**MODERN TIRE DEALER**  25053
341 White Pond Dr.
Akron, OH 44320
Telephone: (216) 867-4401
FAX: (216) 867-0019
Mailing Address:
P.O. Box 3599
Akron, OH 44309-3599
Year Established: 1919
Pub. Frequency: m. plus 2 special editions
Page Size: standard
Subscrip. Rate: $36/yr. US & Canada;
$55/yr. elsewhere
Freelance Pay: avail. upon request
Circulation: 33,000
Circulation Type: controlled
**Owner(s):**
Bill Communications, Inc.
355 Park Ave., S.
New York, NY 10010
Telephone: (212) 592-6200
Ownership %: 100
**Management:**
John Wickiersham ...............................President
Greg Smith ...........................Publisher
Shane Molloy ....................Circulation Manager
Karen Runion ....................Production Manager

**Editorial:**
Robert J. Ulrich ...................Senior Editor
Lloyd R. Stoyer .............................Editor
Lori L. Mavrigian ...........Managing Editor
Roger Slavens ...............Assistant Editor
Jerry White ..............Contributing Writer
Duane DePuy ............Contributing Writer
John P. Kelley ...................Feature Editor
Lori Mavrigian .................Miscellaneous
Ed Wagner ..............................Reporter
Stuart Marshall ........................Reporter

**Desc.:** Circulated to retailers and wholesalers of tires, batteries and accessories; tire retreading and repair shops, brake, wheel, front end, alignment and safety service shops; headquarter offices of discount houses, department stores, wholesalers and retail hardware stores with TBA departments, and headquarter offices of automotive chain store companies.

**Readers:** Retailers and wholesalers of tires, who are involved in most types of automotive services.

## MOTOR
69782

645 Stewart Ave.
Garden City, NY 11530
Telephone: (516) 227-1399
FAX: (516) 227-1405
Year Established: 1903
Pub. Frequency: m.
Page Size: standard
Subscrip. Rate: $18/yr.
Materials: 01,02,05,06,15,21,28,29,30,32,33
Freelance Pay: varies
Circulation: 127,000
**Owner(s):**
Hearst Business Communications
645 Stewart Ave.
Garden City, NY 11530
Telephone: (516) 227-1300
FAX: (516) 227-1405
Ownership %: 100
**Editorial:**
Wade Hoyt .................................Editor
**Desc.:** Technical journal for auto repair industry.
**Readers:** Professional auto mechanics and repair shop owners.
**Deadline:** story-2 mo. prior to pub. date; news-2 mo. prior; photo-2 mo. prior; ads-1 mo. prior to pub. date

## MOTOR AGE
21813

Chilton Way
Radnor, PA 19089-4237
Telephone: (610) 964-4237
FAX: (610) 964-4981
Year Established: 1899
Pub. Frequency: m.
Page Size: standard
Subscrip. Rate: $40/yr. US; $60/2 yrs. US; $90/yr. foreign
Materials: 05,06,28,29,32,33
Freelance Pay: negotiable
Circulation: 139,374
Circulation Type: controlled
**Owner(s):**
Capital Cities/ABC, Inc.
77 W. 66th St.
New York, NY 10023
Telephone: (212) 456-7777
Ownership %: 100
**Management:**
Sarah Frankson .................Vice President
Sarah Frankson .........................Publisher
Donna Borelli ...............Business Manager
Bernard J. Karpinski .........Production Manager
**Editorial:**
Tony Molla .......................Editor in Chief
Shahla Siddiqi .....................Senior Editor
Bill Cannon ..................Managing Editor
Teresa Kuncas .........................Advertising

Lisa Brody ...........Nat'l Sales Manager
Steve Horner ................Technical Editor
**Desc.:** Cover service procedures, technical developments, management techniques, merchandising direction, new designs and other material of use to the automotive service industry. Emphasizing management and merchandising features for automotive aftermarket service professionals. Departments include: New Products, Troubleshooting, Technical features on repair and diagnosis, Tool Topics, Managing The Business, Servicing Imports, Merchandising The Jobs, Factory Bulletins, Motor/Age Mechanic Training Program.
**Readers:** Repair shops, car and truck dealers, service station operators, or owners, and independent businessmen.

## MOTOR MAGAZINE
21812

645 Stewart Ave.
Garden City, NY 11530
Telephone: (516) 227-1399
FAX: (516) 227-1405
Year Established: 1903
Pub. Frequency: m.
Page Size: standard
Subscrip. Rate: $24/yr.
Freelance Pay: $50-$1,000
Circulation: 120,000
Circulation Type: paid
**Owner(s):**
Hearst Business Publishing
959 Eighth Ave.
New York, NY 10019
Ownership %: 100
**Management:**
Michael Bernstein ....................Publisher
Lisa Doherty ...............Broadcast Manager
**Editorial:**
Tom Wilkinson ............................Editor
Paul Eckstein ................Managing Editor
Harold Perry ........................Art Director
Bob Cerullo .............................Columnist
**Desc.:** Features on car service problems.
**Readers:** Management & mechanics at repair shops, service stations, vehicle dealers, fleets, truck stops, specialty shops.

## MOTOR SERVICE
21816

25 N.W. Point Blvd., Ste. 800
Elk Grove Village, IL 60007-1030
Telephone: (708) 427-9512
FAX: (708) 427-2006
Year Established: 1921
Pub. Frequency: m.
Page Size: standard
Subscrip. Rate: $36/yr.
Materials: 01,06,15,25,28,29,30,32,33
Print Process: web offset
Circulation: 175,000
Circulation Type: controlled
**Owner(s):**
Hunter Publishing Limited Partnership
25 N.W. Point
Elk Grove Village, IL 60007
Telephone: (708) 427-9512
FAX: (708) 427-2006
Ownership %: 100
**Management:**
James Pierce ..........................President
Larry Greenberger .....................Publisher
**Editorial:**
James Halloran ............................Editor
Jeanne Belanger ............Managing Editor
James Halloran ................Editorial Editor
George Chmielarz .........Production Director
James Armitage ................Technical Editor

Bob Freudenberger ................Technical Editor
**Desc.:** Technical service magazine serving the car dealer, fleet and independent repair shop operator. Emphasizes "how-to", new products service equipments, and product and equipment field testing.
**Readers:** Automotive service shop operators.
**Deadline:** story-6 wks. prior to pub. date; news-6 wks. prior; photo-6 wks. prior; ads-30 days prior to pub date

## NEW YORK AUTO REPAIR NEWS
21822

P.O. Box 354
Hicksville, NY 11801
Telephone: (516) 422-5521
Year Established: 1948
Pub. Frequency: m.
Page Size: broadsheet
Subscrip. Rate: $19/yr.
Materials: 28,29,30,31,32,33
Print Process: web offset
Circulation: 11,300
Circulation Type: controlled
**Owner(s):**
Van Allen Publishing Co.
P.O. Box 354
Hicksville, NY 11802
Telephone: (516) 422-5521
Ownership %: 100
**Management:**
Richard Van Allen .....................Publisher
**Editorial:**
Walter VanAllen ....................Chief Editor
Francis Church .................Associate Editor
J. A. Mitchel ...................Circulation Editor
**Desc.:** Contains news of value to the automotive trade, especially that relating to metropolitan New York City. Departments include: Automotive Service, New Products, Service and Parts News. Nation/local industry news.
**Readers:** Automotive trade, including independent service stations, warehouse jobbers and wholesalers.

## NORTHWEST MOTOR
21823

31548 State Hwy. 3, N.E.
Poulsbo, WA 98370
Telephone: (206) 697-6200
FAX: (206) 697-4040
Mailing Address:
  P.O. Box 25
  Port Gamble, WA 98364-0025
Year Established: 1909
Pub. Frequency: m.
Page Size: standard
Subscrip. Rate: $12/yr.; $58/lifetime membership
Freelance Pay: $25-$100
Circulation: 5,800
Circulation Type: controlled
**Owner(s):**
Northwest Motor Publishing Co.
P.O. Box 25
Port Gamble, WA 98364-0025
Telephone: (206) 697-6200
Ownership %: 100
**Management:**
Peter D. duPre ........................Publisher
**Editorial:**
J.B. (Jerry) Smith ...................Exec. Editor
Peter D. duPre .............................Editor
Phil Ljunghammar .....................Art Director

**Desc.:** Covers automotive trade of Washington State, Idaho, Montana, Alaska, and Oregon. Features business and personal news of this trade, trade association activities, conventions. Also use new product items and glossies (preferably under 200 woords), new car and truck model announcements and photos, and articles (under 1,000 words) of general automotive interest. Also legislative news and legal views plus product testing.
**Readers:** Manufacturers, wholesalers, car dealers, garages, fleetshops, specialized service shops, parts rebuilders, factory reps, auto parts stores, automotive associations, parts stores, collision repair shops, fleets.

## NOZZLE, THE
21824

9420 Annapolis Rd., Ste. 307
Lanham, MD 20706
Telephone: (301) 577-2875
FAX: (301) 306-0523
Year Established: 1950
Pub. Frequency: m.
Page Size: standard
Subscrip. Rate: membership
Freelance Pay: open
Circulation: 4,000
Circulation Type: controlled
**Owner(s):**
WMDP Service Station & Auto Repair Assn.
9420 Annapolis Rd., Ste. 307
Lanham, MD 20706
Telephone: (301) 577-2875
Ownership %: 100
**Management:**
Roy Littlefield .........................Publisher
**Editorial:**
Brenda M. Judge ...............Assistant Editor
**Desc.:** Service station dealers problems, legislation having to do with the service station industry, advertisements and general news.
**Readers:** Service station dealers, congressmen and legislators.

## NTDRA DEALER NEWS
25054

1250 I St., N.W., Ste. 400
Washington, DC 20005
Telephone: (202) 789-2300
Year Established: 1942
Pub. Frequency: m.
Page Size: standard
Subscrip. Rate: $13/yr.
Circulation: 6,500
Circulation Type: paid
**Owner(s):**
National Tire Dealers & Retreaders Association
Telephone: (202) 789-2300
Ownership %: 100
**Editorial:**
Jim Schepmoes ...............Managing Editor
Tony Hylton ............Communications Director
Kate Hooten ...............Editorial Assistant
Cary Boshammer ......................News Editor
**Desc.:** Devoted to news in tire and rubber industry and business world events affecting the industry. Special articles designed to aid the tire dealer and retreader in running his shop or store, plus association news and services.
**Readers:** Membership of Association (tire dealers).

## PACIFIC AUTOMOTIVE NEWS
21826

31548 St. Hwy. 3, N.E.
Poulsbo, WA 98370
Telephone: (206) 697-6200
FAX: (206) 697-4040

**Materials Accepted/Included:** 01-Business news 02-By-line articles 03-Fashion news 04-Food news 05-Freelance copy 06-Letters to editor 07-Real estate news 08-Sports news 09-Travel news 10-Book rev. 11-Movie rev. 12-Music rev. 13-TV rev. 14-Theater rev. 15-Coming events 16-Obituaries 17-Question & answer 18-Social announcements 19-Artwork 20-Cartoons 21-Photos 22-TV listings 23-Audio rec. 24-Video rec. 25-Books 26-Films/film clips 27-Personnel news 28-Press releases 29-New product news/photos 30-Trade lit. 31-Contracts awarded 32-Display adv. 33-Classified adv.

4-23

Mailing Address:
P.O. Box 25
Port Gamble, WA 98364
Year Established: 1973
Pub. Frequency: q.
Page Size: standard
Subscrip. Rate: $1.25 newsstand; $15/yr.
Freelance Pay: $25-$150/article
Circulation: 16,500
Circulation Type: controlled
**Owner(s):**
Northwest Motor Publishing Co.
P.O. Box 25
Port Gamble, WA 98364
Ownership %: 100
**Management:**
Peter D. DuPre ........................Publisher
**Editorial:**
J.B. Smith ....................Executive Editor
Peter D. DuPre ..............................Editor
Phil Liunghammar ..............Art Director
**Desc.:** Contains local/regional news for
the aftermarket automotive industry in
California, reaching collision repair
shops, garages, service centers, car
dealers, technicians, tire dealers,
rebuilders, fleet operators, reps,
specialists, installers, wholesale
distributors, and jobbers. Each issue
contains news and feature articles
concerning improved merchandising of
automotive products and services.
Content consists of new product
releases, business management tips,
technical articles, event coverage, new
car news, and association news of ASIA,
ASA, APAA, PAS, SEMA and others.
**Readers:** Those engaged in the
automotive aftermarket.

### PARKING
23235
1112 16th St., N.W., Ste. 300
Washington, DC 20036
Telephone: (202) 296-4336
FAX: (202) 331-8523
Year Established: 1952
Pub. Frequency: 10/yr.
Page Size: standard
Subscrip. Rate: $95/yr. US; $125/yr.
foreign
Freelance Pay: negotiable
Circulation: 5,000
Circulation Type: controlled
**Owner(s):**
National Parking Association, Inc.
1112 16th St., N.W., Ste. 2000
Washington, DC 20036
Telephone: (202) 296-4336
Ownership %: 100
**Management:**
Dawn Newman .................Advertising Manager
**Editorial:**
Genilee Swope-Parente ...............Design Editor
**Desc.:** Concerned with the parking
industry. Carries features on the design,
construction, and operation of parking
structures and lots. Also concerned with
parking management. Carries some
human interest material related to
parking and some news of important
members. Spotlight on Washington
affairs interested in news for business
(economics, trends, etc.), taxes levied by
cities; parking meters;
traffic considerations; transportation
issues; pedestrian management.
**Readers:** Members of the National Parking
Association, administrators for cities,
hospitals, colleges and universities,
airports, parking authorities, consultants,
transportation experts; parking owners
and operators of parking lots and
garages, engineers, architects,
designers, parking downtown association
executives.

### PARTS BUSINESS
21806
341 White Pond Dr.
Akron, OH 44320
Telephone: (216) 867-4401
Mailing Address:
P.O. Box 3599
Akron, OH 44309-3599
Year Established: 1977
Pub. Frequency: m.
Page Size: standard
Subscrip. Rate: $60/yr. US & Canada;
$150/yr. elsewhere
Circulation: 32,000
Circulation Type: paid
**Owner(s):**
Bill Communications, Inc.
633 Third Ave.
New York, NY 10017
Telephone: (212) 986-4800
Ownership %: 100
**Management:**
John Wickersham ..............................President
Shane Malloy ...................Circulation Manager
Karen Runion ...................Production Manager
**Editorial:**
David Ogron ...................Senior Editor
Larry Silvey ............................Editor
Linda Arvin ....................Managing Editor
Jeff Torok ............................Art Director
Steve France .......................Sales Director
**Desc.:** A business, marketing trade
magazine edited for automotive parts
jobbers who retail and wholesale auto
parts. The editorial aim is to give
information telling the jobber/warehouse
distributor how to become better and
more competitive in retailing and
wholesaling and how to become more
productive businessmen. Departments
include: products, merchandising aids,
sales promotion, marketing concepts,
technical lines.
**Readers:** Automotive parts jobbers and
warehouse distributors.

### PROFESSIONAL CARWASHING & DETAILING
69161
13 Century Hill Dr.
Latham, NY 12110-2197
Telephone: (518) 783-1281
FAX: (518) 783-1386
Year Established: 1976
Pub. Frequency: m.
Page Size: standard
Subscrip. Rate: $40/yr.
Materials: 01,02,06,15,16,18,27,29,32,33
Circulation: 17,590
Circulation Type: controlled
**Owner(s):**
National Trade Publications, Inc.
13 Century Hill
Latham, NY 12110-2197
Telephone: (518) 783-1281
Ownership %: 100
**Editorial:**
Suzanne Stansbury ................................Editor
Tara Miller ........................................Advertising
**Desc.:** Provides technical, sales and
marketing information.
**Readers:** Investors, owners, operators and
managers of professional carwashing
facilities.

### RESTYLING & ACCESSORIES MARKETING
69162
180 Allen Rd., Ste. 300N
Atlanta, GA 30328-4893
Telephone: (404) 252-8831
FAX: (404) 252-4436
Year Established: 1991
Pub. Frequency: bi-m.
Subscrip. Rate: $50/yr.
Circulation: 11,000

Circulation Type: controlled
**Owner(s):**
Shore Communications, Inc.
180 Allen Rd., Ste. 300N
Atlanta, GA 30328-4893
Telephone: (404) 252-8831
Ownership %: 100
**Editorial:**
Karen Schaffner ..............................Editor
**Desc.:** Focuses on the benefit of
aftermarket restyling and accessorization
of new automobiles.

### SPECIAL INTEREST AUTOS
21831
P.O. Box 196
Bennington, VT 05201-0196
Telephone: (802) 442-3101
FAX: (802) 447-1561
Year Established: 1970
Pub. Frequency: bi-m.
Page Size: standard
Subscrip. Rate: $17.95-$19.95/yr.
Materials: 02,05,06,19,21,24,25,28,32,33
Freelance Pay: negotiable
Print Process: web offset
Circulation: 35,000
Circulation Type: free & paid
**Owner(s):**
Special Interest Publications, Inc.
P.O. Box 196
Bennington, VT 05201
Telephone: (802) 442-3101
Ownership %: 100
**Management:**
Terry Ehrich ..............................Publisher
Lesley Mcfadden ...............Advertising Manager
**Editorial:**
David Brownell ............................Editor
Nancy Bianco ....................Assistant Editor
**Desc.:** Deals with collectable and
interesting older cars-not necessarily
antiques nor classic cars. Approach is
historical, but with a bearing on today's
automobiles, drive reports,
developmental histories, styling trends,
restoration how-to's, engineering,
oddities, personalities, etc.
**Readers:** Collector car owners and
enthusiasts, automotive historians.

### TIRE BUSINESS
52574
1725 Merriman Rd., Ste. 300
Akron, OH 44313-5251
Telephone: (216) 836-9180
FAX: (216) 836-1005
Year Established: 1983
Pub. Frequency: bi-w.
Page Size: tabloid
Subscrip. Rate: $45/yr.
Freelance Pay: $10/col. in.
Circulation: 20,060
Circulation Type: controlled & paid
**Owner(s):**
Crain Communications, Inc.
740 N. Rush St.
Chicago, IL 60611-5251
Telephone: (312) 649-5200
Ownership %: 100
**Bureau(s):**
Washington Bureau
814 National Press Bldg.
Washington, DC 20045-1801
Telephone: (202) 662-7200
Contact: Miles Moore, Reporter

London Bureau
20-22 Bedford Row
London United Kingdom
Contact: Paul Mitchell, Publisher

London Bureau
75-77 Cowcross St., 2nd Fl.
London United Kingdom
Contact: David Shaw, Editor

**Management:**
Robert S. Simmons ........................Publisher
Barb Kisch ...................Circulation Manager
Laureen Beresh .................Production Manager
**Editorial:**
Charles Slaybaugh ...............Executive Editor
David E. Zielasko ............................Editor
Lawrence A. Wingert ...............Managing Editor
Keith Crain ....................Editorial Director
Jennifer L. Poda ...............Marketing Manager
Chris Harris ...............National Sales Manager
Kathy McCarron ........................Reporter
Sigmund Mikolajczyk ........................Reporter
**Desc.:** Publishes news about the tire
industry, tire marketing and retreading,
including news and "how-to" articles
about related auto services and
legislative info.
**Readers:** Edited for independent
dealers/distributors, retreaders, tire
industry management, tire marketers,
mass merchandisers with auto service,
tire company-owned retail stores and
others interested in tire marketing.

### TIRE REVIEW
21835
11 S. Forge St.
Akron, OH 44304
Telephone: (216) 535-6117
FAX: (216) 535-0874
Year Established: 1901
Pub. Frequency: m.
Page Size: standard
Subscrip. Rate: $48/yr.
Circulation: 32,200
Circulation Type: controlled
**Owner(s):**
Babcox Automotive Publications, Inc.
11 S. Forge St.
Akron, OH 44304
Telephone: (216) 535-6117
Ownership %: 100
**Management:**
Tom B. Babcox ..............................President
Jack Hone ..............................Publisher
Cindy Ott ........................Advertising Manager
**Editorial:**
Jim Davis ............................Editor
**Desc.:** Offers readers information germane
to increasingly successful business.
Readers are kept up to date on new
developments, new products, industry
news, merchandising and management
ideas and effective marketing
techniques.
**Readers:** Reaches independent tire
dealers and distributors; independent tire
dealers with retread shops;
safety/service shops; company-owned
tire outlets; oil jobbers; tire equipment
and materials jobbers; mass
merchandiser headquarters offices.

### TOW-AGE
21836
P.O. Box M
Franklin, MA 02038-0907
Telephone: (508) 528-6211
Year Established: 1973
Pub. Frequency: 9/yr.
Page Size: standard
Subscrip. Rate: $21/yr.
Materials: 01,02,03,05,06,07,09,10,11,15,
17,19,20,21,24,25,27,28,29,30,31,32
Freelance Pay: $.20/wd.
Print Process: offset
Circulation: 10,500
Circulation Type: paid
**Owner(s):**
Kruza Kaleidoscopix, Inc.
P.O. Box 389
Franklin, MA 02038
Telephone: (508) 528-6211
Ownership %: 100

**Materials Accepted/Included:** 01-Business news 02-By-line articles 03-Fashion news 04-Food news 05-Freelance copy 06-Letters to editor 07-Real estate news 08-Sports news 09-Travel news 10-Book rev. 11-Movie rev. 12-Music rev. 13-TV rev. 14-Theater rev. 15-Coming events 16-Obituaries 17-Question & answer 18-Social announcements 19-Artwork 20-Cartoons 21-Photos 22-TV listings 23-Audio rec. 24-Video rec. 25-Books 26-Films/film clips 27-Personnel news 28-Press releases 29-New product news/photos 30-Trade lit. 31-Contracts awarded 32-Display adv. 33-Classified adv.

**Bureau(s):**
Chet Spink
San Jose, CA 95120

Dave Ward
Dover, DE 19903-1060

William Mueller
Coralville, IA 52241-5641

Lou Baffa
Brooklyn, NY 11222
**Management:**
J. A. Kruza ...................................President
J. A. Kruza .........................Advertising Manager
**Editorial:**
J. A. Kruza ..........................Executive Editor
Ron Budman ..................................Editor
Richard Jay .....................................Editor
Brian Sawyer ..........................Art Director
Ron Budman ........................Automotive Editor
David Ward ...........................Feature Editor
Beverly Call .......................Research Director
**Desc.:** News and how-to for operators of tow trucks,
**Readers:** High school educated men who work with their hands serving the motorist.
**Deadline:** story-6 wks. prior to pub. date; news-3 wks. prior to pub. date; ads-6 wks. prior

### UNDERCAR DIGEST
21820
3057 E. Cairo
Springfield, MO 65802
Telephone: (417) 866-3917
FAX: (417) 866-2781
Mailing Address:
  P.O. Box 2210
  Springfield, MO 65801
Year Established: 1976
Pub. Frequency: m.
Page Size: standard
Subscrip. Rate: $34/yr.
Freelance Pay: $.10/word
Circulation: 26,180
Circulation Type: paid
**Owner(s):**
M. D. Publications, Inc.
P.O. Box 2210
Springfield, MO 65801
Telephone: (417) 866-3917
Ownership %: 100
**Management:**
Carol Langsford ...........................President
Larry Dixon ................................Publisher
Larry Dixon .........................Advertising Manager
Marylee York ...................Circulation Manager
**Editorial:**
Jim Wilder ......................................Editor
Robert Jacobsmeyer ..................Advertising
Bob Threadgill ...........................Advertising
Bernie Wardlow .........................Art Director
Carolyn Campbell ...........................Artist
Paula Reed ......................................Artist
Lonnie Bolding ...............................Artist
Larry Dixon .........................Marketing Director
Charita Atkins ...................................Sales
**Desc.:** Devoted exclusively to the undercar repair industry. articles include reports on trends in the industry, how-to management articles and profiles on muffler shop operators and industry leaders, special features on manufacturers and legislative news which affects the entire exhaust system industry. Maximum length for articles - 1, 500 words with two or three pix spread. Publicity and new product material is used with pictures of products in automotive or ancilliary product fields as possible
**Readers:** 80.6 percent Muffler Shop Undercar Shop Owners and Operators. 8.5 percent Warehouse Distributors

### USED CAR DEALER
69165
2521 Brown Blvd., Ste. 100
Arlington, TX 76006-5203
Telephone: (817) 640-3838
FAX: (817) 649-5866
Year Established: 1981
Pub. Frequency: m.
Subscrip. Rate: $36/yr.
Circulation: 16,033
Circulation Type: paid
**Owner(s):**
National Independent Automobile Dealers Assn.
2521 Brown Blvd., Ste. 100
Arlington, TX 76006-5203
Telephone: (817) 640-3838
Ownership %: 100
**Editorial:**
Don A. Harris ....................................Editor

### USED CAR MERCHANDISING
69166
125 Edinburgh S.
Cary, NC 27511-6441
Telephone: (919) 469-9911
FAX: (919) 481-2658
Year Established: 1990
Pub. Frequency: bi-m.
Subscrip. Rate: $19.85/yr.
Circulation: 20,000
Circulation Type: paid
**Owner(s):**
Cherokee Publishing Co.
125 Edinburgh S.
Cary, NC 27511-6441
Telephone: (919) 469-9911
Ownership %: 100
**Editorial:**
James Hyatt ......................................Editor
**Desc.:** Reports on changes in the automotive industry and their effects on the buying and selling of used cars. Covers the used car operations of franchised dealers and the preparation of cars for resale.

### USED CARS TODAY NEWSLETTER
65749
2315 Broadway
New York, NY 10024
Telephone: (212) 873-5900
Pub. Frequency: bi-w.
Circulation: 1,650
**Owner(s):**
ATCOM Publishing
2315 Broadway
New York, NY 10024
Telephone: (212) 873-5900
Ownership %: 100
**Editorial:**
Steve Byerers ...................................Editor

### VAN & TRUCK DIGEST
69526
58025 C.R. No. 9 S.
Elkhart, IN 46517
Telephone: (219) 295-1962
FAX: (219) 295-7574
Mailing Address:
  P.O. Box 1805
  Elkhart, IN 46517
Year Established: 1983
Pub. Frequency: bi-m.
Subscrip. Rate: $40/yr.
Circulation: 27,346
Circulation Type: paid
**Owner(s):**
Continental Publishing Company of Indiana, Inc.
58025 C.R. No. 9 S.
Elkhart, IN 46517
Telephone: (219) 295-1962
Ownership %: 100
**Editorial:**
Tom Russell .....................................Editor

**Desc.:** Contains news and business-oriented features on the sales and marketing of vans, custom trucks and accessories.
**Readers:** For the automotive business professionals actively engaged in the manufacture, distribution, or sales or vans, custom trucks and accessories.

### WARD'S AUTO WORLD
21839
3000 Town Center
Ste. 2750
Southfield, MI 48075
Telephone: (810) 357-0800
Year Established: 1965
Pub. Frequency: m.
Page Size: standard
Subscrip. Rate: $47/yr.
Freelance Pay: $250-$750/article
Circulation: 97,621
Circulation Type: controlled
**Owner(s):**
Intertec Publishing Corp.
3000 Town Center
Ste. 2750
Southfield, MI 48075
Telephone: (810) 357-0800
Ownership %: 100
**Management:**
Roger K. Powers ...........................President
Howard E. Johnson .......................Publisher
Rebecca Hughes .............Circulation Manager
**Editorial:**
David C. Smith .......................Editor in Chief
Jon Lowell .............................Senior Editor
Drew Winter ..........................Senior Editor
Majorie A. Sorge ...................Managing Editor
Richard W. West ..........................Advertising
Richard C. Mayer .........................Art Director
Stephen E. Plumb ...................Associate Editor
Elio Parenti ......................Production Director
**Desc.:** Covers the automotive manufacturing industry. Provides in-depth reporting and analysis on every facet of the manufacturer's business, from components to finished vehicles, design to marketing, people to companies.
**Readers:** Executives in auto industry, and auto suppliers.

### WHEELINGS
69528
P.O. Box 389
Franklin, MA 02038
Telephone: (508) 528-6211
Year Established: 1984
Pub. Frequency: 4/yr.
Page Size: tabloid
Subscrip. Rate: $90/yr.
Materials: 01,02,06,10,15,20,21,27,28,32
Print Process: offset
Circulation: 5,641
Circulation Type: controlled & paid
**Owner(s):**
Kruza Kaleidoscopiz, Inc.
P.O. Box 389
Franklin, MA 02038
Telephone: (508) 528-6211
Ownership %: 100
**Bureau(s):**
Chet Spink
San Jose, CA

Ron Budman
Harrisburg, PA

Frank Walker
Atlanta, GA

Charles Rauhauser
Chicago, IL
**Editorial:**
David Ward .....................................Editor

**Readers:** Auto paint specialists and manufacturers.

## Group 018-Aviation & Aerospace

### AERLOG PUBLICATIONS
25656
6290 Willowgate
Dallas, TX 75230
Telephone: (800) 423-7564
FAX: (214) 233-4824
Year Established: 1970
Pub. Frequency: s-a.
Page Size: pocket
Subscrip. Rate: $4.95/issue; $9.90/yr.
Circulation: 12,000
Circulation Type: paid
**Owner(s):**
APO International, Inc.
6290 Willowgate
Dallas, TX 75230
Telephone: (214) 960-9551
Ownership %: 100
**Bureau(s):**
Aerlog Publications
6290 Willowgate
Dallas, TX 75230
Telephone: (214) 960-9551
Contact: Frank Kirmss, Publisher
**Management:**
Frank Kirmss ................................Publisher
Sonya Lee ........................Office Manager
**Editorial:**
Frank Kirmes ........................Managing Editor
C. Norman Nielsen .................Technical Editor
**Desc.:** Tests and evaluations of pilot and flight attendant products and related subjects. Welcomes information on new products and accessories pertaining to matters of aircraft and airline flying. Uses airline industry news of general interest to pilots and flight attendants.
**Readers:** Predominantly male, pilots, flight engineers and flight attendants, median age 25-60.

### AEROSPACE AMERICA
21857
370 L'Enfant Promenade S.W., 10th Fl.
Washington, DC 20024
Telephone: (202) 646-7475
Year Established: 1932
Pub. Frequency: m.
Page Size: standard
Subscrip. Rate: $11 newsstand; $75/yr. US; $85/yr. foreign
Circulation: 68,353
Circulation Type: controlled
**Owner(s):**
American Institute of Aeronautics and Astronautics
370 L'Enfant Promeande, S.W.
Washington, DC 20024
Telephone: (202) 646-7400
Ownership %: 100
**Management:**
Michael Lewis ................................Publisher
Cort Durocher ....................Executive Director
**Editorial:**
Elaine J. Camhi .....................Editor in Chief
Craig S. Byl ....................................Director
**Desc.:** The magazine aerospace industry decision makers turn to first for scientific, engineering and the practitioner's viewpoint. Each issue is written by and for experienced professionals whose pioneering work is advancing aerospace technology around the globe. Every issue features compelling coverage of design electronics, materials, computer applications, science, policy, and products that affect aviation, space, and defense.

---

**Materials Accepted/Included:** 01-Business news 02-By-line articles 03-Fashion news 04-Food news 05-Freelance copy 06-Letters to editor 07-Real estate news 08-Sports news 09-Travel news 10-Book rev. 11-Movie rev. 12-Music rev. 13-TV rev. 14-Theater rev. 15-Coming events 16-Obituaries 17-Question & answer 18-Social announcements 19-Artwork 20-Cartoons 21-Photos 22-TV listings 23-Audio rec. 24-Video rec. 25-Books 26-Films/film clips 27-Personnel news 28-Press releases 29-New product news/photos 30-Trade lit. 31-Contracts awarded 32-Display adv. 33-Classified adv.

**Readers:** Chief engineers, project engineers, design engineers, research and development engineers, production manufacturing engineers, sales engineers, engineering & information specialists, company officers, technical & research directors. Also individuals in related fields including members of the U.S. Congress, retired AIAA members and engineering and science students.

67049

**AIAA JOURNAL**
370 L'Enfant Promenade, S.W.
Washington, DC 20024
Telephone: (202) 646-7400
FAX: (202) 646-7508
Year Established: 1962
Pub. Frequency: m.
Page Size: standard
Subscrip. Rate: $37/yr. members; $370/yr. non-members
Circulation: 5,000
Circulation Type: paid
**Owner(s):**
American Institute of Aeronautics & Astronautics
370 L'Enfant Promenade, S.W.
Washington, DC 20024
Telephone: (202) 646-7400
Ownership %: 100
**Management:**
Robert Fuhrman ...........................President
**Editorial:**
George W. Sutton .........................Editor
**Desc.:** Covers new theoretical developments and experimental results on aeroacoustics, aerodynamics, combustion, fundamentals of propulsion, fluid mechanics, aerospace environment, marine technology, lasers, plasmas, and magnetohydrodynamics, research instrumentation, structural mechanics and thermophysics.

25092

**AIR CARGO GUIDE**
2000 Clearwater Dr.
Hinsdale, IL 60521
Telephone: (708) 654-6000
Year Established: 1957
Pub. Frequency: m.
Page Size: standard
Subscrip. Rate: $117/yr. mailed
Materials: 32,33
Circulation: 7,000
Circulation Type: paid
**Owner(s):**
Official Airline Guides, Inc.
2000 Clearwater Dr.
Hinsdale, IL 60521
Telephone: (708) 574-6000
FAX: (708) 574-6667
Ownership %: 100
**Management:**
Mike Mulligan ...........................President
Richard A. Nelson ......................Publisher
**Editorial:**
Charlene P. Seoane .................Advertising
Gary Ferraro .........................Airline Sales
Alex Igyarto ...............Associate Publisher
**Desc.:** Complete guide to shipping cargo by air.
**Readers:** Airline air freight personnel, air freight forwarders agents & commercial shippers.

21848

**AIR CARGO WORLD**
6151 Powers Ferry Rd., N.W.
Atlanta, GA 30339-2941
Telephone: (404) 955-2500
FAX: (404) 955-0400
Year Established: 1942
Pub. Frequency: m.

Page Size: standard
Subscrip. Rate: $49/yr. US; $109/yr. foreign
Circulation: 25,000
Circulation Type: controlled
**Owner(s):**
Argus Business
6151 Powers Ferry Rd., N.W.
Atlanta, GA 30339-2941
Telephone: (404) 955-2500
Ownership %: 100
**Management:**
David Premo ...........................Publisher
**Editorial:**
Linda Parham ......................Bureau Chief
David Premo .............................Editor
Brian Buxton .......................Art Director
Paul Cohan ............................Reporter
**Desc.:** International magazine devoted to the expeditious movement of goods and information. Serves the fields of transportation, physical distribution, courier and small package shipping, import-export and bulk freight traffic in industries utilizing air as a distribution vehicle.
**Readers:** Primarily manufacturers and freight forwarders (shippers) and those in air transportation (airlines and airports).

68663

**AIR CLASSICS**
7950 Deering Ave.
Canoga Park, CA 91324
Telephone: (818) 887-0550
FAX: (818) 883-1343
Year Established: 1963
Pub. Frequency: m.
Subscrip. Rate: $23.95/yr.
Circulation: 120,000
Circulation Type: paid
**Owner(s):**
Challenge Publications, Inc.
7950 Deering Ave.
Canoga Park, CA 91324
Telephone: (818) 887-0550
Ownership %: 100
**Editorial:**
Michael O'Leary ..........................Editor

67200

**AIRCRAFT TECHNICIAN**
1233 Janesville Ave.
Fort Atkinson, WI 53538
Telephone: (414) 563-6388
FAX: (414) 563-1701
Year Established: 1989
Pub. Frequency: bi-m.
Page Size: tabloid
Subscrip. Rate: $40/yr. US; $55/yr. Canada & Mexico; $120/yr. elsewhere
Circulation: 25,000
Circulation Type: controlled
**Owner(s):**
Johnson Hill Press, Inc.
1233 Janesville Ave.
Fort Atkinson, WI 53558
Telephone: (414) 563-6388
Ownership %: 100
**Management:**
Michael F. Murrell ....................Publisher
Kathy Bailey ...............Advertising Manager
**Editorial:**
Greg Napert ..............................Editor
**Desc.:** Focuses on the technical and mechanical side of the 19-passenger and below aircraft in the airline industry.

21878

**AIRFAIR**
6401 Congress Ave., Ste. 100
Boca Raton, FL 33487
Telephone: (407) 994-4509
Mailing Address:
P.O. Box 5033
Boca Raton, FL 33431

Year Established: 1971
Pub. Frequency: q.
Page Size: standard
Subscrip. Rate: $18/yr.
Freelance Pay: $250/2,500 wds.
Circulation: 55,000
Circulation Type: paid
**Owner(s):**
Airfair Publication Corp.
6401 Congress Ave., Ste. 100
Boca Raton, FL 33487
Telephone: (407) 994-4509
Ownership %: 100
**Management:**
Rob Barrett ...........................Publisher
Andrew Cohen ....................Sales Manager
**Editorial:**
Ratu Kamlani ...........................Editor
Lawrence Glick ...........................Sales
**Desc.:** AIRFAIR is committed to providing comprehensive coverage of world travel geared toward airline employees.
**Readers:** All airline personnel.

65278

**AIRLINERS**
P.O. Box 52-1238
Miami, FL 33152-1238
Telephone: (305) 477-7163
FAX: (305) 599-1995
Year Established: 1987
Pub. Frequency: q.
Page Size: standard
Subscrip. Rate: $15.95/yr.
Circulation: 32,000
Circulation Type: paid
**Owner(s):**
World Transport Press, Inc.
P.O. Box 521238
Miami, FL 33152-1238
Telephone: (305) 477-7163
Ownership %: 100
**Editorial:**
Nick Veronico ...........................Editor
**Desc.:** In-depth features on airlines, airliners, and airports worldwide; related subjects.
**Readers:** Targets airline professionals and enthusiasts.

68665

**AIR MARKET NEWS**
P.O. Box 480
Hatch, NM 87937-0480
Telephone: (505) 267-1030
FAX: (505) 267-1920
Year Established: 1982
Pub. Frequency: bi-m.
Subscrip. Rate: free qualified personnel
Circulation: 18,210
Circulation Type: free
**Owner(s):**
General Publications, Inc.
P.O. Box 480
Hatch, NM 87937-0480
Telephone: (505) 267-1920
Ownership %: 100
**Editorial:**
J. Prill ..............................Editor

66741

**AIRPORTS**
1200 G St. N.W., Ste. 200
Washington, DC 20005
Telephone: (202) 383-2366
FAX: (202) 383-2438
Year Established: 1985
Pub. Frequency: w.
Page Size: standard
Subscrip. Rate: $525/yr.; $345/6 mos.
Circulation: 6,000
Circulation Type: paid

Owner(s):
McGraw-Hill, Inc.
1221 Avenue of the Americas
New York, NY 10020
Telephone: (212) 997-3807
Ownership %: 100
**Editorial:**
Avery Vise ...........................Editor
Holly Arthur ..................Assistant Editor

69316

**AIR POWER HISTORY**
Bldg. 1413, Stop 44
Andrews AFB, MD 20031
Telephone: (301) 736-1959
FAX: (301) 981-4246
Year Established: 1954
Pub. Frequency: q.
Subscrip. Rate: $35/yr. individuals; $45/yr. institutions
Circulation: 3,000
Circulation Type: paid
**Owner(s):**
Air Force Historical Foundation
Bldg. 1413, Stop 44
Andrews AFB, MD 20031
Ownership %: 100
**Editorial:**
Henry S. Bausum ........................Editor
**Desc.:** Includes scholarly articles on subjects focusing on any aspect of air or space history. Includes scholarly articles on subjects focusing on any aspect of air or space history.

21851

**AIR TRANSPORT WORLD**
600 Summer St.
Stamford, CT 06904
Telephone: (203) 348-7531
FAX: (203) 348-4023
Mailing Address:
P.O. Box 1361
Stamford, CT 06904
Year Established: 1964
Pub. Frequency: m.
Page Size: standard
Subscrip. Rate: $50/yr.
Circulation: 41,300
Circulation Type: paid
**Owner(s):**
Penton Publishing
1100 Superior Ave.
Cleveland, OH 44114
Telephone: (216) 696-7000
Ownership %: 100
**Management:**
Sal F. Marino ...............Chairman of Board
Dan Ramella ...........................President
Gere Coffey .............................Publisher
George Emma ..............Advertising Manager
**Editorial:**
J.P. Woolsey ......................Senior Editor
James Donoghue .........................Editor
Robert Moorman ..........................Editor
Kathryn Young ....................Managing Editor
G. Grandstaff .......................Art Director
Lisa Ray Henderson ..............Assistant Editor
Sal F. Marino ...........Chief Executive Officer
Perry Flint ........................Financial Editor
Henry Lefer ...............New Product Editor
**Desc.:** Contains articles on airline industry, new products and trade literature, advertising and marketing, financial and general news.
**Readers:** People in the airline and air transport industry at management level.

21855

**AOPA PILOT**
421 Aviation Way
Frederick, MD 21701
Telephone: (301) 695-2350
Year Established: 1958
Pub. Frequency: m.

**Materials Accepted/Included:** 01-Business news 02-By-line articles 03-Fashion news 04-Food news 05-Freelance copy 06-Letters to editor 07-Real estate news 08-Sports news 09-Travel news 10-Book rev. 11-Movie rev. 12-Music rev. 13-TV rev. 14-Theater rev. 15-Coming events 16-Obituaries 17-Question & answer 18-Social announcements 19-Artwork 20-Cartoons 21-Photos 22-TV listings 23-Audio rec. 24-Video rec. 25-Books 26-Films/film clips 27-Personnel news 28-Press releases 29-New product news/photos 30-Trade lit. 31-Contracts awarded 32-Display adv. 33-Classified adv.

4-26

Page Size: standard
Subscrip. Rate: $12/yr. members; $21/yr.
 qualified organizations
Freelance Pay: $75-$1,000/article
Circulation: 298,715
Circulation Type: controlled
**Owner(s):**
Aircraft Owners & Pilots Association
421 Aviation Way
Frederick, MD 21701
Telephone: (301) 695-2000
Ownership %: 100
**Management:**
R. Anderson Pew ................Chairman of Board
Phil Boyer ..........................................President
Phil Boyer ..........................................Publisher
**Editorial:**
Mark R. Twombly ......................Editor in Chief
Thomas B. Haines ....................Executive Editor
Marc E. Cook ..............................Senior Editor
Julie A. Weinrich ......................Managing Editor
Lee Ann Sansone .......Administrative Assistant
Denis C. Beran ..................Advertising Director
Michael Kline ..................................Art Director
Alton Marsh ..............................Associate Editor
Barry Schiff ......................................Contributor
John S. Yodice ................................Contributor
Bruce Landsberg ..............................Contributor
Art Davis ..............................Creative Director
Thomas A. Horne ....................Editor at Large
Connie F. Iman ....................Editorial Assistant
Janet M. Sappington ...........Editorial Assistant
Mike Fizer ......................................Photographer
**Desc.:** Official publication of the Aircraft
 Owners and Pilots Association. Needs
 factual articles of up to 2,500 words or
 articles of 100-300 words with pictures,
 photos, diagrams or sketches that will
 inform, educate and entertain pilots.
 Contains aircraft maintenance
 information, new or unusual planes or
 aeronautical equipment, how-to features,
 travel articles, pilot reports and general
 aviation policies.
**Readers:** Light airplane, general business
 and corporate pilots and aircraft owners.
 Above average education and income.
 Majority employed in professional,
 managerial, and technical professions.

**25825**
## AVIATION CONSUMER, THE
75 Holly Hill Ln.
Greenwich, CT 06830-2910
Telephone: (203) 661-6111
FAX: (203) 661-4802
Mailing Address:
 P.O. Box 2626
 Greenwich, CT 06836-2626
Year Established: 1971
Pub. Frequency: 24/yr.
Page Size: standard
Subscrip. Rate: $49/yr. US; $108/yr.
 foreign
Freelance Pay: $100-$800/article
Circulation: 37,000
Circulation Type: paid
**Owner(s):**
Belvoir Publications, Inc.
78 Holly Hill Ln.
Greenwich, CT 06830
Telephone: (203) 661-6111
Ownership %: 100
**Management:**
Robert Englander ................Chairman of Board
Donn Smith ........................................President
**Editorial:**
Paul Bertorelli ........................Executive Editor
Andrew Douglas ..........................Senior Editor
Doug Kelly ..........................................Art Director

**Desc.:** No commercial advertising
 accepted. Investigative reporting, aircraft
 and accessory evaluation
 and comparison. Mostly staff written, but
 free-lance work accepted. Use B&W
 photos, illustrations. Departments
 Include: Features, News, Safety, Used
 Aircraft Guide, Queries, Letters,
 Editorials, Sub features on items.
**Readers:** General aviation pilots and
 aircraft owners.

**61618**
## AVIATION DAILY
1200 G St., N.W., Ste. 200
Washington, DC 20005
Telephone: (202) 383-2350
FAX: (202) 383-2438
Year Established: 1940
Pub. Frequency: d.
Page Size: standard
Subscrip. Rate: $830/6 mos.; $1,475/yr.
**Owner(s):**
McGraw-Hill, Inc.
1221 Ave.of the Americas
New York, NY 10020
Telephone: (212) 997-3807
Ownership %: 100
**Editorial:**
Edmund Pinto ............................Editor in Chief
Avery Vice ........................Congressional Editor
Alfhild Winder ..........................Deputy Editor
James Baumgarner ..................Editor at Large
Jennifer Michels ............Federal Agency Editor
Frank Jackman ........................Financial Editor
Frank Jackman ........................International Editor
Grier Graham ..............................Labor Editor
Grier Graham ..........................Marketing Editor
**Readers:** Aviation industry news and
 analysis.

**61617**
## AVIATION EQUIPMENT
## MAINTENANCE
1201 Seven Locks Rd.
Potomac, MD 20854
Telephone: (301) 340-1520
FAX: (301) 340-0542
Year Established: 1982
Pub. Frequency: m.
Page Size: standard
Subscrip. Rate: free; $40/yr.
Materials: 01,02,05,06,17,29,31,32,33
Circulation: 41,500
Circulation Type: controlled
**Owner(s):**
Phillips Business Information, Inc.
1201 Seven Locks Rd
Potomac, MD 20854
Telephone: (301) 340-1520
Ownership %: 100
**Management:**
Richard J. Koulbanis ..........................Publisher
**Editorial:**
Clifton Stroud II ......................................Editor

**21859**
## AVIATION MECHANICS BULLETIN
2200 Wilson Blvd., Ste. 500
Arlington, VA 22201
Telephone: (703) 522-8300
FAX: (703) 525-6047
Year Established: 1952
Pub. Frequency: bi-m.
Page Size: pocket
Subscrip. Rate: $35/yr. US; $40/yr. foreign
Freelance Pay: $100/print page
Circulation: 2,300
Circulation Type: paid
**Owner(s):**
Flight Safety Foundation, Inc.
2200 Wilson Blvd., Ste. 500
Arlington, VA 22201
Telephone: (703) 522-8300
Ownership %: 100
**Management:**
John H. Enders ........................Vice Chairman

Stuart Matthews ............................President
**Editorial:**
Stuart Matthews ..........................Chairman
Stuart Matthews ..........Chief Executive Officer
J. Edward Peery ..........Director of Membership
Roger Rozelle ..................Publication Director
Richard Maginnis ............Senior Vice President
**Readers:** Airlines, aerospace
 manufacturing facilities, professional
 aviation associations.

**21861**
## AVIATION WEEK & SPACE
## TECHNOLOGY
1200 G St.
Ste. 922
Washington, DC 20005
Telephone: (202) 383-2300
FAX: (202) 383-2347
Year Established: 1975
Pub. Frequency: w.
Page Size: standard
Subscrip. Rate: $5 newsstand; $82/yr.
Circulation: 130,000
Circulation Type: paid
**Owner(s):**
McGraw-Hill, Inc.
1221 Ave. of the Americas
New York, NY 10020
Telephone: (212) 997-3807
Ownership %: 100
**Management:**
Kenneth Gazzola ..............................Publisher
**Editorial:**
Donald E. Fink ..................................Editor
David North ........................Managing Editor
**Desc.:** Contains technical developments
 and analysis in the fields of missile
 engineering, air transport, management,
 and finance.
**Readers:** Manufacturers, government
 institutions in relating to areospace
 industry.

**21862**
## BUSINESS & COMMERCIAL
## AVIATION
4 International Dr.
Port Chester, NY 10573
Telephone: (914) 939-0300
FAX: (914) 939-1184
Year Established: 1958
Pub. Frequency: m.
Page Size: standard
Subscrip. Rate: $60/yr. US; $85/yr. foreign
Materials: 01,06,23,24,25,32,33
Freelance Pay: $100-$400/article
Circulation: 53,000
Circulation Type: controlled
**Owner(s):**
McGraw-Hill, Inc.
1221 Ave. of the Americas
New York, NY 10020
Telephone: (212) 512-2000
Ownership %: 100
**Management:**
Joe Dione ......................................President
D.W. Ewald ....................................Publisher
**Editorial:**
Richard N. Aarons ......................Editor in Chief
Jessica Salerno ......................Managing Editor
**Desc.:** Cover business and commercial
 fixed and rotary wing aircraft
 descriptions, operations, service
 operators, overhaul, maintenance, air
 traffic control, piloting, techniques,
 safety, and regional and commuter
 airlines.
**Readers:** Owners and operators of
 business and commercial aircraft.

**68666**
## CAREER PILOT
4959 Massachusetts Blvd.
Atlanta, GA 30337
Telephone: (404) 997-8097
FAX: (404) 997-8111

Year Established: 1983
Pub. Frequency: m.
Page Size: standard
Subscrip. Rate: $39/yr.
Materials: 01,02,05,06,10,15,19,21,29,32,33
Freelance Pay: $.18/wd. & up
Print Process: web
Circulation: 13,500
Circulation Type: paid
**Owner(s):**
Future Aviation Professionals (FAPA)
4959 Massachusetts Blvd.
Atlanta, GA 30337
Telephone: (404) 997-8097
Ownership %: 100
**Editorial:**
David A. Jones ....................................Editor
**Desc.:** Covers career advice and
 information on airlines as employers.

**21863**
## CIVIL AIR PATROL NEWS
CAP-USAF/PAIN
105 South Hansell St.
Maxwell AFB, AL 36112-6332
Telephone: (205) 953-7593
FAX: (205) 953-4245
Year Established: 1968
Pub. Frequency: m.
Page Size: tabloid
Subscrip. Rate: $5/yr.
Circulation: 55,000
Circulation Type: controlled
**Owner(s):**
Civil Air Patrol Corp.
CAP-USAF/PAIN
Montgomery, AL 36112
Telephone: (205) 953-7593
Ownership %: 100
**Editorial:**
Don Thweatt ............................Executive Editor
MSgt. Jeffrey Melvin ..................................Editor
**Desc.:** Stories and photos on CAP
 units and members and their activities.
 Editorials on aerospace developments
 and programs as they affect CAP.
 Stories and photos on search and
 rescue activities and disaster relief
 activities. Stories and photos about
 USAF are also included. Stories on
 developments in Aerospace Educaton.
**Readers:** Aviation Minded CAP Members
 Who Range in Age From 13 on Up

**21867**
## FAA AVIATION NEWS
800 Independence Ave., S.W., AFS-810
Washington, DC 20591
Telephone: (202) 267-8017
FAX: (202) 267-9463
Year Established: 1961
Pub. Frequency: 8/yr.
Page Size: standard
Subscrip. Rate: $15/yr. US; $18.75/yr.
 foreign
Materials: 02,06,15,17,19,20,21,28,29
Freelance Pay: negotiable
Print Process: web
Circulation: 40,000
Circulation Type: paid
**Owner(s):**
FAA/DOT-Superintendent of Documents,
US, GOP
800 Independence Ave., S.W.
Washington, DC 20591
Telephone: (202) 267-8017
Ownership %: 100
**Editorial:**
Phyllis A. Duncan ....................................Editor
Louise Oertly ............................Associate Editor
Dean Chamberlain ..................Associate Editor
**Desc.:** Safety magazine for pilots and
 other airmen. Departments include:
 Editorial, Art and Production.

**Materials Accepted/Included:** 01-Business news 02-By-line articles 03-Fashion news 04-Food news 05-Freelance copy 06-Letters to editor 07-Real estate news 08-Sports news 09-Travel news
10-Book rev. 11-Movie rev. 12-Music rev. 13-TV rev. 14-Theater rev. 15-Coming events 16-Obituaries 17-Question & answer 18-Social announcements 19-Artwork 20-Cartoons 21-Photos 22-TV listings
23-Audio rec. 24-Video rec. 25-Books 26-Films/film clips 27-Personnel news 28-Press releases 29-New product news/photos 30-Trade lit. 31-Contracts awarded 32-Display adv. 33-Classified adv.

4-27

**Readers:** Mainly pilots, others in aviation industry.
**Deadline:** story-3 mos. prior to pub. date; news-3 mos. prior; photo-3 mos. prior

### FLIGHT TRAINING
67214

405 Main St.
Parkville, MO 64152
Telephone: (816) 741-1165
FAX: (816) 741-6458
Year Established: 1989
Pub. Frequency: m.
Page Size: standard
Subscrip. Rate: $2.95 newsstand;
  $19.95/yr.
Materials: 29,32,33,
Freelance Pay: $200-$800
Print Process: web offset
Circulation: 82,000
Circulation Type: controlled & paid
**Owner(s):**
Smooth Propellar Co., Inc.
405 Main St.
Parkville, MO 64152
Telephone: (816) 741-1165
Ownership %: 100
**Management:**
Gary S. Worden ...........................Publisher
**Readers:** New pilots & their instructors;
  flight school owners & managers

### FLYING
21870

500 W. Putnam Ave.
Greenwich, CT 00830
Telephone: (203) 622-2706
FAX: (203) 622-2725
Year Established: 1927
Pub. Frequency: m.
Page Size: standard
Subscrip. Rate: $2.95 newsstand; $24/yr.
Freelance Pay: negotiable
Circulation: 322,039
Circulation Type: paid
**Owner(s):**
Hachette Magazines, Inc.
1633 Broadway
New York, NY 10019
Telephone: (212) 767-6953
Ownership %: 100
**Bureau(s):**
Hachette Magazines, Inc.
1633 Broadway
New York, NY 10019
Telephone: (212) 767-6953
Contact: Patricia Luebke, Vice President
**Management:**
David Pecker ...............................President
Dick Koenig ................................Publisher
Dave Leckey .....................Circulation Manager
Rochelle Togo ............Classified Adv. Manager
**Editorial:**
Mac McClellan ..................Editor in Chief
Nigel Moll ...........................Senior Editor
Mary Hunt ........................Managing Editor
Wayne Lincourt ..................Advertising Director
Nancy Bink ...........................Art Director
Jerry Sablo ..........................Production Editor
**Desc.:** Articles on all aspects of general
  aviation, including fixed and rotary-wing
  aircraft; pilot reports, safety & technique.
  General aviation/personal and business
  flying. Articles range from reports of new
  aircraft, engines and navigational and
  communications equipment to historical
  aviation events. They include ways
  of improving various pilot techniques and
  of building knowledge and promoting
  understanding of the entire aviation field.
**Readers:** Businessman pilots

### FLYING REVIEW MAGAZINE
52639

4801 Charlotte Ct., N.E.
Albuquerque, NM 87109
Telephone: (800) 282-8839
FAX: (505) 298-8093
Mailing Address:
  P.O. Box 9191
  Albuquerque, NM 87119
Year Established: 1969
Pub. Frequency: m.
Page Size: standard
Subscrip. Rate: $25/yr.
Freelance Pay: negotiable
Circulation: 33,000
Circulation Type: paid
**Owner(s):**
J.G. Kinlen
P.O. Box 9191
Albuquerque, NM 87119
Telephone: (505) 842-4184
Ownership %: 100
**Bureau(s):**
CPA Frank Gallo
2698C S. Vaughn Way
Aurora, CO 80014

TPA A1 Shackelford
931 Zachry Dr.
San Antonio, TX 78228
Telephone: (512) 434-7596

Flying Review Magazine
2502 Clark Carr Loop, S.E.
Albuquerque, NM 87106
Telephone: (505) 842-4184
Contact: James G. Kinlen, President
**Management:**
J. G. Kinlen ...........................President
**Editorial:**
R. L. Kinlen ...............................Editor
Bob Worthington .........................Editor
Frank Gallo ................................Editor
M. Young Stokes .................Photographer
Al Santilli Soaring .................Photographer
**Desc.:** A general aviation publication that
  is distributed to and reports on twenty
  West and Southwest states. Official
  publication of the New Mexico,
  Colorado, Texas, Pilots' Associations.
  Lobbies for aviation concerns, informs,
  entertains, pilot safety education, aircraft
  evaluation. Now also represent the
  Kansas-Kentucky-Missouri-North Dakota
  and USPA Pilots Associations. Plus-
  Nebraska, Ohio, Arkansas, North
  Carolina. Now national distribution.
**Readers:** 70% FAA rated pilots from
  student to airline transport rated, 15%
  non-regulated ultralight, sport &
  experimental, soaring pilots, balance
  interested individuals. 65% are college
  graduates, income average $55,000,
  60% own an aircraft, professional
  employment.

### GENERAL AVIATION NEWS & FLYER
21875

P.O. Box 39099
Tacoma, WA 98439
Telephone: (206) 471-9888
FAX: (206) 471-9911
Year Established: 1949
Pub. Frequency: bi-w.
Page Size: tabloid
Subscrip. Rate: $2 newsstand; $24/yr.;
  $41/2 yrs.; $54/3 yrs.
Materials: 01,02,05,06,10,15,25,27,28,29,
  30,32,33
Freelance Pay: up to $3/col. in.
Print Process: web offset
Circulation: 40,000
Circulation Type: paid

**Owner(s):**
Northwest Flyer, Inc.
P.O. Box 39099
Tacoma, WA 98439-0099
Telephone: (206) 471-9888
FAX: (206) 471-9911
Ownership %: 100
**Management:**
David & Marylou Sclair ..................Publisher
Greg O'Neil ...................Advertising Manager
Ron Boydston ...................Circulation Manager
**Editorial:**
David Sclair ..................................Editor
Kirk Gormley .........................Design Editor
**Desc.:** Carries the most current "hard
  news" of the aviation industry plus
  special feature stories about the
  industry, aircraft, products, and general
  aviation businesses of special interest to
  pilots and aircraft owners, news stories
  must be current and of national interest,
  1,000 word features with or without
  pictures on timely subjects. Events are
  staff covered where possible, others
  made on assignment, by-line given on
  assigned or accepted free-lance articles.
  Departments include: New Products,
  Personnel, Financial, Very Interesting
  Pilots, Pilot Reports.
**Readers:** Primarily pilots and aircraft
  owners.
**Deadline:** story-every other Fri.; news-
  every other Fri.; photo-every other Fri.;
  ads-every other Thu.

### JET CARGO NEWS
21881

5353 DeSoto, Ste. 510
Houston, TX 77091
Telephone: (713) 681-4760
FAX: (713) 682-3871
Mailing Address:
  P.O. Box 920952
  Houston, TX 77292
Year Established: 1968
Pub. Frequency: m.
Page Size: tabloid
Subscrip. Rate: $30/yr. US; $45/yr. foreign
Freelance Pay: $4/in.
Circulation: 23,000
Circulation Type: controlled
**Owner(s):**
Hagall Publishing Co.
P.O. Box 920952
Houston, TX 77292
Telephone: (713) 681-4760
Ownership %: 100
**Management:**
Patricia M. Chandler ......................Publisher
Regina P. Michael ...........Advertising Manager
**Editorial:**
Patricia M. Chandler ........................Editor
**Desc.:** Provides the air shipping industry
  with timely, factual news related to
  domestic and international movement of
  goods by air and the purchase of
  shipping equipment, services and
  supplies.
**Readers:** Traffic and distribution
  managers, sales, purchasing agents,
  export managers, and freight forwarders.

### JOURNAL OF AIRCRAFT
64917

370 L'Enfant Promenade, S.W.
Washington, DC 20024-2518
Telephone: (202) 646-7400
Year Established: 1963
Pub. Frequency: bi-m.
Page Size: standard
Subscrip. Rate: $42/yr. members US;
  $72/yr. members foreign; $230/yr. non-
  members US; $285/yr. non-members
  foreign
Circulation: 3,500
Circulation Type: paid

**Owner(s):**
American Institute of Aeronautics &
  Astronautics
370 L'Enfant Promenade, S.W.
Washington, DC 20024-2518
Telephone: (202) 646-7400
Ownership %: 100
**Management:**
John Newbauer ............................Publisher
**Editorial:**
Thomas M. Weeks ..................Editor in Chief
William O'Connor ...................Managing Editor
Norma Brennan ................Publication Director
**Desc.:** Covers design and operations of
  new as well as upgraded military and
  civilian aircraft, Subsonic through
  hypersonic aircraft are included. Papers
  on the integration of control systems
  and propulsion systems are presented,
  with an emphasis on applied
  engineering.
**Readers:** Aeronautical engineers and
  scientists

### JOURNAL OF AIR TRAFFIC CONTROL
21882

2300 Clarendon Blvd.
Ste. 711
Arlington, VA 22201
Telephone: (703) 522-5717
Year Established: 1958
Pub. Frequency: q.
Page Size: standard
Subscrip. Rate: $35/yr. non-member US;
  $45/yr. foreign
Materials: 01,06,10,21,30,32,
Print Process: offset
Circulation: 40,000
Circulation Type: paid
**Owner(s):**
Air Traffic Control Association
2300 Clarendon Blvd.
Ste. 711
Arlington, VA 22201
Telephone: (703) 522-5717
Ownership %: 100
**Management:**
Gabe Hartl .................................President
Gabe Hartl ...........................Executive Director
Judy Gibbons ....................Advertising Manager
**Editorial:**
Suzette Matthews ...................Managing Editor
Suzette Matthews ........................News Editor
Suzette Matthews ...................Technical Editor
**Desc.:** Technical and operational coverage
  of all subjects relating to aviation safety
  and the control of air traffic. Articles:
  2500 word maximum, plus illustrations.
  Departments include: New ATC
  Equipment, International ATC, Book
  Reviews, Flight Safety, Aircraft
  Recognition, Civil and Military.
**Readers:** Air traffic controllers,
  administrators, aviation managers and
  directors, engineers, designers and
  manufacturers of equipments for air
  traffic control.

### JOURNAL OF GUIDANCE, CONTROL & DYNAMICS
56415

370 L'Enfant Promenade, S.W.
Washington, DC 20024-2518
Telephone: (202) 646-7400
Year Established: 1980
Pub. Frequency: bi-m.
Page Size: standard
Subscrip. Rate: $45/yr. members; $250
  non-members; foreign non-members
  $305
Circulation: 3,000
Circulation Type: paid

**Materials Accepted/Included:** 01-Business news 02-By-line articles 03-Fashion news 04-Food news 05-Freelance copy 06-Letters to editor 07-Real estate news 08-Sports news 09-Travel news 10-Book rev. 11-Movie rev. 12-Music rev. 13-TV rev. 14-Theater rev. 15-Coming events 16-Obituaries 17-Question & answer 18-Social announcements 19-Artwork 20-Cartoons 21-Photos 22-TV listings 23-Audio rec. 24-Video rec. 25-Books 26-Films/film clips 27-Personnel news 28-Press releases 29-New product news/photos 30-Trade lit. 31-Contracts awarded 32-Display adv. 33-Classified adv.

**Owner(s):**
American Institute of Aeronautics &
  Astronautics
370 L'Enfant Promenade, S.W.
Washington, DC 20024-2518
Telephone: (202) 646-7400
Ownership %: 100
**Management:**
John Newbauer .................................President
John Newbauer .................................Publisher
**Editorial:**
Kyle T. Alfriend ....................Editor in Chief
William O'Connor ......................Managing Editor
Norma Brennan .................Publication Director
**Desc.:** Covers dynamics, guidance control,
  navigation, optimization, electronics, and
  information processing related to
  aeronautical and astronautical systems.
  Focuses ontechnical knowledge,
  exploratory developments, design
  criteria, and applications.
**Readers:** Engineers, academics, scientists
  interested in aeronautical & astronautical
  guidance & control systems.

## JOURNAL OF PROPULSION & POWER
21883
370 L'Enfant Promenade, S.W.
Washington, DC 20024-2518
Telephone: (202) 646-7400
Year Established: 1984
Pub. Frequency: bi-m.
Page Size: standard
Subscrip. Rate: $38/yr. member US;
  $68/yr. member foreign; $260/yr. non-
  member US; $315/yr. non-member
  foreign
Circulation: 1,900
Circulation Type: paid
**Owner(s):**
American Institute of Aeronautics &
  Astronautics
370 L'Enfant Promenade, S.W.
Washington, DC 20024-2518
Telephone: (202) 646-7400
Ownership %: 100
**Management:**
John Swihart .................................President
John Newbauer .................................Publisher
**Editorial:**
R.H. Woodward Waesche ..........Editor in Chief
William O'Connor ....................Managing Editor
Norma Brennan .................Publication Director
**Desc.:** Covers advances in airbreathing,
  electric and exotic propulsion, solid and
  liquid rockets, fuels and propellants,
  power generation, and the application of
  aerospace technology to terrestrial
  energy systems.
**Readers:** Engineers involved with
  propulsion systems.

## JOURNAL OF SPACECRAFT & ROCKETS
21885
370 L'Enfant Promenade, S.W.
Washington, DC 20024-2518
Year Established: 1964
Pub. Frequency: bi-m.
Page Size: standard
Subscrip. Rate: $33/yr. member US;
  $63/yr. member foreign; $215 non-
  member US; $270/yr. non-member
  foreign
Circulation: 3,500
Circulation Type: paid
**Owner(s):**
American Institute of Aeronautics and
  Astronautics
370 L'Enfant Promenade
Washington, DC 20024-2518
Telephone: (202) 646-7400
Ownership %: 100

**Management:**
John Swihart .................................President
John Newbauer .................................Publisher
**Editorial:**
E. Vincent Zoby ....................Editor in Chief
William F. O'Connor .................Managing Editor
Norma J. Brennan .............Publication Director
**Desc.:** Presents topics on spacecraft and
  tactial and strategic missile systems.
  Covers configuration, design and
  application of systems, subsystems, and
  missions, aerothermodynamics,
  instrumentation, communication,
  manufacturing and operations, data
  processing, space sciences and
  application of space technology to other
  fields.
**Readers:** Aerospace engineers.

## JOURNAL OF THE AMERICAN HELICOPTER SOCIETY
21884
217 N. Washington St.
Alexandria, VA 22314
Telephone: (703) 684-6777
FAX: (703) 739-9279
Year Established: 1956
Pub. Frequency: q.
Page Size: standard
Subscrip. Rate: $35/yr.; $45/yr. foreign
Circulation: 6,000
Circulation Type: paid
**Owner(s):**
American Helicopter Society
217 N. Washington St.
Alexandria, VA 22314
Telephone: (703) 684-6777
Ownership %: 100
**Management:**
Webb Joiner .................................President
Morris E. Flater .................................Publisher
**Editorial:**
Robert J. Huston .................................Editor
Kim Smith .................................Managing Editor
**Desc.:** Theoretical technical articles
  relating to the helicopter and V/STOL
  industry.
**Readers:** All segments of helicopter and
  V/STOL industry.

## NATA NEWS
69167
4226 King St.
Alexandria, VA 22302-1507
Telephone: (703) 845-9000
FAX: (703) 845-8176
Year Established: 1969
Pub. Frequency: m.
Subscrip. Rate: $20/yr. non-members
Circulation: 23,000
Circulation Type: paid
**Owner(s):**
National Air Transportation Association
4226 King St.
Alexandria, VA 22302-1507
Telephone: (703) 845-9000
Ownership %: 100
**Editorial:**
Kai Yee .................................Editor

## PILOT LOG, THE
61716
244 College St.
Macon, GA 31213
Telephone: (912) 743-7403
FAX: (912) 743-2173
Mailing Address:
  P.O. Box 4844
  Macon, GA 31213
Year Established: 1921
Pub. Frequency: 6/yr.
Page Size: standard
Subscrip. Rate: $10/yr. non-member US.;
  $15/yr. foreign
Print Process: web
Circulation: 19,000
Circulation Type: controlled

**Owner(s):**
Pilot International
244 College St.
Macon, GA 31213
Telephone: (912) 743-7403
Ownership %: 100
**Editorial:**
Paige Calvert Henson .................................Editor
Cynthia Mills .................................Executive Director

## PLANE & PILOT MAGAZINE
21892
12121 Wilshire Blvd., Ste. 1220
Los Angeles, CA 90025
Telephone: (310) 820-1500
FAX: (213) 826-5008
Year Established: 1965
Pub. Frequency: m.
Page Size: standard
Subscrip. Rate: $2.95 newsstand;
  $16.95/yr.
Materials: 02,05,15,21,29,20,32,33
Freelance Pay: negotiable
Print Process: offset
Circulation: 135,000
Circulation Type: paid
**Owner(s):**
Werner Publishing Corp.
12121 Wilshire Blvd.
Ste., 1220
Los Angeles, CA 90025
Telephone: (310) 820-1500
Ownership %: 100
**Management:**
Don Werner .................................President
Steve Werner .................................Publisher
**Editorial:**
Steve Werner .................................Editor
Mike McMann .................................Associate Publisher
**Desc.:** Contains articles on flying for
  business and recreation in all types of
  private and executive aircraft other than
  scheduled airline and military flights.
  Feature articles should deal with
  airplanes, equipment for light planes and
  pilot proficiency or matters relating to
  them.
**Readers:** Pilots and plane owners.

## PRIVATE PILOT
25918
2401 Beverly Blvd.
Los Angeles, CA 90057
Telephone: (310) 385-2222
Mailing Address:
  P.O. Box 6050
  Mission Viejo, CA 92690
Year Established: 1965
Pub. Frequency: m.
Page Size: standard
Subscrip. Rate: $23.97/yr.
Materials: 01,02,06,09,10,15,19,20,21
Freelance Pay: $75-$300
Circulation: 100,000
Circulation Type: paid
**Owner(s):**
Fancy Publications, Inc.
2401 Beverly Blvd.
Los Angeles, CA 90057
Telephone: (310) 385-2222
Ownership %: 100
**Management:**
Norman Ridker .................................Publisher
Vera Geuther .................Circulation Manager
Susan McElhaney .............Production Manager
**Editorial:**
Joseph P. O'Leary .................................Editor
Dennis Shattuck .................Editorial Director
Jeff Christian .................................Sales
Chuck Preston .................................Sales

**Desc.:** Edited for the general aviation pilot;
  aimed at the potential pilot as well as
  the man who has earned his private or
  advanced license. Features cover trips
  and budgetary requirements, jobs in
  which the use of a plane is paramount,
  self help articles to improve flying
  proficiency, and serial tests of new
  aircraft. Great emphasis is upon
  encouragement to fly. Technical in
  nature but easy to understand.
  Departments include: Pilot Reports,
  Safety, Navigation, Avionics, Instrument
  Flying.
**Readers:** Affluent group, all flying pilots,
  majoritives, proprietors.

## PROFESSIONAL PILOT
21893
3014 Colvin St.
Alexandria, VA 22314-4544
Telephone: (703) 370-0606
FAX: (703) 370-7082
Year Established: 1967
Pub. Frequency: m.
Page Size: standard
Subscrip. Rate: $36/yr.
Materials: 01,06,15,17,21,27,28,29,30,31,
  32,33
Freelance Pay: varies
Print Process: web offset
Circulation: 32,000
Circulation Type: controlled
**Owner(s):**
Queensmith Communications
3014 Colvin St.
Alexandria, VA 22314
Telephone: (703) 320-0606
Ownership %: 100
**Management:**
Murray Q. Smith .................................President
Murray Q. Smith .................................Publisher
Earlene Chandler .............Advertising Manager
Joan Goveart .................General Manager
Pam Tyrrell .................Production Manager
**Editorial:**
Kirby Harrison .................Managing Editor
Wayne Shipp .................................Art Director
**Desc.:** Articles written for career pilots.
  Departments include: Tiedowns,
  Terminal Checklist, Guest Editorial, New
  Owner, Sideband, News.
**Readers:** Corporate, charter, regional and
  military executive transport pilots.
**Deadline:** story-1 mo.

## PROGRESS IN AEROSPACE SCIENCES
68671
660 White Plains Rd.
Tarrytown, NY 10591-5153
Telephone: (914) 524-9200
FAX: (914) 333-2444
Year Established: 1961
Pub. Frequency: 4/yr.
**Owner(s):**
Pergamon Press, Inc.
660 White Plains Rd.
Tarrytown, NY 10591-5153
Telephone: (914) 524-9200
Ownership %: 100
**Editorial:**
Alec D. Young .................................Editor
**Desc.:** Focuses on the application of
  recent developments and research in
  the aerospace sciences to problems
  encountered in industry, research
  establishments and universities.

## REVISTA AEREA
21895
310 E. 44th St., Ste. 1601
New York, NY 10017
Telephone: (212) 370-1740
FAX: (212) 949-6756
Year Established: 1937
Pub. Frequency: 10/yr.

---

**Materials Accepted/Included:** 01-Business news 02-By-line articles 03-Fashion news 04-Food news 05-Freelance copy 06-Letters to editor 07-Real estate news 08-Sports news 09-Travel news 10-Book rev. 11-Movie rev. 12-Music rev. 13-TV rev. 14-Theater rev. 15-Coming events 16-Obituaries 17-Question & answer 18-Social announcements 19-Artwork 20-Cartoons 21-Photos 22-TV listings 23-Audio rec. 24-Video rec. 25-Books 26-Films/film clips 27-Personnel news 28-Press releases 29-New product news/photos 30-Trade lit. 31-Contracts awarded 32-Display adv. 33-Classified adv.

Page Size: standard
Subscrip. Rate: $50/yr.
Circulation: 10,000
Circulation Type: controlled
**Owner(s):**
Strato Publishing Co., Inc.
310 E. 44th St., Ste. 1601
New York, NY 10017
Telephone: (212) 370-1740
FAX: (212) 949-6756
Ownership %: 100
**Management:**
Elaine Asch ...........................President
Debra Dicker ...............Vice President
Elaine Asch ...........................Publisher
**Editorial:**
Elaine Asch ..............Book Review Editor
Elaine Asch ...........................Columnist
**Desc.:** Covers aviation and aerospace
developments (military, commercial and
business) worldwide for senior Latin
American business executives,
government officials, and other ranking
aerospace decision makers. Printed in
Spanish.
**Readers:** Military and civilian aviation
personnel in Latin America, Spain and
the Portugal.

21896
**ROTOR & WING INTERNATIONAL**
1201 Seven Locks Road
Ste. 300
Potomac, MD 20854
Telephone: (301) 340-1520
FAX: (301) 340-0542
Year Established: 1967
Pub. Frequency: m.
Page Size: standard
Subscrip. Rate: $49/yr.
Materials: 01,05,06,31,32,33
Freelance Pay: varies
Print Process: offset
Circulation: 38,000
Circulation Type: controlled
**Owner(s):**
Phillips Publishing, International
7811 Montrose Rd.
Potomac, MD 20854
Telephone: (301) 340-2100
Ownership %: 100
**Bureau(s):**
R & WI Washington, D.C. Bureau
P.O. Box 12053
Washington, DC 20005
Telephone: (202) 328-8709
FAX: (202) 396-1053
Contact: David Harvey, Bureau Chief

London Rosemount House
Rosemount Ave.
KT14 6NP West Byfleet, Surrey United
Kingdom
Telephone: 44-932-355-515
FAX: 44-932-355-962
Contact: Bill Carey, Bureau Chief
**Management:**
Dick Koulbanis .......................Publisher
**Editorial:**
Kathleen Kocks ...........................Editor
David Jensen ...............Editorial Director
Perry Bradley ....................News Editor
**Desc.:** A controlled subscription magazine
covering civil and military helicopter
operators and companies around the
world.
**Readers:** Owners, operators, and
manufacturers of helicopters, plus
suppliers and services to the rotorcraft
industry.
**Deadline:** story-1 1/2 mo. prior to pub.
date; news-1 1/2 mo. prior; photo-1 1/2
mo. prior; ads-1st of mo. prior to pub.
date

68686
**ULTRALIGHT FLYING!**
1085 Bailey Ave.
Chattanooga, TN 37404
Telephone: (615) 629-5375
FAX: (615) 629-5379
Year Established: 1976
Pub. Frequency: m.
Page Size: tabloid
Subscrip. Rate: $27/yr.
Materials: 05,06,15,19,20,21,24,25,28,29,
30,32,33
Print Process: web offset
Circulation: 14,000
Circulation Type: paid
**Owner(s):**
Glider Rider, Inc.
P.O. Box 6009
Chattanooga, TN 37401
Telephone: (615) 629-5375
Ownership %: 100
**Management:**
Tracy Knauss .......................Publisher
**Editorial:**
Sharon Hill ...............................Editor
**Desc.:** A magazine for enthusiasts of
ultralight and microlight aviation.
**Readers:** People who fly for fun.

21905
**WEEKLY OF BUSINESS AVIATION,
THE**
1200 G St., N.W., Ste. 200
Washington, DC 20005
Telephone: (202) 383-2381
FAX: (202) 383-2438
Year Established: 1965
Pub. Frequency: Mon.
Page Size: standard
Subscrip. Rate: $495/yr.
Circulation: 600
Circulation Type: controlled
**Owner(s):**
McGraw-Hill, Inc., Aerospace & Defense
Group
1221 Ave. of the Americas
New York, NY 10020
Ownership %: 100
**Editorial:**
David Collogan ...........................Editor
Kerry Lynch ....................Assistant Editor
**Desc.:** Weekly newsletter covering news
items of interest to general aviation.
**Readers:** General aviation management,
and manufacturers, flight departments,
fixed-base operators, etc.

21908
**WORLD AVIATION DIRECTORY &
BUYER'S GUIDE**
1200 G. St., N.W.
Ste. 900
Washington, DC 20005
Telephone: (202) 383-2418
FAX: (202) 383-2439
Year Established: 1940
Pub. Frequency: s-a.
Page Size: standard
Subscrip. Rate: $250/yr. US; $310/yr.
foreign
Freelance Pay: none
Circulation: 15,000
Circulation Type: paid
**Owner(s):**
McGraw-Hill, Inc.
1221 Avenue of the Americas
New York, NY 10020
Telephone: (212) 512-2000
Ownership %: 100
**Management:**
Ken Gazzola ..............Executive Vice President
Charles Hull ...........................Publisher
**Editorial:**
Burt H. Shayte ...............Managing Editor
Donna B. Kaulkin ...............Editorial Director
Anne McMahon ...............Circulation Director

Margaret Davis ...............Marketing Director
Bill Orchard ...............Production Director
**Desc.:** Lists over 68,000 names, titles and
7,000 products in over 28,500
aviation/aerospace companies and
organizations in 146 countries.
**Readers:** Aviation and aerospace
executives, managers, purchasers, and
engineers.

61320
**WORLD TRAVELER**
7730 S.W. Mohawk
Tualatin, OR 97062
Telephone: (503) 691-1955
FAX: (503) 691-1275
Year Established: 1992
Pub. Frequency: m.
Page Size: oversize
Subscrip. Rate: $36/yr.
Freelance Pay: $750-$1,100
Circulation: 344,039
Circulation Type: free & paid
**Owner(s):**
Skies America
7730 S.W. Mohawk
Tualatin, OR 97062
Telephone: (503) 636-8679
Ownership %: 100
**Management:**
Sherrill Rullo ...........................Publisher
**Editorial:**
Terri J. Wallo ...........................Editor
**Readers:** Business and vacation travelers

## Group 020-Baking

21911
**BAKERY PRODUCTION &
MARKETING**
455 N. Cityfront Plaza Dr.
Chicago, IL 60611
Telephone: (312) 222-2000
FAX: (312) 222-2026
Year Established: 1966
Pub. Frequency: 15/yr.
Page Size: standard
Subscrip. Rate: $70/yr. US; $130/yr.
foreign
Materials: 32,33
Print Process: web offset
Circulation: 40,052
Circulation Type: controlled
**Owner(s):**
Cahners Publishing Co.
455 N. Cityfront Plaza Dr.
Chicago, IL 60611
Telephone: (312) 222-2000
FAX: (312) 222-2026
Ownership %: 100
**Management:**
Peter Lachapelle ...........................Publisher
Jeanne Sullivan ...............Advertising Manager
Neila Frontier ...............Production Manager
**Editorial:**
Carol Kroskey ...............Senior Editor
Doug Kramrei ...........................Editor
Dan Malovany ...........................Editor
Jean Marie Sullivan ...............Managing Editor
Kathleen Raymer ...............Art Director
Susan Lutzow ...............Assistant Editor
Ray Lahvic ...............Editor Emeritus
Bonnie James ...............Info-Graphics Designer
Rob Mahoney ...............Production Editor

**Desc.:** Serves producers of bakery foods
including wholesale manufacturing
bakeries; grocery chains; multi- unit retail
bakeries; cookie, cracker, pretzel and
snack manufacturers; frozen food and
other food manufacturers producing
bakery foods; bakery cooperatives and
franchise headquarters; retail single-unit
manufacturing bakeries; supermarket in-
store bakeries, food service bakeries,
specialty retail shops, and their
headquarters. Also qualified are dealers,
jobbers, and distributors of bakery
supplies, equipment, and ingredients. A
limited number of copies are also
distributed to manufacturers of bakery
supplies, equipment, and ingredients;
schools, associations, clubs, and
consultants.
**Readers:** General management
production, engineering, technical,
research & development, sanitation,
packaging, fleet operations, sales and
marketing, purchasing, and other
personnel.

61625
**BAKING & SNACK SYSTEMS**
4800 Main St., Ste. 100
Kansas City, MO 64112
Telephone: (816) 756-1000
FAX: (816) 756-0494
Year Established: 1979
Pub. Frequency: 11/yr.
Page Size: standard
Subscrip. Rate: free
Materials: 01,24,25,27,28,29,30,32,33
Print Process: offset,web,web offset
Circulation: 9,390
Circulation Type: controlled
**Owner(s):**
Sosland Publishing Co.
4800 Main St., Ste. 100
Kansas City, MO 64112
Telephone: (816) 756-1000
FAX: (816) 756-0494
Ownership %: 100
**Management:**
Mark Sabo ...........................President
Mike Gude ...........................Publisher
Nora Wages ...............Advertising Manager
**Editorial:**
Laurie Gorton ...........................Editor
Paul Lattan ...........................Sales
Jody Rasch ...........................Sales
Marsha Heckle ...........................Sales
Brenda Barton ...........................Sales
**Desc.:** Written for process, production, and
plant management. Reports new
technologies, ingredients, packaging,
and methods.
**Readers:** Baking and snack food industry
managers.
**Deadline:** story-2 mos. prior to pub. date;
news-2 mos. prior; photo-2 mos. prior;
ads-2 mos. prior

64908
**BAKING BUYER**
4800 Main, Ste. 100
Kansas City, MO 64112
Telephone: (816) 756-1000
FAX: (816) 756-0494
Year Established: 1987
Pub. Frequency: m.
Page Size: tabloid
Subscrip. Rate: free
Materials: 28,29,32,33
Circulation: 30,000
Circulation Type: controlled
**Owner(s):**
Sosland Publishing Co.
4800 Main, Ste. 100
Kansas City, MO 64112
Telephone: (816) 756-1000
Ownership %: 100

**Materials Accepted/Included:** 01-Business news 02-By-line articles 03-Fashion news 04-Food news 05-Freelance copy 06-Letters to editor 07-Real estate news 08-Sports news 09-Travel news 10-Book rev. 11-Movie rev. 12-Music rev. 13-TV rev. 14-Theater rev. 15-Coming events 16-Obituaries 17-Question & answer 18-Social announcements 19-Artwork 20-Cartoons 21-Photos 22-TV listings 23-Audio rec. 24-Video rec. 25-Books 26-Films/film clips 27-Personnel news 28-Press releases 29-New product news/photos 30-Trade lit. 31-Contracts awarded 32-Display adv. 33-Classified adv.

**Management:**
Mark Sabo ...............................President
Mike Gude ..............................Publisher
**Editorial:**
Kerrie Bertz .........................Managing Editor
Carol Kaskie ......................Marketing Director
**Desc.:** New products magazine designed
to update bakers with new ideas for
their businesses.
**Readers:** Retail, instore, food service and
commercial bakers.

## FRESH BAKED
68846
14239 Park Center Dr.
Laurel, MD 20707-5261
Telephone: (301) 725-2149
FAX: (301) 725-2187
Year Established: 1948
Pub. Frequency: m.
Subscrip. Rate: membership
Circulation: 3,300
Circulation Type: paid
**Owner(s):**
Retail Bakers of America
14239 Park Center Dr.
Laurel, MD 20707-5261
Telephone: (301) 725-2149
Ownership %: 100

## MILLING & BAKING NEWS
21913
4800 Main St.
Kansas City, MO 64112
Telephone: (816) 756-1000
FAX: (816) 756-0494
Year Established: 1922
Pub. Frequency: w.
Page Size: standard
Subscrip. Rate: $78/yr.
Materials: 01,02,04,05,06,07,10,16,19,21,
25,27,28,31,32,33
Circulation: 5,000
Circulation Type: paid
**Owner(s):**
Sosland Companies, Inc.
DBA Sosland Publishing Co.
4800 Main St.
Kansas City, MO 64112
Telephone: (816) 756-1000
Ownership %: 100
**Management:**
Mark Sabo ...............................President
Morton I. Sosland ....................Publisher
Melanie Townsend ..............Business Manager
**Editorial:**
Morton I. Sosland ....................Editor in Chief
Gordon L. Davidson ...................Editor
Mike Gude .........................Associate Publisher
Gordon L. Davidson ...................Photo
Mike Gude ...............................Sales
Neil N. Sosland ...................Technical Editor
**Desc.:** Milling & Baking News is a weekly
journal for grain-based food company
managers. Analysis of markets
comprises substantial portion of format.
All news dealing with the industry is
staff-written. Features deal with
developments in milling, baking
and other grain- based food products.
Departments include: Editorials,
Business, Washington, People,
Merchandising, Industry activities,
Education and research, Operations,
Exports and trade issues, Ingredient
week: Bakery flour, Sweeteners, Bakery
shortening, Soy Flour, Milk, Eggs,
Cocoa, Semolina and Durum, Corn Meal,
Wheat Futures, Cas Wheat Premiums,
Millfeed, Feed Grains & Financial
Results, International.
**Readers:** Top executives of all U.S. grain,
milling, and baking companies. Large
international readership.

## MODERN BAKING
68847
2700 River Rd.
Des Plaines, IL 00008
Telephone: (708) 299-4430
FAX: (708) 296-1968
Year Established: 1987
Pub. Frequency: m.
Page Size: standard
Subscrip. Rate: $60/yr.
Materials: 01,06,27,28,29,30,32,33
Print Process: web offset
Circulation: 27,000
Circulation Type: controlled
**Owner(s):**
Donohue-Meehan Publishing Co.
2700 River Rd.
Des Plaines, IL 60018
Telephone: (708) 299-4430
FAX: (708) 296-1968
Ownership %: 100
**Bureau(s):**
Donohue-Meeham Publishing Co.
2 Greenwood Square, Ste. 410
3331 Street Rd.
Bensalem, PA 19020
Telephone: (215) 245-4555
FAX: (215) 245-4060
Contact: John Meeham, Executive Vice
President
**Management:**
William Donohue ...............................Publisher
**Editorial:**
Ed Lee .......................................................Editor
**Desc.:** Mission is to help bakery operations
run their businesses more profitably
through use of articles about successful
bakeries and their operations, as well as
business trends reports on the industry.
**Readers:** Owners and/or operators of
supermarket in-store bakeries,
independent retail bakeries, food service
bakeries, specialty wholesale bakeries,
and bakery supply distributors.
**Deadline:** story-2 mo. prior to pub. date;
news-2 mo.; photo-2 mo.; ads-20th of
mo., prior to pub. date

## Group 022-Banking

## ABA BANKING JOURNAL
21918
345 Hudson St.
New York, NY 10014
Telephone: (212) 620-7200
FAX: (212) 633-1165
Year Established: 1908
Pub. Frequency: m.
Page Size: standard
Subscrip. Rate: $3.25 newsstand; $25/yr.
Freelance Pay: $500-$1500/article
Circulation: 34,652
Circulation Type: paid
**Owner(s):**
American Bankers Association
1120 Connecticut Ave., N.W.
Washington, DC 20036
Telephone: (202) 663-5000
Ownership %: 100
**Management:**
David Bayard .................................Publisher
**Editorial:**
Steve Cocheo ......................Executive Editor
William W. Streeter .......................Editor
John McLaughlin .....................Art Director
Penny Lunt ........................Associate Editor
Harry Waddell ..................Editor Emeritus
Mark Arend ........................Technical Editor
**Desc.:** Business paper covering trends,
products, and developments in financial
services of the banking profession.
**Readers:** Bank officers, directors, and
employees.

## AMERICAN BANKER
21921
One State St. Plz., 31st Fl.
New York, NY 10004
Telephone: (212) 943-5710
FAX: (212) 943-2984
Year Established: 1836
Pub. Frequency: d.
Page Size: tabloid
Subscrip. Rate: $525/yr.
Freelance Pay: negotiable
Circulation: 24,000
Circulation Type: paid
**Owner(s):**
International Thomson Holdings, Inc.
1633 Broadway
New York, NY 10019
Telephone: (212) 956-6000
Ownership %: 100
**Bureau(s):**
Washington Bureau, American Banker
911 National Press Bldg.
Washington, DC 20045
Telephone: (202) 347-5529
Contact: Jim McTague, Bureau Chief

Midwest Bureau
53 W. Jackson Blvd.
Chicago, IL 60604
Telephone: (312) 427-4347
Contact: John Morris, Bureau Chief

West Coast Bureau
235 Montgomery St., Ste. 1204
San Francisco, CA 94104
Telephone: (415) 362-1472
Contact: Geoff Brovillette, Bureau Chief

West Coast Bureau
624 S. Grand Ave., Ste. 2900
Los Angeles, CA 90017
Telephone: (310) 489-6846
Contact: Robert Nile, Bureau Chief

West Coast, American Banker
510 W. Sixth St., Ste. 320
Los Angeles, CA 90014
Telephone: (310) 627-0953
Contact: Robert Luke, Bureau Chief

San Francisco, American Banker
433 California St., Ste. 505
San Francisco, CA 94104
Telephone: (415) 986-8705
Contact: Michael A. Robinson

Southwest, American Banker
8080 N. Central Expy., #1600
Dallas, TX 75206
Telephone: (214) 891-8878
Contact: David LaGesse, Bureau Chief

New England, American Banker
210 South St.
Boston, MA 02111
Telephone: (617) 542-6848
Contact: Michael Weinstein, Bureau Chief
**Management:**
David Branch ...............................President
**Editorial:**
Tom Ferris ..........................Managing Editor
Jeff Kutler ...............Assistant Managing Editor
Pamela Budz ..........................Art Director
Paul S. Nadler ..................Contributing Editor
Patricia Kitchen ...................Feature Editor
**Desc.:** Daily banking/financial services
newspaper to meet the working needs
of the financial services industry.
Includes coverage of marketing,
operations, and technology, regulatory
and legislative change, mortgage
market, thrift industry, human resources,
international banking, executive
changes.
**Readers:** Senior executives and decision
makers in banking and financial services
industry.

## ARKANSAS BANKER, THE
21922
The Carvill Bldg.
1220 W. Third St.
Little Rock, AR 72201-1904
Telephone: (501) 376-3741
Year Established: 1917
Pub. Frequency: m.
Page Size: standard
Subscrip. Rate: $2 newsstand; $15/yr.;
$11.88/yr. group rate
Materials: 01,02,09,32,33
Circulation: 2,400
Circulation Type: paid
**Owner(s):**
Arkansas Bankers Association
The Carvill Bldg.
1220 W. Third St.
Little Rock, AR 72201
Telephone: (501) 376-3741
Ownership %: 100
**Management:**
H.G. "Tres" Williams, ......Advertising Manager
III
**Editorial:**
H.C. Carvill .......................Editor in Chief
H.G. "Tres" Williams, III .........Managing Editor
**Desc.:** Contains educational opportunities
and various feature articles on finances,
conferences, seminars, conventions and
legislative developments.
**Readers:** Banks and banking personnel in
Arkansas and various related industries.
**Deadline:** story-10 days; news-10 days;
photo-10 days; ads-10 days

## BANKCARD CONSUMER NEWS
68675
560 Herndon Pkwy., Ste. 120
Herndon, VA 22070
Telephone: (703) 481-1110
FAX: (703) 481-6037
Year Established: 1986
Pub. Frequency: bi-m.
Subscrip. Rate: $24/yr.
Circulation: 100,000
Circulation Type: paid
**Owner(s):**
Bankcard Holders of America
560 Herndon Pkwy., Ste. 120
Herndon, VA 22070
Telephone: (703) 481-1110
Ownership %: 100
**Editorial:**
Ruth Susswein ...............................Editor

## BANK DIRECTOR
67024
P.O. Box 1603
Brentwood, TN 37024
Telephone: (615) 371-6886
Year Established: 1991
Pub. Frequency: q.
Page Size: oversize
Subscrip. Rate: $85/yr.
Freelance Pay: negotiable
Circulation: 40,000
Circulation Type: controlled & paid
**Owner(s):**
Magellan Financial Corporation
P.O. Box 1603
Brentwood, TN 37024
Telephone: (615) 371-6886
Ownership %: 100
**Management:**
William B. King ...................Chairman of Board
L. William Siedman ...................Publisher
Joan Susie ...................Advertising Manager
**Editorial:**
Deborah Scalley ...................Managing Editor
**Desc.:** Bank Director provides information
on critical banking issues to the
directors of the nation's 12,000 banks
and 2,000 S & Ls. The magazine
focuses on issues relevant to directors
in their board roles.

**Materials Accepted/Included:** 01-Business news 02-By-line articles 03-Fashion news 04-Food news 05-Freelance copy 06-Letters to editor 07-Real estate news 08-Sports news 09-Travel news 10-Book rev. 11-Movie rev. 12-Music rev. 13-TV rev. 14-Theater rev. 15-Coming events 16-Obituaries 17-Question & answer 18-Social announcements 19-Artwork 20-Cartoons 21-Photos 22-TV listings 23-Audio rec. 24-Video rec. 25-Books 26-Films/film clips 27-Personnel news 28-Press releases 29-New product news/photos 30-Trade lit. 31-Contracts awarded 32-Display adv. 33-Classified adv.

4-31

**Readers:** Affluent decisionmakers; most are CEOs of their own companies in addition to being bank directors.

### BANKERS' MAGAZINE, THE
21928

One Penn Plz., 42nd Fl.
New York, NY 10119-4098
Telephone: (212) 971-5001
Year Established: 1846
Pub. Frequency: bi-m.
Page Size: standard
Subscrip. Rate: $115/yr.
Materials: 02,10,25,28,32
Freelance Pay: negotiable
Circulation: 10,000
Circulation Type: paid
**Owner(s):**
Warren, Gorham & Lamont
One Penn Plz.
New York, NY 10119-4098
Telephone: (212) 971-5001
FAX: (212) 971-5215
Ownership %: 100
**Management:**
Blanca Duque ....................Advertising Manager
**Editorial:**
Paul L. Blocklyn ...............................Editor
Kenneth G. Oehlkers ............Managing Editor
**Desc.:** Specialized articles with emphasis on financial controls, strategic planning technology, bank reform, commercial and consumer lending, international human resources, and marketing.
**Readers:** Senior bank executives, and managers.

### BANKERS DIGEST
21927

6440 N. Central Expy., Ste. 215
Dallas, TX 75206
Telephone: (214) 373-4544
FAX: (214) 373-4545
Year Established: 1942
Pub. Frequency: m.
Page Size: standard
Subscrip. Rate: $22/yr.
Materials: 01,02,06,10,15,16,21,27,28,29,
30,32,33
Print Process: web
Circulation: 3,200
Circulation Type: paid
**Owner(s):**
Bonnie J. & R. Gilbert Blackman, Jr.
7515 Greenville Ave., Ste. 901
Dallas, TX 75231-3806
Telephone: (214) 373-4544
Ownership %: 100
**Management:**
Bonnie J. Blackman ..........................Publisher
R. Gilbert Blackman, Jr. .......Business Manager
**Editorial:**
Bonnie J. Blackman ..................................Editor
**Desc.:** Covers news and people in the southwest banking industry. Also covers public relations programs, bank activities. Features run from 750 to 1,000 words. Uses 3 to 10 part series on issues of specific interest to Southwest bankers and related parties. No more than 500 words per part.
**Readers:** Bankers within Southwestern area.
**Deadline:** ads-11 days

### BANK MANAGEMENT
21967

One Franklin St.
Chicago, IL 60606-3401
Telephone: (312) 553-4600
Year Established: 1924
Pub. Frequency: bi-m.
Page Size: standard
Subscrip. Rate: $59/yr. US; $89/yr. foreign
Freelance Pay: negotiable
Circulation: 40,000
Circulation Type: controlled

**Owner(s):**
Bank Administration Institute
One Franklin St.
Chicago, IL 60606
Telephone: (312) 553-4600
Ownership %: 100
**Management:**
Ronald G. Burke ...............................President
Ronald G. Burke ................................Publisher
Joan J. Ritter ....................Associate Publisher
**Editorial:**
Ronald G. Burke ........................Editor in Chief
Christine E. Bailey ...........Advertising Director
J. Christopher Svare .............Consulting Editor
Patricia McKay ...................Sales Administrator
**Desc.:** Covers management and technical subjects generally dealing with investment banking, accounting, automation, technology, audit, control, operations, data processing, payment systems. Other features deal with taxes, personnel, security, & trust. Departments include: Management Software, Systems and Equipment, Banking Applications.
**Readers:** Bankers, supervisory authorities, association members.

### BANK MARKETING MAGAZINE
21923

1120 Connecticut Ave., N.W.
Washington, DC 20036
Telephone: (202) 663-5070
FAX: (202) 828-4540
Year Established: 1916
Pub. Frequency: m.
Page Size: standard
Subscrip. Rate: $60/yr.
Circulation: 7,000
Circulation Type: paid
**Owner(s):**
Bank Marketing Association
120 Connecticut Ave., N.W.
Washington, DC 20036
Telephone: (202) 663-5070
Ownership %: 100
**Management:**
Cindy Wilson ....................................Publisher
Patricia Smith ...................Circulation Manager
**Editorial:**
Tanja Lian ...........................................Editor
Marcia Boggs ..........................Managing Editor
Bob Zeni ......................................Art Director
Hanna Sognnaes .................................Librarian
**Desc.:** Devoted to financial services marketing.
**Readers:** Executives in bank marketing and management, professionals specializing in retail banking, trust and personal banking, service quality, advertising, public relations, research, sales training and sales promotion.

### BANK NETWORK NEWS
53964

118 S. Clinton St.
Ste. 700
Chicago, IL 60606
Telephone: (312) 648-0261
Year Established: 1982
Pub. Frequency: s-m.
Page Size: standard
Subscrip. Rate: $395/yr.
Circulation: 1,200
Circulation Type: paid
**Owner(s):**
Faulkner & Gray, Inc.
11 Penn Plaza
New York, NY 10001
Telephone: (212) 967-7000
Ownership %: 100
**Management:**
Kurt Peters .......................................Publisher
**Editorial:**
Lauri Giesen ........................................Editor

**Desc.:** News and analysis of the retail electronic payments industry including credit cards, automated teller machines, debit cards, video banking and branch automation.
**Readers:** Retail financial services executives, computer vendors.

### BANK NEWS
21924

912 Baltimore Ave.
Kansas City, MO 64105
Telephone: (816) 421-7941
FAX: (816) 472-0397
Year Established: 1901
Pub. Frequency: m.
Page Size: standard
Subscrip. Rate: $54/yr.
Circulation: 8,000
Circulation Type: paid
**Owner(s):**
Bank News, Inc.
912 Baltimore Ave.
Kansas City, MO 64105
Telephone: (816) 421-7941
Ownership %: 100
**Management:**
William F. Baker ..............................Publisher
Kristi Wagner ...................Circulation Manager
**Editorial:**
R.W. Poquette .......................................Editor
Beth Wilson .....................Associate Publisher
**Desc.:** Factual material only, pertaining to almost any aspect of operation of commercial banks. Articles up to 1,500 words. Photo stories acceptable. News of personnel changes, financial news, management news, news of changes in physical facilities.
**Readers:** Chief executive officers of commercial banks in Kansas, Missouri, Nebraska, New Mexico, Colorado, Oklahoma, Texas, Wyoming, Illinois, Arkansas, Iowa, Minnesota, and Wisconsin.

### BANK SECURITIES JOURNAL
68673

40 W. 57th St., Ste. 802
New York, NY 10019
Telephone: (212) 765-5311
FAX: (212) 765-6123
Pub. Frequency: bi-m.
Subscrip. Rate: $36/yr.
Circulation: 10,253
Circulation Type: paid
**Owner(s):**
SDC Publishing
40 W. 57th St., Ste. 802
New York, NY 10019
Telephone: (212) 765-5311
Ownership %: 100
**Editorial:**
Pat Durner ...........................................Editor
**Desc.:** Covers the marketing of securities and other investment products and services to bank customers.

### BANK SECURITY REPORT
66691

One Penn Plz., 42nd Fl.
New York, NY 10119
Telephone: (212) 971-5582
FAX: (212) 971-5215
Year Established: 1973
Pub. Frequency: m.
Page Size: standard
Subscrip. Rate: $137.50/yr.; $187.50/yr. foreign
Materials: 01,10,23,24,25,26,27,28,29,30
Freelance Pay: $1.75/line
Circulation: 2,000
Circulation Type: paid

**Owner(s):**
Warren, Gorham, & Lamont, Inc.
31 St. James Ave.
Boston, MA 02116
Ownership %: 100
**Editorial:**
Ken Feinleib ..........................................Editor
**Desc.:** Informs security operations officers of the latest developments and newest strategies in both physical and data bank security.
**Readers:** Bank security personnel, risk management & information security officers.

### BANK SYSTEMS & TECHNOLOGY
21925

1515 Broadway
New York, NY 10036
Telephone: (212) 869-1300
FAX: (212) 302-6273
Year Established: 1964
Pub. Frequency: m.
Page Size: standard
Subscrip. Rate: free to bank technology mgrs.
Freelance Pay: negotiable
Circulation: 27,000
Circulation Type: controlled
**Owner(s):**
Gralla Publications
1515 Broadway
New York, NY 10036
Telephone: (212) 869-1300
Ownership %: 100
**Management:**
Robert N. Boucher, Jr. ......................President
**Editorial:**
Theodore Iacobuzio .................................Editor
**Desc.:** Provides information on automation, hardware, software, communication systems, word processing, management procedures, security systems, automated teller machines and electronic funds transfer.
**Readers:** Operations & systems officials in banks and thrifts.

### CARDS INTERNATIONAL
66181

2970 Clairmont Rd., Ste. 800
Atlanta, GA 30329
Telephone: (404) 636-6610
FAX: (404) 636-6422
Year Established: 1989
Pub. Frequency: bi-w.
Page Size: oversize
Subscrip. Rate: $995/23 issues
**Owner(s):**
Michael Lafferty
IDA Centre, Pearse St.
Dublin 2 Ireland
Ownership %: 100
**Bureau(s):**
Lafferty Publications (USA)
420 Lexington Ave., Ste. 1745
New York, NY 10170
Contact: Sterett Pope
**Editorial:**
Gerard Lysaght ..............................Senior Editor
**Desc.:** Provides a worldwide briefing on the plastic card industry.
**Readers:** Senior level executives at plastic card organizations (e.g. Mastercard and Visa), and retail banking and consumer group consulting firms.

### CREDIT CARD MERCHANT
68687

217 N. Seacrest Blvd.
Boynton Beach, FL 33425
Telephone: (407) 737-7500
FAX: (407) 737-5800
Mailing Address:
P.O. Box 400
Boynton Beach, FL 33425
Year Established: 1983

Pub. Frequency: m.
Subscrip. Rate: $159/yr. (foreign $199/yr.)
to non-members
Circulation: 2,000
Circulation Type: paid
**Owner(s):**
National Association of Credit Card
Merchants
217 N. Seacrest Blvd.
Boynton Beach, FL 33425
Telephone: (407) 737-7500
**Editorial:**
Larry Schwartz ...........................................Editor
Pearl Sax ....................................................Editor
**Desc.:** Updates readers on chargeback
and fraud control techniques, credit card
problems and solutions, new regulations
of Visa and Mastercard, and protection
against fraud.

66177

**ELECTRONIC PAYMENTS INTERNATIONAL**
2970 Clairmont Rd., Ste. 800
Atlanta, GA 30329
Telephone: (404) 636-6610
FAX: (404) 636-6422
Year Established: 1986
Pub. Frequency: m.
Page Size: oversize
Subscrip. Rate: $879/10 issues
Print Process: desktop
Wire service(s): BW, DJ
**Owner(s):**
Lafferty Publications
The Tower IDA Ctr Pearse St
Dublin 2 Ireland
Ownership %: 100
**Editorial:**
Michael Lafferty ...........................Editor in Chief
Richard Martin ...............................Senior Editor
**Desc.:** To provide expert intelligence on
developments in electronic payments
and financial technology around the
world.
**Readers:** Senior level executives at banks,
card associations, ATM networks, POS
networks, wire transfer networks, and
vendors of financial technology
products.

21952

**FLORIDA BANKING**
214 S. Bronough St.
Tallahassee, FL 32301-1705
Telephone: (904) 224-2265
FAX: (904) 224-2423
Mailing Address:
P.O. Box 1360
Tallahassee, FL 32302-1360
Year Established: 1974
Pub. Frequency: bi-m.
Page Size: standard
Materials: 01,02,05,16,23,25,27,28,29,30,
32,33, PSA
Circulation: 6,700
Circulation Type: controlled
**Owner(s):**
Florida Bankers Association
214 S. Bronough Street
Tallahassee, FL 32301-1705
Telephone: (904) 224-2265
FAX: (904) 224-2423
Ownership %: 100
**Editorial:**
Wendy Barager ..........................................Editor
John Milstead ...........................Editorial Advisor
**Desc.:** Subject matter is banking of
interest to Florida bankers and
personnel in the banking field regionally
and nationally.

**Readers:** Bank officers and employees,
and other financial-oriented business
persons, general business persons.
**Deadline:** story-1st. of mo. prior to pub.
date; news-1st. of mo.; photo-1st. of
mo.; ads-1st. of mo.

21957

**ILLINOIS BANKER**
111 N. Canal, Ste. 1111
Chicago, IL 60606
Telephone: (312) 876-9900
Year Established: 1916
Pub. Frequency: m.
Page Size: standard
Subscrip. Rate: $5 newsstand; $60/yr.
Materials: 02,06,21,32
Freelance Pay: $50-$100/article
Circulation: 2,500
Circulation Type: paid
**Owner(s):**
Illinois Bankers Association
111 N. Canal, Ste. 1111
Chicago, IL 60606
Telephone: (312) 876-9900
Ownership %: 100
**Management:**
William J. Hocter ...............................Publisher
**Editorial:**
Meg Bullock ..............................................Director
Meg Bullock ...........................Marketing Director
Anetta Gauthier ................Production Assistant
Cindy Altman ........................Production Director
**Desc.:** All editorial content pertains to
banks, bankers, banking and finance.
By-lines are given to feature story
writers. No publicity material
used except when submitted by banks
or their agencies, or by current
advertisers. Materials of special interest
to financial community are
considered for publication. Feature
articles run approximately 1,500-2,000
words, covering all phases of banking
and finance.
**Readers:** Bank presidents, vice presidents,
directors.
**Deadline:** story-6 wks. prior to pub. date;
news-6 wks. prior to pub. date; photo-6
wks. prior to pub. date; ads-1st of mo.
prior to pub. date

21958

**INDEPENDENT BANKER, THE**
1168 S. Main St.
Sauk Centre, MN 56378
Telephone: (612) 352-6546
Year Established: 1950
Pub. Frequency: m.
Page Size: standard
Subscrip. Rate: $25/yr.
Materials: 01,02,05
Freelance Pay: $250/1,500 wds.
Print Process: web offset
Circulation: 9,374
Circulation Type: free & paid
**Owner(s):**
The Independent Bankers Association of
America
One Thomas Cir., N.W., Ste. 95
Washington, DC 20005
Telephone: (202) 659-8111
Ownership %: 100
**Management:**
Kenneth A. Guenther .........................Publisher
Faith Moeckel ...................Advertising Manager
**Editorial:**
David Bordewyk ......................................Editor
Elmer Ramos ............................Associate Editor
**Desc.:** Focuses on the nation's
independent banks, mostly the small- to
medium-size commercial banks. Articles
tailored to management of these banks -
success stories, how-to, strategies, etc.
**Readers:** Bank officials and directors.

21962

**INVESTMENT DEALERS' DIGEST**
2 World Trade Ctr., 18th Flr.
New York, NY 10048
Telephone: (212) 227-1200
FAX: (212) 432-1039
Year Established: 1935
Pub. Frequency: w.
Page Size: standard
Subscrip. Rate: $395/yr.
**Owner(s):**
I.D.D. Enterprises, L.P.
2 World Trade Ctr., 18th Flr.
New York, NY 10048
Telephone: (212) 227-1200
**Management:**
Rick Norris ..........................................Publisher
**Editorial:**
Phil Maher ...............................Editor in Chief
Jane Burch ................................................Editor
Janice Fellegara ................Circulation Director
Maxine Marse .....................Production Director
**Desc.:** A professional weekly news
magazine for the investment banking
industry. Each week it carries a feature
story on some industry or some sales
subject relating to securities. By-lines
are used but articles must be down to
earth and sufficiently sophisticated to
appeal to a sophisticated audience. No
market tips or recommendations of
securities. Sections of the publication
are Firms & Exchanges, Street Names,
Corporate Financing Week, Municipal
Financing Week, Mergers &
Acquisrtions, Asset-Backed Finance.
**Readers:** 65 percent professional
investment bankeranks/insurance
companies, corporations.

66014

**JOURNAL OF RETAIL BANKING**
One State St. Plaza, 31st Fl.
New York, NY 10004
Telephone: (212) 943-5908
Year Established: 1979
Pub. Frequency: q.
Subscrip. Rate: $97/yr.
Circulation: 2,800
Circulation Type: paid
**Owner(s):**
American Banker-Bond Buyer
One State St. Plaza
New York, NY 10004
Telephone: (212) 943-5908
Ownership %: 100
**Editorial:**
Leonard Berry .........................................Editor

21965

**KANSAS BANKER, THE**
800 S.W. Jackson St., Ste. 1500
Topeka, KS 66612
Telephone: (913) 232-3444
FAX: (713) 232-3484
Year Established: 1911
Pub. Frequency: m.
Page Size: standard
Subscrip. Rate: $10/yr.
Circulation: 1,100
Circulation Type: paid
**Owner(s):**
Kansas Bankers Association
800 S.W. Jackson St., Ste. 150
Topeka, KS 66612
Telephone: (913) 232-3444
Ownership %: 100
**Management:**
Linda Shinn ......................Advertising Manager
**Editorial:**
Kara Lynch ................................................Editor
**Desc.:** Stories of banks and bankers
activities in Kansas,
**Readers:** Kansas bankers and related
service institutions, dealers and
correspondent banks, etc.

21966

**LOUISIANA BANKER, THE**
666 North St.
Baton Rouge, LA 70802
Telephone: (504) 387-3282
FAX: (504) 343-3159
Mailing Address:
P.O. Box 2871
Baton Rouge, LA 70821
Year Established: 1934
Pub. Frequency: bi-w.
Page Size: standard
Subscrip. Rate: $15/yr.
Circulation: 2,500
Circulation Type: paid
**Owner(s):**
Louisiana Bankers Association
P.O. Box 2871
Baton Rouge, LA 70821
Telephone: (504) 387-3282
Ownership %: 100
**Editorial:**
Heidi Picard ...........................................Editor
Charles Worsham ..............................Advertising
**Desc.:** Pertinent banking information.
**Readers:** Banking personnel.

21971

**MICHIGAN BANKER**
P.O. Box 12236
Lansing, MI 48901
Telephone: (517) 332-7800
FAX: (517) 332-7806
Year Established: 1883
Pub. Frequency: m.
Page Size: standard
Subscrip. Rate: $82.50/yr.
Materials: 01,06,15,28,29,30,32,33
Freelance Pay: varies
Print Process: web offset
Circulation: 600
Circulation Type: paid
**Owner(s):**
Public Relations Enterprises, Inc.
P.O. Box 12236
Lansing, MI 48901
Telephone: (517) 332-7800
Ownership %: 100
**Management:**
J. H. O'Neil ...........................................Publisher
**Editorial:**
J. H. O'Neil ..............................................Editor
Gregory S. O'neil .............................Advertising
**Desc.:** Digest of banking news,
emphasizing vital role of banks, and
their relationship to business enterprise,
in the sustained growth of the state of
Michigan.
**Readers:** Bankers and bank suppliers

61327

**MICROBANKER**
P.O. Box 708
Lake George, NY 12845
Telephone: (518) 745-7071
Year Established: 1982
Pub. Frequency: m.
Page Size: standard
Subscrip. Rate: $246/yr.
**Owner(s):**
Nancy Whelan Davis
P.O. Box 708
Lake George, NY 12845
Telephone: (518) 668-3706
Ownership %: 100
**Management:**
Nancy Whelan Davis ........................Publisher
**Editorial:**
Lisa Valentine ..........................................Editor
Linda Reynolds ...........................Managing Editor
**Desc.:** News and case studies on the use
of personal computers and local area
networks in banking, with concentration
on banking application software.

**Materials Accepted/Included:** 01-Business news 02-By-line articles 03-Fashion news 04-Food news 05-Freelance copy 06-Letters to editor 07-Real estate news 08-Sports news 09-Travel news
10-Book rev. 11-Movie rev. 12-Music rev. 13-TV rev. 14-Theater rev. 15-Coming events 16-Obituaries 17-Question & answer 18-Social announcements 19-Artwork 20-Cartoons 21-Photos 22-TV listings
23-Audio rec. 24-Video rec. 25-Books 26-Films/film clips 27-Personnel news 28-Press releases 29-New product news/photos 30-Trade lit. 31-Contracts awarded 32-Display adv. 33-Classified adv.

4-33

## MISSISSIPPI BANKER
21975

640 N. State St.
Jackson, MS 39202
Telephone: (601) 948-6366
FAX: (601) 355-6466
Mailing Address:
 P.O. Box 37
 Jackson, MS 39205
Year Established: 1914
Pub. Frequency: m.
Page Size: standard
Subscrip. Rate: $15/yr.
Circulation: 1,100
Circulation Type: paid
**Owner(s):**
Mississippi Banker's Association
640 N. State St.
Jackson, MS 39202
Telephone: (601) 948-6366
Ownership %: 100
**Management:**
McKinley W. Deaver ...........................Publisher
**Editorial:**
McKinley W. Deaver ...............................Editor
**Desc.:** Material that will be of interest to banks in state.
**Readers:** Members of Bankers Assn.and businesses serving the banking industry.

## MORTGAGE BANKING
21976

1125 15th St., N.W.
Washington, DC 20005
Telephone: (202) 861-6560
FAX: (202) 861-0736
Year Established: 1939
Pub. Frequency: m.
Page Size: 4 color photos/art
Subscrip. Rate: $42/yr.
Circulation: 12,000
Circulation Type: controlled
**Owner(s):**
Mortgage Bankers Association of America
1125 15th St., N.W.
Washington, DC 20005
Telephone: (202) 861-6500
Ownership %: 100
**Management:**
Mildred Jones ...................Assistant Advertising Manager
**Editorial:**
Janet Hewitt ................................Editor
LaDonna Hale Curzon .............Assistant Editor
**Desc.:** The official publication of the Mortgage Bankers Association of America, the national association of mortgage lenders and investors. Editorially directed to executives of mortgage banking firms, mutual savings banks, pension funds and other institutional investors. Editorial content is primarily coverage of areas encompassing mortgage investment, as well as current news on government regulations and Congressional activity.
**Readers:** Mortgage personnel in commercial and mutual savings banks, title companies, pension and trusteed funds, 1,300 mortgage banking firms.

## OHIO BANKER
21982

37 W. Broad St., Ste. 1001
Columbus, OH 43215-0002
Telephone: (614) 221-5121
FAX: (614) 221-3421
Year Established: 1908
Pub. Frequency: m.
Page Size: standard
Subscrip. Rate: $25/yr. non-members & individual subscriptions
Materials: 15,27,28
Freelance Pay: negotiable
Circulation: 3,960
Circulation Type: paid
**Owner(s):**
Ohio Bankers Association
37 W. Broad St., Ste. 1001
Columbus, OH 43215
Telephone: (614) 221-5121
FAX: (614) 221-3421
Ownership %: 100
**Editorial:**
Melea Wachtman ...................Managing Editor
**Desc.:** Articles covering banking industry changes and trends, as well as official association business are presented with the intent of enhancing the efficiency and effectiveness of the banking profession.
**Readers:** 88 percent bank employees, officers; 8 percent bank product and service providers; 2 percent legislators and government authorities; 2 percent libraries.
**Deadline:** story-15th mo. prior; news-15th mo. prior

## OKLAHOMA BANKER
21983

643 N.E. 41st
Oklahoma City, OK 73105
Telephone: (405) 424-5252
Mailing Address:
 P.O. Box 18246
 Oklahoma City, OK 73154
Year Established: 1909
Pub. Frequency: bi-w.
Page Size: tabloid
Subscrip. Rate: $30/yr.
Circulation: 3,000
Circulation Type: paid
**Owner(s):**
Oklahoma Bankers Association
P.O. Box 18246
Oklahoma City, OK 73154
Telephone: (405) 424-5252
Ownership %: 100
**Editorial:**
D.J. Morrow ....................................Editor
Beth Payne ...............................Advertising
Darrell McClendon ...............Assistant Editor
**Desc.:** News of banking activity, people, new literature, conferences, appointments, trends.
**Readers:** Bank officials and personnel.

## SAVINGS & COMMUNITY BANKERS OF AMERICA
21988

900 19th St., N.W., Ste. 400
Washington, DC 20006
Telephone: (202) 857-3100
Year Established: 1880
Pub. Frequency: m.
Page Size: standard
Subscrip. Rate: $4/issue members; $42/yr. members US; $53/yr. non-members US; $58/yr. Canada & Mexico; $65/yr. elsewhere
Materials: 01,02,05,07,19,20,21,28,29,30,32
Freelance Pay: negotiable
Print Process: offset
Circulation: 13,000
Circulation Type: controlled
**Owner(s):**
U.S. League Of Savings Institutions
900 19th St., N.W., Ste. 400
Washington, DC 20006
Telephone: (202) 857-3100
Ownership %: 100
**Bureau(s):**
U.S. League of Savings Institutions
111 E. Wacker Dr.
Chicago, IL 60601
Telephone: (312) 644-3100
Contact: Robert Bradner, Editor
**Management:**
William T. Marshall ........................Publisher
Carol Najewski .................Advertising Manager
Terry Caudill .....................Circulation Manager

## SECONDARY MARKETING EXECUTIVE
68683

70 Edwin Ave.
Waterbury, CT 06722-2330
Telephone: (203) 755-0158
FAX: (203) 755-3480
Mailing Address:
 P.O. Box 2230
 Waterbury, CT 06722
Year Established: 1986
Pub. Frequency: m.
Page Size: tabloid
Subscrip. Rate: $48/yr.
Materials: 01,02,05,06,19,21,28,29,30,32,33
Circulation: 21,000
Circulation Type: controlled & paid
**Owner(s):**
LDJ Corp.
70 Edwin Ave., Box 2330
Waterbury, CT 06722-2330
Telephone: (203) 755-0158
FAX: (203) 755-3480
Ownership %: 100
**Editorial:**
John Florian .......................Editorial Director
**Desc.:** Provides how-to information and trends analysis for buyers and sellers of mortgage loans and servicing rights on the secondary market.
**Readers:** Secondary marketers and loan production executives at financial institutions nationwide.
**Deadline:** story-1st of the mo.; news-1st of the mo.; photo-1st of the mo.; ads-1st of the mo.

## TARHEEL BANKER, THE
21994

3709 National Dr.
Raleigh, NC 27612
Telephone: (919) 782-6960
Mailing Address:
 P.O. Box 30609
 Raleigh, NC 27622
Year Established: 1922
Pub. Frequency: m.
Page Size: standard
Subscrip. Rate: $12/yr. members; $18/yr. non-members
Circulation: 3,000
Circulation Type: paid
**Owner(s):**
North Carolina Bankers Association
3709 National Dr.
Raleigh, NC 27622
Telephone: (919) 782-6960
Ownership %: 100
**Management:**
A.D. Fuqua, Jr. ...............................Publisher
William E. Stroupe ...........Advertising Manager
**Editorial:**
William E. Stroupe ...............................Editor
Beth O'Kelley ......................Circulation Editor
**Desc.:** Detailed coverage of personnel and activities of N.C. banks, and the N.C. Bankers Association.

**Editorial:**
David Stahl ...........................Senior Editor
Brian Nixon ...................................Editor
Tony Frye ...............................Art Director
Amanda Tirpak .....................Associate Editor
Dana Terwilliger .................Editorial Assistant
Eleanor Hagerup ...............Production Editor
**Desc.:** Written for the key decision makers in the savings institution business - executives, managers and specialists. Aim to inform and educate its readers to meet new business challenges and effectively serve the financial needs of the American public.
**Readers:** Savings institutions management and supervisory personnel in all functional areas of business.

**Readers:** Bankers, bank directors and banking employees.

## TENNESSEE BANKER
21995

201 Venture Cir.
Nashville, TN 37228-1603
Telephone: (615) 244-4871
FAX: (615) 244-0995
Year Established: 1913
Pub. Frequency: m.
Page Size: standard
Subscrip. Rate: $20/yr. members; $30/yr. non-members
Materials: 01,02,15,21,28,29,30,32
Print Process: offset
Circulation: 2,500
Circulation Type: paid
**Owner(s):**
Tennessee Bankers Association
201 Venture Cir.
Nashville, TN 37228
Telephone: (615) 244-4871
FAX: (615) 244-0995
Ownership %: 100
**Management:**
Dianne W. Martin ..............Advertising Manager
**Editorial:**
Bradley L. Barrett ...............................Editor
Dianne W. Martin ...............Managing Editor
**Readers:** Banks, bank directors, attorneys, accountants, securities and investment firms, mortgage and insurance companies.
**Deadline:** ads-1st of mo. prior to pub. date

## TEXAS BANKING
69362

203 W. Tenth St.
Austin, TX 78701
Telephone: (512) 472-8388
FAX: (512) 473-2560
Year Established: 1911
Pub. Frequency: m.
Subscrip. Rate: $25/yr. members; $35/yr. non-members
Circulation: 5,000
**Owner(s):**
Texas Bankers Association
203 W. Tenth St.
Austin, TX 78701
Telephone: (512) 472-8388
Ownership %: 100
**Editorial:**
P. Garrett .........................................Editor

## UNITED STATES BANKER
21999

11 Penn Plz., 17th Fl.
New York, NY 10001
Telephone: (212) 967-7000
FAX: (212) 695-8172
Year Established: 1891
Pub. Frequency: m.
Page Size: standard
Subscrip. Rate: $59/yr.
Materials: 01,06,07,25,28,30,32,33
Freelance Pay: $300-$400/printed page
Circulation: 39,000
Circulation Type: controlled
**Owner(s):**
Faulkner & Gray, Inc.
11 Penn Plz., 17th Fl.
New York, NY 10001
Telephone: (212) 967-7000
Ownership %: 100
**Management:**
John F. Love ................................President
Andrew L. Goodenough .....................Publisher
**Editorial:**
John W. Milligan ...............................Editor
Jeffrey Marshall ...................Managing Editor
Rosemarie Galioto ......................Art Director
**Desc.:** Features current bank methods, problems & opportunities, interviews with top executives, and how-to articles for bankers.

---

**Materials Accepted/Included:** 01-Business news 02-By-line articles 03-Fashion news 04-Food news 05-Freelance copy 06-Letters to editor 07-Real estate news 08-Sports news 09-Travel news 10-Book rev. 11-Movie rev. 12-Music rev. 13-TV rev. 14-Theater rev. 15-Coming events 16-Obituaries 17-Question & answer 18-Social announcements 19-Artwork 20-Cartoons 21-Photos 22-TV listings 23-Audio rec. 24-Video rec. 25-Books 26-Films/film clips 27-Personnel news 28-Press releases 29-New product news/photos 30-Trade lit. 31-Contracts awarded 32-Display adv. 33-Classified adv.

**Readers:** Officers of commercial banks, savings banks, savings and loan associations, credit unions, investment and finance firms.
**Deadline:** story-5 wks.; news-5 wks.; photo-4 wks.; ads-5 wks.

## Group 024-Barbers, Beauty Shops & Cosmetics

**AMERICAN SALON**                              22008
270 Madison Ave.
New Yorknd, NY 10016-0695
Telephone: (212) 951-6600
FAX: (212) 481-6562
Year Established: 1890
Pub. Frequency: m.
Page Size: standard
Subscrip. Rate: $20/yr.
Freelance Pay: negotiable
Circulation: 130,032
Circulation Type: controlled
**Owner(s):**
Advanstar Communications, Inc.
7500 Old Oak Blvd.
Cleveland, OH 44130
Telephone: (216) 826-2839
Ownership %: 100
**Bureau(s):**
American Salon
1544 Wilshire Blvd.
Los Angeles, CA 90017
Telephone: (310) 484-2354
Contact: Maryann Doughtery, Editor
**Management:**
Dick Moller ...............................President
Marianne Dougherty ...............Publisher
**Editorial:**
Kathy McFarland ...............Editor in Chief
**Desc.:** Official publication of the National Hairdressers and Cosmetology Association, with focus on management and technical information emphasizing the full service salon concept.
**Readers:** Salon owners and managers, profession salon industry executives, nail technicians, estheticians.

**BEAUTY EDUCATION JOURNAL**               22018
2 Computer Dr., W.
Albany, NY 12205-1607
Telephone: (800) 836-5239
FAX: (518) 464-0316
Year Established: 1948
Pub. Frequency: m.
Page Size: standard
Subscrip. Rate: free to instructors; $19/yr. US; $27/yr. Canada; $36.50/yr. elsewhere
Freelance Pay: $150/article
Circulation: 4,000
Circulation Type: paid
**Owner(s):**
Milady Publishing Co.
2 Computer Dr., W.
Albany, NY 12205-1607
Telephone: (800) 223-2960
Ownership %: 100
**Management:**
Catherine Frangie ...................Publisher
Jerry Brooks ...........Advertising Manager
Alan Beberwyck ........Production Manager
**Editorial:**
Susan L. Pena ...........................Editor
Alfonso Pena-Ramos ........Associate Editor
Elizabeth Dwyer .............Layout Coordinator
Barb Leto ...................Marketing Manager
Barb Leto ...............................Sales
**Desc.:** Detailed, comprehensive information and techniques for the professional or soon-to-be professional topics include: hairstyling, skin care, nail care, perming, salon management, retailing and more.

**Readers:** A monthly journal serving beauty educators, trainers, and professionals in the cosmetology industry.

**BEAUTY FASHION**                              22725
530 Fifth Ave., 4th Fl.
New York, NY 10036-5101
Telephone: (212) 840-8800
FAX: (212) 840-7246
Year Established: 1916
Pub. Frequency: m.
Page Size: standard
Subscrip. Rate: $25/yr.
Circulation: 18,396
Circulation Type: paid
**Owner(s):**
Beauty Fashion, Inc.
530 Fifth Ave., 4th Fl.
New York, NY 10036-5101
Telephone: (212) 840-8800
Ownership %: 100
**Management:**
John G. Ledes .....................Publisher
**Editorial:**
John G. Ledes ..........................Editor
**Desc.:** Covers the business and lightside of the industry. Features discuss outlook trends, regulations, etc. Departments include: World of Cosmetics, Regional News, Product Preview, Trade Talk, Personal File, Monthly School Program, Counter Points.
**Readers:** Retail cosmetic and perfume trade.

**MODERN SALON MAGAZINE**                    22016
400 Knightsbridge Pkwy.
Lincolnshire, IL 60069
Telephone: (708) 634-2600
FAX: (708) 634-4379
Mailing Address:
    P.O. Box 1400
    Lincolnshire, IL 60069
Year Established: 1924
Pub. Frequency: m.
Page Size: standard
Subscrip. Rate: $20/yr.; $32/2 yrs.
Freelance Pay: negotiable
Circulation: 133,000
Circulation Type: paid
**Owner(s):**
Vance Publishing Corp.
P.O. Box 1400
Lincolnshire, IL 60069
Telephone: (708) 634-2600
Ownership %: 100
**Bureau(s):**
Modern Salon Magazine
122 E. 42nd St.
New York, NY 10168
Telephone: (212) 682-7777
Contact: Tim Murphy, Rick Levine, Sales

Modern Salon Magazine
6800 Owenmouth Ave., Ste. 430
Canoga Park, CA 91303-2091
Contact: Katherine Stadler, Sales
**Management:**
Robert Bellew .......................Publisher
Sherry Fisher .............Operations Manager
**Editorial:**
Mary Atherton .................Editor in Chief
Deborah Ogilvie ............Managing Editor
Howard Krause ............Circulation Director
**Desc.:** Staff-written articles deal with new hairstyles, illustrate styling step-by-step with photos, shop management, etc. Departments include: Industry, Local News, Nationwide News. Bulk of material is staff-produced. Buy very little.
**Readers:** Salon owners, stylists, managers.

**NAILPRO**                                    66289
7628 Densmore Ave.
Van Nuys, CA 91406
Telephone: (818) 782-7328
Year Established: 1990
Pub. Frequency: m.
Page Size: standard
Subscrip. Rate: $31/yr.
Freelance Pay: varies
Circulation: 33,500
Circulation Type: controlled
**Owner(s):**
Creative Age Publications, Inc
7628 Densmore Ave.
Van Nuys, CA 91406
Telephone: (818) 782-7328
**Management:**
Barbara Feiner ...............Associate Publsiher
Barbara Shepherd ...........Circulation Manager
**Editorial:**
Barbara Feiner .................Executive Editor
**Readers:** Nail technicians, salon owners and managers.

**NAILS**                                      66290
2512 Artesia Blvd.
Redondo Beach, CA 90278
Telephone: (310) 376-8788
Year Established: 1983
Pub. Frequency: m.
Page Size: standard
Subscrip. Rate: $38/yr.
Circulation: 53,000
Circulation Type: paid
**Owner(s):**
Bobit Publishing Co.
2512 Artesia Blvd.
Redondo Beach, CA 90278
Telephone: (310) 376-8788
Ownership %: 100
**Management:**
Jay Garbutt ............................Publisher
**Editorial:**
Cyndy Drummey ........................Editor
**Desc.:** Provides business advice and information on new products and application techniques for professional manicurists, nail salon owners, and beauty supply distributors.
**Readers:** Professional manicurists, nail salon owners, and beauty supply distributors.

**NATIONAL BEAUTY NEWS**                       22017
1346 E. Haskell
Tulsa, OK 74106
Telephone: (918) 583-5708
FAX: (918) 582-0099
Year Established: 1976
Pub. Frequency: m.
Page Size: tabloid
Subscrip. Rate: free; $1/issue; $12/Yr.
Freelance Pay: varies
Circulation: 35,500
Circulation Type: controlled & free
**Owner(s):**
Douglas Von Allmen
346 E. Haskell
Tulsa, OK 74106
Telephone: (918) 583-5708
Ownership %: 100
**Management:**
Douglas Von Allmen .....................Owner
**Editorial:**
John Alexander .................Executive Editor
**Desc.:** For the professional beauty industry. Gives news of shows, seminars, product information, interesting guest columns, reports on legislative action by state boards, news of national and state cosmetology associations and special feature articles on all phases of what is happening in the professional beauty industry.

**Readers:** Salon owners, cosmetologists, barber stylers, nail technicians, student.

## Group 026-Beverages

**ALL ABOUT BEER MAGAZINE**                    61304
4764 Galicia Way
Oceanside, CA 92056
Telephone: (619) 724-4447
Year Established: 1979
Pub. Frequency: 6/yr.
Page Size: standard
Subscrip. Rate: $15-$20/yr.
Circulation: 42,000
Circulation Type: paid
**Owner(s):**
Bosak Publishing, Inc.
4764 Galicia Way
Oceanside, CA 92056
Telephone: (619) 724-4447
Ownership %: 100
**Editorial:**
Michael Bosak ..........................Editor
Sandra L. Powers .......................Editor
**Readers:** Up-scale in education & earnings, interested in beer.

**AMERICAN BREWER MAGAZINE**                   22112
P.O. Box 510
Hayward, CA 94543-0510
Telephone: (510) 538-9500
FAX: (510) 538-7644
Year Established: 1986
Pub. Frequency: q.
Page Size: standard
Subscrip. Rate: $4 newsstand; $18/yr.; $30/2 yrs.
Materials: 01
Freelance Pay: $150/1,500 wds.
Print Process: offset
Circulation: 10,000
Circulation Type: paid
**Owner(s):**
American Brewer, Inc.
P.O. Box 510
Hayward, CA 94543
Telephone: (510) 538-9500
Ownership %: 100
**Management:**
Bill Owens ..............................Publisher
**Desc.:** A journal servicing the micro brewing industry. The business of beer.
**Readers:** Individuals interested in starting a brew pub or micro brewery.

**BARTENDER**                                  68691
P.O. Box 158
Liberty Corner, NJ 07938
Telephone: (908) 766-6006
FAX: (908) 766-6607
Year Established: 1979
Pub. Frequency: 4/yr.
Subscrip. Rate: $25/yr.
Materials: 04,05,06,10,19,20,21,29,30
Print Process: web
Circulation: 142,594
Circulation Type: controlled & paid
**Owner(s):**
Foley Publishing Corp.
P.O. Box 158
Liberty Corner, NJ 07938
Telephone: (908) 766-6006
FAX: (908) 766-6607
Ownership %: 100
**Editorial:**
Jaclyn W. Foley .........................Editor
**Desc.:** For the full service on-premise industry.

**Materials Accepted/Included:** 01-Business news 02-By-line articles 03-Fashion news 04-Food news 05-Freelance copy 06-Letters to editor 07-Real estate news 08-Sports news 09-Travel news 10-Book rev. 11-Movie rev. 12-Music rev. 13-TV rev. 14-Theater rev. 15-Coming events 16-Obituaries 17-Question & answer 18-Social announcements 19-Artwork 20-Cartoons 21-Photos 22-TV listings 23-Audio rec. 24-Video rec. 25-Books 26-Films/film clips 27-Personnel news 28-Press releases 29-New product news/photos 30-Trade lit. 31-Contracts awarded 32-Display adv. 33-Classified adv.

4-35

## BEER WHOLESALER
22115

11460 W. 44th Ave., Ste. 4
Wheat Ridge, CO 80033
Telephone: (303) 425-4668
FAX: (303) 425-4701
Year Established: 1968
Pub. Frequency: q.
Page Size: Standard
Subscrip. Rate: $50/Yr.
Freelance Pay: $50-$200
Circulation: 4,400
Circulation Type: controlled
**Owner(s):**
Beverage Management Associates, Inc.
11460 W. 44th Ave., Ste. 4
Wheat Ridge, CO 90033
Ownership %: 100
**Management:**
Vince Ventimiglia .............................Publisher
John Granato ...................Advertising Manager
**Desc.:** "How- to" articles to show nation's
   top prime wholesalers how to do
   something better, faster, more
   economically; how to bolster profits,
   merchandising ideas, features on
   imported beers, wines, trucks and
   warehouse operation.
**Readers:** Beer Wholesalers, Brewery
   Executives and Wine Wholesalers,
   National Retail Management, Imported
   Beer Company Executives

## BEVERAGE & FOOD DYNAMICS
66672

100 Ave. of the Americas
New York, NY 10013-1678
Telephone: (212) 274-7000
FAX: (212) 431-0500
Year Established: 1934
Pub. Frequency: 9/yr.
Page Size: standard
Subscrip. Rate: $35/yr.
Circulation: 50,000
Circulation Type: paid
**Owner(s):**
Jobson Publishing Corp.
100 Ave. of the Americas
New York, NY 10013-1678
Telephone: (212) 274-7000
Ownership %: 100
**Management:**
Seymour L. Leikind .............................Publisher
**Editorial:**
Bob Keane ......................................................Editor

## BEVERAGE ALCOHOL BUSINESS SCENE
69366

15500 Wayzata Blvd., No. 744
Wayzata, MN 55391-1416
Telephone: (612) 449-9446
FAX: (612) 449-9447
Year Established: 1963
Pub. Frequency: 8/yr.
Subscrip. Rate: $30/yr.
Circulation: 26,000
Circulation Type: paid
**Owner(s):**
Diamond Publications
15500 Wayzata Blvd., No. 744
Wayzata, MN 55391-1416
Telephone: (612) 449-9446
Ownership %: 100
**Editorial:**
Gary Diamond ...............................................Editor
**Desc.:** For alcohol beverage licensees
   buying at least $1,000,000 worth of
   liquor, wine or beer at wholesale prices.

## BEVERAGE BULLETIN
22116

8383 Wilshire Blvd., Ste. 345
Beverly Hills, CA 90211
Telephone: (310) 653-4445
Year Established: 1936
Pub. Frequency: m.

Page Size: tabloid
Subscrip. Rate: $24/yr.
Circulation: 16,500
Circulation Type: controlled
**Owner(s):**
California Beverage Publications, Inc.
8383 Wilshire Blvd., Ste. 345
Beverly Hills, CA 90211
Telephone: (310) 653-4445
Ownership %: 100
**Management:**
Max J. Kerstein .............................Publisher
Virginia Greene ................Assistant Advertising
                                                            Manager
**Editorial:**
Michael Lynn .......................Executive Editor
Max J. Kerstein ...............................Editor
Jan Marks ...............................Advertising
Michael Lynn ...................Book Review Editor
Michael Lynn ...............................News Editor
Michael Lynn ...............................Photo
**Desc.:** Covers news, merchandising and
   selling features and people involved in
   licensed beverage industry in Southern
   California.
**Readers:** Licensees, package stores,
   supermarket chains, discount & drug
   store chains, restaurants, hotels and
   bars in Southern California.

## BEVERAGE INDUSTRY
22107

1935 Sherman Rd., Ste. 100
Northbrook, IL 60062
Telephone: (708) 205-5660
FAX: (708) 205-5680
Year Established: 1946
Pub. Frequency: m.
Page Size: standard
Subscrip. Rate: $50/yr.
Materials: 01,04,06,27,28,29,30,32,33
Print Process: web offset
Circulation: 28,987
Circulation Type: controlled
**Owner(s):**
Stagnito Publishing Co.
1935 Shermer Rd., Ste. 100
Northbrook, IL 60062
Telephone: (708) 205-5660
Ownership %: 100
**Management:**
Harry Stagnito ...............................President
Tom Bachman ...............................Publisher
**Editorial:**
John Frank ...............................................Editor
Kristine Portnoy Kelley ............Managing Editor
**Desc.:** Edited for executives in beverage
   markets, with emphasis on marketing,
   technology and distribution activities.
**Readers:** beverage manufacturers,
   bottlers, distributors
**Deadline:** story-1st of mo. prior to pub.
   date; news-1st of mo.; photo-1st of mo.;
   ads-1st of mo.

## BEVERAGE INDUSTRY ANNUAL MANUAL
68692

1935 Chermer Rd., Ste. 100
Northwood, IL 60062
Telephone: (708) 205-5600
FAX: (708) 205-6680
Year Established: 1967
Pub. Frequency: a.
Page Size: standard
Subscrip. Rate: $45/yr.
Circulation: 8,774
Circulation Type: paid
**Owner(s):**
Stagnito Publishing Co.
1935 Shermer Rd., Ste. 100
Northwood, IL 60062
Telephone: (708) 205-5600
Ownership %: 100
**Editorial:**
Gary Hemphill ...............................................Editor

## BEVERAGE MEDIA
22028

161 Ave. of the Americas, 14th Fl.
New York, NY 10013
Telephone: (212) 620-0100
FAX: (212) 255-5684
Year Established: 1935
Pub. Frequency: m.
Page Size: standard
Subscrip. Rate: $69.90/yr.; $130.80/2 yrs.
Freelance Pay: $400/2 pg. article
Circulation: 19,000
Circulation Type: paid
**Owner(s):**
Max J. Slone
161 Ave. of the Americas, 14th
New York, NY 10013
Telephone: (212) 620-0100
Ownership %: 100
**Management:**
Max J. Slone .....................Chairman of Board
William Slone ...............................Publisher
George Gold .................Advertising Manager
**Editorial:**
Jack Kenny ...............................................Editor
Angela Olmeta ...............................Art Director
Alison Hamnersla ...............................Sales
**Desc.:** Covers news and developments of
   interest to liquor retailers, taverns and
   restauranteurs, wholesalers, suppliers,
   vintners and brewers.
**Readers:** Licensed liquor retailers
   (package stores, taverns/restaurants,
   hotels). wholesalers, salesmen, distillers
   and distillery reps, vintners, brewers, and
   importers.

## BEVERAGE RECORD, THE
22029

P.O. Box 310
Lake Arrowhead, CA 92352
Telephone: (909) 337-1666
FAX: (909) 337-6986
Year Established: 1935
Pub. Frequency: m.
Page Size: tabloid
Subscrip. Rate: $10/yr.
Materials: 02,04,06,15,16,21,25,27,28,29,
   30,32
Freelance Pay: varies
Print Process: web offset
Circulation: 3,890
Circulation Type: free
**Owner(s):**
Anderson Publications
P.O. Box 310
Lake Arrowhead, CA 92352
Telephone: (909) 337-1666
FAX: (909) 337-6986
Ownership %: 100
**Management:**
G.L. Anderson ...............................Publisher
**Editorial:**
G.L. Anderson ...............................................Editor
**Desc.:** Technical and features on bottling,
   brewing, distilling and vintners.
   Departments include: Financial, Books.
**Readers:** Alcoholic beverage licensees.

## BEVERAGE REGISTER, THE
22030

P.O. Box 310
Lake Arrowhead, CA 92352
Telephone: (909) 337-1666
FAX: (909) 337-6986
Year Established: 1945
Pub. Frequency: m.
Page Size: tabloid
Subscrip. Rate: $10/yr.
Materials: 02,04,06,15,16,21,25,27,28,29,
   30,32
Freelance Pay: varies
Print Process: web offset
Circulation: 3,640
Circulation Type: free

**Owner(s):**
Anderson Publication
P.O. Box 310
Lk Arrowhead, CA 92352
Telephone: (909) 337-1666
FAX: (909) 337-6986
Ownership %: 100
**Management:**
George Anderson .............................Publisher
**Editorial:**
George Anderson ...............................Editor
**Desc.:** Contains features on bottling,
   brewing, distilled spirits and vintners.
**Readers:** Liquor, beer and wine licensees.

## BEVERAGE WORLD
22108

150 Great Neck Rd.
Great Neck, NY 11021
Telephone: (516) 829-9210
FAX: (516) 829-5414
Year Established: 1882
Pub. Frequency: m.
Page Size: standard
Subscrip. Rate: $39.95/yr. US; $49.95/yr.
   foreign
Freelance Pay: negotiable
Circulation: 34,000
Circulation Type: controlled
**Owner(s):**
Keller International Publishing Corp.
150 Great Neck Rd.
Great Neck, NY 11021
Telephone: (516) 829-9210
Ownership %: 100
**Management:**
G. E. Keller ...............................President
G. E. Keller ...............................Publisher
**Editorial:**
Greg Prince ...............................Senior Editor
Larry Jabbonsky ...............................Editor
Marvin Toben .........................Editorial Director
**Desc.:** Covers a wide range of marketing
   and management subjects, including
   new packaging developments and
   original surveys.
**Readers:** Top management executives of
   firms manufacturing soft drinks, beer,
   bottled waters, fruit juice and juice-type
   drinks. Also food manufacturers and
   wholesalers, beverage distributors,
   franchise and flavor manufacturers.

## BEVERAGE WORLD INTERNATIONAL
22036

150 Great Neck Rd.
Great Neck, NY 11021
Telephone: (516) 829-9210
FAX: (516) 829-5414
Year Established: 1982
Pub. Frequency: bi-m.
Page Size: standard
Subscrip. Rate: $30/yr.
Materials: 01,02,27,28,29,30,31,32,33
Freelance Pay: $200/printed page
Circulation: 30,000
Circulation Type: controlled
**Owner(s):**
Keller International Publishing Corp.
150 Great Neck Rd.
Great Neck, NY 11021
Telephone: (516) 829-9210
FAX: (516) 829-5414
Ownership %: 100
**Management:**
Gerald E. Keller ...............................President
Marvin Toben ............Executive Vice President
Gerald E. Keller ...............................Publisher
**Editorial:**
Havis Dawson ...............................................Editor
Jose Suarez ...............................................Director
**Desc.:** Articles and news relating to
   operations of soft drink plants,
   breweries, wineries, distilleries
   in countries outside U.S.

**Materials Accepted/Included:** 01-Business news 02-By-line articles 03-Fashion news 04-Food news 05-Freelance copy 06-Letters to editor 07-Real estate news 08-Sports news 09-Travel news 10-Book rev. 11-Movie rev. 12-Music rev. 13-TV rev. 14-Theater rev. 15-Coming events 16-Obituaries 17-Question & answer 18-Social announcements 19-Artwork 20-Cartoons 21-Photos 22-TV listings 23-Audio rec. 24-Video rec. 25-Books 26-Films/film clips 27-Personnel news 28-Press releases 29-New product news/photos 30-Trade lit. 31-Contracts awarded 32-Display adv. 33-Classified adv.

**Readers:** Bottling plant owners, executives, wineries, technicians, brewmasters, bottled waters and juice producers.

22117

## BREWERS BULLETIN, THE
8250 W. Holly Rd.
Mequon, WI 53097
Telephone: (414) 242-6105
FAX: (414) 351-5710
Mailing Address:
P.O. Box 677
Thiensville, WI 53092
Year Established: 1907
Pub. Frequency: w.
Page Size: broadsheet
Subscrip. Rate: $80/yr. US.; $85/yr. Canada; $55/yr.+ postage, foreign
Circulation: 650
Circulation Type: paid
**Owner(s):**
Thomas Volke
P.O. Box 677
Thiensville, WI 53092
Telephone: (414) 242-6105
Ownership %: 49
**Management:**
Thomas Volke ........................Publisher
Marjorie Volke ..............Business Manager
**Editorial:**
Cynthia Volke ..........................Editor
**Desc.:** All services, supplies and events relevant to brewing industry and its supply industries.
**Readers:** Upper management.

22118

## BREWERS DIGEST
4049 W. Peterson Ave.
Chicago, IL 60646
Telephone: (312) 463-7484
Year Established: 1926
Pub. Frequency: m.
Page Size: standard
Subscrip. Rate: $25/yr. US.; $40/yr. foreign
Circulation: 2,800
Circulation Type: paid
**Owner(s):**
Anmark Publishing Co., Inc.
4049 W. Peterson Ave.
Chicago, IL 60646
Telephone: (312) 463-7484
Ownership %: 100
**Management:**
Leonard Kay ..........................President
Leonard Kay ..........................Publisher
Leonard Kay ..............Advertising Manager
**Editorial:**
Dori Whitney ............................Editor
**Desc.:** Articles and news of interest to brewery management and to beer wholesalers, including beer manufacturing problems, marketing, public relations, plant maintenance and operation, and administrative problems.
**Readers:** Brewery executives, and beer wholesalers.

58553

## DATABANK
150 Great Neck Rd.
Great Neck, NY 11021
Telephone: (516) 829-9210
Year Established: 1984
Pub. Frequency: a.
Page Size: standard
Subscrip. Rate: membership
Circulation: 33,000
Circulation Type: controlled & paid
**Owner(s):**
Keller International Publishing Corp.
150 Great Neck Rd.
Great Neck, NY 11021
Telephone: (516) 829-9210
Ownership %: 100

**Management:**
Gerald Keller ..........................Publisher
**Editorial:**
Marvin Toben ..........................Editor
**Desc.:** Provides information on all aspects of doing business in the beverage marketplace. Rapid Identification (Buyer's Guide) Charts list current products, equipment and services available. Includes cross-referencing by function in order to help clarify buying decisions, listings of manufacturers/suppliers to the industry as well as franchise companies, government agencies and allied trade associations.
**Readers:** Soft drink franchise company and bottlers, breweries, distributors, wineries, distilleries, bottled water and juice manufacturers.
**Deadline:** ads-Jul. 15

22047

## MODERN BREWERY AGE
50 Day St.
Norwalk, CT 06854
Telephone: (203) 853-6015
Mailing Address:
P.O. Box 5550
Norwalk, CT 06856
Year Established: 1933
Pub. Frequency: bi-m.
Page Size: tabloid
Subscrip. Rate: $85/yr.
Circulation: 2,800
Circulation Type: paid
**Owner(s):**
Business Journals, Inc.
50 Days St.
Norwalk, CT 06856
Telephone: (203) 853-6015
Ownership %: 100
**Management:**
Renfrew Brighton ......................President
Mac Brighton ..........................Publisher
**Editorial:**
Peter V. K. Reid ........................Editor
G. Woodward Schutz ............Assistant Editor
**Desc.:** Contains articles on production, engineering, warehousing, brewing techniques, technical abstracts, chemical abstracts and distribution.
**Readers:** Brewery executives and personnel in wholesaling operations.

58801

## PERISCOPE
150 Great Neck Rd.
Great Neck, NY 11021
Telephone: (516) 829-9210
Year Established: 1982
Pub. Frequency: m.
Page Size: tabloid
Subscrip. Rate: $40/yr. includes Beverage World
Circulation: 33,000
Circulation Type: controlled & paid
**Owner(s):**
Keller International Publishing Corp.
150 Great Neck Rd.
Great Neck, NY 11021
Telephone: (516) 829-9210
Ownership %: 100
**Management:**
Marv Toben ..............Executive Vice President
Gerald Keller ..........................Publisher
**Editorial:**
Greg Prince ............................Editor
**Deadline:** ads-4 wks. prior to pub. date

68693

## QUARTERLY REVIEW OF WINES
24 Garfield Ave.
Winchester, MA 01890
Telephone: (617) 729-7132
FAX: (617) 721-0572
Year Established: 1978

Pub. Frequency: q.
Subscrip. Rate: $3.95 newsstand US; $4.50 Canada; $14.95/yr.
Materials: 04,06,20,28,32
Print Process: web
Circulation: 50,000
Circulation Type: controlled & paid
**Owner(s):**
Q R W, Inc.
24 Garfield Ave.
Winchester, MA 01890
Telephone: (617) 729-7132
Ownership %: 100
**Editorial:**
Richard L. Elia ........................Editor
**Desc.:** Covers wine, food and travel.

22126

## STATEWAYS
100 Ave. of the Americas
New York, NY 10013
Telephone: (212) 274-7000
FAX: (212) 431-0500
Year Established: 1972
Pub. Frequency: bi-m.
Page Size: standard
Subscrip. Rate: $20/yr.
Freelance Pay: varies
Circulation: 10,000
Circulation Type: controlled
**Owner(s):**
Jobson Publishing Corp.
100 Ave. of the Americas
New York, NY 10013
Telephone: (212) 274-7000
Ownership %: 100
**Management:**
Robert A. Amato ......................President
Seymour L. Leikind ..................Publisher
Seymour L. Leikind ..........Advertising Manager
**Editorial:**
David Lynch ............................Editor
**Desc.:** Magazine of the control states.
**Readers:** Commissioners and state officials in control states. State store managers liquor industry members.

66620

## SUDS 'N STUFF MINI MAGAZINE
4764 Galicia Way
Oceanside, CA 92056
Telephone: (619) 724-4447
Year Established: 1979
Pub. Frequency: 6/yr.
Page Size: standard
Subscrip. Rate: $15/yr.
Freelance Pay: $25/page
Circulation: 22,000
Circulation Type: paid
**Owner(s):**
Bosak Publishing, Inc.
4764 Galicia Way
Oceanside, CA 92056
Telephone: (619) 724-4447
Ownership %: 100
**Management:**
Michael Bosak ........................Publisher
**Editorial:**
Sandra Powers ........................Editor
**Desc.:** Provides information for consumers of beer.
**Readers:** People with good education, high earnings, and an interest in beer.

66604

## WINE & SPIRITS
One Academy St., Rd. 6
Princeton, NJ 08540
Telephone: (609) 921-1060
FAX: (609) 921-2566
Mailing Address:
P.O. Box 1548
Princeton, NJ 08542
Pub. Frequency: 8/yr.
Subscrip. Rate: $22/yr.; $38/2 yrs.
Circulation: 60000
Circulation Type: paid

**Owner(s):**
Folio Planning, Inc.
One Academy St., Rd. 6
Princeton, NJ 08540
Telephone: (609) 921-1060
FAX: (609) 921-2566
Ownership %: 100
**Management:**
Joshua Greene ........................Publisher
**Editorial:**
Joshua Greene ........................Editor
Marcy Crimmins ..................Design Editor

68694

## WINE NEWS, THE
353 Alcazar Ave., Ste. 101-B
Coral Gables, FL 33134-4313
Telephone: (305) 444-7250
FAX: (305) 444-5706
Year Established: 1985
Pub. Frequency: bi-m.
Page Size: oversize
Subscrip. Rate: $4 newsstand; $24/yr.
Materials: 04,10,15,17,21,25,28,32
Print Process: offset
Circulation: 46,000
Circulation Type: free & paid
**Owner(s):**
T.E. Smith, Inc.
353 Alcazar Ave., Ste. 101-B
Coral Gables, FL 33134-4313
Telephone: (305) 444-7250
Ownership %: 100
**Management:**
Tom E. Smith ..........................Publisher
**Editorial:**
Elizabeth Smith ................Executive Editor
Kathy Sinnes ..................Managing Editor
**Desc.:** Educates, guides and entertains the reader about wine through interviews, commentary, and historical perspectives. Includes wine pairing and food preparation tips.

66173

## WINE ON LINE
400 E. 59th St., Ste. 9F
New York, NY 10022
Telephone: (212) 755-4363
FAX: (212) 755-4365
Year Established: 1980
Pub. Frequency: w.
Page Size: standard
Subscrip. Rate: $100/yr.
Materials: 01,02,03,04,05,06,07,08,09,10, 11,12,13,14,15,16,17,18,19,21,22,23,24, 25,26,27,
Circulation: 600,000
Circulation Type: controlled
**Owner(s):**
Enterprises Publishing
400 E. 59th St., 9F
New York, NY 10022
Telephone: (212) 755-4363
Ownership %: 100
**Editorial:**
Nancy Preiser ..........................Editor
**Desc.:** Editorial, advertising, data bases and trade and consumer product - review, special international tours and travel section, and evaluation of our wine, special beer, water and gourmet products - also rented products, i.e. wine openers, water filters, etc., articles, features and syndicated columns.
**Readers:** Upper income professionals and trade restaurants. Vineyards-night clubs, entertainment, airlines, restaurants, and railroads.

22065

## WINES & VINES
1800 Lincoln Ave.
San Rafael, CA 94901
Telephone: (415) 453-9700
Year Established: 1919
Pub. Frequency: 13/yr.

**Materials Accepted/Included:** 01-Business news 02-By-line articles 03-Fashion news 04-Food news 05-Freelance copy 06-Letters to editor 07-Real estate news 08-Sports news 09-Travel news 10-Book rev. 11-Movie rev. 12-Music rev. 13-TV rev. 14-Theater rev. 15-Coming events 16-Obituaries 17-Question & answer 18-Social announcements 19-Artwork 20-Cartoons 21-Photos 22-TV listings 23-Audio rec. 24-Video rec. 25-Books 26-Films/film clips 27-Personnel news 28-Press releases 29-New product news/photos 30-Trade lit. 31-Contracts awarded 32-Display adv. 33-Classified adv.

4-37

Page Size: standard
Subscrip. Rate: $77.50/yr.
Materials: 01,06,10,15,16,25,27,28,29,30,
32,33
Freelance Pay: $.05/wd.
Circulation: 4,000
Circulation Type: free & paid
**Owner(s):**
Hiaring Company
1800 Lincoln Ave.
San Rafael, CA 94901
Telephone: (415) 453-9700
Ownership %: 100
**Management:**
Philip E. Hiaring ..............................President
Philip E. Hiaring ..............................Publisher
Dorthy Kubota - ...............Advertising Manager
Cordery
**Editorial:**
Philip E. Hiaring ....................Executive Editor
**Desc.:** Covers current situation in United
States grape and wine industry. Lead
articles deal with industry programs,
marketing situation, trends, prospects,
etc. Technical section devoted to new
production developments and research.
News items of interest to the industry
used. Articles run from 1,000-1,500
words. Pictures and by-lines used.
Material should be of interest to
vintners, grape growers, bottlers,
distributors. Departments include:
Industry Section, Technical section,
Statistical section, News section, State
of the Art, Wine Merchant.
**Readers:** Wine producers, vineyardists,
bottlers and consumers.

## Group 028-Beverages-
## Regional, State, Metro, Local

48950
### ARIZONA BEVERAGE ANALYST
2403 Champa St.
Denver, CO 80205
Telephone: (303) 296-1600
FAX: (303) 295-2159
Year Established: 1936
Pub. Frequency: m.
Page Size: standard
Subscrip. Rate: $15/yr.
Materials: 01,04,05,06,17,19,20,21,27,28,
29,30,32
Freelance Pay: variable
Circulation: 5,240
Circulation Type: paid
**Owner(s):**
Bell Publications
2403 Champa St.
Denver, CO 80205
Telephone: (303) 296-1600
Ownership %: 100
**Bureau(s):**
Arizona Beverage Analyst
P.O. Box 33903
Phoenix, AZ 85067
Telephone: (602) 249-1767
Contact: Carol Dobson
**Management:**
Lawrence Bell ...............................Publisher
Robert Bickley ...................Advertising Manager
Sherri Patterson ................Circulation Manager
**Editorial:**
Sonia Best ...........................Managing Editor
**Desc.:** Features and news covering the
licensed beverage industry, restaurants,
bars, package stores, in Arizona, in
addition to national and regional industry
news, new product information,
personnel changes, and legal/legislative
updates.

**Readers:** Distillery, winery & brewery
personnel; wholesalers and retailers;
restaurant owners and all Arizona
licensees.
**Deadline:** story-15th of the mo.; news-15th
of the mo.; photo-15th of the mo.; ads-
1st of the mo. prior to pub. date

22023
### ATLANTIC CONTROL STATES
### BEVERAGE JOURNAL
3 Twelfth St.
Wheeling, WV 26003
Telephone: (304) 232-7620
Year Established: 1967
Pub. Frequency: m.
Page Size: standard
Subscrip. Rate: $12/yr.
Materials: 01,04,10,21,27,28,29,30,32,33
Circulation: 6,400
Circulation Type: controlled
**Owner(s):**
Club and Tavern, Inc.
3 Twelfth St.
Wheeling, WV 26003
Telephone: (304) 232-7620
Ownership %: 100
**Management:**
Arnold Lazarus ...............................Publisher
Arnold Lazarus ..................Advertising Manager
**Editorial:**
Arnold Lazarus ......................Executive Editor
**Desc.:** Use articles of varying lengths,
pertaining to beverage alcohol field.
**Readers:** Licensees, package stores,
industry representatives.

22114
### BEBIDAS
8575 W. 110th St., Ste. 218
Overland Park, KS 66210
Telephone: (913) 469-8611
Year Established: 1942
Pub. Frequency: bi-m.
Page Size: standard
Subscrip. Rate: $15/yr.
Materials: 01,02,05,016,27,28,29,30,31,32,
33
Freelance Pay: $2/in.; $10/photo
Print Process: offset
Circulation: 8,900
Circulation Type: controlled & paid
**Owner(s):**
International Beverages Publishers
8575 W. 110th St., Ste. 218
Overland Park, KS 66210
Telephone: (913) 469-8611
Ownership %: 100
**Bureau(s):**
Robert S. Windt
225 Sterling Pl.
Brooklyn, NY 11238
Telephone: (718) 789-8898

Rolando Rubalcava
Cerro Compostela 23 Campestre
Churubusco, 04200 Mexico
**Management:**
Floyd Sagesser ..............................President
Robert Gowdy ..........................Vice President
Robert S. Windt ......................Vice President
Robert Gowdy ...................Circulation Manager
**Desc.:** Contributed and staff-written articles
cover Latin American soft drink, wine,
distilled liquor, and brewing
industry/plant operation, management,
growth, sanitation, and sterilization. Also
reports interesting developments; carries
interesting notes; new equipment.
Printed in Spanish. Special Mexican
supplement serves as official publication
for Mexican Soft Drink Association.
(ANPAE)
**Readers:** Bottlers and canners of soft
drinks, beer and wine in Mexico, Central
America, South America, Spain and
Portugal.

61725
### BEVERAGE INDUSTRY NEWS
703 Market St., Ste. 251
San Francisco, CA 94103
Telephone: (415) 495-8984
Year Established: 1935
Pub. Frequency: m.
Page Size: standard
Subscrip. Rate: $63/yr.
Circulation: 11,000
Circulation Type: paid
**Owner(s):**
Philip K. Page, Leroy W. Page, David L.
Page
703 Market St.
San Francisco, CA 94103
Telephone: (415) 986-2360
Ownership %: 100
**Editorial:**
Craig Bystrynski ...............................Editor
**Readers:** Alcoholic beverage industry.

22034
### COLORADO BEVERAGE ANALYST
2403 Champa St.
Denver, CO 80205
Telephone: (303) 296-1600
FAX: (303) 295-2159
Year Established: 1936
Pub. Frequency: m.
Page Size: standard
Subscrip. Rate: $15/yr. in state; $16/yr. in
Denver
Freelance Pay: $1.50/col. in.
Circulation: 3,000
Circulation Type: paid
**Owner(s):**
Bevan, Inc.
2403 Champa St.
Denver, CO 80205
Telephone: (303) 296-1600
Ownership %: 100
**Management:**
Larry Bell ...............................Publisher
Larry Bell ..........................Advertising Manager
Sherri Patterson ................Circulation Manager
**Editorial:**
Susan Sherwood ...............................Editor
**Desc.:** News items and features pertinent
to the alcoholic beverage industry, with
special emphasis on the industry in
Colorado.
**Readers:** Retailers, wholesalers, sales
personnel, distillers.

22035
### CONNECTICUT BEVERAGE
### JOURNAL
2508 Whitney Ave., Ste. C
Hamden, CT 06518
Telephone: (203) 288-3375
FAX: (203) 288-2693
Mailing Address:
P.O. Box 5157
Hamden, CT 06518
Year Established: 1943
Pub. Frequency: m.
Page Size: standard
Subscrip. Rate: $20/yr.
Circulation: 5,636
Circulation Type: paid
**Owner(s):**
Beverage Publications, Inc.
P.O. Box 5157
Hamden, CT 06518
Telephone: (203) 288-3375
Ownership %: 100
**Management:**
Gerald P. Slone ...............................Publisher
Noreen Hartmann ..............Circulation Manager
Laurie Buick ..........Composing Room Manager
**Editorial:**
Loretta Johlman ...............................Art Director

**Desc.:** Covers news, merchandising
techniques, developments, and
government regulations relating to
wholesale and retail liquor, wine and
beer. Includes retail liquor, wine and
beer retailers who sell both on-premise
and off-premise.
**Readers:** Package stores, drug stores,
clubs, hotel restaurants, cafes, night
clubs and liquor industry.

67682
### DELAWARE BEVERAGE MONTHLY
Trolley Sq. 8-C
Wilmington, DE 19806
Telephone: (302) 655-2800
FAX: (302) 655-2805
Year Established: 1984
Pub. Frequency: m.
Page Size: standard
Subscrip. Rate: $19/yr. 3rd class; $38/yr.
1st class
Circulation: 1,800
Circulation Type: controlled
**Owner(s):**
Melton Communications
Trolley Square 8-C
Wilmington, DE 19806
Telephone: (302) 655-2800
Ownership %: 100
**Management:**
Dale Melton ...............................President
Dale Melton ...............................Publisher
Dale Melton ...................Advertising Manager
**Editorial:**
Dale Melton ...............................Editor

22037
### HAWAII BEVERAGE GUIDE
1311 Kapidani Blvd., Ste. 508
Honolulu, HI 96814
Telephone: (808) 591-0049
FAX: (808) 591-0038
Mailing Address:
P.O. Box 853
Honolulu, HI 96808
Year Established: 1949
Pub. Frequency: m.
Page Size: standard
Subscrip. Rate: $4 newsstand; $29/yr.
Materials: 01,04,21,27,28,29,30,32
Print Process: offset
Circulation: 2,000
Circulation Type: controlled & paid
**Owner(s):**
Service Publications, Inc.
P.O. Box 853
Honolulu, HI 96808
Telephone: (808) 591-0049
FAX: (808) 591-0038
Ownership %: 100
**Management:**
Campbell Mansfield ...............................Publisher
**Editorial:**
Campbell Mansfield ...............................Editor
**Desc.:** News of interest to the beverage
industry in Hawaii, both national and
local plus wholesale price listings.
**Readers:** All licensed beverage members
in Hawaii markets. National and
international suppliers in the beverage
industry.
**Deadline:** story-15th of mo.; news-15th of
mo.; photo-15th of mo.; ads-15th of mo.

22119
### ILLINOIS BEVERAGE JOURNAL
550 Frontage Rd.
Ste. 2410
Northfield, IL 60093
Telephone: (708) 441-7776
FAX: (708) 441-7796
Year Established: 1944
Pub. Frequency: m.
Page Size: standard
Subscrip. Rate: $30/yr.
Circulation: 6,000

**Materials Accepted/Included:** 01-Business news 02-By-line articles 03-Fashion news 04-Food news 05-Freelance copy 06-Letters to editor 07-Real estate news 08-Sports news 09-Travel news
10-Book rev. 11-Movie rev. 12-Music rev. 13-TV rev. 14-Theater rev. 15-Coming events 16-Obituaries 17-Question & answer 18-Social announcements 19-Artwork 20-Cartoons 21-Photos 22-TV listings
23-Audio rec. 24-Video rec. 25-Books 26-Films/film clips 27-Personnel news 28-Press releases 29-New product news/photos 30-Trade lit. 31-Contracts awarded 32-Display adv. 33-Classified adv.

4-38

Circulation Type: paid
**Owner(s):**
Illinois Beverage Media, Inc.
550 Frontage Rd.
Ste. 2410
Northfield, IL 60093
Ownership %: 100
**Management:**
Jim O'Brien ................................President
Jim O'Brien ................................Publisher
Jim O'Brien ...................Advertising Manager
**Editorial:**
Nancy Ekstrand ....................Managing Editor
**Desc.:** Covers all branches of beer, wine,
liquor and related products in the
alcoholic beverage field in Illinois,
merchandising developments, people,
new lines, association news, etc.
**Readers:** Liquor licensees. Producers and
manufacturers of liquors, wine, beer.
Sales managers and advertising
agencies.

## INDIANA BEVERAGE JOURNAL    22120
2511 E. 46th St., Ste. A-7
Indianapolis, IN 46205
Telephone: (317) 545-5262
FAX: (317) 545-5263
Year Established: 1945
Pub. Frequency: m.
Page Size: standard
Subscrip. Rate: $20/yr.
Circulation: 2,700
Circulation Type: paid
**Owner(s):**
Indiana Beverage Life, Inc.
2511 E. 46th St.
Indianapolis, IN 46205
Ownership %: 100
**Management:**
Stewart N. Baxter ................................Publisher
**Editorial:**
Stewarta N. Baxter ................................Editor
Richard N. Baxter ........................Columnist
**Desc.:** Company news, local news,
promotions, meetings of the liquor, beer
and wine industry, etc.
**Readers:** Wine, beer, liquor licensee
instate.

## KENTUCKY BEVERAGE JOURNAL    22041
103 Railroad St.
Midway, KY 40347
Telephone: (606) 846-5231
FAX: (606) 846-4378
Mailing Address:
P.O. Box 346
Midway, KY 40347
Year Established: 1948
Pub. Frequency: m.
Page Size: standard
Subscrip. Rate: $18/yr.
Materials: 32
Circulation: 2,000
Circulation Type: controlled & paid
**Owner(s):**
Midway Publications, Inc.
P.O. Box 346
Midway, KY 40347
Telephone: (606) 846-5231
Ownership %: 100
**Management:**
Sharon Turner ....................Circulation Manager
**Editorial:**
John Meyers ................................Editor
**Desc.:** News and developments of general
interest to the beverage industry in
Kentucky.
**Readers:** Individuals operating taverns,
bars and package stores. Industry
officials and other licensees.

## MAIN INGREDIENT, THE    22056
8565 S.W. Salish Ln., Ste. 120
Wilsonville, OR 97070
Telephone: (503) 682-4422
FAX: (503) 682-4455
Year Established: 1975
Pub. Frequency: 10/yr.
Page Size: standard
Subscrip. Rate: members only
Circulation: 2,250
Circulation Type: controlled
**Owner(s):**
Oregon Restaurant Association
85 65 S.W Salish Ln., Ste. 120
Wilsonville, OR 97070
Telephone: (503) 682-4422
Ownership %: 100
**Management:**
Sharyl Parker ................................Publisher
**Editorial:**
Nancy Inman ....................Assistant Publisher
**Desc.:** A publication serving the hospitality
industry of Oregon. Promoting industry
education, legislative and regulatory
oversight and member services.
**Readers:** Tavern, restaurant, lounge, club
operators and hotel/motel operations
with food services as well as purveyors
to the industry.

## MARYLAND-WASHINGTON BEVERAGE JOURNAL    22044
7451 Race Rd.
Hanover, MD 21076
Telephone: (410) 796-5455
Mailing Address:
P.O. Box 1002
Hanover, MD 21076
Year Established: 1938
Pub. Frequency: m.
Page Size: standard
Subscrip. Rate: $30/yr.
Materials: 01,06,25,27,28,29,30,32,33
Freelance Pay: $.10/wd.
Print Process: web offset
Circulation: 8,500
Circulation Type: controlled
**Owner(s):**
Beverage Journal, Inc.
7451 Race Rd.
Hanover, MD 21076
Telephone: (410) 796-5455
Ownership %: 100
**Management:**
Catherine R. Demuth ........................President
Lee W. Murray ....................Vice President
Stephen Patten ................Advertising Manager
Allan Yaker ....................Circulation Manager
**Editorial:**
Michael Spaur ................................Editor
Allan Yaker ....................Associate Publisher
Thomas W. Murray ...........Secretary/Treasurer
**Desc.:** Editorial content deals exclusively
with articles and material covering all
facets of the national and local
beverage industry. Feature articles
consist of profiles of individuals in all
phases of the industry. Also contains
official wholesale beer, wine, and liquor
price lists.
**Readers:** Personnel of restaurants, hotels,
bars, package stores, clubs taverns
brewers, wholesalers, vintners, distillers.
**Deadline:** story-10th of mo. prior to pub.
date; news-10th of mo.; photo-10th of
mo.; ads-10th of mo.

## MASSACHUSETTS BEVERAGE PRICE JOURNAL    22045
31 Memorial Dr.
Avon, MA 02322
Telephone: (508) 580-1710
FAX: (508) 580-1737

Mailing Address:
P.O. Box 608
Avon, MA 02322
Year Established: 1944
Pub. Frequency: m.
Page Size: standard
Subscrip. Rate: $34/yr.; $62/2 yrs.; $81/3
Yrs.
Circulation: 7,600
Circulation Type: paid
**Owner(s):**
New Beverage, Inc.
31 Memorial Dr.
Avon, MA 02322
Telephone: (508) 580-1710
Ownership %: 100
**Management:**
Maury Shugrue ................................Publisher
Lucy Roger ....................Circulation Manager
**Editorial:**
Terry Driscoll ................................Editor
**Desc.:** Covers the field of the alcoholic
beverage industry: liquor, beers, wines,
and affiliated items.
**Readers:** Liquor stores, restaurants,
taverns.

## MID-CONTINENT BOTTLER    22110
8575 W. 110th St., Ste. 218
Overland Park, KS 66210
Telephone: (913) 469-8611
Year Established: 1947
Pub. Frequency: bi-m.
Page Size: standard
Subscrip. Rate: $9/yr.
Materials: 01,02,05,16,27,28,29,30,31,32,33
Freelance Pay: varies
Print Process: offset
Circulation: 3,100
Circulation Type: controlled
**Owner(s):**
Fancy Publications, Inc.
8575 W. 110th St., Ste. 218
Overland Park, KS 66210
Telephone: (913) 469-8611
Ownership %: 100
**Bureau(s):**
Robert S. Windt
225 Sterling Place
Brooklyn, NY 11238
Telephone: (718) 789-8898
Contact: Robert S. Windt
**Management:**
Floyd E. Sageser ................................Publisher
Patricia A. Krisman ...........Circulation Manager
**Editorial:**
Floyd E. Sageser ................................Editor
**Desc.:** Editorial content based mainly on
in-plant interviews with bottlers. From 8
to 15 bottlers in different sections of the
coverage area are interviewed each
month. Main purpose of these interviews
is to report principally on these bottlers'
selling and merchandising successes
or practices. Departments include: In-
plant Interviews; Survey Articles (mail
and direct contact); Technical Articles;
Industry Trend Articles; Bottler and
Franchise News; and Vending News
Articles.
**Readers:** Owners or managers of soft
drink plants.

## NEBRASKA BEVERAGE ANALYST    22050
2403 Champa St.
Denver, CO 80205
Telephone: (303) 296-1600
FAX: (303) 295-2159
Year Established: 1936
Pub. Frequency: m.
Page Size: standard
Subscrip. Rate: $10/yr.
Materials: 01,04,05,06,19,20,21,27,28,29,
30,31,32

Freelance Pay: varies
Circulation: 3,150
Circulation Type: paid
**Owner(s):**
Bell Publications
2403 Champa St.
Denver, CO 80205
Telephone: (303) 296-1600
Ownership %: 100
**Bureau(s):**
Nebraska Beverage Analyst
5809 Pine St.
Omaha, NE 68106
Telephone: (402) 556-4633
Contact: Arthur Grossman
**Management:**
Larry Bell ................................Owner
Larry Bell ................................Publisher
Robert Bickley ...................Advertising Manager
Sherri Patterson ................Circulation Manager
**Editorial:**
Sonia Best ....................Managing Editor
**Desc.:** News items and features pertinent
to the alcoholic beverage industry in the
State of Nebraska, as well as national
and regional industry news.
**Readers:** Retailers, wholesalers, sales
personnel, liquor commission members
and staff, distillers, vintners, breweries
in Nebraska.

## NEW JERSEY BEVERAGE JOURNAL    22123
2414 Morris Ave.
Union, NJ 07083
Telephone: (908) 964-5060
FAX: (908) 964-1472
Year Established: 1949
Pub. Frequency: m.
Page Size: PG: 7 x 10
Subscrip. Rate: $25/yr.
Circulation: 9,000
Circulation Type: controlled
**Owner(s):**
Gem Publishers, Inc.
2414 Morris Ave.
Union, NJ 07083
Telephone: (908) 964-5060
Ownership %: 100
**Bureau(s):**
Associated Beverage Publications
161 Ave. of the Americas
New York, NY 10013
Telephone: (212) 620-0100
Contact: Max J. Slone, Director
**Management:**
Harry Slone ................................Publisher
Angel Wolthers ................Circulation Manager
**Editorial:**
Harry Slone ................................Editor
Max J. Slone ................................Sales
**Desc.:** Merchandising and Sales Help
articles for the retailer, News Features,
Analyses and Trends, Price Information
and Brand Information, Trade Directory,
Monthly Price Changes.
Carries manufacturers News, Personals,
New Products, Appointments.
**Readers:** Retail liquor licensees, bars,
package stores, hotels, restaurants,
seasonal bars. Also, distillers,
wholesalers and salesmen.

## NEW MEXICO BEVERAGE ANALYST    22052
2403 Champa St.
Denver, CO 80205
Telephone: (303) 296-1600
FAX: (303) 295-2159
Year Established: 1947
Pub. Frequency: m.
Page Size: standard
Subscrip. Rate: $10/yr.
Freelance Pay: $1.50/col. in.

---

**Materials Accepted/Included:** 01-Business news 02-By-line articles 03-Fashion news 04-Food news 05-Freelance copy 06-Letters to editor 07-Real estate news 08-Sports news 09-Travel news 10-Book rev. 11-Movie rev. 12-Music rev. 13-TV rev. 14-Theater rev. 15-Coming events 16-Obituaries 17-Question & answer 18-Social announcements 19-Artwork 20-Cartoons 21-Photos 22-TV listings 23-Audio rec. 24-Video rec. 25-Books 26-Films/film clips 27-Personnel news 28-Press releases 29-New product news/photos 30-Trade lit. 31-Contracts awarded 32-Display adv. 33-Classified adv.

4-39

Circulation: 1,250
Circulation Type: paid
**Owner(s):**
Bell Publications, Inc.
2403 Champa St.
Denver, CO 80205
Telephone: (303) 296-1600
Ownership %: 100
**Bureau(s):**
New Mexico Beverage Analyst
1905 San Mateo, N.E.
Albuquerque, NM 87110
Telephone: (505) 255-2721
Contact: William Previtti
**Management:**
Lawrence Bell ........................Publisher
Susan Sherwood ..............Advertising Manager
**Editorial:**
Sherri Patterson ...........................Editor
**Desc.:** Covers news and developments of
interest to the alcoholic beverage
industry in New Mexico as well as the
manufacturers and suppliers in the U.S.
**Readers:** Personnel in alcoholic beverage
industry in New Mexico, including
retailers, restaurant owners, distillers,
wholesalers, and alcohol agencies.

**OBSERVER** 22125
226 N. 12th St.
Philadelphia, PA 19107
Telephone: (215) 567-6221
FAX: (215) 567-4527
Year Established: 1936
Pub. Frequency: m.
Page Size: broadsheet
Subscrip. Rate: $15/yr.; $22/2 yrs.
Freelance Pay: $50-$100/article
Circulation: 18,000
Circulation Type: controlled
**Owner(s):**
Observer Corp.
226 N. 12th St.
Philadelphia, PA 19107
Telephone: (215) 567-6221
Ownership %: 100
**Bureau(s):**
Laurie Rosenstiel
609 Mellon St.
Pittsburgh, PA 15206
Telephone: (412) 361-8396
**Management:**
James J. Curran ........................Publisher
Mark Brakeman ................General Manager
Ruth N. Shapiro ..................Office Manager
**Editorial:**
Mark Brakeman ...........................Editor
**Desc.:** News and politics with an accent
on Pennsylvania and its liquor industry
(beer, wine, spirits).
**Readers:** Pennsylvania liquor licensees,
restaurant owners, tavern owners, food
and beverage director, state, national
and local politicians, public officials,
liquor wholesalers and representatives.

**OHIO BEVERAGE JOURNAL** 22053
3 12th St.
Wheeling, WV 26003
Telephone: (304) 232-7620
Year Established: 1934
Pub. Frequency: m.
Page Size: standard
Subscrip. Rate: $12/yr.
Materials: 01,04,10,21,27,28,29,30,32,33
**Owner(s):**
Midwest Publications, Inc.
3 12th St.
Wheeling, WV 26003
Telephone: (304) 232-6720
Ownership %: 100
**Management:**
Arnold Lazarus ........................Publisher
Arnold Lazarus ..............Advertising Manager

**Editorial:**
Arnold Lazarus ...........................Editor
**Desc.:** Edited for those in the alcoholic
beverage industry responsible for the
sale and distribution of alcoholic
beverages in the state of Ohio. News
articles report on developments and
trends as they pertain to the sale, by the
drink and by the bottle, of alcoholic
beverages for Ohio and elsewhere.

**OHIO TAVERN NEWS** 22054
329 S. Front St.
Columbus, OH 43215
Telephone: (614) 224-4835
FAX: (614) 224-8649
Year Established: 1939
Pub. Frequency: s-m.
Page Size: tabloid
Subscrip. Rate: $14/yr.; $22/2 yrs.
Materials: 01,02,04,05,06,15,21,28,29,30,
32,33
Freelance Pay: $4/in.; $15/photo
Print Process: offset
Circulation: 8,215
Circulation Type: free & paid
**Owner(s):**
Ohio Tavern News, Daily Reporter, Inc.
329 S. Front St.
Columbus, OH 43215
Telephone: (614) 224-4835
Ownership %: 100
**Management:**
Dan Schillingburg ...................General Manager
**Editorial:**
Chris Bailey ...........................Editor
J. Thomas Weeks ........................Advertising
John F. Wilson ...................Production Director
**Desc.:** Governmental regulations, news
and developments affecting liquor permit
and hospitality industries in Ohio.
**Readers:** Taverns, bars, hotels, package
stores, wholesalers and manufacturers.
**Deadline:** story-1st & 3rd Fri.; news-1st &
3rd Fri.; photo-1st & 3rd Fri.; ads-1st &
3rd Tue.

**PATTERSON'S BEVERAGE
JOURNAL** 22058
6055 E. Washington Blvd., Ste. 526
Los Angeles, CA 90040
Telephone: (213) 727-5055
FAX: (213) 727-9496
Year Established: 1941
Pub. Frequency: m.
Page Size: standard
Subscrip. Rate: $48/yr. US; $84/2 yrs. US;
$72/yr. foreign
Circulation: 15,472
Circulation Type: controlled & paid
**Owner(s):**
Wolfer Printing Co., Inc.
6670 Flotilla
Los Angeles, CA 90040
Telephone: (310) 721-5411
Ownership %: 100
**Management:**
Robert Good ........................Publisher
Michael Chu ...................Circulation Manager
Maggie Sharp ...................Production Manager
**Editorial:**
Jean Burggren ...........................Editor
John Colston ...................Finance Director
**Desc.:** News of the alcoholic beverage
industry in the states of California and
Hawaii. Contains market data industry
concerns such as taxation, fair trade
laws, advertising campaigns, new
products and their sources, business
procedures, merchandising, and current
news. Also contains wholesale and retail
price schedules for all brands,
(mandatory under state law).

**RHODE ISLAND BEVERAGE
JOURNAL** 22059
2508 Whitney Ave.
Hamden, CT 06518
Telephone: (203) 288-3375
FAX: (203) 288-2693
Mailing Address:
P.O. Box 5157
Hamden, CT 06518
Year Established: 1945
Pub. Frequency: m.
Page Size: standard
Subscrip. Rate: $20/yr.; $34.50/2 yrs.
Circulation: 1,300
Circulation Type: paid
**Owner(s):**
Beverage Publications, Inc.
P.O. Box 5157
Hamden, CT 06518
Telephone: (203) 288-3375
Ownership %: 100
**Management:**
Gerald P. Slone ........................Publisher
Noreen Hartmann ..............Circulation Manager
Laurie Buick ..........Composing Room Manager
**Editorial:**
Gerald P. Stone ...........................Editor
Loretta Johlman ...................Art Director
**Desc.:** Covers news, merchandising
techniques, and developments relating
to wholesale and retail liquor, wine and
beer.
**Readers:** Package stores, drug stores,
clubs, hotels, restaurants, cafes, night
clubs and liquor industry.

**SOUTHERN BEVERAGE JOURNAL** 22060
13225 S.W. 88th Ave.
Miami, FL 33176
Telephone: (305) 233-7230
FAX: (305) 252-2580
Mailing Address:
P.O. Box 56-1107
Miami, FL 33256
Year Established: 1948
Pub. Frequency: m.
Page Size: standard
Subscrip. Rate: $25/yr.; $40/2 yrs.
Materials: 01,04,32,33
Freelance Pay: $.10/wd.
Print Process: web
Circulation: 25,000
Circulation Type: paid
**Owner(s):**
Southern Beverage Journal
13225 S.W. 88th Ave.
Miami, FL 33176
Telephone: (305) 233-7230
Ownership %: 60

Eliot Levin
Ownership %: 40
**Management:**
Eliot Levin ........................Owner
Eliot Levin ........................Publisher
John Mullin ...................Circulation Manager
**Editorial:**
Jacqueline Preston ...................Managing Editor
**Desc.:** Features primarily written to help
licensees do a better selling job.
Stresses better merchandising and
public relations covers new products,
packages, industry news and
merchandising campaigns.
**Readers:** Package store, bar, restaurant,
hotel-motel managers.
**Deadline:** story-20th of mo., 2 mo. prior to
pub. date; news-20th of mo., 2 mo. prior
to pub. date; photo-20th of mo., 2 mo.
prior to pub. date; ads-varies

**SPIRITS, WINE & BEER
MARKETING IN MINNESOTA,
NORTH & SOUTH DAKOTA** 67032
15500 Wayzata Blvd., Ste. 744
Wayzata, MN 55391
Telephone: (612) 449-9446
FAX: (612) 449-9447
Year Established: 1934
Pub. Frequency: m.
Page Size: standard
Subscrip. Rate: $24/yr.
Circulation: 11,500
Circulation Type: controlled
**Owner(s):**
Diamond Publications
15500 Wayzata Blvd.
Wayzata, MN 55391
Telephone: (612) 449-9446
Ownership %: 100
**Management:**
Gary Diamond ........................Publisher
**Editorial:**
Gary Diamond ...........................Editor

**SPIRITS, WINE & BEER
MARKETING IN MISSOURI** 67033
15500 Wayzata Blvd., Ste. 744
Wayzata, MN 55391-1416
Telephone: (612) 449-9446
FAX: (612) 449-9447
Year Established: 1934
Pub. Frequency: m.
Page Size: standard
Subscrip. Rate: $24/yr. non-members
Circulation: 8,500
Circulation Type: controlled
**Owner(s):**
Diamond Publications
744 12 Oaks Ctr, 15500 Wayzata
Wayzata, MN 55391
Telephone: (612) 449-9446
Ownership %: 100
**Management:**
Gary Diamond ........................Publisher
**Editorial:**
Gary Diamond ...........................Editor

**TEXAS BEVERAGE NEWS** 22061
3500 Williams Rd.
Fort Worth, TX 76116
Telephone: (817) 244-6988
Year Established: 1958
Pub. Frequency: m.
Page Size: standard
Subscrip. Rate: $15/yr.
Circulation: 3,650
Circulation Type: paid
**Owner(s):**
Walter Gray
3500 Williams Rd.
Fort Worth, TX 76116
Ownership %: 100
**Management:**
Walter Gray ........................Publisher
**Editorial:**
Walter Gray ...........................Editor
Beth Gray ...........................Book Editor
**Desc.:** This is the spot journal of the beer,
wine and liquor industry of Texas. Can
use any type of current information of
interest to these businessmen
and women.
**Readers:** Businessmen and women of the
beer, wine and spirits, largely paid retail
subscriptions.

**WINE EAST** 69370
620 N. Pine St.
Lancaster, PA 17603-2824
Telephone: (717) 393-0943
Year Established: 1974
Pub. Frequency: bi-m.

**Materials Accepted/Included:** 01-Business news 02-By-line articles 03-Fashion news 04-Food news 05-Freelance copy 06-Letters to editor 07-Real estate news 08-Sports news 09-Travel news 10-Book rev. 11-Movie rev. 12-Music rev. 13-TV rev. 14-Theater rev. 15-Coming events 16-Obituaries 17-Question & answer 18-Social announcements 19-Artwork 20-Cartoons 21-Photos 22-TV listings 23-Audio rec. 24-Video rec. 25-Films 26-Films/film clips 27-Personnel news 28-Press releases 29-New product news/photos 30-Trade lit. 31-Contracts awarded 32-Display adv. 33-Classified adv.

Page Size: standard
Subscrip. Rate: $18/yr.
Circulation: 1,500
**Owner(s):**
L & H Photojournalism
620 N. Pine St.
Lancaster, PA 17603
Telephone: (717) 393-0943
Ownership %: 100
**Editorial:**
Hudson Cattell ............................Editor
Linda Jones McKee .....................Editor
**Desc.:** Includes features on winemaking, grape growing and marketing. Specializing in grapes and wine east of the Rocky Mountains in North America.

**WISCONSIN BEVERAGE JOURNAL**          22127
550 Frontage St., Ste. 2410
Northfield, IL 60093
Telephone: (708) 441-7771
Year Established: 1942
Pub. Frequency: m.
Page Size: standard
Subscrip. Rate: $8/yr.
Materials: 01,06,15,28,32,33
Circulation: 6,000
Circulation Type: paid
**Owner(s):**
James E. O'Brien
550 Frontage Rd., Ste. 2410
Northfield, IL 60093
Telephone: (708) 441-7776
FAX: (708) 441-7796
Ownership %: 100
**Management:**
James E. O'Brien ................................Publisher
**Editorial:**
Nancy Ekstrand .......................Managing Editor
Herbert D. Zien .......................News Editor
**Desc.:** News about the licensed beverage industry in Wisconsin, nationally and internationally. News about people, new merchandising aids, federal and local regulations.
**Readers:** Retail and wholesale licensees of distilled spirits, wines and brews.
**Deadline:** story-18th of mo. prior to pub. date; news-18th of mo.; photo-18th of mo.; ads-18th of mo.

## Group 029-Biological Sciences

**ABSTRACTS OF ENTOMOLOGY**          52660
2100 Arch St.
Philadelphia, PA 19103
Telephone: (215) 587-4800
Year Established: 1970
Pub. Frequency: m.
Page Size: standard
Subscrip. Rate: $190/yr.
**Owner(s):**
BIOSIS (R)
2100 Arch St.
Philadelphia, PA 19103
Telephone: (215) 587-4800
Ownership %: 100
**Management:**
H.E. Kennedy ..........................President
J.E. Anderson ...........Executive Vice President
D.J. Molitor .............................Vice President
A.W. Elias ...............................Vice President
Maureen Kelly .........................Vice President
D.J. Castagna ..........................Vice President
**Desc.:** Abstracts of Entomology is a monthly current awareness publication containing abstracts and content summaries in English, of pure and applied research studies involving insects, arachnids, and insecticides. Full bibliographic data is provided for each entry.

**Readers:** Professional: scientists, researchers, librarians, students.

**ABSTRACTS OF MYCOLOGY**          49921
2100 Arch St.
Philadelphia, PA 19103
Telephone: (215) 587-4800
Year Established: 1967
Pub. Frequency: m.
Page Size: standard
Subscrip. Rate: $230/yr.
**Owner(s):**
BIOSIS (R)
2100 Arch St.
Philadelphia, PA 19103
Telephone: (215) 587-4800
FAX: (215) 587-2016
Ownership %: 100
**Management:**
J.E. Anderson ...............................President
D.J. Molitor ..............................Vice President
D.J. Hoffman .............................Vice President
M. Kelly ....................................Vice President
D. Castagna ..............................Vice President
**Desc.:** Monthly current awareness publication containing abstracts and content summaries in English of research studies involving fungi, lichens, and fungicides. Full bibliographic data provided for each entry.
**Readers:** Professionals.

**AMERICAN FERN JOURNAL**          24857
Dept. Biology, Univ. Arkansas, Little Rock
Little Rock, AR 72204
Telephone: (501) 569-3505
Year Established: 1910
Pub. Frequency: q.
Page Size: standard
Subscrip. Rate: $20/yr.
Freelance Pay: none
Circulation: 930
Circulation Type: controlled & paid
**Owner(s):**
American Fern Society, Inc.
Richard L. Hauke, Records Trea
456 McGill Pl.
Atlanta, GA 30312-1049
Ownership %: 100
**Editorial:**
J. H. Peck ....................................Editor
C. Haufler ..........................Associate Editor
G. J. Gastony ......................Associate Editor
D. B. Lellinger ....................Associate Editor
R C Moran ..........................Associate Editor
**Desc.:** Scientific journal dealing with ferns of the world and especially those of the United States. Also covers some horticultural aspects.
**Readers:** Professional and amateur botanists, horticulturalists.

**AMERICAN NATURALIST**          68698
5720 S. Woodlawn Ave.
Chicago, IL 60637
Telephone: (312) 753-3347
FAX: (312) 753-0811
Year Established: 1867
Pub. Frequency: m.
Subscrp. Rate: $54/yr.
Circulation: 3,800
Circulation Type: paid
**Owner(s):**
University of Chicago Press
5720 S. Woodlawn Ave.
Chicago, IL 60637
Telephone: (312) 753-3347
Ownership %: 100
**Editorial:**
Mark Rausner ...............................Editor

**ANATOMICAL RECORD**          69399
605 Third Ave.
New York, NY 10158
Telephone: (212) 475-7700
Year Established: 1906
Pub. Frequency: m.
Subscrip. Rate: $1590/yr.
**Owner(s):**
John Wiley & Sons, Inc.
605 Third Ave.
New York, NY 10158
Telephone: (212) 475-7700
Ownership %: 100
**Editorial:**
Aaron Ladman ...............................Editor

**ANIMAL BIOTECHNOLOGY**          70375
270 Madison Ave.
New York, NY 10016
Telephone: (212) 696-9000
FAX: (212) 685-4540
Pub. Frequency: 2/yr.
Page Size: standard
Subscrip. Rate: $127.50/yr. individuals; $255/yr. institutions
Print Process: offset
**Owner(s):**
Marcel Dekker, Inc.
270 Madison Ave.
New York, NY 10016
Telephone: (212) 696-9000
FAX: (212) 685-4540
Ownership %: 100
**Editorial:**
Lawrence B. Shook ..........................Editor
Peter H. Bick ......................Associate Editor
Keith W. Kelley ....................Associate Editor
Harris A. Lewin ...................Associate Editor
Bryan A. White ....................Associate Editor
**Desc.:** Covers the identification and manipulation of genes and their products, stressing applications in domesticated animals. The journal publishes full-length articles, short research communications as well as appropriate reviews. Also provides a forum for regulatory or scientific issues related to cell and molecular biology, immunogenetics, transgenic animals and microbiology.
**Readers:** Directors, managers and researchers in pharmaceutical companies, animal breeders and shippers, reserach scientists, immunologists, molecular biologists, cell biology, academic professionals.

**ANNALS OF THE ENTOMOLOGICAL SOCIETY OF AMERICA**          24862
9301 Annapolis Rd.
Lanham, MD 20706
Telephone: (301) 731-4535
Year Established: 1908
Pub. Frequency: bi-m.
Page Size: standard
Subscrip. Rate: $25/yr. members; $62/yr. non-members; $110/yr. institutions
Circulation: 2,300
Circulation Type: paid
**Owner(s):**
Entomological Society of America
9301 Annapolis Rd.
Lanham, MD 20706
Telephone: (301) 731-4535
Ownership %: 100
**Management:**
W. Darryl Hansen ................Executive Director
Laura Baartz ...................Advertising Manager
**Editorial:**
Carl W. Schaefer ...........................Editor
Leo LaChance ...............................Editor
Raymond L. Everngam, Jr. .....Managing Editor

Lynn Vicchiolla ..........Communications Director
Kathryn O. Meckley .....................Service Editor
**Desc.:** Publishes only technical original research articles in field of basic (not applied) entomology. Chief interests are insect classification, life histories, embryology, physiology.
**Readers:** Primarily professional entomologists, students.

**APPLIED & ENVIRONMENTAL MICROBIOLOGY**          23731
1325 Massachusetts Ave., N.W.
Washington, DC 20005-4171
Telephone: (202) 737-3600
Year Established: 1953
Pub. Frequency: m.
Page Size: standard
Subscrip. Rate: $265/yr. non-member US & Canada
Materials: 02,06,32
Print Process: web offset
Circulation: 8,860
Circulation Type: paid
**Owner(s):**
American Society for Microbiology
1325 Massachusetts Ave., N.W.
Washington, DC 20005
Telephone: (202) 737-3600
Ownership %: 100
**Editorial:**
Lars G. Ljungdahl ....................Editor in Chief
L. M. Illig ................................Director
**Desc.:** Publishes descriptions of all aspects of applied research as well as applied and basic ecological research on bacteria and other microorganisms, including fungi, protozoa, and other simple eukaryotic organisms. Topics include: microbiology in relationship to foods, agriculture, industry, and public health; and basic biological properties of organisms as related to microbial ecology. It is of considerable interest to biotechnologists, since it publishes articles on genetics and molecular biology of microorganisms of commercial importance.
**Readers:** Manufacturers, laboratory workers, ecologists, food microbiologists, and biotechnologists.

**BIO/TECHNOLOGY**          61608
65 Bleecker St.
New York, NY 10012
Telephone: (212) 477-9600
FAX: (212) 505-1364
Year Established: 1983
Pub. Frequency: m.
Page Size: standard
Subscrip. Rate: $59/yr. individuals; $195/yr. institutions
Freelance Pay: $.50/wd.
Circulation: 15,000
Circulation Type: paid
**Owner(s):**
Nature Publishing Co.
65 Bleecker St.
New York, NY 10012
Telephone: (212) 477-9600
Ownership %: 100
**Bureau(s):**
Nature Publishing Co.
582 Market St., Ste. 1408
San Francisco , CA 94104
Telephone: (415) 781-3801
Contact: Lynn Stickrod

Macmillan Magazines, Ltd.
4 Little Essex St.
NC2R 3LF London United Kingdom
Telephone: 011-44-71872-0104
Contact: Ross Sturley

---

**Materials Accepted/Included:** 01-Business news 02-By-line articles 03-Fashion news 04-Food news 05-Freelance copy 06-Letters to editor 07-Real estate news 08-Sports news 09-Travel news 10-Book rev. 11-Movie rev. 12-Music rev. 13-TV rev. 14-Theater rev. 15-Coming events 16-Obituaries 17-Question & answer 18-Social announcements 19-Artwork 20-Cartoons 21-Photos 22-TV listings 23-Audio rec. 24-Video rec. 25-Books 26-Films/film clips 27-Personnel news 28-Press releases 29-New product news/photos 30-Trade lit. 31-Contracts awarded 32-Display adv. 33-Classified adv.

4-41

**Management:**
Andrew Sutherland ...............................Publisher
**Editorial:**
Doug McCormick ......................................Editor
**Desc.:** International monthly magazine for industrial biology.

23751

## BIOLOGICAL ABSTRACTS
2100 Arch St.
Philadelphia, PA 19103-1399
Telephone: (215) 587-4800
FAX: (215) 587-2016
Year Established: 1926
Pub. Frequency: s-m.
Page Size: standard
Subscrip. Rate: $5,650/yr.; $5,000/yr. for universities
**Owner(s):**
BIOSIS
2100 Arch St.
Philadelphia, PA 19103
Telephone: (215) 587-4800
FAX: (215) 587-2016
Ownership %: 100
**Management:**
J.A. Anderson ......................................President
D.J. Molitor ....................................Vice President
D.J. Hoffman ...................................Vice President
D.J. Castagna ..................................Vice President
M. Kelly ...........................................Vice President
**Desc.:** Contains references to basic research papers, notes, short communications and letters that appear in primary biological and medical journals.
**Readers:** Professional.

68699

## BIOS
P.O. Box 670
Madison, NJ 07940-0670
Telephone: (201) 377-8407
Year Established: 1930
Pub. Frequency: q.
Page Size: standard
Subscrip. Rate: $15/yr.; $17/yr. Canada & Mexico; $23/yr. elsewhere
Circulation: 10,500
Circulation Type: paid
**Owner(s):**
Beta Beta Beta
P.O. Box 670
Madison, NJ 07940-0670
Telephone: (201) 377-8407
Ownership %: 100
**Editorial:**
James J. Nagle . .......................................Editor
**Desc.:** Covers biology news reports, juried undergraduate research, grauate reviews and society news.

24866

## BIOSCIENCE
730 11th St., N.W.
Washington, DC 20001-4521
Telephone: (202) 628-1500
FAX: (202) 628-1509
Year Established: 1951
Pub. Frequency: m.
Page Size: standard
Subscrip. Rate: $52/yr. member; $125/yr. institution; $155/yr. foreign institution
Materials: 32,33
Freelance Pay: $300/pg.
Circulation: 11,600
Circulation Type: paid
**Owner(s):**
American Institute of Biological Sciences.
730 11th St., N.W.
Washington, DC 20001
Telephone: (202) 628-1500
Ownership %: 100
**Management:**
Clifford T. Gabriel ...............................Publisher
Robin Zimmerman ...........Advertising Manager

**Editorial:**
Julie Ann Miller ......................................Editor
Christina Thoreson ...................Assistant Editor
Judith S. Weis ....................Book Review Editor
Anna Maria Gillis .........................Feature Editor
Anna Maria Gillis ...........................News Editor
Rachel Russell ...................Production Director
**Desc.:** Contains articles on all areas of biological sciences, including animals, humans, plants, and the environment.
**Readers:** Biologists in research, teaching, industry, and government.

65623

## BIOTECHNOLOGY & BIOENGINEERING
605 Third Ave.
New York, NY 10158
Telephone: (212) 850-6289
Year Established: 1965
Pub. Frequency: 22/yr.
Page Size: standard
Subscrip. Rate: $1,190/yr.
Circulation: 1,773
Circulation Type: controlled
**Owner(s):**
John Wiley & Sons, Inc.
605 Third Ave.
New York, NY 10158
Telephone: (212) 850-6000
Ownership %: 100
**Editorial:**
Elestherios T. Papoutsakis ......................Editor
**Desc.:** Original research on all aspects of biochemical and microbial technology.

58786

## BIOTECHNOLOGY PROGRESS
345 E. 47th St.
New York, NY 10017
Telephone: (212) 705-7327
Mailing Address:
   P.O. Box 3337
   Columbus, OH 43210
Year Established: 1985
Pub. Frequency: bi-m.
Subscrip. Rate: $30/yr. members; $325/yr. non-members
Circulation: 2,800
Circulation Type: paid
**Owner(s):**
American Institute of Chemical Engineers
345 E. 47th St.
New York, NY 10017
Telephone: (212) 705-7330
Ownership %: 100
**Management:**
Maura Mullen ......................................Manager
**Editorial:**
M. L. Shuler ...........................................Editor
Claudia Caruana ....................Associate Editor

24867

## BRYOLOGIST
Dept. of Biology, Univ. of Nebraska at Omaha
Omaha, NE 68182
Telephone: (409) 845-7772
Year Established: 1898
Pub. Frequency: q.
Page Size: standard
Subscrip. Rate: $55/yr. institutions
Materials: 02,10,16,32
Circulation: 900
Circulation Type: paid
**Owner(s):**
American Bryological & Lichenological Society Inc.
Univ. of Nebraska at Omaha
Dept. of Biology
Omaha, NE 68182
Telephone: (409) 845-7772
Ownership %: 100
**Editorial:**
William D. Reese ....................................Editor
Ann Rushing ..................Book Review Editor

**Desc.:** Contributed research papers in the fields of bryology (mosses and hepatics) and lichenology. Reviews books, lists research articles and carries obituaries.
**Readers:** Professional and amateur botanists.

49922

## CA SELECTS
2540 Olentangy River Rd.
Columbus, OH 43202
Telephone: (614) 447-3600
FAX: (614) 447-3713
Mailing Address:
   P.O. Box 3012
   Columbus, OH 43210-0012
Year Established: 1976
Pub. Frequency: bi-w.
Page Size: standard
Subscrip. Rate: $210/subject
**Owner(s):**
Chemical Abstracts Service
P.O. Box 3012
Columbus, OH 43210-0012
Telephone: (614) 447-3600
FAX: (614) 447-3713
Ownership %: 100
**Editorial:**
David W. Weisgerber ..............................Editor
**Desc.:** CA Selects comprises a group of 248 current awareness publications covering specific research topics in the fields of chemistry and related developments in biochemistry, pharmacology and materials science. They contain abstracts with full bibliographic information.
**Readers:** Professional and academic.

68701

## CHRONOBIOLOGY INTERNATIONAL
1185 Ave. of the Americas
New York, NY 10036
Telephone: (212) 930-9500
FAX: (212) 869-3495
Year Established: 1984
Pub. Frequency: bi-m.
Subscrip. Rate: $120/yr. individuals; $270/yr. institutions
**Owner(s):**
Raven Press
1185 Ave. of the Americas
New York, NY 10036
Telephone: (212) 930-9500
Ownership %: 100
**Editorial:**
Alain Rosenberg .........................................Editor
Michael Smolensky .................................Editor
**Desc.:** Publishes original research investigations, short communications and commentaries in chronobiology and related disciplines.

70384

## COMMUNICATIONS IN SOIL SCIENCE & PLANT ANALYSIS
270 Madison Ave.
New York, NY 10016
Telephone: (212) 696-9000
FAX: (212) 685-4540
Year Established: 1970
Pub. Frequency: 20/yr.
Page Size: standard
Subscrip. Rate: $497.50/yr. individuals; $995/yr. institutions
**Owner(s):**
Marcel Dekker, Inc.
270 Madison Ave.
New York, NY 10016
Telephone: (212) 696-9000
Ownership %: 100
**Editorial:**
J. Benton Jones, Jr. ...............................Editor
Harry A. Mills ....................Associate Editor

**Desc.:** Provides a rapid means of publication on important developments in soil science and crop production, with particular reference to elemental content of soils and plants, and plant nutrition. Topics examined include soil chemistry, mineralogy, fertility and testing of soils, soil-crop nutrition, plant analysis, liming and fertilization of soils and techniques for correcting deficiencies.
**Readers:** Agronomists, horticulturists, floriculturists, plant physiologists, soil scientists, agriculturists.

22473

## ENVIRONMENTAL ENTOMOLOGY
9301 Annapolis Rd.
Lanham, MD 20706
Telephone: (301) 731-4535
FAX: (301) 731-4538
Year Established: 1972
Pub. Frequency: bi-m.
Page Size: standard
Subscrip. Rate: $25/yr. members; $75/yr. nonmembers; $150/yr. institutions
Circulation: 3,350
Circulation Type: paid
**Owner(s):**
Entomological Society of America
9301 Annapolis Rd.
Lanham, MD 20706
Telephone: (301) 731-4535
Ownership %: 100
**Management:**
Harry Bradley .........................Executive Director
Paul Moniz ....................................Sales Manager
**Editorial:**
Kaye O. Meckley ...................Assistant Director
Raymond L. Evergam, Jr. ......Assistant Director for Communications
Jennifer Yearwood ..................Communications Director

**Desc.:** Publishes only original research articles on the behavior of insects and their interaction with the biological, chemical and physical constituents of their environment.
**Readers:** Primarily professional entomologists, biologists and students.

58746

## HUMAN BIOLOGY: INTERNATIONAL JOURNAL OF EVOLUTION & GENETICS
5959 Woodward Ave.
Detroit, MI 48202
Telephone: (313) 577-6120
FAX: (313) 577-6131
Year Established: 1929
Pub. Frequency: 6/yr.
Page Size: standard
Subscrip. Rate: $60/yr. individual; $105/yr. institution
Circulation: 1,654
Circulation Type: paid
**Owner(s):**
Wayne State University Press
5959 Woodward Ave.
Detroit, MI 48202
Telephone: (313) 577-6120
Ownership %: 100
**Editorial:**
Michael H. Crawford ...............................Editor
**Desc.:** The new focus of the journal is genetics in the broadest sense. Included under this rubric are population genetics, evolutionary and genetic demography, quantitative genetics, genetic epidemiology, behavioral genetics, molecular genetics, growth and physiology parameters focusing on genetic-environmental interactions.

## INDUSTRIAL BIOPROCESSING
61271

32 N. Dean St.
Englewood, NJ 07631
Telephone: (201) 568-4744
FAX: (201) 568-8247
Mailing Address:
　　P.O. Box 1304
　　Fort Lee, NJ 07024-1304
Year Established: 1978
Pub. Frequency: m.
Page Size: standard
Subscrip. Rate: $545/yr.
Materials: 04,28,29,30,31
**Owner(s):**
Technical Insights, Inc.
P.O. Box 1304
Fort Lee, NJ 07024-1304
Telephone: (201) 568-4744
Ownership %: 100
**Editorial:**
Karen Dean .............................Editor
**Desc.:** We publish short articles about new
technology in the area of biotechnology,
energy, and waste treatment. We also
publish market forecasts for areas in
which biotechnology will have an impact.
**Readers:** Corporate management in
companies involved in biotechnology.

## JOURNAL OF APPLIED BIOMECHANICS (JAB)
58613

1607 N. Market St.
Champaign, IL 61820
Telephone: (217) 351-5076
FAX: (217) 351-2674
Mailing Address:
　　P.O. Box 5076
　　Champaign, IL 61825
Year Established: 1985
Pub. Frequency: q.
Page Size: standard
Subscrip. Rate: $24/yr. students; $36/yr.
individuals; $80/yr. institutions
Materials: 10,25,29
Print Process: offset
Circulation: 1,025
Circulation Type: paid
**Owner(s):**
Human Kinetics Publishers, Inc.
1607 N. Market St.
Champaign, IL 61820
Telephone: (217) 351-5076
FAX: (217) 351-2674
Ownership %: 100
**Management:**
Rainer Martens ............................Publisher
Julie Anderson ............................Manager
**Editorial:**
Robert J. Gregor ...........................Editor
Linda A. Bump ...............Journals Director
**Desc.:** JAB is the single international
source for research, scholarly work and
information concerning the applied
aspects of human biomechanics in
sport, exercise and rehabilitation.
**Readers:** Members of the International
Society for Biomechanics of Sport.

## JOURNAL OF BACTERIOLOGY
23832

1325 Massachusetts Ave., N.W.
Washington, DC 20005-4171
Telephone: (202) 737-3600
Year Established: 1916
Pub. Frequency: s-m.
Page Size: standard
Subscrip. Rate: $378/yr.
Materials: 02,06,32
Print Process: web offset
Circulation: 7,000
Circulation Type: paid

**Owner(s):**
American Society for Microbiology
1325 Massachusetts Ave., N.W.
Washington, DC 20005
Telephone: (202) 737-3600
Ownership %: 100
**Editorial:**
Graham C. Walker .................Editor in Chief
L. M. Illig ...............................Director
**Desc.:** The leading periodical worldwide,
devoted to the advancement of
fundamental knowledge concerning
bacteria and other microorganism,
including fungi and other unicellular,
eukaryotic organisms. Regular features
in this superbly comprehensive journal
include articles on structure and
function, plant microbiology, membranes,
eukaryotic cells, genetics and molecular
biology, population genetics and
evolution, plasmids and transposons,
bacteriophages, physiology and
metabolism, and enzymology.
**Readers:** Laboratory and chemical
researchers, microbiologists,
biotechnologists.

## JOURNAL OF BIOACTIVE & COMPATIBLE POLYMERS
58796

851 New Holland Ave.
Lancaster, PA 17601
Telephone: (717) 291-5609
FAX: (717) 295-4538
Mailing Address:
　　P.O. Box 3535
　　Lancaster, PA 17601
Year Established: 1986
Pub. Frequency: q.
Subscrip. Rate: $260/yr.; $510/2 yrs.;
$760/3 yrs.
Circulation: 225
Circulation Type: paid
**Owner(s):**
Melvyn A. Kohudic
851 New Holland Ave.
Lancaster, PA 17601
Telephone: (717) 291-5609
Ownership %: 100
**Bureau(s):**
Technomic Publishing AG
Missionsstrasse 44
CH-4055 Basel Switzerland
Contact: Frank Versaci, Director
**Editorial:**
Raphael M. Ottenbrite .....................Editor
**Desc.:** The primary emphasis is to provide
a forum for both biological scientists and
polymer chemists to publish refereed
research papers and short
communications in an area that is of
common interest.

## JOURNAL OF BIOMATERIALS APPLICATIONS
58740

851 New Holland Ave.
Lancaster, PA 17601
Telephone: (717) 291-5609
FAX: (717) 295-4538
Mailing Address:
　　P.O. Box 3535
　　Lancaster, PA 17601
Year Established: 1986
Pub. Frequency: q.
Subscrip. Rate: $260/yr.; $510/2 yrs.;
$760/3 yrs.
Circulation: 200
Circulation Type: paid
**Owner(s):**
Melvyn A. Kohudic
851 New Holland Ave.
Lancaster, PA 17601
Telephone: (717) 291-5609

**Bureau(s):**
Technomic Publishing AG
Missionsstrasse 44
CH-4055 Basel Switzerland
Contact: Frank Versaci, Director
**Editorial:**
Michael Szycher ..............................Editor
**Desc.:** Original research and review
articles on biomaterials and their clinical
uses.

## JOURNAL OF BIOMEDICAL MATERIALS RESEARCH
59142

605 Third Ave.
New York, NY 10158
Telephone: (212) 692-6026
Year Established: 1966
Pub. Frequency: 15/yr.
Subscrip. Rate: $405/yr.
**Owner(s):**
James M. Anderson
605 Third Ave.
New York, NY 10158
Telephone: (212) 692-6000
Ownership %: 100
**Management:**
Mary E. Curtis ...........................Publisher
**Editorial:**
A. Norman Cranin .................Editor in Chief
**Desc.:** Evaluates preparation methods and
use of plastics ceramics, metals and
processed animal tissue in fabrication of
equipment and instrumentation used in
medecine and biology.

## JOURNAL OF CLINICAL MICROBIOLOGY
23839

1325 Massachusetts Ave., N.W.
Washington, DC 20005-4171
Telephone: (202) 737-3600
Year Established: 1975
Pub. Frequency: m.
Page Size: standard
Subscrip. Rate: $264/yr. non-member
Materials: 02,06,32
Print Process: web offset
Circulation: 13,600
Circulation Type: paid
**Owner(s):**
American Society for Microbiology
1325 Massachusetts Ave., N.W.
Washington, DC 20005-4171
Telephone: (202) 737-3600
Ownership %: 100
**Editorial:**
Richard C. Tilton ..................Editor in Chief
L.M. Illig ...............................Director
**Desc.:** Concerned with the microbiological
aspects of human and animal infections
and infestations. Particular emphasis is
given to their etiological agents,
diagnosis, and epidemiology. Articles on
quality control procedures, applications
and evaluations of commercially
prepared tests or kits, phage typing
systems, automation, and technological
developments are included.
**Readers:** Clinical microbiologists,
pathologists, laboratory technologists.

## JOURNAL OF PLANT NUTRITION
70385

270 Madison Ave.
New York, NY 10016
Telephone: (212) 696-9000
FAX: (212) 685-4540
Year Established: 1977
Pub. Frequency: 12/yr.
Page Size: standard
Subscrip. Rate: $387.50/yr. individuals;
$775/yr. institutions

**Owner(s):**
Marcel Dekker, Inc.
270 Madison Ave.
New York, NY 10016
Telephone: (212) 696-9000
Ownership %: 100
**Editorial:**
J. Benton Jones, Jr. ........................Editor
Harry A. Mills ..................Associate Editor
**Desc.:** This journal is devoted to the rapid
communication of outstanding papers
exploring the influence of the mineral
elements on plant physiology and
growth.
**Readers:** Horticulturists, botanists, soil
scientists, agronomists, plant
physiologists, phytologists.

## JOURNAL OF VIROLOGY
65662

1325 Massachusetts Ave., N.W.
Washington, DC 20005-4171
Telephone: (202) 737-3600
Year Established: 1967
Pub. Frequency: m.
Page Size: standard
Subscrip. Rate: $380/yr.
Materials: 02,06,32
Print Process: web offset
Circulation: 5,230
Circulation Type: paid
**Owner(s):**
American Society for Microbiology
1325 Massachusetts Ave., N.W.
Washington, DC 20005
Telephone: (202) 737-3600
**Editorial:**
Arnold J. Levine ....................Editor in Chief
Linda M. Illig ...............................Director
**Desc.:** Publishes fundamental new
information concerning the viruses of
bacteria, plants, and animals. The
Journal specifically encourages
publications relating viruses under study
to their host cells or organisms. Sections
include "Viral and Cellular Oncogens,"
"Viral Pathogensis and Immunity," "Virus
- Cell Interactions," "Animal Viruses,"
and "Plant viruses." biologists should
strongly consider a subscription
**Readers:** Virologists, molecular & cellular
biologists, cancer researchers,
immunologists.

## JOURNAL OF WILDLIFE REHABILITATION
68702

4437 Central Pl., Ste. B4
Suisun, CA 94585-1669
Telephone: (707) 864-1761
FAX: (707) 864-3106
Year Established: 1977
Pub. Frequency: q.
Page Size: standard
Subscrip. Rate: $38/yr. to individuals;
institutions $48/yr.
Materials: 10
Print Process: offset lithography
Circulation: 1,500
Circulation Type: paid
**Owner(s):**
International Wildlife Rehabilitation Council
4437 Central Pl., Ste. B4
Suisun, CA 94585-1669
Telephone: (707) 864-1761
FAX: (707) 864-3106
**Editorial:**
Jan White ...................................Editor
**Desc.:** Dedicated to the dissemination of
information related to the field of wildlife
rehabilitation.
**Readers:** Wildlife rehabilitators,
veterinarians, biologists

**Materials Accepted/Included:** 01-Business news 02-By-line articles 03-Fashion news 04-Food news 05-Freelance copy 06-Letters to editor 07-Real estate news 08-Sports news 09-Travel news 10-Book rev. 11-Movie rev. 12-Music rev. 13-TV rev. 14-Theater rev. 15-Coming events 16-Obituaries 17-Question & answer 18-Social announcements 19-Artwork 20-Cartoons 21-Photos 22-TV listings 23-Audio rec. 24-Video rec. 25-Books 26-Films/film clips 27-Personnel news 28-Press releases 29-New product news/photos 30-Trade lit. 31-Contracts awarded 32-Display adv. 33-Classified adv.

4-43

## LIFE SCIENCES
66485

660 White Plains Rd.
Tarrytown, NY 10523
Telephone: (914) 524-9200
FAX: (914) 333-2444
Year Established: 1962
Pub. Frequency: 52/yr.
Page Size: standard
Subscrip. Rate: $296/yr. individuals;
$2140/yr. institutions
Circulation: 1,109
Circulation Type: paid
**Owner(s):**
Elsevier Science, Ltd.
The Boulevard, Langford Lane
Kidlington
OX5 1GB Oxford United Kingdom
Telephone: 44-865-843000
Ownership %: 100
**Bureau(s):**
Univerity of Arizona Health Science
1501 N. Campbell
Tuscon, AZ 85724
Telephone: (602) 626-2449
Contact: Rubin Bressler, Executive Editor

Life Sciences
Synthelabo Recherche (L.R.R.S.)
B.P. 110-31 Avenue Paul Valliant Couturier
92225 Bagneux Cedex France
Contact: Dr. S.Z. Langer, Executive Editor
**Management:**
Roger A. Dunn ......................General Manager
Mike Boswood ....................Managing Director
**Editorial:**
Jay Feinman ..............................Advertising
Christine Giaccone ......Senior Publishing Editor
**Desc.:** This is an international weekly
journal publishing full length on research
in a range of areas in the life sciences.
These areas include molecular and
cellular aspects of cardiovascular &
autonomic mechanisms, endocrinology,
immunology, toxicology, drug
metabolism, growth factors & neoplasia,
neuroscience.

## MICROBIOLOGICAL REVIEWS
23914

1325 Massachusetts Ave., N.W.
Washington, DC 20005-4171
Telephone: (202) 737-3600
Year Established: 1937
Pub. Frequency: q.
Page Size: standard
Subscrip. Rate: $126/yr. US non-member
Materials: 02,32
Print Process: web offset
Circulation: 11,770
Circulation Type: paid
**Owner(s):**
American Society For Microbiology
1325 Massachusetts Ave., N.W.
Washington, DC 20005-4171
Telephone: (202) 737-3600
Ownership %: 100
**Editorial:**
W.K. Joklik ......................Editor in Chief
L.M. Illig ...................................Director
**Desc.:** Provides its wide readership with in-
depth reviews and monographs dealing
with all aspects of microbiology and
other related fields, such as
immunology. Also includes historical
analyses.
**Readers:** Laboratory workers,
microbiologists, virologists, clinicians,
molecular biologists, and immunologists.

## MOLECULAR BIOLOGY & EVOLUTION
68700

5702 S. Woodlawn Ave.
Chicago, IL 60637
Telephone: (312) 753-3347
Year Established: 1983

Pub. Frequency: bi-m.
Subscrip. Rate: $54/yr. individuals;
$275/yr. institutions; $43/yr. students
Circulation: 1000
Circulation Type: paid
**Owner(s):**
University of Chicago Press
5702 S. Woodlawn Ave.
Chicago, IL 60637
Telephone: (312) 753-3347
Ownership %: 100
**Editorial:**
Walter M. Fitch ...........................Editor

## MUSCLE & NERVE
59144

605 Third Ave.
New York, NY 10158-0012
Telephone: (212) 850-6000
FAX: (212) 850-6088
Year Established: 1979
Pub. Frequency: m.
Subscrip. Rate: $530/yr. US; $650/yr.
Canada & Mexico; $695/yr. foreign
Circulation: 3,500
**Owner(s):**
John Wiley & Sons, Inc.
605 Third Ave.
New York, NY 10158-0012
Telephone: (212) 850-6000
Ownership %: 100
**Management:**
Mary E. Curtis ............................Publisher
**Editorial:**
Walter G. Bradley ...........................Editor
Jun Kimura ....................................Editor
Christina Sheperd ...............Managing Editor
Laurel Bernstein ...................Film Buyer
Dora Castiblanco ............................Sales
**Desc.:** Covers muscle, the peripheral
motor and sensory neurons, and the
neuromuscular junction in both health
and disease.

## NAUTILUS
24884

8911 Alton Pkwy.
Silver Spring, MD 20910
Telephone: (202) 786-2073
Mailing Address:
P.O. Box 7279
Silver Spring, MD 20907
Year Established: 1886
Pub. Frequency: q.
Page Size: standard
Subscrip. Rate: $25/yr. individual; $40/yr.
institution
**Owner(s):**
Trophon Corp.
P.O. Box 7279
Silver Spring, MD 20907
Telephone: (202) 786-2073
Ownership %: 100
**Management:**
M. G. Harasewych .........................President
Trophon Corp. ..............................Publisher
J. Harasewych ..................Business Manager
**Editorial:**
M. G. Harasewych ...............Editor in Chief
**Desc.:** Articles devoted to interests of
malacologists. Cover new species, life-
cycles, and reproductive aspects of
mollusks, fresh water, land and marine.
**Readers:** Institutions, professionals,
students.

## NUCLEOSIDES & NUCLEOTIDES
70389

270 Madison Ave.
New York, NY 10016
Telephone: (212) 696-9000
FAX: (212) 685-4540
Year Established: 1981
Pub. Frequency: 10/yr.
Page Size: standard
Subscrip. Rate: $362.50/yr. individuals;
$725/yr. institutions

**Owner(s):**
Marcel Dekker, Inc.
270 Madison Ave.
New York, NY 10016
Telephone: (212) 696-9000
FAX: (212) 685-4540
Ownership %: 100
**Editorial:**
John A. Secrist, III ...........................Editor
**Desc.:** This all-inclusive journal features
research articles; short notices; and
concise, critical reviews of related topics
in the organic and medicinal chemistry
and biochemistry of nucleosides and
nucleotides. Presenting the latest
original research papers with complete
experimental details emphasizing the
synthesis, biological activities, new and
improved synthetic methods, and
significant observations relating to new
compounds.
**Readers:** organic and medicinal chemists,
biochemists, pharmacologists,
reserachers in recombinant DNA
technology.

## PHYTOPATHOLOGY
70423

Washington State University
Plant Pathology Dept.
Pullman, WA 99164-6430
Telephone: (509) 335-1187
FAX: (509) 335-9581
Pub. Frequency: m.
Page Size: standard
Subscrip. Rate: $235/yr. US non-member;
$280/yr. elesewhere
**Owner(s):**
The American Phytopathological Society
3340 Piot Knob Rd.
St. Paul, MN 55121-2097
Telephone: (612) 454-7250
Ownership %: 100
**Management:**
Steven Nelson ............................Publisher
Steve Kronmiller ..........Production Manager
**Editorial:**
Carol Pagel ...............Circulation Coordinator
Jean Rice ....................Editorial Supervisor
Miles Wimer ...............Publication Director

## PROCEEDINGS OF THE ENTOMOLOGICAL SOCIETY OF WASHINGTON
24892

U.S. National Museum of Natural History
Smithsonian Institution NHB 168
Washington, DC 20560
Telephone: (202) 382-1802
Year Established: 1884
Pub. Frequency: q.
Page Size: standard
Subscrip. Rate: $60/yr.; $70/yr. foreign
Materials: 02,10,16
Circulation: 800
Circulation Type: paid
**Owner(s):**
Entomological Society of Washington
US Natl Museum-Natural History
Washington, DC 20560
Ownership %: 100
**Editorial:**
Thomas J. Henry ...........................Editor
**Desc.:** Publishes origianal scientific papers
and reports minutes of society meetings.
Reviews of natural history books
included.
**Readers:** Entomologists, and biologists.

## PROGRESS IN BIO-MEDICAL RESEARCH
5144

7620 N.W. Loop, Rm. 410
San Antonio, TX 78227
Telephone: (210) 674-1410
FAX: (210) 670-3301

Mailing Address:
P.O. Box 28147
San Antonio, TX 78228
Year Established: 1950
Pub. Frequency: q.
Page Size: standard
Subscrip. Rate: free
Freelance Pay: negotiable
Print Process: offset
Circulation: 6,000
Circulation Type: controlled & free
**Owner(s):**
S.W. Foundation for Bio-Medical Research
7620 N.W. Loop, Rm. 410
San Antonio, TX 78227
Telephone: (210) 674-1410
Ownership %: 100
**Editorial:**
Stacey Maloney ...........................Editor

## QUARTERLY REVIEW OF BIOLOGY
69394

5720 S. Woodlawn Ave.
Chicago, IL 60637
Telephone: (312) 753-3347
FAX: (312) 753-0811
Year Established: 1926
Pub. Frequency: q.
Subscrip. Rate: $31/yr. individual; $80/yr.
institution
Circulation: 3,200
**Owner(s):**
University of Chicago Press
5720 S. Woodlawn Ave.
Chicago, IL 60637
Telephone: (312) 753-3347
Ownership %: 100
**Editorial:**
Frank Erk ....................................Editor
George Williams .............................Editor
**Desc.:** Features recent research and
software reviews in the various fields of
the biological sciences.

## SERIAL SOURCES FOR THE BIOSIS PREVIEWS DATABASE
49920

2100 Arch St.
Philadelphia, PA 19103-1399
Telephone: (215) 587-4800
Pub. Frequency: a.
Page Size: standard
Subscrip. Rate: $60/yr.
**Owner(s):**
BioSciences Information Service (BIOSIS)
2100 Arch St.
Philadelphia, PA 19103
Telephone: (215) 587-4800
Ownership %: 100
**Management:**
J.E. Anderson ..............................President
D.J. Molitor ..........................Vice President
D.J. Hoffman .........................Vice President
M. Kelly ...............................Vice President
D. J. Castagna ......................Vice President
**Desc.:** Serial Sources provides a list of all
source materials of a serial nature
monitored by BIOSIS. Includes serial
title, ISSN, CODEN, frequency, and
publisher's address for approximately 6,
5 00 active serials and 11,000 archival
titles published in over 100 countries.
**Readers:** Professional, libraries.

## SOIL BIOLOGY & BIOCHEMISTRY
69404

660 White Plains Rd.
Tarrytown, NY 10591-5153
Telephone: (914) 524-9200
FAX: (914) 333-2444
Year Established: 1969
Pub. Frequency: 12/yr.
Circulation: 1,250

**Materials Accepted/Included:** 01-Business news 02-By-line articles 03-Fashion news 04-Food news 05-Freelance copy 06-Letters to editor 07-Real estate news 08-Sports news 09-Travel news 10-Book rev. 11-Movie rev. 12-Music rev. 13-TV rev. 14-Theater rev. 15-Coming events 16-Obituaries 17-Question & answer 18-Social announcements 19-Artwork 20-Cartoons 21-Photos 22-TV listings 23-Audio rec. 24-Video rec. 25-Books 26-Films/film clips 27-Personnel news 28-Press releases 29-New product news/photos 30-Trade lit. 31-Contracts awarded 32-Display adv. 33-Classified adv.

**Owner(s):**
Pergamon Press, Inc.
660 White Plains Rd.
Tarrytown, NY 10591-5153
Telephone: (914) 524-9200
Ownership %: 100
**Editorial:**
J.S. Waid ..................................Editor
**Desc.:** Provides a forum for research on soil organisms, their biochemical activities, and the influence on the soil environment and plant growth.

53
69445

## WETLANDS
1451 Green Rd.
Ann Arbor, MI 48105
Telephone: (313) 994-3331
FAX: (313) 994-8780
Year Established: 1981
Pub. Frequency: q.
Page Size: standard
Subscrip. Rate: $40/yr. membership; $100/yr. institutions
Materials: 02
Print Process: electronic
Circulation: 3,500
Circulation Type: paid
**Owner(s):**
Society of Wetlands Scientists
P.O. Box 1897.
Lawrence, KS 66044
Telephone: (913) 843-1235
Ownership %: 100
**Editorial:**
Douglas A. Wilcox ..................Editor

23987

## YALE JOURNAL OF BIOLOGY & MEDICINE, THE
333 Cedar St.
New Haven, CT 06510
Telephone: (203) 785-4251
Year Established: 1928
Pub. Frequency: bi-m.
Page Size: standard
Subscrip. Rate: $45/yr. individuals; $90/yr. institutions
Circulation: 500
Circulation Type: paid
**Owner(s):**
Yale Journal of Biology And Medicine, Inc.
333 Cedar St.
New Haven, CT 06510
Telephone: (203) 785-4251
Ownership %: 100
**Management:**
William C. Summers ......................Publisher
**Editorial:**
William C. Summers ..............Editor in Chief
Emile L. Boulpaep ................Editor in Chief
Robert S. Baltimore ................Associate Editor
James F. Jekel ..................Associate Editor
John T. Stitt ......................Associate Editor
Mary G. McCrea Curnen ..........Associate Editor
Larry Scahill ......................Associate Editor
**Desc.:** Carries original contributions in all fields of bio-medical science, and in the history and teaching of these subjects, interesting medical reviews and case reports. Also publishes symposia in related fields. Illustrations used with articles only. Includes book reviews.
**Readers:** Professional.

52663

## ZOOLOGICAL RECORD
2100 Arch St.
Philadelphia, PA 19103
Telephone: (215) 587-4800
FAX: (215) 587-2016
Year Established: 1865
Pub. Frequency: a.
Page Size: standard
Subscrip. Rate: $2,400/yr.

**Owner(s):**
BIOSIS
2100 Arch St.
Philadelphia, PA 19103
Telephone: (215) 587-4800
Ownership %: 100
**Management:**
John E. Anderson ......................President
**Editorial:**
Marcia Edwards ......................Editor
Maureen Kelly ......................Director
D.J. Castagna ......................Director
D.J. Molitor ......................Director
Diane Hoffman ..................Marketing Director
Robert O'Malley ..............Marketing Specialist
**Desc.:** Provides a comprehensive index to zoological publications which have appeared worldwide in the preceding year.
**Readers:** Scientists, researchers, librarians, and students.

# Group 030-Boating Industry

23667

## BOATING INDUSTRY
5 Penn Plz., 13th Fl.
New York, NY 10001-1810
Telephone: (212) 613-9700
FAX: (212) 613-9749
Year Established: 1929
Pub. Frequency: m.
Page Size: standard
Subscrip. Rate: $30/yr.
Materials: 01,02,05,06,19,20,21,27,28,29, 30,32,33
Freelance Pay: negotiable
Print Process: offset
Circulation: 31,248
Circulation Type: controlled & paid
**Owner(s):**
Argus Business
6151 Powers Ferry Rd., N.W.
Atlanta, GA 30339-2941
Telephone: (404) 955-2500
Ownership %: 100
**Bureau(s):**
Ken Silverstein
 Washington
Contact: Ken Silverstein, Editor
**Management:**
Jerry France ......................President
Ted Lotz ......................Publisher
**Editorial:**
Richard W. Porter ......................Editor
**Desc.:** Presents ideas, role models, and guidance for boat and accessory retailers to operate their businesses more effectively and profitably. Includes information on marine management, merchandising and selling, market analysis, industry trends and new products.
**Readers:** Boat and motor dealers, distributors, boat builders and manufacturer reps.
**Deadline:** story-end of mo., two mos. prior to cover mo.; ads-end of mo., two mos. prior to cover mo.

67294

## CANOE & KAYAK INDUSTRY NEWS
P.O. Box 3146
Kirkland, WA 98083
Telephone: (206) 827-6363
FAX: (206) 827-5177
Year Established: 1986
Pub. Frequency: 4/yr.
Page Size: standard
Subscrip. Rate: $30/yr.
Circulation: 3,000
Circulation Type: paid

**Owner(s):**
Canoe America Associates
P.O. Box 3146
Kirkland, WA 98083
Telephone: (206) 827-6363
Ownership %: 100
**Management:**
Dennis Stuhaug ......................Publisher
**Editorial:**
David Harrison ..................Editor in Chief
Glen Bernard ..................Advertising Director

68739

## INTERNATIONAL MARINE BUSINESS
1766 Bay Rd.
Miami Beach, FL 33139
Telephone: (305) 538-0700
Year Established: 1989
Pub. Frequency: s-a.
Circulation: 26,000
Circulation Type: paid
**Owner(s):**
Marine Business Journal
1766 Bay Rd.
Miami Beach, FL 33139
Telephone: (305) 538-0700
Ownership %: 100
**Editorial:**
Andree Conrad ......................Editor
**Desc.:** Covers products and services in the US marine industry.

68740

## MARINE STORE MERCHANDISING
12 Oaks Ctr., Ste. 922
Wayzata, MN 55391
Telephone: (612) 473-5088
FAX: (612) 473-7068
Year Established: 1990
Pub. Frequency: 8/yr.
Page Size: standard
Subscrip. Rate: $24/yr.
Materials: 01,05,06,19,20,21,27,28,29,30, 32,33
Print Process: web offset
Circulation: 15000
Circulation Type: paid
**Owner(s):**
RCM Enterprises, Inc.
Twelve Oaks Center, Ste. 922
Wayzata, MN 55391
Telephone: (612) 473-5088
Ownership %: 100
**Management:**
Robert C. Mead ......................Publisher
**Editorial:**
Scott Heimes ......................Editor

23683

## POWERBOAT MAGAZINE
1691 Spinnaker Dr., Ste. 206
Ventura, CA 93001-4378
Telephone: (805) 639-2222
FAX: (805) 639-2220
Year Established: 1968
Pub. Frequency: m.; Nov.-Dec. combined
Page Size: standard
Subscrip. Rate: $3.95 newsstand; $27/yr. US; $38/yr. foreign
Materials: 01,02,03,05,06,08,15,17,21,23, 24,25,26,27,28,29,30,32,33
Freelance Pay: $300-$1,000
Print Process: web offset
Circulation: 47,000
Circulation Type: controlled & paid
**Owner(s):**
Nordco Publishing, Inc.
Telephone: (818) 989-1820
Ownership %: 100
**Management:**
Gerald Nordskog ......................Publisher
Chris Mornes ..................Sales Manager
**Editorial:**
Eric Colby ..................Managing Editor
Rob Destocki ..................Art Director
Tosh Arimura ..................Marketing Director

**Desc.:** Powerboat reports on news and trends in the performance boating world. Editorial content deals solely with power boats. Departments include: Competition, Features, Technical.
**Readers:** Performance-minded boaters and water skiers.

67680

## PRACTICAL SAILOR
151 Allston Ave.
Middletown, RI 02840
Telephone: (401) 849-8911
FAX: (401) 849-5812
Mailing Address:
 P.O. Box 819
 Newport, RI 02840
Year Established: 1974
Pub. Frequency: bi-w.
Page Size: standard
Subscrip. Rate: $72/yr.
Materials: 24,25,28,29
Circulation: 50,000
Circulation Type: paid
**Owner(s):**
Belvoir Publications, Inc.
P.O. Box 2626
Greenwich, CT 06836
Telephone: (203) 661-6111
Ownership %: 100
**Management:**
Robert Englander ......................President
Robert Englander ......................Publisher
**Editorial:**
Daniel Spurr ......................Editor
**Desc.:** Boats and related gear are tested and evaluated; recommendations are given. Practical Sailor accepts no advertising.
**Readers:** Sailboat owners

67224

## PROFESSIONAL BOATBUILDER
Naskeag Rd.
Brooklin, ME 04616-0078
Telephone: (207) 359-4651
FAX: (207) 359-8920
Mailing Address:
 P.O. Box 78
 Brooklin, ME 04616
Year Established: 1989
Pub. Frequency: bi-m.
Page Size: standard
Subscrip. Rate: free to qualified personnel
Materials: 29,30,32,33
Print Process: offset
Circulation: 20,000
Circulation Type: controlled
**Owner(s):**
Woodenboat Publications, Inc.
Naskeag Rd.
Brooklin, ME 04616-0078
Telephone: (207) 359-4651
FAX: (207) 359-8920
Ownership %: 100
**Management:**
Jon Wilson ......................President
Carl Cramer ......................Publisher
**Editorial:**
Chris Cornell ......................Editor
**Desc.:** For boat construction, repair, design and surveying company executives.

22072

## WORKBOAT
2101B Lakeshore
Mandeville, LA 70448
Telephone: (504) 626-0298
FAX: (504) 624-4801
Mailing Address:
 P.O. Box 1348
 Mandeville, LA 70470
Year Established: 1933
Pub. Frequency: bi-m.
Page Size: standard
Subscrip. Rate: $20/yr.

Materials Accepted/Included: 01-Business news 02-By-line articles 03-Fashion news 04-Food news 05-Freelance copy 06-Letters to editor 07-Real estate news 08-Sports news 09-Travel news 10-Book rev. 11-Movie rev. 12-Music rev. 13-TV rev. 14-Theater rev. 15-Coming events 16-Obituaries 17-Question & answer 18-Social announcements 19-Artwork 20-Cartoons 21-Photos 22-TV listings 23-Audio rec. 24-Video rec. 25-Books 26-Films/film clips 27-Personnel news 28-Press releases 29-New product news/photos 30-Trade lit. 31-Contracts awarded 32-Display adv. 33-Classified adv.

4-45

Freelance Pay: negotiable
Circulation: 16,500
Circulation Type: controlled
**Owner(s):**
Journal Publications
P.O. Box 1348
Mandeville, LA 70470
Telephone: (504) 626-3151
Ownership %: 100
**Management:**
Bruce Cole .............................Publisher
**Editorial:**
Don Nelson ...............................Editor
**Desc.:** News and feature stories relating
directly to commercial boats, gear,
equipment, new developments in these
fields; coverage of new vessel building
with specifications and details of gear;
general articles relating to legislation,
research, etc. In short, coverage of all
phases of commercial work boats and
fields directly related. Departments
include: Items on Organizations, Boats in
the News; People in the Industry.
**Readers:** Commercial boat owners and
operators, documented, on all inland
and coastal waterways.

## Group 032-Building & Construction

**ABC TODAY**
69488
1300 N. 17th St.
Rosslyn, VA 22209
Telephone: (703) 812-2063
FAX: (703) 812-8203
Year Established: 1953
Pub. Frequency: bi-w.
Page Size: tabloid
Subscrip. Rate: $42/yr. members; $60/yr.
non-members
Circulation: 22,000
Circulation Type: paid
**Owner(s):**
Associated Builders & Contractors, Inc.
729 15th St., N.W.
Washington, DC 20005
Telephone: (202) 637-8800
Ownership %: 100
**Editorial:**
Michael Henderson ......................Editor

**ABERDEEN'S CONCRETE
JOURNAL & TRADER**
66763
426 S. Westgate
Addison, IL 60101
Telephone: (708) 543-0870
FAX: (708) 543-5399
Year Established: 1983
Pub. Frequency: m.
Page Size: tabloid
Subscrip. Rate: free to members
Circulation: 15,000
Circulation Type: controlled
**Owner(s):**
Aberdeen Group, The
Ownership %: 100
**Management:**
Mirlam Wuensch ...................Publisher
**Editorial:**
Martha McIntyre ........................Editor
**Readers:** Producers of concrete products
and ready mix.

**ABERDEEN'S CONSTRUCTION
MARKETING TODAY**
66760
426 S. Westgate
Addison, IL 60101
Telephone: (708) 543-0870
FAX: (708) 543-3112
Year Established: 1990
Pub. Frequency: m.

Page Size: tabloid
Subscrip. Rate: $27/yr.
Materials: 01,02,05,06,32
Print Process: sheet fed
Circulation: 3,700
Circulation Type: controlled & paid
**Owner(s):**
Aberdeen Group, The
Ownership %: 100
**Management:**
Diana Granitto ......................Publisher
**Editorial:**
Diana Granitto ........................Editor
**Desc.:** News and feature articles cover
trends in the construction marketplace,
marketing activities of construction
suppliers, product sales and distribution
channels, and principles of marketing
and advertising as applied to the
construction industry.
**Readers:** Manufacturers and others who
market in the construction industry

**ABERDEEN'S PAVEMENT
MAINTENANCE**
66747
426 S. Westgate St.
Addison, IL 60101
Telephone: (708) 543-0870
FAX: (708) 543-3112
Year Established: 1985
Pub. Frequency: 9/yr.
Page Size: standard
Subscrip. Rate: free to qualified personnel
Materials: 01,02,05,06,15,17,23,24,25,27,
28,29,30,32,33
Freelance Pay: negotiable
Print Process: web offset
Circulation: 25,000
Circulation Type: controlled
**Owner(s):**
Aberdeen Group, The
426 S. Westgate St.
Addison, IL 60101
Telephone: (708) 543-0870
Ownership %: 100
**Management:**
Janet E. Doyle ......................Publisher
**Editorial:**
Allan Heydorn ..........................Editor
**Deadline:** story-1st of mo.; news-1st of
mo.; photo-1st of mo.; ads-1st of mo.

**AUTOMATED BUILDER**
22137
4371 Carpinteria Ave.
Carpinteria, CA 93013
Telephone: (805) 684-7659
FAX: (805) 684-1765
Mailing Address:
P.O. Box 120
Carpinteria, CA 93014
Year Established: 1964
Pub. Frequency: m.
Page Size: standard
Subscrip. Rate: $6/copy; $40/yr.
Materials: 01,02,05,06,07,10,15,27,28,29,
30,32,33
Freelance Pay: $300/article with photos
Print Process: web offset
Circulation: 25,000
Circulation Type: controlled
**Owner(s):**
CMN Associates, Inc.
4371 Carpinteria Ave.
Carpinteria, CA 93013
Telephone: (805) 684-7659
FAX: (805) 684-1765
Ownership %: 100
**Management:**
Don O. Carlson .......................President
Don O. Carlson .......................Publisher
Lance Carlson .............Advertising Manager
**Editorial:**
Don O. Carlson .........................Editor
Mark Blocker ..................Associate Editor

Agnes Carlson ...............Secretary & Treasurer
**Desc.:** Articles on manufacturing and
marketing of manufactured homes,
mobile homes, modular homes &
apartments, and big volume home
builders. Covers new & improved
structural building methods (walls, floors,
roofs, and partitions). Departments
include: News, Products, Literature,
Equipment, People, New Home Ideas,
Coming Events.
**Readers:** Management persons in
industrialized/manufactured housing
and volume producers of homes &
apartments.

**BRICK ARCHITECTURE &
LANDSCAPE**
22189
169 Front St.
San Ramone, CA 94583
Year Established: 1964
Pub. Frequency: bi-m.
Page Size: standard
Subscrip. Rate: $6/yr.
Circulation: 11,787
Circulation Type: controlled & paid
**Owner(s):**
California Conference Mason Contractor
Assns., Inc
7844 Madison Ave., #153
Fair Oaks, CA 95628
Telephone: (916) 966-7666
Ownership %: 100
**Management:**
Alan Knapp ..........................Publisher
**Editorial:**
Nancy Michand .......................Editor
Nancy Michaud ..............Editorial Director
Alan Knapp ................New Products Editor
Alan Knapp .........................News Editor
**Desc.:** Any articles, features or news
stories relative to masonry.
**Readers:** Architects, building designers,
structural engineers, masonry
contractors, materials manufacturers,
block plants, dealers.

**BUILDER**
66721
One Thomas Circle
Washington, DC 20005
Telephone: (202) 452-0800
Year Established: 1977
Pub. Frequency: m.
Page Size: standard
Subscrip. Rate: $29.95/yr.
Materials: 01,02,05,06,07,10,15,17,19,20,
21,23,24,25,28,29,30,32,33
Freelance Pay: varies
Print Process: web offset
Circulation: 210,000
Circulation Type: controlled & paid
**Owner(s):**
Hanley-Wood, Inc.
One Thomas Circle, Ste. 600
Washington, DC 20005
Telephone: (202) 452-0800
Ownership %: 100
**Management:**
Mike Tucker ..........................Publisher
**Editorial:**
Noreen S. Welle ................Executive Editor
Mitchell B. Rouda ....................Editor
Lauren Taylor ....................Managing Editor
**Desc.:** For members of the National
Association of Home Builders.
Departments include: Economy (trends
and new laws that affect homebuilding),
Selling, Design, Business and Building
(technical articles and product
descriptions). In April a Buyer's Guide is
published in place of a conventional
issue. A House Plans issue is published
in mid-May.

**Readers:** Builders, developers, architects,
manufacturers, retailers, specialty
contractors, and distributors.
**Deadline:** story-1st of mo., 3 mo. prior to
pub. date; news-1st of mo., 3 mo. prior;
photo-1st of mo., 3 mo. prior; ads-1st of
mo., 1 mo. prior

**BUILDER/ARCHITECT**
22142
801 W. Maryland Ave.
Phoenix, AZ 85013
Telephone: (602) 433-7393
FAX: (602) 433-2963
Mailing Address:
P.O. Box 37707
Phoenix, AZ 85069
Year Established: 1938
Pub. Frequency: m.
Page Size: Standard
Subscrip. Rate: Free to home builders;
$18/yr.
Freelance Pay: $75-300
Circulation: 200,000
Circulation Type: controlled
**Owner(s):**
Sunshine Media, Inc.
801 W. Maryland Ave.
Ste. 100
Phoenix, AZ 85013
Telephone: (602) 433-7393
Ownership %: 100
**Management:**
Robert G. Loveridge ..................President
Keli Heath ................Advertising Manager
**Editorial:**
Marie Vere ...............................Editor
Keli Heath ......................Associate Editor
Marie Vere ..................New Products Editor
**Desc.:** Reports on new residential
construction projects, new products in
the field, people in the news and runs
related editorial for the residential
construction field.
**Readers:** Residential builders, residential
architects, residential remodelers and
suppliers to residential building trade.

**BUILDER INSIDER**
22143
3111 Cole Ave.
Dallas, TX 75204
Telephone: (214) 871-2913
Mailing Address:
P.O. Box 191125
Dallas, TX 75219
Year Established: 1975
Pub. Frequency: m.
Page Size: tabloid
Subscrip. Rate: Free to builders; $12/yr.
Freelance Pay: none
Circulation: 10,000
Circulation Type: controlled
**Owner(s):**
Divibest, Inc.
3111 Cole Ave.
Dallas, TX 75204
Telephone: (214) 871-2913
Ownership %: 100
**Management:**
Michael J. Anderson ..................President
Michael J. Anderson ..................Publisher
Sheryl Bishop ................Advertising Manager
**Editorial:**
Michael J. Anderson ....................Editor
Cindy Anderson ................Assistant Editor
**Desc.:** A business journal circulated to
qualified persons in the residential and
light commercial building industry and
other related fields.
**Readers:** Builders, remodelers,
contractors, architects, and developers.

Materials Accepted/Included: 01-Business news 02-By-line articles 03-Fashion news 04-Food news 05-Freelance copy 06-Letters to editor 07-Real estate news 08-Sports news 09-Travel news
10-Book rev. 11-Movie rev. 12-Music rev. 13-TV rev. 14-Theater rev. 15-Coming events 16-Obituaries 17-Question & answer 18-Social announcements 19-Artwork 20-Cartoons 21-Photos 22-TV listings
23-Audio rec. 24-Video rec. 25-Books 26-Films/film clips 27-Personnel news 28-Press releases 29-New product news/photos 30-Trade lit. 31-Contracts awarded 32-Display adv. 33-Classified adv.

## BUILDER PROFILE

69494

125 E. Lake St., Ste. 103
Bloomingdale, IL 60108
Telephone: (708) 582-8888
FAX: (708) 582-8895
Mailing Address:
 P. O. Box 354
 Bloomingdale, IL 60108
Year Established: 1988
Pub. Frequency: m.
Page Size: standard
Subscrip. Rate: $30/yr.
Materials: 01,06,07,28,29,30,32,33

Circulation: 7,300
Circulation Type: controlled & free

**Owner(s):**
Progressive Publishing
P.O. Box 354
Bloomingdale, IL 60108
Telephone: (708) 582-8888
FAX: (708) 582-8895
Ownership %: 100
**Management:**
Daniel Nugara .......................Publisher
Joseph Nugara ..................Advertising Manager
Joseph Nugara ..................Circulation Manager
Joseph Nugara ..........................Sales Manager
**Editorial:**
Arley Harriman .............................Editor in Chief
**Desc.:** Contains news, industry forecasts, new product information, technology trends and features on residential and light commercial builders.
**Deadline:** story-15th of mo. prior to pub. date; news-15th of mo. prior; photo-15th of mo. prior; ads-15th of mo. prior

## BUILDERS ASSOCIATION NEWS

22144

6464 Brentwood Stair Rd.
Fort Worth, TX 76112
Telephone: (817) 457-2864
FAX: (817) 457-2870
Year Established: 1954
Pub. Frequency: m.
Page Size: tabloid
Subscrip. Rate: $24/yr.
Circulation: 1,700
Circulation Type: controlled
**Owner(s):**
Builders Association of Ft. Worth & Tarrant County
6464 Brentwood Stair Rd.
Fort Worth, TX 76112
Telephone: (817) 457-2864
Ownership %: 100
**Management:**
Jerry Eisner ......................Advertising Manager
**Editorial:**
Jerry Eisner ...............................Executive Editor
**Desc.:** We tend to use only housing industry material. Most is worked on locally in our area and state plus features prepared by NAHB (National Assn. of Home Builders). We do not use new product features nor announcements of promotions elsewhere in the nation. Request no P.R. News Releases: Unable to use.
**Readers:** Members of the Builders Association & building industry.

## BUILDING BUSINESS & APARTMENT MANAGEMENT

22139

30375 Northwestern Hwy.
Ste. 100
Farmington Hills, MI 48334
Telephone: (810) 737-4477
FAX: (810) 737-5741
Year Established: 1936
Pub. Frequency: m.

Page Size: pg: 8 1/2 x 11; col: 2 5/16; photo: yes; mat: yes
Subscrip. Rate: Free to members; $36/yr.
Circulation: 7,500
Circulation Type: controlled
**Owner(s):**
Builders Association of Southeastern Michigan
30375 Northwestern Hwy.
Farmington Hills, MI 48334
Telephone: (810) 569-0644
Ownership %: 100
**Management:**
Susan Adler ......................Advertising Manager
**Editorial:**
Susan Adler ...............................Editor
**Desc.:** Covers all active residential builders of record in Michigan. Assists in expanding the area of home ownership with special articles, programs and home building promotional activities. Covers materials, equipment and services related to new residential construction.
**Readers:** Residential building industry of Michigan.

## BUILDING DESIGN & CONSTRUCTION

22145

1350 E. Touhy
Des Plaines, IL 60018
Telephone: (708) 635-8800
Mailing Address:
 P.O. Box 5080
 Des Plaines, IL 60017
Year Established: 1956
Pub. Frequency: m.
Page Size: standard
Subscrip. Rate: $20/copy (exc. July-$25); $89.95/yr.; $39.95/LOCATOR issue
Materials: 01,02,06,10,21,25,27,28,29,31,32,
Circulation: 78,600
Circulation Type: controlled
**Owner(s):**
Cahners Publishing Co./Div. Reed Holdings
1350 E. Touhy
Des Plaines, IL 60018
Telephone: (708) 635-8800
Ownership %: 100
**Management:**
Jack Hollfelder .............................Publisher
**Editorial:**
Christopher Olson ......................Editor in Chief
Gordon Wright .........................Senior Editor
John Gregerson .......................Managing Editor
Judy Murphy .................Administrative Assistant
Maureen Eaton .......................Associate Editor
Sue Casson .......................Production Editor
**Desc.:** Edited for the building team of owners, architects, engineers and construction management personnel involved in the design, construction and ownership of commercial, industrial and institutional buildings. Editorial stresses business and technology methods in design, construction and management.
**Readers:** Owners, architects, engineers, construction managers, contractors.
**Deadline:** story-3 mos.; news-3 mos.; photo-3 mos.; ads-1st of mo.

## BUILDING INDUSTRY

22146

287 Mokauea St.
Honolulu, HI 96819-3143
Telephone: (808) 848-0711
FAX: (808) 841-3053
Year Established: 1954
Pub. Frequency: m.
Page Size: standard
Subscrip. Rate: $25/yr.
Circulation: 5,000

Circulation Type: paid
**Owner(s):**
Trade Publishing Co.
287 Mokauea St.
Honolulu, HI 96819
Telephone: (808) 848-0711
Ownership %: 100
**Management:**
Carl Hebenstreit ......................President
Carl Hebenstreit ......................Publisher
Sandy Tottori ....................Advertising Manager
Blanche Pestana ....................Production Manager
**Editorial:**
Jim Crabtree .............................Editor
**Desc.:** Contains news and features relating to construction in Hawaii and the Pacific. The weekly supplement contains contract bid specifications and bid results, and is available only by paid subscription.
**Readers:** Hawaii-licensed contractors, architects and engineers, plus selected government agencies, financial institutions, realtors and developers.

## BUILDING OFFICIAL & CODE ADMINISTRATOR, THE

22148

4051 W. Flossmoor Rd.
Country Club Hills, IL 60478-5795
Telephone: (708) 799-2300
Year Established: 1915
Pub. Frequency: bi-m.
Page Size: standard
Subscrip. Rate: $18/yr.; $30/2 yrs.
Circulation: 12,800
Circulation Type: controlled
**Owner(s):**
Building Officials & Code Administrators Int'l
4051 W. Flossmoor Rd.
Country Club Hills, IL 60478-5795
Telephone: (708) 799-2300
Ownership %: 100
**Management:**
Donna L. Murphy ..............Advertising Manager
**Editorial:**
Paul K. Heilstedt ...................Executive Editor
William J. Even .......................Managing Editor
**Desc.:** Articles pertaining to building and related codes and their enforcement; also interested in new construction techniques or materials and factual (illustrated) examples. Departments include: Letters, General News, People, New Products, For Your Bookshelf.
**Readers:** Professional construction code enforcement officials at all levels, as well as architects, engineers and other building industry professionals. (Approx. 90% of readers are members of BOCA International.)

## BUILDINGS, FACILITIES CONSTRUCTION & MANAGEMENT MAGAZINE

22153

427 Sixth Ave., S.E.
Cedar Rapids, IA 52401
Telephone: (319) 364-6167
FAX: (319) 364-4278
Mailing Address:
 P.O. Box 1888
 Cedar Rapids, IA 52406
Year Established: 1906
Pub. Frequency: m.
Page Size: 4 color photos/art
Subscrip. Rate: $60/yr.
Materials: 01,06,07,15,25,27,28,29,30,32,33
Freelance Pay: negotiable
Print Process: web offset
Circulation: 42,000
Circulation Type: controlled

Owner(s):
Stamats Communications, Inc.
P.O. Box 1888
Cedar Rapids, IA 52406
Telephone: (319) 364-6167
Ownership %: 100
**Management:**
Wayne Bayliss ...........................Publisher
**Editorial:**
Linda Monroe ...............................Editor
**Desc.:** Devoted to operating, maintaining, managing, modernizing and constructing of office, shopping center, hotel & motel, healthcare, apartment & other commercial buildings.
**Readers:** Building owners, developers, corporate buying managers, facilities management personnel.
**Deadline:** news-2 mo. prior to pub. date; ads-1 mo. prior to pub. date

## BUILDING STANDARDS

22151

5360 Workman Mill Rd.
Whittier, CA 90601-2298
Telephone: (310) 699-0541
Year Established: 1922
Pub. Frequency: bi-m.
Page Size: standard
Subscrip. Rate: $23/yr.; $39/2 yrs.; $55/3 yrs.
Materials: 28,32
Print Process: web
Circulation: 16,000
Circulation Type: paid
**Owner(s):**
International Conference of Bldg. Officials
5360 Workman Mill Rd.
Whittier, CA 90601-2298
Telephone: (310) 699-0541
Ownership %: 100
**Management:**
Jon S. Traw .............................President
Cheryl Melendez ........................Vice President
**Editorial:**
Cheryl Melendez ....................Managing Editor
**Desc.:** Timely articles covering subjects of vital interest to the building official, architects, engineers, contractors, and all in the construction field. It is also the medium in which proposed code changes and the reports of various committees are communicated to members of the conference. It includes discussion and analysis of interpretations and applications of the uniform codes to special problems, thus reinforcing the uniformity attained through adoption of the codes.
**Readers:** Building officials, building inspectors, architects, engineers, fire officials, and construction industry representatives.

## CALIFORNIA BUILDER

22154

170 S. Spruce Ave., Ste. 120
South San Francisco, CA 94080
Telephone: (415) 588-8832
Year Established: 1959
Pub. Frequency: bi-m.
Page Size: standard
Subscrip. Rate: $19.80/yr.; $29.90/2 yrs.
Materials: 28,29,32
Freelance Pay: varies
Print Process: web offset
Circulation: 10,100
Circulation Type: controlled
**Owner(s):**
Fellom Publishing Co.
170 S. Spruce Ave., Ste. 120
S San Fran, CA 94080
Telephone: (415) 588-8832
Ownership %: 100
**Management:**
Ann Marie Fellom ...........................Publisher

**Materials Accepted/Included:** 01-Business news 02-By-line articles 03-Fashion news 04-Food news 05-Freelance copy 06-Letters to editor 07-Real estate news 08-Sports news 09-Travel news 10-Book rev. 11-Movie rev. 12-Music rev. 13-TV rev. 14-Theater rev. 15-Coming events 16-Obituaries 17-Question & answer 18-Social announcements 19-Artwork 20-Cartoons 21-Photos 22-TV listings 23-Audio rec. 24-Video rec. 25-Books 26-Films/film clips 27-Personnel news 28-Press releases 29-New product news/photos 30-Trade lit. 31-Contracts awarded 32-Display adv. 33-Classified adv.

4-47

Leonie Garrigues ...............Circulation Manager
Leonie Garrigus ......................Office Manager
**Editorial:**
Trisha Smith .......................Managing Editor
Larry Cookson ................................Advertising
Wanda Fellom .................Assistant Publisher
**Desc.:** Industry coverage is to builders and
general contractors engaged in
construction of subdivision and/or
individual homes, apartments,
condominiums, multiple dwelling units,
and light commercial buildings in the
state of California.
**Readers:** Builders and contractors
throughout the state refer to circulation
analysis.

22155
**CALIFORNIA BUILDER &
ENGINEER**
4110 Transport St.
Palo Alto, CA 94303
Telephone: (415) 494-8822
Mailing Address:
P.O. Box 10070
Palo Alto, CA 94303
Year Established: 1969
Pub. Frequency: s-m.
Page Size: standard
Subscrip. Rate: $30/yr.
Freelance Pay: varies
Circulation: 9,944
Circulation Type: controlled
**Owner(s):**
California Builder & Engineer, Inc.
4110 Transport St.
Palo Alto, CA 94303
Telephone: (415) 494-8822
Ownership %: 100
**Management:**
Joseph W. Woods ....................Executive Vice
President
David W. Woods ...................................Publisher
**Editorial:**
David W. Woods ....................................Editor
**Desc.:** Regional trade publication serving
heavy construction industries of
California, Nevada and Hawaii.
**Readers:** Contractors, engineers, public
officials, and suppliers.

22533
**CARTOGRAPHY & GEOGRAPHIC
INFORMATION SYSTEMS**
210 Little Falls St.
Falls Church, VA 22046
Telephone: (703) 920-3058
FAX: (301) 493-8245
Year Established: 1974
Pub. Frequency: 4/yr.
Page Size: standard
Subscrip. Rate: $85/yr. non-members
Materials: 02,25,32
Print Process: web
Circulation: 4,000
Circulation Type: paid
**Owner(s):**
American Congress on Surveying &
Mapping
5410 Grosvenor Ln., Ste. 100
Bethesda, MD 20814
Telephone: (301) 493-0200
FAX: (301) 493-8245
Ownership %: 100
**Management:**
James L. Clapp ...........................President
Joan Martin .........................Advertising Manager
**Editorial:**
Lucia Chambers .....................Executive Editor
Robert McMasters .................................Editor
David Woodward ....................Associate Editor
Richard Groop ..................Book Review Editor
Richard Dorman ...................Executive Director
Joan Martin ........................Publication Director

**Desc.:** Provides current information on GIS
and digital mapping as well as more
traditional cartographic methods.
**Readers:** Members, libraries and
exchanges.

22537
**CIM CONSTRUCTION JOURNAL**
1500 Providence Hwy., Ste.14
Norwood, MA 02062
Telephone: (617) 551-0182
FAX: (617) 551-0916
Mailing Address:
P.O. Box 667
Norwood, MA 02062
Year Established: 1921
Pub. Frequency: w.
Page Size: standard
Subscrip. Rate: free to membership
Circulation: 2,000
Circulation Type: free
**Owner(s):**
Construction Industries of Massachusetts,
Inc.
1500 Providence Hwy., Ste. 14
Norwood, MA 02062
Telephone: (617) 551-0182
Ownership %: 100
**Management:**
John Pourbaix ......................Executive Director
Mark J. Drummey .............Advertising Manager
**Editorial:**
Patricia A. Mikes ...................................Editor
Patricia A. Mikes .................Legislative Director
Martha Stewart ....................................Photo
**Desc.:** Promotes heavy and highway
construction in Massachusetts and New
England. Averages 100 pages with the
format a 20 page weekly
newsletter which informs and
editorializes upon events relevant to the
industry, followed by an 80 page data
section which lists new
construction proposals, items and notes
on advertised jobs, and bid prices by
item on recently let heavy construction
projects.
**Readers:** Members of the association,
advertisers, and highway construction,
state legislators and interested persons.

22538
**CIVIL ENGINEERING**
345 E. 47th St., 16th Fl.
New York, NY 10017
Telephone: (212) 705-7463
Year Established: 1930
Pub. Frequency: m.
Page Size: standard
Subscrip. Rate: $79/yr.; foreign $112
Materials: 01,02,05,06,32,33
Freelance Pay: varies: $10-$1
Circulation: 107,000
Circulation Type: controlled
**Owner(s):**
American Society of Civil Engineers
345 E. 47th St.
New York, NY 10017
Telephone: (212) 705-7490
Ownership %: 100
**Management:**
William H. Jensen ............Advertising Manager
**Editorial:**
Virginia Fairweather ........................Chief Editor
John Prendergast ....................Managing Editor
Al Grossbard ..................................Art Director
James Denning .....................Assistant Editor
Teresa Austin ........................Assistant Editor
Paul Tarricone ......................Associate Editor
John Rassman .....................Editorial Assistant

**Desc.:** Carries contributed by-line articles
on current progress in engineered
construction, new equipment, materials
and methods. Covers news of ASCE
activities; items of current
professional interest for civil engineers;
new publications, books, literature
available, equipment, etc.
**Readers:** Civil engineers.

66606
**CONCRETE REPAIR DIGEST**
426 S. Westgate
Addison, IL 60101
Telephone: (708) 543-0870
Year Established: 1990
Pub. Frequency: 6/yr.
Page Size: standard
Subscrip. Rate: $18/yr.
Circulation: 12,000
Circulation Type: controlled
**Owner(s):**
Aberdeen Group, The
426 S. Westgate St.
Addison, IL 60101
Telephone: (708) 543-0870
Ownership %: 100
**Management:**
Mike Derda .......................................Publisher
**Editorial:**
Bruce Suprenant ...................................Editor
**Desc.:** Provides technical & marketing
information for concrete repair
professionals and contractors.

22543
**CONNSTRUCTION**
62 LaSalle Rd.
Ste. 211
W. Hartford, CT 06107
Telephone: (203) 523-7518
FAX: (203) 231-8808
Mailing Address:
P.O. Box 9768
W. Hartford, CT 06107
Year Established: 1966
Pub. Frequency: q.
Page Size: standard
Subscrip. Rate: $28/yr.
Freelance Pay: negotiable
Circulation: 7,000
Circulation Type: controlled
**Owner(s):**
McHugh Design Advertising & Publishing
62 LaSalle Rd., Ste. 211
W. Hartford, CT 06107
Telephone: (203) 529-6855
Ownership %: 100
**Management:**
Tracy McHugh .....................................Publisher
Janet Hutson ...................Advertising Manager
**Editorial:**
Thomas Jakups .....................Managing Editor
**Desc.:** Edited for the information of every
segment of the construction industry,
both public and private in Connecticut
and Southern New England. Content
of editorials, features and news is
primarily though regional, national and
international events are reported and
editoralized as they relate to
construction in Southern New England.
Departments include: Material submitted
by Conn. Construction Associations,
Legal Constructors in news, Calendar, In
Memorium, State Highway, DPW, EPA,
etc. Departments.
**Readers:** Persons and organizations
interested in the heavy construction,
industry and related businesses.

22546
**CONSTRUCTION BULLETIN**
8401 N. 73rd Ave., #76
Minneapolis, MN 55428
Telephone: (612) 537-7730
Year Established: 1893

Pub. Frequency: w.
Page Size: standard
Subscrip. Rate: $3 newsstand; $125/yr.
Materials: 01,02,05,06,07,08,10,11,15,16,
17,19,20,21,25,26,27,28,29,30,31,32,33
Print Process: web offset
Circulation: 5,800
Circulation Type: paid
**Owner(s):**
Chapin Publishing Co.
8401 N. 73rd Ave.
Brooklyn, MN 55428
Telephone: (612) 537-7730
Ownership %: 100
**Management:**
Chris Casey ........................................President
**Editorial:**
George Rekela .........................Executive Editor
Stew Thornby .............................Field Editor
William J. Lee ..............................News Editor
**Desc.:** Proves advanced and current
information on highway, airport, bridge,
sewer, waterworks and heavy public and
private building construction from the
"call for bids" stage to the finished
structure. Close to 2,200 pages of this
information is published annually, not
including about 1,600 pages of
advertisements for bids, which support
this editorial feature. Editions include:
Forecast, Asphalt, Concrete, Bridges,
Underground, Trucks, New Equipment,
Road Reconstruction, and Aggregates.
**Readers:** Serves heavy, highway and non-
residential construction industry in
Minnesota, North Dakota and South
Dakota.

66670
**CONSTRUCTION DATA & NEWS**
P.O. Box C-9037
Seattle, WA 98109
Telephone: (206) 283-4675
Pub. Frequency: w.
Page Size: standard
Subscrip. Rate: $596/yr.
**Owner(s):**
McGraw-Hill, Inc.
**Management:**
Phil Bridge .......................................Publisher
**Editorial:**
Scott Handley .....................................Editor
**Desc.:** A weekly magazine servicing the
construction and related industries of
Washington, Oregon and Alaska.

22548
**CONSTRUCTION DIGEST**
5295 Lakeview Pkwy., S. Dr.
Indianapolis, IN 46268
Telephone: (317) 329-3100
FAX: (317) 329-3110
Mailing Address:
P.O. Box 6132
Indianapolis, IN 46206-6132
Year Established: 1926
Pub. Frequency: s-m.
Page Size: standard
Subscrip. Rate: $2/copy; $40/yr.
Circulation: 10,800
Circulation Type: controlled
**Owner(s):**
Construction Magazine Group, Inc.
P.O. Box 6132
Indianapolis, IN 46206-6132
Telephone: (317) 329-3100
Ownership %: 100
**Management:**
Fred G. Johnston ................................Publisher
Patricia Wagner .................Production Manager
L. Robert King ..........................Sales Manager
**Editorial:**
William A. Orth ...................................Editor
A. Jane King ....................Associate Publisher

**Materials Accepted/Included:** 01-Business news 02-By-line articles 03-Fashion news 04-Food news 05-Freelance copy 06-Letters to editor 07-Real estate news 08-Sports news 09-Travel news 10-Book rev. 11-Movie rev. 12-Music rev. 13-TV rev. 14-Theater rev. 15-Coming events 16-Obituaries 17-Question & answer 18-Social announcements 19-Artwork 20-Cartoons 21-Photos 22-TV listings 23-Audio rec. 24-Video rec. 25-Books 26-Films/film clips 27-Personnel news 28-Press releases 29-New product news/photos 30-Trade lit. 31-Contracts awarded 32-Display adv. 33-Classified adv.

4-48

**Desc.:** A regional business magazine serving contractors, construction equipment and materials suppliers, architects/engineers and public officials in IL, IN, KY, OH, and eastern MO.
**Readers:** Engaged in construction and allied fields.

22164

## CONSTRUCTION DIMENSIONS
307 E. Annandale Rd. #200
Falls Church, VA 22042-2454
Telephone: (703) 534-8300
FAX: (703) 534-8307
Pub. Frequency: m.
Page Size: standard
Subscrip. Rate: $30/yr.
Materials: 01,02,05,17,27,28,29,30,31,32
Print Process: web
Circulation: 21,000
Circulation Type: free & paid
**Owner(s):**
Association of the Wall & Ceiling Industry, Int'l.
1600 Cameron St.
Alexandria, VA 22314
Telephone: (703) 534-8300
FAX: (703) 534-8307
Ownership %: 100
**Management:**
Brent Stone ......................Advertising Manager
**Editorial:**
Laura M. Porinchak ...............................Editor
**Desc.:** Contains management oriented features and articles. Covers cash flow, collections. Departments include: Construction Trends (news), Safety, New Products, Insurance.
**Readers:** Wall and ceiling construction company owners, contractors, manufacturers and suppliers.
**Deadline:** story-20th of mo., 2 mos. prior pub. date; news-20th of mo., 2 mos. prior; photo-20th of mo., 2 mos. prior; ads-8th of mo. prior

22168

## CONSTRUCTIONEER
26 Long Hill Rd.
Guilford, CT 06437
Telephone: (203) 453-3717
FAX: (203) 453-4390
Mailing Address:
P.O. Box 362
Guilford, CT 06437
Year Established: 1945
Pub. Frequency: s-m.
Page Size: standard
Subscrip. Rate: $50/yr.
Circulation: 14,000
Circulation Type: controlled
**Owner(s):**
Hes, Inc.
26 Long Hill Rd.
Guilford, CT 06437
Telephone: (203) 453-3717
Ownership %: 100
**Management:**
Colleen Tarantino ..............Advertising Manager
**Editorial:**
Brenda L. Carlson .....................Editor in Chief
**Desc.:** News of engineering construction activities in New York, Pennsylvania, New Jersey and Delaware only. Carries new equipment, news about people, calls for bids & awards, meetings.
**Readers:** Contractors, material producers and suppliers and manufacturers.

22549

## CONSTRUCTION EQUIPMENT
1350 E. Touhy Ave.
Des Plaines, IL 60018
Telephone: (708) 635-8800
Mailing Address:
P.O. Box 5080
Des Plaines, IL 60017

Year Established: 1949
Pub. Frequency: m. (plus s-a. issue)
Page Size: standard
Subscrip. Rate: controlled circulation
Materials: 28,29,30,32,33
Circulation: 80,000
Circulation Type: controlled
**Owner(s):**
Reed Publishing (USA) Inc.
275 Washington St.
Newton, MA 02158
Ownership %: 100
**Editorial:**
Kirk Landers ......................................Editor
Pamela Gruebnau ...................Managing Editor
**Desc.:** Serves decision-makers in the purchase, maintenance, use, management and evaluation of their trucks and equipment.
**Readers:** Contractors, material producers, construction forces of industrial companies, utilities, mining, logging; federal, state, county and local government; equipment distributors; persons with known buying influence among users of construction equipment, trucks and related products.
**Deadline:** story-8th of mo., prior to pub. date

22550

## CONSTRUCTION EQUIPMENT DISTRIBUTION
615 W. 22nd St.
Oak Brook, IL 60521
Telephone: (708) 574-0650
FAX: (708) 574-0132
Year Established: 1937
Pub. Frequency: m.
Page Size: standard
Subscrip. Rate: $25/yr.
Freelance Pay: negotiable
Circulation: 4,200
Circulation Type: paid
**Owner(s):**
Associated Equipment Distributors
615 W. 22nd St.
Oak Brook, IL 60521
Telephone: (708) 574-6050
Ownership %: 100
**Management:**
Kathie Zowaski .........Public Relations Manager
**Editorial:**
Edward Salek .....................................Editor
Tom Astrene ..........................Managing Editor
Nancy Hartley .............................Advertising
Thomas Astrene ................Production Director
**Desc.:** Promotes better management practices, keeps members abreast of merchandising trends, association activities and reports news about association members. Most popular articles deal with such subjects as financing, credit policies, service practices, business administration, market conditions, sales practices, insurance, inventory control, employee relations, manufacturer-distributor relations, government activity, and non-technical information about equipment. Three news departments cover distributor membership news, regional and local association news, manufacturer member news. Welcomes news about personnel changes at management level, expansion of facilities, public service programs, training programs, or any human interest material that would be of interest to readers. Does not carry news of appointments or distributorships, introduction of products or product performance. Photos used when they have news value. No limit is placed on length of features but will edit and condense where deemed necessary.

**Readers:** Top management of American and Canadian firms.

22165

## CONSTRUCTION EQUIPMENT GUIDE
2627 Mt. Carmel Ave.
Glenside, PA 19038
Telephone: (215) 885-2900
FAX: (215) 885-2910
Mailing Address:
P.O. Box 156
Glenside, PA 19038
Year Established: 1957
Pub. Frequency: bi-w./each edition; NE & SE alternate
Page Size: tabloid
Subscrip. Rate: free to trade; $60/yr.
Freelance Pay: varies
Circulation: 52,000
Circulation Type: free & paid
**Owner(s):**
Edwin M. McKeon
2627 Mt. Carmel Ave.
Glenside, PA 19038
Telephone: (215) 885-2900
Ownership %: 100
**Bureau(s):**
Construction Equipment Guide Southeast
131 B. W. Broadway
Oviedo, FL 32765
Telephone: (800) 344-3026
Contact: Joel Van Natta, Sales Manager
**Management:**
Edwin M. Mc Keon .............................President
Edwin M. McKeon ..............................Publisher
John Bothwell ........................General Manager
John Pinkerton .................Production Manager
**Editorial:**
Beth Baker .............................Feature Editor
Ted McKeon .......................Marketing Director
Peter Sigmund .........................Senior Reporter
**Desc.:** News items about construction, jobs, people, equipment, labor, government policies concerning construction, equipment sales new and used at auction, new products, personnel changes, current problems, trade shows such as Conexpo are covered in depth over many issues.
**Readers:** Owners of construction companies, principle heavy industrial firms, construction equipment manufacturers and dealers.

22166

## CONSTRUCTION EQUIPMENT OPERATION & MAINTENANCE
829 Second Ave., S.E.
Cedar Rapids, IA 52403
Telephone: (319) 366-1597
FAX: (319) 364-4853
Mailing Address:
P.O. Box 1689
Cedar Rapids, IA 52406
Year Established: 1948
Pub. Frequency: bi-m.
Page Size: tabloid
Subscrip. Rate: $10/yr.
Freelance Pay: $15/cartoon
Circulation: 51,242
Circulation Type: controlled
**Owner(s):**
Construction Publications, Inc.
P.O. Box 1689
Cedar Rapids, IA 52406
Telephone: (319) 366-1597
Ownership %: 100
**Management:**
Clark K. Parks ....................................President
Clark K. Parks ....................................Publisher
Duane R. Anton ...............Advertising Manager
Charles E. Parks, III ..........Production Manager
**Editorial:**
Clark K. Parks .....................................Editor

Gavin McComus ......................Associate Editor
**Desc.:** Primarily "how-to" editorial material relating to the selection, use, operation and maintenance of construction tools and equipment. Also interested in new construction methods, short cuts in construction work, new ideas, etc. CEO & M is now sponsored by individual construction equipment distributors in various territories throughout the U.S. and product publicity is limited to items sold by the sponsoring distributors.
**Readers:** Actual users of construction tools and equipment and their foremen and supervisors. Also equipment owners.

69504

## CONSTRUCTION NEWS
10825 Financial Centre Pkwy
Ste. 133
Little Rock, AR 72211-3555
Telephone: (501) 376-1931
FAX: (501) 375-5831
Year Established: 1934
Pub. Frequency: bi-w.
Subscrip. Rate: $65/yr.
Circulation: 7,500
Circulation Type: paid
**Owner(s):**
Construction News Publishing Company
715 W. Second St.
Little Rock, AR 72203
Telephone: (501) 376-1931
Ownership %: 100
**Editorial:**
Robert Alvey ......................................Editor
**Desc.:** Covers Arkansas, Oklahoma, western Tennessee, Mississippi and Louisiana.

22162

## CONSTRUCTION PAN AMERICANA
9500 S. Dadeland Blvd.
Ste. 550
Miami, FL 33156
Telephone: (305) 670-4818
FAX: (305) 670-4818
Year Established: 1972
Pub. Frequency: m.
Page Size: standard
Subscrip. Rate: $30/yr.
Materials: 01,02,06,28,29,30,31,32,33
Freelance Pay: varies
Print Process: web offset
Circulation: 12,500
Circulation Type: controlled & paid
**Owner(s):**
International Construction Publ. Co.
9500 S. Dadeland Blvd.
Ste. 550
Miami, FL 33156
Telephone: (305) 670-4818
Ownership %: 100
**Management:**
Luis Suao ..........................................President
Luis Suao ..........................................Publisher
**Editorial:**
Juan Escalante ....................................Editor
Adriana Suao .....................Production Director
**Desc.:** Trade magazine printed in Spanish for Latin America. International editions circulate in Central and South America, the Spanish speaking territories of the Caribbean. Editorial content includes news, articles, and special reports on the state of the construction market, engineering projects, light and heavy equipment and general reports on building and construction activity in the aforementioned markets.

---

**Materials Accepted/Included:** 01-Business news 02-By-line articles 03-Fashion news 04-Food news 05-Freelance copy 06-Letters to editor 07-Real estate news 08-Sports news 09-Travel news 10-Book rev. 11-Movie rev. 12-Music rev. 13-TV rev. 14-Theater rev. 15-Coming events 16-Obituaries 17-Question & answer 18-Social announcements 19-Artwork 20-Cartoons 21-Photos 22-TV listings 23-Audio rec. 24-Video rec. 25-Books 26-Films/film clips 27-Personnel news 28-Press releases 29-New product news/photos 30-Trade lit. 31-Contracts awarded 32-Display adv. 33-Classified adv.

4-49

**Readers:** Construction companies, engineers, contractors, importers and distributors.
**Deadline:** story-30 days prior to pub. date; news-30 days; photo-30 days; ads-30 days

22554

## CONSTRUCTION REVIEW
U.S. Dept. of Commerce, Rm. H4039
Washington, DC 20230
Telephone: (202) 482-0132
FAX: (202) 482-3821
Pub. Frequency: q.
Page Size: standard
Subscrip. Rate: $24/yr.
Circulation: 1,500
Circulation Type: controlled & paid
**Owner(s):**
U.S. Dept. of Commerce Intl. Trade Admin.,
Washington, DC 20401
Ownership %: 100
**Management:**
U. S. Government ..............................Publisher
**Editorial:**
Patrick MacAuley ..................................Editor
Robert Shaw ..........................Associate Editor
**Desc.:** Contains current statistical data on variousled data on housing, building permits, constructioemployment and wage rates. Feature articles carried in the publication cover on, especially economic and statistical analysis.
**Readers:** Those interested in construction activity, government officials, architects, bankers and labor.

22167

## CONSTRUCTION SPECIFIER, THE
601 Madison St.
Alexandria, VA 22314
Telephone: (703) 684-0300
Year Established: 1949
Pub. Frequency: m.
Page Size: standard
Subscrip. Rate: $36/yr. individuals; $30/yr. institutions
Materials: 02,06,28,29,30,32
Freelance Pay: $.10-$.20/wd.
Circulation: 17,500
Circulation Type: paid
**Owner(s):**
Construction Specifications Institute
601 Madison St.
Alexandria, VA 22314
Telephone: (703) 684-0300
Ownership %: 100
**Management:**
Jack Reeder ........................................Publisher
Julie Savage ......................Advertising Manager
Edel Finnegan ..................Assistant Advertising Manager
**Editorial:**
Kristina Kessler ....................................Editor
Anne Fobear ..............................Assistant Editor
Peggy Myers ..............................Assistant Editor
Nathan Dotson ..........................Associate Editor
Diane Mossholder ................Editorial Assistant
**Desc.:** Technical articles primarily dealing with construction specifications, building techniques, products, and construction methods and practices.
**Readers:** Architects, engineers, specification writers, product manufacturers, lawyers, contract administrators, sales people, systems analysts.
**Deadline:** story-2 mos. prior to pub. date; news-2 mos. prior; photo-2 mos. prior; ads-2 mos. prior

22169

## CONSTRUCTOR
1957 E St., N.W.
Washington, DC 20006
Telephone: (202) 393-2040
FAX: (202) 628-7369

Year Established: 1919
Pub. Frequency: 12/yr.
Page Size: standard
Subscrip. Rate: $15/yr. to members; $100/yr. to non-members; $148/yr. foreign
Materials: 01,02,06,10,27,28,29,30,31,32,33
Print Process: web
Circulation: 44,000
Circulation Type: paid
**Owner(s):**
AGC Information, Inc.
1957 E. St. N.W.
Washington, DC 20006
Telephone: (202) 393-2040
FAX: (202) 628-7369
Ownership %: 100
**Management:**
Donald A. Scott ..................................Publisher
Jeff Smith ..........................Advertising Manager
Rich Bohan ..........................Production Manager
**Editorial:**
William Heavy ......................................Editor
Ben Harris ..................................Features Editor
**Desc.:** Features new ideas for top management and reviews of management trends in construction. Contains market data and economic analysis, interpretation of government controls and regulations, review of labor and open shop activities, digest of legislative activity, ideas on computers, bidding, purchasing, public relations, insurance, new equipment and materials, safety, education, manpower and training, legal matters and texation. Departments include: Perspective, News Line, Tax & Fiscal Affairs, Occupational Division Outlook, Focus on ERISA Labor Notes, International Outlook, Safety and Health Report.
**Readers:** Owners, presidents, vice presidents of companies which perform more than 80% of all U.S. construction, including buildings, highways, heavy, industrial, underground and environmental construction.
**Deadline:** story-45 days prior to pub. date; news-15 days prior; photo-15th of mo. prior to pub. date

67684

## CONTRACTOR
1350 E. Touhy Ave.
Des Plaines, IL 60018
Telephone: (708) 390-2676
FAX: (708) 390-2690
Year Established: 1954
Pub. Frequency: m.
Page Size: tabloid
Subscrip. Rate: $64.95/yr.
Circulation: 47,000
Circulation Type: controlled
**Owner(s):**
Cahners Publishing Company, Inc.
1350 E. Touhy
Des Plaines, IL 60018
Telephone: (708) 635-8800
Ownership %: 100
**Management:**
William J. Adams ..................................Publisher
**Editorial:**
John Schweizer ....................................Editor
**Desc.:** Presents news, market trends and product developments in plumbing, heating, airconditioning, fire protection and specialty piping along with columns and features on service and contracting management, emerging markets and technologies, jobsite reports and company profiles.
**Readers:** Owners and senior management personnel of mechanical specialties contraction firms.

66013

## CONTRACTOR'S GUIDE
6201 W. Howard St.
Chicago, IL 60714
Telephone: (708) 647-1200
Year Established: 1978
Pub. Frequency: m.
Subscrip. Rate: $26/yr.
Circulation: 26,590
Circulation Type: controlled
**Owner(s):**
Century Communications, Inc.
6201 W. Howard St.
Chicago, IL 60714
Telephone: (708) 647-1200
Ownership %: 100
**Editorial:**
Greg Ettling ........................................Editor
**Desc.:** Serves as a guide to the roofing, insulation, siding, solar and window industries.

68751

## CUSTOM BUILDER
38 Lafayette St.
Yarmouth, ME 04096-0470
Telephone: (207) 846-0970
FAX: (207) 846-1561
Mailing Address:
P.O. Box 998
Yarmouth, ME 04096-0470
Year Established: 1976
Pub. Frequency: bi-m.
Subscrip. Rate: $23/yr.
Circulation: 30000
Circulation Type: controlled
**Owner(s):**
New York Times Co. Magazine Group
38 Lafayette St.
P.O. Box 998
Yarmouth, ME 04096-0470
Telephone: (207) 846-0970
Ownership %: 100
**Editorial:**
John Andrews ......................................Editor
**Desc.:** Covers innovations in building techniques, practices and products for the builder of new homes.

22560

## DAILY CONSTRUCTION SERVICE-LOS ANGELES
2625 Manhattan Beach Blvd.
Rondo, CA 90278
Telephone: (310) 322-2437
FAX: (310) 643-1270
Mailing Address:
P.O. Box 90278
Rondo, CA 90278
Year Established: 1933
Pub. Frequency: 5/wk.; Mon.-Fri.
Page Size: standard
Subscrip. Rate: $1,000/yr.
Circulation: 750
Circulation Type: paid
**Owner(s):**
CMD, Inc.
4126 Pleasantdale Rd., B-102
Doraville, GA 30340
Telephone: (404) 447-0630
Ownership %: 100
**Bureau(s):**
DCS
589 Howard St.
San Francisco , CA 94105
Telephone: (415) 781-8088
Contact: David Yates, Editor
**Management:**
Arol Woodford ....................................Publisher
**Editorial:**
Brian Mulligan ....................................Editor
**Desc.:** Construction news, bid calls, bid opening, contract awards. Engineering construction news.

**Readers:** General and Subcontractors, Material and Equipment Suppliers, Archs., Engrs., and Designers.

22561

## DAILY CONSTRUCTION SERVICE-SAN FRANCISCO
589 Howard St.
San Francisco, CA 94105
Telephone: (415) 781-8088
FAX: (415) 495-4797
Mailing Address:
P.O. Box 193019
San Francisco, CA 94119-3019
Year Established: 1919
Pub. Frequency: d.
Page Size: standard
Subscrip. Rate: $959/yr.
Materials: 01,07,16,23,24,25,26,27,28,29, 30,31,32,33
Print Process: web offset
Circulation: morn. 5,000
Circulation Type: paid
**Owner(s):**
Wade Publishing Co.
P.O. Box 3019
San Francisco, CA 94119
Telephone: (415) 781-8088
Ownership %: 100
**Management:**
W. B. Wallace ......................................Publisher
**Editorial:**
W. B. Wallace ..........................Executive Editor
**Desc.:** Coverage of heavy and general engineering construction.

52679

## DEMOLITION AGE
16 N. Franklin St., Ste. 200-B
Doylestown, PA 18901-0710
Telephone: (215) 348-8282
FAX: (215) 348-8422
Year Established: 1973
Pub. Frequency: m.
Page Size: standard
Subscrip. Rate: $34/yr.
Materials: 01,02,28,29,32,33
Freelance Pay: varies
Print Process: offset
Circulation: 4,400
Circulation Type: paid
**Owner(s):**
National Association of Demolition Contractors
16 N. Franklin St.
Suite 200-B
Doylestown, PA 18901-3529
Telephone: (215) 348-4949
FAX: (215) 348-8422
Ownership %: 100
**Editorial:**
Michael R. Taylor ..................................Editor
**Desc.:** Contains articles that discuss technical aspects of structural demolition and salvage and disposal of contents.
**Readers:** Demolition contractors, equipment and materials service suppliers, government libraries.
**Deadline:** story-1 mo. prior to pub. date; news-1 mo. prior to pub. date; photo-1 mo. prior; ads-1 mo. prior

22567

## DIGGER, THE
2780 S.E. Harrison, Ste. 102
Portland, OR 97222
Telephone: (503) 653-8733
FAX: (503) 653-1528
Year Established: 1956
Pub. Frequency: m.
Page Size: standard
Subscrip. Rate: free in industry
Materials: 02,05,10,15,19,21,25,27,28,29, 30,32,33
Freelance Pay: $100-$300
Print Process: web offset
Circulation: 4,500

Circulation Type: controlled & free
**Owner(s):**
Oregon Association of Nurserymen
2780 S.E. Harrison, Ste. 102
Portland, OR 97222
Telephone: (503) 653-8733
FAX: (503) 653-1528
Ownership %: 100
**Management:**
Don Grey ............................Advertising Manager
**Editorial:**
Don Grey ...................................................Editor
**Desc.:** Feature stories and news regarding the West's nursery, greenhouse and landscape industries. Reports on industry topics and trends. Staff and freelance written. Stories up to 2,000 words.
**Readers:** Nursery, greenhouse, landscape and garden center retailers and professionals in the West.
**Deadline:** story-2 mo. prior to pub. date; news-1 mo. prior; photo-1 mo. prior; ads-1 mo. prior

## DIXIE CONTRACTOR
22568

209-A Swanton Way
Decatur, GA 30030
Telephone: (404) 377-2683
FAX: (404) 371-1509
Mailing Address:
P.O. Box 280
Decatur, GA 30030
Year Established: 1926
Pub. Frequency: s-m.
Page Size: standard
Subscrip. Rate: $20/yr.
Freelance Pay: $75/pg.
**Owner(s):**
Dixie Contractor, Inc.
209A Swanton Way
Decatur, GA 30030
Telephone: (404) 377-2683
Ownership %: 100
**Management:**
J. O. Bowen, III ..............................Publisher
Francis J. Aaron ..............Advertising Manager
**Editorial:**
Steve Hudson .......................................Editor
J. O. Bowen, III ...............Production Director
**Desc.:** New machines, new products applicable to construction field. Architectural and engineering photos of job applications, etc. Features cover active construction work. Carries Southeastern States construction news items.
**Readers:** General and Sub - Contractors, Producers, Public Officials, Engineers, Etc.in Southeast U.S. Equipment Distributors & Manufacturers.

## DODGE CONSTRUCTION NEWS GREEN SHEET
22569

1333 S. Mayflower Ave., 3rd. Fl.
Monrovia, CA 91016
Telephone: (818) 932-6178
Mailing Address:
P.O. Box 5050
Monrovia, CA 91017
Year Established: 1865
Pub. Frequency: Mon.-Fri.
Page Size: standard
Subscrip. Rate: $1460/yr.
Circulation: 2,950
Circulation Type: paid
**Owner(s):**
McGraw-Hill, Inc.
Telephone: (810) 932-6100
Ownership %: 100
**Management:**
Susan K. Miller ................................Publisher
Carol Hauser .....................Business Manager
Dick Uber ...........................Production Manager

**Desc.:** Covers the nation's largest construction market with an annual construction volume in excess of 18.5 billion dollars. Provides comprehensive up-to-the minute construction news for contractors and suppliers, and advance construction project reports from planning stage to award of contract. Supplies credit news and news of equipment and materials purchased by government agencies.
**Readers:** Covering the engineering, public works, principally in Southern California, Arizona, and Southern Nevada.

## ELEVATOR WORLD
22171

354 Morgan Ave.
Mobile, AL 36606
Telephone: (205) 479-4514
FAX: (205) 479-7043
Mailing Address:
P.O. Box 6507
Mobile, AL 36660
Year Established: 1953
Pub. Frequency: m.
Page Size: standard
Subscrip. Rate: $57/yr. US; $90/yr. foreign
Materials: 01,06,07,10,17,20,25,27,28,29, 30,31,32,33
Circulation: 6,200
Circulation Type: paid
**Owner(s):**
William C. Sturgeon
277 N. Walton
Mobile, AL 36606
Telephone: (205) 479-4514
Ownership %: 80

Ricia Sturgeon-Hendrick
2313 Lantern Ln., W.
Mobile, AL 36693
Telephone: (205) 666-5749
Ownership %: 20
**Management:**
William C. Sturgeon ............................President
Ricia Sturgeon-Hendrick ...................Publisher
Patricia Cartee .................Advertising Manager
Rebecca Bates ..................Circulation Manager
Linda A. Williams ....................General Manager
**Editorial:**
William C. Sturgeon ...............................Editor
Richard Yarbourough ..............Education Editor
Linda A. Williams ..................Executive Director
Val Banks .......................................Feature Editor
Lois Peavy ............................Production Director
**Desc.:** Technical publication of elevator and escalator industry and related fields. Departments include: Speaking of Issues (editorials), Monitor, Dateline Washington (current news), Innovations (new equipment), Comments, Patents, Round the Elevator World, Atlantic Cable, Outlook From the Orient, Contact, Court Cases, Independently Speaking, A Matter of Association, Sky Ways, Lighting Up the Shaftway and Another View. On the more technical side, Questions & Answers, Law & Liability, Codes and Standards, Staying on Top (calendar), Past in Retrospect, Horizontal Elevators, The Subcontractor, Government, Labor and Management, Changing Skylines, Link with Latin America, and Column from Continent.
**Readers:** Manufacturers, suppliers, installers, maintainers, inspectors, buyers, architects, engineers, building owners, managers and contractors.
**Deadline:** story-2-3 mos. prior to pub. date; news-2 mos. prior; ads-30-45 days prior

## ENGINEERING NEWS-RECORD
22574

1221 Ave. of Americas
New York, NY 10020-3132
Telephone: (212) 512-2372
FAX: (212) 512-2007
Year Established: 1874
Pub. Frequency: 51/yr., Mon.
Page Size: standard
Subscrip. Rate: $65/yr.
Materials: 01,06,27,28,29,30,31,32,33
Print Process: web offset
Circulation: 86,178
Circulation Type: paid
**Owner(s):**
McGraw-Hill, Inc.
1221 Ave. Of Americas
New York, NY 10020
Telephone: (212) 512-2000
Ownership %: 100
**Management:**
Howard Mager .......................................Publisher
**Editorial:**
Howard Stussman ........................Editor in Chief
Janice L. Tuchman ..................Managing Editor
John J. Kosowatz ..............Assistant Managing Editor
Andrew Wright ....................Computer Editor
Timothy Grogan ....................Economics Editor
Debra Rubin ....................Environmental Editor
William Krizan ...............Managing Senior Editor
**Desc.:** Contributed and staff-written articles cover construction methods, design, applications. Covers construction trends, industry news, personals, labor news, finance, construction reports, new products.
**Readers:** Owners, contractors, engineers, architects, producers of building materials, government, commercial and industrial organizations
**Deadline:** ads-1 mo. prior to pub. date

## EQUIPMENT TODAY
22172

1233 Janesville Ave.
Ft. Atkinson, WI 53538
Telephone: (414) 563-6388
FAX: (414) 563-1699
Mailing Address:
P.O. Box 803
Ft. Atkinson, WI 53538-0808
Year Established: 1966
Pub. Frequency: m.
Page Size: tabloid
Subscrip. Rate: $50/yr. US; 65/yr. Canada & Mexico; $120 elsewhere
Freelance Pay: varies
Circulation: 81,000
Circulation Type: free
**Owner(s):**
Johnson Hill Press, Inc.
1233 Janesville Ave.
Ft. Atkinson, WI 53538
Telephone: (414) 563-6388
FAX: (414) 563-1699
Ownership %: 100
**Management:**
Jonathan Pellegrin .............................President
Tom Swetland .......................................Publisher
**Editorial:**
Jeff Ignaszak ........................................Editor
**Desc.:** Devoted to new products, modifications of products or available material on equipment used in construction. Emphasis on equipment selection application and maintenance.
**Readers:** Construction contractors, dealers and allied fields.

## EQUIPMENT WORLD
22581

3200 Riceman Rd.
Tuscaloosa, AL 35406
Telephone: (800) 633-5953
FAX: (205) 752-0930

Mailing Address:
P.O. Box 2029
Tuscaloosa, AL 35403
Year Established: 1972
Pub. Frequency: bi-m.
Page Size: standard
Subscrip. Rate: $98/yr.
Freelance Pay: varies
Circulation: 95,000
Circulation Type: controlled
**Owner(s):**
Randall Publishing Co.
P.O. Box 2029
Tuscaloosa, AL 35403
Telephone: (800) 633-5953
Ownership %: 100
**Management:**
Terry Kilgore ...............................Vice President
Terry Kilgore .......................................Publisher
Nicole Spiller ....................Circulation Manager
**Editorial:**
Jim Clemens .............................Executive Editor
Marcia Gruver ................................................Editor
**Desc.:** Provides information and insight needed to make business decisions when buying, renting, leasing, selling or using equipment from earthmovers to pickups.
**Readers:** Individual responsible for the selection, specification, purchase, and/or maintenance of equipment used in the off-road market.

## FINE HOMEBUILDING
49802

63 S. Main St.
Newtown, CT 06470
Telephone: (203) 426-8171
FAX: (203) 426-3434
Mailing Address:
P.O. Box 5506
Newtown, CT 06470
Year Established: 1981
Pub. Frequency: 7/yr.
Page Size: oversize
Subscrip. Rate: 29/yr.
Circulation: 243,000
Circulation Type: paid
**Owner(s):**
Taunton Press, Inc.
P.O. Box 5506
Newtown, CT 06470-5506
Telephone: (203) 426-8171
Ownership %: 100
**Management:**
John Lively ..........................................Publisher
Sam Vincent ......................Advertising Manager
**Editorial:**
Charles Miller .............................Senior Editor
Mark Feirer .............................................Editor
Kevin Ireton ......................Managing Editor
Chuck Lockhart .................................Art Director
Bruce Greenlaw ........................Associate Editor
**Desc.:** Designed for builders, architects, contractors and home owners who want to get seriously involved in building new houses or renovating old ones. Empasizes on high-quality workmanship and thoughtful design. Seldom uses material from freelance writers. Departments include letters, tips and techniques, questions and answers, book reviews, calendar of events, reports and great moments in building history.
**Readers:** Buliders, contractors, architects, homeowners, remodelors.

## FLORIDA BUILDER
22174

4703 Lumb Ave.
Tampa, FL 33629
Telephone: (813) 835-4689
FAX: (813) 835-4689

Mailing Address:
  P.O. Box 13167
  Tampa, FL 33681
Year Established: 1946
Pub. Frequency: bi-m.
Page Size: standard
Subscrip. Rate: $18/yr.
Freelance Pay: negotiable
Circulation: 10,125
Circulation Type: controlled
Owner(s):
Peninsula Publishing Co.
P.O. Box 13167
Tampa, FL 33681
Telephone: (813) 835-4689
Ownership %: 100
Management:
Joan B. Antoine ..................................Publisher
Editorial:
Joan B. Antoine ..................................Editor
James McCarthy ..........................Art Director
David J. Neel ...................Financial Editor
Desc.: New products section, new
    literature section, convention calendar,
    feature stories and editorials. Primarily
    features that would be of benefit to
    the architects, builders and contractors,
    and the new products that come out
    that they would use.
Readers: Architects, engineers, builders,
    contractors.

**FLORIDA CONSTRUCTOR** 22175
  **MAGAZINE**
495 E. Summerlin St.
Bartow, FL 33830
Telephone: (813) 533-4835
Mailing Address:
  P.O. Box 89
  Bartow, FL 33830
Year Established: 1945
Pub. Frequency: bi-m.
Page Size: standard
Subscrip. Rate: $10/yr.
Circulation: 21,000
Circulation Type: controlled
Owner(s):
Associated Publications Corp.
P.O. Box 89
Bartow, FL 33830
Telephone: (813) 533-4114
Ownership %: 100
Management:
Richard R. Frisbie ...............................Publisher
Jane Kutler .......................Advertising Manager
Becky Crucet ......................Business Manager
Lisa Frisbie ........................Circulation Manager
Editorial:
Mariann Frisbie .................................Editor
Desc.: Florida Constructor is published
    primarily for members of the
    construction industry and allied decision
    - makers throughout the state of Florida:
    general contractors, specifiers,
    architects, builders, developers,
    heavy construction firms, engineers,
    construction equipment dealers,
    construction materials dealers. The
    magazine includes news, views,
    statistics and trends of residential,
    commercial and heavy construction, as
    well as coverage of architecture and
    design, marketing, management,
    maintenance, financing and mortgaging,
    news of trade and professional
    associations, new products and
    literature, and building permit reports -
    virtually all the activities which reflect
    the growth of Florida. Florida
    Constructor is the official state magazine
    of AGC (Associated General
    Contractors.)

Readers: Architects, engineers, heavy
    contractors, builders and general
    contractors, AGC members, specifiers
    and subcontractors.

**FOUNDATION DRILLING** 69510
P.O. Box 280379
Dallas, TX 75228
Telephone: (214) 343-2091
FAX: (214) 343-2384
Year Established: 1980
Pub. Frequency: 8/yr.
Page Size: standard
Subscrip. Rate: $60/yr. US; $75/yr. foreign
Materials: 01,02,06,15,21,28,29,32,33
Print Process: offset
Circulation: 2,000
Circulation Type: paid
Owner(s):
Assn. of Drilled Shaft Contractors
P.O. Box 280379
Dallas, TX 75228
Telephone: (214) 343-2091
FAX: (214) 343-2384
Ownership %: 100
Editorial:
Scott Litke ..................................Editor
Desc.: For the foundation drilling industry
    worldwide. Includes feature articles,
    news departments, insurance, personnel
    and management reports, and a
    calendar of monthly events.
Deadline: story-1st of issue mo.; news-1st
    of issue mo.; photo-1st of issue mo.;
    ads-1st of issue mo.

**HARDHAT** 69520
P.O. Box 6132
Indianapolis, IN 46206-6132
Telephone: (317) 329-3100
Year Established: 1991
Pub. Frequency: m.
Circulation: 29,869
Owner(s):
Construction Magazine Group, Inc.
P.O. Box 6132
Indianapolis, IN 46206-6132
Telephone: (317) 329-3100
Ownership %: 100
Desc.: For those involved in the purchase,
    sale or related services of new and used
    construction equipment.

**HEAT TRANSFER - JAPANESE** 65617
  **RESEARCH**
605 Third Ave.
New York, NY 10158
Telephone: (212) 850-6000
Year Established: 1980
Pub. Frequency: 8/yr.
Subscrip. Rate: $850/yr.
Circulation: 350
Circulation Type: paid
Owner(s):
John Wiley & Sons, Inc.
605 Third Ave.
New York, NY 10158
Telephone: (212) 850-6289
Ownership %: 100
Editorial:
Thomas F. Irving, Jr. ...................................Editor

**HEAVY EQUIPMENT CATALOG** 22605
P.O. Box 70208
Eugene, OR 97401
Telephone: (503) 342-1201
Year Established: 1958
Pub. Frequency: m.
Page Size: pocket
Subscrip. Rate: $18/yr.;$30/2yrs.
Circulation: 27,000
Circulation Type: controlled & paid

Owner(s):
My Little Salesman, Inc.
Telephone: (503) 342-1201
Management:
Richard E. Pierce ..............................President
Rod Womack ....................Advertising Manager
Nita Agol ........................Circulation Manager
Desc.: No articles are utilized. Editorial
    content consists only of coming events.
    Total content is primarily of paid, display
    advertising which allows our subscribers
    to locate new and used equipment and
    services required in their fields of
    construction, logging, and allied
    industries.
Readers: Users and purchasers of
    equipment; logging industries who are in
    need of up-to-date services.

**INTERIOR CONSTRUCTION** 22208
579 W. North Ave.
Ste. 301
Elmhurst, IL 60126
Telephone: (708) 833-1919
FAX: (708) 833-1940
Year Established: 1955
Pub. Frequency: 6/yr.
Page Size: standard
Subscrip. Rate: $35/yr. US; $45/yr. foreign
Freelance Pay: none
Circulation: 10,000
Circulation Type: controlled & paid
Owner(s):
Ceilings & Interior Systems Construction
    Assn.
579 W. North Ave., Ste. 301
Elmhurst, IL 60126
Telephone: (708) 833-1919
Ownership %: 100
Management:
Jan R. Foxen ........................................Publisher
Sheila Kerrigan ..................Circulation Manager
Editorial:
John Sanger ..................................Editor
Desc.: Designed to keep contractors
    abreast with developments in the interior
    systems market. Covers specific
    problems of acoustical contractors, the
    development of new installation
    techniques, new approaches of providing
    interior treatment for institutions,
    factories, offices, stores. Also covers
    ceiling systems, access floor systems,
    and partition systems with strong
    emphasis on the sound conditioning of
    buildings.
Readers: Contractors, managers, company
    presidents, controllers, office managers,
    foremen, systems materials and
    suspended ceiling manufacturers,
    architects and general and other trade
    contractor. Also architects, engineers,
    construction specifiers and buyers of
    interior construction products and
    services.

**INTERMOUNTAIN CONTRACTOR** 22585
1743 W. Alexander
Salt Lake City, UT 84119
Telephone: (801) 972-4400
FAX: (801) 972-8975
Mailing Address:
  P.O. Box 26237
  Salt Lake City, UT 84126
Year Established: 1950
Pub. Frequency: w.
Page Size: 4 color photos/art
Subscrip. Rate: $381/yr.
Materials: 01,05,06,28,29,30,32,33
Circulation: 4,500
Circulation Type: free & paid

Owner(s):
McGraw Hill, Inc.
1221 Ave. of the Americas
New York, NY 10020
Telephone: (801) 972-4400
Ownership %: 100
Management:
Robert Marshall ..............................Publisher
Karen Warren ...................Business Manager
Albert Vandyk ........................General Manager
Editorial:
Kendall Hanson ..................................Editor
Desc.: Highways, engineering and public
    works, personnel, equipment.
Readers: Management in construction
    industry.
Deadline: story-20 days prior to pub. date;
    news-20 days prior; photo-20 days prior;
    ads-20 days prior

**JOURNAL OF HOUSING** 22182
1320 18th St., N.W., #402
Washington, DC 20036
Telephone: (202) 429-2960
FAX: (202) 429-9684
Year Established: 1943
Pub. Frequency: bi-m.
Page Size: 4 color photos/art
Subscrip. Rate: $4 newsstand; $24/yr.
Materials: 28,29
Circulation: 13,000
Circulation Type: paid
Owner(s):
Natl. Assn. of Housing & Redevelopment
    Officials
1320 18th St., N.W., #402
Washington, DC 20036
Telephone: (202) 429-2960
Ownership %: 100
Management:
Richard Y. Nelson, Jr. ..........Executive Director
Victoria S. Mellin ..............Advertising Manager
Editorial:
Terence K. Cooper ..................................Editor
Pete Hart ..............................Advertising
Pete Hart .............................Production Director
Desc.: Covers national field of publicly
    assisted housing, urban renewal and
    codes enforcement programs & other
    areas of community development.
    Features cover urban aesthetics and
    economics; citizen participation;
    legislative analysis; organizational and
    administrative techniques, etc.
    Departments include: Personals, Letters
    to Editor, City News, State News, Picture
    Reports, Books, Reports & Literature.
Readers: Federal, state, local government
    officials; housing managers, planners,
    developers, architects, academicians,
    maintenance supervisors.

**JOURNAL OF LIGHT** 66315
  **CONSTRUCTION, THE**
Rte. 2, P.O. Box 146
Richmond, VT 05477
Telephone: (802) 434-4747
FAX: (802) 434-4467
Year Established: 1982
Pub. Frequency: m.
Page Size: standard
Subscrip. Rate: 3.95 newsstand;
    $32.50/yr.; $52.50/2 yrs.; $64.50/3 yrs.
Materials: 01,02,17,19,21
Freelance Pay: varies
Print Process: web
Circulation: 40,000
Circulation Type: paid
Owner(s):
Builderburg Partners, Ltd.
Rt. 2, P.O. Box 146
Richmond, VT 05477
Telephone: (802) 434-4747

Materials Accepted/Included: 01-Business news 02-By-line articles 03-Fashion news 04-Food news 05-Freelance copy 06-Letters to editor 07-Real estate news 08-Sports news 09-Travel news 10-Book rev. 11-Movie rev. 12-Music rev. 13-TV rev. 14-Theater rev. 15-Coming events 16-Obituaries 17-Question & answer 18-Social announcements 19-Artwork 20-Cartoons 21-Photos 22-TV listings 23-Audio rec. 24-Video rec. 25-Books 26-Films/film clips 27-Personnel news 28-Press releases 29-New product news/photos 30-Trade lit. 31-Contracts awarded 32-Display adv. 33-Classified adv.

**Management:**
Michael Reitz .............................Publisher
**Editorial:**
Steven Bliss .................................Editor
**Desc.:** Provides practical information on building technology and business management for residential and light commercial building contractors.
**Readers:** Builders, remodelers, & home designers.

22181

## JOURNAL OF THE INTERNATIONAL UNION OF BRICKLAYERS & ALLIED CRAFTSMEN
815 15th St., NW
Washington, DC 20005
Telephone: (202) 783-3788
FAX: (202) 393-0219
Year Established: 1895
Pub. Frequency: m.
Page Size: tabloid
Subscrip. Rate: $.15 newsstand; $1.50/yr.
Circulation: 105,000
**Owner(s):**
Intl. Union of Bricklayers & Allied Craftsmen
815 15th St., N.W.
Washington, DC 20005
Telephone: (202) 783-3788
Ownership %: 100
**Editorial:**
Joan Baggett .............................Executive Editor
Paul Ruffins .............................Associate Editor
**Desc.:** Written for our union members and contractors, materials manufacturers and others interested in masonry construction. Do not use publicity hand-outs unless of particular and specific interest to our readers.
**Readers:** Union members and contractors, materials in masonry construction.

22204

## JOURNEYMAN ROOFERS & WATERPROOFERS
1125 17TH St., NW
Washington, DC 20036
Telephone: (202) 638-3228
FAX: (202) 737-3621
Pub. Frequency: q.
Subscrip. Rate: $6/yr.
Circulation: 21000
Circulation Type: controlled & paid
**Owner(s):**
United Union of Roofers, Waterproofers and Allied
1125 17th St., N.W.
Washington, DC 20036
Telephone: (202) 638-3228
Ownership %: 100
**Editorial:**
Kinsey Robinson .............................Editor
**Desc.:** Covers labor aspects of roofing industry.
**Readers:** Roofing contractors and members of the as

22184

## KITCHEN & BATH BUSINESS
1515 Broadway
New York, NY 10036
Telephone: (212) 869-1300
FAX: (212) 719-3588
Year Established: 1955
Pub. Frequency: m.
Page Size: standard
Subscrip. Rate: $45/yr.
Circulation: 49,956
Circulation Type: paid

**Owner(s):**
Miller Freeman, Inc.
1515 Broadway
New York, NY 10036
Telephone: (212) 869-1300
Ownership %: 100
**Bureau(s):**
Gralla Publications
3525 W. Peterson Ave.
Chicago, IL 60659
Telephone: (312) 463-1102
Contact: Ann Kerstetter

Gralla Publications
6355 Topango Canyon Blvd.
Woodland Hls, CA 91367
Telephone: (818) 348-1943
Contact: Barry Wolfe
**Management:**
Leslie Hart .............................Publisher
Allan Brown .............................Advertising Manager
**Editorial:**
Ed Pell .............................Editor in Chief
Valerie Caruso .............................Managing Editor
Leslie Hart .............................Editorial Director
**Desc.:** Covers industry trends, case history, new products, literature and merchandising ideas for residential kitchen and bathroom dealers or distributors. Also contains factory and shop procedures for kitchen cabinet, countertop and vanity manufacturers.
**Readers:** Kitchen & bath dealers, distributors, contractors, designers, remodelers, manufacturers, fabricators, architects and interior designers.

22591

## LOUISIANA CONTRACTOR
2900 Westfork Dr.
Ste. 345
Baton Rouge, LA 70827-0022
Telephone: (504) 292-8980
FAX: (504) 292-5089
Year Established: 1953
Pub. Frequency: m.
Page Size: standard
Subscrip. Rate: $19.50/yr.
Freelance Pay: $100-$200/article
Circulation: 6,000
Circulation Type: controlled
**Owner(s):**
McGraw-Hill, Inc.
2900 Westfork Dr.
Baton Rouge, LA 70827
Telephone: (504) 292-8980
Ownership %: 100
**Management:**
Kevin Rhodes .............................Publisher
Pat Wells .............................Circulation Manager
**Editorial:**
Sam Barnes .............................Editor
**Desc.:** Features on new construction projects in Louisiana, special techniques in heavy construction, special emphasis on people and speakers at meetings, conventions, seminars related to Louisiana construction industry. News releases on new equipment, new ideas, new methods, special issues, on asphalt, concrete, oil field construction, industrial construction, pile driving.
**Readers:** Licensed Contractors, Architects, Engineers, Suppliers, Industrial Contractors, Sub - Contractors, Suppliers, Government Personnel

22188

## MASONRY
1550 Spring Rd.
Oak Brook, IL 60521
Telephone: (708) 782-6767
FAX: (708) 782-6786
Year Established: 1960
Pub. Frequency: 6/yr.

Page Size: standard
Subscrip. Rate: $20/yr. US; $22/yr. Canada
Materials: 01,02,05,06,10,15,16,17,19,20, 21,23,24,25,26,27,28,29,30,32,33
Freelance Pay: negotiated
Print Process: web offset
Circulation: 7,200
Circulation Type: paid
**Owner(s):**
Mason Contractors Association of America
1550 Spring Rd.
Oak Brook, IL 60521
Telephone: (708) 782-6767
FAX: (708) 782-6786
Ownership %: 100
**Editorial:**
Gene Adams .............................Editor
**Desc.:** Features consist of articles on masonry construction and its application to the building industry plus mason contractor news and related information of the industry.
**Readers:** Mason contractors, architects, allied industries and engineers.
**Deadline:** story-5th of mo. prior to pub. date; news-5th of mo. prior; photo-5th of mo. prior; ads-5th of mo. prior

68753

## METAL CONSTRUCTION NEWS
7450 Skokie Blvd.
Skokie, IL 60077
Telephone: (708) 674-2200
FAX: (708) 390-2690
Pub. Frequency: m.
Subscrip. Rate: $45/yr.
Circulation: 32,800
Circulation Type: paid
**Owner(s):**
Modern Trade Communications
7450 Skokie Blvd.
Skokie, IL 60077
Telephone: (708) 674-2200
Ownership %: 100
**Editorial:**
Shawn Zuver .............................Editor

22192

## MH/RV BUILDERS NEWS
716 Webley Ct.
Schaumburg, IL 60193
Telephone: (708) 893-8872
Mailing Address:
  P.O. Box 72367
  Roselle, IL 60172
Year Established: 1965
Pub. Frequency: 6/yr.
Page Size: tabloid
Subscrip. Rate: $15/yr. US.; $20/yr. Canada
Materials: 01,21,27,28,29,30,32,33
Print Process: offset
Circulation: 10,000
Circulation Type: controlled
**Owner(s):**
Dan Kamrow & Associates, Inc.
P.O. Box 72367
Roselle, IL 60172
Telephone: (708) 893-8872
FAX: (708) 893-8872
Ownership %: 100
**Bureau(s):**
Paul Gilbert
80 Poillon Dr.
Chappaqua, NY 10514
Telephone: (914) 238-8016
Contact: Paul Gilbert, Reporter
**Management:**
Dan Kamrow .............................President
Dan Kamrow .............................Publisher
Dan Kamrow .............................Advertising Manager
Patt Kamrow .............................Circulation Manager
**Editorial:**
Patt Kamrow .............................Managing Editor
Pat Finn .............................New Product Editor

Pat Finn .............................News Editor
**Desc.:** Product stories of items used to build and furnish manufactured homes and travel homes. Also, marine homes. Also any information of value to builders of these homes. Fields reached include mobile homes, manufactured homes, modular homes, marine homes and travel homes.
**Readers:** Builders of all types of manufactured homes; mobile, modular, panelized, park homes, motor homes, van conversions, campers, travel homes and marine homes.

22597

## MICHIGAN CONTRACTOR & BUILDER
1629 W. Lafayette Blvd.
Detroit, MI 48216
Telephone: (313) 962-3337
FAX: (313) 926-3655
Year Established: 1907
Pub. Frequency: w.
Page Size: standard
Subscrip. Rate: $125/yr.
Materials: 01,02,07,15,16,17,24,25,27,28, 29,30,31,32,33
Freelance Pay: $80/page
Print Process: offset
Circulation: 3,455
Circulation Type: paid
**Owner(s):**
Contractor Publishing Co.
1629 W. Lafayette
Detroit, MI 48216
Telephone: (313) 962-3337
FAX: (313) 962-3365
Ownership %: 100
**Management:**
John Mertz .............................Publisher
Roy Jones .............................Advertising Manager
**Editorial:**
Guy Snyder .............................Editor
**Desc.:** Devoted editorially to Michigan's heavy construction industry-highways, roads, streets, underground installations, airports, public works services, public projects and large general projects. Carries maintenance, operating, legal and legislative information of significance to contractors and public officials; Michigan architectural and engineering reports and news; material of consequence to all readers involved in the state's non-home building construction field.
**Readers:** Contractors, engineers, architects, construction equipment and material suppliers; public officials.
**Deadline:** story-Fri., 1 wk. prior to pub. date; news-Fri., 1 wk. prior; photo-Fri., 1 wk. prior; ads-Fri., 1 wk. prior

22598

## MICHIGAN ROADS & CONSTRUCTION
535 N. Clippert St.
Lansing, MI 48912
Telephone: (517) 332-7600
FAX: (517) 332-7336
Mailing Address:
  P.O. Box 25007
  Lansing, MI 48909
Year Established: 1983
Pub. Frequency: w.
Page Size: standard
Subscrip. Rate: $30/yr.
Circulation: 2,000
Circulation Type: paid
**Owner(s):**
Baker Publishing Co.
P.O. Box 25007
Lansing, MI 48909
Telephone: (517) 332-7600
Ownership %: 100

---

**Materials Accepted/Included:** 01-Business news 02-By-line articles 03-Fashion news 04-Food news 05-Freelance copy 06-Letters to editor 07-Real estate news 08-Sports news 09-Travel news 10-Book rev. 11-Movie rev. 12-Music rev. 13-TV rev. 14-Theater rev. 15-Coming events 16-Obituaries 17-Question & answer 18-Social announcements 19-Artwork 20-Cartoons 21-Photos 22-TV listings 23-Audio rec. 24-Video rec. 25-Books 26-Films/film clips 27-Personnel news 28-Press releases 29-New product news/photos 30-Trade lit. 31-Contracts awarded 32-Display adv. 33-Classified adv.

**Management:**
Bud Baker .............................................Publisher
Robert Johnson ................Circulation Manager
**Editorial:**
Bud Baker .................................................Editor
William Trevarthen ...................Managing Editor
**Readers:** Highway and heavy public works industries.

22600
## MIDWEST CONTRACTOR MAGAZINE
5295 Lakeview Pkwy., South Drive
Indianapolis, IN 46268
Telephone: (800) 860-3105
FAX: (317) 329-3110
Mailing Address:
   P.O. Box 6132
   Indianapolis, IN 46206
Year Established: 1901
Pub. Frequency: s-m.
Page Size: standard
Subscrip. Rate: $38/yr. N. & S. editions;
   $62/yr. both
Circulation: 7,000
Circulation Type: controlled
**Owner(s):**
Allied Publications
P.O. Box 603
Indianapolis, IN 46206
Telephone: (317) 297-5500
Ownership %: 100
**Management:**
Kirsten Jackson .....................................Publisher
Pat Wagner .......................Advertising Manager
Laura Haag ........................Circulation Manager
**Editorial:**
William Orth .................................................Editor
**Desc.:** Serves the engineering, construction and public works industries in Iowa, Kansas, Nebraska, and western and northeastern Missouri. Includes bids asked, low bids, awards, planned work, feature articles, new products and literature, legislation, manufacturer and distributor news, industry trends, news of people, and association meetings.
**Readers:** Contractors, highway commissioners and engineers, surveyors, mayors, city managers, manufacturers and distributors.

67645
## MISSISSIPPI CONSTRUCTION
18271 Jefferson Hwy.
Baton Rouge, LA 70817
Telephone: (504) 752-8980
Mailing Address:
   2900 Westfork Dr., Ste. 345
   Baton Rouge, LA 70827-0008
Year Established: 1991
Pub. Frequency: m.
Page Size: standard
Subscrip. Rate: $18/yr.
Freelance Pay: $150-$300
Circulation: 2,000
Circulation Type: controlled
**Owner(s):**
McGraw-Hill, Inc.
2900 Westfork Dr., Ste. 345
Baton Rouge, LA 70827-0008
Telephone: (504) 292-8980
Ownership %: 100
**Management:**
Kevin Rhodes .....................................Publisher
**Editorial:**
Sam Barnes .................................................Editor

22196
## MULTI-HOUSING NEWS
1515 Broadway
New York, NY 10036
Telephone: (212) 869-1300
FAX: (212) 719-3588
Year Established: 1966
Pub. Frequency: bi-m.

Page Size: standard
Subscrip. Rate: $30/yr.
Materials: 01,06,07,15,28,29,30
Freelance Pay: $100-$600
Print Process: offset
Circulation: 30,000
Circulation Type: controlled
**Owner(s):**
Miller Freeman, Inc.
1515 Broadway
New York, NY 10036
Telephone: (212) 869-1300
Ownership %: 100
**Management:**
Peter Watson .......................................Publisher
Laura Rowley .........................Associate Publisher
Kit Reynolds ......................Circulation Manager
**Editorial:**
Laura Rowley ..............................Editor in Chief
Christina Trauthwein ................Managing Editor
Lisa Mancin .........................Production Director
**Desc.:** Articles on multi-housing developments, finance, land planning, design, marketing and management. Departments include: Financial, Senior Living, Remodeling, Property Management, and Marketplace.
**Readers:** Developers, builders, owners, managers, remodelers and financiers.

22230
## NATIONAL HOME CENTER NEWS
425 Park Ave.
New York, NY 10022
Telephone: (212) 756-5000
FAX: (212) 756-5395
Year Established: 1975
Pub. Frequency: s-m.
Page Size: tabloid
Subscrip. Rate: $5 newsstand; $99/yr.
Freelance Pay: negotiable
Circulation: 52,000
Circulation Type: controlled & paid
**Owner(s):**
Lebhar-Friedman, Inc.
425 Park Avenue
New York, NY 10022
Telephone: (212) 756-5000
Ownership %: 100
**Bureau(s):**
Lebhar - Friedman, Inc./National Home Center News
606 N. Larchmont Blvd.
Los Angeles, CA 90004-1309
Telephone: (310) 464-8321
Contact: Robyn Taylor, Associate Editor

Lebhar - Friedman, Inc./NHCN
444 N. Michigan Ave.
Chicago, IL 60611-3984
Telephone: (312) 644-8688
Contact: Gary Ruderman, Senior Editor
**Management:**
J. Roger Friedman ............................President
Wyatt Kash .......................................Publisher
Christopher Harrison .........Advertising Manager
Kenneth Schept .......................Sales Manager
**Editorial:**
John Caulfield .................................Exec. Editor
**Desc.:** Business newspaper serving the retail home improvement market.
**Readers:** Home center, lumber and building material retailers and their suppliers.

22608
## NEW YORK CONSTRUCTION NEWS
1633 Broadway, 13th Fl.
New York, NY 10019-7164
Telephone: (212) 512-4770
FAX: (212) 472-2335
Year Established: 1953
Pub. Frequency: w.
Page Size: standard
Subscrip. Rate: $39/yr.
Circulation: 7,000

Circulation Type: paid
**Owner(s):**
McGraw-Hill Publishing, Inc.
1212 Avenue of the Americas
New York, NY 10019
Ownership %: 100
**Management:**
Mark Kelly .........................................Publisher
Frann Shaw ....................Advertising Manager
**Editorial:**
David Chartock ...........................................Editor
**Desc.:** Covers the design and construction of metropolitan New York, northern New Jersey, and southern Connecticut.
**Readers:** Architects, engineers, general contractors supporting industries in the building trades.

68748
## NORTHWEST KITCHEN & BATH QUARTERLY
P.O. Box 58866
Seattle, WA 98138
Telephone: (206) 248-2064
FAX: (206) 852-4854
Pub. Frequency: q.
Subscrip. Rate: $6/yr.
Circulation: 112,000
Circulation Type: paid
**Owner(s):**
Quarterly Publishing
P.O. Box 58866
Seattle, WA 98138
Telephone: (206) 248-2064
Ownership %: 100
**Editorial:**
Cindee B. Berry ........................................Editor

22613
## OHIO CONTRACTOR
1313 Dublin Rd.
Columbus, OH 43215
Telephone: (614) 488-0724
Mailing Address:
   P.O. Box 909
   Columbus, OH 43216
Year Established: 1928
Pub. Frequency: bi-m.
Page Size: standard
Subscrip. Rate: $1.25 newsstand; $20/yr.
**Owner(s):**
Ohio Contractors Association
1313 Dublin Rd.
Columbus, OH 43215
Telephone: (614) 488-0724
Ownership %: 100
**Editorial:**
Clark Street ...............................................Editor
Carrie Silverstein ...............................Advertising
**Desc.:** Includes job stories, new equipment.
**Readers:** Member and non-member contractors perform construction, sand & gravel producers, connected with or interested in the industry.

22619
## PACIFIC BUILDER & ENGINEER
3000 Northup Way, Ste. 200
Bellevue, WA 98004
Telephone: (206) 827-9900
Mailing Address:
   P.O. Box 96043
   Bellevue, WA 98009
Year Established: 1902
Pub. Frequency: s-m.
Page Size: standard
Subscrip. Rate: $23/yr.
Freelance Pay: negotiable
Circulation: 12,423
Circulation Type: controlled

**Owner(s):**
Vernon Publications, Inc.
3000 Northup Way, Ste. 200
Bellevue, WA 98004
Telephone: (206) 827-9900
Ownership %: 100
**Management:**
Bill R. Vernon ................Chairman of Board
Geoffrey P. Vernon ...........................Publisher
Barry Lawrence .................Advertising Manager
Jan Coates ........................Circulation Manager
**Editorial:**
Michele Dill ..........................Editorial Director
Richard C. Bachus ....................Associate Editor
Charles M. Gordon ........................Field Editor
Jon Flies ...........................Production Director
**Desc.:** Illustrated feature articles - all types heavy construction projects in Oregon, Washington, Alaska, Idaho, and Montana, stress construction methods, engineering design and business management. Departments include: Products, Literature, Washington Report, Bid and Award News, Calendar, Comparative Unit Prices.
**Readers:** Highway, heavy and building contractors, engineers, supervisory personnel.

61717
## PIPELINE & UTILITIES CONSTRUCTION
14515 Brier Hills, Ste. 208
Houston, TX 77077
Telephone: (713) 558-6930
FAX: (713) 558-7029
Mailing Address:
   P.O. Box 219368
   Houston, TX 77218-9368
Year Established: 1945
Pub. Frequency: m.
Page Size: standard
Subscrip. Rate: $50/yr.
Materials: 01,02,05,06,15,21,24,25,27,28,
   29,30,31,32,33
Freelance Pay: $50-$400
Print Process: web offset
Circulation: 62,000
Circulation Type: controlled & paid
**Owner(s):**
Oildom Publishing Co. of Texas, Inc.
P.O. Box 219368
Houston, TX 77218-9568
Telephone: (713) 622-0676
FAX: (713) 558-7029
Ownership %: 100
**Management:**
Michael Speer ...................Circulation Manager
Elizabeth Ross ...................Production Manager
**Editorial:**
Robert Carpenter ....................................Editor
Trey Randalck ............................Assistant Editor
**Desc.:** Covers all aspects of underground systems construction and rehabilitation as applied to pipelines and distribution systems: water, gas, sewers, and storm drains.
**Readers:** Contractors, engineers and professionals related to the oil and gas pipeline industry.
**Deadline:** story-15th of mo.; news-15th of mo.; photo-15th of mo.; ads-15th of mo.

22200
## PROFESSIONAL BUILDER & REMODELER
1350 E. Touhy
Des Plaines, IL 60018
Telephone: (708) 635-8800
FAX: (708) 299-8622
Mailing Address:
   P.O. Box 5080
   Des Plaines, IL 60017-5080
Year Established: 1936
Pub. Frequency: m.

---

**Materials Accepted/Included:** 01-Business news 02-By-line articles 03-Fashion news 04-Food news 05-Freelance copy 06-Letters to editor 07-Real estate news 08-Sports news 09-Travel news 10-Book rev. 11-Movie rev. 12-Music rev. 13-TV rev. 14-Theater rev. 15-Coming events 16-Obituaries 17-Question & answer 18-Social announcements 19-Artwork 20-Cartoons 21-Photos 22-TV listings 23-Audio rec. 24-Video rec. 25-Books 26-Films/film clips 27-Personnel news 28-Press releases 29-New product news/photos 30-Trade lit. 31-Contracts awarded 32-Display adv. 33-Classified adv.

Page Size: 8 1/8 x 10 7/8
Subscrip. Rate: $85/yr.
Freelance Pay: no free lancing accepted
Circulation: 138,091
Circulation Type: controlled & paid
**Owner(s):**
Cahners Publ. Co./Div. of Reed Publ.
  U.S.A.
1350 E. Touhy
P.O. Box 5080
Des Plaines, IL 60017-5080
Telephone: (708) 635-8800
Ownership %: 100
**Management:**
Pete Orsi .............................Publisher
Paul Gillen ..........Advertising Manager
**Editorial:**
Ed Fitch ...................................Editor
Barbara McHatton ...........New Products Editor
**Desc.:** Devoted to the housing and light
  construction industry. Illustrated articles
  cover design, application of new building
  techniques and materials installation,
  industrialized building techniques,
  remodeling and rehabilitation.
  Covers management problems, new
  building equipment, building products,
  literature.
**Readers:** Building contractors of homes
  and apartments, low-rise commercial &
  industrial buildings; remodelers and
  housing & mobile home manufacturers.

---

### PROFESSIONAL ROOFING I.C. MAGAZINE
**22206**
10255 W. Higgins Rd., Ste 600
Rosemont, IL 60018
Telephone: (708) 299-9070
FAX: (708) 299-1183
Year Established: 1962
Pub. Frequency: 12/yr.
Page Size: standard
Subscrip. Rate: $25/yr.
Materials: 01,02,06,07,15,27,28,29,30
Freelance Pay: negotiable
Circulation: 20,000
Circulation Type: controlled
**Owner(s):**
National Roofing Service Corporation
10255 W. Higgins Rd., Ste. 600
Rosemont, IL 60018
Telephone: (708) 299-9070
Ownership %: 100
**Bureau(s):**
National Roofing Contractors Assn.
206 E. St., N.E.
Washington, DC 20002
Telephone: (202) 546-7584
Contact: Craig Brightup, Director
**Editorial:**
Mari Ujka ................................Editor
MaryRo Siewers ................Advertising
Mary Talley ...............Associate Editor
Joan Kriete ...............Circulation Editor
Melissa Ruksakiati ...............Editorial Assistant
**Desc.:** Contains news and features on
  roofing, roof deck and waterproofing
  materials, equipment, services, technical
  data and management information,
  association news, legal news, safety and
  health, and regulatory issues.
  Departments include: News from
  Associate Members, Industry Briefings,
  Technical Developments, Regulatory
  Review, Legal Review, Book
  and Product Reviews, Letters to the
  Editor.
**Readers:** Roofing, roof deck and
  waterproofing contractors, architects,
  specifiers, manufacturers, roof
  consultants, and building owners.

---

### QUALIFIED REMODELER
**22202**
20 E. Jackson Blvd.
Chicago, IL 60604
Telephone: (312) 922-5402
FAX: (312) 922-0856
Year Established: 1975
Pub. Frequency: 14/yr.
Page Size: standard
Subscrip. Rate: free to qualified individuals
Freelance Pay: $100-$300/article
Circulation: 101,000
Circulation Type: controlled & free
**Owner(s):**
PTN Publishing
445 Broad Hollow Rd.
Melville, NY 11747
Telephone: (516) 845-2700
Ownership %: 100
**Management:**
David M. Sauer ......................Founder
David M. Sauer ......................Publisher
**Editorial:**
Mary Buckart ....................Editor in Chief
**Desc.:** Slant essentially is design and
  installation of all remodeling activities,
  homes, apartments and light
  commercial. Preference to 4-color
  transparencies. Departments include:
  Business, News, New Products,
  Association News, New Literature,
  Editorial, Computers, Management.
**Readers:** 130,000 professional remodeling
  contractors and distributors, architects,
  kitchen & bath designers.

---

### REMODELING
**65220**
One Thomas Circle, N.W.
Washington, DC 20005-5701
Telephone: (202) 452-0800
FAX: (202) 785-1974
Year Established: 1985
Pub. Frequency: m.
Page Size: standard
Subscrip. Rate: $24.95/yr.; free to qualified
  personnel
Freelance Pay: $.20/word
Circulation: 95,000
Circulation Type: controlled
**Owner(s):**
Hanley-Wood, Inc.
One Thomas Circle, N.W.
Washington, DC 20005-5701
Telephone: (202) 452-0800
Ownership %: 100
**Management:**
Peter Miller ............................Publisher
Leslie Ensor ...........................Manager
**Editorial:**
Wendy Jordan ..........................Editor
**Desc.:** Gives remodelers the information
  they need to excel in business. Presents
  the best new ideas in remodeling design
  management, marketing,
  construction and products.
**Readers:** Residential and light commercial
  remodeling contractors.

---

### REMODELING NEWS
**68749**
600 Lake St.
Ste. C
Ramsey, NJ 07446
Telephone: (201) 327-1600
FAX: (201) 327-3185
Year Established: 1987
Pub. Frequency: m.
Materials: 01,02,05,06,15,27,28,29,30,31,33
Freelance Pay: negotiable
Print Process: web offset
Circulation: 54,121
Circulation Type: controlled

---

**Owner(s):**
S. R. Sound, Inc.
600 Lake St.
Ste. C
Ramsey, NJ 07446
Telephone: (201) 327-1600
FAX: (201) 327-4909
Ownership %: 100
**Editorial:**
Renee Rewiski ..........................Editor
**Desc.:** News, trends & analysis, product &
  material information important to the
  builder/remodeler.
**Readers:** Builders/remodelers, architects
  and other professionals allied to the
  field.
**Deadline:** story-75 days prior to pub. date;
  news-ASAP; photo-75 days prior to pub.
  date; ads-60 days prior to pub. date

---

### ROCKY MOUNTAIN CONSTRUCTION
**22629**
2403 Champa St.
Denver, CO 80205
Telephone: (303) 295-0630
FAX: (303) 295-2159
Year Established: 1924
Pub. Frequency: bi-w.
Page Size: standard
Subscrip. Rate: $40/yr.
Materials: 01,02,27,28,29,30,31,32,33
Print Process: offset
Circulation: 7,150
Circulation Type: controlled
**Owner(s):**
Rocky Mountain Construction Magazine,
  Inc.
2403 Champa St.
Denver, CO 80205
Telephone: (303) 295-0630
Ownership %: 100
**Management:**
Lawrence Bell .........................Publisher
Don Ludwig ............Advertising Manager
**Editorial:**
F. Hol Wagner, Jr. .....................Editor
**Desc.:** Articles pertinent to heavy
  construction and highway building field.
  Reports on building, engineering, and
  architectural news, legislation as
  affecting building construction and
  highways, new production developments,
  etc. Weekly advance
  construction reports, building and
  engineering.
**Readers:** Highway, heavy, utility and
  building contractors, suppliers, allied
  industries, public officials machinery
  manufacturers and distributors.
**Deadline:** story-60 days prior to pub. date;
  news-30 days prior; photo-30 days prior;
  ads-30 days prior

---

### ROOFING SIDING INSULATION MAGAZINE
**22205**
7500 Old Oak Blvd.
Cleveland, OH 44130
Telephone: (212) 951-6600
FAX: (216) 891-2675
Year Established: 1945
Pub. Frequency: m.
Page Size: standard
Subscrip. Rate: $36/yr. US; $49/yr.
  Canada; $69/yr. foreign
Freelance Pay: $200-$500
Circulation: 21,000
Circulation Type: controlled & paid
**Owner(s):**
Advanstar Communications, Inc.
7500 Old Oak Blvd
Cleveland, OH 44130
Telephone: (216) 826-2839
Ownership %: 100

---

**Editorial:**
Teresa O'Dea ......................Bureau Chief
Mike Russo ...............................Editor
Sharron Conners ............Managing Editor
Mike Russo .............Associate Publisher
**Desc.:** Contains merchandising features,
  technical articles and stories on industry
  events such as conventions, and
  regional meetings. Publicity material
  can be any feature-size length, while
  photos are practically a must.
**Readers:** Serves companies engaged in
  the sale and installation of roofing,
  siding, insulation and solar energy and
  related improvement products.

---

### RURAL BUILDER
**25438**
700 E. State St.
Iola, WI 54990
Telephone: (715) 445-2214
FAX: (715) 445-4087
Year Established: 1967
Pub. Frequency: 8/yr.
Page Size: standard
Subscrip. Rate: $18.95/yr.; $32.25/2 yrs.
Materials: 01,06,15,27,28,29,30,32,33
Freelance Pay: negotiable
Print Process: web offset
Circulation: 35,000
Circulation Type: controlled
**Owner(s):**
Krause Publications, Inc.
700 E. State St.
Iola, WI 54990
Telephone: (715) 445-2214
FAX: (715) 445-4087
Ownership %: 100
**Management:**
Rick Groth ..............................Publisher
**Editorial:**
Erik Stottrup ...........................Editor
Randy Graper ...........................Sales
Claude Ckmiel ..........................Sales
Mary Rolof ..............................Sales
**Desc.:** Editorial features focus on new
  trends in rural buildings, profiles of rural
  builders and on rural building designs.
**Readers:** Small, non-urban building
  contractors active in commercial,
  agricultureal, residential, and light
  industrial markets.
**Deadline:** story-30 days prior to pub. date;
  ads-25 days prior

---

### SHELTER
**22207**
167 Hwy. 72, E.
Collierville, TN 38017
Telephone: (901) 853-7470
FAX: (901) 853-6437
Mailing Address:
  P.O. Box 640
  Collierville, TN 38017
Year Established: 1964
Pub. Frequency: 8/yr.
Page Size: standard
Subscrip. Rate: $15/yr.
Circulation: 25,475
Circulation Type: controlled
**Owner(s):**
Associations Publications, Inc.
P.O. Box 640
Collierville, TN 38017
Telephone: (901) 853-7470
Ownership %: 100
**Management:**
James D. Powell ......................Publisher
**Editorial:**
Joyce Powell ...........................Editor
Owen Proctor ...............Associate Editor
Anissa Anderson ...........Associate Editor
**Desc.:** Contains articles on merchandising
  building supplies.
**Readers:** Wholesale and retail building
  supply dealers.

---

**Materials Accepted/Included:** 01-Business news 02-By-line articles 03-Fashion news 04-Food news 05-Freelance copy 06-Letters to editor 07-Real estate news 08-Sports news 09-Travel news 10-Book rev. 11-Movie rev. 12-Music rev. 13-TV rev. 14-Theater rev. 15-Coming events 16-Obituaries 17-Question & answer 18-Social announcements 19-Artwork 20-Cartoons 21-Photos 22-TV listings 23-Audio rec. 24-Video rec. 25-Books 26-Films/film clips 27-Personnel news 28-Press releases 29-New product news/photos 30-Trade lit. 31-Contracts awarded 32-Display adv. 33-Classified adv.

## SOUTHAM PUBLICATION CONSTRUCTION NEWS
22552

10825 Financial Centre Pky., Ste. 133
Little Rock, AR 72211-3555
Telephone: (501) 227-8551
FAX: (501) 227-6856
Year Established: 1934
Pub. Frequency: s-m.
Page Size: standard
Subscrip. Rate: $65/yr.
Circulation: 7,500
Circulation Type: controlled
**Owner(s):**
Construction Magazine Group
5295 Lakeview Pkwy., South Dr.
Indianapolis, IN 46268
Telephone: (317) 299-3156
Ownership %: 100
**Management:**
Mary Anne Nichol .....................Publisher
Sharon Johnson ...........Advertising Manager
**Editorial:**
William Orth .................................Editor
**Desc.:** Covers construction and
engineering fields in Oklahoma,
Arkansas, western Tennessee,
Louisiana, and Mississippi. Carries news
of industry in 5-state area, national news
of importance to 5-state area, project
information, company news, association
news, new products, personnel
appointments, articles illustrated by on-
the-job pictures, special reports and
highlights and details of new methods,
techniques.
**Readers:** Contractors, engineers, public
officials, et al., in the area covered.

## SOUTHERN BUILDING MAGAZINE
22209

900 Montclair Rd.
Birmingham, AL 35213
Telephone: (205) 591-1853
FAX: (205) 592-7001
Year Established: 1945
Pub. Frequency: bi-m.
Page Size: standard
Subscrip. Rate: $12/yr.
Freelance Pay: none
Circulation: 9,200
Circulation Type: paid
**Owner(s):**
Southern Building Code Congress
International, Inc
900 Montclair Rd.
Birmingham, AL 35213
Telephone: (205) 591-1853
Ownership %: 100
**Editorial:**
Karla Price ..............................Managing Editor
William J. Tangye .........Chief Executive Officer
**Desc.:** Edited for those in the building
code industry. Covers innovations in
building materials, new methods of
construction, code administration and
enforcement.
**Readers:** Architects, engineers,
contractors, municipal building officials.

## ST. LOUIS CONSTRUCTION NEWS & REVIEW
22210

8730 Big Bend Blvd.
St. Louis, MO 63119
Telephone: (314) 961-6644
FAX: (314) 961-4809
Year Established: 1969
Pub. Frequency: m.
Page Size: oversize
Subscrip. Rate: $18/yr.
Materials: 06,07,27,28,32,33,34
Freelance Pay: varies
Print Process: web offset
Circulation: 6,500
Circulation Type: controlled & paid

**Owner(s):**
Finan Publishing Co., Inc.
8730 Big Bend Blvd.
Saint Louis, MO 63119
Telephone: (314) 961-6644
Ownership %: 100
**Management:**
Thomas J. Finan .....................Publisher
Nancy Valentine ...............Advertising Manager
Laura Stackle .................Business Manager
**Editorial:**
Nancy Roenfeldt ...........................Editor
R. D. Richardson .............Production Director
**Desc.:** The voice for the bi-state St. Louis
area construction industry, with coverage
extending throughout Eastern Missouri
and Southern Illinois. Article coverage
includes general interest construction
news as well as special issue themes
monthly. News value and space
availability are criteria for publication.
The right is reserved to edit or rewrite
submitted stories. Departments include:
Building, Education, Construction
Projects, Architects, Engineers,
Contractors, Industry Briefs on People
and Places. Construction Law,
Construction Accounting, Organizations,
Construction News.
**Readers:** Architects, engineers, planners,
contract developers, manufacturers,
building owners, plant managers,
developers, construction managers,
estimators, specifiers, bankers.
Suppliers; state & local government
officials; municipalities; contractors;
trades; associations.

## SUN/COAST ARCHITECT/BUILDER
22199

333 E. Glenoaks Blvd., 204
Glendale, CA 91207-2074
Telephone: (818) 241-0250
FAX: (818) 241-4406
Year Established: 1935
Pub. Frequency: m.
Page Size: standard
Subscrip. Rate: $22/yr.
Materials: 01,02,06,07,10,15,17,20,21,25,
27,28,29,30,31,32
Print Process: web offset
Circulation: 57,000
Circulation Type: controlled
**Owner(s):**
McKellar Publications, Inc.
333 E. Glenoaks Blvd, 204
Glendale, CA 91207
Telephone: (818) 241-0250
Ownership %: 100
**Management:**
James L. McKellar ..............Chairman of Board
James L. McKellar ........................President
James L. McKellar ........................Publisher
Jean Koehler ...................Advertising Manager
Judy Davis ......................Circulation Manager
Mary Ita Smyth ................Office Manager
**Editorial:**
Doyle Peck ..............................Editor
Marla O'Laughlin ..........Administrative Assistant
Bonnie Millard ..........................Sales
Judith McKellar .........................Treasurer
**Desc.:** Edited for architects, builders,
developers, general contractors,
specification writers, designers and
remodelers in 41 Eastern, Mid-Western,
Southern, and Western states. Editorial
deals within single, multi-family,
commercial and remodeling/renovation.
Also covers management, marketing
techniques, trends and statistics, legal
and accounting.
**Readers:** Architects, specification writers,
designers, builders, developers and
general contractors and remodelers.

## TENNESSEE HOME BUILDER
55877

415 Fourth Ave. S.
Nashville, TN 37201-2211
Telephone: (615) 373-5565
FAX: (615) 370-5870
Year Established: 1980
Pub. Frequency: q.
Page Size: standard
Subscrip. Rate: membership
Circulation: 4,000
Circulation Type: controlled
**Owner(s):**
Bracey Campbell Co.
109 W. Park Dr., Ste. 200
Brentwood, TN 37027
Telephone: (615) 373-5565
**Management:**
Betty Webb ...................Advertising Manager
**Editorial:**
Betty Webb ..............................Editor
**Desc.:** The official voice of the Tennessee
housing industry through the Tennessee
Home Builders Association.
**Readers:** Read by all members of the
Tennessee Home Builders Association.

## TEXAS CIVIL ENGINEER
22639

3501 Manor Rd.
Austin, TX 78723
Telephone: (512) 472-8905
FAX: (512) 472-2934
Mailing Address:
    P.O. Box 2161
    Austin, TX 78768
Year Established: 1931
Pub. Frequency: 6/yr.
Page Size: standard
Subscrip. Rate: $30/yr.
Materials: 19,21,28,32,33
Print Process: offset
Circulation: 6,500
Circulation Type: free & paid
**Owner(s):**
Texas Section-ASCE
3501 Manor Rd.
Austin, TX 78723
Telephone: (512) 472-8905
FAX: (512) 472-2934
Ownership %: 100
**Management:**
Billy J. Moreau, Jr. ........................President
Janis M. Meyer ...............Advertising Manager
Janis M. Meyer ...............Circulation Manager
**Editorial:**
Janis M. Meyer ..........................Editor
**Desc.:** American Society of Civil Engineers
regional journal; news, technical papers
and professional practice essays.
**Readers:** Civil engineers in Texas
**Deadline:** story-10th of mo. prior to pub.
date; news-10th; photo-10th; ads-10th

## TEXAS CONTRACTOR
22640

2510 National Dr.
Garland, TX 75041-2329
Telephone: (214) 271-2693
FAX: (214) 278-4652
Mailing Address:
    P.O. Box 551359
    Dallas, TX 75355-1359
Year Established: 1923
Pub. Frequency: w.
Page Size: standard
Subscrip. Rate: $80/yr.
Materials: 01,15,16,27,28,29,32,33
Freelance Pay: $50/page
Print Process: offset
Circulation: 6,730
Circulation Type: controlled & paid

**Owner(s):**
Peters Publishing Co. of Texas
P.O. Box 551359
Dallas, TX 75355-1359
Telephone: (214) 271-2693
FAX: (214) 278-4652
Ownership %: 100
**Management:**
Weldon K. McDonald ........................President
Weldon K. McDonald ........................Publisher
Don Schmidt ...................Advertising Manager
Connie Kirsch ...................Circulation Manager
Linda McMillion ..............Production Manager
**Editorial:**
Wm. B. Morrison ..........................Editor
**Desc.:** Provides news and methods
information to engineered construction,
public works and related industries.
**Readers:** Contractors, public officials, mine
and quarry operators, architects,
engineers, producers and suppliers.

## TRADITIONAL BUILDING
65450

69A Seventh Ave.
Brooklyn, NY 11217
Telephone: (718) 636-0788
FAX: (718) 636-0750
Year Established: 1988
Pub. Frequency: bi-m.
Page Size: tabloid
Subscrip. Rate: $18/yr.
Print Process: web offset
Circulation: 17,250
Circulation Type: controlled & paid
**Owner(s):**
Historical Trends Corp.
69A Seventh Ave.
Brooklyn, NY 11217
Telephone: (718) 636-0788
Ownership %: 100
**Management:**
Clem Labine ..............................Publisher
**Editorial:**
Clem Labine ..............................Editor
Judith Lief ......................Managing Editor
Susan Littman ...............Advertising Director
**Desc.:** Review historical products for
restoration and new construction.
Profiles projects, architects and builders
doing traditional work.
**Readers:** Architects, contractors, interior
designers, and builders specializing in
restoration and new construction in
traditional styles.

## TUNNELLING & UNDERGROUND SPACE TECHNOLOGY
22642

660 White Plains Rd.
Tarrytown, NY 10591-5153
Telephone: (914) 524-9200
FAX: (914) 333-2444
Year Established: 1977
Pub. Frequency: q.
Page Size: standard
Subscrip. Rate: $395/yr.
**Owner(s):**
Elsevier Science Co.
660 White Plains Rd.
Tarrytown, NY 10591-5153
Telephone: (914) 524-9200
Ownership %: 100
**Bureau(s):**
Pergamon Press, Inc.
Maxwell House, Fairview Park
Elmsford, NY 10523
Telephone: (914) 592-7700
Contact: Robert Miranda, President
**Management:**
Robert Miranda ........................President
Arnold Krazler ...................Advertising Manager
**Editorial:**
Dr. Charles Fairhurst ..............Executive Editor
Einar Broch ......................Senior Editor
K. Sale ..............................Editor

**Materials Accepted/Included:** 01-Business news 02-By-line articles 03-Fashion news 04-Food news 05-Freelance copy 06-Letters to editor 07-Real estate news 08-Sports news 09-Travel news 10-Book rev. 11-Movie rev. 12-Music rev. 13-TV rev. 14-Theater rev. 15-Coming events 16-Obituaries 17-Question & answer 18-Social announcements 19-Artwork 20-Cartoons 21-Photos 22-TV listings 23-Audio rec. 24-Video rec. 25-Books 26-Films/film clips 27-Personnel news 28-Press releases 29-New product news/photos 30-Trade lit. 31-Contracts awarded 32-Display adv. 33-Classified adv.

4-56

Keith Cambert ............................................Editor

**Desc.:** Devoted to the broad technical, legal and social aspects of expanding the use of this important resource.

**Readers:** Civil and mining engineers, geologists, excavation engineers, environmentalists, lawyers.

## ULTILITY CONSTRUCTION & MAINTENANCE
68750

P.O. Box 183
Cary, IL 60013
Telephone: (708) 639-2200
FAX: (708) 639-9542
Mailing Address:
P.O. Box 183
Cary, IL 60013-0183
Year Established: 1990
Pub. Frequency: q.
Page Size: standard
Subscrip. Rate: free
Materials: 01,02,05,06,15,24,25,27,29,30, 31,32,33
Print Process: offset
Circulation: 51,000
Circulation Type: controlled & paid
**Owner(s):**
Practical Communications, Inc.
P.O. Box 183
Cary, IL 60013-0183
Telephone: (708) 639-2200
Ownership %: 100
**Management:**
J. Chance ............................................President
L. Jack Stober ....................................Publisher
James Queenan ................Advertising Manager
James Queenan ................Circulation Manager
**Editorial:**
Alan Richter ............................Editor-in-Chief
**Desc.:** Focuses on construction, maintenance, and equipment for managers in the utilities, public works, municipalities, CATV operations industries and related contractors.

## WALLS & CEILINGS
22211

8602 N. 40th St.
Tampa, FL 33604
Telephone: (813) 989-9300
FAX: (813) 980-3982
Year Established: 1938
Pub. Frequency: m.
Page Size: standard
Subscrip. Rate: $24/yr.
Freelance Pay: $25-$125/article
Circulation: 22,000
Circulation Type: controlled & paid
**Owner(s):**
L.M. Rector Corp.
8602 N. 40th St.
Tampa, FL 33604
Telephone: (813) 989-9300
Ownership %: 100
**Bureau(s):**
Walls & Ceilings Magazine - West
P.O. Box 311
Monterey, CA 93942
Telephone: (408) 649-3466
Contact: Bob Welch, Editor
**Management:**
Lee Rector ..........................................Publisher
Mary V. Rector ....................Business Manager
Beth Matteson ..................Circulation Manager
**Editorial:**
Robert F. Welch ......................Executive Editor
Greg Campbell ......................Managing Editor
Barbara Castelli ..........Administrative Assistant
Paula Graham ......................Marketing Director
**Desc.:** Covers wall and ceiling construction techniques. Contains illustrated project stories showing how to improve operating efficiency, cut job costs, achieve better wall and ceiling construction.

**Readers:** Contractors, specifiers, manufacturers, architects and suppliers engaged in drywall, lath, plaster, metal framing, ceiling systems, exterior insulation, acoustics ad fireproofing.

## WESTERN BUILDER
22647

6526 River Pkwy.
Milwaukee, WI 53213
Telephone: (414) 453-7700
FAX: (414) 453-8075
Mailing Address:
P.O. Box 13309
Milwaukee, WI 53213-0309
Year Established: 1902
Pub. Frequency: w.
Page Size: standard
Subscrip. Rate: $83/yr.
Materials: 01,02,10,15,32,33,34
Print Process: web offset
Circulation: 4,650
Circulation Type: free & paid
**Owner(s):**
Western Builder Publishing Co.
6526 River Pkwy.
Milwaukee, WI 53213
Telephone: (414) 453-7700
Ownership %: 100
**Management:**
James E. Keyes ...............................President
John A. Keyes ................................Publisher
James E. Keyes ................Advertising Manager
**Editorial:**
John A. Keyes ......................................Editor
**Desc.:** Contributed and staff-written articles covering construction, public works, progress reports. Reviews and covers new equipment, appointments, company news, new literature, and association news and meetings.
**Readers:** Contractors, architects, engineers, distributors.
**Deadline:** story-1 wk.; ads-10 days

## WEST VIRGINIA CONSTRUCTION NEWS
22646

2114 Kanawha Blvd., E.
Charleston, WV 25311
Telephone: (304) 342-1166
FAX: (304) 342-1074
Year Established: 1937
Pub. Frequency: bi-m.
Page Size: standard
Subscrip. Rate: $8/yr.
Circulation: 1,300
Circulation Type: controlled
**Owner(s):**
Contractors Association of West Virginia
2114 Kanawha Blvd., E.
Charleston, WV 25311
Telephone: (304) 342-1166
Ownership %: 100
**Management:**
Tom Gesner ......................Advertising Manager
**Editorial:**
Mike Clowser ........................................Editor
**Desc.:** Publication covering construction industry in West Virginia. Features on large or unique construction projects, respected individuals and companies, research projects, new products, important meetings, symposiums and conventions. Publicity material used if newsworthy in our region and of interest or benefit to our industry (selective). Very receptive to photos and graphics. By-lines desired.
**Readers:** Representatives of companies involved directly or indirectly in the construction industry - owners, contractors, sales people, state and local governments.

## WRECKING & SALVAGE JOURNAL
22651

P.O. Box 9073
Braintree, MA 02184
Telephone: (617) 848-6150
FAX: (617) 848-6160
Year Established: 1967
Pub. Frequency: m.
Page Size: standard
Subscrip. Rate: $35/yr.
Circulation: 2,500
Circulation Type: paid
**Owner(s):**
Wrecking & Salvage Journal, Inc.
P.O. Box 410
North Conway, NH 03860
Ownership %: 100
**Bureau(s):**
Sue Cellucci
Telephone: (617) 848-6150
Contact: Sue Cellucci, News Coordinator

Karen Duane
Telephone: (516) 757-3025
Contact: Karen Duane, Advertising Manager
**Management:**
Katherine Duane ....................................Owner
Katherine Duane ................................President
Herbert T. Duane, Jr. ..........................Publisher
Karen Duane ....................Advertising Manager
**Editorial:**
H. Tobis Duane ....................................Editor
Sue Cellucci ..........................Circulation Editor
Karen Duane ..............................News Editor
**Desc.:** Contains news articles on jobs: awarded, in process, and upcoming. Feature stories on unusual wrecking jobs, techniques and problems peculiar to the industry. By-line pieces may deal with environmentalism, projections of large-scale demolition possibilities. New equipment is covered and current legal requirements including OSHA requirements.
**Readers:** Owners of wrecking firms devoted to demolition & removal.
**Deadline:** story-10th of mo. prior to pub. date; news-10th of mo. prior; photo-10th of mo. prior; ads-10th of mo. prior

---

## Group 034-Building Management & Real Estate

## APARTMENT OWNER/BUILDER
22215

3220 E. Willow
Long Beach, CA 90806
Telephone: (310) 424-8674
FAX: (213) 636-8353
Year Established: 1959
Pub. Frequency: m.
Page Size: standard
Subscrip. Rate: $9/yr.; $15/2 yrs.
Circulation: 60,000
Circulation Type: controlled & paid
**Owner(s):**
Apartment News Publications, Inc.
3220 E. Willow
Long Beach, CA 90806
Telephone: (310) 424-8674
Ownership %: 100
**Management:**
Donn R. Smeallie ..............................Publisher
**Editorial:**
Chris Callard ........................................Editor
Mark Ladenheim ..............................Advertising

**Desc.:** News and feature stories concerning legislation (state and national), business, financial, construction, maintenance, operation, and new products pertaining to the apartment industry. Includes how-to's of cost-cutting in apartment management. Five separate issues are published for the different areas of Los Angeles and Orange counties.
**Readers:** Apartment owners and managers.

## APPRAISAL JOURNAL, THE
65757

875 N. Michigan Ave., Ste. 2400
Chicago, IL 60611
Telephone: (312) 335-4100
FAX: (312) 335-4400
Year Established: 1932
Pub. Frequency: q.
Page Size: standard
Subscrip. Rate: $30/yr.; $55/2 yrs.; $75/3 yrs.
Materials: 07
Circulation: 36,000
Circulation Type: paid
**Owner(s):**
Appraisal Institute
875 N. Michigan Ave.
Ste. 2400
Chicago, IL 60611-1980
Telephone: (312) 335-4100
Ownership %: 100
**Editorial:**
Richard Marchetelli ................................Editor
Jennifer Roberts ......................Managing Editor
**Readers:** Real estate professionals.

## BUILDING OPERATING MANAGEMENT
22219

2100 W. Florist
Milwaukee, WI 53209
Telephone: (414) 228-7701
FAX: (414) 228-1134
Mailing Address:
P.O. Box 694
Milwaukee, WI 53201
Year Established: 1954
Pub. Frequency: m.
Page Size: standard
Subscrip. Rate: $49/yr.
Circulation: 67,000
Circulation Type: controlled & paid
**Owner(s):**
Trade Press Publishing Corp.
P.O. Box 694
Milwaukee, WI 53201
Telephone: (414) 228-7701
Ownership %: 100
**Bureau(s):**
Trade Press Publishing Corp.
102 E. Main St.
Little Falls, NJ 07424
Contact: Kevin Dahl, Sales Manager
**Management:**
Robert Wisniewski ..............................President
Robert Wisniewski ..............................Publisher
**Editorial:**
Richard Yake ........................................Editor
Edward Sullivan ......................Managing Editor
Richard Yake ........................Editorial Director
David Kozlowski ......................Associate Editor
**Desc.:** Contains features on remodeling, retrofit, maintenance and product oriented subjects. Also contains installation case studies from manufacturers.
**Readers:** Building owners and managers.

## CHIEF ENGINEER
24376

11340 W. 159th St.
Orland Park, IL 60462-4415
Telephone: (708) 403-2444
FAX: (708) 349-4507

---

**Materials Accepted/Included:** 01-Business news 02-By-line articles 03-Fashion news 04-Food news 05-Freelance copy 06-Letters to editor 07-Real estate news 08-Sports news 09-Travel news 10-Book rev. 11-Movie rev. 12-Music rev. 13-TV rev. 14-Theater rev. 15-Coming events 16-Obituaries 17-Question & answer 18-Social announcements 19-Artwork 20-Cartoons 21-Photos 22-TV listings 23-Audio rec. 24-Video rec. 25-Books 26-Films/film clips 27-Personnel news 28-Press releases 29-New product news/photos 30-Trade lit. 31-Contracts awarded 32-Display adv. 33-Classified adv.

4-57

Year Established: 1935
Pub. Frequency: m.
Page Size: standard
Subscrip. Rate: $25/yr.
Materials: 01,02,28,29,30,32
Print Process: offset
Circulation: 1,800
Circulation Type: controlled
**Owner(s):**
Chief Engineers Assoc. of Chicagoland
11340 W. 159th St.
Orland Park, IL 60462
Telephone: (708) 403-2444
FAX: (708) 349-4507
Ownership %: 100
**Editorial:**
Ernest K. Wulff .........................Executive Editor
**Desc.:** Material directed to operating engineer, any material in reference to boilers, maintenance, new products, all related to big and medium buildings and complexes.
**Deadline:** story-30 days prior to pub. date; news-30 days prior; photo-30 days prior; ads-30 days prior

69095

**COMMERCIAL**
138 N. Saginaw
Pontiac, MI 48342-2112
Telephone: (810) 332-9770
FAX: (810) 332-3003
Year Established: 1988
Pub. Frequency: m.
Page Size: standard
Subscrip. Rate: $18/yr.
Materials: 01,02,05,07,15,17,19,21,28,32, 33,34
Print Process: web
Circulation: 37,000
Circulation Type: controlled & paid
**Owner(s):**
Commercial, Inc.
138 N. Saginaw
Pontiac, MI 48342-2112
Telephone: (810) 332-9770
FAX: (810) 332-3003
Ownership %: 100
**Editorial:**
Bonnie M. Taube .........................Editor
**Desc.:** Provides comprehensive, current offerings of commercial real estate and business opportunities for sale or lease in Michigan and reports the latest commercial real estate news, trends, and professional how-to articles.
**Readers:** Over 65% of our readers are at the vice-presidential level or higher. Commercial, Inc. covers 11 of Michigan's most prominent counties. Our subscribers are the top decision makers in the commercial real estate community. Commercial property owners, managers, investors, developers, builders, brokers, financial lenders, architects, attorneys, accountants, appraisers, environmental consultants, economic development officials, corporate real estate executives, and others allied to the field.
**Deadline:** story-10th of the mo.; news-10th of the mo.; ads-25th of the mo.

66024

**COMMERCIAL INVESTMENT REAL ESTATE JOURNAL**
430 N. Michigan Ave., 500
Chicago, IL 60611-4092
Telephone: (312) 321-4530
FAX: (312) 329-8882
Year Established: 1982
Pub. Frequency: q.
Subscrip. Rate: $32/yr.
Circulation: 9,000
Circulation Type: paid

**Owner(s):**
Commercial Investment Real Estate Institute
430 N. Michigan Ave., 500
Chicago, IL 60611-4092
Telephone: (312) 321-4530
Ownership %: 100
**Editorial:**
Lorene Norton Palm .........................Editor
**Desc.:** Provides practical information for professionals on all aspects of commercial real estate.

22225

**CONNECTICUT REAL ESTATE JOURNAL**
57 Washington St.
Norwell, MA 02061
Telephone: (617) 878-4540
FAX: (617) 871-1853
Mailing Address:
   P.O. Box 55
   Accord, MA 02018
Year Established: 1963
Pub. Frequency: s-m.
Page Size: tabloid
Subscrip. Rate: free; $48/yr.
Circulation: 30,000
Circulation Type: free & paid
**Owner(s):**
East Coast Publications, Inc.
P.O. Box 55
Accord, MA 02018
Telephone: (617) 749-6947
Ownership %: 100
**Management:**
Christine Fernald .........................Publisher
**Desc.:** Stories and photos on real estate sales, land investment real estate.
**Readers:** Investors, builders, developers, brokers.

52672

**CONNECTICUT REALTOR, THE**
316 Farmington Ave.
Hartford, CT 06105-3300
Telephone: (203) 522-7255
Pub. Frequency: m.
Page Size: tabloid
Subscrip. Rate: free to members
Materials: 01,02,06,07,20,21
Print Process: web
Circulation: 13,000
Circulation Type: controlled
**Owner(s):**
Connecticut Association of Realtors
Ownership %: 100
**Management:**
Gerald Kunde .........................Executive Vice President
**Editorial:**
Brad Durrell .........................Editor
Lisa Governale .........................Communications Director
**Readers:** Members, and real estate industry in Connecticut.

69400

**CPM ASPECTS**
430 N. Michigan Ave.
Chicago, IL 60611-4090
Telephone: (312) 329-6055
FAX: (312) 661-0217
Mailing Address:
   P.O. Box 109025
   Chicago, IL 60610-9025
Year Established: 1968
Pub. Frequency: bi-m.
Page Size: standard
Subscrip. Rate: membership
Materials: 01,07,28,30
Print Process: offset
Circulation: 12,785
Circulation Type: free & paid

**Owner(s):**
Institute of Real Estate Management
430 N. Michigan Ave.
Chicago, IL 60611-4090
Telephone: (312) 329-6055
FAX: (312) 661-0217
Ownership %: 100
**Management:**
Ronald Vukas .........................Executive Vice President
**Editorial:**
Pamela M. Chwedyk .........................Editor
Martha McGregor .........................Editorial Supervisor
Kathy Forss .........................Graphic Designer
Thom Olson .........................Publications Graphic Arts Supervisor
Joyce Travis Copess .........................Staff VP, Education & Communications
Charles Achilles .........................Staff VP, Legislative Affairs & Special Ser.
J. Stephen Reed .........................Typographer
**Desc.:** Covers IREM policies and programs, news on industry trends, legislation affecting real estate management, HUD, and a job bulletin.

65393

**CRITTENDEN'S WESTERN REAL ESTATE WEEK**
P.O. Box 6119
Novato, CA 94948
Telephone: (415) 382-2400
FAX: (415) 382-2416
Pub. Frequency: s-m.
Page Size: tabloid
Subscrip. Rate: $79/yr.
Circulation: 3,672
Circulation Type: paid
**Owner(s):**
Real Estate Week, Inc.
P.O. Box 6119
Novato, CA 94948
Telephone: (415) 382-2400
Ownership %: 100
**Editorial:**
John N. Goodwin .........................Editor
**Desc.:** Real estate development news in the West; who's building, what's selling and for how much.
**Readers:** Real estate developers and their satellites.

69524

**DEVELOPMENT**
2201 Cooperative Way
Herndon, VA 22071
Telephone: (914) 365-0334
FAX: (914) 365-0503
Mailing Address:
   P.O. Box 8
   Piermont, NY 10968
Year Established: 1978
Pub. Frequency: q.
Page Size: standard
Subscrip. Rate: $50/yr. member; $65/yr. non-member
Materials: 02,07,28,32
Print Process: offset
Circulation: 10,000
Circulation Type: paid
**Owner(s):**
National Assn. of Industrial and Office Parks
2201 Cooperative Way
Herndon, VA 22071
Telephone: (703) 904-7100
FAX: (703) 904-7942
Ownership %: 100
**Editorial:**
Ron Derven .........................Editor
Ellen Rand .........................Editor

**Desc.:** Covers the full range of commercial real estate.
**Deadline:** story-3 mo. prior to pub. date; news-3 mo. prior to pub. date; photo-3 mo. prior to pub. date; ads-1 mo. prior to pub. date

69096

**EMPIRE STATE REALTOR**
130 Washington Ave.
Albany, NY 12210-2298
Telephone: (518) 463-0300
FAX: (518) 462-5474
Year Established: 1970
Pub. Frequency: m.
Subscrip. Rate: $4/yr.
Materials: 07,28,32,33
Circulation: 35,000
Circulation Type: paid
**Owner(s):**
New York State Association of Realtors
130 Washington Ave.
Albany, NY 12210-2298
Telephone: (518) 463-0300
Ownership %: 100
**Editorial:**
Kevin W. LaPoint .......Communications Director
**Desc.:** Provides information about current events in the real estate industry and association activities and programs.
**Deadline:** story-20th of mo. prior to pub. date; ads-10th of mo. prior

49889

**FACILITIES DESIGN & MANAGEMENT**
1515 Broadway
New York, NY 10036
Telephone: (212) 869-1300
FAX: (212) 302-6273
Year Established: 1982
Pub. Frequency: m.
Page Size: standard
Subscrip. Rate: free to members
Circulation: 35,000
Circulation Type: controlled
**Owner(s):**
Miller Freeman, Inc.
1515 Broadway
New York, NY 10036
Telephone: (212) 869-1300

United Newspapers
London United Kingdom
**Editorial:**
Anne Fallucchi .........................Editor
**Desc.:** Subject matter relates to the design, planning, and management of their commercial and institutional facilities. Articles: new corporate offices; interviews with corporate executives on varying topics, office-related articles (productivity, human factors, etc.); new products.
**Readers:** 35,000 corporate facilities executives.

23196

**FACILITY MANAGER**
4425 W. Airport Frwy., Ste. 590
Irving, TX 75062
Telephone: (214) 255-8020
FAX: (214) 255-9582
Year Established: 1985
Pub. Frequency: bi-m.
Page Size: standard
Subscrip. Rate: $45/yr.
Materials: 02,19,28,30
Freelance Pay: negotiable
Print Process: offset
Circulation: 2,200
Circulation Type: paid

---

**Materials Accepted/Included:** 01-Business news 02-By-line articles 03-Fashion news 04-Food news 05-Freelance copy 06-Letters to editor 07-Real estate news 08-Sports news 09-Travel news 10-Book rev. 11-Movie rev. 12-Music rev. 13-TV rev. 14-Theater rev. 15-Coming events 16-Obituaries 17-Question & answer 18-Social announcements 19-Artwork 20-Cartoons 21-Photos 22-TV listings 23-Audio rec. 24-Video rec. 25-Books 26-Films/film clips 27-Personnel news 28-Press releases 29-New product news/photos 30-Trade lit. 31-Contracts awarded 32-Display adv. 33-Classified adv.

**Owner(s):**
Facility Manager
4425 W. Airport Frwy.
Irving, TX 75062
Telephone: (214) 255-8020
FAX: (214) 255-9582
Ownership %: 100
**Management:**
John Swinburn ...................Executive Director
Carole Snyder .................Advertising Manager
**Editorial:**
Julie Herrick ...............................................Editor
**Desc.:** Edited to provide managers of
public assembly facilities such as
arenas, stadiums, auditoriums,
performing arts theaters, convention
centers and exhibit halls with up-to-date
features on industry issues of current
interest. Contains interviews and case
histories, reports on problems and
solutions, analyzes trends and surveys
leaders in related service and product
organizations. Departments
update issues in legislation, marketing
and vendor products and services.
**Readers:** Top executives of public events
facilities including stadiums, arenas,
auditoriums, convention/exhibit halls and
performing arts in US, Canada and other
countries.
**Deadline:** story-1 mo. prior to pub. date;
ads-1 mo. prior

56293

## FLORIDA MARKET UPDATE
P.O. Box 1052
Port Washington, NY 11050
Telephone: (516) 741-8877
Year Established: 1985
Pub. Frequency: m.
Page Size: standard
Subscrip. Rate: $100/yr.; $135/yr.
overseas
Freelance Pay: negotiable
Circulation: 3,000
Circulation Type: controlled
**Owner(s):**
Data Directions, Inc.
P.O. Box 1052
Port Washingtn, NY 11050
Ownership %: 100
**Management:**
Mary Ann Boerner ...............................President
Mary Ann Boerner ...............................Publisher
**Editorial:**
Henry Boerner ......................................Editor
Henry Boerner ................Secretary & Treasurer
**Desc.:** Covers Florida market trends in
economy, politics, demographics,
tourism, agriculture, military, foreign
trade, corporate affairs, banking,
transportation, aviation, real estate &
development.
**Readers:** Senior managers and executives,
business owners, government officials,
libraries, professionals, academicians,
media (editors).

56288

## FLORIDA REAL ESTATE & DEVELOPMENT UPDATE
P.O. Box 1052
Port Washington, NY 11050
Telephone: (516) 741-8877
Year Established: 1986
Pub. Frequency: m.
Page Size: standard
Subscrip. Rate: $100/yr.
Freelance Pay: negotiable
Circulation: 3,000
Circulation Type: paid

**Owner(s):**
Data Directions, Inc.
23 E. Tarpon Ave.
Tarpon Springs, FL 34689
Telephone: (813) 942-1018
Ownership %: 100
**Management:**
Mary Ann Boerner ...............................President
Mary Ann Boerner ...............................Publisher
**Editorial:**
Henry Boerner ......................................Editor
Henry Boerner ................Secretary & Treasurer
**Desc.:** Explores residential, commercial,
industrial, resort, institutional,
governmental and other land use and
development in the State of Florida.
Subjects covered include zoning, real
estate transactions, contracts, financing,
construction, companies, trends,
statistics for real property activities,
government actions, sales and leasing,
among more than 100 topics regularly
monitored by the editors.
**Readers:** Senior management and
business owners. Banks, lenders,
financial institutions; real estate brokers;
serious investors in real property;
government officials;
construction/contracting companies;
attorneys; libraries; area development
agencies and chambers of commerce;
corporate officers (non-real estate);
other media (newspapers, magazines,
wire services); foreign consulates.

22226

## FLORIDA REALTOR
7025 Augusta National Dr.
Orlando, FL 32822
Telephone: (407) 438-1400
FAX: (407) 438-1411
Mailing Address:
P.O. Box 725025
Orlando, FL 32872-5025
Year Established: 1925
Pub. Frequency: 11/yr.
Page Size: 4 Color Photos/Art
Subscrip. Rate: $15/yr.
Circulation: 60,000
Circulation Type: paid
**Owner(s):**
Florida Association Of Realtors
P.O. Box 725025
Orlando, FL 32872-5025
Telephone: (407) 438-1400
FAX: (407) 438-1411
Ownership %: 100
**Management:**
Jeff Zipper ...........................................Publisher
Tracey Lowton .................Advertising Manager
**Editorial:**
Pam Littlefield ...........................Editor in Chief
**Desc.:** Of professional and education
interest to those interested in Florida
real estate from sales - people to
syndicators, investors, and
property managers.
**Readers:** Individuals interested in Florida
real estate.

22228

## JOURNAL OF PROPERTY MANAGEMENT
430 N. Michigan Ave.
Chicago, IL 60611
Telephone: (312) 661-1930
FAX: (312) 661-0217
Mailing Address:
P.O. Box 109025
Chicago, IL 60610
Year Established: 1934
Pub. Frequency: bi-m.
Page Size: standard
Subscrip. Rate: $38.95/yr.
Materials: 01,02,06,07,21,25,29,32
Freelance Pay: negotiable

Circulation: 19,800
Circulation Type: paid
**Owner(s):**
Institute of Real Estate Management
430 N. Michigan Ave.
Chicago, IL 60611
Telephone: (312) 661-1930
Ownership %: 100
**Management:**
Ronald Vukas ........................................President
Carla Eringer ....................Advertising Manager
Carole Hansen ...................Circulation Manager
**Editorial:**
Mariwyn Evans ......................................Editor
Katherine Anderson .................Associate Editor
**Desc.:** Presents articles written by
members of the Institute of Real Estate
Management (CPM's) and other
professionals in the field of real estate.
Topics include asset management,
purchasing, personnel, computer
applications, accounting, maintenance,
construction, leasing, developing, and
software. Departments include: New
Products, Computer Corner, Viewpoint,
Insurance Insights, Investment Corner,
Software Reviews, Tax Corner, Book
Reviews, New Publications, Courses &
Conferences, Legal Insights.
**Readers:** Property managers of
apartments, industrial parks, office
buildings, shopping centers, all types of
residential and commercial property.
**Deadline:** story-3 mos.; news-3 mos.;
photo-3 mos.; ads-2 mos.

52678

## MAINE & NEW HAMPSHIRE REAL ESTATE GUIDE
89 N. Main St.
Andover, MA 01810
Telephone: (508) 475-8732
FAX: (508) 475-6132
Year Established: 1970
Pub. Frequency: m.
Page Size: pocket
Subscrip. Rate: $20/yr.
Circulation: 15,000
Circulation Type: paid
**Owner(s):**
Robert Finlayson
39 Abbot St.
Andover, MA 01810
Telephone: (508) 475-8732
Ownership %: 100
**Management:**
Robert Finlayson ..................................Publisher
**Editorial:**
Gary Finlayson ....................Assistant Publisher
**Desc.:** Includes tax rates & town
information.
**Readers:** Middle & upper income people
looking for real estate.

52606

## MAINE REAL ESTATE GUIDE
89 N. Main St.
Andover, MA 01810
Telephone: (508) 475-8732
Year Established: 1970
Pub. Frequency: m.
Page Size: pocket
Subscrip. Rate: $3 newsstand; $20/yr.
Materials: 32
Circulation: 15,000
Circulation Type: paid
**Owner(s):**
Robert Finlayson
PO Box 999
Andover, MA 01810
Telephone: (508) 475-8732
Ownership %: 100
**Management:**
Robert Finlayson ..................................Publisher
**Editorial:**
Gary Finlayson ....................Assistant Publisher

**Readers:** anyone looking for real estate in
Maine.
**Deadline:** ads-8th of mo. prior to pub. date

69097

## MANAGER'S REPORT
1700 Southern Blvd.
W. Palm Beach, FL 33406
Telephone: (407) 687-4700
Pub. Frequency: m.
Subscrip. Rate: $18/yr.
Circulation: 10,000
Circulation Type: paid
**Owner(s):**
Ivor Thomas & Associates, Inc.
1700 Southern Blvd.
W. Palm Beach, FL 33406
Telephone: (407) 687-4700
Ownership %: 100
**Editorial:**
Ivor Thomas ..........................................Editor
**Desc.:** News and feature articles dealing
with areas of interest to individuals
responsible for the management and
purchasing activities of condominium,
homeowner and co-operative
associations.

22223

## METRO CHICAGO REAL ESTATE
415 N. State St.
Chicago, IL 60610
Telephone: (312) 644-7800
FAX: (312) 644-4255
Year Established: 1913
Pub. Frequency: bi-m.
Page Size: standard
Subscrip. Rate: $20/yr.
Materials: 02,07,32,33
Print Process: web offset
Circulation: 10,000
Circulation Type: controlled & paid
**Owner(s):**
Law Bulletin Pub. Co.
415 N. State
Chicago, IL 60610
Telephone: (312) 644-7800
FAX: (312) 644-4255
Ownership %: 100
**Management:**
Lanning MacFarland ...........................President
Sandy MacFarland ...............................Publisher
**Editorial:**
Kevin Deany ...........................Managing Editor
Linda Seggelke .................Associate Publisher
**Desc.:** Features and photos on new
methods of construction. Mortgage rates
and real estate financing. Chicago area
real estate special editions include
industrial development, new products
and more.
**Readers:** Real estate brokers, mortgage
bankers, real estate appraisers and
investors.

22229

## MISSOURI REALTOR, THE
2601 Bernadette Pl.
Columbia, MO 65203
Telephone: (314) 445-8400
Mailing Address:
P.O. Box 1327
Columbia, MO 65205
Year Established: 1937
Pub. Frequency: 8/yr.
Page Size: standard
Subscrip. Rate: $6/yr.
Circulation: 18,000
Circulation Type: paid
**Owner(s):**
Missouri Association of Realtors
P.O. Box 1327
Columbia, MO 65203
Telephone: (314) 445-8400
FAX: (314) 445-7865
Ownership %: 100

---

**Materials Accepted/Included:** 01-Business news 02-By-line articles 03-Fashion news 04-Food news 05-Freelance copy 06-Letters to editor 07-Real estate news 08-Sports news 09-Travel news
10-Book rev. 11-Movie rev. 12-Music rev. 13-TV rev. 14-Theater rev. 15-Coming events 16-Obituaries 17-Question & answer 18-Social announcements 19-Artwork 20-Cartoons 21-Photos 22-TV listings
23-Audio rec. 24-Video rec. 25-Books 26-Films/film clips 27-Personnel news 28-Press releases 29-New product news/photos 30-Trade lit. 31-Contracts awarded 32-Display adv. 33-Classified adv.

**Editorial:**
Pamela J. Sage .............................Editor
**Desc.:** News, features, articles of up to 1,
500 words pertaining to real estate and
related fields.
**Readers:** Professional real estate brokers,
salesmen.

52669

## NATIONAL REAL ESTATE
INVESTOR SOURCEBOOK

6151 Powers Ferry Rd. N.W.
Atlanta, GA 30339-2941
Telephone: (404) 955-2500
Year Established: 1961
Pub. Frequency: a.
Page Size: standard
Print Process: offset
Circulation: 32,500
Circulation Type: controlled
**Owner(s):**
Argus, Inc.
6151 Powers Ferry Rd., N.W.
Atlanta, GA 30339
Telephone: (404) 955-2500
Ownership %: 100
**Management:**
Jerrold France ............................Publisher
**Editorial:**
Paula Stephens .............................Editor
Barbara Katinsky .........................Editor
Melanie Gibbs .................Managing Editor
Robin Sherman .............Editorial Director
Paula Stephens .............Associate Publisher
John Davis ....................Associate Publisher
**Desc.:** Contains over 7,000 listings of
companies and individuals in 22
categories of real estate services.
**Readers:** The owners, developers,
investors and managers of commercial
or income-producing estates and those
in allied fields.

22232

## NATIONAL REAL ESTATE
INVESTOR, THE

6151 Powers Ferry Rd., N.W.
Atlanta, GA 30339-2941
Telephone: (404) 955-2500
FAX: (404) 618-0343
Year Established: 1959
Pub. Frequency: m.
Page Size: standard
Subscrip. Rate: $70/yr.; $94/2 yrs.
Print Process: web offset
Circulation: 33,012
Circulation Type: controlled
**Owner(s):**
Argus, Inc.
6151 Powers Ferry Rd., N.W.
Atlanta, GA 30339
Telephone: (404) 955-2500
Ownership %: 100
**Management:**
Jerrold France .........................President
Jerrold France .........................Publisher
Terri Hill .......................Production Manager
**Editorial:**
Paula Stephens .............................Editor
Paula Stephens .............Associate Publisher
John Davis ....................Associate Publisher
Martin E. Greene ...........Production Director
**Desc.:** Covers all phases of income-
producing real estate construction,
development, financing, investment and
management.
**Readers:** Builders and developers,
financial institutions, mortgage bankers,
real estate brokers, corporate real estate
executives.

22233

## NEW ENGLAND REAL ESTATE
JOURNAL

57 Washington St.
Norwell, MA 02061
Telephone: (617) 878-4540
FAX: (617) 871-1853
Mailing Address:
P.O. Box 55
Hingham, MA 02018
Year Established: 1963
Pub. Frequency: w.
Page Size: tabloid
Subscrip. Rate: $96/yr.; $172/2 yrs.
Materials: 01,07,28,32,33
Print Process: web offset
Circulation: 10,000
Circulation Type: paid
**Owner(s):**
East Coast Publication, Inc.
P.O. Box 55
Hingham, MA 02018
Telephone: (617) 878-4540
FAX: (617) 871-1853
Ownership %: 100
**Management:**
Roland Hopkins .........................Publisher
Patricia Stone ...............Advertising Manager
Coleman
**Editorial:**
David Denelle ...............Editor in Chief
Benjamin Summers .................Managing Editor
Cheryl Stevenson .........................Art Editor
**Desc.:** Stories and photos on real estate
sales, leases, mortgages and plans on
commercial, industrial and investment
real estate.
**Readers:** Investors, builders, developers,
brokers, bankers.
**Deadline:** ads-Fri. prior to issue date

52677

## NEW HAMPSHIRE REAL ESTATE
GUIDE

89 N. Main St.
Andover, MA 01810
Telephone: (508) 475-8732
Year Established: 1970
Pub. Frequency: m.
Page Size: pocket
Subscrip. Rate: $20/yr.
Circulation: 15,000
Circulation Type: paid
**Owner(s):**
Robert Finlayson
39 Abbot St.
Andover, MA 01810
Telephone: (508) 475-8732
Ownership %: 100
**Management:**
Robert Finlayson ........................Publisher
**Editorial:**
Gary Finlayson ...............Assistant Publisher
**Readers:** Middle & upper income people
looking for real estate.

52601

## NEW HOMES GUIDE

1010 Wisconsin Ave., N.W., #600
Washington, DC 20007
Telephone: (202) 342-0410
FAX: (202) 342-0515
Year Established: 1974
Pub. Frequency: bi-m.
Page Size: pocket
Subscrip. Rate: free
Materials: 07
Print Process: web
Circulation: 50,000
Circulation Type: controlled
**Owner(s):**
William A. Regardie
1010 Wisconsin Ave.
Washington, DC 20007
Telephone: (202) 342-0410
Ownership %: 100

**Management:**
Charles Browning ........................Publisher
**Desc.:** A thorough directory to all of the
new home and condominium
communities in the Washington area;
featuring maps and community
descriptions, plus paid advertising.
**Readers:** Personnel directors, realtors.

69098

## NORTH CAROLINA HOUSING
NETWORK

9607 Gayton Rd., Ste. 201
Richmond, VA 23233
Telephone: (804) 741-6704
FAX: (804) 750-2399
Year Established: 1985
Pub. Frequency: m.
Subscrip. Rate: $39/yr.
Circulation: 23,971
Circulation Type: paid
**Owner(s):**
Leo Douglas, Inc.
9607 Gayton Rd., Ste. 201
Richmond, VA 23233
Telephone: (804) 741-6704
Ownership %: 100
**Editorial:**
D.J. Kingrey ...............................Editor
**Desc.:** Covers the design, construction,
sale and financing of homes in the state.

52671

## OPEN HOUSE

1665 Hot Springs Rd.
Carson City, NV 89710
Telephone: (702) 687-4280
FAX: (702) 687-4868
Year Established: 1976
Pub. Frequency: q.
Page Size: standard
Circulation: 15,550
Circulation Type: free
**Owner(s):**
State of Nevada Real Estate Division
1665 Hot Springs Rd.
Carson City, NV 89710
Telephone: (702) 687-4280
Ownership %: 100
**Readers:** Information relating to law and
regulations in real estate license law and
appraiser license law.

22234

## ORANGE COUNTY APARTMENT
NEWS

12822 Garden Grove Blvd., Ste. D
Garden Grove, CA 92643
Telephone: (714) 638-8743
FAX: (714) 741-9457
Year Established: 1960
Pub. Frequency: m.
Page Size: standard
Subscrip. Rate: $36/yr.
Materials: 01,02,05,06,07,15,17,19,21,32
Circulation: 4,000
Circulation Type: paid
**Owner(s):**
Orange County Multi-Housing Service
Corp.
12822 Garden Grove Blvd.
Garden Grove, CA 92643
Telephone: (714) 638-8743
Ownership %: 100
**Management:**
Ralph Kent .....................Executive Director
**Editorial:**
Erica C. Pierce ...........................Editor
**Readers:** Apartment owners, managers
and developers.
**Deadline:** story-35 days prior to pub. date;
news-35 days prior; photo-35 days prior;
ads-40 days prior

22235

## PROPERTIES

4900 Euclid Ave.
Cleveland, OH 44103
Telephone: (216) 431-7666
Year Established: 1946
Pub. Frequency: m.
Page Size: standard
Subscrip. Rate: $15/yr.
Materials: 02,06,07,10,15,21,27,28,32,33
Print Process: offset
Circulation: 2,100
Circulation Type: controlled & paid
**Owner(s):**
Properties
**Management:**
Gene Bluhm ............................Publisher
**Editorial:**
Gene Bluhm ...............................Editor
**Desc.:** Carries by-line and staff-written
articles covering apartments, homes,
buildings, hotels. Covers management,
construction, financing brokerage,
maintenance, legal, and appraisal.
Typical titles: Component Construction
Cuts Building Time, Why It's Important
to Upgrade Your Property, How to
Reduce Heating Costs, Next Time You
Need a Mortgage.
**Readers:** Builders, owners, and managers
of income property.
**Deadline:** story-15th of mo.; news-15th of
mo.; photo-15th of mo.; ads-15th of mo.

66591

## REAL ESTATE BUSINESS

430 N. Michigan Ave.
Ste. 500
Chicago, IL 60611
Telephone: (312) 670-3780
Year Established: 1982
Pub. Frequency: q.
Page Size: standard
Subscrip. Rate: $20/yr. members
Circulation: 25,000
Circulation Type: controlled
**Owner(s):**
Realtors National Marketing Institute
P.O. Box 300
Wheaton, IL 60189-0300
Telephone: (708) 752-0500
Ownership %: 100
**Editorial:**
Pierce Hollinsgworth ......................Editor
**Desc.:** News and educational articles for
designated realtors.

66020

## REAL ESTATE FINANCE JOURNAL

One Penn Plz., 42nd Fl.
New York, NY 10119
Telephone: (212) 971-5225
Year Established: 1985
Pub. Frequency: q.
Page Size: standard
Subscrip. Rate: $115/yr.
Circulation: 2,500
Circulation Type: paid
**Owner(s):**
Warren Gorham Lamont
One Penn Plz.
New York, NY 10119
Telephone: (212) 971-5000
Ownership %: 100
**Editorial:**
William Zucker ...........................Editor
Janis L. Gibson ...................Managing Editor
**Desc.:** Provides analysis of current real
estate financing events and issues,
giving forecasts on important regulatory
trends.

22237

## REAL ESTATE FORUM

12 W. 37th St.
New York, NY 10018
Telephone: (212) 563-6460

**Materials Accepted/Included:** 01-Business news 02-By-line articles 03-Fashion news 04-Food news 05-Freelance copy 06-Letters to editor 07-Real estate news 08-Sports news 09-Travel news 10-Book rev. 11-Movie rev. 12-Music rev. 13-TV rev. 14-Theater rev. 15-Coming events 16-Obituaries 17-Question & answer 18-Social announcements 19-Artwork 20-Cartoons 21-Photos 22-TV listings 23-Audio rec. 24-Video rec. 25-Books 26-Films/film clips 27-Personnel news 28-Press releases 29-New product news/photos 30-Trade lit. 31-Contracts awarded 32-Display adv. 33-Classified adv.

Year Established: 1946
Pub. Frequency: m.
Page Size: standard
Subscrip. Rate: $65/yr.
Materials: 01,02,06,07,32
Freelance Pay: $10/hr.
Print Process: web offset
Circulation: 30,700
Circulation Type: controlled & paid
**Owner(s):**
Real Estate Forum, Inc.
12 W. 37th St.
New York, NY 10018
Telephone: (212) 563-6460
Ownership %: 100
**Bureau(s):**
Real Estate Forum
122 S. Michigan Ave., Ste. 143
Chicago, IL 60603
Telephone: (312) 986-0445
Contact: Kathleen Schneider, Advertising
**Management:**
Gerald D. Schein ....................................President
Gerald D. Schein ....................................Publisher
**Editorial:**
Michael Desiato ...........................Editor in Chief
Patric Dolan ............................................Editor
Jonathan Schein ................Associate Publisher
**Desc.:** Distributed to building owners, banks, insurance companies, real estate management executives, brokers, corporation real estate officers, maintenance supervisors, architects and builders. Provides national coverage of real estate investment and development news.
**Readers:** Primary "must reading" for the major players in the worldwide commercial real estate business; directed to the nation's top rank decision makers (over 80% vice president and above), including corporate/institutional realty executives, developers, investors, brokers, lenders and asset managers.
**Deadline:** story-2 mos. prior to pub. date; news-1 mo. prior; photo-1 mo. prior; ads-1 mo. prior

22239
## REAL ESTATE NEWS
5525 W. Peterson Ave.
Ste. 103
Chicago, IL 60659
Telephone: (312) 866-9900
FAX: (312) 866-9906
Year Established: 1927
Pub. Frequency: m.
Page Size: standard
Subscrip. Rate: $5 newsstand; $35/yr.
Circulation: 10,000
Circulation Type: paid
**Owner(s):**
Real Estate News Corp.
5525 W. Petersom
Ste. 103
Chicago, IL 60659
Telephone: (312) 866-9900
Ownership %: 100
**Bureau(s):**
St. Louis Real Estate News
St Louis, MO 63155
Telephone: (314) 991-1000
**Editorial:**
Steve Klebba ...........................................Editor
**Desc.:** News items about real estate transactions, trends and market conditions, building projects, financing, personalities, conventions, meetings, activities in allied fields, calendar of events, in Chicago metropolitan area plus remainder of Illinois, Northern Indiana and Southern Wisconsin. Length of articles determined by importance.
**Readers:** Real estate, construction, financial interests.

22240
## REAL ESTATE REVIEW
One Penn Plz.
42nd Fl.
New York, NY 10119
Telephone: (212) 971-5225
FAX: (212) 971-5025
Year Established: 1971
Pub. Frequency: q.
Page Size: standard
Subscrip. Rate: $90/yr.
Circulation: 10,000
Circulation Type: paid
**Owner(s):**
Warren Gorham Lamont
One Penn Plz.
New York, NY 10119
Telephone: (800) 950-1201
Ownership %: 100
**Management:**
Blanca Duque ...................Advertising Manager
**Editorial:**
Jayne Allen ...........................................Editor
Norman Weinberg ..............Book Review Editor
**Desc.:** Specialized articles on trends and developments in real estate, financing, taxation, housing, condominiums, new developments, land use, shopping centers, apartments, office buildings, resorts and second homes, mobile homes and manufactured housing.
**Readers:** Builders, developers, realtors, building real estate attorneys and investors.

52570
## REAL ESTATE TODAY
430 N. Michigan Ave.
Chicago, IL 60611
Telephone: (312) 329-8461
FAX: (312) 329-5978
Year Established: 1968
Pub. Frequency: 10/yr.
Page Size: standard
Subscrip. Rate: $25/yr.
Freelance Pay: negotiable
Circulation: 750,000
Circulation Type: controlled
**Owner(s):**
National Association of Realtors
430 N. Michigan Ave.
Chicago, IL 60611
Telephone: (312) 329-8200
Ownership %: 100
**Management:**
William Adkinson ...........................Vice President
William Adkinson ..............................Publisher
Kathy Marusarz ...................Circulation Manager
Marcia Murton ...................Production Manager
Holly Poe Egge ................Promotion Manager
**Editorial:**
Maureen Glass ......................................Editor
Annette Cohen .................................Advertising
Gabriella Filisko ........................Associate Editor
Debbie Barker ...............Production Coordinator
**Desc.:** A professional, educational magazine that serves as a forum for ideas, opinions and practical applications in all areas of residential and commercial investment, and brokerage/management real estate. Information relating to association activities and interests is also included.
**Readers:** Real estate brokers and salespeople involved in all areas of real estate business, as well as many readers who are members of allied fields; developers, builders, lenders, government agencies.

22242
## REAL ESTATE WEEKLY
One Madison Ave.
New York, NY 10010
Telephone: (212) 679-1234
FAX: (212) 689-2267

Year Established: 1952
Pub. Frequency: w.
Page Size: tabloid
Subscrip. Rate: $49/yr.; $72/2 yrs.; $108/3 yrs.
Circulation: 9,383
Circulation Type: paid
**Owner(s):**
Hagedorn Publishing Co.
One Madison Ave.
New York, NY 10010
Telephone: (212) 679-1234
Ownership %: 100
**Management:**
Alfred Hagedorn, Jr. ...........................President
Alfred Hagedorn, Jr. ...........................Publisher
**Editorial:**
Eric Gerard ...........................................Editor
**Desc.:** The only weekly newspaper in America's No. 1 real estate market, with news, features, pictures, reports on sales, mortgages, leases, appointments and promotions, hard-hitting editorials, legislation wrapups/everything for the owner, broker, managing agent and other professionals in real estate. Departments include: On the Real Estate Scene, Sales, Mortgages and Leases, National Real Estate Transactions, Profiles, Appointments-Promotions, Corporate Earnings.
**Readers:** Owners, brokers, managing agents, bankers involved in apartment houses and commercial real estate.

69099
## REAL ESTATE WEST
825 E. Speer Blvd., Ste. 300
Denver, CO 80218-3719
Telephone: (303) 744-6692
Year Established: 1976
Pub. Frequency: bi-m.
Page Size: tabloid
Subscrip. Rate: $38/yr.; $58/2 yrs.
Materials: 07,32
Print Process: offset
Circulation: 10,675
Circulation Type: free & paid
**Owner(s):**
Grier & Co.
825 E. Speer Blvd., Ste. 300
Denver, CO 80218-3719
Telephone: (303) 744-6692
Ownership %: 100
**Management:**
Bill Grier ...........................................President
Bill Grier ...........................................Publisher
George Wright ...................Advertising Manager
Elizabeth Snook ...............Circulation Manager
**Editorial:**
Marti Kelly ...........................Editor in Chief
Marti Kelly ...........................Managing Editor
**Desc.:** Provides news of income-producing real estate construction, development, financing, investment and marketing in the West, from Midwest to Pacific Coast.
**Readers:** Corporate real estate executives, land developers, builders, investors (pension funds, insurance companies, private partnerships and corporations). Brokers, leasing agents, property and assistant managers, mortgage brokers; managers of products and services of commercial real estate industry.

52643
## REALTOR NEWS
777 14th St., N.W.
Washington, DC 20005
Telephone: (202) 383-1000
FAX: (202) 383-1231
Year Established: 1980
Pub. Frequency: bi-w.
Page Size: standard
Subscrip. Rate: $12/yr.

Circulation: 800,000
Circulation Type: controlled
**Owner(s):**
National Association of Realtors
777 14th St., N.W.
Washington, DC 20005
Telephone: (202) 383-1011
Ownership %: 100
**Management:**
William Adkinson ..............................Publisher
**Editorial:**
Majorie Green ...........................Executive Editor
**Desc.:** News and topical information of use and interest to real estate professionals.
**Readers:** Membership of The National Association of Realtors. (812575 Members as of 4/9/90).

22244
## REALTY
80-34 Jamaica Ave.
Jamaica, NY 11421
Telephone: (718) 296-2200
Year Established: 1950
Pub. Frequency: bi-w.
Page Size: tabloid
Subscrip. Rate: $15/yr.
Circulation: 8,000
Circulation Type: paid
**Owner(s):**
Leader Observer, Inc.
80-34 Jamaica Ave.
Jamaica, NY 11421
Telephone: (718) 296-2200
Ownership %: 100
**Management:**
Norman Cohen ..............................Publisher
**Editorial:**
Andrew Cohen ..........................................Editor
**Desc.:** Covers all aspects in the field of real estate except one-family houses.
**Readers:** Brokers, bankers, developers, investors.

22245
## REALTY & BUILDING
11 E. Hubbard St.
Ste. 3A
Chicago, IL 60611
Telephone: (312) 944-1204
FAX: (312) 467-0225
Year Established: 1888
Pub. Frequency: w.
Page Size: oversize
Subscrip. Rate: $40/yr.; $60/2 yrs.
Circulation: 9,000
Circulation Type: paid
**Owner(s):**
John Cutler
11 E. Hubbard St.
Ste. 3A
Chicago, IL 60611
Telephone: (312) 944-1204
Ownership %: 100
**Management:**
John Cutler ...........................................President
Patricia Nebel ...........................Vice President
John Cutler ...........................................Publisher
**Editorial:**
Bonnie Grota ..........................................Editor
Karen Shadbar ........................Associate Editor
**Readers:** Brokers, leasing agents, and developers.

53943
## REGISTRY REVIEW, THE
36 Bay St.
Manchester, NH 03104-3003
Telephone: (603) 669-3822
Mailing Address:
    P.O. Box 240
    Manchester, NH 03104-0240
Year Established: 1978
Pub. Frequency: w.
Page Size: tabloid
Subscrip. Rate: $145/yr.
Circulation: 3,500

**Materials Accepted/Included:** 01-Business news 02-By-line articles 03-Fashion news 04-Food news 05-Freelance copy 06-Letters to editor 07-Real estate news 08-Sports news 09-Travel news 10-Book rev. 11-Movie rev. 12-Music rev. 13-TV rev. 14-Theater rev. 15-Coming events 16-Obituaries 17-Question & answer 18-Social announcements 19-Artwork 20-Cartoons 21-Photos 22-TV listings 23-Audio rec. 24-Video rec. 25-Books 26-Films/film clips 27-Personnel news 28-Press releases 29-New product news/photos 30-Trade lit. 31-Contracts awarded 32-Display adv. 33-Classified adv.

4-61

Circulation Type: paid
**Owner(s):**
Robert Finlayson
Box 999
Andover, MA 01810
Telephone: (617) 475-8732

Irvin Tolles
83 Bay St.
Manchester, NH 03104
Telephone: (603) 669-3822
**Management:**
Robert Finlayson ..................................Publisher
**Editorial:**
Irvin Tolles ..................................................Editor
**Readers:** Bankers, real estate brokers,
appraisers.

65474
**S/F**
755 Mt. Auburn St.
Watertown, MA 02172
Telephone: (617) 924-5100
Year Established: 1987
Pub. Frequency: m.
Page Size: 4 color photos/art
Subscrip. Rate: $38/yr.
Circulation: 15,000
Circulation Type: paid
**Owner(s):**
Mass Tech Times, Inc.
**Management:**
Douglas Green ......................................Publisher
**Editorial:**
John Heymann ........................................Editor
**Desc.:** Focus on real estate in the New
England area. Covers legislation, foreign
investments, city vs. suburb issues.
**Readers:** New England Real Estate
Developers, Corporate Real Estate
Officers, Architects, Builders,
Contractors and Brokers.

22220
**SKYLINES**
1201 New York Ave., N.W., Ste. 300
Washington, DC 20005
Telephone: (202) 408-2686
FAX: (202) 371-0181
Year Established: 1981
Pub. Frequency: m.
Page Size: standard
Subscrip. Rate: $75/yr. members; $95/yr.
non-members
Materials: 02,07,27,28,32
Circulation: 15,800
Circulation Type: paid
**Owner(s):**
Building Owners & Managers Assn.
International
1201 New York Ave., N.W.
Washington, DC 20005
Telephone: (202) 408-2686
Ownership %: 100
**Management:**
Thomas B. McChesney ......................President
Mark W. Hurwitz ........Executive Vice President
Henry H. Chamberlain .............Public Relations
Manager
**Editorial:**
Jeanie Markel ..........................................Editor
Angelica Nunez ...................Publication Director
**Desc.:** Carries important information on
national issues which can affect the
profitable operation of office buildings.
Featured also are articles on building
operations, systems, and procedures,
trends in commercial real estate, office
building occupancy rates, etc.
**Readers:** Building owners and managers,
commercial real estate investors,
brokers, leasing agents and property
managers.

22246
**SOUTHEAST REAL ESTATE NEWS**
6151 Powers Ferry Rd., N.W.
Atlanta, GA 30339-2941
Telephone: (404) 955-2500
FAX: (404) 955-0400
Year Established: 1974
Pub. Frequency: m.
Page Size: tabloid
Subscrip. Rate: $38/yr. US; $60/2 yrs.;
$98/yr. foreign
Circulation: 19,000
Circulation Type: controlled & paid
**Owner(s):**
Argus Business, Inc.
6151 Powers Ferry Rd., N.W.
Atlanta, GA 30339-2941
Telephone: (404) 955-2500
Ownership %: 100
**Bureau(s):**
Dallas
18601 LBJ Frwy., Ste. 240
Mesquite, TX 75150
Telephone: (214) 348-0739

New York
390 Fifth Ave.
New York, NY 10018
Telephone: (212) 889-1850

Chicago
307 N. Michigan Ave., Ste. 812
Chicago, IL 60601
Telephone: (312) 726-7277

Santa Monica
1424 Fourth St., Ste. 231
Santa Monica, CA 90401
Telephone: (310) 451-5655

Ft. Lauderdale
915 Middle River Dr., Ste. 409
Ft. Lauderdale, FL 33304
Telephone: (305) 561-5553
**Management:**
Jerrold France ......................................President
Dreama McDaniel ................................Publisher
Dreama McDaniel .............Advertising Manager
**Editorial:**
Coles McKagen ........................................Editor
**Desc.:** Covers commercial and industrial
real estate activity in Alabama, Florida,
Georgia, Kentucky, Maryland,
Mississippi, North Carolina, Tennessee,
Virginia, West Virginia, and Washington
D.C.
**Readers:** Realtors, brokers, developers,
builders.

22247
**SOUTHWEST REAL ESTATE NEWS**
310 E. I-30
Ste. 240
Garland, TX 75403
Telephone: (214) 226-1339
FAX: (214) 226-5884
Year Established: 1973
Pub. Frequency: bi-m.
Page Size: tabloid
Subscrip. Rate: $38/yr.
Circulation: 13,000
Circulation Type: paid
**Owner(s):**
Argus Business, Inc.
6151 Powers Ferry Rd., N.W.
Atlanta, GA 30339
Telephone: (404) 955-2500
Ownership %: 100
**Management:**
Jerrold France ......................................President
Dreama McDaniel ................................Publisher
Tammy Orr ........................Circulation Manager
**Editorial:**
Jim Mitchell ..........................Associate Publisher
Nan McDowell ...................Production Director

**Desc.:** Covers the revenue producing real
estate in the seven Southwestern states.
Of particular importance are new
projects, covering all facets: planning,
financing, construction, and tenant
occupation. Every issue has a particular
theme, either a city review or feature
material on a particular topic in the real
estate industry. Departments include:
Mortgages, Sales/Purchases, Shopping
Centers, Industrial Property, Office
Space, Financing, People, Leases.
**Readers:** Developers, financial institutions,
brokers, and corporate real estate
executives of commercial and industrial
real estate.

22248
**TENNESSEE REALTOR**
1910 Adelicia St.
Nashville, TN 37212
Telephone: (615) 321-0515
FAX: (615) 320-0452
Mailing Address:
P.O. Box 121149
Nashville, TN 37212-1149
Year Established: 1961
Pub. Frequency: bi-m.
Page Size: standard
Subscrip. Rate: $5/yr.
Circulation: 12000
Circulation Type: paid
**Owner(s):**
TN Association of Realtors
1910 Adelecia St.
Nashville, TN 37212
Telephone: (615) 321-0515
Ownership %: 100
**Editorial:**
Stephen D. Harding ..............................Editor
Linda Woods .........................Managing Editor
**Desc.:** Articles and features are published
on legislation, current trends, market
analysis, regional news events, meeting
and convention announcements and
reports, general business and economic
news, as they affect the real estate
industry.
**Readers:** Real estate professionals.

22249
**TRI-STATE REAL ESTATE
JOURNAL**
4001 Lincoln Dr. W., Ste. G
Marlton, NJ 08053
Telephone: (609) 988-0092
FAX: (609) 988-0093
Year Established: 1984
Pub. Frequency: w.
Page Size: tabloid
Subscrip. Rate: $84/yr.
Materials: 01,02,07,15,32,33
Freelance Pay: $10/hr.
Print Process: offset
Circulation: 7,500
Circulation Type: paid
**Owner(s):**
Adler Group, Inc., The
8601 Georgia Ave.
Silver Spring, MD 20910
Telephone: (301) 588-0681
Ownership %: 100
**Management:**
Jonathan Adler ......................................Owner
Warren Kolber ...................................Publisher
**Editorial:**
Stephanie Mis ........................................Editor
Priscilla Faragalli ....................Production Editor
**Desc.:** Stories and photos on real estate
sales, land investment and real estate in
New Jersey, Delaware and Eastern
Pennsylvania.
**Readers:** Investors, builders, developers,
and brokers,
**Deadline:** ads-10 days prior to pub. date

52603
**WASHINGTON REAL ESTATE
NEWS**
2424 Bristol Ct., S.W.
Olympia, WA 98502
Telephone: (206) 753-0775
Mailing Address:
P.O. Box 9012
Olympia, WA 98504
Year Established: 1953
Pub. Frequency: q.
Page Size: standard
Subscrip. Rate: free
Circulation: 57,000
Circulation Type: controlled & free
**Owner(s):**
State of Washington/Dept. of Licensing
Highway Licenses Building
Olympia, WA 98504
Telephone: (206) 753-4091
Ownership %: 100
**Management:**
Mary Faulk ..........................Chairman of Board
**Editorial:**
Nancy Botaitis ........................................Editor
Ralph Birkedahl ...........Administrative Assistant
Sydney W. Beckett ......................Administrator
Mary Faulk ..........................................Director
**Desc.:** Professional licensing services
regulating real estate licensees. Provides
information on statute and rules
changes, educational articles, reports
disciplinary and enforcement actions and
recognizes achievements of licensees.
**Readers:** All active and inactive real
estate agents, escrow officers, real
estate educators and other people in
related fields who request a
copy. Regulatory agencies in each state,
Narello & Reea also receive a copy.

69405
**WESTERN REAL ESTATE NEWS**
500 S. Airport Blvd.
S. San Francisco, CA 94080
Telephone: (415) 737-5700
FAX: (415) 737-9080
Year Established: 1964
Pub. Frequency: s-m.
Subscrip. Rate: $80/yr.
Circulation: 125,000
Circulation Type: paid
**Owner(s):**
B.E.B. Publications
500 S. Airport Blvd.
S. San Francisco, CA 94080
Telephone: (415) 737-5700
Ownership %: 100
**Editorial:**
Leila K. Moavero ......................................Editor

## Group 036-Building Materials & Supplies

23650
**BUILDING MATERIAL RETAILER**
40 Ivy St., S.E.
Washington, DC 20003
Telephone: (202) 547-2230
FAX: (202) 547-7640
Year Established: 1984
Pub. Frequency: m.
Page Size: standard
Subscrip. Rate: $18/yr.
Freelance Pay: varies
Circulation: 23,000
Circulation Type: paid
**Owner(s):**
National Lumber & Building Material
Dealers Assn.
40 Ivy St., S.E.
Washington, DC 20003
Telephone: (202) 547-2230
Ownership %: 100
**Management:**
Ray Lorenz ..........................General Manager

**Materials Accepted/Included:** 01-Business news 02-By-line articles 03-Fashion news 04-Food news 05-Freelance copy 06-Letters to editor 07-Real estate news 08-Sports news 09-Travel news
10-Book rev. 11-Movie rev. 12-Music rev. 13-TV rev. 14-Theater rev. 15-Coming events 16-Obituaries 17-Question & answer 18-Social announcements 19-Artwork 20-Cartoons 21-Photos 22-TV listings
23-Audio rec. 24-Video rec. 25-Books 26-Films/film clips 27-Personnel news 28-Press releases 29-New product news/photos 30-Trade lit. 31-Contracts awarded 32-Display adv. 33-Classified adv.

**Editorial:**
Herb Oviatt ....................................Editor
Nancy Baldrica ...............................Editor
Ron Bygness ...................Managing Editor
Jane Burger ...........................Advertising
Denise Pitzl ....................Circulation Editor
**Desc.:** Covers all phases of the retail sales of lumber and building materials as well as home builders, general contractors and architects. Departments include: General Information, People and Places (personal items), New Products, Special Articles, Merchandising.
**Readers:** Owners, buyers, superintendents & management.

### BUILDING PRODUCTS
66312
655 15th St. N.W., Ste. 475
Washington, DC 20005
Telephone: (202) 737-0717
Year Established: 1990
Pub. Frequency: q.
Page Size: tabloid
Subscrip. Rate: $36/yr. US; $48/yr. Canada
Circulation: 80,000
Circulation Type: controlled
**Owner(s):**
Hanley-Wood, Inc.
655 15th St. N.W., Ste. 475
Washington, DC 20005
Telephone: (202) 737-0717
Ownership %: 100
**Management:**
Michael Tucker .............................Publisher
**Editorial:**
Paul Kitzke ....................................Editor
**Readers:** Builders/Remodelers in residential construction.

### BUILDING PRODUCTS DIGEST
52569
4500 Campus Dr., Ste. 480
Newport Beach, CA 92660
Telephone: (714) 852-1990
FAX: (714) 852-0231
Year Established: 1982
Pub. Frequency: m.
Page Size: standard
Subscrip. Rate: controlled circulation
Materials: 01,02,06,15,16,20,21,27,28,29, 30,32,33
Print Process: web
Circulation: 12,750
Circulation Type: controlled
**Owner(s):**
David Cutler/Cutler Publishing, Inc.
4500 Campus Dr., Ste. 480
Newport Beach, CA 92660
Telephone: (714) 852-1990
Ownership %: 100
**Management:**
David Cutler ................................Publisher
Michelle Mondragon ..........Circulation Manager
Alan Wickstrom ......................Sales Manager
**Editorial:**
Juanita Lovret ...............................Editor
David Koenig .....................Assistant Editor
**Desc.:** Serving the lumber and home center markets in 13 Southern states with industry news, profiles, personals, new products, new literature.
**Readers:** Owners, managers of both the retail & wholesale segment of the lumber & home center market.
**Deadline:** story-1st of mo.; news-1st of mo.; photo-1st of mo.; ads-1st of mo.

### BUILDING SUPPLY HOME CENTERS
22152
1350 E. Touhy Ave.
Des Plaines, IL 60018
Telephone: (708) 635-8800
Year Established: 1917
Pub. Frequency: m.

Page Size: standard
Subscrip. Rate: $70/yr. US; $102/yr. Canada
Materials: 01,06,07,27,28,29,30,32,33
Circulation: 46,017
Circulation Type: controlled
**Owner(s):**
Cahners Publishing Co.
275 Washington St.
Newton, MA 02158
Telephone: (617) 964-3030
Ownership %: 100
**Management:**
Robert Krakoff .............................President
Daniel E. Comiskey ......................Publisher
**Editorial:**
William Schober ....................Editor in Chief
Rod Sutton ...........................Managing Editor
Alicia Lasek ......................Associate Editor
Bill McDowell .....................Associate Editor
Patricia Coleman ................Associate Publisher
Rod Sutton ...........................Feature Editor
Rod Sutton ....................New Products Editor
Gay Hooper ...........................Production Editor
**Desc.:** Devoted to improved methods of merchandising and management in the building supply field.
**Readers:** Retailers of lumber, building supplies, home improvement products & hardware.
**Deadline:** story-4 mos. prior to pub. date; news-1 1/2 mos. prior; photo-1 1/2 mos. prior; ads-1 mo. prior

### C/M NEWS
22157
2302 Horse Pen Rd.
Herndon, VA 22071
Telephone: (703) 713-1900
FAX: (703) 713-1910
Year Established: 1961
Pub. Frequency: m.
Page Size: tabloid
Subscrip. Rate: free to trade
Circulation: 5,800
Circulation Type: controlled
**Owner(s):**
National Concrete Masonry Association
P.O. Box 2330
Herndon, VA 22070
Telephone: (703) 435-4900
Ownership %: 100
**Management:**
Lynne Mulston ...........................Publisher
Yvonne Hawk ...............Advertising Manager
**Editorial:**
Scott Ramminger ....................Executive Editor
**Desc.:** News articles report on the development of concrete masonry product manufacturing including equipment, processes and techniques. Other subject matter includes management, promotion and publicity, labor, financial and sales information for the concrete masonry industry.
**Readers:** Owners, operators, supervisors, sales personnel, presidents, plant managers and supervisors in concrete masonry manufacturing plants.

### CONCRETE INTERNATIONAL
22542
22400 W. Seven Mile Rd.
Detroit, MI 48219
Telephone: (313) 532-2600
FAX: (313) 538-0655
Mailing Address:
P.O. Box 19150
Detroit, MI 48219
Year Established: 1979
Pub. Frequency: m.
Page Size: standard
Subscrip. Rate: $104/yr.
Materials: 01,02,06,10,15,16,17,21,27,28, 29,30,32,33
Print Process: offset

Circulation: 20,800
Circulation Type: paid
**Owner(s):**
American Concrete Institute
22400 W. Seven Mile Rd.
Detroit, MI 48219
Telephone: (313) 532-2600
FAX: (313) 538-0655
Ownership %: 100
**Editorial:**
Roger D. Wood .....................Senior Editor
William J. Semioli ......................Editor
Diane Pociask ...........................Advertising
Christine R. Leninger ................Associate Editor
Todd R. Watson ...............Engineering Editor
Franklin S. Kurtz ...............Engineering Editor
Paula Schmalzriedt ................Production Editor
**Desc.:** Features vary from 800-4,000 words. Provides timely reports on construction, products, structural design, and materials related to concrete.
**Readers:** Professional contractors, architects, engineers, design management, specifiers.
**Deadline:** story-6 mo. prior to pub. date; news-6 mo.; photo-6 mo.; ads-2 mo.

### CONCRETE PRODUCTS
22161
29 N. Wacker Dr.
Chicago, IL 60606
Telephone: (312) 726-2802
Year Established: 1947
Pub. Frequency: m.
Page Size: standard
Subscrip. Rate: $31.50/yr. US & Canada; $50/yr. elsewhere
Materials: 01,02,06,19,27,28,29,30,32,33
Print Process: web offset
Circulation: 20,766
Circulation Type: controlled
**Owner(s):**
MacLean-Hunter Publishing Co.
29 N. Wacker Dr.
Chicago, IL 60606
Telephone: (312) 726-2802
Ownership %: 100
**Management:**
John Skeels .............................President
Robert Dimond ...........................Publisher
**Editorial:**
Don Marsh .................................Editor
Kathleen Mrumlinski ...............Administrative Assistant
Kirsten Bedway ...................Assistant Editor
**Desc.:** Staff-written and contributed articles on the production, application, and new markets for ready mix & concrete products. Covers industry news, company news, association news, new literature & equipment.
**Readers:** Producers of ready-mixed concrete, concrete block, pipe, precast & prestress.

### DIMENSIONAL STONE MAGAZINE
68747
6300 Variel Ave.
Ste. I
Woodland Hills, CA 91367
Telephone: (818) 704-5555
FAX: (818) 704-6500
Year Established: 1985
Pub. Frequency: m.
Page Size: standard
Subscrip. Rate: $50/yr.
Materials: 01,02,05,06,10,15,16,18,19,20, 21,24,27,28,29,30,31,32,33
Freelance Pay: negotiable
Print Process: offset
Circulation: 17,500
Circulation Type: paid

**Owner(s):**
Dimensional Stone Institute, Inc.
20335 Ventura Blvd., Ste. 400
Woodland Hills, CA 91364
Telephone: (818) 704-5555
Ownership %: 100
**Management:**
Jerry Fisher .............................Publisher
**Editorial:**
Marc Birenbaum .............................Editor
Jim Burros ......................Advertising Director
Susan Sommer ................Assistant Publisher
**Desc.:** Contains industry trends and events, feature articles on quarrying, installation, fabrication and cutting techniques, sales and marketing, finance, equipment, and new products.
**Readers:** From quarries and processors to importers, marble shops and retail operations.
**Deadline:** story-2 mo. prior to pub. date; news-2 mo. prior; photo-2 mo. prior; ads-1 mo. prior

### DOOR & WINDOW BUSINESS
68752
488 Rte. 24, Bldg. 1, Ste. 1
Hackettstown, NJ 07840
Telephone: (908) 850-8100
Year Established: 1989
Pub. Frequency: bi-m.
Page Size: standard
Subscrip. Rate: $15/yr.
Circulation: 16,000
Circulation Type: paid
**Owner(s):**
Jervis & Associates
488 Rte. 24, Bldg. 1, Ste. 1
Hackettstown, NJ 07840
Telephone: (908) 850-8100
Ownership %: 100
**Editorial:**
John H. Jervis ...............................Editor
**Desc.:** Provides news, technical reports, product descriptions, marketing concepts, trends, opinion and interviews about door and window marketing.

### GEOTECHNICAL FABRICS REPORT
69147
345 Cedar St., Ste. 800
St. Paul, MN 55101
Telephone: (612) 222-2508
FAX: (612) 222-1366
Year Established: 1983
Pub. Frequency: 9/yr.
Page Size: standard
Subscrip. Rate: $30/yr. US; $42/yr. foreign
Materials: 01,02,05,06,10,17,19,20,27,28, 29,30,32,33,34
Print Process: web
Circulation: 14,000
Circulation Type: paid
**Owner(s):**
Industrial Fabrics Association International
345 Cedar St., Ste. 800
St. Paul, MN 55101
Telephone: (612) 222-2508
Ownership %: 100
**Editorial:**
Danette R. Fettig ...............................Editor
**Desc.:** Case histories, technical papers and features related to geosynthetics used in civil engineering applications.
**Readers:** Civil engineers, consulting engineers, geotechnical engineers, academicians and students, manufacturers, installers and distributors of geosynthetics.

### GLASS DIGEST
22516
310 Madison Ave.
New York, NY 10017
Telephone: (212) 682-7681
FAX: (212) 697-8331

**Materials Accepted/Included:** 01-Business news 02-By-line articles 03-Fashion news 04-Food news 05-Freelance copy 06-Letters to editor 07-Real estate news 08-Sports news 09-Travel news 10-Book rev. 11-Movie rev. 12-Music rev. 13-TV rev. 14-Theater rev. 15-Coming events 16-Obituaries 17-Question & answer 18-Social announcements 19-Artwork 20-Cartoons 21-Photos 22-TV listings 23-Audio rec. 24-Video rec. 25-Books 26-Films/film clips 27-Personnel news 28-Press releases 29-New product news/photos 30-Trade lit. 31-Contracts awarded 32-Display adv. 33-Classified adv.

4-63

Year Established: 1922
Pub. Frequency: m.
Page Size: standard
Subscrip. Rate: $6/issue; $40/yr.
Freelance Pay: varies
Circulation: 12,000
Circulation Type: paid
**Owner(s):**
Ashlee Publishing Co., Inc.
310 Madison Ave.
New York, NY 10017
Telephone: (212) 682-7681
Ownership %: 100
**Management:**
B. Lee .................................Chairman of Board
Jordan Wright ...............................President
Jordan Wright ...............................Publisher
Judith Hicks .....................Circulation Manager
Regina Gelman ......................Office Manager
Tina Perez ........................Production Manager
**Editorial:**
Charles B. Cumpston ............................Editor
Bill Haciolek .................................Art Director
Maryanne Polidoro ..........Assistant Production
    Manager
Lowell E. Perrine .....................Associate Editor
John G. Swanson ..................Associate Editor
Ted T. Hart ........................Contributing Editor
Fred S. Steingold ...............Contributing Editor
R. Gelman .....................Secretary & Treasurer
Thomas A. Schwartz ..............Technical Editor
**Desc.:** Uses only material directly
pertaining to the flat glass, architectural
metal, and allied products industries.
Covers new products, news of
industry. Merchandising know-how.
**Readers:** Principals in flat glass
distributorships and dealers,
manufacturers, storefront installers,
curtainwall fabricators, installers.

22515
### GLASS MAGAZINE
8200 Greensboro Dr., Ste. 302
McLean, VA 22102
Telephone: (703) 442-4890
FAX: (703) 442-0630
Year Established: 1948
Pub. Frequency: m.
Page Size: standard
Subscrip. Rate: $34.95/yr.
Freelance Pay: $50-$300
Circulation: 16,500
Circulation Type: controlled & paid
**Owner(s):**
National Glass Association
8200 Greensboro Dr., Ste. 302
McLean, VA 22102
Telephone: (202) 442-4890
Ownership %: 100
**Management:**
Nicole Harris .................................Publisher
**Editorial:**
Mike Gribbin ...................Advertising Director
Michelle Nosko ...............Circulation Director
**Desc.:** Features articles about the
architectural and automotive glass
industries and the related areas of
machinery, metals and supplies. These
include mirrors, storefront/curtainwall,
sealants, doors, windows and entrances,
shower doors and tub enclosures,
skylights, hardware support service, auto
glass repair, replacements and tools.
**Readers:** Key personnel in architectural
glass industry.

22198
### INSULATION OUTLOOK
99 Canal Center Plz., Ste. 222
Alexandria, VA 22314
Telephone: (703) 683-6480
Year Established: 1955
Pub. Frequency: m.

Page Size: standard
Subscrip. Rate: $40/yr.
Materials: 01,02,05,06,15,16,19,21,27,28,
   29,30,32,33
Freelance Pay: negotiable
Print Process: web
Circulation: 6,000
Circulation Type: controlled
**Owner(s):**
National Insulation & Abatement
   Contractors Assn.
99 Canal Center Plz., Ste. 222
Alexandria, VA 22314
Telephone: (703) 683-6480
Ownership %: 100
**Management:**
William Pitkin ............Executive Vice President
Stephanie Goldberg ..........Advertising Manager
**Editorial:**
Stuart C. Hales ......................Executive Editor
Marcia Jonas ........................Production Editor
**Desc.:** A monthly magazine that provides
an industry watch to contractors,
distributors, and manufacturers in the
fields of commercial and industrial
insulation and/or asbestos abatement.
Articles range from technical case
studies to features on labor, finance,
legal and management issues.
**Readers:** Insulation and asbestos
abatement contractor executives of
contracting firms, engineers, energy
users in the process, refining,
petrochemical, power and other
manufacturing industries, subcontractors, manufacturers, NIAC
members and architects/engineers.

58755
### JOURNAL OF THERMAL INSULATION & BUILDING ENVELOPES
851 New Holland Ave., Box 3535
Lancaster, PA 17601
Telephone: (717) 291-5609
FAX: (717) 295-4538
Year Established: 1977
Pub. Frequency: q.
Subscrip. Rate: $205/yr.; $400/2 yrs.;
   $595/3 yrs.
Circulation: 250
Circulation Type: paid
**Owner(s):**
Melvyn A. Kohudic
851 New Holland Ave., Box 3535
Lancaster, PA 17601
Telephone: (717) 291-5609
**Bureau(s):**
Technomic Publishing AG
Missionsstrasse 44
CH-4055 Basel Switzerland
Contact: Paul Versaci, Director
**Editorial:**
Dr. Mark Bomberg ...............................Editor
Charles F. Gilbo ...................Editor Emeritus
**Desc.:** Covers in-depth technical papers
on new developments in materials and
methods and offers results of recent
research from leading international
specialists. Also includes the coverage
of heat, air, and moisture performance
of building envelopes.

22190
### MERCHANT MAGAZINE, THE
4500 Campus Dr., Ste. 480
Newport Beach, CA 92660
Telephone: (714) 852-1990
FAX: (714) 852-0231
Year Established: 1922
Pub. Frequency: m.
Page Size: standard
Subscrip. Rate: $11/yr.
Materials: 01,02,06,07,16,25,27,28,29,30,
   32,33
Print Process: web

Circulation: 5,000
Circulation Type: paid
**Owner(s):**
Merchant Magazine, Inc.
4500 Campus Dr., Ste. 480
Newport Beach, CA 92660
Telephone: (714) 852-1990
Ownership %: 100
**Management:**
David Cutler .................................President
David Cutler .................................Publisher
Alan Wickstrom .............Advertising Manager
Michelle Mondragon ..........Circulation Manager
**Editorial:**
Juanita Lovret ..........................Senior Editor
David Cutler ....................................Editor
David Koenig ...............New Products Editor
**Desc.:** News features, stories covering
market trends, production, regulations,
yard openings, new plants,
merchandising for retail outlets, home
centers, mass merchandisers. Uses
personals, appointments, human interest
material, catalogs, displays and
marketing and merchandising ideas, and
hard news.
**Readers:** Management, executives, yards,
retail outlets, home centers and mass
merchandisers.
**Deadline:** story-1st of mo. prior to pub.
date; news-15th of mo. prior; photo-1st
of mo. prior; ads-15th of mo. prior

22183
### PCI JOURNAL
175 W. Jackson Blvd.
Ste. 1859
Chicago, IL 60604
Telephone: (312) 786-0300
FAX: (312) 786-0353
Year Established: 1956
Pub. Frequency: bi-m.
Page Size: standard
Subscrip. Rate: $7 newsstand; $29/yr. US;
   $40/yr. foreign
Circulation: 6,500
Circulation Type: controlled & paid
**Owner(s):**
Precast/Prestressed Concrete Inst.
175 W. Jackson Blvd.
Ste. 1859
Chicago, IL 60604
Telephone: (312) 786-0300
Ownership %: 100
**Management:**
Brenda S. Banks ...............Production Manager
**Editorial:**
George D. Nasser ......................Editor in Chief
Joe Hoyle .........................Assistant Editor
**Desc.:** Reports new techniques, current
research and project studies in technical
aspects of prestressed and precast
concrete fabrication.
**Readers:** Engineers, architects, plant
managers, contractors, government
officials.

24994
### PIT & QUARRY
7500 Old Oak Blvd.
Cleveland, OH 44130
Telephone: (216) 243-8100
FAX: (216) 891-2675
Year Established: 1916
Pub. Frequency: m.
Page Size: standard
Subscrip. Rate: $38/yr.
Materials: 01,02,05,06,15,27,28,29,32,33,34
Freelance Pay: negotiable
Circulation: 22,000
Circulation Type: controlled

**Owner(s):**
Advanstar Communications, Inc.
7500 Old Oak Blvd.
Cleveland, OH 44130
Telephone: (216) 243-8100
Ownership %: 100
**Management:**
Dean Martin .................................Publisher
**Editorial:**
Robert Drake ....................................Editor
**Desc.:** Covers production methods, new
plant construction, use of equipment for
producers and manufacturers of cement,
crushed stone, gypsum, sand, gravel,
and other non-metallic minerals.
Departments include: News (new
companies, government reports, people),
Cement Production Chart, New
Machinery and Equipment, More
Information Please (literature),
Trade Notes (news of suppliers to the
industry, personnel), Industry Personals,
and Coming Events.
**Readers:** Management and production
executives.

22194
### READY MIX
7500 Old Oak Blvd.
Cleveland, OH 44130
Telephone: (216) 243-8100
FAX: (216) 891-2675
Year Established: 1991
Pub. Frequency: bi-m.
Page Size: standard
Subscrip. Rate: $40/yr. US; $50/yr.
   Canada; $80/yr. foreign
Circulation: 11,500
Circulation Type: controlled & paid
**Owner(s):**
Advanstar Communications, Inc.
7500 Old Oak Blvd.
Cleveland, OH 44130
Telephone: (216) 243-8100
Ownership %: 100
**Management:**
W. Dean Martin .................................Publisher
W. Dean Martin ................Advertising Manager
Dan Weist ....................................Sales Manager
**Editorial:**
Bob Drake ....................................Editor
**Desc.:** Staff-written features covering
concrete blocks, ready-mixed concrete,
pre-stressed concrete and all other
concrete units. Also covers industry
news, new equipment, machinery and
supplies, meetings.
**Readers:** Producers of ready mix concrete,
prestressed, other concrete units.

24995
### ROCK PRODUCTS
29 N. Wacker Dr.
Chicago, IL 60606
Telephone: (312) 726-2802
Year Established: 1896
Pub. Frequency: m.
Page Size: standard
Subscrip. Rate: $31.25/yr. US & Canada;
   $100/yr. foreign
Circulation: 22,016
Circulation Type: controlled
**Owner(s):**
MacLean Hunter Publishing Co.
29 N. Wacker Dr.
Chicago, IL 60606
Telephone: (312) 726-2802
FAX: (312) 726-2574
Ownership %: 100
**Management:**
John Skeels ....................................President
Robert Dimond ...............................Publisher
**Editorial:**
Richard S. Huhta ....................................Editor

**Materials Accepted/Included:** 01-Business news 02-By-line articles 03-Fashion news 04-Food news 05-Freelance copy 06-Letters to editor 07-Real estate news 08-Sports news 09-Travel news 10-Book rev. 11-Movie rev. 12-Music rev. 13-TV rev. 14-Theater rev. 15-Coming events 16-Obituaries 17-Question & answer 18-Social announcements 19-Artwork 20-Cartoons 21-Photos 22-TV listings 23-Audio rec. 24-Video rec. 25-Books 26-Films/film clips 27-Personnel news 28-Press releases 29-New product news/photos 30-Trade lit. 31-Contracts awarded 32-Display adv. 33-Classified adv.

**Desc.:** Covers production processing and marketing of crushed stone, sand and gravel, cement, lime, gypsum, lightweight aggregates, and other non-metallic construction minerals. Articles are technical and practical for the man in the field. Departments include: Rock Newscope, Washington Letter, Industry News, Hints and Help, New Machinery, New Literature, Trends and Ideas, Statistics.

**Readers:** Producers of non-metallic minerals.

### TILE AND DECORATIVE SURFACES
22521

6300 Variel Ave., Ste. I
Woodland Hills, CA 91367-2513
Telephone: (818) 704-5555
FAX: (818) 704-6500
Year Established: 1955
Pub. Frequency: 12/yr.
Page Size: standard
Subscrip. Rate: $50/yr.
Materials: 01,02,06,27,28,29,30,32,33
Freelance Pay: varies
Print Process: web offset
Circulation: 17,029
Circulation Type: controlled & paid
**Owner(s):**
Decorative Surfaces Publishing Co.
6300 Variel Ave., Ste. 1
Woodland Hills, CA 01367
Telephone: (818) 704-5555
Ownership %: 100
**Management:**
Jerry Fisher ................................Owner
Jerry Fisher ..............................President
Jerry Fisher ..............................Publisher
Steve Fisher ...................Advertising Manager
Mark Cross ........Assistant Advertising Manager
Llian Kremar .................Circulation Manager
**Editorial:**
Marc Birenbaum ...............................Editor
Ted Steinberg ...........................Art Director
William Campbell ................Associate Editor
Jerry Fisher ................................Director
William Campbell ................Feature Editor
Linda Evans .................Production Coordinator
**Desc.:** Standard trade paper, standard format. Serves ceramic, marble, granite tile and terrazzo field in United States and Canada. Editorial coverage devoted to manufacturing, installation, etc., of all forms of ceramic tile, marble, granite and terrazzo.
**Readers:** Contractors, architects, designers, manufacturers, distributors, and dealers.
**Deadline:** news-40 days; ads-30 days

### U.S. GLASS, METAL & GLAZING
22522

One Novak Drive
Stafford, VA 22554
Telephone: (703) 720-5584
FAX: (703) 720-5687
Mailing Address:
  P.O. Box 569
  Garrisonville, VA 22463
Year Established: 1966
Pub. Frequency: m.
Page Size: standard
Subscrip. Rate: $5/issue; $35/yr.; $70/2 yrs.; $105/3 yrs.
Freelance Pay: negotiable
Circulation: 20,000
Circulation Type: paid
**Owner(s):**
U.S. Glass Publications, Inc.
Ownership %: 100

**Bureau(s):**
European Bureau
99 Kings Rd.
Westcliff on Sea
 Essex 550 8PH, United Kingdom
Telephone: 44-702-77341
Contact: Patrick Connolly, Advertising

Chicago
4761 W. Touhy Ave.
Lincolnwood, IL 60646
Telephone: (708) 679-1100
Contact: Matt E. McFadden, Manager

New York
122 E. 42nd St., Ste. 2707
New York, NY 10168
Telephone: (212) 953-2121
Contact: Judi Block, Advertising
**Management:**
Deborah Levy ..............................Publisher
**Editorial:**
Deborah Levy ................................Editor
Rebecca Thake ...............Advertising Assistant
Judith Tibbs .............................Art Director
Andrea Karges .................Circulation Director
**Desc.:** Serves the marketing, manufacturing/fabricating, and installation segments of flat glass, architectural metal, and glazing industries with feature stories. Case histories on buildings are included as well. Departments include: Industry News, Trade and Financial news; New Buildings; People; Products and Literature; Coming Events; Question & Answer Section; Washington Report; Labor and Law Columns; Stained Glass Column; Management Column; Auto Glass Column, Contract Glazing Column.
**Readers:** Dealers & distributors, manufacturers, fabricators, and importers of flat glass, architectural metal, and related products.

## Group 038-Business, General

### AMERICAN DEMOGRAPHICS
56376

127 W. State St.
Ithaca, NY 14850
Telephone: (607) 273-6343
FAX: (607) 273-3196
Mailing Address:
  P.O. Box 68
  Ithaca, NY 14851-0068
Year Established: 1979
Pub. Frequency: m.
Page Size: standard
Subscrip. Rate: $62/yr.
Freelance Pay: $300/feature article
Circulation: 35,000
Circulation Type: paid
**Owner(s):**
Dow Jones & Co., Inc.
World Financial Ctr.
New York, NY 10017
Ownership %: 100
**Management:**
Peter Francese ..............................President
Peter Francese ..............................Publisher
Michelle Dechant .............Advertising Manager
Michael Edmondson ..........Circulation Manager
**Editorial:**
Brad Edmondson ................Editor in Chief
Caroline Arthur ................Managing Editor
Jim Keller .............................Art Director
**Desc.:** Reports exclusively on consumer trends and lifestyles.
**Readers:** Marketing directors, advertising agencies, chief executive officers, media buyers, branch managers, marketing research managers, consumer information systems managers, strategic planners.

### ASSOCIATION MANAGEMENT
22258

1575 I St., N.W.
Washington, DC 20005
Telephone: (202) 626-2702
FAX: (202) 408-9634
Year Established: 1949
Pub. Frequency: m.
Page Size: standard
Subscrip. Rate: $4/issue; $30/yr.
Materials: 01,02,05,06,09,10,19,21,23,24, 25,26,27,28,29,30,31,32,33
Freelance Pay: varies
Circulation: 24,500
Circulation Type: paid
**Owner(s):**
American Society of Association Executives
1575 I St., N.W.
Washington, DC 20005
Telephone: (202) 626-2723
FAX: (202) 409-9634
Ownership %: 100
**Management:**
Elissa Myers ..............................Publisher
Karl Ely ..............................Sales Manager
Robert Purdy ..........................Sales Manager
Richard Bahruth .......................Sales Manager
George Moffat .........................Sales Manager
**Editorial:**
Ann Mahoney ...............................Editor
John B. Young ...................Production Director
**Desc.:** Articles on association management, prepared especially for association executives.
**Readers:** Association executives principally. A small percentage is circulated among educators and public libraries.
**Deadline:** story-4 mos.; news-3 mos.; photo-3 mos.; ads-15th of mo. prior to pub. date

### ASSOCIATION MEETINGS
56373

63 Great Rd.
Maynard, MA 01754
Telephone: (508) 897-5552
FAX: (508) 897-6824
Year Established: 1916
Pub. Frequency: bi-m.
Page Size: standard
Subscrip. Rate: $42/yr. US; $64/yr. CN; $96/yr. foreign
Circulation: 22,000
Circulation Type: controlled
**Owner(s):**
Laux Company, Inc.
63 Great Rd.
Maynard, MA 01754
Telephone: (508) 897-5552
Ownership %: 100
**Management:**
Peter Huestis ..............................Publisher
Kristin McHugh .................Circulation Manager
**Editorial:**
Betsy Bair ..........................Editor in Chief
Regina McGee ...............................Editor
**Desc.:** Edited for the association meeting planner.

### ASSOCIATION TRENDS
22259

7910 Woodmont Ave.
Ste. 1150
Bethesda, MD 20814
Telephone: (301) 652-8666
FAX: (301) 656-8654
Year Established: 1973
Pub. Frequency: 50/yr.
Page Size: Tabloid
Subscrip. Rate: $72/yr.; $130/2 yrs.; $195/3 yrs.
Freelance Pay: None
Circulation: 7,500
Circulation Type: controlled & paid

**Owner(s):**
Martineau Corp.
7910 Woodmont Ave.
Ste. 1150
Bethesda, MD 20814
Telephone: (301) 652-8666
Ownership %: 100
**Management:**
Jill M. Cornish ....................Chairman of Board
Jill M. Cornish ..............................President
Jill M. Cornish ..............................Publisher
**Desc.:** Weekly newspaper for paid staff executives of the national, regional & state associations in the U.S., featuring hot news, trends, personnel changes and how - to in association management. 1989 reader survey shows 3.8 readers per copy. Departments include: Washington News, New York News, Chicago News, Executive Changes, Books, Newsletters, & Publications, Letters, Moves & Changes. ASAE News, Freebies, Obituaries.
**Readers:** The top executives in major business, professional, civic service, union and fraternal voluntary organization in the U.S.

### BERKS COUNTY B17
67692

P.O. Box H
Oxford, PA 19363
Telephone: (215) 932-2444
Year Established: 1990
Pub. Frequency: bi-w.
Page Size: tabloid
Materials: 01,06,07,27,28,29,30,31
Circulation: 5,000
Circulation Type: controlled
**Owner(s):**
Ad Pro, Inc.
P.O. Box H
Oxford, PA 19363
Telephone: (215) 932-2444
Ownership %: 100
**Management:**
Randall Lieberman ........................Publisher
**Editorial:**
Steve Ennen ...............................Editor

### BLACK CAREERS
22266

P.O. Box 8214
Philadelphia, PA 19101
Telephone: (215) 387-1600
Year Established: 1965
Pub. Frequency: bi-m.
Page Size: standard
Subscrip. Rate: $20/yr.
Circulation: 275,000
Circulation Type: paid
**Owner(s):**
Project Magazine, Inc.
P.O. Box 8214
Philadelphia, PA 19101
Telephone: (215) 387-1600
Ownership %: 100
**Management:**
Emory W. Washington .......................Publisher
Herbert Bass ...................Advertising Manager
**Editorial:**
Emory W. Washington ..............................Editor
Kingston Nevins ................Managing Editor
Diane Washington .................Associate Editor
Jerusa C. Wilson, .................Book Review Editor
Ph.D
Norman Harris ...................Education Editor
Lance Gooden ...................Industrial Editor
Robert Thomas ..............................News Editor
Ed Piazza ...............................Photo
Bernie Edwards ...................Technical Editor

**Materials Accepted/Included:** 01-Business news 02-By-line articles 03-Fashion news 04-Food news 05-Freelance copy 06-Letters to editor 07-Real estate news 08-Sports news 09-Travel news 10-Book rev. 11-Movie rev. 12-Music rev. 13-TV rev. 14-Theater rev. 15-Coming events 16-Obituaries 17-Question & answer 18-Social announcements 19-Artwork 20-Cartoons 21-Photos 22-TV listings 23-Audio rec. 24-Video rec. 25-Books 26-Films/film clips 27-Personnel news 28-Press releases 29-New product news/photos 30-Trade lit. 31-Contracts awarded 32-Display adv. 33-Classified adv.

4-65

**Desc.:** Provides career guidance to working professionals and graduates and is a ready reference for placement directors, students and others in academe. A useful manual for job hunters and career-changers, offers advice on career planning and advancement, emerging business practices and professional employment market trends.

**Readers:** Working professionals in business, government, and industry, almost exclusively 1-15 years out of college, very mobile; still actively seeking new opportunities; new challenges.

22267

### BLACK ENTERPRISE
130 Fifth Ave.
New York, NY 10011
Telephone: (212) 242-8000
FAX: (212) 886-9610
Year Established: 1970
Pub. Frequency: m.
Page Size: standard
Subscrip. Rate: $15.95/yr.
Freelance Pay: $600-$1200/feature articles
Circulation: 266,406
Circulation Type: paid
**Owner(s):**
Earl G. Graves Publishing Co., Inc.
130 Fifth Ave.
New York, NY 10011
Telephone: (212) 242-8000
FAX: (212) 886-9610
Ownership %: 100
**Management:**
Earl G. Graves .............................President
Earl G. Graves, Jr. ..... Executive Vice President
Sheryl Hillard Tucker ..................Vice President
Earl G. Graves .............................Publisher

**Editorial:**
Sheryl Hillard Tucker ..................Editor in Chief
Earl G. Graves .............................Editor
Aldred Edmond ......................Managing Editor
Earl G. Graves, Jr. ......................Advertising
Gail Williams .............................Art Director
Robert Acquaye .................Circulation Director
Earl G. Graves, Jr. ..............Marketing Director
**Desc.:** Black Enterprise is a business-service magazine for African-American professionals, entrepreneurs and corporate executives.
**Readers:** Primarily black businessmen and women.

22275

### BUSINESS & SOCIETY REVIEW
200 W. 57th St., 15th Fl.
New York, NY 10019
Telephone: (212) 399-1088
FAX: (212) 245-1973
Year Established: 1972
Pub. Frequency: q.
Page Size: standard
Subscrip. Rate: $56/yr.
Freelance Pay: varies
Circulation: 3,000
Circulation Type: paid
**Owner(s):**
Management Reports, Inc.
200 W. 57th St., 15th Fl.
New York, NY 10019
Telephone: (212) 399-1088
FAX: (212) 245-1973
Ownership %: 100
**Editorial:**
Milton Moskowitz .....................Senior Editor
Theodore Cross .............................Editor
Robert Bruce Slater .................Managing Editor

**Desc.:** Original articles dealing with the interaction between business and society/big business, consumerism, environment, discriminations, worker participation, and other questions of corporate social responsibility and ethics.
**Readers:** Executives, business and law professors.

68755

### BUSINESS CONCEPTS
951 S. Oxford, No. 109
Los Angeles, CA 90006
Telephone: (213) 732-3477
Mailing Address:
P.O. Box 75392
Los Angeles, CA 90075
Year Established: 1991
Pub. Frequency: q.
Subscrip. Rate: $29.99/yr.
Materials: 01,02,03,04,05,06,07,08,09,10,
11,12,13,14,15,16,17,18,19,20,21,22,23,
24,25,26,27,28,29,30,31,32,33
Freelance Pay: $.20-.50/word
Print Process: web
Circulation: 120,000
Circulation Type: controlled & paid
**Owner(s):**
Publishing & Business Consultants
951 S. Oxford, No. 109
Los Angeles, CA 90006
Telephone: (213) 732-3477
FAX: (213) 732-9123
Ownership %: 100
**Editorial:**
Andeson Napolean Atia .....................Editor
**Desc.:** Presents money making ideas and new business opportunities.
**Deadline:** story-2 wks. prior to pub. date; news-2 wks.; photo-2 wks.; ads-90 days prior to pub. date

61574

### BUSINESS COUNSEL
1615 H St., N.W.
Washington, DC 20062
Telephone: (202) 463-5337
FAX: (202) 463-5346
Year Established: 1990
Pub. Frequency: q.
Page Size: tabloid
Subscrip. Rate: free to members; $15/yr. non-mebers
Circulation: 1,000
Circulation Type: free & paid
**Owner(s):**
National Chamber Litigation Center
1615 H St., N.W.
Washington, DC 20062
Telephone: (202) 463-5337
Ownership %: 100
**Editorial:**
Cam Esser ..................................Editor

66220

### BUSINESS DRIVER
2512 Artesia Blvd.
Redondo Beach, CA 90278
Telephone: (310) 376-8788
FAX: (310) 376-9043
Pub. Frequency: a.
Page Size: standard
Subscrip. Rate: $5/yr.; free to qualified personnel
**Owner(s):**
Bobit Publishing Co.
2512 Artesia Blvd.
Redondo Beach, CA 90278
Telephone: (310) 376-8788
Ownership %: 100
**Management:**
Ed Bobit ....................................Publisher
Chuck Parker ...................Advertising Manager
**Editorial:**
Mike Antich .................................Editor

**Desc.:** Covers car value and driver safety issues for business car drivers.

65673

### BUSINESS ETHICS MAGAZINE
52 S. Tenth St., Ste. 10
Minneapolis, MN 55318
Telephone: (612) 962-4700
Year Established: 1987
Pub. Frequency: bi-m.
Page Size: standard
Subscrip. Rate: $49/yr. US; $59/yr. foreign
Freelance Pay: call for rates
Circulation: 10,000
Circulation Type: paid
**Owner(s):**
Mavis Publications, Inc.
52 S. Tenth St., Ste. 10
Minneapolis, MN 55318
Telephone: (612) 962-4700
Ownership %: 100
**Management:**
Leila Zima ..............Customer Service Manager
**Editorial:**
Craig Cox ..................................Editor
Margaret Kaeter .......................Assistant Editor
Miriam Kniaz .............................Chief Dir.
**Desc.:** The only national magazine for socially responsible business. News, trends, interviews, management ideas, social investing and book reviews are some of the topics covered. Not an academic or non-profit journal, although academics and non-profit managers can benefit.
**Readers:** Management and executive level in small and large corporations.

69354

### BUSINESS FORUM
5151 State University Dr.
Los Angeles, CA 90032-8120
Telephone: (213) 343-2806
FAX: (213) 343-2813
Year Established: 1975
Pub. Frequency: q.
Page Size: standard
Subscrip. Rate: $5/copy; $16/yr.
Materials: 01,02,10,32
Print Process: offset
Circulation: 5,000
Circulation Type: controlled & paid
**Owner(s):**
California State University, Los Angeles
5151 State University Dr.
Los Angeles, CA 90032
Telephone: (213) 343-2806
Ownership %: 100
**Editorial:**
Thomas H. Woods ..................................Editor
**Desc.:** Interpretative commentary and research by practitioners and academicians on contemporary issues of interest to all business and economics disciplines.
**Readers:** Business executives, academicians and public administrators.

22273

### BUSINESS HORIZONS
Indiana University School of Business
Bloomington, IN 47405
Telephone: (812) 855-6342
FAX: (812) 855-8679
Mailing Address:
55 Old Post Rd., #2
P.O. Box 1678
Greenwich, CT 06836-1636
Year Established: 1958
Pub. Frequency: bi-m.
Page Size: standard
Subscrip. Rate: $60/yr.
Materials: 02,10,32
Circulation: 3,000
Circulation Type: paid

**Owner(s):**
Indiana University, Graduate School of Business
Bloomington, IN 47405
Telephone: (812) 335-6342
Ownership %: 100
**Management:**
Brian Burton .....................Business Manager
**Editorial:**
Harvey C. Bunke .............................Editor
Brian Burton ......................Managing Editor
Michael Parrish ...................Book Review Editor
**Desc.:** Departments include: Practice of Business, Legal Horizons, Editor's Chair, Counterpoint, Focus on Books. A scholarly journal publishing articles of interest to academicians and business people. Articles emphasize significant issues and subjects with broad economic, social, or political implications. They strike a balance between the practical and the theoretical, and are presented in readable, nontechnical language.
**Readers:** Business executives and business faculty.

22274

### BUSINESS IDEAS
1051 Bloomfield Ave.
Clifton, NJ 07012
Telephone: (201) 778-6677
Year Established: 1950
Pub. Frequency: m.
Page Size: standard
Subscrip. Rate: $50/yr.; $65/2 yrs.
Materials: 01,10,20,21,28,29,30
Circulation: 3,000
Circulation Type: paid
**Owner(s):**
Dan Newman Co.
1051 Bloomfield Ave.
Clifton, NJ 07012
Telephone: (201) 778-6677
Ownership %: 100
**Management:**
Dan Newman .............................Publisher
Dan Newman ...................Advertising Manager
**Editorial:**
Peter Newman .....................Executive Editor
Dan Newman ......................Managing Editor
Marc Newman ......................Associate Editor
C. Bromley .....................New Products Editor
Doris Leff .............................News Editor
**Desc.:** Consists of new ideas, techniques, and products of interest to the businessman, and how this information applies to libraries, schools, banks, and institutions.

67029

### BUSINESS INFORMATION ALERT
401 W. Fullerton Pkwy., Ste. 1403E
Chicago, IL 60614-3857
Telephone: (312) 525-7594
FAX: (312) 525-7015
Year Established: 1988
Pub. Frequency: 10/yr.
Page Size: standard
Subscrip. Rate: $142/yr.
**Owner(s):**
Alert Publications, Inc.
401 W. Fullerton Pkwy.
Chicago, IL 60614-3857
Telephone: (312) 525-7594
Ownership %: 100
**Management:**
Donna Tuke Heroy .............................Publisher
**Editorial:**
Donna Tuke Heroy .............................Editor
**Desc.:** Designed to keep librarians and related information professionals informed of new literature, information services and research techniques in the field of business.

**Materials Accepted/Included:** 01-Business news 02-By-line articles 03-Fashion news 04-Food news 05-Freelance copy 06-Letters to editor 07-Real estate news 08-Sports news 09-Travel news 10-Book rev. 11-Movie rev. 12-Music rev. 13-TV rev. 14-Theater rev. 15-Coming events 16-Obituaries 17-Question & answer 18-Social announcements 19-Artwork 20-Cartoons 21-Photos 22-TV listings 23-Audio rec. 24-Video rec. 25-Books 26-Films/film clips 27-Personnel news 28-Press releases 29-New product news/photos 30-Trade lit. 31-Contracts awarded 32-Display adv. 33-Classified adv.

4-66

## BUSINESS OPPORTUNITIES JOURNAL
66219

1050 Rosecrans St., Ste. 8
San Diego, CA 92106
Telephone: (619) 223-5661
FAX: (619) 223-1705
Mailing Address:
P.O. Box 990
Olalla, WA 98359
Year Established: 1969
Pub. Frequency: m.
Page Size: tabloid
Subscrp. Rate: $30/yr.; $48/2 yrs.
Materials: 01,07,32,33
Circulation: 100,000
Circulation Type: controlled & paid
**Owner(s):**
Business Service Corp.
P.O. Box 990
Olalla, WA 98359
Telephone: (206) 857-3720
Ownership %: 100
**Management:**
Maria Nicolaidis .........................Vice President
John Madsen .........................................Manager
**Editorial:**
Gina Petrone .................................................Editor
**Desc.:** The nation's largest journal
specializing in franchising, businesses
for sale, and business opportunities in
the US and Canada.
**Readers:** Individuals and companies
looking to buy a business, franchise or
business opportunity.

## BUSINESS TODAY
24716

305 Aaron Burr Hall
Princeton, NJ 08540
Telephone: (609) 258-1111
Year Established: 1968
Pub. Frequency: 3/yr.
Page Size: standard
Subscrp. Rate: $3.89 newsstand; $12/yr.
Materials: 01,06
Print Process: web offset
Circulation: 200,000
Circulation Type: controlled
**Owner(s):**
Foundation For Student Communication,
Inc.
305 Aaron Burr Hall
Princeton, NJ 08544-1011
Telephone: (609) 258-1111
Ownership %: 100
**Management:**
Dan Rosenthal ...................................President
Adam Bromwich .................................Publisher
**Editorial:**
Bryan Bradford ........................................Editor
Andrew O'Brien .....................Managing Editor
**Desc.:** Topics for articles include social
and political issues of national
significance, business trends and
developments, employment and
career opportunities, particular
professions, new products, students and
education interviews with notable
persons. Departments include features,
non-staff articles, staff articles,
graphics, career survey.
**Readers:** Undergrads at outstanding
American colleges and universities and
businessmen.

## BUSINESS WEEK
26162

1221 Ave. of The Americas, 39th Fl.
New York, NY 10020
Telephone: (212) 512-3040
FAX: (212) 512-4464
Year Established: 1929
Pub. Frequency: w.
Page Size: standard
Subscrp. Rate: $46.95/yr.

Circulation: 883,718
Circulation Type: paid
**Owner(s):**
McGraw-Hill, Inc.
1221 Ave. of The Americas
New York, NY 10020
Telephone: (212) 997-1221
Ownership %: 100
**Management:**
John W. Patten ...................................President
David Ferm .........................................Publisher
**Editorial:**
Stephen B. Shepard ..................Editor in Chief
Mark Morrison .........................Managing Editor
Larry Lippmann ...................Photography Editor
**Desc.:** Reports news, ideas and trends
that have an impact on the economy or
on an industry - or that can provide new
insights for business executives in
the operation of their own businesses.
**Readers:** Executive decision makers in
business, industry, and the professions

## CELLULAR BUSINESS
58793

9800 Metcalf
Overland Park, KS 66282-2901
Telephone: (913) 967-1900
Year Established: 1984
Pub. Frequency: m.
Page Size: standard
Subscrp. Rate: $36/yr.
Freelance Pay: negotiable
Circulation: 20,000
Circulation Type: controlled
**Owner(s):**
Intertec Publishing Corp.
333 W. Hampdon, Ste. 803
Englewood, CO 80110
Telephone: (303) 762-1249
Ownership %: 100
**Management:**
Mercy Contreras ................................Publisher
**Editorial:**
Rhonda Wickham ......................................Editor
**Desc.:** Information for cellular
professionals.
**Readers:** 100 % Cellular

## CHIEF EXECUTIVE MAGAZINE
22280

733 Third Ave.
New York, NY 10017
Telephone: (212) 687-8288
FAX: (212) 687-8456
Year Established: 1977
Pub. Frequency: 9/yr.
Page Size: oversize
Subscrp. Rate: $18/issue; $95/yr.
Freelance Pay: $300-$800
Circulation: 40,000
Circulation Type: controlled
**Owner(s):**
Chief Executive Group. Inc.
733 Third Ave.
New York, NY 10017
Telephone: (212) 687-8288
FAX: (212) 687-8456
Ownership %: 100
**Management:**
Arnold B. Pollard ...............................President
Darcy Miller Donaldson .....................Publisher
**Editorial:**
J.P. Donlon ..............................................Editor
**Desc.:** Seeks to alert them to the views
and valuable insights of other chief
executives in the belief that a
knowledgeable CEO is the best
consultant top management can have.
This is a forum through which top
executives may raise issues, share
concerns and offer solutions to
problems in strategy, management,
finance, administration and matters of
public policy.

Readers: 40,000 CEOs. 98% US, 2%
foreign business and government
leaders

## COMMERCIAL RECORD
22285

435 Buckland Rd., Brandywine Bldg.
South Windsor, CT 06074
Telephone: (203) 644-3489
FAX: (203) 644-7376
Mailing Address:
P.O. Box 902
South Windsor, CT 06074
Year Established: 1882
Pub. Frequency: Fri.
Page Size: tabloid
Subscrp. Rate: $208/yr.
Circulation: 4,000
Circulation Type: paid
**Owner(s):**
Commercial Record Publishing Co., The
435 Buckland Rd.
Brandywine Bldg.
South Windsor, CT 06074
Telephone: (203) 644-3489
Ownership %: 100
**Management:**
Vincent M. Valvo ...............................Publisher
William Samatis ................Production Manager
**Editorial:**
Vincent M. Valvo .......................................Editor
Charles Howes ................Director of Marketing
**Desc.:** Prints official records such as real
estate transfers, mortgages,
attachments, personal property records,
corporations, bankruptcy petitions,
construction news, financial news and
comment. Covers the State of
Connecticut.
**Readers:** Architects, builders, contractors,
construction brokers, building supply
companies, building specification
companies and agents, credit managers,
small businessmen, real estate
brokers & agents, insurance brokers &
agents, bank officials, lawyers, and
professional men in general.

## CONTINUOUS JOURNEY
58666

123 N. Post Oak Ln., 3rd. Fl.
Houston, TX 77024
Telephone: (713) 681-4641
Year Established: 1992
Pub. Frequency: bi-m.
Page Size: standard
Subscrp. Rate: $50/yr. member; $75/yr.
non-member
Materials: 01,02,05,06,10,15,21,28,32,33
Circulation: 10,000
Circulation Type: controlled & paid
**Owner(s):**
American Productivity & Quality Ctr.
123 N. Post Oak Ln.
Houston, TX 77024
Telephone: (713) 681-4020
FAX: (713) 681-8578
Ownership %: 100
**Editorial:**
Steve Scheffler .........................................Editor
Vicki Powers .............................................Editor
**Readers:** Hi-level executives

## CORPORATE CONTROL ALERT
67661

600 Third Ave.
New York, NY 10016
Telephone: (212) 973-2800
FAX: (212) 972-6258
Year Established: 1984
Pub. Frequency: m.
Page Size: standard
Subscrp. Rate: $14.95/yr.
Circulation: 600
Circulation Type: paid

**Owner(s):**
American Lawyer Media
600 Third Ave.
New York, NY 10016
Telephone: (212) 973-2800
Ownership %: 100
**Management:**
Margaret Samson ...............................Publisher
**Editorial:**
Martha Klein .............................................Editor
**Desc.:** News on mergers and acquisitions.

## CORPORATE FINANCE
66218

1328 Broadway, 3rd Fl.
New York, NY 10001
Telephone: (212) 594-5030
FAX: (212) 629-0026
Year Established: 1986
Pub. Frequency: q.
Page Size: standard
Subscrp. Rate: $29.95/yr.
Circulation: 60,560
Circulation Type: controlled
**Owner(s):**
Financial World Partners
1328 Broadway, 3rd Fl.
New York, NY 10001
Telephone: (212) 594-5030
Ownership %: 100
**Management:**
Tom Braun ..........................................Publisher
**Editorial:**
Anthony Baldo ..........................................Editor

## CORPORATE REAL ESTATE EXECUTIVE
69397

440 Columbia Dr.
W. Palm Beach, FL 33409-6685
Telephone: (407) 683-8111
FAX: (407) 697-4853
Year Established: 1986
Pub. Frequency: 9/yr.
Page Size: standard
Subscrp. Rate: $65/yr. US; $95/yr. foreign
Materials: 02,32
Circulation: 3,468
Circulation Type: paid
**Owner(s):**
International Association of Corporate Real
Estate
440 Columbia Dr.
W. Palm Beach, FL 33409-6685
Telephone: (407) 683-8111
Ownership %: 100
**Editorial:**
Kathleen B. Dempsey ...........................Editor
**Desc.:** Provides educational and
informative articles on topics of interest
to heads of real estate departments in
large corporations.

## DISCOUNT STORE NEWS
58639

425 Park Ave.
New York, NY 10022
Telephone: (212) 756-5105
FAX: (212) 756-5125
Year Established: 1962
Pub. Frequency: bi-w.
Page Size: tabloid
Subscrp. Rate: $100/yr.
Circulation: 26,051
Circulation Type: paid
**Owner(s):**
Lebhar-Friedman, Inc.
425 Park Ave.
New York, NY 10022
Telephone: (212) 756-5100
Ownership %: 100
**Management:**
Don Longo ..........................................Manager
**Editorial:**
Tony Lisanti .............................................Editor

**Materials Accepted/Included:** 01-Business news 02-By-line articles 03-Fashion news 04-Food news 05-Freelance copy 06-Letters to editor 07-Real estate news 08-Sports news 09-Travel news
10-Book rev. 11-Movie rev. 12-Music rev. 13-TV rev. 14-Theater rev. 15-Coming events 16-Obituaries 17-Question & answer 18-Social announcements 19-Artwork 20-Cartoons 21-Photos 22-TV listings
23-Audio rec. 24-Video rec. 25-Books 26-Films/film clips 27-Personnel news 28-Press releases 29-New product news/photos 30-Trade lit. 31-Contracts awarded 32-Display adv. 33-Classified adv.

4-67

## DOLLARS & SENSE

22309

One Summer St.
Somerville, MA 02143
Telephone: (617) 628-8411
Year Established: 1974
Pub. Frequency: bi-m.
Page Size: standard
Subscrip. Rate: $3.95 newsstand;
$22.95/yr. individuals; $42/yr.
institutions
Circulation: 7,000
Circulation Type: paid
**Owner(s):**
Economic Affairs Bureau, Inc.
One Summer St.
Somerville, MA 02143
Telephone: (617) 628-8411
Ownership %: 100
**Management:**
Deborah Dover .....................Publisher
**Editorial:**
Betsy Reed ..............................Editor
John Stamm ...............Circulation Director
**Desc.:** Presents popular analysis of broad
range of economic issues from
independent socialist and left
perspectives. Topics include
macroeconomic policy, labor markets,
international economics, industry studies.
**Readers:** Political activists, workers,
teachers and professionals, economists,
students.

## DOWLINE

66854

P.O. Box 300
Princeton, NJ 08543
Telephone: (609) 520-4000
Year Established: 1982
Pub. Frequency: q.
Subscrip. Rate: Dow Jones on-line
subscribers
Circulation: 80,000
Circulation Type: controlled
**Owner(s):**
Dow Jones Company, Inc.
200 Liberty St.
New York, NY 10281
Telephone: (212) 416-2000
**Bureau(s):**
Dow Jones Company, Inc.
200 Liberty St.
New York, NY 10281
Telephone: (212) 416-2000
**Management:**
Carl Valenti ...........................Publisher
**Editorial:**
Catherine Ward ...........................Editor

## EC&M

66505

9800 Metcalf Ave.
Overland Park, KS 66212
Telephone: (913) 341-1300
FAX: (913) 967-1905
Mailing Address:
P.O. Box 12901
Overland Park, KS 66282
Year Established: 1901
Pub. Frequency: m.
Page Size: standard
Subscrip. Rate: free
Freelance Pay: negotiable
Circulation: 103,000
Circulation Type: controlled
**Owner(s):**
Intertec Publishing Corp.
P.O. Box 12901
Shawnee Mission, KS 66282
Ownership %: 100
**Editorial:**
John DeDod ...................Editor in Chief

## ECONOMIC REVIEW

69310

400 S. Akard
Dallas, TX 75202
Telephone: (214) 922-5254
FAX: (214) 922-5268
Mailing Address:
Publications Department
P.O. Box 655906
Dallas, TX 75265-5906
Year Established: 1982
Pub. Frequency: q.
Page Size: standard
Circulation: 20,000
Circulation Type: paid
**Owner(s):**
Federal Reserve Bank of Dallas
P.O. Box 655906
Dallas, TX 75265-5906
Telephone: (214) 922-5268
Ownership %: 100
**Editorial:**
Rhonda Harris ..............................Editor
**Desc.:** Publishes analytical articles on
economic and financial matters, ranging
in scope from international finance to
regional developments.
**Readers:** Academic and special libraries,
schools of business administration and
finance.

## EDUCATIONAL IRM QUARTERLY

67188

1787 Agate St.
Eugene, OR 97403-1923
Telephone: (503) 346-4414
FAX: (503) 346-5890
Year Established: 1991
Pub. Frequency: q.
Page Size: standard
Subscrip. Rate: $29/yr.
Circulation: 10,000
Circulation Type: controlled
**Owner(s):**
International Society for Technology in
Education
1787 Agate St.
Eugene, OR 97403
Telephone: (503) 346-4414
Ownership %: 100
**Management:**
Linda Ferguson .................Advertising Manager
**Editorial:**
Dennis Bybee .................Editor in Chief
Carolyn Knox-Quinn .................Design Editor

## EMERGENCY PREPAREDNESS NEWS

65728

951 Pershing Dr.
Silver Spring, MD 20910
Telephone: (301) 587-6300
FAX: (301) 587-1081
Year Established: 1977
Pub. Frequency: bi-w.
Subscrip. Rate: $261.04/yr.
**Owner(s):**
Business Publishers, Inc.
951 Persing Dr.
Silver Spring, MD 20910
Telephone: (301) 587-6300
**Editorial:**
Bonnie Becker ..............................Editor

## EXECUTIVE EDGE

66673

P.O. Box 37
Corte Madera, CA 94976-0037
Telephone: (415) 924-1612
Year Established: 1970
Pub. Frequency: m.
Page Size: standard
Subscrip. Rate: $69.95/yr.
Materials: 01,02,06,09,10,17,20,28
Print Process: web
Circulation: 10,000
Circulation Type: paid

**Owner(s):**
Select Press
P.O. Box 37
Corte Madera, CA 94976-0037
Telephone: (415) 924-1612
Ownership %: 100
**Management:**
Carolynn Quirici ...................Business Manager
**Editorial:**
Rick Crandall ..............................Editor
Catherine White ...................Design Editor
**Desc.:** Contains information for personal
advancement on and off the job. Covers
time management, communication,
supervision, health and fitness, image,
leadership, marketing, sales and more.
**Readers:** Executives and managers.

## EXECUTIVE FEMALE

66239

127 W. 24th St.
4th Fl.
New York, NY 10011
Telephone: (212) 645-0770
FAX: (212) 633-6489
Year Established: 1972
Pub. Frequency: bi-m.
Page Size: standard
Subscrip. Rate: $29/yr.
Materials: 01,06,27,28,31,32,33
Freelance Pay: varies
Circulation: 200,000
Circulation Type: paid
**Owner(s):**
National Association for Female Executives
30 Irving Pl.
New York, NY 10003
Telephone: (212) 477-2200
Ownership %: 100
**Management:**
George Tunick ...........................Publisher
**Editorial:**
Basia Hellwig ..............................Editor
**Desc.:** Provides readers with sophisticated
service article on managing their own
time, careers and finances.
**Readers:** Readers are managerial or
entrepreneurial women in upper 30's
age.

## FAMILY BUSINESS

66336

229 S. 18th St.
Philadelphia, PA 19103
Telephone: (215) 790-7000
Year Established: 1990
Pub. Frequency: q.
Page Size: standard
Subscrip. Rate: $95/yr.
**Owner(s):**
MLR Enterprises
229 S. 18th St
Philadelphia, PA 19103
Telephone: (215) 790-7000
Ownership %: 100
**Management:**
Leonard Zweig ...........................Publisher
**Editorial:**
Leonard Zweig ..............................Editor
**Desc.:** Covers management concerns
affecting family owned businesses.
**Readers:** Geared toward family owned
businesses.

## FORBES

21953

60 Fifth Ave.
New York, NY 10011
Telephone: (212) 620-2200
Year Established: 1917
Pub. Frequency: bi-w.
Page Size: standard
Subscrip. Rate: $52/yr. US; $90/yr.
Canada; $119/yr. elsewhere
Circulation: 735,000
Circulation Type: paid

**Owner(s):**
Forbes, Inc.
60 Fifth Ave.
New York, NY 10011
Telephone: (212) 620-2200
Ownership %: 100
**Bureau(s):**
Washington, D. C.
399 National Press Bldg.
Washington, DC 20045
Telephone: (202) 628-2344
Contact: Howard Banks, Manager
Chicago
410 N. Michigan Ave.
Chicago, IL 60611
Telephone: (312) 329-1562
Contact: Steve Weiner, Manager

Houston
2 Shell Plaza, Ste. 2410
Houston, TX 77201
Telephone: (713) 228-2272
Contact: William P. Barrett, Manager

Los Angeles
12233 W. Olympic Blvd.
Los Angeles, CA 90064
Telephone: (310) 820-1140
Contact: Kathleen K. Wiegner, Manager
**Management:**
Christopher Forbes .....................Vice Chairman
Leonard H. Yablon .................Executive Vice
President
Stephen G. Nicoll .....................Vice President
**Editorial:**
James Cook ...........................Executive Editor
William Baldwin ...................Executive Editor
Jerry Flint ...........................Senior Editor
Thomas Jaffe ...........................Senior Editor
Peter Brimelow ...........................Senior Editor
Lisa Gubernick ...........................Senior Editor
William G. Flanagan ...................Senior Editor
Merrill Vaughn ...........................Senior Editor
Steve Kichen ...........................Senior Editor
Howard Rudtsky ...........................Senior Editor
Harold Seneker ...........................Senior Editor
Phyllis Berman ...........................Senior Editor
Gary Samuels ...........................Senior Editor
Marlene Mandel ...........................Senior Editor
James R. Norman ...........................Senior Editor
Laura Saunders ...........................Senior Editor
Matthew Schifrin ...........................Senior Editor
James W. Michaels ..............................Editor
Lawrence Minard ...................Managing Editor
Jean A. Briggs .........Assistant Managing Editor
Stewart Pinkerton ...............Assistant Managing
Editor
Subrata N. Chakravarty ...Assistant Managing
Editor
William J. Flatley ...............Advertising Director
Everett Halvorsen ...........................Art Director
Jeffrey M. Cunningham ......Associate Publisher
Bruce H. Rogers .......Communications Director
Bruce H. Rogers ...................Marketing Director
**Desc.:** Covers business, finance,
corporate, market and economic affairs.
**Readers:** Business executives, and
investors.

## FORTUNE

26168

Time/Life Bldg., Rockefeller Ctr.
New York, NY 10020
Telephone: (212) 522-1212
FAX: (212) 522-0024
Year Established: 1930
Pub. Frequency: bi-w.
Page Size: oversize
Subscrip. Rate: $4.50 newsstand; $57/yr.
Circulation: 921,789
Circulation Type: paid
**Owner(s):**
Time, Inc.
Time/Life Bldg., Rockefeller
New York, NY 10020
Telephone: (212) 522-1212
Ownership %: 100

**Materials Accepted/Included:** 01-Business news 02-By-line articles 03-Fashion news 04-Food news 05-Freelance copy 06-Letters to editor 07-Real estate news 08-Sports news 09-Travel news 10-Book rev. 11-Movie rev. 12-Music rev. 13-TV rev. 14-Theater rev. 15-Coming events 16-Obituaries 17-Question & answer 18-Social announcements 19-Artwork 20-Cartoons 21-Photos 22-TV listings 23-Audio rec. 24-Video rec. 25-Books 26-Films/film clips 27-Personnel news 28-Press releases 29-New product news/photos 30-Trade lit. 31-Contracts awarded 32-Display adv. 33-Classified adv.

**Management:**
C. Stuart Arnold ............................Publisher
Susan F. Sachs ...............Associate Publisher
Brian D. Wolfe ...............Circulation Manager
**Editorial:**
Jason McManus ....................Editor in Chief
Allan Demaree .....................Executive Editor
Ann Morrison .......................Executive Editor
Walter Kiechel ......................Managing Editor
Leslie Gaines Ross .............Marketing Director
Guy Gleysteen ...................Production Director
**Desc.:** Staff-written articles devoted to
managing, the economy, corporate
performance, selling, technology, money
& markets, politics & policy,
entrepreneurs. Departments include:
News/Trends, Personal Investing, Office
Hours, Books & Ideas.
**Readers:** Management, executives,
business, etc.

### FRANCHISING INVESTMENTS AROUND THE WORLD
*22321*
6119 Pierce St.
Hollywood, FL 33024-7943
Telephone: (305) 966-1530
Year Established: 1967
Pub. Frequency: m.
Page Size: tabloid
Subscrip. Rate: $10/yr.
Freelance Pay: $25-$100
Circulation: 38,500
Circulation Type: controlled
**Owner(s):**
Sutton Place Publications, Inc.
6119 Pierce St.
Hollywood, FL 33024-7943
Telephone: (305) 966-1530
Ownership %: 100
**Management:**
Edward J. Foley ............................Publisher
**Editorial:**
Edward J. Foley ..............................Editor
Kim Foley ...............................Art Director
**Desc.:** Recognized as the leader in
reporting news on business and
franchising.
**Readers:** Large and small investor.

### GEICO DIRECT
*64901*
2001 Killebrew Dr., Ste. 105
Minneapolis, MN 55425
Telephone: (612) 854-0155
Year Established: 1986
Pub. Frequency: s-a.
Page Size: standard
Materials: 21,28,29,30
Freelance Pay: $200-$800
Print Process: web offset
Circulation: 1,500,000
Circulation Type: controlled
**Owner(s):**
Geico Insurance
5260 Western Ave.
Washington, DC 20076
Telephone: (612) 854-0155
Ownership %: 100
**Management:**
Karel Laing ...............................Publisher
**Editorial:**
Pat Burke ....................................Editor
Kirsten Ford ...............................Art Director
Suesan Ritchie ...............................Photo
Luann Eager ..............Production Coordinator
**Desc.:** Carries six or seven feature stories
per issue in the financial, consumer,
lifestyle, leisure, automotive, and safety
categories. Most stories are written on
assignment.
**Readers:** Geico Insurance policy holders.

### GLOBAL FINANCE
*66237*
11 W. 19th St., 2nd Fl.
New York, NY 10011
Telephone: (212) 337-5900
FAX: (212) 337-5055
Year Established: 1987
Pub. Frequency: m.
Page Size: standard
Subscrip. Rate: $120/yr.
Circulation: 55,000
Circulation Type: controlled
**Owner(s):**
Global Finance Joint Venture
1221 Ave. America
New York, NY 10020
Telephone: (212) 512-2000
**Management:**
Joseph Giarraputo ........................Publisher
**Editorial:**
Carl Burgen .................................Editor
**Readers:** Management and finance
executives at non-financial & financial
corporations.

### HARVARD BUSINESS REVIEW
*22327*
Soldiers Field Rd.
Boston, MA 02163-0199
Telephone: (617) 495-6800
FAX: (617) 495-9933
Year Established: 1922
Pub. Frequency: bi-m.
Page Size: standard
Subscrip. Rate: $145/yr. foreign
Circulation: 216,000
Circulation Type: paid
**Owner(s):**
Harvard Business School Publishing Corp.
Soldiers Field Rd.
Boston, MA 02163-0199
Telephone: (617) 495-6800
Ownership %: 100
**Management:**
Lawrence Allen .............................Publisher
**Editorial:**
Joel Kurtzmann ...............................Editor
Anne Friedman ..................Managing Editor
**Desc.:** Publishes research and case
studies on business related issues such
as corporate strategy, management,
finance, regulatory policy, technology,
international trends. Length: 4,000-6,000
words. Articles should be helpful,
provocative, and with original slants on
the problem discussed.
**Readers:** Senior corporate executives.

### HIGH TECH CERAMICS NEWS
*66134*
25 Van Zant St.
Norwalk, CT 06855
Telephone: (203) 853-4266
Year Established: 1989
Pub. Frequency: m.
Page Size: standard
Subscrip. Rate: $325/yr.
**Owner(s):**
Louis Naturman
25 Van Zant St.
Norwalk, CT 06855
Telephone: (203) 853-4266
**Management:**
Robert Butler ...............................Manager
**Desc.:** Provides monthly new product
news, technology information and
analysis, market data and company
information.
**Readers:** Commercial development-
corporate management, technical
management research & market
research people.

### HIGH TECH SEPARATIONS NEWS
*66130*
25 Van Zant St.
Norwalk, CT 06855
Telephone: (203) 853-4266
FAX: (203) 853-0348
Year Established: 1988
Pub. Frequency: m.
Page Size: standard
Subscrip. Rate: $325/yr.
**Owner(s):**
Louis Naturman
25 Van Zant St.
Norwalk, CT 06855
Telephone: (203) 853-4266
**Management:**
Robert Butler ...............................Manager
**Desc.:** Provides monthly new product
news, technology information and
analysis, market data and company
information.
**Readers:** Commercial development-
corporate management-technical
management/research and market
research people.

### HISPANIC BUSINESS MAGAZINE
*66235*
360 S. Hope Ave., 300c
Santa Barbara, CA 93105
Telephone: (805) 682-5843
FAX: (805) 563-1239
Year Established: 1979
Pub. Frequency: m.
Page Size: standard
Subscrip. Rate: $18/yr.
Materials: 01,02,05,06,10,23,24,28,31,32,33
Freelance Pay: $.25/wd.
Print Process: offset
Circulation: 165,000
Circulation Type: controlled & paid
**Owner(s):**
Jesus Chavarria
360 S. Hope Ave., 300c
Santa Barbara, CA 93105
Telephone: (805) 682-5843
Ownership %: 100
**Editorial:**
Jesus Chavarria ...............................Editor
Hector Canto ......................Managing Editor
**Desc.:** Written for and about Hispanic
CEO's, managers and professionals.
Editorial features include research-based
reports on Hispanic entrepreneurs,
markets and media.
**Readers:** Hispanic business owners,
Hispanic market professionals.
**Deadline:** story-3 mo. prior to pub. date

### HUMAN RESOURCE EXECUTIVE
*66233*
747 Dresher Rd., P.O. Box 980
Horsham, PA 19044
Telephone: (215) 784-0860
FAX: (215) 784-0870
Year Established: 1987
Pub. Frequency: m.
Page Size: tabloid
Subscrip. Rate: $49.95/yr. in US
Materials: 01,06,27,28,29
Circulation: 45,000
Circulation Type: controlled & paid
**Owner(s):**
Axon Group
747 Dresher Rd., P.O. Box 980
Horsham, PA 19044
Telephone: (215) 784-0860
Ownership %: 100
**Management:**
Bernie Trachtenberry ....................Publisher
Al'n Novak ...........................General Manager
**Editorial:**
Dave Shadovitz .....................Editor in Chief
Marilyn Schaefer ...................Managing Editor
Dave Shadovitz ................Associate Publisher
Dawn Schaefer ...............Production Coordinator

**Desc.:** Coverage of key human resource
issues facing organizations today.
**Readers:** Human resource executives,
human resource vice presidents,
directors and managers.

### IB: INDEPENDENT BUSINESS
*67216*
875 S. Westlake Blvd., 211
Westlake Village, CA 91361
Telephone: (805) 496-6156
Year Established: 1990
Pub. Frequency: bi-m.
Page Size: standard
Freelance Pay: $500-$1500
Circulation: 630,000
Circulation Type: controlled
**Owner(s):**
IB Ltd. Group IV Communications, Inc.,
G.P.
875 S. Westlake Blvd., 211
Westlake Village, CA 91361
Telephone: (805) 496-6156
Ownership %: 100
**Management:**
P. Thomas Sargent ...........................President
Michael Carpenter ...........................Publisher
Angus McCauley ...............Advertising Manager
**Editorial:**
Daniel Kehrer .....................................Editor
Don Phillipson ...................Editorial Director
**Desc.:** America's small business magazine.
How-to articles for small business
owners.
**Readers:** Small business owners.

### INC.
*66851*
38 Commercial Wharf
Boston, MA 02110
Telephone: (617) 248-8000
FAX: (617) 248-8040
Year Established: 1979
Pub. Frequency: m.
Page Size: standard
Subscrip. Rate: $19/yr.
Circulation: 640,000
Circulation Type: paid
**Owner(s):**
Goldhirsch Group, The
38 Commercial Wharf
Boston, MA 02110
Telephone: (617) 248-8000
Ownership %: 100
**Management:**
Jay McDonald ................................Publisher
Jay McDonald ...................Advertising Manager
**Editorial:**
George Gendron ...................Editor in Chief
Nancy Lons .........................Executive Editor
Michael Hopkins .....................Executive Editor

### INDUSTRIA ALIMENTICIA
*66751*
1935 Shermer Rd., Ste. 100
Northbrook, IL 60062
Telephone: (708) 205-5660
FAX: (708) 205-5680
Year Established: 1990
Pub. Frequency: m.
Page Size: standard
Subscrip. Rate: $30/yr. US; $100/yr.
foreign
Materials: 04,28,29,33
Circulation: 20,000
Circulation Type: controlled
**Owner(s):**
Stagnito Publishing Co.
1935 Shermer Rd., Ste. 100
Northbrook, IL 60062
Telephone: (708) 205-5660
Ownership %: 100
**Management:**
Mario Schacher ............................Publisher
**Editorial:**
Elsa Torres .....................................Editor

**Materials Accepted/Included:** 01-Business news 02-By-line articles 03-Fashion news 04-Food news 05-Freelance copy 06-Letters to editor 07-Real estate news 08-Sports news 09-Travel news 10-Book rev. 11-Movie rev. 12-Music rev. 13-TV rev. 14-Theater rev. 15-Coming events 16-Obituaries 17-Question & answer 18-Social announcements 19-Artwork 20-Cartoons 21-Photos 22-TV listings 23-Audio rec. 24-Video rec. 25-Books 26-Films/film clips 27-Personnel news 28-Press releases 29-New product news/photos 30-Trade lit. 31-Contracts awarded 32-Display adv. 33-Classified adv.

4-69

**Desc.:** For Latin American food processing manufacturers including meat, poultry, seafood, dairy products, processed fruits and vegetables, bakery and snack foods, beverages, processed meals and specialty foods. Technical information covers food product development and innovative processing systems. Features editorial content reports on major plant visits, supplier product news, convention coverage, plant equipment, ingredients, packaging materials, and distribution. Written in Spanish.

**Readers:** Executives & department heads of processed food companies in Latin America.

66009

## INFORMATION WEEK
600 Community Dr.
Manhasset, NY 11030
Telephone: (516) 562-5000
FAX: (516) 562-3036
Pub. Frequency: w.
Subscrip. Rate: $100/yr.
Circulation: 140,000
Circulation Type: paid
**Owner(s):**
CMP Publications
600 Community Dr.
Manhasset, NY 11030
Telephone: (516) 562-5000
**Management:**
Becky Barna .............................Publisher
**Editorial:**
Joel Dreyfuss ...............................Editor

53965

## JOB OPENINGS FOR ECONOMISTS
2014 Broadway, Ste. 305
Nashville, TN 37203
Telephone: (615) 322-2595
Year Established: 1974
Pub. Frequency: bi-m
Subscrip. Rate: $15/yr. members; $25/yr. non-members
Circulation: 2,500
**Owner(s):**
American Economic Association
2014 Broadway, Ste. 305
Nashville, TN 37203
Telephone: (615) 322-2595
**Editorial:**
Violet Sikes ..................................Editor
**Desc.:** Lists job opportunities for economists.

64719

## JOURNAL OF BUSINESS
1101 E. 58th St.
Chicago, IL 60637
Telephone: (312) 702-7140
FAX: (312) 702-0458
Mailing Address:
  1101 E. 58th St.
  Chicago, IL 60637
Year Established: 1928
Pub. Frequency: q.
Page Size: standard
Subscrip. Rate: $23/yr. individuals; $43/yr. institutions
Circulation: 4,900
Circulation Type: paid
**Owner(s):**
University of Chicago, The
Chicago, IL 60637
Ownership %: 100
**Editorial:**
Abel P. Jeuland ............................Editor
B. Peter Pashigian ........................Editor
Ben S. Bernavine ..........................Editor
Albert Wadansky ...........................Editor
Victor Zarnowitz ...........................Editor
Douglas W. Diamond .............Managing Editor
**Readers:** Business academics.

68760

## JOURNAL OF BUSINESS RESEARCH
655 Ave. of the Americas
New York, NY 10010
Telephone: (212) 989-5800
FAX: (212) 633-3990
Mailing Address:
  Tulane University
  Freeman School of Business
  New Orleans, LA 70118
Year Established: 1973
Pub. Frequency: 9/yr.
Page Size: standard
Subscrip. Rate: $345/yr.
Materials: 02,05,10,32
Circulation: 1,750
Circulation Type: paid
**Owner(s):**
Elsevier Science Publishing Co., Inc.
655 Ave. of the Americas
New York, NY 10010
Telephone: (212) 989-5800
Ownership %: 100
**Editorial:**
Arch G. Woodside ........................Editor
**Desc.:** Applies theory developed from business research to actual business situations.
**Readers:** Scholars at universities and business firms.

66708

## JOURNAL OF BUSINESS STRATEGY, THE
11 Penn Plz., 17th Fl.
New York, NY 10001
Telephone: (212) 967-7000
FAX: (212) 629-7885
Year Established: 1980
Pub. Frequency: bi-m.
Page Size: standard
Subscrip. Rate: $98/yr.
Materials: 01,02,03,05,06,10,11,12,13,14, 16,17,19,20,21,23,24,25,28,29,30,32
Print Process: sheet fed
Circulation: 18,000
Circulation Type: free & paid
**Owner(s):**
Faulkner & Gray, Inc.
11 Penn Plz., 17th Fl.
New York, NY 10001
Telephone: (212) 967-7000
FAX: (212) 967-7155
Ownership %: 100
**Editorial:**
Bristol Voss ..................................Editor
**Desc.:** Articles on strategic planning, corporate case histories, new product development, marketing, competitor intelligence, cost reductions, reengineering, technology, business-to-business, acquisitions, ethics, executive education, research & development, politics, boards and leadership.
**Readers:** Corporate planning and strategy professionals in mid-sized to large companies in the U.S., Canada, and Europe.

68761

## JOURNAL OF BUSINESS VENTURING
655 Ave. of the Americas
New York, NY 10010
Telephone: (212) 989-5800
FAX: (212) 633-3990
Year Established: 1985
Pub. Frequency: bi-m.
Subscrip. Rate: $238/yr.
**Owner(s):**
Elsevier Science Publishing Co., Inc.
655 Ave. of the Americas
New York, NY 10010
Telephone: (212) 989-5800
Ownership %: 100

**Editorial:**
Ian MacMillan ..............................Editor
**Desc.:** Details research on entrepreneurship, either as independent start-ups or within existing corporations.

53950

## JOURNAL OF ECONOMIC LITERATURE
P.O. Box 7320, Oakland Sta.
Pittsburgh, PA 15213
Telephone: (412) 268-3869
FAX: (412) 268-6810
Year Established: 1963
Pub. Frequency: q.
Page Size: standard
Circulation: 26,000
Circulation Type: paid
**Owner(s):**
American Economic Assn.
2014 Broadway 305
Nashville, TN 37203
Telephone: (615) 322-2595
Ownership %: 100
**Editorial:**
John Pencavel ..............................Editor
Drucilla Ekwurzel ..................Associate Editor

68762

## JOURNAL OF ECONOMICS & BUSINESS
655 Ave. of the Americas
New York, NY 10010
Telephone: (212) 989-5800
FAX: (212) 633-3990
Year Established: 1949
Pub. Frequency: q.
Subscrip. Rate: $181/yr.
**Owner(s):**
Elsevier Science Publishing Co., Inc.
655 Ave. of the Americas
New York, NY 10010
Telephone: (212) 989-5800
Ownership %: 100
**Editorial:**
David Meinster ..............................Editor
**Desc.:** Presents scholarly research in applied economics, finance and related disciplines that focus on the domestic and international aspects of business and society.

70967

## JOURNAL OF MANAGEMENT INQUIRY
2455 Teller Rd.
Thousand Oaks, CA 91320
Telephone: (805) 494-9821
FAX: (805) 499-0871
Year Established: 1992
Pub. Frequency: q.
Subscrip. Rate: $45/yr. individuals; $105/yr. institutions
Circulation: 1,500
Circulation Type: controlled & paid
**Owner(s):**
Sage Publications, Inc.
2455 Teller Rd.
Thousand Oaks, CA 91320
Telephone: (805) 499-9821
FAX: (805) 499-0871
Ownership %: 100
**Editorial:**
Thomas G. Cummings .....................Editor
Alan M. Glassman .........................Editor
**Desc.:** Provides a forum for nontraditional research and practice in the fields of management and organization.
**Readers:** Individuals and instititions.

65119

## KIPLINGER WASHINGTON LETTER
1729 H St., N.W.
Washington, DC 20006
Telephone: (202) 887-6400
FAX: (202) 331-1206

Pub. Frequency: m.
Subscrip. Rate: $68/yr.
Circulation: 500,000
Circulation Type: paid
**Owner(s):**
Kiplinger Washington Editors, Inc.
1729 H St., N.W.
Washington, DC 20006
Telephone: (202) 887-6400
Ownership %: 100
**Management:**
Tom Eggleston ..................Circulation Manager
**Editorial:**
Knight A. Kiplinger ...................Editor in Chief
**Desc.:** Weekly news, information, analyses, and forecasts, affecting personal lives and finances.

22349

## LEADERS
59 E. 54th St.
New York, NY 10022
Telephone: (212) 758-0740
FAX: (212) 593-5194
Year Established: 1978
Pub. Frequency: q.
Page Size: oversize
Subscrip. Rate: controlled
Circulation: 33,000
Circulation Type: controlled
**Owner(s):**
Leaders Magazine, Inc.
59 E. 54th St.
New York, NY 10022
Telephone: (212) 758-0740
Ownership %: 100
**Management:**
Henry O. Dormann ..............Chairman of Board
Darrell J. Brown .........................President
David W. Schner ......................Vice President
**Editorial:**
Henry O. Dormann ....................Editor in Chief
Darrell J. Brown ............................Editor
Deanne Vorster ......................Managing Editor
David Snyder ..........................Associate Editor
Darrell J. Brown .................Book Review Editor
David Schner ......................Marketing Director
**Desc.:** Contains general articles which convey the viewpoints and feelings of the respective authors. Articles may cover any subject the author chooses but must be an original composition. Topics generally deal with world issues, policy pronouncements on world problems and proposed solutions to issues of conflict in the world today.
**Readers:** International companies, leaders of nations, world religions, international learning, international labor organizations, chief financial officers, major investors, Nobel laureates, science and arts.

59648

## LIGHTBULB/INVENT
12424 Main St.
Fort Jones, CA 96032
Telephone: (916) 468-2282
FAX: (916) 468-2238
Year Established: 1971
Pub. Frequency: bi-m.
Page Size: standard
Subscrip. Rate: $30/yr. US; $60/yr. foreign air
Circulation: 15,000
Circulation Type: free & paid
**Owner(s):**
M&M Associates
P.O. Box 1020
Fort Jones, CA 96032-9712
Telephone: (916) 468-2282
Ownership %: 100
**Editorial:**
Maggie Weisberg ...........................Editor

Materials Accepted/Included: 01-Business news 02-By-line articles 03-Fashion news 04-Food news 05-Freelance copy 06-Letters to editor 07-Real estate news 08-Sports news 09-Travel news 10-Book rev. 11-Movie rev. 12-Music rev. 13-TV rev. 14-Theater rev. 15-Coming events 16-Obituaries 17-Question & answer 18-Social announcements 19-Artwork 20-Cartoons 21-Photos 22-TV listings 23-Audio rec. 24-Video rec. 25-Books 26-Films/film clips 27-Personnel news 28-Press releases 29-New product news/photos 30-Trade lit. 31-Contracts awarded 32-Display adv. 33-Classified adv.

**Desc.:** International magazine for inventors, innovators, scientists, engineers, designers and entrepreneurs. Provides comprehensive information and resources. Covers the business of inventing.
**Readers:** Inventors and entrepreneurs, plus financial people, manufacturers, professional services, governments, and developers of new products and businesses.

66856

## L.O.M.A. RESOURCE
5770 Powers Ferry Rd.
Atlanta, GA 30327
Telephone: (404) 951-1770
FAX: (404) 984-0441
Year Established: 1974
Pub. Frequency: m.
Page Size: standard
Subscrip. Rate: $36/yr.
Materials: 01,28,29,32
Print Process: offset
Circulation: 26,000
Circulation Type: controlled
**Owner(s):**
L.O.M.A. Association
Atlanta, GA 30327
Telephone: (404) 951-1770
Ownership %: 100
**Management:**
Ron Clark ..........................Advertising Manager
**Editorial:**
Ron Clark ................................Editor in Chief
**Desc.:** Covers news and trends in the management of the life insurance industry.
**Readers:** Upper management of life insurance companies.
**Deadline:** ads-1st of each mo.

23446

## MANAGE
2210 Arbor Blvd.
Dayton, OH 45439
Telephone: (513) 294-0421
FAX: (513) 294-2374
Year Established: 1925
Pub. Frequency: q.
Page Size: standard
Subscrip. Rate: $5/yr.
Materials: 01,02,05,06,09,10,17,19,20,21, 28,29,30,32,33
Freelance Pay: $.05/wd.
Print Process: web offset
Circulation: 151,300
Circulation Type: free & paid
**Owner(s):**
National Management Association
2210 Arbor Blvd.
Dayton, OH 45439
Telephone: (513) 294-0421
Ownership %: 100
**Editorial:**
Douglas E. Shaw ..........................Editor in Chief
Nancy Rice ..................................Advertising
Douglas E. Shaw ...........................Columnist
Douglas E. Shaw ...............New Product Editor
Douglas E. Shaw ...............................Photo
Douglas E. Shaw ..................Technical Editor
**Desc.:** Management information journal published quarterly by world's largest professional management association. By-line articles of general interest to all people in management.
**Readers:** Over 52,000 NMA members and 4,000 others.

66101

## MANAGEMENT REPORT
22 W. 21st St.
New York, NY 10010-1160
Telephone: (212) 645-7880
FAX: (212) 645-1160
Year Established: 1978
Pub. Frequency: m.

Page Size: standard
Subscrip. Rate: $195/yr. US & Canada; $245/yr. foreign
**Owner(s):**
Executive Enterprises Publications Co., Inc.
22 W. 21st St.
New York, NY 10010-1160
Telephone: (212) 645-7880
Ownership %: 100
**Editorial:**
Jane G. Bensahel ........Director, Business Publ.
**Desc.:** Discusses non-union alternatives for organization management.
**Readers:** Human resources managers, labor relations managers, line managers and supervisors.

22354

## MANAGEMENT REVIEW
135 W. 50th St.
New York, NY 10020
Telephone: (212) 903-8393
Year Established: 1923
Pub. Frequency: m.
Page Size: 4 color photos/art
Subscrip. Rate: $45/yr.
Circulation: 75,000
Circulation Type: controlled
**Owner(s):**
American Management Association
135 W. 50th St.
New York, NY 10020
Telephone: (212) 586-8100
Ownership %: 100
**Management:**
Rosemary K. Carlough .......................Publisher
**Editorial:**
Martha H. Peak ...............................Editor
Hilda Tejada ..............................Advertising
**Desc.:** Carries first-rights only by-lined articles running from 1,500 to 2,000 words of general management interest. Articles deal with general management, marketing, international management, organizational development, human resources development.
**Readers:** Business executives and administrators.

24881

## MANAGEMENT SCIENCE
290 Westminster St.
Providence, RI 02903
Telephone: (401) 274-2525
Year Established: 1953
Pub. Frequency: m.
Page Size: standard
Subscrip. Rate: $159/yr. US; $174/yr. foreign
Circulation: 9,100
Circulation Type: paid
**Owner(s):**
Institute of Management Sciences
290 Westminster St.
Providence, RI 02903
Telephone: (401) 274-2525
Ownership %: 100
**Management:**
William R. King ...............................President
**Editorial:**
Gabroel Birtan ...............................Editor
Barbara Sorich ......................Managing Editor
Candita Gerzeuitz ..................Technical Editor
**Desc.:** Seeks to publish significant articles that identify, extend, or unify scientific knowledge pertaining to management.
**Readers:** Managers, educators, practicing management.

61245

## MEETING & CONFERENCE EXECUTIVES ALERT
P.O. Box 24, Prudential Sta.
Boston, MA 02199
Telephone: (617) 267-7151
FAX: (617) 267-6577
Year Established: 1983

Pub. Frequency: m.
Page Size: standard
Subscrip. Rate: $89/yr.
Materials: 01,02,05,06,09,10,15,17,28,29, 30,33,34
Freelance Pay: $50/article
Circulation: 1,000
Circulation Type: paid
**Owner(s):**
Mather Communications, Inc.
P.O. Box 24, Prudential Sta.
Boston, MA 02199
Telephone: (617) 267-7151
FAX: (617) 267-6577
Ownership %: 100
**Management:**
Joan Mather ...............................Publisher
**Editorial:**
Joan Mather ...............................Editor
**Readers:** Members and suppliers of meeting planning field.

61295

## MEETING MANAGER, THE
1950 Stemmons Fwy., Ste. 5018
Dallas, TX 75207
Telephone: (214) 712-7752
FAX: (214) 712-7770
Year Established: 1980
Pub. Frequency: m.
Page Size: standard
Subscrip. Rate: $35/yr. non-members
Freelance Pay: varies
Circulation: 10,500
Circulation Type: controlled
**Owner(s):**
Meeting Planners International
1950 Stemmons Fwy., Ste. 5018
Dallas, TX 75207
Telephone: (214) 712-7752
Ownership %: 100
**Management:**
Edwin L. Griffin, Jr. .......................Publisher
Bridget Heuer ........................Sales Manager
**Editorial:**
Tina Filipski ...............................Editor
**Desc.:** For professionals who plan and manage meetings, conventions, conferences and tradeshows. Articles cover every aspect of meeting management from the basics to the industry's cutting edge.
**Readers:** Meeting professionals.

61323

## MINI-STORAGE MESSENGER
2531 W. Dunlap
Phoenix, AZ 85021
Telephone: (602) 870-1711
FAX: (602) 861-1094
Year Established: 1979
Pub. Frequency: m.
Page Size: standard
Subscrip. Rate: $5.95 newsstand; $59.95/yr.; $109.96/2 yrs.
Materials: 01,02,06,07,19,21,27,28,29,31, 32,33
Freelance Pay: $100-$350
Print Process: offset
Circulation: 4,732
Circulation Type: free & paid
**Owner(s):**
Hardy Good
2531 W. Dunlap
Phoenix, AZ 85021
Telephone: (602) 870-1711
FAX: (602) 861-1094
Ownership %: 100
**Management:**
Bob Rogers ....................Advertising Manager
Bob Rogers ....................Circulation Manager
Carla Love ....................Production Manager
**Editorial:**
Stefan Budricks ...............................Editor
Rhonda L. Baker ..........................Art Director
Randy Tipton ....................Publication Director

**Desc.:** Official publication of the Self-Storage Association. Published for owners, managers and interested parties of the nation's self-storage industry. Aims to help industry professionals better communicate among themselves.
**Readers:** Self-storage developers, owners, operators and industry professionals.
**Deadline:** story-60 days prior to pub. date; news-45 days prior; photo-60 days prior; ads-40 days prior

66230

## MINORITIES & WOMEN IN BUSINESS
441 S. Spring
Burlington, NC 27215
Telephone: (919) 229-1462
FAX: (919) 222-7455
Mailing Address:
P.O. Drawer 210
Burlington, NC 27216
Year Established: 1984
Pub. Frequency: bi-m.
Page Size: standard
Subscrip. Rate: $15/yr.; $25/2 yrs.; $36/3 yrs.
Circulation: 60,000
Circulation Type: controlled & paid
**Owner(s):**
John D. Enoch
441 S. Spring St.
Burlington, NC 27215
Telephone: (919) 229-1462
**Editorial:**
Karin C. Bassler ......................Managing Editor
Cynthia A. McCray .......................Art Director
**Desc.:** Offers insight into the issues and trends affecting minority and female entrepreneurs and executives. Regular columns and departments feature role models and valuable tips which encourage minorities and females to participate more fully in the economy.
**Readers:** Minorities and female entrepreneurs and executives, corporate officers, corporate buyers, and professors and students of business.

69336

## MINORITY BUSINESS ENTREPRENEUR
3528 Torrance Blvd., Ste. 101
Torrance, CA 90503-4803
Telephone: (310) 540-9398
FAX: (310) 792-8263
Year Established: 1984
Pub. Frequency: bi-m.
Page Size: standard
Subscrip. Rate: $15/yr.
Materials: 01,02,09,10,19,21,28,29,20,31, 32,33
Circulation: 30,638
Circulation Type: free & paid
**Owner(s):**
Minority Business Entrepreneur
3528 Torrance Blvd., #101
Torrance, CA 90503-4803
Telephone: (310) 540-9398
FAX: (310) 792-8263
Ownership %: 100
**Management:**
Ginger Conrad ...............................Publisher
**Editorial:**
Jeanie M. Barnett ....................Executive Editor
Barbara Daley ................Assistant to Publisher
**Desc.:** Minority and women business development issues in public/private sectors.
**Readers:** 90% minority and women business owners nationwide. 10% public and private administrators of MWBE programs.
**Deadline:** story-60 days prior; news-30 days prior; photo-30 days prior; ads-2 wks. prior

**Materials Accepted/Included:** 01-Business news 02-By-line articles 03-Fashion news 04-Food news 05-Freelance copy 06-Letters to editor 07-Real estate news 08-Sports news 09-Travel news 10-Book rev. 11-Movie rev. 12-Music rev. 13-TV rev. 14-Theater rev. 15-Coming events 16-Obituaries 17-Question & answer 18-Social announcements 19-Artwork 20-Cartoons 21-Photos 22-TV listings 23-Audio rec. 24-Video rec. 25-Books 26-Films/film clips 27-Personnel news 28-Press releases 29-New product news/photos 30-Trade lit. 31-Contracts awarded 32-Display adv. 33-Classified adv.

4-71

**MR** 67040
50 Day St.
Norwalk, CT 06854
Telephone: (203) 853-6015
FAX: (203) 852-8175
Year Established: 1990
Pub. Frequency: 7/yr.
Page Size: standard
Subscrip. Rate: $24/yr.
Materials: 28,29,30
Circulation: 20,000
Circulation Type: controlled
**Owner(s):**
Business Journals, Inc.
50 Day St.
Norwalk, CT 06854
Telephone: (203) 853-6015
Ownership %: 100
**Management:**
Stuart Nifoussi .......................Publisher
Lorelyn Eaves ..............Advertising Manager
**Editorial:**
Karen Alberg Grossman ..........................Editor

**NATION'S BUSINESS** 26179
1615 H St., N.W.
Washington, DC 20062
Telephone: (202) 463-5650
FAX: (202) 887-3437
Year Established: 1912
Pub. Frequency: m.
Page Size: standard
Subscrip. Rate: $22/yr.
Materials: 01,02,05,06,07,09,21,29,32,33
Freelance Pay: $100/pg. min.
Circulation: 850,000
Circulation Type: paid
**Owner(s):**
U.S. Chamber Of Commerce
1615 H. St. N.W.
Washington, DC 20062
Telephone: (202) 463-5650
FAX: (202) 887-3437
Ownership %: 100
**Management:**
Dr. Richard L. Lesher .......................President
David A. Roe ........................Vice President
Neil Hanlon .......................Advertising Manager
James M. Yandle ..............Advertising Manager
Richard Chalkley ..............Advertising Manager
Robert H. Gotshall ..........Advertising Manager
Tom Bowman ...................Advertising Manager
Jerry V. Camporine ...........Advertising Manager
Richard Topous .................Advertising Manager
Terry Nance .....................Advertising Manager
Joseph Adduci ..................Advertising Manager
Richard Sands ..................Advertising Manager
Mike McNew ....................Advertising Manager
Leonard Rippa ....................Business Manager
**Editorial:**
Albert G. Holzinger .......................Senior Editor
Robert T. Gray .......................................Editor
Mary McElveen ......................Managing Editor
Terry Shea ..............Assistant Managing Editor
Roger Thompson ............Assistant Managing
Editor
Hans A. Baum .......................Art Director
Joan Szabo .......................Associate Editor
El Motaz Sonbol ..................Marketing Director
Laurence Levin .....................Photography Editor
Shiela Yoder .......................Production Director
David Warner .......................Senior Writer
Sharon Nelton ..............Special Correspondent
**Desc.:** Helps owners and/or managers of
smaller to medium sized enterprises do
a better job of running their businesses.
Provides guidance and advice on
effective business management,
business success stories, personal
advice on health, investing, tax matters,
and information on Washington
developments affecting business.

**Readers:** Owners and managers of
businesses of all sizes and types
particularly smaller to medium-sized
businesses, professional people;
government officials.
**Deadline:** story-60 days; news-60 days;
photo-60 days; ads-60 days

**NATIONAL PRODUCTIVITY
REVIEW** 58645
22 W. 21st St.
New York, NY 10010-6904
Telephone: (212) 645-7880
FAX: (212) 645-1160
Year Established: 1981
Pub. Frequency: q.
Page Size: standard
Subscrip. Rate: $168/yr.
**Owner(s):**
Executive Enterprises Publications Co., Inc.
22 W. 21st St.
New York, NY 10010
Telephone: (212) 645-7880
FAX: (212) 645-1160
Ownership %: 100
**Editorial:**
Mary Ann Castronovo Fusco ..................Editor
Jane G. Bensahel .........Business Pub. Director
**Desc.:** Focuses on new techniques for
enhancing productivity and quality to
achieve better performance; case
studies, new trends in measurement
systems, productivity research and
efficiency implementation, worldwide,
and in both the private and public
sectors.
**Readers:** Organization executives,
productivity specialists.

**NEW MIAMI** 67221
100 N.W. 37th Ave.
Miami, FL 33125-4844
Telephone: (305) 372-5000
FAX: (305) 372-1669
Year Established: 1988
Pub. Frequency: m.
Page Size: standard
Subscrip. Rate: $18/yr.
Circulation: 21,000
Circulation Type: paid
**Owner(s):**
New Miami Magazine
444 Brickell Ave., 250
Miami, FL 33131
Telephone: (305) 372-5000
Ownership %: 100
**Management:**
Mona Ignatz .......................President
Mona Ignatz .......................Publisher

**OPPORTUNITY MAGAZINE** 66859
73 Spring St., 303
New York, NY 10012
Telephone: (212) 925-3180
Year Established: 1924
Pub. Frequency: m.
Subscrip. Rate: $19.95/yr.
Circulation: 250,000
Circulation Type: paid
**Owner(s):**
Opportunity Associates
73 Spring St.
New York, NY 10012
Telephone: (212) 925-3180
**Management:**
Sherrill Rhoades .......................Publisher
**Editorial:**
Donna Ruffini .......................................Editor
Greg Poort ..................Advertising Director

**OUTLOOK MAGAZINE** 21933
275 Shoreline Dr.
Redwood City, CA 94065-1412
Telephone: (415) 802-2600
Year Established: 1959
Pub. Frequency: q.
Subscrip. Rate: $26/yr.
Print Process: web offset
Circulation: 60,000
Circulation Type: controlled & paid
**Owner(s):**
California Society of CPA's
275 Shoreline Dr.
Redwood City, CA 94065-1412
Telephone: (415) 802-2600
Ownership %: 100
**Management:**
James R. Kurtz .......................Publisher
Bobbi Petrov ..................Advertising Manager
**Editorial:**
Sheri Pepper .......................................Editor
**Desc.:** Explores in-depth, broad-based
issues, oriented subjects and technical
topics of specific concern to members of
the California Society of CPA's.
**Readers:** Members of the California
Society of CPA's.

**PROFESSIONAL APARTMENT
MANAGEMENT** 65733
149 Fifth Ave., 16th Fl.
New York, NY 10010-6801
Telephone: (212) 473-8200
FAX: (212) 473-8786
Year Established: 1990
Pub. Frequency: m.
Page Size: standard
Subscrip. Rate: $168/yr.
Materials: 07
Print Process: offset
**Owner(s):**
Brownstone Publishers, Inc.
149 Fifth Ave., 16th Fl.
New York, NY 10010-6801
Telephone: (212) 473-8200
Ownership %: 100
**Management:**
Cassie Feng ..................Circulation Manager
**Editorial:**
Mary Ann Hallenborg, Esq. ..................Editor
Mary Lopez .......................Managing Editor

**QUARTERLY JOURNAL OF
ECONOMICS** 22390
Littauer Ctr.
Harvard University
Cambridge, MA 02138
Telephone: (617) 495-2142
Year Established: 1886
Pub. Frequency: q.
Page Size: 5 1/2 x 8 1/2
Subscrip. Rate: $30/yr. individuals; $85/yr.
institutions; $20/yr. students
**Owner(s):**
Harvard University
Cambridge, MA 02138
Telephone: (617) 495-2142
Ownership %: 100
**Desc.:** Professional economics journal
stressing in particular economic theory;
banking and finance, money,
international trade; industrial
organization and control; industrial
fluctuations; economic development,
agricultural economics; labor problems,
etc.
**Readers:** Mostly professional economists,
especially academics.

**R&D CONTRACTS MONTHLY** 58754
1155 Connecticut Ave., N.W.
Washington, DC 20036

Year Established: 1962
Pub. Frequency: m.
Subscrip. Rate: $96/yr.
**Owner(s):**
Government Data Publications, Inc.
1155 Connecticut Ave., N.W.
Washington, DC 20036
Ownership %: 100
**Management:**
Nellie Coreman .......................Manager
**Editorial:**
Siegfried Lobel .......................................Editor
**Desc.:** Coverage of sales as well as
research and development intelligence.
Lists recently awarded government
contracts.

**RESEARCH-IDEAS FOR TODAY'S
INVESTORS** 66225
2201 Third St.
San Francisco, CA 94107
Telephone: (415) 621-0220
Year Established: 1978
Pub. Frequency: m.
Page Size: standard
Subscrip. Rate: $35/yr.
Freelance Pay: negotiable
Circulation: 75,000
Circulation Type: controlled
**Owner(s):**
RSI Holdings, Inc.
2201 Third St.
San Francisco, CA 94107
Telephone: (415) 621-0220
Ownership %: 100
**Management:**
Robert R. Tyndall .......................Publisher
**Editorial:**
Rebecca McReynolds .......................Editor
**Readers:** 100% Stock Brokers/Branch
Managers

**RODALE REPORT, THE** 66724
33 E. Minor St.
Emmaus, PA 18098
Telephone: (215) 967-8343
Pub. Frequency: bi-m.
Page Size: standard
Subscrip. Rate: free
Circulation: 20,000
Circulation Type: controlled & free
**Owner(s):**
Rodale Press, Inc.
33 E. Minor St.
Emmaus, PA 18098
Telephone: (215) 967-5171
**Editorial:**
Sid Kirchheimer .......................................Editor
**Desc.:** Good ideas for your life and
business: health, business and fitness.
**Readers:** Business professionals.

**SMALL BUSINESS PREFERENTIAL
SUBCONTRACTS
OPPORTUNITIES MONTHLY** 58642
1661 McDonald Ave.
Brooklyn, NY 11230
Telephone: (718) 627-0819
Pub. Frequency: m.
Subscrip. Rate: $84/yr.
**Owner(s):**
Government Data Publications, Inc.
1155 Connecticut Ave. N.W.
Washington, DC 20036
**Management:**
Nellie Coreuman .......................Manager
**Editorial:**
Siegfried Lobel .......................................Editor

**Materials Accepted/Included:** 01-Business news 02-By-line articles 03-Fashion news 04-Food news 05-Freelance copy 06-Letters to editor 07-Real estate news 08-Sports news 09-Travel news 10-Book rev. 11-Movie rev. 12-Music rev. 13-TV rev. 14-Theater rev. 15-Coming events 16-Obituaries 17-Question & answer 18-Social announcements 19-Artwork 20-Cartoons 21-Photos 22-TV listings 23-Audio rec. 24-Video rec. 25-Books 26-Films/film clips 27-Personnel news 28-Press releases 29-New product news/photos 30-Trade lit. 31-Contracts awarded 32-Display adv. 33-Classified adv.

## SMALL BUSINESS REPORTS
66224

135 W. 50th St.
New York, NY 10020
Telephone: (212) 903-8103
FAX: (212) 903-8083
Year Established: 1975
Pub. Frequency: m.
Page Size: standard
Subscrip. Rate: $98/yr.
Materials: 01,05
Freelance Pay: $100
Circulation: 10,000
Circulation Type: paid
**Owner(s):**
American Management Association
135 W. 50th St.
New York, NY 10020
Telephone: (212) 903-8103
Ownership %: 100
**Management:**
Rosemary Carlough .....................Publisher
**Desc.:** A monthly publication for the owners and managers of small business (under 15 million in sales) packed with practical, hands-on advice on how to run their businesses more efficiently and profitably. Regular monthly departments cover management, financing, legal issues, sales strategies, compensation, and taxes, as well as tips on personal health and finance. book digest included in each issue. Designed to be a fast read, each issue includes checklists, resource lists, and dozens of how-to suggestions.
**Readers:** Top level executive of small to mid size businesses.

## SPACE NEWS
67192

6883 Commercial Dr.
Springfield, VA 22159
Telephone: (703) 658-8400
FAX: (703) 658-8412
Year Established: 1990
Pub. Frequency: w.
Page Size: tabloid
Subscrip. Rate: $75/yr.
Circulation: 19,161
Circulation Type: paid
**Owner(s):**
Army Times Publishing Co.
6883 Commercial Dr.
Springfield, VA 22159
Telephone: (703) 658-8400
Ownership %: 100
**Management:**
Henry Belder .................................President
Jack Kerrigan ...............................Publisher
**Editorial:**
Elaine Howard ..............Associate Publisher

## SUN BELT JOURNAL, THE
52670

929 W. Port Au Prince
Phoenix, AZ 85023
Telephone: (602) 866-7714
Year Established: 1980
Pub. Frequency: bi-m.
Page Size: tabloid
Subscrip. Rate: $55/yr.
Materials: 01,10,11,12,13,14,28,29,30,32
Freelance Pay: varies
Print Process: offset
Circulation: 104,000
Circulation Type: paid
**Owner(s):**
Wiffden Company
929 W. Port Au Prince
Phoenix, AZ 85023
Telephone: (602) 866-7714
Ownership %: 100
**Editorial:**
Judith Peters ..........................Assistant Editor
Marie Jablonty .....................Circulation Editor
Roxy Andreli .....................Production Editor

Adam Casey .................................Sales
**Readers:** Entertainment, business.

## SURFACE MODIFICATION TECHNOLOGY NEWS
66132

25 Van Zant St.
Norwalk, CT 06855
Telephone: (203) 853-4266
FAX: (203) 853-0348
Year Established: 1991
Pub. Frequency: m.
Page Size: standard
Subscrip. Rate: $295/yr.
**Owner(s):**
Louis Naturman
25 Van Zant St.
Norwalk, CT 06855
Telephone: (203) 853-4266
**Management:**
Robert Butler ..............................Manager
**Desc.:** Provides monthly new product news, technology information and analysis, market data, and company information.
**Readers:** Commercial development, corporate management, technical management and research, and market research people.

## TECHPAK
66784

1221 Ave. of the Americas, 43rd Fl.
New York, NY 10020
Telephone: (212) 512-6779
FAX: (212) 512-2989
Year Established: 1955
Pub. Frequency: bi-w.
Page Size: standard
Subscrip. Rate: $417/yr.
**Owner(s):**
McGraw-Hill, Inc.
1221 Ave. of the Americas
43rd Fl.
New York, NY 10020
Ownership %: 100
**Editorial:**
Robert Martino .................Editorial Director
Patricia Fitzgerald ...............Associate Editor

## TODAYS IMAGE
65321

8888 Thorne Rd.
Horton, MI 49246
Telephone: (517) 563-8133
Pub. Frequency: 10/yr.
Page Size: standard
Subscrip. Rate: $22/yr.
**Owner(s):**
Todays Image
Ownership %: 100
**Management:**
Eileen F. DeVito ............................President
Richard DeVito ..............................Publisher
Jack Stoltz .....................Circulation Manager
Rick Martinec ...............Production Manager
**Editorial:**
John W. Dancer ...............Editorial Director
Monica S. Smiley ..............Editorial Director
Jennifer Caruso ...........Advertising Coordinator
Monica S. Smiley ...........Advertising Director
John W. Dancer ...............Advertising Director
Carol L. Genee .................Contributing Editor
Kath Ann Moilanen ...........Contributing Editor
Noreen Cerino, RN, EdD ......Editorial Advisor
**Desc.:** Focus is on business improvements, new products, industry news & trends, marketing information, and profiles of successful entrepreneurs.
**Readers:** Businesses that serve image-conscious customers; tanning and toning centers, fitness clubs, beauty salons, and resorts.

## TRADESHOW WEEK
65735

12233 W. Olympic Blvd., Ste. 236
Los Angeles, CA 90064-9956
Telephone: (310) 826-5696
Year Established: 1971
Pub. Frequency: a.
Page Size: standard
Subscrip. Rate: $319/yr.
Materials: 01,06,15,17,19,20,21,27,28,29, 31,32,33
Freelance Pay: varies
Circulation: 2,500
Circulation Type: paid
**Owner(s):**
Reed Reference Publishing, Inc.
121 Chanlon Rd.
New Providence, NJ 07974
Telephone: (908) 464-6800
Ownership %: 100
**Management:**
Darlene Gudea .............................Publisher
**Editorial:**
Darlene Gudea ...............................Editor
Carol Andrews ........................Managing Editor
**Desc.:** Published to inform and inspire tradeshow executives with news, surveys and how-to articles on expositions in the US. and abroad.
**Readers:** Corporate exhibit managers, show organizers, and suppliers.
**Deadline:** story-3 wks. prior to pub. date; news-7 days prior to pub. date; photo-7 days prior to pub. date; ads-2 wks. prior to pub. date

## TRIAD BUSINESS NEWS
59145

5601 Roanne Way, Ste. 113
Greensboro, NC 27409
Telephone: (919) 854-3001
Year Established: 1986
Pub. Frequency: w.
Page Size: tabloid
Subscrip. Rate: $42/yr.
Freelance Pay: negotiable
Circulation: 15,000
Circulation Type: paid
**Owner(s):**
Highpoint Enterprises, Inc.
5601 Roanne Way, Ste. 113
Greensboro, NC 27409
Telephone: (919) 854-3001
Ownership %: 100
**Management:**
F.D. Howard ...............................Publisher
**Editorial:**
Richard M. Barron ............................Editor
**Desc.:** Business news and information of the Triad area (Greensboro, Winston Salem, High Point) NC.
**Readers:** Top 15,000 business decision makers in Triad area.

## TRIANGLE BUSINESS JOURNAL
59143

3125 Poplarwood Ct., Ste. 304
Raleigh, NC 27604
Telephone: (919) 878-0010
FAX: (919) 790-6885
Year Established: 1985
Pub. Frequency: w.
Page Size: tabloid
Subscrip. Rate: $.75/copy; $38/yr.
Materials: 01,06,07,08,09,21,23,24,25,27, 28,29,31,32,33
Freelance Pay: $125/story
Print Process: web offset
Circulation: 9,500
Circulation Type: paid
**Owner(s):**
American City Business Journal
128 S. Tryon St., Ste. 2200
Charlotte, NC 28202
Telephone: (704) 375-7404
Ownership %: 100

**Management:**
Ray Shaw .........................Chairman of Board
Charlene Grunwaldt ......................Publisher
**Desc.:** Business to business news and information of the Raleigh-Durham area.
**Readers:** Top 9,500 business decision makers in Raleigh-Durham area.
**Deadline:** news-2 wks. prior to pub. date; ads-10 days prior

## UPSIDE
67226

1159 Triton Dr.
Foster City, CA 94404
Telephone: (415) 377-0950
FAX: (415) 377-1961
Year Established: 1989
Pub. Frequency: m.
Page Size: standard
Subscrip. Rate: $4.95 newsstand; $48/yr.
Materials: 01,02,05,06,10,17,25,28,30,32,33
Print Process: web offset
Circulation: 50,303
Circulation Type: controlled & paid
**Owner(s):**
Upside Publishing Co.
1159 Triton Dr.
Foster City, CA 94404
Telephone: (415) 377-0950
FAX: (415) 377-1961
Ownership %: 100
**Management:**
Susan Scott ................................Publisher
Cheryl Lucanegro ............Advertising Manager
**Editorial:**
Eric Nee .......................................Editor
David Bunnell ..................Editorial Director
**Desc.:** A provocative, insightful magazine that delivers an unflinchingly honest perspective on the people and companies creating the digital revolution.
**Readers:** Technology elite; top executives and senior-level managers whose corporate strategies and technology decisions drive the industry.

## WARFIELD'S BUSINESS RECORD
64931

11 E. Saratoga St.
Baltimore, MD 21202
Telephone: (410) 528-0600
FAX: (410) 752-5469
Year Established: 1986
Pub. Frequency: w.
Page Size: tabloid
Subscrip. Rate: $30/yr.; $48/2 yrs.
Freelance Pay: $5 per col. inch
Circulation: 20,000
**Owner(s):**
Daily Record, The
11 E. Saratoga St.
Baltimore, MD 21202
Telephone: (410) 528-0600
Ownership %: 100
**Management:**
Edwin Warfield, IV .......................Publisher
Bob Dawson ....................Advertising Manager
**Editorial:**
Keith Girard ....................................Editor
**Desc.:** Maryland's business weekly.
**Readers:** Business decision-makers.

## WESTCHESTER COUNTY BUSINESS JOURNAL
66588

22 Saw Mill River Rd.
Hawthorne, NY 10532
Telephone: (914) 347-5200
Year Established: 1968
Pub. Frequency: w.
Page Size: tabloid
Subscrip. Rate: $36/yr.
Freelance Pay: negotiable
Circulation: 12,000
Circulation Type: controlled

---

**Materials Accepted/Included:** 01-Business news 02-By-line articles 03-Fashion news 04-Food news 05-Freelance copy 06-Letters to editor 07-Real estate news 08-Sports news 09-Travel news 10-Book rev. 11-Movie rev. 12-Music rev. 13-TV rev. 14-Theater rev. 15-Coming events 16-Obituaries 17-Question & answer 18-Social announcements 19-Artwork 20-Cartoons 21-Photos 22-TV listings 23-Audio rec. 24-Video rec. 25-Books 26-Films/film clips 27-Personnel news 28-Press releases 29-New product news/photos 30-Trade lit. 31-Contracts awarded 32-Display adv. 33-Classified adv.

4-73

**Owner(s):**
Alfred & Dolores Delbello
Makepeace Hill
Waccabuc, NY 10597
Telephone: (914) 763-3653
Ownership %: 50

Empire Systems
2900 Westchester Ave.
Purchase, NY 10577
Telephone: (914) 251-1555
Ownership %: 50
**Management:**
Dee Delbello ..............................Publisher
**Editorial:**
Mills Korte ......................................Editor
**Desc.:** We are a grass-roots publication bringing in-depth business news and information to our business readership.
**Readers:** A full range of privately-owned business to major corporations located in Westchester and Fairfield counties.

65477

**WNC BUSINESS JOURNAL**
P.O. Box 8204
Asheville, NC 28814
Telephone: (704) 258-1322
FAX: (704) 253-3726
Year Established: 1987
Pub. Frequency: m.
Page Size: tabloid
Subscrip. Rate: $1.25 newsstand; $19/yr. in state; $25/yr. outside state
Materials: 01,15,27,29,30,32
Print Process: web offset
Circulation: 20,000
Circulation Type: controlled
**Owner(s):**
Nason & Associates
P.O. Box 8204
Asheville, NC 28814
Telephone: (704) 258-1322
FAX: (704) 253-3726
Ownership %: 100
**Management:**
Michelle Ramsey ..................Office Manager
**Editorial:**
Marilyn Nason ..............................Editor
Stephen Nason ..............................Editor
**Desc.:** Covers the business news and general news of the 44 chambers of commerce of the 28 counties of western North Carolina. The directors of each chamber report some of the news to the magazine.
**Readers:** Members of the 44 Chambers of Commerce in 28 counties of western North Carolina and other business people.
**Deadline:** story-3rd Fri. of previous mo.; news-3rd Fri. of previous mo.; photo-3rd Fri. of previous mo.; ads-3rd Fri. of previous mo.

22427

**WOMEN IN BUSINESS**
9100 Ward Pkwy.
Kansas City, MO 64114
Telephone: (816) 361-6621
FAX: (816) 361-4991
Mailing Address:
   P.O. Box 8728
   Kansas City, MO 64114-0728
Year Established: 1949
Pub. Frequency: bi-m.
Page Size: standard
Subscrip. Rate: $12/yr. US/ $16/yr. foreign
Freelance Pay: $.15/wd. approx.
Circulation: 100,000
**Owner(s):**
The ABWA Co., Inc.
9100 Ward Pkwy.
Kansas City, MO 64114
Telephone: (816) 361-6621
Ownership %: 100

**Management:**
Belinda Riney ..................Advertising Manager
**Editorial:**
Wendy Myers ..............................Editor
Dawn J. Grubb ..................Associate Editor
**Desc.:** For women in every field, conveying these objectives: improving employee-employer relations, keeping business women informed on new techniques, and current trends. Contains general interest features, new products, legislation that affects women, self-improvement, book reviews, financial advice, small business/entrepreneur updates, etc.
**Readers:** Members of the American Business Women's Association.

67697

**YOUR COMPANY**
1120 Avenue of The Americas
New York, NY 10036
Telephone: (212) 382-5739
Year Established: 1990
Pub. Frequency: q.
Page Size: standard
Circulation: 1,250,000
Circulation Type: controlled
**Owner(s):**
American Express Publishing Corp.
1120 Avenue of Americas
New York, NY 10036
Telephone: (212) 382-5739
Ownership %: 100
**Management:**
Jack Laschever ..............................Publisher
**Editorial:**
Robert W. Casey ..............................Editor
**Readers:** Small business owners.

66229

**YOUR MONEY**
5705 N. Lincoln Ave.
Chicago, IL 60659
Telephone: (312) 275-3590
FAX: (312) 275-7273
Year Established: 1979
Pub. Frequency: bi-m.
Page Size: standard
Subscrip. Rate: $15.97/yr.
Circulation: 150,000
Circulation Type: paid
**Owner(s):**
Arthur Weber
5705 N. Lincoln Ave.
Chicago, IL 60659
Telephone: (312) 275-3590
**Management:**
Randy Weber ..............................Publisher
**Editorial:**
Dennis Fertig ..............................Editor
**Desc.:** Tells readers how to earn more money, how to save it and invest it more profitably, and even how to spend it more wisely.

### Group 040-Business-Regional, State, Metro, Local

61025

**AMS ADVISOR, THE**
8000 Towers Crescent Dr.
Ste. 1180
Vienna, VA 22182
Telephone: (703) 893-0833
Pub. Frequency: m.
Page Size: standard
Subscrip. Rate: $495/yr.
Freelance Pay: negotiable
**Owner(s):**
Government International Data Corp.
Ownership %: 100
**Management:**
Kenneth Kaplan ..............................Publisher
**Editorial:**
Edith Hdines ..............................Editor

Alvin Young ..............................Editor

22262

**ATLANTA BUSINESS CHRONICLE**
1801 Peachtree St. N.E.
Ste. 150
Atlanta, GA 30309
Telephone: (404) 249-1000
FAX: (404) 249-1048
Year Established: 1978
Pub. Frequency: w.
Page Size: tabloid
Subscrip. Rate: $1 newsstand; $51/yr.
Freelance Pay: $2.50/col. in.
Circulation: 35,000
Circulation Type: paid
**Owner(s):**
American City Business Journals
128 S. Tryon St.
Ste. 2200
Charlotte, NC 28202
Telephone: (704) 375-7404
Ownership %: 100
**Management:**
Ed Baker ..............................Publisher
Nancy Kenerly ..................Advertising Manager
Valerie L. Acree ..................Office Manager
**Editorial:**
David Black ..............................Editor
Anita Cambal ..................Circulation Editor
**Desc.:** Designed to inform the business community throughout the Atlanta metropolitan market. Examines various segments of business including finance, real estate, distribution, agribusiness, manufacturing, construction, transportation, marketing, energy and government actions affecting Atlanta business. Features information on listed and over-the-counter Atlanta stocks, in-depth trend reports on Atlanta commerce and detailed analyses of growth in certain industries. Departments include: Finance, Real Estate, Energy, Distribution, Agribusiness, Construction, Wholesale-Retail Trade, Transportation, Marketing, Communications, Government, Manufacturing, Conventions, International Trade, Professions, Memos, Letters to Editor, Commentaries, Personality Profile, Atlanta Gourmet, Automotive Review, Atlanta Barfly, Travel, Executive Image, Entertainment, Book Reviews, Stock Analyses.
**Readers:** Professional/managerial, top management positions, chairmen, college graduates.

61613

**AUSTIN BUSINESS JOURNAL**
1301 S. Capital Texas
Ste. B-224
Austin, TX 78746
Telephone: (512) 328-0180
FAX: (512) 328-7304
Year Established: 1981
Pub. Frequency: w.
Page Size: tabloid
Subscrip. Rate: $1 newsstand; $49/yr.; $99/3yr.
Materials: 01,02,06,07,15,17,19,20,21,
Freelance Pay: $40-150
Circulation: 7,000
Circulation Type: paid
**Owner(s):**
John Winsor
1919 14th St., P.O. Box 187
Ste. 300
Boulder, CO 80302
Telephone: (303) 444-6805
FAX: (303) 443-1842
Ownership %: 100
**Management:**
Rebecca Melanccon ..............................Publisher
Marilyn Hunt ..................Circulation Manager

**Editorial:**
Ken Martin ..............................Editor
**Desc.:** Central Texas's most complete source for local business news.
**Readers:** Executives, managers w/household income of $104,000 plus.

65046

**BATON ROUGE BUSINESS REPORT, THE**
5757 Corporate Blvd., Ste. 402
Baton Rouge, LA 70808
Telephone: (504) 928-1700
FAX: (504) 923-3448
Year Established: 1982
Pub. Frequency: m.
Page Size: tabloid
Subscrip. Rate: $1.35/copy; $36/yr.
Materials: 01,05,06,07,21,28,32
Circulation: 15,000
Circulation Type: paid
**Owner(s):**
Louisiana Business, Inc.
5757 Corporate Blvd., Ste. 402
Baton Rouge, LA 70808
Telephone: (504) 928-1700
FAX: (504) 923-3448
Ownership %: 100
**Management:**
Rolfe H. Mc Collister, Jr. ..................Publisher
Mary Johnson ..................General Manager
**Editorial:**
Paulette W. Senior ..............................Editor

65047

**BIRMINGHAM BUSINESS**
2027 First Ave. N.
Birmingham, AL 35203
Telephone: (205) 323-5461
FAX: (205) 250-7669
Year Established: 1983
Pub. Frequency: m.
Page Size: 11"X5 1/2"
Subscrip. Rate: $6/yr. non-members
Materials: 01,32
Print Process: offset
Circulation: 3,750
Circulation Type: paid
**Owner(s):**
Birmingham Area Chamber of Commerce
2027 First Ave. N.
Birmingham, AL 35203
Telephone: (205) 323-5461
FAX: (205) 250-7669
Ownership %: 100
**Management:**
Don A. Newton ..............................Publisher
**Editorial:**
Kristi Gilmore ..............................Editor
**Desc.:** Reports on chamber activities and programs; provides calendar of events.
**Readers:** Chamber members
**Deadline:** story-1 mo. prior to pub. date

66861

**BOSTON BUSINESS JOURNAL**
200 High St.
Boston, MA 02110-3036
Telephone: (617) 330-1000
FAX: (617) 330-1015
Year Established: 1981
Pub. Frequency: w.
Page Size: standard
Subscrip. Rate: $48/yr.
Circulation: 25,000
Circulation Type: paid
**Owner(s):**
P&L Publications
200 High St.
Boston, MA 02110-3005
Telephone: (617) 330-1000
Ownership %: 100
**Management:**
James C. Menneto ..............................Publisher
**Editorial:**
Bennie DiNardo ..............................Editor
Stephanie Gelston ..................Design Editor

**Materials Accepted/Included:** 01-Business news 02-By-line articles 03-Fashion news 04-Food news 05-Freelance copy 06-Letters to editor 07-Real estate news 08-Sports news 09-Travel news 10-Book rev. 11-Movie rev. 12-Music rev. 13-TV rev. 14-Theater rev. 15-Coming events 16-Obituaries 17-Question & answer 18-Social announcements 19-Artwork 20-Cartoons 21-Photos 22-TV listings 23-Audio rec. 24-Video rec. 25-Books 26-Films/film clips 27-Personnel news 28-Press releases 29-New product news/photos 30-Trade lit. 31-Contracts awarded 32-Display adv. 33-Classified adv.

4-74

## BUSINESS & INDUSTRY
*22272*
172 28th St., #B
Des Moines, IA 50312
Telephone: (515) 225-2547
FAX: (515) 225-2318
Year Established: 1947
Pub. Frequency: m.
Page Size: standard
Subscrip. Rate: $24/yr.
Circulation: 13,500
Circulation Type: controlled
**Owner(s):**
James V. Snyder
R.R. 1 Box 6
Carlisle, IA 50047
Telephone: (515) 223-1226

Robert J. Wagner
4304 82nd
Des Moines, IA 50322
Telephone: (515) 276-9653
**Management:**
James V. Snyder .........................President
Sally J. Wagner .........................Vice President
**Editorial:**
James V. Snyder .........................Editor
Robert J. Wagner ..........Secretary & Treasurer
**Desc.:** An industrial news magazine,
serving the Iowa, Minnesota, Nebraska,
The Dakotas, W. Wisconsin, Quad cities
industrial complex. News features cover
manufacturing; industrial construction;
management methods; plant expansions,
equipment and custom services. Special
features include: Man of the
Month; Introduction of Purchasers; New
Corporations.
**Readers:** Men in management, purchasing,
engineering in Nebraska, Minnesota, the
Dakotas and W. Wisconsin.

## BUSINESS ALABAMA MONTHLY
*61576*
2465 Commercial Park Dr.
Mobile, AL 36606
Telephone: (205) 473-6269
Mailing Address:
P.O. Box 66200
Mobile, AL 36660
Year Established: 1986
Pub. Frequency: m.
Page Size: standard
Subscrip. Rate: $19.95/yr.
Freelance Pay: $50-$200
Circulation: 16,000
Circulation Type: paid
**Owner(s):**
PMT Publishing Co., Inc.
2465 Commercial Park Dr.
Mobile, AL 36606
Telephone: (205) 473-6269
Ownership %: 100
**Management:**
T.J. Potts .........................Manager
**Editorial:**
Matthew Solon .........................Editor
**Desc.:** Primarily serves the business and
professional community throughout
Alabama.
**Readers:** Qualified recipients are chairmen
of the board, chief executive officers,
presidents, partners, owners, vice
presidents, treasurers, corporate
secretaries, general managers, directors
and managers of finance, controllers,
budget directors, trust officers, internal
audit managers, treasurers, accountants,
bookkeepers, department heads,
managers, division heads, professionals,
attorneys, elected officials and staffs.
Also qualified are a limited number
of company and library copies and
others allied to the field.

## BUSINESS FIRST
*65048*
472 Delaware Ave.
Buffalo, NY 14202
Telephone: (716) 882-6200
FAX: (716) 822-3020
Year Established: 1984
Pub. Frequency: w.
Page Size: tabloid
Materials: 01,07,08,09,29
Freelance Pay: negotiable
Circulation: 15,000
Circulation Type: paid
**Owner(s):**
American City Business Journals, Inc.
472 Delaware Ave.
Buffalo, NY 14202
Telephone: (716) 822-6200
**Management:**
Maureen Rose .........................Business Manager
M. J. Wajmer .........................Circulation Manager
Larry Ponzi .........................Production Manager
**Editorial:**
Donna Collins .........................Editor
Bill McMeekin .........................Managing Editor

## BUSINESS JOURNAL OF CHARLOTTE
*65719*
128 S. Tryon St., Ste. 2250
Charlotte, NC 28202
Telephone: (704) 347-2340
FAX: (704) 347-2350
Pub. Frequency: w.
Page Size: standard
Subscrip. Rate: $41/yr.
Circulation: 14,500
Circulation Type: paid
**Owner(s):**
American City Business Journals
128 S. Tryon St., Ste. 2300
Charlotte, NC 28202
Telephone: (704) 375-7404
Ownership %: 100
**Management:**
Mark Ethridge .........................Publisher
**Editorial:**
Joanne Skoog .........................Editor

## BUSINESS JOURNAL OF NEW JERSEY
*61546*
55 Park Pl.
Morristown, NJ 07960
Telephone: (201) 644-5570
FAX: (201) 538-2953
Mailing Address:
P.O. Box 920
Morristown, NJ 07963
Year Established: 1983
Pub. Frequency: m.
Page Size: standard
Subscrip. Rate: $29.95/yr.
Circulation: 25,000
Circulation Type: controlled & paid
**Owner(s):**
Micromedia Affiliates
7 Dumont Pl., P.O. Box 920
Morristown, NJ 07960
Telephone: (201) 644-5570
Ownership %: 100
**Management:**
Richard McComb .........................Publisher
**Editorial:**
Linda Molnor .........................Editor
Lynette Dilbeck .........................Associate Publisher
**Readers:** NJ Business Leaders

## BUSINESS JOURNAL, THE
*64926*
96 N. Third St., Ste. 100
San Jose, CA 95112
Telephone: (408) 295-3800
FAX: (408) 295-5028
Year Established: 1983
Pub. Frequency: w.

Page Size: tabloid
Subscrip. Rate: $49/yr.
Circulation: 17,612
Circulation Type: controlled & paid
**Owner(s):**
City Business-USA Publications, Inc.
96 N. 3rd St., Ste. 100
San Jose, CA 95112
Telephone: (408) 295-3800
Ownership %: 100
**Management:**
Armon Mills .........................Publisher
Natt Toledo .........................Advertising Manager
**Editorial:**
Delbert Schafer .........................Editor

## BUSINESS JOURNAL, THE
*65035*
2910 N. Central Ave.
Phoenix, AZ 85102
Telephone: (602) 230-8400
FAX: (602) 230-9955
Year Established: 1980
Pub. Frequency: w.
Subscrip. Rate: $48/yr.
Circulation: 16,500
Circulation Type: paid
**Owner(s):**
Phoenix Business Journal, Inc.
2910 N. Central Ave.
Phoenix, AZ 85012
Telephone: (602) 230-8400
**Management:**
Diane Craig .........................Advertising Manager
Mary Wegher .........................Sales Manager
**Editorial:**
Thomas Jensen .........................Editor
**Desc.:** Covers all facets of business news
about the Phoenix metropolitan area.

## BUSINESS JOURNAL, THE
*67039*
P.O. Box 14490
Portland, OR 97214
Telephone: (503) 274-8733
FAX: (503) 227-2650
Year Established: 1984
Pub. Frequency: w.
Page Size: tabloid
Subscrip. Rate: $1.25/copy; $48/yr.
Materials: 01,06,07,27,28,32,33,34
Print Process: web offset
Circulation: 15,000
Circulation Type: controlled & paid
**Owner(s):**
Network of City Business Journals
3535 Broadway, Ste. 30
Kansas City, MO 64111
Telephone: (816) 753-4300
Ownership %: 100
**Management:**
Candace Clement .........................General Manager
**Editorial:**
Steve D. Jones .........................Editor
**Desc.:** Covers business and economics in
the Portland area.
**Deadline:** story-1 wk.; news-1 wk.; photo-1
wk.; ads-1 wk.

## BUSINESS NEW HAMPSHIRE MAGAZINE
*61549*
404 Chestnut St., Ste. 201
Manchester, NH 03101-1831
Telephone: (603) 626-6354
FAX: (603) 626-6359
Year Established: 1983
Pub. Frequency: m.
Page Size: standard
Subscrip. Rate: $24/yr.
Materials: 01,02,05,06,15,21,23,24,25,26,
27,28,29,30,31,32
Freelance Pay: $50-$200
Print Process: offset
Circulation: 13,500
Circulation Type: controlled & paid

**Owner(s):**
Laurentian Business Publishing, Inc.
404 Chestnut St., Ste. 201
Manchester, NH 03101-1831
Telephone: (603) 626-6354
Ownership %: 100
**Management:**
B.J. Eckardt .........................Publisher
David Kruger .........................Advertising Manager
**Editorial:**
Robin Baskerville .........................Editor
**Desc.:** Departments including: Letters to
the Editor, Political Beat, Editor's Notes,
Openers, Trends for the Record, Photo
Page. Features, Resource Guides, and
directories all New Hampshire business-
related.
**Readers:** Business decision makers in
New Hampshire
**Deadline:** story-10 wks. prior to pub. date;
news-10 wks.; photo-10 wks.; ads-10
wks.

## BUSINESS NORTH CAROLINA
*61558*
5435 77 Center Dr., Ste. 50
Charlotte, NC 28217-0711
Telephone: (704) 523-6987
FAX: (704) 523-4211
Year Established: 1971
Pub. Frequency: m.
Page Size: standard
Subscrip. Rate: $26/yr.
Materials: 01
Circulation: 26,000
Circulation Type: controlled
**Owner(s):**
News & Observer Publishing Co., The
215 S. McDowell St.
Raleigh, NC 27601
Telephone: (919) 829-4500
Ownership %: 100
**Management:**
Frank Daniels, III .........................Publisher
**Editorial:**
David Kinney .........................Editor
**Readers:** Executives of North Carolina
Companies.

## BUSINESS PEOPLE MAGAZINE OF GREATER FORT WAYNE
*69357*
2410 Coliseum Blvd., #100
Fort Wayne, IN 46805-3140
Telephone: (219) 484-1840
Year Established: 1988
Pub. Frequency: m.
Subscrip. Rate: $15/yr.
Circulation: 8,400
**Owner(s):**
Michiana Business Publications, Inc.
2410 Coliseum Blvd., No. 100
Fort Wayne, IN 46805-3140
Telephone: (219) 484-1840
**Editorial:**
Kelli Rigsby .........................Editor
**Desc.:** Deals with issues and information
affecting business professionals in Allen
County.

## BUSINESS RECORD
*64734*
100 Fourth St.
Des Moines, IA 50309
Telephone: (515) 288-3336
FAX: (515) 288-0309
Year Established: 1983
Pub. Frequency: w.
Page Size: tabloid
Freelance Pay: $75-$150/article
Circulation: 9,200
Circulation Type: paid

**Owner(s):**
Connie Wimer
100 Fourth St.
Des Moines, IA 50309
Telephone: (515) 288-3336
Ownership %: 100
**Management:**
Connie Wimer ................................Publisher
Marilyn Tanious ...................Sales Manager
**Editorial:**
John Peterson .................Managing Editor
**Desc.:** The Business Record is a weekly
journal of business news for Des Moines
and Central Iowa.
**Readers:** Top-level business executives in
Central Iowa

22295
## BUSINESS TIMES
315 Peck St.
New Haven, CT 06513
Telephone: (203) 782-1420
Mailing Address:
P.O. Box 580
New Haven, CT 06513
Year Established: 1978
Pub. Frequency: m.
Page Size: tabloid
Subscrip. Rate: $18/yr.
Freelance Pay: $2/col. in.
Print Process: web
Circulation: 22,000
Circulation Type: controlled
**Owner(s):**
Choice Media
315 Peck St.
New Haven, CT 06513
Telephone: (203) 782-1420
Ownership %: 100
**Management:**
Joel D. MacClaren ...........................Publisher
**Editorial:**
Joel D. MacClaren ...............................Editor
Jennifer Frey .........................Managing Editor
**Desc.:** Circulates in Connecticut and
features financial news and analyses of
businesses located there. Special
sections cover computers, legal matters,
and small business management.
Special issue published four times
annually. Destination Magazine-an
Executive Travel Quarterly.
**Readers:** Chief executives and business
owners.

22277
## CAPITAL DISTRICT BUSINESS
REVIEW
P.O. Box 15081
Albany, NY 12212-5081
Telephone: (518) 437-9855
FAX: (518) 437-0764
Mailing Address:
2 Computer Dr. W.
Albany, NY 12205
Year Established: 1974
Pub. Frequency: w.
Page Size: tabloid
Subscrip. Rate: $1.25/copy; $50/yr.
Materials: 01,06,07,27,28,29,30,32,33
Circulation: 10,000
Circulation Type: paid
**Owner(s):**
American City Business Journals
128 S. Tryon St.
Charlotte, NC 28202
Ownership %: 100
**Management:**
George B. Guthinger ...........................Publisher
**Editorial:**
Marlene Kennedy .................................Editor
**Desc.:** General business and financial
news geared almost exclusively to local
area, including 10 county region
surrounding Albany.

**Readers:** Top business executives in area.
**Deadline:** news-2 wks. prior to pub. date;
ads-10 days prior

68756
## CENTRAL PENN BUSINESS
JOURNAL
409 S. Second St.
Harrisburg, PA 17104-1612
Telephone: (717) 236-4300
FAX: (717) 236-6803
Year Established: 1984
Pub. Frequency: s-m.
Subscrip. Rate: $24/yr.
Circulation: 16,000
Circulation Type: controlled
**Owner(s):**
CPNC, Inc.
1500 N. Second St.
Harrisburg, PA 17102-2527
Telephone: (717) 236-4300
Ownership %: 100
**Editorial:**
Carl Defebo .......................................Editor
**Desc.:** Profiles regional businesses and
professionals and covers the issues and
topics which affect them.

65732
## CINCINNATI BUSINESS COURIER
35 E. Seventh St.
Cincinnati, OH 45202
Telephone: (513) 621-6665
Year Established: 1984
Pub. Frequency: w.
Page Size: tabloid
Subscrip. Rate: $48/yr.
Circulation: 10,000
Circulation Type: paid
**Owner(s):**
American City Business Journals, Inc.
128 S. Tryon St., Ste. 2200
Charlotte, NC 28202
Telephone: (704) 375-7404
Ownership %: 100
**Management:**
Scott Bemis ...................................Publisher
Kim Spangler ...................Operations Manager
**Editorial:**
Brian Settle ...................................Editor
Susan Labonte ...........................Advertising
Joe Hoffelker ...............................Art Director

22278
## CNY BUSINESS JOURNAL
231 Walton St.
Syracuse, NY 13202-1226
Telephone: (315) 472-3104
FAX: (315) 472-3644
Year Established: 1985
Pub. Frequency: bi-w.
Page Size: tabloid
Subscrip. Rate: $2/newsstand; $36/yr.
Materials: 01,02,06,07,20,27,28,31,32,33
Freelance Pay: $75-$1,500
Print Process: web offset
Circulation: 10,000
Circulation Type: controlled & paid
**Owner(s):**
Norman Poltenson
231 Walton St.
Syracuse, NY 13202
Telephone: (315) 472-3104
Ownership %: 100
**Management:**
Norman Poltenson ...........................President
Norman Poltenson ...........................Publisher
**Editorial:**
Don Harting ...............................News Editor

**Desc.:** Articles focus on affairs of
business in central New York, state and
federal legislation affecting central New
York, new products being tested or
marketed in any area. Any article
focused on this area welcome. Publicity
material used on basis of relevance to
local businessmen. Same policy applies
to photos. Articles average 1500 words,
although special reports may reach 5000
words. Special reports appear monthly
and deal with subjects such as health
care, computers, finance,
telecommunications, advertising, and
real estate.
**Readers:** Corporate executives, business
owners, bankers; in general, highest
wage earners in the country.
**Deadline:** story-30 days prior to pub. date;
news-date of sale; ads-13 days prior to
sale date

22281
## COLORADO BUSINESS MAGAZINE
7009 S. Potomac St.
Englewood, CO 80112
Telephone: (303) 397-7600
FAX: (303) 397-7619
Year Established: 1973
Pub. Frequency: m.
Page Size: standard
Subscrip. Rate: $2.95 newsstand; $24/yr.
Materials: 01,06,07,32,33
Freelance Pay: negotiable
Print Process: web
Circulation: 20,800
Circulation Type: controlled
**Owner(s):**
Weisner Publishing
7009 S. Potomac
Englewood, CO 80112
Telephone: (303) 397-7619
Ownership %: 100
**Management:**
Pat Weisner ...................................President
Cynthia Evans ...............................Publisher
**Editorial:**
Julie Hutchinson ...............................Editor
**Desc.:** Monthly business news magazine
analyzes the circumstances and the
trends that have an impact on
the economy and life style in the
Mountain States. Editorial content is
designed to help the reader understand
more thoroughly the events and forces
affecting business developments and
consumerism in Colorado and the Rocky
Mountain West.
**Readers:** Management and professional
business people in Colorado and the
West.
**Deadline:** story-3 mos. prior to pub. date;
news-1 mo. prior; photo-3 mos. prior

68758
## COLORADO SPRINGS BUSINESS
JOURNAL
31 E. Platte Ave., Ste. 200
Colorado Springs, CO 80903-1234
Telephone: (719) 634-5905
FAX: (719) 634-5157
Mailing Address:
P.O. Box 1541
Colorado Springs, CO 80901-1541
Year Established: 1989
Pub. Frequency: w.
Page Size: tabloid
Subscrip. Rate: $.50 newsstand; $29.50/yr.
Materials: 01,02,06,07,28,31
Print Process: web
Circulation: 9,500
Circulation Type: controlled & paid
**Owner(s):**
Colorado Springs Business Journal
**Management:**
Charles B. Sheldon ...........................Publisher

**Editorial:**
Karene Williams ...............................Editor
**Desc.:** Provides local business news and
feature articles of interest to the
business and professional community.
**Readers:** Business executives,
professionals, owners

68759
## COMSTOCK'S
1770 Tribute Rd., Ste. 205
Sacramento, CA 95815
Telephone: (916) 924-9815
FAX: (916) 924-9034
Year Established: 1989
Pub. Frequency: m.
Subscrip. Rate: $30/yr.
Materials: 01,02,05,06,07,08,09,10,15,18,
19,20,21,23,24,25,26,27,28,32,33
Freelance Pay: $50-300; negotiable
Print Process: offset
Circulation: 16,000
Circulation Type: paid
**Owner(s):**
Comstock Publishing, Inc.
1770 Tribute Rd., Ste. 205
Sacramento, CA 95815
Telephone: (916) 924-9815
Ownership %: 100
**Editorial:**
Janice Fillip ...............................Editor
**Desc.:** Profiles business leaders, discusses
issues facing business and industry in
the region.
**Deadline:** story-3 mo. prior to pub. date;
news-3 mo.; photo-3 mo.; ads-1 mo.

66855
## CORPORATE CLEVELAND
1720 Euclid Ave.
Cleveland, OH 44115
Telephone: (216) 621-1644
FAX: (216) 621-5918
Year Established: 1990
Pub. Frequency: m.
Page Size: standard
Subscrip. Rate: $30/yr.
Freelance Pay: negotiable
Circulation: 31,000
Circulation Type: controlled
**Owner(s):**
Business Journal Publishing Co.
1720 Euclid Ave.
Cleveland, OH 44115
Telephone: (216) 621-1644
Ownership %: 100
**Management:**
David John ...................................Publisher
Daniel Rose ...................Advertising Manager
**Editorial:**
Richard Osborne ...............................Editor
Robert Rosenbaum .................Managing Editor
**Desc.:** Covering the northeast Ohio
business community with traditional,
aggressive journalism.
**Readers:** Corporate & small business
executives.

61252
## CORPORATE DETROIT
26111 Evergreen Rd., Ste. 303
Southfield, MI 48076-4499
Telephone: (313) 357-8300
FAX: (313) 357-8308
Year Established: 1984
Pub. Frequency: m.
Page Size: standard
Subscrip. Rate: $30/yr.; free to qualified
personnel
Materials: 01,02,05,06,07,19,21,28,29,30,
31,32
Freelance Pay: by arrangement
Print Process: web offset
Circulation: 32,000
Circulation Type: controlled

**Materials Accepted/Included:** 01-Business news 02-By-line articles 03-Fashion news 04-Food news 05-Freelance copy 06-Letters to editor 07-Real estate news 08-Sports news 09-Travel news 10-Book rev. 11-Movie rev. 12-Music rev. 13-TV rev. 14-Theater rev. 15-Coming events 16-Obituaries 17-Question & answer 18-Social announcements 19-Artwork 20-Cartoons 21-Photos 22-TV listings 23-Audio rec. 24-Video rec. 25-Books 26-Films/film clips 27-Personnel news 28-Press releases 29-New product news/photos 30-Trade lit. 31-Contracts awarded 32-Display adv. 33-Classified adv.

**Owner(s):**
Business Journal Publishing Co.
26111 Evergreen Rd., Ste. 303
Southfield, MI 48076-4499
Telephone: (313) 357-8300
**Bureau(s):**
Michigan Business
40 Pearl St., Ste. 336
Grand Rapids, MI 49503
Telephone: (616) 451-2253
Contact: Eric Whisenhunt, Writer
**Management:**
Jack Bick .........................Publisher
**Editorial:**
Gary Hoffman .........................Editor
**Desc.:** Published monthly for top
executives in Detroit Business
community. Editorial focus is on
manufacturing, finance, communications,
retailing transportion, and real estate.
**Readers:** Senior level executives
**Deadline:** story-2 mo. prior to pub. date;
news-2 mo. prior; photo-2 mo. prior; ads-
1 mo. prior

22298
## CORPORATE REPORT MINNESOTA
5500 Wayzata Blvd., Ste. 800
Minneapolis, MN 55416
Telephone: (612) 591-2500
FAX: (612) 591-2639
Year Established: 1967
Pub. Frequency: m.
Page Size: standard
Subscrip. Rate: $29/yr.
Freelance Pay: varies
Circulation: 20,000
Circulation Type: paid
**Owner(s):**
MCP, Inc.
5500 Wayzata Blvd., 800
Minneapolis, MN 55416
Telephone: (612) 338-3267
Ownership %: 100
**Management:**
Thomas Minnhagen ..................President
Stuart Chamblin ..................Publisher
Mary Carlson ...........Advertising Manager
**Editorial:**
Lee Shater .........................Senior Editor
Kathy Palmquist ...............Senior Editor
Terry Fiedler .........................Editor
**Desc.:** Covers business in Minnesota.
**Readers:** Business owners and managers
in Minnesota.

64741
## CORPORATE REPORT WISCONSIN
N 80 W 12878 Fond du Lac Ave.
P.O. Box 878
Menomonee Falls, WI 53052-0878
Telephone: (414) 255-9077
FAX: (414) 255-3388
Year Established: 1985
Pub. Frequency: m.
Page Size: standard
Subscrip. Rate: $18/yr.
Freelance Pay: $500-$700/feature length
article
Circulation: 27,000
Circulation Type: controlled
**Owner(s):**
Brady Company, Inc.
P.O. Box 878
Menomonee Falls, WI 53051
Telephone: (414) 255-9077
Ownership %: 100
**Management:**
Karl Ohm, Sr. .........................Publisher
Christine Schramek ...............Sales Manager
**Editorial:**
Pete Millard .........................Editor
**Desc.:** Business magazine for executives
in the state of Wisconsin.

**Readers:** Wisconsin business owners,
managers.

22299
## CRAIN'S CHICAGO BUSINESS
740 N. Rush St.
Chicago, IL 60611-2525
Telephone: (312) 649-5270
FAX: (312) 649-5228
Year Established: 1978
Pub. Frequency: Mon.
Page Size: tabloid
Subscrip. Rate: $68/yr.
Freelance Pay: $11.60/col. in.
Circulation: 50,000
Circulation Type: paid
**Owner(s):**
Crain Communications, Inc.
740 N. Rush St.
Chicago, IL 60611
Telephone: (312) 649-5200
Ownership %: 100
**Bureau(s):**
C. W. Communications, Inc.
1273 National Press Bldg.
529 14th St.
Washington, DC 20045
Telephone: (202) 347-6718
Contact: Bryan Wilkins, Writer

C. W. Communications, Inc.
1060 Marsh Rd.
Menlo Park, CA 94025
Telephone: (510) 328-8064
Contact: Jeffry Beeler, Bureau Chief

C. W. Communications, Inc.
140 Rt. 17 N.
Paramus, NJ 07652
Telephone: (201) 967-1350
Contact: Charles Babcock, Writer
**Management:**
Gloria Scoby .........................Publisher
Jill Ittersagen ...............Circulation Manager
**Editorial:**
Rance Crain .........................Editor in Chief
Mark Miller .........................Editor

64738
## CRAIN'S NEW YORK BUSINESS
220 E. 42nd St.
Ste. 1306
New York, NY 10017
Telephone: (212) 210-0277
FAX: (212) 210-0799
Year Established: 1985
Pub. Frequency: w.
Subscrip. Rate: $52/yr.
Circulation: 77,000
Circulation Type: paid
**Owner(s):**
Crain Communications
220 E. 42nd St.
New York, NY 10017
Telephone: (212) 210-0277
FAX: (212) 210-0799
Ownership %: 100
**Management:**
Sam Wender .........................Advertising Manager
**Editorial:**
Steve Malenja .........................Executive Editor
Greg David .........................Editor

64737
## DELAWARE BUSINESS REVIEW
640 James St., Ste. 200A
Wilmington, DE 19804
Telephone: (302) 998-9580
FAX: (302) 998-1276
Mailing Address:
P.O. Box 3350
Wilmington, DE 19804
Year Established: 1978
Pub. Frequency: w.
Page Size: tabloid
Subscrip. Rate: $48/yr.; $78/2 yrs.
Materials: 01,02,05,06,07,15,32,33
Print Process: offset

Circulation: 11,000
Circulation Type: paid
**Owner(s):**
Independent Newspapers, Inc.
P.O. Box 7013
Dover, DE 19903
Telephone: (800) 426-4192
FAX: (302) 674-4752
Ownership %: 100
**Bureau(s):**
Delaware Business Review
240 N. James St.
Ste. 200-A   P.O. Box 3350
Wilmington, DE 19804-9929
Telephone: (302) 998-6580
FAX: (302) 998-1276
Contact: Frank Fantini, Publisher
**Management:**
Frank Fantini .........................Publisher
Sheila Snow .........................Circulation Manager
**Editorial:**
Paul Wilke .........................Editor
**Desc.:** Legal and business journal mailed
to Delaware Valley area business
leaders.
**Readers:** 65% of readers C.E.O.'s, owners
and managers. Average income of
readers $92,215.
**Deadline:** story-Mon., prior to pub. date;
news-Mon., prior to pub. date; photo-
Mon., prior to pub. date; ads-Mon., prior
to pub. date

64735
## DENVER BUSINESS JOURNAL
1700 Broadway, Ste. 515
Denver, CO 80290
Telephone: (303) 837-3500
FAX: (303) 837-3535
Year Established: 1949
Pub. Frequency: w.
Page Size: tabloid
Subscrip. Rate: $49.50/yr.
Freelance Pay: $150-$200/article
Circulation: 15,000
Circulation Type: paid
**Owner(s):**
American City Business Journals
128 S. Tryon St., Ste. 2200
Charlotte, NC 28202
Telephone: (704) 375-7404
Ownership %: 100
**Management:**
Maureen Regan Smith .........................Publisher
Joe Mivshek ...............Assistant Sales Manger
Jill Hess .........................Sales Manager
**Editorial:**
Dougald MacDonald .........................Editor
Christopher Wood ...............Managing Editor
**Readers:** Professional middle to upper
level management and business owners

22306
## DETROITER
600 W. Lafayette
Detroit, MI 48226
Telephone: (313) 596-0352
FAX: (313) 964-0664
Year Established: 1903
Pub. Frequency: m.
Page Size: standard
Subscrip. Rate: $12/yr.
Materials: 01,02,04,05,06,07,15,17,19,21,
28,29,30,32
Freelance Pay: $300/feature
Print Process: web
Circulation: 17,000
Circulation Type: controlled & paid
**Owner(s):**
Greater Detroit Chamber of Commerce
600 W. Lafayette
Detroit, MI 48226
Telephone: (313) 964-4000
Ownership %: 100
**Management:**
Barbara B. Gattorn .........................Vice President

Frank E. Smith .........................Publisher
**Editorial:**
Louise Thomas .........................Editor
Amy Hennes .........................Managing Editor
Robert Smuck .........................Art Director
David Littman .........................Columnist
**Desc.:** Southeastern Michigan business
community magazine.
**Readers:** Chamber of Commerce
members, business community, news
media, and public officials.

54032
## EXECUTIVE REPORT
Three Gateway Center, 5th Fl.
Pittsburgh, PA 15222
Telephone: (412) 471-4585
FAX: (412) 644-3006
Year Established: 1981
Pub. Frequency: m.
Page Size: standard
Subscrip. Rate: free to qualified executives;
$24/yr. others
Freelance Pay: negotiable
Circulation: 27,317
Circulation Type: controlled
**Owner(s):**
Riverview Publications, Inc.
3 Gateway Ctr., 5th Fl.
Pittsburgh, PA 15222
Telephone: (412) 471-4585
Ownership %: 100
**Management:**
Linda A. Dickerson .........................President
Jackie Priddy .........................Office Manager
Karen Schade .........................Sales Manager
**Editorial:**
Patty Tascarella .........................Editor
Rob Mitrick .........................Art Director
Cheryl Forcey .........................Circulation Director
**Desc.:** Executive report carries articles
concerning western Pennsylvania
business, industry, and finance. Feature
stories include corporate and executive
profiles, business trend analysis, and
other related subjects.
**Readers:** Chief executive officers,
presidents, partners, owners, vice-
presidents, treasurers, managers,
directors, and other management of
western Pennsylvania corporations and
businesses.

68763
## EXECUTIVE SUITE
10169 New Hampshire Ave., Ste. 171
Silver Spring, MD 20903
Telephone: (301) 439-7750
FAX: (301) 439-7885
Year Established: 1991
Pub. Frequency: m.
Subscrip. Rate: $24/yr.
Circulation: 10,000
Circulation Type: paid
**Owner(s):**
Eric Communications
10169 New Hampshire Ave.
Silver Spring, MD 20903
Telephone: (301) 439-7750
Ownership %: 100
**Editorial:**
James Eric .........................Editor
**Desc.:** Targets African-American business
owners in the Washington, DC-Baltimore
corridor.

54019
## GEORGIA TREND
P.O. Box 56447
Atlanta, GA 30343
Telephone: (404) 522-7200
FAX: (404) 522-4501
Year Established: 1985
Pub. Frequency: m.
Page Size: standard
Subscrip. Rate: $27/yr.
Freelance Pay: varies

**Materials Accepted/Included:** 01-Business news 02-By-line articles 03-Fashion news 04-Food news 05-Freelance copy 06-Letters to editor 07-Real estate news 08-Sports news 09-Travel news
10-Book rev. 11-Movie rev. 12-Music rev. 13-TV rev. 14-Theater rev. 15-Coming events 16-Obituaries 17-Question & answer 18-Social announcements 19-Artwork 20-Cartoons 21-Photos 22-TV listings
23-Audio rec. 24-Video rec. 25-Books 26-Films/film clips 27-Personnel news 28-Press releases 29-New product news/photos 30-Trade lit. 31-Contracts awarded 32-Display adv. 33-Classified adv.

4-77

Circulation: 39,000
Circulation Type: controlled
**Owner(s):**
Williams Communications, Inc.
P.O. Box 56447
Atlanta, GA 30343
Telephone: (404) 522-7200
Ownership %: 100
**Management:**
Hill Robertson .........................Publisher
Hill Robertson .................Advertising Manager
Leslie Greene .....................Business Manager
Debbie Privett ....................Circulation Manager
Gail Aronoff ......................Production Manager
**Editorial:**
Edward Bean ...............................Editor
**Desc.:** Edited for Georgia executives and
  business leaders. Each issue includes
  features on Georgia companies, industry
  reports, business news and economic
  trends.
**Readers:** Executives with average
  household income exceeding $100,000.
  Active business people with decision-
  making authority in their companies.

64730

**GRAND RAPIDS BUSINESS
  JOURNAL**
549 Ottawa Ave. N.W.
Grand Rapids, MI 49503-1444
Telephone: (616) 459-4545
FAX: (616) 459-4800
Year Established: 1983
Pub. Frequency: w.
Page Size: tabloid
Subscrip. Rate: $42/yr.
Materials: 01,02,05,06,07,20,21,27,28,29,
  30,31,32,33
Freelance Pay: $3.50/in.
Circulation: 6,000
Circulation Type: paid
**Owner(s):**
Gemini Publications
549 Ottawa Ave. N.W.
Grand Rapids, MI 49503-1444
Telephone: (616) 459-4545
Ownership %: 100
**Management:**
Craig R. Rich ...........................Sales Manager
**Editorial:**
Carole Valade Smith ..........................Editor
**Readers:** Executives of the Grand Rapids
  area business community.
**Deadline:** story-2 wks. prior to pub. date;
  news-1 wk. prior; photo-1 wk. prior; ads-
  2 wks. prior

23422

**HAWAII BUSINESS**
P.O. Box 913
Honolulu, HI 96808
Telephone: (808) 946-3978
FAX: (808) 947-8498
Year Established: 1955
Pub. Frequency: m.
Page Size: standard
Subscrip. Rate: $18/yr. HI/Guam; $24/yr.
  US & Canada
Circulation: 8,046
Circulation Type: paid
**Owner(s):**
Hawaii Business Publishing Corp.
Telephone: (808) 946-3978
Ownership %: 100
**Management:**
Kim Jacobsen .........................Publisher
**Editorial:**
Mari Taketa ...............................Editor
Gina Murphy ...............................Art Director

**Desc.:** Covers agriculture, finance,
  construction, engineering, hotel and
  restaurant, manufacturing, maritime
  affairs, labor, government, armed forces,
  general business, foreign investment,
  transportation, development issues.
  Departments include: Hawaii Stocks,
  Real Estate, News, Business Ink, Bishop
  Street.
**Readers:** Owners, managers, presidents.

69314

**HOUSTON BUSINESS**
2200 N. Pearl St.
Dallas, TX 75201
Telephone: (214) 922-5251
FAX: (214) 922-5268
Mailing Address:
  Public Affairs
  P.O. Box 655906
  Dallas, TX 76265-5906
Pub. Frequency: every 6 wks.
Materials: 01
Print Process: offset
**Owner(s):**
Federal Reserve Bank of Dallas
Public Affairs
P.O. Box 65506
Dallas, TX 76265-5906
Telephone: (214) 922-5251
Ownership %: 100
**Editorial:**
Tara Barrett ...............................Editor
**Desc.:** Covers the Texas Gulf Coast
  economy, with emphasis on Houston.
  Each issue contains an economic
  feature and a report about the results of
  the Houston Beige Book Survey.

22329

**HOUSTON BUSINESS JOURNAL**
One W. Loop S., Ste. 650
Houston, TX 77027
Telephone: (713) 688-8811
FAX: (713) 963-0482
Year Established: 1971
Pub. Frequency: w.
Page Size: tabloid
Subscrip. Rate: $49/yr.
Freelance Pay: $3/in.
Circulation: 27,000
Circulation Type: paid
**Owner(s):**
American City Business Journal
One W. Loop S., #650
Houston, TX 77027
Telephone: (713) 688-8811
Ownership %: 100
**Management:**
Tina Carusillo ...........................Publisher
Tina Phillips .................Advertising Manager
**Editorial:**
Bill Schadewald ..........................Editor
**Desc.:** Report on trends, growth and new
  ideas important to the commerce and
  industry in the Houston Metropolitan
  Statistical Area. By-lines used, some
  publicity material and photo spreads are
  used on occasion. Departments include:
  Commentary, Finance, Real Estate-
  Construction, Marketing, Transportation,
  Advertising, International Trade, Natural
  Resources, New Products, Business and
  Pleasure (travel), Automotive Reviews,
  Image, and Health Care.
**Readers:** Decision-making executives.

59579

**IDC JAPAN REPORT**
41 West St.
Boston, MA 02111
Telephone: (617) 423-9030
FAX: (617) 423-0712
Year Established: 1973
Pub. Frequency: m.

Page Size: standard
Subscrip. Rate: $495/yr. US: $535/yr.
  foreign
**Owner(s):**
International Data Corp.
41 West St.
Boston, MA 02111
Telephone: (617) 423-9030
Ownership %: 100
**Editorial:**
Yugi Ogino ...............................Editor
Donald Bellomy ...............Editorial Advisor
**Desc.:** News and information on the fast-
  paced Japanese information technology
  market.

55873

**INDIANAPOLIS BUSINESS
  JOURNAL**
431 N. Pennsylvania St.
Indianapolis, IN 46204
Telephone: (317) 634-6200
FAX: (317) 263-5060
Year Established: 1980
Pub. Frequency: w.
Page Size: tabloid
Subscrip. Rate: $1.25/copy; $59/yr.
Materials: 01,06,07,09,23,25,27,28,31,32,33
Circulation: 14,583
Circulation Type: paid
**Owner(s):**
IBJ Corp.
431 N. Pennsylvania
Indianapolis, IN 46204
Telephone: (612) 634-6200
Ownership %: 100
**Management:**
Chris Katterjohn ...........................Publisher
Greg Morris .................Advertising Manager
**Editorial:**
Tom Harton ...............................Editor
Chip Otte ...............................Art Director
Kim Harlow ...............Marketing Director
**Desc.:** Has established itself as the voice
  of local business in central Indiana. No
  other local medium reaches mid to
  upper management as cost effectively.
  Has an editorial scope that includes real
  estate and stock market reports,
  features on local businesses and
  business people, corporate comings and
  goings, government effects on business,
  etc. In short it offers all that interests
  the people in the local community, from
  a business oriented prospective.
**Readers:** Local business executives thirst
  for pertinent local business news. Our
  writters and editors know their market
  and satisfy the need of business
  executives for local
  business information. Thus, our editorial
  product creates an environment
  conductive to successful
  business advertising.

64944

**INGRAM'S**
306 E. Twelfth St.
Ste. 1014
Kansas City, MO 64106
Telephone: (816) 842-9994
FAX: (816) 474-1111
Year Established: 1975
Pub. Frequency: m.
Page Size: standard
Subscrip. Rate: $18/yr.
Freelance Pay: $50-$1,000
Circulation: 275,000
Circulation Type: controlled & paid
**Owner(s):**
Robert P. Ingram
306 E. Twelfth St.
Kansas City, MO 64106
Telephone: (816) 842-9994
Ownership %: 100

**Management:**
Robert P. Ingram ...........................Publisher
Del Black .....................Circulation Manager
**Editorial:**
Robin Silverman ...............................Editor
**Desc.:** Ingram's is written for Kansas
  citians who are successful and those
  who are aspiring to be. It's target
  audience is business people and
  professionals. The cornerstone of
  Ingram's coverage is emerging business
  trends and profiles of the city's most
  dynamic personalities. It also covers the
  business of enjoying and improving on
  the quality of life in greater Kansas City
  with articles of personal and civic
  interest to its readers. Subjects include:
  cultural activities, dining out, health and
  fitness, personal style, the home,
  politics, education, and
  contemporary issues.
**Readers:** 32,500 Persons in Upper and
  Middle Management Of Business and
  Professional Firms Plus Educational,
  Governmental and Non -
  Profit Organizations.

65257

**INTERNATIONAL BUSINESS**
500 Mamaroneck Ave., Ste. 314
Harrison, NY 10528-1600
Telephone: (914) 381-7700
FAX: (914) 381-7713
Year Established: 1987
Pub. Frequency: m.
Page Size: standard
Subscrip. Rate: $60/yr. US; $120/yr.
  foreign
Freelance Pay: $.65-$.85/wd.
Circulation: 60,000
Circulation Type: paid
**Owner(s):**
American International Publishing Corp.
500 Mamaroneck Ave., Ste. 314
Harrison, NY 10528-1600
Telephone: (914) 381-7700
Ownership %: 100
**Management:**
David Hall ...........................Publisher
Maria DiPlazido .................Circulation Manager
Patricia Hall .....................General Manager
**Editorial:**
Ed Mervash .....................Editor in Chief
David Moore ...............................Editor
David Moore .................Editorial Director
Amy Vischio ...............................Art Director
Steven Rothman .................Production Director
**Desc.:** Covers international finance, trade
  and transportation. Redesigned and
  expanded, the magazine places
  emphasis on international trade,
  manufacturing, marketing, technology,
  management, etc. in a manner
  conducive to the self-taught.
**Readers:** Vice-presidents in large
  corporations and owners/entrepreneurs
  in small US businesses involved with
  the world market.

65054

**KANSAS CITY BUSINESS
  JOURNAL**
324 E. 11th, Ste. 800
Kansas City, MO 64106-2417
Telephone: (816) 421-5900
FAX: (816) 472-4010
Year Established: 1982
Pub. Frequency: w.
Page Size: tabloid
Subscrip. Rate: $1.25 newsstand; $53/yr.
Materials: 01,02,05,06,07,15,19,20,21,32,33
Print Process: web offset
Circulation: 16,354
Circulation Type: free & paid

**Materials Accepted/Included:** 01-Business news 02-By-line articles 03-Fashion news 04-Food news 05-Freelance copy 06-Letters to editor 07-Real estate news 08-Sports news 09-Travel news
10-Book rev. 11-Movie rev. 12-Music rev. 13-TV rev. 14-Theater rev. 15-Coming events 16-Obituaries 17-Question & answer 18-Social announcements 19-Artwork 20-Cartoons 21-Photos 22-TV listings
23-Audio rec. 24-Video rec. 25-Books 26-Films/film clips 27-Personnel news 28-Press releases 29-New product news/photos 30-Trade lit. 31-Contracts awarded 32-Display adv. 33-Classified adv.

**Owner(s):**
American City Business Journals Inc.
128 S. Trion St., Ste. 2200
Charlotte, NC 28202
Telephone: (904) 375-7404
Ownership %: 100
**Management:**
Joyce Hayhow ...............................Publisher
Linda Wilson ....................Circulation Manager
Fawn Fleming ..........................Sales Manager
**Editorial:**
Tammy Tierney ...................................Editor
Kevin Garrity ..........................Associate Editor
**Readers:** Business persons interested in the business news and trends in the Greater Kansas City area
**Deadline:** story-Fri. prior to pub. date

61585

## LEHIGH VALLEY BUSINESS DIGEST
911 N. Jerome St.
Allentown, PA 18103-1968
Telephone: (610) 821-8350
FAX: (610) 437-6776
Year Established: 1982
Pub. Frequency: m.
Page Size: tabloid
Subscrip. Rate: $25/yr.
Materials: 01,02,06,07,09,15,17,18,19,20,
  21,27,28,29,32,33
Print Process: web offset
Circulation: 14,500
Circulation Type: controlled
**Owner(s):**
Daniel J. Lasdon
911 N. Jerome St.
Allentown, PA 18103
Telephone: (215) 477-8620
FAX: (215) 477-7054
Ownership %: 100
**Management:**
Estelle A. Becker ...............................Publisher
**Desc.:** Try to keep editorial coverage on a regional basis as opposed to national. Editorial content must be conducive to daily business operation, no matter what the nature of the service. We focus attention to conducting businesses of small to mid-size range.
**Readers:** Target market readership to only: Owners, Presidents, CEO's, Managers, and Partners.
**Deadline:** story-5th of mo.; news-5th of mo.; photo-5th of mo.; ads-10th of mo. prior to pub. date

65053

## LONG ISLAND BUSINESS NEWS
2150 Smithtown Ave.
Ronkonkoma, NY 11779
Telephone: (516) 737-1700
FAX: (516) 737-1890
Year Established: 1953
Pub. Frequency: w.
Page Size: tabloid
Subscrip. Rate: $59/yr.
Print Process: web offset
Circulation: 10,500
Circulation Type: paid
**Owner(s):**
LI Commercial Review, Inc.
2150 Smithtown Ave.
Ronkonkoma, NY 11779
Ownership %: 100
**Management:**
Wendy Clark Csoka ...................Vice President
Tom Masterson .......................Vice President
Terry Townsend ..............................Publisher
**Editorial:**
Paul Townsend ...................................Editor
Cathy Vrell ...........................Managing Editor

**Desc.:** All business and issues relating to Long Island; realty projects, executive changes in jobs, titles, leisure and philanthropy developments, lists of companies (those with over 100 employees, those in export/import on Long Island, who's who in CEO's), government, colleges & universities, listings of facilities on Long Island, ways to attract business to Long Island, corporate earnings, stocks, dividends. Any news or feature story impacting on L.I. Special books and feature sections on money managements, banking, world trade, freight moving, conventions.
**Readers:** Management of business, financial, government, and educational institutions.

22358

## MERCER BUSINESS MAGAZINE
2550 Kuser Rd.
P.O. Box 8307
Trenton, NJ 08650
Telephone: (609) 586-2056
FAX: (609) 586-8052
Year Established: 1924
Pub. Frequency: m.
Page Size: 8 1/2 x 11
Subscrip. Rate: $2.50 newsstand; $20/yr.
Materials: 01,07,32
Freelance Pay: $75-$125
Print Process: offset
Circulation: 8,100
Circulation Type: free & paid
**Owner(s):**
Mercer County Chamber of Commerce
214 W. State St.
Trenton, NJ 08608
Telephone: (609) 393-4143
Ownership %: 100
**Management:**
Edward F. Meara, III .........................Publisher
Donna L. Hill .....................Advertising Manager
**Editorial:**
Gene J. Sayko ...................................Editor
Ed Tereszczyn, Jr. ........................Art Director
White Eagle, Inc. ..............Publication Manager
**Desc.:** A business features magazine, covering the Princeton-Trenton, NJ market areas.
**Readers:** Business and professional people of the area.
**Deadline:** story-30 days prior to pub. date; ads-30 days prior to pub. date

22363

## MID-AMERICA COMMERCE & INDUSTRY
1824 Cheyenne Rd.
Topeka, KS 66604-3704
Telephone: (913) 272-5280
Year Established: 1973
Pub. Frequency: m.
Page Size: standard
Subscrip. Rate: $18.50/yr.
Materials: 01,02,21,25,27,28,29,30,32
Print Process: offset
Circulation: 10,300
Circulation Type: controlled & free
**Owner(s):**
MACI, Inc.
1824 Cheyenne Rd.
Topeka, KS 66604-3704
Telephone: (913) 272-5280
Ownership %: 100
**Management:**
N. Ray Lippe ...................................Publisher
**Editorial:**
N. Ray Lippe ...................................Editor

**Desc.:** Features success stories of manufacturers and distributors in KS, MO, AR, OK, NE, and Southern Iowa; saving money by using certain methods or equipment, plant expansions, new equipment, 25th, 50th, 100th anniversaries, various types of management ideas, timely topics such as product liability, insurance, computers, robotics and government regulations. Any interesting article that will help a manager run a company better, save money for a purchaser or inspire top executives. Features normally no more than 3 magazine pages. By-lines are used. Staff writes most of the articles. As a regional, we want articles localized so that readers can identify with subject. Like to use photos if good. Send new products if they have a tie-in locally. Helps to tell who the local distributor is. Promotions, any sign of growth are used. Departments include: Main Features, Publishers Column, Purchasing, Safety, News of People, News of Plant Expansions and New Equipment, Purchasing Electronics.
**Readers:** People who make buying decisions. Purchasing managers, presidents, industrial engineers, plant managers and production managers.

65050

## MINNEAPOLIS/ST. PAUL CITY BUSINESS
5500 Wayzata Blvd., Ste. 800
Minneapolis, MN 55416
Telephone: (612) 591-2701
FAX: (612) 591-2639
Year Established: 1983
Pub. Frequency: Fri.
Page Size: tabloid
Subscrip. Rate: $54/yr.
Materials: 01,05,06,07,08,09,27,28,31,32,33
Circulation: 10,000
Circulation Type: paid
**Owner(s):**
MCP, Inc.
5500 Wayzata Blvd., Ste. 800
Minneapolis, MN 55416
Telephone: (612) 591-2701
**Management:**
Stuart Chamblin ...............................Publisher
**Editorial:**
Beth Even ...................................Editor

22377

## NEW JERSEY BUSINESS MAGAZINE
310 Passaic Ave.
Fairfield, NJ 07004
Telephone: (201) 882-5004
Year Established: 1954
Pub. Frequency: m.
Page Size: standard
Subscrip. Rate: $20/yr.
Freelance Pay: $200-$400
Circulation: 17,000
Circulation Type: paid
**Owner(s):**
New Jersey Business & Industry Association
102 W. State St.
Trenton, NJ 08608
Telephone: (609) 393-7707
Ownership %: 100
**Management:**
Bruce Coe ....................................President
Donald Hahnes ...............................Publisher
**Editorial:**
James Prior ..........................Executive Editor
Jacqueline Juster ....................Senior Editor
**Desc.:** Regional industrial, business and financial magazine.

**Readers:** Presidents, vice presidents, officers and owners of industries and financial institutions throughout New Jersey.

22378

## NEW MEXICO BUSINESS JOURNAL
2323 Aztec N.E.
Albuquerque, NM 87107
Telephone: (505) 889-2911
FAX: (505) 889-0822
Mailing Address:
  P.O. Box 30550
  Albuquerque, NM 87190
Year Established: 1976
Pub. Frequency: m.
Page Size: 4 color photos/art
Subscrip. Rate: $2.95/copy; $24/yr.
Materials: 01,02,05,06,07,09,17,19,20,21,
  28,32,33
Freelance Pay: $.05/pub. wd.
Print Process: web offset
Circulation: 3,500
Circulation Type: controlled & paid
**Owner(s):**
Southwest Publications, Inc.
P.O. Box 30550
Albuquerque, NM 87190
Telephone: (505) 889-2911
Ownership %: 100
**Management:**
George Hackler ...............................Publisher
Jeanne Nolan ...................Advertising Manager
**Editorial:**
Jack Hartsfield ........................Editor in Chief
**Desc.:** Our editorial covers New Mexico business and commercial development; new ways to increase profits; management, sales, government policy as it affects business, profiles of business leaders and innovators, finance, taxation, computer utilization, etc. Departments include: People, Real Estate, Management Self-Help, Business Indicators, and briefs on finance and business around the states.
**Readers:** Small and large businesses, realtors, contractors, builders and developers.

22380

## NORTH CAROLINA
225 Hillsborough, #460
Raleigh, NC 27603
Telephone: (919) 828-0758
FAX: (919) 821-4992
Mailing Address:
  P.O. Box 2508
  Raleigh, NC 27602
Year Established: 1943
Pub. Frequency: m.
Page Size: standard
Subscrip. Rate: $21.20/yr.; $37.10/2 yrs.
Circulation: 13,000
Circulation Type: paid
**Owner(s):**
North Carolina Citizens for Business & Industry
P.O. Box 2588
Raleigh, NC 27602
Telephone: (919) 828-0758
Ownership %: 100
**Management:**
Phillip J. Kirk, Jr. ............................President
Phillip J. Kirk, Jr. ...........................Publisher
Charles Couch ..............Advertising Manager
Vikki Faircloth ............Circulation Manager
**Editorial:**
Regina Oliver ........................Senior Editor
Steve A. Tuttle ...................................Editor
Michael Lancaster ..............Production Director

Materials Accepted/Included: 01-Business news 02-By-line articles 03-Fashion news 04-Food news 05-Freelance copy 06-Letters to editor 07-Real estate news 08-Sports news 09-Travel news 10-Book rev. 11-Movie rev. 12-Music rev. 13-TV rev. 14-Theater rev. 15-Coming events 16-Obituaries 17-Question & answer 18-Social announcements 19-Artwork 20-Cartoons 21-Photos 22-TV listings 23-Audio rec. 24-Video rec. 25-Books 26-Films/film clips 27-Personnel news 28-Press releases 29-New product news/photos 30-Trade lit. 31-Contracts awarded 32-Display adv. 33-Classified adv.

4-79

**Desc.:** Serves as an information vehicle for members of N.C. Citizens Association. Originated as an informational vehicle. Deals with business, government and public affairs. Most articles are staff-written.
**Readers:** Members of N.C. Citizens Association (business officials and legislators), school and college libraries.

22383

## ORANGE COUNTY BUSINESS JOURNAL
4590 MacArthur Blvd., Ste. 100
Newport Beach, CA 92660
Telephone: (714) 833-8373
FAX: (714) 833-8751
Year Established: 1978
Pub. Frequency: w.
Page Size: tabloid
Subscrip. Rate: $39/yr.
Circulation: 22,000
Circulation Type: controlled & paid
**Owner(s):**
CBJ, L.P.
1200 Main, Ste. 3800
Kansas City, MO 64105
Telephone: (816) 421-2500
Ownership %: 100
**Management:**
Richard Reisman .................................Publisher
**Editorial:**
Rick Reiff ...........................................Editor
**Desc.:** Business coverage of Orange County, CA.
**Readers:** Business executives and professionals.

65037

## OREGON BUSINESS MAGAZINE
921 S.W. Morrison, Ste. 407
Portland, OR 97205
Telephone: (503) 223-0304
Year Established: 1981
Pub. Frequency: m.
Page Size: standard
Subscrip. Rate: $19.95/yr.
Materials: 06,25,29,32
Print Process: web offset
Circulation: 18,500
Circulation Type: controlled & paid
**Owner(s):**
MediAmerica, Inc.
921 S.W. Morrison, Ste. 407
Portland, OR 97205
Telephone: (503) 223-0304
Ownership %: 100
**Management:**
David Rowe ......................................Publisher
Ken Rapple ...............................Sales Manager
**Editorial:**
Kathy Dimond ...................................Editor
D.C. Jesse Burkhardt ..............Associate Editor
**Desc.:** "Helping Oregon companies grow."
**Readers:** Everyone with an economic stake in the state of Oregon, especially managers, owners and presidents of small and medium-size businesses.

65036

## PACIFIC BUSINESS NEWS
863 Halekauwila St.
Honolulu, HI 96813
Telephone: (808) 521-0021
Mailing Address:
    P.O. Box 833
    Honolulu, HI 96808
Year Established: 1963
Pub. Frequency: w.
Page Size: tabloid
Subscrip. Rate: $48/yr. mainland; $43/yr. HI
Circulation: 14,800
Circulation Type: paid
**Owner(s):**
American City Business Journals, Inc.
Ownership %: 100

**Management:**
George Mason ....................................Publisher
Stephen S. Lent .........................Sales Manager
**Editorial:**
George Mason ....................................Editor
Ann L. Moore ...........................Managing Editor
Tom Leonard .....................Associate Publisher
**Desc.:** Edited for various categories of business and professional readers. Reports New Business, Federal and State tax liens, Real Estate transactions, Bankruptcies, Building Permits, Civil Court cases, Asia - Pacific Business, and features five syndicated columnists. Local business news and features are augmented by editorial positions on local and national issues.
**Readers:** Hawaii Business, Industry, & Professionsl.

22359

## PARTNERSHIP PROGRESS
1 Newark Center, 22nd Fl.
Newark, NJ 07102-5265
Telephone: (201) 242-6237
FAX: (201) 824-6587
Year Established: 1956
Pub. Frequency: 6/yr.
Page Size: tabloid
Subscrip. Rate: free
Freelance Pay: $25 up
Circulation: 10,000
Circulation Type: controlled
**Owner(s):**
Regional Business Partnership
1 Newark Center
Newark, NJ 07102-5265
Telephone: (201) 242-6237
FAX: (201) 824-6587
Ownership %: 100
**Bureau(s):**
Metro Newark Chamber of Commerce
40 Clinton St.
Newark, NJ 07102
Telephone: (201) 242-6237
Contact: Joseph LaMonica, Editor
**Management:**
Sam Crane ....................................President
**Editorial:**
Jean Benish ...................................Editor
**Desc.:** Pieces cover Newark, Essex County and Northern New Jersey - both features and news features. Freelance material used. By - Lines used when due. Occasional photo spreads. Departments include: Chamber News, Around Town, Newsreel, Newsmakers, In The News.
**Readers:** READERS: Chamber members, businessmen and individuals throughout the greater Newark area.

52688

## PITTSBURGH BUSINESS TIMES
2313 E. Carson St., Ste. 200
Pittsburgh, PA 15203
Telephone: (412) 481-6397
Year Established: 1981
Pub. Frequency: w.
Page Size: tabloid
Subscrip. Rate: $54/yr.
Freelance Pay: negotiable
Circulation: 14,000
Circulation Type: paid
**Owner(s):**
Pittsburgh Business Weekly Corp.
2313 E. Carson St., Ste. 200
Pittsburgh, PA 15203
Telephone: (412) 481-6397
Ownership %: 100
**Management:**
Alan Robertson ...............................Publisher
Rick Lindner ...............Advertising Manager
Tom Gagliardi ...............Business Manager
Ana Blanco ...............Circulation Manager

**Editorial:**
Huntley Paton ....................................Editor
Rick Teaff ...........................Managing Editor
Richard Cerilli ...........................Production Director
**Desc.:** Covers business financial topics relevant to Pittsburgh.
**Readers:** High-income business executives and/or owners.

65034

## PORTLAND BUSINESS JOURNAL
P.O. Box 14490
Portland, OR 97214
Telephone: (503) 274-8733
FAX: (503) 227-2650
Year Established: 1984
Pub. Frequency: w.
Subscrip. Rate: $48/yr.
Circulation: 15,000
Circulation Type: controlled & paid
**Owner(s):**
American City Business Jornals, Inc.
P.O. Box 14490
Portland, OR 97214
Telephone: (503) 274-8733
**Management:**
Betsy Leedy ...............Advertising Manager
Betsy Leedy ...............Sales Manager
**Editorial:**
Steven D. Jones ....................................Editor
**Desc.:** Covers business and economics in the Portland area.

69723

## PUERTO RICO BUSINESS REVIEW
P.O. Box 42001
San Juan, PR 00940-2001
Telephone: (809) 729-6433
FAX: (809) 728-0975
Year Established: 1976
Pub. Frequency: q.
Page Size: standard
Subscrip. Rate: free
Print Process: offset
Circulation: 11,000
Circulation Type: controlled & paid
**Owner(s):**
Banco Gubernamental de Fomento para Puerto Rico
P.O. Box 42001
San Juan, PR 00940-2001
Telephone: (809) 729-6433
FAX: (809) 268-5496
Ownership %: 100
**Bureau(s):**
Government Development Bank for Puerto Rico
140 Broadway
New York, NY 10005
Telephone: (212) 422-6420
**Editorial:**
Eunice Pagan-Vega, Esq. .........................Editor
**Desc.:** Provides business-related articles of interest to the financial community, economists, and the private and public sectors.

65043

## ROCHESTER BUSINESS JOURNAL
55 St. Paul St.
Rochester, NY 14604-1343
Telephone: (716) 546-8303
FAX: (716) 546-3398
Pub. Frequency: w.
Page Size: tabloid
Subscrip. Rate: $1.25 newsstand; $52/yr.
Circulation: 10,500
Circulation Type: paid
**Owner(s):**
Susan R. Holiday
55 St. Paul St.
Rochester, NY 14604-1343
Telephone: (716) 546-8303
**Management:**
Susan R. Holiday ...............Sales Manager
**Editorial:**
Paul Erickson ....................................Editor

64732

## SAN DIEGO EXECUTIVE
15 S. Fifth St.
Minneapolis, MN 55402-1013
Telephone: (619) 467-1050
FAX: (619) 467-1154
Year Established: 1983
Pub. Frequency: m.
Page Size: standard
Subscrip. Rate: $18/yr.
Freelance Pay: varies
Circulation: 23,000
Circulation Type: controlled
**Owner(s):**
Magazine Group, Inc.
9449 Balboa Ave., Ste. 111
San Diego, CA 92123
Telephone: (619) 467-1154
Ownership %: 100
**Management:**
Mary Ann Czerwinski ...........................Publisher
Cheri Petiprin ...............Sales Manager
**Editorial:**
David E. Whiteside ...............................Editor
Timothy J. McClain .................Managing Editor

22405

## SOUTHERN CALIFORNIA BUSINESS
404 S. Bixel St.
Los Angeles, CA 90017
Telephone: (213) 629-0671
FAX: (213) 629-0611
Year Established: 1923
Pub. Frequency: m.
Page Size: tabloid
Subscrip. Rate: free membership; $16/yr.
Circulation: 10,000
Circulation Type: controlled
**Owner(s):**
Los Angeles Area Chamber of Commerce
404 S. Bixel St.
Los Angeles, CA 90017
Telephone: (310) 629-0671
Ownership %: 100
**Editorial:**
Christopher J. Volker ...............................Editor
**Desc.:** Devoted to chamber activity and to general business news by-lines. Departments include: Economic Trends, Management Update, Newsmakers, Business Briefs, Sacramento Report, New Members, The Pacific Rim, Small Business, Company Profiles, and a special section monthly on an industry in Southern California.
**Readers:** Business people.

69535

## SOUTHERN ECONOMIC JOURNAL
300 Hanes Hall, CB 3540
Chapel Hill, NC 27599-3540
Telephone: (919) 966-5261
Year Established: 1933
Pub. Frequency: s-m.
Subscrip. Rate: $57/yr.
Circulation: 4,000
**Owner(s):**
University of North Carolina at Chapel Hill
Southern Economic Association
300 Hanes Hall, CB3540
Chapel Hill, NC 27599-3540
Telephone: (919) 966-5261
**Editorial:**
Vincent J. Tarascio ...................................Editor
**Desc.:** Theoretical and empirical research in economics.
**Readers:** Teachers, researchers, other professionals in business, economics and related fields.

64928

## ST. LOUIS BUSINESS JOURNAL
612 N. 2nd St.
St. Louis, MO 63102
Telephone: (314) 421-6200

**Materials Accepted/Included:** 01-Business news 02-By-line articles 03-Fashion news 04-Food news 05-Freelance copy 06-Letters to editor 07-Real estate news 08-Sports news 09-Travel news 10-Book rev. 11-Movie rev. 12-Music rev. 13-TV rev. 14-Theater rev. 15-Coming events 16-Obituaries 17-Question & answer 18-Social announcements 19-Artwork 20-Cartoons 21-Photos 22-TV listings 23-Audio rec. 24-Video rec. 25-Books 26-Films/film clips 27-Personnel news 28-Press releases 29-New product news/photos 30-Trade lit. 31-Contracts awarded 32-Display adv. 33-Classified adv.

Mailing Address:
P.O. Box 647
St. Louis, MO 63188
Year Established: 1980
Pub. Frequency: w.
Page Size: tabloid
Subscrip. Rate: $49.50/yr.
Freelance Pay: negotiable
Circulation: 18,991
Circulation Type: paid
**Owner(s):**
American City Business Journals
128 S. Tryon St., Ste. 2200
Charlotte, NC 28202
Telephone: (704) 375-7404
Ownership %: 100
**Management:**
Ellen Sherberg .............................Publisher
Carol Stolze ....................Advertising Manager
Christee Cook ...............Business Manager
Eric Bartholomew ...........Circulation Manager
**Editorial:**
Tom Wolf .......................................Editor
Brad Cripe ................Production Coordinator
**Readers:** Top and middle management of small, medium and large St. Louis companies.

---

**ST. LOUIS COMMERCE** 22396
100 S. Fourth St., Ste. 500
Saint Louis, MO 63102
Telephone: (314) 231-5555
FAX: (314) 444-1122
Year Established: 1926
Pub. Frequency: m.
Page Size: 4 color photos/art
Subscrip. Rate: $36/yr.
Circulation: 11,000
Circulation Type: paid
**Owner(s):**
St. Louis Regional Commerce & Growth Assn.
100 S. Fourth St., Ste. 500
Saint Louis, MO 63102
Telephone: (314) 231-5555
Ownership %: 100
**Editorial:**
Laura S. Barlow ...............Managing Editor
Karen Clare .............................Advertising
**Desc.:** Provides the region's business, industrial, cultural, governmental, and educational leaders with essential economic, social, management and civic information to help executives meet their responsibilities as community leaders. Also reflects the area's resources and advantages as a place for commerce and industry to grow and prosper.
**Readers:** Business executives, government officials, purchasing agents, community leaders, educators; professionals, sales & marketing executives.

---

**TEXAS BUSINESS REVIEW** 58721
21st & Speedway
Austin, TX 78712
Telephone: (512) 471-1616
FAX: (512) 471-1063
Mailing Address:
P.O. Box 7459
Austin, TX 78713
Year Established: 1927
Pub. Frequency: bi-m.
Page Size: standard
Subscrip. Rate: free
Circulation: 5,500
Circulation Type: free

**Owner(s):**
Bureau of Business Research, Univ. Texas at Austin
P.O. Box 7459
Austin, TX 78713
Telephone: (512) 471-1616
FAX: (512) 471-1063
Ownership %: 100
**Editorial:**
Lois G. Shrout ..................Editor/Associate Dir.
**Desc.:** Focuses on the current condition of the Texas economy and the outlook for the economies of the state and substate areas. Includes employment data and an index of leading economic indicators.
**Readers:** Business professionals, analysts.

---

**VERMONT BUSINESS MAGAZINE** 64929
2 Church St.
Burlington, VT 05302
Telephone: (802) 863-8038
FAX: (802) 863-8069
Year Established: 1972
Pub. Frequency: m.
Page Size: tabloid
Subscrip. Rate: $25/yr. plus special issues
Freelance Pay: varies
Circulation: 12,000
Circulation Type: controlled
**Owner(s):**
Lake Iroquois Publishing, Inc.
2 Church St.
Burlington, VT 05401
Telephone: (802) 863-8038
Ownership %: 100
**Bureau(s):**
Vermont Business Magazine
P.O. Box 6120
Brattleboro, VT 05301
Telephone: (802) 658-7790
Contact: Amy Jenness, Managing Editor
**Management:**
Ann Lurie ....................................President
John Boutin ..................................Publisher
Wendy Ewing ..............Advertising Manager
**Editorial:**
Timothy McQuiston .......................Editor
Amy Jenness ...................Managing Editor
Jim Lurie ...................................Treasurer
**Desc.:** Employee owned; statewide business publication.
**Readers:** Vermont's business community.

---

**VIRGIN ISLANDS BUSINESS JOURNAL** 69715
40 CCC Taarnberg
P.O. Box 1208
St. Thomas, VI 00804-1208
Telephone: (809) 776-0000
FAX: (809) 774-3636
Year Established: 1985
Pub. Frequency: w.
Page Size: tabloid
Subscrip. Rate: $.50 newsstand; $25/yr.
Materials: 01,02,03,04,05,06,07,08,09,10, 17,19,20,21
Freelance Pay: $50-$200 (US)
Circulation: 8,000
Circulation Type: paid
**Owner(s):**
Media Ventures (V.I.), Inc.
69 Krondprindsens
P.O. Box 1208
St. Thomas, VI 00804-1208
Telephone: (809) 776-2874
FAX: (809) 774-3636
Ownership %: 100
**Editorial:**
Christopher B. Garrity .....................Editor
**Deadline:** story-Wed.; news-Wed.; photo-Wed.; ads-Wed.

---

**WASHINGTON BUSINESS JOURNAL** 49892
2000 14th St., N., Ste. 500
Arlington, VA 22201
Telephone: (703) 875-2200
FAX: (703) 875-2231
Year Established: 1982
Pub. Frequency: w.
Page Size: tabloid
Subscrip. Rate: $49/yr.
Freelance Pay: negotiable
Circulation: 20,000
Circulation Type: paid
**Owner(s):**
American City Business Journal
Ownership %: 100
**Management:**
Richard Kreuz ..............................Publisher
Lisa Bormaster .................Advertising Manager
**Editorial:**
David Yochum .................................Editor
Marvin Arth .....................Managing Editor
Susan Stocker ..................Assistant Editor
**Desc.:** Weekly business newspaper with a decided emphasis on local news.
**Readers:** Upscale business people, from CEO's to entrepreneurs, who work in the Greater Washington area.

---

**WESTCHESTER BUSINESS JOURNAL** 22294
22 Saw Mill River Rd.
Hawthorne, NY 10532
Telephone: (914) 347-5200
FAX: (914) 347-5576
Year Established: 1968
Pub. Frequency: w.
Page Size: tabloid
Subscrip. Rate: $1.25 newsstand; $48/yr.; $75/2 yrs.
Materials: 01,02,05,06,07,20,21,28,29,30, 31,32
Freelance Pay: competitive
Print Process: web offset
Circulation: 14,000
Circulation Type: controlled & paid
**Owner(s):**
West Fair Communications, Inc.
22 Saw Mill River Rd.
Hawthorne, NY 10532
Telephone: (914) 347-5200
FAX: (914) 347-5576
Ownership %: 100
**Management:**
Dee Delbello ................................Publisher
**Editorial:**
Mills Korte ....................................Editor
**Desc.:** Features include articles on local business trends and developments, financial reports of the local firms, executive promotions, stock quotes, and feature articles on local businessmen and companies. Departments include: Financial, Business, Transportation, Communications, Advertising and Marketing, Office Equipment, and Data Processing. A recent survey revealed that 82.9 % of the Journal's readers are top executives with an average annual family income of $148,000. They consider the Journal their primary source of local business news. Popular features include: business lists, newsmaker profiles, focus sections, tradetips, industry supplements and records of incorporations, deeds, etc.
**Readers:** Decision-makers in corporations and businesses, executives, professionals and managers, business owners
**Deadline:** story-7 days prior to pub. date; news-5 days prior; photo-7 days prior; ads-10 days prior

---

**WORCESTER MAGAZINE** 61814
172 Shrewsbury St.
Worcester, MA 01604
Telephone: (508) 799-0511
FAX: (508) 755-8860
Mailing Address:
P.O. Box 1000
Worcester, MA 01614
Year Established: 1976
Pub. Frequency: w.
Page Size: tabloid
Subscrip. Rate: free newsstand; $65/yr. 1st class; $26/yr. 3rd class
Circulation: 40,000
Circulation Type: free & paid
**Owner(s):**
Worcester Publishing Ltd.
25 Elm St.
Southbridge, MA 01550
Telephone: (508) 764-4325
Ownership %: 100
**Management:**
Peter Stanton ...............................Publisher
Kathleen Real ...................Sales Manager
**Editorial:**
Walter Crockett ..............................Editor
**Desc.:** Firmly established newsweekly providing commentary, analysis, and investigative pieces on central Massachusetts to our readers.
**Readers:** Educated, 25 - 55, high income, professionals.

---

## Group 042-Candy and Confectionery

**CANDY INDUSTRY** 22720
7500 Old Oak Blvd.
Cleveland, OH 44130
Telephone: (216) 826-2866
FAX: (216) 819-2651
Year Established: 1874
Pub. Frequency: m.
Page Size: standard
Subscrip. Rate: $7/issue; $25/yr.
Freelance Pay: negotiable
Circulation: 4,000
Circulation Type: paid
**Owner(s):**
Advanstar Communications, Inc.
7500 Old Oak Blvd.
Cleveland, OH 44130
Telephone: (216) 826-2866
Ownership %: 100
**Management:**
Pat Magee ..................................Publisher
**Editorial:**
Susan Tiffany ................................Editor
**Desc.:** Interested in editorial material on firms which sell in the national market. Features of 1,000 to 1,250 words on activities of large firms who participate in all phases of the candy industry. Also short news stories on personnel. Covers articles on packaging, production, merchandising, finance, advertising, promotion, etc.
**Readers:** Large scale manufacturers.

---

**CANDY MARKETER** 22719
7500 Old Oak Blvd.
Cleveland, OH 44130
Telephone: (216) 826-2839
FAX: (216) 891-2726
Year Established: 1937
Pub. Frequency: bi-m.
Page Size: standard
Subscrip. Rate: $25/yr. US; $35/yr. Canada; $70/yr. foreign
Circulation: 12,174
Circulation Type: controlled

---

**Materials Accepted/Included:** 01-Business news 02-By-line articles 03-Fashion news 04-Food news 05-Freelance copy 06-Letters to editor 07-Real estate news 08-Sports news 09-Travel news 10-Book rev. 11-Movie rev. 12-Music rev. 13-TV rev. 14-Theater rev. 15-Coming events 16-Obituaries 17-Question & answer 18-Social announcements 19-Artwork 20-Cartoons 21-Photos 22-TV listings 23-Audio rec. 24-Video rec. 25-Books 26-Films/film clips 27-Personnel news 28-Press releases 29-New product news/photos 30-Trade lit. 31-Contracts awarded 32-Display adv. 33-Classified adv.

4-81

**Owner(s):**
Advanstar Communications, Inc.
7500 Old Oak Blvd.
Cleveland, OH 44130
Telephone: (216) 826-2839
Ownership %: 100
**Management:**
Bill Dolan ..............................Publisher
Steve Forster ..........................Publisher
Ken Jordan ......................Sales Manager
**Editorial:**
Teresa Tarantino ...............Editor in Chief
Steve Forster .................Executive Editor
Vern Henry ...............................Editor
**Desc.:** Merchandising articles on candy,
snacks and tobacco covering all
retail/wholesale. Gives specific ideas
readers can adopt. Photos should show
closeup of interesting displays.
Departments include: New Products,
New Packaging, Display Aids.
**Readers:** Volume candy, snack and
tobacco buyers and merchandisers for
supermarkets, convenience stores, drug
stores, wholesale distributors, brokers,
vending and theater concessions.

22723
### CANDY WHOLESALER
1128 16th St., N.W.
Washington, DC 20036
Telephone: (202) 463-2124
FAX: (202) 467-0559
Year Established: 1948
Pub. Frequency: 10/yr.
Page Size: standard
Subscrip. Rate: $36/yr. US; $45/yr. foreign
Freelance Pay: $200-$700/article
Circulation: 12,000
Circulation Type: paid
**Owner(s):**
American Wholesale Marketers
Association, Inc.
1128 16th St., N.W.
Washington, DC 20036
Telephone: (202) 463-2124
Ownership %: 100
**Management:**
Joyce Grimley ...........................Publisher
Maryann Paniccia ...........Assistant Advertising
Manager
Jim Turner ...................Business Manager
**Editorial:**
Joyce Grimley .................Executive Editor
Jessica Johns ..................Associate Editor
Barbara Valakos ..........................Design
Michael Cohen ......................Production
Kelly Madden ......................Staff Writer
**Desc.:** Covers wide range of topics of
interest to the nation's candy, tobacco
and snack distributors including profile
stories, industry trends, how-to features,
legislative analysis, association news,
Washington notes, notes about
wholesalers, manufacturers and sales
people. Most items illustrated.
**Readers:** Wholesaler executives and other
volume buyers, sales staff and
executives of candy and tobacco
companies, plus brokers and other
manufacturers' representatives.

22718
### CANDY WORLD, ILLUSTRATED
13222 - B Admiral Ave.
Marina Del Rey, CA 90292
Telephone: (310) 397-4217
Mailing Address:
P.O. Box 1107
Santa Monica, CA 90406
Year Established: 1914
Pub. Frequency: 3/yr.
Page Size: tabloid
Subscrip. Rate: $18/yr.
Materials: 01,04,06,15,17,27,28,29,30,31,
32,33,34

Freelance Pay: $.01/wd.
Print Process: web
Circulation: 2,000
Circulation Type: controlled & paid
**Owner(s):**
Lott Publishing Co.
P.O. Box 1107
Santa Monica, CA 90406
Telephone: (310) 397-4217
Ownership %: 100
**Management:**
Dave Lott ..............................Publisher
Dave Lott ....................Advertising Manager
**Editorial:**
Dave Lott ..................................Editor
Laurie Lott ..................................Photo
**Desc.:** Coverage of trends, events and
opportunities for increased efficiency
and improvement of sales and
production in candy and tobacco.
Carries articles on merchandising,
display, management, advertising,
promotion, tight fact filled writing
essential. Departments include:
Management That Pays, Covering
Factory Methods, Manufacturers News
Briefs, Candy Camera, New Products,
Promotions, Premiums, Merchandising
That Works. Also covered are
conferences, meetings, committee
reports involving the candy trade. Areas
covered are the entire U.S.
**Readers:** Factory wholesalers, jobbers,
brokers and related trade personnel.

22721
### CONFECTIONER
17400 N. Dallas Pkwy., Ste. 121
Dallas, TX 75287
Telephone: (214) 250-3630
FAX: (214) 250-3733
Year Established: 1916
Pub. Frequency: bi-m.
Page Size: standard
Subscrip. Rate: $35/yr.
Freelance Pay: negotiable
Circulation: 16,500
Circulation Type: controlled
**Owner(s):**
American Publishing Corp.
Ownership %: 100
**Management:**
Lisbeth Echeandia ....................Publisher
**Desc.:** Articles cover wholesale and retail
confectionery and snack trade as well
as allied trades. Reports on outlook,
trends, promotions, company news,
marketing, merchandising, new products,
etc.
**Readers:** Buyers in all channels of
confectionery and snack wholesale and
retail distribution.

22722
### MANUFACTURING CONFECTIONER
175 Rock Rd.
Glen Rock, NJ 07452
Telephone: (201) 652-2655
FAX: (201) 652-2655
Year Established: 1921
Pub. Frequency: m.
Page Size: standard
Subscrip. Rate: $25/yr.
Circulation: 5,000
Circulation Type: paid
**Owner(s):**
Manufacturing Confectioner Publishing Co.
175 Rock Rd.
Glen Rock, NJ 07452
Telephone: (201) 652-2655
Ownership %: 100
**Management:**
Allen R. Allured .......................Publisher
**Editorial:**
Kate Allured ................................Editor

aspect of manufacturing; news of
manufacturers and suppliers; new
equipment and products. Uses staff-
written as well as contributed articles.
**Readers:** Candy manufacturers, chemists,
superintendents, marketing executives.

25060
### U.S. DISTRIBUTION JOURNAL
Seven Penn Plz.
New York, NY 10001
Telephone: (212) 594-4120
FAX: (212) 714-0491
Year Established: 1874
Pub. Frequency: m.
Page Size: tabloid
Subscrip. Rate: $48/yr.
Freelance Pay: $3/in.
Circulation: 18,000
Circulation Type: controlled
**Owner(s):**
T/SF Communications
2407 E. Skelly Dr.
Tulsa, OK 74105
Telephone: (918) 747-2600
Ownership %: 100
**Bureau(s):**
BMT Publications, Inc.
308 W. Erie St., Ste. 710
Chicago, IL 60610
Telephone: (312) 943-0684
Contact: Donna Schauer
**Management:**
Hedy Halpert .............................President
Daniel Petrocelli ...................Vice President
D.N. Petrocelli ..................General Manager
**Editorial:**
Kevin Francella .............................Editor
Kevin Francella ..................Associate Publisher
**Desc.:** Monthly marketing journal serving
every facet of tobacco, confectionery,
and grocery distribution industry.
Directed to management, marketing and
sales among tobacco, confectionary,
grocery, and candy manufactures.
**Readers:** Tobacco, confectionary, grocery
manufacturers and distributors.

## Group 044-Chemical Industries & Chemical Engineering

68765
### ACCOUNTS OF CHEMICAL RESEARCH
1155 16th St., N.W.
Washington, DC 20036
Telephone: (202) 872-4363
FAX: (202) 872-4615
Year Established: 1968
Pub. Frequency: m.
Subscrip. Rate: $28/yr.; $177/yr. non-
members
Circulation: 6,920
Circulation Type: paid
**Owner(s):**
American Chemical Society
1155 16th St., N.W.
Washington, DC 20036
Telephone: (202) 872-4363
Ownership %: 100
**Editorial:**
F.W. McLafferty ............................Editor
**Desc.:** Contains information on major
advances in basic research and
applications. Brief, critical articles cover
various areas of chemical research.

68767
### ADVANCES IN CHEMISTRY SERIES
1155 16th St., N.W.
Washington, DC 20032
Telephone: (202) 872-4363
FAX: (202) 872-4615

Year Established: 1950
Pub. Frequency: irreg.
Subscrip. Rate: varies
**Owner(s):**
American Chemical Society
1155 16th St., N.W.
Washington, DC 20032
Telephone: (202) 872-4363
Ownership %: 100

68771
### AEROSOL SCIENCE AND TECHNOLOGY
655 Ave. of the Americas
New York, NY 10010
Telephone: (212) 989-5800
FAX: (212) 633-3990
Year Established: 1982
Pub. Frequency: 8/yr.
Subscrip. Rate: $529/yr.
**Owner(s):**
Elsevier Science Publishing Co., Inc.
655 Ave. of the Americas
New York, NY 10010
Telephone: (212) 989-5800
Ownership %: 100
**Desc.:** Covers theoretical and experimental
investigations of aerosol and closely
related phenomena.

22454
### AICHE JOURNAL
345 E. 47 St.
New York, NY 10017
Telephone: (212) 705-7649
FAX: (212) 752-3294
Year Established: 1955
Pub. Frequency: m.
Page Size: standard
Subscrip. Rate: $395/yr. non-members;
$60/yr. members
Circulation: 5,000
Circulation Type: paid
**Owner(s):**
American Institute of Chemical Engineers
345 E. 47th St.
New York, NY 10017
Telephone: (212) 705-7649
Ownership %: 100
**Management:**
George Cominsky ............Advertising Manager
**Editorial:**
Matthew V. Tirrell ..........................Editor
Haeja L. Han ...................Managing Editor
Stephen R. Smith .............Publication Director
Haeja L. Han ...................Technical Editor
**Desc.:** As a broad-based journal in
chemical engineering, it provides
comprehensive coverage of the latest
research developments in traditional
chemical engineering as well as fast
expanding areas such as biochemical
engineering, materials, electrochemical
engineering, surface science, and
related fields.
**Readers:** Academics in chemical
engineering and related fields as well as
chemical engineers engaged in research
and development work worldwide.

22455
### ANALYTICAL CHEMISTRY
1155 16th St., N.W.
Washington, DC 20036
Telephone: (800) 333-9511
FAX: (202) 872-4574
Year Established: 1929
Pub. Frequency: s-m.
Page Size: 4 color photos/art
Subscrip. Rate: $78/yr. non-members;
$36/yr. members
Circulation: 27,000
Circulation Type: paid

---

**Materials Accepted/Included:** 01-Business news 02-By-line articles 03-Fashion news 04-Food news 05-Freelance copy 06-Letters to editor 07-Real estate news 08-Sports news 09-Travel news 10-Book rev. 11-Movie rev. 12-Music rev. 13-TV rev. 14-Theater rev. 15-Coming events 16-Obituaries 17-Question & answer 18-Social announcements 19-Artwork 20-Cartoons 21-Photos 22-TV listings 23-Audio rec. 24-Video rec. 25-Books 26-Films/film clips 27-Personnel news 28-Press releases 29-New product news/photos 30-Trade lit. 31-Contracts awarded 32-Display adv. 33-Classified adv.

**Owner(s):**
American Chemical Society
1155 16th St., N.W.
Washington, DC 20036
Telephone: (202) 872-4570
Ownership %: 100
**Management:**
Bruce Poorman .................Advertising Manager
David Schulbaum ..............Circulation Manager
**Editorial:**
Louise Voress ...................Senior Editor
R. W. Murray ....................Editor
Mary Warner ....................Managing Editor
Alan Kahan ......................Art Director
Bob Sargent .....................Art Editor
Peggy Corrigan .................Art Editor
Grace Lee ........................Associate Editor
Felicia Wach ....................Book Review Editor
Elizabeth Wood .................Chief Copy Editor
Robert Marks ....................Director
Leroy Corcoran .................Production Director
Robert Marks ....................Publication Director
**Desc.:** Scientific and technical articles relating to theoretical and applied research in the fields of qualitative and quantitive analysis and instrumentation. Departments include: The Analytical Approach, News, Short Courses, Reviews, Reports, Instrumentation, A/C Interface.
**Readers:** Chemists, scientists, researchers, engineers.

## ANALYTICAL LETTERS
70376
270 Madison Ave.
New York, NY 10016
Telephone: (212) 696-9000
FAX: (212) 685-4540
Year Established: 1967
Pub. Frequency: 15/yr.
Page Size: standard
Subscrip. Rate: $722.50/yr. individuals; $1445/yr. institutions
Print Process: offset
**Owner(s):**
Marcel Dekker, Inc.
270 Madison Ave.
New York, NY 10016
Telephone: (212) 696-9000
FAX: (212) 696-4540
Ownership %: 100
**Editorial:**
George G. Guilbault .........................Editor
**Desc.:** This rapid communication journal provides the fastest, most efficient transmittal of recent advances in all areas of analytical chemistry. Presenting short papers, original ideas, observations, and important analytical discoveries.
**Readers:** Analytical chemists, spectroscopists, electrochemists, environmental scientists, clinical analysts, biochemists.

## BIOTECHNIC & HISTOCHEMISTRY
22504
601 Elmwood Ave., #607, Univ. of Louisville
Louisville, KY 40292
Telephone: (502) 222-1347
Mailing Address:
428 E. Preston St.
Baltimore, MD 21202
Year Established: 1925
Pub. Frequency: bi-m.
Page Size: 4 color photos/art
Subscrip. Rate: $55/yr. individuals; $94/yr. institutions
Circulation: 2,000
Circulation Type: paid

**Owner(s):**
Biological Stain Commission
601 Elmwood Ave.
Rochester, NY 14642
Ownership %: 100
**Management:**
Don Pfarr ..........................Advertising Manager
**Editorial:**
G.S. Nettleton Ph.D. ...........................Editor
**Desc.:** A journal for microtechnic and histochemistry. Articles dealing with the nature and use of dyes, and other staining agents, histological technique and histochemistry and literature reviews.
**Readers:** Subscribers are histologists, pathologists, and histochemists, as well as laboratories, and include members of The Biological Stain Commission.

## CATALYST, THE
22456
Dept. of Chemistry, Univ. of PA.
Philadelphia, PA 19104-6323
Telephone: (215) 382-1589
Year Established: 1916
Pub. Frequency: m. (Sep.-June)
Page Size: 6" X 9"
Subscrip. Rate: $4.25/yr. US; $5.25/yr. foreign
Materials: 02,06,16,20,21,27,32,33
Print Process: offset
Circulation: 5,350
Circulation Type: controlled & paid
**Owner(s):**
Philadelphia Section, ACS
Dept. Chemistry, Univ. of Penn
Philadelphia, PA 19104-6323
Telephone: (215) 382-1589
Ownership %: 100
**Management:**
Victor Tortorelli ..................Advertising Manager
G. F. Cowperthwaite ............Business Manager
**Editorial:**
Deborah Kilmartin .....................................Editor
**Desc.:** Contains advertising and marketing, coming events, letters to the editor, and personnel news.
**Readers:** Chemists and chemical engineers.
**Deadline:** story-2 mos. prior to pub. date; news-2 mos. prior; photo-2 mos. prior; ads-7 wks. prior

## CHAPTER ONE
65476
345 E. 47th St.
New York, NY 10017
Telephone: (212) 705-7661
FAX: (212) 752-3294
Year Established: 1987
Pub. Frequency: q.
Page Size: standard
Subscrip. Rate: $12/yr.
Circulation: 10,000
Circulation Type: paid
**Owner(s):**
American Inst. of Chemical Engineers
345 E. Fourth
New York, NY 10009
Telephone: (212) 705-7661
Ownership %: 100
**Editorial:**
Lois DeLong ..............................Editor
Beth Meyer .............................Advertising
Joseph Roseti ..........................Art Director
**Desc.:** Geared to chemical engineering undergraduates. Covers new technologies within the profession, career choices and profiles of interesting and unusual people and programs on and off campus.
**Readers:** Undergraduate chemical engineering students at 145 schools in the United States, and in 50 countries overseas.

## CHEMICAL & ENGINEERING NEWS
22457
1155 16th St., N.W.
Washington, DC 20036
Telephone: (800) 333-9511
Year Established: 1923
Pub. Frequency: w.
Page Size: standard
Subscrip. Rate: $110/yr.
Circulation: 138,574
Circulation Type: paid
**Owner(s):**
American Chemical Society
1155 16th St., N.W.
Washington, DC 20036
Telephone: (202) 872-4600
Ownership %: 100
**Bureau(s):**
Northeast News Bureau
379 Thornall St.
Edison, NJ 08837
Telephone: (908) 906-8300
Contact: William J. Storck, Assistant Managing Editor

San Francisco Bureau
1408 Shroder St.
San Francisco , CA 94117
Telephone: (415) 665-4971
Contact: Rudy Baum, Bureau Chief

Chicago Bureau
176 W. Adams St., Rm. 1433
Chicago, IL 60603
Telephone: (312) 236-7325
Contact: Ward Worthy, Bureau Chief

Houston Bureau
P.O. Box 19646
Houston, TX 77224
Telephone: (713) 973-8111
Contact: Bruce Greek, Bureau Chief

West Coast News Bureau
261 Capricorn Ave.
Piedmont, CA 94611
Telephone: (510) 653-3630
Contact: Rudy Baum, Bureau Chief

Chicago News Bureau
P.O. Box 845
Arlington Hts , IL 60006
Telephone: (708) 255-3849
Contact: Joseph Haggin, Senior Editor
**Management:**
Benjamin Jones .................Advertising Manager
Arthur Poulos ...................Business Manager
**Editorial:**
Ward Worthy ......................Bureau Chief
Rudy Baum .........................Bureau Chief
Dermot O'Sullivan ...............Bureau Chief
David Hanson .....................Bureau Chief
Joseph Haggin ...................Senior Editor
Rebecca L. Rawls ...............Senior Editor
Doron Dagani .....................Senior Editor
Lois Ember ........................Senior Editor
Pamela Zurer .....................Senior Editor
Stephen Stinson ..................Senior Editor
Carl Anderson ....................Senior Editor
Michael Heylin ...................Editor
Ernest Carpenter ................Editor
W. Lepkowski .....................Editor
Dolores Miner ....................Editor
William Storck ........Assistant Managing Editor
David M. Kiefer .......Assistant Managing Editor
Donald J. Soisson ..............Assistant Managing Editor
James Krieger .......Assistant Managing Editor
Janice Long ..........Assistant Managing Editor
Pat Oates ................Administrative Assistant
Marc Reisch ..........................Assistant Editor
Patricia Layman ...................Associate Editor
Mairin Brennan ....................Associate Editor
Bette Hileman .....................Associate Editor
Richard Seltzer ....................Associate Editor
Stu Borman ........................Associate Editor
Anne Reisberg .....................Editorial Assistant
Arlene Goldberg - Gist .........Editorial Assistant

**Desc.:** News of chemical, science, technology, profession and chemical and process industries and the interaction of chemistry with government and society at large. Business and financial news, technical developments in chemistry and chemical engineering; new products and processes, literature, education.
**Readers:** Chemical and manufacturing executives, research chemists, independent laboratories, professors.

## CHEMICAL BULLETIN, THE
22458
7173 N. Austin
Chicago, IL 60714
Telephone: (708) 647-8405
FAX: (708) 647-8364
Year Established: 1914
Pub. Frequency: 10/yr.
Page Size: standard
Subscrip. Rate: $10/yr. US; $15/yr. foreign
Freelance Pay: volunteer
Circulation: 5,900
**Owner(s):**
American Chemical Society, Chicago Section
7173 N. Austin
Chicago, IL 60714
Telephone: (708) 647-8405
Ownership %: 100
**Management:**
Ronald J. Sykstus ............Advertising Manager
Ronald J. Sykstus .............Business Manager
Ronald J. Sykstus .............Office Manager
**Editorial:**
Fran Knien Kravitz .............................Editor
**Desc.:** Departments include: From the Editor; Letters; Chicago Section News.
**Readers:** Members of the American Chemical Society, supervisory, and miscellaneous pursuits, and area high school science teachers, area colleges.

## CHEMICAL ENGINEERING
22459
1221 Ave. of the Americas
New York, NY 10020
Telephone: (212) 512-2921
FAX: (212) 512-4762
Year Established: 1902
Pub. Frequency: m.
Page Size: 4 color photos/art
Subscrip. Rate: $8 newsstand; $35.50/yr.
Freelance Pay: varies
Circulation: 70,205
Circulation Type: paid
**Owner(s):**
McGraw-Hill, Inc.
1221 Avenue Of The Americas
New York, NY 10020
Telephone: (212) 512-2197
Ownership %: 100
**Management:**
Alan Morris .......................................Publisher
Len Vanderwende ................Business Manager
Maurice Persinni .................Circulation Manager
**Editorial:**
Richard J. Zanetti ......................Editor in Chief
Nicholas Chopey .......................Exec. Editor
Philip M. Kohn ........................Managing Editor
Maureen R. Gleason ................Art Director
Agnes Shanley .......................Associate Editor
Joan Schweikart ....................Book Review Editor
Ellen Coddy .........................Book Review Editor
Gulam Samdani ....................New Products Editor
Jay Chowdhury ....................News

**Materials Accepted/Included:** 01-Business news 02-By-line articles 03-Fashion news 04-Food news 05-Freelance copy 06-Letters to editor 07-Real estate news 08-Sports news 09-Travel news 10-Book rev. 11-Movie rev. 12-Music rev. 13-TV rev. 14-Theater rev. 15-Coming events 16-Obituaries 17-Question & answer 18-Social announcements 19-Artwork 20-Cartoons 21-Photos 22-TV listings 23-Audio rec. 24-Video rec. 25-Books 26-Films/film clips 27-Personnel news 28-Press releases 29-New product news/photos 30-Trade lit. 31-Contracts awarded 32-Display adv. 33-Classified adv.

4-83

**Desc.:** Edited to supply engineers and technical management people, the technical decision-makers of the Chemical Process Industries, with accurate, timely, useful information on the uses of chemicals, chemical engineering principles and techniques and related economic data for use in making technical judgements. Strives to disseminate useful, practical technical information, presents specialized information on costs and economics. The editors assess for their readers the technical and economic impact of world-wide developments affecting the profitable application of chemical technology.

**Readers:** The engineer and technical management people usually work within the broad, overlapping areas of manufacturing, engineering design and construction, research and development.

22460
## CHEMICAL ENGINEERING PROGRESS
345 E. 47th St.
New York, NY 10017
Telephone: (212) 705-7968
FAX: (212) 752-3294
Year Established: 1947
Pub. Frequency: m.
Page Size: standard
Subscrip. Rate: $75/yr.
Materials: 01,02,06,10,15,19,20,21,25,28, 29,30,32,33
Print Process: web offset
Circulation: 55,846
Circulation Type: paid
**Owner(s):**
American Institute of Chemical Engineers
345 E. 47th St.
New York, NY 10017
Telephone: (212) 705-7335
Ownership %: 100
**Management:**
Gary M. Rekstad ...........................Publisher
George E. Cominsky ........Advertising Manager
**Editorial:**
Mark Rosenzweig ......................Editor in Chief
John Howe ...........................Managing Editor
Sally Kilkenny ...........................Adv. Prod. Mng.
Claudia Caruana ......................Associate Editor
Alex G. Santaquilani ................Associate Editor
Elizabeth Meyer ...........Classified Adv. Mng.
Dale Brooks ........................Contributing Editor
Roy V. Hughson ...................Contributing Editor
Karen Simpson ......................Editorial Assistant
Cynthia Favian Mascone .........Technical Editor
**Desc.:** Technical discussions on current developments in the industry, including emphasis on chemical engineering economics and management, as well as technical articles on chemical engineering. news section carries news of the chemical process industries, business and R & D developments.
**Readers:** Chemical engineers in executive positions, research and development, equipment engineering & plant and process design.
**Deadline:** story-1st of mo. prior to pub. date

69609
## CHEMICAL ENGINEERING SCIENCE
660 White Plains Rd.
Tarrytown, NY 10591-5153
Telephone: (914) 524-9200
FAX: (914) 333-2444
Year Established: 1951
Pub. Frequency: 24/yr.
Circulation: 2,000
Circulation Type: paid

**Owner(s):**
Pergamon Press, Inc.
660 White Plains Rd.
Tarrytown, NY 10591-5153
Telephone: (914) 524-9200
Ownership %: 100
**Editorial:**
J. Bridgwater ...........................Editor
**Desc.:** Publishes papers on the fundamentals of chemical engineering, including applications of the basic sciences and mathematics.

22461
## CHEMICAL EQUIPMENT
301 Gibraltar Dr.
Morris Plains, NJ 07950
Telephone: (201) 292-5100
FAX: (201) 539-3476
Mailing Address:
 P.O. Box 650
 Morris Plains, NJ 07950-0650
Year Established: 1962
Pub. Frequency: m.
Page Size: tabloid
Subscrip. Rate: $30/yr.
Circulation: 112,000
Circulation Type: controlled
**Owner(s):**
Gordon Publications, Inc.
P.O. Box 650
Morris Plains, NJ 07950
Telephone: (201) 361-9060
Ownership %: 100
**Management:**
Bud Ramsey ...........................Publisher
Sue Avery ......................Circulation Manager
Maryann Ullrich ......Customer Service Manager
**Editorial:**
Geoff Bridgman ...........................Editor
Judy Petrone ...................Production Director
**Desc.:** Contains product and services information concerning machinery, equipment, instruments, and materials of construction used in the chemical processing industries. Interested in pertinent information.
**Readers:** Engineers, production and plant supervisors in the chemical processing industries.

22464
## CHEMICAL PROCESSING
301 E. Erie St.
Chicago, IL 60611
Telephone: (312) 644-2020
FAX: (312) 644-1131
Year Established: 1938
Pub. Frequency: 15/yr.
Page Size: standard
Subscrip. Rate: $30/yr.
Freelance Pay: $200-$500/article
**Owner(s):**
Putman Publishing Co.
301 E. Erie St.
Chicago, IL 60611
Telephone: (312) 644-2020
Ownership %: 100
**Management:**
Grace Cappelletti ...........................President
John Cappalletti .........................Vice President
John Cappalletti ...........................Publisher
**Editorial:**
Margaret Malochleb ...........................Editor
**Desc.:** Every issue gives broad coverage of development news of interest to operating management. Case histories, photo spreads and diagrams are used. Regular sections on processing equipment and processes, plant engineering and maintenance, corrosion control, instrumentation, pollution control, material handling, and chemical materials are carried.
**Readers:** Operating management in the chemical processing industry.

22467
## CHEMICAL TIMES & TRENDS
810 E. Tenth St.
Lawrence, KS 66044
Telephone: (913) 843-1234
FAX: (913) 843-1244
Mailing Address:
 P.O. Box 1897
 Lawrence, KS 66044-8897
Year Established: 1977
Pub. Frequency: q.
Page Size: standard
Subscrip. Rate: $8/issue US; $10/issue foreign; $27/yr. US; $39/yr. foreign
Circulation: 6,000
Circulation Type: controlled
**Owner(s):**
Chemical Specialties Manufacturers Association
1913 I, NW
Washington, DC 20036
Telephone: (202) 872-8110
Ownership %: 100
**Management:**
Ralph Engel ...........................Publisher
**Editorial:**
Connie Neuman ......................Executive Editor
**Desc.:** Devoted to news and issues concerning the nation's aerosol, antimicrobial, automotive chemicals, home and garden pesticides, detergents and cleaning compounds, and waxes, polishes and floor finishes industries.
**Readers:** Reaches all members of CSMA, as well as members of Congress, the White House staff, top administrators at federal, scientific and regulatory agencies, and key business leaders; also some universities and colleges.

69763
## CHEMICAL WEEK
888 7th Ave.
New York, NY 10106
Telephone: (212) 621-4900
FAX: (212) 621-4949
Year Established: 1914
Pub. Frequency: w.
Page Size: standard
Subscrip. Rate: $99/yr.
Materials: 01,06,15,28,29,32,33
Circulation: 46,440
Circulation Type: controlled & paid
**Owner(s):**
Chemical Week Associates
888 7th Ave.
New York, NY 10106
Telephone: (212) 621-4900
Ownership %: 100
**Bureau(s):**
Ron Bogley
Telephone: (202) 628-3728
FAX: (202) 628-3628

Gregory DL Morris
Telephone: (713) 977-9271
FAX: (713) 953-7074
**Editorial:**
David Hunter ...........................Editor

22469
## CHEMIST, THE
7315 Wisconsin Ave., Ste. 502E
Bethesda, MD 20814
Telephone: (301) 652-2447
FAX: (301) 657-3549
Year Established: 1923
Pub. Frequency: 11/yr.
Page Size: standard
Subscrip. Rate: $25/yr.
Materials: 04,06,19,21,27,28,29,32,33
**Owner(s):**
American Institute of Chemists, Inc.
7315 Wisconsin Ave.
Bethesda, MD 20814
Telephone: (301) 652-2447
Ownership %: 100

**Management:**
Roger P. Maickel ...........................President
Macey Elliott ...................Executive Director
Macey Elliott ...................Advertising Manager
**Editorial:**
Macey Elliott ...........................Editor
**Desc.:** Concerned with the professional, economic and ethical status of chemists and chemical engineers. Interested in articles dealing with these as professions, not with chemistry per se. Reviews new books, lists new bulletins and booklets.
**Readers:** Executives and chemists of qualified background.

22470
## CHEMTECH
1155 16th St., N.W.
Washington, DC 20036
Telephone: (800) 333-9511
Year Established: 1971
Pub. Frequency: m.
Page Size: standard
Subscrip. Rate: $39/yr. members; $79/yr. non-members
Circulation: 9,000
Circulation Type: paid
**Owner(s):**
American Chemical Society
1155 15th St., N.W.
Washington, DC 20005
Telephone: (202) 872-4600
Ownership %: 100
**Editorial:**
Marcia R. Dresner ...........................Senior Editor
Dr. B. J. Luberoff ...........................Editor
Dr. Dorit L. Noether ...........Associate Editor
**Desc.:** Multidisciplinary material of interest to the practicing technologist who is associated with chemistry in all its dimensions. Features are also on engineering, law, government, sociology, medicine, economics, marketing and management. Departments include: View from the Top (high corporate and government officials), Out in the Plant (short practical material), Last Word (relevant humor), Editorials, Heart Cut (short digest type pieces from the current literature).
**Readers:** Industrial and governmental practitioners, managers.

22726
## COSMETICS & TOILETRIES
362 S. Schmale Rd.
Carol Stream, IL 60188-2787
Telephone: (708) 653-2155
FAX: (708) 653-2192
Year Established: 1906
Pub. Frequency: m.
Page Size: standard
Subscrip. Rate: $72/yr. US; $100/yr. Canada; $142/yr. elsewhere
Freelance Pay: varies
Circulation: 3,300
Circulation Type: paid
**Owner(s):**
Allured Publishing Corp.
P.O. Box 318
Wheaton, IL 60189
Telephone: (708) 653-2155
Ownership %: 100
**Management:**
Stanley E. Allured ...........................President
Nancy Allured ...........................Publisher
Maria Tardi ...................Advertising Manager
Susan Rzepka ...................Production Manager
**Editorial:**
Sandra L. Herzog ...........................Editor
Carole Stephanides ...........................Advertising
Betty Lou Allured ...........Circulation Editor
Susan N.C. Price ...................Technical Editor

Materials Accepted/Included: 01-Business news 02-By-line articles 03-Fashion news 04-Food news 05-Freelance copy 06-Letters to editor 07-Real estate news 08-Sports news 09-Travel news 10-Book rev. 11-Movie rev. 12-Music rev. 13-TV rev. 14-Theater rev. 15-Coming events 16-Obituaries 17-Question & answer 18-Social announcements 19-Artwork 20-Cartoons 21-Photos 22-TV listings 23-Audio rec. 24-Video rec. 25-Books 26-Films/film clips 27-Personnel news 28-Press releases 29-New product news/photos 30-Trade lit. 31-Contracts awarded 32-Display adv. 33-Classified adv.

**Desc.:** Covers research, product development, production, management in the cosmetic and toiletries fields. Contributed technical articles and discuss developments in the industry. Also contains how-to articles for manufacturers. Departments include: New Products and Developments, Industry and Association News, Personnel News, Regulatory Status.
**Readers:** Manufacturers of toiletries and cosmetics only. No retailers.

## CRYOGAS INTERNATIONAL
66188

5 Militia Dr.
Lexington, MA 02173
Telephone: (617) 862-0624
FAX: (617) 863-9411
Year Established: 1962
Pub. Frequency: 11/yr.
Page Size: standard
Subscrip. Rate: $150/yr. US; $200/yr. foreign
Materials: 01,02,06,32,33
Freelance Pay: varies
Print Process: offset
Circulation: 470
Circulation Type: paid
**Owner(s):**
J.R. Campbell & Associates, Inc.
5 Militia Dr.
Lexington, MA 02173
Telephone: (617) 862-0624
FAX: (617) 863-9411
Ownership %: 100
**Desc.:** Reports on news & technology relating to the industrial gases and cryogenics industries. Includes interviews with key industry executives. Feature sections: Update, R&D, Equipment & Services, Gas Technology & Gas Applications, US & International Patent Watch, Markets, Citations, Events, Data. Publishes articles written by experts in their fields.
**Readers:** General management, engineers, marketers and sales persons, etc.
**Deadline:** story-10th of mo. prior to pub. date; news-10th of mo. prior; photo-10th of mo. prior; ads-10th of mo. prior

## DEL-CHEM BULLETIN
22472

P.O. Box 4071
Wilmington, DE 19807
Telephone: (302) 994-1931
FAX: (302) 995-2895
Year Established: 1944
Pub. Frequency: 9/yr.
Page Size: standard
Subscrip. Rate: $3/yr.
Circulation: 2,900
Circulation Type: controlled
**Owner(s):**
American Chemical Society-Delaware Section
P.O. Box 4071
Wilmington, DE 19807
Ownership %: 100
**Management:**
Dr. Helmut Engelmann ......Circulation Manager
Dr. Eugene Hamilton .........Circulation Manager
**Editorial:**
Joseph Morello ...........................................Editor
Dr. Dominic Chan ....................Assistant Editor
Debra Banville ................Environmental Editor
Herman Skolnik ...........................Feature Editor
**Desc.:** Includes non-technical general articles, meeting announcements, news of services and courses. Departments: Meeting Announcements, Opinions, People, Local News (chemical), Environment, Education, Editorials.

**Readers:** Professional chemists and chemical engineers, industrial management, sales people, etc.

## DRYING TECHNOLOGY
70404

270 Madison Ave.
New York, NY 10016
Telephone: (212) 696-9000
FAX: (212) 685-4540
Year Established: 1982
Pub. Frequency: 8/yr.
Page Size: standard
Subscrip. Rate: $337.50/yr. individuals; $675/yr. institutions
Print Process: offset
**Owner(s):**
Marcel Dekker, Inc.
270 Madison Ave.
New York, NY 10016
Telephone: (212) 696-9000
FAX: (212) 685-4540
Ownership %: 100
**Editorial:**
Arun S. Mujumdar ................................Editor
Larry R. Genskow ....................Associate Editor
**Desc.:** This journal explores, in depth, the science, technology, and engineering of drying, dewatering, and related topics. Articles cover transport phenomena in porous media, heat and mass transfer in single or miltiphase systems, evaporation, membrane separation, solid/liquid separation, powder technology, fluidization, agglomeration, gas-solid systems, solids mixing, handling, transport and more.
**Readers:** Mechanic, chemical, and agricultural engineers, food scientists and technologists in the fileds of agriculture, biology, physics, pharmaceticals, chemistry, waste management, mineralogy and food processing. Mechanical, chemical, and agricultural engineers, food scientists and technologists in the fileds of agriculture, biology, physics, pharmaceticals, chemistry, waste management, mineralogy and food processing.

## FILTER PRESS, THE
22476

The Coca-Cola Co.
P.O. Drawer 1734
Atlanta, GA 30301-1734
Telephone: (404) 676-2895
FAX: (404) 515-3900
Year Established: 1946
Pub. Frequency: 8/yr.
Page Size: pocket
Subscrip. Rate: membership
Materials: 32,33
Circulation: 1,600
Circulation Type: controlled & free
**Owner(s):**
Georgia Section of the American Chemical Society
Atlanta University, SRI
Atlanta, GA 30309
Telephone: (404) 523-5148
Ownership %: 100
**Management:**
Dr. C.K. Kohlmiller .............Advertising Manager
**Editorial:**
Dr. Cindy Brittain ....................Graphics Design
**Readers:** Georgia section of the American Chemical Society.
**Deadline:** ads-3 wks. prior to pub. date

## I & EC RESEARCH
22480

1155 16th St., N.W.
Washington, DC 20036
Telephone: (202) 872-4542
FAX: (202) 872-6325
Year Established: 1963

Pub. Frequency: m.
Page Size: standard
Subscrip. Rate: $64/yr. members; $567/yr. non members
Circulation: 4,000
Circulation Type: paid
**Owner(s):**
American Chemical Society
1155 16th St., N.W.
Washington, DC 20036
Telephone: (202) 872-4542
Ownership %: 100
**Management:**
T. N. J. Koerwer ..............Advertising Manager
**Editorial:**
Jerome Seiner ...............................Senior Editor
Donald R. Paul ....................................Editor
J. D. Seader .............................Associate Editor
John L. Anderson .................Associate Editor
Milorad P. Dudukovic .............Associate Editor
**Desc.:** Technical articles related to industrial and engineering chemistry. Primary research only.
**Readers:** Industrial and engineering chemists.

## INDICATOR, THE
22483

43 Reservoir Pl.
Cedar Grove, NJ 07009-1620
Telephone: (201) 239-1975
Year Established: 1919
Pub. Frequency: m. (exc. Jul. & Aug.)
Page Size: pocket
Subscrip. Rate: $20/yr.
Circulation: 13,000
Circulation Type: paid
**Owner(s):**
New York-American Chemical Society
St. John's University
Chemistry Dept.
Jamaica, NY 11439
Telephone: (516) 883-7510
FAX: (516) 883-4003
Ownership %: 50

North Jersey-American Chemical Society
34 Maple St.
Summit, NJ 07901
Telephone: (908) 522-1122
Ownership %: 50
**Management:**
Herman Burwasser ...........Advertising Manager
**Editorial:**
Lilian H. Sello ........................Managing Editor
**Desc.:** Relating to chemists.
**Readers:** Science teachers (university, college, high school), chemists, chemical engineers.

## INDUSTRIAL & ENGINEERING CHEMISTRY RESEARCH
65722

1155 16th St. N.W.
Washington, DC 20036
Telephone: (202) 872-4545
Year Established: 1987
Pub. Frequency: m.
Subscrip. Rate: $567/yr.
Circulation: 4,437
Circulation Type: paid
**Owner(s):**
American Chemical Society
1155 16th St., N.W.
Washington, DC 20036
Telephone: (800) 333-9511
Ownership %: 100
**Editorial:**
Donald Paul ....................................Editor
**Desc.:** Focuses on fundamental and theoretical aspects of chemical engineering, recent work on design methods and their application to processes and process equipment. Includes new technology applicable to products involving chemical engineering.

## INFOCHEM
68834

150 Great Neck Rd.
Great Neck, NY 11021
Telephone: (516) 829-9210
Pub. Frequency: bi-m.
Circulation: 26,149 English ed.; 25,399 Spanish ed.
Circulation Type: paid
**Owner(s):**
Keller International Publishing Corp.
150 Great Neck Rd.
Great Neck, NY 11021
Telephone: (516) 829-9210
Ownership %: 100

## INTERNATIONAL JOURNAL OF CHEMICAL KINETICS
65631

605 Third Ave.
New York, NY 10158
Telephone: (212) 850-6000
Year Established: 1969
Pub. Frequency: m.
Page Size: standard
Subscrip. Rate: $730/yr.
Circulation: 700
Circulation Type: paid
**Owner(s):**
John Wiley & Sons, Inc.
Ownership %: 100
**Editorial:**
David Mark Golden ...................................Editor

## INTERNATIONAL JOURNAL OF QUANTUM CHEMISTRY
65633

605 Third Ave.
New York, NY 10158-0012
Telephone: (212) 850-6000
FAX: (212) 850-6088
Year Established: 1967
Pub. Frequency: bi-w.
Page Size: standard
Subscrip. Rate: $24.65/yr.
Circulation: 800
Circulation Type: paid
**Owner(s):**
John Wiley & Sons, Inc.
605 Third Ave.
New York, NY 10158-0012
Telephone: (212) 850-6000
Ownership %: 100
**Editorial:**
Per Olov Lowdin ......................................Editor
**Desc.:** Provides information on quantum mechanics: fundamental concepts; mathematical structure; applications to atoms, molecules, crystals and molecular biology.

## JOURNAL OF AOAC INTERNATIONAL
22986

2200 Wilson Blvd., Ste. 400
Arlington, VA 22201
Telephone: (703) 522-3032
FAX: (703) 522-5468
Year Established: 1915
Pub. Frequency: bi-m.
Page Size: standard
Subscrip. Rate: $160/yr. institutions & non-members; $190/yr. foreign
Freelance Pay: $15-$20/hr.
Circulation: 4,200
Circulation Type: paid
**Owner(s):**
AOAC International
2200 Wilson Blvd., Ste. 400
Arlington, VA 22201
Telephone: (703) 522-3032
Ownership %: 100
**Management:**
Marilyn Blakely ..............Advertising Manager
**Editorial:**
Claire Franklin ....................................Editor
Robert Rathbone ....................Managing Editor

**Materials Accepted/Included:** 01-Business news 02-By-line articles 03-Fashion news 04-Food news 05-Freelance copy 06-Letters to editor 07-Real estate news 08-Sports news 09-Travel news 10-Book rev. 11-Movie rev. 12-Music rev. 13-TV rev. 14-Theater rev. 15-Coming events 16-Obituaries 17-Question & answer 18-Social announcements 19-Artwork 20-Cartoons 21-Photos 22-TV listings 23-Audio rec. 24-Video rec. 25-Books 26-Films/film clips 27-Personnel news 28-Press releases 29-New product news/photos 30-Trade lit. 31-Contracts awarded 32-Display adv. 33-Classified adv.

4-85

Betty Johnson .........................Associate Editor
**Desc.:** The journal of AOAC International publishes fully referred, contributed papers in the field of chemical and biological analysis: documenting original research on new techniques and applications, collaborative studies, authentic data of composition, studies leading to method development, meeting symposia, newly adopted AOAC approved methods and invited reviews.
**Readers:** Chemists and microbiologists in federal, state, provincial & municipal governments; food, agricultural, and drug industries; universities and colleges.

### JOURNAL OF CHEMICAL & ENGINEERING DATA
22488

1155 16th St., N.W.
Washington, DC 20036
Telephone: (800) 333-9511
FAX: (202) 872-4615
Year Established: 1956
Pub. Frequency: q.
Page Size: standard
Subscrip. Rate: $309/yr. non-members; $36/yr. members
Circulation: 1,591
Circulation Type: paid
**Owner(s):**
American Chemical Society
1155 16th St., N.W.
Washington, DC 20036
Telephone: (202) 872-4600
Ownership %: 100
**Management:**
Bruce Poorman .................Advertising Manager
**Editorial:**
Kenneth Marsh .......................Associate Editor
**Desc.:** Technical articles describing chemical and engineers studies - principally data compilations. Primary research only.
**Readers:** Chemists & chemical engineers.

### JOURNAL OF CHEMICAL EDUCATION
22489

Univ. of Texas
Austin, TX 78712
Telephone: (800) 333-9511
FAX: (203) 459-9939
Year Established: 1923
Pub. Frequency: m.
Page Size: standard
Subscrip. Rate: $30/yr. individuals; $60/yr. institutions
Circulation: 20,000
Circulation Type: paid
**Owner(s):**
Div. Of Chemical Education Of American Chem. Soc.
1155 16th St., N.W.
Washington, DC 20036
Telephone: (800) 333-9511
Ownership %: 100
**Management:**
Ed Black .............................Advertising Manager
**Editorial:**
J. J. Lagowski .................................Editor
Angie Valentino ................New Products Editor
**Desc.:** A technical journal edited for chemists in education and industry. Reports technical papers. Reviews for the non-specialist. Covers new books, new equipment, chemistry teaching methodology.
**Readers:** Professors, teachers; industrial chemists.

### JOURNAL OF CHEMICAL VAPOR DEPOSITION
69727

851 New Holland Ave., Box 3535
Lancaster, PA 17604
Telephone: (717) 291-5609
FAX: (717) 295-4538
Year Established: 1992
Pub. Frequency: q.
Page Size: 6 x 9
Subscrip. Rate: $195/yr.; $380/2 yrs.; $565/3 yrs.
Circulation: 100
Circulation Type: paid
**Owner(s):**
Technomic Publishing Co., Inc.
851 New Holland Ave.
Box 3535
Lancaster, PA 17604
Telephone: (717) 291-5609
Ownership %: 100
**Editorial:**
Shojiro Komatsu .............................Editor
**Desc.:** Provides new developments in the science and engineering of CVD and related technologies. Emphasis on experimental, theoretical and applied physics and chemistry of vapor deposition.

### JOURNAL OF CHROMATOGRAPHIC SCIENCE
22490

7800 Merrimac Ave.
Niles, IL 60714
Telephone: (708) 965-0566
FAX: (708) 965-7639
Mailing Address:
    P.O. Box 48312
    Niles, IL 60714
Year Established: 1963
Pub. Frequency: m.
Page Size: standard
Subscrip. Rate: $190/yr.
Materials: 06,25,29,32
Freelance Pay: $100 for cover photographs only
Circulation: 4,500
Circulation Type: paid
**Owner(s):**
Preston Publications, Seaton T. Preston
7800 Merrimac Ave.
Chicago, IL 60714
Telephone: (708) 965-0566
**Management:**
Seaton T. Preston ...........................Publisher
S. Tinsley Preston, III ........Advertising Manager
**Editorial:**
Bert M. Gordon .................................Editor
John Q. Walker .................................Editor
Jennifer Decker .......................Managing Editor
Seaton T. Preston ...................Technical Editor
**Desc.:** A scientific journal published for those scientists, chemists, educators and researchers engaged in the use of any of the analytical chromatographic techniques (gas, liquid, thin layer, gel permeation, etc.), to advance the science of chromatography by bringing together and disseminating technical and theoretical information concerning the chromatographic science. Areas served include: government, military, industrial, medical, university and independent research institutions as well as hospitals and clinics and manufacturers engaged in the manufacture and analysis of chemicals, biologicals, pharmaceuticals, food products, cosmetics, petroleum. Also, information on new instrument developments, new products, and new literature, question-and-answer columns are included. Letters to the Editor and Chromatography Problem Solving and Troubleshooting.

### JOURNAL OF COATED FABRICS
22491

851 New Holland Ave.
Lancaster, PA 17601
Telephone: (717) 291-5609
FAX: (717) 295-4538
Mailing Address:
    P.O. Box 3535
    Lancaster, PA 17601
Year Established: 1971
Pub. Frequency: q.
Page Size: pg.: 6 1/2 x 9 1/2; col.: 4 5/8
Subscrip. Rate: $205/yr.; $400/2 yrs.; $595/3 yrs.
Circulation: 425
Circulation Type: paid
**Owner(s):**
Technomic Publishing Co., Inc.
Telephone: (717) 291-5609
Ownership %: 100
**Bureau(s):**
Technomic Publishing AG
Missionsstrasse 44
CH-4055 Basel Switzerland
Contact: Frank Versaci, Director
**Management:**
Melvyn Kohudic ...........................Publisher
**Editorial:**
William C. Smith .............................Editor
Kier M. Finlayson .............................Editor
**Desc.:** The latest, scientifically based findings and ideas related to the production and use of flexible coated and laminated materials. Areas explored include: polymer chemistry, rheology, fluid dynamics, mechanical engineering, textile technology, applications technology, surface chemistry, adhesion, fibrous reinforcement, mechanics of complex multi-phase systems, materials properties characterization. Results presented in practical terms.
**Readers:** Technical.

### JOURNAL OF COMPUTATIONAL CHEMISTRY
65636

605 Third Ave.
New York, NY 10158
Telephone: (212) 850-6289
Pub. Frequency: 8/yr.
Page Size: standard
Subscrip. Rate: $596/yr.
Circulation: 800
Circulation Type: paid
**Owner(s):**
John Wiley & Sons, Inc.
605 Third Ave.
New York, NY 10158
Telephone: (212) 850-6000
Ownership %: 100
**Editorial:**
Norman L. Allinger ...........................Editor

### JOURNAL OF ELASTOMERS & PLASTICS
23444

851 New Holland Ave., Box 3535
Lancaster, PA 17601
Telephone: (717) 291-5609
FAX: (717) 295-4538
Year Established: 1968
Pub. Frequency: q.
Page Size: pg.: 6 1/2 x 9 1/2; col.: 4 5/8
Subscrip. Rate: $205/yr.; $400/2 yrs.; $595/3 yrs.
Circulation: 400
Circulation Type: paid
**Owner(s):**
Technomic Publishing Co., Inc.
Telephone: (717) 291-5609
Ownership %: 100

**Bureau(s):**
Technomic Publishing AG
Missionsstrasse 44
CH-4055 Basel Switzerland
Contact: Frank Versaci, Director
**Editorial:**
Heshmat Aglanc .............................Editor
**Desc.:** The development, production, application and marketing of synthetic elastomers are presented in this journal. These elastomeric systems are covered: polysulfide rubber, acrylic, flurocarbon, urethane, silicone and butyl.

### JOURNAL OF LIQUID CHROMATOGRAPHY
70377

270 Madison Ave.
New York, NY 10016
Year Established: 1977
Pub. Frequency: 20/yr.
Page Size: standard
Subscrip. Rate: $675/yr. individuals; $1350/yr. institutions
Print Process: offset
**Owner(s):**
Marcel Dekker, Inc.
270 Madison Ave.
New York, NY 10016
Telephone: (212) 696-9000
FAX: (212) 696-4540
Ownership %: 100
**Editorial:**
Jack Cazes .................................Editor
**Desc.:** This journal contains a selection of critical, analytical, and preparative papers involving the application of liquid chromatography to the solution of problems in all areas of science and technology, as well as papers that deal specifically with liquid chromatography as a science within itself. Special topics on liquid chromatography, including an annual directory of LC manufacturers, suppliers and services.
**Readers:** Analytical chemists, biochemists, polymer chemists.

### JOURNAL OF ORGANIC CHEMISTRY, THE
22493

1155 16th St., N.W.
Washington, DC 20036
Telephone: (202) 872-4600
FAX: (202) 872-4615
Pub. Frequency: bi-w.
Page Size: standard
Subscrip. Rate: $785/yr. non-members; $75/yr. members
Circulation: 9,900
Circulation Type: paid
**Owner(s):**
American Chemical Society
1155 16th St., N.W.
Washington, DC 20036
Telephone: (202) 872-4600
Ownership %: 100
**Management:**
Bruce Poorman .................Advertising Manager
**Editorial:**
Clayton H. Heathcock .............................Editor
**Desc.:** Offers the organic chemist bi-weekly critical accounts of original work in all branches of organic chemistry, and interpretative reviews of existing data which present new viewpoints. Areas emphasized include the many facets of organic reaction, natural products, studies of mechanism, theoretical organic chemistry, and the various aspects of spectroscopy related to organic chemistry.
**Readers:** Inorganic, organic, and physical chemists.

---

**Materials Accepted/Included:** 01-Business news 02-By-line articles 03-Fashion news 04-Food news 05-Freelance copy 06-Letters to editor 07-Real estate news 08-Sports news 09-Travel news 10-Book rev. 11-Movie rev. 12-Music rev. 13-TV rev. 14-Theater rev. 15-Coming events 16-Obituaries 17-Question & answer 18-Social announcements 19-Artwork 20-Cartoons 21-Photos 22-TV listings 23-Audio rec. 24-Video rec. 25-Books 26-Films/film clips 27-Personnel news 28-Press releases 29-New product news/photos 30-Trade lit. 31-Contracts awarded 32-Display adv. 33-Classified adv.

4-86

## JOURNAL OF PHYSICAL CHEMISTRY, THE

22494

1155 16th St., N.W.
Washington, DC 20036
Telephone: (202) 872-4600
FAX: (202) 872-4615
Year Established: 1896
Pub. Frequency: w.
Page Size: standard
Subscrip. Rate: $98/yr. members;
$1295/yr. non-members
Circulation: 3,800
Circulation Type: paid
**Owner(s):**
American Chemical Society
1155 16th St., N.W.
Washington, DC 20036
Telephone: (202) 872-4600
FAX: (202) 872-4363
Ownership %: 100
**Management:**
Bruce Poorman ...............Advertising Manager
**Editorial:**
Dr. Mostafa El-Sayed ................................Editor
**Desc.:** Reports both experimental and theoretical research dealing with fundamental aspects of physical chemistry. Topics include those of general interest to physical chemists, especially work involving new concepts, techniques, and interpretations. Containing articles and communications, in addition to the proceeding of selected symposia, JPC offers a comprehensive and authoritative source of important findings in this field.
**Readers:** Physical chemists & chemical physicists.

## JOURNAL OF THE AMERICAN CHEMICAL SOCIETY

22485

1155 16th St., N.W.
Washington, DC 20036
Telephone: (202) 872-4600
Year Established: 1879
Pub. Frequency: bi-w.
Page Size: standard
Subscrip. Rate: $1055/yr. non-members;
$96/yr. members
Circulation: 13,000
Circulation Type: paid
**Owner(s):**
American Chemical Society
1155 Sixteenth St., N.W.
Washington, DC 20036
Telephone: (202) 872-4600
Ownership %: 100
**Management:**
Bruce Poorman ...............Advertising Manager
**Editorial:**
Dr. Allen Bard ...............................................Editor
Paula L. Commodore .........Marketing Assistant
**Desc.:** Contains material of the widest possible interest to research workers and students in all fields of chemistry. All articles have been carefully reviewed by referees prominent in their respective fields. Communications are handled on an accelerated basis to provide readers with earliest possible reports of significant results. Publishes more than 10,000 pages of new chemistry a year, documenting advances in all areas of chemical research. Articles meet the Society's highest standards for quality and relevance. Reviews books and software of special interest to professional chemists.
**Readers:** Inorganic, organic, physical chemists.

## JOURNAL OF THE AMERICAN LEATHER CHEMISTS ASSOCIATION

22486

University of Cincinnati
Cincinnati, OH 45221-0014
Telephone: (513) 556-1197
Mailing Address:
P.O. Box 210014
Cincinnati, OH 45221-0014
Year Established: 1906
Pub. Frequency: m.
Page Size: 6 3/4 x 9 3/4
Subscrip. Rate: $90/yr.
Materials: 06,34
Print Process: offset
Circulation: 1,250
Circulation Type: paid
**Owner(s):**
American Leather Chemists Association
University of Cincinnati
P.O. Box 210014
Cincinnati, OH 45221-0014
Telephone: (513) 556-1197
Ownership %: 100
**Management:**
Russell A. Launder ...........................President
**Editorial:**
Stephen Feairheller ................................Editor
Robert E. Merritt ..................Associate Editor
Alex E. McDonell ..........Secretary & Treasurer
Stephen Feairheller ................Technical Editor
**Desc.:** Technical papers covering research, progress in the chemistry of leather. Carries association news, news of industry wide activities in relation to research.
**Readers:** Chemists, research workers, leather technologists.

## JOURNAL OF THE AMERICAN OIL CHEMISTS' SOCIETY

24210

1608 Broadmoor Dr.
Champaign, IL 61821
Telephone: (217) 359-2344
FAX: (217) 351-8091
Mailing Address:
P.O. Box 3489
Champaign, IL 61826-0489
Year Established: 1909
Pub. Frequency: m.
Page Size: standard
Subscrip. Rate: $185/yr.
Circulation: 4,000
Circulation Type: paid
**Owner(s):**
American Oil Chemists' Society
P.O. Box 3489
Champaign, IL 61826
Telephone: (217) 359-2344
Ownership %: 100
**Management:**
James Lyon ......................................Publisher
**Editorial:**
L.H. Princen ...........................................Editor
Melissa Blankenship ...........Production Director
Mary Lane .........................Publication Director
**Desc.:** Contributed scientific papers and abstracts dealing with oils, fats, surfactants, detergents and other lipids.
**Readers:** Technical managers at manufacturers and processors of foods, surfactants and detergents, also consultants, educators, government, chemists, chemical engineers.

## JOURNAL OF THE ELECTROCHEMICAL SOCIETY

22492

10 South Main St.
Pennington, NJ 08534
Telephone: (609) 737-1902
FAX: (609) 737-2743
Year Established: 1948
Pub. Frequency: m.
Page Size: pg.: 6 1/2 x 10 1/2; col.: 3 1/4 in.
Subscrip. Rate: $400/yr.
Circulation: 8,200
Circulation Type: paid
**Owner(s):**
The Electrochemical Society, Inc.
10 South Main St.
Pennington, NJ 08534
Telephone: (609) 737-1902
FAX: (609) 737-2743
Ownership %: 100
**Editorial:**
Barry Miller ...........................................Editor
Sarah A. Kilfoyle ..........Publications Manager
**Desc.:** A research journal covering the interests of chemistry, physics, electronics, biology, medicine and engineering pertaining to electrochemistry. Publishes contributed papers, notes on original current basic research. Edited in three sections: electrochemical science and technology, solid-state science and technology, reviews and news.
**Readers:** Written for research scientists.

## JOURNAL OF THE SOCIETY OF COSMETIC CHEMISTS

22495

120 Wall St.
Ste. 2400
New York, NY 10005
Telephone: (212) 874-0600
FAX: (212) 668-1504
Year Established: 1947
Pub. Frequency: bi-m.
Page Size: standard
Subscrip. Rate: free with membership;
$110/yr. non-members
Circulation: 4,400
Circulation Type: controlled
**Owner(s):**
Society of Cosmetic Chemists
Telephone: (212) 874-0600
Ownership %: 100
**Management:**
Daniel Weinheimer ............Production Manager
**Editorial:**
Dr. Randall Wickett ................................Editor
**Desc.:** JSCC is a scientific publication publishing papers concerned with cosmetics or one of the sciences underlying cosmetics. Major areas of interest are: New raw materials, safety, efficacy & performance of cosmetics; physical and chemical characteristics of cosmetics, new processing procedures, dermatological, pharmacological and microbiological aspects of cosmetics.
**Readers:** Cosmetic scientists, libraries, universities.

## LIPIDS

22497

1608 Broadmoor Dr.
Champaign, IL 61821
Telephone: (217) 359-2344
FAX: (217) 351-8091
Mailing Address:
P.O. Box 3489
Champaign, IL 61826
Year Established: 1966
Pub. Frequency: m.
Page Size: standard
Subscrip. Rate: $195/yr.
Circulation: 1,800
Circulation Type: paid
**Owner(s):**
American Oil Chemists' Society
P.O. Box 3489
Champaign, IL 61826
Telephone: (217) 359-2344
Ownership %: 100
**Editorial:**
Wolfgang J. Baumann ........................Editor
**Desc.:** Basic research in fats, oils, other lipids and lipid metabolism. No news, features or such. This is strictly a scientific journal.
**Readers:** Scientists and researchers.

## MINNESOTA CHEMIST

22498

2004 Randolph Ave.
Saint Paul, MN 55105
Telephone: (612) 690-6620
Pub. Frequency: 8/yr.
Subscrip. Rate: $5/yr.
**Owner(s):**
American Chemical Society - MN. Section
Ownership %: 100
**Editorial:**
Patricia Fish .........................Managing Editor
John Howe Scott ........................Miscellaneous
**Desc.:** Feature stories and articles of interest to Stories covering activities of the ACS, the MinnesEditorial comment. Book reviews. Also chairman's comment, puzzles.

## NAVAL STORES REVIEW

22499

129 S. Cortez St.
New Orleans, LA 70119
Telephone: (504) 482-3914
FAX: (504) 482-4205
Year Established: 1890
Pub. Frequency: bi-m.
Page Size: standard
Subscrip. Rate: $58/yr.
Circulation: 400
Circulation Type: paid
**Owner(s):**
Kriedt Enterprises, Ltd.
129 S. Cortez St.
New Orleans, LA 70119
Telephone: (504) 482-3914
Ownership %: 100
**Management:**
Romney Kriedt ....................................Publisher
Cyndi Gai ...........................................Manager
**Editorial:**
Don Neighbors .......................................Editor
Romney Kriedt ..............................Advertising
Marilyn Everett .........................Art Department
**Desc.:** Discusses markets, operations, patents, new uses of products. Departments cover Washington, New York Market, International Market.
**Readers:** Naval stores and pine chemical industry, pulp and paper, perfumes, aromas, fragrances.

## PERFUMER & FLAVORIST

22727

362 Schmale Rd.
Carol Stream, IL 60188
Telephone: (708) 653-2155
FAX: (708) 653-2192
Mailing Address:
P.O. Box 318
Wheaton, IL 60189
Year Established: 1906
Pub. Frequency: bi-m.
Page Size: standard
Subscrip. Rate: $105/yr.
Freelance Pay: varies
Circulation: 2,000
Circulation Type: paid
**Owner(s):**
Allured Publishing Corp.
P.O. Box 318
Wheaton, IL 60189
Telephone: (708) 653-2155
Ownership %: 100
**Management:**
Stanley E. Allured .............................Publisher
**Editorial:**
Marian Raney ........................................Editor

**Materials Accepted/Included:** 01-Business news 02-By-line articles 03-Fashion news 04-Food news 05-Freelance copy 06-Letters to editor 07-Real estate news 08-Sports news 09-Travel news 10-Book rev. 11-Movie rev. 12-Music rev. 13-TV rev. 14-Theater rev. 15-Coming events 16-Obituaries 17-Question & answer 18-Social announcements 19-Artwork 20-Cartoons 21-Photos 22-TV listings 23-Audio rec. 24-Video rec. 25-Books 26-Films/film clips 27-Personnel news 28-Press releases 29-New product news/photos 30-Trade lit. 31-Contracts awarded 32-Display adv. 33-Classified adv.

4-87

**Desc.:** Covers research, product development, production, and management in flavor and fragrance fields (published bi-monthly). Technical articles are contributed. News articles and stories discuss developments in the industry and associations. Departments include: News, Personnel, Book Reviews, Patents, Technical Literature.
**Readers:** Manufacturers and compounders of fragrances and flavors.

58722

### PESTICIDE & TOXIC CHEMICAL NEWS
1101 Pennsylvania Ave., S.E.
Washington, DC 20003
Telephone: (202) 544-1980
FAX: (202) 546-3890
Year Established: 1972
Pub. Frequency: w.
Page Size: standard
Subscrip. Rate: $715/yr.
**Owner(s):**
Food Chemical News, Inc.
1101 Pennsylvania Ave., S.E.
Washington, DC 20003
Telephone: (202) 544-1980
Ownership %: 100
**Management:**
Ronald Grandon .....................Manager
**Editorial:**
Cathy Cooper .........................Editor
**Desc.:** Contains information about regulatory and legislative activities governing pesticides, toxic chemicals, and hazardous wastes.

58744

### PESTICIDE CHEMICAL NEW GUIDE
1101 Pennsylvania Ave., S.E.
Washington, DC 20003
Telephone: (202) 544-1980
FAX: (202) 546-3890
Mailing Address:
   4831 Cross Keys Dr.
   Baton Rouge, LA 70817
Year Established: 1973
Pub. Frequency: m.
Page Size: standard
Subscrip. Rate: $395/yr.; $630/yr. new svc.
Circulation: 700
Circulation Type: paid
**Owner(s):**
CRC Press, Inc.
1101 Pennsylvania Ave., S.E.
Washington, DC 20003
Telephone: (202) 544-1980
Ownership %: 100
**Bureau(s):**
Duggan & Associates, Inc.
Rte. 1, Box 3070
Montross, VA 22520
Telephone: (804) 493-8525
**Editorial:**
Patrick D. Duggan .............Chief Editor
**Readers:** Persons and firms impacted by US Government pesticide regulations

61688

### PEST MANAGEMENT
8100 Oak St.
Dunn Loring, VA 22027
Telephone: (703) 573-8330
Year Established: 1981
Pub. Frequency: 11/yr.
Page Size: standard
Subscrip. Rate: $35/yr. non-member
Freelance Pay: $.10/wd.
Circulation: 5,500
Circulation Type: controlled

**Owner(s):**
National Pest Control Association
8100 Oak St.
Dunn Loring, VA 22027
Telephone: (703) 573-8330
Ownership %: 100
**Management:**
Harvey S. Gold .....................Publisher
**Editorial:**
Kathleen Bova .........................Editor
Eileen Griffiths .....................Advertising
Eileen Griffiths ...............Assistant Editor
**Desc.:** The official voice of the National Pest Control Association. The purpose of this magazine is to improve communications within the structural pest control industry and with regulatory officials and to assist pest control operators in the safe, efficient and profitable operation of their businesses. We bring the latest techniques in pest elimination and control; marketing, sales, management, and financial features; news of government legislation and regulations affecting the industry; and the latest news of NPCA, state associations, meetings and sessions, people and events, products and services.
**Readers:** Small business men and owners of pest control companies.

64953

### POLYMER BLENDS, ALLOYS & IPN'S-ABSTRACTS
851 New Holland Ave., Box 3535
Lancaster, PA 17601
Telephone: (717) 291-5609
FAX: (717) 295-4538
Year Established: 1987
Pub. Frequency: m.
Page Size: standard
Subscrip. Rate: $340/yr.; $670/2 yrs.; $1,000/3 yrs.
Circulation: 160
Circulation Type: paid
**Owner(s):**
Melvyn A. Kohudic
851 New Holland Ave., Box 3535
Lancaster, PA 17601
Telephone: (717) 291-5609
Ownership %: 100
**Editorial:**
John W. DeGroot, Jr. ...................Editor
Jean Rhoads .............Marketing Assistant
**Desc.:** Digest of current literature and patents on the rapidly growing fields of polymer technology and product development.

22462

### PROCESSING
301 E. Erie St.
Chicago, IL 60611
Telephone: (312) 644-2020
FAX: (312) 644-1131
Year Established: 1987
Pub. Frequency: m.
Page Size: tabloid
Subscrip. Rate: $30/yr.
Circulation: 110,000
Circulation Type: paid
**Owner(s):**
Putman Publishing Co.
301 E. Erie St.
Chicago, IL 60611
Telephone: (312) 644-2020
Ownership %: 100
**Management:**
Grace Cappelletti ...................President
**Editorial:**
Sandra Herzog ...........................Editor
**Desc.:** A digest of new product developments for the chemical process industries.

**Readers:** Operating Management in The Chemical and Process Related Industries.

22478

### ROCHESTER SECTION CHEMUNICATIONS
75 Oakridge Dr.
Rochester, NY 14617-2507
Telephone: (716) 338-3995
Year Established: 1949
Pub. Frequency: bi-m.
Page Size: standard
Subscrip. Rate: $5/yr.
Materials: 06,15,19,20,21,27,28,32
Print Process: web
Circulation: 1,600
Circulation Type: controlled
**Owner(s):**
Rochester Section of The American Chemical Society
P.O. Box 15571
Rochester, NY 14615-0571
Telephone: (716) 338-3995
Ownership %: 100
**Editorial:**
Susan L. Mattes .........................Editor
**Desc.:** Editorial matter strictly local; articles, meeting notices, personals, etc. Editorial matter is written by a group of assistant editors whose assignments vary from issue to issue.
**Readers:** All members of the Rochester Section, Inc., of the American Chemical Society. Majority employed as research development scientists in companies such as Eastman Kodak, Xerox Corporation and Pennwalt Corp. Also: faculty at Rochester Institute of Technology, University of Rochester, and several SUNY Colleges and private colleges. Also: heads of high school science departments.

22502

### SCALACS
American Chemical Soc.
14934 S. Figueroa
Gardena, CA 90248
Telephone: (310) 327-1216
Year Established: 1945
Pub. Frequency: 7/yr.
Page Size: standard
Subscrip. Rate: free to southern Calif.
Circulation: 3,200
Circulation Type: free
**Owner(s):**
S. California American Chemical Soc.
14934 S. Figueroa St.
Gardina, CA 90248
Telephone: (310) 327-1216
Ownership %: 100
**Editorial:**
Michael Tanouye .........................Editor
Paula Sandoval .........................Editor
Myriam Easton .........Bus. and Fin News Editor
**Desc.:** Anything of interest to chemists or chemistry.
**Readers:** Chemists & chemical engineers.
**Deadline:** story-1st of mo.; news-1st of mo.; photo-1st of mo.; ads-1st of mo.

70388

### SEPARATION SCIENCE & TECHNOLOGY
270 Madison Ave.
New York, NY 10016
Telephone: (212) 696-9000
FAX: (212) 685-4540
Year Established: 1965
Pub. Frequency: 18/yr.
Page Size: standard
Subscrip. Rate: $725/yr. individuals; $1,450/yr. institutions
Print Process: offset

**Owner(s):**
Marcel Dekker, Inc.
270 Madison Ave.
New York, NY 10016
Telephone: (212) 696-9000
FAX: (212) 685-4540
Ownership %: 100
**Editorial:**
J. Calvin Giddings .....................Editor
Jimmy T. Bell .................Associate Editor
J.A. Watson ...................Associate Editor
**Desc.:** This publication reviews the newest concepts and techniques for dealing with problems encountered by professionals and, offers authoritative and critical articles, notes and reviews on all the varied aspects of separation, including separation theory, ultrafiltration, chromatography, electrophoresis, foam fractionation, and ion-exchange.
**Readers:** Analytical chemists, chemical engineers, biochemists, physical chemists, environmental scientists, mechanical engineers, biologists, polymer chemists, colloid scientists.

24928

### SOAP, COSMETICS, CHEMICAL SPECIALTIES
445 Broad Hollow Rd., Ste. 21
Melville, NY 11747
Telephone: (516) 845-2700
Year Established: 1925
Pub. Frequency: m.
Page Size: standard
Subscrip. Rate: $60/yr.
Freelance Pay: negotiable
Circulation: 17,000
Circulation Type: controlled
**Owner(s):**
PTN Publishing Co.
445 Broadhollow Rd., Ste. 21
Melville, NY 11747
Telephone: (516) 845-2700
Ownership %: 100
**Management:**
Stanley Sills .........................Publisher
John Quirk .................Advertising Manager
**Editorial:**
Anita Shaw .............................Editor
Thomas S. Kapinos .............Editorial Director
Suzanne Christiansen ...........Associate Editor
**Desc.:** Covers the use of various chemicals in the manufacturing detergents, chemical specialties, cosmetics, toiletries. Also reports on meetings, seminars, overview of market trends. Departments include: Packaging News, Bulletins & Equipment, Formulations, News (company appointments, acquisitions, expansions, coming events), Production & Engineering (new production techniques, research), What's New (new package-product pictures),Marketing Briefs, Laws and Regulations, International Roundup.
**Readers:** Primarily manufacturers & marketers of soaps, detergents, cosmetics, toiletries, fragrances and household chemical specialties.

70396

### SPECTROSCOPY LETTERS
270 Madison Ave.
New York, NY 10016
Telephone: (212) 696-9000
FAX: (212) 685-4540
Year Established: 1967
Pub. Frequency: 10/yr.
Page Size: standard
Subscrip. Rate: $387.50/yr. individuals; $775/yr. institutions
Print Process: offset

**Materials Accepted/Included:** 01-Business news 02-By-line articles 03-Fashion news 04-Food news 05-Freelance copy 06-Letters to editor 07-Real estate news 08-Sports news 09-Travel news 10-Book rev. 11-Movie rev. 12-Music rev. 13-TV rev. 14-Theater rev. 15-Coming events 16-Obituaries 17-Question & answer 18-Social announcements 19-Artwork 20-Cartoons 21-Photos 22-TV listings 23-Audio rec. 24-Video rec. 25-Books 26-Films/film clips 27-Personnel news 28-Press releases 29-New product news/photos 30-Trade lit. 31-Contracts awarded 32-Display adv. 33-Classified adv.

**Owner(s):**
Marcel Dekker, Inc.
270 Madison Ave.
New York, NY 10016
Telephone: (212) 696-9000
FAX: (212) 685-4540
Ownership %: 100
**Editorial:**
James W. Robinson ......................Editor
**Desc.:** This journal provides vital coverage
of fundamental developments in
spectroscopy. Offering communications
of orginal, experimental, and theoretical
work, this international journal reports
such methods as NMR, ESR,
microwave, IR, Raman, and UV
spectroscopy. In addition, atomic
emission and absorption, X-ray
spectroscopy, mass spectrometry,
lasers, electron microscopy, molecular
fluorescence, and molecular
phosphorescence are discussed.
**Readers:** Spectroscopists, analytical and
physical chemists, biochemists,
physicists.

### SPRAY TECHNOLOGY & MARKETING
23406
389 Passaic Ave.
Fairfield, NJ 07004
Telephone: (201) 227-5151
FAX: (201) 227-9219
Year Established: 1956
Pub. Frequency: m.
Page Size: standard
Subscrip. Rate: $30/yr.; $40/yr. Canada;
$100/yr. other countries
Circulation: 7,000
Circulation Type: controlled
**Owner(s):**
Industry Publications Inc.
389 Passaic Ave.
West Caldwell, NJ 07006
Telephone: (201) 227-5151
Ownership %: 100
**Management:**
Margaret Hundley ...................Publisher
Cynthia Hundley ..............Advertising Manager
**Editorial:**
Michael SanGiovanni ......................Editor
Shirleen Dorman .....................Associate Editor
Lawrence Patrick ....................Columnist
Marie Ferraro ...............Production Coordinator
Montfort A. Johnsen ...............Technical Editor
**Desc.:** Covers aerosol and pump
packaging of cosmetics and other
personal products, chemical specialties,
paints and coatings, pharmaceuticals,
insecticides, automotive and industrial
products and foods/their manufacturing,
formulation, filling, marketing, distribution
and packaging. Covers every aspect
of the spray and pressure packaging
industry. Only U.S. magazine devoted
completely and exclusively to the
aerosol, spray and pressure packaging
industry. Departments include: News,
Personnel, Letters, New Products,
Calendar, Equipment, New Technology,
Pharmaceuticals, Patents, Washington,
Business Outlook, Spray Patterns.
**Readers:** Companies with aerosol filling
equipment;suppliers of raw materials,
components, containers; executives,
marketers, technical people, chemists.

### SYNTHESIS & REACTIVITY IN INORGANIC & METAL-ORGANIC CHEMISTRY
70403
270 Madison Ave.
New York, NY 10016
Telephone: (212) 696-9000
FAX: (212) 685-4540
Year Established: 1970

Pub. Frequency: 10/yr.
Page Size: standard
Subscrip. Rate: $347.50/yr. individuals;
$695/yr. institutions
**Owner(s):**
Marcel Dekker, Inc.
270 Madison Ave.
New York, NY 10016
Telephone: (212) 696-9000
FAX: (212) 685-4540
Ownership %: 100
**Editorial:**
Kur Moedritzer ......................Editor
**Desc.:** Provides rapid dissemination of
important, original research papers as
well as critical, in-depth reviews of
reactions, techniques, and synthetic
methods. Dealing with compounds of
main-group elements and transition
elements, this journal delivers
penetrating, up-to-the-minute coverage
that includes: the synthesis,
characterization, and reactivity of new
compounds; new or improved synthetic
procedures, physical-chemical data, and
reactions for known compounds; and
detailed descriptions of experimental
work.
**Readers:** Inorganic and metal-organic
chemists.

### SYNTHETIC COMMUNICATIONS
70394
270 Madison Ave.
New York, NY 10016
Telephone: (212) 696-9000
FAX: (212) 685-4540
Year Established: 1970
Pub. Frequency: 22/yr.
Page Size: standard
Subscrip. Rate: $525/yr. individuals;
$1050/yr. institutions
Print Process: offset
**Owner(s):**
Marcel Dekker, Inc.
270 Madison Ave.
New York, NY 10016
Telephone: (212) 696-9000
FAX: (212) 685-4540
Ownership %: 100
**Editorial:**
Michael Kolb ......................Editor
James A. Marshall ...............Associate Editor
**Desc.:** This journal presents timely and
extensive coverage on a broad range of
topics, ranging from the synthesis of
natural products and related
intermediates to the synthesis and
utilization of new reagents for functional
group interconversions. Features in-
depth reporting on new experimental
methods and reagents pertaining to
synthetic organic chemistry.
**Readers:** Organic chemists.

### TODAY'S CHEMIST AT WORK
68780
1155 16th St., N.W.
Washington, DC 20036
Telephone: (800) 227-5558
FAX: (202) 872-4615
Year Established: 1988
Pub. Frequency: 9/yr.
Circulation: 100,000
Circulation Type: paid
**Owner(s):**
American Chemical Society
1155 16th St., N.W.
Washington, DC 20036
Telephone: (800) 227-5558
Ownership %: 100
**Editorial:**
Patrick P. McCurdy ......................Editor

### URETHANE ABSTRACTS
21690
851 New Holland Ave.
Lancaster, PA 17601
Telephone: (717) 291-5609
FAX: (717) 295-4538
Mailing Address:
P.O. Box 3535
Lancaster, PA 17601
Year Established: 1971
Pub. Frequency: m.
Page Size: standard
Subscrip. Rate: $195/yr.; $380/2 yrs.;
$565/3 yrs.
Circulation: 200
Circulation Type: paid
**Owner(s):**
Technomic Publishing Co., Inc.
Telephone: (717) 291-5609
Ownership %: 100
**Bureau(s):**
Technomic Publishing AG
Missionsstrasse 44
CH-4055
Basel Switzerland
**Editorial:**
John W. DeGroot, Jr. ......................Editor
**Desc.:** Monthly abstracting service which
provides proceedings, and other reports
on urethane abstracts.

### URETHANE PLASTICS & PRODUCTS
22506
851 New Holland Ave.
Lancaster, PA 17601
Telephone: (717) 291-5609
FAX: (717) 295-4538
Mailing Address:
P.O. Box 3535
Lancaster, PA 17601
Year Established: 1970
Pub. Frequency: m.
Page Size: standard
Subscrip. Rate: $185/yr.; $360/2 yrs.;
$535/3 yrs.
Circulation: 200
Circulation Type: paid
**Owner(s):**
Technomic Publishing Co., Inc.
Telephone: (717) 291-5609
Ownership %: 100
**Bureau(s):**
Technomic Publishing AG
Missionsstrasse 44
CH-4055
Basel Switzerland
Contact: Frank Versaci, Director
**Management:**
Melvyn A. Kohudic ......................Publisher
**Editorial:**
Jerry Pool ......................Editor
**Desc.:** Reports new developments in the
marketing, technology, and applications
of urethanes. All urethanes are covered:
adhesives, coatings, sealants, primers,
elastomers, gums, foams, specialty
urethanes, and water-based urethanes.
Applications in every industry in which
urethanes are or can be used are
explored, including automotive, textile,
packaging, aircraft, construction and
building, and others.

## Group 046-China, Glassware & Ceramics

### AMERICAN CERAMIC SOCIETY BULLETIN
22508
735 Ceramic Pl.
Westerville, OH 43081-8720
Telephone: (614) 890-4700
FAX: (614) 899-6109
Year Established: 1922
Pub. Frequency: m.

Page Size: standard
Subscrip. Rate: free to members; $50/yr.
non-members
Materials: 01,06,15,25,27,28,29,30,31,32,
33, consultants business card ads
Freelance Pay: negotiable
Circulation: 15,600
Circulation Type: free & paid
**Owner(s):**
American Ceramic Society, Inc.
735 Ceramic Pl.
Westerville, OH 43081-8720
Ownership %: 100
**Management:**
W. Paul Holbrook ......................Publisher
Steve Hecker ...............Production Manager
**Editorial:**
Jon Hines ......................Senior Editor
Patricia A. Janeway ......................Editor
Annette Delagrange ...............Advertising Sales
Manager
Linda Lakemacher ......................Director
Cleopatra Eddie ...........Production Coordinator
Diana Contich ...............Publication Designer
**Desc.:** Covers industry and society news,
carries articles covering all aspects of
ceramic technology, including
manufacturing, marketing, engineering
and research and development.
**Readers:** Plant and production
management, research educators.
**Deadline:** news-10th of mo. prior pub.
date; photo-10th of mo. prior; ads-10th
of mo. prior

### AMERICAN GLASS REVIEW
22509
1033 Clifton Ave.
Clifton, NJ 07013
Telephone: (201) 779-1600
FAX: (201) 779-3242
Mailing Address:
P.O. Box 2147
Clifton, NJ 07015
Year Established: 1882
Pub. Frequency: m. & extra Mar. issue
Page Size: standard
Subscrip. Rate: $4/copy; $25/yr. US;
$35/yr. foreign
Freelance Pay: varies
Circulation: 2,000
Circulation Type: paid
**Owner(s):**
Doctorow Communications, Inc.
1003 Clifton Ave.
Clifton, NJ 07013
Telephone: (201) 779-1600
Ownership %: 100
**Management:**
Jeffrey I. Doctorow ......................President
Jeffrey I. Doctorow ......................Publisher
Jon Doctorow ...............Advertising Manager
**Editorial:**
Susan Grisham ......................Editor
**Desc.:** The authoritative monthly magazine
of the American glass industry. Covers
the manufacture, distribution and
processing of flat glass, glass
containers, glass tableware, fiber glass,
industrial glass, scientific and optical
glass, etc. Departments include:
Features on Glass Manufacturing, Plant
Stories, Glass Application, New
Developments, Industry News, Business,
People, World Glass, Events, Products,
Literature.
**Readers:** Goes to every glass
manufacturing plant in U.S. as well as
factories in Canada and throughout the
world. Readership includes top
executives of these companies.

**Materials Accepted/Included:** 01-Business news 02-By-line articles 03-Fashion news 04-Food news 05-Freelance copy 06-Letters to editor 07-Real estate news 08-Sports news 09-Travel news
10-Book rev. 11-Movie rev. 12-Music rev. 13-TV rev. 14-Theater rev. 15-Coming events 16-Obituaries 17-Question & answer 18-Social announcements 19-Artwork 20-Cartoons 21-Photos 22-TV listings
23-Audio rec. 24-Video rec. 25-Books 26-Films/film clips 27-Personnel news 28-Press releases 29-New product news/photos 30-Trade lit. 31-Contracts awarded 32-Display adv. 33-Classified adv.

4-89

## CERAMIC ABSTRACTS
22510

735 Ceramic Pl.
Westerville, OH 43081
Telephone: (614) 890-4700
FAX: (614) 794-5812
Year Established: 1922
Pub. Frequency: bi-m.
Page Size: standard
Subscrip. Rate: $138/yr.
Freelance Pay: $.60/abstract;
$.04/published wd.
Print Process: offset
Circulation: 2,000
Circulation Type: paid
**Owner(s):**
American Ceramic Society
735 Ceramic Pl.
Westerville, OH 43081
Telephone: (614) 890-4700
FAX: (614) 794-5812
Ownership %: 100
**Management:**
W. Paul Holbrook ...............................Publisher
**Editorial:**
Janette L. Boor ......................Editorial Assistant
Christine Schnitzer ...............Product Manager
Linda S. Lakemacher .......Publication Director
John B. Wachtman ......................Society Editor
Patricia A. Polko ......................Society Editor
**Desc.:** Publishes abstracts of ceramic and
related literature published throughout
the world, including patents and book
reviews. No news items carried.
**Readers:** Persons interested in all fields of
ceramics.

## CERAMIC ENGINEERING & SCIENCE PROCEEDINGS
49911

735 Ceramic Pl.
Westerville, OH 43081
Telephone: (614) 890-4700
FAX: (614) 899-6109
Year Established: 1980
Pub. Frequency: bi-m.
Page Size: standard
Subscrip. Rate: $80/yr.
Freelance Pay: offset lithography
Circulation: 1,500
Circulation Type: paid
**Owner(s):**
American Ceramic Society, Inc.
735 Ceramic Pl.
Westerville, OH 43081
Telephone: (614) 890-4700
Ownership %: 100
**Management:**
W. Paul Holbrook ...............................Publisher
**Editorial:**
John B. Wachtman Jr. ...........................Editor
Lori A. Kozey ...............Production Coordinator
Linda Lakemacher ...............Publication Director
**Desc.:** Contains manuscripts presented at
American Ceramic Society-sponsored (or
other professional society-sponsored)
meetings; no unsolicited manuscripts
accepted.
**Readers:** Scientists, managers, sales
personnel, academicians and other
professionals involved in technical
ceramics.

## CERAMIC INDUSTRY
22512

5900 Harper Rd., Ste. 109
Cleveland, OH 44139
Telephone: (216) 498-9214
FAX: (216) 498-9121
Year Established: 1923
Pub. Frequency: m.
Page Size: standard
Subscrip. Rate: $8/issue; $55/yr.
Circulation: 11,700
Circulation Type: paid

**Owner(s):**
Business News Publishing Co.
755 W. Big Beaver Rd.
Ste. 1000
Troy, MI 48084
Telephone: (313) 362-3700
Ownership %: 100
**Management:**
Collien M. Rodriguez ...........................Publisher
Carol Lawrence ...............Advertising Manager
Vance R. Frost ...................Circulation Manager
**Editorial:**
Tobey L. Benedict ...................Associate Editor
**Desc.:** Covers production and marketing in
all branches of the ceramic
industry/porcelain enameling, glass
manufacturing, composites, and whitewares, including electronic ceramics.
Porcelain enameling encompasses such
industries as manufacture of signs,
refrigerators and other major appliances,
holloware, architectural panels, metal
tile, etc. Glass covers the production of
glass in its many forms, i.e., containers,
flat scientific ware, oven ware, technical,
stemware, tubing, fibers, etc.
The newest addition being TV tubes.
Pottery or whitewares covers
dinnerware, both hotel and domestic,
chinaware, sanitaryware and
electrical porcelain. Electronic ceramics
includes all newer applications of
ceramics in electronics,
high temperature work, cutting tools, etc.
Composites cover glass, ceramic and
single crystal fibers, and whiskers in
organic and metal matricies. Covers
company news, appointments, books,
association meetings, people in the
trade news.
**Readers:** Management, executives,
production managers, marketing
executives, engineers and technicians.

## CERAMICS
59139

30595 Eight Mile Rd.
Livonia, MI 48152-1798
Telephone: (313) 477-6650
FAX: (313) 477-6795
Year Established: 1964
Pub. Frequency: m.
Page Size: standard
Subscrip. Rate: $19.60/yr. US; $26.60/yr.
foreign
Freelance Pay: $25 to hobbyists
Circulation: 30,000
Circulation Type: paid
**Owner(s):**
Scott Advertising & Publishing Co.
30595 Eight Mile Rd.
Livonia, MI 48152-1798
Telephone: (313) 477-6650
Ownership %: 100
**Management:**
Bill Thompson ...........................Vice President
Robert H. Keessen ...........................Publisher
Jeanette Foxe ...................................Manager
**Editorial:**
Barbara Campbell ...................Managing Editor
Peggy Austen ...................Associate Editor
William A. Latocki ...................Creative Services
Director
Carmen Qurizzian ...................Editorial Assistant
Tom Grimes ...................Marketing Director
**Desc.:** Decorating ideas and techniques
that span the the entire range of
ceramics, from traditional to trendy,
profiles of interesting people. Extensive
new product section, artist tips and hints
terminology, patterns.
**Readers:** Nationwide show listing,
hobbyist, manufacturers, and
professionals.

## CHINA GLASS & TABLEWARE
22514

1033 Clifton Ave.
Clifton, NJ 07013
Telephone: (201) 779-1600
FAX: (201) 779-3242
Mailing Address:
P.O. Box 2147
Clifton, NJ 07015
Year Established: 1892
Pub. Frequency: m.: twice in Sept.
Page Size: standard
Subscrip. Rate: $20/yr.
Freelance Pay: varies
Circulation: 4,200
Circulation Type: controlled & paid
**Owner(s):**
Doctorow Communications, Inc.
1115 Clifton Avenue
Clifton, NJ 07013
Telephone: (201) 779-1600
Ownership %: 100
**Management:**
Jeffrey I. Doctorow ...........................President
Jeffreu I. Doctorow ...........................Publisher
Jon Doctorow ...................Advertising Manager
**Editorial:**
Amy Stavis ...........................................Editor
**Desc.:** Uses illustrated articles concerning
all phases of dinnerware, glassware and
tableware specialty shop and
department store operation:
merchandising, promotions, display,
sales training, modernization, table
settings, style trends, etc. Covers
trade news, personnel notes, company
news.
**Readers:** Retailers, wholesalers,
manufacturers, importers.

## GLASS FACTORY DIRECTORY
22519

P.O. Box 2267
Hempstead, NY 11551-2267
Telephone: (516) 481-2188
Year Established: 1912
Pub. Frequency: a.
Page Size: pocket
Subscrip. Rate: $18/yr.
Materials: 01,15,27,32
Freelance Pay: varies
Print Process: offset
Circulation: 1,500
Circulation Type: paid
**Owner(s):**
LJV, Inc.
P.O. Box 2267
Hempstead, NY 11551
Telephone: (516) 481-2188
Ownership %: 100
**Editorial:**
Liz Scott ...........................Managing Editor
Anne C. Gaudio ...........................Miscellaneous
**Desc.:** Annual glass factory directory lists
350 glass plants in US, Canada and
Mexico.
**Readers:** Glass industry personnel,
engineering firms, glass industry
suppliers, plant managers, customers.

## JOURNAL OF THE AMERICAN CERAMIC SOCIETY
22518

735 Ceramic Pl.
Westerville, OH 43081
Telephone: (614) 890-4700
FAX: (614) 899-6109
Year Established: 1899
Pub. Frequency: m.
Page Size: standard
Subscrip. Rate: $75/yr. members; $175/yr.
non- members
Circulation: 5,500
Circulation Type: paid

**Owner(s):**
American Ceramic Society, Inc.
735 Ceramic Pl.
Westerville, OH 43081
Telephone: (614) 890-4700
Ownership %: 100
**Management:**
W. Paul Holbrook ...............................Publisher
**Editorial:**
John B. Wachtman, Jr. ...........................Editor
Russell W. Jordan ...................Managing Editor
John C. Webb ...................Associate Editor
Linda S. Lakemacher .........Publication Director
**Desc.:** Publishes only original authentic
research papers. No news items or
advertising are carried.
**Readers:** Persons interested in all fields of
ceramics.

## TILE NEWS
69401

499 Park Ave.
New York, NY 10022
Telephone: (212) 980-1500
FAX: (212) 758-1050
Year Established: 1980
Pub. Frequency: q.
Subscrip. Rate: free
Circulation: 22,000
**Owner(s):**
Italian Trade Commission
499 Park Ave.
New York, NY 10022
Telephone: (212) 758-1050
**Editorial:**
Christine Abbate ...................Marketing Director
**Desc.:** Presents new uses, ideas and
designs for the Italian tile industry in the
U.S.

## Group 048-Chiropractic

## AMERICAN CHIROPRACTOR, THE
56277

5005 Riviera Ct.
Fort Wayne, IN 46825
Telephone: (219) 484-9600
Year Established: 1979
Pub. Frequency: m.
Page Size: standard
Subscrip. Rate: $56/yr.
Circulation: 35,000
Circulation Type: controlled
**Owner(s):**
Busch Publishing
**Management:**
R. E. Busch D.C. ...........................Publisher
Elaine Fortmeyer ...............Advertising Manager
**Editorial:**
Chuck Stairs ...........................Executive Editor
Lana K. Stewart ...................................Editor
**Desc.:** Technical & research articles,
current interviews and news releases,
financial and management features, and
the latest professional findings on
nutrition technique, adjunctives, sport
chiropractic, politics, education, and
diagnostics.
**Readers:** Actively practicing chiropractic
physicians, colleges.

## CALIFORNIA CHIROPRACTIC ASSOCIATION JOURNAL
69209

7801 Folsom Blvd., Ste. 375
Sacramento, CA 95826
Telephone: (916) 387-0177
FAX: (916) 325-4855
Year Established: 1929
Pub. Frequency: m.
Page Size: standard
Subscrip. Rate: $50/yr.
Materials: 06,32,33
Print Process: web
Circulation: 16,100
Circulation Type: controlled & free

**Materials Accepted/Included:** 01-Business news 02-By-line articles 03-Fashion news 04-Food news 05-Freelance copy 06-Letters to editor 07-Real estate news 08-Sports news 09-Travel news 10-Book rev. 11-Movie rev. 12-Music rev. 13-TV rev. 14-Theater rev. 15-Coming events 16-Obituaries 17-Question & answer 18-Social announcements 19-Artwork 20-Cartoons 21-Photos 22-TV listings 23-Audio rec. 24-Video rec. 25-Books 26-Films/film clips 27-Personnel news 28-Press releases 29-New product news/photos 30-Trade lit. 31-Contracts awarded 32-Display adv. 33-Classified adv.

4-90

**Owner(s):**
California Chiropractic Association
7801 Folsom Blvd., Ste. 375
Sacramento, CA 95826
Telephone: (916) 387-0177
Ownership %: 100
**Editorial:**
Leslie Youngstrom ..........Publications Manager
**Desc.:** Promotes chiropractic and general
health progress.

## CHIROPRACTIC PRODUCTS
69210

3510 Torrance Blvd., No. 315
Torrance, CA 90503
Telephone: (310) 316-8112
FAX: (310) 316-8422
Year Established: 1985
Pub. Frequency: 8/yr.
Subscrip. Rate: $16/yr.
Materials: 06,28,29,32
Print Process: web
Circulation: 35,059
Circulation Type: controlled
**Owner(s):**
Novicom, Inc.
3510 Torrance Blvd., No. 315
Torrance, CA 90503
Telephone: (310) 316-8112
FAX: (310) 316-8422
Ownership %: 100
**Editorial:**
Julie Craig ............................................Editor
**Desc.:** Covers news of product releases,
topics of interest to professionals in the
field, and special features.

## CHIROPRACTIC SPORTS MEDICINE
58926

428 E. Preston St.
Baltimore, MD 21202
Telephone: (410) 528-4000
FAX: (410) 528-4312
Year Established: 1987
Pub. Frequency: q.
Subscrip. Rate: $62/yr. individual; $93/yr.
institution
Circulation: 3,000
Circulation Type: paid
**Owner(s):**
Williams & Wilkins Co.
428 E. Preston St.
Baltimore, MD 21202
Telephone: (410) 528-4000
Ownership %: 100
**Management:**
Don Pfarr ..........................Advertising Manager
Alma Wills ..............................................Manager
**Editorial:**
Robert Hazel, D.C. ................................Editor
Nancy Collins ....................Marketing Director

## ICA INTERNATIONAL REVIEW OF CHIROPRACTIC
22527

1110 N. Glebe Rd., Ste. 1000
Arlington, VA 22201
Telephone: (703) 528-5000
Year Established: 1948
Pub. Frequency: bi-m.
Page Size: standard
Subscrip. Rate: $50/yr.
Circulation: 12,000
Circulation Type: paid
**Owner(s):**
ICA
1110 N. Glebe Rd., Ste. 1000
Arlington, VA 22201
Telephone: (703) 528-5000
Ownership %: 100
**Editorial:**
Molly Rangnalh ....................Editor in Chief
Karen Cercone ..................Assistant Editor
Lois M. Johnson ..............................Sales

**Desc.:** Deals with current health care
issues, professional papers, and
information relevant to the chiropractic
profession.

## JOURNAL OF CHIROPRACTIC, THE
22525

8229 Maryland Ave.
St. Louis, MO 63105
Telephone: (314) 862-7800
FAX: (314) 721-5171
Year Established: 1930
Pub. Frequency: m.
Page Size: standard
Subscrip. Rate: $80/yr. US; $100/yr.
foreign
Materials: 06,10,17,28,29,32,33
Freelance Pay: varies
Print Process: offset
Circulation: 24,000
Circulation Type: paid
**Owner(s):**
American Chiropractic Association
1701 Clarendon Blvd.
Arlington, VA 22209
Telephone: (703) 276-8800
Ownership %: 100
**Management:**
Lee Clark ........................Advertising Manager
**Editorial:**
Irvin Davis ..............................................Editor
Steven R. Pezold ....................Art Director
Cheryl Keen ..........................................Artist
Greg Lammert ..................Associate Editor
Steven R. Pezold ..........Production Director
**Desc.:** Contributed and staff-written articles
for the chiropractic profession dealing
with the clinical sciences, news and
developments within the profession,
education, research, legislation,
editorials, council and auxiliary reports,
literature abstracts, book reviews,
college news, convention and seminar
schedules.
**Readers:** Doctors and students of
chiropactic in the U.S. and some foreign
countries, legislators.
**Deadline:** ads-10th of mo. prior to pub.
date

## NEWS & ALUMNI REPORT
22526

16200 E. Amber Valley Dr.
Whittier, CA 90604-1166
Telephone: (310) 947-8755
FAX: (310) 947-5724
Mailing Address:
P.O. Box 1166
Whittier, CA 90609-1166
Year Established: 1977
Pub. Frequency: q.
Page Size: standard
Subscrip. Rate: free
Materials: 30
Freelance Pay: voluntary
Circulation: 4,500
Circulation Type: controlled & free
**Owner(s):**
Los Angeles College of Chiropractic
P.O. Box 1166
Whittier, CA 90609
Telephone: (310) 947-8755
Ownership %: 100
**Management:**
Dr. Reed Phillips ........................President
Dr. John Beckman ..................Vice President
**Editorial:**
Dr. Joseph Laurin ................Editor in Chief
Laura H. Arthur ..................................Editor
**Desc.:** News, announcements, and notes
on the activities and people associated
with the college.
**Readers:** Alumni of Los Angeles College
of Chiropractic, chiropractors and other
health professionals.

## TEXAS JOURNAL OF CHIROPRACTIC
69211

1601 Rio Grande
Ste. 420
Austin, TX 78701-1149
Telephone: (512) 477-9292
FAX: (512) 477-9296
Year Established: 1983
Pub. Frequency: m.
Page Size: standard
Subscrip. Rate: $36/yr.
Materials: 01,06,07,08,19,21,27,28,30,32,33
Print Process: web offset
Circulation: 2,050
Circulation Type: free & paid
**Owner(s):**
Texas Chiropractic Association
1601 Rio Grande, Ste. 420
Austin, TX 78701-1149
Telephone: (512) 477-9292
Ownership %: 100
**Editorial:**
Chris Dalrymple ..................................Editor
**Readers:** Doctor members, affiliate
(distributor) members & student
members.
**Deadline:** story-15th of mo. prior to pub
date; news-15th of mo. prior; photo-15th
of mo. prior; ads-15th of mo. prior

## TODAY'S CHIROPRACTIC
22528

1085 Barclay Cir.
Marietta, GA 30060
Telephone: (404) 499-9824
FAX: (404) 419-0568
Year Established: 1962
Pub. Frequency: bi-m.
Page Size: standard
Subscrip. Rate: $24/yr. US; $28/yr.
Canada; $33/yr. elsewhere
Circulation: 38,000
Circulation Type: controlled
**Owner(s):**
Life Chiropractic College
1269 Barclay Cir.
Marietta, GA 30060
Telephone: (404) 424-0554
Ownership %: 100
**Management:**
Sid E. Williams ..........................President
Cheryl DiDuro ..................Advertising Manager
Sherry Gray ..........................Business Manager
**Editorial:**
James Panter ......................................Editor
Sherry Gray ................Administrative Assistant
Anne Griffin ..................................Art Director
Craig Cannon ......................................Artist
Kim Humphreys ..................Associate Editor
Donna Harris ..................Circulation Director
Cheryl Urbano ....................................Sales
**Desc.:** Articles report on the development
and technical aspects of new scientific
advancements, equipment, techniques
as well as state, local and national
developments of general interest to
the chiropractic profession. Departments
include: sports chiropractic, nutrition, X-
ray, insurance, chiropractic in industry,
clinics, research, law, technique review,
general health, practice management,
finance, chiropractic update, college
news and product news.
**Readers:** Chiropractors, chiropractic
professionals and chiropractic students.

## Group 050-Climate Control

## ALABAMA CONTRACTOR
21697

P.O. Box 36972
Birmingham, AL 35236-6972
Telephone: (205) 987-5100
FAX: (205) 733-1006
Year Established: 1940

Pub. Frequency: a.
Page Size: standard
Subscrip. Rate: free
Freelance Pay: varies
Circulation: 2,000
Circulation Type: free
**Owner(s):**
Assn. of Plmbing, Htng, Clng. Ctrs. of AL.,
Inc.
3 Office Park Cir., 210
Birmingham, AL 35223
Telephone: (205) 870-5802
Ownership %: 100
**Management:**
Conrad Watson ................................President
Bob Mosca ....................Advertising Manager
**Editorial:**
Bob Mosca ..........................Executive Editor
**Desc.:** Contains articles about the
plumbing and heating, cooling
contracting industry.
**Readers:** Heating, plumbing and air
contractors, home builders, mechanical
engineers, and others in related fields.

## ASHRAE JOURNAL
21698

1791 Tullie Cir., N.E.
Atlanta, GA 30329
Telephone: (404) 636-8400
FAX: (404) 321-5478
Year Established: 1959
Pub. Frequency: m.
Page Size: standard
Subscrip. Rate: $49/yr.
Materials: 02,06,15,27,28,29,30,32,33
Print Process: offset, web offset
Circulation: 55,000
Circulation Type: paid
**Owner(s):**
Am. Soc. of Heating, Refrig. & Air Cond.
Engineers
1791 Tullie Cir., NE
Atlanta, GA 30329
Telephone: (404) 636-8400
Ownership %: 100
**Management:**
Frank D. Coda ..................................Publisher
Irene F. Eggeling ..............Advertising Manager
**Editorial:**
Bill Coker ..............................................Editor
**Desc.:** Uses by-line engineering feature
articles describing research, new
developments and application in the
heating, refrigerating, air conditioning
and ventilating industries. Carries news
of the industry/new products,
trade literature, people in the industry.
Experience indicates only practicing
engineers to be qualified to write
technical articles used.
**Readers:** Heating, refrigerating, air
conditioning duct development,
manufacture and applications.
**Deadline:** story-2 mos. prior to pub. date;
news-2 mos. prior; photo-2 mos. prior;
ads-5th of preceding issue

## CAROLINA HVAC NEWS
69533

P.O. Box 830034
Stone Mountain, GA 30083-0001
Telephone: (404) 879-9682
FAX: (404) 879-6791
Year Established: 1992
Pub. Frequency: m.
Page Size: tabloid
Subscrip. Rate: $10/yr.
Circulation: 7,000
Circulation Type: paid
**Owner(s):**
Holco Communications Inc.
P.O. Box 830034
Stone Mountain, GA 30083-0001
Telephone: (404) 879-9682
Ownership %: 100

**Materials Accepted/Included:** 01-Business news 02-By-line articles 03-Fashion news 04-Food news 05-Freelance copy 06-Letters to editor 07-Real estate news 08-Sports news 09-Travel news 10-Book rev. 11-Movie rev. 12-Music rev. 13-TV rev. 14-Theater rev. 15-Coming events 16-Obituaries 17-Question & answer 18-Social announcements 19-Artwork 20-Cartoons 21-Photos 22-TV listings 23-Audio rec. 24-Video rec. 25-Books 26-Films/film clips 27-Personnel news 28-Press releases 29-New product news/photos 30-Trade lit. 31-Contracts awarded 32-Display adv. 33-Classified adv.

4-91

**Desc.:** Contains wholesale and manufacturing news, local distribution news for dealers and contractors/installers of central heating and cooling equipment; residential, light commercial and industrial.

21696

## CONTRACTING BUSINESS
1100 Superior Ave.
Cleveland, OH 44114
Telephone: (216) 696-7000
FAX: (216) 696-7932
Year Established: 1944
Pub. Frequency: m.
Page Size: standard
Subscrip. Rate: $3/copy; $55/yr.; $95/2 yrs.
Freelance Pay: negotiated
Circulation: 52,000
Circulation Type: controlled
**Owner(s):**
Penton Publishing, Division of Pittway Corp.
1100 Superior Ave.
Cleveland, OH 44114
Telephone: (216) 696-7000
Ownership %: 100
**Management:**
Jeff Forker ...............................Publisher
Elaine Brown ...............Circulation Manager
**Editorial:**
Dominick Guarino .....................Editor in Chief
Bob Schwed ..........................Senior Editor
Michael S. Weil ......................Senior Editor
Gwen Hostnik .................Marketing Manager
**Desc.:** Contracting Business serves those contractors engaged in the design, installation and service of mechanical systems in residential, commercial and industrial building. The mechanical systems field includes: air-conditioning (both central and unitary), warm air heating, hydronic heating, refrigeration, ventilation, sheet metal and fiber glass duct fabrication, water treatment/conditioning, and energy management. We are interested in product developments on all types of equipment and components for mechanical systems.
**Readers:** Installing contractors, dealers - distributors within the mechanical systems field; large users of mechanical systems with their own installation or service departments; Design/Build contractors; specifying engineers and architects.

68875

## DISTRIBUTOR
651 W. Washington St., Ste. 300
Chicago, IL 60661
Telephone: (312) 993-0929
FAX: (312) 993-0960
Year Established: 1983
Pub. Frequency: m.
Page Size: standard
Subscrip. Rate: free
Circulation: 17,500
Circulation Type: paid
**Owner(s):**
Palmer Publishing Co.
651 W. Washington St., Ste.300
Chicago, IL 60661
Telephone: (312) 993-0929
Ownership %: 100
**Editorial:**
Mary Dolan ...................................Editor

21699

## ENERGY ENGINEERING
700 Indian Trail
Lilburn, GA 30247
Telephone: (404) 925-9388
Year Established: 1904
Pub. Frequency: bi-m.

Page Size: standard
Subscrip. Rate: $99/yr.
Circulation: 8,300
Circulation Type: paid
**Owner(s):**
Fairmont Press
700 Indian Trail
Lilburn, GA 30247
Telephone: (404) 925-9388
Ownership %: 100
**Bureau(s):**
Randall Scott Sumpter
8140-B Ceberry Dr.
Austin, TX 78759
Telephone: (512) 346-9260
**Management:**
Richard Miller .....................Chairman of Board
**Editorial:**
Randall Scott Sumpter ...............Editor in Chief
**Desc.:** Utilization in building systems energy conservation. Note: energy engineering is technical journal of Association of Energy Engineers, Atlanta.
**Readers:** Engineers who manage utilization of energy in buildings and their consultants.

22176

## FLORIDA FORUM
4111 Metric Dr.
Winter Park, FL 32792
Telephone: (407) 671-3772
Mailing Address:
   P.O. Drawer 4850
   Winter Park, FL 32793
Year Established: 1961
Pub. Frequency: m.
Page Size: standard
Subscrip. Rate: free
Freelance Pay: negotiable
Circulation: 9,500
Circulation Type: free
**Owner(s):**
FRSA Services Corp.
P.O. Drawer 4850
Winter Park, FL 32793
Telephone: (407) 671-3772
Ownership %: 100
**Management:**
Steve Munnell ...........................President
**Editorial:**
Bonnie B. Pierce .........................Feature Editor
Steve Currie .....................New Products Editor
Bonnie B. Pierce .........................News Editor
**Desc.:** Published and edited for members of the roofing, sheet metal, and air conditioning industries in Florida. Covers Industry Social News, Features, New Product Information, Legislative Trends, etc.
**Readers:** Roofing, sheet metal, air conditioning contractors, building officials, and architects.

21707

## FUELOIL & OIL HEAT
389 Passaic Ave.
Fairfield, NJ 07004
Telephone: (201) 227-5151
FAX: (201) 227-9219
Year Established: 1922
Pub. Frequency: 11/yr.
Page Size: standard
Subscrip. Rate: $20/yr.
Print Process: sheet fed
Circulation: 13,500
Circulation Type: controlled
**Owner(s):**
Industry Publications, Inc.
389 Passaic Ave.
Fairfield, NJ 07004
Telephone: (201) 227-5151
Ownership %: 100
**Management:**
Margaret Hundley ...............................Publisher

Donald Farrell ...........................Sales Manager
**Editorial:**
Paul Geiger ...............................Editor
Margaret Mantho .....................Marketing Editor
**Desc.:** Covers all phases of fuel oil and oil heating written to increase the profits of the retail marketer concerned with the sale, installation and servicing of oil heating and air conditioning equipment. Plus supplying the fuel oil used by these units. Includes emphasis on technical developments and application from the standpoint of installation and maintenance techniques; covers management topics; merchandising management and methods; competitive fuels; statistical review and outlook; editorial opinion and provides a journal of discussion for current items of interest. Departments include: Oil Heating Sales Trends, Fuel Oil Markets, Government Influences on Fuels, Names in the News, Manufacturers' Activities, Industry Groups, New Products, Readers' Problems.
**Readers:** Consists basically of fuel oil and oil-heating, dealers who sell equipment and deliver the fuel oil. Also heating and air- conditioning dealers.

21706

## FUEL OIL NEWS
411-B110 W. Lake Lansing Rd.
East Lansing, MI 48823
Telephone: (517) 333-3557
FAX: (517) 337-8041
Year Established: 1935
Pub. Frequency: m.
Page Size: standard
Subscrip. Rate: $26/yr. US; $33/yr. Canada & Mexico; $74/yr. elsewhere
Freelance Pay: $400/article
Circulation: 15,416
Circulation Type: controlled
**Owner(s):**
Premier Inc.
411-B110 W. Lake Lansing Rd.
East Lansing, MI 48823
Ownership %: 100
**Management:**
William Straub ...........................Publisher
Lloyd Schultz .....................Advertising Manager
**Editorial:**
George Schultz ...............................Editor
Jim Wessel .....................Circulation Director
**Desc.:** Covers all phases of fuel oil distribution, sales, installation and servicing of oil heating and air conditioning equipments. Interested in clean dealer operations, and in the manufacture, sale, service, and installation of heating and air conditioning equipments. Uses news and feature stories, by-lining outside features. Stories may run up to 3,000 words; photos required. Departments include: Personalities in the News, New Products, New Literature, Coming Events.
**Readers:** Fuel oil dealers, heating contractors, manufacturers of heating & air conditioning equipment, major oil company executives.

21709

## HEATING/PIPING/AIR CONDITIONING
2 Illinois Ctr., Ste. 1300
Chicago, IL 60601
Telephone: (312) 861-0880
FAX: (312) 861-0874
Year Established: 1929
Pub. Frequency: m.
Page Size: standard
Subscrip. Rate: $45/yr.

Circulation: 51,000
Circulation Type: controlled
**Owner(s):**
Penton Publishing, Inc.
1100 Superior Ave.
Cleveland, OH 44114
Telephone: (216) 696-7000
Ownership %: 100
**Management:**
Perry G. Clark ...............................Publisher
**Editorial:**
Robert T. Korte ...............................Editor
Vicki Daniels .....................Associate Editor
**Desc.:** Covers design, operation, and maintenance of heating, piping, and air conditioning systems in all types of large buildings such as industrial plants, commercial buildings, institutional buildings, etc., as well as the energy management of these systems. Departments include: Editor's page; You'll Want to Know; Open for Discussion (letters from readers); The Law and Your Profits; Equipment Developments; Industry Appointments; Industry Reports; Meetings and Conventions; Books & Reports; Engineering Data.
**Readers:** Mechanical engineers with consulting firms, with mechanical contracting firms, and with owners of commercial, institutional, and industrial buildings.

21711

## ILLINOIS MASTER PLUMBER
821 S. Grand Ave., W.
Springfield, IL 62704
Telephone: (217) 522-7219
FAX: (217) 522-4315
Year Established: 1913
Pub. Frequency: m.
Page Size: standard
Subscrip. Rate: $9/yr.; $25/3 yrs.
Circulation: 1,850
Circulation Type: controlled
**Owner(s):**
Illinois Association of Plumbing, Heating, Cooling
821 S. Grand Ave., W.
Springfield, IL 62704
Telephone: (217) 522-7219
Ownership %: 100
**Management:**
IAPHCC ...............................Publisher
Dorothy Sharpe Clem .......Advertising Manager
Joan Wiessing .....................Assistant Manager
**Editorial:**
Dorothy Sharpe Clem .....Executive Editor
Dorothy Sharpe Clem ...............................Editor
**Desc.:** New products, organization activities, personals, new literature, industry news covered in news briefs and longer articles.
**Readers:** Plumbing and heating contractors, wholesalers, city officials, plumbing inspectors, architects, engineers.

24340

## INDIANA CONTRACTOR
9595 Whitley Dr., Ste. 208
Indianapolis, IN 46240
Telephone: (317) 575-9292
FAX: (317) 575-9378
Year Established: 1957
Pub. Frequency: bi-m.
Page Size: standard
Subscrip. Rate: free
Circulation: 5,100
Circulation Type: controlled

**Owner(s):**
Indiana Assoc. of Plumbing-Heating-
Cooling Contr.
9595 Whitley Pl., Ste. 208
Indianapolis, IN 46240
Telephone: (317) 575-9292
Ownership %: 100
**Management:**
Philip Amodeo .............................Publisher
Philip Amodeo .................Executive Director
Melissa Bloom ...............Advertising Manager
Melissa Bloom .................Circulation Manager
**Editorial:**
Melissa Bloom ...................................Editor

## INDOOR COMFORT NEWS
68877

606 N. Larchmont Blvd., Ste. 4A
Los Angeles, CA 90004
Telephone: (213) 467-1158
FAX: (213) 461-2588
Year Established: 1955
Pub. Frequency: m.
Page Size: tabloid
Subscrip. Rate: $12/yr.
Materials: 01,02,05,06,19,20,21,27,28,29,
30,31,32,33
Circulation: 23,000
Circulation Type: paid
**Owner(s):**
Institute of Heating & Air Conditioning
Industries
606 N. Larchmont Blvd., Ste.4A
Los Angeles, CA 90004
Telephone: (213) 467-1158
FAX: (213) 461-2588
Ownership %: 100
**Editorial:**
Michelle Miller .........................Managing Editor
**Desc.:** Provides industry news and
information on products and equipment
for heating and air conditioning
engineers and contractors in the
western states.
**Deadline:** story-1st of mo.; news-2 mo.
prior to pub. date; photo-2 mo. prior to
pub. date; ads-3rd of mo. prior to pub.
date

## KENTUCKY PLUMBING-HEATING-
COOLING INDEX
24342

1501 Durrett Ln.
Louisville, KY 40213
Telephone: (502) 451-5577
FAX: (502) 451-5551
Year Established: 1950
Pub. Frequency: m.
Page Size: tabloid
Subscrip. Rate: free
Circulation: 1,700
Circulation Type: controlled
**Owner(s):**
KY Assoc. of Plumbing Heating Cooling
Contractors
Ownership %: 100
**Management:**
Woody Yonts ...............................President
Linda Griffey .................Advertising Manager
**Editorial:**
Linda Griffey ...................................Editor
**Desc.:** Official publication of the Kentucky
Association of Plumbing Heating Cooling
Contractors.
**Readers:** All plumbing, heating and cooling
contractors and related industries in
Kentucky.

## MICHIGAN MASTER PLUMBER &
MECHANICAL CONTRACTOR
24345

400 N. Walnut St.
Lansing, MI 48933
Telephone: (517) 484-5500
FAX: (517) 484-5500
Year Established: 1953
Pub. Frequency: m.

Page Size: standard
Circulation: 3,000
Circulation Type: controlled
**Owner(s):**
Michigan Plumbing & Mechanical
Contractors
400 N. Walnut St.
Lansing, MI 48933
Telephone: (517) 484-5500
Ownership %: 100
**Management:**
Cindy Hall .......................Advertising Manager
**Editorial:**
Cindy Hall .....................................Editor
**Desc.:** Editorials are commentaries on
matters of urgency and interest that
apply to the construction industry and
the plumbing and heating and
mechanical trades. Articles of interest
are news releases from manufacturers
and suppliers in the mechanical industry,
news from Dept. of Labor, Construction
Safety Institute, OSHA, American Supply
Association, and news from our local
associations and members. Departments
include: Labor Relations, Association
Participation, Education.
**Readers:** Plumbing, heating, cooling and
mechanical contractors, manufacturers,
wholesalers, architects, inspectors and
builders.

## MID-ATLANTIC HUAC/R NEWS
68882

P.O. Box 80727
Conyers, GA 30208-0727
Telephone: (404) 483-4860
FAX: (404) 483-2447
Year Established: 1993
Pub. Frequency: m.
Page Size: tabloid
Subscrip. Rate: $25/yr.
Materials: 01,02,05,06,27,28,29,30,32
Print Process: web offset
Circulation: 7,500
Circulation Type: free
**Owner(s):**
Holco Communications Inc.
P.O. Box 80727
Conyers, GA 30208-0727
Telephone: (404) 483-4860
FAX: (404) 483-2447
Ownership %: 100
**Management:**
Byron F. Hollingsworth .................President
Byron F. Hollingsworth .................Publisher
**Editorial:**
David M. Hollingsworth ...........Associate Editor
**Desc.:** Provides wholesale and
manufacturing news and local distributor
news for dealers and contractors-
installers of central heating and cooling
equipment: residential, light commercial
and industrial, refrigeration & plumbing.
**Readers:** wholesalers, manufacturers,
dealers, architects, material handlers,
contractors
**Deadline:** story-25th of mo. prior to pub.
date; news-25th of mo. prior; photo-25th
of mo. prior; ads-25th of mo. prior

## MINNESOTA P-H-C CONTRACTOR
24346

8085 Wayzata Blvd., Ste. 109
Minneapolis, MN 55426-1456
Telephone: (612) 546-4448
FAX: (612) 546-4507
Year Established: 1948
Pub. Frequency: m.
Page Size: standard
Subscrip. Rate: $3/yr.; free to members
Circulation: 2,000
Circulation Type: controlled

**Owner(s):**
Minnesota Master Plumber Publishing Co.
8085 Wayzata Blvd., Ste. 109
Minneapolis, MN 55426-1456
Telephone: (616) 546-4448
Ownership %: 100
**Management:**
Jack Tester ...........................Business Manager
**Editorial:**
Donald E. Sullivan ...........................Editor
**Desc.:** News on the plumbing-heating-
cooling industry.
**Readers:** Plumbing-heating-cooling
contractors.

## PALMETTO PIPER
24348

P.O. Box 384
Columbia, SC 29202
Telephone: (803) 772-7834
FAX: (803) 731-0390
Year Established: 1964
Pub. Frequency: bi-m.
Page Size: standard
Subscrip. Rate: free
Circulation: 2,200
Circulation Type: free
**Owner(s):**
Mechanical Contractors Association of S.C.
P.O. Box 384
Columbia, SC 29202
Telephone: (803) 772-7834
Ownership %: 100
**Editorial:**
Reid Hearn ...................................Editor
**Desc.:** News and features in plumbing,
electrical, heating and air conditioning
industry especially as related to South
Carolina firms and personalities.
However, the emphasis is on
personalities and success stories and
events affecting the mechanical
contracting industry.
**Readers:** Mechanical and general
contractors, architects, engineers,
suppliers.

## PENNSYLVANIA CONTRACTOR
24349

4015 Jonestown Rd.
Harrisburg, PA 17109
Telephone: (717) 541-9109
FAX: (717) 541-9823
Year Established: 1949
Pub. Frequency: bi-m.
Page Size: pg.: 8 1/4 x 11; col.: 2 1/8
wide
Subscrip. Rate: free
Materials: 01,02,05,06,19,20.21.28,29,30,
31,32,33
Circulation: 5,000
Circulation Type: controlled
**Owner(s):**
PA Assn. Of Plmg., Htg., Clg. Contractors
4015 Jonestown Rd.
Harrisburg, PA 17109
Telephone: (717) 541-9109
Ownership %: 100
**Management:**
Al Riscito .........................Advertising Manager
Elaine Houser .................Circulation Manager
**Editorial:**
Al Risciuto ...........................Executive Editor
**Desc.:** Covers work that affects or is
associated with plumbing-heating-cooling
industry.
**Readers:** Architects, engineers, all
plumbing, heating and cooling, back
flow, ventilation process piping
contractors (including members and non-
members) and manufacturers.

## PIPELINE
24347

8755 S.W. Citizens Dr., #202
Wilsonville, OR 97070-8405
Telephone: (503) 682-7165
FAX: (503) 682-8009
Mailing Address:
P.O. Box 448
Welches, OR 97067-0448
Year Established: 1965
Pub. Frequency: m.
Page Size: standard
Subscrip. Rate: $12/yr.
Circulation: 500
Circulation Type: controlled
**Owner(s):**
Oregon Plumbing-Heating-Cooling
Contractor
**Management:**
John David .............................Publisher
Linda Lindsten ...............Advertising Manager
**Editorial:**
Linda Lindsten ...................................Editor
**Desc.:** Trade magazine for plumbing-
heating-cooling contractors. Story on
association, members, industry, etc. Ads
relate to industry. Article should be as
brief as possible. Photos used of new
products with firm paying for picture
charge.
**Readers:** Plumbing - heating - cooling
contractors, all government officials,
lobbyists & legislators, industry
wholesalers, suppliers, architects,
engineers, others in construction trade.

## PROGRESS
24352

5 The Mountain Rd.
Framingham, MA 01701
Telephone: (508) 879-6799
FAX: (508) 879-3044
Year Established: 1935
Pub. Frequency: q.
Page Size: standard
Subscrip. Rate: free
Materials: 02,05,32,33
Freelance Pay: varies
Print Process: web offset
Circulation: 5,000
Circulation Type: controlled & free
**Owner(s):**
MA Plumbing, Heating and Cooling
Contractors
Telephone: (617) 879-6802
Ownership %: 100
**Management:**
Carolyn P. Davis .............Advertising Manager
**Editorial:**
Carolyn P. Davis .....................Managing Editor
**Desc.:** Interested in articles dealing with
improvements and new developments in
the fields of plumbing, heating and
cooling or news items concerning the
New England area.
**Readers:** Plumbing contractors in the six
New England states, inspectors,
engineers and architects as well as
other in related fields.

## REEVES JOURNAL, PLUMBING-
HEATING-COOLING
24353

23187 LaCadena Dr., #101
Laguna Hills, CA 92653
Telephone: (714) 830-0881
FAX: (714) 859-7845
Mailing Address:
P.O. Box 30700
Laguna Beach, CA 92654
Year Established: 1920
Pub. Frequency: m.
Page Size: standard
Subscrip. Rate: $36/yr.
Materials: 01,02,05,06,15,16,18,21,32,33
Circulation: 13,658

**Materials Accepted/Included:** 01-Business news 02-By-line articles 03-Fashion news 04-Food news 05-Freelance copy 06-Letters to editor 07-Real estate news 08-Sports news 09-Travel news
10-Book rev. 11-Movie rev. 12-Music rev. 13-TV rev. 14-Theater rev. 15-Coming events 16-Obituaries 17-Question & answer 18-Social announcements 19-Artwork 20-Cartoons 21-Photos 22-TV listings
23-Audio rec. 24-Video rec. 25-Books 26-Films/film clips 27-Personnel news 28-Press releases 29-New product news/photos 30-Trade lit. 31-Contracts awarded 32-Display adv. 33-Classified adv.

4-93

Circulation Type: controlled
**Owner(s):**
Business News Publishing Co.
P.O. Box 7001
Troy, MI 48007
Telephone: (810) 362-3700
FAX: (810) 362-0317
Ownership %: 100
**Management:**
Mary K. Larsoon ................................Publisher
Ellyn Fishman ........................General Manager
**Editorial:**
Scott Marshutz .................................Editor
Scott Marshutz .................................Editor
Janice Upp ....................Production Coordinator
**Desc.:** Articles covering specific contractor
or wholesaler operations in the Western
US.
**Readers:** Contractors and wholesalers in
the plumbing, heating and cooling
industries.
**Deadline:** ads-10th of mo., prior to pub.
date

21714
**REFRIGERATION**
1575 Northside Dr., Bldg. 2-230
Atlanta, GA 30318
Telephone: (800) 849-9677
FAX: (800) 849-8418
Year Established: 1906
Pub. Frequency: m.
Page Size: tabloid
Subscrip. Rate: $25/yr.
Materials: 01,02,06,27,28,29,30,32,33
Print Process: offset
Circulation: 3,000
Circulation Type: paid
**Owner(s):**
John W. Yopp Publications, Inc.
1575 Northside Dr., Bldg. 2-23
Atlanta, GA 30318
Telephone: (800) 849-9677
Ownership %: 100
**Management:**
Mary N. Cromley .................................Publisher
Joseph M. Cromley ..........Advertising Manager
**Editorial:**
Mary N. Cromley .................................Editor
**Readers:** Executives, manufacturers and
suppliers of the the ice industry.
**Deadline:** story-10th of mo. prior to pub.
date; news-10th of mo. prior; photo-10th
of mo. prior

21695
**REFRIGERATION SERVICE &
CONTRACTING**
755 W. Big Beaver Rd., #1000
Troy, MI 48084
Telephone: (810) 362-3700
FAX: (810) 362-0317
Mailing Address:
P.O. Box 7021
Troy, MI 48007
Year Established: 1931
Pub. Frequency: m.
Page Size: standard
Subscrip. Rate: $36/yr.; $72/3 yrs.
Materials: 01,02,06,17,19,21,27,28,29,30,
32,33
Freelance Pay: negotiable
Print Process: web offset
Circulation: 46,038
Circulation Type: paid
**Owner(s):**
Business News Publishing Co.
755 W. Big Beaver, 1000
Troy, MI 48084
Telephone: (810) 362-3700
FAX: (810) 362-0317
Ownership %: 100
**Management:**
James E. Henderson ..........................President
Michael A. Miller ...............................Publisher
Bonnie Kaye ..................Advertising Manager

**Editorial:**
Peter Powell ................................Editor
Barbara Sieg ........................Assistant Editor
Sarah M. Sjobakken ..........Marketing Director
**Desc.:** Industry service magazine/official
journal of RSES. Carries news and
feature articles on all aspects of
HVAC/R equipment installation and
repair. Service, installation, technology,
maintenance, and replacements.
**Readers:** Contractors, manufacturers,
distributors, wholesalers, equipment
users, and engineers engaged in the
manufacture, installation, and
maintenance of air-conditioning, heating,
and refrigeration equipment.

21715
**RSC/REFRIGERATION SERVICE &
CONTRACTING**
3150 River Rd., #115
Des Plaines, IL 60018
Telephone: (708) 297-3450
FAX: (708) 413-9030
Year Established: 1933
Pub. Frequency: m.
Page Size: standard
Subscrip. Rate: $5 newstand; $39/yr.
Circulation: 40,000
Circulation Type: paid
**Owner(s):**
Business News Publishing Co.
P.O. Box 2600
Troy, MI 48007
Telephone: (313) 362-3700
Ownership %: 100
**Management:**
Michael Miller ...............................Publisher
Bonnie Kaye ....................Advertising Manager
Madonna Olah ....................Circulation Manager
**Editorial:**
Peter Powell ................................Editor
Barbara Sieg ....................Associate Editor
**Desc.:** Domestic, commercial and
industrial refrigeration, air conditioning,
heating, and ventilating service,
installation and contracting.
**Readers:** Refrigeration & air conditioning &
heating contractors, distributors,
wholesalers, business owner.

21716
**SERVICE REPORTER**
651 W. Washington, #300
Chicago, IL 60661
Telephone: (312) 993-0929
FAX: (312) 993-0960
Mailing Address:
651 W. Washington, #300
Chicago, IL 60661
Year Established: 1968
Pub. Frequency: m.
Page Size: tabloid
Subscrip. Rate: $15/yr.
Freelance Pay: $.10/wd.
Circulation: 47,000
Circulation Type: controlled & paid
**Owner(s):**
Technical Reporting Corp.
651 W. Washington, #300
Chicago, IL 60661
Telephone: (312) 993-0929
Ownership %: 100
**Management:**
Earl Palmer ................................Owner
Earl Palmer ....................Chairman of Board
Philip Palmer ................................President
Philip Palmer ................................Publisher
Ann Arnold ....................Circulation Manager
**Editorial:**
Ed Schwenn ................................Editor
Bill Turley ....................Managing Editor
Eryn Ferdman ....................Assistant Editor
Evelyn Foltz ....................Secretary & Treasurer

**Desc.:** Contains service data, application
information, notices and new products
for air conditioning, ventilating, heating
and refrigeration industry.
**Readers:** Dealers contractors/service and
installation, inplant maintaince
personnel.

21717
**SNIPS**
1949 Cornell Ave.
Melrose Park, IL 60160
Telephone: (708) 544-3870
FAX: (708) 544-3884
Year Established: 1932
Pub. Frequency: m.
Page Size: standard
Subscrip. Rate: $12/yr.; $19/2 yrs.
Print Process: offset
Circulation: 32,300
Circulation Type: controlled
**Owner(s):**
SNIPS Magazine Inc.
1949 Cornell Ave.
Melrose Park, IL 60160
Telephone: (708) 544-3870
FAX: (708) 544-3884
Ownership %: 100
**Management:**
Nick Carter ...............................Publisher
**Editorial:**
Nick Carter ................................Editor
Bob Murphy ....................Associate Editor
Bill Licht ....................Associate Editor
**Desc.:** Contains articles on advertising and
marketing, book reviews, coming events,
new products news, personnel news,
trade literature, plus illustrated field-
gathered stories of air conditioning,
warm air heating, sheet metal work and
ventilation done by its readers.
**Readers:** Sheet metal, warm air heating,
air conditioning ventilation contractors,
dealers and fabricators, plus the
wholesalers, manufacturers
representatives and manufacturers that
serve these dealer-contractors with
industry products. Also trade
associations, trade schools architects
and other companies allied to the field.

21720
**SOUTHERN PLUMBING, HEATING
& AIR CONDITIONING**
609 Gallimore Dairy Rd.
High Point, NC 27265
Telephone: (910) 454-3516
Mailing Address:
P.O. Box 18343
Greensboro, NC 27419
Year Established: 1946
Pub. Frequency: bi-m.
Page Size: standard
Subscrip. Rate: $10/yr.
Materials: 01,02,05,06,15,17,19,20,21,24,
25,27,28,29,30,31,32,33
Circulation: 8,500
Circulation Type: controlled
**Owner(s):**
Southern Trade Publications Co.
P.O. Box 18343
Greensboro, NC 27419
Telephone: (910) 454-3516
Ownership %: 100
**Management:**
E.D. Atkins ...............................Publisher
**Editorial:**
Mark Blaine ................................Editor

**Desc.:** Interested in product development,
technical, promotional and sales plans
for plumbing, heating and air
conditioning equipment; news of
personnel known by or working with
industry in Southeast and Southwest
and installations in these areas. Covers
installations, practices, sales,
merchandising, and more.
**Readers:** Plumbing, heating, and air
conditioning contractors and wholesalers
in 14 Southern states.
**Deadline:** story-15th of mo. prior to pub.
date; news-15th of mo. prior; photo-15th
of mo. prior; ads-15th of mo. prior

24354
**SUPPLY HOUSE TIMES**
1350 E. Touhy Ave.
Des Plaines, IL 60018
Telephone: (708) 635-8800
FAX: (708) 390-2690
Mailing Address:
P.O. Box 5080
Des Plaines, IL 60017
Year Established: 1958
Pub. Frequency: m.
Page Size: standard
Subscrip. Rate: $65/yr.
Materials: 01,06,16,28,29,32,33
Print Process: web offset
Circulation: 29,441
Circulation Type: controlled
**Owner(s):**
Cahners Publishing Co.
1350 E. Touhy Ave.
Des Plaines, IL 60018
Telephone: (708) 635-8800
FAX: (708) 390-2690
Ownership %: 100
**Management:**
Bill Everham ...............................Publisher
**Editorial:**
John O'Reilly ................................Editor
**Desc.:** Covers all subjects of interest to
plumbing-piping, heating, cooling
wholesalers. Departments include
Materials Handling, Salesmanship,
Industry News, Merchandising, New
Products, Computers and other relevant
technologies.
**Readers:** Executives, buyers, salesmen,
sales managers, distributors of supply
houses of plumbing, heating, pipe,
valves fittings, water systems and well
supplies.
**Deadline:** news-6 wks. prior to pub. date;
photo-6 wks. prior; ads-6 wks. prior

24355
**TEXAS JOURNAL OF PLUMBING-
HEATING-COOLING
CONTRACTING**
2201 N. Lamar, Ste. 102
Austin, TX 78705
Telephone: (512) 472-7422
FAX: (512) 474-2604
Year Established: 1938
Pub. Frequency: s-a.
Page Size: standard
Subscrip. Rate: members only
Circulation: 2,000
Circulation Type: controlled
**Owner(s):**
Texas APHCC
1601 Rio Grande, Ste. 440
Austin, TX 78701
Telephone: (512) 479-0425
Ownership %: 100
**Management:**
Richard Blackmond ..............Executive Director
**Editorial:**
Richard Blackmond ................Editorial Director

**Materials Accepted/Included:** 01-Business news 02-By-line articles 03-Fashion news 04-Food news 05-Freelance copy 06-Letters to editor 07-Real estate news 08-Sports news 09-Travel news 10-Book rev. 11-Movie rev. 12-Music rev. 13-TV rev. 14-Theater rev. 15-Coming events 16-Obituaries 17-Question & answer 18-Social announcements 19-Artwork 20-Cartoons 21-Photos 22-TV listings 23-Audio rec. 24-Video rec. 25-Books 26-Films/film clips 27-Personnel news 28-Press releases 29-New product news/photos 30-Trade lit. 31-Contracts awarded 32-Display adv. 33-Classified adv.

**Desc.:** Runs local interest stories on a variety of subjects from around the state. Reporting is done by the members, in that they send in interesting stories and articles. There is limited use of new product literature, depending on the novelty and pertinence of the products. Also runs business articles of interest to small business owner.

**Readers:** Contractors (members and non-members).

---

24356

**VIRGINIA P-H-C IMAGE**
2103 Lake Ave.
Richmond, VA 23230
Telephone: (804) 288-2080
Year Established: 1964
Pub. Frequency: m.
Page Size: standard
Subscrip. Rate: $3/yr.
Freelance Pay: $100-$300
Circulation: 4,425
Circulation Type: controlled
**Owner(s):**
Va. Assn. of Plumbing-Heating-Cooling Contractors
2103 Lake Ave.
Richmond, VA 23230
Telephone: (804) 288-2080
Ownership %: 100
**Management:**
James B. Muncy, Jr. ............................President
James B. Muncy, Jr. ............................Publisher
James B. Muncy, Jr. ........Advertising Manager
**Editorial:**
James B. Muncy, Jr. .................Executive Editor
**Desc.:** Facts and figures applicable to plumbing, heating, cooling contractors in Virginia and Mid-Atlantic region. Feature stories emphasizes industry business management.
**Readers:** Licensed plumbing, heating and HVAC contractors and manufacturers operating in Virginia, and their associate contacts with the industry, building officials, architects and engineers.

---

21712

**WESTERN HVACR NEWS**
4215 N. Figueroa St.
Los Angeles, CA 90065-3011
Telephone: (213) 225-8034
Year Established: 1981
Pub. Frequency: m.
Page Size: tabloid
Subscrip. Rate: $12/yr.; $23/2 yrs.; $34/3 yrs.
Materials: 01,02,06,10,15,21,27,28,29,30,31
Circulation: 20,000
Circulation Type: controlled & paid
**Owner(s):**
Western HVACR News
1137 Huntington Dr.
S. Pasadena, CA 91030
Telephone: (310) 255-0102
Ownership %: 100
**Management:**
Joen Mascari ......................................Publisher
Chuck Lyons ....................Advertising Manager
**Editorial:**
Joen Mascari ..........................................Editor
**Desc.:** Technical articles, news features, product information, trade literature, association news, features covering the heating, air conditioning, ventilating, solar, sheet metal, refrigeration and some plumbing/in California, Arizona, Nevada, Oregon, Washington, Alaska and Hawaii. In addition carry area news columns by sheet metal, air conditioning and refrigeration contractors throughout the west.

**Readers:** Contractors, Service Personnel, Engineers, Manufacturers, Wholesalers, Distributors in The Heating, Ventilating, Air Conditioning, Refrigeration Solar, Sheet Metal And Some Plumbing Industries.
**Deadline:** story-1st of previous mo.; news-1st of previous mo.; photo-1st of previous mo.

---

21722

**WHOLESALER, THE**
1838 Techny Ct.
Northbrook, IL 60082
Telephone: (708) 564-1127
Year Established: 1944
Pub. Frequency: m.
Page Size: tabloid
Subscrip. Rate: $75/yr.; $130/2 yrs.; $175/yr. foreign
Print Process: offset
Circulation: 32,000
Circulation Type: controlled
**Owner(s):**
TMB Publishing
1838 Techny Ct.
Northbrood, IL 60082
Telephone: (708) 564-1127
Ownership %: 100
**Management:**
Bill Adams ..........................................Publisher
**Editorial:**
John Schweizer ......................................Editor
**Desc.:** Up-to-date news on happenings of wholesalers, manufacturer and sales representatives in the plumbing, piping, heating, cooling and refrigeration industry with meaningful features on industry problem areas. Major emphasis on marketing, with side emphasis on warehousing, sales and general management. Departments are Products, Lit File, Who's Calling, Product Knowledge Notebook, Letters, Viewpoint, Business, and On the Move.
**Readers:** Executives of plumbing, heating, cooling, air conditioning, pipe, valves and fittings, and water systems. Includes wholesalers.

---

## Group 052-Coffee, Tea & Spices

22695

**TEA & COFFEE TRADE JOURNAL**
130 W. 42nd St.
New York, NY 10036
Telephone: (212) 391-2060
FAX: (212) 827-0945
Year Established: 1901
Pub. Frequency: m.
Page Size: standard
Subscrip. Rate: $5/issue; $30/yr.
Freelance Pay: $5.50/in.
Circulation: 9,000
Circulation Type: controlled & paid
**Owner(s):**
Lockwood Trade Journal Co.
130 W. 42nd St.
New York, NY 10036
Telephone: (212) 391-2060
FAX: (212) 827-0945
Ownership %: 100
**Management:**
George Lockwood ..............................Publisher
Robert Lockwood ...............................Publisher
Larry Frank .......................Advertising Manager
Edward Feng ......................Circulation Manager
**Editorial:**
Jane Phillips McCabe ..............................Editor
Fred Lockwood ...................Associate Publisher
Jonathan Bell .............................Foreign Editor
Craig Wang .........................Production Director

**Desc.:** Interested in merchandising articles tea and coffee merchants can use.
**Readers:** Tea and coffee exporters, importers, roasters.

---

22696

**WORLD COFFEE & TEA**
1801 Rockville Pike
Ste. 330
Rockville, MD 20852
Telephone: (301) 984-4000
FAX: (301) 984-7340
Year Established: 1960
Pub. Frequency: m.
Page Size: standard
Subscrip. Rate: $5/issue; $24/yr.; $40/2 yrs. US; $30/yr. in Canada; $90/yr. foreign
Circulation: 8,500
Circulation Type: controlled & paid
**Owner(s):**
Graphic Concepts, Inc.
1801 Rockville Pike, Ste. 330
Rockville, MD 20852
Telephone: (301) 984-4000
Ownership %: 100
**Management:**
Robert Silverstein ...............................President
**Editorial:**
Colin Campbell ........................................Editor
**Desc.:** Articles are generally survey-analysis-trend reports on public feeding, international coffee/tea movements, packaging, equipment, vending, tea, convention reports, and producing country reports. Departments include: Instants, Marketing, Public Feeding, Producing Countries, Processing.
**Readers:** Those in the coffee and tea field.

---

## Group 054-Coin-Operated Machines

22698

**AUTOMATIC MERCHANDISER**
111 E. Wacker Dr.
17th Fl.
Chicago, IL 60601
Telephone: (312) 938-2300
Year Established: 1958
Pub. Frequency: m.
Page Size: standard
Subscrip. Rate: $25/yr.
Circulation: 13,000
Circulation Type: controlled
**Owner(s):**
Johnson Hill Press, Inc.
1233 Janesville Ave.
Ft. Atkinson, WI 53538
Telephone: (414) 563-6388
Ownership %: 100
**Bureau(s):**
American Automatic Merchandiser
7500 Old Oak Blvd.
Cleveland, OH 44130
Telephone: (216) 243-8100
Contact: David R. Stone, Editor
**Management:**
Rebecca Ginsberg ..............................Publisher
**Editorial:**
Mark Dlugoss ..........................................Editor
**Desc.:** Serves the industry of automatic merchandising (vending), including industrial/institutional feeding service, as performed by merchandise vending operators, plus coverage of the coffee service industry.
**Readers:** Individuals or firms actively engaged in vending of merchandise.

---

22699

**PLAY METER MAGAZINE**
6600 Fluer de Lis
New Orleans, LA 70124
Telephone: (504) 488-7003
FAX: (504) 488-7083
Mailing Address:
P.O. Box 24970
New Orleans, LA 70184
Year Established: 1974
Pub. Frequency: m.
Page Size: standard
Subscrip. Rate: $5/issue ;$60/yr.
Freelance Pay: $50-75/pg.
Circulation: 6,500
Circulation Type: paid
**Owner(s):**
Skybird Publishing Co., Inc.
P.O. Box 24970
New Orleans, LA 70184
Telephone: (504) 488-7003
Ownership %: 100
**Management:**
Carol Lally ..........................................President
Carol Lally ..........................................Publisher
Ron Kogos ........................Advertising Manager
Renee Pierson ...................Circulation Manager
**Editorial:**
Valerie Cognevich ...................................Editor
Jane Nisbet ..................................Art Director
**Desc.:** Edited for amusement company owners, content is intended to inform these businessmen on news, new product announcements, interviews, technical advice, and legal problems. Feature stories are slanted to helping amusement operators running their businesses more profitably. Departments include: Operating, Distributing, Manufacturing.
**Readers:** Coin operated amusement machine operators.

---

22700

**VENDING TIMES**
1375 Broadway
New York, NY 10018
Telephone: (212) 302-4700
FAX: (212) 221-3311
Year Established: 1960
Pub. Frequency: m.
Page Size: tabloid
Subscrip. Rate: $30/yr.
Circulation: 15,000
Circulation Type: paid
**Owner(s):**
Vending Times, Inc.
1375 Broadway
New York, NY 10018
Telephone: (212) 302-4700
FAX: (212) 221-3311
Ownership %: 100
**Management:**
Victor Lavay ........................................Publisher
**Editorial:**
T.R. Sanford ................................Exec. Editor
Arthur E. Yohalem .................................Editor
John DeGiovanni ...........................Music Editor
**Desc.:** Covers all areas as they relate to the vending operator; candy, soft drinks, hot foods, ice cream, new vending machine developments, speeches by prominent executives.
**Readers:** Vending operators, suppliers, manufacturers.

---

## Group 056-Computers and Data Processing

66320

**ACCESS TO WANG**
10711 Burnet Rd., Ste. 305
Austin, TX 78758-4459
Telephone: (512) 873-7761
FAX: (512) 873-7782
Year Established: 1983

---

Materials Accepted/Included: 01-Business news 02-By-line articles 03-Fashion news 04-Food news 05-Freelance copy 06-Letters to editor 07-Real estate news 08-Sports news 09-Travel news 10-Book rev. 11-Movie rev. 12-Music rev. 13-TV rev. 14-Theater rev. 15-Coming events 16-Obituaries 17-Question & answer 18-Social announcements 19-Artwork 20-Cartoons 21-Photos 22-TV listings 23-Audio rec. 24-Video rec. 25-Books 26-Films/film clips 27-Personnel news 28-Press releases 29-New product news/photos 30-Trade lit. 31-Contracts awarded 32-Display adv. 33-Classified adv.

4-95

Pub. Frequency: m.
Page Size: standard
Subscrip. Rate: $38/yr; $52/2 yrs.; $64/yr. foreign
Freelance Pay: $150-$300
Circulation: 11,000
Circulation Type: controlled & paid
Owner(s):
Executive Enterprises Publications Co., Inc.
457 N. Harrison St.
Princeton, NJ 08542
Telephone: (609) 924-9394
Ownership %: 100
Management:
Kathy Murphy ........................................Publisher
Editorial:
Patrice Sarath ..............................................Editor
Micheal Burke ....................Advertising Director
Jan Hahn ..........................Advertising Executive
Cindy Leffingwell ................Circulation Director
Desc.: The leading independent magazine in the Wang marketplace; with a broad range of coverage from quick news items about Wang to highly technical user-oriented articles. Covers the latest developments in the Wang marketplace, not only for VS users who plan to stick with their current system, but for those users who are ready to integrate various platforms or move to a new platform, such as the RISC Series. Keeps readers abreast of advances in integration and migration products and services, whether they're provided by Wang Labs or third-party companies. Describes how users can successfully introduce non-VS products into their evolving computing environments.
Readers: Wang Systems users, users of Wang software and services, as well as Wang hardware.

52591
## ACM COMPUTING SURVEYS
1515 Broadway, 17th Fl.
New York, NY 10036-5701
Telephone: (212) 869-7440
FAX: (212) 944-1318
Year Established: 1969
Pub. Frequency: q.
Page Size: standard
Subscrip. Rate: $100/yr to non-members
Circulation: 33,000
Circulation Type: paid
Owner(s):
ACM-Association for Computing Machinery
1515 Broadway, 17th Fl.
New York, NY 10036-5701
Telephone: (212) 869-7440
Ownership %: 100
Management:
Joseph DeBlasi .....................Executive Director
Editorial:
Richard Muntz ..............................................Editor
Roma Simon ...........................Managing Editor
Mark Mandelbaum ..............Publication Director
Desc.: Publishes tutorial and survey papers covering the entire range of special areas included in the field of computing science. The aim of the journal is to help researchers discover new specialities and practitioners to stay abreast of developments in the field.
Readers: Students and practitioners of computing science.

56363
## ACM TRANSACTIONS ON DATABASE SYSTEMS
1515 Broadway, 17th Fl.
New York, NY 10036
Telephone: (212) 869-7440
FAX: (212) 944-1318
Year Established: 1976
Pub. Frequency: q.

Page Size: standard
Subscrip. Rate: $75/yr. members; $175/yr. non-members
Circulation: 9,600
Circulation Type: paid
Owner(s):
Association for Computing Machinery
1515 Broadway, 17th Fl.
New York, NY 10036
Telephone: (212) 869-7440
Ownership %: 100
Editorial:
Gio Wiederhold ..........................Editor in Chief
Desc.: Reports the latest database design and implementation methods.
Readers: Industries involved in CAD-CAM, CIM, CAE, data communications, telecommunications, process control, computers and related equipment.

56365
## ACM TRANSACTIONS ON GRAPHICS
1515 Broadway, 17th Fl.
New York, NY 10036
Telephone: (212) 869-7440
FAX: (212) 944-1318
Year Established: 1982
Pub. Frequency: q.
Page Size: standard
Subscrip. Rate: $32/yr. members; $115/yr. to non-members
Circulation: 6,104
Circulation Type: paid
Owner(s):
Association for Computing Machinery
1515 Broadway, 17th Fl.
New York, NY 10036
Telephone: (212) 869-7440
Ownership %: 100
Management:
Carol Meyer ........................................Publisher
Editorial:
Jim Foley ...................................Editor in Chief
Desc.: ACM Transactions on Graphics features exciting significant and original work in every aspect of the use and development of computer graphics. Leading researchers discuss breakthroughs in computer-aided design, synthetic image generation, rendering, solid modeling and other area. The largest regular section, "Research" is necessary intellectual nourishment for anyone implementing graphics systems. The "Practice and Experience" papers and the "Interaction Technique Notebook" contain accounts of innovative systems, informative applications and novel user interface ideas.
Readers: Industries involved in CAD/CAM/CIM/CAE, and consumer electronics.

56426
## ACM TRANSACTIONS ON MATHEMATICAL SOFTWARE
1515 Broadway, 17th Fl.
New York, NY 10036
Telephone: (212) 869-7440
FAX: (212) 869-0481
Year Established: 1975
Pub. Frequency: q.
Page Size: standard
Subscrip. Rate: $28/yr. members; $114/yr. non-members
Materials: 19
Circulation: 3,114
Circulation Type: paid
Owner(s):
Association for Computing Machinery
1515 Broadway, 17th Fl.
New York, NY 10036
Telephone: (212) 869-7440
Ownership %: 100

Editorial:
Ronald Fl. Boisvert ......................Editor in Chief
Desc.: ACM Transactions on Mathematical Software publishes significant results in fundamental mathematical algorithms and associated software plus thoroughly tested programs in machine-readable form.
Readers: Industries involved in computer/mathematical software.

56367
## ACM TRANSACTIONS ON PROGRAMMING LANGUAGES & SYSTEMS
1515 Broadway, 17th Fl.
New York, NY 10036
Telephone: (212) 869-7440
FAX: (212) 869-0481
Year Established: 1979
Pub. Frequency: bi-m.
Page Size: standard
Subscrip. Rate: $35/yr. members; $150/yr. to non-members
Materials: 19
Circulation: 7,077
Circulation Type: paid
Owner(s):
Association for Computing Machinery
1515 Broadway, 17th Fl.
New York, NY 10036
Telephone: (212) 869-7440
Ownership %: 100
Management:
Carol Meyer ........................................Publisher
Editorial:
Andrew W. Appel ........................Editor in Chief
Desc.: Offers research & technical papers, algorithms, and technical correspondence over the full spectrum of programming languages and systems. Influential research, technical papers, and correspondence relevant to the logic, meaning, correctness and efficiency of programming languages and computing systems. In the process, it addresses systems organization, analysis of algorithms, program complexity, communications networks, operating system, artificial intelligence, software engineering and related topics
Readers: Industries involved in CAD/CAM/CIM/CAE, data communications, telecommunications, process control, computers, and related equipment.

69476
## ADVANCED IMAGING
445 Broad Hollow Rd., Ste. 21
Melville, NY 11747-4722
Telephone: (516) 845-2700
FAX: (516) 845-2797
Year Established: 1986
Pub. Frequency: m.
Subscrip. Rate: free to qualified personnel
Circulation: 42,000
Circulation Type: controlled
Owner(s):
PTN Publishing Co.
445 Broad Hollow Rd.
Melville, NY 11747-4722
Telephone: (516) 845-2700
Ownership %: 100

56272
## AI MAGAZINE
445 Burgess Dr.
Menlo Park, CA 94025-3496
Telephone: (510) 328-3123
FAX: (415) 321-4457
Year Established: 1980
Pub. Frequency: q.

Page Size: standard
Subscrip. Rate: $40/yr. to individuals; $65/yr. corporate & libraries
Materials: 01,02,05,06,10,19,20,21,28,29, 30,32
Freelance Pay: negotiable
Print Process: web offset
Circulation: 10,000
Circulation Type: paid
Owner(s):
American Association for Artificial Intelligence
445 Burgess Dr.
Menlo Park, CA 94025
Telephone: (415) 328-3123
FAX: (415) 321-4457
Ownership %: 100
Bureau(s):
Live Oak Press, The
P.O. Box 60036
Palo Alto, CA 94306
Telephone: (415) 853-0197
Contact: David Hamilton, Consulting Editor
Management:
Mike Hamilton ...................Advertising Manager
Editorial:
Ramesh Patil ...............................................Editor
Ellie Engelmore .......................Managing Editor
Milend Tambe ....................Book Review Editor
David Hamilton .......................Consulting Editor
Carol Hamilton .......................Executive Director
Sunny Ludvik .........................Production Editor
Desc.: The official publication of the American Association for Artificial Intelligence. Its purpose is to disseminate timely and informative articles which represent the current state of the art in artificial intelligence. Articles are selected for appeal to the broad spectrum of researchers in AI and related areas, and are intended to be clear enough to permit specialists to review work outside their particular area of expertise.
Readers: Computer science professionals, business managers, information science professionals, academicians in computer science, psychology, etc., programmers, knowledge engineers, and experts in all fields who have an interest in artificial intelligence theory and application.

65667
## BANK AUTOMATION QUARTERLY
823 Westfield Blvd.
Indianapolis, IN 46220
Telephone: (317) 251-7727
Year Established: 1975
Pub. Frequency: q.
Page Size: standard
Subscrip. Rate: controlled circulation
Circulation: 15,000
Circulation Type: controlled
Owner(s):
Bank Automation Quarterly
823 Westfield Blvd.
Indianapolis, IN 46220
Telephone: (317) 251-7727
Ownership %: 100
Management:
L.A. Welke ..........................................Publisher
Desc.: To report on the software, services, and related products developed to improve operations, products, and profitability for banks and other financial institutions.
Readers: Bank operations and DP/MIS staff.

65298
## BULLETIN, THE
12416 Hymeadow Dr.
Austin, TX 78750
Telephone: (512) 250-9023
FAX: (512) 331-3900
Year Established: 1983

Pub. Frequency: m.
Page Size: tabloid
Subscrip. Rate: $92/yr.
Circulation: 6,000
Circulation Type: paid
**Owner(s):**
Cahners Publishing Co.
275 Washington St.
Newton, MA 02158-1630
Ownership %: 100
**Editorial:**
Sandy Marshal .................................Editor
**Desc.:** Features product news, technical articles and software, hardware reviews for users of Honeywell systems, from the DPS610 to the DPS900 systems.
**Readers:** Users of Bull Information Systems

## BYTE
69738
One Phoenix Mill Ln.
Peterborough, NH 03458
Telephone: (603) 924-9281
FAX: (603) 924-2550
Year Established: 1975
Pub. Frequency: m.
Subscrip. Rate: $29.95/yr.
Materials: 02,06,29,32,33
Circulation: 500,000
Circulation Type: paid
**Owner(s):**
McGraw-Hill, Inc.
One Phoenix Mill Ln.
Peterborough, NH 03458
Telephone: (603) 924-9281
Ownership %: 100
**Bureau(s):**
West Coast
1900 O'Farrell St.
Ste. 200
San Mateo, CA 94403
Telephone: (415) 513-6809
FAX: (415) 513-6950
Contact: Andy Reinhardt, Bureau Chief

New York
1221 Ave. of the Americas
28th Fl.
New York, NY 10020
Telephone: (212) 512-6057
FAX: (212) 512-2075
Contact: Ed Perratore, News Editor
**Editorial:**
Dennis Allen .................................Editor

## CAPACITY MANAGEMENT REVIEW
56281
P.O. Box 82266
Phoenix, AZ 85071
Telephone: (800) 234-2227
FAX: (602) 861-2587
Year Established: 1973
Pub. Frequency: m.
Page Size: standard
Subscrip. Rate: $195/yr.
Circulation: 2,000
Circulation Type: paid
**Owner(s):**
Applied Computer Research, Inc.
P.O. Box 82266
Phoenix, AZ 85071
Telephone: (602) 995-5929
Ownership %: 100
**Management:**
Phillip C. Howard .......................President
Alice Howard .........................Vice President
Suzanne Howard ...........................Manager
**Editorial:**
Phillip C. Howard ............................Editor
Janet Butler ....................Managing Editor
Alan Howard ....................Marketing Director
Karen Hedden ..................Marketing Director

**Desc.:** Includes in-depth tutorial reports and case studies on aspects of performance evaluation, improvement, or management. Typical subjects include capacity planning, user services, job accounting, performance measurement and new products.
**Readers:** Current subscribers include EDP managers, operations managers, capacity planners, tech support managers, and performance analysts.

## CD-ROM ENDUSER
67211
7 Cottonwood Ln.
Hilton Head, SC 29926-1960
Year Established: 1989
Pub. Frequency: m.
Page Size: standard
Subscrip. Rate: free
Circulation: 350,000
Circulation Type: controlled
**Owner(s):**
Disc Co., The
6609 Rosecroft Pl.
Falls Church, VA 22043
Telephone: (703) 237-0682
Ownership %: 100
**Management:**
Linda Helgerson .........................Publisher
Susan Anastase ...............Advertising Manager
**Editorial:**
Linda Helgerson ............................Editor
**Readers:** Users of CD-Rom technology

## CD DATA REPORT
61677
7 Cottonwood Ln.
Hilton Head, SC 29926-1960
Year Established: 1984
Pub. Frequency: m.
Page Size: standard
Subscrip. Rate: $395/yr.
**Owner(s):**
Disc Co., The
6609 Rosecrott Pl.
Falls Church, VA 22043
Telephone: (703) 237-0682
Ownership %: 100
**Editorial:**
Linda W. Helgerson .......................Editor

## CHINA INFORMATICS
59580
5 Speen St.
Framingham, MA 01701
Telephone: (508) 872-8200
Year Established: 1973
Pub. Frequency: 24/yr.
Page Size: standard
Subscrip. Rate: $595/yr.
Circulation: 300
Circulation Type: paid
**Owner(s):**
International Data Corp.
5 Speen St.
Framingham, MA 01701
Telephone: (508) 872-8200
Ownership %: 100
**Bureau(s):**
International Data Corp. China - Hong Kong
12-F Seabird House
Wyndham St., Central,
 Hong Kong Hong Kong
Telephone: 852-8456588
**Management:**
Saiman Hui .................................Publisher
**Editorial:**
David Herbener .............................Editor
**Desc.:** Provides news coverage on China's information technology industry and markets, covers major foreign sales in China, technical process, import policies and marketing profiles.

## COMMUNICATIONS OF THE ACM
22710
1515 Broadway
New York, NY 10036
Telephone: (212) 869-7440
FAX: (212) 869-0481
Year Established: 1958
Pub. Frequency: m.
Page Size: standard
Subscrip. Rate: $79/yr. members; $109/yr. non-members
Circulation: 85,000
Circulation Type: paid
**Owner(s):**
Association for Computing Machinery
1515 Broadway
New York, NY 10036
Telephone: (212) 869-7440
Ownership %: 100
**Management:**
James Maurer .............................Publisher
Roxanne Carcaterra ..........Business Manager
**Editorial:**
Jacques Cohen .......................Editor in Chief
Diane Crawford ..................Executive Editor
Carla V. Roberts ..........Administrative Assistant
Timothy Bennett ..........................Advertising
Walter Andrzejewski .........Advertising Director
Thomas E. Lambert ................Associate Editor
Mark Mandelbaum ............Publication Director
**Desc.:** Main content is refereed articles on all aspects of computer science, including artificial intelligence, graphics, database systems, programming languages and techniques, scientific applications, computer systems, operating systems, computing theory, and management science.
**Readers:** Members of the computing profession.

## COMPUTER DESIGN MAGAZINE
22847
10 Tara Blvd.
5th Fl.
Nashua, NH 03062-2801
Telephone: (603) 891-0123
FAX: (603) 891-0514
Year Established: 1962
Pub. Frequency: m.
Page Size: standard
Subscrip. Rate: $85/yr.
Materials: 28,31,32,33
Freelance Pay: open
Print Process: web offset
Circulation: 102,060
Circulation Type: controlled & paid
**Owner(s):**
PennWell Publishing Co., Advanced Technology Group
10 Tara Blvd.
Nahua, NH 03062-2801
Telephone: (603) 891-0123
FAX: (603) 891-0514
Ownership %: 100
**Management:**
Frank Lauinger ...............Chairman of Board
Joseph Wolking ............................President
John Maney ..........................Vice President
Dr. Morris Levitt ....................Vice President
David L. Allen ...........................Publisher
Ron Kalusha ...................Circulation Manager
Karen Schulz ........Customer Service Manager
Tim Tobeck ..........................Sales Manager
**Editorial:**
John Miklosz .......................Editor in Chief
Warren Andrews ........................Senior Editor
Barbara Tuck .............................Senior Editor
Tom Williams ............................Senior Editor
Michael Donlin ..........................Senior Editor
Jeff Child ...............................Senior Editor
Ray Weiss ..............................Senior Editor
John Miklosz ....................Associate Publisher
Tim Tobeck .....................Associate Publisher
Paul Westervelt ...............Circulation Director
John Maney ........................Finance Director

Joni Montemagno ...............Marketing Director
Richard Sarno ..............Presentation Manager
Cathi Butt .......................................Sales
David Singer ...................................Sales
Diane Palermo ................................Sales
Eric Jeter .......................................Sales
Kelly Rice ...........Special Projects Coordinator
**Desc.:** Serves companies and organizations that design and develop computers, computer peripherals and other electronic equipment that incorporate microprocessors, board-level computers or computers for sale or in-house use, worldwide. The magazine is targeted at senior design engineers and design engineering managers and focuses on technology, design and product information as it affects system performance and integrity.
**Readers:** Engineers and engineering managers involved in the development of computer microprocessor-based systems.
**Deadline:** story-60 days prior to pub. date; ads-30 days prior

## COMPUTER GRAPHICS WORLD
52586
10 Tara Blvd.
5th Fl.
Nashua, NH 03062-2801
Telephone: (603) 891-0123
FAX: (603) 891-0539
Year Established: 1978
Pub. Frequency: m.
Page Size: standard
Subscrip. Rate: $4.95 newsstand; $48/yr.
Materials: 01,06,15,28,29,30,32
Freelance Pay: $0.50/word
Circulation: 70,000
Circulation Type: paid
**Owner(s):**
PennWell Publishing Co.
1421 South Sheridan
Tulsa, OK 74101
Telephone: (918) 835-3161
Ownership %: 100
**Management:**
Robert P. Holton ........................Publisher
Paul Westervelt .................Circulation Manager
**Editorial:**
Stephen Porter .............................Senior Editor
**Desc.:** CGW reports on the use of modeling animation and multimedia in the areas of science and engineering, art, and entertainment, and presentation and training.
**Readers:** Users and developers of computer graphics technology, systems, and software.

## COMPUTER INDUSTRY REPORT ("THE GRAY SHEET")
23418
5 Speen St.
Framingham, MA 01701
Telephone: (508) 935-4760
FAX: (508) 935-4271
Mailing Address:
 P.O. Box 955
 Framingham, MA 01701
Year Established: 1964
Pub. Frequency: s-m.
Page Size: standard
Subscrip. Rate: $495/yr.
**Owner(s):**
International Data Corp.
5 Speen St.
Framingham, MA 01701
Telephone: (508) 935-4760
FAX: (508) 935-4271
Ownership %: 100
**Management:**
Kirk Campbell ............................President
**Editorial:**
Doug McLeod ...............................Editor

**Materials Accepted/Included:** 01-Business news 02-By-line articles 03-Fashion news 04-Food news 05-Freelance copy 06-Letters to editor 07-Real estate news 08-Sports news 09-Travel news 10-Book rev. 11-Movie rev. 12-Music rev. 13-TV rev. 14-Theater rev. 15-Coming events 16-Obituaries 17-Question & answer 18-Social announcements 19-Artwork 20-Cartoons 21-Photos 22-TV listings 23-Audio rec. 24-Video rec. 25-Books 26-Films/film clips 27-Personnel news 28-Press releases 29-New product news/photos 30-Trade lit. 31-Contracts awarded 32-Display adv. 33-Classified adv.

4-97

David Moschella ..................Contributing Editor
Peter Burris ..................Contributing Editor
**Desc.:** Provides original research; identifying and explaining important trends in world wide IT industry.
**Readers:** Executives concerned with the electronic data processing industry.

65688
## COMPUTER INDUSTRY UPDATE
960 N. San Antonio Rd., 130
Los Altos, CA 94022
Telephone: (415) 941-6679
Mailing Address:
 P.O. Box 681
 Los Altos, CA 94023
Year Established: 1979
Pub. Frequency: m.
Page Size: standard
Subscrip. Rate: $345/yr.
**Owner(s):**
IMR, Inc.
Box 681
Los Altos, CA 94023
Telephone: (415) 941-6679
**Editorial:**
George Weiser ..................Editor
**Desc.:** To provide summaries of product announcements, vendor news, and articles of interest from the computer industry tack press. Summaries are organized by market segment: Mainframes, Minicomputers, Workstations, Peripherals, Personal Computers, and Networking. Publications covered: Computerworld, Communications Week, Electronic News, Information Week, Datanation, NetworkWorld, Software Magazine.

58724
## COMPUTER LANGUAGE
600 Harrison St.
San Francisco, CA 94107
Telephone: (415) 905-2200
Year Established: 1984
Pub. Frequency: m.
Page Size: standard
Subscrip. Rate: $29.95/yr.
Freelance Pay: negotiable
Circulation: 65,000
Circulation Type: paid
**Owner(s):**
Miller Freeman, Inc.
600 Harrison St.
San Francisco, CA 94107
Telephone: (415) 905-2200
**Management:**
Regina Starr Ridley ..................Publisher
**Editorial:**
Larrry O'Brien ..................Editor
**Desc.:** Technical editorial for professional software developers.
**Readers:** Professional software developers & engineers.

49807
## COMPUTER RESELLER NEWS
600 Community Dr.
Manhasset, NY 11030
Telephone: (516) 562-5000
FAX: (516) 562-5636
Year Established: 1982
Pub. Frequency: w.
Page Size: tabloid
Subscrip. Rate: controlled
Materials: 01,05,06,10,28,32,33
Circulation: 104,000
Circulation Type: controlled
**Owner(s):**
CMP Publications, Inc.
600 Community Dr.
Manhasset, NY 11030
Telephone: (516) 562-5000
Ownership %: 100

**Bureau(s):**
Al Senia, Sr. Ed.
1849 Sawtelle Blvd.
Los Angeles, CA 90025
Telephone: (310) 204-0337
Contact: Albert Pang, Editor

East Coast
One Hollis St.
Ste. 205
Wellesley, MA 02181
Telephone: (617) 237-5588
**Editorial:**
Bob Faletra ..................Editor in Chief
Bob DeMarzo ..................Executive Editor
Brian Gillooly ..................Editor
Pat Pan ..................Copy Chief
Edie Feldman ..................Production Editor
Albert Pang ..................West Coast Bureau Chief

57277
## COMPUTERS & SECURITY
562 Croydon Rd.
Elmont, NY 11003
Telephone: (516) 488-6868
Year Established: 1982
Pub. Frequency: 8/yr.
Page Size: standard
Subscrip. Rate: $273/yr.
Circulation: 2,500
Circulation Type: paid
**Owner(s):**
Elsevier Advanced Technology Publications
**Management:**
John Meyers ..................Publisher
**Editorial:**
Dr. Harold Highland ..................Editor
**Desc.:** International journal for the professionals involved in computed security, audit, control and data integrity. Official journal of IFIP/TC 11. Feature columns and articles directed toward business, governments and research.
**Readers:** Major corporations over the world, government agencies, etc. Primarily computer security and/or audit directors. Also top corporate management.

52582
## COMPUTERS IN HEALTHCARE
6300 S. Syracuse Wy., Ste. 650
Englewood, CO 80111
Telephone: (303) 220-0600
Year Established: 1980
Pub. Frequency: m.
Page Size: standard
Subscrip. Rate: $24/yr.
Circulation: 17,000
Circulation Type: controlled
**Owner(s):**
Cardiff Publishing Co., Inc.
6300 S. Syracuse Way, Ste. 650
Englewood, CO 80111
Telephone: (303) 220-0600
Ownership %: 100
**Management:**
Robert A. Searle ..................President
**Editorial:**
Carolyn Dunbar ..................Managing Editor
Michael Laughlin ..................Industry Editor
**Desc.:** Features articles on healthcare computing in hospitals, clinics, M.D. offices, HMO's, nursing homes, and home healthcare. Also includes management, finance, ADT, nursing, pharmacy, laboratory, radiology, HIS, CIS, and materials management.
**Readers:** Hospital administration, data processing, ancillary department heads, clinic & HMO management, physicians, medical persons, vendors, consultants, medical school libraries, purchasing, finance, etc.

67694
## COMPUTERS IN PHYSICS
One Physics Ellipse
College Park, MD 20740-3843
Telephone: (301) 209-3001
FAX: (301) 209-0842
Year Established: 1987
Pub. Frequency: bi-m.
Page Size: standard
Subscrip. Rate: $50/yr. members
Materials: 02,06,10,15,21,25,29,32
Circulation: 9,500
Circulation Type: paid
**Owner(s):**
American Institute of Physics
One Physics Ellipse
College Park, MD 20740-3843
Telephone: (301) 209-3000
Ownership %: 100
**Management:**
Rich Kobel ..................Advertising Manager
**Editorial:**
Lewis Holmes ..................Editor
Ed Greeley ..................Advertising Director
D. LaFrenler ..................Marketing Manager
**Desc.:** Foster progress in physics through computing, by facilitating the exchange of ideas on new computer technologies, and reporting on the performance of relevant products.
**Readers:** Physics researchers and educators.
**Deadline:** story-2-1/2 mos.; photo-2-1/2 mos.; ads-2-1/2 mos.

66174
## COMPUTER SURVIVAL MAGAZINE
400 E. 59th St., 9F
New York, NY 10022
Telephone: (212) 755-4363
FAX: (212) 755-4365
Year Established: 1982
Pub. Frequency: m.
Page Size: standard
Subscrip. Rate: $50/yr.
Materials: 01,02,06,17,23,24,25,26,27,28, 29,30
Circulation: 200,000
Circulation Type: controlled
**Owner(s):**
Enterprises Publishing
400 E. 59th St., 9F
New York, NY 10022
Telephone: (212) 755-4363
Ownership %: 100
**Editorial:**
John Edwards ..................Editor
**Desc.:** Computer hardware-software and journals; reviews sales, help-technical support and development of system information. New listings and introductions-testing evaluation of hardware, software, facsimile and all rented outputs, including business and professional equipment, and office machines and supplies.
**Readers:** Outlines professions, consumers, trades and media.
**Deadline:** story-30 days prior to pub. date

22290
## COMPUTERWORLD
375 Cochituate Rd.
Framingham, MA 01701
Telephone: (508) 879-0700
FAX: (508) 875-8931
Mailing Address:
 Box 9171
 Framingham, MA 01701
Year Established: 1967
Pub. Frequency: Mon.
Page Size: tabloid
Subscrip. Rate: $44/yr.
Circulation: 135,568
Circulation Type: paid

**Owner(s):**
Computer World Publishing
P.O. Box 9171
Framingham, MA 01701
Telephone: (617) 879-0700
Ownership %: 100
**Management:**
Fritz Landmann ..................President
Kevin Harold ..................Vice President
Kevin Harold ..................Sales Manager
**Editorial:**
Bill Labaris ..................Editor in Chief
Paul Gillen ..................Exec. Editor
**Desc.:** Edited for MIS/DP and other information systems professionals who are responsible for planning, implementation and management of computer-based information systems, including data and telecomm, in business, government, vendor and educational organizations. Coverage includes latest news, as well as, Features, Spotlight sections, and in-depth articles on everything from PC's to Super computers. Editorial sections include systems and Software, Networking, Microcomputing, Trends, Management, Computer Industry, Computer Careers, Marketplace, and Training.
**Readers:** Executives, managers and technical staff who are responsible for, or involved in the operation of, computer - based management information and data processing systems, including communication systems; executives, marketing and technical staff at companies which supply computer - related products and/or services to computer - using organizations; consultants and other professionals involved with computers and computer - based systems.

22291
## COMPUTING REVIEWS
1515 Broadway, 17th Fl.
New York, NY 10036
Telephone: (212) 869-7440
FAX: (212) 944-1318
Year Established: 1960
Pub. Frequency: m.
Page Size: standard
Subscrip. Rate: $130/yr. non-member
Freelance Pay: varies
Circulation: 7,000
Circulation Type: paid
**Owner(s):**
Association for Computing Machinery
1515 Broadway, 17th Fl.
New York, NY 10036
Telephone: (212) 869-7440
Ownership %: 100
**Management:**
Carol Meyer ..................Publisher
**Editorial:**
Aaron Finerman ..................Editor in Chief
Craig Rodkin ..................Assignment Editor
Vicki Rosenzweig ..................Assistant Editor
Carol Wierzbicki ..................Associate Editor
Mark Mandelbaum ..................Publication Director
**Desc.:** Review articles covering computing. Reviews books, theses, periodicals, films, recordings, etc., pertinent to computing.
**Readers:** Computing and information processing scientists; computing centers, professors. Other professionals closely connected with computers or automation, including computer science degree candidates and librarians.

---

Materials Accepted/Included: 01-Business news 02-By-line articles 03-Fashion news 04-Food news 05-Freelance copy 06-Letters to editor 07-Real estate news 08-Sports news 09-Travel news 10-Book rev. 11-Movie rev. 12-Music rev. 13-TV rev. 14-Theater rev. 15-Coming events 16-Obituaries 17-Question & answer 18-Social announcements 19-Artwork 20-Cartoons 21-Photos 22-TV listings 23-Audio rec. 24-Video rec. 25-Books 26-Films/film clips 27-Personnel news 28-Press releases 29-New product news/photos 30-Trade lit. 31-Contracts awarded 32-Display adv. 33-Classified adv.

## DATA BASED ADVISOR
54061

4010 Morena Blvd., Ste. 200
San Diego, CA 92117
Telephone: (619) 483-6400
FAX: (619) 483-9851
Year Established: 1983
Pub. Frequency: m.
Page Size: standard
Subscrip. Rate: $3.95 newsstand; $35/yr.
Materials: 01,02,05,06,10,15,17,19,21,28,
29,32,33
Freelance Pay: negotiable
Circulation: 41,138
Circulation Type: paid
**Owner(s):**
Larry Eitel
4010 Morena Blvd.
San Diego, CA 92117
Telephone: (619) 483-6400
Ownership %: 62

David Goldberg
4010 Morena Blvd.
San Diego, CA 92117
Telephone: (619) 483-6400
Ownership %: 5

Walter Karasek
4010 Morena Blvd.
San Diego, CA 92117
Telephone: (619) 483-6400
Ownership %: 5

Danny Thiessen
4010 Morena Blvd.
San Diego, CA 92117
Telephone: (619) 483-6400
Ownership %: 5

Frank Lomas
4010 Morena Blvd.
San Diego, CA 92117
Telephone: (619) 483-6400
Ownership %: 21
**Management:**
Bill Ota ............................................Publisher
B. J. Ghiglione ................Advertising Manager
Becky Hitchcock ................Circulation Manager
**Editorial:**
John L. Hawkins ................................Editor
Sharon Mann ...........................Art Director
David Irwin ...........................Miscellaneous
Alicia Rocks ...........................Miscellaneous
**Desc.:** Focuses on solving business
problems with PC-based database
programming products. Each month's
issue includes business applications,
feature articles, software reviews,
useable source code and practical
information that will increase DBMS
knowledge, productivity and effeciency.
**Readers:** Sophisticated database
developers, interested in the latest
hardware, software utilities and
techniques for maximizing computer
efficiency.
**Deadline:** story-1st of mo., 3 mo. prior to
pub. date; news-10th of mo., 3 mo. prior
to pub. date; photo-1st of mo., 3 mo.
prior to pub. date

## DATA BASE DIGEST
67198

P.O. Box 19874
Santa Ana, CA 92713
Telephone: (714) 553-8200
Year Established: 1988
Pub. Frequency: bi-m.
Page Size: standard
Subscrip. Rate: $55/yr.
Circulation: 1,000
Circulation Type: paid

**Owner(s):**
Jes Publishing Co.
P.O. Box 19274
Irvine, CA 92713
Telephone: (714) 553-8200
Ownership %: 100
**Management:**
Jonathan Sisk ...........................President
**Editorial:**
Kathy Burbank ...........................Editor

## DATA BASE PRODUCT REPORTS
58559

401 E. Rte. 70
Cherry Hill, NJ 08034
Telephone: (609) 428-1020
FAX: (609) 428-1683
Mailing Address:
P.O. Box 5062
Cherry Hill, NJ 08034
Pub. Frequency: m.
Page Size: standard
Subscrip. Rate: $721/yr.
**Owner(s):**
Lawrence Feidelman
401 E. Rte. 70
Cherry Hill, NJ 08034
Telephone: (609) 428-1020
Ownership %: 100
**Management:**
Lawrence Feidelman ...........................Publisher
Carol Bell ...........................Manager
**Editorial:**
Mark Kostic ...........................Managing Editor
**Desc.:** Provides evaluations and
competitive analyses of data base
management systems implemented on
microcomputers & medium to large size
mainframe systems. Each product
description contains systems
configuration, operating systems,
program languages, program functions,
communications & pricing. Each month
new products are evaluated and updates
are provided on previously evaluated
products. Service includes initial two
volumes plus monthly reports.
**Readers:** MIS, data processing managers,
vendors, government.

## DATABASE PROGRAMMING & DESIGN
65262

600 Harrison St.
San Francisco, CA 94107
Telephone: (415) 905-2200
FAX: (415) 905-2234
Year Established: 1987
Pub. Frequency: m.
Page Size: standard
Subscrip. Rate: $37/yr.
Freelance Pay: $75/printed pg.
Circulation: 30,000
Circulation Type: paid
**Owner(s):**
Miller Freeman, Inc.
600 Harrison St.
San Francisco, CA 94107
Telephone: (415) 905-2200
Ownership %: 100
**Management:**
Steve Schneiderman ...........................Publisher
**Editorial:**
David B. Stodder ...........................Editor
Annalisa Chamberlain ...........................Managing Editor
**Desc.:** Features technical, how-to articles
covering corporate database
applications development, maintenance,
and management, as well as technical
developments.
**Readers:** Management information system
and data processing managers,
database administrators, application
developers.

## DATACOM READER
67037

P.O. Box 24344
Minneapolis, MN 55424
Telephone: (612) 935-2035
FAX: (612) 829-5871
Year Established: 1982
Pub. Frequency: m.
Page Size: standard
Subscrip. Rate: $175/yr.
Materials: 29
Print Process: offset
**Owner(s):**
Architecture Technology Corp.
P.O. Box 24344
Minneapolis, MN 55424
Telephone: (612) 935-2035
Ownership %: 100
**Management:**
Kenneth Thurber ...........................President
**Editorial:**
Gordy Palzer ...........................Editor
**Desc.:** Newsletter covering important
developments in the field of data
communications.
**Readers:** Professionals involved in the
field of data communications.
**Deadline:** news-2nd Tue.

## DATA ENTRY AWARENESS REPORT
58710

401 E. Rte. 70
Cherry Hill, NJ 08034
Telephone: (609) 428-1020
FAX: (609) 428-1683
Mailing Address:
P.O. Box 5062
Cherry Hill, NJ 08034
Year Established: 1971
Pub. Frequency: m.
Page Size: standard
Subscrip. Rate: $721/yr.
**Owner(s):**
Lawrence Feidelman
MIC-401 E. Rte. 70
Cherry Hill, NJ 08034
Telephone: (609) 428-1020
Ownership %: 100
**Management:**
Lawrence Feidelman ...........................Publisher
Carol Bell ...........................Manager
**Editorial:**
Mark Kostic ...........................Managing Editor
**Desc.:** Provides evaluations of such data
entry products as key-to-disk, intelligent
terminals, optical character readers,
imaging, voice data entry, and direct
data entry. Service includes initial two
volumes plus monthly reports.
**Readers:** MIS, data processing managers,
data entry managers, vendors,
government.

## DATAMATION
24435

275 Washington St.
Newton, MA 02158
Telephone: (617) 964-3030
FAX: (617) 558-4506
Year Established: 1957
Pub. Frequency: s-m.
Page Size: standard
Subscrip. Rate: $75/yr.
Freelance Pay: negotiable
Circulation: 200,000
Circulation Type: controlled & paid
**Owner(s):**
Cahners Publishing Co.
275 Washington St.
Newton, MA 02158
Telephone: (617) 964-3030
Ownership %: 100

**Bureau(s):**
Datamation
595 Market St., Ste. 2500
San Francisco , CA 94105
Telephone: (415) 777-0606
Contact: Jeff Moad, Bureaus Editor
**Management:**
Mak Holdreith ...........................Publisher
**Editorial:**
Kevin Strehlo ...........................Editor in Chief
Steve Paul ...........................Managing Editor
Andrea Ovans ...........Assistant Managing Editor
Cathy McCormick ...........................Assistant Publisher
Regina Twiss ...........................Marketing Manager
**Desc.:** Semi-technical publication
concerned primarily with the use of and
management corporate
information processing resources.
Departments include: Lookahead,
Editorial, and Books; Media Report,
Career Opportunities, Ad Index, Future
Vision, Inside Datamation.
**Readers:** Management and technical
personnel, technical management
people or advisors, independent
consultants, and educators.

## DATA PROCESSING DIGEST
54064

3848 Fredonia Dr.
Los Angeles, CA 90068
Telephone: (310) 851-3156
Mailing Address:
P.O. Box 1249
Los Angeles, CA 90078
Year Established: 1955
Pub. Frequency: m.
Page Size: standard
Subscrip. Rate: $159/yr. US, Canada &
Mexico; $168/yr. elsewhere
**Owner(s):**
Data Processing Digest, Inc.
3848 Fredonia Dr.
Los Angeles, CA 90068
Telephone: (310) 851-3156
**Management:**
Gisela Ilse Wermke ...........Vice President
Margaret Milligan ...........................Publisher
**Editorial:**
Margaret Milligan ...........................Editor
Gisela Ilse Wermke ...........................Miscellaneous
**Desc.:** We review more than 130 scientific,
business, trade, educational & computer
journals each month. We digest articles
selected for specific needs of EDP
Mgmt., computer professionals,
& corporate executives. Books are
reviewed by EDP professionals &
experts. Full reference to original
material is given for each item.
**Readers:** Top mgmt., MIS, EDP, systems
executives in almost every country world
- wide.

## DIGITAL NEWS & REVIEW
66034

275 Washington St.
Newton, MA 02158-1630
Telephone: (617) 964-3030
FAX: (617) 558-4656
Year Established: 1983
Pub. Frequency: bi-w.
Page Size: tabloid
Subscrip. Rate: free to qualified personnel;
$74.95/yr. US; $89.95/yr. Mexico;
$96.25/yr. Canada
Materials: 28,29,30,32,33
Print Process: web
Circulation: 90,000
Circulation Type: controlled

---

**Materials Accepted/Included:** 01-Business news 02-By-line articles 03-Fashion news 04-Food news 05-Freelance copy 06-Letters to editor 07-Real estate news 08-Sports news 09-Travel news 10-Book rev. 11-Movie rev. 12-Music rev. 13-TV rev. 14-Theater rev. 15-Coming events 16-Obituaries 17-Question & answer 18-Social announcements 19-Artwork 20-Cartoons 21-Photos 22-TV listings 23-Audio rec. 24-Video rec. 25-Books 26-Films/film clips 27-Personnel news 28-Press releases 29-New product news/photos 30-Trade lit. 31-Contracts awarded 32-Display adv. 33-Classified adv.

4-99

**Owner(s):**
Cahners Publishing Co.
275 Washington St.
Newton, MA 02158-1630
Telephone: (617) 964-3030
FAX: (617) 558-4656
Ownership %: 100
**Bureau(s):**
Digital News & Review
3031 Tisch Way, Ste. 100
San Jose, CA 95128
Telephone: (408) 345-3030
Contact: Greg Garry, Senior Editor

Digital News & Review
412 North Coast Hwy., Box 357
Laguna Beach, CA 92651
Telephone: (714) 499-6191
Contact: David Simpson, Senior Editor
**Management:**
Backy P. McAdams ...............................Publisher
**Editorial:**
Jack Fegreus, Ph.D. ....................Editor in Chief
Robert Bragdon ..................Marketing Manager
**Desc.:** For Digital Equipment
   microcomputer users. Features articles
   on hardware, software and networking.
**Readers:** Computer software and
   peripheral purchase decision makers at
   DEC sites.
**Deadline:** ads-13 days prior to pub. date.

69231

**DIGITAL SYSTEMS JOURNAL**
101 Witmer Rd.
Horsham, PA 19044
Telephone: (215) 957-1500
FAX: (215) 957-1050
Year Established: 1979
Pub. Frequency: bi-m.
Page Size: standard
Subscrip. Rate: $48/yr. US; $60/yr. foreign
Materials: 02,06
Freelance Pay: $400-800
Circulation: 7,500
Circulation Type: paid
**Owner(s):**
Cardinal Business Media, Inc.
101 Witmer Rd.
Horsham, PA 19044
Telephone: (215) 957-1500
Ownership %: 100
**Editorial:**
Jeff Berman ......................................Advertising
Karen V. Detwiler ........................Editor-in-Chief
**Desc.:** Technical articles on software,
   applications and programming
   techniques.
**Readers:** Programmers for Open VMS,
   OSF/1 and Windows NT operating
   systems.
**Deadline:** story-3 mo. prior to pub. date;
   ads-2 mo. prior

69468

**DIGITAL TECHNICAL JOURNAL**
LJ02/D10
Littleton, MA 01460-1446
Telephone: (508) 486-2544
FAX: (508) 486-2444
Year Established: 1985
Pub. Frequency: q.
Page Size: standard
Subscrip. Rate: $16/copy; $40/yr.
Materials: 10
Print Process: web
Circulation: 12,500
Circulation Type: free & paid
**Owner(s):**
Digital Equipment Corp.
30 Porter Rd.
Littleton, MA 01460
Telephone: (508) 486-2544
Ownership %: 100
**Management:**
Catherine M. Phillips ..........Circulation Manager

**Editorial:**
Jane C. Blake .........................................Editor
**Desc.:** Discusses the application of
   scientific and engineering principles to
   the development of new computer
   technologies and products.
**Readers:** Hardware & software engineers,
   professors of computer science and
   engineering.

56278

**DIRECTORY OF TOP COMPUTER
EXECUTIVES**
P.O. Box 82266
Phoenix, AZ 85071
Telephone: (800) 234-2227
Year Established: 1972
Pub. Frequency: s-a.
Page Size: standard
**Owner(s):**
Applied Computer Research, Inc.
P.O. Box 82266
Phoenix, AZ 85071
Telephone: (602) 995-5929
Ownership %: 100
**Editorial:**
Alan Howard ...........................................Editor
**Desc.:** Lists top DP executives as well as
   second level management in the largest
   user organizations. The directory is
   organized geographically, with an
   industry cross reference. Industry
   segments include manufacturing,
   banking, diversified finance, insurance,
   retail, transportation, education, health
   care and government. Also company
   cross reference. Lists the types of
   mainframe hardware installed at each
   location along with model numbers.
   Over 12000 companies, over 36000
   listed executives.
**Readers:** Sales and marketing
   management, recruiters,
   conference/seminar organizers, DP
   managers, equipment dealers/brokers.

52593

**DR. DOBB'S JOURNAL**
411 Borel Ave.
San Meteo, CA 94402
Telephone: (415) 358-9500
FAX: (415) 358-9749
Year Established: 1976
Pub. Frequency: m.
Page Size: standard
Subscrip. Rate: $29.97/yr.
Freelance Pay: $50/pg.
Circulation: 104,000
Circulation Type: paid
**Owner(s):**
Miller Freeman, Inc.
600 Harrison St.
San Francisco, CA 94107
Telephone: (415) 905-2200
Ownership %: 100
**Management:**
Peter Hutchinson ..................................Publisher
**Editorial:**
John Erickson ...........................Editor in Chief
Monica Berg ...........................Managing Editor
Cyndy Sandor ....................Associate Publisher
**Desc.:** Publishes technical information
   about programming tools & techniques
   that professional software developers
   study & apply in the computer
   marketplace.
**Readers:** Corporate developers,
   consultants, and developers who
   program commercial applications;
   software professionals in management
   positions.

22854

**EDP WEEKLY**
3918 Prosperity Ave., Ste. 310
Fairfax, VA 22031
Telephone: (703) 573-8400
FAX: (703) 573-8594
Year Established: 1958
Pub. Frequency: w.
Page Size: standard
Subscrip. Rate: $495/yr. in country;
   $542/yr. out of country
Materials: 01,02,05,06,10,21,23,24,25,26,
   27,28,29,30,31
Freelance Pay: negotiable
Print Process: offset
Circulation: 1,200
Circulation Type: paid
**Owner(s):**
Computer Age Publications
3918 Prosperity Ave., Ste. 310
Fairfax, VA 22031
Telephone: (703) 573-8400
FAX: (703) 573-8594
Ownership %: 100
**Management:**
S.L. Millin ...........................................Publisher
**Editorial:**
Charles A. Bailey ....................................Editor
Mike Cotter ...........................Managing Editor
Thomas G. Shack III ............Marketing Director
**Desc.:** The nation's oldest independent
   computer publication, reports industry-
   wide corporate and governmental
   announcements, developments and
   strategies, with special twice-monthly
   features on mini and micro computers,
   data communications, robotics,
   electronic funds transfer, and world
   trade.
**Readers:** The makers of high technology
   and users throughout the world; mostly
   chief executives and policy makers.
**Deadline:** story-Thu.; news-Thu.

67673

**GEO INFO SYSTEMS**
7500 Old Oak Blvd.
Cleveland, OH 44130
Telephone: (216) 826-2839
FAX: (216) 891-2726
Year Established: 1990
Pub. Frequency: 10/yr.
Page Size: standard
Subscrip. Rate: $59/yr. US; $117/yr.
   foreign
Circulation: 24,511
Circulation Type: paid
**Owner(s):**
Advanstar Communications, Inc.
7500 Old Oak Blvd.
Cleveland, OH 44130
Ownership %: 100
**Management:**
Brian Langille ........................................Publisher
**Editorial:**
Guy Maynard ...........................................Editor
**Desc.:** Covers practical applications of
   geographic information systems for
   planning, developing and managing
   environments ranging from a local utility
   infrastructure to the North American
   ecosystem.

66592

**GOVERNMENT COMPUTER NEWS**
8601 Georgia Ave., 300
Silver Spring, MD 20910
Telephone: (301) 650-2000
FAX: (301) 650-2111
Year Established: 1982
Pub. Frequency: bi-w.
Page Size: tabloid
Subscrip. Rate: $79.95/yr.
Materials: 02,05,06,15,16,19,21,27,28,29,
   31,32,33
Circulation: 80,000
Circulation Type: controlled & paid

**Owner(s):**
Cahners Publishing Co.
8601 Georgia Ave., 300
Silver Spring, MD 20910
Telephone: (301) 650-2000
FAX: (301) 650-2111
Ownership %: 100
**Management:**
Gary R. Squires ...................................Publisher
**Editorial:**
Thomas R. Temin .....................................Editor
Nancy Ferris ...........................Managing Editor
William A. Klanke ..........National Sales Director
Franke Simon Pass ............Production Director
**Desc.:** The national newspaper of
   government computing.
**Readers:** Government computer
   managers, users and buyers.

65316

**HARLOW REPORT: GEOGRAPHIC
INFORMATION SYSTEMS**
3207 Gatsby Ln.
Montgomery, AL 36106-2669
Telephone: (205) 980-8297
FAX: (205) 991-3877
Year Established: 1978
Pub. Frequency: m.
Page Size: standard
Subscrip. Rate: $190/yr. US; $240/yr.
   foreign
Materials: 01,10,15,24,25,27,28,29
Print Process: offset
Circulation: 2,000
Circulation Type: paid
**Owner(s):**
Advanced Information Management Group
   Inc.
3207 Gatsby Ln.
Montgomery, AL 36106-2669
Telephone: (205) 213-0053
Ownership %: 100
**Editorial:**
Chris Harlow ...........................................Editor
**Desc.:** Newsletter aimed at management
   and technical issues of geographic
   information systems, includes product
   reviewss, advice and editorial reports.
**Readers:** Engineers, municipal plannners,
   utility engineers, computer system
   developers, cartographers, map services
   companies.

52594

**IBM SYSTEMS JOURNAL**
P.O. Box 218
Yorktown Heights, NY 10598-0218
Telephone: (914) 241-4194
Year Established: 1962
Pub. Frequency: q.
Page Size: standard
Subscrip. Rate: $49.50/yr.; $64.50/yr.
   foreign
Materials: 01,10,19,21
Print Process: offset lithography
Circulation: 85,000
Circulation Type: paid
**Owner(s):**
IBM Corp.
Old Orchard Rd.
Armonk, NY 10504
Telephone: (914) 241-4194
Ownership %: 100
**Editorial:**
Gene Hoffnagle .......................................Editor
A.G. Davis ...........................Associate Editor
J.R. Friedman ...........................Associate Editor
C.R. Seddon ...........................Staff Editor
**Desc.:** The objectives of the IBM Systems
   Journal is: to inform and educate its
   readers, provide a bridge between
   computer science and the practical
   application of computing and encourage
   the use of advanced data processing
   technology.

**Materials Accepted/Included:** 01-Business news 02-By-line articles 03-Fashion news 04-Food news 05-Freelance copy 06-Letters to editor 07-Real estate news 08-Sports news 09-Travel news 10-Book rev. 11-Movie rev. 12-Music rev. 13-TV rev. 14-Theater rev. 15-Coming events 16-Obituaries 17-Question & answer 18-Social announcements 19-Artwork 20-Cartoons 21-Photos 22-TV listings 23-Audio rec. 24-Video rec. 25-Books 26-Films/film clips 27-Personnel news 28-Press releases 29-New product news/photos 30-Trade lit. 31-Contracts awarded 32-Display adv. 33-Classified adv.

**Readers:** Computer Science and Systems professionals working in systems, programming, data processing management, and research.

## ID SYSTEMS

52583

174 Concord St.
Peterborough, NH 03458
Telephone: (603) 924-9631
FAX: (603) 924-7408
Mailing Address:
P.O. Box 874
Peterborough, NH 03458-0874
Year Established: 1981
Pub. Frequency: m.
Page Size: standard
Subscrip. Rate: $55/yr. (free to qualified personnel)
Materials: 32
Freelance Pay: approx. $350/article
Circulation: 72,000
Circulation Type: controlled & paid
**Owner(s):**
Helmers Publishing, Inc.
174 Concord St.
Peterborough, NH 03458
Telephone: (603) 924-9631
**Management:**
Kevin Rushalko ..............................Publisher
**Editorial:**
Deborah Navas ..............................Editor
Mary Langen .......................Managing Editor
Carl T. Helmers ...............Editorial Director
Paul Quinn ...........................Feature Editor
Kevin R. Sharp .................Technical Editor
**Desc.:** Covers news and commentary on the state of products and applications involving all keyless data entry technologies-barcode, OCR, touch screen, voice, smart card, RF, etc.
**Readers:** The magazine goes to all industries using or planning to use automatic identification, i.e., manufacturing, warehousing laboratories, retail, government, etc.

## IEEE COMPUTER GRAPHICS & APPLICATIONS

52584

10662 Los Vaqueros Cir.
Los Alamitos, CA 90720
Telephone: (714) 821-8380
Year Established: 1981
Pub. Frequency: bi-m.
Page Size: standard
Subscrip. Rate: $26/yr. members
Freelance Pay: $100/col.
Circulation: 15,000
Circulation Type: paid
**Owner(s):**
IEEE Computer Society
10662 Los Vaqueros Cir.
Los Alamitos, CA 90720
Telephone: (714) 821-8380
Ownership %: 100
**Management:**
True Seaborn ..............................Publisher
Heidi Rex ..........................Advertising Manager
**Editorial:**
Peter Wilson ......................Editor in Chief
Nancy Hays .......................Managing Editor
Marilyn Potes .................Editorial Director
Tony Bird ..........................Assistant Editor
**Desc.:** Is focused on the interests and needs of computer graphics scientists, professional designers and users of computer graphics hardware, software, and systems. It is written and refereed by respected professionals in all areas of the computer graphics field.

**Readers:** Nearly 85% of readers are employed by OEM/end-user firms. Readers purchase, specify, or approve computer systems, components, and peripheral equipment. Readers are highly educated, 54.5% having Master's or Doctorates. 71.2% save their issues for research.

## INDUSTRIAL COMPUTING

67218

67 Alexander Dr,
Research Triangle Park, NC 27709
Telephone: (919) 549-8411
FAX: (919) 549-8288
Year Established: 1989
Pub. Frequency: bi-m.
Page Size: standard
Subscrip. Rate: $55/yr.
Circulation: 45,000
Circulation Type: controlled
**Owner(s):**
ISA Publications
67 Alexander Dr.
Res Triangle Park, NC 27709
Telephone: (919) 549-8411
Ownership %: 100
**Management:**
Richard Simpson ..............................Publisher
Richard Simpson .............Advertising Manager
**Desc.:** Covers technology reports and news on hardware and software products.

## INFORMATION SYSTEMS MANAGEMENT

53971

One Penn Plz.
New York, NY 10119
Telephone: (212) 971-5000
FAX: (212) 971-5024
Year Established: 1983
Pub. Frequency: q.
Page Size: standard
Subscrip. Rate: $134/yr.
Materials: 02,06,10,25,30,32,33
Freelance Pay: varies
Circulation: 8,000
Circulation Type: paid
**Owner(s):**
Auerbach Publications
One Penn Plz.
New York, NY 10119
Telephone: (212) 971-5000
Ownership %: 100
**Editorial:**
Debra Rhoades .......................Managing Editor
**Desc.:** Bridges the gap between management and technically oriented trade and academic publications. Emphasis is on practical information for today's IS manager on current and emerging information systems issues.
**Readers:** IS management and staff.
**Deadline:** story-3 mo. prior to pub. date; ads-3 mo. prior to pub. date

## INFOWORLD

49860

155 Bovet Rd., Ste. 800
San Mateo, CA 94402
Telephone: (415) 572-7341
FAX: (415) 358-1269
Year Established: 1980
Pub. Frequency: w.
Page Size: tabloid
Subscrip. Rate: $110/yr.
Freelance Pay: variable
Circulation: 205,000
Circulation Type: controlled
**Owner(s):**
IDG Communications, Inc.
One Exeter Plz., 15th Fl.
Boston, MA 02116-2851
Telephone: (617) 534-1200
Ownership %: 100

**Management:**
Jonathan Sacks ..............................Publisher
Pat Crotty ....................Circulation Manager
**Editorial:**
Michael J. Miller ................Editor in Chief
Stewart Alsop ..............................Editor
Dennis O'Donnell .............Production Director
**Desc.:** The newsweekly for volume buyers and PC professionals. Publishes news, comprehensive evaluations of software and hardware products, as well as announcements of new products, analyses of trends and profiles of companies and people.
**Readers:** Serious corporate computer buyers.

## INSIDE DPMA

24198

505 Busse Highway
Park Ridge, IL 60068
Telephone: (708) 825-8124
FAX: (708) 825-1693
Year Established: 1988
Pub. Frequency: m.
Page Size: tabloid
Subscrip. Rate: $75/yr.
Circulation: 20,000
Circulation Type: controlled
**Owner(s):**
Data Processing Management Association
505 Busse Highway
Park Ridge, IL 60068
Telephone: (708) 825-8124
Ownership %: 100
**Management:**
Paul Zuziak ..............................Publisher
Michael Wright .................Advertising Manager
**Editorial:**
Paul Zuziak ..............................Editor
**Desc.:** Feature articles are user oriented, dealing with modern data processing concepts, practices, and managerial problems. Departments include latest industry news, new products, meetings and methods information, abstracts of current books and literature. Items of interest regarding members and chapters also are published-OPMA News, Legislative Activity and Special Interest Group News.
**Readers:** Management and supervisory groups in business with responsibility for the installation and efficient operation of information systems.

## JOURNAL OF OBJECT-ORIENTED PROGRAMMING

65327

588 Broadway, Ste. 604
New York, NY 10012
Telephone: (212) 274-0640
FAX: (212) 274-0646
Pub. Frequency: 9/yr.
Page Size: standard
Subscrip. Rate: $59/yr.
Freelance Pay: $200-$250/article
Circulation: 24,000
Circulation Type: paid
**Owner(s):**
SIGS Publications, Inc.
588 Broadway
New York, NY 10012
Telephone: (212) 274-0640
Ownership %: 100
**Management:**
Richard Friedman ..............................Publisher
Margherita Moack .................General Manager
**Editorial:**
Richard S. Weiner ..............................Editor

**Desc.:** Tracks and evaluates the latest advances in object oriented methodology. Features research articles and tutorial papers dealing with problem-solving techniques, re-usable components, applications in artificial intelligence, software maintenance and language development.
**Readers:** High-level software designers and engineers as well as developers and researchers.

## JOURNAL OF ROBOTIC SYSTEMS

65638

605 Third Ave.
New York, NY 10158
Telephone: (212) 850-6000
Pub. Frequency: bi-m.
Page Size: standard
Subscrip. Rate: $525/yr.
Circulation: 700
Circulation Type: paid
**Owner(s):**
John Wiley & Sons, Inc.
605 Third Ave.
New York, NY 10158
Telephone: (212) 850-6000
**Editorial:**
Gerardo Beni ..............................Editor
Susan Hackwood ..............................Editor

## JOURNAL OF SYSTEMS MANAGEMENT

22901

P.O. Box 38370
Cleveland, OH 44138-0370
Telephone: (216) 243-6900
Year Established: 1947
Pub. Frequency: m.
Page Size: standard
Subscrip. Rate: $6/copy; $60/yr.; $110/2 yrs.; $150/3 yrs.
Circulation: 9,000
Circulation Type: paid
**Owner(s):**
Association for Systems Management
P.O. Box 38370
Cleveland, OH 44138
Telephone: (216) 243-6900
FAX: (216) 234-2930
Ownership %: 100
**Management:**
Assoc. for Systems Management .......Publisher
Susan Thornton .................Production Manager
**Desc.:** Covers the tools, techniques and technologies of effective business information systems management. The main goal of the publications is to help business professionals use information technology to improve their organization's efficiency and provide their companies with competitive advantage.
**Readers:** Business professionals who use and manage information systems (including MIS directors and analysts); information systems educators; systems analysts; management consultants specializing in information systems.

## JOURNAL OF THE ACM

56366

1515 Broadway, 17th Fl.
New York, NY 10036
Telephone: (212) 869-7440
FAX: (212) 944-1318
Year Established: 1954
Pub. Frequency: bi-m.
Page Size: standard
Subscrip. Rate: $36/members; $165/yr. to non-members
Circulation: 9,161
Circulation Type: paid

**Materials Accepted/Included:** 01-Business news 02-By-line articles 03-Fashion news 04-Food news 05-Freelance copy 06-Letters to editor 07-Real estate news 08-Sports news 09-Travel news 10-Book rev. 11-Movie rev. 12-Music rev. 13-TV rev. 14-Theater rev. 15-Coming events 16-Obituaries 17-Question & answer 18-Social announcements 19-Artwork 20-Cartoons 21-Photos 22-TV listings 23-Audio rec. 24-Video rec. 25-Books 26-Films/film clips 27-Personnel rev. 28-Press releases 29-New product news/photos 30-Trade lit. 31-Contracts awarded 32-Display adv. 33-Classified adv.

4-101

**Owner(s):**
Association for Computing Machinery
1515 Broadway, 17th Fl.
New York, NY 10036
Telephone: (212) 869-7440
Ownership %: 100
**Editorial:**
F. Thomas Leighton ...................Editor in Chief
**Desc.:** Offers a broad range of scientific
material that keeps computer scientists
aware of the latest issues and
advances. Serves as a venue for careful
presentation of theoretical research in
computing's core areas: complexity of
algorithms, computer architecture,
system modeling, AI, data structures,
database theory and graph theory, to
name a few. The authors are world-class
scientists, writing to other scientists
about advances, methods, and finding
behind the fundamentals.
**Readers:** Industries involved in computers,
CAD-CAM, CIM, CAE, electro-optics &
lasers, fiber optics, semiconductors, and
medical electronics.

69770

**LAN MAGAZINE**
600 Harrison St.
San Francisco, CA 94107-2587
Telephone: (415) 905-2200
FAX: (415) 905-2232
Year Established: 1986
Pub. Frequency: m.
Page Size: standard
Subscrip. Rate: $3.95 newsstand;
$19.97/yr.
Materials: 01,05,06,25,28,29,30,32,33
Print Process: offset
Circulation: 68,000
Circulation Type: paid
**Owner(s):**
Miller Freeman, Inc.
600 Harrison St.
San Francisco, CA 94107
Telephone: (415) 905-2200
FAX: (415) 905-2587
Ownership %: 100
**Editorial:**
Patricia Schnaidt ...........................Editor
**Readers:** MIS, network managers.

69760

**LAN TIMES**
1221 Ave. of the Americas
New York, NY 10020
Telephone: (212) 512-2000
Year Established: 1984
Pub. Frequency: bi-w.
Page Size: tabloid
Subscrip. Rate: free
Materials: 01,02,05,06,10,17,19,20,21,32,33
Freelance Pay: $.50-.70/wd.
Print Process: web offset
Circulation: 153,845
Circulation Type: free & paid
**Owner(s):**
McGraw-Hill, Inc.
1221 Ave. of the Americas
New York, NY 10020
Telephone: (212) 512-2000
Ownership %: 100
**Bureau(s):**
Lexington
24 Hartwell Ave.
Lexington, MA 02173
Telephone: (617) 860-6827
FAX: (617) 860-6899
Contact: Stephen Loudermilk, Associate
Editor

Portland
2083 N.W. Johnson
Ste. 5
Portland, OR 97209
Telephone: (503) 248-4473
FAX: (503) 248-4475
Contact: April Streeter, Senior Editor
**Editorial:**
Susan Breidenbach .................Editor in Chief
Leonard Heymann .......................Editor
**Readers:** Managers and administrators of
PC-based networks. Resellers and
integrators of PC-based networks. MIS
professionals.
**Deadline:** story-2-8 wks. prior to pub. date;
news-2-4 wks. prior to pub. date; photo-
2-8 wks. prior to pub. date; ads-1 mo.
prior to pub. date

67665

**LOCALNETTER, THE**
P.O. Box 24344
Minneapolis, MN 55424
Telephone: (612) 935-2035
FAX: (612) 829-5871
Year Established: 1981
Pub. Frequency: m.
Page Size: standard
Subscrip. Rate: $300/yr. US.
Materials: 01,27,28,29,30,31
Print Process: offset
**Owner(s):**
Architecture Technology Corp.
P.O. Box 24344
Minneapolis, MN 55424
Telephone: (612) 935-2035
Ownership %: 100
**Management:**
Kenneth J. Thurber ......................President
**Editorial:**
Gordy Palzer ................................Editor
**Desc.:** The monthly newsletter covering
important developments in the field of
local computer networks.
**Readers:** Professionals involved in local-
area networks, office systems, and data
communications.
**Deadline:** news-4th Tue.

67208

**MAC ARTIST**
7520 S.W. Schools Ferry Rd.
Beaverton, OR 97005-6581
Telephone: (714) 668-1020
Year Established: 1991
Pub. Frequency: m.
Page Size: standard
Subscrip. Rate: $23.95/yr.
Circulation: 25,000
Circulation Type: controlled & paid
**Owner(s):**
Image Line Publishing Co.
119 E. Alton Ave., Ste. D
Santa Ana, CA 92707
Telephone: (714) 668-1020
Ownership %: 100
**Management:**
Fritz Richard ...............................President
Fritz Richard ...............................Publisher
Belinda Neal .................Advertising Manager
**Editorial:**
Carl Calvert ................................Editor
**Desc.:** Geared to Macintosh graphics
users.

69714

**MACWEEK**
One Park Ave.
New York, NY 10016
Telephone: (415) 243-3500
FAX: (415) 243-3650
Year Established: 1987
Pub. Frequency: w.
Subscrip. Rate: $99/yr. US; $175/yr.
Canada & Mexico; $300/yr. elsewhere
Circulation: 50,000
Circulation Type: paid

**Owner(s):**
Coastal Associates Publishing, L.P.
One Park Ave.
New York, NY 10016
Telephone: (415) 243-3500
Ownership %: 100
**Editorial:**
Daniel Farber ................................Editor

57269

**MANAGING AUTOMATION**
5 Penn Plz.
New York, NY 10001
Telephone: (212) 695-0500
FAX: (212) 629-1564
Year Established: 1986
Pub. Frequency: m.
Page Size: standard
Subscrip. Rate: $60/yr. US; $75/yr.
Canada & Mexico; $125/yr. foreign
Freelance Pay: $500 - $2200/article
Circulation: 100,206
Circulation Type: controlled
**Owner(s):**
Thomas Publishing Co.
One Penn Plz.
New York, NY 10119
Telephone: (212) 695-0500
Ownership %: 100
**Management:**
Ralph E. Richardson ....................Publisher
James Morris ..............................Publisher
**Editorial:**
Robert Malone ....................Editor in Chief
William McIlvaine ...............Managing Editor
**Desc.:** A forum for ideas of interest to
manufacturers employing automation
and suppliers of automation equipment,
as well as for top managers responsible
for implementing manufacturing
technologies and allocating needed
funds to do this. Managing Automation
addresses all the organizational,
financial, and technological issues
engendered by factory automation in the
manufacturing industries.
**Readers:** Carefully selected automation
teams; the individuals responsible for
the key decisions required in automating
manufacturing facilities including:
engineering executives, senior general
management executives at divisional
levels, corporate executives, and
manufacturing executives, including
CEO's and CFO's.

58711

**MIC/TECH-MINI COMPUTERS &
MAINFRAMES**
401 E. Rte. 70
P.O. Box 5062
Cherry Hill, NJ 08034
Telephone: (609) 428-1020
FAX: (609) 428-1683
Pub. Frequency: m.
Page Size: standard
Subscrip. Rate: $1,145/yr.
**Owner(s):**
Lawrence Feidelman
MIC-401 E. Rte. 70
Cherry Hill, NJ 08034
Telephone: (609) 428-1020
Ownership %: 100
**Management:**
Lawrence Feidelman ....................Publisher
Carol Bell .................................Manager
**Editorial:**
Steve Schlanger ...........................Editor

**Desc.:** Provides complete performance
pricing of computer systems from minis
to large scale mainframes. Included with
each product evaluation is a description
of software, peripherals and
communications. Systems are evaluated
in both a stand-alone and networked
configuration. Service is provided on
diskettes.
**Readers:** MIS, data processing managers,
venders, and government.

61256

**MICROCOMPUTER INDUSTRY
UPDATE**
960 N. San Antonio Rd., Ste. 130
Los Altos, CA 94022
Telephone: (415) 941-6679
Mailing Address:
P.O. Box 681
Los Altos, CA 94023
Year Established: 1983
Pub. Frequency: m.
Page Size: standard
Subscrip. Rate: $295/yr.
**Owner(s):**
IMR, Inc.
P.O. Box 681
Los Altos, CA 94023
Telephone: (415) 941-6679
**Editorial:**
George Weiser ............................Editor
**Desc.:** To provide summaries of product
announcements, vendor news, and
articles of interest from the industry
trade press. Summaries are organized
by market segment; personal computers,
high-end systems, software, peripherals,
local area networks, and distribution.
Publications covered: Computer Reseller
News, Computerworld, Infoworld, Byte,
PC Magazine, PC Week, and PC World.
**Readers:** Vendors, consultants, market
researchers and large users.

61592

**MICROCOMPUTER JOURNAL**
76 N. Broadway
Hicksville, NY 11801
Telephone: (516) 681-2922
FAX: (516) 681-2926
Year Established: 1984
Pub. Frequency: bi-m.
Page Size: standard
Subscrip. Rate: $4.95 newsstand;
$29.70/yr.
Materials: 02,05,06,10,15,17,20,25,28,29,
30,32,33
Freelance Pay: $90-150/pub. pg.
Print Process: offset
Circulation: 50,000
Circulation Type: paid
**Owner(s):**
CQ Communications, Inc.
76 N. Broadway
Hicksville, NY 11801
Telephone: (516) 681-2922
FAX: (516) 681-2926
Ownership %: 100
**Management:**
Richard Ross ...............................Publisher
**Editorial:**
Arthur Salsberg ...........................Editor
**Desc.:** Focuses on upgrading, enhancing
and fixing personal computers and
micro-controllers.
**Readers:** Technically inclined do-it-yourself
computer and electronics professionals
and semi-professionals.

61802

**MICROTIMES**
3470 Buskirk Ave.
Pleasant Hill, CA 94523
Telephone: (510) 934-3700
FAX: (510) 934-7351
Year Established: 1984

Pub. Frequency: 13/yr.
Page Size: tabloid
Subscrip. Rate: $32/yr.
Freelance Pay: negotiable
Circulation: 191,440
Circulation Type: free
**Owner(s):**
Dennis Erokan
3470 Buskirk Ave.
Pleasant Hill, CA 94523
Telephone: (510) 934-3700
Ownership %: 100
**Editorial:**
Mary Eisenhart ............................Editor
Michel Rabin ..........................Editorial Assistant
Paul Hoffman ..............................News Editor
**Desc.:** Includes interviews, company profiles, hands on reviews, and new product announcements.
**Readers:** All kinds of PC users-Mac, IBM, Amiga, UHIX, etc.

67027

## MULTIMEDIA WORLD
501 Second St.
San Francisco, CA 94107
Telephone: (415) 281-8650
FAX: (415) 281-3915
Year Established: 1991
Pub. Frequency: m.
Page Size: standard
Subscrip. Rate: $9.95/yr
Circulation: 120,000
Circulation Type: paid
**Owner(s):**
IDG Communications, Inc.
501 Second St.
San Francisco, CA 94107
Telephone: (415) 281-8650
Ownership %: 100
**Management:**
Jonathan Epstein ..............................Publisher
Patricia Navone .................Advertising Manager
**Editorial:**
Don Menn ..............................Editor
**Desc.:** Features informative articles, how-to clinics, new product reviews and special departments on multimedia personal computing.

66322

## NETWARE SOLUTIONS
10711 Burnet Rd., Ste. 305
Austin, TX 78758
Telephone: (512) 873-7761
FAX: (512) 873-7782
Year Established: 1991
Pub. Frequency: m.
Page Size: standard
Subscrip. Rate: $35.40/yr. US; $50/yr. foreign
Freelance Pay: negotiable
Circulation: 40,000
Circulation Type: controlled
**Owner(s):**
DB/Media Publications, Inc.
10711 Burnet Rd., Ste. 305
Austin, TX 78758
Telephone: (512) 873-7761
**Management:**
John V. Moore ..............................Publisher
Kathy Murphy ...................Circulation Manager
Brian Clifton ..............................Sales Manager
**Editorial:**
David J. Nardecchia ..............................Editor
Margaret Mulligan .................Managing Editor
Tony Lopez ..............................Art Director
Jan Kiker ..............................Production Director

**Desc.:** Caters exclusively to the needs of the Novell and compatible marketplace. It provides NetWare system managers and users with how-to articles, reviews, case studies, Q & A columns and product information. Also features Novell industry news and analysis, including Novell corporate and third-party news, plus interviews with Novell officials.
**Readers:** Novell NetWare system managers and users.

66733

## NETWORK COMPUTING
600 Community Dr.
Manhasset, NY 11030
Telephone: (516) 562-5000
FAX: (516) 562-5474
Year Established: 1990
Pub. Frequency: m.
Page Size: standard
Subscrip. Rate: free
Freelance Pay: negotiable
Circulation: 175,000
Circulation Type: controlled
**Owner(s):**
CMP Publications, Inc.
**Management:**
Al Pearlman ..............................Publisher
**Editorial:**
Tony Rizzo ..............................Executive Editor
Gary A. Bolles ..............................Editor
Amy Lipton ..............................Managing Editor
**Readers:** Specifiers of network computing products.

67220

## NETWORK WORLD
161 Worcester Rd.
Framingham, MA 01701
Telephone: (508) 875-6400
FAX: (508) 820-3467
Year Established: 1986
Pub. Frequency: w.
Page Size: tabloid
Subscrip. Rate: controlled for those who qualify
Materials: 01,02,05,06,15,19,20,21,27,28, 29,30,31,32,33
Print Process: web
Circulation: 150,100
Circulation Type: controlled
**Owner(s):**
International Data Group (IDG)
One Exeter Plz.
Boston, MA 02116
Telephone: (617) 534-1200
Ownership %: 100
**Management:**
Colin Ungaro ..............................President
Colin Ungaro ..............................Publisher
**Editorial:**
John Gallant ..............................V. P. Editorial
Deborah Winders .................V.P. Circulation
Mary Fanning ..............................V.P. Finance
Evilee Thibeault ..............................V.P. Marketing
Thomas J. Wilson ..............................V.P. Sales
**Desc.:** Covers enterprise network strategies from corporate backbone networks to developmental departmental LANS including the computers, applications and peripherals that comprise those networks.
**Readers:** Network professionals.

69764

## OPEN COMPUTING
1221 Ave. of the Americas
New York, NY 10020
Telephone: (212) 512-2000
Mailing Address:
1900 O'Farrell St.
San Mateo, CA 94403
Year Established: 1984
Pub. Frequency:

Page Size: standard
Subscrip. Rate: $3 newsstand; $18/yr.
Materials: 06,10,28,29,
Circulation: 48,978
Circulation Type: controlled & paid
**Owner(s):**
McGraw-Hill, Inc.
1221 Ave. of the Americas
New York, NY 10020
Telephone: (212) 512-2000
Ownership %: 100
**Editorial:**
David L. Flack ..............................Editor in Chief

66008

## OPEN SYSTEMS TODAY
600 Community Dr.
Manhasset, NY 11030
Telephone: (516) 562-5000
FAX: (516) 365-4601
Year Established: 1988
Pub. Frequency: bi-w.
Page Size: tabloid
Subscrip. Rate: $69/yr.
Circulation: 100,055
**Owner(s):**
CMP Publications, Inc.
600 Community Dr.
Manhasset, NY 11030
Telephone: (516) 562-5000
Ownership %: 100
**Editorial:**
Mike Azzara ..............................Editor
**Desc.:** Provides news, analysis of news, and feature stories for and about open systems.

67222

## ORACLE WORLD
12416 Hymeadow Dr.
Austin, TX 78750
Telephone: (512) 250-9023
FAX: (512) 331-3900
Year Established: 1990
Pub. Frequency: m.
Page Size: tabloid
Subscrip. Rate: $45.33/yr. US; $75/yr. foreign
Freelance Pay: $150-$250/article
Circulation: 10,000
**Owner(s):**
PCI Publishing
12416 Hymeadow Dr.
Austin, TX 78750
Telephone: (512) 331-6779
Ownership %: 100
**Management:**
Gary Pittman ..............................Publisher
**Editorial:**
Larry Storer ..............................Editor in Chief
Elizabeth Gastwick ..............................Editor
**Desc.:** Provides information about new and existing products in the Oracle market.
**Readers:** Oracle users.

67664

## OSINETTER, THE
P.O. Box 24344
Minneapolis, MN 55424
Telephone: (612) 935-2035
FAX: (612) 829-5871
Year Established: 1986
Pub. Frequency: m.
Page Size: standard
Subscrip. Rate: $372/yr. US.
Materials: 01,27,28,29,30,31
Print Process: offset
**Owner(s):**
Architecture Technology Corp.
P.O. Box 24344
Minneapolis, MN 55424
Telephone: (612) 935-2035
Ownership %: 100
**Management:**
Kenneth J. Thurber ..............................President
**Editorial:**
Gordy Palzer ..............................Editor

**Desc.:** The monthly newsletter covering important developments in the field of open system products.
**Readers:** Local-area networking, office systems, data communications and professionals.

58712

## PACKAGED SOFTWARE REPORTS
401 E. Rte. 70, P.O. Box 5062
Cherry Hill, NJ 08034
Telephone: (609) 428-1020
FAX: (609) 428-1683
Year Established: 1981
Pub. Frequency: m.
Page Size: standard
Subscrip. Rate: $721/yr.
**Owner(s):**
Lawrence Feidelman, Publisher
MIC, 401 E. Rte. 70
Cherry Hill, NJ 08034
Telephone: (609) 428-1020
Ownership %: 100
**Management:**
Carol Bell ..............................Manager
**Editorial:**
Pam Benham ..............................Editor
**Desc.:** Packaged Software Reports provides new announcements of software products and evaluations of CASE products.
**Readers:** MIS, data processing managers, vendors, government.

66018

## PC COMPUTING
950 Tower Ln., 20th Fl.
Foster City, CA 94404
Telephone: (415) 578-7000
FAX: (415) 578-7059
Year Established: 1988
Pub. Frequency: m.
Subscrip. Rate: $19.94/yr.
Circulation: 800,000
Circulation Type: paid
**Owner(s):**
Ziff-Davis Publishing Co.
4 Cambridge Ctr., 9th Fl.
Cambridge, MA 02142
Telephone: (617) 492-7500
**Editorial:**
Mike Edelhart ..............................Editor in Chief

66720

## PC LAPTOP COMPUTERS MAGAZINE
9171 Wilshire Blvd., Ste. 300
Beverly Hills, CA 90210
Telephone: (310) 858-7155
FAX: (310) 274-7985
Year Established: 1989
Pub. Frequency: m.
Page Size: standard
Subscrip. Rate: $24.95/yr.
Materials: 01,02,05,06,17,28,29,32
Freelance Pay: $200-$500
Circulation: 70,000
Circulation Type: paid
**Owner(s):**
L.F.P., Inc.
9171 Wilshire Blvd.
Beverly Hills, CA 90210
Telephone: (310) 858-7100
Ownership %: 100
**Editorial:**
Michael Goldstein ..............................Editor in Chief
Cassandra Cavanah .................Associate Editor
**Desc.:** Devoted to owners and potential buyers of laptop, notebook, and handheld computers with features, articles, reviews, buyers guide and more.
**Readers:** Current and future owners of portable computers.
**Deadline:** story-3 mos. prior; news-3 mos. prior; photo-3 mos. prior; ads-3 mos. prior

---

Materials Accepted/Included: 01-Business news 02-By-line articles 03-Fashion news 04-Food news 05-Freelance copy 06-Letters to editor 07-Real estate news 08-Sports news 09-Travel news 10-Book rev. 11-Movie rev. 12-Music rev. 13-TV rev. 14-Theater rev. 15-Coming events 16-Obituaries 17-Question & answer 18-Social announcements 19-Artwork 20-Cartoons 21-Photos 22-TV listings 23-Audio rec. 24-Video rec. 25-Books 26-Films/film clips 27-Personnel news 28-Press releases 29-New product news/photos 30-Trade lit. 31-Contracts awarded 32-Display adv. 33-Classified adv.

## PC MAGAZINE
65991

One Park Ave.
New York, NY 10016
Telephone: (212) 503-5100
Year Established: 1982
Pub. Frequency: fortn.
Page Size: standard
Subscrip. Rate: $29.97/yr.
Circulation: 448,456
Circulation Type: paid
**Owner(s):**
Ziff-Davis Publishing Co.
One Park Ave.
New York, NY 10016
Telephone: (212) 503-5100
Ownership %: 100
**Editorial:**
Gus Venditto .....................................Exec. Editor
Bill Howard .......................................Exec. Editor
Bill Machrone ...........................................Editor
**Desc.:** A magazine for buyers of PC's
software, peripherals and accessories.
Provides information needed in order to
specify brands of PC related products
and help make those products more
useful in business. Major elements of
the magazine include extensive product
reviews based on lab tests, productivity
enhancement departments, and opinion
and analysis columns.
**Readers:** Brand specifers of PCs and PC
related products, who need in-depth
product information.

## PCNETTER NEWSLETTER
67034

P.O. Box 24344
Minneapolis, MN 55424
Telephone: (612) 935-2035
FAX: (612) 829-5871
Year Established: 1986
Pub. Frequency: m.
Page Size: standard
Subscrip. Rate: $275/yr.
Materials: 01,27,28,29,30,31
Print Process: offset
**Owner(s):**
Architecture Technology Corp.
P.O. Box 24344
Minneapolis, MN 55424
Telephone: (612) 935-2035
Ownership %: 100
**Management:**
Kenneth J. Thurber ..............................President
**Editorial:**
Gordon Palzer ...........................................Editor
**Desc.:** The monthly newsletter covering
important developments in the field of
personal computers and workstations.
**Readers:** Professionals involved in local-
area networking, office systems, and
data communications.
**Deadline:** news-2nd Tue. prior to pub. date

## PC TECHNIQUES
67223

7721 E. Gray Rd., 204
Scottsdale, AZ 85260
Telephone: (602) 483-0192
FAX: (602) 483-0193
Year Established: 1990
Pub. Frequency: bi-m.
Page Size: standard
Subscrip. Rate: $21.95/yr.; $37.95/2 yrs.
Freelance Pay: varies
Circulation: 35,000
Circulation Type: paid
**Owner(s):**
The Coriolis Group
7721 E. Gray Rd., 204
Scottsdale, AZ 85260
Telephone: (602) 483-0192
Ownership %: 100
**Management:**
Keith Weiskamp ..............................Publisher
Tom Mayer ......................Advertising Manager

**Editorial:**
Jeff Duntemann ......................Editor in Chief
Carol Duntemann ..............Financial Controller
Barbara Nicholson ..............Production Director
**Desc.:** Serves the needs of software &
database developers on both DOS &
Windows platforms. Coverage is detail-
oriented and highly PC specific,
balancing the major programming
languages and database development
environments according to their industry
penetration as determined by our
ongoing readership surveys. Seeks to
answer the questions: How does it work
& how do I do it?
**Readers:** Decision-making managers and
technical staff, software engineers,
consultants, programmers, and analysts.

## PC WEEK
66032

Presidents Landing
Medford, MA 02155-5146
Telephone: (617) 393-3000
Pub. Frequency: w.
**Owner(s):**
Ziff-Davis Publishing Co.
Presidents Landing
Medford, MA 02155-5146
Telephone: (617) 393-3000
Ownership %: 100
**Editorial:**
Sam Whitmore ........................Editor in Chief
Wendy Mexfield .......................Managing Editor

## QUARTERLY BYTE, THE
67669

875 N. Michigan Ave., 2400
Chicago, IL 60611-1980
Telephone: (312) 335-4100
FAX: (312) 335-4400
Year Established: 1985
Pub. Frequency: q.
Page Size: standard
Subscrip. Rate: $30/yr.; $55/2 yr.
Materials: 06,10
Circulation: 2,500
Circulation Type: paid
**Owner(s):**
Appraisal Institute
875 N. Michigan Ave., 2400
Chicago, IL 60611
Telephone: (312) 335-4100
Ownership %: 100
**Editorial:**
Mary J. Dum ...........................Editor in Chief
Jennifer McLarin ........................................Editor
**Desc.:** Tips, programs and software
reviews for the computer-using real
estate appraiser.
**Readers:** Real estate professionals.

## RESELLER MANAGEMENT
52590

301 Gibraltar Dr.
Morris Plains, NJ 07950
Telephone: (201) 292-5100
FAX: (201) 898-9281
Mailing Address:
    P.O. Box 650
    Morris Plains, NJ 07950-0650
Year Established: 1976
Pub. Frequency: m.
Page Size: standard
Subscrip. Rate: $60/yr.
Materials: 01,02,29
Freelance Pay: varies
Circulation: 60,000
Circulation Type: controlled
**Owner(s):**
Gordon Publications, Div. of Cahners, Inc.
301 Gibraltar Dr.
P.O. Box 650
Morris Plains, NJ 07950-0650
Telephone: (201) 292-5100
Ownership %: 100

**Management:**
Michael Doyle ...................................Publisher
**Editorial:**
Tom Farre ...............................................Editor
Michael Wald .............................Associate Editor
Elizabeth McDonald .........New Products Editor
**Desc.:** Business management magazine
for computer resellers offering profitable
strategies for value-added reselling.
**Readers:** Resellers, systems integrators
and VADS consultants.

## RIS NEWS
65259

One West Hanover Ave., Ste. 107
Randolph, NJ 07869
Telephone: (201) 895-3300
FAX: (201) 895-7711
Year Established: 1988
Pub. Frequency: 10/yr.
Page Size: tabloid
Subscrip. Rate: $50/yr.
Freelance Pay: varies
Circulation: 16,400
Circulation Type: controlled
**Owner(s):**
Edgell Enterprises, Inc.
Douglas C. Edgell
One West Hanover Ave., Ste 107
Randolph, NJ 07869
Telephone: (201) 895-3300
Ownership %: 50

Edgell Enterprises, Inc.
Gabriele Edgell
One West Hanover Ave., Ste 107
Dover, NJ 07869
Telephone: (201) 895-3300
Ownership %: 50
**Management:**
Douglas C. Edgell .............................Publisher
**Editorial:**
Georgia Colicchio ....................Editor in Chief
Jeff Woosnam ..........................................Editor
Rick Granato ........................Account Manager
Gabriele A. Edgell ..............Associate Publisher
Lisa Strunin ........................Production Director
**Desc.:** Covers applications of retail
information systems across 15 segments
of retail business. The publication
reaches 16,400 financial/corporate
managers and operations managers. It
focuses on the information systems
needs of retailers with corporate view of
new technologies application stories,
new products, industry news and trade
show highlights.
**Readers:** Financial management, MIS/DP
management, corporate management,
operations management, merchandise
management, and distribution center
management.

## SCIENTIFIC COMPUTING & AUTOMATION
54055

301 Gibraltar Dr., Box 650
Morris Plains, NJ 07950
Telephone: (201) 292-5100
FAX: (201) 539-3476
Year Established: 1984
Pub. Frequency: m.
Page Size: standard
Subscrip. Rate: free to qual. professionals;
    $60/yr. US; $90/yr. foreign; $150/yr. air-
    mail
Circulation: 70,000
Circulation Type: controlled
**Owner(s):**
Gordon Publications, Inc.
301 Gibraltar Dr., Box 650
Morris Plains, NJ 07950
Telephone: (201) 292-5100
Ownership %: 100
**Management:**
Jan H. Verleur ................Chairman of Board
William Rakay .....................................President

Calvin Carr ........................................Publisher
**Editorial:**
Dan Brueman ...........................................Editor
Helen Robinson .......................Editorial Director
**Desc.:** Covers computing and automation
products and their applications within
laboratories and laboratory equipment.
Each month 4 feature articles by end-
users.
**Readers:** 70,000 readers in Lab, R & D
and corporate management based in
industry, university, government, clinical,
electrical and hospitals.

## SYS ADMIN
67196

1601 W. 23rd St., Ste. 200
Lawrence, KS 66046
Telephone: (913) 841-1631
Year Established: 1992
Pub. Frequency: bi-m.
Page Size: standard
Subscrip. Rate: $6.50 newsstand; $39/yr.
Materials: 10,17,29,32
Freelance Pay: varies
Print Process: web offset
Circulation: 14,032
Circulation Type: paid
**Owner(s):**
R & D Publications, Inc.
1601 W. 23rd St., Ste. 200
Lawrence, KS 66046
Telephone: (913) 841-1631
Ownership %: 100
**Management:**
Robert Ward .....................................Publisher
Noelle Martin ....................Advertising Manager
**Editorial:**
Robert Ward .............................................Editor
**Desc.:** Provides technical information for
administrators who seek to improve the
performance or extend the capabilities
of their systems; focuses on system-
level processes.
**Deadline:** story-2 mo. prior to pub. date;
news-2 mo. prior to pub. date; photo-2
mo. prior to pub. date; ads-2 mo. prior to
pub. date

## SYSTEM DEVELOPMENT
56280

P.O. Box 82266
Phoenix, AZ 85071
Telephone: (602) 995-5929
Year Established: 1981
Pub. Frequency: m.
Page Size: standard
Subscrip. Rate: $195/yr.
Freelance Pay: $150-$300
Circulation: 1,500
Circulation Type: paid
**Owner(s):**
Applied Computer Research, Inc.
P.O. Box 82266
Phoenix, AZ 85071
Telephone: (602) 995-5929
Ownership %: 100
**Management:**
Phillip C. Howard ..............................President
Alice Howard ...............................Vice President
Alan Howard ...............................Vice President
**Editorial:**
Janet Bytler ..............................................Editor
**Desc.:** A monthly newsletter devoted to
the improvement of quality and
productivity in application development.
Each issue contains several short
articles on managing system
development, plus conference coverage,
book reviews, announcements of new
products and services, other literature
and a calendar of events.
**Readers:** Primarily composed of: director
of DP, programmers, systems analysts,
managers of system development,
project leaders.

## TECHNOLOGY & LEARNING

52592

2169 Francisco Blvd., E., #A-4
San Rafael, CA 94901
Telephone: (415) 457-4333
FAX: (415) 457-4379
Year Established: 1980
Pub. Frequency: 8/yr.
Page Size: standard
Subscrip. Rate: $24/yr.
Materials: 01,02,05,06,15,25,28,29,32
Freelance Pay: varies
Circulation: 83,000
Circulation Type: controlled
**Owner(s):**
Peter Li Education Group
330 Progress Rd.
Dayton, OH 45449
Telephone: (513) 847-5900
Ownership %: 100
**Management:**
Peter Li .................................Publisher
**Editorial:**
Holly Brady ......................Editor in Chief
Judy Salpeter ..........................Managing Editor
Susan McLester ..............Associate Editor
**Desc.:** Designed to reach teachers of
grades k-12 interested in integrating
computers into the classroom. Delivers
issues-oriented feature pieces, class
room activities, software reviews, and
more.
**Readers:** Students
**Deadline:** story-3-4 mos. prior to pub.
date; news-3-4 mos. prior; ads-3-4 mos.
prior

## TOKEN PERSPECTIVES

67036

## NEWSLETTER

P.O. Box 24344
Minneapolis, MN 55424
Telephone: (612) 935-2035
FAX: (612) 829-5871
Year Established: 1983
Pub. Frequency: m.
Page Size: standard
Subscrip. Rate: $312/yr. U.S.
Materials: 01,27,28,29,30,31
Print Process: offset
**Owner(s):**
Architecture Technology Corp.
P.O. Box 24344
Minneapolis, MN 55424
Telephone: (612) 935-2035
Ownership %: 100
**Management:**
Kenneth J. Thurber ......................President
**Editorial:**
Gordy Palzer ...................................Editor
**Desc.:** Newsletter covering important
developments in the field of token-ring
networks.
**Readers:** Professionals involved in local
area networking, office systems, and
data communications.
**Deadline:** news-3rd Tue. prior to pub. date

## TRANSACTIONS ON COMPUTER

56368

## SYSTEMS

1515 Broadway, 17th Fl.
New York, NY 10036
Telephone: (212) 869-7440
FAX: (212) 944-1318
Year Established: 1983
Pub. Frequency: q.
Page Size: standard
Subscrip. Rate: $28/yr. to members;
$115/yr. to non-members
Circulation: 7,259
Circulation Type: paid

**Owner(s):**
Association for Computing Machinery
1515 Broadway, 17th Fl.
New York, NY 10036
Telephone: (212) 869-7440
Ownership %: 100
**Management:**
J.G. Benton .................................Publisher
**Editorial:**
Anita K. Jones ......................Editor in Chief
**Desc.:** Publishes the newest findings of
the computing research field. papers are
theoretical and conceptual explorations
of operating systems, distributed
systems and networks. Readers will find
design principles, case studies and
experiemental results in specification,
processor management, implementation
techniques and protocols. Also
discusses security and reliability, and
offers experienced-based papers on all
these topics.
**Readers:** Industries involved in data
communications, telecommunications,
computers, components, and related
equipment.

## TRANSACTIONS ON

56425

## INFORMATION SYSTEMS

1515 Broadway, 17th Fl.
New York, NY 10036-5701
Telephone: (212) 869-0481
Year Established: 1983
Pub. Frequency: q.
Page Size: standard
Subscrip. Rate: $28/yr. to members;
$115/yr. to non-members
Circulation: 4,573
Circulation Type: paid
**Owner(s):**
Association for Computing Machinery
1515 Broadway, 17th Fl.
New York, NY 10036
Telephone: (212) 869-7440
Ownership %: 100
**Editorial:**
Robert B. Allen ......................Editor in Chief
**Desc.:** For researchers involved with office
information methodologies. Divided into
two sections: Research Contributions,
offering advances in information,
automation and communications; and
Practice and Experience, which supplies
information on incorporating systems in
the office. Topics include integrated
communication systems, workstation
design, productivity measurement,
human interfaces and office automation
systems. No advertising is included.
**Readers:** Industries involved in data
communications, telecommunications,
and consumer electronics.

## UNISYS WORLD

61707

12416 Hymeadow Dr.
Austin, TX 78750-1896
Telephone: (512) 250-9023
FAX: (512) 331-3900
Year Established: 1979
Pub. Frequency: m.
Page Size: tabloid
Subscrip. Rate: $92/yr. US; $140/yr.
foreign
Freelance Pay: $100 flat rate to $.10/wd.
Circulation: 13,500
Circulation Type: paid
**Owner(s):**
Gary Pittman
12416 Hymeadow Dr.
Austin, TX 78750-1896
Telephone: (512) 250-9023
**Management:**
Sylvia Wysocki ...................................Manager

**Editorial:**
Kip Stratton .................................Editor
**Desc.:** Features product news, corporate
news, technical articles and software,
hardware reviews for users of UNISYS
systems. Provides coverage of the
entire range of UNISYS and third party
vendor products.
**Readers:** For users of UNISYS systems.

## UNIX REVIEW

66605

411 Borel Ave., Ste. 100
San Mateo, CA 94402
Telephone: (415) 358-9500
FAX: (415) 358-9739
Year Established: 1983
Pub. Frequency: m.
Page Size: standard
Subscrip. Rate: $3.95 newsstand; $55/yr.
Materials: 02,05,06,28,29
Print Process: web offset
Circulation: 71,000
Circulation Type: controlled
**Owner(s):**
Miller Freeman Publications, Inc.
600 Harrison St.
San Francisco, CA 94107
Telephone: (415) 905-2000
FAX: (415) 905-2232
Ownership %: 100
**Management:**
Katie McGolderick .................................Publisher
**Editorial:**
Andrew Binstock .................................Editor
Lea Ann Bantsari ......................Managing Editor
**Desc.:** Features articles on UNIX
applications as well as compatible
hardware and software coverage.
Editorials and new product
announcements.
**Readers:** For UNIX operating system
users.
**Deadline:** story-6 mos.; photo-6 mos.; ads-
3 mos.

## WORDPERFECT FOR WINDOWS

67084

1555 N. Technology Way
Orem, UT 84057
Telephone: (801) 226-5555
FAX: (801) 227-3479
Year Established: 1992
Pub. Frequency: m.
Page Size: standard
Subscrip. Rate: $3/copy; $24/yr.
Materials: 06,17,28,32,33
Freelance Pay: $500-$1000
Circulation: 963,000
Circulation Type: free & paid
**Owner(s):**
Wordperfect Publishing Corp.
1555 N. Technology Way
Orem, UT 84057
Telephone: (801) 226-5555
FAX: (801) 227-3479
Ownership %: 100
**Management:**
Edie Rockwood .................................Publisher
Maurice Beaujeu ..............Advertising Manager
**Editorial:**
Jeff Hadfield .................................Editor

## WORKSTATION MAGAZINE

69233

12416 Hymeadow Dr.
Austin, TX 78750-1896
Telephone: (512) 250-5518
FAX: (512) 331-6778
Year Established: 1985
Pub. Frequency: m.
Subscrip. Rate: $45/yr.
Circulation: 10,000
Circulation Type: paid

**Owner(s):**
Publications & Communications, Inc.
12416 Hymeadow Dr.
Austin, TX 78750-1896
Telephone: (512) 250-5518
Ownership %: 100
**Editorial:**
John Mitchell .................................Editor
**Readers:** Managers, purchasers and
others responsible for HP Apollo
workstations.

## WORKSTATION NEWS

66318

10711 Burnet Rd., Ste. 305
Austin, TX 78758-4459
Telephone: (512) 873-7761
FAX: (512) 873-7782
Year Established: 1990
Pub. Frequency: m.
Page Size: tabloid
Subscrip. Rate: $48/yr. US; $64/yr. foreign
Freelance Pay: $150-$300
Circulation: 50,000
Circulation Type: controlled
**Owner(s):**
DB Media Publications, Inc.
10711 Burnet Rd., Ste. 305
Austin, TX 78758-4459
Telephone: (512) 873-7761
Ownership %: 100
**Management:**
John V. Moore .................................Publisher
Kathy Murphy ..............Circulation Manager
**Editorial:**
Margaret Mulligan .................................Editor
**Desc.:** Provides industry information for
the UNIX workstation user.
**Readers:** Users of UNIX Workstation
computers and equipment.

## X JOURNAL, THE

67199

588 Broadway, Ste. 604
New York, NY 10012
Telephone: (212) 274-0640
FAX: (212) 274-0646
Year Established: 1991
Pub. Frequency: bi-m.
Page Size: standard
Subscrip. Rate: $39/yr. US individuals;
$79/yr. foreign; $79/yr. US institutions;
foreign $99/yr.)
Circulation: 17,500
Circulation Type: paid
**Owner(s):**
Sigs Publications, Inc.
588 Broadway, Ste. 604
New York, NY 10012
Telephone: (212) 274-0640
Ownership %: 100
**Management:**
Richard Friedman .................................Publisher
Miles E. Silverman ............Advertising Manager
**Editorial:**
Steven Mikes .................................Editor
Brian Keller .................................Editor
**Desc.:** Covers X servers, window
managers, X-based applications, X
education and software engineering in X.

## 68 MICRO JOURNAL

52694

P.O. Box 437
Hixson, TN 37343-0437
Telephone: (615) 842-4600
Year Established: 1979
Pub. Frequency: m.
Page Size: standard
Subscrip. Rate: $24.50/yr.
Freelance Pay: negotiable
Circulation: 10,000
Circulation Type: paid

**Materials Accepted/Included:** 01-Business news 02-By-line articles 03-Fashion news 04-Food news 05-Freelance copy 06-Letters to editor 07-Real estate news 08-Sports news 09-Travel news 10-Book rev. 11-Movie rev. 12-Music rev. 13-TV rev. 14-Theater rev. 15-Coming events 16-Obituaries 17-Question & answer 18-Social announcements 19-Artwork 20-Cartoons 21-Photos 22-TV listings 23-Audio rec. 24-Video rec. 25-Books 26-Films/film clips 27-Personnel news 28-Press releases 29-New product news/photos 30-Trade lit. 31-Contracts awarded 32-Display adv. 33-Classified adv.

4-105

**Owner(s):**
Donald M. Williams, Sr.
5900 Cassandra Smith Rd.
Hixson, TN 37343
Telephone: (615) 842-4600

Larry E. Williams
5900 Cassandra Smith Rd.
Hixson, TN 37343
Telephone: (615) 842-4600
**Management:**
Cheryl Hodge .............................Manager
**Editorial:**
Larry E. Williams ..................Exec. Editor
Donald Williams ..............................Editor
Tom Williams ....................Technical Editor
**Desc.:** Articles dealing with the uses of
Motorola's 6809, 68000 & 68020
processor. Apple MacIntosh
Desktop Publishing.
**Readers:** Users of microcomputers using
the Motorola 6809 or 68000 & 68020
microprocessor.

## Group 058-Dairy Products

22730
### CHEESE REPORTER
4210 E. Washington Rd.
Madison, WI 53704-3742
Telephone: (608) 273-1300
FAX: (608) 273-1302
Year Established: 1876
Pub. Frequency: w.
Page Size: tabloid
Subscrip. Rate: $55/yr.
Freelance Pay: $2/col. in.
Circulation: 2,450
Circulation Type: paid
**Owner(s):**
Cheese Reporter Publishing Co., Inc.
6401 Odana Rd.
Madison, WI 53719-1157
Telephone: (608) 273-1300
Ownership %: 100
**Management:**
Richard Groves .........................President
Richard Groves ..........................Publisher
Kevin M. Thome ..............Advertising Manager
Betty Merkes .................Circulation Manager
**Editorial:**
Richard Groves ............................Editor
**Desc.:** Features covering cheese and
allied products production, company
notes, regulations, association, exhibits,
promotion, marketing, merchandising,
technical and production information
covered.
**Readers:** Butter and cheese
manufacturers, executives and grocery
retailers, distributors, supply firms.

61603
### DAIRY, FOOD & ENVIRONMENTAL SANITATION
6200 Aurora Ave., Ste. 200W
Des Moines, IA 50322-2838
Telephone: (515) 276-3344
FAX: (515) 276-8655
Year Established: 1980
Pub. Frequency: m.
Page Size: standard
Subscrip. Rate: $100/yr.
Materials: 01,04,06
Circulation: 3,500
Circulation Type: paid
**Owner(s):**
IAMFES
6200 Aurora Ave., Ste. 200W
Des Moines, IA 50322
Telephone: (515) 276-3344
FAX: (315) 276-8655
Ownership %: 100
**Management:**
Steven K. Halstead ......................Manager

**Editorial:**
Jeanne A. Lightly ........................Editor
**Desc.:** Practical application of research
findings.
**Readers:** food processors,
acadamicians/research scientists,
regulatory people, quality control
**Deadline:** story-20th of mo. prior to pub.
date; news-20th of mo. prior to pub.
date; photo-20th of mo. prior; ads-20th
of mo. prior

22734
### JOURNAL OF DAIRY SCIENCE
309 W. Clark St.
Champaign, IL 61820
Telephone: (217) 356-3182
FAX: (217) 398-4119
Year Established: 1917
Pub. Frequency: m.
Page Size: pg.: 6 3/4 x 10; col.: 16 x 48
picas
Subscrip. Rate: $120/yr. US; $145/yr.
foreign
Circulation: 5,000
**Owner(s):**
American Dairy Science Association
309 W. Clark St.
Champaign, IL 61820
Telephone: (217) 356-3182
FAX: (217) 398-4119
Ownership %: 100
**Management:**
Carl D. Johnson ...............Advertising Manager
**Editorial:**
John W. Fuquay ...........................Editor
Cheryl Nimz ......................Managing Editor
Carl D. Johnson ....................Miscellaneous
Cheryl Nimz .........................News Editor
Cheryl Nimz ................................Photo
Cheryl Nimz ....................Technical Editor
**Desc.:** Carries original research in dairy
manufacturing, production and extension
submitted by institutional and industry
workers. Papers not limited in length.
Drawings and other illustrative material
should accompany the article. News of
the association.
**Readers:** International coverage of the
dairy industry.

25368
### MILK MARKETER
8257 Dow Cir.
Cleveland, OH 44136-9717
Telephone: (216) 826-4730
FAX: (216) 826-1971
Mailing Address:
P.O. Box 36050
Strongsville, OH 44136
Year Established: 1978
Pub. Frequency: q.
Page Size: standard
Subscrip. Rate: $3/yr. members; $5/yr.
non-member
Circulation: 8,000
Circulation Type: controlled
**Owner(s):**
Milk Marketing Inc.
8257 Dow Cir.
Cleveland, OH 44136
Telephone: (216) 826-4730
Ownership %: 100
**Editorial:**
William Perry ..............................Editor
Jane Spencer Sweet ..............Managing Editor
Agnes Schafer-Kreiser ..............Assistant Editor
**Desc.:** All material relates to dairy
cooperatives and marketing.
**Readers:** Milk producers who are
members of milk marketing inc., dealers,
haulers, county agents, teachers, and
other persons in dairy marketing field.

68845
### NATIONAL DIPPER
1480 Renaissance Dr., Ste. 101
Park Ridge, IL 60068
Telephone: (708) 390-6550
FAX: (708) 390-6558
Year Established: 1985
Pub. Frequency: bi-m.
Page Size: standard
Subscrip. Rate: $55/yr.
Materials: 01,02,04,06,10,15,21,25,27,28,
29,30,32,33
Print Process: offset
Circulation: 20,000
Circulation Type: controlled
**Owner(s):**
United States Exposition Corp.
1480 Renaissance Dr., Ste. 101
Park Ridge, IL 60068
Telephone: (708) 390-6550
FAX: (708) 390-6558
Ownership %: 100
**Management:**
Lynda Utterback .........................Publisher
**Desc.:** Helps find new products for ice
cream dipping stores.

## Group 060-Dentistry, Dental Equipment & Supplies

22741
### ADA NEWS
211 E. Chicago Ave., 2010
Chicago, IL 60611
Telephone: (312) 440-2794
FAX: (312) 440-3538
Year Established: 1970
Pub. Frequency: bi-w.
Page Size: tabloid
Subscrip. Rate: $35/yr.
Materials: 01,06,28,30,32
Print Process: web offset
Circulation: 140,000
Circulation Type: paid
**Owner(s):**
American Dental Association Publishing
Co., Inc.
211 E. Chicago Ave.
Chicago, IL 60611
Telephone: (312) 440-2790
Ownership %: 100
**Bureau(s):**
Washington DC Bureau
1111 14th St. N.W.
Ste. 1200
Washington, DC
Telephone: (202) 898-2400
Contact: Craig Palmer, Editor
**Management:**
Laura Kosden ...........................Publisher
**Editorial:**
James Berry .......................Executive Editor
Dr. Larry Meskin ...........................Editor
Judy Jakush .........................News Editor
**Desc.:** News and feature stories of
dentistry or health subjects which would
interest dentists. Use interviews, stories
on legislative developments, research,
politics, people, campus development,
etc.
**Readers:** Membership of American Dental
Association, also those in the dental
trade, and other subscribers (libraries,
schools, etc.).

56372
### AGD IMPACT
211 E. Chicago Ave., Ste. 1200
Chicago, IL 60611-2670
Telephone: (312) 440-4300
FAX: (312) 440-0559
Year Established: 1973
Pub. Frequency: 11/yr.

Page Size: standard
Subscrip. Rate: $20/yr. individuals; $32/yr.
institutions
Materials: 01,02,06,15,21,28,32,33
Print Process: web offset
Circulation: 33,000
Circulation Type: paid
**Owner(s):**
Academy of General Dentistry
211 E. Chicago Ave., Ste. 1200
Chicago, IL 60611-2670
Telephone: (312) 440-4300
FAX: (312) 440-0559
Ownership %: 100
**Bureau(s):**
The Goldman Group
410 Ware Blvd., Ste. 601
Tampa, FL 33619
Telephone: (813) 664-1355
FAX: (813) 664-1156
Contact: Todd E. Goldman, President
**Management:**
Lisa Stockdale ...................Circulation Manager
Timothy Henney ................Production Manager
**Editorial:**
William W. Howard, D.M.D. .....................Editor
Silvia Foti ........................Managing Editor
Jo-Ellyn Posselt ........Communications Director
**Desc.:** The official news magazine of the
Academy of General Dentistry. It serves
to keep readers informed on issues,
legislation, and trends that affect their
practice and position in the health care
community. Also includes editorial, news,
and continuing education calendar.
**Readers:** Practicing General Dentists,
Dentists in Uniformed Services, and
Dental Students.

66664
### AMERICAN JOURNAL OF ORTHODONTICS AND DENTOFACIAL ORTHOPEDICS
11830 Westline Industrial Dr.
St. Louis, MO 63146
Telephone: (800) 325-4117
FAX: (314) 432-1380
Year Established: 1915
Pub. Frequency: m.
Page Size: standard
Subscrip. Rate: $76/yr. individuals; $99/yr.
foreign; $155/yr. institutions; $178/yr.
foreign; $37/yr. students US; $60/yr.
foreign
Circulation: 15,188
Circulation Type: paid
**Owner(s):**
Times Mirror Co.
11830 Westline Industrial Dr.
St. Louis, MO 63146
Telephone: (314) 872-8370
Ownership %: 100
**Management:**
Carol Trumbold ..........................Publisher
Kathy Erhardt ...................Advertising Manager
**Editorial:**
T.M. Graber, D.M.D. ........................Editor
Kathy Keller .....................Production Director
**Desc.:** International research covering all
phases of orthodontic treatment.

22743
### ANESTHESIA PROGRESS
UCLA School of Dentistry
Los Angeles, CA 90024
Telephone: (310) 825-9300
FAX: (310) 206-5539
Mailing Address:
UCLA School of Dentistry
Los Angeles, CA 90024
Year Established: 1953
Pub. Frequency: q.
Page Size: standard
Subscrip. Rate: $40/yr. US; $64/yr. foreign
Circulation: 4,036
Circulation Type: free

**Materials Accepted/Included:** 01-Business news 02-By-line articles 03-Fashion news 04-Food news 05-Freelance copy 06-Letters to editor 07-Real estate news 08-Sports news 09-Travel news 10-Book rev. 11-Movie rev. 12-Music rev. 13-TV rev. 14-Theater rev. 15-Coming events 16-Obituaries 17-Question & answer 18-Social announcements 19-Artwork 20-Cartoons 21-Photos 22-TV listings 23-Audio rec. 24-Video rec. 25-Books 26-Films/film clips 27-Personnel news 28-Press releases 29-New product news/photos 30-Trade lit. 31-Contracts awarded 32-Display adv. 33-Classified adv.

**Owner(s):**
American Dental Society of Anesthesiology
211 E. Chicago Ave.
Chicago, IL 60611
Telephone: (312) 664-8270
Ownership %: 100
**Editorial:**
John Yagiela .............................Editor
**Desc.:** Original reports and studies on pain
control, anesthesia and patient
managment-methods, equipments, etc.
Also contains reports on the scientific
and business activities of the society,
scientific abstract, book reviews and
announcements.
**Readers:** Members of American Dental
Society of Anesthesiology plus by
subscription.

69502
**ANGLE ORTHODONTIST**
P.O. Box 2577
Appleton, WI 54913-2577
Telephone: (414) 738-2602
Year Established: 1931
Pub. Frequency: bi-m.
Subscrip. Rate: $60/yr. US; $70/yr. foreign
Circulation: 5,000
Circulation Type: paid
**Owner(s):**
Angle Orthodontists Rsrch. & Education
Foundation
P.O. Box 2577
Apppleton, WI 54913-2577
Telephone: (414) 738-2602
FAX: (414) 830-2468
Ownership %: 100
**Editorial:**
Dr. John S. Kloehn .....................Editor
**Desc.:** Covers all phases of orthodontic
treatment as well as the basic sciences
related to orthodontics.

61330
**ASDA NEWS**
211 E. Chicago, #840
Chicago, IL 60611
Telephone: (312) 440-2795
FAX: (312) 440-2820
Year Established: 1981
Pub. Frequency: m.: Sep.-May
Page Size: tabloid
Subscrip. Rate: $5/yr. member; $20/yr.
non-member in US; $30/yr. foreign
Materials: 02,06,20,21,28,32,33
Circulation: 13,500
Circulation Type: paid
**Owner(s):**
American Student Dental Association
211 E. Chicago Ave.
Ste. 840
Chicago, IL 60611
Telephone: (312) 440-2795
FAX: (312) 440-2820
Ownership %: 100
**Editorial:**
Paul Farsai .....................Editor in Chief
Lisa Coghlan .............Managing Editor
Angela Green ..............Associate Editor
**Readers:** More than 80% of all dental
students and new dental professionals.

22744
**CDS REVIEW (CHICAGO DENTAL
SOCIETY)**
401 N. Michigan Ave., Ste. 300
Chicago, IL 60611-4205
Telephone: (312) 836-7300
FAX: (312) 836-7337
Pub. Frequency: 11/yr.
Page Size: standard
Subscrip. Rate: $25/yr. individuals; $30/yr.
institutions; $45/yr. foreign
Freelance Pay: negotiable
Circulation: 8,500
Circulation Type: paid

**Owner(s):**
Chicago Dental Society
401 N. Michigan Ave., Ste. 300
Chicago, IL 60611-4205
Telephone: (312) 836-7300
Ownership %: 100
**Editorial:**
Robert Scholle .............................Editor
E. Giangrego .............Managing Editor
Grant A. MacLean, D.D.S. .........Editor Emeritus
**Desc.:** Original manuscripts, complete
coverage of news and other articles of
interest to dentists. Society programs,
news and programs of 9 branches;
original papers from Midwinter Meetings.
Departments include: Mailbag, Editorial,
President's Message, News &
Announcements, Miniclinic, Branch
News, New Products, Business
Management.
**Readers:** Dentists (general practitioners
and specialists), schools, faculties and
students, dental manufacturers, dental
auxiliaries.

22746
**DENTAL ASSISTANT, THE**
919 N. Michigan Ave., Ste. 3400
Chicago, IL 60611
Telephone: (312) 664-3327
FAX: (312) 664-5288
Mailing Address:
203 N. LaSalle St., Ste. 1320
Chicagoo, IL 60601-1225
Year Established: 1931
Pub. Frequency: q.
Page Size: standard
Subscrip. Rate: $30/yr. US; $35/yr. foreign
Materials: 01,02,05,06,10,21,25,28,29,30,
32,33
Freelance Pay: negotiable
Circulation: 15,500
Circulation Type: controlled
**Owner(s):**
American Dental Assistants Assn.
203 N. LaSalle St. Ste. 1320
Chicago, IL 60601-1225
Telephone: (312) 541-1550
FAX: (312) 541-1496
Ownership %: 100
**Management:**
Kathy Zwieg, CDA, RDA ..................President
Dolores Lopez ...............Advertising Manager
Debbie Wightman .............Production Manager
**Editorial:**
Michael Shaneyfelt .......................Editor
**Desc.:** Emphasizes continuing education in
all phases of dentistry. Written for and
directed to the working dental assistant,
each issue contains technical and
theoretical articles, current technical
advances, national organization news,
coming events, and information
regarding the current status of education
in the dental assisting field.
**Readers:** Members of the American Dental
Assistants Association, working dental
assistants.

22748
**DENTAL ECONOMICS**
1421 S. Sheridan Rd.
Tulsa, OK 74112
Telephone: (918) 835-3161
FAX: (918) 831-9804
Mailing Address:
P.O. Box 3408
Tulsa, OK 74101
Year Established: 1911
Pub. Frequency: m.
Page Size: standard
Subscrip. Rate: $55/yr. US; $72/yr.
foreign; $105/yr. overseas airmail
Materials: 02,05,06,20,28,29,32,33
Freelance Pay: $50-$500
Print Process: web offset

Circulation: 110,000
Circulation Type: controlled
**Owner(s):**
PennWell Publishing Co.
P.O. Box 3408
Tulsa, OK 74101
Telephone: (918) 835-3161
Ownership %: 100
**Management:**
Joseph A. Wolking ........................President
John Ford ...............................Vice President
Dick Hale ......................................Publisher
Vicki Cheeseman ................Business Manager
Juan Roof ....................Circulation Manager
**Editorial:**
Penny Elliott Anderson ................Senior Editor
Dick Hale ........................................Editor
Mike Reeder ..............................Art Director
Melba Koch ..........................Assistant Editor
H. Ronald Combs ..................Associate Editor
Roger J. Harway ................Associate Publisher
Marv Ashworth ............Direct-Mail Services
LaVerne Lewis ..............Production Manager
**Desc.:** Helps dentists combine their clinical
skills and product knowledge with sound
management decisions to help achieve
a more rewarding practice. Articles point
out how areas of clinical expertise and
groups of products can be combined
with available staff, existing office space
and patient demographics to maximize
quality and quantity of care. Articles on
marketing, public relations, finance and
investments supplement dentists' clinical
training so they can profit in a
competitive market.
**Readers:** Dentists and senior dental
students.
**Deadline:** ads-1 mo. prior to pub. date

22751
**DENTAL LAB PRODUCTS**
5 Paragon Dr.
Montvale, NJ 07645
Telephone: (201) 358-7200
FAX: (201) 573-1045
Year Established: 1976
Pub. Frequency: bi-m.
Page Size: tabloid
Subscrip. Rate: $18/yr. U.S.; $24/yr.
foreign
Circulation: 20,430
Circulation Type: controlled
**Owner(s):**
Medical Economics Publishing Co., Inc.
Ownership %: 100
**Management:**
Thomas D. Hoyt ..........................Publisher
**Editorial:**
Jeanne K. Matson ..........................Editor
**Desc.:** New product news and related
feature material. Also cover major dental
laboratory meetings, technical training
aids, and sales promotion aids. All
features are staff written.
**Readers:** Dental laboratory owners and
managers, dental dealers and dental
manufacturers.

22756
**DENTAL PRODUCTS REPORT**
5 Paragon Dr.
Montvale, NJ 07645
Telephone: (201) 358-7246
FAX: (201) 573-0344
Year Established: 1967
Pub. Frequency: 11/yr.
Page Size: tabloid
Subscrip. Rate: $66/yr. US; $88/yr. foreign
Circulation: 147,801
Circulation Type: controlled

**Owner(s):**
Medical Economics Publishing Co., Inc.
5 Paragon Dr.
Montvale, NJ 07645
Telephone: (201) 358-7246
Ownership %: 100
**Editorial:**
Jeanne K. Matson ..........................Editor
**Desc.:** New product news and related
feature material (i.e. maintenance,
technique). Also covers major dental
meetings. All features are staff written.
**Readers:** Dentists in the U.S., Armed
Forces and Canada; senior dental
students; administrators and faculty
members of dental schools without a
DDS or DMD degree; schools for dental
hygienists, assistants and laboratory
technicians; dental supply dealers.

54057
**DENTISTRY TODAY**
26 Park St.
Montclair, NJ 07042
Telephone: (201) 783-3935
Year Established: 1982
Pub. Frequency: 11/yr.
Page Size: tabloid
Subscrip. Rate: $40/yr. US; $50/yr.
Canada; $77/yr. foreign
Freelance Rate: $100/story
Circulation: 149,179
Circulation Type: controlled
**Owner(s):**
Dentistry Today
26 Park St.
Montclair, NJ 07042
**Management:**
Paul Radcliffe ...............................Publisher
**Editorial:**
Ted Fetner ......................................Editor
**Desc.:** The nation's leading clinical and
news magazine for dentists.
**Readers:** Dentists in the US.

68980
**DENTISTRY 1995**
211 E. Chicago Ave., Ste. 840
Chicago, IL 60611
Telephone: (312) 440-2795
FAX: (312) 440-2820
Year Established: 1981
Pub. Frequency: m.
Page Size: standard
Subscrip. Rate: $16/yr. US; $24/yr. foreign
Materials: 06,32,33
Print Process: offset
Circulation: 12,000
Circulation Type: paid
**Owner(s):**
American Student Dental Association
211 E. Chicago Ave., Ste. 840
Chicago, IL 60611
Telephone: (312) 440-2795
FAX: (312) 440-2820
Ownership %: 100
**Management:**
Maggie White ...................Advertising Manager
**Editorial:**
Lisa Coghlan ....................Managing Editor
Paul Farsai ...........................Editor-in-Chief
**Desc.:** Discusses issues, trends and new
developments in dentistry.
**Readers:** Dental students and young
dental professionals.

22760
**GENERAL DENTISTRY**
211 E. Chicago Ave. Ste. 1200
Chicago, IL 60611-2670
Telephone: (312) 440-4300
FAX: (312) 440-0559
Year Established: 1952
Pub. Frequency: bi-m.

---

**Materials Accepted/Included:** 01-Business news 02-By-line articles 03-Fashion news 04-Food news 05-Freelance copy 06-Letters to editor 07-Real estate news 08-Sports news 09-Travel news
10-Book rev. 11-Movie rev. 12-Music rev. 13-TV rev. 14-Theater rev. 15-Coming events 16-Obituaries 17-Question & answer 18-Social announcements 19-Artwork 20-Cartoons 21-Photos 22-TV listings
23-Audio rec. 24-Video rec. 25-Books 26-Films/film clips 27-Personnel news 28-Press releases 29-New product news/photos 30-Trade lit. 31-Contracts awarded 32-Display adv. 33-Classified adv.

4-107

Page Size: standard
Subscrip. Rate: $25/yr., $45/2 yrs.
  individuals; $40/yr., $72/2 yrs.
  institutions
Materials: 02,06,10,21,28,29,30,32
Print Process: web offset
Circulation: 45,500
Circulation Type: paid
**Owner(s):**
Academy of General Dentistry
211 E. Chicago Ave., Ste. 1200
Chicago, IL 60611-2670
Telephone: (312) 440-4300
FAX: (312) 440-0559
Ownership %: 100
**Bureau(s):**
The Goldman Group
410 Ware Blvd., Ste. 601
Tampa, FL 33619
Telephone: (813) 664-1355
FAX: (813) 664-1156
Contact: Todd E. Goldman, President
**Management:**
Lisa Stockdale ..................Circulation Manager
Timothy Henney .................Production Manager
**Editorial:**
William W. Howard, D. M. D. ..................Editor
Janis Forgue ...........................Managing Editor
Jo - Ellyn Posselt ......Communications Director
**Desc.:** Official journal of the Academy of
  General Dentistry. It serves as the
  general dentist's resource for clinical
  data and management information
  applicable in today's practice.
  Departments and features include: case
  reports, reviews, techniques, opinion
  articles, research, clinical reports,
  editorial, abstracts, book reviews, new
  products, self-assessment quizzes, self-
  instruction programs.
**Readers:** Practicing general dentists,
  dental students, dentists in uniformed
  services.

22761
**ILLINOIS DENTAL JOURNAL**
P.O. Box 376
Springfield, IL 62705
Telephone: (217) 525-8872
Year Established: 1931
Pub. Frequency: 7/yr.
Page Size: standard
Subscrip. Rate: $5/copy; $20/yr. member;
  $30/yr. non-member
Materials: 01,05,06,16,18,21,27,28,29,30,
  32,33
Freelance Pay: negotiable
Circulation: 6,000
Circulation Type: controlled & paid
**Owner(s):**
Illinois State Dental Society
1010 S. Second St.
P.O. Box 376
Springfield, IL 62705
Telephone: (217) 525-1406
FAX: (217) 525-8872
Ownership %: 100
**Editorial:**
Dr. D. Milton Salzer ................................Editor
Mary M. Byers ........................Managing Editor
Stefany Buecker ....................Editorial Assistant
**Desc.:** Articles submitted for publication
  should be articles that have not been
  previously published and are submitted
  solely to the Journal. Such published
  articles become one property of the IL
  State Dental Society. Articles
  published in the Illinois Dental Journal
  may be reproduced or reprinted only
  after written permission has been
  granted by the Illinois Dental Journal.
**Readers:** Illinois State Dental Society
  Members
**Deadline:** story-15th of mo. prior to pub.
  date; news-15th of mo.; photo-15th of
  mo.; ads-15th of mo.

65325
**INSIGHT**
413 N. Pearl St.
Albany, NY 12207
Telephone: (800) 888-5868
FAX: (518) 434-1288
Mailing Address:
  P.O. Box 350
  Albany, NY 12201
Year Established: 1989
Pub. Frequency: q.
Page Size: standard
Subscrip. Rate: free
Freelance Pay: negotiable
Circulation: 4,000
Circulation Type: free
**Owner(s):**
Ticonium Co.-CMP Industries
413 N. Pearl St.
Albany, NY 12207
Telephone: (800) 888-5868
Ownership %: 100
**Editorial:**
Dean Quackenbush ..............................Editor
Richard C. Adamson ...............Managing Editor
**Desc.:** Company lab & equipment &
  industry news.
**Readers:** Dental lab owners.

69507
**INTERNATIONAL JOURNAL OF
ORAL & MAXILLOFACIAL
IMPLANTS**
551 Kimberly Dr.
Carol Stream, IL 60188-1881
Telephone: (708) 682-3223
FAX: (708) 682-3288
Year Established: 1986
Pub. Frequency: bi-m.
Subscrip. Rate: $92/yr. US; $116/yr.
  foreign
Circulation: 7,200
Circulation Type: paid
**Owner(s):**
Quintessence Publishing Co., Inc.
551 Kimberly Dr.
Carol Stream, IL 60188-1881
Telephone: (708) 682-3223
Ownership %: 100
**Editorial:**
Dr. William Laney ...............................Editor
**Desc.:** Tracks developments in
  reconstructive dentistry and implantology
  by compiling research, technology,
  clinical applications, symposia
  proceedings and review treatises.

69511
**INTERNATIONAL JOURNAL OF
PROSTHODONTICS**
551 Kimberly Dr.
Carol Stream, IL 60188-1881
Telephone: (708) 682-3223
FAX: (708) 682-3288
Year Established: 1988
Pub. Frequency: bi-m.
Subscrip. Rate: $92/yr. US; $114/yr.
  foreign
Circulation: 5,000
Circulation Type: paid
**Owner(s):**
Quintessence Publishing Co., Inc.
551 Kimberly Dr.
Carol Stream, IL 60188-1881
Telephone: (708) 682-3223
Ownership %: 100
**Editorial:**
Dr. Jack O. Preston ...............................Editor
**Desc.:** Contains articles covering
  interrelated disciplines such as
  periodontics, oral and maxillofacial
  surgery, endodontics and orthodontics.
  Edited by the International College of
  Prosthodontists.

22762
**JOURNAL OF CLINICAL
ORTHODONTICS, THE**
1828 Pearl St.
Boulder, CO 80302
Telephone: (303) 443-1720
FAX: (303) 443-9356
Year Established: 1967
Pub. Frequency: m.
Page Size: standard
Subscrip. Rate: $107/yr. individual;
  $145/yr. institutions
Circulation: 11,000
Circulation Type: paid
**Owner(s):**
JCO, Inc.
1828 Pearl St.
Boulder, CO 80302
Telephone: (303) 443-1720
Ownership %: 100
**Management:**
Lynn Bollinger ..................Advertising Manager
**Editorial:**
Larry White, D.D.S. ...............................Editor
David Vogels ........................Managing Editor
**Desc.:** Stresses the practical aspects of
  everyday orthodontic treatment
  techniques and practice administration.
**Readers:** Orthodontists and others with
  interest in orthodontics.

22763
**JOURNAL OF DENTAL
EDUCATION**
1625 Massachusettes Ave., N.W.
Washington, DC 20036-2212
Telephone: (202) 667-9433
Year Established: 1936
Pub. Frequency: m.
Page Size: standard
Subscrip. Rate: $75/yr.; $125/yr. foreign
Circulation: 4,300
Circulation Type: controlled & paid
**Owner(s):**
American Association of Dental Schools
1625 Massachusetts Ave., N.W.
Washington, DC 20036-2212
Telephone: (202) 667-9433
Ownership %: 100
**Editorial:**
Dr. James D. Bader .............................Editor

22749
**JOURNAL OF DENTAL HYGIENE**
444 N. Michigan Ave., Ste. 3400
Chicago, IL 60611
Telephone: (312) 440-8900
FAX: (312) 440-8929
Year Established: 1927
Pub. Frequency: 9/yr.
Page Size: standard
Subscrip. Rate: $40/yr.; $75/2 yrs.
Freelance Pay: varies
Circulation: 30,000
Circulation Type: paid
**Owner(s):**
American Dental Hygienists' Association
444 N. Michigan Ave.
Chicago, IL 60611
Telephone: (312) 440-8900
Ownership %: 100
**Editorial:**
Rosetta Gervasi ................................Editor
Nancy Sisty ...............Editorial Director
Lisa Moore ......................................Advertising
Linda King ...........................Assistant Editor
Jean Majeski ........................Associate Editor
**Desc.:** Directed to dental hygienists and
  others in the oral health carefield; it
  contains scientific and technical
  manuscripts on clinical practice,
  research, education and community
  dental health.
**Readers:** Dental hygienists and other
  health professionals.

22764
**JOURNAL OF DENTAL RESEARCH**
1111 14th St., N.W., Ste. 1000
Washington, DC 20005
Telephone: (202) 898-1050
FAX: (202) 789-1033
Year Established: 1919
Pub. Frequency: m.
Page Size: standard
Subscrip. Rate: $350/yr. US; $360/yr.
  foreign
Circulation: 7,237
Circulation Type: controlled & paid
**Owner(s):**
American Association for Dental Research
1111 14th St., N.W., Ste. 1000
Washington, DC 20005
Telephone: (202) 898-1050
Ownership %: 100
**Editorial:**
Dr. Mark Hersberg ...............................Editor
**Desc.:** Dedicated to the dissemination of
  new knowledge and information on all
  sciences relevant to dentistry and to the
  oral cavity and associated structures in
  health and disease.
**Readers:** Researchers, teachers, students.

22765
**JOURNAL OF DENTISTRY FOR
CHILDREN**
875 N. Michigan Ave.
Ste. 4040
Chicago, IL 60611-1901
Telephone: (312) 943-1244
FAX: (312) 943-5341
Year Established: 1933
Pub. Frequency: bi-m.
Page Size: standard
Subscrip. Rate: $105/yr. US institutions;
  $135/yr. foreign institutions
Materials: 06,29,30,32,33
Print Process: web
Circulation: 13,700
Circulation Type: controlled & paid
**Owner(s):**
American Society of Dentistry for Children
875 N. Michigan Ave.
Ste. 4040
Chicago, IL 60611-1901
Telephone: (312) 943-1244
FAX: (312) 943-5341
Ownership %: 100
**Editorial:**
Anthony J. Jannetti .....................Miscellaneous
**Desc.:** Covers field of pedodontics. The
  official journal of American Society of
  Dentistry for Children.
**Readers:** Dentists.

22766
**JOURNAL OF ORAL &
MAXILLOFACIAL SURGERY**
Curtis Center
Independence Square W.
Philadelphia, PA 19106
Telephone: (215) 238-7800
FAX: (215) 238-6445
Year Established: 1943
Pub. Frequency: m.
Page Size: standard
Subscrip. Rate: $85/yr. individuals;
  $106/yr. institutions
Circulation: 8,500
Circulation Type: paid
**Owner(s):**
American Assn. of Oral and Maxillofacial
  Surgeons
211 E. Chicago Ave.
Chicago, IL 60611
Telephone: (312) 642-6446
Ownership %: 100
**Management:**
W.B. Saunders ................................Publisher
M.J. Mivica ..................Advertising Manager
  Associates

**Materials Accepted/Included:** 01-Business news 02-By-line articles 03-Fashion news 04-Food news 05-Freelance copy 06-Letters to editor 07-Real estate news 08-Sports news 09-Travel news
10-Book rev. 11-Movie rev. 12-Music rev. 13-TV rev. 14-Theater rev. 15-Coming events 16-Obituaries 17-Question & answer 18-Social announcements 19-Artwork 20-Cartoons 21-Photos 22-TV listings
23-Audio rec. 24-Video rec. 25-Books 26-Films/film clips 27-Personnel news 28-Press releases 29-New product news/photos 30-Trade lit. 31-Contracts awarded 32-Display adv. 33-Classified adv.

4-108

Diana Pesek .............................Manager
**Editorial:**
D.M. Laskin .................................Editor
Pam Fried ..........................Managing Editor
Harry A. Dean, Jr. .............Assistant Publisher
Dr. D.M. Laskin .............Book Review Editor
**Desc.:** Articles in the oral and maxillofacial surgery or pathology field by professional people in the dental field, primarily.
**Readers:** Oral and maxillofacial surgeons, dentists, otolaryngologists, plastic surgeons.

### JOURNAL OF PERIODONTOLOGY
22767

787 N. Michigan Ave., Ste. 800
Chicago, IL 60611
Telephone: (312) 787-5518
FAX: (312) 787-3670
Year Established: 1930
Pub. Frequency: m.
Page Size: standard
Subscrip. Rate: $80/yr.; $90/yr. elsewhere
Circulation: 8,000
Circulation Type: paid
**Owner(s):**
American Academy of Periodontology
787 N. Michigan Ave., Ste. 800
Chicago, IL 60611
Telephone: (312) 787-5518
Ownership %: 100
**Editorial:**
Dr. Robert J. Genco .......................Editor
Rita Shafer .........................Managing Editor
Kate Goss ...............................Advertising
Kelly Wool ..............................Advertising
Alice DeForest .................Executive Director
**Desc.:** Original articles on research and therapy.
**Readers:** Periodontists, dentists, teachers, graduate and undergraduate students, general dental practitioners with an interest in periodontics.

### JOURNAL OF PRACTICAL HYGIENE
68981

70 Hill Top Rd.
Ramsey, NJ 07446
Telephone: (201) 236-0700
FAX: (201) 236-1339
Year Established: 1992
Pub. Frequency: bi-m.
Page Size: standard
Subscrip. Rate: $28/yr.
Materials: 02,06,28,29,32
Print Process: web offset
Circulation: 60,000
Circulation Type: controlled & paid
**Owner(s):**
Montage Media Corp.
70 Hill Top Rd.
Ramsey, NJ 07446
Telephone: (201) 236-0700
FAX: (201) 236-1339
Ownership %: 100
**Desc.:** Disseminates information on practical applications of soft tissue management and oral hygiene, as well as applications in restorative and implant treatments.
**Readers:** 52,000 registered dental hygienists, 3,100 hygienists in periodontal practice, 2,800 requested dental assistants, 2,500 ADA accredited dental hygiene academicians/students.

### JOURNAL OF PROSTHETIC DENTISTRY, THE
56370

11830 Westline Industrial Dr.
St. Louis, MO 63146
Telephone: (314) 872-8370
FAX: (314) 432-1380
Year Established: 1951
Pub. Frequency:

Page Size: standard
Subscrip. Rate: $78/yr. individauls; $147/yr. institutions; $48/yr. students
Circulation: 13,585
Circulation Type: free & paid
**Owner(s):**
Mosby-Year Book Company
11830 Westline Industrial Dr.
St. Louis, MO 63146
Telephone: (314) 872-8370
Ownership %: 100
**Management:**
Carol Trumbold ...........................Publisher
Kathy Preston ...............Advertising Manager
**Editorial:**
Glen P. McGivney, D.D.S. ...............Editor
Kathy Keller .....................Production Director
**Desc.:** Covers the various phases of restorative dentistry. It is edited for prosthodontists and those general practice dentists who include prosthetics as a major portion of their practice. Its practical, clinical orientation emphasizes new techniques, evaluation of dental materials, pertinent basic science concepts and patient psychology.
**Readers:** Prosthodontists and general dentists. Official publication of: The Academy of Denture Prosthetics, The American Prosthodontic Society, The Pacific Coast Society of Prosthodontists.

### JOURNAL OF THE AMERICAN DENTAL ASSOCIATION
22769

211 E. Chicago Ave.
Chicago, IL 60611
Telephone: (312) 440-2740
FAX: (312) 440-3538
Year Established: 1913
Pub. Frequency: m.
Page Size: standard
Subscrip. Rate: $8/issue U.S.; $12/issue foreign; $25/yr. membership; $95/yr. foreign
Materials: 06,10,28,30,32,33
Print Process: web offset
Circulation: 150,000
Circulation Type: paid
**Owner(s):**
ADA Publishing Co., Inc.
211 E. Chicago Ave.
Chicago, IL 60611
Telephone: (312) 440-2785
Ownership %: 100
**Management:**
Laura Kosden ..............................Publisher
Duane Billek .................Advertising Manager
Duane Billek .........................Sales Manager
**Editorial:**
James Berry ................................Editor
James Berry .......................Managing Editor
Judy Jakush .............................News Editor
**Desc.:** Published for members of the dental profession. All scientific or informative articles must apply to some aspect of dental practice. The same applies to news articles, book reviews, illustrations and case reports.
**Readers:** Dentists, plus some dental auxiliaries.

### JOURNAL OF THE MICHIGAN DENTAL ASSOCIATION
69537

230 N. Washington Sq., Ste. 208
Lansing, MI 48933
Telephone: (517) 372-9070
FAX: (517) 372-0008
Year Established: 1919
Pub. Frequency: 9/yr.
Page Size: 8 1/2 x 11
Subscrip. Rate: $5/yr. members; $70/yr. non-members; $15/yr. libraries
Materials: 02,05,06,20,32,33
Print Process: offset

Circulation: 5,300
Circulation Type: paid
**Owner(s):**
Michigan Dental Association
230 N. Washington Sq., Ste.208
Lansing, MI 48933
Telephone: (517) 372-9070
Ownership %: 100
**Editorial:**
Dr. Charles E. Owens ......................Editor
**Readers:** Members of the Michigan Dental Association, their staffs, other dental society executives, members of state and federal government and regulatory agencies.

### MISSOURI DENTAL JOURNAL
22770

230 W. McCarty St.
Jefferson City, MO 65101
Telephone: (314) 634-3436
Mailing Address:
P.O. Box 1707
Jefferson City, MO 65102
Year Established: 1921
Pub. Frequency: bi-m.
Page Size: standard
Subscrip. Rate: $12/yr. US; $18/yr. foreign
Materials: 01,02,06,15,28,31,32,33
Print Process: offset
Circulation: 2,500
Circulation Type: paid
**Owner(s):**
Missouri Dental Association
230 W. McCarty St.
Jefferson City, MO 65101
Telephone: (314) 634-3436
Ownership %: 100
**Management:**
Tammy L. Miller ...............Advertising Manager
**Editorial:**
Dr. Elizabeth Ward ........................Editor
Tammy L. Miller ....................Associate Editor
**Desc.:** Comments on dentistry, government relations, association news, awards.
**Readers:** Dentists and other health care professionals.

### NORTHWEST DENTISTRY
22774

2236 Marshall Ave.
Saint Paul, MN 55104
Telephone: (612) 646-7454
FAX: (612) 646-8246
Year Established: 1930
Pub. Frequency: bi-m.
Page Size: standard
Subscrip. Rate: $20/yr. non-members
Freelance Pay: negotiated
Circulation: 3,400
Circulation Type: controlled
**Owner(s):**
Minnesota Dental Association
2236 Marshall Ave.
Saint Paul, MN 55104
Telephone: (612) 646-7454
Ownership %: 100
**Management:**
Patty Lien ......................Advertising Manager
Claudia L. Kanter ...............Business Manager
**Editorial:**
Richard A. Johnson .......................Editor
Susan Miller ............................News Editor
Susan Miller ..........................Technical Editor
**Desc.:** Original articles, editorials, clinical abstracts, reports on research projects, governments role in health affairs, insurance matters, association news.
**Readers:** Practicing dentists and auxiliary personnel.

### OHIO DENTAL JOURNAL
22775

1370 Dublin Rd.
Columbus, OH 43215
Telephone: (614) 486-2700
FAX: (614) 486-0381
Year Established: 1926
Pub. Frequency: s-a.
Page Size: standard
Subscrip. Rate: $30/yr. includes Focus On Ohio Dentistry
Circulation: 5,300
Circulation Type: controlled
**Owner(s):**
Ohio Dental Association
1370 Dublin Rd.
Columbus, OH 43215
Telephone: (614) 486-2700
Ownership %: 100
**Management:**
Christine Kerstetter ..........Advertising Manager
**Editorial:**
Donald F. Bowers, D.D.S. .................Editor
Dirk Vonderlage .....................Managing Editor
**Desc.:** As the official publication of the Ohio Dental Association, attempts to publish feature articles, general news, announcements, editorials, letters to the editor, advertising, etc. Articles should be clear and concise and directly relevant to the reading audience. Illustration is requested when possible. Advertising must deal with dental products and services, or relate to the practice of dentistry.
**Readers:** Ohio dentists, dental schools, editors.

### ORAL SURGERY, ORAL MEDICINE, ORAL PATHOLOGY
22776

11830 Westline Industrial Dr.
St. Louis, MO 63146
Telephone: (314) 872-8370
FAX: (314) 432-1380
Year Established: 1948
Pub. Frequency: m.
Page Size: standard
Subscrip. Rate: $74/yr. individual; $155/yr. institution
Circulation: 8,421
Circulation Type: paid
**Owner(s):**
Mosby-Year Book, Inc.
11830 Westline Industrial Dr.
St. Louis, MO 63146
Telephone: (314) 872-8370
Ownership %: 100
**Management:**
Carol Trumbold ...........................Publisher
Kathy Preston ...............Advertising Manager
**Editorial:**
Larry J. Peterson, D.D.S .................Editor
Kathy Keller .....................Production Director
**Desc.:** Geared to the medical aspects of dentistry and is edited for oral surgeons, peridontists, endodontists, oral pathologists and dental students. The content is concerned with the diagnostic aids, medical treatment and surgical techniques of dental practice as it is correlated with significant developments in various branches of medicine and dentistry.
**Readers:** Circulation is balanced among oral surgeons, oral pathologists, endodontists, periodontists, and general practitioners whose dental practices include all areas of dentistry covered by the journal. There is also a significant circulation to graduate dental students.

**Materials Accepted/Included:** 01-Business news 02-By-line articles 03-Fashion news 04-Food news 05-Freelance copy 06-Letters to editor 07-Real estate news 08-Sports news 09-Travel news 10-Book rev. 11-Movie rev. 12-Music rev. 13-TV rev. 14-Theater rev. 15-Coming events 16-Obituaries 17-Question & answer 18-Social announcements 19-Artwork 20-Cartoons 21-Photos 22-TV listings 23-Audio rec. 24-Video rec. 25-Books 26-Films/film clips 27-Personnel news 28-Press releases 29-New product news/photos 30-Trade lit. 31-Contracts awarded 32-Display adv. 33-Classified adv.

4-109

## PROOFS
22777

1421 S. Sheridan
Tulsa, OK 74112
Telephone: (918) 835-3161
FAX: (918) 831-9804
Mailing Address:
  P.O. Box 3408
  Tulsa, OK 74101
Year Established: 1917
Pub. Frequency: 10/yr.
Page Size: standard
Subscrip. Rate: $17/yr. US.; $23/yr.
  Canada; $85/yr. overseas airmail
Materials: 01,02,05,06,15,16,27,28,32,33
Freelance Pay: $100-$175
Print Process: web
Circulation: 7,500
Circulation Type: paid
**Owner(s):**
PennWell Publishing Co.
P.O. Box 3408
Tulsa, OK 74101
Telephone: (918) 835-3161
Ownership %: 100
**Management:**
Dick Hale ...............................Publisher
Vicki Cheeseman .................Business Manager
LaVerne Lewis ...................Production Manager
**Editorial:**
Mary Elizabeth Good .....................Editor
Roger Harway .....................Associate Publisher
**Desc.:** Contributed and staff-written
  features for the dental trade. Covers
  employee training, selling,
  merchandising, association news,
  meetings, company news, appointments,
  trade items.
**Readers:** Dental dealers and dental
  manufacturers.
**Deadline:** story-1st of mo. prior to pub.
  date; news-1st of mo. prior; photo-1st of
  mo. prior; ads-10th of mo. prior

## QUINTESSENCE INTERNATIONAL
22778

551 Kimberly Dr.
Carol Stream, IL 60188-1881
Telephone: (708) 682-3223
FAX: (708) 682-3288
Year Established: 1969
Pub. Frequency: m.
Page Size: standard
Subscrip. Rate: $72/yr.
Circulation: 26,412
Circulation Type: paid
**Owner(s):**
Quintessence Publishing Co., Inc.
551 Kimberly Dr.
Carol Stream, IL 60188-1881
Telephone: (708) 682-3223
Ownership %: 100
**Management:**
H.W. Haase ...............................Owner
H.W. Haase ...............................President
L.F. Gustas .................Executive Vice President
T. Tsuchiya .....................Vice President
H.W. Haase ...............................Publisher
L.F. Gustas .....................Advertising Manager
W. Hartman .....................Business Manager
L. Hartman .....................Circulation Manager
**Editorial:**
Richard Simonsen, D.D.S. ..........Editor in Chief
K.M. Vandersteen ...............Production Director
**Desc.:** Articles of practical usefulness to
  dentists. It provides continuing education
  in articles authored by dental authorities
  according to particular dental specialties.
  A new product section is included as
  well.
**Readers:** Practicing dentists.

## RDH: REGISTERED DENTAL HYGIENIST
68978

225 N. New Rd.
Waco, TX 76710
Telephone: (817) 776-9000
Year Established: 1981
Pub. Frequency: m.
Subscrip. Rate: $40/yr.
Circulation: 65,000
Circulation Type: paid
**Owner(s):**
Stevens Publishing Corp.
225 N. New Rd.
Waco, TX 76710
Telephone: (817) 776-9000
Ownership %: 100
**Editorial:**
Kathleen Witherspoon ...............Editor

## SOUTH CAROLINA DENTAL BULLETIN
22779

120 Stonemark Ln.
Columbia, SC 29210
Telephone: (803) 750-2277
FAX: (803) 750-1644
Year Established: 1982
Pub. Frequency: m.
Page Size: tabloid
Subscrip. Rate: $12/yr.
Print Process: offset
Circulation: 1,400
Circulation Type: controlled
**Owner(s):**
South Carolina Dental Association
120 Stonemark Ln.
Columbia, SC 29210
Telephone: (803) 750-2277
Ownership %: 100
**Management:**
Hal Zorn ...............................Advertising Manager
**Editorial:**
Dr. Doug Rawls .....................Editor
**Readers:** Dental staff

## TODAY'S FDA
69539

1111 E. Tennessee St., Ste. 102
Tallahassee, FL 32308-6914
Telephone: (904) 681-3629
FAX: (904) 561-0504
Year Established: 1989
Pub. Frequency: m.
Page Size: tabloid
Subscrip. Rate: $32.10/yr.
Materials: 32,33
Print Process: web
Circulation: 6,800
Circulation Type: paid
**Owner(s):**
Florida Dental Association
1111 E. Tennessee St., Ste. 10
Tallahassee, FL 32308-6914
Telephone: (904) 681-3629
FAX: (904) 561-0504
Ownership %: 100
**Editorial:**
Dr. Bert V. Dannheisser, Jr. .....................Editor
**Desc.:** Contains news, features,
  commentary, and scientific information
  for the Florida Dentist.

## TRENDS & TECHNIQUES IN THE CONTEMPORARY DENTAL LABORATORY
68982

555 E. Braddock Rd.
Alexandria, VA 22314-2161
Telephone: (703) 683-5263
FAX: (703) 549-4788
Year Established: 1954
Pub. Frequency: bi-m.
Subscrip. Rate: $40/yr. US; $50/yr. foreign
Circulation: 17,000
Circulation Type: paid

**Owner(s):**
National Association of Dental Laboratories
3801 Mt. Vernon Ave.
Alexandria, VA 22305
Telephone: (703) 683-5263
Ownership %: 100
**Editorial:**
Douglas W. Newcomb ...............Editor
**Desc.:** Covers technical issues, association
  activities and business management, as
  well as industry news and new products.
**Readers:** Dental technicians and
  laboratory owners.

## WDA JOURNAL
69542

111 E. Wisconsin Ave., Ste. 1300
Milwaukee, WI 53202
Telephone: (414) 276-4520
Pub. Frequency: bi-m.
Subscrip. Rate: $45/yr. libraries US;
  $75/yr. foreign
Materials: 32,33
Circulation: 3,100
Circulation Type: controlled
**Owner(s):**
Wisconsin Dental Association
111 E. Wisconsin Ave., Ste. 1300
Milwaukee, WI 53202
Telephone: (414) 276-4520
Ownership %: 100
**Editorial:**
Mr. Rick Brandtjen ...................Managing Editor

## WEST VIRGINIA DENTAL JOURNAL
22781

300 Capitol St., Ste. 1002
Charleston, WV 25301
Telephone: (304) 925-7201
FAX: (304) 344-5316
Year Established: 1960
Pub. Frequency: q.
Page Size: standard
Subscrip. Rate: $10/yr.
**Owner(s):**
West Virginia Dental Association
300 Capitol St., Ste. 1002
Charleston, WV 25301
Telephone: (304) 344-5246
Ownership %: 100
**Management:**
Richard D. Stevens ..........Advertising Manager
**Editorial:**
Richard D. Stevens .................Managing Editor
Dr. Joseph V. Rice ...................Associate Editor
Dr. Joseph V. Rice ...................Technical Editor
**Desc.:** All articles and editorials pertaining
  to dentistry.
**Readers:** Dental professionals.

## WIRELINE
68979

9550 Forest Ln., Ste. 215
Dallas, TX 75243
Telephone: (214) 343-0805
FAX: (214) 343-1628
Year Established: 1978
Pub. Frequency: q.
Circulation: 15000
Circulation Type: controlled
**Owner(s):**
American Orthodontic Society
9550 Forest Ln., Ste. 215
Dallas, TX 75243
Telephone: (214) 343-0805
Ownership %: 100
**Editorial:**
Bret Cullers ...............................Editor

**Desc.:** Provides information relating to
  changes within the organization, and
  dental and orthodontic information.

## Group 062-Discount Merchandising

## DISCOUNT MERCHANDISER, THE
23165

233 Park Ave., S.
New York, NY 10003
Telephone: (212) 979-4840
FAX: (212) 979-7431
Year Established: 1961
Pub. Frequency: m.
Page Size: standard
Subscrip. Rate: $55/yr. US; $100/yr.
  foreign
Circulation: 35,000
Circulation Type: paid
**Owner(s):**
MacFadden Publishing
Ownership %: 100
**Management:**
Steven Jacober ...............................President
Steven Jacober ...............................Publisher
Vanessa May .....................Advertising Manager
Bob Boston .....................Circulation Manager
**Editorial:**
Jay L. Johnson ...............................Executive Editor
Pat Corwin .....................Senior Editor
Renee Romland .....................Senior Editor
Steven Jacober .....................Editor
Jennifer Pellat .....................Associate Editor
Debra Chanil .....................New Products Editor
**Desc.:** Management publication devoted to
  the discount industry.
**Readers:** Owners, officers, executives,
  buyers, merchants.

## Group 064-Drugs, Pharmaceutical & Pharmacies

## AMERICAN DRUGGIST
22788

60 E. 42nd St., Ste. 449
New York, NY 10165-0449
Telephone: (212) 297-9680
FAX: (212) 286-9886
Year Established: 1871
Pub. Frequency: m.
Page Size: standard
Subscrip. Rate: $3/copy; $44/yr.
Freelance Pay: $100-$500/project
Circulation: 92,000
Circulation Type: controlled
**Owner(s):**
Hearst Corp.
60 E. 42nd St., Ste. 449
New York, NY 10165-0449
Telephone: (212) 297-9680
Ownership %: 100
**Management:**
Frank A. Bennack, Jr. ...............President
Scott E. Pierce .....................Publisher
**Editorial:**
Sandra Rifkin ...............................Editor in Chief
**Desc.:** The complete source for the
  American pharmacist. Articles address
  the interests of pharmacists in the
  following practice settings: independent
  retail, chain, hospital, HMO's, drug
  wholesalers and other specialty areas.
  Covers news and latest development in
  management how-to format. From new
  pharmaceuticals to marketing strategies,
  from appropriate drug use to
  governmental and regulatory changes.
  Also addresses the cultural context in
  which today's pharmacist functions.
**Readers:** Pharmacists (independent, chain,
  hospital, HMO, nursing home), store
  owners, chain headquarters personnel,
  wholesalers, PPO's.

## AMERICAN JOURNAL OF HOSPITAL PHARMACY

22789

7272 Wisconsin Ave.
Bethesda, MD 20814
Telephone: (301) 657-3000
FAX: (301) 657-1615
Year Established: 1943
Pub. Frequency: bi-m.
Page Size: standard
Subscrip. Rate: $133/yr.
Materials: 10,28,29,32,33
Print Process: offset
Circulation: 28,731
Circulation Type: paid
**Owner(s):**
American Society of Hospital Pharmacists
7272 Wisconsin Ave.
Bethesda, MD 20814
Telephone: (301) 657-3000
Ownership %: 100
**Management:**
Wende B. Mack ..................Editorial Production
Manager
**Editorial:**
C. Richard Talley ..........................Editor
Catherine Nichols Klein ...........Managing Editor
William McCausland .........................Advertising
Nasrine L. Sabi ...............................Advertising
**Desc.:** Professional publication edited by
and for hospital pharmacists.
**Readers:** Hospital pharmacists.
**Deadline:** story-1 mo. prior to pub. date;
news-1 mo. prior to pub. date; photo-1
mo. prior to pub. date; ads-1 mo. prior to
pub. date

## AMERICAN PHARMACY

22790

2215 Constitution Ave., N.W.
Washington, DC 20037
Telephone: (202) 628-4410
FAX: (202) 783-2351
Year Established: 1912
Pub. Frequency: m.
Page Size: standard
Subscrip. Rate: $50/yr. non-member;
$110/yr. foreign
Freelance Pay: $.15/wd.
Circulation: 42,646
Circulation Type: paid
**Owner(s):**
American Pharmaceutical Association
2215 Constitution Ave., N. W.
Washington, DC 20037
Telephone: (202) 628-4410
Ownership %: 100
**Management:**
John A. Gans .........................President
**Editorial:**
Joyce Leinberger-Mitchell ............Senior Editor
Marlene Bloom ...........................Editor
Rick Harding ...........................Managing Editor
Mary Jane Hickey ..................Production Editor
**Desc.:** Staff-written articles and articles
authored by outstanding leaders in
health and pharmaceutics on health
care, research, and practices relating to
pharmacy; special reports; editorials;
news. Authored articles are by-lined. All
materials must be approved by the
editor. If appropriate, no limit on length
of articles-most run 2 to 6 pages.
**Readers:** Practicing pharmacists,
prescription specialists, students,
wholesale druggists, association officials,
personnel in drug industry, members of
allied professions.

## AMERICAN PHARMACY TECHNICIAN JOURNAL

69055

330 E. Lakeside St.
Madison, WI 53715
Telephone: (800) 762-8978
FAX: (608) 283-5402

Mailing Address:
P.O. Box 1109
Madison, WI 53715
Year Established: 1991
Pub. Frequency: bi-m.
Subscrip. Rate: $45/yr. non-members;
$60/yr. institutions
**Owner(s):**
American Association of Pharmacy
Technicians
330 E. Lakeside St.
P.O. Box 11109
Madison, WI 53715
Telephone: (800) 762-8978
Ownership %: 100
**Desc.:** Covers scientific and managerial
aspects of pharmacy practice, current
legislative issues affecting technicians,
pharmaceutical hardware and
computer applications, and the
development of professional skills.

## APOTHECARY, THE

22791

95 1st St., #200
Los Altos, CA 94022
Telephone: (510) 941-3955
FAX: (415) 941-2303
Mailing Address:
P.O. Box AP
Los Altos, CA 94023
Year Established: 1888
Pub. Frequency: q.
Page Size: standard
Subscrip. Rate: $12/yr.
Freelance Pay: $50-$250
Circulation: 60,000
Circulation Type: controlled
**Owner(s):**
Health Care Marketing Services
95 First St., #200
Los Altos, CA 94022
Telephone: (510) 941-3955
Ownership %: 100
**Management:**
Eli Traub .............................Publisher
**Editorial:**
Cathryn D. Evans .........................Senior Editor
Jerold K. Karabensh, R.Ph. ...................Editor
Susan Keller ............................Managing Editor
Ronald Goodman ..............................Art Director
Janet Goodman .................Publication Director
**Desc.:** Business management journal for
practicing pharmacists.
**Readers:** Retail and hospital pharmacists.

## ARIZONA PHARMACIST

22792

1845 E. Southern Ave.
Tempe, AZ 85282
Telephone: (602) 838-3385
FAX: (602) 838-3557
Year Established: 1921
Pub. Frequency: bi-m.
Page Size: standard
Subscrip. Rate: free/members; $45/yr.
non-members
Print Process: offset
Circulation: 1,600
Circulation Type: controlled & paid
**Owner(s):**
Arizona Pharmacy Association
1845 E. Southern Ave
Tempe, AZ 85282
Telephone: (602) 838-3385
Ownership %: 100
**Management:**
Kim D. Roberson ..............Advertising Manager
**Editorial:**
Kim D. Roberson ...............Executive Editor
Alfred Duncan .................Consulting Editor

**Desc.:** A publication covering the field of
pharmacy. Carries articles on national
and state (mostly Arizona) basis. New
products of advertisers and news of
advertisers are printed bimonthly in
an effort to cover pharmacy in general.
**Readers:** Pharmacists in Arizona and other
states.

## CALIFORNIA PHARMACIST

22793

1112 I St., Ste. 300
Sacramento, CA 95814
Telephone: (916) 444-7811
FAX: (916) 444-7929
Year Established: 1954
Pub. Frequency: m.
Page Size: standard
Subscrip. Rate: $25/yr.
Freelance Pay: negotiable
Circulation: 7,000
Circulation Type: controlled
**Owner(s):**
California Pharmacists Association
1112 I St., Ste. 300
Sacramento, CA 95814
Telephone: (916) 444-7811
Ownership %: 100
**Management:**
Robert P. Marshall ...............Publisher
Bob Andosca ..................Advertising Manager
**Editorial:**
Robert P. Marshall ........................Editor
Bob Andosca ...........................Managing Editor
Bob Andosca ...........................Advertising
**Desc.:** A professional pharmaceutical
publication devoted to the dissemination
of information relating to the practice of
pharmacy and the dispensing of drugs. It
provides knowledge of professional
practice, legislative reviews, information
on drug products and continuing
education articles.
**Readers:** California pharmacists,
professors of pharmacy, and pharmacy
students.

## DRUG & COSMETIC INDUSTRY

22796

270 Madison Ave.
New York, NY 10016
Telephone: (212) 951-6719
FAX: (212) 481-6562
Year Established: 1914
Pub. Frequency: m.
Page Size: standard
Subscrip. Rate: $32/yr.; $57/2 yrs.
Materials: 01,02,05,06,10,15,16,27,28,30,
32,33
Freelance Pay: $150-$200/2 pg. article
Print Process: web
Circulation: 14,000
Circulation Type: paid
**Owner(s):**
Advantar Communications, Inc.
270 Madison Ave.
New York, NY 10016
Telephone: (212) 951-6700
Ownership %: 100
**Management:**
Roz Markhouse ...........................Publisher
Rick Wilkes ..................Circulation Manager
**Editorial:**
Donald A. Davis ...........................Editor
Karen Hoppe ...........................Associate Editor
Robert L. Goldemberg ..........Consulting Editor

**Desc.:** Contributed and staff-written by-line
articles and news departments covering
industry problems, technical analysis,
discussion of different lines, drugs,
packaging, etc. Articles are written on a
professional and technical level.
Departments include: Keeping Posted,
DCI People, Cosmetic Marketing, Trade
Literature, Industry People, Package of
the Month Washington Letter, Industry's
Books, Bassin on Beauty Biz, The Last
Word, Cosmetic Compounding,
Compounder's Corner. News coverage
includes company activities,
appointments, regulatory information,
etc.
**Readers:** Manufacturers of cosmetics,
pharmaceutical packaged chemical
products, manufacturing wholesalers.
**Deadline:** story-1st of mo. prior to pub.
date; news-12th of mo. prior; photo-15th
of mo. prior; ads-12th of mo. prior

## DRUG METABOLISM & DISPOSITION

55902

428 E. Preston St.
Baltimore, MD 21202
Telephone: (410) 528-4000
FAX: (410) 528-4312
Year Established: 1984
Pub. Frequency: bi-m.
Page Size: standard
Subscrip. Rate: $85/yr. individuals;
$140/yr. institutions
Circulation: 1,075
Circulation Type: paid
**Owner(s):**
Amer. Soc. Pharm. & Experimental
Therapeutics
Ownership %: 100
**Editorial:**
Dr. Vincent G. Zannoni ............................Editor
**Desc.:** Covers metabolism of
pharmacologic agents or drugs and
environmental chemicals, reactants and
preservatives for pharmacologists,
toxicologists, and medicinal chemists.
**Readers:** Subscribers include members of
the American Society for Pharmacology
and Experimental Therapeutics,
pharmacologists, toxicologists,
medicinal chemists, and medical
libraries.

## DRUG STORE NEWS

23280

425 Park Ave.
New York, NY 10022
Telephone: (212) 756-5220
FAX: (212) 756-5250
Year Established: 1928
Pub. Frequency: bi-m.
Page Size: tabloid
Subscrip. Rate: $19.50/yr.
Freelance Pay: negotiable
Circulation: 45,604
Circulation Type: paid
**Owner(s):**
Lebhar-Friedman, Inc.
425 Park Ave.
New York, NY 10022
Telephone: (212) 756-5000
Ownership %: 100
**Bureau(s):**
Lebhar-Friedman, Inc.
One Gateway Ctr.
Newton, MA 02158
Telephone: (617) 527-6394
Contact: Jim Malver, Manager

Lebhar-Friedman, Inc.
444 N. Michigan Ave.
Chicago, IL 60611
Telephone: (312) 644-8688
Contact: Maggie Kaeppel, Manager

**Materials Accepted/Included:** 01-Business news 02-By-line articles 03-Fashion news 04-Food news 05-Freelance copy 06-Letters to editor 07-Real estate news 08-Sports news 09-Travel news 10-Book rev. 11-Movie rev. 12-Music rev. 13-TV rev. 14-Theater rev. 15-Coming events 16-Obituaries 17-Question & answer 18-Social announcements 19-Artwork 20-Cartoons 21-Photos 22-TV listings 23-Audio rec. 24-Video rec. 25-Books 26-Films/film clips 27-Personnel news 28-Press releases 29-New product news/photos 30-Trade lit. 31-Contracts awarded 32-Display adv. 33-Classified adv.

4-111

**Management:**
Jay Forbes .............................Publisher
Mary Lewis ..................Production Manager
**Editorial:**
Marie Griffin ...................Editor in Chief
Jill Manee ...................Associate Publisher
**Desc.:** Contains news-oriented editorial which focuses on retail drug chains, volume independents, wholesale distributors. A regular pharmacy section, Inside Pharmacy, features articles on operations, new product introductions, market trends and federal and state issues. Each issue includes Trends, a magazine section that reports on merchandising of health and beauty aids and general merchandise in drug stores.
**Readers:** Headquarters executives, district managers, buyers, supervisors & store managers of chain drug stores, wholesalers and high volume independent stores.

### DRUG THERAPY
22797

105 Raider Blvd.
Belle Mead, NJ 08502
Telephone: (908) 874-8550
FAX: (908) 874-0707
Year Established: 1971
Pub. Frequency: m.
Page Size: standard
Subscrip. Rate: $50/yr. individual; $66/yr. institution
Freelance Pay: $200-$500/article
Circulation: 112,000
Circulation Type: controlled
**Owner(s):**
Reed Elsevier Medical Publishers, USA
Core Publishing Division
105 Raider Blvd.
Belle Mead, NJ 08502
Telephone: (908) 874-8550
Ownership %: 100
**Management:**
Robert Frattaroli ............................President
Melissa Warner ............................Publisher
**Editorial:**
David MacDougall ...............Editor in Chief
Barbara Ready ...............Managing Editor
Ken Senerth ...............Associate Publisher
**Desc.:** Original articles authored by physicians on the use and action of therapeutic agents. Contents are selected and edited to be practical and clinically relevant to the needs of office based practitioners.
**Readers:** Primary care physicians in general and family practice, internal medicine, cardiology, gastroenterology, and osteopathy.

### DRUG TOPICS
22799

Five Paragon Dr.
Montvale, NJ 07645
Telephone: (201) 358-7200
Year Established: 1857
Pub. Frequency: 23/yr.
Page Size: standard
Subscrip. Rate: $10/copy; $58/yr.; $15/special issue
Circulation: 93,000
Circulation Type: controlled
**Owner(s):**
Medical Economics Publishing Co., Inc.
Five Paragon Dr.
Montvale, NJ 07645
Telephone: (201) 358-7200
Ownership %: 100
**Bureau(s):**
Medical Economics Publishing
20 N. Clark St. Bldg.
Chicago, IL 60602
Telephone: (800) 223-0581
Contact: Chad Alcorn, Manager

**Management:**
Lee A. Maniscalco ............................Publisher
Audra Sharry ...............Promotion Manager
Patrick J. Guiliano ...............Sales Manager
**Editorial:**
Ralph M. Thurlow ...............Executive Editor
Valentine Cardinale ............................Editor
**Desc.:** Keeps retail drug stores fully informed on important news of the retail drug trade-selling, merchandising, store management, national issues, scientific developments. Keeps pharmacy up to date on the latest ideas, trends, and developments affecting its various components, drugstore chains, independents and hospital pharmacies.
**Readers:** Pharmacists at the independent chain, and hospital levels; chain headquarters executives and buyers; and wholesalers.

### HOSPITAL FORMULARY
69054

7500 Old Oak Blvd.
Cleveland, OH 44130
Telephone: (216) 891-2689
FAX: (216) 891-2683
Year Established: 1966
Pub. Frequency: m.
Page Size: standard
Subscrip. Rate: $55/yr.
Materials: 01,02,06,28,29,32,33
Circulation: 39,576, 1013
Circulation Type: controlled
**Owner(s):**
Advanstar Communications, Inc.
7500 Old Oak Blvd.
Cleveland, OH 44130
Telephone: (216) 891-2689
Ownership %: 100
**Editorial:**
Karen Sprague ............................Editor
**Desc.:** Focuses on institutional medicine: drug therapy, drug distribution systems, P & T Committee issues, formulary issues, and pharmacological economics.
**Deadline:** ads-9th-14th of each mo.

### HOSPITAL PHARMACY
23811

227 E. Washington Sq.
Philadelphia, PA 19106
Telephone: (215) 238-4200
Year Established: 1966
Pub. Frequency: m.
Page Size: standard
Subscrip. Rate: $83/yr. US; $108/yr. foreign
Circulation: 28,423
Circulation Type: controlled
**Owner(s):**
J.B. Lippincott Co.
East Washington Sq.
Philadelphia, PA 19105
Telephone: (215) 238-4200
Ownership %: 100
**Management:**
Marcia Serepy ............................Publisher
Joe Baiocco ...............Production Manager
**Editorial:**
Neil M. Davis, M.S., Pharm. D. ...............Editor
Pharmaceutical Media, Inc. ...............Advertising
Beverly Dietrich ...............Circulation Director
Virginia Martin ............................V.P. Journals
**Desc.:** Original articles involving clinical pharmacy and related areas of interest to the professional in hospital pharmacy.
**Readers:** Covers 100 percent of U.S. hospitals with 100 or more beds; directors/chiefs/asst. chiefs of pharmacy service; supervisor/manager pharmacists; staff, clinical and consultant pharmacists.

### ILLINOIS PHARMACIST
22801

223 W. Jackson Blvd., Ste. 1000
Chicago, IL 60606
Telephone: (312) 939-7300
Year Established: 1880
Pub. Frequency: m.
Page Size: standard
Subscrip. Rate: $36/yr.
Freelance Pay: negotiable
Circulation: 3,000
Circulation Type: paid
**Owner(s):**
Illinois Pharmacists Association
223 W. Jackson Blvd., 1400
Chicago, IL 60606
Telephone: (312) 939-7300
Ownership %: 100
**Management:**
Mark Pilkington ...............Executive Director
**Desc.:** News of association activities and drug industry. Company notes, professional articles, legislation and regulations, research findings, college news and related activities in the drug field.
**Readers:** Pharmacists in Illinois.

### INDIANA PHARMACIST
22802

729 N. Pennsylvania St.
Indianapolis, IN 46204-1128
Telephone: (317) 634-4968
FAX: (317) 632-1219
Year Established: 1882
Pub. Frequency: m.
Page Size: standard
Subscrip. Rate: $15/yr.
Circulation: 1,700
Circulation Type: controlled
**Owner(s):**
Indiana Pharmacists Association
156 E. Market St., Ste. 900
Indianapolis, IN 46204
Telephone: (317) 634-4968
Ownership %: 100
**Editorial:**
Lary Sage ............................Editor
**Desc.:** Primarily news publication covering developments of interest to the pharmacist and association news. Departments include pharmaceutical dynamics (new products, research developments carried as an extension service from the Purdue University School of Pharmacy and Pharmaceutical Sciences), biology, chemistry, pharmacy, including technical material from the Butler University College of Pharmacy.
**Readers:** Members of the Indiana Pharmacists Association.

### INTERNATIONAL JOURNAL OF THE ADDICTIONS, THE
70380

270 Madison Ave.
New York, NY 10016
Telephone: (212) 696-9000
FAX: (212) 684-4540
Year Established: 1965
Pub. Frequency: 14/yr.
Page Size: standard
Subscrip. Rate: $575/yr. individuals; $1150/yr. institutions
Print Process: offset
**Owner(s):**
Marcel Dekker, Inc.
270 Madison Ave.
New York, NY 10016
Telephone: (212) 696-9000
FAX: (212) 685-4540
Ownership %: 100
**Editorial:**
Stanley Einstein ............................Editor

**Desc.:** This journal presents authoritative, comprehensive reports on the serious problems facing individuals and communities in the areas of drug, alchohol, and tobacco use, abuse, and dependency. Representing a world-wide network on rsearch, training, and treatment.
**Readers:** Physicians, psychologists, sociologists, social workers, pharmacologists, educators, addiction rehabilitation centers, addiction research centers, law enforement agencies.

### IOWA PHARMACIST
22803

8515 Douglas, Ste. 16
Des Moines, IA 50322
Telephone: (515) 270-0713
FAX: (515) 270-2979
Year Established: 1946
Pub. Frequency: m.
Page Size: standard
Subscrip. Rate: $30/yr.
**Owner(s):**
Iowa Pharmacists Association
8515 Douglas, Ste. 16
Des Moines, IA 50322
Telephone: (515) 270-0713
Ownership %: 100
**Editorial:**
Tom Temple ............................Editor
Joan Stover ...............Managing Editor
**Readers:** Pharmacists, manufacturers, wholesalers.

### JOURNAL MICHIGAN PHARMACIST
22812

815 N. Washington Ave.
Lansing, MI 48906
Telephone: (517) 484-1466
FAX: (517) 484-4893
Year Established: 1963
Pub. Frequency: m.
Page Size: standard
Subscrip. Rate: $40/yr.
Materials: 02,06,15,19,20,21,28,29,30,32, 33
Freelance Pay: $200/continuing education articles
Circulation: 4,304
Circulation Type: controlled
**Owner(s):**
Michigan Pharmacists Association
815 N. Washington Ave.
Lansing, MI 48906
Telephone: (517) 484-1466
FAX: (517) 484-4893
Ownership %: 100
**Editorial:**
Louis M. Sesti, R.Ph. ............................Editor
Debra N. McGuire B.A. ...............Managing Editor
TBA ...............Advertising Coordinator
**Desc.:** Editorial content includes original articles convention and seminar reports, pharmacy continuing education articles and quizzes, practice ideas and concepts, association news and reports, board of pharmacy reports, pharmaco-legal developments and new legislation.
**Readers:** Edited for registered practicing pharmacists and is distributed among Association members and other subscribers. Readers include pharmacy owners, community pharmacy managers, long-term care pharmacists, employee pharmacists, hospital pharmacists, pharmaceutical representatives, pharmacy technicians, pharmacy students and educators, and other members of the health care community.
**Deadline:** ads-1 mo.

Materials Accepted/Included: 01-Business news 02-By-line articles 03-Fashion news 04-Food news 05-Freelance copy 06-Letters to editor 07-Real estate news 08-Sports news 09-Travel news 10-Book rev. 11-Movie rev. 12-Music rev. 13-TV rev. 14-Theater rev. 15-Coming events 16-Obituaries 17-Question & answer 18-Social announcements 19-Artwork 20-Cartoons 21-Photos 22-TV listings 23-Audio rec. 24-Video rec. 25-Books 26-Films/film clips 27-Personnel news 28-Press releases 29-New product news/photos 30-Trade lit. 31-Contracts awarded 32-Display adv. 33-Classified adv.

## JOURNAL OF CLINICAL PSYCHOPHARMACOLOGY
59035

428 E. Preston St.
Baltimore, MD 21202
Telephone: (410) 528-4000
FAX: (410) 528-4312
Year Established: 1979
Pub. Frequency: bi-m.
Page Size: standard
Subscrip. Rate: $84/yr. individual; $129/yr. institution
Circulation: 9,350
Circulation Type: paid
**Owner(s):**
Williams & Wilkins Co.
428 E. Preston St.
Baltimore, MD 21202
Telephone: (410) 528-4000
Ownership %: 100
**Management:**
Don Pfarr ...........................Advertising Manager
Alma Wills ...............................................Manager
Annette Grayson ..............Production Manager
**Editorial:**
Richard I. Shader, M.D. ..........................Editor
Nancy Collins .......................Marketing Director
**Desc.:** Clinical papers for psychiatrists on antipsychotic, antianxiety and antidepressant medications and stimulants.
**Readers:** Psychiatrists and psychiatric residents.

## JOURNAL OF KANSAS PHARMACY
22806

1308 W. Tenth St.
Topeka, KS 66604
Telephone: (913) 232-0439
FAX: (913) 232-3764
Year Established: 1929
Pub. Frequency: q.
Page Size: standard
Subscrip. Rate: $18/yr.
Materials: 02,32
Circulation: 1,300
Circulation Type: controlled
**Owner(s):**
Kansas Pharmacists Association
1308 W. 10th St.
Topeka, KS 66604
Telephone: (913) 232-0439
FAX: (913) 232-3764
Ownership %: 100
**Editorial:**
Jenith Hoover ............................................Editor
Ray Ramirez .............................Managing Editor
**Desc.:** Carries information of interest to pharmacists dealing with store management, advertising, ideas, customer relations, legislation, professional issues, association events & news.
**Readers:** Pharmacists.

## JOURNAL OF PHARMACEUTICAL SCIENCES
22807

2215 Constitution Ave., N.W.
Washington, DC 20037
Telephone: (202) 429-7526
FAX: (202) 783-2351
Year Established: 1912
Pub. Frequency: m.
Page Size: standard
Subscrip. Rate: $85/yr. individuals; $195/yr. institutions
Circulation: 5,793
Circulation Type: paid
**Owner(s):**
American Pharmaceutical Association
2215 Constitution Ave., NW
Washington, DC 20037
Telephone: (202) 628-4410
Ownership %: 100

**Management:**
John A. Gans ........................................President
John Gill .........................Advertising Manager
**Editorial:**
A. Maureen Rouhi, Ph.D. ........Managing Editor
Margaret H. Sickels ..................Assistant Editor
Susan Ysais .........................Editorial Associate
**Desc.:** Devoted exclusively to covering the latest developments in pharmaceutical research, including controlled drug delivery systems, biopharmaceutics and pharmacokinetics, drug metabolism, and disposition, medicinal chemistry, pharmacological studies, novel analytical methods, biotechnological applications to pharmaceutical problems, and all interesting developments in natural products chemistry relating to drug development.
**Readers:** Scientists and management in pharmaceutical industry, pharmacy faculties, research, and allied basic disciplines. Technologists and scientists in pharmaceutical manufacturing, research, regulation, and education in pharmacy, pharmacognosy, pharmaceutical chemistry, pharmacology, instrumentation, production engineering and allied basic disciplines.

## JOURNAL OF PHARMACY TECHNOLOGY
54067

8044 Montgomery Rd., Ste. 415
Cincinnati, OH 45236
Telephone: (513) 793-3555
FAX: (513) 793-3600
Mailing Address:
   P.O. Box 42696
   Cincinnati, OH 45242
Year Established: 1985
Pub. Frequency: bi-m.
Page Size: standard
Subscrip. Rate: $10; $39/yr.
Freelance Pay: negotiable
Circulation: 5,000
Circulation Type: paid
**Owner(s):**
Harvey Whitney Book Company
8044 Montgomery Rd., Ste. 415
Cincinnati, OH 45236
Telephone: (513) 793-3600
Ownership %: 100
**Management:**
Harvey A. K. Whitney .........................President
Carol Redish .....................Circulation Manager
**Editorial:**
Harvey A. K. Whitney ..............................Editor
Donna Thordsen .....................Managing Editor
Dr. Hedva Barenholtz ...............Assistant Editor
Dr. Paul Jaworski ....................Assistant Editor
Dr. Tim Welty .....................Publication Director
**Desc.:** The official journal of the Pharmacy Technician Educators Council. Provides the latest knowledge in the technology of pharmacy with articles covering pharmacy systems, pharmacy operations, patient education, pharmacy personnel training, advances in drug knowledge, updating technical skills, new laws and continuing education.
**Readers:** Pharmacists, pharmacy technicians, physicians, nurses and others who need information about drugs and technology of pharmacy. All members and member schools of the Pharmacy Technician Educators Council.

## KENTUCKY PHARMACIST, THE
22808

1228 U.S. Hwy.
Frankfort, KY 40601
Telephone: (502) 227-2303
FAX: (502) 227-2258
Year Established: 1878

Pub. Frequency: m.
Page Size: standard
Subscrip. Rate: $30/yr.
Circulation: 1,800
Circulation Type: paid
**Owner(s):**
Kentucky Pharmacists Association
1228 U.S. Hwy.
Frankfort, KY 40601
Telephone: (502) 227-2303
Ownership %: 100
**Management:**
Robert L. Barnett, Jr. ...........Executive Director
**Editorial:**
Robert L. Barnett, Jr. ...............................Editor
**Desc.:** News, features and articles pertinent to and of interest to pharmacies and pharmacists.
**Readers:** Pharmacists and people interested in pharmacy.

## MARYLAND PHARMACIST
22809

650 W. Lombard St.
Baltimore, MD 21201
Telephone: (301) 727-0746
FAX: (301) 725-2253
Year Established: 1924
Pub. Frequency: m.
Page Size: standard
Subscrip. Rate: $10/yr.
Circulation: 1,400
Circulation Type: controlled
**Owner(s):**
Maryland Pharmacists Association
650 W. Lombard St.
Baltimore, MD 21201
Telephone: (301) 727-0746
Ownership %: 100
**Editorial:**
David G. Miller ........................................Editor
**Desc.:** Articles and news to help pharmacists professionally and in management. Covers government relations, pharmaceutical sciences, legislation, association news, education, etc.
**Readers:** Pharmacists in Maryland.

## MEDICAL MARKETING & MEDIA
22810

7200 W. Camino Real, Ste. 215
Boca Raton, FL 33433
Telephone: (407) 368-9301
Year Established: 1965
Pub. Frequency: m.
Page Size: standard
Subscrip. Rate: $75/yr. individuals; $96/yr. institutions
Materials: 01,02,06,27,28,29,32,33
Print Process: offset
Circulation: 11,000
Circulation Type: controlled & paid
**Owner(s):**
CPS Communications
7200 W. Camino Real, Ste. 215
Boca Raton, FL 33433
Telephone: (407) 368-9301
Ownership %: 100
**Management:**
David Gideon ......................................Publisher
Beverly Reynolds ...............Associate Publsiher
Suzanne Besse .................Circulation Manager
**Editorial:**
Warren Ross ...........................................Editor
Michael Antonevich .......................Art Director
Ty Schuldner .............................................Sales

**Desc.:** Editorials, abstracts of current literature. Departments include: Washington Update, Business Notes, Industry Reports, New Products Briefs, Update/People, Media, Agency Assignments, New Locations, Calendar, Publications and Services. Editorial Direction: An exclusive vertical professional journal published to and for the pharmaceutical and medical industry, providing intra-industry communication and an information link with other industries and government. September and October issues provide a special focus on advertising promotion. MM7M's Healthcare Advertising Goldbook supplements will provide an in depth review of agency product assignments and promotion expenditures.
**Deadline:** story-1st of mo. prior to pub. date; news-1st of mo. prior to pub. date; photo-1st of mo. prior; ads-1st of mo. prior

## MISSOURI PHARMACIST
22814

410 Madison St.
Jefferson City, MO 65101
Telephone: (314) 636-7522
FAX: (314) 636-7485
, 00 65101
Year Established: 1926
Pub. Frequency: m.
Page Size: standard
Subscrip. Rate: membership; $25/yr. non-members
Circulation: 1,500
Circulation Type: controlled
**Owner(s):**
Missouri Pharmaceutical Association
410 Madison St.
Jefferson City, MO 65101
Telephone: (314) 636-7522
Ownership %: 100
**Editorial:**
Deedie Bedosky ......................................Editor
**Desc.:** A magazine featuring news about Missouri pharmacy, scientific information about pharmaceutical research; new merchandising ideas, improvements and inventions in the profession; continuing education articles for pharmacists.
**Readers:** Pharmacists of Missouri.

## MOLECULAR PHARMACOLOGY
55908

428 E. Preston St.
Baltimore, MD 21202
Telephone: (410) 528-4000
FAX: (410) 528-4312
Year Established: 1984
Pub. Frequency: m.
Subscrip. Rate: $105/yr. individuals; $230/yr. institutions
Circulation: 1,450
Circulation Type: paid
**Owner(s):**
Amer.Soc. Pharmacology & Experimental Therapeutics
**Editorial:**
T. Kendall Harden ...................................Editor
**Desc.:** Covers research on drug action and selective toxicity at the molecular level for pharmacologists and biochemists.
**Readers:** Subscribers include pharmacologists, biochemists and medical libraries. For member subscriber list, contact The American Society for Pharmacology and Experimental Therapeutics, Inc.

## NARD JOURNAL
22815

205 Daingerfield Rd.
Alexandria, VA 22314
Telephone: (703) 683-8200
FAX: (703) 683-3619

---

**Materials Accepted/Included:** 01-Business news 02-By-line articles 03-Fashion news 04-Food news 05-Freelance copy 06-Letters to editor 07-Real estate news 08-Sports news 09-Travel news 10-Book rev. 11-Movie rev. 12-Music rev. 13-TV rev. 14-Theater rev. 15-Coming events 16-Obituaries 17-Question & answer 18-Social announcements 19-Artwork 20-Cartoons 21-Photos 22-TV listings 23-Audio rec. 24-Video rec. 25-Books 26-Films/film clips 27-Personnel news 28-Press releases 29-New product news/photos 30-Trade lit. 31-Contracts awarded 32-Display adv. 33-Classified adv.

Year Established: 1895
Pub. Frequency: m.
Page Size: standard
Subscrip. Rate: $50/yr.
Freelance Pay: negotiable
Circulation: 29,000
Circulation Type: controlled
**Owner(s):**
NARD
205 Daingerfield Rd.
Alexandria, VA 22314
Telephone: (703) 683-8200
Ownership %: 100
**Management:**
Charles M. West ........Executive Vice President
John W. Wharton ..............Advertising Manager
**Editorial:**
Todd Dankmyer ..............................Editor
Marisa Dumas .......................Editorial Assistant
Robert H. Walker ................Production Director
Todd Dankmyer ..................Publication Director
**Desc.:** News stories must pertain to
independent druggists/products sold in
drug stores/progress. Features on
activities of independent druggists/on
ideas that have been proven to sell
merchandise in drug stores. Length of
features up to 2,000 words and usable
photos usually necessary/Washington
news, health and welfare, legal
comments, news and events, new
products, questions answered, letters.
**Readers:** Owners of independent drug
stores and employee pharmacists,
pharmacy students, professors
and deans.

22816
**NEBRASKA MORTAR & PESTLE**
6221 S. 58th St., Ste. A
Lincoln, NE 68516
Telephone: (402) 420-1500
FAX: (402) 420-1406
Year Established: 1937
Pub. Frequency: m.
Page Size: standard
Subscrip. Rate: $15/yr.
Circulation: 1,200
Circulation Type: paid
**Owner(s):**
Nebraska Pharmacists Association
6221 S. 58th St., Ste. A
Lincoln, NE 68516
Telephone: (402) 420-1500
Ownership %: 100
**Management:**
Tom R. Dolan, R.P. ..........Advertising Manager
**Editorial:**
Tom R. Dolan, R.P. ..................Executive Editor
Carol N. Langdon ..........................Editor
**Desc.:** Articles of 1 to 4 page length
relating to pharmacy (professional) plus
articles of commercial nature relating to
improved store operation, layout and
management. Use by-lines, some
pictures depending upon suitability of
picture. Member of State Pharmaceutical
Editorial Assn., groups of 15 state
magazines. Editorial departments
include: articles relating to pharmacy,
President's Page; Board of Pharmacy
Reports, Material Relating to Law,
Booster Page (an index of personnel
calling upon retail members), Convention
Talks of Special Value, Auxiliary and
Articles concerning pharmacy activities
in Nebraska.
**Readers:** Pharmacists, pharmacy
salesmen calling on pharmacies, and
non-pharmacist sales representatives,
pharmacy students.

22817
**NEW JERSEY JOURNAL OF
PHARMACY**
120 W. State St.
Trenton, NJ 08608
Telephone: (609) 394-5596
FAX: (609) 394-7806
Year Established: 1928
Pub. Frequency: m.
Page Size: standard
Subscrip. Rate: $12/yr.
Circulation: 4,200
Circulation Type: paid
**Owner(s):**
New Jersey Pharmaceutical Association
120 W. State St.
Trenton, NJ 08608
Telephone: (609) 394-5596
FAX: (609) 394-7806
Ownership %: 100
**Management:**
Alvin N. Geser ..........................Publisher
Arthur L. Taub ..................Advertising Manager
Alvin N. Geser ..................Business Manager
**Editorial:**
Gilbert E. Finkelstein ......................Editor
Diana S. Herman ................Managing Editor
Albert C. Meyer ..............Book Review Editor
Diana S. Herman .............New Products Editor
Diana S. Herman ..................News Editor
Diana S. Herman ..........................Photo
Gilbert E. Finkelstein ..............Science Editor
Arthur L. Taub ..................Technical Editor
**Desc.:** Features include items pertaining to
the practice of pharmacy, both scientific
and economic. Legal opinions
concerning pharmacy are also included
as well as political activity. Departments
include: Classified, Letters, Opinion, Late
News Briefly, etc.
**Readers:** Pharmacists, libraries,
pharmaceutical companies.

22818
**NEW YORK STATE PHARMACIST**
Pine West Plz. IV
Albany, NY 12205
Telephone: (518) 869-6595
FAX: (518) 464-0618
Year Established: 1879
Pub. Frequency: bi-m.
Page Size: standard
Subscrip. Rate: $10/yr.
Circulation: 2,800
Circulation Type: paid
**Owner(s):**
Pharmaceutical Society of the State of
New York
Pine West Plz. IV
Albany, NY 12205
Telephone: (518) 869-6595
**Editorial:**
Anthony Conte ............................Editor
Craig Burridge ....................Managing Editor
**Desc.:** Chiefly concerned with news
affecting the professional and business
status of pharmacists and pharmacy
owners. Also interested in political and
economic news that may have a bearing
on the field. Uses personals, new
products, news items.
**Readers:** Pharmacists in New York State.

22798
**P & T**
105 Raider Blvd.
Belle Mead, NJ 08502
Telephone: (908) 874-8550
FAX: (908) 874-0700
Year Established: 1975
Pub. Frequency: m.
Page Size: standard
Subscrip. Rate: $50/yr. individuals; $60/yr.
institutions; $28/yr. students
Materials: 28,29,30
Circulation: 49,000

Circulation Type: paid
**Owner(s):**
Reed Elsevier Medical Publishers, USA
Core Publishing Division
105 Raider Blvd.
Belle Mead, NJ 08502
Telephone: (908) 874-8550
Ownership %: 100
**Management:**
William Markowitz ......................Publisher
**Editorial:**
Annette Skiendziel ..........................Editor
David McDougal ..................Group Editor
**Desc.:** Articles authored by physicians
and/or pharmacists focusing on the drug
treatment of conditions commonly
encountered in the hospital setting.
Other articles deal with such issues as
diagnosis-related groups, other cost-
containment strategies, and specific
problems and issues of interest to the
Formulary Committee. Several issues
during the year feature special
symposia, which consist of 2 to 4
articles covering different aspects of the
treatment of a common disorder.
Editorial departments/features:
Compendium Update, New Drugs/Drug
News, State of the Art (Drug
Interactions, Clinical Drug Abstracts),
Formulary Consult (feature column
devoted to reader questions), Grand
Rounds, How Would You Treat...,
Pediatric Case Problems, Geriatric Case
Problems, Emergency Case Problems,
Drug Usage Case Problems.
**Readers:** Pharmacy & therapeutics,
physicians, hospital pharmacists,
administrators & nurses who are
Pharmacy & Therapeutics Committee
members.

22820
**P.A.R.D. BULLETIN**
630 S. 42nd St.
Philadelphia, PA 19104
Telephone: (215) 387-6180
FAX: (215) 387-6180
Year Established: 1898
Pub. Frequency: a.
Page Size: standard
Subscrip. Rate: free/members
Circulation: 400
Circulation Type: controlled
**Owner(s):**
Philadelphia Assn. of Retail Druggists
630 S. 42nd St.
Philadelphia, PA 19104
Telephone: (215) 387-6180
Ownership %: 100
**Editorial:**
Al N. Lehman ............................Editor
Al N. Lehman ..................Executive Director
**Desc.:** Feature articles cover pricing,
management, promotion for the retail
druggist. Departments include: People
and Events (personals), Products and
Services, drug trade notes.
**Readers:** Pharmacists, drug wholesalers,
drug stores.

22822
**PENNSYLVANIA PHARMACIST**
508 N. Third St.
Harrisburg, PA 17101
Telephone: (717) 234-6151
FAX: (717) 236-1618
Year Established: 1878
Pub. Frequency: m.
Page Size: standard
Subscrip. Rate: $75/yr.
Circulation: 2,500
Circulation Type: paid

**Owner(s):**
Pennsylvania Pharmacists Association
508 N. 3rd St.
Harrisburg, PA 17101
Telephone: (717) 234-6151
Ownership %: 100
**Management:**
William R. Seitzinger ......................President
Judy Kleinfelter ................Advertising Manager
**Editorial:**
Carmen A. DiCello ..........................Editor
Ann Fettro ......................Associate Editor
**Desc.:** News of government regulations,
promotions of interest to retail
pharmacists. Covers new products,
merchandising and sales aids,
company news, news of the colleges,
radio merchandising news, etc. Space
available for publicity primarily confined
to advertisers.
**Readers:** Pennsylvania pharmacists.

58586
**PHARMACEUTICAL EXECUTIVE**
7500 Old Oak Blvd.
Cleveland, OH 44130
Telephone: (216) 826-2839
FAX: (216) 891-2726
Year Established: 1980
Pub. Frequency: m.
Page Size: standard
Subscrip. Rate: $59/yr. US; $117/yr.
foreign
Circulation: 14,000
Circulation Type: controlled
**Owner(s):**
Advanstar Communications, Inc.
7500 Old Oak Blvd.
Cleveland, OH 44130
Telephone: (216) 826-2839
Ownership %: 100
**Editorial:**
Wayne Koberstein ..........................Editor
B.K. Krewson ......................Associate Editor
Robin Burke-Madell ..............Associate Editor
**Desc.:** Delivers balanced coverage trends,
sales & promotional strategies & the
legal & regulatory issues influencing
product development and management.
**Readers:** Corporate management,
marketing and sales management,
product management, advertising and
promotion management, account and
media management, market and
marketing research, ad agencies.

54034
**PHARMACEUTICAL PROCESSING**
301 Gibraltar Dr.
Morris Plains, NJ 07950
Telephone: (201) 292-5100
FAX: (201) 539-3476
Mailing Address:
P.O. Box 650
Morris Plains, NJ 07950
Year Established: 1984
Pub. Frequency: m.
Page Size: tabloid
Subscrip. Rate: $36/yr.
Circulation: 26,500
Circulation Type: controlled
**Owner(s):**
Gordon Publications
301 Garalter Dr.
Morris Plains, NJ 07950
Telephone: (201) 292-5100
**Management:**
Mary Gronmeier ..........................Publisher
Joe Kenna ....................Circulation Manager
**Editorial:**
Michael Auerbach ..........................Editor

**Materials Accepted/Included:** 01-Business news 02-By-line articles 03-Fashion news 04-Food news 05-Freelance copy 06-Letters to editor 07-Real estate news 08-Sports news 09-Travel news 10-Book rev. 11-Movie rev. 12-Music rev. 13-TV rev. 14-Theater rev. 15-Coming events 16-Obituaries 17-Question & answer 18-Social announcements 19-Artwork 20-Cartoons 21-Photos 22-TV listings 23-Audio rec. 24-Video rec. 25-Books 26-Films/film clips 27-Personnel news 28-Press releases 29-New product news/photos 30-Trade lit. 31-Contracts awarded 32-Display adv. 33-Classified adv.

4-114

**Desc.:** Editorial contains news of equipment, packaging supplies and materials used by the pharmaceutical and related processing industries. Features new & improved product news, literature and illustrations.
**Readers:** Personnel in processing, engineering, production, R & D, and QC/QA phases of pharmaceutical manufacturing.

22823

## PHARMACEUTICAL REPRESENTATIVE
Two Northfield Plaza, Ste. 300
Northfield, IL 60093-1217
Telephone: (708) 441-3700
FAX: (708) 441-3701
Year Established: 1971
Pub. Frequency: m.: 20th
Page Size: tabloid
Subscrip. Rate: $5/copy; $24.95/yr. US; $34.94/yr. Canada; $39.95/yr. foreign; contact publ. for group & bulk rates
Circulation: 28,500
Circulation Type: paid
**Owner(s):**
McKnight Medical Communications
Two Northfield Plaza, Ste. 300
Northfield, IL 60093
Telephone: (708) 441-3700
Ownership %: 50

Medical Economics Publishing Co., Inc.
5 Paragon Dr.
Montvale, NJ 07645
Telephone: (201) 358-7200
Ownership %: 50
**Management:**
Christopher Bale .........................Vice President
Chris Bale ..................................Publisher
**Editorial:**
Laura Ramos ..............................Editor
Mark Thill ..................................Editorial Director
Karen Roszkowski .......................Art Director
Gregg Haunroth ..................Circulation Director
Bill Briggs ........................Contributing Editor
Sue Powills ......................Contributing Editor
John O'Connor ..................Contributing Editor
Noelle Taras ........................Marketing Director
Constance Heard ...............Production Director
**Desc.:** Written solely for pharmaceutical sales people; contains new product news, trade news, legislative and financial happenings. Departments include: Editorial, Continuing Education, News Capsules, Research Capsules, Data Banks, Financial Updates, Rep. Association
**Readers:** Pharmaceutical sales representatives.

66756

## PHARMACEUTICAL TECHNOLOGY
7500 Old Oak Blvd.
Cleveland, OH 44130
Telephone: (216) 826-2839
FAX: (216) 891-2726
Year Established: 1977
Pub. Frequency: m.
Page Size: standard
Subscrip. Rate: $54/yr.
Circulation: 35,000
Circulation Type: controlled
**Owner(s):**
Advanstar Communications, Inc.
7500 Old Oak Blvd.
Cleveland, OH 44130
Telephone: (216) 826-2839
Ownership %: 100
**Management:**
Ralph Vitaro ..............................Publisher
**Editorial:**
Stefan Schuher ..........................Editor
B.K. Krewson .....................Associate Editor
**Desc.:** The magazine of applied pharmaceutical research & development.

58587

## PHARMACEUTICAL TECHNOLOGY INTERNATIONAL
7500 Old Oak Blvd.
Cleveland, OH 44130
Telephone: (216) 826-2839
FAX: (216) 891-2726
Year Established: 1978
Pub. Frequency: m.
Page Size: standard
Subscrip. Rate: $117/yr. US
Circulation: 20,000
Circulation Type: controlled
**Owner(s):**
Advanstar Communications, Inc.
7500 Old Oak Blvd.
Cleveland, OH 44130
Telephone: (216) 826-2839
Ownership %: 100
**Editorial:**
Martin Rosser ............................Editor
Amy Vickland ........................Associate Editor
**Desc.:** Covers industrial pharmacy for technical staff and management in production/manufacturing, quality control/assurance, applied research and development, and facility engineering at pharmaceutical manufacturing firms.

55906

## PHARMACOLOGICAL REVIEWS
428 E. Preston St.
Baltimore, MD 21202
Telephone: (410) 528-4000
FAX: (410) 528-4312
Year Established: 1949
Pub. Frequency: q.
Subscrip. Rate: $60/yr. individuals; $107/yr. institutions
Circulation: 2,800
Circulation Type: paid
**Owner(s):**
American Soc. Pharm. & Experimental Therapeutics
Baltimore, MD
**Editorial:**
Robert E. Stitzel .........................Editor
**Desc.:** Important review articles on topics of high current interest for pharmacologists, toxicologists and biochemists.
**Readers:** Subscribers include pharmacologists, toxicologists, biochemists and medical libraries. For member subscribers list contact The American Society for Pharmacology and Experimental Therapeutics, Inc.

69058

## PHARMACOTHERAPY
c/o New England Medical Center
171 Harrison Ave.
Boston, MA 02111
Telephone: (617) 956-5390
FAX: (617) 956-5318
Mailing Address:
  P.O. Box 806
  Boston, MA 02111
Year Established: 1981
Pub. Frequency: bi-m.
Page Size: standard
Subscrip. Rate: $95/yr.
Materials: 05,06,32,33
Print Process: offset
Circulation: 4,390
Circulation Type: free & paid
**Owner(s):**
Pharmacotherapy Publications, Inc.
New England Medical Center
171 Harrison Ave.
Boston, MA 02111
Telephone: (617) 956-5390
FAX: (617) 956-5318
Ownership %: 100
**Management:**
Ann E. Chella-Nigl ...............Business Manager

Minhoai Lay ...........................Program Manager
**Editorial:**
Richard T. Scheife .......................Editor
**Desc.:** Covers pharmacology and drug therapy.

61712

## PHARMACY PRACTICE NEWS
148 W. 24th St., 8th Fl.
New York, NY 10011-1916
Telephone: (212) 620-4600
FAX: (212) 620-5928
Pub. Frequency: m.
Page Size: tabloid
Subscrip. Rate: $55/yr.
Materials: 06,25,30,32
Circulation: 25,000
Circulation Type: controlled
**Owner(s):**
Ray McMahon
148 W. 24th St., 8th Fl.
New York, NY 10011-1916
Telephone: (212) 620-4600
FAX: (212) 620-5928
Ownership %: 100
**Editorial:**
Sarah Tilyou ..............................Editor
**Readers:** Hospital/Consultant of home health care pharmacists.
**Deadline:** story-1st of mo. prior to pub. date; news-1st of mo. prior; photo-1st of mo. prior; ads-1st of mo. prior

22825

## PHARMACY TIMES
80 Shore Rd.
Port Washington, NY 11050
Telephone: (516) 883-6350
FAX: (516) 883-6609
Year Established: 1897
Pub. Frequency: m.
Page Size: pg. 7 x 10; col. 4 5/8 x 10
Subscrip. Rate: $30/yr.
Materials: 21
Circulation: 95,000
**Owner(s):**
Romaine Pierson Publishing
80 Shore Rd.
Port Washington, NY 11050
Telephone: (516) 883-6350
Ownership %: 100
**Management:**
William F. Morando ......................President
Harold Cohen ..............................Publisher
**Editorial:**
Bruce Buckley .....................Editor in Chief
**Desc.:** Includes interpretive articles of practical nature of interest to all phases of Pharmacy: retail, hospital, manufacturing and teaching.

69057

## PHARMACY WEEK
668 W. Washington Ave., Ste. 145
Madison, WI 53703
Telephone: (608) 251-1112
FAX: (609) 251-1155
Year Established: 1992
Pub. Frequency: w.
Page Size: standard
Subscrip. Rate: free
Materials: 02,05,32
Freelance Pay: $.05/wd. (up to 500 wds.)
Print Process: offset
Circulation: 12,600
Circulation Type: controlled & free
**Owner(s):**
Pharmacy Week
668 W. Washington Ave., #145
Madison, WI 53703
Telephone: (608) 251-1112
Ownership %: 100
**Management:**
Paul Barnes .................................Publisher
Gail Scherer ..........................Sales Manager

**Desc.:** Publication via its network of professional guest writers provides practical information to hospitals and pharmacists in the area of management, drug information and employment.
**Readers:** Exclusively for hopital and pharmacists.

22826

## PHARMACY WEST
333 W. Hampden Ave.
Ste. 1050
Englewood, CO 80110
Telephone: (303) 761-8818
FAX: (303) 761-2440
Year Established: 1888
Pub. Frequency: m.
Page Size: standard
Subscrip. Rate: $18/yr.; $60/yr. foreign & Canada
Circulation: 15,000
Circulation Type: controlled
**Owner(s):**
Western Communications, Ltd.
333 W. Hampden Ave.
Ste. 1050
Englewood, CO 80110
Telephone: (303) 761-8818
Ownership %: 100
**Management:**
ElRoy FitzSenry ..........................Publisher
John McGinnis .................Advertising Manager
Bernadine Jewell ...............Circulation Manager
Rick Gaither .......................Production Manager
**Editorial:**
Judith D. Lane .......................Executive Editor
ElRoy FitzSenry ..........................Editor
Jennifer Lamb ........................Associate Editor
Candice Cantwell ..............New Products Editor
**Desc.:** An independently-owned regional drug magazine distributed to all pharmacies in the 13 western states, covering news and other events about Pharmacy in the West. Our objective is to provide in depth coverage of the news as it affects all pharmacists practicing at any level in the west. Heavy emphasis is placed on happenings, continuing education programs, general news and photos, legislative information, new products, personnel changes and other items.
**Readers:** Reaches pharmacists throughout the west. The magazine is circulated to all: independent retail pharmacies, hospital pharmacies, chain drug store pharmacies, chain drug store executives & buying offices, department, discount, variety store & supermarket Rx departments, convalescent & nursing home pharmacies, wholesale houses, rack jobbers & manufacturers executives, buyers & sales people, government offices, state boards, & associations, colleges of pharmacy.

61715

## PRIMARY CARE MEDICINE DRUG ALERTS
374 Millburn Ave.
Millburn, NJ 07041
Telephone: (201) 467-4456
Pub. Frequency: m.
Subscrip. Rate: $48/yr.
**Owner(s):**
Michael Powers
374 Millburn
Millburn, NJ 07041
Telephone: (201) 467-4456
**Editorial:**
John Roche ................................Editor

61714

## PSYCHIATRY DRUG ALERTS
347 Millburn Ave.
Millburn, NJ 07041
Telephone: (201) 467-4556

---

**Materials Accepted/Included:** 01-Business news 02-By-line articles 03-Fashion news 04-Food news 05-Freelance copy 06-Letters to editor 07-Real estate news 08-Sports news 09-Travel news 10-Book rev. 11-Movie rev. 12-Music rev. 13-TV rev. 14-Theater rev. 15-Coming events 16-Obituaries 17-Question & answer 18-Social announcements 19-Artwork 20-Cartoons 21-Photos 22-TV listings 23-Audio rec. 24-Video rec. 25-Books 26-Films/film clips 27-Personnel news 28-Press releases 29-New product news/photos 30-Trade lit. 31-Contracts awarded 32-Display adv. 33-Classified adv.

4-115

Pub. Frequency: m.
Subscrip. Rate: $59/yr.
Owner(s):
Michael Powers
374 Millburn
Millburn, NJ 07041
Telephone: (201) 467-4456
Ownership %: 100
Editorial:
John Roche ..............................Executive Editor
Dory Greene ............................................Editor

22829
## SOUTHERN PHARMACY JOURNAL
333 W. Hampden Ave., Ste. 1050
Englewood, CO 80110
Telephone: (303) 761-8818
FAX: (303) 761-2440
Year Established: 1908
Pub. Frequency: 10/yr.
Page Size: standard
Subscrip. Rate: $15/yr.
Circulation: 20,000
Circulation Type: controlled
Owner(s):
Southern Pharmacy Journal
333 W. Hampden Ave., Ste. 1050
Englewood, CO 80110
Telephone: (303) 761-8818
Ownership %: 100
Management:
ElRoy FitzSenry ..............................Publisher
John McGinnis ..............Advertising Manager
Bernadine Jewell ............Circulation Manager
Editorial:
Judith D. Lane ..........................Executive Editor
ElRoy FitzSenry ......................................Editor
Jennifer Lamb ..........................Associate Editor
Chuck Austin ............................Associate Editor
Candice Cantwell ..............New Products Editor
Desc.: An independently-owned regional
drug magazine distributed to all
pharmacies in the 12 southern states
covering news and other events about
Pharmacy in the South, exclusively. Our
objective is to provide in depth coverage
of the news as it affects all pharmacists
practicing at any level in the south.
Heavy emphasis is placed on
happenings, continuing education
programs, general news & photos,
legislative information, new products,
personnel changes and other items.
Continuing professional education
articles published each month, are
approved by American Council on
Pharmaceutical Education.
Readers: Reaches pharmacists
throughout the south. The magazine is
circulated to all independent retail
pharmacies, hospital pharmacies, chain
drug store pharmacies, chain drug store
executives & buying offices, department,
discount, variety store & supermarket Rx
departments, convalescent & nursing
home pharmacies, wholesale houses,
rack jobbers & manufacturer's
executives, buyers & sales people,
government offices, state boards &
associations, colleges of pharmacy.

22830
## TEXAS PHARMACY
1624 E. Anderson Ln.
Austin, TX 78752
Telephone: (512) 836-8350
FAX: (512) 836-0308
Mailing Address:
   P.O. Box 14709
   Austin, TX 78761
Year Established: 1879
Pub. Frequency: m.
Page Size: standard
Subscrip. Rate: $30/yr.
Materials: 02,06,11,16,20
Circulation: 5,000

Circulation Type: controlled
Owner(s):
Texas Pharmaceutical Association
P.O. Box 14709
Austin, TX 78761-4709
Telephone: (512) 836-8350
Ownership %: 100
Editorial:
Paul F. Davis ........................................Editor
Paula Sasser ..........................Managing Editor
Desc.: Illustrated features include:
Scanning the News, covering state and
national developments in the pharmacy
profession; state and federal regulations
governing practice of pharmacy.
Pharmacists Roundup highlights Texas
personals. Components Briefs publish
news of TPA component societies, Post
Graduate Education, Hospital Pharmacy
Practice, Soundoff to the Editor and
Response, Auxiliary Memoranda. Query
editor regarding specific features ideas.
Readers: Pharmacists and auxiliary
members; service wholesalers,
pharmacy students, faculty of schools of
pharmacy.

22831
## U.S. PHARMACIST
100 Ave. of the Americas
New York, NY 10013
Telephone: (212) 274-7000
FAX: (212) 431-0500
Year Established: 1976
Pub. Frequency: m.
Page Size: standard
Subscrip. Rate: $28/yr.
Circulation: 104,500
Circulation Type: controlled
Owner(s):
Jobson Publishing Corp., Robert Amato
100 Ave. of Americas
New York, NY 10013
Telephone: (212) 274-7000
Ownership %: 100
Management:
Edward R. Barnhart ....................Vice President
Edward R. Barnhart ............................Publisher
Editorial:
Allen Schwartz ........................................Editor
Angele D'Angelo ....................Editorial Director
Desc.: Aims to help educate pharmacists
to become more knowledgeable in the
delivery of health care information.
Readers: Pharmacists, retail drug stores
and hospital personnel.

22832
## VIRGINIA PHARMACIST
3119 W. Clay St.
Richmond, VA 23230
Telephone: (804) 355-7941
FAX: (804) 355-7991
Year Established: 1882
Pub. Frequency: m.
Page Size: standard
Subscrip. Rate: $50/yr.
Circulation: 2,000
Circulation Type: paid
Owner(s):
Virginia Pharmaceutical Association
3119 W. Clay St.
Richmond, VA 23230
Telephone: (804) 355-7941
Ownership %: 100
Management:
Kelly Kall ..............................................President
Randy Wampler ....................Executive Director
Peggy McLaughlin ....................Office Manager
Editorial:
Randy Wampler ......................................Editor

Desc.: Articles of current professional and
merchandising interest; fair trade review;
personals; board of pharmacy news;
advertisers and advertisers' product
news; local pharmaceutical news; news
of district pharmaceutical associations;
animal health news; college news;
hospital pharmacy, continuing
educational articles.
Readers: Pharmacists, wholesalers,
retailers, school, drug trade.

22833
## WHOLESALE DRUG MAGAZINE
333 W. Hampden Ave., Ste. 1050
Englewood, CO 80110
Telephone: (303) 761-8818
FAX: (303) 761-2440
Year Established: 1948
Pub. Frequency: 10/yr.
Page Size: standard
Subscrip. Rate: $15/yr.
Owner(s):
Wholesale Drug Magazine, Inc.
333 W. Hampden Ave., Ste. 1050
Englewood, CO 80110
Telephone: (303) 761-8818
Ownership %: 100
Management:
ElRoy FitzSenry ..............................Publisher
Bernadine Jewell ..............Circulation Manager
Rick Gaither ........................Production Manager
Editorial:
Judith D. Lane ..........................Executive Editor
Chuck Austin ............................Associate Editor
Desc.: An independently owned national
magazine providing in depth coverage of
news as it affects the wholesale drug
industry.
Readers: Reaches top executives and
other key personnel involved in the day
to day operations of drug wholesale
houses. The magazine is distributed
nationwide as well as in Canada and
abroad.

22834
## WISCONSIN PHARMACIST, THE
202 Price Pl.
Madison, WI 53705
Telephone: (608) 238-5515
FAX: (608) 238-5546
Year Established: 1930
Pub. Frequency: m.
Page Size: standard
Subscrip. Rate: $60/yr.
Materials: 01,06,28,32,33
Circulation: 1,800
Circulation Type: controlled
Owner(s):
Wisconsin Pharmacists Association
202 Price Pl.
Madison, WI 53705
Telephone: (608) 238-5515
Ownership %: 100
Editorial:
Christopher Decker ..................Executive Editor
Christopher Decker ................................Editor
Mary K. Nowakowski ..............Managing Editor
Readers: Pharmacists and pharmacy
students.
Deadline: story-5th of mo.; news-5th of
mo.; photo-5th of mo.

## Group 066-Electrical

22849
## CEE NEWS
9800 Metcalf
Overland Park, KS 66282-2901
Telephone: (913) 341-1300
FAX: (913) 967-1898
Year Established: 1949
Pub. Frequency: m.
Page Size: tabloid
Subscrip. Rate: free to qualified personnel
Materials: 01,02,06,17,32,33

Circulation: 110,000
Circulation Type: controlled
Owner(s):
Intertec Publishing Corp.
9800 Metcalf
Overland Park, KS 66282-2901
Telephone: (913) 341-1300
Ownership %: 100
Management:
Raymond Maloney ..............................President
Richard A. Hathaway ..........................Publisher
Editorial:
Stuart Lewis ....................................Chief Editor
Michael J. Harrington ..............Managing Editor
Monica Finnigan ......................Associate Editor
Holly Oeltien ............................Associate Editor
Desc.: Editorially designed to serve the
electrical-construction market whose
primary business is concerned with the
erecting, installing, altering, repairing,
servicing, and maintaining of electrical
wiring, devices, appliances, and
equipment. It is circulated to electronic
contractors, electric consulting
engineers, architects, and their electrical
engineers, buying personnel in electric
utilities, in-plant placing electric
personnel, and electrical wholesalers. It
is a tabloid size publication presenting
carefully analyzed feature and new
products material interpreted in terms of
the electrical-construction industry and
presented in a concise, comprehensive
and easy-to-read style.
Readers: Electrical contractors, consulting
electrical engineers, architects, electric
wholesalers in plant/facility electrical
personnel, electrical utility engineers,
etc.

22856
## ELECTRICAL APPARATUS
400 N. Michigan Ave.
Chicago, IL 60611-4198
Telephone: (312) 321-9440
FAX: (312) 321-1288
Year Established: 1948
Pub. Frequency: m.
Page Size: standard
Subscrip. Rate: $3.50/issue; $40/yr.
Materials: 01,06,10,16,17,20,21,25,27,29,
   32,33
Print Process: web offset
Circulation: 17,000
Circulation Type: controlled & paid
Owner(s):
Barks Publications, Inc.
400 N. Michigan Ave., Ste 1016
Chicago, IL 60611-4198
Telephone: (312) 321-9440
FAX: (312) 321-1288
Ownership %: 100
Management:
Horace B. Barks ..................................President
Horace B. Barks ..................................Publisher
Joseph V. Barks ................Associate Publisher
Shannon Cooper ..............Advertising Manager
Mary Kay Gerut ................Circulation Manager
Editorial:
Kevin N. Jones ............................Senior Editor
Horace B. Barks ....................................Editor
Ann Coles ............................Managing Editor
Jacqueline Tithof ....................Assistant Editor
Elsie Dickson ......................Associate Publisher
Lucy Gregor ....................Circulation Assistant

**Materials Accepted/Included:** 01-Business news 02-By-line articles 03-Fashion news 04-Food news 05-Freelance copy 06-Letters to editor 07-Real estate news 08-Sports news 09-Travel news
10-Book rev. 11-Movie rev. 12-Music rev. 13-TV rev. 14-Theater rev. 15-Coming events 16-Obituaries 17-Question & answer 18-Social announcements 19-Artwork 20-Cartoons 21-Photos 22-TV listings
23-Audio rec. 24-Video rec. 25-Books 26-Films/film clips 27-Personnel news 28-Press releases 29-New product news/photos 30-Trade lit. 31-Contracts awarded 32-Display adv. 33-Classified adv.

**Desc.:** Articles include how-to type features dealing with technical aspects of the application, maintenance, repair and servicing of electrical apparatus, principally commercial and industrial motors, generators, and transformers and allied electronic controls. Magazine is about equally divided between industry news and technical articles, exclusively staff-written. Also covers business, management aspects of the industry for the maintenance department, and shop operator. Covers costs, general business conditions, problems, etc. Carries new products information, news of manufacturers, personnel changes, moves, prices, etc. Photos are used liberally, preferably color or black & white glossies showing technical detail.

**Readers:** Electrical apparatus service shops, in-plant and institutional facilities, electrical departments, electrical contractors, electrical consultants, distributors, manufacturers and electrical utilities.

**Deadline:** story-15th of 2nd mo. prior to pub. date; news-15th of 2nd mo. prior; photo-15th of 2nd mo. prior; ads-5th of mo. prior

22858

## ELECTRICAL CONSTRUCTION & MAINTENANCE
9800 Metcalf
Overland Park, KS 66212-2215
Telephone: (913) 341-1300
FAX: (913) 967-1898
Year Established: 1901
Pub. Frequency: m.
Page Size: standard
Subscrip. Rate: $30/yr.
Circulation: 103,000
Circulation Type: controlled
**Owner(s):**
Intertec Publishing Corp.
9800 Metcalf
Overland Park, KS 66212-2215
Telephone: (913) 341-1300
Ownership %: 100
**Bureau(s):**
EC & M
301 Lindenwood Dr., Ste. 1
Malvern, PA 19355
Telephone: (215) 640-3140
Contact: Thomas Esposito, Manager

EC & M
9894 Bissonnet, Ste. 100
Houston, TX 77036
Telephone: (713) 779-1501
Contact: James F. Gombac, Manager

EC & M
5921 Crestbrook Dr.
Morrison, CO 80465
Telephone: (303) 697-1701
Contact: James T. Carahalias, Manager

EC & M
345 Fourth Ave., Ste. 1000
Pittsburgh, PA 15222
Telephone: (412) 391-3277
Contact: W. B. Hicks, Manager

EC & M
945 Concord St.
Framingham, MA 01701
Telephone: (508) 879-9233
Contact: Bob MacArthur, Manager

EC & M
55 E. Jackson Blvd., Ste. 1100
Chicago, IL 60604
Telephone: (312) 435-2342
Contact: Howard Green, Manager

EC & M
600 Houzc Way, Ste. A4
Roswell, GA 30076
Telephone: (404) 552-1098
Contact: Jim Bauschka, Manager

EC & M
395 Matheson Blvd., E.
Stamford, CT 06902
Telephone: (416) 890-1846
Contact: John Kerr, Janet Small, Publisher

EC & M
Rosleigh House, New St.
Pittsburgh, PA 15222
Telephone: (412) 227-3652
Contact: Nicholas Mcgeachin, Manager
**Management:**
Richard A. Hathaway .......................Publisher
Bob MacArthur .......................Sales Manager
**Editorial:**
John DeDad .......................Chief Editor
Frederic Hartwell .......................Editor
Robert Morgan .......................Editor
**Desc.:** Staff-written and contributed features cover electrical design, installation and maintenance for all types of building, design of electrical circuits and systems, maintenance of electrical systems, repairing of equipment. Editorial departments include: Practical Methods, Products News, Code Forum, Reader's Quiz, Your Business, Letters, In the News, What's the Story, Estimating Forum, Quizzes on the Code. All sections fully illustrated. Also covers bulletins and catalogs.
**Readers:** Electrical contractors, electrical engineers, in-plant electrical engineers, consultants.

22860

## ELECTRICAL CONTRACTOR
3 Bethesda Metro Ctr., Ste. 1100
Bethesda, MD 20814
Telephone: (301) 657-3110
FAX: (301) 215-4500
Year Established: 1939
Pub. Frequency: m.
Page Size: standard
Freelance Pay: varies
Circulation: 80,000
Circulation Type: controlled
**Owner(s):**
National Electrical Contractors Assn., Inc.
3 Bethesda Metro Ctr.
Ste. 1100
Bethesda, MD 20814
Telephone: (301) 657-3110
Ownership %: 100
**Management:**
John M. Grau .......................President
Joseph Salimando .......................Publisher
Donna L. Bailey .......................Advertising Manager
**Editorial:**
Thomas Naber .......................Editor
Karin Engelmann .......................Assistant Editor
**Desc.:** Staff-written and contributed by-line articles for electrical contractors. Emphasis is on installation ideas, better management methods and new technical developments in the industry; also covers insurance problems, cost control, taxation, sales promotion and labor relations. Departments include: The National Electric Code, Product Application, New Literature, Estimating.
**Readers:** Electrical contractors, key employees of electrical contractors.

22861

## ELECTRICAL DISTRIBUTOR, THE
45 Danbury Rd.
Wilton, CT 06897
Telephone: (203) 834-1908
FAX: (203) 834-1938
Year Established: 1964

Pub. Frequency: m.
Page Size: standard
Subscrip. Rate: $12/yr. US; $30/yr. foreign
Circulation: 28,510
Circulation Type: controlled
**Owner(s):**
National Association of Electrical Distributors
45 Danbury Rd.
Wilton, CT 06897
Telephone: (203) 834-1908
Ownership %: 100
**Management:**
R.A. Goldrick .......................President
Lynda Healy .......................Publisher
**Editorial:**
Oscar Leiding .......................Executive Editor
Jane Luby .......................Managing Editor
Jack Foster .......................Editorial Director
Ken Best .......................Assistant Editor
Lisa Baron .......................Production Director
**Desc.:** Primarily feature articles aimed at improving the business skills and industrial knowledge of electrical wholesale distributors.
**Readers:** Employees and owners of electrical distributing firms.

56228

## ELECTRICAL NEWS
135 E. La Porte-D
Arcadia, CA 91006
Telephone: (818) 446-8652
FAX: (818) 447-6047
Mailing Address:
  P.O. Box 660760
  Arcadia, CA 91066-0760
Year Established: 1984
Pub. Frequency: m.
Page Size: tabloid
Subscrip. Rate: $20/yr.
Materials: 01,02,06,27,28,29,30,32,33
Circulation: 20,000
Circulation Type: controlled
**Owner(s):**
Mellon & Associates, Inc.
P.O. Box 660760
Arcadia, CA 91066-0760
Telephone: (818) 446-8652
Ownership %: 100
**Editorial:**
Basil Mellon .......................Editor
**Readers:** Electrical wholesale distributors, contractors, engineers-specifiers, manufacturers and utility companies in the western states.
**Deadline:** story-15th of mo., prior to pub. date; news-15th of mo.; photo-15th of mo.; ads-15th of mo.

22865

## ELECTRICAL WHOLESALING
9800 Metcalf Ave.
Overland Park, KS 66212-2215
Telephone: (913) 341-1300
FAX: (913) 967-1898
Year Established: 1920
Pub. Frequency: m.
Page Size: standard
Subscrip. Rate: $12/yr.
Circulation: 20,188
Circulation Type: paid
**Owner(s):**
Intertec Publishing Corp.
P.O. Box 12901
Shawnee Mission, KS 66282-2901
Telephone: (913) 341-1300
Ownership %: 100
**Management:**
Richard Hathaway .......................Publisher
Robert MacArthur .......................Advertising Manager
**Editorial:**
Jim Lucy .......................Chief Editor
Andrea J. Herbert .......................Editorial Director
Tim Kasen .......................Associate Editor
Doug Chandler .......................Associate Editor

Agnieshka Jane .......................Graphic Designer
**Desc.:** Features discuss customer relations, selling to specialized markets, customer and dealer service, outlook. Uses industry news, new products.
**Readers:** Wholesale distributors of electrical apparatus and supplies and include both managers and salespeople.

22866

## ELECTRICAL WORLD
11 W. 19th St., Second Fl.
New York, NY 10011-4285
Telephone: (212) 337-4060
Year Established: 1874
Pub. Frequency: m.
Page Size: standard
Subscrip. Rate: $55/yr. non-members
Materials: 01,15,28,29,32,33
Print Process: web offset
Circulation: 48,258
Circulation Type: controlled & paid
**Owner(s):**
McGraw-Hill, Inc.
1221 Ave. of the Americas
New York, NY 10020
Telephone: (212) 512-2000
Ownership %: 100
**Management:**
John E. Slater .......................Publisher
**Editorial:**
Herbert Cavanaugh .......................Exec. Editor
John Reason .......................Senior Editor
Robert G. Schwieger .......................Editorial Director
**Desc.:** Technical articles cover design, equipment specification, construction, operation and maintenance of facilities for electric generation, transmission, & distribution facilities; also new developments, management problems, etc. Includes new equipment, news about people in the industry, manufacturer news, new construction, sales and service items.
**Readers:** Engineers, management and consultants of the electric utility industry, consulting engineering firms, and others allied to the field.
**Deadline:** ads-1st of mo. prior to pub. date

24380

## ELECTRIC LIGHT & POWER
1421 S. Sheridan
Tulsa, OK 74112
Telephone: (918) 835-3161
Year Established: 1922
Pub. Frequency: m.
Page Size: tabloid
Subscrip. Rate: $45/yr. US; $95/yr. Canada
Circulation: 45,000
Circulation Type: controlled
**Owner(s):**
PennWell Publishing Co.
1421 S. Sheridan
Tulsa, OK 74112
Telephone: (918) 835-3161
Ownership %: 100
**Management:**
Frank Lavinger .......................Chairman of Board
Joseph A. Wolking .......................President
Arthur L. Rice .......................Publisher
Margaret Shake .......................Sales Manager
**Editorial:**
Robert W. Smock .......................Editor
Larry Spiker .......................Production Director
**Desc.:** Covers electric utility business conditions, engineering, management, administrative and marketing developments, new products, regulatory review, new literature, management methods, calendar of events.

---

**Materials Accepted/Included:** 01-Business news 02-By-line articles 03-Fashion news 04-Food news 05-Freelance copy 06-Letters to editor 07-Real estate news 08-Sports news 09-Travel news 10-Book rev. 11-Movie rev. 12-Music rev. 13-TV rev. 14-Theater rev. 15-Coming events 16-Obituaries 17-Question & answer 18-Social announcements 19-Artwork 20-Cartoons 21-Photos 22-TV listings 23-Audio rec. 24-Video rec. 25-Books 26-Films/film clips 27-Personnel news 28-Press releases 29-New product news/photos 30-Trade lit. 31-Contracts awarded 32-Display adv. 33-Classified adv.

**Readers:** Top management, engineering and operating personnel in electric utility (investor owned, REC's, municipals, & govt.) organizations throughout the United States and Canada, plus consulting firms involved in design and construction for electric utilities.

## ELECTROMAGNETOEFFECT
69269

6080 Jericho Tpke., Ste. 207
Commack, NY 11725-2808
Telephone: (516) 499-3103
Year Established: 1992
Pub. Frequency: q.
Subscrip. Rate: $295/yr.
**Owner(s):**
Nova Science Publishers, Inc.
6080 Jericho Tpke., Ste. 207
Commack, NY 11725-2808
Telephone: (516) 499-3103
Ownership %: 100
**Editorial:**
Vladimir N. Ostreiko ........................Editor
**Desc.:** Covers theoretical and experimental investigations of various electromagnetic effects, offering new possibilities or prospects for developing electromagnetic machinery.

## IAEI NEWS
22891

901 Waterfall Way, Ste. 602
Richardson, TX 75080
Telephone: (214) 235-1455
FAX: (214) 235-3855
Year Established: 1929
Pub. Frequency: bi-m.
Page Size: standard
Subscrip. Rate: $30/yr.
Materials: 01,02,06,15,16,17,21,25,27,28, 29,30,32
Print Process: web
Circulation: 23,000
Circulation Type: paid
**Owner(s):**
International Association of Electrical Inspectors
901 Waterfall Way, Ste. 602
Richardson, TX 75080
Telephone: (214) 235-1455
Ownership %: 100
**Editorial:**
J. Philip Simmons ............................Editor
Jerralyn R. Smith ..................Managing Editor
Cathy Burkhead ..............Membership Services Manager
**Desc.:** Objective is to give members of the International Association of Electrical Inspectors up-to-date information in relation to electrical safety; with problems encountered in the inspection field, with greater safety in using better products and wiring methods, with explanations of the more complicated sections and articles of the national electrical code. Also presents current listing of electrical devices, materials and applications. Departments include: Focus on the Code, Reader's Views, A Closer Look, Report of Electrical Accidents Industry News, From the Field, UL Question Corner, Dates Ahead, New Products, Activities of the Chapters of the Association, the Law Involving Electrical Inspection.
**Readers:** Electrical inspectors, electricians, journeymen, field engineers, sales representatives, managers, manufacturers, contractors, electrical utilities, testing laboratories, cities, towns and municipalities.
**Deadline:** story-1st of mo., 2 mo. prior to pub. date; news-1st of mo.; photo-1st of mo.; ads-1st of mo.

## IC MASTER
56291

645 Stewart Ave.
Garden City, NY 11530
Telephone: (516) 227-1300
FAX: (516) 227-1901
Year Established: 1974
Pub. Frequency: a.
Page Size: standard
Subscrip. Rate: $180/yr.
Materials: 29,30
Print Process: offset
Circulation: 30,000
Circulation Type: paid
**Owner(s):**
Hearst Business Communications, Inc.
645 Stewart Ave.
Garden City, NY 11530
Telephone: (516) 227-1300
FAX: (516) 227-1901
Ownership %: 100
**Management:**
Armand Villiger ........................Publisher
Marie Botta ..................Sales Manager
**Editorial:**
Dave Howell ..................Editor in Chief
John H. Remmer ..................Senior Editor
Sal Provenzano ..................Associate Publisher
Georgeann Amsler ..............Marketing Director
Glenn H. Moore ..........Senior Technical Editor
**Desc.:** A reference source for all integrated circuits and related products marketed in the United States. The emphasis is on problem-solution as it relates to electronic engineering design work. Also use for reference to manufactures of all products listed.
**Readers:** Used by specifiers of integrated circuits and related products. Design engineers and design engineering management.
**Deadline:** Sept.

## IC UPDATE
56292

645 Stewart Ave.
Garden City, NY 11530
Telephone: (516) 227-1300
FAX: (516) 227-1901
Pub. Frequency: s-a.: spring & fall
Page Size: standard
Subscrip. Rate: free with IC Master subscription
Materials: 32
Print Process: web offset
**Owner(s):**
Hearst Business Communications, Inc.
645 Stewart Ave.
Garden City, NY 11530
Telephone: (516) 227-1300
FAX: (516) 227-1901
Ownership %: 100
**Management:**
Armand Villiger ........................Publisher
**Editorial:**
Dave Howell ..................Editor in Chief
John H. Remmer ..................Senior Editor
Sal Provenzano ..................Associate Publisher
Georgeann Amsler ..............Marketing Director
Glenn H. Moore ..........Senior Technical Editor
**Desc.:** Reference source for all new integrated circuits and related products announced after IC Master publication.
**Readers:** Used by specifiers of integrated circuits and related products. Design engineers and design engineering management.
**Deadline:** ads-Apr. & Sep.

## JOURNAL OF THE ILLUMINATING ENGINEERING SOCIETY
22900

120 Wall St., 17th Fl.
New York, NY 10005
Telephone: (212) 248-5000
FAX: (212) 248-5017

Year Established: 1972
Pub. Frequency: s-a.
Page Size: standard
Subscrip. Rate: $195/yr.
Circulation: 3,200
**Owner(s):**
Illuminating Engineering Society
120 Wall St., 17th Fl.
New York, NY 10005
Telephone: (212) 248-5000
Ownership %: 100
**Editorial:**
Kevin Heslin ........................Editor
Lois I. Burgner ..................Associate Editor
**Readers:** Lighting designers, engineers, manufacturers.

## NATIONAL ELECTRICAL ESTIMATOR 1995
69531

6058 Corte del Cedro
Carlsbad, CA 92009
Telephone: (800) 829-8123
FAX: (619) 438-0398
Mailing Address:
  P.O. Box 6500
  Carlsbad, CA 92018
Year Established: 1985
Pub. Frequency: a.
Page Size: standard
Subscrip. Rate: $31.75/yr.
Print Process: web
Circulation: 5,000
Circulation Type: paid
**Owner(s):**
Craftsman Book Co.
6058 Corte del Cedro
Carlsbad, CA 92008
Telephone: (800) 829-8123
Ownership %: 100
**Editorial:**
Laurence Jacobs ........................Editor
Edward Tyler ..................Author
**Desc.:** Labor and material costs for installing electrical in residential, commercial, and industrial construction. An annual cost book.

## Group 068-Electronics

## ARCNET NEWS
22927

2460 Wisconsin Ave.
Downers Grove, IL 60515
Telephone: (708) 960-5130
FAX: (708) 963-2122
Year Established: 1966
Pub. Frequency: q.
Page Size: standard
Subscrip. Rate: $15/yr. members
Circulation: 2,000
Circulation Type: paid
**Owner(s):**
ARCNET Trade Association
2460 Wisconsin Ave.
Downers Grove, IL 60515
Telephone: (708) 960-5130
Ownership %: 100
**Editorial:**
Chris Bowbottom ........................Editor
**Desc.:** Features sometimes used as fill. Aimed at arcnet users. Provides electronics and supplier information. Photo stories sometimes used.
**Readers:** All members of arcnet trade association.

## AUTOMATIC I.D. NEWS
61616

7500 Old Oak Blvd.
Cleveland, OH 44130
Telephone: (216) 243-8100
FAX: (908) 549-8927
Year Established: 1985
Pub. Frequency: m.

Page Size: tabloid
Subscrip. Rate: free to qualified subscribers
Materials: 15,24,28,29,32,33
Freelance Pay: $350-$500
Circulation: 72,000
Circulation Type: controlled & paid
**Owner(s):**
Advanstar Communications, Inc.
7500 Old Oak Blvd.
Cleveland, OH 44130
Telephone: (216) 243-8100
Ownership %: 100
**Management:**
Diva Norwood ........................Publisher
**Editorial:**
Mark David ........................Editor
**Desc.:** Serving users of bar code and other automatic identification technologies including radio frequency, voice input/output, magnetic stripe and vision systems, as well as mobile data capture and communications.
**Readers:** End-users of automated data capture technologies as well as systems integrators and VARs.
**Deadline:** news-6 wks. prior to pub. date; ads-5 wks. prior to pub. date

## CIRCUITREE MAGAZINE
69251

700 Gale Dr.
Ste. 200
Campbell, CA 95008
Telephone: (408) 364-3930
FAX: (408) 364-3938
Year Established: 1987
Pub. Frequency: m.
Page Size: standard
Subscrip. Rate: $48/yr. US; $128/yr. foreign
Print Process: offset lithography
Circulation: 8,500
Circulation Type: free & paid
**Owner(s):**
Circuitree
Ownership %: 100
**Editorial:**
Raymond Rasmussen ............................Editor
**Readers:** Owners and operators of printed circuit board facilities worldwide.

## CIRCUITS ASSEMBLY
22845

600 Harrison St.
San Francisco, CA 94107
Telephone: (415) 905-2200
FAX: (415) 905-2232
Year Established: 1961
Pub. Frequency: m.
Page Size: standard
Subscrip. Rate: $80/yr. US & Canada; $135/yr. foreign
Materials: 01,02,06,10,15,17,25,27,28,29, 31,32,33
Freelance Pay: negotiable
Print Process: web
Circulation: 40,535
Circulation Type: controlled
**Owner(s):**
Miller Freeman, Inc.
600 Harrison St.
San Francisco, CA 94107
Telephone: (415) 905-2200
Ownership %: 100
**Management:**
Marshall Freeman ..............................President
Frances Stewart ..............................Publisher
**Editorial:**
Ron Daniels ..............................Editor in Chief
Teresa Gentry ..........................Assistant Editor

**Materials Accepted/Included:** 01-Business news 02-By-line articles 03-Fashion news 04-Food news 05-Freelance copy 06-Letters to editor 07-Real estate news 08-Sports news 09-Travel news 10-Book rev. 11-Movie rev. 12-Music rev. 13-TV rev. 14-Theater rev. 15-Coming events 16-Obituaries 17-Question & answer 18-Social announcements 19-Artwork 20-Cartoons 21-Photos 22-TV listings 23-Audio rec. 24-Video rec. 25-Books 26-Films/film clips 27-Personnel news 28-Press releases 29-New product news/photos 30-Trade lit. 31-Contracts awarded 32-Display adv. 33-Classified adv.

**Desc.:** Functions as a means of communication among manufacturing professionals responsible for the production of board-level electronics. Covers assembly of circuit boards and hybrid circuits.
**Readers:** Managers and engineers engaged in OEM and contract assembly electronics manufacturing from assembly through final assembly.
**Deadline:** story-2 mo. prior to pub. date; news-1 mo.; photo-1 mo.; ads-1 mo.

## DEFENSE ELECTRONICS
52653
6300 S. Syracuse Way, Ste. 650
Englewood, CO 80111
Telephone: (303) 220-0600
Year Established: 1970
Pub. Frequency: m.
Page Size: standard
Subscrip. Rate: $38/yr.
Freelance Pay: varies
Circulation: 50,000
Circulation Type: controlled
**Owner(s):**
Argus Business, Inc.
6300 S. Syracuse, Ste. 650
Englewood, CO 80111
Telephone: (303) 220-0600
Ownership %: 100
**Editorial:**
Roger Lesser ...............................Editor in Chief
David Premo ......................Associate Publisher
**Desc.:** Serves readers involved in the development and procurement of military electronics including Avionics, ASW, Communications, Computers, CI, Electronic Warfare, Electro-optics, IFF, Guided Weapons, Navigation, Radar, Satellites, Software, Test & measurement and Vehicle Electronics. Coverage extends from ICs and Semiconductors, Microprocessors and Components through Subsystem and Stem Integration. Profiles of key DOD and Service procurement agencies are regularly included. Comprehensive staff reports and contributed feature articles are supplemented with news columns, extensive news columns, extensive new product section and Budget and Financial Analysis Sections.
**Readers:** Qualified recipients are individuals in the government: executive and legislative branches; program management; purchasing and procurement; engineering/design and analysis; planning and command; engineering/technical management; agencies and services in the military electronics industry whose job functions are executive and military electronics field in both military and other personnel in the field served.

## ECN (ELECTRONIC COMPONENT NEWS)
22873
Chilton Way
Radnor, PA 19089
Telephone: (215) 964-4000
FAX: (215) 964-4348
Year Established: 1956
Pub. Frequency: m.
Page Size: tabloid
Subscrip. Rate: $60/yr. US.; $75/yr. foreign
Circulation: 125,000
Circulation Type: controlled

**Owner(s):**
Capital Cities-ABC, Inc.
1330 Avenue of the Americas
New York, NY 10019
Telephone: (212) 887-7777
FAX: (610) 964-4348
Ownership %: 100
**Management:**
Joseph Breck ................................Publisher
William Cariello ........................Sales Manager
**Editorial:**
Hy Natkin ...........................................Editor
Suzanne Hayes ..................Production Director
**Desc.:** Provides illustrated information on new electronic and electro-mechanical components sub-assemblies, sub-systems, microcomputers, OEM computer peripherals, test equipment, product packaging and associated hardware, materials and electronic product production equipment. Departments include: New Products, New Literature, Editorial, Special Reports, one full length article/month and software for electronic engineers.
**Readers:** Engineers, department and section heads, buyers, distribution principals, electronic engineers and managers.

## EDN MAGAZINE
22853
275 Washington St.
Newton, MA 02158-1630
Telephone: (617) 964-3030
FAX: (617) 558-4470
Year Established: 1956
Pub. Frequency: 26/yr.
Page Size: standard
Subscrip. Rate: $159.95/yr.
Materials: 01,02,06,28,29,30,32,32
Freelance Pay: negotiable
Print Process: web
Circulation: 161,500
Circulation Type: controlled
**Owner(s):**
Cahners Publishing Co.
275 Washington St.
Newton, MA 02158
Telephone: (617) 964-3030
FAX: (617) 558-4470
Ownership %: 100
**Management:**
Jeff Patterson ................................Publisher
Eric Rutter ........................Circulation Manager
**Editorial:**
Steven H. Leibson ..............................Editor
Joan Morrow - Lynch ..............Managing Editor
Paul Rothkopf ..........Advertising Sales Director
Ken Racicot ...........................Art Director
Kathleen Leonard ....................Assistant to the Ed.-in-Chief
Robert Krakoff ..................Chief Exec. Officer
Andrew Jantz ...................Production Director
**Desc.:** Serves establishments that manufacture, design or develop electronic products, equipment and systems, or that incorporate electronic equipment in their end products. Also included are establishments using and/or incorporating electronic equipment in their manufacturing, research and development activities.
**Readers:** Qualified recipients are individuals who perform an engineering or engineering management function. All qualified recipients must indicate that they authorize or specify designated products used in electronic systems and equipment design.
**Deadline:** story-2 mos. prior to pub. date; news-3 wks. prior; photo-2 mos. & 3 wks. prior; ads-1 mo. prior

## EDN PRODUCTS & CAREERS
65998
275 Washington St.
Newton, MA 02158
Telephone: (617) 964-3030
Year Established: 1986
Pub. Frequency: 22/yr.
Subscrip. Rate: $79/yr. US; $109.95/yr. Mexico; $117.65/yr. Canada; $125.95/yr. elsewhere
Circulation: 131,000
Circulation Type: paid
**Owner(s):**
Cahners Publishing Co.
275 Washington St.
Newton, MA 02158
Telephone: (617) 964-3030
Ownership %: 100
**Editorial:**
John Whitmarsh ...........................Editor
George Stubbs ......................Managing Editor
**Desc.:** Provides news of products and technology. Includes a career news section.
**Readers:** Design engineers and managers in electronics.

## ELECTRONIC BUSINESS BUYER
67047
275 Washington St.
Newton, MA 02158-1630
Telephone: (617) 558-4250
FAX: (617) 558-4470
Year Established: 1993
Pub. Frequency: m.
Page Size: standard
Subscrip. Rate: $80/yr.
**Owner(s):**
Cahners Publishing Co.
275 Washington St.
Newton, MA 02158-1630
Telephone: (617) 558-4250
Ownership %: 100
**Management:**
Bob Block ....................................Publisher
**Editorial:**
John Lineback ........................Executive Editor
**Desc.:** Offers analysis, trends, figures, and forecasts. Examines successful firms and managers, and evaluates marketing strategies and manufacturing methods.
**Readers:** For the management team in the electronics, computer and systems companies.

## ELECTRONIC BUYERS' NEWS
22872
600 Community Dr.
Manhasset, NY 11030
Telephone: (516) 562-5000
FAX: (516) 562-5123
Year Established: 1971
Pub. Frequency: w.
Page Size: tabloid
Subscrip. Rate: free
Circulation: 61,036
Circulation Type: controlled
**Owner(s):**
CMP Publications, Inc.
600 Community Dr.
Manhasset, NY 11030
Telephone: (516) 562-5000
Ownership %: 100
**Management:**
Michael Leeds ................................President
Grace Monahan ........................Vice President
Mark Holdreith ...............................Publisher
**Editorial:**
Paul Hyman ....................................Editor
Jeremy Young ..................................Editor
P. Turner ....................................Treasurer
**Readers:** Purchasing managers, purchasing agents.

## ELECTRONIC DESIGN
22874
P.O. Box 821
Hasbrouck Heights, NJ 07964
Telephone: (201) 393-6060
Year Established: 1952
Pub. Frequency: bi-w.
Page Size: standard
Subscrip. Rate: $95/yr. US; $255/yr. foreign
Freelance Pay: $50/pg.
Circulation: 165,090
Circulation Type: controlled
**Owner(s):**
Penton Publishing
San Jose Gateway, Ste. 354
2025 Gateway Pl.
San Jose, CA 95110
Telephone: (408) 441-0550
Ownership %: 100
**Management:**
John Carroll ................................Publisher
Russ Gerches ........................Sales Manager
**Editorial:**
Deborah Eng ........................Marketing Director
**Desc.:** Carries editorial descriptions of the latest developments in new equipment, component parts, new materials, new sub-assemblies or new services of interest to the electronic design and development engineers. Features articles useful to design engineers or engineering management. Design data sheets, application case histories, new circuits and literature will be reviewed along with significant patent developments and governmental material. Departments include new products, ideas for design, new literature.
**Readers:** Individuals influencing design.

## ELECTRONIC DISTRIBUTION TODAY
69253
7912 Country Ln.
Chagrin Falls, OH 44023
Telephone: (216) 543-9451
FAX: (216) 543-9764
Year Established: 1991
Pub. Frequency: bi-m.
Page Size: standard
Subscrip. Rate: $30/yr.
Materials: 01,06,27,29
Print Process: offset
Circulation: 6,528
Circulation Type: controlled & paid
**Owner(s):**
Custom Media, Inc.
7912 Country Lane.
Chagrin Falls, OH 44023
Telephone: (216) 543-9451
Ownership %: 100
**Editorial:**
Edward J. Walter .................................Editor
**Desc.:** Covers management, sales and marketing, industry trends, purchasing, trade association news and new product information.
**Readers:** Electronics distributors.
**Deadline:** story-1st of mo., prior to pub. date; ads-10th of mo., prior to pub. date

## ELECTRONIC ENGINEERING TIMES
67048
600 Community Dr.
Manhasset, NY 11030
Telephone: (516) 562-5325
FAX: (516) 562-5409
Year Established: 1972
Pub. Frequency: w.
Page Size: tabloid
Subscrip. Rate: $159/yr.
Materials: 06,25,27,28,29,30,31,32,33
Circulation: 125,000

Circulation Type: controlled
**Owner(s):**
CMP Publications, Inc.
600 Community Dr.
Manhasset, NY 11030
Telephone: (516) 562-5000
Ownership %: 100
**Management:**
Girish Mhatre .............................Publisher
**Editorial:**
Richard Wallace ..............................Editor
**Desc.:** Delivers news and analysis of the
week's happenings in electronics and
computers for engineers and technical
management every Monday morning.
**Readers:** Engineering and technical
management

22877

## ELECTRONIC NEWS
488 Madison Ave., 6th Fl.
New York, NY 10022
Telephone: (212) 909-5918
FAX: (212) 755-2801
Year Established: 1957
Pub. Frequency: w.
Page Size: tabloid
Subscrip. Rate: $59/yr. US; $159/yr.
Canada; $289/yr. foreign
Materials: 01,06,21,27,28,29,30,31,32,33
Print Process: web offset
Circulation: 27,000
Circulation Type: paid
**Owner(s):**
International Publishing Corporation
428 Main St.
Hudson, MA 01749
Telephone: (508) 562-5005
FAX: (508) 568-1321
Ownership %: 100
**Management:**
Richard Bambrick ....................President
Richard Bambrick ....................Publisher
**Editorial:**
Frank Barbetta .............................Editor
**Desc.:** Presents news of the electronics
and semiconductor industries in regards
to the management responsibilities in
product design research and
development, production, procurement,
marketing and sales, finance, general
administration, etc. Departments include:
Computers, Components,
Communications, Government Electronic
and Finance. Design, Test and
Manufacturing.
**Readers:** Anyone with the electronics or
semiconductor industry.
**Deadline:** story-1 wk. prior to pub. date;
news-1 wk. prior; photo-1 wk. prior; ads-
1 wk. prior

22878

## ELECTRONIC PACKAGING & PRODUCTION
1350 E. Touhy Ave.
Des Plaines, IL 60018
Telephone: (708) 635-8800
Year Established: 1961
Pub. Frequency: m.
Page Size: standard
Subscrip. Rate: $79.95/yr. US.; $117/yr.
Canada; $144/yr. foreign
Materials: 01,05,28,29,32,33
Freelance Pay: varies
Print Process: web
Circulation: 44,000
Circulation Type: controlled
**Owner(s):**
Cahners Publishing Co.
275 Washington St.
Newtonville, MA 02160
Telephone: (617) 964-3030
Ownership %: 100
**Management:**
Randolph D. King ....................Publisher

**Editorial:**
Tim Hodson .............................Managing Editor
Donald E. Swanson ................Editorial Director
**Desc.:** Covers process by which electronic
components are selected, utilized, and
integrated into an operating electronic
unit that performs the intended task.
Articles are sought covering circuit
packaging techniques or procedures,
and methods by which these parts can
be produced and tested in volume.
Departments include: New Products,
New Literature, and News.
**Readers:** Engineers who specialize in the
conversion of an electronic schematic
into a viable product.
**Deadline:** story-3 mos. prior to pub. date;
ads-1 mo. prior

22879

## ELECTRONIC PRODUCTS
645 Stewart Ave.
Garden City, NY 11530
Telephone: (516) 227-1300
FAX: (516) 227-1444
Year Established: 1957
Pub. Frequency: m.
Page Size: standard
Subscrip. Rate: free/qualified personnel;
$50/yr.
Materials: 28,29,30,32
Print Process: web offset
Circulation: 124,126
Circulation Type: controlled
**Owner(s):**
Hearst Business Communications, Inc.
645 Stewart Ave.
Garden City, NY 11530
Telephone: (516) 227-1300
Ownership %: 100
**Management:**
Frank Egan .............................Publisher
**Editorial:**
Rod Myrvaagnes ....................Associate Editor
Warren Yates ..........................Associate Editor
Richard Pell ...........................Associate Editor
Spencer Chin .........................Associate Editor
Patrick Mannion .....................Associate Editor
**Desc.:** Covers new product data,
specifications, applications, prices,
availability. Feature articles highlight
selection and applications of electronic
components, equipment and methods.
By-lines and credits are always given.
Departments include: Editor's Page,
Outlook (product trends, developments,
etc.), Highlights of the Month, New
Products of the Month, New Products
Literature.
**Readers:** Engineers and engineering
managers engaging in the selection of
electronic components, equipment,
instruments and systems.

22882

## ELECTRONICS
San Jose Gateway, Ste. 354
2025 Gateway Pl.
San Jose, CA 95110
Telephone: (408) 441-0550
Year Established: 1930
Pub. Frequency: s-w.
Page Size: standard
Subscrip. Rate: $98/yr. US; $120/yr.
Canada & Latin America
Freelance Pay: varies
Circulation: 85,061
Circulation Type: paid
**Owner(s):**
Penton Publishing
1100 Superior Ave.
Cleveland, OH 44114
Telephone: (216) 696-7000
Ownership %: 100
**Editorial:**
Jonah McLeod ..............................Editor

**Desc.:** Staff-written and contributed
technical articles deal with design,
production and practical applications of
electronic equipment. Also reviews new
books, carries industry news, new
products.
**Readers:** Executives and managers,
researchers, design and product
manufacturing plants, chief engineers,
operators, control, designs and
production engineers, physicists, and
persons who use electronic equipment.
Business executives and engineers
involved in marketing of electronic
systems.

65601

## ELECTRONICS & COMMUNICATIONS IN JAPAN
605 Third Ave.
New York, NY 10158
Telephone: (212) 850-6289
Pub. Frequency: m.
Page Size: standard
Subscrip. Rate: $1,375/yr.
Circulation: 350
Circulation Type: paid
**Owner(s):**
John Wiley & Sons, Inc.
605 Third Ave.
New York, NY 10158
Telephone: (212) 850-6289
Ownership %: 100
**Editorial:**
Tatsuo Itoh ..............................Editor

56222

## EMMS
1333 H St. N.W., 11th Fl.
Washington, DC 20005
Telephone: (202) 842-3022
FAX: (202) 842-1875
Year Established: 1977
Pub. Frequency: bi-w.
Page Size: standard
Subscrip. Rate: $595/yr. US, Canada,
Mexico; $655/yr. Int'l. air mail
Materials: 01,06,10,15,19,23,24,25,27,28,
29,30,31
Print Process: offset
Circulation: 2,000
Circulation Type: paid
**Owner(s):**
BRP Publications
1333 H St. N.W.
Washington, DC 20005
Telephone: (202) 842-3022
FAX: (202) 842-3023
Ownership %: 100
**Editorial:**
Eric Arnum ..............................Editor
**Desc.:** The oldest and most widely
respected newsletter in the electronic
mail and micro system field. Published
twice a month, it covers all aspects of
the e-mail scene: telex/TWX, teletex,
store-and-forward voice, local area
networks, communicating terminals,
personal computers, etc. Also assesses
effects of these technologies on more
traditional communications players like
the telephone companies, the post
office, and the IRCs.
**Readers:** Telecommunications and
computer executives.

22893

## IEEE ALMANACK
Moore School of E.E., Univ. of PA.
Philadelphia, PA 19104
Telephone: (215) 898-8106
FAX: (215) 898-8134
Year Established: 1958
Pub. Frequency: 8/yr.
Page Size: standard
Subscrip. Rate: free to members; $2/yr.
non-members

Circulation: 65,000
Circulation Type: controlled
**Owner(s):**
IEEE Philadelphia Section
Telephone: (215) 898-8106
Ownership %: 100
**Management:**
Graphic Data, Inc. ....................Publisher
Ed Podell .............................Advertising Manager
Viniti Veish .............................Office Manager
**Editorial:**
Ed Podell .............................Managing Editor
**Desc.:** Edited for electrical and electronics
engineers living in the Philadelphia
Metropolitan Area who are interested in
the activities of the Institute of Electrical
and Electronics Engineers. Primary
function is to serve as a bulletin listing
all of the monthly meetings of the
various professional groups/societies
within IEEE in the Philadelphia Section.
Articles are concerned with honors and
achievements of Philadelphia Section
Members and with developments in
technologies of interest to IEEE
members.
**Readers:** Electrical and electronics
engineers.

22894

## IEEE GRID
701 Welch Rd., Ste. 2205
Palo Alto, CA 94304
Telephone: (415) 327-6622
FAX: (415) 321-9692
Year Established: 1963
Pub. Frequency: 10/yr.
Page Size: standard
Subscrip. Rate: $1/copy; $10/yr.
Circulation: 18,000
Circulation Type: controlled
**Owner(s):**
San Francisco Bay Area Council, IEEE
701 Welch Rd., Ste. 2205
Palo Alto, CA 94304
Telephone: (415) 327-6622
Ownership %: 100
**Management:**
Gerry Helmke .............................Office Manager
**Editorial:**
Doug Davolt ..............................Editor
**Desc.:** Purpose is to announce local IEEE
meetings to the membership. Special
Features include notices of courses,
symposia, etc, of interest to our
members. We accept advertising on a
space available basis.
**Readers:** Members of SFBA Council,
IEEE.

22895

## IEEE SPECTRUM
345 E. 47th St.
New York, NY 10017-2394
Telephone: (212) 705-7555
FAX: (212) 705-7453
Year Established: 1964
Pub. Frequency: m.
Page Size: standard
Subscrip. Rate: $157/yr. non-members
Freelance Pay: negotiable
Circulation: 315,000
Circulation Type: paid
**Owner(s):**
The Institute of Electrical and Electronics
Enrs.
345 E. 47th St.
New York, NY 10017
Telephone: (212) 705-7555
Ownership %: 100
**Management:**
William R. Saunders ........Advertising Manager
Robert T. Russ ................Business Manager
Fran Zappulla ....................Operations Manager
**Editorial:**
Trudy E. Bell .............................Senior Editor

**Materials Accepted/Included:** 01-Business news 02-By-line articles 03-Fashion news 04-Food news 05-Freelance copy 06-Letters to editor 07-Real estate news 08-Sports news 09-Travel news 10-Book rev. 11-Movie rev. 12-Music rev. 13-TV rev. 14-Theater rev. 15-Coming events 16-Obituaries 17-Question & answer 18-Social announcements 19-Artwork 20-Cartoons 21-Photos 22-TV listings 23-Audio rec. 24-Video rec. 25-Books 26-Films/film clips 27-Personnel news 28-Press releases 29-New product news/photos 30-Trade lit. 31-Contracts awarded 32-Display adv. 33-Classified adv.

Alfred Rosenblatt .........................Senior Editor
Telka Perry ...........................................Editor
John Adam ...........................................Editor
Margaret Eastman ...............................Editor
Glenn Zorpette .....................................Editor
Murray Slovick .....................................Editor
Morris Khan ..........................................Artist
William R. Saunders ..........Associate Publisher
Rita Holland ..........................Editorial Assistant
Gadi Kaplan ...........................Technical Editor
**Desc.:** Monthly magazine containing
technical articles on important
developments. Also included are book
reviews, letters, and news of IEEE
activities and the industry and the
profession. Departments include: EES
Tools and Toys, Engineer at Large,
Scanning the Institute, Forum, Calendar,
Special Publications, Book Reviews,
Technically Speaking, Whatever
Happened To, Innovations, Speakout
and Spinoffs.
**Readers:** Electronics and electrical
engineers.

67687

## INSTALLATION NEWS
2512 Artesia Blvd.
Redondo Beach, CA 90278-3210
Telephone: (310) 376-8788
FAX: (310) 376-9043
Year Established: 1983
Pub. Frequency: m.
Page Size: standard
Subscrip. Rate: $35/yr. non-members;
$42/yr. in Canada; $53/yr. elsewhere
Materials: 01,06,15,27,28,29,30,32,33
Print Process: offset
Circulation: 23,500
Circulation Type: controlled
**Owner(s):**
Bobit Publishing Co.
2512 Artesia Blvd.
Redondo Beach, CA 90278-3210
Telephone: (310) 376-8788
Ownership %: 100
**Management:**
Mike'l Dornhecker ............................Publisher
**Editorial:**
Michele Guido .........................Executive Editor
Laura Mueller ...........................Managing Editor
**Desc.:** Technical journal covering
automotive aftermarket electronics.

54074

## INTERCONNECTION
## TECHNOLOGY
17730 W. Peterson Rd.
Libertyville, IL 60048-0159
Telephone: (708) 362-8711
Mailing Address:
P.O. Box 159
Libertyville, IL 60048-0159
Year Established: 1985
Pub. Frequency: m.
Page Size: standard
Subscrip. Rate: $10/copy; $60/yr. US &
Canada; $110/yr. foreign
Materials: 01,15,21,27,28,29,31,32,33
Circulation: 35,000
Circulation Type: controlled
**Owner(s):**
IHS Publishing Group, Inc.
17730 W. Peterson Rd.
Libertyville, IL 60048-0159
Telephone: (708) 362-8711
Ownership %: 100
**Management:**
Kathy Brinkmeier ...............Circulation Manager
**Editorial:**
Brian Taylor ...............................Editor in Chief
James K. Fulcher .....................Managing Editor
Carol Nies .......Advertising Production Manager
Linda K. Becker .........................Assistant Editor
Kevin Hambel ............Creative Services Director
Kari Smith ...............................Editorial Assistant

Marsha J. Robertson ...............Group Publisher
Lauren Guthrie .............National Sales Director
**Desc.:** Any editorial material of any type
will be considered provided it is
applicable to connection and
interconnection technology, is news
worthy & objective.
**Readers:** Electronic & electrical
manufacturing personnel involved with
producing end products incorporating
connection and interconnection
technology.

65614

## JOURNAL OF COMMUNICATIONS
## TECHNOLOGY & ELECTRONICS
605 Third Ave.
New York, NY 10158
Telephone: (212) 850-6000
Year Established: 1971
Pub. Frequency: 16/yr.
Page Size: standard
Subscrip. Rate: $1296/yr.
Circulation: 200
Circulation Type: paid
**Owner(s):**
John Wiley & Sons, Inc.
New York, NY
Ownership %: 100
**Editorial:**
N.D. Devyatkov ...........................Editor in Chief

23886

## LASER FOCUS WORLD
10 Tara Blvd., 5th Fl.
Nashua, NH 03062-2801
Telephone: (603) 891-0123
FAX: (603) 891-0574
Year Established: 1964
Pub. Frequency: m.
Page Size: standard
Subscrip. Rate: $104/yr.; $196/2 yrs.
Freelance Pay: negotiable
Circulation: 66,080
Circulation Type: controlled & paid
**Owner(s):**
PennWell Publishing Co., Advanced
Technology Grp.
1421 South Sheridan
Tulsa, OK 74112
Telephone: (918) 835-3161
Ownership %: 100
**Management:**
William L. Pryor .................................Publisher
**Editorial:**
Jeffrey N. Bairstow ....................Editor in Chief
Barbara Murray ........................Managing Editor
Jerry Hobbs ......................New Products Editor
**Desc.:** News and feature articles that
relate to research & development,
design, manufacturing test &
measurement and applications of laser
and other segments of electro-optical
technologies. Feature articles provide
state-of-the-art reviews on various
aspects of laser, fiberoptic,
optoelectronic and optic materials,
components, instrumentation, sub-
systems and systems. Monthly
departments include: Postdeadline
News, Technical News, Business News,
New Products & Literature, Comment
and Features, Letters to the Editor, and
Washington Report.

**Readers:** Qualified recipients are
engineers, researchers, and scientists
engaged in research, development,
design, application, test and
measurement, and fiberoptic
technologies. Also qualified are
engineering personnel, consultants, and
educators technical, corporate,
production, manufacturing and
purchasing management; other scientific
and systems in the laser, electro-optic,
optic and production of materials,
components, instrumentation, equipment,
sub-systems involved in the field.

61644

## MICROCONTAMINATION
3340 Ocean Park Blvd., Ste. 1000
Santa Monica, CA 90405
Telephone: (310) 392-5509
FAX: (310) 392-4920
Year Established: 1983
Pub. Frequency: 11/yr.
Page Size: standard
Subscrip. Rate: free to qualified readers
Circulation: 35,000
Circulation Type: controlled
**Owner(s):**
Clay Camburn & Evangeline Shears, Publs.
3340 Ocean Park Blvd., 1000
Santa Monica, CA 90405
Telephone: (310) 392-5509
Ownership %: 100
**Editorial:**
Bob Keeley ...........................................Editor
Kim Williamson ........................Managing Editor
**Desc.:** A magazine for ultraclean
manufacturing technology.
**Readers:** Professionals from the
semiconductor, disk drive, aerospace,
biomedical, and related industries
interested in ultra-clean manufacturing
technology and contamination control.

67195

## MICROLITHOGRAPHY WORLD
10 Tara Blvd., Fifth Fl.
Nashua, NH 03062-2801
Telephone: (508) 692-0700
Year Established: 1992
Pub. Frequency: q.
Page Size: standard
Subscrip. Rate: $21.95/yr. US; $27.95/yr.
foreign; $30/yr. US non-qualified;
$45/yr. foreign non-qualified
Materials: 01,28,29
Print Process: offset
Circulation: 2,000
Circulation Type: paid
**Owner(s):**
Penwell Publishing Co.
10 Tara Blvd., 5th Fl.
Nashua, NH 03062-2801
Telephone: (603) 891-0597
FAX: (603) 891-0597
Ownership %: 100
**Management:**
Sidney Marshall ..................................Publisher
Florence Oreiro ................Advertising Manager
**Editorial:**
Sidney Marshall ...................................Editor
**Desc.:** Microlithography in the science of
imaging and generating geometrical
patterns having microscopic dimensions.
Focuses on high-level engineering,
scientific and corporate management
issues, as well as worldwide news of the
microlithography industry.

22906

## MICROWAVE JOURNAL
685 Canton St.
Norwood, MA 02062
Telephone: (617) 769-9750
FAX: (617) 762-9230
Year Established: 1958

Pub. Frequency: m.
Page Size: standard
Subscrip. Rate: $67/yr. US; $120/yr.
foreign
Materials: 01,15,27,28,29,31,32,33
Circulation: 52,000
Circulation Type: controlled
**Owner(s):**
Horizon House Publications, Inc.
685 Canton St.
Norwood, MA 02062
Telephone: (617) 769-9750
Ownership %: 100
**Management:**
William Bazzy ......................................President
Harlan Howe ........................................Publisher
**Editorial:**
Harlan Howe ...........................................Editor
**Desc.:** Covers the technical aspects of
microwave information. Departments
include: Featured Industry News, New
Products, Letters to the Editor, Market
Reports, Technical (applications)
articles.
**Readers:** Engineers, physicists and
scientists.

22908

## MICROWAVES & RF
611 Rte. 46 W.
Hasbrouck Heights, NJ 07604
Telephone: (201) 393-6289
FAX: (210) 393-4297
Year Established: 1962
Pub. Frequency: m.
Page Size: standard
Subscrip. Rate: $60/yr. US; $115/yr.
foreign
Freelance Pay: $50/pg.
Circulation: 61,000
Circulation Type: controlled
**Owner(s):**
Penton Publishing
611 Rte. 46 W.
Hasbrouck Heights, NJ 07604
Telephone: (201) 393-6289
Ownership %: 100
**Management:**
Dan Ramella ........................................President
John G. French .....................................Publisher
Jack Browne ..........................Associate Publisher
**Editorial:**
Ron Schneiderman ...........................Senior Editor
David Begley ..........Associate Managing Editor
Peter Jeziorski ................................Art Director
Bonnie O'Connell ..................Production Editor
Victor Perrote .............................Technical Editor
**Desc.:** Covers the microwave field,
facilities concerned with development
design, research of techinques and
systems involving radiated frequencies
above 50 MHZ.
**Readers:** Design engineers, engineering
managers, research engineers.

66337

## MILITARY & AEROSPACE
## ELECTRONICS
346 Commerce St., 2nd Fl.
Alexandria, VA 22314
Telephone: (703) 739-0007
Year Established: 1990
Pub. Frequency: m.
Page Size: tabloid
Subscrip. Rate: $85/yr.
Materials: 01,06,27,29,30,31,32,33
Circulation: 50,000
Circulation Type: controlled
**Owner(s):**
PennWell Publishing Co.
10 Tara Blvd.
5th Fl.
Nashua, NH 03062-2801
Telephone: (603) 891-0123
FAX: (603) 891-0514
Ownership %: 100

**Materials Accepted/Included:** 01-Business news 02-By-line articles 03-Fashion news 04-Food news 05-Freelance copy 06-Letters to editor 07-Real estate news 08-Sports news 09-Travel news 10-Book rev. 11-Movie rev. 12-Music rev. 13-TV rev. 14-Theater rev. 15-Coming events 16-Obituaries 17-Question & answer 18-Social announcements 19-Artwork 20-Cartoons 21-Photos 22-TV listings 23-Audio rec. 24-Video rec. 25-Books 26-Films/film clips 27-Personnel news 28-Press releases 29-New product news/photos 30-Trade lit. 31-Contracts awarded 32-Display adv. 33-Classified adv.

**Editorial:**
Bruce Rayner .............................Editor
**Desc.:** Includes product and technology applications, military and defense industry news, design development briefs and new product updates.
**Readers:** Designers, buyers and specifiers of electronic components and subsystems.

22618

## OPTICAL ENGINEERING
1000 20th St.
Bellingham, WA 98225
Telephone: (206) 676-3290
Mailing Address:
P.O. Box 10
Bellingham, WA 98227-0010
Year Established: 1962
Pub. Frequency: m.
Page Size: standard
Subscrip. Rate: $195/yr. US; $240/yr. foreign
Print Process: offset
Circulation: 11,500
Circulation Type: controlled
**Owner(s):**
SPIE-The International Society For Optical Eng.
1000 20th St.
Bellingham, WA 98225
Telephone: (206) 676-3290
Ownership %: 100
**Editorial:**
James Pearson .....................Executive Editor
Brian J. Thompson ..........................Editor
Lorretta Palagi ...................Managing Editor
Bonnie Peterson ......................Advertising
Marybeth Manning ..............Publication Director
**Desc.:** Professional journal for optical, electro-optical and optoelectronic engineers containing technical articles and references. Also includes book reviews and meetings and course calendars.
**Readers:** Applied scientists, engineers, skilled technicians in optical, electro-optical, fiber-optic, laser, high speed photographic fields.

64962

## POPULAR ELECTRONICS
500-B Bi County Blvd.
Farmingdale, NY 11735
Telephone: (516) 293-3000
FAX: (516) 293-3115
Year Established: 1988
Pub. Frequency: m.
Page Size: standard
Subscrip. Rate: $3.50/copy US; $3.95/copy Canada; $21.95/yr.
Materials: 05,06,10,28,29,32,33
Freelance Pay: $75-$450
Print Process: web offset
Circulation: 84,015
Circulation Type: paid
**Owner(s):**
Gernsback Publications, Inc.
500-B Bicounty Blvd.
Farmingdale, NY 11735
Telephone: (516) 293-3000
FAX: (516) 293-3115
Ownership %: 100
**Management:**
Larry Steckler .........................President
Larry Steckler .........................Publisher
**Editorial:**
Carl Laron ...............................Editor
John Yacono .....................Associate Editor
Robert A. Young ..................Associate Editor
Jeff Holtzman .....................Contributing Editor
Joe Carr .............................Contributing Editor
Don Jensen ........................Contributing Editor
Marc Ellis ...........................Contributing Editor
Marc Saxon .......................Contributing Editor
Charles Rakes ...................Contributing Editor

**Desc.:** The premier magazine for the person interested in electronics. Contains practical product information, features, articles, and projects of interest and challenge to the reader.

65467

## PRE
8340 Mission Rd., Ste. 106
Prairie Village, KS 66206
Telephone: (913) 642-6611
Year Established: 1990
Pub. Frequency: bi-m.
Page Size: standard
Subscrip. Rate: $45/yr.
Materials: 01,02,06,10,15,19,21,25,28,29, 30,32,33
Freelance Pay: varies
Print Process: web offset
Circulation: 31,100
Circulation Type: controlled
**Owner(s):**
South Wind Publishing Co.
8340 Mission Rd., Ste. 106
Prairie Village, KS 66206
Ownership %: 100
**Management:**
Mike Kreiter ...........................Publisher
**Editorial:**
Howard Fenton ..........................Editor
Maureen Waters ......................Managing Editor
**Desc.:** Covers news, trends, products, and services in the pre-press and pre-publishing industry.
**Readers:** Targets users and buyers of electronic design and pre-press and pre-publishing systems and services.
**Deadline:** story-3 mos.; news-3 mos.; photo-3 mos.

66305

## PRINTED CIRCUIT DESIGN
600 Harrison St.
San Francisco, CA 94107
Telephone: (415) 905-2200
Year Established: 1984
Pub. Frequency: m.
Page Size: standard
Subscrip. Rate: $55/yr.; free to qualified personnel
Materials: 01,05,06,28,29,30,32,33
Circulation: 25,142
Circulation Type: controlled
**Owner(s):**
Miller Freeman, Inc.
600 Harrison St.
San Francisco, CA 94107
Telephone: (415) 905-2200
Ownership %: 100
**Management:**
Frances M. Stewart ..........................Publisher
**Editorial:**
Pete Waddell ......................Editor in Chief
**Readers:** For IC, ASIC, Hybrid and PCB design professionals.

66307

## PRINTED CIRCUIT FABRICATION
600 Harrison St.
San Francisco, CA 94107
Telephone: (415) 905-2200
Mailing Address:
2000 Powers Ferry Ctr., Ste. 450
Marietta, GA 30067
Year Established: 1978
Pub. Frequency: m.
Page Size: standard
Subscrip. Rate: $60/yr.; free to qualified personnel
Materials: 01,02,06,109,24,27,28,29,31,32, 33
Print Process: web
Circulation: 20,000
Circulation Type: controlled

**Owner(s):**
Miller Freeman, Inc.
600 Harrison St.
San Francisco, CA 94107
Telephone: (415) 905-2200
Ownership %: 100
**Editorial:**
Ron Davids ...........................Editor in Chief
Elizabeth Clark ...........................Senior Editor
**Desc.:** Designed for key personnel of the printed circuit board fabricators, both at independent and captive operations.
**Deadline:** story-2 mo. prior; news-1 mo. prior; ads-1 mo. prior

24592

## PROCEEDINGS OF THE IEEE
445 Hoes Ln.
Piscataway, NJ 08855-1331
Telephone: (908) 562-5478
FAX: (908) 562-5456
Year Established: 1913
Pub. Frequency: m.
Page Size: standard
Subscrip. Rate: $22/yr. for members; $325/yr. non-members
Circulation: 30,000
Circulation Type: paid
**Owner(s):**
IEEE
445 Hoes Ln.
Piscataway, NJ 08855
Telephone: (908) 562-5478
Ownership %: 100
**Management:**
John H. Powers ...................General Manager
**Editorial:**
Richard B. Fair ...........................Editor
George F. Watson ...................Managing Editor
Susan Schneiderman ....................Advertising
Richard Faust ...........................Advertising
**Desc.:** Technical papers, especially in-depth reviews, and tutorials on topics of broad significance and long-range interest in all areas of electrical, electronics, and computer engineering.
**Readers:** Engineers and scientists in the electrotechnical and computer fields.

22928

## PROFESSIONAL ELECTRONICS
2708 W. Berry St.
Fort Worth, TX 76109-2397
Telephone: (817) 921-9062
FAX: (817) 921-3741
Year Established: 1975
Pub. Frequency: bi-m.
Page Size: standard
Subscrip. Rate: $12/6 mos.; $20/yr.
Freelance Pay: varies
Circulation: 10,000
Circulation Type: controlled
**Owner(s):**
National Electronics Service Dealers Association
2708 W. Berry St.
Fort Worth, TX 76109-2397
Telephone: (817) 921-9061
Ownership %: 100
**Bureau(s):**
J. E. Publishers Representative
3415 S. Sepulveda Blvd.
Ste. 520
Los Angeles, CA 90034
Telephone: (310) 572-7272
Contact: Jay Eisenberg
**Management:**
Clyde Nabors ...........................Publisher
Barbara Rubin ...................Advertising Manager
Wallace Harrison ...................Operations Manager
**Editorial:**
Wallace Harrison ...........................Editor in Chief
Clyde Nabors ...........................Director

**Desc.:** Edited for professional electronics service dealers and technicians who service radio-TV; 2-way communications, audio-visual equipment, MATV-antenna systems, auto radio video equipment, computer, CCTV-closed circuit TV sound systems, and for other types of businesses in which product and technical electronic service is performed. Primary editorial emphasis is upon business articles aimed at improving the professional sales and service dealer's management skills and technical news of interest to professional technicians. Industry news, technical articles, test equipment reviews, association news and new products make up the balance of editorial content. Departments Include: New Book News; Letters to the Editor, Profitable Service Management, Manufacturing News, Calendar of Events, Test Equipment Reports, Association News.
**Readers:** Professional electronics and service dealers and technicians are the bulk of the readership. Distribution also to manufacturers and representatives, and to electronics instructors.

66005

## SEMICONDUCTOR INTERNATIONAL
1350 E. Touhy Ave.
Des Plaines, IL 60017-5080
Telephone: (708) 635-8800
FAX: (708) 390-2770
Mailing Address:
P.O. Box 5080
Des Plaines, IL 60017-5080
Year Established: 1978
Pub. Frequency: 13/yr.
Page Size: standard
Subscrip. Rate: $84.95/yr. US; $123.95/yr. Canada; $114.95/yr. Mexico; $144.95/yr. elsewhere
Materials: 02,06,15,27,28,29,32,33
Print Process: web offset
Circulation: 49,190
Circulation Type: controlled & paid
**Owner(s):**
Cahners Publishing Co.
1350 E. Touhy Ave.
Des Plaines, IL 60018
Telephone: (708) 635-8800
Ownership %: 100
**Management:**
Laura Peters .................New Products Manager
**Editorial:**
Betty Newboe ...................Managing Editor
**Desc.:** Serves industry specialists whose function is to design, research and develop, wafer processing, testing, and assembly equipment for the semiconductor manufacturing industry.
**Deadline:** story-3 mos.; news-6 wks.; photo-2 mos.; ads-1st of mo.

24078

## SIGNAL
4400 Fair Lakes Ct.
Fairfax, VA 22033
Telephone: (703) 631-6180
FAX: (703) 631-4693
Year Established: 1946
Pub. Frequency: m.
Page Size: standard
Subscrip. Rate: $5/copy; $44/yr. US; $65/yr. foreign
Materials: 01,02,06,15,29,30,31,32
Freelance Pay: negotiable
Print Process: web
Circulation: 39,740
Circulation Type: controlled & paid

**Materials Accepted/Included:** 01-Business news 02-By-line articles 03-Fashion news 04-Food news 05-Freelance copy 06-Letters to editor 07-Real estate news 08-Sports news 09-Travel news 10-Book rev. 11-Movie rev. 12-Music rev. 13-TV rev. 14-Theater rev. 15-Coming events 16-Obituaries 17-Question & answer 18-Social announcements 19-Artwork 20-Cartoons 21-Photos 22-TV listings 23-Audio rec. 24-Video rec. 25-Books 26-Films/film clips 27-Personnel news 28-Press releases 29-New product news/photos 30-Trade lit. 31-Contracts awarded 32-Display adv. 33-Classified adv.

**Owner(s):**
AFCEA
4400 Fair Lakes Ct.
Fairfax, VA 22033
Telephone: (703) 631-6100
Ownership %: 100
**Management:**
Adm. James Busey (Ret.) ...................President
Louise Nelson ...................Advertising Manager
**Editorial:**
Clarence A. Robinson, Jr. .........Editor in Chief
Robert Ackerman ........................Senior Editor
Beverley Mowery .....................Managing Editor
Beverly Schaeffer .............Assistant Managing Editor
Donna Seward ................................Design
Jack Sykes ................................Design
Kit McDuffie ................................Design
Gretchen Kraft ..................Editorial Assistant
**Desc.:** Emphasizes military-industry-government relationship in related communications, electronics, computer sciences, teleprocessing intelligence systems and imagery fields with technical and semi-technical articles on research, development, procurement, design, etc. of systems and equipment. Features about companies and personalities in the field, sections for new products and items of current interest; Capitol Hill and international news. Includes book reviews, associations news.
**Readers:** Military, industry and government managers; personnel in electronics, defense, industry, intelligence and aerospace.
**Deadline:** ads-40 days prior to pub. date

22929
## SOLID STATE TECHNOLOGY
10 Tara Blvd.
5th Fl.
Nashua, NH 03062-2801
Telephone: (603) 891-0123
FAX: (603) 891-0597
Year Established: 1958
Pub. Frequency: m.
Page Size: standard
Subscrip. Rate: $10/issue US; $15/issue foreign; $145/yr. US; $192/yr. foreign
Circulation: 43,633
Circulation Type: paid
**Owner(s):**
PennWell Publishing Co.
One Technology Park Dr.
Westford, NY 01886
Telephone: (508) 692-0700
Ownership %: 100
**Management:**
Adam Japko ................................Publisher
Florence L. Oreiro ...........Advertising Manager
**Editorial:**
Robert Haavind ........................Editor in Chief
Sid Marshall ....................Editorial Director
Sidney Marshall ...................Associate Editor
Selma Uslaner ........Chief Editor, News Bureau
Dr. Morris R. Levitt .......Chief Operating Officer
**Desc.:** Editorial content consists of feature articles on: survey, original verified design, semi-conductor devices, circuits and systems. Also includes descriptions of machinery equipment and processes used in the solid state industry.
**Readers:** Engineers, scientists and other technical staff of solid state materials, equipments, devices.

49874
## TEST & MEASUREMENT WORLD
275 Washington St.
Newton, MA 02158
Telephone: (617) 964-3030
Year Established: 1981
Pub. Frequency: 13/yr.

Page Size: standard
Subscrip. Rate: free to qualified personnel
Circulation: 75,000
Circulation Type: controlled
**Owner(s):**
Cahners Publishing Co.
275 Washington St.
Newton, MA 02158
Telephone: (617) 964-3030
Ownership %: 100
**Management:**
John Kovacs ................................Publisher
**Editorial:**
Charles Masi ................................Editor
Deborah Sargent ...................Managing Editor
Peter Micheli .......................Marketing Director
Dan Romanchik ...................Technical Editor
Martin Rowe ...................Technical Editor
John Flarhety ...................Technical Editor
**Desc.:** Contains information for electronics engineers and managers on the news, products, and technology of test, measurement, and inspection in the electronics industry around the world. Typical issues contain: product news, product & technology features, technology news, staff written columns, measurement and inspection technology.
**Readers:** Circulated to managers, engineers, supervisors, and company executives responsible for the selection specification, recommendation, authorization or cost justification for purchases of equipment, services, and software used for test, measurement, inspection characterization, evaluation, quality assurance, reliability, quality control and related support functions in the electronics industry around the world.

22934
## WHO'S WHO ELECTRONICS BUYER'S GUIDE
2057 Aurora Rd.
Twinsburg, OH 44087
Telephone: (216) 425-9000
Year Established: 1948
Pub. Frequency: a.
Page Size: standard
Subscrip. Rate: $60/yr.
Circulation: 62,000
Circulation Type: paid
**Owner(s):**
Harris Publishing Co., Inc.
2057 Aurora Rd.
Twinsburg, OH 44087
Telephone: (216) 425-9000
Ownership %: 100
**Management:**
Robert A. Harris, Jr. ...........................President
**Editorial:**
Kathi Graeser ................................Editor
Paula Scroggy ................................Advertising
**Desc.:** An industrial directory devoid of editorial content. Contains 18,000 listings of manufacturers, importers, representatives and distributors in the electronics industry.
**Readers:** Buyers and specifying engineers within industries making and/or using electronics component equipment, materials and instruments.

## Group 070-Engineering, College

22536
## ARKANSAS ENGINEER, THE
Bell Engineering Ctr., Rm. 4162A
Fayetteville, AR 72701
Telephone: (501) 575-6016
FAX: (501) 575-4346
Year Established: 1921
Pub. Frequency: a.

Page Size: standard
Subscrip. Rate: free to engineering students
Circulation: 2,000
Circulation Type: free
**Owner(s):**
Engineering Publications
4162 Bell Engineering Ctr.
Fayetteville, AR 72701
Telephone: (501) 575-6016
Ownership %: 100
**Editorial:**
Mary-Ann Bloss ...................Managing Editor
**Desc.:** Features are of engineering interest as often as possible. However, some human interest features are used. News stories are usually covering new developments in the various engineering fields. By-lines are given for features and credit is given for news and development articles. Publicity material is often used when it contains a good news item. Articles are usually 800 to 1,200 words with as much photo spread as possible. Departments include: Copy, Editorials, Features, Reporters and Makeup. Magazine averages 25 pages.
**Readers:** Mostly students of engineering and advertisers.

24717
## CALIFORNIA ENGINEER
221 Bechtel Enr. Ctr., Rm. 221
University of California, Berkeley
Berkeley, CA 94720
Telephone: (510) 642-8679
Year Established: 1923
Pub. Frequency: q.
Page Size: standard
Subscrip. Rate: $5/yr.
Materials: 01,02,06,15,19,21,23,24,25,26, 28,29,30,32,33
Circulation: 10,000
Circulation Type: paid
**Owner(s):**
California Engineer Publishing Co., Inc.
221 Bechtel Engineering Ctr.
University of California, Berkeley
Berkeley, CA 94720
Telephone: (510) 642-8679
Ownership %: 100
**Management:**
Florence Meza ...................Advertising Manager
Ivan Choi ...........................Business Manager
**Editorial:**
David D. Chen ................................Editor
Krishna Kaza .................Production Coordinator
**Desc.:** Published by students for engineering students. Prints semi-technical articles of broad interest.
**Readers:** Engineering students, faculty, and alumni of the University of California.

22558
## CORNELL ENGINEER, THE
217 Carpenter Hall
Ithaca, NY 14853
Telephone: (607) 255-3312
Year Established: 1895
Pub. Frequency: q.
Page Size: standard
Subscrip. Rate: $8/yr.
Circulation: 3,800
Circulation Type: controlled
**Owner(s):**
Cornell Engineer, Inc.
217 Carpenter Hall
Jacksonville, NY 14854
Telephone: (607) 255-3312
Ownership %: 100
**Management:**
Cornell Engineer ................................Publisher

**Desc.:** Articles on technical aspects of engineering, general science, and social implications of technology. Departments include: Alumni News, College News, Book Review, and Editorial Comment. 3,000 word articles, also Humor Page, Engineering Breakthroughs.
**Readers:** Undergraduate and graduate students of Cornell University.

22624
## E-QUAD NEWS
Office C-218, E-Quad
Princeton, NJ 08544
Telephone: (609) 258-3617
Year Established: 1988
Pub. Frequency: q.
Page Size: standard
Subscrip. Rate: free
Materials: 06,27,28
Print Process: offset
Circulation: 12,300
Circulation Type: controlled & free
**Owner(s):**
SEAS Dean's Office
Princeton University
Princeton, NJ 08544
Telephone: (609) 258-3617
Ownership %: 100
**Editorial:**
Ann Haver-Allen ..................Publication Director
**Desc.:** General interest publication. Reports on news, features, research, etc. at SEAS. No advertisements accepted. All published material has a SEAS connection, ie. faculty news, alumni news. Written by publications director and engineering students.
**Readers:** Engineering alumni of Princeton, all undergraduates of Princeton, all engineering graduate students, all engineering faculty members. Corporate sponsors of SEAS.

22575
## ENGINEERING & SCIENCE MAGAZINE
Caltech., 1-71
Pasadena, CA 91125
Telephone: (818) 395-3630
FAX: (818) 577-0636
Year Established: 1937
Pub. Frequency: q.
Page Size: standard
Subscrip. Rate: $8/yr.
Circulation: 16,000
Circulation Type: controlled
**Owner(s):**
California Inst. of Technology & Alumni Assn.
1-71 Caltech
Pasadena, CA 91125
Telephone: (818) 395-3630
Ownership %: 100
**Management:**
Debbie Bradbin ...................Business Manager
Susan Lee ........................Circulation Manager
**Editorial:**
Jane Dietrich ................................Editor
Douglas Smith ...................Managing Editor
Barbara Wirick ................................Artist
Robert Paz ................................Photographer
**Desc.:** Devoted to information about Caltech and the research going on there. All features, articles and news stories are about people at Caltech or people from Caltech who are working elsewhere.
**Readers:** Alumni, faculty, students and general public. The magazine is also sent regularly to companies, libraries, high school, and the science media.

**Materials Accepted/Included:** 01-Business news 02-By-line articles 03-Fashion news 04-Food news 05-Freelance copy 06-Letters to editor 07-Real estate news 08-Sports news 09-Travel news 10-Book rev. 11-Movie rev. 12-Music rev. 13-TV rev. 14-Theater rev. 15-Coming events 16-Obituaries 17-Question & answer 18-Social announcements 19-Artwork 20-Cartoons 21-Photos 22-TV listings 23-Audio rec. 24-Video rec. 25-Books 26-Films/film clips 27-Personnel news 28-Press releases 29-New product news/photos 30-Trade lit. 31-Contracts awarded 32-Display adv. 33-Classified adv.

4-123

## HAWKEYE ENGINEER
22580

4101 EB University of Iowa
Iowa City, IA 52242
Telephone: (319) 335-1538
Year Established: 1880
Pub. Frequency: q.
Page Size: standard
Subscrip. Rate: $10/yr.
Materials: 01,02,05,06,10,11,15,17,18,19,
   20,21,22,27,28,09,30,31,32,33
Freelance Pay: voluntary
Circulation: 1,700
Circulation Type: free & paid
**Owner(s):**
Collegiate Association Council
IMU
Coralville, IA 52242
Telephone: (319) 335-3262
Ownership %: 100

**Management:**
Scott Bishop ....................Circulation Manager
Ken Kauffman ......................General Manager
**Editorial:**
Katherine Tharp ...................................Editor
Darren Farrey ..................................Advertising
Barry Swenka .................................Comptroller
Tamer Selim ..........................Production Editor
**Desc.:** Research at U. of I. articles of
   interest to student engineers and
   undergraduate engineers. Editorials on
   school policy and curriculm, safety and
   pertinent engineering developments.
   Letters to editor welcome on
   controversial material in magazine.
**Readers:** Students and Professors in
   Engineering College. U. of I. Alumni With
   Subscriptions

## ILLINOIS TECHNOGRAPH
22582

57 E. Green St.
Champaign, IL 61820
Telephone: (217) 333-6602
FAX: (217) 244-6616
Year Established: 1885
Pub. Frequency: bi-m.
Page Size: standard
Subscrip. Rate: $12.95/yr.
Freelance Pay: $.35/col. in.
Circulation: 4,100
Circulation Type: free
**Owner(s):**
Illini Media Co.
57 E. Green St.
Champaign, IL 61820
Telephone: (217) 333-3733
Ownership %: 100
**Management:**
Jim McKellar ......................................Publisher
Jack Gidding ......................Advertising Manager
**Editorial:**
John Fultz ...............................Editor in Chief
George Thirurathukal ..........................Editor
Minako Hashimoto ...........................Copy Chief
Rebecca Fagan ....................................Design
Chi - Ting Huang ...................Production Editor
**Desc.:** The feature articles are those that
   appeal specifically to undergraduate
   students. It is the policy to feature
   articles of general interest to students
   rather than featuring purely
   technical material.
**Readers:** Engineering students & faculty

## IOWA ENGINEER
22586

16 G. Hamilton Hall
Iowa State University
Ames, IA 50010
Telephone: (515) 294-9390
Year Established: 1920
Pub. Frequency: q.
Page Size: standard
Subscrip. Rate: free/students
Materials: 28,29,30,32

Freelance Pay: offset
Circulation: 3,200
Circulation Type: free
**Owner(s):**
Campus Magazine, Inc.
16 G. Hamilton Hall
Iowa State University
Ames, IA 50010
Telephone: (515) 294-9390
Ownership %: 100
**Editorial:**
Alan M. Russell ..................................Advisor
**Desc.:** Articles deal with local interest and
   technical subjects which promote
   engineering to students. Technical news
   in the engineering field is welcome.
   Publicity material must generally be of
   some technical interest to warrant
   publication.
**Readers:** University students and alumni
   subscribers.
**Deadline:** story-Aug.1, Nov.1, Jan.1, Mar.1
   of ea. yr.

## KANSAS ENGINEER
22589

University of Kansas
4010 Learned Hall
Lawrence, KS 66045
Telephone: (913) 864-3881
FAX: (913) 864-5445
Year Established: 1914
Pub. Frequency: q.
Page Size: standard
Subscrip. Rate: $10/yr.
Circulation: 2,500
Circulation Type: paid
**Owner(s):**
University of Kansas School of Engineering
University of Kansas
4010 Learned Hall
LAWRENCE, KS 66045
Telephone: (913) 864-3881
Ownership %: 100
**Management:**
Mainline Printers ...............................Publisher
**Editorial:**
Ray Dean ....................Administrative Assistant
**Desc.:** Engineering student publication
   mainly uses research, technical
   development or other subjects of
   interest to engineering students.
**Readers:** College engineering students
   and alumni and industrial
   representatives.

## KANSAS STATE ENGINEER
22590

133 Ward Hall
Kansas State University
Manhattan, KS 66506
Telephone: (913) 532-6026
FAX: (913) 532-6952
Year Established: 1915
Pub. Frequency: q.
Page Size: standard
Subscrip. Rate: $6/yr.
Circulation: 3,200
Circulation Type: paid
**Owner(s):**
College of Engineering
Kansas State University
Manhattan, KS 66506
Telephone: (913) 532-5590
Ownership %: 100
**Management:**
College of Engineering ......................Publisher

**Desc.:** The purpose of the Kansas State
   Engineer is to bring to its readers news
   and interesting developments and
   projects within their college: student,
   faculty and staff profiles, and
   commentaries and observations on life
   from the perspective of the engineering
   student. Main emphasis is placed on
   local feature stories with picture
   illustrations, but news items also play an
   important part in the magazine. Material
   written by college students.
**Readers:** College students majoring in
   engineering.

## MANHATTAN COLLEGE ENGINEER
22594

Manhattan College School of Engineering
Manhattan College Pkwy.
Riverdale, NY 10471
Telephone: (718) 920-0281
FAX: (718) 796-9812
Year Established: 1940
Pub. Frequency: 3/semester
Page Size: standard
Subscrip. Rate: free
Circulation: 2,500
Circulation Type: free
**Owner(s):**
Manhattan College Students
School of Engineering
Riverdale, NY 10471
Telephone: (718) 920-0281
Ownership %: 100
**Editorial:**
Karen Lynn Counes .................................Editor
Dr. Pritchard .................Administrative Assistant
**Readers:** Engineering colleges, students,
   & engineering firms.

## NEBRASKA BLUEPRINT
22606

W181 Nebraska Hall
Univ. of Nebraska College of Engineering
Lincoln, NE 68588-0501
Telephone: (402) 472-9420
FAX: (402) 492-7292
Year Established: 1902
Pub. Frequency: q.
Page Size: standard
Subscrip. Rate: $5/yr.
Circulation: 16,000
Circulation Type: free & paid
**Owner(s):**
Univ. of Nebraska, College of Engineer.
   and Tech.
W181 Nebraska Hall
Lincoln, NE 68588
Telephone: (402) 472-3181
Ownership %: 100
**Management:**
Stan Liberty .......................................Publisher
Kerry Shepherd ......................General Manager
**Editorial:**
Marc Schultz ........................................Editor
**Desc.:** Stories and articles of general
   interest to engineers and engineering
   students.
**Readers:** University of Nebraska
   engineering students, alumni, faculty and
   staff.

## NORTH CAROLINA STATE ENGINEER
22634

10 Page Hall, N.C. State Univ.
Raleigh, NC 27695
Telephone: (919) 737-2240
Mailing Address:
   Box 7901, N.C. State Univ.
   Raleigh, NC 27695
Year Established: 1936
Pub. Frequency: q.
Page Size: standard
Subscrip. Rate: $2/issue; $5/yr.

**Owner(s):**
Engineers' Council
5 Page Hall, N.C.S.U.
Raleigh, NC 27695
Telephone: (919) 737-2240
Ownership %: 100
**Management:**
Engineers' Council, NCSU .................Publisher
**Editorial:**
Steven Freedman ................................Editor
**Desc.:** Features articles on current
   engineering research, faculty profiles,
   technical society reports, and news of
   new product developments.
**Readers:** Undergraduate engineering
   students, graduate students, research
   faculty at North Carolina State
   University.

## NOTRE DAME TECHNICAL REVIEW
24800

257 Fitzpatrick Hall, University of N.D.
Notre Dame, IN 46556
Telephone: (219) 631-4303
Year Established: 1947
Pub. Frequency: 4/yr.
Page Size: standard
Subscrip. Rate: $15/yr.
Circulation: 1,750
Circulation Type: paid
**Owner(s):**
University of Notre Dame
Notre Dame, IN 46556
Telephone: (219) 239-5530
Ownership %: 100
**Editorial:**
Daniel J. Kelly.......................................Editor
Matthew C. Connor .................Managing Editor
David Grover ...........................Associate Editor
Dr. John Lucey ........................................Dean
**Desc.:** Articles dealing with innovations in
   the engineering field and with
   information for the engineer at Notre
   Dame. All features and articles written
   by undergraduate and graduate
   students.
**Readers:** Faculty, student body and
   alumni.

## OLE MISS ENGINEER
68833

University of Mississippi
Department of Engineering
University, MS 38677
Telephone: (601) 232-7407
FAX: (601) 232-7219
Year Established: 1962
Pub. Frequency: s-a.
Subscrip. Rate: $1/yr.
Circulation: 2900
Circulation Type: paid
**Owner(s):**
University of Mississippi, Dept. of
   Engineering
University, MS 38677
Telephone: (601) 232-7407
Ownership %: 100
**Editorial:**
J.G. Vaughn .........................................Editor

## PENNSYLVANIA TRIANGLE
22620

322 Towne Bldg.
University of Pennsylvania
Philadelphia, PA 19104
Telephone: (215) 898-1444
Year Established: 1899
Pub. Frequency: 3/yr.
Page Size: standard
Subscrip. Rate: $5/yr.
Circulation: 3,000
Circulation Type: paid

**Owner(s):**
University of Pennsylvania
Office of Student Life
Philadelphia, PA 19104
Telephone: (215) 898-6533
Ownership %: 100
**Management:**
Mahmud Wazihullah .........Advertising Manager
**Editorial:**
Matt Bednar ..................Editor in Chief
Timothy Z. Chiu .......................Managing Editor
**Desc.:** A college engineering, science and
fine arts magazine, published by and for
the students at the university and also
for the university community at large.
We exchange magazines with other
colleges on a nationwide basis.
Departments include: photo essays,
editorial comments, and interviews with
note-worthy persons, as descriptions of
research and products within the
university. Student articles on their own
research encouraged, also. Regularly
describe new achievements, processes,
and products in a featured column.
**Readers:** Students, alumni and faculty in
engineering and science at the
University of Pennsylvania.

22628

**RENSSELAER ENGINEER**
Rensselaer Union
Troy, NY 12180-3590
Telephone: (518) 276-6515
FAX: (518) 276-6920
Year Established: 1948
Pub. Frequency: s-a.
Page Size: standard
Subscrip. Rate: $10/yr.
Circulation: 4,000
Circulation Type: paid
**Owner(s):**
Rensselaer Engineer
RPI
Troy, NY 12180
Telephone: (518) 266-6505
Ownership %: 100
**Editorial:**
Paul Singh .................................Editor
**Desc.:** Articles of interest to the
Rensselaer community, as students and
future professionals. Articles vary from
the relatively technical to the
interactions of technology and society.
Departments include Editorials,
Engineering in its Social Text,
Mathematical Puzzles and occasionally
hobby sections.
**Readers:** Alumni, students and faculty of
Rensselaer.

22643

**USC ENGINEER**
OHE-300 University Pk.
Los Angeles, CA 90089
Telephone: (310) 743-2502
Year Established: 1950
Pub. Frequency: s-a.
Page Size: 4 color photos/art
Subscrip. Rate: $5/yr.
Circulation: 5,500
Circulation Type: controlled
**Owner(s):**
School of Engineering USC
OHE-300 University Pk.
Los Angeles, CA 90089
Telephone: (310) 743-2502
Ownership %: 100
**Editorial:**
Brian Didier ...........................Miscellaneous
Teresa Drake ...........................Miscellaneous

**Desc.:** Main purpose is to publicize
activities of USC School of Engineering
and to feature articles of interest to
engineers and scientists. Of secondary
importance is the including of features
and articles of interest to the entire USC
student body. Also serves as a
laboratory for developing and
recognizing the literary and
communicative skills of the members.
By-line given in all stories. Length of
articles is at writer's discretion. Four-
color printing employed.
**Readers:** 60% USC students, 30%
business, 10% alumni.

22645

**WAYNE ENGINEER, THE**
Wayne State Univ., College of Engineering
Detroit, MI 48202
Telephone: (313) 577-3829
Year Established: 1934
Pub. Frequency: q.
Page Size: standard
Subscrip. Rate: $.95 issue; $3.80/yr.
**Owner(s):**
Students of the College of Engineering
5050 Anthony Wayne Dr.
Rm. 2200
Detroit, MI 48202
Telephone: (313) 577-3829
Ownership %: 100
**Bureau(s):**
Wayne State University, College of
Engineering
5050 Anthony Wayne Dr. Rm 2200
Detroit, MI 48202
Telephone: (313) 577-3829
Contact: Tarek Kazzi, Editor in Chief
**Desc.:** Articles of interest to College of
Engineering students and the scientific
community as a whole, campus news,
and latest news of
industrial developments.
**Readers:** College of Engineering students,
alumni.

22648

**WISCONSIN ENGINEER**
Mechanical Engineering Bldg.
Madison, WI 53706
Telephone: (608) 262-3494
Year Established: 1896
Pub. Frequency: 5/yr.
Page Size: standard
Subscrip. Rate: $10/yr.
Circulation: 4,000
Circulation Type: paid
**Owner(s):**
WI. Engineering Journal Association
460 Mechanical Engineering
Bldg.
Madison, WI 53706
Telephone: (608) 262-2472
Ownership %: 100
**Desc.:** Topics related to engineering
developments, particularly those
connected with research at University of
Wisconsin-Madison.
**Readers:** Engineering students,
professors, and alumni.

## Group 072-Engineering, General

68840

**ADVANCED COMPOSITES**
7500 Old Oak Blvd.
Cleveland, OH 44130
Telephone: (216) 826-2839
FAX: (216) 891-2726
Year Established: 1986
Pub. Frequency: 7/yr.
Subscrip. Rate: $35/yr.
Circulation: 24,858
Circulation Type: paid

**Owner(s):**
Advanstar Communications, Inc.
7500 Old Oak Blvd.
Cleveland, OH 44130
Telephone: (216) 826-2839
Ownership %: 100
**Editorial:**
Suzanne Witzler ...........................Editor

61335

**AEE ENERGY INSIGHT**
4025 Pleasantdale Rd., Ste. 420
Atlanta, GA 30340-4264
Telephone: (404) 447-5083
FAX: (404) 446-3969
Year Established: 1977
Pub. Frequency: 3/yr.
Page Size: tabloid
Subscrip. Rate: free to members
Circulation: 15,000
Circulation Type: free
**Owner(s):**
AEE Energy
Ownership %: 100
**Management:**
Ruth M. Bennett ...........................Manager
**Editorial:**
Ruth M. Bennett ...........................Editor

61309

**AEROSPACE ENGINEERING**
400 Commonwealth Dr.
Warrendale, PA 15096-0001
Telephone: (412) 776-4841
Year Established: 1983
Pub. Frequency: m.
Page Size: standard
Subscrip. Rate: $48/yr.
Materials: 06,28,29,30,32,33
Circulation: 52,314
Circulation Type: controlled
**Owner(s):**
Society of Auto Engineers, Inc.
400 Commonwealth Dr.
Warrendale, PA 15098
Ownership %: 100
**Management:**
Larry Schneider ...........................Publisher
David Cybak ...................Circulation Manager
Gerry Dunlap ...................Production Manager
Carolyn Taylor ...................Promotion Manager
**Editorial:**
Daniel J. Holt ...........................Editor in Chief
Albert Demmler ...........................Senior Editor
**Desc.:** Written for the engineer involved in
the design and development of
aerospace vehicles.
**Readers:** Design Engineers, Corporate
Managers in Aerospace
**Deadline:** story-2 mos. prior to pub. date;
news-2 mos. prior; ads-1 mo. prior

24434

**ASSEMBLY**
191 S. Gary Ave.
Carol Stream, IL 60188
Telephone: (708) 462-2289
FAX: (708) 462-2225
Year Established: 1958
Pub. Frequency: m.
Page Size: standard
Subscrip. Rate: $50/yr. US.
Circulation: 60,000
Circulation Type: controlled
**Owner(s):**
Hitchcock Publ. Co., Capital Cities/ABC,
Inc.
191 S. Gary Ave.
Carol Stream, IL 60188
Telephone: (708) 665-1000
Ownership %: 100
**Management:**
Don Hegland ...........................Publisher
Nancy Wyman ...................Advertising Manager
**Editorial:**
Allan Benson ...........................Senior Editor
Wesley R. Iversen ...........................Senior Editor

Don Hegland ...........................Editor
Jean McNamara ...........................Art Director
**Desc.:** Covers all phases of products
assembly, from designing for assembly
through the actual assembly techniques
used. Contributed technical articles as
well as staff features. Departments
include: News Line, Coming Events,
New Products, Free Literature, Assembly
in Action, and Ergonomics.
**Readers:** Primarily design, manufacturing,
engineers performing assembly
operations on manufactured products.

66693

**BOUNDARY ELEMENTS
COMMUNICATIONS**
25 Bridge St.
Billerica, MA 01821
Telephone: (508) 667-5841
FAX: (508) 667-7582
Year Established: 1990
Pub. Frequency: bi-m.
Page Size: oversize
Subscrip. Rate: $225/yr.
Materials: 06,10,15,27,28,29,32
**Owner(s):**
Wessex Institute of Technology
Ashurst Lodge
Ashurst
SO4 2AA Southampton United Kingdom
Telephone: (44)(703)293223
FAX:(44)(703)292853
Ownership %: 100
**Editorial:**
Dr. M.H. Aliabadi ...........................Editor
Lance Sucharov ...................Design Editor
Dee Halzack ...................Publications Marketing
Manager
**Desc.:** Purpose is to provide rapid access
to worldwide literature on boundary
element research.
**Readers:** Engineers from all disciplines
who are involved in research,
development, or implementation of
boundary elements methods.

22539

**CES PERSPECTUS**
3100 Chester Ave.
Cleveland, OH 44114-4683
Telephone: (216) 361-3100
FAX: (216) 361-1660
Year Established: 1907
Pub. Frequency: m.
Page Size: standard
Subscrip. Rate: $12/yr. members; $24/yr.
non-members
Circulation: 1,500
Circulation Type: controlled
**Owner(s):**
Cleveland Engineering Society
3100 Chester Ave.
Cleveland, OH 44114
Telephone: (216) 361-3100
Ownership %: 100
**Management:**
Elaine Rybak ...................Advertising Manager
**Editorial:**
Michele O'Keefe ...........................Editor
**Desc.:** Covers engineering society news,
professional items, continuing education,
engineering and technical new books,
accepts page-price articles.
**Readers:** Members of Cleveland
Engineering Society.

52553

**COMPUTER-AIDED ENGINEERING**
1100 Superior Ave.
Cleveland, OH 44114
Telephone: (216) 696-7000
FAX: (216) 696-1309
Year Established: 1982
Pub. Frequency: m.

**Materials Accepted/Included:** 01-Business news 02-By-line articles 03-Fashion news 04-Food news 05-Freelance copy 06-Letters to editor 07-Real estate news 08-Sports news 09-Travel news
10-Book rev. 11-Movie rev. 12-Music rev. 13-TV rev. 14-Theater rev. 15-Coming events 16-Obituaries 17-Question & answer 18-Social announcements 19-Artwork 20-Cartoons 21-Photos 22-TV listings
23-Audio rec. 24-Video rec. 25-Books 26-Films/film clips 27-Personnel news 28-Press releases 29-New product news/photos 30-Trade lit. 31-Contracts awarded 32-Display adv. 33-Classified adv.

4-125

Page Size: standard
Subscrip. Rate: $60/yr.
Materials: 01,06,25,28,29,30,32,33
Freelance Pay: $150/pg.
Circulation: 60,000
Circulation Type: paid
**Owner(s):**
Penton Publishing, Sub. of Pittway Corp.
1100 Superior Ave.
Cleveland, OH 44114
Telephone: (216) 696-7000
Ownership %: 100
**Management:**
John Krouse ..........................................Publisher
**Editorial:**
Bob Mills ........................................................Editor
**Desc.:** Reports on the application of
software and database principles
throughout engineering and
manufacturing.
**Readers:** Engineers, managers, and
others who are concerned with applying
computer technology to engineering
design and manufacturing functions.
Readers represent many technical
disciplines and work in numerous
industries.

22555
## CONSULTING-SPECIFYING ENGINEER
1350 E. Touhy Ave.
Des Plaines, IL 60018-3358
Telephone: (708) 635-8800
FAX: (708) 635-9950
Year Established: 1958
Pub. Frequency: m.
Page Size: standard
Subscrip. Rate: $74.95/yr. in country;
$112.30 Canada; $104.95/yr. Mexico
Materials: 01,15,21,23,24,27,28,29,32,33
Circulation: 47,550
Circulation Type: controlled
**Owner(s):**
Cahners Publishing Co.
1350 E. Touhy Ave.
Des Plaines, IL 60018-3368
Telephone: (708) 635-8800
FAX: (708) 635-9950
Ownership %: 100
**Management:**
Robert Lindsey ..................................Publisher
John Bowman ....................Circulation Manager
Steve Lovisa ......................Production Manager
**Editorial:**
Thomas Klemens ..........................Senior Editor
Randi Campise ............Administrative Assistant
John Hansen ..............................Art Department
Cathryn Hodson ......................Associate Editor
Paul E. Beck ..............................Editor-in-Chief
Ann Kruckmeyes ..................Editorial Assistant
Carol Davies ..........................Production Editor
**Desc.:** Covers mechanical and electrical
equipment and systems in which these
products are applied for commercial,
institutional, industrial, informative,
factual, easy to read and use articles
are published. Length ranges from about
1,000 to 10,000 words, with good
illustrative material. Departments include:
Editor's Viewpoint, Engineer's Briefing,
Engineers At the Bar, Technology- In-
Action, Calendar, Short Takes,
Technology Pipeline, New Products,
New Literature.
**Readers:** Consulting/specifying engineers,
engineers with architectural/engineering
firms, design/construct firms, corporate
engineering departments of large
industrial companies, M/E engineers
with government and utilities.
**Deadline:** story-3 mo. prior to pub. date;
news-8 wks. prior; photo-8 wks. prior;
ads-1 mo. prior

22559
## COST ENGINEERING
209 Prairie Ave., Ste. 100
Morgantown, WV 26505
Telephone: (304) 296-8444
Mailing Address:
P.O. Box 1557
Morgantown, WV 26507
Year Established: 1956
Pub. Frequency: m.
Page Size: standard
Subscrip. Rate: $48/yr. US & Canada;
$64/yr. elsewhere
Circulation: 6,000
Circulation Type: controlled
**Owner(s):**
AACE, Inc.
P.O. Box 1557
Morgantown, WV 26507
Telephone: (304) 296-8444
Ownership %: 100
**Management:**
Kenneth K. Humphreys, PE, CCE .......Publisher
Lauri M. Schiffbauer ..........Advertising Manager
Charla Prager ....................Circulation Manager
Charla Prager ............................Office Manager
**Editorial:**
Lloyd M. English, PE .........Book Review Editor
Betsy Humphreys ..................Editorial Assistant
Cathleen Falvey ........................Technical Editor
**Desc.:** Technical papers and news items
related to cost engineering. Manuscripts
should be limited to 10 typewritten,
double spaced pages.
**Readers:** Cost engineers, estimators,
project managers, planners and
schedulers.

65604
## ELECTRICAL ENGINEERING IN JAPAN
605 Third Ave.
New York, NY 10158
Telephone: (212) 850-6289
Pub. Frequency: bi-m.
Page Size: standard
Subscrip. Rate: $545/yr.
Circulation: 300
Circulation Type: paid
**Owner(s):**
John Wiley & Sons, Inc.
605 Third Ave.
New York, NY 10158
Telephone: (212) 850-6289
Ownership %: 100
**Editorial:**
Yasuji Sekine ..............................................Editor

61749
## ENGINEERED SYSTEMS
755 W. Big Beaver
Ste. 1000
Troy, MI 48084
Telephone: (810) 362-3700
FAX: (810) 362-0319
Mailing Address:
P.O. Box 7016
Troy, MI 48007
Year Established: 1985
Pub. Frequency: 9/yr.
Page Size: standard
Subscrip. Rate: free to qualified
professionals
Freelance Pay: negotiable
Circulation: 57518
Circulation Type: controlled & free
**Owner(s):**
Business News Publishing Co.
755 W. Big Beaver
Ste. 1000
Troy, MI 48084
Telephone: (810) 362-3700
Ownership %: 100
**Management:**
James E. Henderson ..........................President
Peter Moran ......................................Publisher

Kathy Janes ......................Advertising Manager
**Editorial:**
Anne Hayner ................................................Editor
Wayne Johnson ......................Editorial Director
Michael A. Miller ......................Group Publisher
Sarah Sjobakken ..................Marketing Director
**Desc.:** Carries technical featured stories
on all aspects of the non- residential
HVAC/R field. Service, installation
technology & maintenance.
**Readers:** Operating engineers, consulting
engineers, building operators, design
build mechanical contractors, and others
who specify, install, maintain or operate
nonresidential HVACR equipment.

69565
## ENGINEERING MANAGEMENT JOURNAL
1005 Pine St.
Rolla, MO 65401
Telephone: (314) 341-2101
FAX: (314) 341-5522
Year Established: 1989
Pub. Frequency: q.
Subscrip. Rate: $40/yr.
Circulation: 2,300
Circulation Type: paid
**Owner(s):**
American Society for Engineering
Management
1005 Pine St.
Rolla, MO 65401
Telephone: (314) 341-2101
Ownership %: 100
**Editorial:**
Ted Eschenbach ........................................Editor

69573
## ENGINEERING OPTIMIZATION
270 Eighth Ave.
New York, NY 10011
Telephone: (212) 206-8900
FAX: (212) 645-2459
Year Established: 1974
Pub. Frequency: 8/yr.
**Owner(s):**
Gordon & Breach Science Publishers
270 Eighth Ave.
New York, NY 10011
Telephone: (212) 206-8900
Ownership %: 100
**Editorial:**
Andrew Templeman ..................................Editor

49865
## ENGINEERING TIMES
1420 King St.
Alexandria, VA 22314-2794
Telephone: (703) 684-2875
FAX: (703) 836-4875
Year Established: 1979
Pub. Frequency: m.
Page Size: tabloid
Subscrip. Rate: $30/yr.
Freelance Pay: varies
Circulation: 75,000
Circulation Type: controlled
**Owner(s):**
National Society of Professional Engineers
1420 King St.
Alexandria, VA 22314
Telephone: (703) 684-2800
Ownership %: 100
**Editorial:**
Stefan Jaeger ..............................................Editor
**Desc.:** News and commentary of the
profession.
**Readers:** For all those involved in the
engineering community.

22573
## ENGINEER OF CALIFORNIA, THE
626 N. Garfield Ave.
Alhambra, CA 91802
Telephone: (800) 362-3162
FAX: (818) 281-5646

Mailing Address:
P.O. Box 991
Alhambra, CA 91801
Year Established: 1947
Pub. Frequency: 10/yr.
Page Size: standard
Subscrip. Rate: $12/yr.
Materials: 06
Print Process: offset
Circulation: 6,000
Circulation Type: paid
**Owner(s):**
Schilling Graphics
626 W. Garfield
Alhambra, CA 91802
Telephone: (310) 283-1986
Ownership %: 100
**Management:**
Michael Schilling ..............................Publisher
Annette Schilling ................Advertising Manager
**Editorial:**
Annette Schilling ......................................Editor
**Desc.:** Uses more and more feature
material (maximum 2,000 wds.) by-lined
and staff written. Subjects are open to
any and all stories with basic
engineering interest. News coverage
(unless of far reaching effect) is of the
S. California area or are notices of
society meetings and engineers job
changes. Departments include Engineer
Editorial, News of Engineers, Letters,
Coming Events, Society Meeting
Notices.
**Readers:** Engineers of all disciplines,
scientists, manufacturers
**Deadline:** ads-10 days prior to pub. date

22566
## ESD TECHNOLOGY
27241 Harper Ave.
St. Clair Shores, MI 48081
Telephone: (313) 774-3530
FAX: (313) 774-3892
Year Established: 1939
Pub. Frequency: m.
Page Size: 4 color photos/art
Subscrip. Rate: $22/yr.
Freelance Pay: varies
Circulation: 8,000
Circulation Type: paid
**Owner(s):**
Engineering Society of Detroit, The
100 Farnsworth
Detroit, MI 48202
Telephone: (313) 832-5400
Ownership %: 100
**Management:**
Barbara Kelvin ..................Circulation Manager
**Editorial:**
Karen Shellie ..............................................Editor
**Desc.:** 1-4 page technical articles (original
material only) with 1-4 pictures average.
By-line by person in field. Publicity
material used when of technical nature
and not covered by weekly technical
publications or newspapers.
Departments include developments in
pure and applied science.
**Readers:** Members of the Engineering
Society of Detroit; including
professionals in industries; engineering,
construction, automotive, manufacturing,
and utilities.

22577
## EXPONENT
1051 Office Park Rd., Ste. 2
West Des Moines, IA 50265
Telephone: (515) 225-7966
Year Established: 1889
Pub. Frequency: q.
Page Size: standard
Subscrip. Rate: $5/yr. members; $6/yr.
non-members
Circulation: 1,400

**Materials Accepted/Included:** 01-Business news 02-By-line articles 03-Fashion news 04-Food news 05-Freelance copy 06-Letters to editor 07-Real estate news 08-Sports news 09-Travel news 10-Book rev. 11-Movie rev. 12-Music rev. 13-TV rev. 14-Theater rev. 15-Coming events 16-Obituaries 17-Question & answer 18-Social announcements 19-Artwork 20-Cartoons 21-Photos 22-TV listings 23-Audio rec. 24-Video rec. 25-Books 26-Films/film clips 27-Personnel news 28-Press releases 29-New product news/photos 30-Trade lit. 31-Contracts awarded 32-Display adv. 33-Classified adv.

Circulation Type: paid
**Owner(s):**
Iowa Engineering Society
2900 Westown Parkway, Ste. 2
W Des Moines, IA 50265
Telephone: (515) 223-0309
Ownership %: 100
**Management:**
B. J. Bertrand ......................Advertising Manager
**Editorial:**
David Scott ..............................Executive Editor
**Desc.:** Official publication of the Iowa Engineering Society. Covers news concerning engineering personalities and activities but no technical articles. An annual directory issue includes specifying engineers in the state and those in executive positions in industry, education, private practice, government work.

### FLORIDA ENGINEERING SOCIETY JOURNAL
22588

125 S. Gadsden St.
Tallahassee, FL 32301
Telephone: (904) 224-7121
FAX: (904) 222-4349
Mailing Address:
P.O. Box 750
Tallahassee, FL 32302
Year Established: 1917
Pub. Frequency: m.
Page Size: standard
Subscrip. Rate: $50/yr. foreign
Materials: 32,33
Freelance Pay: negotiable
Print Process: offset
Circulation: 4,500
Circulation Type: controlled
**Owner(s):**
Florida Engineering Society Journal
125 S. Gadsden St.
Tallahassee, FL 32301
Telephone: (904) 224-7121
Ownership %: 100
**Management:**
Carol G. Brittain ......................Publisher
Nancy Taylor ....................Advertising Manager
**Editorial:**
Patricia Sunseri ...............................Editor
**Desc.:** Features cover topics of interest to, or about professional engineering activities. About 75% staff-written. Departments include: Legislative Report, New Members, Measure X Measure (current events).
**Readers:** Members of the Florida Engineering Society and government officials.

### GRADUATING ENGINEER
22579

16030 Ventura Blvd., Ste. 560
Encino, CA 91436
Telephone: (818) 789-5293
Year Established: 1979
Pub. Frequency: 8/yr.
Page Size: standard
Subscrip. Rate: $16/yr.
Freelance Pay: $300-$500
Circulation: 70,000
Circulation Type: controlled
**Owner(s):**
Peterson's/COG Publishing
16030 Ventura Blvd., Ste. 560
Encino, CA 91436
Telephone: (818) 789-5293
Ownership %: 100
**Management:**
Bruce D. Matzner ..............................Publisher
**Editorial:**
Charlotte Chandler Thomass ..............Editor in Chief
Terry Bratcher ..............................Art Director

**Desc.:** Career-oriented for senior level and graduate engineering students. Examines the exciting prospects in the job market, but also pauses to look at the whole engineer. Departments include: Editor's Letter, Campus Calendar and Resume Forwarding Service.
**Readers:** Senior level and graduate engineering students.

### HIGH-TECH MARKETING NEWS
67685

600 Community Dr.
Manhasset, NY 11030
Telephone: (516) 562-5607
FAX: (516) 562-7154
Year Established: 1991
Pub. Frequency: 9/yr.
Page Size: tabloid
Subscrip. Rate: $39.95/yr.
Freelance Pay: varies
Circulation: 15,000
Circulation Type: controlled
**Owner(s):**
CMP Pulbications, Inc.
600 Community Dr.
Manhasset, NY 11030
Telephone: (516) 365-4600
Ownership %: 100
**Editorial:**
Robert Henkel ......................Editorial Director
Rachele Greco ..................Marketing Manager

### IAN
23439

One Chilton Way
Radnor, PA 19087
Telephone: (215) 964-4419
FAX: (215) 964-2919
Year Established: 1952
Pub. Frequency: m.
Page Size: tabloid
Subscrip. Rate: free/qualified readers
Circulation: 117,266
Circulation Type: controlled
**Owner(s):**
Chilton Co., Sub. of Cap Cities/ABC
1 Chilton Way
Radnor, PA 19087
Telephone: (215) 964-4419
Ownership %: 100
**Management:**
Richard E. Dute ..............................Publisher
Matt DeJulio ......................Business Manager
Rick Thornton ..................Circulation Manager
**Editorial:**
Patricia Pool ...............................Editor
Midge Regester ......................Associate Editor
Dana Hazelton ..................Production Assistant
Peg Roby ..........................Production Director
**Desc.:** To provide the reader with product information on instruments, industrial control products and control systems. Departments include: New Products, New Literature, Technical Briefs.
**Readers:** Distributed nationally to engineering, technical & management personnel with functions in the areas of design, application, production operations, research & procurement who are responsible for brand selection and purchasing of instruments, industrial controls & control systems in the broad OEM and User Market.

### IEEE COMMUNICATIONS MAGAZINE
52655

345 E. 47th St.
New York, NY 10017
Telephone: (212) 705-7018
Year Established: 1953
Pub. Frequency: m.
Page Size: standard
Subscrip. Rate: $125/yr. to non-members
Circulation: 35,000

Circulation Type: paid
**Owner(s):**
IEEE
345 E. 47th
New York, NY 10017
Telephone: (212) 705-7018
Ownership %: 100
**Management:**
Richard Shippee ..............................Publisher
**Editorial:**
Tom Plevyate ...............................Editor
Joseph Milizzo ......................Managing Editor
Judy Raposa ................Administrative Assistant
Eric Levine ..............................Advertising
**Desc.:** Technical guide with practical applications for working professionals in telecommunications and data communications.
**Readers:** Communications engineers involved in all aspects of communications.

### INDIANA PROFESSIONAL ENGINEER
22583

1810 Broad Ripple Ave.
Ste. 14
Indianapolis, IN 46220
Telephone: (317) 255-2267
Mailing Address:
P.O. Box 20806
Indianapolis, IN 46220
Year Established: 1937
Pub. Frequency: bi-m.
Page Size: tabloid
Subscrip. Rate: $5/yr. non-members
Circulation: 2,500
Circulation Type: controlled
**Owner(s):**
Indiana Society of Professional Engineers, Inc.
P.O. Box 20806
Indianapolis, IN 46220
Telephone: (317) 255-2267
Ownership %: 100
**Management:**
Charles E. Long, PE ......................President
**Editorial:**
J. B. Wilson ...............................Editor
Laurie Howe ..............................Assistant Editor
**Desc.:** Devoted to news affecting the engineering profession in Indiana. Although in recent years few features or by-lined articles have appeared, magazine is now under new editorial policy that actively seeks stories and features about engineering problems and successes in overcoming them, new product developments, and issues currently facing the profession. By-lined articles are welcome. Staff ability to cover field events is limited; accordingly, publicity news releases and other materials will be used if genuinely newsworthy and pertinent to the profession in Indiana. Current max. article length is 500 words. This policy subject to reassessment should advertisements permit an increase in number of pages per issue. Photo spreads are desired.
**Readers:** Professional engineers (P.E.), 350 gratis distribution to engineering, manufacturing agencies and selected libraries, contractors, suppliers, government officials.

### INDUSTRIAL ENGINEERING
22584

25 Technology Pk./Atlanta
Norcross, GA 30092-2988
Telephone: (404) 449-0461
FAX: (404) 263-8532
Year Established: 1969
Pub. Frequency: m.

Page Size: standard
Subscrip. Rate: $49/yr.
Circulation: 36,000
Circulation Type: paid
**Owner(s):**
Institute Of Industrial Engineers
25 Technology Park/Atlanta
Norcross, GA 30092
Telephone: (404) 449-0460
Ownership %: 100
**Management:**
Ellen Snodgrass ..............................Publisher
**Editorial:**
Eric E. Torrey ...............................Editor
Gary Ferguson ......................Associate Editor
Heather Sutton ............Production Coordinator
**Desc.:** Industrial engineering features articles on material handling, computers, quality control, production and inventory control, engineering economics, worker motivation, management strategies and factory automation. Regular departments include application case studies, new technology, products, literature and books.
**Readers:** Engineers and managers who are concerned with slashing operating costs, increasing efficiency, and boosting productivity in business, industry, and government.

### INSTRUMENTATION & CONTROL SYSTEMS
23441

Chilton Way
Radnor, PA 19087
Telephone: (215) 964-4417
Year Established: 1928
Pub. Frequency: m.
Page Size: standard
Subscrip. Rate: $60/yr.
Materials: 01,02,28,29,30
Print Process: web offset
Circulation: 92,600
Circulation Type: controlled
**Owner(s):**
Chilton Co., Cap. Cities/ABC
Chilton Way
Radnor, PA 19087
Telephone: (610) 964-4000
FAX: (610) 964-2919
Ownership %: 100
**Management:**
Richard Dute ..............................Publisher
Matt DeJulio ......................Business Manager
Rick Thornton ..................Circulation Manager
Mike Koehler ..............................Sales Manager
**Editorial:**
Ronald Kuhfeld ......................Managing Editor
Jack Hickey ......................Editorial Director
Monika Kozub ......................Editorial Assistant
Betty Eastlack ......................Marketing Manager
Peg Ruby ..........................Production Director
Wayne Labs ..............................Technical Editor
John Hall ..............................Technical Editor
Peter Cleaveland ......................Technical Editor
**Desc.:** Written to tell readers about techniques and equipment they can design, devise, buy, adapt or otherwise apply to optimize production and processes. Technical and interpretive articles by experts in various fields are presented on the broad spectrum of industrial and process control practices and equipment. Articles tend to be generic rather than particular to a single industry. Feature articles emphasize practical design and applications, and ensure readers will be able to take advantage of new technologies as they develop. Departments in I&CS include: Editor's Views, New Products, New Literature, News, Book Reviews, Coming Events, Letters to the Editor, and Product Applications.

---

**Materials Accepted/Included:** 01-Business news 02-By-line articles 03-Fashion news 04-Food news 05-Freelance copy 06-Letters to editor 07-Real estate news 08-Sports news 09-Travel news 10-Book rev. 11-Movie rev. 12-Music rev. 13-TV rev. 14-Theater rev. 15-Coming events 16-Obituaries 17-Question & answer 18-Social announcements 19-Artwork 20-Cartoons 21-Photos 22-TV listings 23-Audio rec. 24-Video rec. 25-Books 26-Films/film clips 27-Personnel news 28-Press releases 29-New product news/photos 30-Trade lit. 31-Contracts awarded 32-Display adv. 33-Classified adv.

**Readers:** Over 92,600 engineers who design, use, specify and buy industrial and process control devices, equipment and systems.
**Deadline:** story-15th of 2nd mo. prior to pub. date; ads-1st of mo. prior to pub. date

69728

## INTERNATIONAL JOURNAL OF DAMAGE MECHANICS
851 New Holland Ave.
Box 3535
Lancaster, PA 17604
Telephone: (717) 291-5609
FAX: (717) 295-4538
Year Established: 1992
Pub. Frequency: q.
Page Size: 6 x 9
Subscrip. Rate: $215/yr.; $420/2 yrs.; $625/3 yrs.
Circulation: 125
Circulation Type: paid
**Owner(s):**
Technomic Publishing Co., Inc.
851 New Holland Ave.
Box 3535
Lancaster, PA 17604
Telephone: (717) 291-5609
FAX: (717) 295-4538
Ownership %: 100
**Editorial:**
C.L. Chow ................................................Editor
Dusan Krajcinovic .................................Editor
J.L. Chaboche .......................................Editor
S. Murakami ..........................................Editor
**Desc.:** Provides new developments in the science and engineering of fracture and damage mechanics.

69582

## INTERNATIONAL JOURNAL OF ENGINEERING
660 White Plains Rd.
Tarrytown, NY 10591-5153
Telephone: (914) 524-9200
FAX: (914) 333-2444
Year Established: 1963
Pub. Frequency: m.
Circulation: 1,400
**Owner(s):**
Pergamon Press, Inc.
660 White Plains Rd.
Tarrytown, NY 10591-5153
Telephone: (914) 524-9200
Ownership %: 100
**Editorial:**
A.C. Eringen .........................................Editor
**Desc.:** Original research pertaining to the application of the physical, chemical and mathematical sciences to engineering.

69604

## JOURNAL OF MANAGEMENT IN ENGINEERING
345 E. 47th St.
New York, NY 10017-2398
Telephone: (212) 705-7288
FAX: (212) 980-4681
Year Established: 1985
Pub. Frequency: bi-m.
Page Size: standard
Subscrip. Rate: $28/yr. member; $112/yr. non-member
Circulation: 4,900
Circulation Type: paid
**Owner(s):**
American Society of Civil Engineers
345 E. 47th St.
New York, NY 10017-2398
Telephone: (212) 705-7288
Ownership %: 100
**Editorial:**
Gary Bates ............................................Editor

**Desc.:** Examines a broad spectrum of organizations: private and public; design, research, operations and maintenance; large and small.

22344

## JOURNAL OF THE ACOUSTICAL SOCIETY OF AMERICA
500 Sunnyside Blvd.
Woodbury, NY 11797
Telephone: (516) 576-2360
FAX: (516) 349-7669
Year Established: 1929
Pub. Frequency: m.
Page Size: standard
Subscrip. Rate: $855.95/yr.
Circulation: 8,500
Circulation Type: paid
**Owner(s):**
Acoustical Society of America
500 Sunnyside Blvd.
Woodbury, NY 11797
Telephone: (516) 576-2360
Ownership %: 100
**Management:**
Charles E. Schmid ...............Executive Director
**Editorial:**
Daniel W. Martin ...................................Editor
James F. Bartram ...............Book Review Editor
**Readers:** Scientists, engineers, psychologists.

24879

## JOURNAL OF THE FRANKLIN INSTITUTE
20th St. & Pkwy.
Philadelphia, PA 19103
*see Service,Trade,Professional Magazines, Science, General*

23447

## MANUFACTURING ENGINEERING
One SME Dr.
Dearborn, MI 48121
Telephone: (313) 271-1500
Mailing Address:
   P.O. Box 930
   Dearborn, MI 48121
Year Established: 1932
Pub. Frequency: m.
Page Size: standard
Subscrip. Rate: $60/yr.
Circulation: 130,000
Circulation Type: controlled
**Owner(s):**
Society of Manufacturing Engineers
One SME Dr.
P.O. Box 930
Dearborn, MI 48121
Telephone: (313) 271-1500
Ownership %: 100
**Management:**
Thomas J. Drozda .............................Publisher
Vicki Soto ...................Circulation Manager
Dale Michelson ...............Production Manager
**Editorial:**
John R. Coleman ...................Editor in Chief
James R. Koelsch ...............Managing Editor
**Desc.:** Prepare technical articles for manufacturing engineers and manufacturing managers.
**Readers:** Manufacturing engineers and manufacturing managers.

61278

## MARINE LOG
345 Hudson St.
New York, NY 10014
Telephone: (212) 620-7200
Year Established: 1867
Pub. Frequency: m.
Page Size: standard
Subscrip. Rate: $35/yr.
Circulation: 20,000
Circulation Type: controlled

**Owner(s):**
Simmons-Boardman Publishing Corp.
345 Hudson St.
New York, NY 10014
Telephone: (212) 620-7200
Ownership %: 100
**Editorial:**
Nicholas Blankey ................................Editor
**Desc.:** Highlights shipbuilding and ship operations.

23449

## MECHANICAL ENGINEERING
345 E. 47th St.
New York, NY 10017
Telephone: (212) 705-7782
Year Established: 1920
Pub. Frequency: m.
Page Size: standard
Subscrip. Rate: $14/yr. members
Circulation: 110,000
Circulation Type: controlled
**Owner(s):**
American Soc. of Mechanical Engineers
345 E. 47th St.
New York, NY 10017
Telephone: (212) 705-7782
Ownership %: 100
**Bureau(s):**
M. H. Bradley
2029 K St., N.W.
Washington, DC 20006
Telephone: (202) 785-3756
**Management:**
Charles Beardsley ............................Publisher
Janet Rogers ...............Advertising Manager
**Editorial:**
John Falcioni ......................................Editor
Steven Ashley ...................Associate Editor
Michael Valenti ...................Associate Editor
Samuel Walters ....................Miscellaneous
Jennifer Halpern ....................Miscellaneous
Jay O'Leary ...........................News Editor
**Desc.:** Contributed papers discuss concepts of industry and the role of the engineer in society, as well as technical developments. Departments include; Briefing the Record, Photo Briefs, The Roundup, International Focus, ASMENews, Technical Digest, Letters and Comments, Book Reviews, Keep Informed section reporting on new equipment business notes, latest catlogs made up mostly of news releases.
**Readers:** Mechanical engineers.

23452

## MIDWEST ENGINEER
176 W. Adams St.1734
Chicago, IL 60603
Telephone: (312) 372-3760
FAX: (312) 372-3761
Mailing Address:
   649 Hinman Ave.
   Evanston, IL 60202
Year Established: 1948
Pub. Frequency: 9/yr.: Sep.-May
Page Size: standard
Subscrip. Rate: $15/yr.
Materials: 28,30,32,33
Print Process: offset
Circulation: 1,000
Circulation Type: paid
**Owner(s):**
The Western Society of Engineers
176 W. Adams
Chicago, IL 60603
Telephone: (312) 372-3760
FAX: (312) 372-3761
Ownership %: 100
**Management:**
Western Society of Engineers ............Publisher
John LaPlante ...................Executive Director
Margaret Bement ...................Office Manager
**Editorial:**
James A. Kepler ................................Editor

James A. Kepler .........................Photographer
**Desc.:** Midwest engineering news magazine.
**Readers:** Engineers in all areas.

22601

## MILITARY ENGINEER, THE
607 Prince St.
Alexandria, VA 22314-3177
Telephone: (703) 549-3800
FAX: (703) 548-6153
Year Established: 1920
Pub. Frequency: bi-m.
Page Size: standard
Subscrip. Rate: $48/yr.
Materials: 29,32,33
Circulation: 22,000
Circulation Type: free & paid
**Owner(s):**
Society of American Military Engineers
607 Prince St.
P.O. Box 21289
Alexandria, VA 22314-3117
Telephone: (703) 549-3800
FAX: (703) 548-6153
Ownership %: 100
**Management:**
Bruce Beran .......................Executive Director
**Editorial:**
Gordon T. Bratz ...................Editor in Chief
Carol Urban-Pastore .................Assistant Editor
Betty Tihey ...........................Associate Editor
Richard Bilden .....................Contributing Editor
Richard Cunningham .............Contributing Editor
Coralyn Goode .....................Contributing Editor
Vincent Grimes .....................Contributing Editor
Jeffery Walascek ...................Contributing Editor
Lorraine Picott ......................Marketing Director
**Desc.:** Covers all disciplines of engineering--design, heavy construction, environmental, computer use, research and development, technology advancements, management, security and more.
**Readers:** Executives, managers, superintendents, planners, consultants, specifiers and contracting and procurement officials in private and government engineering environment, and manufacturers and suppliers of engineering and engineering-related products.

24096

## MINES MAGAZINE
1811 Elm St.
Golden, CO 80401
Telephone: (303) 273-3291
FAX: (303) 273-3165
Mailing Address:
   P.O. Box 1410
   Golden, CO 80402
Year Established: 1910
Pub. Frequency: bi-m.
Page Size: standard
Subscrip. Rate: $30/yr. US; $35/yr. Canada
Materials: 01,02,05,06,10,16,17,19,20,21, 27,28,29,30,31,32
Freelance Pay: negotiable
Print Process: web offset
Circulation: 6,000
Circulation Type: free & paid
**Owner(s):**
Colo. School Of Mines Alumni Association
P.O. Box 1410
Golden, CO 80402
Telephone: (303) 273-3293
Ownership %: 100
**Management:**
Norman R. Zehr ................................Publisher
**Editorial:**
Richard Haugh .....................................Editor
Richard Haugh ...............................Advertising

**Materials Accepted/Included:** 01-Business news 02-By-line articles 03-Fashion news 04-Food news 05-Freelance copy 06-Letters to editor 07-Real estate news 08-Sports news 09-Travel news 10-Book rev. 11-Movie rev. 12-Music rev. 13-TV rev. 14-Theater rev. 15-Coming events 16-Obituaries 17-Question & answer 18-Social announcements 19-Artwork 20-Cartoons 21-Photos 22-TV listings 23-Audio rec. 24-Video rec. 25-Books 26-Films/film clips 27-Personnel news 28-Press releases 29-New product news/photos 30-Trade lit. 31-Contracts awarded 32-Display adv. 33-Classified adv.

4-128

**Desc.:** Feature articles on alumni, faculty and students of the Colorado School of Mines as well as technical subjects explained to a broad audience in non-technical terms.
**Readers:** Graduates of Colorado School of Mines, who are members of the Alumni Association.
**Deadline:** story-EOM prior to pub. date; news-EOM prior to pub. date; photo-EOM prior to pub. date; ads-15th of mo., prior to pub. date

### MISSOURI ENGINEER, THE
22602
330 E. High St., 2nd Fl.
Jefferson City, MO 65101
Telephone: (314) 636-6949
FAX: (314) 636-5475
Year Established: 1937
Pub. Frequency: 10/yr.
Page Size: tabloid
Subscrip. Rate: $1/yr. member; $12/yr. non-member
Freelance Pay: 15% commission
Circulation: 3,700
Circulation Type: paid
**Owner(s):**
Missouri Society of Professional Engineers
330 E. High St.
Jefferson Cy, MO 65101
Telephone: (314) 636-4861
Ownership %: 100
**Management:**
Paul E. Jobe .........................Publisher
Cherie Bishop ..............Executive Director
**Editorial:**
Cherie Bishop .............................Editor
**Desc.:** Edited for, by and about registered professional engineers in Missouri in all engineering fields-private practice, industry, government, education and construction. News and feature stories of interest to these readers are used each month from local, state and national levels. Features by professional engineers carry by-lines, and articles contributed by those who are not members of the professional engineering society also have by-lines. The majority of news stories and editorial comment is prepared by staff. Photos are used as much as possible. Features are usually 1 or 2 pages in length. Publicity material is used if it has local interest, as space permits.
**Readers:** Members of the Missouri Society of Professional Engineers; Missouri registered engineering, architectural and land surveying corporations; city public works directors; county engineers; selected state and federal agencies; state and federal legislators; members of selected organizations.

### NEW YORK PROFESSIONAL ENGINEER
22609
150 State St.
Albany, NY 12207
Telephone: (518) 465-7386
Year Established: 1943
Pub. Frequency: bi-m.
Page Size: standard
Subscrip. Rate: $.40 issue; $2/yr. members; $4/yr. non-members
Circulation: 4,000
Circulation Type: controlled & paid
**Owner(s):**
NYS Soc. of Prof. Engineers
150 State St.
Albany, NY 12207
Telephone: (518) 465-7386
Ownership %: 100
**Management:**
Jacquelyn M. Creech ........Advertising Manager

**Editorial:**
Christine M. Sikora ..............Managing Editor
Gina Sayward ........................Miscellaneous
Christine M. Sikora ....................News Editor
Christine M. Sikora ..............................Photo
Christine M. Sikora ..............Technical Editor
**Desc.:** Professional features. Brief articles of professional interest. By-lines used for articles prepared by other than staff.
**Readers:** New York state registered and graduate engineers, engineering students.

### NOISE/NEWS INTERNATIONAL
22611
P.O. Box 2469, Arlington Branch
Poughkeepsie, NY 12603
Year Established: 1972
Pub. Frequency: q.
Page Size: standard
Subscrip. Rate: $40/yr.
Materials: 01,06,10,30,32
Print Process: web offset
Circulation: 4,300
Circulation Type: paid
**Owner(s):**
Institute of Noise Control Eng.
P.O. Box 3206, Arlington Brnch
Poughkeepsie, NY 12603
Telephone: (914) 462-4006
Ownership %: 100
**Editorial:**
G. C. Maling .........................Managing Editor
**Desc.:** Articles concerning acoustical noise control. Departments include: Books, Government Reports, Contract Info. & Awards, Product News, and Standard News.
**Readers:** Engineers concerned with noise control.
**Deadline:** story-1 mo.; news-1 mo.; photo-1 mo.; ads-1 mo.

### NOISE CONTROL ENGINEERING JOURNAL
22610
Dept. of Mechanical Engineering
Auburn University
Auburn, AL 36849
Telephone: (205) 844-3306
FAX: (205) 844-3307
Year Established: 1973
Pub. Frequency: bi-m.
Page Size: standard
Subscrip. Rate: $60/yr. US; $87/yr. foreign
Circulation: 2,100
Circulation Type: paid
**Owner(s):**
Institute of Noise Control Engineering
P.O. Box 3206
Poughkeepsie, NY 12603
Telephone: (914) 462-4006
Ownership %: 100
**Editorial:**
Dr. George Maling .........................Editor
Lee Wilkins ..........................Assistant Editor
Rebecca Haack ......................Assistant Editor
**Desc.:** Publishes authoritative, refereed, technical articles which demonstrate effective engineering approaches to a variety of problems involving noise control in transportation, industry, products. Articles combining theoretical and experimental means of efficiently solving noise problems are particularly welcome. An article must either demonstrate a good engineering solution to a noise problem, describe a new approach in the state of the art in a specific noise area, or summarize recent findings, if it is a review. NCEJ will also publish articles in fields that are closely related to the work of noise control engineers (hearing protection, etc.).
**Readers:** Industry 60%; consulting 20%; universities 10%; government 10%.

### OHIO ENGINEERING
22614
445 King Ave.
Columbus, OH 43201
Telephone: (614) 424-6640
FAX: (614) 421-1257
Year Established: 1943
Pub. Frequency: bi-m.
Page Size: standard
Subscrip. Rate: $15/yr. for non-members
Circulation: 3500
Circulation Type: controlled & paid
**Owner(s):**
Ohio Society of Professional Engineers
445 King Ave.
Columbus, OH 43201
Telephone: (614) 424-6640
Ownership %: 100
**Editorial:**
Paula Hammer .............................Editor
**Desc.:** Covers legislative matters, society news, engineering products and design, calendar of upcoming evients and continuing education programs for engineers.
**Readers:** Registered professional engineers, in industry, construction, education, research, environmental protection and private practice; municipal, county and state government officials.

### OKLAHOMA PROFESSIONAL ENGINEER
22616
201 NE 27th St.
Oklahoma City, OK 73105
Telephone: (405) 528-1435
Year Established: 1947
Pub. Frequency: bi-m.
Page Size: tabloid
Subscrip. Rate: $6/yr.
Circulation: 1,000
Circulation Type: paid
**Owner(s):**
Oklahoma Society of Professional Engineers
201 N. E. 27-Room 125
Oklahoma City, OK 73105
Telephone: (405) 528-1435
Ownership %: 100
**Management:**
Ok. Society of Prof. Engineers ...........Publisher
**Editorial:**
Noel Long ..............................Editor in Chief
**Desc.:** Professional society official journal. Member news, society news, features, president's comments, staff columns.
**Readers:** Professional engineer members in construction, industry, government, education and private consulting.

### OPTICAL MATERIALS & ENGINEERING NEWS
66133
25 Van Zant St.
Norwalk, CT 06855
Telephone: (203) 853-4266
FAX: (203) 853-0348
Year Established: 1990
Pub. Frequency: m.
Page Size: standard
Subscrip. Rate: $305/yr.
**Owner(s):**
Louis Naturman
25 Van Zant St.
Norwalk, CT 06855
Telephone: (203) 853-4266
Ownership %: 100
**Management:**
Robert Butler .............................Manager
**Editorial:**
Richard Bryant .............................Editor

**Desc.:** Provides monthly new product news-technology information and analysis-market data-company information.
**Readers:** Commercial development, corporate management, technical management/research and market research people.

### POWDER & BULK ENGINEERING
68841
1300 E. 66th St.
Minneapolis, MN 54230
Telephone: (612) 866-2242
FAX: (612) 866-1939
Year Established: 1987
Pub. Frequency: m.
Page Size: standard
Subscrip. Rate: free to qualified; $60/yr. for non-qualified
Circulation: 35,242
Circulation Type: controlled & paid
**Owner(s):**
CSC Publishing, Inc.
1300 E. 66th St.
Minneapolis, MN 55423
Telephone: (612) 866-2242
Ownership %: 100
**Editorial:**
Sherri Weiss .............................Editor

### QUALITY PROGRESS
23464
611 E. Wisconsin Ave.
Milwaukee, WI 53202
Telephone: (414) 272-8575
Mailing Address:
  P.O. Box 3005
  Milwaukee, WI 53201-3005
Year Established: 1944
Pub. Frequency: m.
Page Size: standard
Subscrip. Rate: $50/yr.
Materials: 02,06,10,15,25,28,29,32,33
Print Process: web
Circulation: 125,000
Circulation Type: controlled & paid
**Owner(s):**
American Society for Quality Control, Inc.
611 E. Wisconsin Ave.
Milwaukee, WI 53202
Telephone: (414) 272-8575
FAX: (414) 272-1734
Ownership %: 100
**Editorial:**
Brad Stratton .............................Editor
Robert Brezenski ......................Advertising
Joan Schuelke ..........................Advertising
Pat Serketich ..........................Advertising
Janelle Dougherty ....................Advertising
Jon Brecka ........................Assistant Editor
Karen Bemowski ...................Associate Editor
Laura Rubach ..................Book Review Editor
Cathy Schnackenberg ...........Production Editor
**Desc.:** Contains articles of a semi-technical nature. Articles discuss techniques and philosophies pertaining to quality control/quality assurance in manufacturing and service industries. Special issues - QA/QC Software Directory(March); Services Directory (August).
**Readers:** Quality sciences professionals, management.
**Deadline:** news-3 mos. prior to pub. date; ads-1 mo. prior

### SMPTE JOURNAL
25034
595 W. Hartsdale Ave.
White Plains, NY 10607
Telephone: (914) 761-1100
Year Established: 1916
Pub. Frequency: m.
Page Size: standard
Subscrip. Rate: $75/yr.
Circulation: 11,000

**Materials Accepted/Included:** 01-Business news 02-By-line articles 03-Fashion news 04-Food news 05-Freelance copy 06-Letters to editor 07-Real estate news 08-Sports news 09-Travel news 10-Book rev. 11-Movie rev. 12-Music rev. 13-TV rev. 14-Theater rev. 15-Coming events 16-Obituaries 17-Question & answer 18-Social announcements 19-Artwork 20-Cartoons 21-Photos 22-TV listings 23-Audio rec. 24-Video rec. 25-Books 26-Films/film clips 27-Personnel news 28-Press releases 29-New product news/photos 30-Trade lit. 31-Contracts awarded 32-Display adv. 33-Classified adv.

4-129

Circulation Type: paid
**Owner(s):**
Society of Motion Picture & Television
Engineers
595 W. Hartsdale Ave.
White Plains, NY 10607
Telephone: (914) 761-1100
Ownership %: 100
**Management:**
Alan Ehrlich .......................Advertising Manager
**Editorial:**
Jeffrey B. Friedman ................................Editor
**Desc.:** Covers technical and scientific
aspects of motion picture and television
engineering, and related fields.
Departments include: News and Reports
Section, New Products Column, Book
Reviews, News of Persons and
Organizations in the Industry.
**Readers:** Members of the Society of
Motion Picture and Television Engineers.

22632

**SOUND & VIBRATION**
27101 E. Oviatt Rd.
Cleveland, OH 44140
Telephone: (216) 835-0101
FAX: (216) 835-9303
Mailing Address:
P.O. Box 40416
Cleveland, OH 44140
Year Established: 1967
Pub. Frequency: m.
Page Size: standard
Subscrip. Rate: free/qualified in US;
$20/yr. US; $25/yr. Canada; $60 yr.
foreign
Circulation: 20,875
Circulation Type: free & paid
**Owner(s):**
Acoustical Publications, Inc.
P.O. Box 40416
Cleveland, OH 44140
Telephone: (216) 835-0101
Ownership %: 100
**Management:**
Jack Mowry ...........................................Publisher
Nancy Ormsby ..................Circulation Manager
**Editorial:**
Jack Mowry ..............................................Editor
Lisa King ........................New Production Editor
Lisa King ....................................News Editor
**Desc.:** Contains technical information on
noise and vibration control, structural
analysis, machinery monitoring, dynamic
measurements and dynamic testing.
**Readers:** Individuals who are concerned
with noise and vibration control.
Individuals in manufacturing industries,
nonmanufacturing industries
and government who are concerned
with one or more of the fields served.

59137

**TV TECHNOLOGY**
5827 Columbia Pike, Ste. 310
Falls Church, VA 22041
Telephone: (703) 998-7600
FAX: (703) 998-2966
Mailing Address:
P.O. Box 1214
Falls Church, VA 22041
Year Established: 1983
Pub. Frequency: m.
Page Size: tabloid
Subscrip. Rate: free to qualified
subscribers
Freelance Pay: negotiable
Circulation: 50,000
Circulation Type: controlled
**Owner(s):**
Stevan B. Dana
P.O. Box 1214
Falls Church, VA 22041
Telephone: (703) 998-7600
Ownership %: 100

**Bureau(s):**
TV Technology-Natl.
64 Eastern Ave.
Ossining, NY 10562
Telephone: (914) 762-3572
FAX: (914) 762-3107
Contact: Michael S. Dahle, Sales Manager

TV Technology
104 Winding Canyon Ln.
Folsom, CA 95630
Telephone: (916) 988-8558
FAX: (916) 988-4052
Contact: Jack Ducart, Sales Manager

TV Technology
2856 N. Burling St., Unit 2
Chicago, IL 60657
Telephone: (312) 327-3192
FAX: (312) 327-3193
Contact: Gene Kinsella, Sales Manager

TV Technology
50 Deanna Dr.
Ste. 140
Somerville, NJ 08876
Telephone: (908) 281-5785
FAX: (908) 281-5795
Contact: Eric Trabb, Sales Manager
**Management:**
Stevan B. Dana ...................................Publisher
Lisa Lyons ........................Production Manager
**Editorial:**
Richard Farrell ......................................Editor
Marlene Lane .....................Editorial Director
Carmel King ......................Associate Publisher
Art Cole ...............................International Editor
**Desc.:** Edited for engineering, operations,
management personnel in professional
video facilities. Features and news are
of a technical nature and cover topics
ranging from high technology
developments through maintenance and
new product introductions.
**Readers:** Engineering, production and
general management personnel at TV
stations, production and post production
houses, corporate and industrial
facilities, and cable companies.

52673

**U.S. WOMAN ENGINEER**
120 Wall St.
New York, NY 10005
Telephone: (212) 509-9577
FAX: (212) 509-0224
Year Established: 1951
Pub. Frequency: bi-m.
Page Size: standard
Subscrip. Rate: $20/yr.
Freelance Pay: negotiable
Circulation: 16,000
Circulation Type: controlled
**Owner(s):**
Society of Women Engineers
120 Wall St.
New York, NY 10005
Telephone: (212) 509-9577
Ownership %: 100
**Management:**
B. J. Harrod ........................Managing Director
**Editorial:**
Anne Perusek ........................Managing Editor
**Readers:** Engineering students,
professional engineers, corporate
engineering staff, engineering firms, and
technical societies.

## Group 074-Entertainment

69001

**AMERICAN PREMIERE MAGAZINE**
8421 Wilshire Blvd., Penthouse Ste.
Beverly Hills, CA 90211
Telephone: (213) 852-0434
Year Established: 1979
Pub. Frequency: bi-m.

Page Size: standard
Subscrip. Rate: $4 newsstand; $16/yr.
Materials: 10,25,32
Circulation: 17,500
Circulation Type: paid
**Owner(s):**
American Premiere, Ltd.
8421 Wilshire Blvd.
Penthouse Ste.
Beverly Hills, CA 90211
Telephone: (213) 852-0434
Ownership %: 100
**Editorial:**
Susan Royal ........................................Editor
**Desc.:** Film industry.

24285

**AMUSEMENT BUSINESS**
49 Music Square, W.
Nashville, TN 37203
Telephone: (615) 321-4267
FAX: (615) 327-1575
Mailing Address:
P.O. Box 24970
Nashville, TN 37202
Year Established: 1894
Pub. Frequency: w.
Page Size: tabloid
Subscrip. Rate: $105/yr.
Freelance Pay: negotiable
Circulation: 11,806
Circulation Type: paid
**Owner(s):**
BPI Communications
P.O. Box 24970
Nashville, TN 37202
Telephone: (615) 321-4250
Ownership %: 100
**Bureau(s):**
Amusement Business
9107 Wilshire Blvd.
Beverly Hills , CA 90210
Telephone: (310) 273-7040
Contact: Linda Deckard

Amusement Business
150 N. Wacker Dr.
Chicago, IL 60606
Telephone: (312) 236-9818
Contact: Louise Zepp, Reporter

Amusement Business
1515 Broadway
New York, NY 10036
Telephone: (212) 536-5188
Contact: Candice Carmel, Reporter
**Management:**
Karen Oertley ...................................Publisher
Beth Jenkins .....................Advertising Manager
Anne Massei .....................Circulation Manager
Ray Pilszak ........................Sales Manager
**Editorial:**
Lisa Zhito ........................Managing Editor
Gina Keena ........................Production Director
Ray Waddell ........................................Reporter
Gary Coffey ..................Special Projects Editor
**Desc.:** Trade publication supplying
management in the sports business and
mass entertainment industry news on
events, attendance, talent, promotions,
spending, as well as news on carnivals
and circuses. Departments include:
Arenas & Auditoriums, Funparks, Fairs,
Talent, Promotions, Food & Drink,
Souvenir/Novelty, Carnivals & Circuses.
Covers everything of importance to
management in the permanently located
amusement-recreation fields, including
auditoriums, arenas, coliseums,
amusement and mobile parks,
kiddieland, tourist attractions,
government parks, circuses, carnivals,
fairs. Departments include: Talent,
Management, Maintenance, Promotion,
General News, Funparks, Shows.

**Readers:** Owner, operators, managers and
concessionaires, fairs, circuses,
carnivals, food, promoters, booking
agents, manufacturers, distributors,
sports franchises.

22136

**AUD ARENA STADIUM
INTERNATIONAL GUIDE**
49 Music Sq. W.
Nashville, TN 37203
Telephone: (615) 321-4250
FAX: (615) 320-5407
Mailing Address:
P.O. Box 24970
Nashville, TN 37202
Pub. Frequency: a.
Page Size: standard
Subscrip. Rate: $75/copy
Circulation: 8,400
Circulation Type: controlled
**Owner(s):**
BPI Communications, Inc.
49 Music Sq. W.
Nashville, TN 37203
Telephone: (615) 321-4250
Ownership %: 100
**Management:**
Karen Oertley ...................................Publisher
Beth Jenkins .....................Advertising Manager
Daniel Bale ........................................Manager
Gina Keena ........................Operations Manager
**Desc.:** Directory of over 6,000 arenas,
auditoriums, stadiums, exhibit halls and
coliseums in the U.S., Canada, most of
Europe, South America, and other
nations. Complete data on
facilities available for concerts, sporting
events, meetings, exhibitions,
demonstrations, etc. Lists provide
contacts, seating capacities, floor size
and services offered. Also included are
listings of companies who offer services
or supplies to facilities.
**Readers:** Top management associated
with arenas & facilities of events,
professional and major college sports,
booking agents & promoters.

25023

**BOXOFFICE**
6640 Sunset Blvd., Ste. 100
Los Angeles, CA 90028
Telephone: (213) 465-1186
FAX: (213) 465-5049
Year Established: 1920
Pub. Frequency: m.
Page Size: standard
Subscrip. Rate: $40/yr.
Freelance Pay: $75-$150/article
Circulation: 8,000
Circulation Type: paid
**Owner(s):**
R.L.D. Publications, Inc.
P.O. Box 25485
Chicago, IL 60625
Telephone: (312) 271-0425
Ownership %: 100
**Management:**
Robert L. Dietmeier ..........................Publisher
Robert Vale ........................Advertising Manager
**Editorial:**
Ray Greene ........................Senior Editor
Harley W. Lond ......................................Editor
Marilyn Moss ........................Associate Editor
Harley W. Lond ..................Associate Publisher

**Materials Accepted/Included:** 01-Business news 02-By-line articles 03-Fashion news 04-Food news 05-Freelance copy 06-Letters to editor 07-Real estate news 08-Sports news 09-Travel news
10-Book rev. 11-Movie rev. 12-Music rev. 13-TV rev. 14-Theater rev. 15-Coming events 16-Obituaries 17-Question & answer 18-Social announcements 19-Artwork 20-Cartoons 21-Photos 22-TV listings
23-Audio rec. 24-Video rec. 25-Books 26-Films/film clips 27-Personnel news 28-Press releases 29-New product news/photos 30-Trade lit. 31-Contracts awarded 32-Display adv. 33-Classified adv.

4-130

**Desc.:** News, developments, legislation, campaigns, new films, personality profiles, articles on movies and movie-makers, regional news of the motion picture industry. The Modern Theatre section covers construction, equipment, maintenance, concessions, new technologies. InVideo supplement covers news and reviews of latest prerecorded videotape movies. Seeking illustrated features on concessions merchandising in theatres; theatre remodeling, new theatres.
**Readers:** Motion picture industry.

22738
### DANCE MAGAZINE
33 W. 60th St.
New York, NY 10023
Telephone: (212) 245-9050
FAX: (212) 956-6487
Year Established: 1926
Pub. Frequency: m.
Page Size: standard
Subscrip. Rate: $3.95 newsstand; $29.95/yr.; $54.90/2 yrs.
Materials: 01,02,06,10,13,14,15,16,21,22, 24,25,28,32,33
Circulation: 54,000
Circulation Type: paid
**Owner(s):**
Dance Magazine, Inc.
33 W. 60th St.
New York, NY 10023
Telephone: (212) 245-9050
FAX: (212) 956-6487
Ownership %: 100
**Management:**
Robert Stern .................................President
Roslyne Paige Stern .....................Publisher
Rita Brandt .......................Advertising Manager
Sondra Weintraub ..............Circulation Manager
**Editorial:**
Richard Philp ....................Editor in Chief
Joan Mischon .................Assistant Chief Editor
Gary Parks ......................Associate Editor
Marian Horosko ...................Associate Editor
Robert Johnson ....................Associate Editor
Marilyn Hunt ......................Associate Editor
Harris Green ......................Associate Editor
Herbert Migdoll ...........................Design
**Desc.:** Regular coverage of dance books, records, television, health, technique, films, travel, fashion/beauty and lifestyle for the dancer. Editorial includes national/international news reports; reviews of dance performances; monthly feature articles on dance companies and their current stars; historical viewpoints on the dance and its pioneer personalities; educational/technical material concerning dance training. Also emphasizes calendar information for upcoming performances and training programs across the country. It is the oldest, continuously published arts publication in the world.
**Readers:** Performers, patrons, educators, students, choreographers in the dance community.
**Deadline:** story-3 mo. prior to pub. date; news-3 mo. prior; photo-3 mo. prior

61600
### DANCE TEACHER NOW
3020 Beacon Blvd.
West Sacramento, CA 95691-1964
Telephone: (916) 373-0201
FAX: (916) 373-0232
Year Established: 1979
Pub. Frequency: 9/yr.
Subscrip. Rate: $24/yr. US; $40/yr. foreign
Circulation: 6,000
Circulation Type: paid

**Owner(s):**
SMW Communications, Inc.
3020 Beacon Blvd.
West Sacramento, CA 95691-1964
Telephone: (916) 373-0201
Ownership %: 100
**Editorial:**
K.C. Patrick ..................................Editor
Diane Wershing ................Production Assistant
Sue Abdi .......................................Sales

49917
### GAMING & WAGERING BUSINESS
Seven Penn Plz.
New York, NY 10001-3900
Telephone: (212) 594-4120
FAX: (212) 714-0514
Year Established: 1980
Pub. Frequency: m.
Page Size: tabloid
Subscrip. Rate: $6/issue; $60/yr.
Freelance Pay: $.15/wd.
Circulation: 10,500
Circulation Type: paid
**Owner(s):**
T/SF Communications
2407 E. Skelly Dr.
Tulsa, OK 74105
Telephone: (918) 747-2600
Ownership %: 100
**Bureau(s):**
BMT Publications, Inc.
221 Mountain View Ave.
Scotch Plains , NJ 07076
Telephone: (908) 889-2376
Contact: Betsy McQuade
**Management:**
Hedy Halpert .............................President
Daniel N. Petrocelli .................Vice President
Bruce Smith ...............................Publisher
Daniel N. Petrocelli ...............General Manager
**Editorial:**
Paul Dworin .................................Editor
Bruce Smith ..................................Sales
**Desc.:** Deals with the major issues, hard news and fast breaking developments affecting the various segments of the legalized gambling and wagering industry. Emphasis is placed on the needs of executives in the areas of business strategy, marketing, finance, licensing, government regulations, security, credit, real estate, food service, entertainment, consumer research and promotional activities.
**Readers:** Serves executives involved in all segments of the legalized gambling and wagering industry as well as financial executives and government legislators and regulators.

69629
### ILLINOIS ENTERTAINER
1319 W. Locust
Fairbury, IL 61739
Telephone: (708) 298-9333
FAX: (708) 298-7973
Year Established: 1974
Pub. Frequency: m.
Subscrip. Rate: $25/yr.
Circulation: 80,000
Circulation Type: paid
**Owner(s):**
Illinois Entertainer
**Editorial:**
Michael Harris ...............................Editor
**Desc.:** Covers the music, film and video industries in the Chicago area and nationally.

69006
### IN MOTION
1201 Seven Locks Rd.
Ste. 300
Potomac, MD 20854-2937
Telephone: (301) 340-1520
FAX: (301) 340-0542

Year Established: 1981
Pub. Frequency: m.
Subscrip. Rate: $27.95/yr.
Materials: 01,06,15,23,24,25,26,27, 28,29,30,31,32,33
Freelance Pay: $300-1200
Circulation: 30,000
Circulation Type: controlled
**Owner(s):**
Phillips Business Information Inc.
1201 Seven Locks Rd.
Ste. 300
Potomac, MD 20854
Telephone: (301) 340-1520
Ownership %: 100
**Bureau(s):**
Southeast Bureau
4514 Chamblee Dunwoody Rd.
Ste. 271
Atlanta, GA 30338
Telephone: (404) 451-4295
FAX: (404) 451-8545
Contact: Diane Butler, Marketing Manager


U.K. Bureau
The Garden Suite, Pinewood Stu
Pinewood Rd.
SLOONH Iner, Heath Bucks United Kingdom
Telephone: 44-753-650-101
FAX: 44-753-650-111
Contact: Alan Lowne, Marketing Manager


Western Bureau
Telephone: (303) 470-0582
Contact: Brian Tellingwisen, Marketing Manager
**Editorial:**
Allison Dollar ................................Editor
**Desc.:** Reports on equipment, trends, people in the film and video production industry. Covers production, postproduction, multimedia, VR, and production support services as well as surveys of segments of the industry.
**Deadline:** story-23rd of mo. prior to pub. date; news-17th of mo. prior; photo-30th of mo. prior; ads-5th of mo. prior

54082
### JOURNAL OF ARTS MANAGEMENT, LAW, & SCIENCE, THE
1319 18th St., N.W.
Washington, DC 20036
Telephone: (202) 296-6267
FAX: (202) 296-5149
Year Established: 1969
Pub. Frequency: q.
Page Size: pocket
Subscrip. Rate: $43/yr. individuals; $86/yr. institutions; add $10 outside of US
Circulation: 509
Circulation Type: paid
**Owner(s):**
Heldref Publications
1319 18th St., N.W.
Washington, DC 20036-1802
Telephone: (202) 296-6267
**Management:**
Walter E. Beach .............................Publisher
Raymond M. Rallo ..........Advertising Manager
Catherine Welker ............Circulation Manager
Kerri P. Kilbane ..............Promotion Manager
**Editorial:**
Zell Rosenfelt ...............................Editor

**Desc.:** Has become an authoritative resource for the field of performing, visual, and media arts in particular and cultural affairs more generally. Articles, commentary, and book reviews address current and ongoing issues in arts policy, management, law and governance from a range of philosophical and national perspectives encompassing diverse disciplinary viewpoints.
**Readers:** Artists, public and private policy makers, cultural administrators, trustees, patrons, scholars, educators and lawyers.

54079
### JOURNAL OF POPULAR FILM & TELEVISION
1319 18th St., N.W.
Washington, DC 20036-1802
Telephone: (202) 296-6267
FAX: (202) 296-5149
Year Established: 1971
Pub. Frequency: q.
Page Size: standard
Subscrip. Rate: $32/yr. individuals; $62/yr. institutions
Circulation: 800
Circulation Type: paid
**Owner(s):**
Heldref Publications
1319 18th St., N.W.
Washington, DC 20036-1802
Telephone: (202) 296-6267
**Management:**
Walter E. Beach .............................Publisher
Raymond M. Rallo ..........Advertising Manager
Catherine Welker ............Circulation Manager
Kerri P. Kilbane ..............Promotion Manager
**Editorial:**
Zell Rosenfelt ...............................Editor
**Desc.:** Reflecting interest in popular culture studies, treats commercial films and television from a socio-cultural perspective. Its editors seek thoughtful articles on stars, directors, producers, studios, networks, genres, series and the audience.
**Readers:** Teachers and students of film & television as well as general appeal to those people interested in all areas of popular culture studies.

69538
### LINKING RING
348 S. Wishire Ln.
Arlington Heights, IL 60004
Telephone: (708) 577-7337
Year Established: 1923
Pub. Frequency: m.
Subscrip. Rate: membership
Circulation: 13,000
Circulation Type: controlled
**Owner(s):**
International Brotherhood of Magicians
348 S. Wishire Ln.
Arlington Heights, IL 60004
Telephone: (708) 577-7337
Ownership %: 100
**Editorial:**
Philip R. Willmarth ..................Executive Editor

69007
### LOCATION UPDATE
2301 Bellevue Ave.
HollywLoLos Angeles, CA 90026-4017
Telephone: (213) 461-8887
FAX: (213) 469-3711
Year Established: 1985
Pub. Frequency: m.
Subscrip. Rate: $25.95/yr. US; $49.95/yr. foreign
Circulation: 30,000
Circulation Type: controlled

---

**Materials Accepted/Included:** 01-Business news 02-By-line articles  03-Fashion news  04-Food news  05-Freelance copy  06-Letters to editor  07-Real estate news  08-Sports news 09-Travel news 10-Book rev. 11-Movie rev. 12-Music rev. 13-TV rev. 14-Theater rev. 15-Coming events 16-Obituaries 17-Question & answer 18-Social announcements 19-Artwork 20-Cartoons 21-Photos 22-TV listings 23-Audio rec. 24-Video rec. 25-Books 26-Films/film clips 27-Personnel news  28-Press releases  29-New product news/photos 30-Trade lit. 31-Contracts awarded 32-Display adv. 33-Classified adv.

**Owner(s):**
Location Update, Inc.
6922 Hollywood Blvd., Ste. 612
Hollywood, CA 90028
Telephone: (213) 461-8887
Ownership %: 100
**Desc.:** Covers elements that evolve when filming and video taping on local and distant location, as well as studios and soundstages.

69008

## MARKEE
655 Fulton St., Ste. Nine
Sanford, FL 32771-1100
Telephone: (407) 324-1733
FAX: (407) 324-1766
Year Established: 1986
Pub. Frequency: m.
Page Size: standard
Subscrip. Rate: $34/yr.
Materials: 01,02,05,06,15,21,28,29,30,31, 32,33
Freelance Pay: varies
Circulation: 16,500
Circulation Type: controlled
**Owner(s):**
HJK Publications, Inc.
655 Fulton St., Ste. 9
Sanford, FL 32771
Telephone: (407) 324-1733
Ownership %: 100
**Editorial:**
Janet Karcher ............................Editor
**Desc.:** For the Southeast and Southwest film and video industries.
**Deadline:** story-10th of mo. prior to pub. date; news-10th of mo. prior to pub. date; photo-10th of mo. prior; ads-10th of mo. prior

25030

## MILLIMETER
826 Broadway
New York, NY 10003
Telephone: (212) 477-4700
Year Established: 1973
Pub. Frequency: m.
Page Size: standard
Subscrip. Rate: $50/yr.
Freelance Pay: $100-$750/article
Circulation: 30,000
Circulation Type: controlled
**Owner(s):**
Penton Publishing
1100 Superior Ave.
Cleveland, OH 44114
Telephone: (216) 696-7000
Ownership %: 100
**Bureau(s):**
Penton Publishing
16255 Ventura Blvd.
Van Nuys, CA 91436
Telephone: (818) 990-9000
Contact: Victoria Stewart

Penton Publishing
233 N. Michigan Ave., Ste 1300
Chicago, IL 60601
Telephone: (312) 861-0880
Contact: Jeff Victor

Millimeter Magazine
501 Santa Monica Blvd.
Santa Monica, CA 90401
Telephone: (310) 393-9285
Contact: Herb Schiff
**Management:**
Philip Hubbard ......................Vice President
Sam Kintzer ...............................Publisher
Jack Rudd ......................Promotion Manager
**Editorial:**
Alison Jones ..................Editor in Chief
Lisa Vincenzi ...................Senior Editor
Greg Solman ...................Senior Editor
Bruce Stockler .................Senior Editor
Mark Lang ...................Managing Editor

John Browning ......................Art Director
Barbara Schwartz ...............Production Editor
Dan Ochiva ..........................Technical Editor
**Desc.:** Feature story magazine devoted to the professionals, producers and creatives, working in films, commercials, TV programs, and other related fields such as animation, documentary, special effects, music, etc. Emphasis is on production techniques, technology and commerce associated with the film and television industry.
**Readers:** Professionals in TV broadcast production, film production & television commercial industries.

69632

## ON PRODUCTION & POST-PRODUCTION
17337 Ventura Blvd., Ste. 226
Encino, CA 91316
Telephone: (818) 907-6682
Year Established: 1992
Pub. Frequency: 8/yr.
Subscrip. Rate: $36/yr. US; $58/yr. foreign
Circulation: 20,000
Circulation Type: paid
**Owner(s):**
On Production, Inc.
17337 Ventura Blvd., Ste. 226
Encino, CA 91316
Telephone: (818) 907-6682
Ownership %: 100
**Editorial:**
Howard Kunin ...........................Editor
**Desc.:** News, trends and feature stories on the latest developments in the production and post-production industry.
**Readers:** Producers, directors, production managers, video facility managers, editors, agents and post-production executives.

69009

## PRODUCER
25 Willowdale Ave.
Port Washington, NY 11050
Telephone: (516) 767-2500
FAX: (516) 767-9335
Year Established: 1990
Pub. Frequency: bi-m.
Page Size: standard
Subscrip. Rate: $4.00 newsstand; $15/yr.
Materials: 01,02,05,21,24,26,27,28,29,30, 31,32
Freelance Pay: $350/1200 wds.
Circulation: 15,000
Circulation Type: paid
**Owner(s):**
Testa Communications, Inc.
25 Willowdale Ave.
Port Washington, NY 11050
Telephone: (516) 767-2500
FAX: (516) 767-9335
Ownership %: 100
**Editorial:**
Randi Altman ...............Executive Editor
Ken McGorry ...........................Editor
**Readers:** Producers, directors, editors, videographers, composers.

25036

## TCI
32 W. 18th St.
New York, NY 10011
Telephone: (212) 229-2965
FAX: (212) 229-2084
Year Established: 1967
Pub. Frequency: 10/yr.
Page Size: tabloid
Subscrip. Rate: $5/copy; $24.95/yr.
Materials: 01,02,05,06,10,11,12,13,14,15, 16,19,21,23,24,25,28,29,30,31,32,33
Freelance Pay: varies
Circulation: 27,000
Circulation Type: paid

**Owner(s):**
Entertainment Technology Communications Corp.
32 W. 18th St.
New York, NY 10011
Telephone: (212) 229-2965
FAX: (212) 229-2084
Ownership %: 100
**Management:**
Patricia J. MacKay ......................Publisher
Harvey Swaine ...............Circulation Manager
**Editorial:**
David Barbour ...........................Editor
Joanne Hixson ......................Art Director
Jacqueline Tien ...............Associate Publisher
John Calhoun ......................Film Editor
Karl Ruling ......................Technical Editor
**Desc.:** Deals with all aspects of theatre, films, TV, video, except acting and directing. 4-5 features per issue deal with lighting, costume, set, and makeup design; theatre architecture and administration. 50% staff and 50% free-lance contributions. Interested in publicity materials in so far as they would be the basis of a story we might assign to someone in the field. General article length about 2,000 words. Photos, sketches, drawings, etc. must accompany. Departments include: News, Notes and Reviews of Theatre Productions, Broadway, Regional Rep, Education, New Products, New Literature, Book Reviews, Shop Talk-Technical Nuts and Bolts, Safety, Working Profiles, Media File, Training, Buying Guides.
**Readers:** Designers and technicians working with lighting and sound, sets and costumes for stage and studio productions.

65267

## TELEVISION BUSINESS INTERNATIONAL
6400 Hollis, Ste. 12
Emeryville, CA 94608
Telephone: (415) 653-3307
Year Established: 1988
Pub. Frequency: m.
Page Size: standard
Subscrip. Rate: $90/yr.
Circulation: 10,000
Circulation Type: paid
**Owner(s):**
Act III Publishing
6400 Hollis, Ste. 12
Emeryville, CA 94608
Telephone: (415) 653-3307

Television Business International
401 Park Ave., S.
New York, NY 10016
Telephone: (212) 545-5100
**Bureau(s):**
Television Business Int'l
531-533 Kings Rd.
London United Kingdom
Contact: Paul Nicholson, Managing Editor
**Management:**
Colby Coates ...........................Publisher
**Editorial:**
Les Brown ......................Editor in Chief
**Desc.:** A monthly business magazine that analyzes and interprets economic and political factors that affect all aspects of television commerce worldwide. Every month TBI provides a Focus section that takes on in-depth look at an important aspect of international television programming; country by country ratings analyses; a People to Watch report; and a Data section providing key financial, production and advertising statistics on television worldwide.

**Readers:** Television industry executives, financiers, investors and acquirers.

25035

## TELEVISION INTERNATIONAL MAGAZINE
P.O. Box 8471
Universal City, CA 91608
Telephone: (818) 795-8386
FAX: (818) 795-8436
Year Established: 1956
Pub. Frequency: bi-m.
Page Size: standard
Subscrip. Rate: $42/yr.
Materials: 06,10,13,21,22,25,28,29,32,33
Freelance Pay: negotiable
Circulation: 16,000
Circulation Type: controlled
**Owner(s):**
Television International Magazine
P.O. Box 8471
Universal City, CA 91608
Telephone: (818) 795-8386
Ownership %: 100
**Bureau(s):**
Television International
P.O. Box 2430
Los Angeles, CA 90028
Telephone: (213) 462-1099
Contact: Josie Cory, Editor
**Management:**
Josie Cory ...........................Publisher
**Editorial:**
Josie Cory ...........................Editor
Alden Stubblefield ......................Editor
Ginger Adams ......................Advertising
**Desc.:** Trade features in depth.
**Readers:** Television industry in 146 countries. Published since 1956.

25038

## THEATRE JOURNAL
2715 N. Charles St.
Baltimore, MD 21218-4319
Telephone: (410) 516-6982
FAX: (410) 516-6968
Year Established: 1949
Pub. Frequency: q.
Page Size: standard
Subscrip. Rate: $21/yr. individuals; $49.50/yr. institutions
Circulation: 4,000
Circulation Type: paid
**Owner(s):**
Johns Hopkins University Press, Journals Div.
2715 N. Charles St.
Baltimore, MD 21218-4319
Telephone: (410) 516-6982
Ownership %: 100
**Management:**
Tara Dorai-Berry ...............Advertising Manager
**Editorial:**
W.B. Worthen ...........................Editor
Janelle Reinelt ...........................Editor
Katherine Kelly ...............Book Review Editor
James S. Moy ......................Miscellaneous
Marie Hansen ...............Publication Director
Kate Devy ......................Theatrical Editor
**Desc.:** Provides an outlet for scholarship and criticism in the theatre arts. 150 pages per issue.
**Readers:** Scholars & educators in theatre studies and performing arts, practitioners in the performing arts, general readers in the field of drama, members of the Association for theatre in Higher Education.

24289

## TOURIST ATTRACTIONS & PARKS
7000 Terminal Sq., Ste. 210
Upper Darby, PA 19082
Telephone: (610) 734-2420
FAX: (610) 734-2423
Year Established: 1972
Pub. Frequency: 7/yr.

**Materials Accepted/Included:** 01-Business news 02-By-line articles 03-Fashion news 04-Food news 05-Freelance copy 06-Letters to editor 07-Real estate news 08-Sports news 09-Travel news 10-Book rev. 11-Movie rev. 12-Music rev. 13-TV rev. 14-Theater rev. 15-Coming events 16-Obituaries 17-Question & answer 18-Social announcements 19-Artwork 20-Cartoons 21-Photos 22-TV listings 23-Audio rec. 24-Video rec. 25-Books 26-Films/film clips 27-Personnel news 28-Press releases 29-New product news/photos 30-Trade lit. 31-Contracts awarded 32-Display adv. 33-Classified adv.

Page Size: standard
Subscrip. Rate: $10 newsstand; $25/yr.
Materials: 01,02,03,04,05,06,07,08,09,10,
　11,12,14,15,16,17,18,19,21,23,24,25,26,
　27,28,29,30
Freelance Pay: $150 max.
Print Process: web
Circulation: 27,000
Circulation Type: controlled & paid
Owner(s):
Kane Communications, Inc.
7000 Terminal Sq.
Upper Darby, PA 19082
Telephone: (610) 734-2420
FAX: (610) 734-2623
Ownership %: 100
Management:
Scott C. Borowsky ............................President
Janice Weiss ....................................Publisher
Janice Weiss ......................Advertising Manager
Editorial:
Sanford Meschkow ..............................Editor
Larry White ..................Associate Publisher
Desc.: Uses articles about tourist
　attractions, amusement parks, state and
　national parks, zoos, arenas, stadiums,
　carnivals, fairgrounds, arcades, concerts.
　Manager or executive is quoted on how
　they solved a particular problem, or
　initiated a significant change, or
　improved a practice. Departments
　include: Operations, Associations,
　Maintenance, New Products, Advertising.
Readers: Owners and managers of tourist
　attractions, carnivals, concert managers,
　concessionaires, arenas, fairgrounds,
　arcades, zoos, museums.
Deadline: story-45 days prior to pub. date;
　ads-30 days prior to pub. date

25039

## VARIETY
475 Park Ave., S.
New York, NY 10016
Telephone: (212) 779-1100
Year Established: 1906
Pub. Frequency: w.
Page Size: oversize
Subscrip. Rate: $149/yr.
Circulation: 55,000
Circulation Type: paid
Owner(s):
Cahners Publishing Co.
475 Park Ave.
New York, NY 10016-6901
Telephone: (212) 779-1100
Ownership %: 100
Bureau(s):
Asia-Pacific Bureau
Contact: Don Groves, Bureau Chief

Amsterdam Bureau
Contact: Chris Fuller, Bureau Chief

Washington, DC Bureau
Contact: Paul Harris, Bureau Chief

Montreal, PQ Bureau
Contact: Leonard Klady, Bureau Chief

Toronto, ON Bureau
Contact: Andy Marx, Bureau Chief

Rome, Italy Bureau
Contact: David Rooney, Bureau Chief
Management:
Gerry Byrne ....................................Publisher
Neal Vitale ..............................General Manager
Editorial:
Stephen West ........................Executive Editor
Max Alexander ......................Executive Editor
Jonathan Taylor ......................Managing Editor
Peter Bart ....................................Editorial Director
Susan Shields ..............Editorial Assistant
Robert Silverman ......................Staff Writer

Desc.: Reviews, critiques, news about
　people and developments. Covers the
　television and radio industry, motion
　picture, vaudeville, night clubs, and
　concerts.
Readers: Show business people, financial
　houses, entry and abroad.

## Group 076-Exports & Imports

22939

### ARTES GRAFICAS
1680 Bayshore Blvd., S.W.
Port St. Lucie, FL 34984-3598
Telephone: (407) 879-6666
FAX: (407) 879-7388
Year Established: 1967
Pub. Frequency: 9/yr.
Page Size: standard
Subscrip. Rate: $50/yr. US; $60/yr.
　elsewhere
Materials: 06,27,28,29,30,32,33,34
Freelance Pay: $150-$250
Print Process: web offset
Circulation: 23,000
Circulation Type: controlled
Owner(s):
Coast Publishing, Inc.
1680 Bayshore Blvd., S.W.
Port St. Lucie, FL 34984-3598
Telephone: (407) 879-6666
FAX: (407) 879-7388
Ownership %: 50

Carvajal International
901 Ponce de Leon Blvd.
Ste. 901
Coral Gables, FL 33134
Telephone: (305) 448-6875
FAX: (305) 448-9942
Ownership %: 50
Bureau(s):
USA/Coast Publishing, Inc.
1680 SW Bayshore Blvd.
Port St. Lucie, FL 34984-3498
Telephone: (407) 879-6666
FAX: (407) 879-7388
Contact: Juan Carlos Gayoso
Editorial:
Miguel Garzon ..................................Editor
Michael Steele ..........................Advertising
Renate Gauf ..............................Advertising
Juan Carlos Cayoso ......................Advertising
Matthew Whitehouse ..................Advertising
Francisco Piedrahita ......................Director
Cindi Schulman ............................Director
David Ashe ....................................Director
Rob Schweiger ............................Director
Juan Carlos Gayoso ............Int'l Sales Director
Desc.: Spanish-language magazine
　published by a joint venture between
　Coast Publishing, Inc. of the USA and
　Carvajal SA of Colombia. It is distributed
　to the printing, newspaper, and graphic
　arts professionals throughout Latin
　America (Mexico, Central, and South
　America).
Readers: Owners, managers,
　superintendents, technical and
　administrative personnels in the field of
　printing, newspaper and
　communications.

22941

### CHINA BUSINESS REVIEW, THE
1818 N. St., N.W., Ste. 500
Washington, DC 20036
Telephone: (202) 429-0340
FAX: (202) 775-2476
Year Established: 1974
Pub. Frequency: bi-m.
Subscrip. Rate: $96/yr.
Materials: 01,25,31
Circulation: 4,500
Circulation Type: paid

Owner(s):
China Business Forum
1818 N. St., N.W., Ste. 500
Washington, DC 20036
Telephone: (202) 429-0340
Ownership %: 100
Bureau(s):
China Business Review, The
18 Fl, Yue Xin Bldng.
160-174 Lockhart Rd, Wanchai
　Hong Kong
Contact: Karina Lam
Management:
Karina Lam ......................Advertising Manager
Caitlin Stewart Harris ........Circulation Manager
Jon Howard ......................Production Manager
Pamela Baldinger ..................Public Relations
　Manager
Editorial:
Pamela Baldinger ..................Editor in Chief
Amy Flynn ..............................Assistant Editor
Vanessa Lide ..........................Associate Editor
Desc.: Business with China and Hong
　Kong in all facets-economic, financial,
　import, export, legal, shipping, news of
　deals, major studies of sectors of
　Chinese economy, details of Sino-US
　trade relations and developments,
　emphasis on reasons for doing business
　with the PRC and Hong Kong.
Readers: Business people, governments,
　academics, financial planners.

22943

### DESARROLLO NACIONAL
25 Sylvan Rd., S.
Westport, CT 06880
Telephone: (203) 226-7463
FAX: (203) 222-8793
Mailing Address:
　P.O. Box 5017
　Westport, CT 06881
Year Established: 1952
Pub. Frequency: bi-m.
Page Size: standard
Subscrip. Rate: $29/issue; $50/yr.
Freelance Pay: $200
Circulation: 22,000
Circulation Type: controlled
Owner(s):
Intercontinental Media, Inc.
P.O. Box 5017
Westport, CT 06880
Telephone: (203) 226-7463
Ownership %: 100
Management:
James R. Coffey ....................................President
James R. Coffey ..................................Publisher
Mike Tomashefsky ..........Advertising Manager
Editorial:
Philip N. Anderson ......................Editor in Chief
Julio De La Torre ..................................Editor
Kathy Seymour ..................Production Director
Desc.: Contains articles on third world
　infrastructure and development including
　public works and planning,
　environmental sanitation, administration,
　public utilities, communications and
　public transportation, public health and
　safety, agricultural development and
　education in Spanish.
Readers: Technocrats and government
　officials in Latin America.

22944

### EXPORT & ESPANOL
25 NW Point Blvd.
Ste. 800
Elk Grove Village, IL 60007-1030
Telephone: (708) 296-0770
Year Established: 1877
Pub. Frequency: bi-m.
Page Size: standard
Subscrip. Rate: $40/yr.; $65/2 yrs.
Freelance Pay: varies
Circulation: 40,000

Circulation Type: controlled
Owner(s):
Johnston International Publishing Corp.
950 Lee St.
Des Plaines, IL 60016
Telephone: (708) 296-0770
Ownership %: 100
Management:
Bob Yarbrough ................................President
Bob Snyder ....................................Publisher
Roger DiGregorio ..............Circulation Manager
Editorial:
Lisa Corbin ..........................................Editor
E.A. Luchetti ........................................Editor
Don Soules ....................................Art Director
Desc.: Reports on new products,
　marketing trends, especially as relates
　to overseas markets in fields of air
　conditioning and refrigeration equipment,
　hardware and tools, home appliances
　and other consumer hardgoods. Can
　use free lance material on new product
　and marketing trends, especially as
　relates to overseas sales. Cover air
　conditioning and refrigeration equipment,
　hardware and tools, home appliances
　and other related consumer hardgoods.
Readers: Importers, dealers and
　distributors in 183 countries, throughout
　the world.

68777

### EXPORTER, THE
34 W. 37th St.
New York, NY 10018
Telephone: (212) 563-2772
FAX: (212) 563-2798
Year Established: 1980
Pub. Frequency: m.
Subscrip. Rate: $144/yr.
Circulation: 8,000
Circulation Type: paid
Owner(s):
Trade Data Reports, Inc.
34 W. 37th St.
New York, NY 10018
Telephone: (212) 563-2772
Ownership %: 100
Editorial:
L. Stroh ..............................................Editor
Desc.: Provides a guide to exporting
　services and resources for people
　involved in the business who need to
　understand and meet foreign import or
　US export requirements.

67045

### FOREIGN TRADE
6849 Old Dominion Dr., Ste. 200
McLean, VA 22101-3705
Telephone: (703) 448-1338
FAX: (703) 448-1841
Year Established: 1991
Pub. Frequency: 10/yr.
Page Size: 4 color photos/art
Subscrip. Rate: $45/yr.
Freelance Pay: $150+
Circulation: 15,000
Circulation Type: paid
Owner(s):
Defense & Diplomacy, Inc.
6849 Old Dominion Dr, Ste. 200
Mc Lean, VA 22101-3705
Telephone: (703) 448-1338
Ownership %: 100
Management:
Denny White ....................................Publisher
William G. Turner ..............Advertising Manager
Editorial:
Russell Goodman ..................Editor in Chief
Desc.: Publishes practical How-to get in on
　the Action articles on international
　trading for the exporters, importers and
　manufacturers of the world.
Readers: Practicing exporters, importers
　and manufacturers.

Materials Accepted/Included: 01-Business news 02-By-line articles 03-Fashion news 04-Food news 05-Freelance copy 06-Letters to editor 07-Real estate news 08-Sports news 09-Travel news 10-Book rev. 11-Movie rev. 12-Music rev. 13-TV rev. 14-Theater rev. 15-Coming events 16-Obituaries 17-Question & answer 18-Social announcements 19-Artwork 20-Cartoons 21-Photos 22-TV listings 23-Audio rec. 24-Video rec. 25-Books 26-Films/film clips 27-Personnel news 28-Press releases 29-New product news/photos 30-Trade lit. 31-Contracts awarded 32-Display adv. 33-Classified adv.

4-133

22938

## GLOBAL TRADE & TRANSPORTATION MAGAZINE
401 N. Broad St., North American Bldg.
Philadelphia, PA 19108
Telephone: (215) 238-5300
FAX: (215) 238-5457
Year Established: 1935
Pub. Frequency: m.
Page Size: standard
Subscrip. Rate: $45/yr.
Materials: 01,02,06,10,23,24,25,26,27,28,
29,30,31,32,33
Freelance Pay: negotiable
Circulation: 19,045
Circulation Type: controlled
**Owner(s):**
North American Publishing Co.
401 N. Broad
Philadelphia, PA 19108
Telephone: (215) 238-5300
Ownership %: 100
**Management:**
Ned S. Borowsky ...............................President
Bennett Zucker ...................................Publisher
Kathy Gilbert ..................Promotion Manager
**Editorial:**
Tery Moran-Lever ...............................Editor
**Desc.:** Key in on international trade,
finance, transportation, government. All
articles, news review, free literature are
aimed at the international trader, broker,
forwarder, banker, manufacturer,
distributor, transporter.
**Readers:** Decision makers involved in
international trade and transport.
**Deadline:** story-1st of mo. 6 wks. prior to
pub. date; news-1st of mo. 6 wks. prior;
photo-1st of mo. 6 wks. prior; ads-1st of
preceding mo.

22951

## INTERNATIONAL BUSINESS OPPORTUNITIES NEWS
17057 Bellflower Blvd., Ste. 205
Bellflower, CA 90706
Telephone: (310) 925-2918
Mailing Address:
P.O. Box 428 - WPN
Bellflower, CA 90707
Year Established: 1976
Pub. Frequency: m.
Page Size: standard
Subscrip. Rate: $89/yr.
Circulation: 2,000
Circulation Type: controlled
**Owner(s):**
U.S. International Marketing Co.
17057 Bellflower Blvd, Ste 205
Bellflower, CA 90706
Telephone: (310) 925-2918
Ownership %: 100
**Management:**
R. Mervyn Heaton ...............................President
Betty Heaton ...................Advertising Manager
**Editorial:**
R. Mervyn Heaton ................Executive Editor
Frances Leneker ...............................Editor
Rosaline Trent ......................Managing Editor
Mervyn Heaton ..............Book Review Editor

**Desc.:** An 8 page newsletter for U.S. and
overseas businessmen and firms who
are looking for business opportunities,
primarily in the import, export, and
international trade fields. Consists of
about 50 classified news releases in
business, consumer, and technical
product classifications. No illustrations,
accepts classified business
opportunities of 30-50 words in length
(including address). Editorial
Departments include: Agencies
Available, Agencies Wanted, Free
Literature, Consumer and Business
Products Wanted, Technical Products
Wanted, Consumer and Business
Products Available, Technical
Products Available, Import-Export Offers,
Business Opportunities, Business
Financing, Business Promotion.
**Readers:** Businessmen looking for
business opportunities, entrepreneurs,
agents looking for lines, manufacturers,
world wide.

22952

## INTERNATIONAL EXECUTIVE, THE
Thunderbird Campus, Box 1700
Glendale, AZ 85306
Telephone: (602) 978-7249
Year Established: 1959
Pub. Frequency: bi-m.
Page Size: pocket
Subscrip. Rate: $57.60/yr. in US & Canada
Freelance Pay: $700
Circulation: 1,000
Circulation Type: paid
**Owner(s):**
American Graduate School of Int'l. Mgmt.
Thunderbird Campus, Box 1700
Glendale, AZ 85306
Telephone: (602) 978-7249
Ownership %: 100
**Editorial:**
Matin H. Sours ...............................Editor
Florence Stone ...............................Editor
Carol LeClaire Klock ................Managing Editor
**Desc.:** A reading service providing an
annotated bibliography of current books,
articles and government reports on
international business, with summaries
of the most significant articles and
research reports. Feature articles,
departments, and reference guide cover,
general management of multinational
corporations, functional fields of
international business (e.g. marketing,
banking, etc.), international economics
(trade, economic development, etc.)
and information on foreign countries
relevant to international business.
Material is geared toward senior
executives and academics. Country/
special topic index added in volume 27,
2 and continuing, cross-references
bibliography entries by country(s) and/or
special topics such as countertrade,
investment, external debt and
technology transfer.
**Readers:** Senior executives interested in
doing business abroad; academics
interested in international business,
university libraries (foreign & US),
corporate libraries, government
agencies, students and researchers.

22953

## INTERNATIONAL NEW PRODUCTS BULLETIN
17057 Bellflower Blvd., Ste. 205
Bellflower, CA 90706
Telephone: (310) 925-2918
Mailing Address:
P.O. Box 428 - WPN
Bellflower, CA 90707
Year Established: 1976

Pub. Frequency: m.
Page Size: standard
Subscrip. Rate: $89/yr.
Circulation: 3,000
Circulation Type: controlled
**Owner(s):**
U.S. International Marketing Co., Inc.
17057 Bellflower Blvd, Ste 205
Bellflower, CA 90706
Telephone: (310) 925-2918
Ownership %: 100
**Management:**
R. Mervyn Heaton ...............................President
U.S. Int'l. Marketing Co, Inc ..............Publisher
Betty Heaton ...................Advertising Manager
**Editorial:**
Frances Leneker ...............................Editor
Rosaline Trent ......................Managing Editor
**Desc.:** An 8-page illustrated newsletter for
the U.S. or overseas manufacturer who
has a new product to promote
worldwide, and for the businessman
or firm who is looking for new products
to sell. Accepts news releases for new
consumer, business, and technical
products. Release should consist of
either a 4 x 5 black and
white photograph and 100 words of
descriptive text, or 40-50 words of
descriptive text. Departments include:
Products from the Far East,
Products from Europe, Products from
the U.S., Gift Ideas from the U.S., New
U.S. Products Available, New Overseas
Products Available,
Business Opportunities Classified, New
U.S. and Overseas Inventions.
**Readers:** Manufacturers, retailers,
wholesalers, importers, exporters,
entrepreneurs, bank
business development departments, U.S.
and overseas.

22955

## JOURNAL OF COMMERCE IMPORT BULLETIN
2 World Trade Center, 7th Fl.
New York, NY 10048
Telephone: (212) 837-7000
FAX: (212) 837-7045
Year Established: 1946
Pub. Frequency: w.
Page Size: tabloid
Subscrip. Rate: $325/yr.
**Owner(s):**
Journal of Commerce, Inc.
2 World Trade Center, 27th Fl.
New York, NY 10048
Telephone: (212) 837-7000
Ownership %: 100
**Management:**
Don C. Becker ...............................Publisher
James Devine ................Advertising Manager
**Editorial:**
Charles Muller ...............................Editor
**Desc.:** The Import Bulletin is a business
service/a functional tool of all those
who import merchandise or who deal in
or compete with imported goods. It
contains a detailed listing of all cargoes
entering the major U.S. ports together
with information on every consignment
of goods/raw materials, semi-finished
goods, manufactured products, bulk
cargoes, directly from ship manifests.
**Readers:** Importers and Exporters.

68778

## TRADE & CULTURE
7127 Hartford Rd.
Baltimore, MD 21234
Telephone: (301) 426-2906
FAX: (301) 444-7837
Year Established: 1992
Pub. Frequency: q.
Subscrip. Rate: $29.95/yr.

Circulation: 10,000
Circulation Type: paid
**Owner(s):**
Key Communications Corp.
7127 Hartford Rd.
Baltimore, MD 21234
Telephone: (301) 426-2906
Ownership %: 100
**Editorial:**
Thomas D. Boettcher .........................Editor
**Desc.:** For executives of small to mid-size
firms that produce competitive products
or services. Includes columns on trade
zones and trade functions.

## Group 078-Farm Equipment & Supplies

61313

## AGRI-EQUIPMENT CHEMICAL
P.O. Box 547
Yakima, WA 98902
Telephone: (800) 869-7923
Mailing Address:
P.O. Box 547
Yakima, WA 98907
Year Established: 1976
Pub. Frequency: m.
Page Size: tabloid
Subscrip. Rate: $12/yr.
Freelance Pay: varies
Circulation: 11,000
Circulation Type: paid
**Owner(s):**
Clinton Publishing
P.O. Box 547
Yakima, WA 98907
Telephone: (800) 869-7923
Ownership %: 100
**Management:**
Marlene Riggan ................Circulation Manager
**Editorial:**
Ken Hodge ...............................Editor
John Lamphiear ...............................Advertising
Kathy Noble ..................Production Director
**Readers:** Wide range of agricultural
operations in WA., OR., ID.

22964

## AGRICULTURA DE LAS AMERICAS
150 Great Neck Rd.
Great Neck, NY 11021
Telephone: (516) 829-9210
FAX: (516) 829-7265
Mailing Address:
P.O. Box 781
Great Neck, NY 11025
Year Established: 1952
Pub. Frequency: bi-m.
Page Size: standard
Subscrip. Rate: free to qualified persons;
$30/yr. others
Freelance Pay: varies
Circulation: 38,144
Circulation Type: controlled
**Owner(s):**
Keller International Publishing Corp.
150 Great Neck Rd.
Great Neck, NY 11021
Telephone: (516) 829-9210
Ownership %: 100
**Management:**
Gerald Keller ...............................President
Marvin Toben ...............................Vice President
Robert Herlihy ...............................Publisher
Jose Suarez ......................Circulation Manager
**Editorial:**
Victor Prieto ...............................Executive Editor
Roslyn Young ...............................Art Director
Felicia Morales ................Editorial Assistant
Jane Mahoney ..................Production Director
**Desc.:** Edited for Latin America, covers
better farming, power farming, farm
mechanization, use of farm machinery
and equipment, maintenance and
overhaul methods, etc. Text in Spanish.

**Materials Accepted/Included:** 01-Business news 02-By-line articles 03-Fashion news 04-Food news 05-Freelance copy 06-Letters to editor 07-Real estate news 08-Sports news 09-Travel news 10-Book rev. 11-Movie rev. 12-Music rev. 13-TV rev. 14-Theater rev. 15-Coming events 16-Obituaries 17-Question & answer 18-Social announcements 19-Artwork 20-Cartoons 21-Photos 22-TV listings 23-Audio rec. 24-Video rec. 25-Books 26-Films/film clips 27-Personnel news 28-Press releases 29-New product news/photos 30-Trade lit. 31-Contracts awarded 32-Display adv. 33-Classified adv.

4-134

**Readers:** Principally large farmers plus government, dealers, farmers, ranchers, planters, and distributors.

68674

## ANTIQUE POWER
P.O. Box 838
Yellow Springs, OH 45387
Telephone: (513) 767-1344
Year Established: 1988
Pub. Frequency: bi-m.
Subscrip. Rate: $18/yr.
**Owner(s):**
Antique Power, Inc.
P.O. Box 838
Yellow Springs, OH 45387
Telephone: (513) 767-1344
Ownership %: 100
**Editorial:**
Patrick W. Ertel ...........................Editor

22966

## FARM EQUIPMENT
1233 Janesville Ave.
Ft. Atkinson, WI 53538
Telephone: (414) 563-6388
FAX: (414) 563-1699
Year Established: 1969
Pub. Frequency: 7/yr.
Page Size: tabloid
Subscrip. Rate: $45/yr.
Materials: 01,06,27,28,29,30,32,33
Print Process: web offset
Circulation: 16,700
Circulation Type: controlled
**Owner(s):**
Johnson Hill Press, Inc.
Telephone: (414) 563-6388
Ownership %: 100
**Management:**
Jonathn Pellegrin .................Chairman of Board
Jim Rank ...........................Vice President
Kevin Lephart ...........................Publisher
**Editorial:**
Bill Fogarty ...........................Exec. Editor
Jim Wedde ...........................Editor
Dale Aspinall ...........................Art Director
Phil Merrick ...........................Sales
Arlette Sambs ...........................Sales
**Desc.:** Product news for the agricultural trade nationally. Concentrating on helping dealers become more profitable.
**Readers:** Farm implement dealers across North America.

22968

## IMPLEMENT & TRACTOR
Hwy. 61 at Hwy. 6
Clarksdale, MS 38614
Telephone: (601) 624-8503
FAX: (601) 627-1977
Mailing Address:
P.O. Box 1420
Clarksdale, MS 38614
Year Established: 1886
Pub. Frequency: 5/yr.
Page Size: tabloid
Subscrip. Rate: $39.50/yr.
Freelance Pay: varies
Circulation: 18,000
Circulation Type: controlled
**Owner(s):**
Argus Agronomics
P.O. Box 1420
Clarksdale, MS 38614
Telephone: (601) 624-8503
Ownership %: 100
**Management:**
John Montandon ...........................President
John Montandon ...........................Publisher
**Editorial:**
Scott McClures ...........................Editor
Hembree Brandon ...........................Editorial Director
Judith Flowers ...........................Marketing Director
**Desc.:** Farm machinery business publication covering supply and demand, new equipment, and industry news.

**Readers:** Farm machinery dealers, distributors, manufacturers, farm managers.

70464

## MY LITTLE SALESMAN HEAVY EQUIPMENT CATALOG
2895 Chad Dr.
Eugene, OR 97401
Telephone: (800) 929-2800
FAX: (503) 342-3598
Mailing Address:
P.O. Box 70208
Eugene, OR 97401
Year Established: 1958
Pub. Frequency: m.
Page Size: pocket
Subscrip. Rate: $2.50/copy
Materials: 06,30,32,33
Print Process: offset
**Owner(s):**
My Little Salesman, Inc.
P.O. Box 70208
Eugene, OR 97401
Telephone: (503) 342-1201
Ownership %: 100
**Management:**
Richard E. Pierce ...........................President
Rod Womack ...................Advertising Manager
Richard E. Pierce ...................General Manager
**Editorial:**
Peter Powell ...................Marketing Director
**Deadline:** ads-Fri. prior to pub.

22970

## NORTHWEST FARM EQUIPMENT JOURNAL
101 W. 29th St., Ste. 102
Marshfield, WI 54449
Telephone: (715) 389-2234
FAX: (715) 389-2380
Mailing Address:
P.O. Box 1210
Marshfield, WI 54449
Year Established: 1887
Pub. Frequency: m.
Page Size: tabloid
Subscrip. Rate: $36/yr.
Materials: 01,29,32
Print Process: web offset
Circulation: 2,800
Circulation Type: controlled
**Owner(s):**
Gerald J. Petcher
101 W. 29th St., Ste. 102
Marshfield, WI 54449
Telephone: (715) 389-2380
Ownership %: 100
**Management:**
Gerald J. Petcher ...........................Publisher
**Editorial:**
Gerald J. Petcher ...........................Editor
**Desc.:** Communication medium for farm equipment associations of Minnesota, South Dakota, North Dakota, Wisconsin, Illinois, Montana, Wyoming, Ohio, Iowa, Michigan, Nebraska, Indiana.
**Readers:** Farm equipment retailers of management & sales personnel of mfrs. and wholesalers, marketing into 12 state regions (Iowa, Minnesota, North Dakota, South Dakota, Montana, Wyoming, Nebraska, Wisconsin, Illinois, Ohio, Michigan and Indiana.

22965

## RESOURCE: ENGINEERING & TECHNOLOGY FOR A SUSTAINABLE WORLD
2950 Niles Rd.
St. Joseph, MI 49085-9659
Telephone: (616) 429-0300
FAX: (616) 429-3852
Year Established: 1920
Pub. Frequency: m.

Page Size: standard
Subscrip. Rate: $7.50/issue non-members; $49.50/yr.
Circulation: 10,000
Circulation Type: paid
**Owner(s):**
American Society of Agricultural Engineers
Telephone: (616) 429-0300
Ownership %: 100
**Management:**
Roger R. Castenson ...........................Publisher
Dee Gunn ...................Advertising Manager
Sandy Nalepa ...................Circulation Manager
**Editorial:**
Denise Sicking ...................Managing Editor
Pam Bakken ...........................Art Director
Dolores Gunn ...........................Assistant Editor
Suzanne Howard ...........Book Review Editor
Bill Thompson ...........................Design
Donna Hull ...........................Marketing Director
Pamela Devore-Hansen ...............New Products Editor
**Desc.:** Professional publication dealing with agricultural progress by means of efficient equipment and methods of producing and handling food, feed, and fiber supplies; managing soil and water resources; and housing and handling livestock. Includes both technical articles and general interest articles on matters affecting agricultural progress around the world. Departments include: AE Update, New Products and Literature announced by advertisers, special news columns.
**Readers:** Engineers, educators, and industry leaders.

## Group 080-Fertilizer

22984

## AG RETAILER MAGAZINE
11701 Borman Dr.
St. Louis, MO 63146
Telephone: (314) 569-2700
FAX: (314) 569-1083
Year Established: 1956
Pub. Frequency: 7/yr.
Page Size: standard
Subscrip. Rate: free
Freelance Pay: negotiable
Circulation: 25,700
Circulation Type: free
**Owner(s):**
AG Retailer Association
11701 Borman Dr.
Manchester, MO 63146
Telephone: (314) 569-2700
FAX: (314) 569-1083
Ownership %: 100
**Management:**
Richard Jarrett ...................Circulation Manager
**Editorial:**
Lynn Henderson ...........................Editor
John Appleton ...........................Sales
**Desc.:** Premier publication providing a broad base of useful purchasing, marketing and management information to successful fertilizer and agricultural chemical dealers.
**Readers:** Fertilizer (dry and liquid) and ag chemical dealers; manufacturers and producers of fertilizers and pesticides; ground and/or aerial applicators.

24856

## AGRONOMY JOURNAL
677 S. Segoe Rd.
Madison, WI 53711
Telephone: (608) 273-8080
FAX: (608) 273-2021
Year Established: 1907
Pub. Frequency: bi-m.
Page Size: standard
Subscrip. Rate: $92/yr.
Materials: 32

Circulation: 7,650
Circulation Type: paid
**Owner(s):**
American Society of Agronomy
677 S. Segoe Rd.
Madison, WI 53711
Telephone: (608) 273-8080
Ownership %: 100
**Management:**
Keith R. Schlesinger ........Advertising Manager
Roger Watkins ...................Circulation Manager
David M. Kral ...................Operations Manager
**Editorial:**
J. L. Hatfield ...........................Editor
William R. Luellen ...................Managing Editor
Gunda Koists ...........................Assistant Editor
**Desc.:** Devoted to exchange of information among professional agronomists. Contents are largely technical articles on research findings about resident education, military land use and management, agroclimatology and agronomic modeling, extension education, environmental quality, international agronomy, and agricultural research station management.
**Readers:** Professional agronomists.

22983

## DEALER PROGRESS
314-The Barn, 15444 Clayton Rd.
Manchester, MO 63011
Telephone: (314) 527-4001
Year Established: 1970
Pub. Frequency: bi-m.
Page Size: standard
Subscrip. Rate: $40/yr. US; $80/yr. foreign
Circulation: 26,000
Circulation Type: controlled
**Owner(s):**
Fertilizer Institute, The
501 Second St., N.E.
Washington, DC 20002
Telephone: (202) 675-8250
Ownership %: 100
**Management:**
Marilyn Richardson ...........Advertising Manager
**Editorial:**
Elliott Nowels ...........................Editor
Polly C. Ligon ...................Managing Editor
Robert Wansel ...................Associate Editor
**Desc.:** The business magazine for the entire fertilizer industry. Editorial policy and content is primarily focused on helping the retail dealer solve short and long term problems and manage a profitable business. In addition, overall industry problems and trends are covered. The magazine provides fertilizer log chemical retailers with cutting edge information critical to achieving success in their businesses and lives.
**Readers:** Dealers/distributors of fertilizer and agricultural chemicals.

61023

## FARM CHEMICAL INTERNATIONAL
37733 Euclid Ave.
Willoughby, OH 44094-5992
Telephone: (216) 942-2000
FAX: (216) 975-3447
Year Established: 1986
Pub. Frequency: q.
Page Size: standard
Subscrip. Rate: $20/yr. US & Canada; $50 foreign airmail only
Print Process: web offset
Circulation: 8,748
Circulation Type: controlled

**Materials Accepted/Included:** 01-Business news 02-By-line articles 03-Fashion news 04-Food news 05-Freelance copy 06-Letters to editor 07-Real estate news 08-Sports news 09-Travel news 10-Book rev. 11-Movie rev. 12-Music rev. 13-TV rev. 14-Theater rev. 15-Coming events 16-Obituaries 17-Question & answer 18-Social announcements 19-Artwork 20-Cartoons 21-Photos 22-TV listings 23-Audio rec. 24-Video rec. 25-Books 26-Films/film clips 27-Personnel news 28-Press releases 29-New product news/photos 30-Trade lit. 31-Contracts awarded 32-Display adv. 33-Classified adv.

4-135

**Owner(s):**
Meister Publishing Co.
37733 Euclid Ave
Willoughby, OH 44094-5992
Telephone: (216) 942-2000
FAX: (216) 975-3447
Ownership %: 100
**Editorial:**
Jim Sulecki ............................Senior Editor
Dale L. Little .................................Editor
Charlotte Sine ...............Editorial Director
Alan C. Strohmaier ...........Advertising Director
Amy Fahnestock ................Assistant Editor
Cheryl Buck ....................Assistant Editor
Alan C. Strohmaier ........Associate Publisher
**Desc.:** Contains articles and research
reports on the production, marketing and
application of crop protection chemicals
and fertilizers worldwide. Material is
edited for the agrochemical
producer/formulator/distributor/ dealer
and fertilizer manufacturer/distributor/
dealer to help him improve his operation
and sell his products and services.
Special emphasis on government
regulation, and new product registration,
label expansions, marketing strategies of
leading companies. Special features
include: Forum in Print covering major
industry issues, GIFAP Report,
Presstime News Report.
**Readers:** Distributed outside the U.S. and
Canada exclusively. It reaches almost 9,
000 international marketers, formulators,
distributors, large resellers, cooperatives,
major buying influences and government
agencies in more than 100 countries
with editorial content tailored
specifically for their informational needs.

**FARM CHEMICALS**                    48967
37733 Euclid Ave.
Willoughby, OH 44094-5992
Telephone: (216) 942-2000
FAX: (216) 975-3447
Year Established: 1894
Pub. Frequency: m.
Page Size: standard
Subscrip. Rate: $20/yr.
Print Process: web offset
Circulation: 32,096
Circulation Type: controlled
**Owner(s):**
Meister Publishing Co.
37733 Euclid Ave.
Willoughby, OH 44094-5992
Telephone: (216) 942-2000
FAX: (216) 975-3447
Ownership %: 100
**Editorial:**
Jim Sulecki ............................Senior Editor
Dale L. Little .................................Editor
Charlotte Sine ...............Editorial Director
Alan C. Strohmaier ...............Advertising
Amy L. Fahnestock ................Assistant Editor
Alan C. Strohmaier ...........Associate Publisher
**Desc.:** Contains articles and staff research
reports on the development, production,
marketing and application of fertilizers
and crop protection chemicals. Material
is edited for the fertilizer bulk
blender/fluid mixer/pesticide-fertilizer
dealer/applicator (both aerial and
ground rig operators) to help him
improve his operation and sell his
products and services. Special emphasis
on government regulations, new product
registrations, crop clearances and
applications. Special features include:
Government and Your Business, New
Products, What's Doing in Industry, FC
Executive Suite, People.

**Readers:** Serves the fertilizer and
pesticide manufacturing, retailing and
distributing fields including
manufacturers, blenders, mixers, dealers,
formulators and commercial applicators
and those in closely allied fields.

**FARM CHEMICALS HANDBOOK**          48964
37733 Euclid Ave.
Willoughby, OH 44094-5992
Telephone: (216) 942-2000
FAX: (216) 975-3447
Year Established: 1913
Pub. Frequency: a.
Page Size: standard
Subscrip. Rate: $69/yr. plus $3 domestic
S&H, $25/yr. foreign
Print Process: web offset
**Owner(s):**
Meister Publishing Co.
37733 Euclid Ave.
Willoughby, OH 44094-5992
Telephone: (216) 942-2000
FAX: (216) 975-3447
Ownership %: 100
**Editorial:**
Stella K. Naegely ............................Editor
Charlotte Sine ...............Editorial Director
Alan C. Strohmaier ...........Advertising Director
Judy Gill ........................Assistant Editor
Bonnie L. Wank ...............Associate Editor
Alan C. Strohmaier ........Associate Publisher
**Desc.:** A reference book on fertilizers, crop
protection chemicals and equipment and
supplies. It contains a Pesticide
Dictionary and product descriptions
of crop protection chemicals throughout
the world; Dictionary of Plant Foods and
a listing of micro-nutrients by producer
or distributor; and a Buyer's Guide with
company listings by product name.
There is also an alphabetical list of
suppliers and manufacturers with
addresses.

**JOURNAL OF AGRICULTURAL &**       22985
**FOOD CHEMISTRY**
1155 16th St., N.W.
Washington, DC 20036
Telephone: (202) 872-4600
Year Established: 1953
Pub. Frequency: m.
Page Size: standard
Subscrip. Rate: $32/yr. members; $85/yr.
foreign; $275/yr. non-members; $388/yr.
foreign
Circulation: 4,300
Circulation Type: paid
**Owner(s):**
American Chemical Society
1155 16th St., N.W.
Washington, DC 20036
Telephone: (202) 872-4600
Ownership %: 100
**Editorial:**
Elliott Nowels ............................Editor
**Desc.:** Technical articles related to
agricultural and food chemistry. Primary
research only.
**Readers:** Scientists, technicians,
academicians.

**NEBRASKA FERTILIZER & AG-**       23270
**CHEMICAL DIGEST**
1111 Lincoln Mall, Ste. 308
Lincoln, NE 68508
Telephone: (402) 476-1528
FAX: (402) 476-1259
Year Established: 1944
Pub. Frequency: q.

Page Size: standard
Subscrip. Rate: $10/yr. member; $20/yr.
non-member
Materials: 06,32,33
Print Process: offset
Circulation: 1,000
Circulation Type: free & paid
**Owner(s):**
Chemical Institute, Inc
1111 Lincoln Mall, Ste. 308
Lincoln, NE 68508
Telephone: (402) 476-1528
Ownership %: 100
**Management:**
Rebecca Barker ...............Advertising Manager
Robert L. Anderson ...........Circulation Manager
**Editorial:**
Robert L. Anderson ................Executive Editor
Alice L. Licht ...................Managing Editor
**Desc.:** News and features cover
advertising, nutrition, management,
research, new products,
government regulations, appointments,
dealer news, new literature.
**Readers:** Fertilizer & Ag-chemical retailers.

## Group 082-Finance

**AGRI FINANCE**                     21920
6201 Howard St.
Niles, IL 60714-3403
Telephone: (708) 647-1200
FAX: (708) 647-7055
Year Established: 1959
Pub. Frequency: 10/yr.
Page Size: standard
Subscrip. Rate: $5 newsstand; $30/yr.
Materials: 02,05,32,33
Freelance Pay: $200-$1,000
Circulation: 15,000
Circulation Type: controlled & paid
**Owner(s):**
Century Communications, Inc.
6201 Howard St.
Niles, IL 60714-3403
Telephone: (708) 647-1200
Ownership %: 100
**Management:**
Philip C. Miller ............................President
Marilyn M. Miller ...............Vice President
Philip C. Miller ............................Publisher
Carroll Merry ...............Advertising Manager
Gordon Behtards ...........Circulation Manager
**Editorial:**
Jim Baxter ............................Editor
Kris Myszka ...............Managing Editor
Christine Waligorski .......Secretary & Treasurer
**Desc.:** Covers key financial, marketing and
production aspects of American farm
business management. Departments
include Farm Manager Forum, Farmland
Markets, Focus on Finance, Crop
Consltant Briefings, Management Edge
and Bottom Line Marketing.
**Readers:** Loan officers of banks and farm
credit system, professional farm
managers, commercial farmers and
independent crop consultants.
**Deadline:** story-1 mo. prior to pub. date;
news-1 mo. prior to pub. date; photo-1
mo. prior to pub. date; ads-1 mo. prior to
pub. date

**BANKER & TRADESMAN**              21926
210 South St.
Boston, MA 02111
Telephone: (617) 426-4495
FAX: (617) 357-5215
Year Established: 1872
Pub. Frequency: Mon.
Page Size: tabloid
Subscrip. Rate: $4 newsstand; $176/yr.
Freelance Pay: $150 - $200
Circulation: 5,000

Circulation Type: paid
**Owner(s):**
Warren Publishing Corp.
Telephone: (617) 426-4495
Ownership %: 100
**Management:**
Timothy M. Warren ............................President
Timothy M. Warren, Jr. .................Publisher
Jeffrey Keller ...............Advertising Manager
**Editorial:**
Nena Groskind ...............Executive Editor
W. A. Mallard ...................Technical Editor
**Desc.:** Except for editorials and general
news pages, all pages are devoted to
recording official records from registries,
courts, state, city and town offices.
Prints real estate deeds, mortgages,
attachments, etc., records of new
corporations, probate reports, personnel
of firms, etc., news of financial and real
estate interest. We will accept outside
material.
**Readers:** Banks, real estate brokers and
business executives.

**BARRON'S NATIONAL BUSINESS**      54047
**& FINANCIAL WEEKLY**
200 Liberty St.
New York, NY 10281
Telephone: (212) 416-2700
FAX: (212) 416-2829
Year Established: 1921
Pub. Frequency: w.
Page Size: tabloid
Subscrip. Rate: $109/yr.
Freelance Pay: varies
Circulation: 235,600
Circulation Type: paid
**Owner(s):**
Dow Jones & Company, Inc.
200 Liberty St.
New York, NY 10281
Ownership %: 100
**Management:**
Robert R. Paradise ............................Publisher
**Editorial:**
James P. Meagher ............................Editor
Richard Rescigno ...............Assistant Managing
Editor
Kathryn M. Welling ...............Associate Editor
Peter C. Du Bois ...............Foreign Editor
**Desc.:** Barron's contains industry wide
studies and individual company
analyses. Features and columns closely
examine various segments of the market
and/or the financial world in general.
Each issue also contains a complete
listing of prices and other data on
stocks, bonds, commodities, futures
contracts and other securities, plus
various economic indicators.
**Readers:** Businesses, professionals and
individual investors.

**BOND BUYER**                      22371
One State Street Plz.
New York, NY 10004
Telephone: (212) 943-8549
FAX: (212) 943-2983
Year Established: 1891
Pub. Frequency: d.
Page Size: broadsheet
Subscrip. Rate: $189/yr.
Freelance Pay: $250-$7000
Circulation: 39,000
Circulation Type: controlled
**Owner(s):**
International Thomson, The Bond Buyer
One State St. Plz.
New York, NY 10004
Telephone: (212) 943-8200
Ownership %: 100
**Management:**
David Branch ............................President

**Materials Accepted/Included:** 01-Business news 02-By-line articles 03-Fashion news 04-Food news 05-Freelance copy 06-Letters to editor 07-Real estate news 08-Sports news 09-Travel news 10-Book rev. 11-Movie rev. 12-Music rev. 13-TV rev. 14-Theater rev. 15-Coming events 16-Obituaries 17-Question & answer 18-Social announcements 19-Artwork 20-Cartoons 21-Photos 22-TV listings 23-Audio rec. 24-Video rec. 25-Books 26-Films/film clips 27-Personnel news 28-Press releases 29-New product news/photos 30-Trade lit. 31-Contracts awarded 32-Display adv. 33-Classified adv.

Joe Hysak .................................Publisher
**Editorial:**
John Allen .................................Executive Editor
Joe Hysak .................................Managing Editor
William J. Ryan .......................Associate Editor
**Desc.:** Aimed at professionals in finance and investments, nationally and abroad. Covers all money and capital markets, domestic and international developments in finance. Complete news reports and analysis, with largely staff-written features of developing trends and events affecting the financial and economic situation and the major securities markets.
**Readers:** Senior financial officers of corporations, savings & loan, pension funds, and other such bond houses.

**BUSINESS CREDIT**    21939
8815 Centre Park Dr., Ste. 200
Columbia, MD 21045
Telephone: (301) 740-5560
FAX: (301) 410-7404
Year Established: 1898
Pub. Frequency: m.
Page Size: standard
Subscrip. Rate: $5/copy; $33/yr.
Materials: 01,02,05,06
Freelance Pay: voluntary
Print Process: web
Circulation: 40,000
Circulation Type: controlled
**Owner(s):**
National Association of Credit Management
8815 Center Rd., 200
Columbia, MD 21045
Telephone: (301) 740-5560
Ownership %: 100
**Management:**
Cindy Tursman .....................................Publisher
**Editorial:**
Katharine Jeschke ...................Managing Editor
Robert Lightman ...............................Advertising
Kimberly Howard .......................Associate Editor
**Desc.:** Special issues on education, legislation, accounting, factoring, banking and credit automation.
**Readers:** Top management, credit and financial executives, banking and financial institutions.
**Deadline:** story-1st of mo., 2 mos. prior; ads-15th of mo., 2 mos. prior

**CHEKLIST**    68677
50 Nassau St., Ste. 2030
New York, NY 10038
Telephone: (212) 267-7712
FAX: (212) 267-7726
Year Established: 1989
Pub. Frequency: q.
Page Size: standard
Subscrip. Rate: $25/yr.
Materials: 01,02,06,25,28,29,32,33
Freelance Pay: varies
Circulation: 4,517
Circulation Type: paid
**Owner(s):**
BKB Publications, Inc.
150 Nassau St., Ste. 2030
New York, NY 10038
Telephone: (212) 267-7712
Ownership %: 100
**Editorial:**
Charlene Komar Storey ...........................Editor
**Desc.:** Covers the management in the check-cashing industry.
**Readers:** Check cashiers.
**Deadline:** story-1st of mo. prior to pub.; news-1st of mo. prior; photo-1st of mo. prior; ads-1st of mo. prior

**COLLECTOR**    21934
4040 W. 70th St.
Minneapolis, MN 55435
Telephone: (612) 926-6547
FAX: (612) 926-1624
Mailing Address:
   P.O. Box 39106
   Minneapolis, MN 55439
Year Established: 1939
Pub. Frequency: m.
Page Size: standard
Subscrip. Rate: $25/yr. members; $50/yr. non members
Materials: 01,02,29,32,33
Print Process: offset
Circulation: 5,000
Circulation Type: paid
**Owner(s):**
American Collectors Association, Inc.
4040 W. 70th St.
Edina, MN 55435
Telephone: (612) 926-6547
FAX: (612) 926-1624
Ownership %: 100
**Editorial:**
John W. Johnson .....................................Editor
Kira Marsyla ..............................Managing Editor
Shinobu Garrigues ...................Associate Editor
**Desc.:** News and by-line articles cover all phases of consumer debt collections and association activities. Readers interested in how-to articles and new developments in collection industry. Articles run up to 1,500 words, news to 250. Photographs and line drawings used to illustrate features. Departments include: ACA News, ACA Continuing Education, People, Unit News, Business Briefs, Membership, Calendar, Letters.
**Readers:** Association members; others in finance and consumer credit & collections.
**Deadline:** story-1st of mo. prior to pub. date; ads-1st of mo. prior to pub. date

**CREDIT UNION MANAGEMENT**    69353
P.O. Box 14167
Madison, WI 53714-0167
Telephone: (608) 271-2664
FAX: (608) 271-2303
Year Established: 1978
Pub. Frequency: m.
Page Size: standard
Subscrip. Rate: $5 newsstand; $40/yr. members; $60/yr. non-members
Materials: 02,05,06,10,17,19,20,21,25,28, 29,32
Print Process: offset
Circulation: 4,950
Circulation Type: controlled & paid
**Owner(s):**
Credit Union Executives Society
P.O. Box 14167
Madison, WI 53714-0167
Telephone: (608) 271-2664
Ownership %: 100
**Editorial:**
Paula Symons ..............................Senior Editor
Mary Auestad Arnold ................................Editor
Jill Molbeck .........Advertising & Sales Manager
**Desc.:** Feature articles and departments pertaining to the legislative, financial, technological, human resources, marketing lending, and policy issues affecting credit union management.
**Deadline:** story-15th of 2nd mo. prior to pub. date; news-2 mo. prior to pub. date; photo-15th of 2nd mo. prior to pub. date; ads-1st of mo prior to pub. date

**EQUITIES**    22385
145 49th St., Rm. 5-B
New York, NY 10017
Telephone: (212) 832-7800

Year Established: 1951
Pub. Frequency: m.
Page Size: standard
Subscrip. Rate: $36/yr.
Freelance Pay: varies
Circulation: 5,000
Circulation Type: paid
**Owner(s):**
Equities Magazine, Inc.
145 49th St., Rm. 5-B
New York, NY 10017
Telephone: (212) 832-7800
Ownership %: 100
**Management:**
Doreen Flaherty .................Circulation Manager
**Editorial:**
Robert J. Flaherty ....................................Editor
**Desc.:** All types of financial information regarding OTC companies.
**Readers:** Institutional and private investors, brokers, corporate executives and other key influences of the financial world.

**FINANCIAL ANALYSTS JOURNAL**    21945
P.O. Box 3668
Charlottesville, VA 22903
Telephone: (804) 980-9775
Year Established: 1945
Pub. Frequency: bi-m.
Page Size: standard
Subscrip. Rate: $150/yr.
Circulation: 24,000
Circulation Type: paid
**Owner(s):**
Association for Investment Management & Research
P.O. Box 3668
Charlottesvle, VA 22903
Telephone: (804) 977-6600
Ownership %: 100
**Management:**
John V. Farley ...................Advertising Manager
**Editorial:**
W. Van Harlow III ........................Editor in Chief
Judith Kimball ...........................Managing Editor
**Desc.:** Financial, security or investment analysis, representing both buyers and sellers of securities. Articles in various areas of finance such as economic outlook, investment management, industry studies, investment analysis, accounting analysis, etc.
**Readers:** Securities analysts and portfolio managers.

**FINANCIAL EXECUTIVE**    57264
10 Madison Ave.
Morristown, NJ 07962-1938
Telephone: (201) 898-4621
FAX: (201) 267-4031
Mailing Address:
   P.O. Box 1938
   Morristown, NJ 07962-1938
Year Established: 1934
Pub. Frequency: bi-m.
Page Size: standard
Subscrip. Rate: $45/yr.
Materials: 01,02,06,28,32
Freelance Pay: $1,000/major feature
Circulation: 18,000
Circulation Type: paid
**Owner(s):**
Financial Executives Institution
P.O. Box 1938
Morristown, NJ 07962-1938
Telephone: (201) 898-4600
FAX: (201) 898-4649
Ownership %: 100
**Editorial:**
Robin Couch Cardillo ..............................Editor
James Cardillo ................................Art Director

**Desc.:** Addresses technical and professional issues of concern to the senior financial executives in major corporations. It covers both their day-to-day and long range responsibilities in matters of corporate finance and financial management. It is written by these senior executives and experts in the field.
**Readers:** Senior financial executives in 8, 000 largest corporations.
**Deadline:** story-4 mos. prior to pub. date; ads-1 mo. prior

**FINANCIAL INDUSTRY ISSUES**    69312
2200 N. Pearl St.
Dallas, TX 75201
Telephone: (214) 922-5251
FAX: (214) 922-5268
Mailing Address:
   Public Affairs
   P.O. Box 655906
   Dallas, TX 76265-5906
Pub. Frequency: q.
Page Size: standard
Materials: 01
Print Process: offset
Circulation: 10,000
Circulation Type: controlled & free
**Owner(s):**
Federal Reserve Bank of Dallas
Public Affairs
P.O. Box 655906
Dallas, TX 76265-5906
Telephone: (214) 922-5251
FAX: (214) 922-5268
Ownership %: 100
**Editorial:**
Tara Barrett ...............................................Editor
**Desc.:** A newsletter that presents research about the financial industry in the Eleventh District.

**FINANCIAL INDUSTRY STUDIES**    69313
2200 N. Pearl St.
Dallas, TX 75201
Telephone: (214) 922-5251
FAX: (214) 922-5268
Year Established: 1988
Pub. Frequency: s-a.
Subscrip. Rate: free
Materials: 01,07
Print Process: offset
Circulation: 15,000
Circulation Type: controlled & free
**Owner(s):**
Federal Reserve Bank of Dallas
P.O. Box 655906
Dallas, TX 76265-5906
Telephone: (214) 922-5251
Ownership %: 100
**Editorial:**
Tara Barrett ...............................................Editor
**Desc.:** Presents research on economic and financial topics with emphasis on the financial industry at regional, national and international levels.

**FINANCIAL PLANNING**    21947
40 W. 57th St., 11th Fl.
New York, NY 10019
Telephone: (212) 765-5311
FAX: (212) 765-6123
Year Established: 1972
Pub. Frequency: m.
Page Size: standard
Subscrip. Rate: $9/issue; $79/yr.
Materials: 32
Freelance Pay: varies
Circulation: 40,000
Circulation Type: controlled & paid

---

**Materials Accepted/Included:** 01-Business news 02-By-line articles 03-Fashion news 04-Food news 05-Freelance copy 06-Letters to editor 07-Real estate news 08-Sports news 09-Travel news 10-Book rev. 11-Movie rev. 12-Music rev. 13-TV rev. 14-Theater rev. 15-Coming events 16-Obituaries 17-Question & answer 18-Social announcements 19-Artwork 20-Cartoons 21-Photos 22-TV listings 23-Audio rec. 24-Video rec. 25-Books 26-Films/film clips 27-Personnel news 28-Press releases 29-New product news/photos 30-Trade lit. 31-Contracts awarded 32-Display adv. 33-Classified adv.

**Owner(s):**
Securities Data Publishing
40 W. 57th St., 11th Fl.
New York, NY 10019
Telephone: (212) 765-5311
Ownership %: 100
**Management:**
Bruce Morris .............................................Publisher
John Voss ...................Circulation Manager
**Editorial:**
Evan Simonoff ..........................Editor in Chief
Cerry Capell .........................Managing Editor
**Readers:** Business magazine for
professionals in the financial services
industry-financial planners, bankers,
insurance agents, stock brokers,
lawyers, accountants, securities
broker/dealers.

21950
### FINANCIAL WORLD
1328 Broadway, 3rd Fl.
New York, NY 10001
Telephone: (212) 594-5030
FAX: (212) 629-0026
Year Established: 1902
Pub. Frequency: bi-w.
Page Size: standard
Subscrip. Rate: $3.95/issue; $39/yr.
Freelance Pay: $1,500-$2,000/article
Circulation: 500,000
Circulation Type: paid
**Owner(s):**
Financial World Partners
1328 Broadway
New York, NY 10001
Telephone: (212) 594-5030
Ownership %: 100
**Bureau(s):**
Chicago/Financial World
203 N. Wabash
Chicago, IL 60601
Telephone: (310) 286-1741
Contact: Jim Armstrong

Los Angeles/Financial World
1801 Ave. of the Stars
Los Angeles, CA 90089
Telephone: (213) 286-1741
Contact: Jim Smith

Detroit/Finanicial World
44 E. Long Lake
Bloomfield, MI 48304
Telephone: (313) 647-7060
Contact: Jeff Ahl
**Management:**
Mark Meagher ..................Chairman of Board
Douglas McIntyre .............................President
Willard Rappleye ............Advertising Manager
Ned Bixler .........................Circulation Manager
**Editorial:**
Geoffrey Smith ..............................................Editor
Lawrence Gendron ....................Art Department
Paul Brown ..........................................News Editor
Steve Mussman ...................Research Director
**Desc.:** Staff-written features and analysis
for private and professional investors
and senior corporate management.
Covers industries, companies, outlook.
**Readers:** Businessmen, executives,
investors, brokers, institutional & private
investors.

21951
### FINANCIER MAGAZINE
One Franklin St.
Chicago, IL 60606-3401
Year Established: 1977
Pub. Frequency: m.
Page Size: standard
Subscrip. Rate: $60/yr.
Circulation: 26,000
Circulation Type: controlled

**Owner(s):**
Financier Bank Administration Institute
1 N. Franklin St.
Chicago, IL 60606-3401
Ownership %: 100
**Management:**
H. David Grace ......................................President
**Editorial:**
Nat Gilbert ......................................................Editor
**Desc.:** Provides a forum of ideas for the
private sector.
**Readers:** Executives who bear
responsibility for policy judgment in the
private sector and those whose
judgments and actions affect that
community.

25666
### FUTURES MAGAZINE
250 S. Wacker Dr.
Ste. 1150
Chicago, IL 60606
Telephone: (312) 977-0999
FAX: (312) 977-1042
Year Established: 1972
Pub. Frequency: m.
Page Size: 4 color photos/art
Subscrip. Rate: $4.50/copy; $39/yr.
Freelance Pay: $50-$1,000
Circulation: 60,000
Circulation Type: controlled & paid
**Owner(s):**
Oster Communications, Inc.
219 Parkade
Cedar Falls, IA 50613
Telephone: (319) 277-6341
Ownership %: 100
**Management:**
Joseph Bernardo ..................................President
Merrill Oster ..........................................Publisher
**Editorial:**
Dave Nusbaum ...........................Senior Editor
Ginger Szala ....................................................Editor
Kristin Beane Sullivan ..............Managing Editor
Leah Rippe ..........................Assistant Publisher
Mark Etzkorn ............................Associate Editor
**Desc.:** Analysis and education on futures,
options, and derivative financial and
commodity markets. Interviews, book
and software reviews.
**Readers:** Commodity and financial futures,
options, and derivatives traders, brokers,
etc.

21955
### GOVERNMENT FINANCE REVIEW
180 N. Michigan Ave., Ste. 800
Chicago, IL 60601-7476
Telephone: (312) 977-9700
Year Established: 1926
Pub. Frequency: bi-m.
Page Size: standard
Subscrip. Rate: $30/yr.
Materials: 32
Circulation: 14,000
Circulation Type: paid
**Owner(s):**
Government Finance Officers Assn. of U.S.
& Canada
180 N. Michigan, Ste. 800
Chicago, IL 60601
Telephone: (312) 977-9700
Ownership %: 100
**Management:**
Jeffrey L. Esser ...................................Publisher
Sharon Fucone ................Advertising Manager
**Editorial:**
Barbara Weiss ..............................................Editor
Karen Utterback ......................Associate Editor
**Desc.:** Devoted to technical, practical,
theoretically leading authorities.
**Readers:** Public finance and other officials
in U.S. and Canada, professional
accountants, municipal bond dealers,
commercial bankers, trust officers, and
economists.

69335
### INFRASTRUCTURE FINANCE
488 Madison Ave.
New York, NY 10022
Telephone: (212) 303-3570
FAX: (212) 303-3592
Year Established: 1992
Pub. Frequency: q.
Page Size: standard
Subscrip. Rate: free to qualified personnel
Circulation: 15,000
Circulation Type: controlled
**Owner(s):**
Institutional Investor, Inc.
488 Madison Ave.
New York, NY 10022
Telephone: (212) 303-3570
**Editorial:**
Elizabeth Bailey ..........................................Editor
Dan Kramer ..........................................Advertising
**Desc.:** Covers global development issues
pertaining to infrastructure investment
and maintenance.

21960
### INSTITUTIONAL INVESTOR
488 Madison Ave.
New York, NY 10022
Telephone: (212) 303-3300
FAX: (212) 303-3592
Year Established: 1967
Pub. Frequency: m.
Page Size: standard
Subscrip. Rate: $45/copy; $375/yr.
Freelance Pay: varies
Circulation: 103,788
Circulation Type: controlled
**Owner(s):**
Capital Cities/ABC, Inc.
77 W. 66th St.
New York, NY 10023
Telephone: (212) 456-7777
Ownership %: 100
**Management:**
Peter A. Derow ......................................President
David Wachtel ......................................Publisher
**Editorial:**
Gilbert E. Kaplan ..........................Editor in Chief
Barbara Bent ...............................Senior Editor
Hilary Rosenberg ...........................Senior Editor
Robert Teitelman ...........................Senior Editor
Kenneth Klee ...............................................Editor
David Cudebaca .............................................Editor
Laurie Meisler ...............................................Editor
Fran Hawthorne .............................................Editor
Firth Calhoun ........................Managing Editor
Tina Aridas ..............Assistant Managing Editor
Clem Morgello ..........Assistant Managing Editor
Chel S. Dong .............................Art Director
Wendy Cooper .....................Contributing Editor
Kevin Muehring ...............Senior Correspondent
Ida Picker ...........................................Staff Writer
**Desc.:** Financial articles assigned to and
freelance writers about institutional
investing, corporate and government
financing, pensions, banking, and
insurance.
**Readers:** Financial and investment
professionals.

66096
### JOURNAL OF CORPORATE ACCOUNTING & FINANCE
22 W. 21st St.
New York, NY 10010-6990
Telephone: (212) 645-7880
FAX: (212) 645-1160
Year Established: 1989
Pub. Frequency: q.
Page Size: standard
Subscrip. Rate: $152/yr. US & Canada;
$182/yr. elsewhere

**Owner(s):**
Executive Enterprises Publications Co., Inc.
22 W 21st St.
New York, NY 10010-6990
Telephone: (212) 645-7880
Ownership %: 100
**Editorial:**
Edward J. Stone ..........................................Editor
Jane G. Bensahel ..........Dir., Bus. Publications
**Desc.:** Provides authoritative advice on
how to deal with current issues affecting
corporate accounting practices &
policies. Analyzes existing and proposed
regulatory rulings, statements and tax
code changes.
**Readers:** Corporate controllers, other
accounting and finance executives,
public accountants.

68682
### JOURNAL OF FINANCIAL PLANNING TODAY
P.O. Box 5359
Lake Worth, FL 33461
Telephone: (407) 434-0100
FAX: (407) 641-4801
Year Established: 1977
Pub. Frequency: q.
Subscrip. Rate: $80/yr.
**Owner(s):**
New Directions Publications, Inc.
Box 5359
Lake Worth, FL 33461
Telephone: (407) 434-0100
Ownership %: 100
**Editorial:**
B.E. Newmark ...............................................Editor

21964
### JOURNAL OF MONEY, CREDIT, & BANKING
1945 N. High St.
Columbus, OH 43210
Telephone: (614) 292-7834
Mailing Address:
1070 Carmack Rd.
Columbus, OH 43210
Year Established: 1969
Pub. Frequency: q.
Page Size: standard
Subscrip. Rate: $35/yr. individuals; $70/yr.
library
Circulation: 3,500
Circulation Type: paid
**Owner(s):**
Ohio State University Press
1070 Carmack Rd.
Columbus, OH 43210
Telephone: (614) 292-6930
Ownership %: 100
**Management:**
Margaret Starbuck ............Advertising Manager
**Editorial:**
Stephen G. Cecchetti ..................................Editor
Paul D. Evans .................................................Editor
Margaret Starbuck ..................Managing Editor
**Desc.:** A professional, scientific journal for
scholars, researchers, and policy-makers
in the areas of money and banking,
credit markets, regulation of financial
institutions, international payments,
portfolio management, and monetary
and fiscal policy.
**Readers:** Professors, economists,
researchers, bankers.

67595
### MORNINGSTAR VARIABLE ANNUITY: LIFE PERFORMANCE REPORT
225 W. Wacker Dr.
Chicago, IL 60606-1224
Telephone: (800) 876-5005
FAX: (312) 697-6558
Year Established: 1991
Pub. Frequency: m.

Page Size: broadsheet
Subscrip. Rate: $15/issue; $55/q.
Circulation: 1,769
Circulation Type: paid
**Owner(s):**
Morningstar
53 W. Jackson Blvd.
Chicago, IL 60604
Telephone: (800) 876-5005
Ownership %: 100
**Management:**
Joe Mansueto ......................................President
Don Phillips ........................................Publisher
Susan Bray ........................Advertising Manager
**Editorial:**
Jennifer Strickland ...................................Editor
**Readers:** Insurance agents, planners and
individual investors.

65294

**MORTGAGE & REAL ESTATE
EXECUTIVES REPORT, THE**
One Penn Plz., 42nd Fl.
New York, NY 10119
Telephone: (800) 950-1201
FAX: (212) 971-5240
Year Established: 1969
Pub. Frequency: s-m.
Page Size: standard
Subscrip. Rate: $140/yr.
Circulation: 5,000
Circulation Type: paid
**Owner(s):**
Warren Gorham Lamont
One Penn Plz., 42nd Fl.
New York, NY 10119
Telephone: (800) 922-0066
Ownership %: 100
**Editorial:**
Alvin Arnold ............................................Editor
**Desc.:** Covers legal, regulatory & tax
issues that relate to ownership,
investment, development & operation of
real estate.

67597

**MUTUAL FUND PERFORMANCE
REPORT**
225 W. Wacker Dr.
Chicago, IL 60606-1224
Telephone: (800) 876-5005
Year Established: 1990
Pub. Frequency: m.
Page Size: standard
Subscrip. Rate: $125/yr.
Circulation: 2,000
Circulation Type: paid
**Owner(s):**
Morningstar
53 W. Jackson Blvd.
Chicago, IL 60604
Telephone: (800) 876-5005
Ownership %: 100
**Management:**
Joe Mansueto ......................................President
Don Phillips ........................................Publisher
Susan Newsome ................Advertising Manager
**Editorial:**
Michelle Levell .........................................Editor
**Readers:** Individual and professional
investors.

67591

**MUTUAL FUND SOURCEBOOK**
225 W. Wacker
Chicago, IL 60606
Telephone: (800) 876-5005
Year Established: 1986
Pub. Frequency: a.
Page Size: standard
Subscrip. Rate: $225/yr.
Circulation: 2,000
Circulation Type: paid

**Owner(s):**
Morningstar
225 W. Wacker
Chicago, IL 60606
Telephone: (800) 876-5005
Ownership %: 100
**Management:**
Joe Mansueto ......................................President
Don Phillips ........................................Publisher
Susan Newsome ...............Advertising Manager
**Editorial:**
Patty Dutile ..............................................Editor
**Readers:** Individual and professional
investors.

65681

**NFR COMMUNICATIONS**
2850 Metro Dr., Ste. 524
Minneapolis, MN 55425
Telephone: (612) 854-2177
FAX: (612) 854-2627
Year Established: 1894
Pub. Frequency: w.
Page Size: standard
Subscrip. Rate: $59/yr.; $36/6 mos.
Materials: 06,15,16,27,32,33,34
Circulation: 4,000
Circulation Type: free & paid
**Owner(s):**
NFR Communications, Inc.
2850 Metro Dr., 524
Minneapolis, MN 55425
Telephone: (612) 854-2177
Ownership %: 100
**Bureau(s):**
Northwestern Financial Review
8450 Hickman Rd., Ste. 15C
Des Moines, IA 50325
Telephone: (515) 252-1713
Contact: Robert Cronin, President
**Management:**
Robert Cronin ......................................President
Tom Bengtson ....................................Publisher
**Editorial:**
Tom Bengtson ..........................................Editor
**Desc.:** Feature section devoted to
management, operational, and employee
training ideas. Usually written by bankers
or by our staff based on personal
interviews. Also, special articles
concerning agricultural advances of
interest to country bankers. Individual
news sections for each of eight states
covering prime circulation area. If news
material is of general concern to our
readership, we try to use it, particularly if
it contains information on people
traveling this area.
**Readers:** Bankers doing business in this
area, and approximately 4,000 banks in
9 state areas.
**Deadline:** ads-8 days

21986

**PENSIONS & INVESTMENTS**
220 E. 42nd St., Ste. 930
New York, NY 10017
Telephone: (212) 210-0114
FAX: (212) 210-0117
Year Established: 1973
Pub. Frequency: bi-w.
Page Size: tabloid
Subscrip. Rate: $180/yr.
Freelance Pay: varies
Circulation: 51,000
Circulation Type: paid
**Owner(s):**
Crain Communications, Inc.
220 E. 42nd St.
New York, NY 10017-5806
Telephone: (212) 210-0100
Ownership %: 100

**Bureau(s):**
Pensions & Investments
740 Rush St.
Chicago, IL 60611
Telephone: (312) 649-5280
Contact: Mark Ganchiff, Advertising

Pensions & Investments
6404 Wilshire Blvd.
Los Angeles, CA 90048
Telephone: (213) 655-8157
Contact: Marta Stevens, Advertising

Pensions & Investments
199 State St., 7th Fl.
Boston, MA 02109
Telephone: (310) 655-8157
Contact: Jane Howell, Advertising
**Management:**
Keith E. Crain ......................................President
William T. Bisson, Jr. ...........................Publisher
Carolyn Simpson ..............Circulation Manager
Jeanne Delagardelle ................Classified Adv.
Manager
Julie Hunt ...........................Promotion Manager
**Editorial:**
Michael Clowes .......................................Editor
Nancy Webman ......................Managing Editor
Jay Territo ..........................................Advertising
Tony Ficke ........................................Art Director
Steve Hemmerick ....................Associate Editor
Joel Chernoff ..........................Associate Editor
**Desc.:** News magazine covering
developments affecting the investment
and management of the $4 trillion
institutional investment marketplace.
**Readers:** Financial executives of
corporations, officers of financial
institutions, and investment
professionals.

24510

**PENSION WORLD**
6151 Powers Ferry Rd., N.W.
Atlanta, GA 30339
Telephone: (404) 955-2500
Year Established: 1964
Pub. Frequency: m.
Page Size: standard
Subscrip. Rate: $6/copy; $60/yr.
Freelance Pay: $125/pg.
Circulation: 28,000
Circulation Type: controlled
**Owner(s):**
Communication Channels, Inc.
6151 Powers Ferry Rd., N.W.
Atlanta, GA 30339
Ownership %: 100
**Bureau(s):**
Communication Channels, Inc.
214 Massachusetts Ave.
Washington, DC
Telephone: (202) 544-0304
Contact: Ken Silverstein

Communication Channels, Inc.
390 Fifth Ave.
New York, NY 10018
Telephone: (212) 613-9700
**Management:**
Jerrold France ......................................President
Andrew Farris .....................................Publisher
Walter Coward ...................Circulation Manager
Jamie Hood .......................Promotion Manager
**Editorial:**
Ed LaBorwit ............................................Editor
Robin Sherman .......................Editorial Director
Roxanne Starr ..................................Art Director
Steven E. Schanes .................Editorial Advisor
Donna Guest ........................Editorial Assistant
Peter Ward ...........................Marketing Director
Marty Greene .......................Production Director
**Desc.:** Covers field of pensions/employee
benefits legislation, administration,
investments.

**Readers:** CEO's, CFO's, administrators of
employee benefit plans, institutional
investors, consultants, & investment
managers.

68688

**PUBLIC BUDGETING & FINANCIAL
MANAGEMENT**
270 Madison Ave.
New York, NY 10016
Telephone: (212) 696-9000
Year Established: 1989
Pub. Frequency: 3/yr.
Subscrip. Rate: $137.50/yr. to individuals;
$275/yr. to institutions
**Owner(s):**
Marcel Dekker, Inc.
270 Madison Ave.
New York, NY 10016
Telephone: (212) 696-9000
Ownership %: 100
**Editorial:**
Jack Rabin ...............................................Editor
**Desc.:** Provides a forum in which public
administration professionals can share
issues and their applications in the
public, private and nonprofit
communities.

65009

**PUBLIC FINANCE QUARTERLY**
2455 Teller Rd.
Thousand Oaks, CA 91320
Telephone: (805) 499-0721
FAX: (805) 499-0871
Year Established: 1973
Pub. Frequency: q.
Page Size: standard
Subscrip. Rate: $59/yr. individuals;
$177/yr. institutions
Circulation: 1,400
Circulation Type: paid
**Owner(s):**
Sage Publications, Inc.
2455 Teller Rd.
Thousand Oaks, CA 91320
Telephone: (805) 499-0721
Ownership %: 100
**Management:**
Cris Anderson ....................Circulation Manager
**Editorial:**
J. Ronnie Davis ........................................Editor
**Desc.:** Studies the theory, policy, and
institutions related to the allocation,
distribution, and stabilization functions
within the public sector of the economy.

21987

**REGISTERED REPRESENTATIVE,
THE**
18818 Teller Ave., Ste. 280
Irvine, CA 92715
Telephone: (714) 851-2220
FAX: (714) 851-1636
Year Established: 1976
Pub. Frequency: m.
Page Size: standard
Subscrip. Rate: $21/yr.
Materials: 02,06,10,20,32,33
Freelance Pay: $.20/wd.
Print Process: web offset
Circulation: 90,000
Circulation Type: controlled
**Owner(s):**
Plaza Communications, Inc.
18818 Teller Ave., Ste. 280
Irvine, CA 92715
Telephone: (714) 979-3699
Ownership %: 100
**Management:**
Tolman Farrah Geffs .........................Publisher
Sharon Bauman .................Circulation Manager
Carol Lawrence .....................Office Manager
**Editorial:**
Tolman Farrah Geffs ..................Editor in Chief
Dan Jamison ...............................Senior Editor
Chuck LeBresh .............................Art Director

---

**Materials Accepted/Included:** 01-Business news 02-By-line articles 03-Fashion news 04-Food news 05-Freelance copy 06-Letters to editor 07-Real estate news 08-Sports news 09-Travel news
10-Book rev. 11-Movie rev. 12-Music rev. 13-TV rev. 14-Theater rev. 15-Coming events 16-Obituaries 17-Question & answer 18-Social announcements 19-Artwork 20-Cartoons 21-Photos 22-TV listings
23-Audio rec. 24-Video rec. 25-Books 26-Films/film clips 27-Personnel news 28-Press releases 29-New product news/photos 30-Trade lit. 31-Contracts awarded 32-Display adv. 33-Classified adv.

Adele Wodack ..............Vice President, Finance
Myrna Shinbaum ..............Vice President, Sales
**Desc.:** Helps educate the broker in all phases of the securities industry, by publishing stories on successful brokers and their selling, prospecting techniques. We help motivate the broker to deal with his clients in a more professional and successful manner.
**Readers:** Readership of 81,756 retail stock brokers.

66027
## SECURITIES WEEK
1221 Ave. of the Americas, 36th Fl.
New York, NY 10020
Telephone: (212) 512-6148
Year Established: 1973
Pub. Frequency: w.
Subscrip. Rate: $1350/yr. US; $1375/yr. foreign
Print Process: offset
Circulation: 1,300
Circulation Type: paid
**Owner(s):**
McGraw-Hill, Inc.
1221 Ave. of the Americas
New York, NY 10020
Telephone: (212) 512-6148
FAX: (212) 512-3435
Ownership %: 100
**Editorial:**
Michael Ocrant ........................Managing Editor
**Desc.:** Contains news and analysis of the securities industry, futures and options industries.
**Readers:** Senior executives at Securities and Futures Exchanges and firms; law firms; regulators, other financial services professionals.

69358
## SERVICING MANAGEMENT
P.O. Box 2330
Waterbury, CT 06722-2330
Telephone: (203) 755-0158
FAX: (203) 755-3480
Year Established: 1989
Pub. Frequency: m.
Page Size: tabloid
Subscrip. Rate: $48/yr.
Materials: 01,02,05,06,07,19,20,21,25,27, 28,29,30,32
Freelance Pay: $50-$500/article
Print Process: offset
Circulation: 23,000
Circulation Type: free & paid
**Owner(s):**
LDJ Corp.
P.O. Box 2330
Waterbury, CT 06722-2330
Telephone: (203) 755-0158
FAX: (203) 755-3480
Ownership %: 100
**Editorial:**
Ruth Guillet Fields ..............................Editor
**Desc.:** Provides how-to and trends analysis for executives and managers of mortgage servicing operations.
**Deadline:** story-2 mos.; news-2 mos.; photo-2 mos.; ads-2 mos.

21998
## TRUSTS & ESTATES
6151 Powers Ferry Rd., N.W.
Atlanta, GA 30339
Telephone: (404) 955-2500
FAX: (404) 618-0348
Year Established: 1904
Pub. Frequency: m.
Page Size: standard
Subscrip. Rate: $75/yr.
Materials: 02,06,15,32,33
Freelance Pay: $250/article
Circulation: 14,000
Circulation Type: paid

**Owner(s):**
Argus Business, Inc.
6151 Powers Ferry Rd., N.W.
Atlanta, GA 30339
Telephone: (404) 955-2500
Ownership %: 100
**Management:**
Jerrold France ..............................President
Charles E. Lloyd ..............................Publisher
**Editorial:**
Michael S. Klim ..............................Editor
Allison Warren ..............................Associate Editor
Michael S. Klim ..............................Associate Publisher
Martin Greene ..............................Production Director
**Desc.:** Published articles on estate planning and administration, institutional investments, employee benefits and bank trust department operation, philanthropy, taxes, accounting, life insurance and all disciplines related to estate planning and/or estate administration. Departments include: Law and Life Insurance, Philanthropy and Estate Planning. Trends & Developments, Meetings & Conventions, Litigation Notes, Questions and Answers on Estate Planning.
**Readers:** Trust officers, estate attorneys, life insurance, CPA's, fund raisers.

## Group 084-Fire Protection

23003
## AMERICAN FIRE JOURNAL
9072 E. Artesia Blvd., Ste. 7
Bellflower, CA 90706
Telephone: (310) 866-1664
FAX: (310) 867-6434
Year Established: 1952
Pub. Frequency: m.
Page Size: standard
Subscrip. Rate: $3 newsstand; $19.95/yr.
Freelance Pay: $1.50/col. in.
Circulation: 6,000
Circulation Type: paid
**Owner(s):**
Fire Publications, Inc.
9072 E. Artesia Blvd.
Bellflower, CA 90706
Telephone: (310) 866-1664
Ownership %: 100
**Management:**
John A. Ackerman ..............................President
John A. Ackerman ..............................Publisher
John A. Ackerman ..............Business Manager
Anjli Chudasame ..............Circulation Manager
**Editorial:**
Carol Carlsen Brooks ..............................Editor
R.E. Dundant ..............................Design Director
**Desc.:** All news dealing with the fire service is welcome and may or may not be edited. Of particular interest are news stories from doctors, scientists, college instructors dealing with first aid, rescue, fire behavior, fire research, etc.
**Readers:** Fire service personnel, chief officers, persons with active interest in the fire service.

22991
## FIRE CHIEF
35 E. Wicker Dr.
Ste. 700
Chicago, IL 60601-2198
Telephone: (312) 726-7277
FAX: (312) 726-0241
Year Established: 1956
Pub. Frequency: m.
Page Size: standard
Subscrip. Rate: $52/yr.
Freelance Pay: $40-$50/pg.
Circulation: 39,800
Circulation Type: controlled

**Owner(s):**
Argus Business
6151 Powers Ferry Rd., N.W.
Atlanta, GA 30339
Telephone: (404) 955-2500
Ownership %: 100
**Management:**
Anthony Parrino ..............................Publisher
**Editorial:**
Scott Baltic ..............................Editor
Sarah Johnston ..............Assistant Editor
Lauren Spain ..............Assistant Editor
John D. Rukavina ..............Legal Correspondant
Vince Brannigan ..............Legal Correspondant
Philip Stittleburg ..............Legal Correspondant
Colin A. Campbell ......................Washington Correspondant
**Desc.:** Feature articles directed to the needs and interests of fire chiefs on management, administration, fire fighting operations, and training. Factual and technical stories of fires fought and/or extinguished by volunteer or paid fire departments. By-line of a fire chief or fire officer preferred. Departments include: News and Trends, New Equipment, Free Literature, Books/Video, Calendar of Events, Washington Report, and a legal column.
**Readers:** Chiefs of America's fire departments.

22993
## FIRE ENGINEERING
Park 80 W. Plz. 2, 7th Fl.
Rochelle Park, NJ 07662
Telephone: (201) 845-0800
FAX: (201) 845-6275
Year Established: 1877
Pub. Frequency: m.
Page Size: standard
Subscrip. Rate: $21.95/yr.
Freelance Pay: varies
Circulation: 42,006
Circulation Type: paid
**Owner(s):**
Pennwell Publishing Co.
Park 80 W. Plz. 2, 7th Fl.
Rochelle Park, NJ 07662
Telephone: (201) 845-0800
Ownership %: 100
**Management:**
Henry H. Dinneen ..............................Publisher
**Editorial:**
William A. Manning ..............................Editor
**Desc.:** Reports on fire fighting techniques, use of equipment, tests, etc. Departments include: news, of the manufacturers, persons in the news, books, coming events.
**Readers:** Municipal fire chiefs & officials, industrial engineers, etc.

69212
## FIREFIGHTER'S NEWS
1111 Hwy. 1
Nassau, DE 19969
Telephone: (302) 645-5600
FAX: (302) 645-8747
Mailing Address:
P.O. Box 100
Nassau, DE 19969
Year Established: 1983
Pub. Frequency: bi-m.
Page Size: tabloid
Subscrip. Rate: $2.50 newsstand; $15/yr.
Materials: 01,02,05,06,15,28,30,32,33
Print Process: web
Circulation: 42,000
Circulation Type: controlled & paid
**Owner(s):**
Lifesaving Communications
1111 Hwy. 1
Nassau, DE 19969
Telephone: (302) 645-5600
Ownership %: 100

**Management:**
David McLaughlin ..............................Publisher
**Editorial:**
W.H. Stevenson ..............................Editor
**Desc.:** Provides information and skills for fire service decision makers.

22996
## FIREHOUSE MAGAZINE
445 Broad Hollow Rd.
Ste. 21
Melville, NY 11747
Telephone: (516) 845-2700
Year Established: 1976
Pub. Frequency: m.
Page Size: standard
Subscrip. Rate: $3.25 newsstand; $24/yr.
Circulation: 116,000
Circulation Type: paid
**Owner(s):**
PTN Publishing Co.
445 Broad Hollow Rd.
Melville, NY 11747
Telephone: (516) 845-2700
Ownership %: 100
**Management:**
Stanley Sills ..............................President
Bruce T. Bowling ..............................Publisher
**Editorial:**
Barbara Dunleavy ..............................Editor
Angela Bellucci ..............................Editor
**Desc.:** Feature stories on fires, firefighters, and related fields of law, insurance and equipment industries, architectural trends, ambulance services. Also consumer-oriented columns on new products including areas of home repair and appliances, sports, recreation, camping, and family activities.
**Readers:** Firefighters, paid and volunteer, and others interested in the industry.

22995
## FIRE TECHNOLOGY
One Batterymarch Pk.
Quincy, MA 02269-9101
Telephone: (617) 984-7565
FAX: (617) 471-5231
Year Established: 1965
Pub. Frequency: q.
Page Size: pocket
Subscrip. Rate: $44.50/yr.
Circulation: 2,500
Circulation Type: paid
**Owner(s):**
National Fire Protection Association
One Batterymarch Pk.
Boston, MA 02109
Telephone: (617) 770-3000
Ownership %: 100
**Management:**
Kelli Riccardi ..............Circulation Manager
**Editorial:**
John M. Watts, Jr., Ph.D. ..............................Editor
Gene A. Moulton ..............Managing Editor
Gene A. Moulton ..............Production Director
**Desc.:** By-lined and referred articles on fire protection research and engineering subjects and allied fields with fire protection association; theory, concepts, techniques and equipment. Manuscript length/25-40 double spaced, typewritten pages including tables and illustrations, Departments include: Articles, Book Reviews, Software Reviews, Letters, Viewpoints, Technical Notes, Current Research News, Meeting Notices.
**Readers:** Fire protection engineers, fire department officers, practitioners, researchers, safety engineers and directors, scientists, academics, engineering consultants, insurance concerns, etc.

Materials Accepted/Included: 01-Business news 02-By-line articles 03-Fashion news 04-Food news 05-Freelance copy 06-Letters to editor 07-Real estate news 08-Sports news 09-Travel news 10-Book rev. 11-Movie rev. 12-Music rev. 13-TV rev. 14-Theater rev. 15-Coming events 16-Obituaries 17-Question & answer 18-Social announcements 19-Artwork 20-Cartoons 21-Photos 22-TV listings 23-Audio rec. 24-Video rec. 25-Books 26-Films/film clips 27-Personnel news 28-Press releases 29-New product news/photos 30-Trade lit. 31-Contracts awarded 32-Display adv. 33-Classified adv.

## FLORIDA FIREMAN
22998

P.O. Box 968
Avon Park, FL 33825
Telephone: (813) 453-4817
FAX: (813) 453-7450
Year Established: 1925
Pub. Frequency: m.: July-May
Page Size: standard
Subscrip. Rate: $15/yr.
Circulation: 5,800
Circulation Type: controlled
**Owner(s):**
Florida State Firemen's Assoc., Inc.
P.O. Box 968
Avon Park, FL 33825
Telephone: (813) 453-4817
Ownership %: 100
**Management:**
David Caulfield .............................President
**Editorial:**
Dale Oswalt ...............................Editor in Chief
**Desc.:** Devoted to the advancement of the
fire service, especially in Florida.
**Readers:** Officers, rank and file members
of Florida.

## IAFC ON SCENE
69215

4025 Fair Ridge Dr.
Fairfax, VA 22033-2868
Telephone: (703) 273-0911
FAX: (703) 273-9363
Year Established: 1934
Pub. Frequency: s-m.
Subscrip. Rate: $60/yr.
Circulation: 10,000
Circulation Type: paid
**Owner(s):**
International Association of Fire Chiefs
4025 Fair Ridge Dr.
Fairfax, VA 22033-2868
Telephone: (703) 273-0911
Ownership %: 100
**Editorial:**
Tim Elliot .........................................Editor
**Desc.:** Provides and overview of the types
of things that will affect change in the
fire service and gives specifics about
where to obtain useful references.
**Readers:** Fire service leaders.

## INDUSTRIAL FIRE CHIEF
69213

6151 Powers Ferry Rd., N.W.
Atlanta, GA 30339-2941
Telephone: (404) 955-2500
FAX: (404) 955-0400
Year Established: 1992
Pub. Frequency: bi-m.
Page Size: standard
Subscrip. Rate: $24/yr.
Circulation: 18,000
Circulation Type: paid
**Owner(s):**
Communication Channels, Inc.
6151 Powers Ferry Rd., N.W.
Atlanta, GA 30339-2941
Telephone: (404) 955-2500
Ownership %: 100
**Readers:** Industrial fire service executives
and emergency management personnel
responsible for industrial fire and safety
prevention, protection and suppression
operations in industrial plants, field
operations and commercial buildings.

## IOWA SMOKE-EATER
22999

109 E. Main
Pierce, NE 68767
Telephone: (402) 329-4665
FAX: (402) 329-6337
Mailing Address:
P.O. Box 129
Pierce, NE 68767
Year Established: 1954

Pub. Frequency: m.
Page Size: tabloid
Subscrip. Rate: $10/yr.
Circulation: 8,887
Circulation Type: paid
**Owner(s):**
Smoke-Eater Publications
109 E. Main
Pierce, NE 68767
Telephone: (402) 329-4665
Ownership %: 100
**Management:**
Leslie Falter ...............................Publisher
Randee Falter ..............................Publisher
**Editorial:**
Randee Falter ..................................Editor
**Desc.:** Covers all major fires in Iowa,
training features, other bylines, new
equipment ideas, etc. Departments
include: Fire Marshal Office Notes,
Hoseman Hank Reports, Remarks from
your President, Secretary's Notes,
Editorial.
**Readers:** Volunteer firemen in the state of
Iowa.

## JOURNAL OF FIRE SCIENCES
23000

851 New Holland Ave., Box 3535
Lancaster, PA 17601
Telephone: (717) 291-5609
FAX: (717) 295-4538
Year Established: 1983
Pub. Frequency: bi-m.
Page Size: tabloid
Subscrip. Rate: $295/yr.; $580/2 yrs.;
$865/3 yrs.
Circulation: 500
Circulation Type: paid
**Owner(s):**
Technomic Publishing Co., Inc.
Telephone: (717) 291-5609
Ownership %: 100
**Bureau(s):**
Technomic Publishing AG
Missionsstrasse 44
CH-4055 Basel Switzerland
Contact: Frank Versaci, Director
**Management:**
Melvyn A. Kohudic ......................Publisher
**Editorial:**
Gordon E. Hartzell ..................Editor in Chief
**Desc.:** Flammability of various materials,
fire and flammability in various
environments, and fire exposures and
characteristics are explored by the
foremost authorities in the field.
Pertinent test methods and apparatus,
theories and techniques of fire
prevention, retardation, and
extinguishment, as well as fire retardants
and extinguishing agents, are also
reported.

## MINNESOTA SMOKE-EATER
23001

109 E. Main
Pierce, NE 68767
Telephone: (402) 329-4665
FAX: (402) 329-6337
Mailing Address:
P.O. Box 129
Pierce, NE 68767
Year Established: 1949
Pub. Frequency: m.
Page Size: tabloid
Subscrip. Rate: $10/yr.
Circulation: 12,028
Circulation Type: paid
**Owner(s):**
Smoke-Eater Publications
Box 129
Pierce, NE 68767
Telephone: (402) 329-4665
Ownership %: 100

**Management:**
Leslie Falter ...............................Publisher
Randee Falter ..............................Publisher
**Editorial:**
Randee Falter ..................................Editor
**Desc.:** Covers all major fires in Minnesota,
training features, other bylines, new
equipment ideas, etc. Departments
include: Fire Marshal Division Notes,
Hoseman Hank Reports, Remarks from
your President, Editorial.
**Readers:** Volunteer firemen in the state of
Minnesota.

## NATIONAL FIRE & ARSON REPORT
69216

P.O. Box 411087
Charlotte, NC 28241-1087
Telephone: (800) 488-6327
FAX: (704) 588-1248
Year Established: 1982
Pub. Frequency: q.
Page Size: standard
Subscrip. Rate: $28/yr. US; $36/yr.
Canada; $55/yr. elsewhere
Materials: 02,06,10,15,17,21,25,28,30,32,33
Circulation: 10,000
Circulation Type: paid
**Owner(s):**
Investigative Research International, Inc.
P.O. Box 411087
Charlotte, NC 28241-1087
Telephone: (800) 488-6327
Ownership %: 100
**Editorial:**
Barbara P. Goodnight ..........................Editor
**Desc.:** Provides comprehensive information
and training materials pertinent to
professionals concerned with fire, arson
and fraud investigation as well as
general investigative resources.
**Readers:** Insurance industry, fire service,
law enforcement, legal, armed forces,
educational, engineering firms & labs,
private sector.

## NEBRASKA SMOKE-EATER
23002

109 E. Main
Pierce, NE 68767
Telephone: (402) 329-4665
FAX: (402) 329-6337
Mailing Address:
P.O. Box 129
Pierce, NE 68767
Year Established: 1946
Pub. Frequency: m.
Page Size: tabloid
Subscrip. Rate: $10/yr.
Circulation: 10,350
Circulation Type: paid
**Owner(s):**
Smoke-Eater Publications
Box 129
Pierce, NE 68767
Telephone: (402) 329-4665
Ownership %: 100
**Management:**
Leslie Falter ...............................Publisher
Randee Falter ..............................Publisher
**Editorial:**
Randee Falter ..................................Editor
**Desc.:** Full report each month of all major
Nebraska fires, training features, other
by-lines, new equipment ideas, etc.
**Readers:** Volunteer firemen in the state of
Nebraska.

## NFPA JOURNAL
22994

One Batterymarch Pk.
Boston, MA 02109
Telephone: (617) 770-3000
FAX: (617) 984-7054
Year Established: 1965
Pub. Frequency: bi-m.

Page Size: standard
Subscrip. Rate: $95/yr. members
Materials: 32,33
Freelance Pay: $400/article
Print Process: web
Circulation: 64,000
Circulation Type: controlled
**Owner(s):**
National Fire Protection Association
One Batterymarch Pk.
Boston, MA 02269
Telephone: (617) 770-3000
FAX: (617) 984-7090
Ownership %: 100
**Management:**
George Miller ...............................President
Marilyn Freel .............Advertising Manager
**Editorial:**
Kathleen M. Robinson ...........Editorial Director
Jane Dashfeld ..........................Art Director
Shirley Sherad .....................Associate Editor
Kriston Anderson ..................Associate Editor
**Desc.:** Official publication of the National
Fire Protection Association, designed to
provide its members with latest technical
information in fire protection and fire
prevention, new developments in the fire
engineering field, reviews of important
fires and their lessons, studies of
research and field tests affecting fire
safety and feature articles on fire
protection problems, and national loss
figures useful to stimulate loss
prevention programs for industry, public
officials and fire departments.
Departments Include: Fire Record.
**Readers:** Organizations, companies and
individuals

## TODAY'S FIREMAN
69214

P.O. Box 875108
Los Angeles, CA 90087
Telephone: (213) 960-5776
Year Established: 1960
Pub. Frequency: q.
Page Size: tabloid
Subscrip. Rate: $9/yr.
Circulation: 15500
Circulation Type: paid
**Owner(s):**
Towerhigh Publications, Inc.
P.O. Box 875108
Los Angeles, CA 90087
Telephone: (213) 960-5776
Ownership %: 100
**Editorial:**
Donald Mack ...................................Editor
**Desc.:** Covers the fire service and fire
fighting for both public and professional
fighters.

## Group 086-Fishing & Fisheries

## AQUACULTURE MAGAZINE
23005

31 College Pl.
Asheville, NC 28801
Telephone: (704) 254-7334
FAX: (704) 253-0677
Mailing Address:
P.O. Box 2329
Asheville, NC 28802
Year Established: 1974
Pub. Frequency: bi-m.
Page Size: standard
Subscrip. Rate: $17/yr.
Freelance Pay: negotiable
Circulation: 7,392
Circulation Type: paid

**Materials Accepted/Included:** 01-Business news 02-By-line articles 03-Fashion news 04-Food news 05-Freelance copy 06-Letters to editor 07-Real estate news 08-Sports news 09-Travel news 10-Book rev. 11-Movie rev. 12-Music rev. 13-TV rev. 14-Theater rev. 15-Coming events 16-Obituaries 17-Question & answer 18-Social announcements 19-Artwork 20-Cartoons 21-Photos 22-TV listings 23-Audio rec. 24-Video rec. 25-Books 26-Films/film clips 27-Personnel news 28-Press releases 29-New product news/photos 30-Trade lit. 31-Contracts awarded 32-Display adv. 33-Classified adv.

4-141

**Owner(s):**
Richard Gallagher
P.O. Box 2329
Asheville, NC 28802
Telephone: (704) 254-7334
Ownership %: 100
**Management:**
Richard V. Gallagher ..........................Publisher
**Editorial:**
Greg Gallagher ..........................Editor
Steven Hart ..........................Marketing Director
**Desc.:** Gives in depth news and feature
coverage of all commercial species of
aquaculture throughout the United
States and the world. We make
generous use of photography, how-to
articles, new product information,
research, and special projects. By-lines
are used on guest articles and columns,
with a considerable amount of articles
being staff written. Publicity material is
carefully screened for news information
and educational value, and the length of
all articles is variable. In addition, we
give comprehensive coverage of all
aquaculture trade association's events,
etc., and extensive coverage of college-
university developments in aquaculture
research.
**Readers:** Aquaculturists (commercial fish
farmers) engaged in the production of
finfish, shellfish, crustaceans, and
aquatic plants. Scientists, academicians
and government personnel involved in
research, production, and service.
Readership is worldwide.

23672
**FISHERMEN'S NEWS, THE**
Fishermen's Terminal
4005 20th Ave. W.
Seattle, WA 98199
Telephone: (206) 282-7545
FAX: (206) 282-5125
Year Established: 1945
Pub. Frequency: m.
Page Size: tabloid
Subscrip. Rate: $1.75 newsstand; $16/yr.
Circulation: 15,000
Circulation Type: paid
**Owner(s):**
The Fishermen's News, Inc.
Fishermens Terminal Bld C3 110
Seattle, WA 98119
Telephone: (206) 282-7545
Ownership %: 100

Walter M. Kisner, Jr.
833 N.W. 116th St.
Seattle, WA 98177
**Management:**
Walter M. Kisner, Jr. ..........................President
Walter M. Kisner, Jr. ..........................Publisher
Eleanor Gallagher ..............Circulation Manager
**Editorial:**
Sam Smith ..........................Editor
**Desc.:** Tells story of Pacific Coast
commercial fishing fleets to the men in
the fleets. Articles on new developments
in boat building, engines
and applications, electronic gear, netting,
etc.
**Readers:** Commercial fisherman of the
Pacific Coast.

69618
**FISHERY BULLETIN**
7600 Sandpoint Way, N.E.
Seattle, WA 98115
Telephone: (206) 526-6107
FAX: (206) 526-6426
Year Established: 1881
Pub. Frequency: q.
Subscrip. Rate: $16/yr. US; $20/yr. foreign
Circulation: 2,000
Circulation Type: paid

**Owner(s):**
U.S. National Marine Fisheries Service
7600 Sandpoint Way N.E.
Seattle, WA 98115
Telephone: (206) 526-6107
Ownership %: 100
**Editorial:**
Nancy Peacock ..........................Editor
**Desc.:** Original research reports and
technical notes on investigations in
fishery science.

65745
**FISHING TACKLE RETAILER**
5845 Carmichael Rd.
Montgomery, AL 36117
Telephone: (205) 272-9530
FAX: (205) 279-7148
Mailing Address:
P.O. Box 17151
Montgomery, AL 36141
Year Established: 1980
Pub. Frequency: 11/yr.
Page Size: standard
Subscrip. Rate: free to members
Freelance Pay: $.15-$.20/wd.
Circulation: 22,000
Circulation Type: controlled
**Owner(s):**
B.A.S.S. Publications
5845 Carmichael Rd.
Montgomery, AL 36117
Telephone: (202) 272-9530
Ownership %: 100
**Editorial:**
Dave Ellison ..........................Editor
Deborah Johnson ..................Managing Editor
Donna Speir ................Administrative Assistant
Deborah Johnson ..............New Products Editor
**Desc.:** To strengthen the business acumen
of tackle retailers and to disseminate
timely news of general interest to the
sport fishing industry.
**Readers:** Fishing tackle retailers,
manufacturers, wholesalers, and
representatives.

69138
**FLY TACKLE DEALER**
P.O. Box 370
Camden, ME 04843
Telephone: (207) 594-9544
FAX: (207) 594-7215
Pub. Frequency: bi-m.
Circulation: 10,500
Circulation Type: paid
**Owner(s):**
Down East Enterprises, Inc.
P.O. Box 370
Camden, ME 04843
Telephone: (207) 594-9544
Ownership %: 100
**Editorial:**
Silvid Calan ..........................Editor
**Readers:** Makers and sellers of fly-fishing
equipment.

65646
**JOURNAL OF ICHTHYOLOGY**
605 Third Ave.
New York, NY 10158
Telephone: (212) 850-6000
Pub. Frequency: 8/yr.
Page Size: standard
Subscrip. Rate: $996/yr.
Circulation: 425
Circulation Type: paid
**Owner(s):**
John Wiley & Sons, Inc.
605 Third Ave.
New York, NY 10158
Telephone: (212) 850-6000
Ownership %: 100
**Editorial:**
Robert J. Behnke ..........................Editor

69622
**MARINE FISH MANAGEMENT**
1201 National Press Bldg.
Washington, DC 20045
Telephone: (202) 347-6643
Year Established: 1975
Pub. Frequency: m.
Subscrip. Rate: $87.50/yr. US; $92.50/yr.
foreign
**Owner(s):**
Nautilus Press, Inc.
1201 National Press Bldg.
Washington, DC 20045
Telephone: (202) 347-6643
Ownership %: 100
**Editorial:**
John Botzum ..........................Editor
**Desc.:** Reports on U.S. fisheries policies in
the U.S. 200-mile zone.

23008
**NATIONAL FISHERMAN**
120 Tillson Ave.
Rockland, ME 04841
Telephone: (207) 594-6222
FAX: (207) 594-8978
Year Established: 1903
Pub. Frequency: 13/yr.
Page Size: tabloid
Subscrip. Rate: $2.50 issue; $22.95/yr.
Freelance Pay: $.05/wd. min.
Circulation: 44,000
Circulation Type: paid
**Owner(s):**
Diversified Communications
465 Congress St.
Portland, ME 04101
Telephone: (207) 774-5981
Ownership %: 100
**Bureau(s):**
National Fisherman
4215 21st Ave. W.
Seattle, WA 98199
Telephone: (206) 283-1150
Contact: Brad Matsen, Editor
**Management:**
Wade Leftwich ..........................Sales Manager
**Editorial:**
James W. Fullilove ..........................Editor
Hugh McKellar ..........................Managing Editor
**Desc.:** Monthly tabloid format covering
commercial fishing, boat building,
general marine news, and features along
such lines as new fishing boats, fishing
techniques, proven designs in pleasure
boats. National circulation.
**Readers:** Fishermen, fishing companies,
charter boat owners, power boat
owners, manufacturers, and consumers.

58761
**NMFS FISHERIES MARKET NEWS
REPORT**
182 Queens Blvd.
Bayville, NJ 08721
Telephone: (908) 240-5330
Mailing Address:
P.O. Box 389
Toms River, NJ 08754
Year Established: 1981
Pub. Frequency: w.
Page Size: tabloid
Subscrip. Rate: $184/yr.
Circulation: 633
Circulation Type: paid
**Owner(s):**
Urner Barry Publications, Inc.
P.O. Box 389
Toms River, NJ 08754
Telephone: (908) 240-5330
Ownership %: 100
**Editorial:**
Joseph T. Soja ..........................Editor

23009
**PACIFIC FISHING**
1515 N.W. 51st
Seattle, WA 98107
Telephone: (206) 789-5333
FAX: (206) 784-5545
Year Established: 1979
Pub. Frequency: m.
Page Size: standard
Subscrip. Rate: $2.50/copy; $24/yr.
Materials: 01,02,05,06,10,15,16,17,28,29,
30,32,33
Freelance Pay: $.15/wd.
Print Process: web offset
Circulation: 10,000
Circulation Type: paid
**Owner(s):**
Salmon Bay Communications
1515 N.W. 51st
Seattle, WA 98107
Telephone: (206) 789-5333
Ownership %: 100
**Management:**
Duane Kelly ..........................Publisher
Gerry Davis ..........................Advertising Manager
Valerie A. McNeil ..........................Office Manager
**Editorial:**
Steve Shapiro ..........................Managing Editor
Connie Bollen ..........................Art Director
**Desc.:** A monthly business magazine for
the US and Canadian west coast fishing
industry. Covers the catching,
processing, and marketing of seafood by
the industry. In-depth feature articles are
the basis of the magazine. Reports on
new seafood products made from west
coast fish, new products for the fishing
industry, and christenings of new fishing
vessels.
**Readers:** Fishermen, processors, seafood
traders, and suppliers.

58751
**SEAFOOD PRICE CURRENT**
182 Queens Blvd.
Bayville, NJ 08721
Telephone: (908) 240-5330
Mailing Address:
P.O. Box 389
Toms River, NJ 08754
Pub. Frequency: s.: Tue. & Thu.
Page Size: tabloid
Subscrip. Rate: $240/yr.
Circulation: 1,150
Circulation Type: paid
**Owner(s):**
Urner Barry Publications, Inc.
182 Queens Blvd.
Bayville, NJ 08721
Telephone: (908) 240-5330
Ownership %: 100
**Management:**
Lisa Sharkus ..........................Advertising Manager
**Editorial:**
Paul B. Brown, Jr. ..........................Editor
Joseph T. Soja ..........................Associate Editor

68838
**SHRIMP NEWS INTERNATIONAL**
9434 Kearny Mesa Rd
San Diego, CA 92131
Telephone: (619) 271-6354
FAX: (619) 271-0324
Year Established: 1976
Pub. Frequency: bi-m.
Page Size: standard
Subscrip. Rate: $95/yr.
Materials: 01,04,05,06,09,10,15,16,17,23,
24,25,26,27,28,29,30,31,32,33
**Owner(s):**
Aqaculture Digest
11057 Negley Ave.
San Diego, CA 92131
Telephone: (619) 271-6354
Ownership %: 100
**Editorial:**
Robert Rosenberry ..........................Editor

**Materials Accepted/Included:** 01-Business news 02-By-line articles 03-Fashion news 04-Food news 05-Freelance copy 06-Letters to editor 07-Real estate news 08-Sports news 09-Travel news
10-Book rev. 11-Movie rev. 12-Music rev. 13-TV rev. 14-Theater rev. 15-Coming events 16-Obituaries 17-Question & answer 18-Social announcements 19-Artwork 20-Cartoons 21-Photos 22-TV listings
23-Audio rec. 24-Video rec. 25-Books 26-Films/film clips 27-Personnel news 28-Press releases 29-New product news/photos 30-Trade lit. 31-Contracts awarded 32-Display adv. 33-Classified adv.

4-142

**Desc.:** Publishes a bi-monthly report, on the Shrimp industry. Subscribers receive a directory and annual report.

## Group 088-Floor Coverings

**EASTERN FLOORS** 71286
17835 Ventura, #312
Encino, CA 91316
Telephone: (818) 345-3550
Year Established: 1991
Pub. Frequency: bi-m.
Subscrip. Rate: $23/yr.
Circulation: 17,000
**Owner(s):**
Specialist Publications, Inc.
17835 Ventura Blvd.
Encino, CA 91316
Telephone: (310) 873-1411
Ownership %: 100
**Management:**
Howard Olansky .....................Publisher
**Editorial:**
Howard Olansky ...........................Editor
Jeff Golden ...................Managing Editor
Jeff Golden ....................Associate Editor
Harold B. Arkoff .................Marketing Manager
Harold B. Arkoff ...........Secretary & Treasurer

**FLOOR FOCUS** 68936
10 S. Division St.
New Rochelle, NY 10805
Telephone: (914) 636-0633
FAX: (914) 636-0809
Year Established: 1992
Pub. Frequency: 10/yr.
Page Size: standard
Subscrip. Rate: $29.95/yr.
Materials: 01,02,06,23,24,25,27,28,29,30,31
Print Process: web offset
Circulation: 7,000
Circulation Type: controlled & paid
**Owner(s):**
Floor Focus, Inc.
10 S. Division St.
New Rochelle, NY 10805
Telephone: (914) 636-0633
Ownership %: 100
**Management:**
Frank O'Neill ...........................Publisher
Maurie O'Neill ...................Associate Publisher
**Editorial:**
Cynthia Williamson-Powers ................Managing Editor
**Deadline:** story-1st of mo. prior to pub. date; news-1st of mo. prior; photo-1st of mo. prior; ads-8th of mo. prior

**FLOORING** 22173
9609 Gayton Rd. Ste. 100
Richmond, VA 23233
Telephone: (804) 741-6704
FAX: (804) 750-2399
Year Established: 1932
Pub. Frequency: m.
Page Size: standard
Subscrip. Rate: $37/yr. US; $45/yr. CN; $97/yr. foreign
Freelance Pay: $200-$500
Circulation: 25,000
Circulation Type: controlled
**Owner(s):**
Leo Douglas, Inc.
9609 Gayton Rd., Ste. 100
Richmond, VA 23233
Telephone: (804) 741-6704
Ownership %: 100
**Management:**
Mike Krisonsky ...........................Publisher
Carolyn Ward ...................Advertising Manager
Theodore Brosseau ..........Advertising Manager
**Editorial:**
Greg Valero ...........................Editor

**Desc.:** Contains articles on how-to, new product, marketing, and merchadising and other aspects of flooring industry.
**Readers:** Floor covering retailers, contractors, distributors, manufacturers.

**FLOORING BUYING GUIDE** 69447
9607 Gayton Rd., Ste. 201
Richmond, VA 23233
Telephone: (804) 741-6704
FAX: (804) 750-2399
Pub. Frequency: a.
Subscrip. Rate: $20/yr.; free to convention attendees
Circulation: 4,570
Circulation Type: paid
**Owner(s):**
Leo Douglas, Inc.
9607 Gayton Rd., Ste. 201
Richmond, VA 23233
Telephone: (804) 741-6704
**Editorial:**
Dan Alaimo .........................Editor

**INSTALLATION & CLEANING SPECIALIST** 23012
17835 Ventura, #312
Encino, CA 91316
Telephone: (818) 345-3550
Year Established: 1963
Pub. Frequency: m.
Page Size: standard
Subscrip. Rate: $38/yr.
Circulation: 20,000
**Owner(s):**
Specialist Publications, Inc.
17835 Ventura Blvd.
Encino, CA 91316
Telephone: (310) 873-1411
**Management:**
Howard Olansky .....................Publisher
**Editorial:**
Howard Olansky ...........................Editor
Jeff Golden ...................Managing Editor
Jeff Golden ....................Associate Editor
Harold B. Arkoff .................Marketing Manager
Harold B. Arkoff ...........Secretary & Treasurer
**Desc.:** Feature articles on installation cleaning, & maintenance of floor coverings. Magazine highlights a rundown of new tools, cleaning equipment, accessories & equipment, installation books and catalogs. Departments include: Product Tools Equipment; Industry News & Calendar of Events.
**Readers:** Floor covering installers, cleaners & maintenance personnel.

**STORE WORLD** 65264
One Kalisa Way, Ste. 205
Paramus, NJ 07652-3508
Telephone: (201) 599-0136
FAX: (201) 599-2378
Year Established: 1984
Pub. Frequency: m.
Page Size: standard
Subscrip. Rate: $60/yr.
Materials: 01,02,05,06,07,10,17,21,27,28, 29,30,32,32,33
Freelance Pay: $4/col. in.
Print Process: web
Circulation: 15,400
Circulation Type: controlled & paid
**Owner(s):**
Business News Publishing Co.
755 W. Big Beaver Rd., Ste. 10
Troy, MI 48084
Telephone: (810) 362-3700
FAX: (810) 362-0317
Ownership %: 100
**Management:**
Myra Smitley ...........................Publisher

**Editorial:**
John Sailer .....................Editorial Director
**Desc.:** Features project case histories, covers installations, techniques, and new products.
**Readers:** Users and specifiers of natural store, including architects, interior designers, building owners, quarries, fabricators, dealers, and importers/exporters.
**Deadline:** story-6 wks.

**WESTERN FLOORS** 23015
17835 Ventura Blvd., #312
Encino, CA 91316
Telephone: (818) 345-3550
Year Established: 1952
Pub. Frequency: m.
Page Size: standard
Subscrip. Rate: $40/yr.
Circulation: 16,000
**Owner(s):**
Specialist Publications, Inc.
17835 Ventura Blvd.
Encino, CA 91316
Telephone: (310) 873-1411
Ownership %: 100
**Management:**
Howard Olansky .....................Publisher
**Editorial:**
Howard Olansky ...........................Editor
Jeff Golden ....................Associate Editor
Harold B. Arkoff .................Marketing Manager
Harold B. Arkoff ...........Secretary & Treasurer
**Desc.:** Feature stories are assigned and prepared directly by the staff. Publicity material used when pertaining to floor news, market developments. Feature stories concentrate on floor and wall coverings, etc. Departments include: News, What's New (new products), Promote for Profit, Installation Techniques.
**Readers:** Floor covering & tile dealers, contractors, distributors, manufacturers.

## Group 090-Florists & Floriculture

**AMERICAN ROSE MAGAZINE, THE** 23017
P.O. Box 30000
Shreveport, LA 71130
Telephone: (318) 938-5402
FAX: (318) 938-5405
Year Established: 1892
Pub. Frequency: m.
Page Size: standard
Subscrip. Rate: $32/yr.
Freelance Pay: negotiable
Circulation: 23,500
Circulation Type: controlled
**Owner(s):**
American Rose Society
P.O. Box 30000
Shreveport, LA 71130
Telephone: (318) 938-5402
Ownership %: 100
**Management:**
Norman Winter .....................Executive Director
Joseph Carmody ...............Advertising Manager
**Editorial:**
Ed Gage ...........................Editor
Beth Horstman .....................Assistant Editor
**Desc.:** For advanced and amateur gardeners interested in roses. Covers growing experiences of others, new products, new varieties, hybridizing, exhibitions, and regional seasonal growing tips.
**Readers:** Homeowners who raise roses.

**FLORACULTURE INTERNATIONAL** 66776
335 N. River St.
Batavia, IL 60510
Telephone: (708) 208-9080
FAX: (708) 208-9350
Mailing Address:
P.O. Box 9
Batavia, IL 60510-0009
Year Established: 1990
Pub. Frequency: 8/yr.
Page Size: standard
Subscrip. Rate: $22/yr.; $39/yr. airmail
Materials: 01,02,05,06,15,25,28,30,32,33
Print Process: web offset
Circulation: 11,100
Circulation Type: controlled
**Owner(s):**
International Horticulture Publications Co.
P.O. Box 9
Batavia, IL 60510-0009
Telephone: (708) 208-9080
FAX: (708) 208-9350
Ownership %: 100
**Management:**
Debbie Hamrick ...........................Publisher
**Editorial:**
Debbie Hamrick ...........................Editor
**Readers:** Commercial producers of Floriculture products worldwide.

**FLORAL MASS MARKETING** 49862
120 S. Riverside Plz.
Ste. 464
Chicago, IL 60606-3908
Telephone: (312) 236-8648
FAX: (312) 238-8891
Year Established: 1982
Pub. Frequency: bi-m.
Page Size: tabloid
Subscrip. Rate: $15/yr.; $28/2 yrs.
Materials: 01,06,15,16,21,28,29,32,33
Freelance Pay: negotiable
Print Process: web offset
Circulation: 18,000
Circulation Type: paid
**Owner(s):**
Cenflo Publications, Inc.
120 S. Riverside Plz.
Ste. 464
Chicago, IL 60606
Telephone: (312) 236-8648
FAX: (312) 238-8891
Ownership %: 100
**Management:**
Kenneth M. Benjamin ...........................Publisher
Eric J. Benjamin ...............Advertising Manager
**Editorial:**
Rosemary C. Baldwin .....................Editor
**Desc.:** Editorial content focuses on how to improve floral and nursery product sales at the retail level with regular features including care and handling, quick 'n easy tips for mass production, marketing tips for major holidays and time sales, viewpoints from prominent industry members on ideas, problems, solutions, techniques and tips. Consumer and industry research is also presented.
**Readers:** Published for floral and nursery products buyers at supermarket chains, discount, variety, department and convenient store chains.

**FLOWER NEWS** 23021
120 S. Riverside Plz., Ste. 464
Chicago, IL 60606
Telephone: (312) 258-8500
FAX: (312) 258-8558
Year Established: 1947
Pub. Frequency: w.

**Materials Accepted/Included:** 01-Business news 02-By-line articles 03-Fashion news 04-Food news 05-Freelance copy 06-Letters to editor 07-Real estate news 08-Sports news 09-Travel news 10-Book rev. 11-Movie rev. 12-Music rev. 13-TV rev. 14-Theater rev. 15-Coming events 16-Obituaries 17-Question & answer 18-Social announcements 19-Artwork 20-Cartoons 21-Photos 22-TV listings 23-Audio rec. 24-Video rec. 25-Books 26-Films/film clips 27-Personnel news 28-Press releases 29-New product news/photos 30-Trade lit. 31-Contracts awarded 32-Display adv. 33-Classified adv.

4-143

Page Size: tabloid
Subscrip. Rate: $20/yr.; $28/2 yrs.;
$39/3yrs.
Materials: 01,02,05,06,10,15,16,21,27,28,
29,32,33
Freelance Pay: negotiable
Print Process: web offset
Circulation: 18,724
Circulation Type: paid
**Owner(s):**
Cenflo Publications, Inc.
120 S. Riverside Plaza, Ste. 4
Chicago, IL 60606
Telephone: (312) 258-8500
FAX: (312) 258-8558
Ownership %: 100
**Management:**
Kenneth M. Benjamin .......................Publisher
Eric J. Benjamin ...............Advertising Manager
**Editorial:**
Rosemary C. Baldwin .........................Editor
**Desc.:** How to merchandising helps and
hints for florists. How to sell more, cut
costs, improve profit picture. Carry new
products section, "hot" important
industry news on national and
international basis of coverage.
**Readers:** Retail florists, wholesale florists,
floral plant growers, allied tradesmen,
floral mass market buyers, etc. Buyers
and sellers of greenhouse-grown and
field-produced bedding plants, green
plants, blooming plants, cut flowers,
foliage and nursery products.

23023
**MICHIGAN FLORIST**
5815 Executive Dr.
Lansing, MI 48909
Telephone: (517) 394-2900
FAX: (517) 394-2900
Mailing Address:
P.O. Box 24065
Lansing, MI 48909-4065
Year Established: 1942
Pub. Frequency: bi-m.
Page Size: standard
Subscrip. Rate: $50/yr.
Materials: 01,02,21,27,28,29,32
Circulation: 3,500
Circulation Type: controlled
**Owner(s):**
Michigan Floral Association
5815 Executive Dr.
Lansing, MI 48909-4065
Telephone: (517) 394-2900
FAX: (517) 394-3011
Ownership %: 100
**Management:**
Barb Doyal .........................Advertising Manager
Marsha Gray ...................................Manager
**Editorial:**
Sue Stuever ...........................Managing Editor
**Desc.:** A publication for the Michigan and
Great Lakes floriculture industry. It aims
to inform and educate members about
industry news, events and new products,
both in editorial and advertising.
**Readers:** Florists, growers, wholesalers,
garden centers, etc.
**Deadline:** story-2 mo. prior to pub. date;
news-2 mo. prior; photo-2 mo. prior; ads-
2 mo. prior

23025
**NURSERY MANAGER**
120 St. Louis
Fort Worth, TX 76104
Telephone: (817) 332-8236
FAX: (817) 877-1862
Mailing Address:
P.O. Box 1868
Fort Worth, TX 76101
Year Established: 1915
Pub. Frequency: m.

Page Size: standard
Subscrip. Rate: $24/yr.
Freelance Pay: $1.50/publ. in.
Circulation: 15,000
Circulation Type: controlled
**Owner(s):**
Branch-Smith Publishing
P.O. Box 1868
Fort Worth, TX 76101
Telephone: (817) 332-8236
Ownership %: 100
**Management:**
James O. Branch .................Chairman of Board
Mike Branch ..............................President
Catey Benarz ..............Classified Adv. Manager
**Editorial:**
David Morgan ...............................Editor
Dan Roberts ...............................Advertising
Gina Gilbert ...............................Advertising
**Desc.:** Features primarily consist of articles
about garden center management, plant
production, disease and insect control.
Coverage of nursery conventions.
Complete coverage of the nursery
& garden centers on a national level.
**Readers:** Nurserymen, landscapers &
garden centers.

## Group 092-Foods & Food Processing

22733
**ALIMENTOS PROCESADOS**
455 N. City Front Plz. Dr.
Chicago, IL 60611
Telephone: (312) 222-2000
FAX: (312) 222-2026
Year Established: 1951
Pub. Frequency: m.
Page Size: standard
Subscrip. Rate: free/qualified readers;
$53/yr. others
Print Process: web offset
Circulation: 20,563
Circulation Type: controlled
**Owner(s):**
Cahner's Publishing Co.
1350 E. Touhy Ave.
Des Plaines, IL 60018
Telephone: (708) 635-8800
Ownership %: 100
**Management:**
Sally Schofield .............................Publisher
**Editorial:**
Julia Gallo-Torres ...........................Editor
Nacho Helguera .......................Assistant Editor
**Desc.:** Spanish language publication
reaching over 20,000 food and beverage
processors in Latin America. The
editorial includes news stories, company
profiles, plant tours, new technologies,
trade show coverage, etc.
**Readers:** Food processors in Mexico,
Central America and South America.

70368
**CARROT COUNTRY**
2809-A Fruitvale Blvd.
Yakima, WA 98902
Telephone: (509) 248-2453
Mailing Address:
P.O. Box 1467
Yakima, WA 98907
Year Established: 1993
Pub. Frequency: q.
Page Size: standard
Subscrip. Rate: $6/yr. US; $14/yr. Canada;
$18/yr. foreign
Materials: 01,02,05,06,15,16,20,21,28,29,
20,32,33
Freelance Pay: $100-$150
Print Process: offset
Circulation: 2,051
Circulation Type: controlled & paid

**Owner(s):**
D. Brent Clement
681 Ames Rd.
Selah, WA 98942
Telephone: (509) 697-3070
Ownership %: 50

J. Mike Stoker
4705 W. Powerhouse Rd.
Yakima, WA 98908
Telephone: (509) 966-7731
Ownership %: 50
**Management:**
J. Mike Stoker ...............................Publisher
Beverly Stoker .................Circulation Manager
J. Mike Stoker ...............................Manager
**Editorial:**
Brent Clement ...............................Editor
J. Mike Stoker ...............................Advertising
Kathy Noble .......................Production Director
**Desc.:** Editorial focus is on production and
marketing challanges unique to the
carrot industry. Names were carefully
researched from sources in both
countries.
**Readers:** Carrot producers, packers and
shippers in the U.S. and Canada.
**Deadline:** story-2 mos.; news-2 mos.;
photo-2 mos.; ads-1 mo.

23031
**CEREAL CHEMISTRY**
3340 Pilot Knob Rd.
St. Paul, MN 55121
Telephone: (612) 454-7250
FAX: (612) 454-0766
Year Established: 1915
Pub. Frequency: bi-m.
Page Size: standard
Subscrip. Rate: $200/yr. US; $220/yr.
foreign
Circulation: 3,600
Circulation Type: paid
**Owner(s):**
American Assn. of Cereal Chemists
3340 Pilot Knob Rd.
St. Paul, MN 55121
Telephone: (612) 454-7250
Ownership %: 100
**Management:**
Steven C. Nelson ...........................Publisher
Steven C. Nelson ...................General Manager
Miles Wimer ...............................Manager
**Editorial:**
V. Rasper ...........................Editor in Chief
Greg Grabek .......................Marketing Manager
Phyllis Albertz ........................Technical Editor
**Desc.:** Reports current fundamental
research on raw materials, processes,
and products of the cereal, oilseeds,
pulse, and related industries. Includes
contributions from research scientists
worldwide.
**Readers:** Research scientists working in
the field.

23032
**CEREAL FOODS WORLD**
3340 Pilot Knob Rd.
St. Paul, MN 55121-2097
Telephone: (612) 454-7250
Year Established: 1956
Pub. Frequency: m.
Page Size: 4 color photos/art
Subscrip. Rate: $80/yr.,U.S.; $120/yr.,
overseas
Materials: 32
Circulation: 4,660
Circulation Type: controlled & paid
**Owner(s):**
American Assn. of Cereal Chemists
3340 Pilot Knob Rd.
St. Paul, MN 55121-2097
Telephone: (612) 454-7250
FAX: (612) 454-0766
Ownership %: 100

**Management:**
Steven Nelson ...............................Publisher
Leslie Schoenecker .........Advertising Manager
**Editorial:**
Jody Grider ...............................Editor
Linda Kadlec ...............................Assistant Editor
Dr. Y. Pomeranz .................Book Review Editor
Miles Wimer ....................Publication Director
**Desc.:** Concentrates on use, processing,
marketing, etc., of cereal grains and
cereal-based foods; association news,
research abstracts, book reviews,
cereal industry newsletter, technical and
feature articles.
**Readers:** Cereal and other food scientists,
professionals, managers.

68842
**CORRECTIONAL FOODSERVICE MAGAZINE**
665 La Villa Dr.
Miami Springs, FL 33166
Telephone: (305) 887-1700
FAX: (305) 885-1923
Year Established: 1991
Pub. Frequency: bi-m.
Subscrip. Rate: $25/yr.
Circulation: 10,193
Circulation Type: paid
**Owner(s):**
International Publishing Co. of America
665 La Villa Dr.
Miami Springs, FL 33166
Telephone: (305) 887-1700
Ownership %: 100
**Management:**
George Mazola .....................Managing Director
**Editorial:**
Raymond G. Felman ...........................Editor
**Readers:** Foodservice personnel employed
in prisons, jails, and other correction
institutions in the US and Canada.

58745
**FOOD CHEMICAL NEWS**
1101 Pennsylvania Ave., S.E.
Washington, DC 20003
Telephone: (202) 544-1980
FAX: (202) 546-3890
Year Established: 1959
Pub. Frequency: w.
Page Size: standard
Subscrip. Rate: $875/yr.
**Owner(s):**
CRC Press, Inc.
2000 Corporate Blvd., N.W.
Boca Raton, FL 33431
Telephone: (407) 994-0555
Ownership %: 100
**Management:**
Natalie Pargus ...............................Manager
**Editorial:**
Raymond Galant ...................Executive Editor
Louis Rothschild, Jr. ...........................Editor
**Desc.:** A weekly publication providing in-
depth information regarding regulation of
food, including additives, microbiology,
standards, contaminants, and feed.

23036
**FOOD ENGINEERING**
Chilton Way
Radnor, PA 19087
Telephone: (215) 964-4000
Year Established: 1928
Pub. Frequency: m.
Page Size: standard
Subscrip. Rate: $55/yr.
Circulation: 60,000
Circulation Type: controlled
**Owner(s):**
Chilton Co. Division ABC Pblshng Cptl.
Cities/ABC
Chilton Way
Radnor, PA 19087
Telephone: (215) 964-4000
Ownership %: 100

**Materials Accepted/Included:** 01-Business news 02-By-line articles 03-Fashion news 04-Food news 05-Freelance copy 06-Letters to editor 07-Real estate news 08-Sports news 09-Travel news 10-Book rev. 11-Movie rev. 12-Music rev. 13-TV rev. 14-Theater rev. 15-Coming events 16-Obituaries 17-Question & answer 18-Social announcements 19-Artwork 20-Cartoons 21-Photos 22-TV listings 23-Audio rec. 24-Video rec. 25-Books 26-Films/film clips 27-Personnel news 28-Press releases 29-New product news/photos 30-Trade lit. 31-Contracts awarded 32-Display adv. 33-Classified adv.

**Management:**
Peter N. Havens .................................Publisher
Jerry Clark .........................Circulation Manager
Richard Stettler ..........Classified Adv. Manager
Rick Biros .................................Sales Manager
**Editorial:**
Ann Pryzbyla .................................Senior Editor
Charles Haberstroh .................................Editor
Joyce Fassl .............................Managing Editor
Margie Russel .............................Feature Editor
Marla Feder .........................Marketing Director
Susan Rothrock .............................Miscellaneous
Anne Hartnett .............................Miscellaneous
Maryellen Murrin .............................Miscellaneous
A. Wallace Root .............................Miscellaneous
Judith Babcock .............................Miscellaneous
Patrick O'Donnell .............................Miscellaneous
Diane Drennan .........................Production Editor
Peggy Georges .............................Sales
James Wagner .........................Technical Editor
Pat Dillon .........................Technical Editor
**Desc.:** How to by-line articles for corporate
officials, plant managers, engineers,
quality control men, food technologists
in the food manufacturing and
processing industry. Stresses advances
and trends in food manufacturing.
Departments include: Events,
Washington Report, New Equipment &
Supplies, New Packages and Products,
the supply line, just off the press (free
new catalog and bulletins issued by
equipment and supplies manufacturers),
Packaging Pointers, Ingredients and
additives.
**Readers:** People in all branches of food
manufacturing operations.

23038
## FOOD PROCESSING MAGAZINE
301 E. Erie St.
Chicago, IL 60611
Telephone: (312) 644-2020
FAX: (312) 644-7870
Year Established: 1940
Pub. Frequency: 13/yr.
Page Size: standard
Subscrip. Rate: $10 copy
Freelance Pay: negotiable
Circulation: 66,000
Circulation Type: controlled
**Owner(s):**
Putman Publishing Co.
Telephone: (312) 644-2020
Ownership %: 100
**Management:**
Grace Cappelletti .............................President
John M. Cappelletti .....................Vice President
Peggy Stath .............................Publisher
**Editorial:**
Charles J. Maurer .........................Editor in Chief
Dean D. Duxbury .................................Editor
Judy Rice .................................Editor
Frances W. LaBell .................................Editor
Harold V. Semling .............................Miscellaneous
**Desc.:** New product reports and "case
history" articles describe new
developments in the food processing
industry. Regular monthly sections cover
the many areas of operations:
Processing Systems and Equipment;
Ingredients; Packaging Equipment and
Materials; Sanitation and Cleaning;
Material Handling; Distribution and
Transportation; Controls, Regulators and
Laboratory Instruments; and
Governmental Regulations affecting food
operations. Foods of Tomorrow bi-
monthly section presents new
developments for creating new food
products. FP packaging covers
packaging innovations.
**Readers:** Executive & operating
management in the food processing
industries.

22441
## FOOD PRODUCTION/MANAGEMENT
2619 Maryland Ave.
Baltimore, MD 21218
Telephone: (410) 467-3338
FAX: (410) 467-7434
Year Established: 1878
Pub. Frequency: m.
Page Size: standard
Subscrip. Rate: $25/yr., $45/2 yrs. US;
$40/yr., $75/2 yrs. foreign
Materials: 01,04,27,28,29,30,32,33
Print Process: offset
Circulation: 5,200
Circulation Type: controlled & paid
**Owner(s):**
CTI Publications, Inc.
2619 Maryland Ave.
Baltimore, MD 21218
Telephone: (410) 467-3338
FAX: (410) 467-7434
Ownership %: 100
**Management:**
W. Randall Gerstmyer .........................President
W. Randall Gerstmyer .........................Publisher
W. Randall Gerstmyer .......Advertising Manager
**Editorial:**
Arthur I. Judge, II .........................Executive Editor
Randy Gerstmyer .........................Associate Editor
Arthur I. Judge, II .................New Product Editor
Arthur I. Judge, II .........................News Editor
Arthur I. Judge, II .........................Photo
**Desc.:** Covers canning, glass packing,
frozen, and allied industries, meetings,
market conditions, news and personals,
government regulations, new literature,
products.
**Readers:** Processing plant managers,
officers, quality control people, owners.
**Deadline:** story-5th of mo. prior to pub.
date; news-5th of mo. prior; photo-5th of
mo. prior; ads-5th of mo. prior

24041
## FOOD SERVICE NEWS
2233 Hamline Ave. N., 615
St. Paul, MN 55113
Telephone: (612) 639-9026
FAX: (612) 639-9029
Year Established: 1990
Pub. Frequency: m.
Page Size: tabloid
Subscrip. Rate: free to members
Materials: 01,02,04,05,06,10,15,25,27,28,
29,32
Print Process: web offset
Circulation: 21,000
Circulation Type: controlled
**Owner(s):**
Food Service News
2233 Hamline Ave. N., 615
St. Paul, MN 55113
Telephone: (612) 639-9026
Ownership %: 100
**Management:**
Chuck Weber .................................Publisher
**Editorial:**
Steven Weber .................................Editor
Frank Przybilla .................................Sales
**Desc.:** A regional trade publication
covering news items pertinent to the
food service industry of the Upper
Midwest. Designed to provide food
service operators with information
relating to new products, operational
management personnel development
and long-range planning.
**Readers:** Restaurants, school food
service, dietitians, food service
installations.

23041
## FOOD TECHNOLOGY
221 N. LaSalle St.
Chicago, IL 60601
Telephone: (312) 782-8424
Year Established: 1947
Pub. Frequency: m.
Page Size: standard
Subscrip. Rate: $12 copy; $82/yr. US,
Canada, Mexico; $92/yr. elsewhere
Circulation: 26,000
Circulation Type: paid
**Owner(s):**
Institute of Food Technologists
221 N. LaSalle St.
Chicago, IL 60601
Telephone: (312) 782-8424
Ownership %: 100
**Management:**
Daniel Weber .................................Publisher
Calvin Trout .........................Advertising Manager
Joan Nolan .........................Circulation Manager
**Editorial:**
John B. Klis .................................Editor
Bernard Schukraft .....................Managing Editor
James Giese .........................Associate Editor
Donald E. Pszczola .................Associate Editor
Betsy Baird .................................News Editor
Neil H. Mermelstein ...............Senior Associate
Editor
**Desc.:** Features articles on trends in food
processing and marketing; human
nutrition and public health; food
engineering; new product and
process development; storage of foods
and other technological subjects;
editorials and commentaries on subjects
of professional interest to food
technologists (education,
organization and management,
promotion of food technology as
a profession, etc.); news and notes
concerning IFT activities as well as
those of related technical societies, and
reviews and abstracts of
current technical literature relating to
foods and human nutrition.
**Readers:** Members are food
technologists, food scientists, food
engineers, and food industry managers
and executives, as well as government
personnel and educators in the field of
food science and technology, and other
individuals working in closely related
fields.

65739
## FOOD WORLD
5537 Twin Knolls Rd., 438
Columbia, MD 21045
Telephone: (301) 730-5013
Year Established: 1945
Pub. Frequency: m.
Page Size: tabloid
Subscrip. Rate: $36/yr.
Circulation: 21,000
Circulation Type: paid
**Owner(s):**
Richard Bestany, Jeffrey Metzger
5537 Twin Knolls Rd., 438
Columbia, MD 21045
Telephone: (301) 730-5013
Ownership %: 100
**Editorial:**
Jackie A. Mansfield .................................Editor
**Desc.:** Regional food trade newspaper
reporting on food news in Mid-Atlantic
region. Covers retail & food service
segments.

69634
## FROZEN FOOD EXECUTIVE
P.O. Box 6069
Harrisburg, PA 17112-0069
Telephone: (717) 657-8601
FAX: (717) 657-9862
Year Established: 1983

Pub. Frequency: m.
Page Size: standard
Subscrip. Rate: $60/yr.
Materials: 01,02,04,05,15,16,18,21,27,28,
29,30,31,32,33
Print Process: offset
Circulation: 3,500
Circulation Type: paid
**Owner(s):**
National Frozen Food Association
P.O. Box 6069
Harrisburg, PA 17112-0069
Telephone: (717) 657-8601
FAX: (717) 657-9862
Ownership %: 100
**Editorial:**
Lori Perle Pohlman .................................Editor
Lori Perle Pohlman .......Director of Publications
**Desc.:** News about the frozen food
industry with information on NFFA, new
products, member companies, legislation
and statistics.
**Deadline:** story-mid-mo. 1 1/2 mos. prior
to pub. date; news-mid-mo. 1 1/2 mos.
prior; photo-mid-mo. 1 1/2 mos. prior;
ads-mid-mo. 1 1/2 mos. prior

69637
## FROZEN FOOD REPORT
1764 Old Meadow Ln., Ste. 350
McLean, VA 22102
Telephone: (703) 821-0770
FAX: (703) 821-1350
Year Established: 1973
Pub. Frequency: bi-m.
Subscrip. Rate: membership
Circulation: 5,300
Circulation Type: controlled
**Owner(s):**
American Frozen Food Institute
1764 Old Meadow Ln., Ste. 350
McLean, VA 22102
Telephone: (703) 821-0770
Ownership %: 100
**Editorial:**
Traci Carneal .................................Editor

52599
## GOURMET NEWS
38 Lafayette St.
Yarmouth, ME 04096
Telephone: (207) 846-0600
FAX: (207) 846-0657
Mailing Address:
P.O. Box 1056
Yarmouth, ME 04096
Year Established: 1990
Pub. Frequency: m.
Page Size: tabloid
Subscrip. Rate: free qualified subscribers;
$35/yr. non-subscribers US; $125/yr.
foreign
Circulation: 20,100
Circulation Type: controlled
**Owner(s):**
United Publications
**Editorial:**
Lafe Low .................................Editor
Brook Taliaferro .....................Editorial Director
Hilary Nangle .........................Associate Editor
**Desc.:** For the gourmet industry reporting
all the news for and about the different
segments of the trade: specialty
retailers, supermarkets and department
stores, brokers, distributors, importers
and manufacturers.
**Readers:** All businesses involved in the
retailing of gourmet foods and
hardgoods, including independent
retailers, specialty department buyers,
brokers, distributors, importers, and
manufacturers.

---

Materials Accepted/Included: 01-Business news 02-By-line articles 03-Fashion news 04-Food news 05-Freelance copy 06-Letters to editor 07-Real estate news 08-Sports news 09-Travel news
10-Book rev. 11-Movie rev. 12-Music rev. 13-TV rev. 14-Theater rev. 15-Coming events 16-Obituaries 17-Question & answer 18-Social announcements 19-Artwork 20-Cartoons 21-Photos 22-TV listings
23-Audio rec. 24-Video rec. 25-Books 26-Films/film clips 27-Personnel news 28-Press releases 29-New product news/photos 30-Trade lit. 31-Contracts awarded 32-Display adv. 33-Classified adv.

## GOURMET RETAILER, THE
66284
3301 Ponce de Leon Blvd.
Coral Gables, FL 33134
Telephone: (305) 446-3388
Year Established: 1979
Pub. Frequency: m.
Page Size: standard
Subscrip. Rate: free
Materials: 01,04
Freelance Pay: $400-$600/2,200 wd.
   feature
Circulation: 21,000
Circulation Type: controlled
**Owner(s):**
Specialty Media, Inc.
3301 Ponce de Leon Blvd.
Coral Gables, FL 33134
Telephone: (305) 731-0000
Ownership %: 100
**Management:**
Edward R. Loeb ..........................Publisher
**Editorial:**
Nancy Moore ...........................Executive Editor
**Desc.:** Highly targeted coverage of
   specialty food and housewares. Written
   for retailers by experienced writers.
**Readers:** Specialty retailers.

## HEALTHCARE FOODSERVICE
   MAGAZINE
68843
665 La Villa Dr.
Miami Springs, FL 33166
Telephone: (305) 887-1700
FAX: (305) 885-1923
Year Established: 1991
Pub. Frequency: m.
Subscrip. Rate: $25/yr.
Circulation: 29,215
Circulation Type: paid
**Owner(s):**
International Publishing Co. of America
665 La Villa Dr.
Miami Springs, FL 33166
Telephone: (305) 887-1700
Ownership %: 100
**Readers:** Foodservice professionals in
   hospitals, nursing homes, hospices and
   treatment centers, contract caterers and
   restaurant and cafeteria operators in
   healthcare facilities in the US and
   Canada.

## JOURNAL OF FOOD SCIENCE
23049
221 N. LaSalle St.
Chicago, IL 60601
Telephone: (312) 782-8424
Year Established: 1936
Pub. Frequency: bi-m.
Page Size: standard
Subscrip. Rate: $12/copy; $72/yr. US,
   Canada, Mexico; $82/yr. foreign
Circulation: 12,000
Circulation Type: paid
**Owner(s):**
Institute of Food Technologists
221 N. LaSalle St.
Chicago, IL 60601
Telephone: (312) 782-8424
Ownership %: 100
**Management:**
Daniel Weber ..............................Publisher
John B. Klis ..............................Publisher
**Editorial:**
Dr. Robert E. Berry ......................Editor
B. Schukraft ............................Managing Editor

**Desc.:** Publishes research articles in food
   science on the following subjects:
   physical and chemical studies on the
   separation, isolation, and identification of
   components of foods; chemical
   composition and nutritive value of foods;
   microbiology, toxicology, and nutrition;
   the sensory evaluation of foods; food
   processing and engineering.
**Readers:** Research specialists in food and
   related fields.

## MODERN FOOD SERVICE NEWS
68839
15 Emerald St.
Hackensack, NJ 07601
Telephone: (201) 488-1800
Year Established: 1989
Pub. Frequency: m.
Page Size: tabloid
Subscrip. Rate: $30/yr.
Materials: 01,04,27,28,29,30,32,33
Print Process: web offset
Circulation: 24,639
Circulation Type: paid
**Owner(s):**
Grocers Publishing Co., Inc.
15 Emerald St.
Hackensack, NJ 07601
Telephone: (201) 488-1800
Ownership %: 100
**Editorial:**
Mark LeFens ............................Editor
**Readers:** Food service directors, buyers
   and end users in New York, New Jersey
   and Connecticut.

## NATIONAL CULINARY REVIEW
68844
10 San Bartola Dr.
St. Augustine, FL 32086
Telephone: (904) 824-4468
FAX: (904) 825-4758
Mailing Address:
   P.O. Box 3466
   St. Augustine, FL 32086
Year Established: 1929
Pub. Frequency: m.
Page Size: standard
Subscrip. Rate: $2 newsstand; $35/yr.
Materials: 04,05,06,10,17,19,20,21,23,24,
   25,26,28,29,30,32,33
Freelance Pay: $50-$75/article
Print Process: offset
Circulation: 20,000
Circulation Type: controlled & paid
**Owner(s):**
American Culinary Federation, Inc.
10 San Bartola Dr.
St. Augustine, FL 32086
Telephone: (904) 824-4468
FAX: (904) 825-4758
Ownership %: 100
**Bureau(s):**
Suzzane B. Hall
13411 Bellacoola Rd.
Soddy-Daisy, TN 37279-8070
Telephone: (615) 332-4953
FAX: (615) 332-3596
**Editorial:**
Brent T. Frei ............................Editor
**Desc.:** Focus on food and the movers and
   shakers in the food service industry;
   plus industry news and trends.
**Deadline:** story-6 wks.; news-6 wks.;
   photo-6 wks.; ads-4 wks.

## OIL MILL GAZETTEER
24211
17000 El Camino Real
Ste. 210A
Houston, TX 77058
Telephone: (713) 480-7889
FAX: (713) 338-2345
Year Established: 1895
Pub. Frequency: m.

Page Size: standard
Subscrip. Rate: $13/yr.
Materials: 01,04,28,29,32,33
Print Process: offset
Circulation: 1,400
Circulation Type: paid
**Owner(s):**
Oil Mill Gazetteer
17000 El Camino Real
Ste. 210A
Houston, TX 77058
Telephone: (713) 480-7889
FAX: (713) 338-2345
Ownership %: 100
**Management:**
Paula Kolmar ..............................Publisher
Denise Whitson ...............Circulation Manager
**Editorial:**
Paula Kolmar ..............................Editor
**Desc.:** Technical magazine for vegetable
   oilseeds processing industry
   emphasizing processes, equipment and
   production techniques. Covers anything
   pertaining to oil milling worldwide.
**Readers:** Plant managers &
   superintendents of the vegetable oils
   industry.

## ONION WORLD
61591
2809-A Fruitvale Blvd.
Yakima, WA 98902
Telephone: (509) 248-2452
Mailing Address:
   P.O. Box 1467
   Yakima, WA 98907
Year Established: 1993
Pub. Frequency: 8/yr.
Page Size: standard
Subscrip. Rate: $15/yr. US; $27/yr.
   Canada & Mexico; $45/yr. foreign
Materials: 01,02,05,06,15,16,20,21,28,29,
   30,32,33
Freelance Pay: $100-$150
Print Process: offset
Circulation: 6,082
Circulation Type: controlled & paid
**Owner(s):**
D. Brent Clement
681 Ames Rd.
Selah, WA 98942
Telephone: (509) 697-3070
Ownership %: 50

J. Mike Stoker
4705 W. Power House Rd.
Takima, WA 98908
Telephone: (509) 966-7731
Ownership %: 50
**Management:**
J. Mike Stoker ..........................Publisher
Beverly Stoker ...............Circulation Manager
**Editorial:**
Brent Clement ...........................Editor
J. Mike Stoker ..........................Advertising
Kathy Noble ...............Production Director
**Desc.:** Editorial focus is on production and
   marketing challenges unique to the
   onion industry. Names were carefully
   researched from sources in both
   countries.
**Readers:** Onion producers, packers and
   shippers.
**Deadline:** story-2 mos. prior to pub. date;
   news-2 mos. prior; photo-2 mos. prior;
   ads-1 mo. prior

## PASTA JOURNAL
23050
2101 Wilson Blvd., Ste. 920
Arlington, VA 22201
Telephone: (703) 841-0818
FAX: (703) 528-6507
Year Established: 1919
Pub. Frequency: bi-m.

Page Size: standard
Subscrip. Rate: $28/yr. US; $38.50/yr.
   foreign
Materials: 04
Print Process: offset
Circulation: 750
Circulation Type: paid
**Owner(s):**
National Pasta Association
2101 Wilson Blvd., Ste. 920
Arlington, VA 22201
Telephone: (703) 841-0818
Ownership %: 100
**Editorial:**
Donna Chowning Reid ..........Executive Editor
Jennifer L. Rakowsky ...........Communications
                                        Assistant
**Desc.:** Contributed features deal with
   pasta promotion, manufacturing
   techniques, new equipment. reports
   on new packages, company news
   appointments, trade activities.
**Readers:** Pasta manufacturers, millers,
   egg processors, packaging & equipment
   suppliers, distributors.

## PREPARED FOODS
23055
455 N. Cityfront Plz. Dr.
Chicago, IL 60611
Telephone: (312) 222-2000
FAX: (312) 222-2026
Year Established: 1895
Pub. Frequency: 13/yr.
Page Size: standard
Subscrip. Rate: $75/yr. US; $130/yr.
   foreign
Materials: 32,33
Print Process: web offset
Circulation: 71,815
Circulation Type: controlled
**Owner(s):**
Cahners Publishing Co.
455 N. Cityfront Plz. Dr.
Chicago, IL 60611
Telephone: (312) 222-2000
FAX: (312) 222-2026
Ownership %: 100
**Management:**
Roy Hlavacek .....................Vice President
Roy Hlavacek .........................Publisher
Cheryl Kwiatkowski ...........Production Manager
**Editorial:**
Jack Mans ...........................Senior Editor
Nancy McCue ........................Senior Editor
Fran LaBell ..........................Senior Editor
Bob Swientek ...........................Editor
Dave Fusaro .......................Managing Editor
Betty Mohr ........................Assistant Editor
Steve Berne .......................Associate Editor
Katherine Hauck ...........Contributing Business
                                        Editor
Louis Richard ....................Contributing Editor
Ala Ennes .....................Corporate Art Director
Rob Mahoney ...............Electronic Production
                                        Manager
Lynn Dornblaser .........New Product Publisher
Martin Friedman ...............New Products Editor
Claudia Dziuk O'Donnell .......Technical Director
Donna Gorski ..........................Technical Editor
Diane Jacobs ..........Vice President, Production

**Materials Accepted/Included:** 01-Business news 02-By-line articles 03-Fashion news 04-Food news 05-Freelance copy 06-Letters to editor 07-Real estate news 08-Sports news 09-Travel news 10-Book rev. 11-Movie rev. 12-Music rev. 13-TV rev. 14-Theater rev. 15-Coming events 16-Obituaries 17-Question & answer 18-Social announcements 19-Artwork 20-Cartoons 21-Photos 22-TV listings 23-Audio rec. 24-Video rec. 25-Books 26-Films/film clips 27-Personnel news 28-Press releases 29-New product news/photos 30-Trade lit. 31-Contracts awarded 32-Display adv. 33-Classified adv.

**Desc.:** Serves firms that develop, manufacture, process, package, and market high value-added food and beverage products. Among foods included are prepared foods and specialties, prepared fruits and vegetables, prepared meat, seafood and poultry, dairy foods, bakery foods, alcoholic and non-alcoholic beverages, snack foods and candy. Also served are food research centers and sales agents, including independent labs, research and development facilities, university food science departments/research institutes, distributors, dealers, jobbers & brokers servicing food manufacturers. A limited number of copies are also distributed to consultants, manufacturers of ingredients, equipment, and supplies and trade associations.
**Readers:** Qualified recipients are executives, management and staff personnel in administration, plant operations, plant production, engineering, packaging, technical, research & development, purchasing, marketing and sales and other titled personnel.

### PROCESSED POULTRY
65318

Sandstone Bldg.
Mount Morris, IL 61054
Telephone: (815) 734-4171
FAX: (815) 734-4201
Pub. Frequency: bi-m.
Page Size: standard
Subscrip. Rate: $18/yr.
Circulation: 15,000
Circulation Type: paid
**Owner(s):**
Watt Publishing Co.
Sandstone Bldg.
Mount Morris, IL 61054
Telephone: (815) 734-4171
Ownership %: 100
**Management:**
Dr. Charles Olintine .............................Publisher
**Editorial:**
Virginia Lazar ............................................Editor
**Desc.:** Editorial familiarizes marketers & distributors with the latest products & technologies relating to value added poultry products.
**Readers:** Processing plant managers, marketers, purchasers, and restaurant managers.

### QUICK FROZEN FOODS INTERNATIONAL
65324

2125 Center Ave., Ste. 305
Fort Lee, NJ 07024
Telephone: (201) 592-7007
FAX: (201) 592-7171
Year Established: 1959
Pub. Frequency: q.
Page Size: standard
Subscrip. Rate: $24/yr. US; $42/yr. foreign
Materials: 01,02,04,05,06,24,27,28,29,30,
31,32,33
Freelance Pay: $.10/wd.
Print Process: offset
Circulation: 11,440
Circulation Type: controlled & paid
**Owner(s):**
E.W. Williams Publications Co.
2125 Center Ave., Ste. 305
Fort Lee, NJ 07024
Telephone: (201) 592-7007
Ownership %: 100
**Management:**
Ed Williams ............................................President
**Editorial:**
John M. Saulnier ........................................Editor

**Desc.:** The editorial concept is to promote frozen foods throughout the world; to review the latest developments in the frozen food industry, both in the U.S. and other principal countries; and to encourage the export and import of frozen products and equipment internationally.
**Readers:** Leading decision makers and equipment purchasers in the global frozen food and ice cream production sector as well as cold stores, transportation, retail and food-service operators.
**Deadline:** story-Feb. 15; May 15; photo-Aug. 15; Nov. 15; ads-Mar. 15; June 15; Sep. 15; Dec. 15

### REFRIGERATED & FROZEN FOODS
66752

1935 Shermer Rd., Ste. 100
Northbrook, IL 60062
Telephone: (708) 205-5660
FAX: (708) 205-6680
Year Established: 1990
Pub. Frequency: m.
Page Size: standard
Subscrip. Rate: $55/yr.; $110/yr. foreign; free to qualified personnel
Circulation: 35,000
Circulation Type: controlled
**Owner(s):**
Stagnito Publishing Co.
1935 Shermer Rd., Ste. 100
Northbrook, IL 60062
Ownership %: 100
**Management:**
Harry Stagnito ...............................Publisher
**Editorial:**
Wendy Kimbrell .................................Editor
**Desc.:** Aimed at management and employees in the US and Canadian refrigerated and frozen food industries. Covers in-plant visits and news and analysis of business and consumer trends.

### SEAFOOD BUSINESS
49893

120 Tillson Ave.
Rockland, ME 04841
Telephone: (207) 594-6222
Year Established: 1982
Pub. Frequency: 7/yr.
Page Size: standard
Subscrip. Rate: $30/yr.
Circulation: 15,000
Circulation Type: controlled
**Owner(s):**
Diversified Communications
P.O. Box 7437 (DTS)
Portland, ME 04112
Telephone: (207) 774-5981
Ownership %: 100
**Bureau(s):**
Seafood Business
4055 21st Ave., W.
Seattle, WA 98199
Telephone: (206) 283-1150
Contact: Katherine Morris, Editor

Seafood Business
875 Massachusetts Ave., #41
Cambridge, MA 02139
Telephone: (617) 547-8366
Contact: Sally Webb, Advertising Manager
**Desc.:** The magazine for marketing success. Committed to promoting the long-term health and growth of the seafood market by being a credible and reliable resource for seafood buyers.
**Readers:** Seafood buyers (commercial).

### SNACK FOOD
21915

1935 Shermer Rd., Ste. 100
Northbrook, IL 60062
Telephone: (708) 205-5660
FAX: (708) 205-5680
Year Established: 1912
Pub. Frequency: m.
Page Size: standard
Subscrip. Rate: $45/yr. US; $70/yr. foreign
**Owner(s):**
Stagnito Publishing Co.
1935 Shermer Rd., Ste. 100
Northbrook, IL 60062
Telephone: (708) 205-5660
Ownership %: 100
**Bureau(s):**
Edgell Communications, Inc.
7500 Old Oak Blvd.
Cleveland, OH 44130
Telephone: (216) 243-8100
**Management:**
Tom Bachman ...............................Publisher
**Editorial:**
John Frank .............................Editor in Chief
Kristine Kelley ......................Managing Editor
**Desc.:** Covers producers of manufactured and packaged cookie and crackers, extruded snacks, baked snacks, crackers, potato chips, corn snacks, pretzels, popcorn, nut processing and frozen snacks. Text pages deal with all phases of management, production, packaging and marketing.
**Readers:** Top executives in the field of sales, marketing, production & packaging of biscuit, cracker, chip, pretzel, popcorn.

### SNACK WORLD
23033

1711 King St.
Alexandria, VA 22314
Telephone: (703) 836-4500
Year Established: 1939
Pub. Frequency: m.
Page Size: standard
Subscrip. Rate: $60/yr.
Print Process: web
Circulation: 5,400
Circulation Type: paid
**Owner(s):**
Snack Food Association
1711 King St.
Alexandria, VA 22314
Telephone: (703) 836-4500
Ownership %: 100
**Management:**
Jim Shufelt ...............................Publisher
**Editorial:**
Al Rickard ....................................Editor
Jane Schultz ......................Managing Editor
Gina Barrett ........................Assistant Editor
Bill Levy ........................Contributing Editor
Judith M. Barth ...............Marketing Director
**Desc.:** The editorial voice of the snack industry (popcorn, potato chips, pretzels, savory pork rinds, cheese curls, meat snacks, and tortilla chips). Published to inform executives of trends and new production methods within the industry.
**Readers:** 5,400 executives of snack manufacturing companies and suppliers to the snack food industry.

## Group 094-Funeral Service Business

### AMERICAN CEMETERY
22443

1501 Broadway
New York, NY 10023
Telephone: (212) 398-9266
FAX: (212) 768-9140
Year Established: 1928
Pub. Frequency: m.

Page Size: standard
Subscrip. Rate: $18/yr.; $30/2 yrs. US; $20/yr.; $34/2 yrs. foreign
Materials: 01,02,06,28,29,32,33
Print Process: offset
Circulation: 6,000
Circulation Type: controlled & paid
**Owner(s):**
The American Cemetery
New York, NY
Ownership %: 100
**Management:**
Adrian F. Boylston .............................Publisher
**Editorial:**
Nicholas Verastro ..................................Editor
Xavier Cronin ..........................Associate Editor
**Desc.:** Staff-written features cover public relations; cemetery design, construction and management. Carries association and trade news, new products and supplies, personals.
**Readers:** Cemetery owners, executives.
**Deadline:** news-25th of 2nd mo. prior to pub. date; ads-25th of 2nd mo. prior

### AMERICAN FUNERAL DIRECTOR
24109

1501 Broadway
New York, NY 10023
Telephone: (212) 398-9266
FAX: (212) 768-9140
Year Established: 1878
Pub. Frequency: m.
Page Size: standard
Subscrip. Rate: $23/yr.; $32/2 yrs. US; $29/yr.; $48/2 yrs. foreign
Materials: 01,02,06,28,29,32,33
Print Process: offset
Circulation: 11,226
Circulation Type: paid
**Owner(s):**
Kates-Boylston Publications, Inc.
Telephone: (212) 398-9266
**Management:**
Rucker Burks ....................Advertising Manager
Eli Kerins ...........................Production Manager
**Editorial:**
Nick Verrastro ..........................................Editor
Xavier Cronin ..........................Associate Editor
**Desc.:** Staff-written articles on the professional and busines side of the funeral field. Discusses management, advertising, public relations education. Uses supplier news, appointments, trade news, new products and equipment. Departments include News of the Profession, Association News, News of the Supply Trade.
**Readers:** Funeral directors.
**Deadline:** ads-20th of 2nd mo. prior to pub. date

### CATHOLIC CEMETERY, THE
22444

710 N. River Rd.
Des Plaines, IL 60016
Telephone: (708) 824-8131
Year Established: 1949
Pub. Frequency: m.
Page Size: standard
Subscrip. Rate: $35/yr.
Materials: 02,28,29,30,33
Circulation: 2,300
Circulation Type: controlled
**Owner(s):**
Catholic Cemetery
Ownership %: 100
**Editorial:**
Leo A. Droste .........................................Editor
**Deadline:** ads-2 mos. prior to pub. date

### CFSA NEWSLETTER
69217

708 Church St.
Evanston, IL 60201
Telephone: (708) 866-8383
FAX: (708) 866-0901

**Materials Accepted/Included:** 01-Business news 02-By-line articles 03-Fashion news 04-Food news 05-Freelance copy 06-Letters to editor 07-Real estate news 08-Sports news 09-Travel news 10-Book rev. 11-Movie rev. 12-Music rev. 13-TV rev. 14-Theater rev. 15-Coming events 16-Obituaries 17-Question & answer 18-Social announcements 19-Artwork 20-Cartoons 21-Photos 22-TV listings 23-Audio rec. 24-Video rec. 25-Books 26-Films/film clips 27-Personnel news 28-Press releases 29-New product news/photos 30-Trade lit. 31-Contracts awarded 32-Display adv. 33-Classified adv.

4-147

Year Established: 1953
Pub. Frequency: m.
Subscrip. Rate: $36/yr.
Circulation: 550
Circulation Type: paid
**Owner(s):**
Casket & Funeral Supply Association of America
708 Church St.
Evanston, IL 60201
Telephone: (708) 866-8383
Ownership %: 100
**Editorial:**
George Lemke ..............................Editor

24111
**DIRECTOR, THE**
11121 W. Oklahoma Ave.
Milwaukee, WI 53227-0641
Telephone: (414) 541-2500
FAX: (414) 541-1909
Year Established: 1930
Pub. Frequency: m.
Page Size: standard
Subscrip. Rate: $24/yr. US; $30/yr. foreign
Circulation: 14,559
Circulation Type: paid
**Owner(s):**
NFDA Publications
11121 W. Oklahoma Ave.
Milwaukee, WI 53227-0641
Telephone: (414) 541-2500
Ownership %: 100
**Management:**
Kellie Schilling ..................Advertising Manager
**Editorial:**
Sue Simon ..............................Editor
Gordon Mason ..........................Art Director
**Desc.:** Informs on any and all aspects relating to the funeral service profession, including subjects relating to dying, death, and bereavement; governmental activities, such as veterans' affairs; association projects and programs; and the overall place of the funeral and the role of the funeral director in contemporary America. Feature subjects include counselling, funeral service education, management, public relations, the history of funeral practices, and comments and expressions of thought from leaders of the profession.

24112
**MORTICIANS OF THE SOUTHWEST**
2514 National Dr.
Garland, TX 75041-2329
Telephone: (214) 840-1060
Year Established: 1947
Pub. Frequency: m.
Page Size: standard
Subscrip. Rate: $18/yr., $34/2 yrs. US; $22/yr., $42/2 yrs. foreign
Circulation: 3,600
Circulation Type: paid
**Owner(s):**
Farring, Inc.
2514 National Dr.
Garland, TX 75041
Telephone: (214) 840-1060
Ownership %: 100
**Management:**
Hugh J. Farrell ..............................Publisher
Nancy E. Farrell ..............................Publisher
**Desc.:** Morticians of the Southwest is an independent funeral service journal reporting on activities, products and services, state and national governmental regulatory trends, business and financial news, and personal involvement articles for funeral industry practicioners throughtout the Southwest, including the Republic of Mexico.

**Readers:** Funeral directors and related industries.

24113
**MORTUARY MANAGEMENT**
315 Silverlake Blvd.
Los Angeles, CA 90026
Telephone: (310) 665-0101
FAX: (213) 665-3068
Year Established: 1914
Pub. Frequency: 11/yr.
Page Size: standard
Subscrip. Rate: $27/yr.; $45/2 yrs. US; $30/yr. foreign
Circulation: 7,100
Circulation Type: paid
**Owner(s):**
Berg Publications, Inc.
315 Silverlake Blvd.
Los Angeles, CA 90026
Telephone: (310) 665-0101
Ownership %: 100
**Management:**
William Berg ..............................Founder
Ronald A. Hast ..............................Publisher
Michael Abbott ..................Advertising Manager
Gregory Abbott ..................Circulation Manager
Michael Abbott ..............................Manager
**Editorial:**
Ronald A. Hast ..................Executive Editor
Steve Nimz ..................Managing Editor
Jon St. John ..............................Art Director
Suzanne Nagle ..............................Artist
Steve Nimz ..................Associate Editor
Allan Abbott ..................Associate Publisher
Bud Noakes ..................Contributing Writer
Tom Fisher ..................Contributing Writer
Gregory W. Motzkin ..........Contributing Writer
Brian Porteous ..................Contributing Writer
**Desc.:** Material of interest to funeral directors or embalmers. Will pay for material if it is of direct interest to the field. Material on prominent funerals, association activities, trends and thoughts in the industry, public opinion about funeral directors and their activities is readily accepted. Will use by-lines and photos. Departments include News, Feature, Opinion, Publicity and New Funeral Homes.
**Readers:** Funeral directors, embalmers and their survices.

22446
**SOUTHERN CEMETERY**
P.O. Box 19919
Atlanta, GA 30325
Telephone: (404) 351-1276
FAX: (404) 351-1584
Year Established: 1958
Pub. Frequency: bi-m.
Subscrip. Rate: $21/yr.
Circulation: 2,293
Circulation Type: paid
**Owner(s):**
John W. Yopp Publications, Inc.
P.O. Box 19919
Atlanta, GA 30325
Telephone: (404) 351-1276
Ownership %: 100
**Management:**
Mary Cronley ..............................Publisher
**Editorial:**
Mary Cronley ..............................Editor
John W. Yopp ..................Editor Emeritus
**Desc.:** Serving modern type and traditional cemeteries and memorial parks in 18 Southeast and Southwest states.

24114
**SOUTHERN FUNERAL DIRECTOR**
P.O. Box 1147
Beaufort, SC 29901
Telephone: (803) 521-0239
FAX: (803) 521-1398
Year Established: 1919
Pub. Frequency: m.

Page Size: standard
Subscrip. Rate: $25/yr.; $45/2 yrs.
Materials: 01,02,06,16,21,28,29,32,33
Circulation: 5,000
Circulation Type: controlled
**Owner(s):**
John W. Yopp Publications, Inc.
P.O. Box 1147
Beaufort, SC 29901
Telephone: (803) 521-0239
FAX: (803) 521-1398
Ownership %: 100
**Management:**
Mary Cronley ..............................Publisher
**Editorial:**
Mary Cronley ..............................Editor
J.W. Yopp ..................Editor Emeritus
**Desc.:** Business and professional journal covering developments in the industry and association news. Carries company news, new appointments, personal items about funeral directors in the South and Southwest. Articles cover new funeral homes, management, merchandising.
**Readers:** Funeral directors in the South and Southwest.

22447
**STONE IN AMERICA**
30 Eden Alley, Ste. 301
Columbus, OH 43215
Telephone: (614) 885-2713
FAX: (614) 885-9133
Year Established: 1892
Pub. Frequency: m.
Page Size: standard
Subscrip. Rate: $30/yr.; $56/2 yrs.
Freelance Pay: $150-300
Circulation: 2,100
Circulation Type: paid
**Owner(s):**
American Monument Assn.
933 High St., #220
Worthington, OH 43085
Telephone: (614) 461-5852
Ownership %: 100
**Management:**
Pennie Sabel ..............................Publisher
**Editorial:**
Linda Gambiani ..................Managing Editor
Gale Martin ..............................Advertising
**Desc.:** Editorial content pertinent to manufacturers, distributors, suppliers of granite and marble memorial products. Contains trade literature. General information: a monthly magazine for retail memorialists in the United States and Canada. It is published by the American Monument Association, a national trade association representing the quarriers and manufacturers of memorial stone products. Articles are designed to meet the following editorial objectives: (1) assist memorialists in marketing upright granite and marble memorials; (2) help memorialists become better businessmen; (3) assist memorialists in promoting the concept of upright memorialization; (4) help memorialists improve their relations with cemeteries; (5) help memorialists improve their monument design capabilities.
**Readers:** Monument retailers & manufacturers in United States & Canada.

69218
**TEXAS DIRECTOR**
P.O. Box 14667
Austin, TX 78761
Telephone: (512) 454-5262
FAX: (512) 451-9556
Year Established: 1964
Pub. Frequency: m.
Page Size: standard

Circulation: 1,000
Circulation Type: controlled
**Owner(s):**
Rector-Duncan & Associates
P.O. Box 14667
Austin, TX 78761
Telephone: (512) 454-5262
Ownership %: 100
**Editorial:**
Jeannette Brown ..............................Editor

## Group 096-Fur Farming & Trapping

23099
**BLUE BOOK OF FUR FARMING**
9995 W. 69th St.
Ste. 201
Eden Prairie, MN 55344-3408
Telephone: (612) 941-5820
FAX: (612) 941-1708
Year Established: 1950
Pub. Frequency: a.
Page Size: standard
Subscrip. Rate: $20/copy
Circulation: 816
Circulation Type: paid
**Owner(s):**
Communications Marketing, Inc.
999 SW 69th St.
Ste. 201
Eden Prairie, MN 55344-3408
Telephone: (612) 941-5820
FAX: (612) 941-1708
Ownership %: 100
**Management:**
Spencer M. Dean ..............................President
Spencer M. Dean ..............................Publisher
James Laird ..................Advertising Manager
**Editorial:**
Frank Zaworski ..................Editorial Director
**Desc.:** Annual directed at mink and fox farmers, throughout the world, photos of mink and fox garments of fine quality, feed and medicinal products applicable to fur-bearing animals. Technical advice on health, feeding, and breeding.
**Readers:** Fur farmers and fur industries in the United States, Canada, and elsewhere.

23100
**EMPRESS CHINCHILLA BREEDER**
575 Union Blvd.
Ste. 209
Morrison, CO 80465
Telephone: (503) 332-3222
FAX: (503) 332-4704
Mailing Address:
 P.O. Box 318
 Sixes, OR 97476
Year Established: 1945
Pub. Frequency: m.
Page Size: standard
Subscrip. Rate: $25/yr. US; $30/yr.foreign
Materials: 01,02,03,30,32,33
Print Process: offset
Circulation: 400
Circulation Type: controlled
**Owner(s):**
Empress Chinchilla Breeders Co-Op., Inc.
575 Union Blvd.
Ste. 209
Morrison, CO 80465
Telephone: (503) 332-3222
FAX: (503) 322-4704
Ownership %: 100
**Editorial:**
Wendell Bird ..............................Editor

**Desc.:** Devoted to the dissemination of information regarding ranching, husbandry and general care of chinchillas. General policies of association, legal articles, how-to-do-it articles, news from the fur trade, advertising methods for the establishment of chinchilla on fur market, etc.

**Readers:** Comprised of Empress co-op members. Circulation covers entire United States and 20 foreign countries.

**Deadline:** story-1st of mo. prior to mo. pub.

### FUR AGE WEEKLY
23101

P.O. Box 868
Glenwood Landing, NY 11547
Telephone: (516) 484-0631
FAX: (516) 676-3130
Year Established: 1918
Pub. Frequency: w.
Page Size: tabloid
Subscrip. Rate: $2/copy; $68/yr.
**Owner(s):**
Fur Vogue Publishing Co., Inc.
Telephone: (516) 484-0631
Ownership %: 100
**Management:**
Marc L. Rubman ...............................Publisher
Marc Rubman ....................Advertising Manager
**Editorial:**
Lisa Marcinek .......................................Editor
Simon Clayton ..................................Columnist
Marc Rubman ...................................Columnist
Henry Foner ......................................Columnist
Lisa Marcinek .............................Fashion Editor
**Desc.:** Anything referring to phases of the fur industry from animals to consumers of fur garments.
**Readers:** Firms in every segment of the fur industry.

### FUR RANCHER
23102

9995 W. 69th St.
Ste. 201
Eden Prairie, MN 55344-3408
Telephone: (612) 941-5820
FAX: (612) 941-1708
Year Established: 1921
Pub. Frequency: bi-m.
Page Size: standard
Subscrip. Rate: $20/yr.
Circulation: 800
Circulation Type: paid
**Owner(s):**
Communications Marketing, Inc.
9995 W. 69th St.
Ste. 201
Eden Prairie, MN 55344
Telephone: (612) 941-5820
Ownership %: 100
**Management:**
Spencer M. Dean ...............................President
Spencer M. Dean ...............................Publisher
James Laird ......................Advertising Manager
**Editorial:**
Frank Zaworski .......................Editorial Director
**Desc.:** Bi-monthly magazine on breeding, feeding, health equipment, and marketing of mink and fox pelts.
**Readers:** Fur farmers all over the world raising mink & foxes.

### Group 098-Furniture & Upholstery

### BEDTIMES
23080

333 Commerce St.
Alexandria, VA 22314
Telephone: (703) 683-8371
FAX: (703) 683-4503
Year Established: 1917

Pub. Frequency: m.
Page Size: 4 color photos/art
Subscrip. Rate: $35/yr. US; $40/yr. foreign; $60/2 yrs. US; $70/2 yrs. foreign
Freelance Pay: $100-$750
Circulation: 2,900
Circulation Type: free & paid
**Owner(s):**
International Sleep Products Assn.
333 Commerce St.
Alexandria, VA 22314
Telephone: (703) 683-8371
Ownership %: 100
**Management:**
Andrea Herman ................................Publisher
Susan Perry ......................Advertising Manager
Sandy Stewart ..................Circulation Manager
**Desc.:** Articles covering the manufacture and marketing of mattresses, foundations and other sleep equipment. Stories on management for the bedding industry. Uses new products, machinery, equipment and articles.
**Readers:** Primarily bedding manufacturers and their suppliers.

### FDM
23083

455 N. Cityfront Plz. Dr.
Chicago, IL 60611-5503
Telephone: (312) 222-2000
FAX: (312) 222-2026
Year Established: 1958
Pub. Frequency: m.
Page Size: standard
Subscrip. Rate: $55/yr.
Materials: 01,10,15,27,28,29,30,32,33
Freelance Pay: $300-$450
Circulation: 52,000
Circulation Type: controlled
**Owner(s):**
Cahners Publishing Co.
275 Washington St.
Newton, MA 02158
Telephone: (617) 964-3030



Delta Communications, Inc.
455 N. Cityfront Plz. Dr.
Chicago, IL 60611-5503
Telephone: (312) 222-2000
FAX: (312) 222-2026
**Management:**
Charles E. Moodhe ...........................President
Sandy Berliner ..................................Publisher
Julie Okun ........................Advertising Manager
Rick Ellis .........................Circulation Manager
Vicky Dillon ......................Promotion Manager
**Editorial:**
Bruce Plantz ...........................Executive Editor
James D. Saul .........................Managing Editor
Michael Chazin ........................Editorial Director
Renee Le Tourneau Gattone .........Art Director
Jean Hyland ...............................Design Editor
Gina Doulin ................................Design Editor
Rob Roszell ...........................Marketing Director
Andrew Mykytiuk ..............New Products Editor
Betty McCarthy ...............Production Coordinator
**Desc.:** Contains technical information concerning the use of materials, equipment and supplies as they pertain to the design and manufacturing of furniture, cabinets, seating, interior fixtures. Information either staff-written or contributed by recognized authorities as it pertains to the field of management and production. Monthly technical and management columns by recognized authorities are included. Departments include: Computer Concepts, Finishing Forum, Cutting Tool Technology, Technology of Laminating, Technology Watch, Economic Watch.

**Readers:** Production management, engineering, and product designers in the woodworking, furniture, and cabinet manufacturing industry.
**Deadline:** story-1st of the mo. 2 mos. prior to pub. date; news-15th of mo. 2 mos. prior

### FLOWER & GARDEN MAGAZINE
23020

700 W. 47th St., Ste. 310
Kansas City, MO 64112
Telephone: (816) 531-5730
Year Established: 1957
Pub. Frequency: bi-m.
Page Size: standard
Subscrip. Rate: $2.95 issue; $12.95/yr.
Freelance Pay: negotiable
Circulation: 600,000
Circulation Type: paid
**Owner(s):**
KC Publishing, Inc.
700 W. 47th St., Ste. 310
Kansas City, MO 64112
Telephone: (816) 531-5730
Ownership %: 100
**Bureau(s):**
North Carolina
1 Westchester Dr.
Asheville, NC 28803
Telephone: (704) 253-3558
Contact: Catherine Agger, Manager

Chicago Bureau
230 N. Michigan Ave., 1025
Chicago, IL 60601
Telephone: (312) 726-7012
Contact: Bill Siddon, Manager

Los Angeles Bureau
456 Schooner Wy.
Seal Beach, CA 90740
Telephone: (310) 598-5676
Contact: Les Gage, Manager

Kansas City
4251 Pennsylvania Ave.
Kansas City, MO 64111
Telephone: (816) 756-3838
Contact: Everett Knapp, Manager

Detroit
33975 Dequindre, Ste. 100
Troy, MI 48083
Telephone: (313) 585-8266
Contact: Dave Jackson, Manager
**Management:**
John C. Prebich ................................Publisher
**Editorial:**
Kay M. Olson ..........................Executive Editor
**Desc.:** Practical how-to information written by leading authorities in the horticulture field. Edited for home gardening enthusiasts concentrating on upkeep, planting problems, trees, shrubs, lawns, flower and vegetable gardens as well as other activities related to horticulture.
**Readers:** Enthusiastic home gardeners, outdoors, indoors, and nationwide.

### FURNITURE/TODAY
23086

7025 Albert Pick Rd.
Greensboro, NC 27249
Telephone: (910) 605-0121
FAX: (910) 605-1143
Mailing Address:
P.O. Box 2754
High Point, NC 27261
Year Established: 1976
Pub. Frequency: w.
Page Size: tabloid
Subscrip. Rate: $89.97/yr.
Materials: 01,32,33
Freelance Pay: negotiable
Print Process: offset
Circulation: 25,665
Circulation Type: paid

**Owner(s):**
Cahners Publishing Co.
199 Wells Ave.
Newton Center, MA 02159
Telephone: (617) 964-3730
Ownership %: 100
**Management:**
Robert F. Steimel .......................Vice President
Joseph F. Carroll ..............................Publisher
Mary Rulli ......................Circulation Manager
Robin Craven .............Classified Adv. Manager
Jean Bushawn ..................................Manager
**Editorial:**
Lester Craft ...............................Editor in Chief
Carole Sloan ...............................Senior Editor
Anthony E. Bengel .......................Senior Editor
David Perry .............................Managing Editor
Judith Z. Cushman ....................Associate Editor
Cindy Sheaffer ........................Associate Editor
Jay McIntosh ..............................Business Editor
Michael Greene ...............................Columnist
Kim D. Shaver ......................Contributing Editor
Susan Andrews ...............................Copy Editor
Tom Mehalko ..................Director of Advertising
Timothy McCulloch ..............Director of Circulation
Kay Anderson ......Director of Market Research
Larry Thomas .........................Editor, Bedding
Vicky Jarrett ..................................Editor, Page
Jaci Ponzon ..................................Editor, Page
Lee Buchanan .......................Editor, Upholstery
Charles J. L. ..........Government Affairs Editor
McKee
T. Scott McIlhenny ..........Group Vice President & General Manager
Thomas Weber ....................Production Manager
Fred Haley ...........................Production Manager
Gary James ....................Special Projects Editor
Mark T. McMenamin .......................Staff Writer
Tom Edmonds ..................................Staff Writer
Brian Carroll ....................................Staff Writer
Clint Engel .......................................Staff Writer
Connie C. Lineberry ..................Vice President, Marketing Services
**Desc.:** The business newspaper of the furniture industry. Publishes all information that impacts on the profitability of retailers, manufacturers and suppliers. This includes new products, style and merchandising trends, industry performance analysis and industry people with emphasis on key decision-makers. Stories almost 100% staff written but rely on P.R. Agencies/Departments to help keep us informed on new products and personnel changes. Departments include: General Industry, New Marketing and Merchandising, Opinion/Today; which includes staff-written columns and Letters to Editor, People/Today, Bedding/Today, Manufacturing/Today, Timely Tips, (shorts about industry people) and Business/Today.
**Readers:** Approximately 25,000 furniture retailers, advertising/P.R. execs., The financial community, furniture manufacturers and suppliers.

### FURNITURE EXECUTIVE, THE
68855

P.O. Box HP-7
High Point, NC 27261
Telephone: (919) 884-5000
Year Established: 1983
Pub. Frequency: m.
Subscrip. Rate: membership
Circulation: 2,500
Circulation Type: controlled & paid
**Owner(s):**
American Furniture Manufacturers Assn.
P.O. Box HP-7
High Point, NC 27261
Telephone: (919) 884-5000
Ownership %: 100

**Materials Accepted/Included:** 01-Business news 02-By-line articles 03-Fashion news 04-Food news 05-Freelance copy 06-Letters to editor 07-Real estate news 08-Sports news 09-Travel news 10-Book rev. 11-Movie rev. 12-Music rev. 13-TV rev. 14-Theater rev. 15-Coming events 16-Obituaries 17-Question & answer 18-Social announcements 19-Artwork 20-Cartoons 21-Photos 22-TV listings 23-Audio rec. 24-Video rec. 25-Books 26-Films/film clips 27-Personnel news 28-Press releases 29-New product news/photos 30-Trade lit. 31-Contracts awarded 32-Display adv. 33-Classified adv.

4-149

**Editorial:**
Nancy High .................................................Editor

## FURNITURE WORLD
23089
530 Fifth Ave.
Pelham, NY 10803
Telephone: (914) 738-6744
FAX: (914) 738-6820
Year Established: 1870
Pub. Frequency: 13/yr.
Page Size: standard
Subscrip. Rate: $16/yr.; $36/3 yrs.
Freelance Pay: $100/pg.
Circulation: 20,000
Circulation Type: controlled & paid
**Owner(s):**
Towse Publishing Co.
530 Fifth Ave.
Pelham, NY 10803
Telephone: (914) 738-6744
Ownership %: 100
**Management:**
Russell Bienenstock ...........................President
Barbara Bienenstock .................Vice President
Barton Bienenstock ...........................Publisher
Teresa Fowler ....................Circulation Manager
**Editorial:**
Russell Bienenstock ....................Editor in Chief
Elaine Saum .......................................Editor
S. T. Lebovic ...........................Production Director
**Desc.:** In business to further the financial
growth of our retail community. We have
become a business tool for every store
doing over 1 million dollars in sales.
**Readers:** Target audience is the top
management, merchandise managers
and buyers in retail furniture stores,
department stores, warehouse
showrooms, mass merchants and home
furnishings wholesalers.

## HOME FURNISHINGS EXECUTIVE
23082
1301 Carolina St.
Greensboro, NC 27401
Telephone: (919) 378-6065
FAX: (919) 275-2864
Year Established: 1989
Pub. Frequency: m.
Page Size: standard
Subscrip. Rate: $48/yr. US; $60/yr.
Canada; $90/yr. overseas
Circulation: 12,795
Circulation Type: paid
**Owner(s):**
Pace Communications, Inc.
1301 Carolina St.
Greensboro, NC 27401
Telephone: (919) 378-6065
Ownership %: 100
**Management:**
Edward Calso ....................................Publisher
**Editorial:**
Patricia Bowling ...................................Editor
Kenneth Gonzalez .............Advertising Director
Jim DeCata .........................Production Director
**Desc.:** Edited for the executive and
management level of home furnishings
retail stores. Editorial covers
management, merchandising, and store
operations, relating each to profit and
growth.
**Readers:** Home furnishings dealers and
buyers, manufacturers.

## OR REPORTS
70424
P.O. Box 17487
Boulder, CO 80303-0487
Telephone: (303) 442-1661
FAX: (303) 442-5960
Year Established: 1992
Pub. Frequency: bi-m.

Page Size: 8 1/2 x 11 1/2
Subscrip. Rate: $88/yr. U.S.; $98/yr.
Canada; $108/yr. foreign
Print Process: offset
Circulation: 1,000
Circulation Type: paid
**Owner(s):**
OR Manager, Inc.
P.O. Box 17487
Boulder, CO 80308-0487
Telephone: (303) 442-1661
FAX: (303) 442-5960
Ownership %: 100
**Management:**
Elinor S. Schrader ..............................Publisher
**Editorial:**
Pat Patterson ...........................Executive Editor
Judy Mathias, RN, MA ...........................Editor
William C. Beck, MD, ............Consulting Editor
FACS

## PACIFIC MARKETER
23091
121 Boren Ave., N.
Seattle, WA 98109
Telephone: (206) 622-4515
Year Established: 1926
Pub. Frequency: bi-m.
Page Size: 4 Color Photos/Art
Subscrip. Rate: $6/yr.
Freelance Pay: 0004100
**Owner(s):**
Northwest Furniture Retailers' Assoc.
121 Boren Ave. N
Seattle, WA 98109
Telephone: (206) 622-4515
Ownership %: 100
**Management:**
Bob Kraski ........................................President
Bob Masin ........................................President
Northwest Furniture Retailers .............Publisher
E. Michael Allen ................Advertising Manager
E. Michael Allen ..................Business Manager
**Editorial:**
E. Michael Allen ...................................Editor
**Desc.:** Accept publicity stories of interest
to Northwest retailers, rewrite most
national releases to one paragraph
length, unless particularly noteworthy.
Use pictures of products and persons.
Editorial and feature material almost
exclusively of furniture. Prefer
controversial articles by credible
personalities when available.
**Readers:** Primarily retail furniture stores,
wholesalers, all members of the home
furnishings industry and exchange group.

## UDM
68857
455 N. Cityfront Dr., 24th Fl.
Chicago, IL 60611
Telephone: (312) 222-2000
FAX: (312) 222-2026
Year Established: 1988
Pub. Frequency: m.
Materials: 01,02,10,15,27,28,29,30,32,33
Print Process: web offset
Circulation: 12,000
Circulation Type: controlled
**Owner(s):**
Reed Publishing (USA) Inc.
275 Washington St.
Newton, MA 02158
Telephone: (617) 964-3030
Ownership %: 100
**Management:**
S.L. Berlinger ....................................Publisher
Rick Ellis ..........................Circulation Manager
Carl Johnson ....................Production Manager
**Editorial:**
Bruce Plantz ...........................Senior Editor
Jean C. Hyland ...........................Senior Editor
Gina Donlin ...........................Senior Editor
Michael Chazin ...................................Editor
James D. Saul .........................Managing Editor

Michael Chazin .......................Editorial Director
Julie Okon ................Advertising Services Mgr.
Curt Snyder ...................................Art Director
Sacha Cohen ...................New Products Editor
**Desc.:** Edited for top management,
production management and designers
of upholstered furniture and
seating including household furniture,
office/contract furniture, institutional
furniture, automotive and recreational
vehicle seating, marine seating. Editorial
covers mfg. processes, materials and
equipment selection. Product design,
and other production related issues.

## Group 100-Gardening, Landscaping & Nursery Trades

## AMERICAN NURSERYMAN
26027
77 W. Washington, Ste. 2100
Chicago, IL 60602-2904
Telephone: (312) 782-5505
FAX: (312) 782-3232
Year Established: 1904
Pub. Frequency: s-m.
Page Size: standard
Subscrip. Rate: $45/yr.; $80/2 yrs. US;
$75/yr. foreign
Materials: 01,02,06,10,15,16,21
Freelance Pay: $200/article
Circulation: 14,883
Circulation Type: paid
**Owner(s):**
American Nurseryman Pub. Co.
77 W. Washington, Ste. 2100
Chicago, IL 60602-2904
Telephone: (312) 782-5505
FAX: (312) 782-3232
Ownership %: 100
**Management:**
Allen W. Seidel ...................................President
Allen W. Seidel ...................................Publisher
**Editorial:**
Julie S. Higginbotham ...........................Editor
Carole Beeson Turner .............Managing Editor
Timothy Schaedel .............Advertising Director
Lee Geistlinger .......................Assistant Editor
Irene Z. Swiderski ................Circulation Director
Romy Schafer ....................Editorial Associate
Jennifer L. Misek ................Production Director
Christine Brown ...................................Sales
Lorraine Romanek ...................................Sales
**Desc.:** Articles on woody ornamental
nursery stock, landscape contracting
and design, garden center operation,
nursery production, personnel
and financial management, computers,
international horticulture, and disease,
weed and pest control. Covers industry
news and meetings. Research reports,
profiles & case studies, trends, how -
to's, recommendations, etc.
**Readers:** Landscapers, garden center
operators, re-wholesalers, field and
container nurserymen.

## BUSINESS OF HERBS
68863
P.O. Box 246
Shevlin, MN 56676-9535
Telephone: (218) 657-2478
FAX: (218) 657-2447
Year Established: 1983
Pub. Frequency: bi-m.
Page Size: standard
Subscrip. Rate: $20/yr. US; $23/yr.
Canada; $28/yr. elsewhere
Materials: 01,04,05,15,25,28,29,30,32,33
Circulation: 2200
Circulation Type: paid

**Owner(s):**
Northwind Farm Publications
P.O. Box 246
Shevlin, MN 56676
Telephone: (218) 657-2478
Ownership %: 100
**Editorial:**
Paula Oliver ...................................Editor
David Oliver ...................................Editor
**Desc.:** Profiles successful herb growers
and business owners and lists useful
resources and news for the small herb
grower and seller.
**Deadline:** story-10th of mo. prior to pub.
date; ads-10th of mon. prior to pub. date

## FOLIAGE DIGEST
69300
1331 N. Mills Ave.
Orlando, FL 32803
Telephone: (407) 894-6522
Year Established: 1967
Pub. Frequency: m.
Page Size: standard
Subscrip. Rate: $35/yr. in state; $45/yr.
out of state; $60/yr. foreign
Circulation: 1,200
Circulation Type: paid
**Owner(s):**
FGR, Inc.
1331 N. Mills Ave.
Orlando, FL 32803
Telephone: (407) 894-6522
Ownership %: 100
**Management:**
Sondra G. Abrahamson .......................Publisher
Sharon L. Butler ...................Business Manager
**Editorial:**
Kathy Phillips ...................................Editor
**Desc.:** Prepared by the National Foliage
Foundation to be a technical resource
for growers in the foliage industry.
**Readers:** Nursery personnel and foliage
growers in Florida, the U.S. and
throughout the world.

## GROUNDS MAINTENANCE
23068
9800 Metcalf
Overland Park, KS 66212-2215
Telephone: (913) 341-1300
Mailing Address:
P.O. Box 12901
Overland Park, KS 66282-2901
Year Established: 1966
Pub. Frequency: m.
Page Size: standard
Subscrip. Rate: $30/yr.
Circulation: 48,006
Circulation Type: controlled
**Owner(s):**
Intertec Publishing Corp.
9800 Metcalf
Overland Park, KS 66212-2215
Telephone: (913) 341-1300
Ownership %: 100
**Management:**
Ray Maloney ...................................President
Ron Wall ...........................Vice President
Brian Agnes ...................................Publisher
Sonja Shaffer ....................Production Manager
**Editorial:**
Dr. Mark Welterlen ...........................Editor
Gina Kellogg Hogan .............Managing Editor
Jeralyn Lutz ...........................Assistant Editor
Sandra Milan ................Circulation Director
Marilyn Roger ...........................Technical Editor

**Materials Accepted/Included:** 01-Business news 02-By-line articles 03-Fashion news 04-Food news 05-Freelance copy 06-Letters to editor 07-Real estate news 08-Sports news 09-Travel news 10-Book rev. 11-Movie rev. 12-Music rev. 13-TV rev. 14-Theater rev. 15-Coming events 16-Obituaries 17-Question & answer 18-Social announcements 19-Artwork 20-Cartoons 21-Photos 22-TV listings 23-Audio rec. 24-Video rec. 25-Books 26-Films/film clips 27-Personnel news 28-Press releases 29-New product news/photos 30-Trade lit. 31-Contracts awarded 32-Display adv. 33-Classified adv.

**Desc.:** Covers problems of the professional grounds superintendent of golf courses, industrial parks and plants, institutions and recreational areas, as well as landscape contractors and other grounds specialists. Technical problems include such topics as recognition and treatment of plant diseases, turf care, tree and ornamentals. Business operating problems include such topics as personnel management, time and cost of jobs, equipment selection and maintenance. Departments include: Researching Maintenance, Almost News, Trade Secrets, Chemical Hotline, Products In Practice, Product Parade.

**Readers:** Landscape contractors, professional grounds superintendents, and lawn care companies.

## GROWER TALKS MAGAZINE
68859

P.O. Box 532
Geneva, IL 60134
Telephone: (708) 208-9080
FAX: (708) 208-9350
Year Established: 1937
Pub. Frequency: m.
Page Size: standard
Subscrip. Rate: $22/yr. US; $28/yr. Canada & Mexico; $75/yr. elsewhere
Materials: 27,29,32,33
Circulation: 10,238
Circulation Type: paid
**Owner(s):**
Geo J. Ball Publishing
P.O. Box 9
Batavia, IL 60510-0009
Telephone: (708) 208-9080
FAX: (708) 208-9350
Ownership %: 100
**Editorial:**
Chris Beytes ...................................Editor
**Readers:** Commercial growers of horticultural plants.

## HORTTECHNOLOGY
69556

113 S. West St., Ste. 400
Alexandria, VA 22314-2824
Telephone: (703) 836-4606
FAX: (703) 836-2024
Year Established: 1991
Pub. Frequency: q.
Subscrip. Rate: $40/yr.
Circulation: 6,000
Circulation Type: paid
**Owner(s):**
American Society for Horticultural Science
Ownership %: 100
**Management:**
Skip McAfee ..................Executive Director
**Editorial:**
John F. Kelly ...................................Editor
**Desc.:** Provides applied science-based subjects. Includes original research reports on technologically based subjects of potential or immediate value to horticultural practitioners.
**Readers:** Professional horticulturists and practitioners.

## INTERIOR LANDSCAPE
66105

77 W. Washington St., Ste. 2100
Chicago, IL 60602-2904
Telephone: (312) 782-5505
FAX: (312) 782-3232
Year Established: 1984
Pub. Frequency: q.
Page Size: standard
Subscrip. Rate: $16/yr. in US.; $24/yr. foreign
Materials: 01,02,05,06,10,15,16,32,33
Freelance Pay: $2/pub. in.
Circulation: 4,500
Circulation Type: paid

**Owner(s):**
American Nurse Publishing Co.
77 W. Washington St.
Ste. 2100
Chicago, IL 60602-2904
Telephone: (312) 782-5505
FAX: (312) 782-3232
Ownership %: 100
**Management:**
Allen W. Seidel ..........................President
Allen W. Seidel ..........................Publisher
**Editorial:**
Julie S. Higginsotham ...................Editor
Tomothy Schaedel ...........Advertising Director
Irene Z. Swiderski ..............Circulation Director
**Desc.:** Magazine for designing minds and growing businesses, features technical articles, columns and departments for professionals in the indoor horticulture market, particularly those working for commercial interior landscape contracting companies. Technical articles cover everything from design through installation and maintenance, as well as specifics on the plants and related accessories used.
**Readers:** Principally interior landscape contractors, those who design, install and maintain interior landscaping projects. Also the producers of foliage and flowering plants used indoors; interior landscape design professionals, including architects, landscape architects and interior designers; property developers and facility managers; and the suppliers and manufacturers of interior design accessories and indoor horticulture equipment and supplies.

## INTERIORSCAPE
71292

3023 Eastland Blvd., 103
Clearwater, FL 34621
Telephone: (813) 796-3877
FAX: (813) 791-4126
Year Established: 1990
Pub. Frequency: bi-m.
Subscrip. Rate: $12/yr.; $30/3 yrs.
**Owner(s):**
Brantwood Publications, Inc.
3023 Eastland Blvd., 103
Clearwater, FL 34621
Telephone: (813) 796-3877
Ownership %: 100
**Management:**
Jeff Morey .................................Publisher
**Editorial:**
Jeff Morey ....................................Editor

## JOURNAL OF HOME & CONSUMER HORTICULTURE
69559

10 Alice St.
Binghamton, NY 13904
Telephone: (800) 342-9678
FAX: (607) 722-1424
Year Established: 1993
Pub. Frequency: q.
Subscrip. Rate: $24/yr.
**Owner(s):**
Haworth Press, Inc.
10 Alice St.
Binghamton, NY 13904
Telephone: (800) 342-9678
Ownership %: 100
**Editorial:**
Ray Poincelot ...............................Editor
**Desc.:** Covers home and consumer horticulture.
**Readers:** For academics and business professionals.

## LAND & WATER
23073

900 Central Ave.
Ste. 21
Fort Dodge, IA 50501
Telephone: (515) 576-3191
FAX: (515) 576-2606
Mailing Address:
P.O. Box 1197
Fort Dodge, IA 50501
Year Established: 1956
Pub. Frequency: bi-m.
Page Size: standard
Subscrip. Rate: $2.50/issue; $14.40/yr. US; $26.40/yr. foreign
Materials: 01,02,06,10,15
Print Process: web offset
Circulation: 20,000
Circulation Type: controlled & paid
**Owner(s):**
Land and Water, Inc.
900 Central Ave.
Ste. 21
Fort Dodge, IA 50501
Telephone: (515) 576-3191
FAX: (515) 576-2606
Ownership %: 100
**Management:**
Kenneth Rasch ...........................President
Amy Dencklau ............................Publisher
Ann Crouse .....................Circulation Manager
**Editorial:**
Teresa Doyle ......................Managing Editor
Teresa Doyle ...........................Art Director
Teresa Doyle ...................Book Review Editor
Teresa Doyle ..................New Products Editor
Teresa Doyle ...........................News Editor
Gail Henry ........................................Sales
D. L. (Gina) Kuhn ...............................Sales
**Desc.:** Published for those individuals involved in natural resource management and restoration. We help our readers gain access to this market by publishing job site stories, case histories, and the information on the latest developments in the industry.
**Readers:** Contractors, engineers, architects, government officials and those working in the field of natural resource management and restoration from idea stage through project completion and maintenance.
**Deadline:** story-2 mo. prior to pub. date; ads-2 mo. prior to pub. date

## LANDSCAPE & IRRIGATION
24166

68-860 Perez Rd. J
Cathedral City, CA 92234-7248
Telephone: (818) 781-8300
Year Established: 1977
Pub. Frequency: m.
Page Size: standard
Subscrip. Rate: $33/yr.
Freelance Pay: negotiable
Circulation: 37,000
Circulation Type: paid
**Owner(s):**
Adams Communications
109 Bushaway Rd.
Wayzata, MN 55391
Ownership %: 100
**Management:**
Denne Goldstein ..........................President
Mark Adams ..........................Vice President
Denne Goldstein ..........................Publisher
Denise Allen .....................Circulation Manager
**Editorial:**
Holly Gibson ..................................Editor
James Gregory ....................Associate Editor
Bruce F. Shank ...................Associate Editor

**Desc.:** A trade publication of the landscape & irrigation industry. Articles on technical and informational interest are published each issue. By-lines on articles used. Concentrating on all landscapes and irrigation systems.
**Readers:** Landscape contractors and irrigation contractors, and lawn care specialists.

## LANDSCAPE ARCHITECTURE
24165

4401 Connecticut Ave., N.W.
Washington, DC 20008-2302
Telephone: (202) 686-2752
FAX: (202) 686-1001
Year Established: 1910
Pub. Frequency: m.
Page Size: oversize
Subscrip. Rate: $44/yr.; $84/2 yrs.
Freelance Pay: $.50/wd. and up
Circulation: 18,000
Circulation Type: paid
**Owner(s):**
American Society of Landscape Architects
4401 Connecticut Ave., N.W.
Washington, DC 20008-2302
Telephone: (202) 686-2752
Ownership %: 100
**Management:**
James G. Trulove ..........................Publisher
Lee Ann Moody ...............Advertising Manager
Patrick Baggata .................Circulation Manager
**Editorial:**
James G. Trulove .......................Editor in Chief
**Desc.:** Medium for the publication of major new developments, and for the exchange of thought and experience within the landscape architectual profession and its allied fields of architecture, city planning, housing, park planning, landscape design, etc. Departments include: News, Book Reviews, Construction, In Practice, Education, Profile, Computers, Product News.
**Readers:** Members of the ASLA, landscape architects, architects, engineers, city planners, contractors.

## LANDSCAPE CONTRACTOR MAGAZINE, THE
24164

2200 S. Main St., Ste. 304
Lombard, IL 60148
Telephone: (708) 932-8443
Year Established: 1959
Pub. Frequency: m.
Page Size: standard
Subscrip. Rate: $65/yr.
Materials: 29,30,32,33
Freelance Pay: negotiable
Circulation: 2,200
Circulation Type: controlled
**Owner(s):**
Illinois Landscape Contractors Assn.
2200 S. Main St.
Ste. 304
Lombard, IL 60148
Telephone: (708) 932-8443
Ownership %: 100
**Management:**
Maury Boyd & Assocs., Inc. ...............Publisher
Esther Baricza ...........................Sales Manager
**Editorial:**
Deborah Quinto ...............................Editor
**Desc.:** We are extremely interested in getting good case history features on outstanding landscape projects in the Midwest, and new and interesting insights into plant material in all its phases of propagation, planting and care.

**Materials Accepted/Included:** 01-Business news 02-By-line articles 03-Fashion news 04-Food news 05-Freelance copy 06-Letters to editor 07-Real estate news 08-Sports news 09-Travel news 10-Book rev. 11-Movie rev. 12-Music rev. 13-TV rev. 14-Theater rev. 15-Coming events 16-Obituaries 17-Question & answer 18-Social announcements 19-Artwork 20-Cartoons 21-Photos 22-TV listings 23-Audio rec. 24-Video rec. 25-Books 26-Films/film clips 27-Personnel news 28-Press releases 29-New product news/photos 30-Trade lit. 31-Contracts awarded 32-Display adv. 33-Classified adv.

4-151

**Readers:** Landscape contractors, landscape nurserymen, sod producers, garden centers, horticulture college educators, state legislators, landscape architects, and suppliers.

68860

## LANDSCAPE DESIGN
68-860 Perez Rd., #J
Cathedral City, CA 92234-7248
Telephone: (818) 781-8300
Year Established: 1988
Pub. Frequency: bi-m.
Subscrip. Rate: $25/yr.
Circulation: 13000
Circulation Type: paid
**Owner(s):**
Gold Trade Publications, Inc.
P.O. Box 8420
Van Nuys, CA 91409
Telephone: (818) 781-8300
Ownership %: 100
**Editorial:**
Matthew Trulio .............................................Editor

24173

## LANDSCAPE MANAGEMENT
7500 Old Oak Blvd.
Cleveland, OH 44130
Telephone: (216) 243-8100
FAX: (216) 891-2675
Year Established: 1962
Pub. Frequency: m.
Page Size: standard
Subscrip. Rate: $3/issue; $55/yr. US.;
$75/yr. foreign
Materials: 01,02,21,29,32,33
Freelance Pay: $100-$300
Print Process: web offset
Circulation: 47,000
Circulation Type: controlled
**Owner(s):**
Advanstar Communications, Inc.
7500 Old Oak Blvd.
Cleveland, OH 44130
Telephone: (216) 243-8100
Ownership %: 100
**Editorial:**
Jerry Roche ...............................Editor in Chief
Ron Hall ....................................Senior Editor
Terry McIver ............................Managing Editor
**Desc.:** Covers weed control, turf
maintenance, tree care, landscape
contracting, park maintenance, lawn
care, and golf course management.
**Readers:** Municipalities park
superintendents, golf course
superintendents, landscape contractors,
and professional lawn care operators.

65674

## LAWN & LANDSCAPE
## MAINTENANCE
4012 Bridge St.
Cleveland, OH 44113
Telephone: (216) 961-4130
FAX: (216) 961-0364
Year Established: 1980
Pub. Frequency: m.
Page Size: standard
Subscrip. Rate: $25/yr. US; $29/yr.
Canada; $82/yr. foreign
Circulation: 43,675
Circulation Type: controlled
**Owner(s):**
GIE, Inc.
4012 Bridge Ave.
Cleveland, OH 44113
Telephone: (216) 961-4130
Ownership %: 100
**Editorial:**
Cindy Code ..................................Editor

**Desc.:** Circulated nationally to landscape
contractors; chemical lawn services;
mowing/maintenance contractors;
ornamental shrub and tree services and
grounds superintendents of commercial,
industrial and health care institutions,
government parks and recreational
facilities. The exclusive forum for
technical research relating to the lawn
landscape maintenance field, and turf
and ornamental facilities; as well as a
timely business news magazine with a
reputation for its coverage of in-depth
business/management subjects.

66679

## NORTHERN TURF MANAGEMENT
P.O. Box 1420
Clarksdale, MS 38614
Telephone: (601) 624-8502
FAX: (601) 627-1977
Year Established: 1990
Pub. Frequency: m.
Page Size: standard
Subscrip. Rate: $25/yr.
Circulation: 20,000
Circulation Type: paid
**Owner(s):**
Farm Press Publications, Inc.
P.O. Box 1420
Clarksdale, MS 38614
Telephone: (652) 624-8502
Ownership %: 100
**Management:**
Tommy L. Keith ...............................Publisher
**Editorial:**
Edward Phillips ...............................Editor
Edward Phillips ...........................Design Editor
**Desc.:** For the northern turf market
including golf course superintendents,
professional lawn care operators,
municipal parks and recreational areas,
sod producers, sports turf managers and
others.

71290

## NURSERY BUSINESS GROWER
3023 Eastland Blvd., 103
Clearwater, FL 34621
Telephone: (813) 796-3877
FAX: (813) 791-4126
Year Established: 1990
Pub. Frequency: bi-m.
Subscrip. Rate: $15/yr.; $35/3 yrs.
**Owner(s):**
Brantwood Publications, Inc.
3023 Eastland Blvd., 103
Clearwater, FL 34621
Telephone: (813) 796-3877
Ownership %: 100
**Management:**
Richard W. Morey ...............................Publisher
**Editorial:**
Richard W. Morey ..............................Editor
Jeffrey Parnau .........................Managing Editor

71289

## NURSERY BUSINESS RETAILER
3023 Eastland Blvd., 103
Clearwater, FL 34621
Telephone: (813) 796-3877
FAX: (813) 791-4126
Year Established: 1990
Pub. Frequency: bi-m.
Subscrip. Rate: $30/yr.
Circulation: 35,000
Circulation Type: paid
**Owner(s):**
Brantwood Publications, Inc.
3023 Eastland Blvd., 103
Clearwater, FL 34621
Telephone: (813) 796-3877
Ownership %: 100
**Management:**
Richard W. Morey ...............................Publisher
**Editorial:**
Richard W. Morey ..............................Editor

Jeffrey Parnau ............................Managing Editor

66012

## NURSERY NEWS
120 S. Riverside Plaza #464
Chicago, IL 60606-3908
Telephone: (312) 258-8500
FAX: (312) 258-8558
Year Established: 1986
Pub. Frequency: m.
Page Size: tabloid
Subscrip. Rate: $15/yr.
Materials: 01,06,15,16,21,28,29
Freelance Pay: varies
Print Process: web offset
Circulation: 19,466
Circulation Type: paid
**Owner(s):**
Cenflo Publications, Inc.
120 Riverside Plaza
Ste. 464
Chicago, IL 60606
Telephone: (312) 258-8500
FAX: (312) 258-8558
Ownership %: 100
**Editorial:**
Rosemary Baldwin ...............................Editor
**Desc.:** Carries articles on current
horticultural research and production
techniques, exterior
landscaping; effective retailing;
marketing and promotion techniques and
various other facets of the industry. Also
regularly publishes special issues in
cooperation with national, state, and
regional organizations covering their
meetings and conventions.
**Readers:** Growers, wholesalers,
rewholesalers of ornamental plant
material, retail nurseryman, garden
center operators, exterior landscape
contractors, architects, and designers,
mass market buyers for hardware, lawn
and garden, chain, convenience and
variety stores, and various arborists.

24171

## PACIFIC COAST NURSERYMAN &
## GARDEN SUPPLY DEALER
306 W. Foothill Blvd.
Glendora, CA 91740
Telephone: (818) 914-3916
FAX: (818) 914-3751
Mailing Address:
P.O. Box 1477
Glendora, CA 91740
Year Established: 1941
Pub. Frequency: m.
Page Size: standard
Subscrip. Rate: $20/yr.
Circulation: 10,500
Circulation Type: controlled
**Owner(s):**
John C. Chiapelone
306 W. Foothill Blvd.
Glendora, CA 91740
Telephone: (818) 914-3916
Ownership %: 17

Leo M. Dupuich
306 W. Foothill Blvd.
Glendora, CA 91740
Telephone: (818) 914-3916
Ownership %: 33

Harold R. Young
306 W. Foothill Blvd.
Glendora, CA 91740
Telephone: (818) 914-3916
Ownership %: 33

Janice Chiapelone
306 W. Foothill Blvd.
Glendora, CA 91740
Telephone: (818) 914-3916
Ownership %: 17
**Management:**
Harold R. Young ...........................Publisher

Jeffrey Parnau ...........................Managing Editor

66012

**Editorial:**
Harold R. Young ...............................Editor
John Humes ...........................Associate Editor
**Desc.:** Staff written articles covering
production, wholesale and retail
marketing of nursery stock and garden
supplies, new growing techniques, and
new laws and regulations affecting the
field. Regularly carries news of new
plants, garden supplies and equipment.
Reviews new books, carries company
news, appointments, association news.
**Readers:** Growers, retailers, and
landscape professionals throughout the
western states.

68862

## PUBLIC GARDEN
786 Church Rd.
Wayne, PA 19087
Telephone: (215) 688-1120
FAX: (215) 293-0149
Year Established: 1950
Pub. Frequency: q.
Page Size: standard
Subscrip. Rate: $24/yr.
Materials: 10,32
Print Process: offset lithography
Circulation: 5,000
Circulation Type: free & paid
**Owner(s):**
American Assn. of Botanical Gardens and
Aboreta
786 Church Rd.
Wayne, PA 19087
Telephone: (610) 688-1120
FAX: (610) 293-0149
Ownership %: 100
**Editorial:**
Sharon Lee .......................................Editor
**Desc.:** Themed issues on topics of current
concern to those working in public
horticulture.

24913

## SEED TRADE NEWS
9995 W. 69th St.
Eden Prairie, MN 55344-3497
Telephone: (612) 941-5820
FAX: (612) 941-1708
Year Established: 1923
Pub. Frequency: 14/yr.
Page Size: tabloid
Subscrip. Rate: $25/yr.
Materials: 01,02,15,21,27,28,29,32,33
Print Process: offset
Circulation: 3,800
Circulation Type: paid
**Owner(s):**
Dean Enterprises, Inc.
9995 W. 69th St.
Eden Prairie, MN 55344-3497
Telephone: (612) 941-5820
Ownership %: 100
**Management:**
Spencer M. Dean ...............................Publisher
Jim Laird ..........................Advertising Manager
Julie Lindeman .................Circulation Manager
**Editorial:**
Frank Zaworski ...................................Editor
Rose McCormick ................Production Director
**Desc.:** Covers all methods of seed
production and merchandising for
growers, wholesalers, catalog, mail
order, and retail seedsmen.
**Deadline:** story-15th of mo. prior to pub.
date; ads-15th of mo. prior

24172

## SEED WORLD
380 E. Northwest Hwy.
Des Plaines, IL 60016
Telephone: (708) 298-6622
FAX: (708) 390-0408
Year Established: 1915
Pub. Frequency: m.

**Materials Accepted/Included:** 01-Business news 02-By-line articles 03-Fashion news 04-Food news 05-Freelance copy 06-Letters to editor 07-Real estate news 08-Sports news 09-Travel news 10-Book rev. 11-Movie rev. 12-Music rev. 13-TV rev. 14-Theater rev. 15-Coming events 16-Obituaries 17-Question & answer 18-Social announcements 19-Artwork 20-Cartoons 21-Photos 22-TV listings 23-Audio rec. 24-Video rec. 25-Books 26-Films/film clips 27-Personnel news 28-Press releases 29-New product news/photos 30-Trade lit. 31-Contracts awarded 32-Display adv. 33-Classified adv.

Page Size: standard
Subscrip. Rate: $25/yr.
Freelance Pay: negotiable
Circulation: 5,505
Circulation Type: paid
**Owner(s):**
Scranton Gillette Communications, Inc.
380 E. Northwest Hwy.
Des Plaines, IL 60016
Telephone: (708) 298-6622
Ownership %: 100
**Management:**
Gene H. McCormick ..........................Publisher
Doug O'Gorden .................Advertising Manager
**Editorial:**
Lynn Whitmore-Grooms ..........................Editor
Judith Schmueser ...............Production Director
**Desc.:** Features on seed growing and
wholesaling; crop and market
information; news of people, firms and
products; convention and meeting
announcements and reports.
Departments include: Company News,
People in the News, New Products and
Varieties, Managing Information.
**Readers:** Retailers, wholesalers and
growers of all seeds.

71288
**SOUTHERN GOLF**
3023 Eastland Blvd., 103
Clearwater, FL 34621
Telephone: (813) 796-3877
FAX: (813) 791-4126
Year Established: 1990
Pub. Frequency: bi-m.
Subscrip. Rate: $9/yr.; $20/3 yrs.
**Owner(s):**
Brantwood Publications, Inc.
3023 Eastland Blvd., 103
Clearwater, FL 34621
Telephone: (813) 796-3877
Ownership %: 100
**Management:**
Richard W. Morey ...............................Publisher
**Editorial:**
Richard W. Morey ..............................Editor
Jeffrey Parnau ...........................Managing Editor

66677
**SOUTHERN TURF MANAGEMENT**
P.O. Box 1420
Clarksdale, MS 38614
Telephone: (601) 624-8503
FAX: (601) 627-1977
Year Established: 1990
Pub. Frequency: m.
Page Size: standard
Subscrip. Rate: $25/yr.
Circulation: 15,000
Circulation Type: paid
**Owner(s):**
Farm Press Publications, Inc.
P.O. Box 1420
Clarksdale, MS 38614
Telephone: (601) 624-8503
Ownership %: 100
**Management:**
Tommy L. Keith ...................................Publisher
**Editorial:**
Ron Smith ...............................................Editor
Scott McClure ...............................Design Editor
**Desc.:** Covers the production and
maintenance of turf in the US.

68861
**TURF NORTH**
50 Bay St.
St. Johnsbury, VT 05819
Telephone: (802) 748-8908
FAX: (802) 748-1866
Mailing Address:
P.O. Box 391
St. Johnsbury, VT 05819-0391
Year Established: 1988
Pub. Frequency: m.

Page Size: tabloid
Subscrip. Rate: free
Materials: 01,02,05,06,15,27,28,29,32,33
Freelance Pay: $225
Print Process: web offset
Circulation: 17,500
Circulation Type: controlled & free
**Owner(s):**
NEF Publishing Co.
50 Bay St.
P.O. Box 391
St. Johnsbury, VT 05819-0391
Telephone: (802) 748-8908
FAX: (802) 748-1866
Ownership %: 100
**Editorial:**
Daniel Hurley .........................................Editor
Francis Carlet ........................................Editor
**Desc.:** Focuses on the greenspace
industry, including research
developments and new technology.
**Readers:** Professionals in the greenspace
industry, including landscape and lawn
care companies, golf courses,
cemeteries, municipalities and parks,
private, public and government
installations, headquarters and estates,
schools and universities, airports, sport
complexes, landscape architects, sod
growers, seed companies, nurseries,
dealers, distributors and suppliers.
**Deadline:** story-1st of mo. preceding cover
date; ads-1st of mo. preceding cover
date

69563
**TURF SOUTH**
50 Bay St.
St. Johnsbury, VT 05819-0391
Telephone: (802) 748-8908
FAX: (802) 748-1866
Mailing Address:
P.O. Box 391
St. Johnsbury, VT 05819
Year Established: 1989
Pub. Frequency: m.
Page Size: tabloid
Subscrip. Rate: free
Materials: 01,02,05,15,28,29,32,33
Freelance Pay: $225
Print Process: web offset
Circulation: 16,000
Circulation Type: controlled & free
**Owner(s):**
NEF Publishing Co.
P.O. Box 391
50 Bay St.
St. Johnsbury, VT 05819
Telephone: (802) 748-8908
FAX: (802) 748-1866
Ownership %: 100
**Management:**
Francis Carlet .....................................President
Francis Carlet ......................................Publisher
Daniel Hurley .......................................Publisher
Johanna Myers .................Advertising Manager
Shellie Beauparlant ..........Advertising Manager
Elizabeth Brown .................Circulation Manager
**Editorial:**
Francis Carlet ...............................Editor in Chief
Daniel Hurley ...............................Editor in Chief
Robert Hookway .......................Managing Editor
**Desc.:** Focuses on the greenspace
industry, including research
developments and new technology.

**Readers:** Professionals in the greenspace
industry, including landscape and lawn
care companies, golf courses,
cemeteries, municipalities and parks,
private, public and government
installations, headquarters and estates,
schools and universities, airports, sport
complexes, landscape architects, sod
growers, seed companies, nurseries,
dealers, distributors and suppliers.
**Deadline:** story-1st of mo. preceding cover
date; ads-1st of mo. preceding cover
date

69568
**TURF WEST**
50 Bay St.
St. Johnsbury, VT 05819
Telephone: (802) 748-8908
FAX: (802) 748-1866
Mailing Address:
P.O. Box 391
St. Johnsbury, VT 05819-0391
Year Established: 1991
Pub. Frequency: m.
Page Size: tabloid
Subscrip. Rate: free
Materials: 01,02,05,15,28,29,32,33
Freelance Pay: $225
Print Process: web offset
Circulation: 8,333
Circulation Type: controlled & free
**Owner(s):**
NEF Publishing Co.
50 Bay St.
P.O. Box 391
St. Johnsbury, VT 05819
Telephone: (802) 748-8908
FAX: (802) 748-1866
Ownership %: 100
**Management:**
Francis Carlet ......................................Publisher
Daniel Hurley .......................................Publisher
Johanna Myers .................Advertising Manager
Shellie Beauparlant ..........Advertising Manager
Elizabeth Brown .................Circulation Manager
**Editorial:**
Francis Carlet ...............................Editor in Chief
Daniel Hurley ...............................Editor in Chief
Robert Hookway .......................Managing Editor
**Desc.:** Focuses on the greenspace
industry, including research
developments and new technology.
**Readers:** Professionals in the greenspace
industry, including landscape and lawn
care companies, golf courses,
cemeteries, municipalities and parks,
private, public and government
installations, headquarters and estates,
schools and universities, airports, sport
complexes, landscape architects, sod
growers, seed companies, nurseries,
dealers, distributors and suppliers.

66678
**WESTERN TURF MANAGEMENT**
P.O. Box 1420
Clarksdale, MS 38614
Telephone: (601) 624-8503
FAX: (601) 627-1977
Year Established: 1990
Pub. Frequency: m.
Page Size: standard
Subscrip. Rate: $25/yr.
Circulation: 9,000
Circulation Type: paid
**Owner(s):**
Farm Press Publications, Inc.
P.O. Box 1420
Clarksdale, MS 38614
Telephone: (601) 624-8503
Ownership %: 100
**Management:**
Tommy L. Keith ...................................Publisher
**Editorial:**
Ed Phillips ..............................................Editor

**Desc.:** For golf course superintendents,
professional lawn care service
operators, supervisors of municipal parks
and other recreational areas, sod
producers and sports turf managers in
the western states.

24175
**YARD & GARDEN**
1233 Janesville Ave.
Fort Atkinson, WI 53538
Telephone: (414) 563-6388
FAX: (414) 563-1701
Year Established: 1977
Pub. Frequency: 9/yr.
Page Size: tabloid
Subscrip. Rate: $40/yr. US; $55/yr.
Canada; $120/yr. elsewhere
Circulation: 33,000
Circulation Type: controlled
**Owner(s):**
Johnson Hill Press, Inc.
1233 Janesville Ave.
Fort Atkinson, WI 53538
Telephone: (414) 563-6388
Ownership %: 100
**Management:**
Patrick Nadler ......................................Publisher
Julie Nachtical ...................Circulation Manager
**Editorial:**
Dan Kirkpatrick ......................................Editor
July Whitty ...................................Art Director
Cindy Rusch .................Production Coordinator
Linda Stevlingson ...................................Sales
Rick Monogue ..........................................Sales
**Desc.:** Provides information concerning
new products and supplies for retailers
and wholesalers whose primary business
is the sale of yard and garden products,
including power equipment. In-depth
marketing & merchandising features are
designed to enhance the sales &
marketing skills of the yard & garden
retailer.
**Readers:** Dealers, distributors and
manufacturers whose primary products
and services are yard and garden
product and merchandising related.
Retailer interviews.

## Group 102-Gas, Oil & Petroleum

23105
**AAPG EXPLORER**
1444 S. Boulder Ave.
Tulsa, OK 74119
Telephone: (918) 584-2555
FAX: (918) 584-0469
Mailing Address:
P.O. Box 979
Tulsa, OK 74101-0979
Year Established: 1979
Pub. Frequency: m.
Page Size: tabloid
Subscrip. Rate: $3 newsstand; $45/yr.
Materials: 01,06,16,21,32,33
Freelance Pay: $50/col.
Circulation: 44,000
Circulation Type: paid
**Owner(s):**
American Association of Petroleum
Geologists
P.O. Box 979
Tulsa, OK 74101
Telephone: (918) 584-2555
Ownership %: 100
**Editorial:**
Vern Stefanic ...........................Managing Editor
Larry M. Nation .........Communications Director
**Desc.:** Primary communications tool of the
largest professional geological
association in the world at over 34,000
members.

**Materials Accepted/Included:** 01-Business news 02-By-line articles 03-Fashion news 04-Food news 05-Freelance copy 06-Letters to editor 07-Real estate news 08-Sports news 09-Travel news 10-Book rev. 11-Movie rev. 12-Music rev. 13-TV rev. 14-Theater rev. 15-Coming events 16-Obituaries 17-Question & answer 18-Social announcements 19-Artwork 20-Cartoons 21-Photos 22-TV listings 23-Audio rec. 24-Video rec. 25-Books 26-Films/film clips 27-Personnel news 28-Press releases 29-New product news/photos 30-Trade lit. 31-Contracts awarded 32-Display adv. 33-Classified adv.

4-153

**Readers:** Trained geologists, geophysicists, oceanographers and all geoscientists worldwide.

23107

## AMERICAN OIL & GAS REPORTER, THE
P.O. Box 343
Derby, KS 67037-0343
Telephone: (316) 788-1835
Year Established: 1958
Pub. Frequency: m.
Page Size: standard
Subscrip. Rate: $28/yr.
Materials: 01,02,06,27,28,29,30,31,32,33
Freelance Pay: $6/in.
Print Process: web offset
Circulation: 11,228
Circulation Type: paid
**Owner(s):**
National Publishers Group
P.O. Box 343
Derby, KS 67037
Telephone: (316) 681-3560
Ownership %: 100
**Management:**
Charlie Cookson ..................................Publisher
Charlie Cookson ..............Advertising Manager
**Editorial:**
Bill Campbell .............................Managing Editor
Luanne Pierce ....................Production Director
Tim Beims ....................Special Sections Editor
**Desc.:** The focus of the publication's editorial effort is the business side of the exploratory/drilling/production industry. Major topics include: economics, legislative and regulatory problems, judicial rulings and their implications, and taxing jurisdiction difficulties; all matters which daily affect the oil executive.
**Readers:** Owners and top management of producer/operator firms and the drilling and well servicing contractors serving them. The American Reporter is designed exclusively for these firms.

23108

## ARKANSAS PROPANE GAS NEWS
103 E. Seventh St., Ste. 1012
Little Rock, AR 72201
Telephone: (501) 374-8396
Pub. Frequency: bi-m.
Page Size: standard
Subscrip. Rate: $2/yr.
Circulation: 600
Circulation Type: controlled
**Owner(s):**
Arkansas Propane Gas Association
103 E. Seventh St., Ste 1012
Little Rock, AR 72201
Telephone: (501) 374-8396
Ownership %: 100
**Editorial:**
J.P. Lybrand, Jr. ...........................................Editor
**Desc.:** LP Gas Industry, Facts and Development, New Products, Promotional Methods, Small Business Information.
**Readers:** Dealers, employees, trade.

23109

## BULLETIN OF THE AMERICAN ASSOCIATION OF PETROLEUM
1444 S. Boulder Ave.
Tulsa, OK 74119
Telephone: (918) 584-2555
FAX: (918) 584-0469
Mailing Address:
P.O. Box 979
Tulsa, OK 74101
Year Established: 1917
Pub. Frequency: m.
Page Size: standard
Subscrip. Rate: $8/issue members;
$12/issue non-members; $135/yr. US;
$160/yr. foreign
Circulation: 34,000

Circulation Type: paid
**Owner(s):**
The American Association of Petroleum Geologists
Ownership %: 100
**Management:**
Fred A. Dix ..........................Executive Director
Brenda Merideth ..............Advertising Manager
Rusty Johnson ....................Assistant Manager
**Desc.:** News and features on new exploration techniques, technical literature on geology, oceanography and geophysics world-wide, and news of the profession. Publication aids the association in accomplishing its objectives. Much of the editorial content is technical material, unsolicited and provided by members. Additional material includes news of conventions, activities of members, and other related association business.
**Readers:** Made up of AAPG members, including oil company management, service companies, colleges, governmental agencies, foreign governments.

23110

## BUTANE-PROPANE NEWS
338 E. Foothill Blvd.
Arcadia, CA 91006
Telephone: (818) 357-2168
FAX: (818) 303-2854
Mailing Address:
P.O. Box 660698
Arcadia, CA 91066-0698
Year Established: 1939
Pub. Frequency: m.
Page Size: standard
Subscrip. Rate: $20/yr. to qualified personnel; $30/yr. others
Materials: 01,06,16,21,27,29,30,31,32,33
Freelance Pay: $90/pg.
Circulation: 18,000
Circulation Type: controlled
**Owner(s):**
Butane-Propane News, Inc.
338 E. Foothill Blvd.
Arcadia, CA 91006
Telephone: (818) 357-2168
Ownership %: 100
**Management:**
Natalie Peal ........................................Publisher
Kurt Ruhl .........................Advertising Manager
Natalie Peal ........Editorial Production Manager
**Editorial:**
Chuck Elliott ...............................................Editor
Ann Rey .......................................................Editor
William W. Clark ...................Editorial Director
Sheri Sinske ...........................Circulation Editor
Natalie Peal ..............................Production Director
**Desc.:** Contributed articles on merchandising, customer relations, practical management, marketing, etc., dealing with liquefied petroleum gas industry. Covers personnel changes, association news, trade news, new products.
**Readers:** Transporters, wholesalers, and pipeline companies, LPG distributor dealers, LPG producers.

23113

## DRILLING CONTRACTOR
15810 Pk. Ten Pl., Ste. 222
Houston, TX 77084
Telephone: (713) 578-7171
Mailing Address:
P.O. Box 4287
Houston, TX 77210
Year Established: 1944
Pub. Frequency: bi-m.
Page Size: standard
Subscrip. Rate: free
Circulation: 17,500
Circulation Type: controlled

**Owner(s):**
IADC
15810 Pk. 10 Pl.
Houston, TX 77084
Telephone: (713) 578-7171
Ownership %: 100
**Management:**
Alvaro Franco ....................................President
Alvaro Franco ....................................Publisher
Bridget S. Rives ................Circulation Manager
Cindy McManus ........................Office Manager
**Editorial:**
Alvaro Franco ...............................................Editor
Bill Wageneck ................................Advertising
Hager Patton ..................................Advertising
Mike Killalea ..........................Associate Editor
**Desc.:** Contributed and staff-developed articles cover drilling and production operations, industry outlook. Carries association news, personalities, new equipment.
**Readers:** Readers active in the drilling/production segment of the oil industry.

69039

## FUEL REFORMULATION
4545 Post Oak Rd., Ste. 210
Houston, TX 77027
Telephone: (713) 993-9320
FAX: (713) 840-8585
Year Established: 1991
Pub. Frequency: bi-m.
Subscrip. Rate: $149/yr.
Materials: 01,02,21
Circulation: 8,000
Circulation Type: paid
**Owner(s):**
Hart Publications, Inc.
4545 Post Oak Rd.
Ste. 210
Houston, TX 77027
Telephone: (713) 993-9320
FAX: (713) 840-8585
Ownership %: 100
**Editorial:**
Rene Gonzalez ...........................................Editor
**Desc.:** Analyzes the business, technical and regulatory circumstances associated with the manufacture, supply and use of transportation fuels, reformulated to improve air quality worldwide.

23116

## GAS DIGEST
11246 S. Post Oak Rd.
Houston, TX 77035
Telephone: (713) 723-7456
FAX: (713) 723-3807
Mailing Address:
P.O. Box 35819
Houston, TX 77235
Year Established: 1975
Pub. Frequency: bi-m.
Page Size: standard
Subscrip. Rate: $8/yr.
Circulation: 10,500
Circulation Type: controlled
**Owner(s):**
Tri Plek Productions
P.O. Box 35819
Houston, TX 77235
Telephone: (713) 723-7456
Ownership %: 100
**Management:**
Ken Kridner ........................................Publisher
Mike Kridner ....................Advertising Manager
**Editorial:**
Ken Kridner ...............................................Editor
**Desc.:** Departments include: Gas News, Washington Memo, Gas Meetings, Measurement Corner, New Products, Literature, People.
**Readers:** In the operating area of the gas industry.

23117

## GAS INDUSTRIES MAGAZINE
6300 N. River Rd.
Des Plaines, IL 60018
Telephone: (708) 693-3682
Mailing Address:
6333 E. Mockingbird Ln., 147
Dallas, TX 75214
Year Established: 1956
Pub. Frequency: m.
Page Size: standard
Subscrip. Rate: $20/yr.; $90/yr. foreign
Circulation: 11,000
Circulation Type: controlled
**Owner(s):**
Better Roads
P.O. Box 558
Park Ridge, IL 60068
Telephone: (708) 693-7710
Ownership %: 100
**Management:**
Wm. Dannhausen ................................Publisher
**Editorial:**
Ruth Stidger ...................Editorial Director
Paul Lady ....................Associate Publisher
**Desc.:** Management of gas energy pipelines-utility distribution and transmission/distribution operations. Features & items for natural gas pipelines, transmission processing, and utility distribution. Contains news & methods of construction, maintenance, equipment, and materials; illustrated with photos or diagrams. Departments include: Products, Literature, Manufacturing News, Personnel, Associations, Washington Legislation, Supplemental Gas Projects, CNG Carburation, Commercial, Industrial, & Residential Gas Applications, Co-Generation.
**Readers:** Management, engineering operations, equipment management, materials fleet, and marketing.

23118

## GEOPHYSICS
8801 S. Yale
Tulsa, OK 74137
Telephone: (918) 493-3516
FAX: (918) 493-2074
Mailing Address:
P.O. Box 702740
Tulsa, OK 74170
Year Established: 1936
Pub. Frequency: m.
Page Size: standard
Subscrip. Rate: $250/yr. US; $260/yr. foreign
Circulation: 15,000
Circulation Type: paid
**Owner(s):**
Society of Exploration Geophysicists
P.O. Box 702740
Tulsa, OK 74170
Telephone: (918) 493-3516
Ownership %: 100
**Management:**
John Hyden ...........................Executive Director
John Daubenspeck ............Advertising Manager
John Hyden ...........................General Manager
**Editorial:**
Bob Hardage ...............................................Editor
Michael D. McCormack ...............Book Review Editor
Jerry W. Henry ....................Publication Director
J.R. Salas ....................Special Events Director

**Materials Accepted/Included:** 01-Business news 02-By-line articles 03-Fashion news 04-Food news 05-Freelance copy 06-Letters to editor 07-Real estate news 08-Sports news 09-Travel news 10-Book rev. 11-Movie rev. 12-Music rev. 13-TV rev. 14-Theater rev. 15-Coming events 16-Obituaries 17-Question & answer 18-Social announcements 19-Artwork 20-Cartoons 21-Photos 22-TV listings 23-Audio rec. 24-Video rec. 25-Books 26-Films/film clips 27-Personnel news 28-Press releases 29-New product news/photos 30-Trade lit. 31-Contracts awarded 32-Display adv. 33-Classified adv.

**Desc.:** Professional papers dealing with geophysical exploration in the petroleum and mining industries. Abstracts must accompany article submitted for publication. Line drawings and halftones used to illustrate material and must be prepared in accordance with publication's requirements. Departments include: Reviews, Patent Abstracts, Titles of Papers from other Journals, and International Advances in Geophysics.
**Readers:** Members of the Society of Exploration Geophysicists, and others interested in applied geophysics.

### GLOBAL OIL STOCKS & BALANCES
69041

575 Broadway, 4th Fl.
New York, NY 10012-3230
Telephone: (212) 941-5500
FAX: (212) 941-5508
Year Established: 1990
Pub. Frequency: m.
Subscrip. Rate: $745/yr.
**Owner(s):**
Petroleum & Energy Intelligence Weekly, Inc.
575 Broadway, 4th Fl.
New York, NY 10012-3220
Telephone: (212) 941-5500
FAX: (212) 941-5508
Ownership %: 100
**Editorial:**
Jay Bhutani .....................................Senior Editor
Tom Wallin ...................................Group Editor
**Desc.:** Reports and analyzes international oil inventories and supply-demand trends.

### GRID: GAS RESEARCH INSTITUTE DIGEST
69040

8600 W. Bryn Mawr Ave.
Chicago, IL 60631
Telephone: (312) 399-8100
FAX: (312) 399-8170
Year Established: 1976
Pub. Frequency: q.
Subscrip. Rate: free
Materials: 01,15,28
Circulation: 11,000
Circulation Type: controlled
**Owner(s):**
Gas Research Institute, Member Rela. and Comm.
8600 W. Bryn Mawr Ave.
Chicago, IL 60631
Telephone: (312) 399-8100
Ownership %: 100
**Editorial:**
Cheryl G. Drugan ...............................Editor
**Desc.:** Natural gas research of a technical nature, explained in simplified terms.

### GULF COAST OIL WORLD
49845

1900 Grant St., Ste. 400
Denver, CO 80203
Telephone: (303) 837-1917
Mailing Address:
P.O. Box 1917
Denver, CO 80201
Year Established: 1981
Pub. Frequency: m.
Page Size: standard
Subscrip. Rate: $39/yr.; $89/3 yrs.
Circulation: 4,000
Circulation Type: paid
**Owner(s):**
Hart Publications, Inc.
P.O. Box 1917
Denver, CO 80201
Telephone: (303) 837-1917
Ownership %: 20

Phillips Publishing International Inc.
7811 Montrose Rd.
Potomac, MD 20854
Telephone: (301) 340-2100
**Bureau(s):**
Gulf Coast Oil World
4545 Post Oak Pl., Ste. 210
Houston, TX 77027
Telephone: (713) 993-9320
Contact: Robert G. Burke, Senior Editor
**Management:**
Donald Hart ..................................Publisher
Stephen Steeves ...............Advertising Manager
**Editorial:**
Don Lyle ..........................................Editor
**Desc.:** Edited for management onshore and offshore in the Gulf Coast region including southeast and east Texas, Louisiana, southern Arkansas, Mississippi, Alabama and Florida and federal and state waters in the Gulf of Mexico. News and feature articles cover exploration, drilling, production engineering, natural gas processing, refining, pipelining and marine support activities in the region. Part of the Oil World Network group of regional petroleum magazines.
**Readers:** Readership backgrounds vary from those with only a H.S. diploma to those with doctorates. Numerous technical disciplines are involved. Major classifications of readers are: drilling & reservoir engineer; oil company executive; toolpusher; production foreman; geologist/geophysicist; landman; independent operator; service & supply company personnel; and investors.

### HART'S OIL & GAS WORLD
23112

1900 Grant St., Ste. 400
Denver, CO 80203
Telephone: (303) 837-1917
FAX: (303) 837-8585
Mailing Address:
P.O. Box 1917
Denver, CO 80201
Year Established: 1953
Pub. Frequency: m.
Page Size: standard
Subscrip. Rate: $10/issue; $59/yr.
Circulation: 5,000
Circulation Type: paid
**Owner(s):**
Hart Publications, Inc.
1900 Grant St. 400
P.O. Box 1917
Denver, CO 80203
Telephone: (303) 837-1917
Ownership %: 20

Phillips Publishing International
P.O. Box 59805
Potomac, MD 20859-2100
Telephone: (301) 340-2100
Ownership %: 80
**Management:**
Kathy Walsh ....................................Publisher
**Editorial:**
Don Lyle ..............................Managing Editor
Ray Hedman ......................................Sales
**Desc.:** Regional oil and gas magazine for Western and Central Texas and Southeast New Mexico. Part of the Oil World Network group of regional petroleum magazines.
**Readers:** Oil and gas operators, drilling contractors, geologists, geophysicists, engineers, landsmen, oil field suppliers, and service personnel.

### HOOSIER INDEPENDENT
23119

101 W. Washington St., Ste. 1338
Indianapolis, IN 46204-4662
Telephone: (317) 633-4662
FAX: (317) 630-1827
Year Established: 1924
Pub. Frequency: q.
Page Size: standard
Subscrip. Rate: free to members
Circulation: 1,200
Circulation Type: free
**Owner(s):**
Indiana Oil Marketers Assn. Inc.
101 Washington St., Ste. 1338
Indianapolis, IN 46204-3413
Telephone: (317) 633-4662
Ownership %: 100
**Management:**
Tom Fair ........................................President
C. Michael Pitts ....................Executive Director
Robert E. Hillman ............Advertising Manager
**Editorial:**
Charlene Hillman ....................Managing Editor
Charlene Hillman ................New Product Editor
Charlene Hillman .......................News Editor
Robert E. Hillman ..............................Sales
**Desc.:** Covers petroleum industry news generally, as well as feature material, including new products and services.
**Readers:** Individual oil marketer members, associate members, other industry people throughout the country.

### HYDROCARBON PROCESSING
23121

Street 3301 Allen Pkwy.
Houston, TX 77019-1896
Telephone: (713) 529-4301
FAX: (713) 520-4433
Mailing Address:
P.O. Box 2608
Houston, TX 77252-2608
Year Established: 1922
Pub. Frequency: m.
Page Size: standard
Subscrip. Rate: $22/yr; $47/3 yrs. US; $34/yr. foreign; $73/3 yrs. foreign
Materials: 27,28,29,30,31,32,33
Print Process: web offset
Circulation: 34,172
Circulation Type: paid
**Owner(s):**
Gulf Publishing Co.
P.O. Box 2608
Houston, TX 77252-2608
Telephone: (713) 529-4301
FAX: (713) 520-4433
Ownership %: 100
**Management:**
Ray D. Cashman ..............................President
Lanie Finlayson .........................Vice President
Ray D. Cashman ..............................Publisher
**Editorial:**
Charles Vervalin ................................Editor
Bob Scott ...........................Editorial Director
Gene Swantek ....................Associate Publisher
Les A. Kane ........................Engineering Editor
LeAnn Dunn ......................Management Editor
Joe D. Woods ...................Marketing Manager
Les A. Kane .....................New Product Editor
David Nakamura ......................Process Editor
Stephany Romanow-Garcia ....................Senior
**Desc.:** Specialized for the hydrocarbon processing management. Carries contributed technical articles dealing with departments include: H.P. Impact; HPI Construction Literature; New Equipment; Book Reviews; Profusely
**Readers:** Management, technical personnel in the hydrocarbon processing industry.

### INTERNATIONAL OIL NEWS: MANAGEMENT EDITION
23122

111 Cloister Ct., Ste. 114
Chapel Hill, NC 27514
Telephone: (919) 490-0700
FAX: (919) 490-3002
Mailing Address:
P.O. Box 16666
Chapel Hill, NC 27516-6666
Year Established: 1953
Pub. Frequency: w.
Page Size: standard
Subscrip. Rate: $455/yr.
Materials: 01,05,15,28,31
Print Process: offset
**Owner(s):**
William F. Bland Co.
111 Cloister Ct., Ste. 114
Chapel Hill, NC 27514
Telephone: (919) 490-0700
Ownership %: 100
**Management:**
William F. Bland ..............................President
William F. Bland ..............................Publisher
Mollie B. Sandor ...............Circulation Manager
**Editorial:**
Chris R. Schultz ................................Editor
**Desc.:** Covers significant developments in all areas of the international petroleum industry: exploration, development, production, refining, transportation and marketing.
**Deadline:** story-10:00 am, Fri.

### JOURNAL OF PETROLEUM TECHNOLOGY
23123

222 Palisades Creek Dr.
Richardson, TX 75080
Telephone: (214) 952-9393
FAX: (214) 952-9435
Mailing Address:
P.O. Box 833836
Richardson, TX 75083
Year Established: 1949
Pub. Frequency: m.
Page Size: standard
Subscrip. Rate: $40/yr. members; $60/yr. non-members
Circulation: 52,000
Circulation Type: paid
**Owner(s):**
Society of Petroleum Engineers, Inc.
P.O. Box 833836
Richardson, TX 75083
Telephone: (214) 952-9393
Ownership %: 100
**Management:**
Doris Tolman ..............Classified Adv. Manager
**Editorial:**
Georgeann Bilich .................................Editor
Dan K. Adamson ...............................Director
Ann Gibson ........................Production Director
**Desc.:** Features articles on oil and gas drilling, exploration, and production management and technology. Indexed annually.
**Readers:** Petroleum engineers, geologists, & managers; drilling, production, & exploration executives & engineers.

### LP-GAS
23124

131 W. First St.
Duluth, MN 55802
Telephone: (218) 723-9275
FAX: (218) 723-9683
Pub. Frequency: m.
Page Size: standard
Subscrip. Rate: $24/yr. in U.S.; $40/yr. in Canada
Freelance Pay: negotiable
Circulation: 16,000
Circulation Type: controlled & paid

**Materials Accepted/Included:** 01-Business news 02-By-line articles 03-Fashion news 04-Food news 05-Freelance copy 06-Letters to editor 07-Real estate news 08-Sports news 09-Travel news 10-Book rev. 11-Movie rev. 12-Music rev. 13-TV rev. 14-Theater rev. 15-Coming events 16-Obituaries 17-Question & answer 18-Social announcements 19-Artwork 20-Cartoons 21-Photos 22-TV listings 23-Audio rec. 24-Video rec. 25-Books 26-Films/film clips 27-Personnel news 28-Press releases 29-New product news/photos 30-Trade lit. 31-Contracts awarded 32-Display adv. 33-Classified adv.

4-155

**Owner(s):**
Advanstar Communications, Inc.
7500 Old Oak Blvd.
Cleveland, OH 44130
Telephone: (216) 243-8100
Ownership %: 100
**Management:**
Robert Earley ...............Vice President
Zane Chastain .....................Publisher
**Editorial:**
Zane Chastain ...........Executive Editor
Don Mason ................Assistant Editor
**Desc.:** Carries articles concerning
   merchandising, management and
   operation of LP gas retail companies
   including propane motor fuel. Carries
   news, new products, meetings, and
   association news.
**Readers:** LP gas dealers, plant managers,
   distributors and providers of LP
   equipment.

23135
### MICHIGAN OIL & GAS NEWS
206 W. Michigan
Suite 200
Mt. Pleasant, MI 48858
Telephone: (517) 772-5181
FAX: (517) 773-2970
Mailing Address:
   P.O. Box 250
   Mt. Pleasant, MI 48804-0250
Year Established: 1932
Pub. Frequency: w.
Page Size: standard
Subscrip. Rate: $100/yr.
Materials: 01,06,07,27,28,30,31,32,33
Print Process: offset
Circulation: 1,974
Circulation Type: paid
**Owner(s):**
Michigan Oil & Gas Association
1610 Michigan National Tower
Lansing, MI 48933
Telephone: (517) 772-5181
Ownership %: 100
**Management:**
Jack R. Westbrook ...........Advertising Manager
Jack R. Westbrook ...........Circulation Manager
**Editorial:**
Scott Bellinger ...................Senior Editor
Jack R. Westbrook .................Managing Editor
**Desc.:** State wide news coverage of the oil
   industry in Michigan; production, leasing,
   refining, transportation, finance. Annual
   Michigan Petroleum Directory published
   in June.
**Readers:** Producers, refiners, contractors.

54063
### MIDCONTINENT OIL WORLD
1900 Grant St., Ste. 400
Denver, CO 80203
Telephone: (303) 837-1917
Mailing Address:
   P.O. Box 1917
   Denver, CO 80201
Year Established: 1985
Pub. Frequency: bi-m.
Subscrip. Rate: $39/yr; $89/3 yrs.
**Owner(s):**
Hart Publications, Inc.
P.O. Box 1917
Denver, CO 80201
Telephone: (303) 837-1917

Philips Publishing International, Inc.
7811 Montrose Rd.
Potomac, MD 20854
Telephone: (301) 340-2100
Ownership %:  80
**Management:**
Lavryn Franzoni ......................Publisher
Scott Herman ...................Advertising Manager
**Editorial:**
June C. Younger .....................Managing Editor

**Desc.:** Edited for management & technical
   petroleum industry personnels. Covers
   exploration, drilling, production,
   processing & transmission in mid-
   continent states.
**Readers:** Geologists, geophysicists,
   engineers, operators, drilling contractors,
   tool pushers.

23126
### MISSOURI PIPELINE
238 E. High St.
Jefferson Cy, MO 65101
Telephone: (314) 635-7117
FAX: (314) 635-3575
Year Established: 1937
Pub. Frequency: 14/yr.
Page Size: standard
Subscrip. Rate: free to members; $25/yr.
   non-members
Circulation: 8,000
Circulation Type: controlled
**Owner(s):**
Missouri Petroleum Marketers
238 E. High St.
Jefferson Cy, MO 65101
Telephone: (314) 635-7117
Ownership %: 100
**Management:**
John Pelzer ............................Publisher
**Editorial:**
John Pelzer .................................Editor
**Desc.:** News stories pertaining to all facets
   of the petroleum marketing field.
**Readers:** All directly related to petroleum
   marketing.

23129
### NATIONAL PETROLEUM NEWS
25 NW Point Blvd.
Ste. 800
Elk Grove Village, IL 60007
Telephone: (708) 427-9512
FAX: (708) 296-8821
Year Established: 1909
Pub. Frequency: m.
Page Size: standard
Subscrip. Rate: $60/yr.
Circulation: 18,000
Circulation Type: paid
**Owner(s):**
Hunter Publishing
Ownership %: 100
**Management:**
Arleigh Hupp .........................Publisher
**Editorial:**
Peggy Smedley ...........................Editor
Bernie Pacyniack .............Managing Editor
Lloyd Schultz .......................Advertising
Greg Lindenberg ...............Copy Editor
Angel Abcede ..........................Reporter
Howard Shingle .......................Reporter
Steve Dwyer ............................Reporter
Mark Emond ............................Reporter
George Schultz ........................Reporter
**Desc.:** Reports news, market
   developments and trends in petroleum
   marketing. Features cover
   merchandising, distribution, storage,
   transportation and management.
   Departments include: About Oil People,
   Catching Up, Statistics, Oil Market
   Review.

23130
### NEBRASKA PETROLEUM MARKETER
1320 Lincoln Mall
Lincoln, NE 68508
Telephone: (402) 474-6691
FAX: (402) 474-2510
Year Established: 1917
Pub. Frequency: m.
Page Size: standard
Subscrip. Rate: $25/yr.
Freelance Pay: negotiable
Circulation: 1,900

Circulation Type: paid
**Owner(s):**
Nebraska Petroleum Marketers, Inc.
1320 Lincoln Mall
Lincoln, NE 68508
Telephone: (402) 474-6691
Ownership %: 100
**Editorial:**
Fred R. Stone ..............................Editor
**Desc.:** Staff-written news features cover
   marketing, legislation, financing,
   important company developments in the
   petroleum industry as well as
   association news.
**Readers:** Licensed oil jobbers, importing
   dealers, new car dealers, convenience
   stores, service stations.

23111
### NORTH CAROLINA PROPANE GAS NEWS
5112 Bur Oak Cir.
Raleigh, NC 27612
Telephone: (919) 787-8485
FAX: (919) 781-7481
Year Established: 1948
Pub. Frequency: m.
Page Size: Standard
Subscrip. Rate: $15/yr.
Circulation: 800
Circulation Type: controlled
**Owner(s):**
Carolina Propane Gas Assoc.
5112 Bur Oak Cir.
Raleigh, NC 27612
Telephone: (919) 787-8485
Ownership %: 100
**Editorial:**
Romaine Holt .............Executive Editor
**Desc.:** Articles on safety, selling, items of
   interest to LP-GAS dealers and
   suppliers, legislative matters.
**Readers:** LP gas dealers in North
   Carolina, South Carolina & Virginia.

49844
### NORTHEAST OIL WORLD
7811 Montrose Rd.
Potomac, MD 20854
Telephone: (301) 340-2100
Mailing Address:
   P.O. Box 59805
   Potomac, MD 20859-9805
Year Established: 1980
Pub. Frequency: m.
Page Size: standard
Subscrip. Rate: $39/yr.; $89/3 yrs.
Circulation: 6,000
Circulation Type: paid
**Owner(s):**
Hart Publications, Inc.
P.O. Box 1917
Denver, CO 80201
Telephone: (303) 837-1917
Ownership %:  20

Phillips Publishing International Inc.
7811 Montrose Rd.
Potomac, MD 20854
Telephone: (301) 340-2100
Ownership %:  80
**Management:**
Lauryn Franzoni .....................Publisher
Joel Gregg ........................Sales Manager
**Editorial:**
Timothy Burn ...................Managing Editor
**Desc.:** Edited for management on and off
   the oilfield. The publication covers
   petroleum drilling, exploration,
   production, transportation and refining in
   the Northeast, which encompasses the
   Illinois, Michigan and Appalachian
   basins. Part of the Oil World Network
   group of regional petroleum magazines.

**Readers:** Educational backgrounds vary
   from those with only  a H.S. diploma to
   those with doctorates. Numerous
   technical disciplines are involved. Some
   major classifications of readers are:
   drilling & completion engineer;
   production & reservoir engineer; oil
   company executive; toolpusher;
   production foreman;
   geologist/geophysicist; landman;
   independent operator; service & supply
   company personnel; investors.

23131
### O&A MARKETING NEWS
1037 N. Lake Ave.
Pasadena, CA 91104
Telephone: (818) 398-6848
FAX: (818) 398-6840
Year Established: 1966
Pub. Frequency: 7/yr.
Page Size: tabloid
Subscrip. Rate: $20/yr.
Materials: 01,06,15,16,18,20,21,23,24,25,
   27,28,29,30,31,32,33
Freelance Pay: $1.25/col. in.
Print Process: web
Circulation: 7,000
Circulation Type: paid
**Owner(s):**
KAL Publishing, Inc.
1037 N. Lake Ave.
Pasadena, CA 91104
Telephone: (818) 398-6848
Ownership %: 100
**Management:**
Kathy Laderman .......................Publisher
Lynne Kenworthy .............Advertising Manager
Cathy Wacker ....................Business Manager
**Editorial:**
Kathy Laderman .............................Editor
**Desc.:** Coverage of movement of finished
   petroleum products, fuels, lubricants and
   automotive products. The editorial scope
   covers management, merchandising and
   service of markets and marketers within
   13 western states.
**Readers:** Service station dealers,
   garagemen, TBA distributors, automotive
   jobbers, marketers in major and
   independent oil companies, oil jobbers
   and distributors, equipment
   manufacturers and distributors,
   alternative fuel manufacturers and
   distributors.

23133
### OFFSHORE
3050 Post Oak Blvd.
Houston, TX 77056
Telephone: (713) 621-9720
Year Established: 1954
Pub. Frequency: m.
Page Size: standard
Subscrip. Rate: $55/yr.; $72/yr. foreign
Materials: 01,27,28,29,30,31,32,33
Freelance Pay: negotiable
Print Process: web offset
Circulation: 38,500
Circulation Type: controlled & paid
**Owner(s):**
PennWell Publishing Co.
3050 Post Oak Blvd.
Houston, TX 77056
Telephone: (713) 621-9720
Ownership %: 100
**Management:**
John R. Schirra .........................Publisher
**Editorial:**
Leonard LeBlanc ..........................Editor
Barbara Henderson ...................Art Director
Michael Crowden .................News Editor

Materials Accepted/Included: 01-Business news 02-By-line articles  03-Fashion news  04-Food news  05-Freelance copy  06-Letters to editor  07-Real estate news  08-Sports news 09-Travel news 10-Book rev. 11-Movie rev. 12-Music rev. 13-TV rev. 14-Theater rev. 15-Coming events 16-Obituaries 17-Question & answer 18-Social announcements 19-Artwork 20-Cartoons 21-Photos 22-TV listings 23-Audio rec. 24-Video rec. 25-Books 26-Films/film clips 27-Personnel news 28-Press releases 29-New product news/photos 30-Trade lit. 31-Contracts awarded 32-Display adv. 33-Classified adv.

**Desc.:** Covers marine activities relating to oil and gas operations at sea. Departments include: News, Marine Construction, Marine Services, Exploration Section, Industry Items, Service Personalities, New Products and Financial Department.

**Readers:** Oil companies, offshore operators, drilling contractors, marine and oilfield equipment operators.

24888

**OFFSHORE FIELD DEVELOPMENT INTERNATIONAL**
3200 Wilcrest, #170
Houston, TX 77042
Telephone: (713) 781-2713
Mailing Address:
P.O. Box 19909
Houston, TX 77224
Year Established: 1974
Pub. Frequency: m.
Page Size: standard
Subscrip. Rate: $445/yr. US; $480/yr. foreign
Freelance Pay: $25/article
Circulation: 900
Circulation Type: paid
Owner(s):
Offshore Data Services, Inc.
P.O. Box 19909
Houston, TX 77224
Telephone: (713) 781-2713
Ownership %: 100
Management:
Loran R. Sheffer ...................................Publisher
Editorial:
Paul Hillegeist .........................................Editor
**Desc.:** A weekly periodical that summarizes the latest news affecting the offshore oil, gas and marine construction market on a worldwide basis. Lists information on all offshore platform, pipeline, and mooring terminal projects worldwide, from the planning stages to final installation.
**Readers:** Those interested in offshore oil field development.

61589

**OHIO PIPELINE**
17 S. High St., Ste. 1200
Columbus, OH 43215
Telephone: (614) 221-1900
Pub. Frequency: 8/yr.
Page Size: standard
Subscrip. Rate: controlled
Circulation: 300
Circulation Type: paid
Owner(s):
O.S.A.P.H.C.C.
17 High St., Ste. 1200
Columbus, OH 43215
Telephone: (614) 221-1900
Ownership %: 100
Editorial:
Kathy Laraway ........................................Editor

49873

**OIL & GAS INVESTOR**
1900 Grant St., Ste. 400
Denver, CO 80203
Telephone: (303) 832-1917
FAX: (303) 837-8585
Year Established: 1981
Pub. Frequency: m.
Page Size: standard
Subscrip. Rate: $195/yr.
Materials: 01,06,32,33
Circulation: 4,000
Circulation Type: paid
Owner(s):
Phillips Publishing International, Inc.
7811 Montrose Rd.
Potomac, MD 20854
Telephone: (301) 340-2100
Ownership %: 100

**Management:**
Richard Eichler ...................................Publisher
Verna Ray .........................Advertising Manager
**Editorial:**
Leslie Haines ...........................................Editor
Susan Klann .............................Managing Editor
**Desc.:** Explores investment and exploration opportunities (energy stocks, acquisitions, royalties, leases, drilling activity) of the oil and gas industry, and features interviews with oil and gas executives and analysts.
**Readers:** Chief and financial executives of oil companies; institutional fund managers; financial advisors; wealthy individuals; petroleum analysts.
**Deadline:** story-2 mos. prior; news-2 mos.; photo-2 mos.; ads-1 mo. prior

23134

**OIL & GAS JOURNAL**
3050 Post Oak Blvd., Ste. 200
Houston, TX 77056
Telephone: (713) 621-9720
Mailing Address:
P.O. Box 1941
Houston, TX 77251
Year Established: 1902
Pub. Frequency: w.
Page Size: standard
Subscrip. Rate: $69/yr.
Materials: 01,02,06,15,16,27,28,29,20,31, 32,33
Print Process: web offset
Circulation: 42,000
Circulation Type: paid
Owner(s):
PennWell Publishing Co.
P.O. Box 1260
Tulsa, OK 74101
Telephone: (918) 835-3161
Ownership %: 100
Bureau(s):
Pittsburgh Bureau
429 Fourth Ave., Rm. 2004
Pittsburgh, PA 15219
Telephone: (412) 471-5847
FAX: (412) 471-9114
Contact: Robert S. McGinnis

Dallas Bureau
4849 Greenville Ave., Ste. 660
Dallas, TX 75206
Telephone: (214) 739-3338
FAX: (214) 739-2033
Contact: Ron Higgins
**Management:**
Frank T. Lauinger .............Chairman of Board
Joseph A. Wolking .............................President
Tom Terrell ...............................Vice President
Tom Terrell .................................Publisher
Larry Lofton ......................Circulation Manager
LaVerne Caffey ..........Classified Adv. Manager
**Editorial:**
John L. Kennedy .....................................Editor
Jim West .................................Managing Editor
Bob Tippee ..............................Managing Editor
Leo Aalund ..............................Managing Editor
Jo Jeanne London .........................Art Director
Nancy Hamilton ...............Marketing Director
Jim Stilwell .......................New Product Editor
Larry Spiker ..........................Production Director
**Desc.:** Provides all news and technical developments of significance to every division of the petroleum industry.
**Readers:** Circulated to managers and engineers engaged in one or more operating phases of the world-wide petroleum industry.

23136

**OIL CAN, THE**
P.O. Box 12020
Springfield, IL 62791
Telephone: (217) 544-4609
FAX: (217) 789-0222
Year Established: 1926

Pub. Frequency: bi-m.
Page Size: standard
Subscrip. Rate: $18/yr.
Materials: 27,28,29,30,32,33
Circulation: 1,250
Circulation Type: paid
Owner(s):
Illinois Association of Convenience Stores (IACS)
Ownership %: 100
Management:
Elizabeth Kennedy ...........Advertising Manager
Editorial:
Wm. R. Deutsch ...................Executive Editor
Elizabeth Kennedy ..................Managing Editor
Wm. R. Deutsch ................New Product Editor
Elizabeth Kennedy ....................News Editor
**Desc.:** Feature articles concerning petroleum marketers of the State of Illinois, problems which face them - both on federal and state levels. Aims to keep them informed on important dates and changes in both state and federal regulations.
**Readers:** Petroleum marketers & convenience store operators-primarily membership of Assn. in IL and other states.

61588

**OIL DAILY, THE**
1401 New York Ave., N.W., Ste. 500
Washington, DC 20005
Telephone: (202) 662-0700
FAX: (202) 783-8320
Year Established: 1951
Pub. Frequency: d.
Page Size: tabloid
Subscrip. Rate: $597/yr.
Owner(s):
Oil Daily Co.
1401 New York Ave N.W. Ste 500
Washington, DC 20005
Telephone: (202) 662-0700
Ownership %: 100
Management:
Richard G. Graham ...................Vice President
Marshall Thomas ...........................Publisher
Editorial:
Marshall Thomas .....................................Editor
Michael K. Zastudil ................Managing Editor
**Readers:** Oil & gas company executives/managers.

23137

**OIL, GAS & PETROCHEM EQUIPMENT**
1421 S. Sheridan Rd.
Tulsa, OK 74112
Telephone: (918) 835-3161
FAX: (918) 832-9201
Mailing Address:
P.O. Box 1260
Tulsa, OK 74101
Year Established: 1954
Pub. Frequency: m.
Page Size: tabloid
Subscrip. Rate: $32/yr. US, Canada & Mexico; $70/yr. Europe & S. America; $89/yr. Africa, Asia, Middle East
Materials: 23,24,28,29,30,32
Print Process: web offset
Circulation: 36,000
Circulation Type: controlled
Owner(s):
PennWell Publishing Co.
P.O. Box 1260
Tulsa, OK 74101-1260
Telephone: (918) 835-3161
FAX: (918) 832-9201
Ownership %: 100

**Bureau(s):**
Publisher Hdqtrs.
3050 Post Oak Blvd., Ste. 200
Houston, TX 77056
Telephone: (713) 621-9720
Contact: John R. Schirra, Publisher

Editorial Headquarters
1421 S. Sheridan Rd.
Tulsa, OK 74112
Telephone: (918) 835-3161
FAX: (918) 832-9201
Contact: J.B. Avants, Editor
**Management:**
John R. Schirra ...................................Publisher
John R. Schirra ..................Advertising Manager
Larry Spiker ........................Production Manager
**Editorial:**
J. B. Avants ...........................................Editor
John Tabor ..............................Associate Editor
Marcella Hanson ...............Editorial Assistant
Jim McManus-OK. ................................Sales
David Davis-TX. ...................................Sales
Bruce Berkey-CA. ...............................Sales
Gil Tottem-IL. ......................................Sales
**Desc.:** The editorial content deals solely with new, significant, commercially available equipment products and services for oil, gas, and petrochemical operations. Edited primarily for those who buy, specify, design, requisition, install, and maintain all kinds of equipment in petroleum operations. Reader service card provides inquiry printout data on all persons requesting information on editorial or advertising. Editorial content is divided into two types of material: new products, new literature. Departments include: New Products and New Literature with the special reports throughout the the year on such equipment topics as they apply to safety, environmental, health, pollution-control, drilling/production, refining/petrochemical, valves, pumps, instrumentation, heating and cooling, maintenance, pumps offshore and pipeline, environmental compliance.
**Readers:** Those who buy, specify, install and operate within the industry. Engineers, operating managers, superintendents and foremen with influence to specify and/or purchase products and services for application in producing, drilling, pipeline, petrochemical manufacturing, refining, and gas processing.
**Deadline:** story-15th of mo.; news-15th of mo.; ads-15th of mo.

23138

**OIL MARKETER, THE**
5115 N. Western
Oklahoma City, OK 73118
Telephone: (405) 842-6625
FAX: (405) 842-9564
Year Established: 1958
Pub. Frequency: q.
Page Size: standard
Subscrip. Rate: free to members
Circulation: 600
Circulation Type: free
Owner(s):
Oklahoma Oil Marketers Assn, Inc.
5115 N. Western
Oklahoma City, OK 73118
Telephone: (405) 842-0344
Ownership %: 100
Management:
Kelly Kyle ........................Advertising Manager
Editorial:
Kelly Kyle ..............................Managing Editor
**Desc.:** Trade publication for companies which own chains of service stations, and wholesale gasoline and convenience stores.

**Materials Accepted/Included:** 01-Business news 02-By-line articles 03-Fashion news 04-Food news 05-Freelance copy 06-Letters to editor 07-Real estate news 08-Sports news 09-Travel news 10-Book rev. 11-Movie rev. 12-Music rev. 13-TV rev. 14-Theater rev. 15-Coming events 16-Obituaries 17-Question & answer 18-Social announcements 19-Artwork 20-Cartoons 21-Photos 22-TV listings 23-Audio rec. 24-Video rec. 25-Books 26-Films/film clips 27-Personnel news 28-Press releases 29-New product news/photos 30-Trade lit. 31-Contracts awarded 32-Display adv. 33-Classified adv.

4-157

**Readers:** Oil jobbers, commissions agents and suppliers.

23140

## PETROLEO INTERNACIONAL
150 Greatneck Rd.
Great Neck, NY 11021
Telephone: (516) 829-9210
FAX: (516) 829-5414
Year Established: 1943
Pub. Frequency: bi-m.
Page Size: standard
Subscrip. Rate: $32/yr.
Materials: 02,28,29,32,33,34
Freelance Pay: varies
Circulation: 8,810
Circulation Type: controlled
**Owner(s):**
Keller International Publishing Co.
150 Greatneck Rd.
Great Neck, NY 11021
Telephone: (516) 829-9210
Ownership %: 100
**Management:**
Gerald Keller ..............................President
Bob Herlicky ..............................Publisher
Orlando Llerandi ...........Advertising Manager
**Editorial:**
Vivtor Prieto ..............................Editor
**Desc.:** Devoted to the oil and gas industries in Latin America, news, technical developments, and equipment. Editorial material in Spanish (no English abstracts).
**Readers:** Oil industry companies, personnel, affiliates, distributors.

23142

## PETROLEUM INDEPENDENT
1101 16th St., N.W.
Washington, DC 20036
Telephone: (202) 857-4774
FAX: (202) 857-4799
Year Established: 1930
Pub. Frequency: bi-m.
Page Size: standard
Subscrip. Rate: $100/yr.
Materials: 01,15,27,28,29,30,32
Freelance Pay: $.20/wd.
Print Process: offset
Circulation: 7,000
Circulation Type: paid
**Owner(s):**
Petroleum Independent Publisher, Inc.
1101 16th St., N.W.
Washington, DC 20036
Telephone: (202) 857-4774
Ownership %: 100
**Management:**
Denise Bode ..............................President
Rick Carbo ...........Advertising Manager
**Editorial:**
Bruce Wells ..............................Managing Editor
Deborah Rowell ...........Economics Editor
**Desc.:** Contributed articles on the economics of the industry, trends, broad outlook. Uses personals, announcements. Keep latter copy brief. Query editor before submitting features.
**Readers:** Petroleum-drilling-producing.

61711

## PETROLEUM INTELLIGENCE WEEKLY
575 Broadway, 4th Fl.
New York, NY 10012-3230
Telephone: (212) 941-5500
FAX: (212) 941-5508
Year Established: 1961
Pub. Frequency: w.
Page Size: pocket
Subscrip. Rate: $1475/yr.

**Owner(s):**
Petroleum & Energy Intelligence Weekly, Inc.
575 Broadway, 4th Fl.
New York, NY 10012-3230
Telephone: (212) 941-5500
Ownership %: 100
**Management:**
Edward L. Morse ..............................Publisher
**Editorial:**
Sarah Miller ..............................Editor
**Desc.:** Provides market insights for oil and natural gas executives and government leaders. Includes information and analysis of major industry developments, issues and trends.
**Readers:** Top international oil & gas execs.

23143

## PETROLEUM MARKETER
1801 Rockville Pike, Ste. 330
Rockville, MD 20852
Telephone: (301) 984-4000
FAX: (301) 984-7340
Year Established: 1933
Pub. Frequency: bi-m.
Page Size: standard
Subscrip. Rate: $24/yr.
Circulation: 20,000
Circulation Type: controlled
**Owner(s):**
G.C.I. Publishing
Ownership %: 100
**Editorial:**
Louise Classon ..............................Editor
**Desc.:** Contains marketing information for people directly involved in sales, sales promotion, advertising and marketing development. Also contains news, features, and departments.
**Readers:** Marketing executives, managers, major oil company operations/engineering supervisory personnel & management, jobbers companies and Petroleum marketing equipment manufacturers and distributers.

23144

## PIPELINE & GAS JOURNAL
P.O. Box 219368
Houston, TX 77218-9368
Telephone: (713) 558-6930
Year Established: 1859
Pub. Frequency: m.
Page Size: standard
Subscrip. Rate: $22/yr. within industry; $75/yr. outside industry
Materials: 01,02,05,06,15,21,27,28,29,30,31
Freelance Pay: $100/printed pg.
Print Process: web offset
Circulation: 26,000
Circulation Type: controlled
**Owner(s):**
Oildom Publishing Co. of Texas
P.O. Box 219368
Houston, TX 77218-9368
Telephone: (713) 558-6930
Ownership %: 100
**Management:**
Oliver Klinger, III ..............................Publisher
**Editorial:**
James Watts ..............................Executive Editor
Mark Babineck ...........New Products Editor
**Desc.:** Serves pipeline industry. Covers design, operation, and management of oil, natural gas, gas distribution and products, with specialized departments on communications and corrosion as applied to the pipeline field.
**Readers:** Officials, engineers, operating heads of pipeline and gas companies.
**Deadline:** story-2 mos. prior to pub. date; news-2 mos. prior; photo-2 mos. prior; ads-1 mo. prior

57802

## PIPELINE DIGEST
1900 Grant St., Ste. 400
Denver, CO 80201
Telephone: (303) 837-1917
FAX: (303) 837-8585
Mailing Address:
P.O. Box 1917
Denver, CO 80201
Year Established: 1963
Pub. Frequency: s-m.
Page Size: standard
Subscrip. Rate: $57/yr.
Circulation: 27,000
Circulation Type: paid
**Owner(s):**
Phillips Publishing International, Inc.
7811 Montrose Rd.
Potomac, MD 20854
Telephone: (301) 340-2100
Ownership %: 100
**Management:**
H. M. Stemmer ..............................Publisher
Norma Babbitt ...........Advertising Manager
Alice Pouliadis ...........Circulation Manager
Rick Minett ..............................General Manager
**Editorial:**
Judy R. Clark ..............................Editor
Rosalie Milton ...........Production Director
**Desc.:** Edited for companies and their personnel involved in the worldwide construction and operation of pipelines transporting crude oil, natural gas, synthetic gas, liquid products, water and slurry. It also covers distribution, gathering and utility systems, stations, plants, as well as industry news, personals, technology, etc.

23145

## PIPE LINE INDUSTRY
3301 Allen Pkwy.
Houston, TX 77019-1896
Telephone: (713) 529-4301
FAX: (713) 520-4433
Mailing Address:
P.O. Box 2608
Houston, TX 77252-2608
Year Established: 1954
Pub. Frequency: m.
Page Size: standard
Subscrip. Rate: $20-$24/yr.
Materials: 27,28,29,30,31,32,33
Print Process: web offset
Circulation: 27,499
Circulation Type: controlled
**Owner(s):**
Gulf Publishing Co.
P.O. Box 2608
Houston, TX 77252
Telephone: (713) 520-4433
Ownership %: 100
**Management:**
Ray Cashman ..............................President
Lanie Finlayson ...........Vice President
Ray D. Cashman ..............................Publisher
**Editorial:**
Buddy Ives ..............................Editor
Robert Scott ...........Editorial Director
Lew Bullion ...........Associate Editor
Rusty Meador ...........Associate Publisher
Leonard Parent ...........Contributing Editor
Joseph Caldwell ...........Contributing Editor
Megan Stevens ...........Editorial Assistant
**Desc.:** To help industry personnel arrive at decisions or formulate policies that will improve company operations and their own personal positions.
**Readers:** People responsible for buying, specifying, recommending, or approving purchases of equipment, materials, or services used in the construction, operation, or maintenance of gas transmission and distribution systems, oil and product pipe lines and pipe lines for water, slurries, or fluidized solids.

23148

## SERVICE QUARTERLY
200 N. Capitol, Ste. 420
Lansing, MI 48933
Telephone: (517) 484-4096
FAX: (517) 484-5705
Year Established: 1929
Pub. Frequency: q.
Page Size: tabloid
Subscrip. Rate: $40/yr.
Circulation: 2,500
Circulation Type: paid
**Owner(s):**
SSDA - MI
Ownership %: 100
**Editorial:**
Letitia A. Skeen ..............................Editor
**Desc.:** Covers all phases of retail petroleum marketing. Editorials cover activities in fields of industry relations, public relations, legislation and law enforcement. Departments include: New Products, state legislation, national legislation, EPA mandates, legal news, healthcare news.
**Readers:** Service Station Operators/Owners.

23150

## SOONER LPG TIMES
4200 N. Lindsay
Oklahoma City, OK 73105
Telephone: (405) 424-1775
FAX: (405) 424-1781
Year Established: 1945
Pub. Frequency: bi-m.
Page Size: PG: 8 1/2 x 11; COL: 2 3/8; PHOTO: Yes; MAT: No; C
Subscrip. Rate: free to industry
Circulation: 1,600
Circulation Type: controlled
**Owner(s):**
Oklahoma Propane Gas Association
4200 N. Lindsay
Oklahoma City, OK 73105
Telephone: (405) 424-1775
Ownership %: 100
**Management:**
Dawn Chelton ...........Advertising Manager
**Editorial:**
Richard Hess ..............................Editor
**Readers:** Retail dealers and suppliers of LP-gas, pnterested dealers in the surrounding states.

23153

## TEXAS OIL MARKETER
701 W. 15th
Austin, TX 78701
Telephone: (512) 476-9547
FAX: (512) 477-4239
Year Established: 1951
Pub. Frequency: q.
Page Size: standard
Subscrip. Rate: $5/issue; $20/yr.
Circulation: 1,400
Circulation Type: controlled & paid
**Owner(s):**
Texas Oil Marketers Association
701 W. 15th St.
Austin, TX 78701
Telephone: (512) 476-9547
Ownership %: 100
**Management:**
R.C. Harris ..............................President
Jerdy Gary ...........Executive Vice President
Robin Mayhall ...........Advertising Manager
**Editorial:**
Cheryl Lockhart ..............................Editor
Robin Mayhall ...........Assistant Editor

**Materials Accepted/Included:** 01-Business news 02-By-line articles 03-Fashion news 04-Food news 05-Freelance copy 06-Letters to editor 07-Real estate news 08-Sports news 09-Travel news 10-Book rev. 11-Movie rev. 12-Music rev. 13-TV rev. 14-Theater rev. 15-Coming events 16-Obituaries 17-Question & answer 18-Social announcements 19-Artwork 20-Cartoons 21-Photos 22-TV listings 23-Audio rec. 24-Video rec. 25-Books 26-Films/film clips 27-Personnel news 28-Press releases 29-New product news/photos 30-Trade lit. 31-Contracts awarded 32-Display adv. 33-Classified adv.

4-158

**Desc.:** News of the oil industry with emphasis on developments affecting members of the Texas Oil Marketers Assn. Staff-written articles cover new methods of fuel dispensing, marketing, etc. Reports on important personnel appointments in the area covered.

**Readers:** Wholesale marketing branch of petroleum. Primary circulation in Texas. Some in New Mexico.

### TEXAS PROPANE
23152

8408 N. Interregional
Austin, TX 78753
Telephone: (512) 836-8620
FAX: (512) 834-0758
Mailing Address:
  P.O. Box 140735
  Austin, TX 78714-0735
Year Established: 1944
Pub. Frequency: 11/yr.
Page Size: standard
Subscrip. Rate: $36/yr.
Materials: 01,02,06,28,29,32,33
Print Process: offset
Circulation: 1,300
Circulation Type: controlled & free
**Owner(s):**
Texas Propane Gas Association
8408 N. Interregional
Austin, TX 78753
Telephone: (512) 836-8620
Ownership %: 100
**Management:**
John Danks ................Executive Vice President
Ellen Terry .........................Advertising Manager
John Danks ............................General Manager
**Editorial:**
Ellen Terry ......................................................Editor
**Desc.:** Staff-written features and news cover the propane-Gas industry in the state, including association activities, industry personnel and products. Other subjects include safety news, promotion ideas, and use of propane.
**Readers:** All licensed retail LPG dealers in the state of Texas. who are members of the Texas Propane Gas Assn.
**Deadline:** story-2 mo. prior to pub. date; news-2 mo. prior to pub. date; photo-2 mo. prior; ads-10th of mo. prior to pub. date

### TODAY'S REFINERY
69042

170 King St.
Chappaqua, NY 10514
Telephone: (914) 238-0205
FAX: (914) 238-0210
Mailing Address:
  P.O. Box 287
  Chappaqua, NY 10514-0287
Year Established: 1987
Pub. Frequency: m.
Subscrip. Rate: $25/yr. US & Canada; $60/yr. elsewhere
Print Process: offset
Circulation: 9,400
Circulation Type: controlled & paid
**Owner(s):**
Percy Publishing Co., Inc.
170 King St.
P.O. Box 287
Chappaqua, NY 10514
Telephone: (914) 238-0205
FAX: (914) 238-0210
Ownership %: 100
**Editorial:**
James D. Wall .......................Editorial Director
**Desc.:** Contains articles, columns, abstracts and reviews of interest to petroleum refiners in the USA and Canada.

### WELL SERVICING
69043

6060 N. Central Expy., Ste. 428
Dallas, TX 75206
Telephone: (214) 692-0771
Year Established: 1961
Pub. Frequency: bi-m.
Page Size: standard
Subscrip. Rate: free
Materials: 01,05,15,21,28,29,30,32
Freelance Pay: negotiable
Circulation: 10,000
Circulation Type: controlled
**Owner(s):**
Workover-Well Servicing Publications, Inc.
6060 N. Central Expy., Ste.428
Dallas, TX 75206
Telephone: (214) 692-0771
Ownership %: 100
**Editorial:**
Polly Fisk ........................................................Editor
**Deadline:** story-1 mo. prior to pub. date; news-1 mo. prior; photo-1 mo. prior; ads-20th of mo. prior

### WESTERN OIL WORLD
23155

1900 Grant St., Ste. 400
Denver, CO 80203
Telephone: (303) 837-1917
Mailing Address:
  P.O. Box 1917
  Denver, CO 80201
Year Established: 1944
Pub. Frequency: m.
Page Size: standard
Subscrip. Rate: $36/yr.; $81/3 yrs.
Circulation: 17,000
Circulation Type: paid
**Owner(s):**
Hart Publications, Inc.
1900 Grant St.
Denver, CO 80201
Telephone: (303) 892-1164
Ownership %: 100
**Bureau(s):**
Houston
4545 Post Oak Place
Suite 210
Houston, TX 77027
Telephone: (713) 993-9320
**Management:**
Joel Gregg ................................................Publisher
Joel Gregg .........................Advertising Manager
**Editorial:**
Don Lyle ..........................................................Editor
**Desc.:** Regional oil and gas magazine for Rocky Mountain states. Edited for management and technical petroleum industry personnel. Covers exploration, drilling, production, processing, and transmission in the region. Part of the Oil World Network group of regional petroleum magazines.
**Readers:** Operators, drilling contractors, tool pushers, geologists, geophysicists, and engineers.

### WORLD GAS INTELLIGENCE
69044

575 Broadway, 4th Fl.
New York, NY 10012-3230
Telephone: (212) 941-5500
FAX: (212) 941-5508
Year Established: 1990
Pub. Frequency: m.
Subscrip. Rate: $685/yr.
**Owner(s):**
Petroleum & Energy Intelligence Weekly, Inc.
575 Broadway, 4th Fl.
New York, NY 10012-3230
Telephone: (212) 941-5500
Ownership %: 100
**Editorial:**
Patrick Heren ..................................................Editor

**Desc.:** Provides concise news and analysis of developments in the international gas industry.

### WORLD OIL
23156

3301 Allen Pkwy.
Houston, TX 77019-2608
Telephone: (713) 529-4301
FAX: (713) 520-4433
Mailing Address:
  P.O. Box 2608
  Houston, TX 77252-2608
Year Established: 1916
Pub. Frequency: m.
Page Size: standard
Subscrip. Rate: $24-$30/yr.
Materials: 27,28,29,30,31,32,33
Print Process: web offset
Circulation: 39,871
Circulation Type: controlled & paid
**Owner(s):**
Gulf Publishing Co.
P.O. Box 2608
Houston, TX 77252-2608
Telephone: (713) 529-4301
FAX: (713) 520-4433
Ownership %: 100
**Management:**
Ray D. Cashman ...........................President
Lanie Finlayson ........................Vice President
Ray D. Cashman ...........................Publisher
**Editorial:**
Robert Snyder .................................Editor
Bob Scott ..........................Editorial Director
Lanie Finlayson ...................Associate Publisher
David LeLeux .....................Engineering Editor
William Pike ........................Foreign Editor
**Desc.:** Covers new management ideas, economics, technology, drilling, exploration, production, international articles and current outlook. Departments include: Looking Ahead, Editorial Page, Hot Line, Gas and Oil Washington, World of Oil, What's New in Drilling, What's New in Exploration, What's New in Production, Drilling Activities, Who's Meeting Where, Your Industry at Work, Men in the Industry, Associations, Suppliers' Notes, Trading Post, Classified Advertising, New Equipment, New Literature, Advertisers.
**Readers:** Oil company officials, engineers, drilling contractors, geologists and geophysicists.

### YANKEE OILMAN
23157

23 Greystone Pk., c/o Greystone Services
Swampscott, MA 01902
Telephone: (617) 598-2074
Mailing Address:
  P.O. Box 457
  Swampscott, MA 01907
Year Established: 1955
Pub. Frequency: m.
Page Size: standard
Subscrip. Rate: $15/yr.
Materials: 01,05,06,27,28,29,30
Circulation: 7,000
Circulation Type: paid
**Owner(s):**
New England Fuel Institute
20 Summer St., P.O. Box 888
Watertown, MA 02172
Telephone: (617) 924-1000
Ownership %: 100
**Management:**
Bernard Smith ...................................President
Catherine Armao ..............Advertising Manager
**Editorial:**
Scott Rolph ..........................Managing Editor

**Desc.:** Devoted to New England fuel oil dealers, suppliers, and refiners with additional information for manufacturers of oil heating equipment. Departments include: New Products, Association Activities, N.E. Energy News, Degree Day Report, NEFI Newsline, Futures Report.
**Readers:** Those in northern & mid-Atlantic regions in fuel oil, oil heating. Major oil companies, including such job titles as manager, service manager, division or regional managers, oil distribution personnel.

## Group 104-Gifts, Novelties & Greeting Cards

### BALLOONS & PARTIES TODAY
69235

1205 W. Forsyth St.
Jacksonville, FL 32204
Telephone: (904) 634-1902
FAX: (904) 633-8764
Year Established: 1986
Pub. Frequency: m.
Page Size: standard
Subscrip. Rate: $29.95/yr.
Circulation: 18,000
Circulation Type: paid
**Owner(s):**
Festivities Publications, Inc.
1205 W. Forsyth St.
Jacksonville, FL 32204
Telephone: (904) 634-1902
Ownership %: 100
**Editorial:**
April Anderson ....................................Editor
**Desc.:** Presents full color designs and decorations using balloons.
**Readers:** Balloon retailers and trade managers.

### GIFT & STATIONERY BUSINESS
23182

1515 Broadway, 32nd Fl.
New York, NY 10036
Telephone: (212) 869-1300
FAX: (212) 302-6273
Year Established: 1964
Pub. Frequency: m.
Page Size: tabloid
Subscrip. Rate: $29.25/yr.
Circulation: 34,476
Circulation Type: paid
**Owner(s):**
Gralla Publications
1515 Broadway
New York, NY 10036
Telephone: (212) 869-1300
Ownership %: 100
**Management:**
Steve Silberberg ...............................Publisher
Diana Judelson .................Circulation Manager
**Editorial:**
Katherine Krassner ................Associate Editor
Carrie Chesloff .....................Associate Editor
**Desc.:** For retailers and suppliers of gifts, stationery, and accessories providing news, product, trend, and merchandising information.
**Readers:** Owners, managers, buyers of gift shops, jewelry, furniture, and department stores, catalog showrooms, catalog & mail order operations, stationery shops, florists, and other retail stores.

### GIFT BASKET REVIEW
69242

1205 W. Forsythe St.
Jacksonville, FL 32204
Telephone: (904) 634-1902
FAX: (904) 633-8764
Year Established: 1990
Pub. Frequency: m.

**Materials Accepted/Included:** 01-Business news 02-By-line articles 03-Fashion news 04-Food news 05-Freelance copy 06-Letters to editor 07-Real estate news 08-Sports news 09-Travel news 10-Book rev. 11-Movie rev. 12-Music rev. 13-TV rev. 14-Theater rev. 15-Coming events 16-Obituaries 17-Question & answer 18-Social announcements 19-Artwork 20-Cartoons 21-Photos 22-TV listings 23-Audio rec. 24-Video rec. 25-Books 26-Films/film clips 27-Personnel news 28-Press releases 29-New product news/photos 30-Trade lit. 31-Contracts awarded 32-Display adv. 33-Classified adv.

4-159

Page Size: standard
Subscrip. Rate: $29.95/yr.
Materials: 01,04,06,25,27,28,29,30,32,33
Print Process: web offset
Circulation: 15,000
Circulation Type: paid
**Owner(s):**
Festivities Publications, Inc.
1205 W. Forsyth St.
Jacksonville, FL 32204
Telephone: (904) 634-1902
Ownership %: 100
**Management:**
Debra Paulk .......................................Publisher
Ann Saparito .....................Advertising Manager
Paula Irvin ........................Circulation Manager
**Editorial:**
Elizabeth Skelton .........................Editor in Chief
Kelly Morton ...............................News Editor
**Desc.:** Features full color design ideas for
   gift baskets, business and marketing
   tips, small business ideas, new product
   information.
**Readers:** Creative small business owners;
   own gift basket shops, gift shops,
   gourmet food stores, florists, balloon
   shops & related businesses.

23180
## GIFTS & DECORATIVE ACCESSORIES
51 Madison Ave.
New York, NY 10010
Telephone: (212) 689-4411
FAX: (212) 683-7929
Year Established: 1917
Pub. Frequency: m.
Page Size: standard
Subscrip. Rate: $39/yr.
Circulation: 33,000
Circulation Type: paid
**Owner(s):**
Geyer-McAllister Publications
Telephone: (212) 689-4411
**Management:**
Robert Chiara ...............................Publisher
Phyllis Sweed ................................Publisher
**Editorial:**
Phyllis Sweed ....................................Editor
Jack Smith ...............................Managing Editor
David Gooding .........................Associate Editor
Kimberly Solomon ......................Market Editor
Janet Henry .................................News Editor
**Desc.:** Use feature stories about quality
   gift and home accessory retailers; their
   activites, promotions, displays, new
   openings, etc. Particularly interested in
   stories conveying solid merchantising
   angles. They should illustrate how a
   particular retailer profited or benefited
   from some business activity. We do not
   cover souvenir trade, preferring stories
   of better shops departments, rather than
   adjuncts to motels, hospitals, clubs, or
   similar organizations.

23183
## GIFTWARE NEWS
20 No. Wacker Dr.
Ste. 3230
Chicago, IL 60606
Telephone: (312) 849-2220
Mailing Address:
   P.O. Box 5398
   Deptford, NJ 08096
Year Established: 1976
Pub. Frequency: m.
Page Size: tabloid
Subscrip. Rate: $32/yr.
Materials: 01,02,03,04,05,06,16,17,19,20,
   21,23,24,25,26,27,28,29,30,31,32,33
Freelance Pay: negotiable
Circulation: 45,000
Circulation Type: controlled & paid

**Owner(s):**
Talcott Communications Co.
20 N. Wacker Dr.
Chicago, IL 60606
Telephone: (312) 849-2220
Ownership %: 100
**Management:**
Daniel Von Rabinau .......................Publisher
**Editorial:**
Anthony DeMasi ...............................Editor
**Desc.:** Features new product news.
   Editorial features cover merchandising
   and management. Editorial emphasis is
   on promoting product availability,
   awareness, and profitability.
   Departments include: Tops in Tabletops,
   New & Noteworthy, Dateline Imports
   U.S.A., Crystal Classics, Stationery-
   Greeting Cards and Paper Products.
   Regional news including Los Angeles,
   Chicago, Dallas, Atlanta, and New York.
**Readers:** Buyers of gift and decorative
   items, collectibles, tabletop accessories,
   social stationery.
**Deadline:** story-6 wks. prior to pub. date;
   news-6 wks. prior; photo-6 wks. prior;
   ads-1 mo. prior to pub. date

24158
## GREETINGS MAGAZINE
309 Fifth Ave.
New York, NY 10016
Telephone: (212) 679-6677
Year Established: 1960
Pub. Frequency: m.
Page Size: standard
Subscrip. Rate: $15/yr.; $30/3 yrs.
Materials: 01,02,06,10,15,16,17,18,19,21,
   27,28,29,30,32,33
Print Process: offset
Circulation: 9,500
Circulation Type: controlled & paid
**Owner(s):**
Mackay Publishing Corp.
309 Fifth Ave.
New York, NY 10016
Telephone: (212) 679-6677
Ownership %: 100
**Management:**
M. J. Kristt .....................................President
M. J. Kristt .....................................Publisher
Alan Szydlowski ...............Advertising Manager
**Editorial:**
M. J. Kristt .......................................Editor
**Desc.:** Feature stories about successful
   store operations, about ideas that
   retailers use to stimulate business,
   industry opinions and forecasts. We use
   news stories about retailers (new shops,
   etc.), manufacturers, suppliers to these
   manufacturers, sales managers. New
   product information is always welcome.
   Departments include: News of Industry,
   News of Suppliers, New Products,
   Obituary Notices, Personnel Changes,
   Calendar of Events, Promotional News.
**Readers:** Retailers of greeting cards,
   social stationery products and their
   salesmen, designers, publishers.
**Deadline:** story-1st of mo. prior to pub.
   date; news-1st of mo. prior; photo-1st of
   mo. prior; ads-10th of mo. prior

67592
## PARTY SOURCE
1515 Broadway
New York, NY 10036
Telephone: (212) 869-1300
FAX: (212) 302-6273
Year Established: 1991
Pub. Frequency: q.
Page Size: standard
Subscrip. Rate: free to qualified retailers
Circulation: 11,000
Circulation Type: paid

**Owner(s):**
Miller Freeman, Inc.
1515 Broadway
New York, NY 10036
Telephone: (212) 869-1300
Ownership %: 100
**Management:**
Steve Silberberg ............................Publisher
**Editorial:**
Maria Cagurton ...............................Editor

24160
## SOUVENIRS & NOVELTIES MAGAZINE
7000 Terminal Sq.
Upper Darby, PA 19082
Telephone: (610) 734-2420
FAX: (610) 734-2423
Year Established: 1962
Pub. Frequency: 7/yr.
Page Size: pocket
Subscrip. Rate: $25/yr.; $40/2 yrs.
Materials: 01,02,03,04,05,06,07,08,09,10,
   15,16,17,18,19,21,23,24,25,27,28,29,30,
   31,32,33
Freelance Pay: $150/article
Print Process: web
Circulation: 29,000
Circulation Type: controlled & paid
**Owner(s):**
Kane Communications, Inc.
7000 Terminal Sq.
Upper Darby, PA 19082
Telephone: (619) 734-2420
FAX: (613) 000-0000
Ownership %: 100
**Management:**
Scott C. Borowsky ............................President
Janice Weiss .................................Publisher
**Editorial:**
Sandy Meschkow ...............................Editor
Linda Eckland .............................Art Director
Mary Anne Peacock ...........Circulation Editor
Larry White ..........................Marketing Director
Dorthory Higgins .................................Sales
David Kagan .......................................Sales
**Desc.:** Serves the resort-gift industry,
   souvenir and T-Shirt shops.
**Readers:** Owners and managers of resort-
   gift shops, souvenir, T-Shirt stores,
   outlets at amusement parks and
   attractions, postcard distributors and
   novelty jobbers.

## Group 106-Government - Municipal, County, State, Federal
23193
## ALABAMA MUNICIPAL JOURNAL
535 Adams Ave.
Montgomery, AL 36104
Telephone: (205) 263-1042
FAX: (205) 263-0200
Mailing Address:
   P.O. Box 1270
   Montgomery, AL 36102-1270
Year Established: 1940
Pub. Frequency: m.
Page Size: standard
Subscrip. Rate: $1.20/issue; $12/yr.
Materials: 02,32
Freelance Pay: payment in copies
Print Process: offset
Circulation: 4,500
Circulation Type: controlled & paid
**Owner(s):**
Alabama League of Municipalities
535 Adams Ave.
Montgomery, AL 36104
Telephone: (205) 262-2566
Ownership %: 100
**Management:**
Perry C. Roquemore, Jr. ..................Publisher
Anne Roquemore ...........Advertising Manager

**Editorial:**
Anne Roquemore .....................Executive Editor
**Desc.:** Devoted exclusively to municipal
   government, its problems, solutions,
   trends, legal information, news of city
   and town governments statewide. Little
   outside material except reprints of
   speeches and articles from other
   publications. Fillers provided by public
   service organizations such as public
   safety, fire prevention, and anti-litter.
   Departments Include: Revenue &
   Finance, Public Safety, State and
   Federal Legislation, Community
   Development, Human Resources
   Development, Intergovernmental
   Relations, Natural Resources,
   Transportation and Communication,
   Public Relations.
**Readers:** Elected public officials,
   universities and colleges.
**Deadline:** story-20th of mo.; news-20th of
   mo.; photo-20th of mo.; ads-1st of mo.
   of pub. date

23194
## AMERICAN CITY & COUNTY
6151 Powers Ferry Rd., N.W.
Atlanta, GA 30339-2941
Telephone: (404) 955-2500
FAX: (404) 955-0400
Year Established: 1909
Pub. Frequency: m.
Page Size: 4 color photos/art
Subscrip. Rate: $56/yr.; $116/yr. foreign
Materials: 01,02,28,29,30,32,33
Freelance Pay: $110/pg.
Circulation: 71,000
Circulation Type: controlled
**Owner(s):**
Argus Business, Division of Argus Inc.
6151 Powers Ferry Rd., N.W.
Atlanta, GA 30339-2941
Telephone: (404) 955-2500
Ownership %: 100
**Management:**
Pat Greene ........................Production Manager
**Editorial:**
Janet Ward .......................Assoc. Publ./EditorL
Karen Letterman .............Assoc. Publ./National
   Sales Mgr.
Gregg Herring ................Vice President/ Group
   Publisher
**Desc.:** American City & County features
   news and in-depth reports on a range of
   topics of interest to local government
   administrators, department heads and
   engineers. Areas of interest include
   financial management, computer
   applications, mass transit, street and
   highway construction and maintenance,
   water supply, wastewater collection and
   treatment, solid waste collection and
   disposal, parks and recreation, fleet
   vehicle and building maintenance,
   equipment and services.
**Readers:** Municipal and county
   government administrative, engineering
   and operating personnel including
   mayors, city and county managers,
   public works directors, city and county
   engineers, water and wastewater
   superintendents, state government
   legislative and  administrative personnel
   as well as consulting engineers and
   other independent contractors to the
   federal government.

69091
## AMERICAN PROSPECT
P.O. Box 383080
Cambridge, MA 02238-3080
Telephone: (617) 547-2950
FAX: (617) 547-3896
Year Established: 1990

**Materials Accepted/Included:** 01-Business news 02-By-line articles 03-Fashion news 04-Food news 05-Freelance copy 06-Letters to editor 07-Real estate news 08-Sports news 09-Travel news 10-Book rev. 11-Movie rev. 12-Music rev. 13-TV rev. 14-Theater rev. 15-Coming events 16-Obituaries 17-Question & answer 18-Social announcements 19-Artwork 20-Cartoons 21-Photos 22-TV listings 23-Audio rec. 24-Video rec. 25-Books 26-Films/film clips 27-Personnel news 28-Press releases 29-New product news/photos 30-Trade lit. 31-Contracts awarded 32-Display adv. 33-Classified adv.

Pub. Frequency: q.
Subscrip. Rate: $7.95 newsstand; $25/yr.
 individuals; $60/yr. instn.
Materials: 06,10,19,32
Circulation: 12000
Circulation Type: paid
**Owner(s):**
New Prospect, Inc.
P.O. Box 383080
Cambridge, MA 02238-3080
Telephone: (617) 547-2950
Ownership %: 100
**Editorial:**
Robert Kuttner ............................Editor
Paul Starr ....................................Editor

**CALIFORNIA PRIDE** 23197
1108 O St.
Sacramento, CA 95814
Telephone: (916) 326-4293
FAX: (916) 326-4215
Year Established: 1987
Pub. Frequency: bi-m.
Page Size: broadsheet
Subscrip. Rate: $10/yr.
Materials: 06,10,11,21,25,28,32
Freelance Pay: negotiable
Print Process: web offset
Circulation: 60,000
Circulation Type: controlled
**Owner(s):**
California State Employees' Association
1108 O St.
Sacramento, CA 95814
Telephone: (916) 444-8134
FAX: (916) 326-4215
Ownership %: 100
**Editorial:**
Robert C. Striegel ......................Editor
**Desc.:** Articles deal with salary, hours,
 working conditions, institution practices,
 public attitudes, etc., as related to the
 California State employee.
**Readers:** State civil service and
 legislators.

**CITY & TOWN** 23199
P.O. Box 38
N. Little Rock, AR 72115
Telephone: (501) 374-3484
FAX: (501) 374-0541
Year Established: 1934
Pub. Frequency: m.
Page Size: standard
Subscrip. Rate: $15/yr.
Circulation: 6,400
Circulation Type: paid
**Owner(s):**
Arkansas Municipal League
P.O. Box 38
N. Little Rock, AR 72115
Telephone: (501) 374-3484
Ownership %: 100
**Management:**
Harry J. Hamner ...............Advertising Manager
**Editorial:**
Harry J. Hamner ..........................Editor
John Woodruff .............................Editor
**Desc.:** Devoted exclusively to municipal
 governments. Articles about municipal
 governments and the laws that affect
 them, problems and suitable solutions,
 etc.
**Readers:** Municipal officials of Arkansas.

**COUNTY PROGRESS** 69090
P.O. Box 519
Brownwood, TX 76804
Telephone: (915) 643-2995
FAX: (915) 643-2995
Year Established: 1923
Pub. Frequency: m.

Page Size: standard
Subscrip. Rate: $17.50/yr.
Materials: 01,06,16,32,33
Print Process: offset
Circulation: 1,800
Circulation Type: paid
**Owner(s):**
County Judges and Commissioners Assoc.
 of Texas

Coursey Publishing Co.
P.O.Box 519
Brownwood, TX 76804
Telephone: (915) 643-2995
FAX: (915) 643-2995
Ownership %: 100
**Management:**
Pat Coursey ...........................Publisher
Sam Coursey ..........................Publisher
**Editorial:**
Robert Tindol ..............................Editor
**Readers:** County and state government
 officials.
**Deadline:** story-20th of previous mo.; ads-
 20th of previous mo.

**EMPIRE STATE REPORT** 23203
 **MAGAZINE**
Four Central Ave., Third Fl.
Albany, NY 11210
Telephone: (518) 465-5502
FAX: (518) 465-9822
Year Established: 1974
Pub. Frequency: m.
Page Size: standard
Subscrip. Rate: $3.50 newsstand; $35/yr.
Materials: 01,05,06,15,19,21,27,28,31,32
Freelance Pay: varies
Circulation: 12,500
Circulation Type: controlled
**Owner(s):**
Empire State Report Magazine, Inc.
545 Eighth Ave.
New York, NY 10018
Telephone: (212) 239-9797
Ownership %: 100
**Management:**
Floyd Weintraub ......................Publisher
Kathryn Donovan ..............Circulation Manager
**Editorial:**
Jeff Plungis ................................Editor
Jeff Jones ...........................Associate Editor
David Bulmer ...................Marketing Director
**Desc.:** Devoted to the government and
 politics of New York State. Feature
 articles on significant current and
 projected issues. Political profiles of key
 people in and around the State
 Government. Regular service features
 such as behind-the scenes coverage of
 Albany. Intelligence reports upcoming
 issues as reflected in trends and
 developments at State regulatory
 agencies and the legislature.
**Readers:** Business, government, officials,
 and lobbyists.
**Deadline:** story-1st of mo. prior to pub.
 date; news-1st of mo. prior; photo-1st of
 mo. prior; ads-7th of mo. prior

**FEDERAL TIMES** 25687
6883 Commercial Dr.
Springfield, VA 22159
Telephone: (703) 750-9000
FAX: (703) 750-8622
Year Established: 1965
Pub. Frequency: w.
Page Size: tabloid
Subscrip. Rate: $48/yr.
Circulation: 33,628
Circulation Type: paid

**Owner(s):**
Army Times Publishing Co.
6883 Commercial Dr.
Springfield, VA 22159
Telephone: (703) 750-9000
Ownership %: 100
**Management:**
William F. Donnelly ...........Chairman of Board
Henry Belber ...........................President
**Editorial:**
Marianne Lester ..........................Editor
Susan Fourney ...................Managing Editor
Nat Cornfeld ...................Advertising Director
**Desc.:** Weekly national newspaper
 covering federal bureaucracy with
 special emphasis on personnel policies,
 employee problems.
**Readers:** Federal government and postal
 service employees.

**FOREIGN SERVICE JOURNAL** 23208
2101 E St., N.W.
Washington, DC 20037
Telephone: (202) 338-4045
FAX: (202) 338-8244
Year Established: 1924
Pub. Frequency: m.
Page Size: standard
Subscrip. Rate: $3.50/newsstand; $40/yr.
Materials: 01,02,05,06,10,14,16,19,20,21,
 32,33
Freelance Pay: $50-$750
Print Process: web offset
Circulation: 11,500
Circulation Type: paid
**Owner(s):**
American Foreign Service Association
2101 E St., N.W.
Washington, DC 20037
Telephone: (202) 338-4045
Ownership %: 100
**Management:**
F.A. (Tex) Harris ......................President
Tina Dreyfus ...................Advertising Manager
**Editorial:**
Karen Kiebsbach ..........................Editor
Nancy Johnson ...................Associate Editor
Liz Allan ........................Editorial Assistant
**Desc.:** The magazine for professionals in
 foreign affairs. Covers foreign policy,
 history and foreign service concerns.
**Readers:** Foreign affairs personnel of the
 U.S. government, journalists, lobbyists,
 legislatives and companies doing
 business abroad.
**Deadline:** story-1st of mo. prior to pub.
 date; news-1st of mo. prior; ads-1st of
 mo. prior

**GEOGRAPHICAL ANALYSIS** 23209
1070 Carmack Rd.
Columbus, OH 43210-1002
Telephone: (614) 292-6930
Year Established: 1969
Pub. Frequency: q.
Subscrip. Rate: $30/yr. individuals; $75/yr.
 instn.
Circulation: 900
Circulation Type: paid
**Owner(s):**
Ohio State University Press
1070 Carmack Rd.
Columbus, OH 43210
Telephone: (614) 292-6930
Ownership %: 100
**Management:**
Margaret Starbuck ...........Advertising Manager
**Editorial:**
Emilio Casetti ..............................Editor
Margaret Starbuck ...................Managing Editor
**Desc.:** Theoretical modeling of spatial
 behavior and planning, treating land use,
 transportation, consumer behavior, urban
 and regional planning, and ecology.

**Readers:** Academicians, researchers,
 planners.

**GOVERNING** 65249
2300 N. St., N.W.
Washington, DC 20037
Telephone: (202) 862-8802
Year Established: 1987
Pub. Frequency: m.
Page Size: standard
Subscrip. Rate: $48/yr.
Freelance Pay: $500-$2500
Circulation: 75,000
Circulation Type: controlled & paid
**Owner(s):**
Congressional Quarterly, Inc.
1414 22nd St., N.W.
Washington, DC 20037
Telephone: (202) 887-8500
Ownership %: 100
**Management:**
Peter Harkness .......................Publisher
**Editorial:**
Alan Ehrenhalt ...................Executive Editor
Peter Harkness ..........................Editor
John Martin ......................Managing Editor
**Desc.:** A professional management
 magazine covering trends and issues,
 people and places in state and
 local government.
**Readers:** Distributed to governors, mayors,
 county executives, city-county council
 representatives, state legislators and
 executive branch officials at all levels of
 government.

**GOVERNMENT PRIME** 58756
 **CONTRACTS MONTHLY**
1155 Connecticut Ave., N.W.
Washington, DC 20036
Year Established: 1976
Pub. Frequency: m.
Subscrip. Rate: $96/yr.
**Owner(s):**
Government Data Publications, Inc.
1155 Connecticut Ave., N.W.
Washington, DC 20036
Ownership %: 100
**Management:**
Nellie Coreman ..........................Manager
**Editorial:**
Siegfried Lobel ..........................Editor

**GOVERNMENT PRODUCT NEWS** 23211
1100 Superior Ave.
Cleveland, OH 44114
Telephone: (216) 696-7000
FAX: (216) 696-7658
Year Established: 1962
Pub. Frequency: m.
Page Size: tabloid
Subscrip. Rate: $45/yr.
Materials: 29
Freelance Pay: $100/pub. pg.
Print Process: web
Circulation: 85,000
Circulation Type: controlled
**Owner(s):**
Penton Publishing
1100 Superior Ave.
Cleveland, OH 44114
Telephone: (216) 696-7000
FAX: (216) 696-7658
Ownership %: 100
**Management:**
Vaughn Rockhold .......................Publisher
Catherine Anthony ..........Advertising Manager
Catherine Anthony ..........Production Manager
**Editorial:**
Leslie Drahos ...................Editor in Chief
Kate Frisch .......................Senior Editor
Kristin Atwater ..................Managing Editor
Geraldine Zachary ......................Advertising
Sharon Shiplett ..................Assistant Editor

**Materials Accepted/Included:** 01-Business news 02-By-line articles 03-Fashion news 04-Food news 05-Freelance copy 06-Letters to editor 07-Real estate news 08-Sports news 09-Travel news 10-Book rev. 11-Movie rev. 12-Music rev. 13-TV rev. 14-Theater rev. 15-Coming events 16-Obituaries 17-Question & answer 18-Social announcements 19-Artwork 20-Cartoons 21-Photos 22-TV listings 23-Audio rec. 24-Video rec. 25-Books 26-Films/film clips 27-Personnel news 28-Press releases 29-New product news/photos 30-Trade lit. 31-Contracts awarded 32-Display adv. 33-Classified adv.

4-161

Pam Studier ........................Business Secretary
Ivan Weinstock .......................Group President
Robert Marinez ..........National Sales Manager
Wendy Weber ..................Production Assistant
**Desc.:** News releases and brochures on products purchased by public sector employees at all government levels. Case history stories on public servants using a product.
**Readers:** Public employees who specify or procure products and services for government use at the municipal, county, special district, state and federal levels. Specific readers are mayors, city managers, commissioners, department officials, purchasing directors, engineering officials, police and fire administrators and operational officials.

### ILLINOIS COUNTY & TOWNSHIP OFFICIAL
23214

P.O. Box 409
Astoria, IL 61501
Telephone: (309) 329-2101
FAX: (309) 329-2133
Year Established: 1946
Pub. Frequency: 11/yr.
Page Size: standard
Subscrip. Rate: $15/yr.
Circulation: 13,000
Circulation Type: paid
**Owner(s):**
Township Officials of Illinois
P.O. Box 455
Astoria, IL 61501
Telephone: (309) 329-2101
Ownership %: 100
**Management:**
Township Official Of Illinois ................Publisher
Bryan E. Smith ..................Advertising Manager
**Editorial:**
George H. Miller ...........................Editor
Lynette Rhodes ........................Associate Editor
**Desc.:** General and technical news of local governmental nature for membership of 18 county and township non-partisan associations representing 1,433 townships and 102 counties.
**Readers:** Township officials (supervisors, town clerks, coroners, auditors, county board members, board chairmen, board members, court clerks, assessors, collectors,) County Officials (county trustees, road commissioners). Trustees, officers of county fairs.

### ILLINOIS MUNICIPAL REVIEW
23215

P.O. Box 3387
Springfield, IL 62708
Telephone: (217) 525-1220
Mailing Address:
 P.O. Box 3387
 Springfield, IL 62708
Year Established: 1912
Pub. Frequency: m.
Page Size: standard
Subscrip. Rate: $5/yr.
**Owner(s):**
Illinois Municipal League
500 E. Capitol Ave.
Springfield, IL 62701
Telephone: (217) 525-1220
Ownership %: 100
**Editorial:**
Tom Fitzsimmons ....................Managing Editor
**Desc.:** Municipal government.
**Readers:** Municipal officials: elected and appointe

### IMSA JOURNAL MAGAZINE
23216

165 E. Union St.
Newark, NY 14513
Telephone: (315) 331-2182
FAX: (315) 331-8205

Mailing Address:
 P.O. Box 539
 Newark, NY 14513
Year Established: 1965
Pub. Frequency: bi-m.
Page Size: standard
Subscrip. Rate: $5/issue members; $40/yr. non-members
Materials: 06,19,21,27,28,29,30,33
Print Process: offset
Circulation: 5,125
Circulation Type: free & paid
**Owner(s):**
International Municipal Signal Assn.
165 E. Union St.
Newark, NY 14513
Telephone: (315) 331-2182
FAX: (315) 331-8205
Ownership %: 100
**Management:**
Harold Glerum ...................................Publisher
Sharon Earl .......................Advertising Manager
**Editorial:**
Harold Glerum ...................................Editor
Debbie Smith ........................Associate Editor
Linda Rogers ..................Editorial Assistant
**Desc.:** Contains articles to serve the Government Public Safety Field in fire and police fire alarms, traffic control, maintenance and installation, radio communications, civil defense, electrical street lighting, wire and cable, signs and markings, parking, emergency medical services & dispatching, fire & police & Emergency Medical Street Signs & Markings.
**Readers:** Persons legitimately affiliated in some manner for the installation; maintenance equipment, public safety personnel. Municipal, valleys, town, city government employees, electrical contractors.
**Deadline:** story-20th of mo. prior to pub. date; news-20th of mo. prior; photo-20th of mo. prior; ads-20th of mo. prior

### INTERNATIONAL JOURNAL OF PUBLIC ADMINISTRATION
69092

270 Madison Ave.
New York, NY 10016
Telephone: (212) 696-9000
FAX: (212) 685-4540
Year Established: 1979
Pub. Frequency: m.
Page Size: standard
Subscrip. Rate: $417.50/yr. individuals; $835/yr. instn.
Print Process: offset
**Owner(s):**
Marcel Dekker, Inc.
270 Madison Ave.
New York, NY 10016
Telephone: (212) 696-9000
FAX: (212) 685-4540
Ownership %: 100
**Editorial:**
Jack Rabin .................................Editor
Thomas Vocino ...........................Editor
**Desc.:** Journal is blind-refered, scholarly publication which presents a forum for academicians and practitioners in manaagement and administration to share theoretical issues, as well as applications of concepts and theories. This journal concentrates primarily on American theory and practice.
**Readers:** Public administrators and manaagers, civil servants, public policy specialists, political scientists, and students of public administration.

### I.T.E. JOURNAL
25097

525 School St., S.W.
Ste. 410
Washington, DC 20024
Telephone: (202) 554-8050
FAX: (202) 863-5486
Year Established: 1930
Pub. Frequency: m.
Page Size: standard
Subscrip. Rate: $50/yr.
Circulation: 12,000
Circulation Type: paid
**Owner(s):**
Institute of Transportation Engineers
525 School St., S.W.
Ste. 410
Washington, DC 20024
Telephone: (202) 554-8050
Ownership %: 100
**Management:**
Shannon Gore Peters .......Advertising Manager
**Editorial:**
Eduardo Dalere .............................Editor
**Desc.:** Articles and technical papers dealing with all phases and modes of surface traffic transportation engineering with emphasis on safe, convenient, efficient, and economic private and public transportation via highway, roads, streets, rail, planning and geometric design of related facilities, vehicles and abutting lands in rural, suburban and urban areas; human and enviornmental factors. Authors' guide available, queries welcome. Departments include: Service Directory, Products. People, Calendar, Publications, Professional Service Directory, Products.
**Readers:** Members of the Institute of Transportation Engineers and people interested in all forms of surface transportation.

### JOURNAL OF PLANNING LITERATURE
59141

2455 Teller Rd.
Thousand Oaks, CA 91320
Telephone: (805) 499-0721
FAX: (805) 499-0871
Year Established: 1986
Pub. Frequency: q.
Page Size: standard
Subscrip. Rate: $44/yr. individuals; $113/yr. libraries
Circulation: 900
Circulation Type: paid
**Owner(s):**
Sage Publications, Inc.
2455 Teller Rd.
Thousand Oaks, CA 91320
Telephone: (805) 499-0721
**Editorial:**
Kenneth Pearlman ...........................Editor
**Desc.:** A comprehensive source of up-to-date information on the literature of city and regional planning, with review articles on major issues, abstracts of hundreds of books and articles, and title listings of several hundred additional publications.
**Readers:** Planning professionals-city, county and state planners, planning consultants, university faculty, government officials.

### JOURNAL OF THE AMERICAN PLANNING ASSOCIATION
23218

Virginia Commonwealth University
919 W. Franklin St.
Richmond, VA 23284-2504

Mailing Address:
 Virginia Commonwealth University
 P.O. Box 2504
 Richmond, VA 23284-2504
Year Established: 1925
Pub. Frequency: q.
Page Size: 4 color photos/art
Subscrip. Rate: $30/yr. US members-APA; $23/yr. foreign members-APA
Circulation: 13,000
Circulation Type: paid
**Owner(s):**
American Planning Association
1313 E. 60th St.
Chicago, IL 60637
Telephone: (312) 955-9100
Ownership %: 100
**Management:**
Raquel Lavin ......................Advertising Manager
**Editorial:**
Eugenie L. Birch ..............................Editor
Peter D. Salins ...............................Editor
Linda Mandeville ...............Managing Editor
Christopher Silver .............Book Review Editor
Gary Johnson ....................Book Review Editor
**Desc.:** A quality professional and scholarly journal in the field of planning, environmental and urban affairs. It addresses a full range of planning interests: histories, empirical analyses, reviews, and practical contributions to theory.
**Readers:** Practicing planners and academics.

### KANSAS GOVERNMENT JOURNAL
23219

112 S.W. Seventh St.
Topeka, KS 66603
Telephone: (913) 354-9565
FAX: (913) 354-4186
Year Established: 1914
Pub. Frequency: m.
Page Size: standard
Subscrip. Rate: $18/yr.
Circulation: 7,700
Circulation Type: paid
**Owner(s):**
League of Kansas Municipalities
112 S.W. Seventh St.
Topeka, KS 66603
Telephone: (913) 354-9565
Ownership %: 100
**Editorial:**
Paula Drummond ..............................Editor
Wendy A. Murray ....................Managing Editor
**Readers:** Local and state government officials.

### KENTUCKY CITY, THE
23220

2201 Regency Rd.
Ste. 100
Lexington, KY 40503
Telephone: (606) 277-2886
FAX: (606) 278-5766
Year Established: 1927
Pub. Frequency: m.
Page Size: tabloid
Subscrip. Rate: $11/yr.
Circulation: 5,000
Circulation Type: paid
**Owner(s):**
Kentucky League of Cities
2201 Regency Rd., #100
Lexington, KY 40503
Telephone: (606) 277-2886
Ownership %: 100
**Management:**
Ellen Razar .......................Advertising Manager
**Editorial:**
Sylvia L. Lovely ...........................Editor in Chief

---

**Materials Accepted/Included:** 01-Business news 02-By-line articles 03-Fashion news 04-Food news 05-Freelance copy 06-Letters to editor 07-Real estate news 08-Sports news 09-Travel news 10-Book rev. 11-Movie rev. 12-Music rev. 13-TV rev. 14-Theater rev. 15-Coming events 16-Obituaries 17-Question & answer 18-Social announcements 19-Artwork 20-Cartoons 21-Photos 22-TV listings 23-Audio rec. 24-Video rec. 25-Books 26-Films/film clips 27-Personnel news 28-Press releases 29-New product news/photos 30-Trade lit. 31-Contracts awarded 32-Display adv. 33-Classified adv.

**Desc.:** Solely intended to serve as a news and information source for city officials, to guide and lead in thought concerning local, state and federal government policies that affect municipal government in the state of Kentucky.
**Readers:** Local governmental officials throughout Kentucky, councilmembers, police and fire chiefs, state legislators, congressional delegation, etc.

## KENTUCKY JOURNAL
69094
167 W. Main St., Ste. 310
Lexington, KY 40507
Telephone: (606) 255-5361
FAX: (606) 233-0760
Year Established: 1989
Pub. Frequency: 8/yr.
Subscrip. Rate: $20/yr.
Circulation: 3000
Circulation Type: paid
**Owner(s):**
Kentucky Center for Public Issues
167 W. Main St., Ste. 310
Lexington, KY 40507
Telephone: (606) 255-5361
Ownership %: 100
**Editorial:**
David G. Mudd ...............................Editor
**Desc.:** Features ideas, research and current information on public policy in Kentucky.

## MAINE TOWNSMAN
23221
37 Community Dr.
Augusta, ME 04330
Telephone: (207) 623-8428
FAX: (207) 626-5947
Year Established: 1937
Pub. Frequency: m.
Page Size: standard
Subscrip. Rate: $15/yr.
Print Process: offset
Circulation: 4,400
Circulation Type: paid
**Owner(s):**
Maine Municipal Association
37 Community Dr.
Augusta, ME 04330
Telephone: (207) 623-8429
**Management:**
Michael L. Starn ...............Advertising Manager
**Editorial:**
Michael Starn ...............................Editor
Marilyn Josephson ...............Editorial Assistant
**Desc.:** Appropriate items of municipal interest.
**Readers:** Municipal
**Deadline:** ads-1st of mo. prior to pub. date

## MICHIGAN MUNICIPAL REVIEW
23222
1675 Green Rd.
Ann Arbor, MI 48105
Telephone: (313) 662-3246
FAX: (313) 662-8083
Mailing Address:
P.O. Box 1487
Ann Arbor, MI 48106
Year Established: 1928
Pub. Frequency: 10/yr.
Page Size: standard
Subscrip. Rate: $24/yr.
Circulation: 9,600
Circulation Type: controlled
**Owner(s):**
Michigan Municipal League
P.O. Box 1487
Ann Arbor, MI 48106
Telephone: (313) 662-3246
Ownership %: 100
**Editorial:**
Judi Campbell ...............................Editor

**Desc.:** Covers municipal government in Michigan. Written by persons in municipal government, governmental agencies, Michigan Municipal League staff, and consultants in the field.
**Readers:** Elected and appointed officials in Michigan cities, villages and some townships and selected state administrative personnels.

## MINNESOTA CITIES
23223
3490 Lexington Ave. N.
St. Paul, MN 55126-8044
Telephone: (612) 490-5600
FAX: (612) 490-0072
Year Established: 1916
Pub. Frequency: m.
Page Size: standard
Subscrip. Rate: $18/yr.
Materials: 02,06,19,20,21,32,33
Print Process: offset
Circulation: 10,000
Circulation Type: controlled
**Owner(s):**
League of Minnesota Cities
3490 Lexington Ave., N.
St. Paul, MN 55126
Telephone: (612) 490-5600
FAX: (612) 490-0072
Ownership %: 100
**Management:**
Tim Busse ...................Advertising Manager
**Editorial:**
Jean Mehle Goad ...............................Editor
Tim Busse ...............Managing Editor
**Desc.:** By-line articles are written by authorities in the municipal field and cover such subjects as intergovernmental relations, municipal planning, etc.
**Readers:** Members of the League of Minnesota Cities in member municipalities receive the magazine.
**Deadline:** story-1st of mo., prior to pub. date; news-1st of mo.; photo-1st of mo.; ads-1st of mo.

## MISSOURI MUNICIPAL REVIEW
23224
1727 Southridge Dr.
Jefferson City, MO 65109
Telephone: (314) 635-9134
FAX: (314) 635-9009
Year Established: 1936
Pub. Frequency: 10/yr.
Page Size: standard
Subscrip. Rate: $18/yr.
Circulation: 5,600
Circulation Type: paid
**Owner(s):**
Missouri Municipal League
1727 Southridge Dr.
Jefferson City, MO 65109
Telephone: (314) 635-9134
Ownership %: 100
**Management:**
Gary S. Markenson ...............Publisher
Dolores Schulte ...............Advertising Manager
**Editorial:**
Dolores Schulte ...............................Editor
Gary Markenson ...............Associate Editor
Bill Johnson ...............Associate Editor
Beth Storm ...............Book Review Editor

## MUNICIPALITY, THE
23226
202 State St., Ste. 300
Madison, WI 53703-2215
Telephone: (608) 267-2380
FAX: (608) 267-0645
Year Established: 1900
Pub. Frequency: m.
Page Size: standard
Subscrip. Rate: $18/yr.
Materials: 10,32
Print Process: web offset

Circulation: 9,642
Circulation Type: controlled & paid
**Owner(s):**
League of Wisconsin Municipalities
202 State St., Ste. 300
Madison, WI 53703-2215
Telephone: (608) 267-2380
Ownership %: 100
**Management:**
John Kirkpatrick ...............Advertising Manager
**Editorial:**
Daniel R. Thompson ...............................Editor
Kathy Bull ...............Managing Editor
**Desc.:** Articles cover everyday problems of municipal government, offer legal advice to local officials, review new and proposed legislation in the state level, publish surveys on municipal practices. Reviews new publications; carries notes about local developments.
**Readers:** Mayors, village presidents and managers, city aldermen, village trustees, assessors, engineers, and public commission and board of public works, inspectors of zoning and planning, parks and local government officials.

## NATION'S CITIES WEEKLY
23230
1301 Pennsylvania Ave., N.W.
Washington, DC 20004-1763
Telephone: (202) 626-3040
FAX: (202) 626-3043
Year Established: 1978
Pub. Frequency: w.
Page Size: tabloid
Subscrip. Rate: $80/yr.; $125/2 yrs.; $160/3 yrs.
Materials: 01,02,05,06,28,29,30,32,33
Freelance Pay: negotiable
Print Process: offset
Circulation: 31,000
Circulation Type: paid
**Owner(s):**
National League of Cities
1301 Pennsylvania Ave., N.W.
Washington, DC 20004
Telephone: (202) 626-3000
Ownership %: 100
**Management:**
Donald J. Borut ...............................Publisher
Al Junge ...............Advertising Manager
**Editorial:**
Jeff Fletcher ...............................Editor
Julianne Ryan Ryder ...............Managing Editor
**Desc.:** Developments in urban affairs, administration, planning, federal legislation, technology and research, and urban conservation. All material is in a general-interest, illustrated format. We are topical, but not a news magazine.
**Readers:** Municipal officials, and civic leaders.
**Deadline:** story-1 wk. prior to pub. date; news-1 wk. prior; photo-1 wk. prior; ads-2 wks. prior

## NATIONAL CIVIC REVIEW
23228
1445 Market St., Ste 300
Denver, CO 80202-1728
Telephone: (303) 571-4343
FAX: (303) 571-4404
Year Established: 1912
Pub. Frequency: q.
Page Size: standard
Subscrip. Rate: $8 newsstand; $30/yr.
Materials: 02,10,28,31,32
Print Process: offset lithography
Circulation: 3,500
Circulation Type: paid

**Owner(s):**
National Civic League, Inc.
1445 Market St., Ste. 300
Denver, CO 80202
Telephone: (303) 571-4343
FAX: (303) 571-4404
Ownership %: 100
**Management:**
John Parr ...................Chairman Editorial Board
**Editorial:**
David Lampe ...............................Editor
**Desc.:** Contributed papers discuss governmental issues and structures, training, citizenship, taxation, etc. Contributing editors responsible for news in their respective fields. Reviews new books, lists books and pamphlets.
**Readers:** Citizens and officials interested in good government.

## NATIONAL DEVELOPMENT
23229
25 Sylvan Rd., S., Section R
Westport, CT 06880
Telephone: (203) 226-7463
FAX: (203) 222-8793
Mailing Address:
P.O. Box 5017
Westport, CT 06881-5017
Year Established: 1955
Pub. Frequency: bi-m.
Page Size: standard
Subscrip. Rate: $20/yr.
Materials: 02,05,19,21,28,29,30,31,32
Freelance Pay: $100-$450/article
Print Process: web offset
Circulation: 20,000
Circulation Type: controlled
**Owner(s):**
Intercontinental Media, Inc.
P.O. Box 5017
Westport, CT 06881
Telephone: (203) 226-7463
FAX: (203) 222-8793
Ownership %: 100
**Management:**
James Coffey ...............................Publisher
Sharon Saccary ...............Circulation Manager
**Editorial:**
Phil Anderson ...............Exec. Editor
Kathy Seymour ...............Production Director
Michael Tomashefsky .........Vice Pres. Sales & Marketing
**Desc.:** Contains articles on public works and planning, engineering technologies, administration, public utilities, communications and public transportations, public health and safety, agricultural development, education, and other areas of Third World development.
**Readers:** Government officials and technocrats in Africa, Middle East and Asia.

## NATIONAL RURAL LETTER CARRIER
25698
1630 Duke St.
Alexandria, VA 22314
Telephone: (703) 684-5545
Year Established: 1903
Pub. Frequency: w.
Page Size: standard
Subscrip. Rate: $15/yr.
Freelance Pay: $.05/wd.
Circulation: 88,000
Circulation Type: paid
**Owner(s):**
National Rural Letter Carriers Association
1630 Duke St.
Alexandria, VA 22314
Telephone: (703) 684-5545
Ownership %: 100
**Editorial:**
William R. Brown, Jr. ...............................Editor
Ruthann Saenger ...................Managing Editor

---

**Materials Accepted/Included:** 01-Business news 02-By-line articles 03-Fashion news 04-Food news 05-Freelance copy 06-Letters to editor 07-Real estate news 08-Sports news 09-Travel news 10-Book rev. 11-Movie rev. 12-Music rev. 13-TV rev. 14-Theater rev. 15-Coming events 16-Obituaries 17-Question & answer 18-Social announcements 19-Artwork 20-Cartoons 21-Photos 22-TV listings 23-Audio rec. 24-Video rec. 25-Books 26-Films/film clips 27-Personnel news 28-Press releases 29-New product news/photos 30-Trade lit. 31-Contracts awarded 32-Display adv. 33-Classified adv.

Ruthann Saenger .......................Advertising
Scottie B. Hicks ...................Associate Editor
**Desc.:** Informs rural mail carriers.
**Readers:** Rural mail carriers and their
families.

23231

### NEW JERSEY MUNICIPALITIES
407 W. State St.
Trenton, NJ 08618
Telephone: (609) 695-3481
FAX: (609) 695-0151
Year Established: 1917
Pub. Frequency: 9/yr.
Page Size: standard
Subscrip. Rate: $9/yr. league members;
$12/yr. non-members
Freelance Pay: in copies
Circulation: 8,500
Circulation Type: controlled
**Owner(s):**
N.J. State League of Municipalities,
Trenton
Telephone: (609) 695-3481
Ownership %: 100
**Management:**
Michael Darcy ..................Advertising Manager
Margaret T. Palinski ..........Circulation Manager
**Editorial:**
John E. Trafford ...............................Editor
**Desc.:** Covers New Jersey municipalities,
state, county and national.
**Readers:** Municipal officials and
administrative personnel.

23232

### OFFICIAL MICHIGAN
3078 S. Main St.
Marlette, MI 48453
Telephone: (517) 635-3000
FAX: (517) 635-3000
Mailing Address:
P.O. Box 275
Marlette, MI 48453
Year Established: 1949
Pub. Frequency: w.
Page Size: tabloid
Subscrip. Rate: $79.95/yr.
Circulation: 9,000
Circulation Type: paid
**Owner(s):**
Sanilac Publishing, Inc.
432 S. Sandusky Rd.
Sandusky, MI 48471
Telephone: (313) 648-4000
Ownership %: 100
**Management:**
John D. Johnson .......................Publisher
Karen Schalau ..................Advertising Manager
**Desc.:** Government news.
**Readers:** Officials, statewide and business.

23233

### OHIO CITIES & VILLAGES
175 S. Third, Ste. 510
Columbus, OH 43215
Telephone: (614) 221-4349
FAX: (614) 221-4390
Year Established: 1953
Pub. Frequency: 10/yr.
Page Size: standard
Subscrip. Rate: $2/issue; $10/yr.
Circulation: 9,400
Circulation Type: paid
**Owner(s):**
Ohio Municipal League, The
40 S. Third St., Ste. 540
Columbus, OH 43215
Telephone: (614) 221-4349
Ownership %: 100
**Management:**
John P. Coleman .......................Publisher
John K. Mahoney ..........Advertising Manager
Connie Retherford ...................Office Manager
**Editorial:**
John K. Mahoney ..................Managing Editor

**Desc.:** All types of features and news
articles dealing with municipal
government in any form. Maximum
length for feature article is 2,500 words
plus illustrations. By-lines will be used in
some cases on feature articles. By-lines
of Ohio municipal officials preferred. All
material should be prepared with the
fact in mind that only municipal officials
will be reading the material.
**Readers:** Mayors, city managers, finance
officers, councilmen, legal officers,
municipal utility and park managers.

23236

### PENNSYLVANIAN
2941 N. Front St.
Harrisburg, PA 17110
Telephone: (717) 236-9526
FAX: (717) 236-8164
Mailing Address:
2941 N. Front St.
Harrisburg, PA 17110
Year Established: 1962
Pub. Frequency: m.
Page Size: standard
Subscrip. Rate: $18/yr.
Materials: 02,06,15,17,21,32,33
Freelance Pay: negotiable
Print Process: offset
Circulation: 7,000
Circulation Type: paid
**Owner(s):**
Pennsylvania State Assn. Of Township
Commissioners
2608 N. Third St.
Harrisburg, PA 17110
Telephone: (717) 236-9469
Ownership %: 18

Assessors Association of Pennsylvania
2941 N. Front St.
Harrisburg, PA 17110
Telephone: (717) 236-9526
Ownership %: 8

Pennsylvania Local Government
Secretaries Assn.
2941 N. Front St.
Harrisburg, PA 17110
Telephone: (717) 236-9526
Ownership %: 8

Penn. State Association of Borough
2941 N. Front St.
Harrisburg, PA 17110
Telephone: (717) 236-9526
Ownership %: 50

Assn. of Mayors of the Boroughs of Penn.
2941 N. Front St.
Harrisburg, PA 17110
Telephone: (717) 236-9526
Ownership %: 8

Borough Councilmen's Assn. of Penn.
2941 N. Front St.
Harrisburg, PA 17110
Telephone: (717) 236-9526
Ownership %: 8
**Management:**
Samuel Black ...........................President
Robert C. Edwards .......................Publisher
Susan E. Wolfe ...............Advertising Manager
Georgann Rhoads ...................Office Manager
**Editorial:**
Susan E. Wolfe ...........................Editor
Georgann Rhoads ...............Editorial Assistant
**Desc.:** Directed towards meeting the
educational and informational needs of
local government officials, particularly
pertaining to the practical application of
new administrative and program
developments and legislative findings to
their municipality.
**Readers:** Local government officials and
legislators.

23237

### PENNSYLVANIA TOWNSHIP NEWS
3001 Gettysburg Rd.
Camp Hill, PA 17011
Telephone: (717) 763-0930
FAX: (717) 763-9732
Year Established: 1948
Pub. Frequency: m.
Page Size: standard
Subscrip. Rate: $27/yr.
Freelance Pay: varies
Circulation: 11,660
Circulation Type: controlled
**Owner(s):**
Pennsylvania State Assoc. of Township
Supervisors
3001 Gettysburg
Camp Hill, PA 17011
Telephone: (717) 763-0930
Ownership %: 100
**Management:**
B. Kenneth Greider .......................Publisher
Ginni Linn Gustavson .......Advertising Manager
**Editorial:**
Ginni Linn Gustavson .......................Editor
Amy Lehman Bobb ..................Associate Editor
Scott McQuinn ...................Editorial Assistant
Steven Robinson ..................Editorial Assistant
**Desc.:** Contains news of the purchasing
potential of 1,458 second class
townships, proserous and
individual municipalities that own or rent
thier own equiptment and are
responsible for the welfare of their
citizens.
**Readers:** Township Supervisors and
Employees, Solicitors, Engineers,
Auditors, Legislators, Universities, Etc.

23238

### PLANNING
1313 E. 60th St.
Chicago, IL 60637
Telephone: (312) 955-9100
FAX: (312) 955-8312
Year Established: 1972
Pub. Frequency: m.
Page Size: standard
Subscrip. Rate: $40/yr. US; $50/yr. foreign
Materials: 02,06,10,20,21,32
Freelance Pay: news & features-$50-$800
Print Process: web
Circulation: 30,000
Circulation Type: paid
**Owner(s):**
American Planning Association
1313 E. 60th St.
Chicago, IL 60637
Telephone: (312) 955-9100
FAX: (312) 955-8312
Ownership %: 100
**Management:**
Raquel Lavin ...............Advertising Manager
**Editorial:**
Ruth Knack ...........................Senior Editor
Sylvia Lewis ...........................Editor
Mary Lou Gallagher ..................News Editor
Richard Sessions ...........................Photo

23237

**Desc.:** Carry feature and news articles on
city planning and urban affairs. Topics
include land-use planning, zoning,
transportation, housing, neighborhoods,
energy, the environment, downtown
redevelopment. Articles are of national
interest and are written in magazine
feature style. About 25 percent of
our articles are staff written; the rest are
written by free-lancers on assignment,
generally after they have submitted a
query. All articles except staff-written
news items carry by-lines. Rarely do we
reprint press releases, though they may
be used as the basis of followup stories.
Departments include: News, Planners
Library (book reviews), Tech (new
products), full-length feature articles,
Planning Practice (planning techniques),
Viewpoint (opinion essays).
**Readers:** Most are professional city
planners who work for government
agencies; about 1/3 work for private
planning consulting firms; the remainder
teach planning at the university level or
serve on zoning and planning boards.
**Deadline:** story-1st of mo., 2 mos. prior to
pub. date; news-1st of mo., 2 mos. prior;
photo-1st of mo., 2 mos. prior; ads-25th
of mo. prior

58649

### POPULAR GOVERNMENT
Inst. of Government
CB 3330 Knapp Bldg., UNC-CH
Chapel Hill, NC 27599
Telephone: (919) 966-4119
FAX: (919) 962-2707
Year Established: 1931
Pub. Frequency: q.
Page Size: standard
Subscrip. Rate: $12/yr.
Freelance Pay: varies
Circulation: 7,700
Circulation Type: free & paid
**Owner(s):**
Institute of Government
CB 3330 Knapp Bldg., UNC-CH
Chapel Hill, NC 27599
Telephone: (919) 966-4119
FAX: (919) 962-2707
Ownership %: 100
**Management:**
Marilyn E. Penrod ...............................Manager
**Editorial:**
Robert P. Joyce ...........................Editor
Carol Offen ...............Managing Editor
Michael Brady ...........................Art Director
**Readers:** State and local government
officials and educators.

69093

### PUBLIC ADMINISTRATION
### QUARTERLY
Penn State Univ. at Harrisburg
Div. of Public Affairs
Middletown, PA 17057
Telephone: (717) 948-6363
FAX: (717) 540-1383
Year Established: 1977
Pub. Frequency: q.
Subscrip. Rate: $25/yr. individuals; $40/yr.
libraries
Circulation: 1,300
Circulation Type: paid
**Owner(s):**
Southern Public Administration Education
Foundtn.
Ownership %: 100
**Editorial:**
Jack Rabin ...........................Editor
Thomas Vocino ...........................Editor

**Materials Accepted/Included:** 01-Business news 02-By-line articles 03-Fashion news 04-Food news 05-Freelance copy 06-Letters to editor 07-Real estate news 08-Sports news 09-Travel news 10-Book rev. 11-Movie rev. 12-Music rev. 13-TV rev. 14-Theater rev. 15-Coming events 16-Obituaries 17-Question & answer 18-Social announcements 19-Artwork 20-Cartoons 21-Photos 22-TV listings 23-Audio rec. 24-Video rec. 25-Books 26-Films/film clips 27-Personnel news 28-Press releases 29-New product news/photos 30-Trade lit. 31-Contracts awarded 32-Display adv. 33-Classified adv.

## PUBLIC ADMINISTRATION REVIEW
23244

1120 G St., N.W., Ste. 700
Washington, DC 20005
Telephone: (202) 393-7878
FAX: (202) 638-4952
Year Established: 1940
Pub. Frequency: bi-m.
Page Size: standard
Subscrip. Rate: $100/yr. US instn. only
Circulation: 18,000
Circulation Type: paid
**Owner(s):**
American Society for Public Administration
1120 G St., N.W., Ste. 700
Washington, DC 20005
Telephone: (202) 393-7878
Ownership %: 100
**Management:**
Sheila McCormick ...........Advertising Manager
Patricia Woodward ...............Customer Service
Manager
Sheila McCormick .............Promotion Manager
**Editorial:**
David Rosenbloom ......................Editor in Chief
John P. Thomas .....................................Director
John Larkin ...............................Production Editor
**Desc.:** Carries articles on current
administrative problems and techniques;
essay-reviews of books and public
documents significant in the field of
public administration. Articles are written
by professors of government and social
science, government administrators, and
researchers; and run from 2,000-6,000
words. Book reviews run from 1,000-4,
000 words.
**Readers:** Members of the American
Society for public, federal, state, and
local officials, research workers,
educators and students in the social
sciences and science of public
administration, including library.

## PUBLIC MANAGEMENT/PM
23245

777 N. Capitol St., N.E., Ste. 500
Washington, DC 20002-4201
Telephone: (202) 962-3619
Year Established: 1919
Pub. Frequency: m.
Page Size: standard
Subscrip. Rate: $30/yr.
Materials: 32
Print Process: web
Circulation: 14,000
Circulation Type: paid
**Owner(s):**
International City/County Mgmnt.
Association
777 N. Capitol St., N.E.
Ste. 500
Washington, DC 20002
Telephone: (202) 962-3619
FAX: (202) 962-3500
Ownership %: 100
**Management:**
William H. Hansell, Jr. ..........Executive Director
Beth Payne ......................Advertising Manager
Elena Mina ......................Advertising Manager
**Editorial:**
Beth Payne ...............................................Editor
**Desc.:** Each issue carries three or four 2,
000-2,500 word articles dealing with the
administration of local government. New
sections deal mainly with methods and
techniques used by local governments
to improve the administration of local
services.
**Readers:** Circulation is among local
government figures including managers,
assistants, department heads, mayors,
councilmembers, professors of
government, and other key individuals.

## PUBLIC WORKS MAGAZINE
23247

200 S. Broad St.
Ridgewood, NJ 07450
Telephone: (201) 445-5800
Mailing Address:
P.O. Box 688
Ridgewood, NJ 07451
Year Established: 1896
Pub. Frequency: m.
Page Size: standard
Subscrip. Rate: $45/yr.
Materials: 01,06,10,19,21,27,28,30
Freelance Pay: varies
Circulation: 51,286
Circulation Type: controlled
**Owner(s):**
Public Works Journal Corp.
200 S. Broad St.
Ridgewood, NJ 07450
Telephone: (201) 445-5800
Ownership %: 100
**Management:**
James P. Spollen ........................Vice President
**Editorial:**
Edward B. Rodie .......................................Editor
James R. Kircher ......................Assistant Editor
Gary W. Szelc ........................Book Review Editor
Paul S. Kobelt ....................New Products Editor
James R. Kircher ..............................News Editor
Jerry Kilmnick ..............Production Coordinator
**Desc.:** Verified technical articles on city,
county, and state engineering; water
supply and purification, sewage and
sewage treatment; highways, streets,
refuse collection and disposal; lighting
and traffic control; airports, civil defense
and disaster control.
**Readers:** City, county, state engineering &
technical administrators.

## QUALITY CITIES
23207

201 W. Park Ave.
Tallahassee, FL 32301
Telephone: (904) 222-9684
FAX: (904) 222-3806
Mailing Address:
P.O. Box 1757
Tallahassee, FL 32302-1757
Year Established: 1928
Pub. Frequency: 11/yr.
Page Size: standard
Subscrip. Rate: $20/yr.
Materials: 02,06,28,30,32,33
Circulation: 5,300
Circulation Type: paid
**Owner(s):**
Florida League of Cities
P.O. Box 1757
Tallahassee, FL 32302-1757
Telephone: (904) 222-9684
FAX: (904) 222-3806
Ownership %: 100
**Management:**
Raymond C. Sittig ...............................Publisher
**Editorial:**
Cecka R. Trueblood .................................Editor
Priscilla Dawson ...............................Advertising
Mary Smith Judd ..............Publication Assistant
**Desc.:** Reports on legislation impacting
cities, current issues affecting
municipalities, innovative local
government ideas. Includes personnel
changes, positions open, Attorney
General's opinions and Commission on
Ethics opinions.
**Readers:** City, county, state, school
officials in Florida.
**Deadline:** ads-1st of mo. prior to mo. of
pub.

## SOUTH DAKOTA MUNICIPALITIES
23250

214 E. Capitol
Pierre, SD 57501
Telephone: (605) 224-8654

Year Established: 1934
Pub. Frequency: m.
Page Size: standard
Subscrip. Rate: $20/yr.
Materials: 17,19,20,28
Circulation: 2,700
Circulation Type: paid
**Owner(s):**
South Dakota Municipal League
214 E. Capitol
Pierre, SD 57501
Telephone: (605) 224-8654
Ownership %: 100
**Management:**
Marla Geinger ...................Advertising Manager
**Editorial:**
Yvonne A. Vik .............................................Editor
**Desc.:** Stories and articles of interest to
municipalities/water and sewage, waste
disposal, city government, property tax
reform and taxes in general and other
professional subjects.
**Readers:** Mayor, auditors, attorneys,
elected and appointed municipal
officials.
**Deadline:** story-10th of mo. prior to pub.
date; news-10th of mo. prior; photo-10th
of mo. prior; ads-10th of mo. prior

## TENNESSEE TOWN & CITY
23253

226 Capitol Blvd., Rm. 710
Nashville, TN 37219
Telephone: (615) 255-6416
FAX: (615) 255-7428
Year Established: 1950
Pub. Frequency: s-m.
Page Size: broadsheet
Subscrip. Rate: $1/issue; $10/yr.
Materials: 06,20,21
Print Process: web
Circulation: 5,400
Circulation Type: controlled
**Owner(s):**
Tennessee Municipal League
226 Capitol Blvd.
Nashville, TN 37219
Ownership %: 100
**Management:**
Joseph Sweat .......................................Publisher
**Editorial:**
Beverly Bruninga .....................Managing Editor
**Readers:** Elected and appointed municipal
officials in Tennessee.

## TEXAS TOWN & CITY
23255

1821 Rutherford Lane., Ste. 400
Austin, TX 78754
Telephone: (512) 719-6300
FAX: (512) 719-6390
Year Established: 1913
Pub. Frequency: m.
Page Size: standard
Subscrip. Rate: $20/yr.
Circulation: 11,800
Circulation Type: controlled
**Owner(s):**
Texas Municipal League
1020 S.W. Tower
Austin, TX 78701
Telephone: (512) 478-6601
Ownership %: 100
**Management:**
Karla Vining ..........................................Publisher
**Editorial:**
Karla Vining ................................................Editor
**Desc.:** Contributed articles by municipal
officials, controllers, city planning and all
other areas of municipal departments.
**Readers:** City managers, city attorneys,
personnel officers, and mayors.

## VIRGINIA REVIEW
23257

3800 S. Middlebrook Ct.
Chester, VA 23831
Telephone: (804) 748-6351
FAX: (804) 796-6931
Mailing Address:
P.O. Box 860
Chester, VA 23831
Year Established: 1923
Pub. Frequency: bi-m.
Page Size: standard
Subscrip. Rate: $14/yr.
Materials: 02,06,10,25,27,28,32
Freelance Pay: negotiable
Print Process: offset
Circulation: 10,000
Circulation Type: paid
**Owner(s):**
Review Publications, Inc.
P.O. Box 860
Chester, VA 23831
Telephone: (804) 748-6351
FAX: (804) 796-6931
Ownership %: 100
**Management:**
Roger H. Habeck ...................................Publisher
Roger H. Habeck ...........Advertising Manager
Whitley Blake ....................Circulation Manager
**Editorial:**
Alyson L. Taylor-White ...........Executive Editor
**Desc.:** All contributed articles are of
interest to municipal and other state and
local officials in Virginia. Covers
management, waste management,
governmental law and finance, focus on
localities in each issue and profiles of
leaders, mentors and personalities in the
field. Departments include: Elucidations,
Counselor's Corner, Ecotech Network,
Commonwealth Contact, and
Management Matters, Currents, of Note,
Professional Directory.
**Readers:** State, city, town, and county and
federal elected and appointed
government officials, and consultants
who work with them to solve their
problems, in addition to academics,
private sector leaders, government
students and interns. Also, professionals
in government law, corrections,
emergency services, and training.
**Deadline:** ads-1st working day of the mo.
prior to pub. date

## VIRGINIA TOWN & CITY
23258

13 E. Franklin St.
Richmond, VA 23219
Telephone: (804) 649-8471
FAX: (804) 343-3758
Mailing Address:
P.O. Box 12164
Richmond, VA 23241
Year Established: 1966
Pub. Frequency: m.
Page Size: standard
Subscrip. Rate: $8/yr.
Materials: 01,02,05,06,10,15,17,19,20,21,
25,27,28,29,30,31,32,33
Print Process: offset
Circulation: 5,000
Circulation Type: controlled & paid
**Owner(s):**
Virginia Municipal League
P.O. Box 12164
Richmond, VA 23241
Telephone: (804) 649-8471
FAX: (804) 343-3758
Ownership %: 100
**Management:**
Beth McDonald .................Advertising Manager
Christine A. Everson ...........Business Manager
Peggy S. Blunt ....................Circulation Manager
**Editorial:**
Christine A. Everson ................................Editor

Materials Accepted/Included: 01-Business news 02-By-line articles 03-Fashion news 04-Food news 05-Freelance copy 06-Letters to editor 07-Real estate news 08-Sports news 09-Travel news
10-Book rev. 11-Movie rev. 12-Music rev. 13-TV rev. 14-Theater rev. 15-Coming events 16-Obituaries 17-Question & answer 18-Social announcements 19-Artwork 20-Cartoons 21-Photos 22-TV listings
23-Audio rec. 24-Video rec. 25-Books 26-Films/film clips 27-Personnel news 28-Press releases 29-New product news/photos 30-Trade lit. 31-Contracts awarded 32-Display adv. 33-Classified adv.

4-165

**Desc.:** Trade publication for Virginia Municipal Government, focusing on local government problems, solution and services. News items include promotions and retirements of state and local leaders. Research articles wanted, but not with an academic slant. Feature articles cover topics of legislation, innovative municipal services, and management techniques. Departments include: people, calendar, letters to the editor, marketplace, legal guidelines, commentary, directories, guest editorial, book reviews, environmental corner, Q & A, and Stateline.

**Readers:** Mayors, council members, managers, city department heads, state and federal administrators, public works directors, Virginia congressional delegations, librarians, fire chiefs, building officials, and electric utility managers.

**Deadline:** story-10th of mo. prior to pub. date; news-10th of mo. prior; photo-10th of mo. prior; ads-10th of mo. prior

23259

## WESTERN CITY
1400 K St.
Sacramento, CA 95814
Telephone: (916) 444-5790
FAX: (916) 444-5129
Year Established: 1932
Pub. Frequency: m.
Page Size: standard
Subscrip. Rate: $3 newsstand; $30/yr.; $49/2 yr; $29/student; $40/yr. foreign
Materials: 32,33
Print Process: sheet fed
Circulation: 10,600
Circulation Type: controlled & paid
**Owner(s):**
League of California Cities
1400 K St.
Sacramento, CA 95814
Telephone: (916) 444-5790
Ownership %: 100
**Management:**
Don Benninghoven ..............Executive Director
Jehan Flagg ......................Advertising Manager
Dan Harrison ........................Business Manager
**Editorial:**
Victoria Clark ..................................Editor
**Desc.:** Covers how to more effectively and efficiently provide city services, including: water, sewage, public works, city planning, labor relations, municipal finance, energy management; how to make the most of city budgets, activities of California Governor and legislature and their impact on city government. Also carries association news, new literature and other short material of direct interest to the field. Federal legislation affecting cities in California.

**Readers:** Mayors, city managers, city engineers, public works, directors, council members, fire and police chief, finance officers, city clerks, purchasing agents, energy coordinators, park and recreation directors, urban planners, personnel directors, senators, assembly members, congressional delegations, and other major department heads.

## Group 108-Grains, Feed & Milling

25406

## AG FOCUS
420 E. Main St.
Batavia, NY 14020
*see Farm and Agriculture Magazines, Farm Organizations & Cooperatives*

23262

## COMMERCIAL REVIEW
1725 N.W. 24th St.
Portland, OR 97210
Telephone: (503) 226-2758
FAX: (503) 224-0947
Year Established: 1890
Pub. Frequency: w.
Page Size: standard
Subscrip. Rate: $28/yr.
Circulation: 1,500
Circulation Type: paid
**Owner(s):**
Commercial Review, Inc.
1725 N.W. 24th St.
Portland, OR 92710-2507
Telephone: (503) 226-2758
Ownership %: 100
**Management:**
Dennis Hays ..........................Publisher
**Editorial:**
Dennis Hays ..............................Editor
**Desc.:** Emphasis on news coverage of the grain, feed, seed, fertilizer and garden supply milling industries of the Pacific Coast slopes. Publishes only material that will appeal to readers in these fields. Prefers short, terse articles. Covers export markets, domestic markets, crop estimates, associations, etc.
**Readers:** Executives in the fields of agriculture.

23264

## FEED & GRAIN
1233 Janesville Ave.
Ft. Atkinson, WI 53538
Telephone: (414) 563-6388
FAX: (414) 563-1699
Year Established: 1966
Pub. Frequency: 7/yr.
Page Size: tabloid
Subscrip. Rate: $40/yr. US; $55/yr. Canada & Mexico; $120/yr. elsewhere
Materials: 01,05,15,27,27,29,32,33
Freelance Pay: varies
Print Process: web
Circulation: 19,300
Circulation Type: controlled
**Owner(s):**
Johnson Hill Press, Inc.
1233 Janesville Ave.
Fort Atkinson, WI 53538
Telephone: (414) 563-6388
Ownership %: 100
**Management:**
Jonathan Pellegrin ....................President
Mike Martin ............................Publisher
**Editorial:**
Kay Jensen ...............................Editor
Arlette Sambs ...............Associate Publisher
**Desc.:** New product news for all feed, grain and allied grain processing industries. Business management information for owners, managers and operators of feed, grain, and grain processing facilities.
**Readers:** Grain and feed handlers and processors. business engaged in purchase, handling, processing, sale and/or shipping of grain and feed.

23266

## FEED MANAGEMENT
122 S. Wesley Ave.
Mt. Morris, IL 61054
Telephone: (815) 734-4171
FAX: (315) 734-4201
Year Established: 1950
Pub. Frequency: m.
Page Size: standard
Subscrip. Rate: $48/yr.
Freelance Pay: varies
Circulation: 22,000
Circulation Type: controlled

**Owner(s):**
Watt Publishing Co.
122 S. Wesly Ave.
Mt. Morris, IL 61054
Telephone: (815) 734-4171
Ownership %: 100
**Management:**
James W. Watt .........................President
Clay Schreiber .........................Publisher
Dee Lene Henson ..........Editorial Production Manager
**Editorial:**
Clayton Gill ...............................Editor
Laurance Laskos ......................Art Director
**Desc.:** Written for animal feed trade. Carries technical merchandising, plant management by-line articles. Departments include: speaking of nutrition, mill management, Washington comments, international feedback, AFIA News, research highlights, NFIA report product news, up-from-the minors, and movers and shakers.
**Readers:** Commercial and integrated feed manufacturers, mixers, and retailers of feeds for livestock and poultry.

23267

## FEEDSTUFFS
12400 Whitewater Dr.
Minnetonka, MN 55343
Telephone: (612) 931-0211
FAX: (612) 938-1832
Mailing Address:
P.O. Box 2400
Minnetonka, MN 55343
Year Established: 1929
Pub. Frequency: w.
Page Size: tabloid
Subscrip. Rate: $89.95/yr.
Materials: 01,02,05,06,28,29,32,33
Freelance Pay: $2/col. in.
Circulation: 16,545
Circulation Type: paid
**Owner(s):**
Miller Publishing Co.
P.O. Box 2400
Minnetonka, MN 55343
Telephone: (612) 931-0211
FAX: (612) 938-1832
Ownership %: 100
**Management:**
Allan R. Johnson ...................General Manager
**Editorial:**
Jon Schied ...............................Editor
Sarah Muirhead ..................Managing Editor
**Desc.:** Primarily presenting coverage of all phases of the feed manufacturing and distributing industry and large feeding operations. Washington news is provided by two correspondents with news and market correspondents in all of the key distribution centers. Feature material runs heavily to developments in animal nutrition research, with merchandising, manufacturing and general business operations also getting feature attention. Departments Include: Feed Ingredient Markets, Formula Feed Market Review, Nutrition Research, New Products and Literature, Management Tips, Market Analysis, Cattle, Poultry, Pork.
**Readers:** Feed manufacturers, grain handlers and processors, merchandisers, nutritionists, financial and marketing.

23268

## GRAIN AGE
9995 W. 69th St.
Eden Prairie, MN 55344-3408
Telephone: (612) 941-5820
FAX: (612) 941-6746
Year Established: 1959
Pub. Frequency: bi-m.

Page Size: standard
Subscrip. Rate: $15/yr.
Circulation: 9,375
Circulation Type: controlled
**Owner(s):**
Communications Marketing, Inc.
9995 W. 69th St.
Eden Prairie, MN 55344-3408
Telephone: (612) 941-5820
Ownership %: 100
**Management:**
Spencer M. Dean ...............................Publisher
John F. Cooney ...............Advertising Manager
**Editorial:**
Bruce W. Smith ......................Editorial Director
**Desc.:** Technical, processing and handling information for grain and oilseed elevator firms with minimum of 100,000 bushels storage. New products, techniques, government regulations, merchandising ideas.
**Readers:** Grain firm management.

54073

## GRAIN JOURNAL
2490 N. Water St.
Decatur, IL 62526
Telephone: (217) 877-9660
FAX: (217) 877-6647
Year Established: 1972
Pub. Frequency: bi-m.
Page Size: standard
Subscrip. Rate: $25/yr.
Materials: 01,02,25,27,28,29,30,31,32,33
Freelance Pay: $50-$100/article
Circulation: 11,444
Circulation Type: controlled
**Owner(s):**
Grain Journal/Helen Reeter
2490 N. Water St.
Decatur, IL 62526
Telephone: (217) 877-9660
Ownership %: 33

Grain Journal/Sam Koehl
2490 N. Water St.
Decatur, IL 62526
Telephone: (217) 877-9660
Ownership %: 33

Grain Journal/Mark Avery
2490 N. Water St.
Decatur, IL 62526
Telephone: (217) 877-9660
Ownership %: 33
**Management:**
Sam Koehl ...............................President
Helen Reeter ..............................Vice President
**Editorial:**
Mark Avery ...............................Treasurer
**Desc.:** Dedicated to bringing useful and innovative news to the grain industry.
**Readers:** Grain elevator managers across U.S.

64907

## WORLD GRAIN
4800 Main St., Ste. 100
Kansas City, MO 64112
Telephone: (816) 756-1000
FAX: (816) 756-0494
Year Established: 1982
Pub. Frequency: 10/yr.
Page Size: standard
Subscrip. Rate: $32/yr.; $56/2 yrs.
Materials: 28,29,32
Freelance Pay: $250-$300
Circulation: 10,000
Circulation Type: free & paid
**Owner(s):**
Sosland Publishing Co.
4800 Main St., Ste. 100
Kansas City, MO 64112
Telephone: (816) 756-1000
Ownership %: 100
**Management:**
Charles Sosland ...............................Publisher

**Materials Accepted/Included:** 01-Business news 02-By-line articles 03-Fashion news 04-Food news 05-Freelance copy 06-Letters to editor 07-Real estate news 08-Sports news 09-Travel news 10-Book rev. 11-Movie rev. 12-Music rev. 13-TV rev. 14-Theater rev. 15-Coming events 16-Obituaries 17-Question & answer 18-Social announcements 19-Artwork 20-Cartoons 21-Photos 22-TV listings 23-Audio rec. 24-Video rec. 25-Books 26-Films/film clips 27-Personnel news 28-Press releases 29-New product news/photos 30-Trade lit. 31-Contracts awarded 32-Display adv. 33-Classified adv.

Nora Wages .......................Advertising Manager
Vance Spearman ...............Editorial Production
                                                    Manager
**Editorial:**
Melissa Cordonier ......................................Editor
Mark Sabo ..............President & Publishing Dir.
**Readers:** Company and operations
  management in the grain and grain
  processing industries world wide.

## Group 110-Grocery & Food Marketing

23278
**ARIZONA GROCER**
120 E. Pierce St.
Phoenix, AZ 85004
Telephone: (602) 252-9761
Year Established: 1944
Pub. Frequency: m.
Page Size: standard
Subscrip. Rate: $50/yr.
Materials: 01,06,21,27,28,29,30,32
Print Process: offset
Circulation: 2,500
Circulation Type: controlled
**Owner(s):**
Arizona Grocers Publishing Co.
120 E. Pierce St.
Phoenix, AZ 85004
Telephone: (602) 252-9761
Ownership %: 100
**Editorial:**
Rodney K. Platt ...................................Editor
**Desc.:** Confined to retail food industry.
  Covers merchandising and sales ideas,
  new lines, contests, legislation, local
  news, and people in the trade.
  Publication of the Retail Grocers
  Association of Arizona.
**Readers:** Retail and wholesale grocers,
  factory or companies engaged in the
  distribution or manufacturing grocer
  channels; hotel, public officials,
  convenience stores, drug stores, and
  libraries.

23030
**CAROLINA FOOD DEALER**
One Charlottetown Ctr., Rm. 217
Charlotte, NC 28207
Telephone: (704) 334-3935
FAX: (704) 334-9126
Pub. Frequency: bi-m.
Page Size: standard
Subscrip. Rate: $1/yr.
Circulation: 2,500
Circulation Type: paid
**Owner(s):**
North Carolina Food Dealers Association,
  Inc.
1 Charlottetown Ctr., Rm. 217
Charlotte, NC 28207
Telephone: (704) 334-3935
Ownership %: 100
**Management:**
G. Everett Suddreth .........Advertising Manager
**Editorial:**
G. Everett Suddreth ...................................Editor
**Desc.:** Covers food and grocery news,
  merchandising, new products,
  promotions, plant expansions and News
  of the Month department reports on new
  sales personnel.

23281
**CLEVELAND FOOD DEALER, THE**
4204 Detroit Ave.
Cleveland, OH 44113
Telephone: (216) 961-4836
FAX: (216) 961-9302
Year Established: 1959
Pub. Frequency: bi-m.
Page Size: standard
Subscrip. Rate: $1.25 newsstand; $12/yr.
Materials: 04,21,28,29,30

Circulation: 1,400
Circulation Type: controlled & paid
**Owner(s):**
Cleveland Food Dealers Assn., Inc.
4204 Detroit Ave.
Cleveland, OH 44113
Telephone: (216) 961-4836
Ownership %: 100
**Management:**
Alvin J. Palack ......................Executive Director
Karen L. Curtin ..................Advertising Manager
Alvin J. Palack ..................................Manager
William Morley ..........Public Relations Manager
**Editorial:**
Alvin J. Palack ......................Executive Editor
Karen L. Curtin ......................Associate Editor
Alvin J. Palack ..........Communications Director
Karen L. Curtin ..........Communications Director
Joan Sanford ..........Executive Editor Assistant
Alvin J. Palack ..................................News Editor
**Desc.:** Important news of the trade
  accepted and run at no charge. News
  must be timely. Covers the Cleveland &
  Cuyahoga County retail food field.
**Readers:** Mailed to every market operator
  and wholesaler. Official publication of
  The Cleveland Food Dealers
  Association.
**Deadline:** story-20th of mo. prior to pub.
  date

23283
**CONVENIENCE STORE NEWS**
Seven Penn Plz.
New York, NY 10001-3900
Telephone: (212) 594-4120
FAX: (212) 714-0514
Year Established: 1969
Pub. Frequency: 16/yr.
Page Size: tabloid
Subscrip. Rate: $48/yr.
Freelance Pay: $3/in.
Circulation: 118,260
Circulation Type: controlled
**Owner(s):**
T/SF Communications
2407 E. Skelly Dr.
Tulsa, OK 74105
Telephone: (918) 747-2600
Ownership %: 100
**Bureau(s):**
BMT Publications, Inc.
308 W. Erie St., Ste. 710
Chicago, IL 60610
Telephone: (312) 943-0684
Contact: Michael Walsh


Marritt & Co.
16133 Ventura Blvd., Ste. 1270
Van Nuys, CA 91436
Telephone: (818) 783-5888
Contact: Sue Marritt

BMT Publications, Inc.
4522 Spruce St., Ste. 200
Tampa, FL 33607
Telephone: (813) 878-2277
Contact: Patricia Hincher
**Management:**
Hedy Halpert ...................................President
Daniel N. Petrocelli ...................Vice President
Joan Toth ...................................Publisher
Daniel N. Petrocelli ..............General Manager
**Editorial:**
Maureen Azzato ...................................Editor
**Desc.:** News or feature stories relating to
  convenience stores and their operations.
  Covers all product categories of a
  convenience store. Feature stories
  emphasize successful or unusual
  merchandising, promotions, displays,
  and advertising in C-stores.

**Readers:** Comprised of executives, buyers,
  owners of chain, franchises, petroleum
  marketer and independent convenience
  stores. Also, suppliers, wholesalers and
  distributors selling to convenience
  stores.

23286
**FLORIDA FOOD DEALER**
105 Live Oak Gardens, 101
Casselberry, FL 32707
Telephone: (407) 339-7423
FAX: (407) 339-1268
Year Established: 1947
Pub. Frequency: bi-m.
Page Size: standard
Subscrip. Rate: $15/yr. members; $18/yr.
  non-members
Freelance Pay: varies
Circulation: 3,500
Circulation Type: controlled
**Owner(s):**
Florida Food Industries, Inc.
105 Live Oak Gardens, Ste. 101
Casselberry, FL 32707
Telephone: (407) 339-7423
Ownership %: 100
**Management:**
John B. Pearman ......................President
**Editorial:**
Andy Williams ...................................Editor
**Desc.:** General news, product and
  promotion news pertaining to the
  grocery business.
**Readers:** Retail grocers, convenience
  store operators.

23288
**FLORIDA GROCER**
2828 Coral Way- East Entrance
Ste. 102
Miami, FL 33145
Telephone: (305) 441-1138
FAX: (305) 661-6720
Mailing Address:
  P.O. Box 430760
  South Miami, FL 33243
Year Established: 1956
Pub. Frequency: m.
Page Size: broadsheet
Subscrip. Rate: $29/yr.
Circulation: 16,000
Circulation Type: controlled
**Owner(s):**
Florida Grocer Publications, Inc.
P.O. Box 430760
S. Miami, FL 33243
Telephone: (305) 441-1138
Ownership %: 100
**Management:**
Jack Nobles ...................................Publisher
**Editorial:**
Dennis M Kane ...................................Editor
Minnie Nobles ............Administrative Assistant
**Desc.:** Newspaper style treatment,
  emphasizing factual reporting of local,
  state and national news of interest to
  Florida wholesale and retail grocery
  industry. News releases from buyers &
  sellers, including manufacturers, brokers,
  chain, government agencies regarding
  new products, ownership & personnel
  changes, financial information, meetings,
  conventions. Special features &
  columns: Editorial, New Products Page,
  Equipment News Page, Letter to Editor,
  Upcoming Events Calendar, Financial,
  People, Places & Things, Obituary,
  Spanish Section.
**Readers:** Chain stores, independent
  stores, food brokers, manufacturing
  representatives, wholesalers, distributors
  and members of allied industries.

23034
**FOOD DISTRIBUTION MAGAZINE**
406 Water St.
Warren, RI 02885
Telephone: (401) 245-4500
FAX: (401) 245-4699
Mailing Address:
  P.O. Box 87
  Barrington, RI 02806
Year Established: 1960
Pub. Frequency: m.
Page Size: standard
Subscrip. Rate: $49/yr.; $75/2 yrs.
Freelance Pay: varies
Circulation: 35,000
Circulation Type: controlled
**Owner(s):**
National Food Distribution Network
406 Water St.
Warren, RI 02885
Telephone: (401) 245-4500
Ownership %: 100
**Management:**
Brad McDowell ...................................Publisher
Dana McDowell ...................................Publisher
Dana McDowell ...................Business Manager
**Editorial:**
Dara Chadwick ...................Executive Editor
**Desc.:** Stories and articles on the food
  distributors business, slanted toward
  management, including internal
  management, marketing, promotions,
  general industry climate articles, case
  history stories, personnel changes, news
  items.
**Readers:** National food distributors,
  specialty food store buyers, natural food
  store buyers, supermarket headquarters
  & buying offices, convenience store
  headquarters & buying offices, brokers,
  manufacturers and importers.

23289
**FOOD HERALD**
3001 LBJ Fwy. Ste. 133
Dallas, TX 75234-7756
Telephone: (214) 243-5885
FAX: (214) 243-5886
Mailing Address:
  3001 LBJ Fwy. Ste. 133
  Dallas, TX 75234
Year Established: 1947
Pub. Frequency: 8/yr.
Page Size: standard
Subscrip. Rate: $20/yr.
Materials: 01,02,04,06,15,21,27,28,29,30,32
Print Process: offset
Circulation: 1,000
Circulation Type: controlled
**Owner(s):**
Dallas/Fort Worth Grocers Association
3001 LBJ Fwy. Ste. 133
Dallas, TX 75234
Telephone: (214) 243-5885
Ownership %: 100
**Editorial:**
Valerie A. Schenewerk ............Executive Editor
**Desc.:** Reports on social and business
  activities of local, state, and national
  grocers' associations. Covers food
  retailing; food safety; government
  regulations on food, grocery, or
  convenience stores, as well as business
  trends and employee relations.
**Readers:** Food retailers, wholesalers,
  manufacturers, and suppliers to same.
**Deadline:** story-20th of mo. prior to pub.
  date; news-20th of mo. prior; photo-20th
  of mo. prior; ads-20th of mo. prior

23042
**FOOD TRADE NEWS**
2 Elm St.
Conshohocken, PA 19003
Telephone: (215) 834-3760
FAX: (215) 834-3765
Year Established: 1945

**Materials Accepted/Included:** 01-Business news 02-By-line articles  03-Fashion news 04-Food news 05-Freelance copy 06-Letters to editor 07-Real estate news 08-Sports news 09-Travel news
10-Book rev. 11-Movie rev. 12-Music rev. 13-TV rev. 14-Theater rev. 15-Coming events 16-Obituaries 17-Question & answer 18-Social announcements 19-Artwork 20-Cartoons 21-Photos 22-TV listings
23-Audio rec. 24-Video rec. 25-Books 26-Films/film clips 27-Personnel news 28-Press releases 29-New product news/photos 30-Trade lit. 31-Contracts awarded 32-Display adv. 33-Classified adv.

4-167

Pub. Frequency: m.
Page Size: tabloid
Subscrip. Rate: $3/issue; $36/yr.
Materials: 01,02,04,06,16,17,32,33
Print Process: web offset
Circulation: 22,342
Circulation Type: controlled
**Owner(s):**
Best-Met Publishing Co., Inc.
5537 Twin Knolls Rd., Ste. 438
Columbia, MD 21045
Telephone: (410) 730-5013
FAX: (410) 740-4680
Ownership %: 100
**Management:**
Richard J. Bestany .............................President
Jeffrey W. Metzger .............................Publisher
Richard J. Bestany .............................Publisher
Richard J. Bestany ..........Advertising Manager
James Kinney .........................General Manager
**Editorial:**
Meg Major .............................................Editor
**Readers:** Food marketing people in
Pennsylvania, New Jersey, Delaware
and Maryland, including chain and
independent supermarket and grocery
store operators and managers, buyers,
merchandisers and sales executives at
chain headquarters and wholesale
buying offices.
**Deadline:** story-1st Mon. of mo.; news-1st
Mon. of mo.; photo-1st Mon. of mo.;
ads-1st Mon. of mo.

23044
**FROZEN FOOD AGE**
263 Tresser Blvd.
Stamford, CT 06901-3218
Telephone: (203) 325-3500
FAX: (203) 325-8423
Year Established: 1952
Pub. Frequency: m.
Page Size: tabloid
Subscrip. Rate: $70/yr.
Materials: 01,02,06,27,28,29,30,31,32,33
Print Process: web offset
Circulation: 19,800
Circulation Type: controlled
**Owner(s):**
McClean-Hunter Media
263 Tresser Blvd.
Stamford, CT 06901-3218
Telephone: (203) 325-3500
Ownership %: 100
**Management:**
Steve Lichtenstein ...............................Publisher
**Editorial:**
Warren Thayer ...............................Editor in Chief
Len Lewis ....................................Executive Editor
Mike Friedman ...........................Managing Editor
**Desc.:** Articles are slanted to material
meant to help retail and institutional
management market frozen foods.
Covers products, transportation,
warehousing, etc.
**Readers:** Firms and their executives
engaged in the processing, distribution,
and sale of frozen foods.
**Deadline:** news-10th of mo. prior to pub.
date; photo-10th of mo. prior; ads-5th of
mo. prior

23294
**GEORGIA FOOD CONNECTION**
3200 Highlands Pkwy., Ste. 210
Smyrna, GA 30082
Telephone: (404) 438-7744
Pub. Frequency: s-a.
Page Size: standard
Subscrip. Rate: $25/yr. non-members
Materials: 04,28,29,30
Circulation: 1,600
Circulation Type: controlled

**Owner(s):**
Georgia Food Industry Association
3200 Highlands Pkwy., Ste. 210
Smyrna, GA 30082
Telephone: (404) 438-7744
Ownership %: 100
**Management:**
Kathy Kuzava ......................Executive Director
Nancy Pruitt ......................Advertising Manager
**Editorial:**
Kathy Kuzava .........................................Editor
**Desc.:** Covers merchandising campaigns,
new lines, association news, government
regulations.
**Readers:** Independent and chain retail and
wholesale grocers and associate
members.

23295
**GRIFFIN REPORT OF FOOD
MARKETING**
1099 Hingham St.
Rockland, MA 02370
Telephone: (617) 878-5300
FAX: (617) 871-4721
Year Established: 1966
Pub. Frequency: m.
Page Size: tabloid
Subscrip. Rate: $36/yr.
Materials: 01,04,15,16,21,27,28,29,30,32,33
Circulation: 15,230
Circulation Type: controlled
**Owner(s):**
Griffin Publishing Co., Inc.
1099 Hingham St.
Rockland, MA 02370
Telephone: (617) 878-5300
Ownership %: 100
**Management:**
Stephen M. Griffin ...............................President
John H. Griffin ...................................Publisher
**Editorial:**
Kevin Griffin ...............................V.P. of Sales
**Desc.:** Features covering supermarkets,
superettes and the people who supply
them. Regulations, new lines, new
products, trade news, trends, market
outlook, etc. Page 1 devoted to news
and photos.
**Readers:** Retail and wholesale grocery
trade in New England and superettes.
Also manufacturers, brokers, and
salesmen.

23301
**GROCERY DISTRIBUTION
MAGAZINE**
455 S. Frontage Rd., 116
Burr Ridge, IL 60521
Telephone: (708) 986-8767
FAX: (708) 986-0206
Year Established: 1975
Pub. Frequency: bi-m.
Page Size: standard
Subscrip. Rate: $30/yr.; $40/2 yrs.
Materials: 01,15,27,28,29,30,32,33
Freelance Pay: $250-$400
Circulation: 16,000
Circulation Type: controlled
**Owner(s):**
Grocery Market Publications
455 S. Frontage Rd., 116
Burr Ridge, IL 60521
Telephone: (708) 986-8767
Ownership %: 100
**Management:**
Richard W. Mulville ...............................Publisher
Richard W. Mulville ...........Advertising Manager
Margaret Donohue ...............Business Manager
**Editorial:**
Richard W. Mulville .............................Editor
Thomas Smith ...................Contributing Editor
Henry Rockwell ...................Contributing Editor

**Desc.:** Interested in factual material related
to physical distribution systems
employed in food warehousing
operations. Product releases should be
on literature, equipment, fixtures, etc.
Prefer releases with photos. Also want
feature articles from equipment
manufacturers but suggest inquiry first.
Free lancers should inquire as most
articles are on assignment basis. Do not
use bylines. Very interested in working
with equipment/fixture manufacturers'
publicity staff to develop articles on
cooperative basis. Departments include:
Literature/Equipment/Fixtures, Industry
News, Supervisors' Section.
**Readers:** Operations managers/executives
responsible for operating warehouses
owned by food wholesalers, food
chains, food manufacturers,
convenience food store chains. Does
not include food buyers, merchandisers.
**Deadline:** story-varies; news-varies; photo-
varies; ads-15th of mo. prior to pub.
date

23298
**GROCERY MARKETING**
625 N. Michigan Ave.
Ste. 2500
Chicago, IL 60611-3109
Telephone: (312) 222-2000
FAX: (312) 222-2026
Year Established: 1933
Pub. Frequency: m.
Page Size: tabloid
Subscrip. Rate: $75/yr. US; $145/yr.
elsewhere
Materials: 01,02,04,06,15,21
Circulation: 63,000
Circulation Type: controlled
**Owner(s):**
Trend Publishing
625 N. Michigan Ave.
Ste. 2500
Chicago, IL 60611-3109
Telephone: (312) 654-2300
FAX: (312) 654-2323
Ownership %: 100
**Bureau(s):**
Gatty Communications
5460 Harris Farm Lane
Clarksville, MO 21029
Telephone: (301) 854-0660
FAX: (301) 854-0662
Contact: Bob Gatty
**Management:**
William J. D'Alexander ......................Publisher
Linda Teer .........................Production Manager
**Editorial:**
Bob Gatty ...............................Bureau Chief
Ryan Mathews .............................................Editor
Joanne Friedrick ...................Managing Editor
Bob Begley ......................Advertising Director
Debbie Ford .......Advertising Services Manager
Tracy Dougherty ...............................Art Director
Ryan Mathews .................Associate Publisher
**Desc.:** Serves the grocery industry
including chain headquarters and their
stores; independent grocery store
operators; grocery and general
merchandise wholesalers; cooperatives
and voluntaries; convenience chain
headquarters, food brokers, and
manufacturers.

**Readers:** Chain executives, buyers, store
managers and supervisors; wholesale
grocers (including voluntary and
cooperative) headquarters executives,
buyers and store supervisors;
executives, owners and managers of
independent supermarkets and
superettes; rack jobbers/service
merchandisers; food brokers and
manufactures.
**Deadline:** story-2 mos. prior to pub. date;
news-2 mos. prior; photo-2 mos. prior

23302
**GULF COAST GROCERY JOURNAL**
1300 Shepherd Dr.
Houston, TX 77007
Telephone: (713) 862-3001
FAX: (713) 862-5296
Mailing Address:
P.O. Box 7650
Houston, TX 77270
Year Established: 1940
Pub. Frequency: m.
Page Size: standard
Subscrip. Rate: free
Circulation: 2,000
Circulation Type: controlled & free
**Owner(s):**
Gulf Coast Grocery Association of Texas
1300 Shepherd Dr.
Houston, TX 77007
Telephone: (713) 862-3001
Ownership %: 100
**Editorial:**
Joe Williams ...............................Executive Editor
Kim Reister ...............................Associate Editor
**Desc.:** News of interest to store owners in
Gulf Coast. National rundown on
legislative matters, etc. Strictly news and
not in-depth features.
**Readers:** Store owners (grocers), food
manufacturers, distributors, rack jobbers,
etc.

23046
**HEALTH FOODS BUSINESS**
567 Morris Ave.
Elizabeth, NJ 07208
Telephone: (908) 353-7373
FAX: (908) 353-8221
Pub. Frequency: m.
Page Size: standard
Subscrip. Rate: $33/yr.
Materials: 01,02,05,06,10,15,25,28,29,32,33
Circulation: 12,000
Circulation Type: controlled & paid
**Owner(s):**
PTN Publishing Co.
445 Broad Hollow Rd.
Melville, NY 11747
Telephone: (516) 845-2700
Ownership %: 100
**Management:**
Howard Wasserman ...............................Publisher
**Editorial:**
Gina Geslewitz ...............................Editor
Mark Boles ...............................Managing Editor
Russ Fields ...............................Advertising

---

Materials Accepted/Included: 01-Business news 02-By-line articles 03-Fashion news 04-Food news 05-Freelance copy 06-Letters to editor 07-Real estate news 08-Sports news 09-Travel news 10-Book rev. 11-Movie rev. 12-Music rev. 13-TV rev. 14-Theater rev. 15-Coming events 16-Obituaries 17-Question & answer 18-Social announcements 19-Artwork 20-Cartoons 21-Photos 22-TV listings 23-Audio rec. 24-Video rec. 25-Books 26-Films/film clips 27-Personnel news 28-Press releases 29-New product news/photos 30-Trade lit. 31-Contracts awarded 32-Display adv. 33-Classified adv.

**Desc.:** Geared primarily towards the needs and interests of health food retailers with news and features designed to relate to those interests. Want business-oriented material not consumer or philosophically oriented copy. Mostly staff-written. Include freelance (mostly feature) articles and some by-line pieces by authorities or people of note in the industry. Unless exclusive to us, all P.R. releases are re-written. Want good, B&W glossy photos with news, new product and feature articles. Query first on features. Key criterion for everything is: Is this information important to retailers, will it help them do a better merchandising job and function better as businessmen. Departments include: News, New Products, Calendar of Events, Columnists, Consumer Education Series, Features.

### IGA GROCERGRAM
23303

1301 Carolina St.
Greensboro, NC 27401
Telephone: (910) 378-6065
FAX: (910) 275-2864
Year Established: 1926
Pub. Frequency: m.
Page Size: standard
Subscrip. Rate: $40/yr.
Circulation: 18,000
Circulation Type: paid
**Owner(s):**
Pace Communications, Inc.
1301 Carolina St.
Greensboro, NC 27401
Telephone: (910) 378-6065
Ownership %: 100
**Management:**
Bonnie McElveen-Hunter ....................Publisher
Mickey McLean .................Advertising Manager
**Editorial:**
Bill Hayes .......................................Editor in Chief
Mickey McLean ........................Managing Editor
Andy Lindsay .....................................Art Director
**Desc.:** Articles deal with retail food store operations, store engineering, supervision, as well as all phases of merchandising with emphasis on meat, produce, frozen foods, etc. Departments include: New Products, National Promotions, News.
**Readers:** IGA members, retail grocers, wholesalers, manufacturers.

### ILLINOIS FOOD RETAILERS' ASSOCIATION
23304

1919 S. Highland Ave.
Lombard, IL 60148
Telephone: (708) 627-8100
FAX: (708) 627-8106
Year Established: 1925
Pub. Frequency: a.
Page Size: standard
Subscrip. Rate: $4/issue
Circulation: 5,103
Circulation Type: controlled & free
**Owner(s):**
Illinois Food Retailers Association
1919 S. Highland Ave.
Lombard, IL 60148
Telephone: (708) 627-8100
Ownership %: 100
**Management:**
Brian R. Jordan .....................................Publisher
**Editorial:**
Brian R. Jordan .........................Managing Editor

**Desc.:** Retail food merchandising feature stories, information on sales techniques, new methods, store layouts, general food information, legislation pertaining to food store operators, product supply information, new trends in cookery. General information on association activities. Food Foto page; photos of new stores and remodelings. Short articles on supplier personnel/promotions, etc.
**Readers:** Retail food stores in Illinois.

### INFORMER, THE
23311

14 Commerce St.-Dundalk Ctr.
Baltimore, MD 21222
Telephone: (410) 285-6777
FAX: (410) 285-6404
Year Established: 1958
Pub. Frequency: q.
Page Size: standard
Subscrip. Rate: $15/yr.
Freelance Pay: negotiable
Circulation: 7,000
Circulation Type: controlled & paid
**Owner(s):**
Mid-Atlantic Food Dealers Association
14 Commerce St.-Dundalk Ctr.
Baltimore, MD 21222
Telephone: (410) 285-6777
Ownership %: 100
**Management:**
Carol McVey .........................................Publisher
**Editorial:**
Carol McVey ..............................................Editor
Roy Hobbs ........................................Advertising
Michael L. Spaur .............................News Editor
**Desc.:** Features factual, informative, topical news stories related to the mid-Atlantic area encompassing Maryland, Delaware, Washington, D.C., Northern Virginia and Southern New Jersey concerning the food distribution industry, including legislative activity. We charge for publicity material such as a product news release.
**Readers:** Independent and chain retailers, suppliers, distributors, top executives and sales staff. Convience stores, manufacturers and food brokers.

### INTERMOUNTAIN RETAILER
23305

1578 W. 1700 S., Ste. 200
Salt Lake City, UT 84104-3470
Telephone: (801) 973-9517
Year Established: 1924
Pub. Frequency: bi-m.
Page Size: standard
Subscrip. Rate: $12/yr.
Circulation: 1,200
Circulation Type: paid
**Owner(s):**
Utah Food Industry Association
1578 W. 1700 S., Ste. 200
Salt Lake Cty, UT 84104-3470
Telephone: (801) 973-9517
Ownership %: 100
**Editorial:**
James V. Olsen .........................................Editor
**Desc.:** Material of interest to Utah's food industry. The retailer is used as the paramount communication vehicle for Utah's food industry. Local news, new store openings, personnel promotions, social events, national news, operating ideas, legislative matters, trade releases.
**Readers:** Chain and Independent Retail Grocers, Convenience Store Owners and Operators, Food Industry Suppliers.

### IOWA GROCER
23306

2894 106th, Ste. 102
Des Moines, IA 50322
Telephone: (515) 270-2628
FAX: (515) 270-0316
Year Established: 1932
Pub. Frequency: s-m.
Page Size: standard
Subscrip. Rate: $25/yr.
Circulation: 2,000
Circulation Type: paid
**Owner(s):**
Grocers Services Co.
2894 106th, Ste. 102
Des Moines, IA 50322
Telephone: (515) 270-2628
Ownership %: 100
**Management:**
Trish Smallenberger ...........................Publisher
Chris Killough ...................Advertising Manager
Carol Popken .........................Office Manager
**Editorial:**
Chris Killough ...........................................Editor
Chris Killough .........................Circulation Editor
Trish Smallenberger ..........Legislative Director
Chris Killough .....................New Products Editor
Chris Killough .........................................Photo
**Desc.:** Articles on new regulations, management, sales techniques for the food members. Some new products, new lines coverage.
**Readers:** Retail food dealers, wholesale grocers, related food industry personnel.

### KANSAS CITY GROCER
23307

2809 W. 47th St.
Shawnee Mission, KS 66205
Telephone: (913) 384-3830
FAX: (913) 384-3868
Year Established: 1913
Pub. Frequency: m.
Subscrip. Rate: $25/yr.
Circulation: 1,825
Circulation Type: paid
**Owner(s):**
Kansas City Grocer
**Editorial:**
James G. Sheehan ....................................Editor
Mary Ann Gunn .......................Assistant Editor

### MAINE GROCER, THE
23310

1 Weston Ct.
Augusta, ME 04330
Telephone: (207) 622-4461
FAX: (207) 622-4461
Mailing Address:
   P.O. Box 5460
   Augusta, ME 04332
Year Established: 1987
Pub. Frequency: m.
Page Size: standard
Subscrip. Rate: free to members
Circulation: 1,200
Circulation Type: controlled
**Owner(s):**
Maine Grocers Association, Inc.
1 Weston Ct.
Augusta, ME 04330
Telephone: (207) 773-0968
Ownership %: 100
**Management:**
John Joyce ...........................................Publisher
Annie Lawrence ...............Advertising Manager
**Editorial:**
John Joyce .............................Managing Editor

**Desc.:** Reports on marketing developments, distributor expansion, price structure changes, government regulations, meetings, sales promotion developments. Interested in news with a Maine angle, as it affects the retail grocer. Has a publicity follow-up in monthly bulletin to association membership. Directory of business trade in Miami wholesale & retail stores.
**Readers:** Maine retail grocers, supermarket managers, trade suppliers.

### MICHIGAN FOOD NEWS
23312

221 N. Walnut
Lansing, MI 48933
Telephone: (517) 372-6800
FAX: (517) 372-3002
Year Established: 1946
Pub. Frequency: m.
Page Size: tabloid
Subscrip. Rate: $25/yr.
Circulation: 6,000
Circulation Type: controlled
**Owner(s):**
Michigan Grocers Service Corp.
221 N. Walnut
Lansing, MI 48933
Telephone: (517) 372-6800
Ownership %: 100
**Management:**
Cherie Smith .........................................Publisher
Cherie Smith ....................Advertising Manager
**Desc.:** News and news features of interest to the Michigan retail food merchant, including c-stores. Carries success stories of retailers who have built profitable business. Uses articles about suppliers based on tie-in with local dealer. Reports on new promotions, new lines and displays.
**Readers:** Retail grocery food merchants, convenience store owners, operators, wholesalers and brokers.

### MILITARY GROCER
26601

4800 Montgomery Ln.
Bethesda, MD 20814
Telephone: (301) 718-7600
FAX: (301) 710-7652
Year Established: 1991
Pub. Frequency: bi-m.
Page Size: standard
Subscrip. Rate: $40/yr.
Materials: 02,04,05,19,20,21,27,28,29,30,32
Freelance Pay: $150-$750
Print Process: web offset
Circulation: 12,000
Circulation Type: controlled
**Owner(s):**
Downey Communications, Inc.
4800 Montegomery Ln.
Bethesda, MD 20814
Telephone: (301) 718-7600
Ownership %: 100
**Management:**
Loretta M. Downey ..............................Publisher
Edward M. Douney ..............................Publisher
**Editorial:**
C.J. Moore III .............................................Editor
Karen Sulmonetti ....................Design Director
F. Clifton Smith ...........Regional Sales Manager
Michael J. Jennings .................V.P. Advertising
**Desc.:** Emphasizes on the "how to" or operational side of the commissary business as well as up to date news and policy information. Covers the latest concepts in store planning, stocking, merchandising and customer service.

**Materials Accepted/Included:** 01-Business news 02-By-line articles 03-Fashion news 04-Food news 05-Freelance copy 06-Letters to editor 07-Real estate news 08-Sports news 09-Travel news 10-Book rev. 11-Movie rev. 12-Music rev. 13-TV rev. 14-Theater rev. 15-Coming events 16-Obituaries 17-Question & answer 18-Social announcements 19-Artwork 20-Cartoons 21-Photos 22-TV listings 23-Audio rec. 24-Video rec. 25-Books 26-Films/film clips 27-Personnel news 28-Press releases 29-New product news/photos 30-Trade lit. 31-Contracts awarded 32-Display adv. 33-Classified adv.

4-169

**Readers:** Managers of U.S. military commissaries at headquarters, region and state level.
**Deadline:** story-60 days prior to pub. date; photo-30 days prior to pub. date; ads-45-60 days prior to pub. date

## MODERN GROCER
23315

15 Emerald St.
Hackensack, NJ 07601
Telephone: (201) 488-1800
Year Established: 1933
Pub. Frequency: s-m.
Page Size: tabloid
Subscrip. Rate: $32/yr.
Materials: 01,04,05,06,10,11,15,27,28,29, 30,32,33
Freelance Pay: negotiable
Print Process: web offset
Circulation: 19,613
Circulation Type: paid
**Owner(s):**
Grocers Publishing Co., Inc.
15 Emerald St.
Hackensack, NJ 07601
Telephone: (201) 488-1800
Ownership %: 100
**Management:**
Howard Ackerman ..............................Publisher
Milton Melendez ...............Production Manager
**Editorial:**
Howard Ackerman ..................................Editor
Robert Reiss ...........................Managing Editor
Marcia White .......Sales Manager/Food Service
Kevin Gallagher .................V.P./Sales Manager
**Desc.:** Twice monthly tabloid food trade publication, covering news pertinent to the retail trade. Also publishes monthly edition in Spanish, similar format and distribution.
**Readers:** Independent retail food operators, chains, distributors, buyers, executives, wholesalers, manufacturers and packers, and food brokers.
**Deadline:** story-14th & 15th of mo. prior to pub. date; news-14th & 15th of mo. prior; photo-14th & 15th of mo. prior; ads-14th & 15th of mo. prior

## MONTANA FOOD DISTRIBUTOR
23053

2700 Airport Way, Unit A
Helena, MT 59601
Telephone: (406) 449-6394
FAX: (406) 449-0647
Mailing Address:
P.O. Box 5775
Helena, MT 59604
Year Established: 1940
Pub. Frequency: m.
Page Size: 4 color photos/art
Subscrip. Rate: $1/newsstand; $10/yr.
Materials: 04,06,27,28,29,30,32,33
Freelance Pay: negotiable
Print Process: offset lithography
Circulation: 1,000
Circulation Type: free & paid
**Owner(s):**
Montana Food Distributors Association
2700 Airport Way, Unit A
Helena, MT 59601
Telephone: (406) 449-6394
Ownership %: 100
**Editorial:**
Harry Black ...........................................Editor
**Desc.:** Montana grocery news, news stories covering retail food trends, food news, Association news, featured articles.
**Readers:** Retail grocers, wholesalers, brokers, manufacturers, bottlers, food distributors, C-stores.
**Deadline:** story-25th of mo. prior to pub. date; news-25th of mo. prior; photo-25th of mo. prior; ads-25th of mo. prior

## NEBRASKA RETAILER
23317

11902 Elm St.
Omaha, NE 68144-4362
Telephone: (402) 333-4421
FAX: (402) 333-4336
Year Established: 1902
Pub. Frequency: bi-m.
Subscrip. Rate: $25/yr.
Circulation: 400
Circulation Type: paid
**Owner(s):**
Nebraska Retail Grocers Association, Inc.
Telephone: (402) 572-8991
Ownership %: 100
**Editorial:**
Kathy Siesken ......................................Editor
**Desc.:** Company development, market trends, merchandising ideas, promotion plans, government regulations.
**Readers:** Retail grocers.

## NEWS & FOOD REPORT
23319

110 Stark St.
Manchester, NH 03101-1977
Telephone: (603) 669-9333
Year Established: 1933
Pub. Frequency: bi-w.
Page Size: standard
Subscrip. Rate: $18/yr.
Materials: 01,02,04,06,15,16,17,18,19,20, 21,27,28,29,30,32,33
Print Process: offset
Circulation: 1,200
Circulation Type: paid
**Owner(s):**
New Hampshire Retail Grocers Association
110 Stark St.
Manchester, NH 03101-1977
Telephone: (603) 669-9333
Ownership %: 100
**Management:**
John M. Dumais ...................................President
Patricia Houde ...................Advertising Manager
**Editorial:**
John M. Dumais ....................................Editor
**Desc.:** Features, articles or stories which pertain to any segment of the food industry, especially retail grocers. Items may include subjects of promotion, sales trends, management ideas, financial assistance, interpretation of government regulations and stories relating to other retailers or suppliers.
**Readers:** For the New Hampshire area: retail chains, independent and convenience food stores. Most distribution establishments.
**Deadline:** story-15 days; news-15 days; photo-15 days

## OKLAHOMA GROCERS JOURNAL
23054

25 N.E. 52nd St.
Oklahoma City, OK 73105
Telephone: (405) 525-9419
Mailing Address:
P.O. Box 18716
Oklahoma City, OK 73154
Year Established: 1940
Pub. Frequency: m.
Page Size: standard
Subscrip. Rate: $5/yr.
Circulation: 1,500
Circulation Type: controlled
**Owner(s):**
Oklahoma Grocers Association
25 N.E. 52nd St.
Oklahoma City, OK 73105
Telephone: (405) 525-9419
Ownership %: 100
**Editorial:**
Elden G. Roscher ..................................Editor
Dianna L. Jones ........................Managing Editor

**Desc.:** Magazine is confined to food industry and their interests. Covers food store operation, market trends, new products, advertising promotions, and related subjects.
**Readers:** Our readers consist of independent retailers, food manufacturers, brokers, and wholesalers.

## PROGRESSIVE GROCER
23320

Four Stamford Forum
Stamford, CT 06901
Telephone: (203) 325-3500
FAX: (203) 325-4377
Mailing Address:
P.O. Box 10246
Stamford, CT 06904
Year Established: 1922
Pub. Frequency: m.
Page Size: standard
Subscrip. Rate: $75/yr.
Freelance Pay: varies
Circulation: 72,500
Circulation Type: paid
**Owner(s):**
Progressive Grocer Co.
Mclean Hunter Media Div.
4 Stamford Forum
Stamford, CT 06901
Telephone: (203) 325-3500
Ownership %: 100
**Bureau(s):**
Progressive Grocer
53 W. Jackson Blvd., Ste. 600
Chicago, IL 60604
Telephone: (312) 663-5560

Progressive Grocer
2015 Bridgeway-#301
Sausalito, CA 94965
Telephone: (510) 332-5121
Contact: Donald L. Raggio, Vice President
**Management:**
John W. Skeels ..................................President
Richard K. Hofler ......Executive Vice President
Walter H. Heller ......................Vice President
**Editorial:**
Steve Weinstein ....................Editor in Chief
Edgar B. Walzer ........................Editor in Chief
Glenn H. Snyder ........................Senior Editor
Michael Sansolo ................................Editor
Lee Dyer ..................................................Editor
Mary Ann Linsen ....................Managing Editor
Priscilla Donegan ...............Assistant Managing Editor
Jean B. DeVito ...................................Art Editor
Marjorie Wold ........................Assistant Editor
Warren Thayer ......................Associate Editor
Stephen Bennett ......................Associate Editor
Richard M. Petreycik ............Associate Editor
Lisa Caliendo ........................Editorial Assistant
Peter Rigney ....................................Field Editor
Lee W. Dyer ................Merchandising Director
**Desc.:** For executives of the food distribution industry and supermarket operators; practical articles on management, marketing and merchandising. Articles have case history approach. Profusely illustrated. Depth studies of product categories, store and corporate operations. Covers and illustrates new technology, new advertising, new products, point of sale display, new store formats, and packages.
**Readers:** Executives of chain and wholesale grocery companies, owners and managers of supermarkets.

## ROCKY MOUNTAIN FOOD DEALER
23321

1370 Pennsylvania St.
Ste. 320
Denver, CO 80203-5022
Telephone: (303) 830-7001
FAX: (303) 830-7040
Year Established: 1897
Pub. Frequency: q.
Page Size: standard
Subscrip. Rate: $15/yr.
Freelance Pay: $25-$35/article
Circulation: 1,500
Circulation Type: paid
**Owner(s):**
Rocky Mountain Food Dealers Assn.
Ownership %: 100
**Management:**
Mary Lou Chapman ............................Publisher
Mary Lou Chapman ...........Executive Director
**Editorial:**
Steve Byrne ...........................Managing Editor
**Desc.:** Covers food, food products, fixtures and food handling equipment. Legislative coverage on a local and national level of extreme importance to retailers. Merchandising ideas, money-saving techniques and other material of direct importance to the reader. Covers states of Colorado and Wyoming.
**Readers:** Retail grocers, food dealers, wholesalers, food brokers.

## SHELBY REPORT OF THE SOUTHEAST, THE
23322

517 Green St.
Gainesville, GA 30501
Telephone: (404) 534-8380
FAX: (404) 535-0110
Year Established: 1967
Pub. Frequency: m.
Page Size: tabloid
Subscrip. Rate: $25/yr.; $45/2 yrs.; $65/3 yrs.
Freelance Pay: negotiable
Circulation: 20,100
Circulation Type: paid
**Owner(s):**
Shelby Publishing Co., Inc.
517 Green St.
Gainesville, GA 30501
Telephone: (404) 534-8380
Ownership %: 100
**Management:**
Gary Shelby ......................................Founder
Gary G. Shelby ................................Publisher
Geri Reynolds ..................Circulation Manager
Karen Crowe ....................Office Manager
**Editorial:**
Chuck Gilmer ......................................Editor
Ileen Bloch ........................................Advertising
Ron Johnston ....................Assistant Publisher
Lorrie Griffith ....................Associate Editor
Diane Heller .....................Publication Director
Karen Kirkpatrick .................................Reporter
Stormie Elwanger ..................................Sales
Joye Jones ..............................................Sales
**Desc.:** News and features of retail food industry. Covers dairy & deli, general merchandise, health and beauty aids, produce, pet supplies, convenience stores, snacks, beverages, meats, ethnic foods, frozen foods, bakery, new products, supermarket & warehouse technology, and breakfast foods.
**Readers:** Food distributors, food brokers, food retailers, food wholesalers, food co-ops, food headquarter accounts, food manufacturers, advertising agencies.

## SUPERMARKET BUSINESS
23328

1086 Teaneck Rd.
Teaneck, NJ 07666-4838
Telephone: (201) 833-1900
FAX: (201) 833-1273
Year Established: 1945
Pub. Frequency: m.
Page Size: tabloid
Subscrip. Rate: $70/yr.
Circulation: 76,693
Circulation Type: paid
**Owner(s):**
Howfrey Communications
1086 Teaneck Rd.
Teaneck, NJ 07666-4838
Telephone: (201) 833-1900
FAX: (201) 833-1273
Ownership %: 100
**Management:**
Jeffrey Schaeffer ......................President
Catherine Cahill ..........................Vice President
Jeffrey Schaeffer ......................Publisher
**Editorial:**
Kenneth P. Partch .....................Editor in Chief
Amy Lipton ...............................Senior Editor
Mike Duff ...............................Senior Editor
Tom Weir ...............................Managing Editor
Lauren Lekoski ........................Associate Editor
Carol Fensholt .........................Associate Publisher
Robert Dietrich .........................Contributing Editor
Barney McClure ........................Contributing Editor
Richard Shulman ......................Contributing Editor
John Baskin ...............................Contributing Editor
David Litwak ...........................Research Director
**Desc.:** All news of the food field of interest
to food retailers, particularly if slanted to
retailers or expressing their viewpoint.
Audience is food store operators,
supermarkets, including chains,
wholesalers and independents. Covers
government regulations, trade news,
trends department management.
Sections include: Equipment and
Supplies, General Merchandise/HBA,
New Products, Promotions and
Packaging. Columns include:
Management, Technology, Engineering,
Business Development, Meat, Produce,
Deli/Bakery, Store Planning, Marketing.
New products and packages pictures
are used in special department/ should
be stills without models. Display
pictures should have store background,
with more than one manufacturers
products shown. News pictures
should be candid as possible.
**Readers:** Retail grocery stores,
supermarkets, chains, wholesalers.

## TEXAS FOOD MERCHANT
23059

7333 Hwy. 290 E.
Austin, TX 78723
Telephone: (512) 926-9285
FAX: (512) 926-0917
Year Established: 1934
Pub. Frequency: bi-m.
Page Size: 8 1/2 x 11
Subscrip. Rate: $24/yr.
Materials: 01,02,04,15,23,25,27,28,29,30
Print Process: offset
Circulation: 3,600
Circulation Type: paid
**Owner(s):**
Texas Food Industry Association
7333 Hwy. 290 E.
Austin, TX 78723
Telephone: (512) 926-9285
Ownership %: 100
**Bureau(s):**
K. Celeste Seay
**Management:**
Rick Johnson ...............................Publisher
K. Celeste Seay ......................Advertising Manager

**Editorial:**
K. Celeste Seay .....................Executive Editor
K. Celeste Seay .....................New Products Editor
**Desc.:** News articles and self-help articles
for the retail grocer and others in the
food industry. Covers management,
stock analysis, fire insurance and
control, credit, inventory keeping, trends,
association news. Also reports on new
products, advertising campaigns, political
activity influencing grocers, government
regulations, etc.
**Readers:** Retail grocer; food industry
suppliers.
**Deadline:** story-10th of mo. prior to pub.
date; news-10th of mo. prior to pub.
date; photo-10th of mo. prior

## TRI-STATE FOOD NEWS
23060

P.O. Box 6429
Pittsburgh, PA 15212
Telephone: (412) 856-7400
FAX: (412) 856-7954
Year Established: 1955
Pub. Frequency: m.
Page Size: tabloid
Subscrip. Rate: $10/yr.
Freelance Pay: negotiable
Circulation: 26,341
Circulation Type: paid
**Owner(s):**
Bill Heufelder
P.O. Box 6429
Pittsburgh, PA 15212
Telephone: (412) 856-7400
Ownership %: 100
**Management:**
Bill Heufelder ...............................Publisher
**Desc.:** Carries news features, product
information of interest having effect on
the retail and wholesale food industry.
Departments include: News, Features,
People, Products and Promotions,
Equipment, Financial.
**Readers:** Food store owners, managers
and supervisors, purchasing agents of
chain warehouses, wholesale grocers,
food brokers, and manufacturers.

## WASHINGTON FOOD DEALER MAGAZINE
23330

480 E. 19th St.
Tacoma, WA 98421
Telephone: (800) 732-1889
FAX: (206) 272-2723
Mailing Address:
480 E. 19th St.
Tacoma, WA 98421
Year Established: 1905
Pub. Frequency: q.
Page Size: 4 Color Photos/Art
Subscrip. Rate: $20/yr.
Circulation: 5,200
Circulation Type: paid
**Owner(s):**
Washington State Food Dealers Assn.
480 E. 19th St.
Tacoma, WA 98421
Ownership %: 100
**Management:**
Doug Henken .....................Executive Director
**Editorial:**
Bob Sheffels .....................Managing Editor
Bob Sheffels .....................Advertising

**Desc.:** Devoted to providing valuable
information to independent and chain
retail food dealers and the grocery
industry as a whole with a relevant,
regionalized perspective. Covers new
products, company news, government
regulations, local, regional and national
news affecting the industry, association
activities, trends, store operations,
technology for grocers,
convenience stores.
**Readers:** Retail grocers, grocery buyers,
brokers, wholesalers and suppliers in
Washington State and Alaska.

## Group 112-Hardware

### DO-IT-YOURSELF RETAILING
23338

5822 W. 74th St.
Indianapolis, IN 46278
Telephone: (317) 297-1190
FAX: (317) 328-4354
Year Established: 1901
Pub. Frequency: m.
Page Size: standard
Subscrip. Rate: $15/yr.
Freelance Pay: negotiable
Circulation: 70,000
Circulation Type: paid
**Owner(s):**
National Retail Hardware Association
5822 W. 74th St.
Indianapolis, IN 46278
Telephone: (317) 290-0338
Ownership %: 100
**Management:**
John P. Hammond ...............................Publisher
Vicky Ramage .....................Circulation Manager
**Editorial:**
Mark Parrott ...............................Editor
Chris Jensen .....................Managing Editor
Ellen E. Hackney .......Communications Director
Vicky Ramage .....................Production Director
**Desc.:** Emphasis on merchandising
management and marketing in the retail
hardware and home center field.
Contributed features stress practical
approach to better selling and
management. Develops original
research, emphasizes creative editing to
illustrate "how- to" in sales building and
promotion. Reports industry news, new
products, displays, literature. Heavily
staff-written.
**Readers:** Hardware and home center
retailers, store personnel, wholesale
representatives.

### DOORS & HARDWARE
23333

14170 Newbrook Dr.
Chantilly, VA 22021-2223
Telephone: (703) 222-2010
FAX: (703) 222-2410
Year Established: 1936
Pub. Frequency: m.
Page Size: standard
Subscrip. Rate: $4/issue; $45/yr.
Freelance Pay: $250-$350
Circulation: 9,500
Circulation Type: controlled
**Owner(s):**
Door and Hardware Institute
14170 Newbrook Dr.
Chantilly, VA 22021-2223
Telephone: (703) 222-2010
Ownership %: 100
**Management:**
Shari Monro .....................Advertising Manager
Wanda Krupinski ...............Production Manager
**Editorial:**
Richard M. Hornaday ...............Executive Editor
Cameron Bishopp .....................Associate Editor
Marta Robinson .....................Creative Director
A. Michie Shaw .....................Publication Director

Kristina Cooper ...............Publications Assistant
**Desc.:** Technical and professional news
exchange about the commercial builders
hardware field, including educational,
informational and opinion pieces about
the trade.
**Readers:** 60% hardware distributors, 30%
other industry personnel, 10%
architects.

### HARDWARE TRADE
23340

10510 France Ave. N.
Ste. 225
Bloomington, MN 55431
Telephone: (612) 944-3172
FAX: (612) 941-3543
Year Established: 1890
Pub. Frequency: bi-m.
Page Size: standard
Subscrip. Rate: $12/yr.
Circulation: 17,242
Circulation Type: paid
**Owner(s):**
Screened Porch Publishing Co.
10510 France Ave. S.
Ste. 225
Bloomington, MN 55431
Telephone: (612) 944-3172
FAX: (612) 941-3543
Ownership %: 100
**Bureau(s):**
Master Publishers, Inc.
2965 Broadmore Vly. Rd., Ste B
Colorado Spgs , CO 80906
Contact: Edward Gonzales, Editor
**Management:**
Sue Connelly ...............................Publisher
**Editorial:**
Sue Connelly ...............................Editor
James Lange .....................Advertising Director
Ken Peterson .....................Circulation Director
**Desc.:** Case history type stories on
successful hardware, lumber, sporting
goods, and home center
dealers. Departments include new
products, general news on hardware
manufacturers, wholesalers and dealers,
readers' viewpoint column,
feature articles on manufacturers,
wholesalers, dealers.
**Readers:** Home Centers, Do - It - Yourself
Stores. Hardware wholesalers, home
center headquarters lumberyard,
discount stores, hardware stores, in 23
Northern, Northwestern States.

### LOCKSMITH LEDGER INTERNATIONAL
23339

850 Busse Hwy.
Park Ridge, IL 60068
Telephone: (708) 692-5940
FAX: (708) 692-4604
Year Established: 1939
Pub. Frequency: 13/yr.
Page Size: standard
Subscrip. Rate: $36/yr.
Materials: 01,02,05,06,27,28,29,30,31,32,33
Freelance Pay: $2.50/col. in.; $5/photo
Print Process: offset
Circulation: 24,000
Circulation Type: paid
**Owner(s):**
Locksmith Publishing Corp.
850 Busse Hwy.
Park Ridge, IL 60068
Telephone: (708) 692-5940
Ownership %: 100
**Management:**
Steven Lasky ...............................Publisher
Robert Swoope .....................Advertising Manager
Dan Koch .....................Circulation Manager
**Editorial:**
Gale Johnson ...............................Editor
Pam Anderson ...............................Editor

Gale Porter ..................................Advertising
Denise Covelli ......................Associate Editor
Steven Lasky ..................................Director
Alyssa Proksa ........................Graphics Editor
Maria Sofierman ....................Marketing Director
Jerry Levine ..........................Technical Editor
**Desc.:** Technical news magazine for the physical and electronic security industry worldwide. It is the "Technical How-To" publication edited to serve the beginner as well as the seasoned professional. Editorial presents material on various security equipment and devices involved in residential, commercial, industrial, government and municipal applications. Editorial covers locksmith techniques, alarms, safes, codes, tools, shop management, padlocks, key machines, Tricks of the Trade, security standards, door closures. Included is coverage on new products, legislation, trade and industry news, personnel, technical tips, wholesale directory, calendar of events, question & answer column, association news.
**Readers:** Locksmiths, keymakers, hardwaremen, alarm installers, and security professionals.
**Deadline:** story-2 mo. prior to pub. date; news-2 mo. prior; photo-2 mo. prior; ads-2 mo. prior

23335
**OUTDOOR POWER EQUIPMENT**
One Chilton Way
Radnor, PA 19087
Telephone: (215) 964-4275
Year Established: 1950
Pub. Frequency: m.
Page Size: 6 X 9
Subscrip. Rate: $16/yr.
Materials: 01,06,15,16,19,21,27,28,29,32,33
Freelance Pay: varies
Circulation: 21,000
Circulation Type: controlled
**Owner(s):**
Capital Cities-ABC, Inc.
77 W. 66th St.
New York, NY 10023
Telephone: (212) 456-7771
Ownership %: 100
**Management:**
Thomas L. Delph ............................Publisher
Ken Battista ....................Circulation Manager
**Editorial:**
Terrence V. Gallagher ..........................Editor
Richard L. Carter ....................Managing Editor
Kristen Wright ..............................Art Director
Karen Lallone ....................Production Director
Janet Baldwin ............Senior Associate Editor
Jon Hoover ..................Senior Associate Editor
**Desc.:** Articles on store management, successful merchandising methods, display and modernization for the outdoor power equipment dealer. Uses case histories illustrating successful volume-building techniques, improved store layouts, displays, etc. Carries trade news, personnel appointments, new product information.
**Readers:** Cross-section of outdoor power equipment industry.

23336
**WESTERN RETAILER**
P.O. Box 419264
Kansas City, MO 64141
Telephone: (816) 561-5323
FAX: (816) 561-1249
Year Established: 1897
Pub. Frequency: m.
Page Size: standard
Subscrip. Rate: $12/yr.
Materials: 01,05
Print Process: 01
Circulation: 1,560

Circulation Type: controlled & paid
**Owner(s):**
Western Retail Implement & Hardware Assn.
P.O. Box 19264
Kansas City, MO 64141
Telephone: (816) 561-5323
**Management:**
Jeffrey H. Flora ..............................Publisher
**Editorial:**
Mike Griffith ..................................Editor
**Desc.:** Carries trade news, helpful feature articles on management, and merchandising in Missouri, Kansas, Nebraska, Oklahoma, and Arkansas. News releases used only in trade topics and new products review. Must relate to products available through midwest jobbers and to midwest trade news. Uses localized "dealers' doings" items.
**Readers:** Composed mainly of hardware and farm equipment dealers in Missouri, Nebraska, Arkansas, Kansas, and Oklahoma. Balance to jobber executives.

## Group 114-Health Care & Hospital Management

67031
**AHA NEWS**
737 N. Michigan Ave.
Chicago, IL 60611-2615
Telephone: (312) 440-6800
FAX: (312) 951-8491
Year Established: 1987
Pub. Frequency: w.
Page Size: tabloid
Subscrip. Rate: $100/yr. non-member
Materials: 32
Print Process: web offset
Circulation: 30,000
Circulation Type: controlled
**Owner(s):**
American Hospital Publishing Inc.
737 N. Michigan Ave.
Chicago, IL 60611
Telephone: (312) 440-6800
Ownership %: 100
**Management:**
John Sheehy ..............................Publisher
**Editorial:**
Barbara Varro ..............................Editor
**Readers:** Administration, governing board members, allied associations, AHA House of Delegates, Congress (House & Senate), libraries, schools, government agencies, manufacturers of hospital equipment, commercial service organizations, other health care professionals.
**Deadline:** ads-2 wks. prior to pub. date

23370
**AOHA PROGRESS**
5301 Wisconsin Ave., NW, Ste. 630
Washington, DC 20015
Telephone: (202) 686-1700
FAX: (202) 686-7615
Year Established: 1955
Pub. Frequency: m.
Page Size: standard
Subscrip. Rate: $25/yr.
Freelance Pay: negotiable
Circulation: 2,300
Circulation Type: paid
**Owner(s):**
American Osteopathic Healthcare Association
5301 Wisconsin Ave. N.W., Ste. 630
Washington, DC 20015
Telephone: (202) 686-1700
FAX: (202) 686-7615
Ownership %: 100
**Management:**
David Kushner ..............................Publisher

**Editorial:**
Susan Sagusti ..............................Editor
**Desc.:** Covers wide range of osteopathic hospital administrative material to increase understanding of issues, suggest improved management technique. Association news, information on member hospitals, statistical reports on osteopathic hospital activity, interpretation of significant data, information on osteopathic accreditation program, legislative and regulatory issues. 8 - 12 double - spaced typwritten pages. Black and white photos only. Departments include: Chairman's Letter, President's Page, Osteopathic Trends, Washington Outlook, People, Making the Rounds, & Hospital Literature, Letters.
**Readers:** Osteopathic hospital CEOs, trustees and other health care executives.

61577
**BUSINESS & HEALTH**
5 Paragon Dr.
Montvale, NJ 07645
Telephone: (201) 358-7208
FAX: (201) 573-1045
Year Established: 1983
Pub. Frequency: 14/yr.
Page Size: standard
Subscrip. Rate: $99/yr.; $136/yr. foreign
Circulation: 35,299
Circulation Type: controlled & paid
**Owner(s):**
Medical Economics Publishing Co., Inc.
5 Paragon Dr.
Montvale, NJ 07645
Telephone: (201) 358-7200
**Management:**
Elizabeth Clifford ..............................Publisher
**Editorial:**
Joe Burnes ..............................Editor
Phil Beninato ..............................Advertising
Bill Nelligan ..............................Advertising
**Desc.:** Covers the health policy and cost management aspects of a broad range of health care issues. Such as employee and retiree benefits, disability, and rehabilitation management and health promotion.
**Readers:** Corporate employers.

67683
**CONTEMPORARY LONG-TERM CARE**
355 Park Ave. S.
3rd Fl.
New York, NY 10010-1706
Year Established: 1977
Pub. Frequency: m.
Page Size: standard
Subscrip. Rate: $35/yr.
Circulation: 36,000
Circulation Type: controlled
**Owner(s):**
Bill Communications, Inc.
633 Third Ave.
Akron, OH 44309
Telephone: (216) 867-4401
Ownership %: 100
**Management:**
Russell Piersons ..............................Publisher
Vince Cavaseno ............Advertising Manager
**Editorial:**
Jim Bowe ..............................Editor

66614
**DERMATOLOGY TIMES**
7500 Old Oak Blvd.
Cleveland, OH 44130
Telephone: (216) 826-2839
FAX: (216) 891-2726
Year Established: 1979
Pub. Frequency: m.

Page Size: tabloid
Subscrip. Rate: $75/yr.
Print Process: offset
Circulation: 7,562
Circulation Type: paid
**Owner(s):**
Advanstar Communications, Inc.
7500 Old Oak Blvd.
Cleveland, OH 44130
Telephone: (216) 826-2839
Ownership %: 100
**Bureau(s):**
Edgell Communications, Inc.
7500 Old Oak Blvd.
Cleveland, OH 44130
Telephone: (216) 243-8100
Contact: Dean Celia, Editor in Chief
**Management:**
Bern Rogers ..............................President
Roger Soderman ..............................Publisher
**Editorial:**
Dean Celia ..............................Editor in Chief
Bruce Millar ..............................Executive Editor
Norman Levine ..............................Consulting Editor
**Desc.:** A scientific specialty tabloid newspaper providing fast, accurate news of dermatology.
**Readers:** All dermatologists involved in patient care.

64986
**EVALUATION & THE HEALTH PROFESSIONS**
2455 Teller Rd.
Thousand Oaks, CA 91320
Telephone: (805) 499-0721
FAX: (805) 499-0871
Year Established: 1975
Pub. Frequency: q.
Page Size: standard
Subscrip. Rate: $144/yr. individuals; $50/yr. institutions
Circulation: 1,100
Circulation Type: paid
**Owner(s):**
Sage Publications, Inc.
2455 Teller Rd.
Thousand Oaks, CA 91320
**Editorial:**
R. Barker Bausell ..............................Editor
**Desc.:** Provides a forum for all health professionals interested or engaged in the development, implementation, and evaluation of health programs.
**Readers:** Academic communities.

23798
**FACETS**
515 N. State St.
Chicago, IL 60610
Telephone: (312) 464-4470
FAX: (312) 464-5839
Year Established: 1965
Pub. Frequency: bi-m.
Page Size: Standard
Subscrip. Rate: $7/yr.
Freelance Pay: $500-$800
Circulation: 57,000
Circulation Type: controlled
**Owner(s):**
AMA Alliance
515 N. State St.
Chicago, IL 60610
Telephone: (312) 464-4470
Ownership %: 100
**Management:**
Barabara Tippins ..............................President
Hazel J. Lewis ..............................Executive Director
**Editorial:**
Kathleen T. Jordan ..............................Editor

**Materials Accepted/Included:** 01-Business news 02-By-line articles 03-Fashion news 04-Food news 05-Freelance copy 06-Letters to editor 07-Real estate news 08-Sports news 09-Travel news 10-Book rev. 11-Movie rev. 12-Music rev. 13-TV rev. 14-Theater rev. 15-Coming events 16-Obituaries 17-Question & answer 18-Social announcements 19-Artwork 20-Cartoons 21-Photos 22-TV listings 23-Audio rec. 24-Video rec. 25-Books 26-Films/film clips 27-Personnel news 28-Press releases 29-New product news/photos 30-Trade lit. 31-Contracts awarded 32-Display adv. 33-Classified adv.

**Desc.:** Features related to community health issues and project activities of AMA Auxiliary members (doctors' spouses), plus physician-spouse-family relationships and financial concerns. Articles run 1,500-2,000 words. Bylines given on all articles. Departments include: Issues of Health Concerns, Events of Auxiliary Concern, People--Doctors' Spouses, Legislative Update, new literature pertaining to health.
**Readers:** All doctors' spouses; most are members of AMA Auxiliary.

58735
### FAMILY & COMMUNITY HEALTH
200 Orchard Ridge Dr.
Gaithersburg, MD 20878
Telephone: (301) 417-7500
FAX: (301) 417-7550
Year Established: 1978
Pub. Frequency: q.
Page Size: standard
Subscrip. Rate: $95/yr.
Circulation: 1,900
Circulation Type: paid
**Owner(s):**
Aspen Publishers, Inc.
200 Orchard Ridge Dr.
Gaithersburg, MD 20878
Telephone: (301) 417-7500
Ownership %: 100
**Editorial:**
Donald Delauter ...........................Senior Editor
Jack Bruggeman ......................Editorial Director
Donna Selig ...............................Assistant Editor
Lorraine Davis ..............Senior Managing Editor
**Desc.:** Peer-reviewed journal providing practical information that addresses the common goals of health care practitioners, regardless of area of practice, in teaching the essentials of self-care, family and community health care, and health promotion and maintenance.
**Readers:** Health care professionals with an interest in prevention and maintenance, public health nurses and educators, and health policymakers.

66714
### FAULKNER & GRAY'S MEDICINE & HEALTH
1133 15th St., N.W., Ste. 450
Washington, DC 20005
Telephone: (202) 828-4148
FAX: (202) 828-2352
Year Established: 1946
Pub. Frequency: w.
Subscrip. Rate: $450/yr.
**Owner(s):**
Faulkner & Gray, Inc., Thomson Publishing Group
1133 15th St., N.W., Ste. 450
Washington, DC 20005
Telephone: (202) 828-4150
Ownership %: 100
**Editorial:**
Janet Firshein ...............................Editor

69594
### FRONTIERS OF HEALTH SERVICES MANAGEMENT
1021 E. Huron St.
Ann Arbor, MI 48104-9990
Telephone: (312) 943-0544
Year Established: 1984
Pub. Frequency: q.
Page Size: standard
Subscrip. Rate: $60/yr.
Circulation: 2,500
Circulation Type: paid

**Owner(s):**
Health Administration Press
1021 E. Huron St.
Ann Arbor, MI 48104-9990
Telephone: (312) 943-0544
Ownership %: 100
**Editorial:**
Douglas A. Conrad ......................................Editor
**Desc.:** Focuses on directions in health services management and policies. Each issue examines a single topic in depth.

66715
### HEALTH BUSINESS
1133 15th St., N.W., Ste. 450
Washington, DC 20005
Telephone: (202) 828-4148
Year Established: 1985
Pub. Frequency: w.
Subscrip. Rate: $595/yr.
**Owner(s):**
Faulkner & Gray, Inc., Thomson Publishing Group
1133 15th St., N.W., Ste. 450
Washington, DC 20005
Telephone: (202) 828-4150
**Editorial:**
John Reichard .............................................Editor

56409
### HEALTHCARE EXECUTIVE
840 N. Lake Shore Dr.
Chicago, IL 60611
Telephone: (312) 943-0544
FAX: (312) 943-3791
Year Established: 1985
Pub. Frequency: bi-m.
Page Size: standard
Subscrip. Rate: $35/yr. in US; $47/yr. foreign
Materials: 02,05,06,27,28,32
Freelance Pay: varies
Print Process: web offset
Circulation: 28,000
Circulation Type: controlled
**Owner(s):**
American College of Healthcare Executives
840 N. Lake Shore Dr.
Chicago, IL 60611
Telephone: (312) 943-0544
Ownership %: 100
**Management:**
Lynn D. Kahn ..........................................Publisher
Joan Diekman ......................Business Manager
**Editorial:**
Walter Wachel ...........................Editor in Chief
Lynn D. Kahn ..............Communications Director
**Desc.:** Written and edited for healthcare executives in hospitals, ambulatory care centers, managed care settings, universities, and consulting firms. Each issue focuses on a single topic such as human resources, careers, physicians, or governance. Articles focus on new and emerging healthcare trends case studies, practical solutions to management problems.
**Readers:** Healthcare experts who operate/manage hospitals, healthcare agencies; consultants, university program faculty.

23359
### HEALTHCARE FINANCIAL MANAGEMENT
Two Westbrook Corporate Ctr.
Westchester, IL 60154-5700
Telephone: (708) 531-9600
FAX: (708) 531-0032
Year Established: 1946
Pub. Frequency: m.
Page Size: standard
Subscrip. Rate: $70/yr. non-members
Materials: 06,20,28,29,32,33
Circulation: 33,000
Circulation Type: controlled

**Owner(s):**
Healthcare Financial Management Assn.
Two Westbrook Corporate Ctr.
Westchester, IL 60154
Telephone: (708) 531-9600
Ownership %: 100
**Bureau(s):**
Healthcare Financial Management Assn.
1050 17th St., NW, Ste. 700
Washington, DC 20036
Telephone: (202) 296-2920
Contact: Wendy W. Herr, Bureau Chief
**Management:**
Dianne Lach ....................Advertising Manager
Ralph Gutierrez ................Production Manager
**Editorial:**
Jake Jaquet .........................Managing Editor
Cheryl Stachura ..............Editor & Publisher
Paul Manus .........................Feature Editor
Bill Siwicki ...............................News Editor
**Desc.:** Editorial material covers the following areas in depth: technical articles covering the management and financial operations inherent in healthcare administration; Association news; articles on the applications of new procedures and systems in accounting, financial management, electronic data processing, communications and financial reporting.
**Readers:** Members of the Association who include hospital administrators, chief financial officers, office managers, accountants and related persons involved with the administrative and financial procedures of healthcare management.
**Deadline:** ads-20th of mo., 2 mo. prior to pub. date

23360
### HEALTHCARE FORUM JOURNAL
830 Market St., 8th Fl.
San Francisco, CA 94102
Telephone: (415) 421-8810
FAX: (415) 421-8837
Year Established: 1958
Pub. Frequency: bi-m.
Page Size: standard
Subscrip. Rate: $45/yr.; $80/2 yrs.
Freelance Pay: varies
Circulation: 26,400
Circulation Type: controlled & paid
**Owner(s):**
Healthcare Forum, The
830 Market St.
San Francisco, CA 94102
Telephone: (415) 421-8810
Ownership %: 100
**Management:**
Kathryn E. Johnson ............................Publisher
M. Gayle Samuelson ........Advertising Manager
**Editorial:**
Susan Anthony ...............................Editor
Susan Sasenick ......................Managing Editor
Lance B. Levy .........Advertising Account Exec.
**Desc.:** Informative articles written by experts in the field on current healthcare trends and practices. Recent editions focused on quality, benchmarking and integrated healthcare systems. Articles submitted usually run from five to ten typewritten, double-spaced pages.
**Readers:** Hospital CEO's and top-level healthcare executives nationwide.

58726
### HEALTH CARE MANAGEMENT REVIEW
200 Orchard Ridge Dr.
Gaithersburg, MD 20878
Telephone: (301) 417-7500
FAX: (301) 417-7550
Year Established: 1975
Pub. Frequency: q.

Page Size: standard
Subscrip. Rate: $99/yr.
Circulation: 2,400
Circulation Type: paid
**Owner(s):**
Aspen Publishers, Inc.
200 Orchard Ridge Dr.
Gaithersburg, MD 20878
Telephone: (301) 417-7500
Ownership %: 100
**Editorial:**
Lenda Hill ...............................Managing Editor
Jack Bruggeman .......................Editorial Director
**Desc.:** Provides health care administrators with savvy, on-target information and key developments in the health care field. Each issue features hard-hitting, practical information from leading practitioners who share their insights and expertise on the key aspects of health care finance, marketing, management policy, operations, reimbursement, regulations, corporate restructuring, health planning, cost containment, antitrust laws, quality control, labor relations, and new technology.
**Readers:** Hospital and health care administrators, assistant administrators, CEO's, financial managers, board members, consultants, and other health care executives.

69600
### HEALTH CARE STRATEGIC MANAGEMENT
5350 S. Roslyn St., Ste. 400
Englewood, CO 80111-2145
Telephone: (303) 290-8500
FAX: (303) 290-9025
Year Established: 1983
Pub. Frequency: m.
Subscrip. Rate: $187/yr.
Circulation: 1,500
Circulation Type: paid
**Owner(s):**
Business World, Inc.
5350 S. Roslyn St., Ste. 400
Englewood, CO 80111-2145
Telephone: (303) 290-8500
Ownership %: 100

58693
### HEALTH CARE SUPERVISOR, THE
200 Orchard Ridge Dr.
Gaithersburg, MD 20878
Telephone: (301) 417-7500
FAX: (301) 417-7550
Year Established: 1982
Pub. Frequency: q.
Page Size: standard
Subscrip. Rate: $99/yr. US; $119/yr. foreign
Materials: 06,10,15,17,32
Print Process: DTP
Circulation: 3,500
Circulation Type: paid
**Owner(s):**
Aspen Publishers, Inc.
200 Orchard Ridge Dr.
Gaithersburg, MD 20878
Telephone: (301) 417-7500
Ownership %: 100
**Editorial:**
Charles R. McConnell ...........................Editor
Lenda Hill ...............................Managing Editor
Jack Bruggeman .................Associate Publisher
**Desc.:** Provides ready-to-use, cost-effective solutions and expert guidance for all health care supervisors, focusing directly on supervisory management skills. Each topical issue features valuable insights and practical information from a team of distinguished health care authorities on how to become a more effective supervisor.

**Materials Accepted/Included:** 01-Business news 02-By-line articles 03-Fashion news 04-Food news 05-Freelance copy 06-Letters to editor 07-Real estate news 08-Sports news 09-Travel news 10-Book rev. 11-Movie rev. 12-Music rev. 13-TV rev. 14-Theater rev. 15-Coming events 16-Obituaries 17-Question & answer 18-Social announcements 19-Artwork 20-Cartoons 21-Photos 22-TV listings 23-Audio rec. 24-Video rec. 25-Books 26-Films/film clips 27-Personnel news 28-Press releases 29-New product news/photos 30-Trade lit. 31-Contracts awarded 32-Display adv. 33-Classified adv.

4-173

**Readers:** Administrators, directors, managers, and supervisors in all hospital administrative and clinical departments.

### HEALTH EDUCATION QUARTERLY
65603

605 Third Ave.
New York, NY 10158
Telephone: (212) 850-6000
Year Established: 1973
Pub. Frequency: q.
Subscrip. Rate: $205/yr.
Circulation: 2,000
Circulation Type: paid
**Owner(s):**
John Wiley & Sons, Inc.
605 Third Ave.
New York, NY 10158
Telephone: (212) 850-6289
**Editorial:**
Noreen M. Clark ...........................................Editor

### HEALTH MANAGEMENT QUARTERLY
68918

One Baxter Pkwy.
Deerfield, IL 60015-4633
Telephone: (708) 948-2000
FAX: (708) 948-2887
Year Established: 1979
Pub. Frequency: q.
Subscrip. Rate: free
Circulation: 10,000
Circulation Type: controlled & free
**Owner(s):**
The Baxter Foundation
One Baxter Pkwy.
Deerfield, IL 60015
Telephone: (708) 948-2000
FAX: (708) 948-2887
Ownership %: 100
**Editorial:**
Philip J. Smith ..........................................Editor
**Readers:** Healthcare managers in hospitals and other medical facilities.

### HEALTH PROGRESS
23361

4455 Woodson Rd.
St. Louis, MO 63134
Telephone: (314) 427-2500
FAX: (314) 427-0029
Year Established: 1920
Pub. Frequency: 10/yr.
Page Size: standard
Subscrip. Rate: $40/yr.
Freelance Pay: varies
Circulation: 13,800
Circulation Type: paid
**Owner(s):**
Catholic Health Association
4455 Woodson Rd.
St. Louis, MO 63134
Telephone: (314) 427-2500
Ownership %: 100
**Bureau(s):**
CHA Washington Office
1776 K St.
Washington, DC 20006
Telephone: (202) 296-3993
Contact: William Cox, Vice President
**Management:**
John E. Curley, Jr. ...........................President
Michael F. McCauley ...............Vice President
Kim Hewitt .....................Circulation Manager
**Editorial:**
Michael F. McCauley ...........Executive Editor
Judy Cassidy ......................................Editor
Susan Hume ...................Managing Editor
Lisa Mathieson ...........................Advertising
Michelle Hey ..........................Assistant Editor
Gordon Burnside ..................Assistant Editor
Sandy Best ..................Production Coordinator

**Desc.:** Coverage of legislative, ethical, administrative, and legal issues among others for administrators, religious sponsors, department heads, trustees, physicians, nurses and other personnel in US Catholic health facilities.
**Readers:** Hospital administrators, department heads, sponsoring groups, boards of trustees.

### HEALTH TEXAS
23373

6225 U.S. Hwy. 290 E.
Austin, TX 78723
Telephone: (512) 465-1050
FAX: (512) 465-1090
Mailing Address:
    P.O. Box 15587
    Austin, TX 78761-5587
Year Established: 1944
Pub. Frequency: m.
Page Size: standard
Subscrip. Rate: $26/yr. members; $36/yr. non-members
Materials: 32,33
Circulation: 7,000
Circulation Type: paid
**Owner(s):**
Texas Hospital Association
6225 U.S. Hwy. 290 E.
Austin, TX 78761-5587
Telephone: (512) 465-1050
Ownership %: 100
**Management:**
Terry Townsend ...................President
**Editorial:**
Margaret Harrist ...........................Editor
**Desc.:** Content is designed to be of assistance and interest to persons in the health care industry in Texas.
**Readers:** Hospital administration and department managers, hospital trustees, health care consultants, and state legislators.

### HEARING INSTRUMENTS
23809

370 Ardmore Rd.
Des Plaines, IL 60016
Telephone: (708) 296-2908
FAX: (708) 296-5875
Year Established: 1951
Pub. Frequency: m.
Page Size: standard
Subscrip. Rate: $50/yr.
Materials: 01,02,06,15,16,21,27,29,32,33
Print Process: offset
Circulation: 19,800
Circulation Type: controlled
**Owner(s):**
Advanstar Communications, Inc.
7500 Old Oak Blvd.
Cleveland, OH 44130
Telephone: (216) 826-2839
Ownership %: 100
**Management:**
Bernard Rogers ...........................President
Ronald Ziegler ...........................Publisher
Kathy Tarnowski ...........................Manager
**Editorial:**
Karen Cranmer-Briskey ...........................Editor
Sheryl Stevenson ...............Managing Editor
**Desc.:** Articles of interest dealing with industry questions, sales techniques, fitting techniques, ethical issues, new developments in hearing health care. Most feature and news material staff-written. By-lines issued at discretion of editor. Departments include: News, Products/Bulletins, People, Continuing Education, News from Associations.

**Readers:** Retailers, manufacturers and suppliers, audiologists, otologists, hearing aid specialists.
**Deadline:** story-1st of mo. prior to pub. date; news-1st of mo. prior; photo-1st of mo. prior; ads-25th of mo. prior

### HOME CARE MAGAZINE
70371

P.O. Box 3640
Culver City, CA 90231
Telephone: (310) 337-9717
FAX: (310) 337-1041
Year Established: 1978
Pub. Frequency: m.
Page Size: standard
Subscrip. Rate: $48/yr.
Materials: 01,02,05,06,10,27,28,29,32,33
Circulation: 16,500
Circulation Type: controlled
**Owner(s):**
Miramar Publishing Co.
P.O. Box 3640
Culver City, CA 90231
Telephone: (310) 337-9717
Ownership %: 100
**Management:**
Andria Segedy ...........................Publisher
Doug Garcia ...............Advertising Manager
**Editorial:**
Janis Samaripa ...........................Editor
**Readers:** People who sell or rent rehab or home healthcare products to the consumer.
**Deadline:** story-3 mos. prior to pub. date; news-3 mos. prior; photo-3 mos. prior; ads-25th of mo., 2 mos. prior

### HOSPITAL & COMMUNITY PSYCHIATRY
23356

1400 K Street, N.W.
Washington, DC 20005
Telephone: (202) 682-6070
FAX: (202) 682-6114
Year Established: 1950
Pub. Frequency: m.
Page Size: standard
Subscrip. Rate: $40/yr. individual; $60/yr. institution; $20/yr. students; $60/yr. individual outside US
Materials: 06,10,11,24,25,28,30,32,33
Print Process: web offset
Circulation: 22,500
Circulation Type: paid
**Owner(s):**
American Psychiatric Association
1400 K Street, N.W.
Washington, DC 20005
Telephone: (202) 682-6000
Ownership %: 100
**Management:**
Ray J. Purkis ...................Advertising Manager
Beth Prester ...................Circulation Manager
Nancy Frey ...................General Manager
**Editorial:**
John A. Talbott, M.D. ...........................Editor
Teddye Clayton ...................Managing Editor
Betty Cochran .........Assistant Managing Editor
Laura Abedi ...........................Advertising
Martin Kesselman, ...........Book Review Editor
M.D.
Laura Abedi ...................Production Director
**Desc.:** Professional and administrative materials covering treatment programs and operations in all types of psychiatric facilities, directed to those who work in programs treating mental illness, mental retardation, alcoholism, drug abuse. All editorial materials must be related to the treatment and welfare of psychiatric patients or the prevention of mental illness. Departments include: Calendar, Film Reviews, Book Reviews, News, Notes, Miscellany, Classified Advertisements.

**Readers:** Multidisciplinary-administrators, clinicians, and educators in psychiatric services.

### HOSPITAL & HEALTH SERVICES ADMINISTRATION
23357

1021 E. Huron
Ann Arbor, MI 48104
Telephone: (313) 764-1380
FAX: (313) 763-1105
Year Established: 1955
Pub. Frequency: q.
Page Size: pocket
Subscrip. Rate: $50/yr.
Materials: 10,25
Circulation: 26,000
Circulation Type: paid
**Owner(s):**
Fdn. of Amer. Clg. of Healthcare Exec.
840 N. Lake Shore Dr.
Chicago, IL 60611
Telephone: (312) 943-0544
Ownership %: 100
**Management:**
Thomas C. Dolan, Ph. D. ...................Publisher
**Editorial:**
Richard S. Kurz, Ph. D. ...........................Editor
Kelly Sippell ...........................Managing Editor
**Desc.:** This journal keeps hospital and healthcare executives informed of new developments in management with relevance to the healthcare delivery system. Emphasis is on research and management analysis rather than news items.
**Readers:** Assistant Administrators, Chief Executive Officers.

### HOSPITAL, EL
69491

5790 Eaglesridge Ln.
Cincinnati, OH 45230
Telephone: (513) 232-0511
FAX: (513) 232-0662
Year Established: 1944
Pub. Frequency: bi-m.
Subscrip. Rate: $35/yr.
Circulation: 14,850
Circulation Type: controlled
**Owner(s):**
Gregory Loomis
5790 Eaglesridge Ln.
Cincinnati, OH 45230
Telephone: (513) 232-0511
Ownership %: 100
**Desc.:** Reports on the latest developments in medical technology, equipment, and supplies. Written in Spanish.

### HOSPITAL EMPLOYEE HEALTH
65705

3525 Piedmont Rd., Ste. 400
Atlanta, GA 30305
Telephone: (404) 262-7436
FAX: (404) 262-7837
Mailing Address:
    P.O. Box 740059
    Atlanta, GA 30374
Pub. Frequency: m.
Page Size: standard
Subscrip. Rate: $299/yr. w/ce credits; $259/yr. w/out ce credits
Freelance Pay: $125/pg.
Circulation: 2,535
Circulation Type: paid
**Owner(s):**
American Health Consultants
**Management:**
Robert Williford ...........................President
David Schwartz ...........................Publisher
**Editorial:**
Don Johnston ...................Executive Editor
Barrie Rissman ...........................Editor
Christi Reynolds ...................Managing Editor
**Readers:** Hospital employee heath practitioners.

**Materials Accepted/Included:** 01-Business news 02-By-line articles 03-Fashion news 04-Food news 05-Freelance copy 06-Letters to editor 07-Real estate news 08-Sports news 09-Travel news 10-Book rev. 11-Movie rev. 12-Music rev. 13-TV rev. 14-Theater rev. 15-Coming events 16-Obituaries 17-Question & answer 18-Social announcements 19-Artwork 20-Cartoons 21-Photos 22-TV listings 23-Audio rec. 24-Video rec. 25-Books 26-Films/film clips 27-Personnel news 28-Press releases 29-New product news/photos 30-Trade lit. 31-Contracts awarded 32-Display adv. 33-Classified adv.

4-174

## HOSPITAL HOME HEALTH
65704

P.O. Box 740056
Atlanta, GA 30374
Telephone: (404) 262-7436
Year Established: 1983
Pub. Frequency: m.
Page Size: standard
Subscrip. Rate: $259/yr.
**Owner(s):**
American Health Consultants
Ownership %: 100
**Editorial:**
Joyce Case ....................................Editor
Kathy Cline, Mng. Ed. ..........Managing Editor
**Desc.:** We are dedicated to providing
material important to and of interest to
the hospital-based home health agency.
**Readers:** Directors and administrators of
hospital-based Home Health Agencies.

## HOSPITAL MATERIEL MANAGEMENT QUARTERLY
58606

200 Orchard Ridge Dr.
Gaithersburg, MD 20878
Telephone: (301) 417-7500
FAX: (301) 417-7550
Year Established: 1979
Pub. Frequency: q.
Page Size: standard
Subscrip. Rate: $101/yr.
Circulation: 2,000
Circulation Type: paid
**Owner(s):**
Aspen Publishers, Inc.
200 Orchard Ridge Dr.
Gaithersburg, MD 20878
Telephone: (301) 417-7531
**Editorial:**
Charles E. Housely ..........................Editor
Lorraine Davis ..........................Managing Editor
Jack Bruggeman ....................Editorial Director
**Desc.:** Explores timely, conceptual, and
critical issues to help hospital
purchasing professionals tackle the
complex challenge of purchasing and
material management. A unique,
professional journal that emphasizes the
application of practical and cost-effective
techniques and produces to everyday
practice.
**Readers:** Directors of material
management, material managers, and
purchasing directors in hospitals.

## HOSPITAL PATIENT RELATIONS REPORT
67659

951 Pershing Dr.
Silver Spring, MD 20910-4464
Telephone: (301) 587-6300
FAX: (301) 585-9075
Year Established: 1980
Pub. Frequency: m.
Page Size: standard
Subscrip. Rate: $264.48/yr.
Materials: $276/yr.
**Owner(s):**
Business Publications, Inc.
951 Pershing Dr.
Silver Spring, MD 20910-4464
Telephone: (301) 587-6300
Ownership %: 100
**Management:**
Lawrence Fishbein ..............................Publisher
**Editorial:**
Terry Hartnett ....................................Editor
**Desc.:** Advice for hospital administrators
on methods to improve satisfaction of
patients and patients' families.

## HOSPITAL PURCHASING NEWS
23371

Two Northfield Plaza
Ste. 300
Northfield, IL 60093-1213
Telephone: (708) 441-3700
FAX: (708) 441-3701
Year Established: 1977
Pub. Frequency: m.
Page Size: tabloid
Subscrip. Rate: $5/issue; $44.95/yr. in
US.; $54.95/yr. in Canada; $59.95/yr.
foreign
Print Process: offset
Circulation: 27,509
Circulation Type: controlled & paid
**Owner(s):**
McKnight Medical Communications Co.
Two Northfield Plaza
Ste. 300
Northfield, IL 60093-1213
Telephone: (800) 451-7838
Ownership %: 50

Medical Economics Publishing Co., Inc.
Five Paragon Dr.
Montvale, NJ 07645-1742
Telephone: (201) 358-7200
Ownership %: 50
**Management:**
Paul Konowitch ..............................President
Christopher Bale ......................Vice President
Stephanie A. Ellis ..............................Publisher
**Editorial:**
John Hall ..............................Senior Editor
Mark Thill ....................................Editor
Rick Barlow ..........................Associate Editor
Gregg Hanrouth ..................Circulation Director
Chris Colatriano ......Eastern Account Manager
Donald B. Holbrook ..............Midwest Account Manager
Nick Kosan ..............Western Account Manager
**Desc.:** Written expressly for the director of
hospital purchasing (materials
management) who-together with the
central supply supervisor-makes a vital
link in the buying chain.
**Readers:** Hospital-based purchasing-
materials managers, supervisors in
larger hospitals. In smaller hospitals as
is indicated, the administrator receives
our publications.

## HOSPITALS & HEALTH NETWORKS
23364

737 N. Michigan Ave., Ste. 700
Chicago, IL 60611
Telephone: (312) 440-6800
FAX: (312) 951-8491
Year Established: 1936
Pub. Frequency: bi-w.
Page Size: standard
Subscrip. Rate: $65/yr. US; $110/yr.
foreign
Materials: 01,06,19,20,21,32,33
Freelance Pay: negotiable
Circulation: 119,000
Circulation Type: controlled
**Owner(s):**
American Hospital Assn. Co.
737 N. Michigan Ave., Ste. 700
Chicago, IL 60611
Telephone: (312) 440-6800
Ownership %: 100
**Management:**
John Sheehy ..............................Publisher
Kate Confer ..................Circulation Manager
Martin Weitzel ..................Editorial Production Manager
**Editorial:**
Kevin Lumsdon ..........................Senior Editor
Mary Grayson ....................................Editor
Terese Hudson ....................................Editor
Mark Hagland ..........................Managing Editor
Mary Grayson ....................Editorial Director

Fred Haas ..................Administrative Assistant
Charles Lazar ....................................Artist
Emily Friedman ..................Contributing Editor
Alden Solovy ..................Contributing Editor
Marcia Kuhr ..........................Design Director
Martin Weitzel ....................Production Director
**Desc.:** Articles cover strategic issues
related to reshaping the delivery system.
**Readers:** Hospital administrators, chief
executive officers and members of the
administrative staff; heads of
professional, business and service
departments; medical directors,
physicians, managed care executives,
and insurance executives.

## HOSPITAL TOPICS
23362

1319 18th St., N.W.
Washington, DC 20036-1802
Telephone: (202) 296-6267
FAX: (202) 296-5149
Year Established: 1922
Pub. Frequency: q.
Page Size: standard
Subscrip. Rate: $28/yr. individuals; $51/yr.
instn.; $61/yr. foreign
Circulation: 1,230
Circulation Type: paid
**Owner(s):**
Heldref Publications
1319 18th St., N.W.
Washington, DC 20036-1802
Telephone: (202) 296-6267
Ownership %: 100
**Management:**
Walter E. Beach ..............................Publisher
Raymond M. Rollo ..........Advertising Manager
Catherine Welker ................Circulation Manager
Kerri P. Kilbane ..................Promotion Manager
**Editorial:**
Lisa Culp Neikirk ....................................Editor
**Desc.:** Addresses many of the concerns of
today's healthcare manager.
Management issues covered include
planning, organizing, staffing, controlling,
directing, and decision making.
**Readers:** Administrative personnel of
hospitals, directors, supervisors,
pharmacists, other department heads.

## INQUIRY
69467

676 N. St. Clair St.
Chicago, IL 60612
Telephone: (312) 440-5575
FAX: (312) 440-5705
Year Established: 1963
Pub. Frequency: q.
Subscrip. Rate: $40/yr. individuals; $45/yr.
instn.; $55/yr. foreign
Circulation: 3,500
Circulation Type: paid
**Owner(s):**
Blue Cross & Blue Shield Association
676 N. St. Clair St.
Chicago, IL 60611
Telephone: (312) 440-5575
Ownership %: 100
**Editorial:**
Jack Hadley ....................................Editor

## INTERNATIONAL JOURNAL OF HEALTH SERVICES
69590

26 Austin Ave.
Amityville, NY 11701
Telephone: (516) 691-1270
FAX: (516) 691-1770
Mailing Address:
P.O. Box 337
Amityville, NY 11701
Year Established: 1970
Pub. Frequency: q.
Subscrip. Rate: $36/yr. individuals;
$114/yr. instn.

**Owner(s):**
Baywood Publishing Co., Inc.
26 Austin Ave.
P.O. Box 337
Amityville, NY 11701
Telephone: (516) 691-1270
FAX: (516) 691-1770
**Management:**
Stuart Cohen ....................................Publisher
**Editorial:**
Dr. Vicente Navarro ..............................Editor
**Desc.:** Contains current and authoritative
information on the development of the
health care industry worldwide.

## JOURNAL OF AMBULATORY CARE MANAGEMENT, THE
58709

200 Orchard Ridge Dr.
Gaithersburg, MD 20878
Telephone: (301) 417-7500
FAX: (301) 417-7550
Year Established: 1977
Pub. Frequency: q.
Page Size: standard
Subscrip. Rate: $105/yr. US; $126/yr.
foreign
Materials: 06,10,15,32
Print Process: DTP
Circulation: 3,178
Circulation Type: paid
**Owner(s):**
Aspen Publishers, Inc.
200 Orchard Ridge Dr.
Gaithersburg, MD 20878
Telephone: (301) 417-7500
Ownership %: 100
**Editorial:**
Lenda Hill ..........................Managing Editor
Jack Bruggeman ....................Editorial Director
Sandra Lunsford ..................Associate Editor
**Desc.:** Features the latest, most reliable
information to help ambulatory care
professionals keep up-to-date in this
fast-changing health service field. It is
the only quarterly publication devoted
exclusively to the management
information needs of professionals in
ambulatory care.
**Readers:** Directors of ambulatory care,
hospital administrators, department
heads, directors of outpatient services,
and directors of emergency services.

## JOURNAL OF HEALTHCARE MATERIAL MANAGEMENT
68919

507 N. Milwaukee Ave.
Libertyville, IL 60048-2018
Telephone: (708) 680-7878
FAX: (708) 680-8180
Year Established: 1983
Pub. Frequency: m.
Page Size: standard
Subscrip. Rate: $39/yr. US; $50/yr.
Canada; $98/yr. elsewhere
Materials: 01,02,06,28,29,20,32,33
Print Process: web offset
Circulation: 23,000
Circulation Type: controlled & paid
**Owner(s):**
Mayworm Associates, Inc.
507 N. Milwaukee Ave.
Libertyville, IL 60048-2018
Telephone: (708) 680-7878
FAX: (708) 680-8180
Ownership %: 100
**Editorial:**
Marilyn Ferdinand ....................................Editor

---

**Materials Accepted/Included:** 01-Business news 02-By-line articles 03-Fashion news 04-Food news 05-Freelance copy 06-Letters to editor 07-Real estate news 08-Sports news 09-Travel news 10-Book rev. 11-Movie rev. 12-Music rev. 13-TV rev. 14-Theater rev. 15-Coming events 16-Obituaries 17-Question & answer 18-Social announcements 19-Artwork 20-Cartoons 21-Photos 22-TV listings 23-Audio rec. 24-Video rec. 25-Books 26-Films/film clips 27-Personnel news 28-Press releases 29-New product news/photos 30-Trade lit. 31-Contracts awarded 32-Display adv. 33-Classified adv.

**Desc.:** Serves the specific educational and information needs of materiel management, central service, purchasing, operating room, infection control and other personnel charged with the responsibility of purchasing, reprocessing and distributing supplies and equipment throughout the healthcare facility.

**Readers:** Hospital personnel, ambulatory care centers, surgery centers, purchasing groups, nrsing homes.

**Deadline:** ads-5th of mo. prior to pub. date

69603

## JOURNAL OF HEALTHCARE RISK MANAGEMENT
840 N. Lake Shore Dr.
Chicago, IL 60611
Telephone: (312) 280-6198
FAX: (312) 280-6228
Year Established: 1981
Pub. Frequency: q.
Subscrip. Rate: membership only
Circulation: 3,200
Circulation Type: controlled
**Owner(s):**
American Hospital Association
840 N. Lake Shore Dr.
Chicago, IL 60611
Telephone: (312) 280-6198
Ownership %: 100
**Editorial:**
Margaret Veach .......................................Editor
**Desc.:** Contains information on quality assurance, professional liability claims management, loss prevention, risk financing, risk management program development, workers' compensation, and risk management legislation and legal issues.

68920

## JOURNAL OF LONG-TERM CARE ADMINISTRATION
325 S. Patrick St.
Alexandria, VA 22314-3571
Telephone: (703) 549-5822
FAX: (703) 739-7901
Year Established: 1972
Pub. Frequency: q.
Page Size: standard
Subscrip. Rate: $70/yr. non-members US; $80/yr. foreign
Materials: 02,05,06,10,21,23,24,25,28,29, 30,32,33
Print Process: offset
Circulation: 6,500
Circulation Type: free & paid
**Owner(s):**
American College of Health Care Administrators
325 S. Patrick St.
Alexandria, VA 22314-3571
Telephone: (703) 549-5822
FAX: (703) 739-7901
Ownership %: 100
**Editorial:**
Jan Lamoglia .........................................Editor
**Desc.:** A four-color, peer-reviewed journal that publishes original research on current industry trends such as specialty care, dementia, HR management, ethics & examples of excellence in administration. Other features include practical strategies for the equality-minded administrator, commentaries, how-to articles, essays, book reviews and annual index.

65721

## JOURNAL OF MEDICINAL CHEMISTRY
1155 16th St. N.W.
Washington, DC 20036
Telephone: (202) 872-4600
Year Established: 1958

Pub. Frequency: bi-w.
Subscrip. Rate: $54/yr. members US; $136/yr. foreign; $586/yr. non-members US; $668/yr. foreign
Circulation: 4,272
Circulation Type: paid
**Owner(s):**
American Chemical Society
1155 16th St., N.W.
Washington, DC 20036
Telephone: (800) 333-9511
Ownership %: 100
**Editorial:**
Philip S. Portoghese ..........................Editor
**Desc.:** Focuses on the relationship of chemistry of biological activity. Provides valuable research findings and comprehensive book reviews on medicinal chemistry and related fields.

24497

## JOURNAL OF N.Y. STATE NURSES ASSOCIATION
2113 Western Ave.
Guilderland, NY 12084-9501
*see Service,Trade,Professional Magazines, Nursing*

66176

## MCKNIGHT'S LONG-TERM CARE NEWS
Two Northfield Plaza
Ste. 300
Northfield, IL 60093-1217
Telephone: (708) 441-3700
FAX: (708) 441-3701
Year Established: 1978
Pub. Frequency: m.
Page Size: tabloid
Subscrip. Rate: $44.95/yr. US; $54.95/yr. Canada; $59.95/yr. elsewhere
Print Process: offset
Circulation: 40,374
Circulation Type: controlled & paid
**Owner(s):**
Medical Economics Publishing Company, Inc.
5 Paragon Dr.
Montvale, NJ 07645-1742
Telephone: (201) 358-7200

McKnight Medical Communications Co.
Two Northfield Plaza
Ste. 300
Northfield, IL 60093-1217
Telephone: (708) 441-3700
FAX: (708) 441-3701
**Management:**
Paul Konowitch .............................President
Elaine Purnell ...............................Publisher
**Editorial:**
Suzanne Powills ....................Editor in Chief
John OConnor .....................Associate Editor
Gregg Haunroth .................Circulation Director
Danny Murphy .................Production Director
Sandy Davis .......................................Sales
Irene Onesto .......................................Sales
Bob Santini .......................................Sales
**Desc.:** Long-term care industry news pertaining to homes, retirement housing centers, extended care and home care.
**Readers:** Nursing homes and hospitals with long-term care facilities, and executive directors of retirement housing centers.

23368

## MODERN HEALTHCARE
740 N. Rush St.
Chicago, IL 60611
Telephone: (312) 649-5350
Year Established: 1976
Pub. Frequency: w.
Page Size: standard
Subscrip. Rate: $110/yr. US; $144/yr. foreign
Materials: 01,27,28,32,33

Freelance Pay: varies
Print Process: web offset
Circulation: 83,000
Circulation Type: controlled & paid
**Owner(s):**
Crain Communications, Inc.
740 N. Rush St.
Chicago, IL 60611
Telephone: (312) 649-5200
Ownership %: 100
**Bureau(s):**
Modern Healthcare
220 E. 42nd St.
New York, NY 10017
Telephone: (212) 210-0208
Contact: Karen Pallarito, Reporter

Modern Healthcare
6500 Wilshire Blvd.
Los Angeles, CA 90048
Telephone: (213) 651-3710
Contact: Della De Lafuente, Reporter

Modern Healthcare
814 National Press Bldg.
Washington, DC 20045
Telephone: (202) 662-7207
Contact: Eric Weissenstein, Reporter

Modern Healthcare
1 Northpark E., 8950 N. Cntrl.
Telephone: (214) 363-1686
Contact: Sandy Lutz, Reporter

Modern Healthcare
814 National Press Bldg.
Washington, DC 20045
Telephone: (202) 662-7215
Contact: Lynn Wagner

Modern Healthcare
410 Ware Blvd.
Park Central
Tampa, FL 33619
Telephone: (813) 620-4088
Contact: Jay Greene
**Management:**
Charles Lauer ..........................Vice President
Charles Lauer .............................Publisher
Atina Majewski .................Circulation Manager
Mary Chamberlain ..............Promotion Manager
Sheryl Bull .......................Sales Manager
**Editorial:**
Clark Bell ...............................Editor
Karen Petitte ...................Managing Editor
Cathy Sommario ........Administrative Assistant
Sheryl Bull ...........................Advertising
Robert Bersin ...............Marketing Director
John Burns ...............................Reporter
Bruce Japsen ...........................Reporter
John Morrissey ...........................Reporter
David Burda ...............................Reporter
Lisa Scott ...............................Reporter
**Desc.:** Contains articles dealing with hospital administration, as well as HMO's home healthcare and alternative services.
**Readers:** Qualified receipients include administrative executives, professional department heads, and service department heads in the field served.

66730

## OBG MANAGEMENT
110 Summit Ave.
Montvale, NJ 07645
Telephone: (201) 391-9100
FAX: (201) 391-2778
Year Established: 1989
Pub. Frequency: m.
Page Size: standard
Subscrip. Rate: $65/yr. US; $80/yr. foreign
Materials: 01,05,06,20,25,28,29,30,32,33
Freelance Pay: $.50/wd.
Print Process: web offset
Circulation: 31,500
Circulation Type: controlled

**Owner(s):**
Dowden Publishing Co.
110 Summit Ave.
Montvale, NJ 07645
Telephone: (201) 391-9100
FAX: (201) 391-2778
Ownership %: 100
**Editorial:**
Mark Dowden ..............................Editor
**Desc.:** The mission of this publication is provide OB/GYNs with specialty-specific information and advice to enable them to better manage their practices, their professional lives and their delivery of patient care. When discussing delivery of care, the magazine overlays clinical information with nonclinical, helping OB/GYNs make clinical decisions that take into account socioeconomic factors such as cost, time, patient wishes, potential liability and personal expertise. The magazine's editors place emphasis on interpreting for readers the newest trends in patient management, payment mechanisms, practice patterns, technology, legislation and regulation.

69589

## OR MANAGER
P.O. Box 17487
Boulder, CO 80308-0487
Telephone: (303) 442-1661
FAX: (303) 442-5960
Year Established: 1985
Pub. Frequency: m.
Page Size: 8 1/4 x 11 1/2
Subscrip. Rate: $68/yr. US; $78/yr. foreign
Materials: 01,02,10,15,32,33
Print Process: offset
Circulation: 3,000
Circulation Type: paid
**Owner(s):**
OR Manager, Inc.
P.O. Box 17487
Boulder, CO 80308-0487
Telephone: (303) 442-1661
FAX: (303) 442-5960
Ownership %: 100
**Management:**
Elinor S. Schrader ..............................Publisher
**Editorial:**
Pat Pattersoon ...............................Editor
**Desc.:** Covers personnel management, budgeting and financial management, equipment and supplies, new technology, operating room nursing issues, and professional development.
**Readers:** OR managers.

69305

## QUALITY MANAGEMENT IN HEALTH CARE
200 Orchard Ridge Dr.
Gaithersburg, MD 20878
Telephone: (301) 417-7500
FAX: (301) 417-7550
Year Established: 1993
Pub. Frequency: q.
Page Size: standard
Subscrip. Rate: $129/yr.
**Owner(s):**
Aspen Publishers, Inc.
200 Orchard Dr.
Gaithersburg, MD 20878
Telephone: (301) 417-7500
Ownership %: 100
**Management:**
Michael B. Brown .......................Vice President
Ernest V. Manzella ....................Vice President
**Editorial:**
Jane Coyle Garwood ...............Executive Editor
Lenda P. Hill ......................Managing Editor
Jack Bruggeman ...................Editorial Director
David A. Uffelman ...................Assistant Editor
A. Maria R. ...................Production Coordinator

**Materials Accepted/Included:** 01-Business news 02-By-line articles 03-Fashion news 04-Food news 05-Freelance copy 06-Letters to editor 07-Real estate news 08-Sports news 09-Travel news 10-Book rev. 11-Movie rev. 12-Music rev. 13-TV rev. 14-Theater rev. 15-Coming events 16-Obituaries 17-Question & answer 18-Social announcements 19-Artwork 20-Cartoons 21-Photos 22-TV listings 23-Audio rec. 24-Video rec. 25-Books 26-Films/film clips 27-Personnel news 28-Press releases 29-New product news/photos 30-Trade lit. 31-Contracts awarded 32-Display adv. 33-Classified adv.

**Desc.:** Provides a forum to explore the theoretical, technical, and strategic elements of quality management, and to assist those who wish to implement this discipline in health care.

65013

## RESEARCH ON AGING
2455 Teller Rd.
Thousand Oaks, CA 91320
Telephone: (805) 499-0721
FAX: (805) 499-0871
Year Established: 1979
Pub. Frequency: q.
Page Size: standard
Subscrip. Rate: $49/yr. individuals; $144/yr. instn.
Circulation: 1,500
Circulation Type: paid
**Owner(s):**
Sage Publications, Inc.
2455 Teller Rd.
Thousand Oaks, CA 91320
Telephone: (805) 499-0721
Ownership %: 100
**Editorial:**
Rhonda J. V. Montgomery ......................Editor
**Desc.:** A journal of interdisciplinary research on current issues, methodological and research problems in the study of the aged.

23372

## SOUTHERN HOSPITALS MAGAZINE
1575 Northside Dr., N.W.
Atlanta, GA 30318
Telephone: (404) 351-1276
FAX: (404) 351-1584
Mailing Address:
P.O. Box 19919
Atlanta, GA 30325
Year Established: 1934
Pub. Frequency: bi-m.
Page Size: standard
Subscrip. Rate: free qualified members; $15/yr. non-members
Freelance Pay: negotiable
Circulation: 18,800
Circulation Type: controlled
**Owner(s):**
John W. Yopp Publications, Inc.
P.O. Box 19919
Atlanta, GA 30325
Telephone: (404) 350-8975
Ownership %: 100
**Management:**
Joseph Cronley ......................Publisher
Joseph Cronley ................Advertising Manager
Joseph Cronley ..................Circulation Manager
**Editorial:**
Fran Bonau ................................Editor
**Desc.:** Trade journal of the Southern health care market covers management, industry issues and trends, association news, conventions, legislation, finance, etc.
**Readers:** Administrators, CEO's and other health care executives, board members, department heads.

67026

## STRAIGHT TALK, A MAGAZINE FOR TEENS
394 Bedford Rd.
Pleasantville, NY 10570
Telephone: (914) 769-0055
FAX: (914) 769-5676
Mailing Address:
P.O. Box 199
Pleasantville, NY 10570
Year Established: 1991
Pub. Frequency: irreg.
Page Size: standard
Subscrip. Rate: $16.80/single series
Materials: 02,05,17,19,20,21

Freelance Pay: $100-$1000
Print Process: offset lithography
**Owner(s):**
Learning Partnership, The
394 Bedford Rd.
Pleasantville, NY 10570
Telephone: (914) 769-0055
Ownership %: 100
**Management:**
John Fisher ............................President
John Fisher ............................Publisher
**Editorial:**
Rita Fisher ....................Editor in Chief
**Desc.:** Deals with health and behavior topics of concern to adolescents.
**Readers:** Adolescents.
**Deadline:** story-per contract; photo-per contract

58597

## TOPICS IN HEALTH CARE FINANCING
200 Orchard Ridge Dr.
Gaithersburg, MD 20878
Telephone: (301) 417-7500
FAX: (301) 417-7550
Year Established: 1974
Pub. Frequency: q.
Page Size: standard
Subscrip. Rate: $105/yr.
Circulation: 3,700
Circulation Type: paid
**Owner(s):**
Aspen Publishers, Inc.
200 Orchard Ridge Dr.
Gaithersburg, MD 20878
Telephone: (301) 417-7500
Ownership %: 100
**Editorial:**
Don Delanter ......................Senior Editor
Lorraine Davis ......................Managing Editor
Jack Bruggeman ................Editorial Director
Sandra L. Lunsford ................Assistant Editor
**Desc.:** Provides authoritative, comprehensive coverage of key issues in health care financial management. Written by the country's top health care legal and financial experts, THCF offers expert advice, effective management strategies, and the latest information on new financing alternatives for competing in today's health care financial environment.
**Readers:** Hospital CFOs, controllers, and executives.

58578

## TOPICS IN HEALTH INFORMATION MANAGEMENT
200 Orchard Ridge Dr.
Gaithersburg, MD 20878
Telephone: (301) 417-7500
FAX: (301) 417-7550
Year Established: 1980
Pub. Frequency: q.
Page Size: standard
Subscrip. Rate: $84/yr.
Circulation: 3,000
Circulation Type: paid
**Owner(s):**
Aspen Publishers, Inc.
200 Orchard Ridge Dr.
Gaithersburg, MD 20878
Telephone: (301) 417-7500
**Editorial:**
Carole Estey ............................Editor

**Desc.:** Focuses entirely on the unique information needs of the medical information practitioner. Each in-depth, topical issue presents original articles by medical information directors and other leaders in the field that provides a practical look at significant issues such as DRGs, cost control, quality control, ambulatory care, legal responsibilities, patient privacy, computer operations, etc.
**Readers:** Directors of medical records and medical records administrators and technicians, and other health care professionals involved in medical information management.

58596

## TOPICS IN HOSPITAL PHARMACY MANAGEMENT
200 Orchard Ridge Dr.
Gaithersburg, MD 20878
Telephone: (301) 417-7500
FAX: (301) 417-7550
Year Established: 1981
Pub. Frequency: q.
Page Size: standard
Subscrip. Rate: $107/yr. US; $128/yr. foreign
Materials: 06,10,15,32
Circulation: 1,500
Circulation Type: paid
**Owner(s):**
Aspen Publishers, Inc.
200 Orchard Ridge Dr.
Gaithersburg, MD 20878
Telephone: (301) 417-7500
**Editorial:**
Lenda Hill ............................Managing Editor
Jack Bruggeman ................Editorial Director
Amy Martin ............................Assistant Editor
**Desc.:** The only topical professional journal devoted entirely to the management of hospital pharmacy services. Provides practical, up-to-date applications, strategies, and valuable insights needed by pharmacy directors to deal successfully with day-to-day management issues.
**Readers:** Directors and managers of hospital pharmacies.

23374

## TRUSTEE
737 N. Michigan Ave., Ste. 700
Chicago, IL 60611
Telephone: (312) 440-6800
FAX: (312) 951-8491
Year Established: 1947
Pub. Frequency: m.
Page Size: standard
Subscrip. Rate: $25/yr.
Materials: 32,33
Freelance Pay: negotiable
Print Process: web offset
Circulation: 40,000
Circulation Type: paid
**Owner(s):**
American Hospital Publ., Inc.
737 N. Michigan Ave., Ste. 700
Chicago, IL 60611
Telephone: (312) 440-6800
Ownership %: 100
**Management:**
John Sheehy ............................President
John Sheehy ............................Publisher
Kate Confer ....................Circulation Manager
David McNamara ........Classified Adv. Manager
Pat Foy ............................Promotion Manager
Jim Dozois ............................Sales Manager
**Editorial:**
Mary A. Grayson ................Executive Editor
Karen Gardner ......................Managing Editor
Jim Dozois ............................Advertising
Marcia Kuhr ............................Art Director
Mark Harju ....................Marketing Director

Martin Weitzel ......................Production Director
**Desc.:** Educational and informational articles on subjects relating to the hospital and health fields and to the role and responsibilities of hospital trustees in the health care delivery system.
**Readers:** Hospital trustees and governing board members.
**Deadline:** ads-10th of mo. prior to pub. date

25711

## VOLUNTEER LEADER, THE
737 N. Michigan Ave., Ste. 700
Chicago, IL 60611
Telephone: (312) 440-6800
FAX: (312) 951-8491
Year Established: 1960
Pub. Frequency: q.
Page Size: standard
Subscrip. Rate: $8/yr.; $10/yr. foreign
Circulation: 6,000
Circulation Type: paid
**Owner(s):**
American Hospital Publishing, Inc.
737 N. Michigan Ave., Ste. 700
Chicago, IL 60611
Telephone: (312) 440-6800
Ownership %: 100
**Management:**
Frank Sabatino ......................Publisher
Richard M. Dudley ....................Sales Manager
**Editorial:**
Daniel S. Schechter ................Editor in Chief
Karen M. Sandrick ..................Managing Editor
**Desc.:** Articles and feature stories of particular interest to hospital auxiliaries and volunteer directors. Articles should be brief, not more than 1,500 words. Case histories of successful auxiliary projects, and project ideas in areas such as fund raising, services for patients, and public relations are special features. Some photos used. Articles accepted for publication are by-lined. Covers all phases of hospital auxiliary and hospital volunteer operation. Hospital auxiliary members, hospital directors of volunteers are principal audience.
**Readers:** Volunteers, directors of volunteers, and hospital auxiliary officers.

58637

## WORLD SMOKING & HEALTH
1599 Clifton Rd., N.E.
Atlanta, GA 30329
Telephone: (404) 329-7936
Year Established: 1976
Pub. Frequency: 3/yr.
Page Size: standard
Subscrip. Rate: free
Circulation: 15,000
Circulation Type: free
**Owner(s):**
American Cancer Society
1599 Clifton Rd., N.E.
Atlanta, GA 30329
Telephone: (404) 329-7936
Ownership %: 100
**Management:**
Jerie Jordan ............................Manager
**Readers:** Smoking control activists worldwide.

## Group 116-Home Economics

23343

## AAFCS ACTION
1555 King St.
Alexandria, VA 22314
Telephone: (703) 706-4600
FAX: (703) 706-4663
Year Established: 1974
Pub. Frequency: 5/yr.

**Materials Accepted/Included:** 01-Business news 02-By-line articles 03-Fashion news 04-Food news 05-Freelance copy 06-Letters to editor 07-Real estate news 08-Sports news 09-Travel news 10-Book rev. 11-Movie rev. 12-Music rev. 13-TV rev. 14-Theater rev. 15-Coming events 16-Obituaries 17-Question & answer 18-Social announcements 19-Artwork 20-Cartoons 21-Photos 22-TV listings 23-Audio rec. 24-Video rec. 25-Books 26-Films/film clips 27-Personnel news 28-Press releases 29-New product news/photos 30-Trade lit. 31-Contracts awarded 32-Display adv. 33-Classified adv.

4-177

Page Size: tabloid
Subscrip. Rate: free to members; $7.50/yr. non-members
Circulation: 25,000
Circulation Type: paid
**Owner(s):**
American Association of Family & Consumer Sciences
1555 King St.
Alexandria, VA 22314
Telephone: (703) 706-4600
Ownership %: 100
**Management:**
Mary Jean Kolar ..................Executive Director
**Editorial:**
Larry Hoffer ..............Communications Director
**Desc.:** Letters to editor, letters to AHEA president, public affairs, professional meetings, and employment opportunities, association and professional news.
**Readers:** Mostly members of the American Home Economics Assn.

68905

## HOME ECONOMICS RESEARCH JOURNAL
2455 Teller Rd.
Newbury Park, CA 91320
Telephone: (805) 499-0721
FAX: (805) 706-0871
Year Established: 1972
Pub. Frequency: q.
Subscrip. Rate: $40/yr. individuals; $65/yr. instn.
Circulation: 2,924
Circulation Type: paid
**Owner(s):**
Sage Publications, Inc.
2455 Teller Rd.
Newbury Park, CA 91320
Telephone: (805) 499-0721
Ownership %: 100
**Desc.:** Scholarly articles on a variety of issues and research in home economics. Sponsored by the American Home Economics Association.

23344

## JOURNAL OF HOME ECONOMICS
1555 King St.
Alexandria, VA 22314
Telephone: (703) 706-4600
FAX: (703) 706-4663
Year Established: 1909
Pub. Frequency: q.
Page Size: standard
Subscrip. Rate: $20/yr.
Circulation: 25,000
Circulation Type: paid
**Owner(s):**
American Association of Family & Consumer Sciences
1555 King St.
Alexandria, VA 22314
Telephone: (703) 706-4600
Ownership %: 100
**Management:**
Mary Jean Kolar ..................Executive Director
**Editorial:**
Larry Hoffer ..............Communications Director
**Desc.:** Covers family relations, children, food and nutrition, household affairs, and teaching methods.
**Readers:** Professional home economists/including home economists in business, extension, human health.

23345

## WHAT'S NEW IN HOME ECONOMICS
1429 Walnut St.
Philadelphia, PA 19102
Telephone: (215) 563-3501
FAX: (215) 563-1588
Year Established: 1936
Pub. Frequency: 5/yr.

Page Size: standard
Subscrip. Rate: $29/yr.; $47/yr. foreign
Freelance Pay: varies
Circulation: 17,000
Circulation Type: paid
**Owner(s):**
University Publishing
1429 Walnut, 4th Fl.
Philadelphia, PA 19102
Telephone: (215) 574-9600
Ownership %: 25
**Management:**
Christine Weiser ..................Publisher
Michele Sokoloff ..............Advertising Manager
**Editorial:**
Christine Weiser ..................Editor
**Desc.:** For high school and college teachers, contains short articles and abstracts of publications of interest.
**Readers:** Home economics teachers, extension home economists in business, editors of food, clothing.

## Group 118-Hotels, Motels & Resorts

68930

## CALIFORNIA INNTOUCH
P.O. Box 160405
Sacramento, CA 95816-0405
Telephone: (916) 444-5780
FAX: (916) 444-5848
Year Established: 1981
Pub. Frequency: s-a.
Page Size: standard
Subscrip. Rate: $35/yr. non-members
Materials: 01,04,05,06,07,09,15,16,17,19, 21,27,28,29,30,31,32,33
Print Process: web
Circulation: 7,100
Circulation Type: paid
**Owner(s):**
California Hotel & Motel Association
P.O. Box 160405
Sacramento, CA 95816-0405
Telephone: (916) 444-5780
FAX: (916) 444-5848
Ownership %: 100
**Editorial:**
William Howe ...............................Editor
Michael Wortell ..........................Advertising
**Desc.:** Features industry news, legislative updates, industry product information, industry events, industry developments.
**Deadline:** story-2 mo. prior to pub. date; news-2 mo.; photo-2 mo.

23377

## CLUB MANAGEMENT
8730 Big Bend Blvd.
St. Louis, MO 63119
Telephone: (314) 961-6644
FAX: (314) 961-4809
Year Established: 1922
Pub. Frequency: bi-m.
Page Size: standard
Subscrip. Rate: $21.95/yr.
Freelance Pay: $150-$600
Circulation: 15,000
Circulation Type: paid
**Owner(s):**
Finan Publishing Co., Inc.
8730 Big Bend Blvd.
St. Louis, MO 63119
Telephone: (314) 961-6644
Ownership %: 100
**Management:**
Thomas J. Finan ........................President
Thomas J. Finan ........................Publisher
Thomas J. Finan ..............Advertising Manager
**Editorial:**
Dee Kaplan .........................Advertising
**Desc.:** Designed to help managers of private clubs that serve food and beverages.

**Readers:** Executives, managers, officers of private clubs and resorts.

23380

## FLORIDA HOTEL & MOTEL JOURNAL
200 W. College Ave.
Tallahassee, FL 32301
Telephone: (904) 224-2888
FAX: (904) 222-3462
Mailing Address:
　P.O. Box 1529
　Tallahassee, FL 32302-1529
Year Established: 1978
Pub. Frequency: m.
Page Size: standard
Subscrip. Rate: $24/yr.
Materials: 01,02,05,06,07,10,16,17,19,20, 21,27,28,29,30,32,33
Freelance Pay: base $.10/wd.
Print Process: web offset
Circulation: 5,000
Circulation Type: controlled & paid
**Owner(s):**
Florida Hotel & Motel Assn.
P.O. Box 1529
Tallahassee, FL 32302
Telephone: (904) 224-2888
Ownership %: 100
**Management:**
Thomas A. Waits ........................Publisher
Helen Sanders ..................Advertising Manager
Herschel Kelly ..................Business Manager
Gayle Jungling ..................Circulation Manager
**Editorial:**
Jayleen Woods ...........................Editor
Janet Litherland ..................Editorial Associate
**Desc.:** The business publication of Florida hotel and motel owners, managers and investors. Energy-saving and cost-effectiveness of management techniques, articles on hospitality, housekeeping, accounting, technology at the front desk, marketing tips and the travel industry, investment and building, operation, promotion, advertising, Florida attraction news, local hotel and motel association news, labor law and equal opportunity employment law, unemployment compensation law and administrative procedures. Departments include: Management Monographs; UP-Dates and Innovations (opening dates and construction/renovation); switchboard (lodging personnel changes); Inn-keeping with the Law; Local, State and national association news; Hotel strata-gees! (marketing ideas).
**Readers:** Owners, investors, managers of Florida hotels, and buyers of services to hotel and motels. CEO's of Florida based trade associations. Florida Tourism and Education Officials.
**Deadline:** story-6 wks. prior to pub. date; news-6 wks. prior; photo-6 wks. prior; ads-6 wks. prior

23384

## HOTEL & MOTEL MANAGEMENT
7500 Old Oak Blvd.
Cleveland, OH 44130
Telephone: (216) 243-8100
FAX: (216) 891-3120
Year Established: 1875
Pub. Frequency: 21/yr.
Page Size: tabloid
Subscrip. Rate: $35/yr.; $50/2 yrs.
Freelance Pay: $100-$500
Circulation: 46,000
Circulation Type: controlled

**Owner(s):**
Advanstar Communications, Inc.
7500 Old Oak Blvd.
Cleveland, OH 44130
Telephone: (216) 243-8100
Ownership %: 100
**Management:**
Alex DeBart ...........................Publisher
Mary Ann Wiberg ..............Circulation Manager
Bernice Geisert ..................Production Manager
**Editorial:**
Robert A. Nozar ..........................Editor in Chief
Bill Gillette ..............................Executive Editor
Lauren Drier ..............................Art Director
Mary Lindskog Rindahl .......Production Director
**Desc.:** Up-to-date news, tips, trends and how-to's; new product and design information for the hotel, motel and resort industry.
**Readers:** Corporate executives, owners, managers, investors, department heads, purchasing agents and other decision makers in the hotel, motel and resort industry.

68923

## HOTEL & RESORT INDUSTRY
488 Madison Ave.
New York, NY 10022
Telephone: (212) 888-1500
FAX: (212) 888-8008
Year Established: 1978
Pub. Frequency: m.
Subscrip. Rate: $50/yr.
Circulation: 49,494
Circulation Type: controlled
**Owner(s):**
Coastal Communications Corp.
488 Madison Ave.
New York, NY 10022
Telephone: (212) 888-1500
Ownership %: 100
**Editorial:**
Stefani O'Connor ...........................Editor

66002

## HOTELS
1350 E. Touhy Ave.
Des Plaines, IL 60018-5080
Telephone: (708) 635-8800
FAX: (708) 635-6856
Mailing Address:
　P.O. Box 5080
　Des Plaines, IL 60017-5080
Year Established: 1966
Pub. Frequency: m.
Page Size: standard
Subscrip. Rate: $75/yr. in US
Materials: 01,04,06,07,27,28,29,32,33
Print Process: offset
Circulation: 60,000
Circulation Type: controlled
**Owner(s):**
Cahners Publishing Co.
1350 E. Touhy
Des Plaines, IL 60018-5080
Telephone: (708) 635-8800
FAX: (708) 635-6856
Ownership %: 100
**Management:**
Don Lock ..................................Publisher
Dan Hogan ..............................Sales Manager
**Editorial:**
Jim Carper .................................Editor
Fran Martin ..............................Managing Editor
**Desc.:** Written for owners and operators of large full service hotels. Editorial includes: design, food & beverage, company profile, development focus and managing and marketing articles.
**Readers:** Managers and operators of hotels
**Deadline:** news-3 mos. prior to pub. date; photo-3 mos. prior; ads-15th of mo.; 2 mos. prior

**Materials Accepted/Included:** 01-Business news 02-By-line articles 03-Fashion news 04-Food news 05-Freelance copy 06-Letters to editor 07-Real estate news 08-Sports news 09-Travel news 10-Book rev. 11-Movie rev. 12-Music rev. 13-TV rev. 14-Theater rev. 15-Coming events 16-Obituaries 17-Question & answer 18-Social announcements 19-Artwork 20-Cartoons 21-Photos 22-TV listings 23-Audio rec. 24-Video rec. 25-Books 26-Films/film clips 27-Personnel news 28-Press releases 29-New product news/photos 30-Trade lit. 31-Contracts awarded 32-Display adv. 33-Classified adv.

4-178

**LODGING HOSPITALITY**     23390
1100 Superior Ave.
Cleveland, OH 44114-2543
Telephone: (216) 696-7000
FAX: (216) 696-7658
Year Established: 1949
Pub. Frequency: m.
Page Size: standard
Subscrip. Rate: $60/yr.
Materials: 01,04,06,07,09,15,16,25,27,28,
   29,30,32,33
Freelance Pay: $100-1000/story
Print Process: web offset
Circulation: 50,000
Circulation Type: controlled
Owner(s):
Penton Publishing
1100 Superior Ave.
Cleveland, OH 44114
Telephone: (216) 696-7000
Ownership %: 100
Management:
Gary Dietz ...............................Publisher
Editorial:
Megan Rowe .....................Senior Editor
Edward Watkins ............................Editor
Carlo Wolff ................................Associate Editor
Grace Wagner ...............Associate Editor
Sharon Estep ................Production Editor
Desc.: Coverage of lodging operations,
   their facilities, including maintenance,
   remodeling, advertising, heating,
   building, furnishing, decorating,
   merchandising, etc. All articles are staff-
   written.
Readers: Owners, managers, operators,
   and purchasing.
Deadline: story-15th of mo., 2 mo. prior to
   pub. date; news-15th of mo.; photo-15th
   of mo.; ads-15th of mo.

**LODGING MAGAZINE**     23388
1201 New York Ave., N.W.
Ste. 600
Washington, DC 20005-3931
Telephone: (202) 289-3100
Year Established: 1975
Pub. Frequency: 11/yr.
Page Size: standard
Subscrip. Rate: $35/yr.
Circulation: 28,194
Circulation Type: paid
Owner(s):
American Hotel Assn. Dir. Corp.
1201 New York Ave., N.W.
Ste. 600
Washington, DC 20005-3931
Telephone: (202) 289-3164
Ownership %: 100
Management:
Laurence E. Wilholm ..............Publisher
Editorial:
Philip Hayward ............................Editor
Paul Cohen ...................................Sales
Desc.: Technical articles on hotel/motel
   management.
Readers: Hotel owners and general
   managers; hotel company executives.

**SUCCESSFUL HOTEL MARKETER**     68931
2718 Dryden Dr.
Madison, WI 53704
Telephone: (608) 246-3580
FAX: (608) 249-0355
Year Established: 1988
Pub. Frequency: m.
Subscrip. Rate: $119/yr.
Circulation: 500
Circulation Type: paid

Owner(s):
Magna Publications, Inc.
2718 Dryden Dr.
Madison, WI 53704
Telephone: (608) 246-3580
Ownership %: 100
Editorial:
Tim Kelley ..................................Editor
Desc.: Offers practical hotel marketing
   strategies, creative ideas, and innovative
   techniques.

## Group 120-Housewares &
## Home Furnishings

**CONTACT**     69548
209 S. Main St., Space M1215
High Point, NC 27261
Telephone: (910) 889-3920
Mailing Address:
   P.O. Box 670
   High Point, NC 27261
Pub. Frequency: m.
Subscrip. Rate: $18/yr.
Owner(s):
International Home Furnishings
   Representatives Asn
209 S. Main St., Space M1215
Box 670
High Point, NC 27261
Telephone: (919) 889-3920
Editorial:
Kelly R. Crisco ..........................Editor
Desc.: Gives facts on taxes, markets,
   legislation and membership benefits and
   ideas on how to enhance sales.
Readers: Home furnishings representative.

**DECORATIVE RUG**     68853
P.O. Box 709
Meredith, NH 03253
Telephone: (603) 744-9191
FAX: (603) 744-6933
Year Established: 1987
Pub. Frequency: m.
Page Size: standard
Subscrip. Rate: $48/yr.
Materials: 01,06,15,17,21,27,28,29,30,32,33
Print Process: web
Circulation: 10,000
Circulation Type: paid
Owner(s):
Oriental Rug Auction Review, Inc.
P.O. Box 709
Meredith, NH 03253
Telephone: (603) 744-9191
Ownership %: 100
Editorial:
Ron O'Callaghan ........................Editor
Desc.: Covers new oriental rugs at the
   wholesale and retail levels.

**DESIGN LINES**     23096
1355 Market St., Ste. 460
San Francisco, CA 94103
Telephone: (415) 552-2311
Year Established: 1988
Pub. Frequency: s-a.
Page Size: tabloid
Subscrip. Rate: free
Circulation: 16,000
Circulation Type: free
Owner(s):
SFM
1355 Market St.
San Francisco, CA 94103
Telephone: (415) 552-2311
Ownership %: 100
Management:
Susan Kuchinskas ..................Publisher
Editorial:
Susan Kuchinskas ......................Editor

Desc.: Trade publication chronicling news
   and information on the Winter &
   Summer Home Furnishing Markets in
   San Francisco at the SF Mart. Editorial
   includes photos and features on new
   products, promotions, seminar programs
   and social events during Market and
   throughout the year. Features products
   sold at SFM only.
Readers: Retail buyers, manufacturers,
   interior designers and architects.

**DRAPERIES & WINDOW**     68935
**COVERINGS**
450 Skokie Blvd., Ste. 507
Northbrook, IL 60062
FAX: (407) 627-3447
Year Established: 1981
Pub. Frequency: 13/yr.
Page Size: standard
Subscrip. Rate: $30/yr.
Circulation: 25,115
Circulation Type: paid
Owner(s):
L.C. Clark Publishing Co., Inc.
450 Skokie Blvd., Ste. 507
Northbrook, IL 60062
Ownership %: 100
Editorial:
Katie Sosnowchik .......................Editor

**LDB/INTERIOR TEXTILES**     23402
370 Lexington Ave.
New York, NY 10017
Telephone: (212) 532-9290
FAX: (212) 779-8345
Year Established: 1927
Pub. Frequency: m.
Page Size: standard
Subscrip. Rate: $40/yr.; $55/2 yrs.; $95/yr.
   foreign
Freelance Pay: varies
Circulation: 13,000
Circulation Type: controlled
Owner(s):
E.W. Williams Publications Co.
2125 Center Ave.
Ft. Lee, NJ 07024
Ownership %: 100
Management:
Philippa Schoenfeld .................Publisher
Editorial:
Renee Bennett ...........................Editor
Desc.: Magazine covers merchandising,
   marketing and design trends in the
   home fashions industry. Meeting the
   information needs of buyers and top
   retail management at department stores,
   mass merchants, discounters, and
   specialty chains. Product coverage
   includes linens, domestics, bath, window
   treatments, bedspreads, fabrics and
   giftware.
Readers: Retailers and manufacturers of
   bed, bath, linen, window treatments,
   bedspreads, fabrics and giftware.
   Circulation is BPA audited.

**MIRROR NEWS MAGAZINE**     23403
103 Second St. N.
Hopkins, MN 55343
Telephone: (612) 935-3666
Mailing Address:
   P.O. Box 471
   Hopkins, MN 55343
Year Established: 1960
Pub. Frequency: q.
Page Size: standard
Subscrip. Rate: $16/yr.
Circulation: 9,610
Owner(s):
Market Power, Inc.
Telephone: (612) 935-3666
Ownership %: 100

Management:
Wil L. Tiller .................................President
Marianna Lee ...........Executive Vice President
Howard Rassier .........................Controller
Wil L. Tiller ................................Publisher
W. Douglas Chandler ........Advertising Manager
Deloris Krois ...............Circulation Manager
Howard Rassier ................Operations Manager
Doug Chandler ...............Sales Manager
Editorial:
Wil L. Tiller .....................Executive Editor
Wil L. Tiller .....................Managing Editor
S. D. Meulpolder ..................Art Director
Douglas Chandler .............Associate Editor
Wil L. Tiller ...............Book Review Editor
Wil L. Tiller .........................Feature Editor
C. Gregory ................New Product Editor
W. Douglas Chandler .............News Editor
S. D. Meulpolder ..........................Photo
S. D. Meulpolder ................Production Director
Marianna Lee ..........Secretary & Treasurer
Lucille Neuberger ............Technical Editor
Howard Rassier .........................Treasurer
Desc.: Six special feature issues each year
   (1) Mirror Promotions by mirror
   manufacturers, heavy-glass mfg., glass
   and mirror industry suppliers
   and manufacturers of related
   accessories and fabrication machinery.
   This is an announcement of activities
   retailers can expect for the year;
   (2) Merchandising Ideas on Sales
   Promotion, advertising, display, etc.; (3)
   New Products announced; (4) National
   Programs for Fall by mirror and heavy-
   glass manufacturers; (5) Creativity in
   Mirror Uses by architects, builders,
   interior designers, furniture builders, etc.;
   (6) Holiday Mirror Retailing
   Ideas. Articles and news stories
   supporting these theme categories are
   most welcomed. Articles should
   be informative and identify their product
   with heavy-glass or mirror superiority
   when applicable. Departments include:
   Retailing Mirrors and Wall Accessories,
   Industrial Production of Heavy-Glass,
   Mirrors and Related Products, National
   Mirror Activity to Consumers via Glass
   and Mirror Manufacturers
   (individually and through NAMM). Heavy-
   Glass and Plate Glass Mirror fabrication,
   Machinery and Tools that benefit
   Custom Mirror and Glass Shops
   with Time/Profit efficiencies; increase
   quality, safety, durability of heavy-glass
   and mirror fabricated products.
Readers: Department store buyers and
   merchandising, mirror manufacturers,
   glass manufacturers, builders and
   contractors, mirror machine and tool,
   interior designers, custom mirrors shops,
   architects, manufacturers of products
   allied with the mirror industry and interior
   decorative glass, educational institutions.

**WALL PAPER, THE**     68939
570 Seventh Ave., Ste. 500
New York, NY 00008
Telephone: (212) 869-4960
FAX: (212) 869-1141
Year Established: 1980
Pub. Frequency: m.
Subscrip. Rate: $21/yr. US; $35/yr.
   Canada; $65/yr. elsewhere
Circulation: 18,000
Circulation Type: paid
Owner(s):
Wall Publications, Inc.
570 Seventh Ave., Ste. 500
New York, NY 10018
Telephone: (212) 869-4960
Ownership %: 100
Editorial:
Marita Thomas ...........................Editor

Materials Accepted/Included: 01-Business news 02-By-line articles 03-Fashion news 04-Food news 05-Freelance copy 06-Letters to editor 07-Real estate news 08-Sports news 09-Travel news
10-Book rev. 11-Movie rev. 12-Music rev. 13-TV rev. 14-Theater rev. 15-Coming events 16-Obituaries 17-Question & answer 18-Social announcements 19-Artwork 20-Cartoons 21-Photos 22-TV listings
23-Audio rec. 24-Video rec. 25-Books 26-Films/film clips 27-Personnel news 28-Press releases 29-New product news/photos 30-Trade lit. 31-Contracts awarded 32-Display adv. 33-Classified adv.

4-179

**Desc.:** Reports on product selling, merchandising, sales training, advertising, promotions, new products and procedures.
**Readers:** Wallcovering dealers and others in the industry.

## Group 122-Industrial Distribution

**AMERICAN SHIPPER**                                    22255
33 S. Hogan St., Ste. 230
Jacksonville, FL 32202-5131
Telephone: (904) 355-2601
FAX: (904) 791-8836
Mailing Address:
P.O. Box 4728
Jacksonville, FL 32201-4728
Year Established: 1959
Pub. Frequency: m.
Page Size: standard
Subscrip. Rate: $90/yr. air; $36/yr. surface
Materials: 30,32
Freelance Pay: none
Print Process: web offset
Circulation: 14,362
Circulation Type: controlled & paid
**Owner(s):**
Howard Publications
P.O. Box 4728
Jacksonville, FL 32201-4728
Telephone: (904) 355-2601
FAX: (904) 791-8836
Ownership %: 100
**Bureau(s):**
American Shipper
National Press Bldg., Rm. 1269
Washington DC , DC 20045-2201
Telephone: (202) 347-1678
FAX: (202) 347-1678
Contact: E. Anthony Beargie, Associate Editor

American Shipper
5 Third St., Rm. 910
San Francisco , CA 94103-3210
Telephone: (415) 421-9815
FAX: (415) 495-6750
Contact: Richard Knee, Associate Editor

American Shipper
5 World Trade Center
Ste. 9259
New York, NY 10048
Telephone: (212) 912-1077
FAX: (212) 912-1244
Contact: Leslie Wines, Associate Editor

American Shipper
33 S. Hogan St., Ste.230
Jacksonville, FL 32202-5131
Telephone: (904) 355-2601
FAX: (904) 791-8836
Contact: Joseph A. Bonney, Editor
**Management:**
David A. Howard ............................President
Hayes H. Howard ..............................Publisher
Bill Barrs ..........................Advertising Manager
Nancy L. Barry ................Assistant Advertising Manager
Karyl DeSousa ..................Circulation Manager
**Editorial:**
David A. Howard ................................Editor
Joseph A. Bonney ..............Managing Editor
C. Anthony Beargie ................Associate Editor
Richard Knee ......................Associate Editor
Gary Burrows ......................Associate Editor
Clinton W. Alphen ..........Associate Publisher
Elizabeth Canna ....................Deputy Editor
**Desc.:** Covers developments in international transportation and logistics with a focus on regulatory and policy issues and on the relationship between importers, exporters, as well as sea and air cargo carriers and analyses of trends affecting both.

**Readers:** Top corporate, operational & marketing managers with firms involved in international transportation & their customers-traffic & logistics managers with manufacturers, growers, miners, wholesalers, and retailers who buy or sell goods in the global marketplace.
**Deadline:** story-1st of mo., prior to pub. date; news-1st of mo.; photo-1st of mo.; ads-1st of mo.

**DEFENSE TRANSPORTATION JOURNAL**                                    25096
50 S. Pickett St.
Ste. 220
Alexandria, VA 22304-3008
Telephone: (703) 751-5011
FAX: (703) 823-8761
Year Established: 1946
Pub. Frequency: bi-m.
Page Size: standard
Subscrip. Rate: $35/yr.
Circulation: 8,100
Circulation Type: paid
**Owner(s):**
National Defense Transportation Assn.
50 S. Pickett St.
Ste. 220
Alexandria, VA 22304
Telephone: (703) 751-5011
Ownership %: 100
**Management:**
Edward Honor ..........................President
Kim Bottoms ..................Circulation Manager
**Editorial:**
Dr. Joseph G. Mattingly, Jr. ................Editor
Col. Denny Edwards ............Managing Editor
**Desc.:** Objectives of the journal are to advance knowledge and science in defense transportation (defense transportation is the partnership between the commercial transportation industry and the military transporter) and to stimulate greater thought and effort in the area of defense transportation and logistics by providing readers with new and helpful information about defense transportation issues.
**Readers:** 30 percent military, 70 percent civilian.

**FASTENER TECHNOLOGY INTERNATIONAL**                                    56226
3869 Darrow Rd., Ste. 101
Stow, OH 44224
Telephone: (216) 686-9544
Year Established: 1979
Pub. Frequency: bi-m.
Page Size: standard
Subscrip. Rate: $30/yr. US & Canada; $55/yr. foreign
Materials: 01,02,06,10,15,16,28,29,30,32,33
Circulation: 13,000
Circulation Type: controlled
**Owner(s):**
Initial Publications, Inc.
3869 Darrow Rd., Ste. 101
Stow, OH 44224
Telephone: (216) 686-9544
Ownership %: 100
**Management:**
John L. Jones ..........................President
John L. Jones ..........................Publisher
**Editorial:**
Thomas H. Dreher ........................Editor
James C. Keebler ..............Technical Director

**Desc.:** Qualified recipients are involved in general management, operations management, technical/production/engineering, purchasing sales & marketing in companies producing, distributing & using fasteners. Also included are a limited number of consulting & design engineering firms, governmental agencies, libraries & others allied to the field.
**Readers:** Serves the manufacturing, distribution & application of mechanical fasteners and custom-formed parts.

**INDUSTRIAL DISTRIBUTION**                                    23485
275 Washington St.
Newton, MA 02158
Telephone: (617) 964-3030
Year Established: 1911
Pub. Frequency: m.
Page Size: standard
Subscrip. Rate: $75/yr.
Freelance Pay: varies
Circulation: 41,500
Circulation Type: controlled
**Owner(s):**
Cahners Publishing Co.
275 Washington St.
Newton, MA 02158
Telephone: (617) 964-3030
Ownership %: 100
**Management:**
John R. Kovacs ..........................Publisher
Dorothy Bannister ............Circulation Manager
Harvey Solomon ..............Production Manager
**Editorial:**
John J. Keough ......................Editor in Chief
George Fodor ......................Managing Editor
Katherine Zwald ......Assistant Managing Editor
Louise King ........................Associate Editor
John Johnson ......................Associate Editor
Michael O'Leary ....................Design Director
**Desc.:** Staff-Written practical "how-to" features cover new resources, business getting, customer relations, sales management in industrial distributor firms, warehouses, operations.
**Readers:** Industrial distributors, management, sales executives and sales personnel.

**INTERMODAL SHIPPING**                                    24250
6151 Powers Ferry Rd., N.W.
Atlanta, GA 30339-2941
Telephone: (404) 955-2500
FAX: (404) 618-0348
Year Established: 1966
Pub. Frequency: m.
Page Size: standard
Subscrip. Rate: $38/yr. US; $98/yr. foreign
Freelance Pay: negotiable
Circulation: 22,000
Circulation Type: controlled
**Owner(s):**
Argus Business
6151 Powers Ferry Rd., N.W.
Atlanta, GA 30339-2941
Telephone: (404) 955-2500
Ownership %: 100
**Management:**
Jerrold France ..........................President
Herb Schild ..........................Publisher
Steve Prince ......................Associate Publsiher
**Editorial:**
Herb Schild ................................Editor
Teri Alger ........................Associate Editor
**Desc.:** Prime focus is on the use of containerized, intermodal transportation by air, sea, land, rail. Concerned with methods, costs, equipment for shipping, insurance, etc.

**Readers:** Manufacturers, carriers; port authorities and freight equipment and services.

**MATERIAL HANDLING ENGINEERING**                                    23661
1100 Superior Ave.
Cleveland, OH 44114-2543
Telephone: (216) 696-7000
FAX: (216) 696-7658
Year Established: 1945
Pub. Frequency: 13/yr.
Page Size: standard
Subscrip. Rate: $5/issue; $50/yr.; $80/2 yrs.
Materials: 24,25,27,28,29,30,32,33
Print Process: web offset
Circulation: 102,251
Circulation Type: controlled
**Owner(s):**
Penton Publishing
1100 Superior Ave.
Cleveland, OH 44114
Telephone: (216) 696-7000
Ownership %: 100
**Management:**
John Davis ..........................Publisher
Mel Burke ....................Business Manager
**Editorial:**
Gene Schwind ......................Executive Editor
C. Witt ................................Senior Editor
B. Knill ................................Editor
C. Trunk ........................Managing Editor
Pet Keefe ........................Group President
**Desc.:** Features cover all phases of material handling and industrial packaging with special emphasis on control of material flow & systems integration.
**Readers:** Management & engineering personnel in material handling and distribution throughout all SIC's.

**MODERN MATERIALS HANDLING**                                    23662
275 Washington St.
Newton, MA 02158
Telephone: (617) 964-3030
FAX: (617) 558-4402
Year Established: 1946
Pub. Frequency: 14/yr.
Page Size: standard
Subscrip. Rate: $20/issue; $80/yr.
Circulation: 105,852
Circulation Type: controlled
**Owner(s):**
Cahners Publishing Co.
275 Washington St.
Newton, MA 02158
Telephone: (617) 964-3030
Ownership %: 100
**Management:**
William G. Sbordon ..........................Publisher
Cynthia C. Clark ................Business Manager
Christine Distler ................Circulation Manager
Melissa Carman ................Production Manager
Amy Schaefer ..................Promotion Manager
**Editorial:**
Ray Kulwiec ......................Editor in Chief
Gary Forger ........................Senior Editor
Karen Auguston ....................Senior Editor
Nancy Staples ............................Editor
Jennifer Mullare ........................Editor
Tom Feare ........................Managing Editor
Ellen Greenblatt ....................Production Editor

Materials Accepted/Included: 01-Business news 02-By-line articles 03-Fashion news 04-Food news 05-Freelance copy 06-Letters to editor 07-Real estate news 08-Sports news 09-Travel news 10-Book rev. 11-Movie rev. 12-Music rev. 13-TV rev. 14-Theater rev. 15-Coming events 16-Obituaries 17-Question & answer 18-Social announcements 19-Artwork 20-Cartoons 21-Photos 22-TV listings 23-Audio rec. 24-Video rec. 25-Books 26-Films/film clips 27-Personnel news 28-Press releases 29-New product news/photos 30-Trade lit. 31-Contracts awarded 32-Display adv. 33-Classified adv.

4-180

**Desc.:** Serves materials handling and packaging personnel in manufacturing and distribution industries. Serves the field of managers, engineers and supervisors involved in planning and selecting materials handling equipment & systems throughout manufacturing and distribution including wholesale, retail, durable and non-durable warehousing locations and other non-manufacturing industries.

## MOVERS NEWS
25234
132 State St.
Albany, NY 12207
Telephone: (518) 449-8833
Year Established: 1937
Pub. Frequency: m.
Page Size: oversize
Subscrip. Rate: $39/yr.
Materials: 01,27,28,32,33
Circulation: 550
Circulation Type: paid
**Owner(s):**
NY State Movers & Warehousemen Association
132 State St.
Albany, NY 12207
Telephone: (518) 449-8833
Ownership %: 100
**Editorial:**
Carolyn Morgenstern ..............................Editor
Kelly Maynard ...............................Advertising
Donald J. Boyle ..................Editor-in-Chief
**Desc.:** Concentrates on the moving and storage industry.
**Readers:** Managers mostly; also suppliers, bureaucrats.
**Deadline:** story-1st of mo. prior to pub. date; news-1st of mo. prior; photo-1st of mo. prior; ads-1st of mo. prior

## NETWORK
69155
252 E. Washington
East Peoria, IL 61611
Telephone: (309) 669-4431
FAX: (309) 698-0801
Mailing Address:
  P.O. Box 2338
  East Peoria, IL 61611
Year Established: 1980
Pub. Frequency: m.
Page Size: tabloid
Subscrip. Rate: $65/yr. US; $125/yr. foreign
Materials: 01,02,05,06,15,19,21,27,28,29, 30,32,33
Circulation: 15,250
Circulation Type: free & paid
**Owner(s):**
Woodward Communications
252 E. Washington
P.O. Box 2338
E. Peoria, IL 61611
Telephone: (309) 669-4431
Ownership %: 100
**Desc.:** Covers news, manufacturers, new products, feature stories and people profiles in the field of materials handling.
**Deadline:** story-10th of mo.; news-10th of mo.; photo-10th of mo.; ads-15th of mo

## REFRIGERATED TRANSPORTER
25106
4200 S. Shepherd Dr.
Ste. 200
Houston, TX 77098
Telephone: (713) 523-8124
FAX: (713) 523-8384
Mailing Address:
  P.O. Box 66010
  Houston, TX 77266
Year Established: 1964
Pub. Frequency: m.

Page Size: standard
Subscrip. Rate: free to qualified members; $25/yr. non-members
Freelance Pay: varies
Circulation: 15,000
Circulation Type: controlled & paid
**Owner(s):**
Tunnell Publications, Inc.
4200 S. Shepherd Dr.
Ste. 200
Houston, TX 77098
Telephone: (713) 523-8124
Ownership %: 100
**Management:**
W.L. Tunnell .......................Advertising Manager
**Editorial:**
Gary Macklin ...................................Editor
Charles Wilson ...................Managing Editor
Paul Schenck ...................Editorial Director
Paul Schenck ...................Associate Editor
**Desc.:** Staff written and contributed articles covers technical and management, equipment and operations stories for all types of temperature controlled transporters. Departments include: New Products and Names in the News.
**Readers:** Company owners, presidents, transportation, and fleet owners.

## SHIPPING DIGEST
25107
51 Madison Ave.
New York, NY 10010
Telephone: (212) 689-4411
FAX: (212) 683-7929
Year Established: 1923
Pub. Frequency: w.
Page Size: standard
Subscrip. Rate: $38/yr.
Circulation: 4,893
Circulation Type: paid
**Owner(s):**
Geyer-McAllister Publications, Inc.
51 Madison Ave.
New York, NY 10010
Telephone: (212) 689-4411
Ownership %: 100
**Bureau(s):**
Western Representative, The R.W. Walker Co., Inc.
2716 Ocean Park Blvd.
Santa Monica, CA 90405
Telephone: (310) 450-9001
Contact: Terry Casaus


R. W. Walker Co., The
24301 Southland Dr., Ste. 216
Hayward, CA 94545
Telephone: (310) 245-1843
Contact: Patricia B. Macsata


Ken Lehman & Assoc.
517 E. Wilson Ave. Ste. 203b
Glendale, CA 91206
Telephone: (510) 786-2198
Contact: Ken Lehman, President
**Management:**
Richard A. Duffy ...................................President
Douglas P. Caffarone .................Executive Vice President
Cal Stein ...................................Publisher
Martin Horan ...................Circulation Manager
**Editorial:**
Maria Reines ...................................Editor
Jim Dow ...................................News Editor
Richard Norman .................Production Director

**Desc.:** News publication reporting on trends, developments, activities within the shipping industry, foreign trade economics, American and Canadian ports, the steamship, railroad and aviation industries, including containerization, intermodal and land bridge developments, foreign exchange rates as well as steamship sailings from U.S. Atlantic and Gulf, Great Lakes, Canadian sailings, Pacific Coast sailings, foreign freight forwarders, customs brokers, steamship companies and agencies and intercoastal sailings, air shipping section weekly, handbook for international trade published twice a year, May & November.
**Readers:** Manufacturers, freight forwarders, brokers and export traders.

## SOUTHERN INDUSTRIAL SUPPLIER
23486
P.O. Box 18343
Greensboro, NC 27419
Telephone: (919) 454-3516
Year Established: 1952
Pub. Frequency: m.
Page Size: standard
Subscrip. Rate: $22/yr.
Circulation: 4,000
Circulation Type: paid
**Owner(s):**
Southern Trade Publications Co.
P.O. Box 18343
Greensboro, NC 27419
Telephone: (919) 454-3516
Ownership %: 100
**Management:**
E.D. Atkins ...................................Publisher
**Editorial:**
E.D. Atkins ...................................Editor
**Desc.:** Serves industrial supply distributor organizations in 14 southern states.
**Readers:** Key personnel in charge of distribution.

## TODAY'S DISTRIBUTOR
65258
1233 Janesville Ave.
Fort Atkinson, WI 53538
Telephone: (414) 563-1701
Year Established: 1988
Pub. Frequency: bi-m.
Page Size: tabloid
Subscrip. Rate: $40/yr. US; $55/yr. Canada and Mexico; $120/yr. elsewhere; free to qualified personnel
Materials: 01,06,15,27,28,29,30,31,32,33
Print Process: offset
Circulation: 42,000
Circulation Type: controlled
**Owner(s):**
Johnson Hill Press, Inc.
1233 Janesville Ave.
Fort Atkinson, WI 53538
Telephone: (414) 563-1701
**Management:**
Robert Lederer ...................................Publisher
**Editorial:**
Greg Udelhoen ...................................Editor
**Desc.:** Profiles distributors, suppliers, sales managers, marketing executives, economics and customers.
**Readers:** Covers industrial and construction distributors.

## TRAFFIC MANAGEMENT
25110
275 Washington St.
Newton, MA 02158
Telephone: (617) 964-3030
Year Established: 1962
Page Size: 4 color photos/art
Subscrip. Rate: $64.95/yr.
Circulation: 73,250

Circulation Type: controlled
**Owner(s):**
Cahners Publishing Co.
275 Washington St.
Newton, MA 02158
Telephone: (617) 964-3030
Ownership %: 100
**Management:**
Robert Krakoff ...................................President
Ronald Bondlow ...................................Publisher
Debbie Sellin ...................Circulation Manager
Bonnie Keller ...................Circulation Manager
Mike Wisher ...................General Manager
**Editorial:**
Francis J. Quinn ...................Senior Editor
James Aaron Cooke ...................................Editor
Martha Spizziri ...................................Editor
Mitchell MacDonald ...................................Editor
Karen Bachrach ...................Managing Editor
Nancy Null ...................Art Director
Jack Farrell ...................Editor Emeritus
Stephen Tinghitella ...................Editor Emeritus
Mary Gregory ...................Marketing Director
Laura H. Diviney .........Production Coordinator
John Sanders ...................Production Director
Alice J. Dorsey ...................Production Director
Laura H. Diviney ...................................Sales
**Desc.:** Articles deal with freight transportation and physical distribution, including related subjects, such as materials handling, warehousing, protective packaging. All articles are staff-written, from the viewpoint of the user of transportation services. Departments include: Report From Washington, Transportation/ Distribution News, New Products, Computer Column, Hazardous Materials Column, Editorial, Negotiating Column, Economic Forecasts.
**Readers:** Industrial traffic managers, warehousing with transportation and distribution; sales executives, buyers of domestic and international transportation services and equipment.

## TRAFFIC WORLD
25112
741 National Press Bldg.
Washington, DC 20045
Telephone: (202) 383-6140
FAX: (202) 737-3349
Year Established: 1907
Pub. Frequency: w.
Page Size: standard
Subscrip. Rate: $159/yr.
Freelance Pay: $300
Circulation: 10,000
Circulation Type: paid
**Owner(s):**
Journal of Commerce, Inc.
741 National Press Bldg.
Washington, DC 20045
Telephone: (202) 383-6140
Ownership %: 100
**Management:**
Patrick Keleher ...................................President
Stanford Erickson ...................................Publisher
**Editorial:**
Jean Murphy ...................................Editor
**Readers:** Shippers & carriers, and related fields.

## TRANSPORTATION & DISTRIBUTION
23484
1100 Superior Ave.
Cleveland, OH 44114
Telephone: (216) 696-7000
FAX: (216) 696-4135
Year Established: 1960
Pub. Frequency: m.
Page Size: standard
Subscrip. Rate: $45/yr.; $75/2 yrs.
Circulation: 75,000
Circulation Type: controlled

**Materials Accepted/Included:** 01-Business news 02-By-line articles 03-Fashion news 04-Food news 05-Freelance copy 06-Letters to editor 07-Real estate news 08-Sports news 09-Travel news 10-Book rev. 11-Movie rev. 12-Music rev. 13-TV rev. 14-Theater rev. 15-Coming events 16-Obituaries 17-Question & answer 18-Social announcements 19-Artwork 20-Cartoons 21-Photos 22-TV listings 23-Audio rec. 24-Video rec. 25-Books 26-Films/film clips 27-Personnel news 28-Press releases 29-New product news/photos 30-Trade lit. 31-Contracts awarded 32-Display adv. 33-Classified adv.

4-181

**Owner(s):**
Penton Publishing
1100 Superior Ave.
Cleveland, OH 44114
Telephone: (216) 696-7000
Ownership %: 100
**Management:**
Robert F. Eck, III .........................Publisher
Christine Marinez ...............Business Manager
**Editorial:**
Perry Trunick ..................................Editor
**Desc.:** Covers physical distribution and logistics field (transportation, material handling, protective packaging, warehousing, and inventory control). Departments include: Product/Lit Review, Services, People, Issues & Trends, Commentary, Legal Briefs, Computer Systems, Logistics Trends, Human Resources.
**Readers:** Physical distribution managers, traffic managers, purchasing managers, warehouse managers, corporate and operating executives.

## Group 124-Industrial Plant Engineering,Maintenance & Operations

23408
### AIPE FACILITIES
8180 Corporate Park Dr. #305
Cincinnati, OH 45242-3309
Telephone: (513) 489-2473
FAX: (513) 247-7422
Year Established: 1974
Pub. Frequency: bi-m.
Page Size: standard
Subscrip. Rate: $42/yr. non-member; $50/yr. foreign
Freelance Pay: negotiable
Circulation: 10,500
Circulation Type: paid
**Owner(s):**
American Institute of Plant Engineers
3975 Erie Ave.
Cincinnati, OH 45208
Telephone: (513) 561-6000
Ownership %: 100
**Management:**
Michael J. Tillar ...............................Publisher
Michael J. Tillar ....................Executive Director
Joseph H. Greil .........Chairman Editorial Board
**Editorial:**
Mike Frening ....................................Editor
**Desc.:** Edited for the field of plant engineering. In both manufacturing and non - manufacturing facilities. Articles report technical updates, management development information, and how - to problem solving ideas. Geared for managers of plant engineering and facilities.
**Readers:** Members of the American Institute of Plant Engineers/Engineering, curriculum graduates, Facilities, Directors/Managers.

23415
### COMPRESSED AIR
253 E. Washington Ave.
Washington, NJ 07882-2495
Telephone: (908) 850-7818
FAX: (908) 689-5576
Year Established: 1896
Pub. Frequency: 8/yr.
Page Size: standard
Subscrip. Rate: $15/yr., $1.50/issue
Materials: 01,05,10,28,29,30
Freelance Pay: $900
Print Process: web offset
Circulation: 145,000
Circulation Type: controlled & paid

**Owner(s):**
Ingersoll-Rand Co.
Ownership %: 100
**Management:**
J. A. McCormick .........................Publisher
M. T. Zayle .........................Business Manager
**Editorial:**
S. M. Parkhill .................................Editor
J. G. Wilcox ...............................Art Director
S. M. Parkhill ....................Publication Director
**Desc.:** Need factual articles on the management of industrial operations and technology as applied to industries as well as articles on subjects that interest a general industrial management audience. Material must be approved for accuracy by someone in authority in the concern written about. Dry, technical descriptions of new products and case histories are not wanted. Prefers to tell what products do rather than give details of their construction. Article concepts should be approved by editor before research and writing begins.
**Readers:** Companies and individuals in executive, production, engineering, consulting or supervisory capacity in industries concerned with applications of pneumatics, hydraulics, and associated energy forms, processes and equipment.

23420
### ENERGY USER NEWS
Chilton Way
Radnor, PA 19089
Telephone: (215) 964-4278
FAX: (215) 964-4647
Year Established: 1976
Pub. Frequency: m.
Page Size: tabloid
Subscrip. Rate: $69.50/yr.
Circulation: 40,000
Circulation Type: paid
**Owner(s):**
Chilton Co.
Chilton Way
Radnor, PA 19089
Telephone: (215) 964-4278
Ownership %: 100
**Management:**
George Hutter .............................Publisher
Jennifer Butler ...................Business Manager
Jack Jones .........................Circulation Manager
**Editorial:**
Virginia Hines ......................Editor in Chief
**Desc.:** Provides in-depth features designed to aid the energy related business decisions of anyone in any industrial or commercial facility responsible for conserving, managing, controlling or purchasing energy. Departments include: General News, Energy Technology, Products, Conservation and Management Applications, Fuel & Power, Price and Availability, Government News, Laws, Regulations, Standards, Codes.
**Readers:** Energy concerned managers and top managers and management of commercial and industrial energy.

23459
### ENGINEER'S DIGEST
29100 Aurora Rd.
Ste. 200
Cleveland, OH 44139
Telephone: (216) 248-1125
FAX: (216) 248-0187
Year Established: 1973
Pub. Frequency: m.
Page Size: digest
Subscrip. Rate: free/qualified
Materials: 02,06,
Freelance Pay: varies

Circulation: 123,250
Circulation Type: controlled
**Owner(s):**
Huebcore Communications, Inc.
29100 Aurora Rd.
Ste. 200
Cleveland, OH 44139
Telephone: (216) 248-1125
FAX: (216) 247-0187
Ownership %: 100
**Management:**
Thomas J. Corcoran .........................President
Gar Blight ..................................Publisher
Holly Penrose ...................Production Manager
**Editorial:**
Larry Beck ....................................Editor
**Desc.:** The editorial purpose of this publication is to provide plant and facilities engineers with a comprehensive, service that keeps them informed on products, equipment and services that they can put to use in the operation and maintenance of their plants to increase efficiency and/or reduce costs. The editorial approach of this publication is to utilize a combination of brief, illustrated technical product reports and full-length, staff written feature articles--presented in a digest format--to fulfill the editorial purpose stated above.
**Readers:** Plant engineers, facilities engineers, maintenance plant managers.

23430
### INDUSTRIAL MAINTENANCE & PLANT OPERATION
One Chilton Way
Radnor, PA 19089
Telephone: (610) 964-4041
FAX: (610) 964-4947
Year Established: 1940
Pub. Frequency: m.
Page Size: tabloid
Subscrip. Rate: $50/yr. US; $79/yr. foreign
Materials: 01,02,28,29,30,32,33
Print Process: web offset
Circulation: 127,000
Circulation Type: controlled
**Owner(s):**
Chilton Co.
One Chilton Way
Radnor, PA 19087
Telephone: (215) 964-4041
Ownership %: 100
**Management:**
Lee Hufnagel ..............................President
Scott Sward ...............................Publisher
Theresa Deal ....................Production Manager
**Editorial:**
Jerry Steinbrink .........................Chief Editor
James McCanney ...................Managing Editor
Hank Pendrak .....................Marketing Director
**Desc.:** Feature articles on all types of industrial plant maintenance and operations topics. Editorial staff recognizes need for fast readership and gives the reader helpful how-to-do-it articles. Inside pages, in typical 1/9 page units, carry the latest news on products, equipment, processes and techniques from all industrial fields. These product news articles gathered from a wide variety of sources, help keep the plant operations and service group up-to-the-minute on new developments without voluminous reading in many periodicals/give busy plant personnel an accurate basis for determining which new developments in their field require more detailed study. We cover 31 basic industries. Each plant to qualify must employ 50 or more employees.

**Readers:** 127,000 maintenance, engineering, operations and purchasing executive in 69,000 industrial plants. Our readership is very high, 100 percent direct request.
**Deadline:** story-6 wks. prior to pub. date; news-6 wks. prior to pub. date; photo-6 wks. prior to pub. date; ads-1st of mo. prior to pub. date

65460
### MAINTENANCE TECHNOLOGY
1300 S. Grove Ave.
Barrington, IL 60010
Telephone: (708) 382-8100
FAX: (708) 304-8603
Year Established: 1988
Pub. Frequency: m.
Page Size: standard
Subscrip. Rate: $75/yr.
Materials: 02,05,06,10,15,21,25,28,29,30, 32,33
Freelance Pay: negotiable
Print Process: web offset
Circulation: 80,000
Circulation Type: controlled
**Owner(s):**
Applied Tech Publications, Inc.
1300 S. Grove Ave.
Barrington, IL 60010
Telephone: (708) 382-8100
Ownership %: 100
**Management:**
Ciro A. Buttacavoli ..........................Publisher
**Editorial:**
Robert C. Baldwin ...............................Editor
**Desc.:** Serves technical and business information needs of engineers, managers, and supervisors responsible for equipment maintenance and reliability in all industries and facilities.
**Readers:** Maintenance professionals, including supervisors, engineers, managers and technicians in all major facilities industrial plants.
**Deadline:** story-8 wks. prior to pub. date; news-6 wks. prior; photo-6 wks. prior; ads-4 wks. prior

61285
### MAYFLOWER WAREHOUSEMAN, THE
9247 N. Meridian, Ste. 120
Indianapolis, IN 46260
Telephone: (317) 844-6226
FAX: (317) 848-3744
Year Established: 1932
Pub. Frequency: bi-m.
Page Size: standard
Subscrip. Rate: $12/yr.
Materials: 01,02,05,06,15,16,20
Freelance Pay: varies
Print Process: offset
Circulation: 2,400
Circulation Type: controlled
**Owner(s):**
Mayflower Warehouseman Association
9247 N. Meridian
Indianapolis, IN 46260
Telephone: (317) 844-6226
**Management:**
G. B. Urias .................................Publisher
**Editorial:**
Julie M. Foster ..................................Editor
**Desc.:** A blend of hard-hitting technical articles dealing with issues that affect the moving and storage industry and general business pieces that enable readers to maximize job performance. Reports and comments on industry affairs and member accomplishments. It offers advice on sales, diversification and management. More than 550 agents of Mayflower Transit, Inc. in United States and Canada.

**Materials Accepted/Included:** 01-Business news 02-By-line articles 03-Fashion news 04-Food news 05-Freelance copy 06-Letters to editor 07-Real estate news 08-Sports news 09-Travel news 10-Book rev. 11-Movie rev. 12-Music rev. 13-TV rev. 14-Theater rev. 15-Coming events 16-Obituaries 17-Question & answer 18-Social announcements 19-Artwork 20-Cartoons 21-Photos 22-TV listings 23-Audio rec. 24-Video rec. 25-Books 26-Films/film clips 27-Personnel news 28-Press releases 29-New product news/photos 30-Trade lit. 31-Contracts awarded 32-Display adv. 33-Classified adv.

**Readers:** Mayflower agency owners and staff.
**Deadline:** story-1st of mo. prior to pub. date; news-1st of mo. prior; photo-1st of mo. prior; ads-1st of mo. prior

66749
## PI QUALITY
191 S. Gary Ave.
Carol Stream, IL 60188
Telephone: (708) 665-1000
FAX: (708) 462-2225
Year Established: 1991
Pub. Frequency: bi-m.
Page Size: standard
Subscrip. Rate: free
Materials: 01,02,06,25,28,29,30,31,32,33
Circulation: 42,000
Circulation Type: controlled & free
**Owner(s):**
Hitchcock Publishing, Div. of Capital Cities/ABC
191 S. Gary Ave.
Carol Stream, IL 60188
Telephone: (708) 665-1000
Ownership %: 100
**Management:**
Richard A. Templeton ...........................Publisher
**Editorial:**
Daniel J. Byrnes ....................................Editor
Margie Gonzalez .....................Managing Editor
Chris Bohentin ..........................Associate Editor
James Losh ..............................Group Publisher
**Desc.:** Our mission is to bring readers the most useful information on proved and developing techniques, concepts, and innovations to help maintain and improve both operational and product quality within the process industries. As such, the magazine reports advances in management, analytical instruments and their applications, associated information management systems, and related technologies that drive the process industries' quality efforts. These quality efforts incorporate many facets, including statistical quality control (SQC), product test and inspection, process monitoring, quality and reliability engineering, and the development of analytical instruments especially designed for QA/QC.
**Readers:** Edited for those having the responsibility of measuring and managing product and process quality, reliability, and efficiency, as well as regulatory compliance in the process industries-that is, the chemical, food and beverage, metallurgical, petrochemical, pharmaceutical, pulp and paper, and textile industries.

58684
## PLANT/OPERATIONS PROGRESS
345 E. 47th St.
New York, NY 10017
Telephone: (212) 705-7327
FAX: (212) 752-3294
Year Established: 1982
Pub. Frequency: q.
Subscrip. Rate: $125/yr. to non-members
Circulation: 1,991
Circulation Type: paid
**Owner(s):**
American Institute of Chemical Engineers
345 E. 47th St.
New York, NY 10017
Telephone: (212) 705-7330
**Management:**
Gary Rekstad ........................................Publisher
Maura Mullen ........................................Manager
**Editorial:**
T.A. Ventrone ........................................Editor
**Desc.:** Discusses the design, operation, maintenance and management of chemical plants, including safety issues.

22621
## PLANT ENGINEERING
1350 E. Touhy Ave.
Des Plaines, IL 60018-6007
Telephone: (708) 635-8800
FAX: (708) 390-2770
Year Established: 1947
Pub. Frequency: m.
Page Size: standard
Subscrip. Rate: $69.95/yr.
Materials: 02,06,10,28,29
Freelance Pay: $50/pg.
Circulation: 128,600
Circulation Type: controlled
**Owner(s):**
Reed Publishing (USA) Inc.
275 Washington St.
Newton, MA 02158
Ownership %: 100
**Management:**
Timothy Kelly ........................................Publisher
**Editorial:**
Ed Palko ...............................................Senior Editor
Jeanine Katzel ......................................Senior Editor
Joseph Foszcz ......................................Senior Editor
Richard Dunn .........................................Editor
Ron Holzhauer .......................Managing Editor
Cheryl Firestone .....................Production Editor
**Desc.:** Technical articles on industrial plant electric power distribution systems; heating, ventilating, and air conditioning systems; gas and fluid handling equipment; material handling; construction; maintenance; safety, security and fire protection; mechanical and fluid power transmission; pollution control; energy conservation; instrumentation & controls, and other subjects of interest to plant engineering personnel.
**Readers:** Personnel performing plant engineering functions; specifying, integrating, and maintaining plant facilities, equipment and systems.

## Group 126-Industrial Products & Equipment

65293
## ABERDEEN'S MAGAZINE OF MASONRY CONSTRUCTION
426 S. Westgate
Addison, IL 60101
Telephone: (708) 543-0870
FAX: (708) 543-3112
Pub. Frequency: m.
Page Size: standard
Subscrip. Rate: $24/yr.
Circulation: 42,046
Circulation Type: paid
**Owner(s):**
Aberdeen Group, The
426 S. Westgate St.
Addison, IL 60101
Telephone: (708) 543-0870
Ownership %: 100
**Editorial:**
Caroline Schierhorn ................Executive Editor
Ken Hooker ...........................................Editor

21702
## DISTRICT ENERGY
1200 19th St. N.W.
Ste. 300
Washington, DC 20036-2401
Telephone: (202) 429-5111
FAX: (202) 429-5113
Year Established: 1915
Pub. Frequency: q.
Page Size: standard
Subscrip. Rate: $40/yr. US; $75/yr. foreign
Circulation: 3,800
Circulation Type: paid

**Owner(s):**
International District Energy
1200 19th St., N.W.
Ste. 300
Washington, DC 20036-2401
Telephone: (202) 429-5111
Ownership %: 100
**Management:**
John L. Fiegel ......................................Publisher
Tammie Jackson ...............Advertising Manager
Tanya Vetter ......................Circulation Manager
**Editorial:**
Jack Kattner ........................................Editor
**Desc.:** Carries articles and technical information covering district heating and cooling (supply and delivery of energy via an extensive distribution system by means of steam, hot water, chilled water or other transport medium for the one or more utilization purposes comprising space conditioning, refrigeration, water heating, process use, etc.) As well as news of the International District Heating Association. Departments include: Products and Publications, Questions and Answers, and International Industry News, Measurement Topics, Capitol Comments.
**Readers:** Leaders in the district heating and cooling consulting engineers, architecture sale of equipment pertaining to district heating plants or distribution systems.

22862
## EE PRODUCT NEWS
707 Westchester Ave.
White Plains, NY 10604
Telephone: (914) 949-8500
FAX: (914) 682-0922
Year Established: 1940
Pub. Frequency: m.
Page Size: tabloid
Subscrip. Rate: $52/yr. US.; $92/yr. foreign
Circulation: 102,000
Circulation Type: controlled
**Owner(s):**
Intertec Publishing Corp.
707 Westchester Ave.
White Plains, NY 10604
Telephone: (914) 949-8500
Ownership %: 100
**Management:**
Matthew Reseska ................................Publisher
**Editorial:**
Joseph DelGatto ....................Editorial Director
Christopher Ricci ...............................Art Director
Joseph Spadaro ..................Editor- East Coast
Ron Shinn ............................Editor- West Coast
Leland Paterson .................Production Director
Patrick Walsh ...............................Systems Editor
**Desc.:** Completely devoted to new products, equipment, parts, material, applications, literature, in the electrical/electronic and electromechanical engineering/manufacturing and application fields.
**Readers:** Engineering electrical/electronic/electro, plant engineer, superintendents, chief engineers, design and prototype engineers.

65602
## FLUID MECHANICS RESEARCH
605 Third Ave.
New York, NY 10158
Telephone: (212) 850-6000
FAX: (212) 850-6088
Year Established: 1975
Pub. Frequency: bi-m.
Subscrip. Rate: $896/yr.

**Owner(s):**
John Wiley & Sons, Inc.
605 Third Ave.
New York, NY 10158
Telephone: (212) 850-6000
**Editorial:**
Novak Zuber ........................................Editor
Ivan Catton ..........................................Editor
M. S. Plesset .......................................Editor

22479
## HAPPI-HOUSEHOLD & PERSONAL PRODUCTS INDUSTRY
17 S. Franklin Tpke.
Ramsey, NJ 07446
Telephone: (201) 825-2552
FAX: (201) 825-0553
Mailing Address:
P.O. Box 555
Ramsey, NJ 07446
Year Established: 1964
Pub. Frequency: m.
Page Size: standard
Subscrip. Rate: $10/issue; $48/yr.
Circulation: 17,000
Circulation Type: controlled
**Owner(s):**
Rodman Publishing Co.
17 S. Franklin Tpke.
Ramsey, NJ 07446
Telephone: (201) 825-2552
Ownership %: 100
**Management:**
Rodman J. Zilenziger, Jr. ......................President
Matthew Montgomery .........................Publisher
**Editorial:**
Tom Branna ........................................Editor
Christine Canning ....................Associate Editor
Andy Teng ..............................Associate Editor
**Desc.:** Seek articles, news about manufacturers of products in field served (U.S. and foreign). Manufacturing, marketing, new product development. Departments include: Washington Report, International Report, Personnel, News, New Products, Formula, Photonews, Reader Service.
**Readers:** Manufacturers of soaps, detergents, cosmetics, toiletries, aerosols, and related chemical specialties.

65260
## HAZMAT WORLD
800 Roosevelt Rd., Ste. E300
Glen Ellyn, IL 60137-5868
Telephone: (708) 858-1888
Year Established: 1988
Pub. Frequency: m.
Page Size: standard
Subscrip. Rate: $40/yr. for non qualified recipients in US
Freelance Pay: $12/col. in.
Circulation: 45,000
Circulation Type: controlled
**Owner(s):**
Advanstar Communications, Inc.
800 Roosevelt Rd., Bldg. C.,
Ste. 206
Glen Ellyn, IL 60137
Telephone: (708) 858-1888
Ownership %: 100
**Management:**
Sheldon G. Schultz ..............................Publisher
**Editorial:**
Jim Bishop ...........................................Editor
**Desc.:** A business/new publication dedicated to environmental management.
**Readers:** Targets persons who specify and purchase products, systems, equipment and services used for hazardous materials and waste management, air and water pollution control.

**Materials Accepted/Included:** 01-Business news 02-By-line articles 03-Fashion news 04-Food news 05-Freelance copy 06-Letters to editor 07-Real estate news 08-Sports news 09-Travel news 10-Book rev. 11-Movie rev. 12-Music rev. 13-TV rev. 14-Theater rev. 15-Coming events 16-Obituaries 17-Question & answer 18-Social announcements 19-Artwork 20-Cartoons 21-Photos 22-TV listings 23-Audio rec. 24-Video rec. 25-Books 26-Films/film clips 27-Personnel news 28-Press releases 29-New product news/photos 30-Trade lit. 31-Contracts awarded 32-Display adv. 33-Classified adv.

4-183

## INDUSTRIAL EQUIPMENT NEWS
23428
Five Penn Plaza
New York, NY 10001
Telephone: (212) 695-0500
FAX: (212) 629-1170
Year Established: 1933
Pub. Frequency: m.
Page Size: tabloid
Subscrip. Rate: free for qualified people;
 $35/yr. US; $50/yr. Canada & Mexico;
 $115/yr. foreign
Circulation: 210,000
Circulation Type: controlled
**Owner(s):**
Thomas Publishing Co.
One Penn Plaza
New York, NY 10119
Telephone: (212) 695-0500
Ownership %: 100
**Management:**
C. T. Holst-Knudsen .........................President
Ralph E. Richardson ...........................Publisher
James A. Vick ......................................Publisher
**Editorial:**
Mark F. Devlin ..................Editor in Chief
L. Bernstein ....................Executive Editor
Deborah Maskin .....................Senior Editor
Virginia Posner ..................Circulation Director
Margaret Wormley ...............Marketing Director
**Desc.:** The original product news
 magazine. Publishes staff-written
 editorial descriptions of equipment, parts
 and materials, for use throughout the
 manufacturing and allied industries.
 These products are certified as new or
 recently improved within two months as
 far as general publicity is concerned.
 Also reviews manufacturer's new
 literature as well as applications and
 custom products. Especially interested in
 useful how-to-do-it literature from
 product manufacturers. Editorial
 coverage consists mainly of new and
 improved products. Departments include:
 Editor's Choice, Free Catalog Shelf,
 Free Tech Tips, Solutions File, Custom
 Shop, Late Breaking Product News, In-
 Depth Spotlights, Automation Features,
 Free Test Samples.
**Readers:** Engineering (plant and product)
 and corporate management personnel in
 industry.

## INDUSTRIAL LASER REVIEW
66743
10 Tara Blvd.
5th Fl.
Nashua, NH 03062-2801
Telephone: (603) 891-0123
FAX: (603) 891-0574
Year Established: 1986
Pub. Frequency: m.
Page Size: standard
Subscrip. Rate: $225/yr. US; $265/yr.
 foreign
Materials: 01,29,32
Circulation: 11,100
**Owner(s):**
Pennwell Publishing Co.
1421 Sheridan
Tulsa, OK 74112
Telephone: (918) 831-9497
**Management:**
Linda Wright ...................................Publisher
**Editorial:**
David Belforte .................................Editor
Laureen Belleville .................Design Editor
**Desc.:** Covers applications of lasers in
 industry, including production line laser
 news, actual applications, new systems
 and products, technical and economic
 analyses, marketing trends, and reports
 of industry conferences.

**Readers:** Manufacturers and users of
 industrial lasers and laser industry
 suppliers.

## INDUSTRIAL PRODUCT BULLETIN
24007
301 Gibraltar Dr.
Morris Plains, NJ 07950
Telephone: (201) 361-9060
Mailing Address:
 P.O. Box 650
 Morris Plains, NJ 07950
Year Established: 1942
Pub. Frequency: m.
Page Size: tabloid
Subscrip. Rate: $48/yr.
Materials: 29,30,32,33
Print Process: web offset
Circulation: 200,050
Circulation Type: controlled
**Owner(s):**
Gordon Publications, Inc.
P.O. Box 650
Morris Plains, NJ 07950
Telephone: (201) 361-9060
Ownership %: 100
**Management:**
Bill Rakay ........................................President
Steve Koppelman ..............Circulation Manager
**Editorial:**
Anita LaFond ....................................Editor
Todd Baker ..................Associate Publisher
Dave Esola .......................Group Publisher
Susan Frank ....................Production Director
**Desc.:** Releases and illustrations covering
 new products, and new literature for all
 manufacturing industries.
**Readers:** Production, operating,
 engineering, administration,
 maintenance, purchasing facilities.

## MATERIAL HANDLING PRODUCT NEWS
61283
301 Gibraltar Dr.
Morris Plains, NJ 07950-0650
Telephone: (201) 292-5100
FAX: (201) 898-9281
Mailing Address:
 P.O. Box 650
 Morris Plains, NJ 07950
Year Established: 1979
Pub. Frequency: 10/yr.
Page Size: tabloid
Subscrip. Rate: $25/yr.
Circulation: 100,500
Circulation Type: paid
**Owner(s):**
Gordon Publications, Inc.
301 Gibraltar Dr.
Morris Plains, NJ 07950-0650
Telephone: (201) 292-5100
Ownership %: 100
**Editorial:**
Dolly Grobstein ...................................Editor
**Desc.:** Provides a listing of equipment and
 systems available for the material
 handling industry, storage areas and
 warehouses.

## NEW EQUIPMENT DIGEST
23454
1100 Superior Ave.
Cleveland, OH 44114
Telephone: (216) 696-7000
FAX: (216) 696-8208
Year Established: 1936
Pub. Frequency: m.
Page Size: tabloid
Subscrip. Rate: $50/yr. in US.; $75/yr.
 Canada; $100/yr. elsewhere
Materials: 29,30,32,33
Circulation: 211,050
Circulation Type: controlled

**Owner(s):**
Penton Publishing
1100 Superior Ave.
Cleveland, OH 44114
Telephone: (216) 696-7000
Ownership %: 100
**Management:**
Dan Ramella .........................President
Russell S. Carson .......................Publisher
Donna Trout ...............Circulation Manager
Jim Lucas ..................Production Manager
Michael W. Kanyok ...........Promotion Manager
**Editorial:**
Robert F. King ..................................Editor
Steven R. Bush .................................Editor
Marci Bushek .............................Advertising
Nancy McCourt ....................Assistant Editor
Paul Farace ....................Associate Editor
Tom R. Sockel ..................Associate Editor
Jeanne M. Ribiniskas .........Associate Editor
Robert P. Bacon ........National Sales Manager
Sal F. Marino .......................President/CEO
Joyce Holmes ...............Research Manager
**Desc.:** Editorial content is composed
 entirely of new industrial products,
 materials, components, equipment, and
 industrial literature and catalog reviews.
 News releases are furnished by
 advertising agencies, public relations
 firms and manufacturers of industrial
 products.
**Readers:** Engineering, design
 management, plant maintenance,
 engineering and design, and
 administrative, production, plant
 operation and purchasing personnel
 throughout the general industrial field.

## OFFICE PRODUCTS INDUSTRY REPORT
61586
301 N. Fairfax St.
Alexandria, VA 22314
Telephone: (703) 549-9040
FAX: (703) 683-7552
Year Established: 1970
Pub. Frequency: bi-w.
Page Size: standard
Subscrip. Rate: $36/yr. non-member;
 $10/yr. member
Circulation: 9,000
Circulation Type: controlled
**Owner(s):**
National Office Products Association
301 N. Fairfax
Alexandria, VA 22314
Telephone: (703) 549-9040
Ownership %: 100
**Editorial:**
Sandra Selva ...................................Editor
**Readers:** Members of office products
 industry, including supplies, furnishings
 and machines.

## PETROLEUM/C-STORE PRODUCTS
61689
950 Lee St.
Des Plaines, IL 60016
Telephone: (708) 296-0770
FAX: (708) 296-8821
Pub. Frequency: 10/yr.
Page Size: tabloid
Subscrip. Rate: $18/yr. US; $27/yr.
 Canada; $478/yr. foreign
Circulation: 13,700
Circulation Type: controlled
**Owner(s):**
Hunter Publishing Co., Inc.
950 Lee St.
Des Plaines, IL 60016
Telephone: (708) 296-0770
Ownership %: 100
**Editorial:**
Howard Shingle ...................................Editor
Bernard Pacyniak ..................Managing Editor

Greg Lindenberg ...........................Copy Editor
Kris Zulaski ....................Production Editor
**Readers:** Petroleum, convenience store
 equipment and product buyers.

## POWDER/BULK SOLIDS
49870
301 Gibralta Dr.
Morris Plains, NJ 07950
Telephone: (201) 292-5100
FAX: (201) 539-3476
Year Established: 1983
Pub. Frequency: m.
Page Size: tabloid
Subscrip. Rate: free to qualified; $35/yr.
 US & Canada
Circulation: 48,000
Circulation Type: controlled & paid
**Owner(s):**
Gordon Publications, Inc.
301 Gibraltar Dr.
Morris Plains, NJ 07950
Telephone: (201) 292-5100
Ownership %: 100
**Management:**
Don Ransdell ...................................Publisher
**Editorial:**
Kevin Cronin ...................................Editor
Christine Hagopalis .......Production Coordinator
**Desc.:** A product news tabloid edited for
 engineers and others concerned with
 processing, handling, and packaging of
 dry particulates and bulk solids. The
 editorial consists of news of equipment
 and supplies used in chemicals, food,
 plastics, coal, cement, pharmaceuticals,
 cosmetics and other industries.
**Readers:** Plant managers, engineers,
 administrative and purchasing executives
 in industries involved with processing
 and handling powders, bulk solids - dry
 particulates of all types.

## POWER EQUIPMENT TRADE
23640
P.O. Box 2268
Montgomery, AL 36102-2268
Telephone: (205) 834-1170
FAX: (205) 834-4525
Year Established: 1952
Pub. Frequency: 10/yr.
Page Size: standard
Subscrip. Rate: $24/yr.
Materials: 01,02,06,28,29,30,32,33
Freelance Pay: $.05/wd.
Print Process: web offset
Circulation: 22,460
Circulation Type: controlled
**Owner(s):**
Hatton-Brown Publishers, Inc.
P.O. Box 2268
Montgomery, AL 36102-2268
Telephone: (205) 834-1170
FAX: (205) 834-4525
Ownership %: 100
**Management:**
David H. Ramsey ...............................Publisher
David E. Knight ...................................Publisher
Eve Dodd ...................Circulation Manager
Dianne Sullivan .................General Manager
**Editorial:**
Dan Shell ...................Managing Editor
Ken Morrison ...................Technical Editor
**Desc.:** Dedicated to the international chain
 saw-portable power equipment industry.
 To serve this audience, it contains
 features on new products, personnel
 changes, industry events and issues,
 technical topics, business management,
 market trends, successful dealers,
 unique product applications, logging
 sports and other areas of interest to
 power equipment retailers.

**Materials Accepted/Included:** 01-Business news 02-By-line articles 03-Fashion news 04-Food news 05-Freelance copy 06-Letters to editor 07-Real estate news 08-Sports news 09-Travel news
10-Book rev. 11-Movie rev. 12-Music rev. 13-TV rev. 14-Theater rev. 15-Coming events 16-Obituaries 17-Question & answer 18-Social announcements 19-Artwork 20-Cartoons 21-Photos 22-TV listings
23-Audio rec. 24-Video rec. 25-Books 26-Films/film clips 27-Personnel news 28-Press releases 29-New product news/photos 30-Trade lit. 31-Contracts awarded 32-Display adv. 33-Classified adv.

4-184

**Readers:** Manufacturers, dealers, distributors and some professional users.
**Deadline:** story-5th of mo. prior to pub. date; news-5th of mo. prior; photo-5th of mo. prior

## PULSO DEL PERIODISMO
68945

3000 N.E. 145th St.
North Miami, FL 33181-3601
Telephone: (305) 940-5672
FAX: (305) 956-5498
Year Established: 1990
Pub. Frequency: q.
Page Size: 8 1/2 x 11
Subscrip. Rate: $15/yr.
Materials: 01,02,05,06,10,16,17,20,21,25, 27,29,32
Circulation: 4500
Circulation Type: controlled
**Owner(s):**
Florida International University
Latin American Journalism Prog
3000 N.E. 145th St.
North Miami, FL 33181-3601
Telephone: (305) 940-5672
FAX: (305) 956-5498
Ownership %: 100
**Management:**
John Virtue ...............................................Publisher
**Editorial:**
Mario Diament ...........................................Editor
Maria Munoz Blanco .................Assistant Editor
**Desc.:** Covers problems in journalism emphasizing Latin American media. Written in Spanish. English language summary of content included to English-speaking subscribers.

## REPORTERO INDUSTRIAL
23469

150 Great Neck Rd.
Great Neck, NY 11021
Telephone: (516) 829-9210
FAX: (516) 829-7265
Mailing Address:
    P.O. Box 918
    Great Neck, NY 11025
Year Established: 1945
Pub. Frequency: 9/yr.
Page Size: tabloid
Subscrip. Rate: free
Freelance Pay: varies
Circulation: 38,428
Circulation Type: controlled
**Owner(s):**
Keller International Publishing Corp.
150 Great Neck Rd.
Great Neck, NY 11021
Telephone: (516) 829-9210
Ownership %: 100
**Management:**
Gerald E. Keller ......................................President
Robert Herlihy ..........................................Publisher
Jose Suarz ........................Circulation Manager
**Editorial:**
Felicia M. Morales ......................................Editor
**Desc.:** New industrial products illustrated and described for export. Covers new literature and catalogues, procedures. Printed in Spanish.
**Readers:** Production and purchasing executives, importers, distributors, representatives in petroleum, metalworking, chemical and food processing industries in Latin America.

## SUPERVISION
23476

P.O. Box 1
Burlington, IA 52601-0001
Telephone: (319) 752-5415
FAX: (319) 752-3421
Year Established: 1939
Pub. Frequency: m.

Page Size: standard
Subscrip. Rate: $40.60/yr.
Materials: 02,05
Freelance Pay: $.04/wd.
Print Process: offset
Circulation: 3,658
Circulation Type: paid
**Owner(s):**
National Research Bureau
P.O. Box 1
200 N. Fourth
Burlington, IA 52601
Telephone: (319) 752-5415
FAX: (319) 752-3421
Ownership %: 100
**Management:**
Michael S. Darnall ...............................Publisher
**Editorial:**
Barbara Boeding ........................................Editor
**Desc.:** Industrial relations magazine covering human relations, supervisory training, office and personnel, health and safety, training and self-development for the factory and/or office firstline supervisor. Including: delegation, motivation, cost control, productivity, safety, labor law, etc. Buy all rights. Send a biography or by-line to accompany manuscript. Author photos are requested upon acceptance. Pay upon publication. Uses AP style book. Desk-top publishing. Articles must be scannable.
**Readers:** Foreman, supervisors and department head.

## SURPLUS RECORD, THE
23477

20 N. Wacker Dr.
Chicago, IL 60606
Telephone: (312) 372-9077
FAX: (312) 372-6537
Year Established: 1924
Pub. Frequency: m.
Page Size: standard
Subscrip. Rate: $4 newssstand; $30/yr.; $50/2 yrs.; $65/3 yrs.
Freelance Pay: varies
Circulation: 140,000
Circulation Type: controlled
**Owner(s):**
Surplus Record, Inc.
20 N. Wacker Dr.
Chicago, IL 60606
Telephone: (312) 372-9077
Ownership %: 100
**Management:**
Thomas C. Scanlan ...........................Publisher
Thomas C. Scanlan ..........Advertising Manager
**Editorial:**
Thomas C. Scanlan ................Managing Editor
Joyce Goldenstern ..................Associate Editor
**Desc.:** Promoting sale of rebuilt and reconditioned industrial plant machinery-metal forming, power plant, electrical, chemical, plastic, construction, mining. Editorial section presents articles on developments, opinions and conditions in U.S. industry and business. Also included are political trends; safety, health and other topics pertinent to industry; and messages by top figures in business and government.

## UTILITY FLEET MANAGEMENT
55972

2111 Wilson Blvd., Ste. 200
Arlington, VA 22201
Telephone: (703) 243-7000
FAX: (703) 527-5829
Year Established: 1982
Pub. Frequency: 9/yr.
Page Size: standard
Subscrip. Rate: $15/yr.; free to qualified personnel
Circulation: 5,100

Circulation Type: controlled
**Owner(s):**
Public Utilities Reports, Inc.
2111 Wilson Blvd., Ste. 200
Arlington, VA 22201
Telephone: (703) 243-7000
Ownership %: 100
**Management:**
Parm Pritchard ........................................Publisher
Jerry Boswell ....................Circulation Manager
Patricia Pritchard ...............Customer Service Manager
Al Gravenhorst .........................Sales Manager
**Editorial:**
Nancy Coe Bailey ......................................Editor
**Desc.:** Interested in articles on management and operation of utility fleets, field applications of equipment maintained by fleet departments. Special emphasis in fleet equipment designs. Departments include: The In-File, Automotive News, Service Engineering, Shopwise, Field Operations, Fleet Management News and Fleet Equipment Designs.
**Readers:** Fleet managers and their staff, construction and maintenance managers, purchasing managers and equipment buyers, suppliers, distributors and dealers of equipment and components.

## WORLD INDUSTRIAL REPORTER
22961

150 Great Neck Rd.
Great Neck, NY 11021
Telephone: (516) 829-9210
FAX: (516) 829-5414
Year Established: 1964
Pub. Frequency: 9/yr.
Page Size: tabloid
Subscrip. Rate: free
**Owner(s):**
Keller International Publishing Corp.
150 Great Neck Rd.
Great Neck, NY 11021
Telephone: (516) 829-9210
Ownership %: 100
**Management:**
Gerald E. Keller ......................................President
Robert Herlihy ..........................................Publisher
Robert Herlihy ..................Advertising Manager
**Editorial:**
Felicia M. Morales ......................................Editor
**Desc.:** New industrial products illustrated and described for export. Covers new literature and catalogues procedures. Printed in English.
**Readers:** Production and purchasing executives, in manufacturing, mining, petroleum, transport, construction, engineering; importers, representatives and distributors of industrial equipment. Europe, East Europe, Africa/Middle East, Asia/Pacific.

## Group 128-Industry, General

## ADHESIVES AGE
23405

6151 Powers Ferry Rd.
Atlanta, GA 30339-2941
Telephone: (404) 955-2500
FAX: (404) 618-0348
Year Established: 1958
Pub. Frequency: 13/yr.
Page Size: standard
Subscrip. Rate: $52/yr. US; $79/2 yrs.; $112/yr. airmail
Circulation: 25,505
Circulation Type: controlled

**Owner(s):**
Argus Press Holdings
6151 Powers Ferry Rd.
Atlanta, GA 30334-2941
Telephone: (404) 955-2500
Ownership %: 100
**Management:**
Larry Anderson ...............................Publisher
Chuck Bacon ...................Advertising Manager
**Editorial:**
Larry Anderson ...........................................Editor
**Desc.:** Provides news of the latest in technology, research, manufacture, application, and marketing of adhesives and sealants. Departments include: New Adhesives, New Equipment, News of the Industry, Patents, Coming Events, Classified Advertising, People on the Move, Book and Literature Reviews, Foreign News, Advice Column, Editorial.
**Readers:** Adhesive and sealant manufacturers and industrial end-users.

## AI EXPERT
61721

600 Harrison St.
San Francisco, CA 94107
Telephone: (415) 905-2200
FAX: (415) 905-2232
Year Established: 1986
Pub. Frequency: m.
Page Size: standard
Subscrip. Rate: $34/yr.
Circulation: 28,000
Circulation Type: paid
**Owner(s):**
United Newspapers
600 Harrison St.
San Francisco, CA 94107
Telephone: (415) 905-2200
Ownership %: 100
**Editorial:**
Larry O'Brien ...........................................Editor
Kay Kepler .............................Managing Editor
**Desc.:** The magazine of practical AI for people developing and deploying AI technology in commercial environments. Features articles on practical techniques in artificial intelligence programming.
**Readers:** For AI programmers, conventional programmers and AI managers.

## AMERICAN INDUSTRY
23410

21 Russell Woods Rd.
Great Neck, NY 11021
Telephone: (516) 487-0990
FAX: (516) 487-0809
Year Established: 1946
Pub. Frequency: m.
Page Size: tabloid
Subscrip. Rate: $25/yr.
Materials: 01,02,10,12,19,21,23,24,25,27, 28,29,30,31,32
Print Process: offset
Circulation: 28,000
Circulation Type: controlled
**Owner(s):**
Publications for Industry
21 Russell Woods Rd.
Great Neck, NY 11021
Telephone: (516) 487-0990
FAX: (516) 487-0809
Ownership %: 100
**Management:**
Jack S. Panes ......................................President
Jack S. Panes ..........................................Publisher
B. Grillo ..........................Advertising Manager
**Editorial:**
Jack S. Panes ...........................................Editor
P. Shaine ...............................Managing Editor

---

**Materials Accepted/Included:** 01-Business news 02-By-line articles 03-Fashion news 04-Food news 05-Freelance copy 06-Letters to editor 07-Real estate news 08-Sports news 09-Travel news 10-Book rev. 11-Movie rev. 12-Music rev. 13-TV rev. 14-Theater rev. 15-Coming events 16-Obituaries 17-Question & answer 18-Social announcements 19-Artwork 20-Cartoons 21-Photos 22-TV listings 23-Audio rec. 24-Video rec. 25-Books 26-Films/film clips 27-Personnel news 28-Press releases 29-New product news/photos 30-Trade lit. 31-Contracts awarded 32-Display adv. 33-Classified adv.

4-185

**Desc.:** Majority of news content is new products and processes. Case histories report and feature articles include news, financial, government, how-to articles, etc., of interest to industry. New product releases, cost saving, time saving, labor saving, time and motion studies, personnel relations, materials handling and new literature copy given top space. Also general interest section maintained to report on general news of interest to the trade in addition to new products releases. Special sections on new brochures, booklets, and other company literature.
**Readers:** Top management executives in largest manufacturing plants.
**Deadline:** story-1st of mo.; news-1st of mo.; photo-1st of mo.; ads-1st of mo.

## AREA DEVELOPMENT SITES & FACILITY PLANNING
22135

400 Post Ave.
Westbury, NY 11590
Telephone: (516) 338-0900
Year Established: 1965
Pub. Frequency: m.
Page Size: standard
Subscrip. Rate: free to business trade; $65/yr. US & Canada; $85/yr. foreign
Freelance Pay: varies
Circulation: 42,500
Circulation Type: controlled
**Owner(s):**
SH Publications, Inc.
525 Northern Blvd.
Great Neck, NY 11021
Telephone: (516) 829-8990
Ownership %: 100
**Management:**
Dennis Shea .......................Chairman of Board
Dennis Shea .....................................President
Rich Bodo .................................Vice President
Dennis Shea ...................................Publisher
**Editorial:**
Tom Bergeron ......................................Editor
Geraldine Gambale .................Managing Editor
Susan DePierro ..................Production Director
**Desc.:** Directed to executives of the nation's manufacturing companies. Dealing with the problems involved in finding new sites, building new plants and/or office facilities, or completely relocating present facilities. Topics cover all phases of facility planning and site selection, worldwide. Subject matter includes the selection of new plant locations; community and employee relations; the political or community climate; transportation, recreational and educational facilities; financing; insurance, plant design and layout; safety factors; water and air pollution controls, and case histories of companies which have moved or opened new plants. They must avoid discussing the merits or disadvantages of any particular areas or communities. Articles can be of any length necessary to tell the whole story. Pictures (art work or glossies) are paid at the same space rate as copy. Bylines used. Editorial space is NOT for sale. Departments include: Editorial; Activities; Of Current Interest; Letters From Readers; Book Reviews.
**Readers:** Chief executives of manufacturing companies, plus real estate managers.

## ASIAN INDUSTRIAL REPORTER
58550

150 Great Neck Rd.
Great Neck, NY 11021
Telephone: (516) 829-9210

Year Established: 1983
Pub. Frequency: 6/yr.
Page Size: tabloid
Circulation: 20,188
Circulation Type: controlled
**Owner(s):**
Keller International Publishing Corp.
150 Great Neck Rd.
Great Neck, NY 11021
Telephone: (516) 829-9210
**Editorial:**
Felicia Morales ....................................Editor

## ASTM STANDARDIZATION NEWS
23411

1916 Race St.
Philadelphia, PA 19103
Telephone: (215) 299-5420
FAX: (215) 299-5511
Year Established: 1921
Pub. Frequency: m.
Page Size: standard
Subscrip. Rate: $5 newsstand; $18/yr.
Materials: 01,06,28,29,30
Circulation: 34,000
Circulation Type: paid
**Owner(s):**
American Society for Testing and Materials
1916 Race St.
Philadelphia, PA 19103
Telephone: (215) 299-5400
Ownership %: 100
**Management:**
James A. Thomas ...............................President
R. L. Meltzer ....................................Publisher
Ellen McGlinchey .............Advertising Manager
**Editorial:**
Barbara Schindler ..................................Editor
Carla Juliani ...........................Assistant Editor
Maryann Gorman ....................Assistant Editor
Bridget McQuate ....................Assistant Editor
Ellen McGlinchey .............New Products Editor
Maryann Gorman ........................News Editor
Carla Juliani ...........................................Photo
Bruce Vieth .........................Production Director
**Desc.:** News and information relating to voluntary consensus standards for materials, products, systems, and services. Departments include: Society News, International and National News on Standards, Feature Articles, New ASTM Publications, Technical Committee Activities, News Notes on Laboratory Apparatus, Supplies and Literatures, Personals, New Members, Deaths, Calendar of Society Events, Other Society Calendar and Seminars. Society Ballot, Standards Actions.
**Readers:** Evaluation, performance and engineering personnel, and associated technical personnel.
**Deadline:** story-8 wks. prior to 1st of pub. mo.; news-6 wks. prior; photo-2 wks. prior; ads-6 wks. prior

## BUSINESS FACILITIES
22133

121 Monmouth St.
Red Bank, NJ 07701
Telephone: (908) 842-7433
FAX: (908) 758-6634
Mailing Address:
P.O. Box 2060
Red Bank, NJ 07701
Year Established: 1968
Pub. Frequency: m.
Page Size: standard
Subscrip. Rate: $30/yr. unqualified
Materials: 01,02,05,06,07,10,17,19,20,21, 27,28,30,32,33
Freelance Pay: $.25/wd. average
Print Process: web
Circulation: 40,000
Circulation Type: controlled & free

**Owner(s):**
Group C Communications, Inc.
P.O. Box 2060
Red Bank, NJ 07701
Telephone: (908) 842-7433
FAX: (908) 758-6634
Ownership %: 100
**Management:**
Ed T. Coene ...................................President
Susan Coene ...................................Publisher
Clarissa McNab ..................Business Manager
**Editorial:**
Eric Peterson .......................................Editor
Mary Lou Lang ......................Managing Editor
Jodi Dash .......................................Art Director
Eric Peterson ....................Associate Publisher
Allyn Tracy Heck ................Marketing Director
Luanne Rathemacher ........Production Director
**Desc.:** Edited for corporate executives with responsibility for their companies' expansion and relocation plans. Features articles covering economics of site selection, case histories, lists of literature offered by various states, counties, utilities, etc., to aid in site selection. Plus articles on business angle of environment, government, finance, export - import, labor, energy, area reviews, transportation, and urban affairs.
**Readers:** Corporate site selectors and real estate execs., economic development practitioners.
**Deadline:** story-5th of mo. prior to pub. date; news-5th of mo.; photo-5th of mo.; ads-10th of mo.

## CABLE INSTALLATION & MAINTENANCE
70436

Ten Tara Blvd.
5th Fl.
Nashua, NH 03062
Telephone: (603) 891-9144
FAX: (603) 891-0587
Year Established: 1993
Pub. Frequency: m.
Page Size: standard
Subscrip. Rate: $10/copy; $42/yr. US; $53/yr. Canada & Mexico; $63/yr. foreign
Materials: 01,02,06,15,17,20,21,27,28,29, 30,32,33
Print Process: web offset
Circulation: 17,974
Circulation Type: free
**Owner(s):**
PennWell Publishing Co.
Ten Tara Blvd.
5th Fl.
Nashua, NH 03062
Telephone: (603) 891-0123
FAX: (603) 891-0587
Ownership %: 100
**Editorial:**
Arlyn Powell ...............................Senior Editor
Kathleen Brady ................Ad Traffic Mananger
Barbara Thompson ...................Associate Editor
Lucas Garofalo ...................Associate Publisher
Stacy Porath ...................District Sales Manager
George Miller ..............Group Editorial Director
Dave Janoff ..............................Group Publisher
Andrea Rollins ....................Marketing Manager
Philip Davis ..................Regional Sales Manager
Jo-Ann Pellegrini .......Regional Sales Manager
Anne Graceffa ..............................Telemarketing
**Desc.:** Provides peer-to-peer perspective in its interpretation of standards and technology, its presentation of installation techniques and in the selection and use of products in premises communications.
**Readers:** Geared to all professionals involved in the installation of fiber and copper communications systems.

## DYNAMIC BUSINESS
23475

1400 S. Braddock Ave.
Pittsburgh, PA 15218
Telephone: (412) 371-1500
FAX: (412) 371-0460
Year Established: 1945
Pub. Frequency: 10/yr.
Page Size: standard
Subscrip. Rate: $25/yr. non-members; $15/yr. members; $45/yr. foreign
Materials: 01,02,06,10,25,27,28,29,30,32,33
Print Process: offset
Circulation: 5,000
Circulation Type: controlled
**Owner(s):**
TEC/Pennsylvania Small Business United
1400 S. Braddock Ave.
Pittsburgh, PA 15218
Telephone: (412) 371-1500
FAX: (412) 371-0460
Ownership %: 100
**Management:**
Terry Mohr .......................Advertising Manager
**Editorial:**
Mary Heindl ..........................................Editor
Mary Heindl ......................Book Review Editor
Mary Heindl ......................Publication Director
**Desc.:** Articles covering individual and collective productivity and profitability for the businessmen involved in manufacturing and all other small businessmen. Dynamic Business is "the voice of small business."
**Readers:** Purchasing agents, schools, companies, association members, key CEO's, small business entrepreneurs.
**Deadline:** story-6 wks. prior to pub. date; news-6 wks. prior; photo-6 wks. prior; ads-6 wks. prior

## GAMING PRODUCTS & SERVICES
70362

12 Oaks Center
Ste. 922
Wayatza, MN 55391
Telephone: (612) 473-5088
FAX: (612) 473-7068
Pub. Frequency: m.
Materials: 06,21,28,32
**Owner(s):**
RCM Enterprises, Inc.
12 Oaks Center
Suite 922
Wayzata, MN 55391
Telephone: (612) 473-5088
FAX: (612) 473-7068
Ownership %: 100
**Management:**
Robert C. Mead ................................Publisher
Jim Pennigroth .................Advertising Manager
**Editorial:**
Jeff Borowicz ........................................Editor
**Readers:** Gaming establishment owners, managers and suppliers.
**Deadline:** story-4 wks. prior to pub. date; news-4 wks.; photo-4 wks.; ads-40 days

## INTEGRATED WASTE MANAGEMENT
66029

1221 Ave. of the Americas, 36th Fl.
New York, NY 10020
Telephone: (212) 512-6310
Pub. Frequency: bi-w.
Subscrip. Rate: $745/yr. US; $770/yr. foreign
**Owner(s):**
McGraw Hill, Inc.
1221 Ave. of Americas, 36th Fl
New York, NY 10020
Telephone: (310) 512-6310
Ownership %: 100
**Editorial:**
Kevin J. Hamilton ................................Editor
Steve Lang .............................Managing Editor

**Desc.:** Provides comprehensive coverage of the worldwide conversion of municipal, industrial and agricultural waste.

## LUBRICATION ENGINEERING
23445

840 Busse Hwy.
Park Ridge, IL 60068
Telephone: (708) 825-5536
Year Established: 1944
Pub. Frequency: m.
Page Size: 4 color photos/art
Subscrip. Rate: $10/issue; $61/yr.
Circulation: 6,100
Circulation Type: paid
**Owner(s):**
Society of Tribologists & Lubrication Engineers
840 Busse Hwy.
Park Ridge, IL 60068
Telephone: (708) 825-5536
Ownership %: 100
**Management:**
Karen J. Vander ..............Advertising Manager
Heyden
**Desc.:** By-line technical papers dealing with lubricants, lubrication devices, hydraulics and other phases of industrial lubrication; tribology. Carries society news, book reviews, news of the industry.
**Readers:** Primarily lubrication engineers, maintenance, manufacturing, & production engineers as well as managers of manufacturing engineering, plants, operations, production. Also marketing service personnel technical service to customers, sales/marketing.

## MANUFACTURERS' MART
61275

16 High St.
Westerly, RI 02891
Telephone: (401) 348-0797
Year Established: 1978
Pub. Frequency: m.
Page Size: tabloid
Subscrip. Rate: $12/yr. out of state
Circulation: 30,000
Circulation Type: paid
**Owner(s):**
Manufacturers' Mart
16 High St.
Westerly, RI 02891
Telephone: (401) 348-0797
Ownership %: 100
**Editorial:**
Ilse Cannon ..................................Editor
Jean Gerescatas ...............Production Manager
**Desc.:** Manfacturers Mart seeks to show plant managers how to more effectively run their plants. Wide gamut of ads provide local distributors of products.
**Readers:** Plant managers, production managers, plant and production engineers, maintenance managers, and purchasing agents in larger plants, owners, partners, presidents in smaller plants.

## MARKING INDUSTRY MAGAZINE
24989

113 Adell Pl.
Elmhurst, IL 60126-3301
Telephone: (708) 832-5200
FAX: (708) 832-5206
Year Established: 1907
Pub. Frequency: m.
Page Size: standard
Subscrip. Rate: $38/yr.
Freelance Pay: negotiable
Circulation: 1,500
Circulation Type: paid

**Owner(s):**
Marking Devices Publishing Co.
113 Adell Pl.
Elmhurst, IL 60126
Telephone: (708) 832-5200
Ownership %: 100
**Management:**
David Hachmeister ..............................Publisher
David Hachmeister ...........Advertising Manager
Carol Lundin ..............................Office Manager
**Editorial:**
Terri Andrews ..................................Editor
Jeanette Hachmeister ............Associate Editor
Barb Makinen ........................Production Editor
**Desc.:** Designed for firms engaged in the manufacturing, distribution and sales of marking products: rubber stamps and dies, steel stamps and dies, engraved plates and signs - plastics or metal.
**Readers:** Manufacturers and dealers.

## MIDWEST PLAYERS
70363

12 Oaks Center
Ste. 922
Wayzata, MN 55391
Telephone: (612) 473-5088
FAX: (612) 473-7068
Pub. Frequency: bi-m.
Materials: 06,21,28,32
Circulation: 44,000
**Owner(s):**
RCM Enterprises, Inc.
12 Oaks Center
Ste. 922
Wayzata, MN 55391
Telephone: (612) 473-5088
FAX: (612) 473-7068
Ownership %: 100
**Management:**
Robert C. Meade ..........................Publisher
**Editorial:**
Joe Pawlowski ..................................Editor
**Desc.:** Focuses on the gaming industry and news useful to the gaming public; information about midwest casinos, tracks and the gaming industry.
**Readers:** Gambling enthusiasts, casino operators and the gaming industry in general.
**Deadline:** story-2 wks. prior to pub. date; news-2 wks.; photo-2 wks.; ads-1 wk.

## NLGI SPOKESMAN
23455

4635 Wyandotte St.
Kansas City, MO 64112
Telephone: (816) 931-9480
FAX: (816) 753-5026
Year Established: 1937
Pub. Frequency: m.
Page Size: standard
Subscrip. Rate: $24/yr.; $56/yr. surface mail foreign; $86/yr. airmail foreign
Circulation: 6,000
Circulation Type: paid
**Owner(s):**
National Lubricating Grease Inst.
4635 Wyandotte
Kansas City, MO 64112
Telephone: (816) 931-9480
Ownership %: 100
**Editorial:**
Duane J. Fike ..................................Editor
Marchand Zade ...........Administrative Assistant

**Desc.:** Complete coverage of the international lubricating grease industry, with technical and marketing features, new products, patents and developments, and general news about the industry included in this journal each month.
Departments include: Technical Features, Marketing Features, Technical Committee Column, Patents and Developments, People in the Industry, Industry News, Future Meetings, Membership Profiles.
**Readers:** Lubrication technician, lubricant salesmen, leaders among lubricant manufacturing companies and allied industries.

## NORTH CAROLINA PLUMBING, HEATING & COOLING FORUM
61632

413 Glenwood Ave.
Raleigh, NC 27603
Telephone: (919) 833-0372
FAX: (919) 833-0921
Year Established: 1942
Pub. Frequency: m.
Page Size: standard
Subscrip. Rate: $4/yr.
Materials: 01,30
Circulation: 4,000
Circulation Type: controlled
**Owner(s):**
North Carolina Association of PHCC, Inc.
413 Glenwood Ave.
Raleigh, NC 27603
Telephone: (919) 833-0372
Ownership %: 100
**Management:**
Annette T. Forsythe .........Advertising Manager
**Editorial:**
Tom Elkins ..................................Editor
Belinda S. Hodde ...................Associate Editor
**Readers:** Construction industry.
**Deadline:** story-10th of prior mo.; news-10th of prior mo.; photo-10th of prior mo.; ads-10th of prior mo.

## OIL DAILY'S LUBRICANTS WORLD
69038

1401 New York Ave. N.W., No. 500
Washington, DC 20005
Telephone: (800) 621-0050
FAX: (202) 783-5918
Year Established: 1991
Pub. Frequency: m.
Subscrip. Rate: $150/yr. US; $175/yr. Canada & Mexico; $220/yr. elsewhere
Circulation: 10,000
Circulation Type: controlled
**Owner(s):**
Oil Daily Co.
1401 New York Ave. N.W., #500
Washington, DC 20005
Telephone: (800) 621-0050
Ownership %: 100
**Editorial:**
John A. Moore ..........................................Editor
**Desc.:** Covers the lubricants business for users and suppliers, buyers and sellers of lubricants and related products.

## PENNSYLVANIA BUSINESS & TECHNOLOGY
66310

4516 Henry St.
Pittsburgh, PA 15213-9916
Telephone: (412) 687-2700
Year Established: 1990
Pub. Frequency: q.
Page Size: standard
Subscrip. Rate: $19.95/yr.; $34.95/2 yrs.; $42.95/3 yrs.
Circulation: 25,000
Circulation Type: controlled

**Owner(s):**
Pittsburgh High Technology Council
4516 Henry St.
Pittsburgh, PA 15213
Telephone: (412) 687-2700
Ownership %: 100
**Management:**
Tim Parks ..............................Publisher
Kevin O'Neil ..............Advertising Manager
Glenn Brooks ..............Circulation Manager
Mary Catherine McKee ........Managing Director
Ralph Keenan ........Production Manager
**Editorial:**
Betsy Momich ..............................Editor
**Readers:** Influential management in technology, and technology support industries.

## PLANTS, SITES & PARKS
24288

10100 W. Sample Rd.
Ste. 201
Coral Springs, FL 33065
Telephone: (305) 753-2660
FAX: (305) 755-7048
Year Established: 1974
Pub. Frequency: bi-m.
Page Size: standard
Subscrip. Rate: $5/copy; $30/yr.
Materials: 01,02,05,06,07
Freelance Pay: negotiable
Circulation: 40,500
Circulation Type: controlled
**Owner(s):**
BPI Communications, Inc.
1515 Broadway
New York, NY 10036
Telephone: (212) 764-7300
Ownership %: 100
**Management:**
Len Scaffidi ..............................Publisher
Nancy Kay ..............................Sales Manager
**Editorial:**
Ken Ibold ..............................Editor
Karen King ..............Managing Editor
Anne Hardy ..............................Sales
Harvey Jefferbaum ..............................Sales
Patrick Joyce ..............................Sales
Jack Sandler ..............................Sales
Karen Orange ..............................Sales
Web Bromley ..............................Sales
**Desc.:** Editorial slant addresses both North American and foreign industrial, office & economic development activity, including office space site location and future development, in-depth reviews of state economic growth, and those factors affecting development site location, expansion and relocation.
**Readers:** Top corporate executives, owners and others involved in site selection process.
**Deadline:** story-3 mos. prior to pub. date; ads-6 wks. prior

## SCRAP PROCESSING & RECYCLING
25237

1325 G St., N.W., Ste. 1000
Washington, DC 20005
Telephone: (202) 466-4050
FAX: (202) 775-9109
Year Established: 1988
Pub. Frequency: bi-m.
Page Size: standard
Subscrip. Rate: $7.50/copy; $26/yr. US; $30/yr. Canada & Mexico
Materials: 01,06,15,16,21,27,28,29,30,32,33
Print Process: web offset
Circulation: 6,132
Circulation Type: paid

---

**Materials Accepted/Included:** 01-Business news 02-By-line articles 03-Fashion news 04-Food news 05-Freelance copy 06-Letters to editor 07-Real estate news 08-Sports news 09-Travel news 10-Book rev. 11-Movie rev. 12-Music rev. 13-TV rev. 14-Theater rev. 15-Coming events 16-Obituaries 17-Question & answer 18-Social announcements 19-Artwork 20-Cartoons 21-Photos 22-TV listings 23-Audio rec. 24-Video rec. 25-Books 26-Films/film clips 27-Personnel news 28-Press releases 29-New product news/photos 30-Trade lit. 31-Contracts awarded 32-Display adv. 33-Classified adv.

**Owner(s):**
Institute of Scrap Recycling Industries
1325 G St., NW, Ste. 1000
Washington, DC 20005
Telephone: (202) 466-4050
Ownership %: 100
**Management:**
James E. Fowler .................................Publisher
Jacqueline L. Tyler ............Circulation Manager
**Editorial:**
Elise Browne .........................................Editor
James E. Fowler ..............................Advertising
Kent Kiser ..............................Assistant Editor
Jeff Borsecnik ........................Assistant Editor
Nancy Gast ............................Assistant Editor
Ellen Ross ............................Production Editor
Nancy Petersen .............Publication Consultant
**Desc.:** Covers all phases of the scrap
processing and recycling industries.
Objective is to provide practical and
useful information to the ISRI
Membership through articles and
departments that will increase the
profitability of their businesses.
**Readers:** Scrap and secondary material
dealers, processors, brokers,
consumers and manufacturers of
recycling equipment.

67688
**SECURITY SALES**
2512 Artesia Blvd.
Redondo Beach, CA 90278
Telephone: (310) 376-8788
FAX: (213) 376-9043
Year Established: 1979
Pub. Frequency: m.
Page Size: standard
Subscrip. Rate: $35/yr. US, $42/yr.
Canada; $52/yr. foreign
Materials: 01,02,05,06,15,17,27,28,29,30,
32,33
Freelance Pay: $50-$300
Print Process: web offset
Circulation: 23,000
Circulation Type: controlled
**Owner(s):**
Bobit Publishing Co.
2512 Artesia Blvd.
Redondo Beach, CA 90278
Telephone: (310) 376-8788
Ownership %: 100
**Management:**
Craig Knauf ........................................Publisher
Charles Oser .....................Production Manager
**Editorial:**
Jason Knott .............................Executive Editor
Joan Christopher ...............Associate Publisher
**Desc.:** News, features, new technology
updates for the security installing dealer.
Editorial is sales, marketing and
management focused in regard to
features.
**Readers:** Installing security dealers and
others allied to the field.
**Deadline:** story-25th of each mo.; news-
25th of each mo.; photo-25th of each
mo.; ads-1st of each mo.

61254
**SERVICE & SUPPORT
MANAGEMENT**
12416 Hymeadow Dr.
Austin, TX 78750
Telephone: (512) 250-9023
FAX: (512) 331-3900
Year Established: 1985
Pub. Frequency: m.
Page Size: standard
Subscrip. Rate: $3 newsstand; free to
qualified subscribers
Materials: 01,02,05,06,15,21,27,28,29,30,
31,32,33
Freelance Pay: negotiable
Print Process: web offset
Circulation: 35,000

Circulation Type: controlled
**Owner(s):**
Publication & Communications, Inc.
12416 Hymeadow Dr.
Austin, TX 78750
Telephone: (512) 250-9023
FAX: (512) 331-3900
Ownership %: 100
**Management:**
Gary Pittman .......................................Publisher
**Editorial:**
Christina Maloof .....................................Editor
**Desc.:** International publication that serves
the needs of service management with
practical solutions-oriented editorial that
shows the service manager how to
increase productivity, customer
satisfaction, and profits.
**Readers:** Management-level at facilities or
businesses servicing computers,
networks and high-tech systems.
**Deadline:** story-1st of each mo.; ads-6th of
each mo.

23426
**SITE SELECTION MAGAZINE**
40 Technology Pk., Ste. 200
Norcross, GA 30092
Telephone: (404) 446-6996
FAX: (404) 263-8825
Year Established: 1956
Pub. Frequency: bi-m.
Page Size: standard
Subscrip. Rate: $75/yr. US; $87/yr. foreign
Materials: 01,02,05,06,07,10,19,20,21,25,
27,28,29,30,31,32
Freelance Pay: negotiable
Print Process: web offset
Circulation: 40,501
Circulation Type: controlled & paid
**Owner(s):**
Conway Data, Inc.
40 Technology Pk., Ste. 200
Norcross, GA 30092
Telephone: (404) 446-6996
Ownership %: 70

Industrial Dev Research Foundation
Ownership %: 30
**Management:**
H. McKinley Conway ...........................Owner
Dan Kinney ................................Vice President
H. McKinley Conway ........................Publisher
**Editorial:**
Jack Lyne ..............................................Editor
Mary Dixon ....................................Advertising
Tim Venable ......................Coordinating Editor
Barbara Baez .........................European Editor
Harry Benedict ....................Marketing Director
Paul Newman ......................Marketing Director
Scott Wilson .......................Marketing Director
Ed Willard ...........................Marketing Director
**Desc.:** Serves the field of industrial
development, area analysis, expansion
planning and business site selection.
Four European issues are now also
published.
**Readers:** Readers are corporate
presidents, corporate facility planners,
location analysts, site selection
specialists, real estate managers and
other executives having responsibilities
for corporate properties.

70361
**UPHOLSTERY JOURNAL**
12 Oaks Center
Ste. 922
Wayzata, MN 55391
Telephone: (612) 473-5088
FAX: (612) 473-7068
Pub. Frequency: m.
Materials: 21,28
Circulation: 20,000

**Owner(s):**
RCM Enterprises, Inc.
12 Oaks Center
Ste. 922
Wayzata, MN 55391
Telephone: (612) 473-5088
FAX: (612) 473-7068
Ownership %: 100
**Management:**
Robert C. Mead ..................................Publisher
**Editorial:**
Thomas M. Faust ...................................Editor
**Desc.:** Product information, upholstery
techniques and industry
commentary. Product information,
upholstery techniques and industry
commentary. Focuses on products and
techniques used by professional custom
upholsterers as well as business tips.
**Readers:** Professional custom upholsterers
in the residential, marine, automotive,
RV, aircraft and commercial markets.
**Deadline:** story-6 wks. prior to pub. date;
news-6 wks.; photo-6 wks.; ads-60 days
prior to pub. date

70365
**WINDOW TECHNOLOGY**
12 Oaks Center
Ste. 922
Wayzata, MN 55391
Telephone: (612) 473-5088
FAX: (612) 473-7068
Pub. Frequency: 9/yr.
Materials: 06,21,28,32
Circulation: 6,000
**Owner(s):**
RCM Enterprises, Inc.
P.O. Box 720
Wayzata, MN 55391
Telephone: (612) 473-5088
FAX: (612) 473-7068
Ownership %: 100
**Management:**
Robert Mead .......................................Publisher
Jim Penningroth ................Advertising Manager
**Editorial:**
Joe Pawlowski .......................................Editor
**Desc.:** New product and technology
information. Focuses on emerging
window-covering and related products,
and technology.
**Readers:** Fabricators, workrooms,
installers and retailers of window
coverings, as well as related suppliers,
manufacturers, importers, distributors,
consultants, architectural and
construction professionals, and technical
experts.
**Deadline:** story-6 wks. prior to pub. date;
news-6 wks.; photo-6 wks.; ads-60 days

## Group 130-Instrumentation & Control System

65469
**CONTROL**
301 E. Erie St.
Chicago, IL 60611
Telephone: (312) 644-2020
Year Established: 1988
Pub. Frequency: 12/yr.
Page Size: standard
Circulation: 75,000
Circulation Type: controlled
**Owner(s):**
Putman Publishing Co.
301 E. Erie St.
Chicago, IL 60611
Telephone: (312) 644-2020
Ownership %: 100
**Management:**
Nick Cappelletti ..................................Publisher
**Editorial:**
Peggy Smedley .........................Editor in Chief

**Desc.:** Covers all aspects of
instrumentation and process control in
the process industries.
**Readers:** Serves professionals in the area
of instrumentation and control systems.

22557
**CONTROL ENGINEERING**
1350 E. Touhy
Des Plaines, IL 60018
Telephone: (708) 390-2783
FAX: (708) 390-2618
Year Established: 1954
Pub. Frequency: m.
Page Size: standard
Subscrip. Rate: $74.95/yr. US; $117.65/yr.
Canada
Materials: 01,06,28,29,30,32,33
Print Process: web offset
Circulation: 99,500
Circulation Type: controlled & paid
**Owner(s):**
Reed Publishing (USA) Inc.
275 Washington Street
Newton, MA 02158
Ownership %: 100
**Bureau(s):**
L.A. News Bureau
12233 W. Olympic Blvd.
Los Angeles, CA 90064
Telephone: (310) 826-5818
Contact: Tom McCusker, Writer
**Management:**
Charles Moodhe .................................President
Dave Harvey .......................................Publisher
Kate Smith ...........................Business Manager
Michael Babb .......................General Manager
Susan Johnson ...................Production Manager
**Editorial:**
Michael Babb .........................................Editor
Matt Wilhem ................................Art Director
**Desc.:** For designers and users of control
and instrumentation equipment and
systems worldwide.
**Readers:** Engineers and technical
management personnel.

22888
**EVALUATION ENGINEERING**
2504 N. Tamiami Trail
Nokomis, FL 34275
Telephone: (813) 966-9521
FAX: (813) 966-2590
Year Established: 1962
Pub. Frequency: m.
Page Size: standard
Subscrip. Rate: $95/yr. US; $135/yr.
foreign; free to qualified subscribers
Freelance Pay: varies
Circulation: 75,525
Circulation Type: controlled
**Owner(s):**
Nelson Publishing
2504 N. Tamiami Trail
Nokomis, FL 34275
Telephone: (813) 966-9521
Ownership %: 100
**Management:**
A.V. Nelson .........................................Publisher
John A. Dold ........................................Publisher
**Editorial:**
Paul Milo .......................................Exec. Editor
Debra Beebe ........................Associate Editor
Paul O'Shea .........................Associate Editor
Kristine Russell ....................Circulation Director
Gerald Jacob ..........................Technical Editor
**Desc.:** All editorial is aimed evaluation at
test and component engineers; topics
include: standards, reliability, QA/QC,
etc. and is targeted towards engineers
and other evaluation engineers in
electronics and allied industries. Stories
include State-of-Art features on product
plus methods articles related to own
field.

**Materials Accepted/Included:** 01-Business news 02-By-line articles 03-Fashion news 04-Food news 05-Freelance copy 06-Letters to editor 07-Real estate news 08-Sports news 09-Travel news 10-Book rev. 11-Movie rev. 12-Music rev. 13-TV rev. 14-Theater rev. 15-Coming events 16-Obituaries 17-Question & answer 18-Social announcements 19-Artwork 20-Cartoons 21-Photos 22-TV listings 23-Audio rec. 24-Video rec. 25-Books 26-Films/film clips 27-Personnel news 28-Press releases 29-New product news/photos 30-Trade lit. 31-Contracts awarded 32-Display adv. 33-Classified adv.

4-188

**Readers:** Management and individuals involved in test, design/development, QC/QA, production/manufacturing product assurances and support in engineering functions for electronic products and allied industries.

21801

## EXPERIMENTAL MECHANICS
Seven School St.
Bethel, CT 06801
Telephone: (203) 790-6373
FAX: (203) 790-4472
Year Established: 1943
Pub. Frequency: q.
Page Size: standard
Subscrip. Rate: $79/yr. US; $87/yr. foreign
Circulation: 4,000
Circulation Type: controlled & paid
**Owner(s):**
Society for Experimental Mechanics
Seven School St.
Bethel, CT 06801
Telephone: (203) 790-6373
Ownership %: 100
**Management:**
Gary L. Cloud ...............................President
K. A. Galione ................................Publisher
**Editorial:**
M. E. Yergin ......................Managing Editor
**Desc.:** A peer-reviewed, archival journal containing original researches, applications and review papers relating to experimental mechanics.
**Readers:** Engineers and scientists in industry.

58551

## INSTRUMENTOS Y CONTROLES INTERNACIONALES
150 Great Neck Rd.
Great Neck, NY 11021
Telephone: (516) 829-9210
Pub. Frequency: 3/yr.
Page Size: tabloid
Circulation: 25,096
Circulation Type: controlled
**Owner(s):**
Gerald E. Keller
150 Great Neck Rd.
Great Neck, NY 11021
Telephone: (516) 829-9210
**Editorial:**
Felicia Morales ..............................Editor
**Desc.:** Written in Spanish.

23440

## INTECH
P. O. Box 12277
67 Alexander Dr.
Research Triangle Park, NC 27709
Telephone: (919) 990-9286
FAX: (919) 549-8288
Year Established: 1954
Pub. Frequency: m.
Page Size: standard
Subscrip. Rate: $75/yr.; $135/2 yrs.; $185/3 yrs.
Materials: 01,02,06,15,28,29,32,33
Circulation: 53,275
Circulation Type: controlled & paid
**Owner(s):**
Instrument Society of America
67 Alexander Dr.
Research Triangle Park, NC 27709
Telephone: (919) 549-8411
FAX: (919) 548-8288
Ownership %: 100
**Management:**
Richard T. Simpson ......................Publisher
**Editorial:**
Robert C. Waterbury ..............Senior Editor
Valerie A. Price ...................Assistant Editor
Susan M. Organ .........Production Administratot
Debbie Jackson ..........Production Coordinator

**Desc.:** Will accept technical, scientific and news articles devoted to theory, testing, operation, use and maintenance of industrial instruments for measurement, telemetering, indicating, recording, control, computation and information processing. By-line stories and illustrations desired for front-of-book departments. New Product and New Literature items desired for monthly listing. Short technical articles on instrument applications desired. News releases on personalities, sales figures, speeches, annual reports, etc. Departments include Technical Feature Editorial; New Product and New Literature Editorial; Industry Personalities; New Books; Coming Events; News Developments in the Instrument Industry, including major contract awards, unique or significant product installations and applications; Instrument Society of America News.
**Readers:** Users and manufacturers of industrial controls and instrumentation in the process industries.
**Deadline:** ads-10th of mo. prior to pub. date

22339

## INTERNATIONAL INSTRUMENTATION & CONTROLS
150 Great Neck Rd.
Great Neck, NY 11021
Telephone: (516) 829-9210
FAX: (516) 824-5414
Mailing Address:
 P.O. Box 781
 Great Neck, NY 11025
Year Established: 1975
Pub. Frequency: bi-m.
Page Size: tabloid
Subscrip. Rate: controlled
Circulation: 30,034
Circulation Type: controlled & free
**Owner(s):**
Keller International Publishing Corp.
150 Great Neck Road
Great Neck, NY 11021
Telephone: (516) 829-9210
Ownership %: 100
**Management:**
Gerald E. Keller ..........................President
Bob Herlihy ................................Publisher
**Editorial:**
Felicia Morales ................Editorial Director
**Desc.:** New product/new process tabloid for the instrument, control and laboratory fields. Markets include metalworking, processing, chemical, research, and government/educational. Also: certain business information and reporting on trade shows, when possible.
**Readers:** Middle management-operating, engineering.

24441

## MEASUREMENTS & CONTROL
2994 W. Liberty Ave.
Pittsburgh, PA 15216
Telephone: (412) 343-9666
FAX: (412) 343-9685
Year Established: 1967
Pub. Frequency: bi-m.
Page Size: standard
Subscrip. Rate: $22/yr.
Circulation: 100,000
Circulation Type: paid
**Owner(s):**
Measurements & Data Corp.
2994 W. Liberty Ave.
Pittsburgh, PA 15216
Telephone: (412) 343-9666
Ownership %: 100

**Management:**
Milton H. Aronson ........................Publisher
**Editorial:**
Milton H. Aronson ............................Editor
Harish C. Saluja ...................Managing Editor
Nancy Gordon ..........................Advertising
**Desc.:** Features include professional courses, mass circulation of news section in which all news is reported by variable under following specific categories: electrical measurements, temperature, pressure mass, force, strain, torque, flow, level, timing, counting, programming, frequency, dimension, velocity, acceleration, vibrations, analysis, bio-medical, data acquisition, etc.
**Readers:** Engineering, scientific and technical personnel involved in control of physical and chemical variables.

65216

## SENSORS
174 Concord St.
Peterborough, NH 03458
Telephone: (603) 924-9631
FAX: (603) 924-7408
Year Established: 1984
Pub. Frequency: m.
Page Size: standard
Subscrip. Rate: $55/yr.
Freelance Pay: negotiable
Circulation: 63,000
Circulation Type: controlled
**Owner(s):**
Helmers Publishing, Inc.
174 Concord St.
Peterborough, NH 03458
Telephone: (603) 924-9631
Ownership %: 100
**Management:**
John E. Hayes ............................Publisher
Shari Courser .................Circulation Manager
**Editorial:**
Stephanie Henkel .......................Senior Editor
Dorothy Rosa .................................Editor
Margaret Gurney .....................Associate Editor
**Desc.:** A magazine produced for design, production and manufacturing engineers who specify sensors and sensing systems. Editorial content focuses on the use of sensors to increase efficiency, economy and productivity in manufacturing and industrial applications. Special emphasis is placed on new developments in sensing technology and innovative applications of existing sensing methods.
**Readers:** Engineers who specify, recommend, or buy sensors.

57274

## TECHNOLOGY FORECASTS & TECHNOLOGY SURVEYS
205 S. Beverly Dr., Ste. 208
Beverly Hills, CA 90212
Telephone: (310) 273-3486
Year Established: 1969
Pub. Frequency: m.
Page Size: standard
Subscrip. Rate: $160/yr.
**Owner(s):**
Technology Forecasts
205 S. Beverly Dr., Ste. 208
Beverly Hills, CA 90212
Telephone: (310) 273-3486
Ownership %: 100
**Management:**
Susan Nemiroff ..................Circulation Manager
**Editorial:**
Irwin Stambler ..............................Editor
Willard Wilks ....................Associate Publisher
Irwin Stambler ................Associate Publisher

**Desc.:** Presents information about major advances in many areas of advanced technology likely to have great impact on future applications in many fields including energy, electronics (computers, VLSI, etc.), chemical systems, etc. Also reports on developments in methodology used to forecast future technology trends.
**Readers:** Company presidents, chief scientists, chief engineers, head of research and development departments, vice president acquisitions, strategic planners, forecasters, economists.

23480

## WEIGHING & MEASUREMENT
P.O. Box 5867
Rockford, IL 61125
Telephone: (815) 229-1818
FAX: (815) 229-4086
Year Established: 1914
Pub. Frequency: bi-m.
Page Size: standard
Subscrip. Rate: $25/yr.
Materials: 02,05,06,28,29,30,32,33
Freelance Pay: $75-$250
Print Process: web offset
Circulation: 15,000
Circulation Type: controlled
**Owner(s):**
Key Markets Publishing
P.O. Box 5867
Rockford, IL 61125
Telephone: (815) 229-1818
FAX: (815) 229-4086
Ownership %: 100
**Management:**
David M. Mathieu ........................President
David M. Mathieu ........................Publisher
Ruby Mathiew ...............Advertising Manager
**Editorial:**
David M. Mathieu ............................Editor
**Desc.:** The main editorial text consists of articles designed to assist owners, executives, engineers, supervisors, and foremen in the performance of their job. Departments include: New Products, Applications, News, New Literature, Features, Coming Events and Letters to the Editor.

### Group 132-Insurance

23492

## AMERICAN AGENT & BROKER
330 N. Fourth St.
St. Louis, MO 63102-2036
Telephone: (314) 421-5445
Year Established: 1929
Pub. Frequency: m.
Page Size: standard
Subscrip. Rate: $1/issue; $12/yr.
**Owner(s):**
Commerce Publishing Co.
330 N. Fourth St.
St. Louis, MO 63102-2036
Telephone: (314) 421-5445
Ownership %: 100
**Management:**
James T. Poor ............................President
David A. Baetz ............................Publisher
**Editorial:**
George Williams ..............................Editor
Marge Bottiaux ..................Production Director
**Desc.:** Provides sales management information to help multi-line independent insurance agents serve their clients better.
**Readers:** Primarily general insurance agents and brokers.

---

Materials Accepted/Included: 01-Business news 02-By-line articles 03-Fashion news 04-Food news 05-Freelance copy 06-Letters to editor 07-Real estate news 08-Sports news 09-Travel news 10-Book rev. 11-Movie rev. 12-Music rev. 13-TV rev. 14-Theater rev. 15-Coming events 16-Obituaries 17-Question & answer 18-Social announcements 19-Artwork 20-Cartoons 21-Photos 22-TV listings 23-Audio rec. 24-Video rec. 25-Books 26-Films/film clips 27-Personnel news 28-Press releases 29-New product news/photos 30-Trade lit. 31-Contracts awarded 32-Display adv. 33-Classified adv.

## BEST'S REVIEW (LIFE/HEALTH)
23493

Ambest Rd.
Oldwick, NJ 08858
Telephone: (908) 439-2200
FAX: (908) 439-3363
Year Established: 1906
Pub. Frequency: m.
Page Size: 4 color photos/art
Subscrip. Rate: $21/yr.
Freelance Pay: free lance material not
  generally accepted
Circulation: 47,289
Circulation Type: paid
**Owner(s):**
A.M. Best Co., Inc.
Ambest Rd.
Oldwick, NJ 08858
Telephone: (908) 439-2200
Ownership %: 100
**Management:**
Arthur Snyder ..................................President
Richard L. Hall ......................Vice President
Arthur Snyder ................................Publisher
Nora Godown ..................Advertising Manager
Pamela Loos ....................Production Manager
**Editorial:**
Marian Freedman ........................Senior Editor
Mark L. Schussel ................................Editor
Neil Crescenti ................................Art Director
**Desc.:** Contributed and staff-written articles
  and features cover insurance trends and
  developments, technologic advances in
  the industry, statistical studies, new
  policies, company news, financial
  planning, marketing, insurance industry
  meetings, new literature, executive
  promotions. Special emphasis themes
  each month. Also publishes
  property/casualty edition, as well as two
  weekly newsletters.
**Readers:** Agents, managers and company
  personnel and executives.

## BEST'S REVIEW (PROPERTY/CASUALTY)
23494

Ambest Rd.
Oldwick, NJ 08858
Telephone: (908) 439-2200
FAX: (908) 439-3363
Year Established: 1900
Pub. Frequency: m.
Page Size: 4 color photos/art
Subscrip. Rate: $21/yr.
Circulation: 44,793
Circulation Type: paid
**Owner(s):**
A.M. Best Co., Inc.
Ambest Rd.
Oldwick, NJ 08858
Telephone: (908) 439-2200
Ownership %: 100
**Management:**
Arthur Snyder ..................................President
Richard L. Hall ......................Vice President
Arthur Snyder ................................Publisher
Nora Godown ..................Advertising Manager
**Editorial:**
Marian Freedman ........................Senior Editor
Mark L. Schussel ................................Editor
Neil Crescenti ......................Advertising Editor
Pamela Loos ....................Production Director
**Desc.:** Contributed and staff-written articles
  and features cover insurance trends and
  developments, company developments,
  technological advances in the industry,
  loss control and underwriting, company
  news, new literature, insurance industry
  meetings, statistical studies, the same
  world insurance & executive promotions.
  Special emphasis themes each month.
  Also publishes life edition, as well as
  two weekly newsletters.
**Readers:** Agents, brokers, managers,
  company personnel and executives.

## BROKER WORLD
61319

10709 Barkley, Ste. 3
Shawnee Mission, KS 66211
Telephone: (913) 383-9191
FAX: (913) 383-1247
Mailing Address:
  P.O. Box 11310
  Shawnee Mission, KS 66207
Year Established: 1980
Pub. Frequency: m.
Page Size: standard
Subscrip. Rate: $6/yr.
Circulation: 26,542
Circulation Type: paid
**Owner(s):**
William S. Howard
10709 Barkley, Ste. 3
Shawnee Mission, KS 66211
Telephone: (913) 383-9191
Ownership %: 100
**Management:**
William S. Howard ..............................Publisher
Elizabeth E. Coleman ........Production Manager
**Editorial:**
Sharon A. Chace ..................................Editor
Stephen A. Howard ..............Assistant Publisher
Catherine A. Fritz ..................Circulation Editor
**Desc.:** Editorial policy is to cover
  developments of significance to the
  brokerage life and health insurance
  community.
**Readers:** Life & health insurance agents,
  brokers and financial planners.

## BUSINESS INSURANCE
23495

740 Rush St.
Chicago, IL 60611
Telephone: (312) 649-5398
FAX: (312) 280-3174
Year Established: 1967
Pub. Frequency: w.
Page Size: tabloid
Subscrip. Rate: $80/yr.
Freelance Pay: $10.00/inch
Circulation: 53,000
Circulation Type: paid
**Owner(s):**
Crain Communications Inc.
740 N. Rush
Chicago, IL 60611
Telephone: (312) 649-5200
Ownership %: 100
**Bureau(s):**
Business Insurance
220 E. 42nd St., Ste. 930
New York, NY 10017
Telephone: (212) 210-0139
Contact: Stacy Gordon, Bureau Chief

Los Angeles
6404 Wilshire Blvd.
Los Angeles, CA 90048
Telephone: (310) 651-3710
Contact: Joanne Wojcik, Bureau Chief

Washington, D. C.
Ste. 814 Natl. Press Bldg.
Washington, DC 20004
Telephone: (202) 638-3155
Contact: Jerry Geisel, Senior Editor

Business Insurance
1 Northpark E. Ste. 114
Dallas, TX 75231
Telephone: (214) 363-1066
Contact: Michael Bradford, Associate
  Editor

Los Angeles
6500 Wilshire Blvd.
Los Angeles, CA 90048
Telephone: (213) 651-3710
Contact: Joanne Wojcik, Bureau Chief

Business Insurance
Nat'l. Press Bldg., Ste. 814
Washington, DC 20004
Telephone: (310) 651-3710
Contact: Jerry Geisel, Editor in Chief

Business Insurance
8950 N. Central Expy. Ste. 114
Dallas, TX 75231
Telephone: (214) 363-1066
Contact: Michael Bradford, Associate
  Editor

Business Insurance
540 Latimer Cir.
Campbell, CA 95008
Telephone: (408) 379-1790
Contact: Judy Greenwald, Associate Editor
**Management:**
Gertrude Crain ..................Chairman of Board
Keith Crain ..........................Vice Chairman
Rance Crain ..................................President
Kathryn J. McIntyre ..........................Publisher
**Editorial:**
James Burcke ................................Editor
James Burcke ..........................Managing Editor
Kathryn J. McIntyre ............Editorial Director
**Desc.:** The weekly newsmagazine for
  corporate risk, employee benefit and
  financial executives. The publication
  carries news of changes and
  revisions of insurance plans of
  corporations of all sizes with comments
  from insurance manager or
  employee benefits director involved.
  Reports on all developments in the
  commercial insurance business,focusing
  on how the developments will affect
  the buyer of commercial insurance.
**Readers:** Corporate Risk, Employee
  Benefit & Financial Executives;
  Insurance Companies; Agents
  And Brokers; Consultants; HMO's;
  Attorneys; Third-Party Administrators.

## CLAIMS
23502

1001 Fourth Ave. Plz., Ste. 3029
Seattle, WA 98154
Telephone: (206) 624-6965
Year Established: 1953
Pub. Frequency: m.
Page Size: standard
Subscrip. Rate: $38/yr.
Circulation: 8,000
Circulation Type: paid
**Owner(s):**
InsuranceWeek
1001 Fourth Ave. Plz., #3029
Seattle, WA 98154
Telephone: (206) 624-6965
Ownership %: 100
**Management:**
Doug Canfield ................................Publisher
**Editorial:**
Ronald Gillmeister ..................Executive Editor
Bill Thorness ................................Editor
**Desc.:** Editorials and news relating to the
  claims/loss field includes personnel
  changes, appointments, changes in
  insurance policy coverage.
  Strong emphasis is placed on legal
  decisions of importance to the insurance
  adjuster.
**Readers:** Independent adjusters, company
  claims examiners, and loss field
  managers.

## CONTINGENCIES
67203

7120 I St., N.W., 7th Fl.
Washington, DC 20006
Telephone: (202) 223-8196
FAX: (202) 872-1948
Year Established: 1989
Pub. Frequency: bi-m.

Page Size: standard
Subscrip. Rate: $24/yr.
Materials: 01,02,05,06,10,17,19,20,21,28,
  29,30,32,33
Print Process: web offset
Circulation: 22,000
Circulation Type: controlled
**Owner(s):**
American Academy of Actuaries
1720 I St., N.W., 7th Fl.
Washington, DC 20006
Telephone: (202) 223-8196
FAX: (202) 872-1948
Ownership %: 100
**Management:**
Jeff Leonard & ................Advertising Manager
Assoc.
**Editorial:**
Erich Parker ..........................Editor in Chief
Dana Murphy ................................Editor
**Desc.:** Reports on and analyzes actuarial
  trends in insurance and business.
**Readers:** Actuaries, business executives,
  insurance executives, CPA's, state and
  federal legislators and regulators.
**Deadline:** story-1st of mo. prior to pub.
  date; news-10th of mo. prior; photo-10th
  of mo. prior; ads-10th of mo. prior

## GENERAL INSURANCE GUIDE
68933

20 Oser Ave.
Hauppauge, NY 11788-3813
Telephone: (516) 234-1114
Year Established: 1936
Pub. Frequency: q.
Subscrip. Rate: $110/yr. initial; $52/yr.
  renewal
Circulation: 3,500
Circulation Type: paid
**Owner(s):**
Werbel Publishing Co., Inc.
20 Oser Ave.
Hauppauge, NY 11788-3813
Telephone: (516) 234-1114
Ownership %: 100
**Editorial:**
Harold Luckstone, Jr. ................................Editor

## HEALTH INSURANCE UNDERWRITER, THE
23499

1000 Connecticut Ave., N.W.
Ste. 810
Washington, DC 20036
Telephone: (202) 223-5533
FAX: (202) 285-2274
Year Established: 1930
Pub. Frequency: 11/yr.
Page Size: standard
Subscrip. Rate: $18/yr. members including
  dues; $40/yr. non-members
Circulation: 13,000
Circulation Type: controlled & paid
**Owner(s):**
National Association of Health
  Underwriters
1000 Connecticut Ave., N.W.
Ste. 810
Washington, DC 20036
Telephone: (202) 223-5533
Ownership %: 100
**Management:**
Mark Lappin ..............Executive Vice President
Pat Tyler ..........................Advertising Manager
**Editorial:**
Marsha Jonas ................................Editor
**Desc.:** Covers all phases of the health
  insurance field. Feature articles, new
  policy coverage, promotions, helpful
  information, covers conventions, and
  carries advertisements by many of the
  prominent insurance companies.
**Readers:** Has a readership of 10,000
  health insurance underwriters in the
  United States, Canada, and Hawaii.

**Materials Accepted/Included:** 01-Business news 02-By-line articles 03-Fashion news 04-Food news 05-Freelance copy 06-Letters to editor 07-Real estate news 08-Sports news 09-Travel news 10-Book rev. 11-Movie rev. 12-Music rev. 13-TV rev. 14-Theater rev. 15-Coming events 16-Obituaries 17-Question & answer 18-Social announcements 19-Artwork 20-Cartoons 21-Photos 22-TV listings 23-Audio rec. 24-Video rec. 25-Books 26-Films/film clips 27-Personnel news 28-Press releases 29-New product news/photos 30-Trade lit. 31-Contracts awarded 32-Display adv. 33-Classified adv.

## INDEPENDENT AGENT
23501

127 S. Peyton St.
Alexandria, VA 22314
Telephone: (703) 706-5411
FAX: (703) 683-7556
Year Established: 1903
Pub. Frequency: m.
Page Size: standard
Subscrip. Rate: $24/yr.
Freelance Pay: $750/article (2000 wds.)
Circulation: 45,000
Circulation Type: controlled
**Owner(s):**
Independent Insurance Agents of America, Inc.
127 S. Paxton St.
Alexandria, VA 22304
Telephone: (703) 683-4422
Ownership %: 100
**Management:**
Russell Burnett ......................................Publisher
**Editorial:**
Maureen Wall ..........................................Editor
Mary Hall ............................Managing Editor
Greg Smith ..........................Advertising Editor
Mary M. Hall ......................Production Director
**Desc.:** Deals with agency management, marketing and sales, new products and services and IIAA's latest news.
**Readers:** Primarily owners of insurance agencies.

## INSURANCE ADVOCATE
23503

P.O. Box 9001
Mount Vernon, NY 10552
Telephone: (914) 699-2020
FAX: (914) 664-1503
Year Established: 1889
Pub. Frequency: w.
Page Size: standard
Subscrip. Rate: $1/copy; $40/yr.
Freelance Pay: varies
Circulation: 11,660
Circulation Type: paid
**Owner(s):**
Chase Communications, Ltd.
25-35 Beechwood Ave.
Mount Vernon, NY 10553
Telephone: (914) 699-2020
Ownership %: 100
**Management:**
Stephen Acunto ....................................President
Stephen Acunto ....................................Publisher
Art Shea ..........................Advertising Manager
**Editorial:**
Emanuel Levy ..........................................Editor
Vito Pasquali ..........................Managing Editor
Neil Carter ..........................Book Review Editor
Michael Carbajal, Jr., CPCU ..............Columnist
Arthur I. Moll ......................................Columnist
David F. Twomey ................................Columnist
Edwin Nadel ........................................Columnist
**Desc.:** News and articles covering various aspects of insurance and finance. Also covers new products of use to the field, books, other publications, association news, appointments.
**Readers:** Insurance agents, brokers and company execs., attorneys, adjusters, libraries.

## INSURANCE JOURNAL, THE
23504

9191 Town Center Dr., Ste. 550
San Diego, CA 92122
Telephone: (619) 455-7717
FAX: (619) 546-1462
Year Established: 1923
Pub. Frequency: bi-w.
Page Size: standard
Subscrip. Rate: $78/yr. US; $156/yr. foreign
Circulation: 11,000
Circulation Type: controlled

**Owner(s):**
Mark Wells
9191 Town Center Dr., Ste. 550
San Diego, CA 92122
Telephone: (619) 455-7717
Ownership %: 100
**Bureau(s):**
Insurance Journal
Telephone: (510) 777-4238
Contact: John McCann, Editor
**Management:**
Mark Wells ..........................................Publisher
Dena Kaplan ......................Advertising Manager
Katie Robley ........................Circulation Manager
Karyn Howard ..........................Office Manager
Ed Richards ..........................Production Manager
**Editorial:**
Denise Carabet ......................Managing Editor
Dena Kaplan ......................Associate Publisher
**Desc.:** INSURANCE journal is edited for property casualty independent agents and brokers of the WEST. EDITORIAL content includes news, features, interviews with insurance industry figures, EDITORIAL content covers company experience, court rulings, legislation, financial information, meetings, personnel changes, associations, actions of regulatory agencies and other activities.
**Readers:** Property/casualty insurance brokers in California & the West.

## INSURANCE MARKETPLACE, THE
48212

1200 N. Meridian
Indianapolis, IN 46204
Telephone: (800) 428-4384
FAX: (317) 634-1041
Year Established: 1878
Pub. Frequency: m.
Page Size: standard
Materials: 32
Print Process: web offset
Circulation: 44,000
Circulation Type: controlled & paid
**Owner(s):**
Rough Notes Co.
1200 N. Meridian
P.O. Box 564
Indianapolis, IN 46206
Telephone: (800) 428-4384
Ownership %: 100
**Editorial:**
Thomas A. McCoy ..................................Editor
Arnold Sherman ..............................Advertising
**Desc.:** Serves specialized forms of insurance called nonstandard-specialty lines and their national/regional markets. Also, editorial sections on aviation, marine and international insurance; the major US insurance exchanges, and aspects of commercial risk management.
**Readers:** Property-casualty agents and brokers and selected buyers.

## INSURANCE RECORD, THE
23506

2730 Stemmons Frwy., Ste. 507
Dallas, TX 75207
Telephone: (214) 630-0687
FAX: (214) 631-2476
Mailing Address:
P.O. Box 225770
Dallas, TX 75222
Year Established: 1934
Pub. Frequency: bi-w.
Page Size: standard
Subscrip. Rate: $15/yr.
Freelance Pay: $1.25/col. in.
Circulation: 2,000
Circulation Type: paid

**Owner(s):**
Record Publishing Co.
P.O. Box 225770
Dallas, TX 75222
Telephone: (214) 630-0687
Ownership %: 100
**Management:**
Mrs. John C. Leslie ..............................President
John H. Leslie ..............................Vice President
Mrs. John C. Leslie ..............................Publisher
Carol J. Leslie Hargis ......Advertising Manager
**Editorial:**
Glen E. Hargis ......................................Editor
Carol J. Leslie Hargis ..............Managing Editor
John H. Leslie ......................................Director
**Desc.:** Published bi-weekly in the interest of sound insurance in the Southwest.
**Readers:** Insurance agents (all kinds) and insurance company personnel as well as by insurance adjusters, actuaries, accountants, attorneys, suppliers, and others in related fields.

## INSURANCEWEEK
23508

1001 Fourth Ave. Plz., Ste. 3029
Seattle, WA 98154
Telephone: (206) 624-6965
FAX: (206) 624-5021
Year Established: 1933
Pub. Frequency: w.
Page Size: standard
Subscrip. Rate: $20/yr. US; $45/yr. CN; $85/yr. foreign
Freelance Pay: varies
Circulation: 8,000
Circulation Type: paid
**Owner(s):**
InsuranceWeek Inc.
1001 Fourth Ave. Plz., #3029
Seattle, WA 98154
Telephone: (206) 624-6965
Ownership %: 100
**Management:**
Doug Canfield ......................................Publisher
Doug Canfield ..................Advertising Manager
**Editorial:**
Ronald J. Gillmeister ..............Executive Editor
Richard Rambeck ..................................Editor
**Desc.:** Provides independent agents and brokers in the Western States (Alaska, Ariz., Calif., Colo., Hawaii, Idaho, Mont., Nev., New Mexico, Utah, Wash., Wyo.) with news of multiline insurance, emphasis being on developments in the west.
**Readers:** Independent Insurance Agents & Brokers, & Intermediaries. Insurance Company Personnel, Attorneys

## JOURNAL OF RISK & INSURANCE, THE
23511

3641 Locust Walk
Wharton School, University of Pennsylvania
Philadelphia, PA 19104-6218
Telephone: (215) 898-9631
FAX: (215) 898-0310
Year Established: 1932
Pub. Frequency: q.
Page Size: standard
Subscrip. Rate: $90/yr. US & Canada; $95/yr. foreign; $105/yr. foreign airmail
Circulation: 1,600
Circulation Type: paid
**Owner(s):**
American Risk and Insurance Association
California State University
Sacramento, CA 95819-6088
Telephone: (916) 278-6609
FAX: (916) 278-5437
Ownership %: 100
**Management:**
Jerry Jorgensen ....................................President

**Editorial:**
J. David Cummins ..................................Editor
Dr. Jerry Jorgensen ..............Managing Editor
Caryl Knutsen ......................Assistant Editor
Dr. Mary A. Weiss ............Book Review Editor
**Desc.:** Primary purpose is to present scholarly articles on theory and practice relevant to insurance and related areas. Articles report both on research which expands the knowledge of risk and insurance and describe methods and procedures related to risk managers and various segments of the insurance business. A forum is also provided for manuscripts devoted to the theoretical concepts pertinent to risk and insurance. All articles are refereed; book reviews, communications, and other features are also a part of the journal. Any library or organization may subscribe by paying the annual subscription rate. All subscriptions are for the calendar year.
**Readers:** Almost all college teachers of insurance & many professors in other fields, risk managers and insurance industry personnel.

## JOURNAL OF THE AMERICAN SOCIETY OF CLU & CHFC
23497

270 Bryn Mawr Ave.
Bryn Mawr, PA 19010-2195
Telephone: (610) 526-2500
FAX: (610) 527-2538
Year Established: 1946
Pub. Frequency: bi-m.
Page Size: standard
Subscrip. Rate: $32/yr.
Materials: 02,10
Print Process: web offset
Circulation: 40,000
Circulation Type: paid
**Owner(s):**
American Society of CLU & CHFC
270 Bryn Mawr Ave.
Bryn Mawr, PA 19010-2195
Telephone: (610) 526-2500
Ownership %: 100
**Management:**
Ray A. Silva ......................................President
Elizabeth M. ..................Advertising Manager
Thomson
**Editorial:**
Dr. Kenneth Black, Jr. ..............Executive Editor
Deanne L. Sherman ..............Managing Editor
Elizabeth M. Thomson ........Assistant Managing Editor
Dr. Kenneth Black, Jr. ........Book Review Editor
**Desc.:** Edited to serve the public interest by providing continuing education, ethical guidance and public recognition for members of the American Society of CLU & CHFC.

## LIFE & HEALTH INSURANCE SALES
23507

Telephone: (606) 277-6135
FAX: (606) 277-8059
Mailing Address:
98 Dennis Drive
Lexington, KY 40503
Year Established: 1917
Pub. Frequency: m.
Subscrip. Rate: $3 newsstand; $25/yr.
Materials: 01,06,10,20
Circulation: 22,000
Circulation Type: paid
**Owner(s):**
Rough Notes Co.
P.O. Box 564
Indianapolis, IN 46206
Telephone: (317) 634-1041
Ownership %: 100
**Management:**
Walter J. Gdowski ................................President

Arnold B. Sherman ............Advertising Manager
**Editorial:**
Phil Zinkewicz ....................................Editor
Evelyn T. Egan ................Book Review Editor
Kenneth L. Meyer ..........................Columnist
James A. Ballew ............................Columnist
Thomas C. Eusebio ......................Columnist
Matt Oechsli ..................................Columnist
**Desc.:** Articles aimed at furthering the
education of salespeople in the life,
health insurance and equities field. Also
articles which discuss techniques for
selling insurance to specific occupational
and age groups. Departments include:
Monthly Features, Health Insurance,
Insurance Court Decisions, Directmail
Marketing, Advanced Underwriting, New
Books And Recordings, New Life
/Health Insurance Product Profiles,
Prospecting, Agency Management,
Insurance Scene, Automation.
**Readers:** 98% life insurance agents,
general agents, managers and brokers;
2% home office executives.
**Deadline:** story-1 mo. prior to pub. date;
ads-1 mo. prior to pub. date

23512
## LIFE ASSOCIATION NEWS
1922 F Street, N.W.
Washington, DC 20006
Telephone: (202) 331-6070
FAX: (202) 835-9608
Year Established: 1906
Pub. Frequency: m.
Page Size: 4 Color Photos/Art
Subscrip. Rate: $6/yr. US; $22/yr. foreign
Freelance Pay: Is By Arrangement
Circulation: 140,000
Circulation Type: controlled
**Owner(s):**
The National Assn. of Life Underwriters
1922 F Street, N.W.
Washington, DC 20006
Telephone: (202) 331-6000
Ownership %: 100
**Management:**
Ian MacKenzie ..............................Publisher
**Editorial:**
Joseph C. Razza, CLU ................Senior Editor
Ian MacKenzie ..................................Editor
Jane Goforth ..............Administrative Assistant
Jeane Molz ..................................Advertising
Dee Lichtenstein ......................Art Director
George A. Norris ....................Associate Editor
Melissa Sprott ....................Production Director
**Desc.:** Contains articles which are specific
how-to pieces, reports news of NALU
and its 958 affiliated local and state
associations, assays trends and
developments in life insurance and allied
fields, feature educational, training,
and sales material, etc. Departments
include: Management and supervision,
training and news of the life insurance
industry, news of allied education,
legislation, sales and selling techniques,
fields (finance, business, public relations,
etc.).
**Readers:** Life, Health and Multiline
Insurance Salesmen In The Country
Who Are Members of Local Life
Underwriting Associations

23513
## LIFE INSURANCE SELLING
330 N. Fourth St.
Saint Louis, MO 63102-2036
Telephone: (314) 421-5445
FAX: (314) 421-1070
Year Established: 1926
Pub. Frequency: m.
Page Size: Standard
Subscrip. Rate: $12/yr.
Circulation: 45,616
Circulation Type: paid

**Owner(s):**
Commerce Publishing Co.
330 N. Fourth St.
Saint Louis, MO 63102
Telephone: (314) 421-5445
Ownership %: 100
**Management:**
James T. Poor ................................President
Larry Albright ................................Publisher
Sue Bohnsack ..............Advertising Manager
**Editorial:**
Gail Waisanen ............................Senior Editor
Larry Albright ....................................Editor
Charles K. Hirsch ..................Managing Editor
**Desc.:** Most of the articles are bylined by
life insurance agents who describe the
ideas and techniques they have used to
achieve success in the life insurance
business. This is not a "News"
publication, other than the
departments that describe new office
and sales aids, books, and life and
health insurance policies. Departments
include: What's Going on in
the Insurance Business, Million Dollar
Sales Ideas, Sales Sizzlers, Remember
the Basics, Letters, Speaking of Books,
Office Aids, Sales Aids, etc.
**Readers:** Life insurance agents.

23514
## LIFETIMES
500 Interstate Blvd. S.
Nashville, TN 37210
Telephone: (615) 256-8262
FAX: (615) 256-8262
Mailing Address:
P.O. Box 100745
Nashville, TN 37224
Year Established: 1962
Pub. Frequency: bi-m.
Page Size: standard
Subscrip. Rate: $12/yr. non-members
Circulation: 4,000
Circulation Type: paid
**Owner(s):**
Tennessee Association of Life
Underwriters
P.O. Box 100745
Nashville, TN 37224
Telephone: (615) 256-8258
Ownership %: 100
**Editorial:**
Terry D. McBride ..............................Editor
**Desc.:** Includes features on activities of
the TALU and articles of interest to
members.
**Readers:** Primarily members of the TALU,
including some home office personnel.

53960
## LIMRA'S MARKETFACTS
Eight Farm Springs
Farmington, CT 06032-2594
Telephone: (203) 677-0033
FAX: (203) 678-0187
Mailing Address:
P.O. Box 208
Hartford, CT 06141-0208
Year Established: 1982
Pub. Frequency: bi-m.
Subscrip. Rate: $50/yr. members; $95/yr.
others; $60/yr. foreign members;
$105/yr. non-members
Materials: 01,02,06,19,21,28,30,32
Print Process: web
Circulation: 8,500
Circulation Type: controlled & paid
**Owner(s):**
Life Insurance Marketing & Research
Assoc.
Eight Farm Springs
Farmington, CT 06032
Telephone: (203) 677-0033
FAX: (203) 678-0187
Ownership %: 100

**Editorial:**
Heather C. Waldron ............................Editor
**Desc.:** Providing news and features on all
phases of insurance product marketing.
**Readers:** Chief marketing executives &
presidents of major North American and
international life insurers, plus staff of
marketing departments.
**Deadline:** story-60 days prior to pub. date;
ads-30 days prior to pub. date

23515
## MANAGERS MAGAZINE
8 Farm Springs
Farmington, CT 06032-0208
Telephone: (203) 677-0033
Mailing Address:
P.O. Box 208
Hartford, CT 06141-0208
Year Established: 1926
Pub. Frequency: m.
Page Size: standard
Subscrip. Rate: $45/yr. members; $65/yr.
non-members
Materials: 01,02,06,10,20,21,23,24,25,28,
29,30
Print Process: web
Circulation: 9,000
Circulation Type: paid
**Owner(s):**
Life Insurance Marketing & Research
Association
P.O. Box 208
Hartford, CT 06141
Telephone: (203) 677-0033
Ownership %: 100
**Editorial:**
Daniel J. Nahorney ............................Editor
**Desc.:** Covers various aspects of life
insurance agency management-training,
public relations, recruiting, etc.
Departments include: Managers
Handbook and Guest Editorials. Does
not carry news.
**Readers:** Life insurance agency managers
and general agents.
**Deadline:** story-3 mo. prior to pub. date;
news-3 mo. prior; photo-3 mo. prior

23516
## MID-AMERICA INSURANCE
10709 Barkley, Ste. 3
Shawnee Mission, KS 66211
Telephone: (913) 383-9191
FAX: (913) 383-1247
Mailing Address:
P.O. Box 11310
Shawnee Mission, KS 66207
Year Established: 1888
Pub. Frequency: Monthly
Page Size: Standard
Subscrip. Rate: $10/Yr.
Freelance Pay: No Fees Paid for Articles
Circulation: 13,196
Circulation Type: controlled
**Owner(s):**
William S. Howard
10709 Barkley, Ste. 3
Shawnee Msn, KS 66211
Telephone: (913) 383-9191
Ownership %: 100
**Management:**
William S. Howard ........................Publisher
Carole A. Howard ................Business Manager
**Editorial:**
Jim Willman ....................................Editor
Robert F. Edwards ..............Associate Publisher
Catherine Fritz ..................Marketing Director
Elizabeth E. Goodnow ........Production Director
**Desc.:** News and features of interest to
producers and other insurance
professionals.
**Readers:** Insurance Agents

23518
## NATIONAL UNDERWRITER (LIFE, HEALTH, FINANCIAL SERVICES)
47 Newark St.
Hoboken, NJ 07030
Telephone: (201) 963-2300
FAX: (201) 963-3632
Year Established: 1897
Pub. Frequency: w.
Page Size: Tabloid
Subscrip. Rate: $75/yr.
Circulation: 42,000
Circulation Type: paid
**Owner(s):**
National Underwriter Co.
505 Gest St.
Cincinnati, OH 45203
Telephone: (513) 721-2140
Ownership %: 100
**Management:**
Clarence W. Barnes ........................President
Thomas J. Slattery ........................Publisher
Dolores Bruschaber ..........Advertising Manager
Barbara E. Swisher ..........Production Manager
**Editorial:**
Sam Friedman ....................................Editor
Linda Jones ..............Administrative Assistant
**Desc.:** Carries material on national scale
and developments in life, health,
financial services field. Reports policy
changes, company news, comment and
trend articles, and sales ideas in the
industry.
**Readers:** Insurance Agents, Brokers and
Financial Planners And Health Insurance
Companies and Home Office Services.

23517
## NATIONAL UNDERWRITER (PROPERTY, CASUALTY)
47 Newark St.
Hoboken, NJ 07030
Telephone: (201) 963-2300
FAX: (201) 963-3632
Year Established: 1897
Pub. Frequency: w.
Page Size: tabloid
Subscrip. Rate: $79/yr.
Circulation: 44,273
Circulation Type: paid
**Owner(s):**
National Underwriter Co., The
505 Gest St.
Cincinnati, OH 45203
Telephone: (513) 721-2140
Ownership %: 100
**Management:**
Clarence W. Barnes ........................President
Thomas J. Slattery ........................Publisher
Dolores J. Bruschaber ......Advertising Manager
**Editorial:**
Sam Friedman ....................................Editor
Linda Jones ................Administrative Assistant
Barbara Swisher ..............Executive Production
Manager
**Desc.:** Carries material on national scale
and developments in fire, casualty,
accident, sickness, risk and benefits
management. Reports policy changes,
company news, convention news,
comment and trend articles, and sales
ideas in the industry.
**Readers:** Insurance agents, brokers, risk
managers and insurance companies.

23525
## OHIO UNDERWRITER, THE
505 Gest St.
Cincinnati, OH 45203
Telephone: (513) 345-4083
FAX: (513) 721-0126
Year Established: 1967
Pub. Frequency: m.
Page Size: standard
Subscrip. Rate: $16.50/yr.
Circulation: 10,200

**Materials Accepted/Included:** 01-Business news 02-By-line articles 03-Fashion news 04-Food news 05-Freelance copy 06-Letters to editor 07-Real estate news 08-Sports news 09-Travel news 10-Book rev. 11-Movie rev. 12-Music rev. 13-TV rev. 14-Theater rev. 15-Coming events 16-Obituaries 17-Question & answer 18-Social announcements 19-Artwork 20-Cartoons 21-Photos 22-TV listings 23-Audio rec. 24-Video rec. 25-Books 26-Films/film clips 27-Personnel news 28-Press releases 29-New product news/photos 30-Trade lit. 31-Contracts awarded 32-Display adv. 33-Classified adv.

Circulation Type: controlled
**Owner(s):**
National Underwriter Co.
505 Gest St.
Cincinnati, OH 45203
Telephone: (513) 721-2140
Ownership %: 100
**Management:**
Clarence Barnes .....................................President
Dolores Brusehaber ..........Advertising Manager
**Editorial:**
Joe Diamond ...............................Editor in Chief
Gil McLean ...............................................Editor
**Desc.:** Newspaper for the state of Ohio
dealing exclusively with insurance news.
**Readers:** Insurance people in the state of
Ohio.

68932

## PRODUCER NEWS
1812 Production Ct.
Louisville, KY 40299
Telephone: (502) 491-5857
FAX: (502) 491-5905
Year Established: 1976
Pub. Frequency: m.
Subscrip. Rate: $27/yr.
Circulation: 16,350
Circulation Type: paid
**Owner(s):**
Insurance Field Co.
1812 Production Ct.
Louisville, KY 40299
Telephone: (502) 491-5857
Ownership %: 100
**Editorial:**
George V.R. Smith .................................Editor
**Readers:** Independent insurance agents.

23520

## PROFESSIONAL AGENT
400 N. Washington St.
Alexandria, VA 22314
Telephone: (703) 836-9340
FAX: (703) 836-1279
Year Established: 1934
Pub. Frequency: m.
Page Size: standard
Subscrip. Rate: $20/yr. non-members;
$12/yr. members of PIA
Materials: 01,06,28,32,33
Freelance Pay: $950
Circulation: 30,000
Circulation Type: paid
**Owner(s):**
National Assn. of Professional Insurance
Agents
400 N. Washington St.
Alexandria, VA 22314
Telephone: (703) 836-9340
Ownership %: 100
**Management:**
Richard H. Freeman ..........................Publisher
Richard Ryan ...................Advertising Manager
**Editorial:**
Alan Prochoroff ......................................Editor
Patty Hashmi ....................................Advertising
**Desc.:** News of developments in property
and casualty insurance. Features contain
helpful information for selling insurance
and managing insurance agencies.
**Readers:** Independent insurance agents.
**Deadline:** ads-1st of mo. prior to pub. date

56407

## PROFESSIONAL INSURANCE
AGENTS OF NEW YORK-NEW
JERSEY-CONNECTICUT
P.O. Box 997
Glenmont, NY 12077
Telephone: (518) 434-3111
FAX: (518) 434-2342
Year Established: 1958
Pub. Frequency: 11/yr.
Page Size: standard
Subscrip. Rate: $25 to non-members
Freelance Pay: negotiable

Circulation: 5,000
Circulation Type: paid
**Owner(s):**
Professional Insurance Agents Association
NY,NJ,CT
P.O. Box 997
Glenmont, NY 12077
Telephone: (518) 434-3111
Ownership %: 100
**Bureau(s):**
PIA of New Jersey
130 W. State St.
Trenton, NJ 08608
Telephone: (609) 393-2228
Contact: Leon Zimmerman
**Editorial:**
Mary Vanniere .......................................Editor
Nancy Zucchino ................Publication Director
**Desc.:** Dedicated to the advancement of
knowledge and informed opinion for the
professional enlightenment and growth
of the men & women of the insurance
industry.
**Readers:** Primarily independent, property-
casualty insurance agents, government
executives, professionals.

66611

## RISK & INSURANCE
747 Dresher Rd., Ste. 500
Horsham, PA 19044
Telephone: (215) 784-0860
FAX: (215) 784-0870
Mailing Address:
P.O. Box 980
Horsham, PA 19044
Year Established: 1990
Pub. Frequency: bi-m.
Page Size: tabloid
Subscrip. Rate: $59.95/yr.
Freelance Pay: negotiable
Print Process: web
Circulation: 40,000
Circulation Type: paid
**Owner(s):**
Axon Group
747 Dresher Rd.
Horsham, PA 19044
Telephone: (215) 784-0860
Ownership %: 100
**Management:**
Al Novak ..............................................Publisher
**Editorial:**
Linda Wasserman ......................Editor in Chief
**Desc.:** Covers professional liability,
environmental liability, captive
administration, health benefits
and workers' compensation.
**Readers:** Risk managers and other
corporate insurance decision makers;
selected insurance company executives.

23521

## RISK MANAGEMENT
205 E. 42nd St.
New York, NY 10017
Telephone: (212) 286-9364
Year Established: 1954
Pub. Frequency: m.
Page Size: standard
Subscrip. Rate: $54/yr.
Freelance Pay: varies
Circulation: 10,700
Circulation Type: paid
**Owner(s):**
Risk and Insurance Management Society
205 E. 42nd St.
New York, NY 10017
Telephone: (212) 286-9364
Ownership %: 100
**Management:**
Edward Donovan ..............Advertising Manager
Nancy Saxe .......................Advertising Manager
Allen Marks ........................Circulation Manager
**Editorial:**
Alice Oshins ..........................................Editor

Craig Goldberg ...............................Art Director
Orin Kurland ...........................Associate Editor
Ann Lem ...............................Production Director
**Desc.:** Official publication of the Risk and
Insurance Management Society with
how-to and interpretive articles relating
to risk analysis and funding techniques,
safety and loss prevention, employees
benefits planning, and federal/state
legislative and regulatory developments.
**Readers:** Corporate risk and insurance
managers, employee benefits managers
and insurance and financial executives.

48213

## ROUGH NOTES
1200 N. Meridian
Indianapolis, IN 46204
Telephone: (800) 428-4384
FAX: (317) 634-1041
Mailing Address:
P.O. Box 564
Indianapolis, IN 46206
Year Established: 1878
Pub. Frequency: m.
Page Size: standard
Subscrip. Rate: $25/yr.
Materials: 01,02,06,17,20,25,28,29,30,32
Circulation: 40,000
Circulation Type: paid
**Owner(s):**
Rough Notes Co.
1200 N. Meridian, Box 564
Indianapolis, IN 46204
Telephone: (800) 428-4384
Ownership %: 100
**Management:**
Arnold Sherman .................Advertising Manager
Nancy Doucette ...........New Products Manager
**Editorial:**
Nancy Doucette ...........................Senior Editor
Tom Mc Coy ..........................................Editor
Tom Mc Coy ..............................News Editor
Tom Mc Coy ......................Photography Editor
Tom Mc Coy ............................Technical Editor
**Desc.:** A monthly magazine for property-
casualty agents and brokers-
management, client services, policy
forms, risk analysis, life insurance and
specialized forms through brokerage,
client service, business acquisition and
retention.
**Readers:** Property-casualty agents and
brokers.
**Deadline:** ads-1st of mo. prior to pub. date

23523

## SOUTHERN INSURANCE
2535 Beechwood Ave.
Mount Vernon, NY 10553
Telephone: (914) 699-2020
FAX: (914) 699-2025
Mailing Address:
P.O. Box 90001
Mount Vernon, NY 10552
Year Established: 1888
Pub. Frequency: m.
Page Size: standard
Subscrip. Rate: $6/yr.
Circulation: 2,000
Circulation Type: paid
**Owner(s):**
Chase Communications
P.O. Box 9001
Mount Vernon, NY 10552
Ownership %: 100
**Management:**
Stephen H. Acunto ...........................Publisher
Matthew Scampoli ............Advertising Manager
**Editorial:**
Stephen H. Acunto ...............................Editor
**Desc.:** Features deal with trends and
regulations affecting fire, life, casualty
and marine insurance fields. Carries
personnel announcements and company
news.

**Readers:** Predominantly insurance agents.
Also includes adjusters, home offices,
attorneys and supervisors.

23524

## STANDARD, THE
155 Federal St.
Boston, MA 02110-1727
Telephone: (617) 457-0604
FAX: (617) 482-7820
Year Established: 1865
Pub. Frequency: w.; bi-w. July & Aug.
Page Size: standard
Subscrip. Rate: $40/yr.
Circulation: 5,675
Circulation Type: paid
**Owner(s):**
Standard Publishing Co.
155 Federal St.
Boston, MA 02110-1727
Telephone: (617) 482-7820
Ownership %: 100
**Management:**
John C. Cross ......................................Publisher
Barbara Crockett ..............Advertising Manager
**Editorial:**
Frank R. Pote, Jr. ..................................Editor
**Desc.:** Concentrates on important national
news and covers company news,
association news, appointments.
**Readers:** New England, New York
insurance people.

68934

## TITLE MANAGEMENT TODAY
901 Church St.
Nashville, TN 37203-3411
Year Established: 1991
Pub. Frequency: m.
Subscrip. Rate: $189/yr.
Materials: 01,20,25,27,30
**Owner(s):**
Lewis Laska
901 Church St.
Nashville, TN 37203-3411
Telephone: (615) 255-6288
FAX: (615) 255-6289
Ownership %: 100
**Editorial:**
Lewis Laska ..........................................Editor
**Desc.:** Covers litigation, regulation,
marketing, and management of title
insurance offices.

23527

## UNDERWRITERS' REPORT
657 Mission St.
Ste. 300
San Francisco, CA 94105-4113
Telephone: (415) 896-2660
FAX: (415) 974-5041
Year Established: 1905
Pub. Frequency: w.
Page Size: standard
Subscrip. Rate: $45/yr.; $120/3 yrs.;
Foreign $90/yr; $240/3 yrs.
Materials: 01,02,05,06,15,16,27,28,29,32,33
Print Process: offset
Circulation: 520,500
Circulation Type: paid
**Owner(s):**
Underwriters' Report, Inc.
657 Mission St.
Ste. 300
San Francisco, CA 94105-4113
Telephone: (415) 981-3221
Ownership %: 100
**Management:**
Roy Pasini ..........................................Publisher
**Editorial:**
Roy Pasini ............................................Editor
Heinz Pulverman ...................Assistant Editor
Ron Lent ..............................Associate Editor
Juanita Timmons ...................Circulation Editor
Chuck Morrisey .......Community Affairs Director
Chuck Morrisey ...................Marketing Director
Bill Harvey ....................................Photographer

**Materials Accepted/Included:** 01-Business news 02-By-line articles 03-Fashion news 04-Food news 05-Freelance copy 06-Letters to editor 07-Real estate news 08-Sports news 09-Travel news 10-Book rev. 11-Movie rev. 12-Music rev. 13-TV rev. 14-Theater rev. 15-Coming events 16-Obituaries 17-Question & answer 18-Social announcements 19-Artwork 20-Cartoons 21-Photos 22-TV listings 23-Audio rec. 24-Video rec. 25-Books 26-Films/film clips 27-Personnel news 28-Press releases 29-New product news/photos 30-Trade lit. 31-Contracts awarded 32-Display adv. 33-Classified adv.

Michael Pasini ...................Production Assistant
**Desc.:** News magazine, reporting on developments, company news, appointments, activities. Departments listed above cover all fields of insurance.
**Readers:** Agents, brokers and company men.

## Group 134-Interior Design & Decorating

### COLOR RESEARCH & APPLICATION
65632

605 Third Ave.
New York, NY 10158
Telephone: (212) 850-6000
FAX: (212) 850-8888
Pub. Frequency: bi-m.
Subscrip. Rate: $240/yr.
Circulation: 1,500
Circulation Type: paid
**Owner(s):**
John Wiley & Sons, Inc.
605 Third Ave.
New York, NY 10158
Ownership %: 100
**Editorial:**
Ellen C. Carter ......................................Editor

### CONTRACT DESIGN
23398

1515 Broadway
New York, NY 10036
Telephone: (212) 869-1300
FAX: (212) 302-2905
Year Established: 1958
Pub. Frequency: m.
Page Size: standard
Subscrip. Rate: $35-$65/yr.
Circulation: 29,000
Circulation Type: controlled
**Owner(s):**
Miller Freeman, Inc.
1515 Broadway
New York, NY 10036
Telephone: (212) 869-1300
Ownership %: 100
**Management:**
Rich Ancas .....................Advertising Manager
**Editorial:**
Roger Yee ...............................Editor in Chief
Jennifer Theile .......................Managing Editor
Cristina Haughton ..........................Art Director
Amy Milshtein ........................Associate Editor
Hally Richmond ..............Junior Assistant Editor
Phillip Russo ...................Publication Director
**Desc.:** The business magazine of commercial furnishings, interior design, and architecture, contains information and articles specifically related to the contract trade. Accepts editorial contributions form people in contract work of all kinds. Articles cover offices, hotels, motels, restaurants, transportations, Federal Government procurement, real estate management, other large installations (non-residential). Also specialized features such as lighting, carpeting, flooring, fabrics, hotel-motel furnishings, etc. Articles run 1-6 pages, sometimes more. Photo features on trends in furniture, typical showrooms, installations, etc. Pictures almost always wanted. Departments include: Calendar of Contract Events, Letters, Contract News. Uses publicity material, manufacturers' literature.
**Readers:** Commercial interior designers, architects, space planners and dealers.

### DECORATING RETAILER
23533

1050 N. Lindbergh Blvd.
St. Louis, MO 63132
Telephone: (314) 991-3470
FAX: (314) 991-5039
Year Established: 1964
Pub. Frequency: m.
Page Size: standard
Subscrip. Rate: $20/yr.
Circulation: 30,469
Circulation Type: controlled
**Owner(s):**
National Decorating Products Assn.
1050 N. Lindbergh Blvd.
St. Louis, MO 63132
Telephone: (314) 991-3470
Ownership %: 100
**Management:**
Ernest Stewart ......................................Publisher
Ernest Stewart .................Advertising Manager
**Editorial:**
Diane Capuano .................................Editor
Tamela Adamson-McMullen ..............Managing Editor
**Desc.:** Contains advertising and marketing, staff articles, coming events, financial, general news, new product news, personnel news, and trade literature. Departments include: Newsmakers, What's New, Worth Reading, Government Scope, On the Calendar.
**Readers:** Paint, wallpaper and allied decorating retailers.

### DESIGNERS WORLD
69296

3255 Wilshire Blvd., Ste. 1100
Los Angeles, CA 90010-1415
Telephone: (310) 657-8231
FAX: (310) 657-3673
Los Angeles, CA 90069
Year Established: 1991
Pub. Frequency: m.
Page Size: standard
Subscrip. Rate: $30/yr.; $50/2 yrs.; $75/3 yrs.
Circulation: 45,000
Circulation Type: controlled & paid
**Owner(s):**
Designers World Corp.
P.O. Box 69660
Los Angeles, CA 90069
Telephone: (310) 657-8231
Ownership %: 100
**Management:**
Walton E. Brown ...............................Publisher
Walton E. Brown, Jr. ...........Business Manager
**Editorial:**
Carol Soucek King ......................Editor in Chief
Ken de Bie ..............................Art Director
Theodora Wade ..................................Director
**Desc.:** Covers the interior design industry in the South and Southwest. Each issue features in-depth, full color sections on residential and contract interiors, plus new product news, industry updates, answers to legal questions and articles on antique treasues and art creations.
**Readers:** Individuals and companies engaged in interior design, architecture, contract specification and facility management.

### DISPLAY & DESIGN IDEAS
69402

6255 Barfield Rd., Ste. 200
Atlanta, GA 30328
Telephone: (404) 252-8831
FAX: (404) 252-4436
Year Established: 1988
Pub. Frequency: 13/yr.
Page Size: tabloid
Subscrip. Rate: $54/yr.
Materials: 01,02,05,06,29,30,32,33
Circulation: 18,039
Circulation Type: controlled

**Owner(s):**
Shore Communications, Inc.
180 Allen Rd., N.E., Ste. 300N
Atlanta, GA 30328
Telephone: (404) 252-8831
Ownership %: 100
**Editorial:**
Karl Hudson, Ed. ..............................Editor
**Desc.:** Discusses new products and display ideas in the visual merchandising and store design field.

### HAUT DECOR
68937

3290 N.E. 12th Ave.
Oakland Park, FL 33334
Telephone: (305) 568-9444
FAX: (305) 568-9445
Mailing Address:
P.O. Box 70126
Oakland Park, FL 33307-0126
Year Established: 1990
Pub. Frequency: bi-m.
Subscrip. Rate: $14.95/yr.
Circulation: 15,000
Circulation Type: paid
**Owner(s):**
Haut Decor, Inc.
3290 N.E. 12th Ave.
Oakland Park, FL 33334
Telephone: (305) 568-9444
Ownership %: 100
**Editorial:**
Janet Verdeguer ..............................Editor
**Desc.:** Reports on the upper-end furnishing community, both residential and commerical, for professional designers.

### INTERIOR DECORATORS' HANDBOOK
23536

370 Lexington Ave.
New York, NY 10017
Telephone: (212) 532-9290
FAX: (212) 779-8345
Year Established: 1922
Pub. Frequency: 3/yr.
Page Size: 5 1/2 x 8 1/2
Subscrip. Rate: $30/yr.
Materials: 19,21,30,32
Circulation: 25,000
Circulation Type: controlled & paid
**Owner(s):**
Columbia Communications, Inc.
370 Lexington Ave.
New York, NY 10017
Telephone: (212) 532-9290
Ownership %: 100
**Management:**
Joseph D. Feldmann ...........................President
Joseph D. Feldmann ...........................Publisher
Desi Leon ...........................Business Manager
**Editorial:**
David Whitten ..............................Art Director
Janet Whitcomb .......Dir. of Mktg. & Advertising
Eileen Roether .........Directory Computerization
Laura Hoffman ...................Production Director
**Desc.:** Solely a directory for the interior decorator and architectural firms with designers on staff. No editorial material except for categories of every facet of the decorative industry necessary to decorator. These consist of furniture, decorative accessories, lighting fixtures, fabrics, wallcoverings, floor coverings, services, etc. These main categories are broken down to many sub-categories and provide a comprehensive coverage of the entire industry. 50,000 listings in 800 product categories.
**Readers:** Interior decorators, designers, architects, artists, antique dealers, workrooms.
**Deadline:** story-Apr. 1; Oct. 1

### INTERIOR DESIGN
23537

249 W. 17th St.
New York, NY 10011
Telephone: (212) 645-0067
Year Established: 1932
Pub. Frequency: 15/yr.
Page Size: standard
Subscrip. Rate: $47.97/yr. US; $63.97/yr. Canada
Circulation: 54,156
Circulation Type: paid
**Owner(s):**
Cahners Publishing Co.
249 W. 17th St.
New York, NY 10011
Ownership %: 100
**Management:**
Mark Strauss ..............................Publisher
Don W. Gross ...................Advertising Manager
George Slowik, Jr. ..............Business Manager
**Editorial:**
Stanley Abercrombie .................Editor in Chief
Jerry Cooper ...........................Senior Editor
Natalie Rakow ..............................Editor
**Desc.:** Staff written features reflect trends in design funishings in both contract and residential installations. Heavily illustrated in 4-color installations, furniture, wall coverings, lighting, floor coverings, and all interior furnishings.
**Readers:** Professional interior designers/specifiers, architects, industrial designers.

### INTERIOR DESIGN MARKET
67649

249 W. 17th St.
New York, NY 10011
Telephone: (212) 645-0067
FAX: (212) 645-6470
Year Established: 1986
Pub. Frequency: s-a.
Page Size: tabloid
Circulation: 57,000
Circulation Type: paid
**Owner(s):**
Cahners Publishing Company, Inc.
249 W. 17th St.
New York, NY 10011
Telephone: (212) 645-0067
Ownership %: 100
**Management:**
Cara S. David ..............................Publisher
John Teefy .......................Advertising Manager
**Editorial:**
Andrea Loukin ..............................Editor
**Desc.:** Survey of new and classic products for the interior design trade.

### INTERIORS
58544

1515 Broadway
New York, NY 10036
Telephone: (212) 764-7300
FAX: (212) 536-5357
Year Established: 1888
Pub. Frequency: m.
Page Size: standard
Subscrip. Rate: $35/yr.
Freelance Pay: $900-$1150/story
Circulation: 30,000
Circulation Type: paid
**Owner(s):**
Billboard Publications, Inc.
1515 Broadway
New York, NY 10036
Telephone: (212) 764-7300
Ownership %: 100
**Editorial:**
Jean Gorman ...........................Executive Editor
Paula Jackson ..............................Editor
Chris Howard ..............................Art Director

**Desc.:** Devoted to the profession of interior design in the commercial field. It is directed to consultant designers, architects, space planners, dealers and in-house corporate design decision makers. It keeps its audience informed about the various aspects of the technical aspects of design and space planning.

**Readers:** Professional designers, buyers, end users, and specifiers of contract interiors.

## PULSE REPORT
1050 N. Lindbergh Blvd.
St. Louis, MO 63132
Telephone: (314) 991-3470
Pub. Frequency: q.
Subscrip. Rate: membership
Circulation: 500
Circulation Type: controlled
**Owner(s):**
National Decorating Products Assn.
1050 Lindbergh Blvd.
St. Louis, MO 63132
Telephone: (314) 991-5039
Ownership %: 100
**Editorial:**
Donald A. Boettcher ..................................Editor
**Desc.:** Marketing newsletter for marketing products.
**Readers:** Decorating products industry.

## TODAY'S FACILITY MANAGER
121 Monmouth St.
Red Bank, NJ 07701
Telephone: (908) 842-7433
FAX: (908) 758-6634
Mailing Address:
P.O. Box 2060
Red Bank, NJ 07701
Year Established: 1988
Pub. Frequency: 10/yr.
Page Size: tabloid
Subscrip. Rate: $30/yr.
Materials: 01,02,06,07,10,15,21,25,27,28, 29,30,31,32
Freelance Pay: varies
Circulation: 35,000
Circulation Type: controlled
**Owner(s):**
Group C Communications, Inc.
121 Monmouth St.
Red Bank, NJ 07701
Telephone: (908) 842-7433
Ownership %: 100
**Management:**
Susan L. Coene ....................................Publisher
**Editorial:**
Heidi Schwartz ..........................................Editor
**Desc.:** Reports on trends in office planning and design. Includes information on new products and updates on legislation affecting the office.
**Readers:** Targets those in-house professionals involved with design and management of interiors for businesses.
**Deadline:** story-2 mo. prior to pub. date; news-2 mo. prior; photo-2 mo. prior; ads-2 mo. prior

## WALLCOVERINGS, WINDOWS, & INTERIOR FASHION
15 Bank St.
Stamford, CT 06901
Telephone: (203) 357-0028
FAX: (203) 357-0075
Year Established: 1918
Pub. Frequency: m.
Page Size: Standard
Subscrip. Rate: $18/yr.
Freelance Pay: Varies
Circulation: 17,500
Circulation Type: paid

**Owner(s):**
Publishing Dynamics-Martin A. Johnson
15 Bank St.
Stamford, CT 06901
Telephone: (203) 357-0028
Ownership %: 100
**Management:**
Diane Johnson ....................................President
Martin A. Johnson ..............................Publisher
Diane Johnson ......................General Manager
**Editorial:**
Sarah Johnson ........................Associate Editor
**Desc.:** Edited primarily for retailers who market through cross - merchandising the "total concept" of residential and commercial fashion products. The objective is to demonstrate how the sale of ancillary products such as window treatments and fabrics enhance wallcoverings sales and, reciprocally, how the promotion of wallcoverings increases exposure for all fashion products.
**Readers:** Wallcovering retailers, distributers, manufacturers, contract architects, contract interior designers.

## WALLPAPER REPRODUCTION NEWS
P.O. Box 187
Lee, MA 01238-0187
Year Established: 1990
Pub. Frequency: q.
Subscrip. Rate: $20/yr.
**Owner(s):**
Wallpaper Reproduction News
P.O. Box 187
Lee, MA 01238
Telephone: (314) 991-3470
Ownership %: 100
**Editorial:**
Robert Kelly ...............................................Editor
**Desc.:** Reports on new methods.
**Readers:** Primarily for the professional markets dealing with reproduction wallpaper including: screen printers, decorators, designers, architects and museum professionals.

## Group 136-Jewelry & Watchmaking

## ACCENT
100 Wells Ave.
Newton, MA 02159
Telephone: (617) 964-5100
FAX: (617) 964-2752
Year Established: 1976
Pub. Frequency: m.
Page Size: standard
Subscrip. Rate: $3.50; $36/yr.; $44/2 yrs.; $58/3 yrs.; $10/Dec. issue
Materials: 03,06,16,28,29,32,33
Freelance Pay: $100 - $400
Print Process: web offset
Circulation: 14,500
Circulation Type: free & paid
**Owner(s):**
The Larkin Group
100 Wells Ave.
Newton, MA 02159
Telephone: (617) 964-5100
Ownership %: 100
**Management:**
A.J. Larkin ..........................................President
A.J. Larkin ..........................................Publisher
Janice P. Lipof ................Advertising Manager
**Editorial:**
Lauren Parker ...........................................Editor
Joanna Drew ......................Art Department
Joyceann Cooney ....................Assistant Editor
Sidney L. Davis ....................Associate Publisher

**Desc.:** Edited for wholesalers of fashion jewelry, watches, displays, packaging and related products, as well as for jewelry buyers and merchandise managers of large volume jewelry sales establishments such as catalog showrooms, department stores, woman's specialty stores, and discount stores. Each issue reports on sales and style trends, market developments, new products, industry events, and the activities, opinions and accomplishments of the people involved in the design, manufacture, distribution and retailing of fashion accessories. Concise feature articles cover new developments and offer new ideas on merchandising, promotion, sales techniques, inventory control, management and other topics of interest to those in the jewelry and watch business.
**Readers:** Jewelry retailers and wholesalers, manufacturers & designers.

## AMERICAN JEWELRY MANUFACTURER
100 India St.
Providence, RI 02903
Telephone: (401) 274-3840
FAX: (401) 274-0265
Year Established: 1956
Pub. Frequency: m.
Page Size: standard
Subscrip. Rate: $36/yr. US; $74/yr. foreign
Freelance Pay: $50/Page; Up to $500 for Major Piece
Circulation: 5,000
Circulation Type: paid
**Owner(s):**
Mfg. Jewelers & Silversmiths Of America Inc.
100 India St.
Providence, RI 02903
Telephone: (401) 274-3840
Ownership %: 100
**Management:**
Matthew Runci ....................................Publisher
**Editorial:**
Clark Heideger ...........................................Editor
David LeFleur ........................Assistant Editor
**Desc.:** Covers all topics of interest to the jewelry and silverware manufacturer. Departments include: Editorial, News of the Industry, Events to Note, Product News, Financial Front, Personals and Personnel, Foreign Trade News, Index to Advertisers.
**Readers:** Jewelry manufacturers.

## COLORED STONE
60 Chestnut Ave., Ste. 201
Devon, PA 19333
Telephone: (610) 293-1112
FAX: (610) 293-1717
Year Established: 1988
Pub. Frequency: bi-m.
Page Size: standard
Subscrip. Rate: $18/yr.
Circulation: 10,000
Circulation Type: controlled & paid
**Owner(s):**
Lapidary Journal, Inc.
60 Chestnut Ave., Ste. 201
Devon, PA 19333
Telephone: (215) 293-1112
Ownership %: 100
**Management:**
Sonia Gilbert ...............................................Owner
Leif Owen Klein ..................................Publisher
Paul Salotto ..............................Sales Manager
**Editorial:**
Elana Verbin ...............................................Editor
Suzanne Wade ......................Managing Editor
Adam Samson ................Associate Publisher

Moskow
Cindi Wilcox ........................Circulation Director
**Desc.:** The exclusive international publication of the colored stone trade.

## FASHION ACCESSORIES
256 S. Robertson Blvd., Ste. 789
Beverly Hills, CA 90211
Telephone: (213) 658-6063
FAX: (213) 658-6063
Year Established: 1951
Pub. Frequency: m.
Page Size: tabloid
Subscrip. Rate: $22/yr.; $38/2 yrs.
Materials: 03,06,15,19,21,27,28,29,30,32,33
Freelance Pay: negotiable
Print Process: web offset
Circulation: 8,000
Circulation Type: controlled & paid
**Owner(s):**
S.C.M. Publications, Inc.
65 W. Main St.
Bergenfield, NJ 07621
Telephone: (201) 384-3336
FAX: (201) 384-6776
Ownership %: 100
**Management:**
Samuel Mendelson ..............................Publisher
Carolyn Raftery ................Circulation Manager
**Editorial:**
Melda Marino ...........................................Editor
**Desc.:** Serves the manufacturing, wholesale and volume buyers of the costume jewelry, semi-precious and watch industries, gift and boutique and related novelty fields with relation to latest styles, motifs, treatments, colors, etc. Also includes sources for basic material, technical information, personnel news, editorials and news pertaining to new products.
**Readers:** Manufacturers, wholesalers and volume buyers of all fashion jewelry & accessories.
**Deadline:** story-1 mo. prior to pub. date; news-1 mo. prior; photo-1 mo. prior; ads-1 mo. prior

## HOROLOGICAL TIMES
3700 Harrison Ave.
Cincinnati, OH 45211
Telephone: (513) 661-3838
FAX: (513) 661-3131
Mailing Address:
P.O. Box 11011
Cincinnati, OH 45211
Year Established: 1977
Pub. Frequency: m.
Subscrip. Rate: $45/yr.
Materials: 28,29,30,32,33
Circulation: 6,000
Circulation Type: paid
**Owner(s):**
American Watchmakers Institute
3700 Harrison Ave.
P.O. Box 11011
Cincinnati, OH 45211
Telephone: (513) 661-3838
Ownership %: 100
**Editorial:**
Milton C. Stevens ....................................Editor

## JEWELERS' CIRCULAR-KEYSTONE
Chilton Way
Radnor, PA 19089
Telephone: (610) 964-4000
FAX: (610) 964-4481
Year Established: 1869
Pub. Frequency: m.
Page Size: standard
Subscrip. Rate: $31.95/yr.
Materials: 01,06,15,16,27,28,29,30,32,33
Freelance Pay: negotiable
Circulation: 30,944

**Materials Accepted/Included:** 01-Business news 02-By-line articles 03-Fashion news 04-Food news 05-Freelance copy 06-Letters to editor 07-Real estate news 08-Sports news 09-Travel news 10-Book rev. 11-Movie rev. 12-Music rev. 13-TV rev. 14-Theater rev. 15-Coming events 16-Obituaries 17-Question & answer 18-Social announcements 19-Artwork 20-Cartoons 21-Photos 22-TV listings 23-Audio rec. 24-Video rec. 25-Books 26-Films/film clips 27-Personnel news 28-Press releases 29-New product news/photos 30-Trade lit. 31-Contracts awarded 32-Display adv. 33-Classified adv.

4-195

Circulation Type: paid
**Owner(s):**
Capital Cities-ABC, Inc.
77 W. 66 St.
New York, NY 10023
Ownership %: 100
**Management:**
Charles M. Bond ............................Publisher
Jennifer Rice ................Promotion Manager
Lee Lawrence .......................Sales Manager
**Editorial:**
George Holmes ..........................Editor in Chief
Deborah Holmes ..................Managing Editor
Donald S. McNeil ...........Book Review Editor
Donald S. McNeil ...............Editor Emeritus
Linda Whitfield ...................Marketing Director
Miriam Whalen .................Production Director
**Desc.:** Articles on merchandising, store
operation, case histories, customer
relations for retailers of diamonds,
precious stones, jewelry, watches,
clocks, silverware, china, crystal and
other jewelry store merchandise. Carries
news of the trade, new products,
personnel changes, company news,
regional news, new promotions.
**Readers:** The primary readers are retail
jewelers. Other readers include
wholesalers & manufacturers.

23546
### MODERN JEWELER
7950 College Blvd.
Overland Park, KS 66210
Telephone: (913) 451-2200
FAX: (913) 451-5821
Mailing Address:
  P.O. Box 2939
  Shawnee Mission, KS 66201
Year Established: 1901
Pub. Frequency: m.
Page Size: standard
Subscrip. Rate: $25/yr.
Materials: 01,03,06,15,16,27,28,29,32,33
Print Process: web offset
Circulation: 36,000
Circulation Type: controlled
**Owner(s):**
Vance Publishing Corp.
400 Knightsbridge Parkway
Lincolnshire, IL 60069
Telephone: (708) 634-2600
Ownership %: 100
**Bureau(s):**
Modern Jeweler
370 Lexington Ave. #2001
New York, NY 10017
Telephone: (212) 682-7777
Contact: Timothy Murphy, Editor
**Management:**
Timothy S. Murphy ................................Publisher
George Sefranek ..............Circulation Manager
Grace E. Bales ................Operations Manager
**Editorial:**
David Federman .....................Executive Editor
Joseph Thompson ...............................Editor
Norma Buchanan .....................Managing Editor
Marcia Young ......................Graphics Editor
Amy Smith ....................Production Coordinator
Joseph Thompson ..............Publication Director
**Desc.:** Articles about retail jewelers slanted
to some phase of their store operation.
All stories must be factual and illustrated
in the 50 states.
**Readers:** Retail jewelers and watchmakers
in US.

23547
### NATIONAL JEWELER
1515 Broadway
New York, NY 10036
Telephone: (212) 626-2380
FAX: (212) 944-7164
Year Established: 1906
Pub. Frequency: s-m.

Page Size: tabloid
Subscrip. Rate: $39/yr.; $62/2 yrs.
Materials: 01,03,05,06,15,16,19,20,21,27,
  28,29,30,32,33,34
Freelance Pay: $200-$500/article
Circulation: 36,000
Circulation Type: controlled & paid
**Owner(s):**
Miller Freeman, Inc.
600 Harrison St.
San Francisco, CA
Telephone: (415) 905-2200
Ownership %: 100
**Management:**
Howard Hauben ................................Publisher
**Editorial:**
S. Lynn Diamond ........................Editor in Chief
S. Lynn Diamond ...............Associate Publisher
**Desc.:** Edited for the retail jewelers, covers
news, promotions, merchandise.
Features articles on all matters relating
to selling jewelry and watches. Also
carries local news, association news,
merchandise news, business news.
**Readers:** Primarily retail jewelers.

68941
### ORNAMENT
P.O. Box 2349
San Marcos, CA 92079-2349
Telephone: (619) 559-0222
FAX: (619) 559-0228
Year Established: 1974
Pub. Frequency: q.
Page Size: standard
Subscrip. Rate: $6.50 newsstand; $26/yr.
  US; $30/yr. foreign
Materials: 02,03,06,15,21,25,28
Print Process: web offset
Circulation: 45,000
Circulation Type: paid
**Owner(s):**
Ornament, Inc.
P.O. Box 2349
San Marcos, CA 92079-2349
Telephone: (619) 559-0222
Ownership %: 100
**Editorial:**
Robert K. Liu ..............................Co-Editor
Carolyn L.E. Benesh ...................Co-Editor
**Desc.:** Covers ancient, ethnic and
contemporary jewelry, costumes and
artist-made clothing.

23542
### WATCH & CLOCK REVIEW
2403 Champa St.
Denver, CO 80205
Telephone: (303) 296-1600
FAX: (303) 295-2159
Year Established: 1933
Pub. Frequency: m.
Page Size: Standard
Subscrip. Rate: $19.50/yr.
Freelance Pay: $.10/word
Circulation: 15,500
Circulation Type: controlled
**Owner(s):**
Golden Bell Press, Inc.
2403 Champa St.
Denver, CO 80205
Telephone: (303) 296-1600
Ownership %: 100
**Bureau(s):**
Bert Kalisher
257 Adams Ln.
Hewlett, NY 11557
Telephone: (516) 295-2516
**Management:**
Lawrence Bell ................................Publisher
Lawrence Bell .............Advertising Manager
Sharon Patterson ...............Circulation Manager
**Editorial:**
Lawrence Bell ...............................Editor
Ted Darhinshaw ..................Managing Editor

**Desc.:** Watch & Clock Marketing, Sales
and Service. Articles cover timepiece
manufacturing and marketing, new
product development, current pricing,
styling trends, retail sales,
company developments. Departments
cover sales, retail management,
timepiece servicing.
**Readers:** Manufacturers, marketers, and
retailers of timepieces.

## Group 138-Laundry, Cleaning & Dyeing

22653
### AMERICAN COIN-OP
500 N. Dearborn St.
Chicago, IL 60610
Telephone: (312) 337-7700
FAX: (312) 337-8654
Year Established: 1960
Pub. Frequency: m.
Page Size: standard
Subscrip. Rate: $33/yr.
Circulation: 20,000
Circulation Type: controlled
**Owner(s):**
Crain Associated Enterprises, Inc.
500 N. Dearborn St.
Chicago, IL 60610
Telephone: (312) 337-7700
Ownership %: 100
**Management:**
Ed Goldstein ................................President
Ed Goldstein ................................Publisher
**Editorial:**
Laurence Cohen ...............................Editor
Richard Traybsza .............Art Director
Jim Miller ......................Associate Editor
Roy Camphouse ................Production Director
**Desc.:** Feature articles fall into two
categories: think-piece, usually staff
researched and written (discusses an
industry problem, e.g.,
gas conservation), specific articles,
usually about a plant (detailing the
success the store had in promotion or in
advancing unusual services). Also a
single theme (air conditioning, publicity,
etc.). Departments include: Editor's
Note, Events & Trends, Business Aids,
Product News, Industry News, Store
Design, Maintenance, Customer Service.
**Readers:** Owners & operators of coin -
operated laundries under controlled
circulation.

22654
### AMERICAN DRYCLEANER
500 N. Dearborn St.
Chicago, IL 60610
Telephone: (312) 337-7700
FAX: (312) 337-8654
Year Established: 1934
Pub. Frequency: m.
Page Size: pocket
Subscrip. Rate: $33/yr.
Circulation: 26,000
Circulation Type: controlled
**Owner(s):**
Crain Associated Enterprises, Inc.
500 N. Dearborn St.
Chicago, IL 60610
Telephone: (312) 337-7700
Ownership %: 100
**Management:**
Ed Goldstein ................................President
Ed Goldstein ................................Publisher
**Editorial:**
Earl Fischer ................................Editor
Dick Traybsza ..................Art Director
Jim Miller ......................Assistant Editor

**Desc.:** There are no limitations as to
length. Prefer to be queried before an
article is prepared so that suggestions
may be made. All contributions must be
significant. Case histories are only useful
if they represent the application of ideas
which may be adopted by other readers.
Departments include: News of the
Month, Product News, Letters,
Conventions, Advertising Clinic, Over
the Counter, Talk of the Trade, Thirty
Second Reader, Analyst's Notebook,
Finishing Forum, Productive
Management, Marketing Methods.
**Readers:** A small businessman operation.

22655
### AMERICAN LAUNDRY DIGEST
500 N. Dearborn St.
Chicago, IL 60610
Telephone: (312) 337-7700
FAX: (312) 337-8654
Year Established: 1936
Pub. Frequency: m.
Page Size: pocket
Subscrip. Rate: $33/yr.
**Owner(s):**
Crain Associated Enterprises, Inc.
500 N. Dearborn St.
Chicago, IL 60610
Telephone: (312) 337-7700
Ownership %: 100
**Management:**
Ed Goldstein ................................President
Ed Goldstein ................................Publisher
**Editorial:**
Larry Ebert ................................Editor
Paul Partyka ..................Managing Editor
Jim Miller ......................Assistant Editor
**Desc.:** Articles on sales, production,
employee relations, incentives, changes
in workflow or equipment and supplies,
diversification, etc. pertaining to family
laundries, hotel and hospital laundries,
linen supply laundries, wiping cloth and
industrial laundries. Open discussion
from all points of view on such industry-
related subjects as linen control,
washroom production, labor relations,
and new concepts of marketing and
service to all types of laundry/linen
users. Plant case histories and how-to
ideas, fully illustrated with in-action pix.
**Readers:** Laundry owners, operators, &
institution laundry managers.

22667
### CLEANING & RESTORATION
10830 Annapolis Junction Rd., Ste. 312
Annapolis Junction, MD 20701-1120
Telephone: (301) 604-4411
FAX: (301) 604-4713
Year Established: 1962
Pub. Frequency: m.
Page Size: standard
Subscrip. Rate: $27/yr.; $36/yr. foreign
Materials: 01,02,06,15,28,29,30,32,33
Circulation: 2,500
Circulation Type: paid
**Owner(s):**
The Assn. of Specialists in Cleaning &
  Rest., Inc.
10830 Annapolis Junction Rd.
Ste. 312
Annapolis Junction, MD 20701-1120
Telephone: (301) 604-4411
FAX: (301) 604-4713
Ownership %: 100
**Management:**
Claudia L. Ramirez ............................Publisher
Coleen Carpenter ..............Advertising Manager
**Editorial:**
Janice R. Gerde, Ph.D. .........Executive Editor
Dr. Steven Spivak ..................Technical Editor
Pat A. Slaven ...................Technical Editor
Martin I. King, CR, ASA ............Technical Editor

**Materials Accepted/Included:** 01-Business news 02-By-line articles 03-Fashion news 04-Food news 05-Freelance copy 06-Letters to editor 07-Real estate news 08-Sports news 09-Travel news 10-Book rev. 11-Movie rev. 12-Music rev. 13-TV rev. 14-Theater rev. 15-Coming events 16-Obituaries 17-Question & answer 18-Social announcements 19-Artwork 20-Cartoons 21-Photos 22-TV listings 23-Audio rec. 24-Video rec. 25-Books 26-Films/film clips 27-Personnel news 28-Press releases 29-New product news/photos 30-Trade lit. 31-Contracts awarded 32-Display adv. 33-Classified adv.

4-196

**Desc.:** Subject matter relating to rug, carpet, upholstery, drapery cleaning and repair retail sales; carpet installation; oriental rugs; fire and water damage restoration; restoration relating to other perils; home, building, and office maintenance; mechanical systems (i.e. HVAC) hygiene. Departments: Commentary, Technical Topics, Notes from the lab, Restoration Corner, News Briefs, Affiliate News,m Industry Events, New Products, Calendar, Classified.
**Readers:** Firms involved in the cleaning and restoration of carpets, rugs, upholstery and drapery; fire, smoke, water, vandal damage restoration, mechanical systems hygiene (i.e., HVAC).
**Deadline:** story-2 mo. prior to pub. date; news-2 mo. prior to pub. date; photo-2 mo. prior to pub. date; ads-45 days prior to pub. date

### COIN LAUNDERER & CLEANER
22657

4512 Lindenwood Ln.
Northbrook, IL 60062
Telephone: (708) 272-8490
Pub. Frequency: m.
Subscrip. Rate: free to qualified persons
Circulation: 21,000
Circulation Type: controlled & free
**Owner(s):**
Scheilko Corp.
4512 Lindenwood Ln.
Northbrook, IL 60062
Telephone: (708) 272-8490
Ownership %: 100
**Management:**
Hy H. Schwartz ..............................Publisher
**Editorial:**
Hy H. Schwartz .................................Editor

### DRYCLEANERS NEWS
22659

70 Edwin Ave.
Waterbury, CT 06708
Telephone: (203) 755-0158
FAX: (203) 755-3480
Mailing Address:
P.O. Box 2180
Waterbury, CT 06722
Year Established: 1950
Pub. Frequency: m.
Page Size: tabloid
Subscrip. Rate: $36/yr.
Materials: 01,02,05,06,19,20,21,27,28,29, 30,32,33
Freelance Pay: $50-$100
Print Process: web offset
Circulation: 10,500
Circulation Type: controlled
**Owner(s):**
Zackin Publications, Inc.
P.O. Box 2180
Waterbury, CT 06722
Telephone: (203) 755-0158
FAX: (203) 755-3480
Ownership %: 100
**Management:**
David R. Zackin ...........................President
David R. Zackin ...........................Publisher
Linda Zackin ..................Advertising Manager
Silvia Purcaro ...........................Office Manager
Henry Pacyna ...................Production Manager
**Editorial:**
Dave Johnston ...............................Editor
John Florian ......................Editorial Director
Amy Williams ...................Account Executive

**Desc.:** Published regionally for Northeastern owners and managers of professional drycleaning plants and drycleaning establishments. Each issue following a general news format reports on new products of interest to the industry, technical articles by industry experts, as well as general news items regarding people and events. News articles include such subjects as new methods and techniques, management and sales tips, case histories and success stories, and convention coverage.
**Readers:** Drycleaners.
**Deadline:** story-1st of mo. prior to pub. date; news-1st of mo. prior; photo-1st of mo. prior; ads-1st of mo. prior

### INDUSTRIAL LAUNDERER
22662

1730 M St., N.W.
Ste. 610
Washington, DC 20036
Telephone: (202) 296-6744
FAX: (202) 296-2309
Year Established: 1950
Pub. Frequency: m.
Page Size: 4 color photos/art
Subscrip. Rate: $30/yr. for members; $50/yr. non-members
Freelance Pay: negotiable
Circulation: 3,000
Circulation Type: paid
**Owner(s):**
Uniform & Textile Service Assn.
1730 M St., N.W.
Ste. 610
Washington, DC 20036
Telephone: (202) 296-6744
Ownership %: 100
**Management:**
Mittie Spruill ...................Advertising Manager
**Editorial:**
Kenneth E. Koepper ...........................Editor
**Desc.:** News and feature stories on new products, equipment, procedures in laundering and drycleaning, material handling, waste water and air purification, new plant design as they apply to industrial launderers. Feature stories also on members and suppliers, articles on route sales, sales and marketing, columns, government regulations and general interest stories for the industry. Focus Interviews.
**Readers:** Industrial launderer owners and managers: predominantly renting, delivering, and cleaning work uniforms, executive shirts and slacks, wiping towels, walk-off mats, and other dust control products.

### LAUNDRY NEWS
22663

19 W. 21st St.
New York, NY 10010
Telephone: (212) 741-2095
FAX: (212) 924-6305
Year Established: 1975
Pub. Frequency: m.
Page Size: tabloid
Subscrip. Rate: free
Materials: 01,02,06,10,15,21,24,25,27,28, 29,30,31,32,33
Freelance Pay: varies
Print Process: offset
Circulation: 15,539
Circulation Type: controlled
**Owner(s):**
Mill Hollow Corp.
19 W. 21st St.
New York, NY 10010
Telephone: (212) 741-2095
Ownership %: 100

**Management:**
Adrian Courtenay ...........................President
Adrian Courtenay ...........................Publisher
**Editorial:**
Richard Merli ...........................Editor in Chief
Elizabeth Negus ...................Assistant Editor
Al D'Alessandro ...............................Sales
**Desc.:** Editorial content includes pictorial coverage of news and events pertaining to institutional laundering, including case histories, new products, coverage of meeting and conventions, features dealing with issues such as unionization, legislation, comparison of in- house laundries vs. commercial laundries vs. central laundries, news of trade associations involved with institutional laundering, and other news as it happens. Departments include: Coming Events, Columns by Industry Experts, Interviews with Industry Figures, New Products, Distributor News , Allied Tradesmen, and other News Features. Plant openings closings, renovations and expansions. Governmental and environmental regulations.
**Readers:** Written for those involved in installing and operating laundries in hospitals and nursing homes, hotels and motels, correctional institutions including central laundries and primarily laundry management.
**Deadline:** story-10th of each month; news-10th; photo-10th; ads-10th

### TEXTILE RENTAL
22666

1130 E. Hallandale Bch. Blvd.
Hallandale, FL 33009
Telephone: (305) 457-7555
FAX: (305) 457-3890
Mailing Address:
P.O. Box 1283
Hallandale, FL 33008-1283
Year Established: 1917
Pub. Frequency: m.
Page Size: standard
Subscrip. Rate: $90/yr.
Circulation: 6,200
Circulation Type: paid
**Owner(s):**
Textile Rental Services Association of America
P.O. Box 1283
Hallandale, FL 33008
Telephone: (305) 457-7555
Ownership %: 100
**Management:**
Steven Feldman ...............Advertising Manager
Eileen Engel ...........................Traffic Manager
**Editorial:**
Christine Seaman ...................Executive Editor
Virginia Sowers ...................Managing Editor
**Desc.:** Contains news (general about the industry, plants, personnel, their activities), along with in-depth articles to foster and promote markets and better production techniques, how-to articles and reports on association activities.
**Readers:** Executives, owners, top management, key personnel in linen supply/industrial laundering.

### WESTERN CLEANER & LAUNDERER
22668

100 N. Hill Ave., C
Pasadena, CA 91106
Telephone: (818) 793-2911
FAX: (818) 793-5540
Year Established: 1960
Pub. Frequency: m.
Page Size: tabloid
Subscrip. Rate: free
Freelance Pay: $.05/wd.; $5/photo

Circulation: 14,500
Circulation Type: controlled & free
**Owner(s):**
Randy and Albane Wente
100 N. Hill Ave., C.
Pasadena, CA 91106
Telephone: (818) 793-2911
FAX: (818) 793-5540
Ownership %: 100
**Management:**
Albane Wente ...........................President
Albane Wente ...........................Publisher
Randy Wente ...................Advertising Manager
Hazel Brewster ...................Circulation Manager
**Editorial:**
Randy Wente ...............................Editor
**Desc.:** Feature stories on drycleaning plants, laundries, coin-op stores with new innovations and modern merchandising practices. Success stories. Departments include: New Products, Allied Trades News, and Notes.
**Readers:** Owners and managers of drycleaning and laundry establishments and distributors of laundry and drycleaning equipment.

## Group 140-Law Enforcement

### ADMINISTRATION OF JUSTICE MEMORANDA
69624

Knapp Bldg., CB 3330
Chapel Hill, NC 27599-3330
Telephone: (919) 966-4119
FAX: (919) 962-2707
Year Established: 1975
Pub. Frequency: irreg.
Subscrip. Rate: varies
Circulation: 400
Circulation Type: free & paid
**Owner(s):**
University of North Carolina at Chapel Hill
Knapp Bldg., CB 3330
Chapel Hill, NC 27599-3330
Telephone: (919) 966-4119
Ownership %: 100
**Editorial:**
Robert L. Farb ...............................Editor
**Desc.:** Discusses current issues of concern to North Carolina law enforcement and judicial officials.

### CALIFORNIA HIGHWAY PATROLMAN, THE
25830

2030 V St.
Sacramento, CA 95818
Telephone: (916) 452-6751
FAX: (916) 457-3398
Mailing Address:
P.O. Box 161209
Sacramento, CA 95816
Year Established: 1937
Pub. Frequency: m.
Page Size: standard
Subscrip. Rate: $15/yr.; $28/2 yrs.; $38/3 yrs.
Materials: 05,06,09,20,32
Freelance Pay: $.25/wd.
Print Process: web
Circulation: 20,000
Circulation Type: paid
**Owner(s):**
California Association of Highway Patrolmen
2030 V Street
Sacramento, CA 95818
Telephone: (916) 452-6751
Ownership %: 100
**Management:**
Jon Hamm ...........................Publisher
Diane Wolff ...................Advertising Manager
Diane Wolff ...................Circulation Manager

**Materials Accepted/Included:** 01-Business news 02-By-line articles 03-Fashion news 04-Food news 05-Freelance copy 06-Letters to editor 07-Real estate news 08-Sports news 09-Travel news 10-Book rev. 11-Movie rev. 12-Music rev. 13-TV rev. 14-Theater rev. 15-Coming events 16-Obituaries 17-Question & answer 18-Social announcements 19-Artwork 20-Cartoons 21-Photos 22-TV listings 23-Audio rec. 24-Video rec. 25-Books 26-Films/film clips 27-Personnel news 28-Press releases 29-New product news/photos 30-Trade lit. 31-Contracts awarded 32-Display adv. 33-Classified adv.

4-197

**Editorial:**
Carol Perri ...............................Editor
**Desc.:** We are currently in the market for articles on transportation safety, driver education, consumer awareness, travel pieces and articles on early California. Illustrated articles always receive preference. We are a general interest magazine.
**Readers:** The magazine is available to the public and association members.

24427

## CORRECTIONS TODAY
8025 Laurel Lakes Ct.
Laurel, MD 20707
Telephone: (301) 206-5100
FAX: (301) 206-5061
Year Established: 1939
Pub. Frequency: 7/yr.
Page Size: standard
Subscrip. Rate: $36/yr.
Circulation: 20,000
Circulation Type: paid
**Owner(s):**
American Correctional Association
8025 Laurel Lakes Ct.
Laurel, MD 20707
Telephone: (301) 206-5100
Ownership %: 100
**Management:**
Marge Restivo ..................Advertising Manager
**Editorial:**
Linda Acorn ..............................Editor
Alonzo Winfield ...............................Art Director
**Desc.:** Official publication of the American Correctional Association and affiliates. Covers correctional field (not law enforcement).
**Readers:** Administrative personnel, faculties, and interested citizens.

24358

## CRIME & DELINQUENCY
2455 Teller Rd.
Newbury Park, CA 91320
Telephone: (805) 499-0721
FAX: (805) 499-0871
Year Established: 1963
Pub. Frequency: q.
Page Size: standard
Subscrip. Rate: $46/yr. individual; $123/yr. institutions
Circulation: 3,250
**Owner(s):**
Sage Publications, Inc.
2455 Teller Rd.
Newbury Park, CA 91320
Telephone: (805) 499-0721
Ownership %: 100
**Editorial:**
Don C. Gibbons, Ph.D ...............Editor
Diane L. Irwin ..........................Assistant Editor
**Readers:** Probation and parole executives and officers, criminologists, lawyers.

66019

## CRIMINAL LAW BULLETIN
One Penn Plz., 40th Fl.
New York, NY 10119
Telephone: (212) 971-5216
Year Established: 1965
Pub. Frequency: bi-m.
Page Size: standard
Subscrip. Rate: $120/yr.
Circulation: 3,000
Circulation Type: paid
**Owner(s):**
Warren Gorham Lamont
One Penn Plz., 40th Fl.
New York, NY 10119
Telephone: (212) 971-5000
Ownership %: 100
**Editorial:**
Fred Cohen ..............................Editor
Rosanne Cohen ....................Managing Editor

**Readers:** Criminal justice, criminal law personnel and law enforcement.

24360

## LAW & ORDER
1000 Skokie Blvd.
Wilmette, IL 60091
Telephone: (708) 256-8555
FAX: (708) 256-8574
Year Established: 1952
Pub. Frequency: m.
Page Size: standard
Subscrip. Rate: $20/yr.
Materials: 20,26,28,29,30
Freelance Pay: $.05-$.10/wd.
Print Process: offset
Circulation: 30,000
Circulation Type: controlled
**Owner(s):**
Hendon, Inc.
1000 Skokie Blvd.
Wilmette, IL 60091
Telephone: (708) 256-8555
Ownership %: 100
**Bureau(s):**
Waller Co.
2933 W. Germantown Pike
Norristown, PA 19403
Telephone: (215) 630-6300
Contact: Mike Garwood
**Management:**
H. Scott Kingwill ...............................President
H. Scott Kingwill ...............................Publisher
Karen Franco .................Advertising Manager
Pete Kingwill .................Advertising Manager
Jim Kuchinsky ...............Circulation Manager
**Editorial:**
Alan Harman ..............................Editor
Bruce Cameron ..............Editorial Director
Chris Geimer ...........................Art Director
Lynnette Johnson ..............Associate Editor
Bill Clede ...........................Technical Editor
Tom Yates .........................Vehicle Specialist
**Desc.:** Designed especially for the law enforcement executive and its editorial objective is to help him do his job in the best possible manner. Most of the articles are of the how-to type. They cover traffic, juvenile problems, police science, communications management, weapons, narcotics, etc. New police equipment is surveyed and frequently evaluated. Departments include: Traffic, Computer Chatter, Inside Justice, Police Equipment News, Training and Fitness.
**Readers:** Law enforcement executives/managers.

64736

## LAW ENFORCEMENT PRODUCT NEWS
100 Garfield St.
Denver, CO 80206-5550
Telephone: (303) 322-6400
FAX: (303) 322-0627
Year Established: 1978
Pub. Frequency: bi-m.
Page Size: Tabloid
Subscrip. Rate: free to qualified personnel
Freelance Pay: $100/published article
Circulation: 40,000
Circulation Type: controlled
**Owner(s):**
General Communications, Inc.
100 Garfield St.
Denver, CO 80206-5550
Telephone: (303) 322-6400
Ownership %: 100
**Management:**
Toni Stephenson ..............................Manager
Michael L. George ....................Sales Manager
**Editorial:**
Toni Stepheson ..............................Editor

**Desc.:** New products designed to increase the effectiveness of law enforcement. Departments and protection of public and high security facilities are published quarterly with reader response service designed to help our advertisers sell their products.
**Readers:** Heads of law enforcement agencies, correctional facilities, corporate security departments.

69625

## NARC OFFICER
112 State St., Ste. 1200
Albany, NY 12207
Telephone: (518) 463-6232
Year Established: 1985
Pub. Frequency: m.
Subscrip. Rate: $35
Materials: 02,06,10,21,28,30,32
Print Process: offset lithography
Circulation: 12,000
Circulation Type: controlled
**Owner(s):**
International Narcotic Enforcement Officers Assoc.
112 State St., Ste. 1200
Albany, NY 12207
Telephone: (518) 463-6232
Ownership %: 100
**Editorial:**
Celeste Morga ..............................Editor
**Deadline:** story-30 days prior to pub. date; news-15 days prior to pub. date; photo-30 days prior to pub. date; ads-30 days prior to pub. date

24364

## POLICE CHIEF, THE
515 N. Washington St. #400
Alexandria, VA 22314-2354
Telephone: (703) 836-6767
FAX: (703) 836-4543
Year Established: 1934
Pub. Frequency: m.
Page Size: 4 color photos/art
Subscrip. Rate: $25/yr.
Materials: 02,29,32
Print Process: web offset
Circulation: 20,848
Circulation Type: free & paid
**Owner(s):**
International Association of Chiefs of Police
515 N. Washington St.
Arlington, VA 22314-2357
Telephone: (703) 836-6767
FAX: (703) 836-4543
Ownership %: 100
**Management:**
B.J. Hendrickson ...............Advertising Manager
**Editorial:**
Dan Rosenblatt ..................Editor in Chief
Charles E. Higginbothem ...............Editor
Rebecca Hoeckele ...................Design Editor
**Desc.:** Edited for the profession to give authoritative information on police practices, standard procedures, and new concepts for increased operational efficiency and effectiveness.
**Readers:** Law enforcement practitioners-all ranks.
**Deadline:** story-60 days prior to pub. date; news-60 days prior; photo-60 days prior; ads-1st of mo. prior

24366

## POLICE MAGAZINE
6300 Yarrow Dr.
Carlsbad, CA 92009
Telephone: (619) 438-2511
FAX: (619) 931-5809
Year Established: 1977
Pub. Frequency: m.
Page Size: standard
Subscrip. Rate: $21.95/yr.
Materials: 05,10,21,24,25,29,32,33

Freelance Pay: $50-$400
Print Process: offset lithography
Circulation: 59,000
Circulation Type: paid
**Owner(s):**
Dyna Industries
6300 Yarrow Dr.
Carlsbad, CA 92009
Telephone: (619) 438-2511
Ownership %: 100
**Management:**
Glenn Hare ..............................President
Glenn Hare ..............................Publisher
Marshall Spevak ....................Sales Manager
**Editorial:**
Dan Burger ..............................Editor
Marry Sorenson ...................Assistant Editor
Amy Little ..........................Associate Editor
Gerald Mortimer .................Associate Publisher
**Desc.:** A professional journal for law enforcement officers. Informational features and monthly departments touch on the many aspects of the law enforcement field.
**Readers:** Law enforcement professionals worldwide

24363

## SHERIFF
1450 Duke St.
Alexandria, VA 22314-3490
Telephone: (703) 836-7827
FAX: (703) 683-6541
Year Established: 1940
Pub. Frequency: bi-m.
Page Size: 4 color photos/art
Subscrip. Rate: $5/newsstand; $25/yr.
Materials: 02,06,15,16,19,20,21,27,28,32,33
Circulation: 20,300
Circulation Type: free & paid
**Owner(s):**
National Sheriffs' Association
1450 Duke St.
Alexandria, VA 22314-3490
Telephone: (703) 836-7827
FAX: (703) 683-6541
Ownership %: 100
**Editorial:**
Suzanne D. Bacon ..............................Editor
Suzanne D. Bacon ..............Publication Director
**Desc.:** General news on sheriffs and deputies and new law enforcement techniques. Emphasizes the human interest stories-articles about sheriffs and deputies in action.
**Readers:** Sheriffs, deputies and other law enforcement and corrections personnels at federal, state and local levels.

## Group 142-Legal

23587

## ABA JOURNAL
750 N. Lake Shore Dr.
Chicago, IL 60611
Telephone: (312) 988-6018
Year Established: 1915
Pub. Frequency: m.
Page Size: standard
Subscrip. Rate: $5.50/yr. members; $66/yr. non-members
Freelance Pay: negotiable
Circulation: 380,000
Circulation Type: paid
**Owner(s):**
American Bar Assn.
750 N. Lake Shore Dr.
Chicago, IL 60611
Telephone: (312) 988-5000
Ownership %: 100
**Management:**
Allen E. Brennecke ............Chairman of Board
Gary A. Hengstler ...................Publisher
**Editorial:**
Gary A. Hengstler ..............................Editor
Kerry Klumpe ....................Managing Editor

**Materials Accepted/Included:** 01-Business news 02-By-line articles 03-Fashion news 04-Food news 05-Freelance copy 06-Letters to editor 07-Real estate news 08-Sports news 09-Travel news 10-Book rev. 11-Movie rev. 12-Music rev. 13-TV rev. 14-Theater rev. 15-Coming events 16-Obituaries 17-Question & answer 18-Social announcements 19-Artwork 20-Cartoons 21-Photos 22-TV listings 23-Audio rec. 24-Video rec. 25-Books 26-Films/film clips 27-Personnel news 28-Press releases 29-New product news/photos 30-Trade lit. 31-Contracts awarded 32-Display adv. 33-Classified adv.

Colleen Dolan Evans .....................Advertising
Marianne Kaiser .........................Advertising
Bob Fernandez ..........................Art Director
Stephanie Goldberg .................Assistant Editor
Steve Keeva ........................Assistant Editor
Susan Holland ...................Associate Publisher
Stephanie Goldberg ..........Book Review Editor
David Jendras ................Graphics Coordinator
Debra Cassens Moss ...................News Editor
Beverly Lane ....................Photography Editor
**Desc.:** News and trends on law, lawyers, & efficient operation of law firms. Maximum length for articles is 3,000 words. Includes new law books reviews. Departments include: Supreme Court Preview, Trends in the Law, At Issue (debate), Litigation, Ethics, Law Office Management, Books for Lawyers, War Stories, New Products.
**Readers:** Legal profession.

## ACCIDENT RECONSTRUCTION JOURNAL
69620
3004 Charleton Ct.
Waldorf, MD 20602-2527
Telephone: (301) 842-1371
Mailing Address:
P.O. Box 234
Waldorf, MD 20604-0234
Year Established: 1989
Pub. Frequency: bi-m.
Page Size: standard
Subscrip. Rate: $39/yr.
Circulation: 3,000
Circulation Type: paid
**Owner(s):**
Victor T. Craig
3004 Charleton Ct.
Waldorf, MD 20602-2527
Telephone: (301) 834-1371
Ownership %: 100
**Editorial:**
Victor T. Craig ..................................Editor

## ADMINISTRATIVE LAW REVIEW
67059
750 N. Lake Shore Dr.
Chicago, IL 60611
Telephone: (312) 988-6068
FAX: (312) 988-6081
Year Established: 1949
Pub. Frequency: q.
Page Size: broadsheet
Subscrip. Rate: $35/yr. non-members
Circulation: 7,500
Circulation Type: controlled & paid
**Owner(s):**
American Bar Assn.
541 N. Fairbanks
Chicago, IL 60611
Telephone: (312) 988-6068
Ownership %: 100
**Management:**
Nora Whitford ...................Advertising Manager
**Editorial:**
Charles H. Koch, Jr. ...............Editor in Chief
**Readers:** Members of ABA Section of Administrative Law & Regulatory Practice.

## AKRON LAW REVIEW
69645
School of Law
Akron, OH 44325
Telephone: (216) 972-7335
FAX: (216) 258-2343
Year Established: 1967
Pub. Frequency: 4/yr.
Subscrip. Rate: $20/yr.
Circulation: 1,500
Circulation Type: paid

**Owner(s):**
University of Akron
School of Law
Akron, OH 44325
Telephone: (216) 972-7335
Ownership %: 100

## AMERICAN LAWYER
23588
600 Third Ave., 2nd Fl.
New York, NY 10016
Telephone: (212) 973-2800
FAX: (212) 972-6258
Year Established: 1978
Pub. Frequency: 10/yr.
Page Size: tabloid
Subscrip. Rate: $565/yr.
Circulation: 17,000
Circulation Type: paid
**Owner(s):**
American Lawyer Media, L.P.
600 Third Ave.
New York, NY 10016
Telephone: (212) 973-2800
Ownership %: 100
**Management:**
Steve Brill ..................................President
Margaret E. Samson .....................Publisher
Amy Doering ...............Advertising Manager
Barbara Eskin ...............Circulation Manager
**Editorial:**
Steven Brill .........................Editor in Chief
Michael Orey .....................Executive Editor
Melissa Feldman ...................Art Director
**Desc.:** News and feature stories about the nation's leading people in the business of lawyering.
**Readers:** Lawyers in law firms and corporate general counsel across the country.

## AMERICAN NOTARY
68946
918 16th St., N.W.
Washington, DC 20006
Telephone: (202) 955-6162
Year Established: 1965
Pub. Frequency: bi-m.
Subscrip. Rate: $9/yr.
Circulation: 27,000
Circulation Type: controlled
**Owner(s):**
American Society of Notaries
918 16th St., N.W.
Washington, DC 20006
Telephone: (202) 955-6162
Ownership %: 100
**Editorial:**
Eugene E. Hines ..........................Editor

## ARBITRATION JOURNAL, THE
59656
140 W. 51st St.
New York, NY 10020
Telephone: (212) 484-4011
FAX: (212) 541-4841
Year Established: 1937
Pub. Frequency: q.
Page Size: standard
Subscrip. Rate: $55/yr.
Circulation: 10,000
Circulation Type: paid
**Owner(s):**
American Arbitration Association
140 W. 51st St.
New York, NY 10020-1203
Telephone: (212) 484-4011
Ownership %: 100
**Management:**
Robert Coulson ...........................President
Susan E. Klein ......................Vice President
**Editorial:**
Jack A. Smith ...............................Editor
**Desc.:** Publishes articles and opinion pages on all forms of dispute resolution in the commercial, construction, labor, and insurance fields, among others.

**Readers:** Lawyers, arbitrators, and academics.

## ARIZONA ATTORNEY
68947
111 W. Monroe, Ste. 1800
Phoenix, AZ 85003-1742
Telephone: (602) 252-4804
FAX: (602) 271-4930
Year Established: 1965
Pub. Frequency: 11/yr.
Subscrip. Rate: $30/yr.
Circulation: 12,000
Circulation Type: paid
**Owner(s):**
State Bar of Arizona
111 W. Monroe, Ste. 1000
Phoenix, AZ 85003
Telephone: (602) 252-4804
Ownership %: 100
**Editorial:**
Patricia Gannon .........................Editor

## BANKING LAW JOURNAL, THE
21930
One Penn Plz.
New York, NY 10119
Telephone: (212) 971-5218
FAX: (212) 971-5215
Year Established: 1889
Pub. Frequency: bi-m.
Page Size: pocket
Subscrip. Rate: $120/yr.
Materials: 02
Circulation: 4,000
Circulation Type: paid
**Owner(s):**
Warren, Gorham & Lamont, Inc.
31 St. James Ave.
Boston, MA 02116-4112
Telephone: (617) 423-2020
Ownership %: 100
**Editorial:**
Gerald T. Dunne .........................Editor
Peter Knopp ...............Managing Editor
**Desc.:** Contains special articles on subjects pertinent to banking law, bank taxation, and to the law of negotiable instruments.
**Readers:** Bankers, and bank attorneys.

## BANKRUPTCY LAW LETTER
66033
One Penn Plz.
New York, NY 10119
Telephone: (212) 971-5284
Year Established: 1981
Pub. Frequency: m.
Subscrip. Rate: $135/yr.
Circulation: 5,000
Circulation Type: paid
**Owner(s):**
Warren, Gorham & Lamont
One Penn Plz.
New York, NY 10119
Telephone: (212) 971-5218
Ownership %: 100
**Editorial:**
Rena Pirsos ...............................Editor
**Readers:** Bankruptcy attorneys.

## BARRISTER
65740
750 N. Lake Shore Dr.
Chicago, IL 60611-4497
Telephone: (312) 988-6068
Year Established: 1972
Pub. Frequency: q.
Page Size: 4 color photos/art
Subscrip. Rate: $19.95/yr.
Freelance Pay: negotiable
Circulation: 175,000
Circulation Type: controlled

**Owner(s):**
American Bar Assn.
750 N. Lake Shore Dr.
Chicago, IL 60611-4497
Telephone: (312) 988-6068
Ownership %: 100
**Editorial:**
Cie Brown-Armstead .......................Editor
**Desc.:** A feature-oriented publication focusing on the career, social, and personal concerns of young lawyers.
**Readers:** Members of the ABA who are 36 years old or younger.

## BARRISTER
69647
121 S. Broad St., Ste. 800
Philadelphia, PA 19107-4594
Telephone: (215) 546-6451
FAX: (215) 546-5430
Year Established: 1970
Pub. Frequency: q.
Page Size: standard
Subscrip. Rate: $32/yr.
Circulation: 4,000
Circulation Type: paid
**Owner(s):**
Pennsylvania Trial Lawyers Association
121 S. Broad St., Ste. 800
Philadelphia, PA 19107-4594
Telephone: (215) 546-6451
FAX: (215) 546-5430
Ownership %: 100
**Editorial:**
Lee C. Swartz ...............................Editor
**Desc.:** Covers practicing trial law in Pennsylvania.

## BENEFITS LAW JOURNAL
66098
22 W. 21st St.
New York, NY 10010-6990
Telephone: (212) 645-7880
FAX: (212) 645-1160
Year Established: 1988
Pub. Frequency: q.
Page Size: standard
Subscrip. Rate: $198/yr. US; $248/yr. foreign
**Owner(s):**
Executive Enterprises Publications Co., Inc.
22 W 21st St.
New York, NY 10010-6990
Telephone: (212) 645-7880
Ownership %: 100
**Editorial:**
Isabelle Cohen ...............................Editor
**Desc.:** Contains information on new types of benefits, new methods of benefit delivery & new legal requirements. Covers welfare benefits, changes in federal tax & labor laws, structuring, restructuring plans, judicial developments, & pending legislative proposals.

## BEVERLY HILLS BAR ASSOCIATION JOURNAL
69654
300 S. Beverly Dr., Ste. 201
Beverly Hills, CA 90212
Telephone: (213) 553-6644
FAX: (213) 284-8290
Year Established: 1962
Pub. Frequency: q.
Page Size: standard
Subscrip. Rate: $40/yr. US.; $50/yr. foreign
Materials: 02
Circulation: 3,000
Circulation Type: paid
**Owner(s):**
Beverly Hills Bar Association
300 S. Beverly Dr., Ste. 201
Beverly Hills, CA 90212
Telephone: (213) 553-6644
Ownership %: 100

**Materials Accepted/Included:** 01-Business news 02-By-line articles 03-Fashion news 04-Food news 05-Freelance copy 06-Letters to editor 07-Real estate news 08-Sports news 09-Travel news 10-Book rev. 11-Movie rev. 12-Music rev. 13-TV rev. 14-Theater rev. 15-Coming events 16-Obituaries 17-Question & answer 18-Social announcements 19-Artwork 20-Cartoons 21-Photos 22-TV listings 23-Audio rec. 24-Video rec. 25-Books 26-Films/film clips 27-Personnel news 28-Press releases 29-New product news/photos 30-Trade lit. 31-Contracts 32-Display adv. 33-Classified adv.

4-199

**Desc.:** Deals with substantive and procedural issues in law.

61272

## BIOTECHNOLOGY LAW REPORT
20 W. Third St.
Media, PA 19063-2824
Telephone: (610) 892-9580
FAX: (610) 892-9577
Year Established: 1982
Pub. Frequency: bi-m.
Page Size: standard
Subscrip. Rate: $460/yr. US; $495
   overseas air
Materials: 02,10,15,27,28,32
Print Process: offset lithography
**Owner(s):**
Mary Ann Liebert, Inc.
1651 Third Ave.
New York, NY 10128
Telephone: (212) 289-2300
Ownership %: 100
**Bureau(s):**
Stem Line Publishing Services, Inc.
P.O. Box 141150
Minneapolis, MN 55414
Telephone: (612) 633-7918
Contact: Judith Gunn Bronson, Managing
    Editor
**Editorial:**
Gerry J. Elman .............................Editor in Chief
Steve Bentkin .............................Senior Editor
Judith Gunn Bronson ..............Managing Editor
**Desc.:** Covers patent, regulatory, product
liability, biomedical, tax, securities,
contract, licensing and international law
as it applies to biotechnology. Includes
reports and full text of major
developments in litigation, legislation &
administrative regulations.
**Readers:** Lawyers, regulatory affairs
professionals involved with
biotechnology.

69652

## BROOKLYN BARRISTER
123 Remsen St.,
Brooklyn, NY 11201
Year Established: 1950
Pub. Frequency: q.
Subscrip. Rate: $15/yr. includes
   membership
Circulation: 2,600
**Owner(s):**
Brooklyn Bar Association
23 Remsen St.,
Brooklyn, NY 11201
Ownership %: 100
**Editorial:**
John L. Leventhal .......................................Editor

69648

## BROOKLYN LAW REVIEW
250 Joralemon St.
Brooklyn, NY 11201
Telephone: (718) 780-7968
Year Established: 1935
Pub. Frequency: 4/yr.
Subscrip. Rate: $18/yr.
Circulation: 3,000
**Owner(s):**
Brooklyn Law School
250 Joralemon St.
Brooklyn, NY 11201
Telephone: (718) 780-7968
Ownership %: 100
**Desc.:** Analyzes a wide variety of legal
topics.

65669

## CALIFORNIA SCHOOL LAW DIGEST
313 South Ave.
Fanwood, NJ 07023
Telephone: (908) 889-6336
FAX: (908) 889-6339

Mailing Address:
   P.O. Box 340
   Fanwood, NJ 07023
Year Established: 1974
Pub. Frequency: m.
Page Size: standard
Subscrip. Rate: $125/yr.
Materials: 01,06,28
Print Process: photocopy
**Owner(s):**
Whitaker Newsletters, Inc.
313 South Ave., P.O. Box 340
Fanwood, NJ 07023
Telephone: (908) 889-6336
FAX: (908) 889-6339
Ownership %: 100
**Management:**
Joel Whitaker ......................................Publisher
Sandra Smith ..................Circulation Manager
**Editorial:**
Fred Rossi ..............................................Editor
**Desc.:** Covers news, administrative law
and court decisions affecting California
schools.
**Readers:** School superintendents,
principals, school union leaders, etc.
**Deadline:** story-1 mo. prior to pub. date;
news-1 mo. prior to pub. date

69651

## CASE WESTERN RESERVE LAW REVIEW
11075 East Blvd.
Cleveland, OH 44106-7148
Telephone: (216) 368-3304
FAX: (216) 368-3310
Year Established: 1948
Pub. Frequency: 4/yr.
Page Size: journal
Subscrip. Rate: $25/yr.
Print Process: offset
Circulation: 800
Circulation Type: free & paid
**Owner(s):**
Case Western Reserve University School
   of Law
11075 East Blvd.
Cleveland, OH 44106
Telephone: (216) 368-3304
FAX: (216) 368-3310
Ownership %: 100
**Desc.:** Law journal/student-edited/broad
range of legal issues and articles.
**Readers:** Law professors and law libraries.

54070

## CHAMPION JOURNAL OF THE NATIONAL ASSOCIATION OF CRIMINAL DEFENSE LAWYERS
1110 Vermont Ave., N.W., Ste. 1150
Washington, DC 20005
Telephone: (202) 872-8688
Year Established: 1958
Pub. Frequency: m. exc. Jan. & Sep.
Page Size: standard
Subscrip. Rate: $25/yr.
Circulation: 4,000
Circulation Type: paid
**Owner(s):**
National Association of Criminal Defense
   Lawyers
1110 Vermont Ave., N.W., #1150
Washington, DC 20005
Telephone: (202) 872-8688
Ownership %: 100
**Management:**
Allen Connally ..................Advertising Manager
**Editorial:**
Jim O'Haver ...........................................Editor
**Desc.:** Serves as a national forum for the
exchange of information of interest and
benefit to criminal defense lawyers.
**Readers:** Members of a professional
association.

68948

## COLORADO LAWYER
1900 Grant St., Ste. 940
Denver, CO 80203-4309
Telephone: (303) 860-1118
FAX: (303) 830-3990
Year Established: 1971
Pub. Frequency: m.
Page Size: standard
Subscrip. Rate: $85/yr. individuals; $35/yr.
   libraries
Materials: 32,33
Print Process: web offset
Circulation: 12,000
Circulation Type: paid
**Owner(s):**
Colorado Bar Association, Inc.
1900 Grant St., Ste. 940
Denver, CO 80203-4309
Telephone: (303) 860-1118
FAX: (303) 830-3990
Ownership %: 100
**Editorial:**
Arlene Abady ............................................Editor
**Desc.:** Includes articles on substantive law,
full appellate opinions, law-related
features and certain federal court
opinion summaries.

69659

## COLUMBIA LAW REVIEW
435 W. 116th St.
Box A-26
New York, NY 10027
Telephone: (212) 854-4398
Year Established: 1901
Pub. Frequency: 8/yr.
Page Size: book; soft cover
Subscrip. Rate: $8.50 newsstand; $40/yr.;
   $46/yr. foreign
Materials: 10
Circulation: 3,000
Circulation Type: paid
**Owner(s):**
Columbia Law Review Association
435 W. 116th St.
New York, NY 10027
Telephone: (212) 854-4398
Ownership %: 100
**Editorial:**
Susan Stagn ............................................Editor
**Desc.:** Publishes articles on current legal
issues by members of the academic and
legal professions.
**Readers:** Professional and academic
members of the legal profession.

23590

## COMMERCIAL LAW JOURNAL
150 N. Michigan Ave.
Ste. 600
Chicago, IL 60601-2703
Telephone: (312) 781-2000
FAX: (312) 781-2010
Year Established: 1895
Pub. Frequency: m.: 10/yr.
Page Size: standard
Subscrip. Rate: $75/yr.
Circulation: 7,000
Circulation Type: paid
**Owner(s):**
Commercial Law League of America
150 N. Michigan Ave.
Ste. 600
Chicago, IL 60601-2703
Telephone: (312) 781-2000
FAX: (312) 781-2010
Ownership %: 100
**Management:**
Linda Saghir .......................................Publisher
**Editorial:**
Linda Saghir .........................Managing Editor
**Desc.:** Discusses legal aspects of
business.
**Readers:** Commercial lawyers, law list
representatives, commercial collection
agencies, law libraries and colleges.

65734

## COMMERCIAL LEASE LAW INSIDER
Commercial Lease Law Insider
New York, NY 10010
Telephone: (212) 473-8200
FAX: (212) 995-9205
Mailing Address:
   P.O. Box 3599
   New York, NY 10163
Year Established: 1982
Pub. Frequency: m.
Page Size: standard
Subscrip. Rate: $227/yr.
**Owner(s):**
Brownstone Publishers, Inc.
P.O. Box 3599
New York, NY 10163
Telephone: (212) 473-8200
**Editorial:**
Seth Ross, Esq. ......................................Editor
Mary V. Lopez ..........................Managing Editor
**Readers:** Commercial real estate
professionals.

22708

## COMMUNICATIONS & THE LAW
10368 W. Centennial Rd.
Littleton, CO 80127-4200
Telephone: (800) 457-1986
FAX: (303) 978-1457
Year Established: 1978
Pub. Frequency: q.
Page Size: standard
Subscrip. Rate: $95/yr. in US.; $105/yr.
   foreign
Materials: 02,10,32
Circulation: 800
Circulation Type: paid
**Owner(s):**
Fred B. Rothman & Co.
10368 W. Centennial Rd.
Littleton, CO 80127
Telephone: (800) 457-1986
FAX: (303) 978-1457
Ownership %: 100
**Management:**
Fred B. Rothman ...............................Publisher
**Editorial:**
Theodore R. Kupferman ............Editor in Chief
Sheila Jarrett ............................Managing Editor
**Desc.:** Expanding technologies, aggressive
use of the media of business,
censorship, public opinion formation by
government; these and scores of
communications issues have daily
impact upon legislative, legal and judicial
affairs. Devoted to the study of these
issues. Articles should average 5000-
10000 words, by-lines always given.
Departments include: Book Reviews.

69649

## COMPARATIVE LABOR LAW JOURNAL
2203 Steinberg-Deitrich Hall
Philadelphia, PA 19104-6369
Telephone: (215) 898-6851
FAX: (215) 898-2400
Year Established: 1976
Pub. Frequency: q.
Subscrip. Rate: $30/yr.
Materials: 05,10
Circulation: 700
Circulation Type: paid
**Owner(s):**
International Society for Law and Social
   Security
U. Penn, Wharton School of Bus
2203 Steinberg-Deitrich Hall
Philadelphia, PA 19104-6369
Telephone: (215) 898-6851
Ownership %: 100
**Editorial:**
Benjamin Aaron ......................................Editor

**Materials Accepted/Included:** 01-Business news 02-By-line articles 03-Fashion news 04-Food news 05-Freelance copy 06-Letters to editor 07-Real estate news 08-Sports news 09-Travel news 10-Book rev. 11-Movie rev. 12-Music rev. 13-TV rev. 14-Theater rev. 15-Coming events 16-Obituaries 17-Question & answer 18-Social announcements 19-Artwork 20-Cartoons 21-Photos 22-TV listings 23-Audio rec. 24-Video rec. 25-Books 26-Films/film clips 27-Personnel news 28-Press releases 29-New product news/photos 30-Trade lit. 31-Contracts awarded 32-Display adv. 33-Classified adv.

4-200

**Desc.:** Comparative studies of various aspects of labor, employment and labor-related matters.

## COMPLEAT LAWYER, THE
65741

750 N. Lake Shore Dr.
Chicago, IL 60611
Telephone: (312) 988-6069
Year Established: 1984
Pub. Frequency: q.
Page Size: standard
Subscrip. Rate: $39.30/yr.
Circulation: 44,000
Circulation Type: paid
**Owner(s):**
American Bar Assn.
750 N. Lake Shore Dr.
Chicago, IL 60611
Telephone: (312) 988-5000
Ownership %: 100
**Editorial:**
Ray DeLong ..................................Editor
**Desc.:** Designed to help GP's attract and retain clients by providing quality service in a sophisticated legal marketplace. Topics range from using a legal assistant in a family-law case and managing cash flow to keeping abreast with trends and substantive or procedural changes in specialized areas of the law.

## CORPORATE SECURITY
67663

1333 H St. N.W.
Washington, DC 20005
Telephone: (202) 842-3022
FAX: (202) 842-3023
Pub. Frequency: s-m.
Page Size: standard
Subscrip. Rate: $225/yr.
Materials: 28,29,30
Print Process: offset
**Owner(s):**
Business Research Publications, Inc.
817 Broadway
New York, NY 10003
Telephone: (212) 673-4700
Ownership %: 100
**Management:**
John Roche ...............................Publisher
**Editorial:**
Gail Hayden ...................................Editor
**Desc.:** Examines current security issues such as employee theft, access control, computer security, industrial espionage, employee substance abuse, arson, wiretapping and disaster control.

## DETROIT LAWYER, THE
23592

2380 Penobscot Bldg.
Detroit, MI 48226-4811
Telephone: (313) 961-6120
FAX: (313) 965-0842
Pub. Frequency: q.
Page Size: standard
Subscrip. Rate: $10/yr. non-members
Circulation: 4,500
Circulation Type: paid
**Owner(s):**
Detroit Bar Association
2380 Penobscot Bldg.
Detroit, MI 48226-4811
Ownership %: 100
**Management:**
James T. Maunders .........Advertising Manager
**Editorial:**
Jeffery J. Alderman ...........................Editor
**Desc.:** By-line articles by members of the Detroit Association news. Official publication of the Detroit Bar Association.
**Readers:** Members of the bar.

## ETHICS
64723

University Hall
Chicago, IL 60607-7114
Telephone: (312) 413-2087
FAX: (312) 413-2093
Mailing Address:
Univ. of IL.
601 So. Morgan St.
Chicago, IL 60607
Year Established: 1890
Pub. Frequency: q.
Page Size: standard
Subscrip. Rate: $29/yr.
Materials: 10,32
Circulation: 3,900
Circulation Type: paid
**Owner(s):**
University of Chicago Press
5720 Woodlawn
Chicago, IL 60637
Telephone: (312) 702-7600
Ownership %: 100
**Editorial:**
Gerald Dworkin ..............................Editor
Timothy A. Stelzig ...................Managing Editor
**Readers:** Academic

## FEDERAL BAR NEWS & JOURNAL
68949

1815 H St., N.W., Ste. 408
Washington, DC 20006-3697
Telephone: (202) 638-0252
FAX: (202) 775-0295
Year Established: 1981
Pub. Frequency: 10/yr.
Page Size: standard
Subscrip. Rate: $25/yr. non-members;
$35/yr. foreign non-members
Materials: 06,10,21,25,28,32,33
Print Process: web
Circulation: 15,000
Circulation Type: paid
**Owner(s):**
Federal Bar Association
1815 H St., N.W. Ste. 408
Washington, DC 20006-3697
Telephone: (202) 638-0252
FAX: (202) 775-0295
Ownership %: 100
**Editorial:**
Joryn Jenkins ................................Editor
Beth Kemper ...........................Managing Editor
**Desc.:** News items about association events and activities, federal practice, and items of practical interest to federal attorneys. Feature articles on the latest topics in the federal area, legislative updates and comparisons as well as legal analysis.
**Readers:** Anyone practicing federal law, judges, paralegals, and other interested attorneys.
**Deadline:** all copy/ads 8 wks. prior to pub. date

## FLORIDA BAR JOURNAL, THE
23593

650 Apalachee Pkwy.
Tallahassee, FL 32399-2300
Telephone: (904) 561-5600
FAX: (904) 681-3859
Year Established: 1927
Pub. Frequency: m.: Sep.-Jun.
Page Size: standard
Subscrip. Rate: $30/yr.
Materials: 10,20,29,32
Print Process: web offset
Circulation: 50,000
Circulation Type: paid
**Owner(s):**
Florida Bar, The
Florida Bar Ctr.
Tallahassee, FL 32399-2300
Telephone: (904) 561-5600
Ownership %: 100

**Management:**
John F. Harkness, Jr. ......................Publisher
Javier Cano ....................Advertising Manager
**Editorial:**
Judson H. Orrick ...........................Editor
Cheryle Dodd ..........................Managing Editor
Judith Nable ..................................Artist
Paul F. Hill ...............Communications Director
**Desc.:** Substantive articles about Florida law of general interest, and specialized law columns. Departments include: Labor Law, Tax Law, Real Property Law, Corporation and Banking Law, Reviews of Law Books, etc., Criminal Law, Admiralty Law, Family Law, Workers' Compensation, Administrative Law, Probate and Trust Law, and Environmental Law.
**Readers:** All lawyers and judges who are members of the Florida Bar (includes 50,000 nationally), interested law students, and subscribers.
**Deadline:** ads-6 wks. prior to pub. date

## GEORGIA STATE BAR JOURNAL
23594

800 The Hurt Bldg.
Atlanta, GA 30303
Telephone: (404) 527-8700
FAX: (404) 527-8717
Year Established: 1964
Pub. Frequency: q.
Page Size: standard
Subscrip. Rate: $10/yr. non-members
Circulation: 25,000
Circulation Type: paid
**Owner(s):**
State Bar of Georgia
800 The Hurt Bldg.
Atlanta, GA 30303
Telephone: (404) 527-8700
Ownership %: 100
**Management:**
Lynn Carpentier .................Advertising Manager
**Editorial:**
Stephanie Manis .............................Editor
Lynne Carpentier ......................Managing Editor
Diane Morgan ...........Administrative Assistant
**Desc.:** Basically legal articles, features, law notes, and comments.
**Readers:** State Bar of Georgia members, law and court associations, individuals interested in the legal profession.

## INDEX TO PERIODICAL ARTICLES RELATED TO LAW
58643

75 Main St.
Dobbs Ferry, NY 10522-1632
Telephone: (914) 693-8100
FAX: (914) 693-0402
Year Established: 1958
Pub. Frequency: q.
Page Size: standard
Subscrip. Rate: $65/yr.
Circulation: 500
Circulation Type: paid
**Owner(s):**
Glanville Publishers, Inc.
75 Main St.
Dobbs Ferry, NY 10522
Telephone: (914) 693-8100
FAX: (914) 693-0402
Ownership %: 100
**Management:**
Fay Cohen .................................President
Alden W. Domizio .........................Manager
**Editorial:**
J. Myron Jacobstein .........................Editor
Roy M. Mersky ...............................Editor
Donald J. Dunn ..............................Editor

**Desc.:** A quarterly journal that indexes articles classified as non-legal but related to legal subjects such as articles in political science, sociology, psychology, medicine and international relations.
**Readers:** Universities, law and non-law libraries.

## JOURNAL OF COURT REPORTING
24203

8224 Old Courthouse Rd.
Vienna, VA 22182
Telephone: (703) 556-6272
FAX: (703) 556-6291
Year Established: 1899
Pub. Frequency: 10/yr.
Page Size: standard
Subscrip. Rate: $35/yr.
Freelance Pay: varies
Circulation: 30,000
Circulation Type: paid
**Owner(s):**
National Court Reporters Association
8224 Old Courthouse Rd.
Vienna, VA 22182
Telephone: (703) 556-6272
Ownership %: 100
**Management:**
Brian E. Cartier ...........................Publisher
**Editorial:**
Benjamin M. Rogner ..........................Editor
Marshall S. Jorpeland .............Managing Editor
Nancy Hodges .....................Production Director
**Desc.:** Articles deal with the history of court reporting, discussions of techniques, developments in computer - aided transcription technology, association news, contests, etc. Publication of the National Shorthand Reporters' Association. Publicity photos not used.
**Readers:** Court and freelance reporters, students, and schools.

## JOURNAL OF LEGAL PLURALISM & UNOFFICIAL LAW
69653

10368 W. Centennial Rd.
Littleton, CO 80127
Telephone: (303) 979-5657
FAX: (303) 978-1457
Year Established: 1969
Pub. Frequency: a.
Subscrip. Rate: $20/yr. individuals; $35/yr. institutions
**Owner(s):**
Fred B. Rothman & Co.
10368 Centennial Rd.
Littleton, CO 80127
Telephone: (303) 979-5657
**Editorial:**
John Griffiths ...............................Editor

## JOURNAL OF LEGAL STUDIES
69655

5720 Woodlawn Ave.
Chicago, IL 60637
Telephone: (312) 753-3347
FAX: (312) 753-0811
Mailing Address:
P.O. Box 37005
Chicago, IL 60637
Year Established: 1972
Pub. Frequency: s-a
Subscrip. Rate: $26/yr. individuals; $39/yr. institutions; $15/yr. students
Circulation: 1,500
**Owner(s):**
University of Chicago Press
5720 Woodlawn Ave.
Chicago, IL 60637
Telephone: (312) 753-3347
Ownership %: 100
**Editorial:**
William M. Landes ...........................Editor

**Materials Accepted/Included:** 01-Business news 02-By-line articles 03-Fashion news 04-Food news 05-Freelance copy 06-Letters to editor 07-Real estate news 08-Sports news 09-Travel news 10-Book rev. 11-Movie rev. 12-Music rev. 13-TV rev. 14-Theater rev. 15-Coming events 16-Obituaries 17-Question & answer 18-Social announcements 19-Artwork 20-Cartoons 21-Photos 22-TV listings 23-Audio rec. 24-Video rec. 25-Books 26-Films/film clips 27-Personnel news 28-Press releases 29-New product news/photos 30-Trade lit. 31-Contracts awarded 32-Display adv. 33-Classified adv.

4-201

**Desc.:** Presents theoretical and empirical research on law and legal institutions, emphasizing the use of social science research techniques to obtain new information about the actual functioning of the legal system.

69657

## JOURNAL OF LEGISLATION
Notre Dame Law School
Notre Dame, IN 46556
Telephone: (219) 631-5918
FAX: (219) 631-6371
Year Established: 1974
Pub. Frequency: 2/yr.
Subscrip. Rate: $16/yr.
Materials: 02,10
Circulation: 1,500
**Owner(s):**
Notre Dame Law School
Notre Dame, IN 46556
Telephone: (219) 631-5918
FAX: (219) 631-6371
Ownership %: 100
**Editorial:**
Vincent A. Sanchez ................................Editor
**Desc.:** Studies current public policy issues facing state, national and international legislative bodies.

23596

## JUDICATURE, THE JOURNAL OF THE AMERICAN JUDICATURE SOCIETY
25 E. Washington, Ste. 1600
Chicago, IL 60602
Telephone: (312) 558-6900
FAX: (312) 558-9175
Year Established: 1917
Pub. Frequency: bi-m.
Page Size: standard
Subscrip. Rate: $48/yr.
Materials: 02,06,10,20,21,23,24,25,32
Print Process: web offset
Circulation: 15,000
Circulation Type: paid
**Owner(s):**
American Judicature Society
Telephone: (312) 558-6900
Ownership %: 100
**Editorial:**
David R. Richert ................................Editor
Ira Pilchen ................................Assistant Editor
Mary-Ann Lupa ................................Design
**Desc.:** News and articles about the administration of justice and its improvement. Departments include: Editorial, News Briefs, Readers' Viewpoint, Literature of Judicial Administration (books, articles).
**Readers:** Lawyers, judges, public officials, professors.
**Deadline:** ads-1st of May, Jul., Sep., Nov., Jan., Mar.

58780

## LAW BOOKS IN REVIEW
75 Main St.
Dobbs Ferry, NY 10522-1632
Telephone: (914) 693-8100
FAX: (914) 693-0402
Year Established: 1974
Pub. Frequency: q.
Page Size: standard
Subscrip. Rate: $55/yr.
Materials: 02,10
Print Process: offset
Circulation: 250
Circulation Type: paid
**Owner(s):**
Glanville Publishers, Inc.
75 Main St.
Dobbs Ferry, NY 10522
Telephone: (914) 693-8100
FAX: (914) 693-0402
Ownership %: 100

**Management:**
Fay Cohen ................................President
**Editorial:**
Alden W. Domizio ................................Editor
Lorraine Wallis ................................Assignment Editor
**Desc.:** Journal of reviews of current publications in law and related areas.
**Readers:** Members of the legal profession, libraries, and law students.

58779

## LAW BOOKS PUBLISHED
75 Main St.
Dobbs Ferry, NY 10522-1632
Telephone: (914) 693-8100
FAX: (914) 693-0402
Year Established: 1965
Pub. Frequency: 2/yr.
Page Size: standard
Subscrip. Rate: $140/yr.
Circulation: 800
Circulation Type: paid
**Owner(s):**
Glanville Publishers, Inc.
75 Main St.
Dobbs Ferry, NY 10522
Telephone: (914) 693-8100
FAX: (914) 693-0402
Ownership %: 100
**Management:**
Fay Cohen ................................President
Alden W. Domizio ................................Manager
**Editorial:**
Nicholas Triffin ................................Editor
Alice Pidgeon ................................Administrative Assistant
**Desc.:** Lists by author/title, subjects by series, and by publisher, all law books published in the English language in the given year. It is a supplement to The Master Work-Law Books in Print.
**Readers:** Members of the legal profession, students, and librarians.

23598

## LAW OFFICE ECONOMICS & MANAGEMENT
139 Grand St.
Croton-Hudson, NY 10520
Telephone: (914) 271-5191
Mailing Address:
P.O. Box 40
Croton-Hudson, NY 10520-0040
Year Established: 1960
Pub. Frequency: q.
Page Size: standard
Subscrip. Rate: $115/yr.
Materials: 28,29
Freelance Pay: contributions only
Circulation: 1,500
Circulation Type: paid
**Owner(s):**
Clark Boardman Callaghan
155 Pfingstom Rd.
Deerfield, IL 60015
Telephone: (708) 948-7000
Ownership %: 100
**Editorial:**
Paul S. Hoffman ................................Editor
Julie M. Rosso ................................Assistant Editor
**Desc.:** Criterion for publication: "Will this item or article be helpful to the man or woman running the law office?" Departments include: Taxes, News, Book Reviews, Word Processing, Law Office Forms, Computers, Short Items of All Types, Cartoons, Letters.
**Readers:** Managers of large and small law offices-both lawyer and non-lawyer.

67061

## LAW PRACTICE MANAGEMENT
P.O. Box 11418
Columbia, SC 29211-1418
Telephone: (803) 754-3563
Year Established: 1975
Pub. Frequency: 8/yr.

Page Size: 8 3/8 x 10 7/8
Subscrip. Rate: $24/yr. members; $48/yr. others
Materials: 02,06,10,15,19,20,21,25,29,32
Freelance Pay: $.15-$.20/wd.
Print Process: web offset
Circulation: 22,234
Circulation Type: paid
**Owner(s):**
American Bar Assn.
750 N. Lake Shore Dr.
Chicago, IL 60611-4497
Telephone: (312) 988-6048
Ownership %: 100
**Management:**
Robert Brouwer ................................Advertising Manager
**Editorial:**
John C. Tredennick ................................Articles Editor
Donna Bausch ................................Books Editor
Delmar Roberts ................................Design Editor
Margo Lynn Hablutzel ................................New Products Editor
G. Burgess Allison ................................Technical Editor
**Readers:** Anyone concerned with day-to-day operations of a law practice.

66502

## LAWYERS PC, THE
334 Old Chapin Rd.
Lexington, SC 29072
Telephone: (803) 359-9941
Mailing Address:
P.O. Box 1108
Lexington, SC 29071
Year Established: 1983
Pub. Frequency: s-m.
Page Size: standard
Subscrip. Rate: $115/yr.
Materials: 05,06,15,25,28,29,32
Freelance Pay: $35-50/pg.
Circulation: 4,000
Circulation Type: paid
**Owner(s):**
Shepherd's McGraw-Hill, Inc.
555 Middle Creek Pkwy.
Colorado Springs, CO 80921
Telephone: (719) 488-3000
Ownership %: 100
**Editorial:**
Robert P. Wilkims ................................Editor
Dan Harmon ................................Design Editor
**Readers:** Lawyers who use personal computers.
**Deadline:** story-open

68950

## LEGAL ASSISTANT TODAY
3520 Cadillac Ave., Ste. F
Costa Mesa, CA 92626-1419
Telephone: (714) 755-5450
Year Established: 1983
Pub. Frequency: bi-m.
Subscrip. Rate: $39.98/yr.
Circulation: 16,500
Circulation Type: paid
**Owner(s):**
James Publishing Group, Inc.
3520 Cadillac Ave., Ste. E
Costa Mesa, CA 92626-1419
Telephone: (714) 755-5450
Ownership %: 100
**Desc.:** Provides information on the day-to-day activities of paralegals, practical advice on working with attorneys, how to handle the case load, and how to get ahead in their careers.

69631

## LEGAL PUBLISHING REVIEW
121 Chanlon Rd.
New Providence, NJ 07974
Telephone: (908) 464-6800
FAX: (908) 665-6688
Year Established: 1989
Pub. Frequency: 6/yr.
Subscrip. Rate: $99.95/yr.
Circulation: 5,000
Circulation Type: controlled

**Owner(s):**
R.R. Bowker
121 Chanlon Rd.
New Providence, NJ 07974
Telephone: (908) 464-6800
Ownership %: 100
**Editorial:**
Lucille Boorstein ................................Editor
**Desc.:** Written for law librarians and legal researchers in both the academic and business communities. Provides authoritative reviews of new and forthcoming legal materials, including books, audio and video cassettes, and specialized software.

67030

## LEGAL TIMES
1730 M St., N.W., Ste. 802
Washington, DC 20036
Telephone: (202) 457-0686
FAX: (202) 457-0718
Year Established: 1978
Pub. Frequency: w.
Page Size: oversize
Subscrip. Rate: $195/yr. individuals; corporations $475/yr.
Circulation: 10,000
Circulation Type: paid
**Owner(s):**
American Lawyer Media, L.P.
1730 M St., N.W., Ste. 802
Washington, DC 20036
Telephone: (202) 457-0686
Ownership %: 100
**Management:**
Eric Effron ................................Publisher
**Editorial:**
Eric Effron ................................Editor
**Desc.:** Covers law, lobbying, and politics in Washington, DC.

59546

## LEGISLATIVE SURVEY
8158 Palm St.
Lemon Grove, CA 91945
Telephone: (619) 460-4480
Year Established: 1965
Pub. Frequency: m.
Subscrip. Rate: $15/yr.
Circulation: 1,000
Circulation Type: paid
**Owner(s):**
William Shearer
8158 Palm St.
Lemon Grove, CA 91945
Telephone: (619) 460-4480
Ownership %: 100
**Management:**
W.K. Shearer ................................Publisher
W.K. Shearer ................................Manager
**Editorial:**
W.K. Shearer ................................Editor
**Desc.:** Covers the national and California political scene.
**Readers:** American Independent Party and US Taxpayer Party Leadership; other subscribers.

23600

## MASSACHUSETTS LAWYERS WEEKLY
41 West St.
Boston, MA 02111
Telephone: (617) 451-7300
Year Established: 1972
Pub. Frequency: w.: Mon.
Page Size: tabloid
Subscrip. Rate: $6 newsstand; $225/yr.
Materials: 32,33
Circulation: 10,200
Circulation Type: paid

**Materials Accepted/Included:** 01-Business news 02-By-line articles 03-Fashion news 04-Food news 05-Freelance copy 06-Letters to editor 07-Real estate news 08-Sports news 09-Travel news 10-Book rev. 11-Movie rev. 12-Music rev. 13-TV rev. 14-Theater rev. 15-Coming events 16-Obituaries 17-Question & answer 18-Social announcements 19-Artwork 20-Cartoons 21-Photos 22-TV listings 23-Audio rec. 24-Video rec. 25-Books 26-Films/film clips 27-Personnel news 28-Press releases 29-New product news/photos 30-Trade lit. 31-Contracts awarded 32-Display adv. 33-Classified adv.

**Owner(s):**
Lawyers Weekly Publications
41 West St.
Boston, MA 02111
Telephone: (617) 451-7300
Ownership %: 100
**Management:**
Samuel B. Spencer .............................Publisher
Laurie Zamparelli .............Advertising Manager
**Editorial:**
Paul J. Martinek ....................................Editor
**Desc.:** Digest which publishes all opinions
written in the courts of Massachusetts.
Publishes general legal news of interest
to legal community.
**Readers:** 22,000 readers, 84 percent of
the total market.
**Deadline:** ads-6 days

23601
## METROPOLITAN NEWS-ENTERPRISE
210 S. Spring St.
Los Angeles, CA 90012
Telephone: (213) 628-4384
FAX: (213) 687-3886
Mailing Address:
  P.O. Box 60859
  Los Angeles, CA 90060
Pub. Frequency: Mon.-Fri.
Page Size: tabloid
Subscrip. Rate: $172.12/yr.
Circulation: 2,500
Circulation Type: paid
**Owner(s):**
Grace Communications, Inc.
210 S. Spring St.
Los Angeles, CA 90012
Telephone: (213) 628-4384
Ownership %: 100
**Management:**
Roger M. Grace .................................Publisher
**Editorial:**
Roger M. Grace .......................................Editor
**Desc.:** News of interest to the legal
profession, laws, new legislation
affecting the legal profession.
**Readers:** Legal profession, business
community, secretaries, paralegals, etc.

23602
## MICHIGAN LAW REVIEW
Hutchins Hall
Ann Arbor, MI 48109-1215
Telephone: (313) 763-5870
FAX: (313) 764-8309
Year Established: 1902
Pub. Frequency: 8/yr.
Page Size: standard
Subscrip. Rate: $40/vol.
Materials: 02,06,10,32
Circulation: 2,561
Circulation Type: paid
**Owner(s):**
Michigan Law Review Association
Hutchins Hall
Ann Arbor, MI 48109
Telephone: (313) 763-5870
FAX: (313) 764-8309
Ownership %: 100
**Management:**
Jenne S. Moldovan ..............Business Manager
**Desc.:** Articles by legal scholars discuss
trends, analyze court decisions.
Departments include: notes (prepared by
students of the law school), articles,
book reviews, legal periodical index.
**Readers:** Members of the bar, law
students.

64955
## NATIONAL JURY VERDICT REVIEW AND ANALYSIS
24 Commerce St., Ste. 1722
Newark, NJ 07102
Telephone: (201) 624-1665
FAX: (201) 624-5176

Year Established: 1985
Pub. Frequency: m.
Page Size: standard
Subscrip. Rate: $250/yr.
Circulation: 17,000
Circulation Type: paid
**Owner(s):**
Jury Verdict Review Publications, Inc.
24 Commerce St., Ste. 1722
Newark, NJ 07102
Telephone: (908) 679-0079
Ownership %: 100
**Management:**
Ira J. Zarin, Esq. ..............................Publisher
Ellen Loren ........................Circulation Manager
Jed M. Zarin ..........................General Manager
**Editorial:**
Lisa Weitzman, Esq. ...............................Editor
**Desc.:** A nationwide review of plaintiff and
defendant civil jury verdicts, with
complete factual summaries, reference
information, and a continuous recording
of all pertinent trial data including the
names of expert witnesses.

23603
## NATIONAL NOTARY, THE
8236 Remmet Ave.
Canoga Park, CA 91304
Telephone: (818) 713-4000
Mailing Address:
  P.O. Box 7184
  Canoga Park, CA 91309
Year Established: 1957
Pub. Frequency: bi-m.
Page Size: 4 color photos/art
Subscrip. Rate: $26/yr. includes NNA
  membership
Freelance Pay: negotiable
Circulation: 80,000
Circulation Type: paid
**Owner(s):**
National Notary Association
8236 Remmet Ave.
Canoga Park, CA 91304
Telephone: (818) 713-4000
Ownership %: 100
**Management:**
Raymond C. Rothman .........................Founder
Milton G. Valera ...............................President
Charles N. Faerber ....................Vice President
Deborah M. Thaw ............................Publisher
**Editorial:**
Charles N. Faerber ................................Editor
**Desc.:** Features and articles dealing with
the notary public, his office and his
duties. Articles generally are not more
than five double-spaced typewritten
pages, providing informative, educational
and entertaining stories directed to the
association's membership which
includes notaries, and those working in
the law, business, real estate, and
banking and finance. Format includes
eye-catching but simple art (drawings
and photographs acceptable). By-lines
accompany articles. Editorial policy
toward publicity is receptive but editors
do not actively solicit materials of that
nature. Departments include: Letters
(letters to the editor), Comment
(editorials), Profile (feature on interesting
notaries), Notary News (news items
affecting notaries), Advisor (question and
answer format), NNA Notes (association
news), and Court Report (synopses of
court cases affecting notaries).
**Readers:** More women than men
representing several fields - real estate,
insurance, finance, law and government.

23605
## NEW JERSEY LAW JOURNAL
238 Mulberry St.
Newark, NJ 07102
Telephone: (201) 642-0075
FAX: (201) 642-0920
Mailing Address:
  P.O. Box 20081
  Newark, NJ 07101-6081
Year Established: 1878
Pub. Frequency: w.
Page Size: tabloid
Subscrip. Rate: $7.00 newsstand; $272/yr.
Materials: 32,33
Print Process: web offset
Circulation: 12,138
Circulation Type: controlled & paid
**Owner(s):**
American Lawyer Media, L.P.
600 Third Ave.
New York, NY 10016
Telephone: (212) 973-2800
Ownership %: 100
**Management:**
Robert S. Steinbaum .........................Publisher
Vivian Distaso ..................Advertising Manager
Kathleen Schroeder ..........Circulation Manager
Jane Sydney ...............Classified Adv. Manager
**Editorial:**
Pamela Brownstein .................Executive Editor
Ronald J. Flevry .....................................Editor
Jeffrey Kanige ..........................Associate Editor
**Desc.:** Articles, treaties, news, stories and
information of interest to the legal
profession. An official publication of the
federal and state courts of New Jersey
and of the New Jersey State Bar
Association.
**Readers:** Practicing attorneys in state.
Also, some circulation outside the state.

64911
## NEW YORK EDUCATION LAW REPORT
313 South Ave.
Fanwood, NJ 07023-0340
Telephone: (201) 889-6336
Mailing Address:
  P.O. Box 340
  Fanwood, NJ 07023-0340
Year Established: 1987
Pub. Frequency: m.
Page Size: standard
Subscrip. Rate: $125/yr.
Freelance Pay: varies
Print Process: duplication
**Owner(s):**
Whitaker Newsletters, Inc.
313 South Ave.
Fanwood, NJ 07023
Telephone: (908) 889-6336
FAX: (908) 889-6339
Ownership %: 100
**Management:**
Joel Whitaker .....................................President
Sandy Smith ....................Operations Manager
**Editorial:**
Fred T. Rossi .........................................Editor
**Desc.:** A monthly report on schools, courts
and New York State.
**Readers:** School superintendents,
principals, teachers, and unions.

48945
## NLADA CORNERSTONE
1625 K St., N.W., 8th Fl.
Washington, DC 20006
Telephone: (202) 452-0620
Year Established: 1979
Pub. Frequency: 4/yr.
Page Size: standard
Subscrip. Rate: $20/yr.
Freelance Pay: negotiable
Circulation: 4,000
Circulation Type: paid

**Owner(s):**
NLADA
1625 K St., N.W.
Washington, DC 20006
Telephone: (202) 452-0620
Ownership %: 100
**Editorial:**
Melanie Herman ....................................Editor
**Desc.:** Contains news, events, opinions on
legal aid for the poor. Also carries public
interest job listings.
**Readers:** Principally lawyers and other
people interested in providing legal aid
to the poor in civil and criminal matters.

69656
## NOTARY BULLETIN
8236 Remmet Ave.
P.O. Box 7184
Canoga Park, CA 91309-7184
Telephone: (818) 713-4000
FAX: (818) 713-9061
Year Established: 1973
Pub. Frequency: bi-m.
Subscrip. Rate: $26/yr. includes NNA
  membership
Circulation: 80,000
Circulation Type: paid
**Owner(s):**
National Notary Association
8236 Remmet Ave.
P.O. Box 7184
Canoga Park, CA 91309-7184
Ownership %: 100
**Editorial:**
Charles N. Faerber ................................Editor

23607
## OHIO STATE BAR ASSOCIATION REPORT
P.O. Box 16562
Columbus, OH 43216-6562
Telephone: (614) 487-2050
Year Established: 1928
Pub. Frequency: w.
Page Size: pocket
Subscrip. Rate: $135/yr.
Materials: 32,33
Print Process: web
Circulation: 24,000
Circulation Type: paid
**Owner(s):**
Ohio State Bar Association
P.O. Box 16562
Columbus, OH 43216
Telephone: (614) 487-2050
Ownership %: 100
**Management:**
Lynn Smith .......................Advertising Manager
**Editorial:**
Kate Hagan ...........................................Editor
**Desc.:** Editorial policy is strictly material of
interest to the legal progression. (Almost
all material generated by association
staff or special agencies.)
**Readers:** Readership is by membership in
the Ohio State Bar Association
members, 95% in Ohio.

23608
## OREGON STATE BAR BULLETIN
5200 S.W. Meadows Rd.
Lake Oswego, OR 97035-0889
Telephone: (503) 620-0222
FAX: (503) 684-1366
Year Established: 1935
Pub. Frequency: 10/yr.
Page Size: standard
Subscrip. Rate: $45/yr.
Materials: 06,16,18,21,32,33
Circulation: 12,250
Circulation Type: paid

**Materials Accepted/Included:** 01-Business news 02-By-line articles 03-Fashion news 04-Food news 05-Freelance copy 06-Letters to editor 07-Real estate news 08-Sports news 09-Travel news 10-Book rev. 11-Movie rev. 12-Music rev. 13-TV rev. 14-Theater rev. 15-Coming events 16-Obituaries 17-Question & answer 18-Social announcements 19-Artwork 20-Cartoons 21-Photos 22-TV listings 23-Audio rec. 24-Video rec. 25-Books 26-Films/film clips 27-Personnel news 28-Press releases 29-New product news/photos 30-Trade lit. 31-Contracts awarded 32-Display adv. 33-Classified adv.

4-203

**Owner(s):**
Oregon State Bar
5200 S.W. Meadows Rd.
Lake Oswego, OR 97035-0889
Telephone: (503) 620-0222
FAX: (503) 684-1366
Ownership %: 100
**Editorial:**
Paul Nickell ...................................Editor
**Desc.:** News stories covering Bar
Association events, appointments,
personals, legal and state
developments. Special inserts of special
bar instruction material, etc.
**Readers:** Members of the Oregon State
Bar, other miscellaneous paid
subscribers.
**Deadline:** story-6 wks. prior to pub. date;
news-6 wks. prior; photo-6 wks. prior;
ads-6 wks. prior

69658

**PAPER BOOK**
666 High St., Ste. 201
Worthington, OH 43085-4135
Telephone: (800) 783-2600
FAX: (614) 888-7680
Year Established: 1913
Pub. Frequency: 4/yr.
Page Size: standard
Subscrip. Rate: $1/yr.
Materials: 10,16
Circulation: 15,000
Circulation Type: free & paid
**Owner(s):**
Delta Theta Phi Law Fraternity, Int'l.
666 High St., Ste. 201
Worthington, OH 43085-4135
Telephone: (800) 783-2600
FAX: (614) 888-7680
Ownership %: 100
**Editorial:**
Michele Shuster ..........................Editor

23609

**PRACTICAL LAWYER, THE**
4025 Chestnut St.
Philadelphia, PA 19104-3099
Telephone: (215) 243-1604
FAX: (215) 243-1664
Year Established: 1955
Pub. Frequency: 8/yr.
Page Size: 7 1/2 x 5 1/2
Subscrip. Rate: $35/yr.
Print Process: offset
Circulation: 7,500
Circulation Type: paid
**Owner(s):**
American Law Institute-American Bar
Association
4025 Chestnut St.
Philadelphia, PA 19104
Telephone: (215) 243-1600
Ownership %: 100
**Management:**
Kathleen H. Lawner .........Advertising Manager
**Editorial:**
Mark T. Carroll .............................Editor
**Desc.:** Articles are chosen for practical
utility; conveying information rapidly,
succinctly, and clearly. Many articles
contain forms, checklists, and other aids.
They are written by experienced
attorneys, law professors, and other
leading authorities. Departments include
all fields of law.
**Readers:** Lawyers.

69650

**PROSECUTOR**
99 Canal Center Plaza, Ste. 510
Alexandria, VA 22314
Telephone: (703) 549-9222
Year Established: 1965
Pub. Frequency: 6/yr.
Subscrip. Rate: membership
Circulation: 7,500

Circulation Type: paid
**Owner(s):**
National District Attorneys Association
99 Canal Center Plaza
Ste. 510
Alexandria, VA 22314
Telephone: (703) 549-9222
Ownership %: 100
**Editorial:**
Newman Flanagan .......................Editor

67695

**RECORDER, THE**
625 Polk St. 500
San Francisco, CA 94102
Telephone: (415) 749-5400
Year Established: 1877
Pub. Frequency: d.
Page Size: tabloid
Subscrip. Rate: $175/yr.
Circulation: 6,200
Circulation Type: paid
**Owner(s):**
American Lawyer Media
625 Polk St., 500
San Francisco, CA 94102
Telephone: (415) 749-5400
Ownership %: 100
**Management:**
Peter Scheer ..........................Publisher
**Editorial:**
Peter Scheer ..............................Editor

23610

**RECORD OF THE ASSOCIATION
OF THE BAR OF THE CITY OF
NEW YORK**
42 W. 44th St.
New York, NY 10036
Telephone: (212) 382-6650
FAX: (212) 768-8630
Year Established: 1946
Pub. Frequency: 8/yr.
Page Size: pocket
Subscrip. Rate: $10/copy; $60/yr.
Circulation: 20,500
Circulation Type: paid
**Owner(s):**
The Association of the Bar of the City of
New York
42 W. 44th St.
New York, NY 10036
Telephone: (212) 382-6650
Ownership %: 100
**Management:**
Barbara Paul Robinson ...................President
**Editorial:**
Lilou Irvine .................................Editor
B. Tion Kwa ...............................Editor
**Desc.:** Association news, selected
association committee reports and text
of selected lectures. New Member and
Association Events. Bibliography, Annual
Index.
**Readers:** Members of the New York City
Bar, libraries and subscribers.

23611

**STUDENT LAWYER**
750 N. Lake Shore Dr.
Chicago, IL 60611-4403
Telephone: (312) 988-6048
Year Established: 1972
Pub. Frequency: m.
Page Size: standard
Subscrip. Rate: $19/yr.
Materials: 02,06,28,32,33
Freelance Pay: $150-$800/article
Circulation: 33,000
Circulation Type: paid
**Owner(s):**
American Bar Assn.
750 N. Lake Shore Dr.
Chicago, IL 60611
Telephone: (312) 988-5000
Ownership %: 100

**Management:**
Robert Brouwer ...............Advertising Manager
**Editorial:**
Sarah Hoban ..............................Editor
Mirian R. Krasno ...............Managing Editor
Rafi Kushmir ...........................Art Director
**Desc.:** Contains non-technical articles
dealing with legal topics of current
interest to law students. Recent articles
discussed pro-bono work in law school,
DNA testing, faculty diversity, advocacy
for the homeless, law and the arts,
substance abuse in law school, law
school stress, child abuse, legal
malpractice, legal clinics, legal
specialties, minority hiring. Also included
are practical articles on career
opportunities and legal education.
Meetings and activities of the ABA law
student division are reported. Regular
features include: Briefly (short news
items on the profession), Letters to the
Editor, Pro Se (opinion pieces), Esq.
(profiles of interesting lawyers), and Et.
Al (general legal world features).
**Readers:** All law student members of ABA
law student dues, law school libraries,
newspapers, and other media.

61004

**TEXAS INTERNATIONAL LAW
JOURNAL**
727 E. 26th St.
Austin, TX 78705
Telephone: (512) 471-5453
FAX: (512) 471-6988
Year Established: 1965
Pub. Frequency: 4/yr.
Page Size: standard
Subscrip. Rate: $25/yr. US.; $28/yr.
foreign
Materials: 10,25,32
Circulation: 700
Circulation Type: paid
**Owner(s):**
Univ. of Texas at Austin, School-Law Publ.,
Inc.
727 E. 26th St.
Austin, TX 78705
Telephone: (512) 471-5453
Ownership %: 100
**Editorial:**
Johanna Oliver .....................Editor in Chief
Heath Esterak ................Managing Editor
**Desc.:** Publication of the School of Law,
University of Texas. Carries articles and
book reviews analyzing legal
developments in public and private
international law.
**Readers:** Judges, attorneys, law students,
government officials.

23612

**TEXAS LAW REVIEW**
727 E. 26th St.
Austin, TX 78705
Telephone: (512) 471-3164
FAX: (512) 471-3282
Year Established: 0922
Pub. Frequency: 7/yr.
Page Size: standard
Subscrip. Rate: $32/yr.
Circulation: 2,100
Circulation Type: paid
**Owner(s):**
Texas Law Review Association
727 E. 26th St.
Austin, TX 78705
Telephone: (512) 471-3164
Ownership %: 100
**Management:**
Denny Peters ...................Business Manager
**Editorial:**
William Christian .................Editor in Chief
Jeffrey Harper ...................Managing Editor

**Desc.:** Carries articles and book reviews
analyzing legal developments.
**Readers:** Judges, attorneys and law
students.

24292

**TRADEMARK REPORTER**
1133 Ave. of the Americas
New York, NY 10036-6710
Telephone: (212) 768-9887
Year Established: 1911
Pub. Frequency: bi-m.
Page Size: standard
Subscrip. Rate: $50/yr. schools &
government agencies
Materials: 06
Print Process: offset
Circulation: 3,200
Circulation Type: controlled & paid
**Owner(s):**
International Trademark Association
1133 Ave. of the Americas
New York, NY 10036-6710
Telephone: (212) 768-9887
Ownership %: 100
**Management:**
Robin A. Rolfe ...............Executive Director
**Editorial:**
Steven M. Weinberg ..............Editor in Chief
Charlotte Jones ...................Managing Editor
**Desc.:** Carries original articles on various
phases of trademarks and major case
reports in full or with commentary.
**Readers:** Trademark owners; lawyers and
law firms, market researchers,
universities, libraries, and government
agencies.

23613

**TRIAL MAGAZINE**
1050 31st St., N.W.
Washington, DC 20007
Telephone: (202) 965-3500
FAX: (202) 965-0030
Year Established: 1964
Pub. Frequency: m.
Page Size: standard
Subscrip. Rate: $48/yr.
Materials: 02,06,10,32,33
Circulation: 65,000
Circulation Type: paid
**Owner(s):**
Assn. of Trial Lawyers of America
1050 31st St., N.W.
Washington, DC 20007
Telephone: (202) 965-3500
Ownership %: 100
**Management:**
Judith Fair ......................Advertising Manager
**Editorial:**
Marion Goldberg ..............Managing Editor
Georgia Sargeant ...............Associate Editor
Donald C. Dilworth ............Associate Editor
Julia Gannon Shoop ...........Associate Editor
**Desc.:** Includes in-depth articles by
lawyers, judges, and law professors on
trial techniques, legal issues.
**Readers:** Members of The Association of
Trial Lawyers of America, who are
primarily plaintiffs' lawyers concerned
with the rights of victims; judges; law
professors; some prosecutors; some
defense counsel; and law students.

23614

**VIRGINIA LAW REVIEW**
School of Law, University of Virginia
Charlottesville, VA 22903
Telephone: (804) 924-3079
Year Established: 1913
Pub. Frequency: 8/yr.
Page Size: 45 x 71
Subscrip. Rate: $9/copy; $40/yr.
Circulation: 2,000
Circulation Type: paid

**Owner(s):**
Virginia Law Review Association
School of Law
University of Virginia
Charlottesville, VA 22901
Telephone: (804) 924-3079
Ownership %: 100
**Editorial:**
Erik Lillquist .............................Editor in Chief
Brad Handler .........................Managing Editor
Elizabeth Magill .........................Articles Editor
Paul Hourihan .....................Book Review Editor
Anthony Picarello .......................Essays Editor
Hilda S. Nordenson .................Miscellaneous
Jessica Dixon ........................Research Editor
**Desc.:** Papers discussing the legal, economic and social policy implications of current questions. Departments include: Articles, Essays, Book Reviews, and Notes.
**Readers:** Attorneys, law faculties, jurists, law students.

## VIRGINIA LAWYER
68951
707 E. Main St., Ste. 1500
Richmond, VA 23219
Telephone: (804) 775-0500
FAX: (804) 786-3036
Year Established: 1953
Pub. Frequency: m.
Subscrip. Rate: $18/yr.
Circulation: 26,000
Circulation Type: paid
**Owner(s):**
Virginia State Bar
707 E. Main St., Ste. 1500
Richmond, VA 23219
Telephone: (804) 775-0500
Ownership %: 100
**Editorial:**
Caroline B. Bolte ................................Editor

## WESTCHESTER LAW JOURNAL
23615
175 Main St.
White Plains, NY 10601
Telephone: (914) 948-0715
Year Established: 1936
Pub. Frequency: w.
Page Size: standard
Subscrip. Rate: $40/yr.
Circulation: 226
Circulation Type: paid
**Owner(s):**
Westchester Law Journal, Inc.
175 Main St.
White Plains, NY 10601
Telephone: (914) 978-0715
Ownership %: 100
**Editorial:**
Jacquelyn Ray ..................................Editor
**Desc.:** Articles dealing with court opinions, court laws, news items.
**Readers:** Lawyers, representatives, bankers, realtors.

## WISCONSIN LAW REVIEW
23616
975 Bascom Mall
Madison, WI 53706-1399
Telephone: (608) 262-5815
FAX: (608) 262-5485
Year Established: 1920
Pub. Frequency: bi-m.
Page Size: standard
Subscrip. Rate: $30/yr.
Materials: 06,10,32
Print Process: offset
Circulation: 2,150
Circulation Type: paid
**Owner(s):**
University of Wisconsin Law School
975 Bascom Mall
Madison, WI 53706-1399
Telephone: (608) 262-5815
Ownership %: 100

**Editorial:**
Sue Ehrmann .........................Editor in Chief
Kendall Harrison ........................Senior Editor
Susan Collins ...........................Senior Editor
Lawrence Glusman .....................Senior Editor
Andrew Clarkowski .....................Senior Editor
**Desc.:** Forum for analysis and discussions of various subjects related to law.
**Readers:** Law students, law professors, lawyers, judges, and others, with an interest in the law.

## WOMEN LAWYERS JOURNAL
71276
750 N. Lake Shore Dr.
Chicago, IL 60611
Telephone: (312) 988-6186
FAX: (312) 988-6281
Mailing Address:
   2027 B Beyer Ave.
   Philadelphia, PA 19115-4704
Year Established: 1911
Pub. Frequency: 4/yr.
Page Size: standard
Subscrip. Rate: $16/yr. in US; $18/yr. foreign
Materials: 01,02,06,07,09,10,11,14,15,16, 17,19,21,25,27,28,30,32,33
Print Process: offset lithography
Circulation: 1500
Circulation Type: free & paid
**Owner(s):**
NAt'l Assn. of Women Lawyers
750 N. Lake Shore Dr.
Chicago, IL 60611
Telephone: (312) 988-6281
FAX: (312) 988-6281
Ownership %: 100
**Editorial:**
Veronica C. Boda .....................Editor in Chief
Grace C. Kennedy ..................Associate Editor
**Desc.:** Commentary and documented policy with regard to the legal profession on issues concerning women worldwide.
**Readers:** Attorneys, judges, law students, and other legal professionals interested in legal issues concerning women worldwide.

## Group 144-Libraries

## AMERICAN ARCHIVIST, THE
23619
600 S. Federal St., Ste. 504
Chicago, IL 60605
Telephone: (312) 922-0140
FAX: (312) 347-1452
Year Established: 1938
Pub. Frequency: q.
Page Size: standard
Subscrip. Rate: $75/yr.
Circulation: 4,800
Circulation Type: paid
**Owner(s):**
Society of American Archivists
600 S. Federal, Ste. 504
Chicago, IL 60605
Telephone: (312) 922-0140
Ownership %: 100
**Management:**
Maygene Daniels ................................President
**Editorial:**
Richard J. Cox .................................Editor
Teresa M. Brinati ...................Managing Editor
Barbara Craig ....................Book Review Editor
**Desc.:** Essays on archival theory and practice in North America, as well as the international scene. Book reviews also included.
**Readers:** Archivists in libraries, universities, museums, historical societies, religious organizations, government, businesses & other special collections, as well as others with interest in cataloging & preserving documents.

## AMERICAN LIBRARIES
23618
50 E. Huron St.
Chicago, IL 60611-2795
Telephone: (312) 280-4216
FAX: (312) 440-0901
Year Established: 1907
Pub. Frequency: 11/yr.
Page Size: 4 color photos/art
Subscrip. Rate: $60/yr.
Freelance Pay: $25-$300
Circulation: 56,000
Circulation Type: paid
**Owner(s):**
American Library Association
50 E. Huron St.
Chicago, IL 60611
Telephone: (312) 944-6780
Ownership %: 100
**Editorial:**
Edith McCormick ........................Senior Editor
Thomas Gaughan ..............................Editor
Leinard Kniffel ........................Managing Editor
Yolanda Spann ...........Administrative Assistant
Carol Kristal .......................Assistant Editor
Beverly Goldberg ....................Associate Editor
**Desc.:** Provides current news and information concerning the library industry. June issue previews annual conference of the American Library Association; September "back-to-work" issue features appropriate material. Departments include: "Quick Bibs" Book Reviews, Datebook, Dedicated Line (actomation developments). In the News, Action Exchange, Reader Forum (letters). Bulletin board (brief supplier ratios). The Source-A Clearinghouse (approx. 18 sections). Facilities and Design (library architecture), Youth-reach (services to young people), and 24 page Classified Advertising. May Issue highlights best reference books.
**Readers:** The 50,000 members of the American Library Association, 2,900 libraries subscribing separately.

## BOOKLIST
24711
50 E. Huron St.
Chicago, IL 60611
Telephone: (312) 944-6780
FAX: (312) 337-6787
Year Established: 1905
Pub. Frequency: 22/yr.
Page Size: standard
Subscrip. Rate: $60/yr. US; $75/yr. foreign
Materials: 23,24,25,26,28,29,30,32
Freelance Pay: negotiable
Circulation: 32,000
Circulation Type: paid
**Owner(s):**
American Library Association
50 E. Huron St.
Chicago, IL 60611
Telephone: (312) 944-6780
Ownership %: 100
**Management:**
Art Beck ......................Advertising Manager
**Editorial:**
Bill Ott ...............................Editor in Chief
Stuart Whitwell ......................Managing Editor
Bill Ott ....................................Art Director
John Mort .........................Book Review Editor
Sally Estes .......................Book Review Editor
Sandy Whiteley ...................Book Review Editor
Irene Wood ................................Film Editor

**Desc.:** Booklist is a program of the American Library Association's Publishing Committee. The purpose is to provide a current guide to materials worthy of consideration for purchase by small and medium-sized public libraries, school media centers, and community college libraries. Materials considered for review, with the exception of books in the non-English-language bibliographies, are limited to works published in English and distributed in the US. Textbooks may be evaluated and selected when relevant for library use. Materials which are highly technical, sectarian, or parochial in character, free materials, and pamphlets are outside the scope of the regular reviewing program. Standard selection criteria consonant with the Library Bill of Rights and its various interpretations as adopted by the Council of the American Library Association are followed. A review in Booklist constitutes a recommendation for library purchase. An * beside a title is a mark of quality, not necessarily of wide appeal or usefulness, and indicates an item selected by the staff as particularly good in its genre. YA at the end of an imprint indicates a book also recommended in the Books for Young Adults section. The editorial and reviewing staff has the responsibility for selection and review of books and audiovisual materials. Editors also assign materials to carefully selected field librarians and media and subject specialists. Selection and annotation of items in special lists are the responsibility of the reviewer.
**Readers:** Public librarians, school librarians & media specialists, college and university librarians, trade book publishers, reading teachers, professors of children's literature, library science and education courses.

## BULLETIN OF BIBLIOGRAPHY
23620
88 Post Rd., W.
Westport, CT 06880
Telephone: (203) 226-3571
FAX: (203) 222-1502
Mailing Address:
   P.O. Box 5007
   Westport, CT 06881
Year Established: 1897
Pub. Frequency: q.
Page Size: standard
Subscrip. Rate: $95/yr.
Circulation: 1,300
Circulation Type: paid
**Owner(s):**
Greenwood Publishing Group, Inc.
88 Post Rd. W.
Westport, CT 06880
Telephone: (203) 226-3571
Ownership %: 100
**Editorial:**
Bernard McTigue ....................Editor in Chief
**Desc.:** A unique publication of bibliographies in the humanities and the social sciences; specializes in topics which contain bibliographical material not accessible through published sources. Advertising rates and specifications available on request from the editor.
**Readers:** Librarians, college students, teachers.

**Materials Accepted/Included:** 01-Business news 02-By-line articles 03-Fashion news 04-Food news 05-Freelance copy 06-Letters to editor 07-Real estate news 08-Sports news 09-Travel news 10-Book rev. 11-Movie rev. 12-Music rev. 13-TV rev. 14-Theater rev. 15-Coming events 16-Obituaries 17-Question & answer 18-Social announcements 19-Artwork 20-Cartoons 21-Photos 22-TV listings 23-Audio rec. 24-Video rec. 25-Books 26-Films/film clips 27-Personnel news 28-Press releases 29-New product news/photos 30-Trade lit. 31-Contracts awarded 32-Display adv. 33-Classified adv.

4-205

## BULLETIN OF THE MEDICAL LIBRARY ASSOCIATION
23621

6 N. Michigan Ave., #300
Chicago, IL 60602-4805
Telephone: (312) 419-9094
FAX: (312) 419-8950
Year Established: 1911
Pub. Frequency: q.
Page Size: standard
Subscrip. Rate: $42.50/copy N. America;
   $45/copy foreign; $136/yr. N. America;
   $174/yr. foreign
Materials: 02,06,10,16,25,27,28,29,32
Print Process: web offset
Circulation: 6,300
Circulation Type: paid
**Owner(s):**
Medical Library Association
6 N. Michigan Ave., Ste. 300
Chicago, IL 60602-4805
Telephone: (312) 419-9094
FAX: (312) 419-8950
Ownership %: 100
**Management:**
Jacqueline Bastille ...............................President
Carla J. Funk ..................................Publisher
Carla J. Funk ......................Business Manager
**Editorial:**
Naomi Broering ......................Executive Editor
Helen Bagdoyan ....................Associate Editor
Connie Poole ......................Book Review Editor
Logan Ludwig ...............Building Projects Editor
Kimberly Pierceall ..........................Director of
Fred W. Roper ....................Proceedings Editor
Janis F. Brown ..............Software Review Editor
**Desc.:** Valuable resource and desk
   reference on the latest technologies and
   products in the health information field.
   Every issue features noted experts
   addressing critical topics in information
   management.
**Readers:** Libraries and librarians, including
   library directors and instructors, health
   sciences professionals.
**Deadline:** ads-1st of 2nd. mo. prior to pub.
   date

## CATHOLIC LIBRARY WORLD
23622

Duchesne Academy
10202 Memorial Dr.
Houston, TX 77024
Telephone: (713) 468-8211
Year Established: 1929
Pub. Frequency: q.
Page Size: standard
Subscrip. Rate: free to members; $60/yr.
Circulation: 950
Circulation Type: controlled & paid
**Owner(s):**
Catholic Library Association
461 W. Lancaster Ave.
Haverford, PA 19041
Telephone: (215) 649-5250
Ownership %: 100
**Management:**
Barbara Weathers ................Chairman Editorial
                                                           Board
**Editorial:**
Allen Gruenke ......................................Editor
**Desc.:** Covers media of Catholic interest,
   professional, children's and young adult
   books. Articles on libraries, library
   methods, library education and literature
   and library professionalism. Departments
   include book reviews for grade school
   libraries and high school libraries and
   professional. Also review reference
   books, books for parish libraries,
   professional titles, adult titles, and A/V
   materials.
**Readers:** Members of Catholic Library
   Association, professional librarians.

## CHOICE
23623

100 Riverview Center
Middletown, CT 06457
Telephone: (203) 347-6933
Year Established: 1964
Pub. Frequency: 11/yr.
Page Size: standard
Subscrip. Rate: $160/yr. domestic;
   $180/yr. foreign
Materials: 10
Circulation: 4,800
Circulation Type: paid
**Owner(s):**
American Library Association
50 E. Huron St.
Chicago, IL 60611
Telephone: (312) 944-6780
Ownership %: 100
**Management:**
Patricia E. Sabosik ..........................Publisher
Art Beck ....................................Sales Manager
**Editorial:**
Terry Farish ....................................Editor
Judith Douville ....................................Editor
Kenneth McLintock ....................................Editor
Helen MacLam ....................................Editor
Robert Balay ....................................Editor
Rebecca Bartlett Fischer ....................Editor
Francine Graf ......................Managing Editor
Dolores LaPointe ......................Advertising
Clare M. Hoover ...............Production Director
**Desc.:** Publishes reviews of books,
   periodicals, audiovisual material and
   microcomputer software suitable for
   college and university libraries with a
   selection emphasis on titles suitable for
   undergraduate library collections. More
   than 6,500 reviews are published
   annually from US and other English-
   language publishers. Reviews are written
   by teaching faculty in US and Canadian
   academic institutions and cover
   publications in the Humanities, Social
   Sciences, and Science & Technology.
   Choice is used by faculty and by
   librarians for collection development and
   acquisition; circulation is international.
**Readers:** College, university and
   community college graduates;
   community college, public and school
   libraries; also federal, foreign and
   national libraries, private individuals,
   publishers, and wholesalers.

## COLLEGE & RESEARCH LIBRARIES
23624

50 E. Huron St.
Chicago, IL 60611-2795
Telephone: (312) 944-6780
FAX: (312) 440-9374
Year Established: 1939
Pub. Frequency: bi-m.
Page Size: tabloid
Subscrip. Rate: $50/yr. U.S.; $55/yr. in
   Canada, Spain; $60/yr. elsewhere
Circulation: 13,000
Circulation Type: paid
**Owner(s):**
American Library Association
50 E. Huron St.
Chicago, IL 60611
Telephone: (312) 944-6780
Ownership %: 100
**Management:**
Tom Kirk ..........................................President
Stuart Foster ....................Advertising Manager
**Editorial:**
Gloriana St. Clair ..............................Editor
Stephen Lehmann ...........Book Review Editor
Bob Walther ......................Book Review Editor
**Desc.:** Articles of interest to college and
   research libraries.

**Readers:** Librarians and library
   administrators academic and research
   libraries.

## DOCUMENT IMAGE AUTOMATION
61564

11 Ferry Ln., W.
Westport, CT 06880
Telephone: (203) 226-6967
Year Established: 1982
Pub. Frequency: 6/yr.
Page Size: standard
Subscrip. Rate: $125/yr.
Circulation: 800
Circulation Type: paid
**Owner(s):**
Meckler Publishing Corp.
11 Ferry Ln., W.
Westport, CT 06880-5808
Telephone: (203) 226-6967
Ownership %: 100
**Management:**
Lise Despres ....................................Manager
**Editorial:**
Judith Roth ......................................Editor

## EMERGENCY LIBRARIAN
57280

Dept. 284
P.O. Box C34069
Seattle, WA 98124-1069
Telephone: (604) 925-0266
FAX: (604) 925-0566
Year Established: 1973
Pub. Frequency: 5/yr.
Page Size: standard
Subscrip. Rate: $47/yr. Canada
Circulation: 10,000
Circulation Type: paid
**Owner(s):**
Ken Haycock & Associates, Inc.
P.O. Box 284
810 W. Broadway
Vancouver BC, V52 4C9, Canada CN
Telephone: (604) 925-0266
FAX: (604) 925-0566
Ownership %: 100
**Management:**
Ken Haycock ....................................Publisher
**Editorial:**
Ken Haycock ......................................Editor
Michele Farquharson ...............Associate Editor
**Desc.:** A professional journal for teachers
   and librarians with children and young
   adults in school and public libraries.

## GOVERNMENT PUBLICATIONS REVIEW
66479

660 White Plains Rd.
Tarrytown, NY 10591-5153
Telephone: (914) 524-9200
FAX: (914) 333-2444
Year Established: 1974
Pub. Frequency: bi-m.
Subscrip. Rate: $180/yr.
Circulation: 1,500
Circulation Type: paid
**Owner(s):**
Pergamon Press, Inc.
660 White Plains Rd.
Tarrytown, NY 10591-5153
Telephone: (914) 524-9200
Ownership %: 100
**Editorial:**
Steven Zink ......................................Editor
**Desc.:** Covers production, distribution,
   library handling, bibliographic control,
   accessibility and use of government
   information in all formats and at all
   levels.

## HORN BOOK GUIDE, THE
70356

11 Beacon St.
Ste. 1000
Boston, MA 02108
Telephone: (617) 227-1555
FAX: (617) 523-0299
Pub. Frequency: s-a.
Materials: 10
**Owner(s):**
The Horn Book, Inc.
11 Beacon St.
Ste. 1000
Boston, MA 02108
Telephone: (617) 227-1555
Ownership %: 100
**Management:**
Thomas Todd ....................................President
Thomas Todd ..................................Publisher
Eden Edwards ...............Advertising Manager
**Editorial:**
Laren Adams ....................Managing Editor
Anita Silvey ......................Book Review Editor
**Desc.:** Reviews 2,000 books per issue.

## HORN BOOK MAGAZINE, THE
24756

11 Beacon St.
Ste. 1000
Boston, MA 02108
Telephone: (617) 227-1555
FAX: (617) 523-0299
Year Established: 1924
Pub. Frequency: bi-m.
Page Size: standard
Subscrip. Rate: $6.95/issue; $35/yr. for
   individuals; $42/yr. for institutions
Materials: 32,33
Circulation: 20,000
Circulation Type: paid
**Owner(s):**
The Horn Book, Inc.
11 Beacon St.
Ste. 1000
Boston, MA 02108
Telephone: (617) 227-1555
Ownership %: 100
**Management:**
Thomas Todd ....................................President
Thomas Todd ..................................Publisher
Eden Edwards ...............Advertising Manager
**Editorial:**
Anita Silvey ......................................Editor
Lauren Adams ....................Managing Editor
Anita Silvey ......................Book Review Editor
**Desc.:** Concerns children's and young
   people's books. Features reviews of
   children's books; lists of recommended
   paperbacks; and articles about children's
   literature.
**Readers:** Children's and school librarians,
   professionals; parents, booksellers,
   children's book editors, writers and
   teachers.

## INFORMATION RETRIEVAL & LIBRARY AUTOMATION
59133

P.O. Box 88
Mount Airy, MD 21771
Telephone: (301) 829-1496
Year Established: 1965
Pub. Frequency: m.
Page Size: standard
Subscrip. Rate: $66/yr. US; $79.50/yr.
   foreign
Freelance Pay: negotiable
Circulation: 1,160
Circulation Type: paid
**Owner(s):**
Lomond Publishing, Inc.
P.O. Box 88
Mount Airy, MD 21771
Telephone: (301) 829-1496
Ownership %: 100

**Materials Accepted/Included:** 01-Business news 02-By-line articles 03-Fashion news 04-Food news 05-Freelance copy 06-Letters to editor 07-Real estate news 08-Sports news 09-Travel news 10-Book rev. 11-Movie rev. 12-Music rev. 13-TV rev. 14-Theater rev. 15-Coming events 16-Obituaries 17-Question & answer 18-Social announcements 19-Artwork 20-Cartoons 21-Photos 22-TV listings 23-Audio rec. 24-Video rec. 25-Books 26-Films/film clips 27-Personnel news 28-Press releases 29-New product news/photos 30-Trade lit. 31-Contracts awarded 32-Display adv. 33-Classified adv.

**Editorial:**
Susan W. Johnson .................................Editor
Maxine Hattery ..........................Managing Editor
**Desc.:** News, articles, and announcements on new techniques, equipment and software in information services for both the public and private sectors.
**Readers:** Librarians and information system specialists.

## INFORMATION TECHNOLOGY & LIBRARIES (ITAL)
23626

50 E. Huron St.
Chicago, IL 60611
Telephone: (312) 280-5413
FAX: (312) 944-8741
Year Established: 1968
Pub. Frequency: q.
Page Size: standard
Subscrip. Rate: $40/yr. non-members; free to members
Materials: 02,06,10,28,32
Circulation: 7,000
Circulation Type: controlled
**Owner(s):**
American Library Association (ALA)
50 E. Huron St.
Chicago, IL 60611
Telephone: (312) 944-6780
Ownership %: 100
**Management:**
Tamara Miller .........................................President
Stuart Foster ......................Advertising Manager
**Editorial:**
Tom Leonhardt ...........................................Editor
**Desc.:** Editorials and articles are concerned with library automation systems, telecommunications, information networks, and the use of audiovisual and video techniques, equipment and systems in libraries. Special features include: Communications News Notes, Announcements and Reviews.
**Readers:** Librarians and others interested in or working with automation, video, telecommunications or audiovisual systems as used in libraries.

## JOURNAL OF YOUTH SERVICES IN LIBRARIES
23631

50 E. Huron St.
Chicago, IL 60611
Telephone: (312) 280-2163
FAX: (312) 280-3257
Year Established: 1987
Pub. Frequency: q.
Page Size: standard
Subscrip. Rate: $40/yr.
Circulation: 9,500
Circulation Type: paid
**Owner(s):**
American Library Association
50 E. Huron St.
Chicago, IL 60611
Telephone: (312) 280-2163
FAX: (312) 280-3257
Ownership %: 100
**Management:**
Ann Weeks .........................Business Manager
Susan Roman .....................Business Manager
**Editorial:**
Donald Kenney ...........................................Editor
Linda Wilson ...............................................Editor
**Desc.:** New and articles of interest to children and young adult librarians.
**Readers:** Children's and young adult librarians in schools, public and institutional libraries; teachers of children's and young adult literature in colleges, and publishers of children's and young adult media.

## LAW LIBRARY JOURNAL
23627

American Assn. of Law Libr. Hdq.
53 W. Jackson
Chicago, IL 60604
Telephone: (312) 939-4764
FAX: (312) 431-1097
Mailing Address:
    Duke Univ. Sch. of Law Library
    Durham, NC 27706
Year Established: 1907
Pub. Frequency: q.
Page Size: standard
Subscrip. Rate: $12.50/issue; $50/yr.
Circulation: 5,400
Circulation Type: paid
**Owner(s):**
American Assn. of Law Libraries
63 W. Jackson Blvd.
Chicago, IL 60604
Telephone: (312) 939-4764
Ownership %: 100
**Management:**
Roger H. Parent ....................Executive Director
Peter Beck ..........................Advertising Manager
Peter Beck ...........................Business Manager
**Editorial:**
Richard A. Danner ......................................Editor
**Desc.:** Carries articles on law librarianship of an educational, scientific and research character; contains bibliographies in the field of law, information on the work of the American Association of Law Libraries and biographical data concerning the members of the association.
**Readers:** Law librarians, book dealers, legal scholars, general librarians.

## LIBRARY ADMINISTRATION & MANAGEMENT
67050

50 E. Huron St.
Chicago, IL 60611-2795
Telephone: (312) 944-6780
FAX: (312) 440-9374
Year Established: 1975
Pub. Frequency: q.
Page Size: standard
Subscrip. Rate: $50/yr. US.; $60/yr. foreign
Circulation: 6,000
Circulation Type: paid
**Owner(s):**
American Library Association
50 E. Huron St.
Chicago, IL 60611-2795
Telephone: (312) 944-6780
Ownership %: 100
**Management:**
Sue Stroyan .........................................President
Pat Sabosik ......................Advertising Manager
**Editorial:**
Fred Heath ................................................Editor

## LIBRARY JOURNAL
23628

249 W. 17th St.
New York, NY 10011
Telephone: (212) 463-6819
FAX: (212) 463-6734
Year Established: 1876
Pub. Frequency: 20/yr.
Page Size: standard
Subscrip. Rate: $87.50/yr.
Freelance Pay: negotiable
Circulation: 24,460
Circulation Type: paid
**Owner(s):**
Reed Publishing, U.S.A./Cahners Magazine Division
275 Washington St.
Newton, MA 02158
Telephone: (617) 964-3030
Ownership %: 100

**Management:**
Fred Ciporen .......................................Publisher
**Editorial:**
John N. Berry, III ......................Editor in Chief
Francine Fialkoff .....................Executive Editor
Bette - Lee Fox ....................Managing Editor
Barbara Hoffert ................Book Review Editor
**Desc.:** Full service publication addressed to the needs and interests of those who buy book and non-book materials and equipment for public & academic libraries. 6,100 critical book reviews per annum. Departments include: Magazines & Professional Reading. Carries appointments, association news, short features on library developments, etc.
**Readers:** Public, academic, business, and special libraries.

## LIBRARY RESOURCES & TECHNICAL SERVICES
23629

50 E. Huron St.
Chicago, IL 60611
Telephone: (312) 280-5034
Year Established: 1957
Pub. Frequency: q.
Page Size: standard
Subscrip. Rate: $12 newsstand; free to members; $45/yr. others
Circulation: 9,000
Circulation Type: free & paid
**Owner(s):**
Assn. for Library Collections & Tech. Services
50 E. Huron St.
Chicago, IL 60611
Telephone: (312) 280-5031
Ownership %: 100
**Management:**
Stuart Foster ......................Advertising Manager
**Editorial:**
Richard P. Smiraglia ...............Executive Editor
Karen Muller .......................Managing Editor
**Desc.:** Articles of interest to technical services librarians on library acquisitions, library cataloging and classification, serials acquisitions and cataloging, reproduction of library materials, and library collection development. Preservation of library materials.
**Readers:** Library technical services personnel in the US and abroad.

## LIBRARY TRENDS
58611

1325 South Oak St.
Champaign, IL 61820-6903
Telephone: (217) 333-8935
Year Established: 1952
Pub. Frequency: q.
Page Size: standard
Subscrip. Rate: $75/yr.; $82/yr. foreign
Materials: 02,10,32
Print Process: offset
Circulation: 3,800
Circulation Type: paid
**Owner(s):**
School of Library & Information Science
Library & Information Science
Urbana, IL 61801-1359
Telephone: (217) 333-3280
Ownership %: 100
**Management:**
James Dowling ......................................Manager
**Editorial:**
F.W. Lancaster .........................................Editor

**Desc.:** A journal of librarianship, which provides a medium for valuative recapitulation of current thought and practice, searching for those ideas and procedures which hold the greatest potentialities for the future. Focuses on library and information science topics of interest primarily to practicing librarians and information scientists and secondarily to educations and students.
**Readers:** Librarians and library science teachers.

## PUBLIC LIBRARIES
65756

50 E. Huron St.
Chicago, IL 60611
Telephone: (312) 944-6780
Year Established: 1970
Pub. Frequency: bi-m.
Subscrip. Rate: $50/yr.
Circulation: 5,781
Circulation Type: paid
**Owner(s):**
Public Library Association
50 E. Huran St.
Chicago, IL 60611
Telephone: (312) 944-6780
Ownership %: 100
**Editorial:**
Sandra Garrison ........................................Editor
**Desc.:** Contains news and articles of interest to public libraries.

## REFERENCE & RESEARCH BOOK NEWS
59135

5606 N.E. Hassalo St.
Portland, OR 97213
Telephone: (503) 281-9230
FAX: (503) 284-8859
Year Established: 1986
Pub. Frequency: 8/yr.
Page Size: standard
Subscrip. Rate: $40/yr. individual; $58/yr. institution
Freelance Pay: $.03/wd.
Circulation: 1,700
Circulation Type: paid
**Owner(s):**
Book News, Inc.
5606 N.E. Hassalo St.
Portland, OR 97213
Telephone: (503) 281-9230
Ownership %: 100
**Management:**
Fred Gullette ......................................Publisher
**Editorial:**
Jane Erskine ..............................................Editor
**Desc.:** Concise, subject-arranged reviews of new scholarly and reference books appropriate for academic and public libraries and librarians.
**Readers:** Librarians and faculty responsible for book selection and acquisition.

## RQ
24815

50 E. Huron St.
Chicago, IL 60611
Telephone: (312) 280-4398
FAX: (312) 944-8085
Year Established: 1960
Pub. Frequency: q.
Page Size: standard
Subscrip. Rate: $12/issue; $42/yr.
Circulation: 6,800
Circulation Type: paid
**Owner(s):**
American Library Assn., Ref. & Adult Svcs. Div.
50 East Huron St.
Chicago, IL 60611
Telephone: (312) 280-4398
Ownership %: 100

**Materials Accepted/Included:** 01-Business news 02-By-line articles 03-Fashion news 04-Food news 05-Freelance copy 06-Letters to editor 07-Real estate news 08-Sports news 09-Travel news 10-Book rev. 11-Movie rev. 12-Music rev. 13-TV rev. 14-Theater rev. 15-Coming events 16-Obituaries 17-Question & answer 18-Social announcements 19-Artwork 20-Cartoons 21-Photos 22-TV listings 23-Audio rec. 24-Video rec. 25-Books 26-Films/film clips 27-Personnel news 28-Press releases 29-New product news/photos 30-Trade lit. 31-Contracts awarded 32-Display adv. 33-Classified adv.

4-207

**Editorial:**
Danny P. Wallace .........................................Editor
Connie Van Fleet .........................................Editor
David Kohl ..........................Book Review Editor
Danny P. Wallace ........................Miscellaneous
Judy Dye ..........................................Review Editor

**Desc.:** The official journal of the reference and Adult Services Division of the American Library Association. The purpose of RQ is to disseminate information of interest to reference librarians, bibliographers, adult services librarians, those in collection departments and selection, and others interested in public services. The scope of the journal includes all aspects of library service to adults, and reference service and collection development at every level and for all types of libraries. The journal follows a policy of double-blind referencing of articles in advance of publication.

**Readers:** Subscribers and membership of the division.

---

23630

## SCHOOL LIBRARY JOURNAL
249 W. 17th St.
New York, NY 10011
Telephone: (212) 463-6759
FAX: (212) 242-6987
Year Established: 1954
Pub. Frequency: m.
Page Size: standard
Subscrip. Rate: $67/yr.
Circulation: 41,265
Circulation Type: paid
**Owner(s):**
Cahners Magazine Division
249 W. 17th St.
New York, NY 10011
Telephone: (212) 463-6759
Ownership %: 100
**Management:**
Neil A. Perlman .........................................Publisher
Carlton H. Thiele ...............Advertising Manager
**Editorial:**
Lillian N. Gerhardt .......................Editor in Chief
Bertha M. Cheatham ...............Managing Editor
Trevelyn E. Jones .............Book Review Editor
**Desc.:** For librarians serving children and young adults in schools and public libraries.
**Readers:** Librarians who work with children and youth in public libraries and school media centers.

---

24824

## SCHOOL LIBRARY MEDIA QUARTERLY
50 E. Huron St.
Chicago, IL 60611
Telephone: (312) 944-6780
FAX: (312) 664-7459
Year Established: 1981
Pub. Frequency: q.
Page Size: standard
Subscrip. Rate: $40/yr. non-members; $20/yr. members
Circulation: 8,220
Circulation Type: paid
**Owner(s):**
American Library Association
50 E. Huron St.
Chicago, IL 60611
Telephone: (312) 944-6780
Ownership %: 100
**Editorial:**
Mary Kay Biagini .........................................Editor
Michael B. Eisenberg .......................Columnist
Thomas L. Hart .................................Columnist
Gloria McClannahan .........................Columnist
Virginia Kalb ......................................Columnist
Eileen D. Cooke ...............................Columnist

---

**Desc.:** Official journal of the American Association of School Librarians. The purpose of the journal is to publish substantive articles to inform, inspire motivate, and assist school library media practitioners in integrating theory and practice; to encourage scholarship and research in the school library media field and to provide information on new developments in the library media field, education, psychology, and other related disciplines.
**Readers:** Building-level library media specialists, supervisors, library educators, and others concerned with the development of library media programs and services from preschool through high school.

---

66000

## UNIVERSITY PRESS BOOK NEWS
5600 N.E. Hassalo St.
Portland, OR 97213
Telephone: (503) 281-9230
Year Established: 1989
Pub. Frequency: 8/yr.
Page Size: standard
Subscrip. Rate: $40/yr.
Freelance Pay: $.03/wd.
Circulation: 1,700
Circulation Type: paid
**Owner(s):**
Book News, Inc.
5600 N.E. Hassalo St.
Portland, OR 97213
Telephone: (503) 281-9230
Ownership %: 100
**Management:**
Fred Gullette .........................................Publisher
**Editorial:**
Jane Grskine .........................................Editor
**Desc.:** Concise reviews of new books from the world's university presses.
**Readers:** Librarians and faculty responsible for book selection and acquisition, bookstore customers.

---

23632

## WILSON LIBRARY BULLETIN
950 University Ave.
Bronx, NY 10452-4221
Telephone: (718) 588-8400
FAX: (718) 681-1511
Year Established: 1914
Pub. Frequency: m.
Page Size: standard
Subscrip. Rate: $52/yr. US & Canada; $58/yr. foreign
Materials: 01,02,06,19,20,21,23,24,25,28, 29,32,33
Freelance Pay: $100-$500
Circulation: 10,036
Circulation Type: paid
**Owner(s):**
The H.W. Wilson Co.
950 University Ave.
Bronx, NY 10452
Telephone: (718) 588-8400
FAX: (718) 579-3610
Ownership %: 100
**Management:**
Leo Weins .........................................President
Leo Weins .........................................Publisher
**Editorial:**
Linda Mark ...................................Senior Editor
GraceAnne DeCandido .........................Editor
Raissa Fomerand ..........................Advertising
Michael O'Connor ..........................Advertising
Lynn Amos .................................Art Director
Irene Astorga .................Assistant Art Director
Janine Stanley - Dunham ........Associate Editor
Alan Mahony .......................Associate Editor
Karen Moller ..................Editorial Assistant

---

**Desc.:** Contains news, articles, features, and special reports on matters of interest to librarians and information specialists working in all kinds of assignments in both profit and nonprofit organizations. The magazine is particularly interested in technological advances in communications, WLB reviews books, films, recordings, software, databases and CD-ROMs.
**Readers:** Librarians in public, school, special, college and university libraries.
**Deadline:** story-3 mo. prior to pub. date; news-2 mo. prior; photo-2 mo. prior; ads-2 mo. prior

---

## Group 146-Lighting

23634

## HOME LIGHTING & ACCESSORIES
1033 Clifton Ave.
Clifton, NJ 07013
Telephone: (201) 779-1600
FAX: (201) 779-3242
Mailing Address:
P.O. Box 2147
Clifton, NJ 07015
Year Established: 1923
Pub. Frequency: m.
Page Size: standard
Subscrip. Rate: $6/copy; $30/yr.; $60/3 yrs.
Freelance Pay: $60/printed pg.
Circulation: 10,000
Circulation Type: paid
**Owner(s):**
Doctorow Communications, Inc.
1033 Clifton Avenue
Clifton, NJ 07013
Telephone: (201) 779-1600
Ownership %: 100
**Management:**
Donald Doctorow .................................President
Jeff Doctorow .........................................Publisher
**Editorial:**
Linda Longo .........................................Editor
Jon Doctorow ....................Circulation Director
Deborah Schwartz .............Production Director
**Desc.:** Covers various marketing and retailing aspects as applied to portable lamps, lamp shades, decorative accessories and residential lighting fixtures/customer relations, sales training, trends, shop layout, design and operation. Carries industry and company news, new promotions, appointments, literature, patents.
**Readers:** Retailers of lamps and residential lighting. Manufacturers of residential lighting.

---

23635

## LIGHTING DESIGN & APPLICATION
345 E. 47th St.
New York, NY 10017
Telephone: (212) 705-7000
Year Established: 1971
Pub. Frequency: m.
Page Size: standard
Subscrip. Rate: $4/issue; $35/yr.
Circulation: 10,838
Circulation Type: paid
**Owner(s):**
Illuminating Engineering Society/Exec. Dir. Publ.
345 E. 47th St.
New York, NY 10017
Telephone: (212) 705-7913
Ownership %: 100
**Management:**
Beth Bay .........................Advertising Manager
**Editorial:**
Kevin Heslin .........................................Editor
Roslyn Lowe ...............Administrative Assistant
Tony Picco .........................................Art Director

---

Lois Burgner .........................Editorial Associate
**Desc.:** Coverage on practical and interesting lighting developments and ideas, including technical material. Details of fascinating new concepts in lighting installations. Discussions of lighting for environmental conditioning, art and esthetics, and energy utilization (lighting). New products for the lighting field. Economics and legal considerations in lighting. News of people and company activities. Feature articles on current lighting applications including Health Care, Industrial, Theater, Television, Recreation, Outdoor, Indoor, Education, Behavior, Office and Computerized Lighting. Book Reviews; Surveys of Lighting Manufacturers; Projects in Progress; "Reflections on the Past"; Lighting Design in Retrospect; "Views on the Visual Environment".
**Readers:** Lighting designers, engineers, architects, engineering colleges; lighting manufacturers and marketing personnel.

---

23636

## LIGHTING DIMENSIONS
32 W. 18th St.
New York, NY 10011-4612
Telephone: (212) 229-2965
FAX: (212) 229-2084
Year Established: 1977
Pub. Frequency: 9/yr.
Page Size: standard
Subscrip. Rate: $24.95/yr.
Materials: 01,05,06,10,11,13,14,21,23,24, 25,26,29,32,33
Freelance Pay: $100-$400/article
Print Process: offset
Circulation: 10,000
Circulation Type: paid
**Owner(s):**
Entertainment Technology Communications Corp.
32 W. 18th St.
New York, NY 10011-4612
Telephone: (212) 229-2965
Ownership %: 100
**Management:**
Patricia MacKay .........................................Publisher
**Editorial:**
Denise Tilles ...............................Managing Editor
Jacqueline Tien .................Associate Publisher
R. Harvey Swaine ...............Circulation Director
**Desc.:** Serves lighting professionals active in all areas of the lighting industry including manufacturing, designing & specifying. Editorial coverage includes problem-solving articles on both entertainment & architectural-related lighting topics, as well as general industry & product news.
**Readers:** Lighting professionals active in entertainment lighting & architectural or interior design lighting. Also, manufacturers & designers of lighting products.
**Deadline:** story-4 mos. prior to pub. date; news-4 mos.; photo-4 mos.; ads-1 mo.

---

69702

## LIGHTING MANAGEMENT & MAINTENANCE
34-C Washington Rd.
Princeton Junction, NJ 08550
Telephone: (609) 799-4900
FAX: (609) 799-7032
Year Established: 1953
Pub. Frequency: m.
Page Size: standard
Subscrip. Rate: $110/yr.
Materials: 02,06,27,28,29,30,32
Circulation: 1,000
Circulation Type: paid

---

**Materials Accepted/Included:** 01-Business news 02-By-line articles 03-Fashion news 04-Food news 05-Freelance copy 06-Letters to editor 07-Real estate news 08-Sports news 09-Travel news 10-Book rev. 11-Movie rev. 12-Music rev. 13-TV rev. 14-Theater rev. 15-Coming events 16-Obituaries 17-Question & answer 18-Social announcements 19-Artwork 20-Cartoons 21-Photos 22-TV listings 23-Audio rec. 24-Video rec. 25-Books 26-Films/film clips 27-Personnel news 28-Press releases 29-New product news/photos 30-Trade lit. 31-Contracts awarded 32-Display adv. 33-Classified adv.

**Owner(s):**
Creative Marketing Alliance, Inc.
34-C Washington Rd.
Princeton Junction, NJ 08550
Telephone: (609) 799-4900
Ownership %: 100
**Editorial:**
Jeff Barnhart .............................Editor in Chief
Craig DiLouie ...........................Managing Editor
Diane Knott ..............................Art Director
Natalie Heringes .........Publications Coordinator
**Desc.:** Official publication of the
InterNational Association of Lighting
Management Companies. Supports,
promotes and encourages the success
and growth of companies and
organizations which participate in the
strategic management of lighting
systems.
**Readers:** Lighting management
companies, manufacturers end users,
utilities and other interested parties.
**Deadline:** story-1 mo. prior to pub. date

**LIGHTWAVE**                                      66619
10 Tara Blvd.
5th Fl.
Nashua, NH 03062-2801
Telephone: (603) 891-9212
FAX: (603) 891-0587
Year Established: 1984
Pub. Frequency: m.
Page Size: tabloid
Subscrip. Rate: $59/yr. US.; $81/yr.
Canada; $99/yr. elsewhere
Materials: 01,02,06,15,20,27,28,29,30,32,
33,
Print Process: web offset
Circulation: 28,211
Circulation Type: controlled & paid
**Owner(s):**
Pennwell Publishing Co.
Ten Tara Blvd.
Fifth Fl.
Nashua, NH 03062-2801
Telephone: (603) 891-9212
Ownership %: 100
**Editorial:**
George Kotelly ...........................Senior Editor
Mary Koff ..................................Assistant Editor
**Desc.:** Fiber optics technology and
applications worldwide (telecomm,
datacomm, video).
**Readers:** Corporate and technical
management.

**TODAY'S LIGHTING DISTRIBUTOR**          69705
2207 Elmwood Ave.
Buffalo, NY 14216
Telephone: (716) 875-3670
FAX: (716) 875-0734
Year Established: 1979
Pub. Frequency: m.
Page Size: standard
Subscrip. Rate: $110/yr.
Circulation: 1,000
Circulation Type: paid
**Owner(s):**
Creative Marketing Alliance, Inc.
34-C Washington Rd.
Princeton Junction, NJ 08550
Telephone: (609) 799-7900
Ownership %: 100
**Editorial:**
Russ MyKytyn ...........................Editor in Chief
Craig DiLouie ...........................Managing Editor
Diane Knott ..............................Art Director
Natalie Heringes .........Publications Coordinator
**Desc.:** Forum for issues concerning the
development, specification, marketing
and sale of advanced lighting products.

**Readers:** Lighting distributors and allied
manufacturers.

## Group 148-Lumber & Forestry

**AMERICAN FORESTS**                               23064
1516 P. St., N.W.
Washington, DC 20005
Telephone: (202) 667-3300
FAX: (202) 667-2407
Mailing Address:
P.O. Box 2000
Washington, DC 20013
Year Established: 1875
Pub. Frequency: bi-m.
Page Size: standard
Subscrip. Rate: $30/yr.
Freelance Pay: $300-$700/article
Circulation: 30,000
Circulation Type: paid
**Owner(s):**
American Forest
P.O. Box 2000
Washington, DC 20005
Telephone: (202) 667-3300
Ownership %: 100
**Management:**
Donald C. Willeke .......................President
R. Neil Sampson ........................Publisher
**Editorial:**
Bill Rooney .................................Editor
Michelle Robbins ...........Managing Editor
Cindy Krick .................Advertising Director
Gerald Fox ..................Assistant Editor
Tricia Taylor ................Assistant Editor
**Desc.:** The magazine of trees and forests.
Runs from 500-2,000 words with black
and white and color photos.
**Readers:** Those interested in conservation
and forests.

**BAROMETER**                                      68849
522 S.W. Fifth Ave.
Portland, OR 97204-2122
Telephone: (503) 224-3930
FAX: (503) 224-3934
Pub. Frequency: w.
Page Size: standard
Subscrip. Rate: $48/yr.
**Owner(s):**
Western Wood Products Association
522 S.W. Fifth Ave.
Portland, OR 97204-2122
Telephone: (503) 224-3930
Ownership %: 100
**Desc.:** Reports lumber statistics for 12
western states.

**CROW'S WEEKLY REPORT &**                         23642
**FOREST INDUSTRY JOURNAL**
9550 S.W. Beaverton-Hillsdale Hwy.
Portland, OR 97225
Telephone: (503) 646-8075
FAX: (503) 646-9971
Mailing Address:
P.O. Box 25749
Portland, OR 97225
Year Established: 1921
Pub. Frequency: w.
Page Size: standard
Subscrip. Rate: $225/yr.
Materials: 01,28,32
Freelance Pay: varies
**Owner(s):**
C.C. Crow Publications, Inc.
Telephone: (503) 297-1535
Ownership %: 100
**Management:**
Frank J. Vetorino ...........................Publisher
**Editorial:**
Sam Sherrill ...........................Executive Editor
Linda Barr ..............................Assistant Editor

Rich Nelson .......................Marketing Manager
**Desc.:** Features concern manufacturing
and marketing of wood products.
Includes 5 pages of prices as a guide to
trading levels reported that week on
lumber and plywood items,
transportation, marketing and promotion,
wholesale and retail activities, end-use
applications of wood. Publicity material
is welcomed and considered on basis of
reader interest. Editorial departments
include: industry news, people, calendar,
futures.
**Readers:** Marketing executives and
management of lumber and wood
products manufacturers, lumber,
plywood railroads, prefab home
manufacturers.

**FOREST FARMER MAGAZINE**                         23066
P.O. Box 95385
Atlanta, GA 30347
Telephone: (404) 325-2954
FAX: (404) 325-2955
Year Established: 1941
Pub. Frequency: 6/yr.
Page Size: standard
Subscrip. Rate: $40/yr.
Materials: 01,15,21,24,25,27,28
Print Process: offset
Circulation: 5,500
Circulation Type: paid
**Owner(s):**
Forest Farmers Association
P.O. Box 95385
Atlanta, GA 30347
Telephone: (404) 325-2954
Ownership %: 100
**Editorial:**
B. Jack Warren ...................Managing Editor
Harry Rossoll .....................Art Director
Kay Morgareidge ...............Assistant Editor
**Desc.:** A how-to-do-it magazine on forestry
in practice, edited primarily for the
private nonindustrial timberland owner
and operator. Departments include:
National Legislative Roundup, General
News of Forestry Activities in the 16
Southern States, New Products and
Equipment of interest to timberland
owners and operators.
**Readers:** The owners and operators of 40
million acres of timberland in the South
and persons interested in forestry
activities.

**FOREST PRODUCTS JOURNAL**                        23067
2801 Marshall Ct.
Madison, WI 53705
Telephone: (608) 231-1361
FAX: (608) 231-2152
Year Established: 1947
Pub. Frequency: 10/yr.
Page Size: standard
Subscrip. Rate: $115/yr. US; $125/yr.
Canada & Mexico; $155/yr. elsewhere
Materials: 01,02,05,06,10,15,17,25,27,28,
29,30,31,32,33
Circulation: 4,500
Circulation Type: paid
**Owner(s):**
Forest Products Society
2801 Marshall Ct.
Madison, WI 53705
Telephone: (608) 231-1361
FAX: (608) 231-2152
Ownership %: 100
**Management:**
Arthur B. Brauner ......Executive Vice President
Gwen A. Evans ................Advertising Manager
Arthur B. Brauner ................Business Manager
**Editorial:**
Arthur B. Brauner .........................Exec. Editor
Gwen A. Evans ...........................Managing Editor

Erin Bosch ..............................Associate Editor
Gwen A. Evans ............................News Editor
**Desc.:** Editorial content devoted to
production, development, utilization, and
distribution of all phases of forest
products industry. Balance maintained
between technical and non-technical
material. Features current industry news,
society news, etc. Departments include:
Guest Editorial; FPRS Bulletin Board
(member news); Names in News;
Industry News; Employment Referral
Service.
**Readers:** Academic, government, industrial
& research people.
**Deadline:** story-6 wks. prior to mo. of pub.;
news-6 wks. prior; photo-6 wks. prior;
ads-6 wks. prior

**FORESTS & PEOPLE**                               23644
2316 S. MacArthur Dr.
Alexandria, LA 71301
Telephone: (318) 443-2558
FAX: (318) 443-1713
Mailing Address:
P.O. Drawer 5067
Alexandria, LA 71307
Year Established: 1951
Pub. Frequency: q.
Page Size: standard
Subscrip. Rate: $11/yr.
Freelance Pay: $100/story
Circulation: 7,500
Circulation Type: controlled & paid
**Owner(s):**
Louisiana Forestry Association
P.O. Drawer 5067
Alexandria, LA 71307
Telephone: (318) 443-2558
Ownership %: 100
**Management:**
Janet Tompkins ...............Advertising Manager
**Editorial:**
Janet Tompkins ...........................Editor
**Desc.:** Covers the interests and needs of
Louisiana's forest resource, the industry
it supports, and the total forestry
community which benefits from the
forest and its products. Feature material
is on phases of forestry, wood products,
people of the forestry community and
general interest pieces.
**Readers:** Association members, loggers,
land owners, foresters, and general
public.

**ILMDA ADVANTAGE**                                22180
932 S. Spring St.
Springfield, IL 62704
Telephone: (217) 544-5405
FAX: (217) 544-4206
Year Established: 1932
Pub. Frequency: m.
Page Size: standard
Subscrip. Rate: $15/yr.
Circulation: 1,000
Circulation Type: controlled
**Owner(s):**
Illinois Lumber & Material Dealers Assn.
932 S. Spring St.
Springfield, IL 62704
Telephone: (217) 544-5405
Ownership %: 100
**Management:**
Tamiko Kinkade ...............Advertising Manager
**Editorial:**
Tamiko Kinkade ...........................Editor
**Desc.:** Directed to the informational
improvement of lumber and building
material merchants in Illinois and fringe
counties of adjacent states.
**Readers:** Retail lumber & building material
dealers.

**Materials Accepted/Included:** 01-Business news 02-By-line articles 03-Fashion news 04-Food news 05-Freelance copy 06-Letters to editor 07-Real estate news 08-Sports news 09-Travel news
10-Book rev. 11-Movie rev. 12-Music rev. 13-TV rev. 14-Theater rev. 15-Coming events 16-Obituaries 17-Question & answer 18-Social announcements 19-Artwork 20-Cartoons 21-Photos 22-TV listings
23-Audio rec. 24-Video rec. 25-Books 26-Films/film clips 27-Personnel news 28-Press releases 29-New product news/photos 30-Trade lit. 31-Contracts awarded 32-Display adv. 33-Classified adv.

4-209

## INNER VOICE
68848

1175 Charnelton
Eugene, OR 97441
Telephone: (503) 484-2692
FAX: (503) 484-3004
Mailing Address:
PO Box 11615
Eugene, OR 97440
Year Established: 1989
Pub. Frequency: bi-m.
Page Size: tabloid
Subscrip. Rate: $2 newsstand; $25/yr.
Materials: 06,20,21
Print Process: web
Circulation: 17,000
Circulation Type: controlled & paid
**Owner(s):**
Assn. Forest Serv. Employees
Environmental Ethics
P.O. Box 11615
Eugene, OR 97440
Telephone: (503) 484-2692
FAX: (503) 484-3004
Ownership %: 100
**Desc.:** Looks at national forest
management, with articles by forest
service employees who are concerned
with environmental ethics. Explores a
variety of topic areas relating to public
land management.

## JOURNAL OF FORESTRY
23071

5400 Grosvenor Ln.
Bethesda, MD 20814
Telephone: (301) 897-8720
FAX: (301) 897-3690
Year Established: 1902
Pub. Frequency: m.
Page Size: standard
Subscrip. Rate: $100/yr. US & Canada;
$130/yr. foreign
Freelance Pay: varies
Circulation: 20,000
Circulation Type: controlled
**Owner(s):**
Society of American Foresters
5400 Grosvenor La.
Bethesda, MD 20814
Telephone: (301) 897-8720
Ownership %: 100
**Editorial:**
Rebecca Staebler ........................Editor
Amy Wainright ..........................Managing Editor
Sandy Brabick ........Advertising Representative
**Desc.:** Principal interests are in technical
advancement in forestry, results and
applications of research, significant
explorations of conservation policy. The
journal is a professional publication and
is in part refereed. Will consider any
material contributing to the knowledge
and advancement of the forestry
profession. Departments include: Society
Affairs, Policy Watch Letters, In Review,
News Briefs, Classifieds, Opinion.
**Readers:** Professional foresters and
conservationists.

## LOGGERS WORLD
23647

4206 Jackson Hwy.
Chehalis, WA 98532-8425
Telephone: (206) 262-3376
FAX: (206) 262-3337
Year Established: 1964
Pub. Frequency: m.
Page Size: tabloid
Subscrip. Rate: $10/yr.; $18/2 yrs.
Circulation: 16,000
Circulation Type: controlled
**Owner(s):**
Loggers World Publications
Telephone: (206) 262-3376
Ownership %: 100

**Management:**
Michael P. Crouse ......................Publisher
**Editorial:**
Michael P. Crouse ..................Managing Editor
Kevin Core ...............................Advertising
Bill Palmroth ..........................Associate Editor
Finley Hays ............................Editor Emeritus
**Desc.:** A trade magazine concerned with
the logging industry. We have our own
staff writers. We always have 50% or
more editorial. It is a regional
magazine. Our biggest circulation is in
the Pacific Northwest States, but we do
have some circulation in each state. Our
biggest circulation areas are:
Washington, Oregon, California, Idaho,
Montana and Alaska.
**Readers:** Loggers, mill owners, contract
loggers, Weyerhaeuser, Louisiana
Pacific, Georgia Pacific. Also teachers
and many others.

## LOG TRUCKER
68852

4206 Jackson Hwy.
Chehalis, WA 98532
Telephone: (206) 262-3376
Pub. Frequency: m.
Subscrip. Rate: $10/yr.
Circulation: 12,000
Circulation Type: paid
**Owner(s):**
Loggers World Publications
4206 Jackson Hwy.
Chehalis, WA 98532
Telephone: (206) 262-3376
Ownership %: 100
**Editorial:**
Bill Palmroth ..............................Editor
**Desc.:** Logging information for the Western
US, including items for sale, news of log
truck drivers, truck parades and logging
conferences.

## NORTHERN JOURNAL OF
## APPLIED FORESTRY
61631

5400 Grosvenor Ln.
Bethesda, MD 20814-2198
Telephone: (301) 897-8720
FAX: (301) 897-3690
Year Established: 1983
Pub. Frequency: q.
Page Size: standard
Subscrip. Rate: $30/yr. non-members;
$15/yr. members; $75/yr. institutions
Circulation: 14,000
Circulation Type: paid
**Owner(s):**
Society of American Foresters
5400 Grosvenor Ln.
Bethesda, MD 20814
Telephone: (301) 897-8720
Ownership %: 100
**Editorial:**
Harry V. Wiant, Jr. ......................Editor

## NORTHERN LOGGER & TIMBER
## PROCESSER, THE
23649

Eagle Bay Rd.
Old Forge, NY 13420
Telephone: (315) 369-3078
Mailing Address:
P.O. Box 69
Old Forge, NY 13420
Year Established: 1952
Pub. Frequency: m.
Page Size: standard
Subscrip. Rate: $1 newsstand; $10/yr.
Freelance Pay: $.10/wd.
Print Process: offset
Circulation: 13,600
Circulation Type: paid

**Owner(s):**
The Northeastern Logger Association, Inc.
Eagle Bay Rd.
P.O. Box 69
Old Forge, NY 13420
Telephone: (315) 369-3078
Ownership %: 100
**Management:**
George F. Mitchell ..............Business Manager
**Editorial:**
Eric A. Johnson ..............................Editor
George F. Mitchell ..................Managing Editor
**Desc.:** Includes technical and other
material concerning all phases of the
forest products industry such as: forest
management, logging, saw milling, wood
products manufacture. Broad coverage
is given operational and management
problems, research and development,
utilization and marketing, safety. Covers
the Northeastern/Lake States. Monthly
features include: late industry news,
recent publications.
**Readers:** Those in occupation of logging,
sawmilling and forest management.

## OHIO WOODLANDS /
## CONSERVATION IN ACTION
23658

1335 Dublin Rd., Ste. 203D
Columbus, OH 43215
Telephone: (614) 486-6767
FAX: (614) 486-6769
Year Established: 1903
Pub. Frequency: q.
Page Size: standard
Subscrip. Rate: $8/yr.
Circulation: 4,000
**Owner(s):**
Ohio Forestry Association
1335 Dublin Rd., Ste. 203D
Columbus, OH 43215
Telephone: (614) 486-6767
Ownership %: 100
**Management:**
Ron Cornell ..............................Publisher
**Editorial:**
Ron Cornell ..............................Editor
**Desc.:** It is aimed at Ohio's forest
industries, woodland owners, and
individuals interested in our
natural resources and its use and
management. The magazine is placed in
all Ohio school libraries. Contains a
center section aimed at teachers to help
in teaching conservation and the wise
use of our natural resources.
**Readers:** Woodland owners.

## PENNSYLVANIA FORESTS
61710

56 E. Main St.
Mechanicsburg, PA 17055
Telephone: (717) 766-5371
Year Established: 1886
Pub. Frequency: q.
Page Size: standard
Subscrip. Rate: $20/yr. individuals.; $25/yr.
institutions.; $10/yr. student libraries
Materials: 01,02,06,15,27,28,32,33
Print Process: offset
Circulation: 3,200
Circulation Type: paid
**Owner(s):**
Pennsylvania Forestry Association
56 E. Main
Mechanicsburg, PA 17055
Telephone: (717) 766-5371
Ownership %: 100
**Editorial:**
Sue Haskins ..............................Editor
**Desc.:** Dedicated to environmental
protection and wise natural resource
use.
**Readers:** General audience.
**Deadline:** story-Jan., Apr., Jul., & Oct. 15

## RANDOM LENGTHS LOCATOR
69544

P.O. Box 867
Eugene, OR 97440-0867
Telephone: (503) 686-9925
FAX: (503) 686-9629
Year Established: 1983
Pub. Frequency: m.
Subscrip. Rate: $30/yr.
Circulation: 13,000
Circulation Type: paid
**Owner(s):**
Random Lengths Publications, Inc.
P.O. Box 867
Eugene, OR 97440-0867
Telephone: (503) 686-9925
Ownership %: 100
**Management:**
John P. Anderson ......................Publisher

## SOUTHERN LOGGIN' TIMES
23075

225 Hanrick St.
Montgomery, AL 36102
Telephone: (205) 834-1170
FAX: (205) 834-4525
Mailing Address:
P.O. Box 2268
Montgomery, AL 36102
Year Established: 1972
Pub. Frequency: m.
Page Size: tabloid
Subscrip. Rate: $30/yr. US; $40/yr.
Canada; $55/yr. surface mail foreign;
$75/yr. airmail foreign
Circulation: 12,839
Circulation Type: controlled
**Owner(s):**
Hatton-Brown Publishers, Inc.
225 Hanrick St.
Montgomery, AL 36102
Telephone: (205) 834-1170
Ownership %: 100
**Management:**
D.K. Knight ..............................Publisher
Dave Ramsey ..............................Publisher
**Editorial:**
Rich Donnell ..........................Managing Editor
**Desc.:** We cover logging and lumber
industry in the Southeast states. Focus
on loggers, sawmills, timber machinery
dealers, and news as it relates to these
interests.
**Readers:** Loggers, timber dealers, timber
machinery dealers.

## SOUTHERN LUMBERMAN
23652

128 Holiday Ct., Ste. 116
Franklin, TN 37064
Telephone: (615) 791-1961
FAX: (615) 790-6185
Mailing Address:
P.O. Box 681629
Franklin, TN 37068
Year Established: 1881
Pub. Frequency: m.
Page Size: standard
Subscrip. Rate: $18/yr.
Freelance Pay: $150-$250/article
Circulation: 12,000
Circulation Type: controlled & paid
**Owner(s):**
Greysmith Publishing, Inc.
128 Holiday Ct., Ste. 116
Franklin, TN 37064
Telephone: (615) 791-1961
Ownership %: 100
**Management:**
William D. Smith ..............................President
Nanci P. Gregg ..........................Vice President
Amy Tomlin ......................Circulation Manager
Lori Fisher ..............................Sales Manager
**Editorial:**
Nanci P. Gregg ..........................Managing Editor
Missy Estes ..............................Art Director
J. Holly McCall ......................Associate Editor

**Materials Accepted/Included:** 01-Business news 02-By-line articles 03-Fashion news 04-Food news 05-Freelance copy 06-Letters to editor 07-Real estate news 08-Sports news 09-Travel news 10-Book rev. 11-Movie rev. 12-Music rev. 13-TV rev. 14-Theater rev. 15-Coming events 16-Obituaries 17-Question & answer 18-Social announcements 19-Artwork 20-Cartoons 21-Photos 22-TV listings 23-Audio rec. 24-Video rec. 25-Books 26-Films/film clips 27-Personnel news 28-Press releases 29-New product news/photos 30-Trade lit. 31-Contracts awarded 32-Display adv. 33-Classified adv.

**Desc.:** Publishes articles, features and news on all phases of the lumber manufacturing industry.
**Readers:** Owners and operators of saw mills and secondary wood manufactuers.

**TIMBER-WEST** 68851
P.O. Box 610
Edmonds, WA 98020
Telephone: (206) 778-3388
FAX: (206) 771-3623
Year Established: 1975
Pub. Frequency: m.
Subscrip. Rate: $20/yr.
Circulation: 10,000
Circulation Type: controlled
**Owner(s):**
Timber-West Publications, Inc.
P.O. Box 610
Edmonds, WA 98020
Telephone: (206) 778-3388
Ownership %: 100
**Editorial:**
John L. Nederlee .........................Editor

**TIMBER HARVESTING** 23654
225 Hanrick St.
Montgomery, AL 36104
Telephone: (205) 834-1170
FAX: (205) 834-4525
Mailing Address:
   P.O. Box 2268
   Montgomery, AL 36102
Year Established: 1953
Pub. Frequency: m.
Page Size: standard
Subscrip. Rate: $24/yr. US.; $40/yr. foreign
Freelance Pay: $200/accepted
Circulation: 23,000
Circulation Type: controlled
**Owner(s):**
Hatton-Brown Publishers, Inc.
P.O. Box 2268
Montgomery, AL 36102
Telephone: (205) 834-1170
Ownership %: 100
**Management:**
D. K. Knight .........................Publisher
Dave Ramsey .........................Publisher
Dave Ramsey ..................Advertising Manager
**Editorial:**
D. K. Knight .........................Editor
Rich Dunnell .........................Managing Editor
**Desc.:** Reports on wood harvesting industry in the United States.
**Readers:** Logging contractors, logging managers and supervisors, wood dealers, equipment manufacturers and vendors, foresters, etc.

**TIMBER PROCESSING** 23655
225 Hanrick St.
Montgomery, AL 36104
Telephone: (205) 834-1170
FAX: (205) 834-4525
Mailing Address:
   P.O. Box 2268
   Montgomery, AL 36102
Year Established: 1976
Pub. Frequency: m.

Page Size: standard
Subscrip. Rate: $30/yr.
Freelance Pay: $200
Circulation: 15,000
Circulation Type: paid
**Owner(s):**
Hatton-Brown Publishers, Inc.
225 Hanrick St.
Montgomery, AL 36104
Telephone: (205) 834-1170
Ownership %: 100
**Management:**
David E. Knight .........................Publisher
Dave Ramsey .........................Publisher
David Ramsey ..................Advertising Manager
**Editorial:**
David E. Knight .........................Editor
Rich Donnell .........................Managing Editor
**Desc.:** Geared to lumber and other wood products manufacturing operations in North America.
**Readers:** Management and supervisory personnel at sawmills, wood products plants, pole treating plants, specialty mills.

**TIMBER PRODUCER, THE** 23656
P.O. Box 39
Tomahawk, WI 54487
Telephone: (715) 453-5159
Year Established: 1959
Pub. Frequency: m.
Page Size: standard
Subscrip. Rate: $15/yr.
Materials: 01,02,07,28,29
Circulation: 3,500
Circulation Type: paid
**Owner(s):**
Timber Producer
P.O. Box 39
Tomahawk, WI 54487
Telephone: (715) 453-5159
Ownership %: 100
**Management:**
David (Bimbo) Alexa .........................President
George Brunette .........................Vice President
**Editorial:**
Carl F. Theiler .........................Managing Editor
**Desc.:** Departments include a wide range in general timber industry.
**Readers:** Operators of saw mills, veneer mills, papers, farmers.

**WOOD TECHNOLOGY** 23643
600 Harrison St.
San Francisco, CA 94107
Telephone: (415) 905-2200
FAX: (415) 905-2232
Year Established: 1889
Pub. Frequency: bi-m.
Page Size: standard
Subscrip. Rate: $85/yr.; free to qualified personnel
Freelance Pay: $50-$250
Print Process: offset
Circulation: 23,500
Circulation Type: controlled
**Owner(s):**
Miller Freeman, Inc.
600 Harrison St.
San Francisco, CA 94107
Telephone: (415) 905-2200
FAX: (415) 905-2630
Ownership %: 100
**Bureau(s):**
Atlanta Branch Office

2000 Powers Ferry Ctr, Ste.450
Marietta, GA 30067
Telephone: (404) 952-1303
FAX: (404) 933-0666
Contact: Jay Schlosser, Sales Manager
**Management:**
Paula J. Irons .........................Publisher
**Editorial:**
Ted Blackman .........................Senior Editor
David A. Pease .........................Editor
Jennifer A. Sowle .........................Managing Editor
Peter G. Sutton .........................Group Publisher
Andrew A. Mickus .........................Production Director
**Desc.:** Articles on various phases of logging, forestry, woods management and log transportation, lumber manufacture, plywood, hardboard, particle board and other wood products. Departments include: Management, Logging and Forestry, Mill & Plant Operation, Equipment, Energy, News.
**Readers:** Logging & lumber and wood-based panel manufacturers in U.S.A. and Canada.

**WOODWORKER, THE** 25266
25 Cornell Ave.
Gladstone, OR 97027
Telephone: (503) 656-1475
FAX: (503) 657-2254
Mailing Address:
   25 Cornell Ave.
   Gladstone, OR 97027
Year Established: 1937
Pub. Frequency: m.
Page Size: tabloid
Subscrip. Rate: $6/yr.
Materials: 06,20,21,28,30
Circulation: 26,000
Circulation Type: controlled
**Owner(s):**
International Woodworkers of America,
   U.S. AFL-CIO
25 Cornell Ave.
Gladstone, OR 97027
Telephone: (503) 656-1475
FAX: (503) 657-2254
Ownership %: 100
**Editorial:**
Glenn Blaylock .........................Editor
**Desc.:** Covers all aspects of lumber, logging, milling, plywood, etc., from the workers' angle rather than from a production and marketing approach.
**Readers:** Loggers, plywood workers, millhands, retirees & companies forest products & management consultants.

**Group 150-Machinery, Metals & Metalworking**

**ABRASIVE ENGINEERING SOCIETY MAGAZINE** 23407
108 Elliott Dr.

Butler, PA 16001
Telephone: (412) 282-6210
Year Established: 1957
Pub. Frequency: q.
Page Size: standard
Subscrip. Rate: $40/yr. US; $65/yr. foreign
Circulation: 2,500
Circulation Type: paid
**Owner(s):**
Abrasive Engineering Society
108 Elliott Dr.
Butler, PA 16001
Telephone: (412) 282-6210
Ownership %: 100
**Editorial:**
Theodore Giese .........................Editor
**Desc.:** For users and manufacturers of all types of abrasive products, equipment, and techniques in metalworking applications. Magazine features include technical articles, new products and literature, and news related to industry personnel.
**Readers:** Abrasive field-users, suppliers and manufacturers.

**ADVANCED MATERIALS & PROCESSES** 24024
ASM International
Materials Park, OH 44073
Telephone: (216) 338-5151
FAX: (216) 338-4634
Year Established: 1930
Pub. Frequency: m.
Page Size: standard
Subscrip. Rate: free to members in US; $103/yr. non-members; $145/yr. foreign
Circulation: 50,000
Circulation Type: paid
**Owner(s):**
ASM International
Materials Park, OH 44073
Telephone: (216) 338-5151
Ownership %: 100
**Management:**
Patricia E. Brooks .........................Publisher
Patricia E. Brooks .........................Production Manager
**Editorial:**
Donald F. Baxter, Jr. .........................Editor
Margaret Hunt .........................Managing Editor
Barbara L. Brody .........................Art Director
Fay Balser .........................Editorial Coordinator
**Desc.:** Articles and departments cover capabilities of high-performance engineered materials, processes that enhance materials properties, equipments used to manufacture products with critical service requirements, and more.
**Readers:** Engineers and engineering managers with strong background in materials, chemistry or metallurgy.

**AMERICAN MACHINIST** 23990
Penton Publishing
1100 Superior Ave.
Cleveland, OH 44114
Year Established: 1877
Pub. Frequency: m.
Page Size: standard
Subscrip. Rate: $65/yr.
Freelance Pay: negotiable
Circulation: 82,000
Circulation Type: controlled

**Materials Accepted/Included:** 01-Business news 02-By-line articles 03-Fashion news 04-Food news 05-Freelance copy 06-Letters to editor 07-Real estate news 08-Sports news 09-Travel news 10-Book rev. 11-Movie rev. 12-Music rev. 13-TV rev. 14-Theater rev. 15-Coming events 16-Obituaries 17-Question & answer 18-Social announcements 19-Artwork 20-Cartoons 21-Photos 22-TV listings 23-Audio rec. 24-Video rec. 25-Books 26-Films/film clips 27-Personnel news 28-Press releases 29-New product news/photos 30-Trade lit. 31-Contracts awarded 32-Display adv. 33-Classified adv.

4-211

**Owner(s):**
Penton Publishing
1100 Superior Ave.
Cleveland, OH 44114
Telephone: (216) 696-7000
Ownership %: 100
**Management:**
Art Hatcher ............................Publisher
Robert DeSan ...............Business Manager
Bob Clark ....................Circulation Manager
**Editorial:**
John A. Vaccari ....................Senior Editor
Fred Mason ..........................Senior Editor
George Weimer ...............................Editor
Leslie Jasany .....................Managing Editor
Douglas Torok .....................Associate Editor
Robert Hatschek ...............Contributing Editor
Anderson Ashburn ............Contributing Editor
Lynn Hazlewood ..................Editorial Assistant
Sandra Buckley .....................Editorial Assistant
Bonnie Velikonya ..............Production Director
**Desc.:** Technical coverage of machining,
forging, forming, molding, die casting,
welding, tooling, laser, cutting tools,
finishing, materials handling, robotics,
computer integration, assembly,
materials, personnel. Photos must
be broadly applicable in metalworking
production shops or toolrooms. Covers
production equipment.
**Readers:** Manufacturing management and
engineering in the durable-goods-
producing industries from airplanes to
appliances to ashtrays.

54020
**AMERICAN METAL MARKET**
825 Seventh Ave.
New York, NY 10019
Telephone: (212) 887-8580
FAX: (212) 887-8493
Year Established: 1882
Pub. Frequency: Mon-Fri.
Page Size: tabloid
Subscrip. Rate: $545/yr.; $1000/yr. Central
& S. America, Europe; $1170 others
Circulation: 13,000
Circulation Type: paid
**Owner(s):**
Capital Cities-ABC, Inc.
Metals Publishing Group
825 Seventh Ave.
New York, NY 10001
Telephone: (212) 887-8560
Ownership %: 100
**Management:**
J. Lindsey ...............................Publisher
**Editorial:**
Michael G. Botta ..................Editor in Chief
B. Teplitz .........................Executive Editor
G. La Rue .........................Managing Editor
Maureen Hyland ...............Marketing Manager
**Desc.:** Daily newspaper of the metals
industry, written for and read by top
executives and managers. Includes over
1700 price quotations and is the pre-
eminent source for industry information
for metal users, producers, distributors,
and recyclers.

23991
**AMERICAN TOOL, DIE &
STAMPING NEWS**
42400 Nine Mile Rd., Ste. B
Novi, MI 48375
Telephone: (313) 347-3487
FAX: (313) 347-3492
Year Established: 1973
Pub. Frequency: bi-m.
Page Size: standard
Subscrip. Rate: $9.80 US (1-time fee);
$60/yr. foreign
Circulation: 27,000
Circulation Type: paid

**Owner(s):**
Eagle Corporation, Inc.
42400 Nine Mile Rd., Ste. B
Novi, MI 48375
Telephone: (313) 347-3487
Ownership %: 100
**Management:**
Art Brown ..............................Publisher
Art Brown ....................Advertising Manager
Joan Oakley ..................Circulation Manager
**Editorial:**
Gail Dawson ...............................Editor
Gail Dawson ..........................Art Director
**Desc.:** New product releases concerning
the tool, die and stamping industry, and
electric discharge machining.
**Readers:** Middle management and owners.

23992
**AUTOMATIC MACHINING**
100 Seneca Ave.
Rochester, NY 14621
Telephone: (716) 338-1522
FAX: (716) 338-2625
Year Established: 1939
Pub. Frequency: m.
Page Size: standard
Subscrip. Rate: $40/yr.
Circulation: 13,000
Circulation Type: controlled
**Owner(s):**
Screw Machine Publishing Co.
100 Seneca Ave.
Rochester, NY 14621
Telephone: (716) 338-1522
Ownership %: 100
**Management:**
Donald E. Wood .........................President
Donald E. Wood .........................Publisher
Linda LoBiondo ...............Advertising Manager
**Editorial:**
Donald E. Wood ...........................Editor
W.A. Wood .........................Editorial Director
**Desc.:** Technical articles on tooling and
production problems, newest techniques
and developments in metal turning field
on automatic screw machines, turret
lathes, automatic chucking machines,
automatic turret lathes, cold heading
machines, and related secondary
equipment. Carries news, new products
and equipment, new literature, special
features, appointments and plant news.

23994
**CASTING WORLD**
1536 Main St.
Stratford, CT 06497
Telephone: (203) 377-5566
Mailing Address:
P.O. Box 1919
Bridgeport, CT 06601
Year Established: 1969
Pub. Frequency: q.
Page Size: standard
Subscrip. Rate: $24/yr.
Circulation: 35,000
Circulation Type: controlled & paid
**Owner(s):**
Continental Communications, Inc.
1536 Main St.
Stratford, CT 06497
Telephone: (203) 377-5566
FAX: (203) 377-7230
Ownership %: 100
**Management:**
W. W. Troland .........................President
W. W. Troland .........................Publisher
W. W. Troland ...............Advertising Manager
**Editorial:**
W. W. Troland ...........................Editor
**Desc.:** Written expressly for the men who
produce, design, process and purchase
castings.

**Readers:** Design engineers, production
engineers, purchasing and foundry
management.

23995
**CUTTING TOOL ENGINEERING**
400 Skokie Blvd., Ste. 395
Northbrook, IL 60062
Telephone: (708) 498-9100
FAX: (708) 559-4444
Year Established: 1955
Pub. Frequency: 9/yr.
Page Size: standard
Subscrip. Rate: $40/yr. in US; $105/yr.
foreign
Freelance Pay: varies
Circulation: 36,000
Circulation Type: controlled
**Owner(s):**
CTE Publications, Inc.
400 Skokie Blvd., Ste. 395
Northbrook, IL 60062
Telephone: (708) 498-9100
Ownership %: 100
**Management:**
John Wm. Roberts .........................President
Stacy Stiglic ..................Circulation Manager
**Editorial:**
Phillip Craig ...............................Editor
Victoria de McInerney .........Production Director
**Desc.:** Concerned with metal-cutting,
metal-removal and abrasive machining.
Features on metalworking involving
cutting tools, grinding wheels, machines,
accessories, etc.
**Readers:** Design, production, engineering.

23997
**DIE CASTING ENGINEER BI-
MONTHLY**
9701 W. Higgins Rd., Ste. 880
Des Plaines, IL 60018-4721
Telephone: (708) 292-3600
FAX: (708) 292-3620
Year Established: 1957
Pub. Frequency: bi-m.
Page Size: 8 1/4 x 11 1/4
Subscrip. Rate: $8/copy; $52/yr.; $65/yr.
outside N. America
Materials: 01,02,06,10,15,16,24,25,27,28,
29,30,32,33
Freelance Pay: negotiable
Print Process: offset lithography
Circulation: 3,600
Circulation Type: paid
**Owner(s):**
North American Die Casting Assn.
9701 W. Higgins Rd., Ste. 880
Des Plaines, IL 60018-4721
Telephone: (708) 292-3600
Ownership %: 100
**Management:**
Jeffry Raynes .........................Publisher
Paul Bralower ...............Advertising Manager
Karen Zalesny ..................Circulation Manager
**Editorial:**
Sally Cunningham ...............Assistant Editor
**Desc.:** Material concerned with the die
casting process and finishing processes
of a practical nature. Any length justified
by the material, any number of photos if
good and informative. Departments
include: New Products, New Literature,
Industry News, NADCA Reports,
Education & Technology, Peoples in Die
Casting, Safety & Environmental.
**Readers:** Plant owners, managers and
engineers engaged in making, designing,
specifying die castings, and/or die
casting dies...and anyone else
interfacing with the industry.
**Deadline:** news-1 mo. prior to pub. date;
ads-6 wks. prior

23998
**FABRICATOR, THE**
833 Featherstone Rd.
Rockford, IL 61107-6302
Telephone: (815) 399-8700
FAX: (815) 399-7279
Year Established: 1971
Pub. Frequency: 10/yr.
Page Size: tabloid
Subscrip. Rate: $30/yr. US; $50/yr.
Canada & Mexico; $125/yr. elsewhere;
free/qualified personnel
Materials: 02,17,21,28,29,30,31,32,33
Print Process: web offset
Circulation: 55,000
Circulation Type: controlled
**Owner(s):**
Croydon Group Ltd., The
833 Featherstone Rd.
Rockford, IL 61107-6302
Telephone: (815) 399-8700
FAX: (815) 399-7279
Ownership %: 100
**Management:**
John Nandzik ...............................Publisher
Mary Poirier-Gasaway ........Circulation Manager
Jack Broughton ..................Sales Manager
**Editorial:**
Kathy Velasco ....................Executive Editor
Theresa Olmsted ...........................Editor
Amy Nickel ........................Associate Editor
David Jackson ....................Associate Editor
Deb Strout ........................Production Director
**Desc.:** Contains material for managers and
engineers of the metal fabricating
industry. Emphasis given to sheet metal,
tube & pipe, stamping, coil, roll forming,
welding, finishing, and plate and
structural fabrication.
**Readers:** Management type personnel,
V.P's., manufacturing job shops,
manufacturing engineers, shop
managers.
**Deadline:** story-4 mos. prior to pub. date;
news-2 mos. prior; ads-6 wks. prior

24000
**FINISHERS MANAGEMENT**
4350 DiPaolo Ctr./Dearlove Rd.
Glenview, IL 60025
Telephone: (708) 699-1706
Year Established: 1957
Pub. Frequency: 10/yr.
Page Size: standard
Subscrip. Rate: $28/yr.
Materials: 01,02,05,06,15,16,17,19,20,21,
27,28,29,30,31,32,33
Print Process: offset
Circulation: 10,000
Circulation Type: controlled & paid
**Owner(s):**
Publication Management, Inc.
4350 DiPaolo Ctr.
Glenview, IL 60025
Telephone: (708) 699-1706
Ownership %: 100
**Management:**
Hugh Morgan ...............................President
Hugh Morgan ...............................Publisher
John McConnel ...............Advertising Manager
Luba Melendez ..................Circulation Manager
**Editorial:**
Barbara Hedrich ...........................Editor
**Desc.:** Covers all phases of management
within metal finishing industry, especially
job shop plating-electroplating,
anodizing, metallizing, electrogalvanizing,
phosphating, electroforming,
handchroming, rust proofing, organic
coating, polishing, buffing, plating on
plastic, powder coating, painting,
lacquering, et al. Departments include:
Names in the News, Labor, Law,
Industry News, New Products &
Equipment, Literature, Editorial,
Management.

**Materials Accepted/Included:** 01-Business news 02-By-line articles 03-Fashion news 04-Food news 05-Freelance copy 06-Letters to editor 07-Real estate news 08-Sports news 09-Travel news 10-Book rev. 11-Movie rev. 12-Music rev. 13-TV rev. 14-Theater rev. 15-Coming events 16-Obituaries 17-Question & answer 18-Social announcements 19-Artwork 20-Cartoons 21-Photos 22-TV listings 23-Audio rec. 24-Video rec. 25-Books 26-Films/film clips 27-Personnel news 28-Press releases 29-New product news/photos 30-Trade lit. 31-Contracts awarded 32-Display adv. 33-Classified adv.

4-212

**Readers:** Owners and managers in job & captive metal finishing-shops.
**Deadline:** story-45 days prior to pub. date; news-45 days; photo-45 days; ads-20 days

### FOUNDRY MANAGEMENT & TECHNOLOGY
24002

1100 Superior Ave.
Cleveland, OH 44114
Telephone: (216) 696-7000
FAX: (216) 696-8765
Year Established: 1892
Pub. Frequency: m.
Page Size: standard
Subscrip. Rate: $4/issue; $35/yr.
**Owner(s):**
Penton Publishing
1111 Chester Ave.
Cleveland, OH 44114
Telephone: (216) 696-7000
Ownership %: 100
**Management:**
David Robinson ...................................Publisher
Sally R. Crooks ................Advertising Manager
James C. Forthofer .............Business Manager
**Editorial:**
J. C. Miske ...............................................Editor
Robert Rodgers ........................Managing Editor
Donna Pokarny ...............................News Editor
H. J. Heine ...............................Technical Editor
**Desc.:** Editorial material relates to techniques employed in production of metal castings, to the operation of foundries, and to activities of the industry's trade and technical societies. Also includes personnel news. Feature articles 500-3,000 words. Departments include: Technical Developments; Environment and Safety; Washington Report; News Briefs; late news; Men of Industry; Products in Action; New Equipment; Literature.
**Readers:** Producers of metal castings.

### IMPACT PUMP NEWS & PATENTS
69432

P.O. Box 3113
Ketchum, ID 83340-3113
Telephone: (208) 726-2133
FAX: (208) 726-2115
Year Established: 1971
Pub. Frequency: 10/yr.
Subscrip. Rate: $100/yr.
Materials: 01,28,29,30,31
**Owner(s):**
Impact Publications
P.O. Box 3113
Ketchum, ID 83340-3113
Telephone: (208) 726-2133
Ownership %: 100
**Editorial:**
Mary Jo Helmeke ....................................Editor
**Desc.:** Contains recent patent gazette summaries, new product information, current technical articles, new books and future seminars.
**Deadline:** story-1st of mo.; news-1st of mo.; photo-1st of mo.; ads-1st of mo.

### INDUSTRIAL HEATING
24008

1910 Cochran Rd., 630
Pittsburgh, PA 15220
Telephone: (412) 531-3370
FAX: (412) 531-3375
Year Established: 1934
Pub. Frequency: m.
Page Size: standard
Subscrip. Rate: $44/yr.
Circulation: 23,000
Circulation Type: paid

**Owner(s):**
Business News Publishing Co.
755 W. Big Beaver Rd. Ste 1000
Troy, MI 48084
Telephone: (313) 362-3700
Ownership %: 100
**Bureau(s):**
R. B. Ashby Bureau Chief
1140 Connecticut Ave. N.W.
Washington, DC 20036
Telephone: (202) 296-3840
**Management:**
James Henderson ...............................President
David Lurie .........................................Publisher
**Editorial:**
S.B. Lasday ...............................................Editor
Kathy Pisano .....................Advertising Director
E. Mcclelland ............................Associate Editor
E. Mcclelland .................................News Editor
**Desc.:** Editorial emphasis is engineering/Management oriented, focusing on advancements in thermal technology discussed definitively in terms of its practical application - encompassing entire industry systems involved in primary metals producing, metals heat treating, brazing, forging, casting, cleaning and finishing, as well as specific analysis of thermal processing control and heat containment. Contains short features on innovations, industry-related economic and legislative analysis, industry and technical society news, literature and book reviews, personnel announcements.
**Readers:** Operating and engineering management personnel.

### INDUSTRIAL MACHINE TRADER
69438

1003 Central Ave.
Fort Dodge, IA 50501
Telephone: (515) 955-1600
Year Established: 1982
Pub. Frequency: w.
Page Size: standard
Subscrip. Rate: $79/yr.
Print Process: web
Circulation: 12,000
Circulation Type: controlled & paid
**Owner(s):**
Heartland Communications, Inc.
1003 Central Ave.
Fort Dodge, IA 50501
Telephone: (515) 955-1600
Ownership %: 100
**Management:**
Joe Peed .............................................President
Steve Scanlan .....................................Publisher
**Desc.:** Keeps potential buyers and sellers current on supply and demand of machinery in the machine tool industry.

### INTERNATIONAL JOURNAL OF MACHINE TOOLS & MANUFACTURE
69258

660 White Plains Rd.
Tarrytown, NY 10591-5153
Telephone: (914) 524-9200
FAX: (914) 333-2444
Year Established: 1961
Pub. Frequency: 6/yr.
Circulation: 1,000
Circulation Type: paid
**Owner(s):**
Pergamon Press, Inc.
660 White Plains Rd.
Tarrytown, NY 10591-5153
Telephone: (914) 524-9200
Ownership %: 100
**Editorial:**
R. Davies ...................................................Editor
T.A. Dean ..................................................Editor

### INTERNATIONAL JOURNAL OF POWDER METALLURGY
24011

105 College Rd., E.
Princeton, NJ 08540-6692
Telephone: (609) 452-7700
FAX: (609) 987-8523
Year Established: 1965
Pub. Frequency: q.
Page Size: standard
Subscrip. Rate: $70/yr. individuals; $145/yr. institutions
Materials: 02,06,10,15,28,29,30,32
Circulation: 3,500
Circulation Type: paid
**Owner(s):**
American Powder Metallurgy Institute
Telephone: (609) 452-7700
Ownership %: 100
**Management:**
Donald G. White ...............................Publisher
**Editorial:**
Alan Lawley ....................................Editor in Chief
Peter K. Johnson ....................Managing Editor
**Desc.:** We cover technical and marketing developments in the international powder metallurgy and particulate materials industry. Metal powder characteristics and properties, the production of powder metallurgy components and products, and applications of powders are reviewed. Articles generally run from six to ten pages.
**Readers:** Metallurgists, engineers, scientists, educators.

### IRON & STEEL ENGINEER
24013

3 Gateway Ctr., Ste. 2350
Pittsburgh, PA 15222
Telephone: (412) 281-6323
FAX: (412) 281-4657
Year Established: 1924
Pub. Frequency: m.
Page Size: standard
Subscrip. Rate: $50/yr. US, Canada, Mexico; $72/yr. elsewhere
Circulation: 12,000
Circulation Type: paid
**Owner(s):**
Assn. of Iron & Steel Engineers
3 Gateway Center, #2350
Pittsburgh, PA 15222
Telephone: (412) 281-6323
Ownership %: 100
**Management:**
Lawrence Malone ...............................Publisher
Samuel H. Seem ...............Advertising Manager
Lawrence Malone ...............Managing Director
**Editorial:**
Dennis Fuga ................................Editor in Chief
Barbara Zeff ..............................Assistant Editor
Norman L. Samways ...............Technical Editor
**Desc.:** Articles cover the producing end of the iron and steel industry and the equipment serving that industry: design, construction, operation and maintenance of plants and equipment for the production and processing of iron and steel. Departments include: Industry News, Personnel News, Equipment News, Technical Literature.
**Readers:** Managers, engineers, operators of steel industry equipment.

### JOM
24015

420 Commonwealth Dr.
Warrendale, PA 15086-9928
Telephone: (412) 776-9000
FAX: (412) 776-3770
Year Established: 1949
Pub. Frequency: m.
Page Size: standard
Subscrip. Rate: $90/yr.

Circulation: 14,000
Circulation Type: paid
**Owner(s):**
TMS
420 Commonwealth Dr.
Warrendale, PA 15086
Telephone: (412) 776-9000
Ownership %: 100
**Management:**
Alexander R. Scott ...........................Publisher
Dan Steighner ..................Advertising Manager
**Editorial:**
James J. Robinson ..................................Editor
Robert Makowski ..............Publication Director
Mark C. Munson ......................Technical Editor
**Desc.:** Written for the professional metallurgical and materials engineers and scientists covering the entire span of interest from extraction of metals from their ores to the study of theoretical metal physics. New products and processes, metaleaders, industry & business news, international report, helpful literature, call for papers, meetings calendar, campus newsletter, help wanted.
**Readers:** Readers hold key positions in management, engineering, research and development, and operations in industrial companies, engineering construction and consulting firms, research organizations, and government agencies which are the principal users of metals and metallurgical products and processes.

### LIGHT METAL AGE
24016

170 S. Spruce Ave., Ste. 120
S. San Francisco, CA 94080
Telephone: (415) 588-8832
FAX: (415) 588-0907
Year Established: 1943
Pub. Frequency: bi-m.
Page Size: standard
Subscrip. Rate: $35/yr.
Circulation: 5,058
Circulation Type: controlled
**Owner(s):**
Fellom Publishing Co.
170 S. Spruce Ave., Ste. 120
S. San Francisco, CA 94080
Telephone: (415) 588-8832
Ownership %: 100
**Management:**
Ann Marie Fellom ............................Publisher
**Editorial:**
Wanda Belland ........................................Editor
**Desc.:** Magazine exclusively devoted to primary reduction and semi-fabrication of light metals. Covers smelting, refining billet and ingot casting, extrusion, rolling and anodizing and heat treatment. Also covers allied subjects including, alloying compositing, powder metallurgy, rapid solidification, die making and forging.
**Readers:** Production & operational management in the basic primary mills and primary plants of the aluminum and non-ferrous metals industry, rolling mills, extrusion plants, smelters and retineries, diecasting plants & foundries.

### LOCATOR OF USED MACHINERY, EQUIPMENT & PLANT SERVICES
68959

1110 Spring St.
Silver Spring, MD 20910
Telephone: (301) 585-9498
FAX: (301) 585-9460
Year Established: 1969
Pub. Frequency: m.
Subscrip. Rate: $38/yr. first class; $22/yr. 3rd class
Materials: 19,32,33
Circulation: 83,000

Circulation Type: controlled & paid
**Owner(s):**
Machinery Information Systems, Inc.
1110 Spring St.
Silver Spring, MD 20910
Telephone: (301) 585-9498
Ownership %: 100
**Management:**
Mark Rogo ..............................President
Rick Shontz ...............................Publisher
Sylvia Sierra ...............Circulation Manager
Bill Wood ....................Sales Manager
**Editorial:**
Mark Bradshaw ..............Associate Editor
**Desc.:** Directory of used metalworking
machinery and manufacturing plant
supplies.

24019
## MATERIALS PERFORMANCE
1440 South Creek Dr.
Houston, TX 77084-4906
Telephone: (713) 492-0535
FAX: (713) 492-8254
Mailing Address:
P. O. Box 218340
Houston, TX 77218-8340
Year Established: 1962
Pub. Frequency: m.
Page Size: standard
Subscrip. Rate: $65/yr. US; $80/yr. foreign
Circulation: 16,000
Circulation Type: paid
**Owner(s):**
National Assn. of Corrosion Engineers
P.O. Box 218340
Houston, TX 77218-8340
Telephone: (713) 492-0535
Ownership %: 100
**Management:**
Aunee Pierce ..............................Publisher
**Editorial:**
Theresa Baer ..............Managing Editor
Peggy Parsons ..............................Director,
Jaime Nunez ...............Graphics Coordinator
Gus Gabino .........Supervisor, Support Services
**Desc.:** Focuses on practical engineering
and case history studies on the
protection and performance of materials
in corrosive environments. Articles peer
reviewed for technical-validity, address
corrosion problems experienced in
marine, underground, atmospheric, and
industrial environments and offer
solutions to these problems. Information
is presented in four sections: protective
coatings and linings, cathodic and
anodic protection, materials selection
and design. Other coverage includes
NACE news and standards, plus
departments featuring new products,
people and places, literature and
software announcements, a problem-
solving clinic, basic corrosion prevention
tips, and news and activities of
worldwide corrosion control and
engineering societies.
**Readers:** Engineers & managers
concerned with corrosive environments.

24026
## METAL/CENTER NEWS
191 S. Gary Ave.
Carol Stream, IL 60188
Telephone: (708) 665-1000
FAX: (708) 462-2862
Year Established: 1961
Pub. Frequency: m.
Page Size: standard
Subscrip. Rate: $55/yr.
Freelance Pay: $300/article
Circulation: 15,000
Circulation Type: controlled

**Owner(s):**
Chilton Publishing
Radnor, PA
Ownership %: 100
**Management:**
Robert Hittins ..............................Publisher
**Editorial:**
Joseph C. Marino ..............................Editor

24021
## METAL FABRICATING NEWS
P.O. Box 1178
Rockford, IL 61105-1178
Telephone: (815) 965-4031
FAX: (815) 964-3175
Year Established: 1968
Pub. Frequency: q.
Page Size: tabloid
Subscrip. Rate: free
Materials: 01,02,05,06,10,15,19,21,28,29,
32,33
Print Process: web offset
Circulation: 39,720
Circulation Type: free
**Owner(s):**
Metal Fabricating News
Telephone: (815) 965-4031
Ownership %: 100
**Management:**
Bonnie Fisher ..............Advertising Manager
Bonnie Fisher ..............Circulation Manager
**Editorial:**
Ron Fowler ..............Executive Editor
Sue Lackner ..............Associate Editor
**Desc.:** News and feature stories covering
new developments, new methods,
industry news, as well as basic
technology of metalworking operations.
Focuses on management's position,
competitive free enterprise systems of
the industry.
**Readers:** US and foreign metal fabricators
in administrative and productions.
**Deadline:** story-3 mos. prior to pub. date;
news-3 mos. prior; photo-3 mos. prior;
ads-3 mos. prior

24023
## METAL FINISHING
3 University Plaza
Hackensack, NJ 07601
Telephone: (201) 487-3700
FAX: (201) 487-3705
Year Established: 1903
Pub. Frequency: m.
Page Size: standard
Subscrip. Rate: $40/yr. US; $61/yr.
Canada & Mexico; $108/yr. elsewhere
Freelance Pay: $55/pg.
Circulation: 13,000
Circulation Type: paid
**Owner(s):**
Elsevier Science, Inc.
655 Ave. of Americas
New York, NY 10010
Telephone: (212) 989-5800
Ownership %: 100
**Management:**
Eugene B. Nadel ..............................Publisher
Nancy Axelrod ..............Circulation Manager
**Editorial:**
Michael Murphy ..............................Editor
Patti Ann Frost ..............Assistant Editor
Bill Dey ..............Regional Manager
Lawrence A. Post ..............Regional Manager
**Desc.:** Contributed articles focus
exclusively on the treatment of metallic
surfaces in various industries. Discusses
specific industry problems and
techniques, new methods, and
processes. Departments include:
Patents; Recent Developments (covering
new methods, material and equipment);
Technical Literature; Manufacturers
Literature; Business Items; Associations
and Societies; Industry Activities.

**Readers:** Chemists, chemical engineers.

24025
## METAL FORMING
27027 Chardon Rd.
Richmond Hts., OH 44143
Telephone: (216) 585-8800
Year Established: 1967
Pub. Frequency: m.
Page Size: standard
Subscrip. Rate: free to qualified personnel
Circulation: 52,000
Circulation Type: free
**Owner(s):**
Precision Metal Forming Association
27027 Chardon Rd.
Richmond Hts., OH 44143
Telephone: (216) 585-8800
Ownership %: 100
**Management:**
Jon Jenson ..............................Publisher
Elaine Bastick ..............Circulation Manager
**Editorial:**
Richard Green ..............................Editor
Beth Vosmik ..............Art Director
Kathy DeLollis ..............Associate Publisher
Marlene Rath ..............New Products Editor
Richard Green ..............News Editor
Beth Vosmik ..............Photo
Kathy DeLollis ..............Production Director
**Desc.:** Readers are interested in and are
influential in purchases of new
equipment, materials and accessory
supplies used in the production of metal
stampings, metal spinnings, fabrications
and washers.
**Readers:** Metal forming managers and
their key employees.

24027
## METALLURGICAL TRANSACTIONS
420 Commonwealth Dr.
Warrendale, PA 15086
Telephone: (412) 776-9080
Pub. Frequency: "A"/m.; "B"/bi-m.
Page Size: standard
Subscrip. Rate: $696/yr. "A"; $498/yr. "B"
Circulation: 7,000
Circulation Type: paid
**Owner(s):**
Minerals, Metals & Materials Society, The,
and ASM
420 Commonwealth Dr.
Warrendale, PA 15086
Telephone: (412) 776-9000
Ownership %: 100
**Management:**
Linda L. Gibb ..............Business Manager
**Editorial:**
David E. Laughlin ..............................Editor
Gerhard Derge ..............Associate Editor
**Desc.:** The editorial objective is to provide
a single journal of recognized
professional stature devoted to all
aspects of research and significant
engineering advances in material
science and metallurgy.
**Readers:** Metallurgists, libraries, technical
institutions.

69243
## METALSMITH
5009 Londonderry Dr.
Tampa, FL 32647
Telephone: (813) 977-5326
FAX: (813) 977-8462
Year Established: 1979
Pub. Frequency: q.
Page Size: standard
Subscrip. Rate: $26/yr. non-members US;
$38/yr. foreign
Circulation: 4,600
Circulation Type: paid

**Owner(s):**
Society of North American Goldsmiths
5009 Londonderry Dr.
Tampa, FL 32647
Telephone: (813) 977-5326
Ownership %: 100
**Editorial:**
Frank Lewis ..............................Editor
**Desc.:** Devoted to the metal arts.

24028
## METALWORKING DIGEST
301 Gilbraltar Dr.
Morris Plains, NJ 07950-0650
Telephone: (201) 292-5100
FAX: (201) 898-9281
Mailing Address:
P.O. Box 650
Morris Plains, NJ 07950-0650
Year Established: 1966
Pub. Frequency: m.
Page Size: tabloid
Subscrip. Rate: $48/yr.
Materials: 29,30,32,33
Print Process: web offset
Circulation: 115,000
Circulation Type: controlled
**Owner(s):**
Gordon Publications, Inc.
301 Gilbraltar Dr.
Morris Plains, NJ 07950-0650
Telephone: (201) 292-5100
Ownership %: 100
**Bureau(s):**
Gordon Publications, Inc.
10600 W. Higgins Rd., Ste. 310
Rosemont, IL 60018
Telephone: (708) 803-5300
FAX: (708) 803-4783
Contact: Mike Cornelo, Sales Manager

Gordon Publications, Inc.
11201 Richmond Ave.
Houston, TX 77082
Telephone: (713) 558-5328
Contact: Donna Cuny, Sales Manager

Gordon Publications, Inc.
10568 Ravenna Rd.
Twinsburg, OH 44087
Telephone: (216) 425-3443
Contact: Tim Kasperovich, Sales Manager

Gordon Publications, Inc.
6520 Powers Ferry Rd., Ste. 39
Atlanta, GA 30339
Telephone: (404) 956-9106
Contact: Mark Davis

Betty Cretara & Assoc.
11288 Urntura Blvd., Ste. 373
Studio City, CA 91604
Telephone: (818) 508-1900
Contact: Betty Cretara, Sales Manager

Gordon Publications, Inc.
74 Main St.
Marlborough, MA 01752
Telephone: (508) 624-4399
Contact: Joe May, Sales Manager
**Management:**
William R. Rakay ..............................President
Dave Esola ..............................Publisher
Claire Mandala .......Customer Service Manager
**Editorial:**
Rich Stevancsecz ..............................Editor
Pete Hernandez ..............Associate Publisher
Sheila Rodgers ..............Production Director
**Desc.:** Editorial consists of new products
and new literature briefs of interest to
the metalworking industry. Departments
include: New Literature.
**Readers:** Those with authority to specify
and/or purchase materials.

## METLFAX MAGAZINE
24030

29100 Aurora Rd., 200
Cleveland, OH 44139
Telephone: (216) 248-1125
FAX: (216) 248-0187
Year Established: 1956
Pub. Frequency: m.
Page Size: 4 color photos/art
Subscrip. Rate: $45/yr.
Circulation: 102,601
Circulation Type: controlled
**Owner(s):**
Huebcore Communications, Inc.
29100 Aurora Rd., Suite 200
Cleveland, OH 44139
Telephone: (216) 248-1125
Ownership %: 100
**Management:**
Thomas J. Corcoran .............................President
Greg Jones .........................................Publisher
Diane Dobies ....................Advertising Manager
Dick Benson .......................Circulation Manager
Georgenne Retych .............Production Manager
**Editorial:**
Jim Destefani ...............................Editor in Chief
Paul C. Miller ........................................Editor
Nancy L. Leape .......................Managing Editor
Andrew M. Shive ...........................Art Editor
**Desc.:** Covers news of products, plants, processes, and production relating to the metal working and manufacturing industries.
**Readers:** Metalworking manufacturing management, line and staff.

## MODERN APPLICATIONS NEWS
22604

2504 N. Tamiami Trail
Nokomis, FL 34275-3476
Telephone: (813) 966-9521
FAX: (813) 966-2590
Year Established: 1967
Pub. Frequency: m.
Page Size: standard
Subscrip. Rate: $10 copy; $104/yr.
Materials: 01,02,15,28,29,30,32,33
Freelance Pay: varies
Circulation: 75,000
Circulation Type: controlled
**Owner(s):**
Nelson Publishing
2504 N. Tamiami Trail
Nokomis, FL 34275-3476
Telephone: (813) 966-9521
FAX: (813) 966-2590
Ownership %: 100
**Management:**
H. Pete Petersen .............................Publisher
**Editorial:**
Larry Olson ....................................Senior Editor
Larry Olson ........................................Editor
Terrence A. Freeman .............Consulting Editor
Janice Titus ..................Special Projects Editor
**Desc.:** Covers materials, components, process and equipment applications, case histories.
**Readers:** Metalworking corp. management, production manufacturing engineers, product design & development personnel.

## MODERN CASTING
24032

505 State St.
Des Plaines, IL 60016
Telephone: (708) 824-0181
FAX: (708) 824-7848
Year Established: 1938
Pub. Frequency: m.
Page Size: standard
Subscrip. Rate: $40/yr. US; $50/yr. foreign; $75/yr. air-mail
Circulation: 25,000
Circulation Type: controlled

**Owner(s):**
American Foundrymen's Society, Inc.
505 State St.
Des Plaines, IL 60016
Telephone: (708) 824-0181
Ownership %: 100
**Bureau(s):**
W.G. Holdsworth & Assoc.
625 E. Seegers Rd.
Des Plaines, IL 60016
Telephone: (708) 803-0500
Contact: Wally Holdsworth, Advertising

Albert D. Shonk Co.
3156 Wilshire Blvd.
Los Angeles, CA 90010
Telephone: (310) 388-7891
Contact: Albert Shonk, President
**Management:**
Charles H. Jones ......................Vice President
Dick Reynolds ..................Advertising Manager
Mary Ann Bogdanske ........Circulation Manager
Dick Reynolds .............Classified Adv. Manager
Dick Reynolds .......Customer Service Manager
Charles H. Jones ..................General Manager
**Editorial:**
Tom Bex .....................................Senior Editor
David P. Kanicki ...................................Editor
Eileen Vukmanic ...........................Art Director
Susan P. Thomas .......................Associate Editor
Martha K. Siebel .......................Miscellaneous
Nancy Davies .................................News Editor
Dick Reynolds ...........................Production Director
**Desc.:** Technical, management and operating articles on foundries and foundry practices. News, new developments, products and processes, literature, book reviews, general news coverage of entire metalcasting industry.
**Readers:** Operation personnel, management, & technical foundrymen, & equipment & supply manufacturers, industry.

## MODERN MACHINE SHOP
24033

6600 Clough Pike
Cincinnati, OH 45244-4090
Telephone: (513) 231-8020
FAX: (513) 231-2818
Year Established: 1928
Pub. Frequency: m.
Page Size: pocket
Subscrip. Rate: $42/yr. US; $50/yr. Canada; $72/yr. elsewhere
Materials: 01,02,20,28,29,30,32,33
Freelance Pay: $100-$600
Circulation: 106,000
Circulation Type: controlled
**Owner(s):**
Gardner Publications, Inc.
6600 Clough Pike
Cincinnati, OH 45244
Telephone: (513) 231-8020
Ownership %: 100
**Management:**
Richard G. Kline ..............................President
Richard G. Kline ..............................Publisher
Don Kline ...........................Advertising Manager
Christopher Felix ................Promotion Manager
**Editorial:**
Mark Albert .................................Exec. Editor
Thomas Beard ...................................Editor
John Jordan .................................Assistant Editor
Johanna Bradbury ...................Assistant Editor
G. Christopher Koepfer ...........Associate Editor
Christopher Felix ................Book Review Editor
**Desc.:** Contributed and staff-written practical "how-to" articles dealing with machine shop methods, equipment use, shortcuts, etc. Departments include: News of the Industry, New Shop Equipment. Covers new literature.

**Readers:** Production and shop operating executives, managers, master mechanics, superintendents, shop foremen.
**Deadline:** story-6 mos. prior to pub. date; news-3 mos. prior to pub. date; ads-5 wks. prior to pub. date

## MODERN METALS
24034

625 N. Michigan Ave.
Chicago, IL 60611
Telephone: (312) 654-2300
Year Established: 1945
Pub. Frequency: m.
Page Size: standard
Subscrip. Rate: $65/yr.
Materials: 01,15,28,29,30,32,33
Circulation: 42,500
Circulation Type: controlled
**Owner(s):**
Trend Publications
625 N. Michigan Ave.
Chicago, IL 60611
Telephone: (312) 654-2300
Ownership %: 100
**Management:**
William J. D'Alexander ......................President
Scott Walker .....................................Publisher
**Editorial:**
Victor M. Cassidy .................................Editor
**Desc.:** Covers all phases of metals production, processing, finishing, fabricating, joining, and manufacturing of end products. Departments include New Products, New Literature, News And Coming Events.
**Readers:** Presidents, owners, vice presidents, also chief engineers, metallurgists, designers, plant managers, department managers, purchasing managers.

## MOTION CONTROL
67193

7500 Old Oak Blvd.
Cleveland, OH 44130
Telephone: (216) 826-2839
FAX: (216) 891-2726
Year Established: 1990
Pub. Frequency: 10/yr.
Page Size: standard
Subscrip. Rate: $50/yr.; $90/yr. foreign
Circulation: 35,000
Circulation Type: paid
**Owner(s):**
Advanstar Communications, Inc.
7500 Old Oak Blvd.
Cleveland, OH 44130
Telephone: (216) 826-2839
Ownership %: 100
**Management:**
Sheldon G. Schultz ............................Publisher
Emma Lou Heitbrink ............Business Manager
**Editorial:**
Daniel P. Miller .....................................Editor
**Desc.:** Covers new and developing techniques and the practical applications of new and existing technologies for motion control; includes sections on industry news and new products.

## ORNAMENTAL-MISCELLANEOUS METAL FABRICATOR
24035

804-10 Main St., Ste. E
Forest Park, GA 30050
Telephone: (404) 363-4009
FAX: (404) 366-1852
Year Established: 1959
Pub. Frequency: bi-m.
Page Size: standard
Subscrip. Rate: $15/yr. US.; $25/yr. Canada & Mexico; $75/yr. others
Materials: 01,02,05,06,10,15,17,19,20,21

Freelance Pay: $125/1200 wds.; $150/1500 wds.
Print Process: offset
Circulation: 7,900
Circulation Type: free & paid
**Owner(s):**
National Ornamental & Misc. Metals Assn. (NOMMA)
804-10 Main St., Ste. E
Forest Park, GA 30050
Telephone: (404) 363-4009
Ownership %: 100
**Management:**
Todd Daniel ......................................Manager
**Editorial:**
Todd Daniel ..........................................Editor
**Desc.:** Targeted to managers and owners of ornamental and miscellaneous metal fabrication shops. Covers trends, technologies, outstanding jobs, and industry news.
**Readers:** Designers and fabricators of ornamental and miscellaneous metal products.

## PLATING & SURFACE FINISHING
24036

12644 Research Pkwy.
Orlando, FL 32826
Telephone: (407) 281-6441
FAX: (407) 281-6446
Year Established: 1909
Pub. Frequency: m.
Page Size: standard
Subscrip. Rate: $60/yr. US., Canada & Mexico; $71/yr. foreign
Circulation: 9,000
Circulation Type: controlled
**Owner(s):**
American Electroplaters/Surface Finishers Society
12644 Research Pkwy.
Orlando, FL 32826
Telephone: (407) 281-6441
Ownership %: 100
**Management:**
Ted Witt .............................................Publisher
Ted Witt .................................Executive Director
Steve Rigo .......................Advertising Manager
**Editorial:**
Sylvia L. Baxley .....................................Editor
Liz Moran .................................Managing Editor
Kathy Schumacher .......Advertising Coordinator
Debbie Swank .......................Publication Director
Robert Herring, CEF ................Technical Editor
**Desc.:** An international, individual-membership, non-profit professional association dedicated to advancement of the science of electroplating and surface finishing. AESF fosters this advancement through broad research and comprehensive educational programs, benefiting not only its members, but all persons involved in this widely diversified industry, as well as government agencies and the general public. AESF disseminates technical and practical information through reports, other publications, meetings, conferences, symposia, and this journal. Membership in AESF is open to all surface finishing professionals as well as to those who provide services, supplies, equipment, and support to the industry.
**Readers:** Electroplating, surface finishing, industry engineers, specifiers, buyers, consultants, captive & job shop management.

## PRODUCTION
23462

6600 Clough Pike
Cincinnati, OH 45244-4090
Telephone: (513) 231-8020
FAX: (513) 231-2818
Year Established: 1934

---

Pub. Frequency: m.
Page Size: standard
Subscrip. Rate: $48/yr. US; $84/yr.
surface mail foreign; $156/yr. airmail
foreign
Circulation: 75,003
Circulation Type: paid
**Owner(s):**
Gardner Publications, Inc.
6600 Clough Pike
Cincinnati, OH 45244
Telephone: (513) 231-8020
Ownership %: 100
**Management:**
Richard G. Kline ................................President
Daniel Luciano ...............................Publisher
**Editorial:**
Gary S. Vasilash .................Senior Editor
Jann Dunn ...............................Managing Editor
**Desc.:** Directed to all plants in country
(approx. 20,000) engaged in repetitive,
metal working manufacturing.
**Readers:** Manufacturing managers and
engineers in metal working plants.

24037
## PRODUCTS FINISHING
6600 Clough Pike
Cincinnati, OH 45244
Telephone: (513) 231-8020
Year Established: 1936
Pub. Frequency: m.
Page Size: pocket
Subscrip. Rate: $36/yr.
Freelance Pay: varies
Circulation: 46,395
Circulation Type: controlled
**Owner(s):**
Gardner Publications, Inc.
6600 Clough Pike
Cincinnati, OH 45244
Telephone: (513) 231-8020
Ownership %: 100
**Management:**
Richard G. Kline ................................President
G. Thomas Robison ........................Publisher
Donald E. Kline ................Advertising Manager
**Editorial:**
Beverly A. Graves ...............................Editor
Barbara Dunn ........................Managing Editor
Mary Poll .....................Administrative Assistant
**Desc.:** Main interests include electroplating
and painting of metal and plastics.
Contributed articles should contain
specific data concerning processes and
equipment described. Departments
Include: New Products, News of the
Industry, etc. Uses personnel notes,
promotions, etc.
**Readers:** Managing personnel and
engineers.

68961
## SERVICING DEALER
206 S. Galena Ave., Ste. 90
Freeport, IL 61032-5177
Telephone: (815) 232-5176
FAX: (815) 232-1363
Year Established: 1987
Pub. Frequency: 8/yr.
Subscrip. Rate: $30/yr.
Circulation: 23,000
Circulation Type: controlled
**Owner(s):**
Communications Group, Inc.
206 S. Galena Ave., Ste. 90
Freeport, IL 61032-5177
Telephone: (815) 232-5176
Ownership %: 100
**Editorial:**
A.D. Horn ...............................................Editor
**Desc.:** Includes articles on technical,
management and industry news topics.
**Readers:** Outdoor power equipment
servicing dealers.

24040
## TOOLING & PRODUCTION MAGAZINE
29100 Aurora Rd., Ste. 200
Solon, OH 44139
Telephone: (216) 248-1125
FAX: (216) 686-0214
Year Established: 1934
Pub. Frequency: m.
Page Size: standard
Subscrip. Rate: $90/yr. US; $125/yr.
Canada; $195/yr. elsewhere
Circulation: 80,000
Circulation Type: controlled
**Owner(s):**
Huebcore Communications, Inc.
29100 Aurora Rd., Ste. 200
Solon, OH 44139
Telephone: (216) 248-1125
Ownership %: 100
**Management:**
Thomas J. Corcoran ..........................President
Stanley J. Modic ..............................Publisher
**Editorial:**
Stanley J. Modic ...................Editor in Chief
Jim Lorincz ............................Senior Editor
John Davison ..........................Senior Editor
John W. Sheridan .................Economics Editor
Elizabeth Engler ..................Editorial Assistant
John R. Coleman ......................Miscellaneous
Eugene E. Sprow ..........Special Projects Editor
**Desc.:** Use contributed (by-lined and non-
by-lined) and staff-written technical
know-how articles on equipment and
methods for tooling of, production in and
management of metalworking plants and
departments. Departments include:
Coming Events, Literature, Book
Reviews, Presstime Notes, Management
Update, Quality in Manufacturing,
Manufacturing in Action, Computer
Hardware and Software, Product News,
Speaking Out.
**Readers:** Manufacturing engineers and
manufacturing managers in the
metalworking industries.

66740
## TPQ, THE TUBE & PIPE QUARTERLY
833 Featherstone Rd.
Rockford, IL 61107-6302
Telephone: (815) 399-8700
FAX: (815) 399-7279
Year Established: 1990
Pub. Frequency: q.
Page Size: standard
Subscrip. Rate: $15/yr. non-qualified;
$45/yr. foreign; $25/yr. Canada &
Mexico
Materials: 01,02,27,28,29,30,32,33
Print Process: web offset
Circulation: 30,000
Circulation Type: controlled
**Owner(s):**
Croydon Group, The
833 Featherstone Rd.
Rockford, IL 61107-6302
Telephone: (815) 399-8700
Ownership %: 100
**Management:**
John Nandzik ...................................Publisher
**Editorial:**
Kathy Velasco ..........................Executive Editor
Theresa Olmsted ...............................Editor
David Jackson ......................Assistant Editor
Amy Boeselager ......................Associate Editor
Mary Puckett-Lindquist ..........Associate Editor
Deb Strout ...........................Production Director
Mike Lacny ...........................................Sales

**Desc.:** Disseminates new and complete
information relating to the producing and
fabricating of metal tube and pipe. The
main editorial consists of articles and
news releases designed to assist
owners, managers, manufacturing
engineers, supervisors, and foremen in
the evaluation of new methods and
techniques.
**Readers:** Metal tube & pipe producers and
fabricators; tube & pipe equipment
builders-suppliers.
**Deadline:** story-3 1/2 mos. prior to pub.
date; news-6 wks. prior; ads-2 1/2 mos.
prior

68960
## USED EQUIPMENT DIRECTORY
P.O. Box 823
Hasbrouck Heights, NJ 07604
Telephone: (800) 526-6052
FAX: (201) 393-9553
Year Established: 1949
Pub. Frequency: m.
Page Size: 8 1/2*10 1/2
Subscrip. Rate: $30/yr. US; $100/yr.
foreign
Print Process: web offset
Circulation: 75,000
Circulation Type: controlled & paid
**Owner(s):**
Penton Publishing, Div. Pittway Corp.
P.O. Box 823
Hasbrouck Heights, NJ 07604
Telephone: (800) 526-6052
FAX: (201) 393-9553
Ownership %: 100
**Management:**
James J. Mack ...................................Publisher
**Editorial:**
Robert L. Tannen ................Associate Publisher
**Desc.:** Lists over 34,000 available used
machines and equipment from more
than 800 dealers.
**Readers:** 130,000 manufacturing plant
managers and purchasing managers
(Rotational circ. to 75,000 monthly).
2300 used equipment dealers selling
manufacturing equipment and
machinery.

66593
## 33 METALPRODUCING
1100 Superior Ave.
Cleveland, OH 44114
Telephone: (216) 696-7000
Year Established: 1962
Pub. Frequency: m.
Page Size: standard
Subscrip. Rate: $50/yr.
Materials: 01,02,06,27,28,29,30,31,32,33
Freelance Pay: negotiable
Print Process: web offset
Circulation: 23,000
Circulation Type: controlled
**Owner(s):**
Penton Publishing
1100 Superior Ave.
Cleveland, OH 44114
Telephone: (216) 696-7000
FAX: (216) 696-7658
Ownership %: 100
**Editorial:**
Wallace Huskonen ...............................Editor
James Forthoter ...............Publication Director

**Readers:** Operating management at
metalproducing plants.
**Deadline:** story-2 mos. prior to pub. date;
news-2 mos. prior; photo-2 mos. prior;
ads-1st of mo. prior

## Group 152-Maintenance & Cleaning-Equipment & Supplies

69337
## AMERICAN WINDOW CLEANER MAGAZINE
27 Oak Creek Rd.
El Sobrante, CA 94803-3505
Telephone: (510) 222-7080
FAX: (510) 223-7080
Year Established: 1986
Pub. Frequency: bi-m.
Page Size: standard
Subscrip. Rate: $6 newsstand; $35/yr.
individuals; $60 institutions
Materials: 01,15,17,19,20,21,28,29,30,32,33
Print Process: web offset
Circulation: 9,000
Circulation Type: free & paid
**Owner(s):**
Richard Fabry
27 Oak Creek Rd.
El Sobrante, CA 94803
Telephone: (510) 222-7080
FAX: (510) 223-7080
Ownership %: 100
**Management:**
Richard Fabry ...................................Publisher
**Editorial:**
Richard Fabry ......................................Editor
**Desc.:** Everything that helps
professionalize and encourage safety in
the professional window cleaning
industry. Articles designed to save
window cleaners both time and money;
new products, bidding, add-on
businesses, association news, upcoming
events and more.
**Readers:** Professional window cleaners,
both beginners and advanced, from
around the world, their suppliers,
manufacturers, some janitorial
companies, and members of the
International Window Cleaning
Association (IWCA) as well as some
media.
**Deadline:** story-2 mos. prior to pub. date;
news-2 mos. prior; photo-2 mos. prior;
ads-2 wks. prior to pub. date

22129
## BROOM, BRUSH & MOP
118 E. Main
Arcola, IL 61910
Telephone: (217) 268-4950
Mailing Address:
P.O. Box 130
Arcola, IL 61910
Year Established: 1912
Pub. Frequency: m.
Page Size: standard
Subscrip. Rate: $20/yr.
Freelance Pay: varies
Circulation: 1,200
Circulation Type: paid
**Owner(s):**
Don Rankin
118 E. Main
Arcola, IL 61910
Telephone: (217) 268-4950
Ownership %: 100
**Management:**
Linda Rankin ...................................Publisher
Don Rankin ......................................Publisher
**Editorial:**
Don Rankin ........................................Editor

**Materials Accepted/Included:** 01-Business news 02-By-line articles 03-Fashion news 04-Food news 05-Freelance copy 06-Letters to editor 07-Real estate news 08-Sports news 09-Travel news 10-Book rev. 11-Movie rev. 12-Music rev. 13-TV rev. 14-Theater rev. 15-Coming events 16-Obituaries 17-Question & answer 18-Social announcements 19-Artwork 20-Cartoons 21-Photos 22-TV listings 23-Audio rec. 24-Video rec. 25-Books 26-Films/film clips 27-Personnel news 28-Press releases 29-New product news/photos 30-Trade lit. 31-Contracts awarded 32-Display adv. 33-Classified adv.

**Desc.:** Covers industry news, sales analysis, market conditions, supplier's surveys, new product news and monthly import and export figures on both raw materials and finished products.
**Readers:** Manufacturers of brooms, broom suppliers, brush factories, etc.

22130
## BRUSHWARE
Rt. 3
Huddleston, VA 24104
Telephone: (703) 297-1517
FAX: (703) 297-1519
Mailing Address:
 P.O. Box 165
 Huddleston, VA 24104
Year Established: 1898
Pub. Frequency: bi-m.
Page Size: standard
Subscrip. Rate: $35/yr.
Freelance Pay: negotiable
Circulation: 2,200
Circulation Type: paid
**Owner(s):**
Centaur & Co.
P.O. Box 165
Huddleston, VA 24104
Ownership %: 100
**Management:**
Carl H. Wurzer .........................Publisher
**Editorial:**
Thomas Goldberg .........Editor in Chief
**Desc.:** Edited for the applicator industry, which includes brushes, rollers, mops, pads, mitts and products that apply materials, clean or polish general surfaces. Articles of 1,000 words, about brushes, brooms and mops. By-line, black and white photos. Emphasis is given to applicator techniques, new applicator materials and methods. General news and new product information is carried equally for all members of the applicator, cleaning and polishing industries. Departments include: Personalities, Plant Stories and Market Reports.
**Readers:** Brush, roller and applicator manufacturers, libraries and miscellaneous.

22656
## CLEANING BUSINESS
1512 Western Ave.
Seattle, WA 98101
Telephone: (206) 622-4241
FAX: (206) 622-6876
Mailing Address:
 P.O. Box 1273
 Seattle, WA 98111
Year Established: 1980
Pub. Frequency: 4/yr.
Page Size: standard
Subscrip. Rate: $20/yr.; $36/2 yrs.
Materials: 01,02,05,06,10,15,16,17,19,20,
 21,25,27,28,29,30,31,32,33
Freelance Pay: varies
Print Process: web offset
Circulation: 5,000
Circulation Type: free & paid
**Owner(s):**
Cleaning Consultant Service, Inc.
1512 Western Ave.
P.O. Box 1273
Seattle, WA 98101
Telephone: (206) 682-9748
Ownership %: 100
**Management:**
Wm. R. Griffin .........................President
Wm. R. Griffin .........................Publisher
Betty Saunders ..........Advertising Manager
Betty Saunders ..........Sales Manager
**Editorial:**
Phil Johnson ......................Art Director
Jim Saunders ..............Associate Editor

Thomas Arron ......................Production Director
**Desc.:** We publish and are interested in material that will be of value to the owners of small service businesses that specialize in the cleaning & maintenance of residences, buildings, areas and surfaces. We welcome all types of related articles, photos, news releases, etc. Departments include: Products, Feature Articles, Book and Seminar Reviews, Technical, Educational, Safety. We publish Technical How To, Interviews and Management Subject articles. Our publication goes to cleaning related service businesses, specifically janitorial, window washing, carpet cleaning, house cleaning, fire damage and water restoration contractors.
**Readers:** Self employed small business owners who clean carpets, upholstery, floors in office buildings and homes, suppliers, janitorial services and contract cleaners, maintenance professionals.

66291
## CLEANING MANAGEMENT
13 Century Hill Dr.
Latham, NY 12110-2197
Telephone: (518) 783-1281
FAX: (518) 783-1386
Year Established: 1964
Pub. Frequency: m.
Page Size: standard
Subscrip. Rate: $40/yr.
Materials: 01,02,05,06,27,28,29,30,31,32,33
Freelance Pay: varies
Circulation: 40,000
Circulation Type: controlled & paid
**Owner(s):**
National Trade Publications, Inc.
13 Century Hill Dr.
Latham, NY 12110
Telephone: (518) 783-1281
Ownership %: 100
**Management:**
Humphrey Tyler ......................President
Alice Savino .........................Publisher
Jean Rench ..............Circulation Manager
**Editorial:**
Steve Kane ...............Executive Editor
Tom Williams ......................Editor
**Desc.:** Editorial emphasis in Cleaning Management Magazine is on educational, instructional and informational material specifically designed to assist those responsible for building cleaning maintenance operations and sanitation to improve efficiency, increase economy and upgrade work performance. Cleaning Management Magazine is the "how-to" educational reference publication for the building cleaning maintenance industry.
**Readers:** In-house custodial/housekeeping managers, and cleaning contractors.
**Deadline:** story-1st of mo. prior to pub. date; news-1st of mo. prior to pub. date; photo-1st of mo. prior; ads-1st of mo. prior

66345
## CLEANROOMS
84 Park Ave.
Flemington, NJ 08822
Telephone: (908) 788-0343
FAX: (908) 788-3782
Year Established: 1988
Pub. Frequency: m.
Page Size: tabloid
Subscrip. Rate: free
Materials: 29
Circulation: 42,500
Circulation Type: controlled & free

**Owner(s):**
Witter Publishing Co., Inc.
84 Park Ave.
Flemington, NJ 08822
Telephone: (908) 788-0343
FAX: (908) 788-3782
Ownership %: 100
**Management:**
Robert A. Witter .........................Publisher
Jennifer Perna ..............Circulation Manager
**Editorial:**
Thomas M. Brotzman ......................Editor
Rita C. Peters ..............Editorial Director
**Desc.:** Discusses engineering, management and quality control issues relating to controlled environment manufacturing.

24923
## MAINTENANCE SUPPLIES
445 Broad Hollow Rd., Ste. 21
Huntington Station, NY 11747
Telephone: (516) 845-2700
FAX: (516) 845-7109
Year Established: 1956
Pub. Frequency: m.
Page Size: standard
Subscrip. Rate: $45/yr. US, Canada;
 $80/yr. foreign
Freelance Pay: $150-$300/article
Circulation: 21,603
Circulation Type: controlled
**Owner(s):**
PTN Publishing Co.
445 Broadhollow Rd., Ste. 21
Melville, NY 11747
Telephone: (516) 845-2700
Ownership %: 100
**Management:**
Stanley Sills .........................President
Mike Rossi .........................Publisher
Susan A. Brady ..............Advertising Manager
**Editorial:**
Linda Bruder ......................Editor
**Desc.:** Desires merchandising articles with detail on how sanitary supply firms have increased volume; articles on how specific cleaning products' sales can be increased. Use occasional historical pieces on products, companies and personalities in the sanitary supply industry. Departments include New Products; Trade News; New Literature; Light Comment.
**Readers:** Jobbers, dealers and distributors of sanitary supplies, chemicals and equipment.

24925
## PEST CONTROL
7500 Old Oak Blvd.
Cleveland, OH 44130
Telephone: (216) 243-8100
FAX: (216) 891-2675
Year Established: 1933
Pub. Frequency: m.
Page Size: standard
Subscrip. Rate: $5/copy; $22/yr.; $35/2 yrs.
Materials: 02,05,06,15,21,27,28,29,30,32,33
Freelance Pay: $200-$500
Print Process: offset
Circulation: 16,000
Circulation Type: controlled
**Owner(s):**
Advanstar Communications, Inc.
7500 Old Oak Blvd.
Cleveland, OH 44130
Telephone: (216) 243-8100
Ownership %: 100
**Management:**
Richard Swank ..............Chairman of Board
Ed Aster .........................President
Bob Earley ......................Vice President
Jerry Mix .........................Publisher
Jim Gillespie ......................Sales Manager

**Editorial:**
Tom Johnson ......................Editor
Lisa Shaheen ..............Managing Editor
Vern Walter .........................Columnist
Douglas Mampe, Ph.D. .........................Columnist
Linda O'Hara ..............Production Coordinator
Douglas Mampe, Ph.D. ............Technical Editor
**Desc.:** Interested only in news, articles, stories, or new product releases dealing with urban and structural insect & rodent control, environmental sanitation, public health pest control, and food processing/handling industry pest control. Publication also deals with structural pest control related business, financial management, personnel training, fleet maintenance, etc. Departments include: Calendar, Regional, National, & Government News, Question & Answer Column, New Products, Letters, Tips, Research.
**Readers:** Pest control industry manufacturers, distributors, business operators, industrial and food industry sanitarians, military pest control officers.
**Deadline:** story-2 mos. prior to pub. date

24926
## PEST CONTROL TECHNOLOGY
4012 Bridge Ave.
Cleveland, OH 44113
Telephone: (216) 961-4130
Year Established: 1972
Pub. Frequency: m.
Page Size: standard
Subscrip. Rate: $30/yr.
Freelance Pay: $200-$300/article
Circulation: 18,100
Circulation Type: paid
**Owner(s):**
Richard J.W. & Nancy Foster
15510 Garfield Rd.
Wakeman, OH 44889
Ownership %: 100
**Management:**
Richard J.W. Foster .........................President
Richard J.W. Foster .........................Publisher
**Editorial:**
Pete Fehrenback ......................Editor
Charlotte Turcotte ..............Art Director
Dan Moreland ..............Associate Publisher
Rosalie Slusher ..............Circulation Director
Jami Childs ..............Production Director
**Desc.:** Serving urban/industrial pest control service industry, with business and technical subject matter.
**Readers:** 90% owners & presidents, 10% branch managers, other managers, technical directors

24927
## SANITARY MAINTENANCE
2100 W. Florist Ave.
Milwaukee, WI 53209
Telephone: (414) 228-7701
FAX: (414) 228-1134
Mailing Address:
 P.O. Box 694
 Milwaukee, WI 53201
Year Established: 1943
Pub. Frequency: m.
Page Size: standard
Subscrip. Rate: $49/yr.; $89/2 yrs.
Freelance Pay: varies
Circulation: 18,000
Circulation Type: controlled
**Owner(s):**
Trade Press Publishing Corp.
2100 W. Florist Ave.
Milwaukee, WI 53209
Telephone: (414) 228-7701
Ownership %: 100
**Management:**
Robert J. Wisniewski .........................Publisher
Brad R. Ehlert .........................Sales Manager

**Materials Accepted/Included:** 01-Business news 02-By-line articles 03-Fashion news 04-Food news 05-Freelance copy 06-Letters to editor 07-Real estate news 08-Sports news 09-Travel news 10-Book rev. 11-Movie rev. 12-Music rev. 13-TV rev. 14-Theater rev. 15-Coming events 16-Obituaries 17-Question & answer 18-Social announcements 19-Artwork 20-Cartoons 21-Photos 22-TV listings 23-Audio rec. 24-Video rec. 25-Books 26-Films/film clips 27-Personnel news 28-Press releases 29-New product news/photos 30-Trade lit. 31-Contracts awarded 32-Display adv. 33-Classified adv.

**Editorial:**
Austin Weber ..............................Managing Editor
Dick Yake ...................................Editorial Director
Austin Weber .....................New Products Editor
**Desc.:** Edited for business executives actively engaged in the distribution of janitorial supplies, maintenance equipment, cleaning chemicals, paper products, and food service disposables.
**Readers:** Sanitary supply houses and paper merchants.

## Group 154-Marine, Maritime & Shipbuilding

### BOAT & MOTOR DEALER
23666
7800 Merrimac Ave.
Niles, IL 60714
Telephone: (708) 967-1810
FAX: (708) 965-7639
Year Established: 1958
Pub. Frequency: m.
Page Size: standard
Subscrip. Rate: $30/yr.
Freelance Pay: varies
Circulation: 32,000
Circulation Type: paid
**Owner(s):**
Preston Publications
7800 Merrimac Ave.
Niles, IL 60714
Telephone: (708) 982-1810
Ownership %: 100
**Management:**
G. Van Zevern ...............................Publisher
Jerry Burns .....................Advertising Manager
Kit Hatcher ........................Circulation Manager
**Editorial:**
Larry Hooper ...................................Editor
Diana Weaver .........................Managing Editor
Lisa Venus ...............................Assistant Editor
Charles Marcussen .......Merchandising Director
**Desc.:** Carries successful dealer's stories each month; these are keyed to dealers with specialized approaches in selling pleasure boat marine equipment and accessories. Departments include: a news section, new products, literature, industry and distributor news, executives on the move. Most of our material is staff covered but publicity material for ideas, news, etc., is welcomed.
**Readers:** Pleasure boat marine equipment dealers, distributors, sales executives, and manufacturers.

### ENSIGN, THE
23671
1504 Blue Ridge Rd.
Raleigh, NC 27607
Telephone: (919) 821-0892
Mailing Address:
   P.O. Box 31664
   Raleigh, NC 27622
Year Established: 1914
Pub. Frequency: m.
Page Size: standard
Subscrip. Rate: $10/yr.; $16/2 yrs.
Circulation: 50,000
Circulation Type: paid
**Owner(s):**
United States Power Squadrons
1504 Blue Ridge
Raleigh, NC 27607
Telephone: (919) 821-0281
Ownership %: 100
**Editorial:**
Carol A. Eddy ...................................Editor
Jayne Potter Teel ...................Associate Editor
**Desc.:** Official publication of United States Power Squadrons. A private, non-profit boating safety and education organization.
**Readers:** Association members and families.

### JOURNAL OF MARITIME LAW & COMMERCE
69261
2035 Reading Rd.
Cincinnati, OH 45202
Telephone: (513) 421-4142
FAX: (513) 562-8116
Year Established: 1969
Pub. Frequency: q.
Subscrip. Rate: $95/yr. US; $195/yr. foreign
Circulation: 2,500
Circulation Type: paid
**Owner(s):**
Anderson Publishing Co.
2035 Reading Rd.
Cincinnati, OH 45202
Telephone: (513) 421-4142
Ownership %: 100
**Editorial:**
John P. McMahon ...................................Editor

### MARITIME REPORTER & ENGINEERING NEWS
23677
118 E. 25th St.
New York, NY 10010
Telephone: (212) 477-6700
FAX: (212) 254-6271
Year Established: 1939
Pub. Frequency: m.
Page Size: tabloid
Subscrip. Rate: free to industry
Circulation: 28,600
Circulation Type: controlled
**Owner(s):**
Maritime Activity Reports
Ownership %: 100
**Management:**
John E. O'Malley .............................Publisher
Charles P. O'Malley .........................Publisher
John C. O'Malley .............................Publisher
**Editorial:**
Erin O'Driscoll ...................................Editor
Greg Trauthwein ...................Assistant Editor
**Desc.:** Commercial vessel design, construction operation and repair and navy - current technical articles, business news, personnel appointments, contract awards, new vessel articles, industry trends.
**Readers:** Shoreside management and engineering people.

### NORTHEAST JOURNAL OF TRANSPORTATION
23668
31 Fargo St.
South Boston, MA 02127
Telephone: (617) 695-1660
FAX: (617) 695-1665
Year Established: 1918
Pub. Frequency: w.
Page Size: tabloid
Subscrip. Rate: $82/yr.
Circulation: 1,500
Circulation Type: paid
**Owner(s):**
Northeast Journal of Transportation
31 Fargo St.
South Boston, MA 02127
Telephone: (617) 695-1660
Ownership %: 100
**Management:**
William Bourbon ...............................Publisher
**Editorial:**
George Lauriat ...................................Editor
**Desc.:** Carries sailing schedules as well as brief reports on transportation, export, import, shipping developments.
**Readers:** Industrial firms, importers, exporters, shipping agents, custom house brokers

### OCEAN ENGINEERING
23132
660 White Plains Rd., Second Fl.
Tarrytown, NY 10591-5193
Telephone: (914) 592-7700
Year Established: 1968
Pub. Frequency: bi-m.
Page Size: standard
Subscrip. Rate: $385/yr.; $731.50/2 yrs.
Circulation: 1,200
Circulation Type: paid
**Owner(s):**
Pergamon Press, Inc.
Maxwell House, Fairview Park
Elmsford, NY 10523
Telephone: (914) 592-7700
Ownership %: 100
**Management:**
Robert N. Miranda ...........................President
Robert Maxwell ...............................Publisher
A. Kranzler ......................Advertising Manager
**Editorial:**
Michael E. McCormick ................Editor in Chief
Rameswar Bhattacharyya ...........Editor in Chief
**Desc.:** A medium for original research and development work in all areas of ocean engineering. Also includes material on marine resources.

### OCEAN OIL WEEKLY REPORT
61634
3050 Post Oak, Ste. 200
Houston, TX 77056
Telephone: (713) 621-9720
FAX: (713) 963-6285
Year Established: 1965
Pub. Frequency: w.
Page Size: broadsheet
Subscrip. Rate: $335/yr.; $395/yr. foreign
Circulation: 1,000
Circulation Type: paid
**Owner(s):**
PennWell Publishing Co.
1421 S. Sheridan Rd.
Tulsa, OK 74112
Telephone: (918) 835-3161
Ownership %: 100
**Editorial:**
Michael Crowden ...................................Editor
**Desc.:** Coverage is focused on global activity concerning oil and gas exploration and development, as well as related activities, such as rig building.
**Readers:** Offshore oil and gas company management.

### PACIFIC SHIPPER
25103
424 W. 33rd St.
New York, NY 10001
Telephone: (800) 221-5488
FAX: (212) 695-5025
Year Established: 1926
Pub. Frequency: w.
Page Size: pocket
Subscrip. Rate: $120/yr. US.; $155/yr. foreign
Circulation: 7,000
Circulation Type: paid
**Owner(s):**
K-III Directory Corp.
424 W. 33rd St.
New York, NY 10001
Telephone: (212) 714-3100
Ownership %: 100
**Management:**
Allan Glass ...............................Publisher
**Editorial:**
Erik McMahon ...................................Editor
**Desc.:** Primary field, ocean shipping and traffic, rates. Also covers port development, foreign trade.
**Readers:** Shippers, freight forwarders, etc.

### PORT OF NEW ORLEANS RECORD
24369
2 Canal St., WTC Bldg., Ste. 2600
New Orleans, LA 70130
Telephone: (504) 528-3249
Mailing Address:
   P.O. Box 60046
   New Orleans, LA 70160
Year Established: 1942
Pub. Frequency: m.
Page Size: standard
Subscrip. Rate: free to qualified subscribers
Materials: 01
Freelance Pay: $5/col. in.
Circulation: 12,000
Circulation Type: controlled
**Owner(s):**
Board of Commissioners, Port of New Orleans
P.O. Box 60046
New Orleans, LA 70160
Telephone: (504) 522-2551
Ownership %: 100
**Bureau(s):**
New Orleans Publishing Group
111 Veterans Blvd., Ste. 1810
Metairie, LA 70005
Telephone: (504) 834-9292
Contact: Carolyn McLellan, Vice President
**Management:**
Carolyn McLellan ...............................Publisher
Coco Evans ......................Advertising Manager
**Editorial:**
Carolyn McLellan ....................Editorial Director
Mitch Rubin ...................................Art Director
Janina F. ...............Corporate Communications
Simmons                                     Manager
Mitch Rubin ....................Photography Editor
Don Hoffman ...................................Staff Writer
**Desc.:** Published primarily for maritime interests and world market as related to the Port of New Orleans.
**Readers:** Shipping executives, members of export/import, traffic managers, other maritime associates.

### SEA FRONTIERS
24905
400 S.E. Second Ave., 4th Fl.
Miami, FL 33131
Telephone: (305) 375-8285
FAX: (305) 375-9188
Year Established: 1954
Pub. Frequency: bi-m.
Page Size: standard
Subscrip. Rate: $24/yr.
Materials: 02,04,05,06,08,098,10,15,17,19, 21,29
Freelance Pay: $.25/wd.
Print Process: web offset
Circulation: 55,000
Circulation Type: paid
**Owner(s):**
Intl. Oceanographic Foundation (Univ. of Miami)
4600 Rickenbacker Causeway
Miami, FL 33149
Telephone: (305) 361-5786
Ownership %: 49

Nature Publishing Co.
65 Bleecker St.
New York, NY 10012
Telephone: (212) 477-9600
Ownership %: 51
**Editorial:**
Rosemary Sullivant ......................Senior Editor
Bonnie Bilyeu Gordon ...............................Editor
Faith Schaefer ....................Associate Editor

**Desc.:** General articles describing interesting life or phenomena of sea economic engineering and industrial applications of marine sciences; historical expeditions and scientists distinguished in the history of marine biology and oceanography.
**Readers:** All who are interested in the sea.

### SEA TECHNOLOGY
23684
1117 N. 19th St., Ste. 1000
Arlington, VA 22209
Telephone: (703) 524-3136
FAX: (703) 841-0852
Year Established: 1960
Pub. Frequency: m.
Page Size: standard
Subscrip. Rate: $25/yr.
Materials: 01,02,06,10,15,21,25,27,28,29, 30,31,32,33
Freelance Pay: negotiable
Circulation: 23,494
Circulation Type: controlled
**Owner(s):**
Compass Publishing, Inc.
1117 N. 19th St., Ste. 1000
Arlington, VA 22209
Telephone: (703) 524-3136
Ownership %: 100
**Management:**
Chas. H. Bussmann ..............................Publisher
Amos Bussmann ................Advertising Manager
**Editorial:**
David M. Graham ..............................Editor
Richard F. Burns ......................Associate Editor
**Desc.:** Serves the underwater defense, marine sciences and ocean/marine/offshore fields. Covers all aspects of undersea research, design, and operations. Departments include: Editorial; Soundings; Letters to the Editor; Capital Report; New Products; People/Employment; New Literature; Book Reviews.
**Readers:** Administrators, engineering management, designers, engineers, scientists, purchasing and sales personnel.

### SEAWAY REVIEW
23685
221 Water St.
Boyne City, MI 49712
Telephone: (616) 582-2814
FAX: (616) 582-3392
Year Established: 1970
Pub. Frequency: q.
Page Size: standard
Subscrip. Rate: $20/yr.
Freelance Pay: $25-$300
Circulation: 8,500
Circulation Type: controlled & paid
**Owner(s):**
Jacques LesStrang, Publ.
221 Water St.
Boyne City, MI 49712
Telephone: (616) 582-2814
Ownership %: 100
**Management:**
Jacques LesStrang ..............................Publisher
Elizabeth Talboys ..............Circulation Manager
**Editorial:**
Michelle Cortright ....................Managing Editor
Dave Knight ..........................Editorial Director

**Desc.:** Serves the economic interests of the Great Lakes-St. Lawrence Seaway region, internodal transportation, lake ports and the Mid-continent maritime industry including the shipbuilding industry and Great Lakes fleet. Articles by experts in economics, government, transportation, ships and maritime affairs combine with late region news and special in-depth reports to bring readers an up-to-the-minute, highly authoritative report on the events and the vital areas of importance to the mid-continent and Great Lakes.
**Readers:** Entire Great Lakes maritime community including international, federal and state government, as well as heads of firms shipping into and out of the Midcontinent.

### UNDERWATER MAGAZINE
69731
5222 FM 1960 W., Ste. 112
Houston, TX 77069
Telephone: (713) 440-0278
FAX: (713) 580-4433
Year Established: 1989
Pub. Frequency: q.
Page Size: 8 1/2 x 11
Subscrip. Rate: n/a.
Materials: 01,02,06,27,28,29,32,33
Print Process: offset
Circulation: 15,000
Circulation Type: controlled
**Owner(s):**
Doyle Publishing Co.
5222 FM 1960 W., Ste. 112
Houston, TX 77069
Telephone: (713) 440-0278
Ownership %: 100
**Management:**
William H. Doyle ..............................Publisher
**Editorial:**
Ross Saxon ..............................Executive Editor
Dee Hoffman ........................Managing Editor
Barbara Treadway ..............Circulation Director
**Readers:** Buyers of commercial diving and underwater services, service and supply companies, and the members of the Association of Diving Contractors.
**Deadline:** news-45 days prior to pub. date; ads-45 days prior

### WATERWAYS JOURNAL
23686
319 N. Fourth St.
650 Security Bldg.
St. Louis, MO 63102
Telephone: (314) 241-7354
FAX: (314) 241-4207
Year Established: 1887
Pub. Frequency: w.
Page Size: standard
Subscrip. Rate: $28/yr.
Circulation: 5,800
Circulation Type: paid
**Owner(s):**
Waterways Journal, Inc.
319 N. Fourth St.,
650 Security Bldg.
St. Louis, MO 63102
Telephone: (314) 241-7354
Ownership %: 100
**Management:**
H. Nelson Spencer III ........................Publisher
Rick Bensinger ..................Advertising Manager
**Editorial:**
Jack R. Simpson ..............................Editor
John Shoulberg ..................Assistant Editor
Daniel C. Owen ........................Associate Editor
John Shoulberg ..............New Products Editor
Jack R. Simpson ..............................News Editor
Jack R. Simpson ..............................Photo

**Desc.:** Main field of interest in inland marine/Mississippi River and tributaries, Gulf intracoastal canal, harbor craft, coastal towing companies. Covers new equipment and appliances, marine supplies, shipyards, engine manufacturers, boat crews, barge lines, dredgers, terminals, U.S. engineers and coast guard activities, improvement associations.

### WAVES
56229
9825 Bonnie Vista Dr.
La Mesa, CA 91941
Telephone: (619) 660-0402
Mailing Address:
P.O. Box 368
Spring Valley, CA 91976
Year Established: 1981
Pub. Frequency: bi-m.
Page Size: standard
Subscrip. Rate: $45/yr. US, Canada, Mexico; $75/yr. elsewhere
Circulation: 5,000
Circulation Type: paid
**Owner(s):**
Windate Enterprises, Inc.
9825 Bonnie Vista Dr.
La Mesa, CA 91941
Telephone: (619) 660-0402
Ownership %: 100
**Management:**
Deam Given ..............................President
Catherine Marley ..............................Manager
**Editorial:**
Deam Given ..............................Editor
Deam Given ..............................Advertising
Kelly Watkins ............Communications Director
**Desc.:** International news about marine technology presented in a quick-read format. Most up-to-date publication in the ocean industry. Includes sections about new products, contracts, coming events, subsea defense, manned submersibles, ocean instrumentation, and the diving industry.
**Readers:** Top level executives & engineers, undersea technology manufacturers, offshore & inshore contractors, military & government installations, scientific institutions. Readers from USA, Europe, Asia, Australia & Canada.

### WORLD DREDGING MINING & CONSTRUCTION
23688
17951 Sky Park Cir., Ste. C
Irvine, CA 92714
Telephone: (714) 553-0836
Mailing Address:
P.O. Box 17479
Irvine, CA 92713-7479
Year Established: 1965
Pub. Frequency: m.
Page Size: standard
Subscrip. Rate: $28/yr.; $48/2 yrs.; $62/3 yrs.
Materials: 01,06,10,15,21,25,27,28,29,30, 31,32,33
Print Process: offset
Circulation: 3,400
Circulation Type: controlled & paid
**Owner(s):**
Placer Management Corp.
P.O. Box 17479
Irvine, CA 92713-7479
Telephone: (714) 553-0836
FAX: (714) 863-9261
Ownership %: 100

**Bureau(s):**
World Dredging European Editorial & Adver. Office
South Place, Derby Rd.
Haslemere, Surrey GU27 1AH, United Kingdom
Telephone: 0428-64-2208
Contact: D. Mark Carter, European Editor
**Management:**
M. J. Richardson ..............................President
M. J. Richardson ..............................Publisher
Steve Richardson ................Business Manager
**Editorial:**
Ron Bowman ..............................Editor
**Desc.:** The only U.S. publication exclusively serving the world-wide dredging, mining and marine construction industry. Editorial emphasis on dredge design, operation and maintenance; port and harbor construction; waterways; dredge mining; precious minerals, tin, sand, shell, gravel and aggregate production; construction of piers, wharves, and jetties; land creation and reclamation; submarine pipelining and ocean mining; public works.
**Readers:** Executive, management, operating personnel. Consulting engineers, government agencies.
**Deadline:** story-5th of mo.; news-10th of mo.; photo-5th of mo.; ads-5th of mo.

## Group 156-Meats & Meat Processing

### MEAT & POULTRY
23691
90 Throckmorton Ave.
Mill Valley, CA 94941
Telephone: (415) 388-7575
Mailing Address:
P.O. Box 1059
Mill Valley, CA 94942
Year Established: 1955
Pub. Frequency: m.
Page Size: standard
Subscrip. Rate: $40/yr. US.; $75/yr. foreign
Materials: 01,02,05,06,15,19,21,27,28,29, 30,32,33
Freelance Pay: negotiable
Print Process: web offset
Circulation: 18,850
Circulation Type: controlled & paid
**Owner(s):**
Oman Publishing, Inc.
90 Throckmorton Ave.
Mill Valley, CA 94942
Telephone: (415) 388-7575
Ownership %: 100
**Management:**
Michael J. Alaimo ..............................President
**Editorial:**
Steve Bjerklie ..............................Editor in Chief
**Desc.:** General business and technical industry information.
**Readers:** Management of meat and poultry processing.

### MEAT BUSINESS MAGAZINE
23051
109 W. Washington
Millstadt, IL 62260
Telephone: (314) 621-0170
FAX: (618) 476-1616
Mailing Address:
P.O. Box 28830
St. Louis, MO 63123
Year Established: 1939
Pub. Frequency: m.
Page Size: standard
Subscrip. Rate: $2/copy; $19/yr.
Circulation: 9,100
Circulation Type: controlled

**Materials Accepted/Included:** 01-Business news 02-By-line articles 03-Fashion news 04-Food news 05-Freelance copy 06-Letters to editor 07-Real estate news 08-Sports news 09-Travel news 10-Book rev. 11-Movie rev. 12-Music rev. 13-TV rev. 14-Theater rev. 15-Coming events 16-Obituaries 17-Question & answer 18-Social announcements 19-Artwork 20-Cartoons 21-Photos 22-TV listings 23-Audio rec. 24-Video rec. 25-Books 26-Films/film clips 27-Personnel news 28-Press releases 29-New product news/photos 30-Trade lit. 31-Contracts awarded 32-Display adv. 33-Classified adv.

4-219

**Owner(s):**
Meat Business Magazine
Telephone: (314) 638-4050
Ownership %: 100
**Management:**
Tony Nolan ................................................Publisher
Bernie Backer ....................Advertising Manager
**Editorial:**
Louise King ....................................................Editor
Janet McMurty ..............Production Coordinator
**Desc.:** Covers operational management of
meat processors and portion control
operators, new merchandising aids,
trade news, government regulations,
processing equipment. Monthly topics
include: injectors, display cases,
smokehouses, tumblers, sanitation,
sausage, seasonings, packaging, mail
order, casings, developing new products,
refrigeration, deli & catering. Special
issues: May (literature showcase), June
(convention preview), July (exhibits in
print), September (source book),
October (convention review).
**Readers:** Meat plant operators, freezer
provisioner dealers and food service
(food plan operators). Supermarket meat
dept. managers, meat market owners,
delis, catering facilities, HRI operations.

23693
**MEAT PROCESSING**
Sandstone Bldg.
Mt. Morris, IL 61054
Telephone: (815) 734-4171
FAX: (815) 734-4201
Year Established: 1962
Pub. Frequency: m.
Page Size: standard
Subscrip. Rate: $25/yr. US; $35/yr.
Canada; $70/yr. foreign
Freelance Pay: $100-$1000
Circulation: 16,000
Circulation Type: controlled
**Owner(s):**
Watt Publishing Co.
Sandstone Bldg.
Mt. Morris, IL 61054
Telephone: (815) 734-4171
Ownership %: 100
**Bureau(s):**
Meat Processing
P.O. Box 947
Cullman, AL 35056
Telephone: (205) 734-6800
Contact: David Amey, Editorial Director
**Management:**
Dr. Charles Olentine ............................Publisher
**Editorial:**
Greg Smith ....................................................Editor
David Amey ............................Editorial Director
**Desc.:** Technically oriented articles cover
each phase of the meat industry
functions from slaughtering to
processing, to transportation. Features
dealing with in-plant stories, conventions
meat science, merchandising, packaging,
equipment, production, industry news,
personnel, and management.
Departments include: Transportation,
Import/Export, Meat Science, Rendering,
News of Suppliers, Industry Bulletin
Board, Editor's Desk, USDA Regulations.
**Readers:** Individuals active in meat
packing, sausage making, wholesaling,
rendering, and supermarket meat
management.

23694
**NATIONAL PROVISIONER, THE**
1935 Shermer Rd.
Northwood, IL 60062
Telephone: (708) 205-5660
FAX: (708) 205-6680
Year Established: 1891
Pub. Frequency: m.

Page Size: standard
Subscrip. Rate: $50/yr. in US.; $100/yr.
foreign; free to qualified personnel
Freelance Pay: negotiable
Circulation: 10,000
Circulation Type: controlled
**Owner(s):**
Stagnito Publishing Co.
1935 Shermer Rd.
Northwood, IL 60062
Telephone: (708) 205-5660
Ownership %: 100
**Editorial:**
Barbara Young ............................Editor in Chief
Michelle Willman ..............New Products Editor
Dan Murphy ............................Technical Editor
**Desc.:** For executives and department
heads in the meat, poultry and seafood
processing industry.
**Readers:** Meat & poultry packers,
processors, provisioners & seafood
processors.

## Group 158-Medical & Surgical

58595
**AAC: AUGMENTATIVE & ALTERNATIVE COMMUNICATION**
P.O. Box 785
Lewiston, NY 14092-0785
FAX: (416) 522-7839
Pub. Frequency: q.
Subscrip. Rate: $67/yr. individuals;
$105/yr. institutions
Circulation: 1,600
Circulation Type: paid
**Owner(s):**
Intl Soc. Augmentative & Alternative
Communication
Ownership %: 100
**Bureau(s):**
Canadian Office
1 James St., S.
P.O. Box 620, LCD 1
Hamilton ON, L8N 3K7, Canada
Contact: Lyle L. Lloyd, Editor
**Editorial:**
Lyle Lloyd, Ph.D. ........................................Editor

23859
**ACADEMIC MEDICINE**
2450 N St., N.W.
Washington, DC 20037-1126
Telephone: (202) 828-0590
FAX: (202) 828-1123
Year Established: 1926
Pub. Frequency: m.
Page Size: standard
Subscrip. Rate: $60/yr. US; $30/yr.
students; $70/yr. foreign
Materials: 06,32
Circulation: 6,000
Circulation Type: paid
**Owner(s):**
Association of American Medical Colleges
2450 N St., N.W.
Washington, DC 20037
Telephone: (202) 828-0400
Ownership %: 100
**Management:**
Jordon J. Cohen, M.D. ........................President
Diane Sherel ....................Advertising Manager
**Editorial:**
Addeane Caelleigh ................Executive Editor
Albert Bradford ............................................Editor
Philip Diamond ............................................Editor
Lisa Dittrich ..................................................Editor
John Rose, M.D. ................Book Review Editor

**Desc.:** Contributed professional articles
dealing with the training of physicians,
the academic medicine community, and
its institutions. Departments include:
Letters to the Editor, Book Reviews.
One third of each issue is devoted to
invited articles and commentaries on the
full spectrum of issues affecting medical
education and academic medical
centers, written by medical and gov't.
leaders and policy makers. A major
portion of each issue is devoted
to research reports (peer-reviewed
articles). Also included are regular
features on international medical
education, medical informatics,
innovations in medical education,
academic computing in medicine, and
national health care policies.
**Readers:** Medical school and teaching
hospital administrators, faculty, &
trainees; policy makers; libraries.

65254
**ADOLESCENT AND PEDIATRIC GYNECOLOGY**
175 Fifth Ave.
New York, NY 10010
Telephone: (212) 460-1612
Year Established: 1987
Pub. Frequency: 4/yr.
Page Size: standard
Subscrip. Rate: $157/yr.
Materials: 10,18,21,32
Circulation: 800
Circulation Type: paid
**Owner(s):**
Springer-Verlag Publishers
175 Fifth Ave.
New York, NY 10010
Telephone: (212) 460-1500
FAX: (212) 473-6272
**Editorial:**
Joseph S. Sanfilippo ................................Editor
**Desc.:** Covers case reports, reviews of
literature, and terntds in this area of
medicine.
**Readers:** Physicians in the field of
adolescent and pediatric gynecology.

69302
**ADVANCES: THE JOURNAL OF MIND-BODY HEALTH**
9292 W. KL Ave.
Kalamazoo, MI 49009-9398
Telephone: (616) 375-2000
FAX: (616) 372-2163
Year Established: 1983
Pub. Frequency: q.
Page Size: standard
Subscrip. Rate: $39/yr.; $67/2 yrs.; $89/3
yrs. individuals; $19/yr. students &
seniors; $79/yr. institutions
Materials: 06,10,15,34
Circulation: 5,553
Circulation Type: free & paid
**Owner(s):**
Fetzer Institute
9292 W. KL Ave.
Kalamazoo, MI 49009-9398
Telephone: (616) 375-2000
FAX: (616) 372-2163
Ownership %: 100
**Management:**
Robert F. Lehman ................................President
Fetzer Institute ......................................Publisher
**Editorial:**
Harris Dienstfrey ........................................Editor
Linda Grdina ............................Managing Editor
Randy Dean ............................Circulation Editor
Michelle M. Alberty ........Publications Assistant
**Desc.:** Examines developments in the
study and understanding of mind-body
health. Encourages discussions and
exchanges among researchers and
health-care professionals.

**Readers:** Researchers, educators,
clinicians, health-care professionals.

58593
**ADVANCES IN ORTHOPAEDIC SURGERY**
1185 Ave. of the Americas
New York, NY 10036
Telephone: (212) 930-9500
FAX: (212) 869-3495
Year Established: 1977
Pub. Frequency: bi-m.
Page Size: standard
Subscrip. Rate: $58/yr. individuals US;
$125 institutions US; $88/yr. individuals
foreign; $155/yr. institutions foreign
Materials: 32
Print Process: offset lithography
Circulation: 2,800
Circulation Type: paid
**Owner(s):**
Raven Press, Inc.
1185 Avenue of the Americas
New York, NY 10036
Telephone: (212) 930-9500
FAX: (212) 869-3495
Ownership %: 100
**Editorial:**
William Cooney, M.D. ................................Editor
**Desc.:** Broad-focus periodical that deals
with all areas pertinenet to orthopedics,
including but not limited to: arthroplasty,
biomechanics, foot and ankle, hand and
upper extremities, hip, knee, pathology,
pediatric orthopedics, spine, sports
medicine, and trauma. Contributions are
divided into the following categories:
1)submitted longer review articles,
2)submitted original manuscripts,
3)invited condensations/commentaries.
**Readers:** Medical doctors who specialize
in orthopedic surgery, medical library
personnel.

61800
**AIR MEDICAL JOURNAL**
1947 Camino Vida Roble, Ste. 200
P.O. Box 2789
Carlsbad, CA 92008
Telephone: (619) 431-9797
FAX: (619) 431-8176
Year Established: 1986
Pub. Frequency: bi-m.
Page Size: standard
Subscrip. Rate: $19.95/yr.
Materials: 05,29,32,33
Freelance Pay: $100-$300
Circulation: 10,000
Circulation Type: paid
**Owner(s):**
JEMS Communications
1947 Camino Vida Roble, #200
P.O. Box 2789
Carlsbad, CA 92008
Telephone: (619) 431-9797
**Editorial:**
William Rutherford, MD ............................Editor
Tara Regan ............................Managing Editor
**Desc.:** Provides its readers with industry
news, safety tips, product information,
treatment techniques and continuing
medical education features pertinent to
improving medical skills and performing
as a flight nurse, flight paramedic,
medical director, instructor or
administrator of emergency air medical
services.
**Readers:** Individuals involved in airborne
emergency care; the official publication
of ASHBEAMS, the National Flight
Nurses Assn. (NFNA), and the National
Flight Paramedics Assn.

**Materials Accepted/Included:** 01-Business news 02-By-line articles 03-Fashion news 04-Food news 05-Freelance copy 06-Letters to editor 07-Real estate news 08-Sports news 09-Travel news 10-Book rev. 11-Movie rev. 12-Music rev. 13-TV rev. 14-Theater rev. 15-Coming events 16-Obituaries 17-Question & answer 18-Social announcements 19-Artwork 20-Cartoons 21-Photos 22-TV listings 23-Audio rec. 24-Video rec. 25-Books 26-Films/film clips 27-Personnel news 28-Press releases 29-New product news/photos 30-Trade lit. 31-Contracts awarded 32-Display adv. 33-Classified adv.

4-220

## AJNR: AMERICAN JOURNAL OF NEURORADIOLOGY
58615

428 E. Preston St.
Baltimore, MD 21202
Telephone: (410) 528-4000
FAX: (410) 528-4312
Year Established: 1980
Pub. Frequency: bi-m.
Page Size: standard
Subscrip. Rate: $133/yr. individuals;
 $160/yr. institutions
Circulation: 4,150
Circulation Type: paid
**Owner(s):**
American Society of Neuroradiology
(ASNR)
Superior St. & Fairbanks Ct.
Chicago, IL 60611
Telephone: (312) 649-2462
**Management:**
Don Pfarr ...........................Advertising Manager
Alma Wills ...................................Manager
**Editorial:**
Michael I. Huckman ..............................Editor
Claudia Brookes ...................Marketing Director

## ALCOHOL
66472

660 White Plains Rd.
Tarrytown, NY 10591-5153
Telephone: (914) 524-9200
FAX: (914) 333-2444
Pub. Frequency: bi-m.
Page Size: standard
Subscrip. Rate: $590/yr. US; varies in
 foreign countries
Circulation: 2,500
Circulation Type: paid
**Owner(s):**
Elsevier Science, Ltd.
The Boulevard, Landford Lane
Kidlington
 Oxford OX5 1GB, United Kingdom
Telephone: 44-865-843000
FAX:44-864-8430101
Ownership %: 100
**Management:**
Michael Boswood ...............................President
Roger A. Dunn ......................General Manager
**Editorial:**
Jay Feinman .......................................Advertising
Christine Giaccone ......Senior Publishing Editor
**Desc.:** A major international journal
 devoted soley to biomedical research on
 alcohol and alcoholism. Appearing bi-
 monthly, features original research
 articles, reviews, theoretical papers, and
 rapid communications.

## ALCOHOL & ALCOHOLISM
69281

660 White Plains Rd.
Tarrytown, NY 14051-5153
Telephone: (914) 524-9200
FAX: (914) 333-2444
Year Established: 1963
Pub. Frequency: 6/yr.
Circulation: 26,000
Circulation Type: paid
**Owner(s):**
Pergamon Press, Inc.
660 White Plains Rd.
Tarrytown, NY 10591-5153
Telephone: (914) 524-9200
Ownership %: 100
**Editorial:**
Timothy J. Peters ....................................Editor
**Desc.:** Publishes research from all clinical
 disciplines of medicine, and psychology,
 sociology, and epidemiology.

## AMERICAN COLLEGE OF PHYSICIANS OBSERVER
23803

Independence Mall W.
Sixth St. at Race
Philadelphia, PA 19106-1572
Telephone: (215) 351-2400
FAX: (215) 351-2644
Year Established: 1981
Pub. Frequency: m.
Page Size: tabloid
Subscrip. Rate: $14/yr.
Freelance Pay: $.25-$.60/wd.
Circulation: 66,000
Circulation Type: controlled
**Owner(s):**
American College Of Physicians
Independence Mall W.
Sixth St. at Race
Philadelphia, PA 19106
Telephone: (215) 351-2400
Ownership %: 100
**Management:**
Dr. John R. Ball, M.D., J.D. .................Publisher
Thomas J. Gillen ................Advertising Manager
Tamara Nixon ....................Circulation Manager
**Editorial:**
Robert Spanier .......................................Editor
Paula Katz ..............................Managing Editor
**Desc.:** Prints primarily nonclinical articles
 and editorials on issues in health care,
 and reports on college activities in
 health and public policy, and education
 with some brief clinical features.
**Readers:** Members of the American
 College of Physicians (doctors of
 internal medicine and its subspecialties).

## AMERICAN FAMILY PHYSICIAN
23700

8880 Ward Pkwy.
Kansas City, MO 64114
Telephone: (816) 333-9700
FAX: (816) 333-0303
Year Established: 1950
Pub. Frequency: 16/yr.; Feb., May, Sep. &
 Nov. 2/mo.
Page Size: standard
Subscrip. Rate: $65/yr.; $90/yr. foreign;
 $80/yr. US institutions; $110/yr. foreign;
 $40/yr. US students; $60/yr. foreign
 students
Materials: 06,10,32,33
Print Process: web offset
Circulation: 149,000
Circulation Type: controlled
**Owner(s):**
American Academy of Family Physicians
8880 Ward Pkwy.
Kansas City, MO 64114
Telephone: (816) 333-9700
Ownership %: 100
**Management:**
Clayton Raker Hasser ..........................Publisher
Joetta Melton ......................Associate Publisher
H. Robert Hogg ..........................Sales Manager
**Editorial:**
Janis Reece ...............................Senior Editor
Jay Siwek, M.D. ......................................Editor
Sharon Scott Morey ...............Managing Editor
**Desc.:** Content is essentially scientific.
**Readers:** Physicians in active family
 practice, AAFP members and selected
 non-member family physicians general
 practitioners, internists and osteopaths.

## AMERICAN HEART JOURNAL
23701

11830 Westline Industrial Dr.
St. Louis, MO 63146
Telephone: (314) 872-8370
Year Established: 1925
Pub. Frequency: m.
Page Size: standard
Subscrip. Rate: $84/yr.
Circulation: 11,837

Circulation Type: paid
**Owner(s):**
The C.V. Mosby Company
11830 Westline Industrial Dr.
St. Louis, MO 63146
Telephone: (314) 872-8370
Ownership %: 100
**Management:**
Carol Trumbold ...................................Publisher
Kathy Erhardt ....................Advertising Manager
**Editorial:**
Dean T. Mason, M.D. ..............................Editor
Kathy Keller ......................Production Director
**Desc.:** Devoted to cardiology and to
 diseases of the peripheral vascular
 system. Published for cardiologists,
 internists, and general practitioners.
**Readers:** Cardiologists, internists, and
 general practitioners.

## AMERICAN JOURNAL OF CARDIOLOGY, THE
23703

105 Raider Blvd.
Belle Mead, NJ 08052
Telephone: (908) 874-8550
FAX: (908) 874-8419
Year Established: 1958
Pub. Frequency: s-m.
Page Size: standard
Subscrip. Rate: $66/yr. US; $105/yr.
 Canada & Mexico; $175/yr. elsewhere
Freelance Pay: $15-$20/hr.
Circulation: 30,717
Circulation Type: paid
**Owner(s):**
Reed Elsevier Medical Publishers, USA
249 W. 17 St.
New York, NY 10011
Telephone: (212) 463-6442
Ownership %: 100
**Management:**
Ronald H. Schlosser ...........................President
Steven V. Claps ..................................Publisher
Robert Weidner .................................Publisher
**Editorial:**
William C. Roberts, M.D. ...........Editor in Chief
Judith Wagner .........................Managing Editor
**Desc.:** Independent, and indexed-
 referenced scientific journal of original
 articles that focus on practical, clinical
 approaches to diagnosis and treatment
 of cardiovascular disease. Features
 report on systemic hypertension,
 methology, drugs, pacing, and
 arrhythmia. Also included are case and
 brief reports, readers comments,
 editorials and symposia.
**Readers:** Physicians specializing in
 cardiology or internal medicine,
 residents, fellows, interns.

## AMERICAN JOURNAL OF CLINICAL PATHOLOGY
23704

227 E. Washington Sq.
Philadelphia, PA 19106
Telephone: (215) 238-4200
FAX: (215) 238-4227
Year Established: 1931
Pub. Frequency: m.
Page Size: 4 color photos/art
Subscrip. Rate: $150/yr. individuals;
 $245/yr. institutions
Circulation: 14,457
Circulation Type: paid
**Owner(s):**
American Society Of Clinical Pathologists
227 E. Washington Sq.
Philadelphia, PA 19106
Telephone: (215) 238-4200
Ownership %: 100
**Management:**
Marcia E. Serapy ................................Publisher
Beth McGee ......................Advertising Manager
Joe Baiocco ......................Production Manager

**Editorial:**
Joseph Lippincott, III ..............................Director
Marcia Serepy .....................Marketing Director
**Desc.:** Devoted to original investigations
 and observations in clinical pathology.
**Readers:** Pathologists, clinics, hospitals,
 researchers and investigators.

## AMERICAN JOURNAL OF GASTROENTEROLOGY, THE
23706

428 E. Preston St.
Baltimore, MD 21202
Telephone: (410) 528-4000
FAX: (410) 528-4312
Year Established: 1934
Pub. Frequency: m.
Page Size: standard
Subscrip. Rate: $110/yr. individuals;
 $156/yr. institutions
Circulation: 5,900
Circulation Type: paid
**Owner(s):**
American College of Gastroenterology, Inc.
Williams & Wilkins
428 E. Preston St.
Baltimore, MD 21202
Telephone: (410) 528-4000
Ownership %: 100
**Management:**
Don Pfarr ...........................Advertising Manager
**Editorial:**
R. K. Zetterman .....................................Editor
**Desc.:** Medical journal pertaining to
 disorders of the digestive system and
 organs.
**Readers:** Primarily gastroenterologists
 including members of The American
 College of Gastroenterology.

## AMERICAN JOURNAL OF INFECTION CONTROL
56421

11830 Westline Industrial Dr.
St. Louis, MO 63146
Telephone: (314) 872-8370
Year Established: 1973
Pub. Frequency: bi-m.
Page Size: standard
Subscrip. Rate: $34/yr. individuals
Circulation: 10,050
Circulation Type: paid
**Owner(s):**
Association for Practitioners in Infection
 Control
505 E. Hawley St.
Mundelein, IL 60060
Telephone: (708) 949-6052
Ownership %: 100
**Management:**
Carol Trumbold ...................................Publisher
Kathy Erhardt ....................Advertising Manager
**Editorial:**
Mary Castle White ..................................Editor
Kathy Keller ......................Production Director
**Desc.:** Serves an international network of
 infection control practitioners united by a
 common concern for control of infection
 associated with hospitals and other
 health care facilities.
**Readers:** Infection control practioners,
 nurses, physicians. Official publication
 for the Association for Practioners in
 Infection Control.

## AMERICAN JOURNAL OF KNEE SURGERY, THE
65452

6900 Grove Rd.
Thorofare, NJ 08086
Telephone: (609) 848-1000
FAX: (609) 853-5991
Year Established: 1988
Pub. Frequency: q.
Page Size: standard
Subscrip. Rate: $90/yr.
Materials: 32,33

**Materials Accepted/Included:** 01-Business news 02-By-line articles 03-Fashion news 04-Food news 05-Freelance copy 06-Letters to editor 07-Real estate news 08-Sports news 09-Travel news 10-Book rev. 11-Movie rev. 12-Music rev. 13-TV rev. 14-Theater rev. 15-Coming events 16-Obituaries 17-Question & answer 18-Social announcements 19-Artwork 20-Cartoons 21-Photos 22-TV listings 23-Audio rec. 24-Video rec. 25-Books 26-Films/film clips 27-Personnel news 28-Press releases 29-New product news/photos 30-Trade lit. 31-Contracts awarded 32-Display adv. 33-Classified adv.

4-221

Circulation: 1,250
Circulation Type: paid
**Owner(s):**
Slack, Inc.
**Management:**
Richard Roash .......................Publisher
**Editorial:**
Mary L. Jerrell .........................Managing Editor
Randi Kershaw ......................Associate Editor
**Desc.:** Covers surgery and rehabilitation.
**Readers:** Focuses on knee surgery and
sports trainers.

59044
## AMERICAN JOURNAL OF
## MEDICAL QUALITY
428 E. Preston St.
Baltimore, MD 21202
Telephone: (410) 528-4000
FAX: (410) 528-4312
Year Established: 1986
Pub. Frequency: q.
Page Size: standard
Subscrip. Rate: $82/yr. individual; $103/yr.
institution
Circulation: 2,850
Circulation Type: paid
**Owner(s):**
American College of Medical Quality
1531 S. Tamiami Trl., Ste. 703
Venice, FL 34292
Telephone: (813) 497-3340
Ownership %: 100
**Editorial:**
Dr. David Jones .........................Editor
**Desc.:** Covers case studies, literature
reviews and original papers regarding
quality assurance, utilization review, cost
containment, and risk management.
**Readers:** Physicians, hospital
administrators, QA/UR professional
staff.

23709
## AMERICAN JOURNAL OF
## MEDICINE, THE
105 Raider Blvd.
Belle Mead, NJ 08502
Telephone: (908) 874-8550
FAX: (908) 874-8550
Year Established: 1946
Pub. Frequency: m.
Page Size: standard
Subscrip. Rate: $66/yr.
Circulation: 57,000
Circulation Type: paid
**Owner(s):**
Reed Elsevier Medical Publishers, USA
249 W. 17th St.
New York, NY 10011
Telephone: (212) 463-6463
Ownership %: 100
**Management:**
Randy Nanna .........................Publisher
Leni Teaman ...............Classified Adv. Manager
**Editorial:**
J. Claude Bennett, M.D. .............Editor in Chief
Kathleen Murphy ............................Editor
Elizabeth A. McDonald ...........Managing Editor
Michael A. Pepper ...........Associate Publisher
Louis A Schiavone ........................Sales
**Desc.:** Edited to meet the total clinical and
scientific needs and interests of the
internist. Designed to be a key element
in his or her continuing medical
education. Publication of fully
documented, well-researched clinical
reports, review articles in depth, detailed
case reports and clinicopathological
conference reports. Departments
include: Clinical Studies, Review Articles,
Clinicopathologic Case Reports, Special
Symposia, Index, Editorial, Letters to the
Editor.
**Readers:** All physicians with an interest in
internship.

23710
## AMERICAN JOURNAL OF
## OBSTETRICS & GYNECOLOGY
11830 Westline Industrial Dr.
St. Louis, MO 63146
Telephone: (314) 872-8370
FAX: (314) 432-1380
Year Established: 1920
Pub. Frequency: m.
Page Size: standard
Subscrip. Rate: $116/yr. individuals;
$202/yr. institutions; $52/yr. residents
Circulation: 20,951
Circulation Type: paid
**Owner(s):**
Mosby-Year Book, Inc.
11830 Westline Industrial Dr.
St. Louis, MO 63146
Telephone: (314) 872-8370
Ownership %: 100
**Management:**
Carol Trumbold .......................Publisher
Kathy Preston ..................Advertising Manager
**Editorial:**
Frederick P. Zuspan, M.D. ...................Editor
E.J. Quilligan, M.D. ........................Editor
Kathy Keller ...................Production Director
**Desc.:** Devoted to obstetrics and
gynecology; published for specialists and
general practitioners. Scientific material
published represents
original contributions. Clinical and
investigative reports are balanced in the
presentation of editorial material each
year.
**Readers:** Obstetricians, surgeons,
gynecologists. Official publication of:
American Gynecological and Obstetrical
Society and American Board
of Obstetrics and Gynecology.

23712
## AMERICAN JOURNAL OF
## OPHTHALMOLOGY
77 W. Wacker Dr., Ste. 660
Chicago, IL 60601-1632
Telephone: (312) 629-1690
FAX: (312) 629-1744
Year Established: 1884
Pub. Frequency: m.
Page Size: standard
Subscrip. Rate: $62/yr.
Materials: 06,10,15,16,29,30,32,33
Freelance Pay: $18/hr.
Print Process: offset
Circulation: 17,500
Circulation Type: paid
**Owner(s):**
Ophthalmic Publishing Co.
77 W. Wacker Dr.
Ste. 660
Chicago, IL 60601-1632
Telephone: (312) 629-1690
FAX: (312) 629-1744
Ownership %: 100
**Management:**
Edward W.D. Norton, M.D. ...............President
Frank W. Newell, M.D. ....................Publisher
Linda G. Clausen ...............Circulation Manager
**Editorial:**
Mary L. Borysewicz ...............Executive Editor
Susan Augustine .........................Advertising
Frank W. Newell, ...........Secretary & Treasurer
M.D.
**Desc.:** Contains original articles, letters to
the editor, coming events, book reviews,
advertising, editorials, notes, cases,
instruments, abstracts, etc.
**Readers:** Physicians and technicians in
the field of ophthalmology.
**Deadline:** ads-20th of 2nd mo. prior to
pub. date

23713
## AMERICAN JOURNAL OF
## PATHOLOGY, THE
9650 Rockville Pike
Bethesda, MD 20814
Telephone: (301) 571-0107
FAX: (301) 571-0108
Year Established: 1901
Pub. Frequency: m.
Page Size: 4 color photos/art
Subscrip. Rate: $160/yr. US; $230/yr.
foreign
Circulation: 6,000
Circulation Type: paid
**Owner(s):**
American Association of Pathologists, The
9650 Rockville Pike
Bethesda, MD 20814
Telephone: (301) 530-7130
Ownership %: 100
**Editorial:**
Marshall Robinson ......................Editor
Terri Chingwa .........................Assistant Editor
**Desc.:** Publishes original experimental and
clinical studies in the field of diagnostic
and experimental pathology. Each issue
includes first hand reports of major
advances and insights into such topics
as cell and tissue injury inflammation,
the mechanisms of atherosclerosis;
immunology, modern concepts of host-
parasite interactions and all aspects of
neoplasia. Articles are complemented by
numerous charts and illustrations
including many outstanding micrographs.
**Readers:** Pathologists at hospitals,
medical universities & research
laboratories.

23714
## AMERICAN JOURNAL OF
## PHYSICAL MEDICINE &
## REHABILITATION
428 E. Preston St.
Baltimore, MD 21202
Telephone: (301) 528-4000
FAX: (301) 528-4312
Year Established: 1921
Pub. Frequency: bi-m.
Page Size: standard
Subscrip. Rate: $75/yr. individuals;
$125/yr. institutions
Circulation: 3,400
Circulation Type: paid
**Owner(s):**
Association of Academic Physiatrists
Williams & Wilkins
428 E. Preston St.
Baltimore, MD 21202
Telephone: (301) 528-4000
Ownership %: 100
**Management:**
Donald Pfarr ...................Advertising Manager
**Editorial:**
Ernest Johnson, M.D. ........................Editor
David Jones ...................Advertising Editor
**Desc.:** Facilitates the dissemination of
scholarly work on the practice, research
and educational aspects of physical
medicine and rehabilitation. Engenders
interest in physiatric research. Its scope
emphasizes all aspects of physiatry,
including physical medicine, rehabilitation
and electrodiagnosis. The focus is on
the clinical and administrative aspects of
physical medicine, rehabilitation and
electrodiagnosis. The research focus
includes both basic science and clinical
inquiry. The educational focus is on the
application of modern teaching
techniques/technology to graduate,
Undergraduate and postgraduate
physiatric instructional programs.
**Readers:** Physicians in-training students,
and allied health professionals in the
field of PM & research.

69477
## AMERICAN JOURNAL OF
## PREVENTIVE MEDICINE
200 Madison Ave.
New York, NY 10016
Telephone: (212) 679-7300
FAX: (212) 689-5312
Year Established: 1984
Pub. Frequency: bi-m.
Page Size: standard
Subscrip. Rate: $79/yr. individuals;
$158/yr. institutions
Circulation: 3,000
Circulation Type: paid
**Owner(s):**
Oxford University Press
200 Madison Ave.
New York, NY 10016
Telephone: (212) 679-7300
Ownership %: 100
**Editorial:**
Charles H. Hennekens, M.D. ......Editor in Chief
Heather Tosteson, Ph.D. .........Executive Editor
Julie E. Buring, Sc.D. .........................Co-Editor
**Desc.:** Original articles and
correspondence on all aspects of
practice, teaching, and research in
preventive medicine.

23721
## AMERICAN JOURNAL OF
## RESPIRATORY & CRITICAL
## CARE MEDICINE
1740 Broadway
New York, NY 10019
Telephone: (212) 315-8700
FAX: (212) 265-5642
Year Established: 1917
Pub. Frequency: m.
Page Size: standard
Subscrip. Rate: $130/yr. individuals;
$220/yr. libraries & institutions
Circulation: 17,300
Circulation Type: controlled
**Owner(s):**
American Lung Assn.
1740 Broadway
New York, NY 10019
Telephone: (212) 315-8700
Ownership %: 100
**Editorial:**
Alan Leff .........................................Editor
Christina Shepherd .................Managing Editor
Cunningham Associates .................Advertising
Lori S. Carlin .................................Director
**Desc.:** Original articles, case reports and
notes on significant work in every aspect
of diseases of the respiratory tract.
**Readers:** Primarily physicians and
scientists.

23716
## AMERICAN JOURNAL OF
## ROENTGENOLOGY
1891 Reston White Dr.
Reston, VA 22091
Telephone: (800) 438-2777
FAX: (703) 264-8863
Year Established: 1906
Pub. Frequency: m.
Page Size: standard
Subscrip. Rate: $125/yr. individuals;
$170/yr. institutions
Circulation: 22,500
Circulation Type: paid
**Owner(s):**
American Roentgen Ray Society
428 E. Preston St.
Baltimore, MD 21202
Telephone: (301) 528-4000
Ownership %: 100
**Editorial:**
Robert N. Berk, M.D. ........................Editor
Karim Valji ...................Associate Editor
Tony DiBiase ...................Production Editor
Susan Brown Cappitelli ...............Publication Director

**Materials Accepted/Included:** 01-Business news 02-By-line articles 03-Fashion news 04-Food news 05-Freelance copy 06-Letters to editor 07-Real estate news 08-Sports news 09-Travel news
10-Book rev. 11-Movie rev. 12-Music rev. 13-TV rev. 14-Theater rev. 15-Coming events 16-Obituaries 17-Question & answer 18-Social announcements 19-Artwork 20-Cartoons 21-Photos 22-TV listings
23-Audio rec. 24-Video rec. 25-Books 26-Films/film clips 27-Personnel news 28-Press releases 29-New product news/photos 30-Trade lit. 31-Contracts awarded 32-Display adv. 33-Classified adv.

4-222

**Desc.:** Publishes original and timely contributions to diagnosis and treatment. Each issue features 35-40 articles by various authors. Illustrations are presented every year. Departments include: Editorials, News Items, Book Radiological literature which is indexed for consumer use.
**Readers:** Diagnostic radiologists and radiology residents, including members of the American Roentgen Ray Society.

69234
### AMERICAN JOURNAL OF SPORTS MEDICINE
230 Calvary St.
Waltham, MA 02154
Telephone: (617) 736-0707
FAX: (617) 736-0607
Year Established: 1972
Pub. Frequency: bi-m.
Page Size: standard
Subscrip. Rate: $80/yr. US; $95/yr. foreign
Materials: 06,32
Circulation: 11,000
Circulation Type: paid
**Owner(s):**
American Orthopaedic Society for Sports Medicine
230 Calvary St.
Waltham, MA 02154
Telephone: (617) 736-0707
FAX: (617) 736-0607
Ownership %: 100
**Editorial:**
Dr. Robert E. Leach ...........................Editor
E. Ann Donaldson, ELS ..........Managing Editor
**Desc.:** Peer-reviewed clinical papers dealing with surgery and related topics for orthopaedic surgeons.
**Readers:** Predominantly physicians and allied health professionals.

23717
### AMERICAN JOURNAL OF SURGERY, THE
105 Raider Blvd.
Belle Mead, NJ 08502
Telephone: (908) 281-3720
FAX: (908) 874-8419
Year Established: 1891
Pub. Frequency: m.
Page Size: standard
Subscrip. Rate: $76/yr.
Materials: 10,28,29,32,33
Circulation: 15,500
Circulation Type: paid
**Owner(s):**
Excerpta Medica, Inc.
105 Raider Blvd.
Belle Mead, NJ 08502
Telephone: (908) 874-8550
FAX: (908) 874-8419
Ownership %: 100
**Management:**
Randolph A. Nanna ...........................Publisher
**Editorial:**
Hiram C. Polk, Jr. ..............................Editor
Geraldine Rossetti ...................Managing Editor
Helena Kravitz ...................................Sales
**Desc.:** Provide surgeons and those physicians with an interest in surgery with highly clinical, practical materials. Contains full original papers recording new clinical and operative techniques and surgical proceedings.
**Readers:** Serves the general surgeon, head and neck and all other physicians performing surgeries.
**Deadline:** ads-1 mo. prior to pub. date

61789
### AMERICAN JOURNAL OF THE MEDICAL SCIENCES, THE
227 E. Washington Sq.
Philadelphia, PA 19106
Telephone: (215) 238-4200

Pub. Frequency: m.
Page Size: standard
Subscrip. Rate: $105/yr. individuals; $200/yr. institutions
Circulation: 2,640
Circulation Type: paid
**Owner(s):**
J.B. Lippincott Co.
227 E. Washington Sq.
Philadelphia, PA 19106
Telephone: (215) 238-4200
Ownership %: 100
**Management:**
Marcia E. Serepy ............................Publisher
Monica Brent ....................Advertising Manager
**Editorial:**
Suzanne Oparil .................................Editor

23720
### AMERICAN MEDICAL NEWS
515 N. State St.
Chicago, IL 60610
Telephone: (312) 464-5000
FAX: (312) 464-4184
Year Established: 1958
Pub. Frequency: w.
Page Size: tabloid
Subscrip. Rate: $99/yr.
Freelance Pay: $400-$750
Circulation: 300,000
Circulation Type: paid
**Owner(s):**
American Medical Association
515 N. State St.
Chicago, IL 60610
Telephone: (312) 464-0183
Ownership %: 100
**Management:**
James S. Todd, ........Executive Vice President
M.D.
Robert Kennett ...........................Vice President
**Editorial:**
Barbara Bolsen .................................Editor
Ben Mindell ....................Communications Editor
Robert McAsee, M.D. .........Production Director
**Desc.:** Its editorial content is non-technical and reports on legislation, business trends, legal decisions, tax rulings, and other forces that affect the practice of medicine. Departments include: Editorial Page, Washington News, Practice Management, Medicine's Week, Medicolegal, Questions and Answers, Photographs and Cartoons, Chart and Graph.
**Readers:** Members of AMA plus selected MD's.

23827
### AMT EVENTS
710 Higgins Rd.
Park Ridge, IL 60068-5765
Telephone: (708) 823-5169
FAX: (708) 823-0458
Year Established: 1939
Pub. Frequency: 6/yr.
Page Size: standard
Subscrip. Rate: $35/yr. US; $45/yr. foreign
Materials: 28,32,33
Freelance Pay: none
Circulation: 21,700
Circulation Type: paid
**Owner(s):**
American Medical Technologists
710 Higgins Rd.
Park Ridge, IL 60068
Telephone: (708) 823-5169
Ownership %: 100
**Editorial:**
Eleanore Bors ....................Managing Editor
David Kellner ....................Assistant Editor
Robert G. Martinek ................Associate Editor
Eleanore Bors ..........................News Editor
Eleanore Bors ...............................Photo

**Desc.:** Contains feature articles, book reviews, news of product, equipment, and technique development of interest to clinical laboratory personnel.
**Readers:** Medical laboratory personnel from administrative through technician and assistant levels.
**Deadline:** ads-1st of prior mo.

23724
### ANESTHESIOLOGY
227 E. Washington Sq.
Philadelphia, PA 19106
Telephone: (215) 238-4200
Year Established: 1940
Pub. Frequency: m.
Page Size: standard
Subscrip. Rate: $22/copy; $180/yr.
Circulation: 39,530
Circulation Type: paid
**Owner(s):**
American Society of Anesthesiologists
227 E. Washington Sq.
Philadelphia, PA 19106
Telephone: (215) 238-4200
Ownership %: 100
**Management:**
Monica Brent ....................Advertising Manager
Beverly Dietrich ..................Circulation Manager
Joe Baiocco .......................Production Manager
**Editorial:**
Lawrence J. Saidman, M.D. ........Editor in Chief
Susan E. Edison ....................Advertising Sales
Suzann Graff ..........Senior Marketing Manager
Virginia Martin ...............................V.P.-Journals
**Desc.:** Scientific medical journal. Original articles concerning current practice of Anesthesiology. Special Editorial Features: Editorials; Review Articles; Laboratory Reports; Special Articles; Clinical Reports; Case Reports, Correspondence; Book Reviews; Reports from Scientific Meetings.
**Readers:** Physicians specializing in anesthesiology, anesthesiology & related medical & scientific.

23725
### ANESTHESIOLOGY REVIEW
105 Raider Blvd.
Belle Mead, NJ 08502
Telephone: (908) 874-8550
FAX: (908) 874-8419
Year Established: 1973
Pub. Frequency: bi-m
Page Size: standard
Subscrip. Rate: $55/yr. US.; $82/yr. foreign & Canada
Materials: 02,06,32,33
Circulation: 18,045
Circulation Type: controlled
**Owner(s):**
Reed Elsevier Medical Publishers, USA
Core Publishing Division
105 Raider Blvd.
Belle Mead, NJ 08502
Telephone: (908) 874-8550
Ownership %: 100
**Management:**
Linda Nelson Fox ...........................Publisher
Georgann Carter ................Circulation Manager
Susan Levey ......................Sales Manager
**Editorial:**
Glenn Williams ............Associate Group Editor
Susan Lusty ...................Classified Advertising
Kathleen Dallessio .......................Group Editor
**Desc.:** Designed to further continuing education in clinical anesthesiology.

23726
### ANGIOLOGY
708 Glen Cove Ave.
Glen Head, NY 00545
Telephone: (516) 759-0025
FAX: (516) 759-5524
Year Established: 1950
Pub. Frequency: m.

Page Size: standard
Subscrip. Rate: $120/yr.
Print Process: offset
Circulation: 6,028
Circulation Type: paid
**Owner(s):**
Westminster Publications, Inc.
708 Glen Cove Ave.
Glen Head, NY 11545
Telephone: (516) 759-0025
FAX: (516) 759-5524
Ownership %: 100
**Management:**
T.R. McLaughlin ...............Advertising Manager
**Editorial:**
Lawrence Gould, MD ...............................Editor
**Desc.:** Features original papers relating to cerebrovascular, cardiovascular and peripheral vascular diseases, including clinical or laboratory research, etiology, diagnosis, rediology, pathology, operative procedures and non-operative treatment, instrumentation and editorials.
**Readers:** Cardiologists, internists, pathologists, medical libraries, hospitals, clinics, research institutes, radiologists, nuclear medicine, neurosurgeons & vascular surgeons.

23727
### ANNALS OF ALLERGY
P.O. Box 3369
Falls Church, VA 22043
Telephone: (703) 821-5461
Year Established: 1943
Pub. Frequency: m.
Page Size: standard
Subscrip. Rate: $42.50/yr.
Print Process: offset
Circulation: 6,100
Circulation Type: paid
**Owner(s):**
American College of Allergy & Immunology
85 Algonquin Rd
Arlington Heights, IL 60005
Telephone: (708) 427-1200
Ownership %: 100
**Editorial:**
R. Michael Sly, M.D. ...........................Editor
Susan Reilly .......................Publication Director
**Desc.:** Original articles, clinical notes, case reports, editorials, news, book reviews, Allergy Abstracts and letters to the Editor.
**Readers:** Physicians concerned with allergy and immunology.

23728
### ANNALS OF INTERNAL MEDICINE
Independence Mall W.
Sixth St. at Race
Philadelphia, PA 19106-1572
Telephone: (215) 351-2400
FAX: (215) 351-2644
Year Established: 1922
Pub. Frequency: s-m.
Page Size: standard
Subscrip. Rate: $84/yr.
Circulation: 95,000
Circulation Type: paid
**Owner(s):**
American College of Physicians
Independence Mall W.
Sixth St. at Race
Philadelphia, PA 19106
Telephone: (215) 351-2400
Ownership %: 100
**Management:**
Lawrence Moore ................Circulation Manager
**Editorial:**
Pam Fried ...........................Managing Editor
Thomas J. Gillen ................Advertising Director
Edward Huth, M.D. ...................Interim Editor
Joseph Johnson ...........Interim Executive Vice President
Ara H. Eloian ...............................Supervisor

**Materials Accepted/Included:** 01-Business news 02-By-line articles 03-Fashion news 04-Food news 05-Freelance copy 06-Letters to editor 07-Real estate news 08-Sports news 09-Travel news 10-Book rev. 11-Movie rev. 12-Music rev. 13-TV rev. 14-Theater rev. 15-Coming events 16-Obituaries 17-Question & answer 18-Social announcements 19-Artwork 20-Cartoons 21-Photos 22-TV listings 23-Audio rec. 24-Video rec. 25-Books 26-Films/film clips 27-Personnel news 28-Press releases 29-New product news/photos 30-Trade lit. 31-Contracts awarded 32-Display adv. 33-Classified adv.

4-223

**Desc.:** Provides education on internal medicine and sub-specialties; original papers, exclusive reports on NIH & UCLA clinical staff conferences; special case reports, comprehensive reviews, editorials and notes, book reviews, approved advertising.

**Readers:** Internists and physicians in related sub-specialties.

22804

## ANNALS OF PHARMACOTHERAPY, THE

8044 Montgomery Rd., Ste. 415
Cincinnati, OH 45236
Telephone: (513) 793-3555
FAX: (513) 793-3600
Year Established: 1967
Pub. Frequency: m.
Page Size: standard
Subscrip. Rate: $63/yr.
Print Process: offset
Circulation: 8,500
Circulation Type: paid
**Owner(s):**
Harvey Whitney Book Company
P.O. Box 42696
Cincinnati, OH 45242
Telephone: (513) 793-3555
Ownership %: 100
**Management:**
Harvey A. K. Whitney ..........................President
**Editorial:**
Dr. Milap C. Nahata ......................Senior Editor
Harvey A. K. Whitney ..............................Editor
Donna S. Thordsen .................Editorial Director
Kelly Turner .......Assistant Circulation Manager
Hedva A. Barenholtz ................Assistant Editor
Holly Smith ...........................Manuscript Editor
Don Thompson .....................Manuscript Editor
**Desc.:** A multidisciplinary journal for health professionals involved with drug therapy. Journal provides information to enable them to enhance their knowledge of drugs, drug research, drug-use control, new patterns of practice. Articles include: research reports, reviews of new drugs, clinical case studies, pharmacoeconomics, pharmacoepidemiology and related matters. All articles submitted are refereed to provide the reader with articles of high quality.
**Readers:** Physicians, pharmacists, nurses and others involved or interested in pharmacotherapy, and who need information about prescribing, administering and evaluating drugs.

23729

## ANNALS OF PLASTIC SURGERY

34 Beacon St.
Boston, MA 02108
Telephone: (617) 859-5500
FAX: (617) 859-0629
Year Established: 1978
Pub. Frequency: m.
Page Size: standard
Subscrip. Rate: $149/yr.; $227/yr. foreign; $288/yr. insts.; $225/yr. foreign insts.
Circulation: 4,000
Circulation Type: paid
**Owner(s):**
Little, Brown And Co.
34 Beacon St.
Boston, MA 02108
Telephone: (617) 859-5500
Ownership %: 100
**Management:**
Ann Orens ..........................Advertising Manager
**Editorial:**
William Morain ......................................Editor
Sherry Frank ........................Managing Editor
**Desc.:** Contains original articles, case reports, collective reviews, editorials, book reviews, correspondence, notices.

**Readers:** Plastic surgeons & hospitals.

23730

## ANNALS OF SURGERY

227 E. Washington Sq.
Philadelphia, PA 19106
Telephone: (215) 238-4200
Year Established: 1885
Pub. Frequency: m.
Page Size: standard
Subscrip. Rate: $88/yr. US individuals; $148/yr. foreign individual
Circulation: 15,247
Circulation Type: paid
**Owner(s):**
J.B. Lippincott Co.
227 E. Washington Sq.
Philadelphia, PA 19105
Telephone: (215) 238-4200
Ownership %: 100
**Management:**
Marcia Serepy ..................................Publisher
David C. Sabiston, Jr., ........Chairman Editorial M.D. Board
Beverly Dietrich ...................Circulation Manager
Joe Baiocco ....................Production Manager
**Editorial:**
David C. Sabiston, Jr., M.D. .....................Editor
Thomas Heitzman ................Advertising Sales Representative
Virginia Martin ..........................V.P.-Journals
**Desc.:** Review of surgical science and practice. An official publication for the American Surgical Association, Southern Surgical Association and The Philadelphia Academy of Surgery.
**Readers:** Surgeons and physicians interested in surgery.

65689

## ANTIMICROBIAL AGENTS & CHEMOTHERAPY

1325 Massachusetts Ave., N.W.
Washington, DC 20005-4171
Telephone: (202) 737-3600
Year Established: 1972
Pub. Frequency: m.
Page Size: standard
Subscrip. Rate: $263/yr.
Materials: 02,06,32
Print Process: web offset
Circulation: 8,860
Circulation Type: paid
**Owner(s):**
American Society for Microbiology
1325 Massachusetts Ave., N.W.
Washington, DC 20005-4171
Telephone: (202) 737-3600
**Editorial:**
R. C. Moellering, Jr. ...................Editor in Chief
L. M. Illig ......................................Director
**Desc.:** Covers antimicrobial, antiviral, antiparasitic, and anticancer agents and chemotherapy. Subjects of particular interest include mechanisms of resistance, chemistry and biosynthesis, susceptibility, experimental and clinical therapeutics, and pharmacology.
**Readers:** Pharmacologists, chemotherapy and infectious disease specialists, and clinicians.

68970

## APPLIED CLINICAL TRIALS

P.O. Box 10460
Eugene, OR 97440
Telephone: (503) 343-1200
FAX: (503) 344-3514
Year Established: 1991
Pub. Frequency: 12/yr.
Page Size: standard
Subscrip. Rate: $97/yr. US; $197/yr. foreign
Materials: 02,06,15,25,28,32,33
Print Process: offset
Circulation: 10,000
Circulation Type: controlled & paid

**Owner(s):**
Advanstar Communications, Inc.
7500 Old Oak Blvd.
Cleveland, OH 44130
Telephone: (216) 826-2839
Ownership %: 100
**Editorial:**
Jennifer Lindsey ..................................Editor
**Desc.:** Offers practical, hands-on information that helps clinical research scientists develop, execute and file new drug applications and expedite the drug approval process.
**Readers:** Clinical research professionals in the US, Western Europe and Japan.
**Deadline:** story-3 mos. prior to pub. date; news-2 mos. prior; ads-10th of mo. prior

23733

## ARCHIVES OF DERMATOLOGY

515 N. State St.
Chicago, IL 60610
Telephone: (312) 464-5000
FAX: (312) 464-2580
Year Established: 1882
Pub. Frequency: m.
Page Size: standard
Subscrip. Rate: $120/yr. US; $155/yr. foreign
Circulation: 14,000
Circulation Type: controlled
**Owner(s):**
American Medical Association
515 N. State St.
Chicago, IL 60610
Ownership %: 100
**Management:**
Robert L. Kennett ..............................Publisher
John P. Cahill ........................Sales Manager
**Editorial:**
Kenneth A. Arndt, M.D. ..........................Editor
Michael D. Springer ..........Associate Publisher
Geoffrey Flick .........Marketing Service Manager
**Desc.:** Enhances the understanding of skin and its diseases by publishing practical, peer-reviewed original articles. The journal has been characterized as an investigative journal for clinicians.
**Readers:** Dermatologists and other physicians.

23734

## ARCHIVES OF ENVIRONMENTAL HEALTH

1319 18th St., NW
Washington, DC 20036-1802
Telephone: (202) 296-6267
FAX: (202) 296-5149
Year Established: 1950
Pub. Frequency: bi-m.
Page Size: standard
Subscrip. Rate: $105/yr. US; $121/yr. foreign
Freelance Pay: complimentary copies (2)
Circulation: 1,872
Circulation Type: paid
**Owner(s):**
Heldref Publications
1319 18th St., NW
Washington, DC 20036-1802
Telephone: (202) 296-6267
Ownership %: 100
**Management:**
Walter E. Beach ...............................Publisher
Raymond M. Rallo ............Advertising Manager
Catherine Welker ..............Circulation Manager
Kerri P. Kilbane .................Promotion Manager
**Editorial:**
Patricia McCready ....................Managing Editor
**Desc.:** Provides objective documentation of the effects of environmental agents on human health. Consolidates the latest research from such varying fields as epidemiology, toxicology, biostatistics and biochemistry.

**Readers:** People concerned with the world environment and the effects of airborne agents on human health.

69303

## ARCHIVES OF FAMILY MEDICINE

515 N. State St.
Chicago, IL 60610
Year Established: 1992
Pub. Frequency: m.
Page Size: standard
Subscrip. Rate: $80/yr. US; $115/yr. foreign
Circulation: 880,000
**Owner(s):**
American Medical Association
515 N. State St.
Chicago, IL 60610
Ownership %: 100
**Management:**
Robert L. Kennett ..............................Publisher
John P. Cahill ....................Advertising Manager
**Editorial:**
Dr. Marjorie A. Bowman ...........................Editor
Michael D. Springer ...........Associate Publisher
**Desc.:** Peer-reviewed original articles that are applicable to everyday patient care. Articles are current and concise, yet provide the theoretical background essential to sound clinical decision making.
**Readers:** Physicians in family practice, general practice, and osteopathic physicians in primary care specialties.

23736

## ARCHIVES OF INTERNAL MEDICINE

515 N. State St.
Chicago, IL 60610
Telephone: (312) 464-5000
FAX: (312) 464-2580
Year Established: 1908
Pub. Frequency: s-m.
Page Size: standard
Subscrip. Rate: $110/yr. US; $145/yr. foreign
Circulation: 90,000
Circulation Type: controlled
**Owner(s):**
American Medical Association
515 N. State St.
Chicago, IL 60610
Ownership %: 100
**Management:**
Robert L. Kennett ..............................Publisher
John P. Cahill ....................Advertising Manager
**Editorial:**
James E. Dalen, MD ..............................Editor
Michael D. Springer ...........Associate Publisher
**Desc.:** Publishes peer-reviewed original articles that are applicable to everyday patient care. Articles are current and concise, yet provide the theoretical background essential to sound clinical decision making.
**Readers:** Internists, cardiologists, gastroenterologists, pulmonologists, rheumatologists, allergists and other physicians.

23737

## ARCHIVES OF NEUROLOGY

515 N. State St.
Chicago, IL 60610
Telephone: (312) 464-5000
FAX: (312) 464-2580
Year Established: 1919
Pub. Frequency: m.
Page Size: standard
Subscrip. Rate: $125/yr. in US; $160/yr. foreign
Circulation: 15,000
Circulation Type: controlled

**Owner(s):**
American Medical Association
515 N. State St.
Chicago, IL 60610
Ownership %: 100
**Management:**
Robert L. Kennett ...............................Publisher
John P. Cahill ....................Advertising Manager
**Editorial:**
Robert J. Joynt, M.D., Ph.D. ......................Editor
Michael D. Springer ...........Associate Publisher
**Desc.:** Publishes peer-reviewed original
contributions of interest to clinicians.
Controversies in Neurology is a unique
forum with differing viewpoints on
a single subject area. Special features-
Practice of Neurology, History of
Neurology, and Neurological Review-
serve intellectual interests as well as
clinical needs.
**Readers:** Neurologists, child neurologists,
and other physicians.

### ARCHIVES OF OPHTHALMOLOGY
23738
515 N. State St.
Chicago, IL 60610
Telephone: (312) 464-5000
FAX: (312) 464-2580
Year Established: 1929
Pub. Frequency: m.
Page Size: standard
Subscrip. Rate: $100/yr. in US; $135/yr.
foreign
Circulation: 20,000
Circulation Type: controlled
**Owner(s):**
American Medical Association
515 N. State St.
Chicago, IL 60610
Ownership %: 100
**Management:**
Robert L. Kennett ...............................Publisher
John P. Cahill ............................Sales Manager
**Editorial:**
Daniel M. Albert, M.D. ............................Editor
Michael D. Springer ...........Associate Publisher
**Desc.:** Archives of Ophthalmology
addresses many needs and interests of
the busy practitioner. Special
departments provide in-depth peer-
reviewed original articles form the core
editorial information on new instruments,
surgical techniques, socioeconomics,
epidemiology, and biostatistics.
**Readers:** Ophthalmologists and other
physicians.

### ARCHIVES OF OTOLARYNGOLOGY-HEAD & NECK SURGERY
23739
515 N. State St.
Chicago, IL 60610
Telephone: (312) 464-5000
FAX: (312) 464-2580
Year Established: 1925
Pub. Frequency: m.
Page Size: standard
Subscrip. Rate: $115/yr. in US; $150/yr.
foreign
Circulation: 12,000
Circulation Type: controlled
**Owner(s):**
American Medical Association
515 N. State St.
Chicago, IL 60610
Ownership %: 100
**Management:**
Robert L. Kennett ...............................Publisher
John P. Cahill ....................Advertising Manager
**Editorial:**
Michael E. Johns, M.D. ............................Editor
Michael D. Springer ...........Associate Publisher

**Desc.:** Publishes peer-reviewed original
articles and clinical notes of interest to
practitioners. Publishes high-quality
manuscripts from around the world.
Serves the diverse needs of a
fragmented specialty as the official
publication of three societies.
**Readers:** Otolaryngologists and other
physicians.

### ARCHIVES OF PATHOLOGY & LABORATORY MEDICINE
23740
515 N. State St.
Chicago, IL 60610
Telephone: (312) 464-5000
FAX: (312) 464-2580
Year Established: 1926
Pub. Frequency: m.
Page Size: standard
Subscrip. Rate: $125/yr. in US; $160/yr.
foreign
Circulation: 16,000
Circulation Type: controlled
**Owner(s):**
American Medical Association
515 N. State St.
Chicago, IL 60610
Ownership %: 100
**Management:**
Robert L. Kennett ...............................Publisher
John P. Cahill ............................Sales Manager
**Editorial:**
William W. McLendon, M.D. ......................Editor
Michael D. Springer ...........Associate Publisher
**Desc.:** Publishes original, peer-reviewed
articles covering every aspect of
anatomic and clinical pathology.
Emphasis is given to the evaluation and
introduction of new knowledge and new
technology in the active clinical arena.
**Readers:** Pathologists and other
physicians, members of College of
American Pathologists (CAP).

### ARCHIVES OF PHYSICAL MEDICINE & REHABILITATION
23741
78 E. Adams St.
Chicago, IL 60603
Telephone: (312) 922-9371
FAX: (312) 922-6754
Year Established: 1920
Pub. Frequency: m.
Page Size: standard
Subscrip. Rate: $130/yr.; $156/yr.
institutions; $154/yr. foreign; $175/yr.
foreign institutions
Circulation: 9,000
Circulation Type: paid
**Owner(s):**
American Academy of Physical Medicine &
Rehab.
122 S. Michigan Ave., Ste. 130
Chicago, IL 60603
Telephone: (312) 922-9368
Ownership %: 100
**Editorial:**
Nicolas E. Walsh, M.D. ...............Editor in Chief
**Desc.:** Official journal of the American
Congress of Rehabilitation Medicine and
the American Academy of Physical
Medicine and Rehabilitation.
Departments include: Abstracts, and
Letters to the Editor.
**Readers:** Doctors and health care
professionals in the field of
rehabilitation, and physical medicine,
including physical therapists,
occupational therapists, speech
therapists, psychologists, and schools
and librians.

### ARCHIVES OF SURGERY
23742
515 N. State St.
Chicago, IL 60610
Telephone: (312) 464-5000
FAX: (312) 464-2580
Year Established: 1920
Pub. Frequency: m.
Page Size: standard
Subscrip. Rate: $90/yr. in US; $125/yr.
foreign
Circulation: 32,000
Circulation Type: controlled
**Owner(s):**
American Medical Association
515 N. State St.
Chicago, IL 60610
Ownership %: 100
**Management:**
Robert L. Kennett ...............................Publisher
John P. Cahill ............................Sales Manager
**Editorial:**
Claude H. Organ, Jr., M.D. ......................Editor
Michael D. Springer ...........Associate Publisher
**Desc.:** An influential general surgery
journal in a fragmented field. It is able to
represent a full range of regional and
specialty interests as the official
publication of six societies. Publishes
peer-reviewed original submissions in
addition to the best papers from the
societies. Stringent statistical review sets
a standard for all surgical publications.
**Readers:** General surgeons and surgical
specialists.

### ASAIO JOURNAL
61788
227 E. Washington Sq.
Philadelphia, PA 19106
Telephone: (215) 238-4200
FAX: (215) 238-4493
Pub. Frequency: q.
Page Size: standard
Subscrip. Rate: $235/yr. institution;
$170/yr. individual; $75/yr. student
Circulation: 2,629
Circulation Type: paid
**Owner(s):**
J.B. Lippincott Co.
227 E. Washington Sq.
Philadelphia, PA 19106
Telephone: (215) 238-4273
Ownership %: 100
**Management:**
Marcia E. Serepy ...............................Publisher
**Editorial:**
Eli A. Friedman, MD ...............................Editor
Kathleen Phelan .......Advertising Repesentative
Beverly Dietrich ...................Circulation Director
Suzann Graff ..........Senior Marketing Manager

### AUDECIBEL
23746
20361 Middlebelt
Livonia, MI 48152
Telephone: (810) 478-2610
FAX: (810) 478-4520
Year Established: 1952
Pub. Frequency: q.
Page Size: standard
Subscrip. Rate: $25/yr. US; $35/yr. foreign
Freelance Pay: $25 minimum
Circulation: 21,051
Circulation Type: controlled
**Owner(s):**
International Hearing Society
20361 Middlebelt
Livonia, MI 48152
Telephone: (810) 478-2610
Ownership %: 100
**Editorial:**
Richard I. Divelbiss ...................Managing Editor

**Desc.:** Four broad groups in the hearing
field are reached: hearing aid specialists,
manufacturers and clinical audiologists,
medical ear specialists and others
working with the hard of hearing in
hospitals and schools. Interested
in technical articles on human hearing,
hearing aids, hearing aid specialists,
etc., but articles dealing with sales or
merchandising are not used. Also print
practical business advice for the hearing
aid specialist.
**Readers:** Hearing aid specialists,
physicians, clinics & others interested in
or working with hard of hearing.

### AVIATION, SPACE, & ENVIRONMENTAL MEDICINE
23748
320 S. Henry St.
Alexandria, VA 22314-3579
Telephone: (703) 739-2240
Year Established: 1930
Pub. Frequency: m.
Page Size: standard
Subscrip. Rate: $100/yr.; $110/yr. foreign
Materials: 06,32,33
Print Process: offset
Circulation: 5,100
Circulation Type: paid
**Owner(s):**
Aerospace Medical Assn.
320 S. Henry St.
Alexandria, VA 22314
Telephone: (703) 739-2240
Ownership %: 100
**Bureau(s):**
Aviation, Space, and Environmental
Medicine
P.O. Box 39788
San Antonio, TX 78218-6788
Contact: David R. Jones, M.D., Editor
**Management:**
Bob Silverstein ..................Advertising Manager
**Editorial:**
David R. Jones, M.D. ...............................Editor
Pamela Day ............................Managing Editor
William H. Johnson, .........Book Review Editor
M.D.
Pamela Day ...............................News Editor
Pamela Day ...............................Photo
**Desc.:** Devoted to scientific articles on
teaching, practice, and research in
aviation, space, and undersea medicine,
and to original articles related to these
specialties. Also publishes obituary
notices of members, news of members,
minutes of annual meetings, book
reviews.
**Readers:** Physicians, bioscientists and
aeronautical engineers working in flight,
and related subjects, including
physicians who are airline medical
directors or Federal Aeronautics
Administration medical examiners.
**Deadline:** ads-2 mos. prior to pub. date

### BIOMEDICAL INSTRUMENTATION & TECHNOLOGY
23901
3330 Washington Blvd., Ste. 400
Arlington, VA 22201
Telephone: (703) 525-4890
FAX: (703) 276-0793
Mailing Address:
210 S. 13th St.
Philadelphia, PA 19107
Year Established: 1966
Pub. Frequency: bi-m.
Page Size: standard
Subscrip. Rate: $66/yr. US; $76/yr. foreign
Freelance Pay: negotiable
Circulation: 6,000
Circulation Type: paid

---

**Materials Accepted/Included:** 01-Business news 02-By-line articles 03-Fashion news 04-Food news 05-Freelance copy 06-Letters to editor 07-Real estate news 08-Sports news 09-Travel news
10-Book rev. 11-Movie rev. 12-Music rev. 13-TV rev. 14-Theater rev. 15-Coming events 16-Obituaries 17-Question & answer 18-Social announcements 19-Artwork 20-Cartoons 21-Photos 22-TV listings
23-Audio rec. 24-Video rec. 25-Books 26-Films/film clips 27-Personnel news 28-Press releases 29-New product news/photos 30-Trade lit. 31-Contracts awarded 32-Display adv. 33-Classified adv.

4-225

**Owner(s):**
Assn. For Advancement of Medical
Instrumentation
3330 Washington Blvd. Ste. 400
Arlington, VA 22201
Telephone: (703) 525-4890
Ownership %: 100
**Management:**
Michael J. Miller .........................President
Diane Sherel ..............Advertising Manager
**Editorial:**
Mary Beth Hatem .............Editor in Chief
Michael Kallok, Ph.D. .....................Editor
Sandy Lovegrove ..................Art Director
Sandy Lovegrove ...........Production Editor

23350

**BIOMEDICAL TECHNOLOGY
INFORMATION SERVICE**
1351 Titan Way
Brea, CA 92621
Telephone: (714) 738-6400
FAX: (714) 525-6258
Year Established: 1974
Pub. Frequency: s-m.: 1st & 15th
Page Size: standard
Subscrip. Rate: $246/yr. US, Canada, &
Mexico; $284/yr. foreign via air mail
**Owner(s):**
Raven Press Ltd.
1185 Ave. of the Americas
New York, NY 10036
Ownership %: 100
**Management:**
Allan F. Pacela .........................Publisher
**Editorial:**
Marty Matisoff ..................Senior Editor
Gregory Nighswonger ..........Managing Editor
**Desc.:** Information service reporting on
high-technology advances in medicine.
Covers medical instrumentation,
biomedical engineering, and clinical
engineering. New inventions are
described and government documents
reviewed. We welcome new product &
new technology news releases in the
health care field.
**Readers:** Hospital engineers, technicians,
administrators, clinical personnel,
manufacturing engineers,
and executives.

23755

**BLOOD**
1018 Beacon St. W.
Brookline, MA 02146
Telephone: (617) 738-9080
FAX: (617) 738-9868
Year Established: 1946
Pub. Frequency: s-m.
Page Size: standard
Subscrip. Rate: $238/yr. to individuals;
$347/yr. foreign; $351/yr. to institutions;
$405/yr. foreign
Print Process: web
Circulation: 11,540
Circulation Type: paid
**Owner(s):**
American Society of Hematology
1101 Connecticut Ave. N.W.
7th Fl.
Washington, DC 20036
Telephone: (202) 857-1118
FAX: (202) 857-1164
Ownership %: 100
**Management:**
Charles C. Cunningham ..............Advertising
Manager
**Editorial:**
James D. Griffin, M.D. ..................Editor
Ken Kornfield ..................Managing Editor
Diane Pesek ..................Production Director
**Desc.:** Reports of original laboratory and
clinical research in hematology and
related fields.
**Readers:** Medical specialists.

66475

**BRAIN RESEARCH BULLETIN**
660 White Plains Rd.
Tarrytown, NY 10591-5153
Telephone: (914) 524-9200
FAX: (914) 333-2444
Year Established: 1976
Pub. Frequency: 18/yr.
Page Size: standard
Subscrip. Rate: $1385/yr. institutions
**Owner(s):**
Elsevier Science, Ltd.
The Boulevard, Langford Lane
Kidlington
Oxford OX5 1GB, United Kingdom
Telephone: 44-865-843000
FAX:44-865-843010
Ownership %: 100
**Bureau(s):**
Division of Life Sciences
University of Texas at San Ant
6900 North Loop 1604 W.
San Antonio, TX 78249-0662
Telephone: (210) 691-4481
FAX: (210) 691-4510
Contact: Matthew J. Wayner
**Editorial:**
Christine Scannell ........Senior Publishing Editor
**Desc.:** Publishes original reports of new
and significant information concerning all
aspects of the nervous system:
biochemistry, physiology, anatomy,
ultrastructure, neurology, pathology, and
behavior. Behavioral studies will not be
published unless they are pertinent and
make a significant contribution to one of
the other fields. Brief communications
which describe a new method,
technique, or apparatus and results of
experiments which can be reported
briefly with limited figures and tables will
be included.

23759

**BULLETIN OF THE HENNEPIN
COUNTY MEDICAL SOCIETY**
3433 Broadway St. N.E., Ste. 325
Minneapolis, MN 55413-1761
Telephone: (612) 623-3030
FAX: (612) 623-2888
Year Established: 1859
Pub. Frequency: bi-m.
Page Size: standard
Subscrip. Rate: $15/yr.
Circulation: 3,500
Circulation Type: controlled & paid
**Owner(s):**
Hennepin County Medical Society
Ownership %: 100
**Editorial:**
Doreen Hines ..................................Editor
Nancy Bauer ..................Managing Editor
Nancy Bauer ..................Associate Director
**Readers:** Physicians-Employees, members
of the Hennepin County Medical Society.

23758

**BULLETIN OF THE NEW YORK
ACADEMY OF MEDICINE**
1216 Fifth Ave.
New York, NY 10029
Telephone: (212) 876-8200
FAX: (212) 876-6620
Year Established: 1925
Pub. Frequency: s-a.
Page Size: standard
Subscrip. Rate: $35/yr.; $40/yr. foreign
Circulation: 3,500
Circulation Type: paid
**Owner(s):**
New York Academy of Medicine
1216 Fifth Ave.
New York, NY 10029
Telephone: (212) 876-8200
Ownership %: 100

**Editorial:**
Robert J. Haggerty, M.D. .........................Editor
**Desc.:** General medical journal publishing
papers presented at the meetings of the
Academy and its affiliated societies,
case reports and scientific
communications and additional papers-
chiefly historical-of acceptable scholarly
and scientific quality. Submitted
manuscripts are reviewed by experts
and, usually, edited heavily.
**Readers:** Physicians and most major
medical libraries.

23760

**CALIFORNIA FAMILY PHYSICIAN**
114 Sansome St., Ste. 1305
San Francisco, CA 94104
Telephone: (415) 394-9121
FAX: (415) 394-9119
Year Established: 1949
Pub. Frequency: 6/yr.
Page Size: standard
Subscrip. Rate: $35/yr.
Circulation: 7,000
Circulation Type: controlled
**Owner(s):**
California Academy of Family Physicians
114 Sansome St., Ste. 1305
San Francisco, CA 94104
Telephone: (415) 394-9121
Ownership %: 100
**Management:**
Matt Harris ..................................President
**Editorial:**
Ransom B. Turner, M.D. ..................Editor
Sheri Cardo ..................Managing Editor
**Desc.:** Designed for family physicians in
practice in California. Editorials deal with
issues of socioeconomic importance to
FP's, including malpractice, training
information on hospitals, residencies and
interviews with different professionals.
**Readers:** Family physicians in California.

23761

**CANCER**
227 E. Washington Sq.
Philadelphia, PA 19106
Telephone: (215) 238-4200
Year Established: 1948
Pub. Frequency: s-m.
Page Size: standard
Subscrip. Rate: $125/yr. individuals;
$205/yr. institutions
Circulation: 17,127
Circulation Type: paid
**Owner(s):**
American Cancer Society, Inc.
227 E. Washington Sq.
Philadelphia, PA 19106
Ownership %: 100
**Management:**
J. B. Lippincott Co. ..................Publisher
**Editorial:**
Robert V.P. Hutter ..................Editor in Chief
Diane Scott-Lichter ..................Managing Editor
Joseph W. Lippincott, III ..................Director
**Desc.:** Articles describing original work and
original articles concerning research,
diagnosis and therapy of cancer
authorized by medical and research
professionals. A journal of the American
Cancer Society.
**Readers:** Oncologists, radiologists,
surgeons and pathologists.

70379

**CANCER PRACTICE**
227 East Washington Sq.
Philadelphia, PA 19106-3780
Telephone: (215) 238-4200
FAX: (215) 238-4227
Year Established: 1993
Pub. Frequency: bi-m.

Page Size: standard
Subscrip. Rate: $35/yr. individuals; $70/yr.
institutions
Freelance Pay: varies
Print Process: web offset
Circulation: 10,000
Circulation Type: paid
**Owner(s):**
J.B. Lippincott Co.
227 East Washington Sq.
Philadelphia, PA 19106
Telephone: (215) 238-4492
FAX: (215) 238-4461
Ownership %: 100
**Management:**
Lisa R. Marshall ..................Publisher
Beverly Dietrich ..................Circulation Manager
**Editorial:**
Genevieve V. Foley ..................Editor
Franklin Cox ..................Advertising Sales Rep.
Michael Fiorillo ..................Advertising Sales Rep.
Suzann Graff ..................Marketing Manager
**Desc.:** A unique multidisciplinary focus on
all aspects of cancer patient care,
including prevention and detection,
treatment, pain management, quality of
life, psychosocial interventions, coping
skills, rehabilitation and continuing care.
**Readers:** Oncology nurses, oncology
social workers, physicians, psychosocial
professionals and other members of the
cancer patient care team.

23936

**CAP TODAY**
325 Waukegan Rd.
Northfield, IL 60093-2750
Telephone: (708) 446-8800
FAX: (708) 446-3563
Year Established: 1987
Pub. Frequency: m.
Page Size: tabloid
Subscrip. Rate: $40/yr. US; $65/yr. N.
America; $95/yr. foreign
Materials: 02,05,06,17,21,29,31,32,33
Freelance Pay: varies
Print Process: web
Circulation: 46,000
Circulation Type: controlled & paid
**Owner(s):**
College Of American Pathologists
325 Waukegan Rd.
Northfield, IL 60093-2750
Telephone: (708) 446-8800
Ownership %: 100
**Management:**
Robert McGonnagle ..................Publisher
**Editorial:**
Sherrie Rice ..................................Editor
Kimberly Carey ..................Managing Editor
Robert McGonnagle ..................Advertising
Sherrie Rice ..................................Photo
**Desc.:** Brings essential news to all key
decision-makers responsible for clinical
lab purchases. This news includes
advances in tests and equipment, trends
in management and clinical operation,
regulatory changes, and finance.
**Readers:** MD pathologists, lab directors
and managers, supervisory
technologists, hospital administrators,
purchasing officers, and hospital
information system managers.
**Deadline:** ads-4th of mo. prior to pub. mo.

61262

**CARDIO**
600 Harrison St.
San Francisco, CA 94107
Telephone: (415) 905-2200
FAX: (415) 905-2235
Year Established: 1984
Pub. Frequency: m.

Page Size: standard
Subscrip. Rate: $90/yr.; free to
cardiologists & internal medicine
physicians working in cardiology
Materials: 01,02,28,29,32,33
Print Process: web offset
Circulation: 31,194
Circulation Type: controlled
**Owner(s):**
Miller Freeman, Inc.
600 Harrison St.
San Francisco, CA 94107
Telephone: (415) 905-2200
FAX: (415) 905-2235
Ownership %: 100
**Bureau(s):**
Miller Freeman Inc.
1515 Broadway
New York, NY 10036
Telephone: (212) 626-2535
FAX: (212) 869-0901
Contact: Bob Grossman, Associate
　　Publisher
**Editorial:**
Joseph Kornfeld ...........................Editor in Chief
Lisle Peterson ...........................Managing Editor
Tracie Thompson ...........................Assistant Editor
Steve Stiles ...........................Associate Editor
Catherine Carrington ...........Associate Editor
Cecile Jackson ...................Editorial Assistant
**Desc.:** Provides news, analysis and news
perspective on all aspects of the
specialty of cardiovascular medicine.
Clinical news, research developments,
socioeconomic coverage, meeting
reports, clinical overviews, drug updates,
regulatory information, technology news,
and current issues are regularly
reported.
**Readers:** Cardiologists, cardiac surgeons,
internal medicine physicians who work in
cardiology.
**Deadline:** story-1 mo. prior to pub. date;
news-1 mo. prior; photo-1 mo. prior; ads-
1 mo. prior

**CARDIOLOGY BOARD REVIEW**　61260
3 Greenwich Office Park
Greenwich, CT 06831-5133
Telephone: (203) 629-3550
FAX: (203) 629-2536
Year Established: 1984
Pub. Frequency: m.
Page Size: standard
Subscrip. Rate: $60/yr.
Materials: 06,15,
Circulation: 33,000
Circulation Type: controlled
**Owner(s):**
MRA Publications, Inc.
3 Greenwich Office Park
Greenwich, CT 06831
Telephone: (203) 629-3550
Ownership %: 100
**Editorial:**
Patricia H. Brenner ...........................Exec. Editor
Dr. Peter F. Cohn .............................Editor
**Readers:** Cardiologists and physicians in
internal medicine.

**CARDIOVASCULAR REVIEWS &**　61263
**REPORTS**
777 W. Putnam Ave.
Greenwich, CT 06830
Telephone: (203) 531-0450
FAX: (203) 531-0533
Year Established: 1980
Pub. Frequency: m.
Page Size: standard
Subscrip. Rate: $60/yr. individuals; $75/yr.
institutions
Circulation: 72,000
Circulation Type: paid

**Owner(s):**
Cardiovascular Reviews & Reports
777 W. Putnam Ave.
Greenwich, CT 06830
Telephone: (203) 531-0450
Ownership %: 100
**Editorial:**
Suzanne DelGallo ...................Managing Editor

**CHEST**　23762
3300 Dundee Rd.
Northbrook, IL 60062
Telephone: (708) 498-1400
FAX: (708) 498-5460
Year Established: 1935
Pub. Frequency: m.
Page Size: standard
Subscrip. Rate: $108/yr. individuals;
$144/yr. institutions
Materials: 02,06,10,28,29,32,33
Freelance Pay: $15/hr.
Print Process: web
Circulation: 23,000
Circulation Type: paid
**Owner(s):**
American College of Chest Physicians
3300 Dundee Rd.
Northbrook, IL 60062
Telephone: (708) 498-7400
Ownership %: 100
**Management:**
Alvin Lever, M.D. ...............................Publisher
Garand Catlin ...................Advertising Manager
**Editorial:**
Mrs. Sylvia Peterson ................Executive Editor
A. Jay Block, M.D. ...........................Editor
Nancy A. Collop, M.D. ...........Associate Editor
Douglas Mann, M.D. ...............Associate Editor
Patricia A. Micek ...............New Products Editor
**Desc.:** Carries original research medical
papers dealing with respiration and
circulation. Illustrations used with
articles.
**Readers:** Clinicians and surgeons.
**Deadline:** ads-1 mo. prior to pub. date

**CHICAGO MEDICINE**　23763
515 N. Dearborn
Chicago, IL 60610
Telephone: (312) 670-2550
Year Established: 1914
Pub. Frequency: s-m.
Page Size: standard
Subscrip. Rate: $15/yr. members; $30/yr.
non-members
Materials: 06,10,15,16,28,29
Circulation: 11,100
Circulation Type: controlled
**Owner(s):**
Chicago Medical Society
515 N. Dearborn
Chicago, IL 60610
Telephone: (312) 670-2550
Ownership %: 100
**Management:**
Kristi Zernia .................Classified Adv. Manager
**Editorial:**
J. Gregory Wiezorek ...............................Editor
Cynthia Petrucci ...................Associate Editor
Scott J. Warner ...................Production Editor
**Desc.:** A publication for physicians and
other members of the Chicago Medical
Society. It reports on activities of the
Society and on events and issues of
importance to the profession. It provides
a forum for the discussion of medical,
ethical, legal, socioeconomic, and other
concerns affecting physicians in Chicago
and Cook County.
**Readers:** Members of the Chicago Medical
Society in Chicago and Cook County.
**Deadline:** story-2 mos. prior to pub. date;
news-2 mos. prior; photo-2 mos. prior;
ads-6 wks. prior

**CINCINNATI MEDICINE**　23764
320 Broadway
Cincinnati, OH 45202
Telephone: (513) 421-7010
FAX: (513) 721-4378
Year Established: 1978
Pub. Frequency: q.
Page Size: standard
Subscrip. Rate: $15/yr.
Freelance Pay: negotiable
Circulation: 3,500
Circulation Type: controlled

**Owner(s):**
Academy of Medicine Cincinnati
320 Broadway
Cincinnati, OH 45202-4292
Telephone: (513) 421-7010
FAX: (513) 721-4378
Ownership %: 100

**Editorial:**
Rhonda Tepe ...........................Editor
Kim Weaver ...............Advertising Sales Manager
Pamela G. Fairbanks ...........Consulting Editor
Pamela G. Fairbanks ...................Miscellaneous

**Desc.:** Carries socio-economic articles of
interest to Cincinnati physicians in
various fields of medicine.

**Readers:** Physicians of Hamilton County,
as well as other allied health
professionals.

**CIRCULATION**　23765
7272 Greenville Ave.
Dallas, TX 75231
Telephone: (214) 706-1310
FAX: (214) 691-6342
Year Established: 1950
Pub. Frequency: bi-w.
Page Size: standard
Subscrip. Rate: 150/yr. individuals;
$224/yr. US institutions
Freelance Pay: $10-$15/hr. proofing
Circulation: 26,500
Circulation Type: paid
**Owner(s):**
American Heart Association
7272 Greenville Ave.
Dallas, TX 75231
Telephone: (214) 373-6300
Ownership %: 100
**Management:**
Margaret Levene ...............Production Manager
Linda Johnston ...................Promotion Manager
**Editorial:**
James T. Willerson ...........................Editor
Mary Ann McNeely ...............Editorial Manager
Krista Curnutt ...............Production Coordinator
Vicki Sullivan ...................Publishing Director
**Desc.:** Devoted to clinical research and
advances in the cardiovascular field.
Presents original articles, symposia,
radiology, case reports, letters to the
editor, clinco-pathologic correlations, and
clinical progress. Approx. 3 supplements
a year are included in the subscription.
**Readers:** Cardiologists, internists,
researchers.

**CIRCULATION RESEARCH**　23766
7272 Greenville Ave.
Dallas, TX 75231
Telephone: (214) 706-1310
FAX: (214) 691-6342
Year Established: 1953
Pub. Frequency:

Page Size: standard
Subscrip. Rate: $190/yr. individual;
$270/yr. institution
Freelance Pay: copy readers $10-$15/hr.;
copy editor $15-$20/hr.
Circulation: 4,000
Circulation Type: paid
**Owner(s):**
American Heart Association
7272 Greenville Ave.
Dallas, TX 75231
Telephone: (214) 373-6300
Ownership %: 100
**Management:**
Margaret Levene ...............Production Manager
Linda Johnston ...................Promotion Manager
**Editorial:**
Stephen Vatner, M.D. ...........................Editor
Mary Ann McNeely ...............Editorial Manager
Krista Curnutt ...............Production Coordinator
Vicki Sullivan ...................Publishing Director
**Desc.:** Provides a medium for bringing
together basic research on the
cardiovascular system from various
disciplines including biology,
biochemistry, biophysics, cellular biology,
molecular biology, morphology,
pathology, physiology, and
pharmacology. The journal also will
accept publication manuscripts
on clinical research that contribute to an
understanding of fundamental problems.
**Readers:** Basic scientists, physicians,
clinicians.

**CLINICAL CHEMISTRY**　22471
2101 L St., N.W.
Ste. 202
Washington, DC 20037
Telephone: (202) 857-0717
Year Established: 1953
Pub. Frequency: m.
Page Size: standard
Subscrip. Rate: $70/yr. individuals;
$150/yr. institutions
Circulation: 14,650
Circulation Type: paid
**Owner(s):**
American Association for Clinical
Chemistry, Inc.
2101 L St., N.W.
Ste. 202
Washington, DC 20037
Telephone: (800) 892-1900
Ownership %: 100
**Management:**
JoAnne Thyken ...................Business Manager
Lenne P. Miller ...............Circulation Manager
**Editorial:**
David E. Bruns ...........................Executive Editor
Virginia Marcum ...................Assistant Editor
David E. Bruns ...............Book Review Editor
David E. Bruns ...........................Columnist
**Desc.:** Scientific articles and professional
news.
**Readers:** Clinical and bio-chemists, clinical
pathologists.

**CLINICAL DIABETES**　58590
1660 Duke St.
Alexandria, VA 22314
Telephone: (703) 549-1500
FAX: (703) 683-2890
Year Established: 1983
Pub. Frequency: bi-m.
Page Size: standard
Subscrip. Rate: $15/yr. in U.S.
Materials: 28,29,32
Circulation: 50,000
Circulation Type: controlled & paid

**Materials Accepted/Included:** 01-Business news 02-By-line articles 03-Fashion news 04-Food news 05-Freelance copy 06-Letters to editor 07-Real estate news 08-Sports news 09-Travel news
10-Book rev. 11-Movie rev. 12-Music rev. 13-TV rev. 14-Theater rev. 15-Coming events 16-Obituaries 17-Question & answer 18-Social announcements 19-Artwork 20-Cartoons 21-Photos 22-TV listings
23-Audio rec. 24-Video rec. 25-Books 26-Films/film clips 27-Personnel news 28-Press releases 29-New product news/photos 30-Trade lit. 31-Contracts awarded 32-Display adv. 33-Classified adv.

4-227

**Owner(s):**
American Diabetes Association, Inc.
1660 Duke St.
Alexandria, VA 22314
Telephone: (703) 549-1500
FAX: (703) 683-2890
Ownership %: 100
**Management:**
Debbie Fentress ........................Manager
**Editorial:**
Alan J. Garber ...............................Editor
**Desc.:** Provides state-of-the-art articles about recent advances in the clinical care of people with diabetes.
**Readers:** Diabetologists, endocrinologists, and primary-care health professionals.
**Deadline:** ads-1 mo. prior to pub. date

58923

## CLINICAL LABORATORY MANAGEMENT REVIEW
428 E. Preston St.
Baltimore, MD 21202
Telephone: (410) 528-4000
Year Established: 1987
Pub. Frequency: bi-m.
Subscrip. Rate: $50/yr. individual; $80/yr. institution
Circulation: 7,500
Circulation Type: paid
**Owner(s):**
Clinical Laboratory Management Association, Inc.
9 Old LIncoln Hwy., Ste. 201
Malvern, PA 19355-2135
Telephone: (215) 647-8970
Ownership %: 100
**Management:**
Don Pfarr ....................Advertising Manager
Alma Wills ..................................Manager
**Editorial:**
William O'Neil ...............................Editor
Nancy Collins ..............Marketing Director

23351

## CLINICAL LAB PRODUCTS
89 Rt. 101A
Amherst, NH 03031
Telephone: (603) 673-7555
FAX: (603) 672-5625
Mailing Address:
P.O. Box 69
Amherst, NH 03031
Year Established: 1972
Pub. Frequency: m.
Page Size: tabloid
Subscrip. Rate: $6/copy; $60/yr.
Circulation: 62,000
Circulation Type: controlled
**Owner(s):**
Clinical Lab Products, Inc.
Telephone: (603) 673-7555
Ownership %: 100
**Management:**
R.M. Ezequelle ...........................President
R.M. Ezequelle ...........................Publisher
Barbara Troian ...............Production Manager
**Editorial:**
Jane D. Osborne ...........................Editor
**Desc.:** News items concerning instruments, diagnostics and supplies used in clinical laboratory. Features and exceptional new products covered with 4 - color photos. Any legitimate new products will be covered, with photos. Departments include: New products, new literature, available products and literature.
**Readers:** Managers & supervisors in all U.S. & Canadian medical laboratories.

23768

## CLINICAL NUCLEAR MEDICINE
227 E. Washington Sq.
Philadelphia, PA 19106
Telephone: (215) 238-4200
Year Established: 1976
Pub. Frequency: m.

Page Size: standard
Subscrip. Rate: $118/yr. individual; $163/yr. institution
Circulation: 3,197
Circulation Type: paid
**Owner(s):**
J.B. Lippincott Co.
227 E. Washington Sq.
Philadelphia, PA 19106
Telephone: (215) 238-4200
Ownership %: 100
**Management:**
Marcia Serepy ...........................Publisher
Beverly Dietrich .............Circulation Manager
Joe Baiocco ..............Production Manager
**Editorial:**
Sheldon Baum, M.D. ........................Editor
Jennifer Bass ................Advertising Sales
Suzann Graff ..........Senior Marketing Manager
Virginia Martin ...................V.P. Journals
**Desc.:** Original articles involving scanning, imaging, and related subjects concerning the clinical techniques and procedures of nuclear medicine.
**Readers:** Nuclear medicine, radiology and related technologists, and hospital departments.

23770

## CLINICAL PHARMACOLOGY & THERAPEUTICS
11830 Westline Industrial Dr.
St. Louis, MO 63146
Telephone: (314) 872-8370
FAX: (314) 432-1380
Year Established: 1960
Pub. Frequency: m.
Page Size: standard
Subscrip. Rate: $92/yr.
Circulation: 5,326
Circulation Type: paid
**Owner(s):**
Mosby-Year Book, Inc.
11830 Westline Industrial Dr.
Saint Louis, MO 63146
Telephone: (314) 872-8370
Ownership %: 100
**Management:**
Carol Trumbold ...........................Publisher
Kathy Preston ...............Advertising Manager
**Editorial:**
Marcus M. Reidenberg, M.D. ...............Editor
Kathy Keller ....................Production Director
**Desc.:** Devoted to the clinical study of the nature, action, efficacy and total evaluation of drugs, both new and established, as they are used in man. It is edited for those clinical pharmacologists and other physicians primarily concerned and responsible for the appropriate selection and use of drugs.
**Readers:** Clinical pharmacologists and internists. Official publication of American Society of Clinical Pharmacology and Therapeutics, American Society for Pharmacology and Experimental Therapeutics.

23963

## COLORADO MEDICINE
7800 E. Dorado Pl.
Englewood, CO 80111
Telephone: (303) 779-5455
Mailing Address:
P.O. Box 17550
Denver, CO 80217-0550
Year Established: 1980
Pub. Frequency: m.
Page Size: standard
Subscrip. Rate: $35/yr.
Circulation: 5,000
Circulation Type: paid

**Owner(s):**
Colorado Medical Society
7800 E. Dorado Pl.
Englewood, CO 80111
Telephone: (303) 779-5455
Ownership %: 100
**Management:**
Dr. David Martz ...........................President
Michael Thompson ..........Advertising Manager
**Editorial:**
Sandra L. Maloney ...............Executive Editor
William Pierson ................Managing Editor
**Desc.:** Reports on society developments, news within the states and national affairs of interest to the profession.
**Readers:** Official journal for Colorado Medical Society.

66477

## COMPUTERIZED MEDICAL IMAGING AND GRAPHICS
Pergamon Press
660 White Plains Rd.
Tarrytown, NY 10591-5153
Telephone: (914) 524-9200
FAX: (914) 333-2444
Year Established: 1977
Pub. Frequency: bi-m.
Page Size: standard
Subscrip. Rate: $114/yr. individual; $650/yr. institution
Circulation: 700
Circulation Type: paid
**Owner(s):**
Pergamon Press, Inc.
660 White Plains Rd.
Tarrytown, NY 10591-5153
Telephone: (914) 524-9200
**Editorial:**
Robert S. Ledley ...............Editor in Chief
William R. Ayers ...........................Editor

55894

## CONTEMPORARY DIAGNOSTIC RADIOLOGY
428 E. Preston St.
Baltimore, MD 21202
Telephone: (410) 528-4000
FAX: (410) 528-4132
Year Established: 1977
Pub. Frequency: bi-w
Subscrip. Rate: $230/yr.
Circulation: 1,590
Circulation Type: paid
**Owner(s):**
Williams & Wilkins Co.
428 E. Preston Dr.
Baltimore, MD 21202
Telephone: (410) 528-4000
Ownership %: 100
**Editorial:**
Dr. Robert E. Campbell ...........................Editor
**Desc.:** Features original articles offering an overview of radiology.
**Readers:** Highly motivated radiologists interested in continuing medical education.

58925

## CONTEMPORARY NEUROSURGERY
428 E. Preston St.
Baltimore, MD 21202
Telephone: (410) 528-4000
FAX: (410) 528-4312
Pub. Frequency: 27/yr.; 26 scored
Subscrip. Rate: $235/yr. scored; $215/yr. non-scored
Circulation: 1,087
Circulation Type: paid
**Owner(s):**
Williams & Wilkins Co.
428 E. Preston St.
Baltimore, MD 21202
Telephone: (410) 528-4000
Ownership %: 100

**Management:**
Don Pfarr ....................Advertising Manager
Alma Wills ..................................Manager
**Editorial:**
George T. Tindall, M.D. .....................Editor
Nancy Collins ..............Marketing Director

23773

## CONTEMPORARY OB/GYN
Five Paragon Dr.
Montvale, NJ 07645
Telephone: (800) 526-4870
FAX: (201) 573-8979
Year Established: 1973
Pub. Frequency: m.
Page Size: standard
Subscrip. Rate: $79/yr.; $109/yr. foreign
Circulation: 39,255
Circulation Type: paid
**Owner(s):**
Medical Economics Publishing Co., Inc.
Five Paragon Dr.
Montvale, NJ 07645
Telephone: (800) 526-4870
Ownership %: 100
**Management:**
Barbara M. Pritchard ...................Publisher
Peggy Jacobsen ...........Circulation Manager
Jean DiPietro ..............Classified Adv. Manager
Monique Michowski ..........Promotion Manager
Robert J. Osborn ...............Sales Manager
**Editorial:**
John T. Queenan ...............Editor in Chief
Mary Hale ...............................Editor
James E. Swan ...............Editorial Director
Rose Abruzzo ...........................Advertising
Barbara Kleppe ...............Research Director
Claine Coutsouridis ...........................Sales
Carl Olsen ...............................Sales
**Desc.:** Practical clinical articles for obstetricians and gynecologists.
**Readers:** Obstetricians and gynecologists.

67051

## CONTEMPORARY ORTHOPAEDICS
2512 Artesia Blvd.
Redondo Beach, CA 90278-3210
Telephone: (310) 376-8788
FAX: (213) 376-9043
Year Established: 1979
Pub. Frequency: m.
Page Size: standard
Subscrip. Rate: $53/yr. US; $63/yr. Canada; $80/yr. elsewhere
Circulation: 30,000
Circulation Type: controlled
**Owner(s):**
Bobit Publishing Company
2512 Artesia Blvd.
Redondo Beach, CA 90278-3210
Telephone: (310) 376-8788
Ownership %: 100
**Management:**
Thomas Bender ...........................Publisher
Thomas Bender ...............Advertising Manager
**Editorial:**
Judith Prow ...............................Editor
**Desc.:** Practical "how-to" clinical information for the teaching and practicing orthopaedic surgeon.

23774

## CONTEMPORARY SURGERY
2512 Artesia Blvd.
Redondo Beach, CA 90278
Telephone: (310) 376-8788
FAX: (310) 374-7878
Year Established: 1972
Pub. Frequency: m.
Page Size: 4 color photos/art
Subscrip. Rate: $5/issue; $53/yr. US; $64/yr. Canada; $80/yr. foreign
Materials: 05,32
Freelance Pay: $150/MD's
Circulation: 50,364
Circulation Type: controlled

**Owner(s):**
Bobit Publishing Co.
2512 Artesia Blvd.
Redondo Beach, CA 90278
Telephone: (310) 376-8788
Ownership %: 100
**Bureau(s):**
Bobit Publishing Co.
49 S. Maple Ave.
Marlton, NJ 08053
Telephone: (609) 596-0999
Contact: Tom Bender, Publisher
**Management:**
Edward J. Bobit ..................Chairman of Board
Ty Bobit ...........................................President
Thomas Bender ................................Publisher
Thomas Bender ...............Advertising Manager
**Editorial:**
Gregg Rogers .......................Managing Editor
Peggy Plendl .....................Book Review Editor
**Desc.:** Practical clinical articles for general
surgeons and other surgical disciplines.
**Readers:** Surgeons.
**Deadline:** story-3rd of mo. prior to pub.
date

67231
**CONTEMPORARY UROLOGY**
Five Paragon Dr.
Montvale, NJ 07645
Telephone: (201) 358-7200
FAX: (201) 358-8979
Year Established: 1989
Pub. Frequency: m.
Page Size: standard
Subscrip. Rate: $89/yr. US; $109/yr.
foreign
Circulation: 9,075
Circulation Type: paid
**Owner(s):**
Medical Economics Publishing Co., Inc.
Five Paragon Dr.
Montvale, NJ 07645
Telephone: (201) 358-7200
Ownership %: 100
**Management:**
Thomas C. Pizor ..............................Publisher
Julianne Asterita ...............Advertising Manager
**Editorial:**
Deborah Kaplan .....................................Editor
**Desc.:** Includes news and features on
solving clinical problems.
**Readers:** For office and hospital-based
urologists.

69444
**CORNHUSKER FAMILY PHYSICIAN**
7101 Newport Ave., No. 201
Omaha, NE 68152-2158
Telephone: (402) 572-3530
FAX: (402) 572-3532
Pub. Frequency: q.
Subscrip. Rate: $5/yr.
Circulation: 3,000
Circulation Type: controlled
**Owner(s):**
Nebraska Academy of Family Physicians
7101 Newport Ave., No. 201
Omaha, NE 68152-2158
Telephone: (402) 572-3530
Ownership %: 100
**Editorial:**
Dr. David H. Filipi .................................Editor

23776
**CRITICAL CARE MEDICINE**
428 E. Preston St.
Baltimore, MD 21202
Telephone: (301) 528-4000
Year Established: 1973
Pub. Frequency: m.
Page Size: standard
Subscrip. Rate: $99/yr. individuals;
$157/yr. institutions
Circulation: 14,000
Circulation Type: paid

**Owner(s):**
Williams & Wilkins Co.
428 E. Preston St.
Baltimore, MD 21202
Telephone: (301) 528-4000
Ownership %: 100
**Management:**
Gary Walchli ......................Advertising Manager
**Editorial:**
Bart Chernow ........................................Editor
**Desc.:** Publishes original articles, abstracts
from international literature and in-depth
studies of issues of particular concern to
members of the critical care team.
**Readers:** Subscribers, including members
of The Society of Critical Care Medicine

23777
**CRYOBIOLOGY**
NYU Med. Ctr. Lemsip
Long Meadow Rd.
Tuxedo Park, NY 10987
*see Service, Trade, Professional
Magazines, Biological Sciences*

23778
**CURRENT SURGERY**
428 E. Preston St.
Baltimore, MD 21202
Telephone: (410) 528-4000
FAX: (410) 528-8596
Year Established: 1991
Pub. Frequency: 9/yr.
Page Size: standard
Subscrip. Rate: $72/yr.
Materials: 06,10,32
Circulation: 1,275
Circulation Type: paid
**Owner(s):**
Williams & Wilkins Co.
428 E. Preston St.
Baltimore, MD 21202
Ownership %: 100
**Management:**
Gary Walchli ......................Advertising Manager
Frank Rodan ......................Circulation Manager
**Editorial:**
Walter J. Pories, M.D. ...........................Editor
Walter J. Pories, M.D. .........................Director
**Desc.:** Presents abstracts-current,
dependable and commented upon by
members of the Editorial Board-and at
least one review article each issue. Only
material of medical and technical
importance is accepted.
**Readers:** Surgeons, general surgeons,
medical schools.

23780
**CUTIS**
105 Raider Blvd.
Belle Mead, NJ 08502
Telephone: (908) 281-3702
FAX: (908) 874-8419
Year Established: 1965
Pub. Frequency: m.
Page Size: standard
Subscrip. Rate: $75/yr. to physicians;
$90/yr. in Canada & Mexico; $105/yr.
elsewhere; $45/yr. to students; $74/yr.
in Canada & Mexico; $85/yr. elsewhere
Materials: 01,02,15,28,29,30
Circulation: 49,300
Circulation Type: paid
**Owner(s):**
Reed Elsevier Medical Publishing, USA
249 W. 17th St.
New York, NY 10011
Telephone: (212) 645-0067
Ownership %: 100
**Management:**
Steven V. Claps .................................Publisher
**Editorial:**
Sharon Finch ........................................Editor
Sharon Mares ......................Managing Editor
Wyman F. Carey ...............Marketing Director
Claudia A. Shayne ...............Marketing Director

Marge Hisen ......................................Sales
**Desc.:** Original clinical articles and useful
information to populated areas
pertaining to the practical side of
practicing physicians. Provides brief
articles, limited to common diseases
faced by physicians. Departments
include: Clinical or Scientific, Abstracts,
Other (Index), Letters to Editor.
**Readers:** Controlled circulation to
dermatologists, allergists, pediatric
allergists, osteopathic physicians and
physicians interested in cutaneous
medicine.
**Deadline:** story-1st of mo.; news-1st of
mo.; photo-1st of mo.; ads-1st of mo.

69446
**DALLAS MEDICAL JOURNAL**
P.O. Box 4680, Sta. A
Dallas, TX 75208
Telephone: (214) 948-3622
FAX: (214) 946-5805
Year Established: 1914
Pub. Frequency: m.
Subscrip. Rate: membership
Circulation: 5,000
Circulation Type: paid
**Owner(s):**
Dallas County Medical Society
P.O. Box 4680, Sta. A
Dallas, TX 75208
Telephone: (214) 948-3622
Ownership %: 100
**Editorial:**
Linda C. Chandler ................................Editor

23782
**DELAWARE MEDICAL JOURNAL**
1925 Lovering Ave.
Wilmington, DE 19806-2147
Telephone: (302) 658-3957
FAX: (302) 658-9669
Year Established: 1929
Pub. Frequency: m.
Page Size: standard
Subscrip. Rate: $20/yr. US; $25/yr. foreign
Circulation: 1,640
Circulation Type: paid
**Owner(s):**
Medical Society of Delaware
1925 Lovering Ave.
Wilmington, DE 19806-2147
Telephone: (302) 658-3957
Ownership %: 100
**Management:**
Thomas J. Maxwell, MD ....................President
Laurel A. Haring ...............Advertising Manager
**Editorial:**
E. Wayne Martz ...................................Editor
Laurel A. Haring ...................Managing Editor
Sharon Swayne ...................Associate Editor
**Desc.:** Departments include: President's
Page, Scientific Articles, Editorials,
Medical Features, Book Reviews, In
Brief.
**Readers:** Physicians and related health
professionals.

23783
**DETROIT MEDICAL NEWS**
1010 Antietam
Detroit, MI 48207-2899
Telephone: (313) 567-1640
FAX: (313) 567-2065
Year Established: 1902
Pub. Frequency: w.
Page Size: standard
Subscrip. Rate: $40/yr.
Materials: 06,16,32,33
Print Process: offset
Circulation: 4,500
Circulation Type: paid

**Owner(s):**
Wayne County Medical Society
1010 Antietam
Detroit, MI 48207-2899
Telephone: (313) 567-1640
FAX: (313) 567-2065
Ownership %: 100
**Editorial:**
Susan Adelman, M.D. .............................Editor
M. A. Michael ........................Managing Editor
M. A. Michael ................Advertising Circulation
Manager
**Readers:** The medical field in the Detroit
tri-county area.
**Deadline:** ads-2 wks. prior to pub. date

23784
**DIABETES**
1660 Duke St.
Alexandria, VA 22314
Telephone: (703) 549-1500
FAX: (703) 836-7439
Year Established: 1952
Pub. Frequency: m.
Page Size: standard
Subscrip. Rate: $125/yr.; $156/yr. foreign
Circulation: 10,000
Circulation Type: paid
**Owner(s):**
American Diabetes Association
1660 Duke St.
Alexandria, VA 22314
Telephone: (703) 549-1500
Ownership %: 100
**Management:**
Susan Hayes Lau ...............................Publisher
**Editorial:**
Philip Cryer ...........................................Editor
Matt Petersen .......................Managing Editor
Karen Ingle ..............Assistant Managing Editor
Peter Banks .........................Editorial Director
Carol Flynn ......................................Advertising
**Desc.:** Covers major scientific papers and
review articles and abstracts of papers
published throughout the world.
Departments include: Review Articles,
Rapid Publications, Original Articles.
**Readers:** Researchers, physicians, &
those in related fields.

65645
**DIABETES/METABOLISM
REVIEWS**
605 Third Ave.
New York, NY 10158
Telephone: (212) 850-6289
Year Established: 1905
Pub. Frequency: 8/yr.
Subscrip. Rate: $195/yr.
Circulation: 499
Circulation Type: paid
**Owner(s):**
John Wiley & Sons, Inc.
605 Third Ave.
New York, NY 10158
Ownership %: 100
**Editorial:**
D. Andreani ...........................................Editor
**Desc.:** Covers clinical and basic scientific
advances in endocrinology, insulin
secretion, resistance, ketone
metabolism, obesity and lipid
metabolism, pathogenesis and cellular
action of insulin.

46872
**DIABETES CARE**
1660 Duke St.
Alexandria, VA 22314
Telephone: (703) 549-1500
Year Established: 1978
Pub. Frequency: m.
Page Size: standard
Subscrip. Rate: $75/yr.
Materials: 01,02,06,10,15,16,21,27,28,29,
32,33
Print Process: offset

**Materials Accepted/Included:** 01-Business news 02-By-line articles 03-Fashion news 04-Food news 05-Freelance copy 06-Letters to editor 07-Real estate news 08-Sports news 09-Travel news
10-Book rev. 11-Movie rev. 12-Music rev. 13-TV rev. 14-Theater rev. 15-Coming events 16-Obituaries 17-Question & answer 18-Social announcements 19-Artwork 20-Cartoons 21-Photos 22-TV listings
23-Audio rec. 24-Video rec. 25-Books 26-Films/film clips 27-Personnel news 28-Press releases 29-New product news/photos 30-Trade lit. 31-Contracts awarded 32-Display adv. 33-Classified adv.

4-229

Circulation: 4,500
Circulation Type: paid
**Owner(s):**
American Diabetes Association
1660 Duke St.
Alexandria, VA 22314
Telephone: (703) 549-1500
Ownership %: 100

**Management:**
Susan Hayes Lau ....................Publisher

**Editorial:**
Alan Drash, M.D. .........................Editor
Matt Petersen ...............Managing Editor
Karen Ingle .......Assistant Managing Editor
Peter Banks .............Editorial Director
Carol Flynn .........................Advertising
**Desc.:** Articles dealing with research,
etiology, and treatment of diabetes.
Contributions must be relevant to clinical
practice and care, management, and
patient education. Features include
Original Articles, Brief Communications,
Special Articles, Case Reports, Reviews,
Editorials, Letters to the Editor. Length
of articles variable. All articles submitted
must first be reviewed by the editor.
**Readers:** Research scientists, clinicians,
podiatrists, dietitians, nurses,
technicians, educators.
**Deadline:** story-10 wks. prior to pub. date;
news-10 wks. prior; photo-10 wks. prior;
ads-10 wks. prior

23785
**DIAGNOSTIC IMAGING**
600 Harrison St.
San Francisco, CA 94107
Telephone: (415) 905-2200
FAX: (415) 905-2235
Year Established: 1979
Pub. Frequency: m.
Page Size: standard
Subscrip. Rate: $95/yr.; free to qualified
personnel
Freelance Pay: $.20-$.25/wd.
Circulation: 31,548
Circulation Type: paid
**Owner(s):**
Miller Freeman, Inc.
600 Harrison St.
San Francisco, CA 94107
Telephone: (415) 905-2200
Ownership %: 100
**Bureau(s):**
Miller Freeman Publications
370 Lexington Ave.
New York, NY 10017
Telephone: (212) 683-9294
Contact: Jennifer Naughton, Sales
Manager
**Management:**
Marshall W. Freeman ...............President
Vicki Masseria ...........................Publisher
**Editorial:**
Peter L. Ogle ...........................Editor
Andrea Wheeler ..............Managing Editor
Brian Casey ...............Business Editor
Jennifer Cox ..............Production Editor
**Desc.:** A news publication dealing with
professionals in the fields of radiology,
nuclear medicine, and ultrasound
imaging.
**Readers:** 24,000 physicians and
technologists involved in the radiology,
nuclear medicine, computed
tomography, ultrasound and magnetic
resonance fields.

69449
**DIAGNOSTIC MOLECULAR
PATHOLOGY**
1185 Ave. of the Americas
New York, NY 10036
Telephone: (212) 930-9500
FAX: (212) 869-3495

Year Established: 1992
Pub. Frequency: q.
Subscrip. Rate: $80/yr. individuals; $95/yr.
institutions
**Owner(s):**
Raven Press
1185 Ave. of the Americas
New York, NY 10036
Telephone: (212) 930-9500
Ownership %: 100
**Editorial:**
Ronald A. DeLellis .....................Editor
Hubert J. Wolfe .......................Editor
**Desc.:** Publishes contributions on
molecular probes for diagnosis, such as
tumor suppressor genes, oncogenes, the
polymerade chain reactions, and in situ
hybridization.

23787
**DIALYSIS & TRANSPLANTATION**
7628 Densmore Ave.
Van Nuys, CA 91406-2088
Telephone: (818) 782-7328
FAX: (818) 782-7450
Year Established: 1972
Pub. Frequency: m.
Page Size: standard
Subscrip. Rate: $35/yr.
Circulation: 17,700
**Owner(s):**
Creative Age Publications, Inc.
7628 Densmore Ave.
Van Nuys, CA 91406
Telephone: (818) 782-7328
Ownership %: 100
**Management:**
Deborah Carver ........................Publisher
Tom Blackstone ...........Advertising Manager
Mindy Rosiejka ..............Business Manager
**Editorial:**
Susan K. Hansen ..................Exec. Editor
Marie Nordberg ........................Editor
Garnet Blair .............Production Director
**Desc.:** Edited for medical, technical and
administrative personnel involved in
renal dialysis and transplantation in
hospitals, centers and homes. Technical
articles report on development and
technical aspects of new procedures,
techniques, equipment, materials,
processes and systems. In a year, the
editorial content covers: new techniques
(40 percent); facility reports (10 percent);
new material and equipment (25
percent); legislation (5 percent); other
(20 percent). Special features include:
new literature, positions sought and
available, commentary. Departments
include: Nephrology Nurse, Dialysis
Technician, Legislation, Dietitian, Renal
Social Worker.
**Readers:** Physicians, nurses and
technicians, hospital administrators,
organ preservation technicians, scientific
and engineering personnel, universities
and labs, libraries and others.

23789
**DIGESTIVE DISEASES &
SCIENCES**
233 Spring St.
New York, NY 10013
Telephone: (212) 620-8000
Mailing Address:
DeSoto at O'Hara Sts.
Pittsburgh, PA 15213
Year Established: 1934
Pub. Frequency: m.
Page Size: standard
Subscrip. Rate: $295/yr.; $405/yr. foreign
Circulation: 6,500
Circulation Type: paid

**Owner(s):**
Plenum Publishing Corp.
233 Spring St.
New York, NY 10013
Telephone: (212) 620-8000
Ownership %: 100
**Editorial:**
Robert R. Schade, M.D. .................Editor
Richard L. Wechsler, M.D. ..............Editor
David Van Thiel, M.D. ..................Editor
Michael Dustevich ..............Assistant Editor
**Desc.:** Original articles, case reports,
progress reports, and subspecialty
articles directed toward
gastroenterologists.
**Readers:** Gastroenterologists, researchers
in digestive diseases & hepatology.

23788
**DISEASES OF THE COLON &
RECTUM**
San Pablo St.
Los Angeles, CA 90033-4612
Telephone: (213) 342-5751
Year Established: 1958
Pub. Frequency: m.
Page Size: 4 color photos/art
Subscrip. Rate: $125/yr. individuals;
$188/yr. institutions
Circulation: 4,804
Circulation Type: paid
**Owner(s):**
American Society of Colon & Rectal
Surgeons
Williams & Wilkins
428 E. Preston St.
Baltimore, MD 21202
Ownership %: 100
**Editorial:**
Robert W. Beart Jr., M.D. ................Editor
Michele Hewlitt ...............Managing Editor
**Desc.:** Devoted to review of proctologic
diseases and surgery. Special editorial
features include: Abstracts, Book
Reviews, and Bibliographies.
**Readers:** All physicians interested in all
branches of colon and rectal disease.

69369
**DRUG DEVELOPMENT &
INDUSTRIAL PHARMACY**
270 Madison Ave.
New York, NY 10016
Telephone: (212) 696-9000
FAX: (212) 685-4540
Mailing Address:
P.O. Box 5017
Monticello, NY 12701
Year Established: 1974
Pub. Frequency: 20/yr.
Page Size: standard
Subscrip. Rate: $597.50/yr. individuals;
$1195/yr. institutions
**Owner(s):**
Marcel Dekker, Inc.
1270 Madison Ave.
New York, NY 10016
Telephone: (212) 685-4540
Ownership %: 100
**Editorial:**
Christopher T. Rhodes ...................Editor
**Desc.:** Covering aspects of the
development, production, and evaluation
of drugs and pharmaceutical products,
this international journal highlights both
the technical and regulatory facets of
industrial pharmacy. Topics include
computerization of production, quality
control, export problems,
pharmacokinetics and biopharmaceutics,
drug regulatory affairs, and successful
manufacturing practices.

**Readers:** Managers and scientists in
pharmaceutical research and
development, quality control, process
develoment, and product manufacturing,
pharmaceutical engineers,
pharmacologists, pharmaceutical
chemists.

58920
**EAR & HEARING**
428 E. Preston St.
Baltimore, MD 21202
Telephone: (410) 528-4000
FAX: (410) 528-4312
Year Established: 1979
Pub. Frequency: bi-m.
Page Size: standard
Subscrip. Rate: $48/yr. individual; $85/yr.
institution
Circulation: 5,100
Circulation Type: paid
**Owner(s):**
American Auditory Society
University of Cincinnati
Medical Center
Cincinnati, OH 45267
Telephone: (513) 872-4893
Ownership %: 100
**Management:**
Don Pfarr ...............Advertising Manager
Alma Wills ...........................Manager
**Editorial:**
Robert W. Keith, Ph.D. .................Editor
Nancy Collins ...............Marketing Director
**Desc.:** Covers assessment, diagnosis and
management of auditory disorders.

23790
**EAR, NOSE & THROAT JOURNAL**
629 Euclid Ave., Ste. 500
Cleveland, OH 44114-3003
Telephone: (216) 522-9700
FAX: (216) 522-9707
Year Established: 1922
Pub. Frequency: m.
Page Size: standard
Subscrip. Rate: $12 newsstand; $100/yr.
individuals; $125/yr. institutions;
$160/yr. foreign
Materials: 01,06,10,28,29,32,33
Print Process: offset
Circulation: 11,000
Circulation Type: paid
**Owner(s):**
Medquest Communications, Inc.
629 Euclid Ave., Ste. 500
Cleveland, OH 44114-3003
Telephone: (216) 522-9700
FAX: (216) 522-9707
Ownership %: 100
**Management:**
John H. Whaley, III ...................Publisher
Mark Goodman ...........Advertising Manager
**Editorial:**
Jack Pulec, M.D. .........................Editor
Jack Pulec, M.D. ...............Managing Editor
**Desc.:** Provides a continuum of
educational clinical material to the
otorhinolaryngologist, including the
subspecialties of otology, laryngology,
and rhinology. Covers allergists, pediatric
allergists, head and neck surgeons,
plastic surgeons and all M.D.'s with a
secondary interest in these specialties.
In addition to individual articles of major
interest in areas involving the ear, nose
and/or throat, there will be a number of
issues devoted entirely to a single
subject theme. Departments include:
Editorial Director's Page, Original
Articles, Book Reviews, Calendar of
Coming Events. Five practical hands on
clinics, classified, CME Test, and a
reader service card program.

**Materials Accepted/Included:** 01-Business news 02-By-line articles 03-Fashion news 04-Food news 05-Freelance copy 06-Letters to editor 07-Real estate news 08-Sports news 09-Travel news 10-Book rev. 11-Movie rev. 12-Music rev. 13-TV rev. 14-Theater rev. 15-Coming events 16-Obituaries 17-Question & answer 18-Social announcements 19-Artwork 20-Cartoons 21-Photos 22-TV listings 23-Audio rec. 24-Video rec. 25-Books 26-Films/film clips 27-Personnel news 28-Press releases 29-New product news/photos 30-Trade lit. 31-Contracts awarded 32-Display adv. 33-Classified adv.

4-230

**Readers:** Physicians in otorhinolaryngology with secondary interest in these specialties, paramedical including office based physician, hospitals and medical schools.

## EMERGENCY
23792

6300 Yarrow Dr.
Carlsbad, CA 92009-1597
Telephone: (619) 438-2511
FAX: (619) 931-5809
Mailing Address:
P.O. Box 159
Carlsbad, CA 92018
Year Established: 1969
Pub. Frequency: m.
Page Size: standard
Subscrip. Rate: $3/newsstand; $21.95/yr.
Materials: 02,06,15,21,28,29,30,32,33
Freelance Pay: varies
Circulation: 30,000
Circulation Type: controlled & paid
**Owner(s):**
Dyna Corporation
6300 Yarrow Dr.
Carlsbad, CA 92009
Telephone: (619) 438-2511
Ownership %: 100
**Management:**
Robert DeBussey .............................President
Gerald Mortimer ........................Vice President
Robert DeBussey .............................Publisher
Patricia Colatarci ..............Advertising Manager
**Editorial:**
Doug Fiske ............................................Editor
Patricia Colatarci ..........................Advertising
Heidi Saucier ...........................Art Department
Julie Fadda ..............................Associate Editor
Advisory Board ........................Editorial Advisor
Patricia Colatarci ..............New Products Editor
**Desc.:** A journal for emergency medical services personnel. Uses articles dealing with pre-hospital, emergency treatment of accident, injury or ill victims, with the setting up and operation of emergency medical services systems, search and rescue and stories of a factual and constructive nature. Articles are from four to twelve typewritten double-spaced pages. Photos, either black and white glossies or color transparancies are purchased. Departments include: Letters, Open Forum, EMS Gear, Open Airways (news of interest to our readers), Drug Watch, Rescue Call, EMS Quiz, and Skills Primer.
**Readers:** Paramedic, emergency medical technicians. Organizations devoted to EMS and SAR, flight nurses, EMS physicians.
**Deadline:** story-5 mos. prior to pub. date; news-4 mos. prior; photo-2-3 mos. prior; ads-1 mo. prior

## EMERGENCY MEDICAL SERVICES
23793

7626 Densmore Ave.
Van Nuys, CA 91406-2088
Telephone: (818) 759-4367
Year Established: 1972
Pub. Frequency: m.
Page Size: standard
Subscrip. Rate: $18.95/yr.
Materials: 02,05,06,20,21,28,29,30,32,33
Freelance Pay: varies
Circulation: 45,000
Circulation Type: controlled & paid
**Owner(s):**
Summer Communications, Inc.
7626 Densmore Ave.
Van Nuys, CA 91406-2088
Telephone: (818) 786-4367
Ownership %: 100
**Management:**
Carol Summer .....................................Publisher

Warren Kaufman ...............Advertising Manager
Gloria Berumen-Heim .........Circulation Manager
**Editorial:**
Barbara Feiner ..................................Exec. Editor
Karen Bruschette ................Production Director
**Desc.:** Edited for personnel responsible for emergency medical systems and services. Articles report on procedures and methods of establishing, staffing, equipping and coordinating emergency systems, departments and emergency transport vehicles.
**Readers:** Paramedics, EMTs, EMS administrators, chiefs, rescue operations, purchasing agents, engineering personnel.

## EMERGENCY MEDICINE
23794

105 Raider Blvd.
Belle Mead, NJ 08502
Telephone: (908) 874-8550
FAX: (908) 874-6096
Year Established: 1969
Pub. Frequency: m.
Page Size: standard
Subscrip. Rate: $60/yr.; $50/yr. to physicians
Freelance Pay: $200/pg.
Circulation: 128,000
Circulation Type: controlled
**Owner(s):**
Excerpta Medica
195 Raider Blvd.
Belle Mead, NJ 08502
Telephone: (908) 874-6096
Ownership %: 100
**Management:**
Michael Pepper ...................................Publisher
**Editorial:**
Harry A. Atkins ...................................Editor
Mary Sheeran .........................Managing Editor
**Desc.:** Brings its readers information in the most readable and accessible form on how to deal with medical problems that require immediate attention to prevent further injury, illness, or death. It also covers new and critical problems in medical care that, although emergent in nature, must still be understood to be properly diagnosed and treated by the primary-care physician.
**Readers:** General and family practitioners, internists, emergency physicians, doctors of osteopathy, and cardiologists.

## EMERGENCY MEDICINE NEWS
65286

E. Washington Sq.
Philadelphia, PA 19105
Telephone: (215) 238-4270
Year Established: 1979
Pub. Frequency: m.
Subscrip. Rate: $69/yr. individuals; $95/yr. instn.; $80/yr. foreign; $118/yr. foreign instn.
Circulation: 21,000
Circulation Type: paid
**Owner(s):**
J.B. Lippincott Co.
E. Washington Sq.
Philadelphia, PA 19106
Telephone: (215) 238-4200
Ownership %: 100
**Management:**
John M. Wehner, Jr. ..........................Publisher
**Editorial:**
James R. Roberts .................................Editor
Beth Hanson ..........................Associate Editor
**Desc.:** Disseminates information in all areas of emergency medicine, as well as emergency departments and ambulatory care centers.

## ENDOCRINE REVIEWS
55898

428 E. Preston St.
Baltimore, MD 21202
Telephone: (410) 528-4000
FAX: (410) 528-4312
Year Established: 1980
Pub. Frequency: q.
Subscrip. Rate: $65/yr. individuals; $85/yr. institutions
Circulation: 3,970
Circulation Type: paid
**Owner(s):**
Endocrine Society, The
**Editorial:**
Dr. Andres Negro Vilar ...........................Editor
**Desc.:** Clinical and experimental endocrinology covered through in-depth review articles focusing on current topics of high interest.
**Readers:** Members of The Endocrine Society; endocrinologists, internists, physiologists and biochemists with an interest in the endocrine glands and their hormones.

## EUROPEAN JOURNAL OF CANCER
23797

660 White Plains Rd.
Tarrytown, NY 10591-5153
Telephone: (914) 592-7700
FAX: (914) 333-3244
Year Established: 1965
Pub. Frequency: 20/yr.
Page Size: standard
Subscrip. Rate: $1525/yr. institutions
Circulation: 3,500
Circulation Type: paid
**Owner(s):**
Pergamon Press, Inc.
660 White Plains Rd.
Tarrytown, NY 10591-5153
Telephone: (914) 524-9200
Ownership %: 100
**Management:**
Roger A. Dunn ....................General Manager
Mike Boswood ....................Managing Director
**Editorial:**
Ian Hart ..............................................Editor
**Desc.:** Provides a forum for the exchange of ideas and information among scientists and researchers belonging to all disciplines concerned with cancer. It encourages the collaboration among scientists and among clinical investigators in the broad field of cancer research and publishes papers pertinent to oncology in its broadest sense, including chemistry, biochemistry, biology, epidemiology, pathology, virology, genetics and clinical medicine, provided these disciplines study normal and abnormal growth. Several European work groups have been created following the foundation of this journal in 1964.
**Readers:** Cancer research scientists, physicians, pathologists, virologists, immunologists.

## EXPERT SYSTEMS WITH APPLICATIONS
66478

660 White Plains Rd.
Tarrytown, NY 10591-5153
Telephone: (914) 524-9200
FAX: (914) 333-2444
Year Established: 1990
Pub. Frequency: q.
Subscrip. Rate: $230/yr.

**Owner(s):**
Pergamon Press, Inc.
660 White Plains Rd.
Tarrytown, NY 10591-5153
Telephone: (914) 524-9200
Ownership %: 100
**Editorial:**
J. Liebowitz ...........................................Editor
**Desc.:** Focuses on the exchange of information relating to expert systems worldwide.
**Readers:** Engineers, developers, researchers, scientists and consultants.

## FAMILY MEDICINE
69479

P.O. Box 8729
8880 Ward Pkwy.
Kansas City, MO 64114
Telephone: (816) 333-9700
FAX: (816) 333-3884
Year Established: 1967
Pub. Frequency: 10/yr.
Page Size: standard
Subscrip. Rate: $75/yr. individuals; $100/yr. institutions
Circulation: 4,500
Circulation Type: paid
**Owner(s):**
Society of Teachers of Family Medicine
P.O. Box 8729
8880 Ward Pkwy.
Kansas City, MO 64114
Telephone: (816) 333-9700
Ownership %: 100
**Editorial:**
Barry Weiss ..........................................Editor
**Desc.:** Presents research studies and teaching methods.
**Deadline:** ads-1st of mo. prior to pub. date

## FAMILY PLANNING PERSPECTIVES
24480

120 Wall St.
New York, NY 10005
Telephone: (212) 248-1111
FAX: (212) 248-1951
Year Established: 1969
Pub. Frequency: bi-m.
Page Size: standard
Subscrip. Rate: $32/yr. individuals; $42/yr. institutions
Circulation: 15,000
Circulation Type: free & paid
**Owner(s):**
Alan Guttmacher Institute
120 Wall St.
New York, NY 10005
Telephone: (212) 248-1111
Ownership %: 100
**Management:**
Jeannie I. Rosoff ................................President
Brian Byrd ..........................Circulation Manager
Kathleen Randall ..............Production Manager
**Editorial:**
Jeanette Johnson .................Executive Editor
Michael Klitsch ....................................Editor
Olivia Nordberg ...................Publication Director
**Desc.:** Professional journal in field of family planning and population.
**Readers:** Clinicians, family planning professionals, social scientists.

## FAMILY PRACTICE NEWS
23799

12230 Wilkins Ave.
Rockville, MD 20852
Telephone: (301) 816-8700
Year Established: 1971
Pub. Frequency: s-m.
Page Size: tabloid
Subscrip. Rate: $96/yr.
Freelance Pay: negotiable
Circulation: 72,488
Circulation Type: controlled

**Owner(s):**
Capital Cities Communications, Inc.
7 E. 12th St.
New York, NY 10003
Ownership %: 100
**Management:**
Tom Fowler ...............................Publisher
Gary Gyss .........................Advertising Manager
**Editorial:**
Johanna Weekley .......................Editor in Chief
Mary Jo. Dales ...............................Editor
**Desc.:** Provides comprehensive reporting of information of interest to the family practitioner and osteopath. Concentrates on in person coverage of clinical meetings, symposia, and conventions to inform the interested physician of clinical developments taking place in the field of family medicine.
**Readers:** Family practioners, general practitioners, and osteopaths in patient care, including residents.

### FAMILY PRACTICE RECERTIFICATION
68971
Three Greenwich Office Pk.
Greenwich, CT 06831-5154
Telephone: (203) 629-3550
FAX: (203) 629-2536
Year Established: 1979
Pub. Frequency: m.
Page Size: standard
Subscrip. Rate: $60/yr.
Freelance Pay: varies
Print Process: web offset
Circulation: 84,205
Circulation Type: controlled
**Owner(s):**
Medical Recertification Associates Publications
3 Greenwich Office Pk.
Greenwich, CT 06831-5154
Telephone: (203) 629-3550
Ownership %: 100
**Editorial:**
Jane C. Monaghan ...............................Editor
Paul Dishart ...............................Editor
**Desc.:** Includes articles on new developments in medicine, clinical issues and family practice skills.
**Readers:** Family physicians.

### FAMILY PRACTICE RESEARCH JOURNAL
69459
233 Spring St.
New York, NY 10013-1578
Telephone: (212) 620-8000
FAX: (212) 463-0742
Year Established: 1981
Pub. Frequency: q.
Subscrip. Rate: $130/yr. US; $150/yr. foreign
**Owner(s):**
Human Sciences Press, Inc.
233 Spring St.
New York, NY 10013-1578
Telephone: (212) 620-8000
Ownership %: 100
**Editorial:**
Leif Solberg ...............................Editor
**Desc.:** Fosters clinical research in family practice and encourages the training of family physicians in research philosophy, methodology, and research.

### FERTILITY & STERILITY
23802
200 First St. S.W., 505 N.W.
Rochester, MN 55905
Telephone: (507) 284-3850
FAX: (507) 284-0780
Year Established: 1950
Pub. Frequency: m.

Page Size: standard
Subscrip. Rate: $110/yr. individuals; $175/yr. for institutions
Circulation: 14,500
Circulation Type: paid
**Owner(s):**
American Fertility Society
1209 Montgomery Hwy.
Birmingham, AL 35216
Telephone: (205) 978-5000
Ownership %: 100
**Management:**
Roger D. Kempers, .............Chairman of Board M.D.
Joyce Zeitz ...................Circulation Manager
Joyce Zeitz .................Classified Adv. Manager
Carol Olson ...................Production Manager
**Editorial:**
Roger D. Kempers, M.D. ............Editor in Chief
Edward E. Wallach ...................Associate Editor
Steven J. Ory, M.D. ...........Book Review Editor
Deborah Markham ...............Editorial Associate
**Desc.:** Contents include original manuscripts, abstracts and book reviews. Original papers are contributed solely to fertility & sterility and are limited to the fields of fertility, sterility, or the physiology of reproduction.
**Readers:** Obstetricians, gynecologists, urologists, endocrinologists investigating problems of infertility and human reproduction.

### FOOT & ANKLE
58932
428 E. Preston St.
Baltimore, MD 21202
Telephone: (410) 528-4000
FAX: (410) 528-4312
Year Established: 1980
Pub. Frequency: 9/yr.
Page Size: standard
Subscrip. Rate: $75/yr. individual; $89/yr. institution
Circulation: 3,800
Circulation Type: paid
**Owner(s):**
American Orthopaedic Foot & Ankle Society, Inc.
3750 N. Lakeshore Dr., Ste. 14
Chicago, IL 60613
Ownership %: 100
**Management:**
Don Pfarr ...................Advertising Manager
Alma Wills ...............................Manager
**Editorial:**
Melvin H. Jahss, M.D. ...............................Editor
Kenneth Johnson ...............Marketing Director

### GASTROENTEROLOGY & ENDOSCOPY NEWS
23715
148 W. 24th St., 8th Fl.
New York, NY 10011
Telephone: (212) 620-4600
FAX: (212) 620-5982
Year Established: 1950
Pub. Frequency: m.
Page Size: tabloid
Subscrip. Rate: $46/yr.
Circulation: 8,261
Circulation Type: controlled
**Owner(s):**
Ray McMahon
148 W. 24th St., 8th Fl.
New York, NY 10011
Telephone: (212) 620-4600
Ownership %: 100
**Management:**
Raymond E. McMahon ...................Publisher
**Editorial:**
Tatiana Chillrud ...............................Editor
**Desc.:** Gastroenterology and endoscopy subjects.
**Readers:** All gastros, gastro fellows & C&R surgeons in U.S.

### GASTROENTEROLOGY NURSING
59045
428 E. Preston St.
Baltimore, MD 21202
Telephone: (410) 528-4000
FAX: (410) 528-4312
Year Established: 1977
Pub. Frequency: bi-m.
Subscrip. Rate: $58/yr. individual; $85/yr. institution
Circulation: 7,500
Circulation Type: paid
**Owner(s):**
Society of Gastroenterology Nurses and Associates
1070 Sibley Tower
Rochester, NY 14604
Telephone: (716) 546-7241
Ownership %: 100
**Management:**
Don Pfarr ...................Advertising Manager
Alma Wills ...............................Manager
**Editorial:**
Susan Trivits, R.M.T., G.I.A. ...............................Editor
Nancy Collins ...............Marketing Director
**Desc.:** Describes new procedures, techniques and equipment for gastroenterology nurses and associates.

### GASTROINTESTINAL ENDOSCOPY
70399
11830 Westline Industrial Dr.
St. Louis, MO 63146
Telephone: (314) 872-8370
FAX: (314) 872-9146
Pub. Frequency: bi-m.
Subscrip. Rate: $16/copy; $30/yr. student; $73/yr. individual; $97/yr. institutional
Circulation: 8,000
Circulation Type: controlled
**Owner(s):**
Mosby-Year Book, Inc.
11830 Westline Industrial Dr.
St. Louis, MO 63146
Telephone: (314) 872-8370
FAX: (314) 872-9146
Ownership %: 100
**Desc.:** Publishes original papers on investigations and observations relating to endoscopic procedures used in the study and treatment of digestive diseases. Peer-reviewed articles cover new instruments and methods, applications of endoscopy, analyses of experience, and relevant case reports.
**Readers:** Offers the perfect mix of high readership among gastroenterologists and a low cost-per-thousand.

### GENERAL SURGERY & LAPAROSCOPY NEWS
23876
148 W. 24th St., 8th Fl.
New York, NY 10011
Telephone: (212) 620-4600
FAX: (212) 620-5928
Year Established: 1980
Pub. Frequency: m.
Page Size: tabloid
Subscrip. Rate: $55/yr.
Circulation: 32,118
Circulation Type: free
**Owner(s):**
McMahon Group
148 W. 24th St., 8th Fl.
New York, NY 10011
Telephone: (212) 620-4600
Ownership %: 100
**Management:**
Raymond E. McMahon ...................Publisher
**Editorial:**
Cornelia Kean ...............................Editor
**Desc.:** Devoted to bringing the physician the latest developments in the field of surgery and laparoscopy.

**Readers:** General and hospital-based surgeons.

### GERIATRIC NURSING
70402
11830 Westline Industrial Dr.
St. Louis, MO 63146
Telephone: (314) 872-8370
FAX: (314) 872-9146
Year Established: 1980
Pub. Frequency: bi-m.
Subscrip. Rate: $5.50/copy; $18/yr. student; $26/yr. individual; $38/yr. institutional
Circulation: 18,000
Circulation Type: controlled
**Owner(s):**
Mosby-Year Book, Inc.
11830 Westline Industrial Dr.
St. Louis, MO 63146
Telephone: (314) 872-8370
FAX: (314) 872-9146
Ownership %: 100
**Desc.:** Written and edited for all nurses and nurse managers who care for older adults in hospitals, nursing homes, senior centers, or private homes. This peer-reviewed journal has become an indispensable source of clinical information and management advice in the area of long-term nursing care.
**Readers:** The majority of the responding subscribers work in either long-term care (64%), hospital (9%), or nursing education settings (7%). More than 25% work as a director or assistant director of nursing administration; nearly 14% are head nurses or supervisors, and 14% are staff nurses.

### GERIATRICS
68866
7500 Old Oak Blvd.
Cleveland, OH 44130
Telephone: (216) 243-8100
FAX: (216) 891-2683
Year Established: 1960
Pub. Frequency: m.
Page Size: standard
Subscrip. Rate: $55/yr. US; $80/yr. Canada; $115/yr. foreign
Materials: 06
Print Process: web
Circulation: 55,571
Circulation Type: paid
**Owner(s):**
Advanstar Communications, Inc.
7500 Old Oak Blvd.
Cleveland, OH 44130
Telephone: (216) 243-8100
Ownership %: 100
**Editorial:**
Alice V. Luddington ...............................Editor

### GROUP PRACTICE JOURNAL
23806
1422 Duke St.
Alexandria, VA 22314-3430
Telephone: (703) 838-0033
FAX: (703) 548-1890
Year Established: 1951
Pub. Frequency: bi-m.
Page Size: standard
Subscrip. Rate: $65/yr.
Freelance Pay: none
Circulation: 47,000
Circulation Type: paid
**Owner(s):**
American Group Practice Association
1422 Duke St.
Alexandria, VA 22314-3430
Telephone: (703) 838-0033
Ownership %: 100
**Management:**
Donald W. Fisher, Ph.D. ...................Publisher
Fred Haag ...................Advertising Manager

**Materials Accepted/Included:** 01-Business news 02-By-line articles 03-Fashion news 04-Food news 05-Freelance copy 06-Letters to editor 07-Real estate news 08-Sports news 09-Travel news 10-Book rev. 11-Movie rev. 12-Music rev. 13-TV rev. 14-Theater rev. 15-Coming events 16-Obituaries 17-Question & answer 18-Social announcements 19-Artwork 20-Cartoons 21-Photos 22-TV listings 23-Audio rec. 24-Video rec. 25-Books 26-Films/film clips 27-Personnel news 28-Press releases 29-New product news/photos 30-Trade lit. 31-Contracts awarded 32-Display adv. 33-Classified adv.

**Editorial:**

Laura Johnson ............................Editor

**Desc.:** Contains exclusive articles written for, by and about AGPA members and other specialists in healthcare to provide analytical and enlightening reports on current issues and trends in medical care delivery systems.

**Readers:** MD-CEO's, administrators and thousands of physicians in every group practice as defined by AGPA and AMA. This involves group practices, free-standing ambulatory care centers, HMO's and PPO's.

68972

## GROUP PRACTICE MANAGED HEALTHCARE NEWS

201 Littleton Rd.
Ste. 100
Morris Plains, NJ 07950-2932
Telephone: (201) 285-0855
FAX: (201) 285-1472
Year Established: 1986
Pub. Frequency: 12/yr.
Page Size: tabloid
Subscrip. Rate: $60/yr.
Materials: 01,02,05,06,15,27,28,29,32,33,34
Print Process: web
Circulation: 68,721
Circulation Type: controlled & paid
**Owner(s):**
Medical Communique, Inc.
201 Littleton Rd.
Ste. 100
Morris Plains, NJ 07950-2932
Telephone: (201) 285-0855
FAX: (201) 285-1472
Ownership %: 100
**Editorial:**
Donald M. Pizzi ............................Editor
**Desc.:** Dedicated to providing useful information for physicians, administrators, pharmacists and key HMO/PPO professionals in group practice or managed healthcare settings.
**Readers:** Group practice office-based primary care physicians, National Association of Managed Care Physicians, group medical directors, HMO/PPO managed healthcare administration professionals including HMO medical directors, HMO executives, PPO executives, utilization review companies' CEOs. Managed care pharmacists, pharmacy benefits managers and drug chain pharmacy program managers. HMO formulary committee members and group practice administrators.
**Deadline:** story-1st of prior mo.; news-1st of prior mo.; photo-1st of prior mo.; ads-15th of prior mo.

70397

## HARVARD REVIEW OF PSYCHIATRY

11830 Westline Industrial Dr.
St. Louis, MO 63146
Telephone: (314) 872-8370
FAX: (314) 872-9164
Year Established: 1993
Pub. Frequency: bi-m.
Subscrip. Rate: $12/copy; $40/yr. students; $65/yr. individual; $85/yr. institutional
Circulation: 3,000
Circulation Type: controlled
**Owner(s):**
Mosby-Year Book, Inc.
11830 Westline Industrial Dr.
St. Louis, MO 63146
Telephone: (314) 872-8370
FAX: (314) 872-9164
Ownership %: 100

**Desc.:** Examines a wide range of topics, with emphasis on the integration of research findings and clinical care. Articles cover diagnosis and treatment of a full range of psychiatric disorders; also covered are important issues in forensic psychiatry, medical ethics, practice managemnt, psychopharmacology, and the neurosciences.

23807

## HAWAII MEDICAL JOURNAL

1360 S. Beretania St., 2nd Fl.
Honolulu, HI 96814
Telephone: (808) 536-7702
FAX: (808) 528-2376
Year Established: 1941
Pub. Frequency: m.
Page Size: standard
Subscrip. Rate: $25/yr.
Circulation: 1,800
Circulation Type: paid
**Owner(s):**
Hawaii Medical Association
1360 S. Beretania St.
Honolulu, HI 96814
Telephone: (808) 536-7702
Ownership %: 100
**Editorial:**
Norman Goldstein, M.D. ...............Exec. Editor
Heidi Swanson ....................Editorial Assistant
Henry Yokoyama, M.D. .................News Editor
**Desc.:** Professional articles on health, diagnosis, case studies, research, etc. Departments include: Book Reviews, County Society Reports, Notes and News, Continuing Medical Education, Legislative, Letters to the Editor, Official Proceedings of the Association, Hawaii Academy of Family Physicians Newsletter, Hospital News, Announcements, etc. All Hawaii oriented, including the scientific material.
**Readers:** Members of the Hawaii Medical Association as well as libraries, medical schools, subscribers, other health organizations.

65612

## HEAD & NECK

605 Third Ave.
New York, NY 10158
Telephone: (212) 850-6047
FAX: (212) 850-6052
Year Established: 1979
Pub. Frequency: bi-m.
Subscrip. Rate: $295/yr.
Materials: 06
Circulation: 1,799
Circulation Type: paid
**Owner(s):**
John Wiley & Sons, Inc.
605 Third Ave.
New York, NY 10158
Ownership %: 100
**Editorial:**
Randal S. Weber .......................Editor

68975

## HEALTHFACTS

237 Thompson St.
New York, NY 10012
Telephone: (212) 674-7105
FAX: (212) 674-7100
Year Established: 1976
Pub. Frequency: m.
Subscrip. Rate: $21/yr. US; $24/yr. Canada & Mexico; $33/yr. Asia and Europe
Circulation: 12,000
Circulation Type: paid

**Owner(s):**
Center for Medical Consumers
237 Thompson St.
New York, NY 10012
Telephone: (212) 674-7105
Ownership %: 100
**Editorial:**
Maryann Napoli ........................Editor
**Desc.:** Designed for informed medical decision making.

23800

## HEALTH SYSTEMS REVIEW

1405 N. Pierce St., Ste. 308
Little Rock, AR 72207
Telephone: (501) 661-9555
FAX: (501) 663-4903
Mailing Address:
  P.O. Box 8708
  Little Rock, AR 72217-8708
Year Established: 1968
Pub. Frequency: bi-m.
Page Size: standard
Subscrip. Rate: $20/yr. US.; $25/yr. Canada & Mexico; $45/yr. foreign
Freelance Pay: varies
Circulation: 30,000
Circulation Type: controlled
**Owner(s):**
Federation of American Heallth Systems
1405 N. Pierce St., Ste. 311
Little Rock, AR 72207
Telephone: (501) 661-9555
Ownership %: 100
**Bureau(s):**
Federation of Amer. Health Systems
1111 19th St., N.W., Ste. 402
Washington, DC 20036
Telephone: (202) 833-3090
Contact: Pat Carmack, Senior Writer
**Management:**
Jim Brader ....................Advertising Manager
Wy Bonne ....................Circulation Manager
Bonnie Moneypenny .............General Manager
**Editorial:**
John Herrmann .......................Editor
**Desc.:** The official publication of the nation's investor-owned hospitals - with in-depth coverage of legislation and regulation at the national and state levels for the entire health care industry. Other coverage includes technology and business issues.
**Readers:** Executive personnel of hospitals, hospital management companies, health systems, and alternative care groups.

23808

## HEARING JOURNAL

428 E. Preston St.
Baltimore, MD 21202
Telephone: (410) 528-4000
FAX: (410) 528-4312
Mailing Address:
  P.O. Box 285
  Newcastle, ME 04553
Year Established: 1947
Pub. Frequency: m.
Page Size: standard
Subscrip. Rate: $36/yr.
Circulation: 22,000
Circulation Type: controlled
**Owner(s):**
William & Wilkins
428 E. Preston St.
Baltimore, MD 21202
Telephone: (410) 528-4000
Ownership %: 100
**Management:**
Jerrold R. Laux ......................Publisher
**Editorial:**
David H. Kirkwood ....................Editor

**Desc.:** By-line articles cover hearing problems, developments in the field of sound, marketing of hearing aids. Written to assist the retail hearing aid dealer, audiologists and otolaryngologists and others in the hearing, health community. Uses company, dealer, association, new product news.

**Readers:** Owners, managers and sales and service personnel, manufacturers of replacement parts and accessories, audiologists and otolaryngologists, personnel in hearing clinics, hospitals, and schools and societies. Manufacturers and suppliers of hearing aids.

66553

## HEPATOLOGY

11830 Westline Industiral Dr.
St. Louis, MO 63146
Telephone: (314) 872-8370
FAX: (314) 872-9146
Year Established: 1981
Pub. Frequency: m.
Page Size: standard
Subscrip. Rate: $17/copy; $60/yr. student; $185/yr. individual; $288/yr. institutional
Circulation: 5,134
Circulation Type: paid
**Owner(s):**
Mosby-Year Book, Inc.
Times Mirror Co.
St. Louis, MO 63146
Telephone: (314) 872-8370
Ownership %: 100
**Bureau(s):**
C.V. Mosby Co., The, Eastern Sales Office
535 Fiifth Ave., Ste. 805
New York, NY 10017
Telephone: (212) 986-7325
Contact: Edward Fox

C.V. Mosby Co., The, Midwest Sales Office
550 Frontage Rd 378 Willow Hll
Northfield, IL 60093
Telephone: (708) 446-9253
Contact: James Kakarakis
**Management:**
Carol Trumbold ......................Publisher
**Editorial:**
Paul D. Berk ........................Editor
**Desc.:** Publishes original, peer-reviewed articles concerning all aspects of liver structure, function, and disease. Articles cover developments in: viral hepatitis, chronic hepatitis, gallstones, cirrhosis, cancer of the liver, liver transplantations, and more.
**Readers:** Physicians and researchers in the specialties of hepatology, gastroenterology, internal medicine, pathology, general surgery, pediatrics, and the basic sciences.

61794

## HMO PRACTICE

900 Guaranty Bldg.
Buffalo, NY 14214
Telephone: (716) 847-1480
FAX: (716) 847-0047
Year Established: 1987
Pub. Frequency: q.
Page Size: standard
Subscrip. Rate: $150/yr.
Circulation: 15,000
Circulation Type: paid
**Owner(s):**
The HMO Group
100 Albany St., Ste. 230
New Brunswick, NJ 08901
Telephone: (908) 220-1388
Ownership %: 100
**Management:**
Daniel B. Wolfson ....................Publisher

**Materials Accepted/Included:** 01-Business news 02-By-line articles 03-Fashion news 04-Food news 05-Freelance copy 06-Letters to editor 07-Real estate news 08-Sports news 09-Travel news 10-Book rev. 11-Movie rev. 12-Music rev. 13-TV rev. 14-Theater rev. 15-Coming events 16-Obituaries 17-Question & answer 18-Social announcements 19-Artwork 20-Cartoons 21-Photos 22-TV listings 23-Audio rec. 24-Video rec. 25-Books 26-Films/film clips 27-Personnel news 28-Press releases 29-New product news/photos 30-Trade lit. 31-Contracts awarded 32-Display adv. 33-Classified adv.

4-233

**Editorial:**
Leonard A. Katz, M.D. ...............Editor
Susan Yox, RN, EdD ........Managing Editor
Jerome Beekman, MD ..........Associate Editor
Stephen Schoenbaum, ..........Associate Editor
M.D.
**Desc.:** Strives to be the leading medical journal for the dissemination of information in prepaid group practice. This information includes discussions of health services research, clinical and program innovations, health policy and opinions and resource management, including new technology. The journal also serves as a forum and communication resource for health professionals concerned with continuous quality improvement in patient care and practice management.
**Readers:** Physicians, other clinicians & clinical managers who practice in group/staff model HMO's.

## HOSPITAL MEDICINE
23810
105 Raider Blvd.
Belle Mead, NJ 08502-1510
Telephone: (908) 874-8550
FAX: (908) 874-6096
Year Established: 1964
Pub. Frequency: m.
Page Size: standard
Subscrip. Rate: $50/yr.; $36/yr. physicians
Circulation: 120,000
Circulation Type: controlled & paid
**Owner(s):**
Excerpta Medica
105 Raider Blvd.
Belle Mead, NJ 08502
Ownership %: 100
**Management:**
Barry J. Murphy .....................Publisher
**Editorial:**
Vymtna Burkhart ......................Editor
**Desc.:** A peer-reviewed illustrated journal for primary care physicians.
**Readers:** Serves, primary care, physicians in selected specialities GP, FP, IM, DO's.

## HOSPITAL PRACTICE
23812
55 Fifth Ave.
New York, NY 10003
Telephone: (212) 989-2100
FAX: (212) 727-7316
Year Established: 1966
Pub. Frequency: m.
Page Size: standard
Subscrip. Rate: $54/yr.
Circulation: 175,000
Circulation Type: controlled
**Owner(s):**
Maclean Hunter, Ltd.
Maclean Hunter Bldg.
777 Bay St.
Toronto ON, Canada
Ownership %: 100
**Management:**
Milton Liebman .....................Publisher
Rita Beale ...........Advertising Manager
**Editorial:**
Samuel C. Bukantz .....................Editor
Dan Radebaugh ........Production Director
**Desc.:** A publication for physicians, consists primarily of articles and features on clinical medicine and research in medicine and the biological sciences, by-lined by leading authorities. Contains departments on news, clinical cases, history of medicine, essays.
**Readers:** Physicians in active medical practice.

## HYPERTENSION
67055
7272 Greenville Ve.
Dallas, TX 75231
Telephone: (214) 706-1310
FAX: (214) 691-6342
Year Established: 1979
Pub. Frequency: m.
Page Size: standard
Subscrip. Rate: $112/yr. institute; $156/yr. international
Freelance Pay: $10-$15/hr. copyreaders; $15-$20/hr. copy editors
Circulation: 4,300
Circulation Type: paid
**Owner(s):**
American Heart Association
7272 Greenville Ave.
Dallas, TX 75231
Telephone: (214) 706-1310
Ownership %: 100
**Management:**
Vicki Sullivan .....................Publisher
Margaret Levene ...........Advertising Manager
Mary Kappel ..........Customer Service Manager
Mary Ann McNeely ...........Editorial Production Manager
**Editorial:**
Allyn Mark .....................Editor
Krista Curnutt ..............Production Coordinator
**Desc.:** Hypertension is a forum for the presentation of scientific investigation of the highest quality in the broad field of cardiovascular regulation as it may affect high blood pressure research. The Editors are interested in receiving original articles that deal with either basic or clinical research in the fields of Biochemistry, Cellular, and Molecular biology, immunology Ditysidogy, Pharmacology, and Epidemiology. In addition, an important part of the journal is reserved for articles on clinical investigation that yield insight into the mechanisms of high blood regulation.
**Readers:** Cardiologists, internists, researchers.

## ILLINOIS MEDICINE
65661
20 N. Michigan Ave., #700
Chicago, IL 60602
Telephone: (312) 782-1654
FAX: (312) 782-2033
Year Established: 1989
Pub. Frequency: bi-w.
Page Size: tabloid
Subscrip. Rate: $12/yr.
Freelance Pay: $.40/wd.
Print Process: web
Circulation: 20,000
Circulation Type: controlled
**Owner(s):**
Illinois State Medical Society
20 N. Michigan, #700
Chicago, IL 60602
Telephone: (312) 782-1654
Ownership %: 100
**Editorial:**
Lynn Koslowsky .....................Editor
Carla Nolan ..........Production/Design Manager
**Desc.:** Published by the Illinois State Medical Society to bring Illinois physicians balanced, accurate news and comment on health care issues and professional concerns. Circulation to community leaders intended to stimulate dialogue and articulate timely, relevant information on public policy matters. Content is structured to challenge, motivate and assist physicians in communicating with patients, colleagues and the public.

**Readers:** MD Society members in Illinois, plus government, hospitals, health facilities, health media.

## INDIANA MEDICINE
23851
322 Canal Walk
Indianapolis, IN 46202-3252
Telephone: (317) 261-2060
FAX: (317) 261-2076
Year Established: 1908
Pub. Frequency: bi-m.
Page Size: standard
Subscrip. Rate: $15/yr. US; $17/yr. Canada; $18/yr. foreign
Materials: 32,33
Circulation: 7,000
Circulation Type: paid
**Owner(s):**
Indiana State Medical Association
322 Canal Walk
Indianapolis, IN 46202
Telephone: (317) 261-2060
Ownership %: 100
**Editorial:**
Tina Sims .....................Managing Editor
Rosanna Iler .................Subscriptions
**Desc.:** Edited for Indiana physicians in general practice, specialists, and those in research and on medical school faculties. Scientific articles comprise previously unpublished case reports and clinical, review and investigative articles. News articles cover organizational, economic, political, legislative, social and personal medical activities. Continuing medical education courses are listed. Columns include national and state medical news, medical history, letters, editorials, and obituaries.
**Readers:** Physicians, hospital staff and medical students.
**Deadline:** ads-1st of mo., prior to pub. date

## INFECTION & IMMUNITY
65682
1325 Massachusetts Ave., N.W.
Washington, DC 20005-4171
Telephone: (202) 737-3600
Year Established: 1970
Pub. Frequency: m.
Page Size: standard
Subscrip. Rate: $368/yr.
Materials: 02,06,32
Print Process: web offset
Circulation: 6,700
Circulation Type: paid
**Owner(s):**
American Society for Microbiology
1325 Massachusetts Ave., N.W.
Washington, DC 20005-4171
Telephone: (202) 737-3600
Ownership %: 100
**Editorial:**
V.A. Fischetti .............Editor in Chief
L.M. Illig .................Director
**Desc.:** Covers topics directed toward immunologists, microbiologists, epidemiologists, pathologists, and clinicians. Subjects include infections caused by pathogenic bacteria, fungi, and unicellular parasites; ecology and epidemiology of pathogenic microbes; virulence factors such as toxins and surface structures; nonspecific factors in host resistance and susceptbility to infection; vaccines; and immunology of microbial infection.
**Readers:** Researchers in the area of infectious disease, microbiology, immunology.

## INFECTIOUS DISEASES IN CLINICAL PRACTICE
55916
428 E. Preston St.
Baltimore, MD 21202
Telephone: (410) 361-8018
FAX: (410) 528-4312
Year Established: 1992
Pub. Frequency: bi-m.
Page Size: standard
Subscrip. Rate: $80/yr. individuals; $125/yr. institutions; $49/yr. in-training
Circulation: 5,398
Circulation Type: paid
**Owner(s):**
Williams & Wilkins Co.
428 E. Preston St.
Baltimore, MD 21202
Telephone: (410) 528-4000
Ownership %: 100
**Management:**
Carol Miranda ...........Production Manager
**Editorial:**
Sherwood L. Gorbach, M.D. ...........Chief Editor
Elizabeth Nolan ...........Marketing Manager
**Desc.:** Articles for pediatricians, internists, surgeons, and infectious disease specialists cover the treatment and prevention of adult infectious diseases.
**Readers:** Subscribers are pediatricians, infectious disease specialists, internists, surgeons, and ob/gyns.

## INTERNAL MEDICINE NEWS & CARDIOLOGY NEWS
54022
12230 Wilkins Ave.
Rockville, MD 20852
Telephone: (301) 770-6170
FAX: (301) 984-3927
Year Established: 1968
Pub. Frequency: s-m.
Page Size: tabloid
Subscrip. Rate: $96/yr.
Circulation: 102,500
Circulation Type: controlled
**Owner(s):**
International Medical News Group
12230 Wilkins Ave.
Rockville, MD 20852
Telephone: (301) 770-6170
Ownership %: 100
**Management:**
George Lister .....................Publisher
**Editorial:**
Johanna H. Weekley .....................Editor

## INTERNATIONAL JOURNAL OF RADIATION: ONCOLOGY/BIOLOGY/PHYSICS
66481
660 White Plains Rd.
Tarrytown, NY 10591
Telephone: (914) 524-9200
FAX: (914) 333-2444
Year Established: 1975
Pub. Frequency: 15/yr.
Page Size: standard
Subscrip. Rate: $1425/yr. institutions
Circulation: 6,500
Circulation Type: paid
**Owner(s):**
Elsevier Science
660 White Plains Rd.
Tarrytown, NY 10591-5153
Telephone: (914) 524-9200
Ownership %: 100
**Management:**
Roger A. Dunn ...........General Manager
Mike Boswood ...........Managing Director
**Editorial:**
Jay Feinman .....................Advertising

**Desc.:** An international journal publishing full length reports on research in a range of areas in the life sciences. These areas include molecular and cellular aspects of: cardiovascular & autonomic mechanisms, drug metabolism, endocrinology, growth factors & neoplasia, immunology, neuroscience and toxicology. Publishes original research rapidly. Although full-length manuscripts are favored, exciting new results requiring rapid dissemination in shorter form will also be considered. These shorter submissions may be considered for either "Life Sciences" or for the ultra-rapid communications section Pharmacology Letters.

## INTERNATIONAL JOURNAL OF SYSTEMATIC BACTERIOLOGY
65660
1325 Massachusettes Ave, N.W.
Washington, DC 20005-4171
Telephone: (202) 737-3600
Year Established: 1951
Pub. Frequency: q.
Page Size: standard
Subscrip. Rate: $158/yr. non-members in US
Materials: 02,06,10,32
Print Process: web offset
Circulation: 1,900
Circulation Type: paid
**Owner(s):**
International Union of Microbiological Societies
c/o Amer. Soc. for Microbiolog
Ownership %: 100
**Editorial:**
R. G. E. Murray ..............................Editor
**Desc.:** Official journal of the International Committee in Systematic Bacteriology of the International Union of Microbiological Societies. Publishes papers concerned with the systematics of bacteria, yeasts, and yeast like organisms, including taxonomy, nomenclature, identification characterization, and culture preservation. Published by ASM as a service to the International Union of Microbiological Societies.
**Readers:** Research & clinical laboratory personnel interested in or engaged in classification and taxonomy of microorganisms.

## INTERNATIONAL REHABILITATION REVIEW
23816
25 E. 21st St.
New York, NY 10010
Telephone: (212) 420-1500
FAX: (212) 505-0871
Year Established: 1949
Pub. Frequency: 3/yr.
Page Size: tabloid
Subscrip. Rate: $30/yr.
Circulation: 6,000
Circulation Type: paid
**Owner(s):**
Rehabilitation International
25 E. 21st St.
New York, NY 10010
Ownership %: 100
**Editorial:**
Barbara Duncan ...............................Editor

**Desc.:** Deals with problems in the rehabilitation of the physically and mentally disabled all over the world, and methods of solving the problems. News of activities throughout the world, feature articles by international experts, and staff reports of the programs. Regular features: Editorial, Professional, International and National News, Progress Reports on Trends in the Field, Publications Page and International Calendar.
**Readers:** Professional and lay rehabilitation workers and disabled persons.

## INVESTIGATIVE OPHTHALMOLOGY & VISUAL SCIENCE
61795
227 E. Washington Sq.
Philadelphia, PA 19106
Telephone: (215) 238-4200
Pub. Frequency: m.
Page Size: standard
Subscrip. Rate: $165/yr. US individual; $220/yr. US instn.; $220/yr. foreign individual; $270/yr. foreign instn.
Circulation: 9,186
Circulation Type: paid
**Owner(s):**
J.B. Lippincott Co.
227 E. Washington Sq.
Philadelphia, PA 19105
Telephone: (215) 238-4273
Ownership %: 100
**Management:**
Lisa Marshall .............................Publisher
**Editorial:**
Harry A. Quigley, M.D. ....................Editor
Susan Eidson .....................Advertising Sales
Beverly Dietrich ...........Circulation Director
Suzann Graff ..........Senior Marketing Manager

## IOWA MEDICINE
23853
1001 Grand Ave.
W Des Moines, IA 50265
Telephone: (515) 223-1401
Year Established: 1910
Pub. Frequency: m.
Page Size: standard
Subscrip. Rate: $20/yr.
Circulation: 5,300
Circulation Type: paid
**Owner(s):**
Iowa Medical Society
1001 Grand Ave.
W Des Moines, IA 50265
Telephone: (515) 223-1401
Ownership %: 100
**Management:**
Jane I. Nieland ..............Advertising Manager
Jane I. Nieland ................Production Manager
**Editorial:**
Eldon E. Huston ..................Executive Editor
Marion E. Alberts, M.D. ......................Editor
Christine K. Clark ...................Managing Editor
**Desc.:** Publishes 1 or 2 technical medical articles, socioeconomic feature articles, and departments such as practice management, medical economics, legislative affairs, health system reform, and editorials in each issue. The scientific articles published are ones written and sent in by the members of our society.
**Readers:** Approximately 90 percent of the doctors of Iowa.

## JAMA: JOURNAL OF THE AMERICAN MEDICAL ASSOCIATION
23826
515 N. State St.
Chicago, IL 60610
Telephone: (312) 464-5000
FAX: (312) 464-4184
Year Established: 1883
Pub. Frequency: 48/yr.
Page Size: standard
Subscrip. Rate: $110/yr. US; $150/yr. foreign
Circulation: 258,000
Circulation Type: paid
**Owner(s):**
American Medical Association
515 N. State St.
Chicago, IL 60610
Telephone: (312) 464-5000
Ownership %: 100
**Management:**
James S. Todd ..........Executive Vice President
Robert L. Kennett ......................Vice President
**Editorial:**
George D. Lundberg, MD .......................Editor
Richard Fleming ................Marketing Manager
**Desc.:** Publication covers progress in clinical medicine, pertinent research and landmark evolutions in the political and social interfaces of medicine.
**Readers:** Medical profession.

## JMPT: JOURNAL OF MANIPULATIVE & PHYSICAL THERAPUTICS
59037
428 E. Preston St.
Baltimore, MD 21202
Telephone: (410) 528-4000
FAX: (410) 528-4312
Year Established: 1979
Pub. Frequency: 9/yr.
Subscrip. Rate: $78/yr. individual; $104/yr. institution
Circulation: 3,850
Circulation Type: paid
**Owner(s):**
National College of Chiropractic
200 E. Roosevelt Rd.
Lombard, IL 60148
Telephone: (708) 629-2000
Ownership %: 100
**Management:**
Don Pfarr ........................Advertising Manager
Alma Wills ..................................Manager
**Editorial:**
Dana J. Lawrence, D.C. ......................Editor
Nancy Collins .....................Marketing Director

## JOURNAL OF ADDICTIVE DISEASES
69498
10 Alice St.
Binghamton, NY 13904
Telephone: (800) 342-9678
FAX: (607) 722-1424
Year Established: 1981
Pub. Frequency: q.
Page Size: standard
Subscrip. Rate: $45/yr. individuals; $95/yr. institutions; $240/yr. libraries
Circulation: 3,506
Circulation Type: paid
**Owner(s):**
Haworth Press, Inc.
10 Alice St.
Binghamton, NY 13904
Telephone: (800) 342-9678
Ownership %: 100
**Editorial:**
Dr. Barry Stimmel ............................Editor
**Desc.:** Covers current topics in alcoholism and substance abuse field. Devotes an entire issue to each topic.

## JOURNAL OF AGING & PHYSICAL ACTIVITY (JAPA)
70430
1607 N. Market St.
Champaign, IL 61820
Telephone: (217) 351-5076
FAX: (217) 351-2674
Year Established: 1993
Pub. Frequency: q.
Page Size: standard
Subscrip. Rate: $24/yr. students; $40/yr. individuals; $90/yr. institutions
Materials: 10,25,29
Print Process: offset
Circulation: 500
Circulation Type: paid
**Owner(s):**
Human Kinetics
1607 N. Market
Champaign, IL 61820
Telephone: (217) 351-5076
FAX: (217) 351-2674
Ownership %: 100
**Management:**
Rainer Martens ...........................Publisher
Peg Goyette ...............................Manager
**Editorial:**
Wojtek Chodzko-Zajko .....................Editor
Linda A. Bump ...................Journal Director
**Desc.:** Multidisciplinary journal focusing on the relationship between physical activity and the aging process.
**Readers:** gerontologists, physical therapists, medical doctors, recreation directors, and other researchers.

## JOURNAL OF ALLERGY & CLINICAL IMMUNOLOGY, THE
23822
11830 Westline Industrial Dr.
St. Louis, MO 63146
Telephone: (800) 325-4117
FAX: (314) 432-1380
Year Established: 1929
Pub. Frequency: m.
Page Size: standard
Subscrip. Rate: $9.50/copy; $96/yr. individuals; $182/yr. institutions
Circulation: 11,541
Circulation Type: paid
**Owner(s):**
Mosby-Year Book, Inc.
11830 Westline Industrial Dr.
St. Louis, MO 63146
Telephone: (314) 872-8370
Ownership %: 100
**Management:**
Carol Trumbold .............................Publisher
Kathy Preston ..................Advertising Manager
**Editorial:**
Philip S. Norman ......................Editor in Chief
Ruth Kaufman .............................Copy Chief
Kathy Keller ....................Production Director
**Desc.:** Serves the needs of the clinical allergist as well as those of the dermatologists, internists, general practitioners, and pediatricians concerned with clinical manifestations of allergies in their practice.
**Readers:** Dermatologists, allergists, general practitioners. Official publication of the American Academy of Allergy and Immunology.

## JOURNAL OF AMERICAN GERIATRICS SOCIETY
23825
66 N. Pauline St.
Ste. 232
Memphis, TN 38105
Telephone: (901) 448-5567
FAX: (901) 448-7041
Year Established: 1953
Pub. Frequency: m.

**Materials Accepted/Included:** 01-Business news 02-By-line articles 03-Fashion news 04-Food news 05-Freelance copy 06-Letters to editor 07-Real estate news 08-Sports news 09-Travel news 10-Book rev. 11-Movie rev. 12-Music rev. 13-TV rev. 14-Theater rev. 15-Coming events 16-Obituaries 17-Question & answer 18-Social announcements 19-Artwork 20-Cartoons 21-Photos 22-TV listings 23-Audio rec. 24-Video rec. 25-Books 26-Films/film clips 27-Personnel news 28-Press releases 29-New product news/photos 30-Trade lit. 31-Contracts awarded 32-Display adv. 33-Classified adv.

4-235

Page Size: standard
Subscrip. Rate: $16/copy; $100/yr.
 individuals; $170/yr. institutions
Circulation: 9,420
Circulation Type: paid
**Owner(s):**
American Geriatrics Society
Williams & Wilkins
428 E. Preston St.
Baltimore, MD 21202
Telephone: (410) 528-4000
Ownership %: 100
**Editorial:**
William Applegate .......................Editor in Chief
Elizabeth Webb ..................Coordinating Editor
**Desc.:** Professional publication dealing
 with problems of the aged and aging
 patient, study of causes, prevention and
 treatment of diseases of advancing
 years, and rehabilitation of patients.
**Readers:** Geriatricians, internists,
 cardiologists, gastroenterologists,
 rheumatologists, psychiatrists,
 endocrinologists, family practitioners,
 nurse practitioners, and other
 professionals who treat older patients.

22487
## JOURNAL OF ANALYTICAL TOXICOLOGY
7800 Merrimac Ave.
Niles, IL 60714
Telephone: (708) 965-0566
FAX: (708) 965-7639
Mailing Address:
 P.O. Box 48312
 Niles, IL 60714
Year Established: 1977
Pub. Frequency: 7/yr.
Page Size: standard
Subscrip. Rate: $50/issue; $220/yr.
Circulation: 1,355
Circulation Type: paid
**Owner(s):**
Preston Industries, Inc.
Preston Publications Division
7800 N. Merrimac
Niles, IL 60714
Telephone: (708) 965-0566
Ownership %: 100
**Management:**
Seaton T. Preston ...............................Publisher
Kit Hatcher ........................Circulation Manager
**Editorial:**
Susan Buksa ...........................Managing Editor
Randall C. Baselt .....................Technical Editor
**Desc.:** A refereed journal with articles
 submitted by research and technical
 staff chemists. Articles are 2-10 pages
 long (average length 3-4 pages), with
 graphs and tables. Publish all new
 product and literature descriptions that
 are applicable to the field. Departments
 include: Letters to the Editor,
 New Books, News, Meetings and Short
 Courses, New Literature, New Products.
**Readers:** Research and technical staff
 chemists and toxiologists employed by
 industrial manufacturing laboratories,
 independent analytical laboratories,
 university laboratories and government
 forensic labs.

61792
## JOURNAL OF ANDROLOGY
c/o Dept. of Urology Research
Guggenheim 1711, Mayo Clinic, 200 1st.
 St. S.W.
Rochester, MN 55905
Telephone: (507) 284-2423
Year Established: 1980
Pub. Frequency: bi-m.
Page Size: standard
Subscrip. Rate: $225/yr. institutions;
 $245/yr. foreign
Circulation: 1,300

Circulation Type: paid
**Owner(s):**
American Society of Andrology
c/o Dept. of Urology Research
Guggenheim 1711, Mayo Clinic, 200 First
 St., S.W.
Rochester, MN 55905
Telephone: (507) 284-2423
Ownership %: 100
**Management:**
Marcia E. Serepy ...............................Publisher
**Editorial:**
Claude Desjardins .......................Editor in Chief
Dr. Donald Tindall ...............................Editor
**Desc.:** Publishes significant new findings of
 basic and clinical research on human
 and animal male reproductive tracts.

23830
## JOURNAL OF APPLIED PHYSIOLOGY
9650 Rockville Pike
Bethesda, MD 20814
Telephone: (301) 530-7071
FAX: (301) 571-1814
Year Established: 1948
Pub. Frequency: m.
Page Size: standard
Subscrip. Rate: $385/yr. individual;
 $465/yr. Canada & Mexico; $510/yr.
 elsewhere; $528/yr. instn.; $583/yr.
 Canada & Mexico; $660/yr. elsewhere
Materials: 15,30,32,33
Print Process: web
Circulation: 3,400
Circulation Type: paid
**Owner(s):**
The American Physiological Society
9650 Rockville Pike
Bethesda, MD 20814
Telephone: (301) 530-7071
FAX: (301) 530-1814
Ownership %: 100
**Editorial:**
J. Remmers ...............................................Editor
**Desc.:** Accepts articles that contribute
 significant insights into respiratory
 physiology, environmental physiology,
 exercise physiology, new and useful
 techniques, equipment. Departments
 include: Abstracts of Important Papers
 from other journals, Editorials, Letters to
 the Editor, Controversies, Book Reviews.
**Readers:** Physiologists, doctors and
 students.

22261
## JOURNAL OF ATHLETIC TRAINING
2952 Stemmons Frwy.
Dallas, TX 75247
Telephone: (214) 637-6282
FAX: (214) 637-2206
Year Established: 1956
Pub. Frequency: q.
Page Size: standard
Subscrip. Rate: $32/yr.
Freelance Pay: donations
Circulation: 18000
Circulation Type: controlled & paid
**Owner(s):**
National Athletic Trainers Association, Inc.
2952 Stemmons Frwy.
Ste. 200
Dallas, TX 75247
Telephone: (214) 637-6282
Ownership %: 100
**Management:**
Hunter Press .......................................Publisher
Teresa Foster ....................Circulation Manager
**Editorial:**
Ken Knight .................................Editor in Chief
Ron Cunningham ....................Managing Editor

**Desc.:** Editorials are related to sports
 medicine and related duties of the
 athletic trainer. The journal of the
 National Athletic Trainers Association.
**Readers:** Sports medicine related.

23833
## JOURNAL OF BIOLOGICAL CHEMISTRY
9650 Rockville Pike
Bethesda, MD 20814
Telephone: (301) 530-7150
FAX: (301) 571-1824
Year Established: 1905
Pub. Frequency: w.
Page Size: standard
Subscrip. Rate: $790/yr.
Circulation: 6,400
Circulation Type: paid
**Owner(s):**
Amer. Soc. for Biochemistry & Molecular
 Biology
9650 Rockville Pike
Bethesda, MD 20814
Telephone: (301) 530-7150
Ownership %: 100
**Management:**
Charles C. Hancock .............................Manager
**Editorial:**
Herbert Tabor .........................................Editor
Pete Farnham .................Public Affairs Director
**Desc.:** Designed for the prompt publication
 of origilogical sciences.
**Readers:** Chemists, physicians, personnel
 of hospitals.

65664
## JOURNAL OF BURNCARE & REHABILITATION
11830 Westline Industrial Dr.
St. Louis, MO 63146
Telephone: (314) 872-8370
FAX: (314) 432-1380
Year Established: 1980
Pub. Frequency: m.
Page Size: standard
Subscrip. Rate: $41/yr. individuals; $75/yr.
 institutions; $24/yr. students
Circulation: 3,902
Circulation Type: free & paid
**Owner(s):**
American Burn Association
5323 Harry Hines Blvd.
Dallas, TX 75235
Ownership %: 100
**Management:**
Carol Trumbold ...................................Publisher
Kathy Preston ....................Advertising Manager
Kate Carter ........................Circulation Manager
**Editorial:**
Charles R. Baster, M.D. .........................Editor
**Desc.:** Offers clinical and research articles
 concerned with advances in burn
 prevention, research education acute-
 care delivery, surgical techniques and
 rehabilitation. The peer-reviewed journal
 includes editorials, historical and current
 reviews, case reports, abstracts and the
 ABA newsletter.
**Readers:** Members of the burn team
 including physicians, nurses, physical
 therapists, occupational therapists,
 psychologists, counselors, research
 personnel and nutritionists. Official
 publication of the American Burn
 Association.

23836
## JOURNAL OF CLINICAL ENDOCRINOLOGY & METABOLISM
525 E. 68th St.
New York, NY 10021
Telephone: (212) 746-4970
FAX: (212) 746-4978
Year Established: 1941

Pub. Frequency: m.
Page Size: standard
Subscrip. Rate: $140/yr. individuals,
 $215/yr. institutions US; $180/yr.
 individuals, foreign
Circulation: 9,500
Circulation Type: paid
**Owner(s):**
Endocrine Society, The
9650 Rockville Pike
Bethesda, MD 20814
Telephone: (301) 571-1802
Ownership %: 100
**Editorial:**
Maria New ...................................Editor in Chief
Elizabeth Kitzinger ...................Managing Editor
**Desc.:** Original articles devoted to clinical
 endocrinology and metabolism in man.
 Stress is on current clinical and
 laboratory methods. A journal of the
 Endocrine Society.
**Readers:** Subscribers, including
 endocrinologists, internists, Ob/Gyn's,
 physiologists, and biochemists with an
 interest in the endocrine glands and
 their hormones, including members of
 The Endocrine Society.

23837
## JOURNAL OF CLINICAL ENGINEERING
1351 Titan Way
Brea, CA 92621
Telephone: (714) 738-6400
FAX: (714) 525-6258
Year Established: 1976
Pub. Frequency: bi-m.
Page Size: standard
Subscrip. Rate: $130/yr. US; $170/yr.
 foreign
Circulation: 3,000
Circulation Type: paid
**Owner(s):**
Quest Publishing Co., Div. of Raven Press
1351 Titan Way
Brea, CA 92621
Telephone: (714) 738-6400
Ownership %: 100
**Management:**
Allan F. Pacela ...................................Publisher
**Editorial:**
Gregory Nighswonger ..............Executive Editor
Allan F. Pacela .......................................Editor
Linnea Brush ...........................Managing Editor
Tyra Childs ........................................Advertising
**Desc.:** A professional publication devoted
 to the communication of information
 essential to the practice of clinical and
 biomedical engineering. Manuscripts
 may be authorized by engineers,
 EMET's, clinical personnel, MD's,
 managers, or others concerned
 with technology or engineering in the
 broad field of health care. Departments
 include: Letters to the Editor, Clinical
 Engineering Forum, Technology &
 Trends, Washington Scene, Directory of
 Local & Regional Biomedical
 Organizations, Reference Library,
 Editorial, Calendar of Events, For Your
 Information, and Service Training
 Programs, Software Reviews.
**Readers:** Biomedical engineers, clinical
 engineers, hospital administrators,
 clinical personnel & manufacturing
 professionals.

23835
## JOURNAL OF CLINICAL EPIDEMIOLOGY
333 Cedar St.
Yale University School of Medicine
New Haven, CT 06510
Telephone: (203) 785-4145
FAX: (203) 785-3641

Mailing Address:
Yale University School of Medicine
P.O. Box 33333
New Haven, CT 06510-8025
Year Established: 1966
Pub. Frequency: m.
Page Size: tabloid
Circulation: 2,200
Circulation Type: paid
**Owner(s):**
Pergamon Journals, Inc.
660 White Plains Rd.
Tarrytown, NY 10591-5153
Telephone: (914) 594-9200
Ownership %: 100
**Editorial:**
Alvan R. Feinstein ................................Editor
Walter D. Spitzer ................................Editor
**Desc.:** Original articles in the field; review articles and editorials in the field; symposia. Concerned with research in chronic illness, and in the domain sometimes called clinical epidemiology.
**Readers:** General practitioners, internists, and biologists, radiologists.

23838
## JOURNAL OF CLINICAL INVESTIGATION
222 E. 70th St.
New York, NY 10021
Telephone: (212) 327-7938
FAX: (212) 327-7944
Mailing Address:
P.O. Box 1500
University of California
San Francisco, CA 94143
Year Established: 1924
Pub. Frequency: m.
Page Size: standard
Subscrip. Rate: $130/yr. individual;
$225/yr. institution
Circulation: 5,768
Circulation Type: paid
**Owner(s):**
American Society for Clinical Investigation
San Diego, CA 92161
Ownership %: 100
**Bureau(s):**
Rockefeller University Press
222 E. 70th St.
New York, NY 10021
Telephone: (212) 327-7938
Contact: Raymond Fastiggi, Business Manager
**Management:**
Stuart M. Orkin, M.D. ...........................President
**Editorial:**
Ajit Varki ................................Editor
E. Kay Meschko ......................Managing Editor
**Desc.:** Publishes manuscripts by clinical and basic researchers. News releases are not accepted and books are not reviewed.
**Readers:** Researchers, medical library personnel.

23841
## JOURNAL OF CLINICAL ULTRASOUND
605 Third Ave.
New York, NY 10158
Telephone: (212) 850-6000
Year Established: 1973
Pub. Frequency: 9/yr.
Page Size: standard
Subscrip. Rate: $210/yr.
Circulation: 4,500
Circulation Type: paid
**Owner(s):**
John Wiley & Sons, Inc.
605 Third Ave.
New York, NY 10157
Telephone: (212) 692-6000
Ownership %: 100

**Management:**
Joseph H. Holmes ......................Founder
W. Bradford Wiley ......................President
Virginia Martin ......................Publisher
**Editorial:**
Russell L. Deter, M.D. ................Editor
Dora Castiblanco ......................Advertising
Christina Shepherd ..........Production Director
**Desc.:** Devoted exclusively to the clinical applications of ultrasound. indispensable as a central forum for up-to-date discussion of the current work in diagnostic ultrasound, it features original articles on new procedures and innovative techniques as well as review articles on specific applications. Also includes a calendar of events, classified, and announcements. The editor invites original articles from those working in the field.
**Readers:** Radiologists, obstetricians, gynecologists, sonographers, pediatricians, cardiologists.

23842
## JOURNAL OF DERMATOLOGIC SURGERY & ONCOLOGY, THE
655 Ave. of the Americas
New York, NY 10010
Telephone: (212) 989-5800
FAX: (212) 633-3990
Year Established: 1975
Pub. Frequency: m.
Page Size: standard
Subscrip. Rate: $125/yr. institutional;
$178/yr. foreign
Circulation: 13,015
Circulation Type: paid
**Owner(s):**
Elsevier Science Publishing Co., Inc.
655 Ave. of the Americas
New York, NY 10010
Ownership %: 100
**Management:**
Janet D. Bailey ......................Publisher
Richard Geyer ..................Advertising Manager
Margot Russell ..................Circulation Manager
**Editorial:**
Leonard Denbow, MD ..........Editor in Chief
C. William Hanke ......................Editor
Thomas J. Easley ..................Managing Editor
Graeme Whitley ......................Production Editor
**Desc.:** Journal concerning skin surgery, oncology, and dermatology. Begun in April, 1975 to fill gap in dissemination of information on dermatologic surgery and oncology.
**Readers:** Dermatologists, dermatology residents, high-prescribing GP's and FP's, medical libraries.

55901
## JOURNAL OF DEVELOPMENTAL & BEHAVIORAL PEDIATRICS
428 E. Preston St.
Baltimore, MD 21202
Telephone: (410) 528-4000
FAX: (410) 528-4312
Year Established: 1980
Pub. Frequency: bi-m.
Subscrip. Rate: $98/yr. individuals;
$138/yr. institutions
Circulation: 1,500
Circulation Type: paid
**Owner(s):**
Society for Behavioral Pediatrics
**Editorial:**
Dr. Stanford B. Friedman ......................Editor
**Desc.:** Articles cover learning disabilities behavioral reactions of childhood and family dynamics for pediatricians, child psychiatrists, and special educators.

**Readers:** Subscribers include pediatricians, child psychiatrists, developmental psychologists, child neurologists, pediatric nurse practioners and health science professionals, and members of The Society for Behavioral Pediatrics.

61793
## JOURNAL OF DIAGNOSTIC MEDICAL SONOGRAPHY, THE
227 E. Washington Sq.
Philadelphia, PA 19106
Telephone: (215) 238-4200
Pub. Frequency: bi-m.
Subscrip. Rate: $62/yr. individuals; $95/yr. institutions
Circulation: 11,514
Circulation Type: paid
**Owner(s):**
J.B. Lippincott Co.
227 E. Washington Sq.
Philadelphia, PA 19106
Telephone: (215) 238-4200
**Management:**
Joe Baiocco ......................Manager
**Editorial:**
Jean Lea Spitz, MPH, RDMS ..................Editor

66482
## JOURNAL OF EMERGENCY MEDICINE
660 White Plains Rd.
Tarrytown, NY 10591-5153
Telephone: (914) 524-9200
FAX: (914) 333-2444
Year Established: 1983
Pub. Frequency: 6/yr.
Subscrip. Rate: $280/yr.
**Owner(s):**
Pergamon Press, Inc.
660 White Plains Rd.
Tarrytown, NY 10591-5153
Telephone: (914) 524-9200
Ownership %: 100
**Editorial:**
Peter Rosen ......................Editor

55903
## JOURNAL OF ENDODONTICS
428 E. Preston St.
Baltimore, MD 21202
Telephone: (410) 528-4000
FAX: (410) 528-4312
Year Established: 1983
Pub. Frequency: m.
Subscrip. Rate: $57/yr. individuals; $90/yr. institutions
Circulation: 5,300
Circulation Type: paid
**Owner(s):**
American Association of Endodontics
**Editorial:**
Dr. Henry J. Van Hassell ......................Editor
**Desc.:** Latest methods of pulp conservation, root canal instrumentation and endodontic treatment for endodontists and general dentists.
**Readers:** Subscribers, including members of the American Association of Endodontists, specialists in root canal, as well as general dentists and dental students.

23844
## JOURNAL OF FAMILY PRACTICE
25 Van Zant St.
Norwalk, CT 06855
Telephone: (203) 838-4400
FAX: (203) 854-9486
Year Established: 1974
Pub. Frequency: m.
Page Size: 4 color photos/art
Subscrip. Rate: $80/yr. individuals;
$120/yr. institutions
Circulation: 76,000
Circulation Type: controlled & paid

**Owner(s):**
Appleton & Lange
25 Van Zant St.
Norwalk, CT 06855
Telephone: (203) 838-4400
Ownership %: 100
**Management:**
Chris J. Rawlins ......................Vice President
Marketta Pettway ..................Customer Service Manager
Patricia Fogle ..................Production Manager
**Editorial:**
Paul M. Fischer, MD ......................Editor
Patricia Delano ..................Managing Editor
Nancy Graves ..................Advertising Director
John W. Richards, Jr., MD ......Associate Editor
L. Paul M. Fischer, MD ..........Book Review Editor
Dorothea L. Robinson ..........Circulation Coordinator
Peg Cameron ......................Copy Director
**Desc.:** Clinical peer review literature which deals with the specialty of family practice.
**Readers:** Family physicians, general practitioners and osteopathic physicians.

58934
## JOURNAL OF FOOT SURGERY, THE
428 E. Preston St.
Baltimore, MD 21202
Telephone: (410) 528-4000
FAX: (410) 528-4312
Year Established: 1960
Pub. Frequency: bi-m.
Subscrip. Rate: $91/yr. individual; $119/yr. institution
Circulation: 6,200
Circulation Type: paid
**Owner(s):**
American College of Foot Surgeons, Inc.
1601 Dolores St.
San Francisco, CA 94110
Ownership %: 100
**Management:**
Don Pfarr ..................Advertising Manager
Alma Wills ......................Manager
**Editorial:**
Richard P. Reinherz, D.P.M. ..................Editor
Nancy Collins ..................Marketing Director
**Desc.:** Clinical advances in foot surgery for podiatrists and orthopedic foot surgeons.

23847
## JOURNAL OF HAND SURGERY, THE
11830 Westline Industrial Dr.
St. Louis, MO 63146
Telephone: (800) 325-4117
FAX: (314) 432-1380
Year Established: 1976
Pub. Frequency: bi-m.
Page Size: standard
Subscrip. Rate: $72/yr. individual; $82/yr. foreign; $141/yr. institution; $156/yr. foreign; $32/yr. student; $47/yr. foreign
Circulation: 7,738
Circulation Type: paid
**Owner(s):**
American Society for Surgery of the Hand
11830 Westline Industrial Dr.
St. Louis, MO 63146
Ownership %: 100
**Management:**
Carol Trumbold ......................Publisher
Kathy Preston ..................Advertising Manager
**Editorial:**
F. William Bora, Jr., M.D. ..................Editor
Kathy Keller ..................Production Director
**Desc.:** Edited for hand, orthopaedic, plastic and reconstructive and general surgeons who seek to restore function of the hand and upper extremity, regardless of the cause of the impairment.

**Materials Accepted/Included:** 01-Business news 02-By-line articles 03-Fashion news 04-Food news 05-Freelance copy 06-Letters to editor 07-Real estate news 08-Sports news 09-Travel news 10-Book rev. 11-Movie rev. 12-Music rev. 13-TV rev. 14-Theater rev. 15-Coming events 16-Obituaries 17-Question & answer 18-Social announcements 19-Artwork 20-Cartoons 21-Photos 22-TV listings 23-Audio rec. 24-Video rec. 25-Books 26-Films/film clips 27-Personnel news 28-Press releases 29-New product news/photos 30-Trade lit. 31-Contracts awarded 32-Display adv. 33-Classified adv.

4-237

**Readers:** Hand surgeons, orthopedic surgeons, plastic surgeons. Official publication of the American Society for Surgery of the Hand.

58604

## JOURNAL OF HEAD TRAUMA REHABILITATION, THE

200 Orchard Ridge Dr.
Gaithersburg, MD 20878
Telephone: (301) 417-7500
FAX: (301) 417-7550
Year Established: 1986
Pub. Frequency: 6/yr.
Page Size: standard
Subscrip. Rate: $80/yr. US; $96/yr. foreign
Materials: 06,10,15,32,34
Print Process: DTP
Circulation: 7,400
Circulation Type: paid
**Owner(s):**
Aspen Publishers, Inc.
200 Orchard Ridge Dr.
Gaithersburg, MD 20878
Telephone: (301) 417-7500
Ownership %: 100
**Management:**
Frances Ray .....................Advertising Manager
**Editorial:**
Lenda Hill ...............................Managing Editor
Stephen M. Zollo ...............Senior Requisitions Editor
**Readers:** Practicing professionals interested in clinical management and rehabilitation of the head injured.

61033

## JOURNAL OF HEART & LUNG TRANSPLANTATION, THE

11830 Westline Industrial Dr.
St. Louis, MO 63146
Telephone: (314) 872-8370
FAX: (314) 432-1380
Year Established: 1981
Pub. Frequency: bi-m.
Page Size: standard
Subscrip. Rate: $65/yr. individuals; $99/yr. institutions; $32/yr. students
Circulation: 2,629
Circulation Type: free & paid
**Owner(s):**
International Society for Heart Transplantation
435 N. Michigan, Ste. 1717
Chicago, IL 60611
Telephone: (312) 644-0828
Ownership %: 100
**Management:**
Carol Trumbold ...............................Publisher
Kathy Preston ...................Advertising Manager
**Editorial:**
Michael P. Kaye, M.D. ........................Editor
Kathy Keller ...............Production Director
**Desc.:** Contains information about the rapidly evolving field of heart transplantation. Each issue reports on procedures, statistical and research method information as well as relevant aspects of artificial organs, especially the development of the artificial heart & includes peer-reviewed articles & scientific abstracts from annual meeting papers.
**Readers:** Thoracic & cardiovascular surgeons, general surgeons & cardiologists. Official publication of the International Society for Heart Transplantation.

23849

## JOURNAL OF HISTOCHEMISTRY & CYTOCHEMISTRY

1 Gustavel L. Levy Pl.
Mt. Sinai School of Medicine
New York, NY 10029
Telephone: (212) 362-1801
FAX: (212) 874-8313

Mailing Address:
P.O. Box 1045, Mt. Sinai School
New York, NY 10211
Pub. Frequency: m.
Page Size: standard
Subscrip. Rate: $110/yr. US; $180/yr. institution; $135/yr. foreign; $215/yr. foreign institution
Circulation: 2,800
Circulation Type: paid
**Owner(s):**
Histochemical Society
Ownership %: 100
**Management:**
Kim Borroni .......................Advertising Manager
**Editorial:**
Paul J. Anderson ...............................Editor
**Desc.:** Publishes original investigations and review articles relating to development, evaluation and application of histochemical methods. Special features include: letters to the editor, book reviews, announcements, current article listings.
**Readers:** Histochemists, cytochemists, medical doctors.

23850

## JOURNAL OF IMMUNOLOGY

9650 Rockville Pike
Bethesda, MD 20814
Telephone: (301) 530-7178
FAX: (301) 571-1831
Year Established: 1916
Pub. Frequency: bi-m.
Page Size: standard
Subscrip. Rate: $170/yr. personal; $190/yr. institution
Circulation: 8,900
Circulation Type: paid
**Owner(s):**
AAI
Telephone: (301) 530-7178
Ownership %: 100
**Management:**
Ally Potter ...........................Production Manager
**Editorial:**
Dr. Peter Lipsky ...........................Editor in Chief
Johanna Matthews ...................Executive Editor
**Desc.:** Original articles dealing with all phases of immunology progress and virus research. The nature of the subject matter includes: immunochemistry, cellular immunology, cytokines, tumor immmology, molecular genetics, clinical immunology and immunopathonly.
**Readers:** Immunologists, virologists, pathologists, allergists.

65468

## JOURNAL OF INVASIVE CARDIOLOGY, THE

550 America Ave.
King of Prussia, PA 19406
Telephone: (215) 337-4466
FAX: (215) 337-0890
Year Established: 1988
Pub. Frequency: 9/yr.
Page Size: standard
Subscrip. Rate: $960/yr.
Circulation: 13,000
Circulation Type: controlled
**Owner(s):**
Health Management Publicaitons
550 America Ave.
King of Prussia, PA 19406
Telephone: (215) 337-4466
**Management:**
Peter A. deTreville ...............................Publisher
**Editorial:**
Richard E. Shaw, Ph.D. ........................Editor
Laurie Gustafson ...................Managing Editor
**Desc.:** Clinical papers, long term case studies, product reports and guest columns.

**Readers:** Serves cardiologists and cardiovascular surgeons.

23771

## JOURNAL OF INVESTIGATIVE MEDICINE

6900 Grove Rd.
Thorofare, NJ 08086
Telephone: (609) 848-1000
FAX: (609) 853-5991
Year Established: 1939
Pub. Frequency: bi-m.
Page Size: standard
Subscrip. Rate: $95/yr. individuals; $100/yr. institutions; $120/yr. foreign
Circulation: 14,000
Circulation Type: controlled
**Owner(s):**
American Federation for Clinical Research
6900 Grove Rd.
Thorofare, NJ 08086
Telephone: (609) 848-1000
Ownership %: 100
**Management:**
Roy Silverstein .......................President
Peter Slack .......................Publisher
Richard Roash ...................Associate Publsiher
**Editorial:**
Barbara Hempstead, PHD .......................Editor
Jonathon Weisler, MD ...........................Editor
Kaye Coraluzzo ...................Managing Editor
Susan Waters .......................Advertising
**Readers:** Medical research staff, medical school faculty.

23819

## JOURNAL OF INVESTIGATIVE RADIOLOGY

E. Washington Square
Philadelphia, PA 19105
Telephone: (215) 238-4273
FAX: (215) 238-4310
Year Established: 1966
Pub. Frequency: m.
Page Size: standard
Subscrip. Rate: $178/yr. individuals US.; $238/yr. foreign; $253/yr. institutions US; $323/yr. foreign
Materials: 32,33
Circulation: 2,603
Circulation Type: paid
**Owner(s):**
Association of University Radiologists
East Washington Square
Philadelphia, PA 19105
Telephone: (215) 238-4273
Ownership %: 100
**Management:**
Marcia Serepy .......................Publisher
Jennifer Bass ...................Advertising Manager
Beverly Dietrich ...................Circulation Manager
**Editorial:**
Bruce Hillman .......................Editor
Peter Stevenson ...........Production Coordinator
Suzann Graff ...................Senior Marketing Manager
**Desc.:** Original reports of investigations in diagnostic radiology, the diagnostic use of radioisotopes, ultrasound, infrared, and related modalities.
**Readers:** Radiologists, residents, libraries and research personnel.

23855

## JOURNAL OF LABORATORY & CLINICAL MEDICINE, THE

11830 Westline Industrial Dr.
St. Louis, MO 63146
Telephone: (314) 872-8370
FAX: (314) 432-1380
Year Established: 1915
Pub. Frequency: m.
Page Size: standard
Subscrip. Rate: $97/yr. individuals; $183/yr. institutions; $44/yr. students
Circulation: 3,942
Circulation Type: free & paid

**Owner(s):**
Mosby-Year Book, Inc.
11830 Westline Industrial Dr.
Saint Louis, MO 63146
Telephone: (314) 872-8370
Ownership %: 100
**Management:**
Carol Trumbold .......................Publisher
Kathy Preston ...................Advertising Manager
**Editorial:**
Harry S. Jacob, MD .......................Editor
Kathy Keller .......................Production Director
**Desc.:** Covers cardiovascular and gastrointestinal diseases, hematology, immunology, endocrinology, oncology, nephrology, organ transplantation, gene therapy.
**Readers:** Pathologists, internists, general practitioners. Official publication of the Central Society for Clinical Research.

55909

## JOURNAL OF MEDICAL PRACTICE MANAGEMENT

428 E. Preston St.
Baltimore, MD 21202
Telephone: (410) 528-4000
FAX: (410) 528-4312
Year Established: 1985
Pub. Frequency: q.
Page Size: standard
Subscrip. Rate: $79/yr. individual; $90/yr. institution
Circulation: 2,200
Circulation Type: paid
**Owner(s):**
Williams & Wilkins Co.
428 E. Preston St.
Baltimore, MD 21202
Telephone: (410) 528-4000
Ownership %: 100
**Management:**
Don Pfarr .......................Advertising Manager
Nancy Collins .......................Manager
**Editorial:**
Marcel Frenkel, M.D. .......................Editor
Leslie Kendrick ...................Marketing Director
**Desc.:** Perspectives on legislation, litigation, office management and other key issues that affect the medical practice of office-based physicians, business managers, administrators and health care professionals.
**Readers:** Subscribers are office managers, business managers, administrators and office-based physicians across all specialties with a high interest in practice management.

65619

## JOURNAL OF NEUROBIOLOGY

605 Third Ave.
New York, NY 10158
Telephone: (212) 850-6000
Pub. Frequency: 8/yr.
Page Size: standard
Subscrip. Rate: $646/yr.
Circulation: 700
Circulation Type: paid
**Owner(s):**
John Wiley & Sons, Inc.
605 Third Ave.
New York, NY 10158
Telephone: (212) 850-6000
Ownership %: 100
**Editorial:**
Darcy B. Kelley .......................Editor
Eduardo Macagno .......................Editor

23863

## JOURNAL OF NEUROPHYSIOLOGY

9650 Rockville Pike
Bethesda, MD 20814
Telephone: (301) 530-7164
FAX: (301) 571-1814
Year Established: 1938
Pub. Frequency: m.

Materials Accepted/Included: 01-Business news 02-By-line articles 03-Fashion news 04-Food news 05-Freelance copy 06-Letters to editor 07-Real estate news 08-Sports news 09-Travel news 10-Book rev. 11-Movie rev. 12-Music rev. 13-TV rev. 14-Theater rev. 15-Coming events 16-Obituaries 17-Question & answer 18-Social announcements 19-Artwork 20-Cartoons 21-Photos 22-TV listings 23-Audio rec. 24-Video rec. 25-Books 26-Films/film clips 27-Personnel news 28-Press releases 29-New product news/photos 30-Trade lit. 31-Contracts awarded 32-Display adv. 33-Classified adv.

4-238

Page Size: standard
Subscrip. Rate: $310/yr. individual;
　　$345/yr. Canada & Mexico; $380/yr.
　　elsewhere; $435/yr. institution; $155/yr.
　　members
Circulation: 1,800
Circulation Type: paid
**Owner(s):**
American Physiological Society
91650 Rockville Pike
Bethesda, MD 20814
Telephone: (301) 530-7071
Ownership %: 100
**Editorial:**
Gordon Shepherd ...............................Editor
**Desc.:** Basic research articles on the
　　nervous system.
**Readers:** Neurophysiologists.

23864
## JOURNAL OF NEUROSURGERY
1224 W. Main St., Ste. 450
Charlottesville, VA 22903
Telephone: (804) 824-5503
FAX: (804) 924-2702
Year Established: 1944
Pub. Frequency: m.
Page Size: standard
Subscrip. Rate: $120/yr.
Circulation: 11,500
Circulation Type: paid
**Owner(s):**
American Association of Neurological
　　Surgeons
22 S. Washington St.
Park Ridge, IL 60068
Telephone: (708) 692-9500
Ownership %: 100
**Management:**
Keenan Jones ...................Advertising Manager
**Editorial:**
John A. Jane, M.D., Ph.D. .......................Editor
Keller Kaufmonfox ...................Managing Editor
**Desc.:** An international medical journal that
　　accepts for publication unsolicited
　　medical articles of the highest caliber in
　　the field of neurosurgery and the
　　neurosciences. Departments include:
　　Articles, Case Reports, Technical Notes,
　　Book Reviews, Notices, Letters to the
　　Editor (Forum).
**Readers:** Neurosurgeons, neurologists and
　　related specialists, librarians.

67219
## JOURNAL OF NIH RESEARCH
1444 I. St., N.W.
Ste. 1000
Washington, DC 20005
*see Service,Trade,Professional*
*Magazines, Science, General*

23865
## JOURNAL OF NUCLEAR MEDICINE, THE
136 Madison Ave.
New York, NY 10016
Telephone: (212) 889-0717
FAX: (212) 545-0221
Year Established: 1960
Pub. Frequency: m.
Page Size: standard
Subscrip. Rate: $120/yr.
Materials: 02,06,10,16,30,32,33
Freelance Pay: negotiable
Print Process: web
Circulation: 13,600
Circulation Type: paid
**Owner(s):**
Society of Nuclear Medicine
136 Madison
New York, NY 10016
Telephone: (212) 889-0717
Ownership %: 100
**Management:**
Peter Walsh ...................Advertising Manager

**Editorial:**
Stanley J. Goldsmith, M.D. ....................Editor
Ellie Nigretto .................................Art Director
Chaitanya Divgi, M.D. .........Book Review Editor
Leigh Silverman ...............Editorial Assistant
Lantz Miller ...........................News Editor
Steve Klein ..................Production Coordinator
John Childs, Ph.D. ............Publication Director
Eleanore Tapscott .......Senior Managing Editor
**Desc.:** Contains peer-reviewed articles in
　　clinical medicine, basic and clinical
　　medical research, physics and chemistry
　　dealing with the use of isotopes in
　　humans and articles on related subjects.
　　Newsline section includes general
　　articles on news & issues of interest to
　　imaging professionals.
**Readers:** Physicians, physicists, chemists,
　　and related professionals; institutions,
　　nuclear medicine and radiologic
　　professionals.

23868
## JOURNAL OF OCCUPATIONAL MEDICINE
P.O. Box 370
Bryn Mawr, PA 19010
Telephone: (215) 649-5756
FAX: (215) 649-5756
Year Established: 1959
Pub. Frequency: m.
Page Size: standard
Subscrip. Rate: $77/yr.
Materials: 06,32,33
Freelance Pay: none
Circulation: 9,300
Circulation Type: paid
**Owner(s):**
American College of
　　Occuptnl/Environmntal Medicine
55 W. Seegers Rd.
Arlington Heights, IL 60005
Telephone: (708) 228-6850
Ownership %: 100
**Management:**
Williams & Wilkins ............Advertising Manager
Maria Reid .........................Circulation Manager
**Editorial:**
Paul W. Brandt-Rauf, MD ...................Editor
Elizabeth Popper, MA ..............Managing Editor
Charles F. Reinhardt, MD ........Associate Editor
Charles E. Becker, MD ..........Associate Editor
Roy L. DeHart, MD ................Associate Editor
David C. Deubner, MD ...........Associate Editor
Theda Harris .....................Production Director
Marianne Dreger .................Publication Editor
**Desc.:** Scientific articles and reports of
　　research by physicians and other health
　　profession personnel on various aspects
　　of the practice of medicine and
　　maintenance of health of an employed
　　population.
**Readers:** Primarily physicians in the field
　　of occupational medicine with
　　responsibility for industrial health,
　　environmental medicine, health
　　promotion, and related research and
　　administration.

55912
## JOURNAL OF ORTHOPAEDIC & SPORTS PHYSICAL THERAPY
428 E. Preston St.
Baltimore, MD 21202
Telephone: (410) 528-4000
FAX: (410) 528-4312
Year Established: 1979
Pub. Frequency: m.
Page Size: standard
Subscrip. Rate: $70/yr. individuals;
　　$105/yr. institutions
Circulation: 17,600
Circulation Type: paid
**Owner(s):**
American Physical Therapy Association
Ownership %: 100

**Editorial:**
Gary L. Smidt .................................Editor
**Desc.:** The latest clinical developments in
　　sports medicine for practicing PTs,
　　athletic trainers, and orthopaedic
　　surgeons.
**Readers:** Subscribers, primarily physical
　　therapists, also including athletic
　　trainers, coaches, and orthopaedic
　　surgeons. For member subscriber
　　list contact The American Orthopaedic &
　　Sports Medicine Sections of the
　　American Physical Therapy Assoc.

61005
## JOURNAL OF PEDIATRIC HEALTH CARE
11830 Westline Industrial Dr.
St. Louis, MO 63146
Telephone: (314) 872-8370
FAX: (314) 432-1380
Year Established: 1987
Pub. Frequency: bi-m.
Page Size: standard
Subscrip. Rate: $36/yr. individual; $46/yr.
　　foreign; $68/yr. instn.; $78/yr. foreign;
　　$20/yr. student; $30/yr. foreign
Circulation: 4,723
Circulation Type: paid
**Owner(s):**
National Association of Pediatric Nurse
　　Associates
1101 Kings Highway N. Ste. 206
Cherry Hill, NJ 08034
Telephone: (609) 667-1773
Ownership %: 100
**Management:**
Carol Trumbold ........................Publisher
Kathy Preston ...................Advertising Manager
**Editorial:**
Bobbie C. Nelms, PhD, RN, CPNP .........Editor
Kathy Keller .........................Production Director
**Desc.:** Contains original peer-reviewed
　　articles of interest to Pediatric Nurse
　　Associates and Practitioners as well as
　　information on pediatric pharmacology,
　　patient education, practice management,
　　and legislative news.
**Readers:** Pediatric nurse practitioners
　　associates. The official publication of the
　　National Association of Pediatric Nurse
　　Associates and Practitioners (NAPNAP).

24224
## JOURNAL OF PEDIATRIC OPHTHALMOLOGY & STRABISMUS
6900 Grove Rd.
Thorofare, NJ 08086
Telephone: (609) 848-1000
Year Established: 1964
Pub. Frequency: bi-m.
Page Size: standard
Subscrip. Rate: $88/yr.
Materials: 06,10,15,29,30,32,33
Circulation: 21,000
Circulation Type: paid
**Owner(s):**
Slack, Inc.
6900 Grove Rd.
Thorofare, NJ 08086
Telephone: (609) 848-1000
Ownership %: 100
**Management:**
Peter Slack ...................................President
Richard N. Roash ...........................Publisher
Donna Carpenter ..............Associate Publisher
Les Robeson ...................Circulation Manager
**Editorial:**
Marilyn Miller, M.D. ...........................Editor
Patricia A. Perry ...................Managing Editor
Jeff Walmsley ...........................Advertising Rep.
**Desc.:** Original research articles geared
　　toward providing clinically useful
　　information on pediatric ophthalmology
　　and strabismus in adults and children.

**Readers:** Pediatric ophthalmologists and
　　surgeons.

23871
## JOURNAL OF PEDIATRICS, THE
11830 Westline Industrial Dr.
St. Louis, MO 63146
Telephone: (314) 872-8370
FAX: (314) 432-1380
Year Established: 1932
Pub. Frequency: m.
Page Size: standard
Subscrip. Rate: $88/yr. individuals;
　　$178/yr. institutions; $43/yr. students
Circulation: 21,673
Circulation Type: free & paid
**Owner(s):**
Mosby-Year Book, Inc.
11830 Westline Industrial Dr.
St. Louis, MO 63146
Telephone: (314) 872-8370
Ownership %: 100
**Management:**
Carol Trumbold ........................Publisher
Kathy Preston ...................Advertising Manager
**Editorial:**
Joseph M. Garfunkel, MD .......................Editor
Kathy Keller .........................Production Director
**Desc.:** A clinical publication devoted to
　　diseases of infants and children. Edited
　　to serve the clinical information needs of
　　physicians engaged in pediatric practice
　　as either a primary or secondary
　　specialty, as well as those in allied
　　medical practice.
**Readers:** Pediatricians and general
　　practitioners.

70393
## JOURNAL OF PERINATOLOGY
11830 Westline Industrial Dr.
St. Louis, MO 63146
Telephone: (314) 872-8370
FAX: (314) 872-9164
Year Established: 1981
Pub. Frequency: bi-m.
Subscrip. Rate: $13/copy; $30/yr.
　　students; $50/yr. individuals; $75/yr.
　　institutional
Circulation: 3,803
Circulation Type: controlled
**Owner(s):**
Mosby-Year Book, Inc.
11830 Westline Industrial Dr.
St. Louis, MO 63146
Telephone: (314) 872-8370
FAX: (314) 872-9164
Ownership %: 100

23872
## JOURNAL OF PHARMACOLOGY & EXPERIMENTAL THERAPEUTICS, THE
MCP/EPPI Campus
3200 Henry Ave., Ste. 129
Philadelphia, PA 19129
Telephone: (215) 842-4061
FAX: (215) 843-0690
Year Established: 1909
Pub. Frequency: m.
Page Size: standard
Subscrip. Rate: $190/yr. individuals;
　　$340/yr. institutions
Circulation: 2,700
Circulation Type: paid
**Owner(s):**
Amer. Soc. Pharmacology & Experimntl.
　　Therapeutics
c/o Williams & Wilkins
428 E. Preston St.
Baltimore, MD 21202
Telephone: (410) 528-4000
Ownership %: 100
**Management:**
Don Pfarr ...................Advertising Manager
**Editorial:**
J.A. Harvey ..............................................Editor

**Materials Accepted/Included:** 01-Business news 02-By-line articles 03-Fashion news 04-Food news 05-Freelance copy 06-Letters to editor 07-Real estate news 08-Sports news 09-Travel news 10-Book rev. 11-Movie rev. 12-Music rev. 13-TV rev. 14-Theater rev. 15-Coming events 16-Obituaries 17-Question & answer 18-Social announcements 19-Artwork 20-Cartoons 21-Photos 22-TV listings 23-Audio rec. 24-Video rec. 25-Books 26-Films/film clips 27-Personnel news 28-Press releases 29-New product news/photos 30-Trade lit. 31-Contracts awarded 32-Display adv. 33-Classified adv.

4-239

Roland E. Keve ..............................Advertising
Carole Pippin .....................Production Editor
**Desc.:** Articles describing investigations in
  pharmacology and experimental
  therapeutics, defined in the broadest
  sense. Specific fields covered include
  biochemical and cellular pharmacology,
  renal pharmacology and electrolytes,
  cardiovascular pharmacology, autonomic
  pharmacology, behavioral pharmacology,
  clinical pharmacology, and toxicology.
**Readers:** Physicians, pharmacologists,
  hospitals.

**JOURNAL OF REHABILITATION** ^24944
633 S. Washington St.
Alexandria, VA 22314
Telephone: (703) 836-0850
FAX: (703) 836-0848
Year Established: 1946
Pub. Frequency: q.
Page Size: standard
Subscrip. Rate: $40/yr. US; $50/yr.
  Canada; $60/yr. foreign
Circulation: 16,500
Circulation Type: controlled
**Owner(s):**
National Rehabilitation Association
633 S. Washington St.
Alexandria, VA 22314
Telephone: (703) 836-0850
Ownership %: 100
**Management:**
Ronald J. Acquavita ..........Advertising Manager
**Editorial:**
Paul Leung ...............................................Editor
Ronald J. Acquavita .................Managing Editor
Ann Ward Tourigny, Ph.D., CAE ......Executive
                                          Director
**Desc.:** Concerned with counseling,
  restorative services, retraining, and
  placement of persons handicapped by
  physical, mental, emotional or social
  disabilities. Articles deal with supervisory
  role, legislative concerns, consumer,
  current trends in rehab. (e.g. barrier free
  architecture). Classified news items,
  short feature stories, book reviews,
  professional articles, research, abstracts.
**Readers:** Physicians, therapists, social
  workers, rehabilitation center personnel.

**JOURNAL OF REPRODUCTIVE** ^23874
**MEDICINE, THE**
8342 Olive Blvd.
St. Louis, MO 63132
Telephone: (314) 991-4440
FAX: (314) 991-4654
Mailing Address:
  P.O. Drawer 12425
  St. Louis, MO 63132
Year Established: 1968
Pub. Frequency: m.
Page Size: standard
Subscrip. Rate: $105/yr. US; $131/yr.
  foreign
Circulation: 32,000
Circulation Type: controlled & paid
**Owner(s):**
Journal of Reproductive Medicine, Inc.
8342 Olive Blvd.
P.O. Drawer 12425
St. Louis, MO 63132
Telephone: (314) 991-4440
Ownership %: 100
**Management:**
Jim Brady .............................Advertising Manager
**Editorial:**
George L. Wied, M.D. .................Editor in Chief
Donna Kessel ............................Managing Editor
**Desc.:** National publication serving the
  audience of specialists and residents in
  the field of obstetrics and gynecology.

**Readers:** Residents and doctors of
  obstetrics and gynecology.

**JOURNAL OF STUDIES ON** ^24945
**ALCOHOL**
Rutgers University, Center of Alcohol
  Studies
Piscataway, NJ 08855
Telephone: (908) 932-2190
Mailing Address:
  P.O. Box 969
  Piscataway, NJ 08855
Year Established: 1940
Pub. Frequency: bi-m.
Page Size: standard
Subscrip. Rate: $120/yr.; $230/2 yrs.;
  $335/3 yrs.
Materials: 25,29,30,32
Print Process: offset
Circulation: 2,700
Circulation Type: paid
**Owner(s):**
Alcohol Research Documentation, Inc.
Rutgers University
Ctr. of Alcohol Studies
New Brunswick, NJ 08903
Telephone: (908) 932-2190
Ownership %: 100
**Management:**
Charles B. Rouse .................Business Manager
**Editorial:**
Marc A. Schuckit .......................................Editor
Alex Fundock, III .....................Managing Editor
Deirdre M. English ...................Assistant Editor
Mark Keller ............................Editor Emeritus
Penny Page ...........................................Librarian
**Desc.:** Issues contain original reports and
  analyses of all aspects of alcohol-
  related problems and research, and
  book reviews. Uses photos for technical
  illustration.
**Readers:** Physicians, psychiatrists,
  psychologists, social workers, personnel
  officers.

**JOURNAL OF THE AMERICAN** ^23823
**ACADEMY OF DERMATOLOGY**
11830 Westline Industrial Dr.
St. Louis, MO 63146
Telephone: (314) 872-8370
FAX: (314) 432-1380
Year Established: 1979
Pub. Frequency: m.
Page Size: standard
Subscrip. Rate: $103/yr. individuals;
  $172/yr. institutions; $51/yr. students
Circulation: 16,357
Circulation Type: free & paid
**Owner(s):**
American Academy of Dermatology
1567 Maple Ave.
Evanston, IL 60201
Telephone: (708) 869-3954
Ownership %: 100
**Management:**
Carol Trumbold .......................................Publisher
Kathy Preston ....................Advertising Manager
**Editorial:**
Richard L. Dobson, M.D. ..........................Editor
Kathy Keller ..........................Production Director
**Desc.:** Provides for the clinical and
  continuing education needs of
  dermatologists as well as those family
  practitioners, internists, and pediatricians
  concerned with clinical manifestations of
  skin diseases in their practice.
**Readers:** Dermatologists, allergists,
  general practitioners. Official publication
  of the American Academy of
  Dermatology.

**JOURNAL OF THE AMERICAN** ^64867
**ACADEMY OF PHYSICIAN**
**ASSISTANTS**
11830 Westline Industrial Dr.
St. Louis, MO 63146
Telephone: (314) 872-8370
FAX: (314) 432-1380
Year Established: 1988
Pub. Frequency: bi-m
Page Size: standard
Subscrip. Rate: $35/yr.
Circulation: 29,409
**Owner(s):**
American Academy of Physicians
  Assistants
950 N. Washington St.
Alexandria, VA 22314
Telephone: (703) 836-2272
Ownership %: 100
**Management:**
Carol Trumbold .......................................Publisher
Kathy Preston ....................Advertising Manager
**Editorial:**
Leslie Kole, PA-C ......................................Editor
Kathy Keller ..........................Production Director
**Desc.:** Publishes articles relevant to the
  practicing physician assistant. Articles
  focus on the etiology, diagnosis, and
  treatment of the wide array of medical
  and surgical conditions in the primary
  care and subspecialty settings in which
  physician assistants practice. Nonclinical articles emphasize socioeconomic and ethical health issues and
  discuss the present and future role of
  the physician assistant in the health
  care system.
**Readers:** Physician assistants. Official
  publication of the American Academy of
  Physician Assistants.

**JOURNAL OF THE AMERICAN** ^23972
**COLLEGE OF SURGEONS**
54 E. Erie St.
Chicago, IL 60611-2796
Telephone: (312) 787-9282
FAX: (312) 440-7026
Year Established: 1905
Pub. Frequency: m.
Page Size: standard
Subscrip. Rate: $60/yr. individual; $70/yr.
  institution
Materials: 06,10,32,33
Print Process: web offset
Circulation: 16,500
Circulation Type: paid
**Owner(s):**
American College of Surgeons
54 E. Erie St.
Chicago, IL 60611
Telephone: (312) 787-9282
FAX: (312) 440-7026
Ownership %: 100
**Management:**
Lloyd D. MacLean, M.D. .....................President
Sean Griskenas ......................General Manager
**Editorial:**
Dr. Samuel A. Wells, Jr. ...........................Editor
**Desc.:** Peer reviewed journal containing
  original manuscripts of leading surgical
  articles from authors throughout the
  world. Departments include:
  Collective Reviews, Editorials, The
  Surgeon at Work, Letters to the Editor
  and Book Reviews.
**Readers:** Medical, surgical and hospital
  fields.
**Deadline:** ads-1st of mo., prior to pub.
  date

**JOURNAL OF THE AMERICAN** ^23905
**HEALTH INFORMATION**
**MANAGEMENT ASSOCIATION**
919 N. Michigan Ave., Ste 1400
Chicago, IL 60611
Telephone: (312) 787-2672
FAX: (312) 787-9793
Year Established: 1929
Pub. Frequency: m.
Page Size: standard
Subscrip. Rate: $72/yr.
Materials: 01,02,06
Print Process: web offset
Circulation: 34,000
Circulation Type: paid
**Owner(s):**
Amer. Health Information Management
  Association
919 N. Michigan Ave., Ste 1400
Chicago, IL 60611
Telephone: (312) 787-2672
Ownership %: 100
**Management:**
Robert Portillo ...................Advertising Manager
Julia Wixtrom ....................Production Manager
**Editorial:**
Gary Baldwin ...........................................Editor
Mary Campbell ...........Administrative Assistant
Steve Mckenzie .....................................Director
Susan Connors ...............Graphics Coordinator
**Desc.:** Includes all copy and pictorial
  material of technical, professional and
  human interest in healthcare information
  management, activities of national and
  component organizations of these health
  field professionals.
**Readers:** Members of the American Health
  Information Management Association,
  hospital administrators, health facility
  managers, quality assurance and
  utilization review monetary agencies,
  government healthcare related
  agencies.

**JOURNAL OF THE AMERICAN** ^23828
**MEDICAL WOMEN'S**
**ASSOCIATION**
801 N. Fairfax St.
Alexandria, VA 22314
Telephone: (703) 838-0500
Year Established: 1945
Pub. Frequency: bi-m.
Page Size: standard
Subscrip. Rate: $45/yr. US; $50/yr. foreign
Materials: 06,32,33
Circulation: 13,000
Circulation Type: paid
**Owner(s):**
American Medical Women's Association
801 N. Fairfax St.
Alexandria, VA 22314
Telephone: (703) 838-0500
Ownership %: 100
**Bureau(s):**
Chemical Dependency Institute
Beth Israel Medical Center
1st Ave. at 16th St.
New York, NY 10003
Telephone: (212) 387-3864
Contact: Wendy Chavkin, MD. MPH, Editor
  in Chief
**Management:**
Eileen McGrath ....................Executive Director
**Editorial:**
Wendy Chavkin, MD., MPH ......................Editor
Jane Williamson ......................Managing Editor

**Materials Accepted/Included:** 01-Business news 02-By-line articles 03-Fashion news 04-Food news 05-Freelance copy 06-Letters to editor 07-Real estate news 08-Sports news 09-Travel news 10-Book rev. 11-Movie rev. 12-Music rev. 13-TV rev. 14-Theater rev. 15-Coming events 16-Obituaries 17-Question & answer 18-Social announcements 19-Artwork 20-Cartoons 21-Photos 22-TV listings 23-Audio rec. 24-Video rec. 25-Books 26-Films/film clips 27-Personnel news 28-Press releases 29-New product news/photos 30-Trade lit. 31-Contracts awarded 32-Display adv. 33-Classified adv.

4-240

**Desc.:** Focuses on women in medicine and women's health issues. It is the official organ of the American Medical Women's Association. Original manuscripts, case reports and medical news, editorials, coverage of news and history of women in medicine, and book reviews of medical nature.

**Readers:** Women doctors all over the world in all fields, including resident interns and undergraduate women in medicine.

---

**JOURNAL OF THE AMERICAN PODIATRIC MEDICAL ASSOCIATION**                               23829

9312 Old Georgetown Rd.
Bethesda, MD 20814-1621
Telephone: (301) 571-9200
FAX: (301) 530-2752
Year Established: 1907
Pub. Frequency: m.
Page Size: standard
Subscrip. Rate: $29/yr. members; $75/yr. non-members
Circulation: 15,000
Circulation Type: paid
**Owner(s):**
American Podiatric Association
9312 Old Georgetown Rd.
Bethesda, MD 20814
Ownership %: 100
**Editorial:**
Warren Joseph ...........................Editor
Alice Overton ............................Associate Editor
**Desc.:** Professional papers by podiatrists and others in the health professions. Sections on case histories, surgery, new technique, new drugs, footwear, and related subjects. Covers activities of specialty and state organizations engaged in care of feet. Photographs used with articles. Departments include: Clinically Speaking, Clinically Illustrated, Practice Management, Special Communications, Pro and Con, Digests from the Literature, Letters to the Editor, Book Reviews, Sports Medicine, Podiatric Roentgenology, Clinical Conference and Guest Editorials.
**Readers:** Professionals.

---

**JOURNAL OF THE AMERICAN SOCIETY OF ECHOCARDIOGRAPHY**                               64870

11830 Westline Industrial Dr.
St. Louis, MO 63146
Telephone: (314) 872-8370
FAX: (314) 432-1380
Year Established: 1988
Pub. Frequency: bi-m.
Page Size: standard
Subscrip. Rate: $62/yr. individuals; $81/yr. institutions; $32/yr. students
Circulation: 68,672
Circulation Type: free & paid
**Owner(s):**
American Society of Echocardiography
1100 Raleigh Bldg.
P.O. Box 2598
Raleigh, NC 27610
Telephone: (919) 821-1435
Ownership %: 100
**Management:**
Carol Trumbold ...........................Publisher
Terry Van Schaik ................Associate Publisher
Kathy Preston ...................Advertising Manager
**Editorial:**
Harvey Feigenbaum, M.D. ..........Editor
Kathy Keller ..................Production Director

**Desc.:** Edited for cardiologists and technician-sonographers working in the field of echocardiography. The journal features peer-reviewed, original articles on the use of cardiac ultrasound, as well as review articles and case studies.
**Readers:** Targets physicians and sonographers responsible for purchasing echocardiographic equipment and supplies. Official publication of the American Society of Echocardiography.

---

**JOURNAL OF THE ARKANSAS MEDICAL SOCIETY**                               23831

#10 Corporate Hill Dr.
Little Rock, AR 72205
Telephone: (501) 224-8967
FAX: (501) 224-6489
Mailing Address:
    P.O. Box 5776
    Little Rock, AR 72215
Year Established: 1903
Pub. Frequency: m.
Page Size: standard
Subscrip. Rate: $30/yr. US; $40/yr. foreign
Circulation: 3,400
Circulation Type: controlled
**Owner(s):**
Arkansas Medical Society
#10 Corporate Hill Dr.
Little Rock, AR 72205
Telephone: (501) 224-8967
Ownership %: 100
**Management:**
Arkansas Medical Society .................Publisher
David Wroten ...................Advertising Manager
Ken LaMastus .....................Business Manager
**Editorial:**
Cindy Sawrie ...........................Managing Editor
**Desc.:** Original scientific articles by members of the medical profession; editorials cover subjects of interest to medical profession such as legislation, new developments in medicine.
**Readers:** Members of the medical profession.

---

**JOURNAL OF THE FLORIDA MEDICAL ASSOCIATION, INC.**                               23845

760 Riverside Ave.
Jacksonville, FL 32204
Telephone: (904) 356-1571
FAX: (904) 353-1247
Mailing Address:
    P.O. Box 2411
    Jacksonville, FL 32203
Year Established: 1914
Pub. Frequency: m.
Page Size: standard
Subscrip. Rate: $30/yr.
Materials: 06,10,32,33
Circulation: 17,200
Circulation Type: paid
**Owner(s):**
Florida Medical Association, Inc.
760 Riverside Ave.
Jacksonville, FL 32204
Telephone: (904) 356-1571
Ownership %: 100
**Editorial:**
Gerry Soud ...........................Executive Editor
Jacques R. Caldwell, M.D. ...............Editor
Joy Batteh-Freiha .................Managing Editor
F. Norman Vickers, ..........Book Review Editor
M.D.
**Desc.:** Scientific articles and news covering all phases of the medical field. Departments include: Scientific, Editorial, President's Page, Comment, Organization, Classified Feature. Scientific articles are all peer - reviewed.
**Readers:** Physicians, advertisers.
**Deadline:** ads-1st of mo. prior to pub. date

---

**JOURNAL OF THE LOUISIANA STATE MEDICAL SOCIETY**                               23856

3501 N. Causeway Blvd., Ste. 800
Metairie, LA 70002-3625
Telephone: (504) 832-9815
Year Established: 1844
Pub. Frequency: m.
Page Size: standard
Subscrip. Rate: $18/yr. US; $21/yr. foreign
Print Process: web offset
Circulation: 6,300
Circulation Type: paid
**Owner(s):**
Journal of the Louisiana State Medical Soc., Inc.
3501 N. Causeway Blvd.
Ste. 800
Metairie, LA 70002
Telephone: (504) 832-9815
Ownership %: 100
**Bureau(s):**
State Journal Group
11437 W. 106th St.
Overland Park , KS 66214
Telephone: (913) 888-8781
FAX: (913) 888-3758
Contact: Lance Kincaid
**Management:**
Anne Gooch ....................Advertising Manager
Gene G. Bailey .................Circulation Manager
Rene Abadie .........................General Manager
**Editorial:**
Conway S. Magee, M. D. ...................Editor
Gene G. Bailey ....................Managing Editor
**Desc.:** Publishes professional articles by practitioners in the medical and surgical field. Illustrations used with articles and advertisements. Departments include: Editorial, Electrocardiogram of the Month, Auxiliary Report, Medical Student Section, New Members, Otolaryngology/Head and Neck Surgery Report, Book Review, Calendar.
**Readers:** Professional.
**Deadline:** ads-1st of mo.

---

**JOURNAL OF THE MEDICAL ASSOCIATION OF GEORGIA**                               23858

938 Peachtree St., N.E.
Atlanta, GA 30309
Telephone: (404) 876-7535
FAX: (404) 874-8651
Year Established: 1911
Pub. Frequency: m.
Page Size: standard
Subscrip. Rate: $40/yr. in Georgia; $60/yr. elsewhere
Circulation: 7,000
Circulation Type: paid
**Owner(s):**
Medical Association of Georgia
938 Peachtree St., N.E.
Atlanta, GA 30309
Telephone: (404) 876-7535
Ownership %: 100
**Editorial:**
Charles R. Underwood, M.D. ...............Editor
Susan T. Johnson ...............Managing Editor
**Desc.:** Articles and features are primarily medical or related to everyday interests of physicians. By-line is used.
**Readers:** Georgia M.D.s.

---

**JOURNAL OF THE MISSISSIPPI STATE MEDICAL ASSOCIATION**                               23861

735 Riverside Dr.
Jackson, MS 39202
Telephone: (601) 354-5433
FAX: (601) 352-4834
Mailing Address:
    P.O. Box 5229
    Jackson, MS 39296-5229
Year Established: 1960

Pub. Frequency: m.
Page Size: standard
Subscrip. Rate: $35/yr. US; $45/yr. foreign
Materials: 06,34
Circulation: 2,700
Circulation Type: controlled & paid
**Owner(s):**
Mississippi State Medical Association
735 Riverside Dr.
Jackson, MS 39202
Telephone: (601) 354-5433
Ownership %: 100
**Management:**
Charles L. Mathews ............Executive Director
Ginger Cocke ....................Advertising Manager
**Editorial:**
Dr. Myron W. Lockey ...............................Editor
Ginger Cocke ....................Managing Editor
Dr. George Abraham ..............Associate Editor
Dr. Lee England ..................Associate Editor
**Desc.:** Up-to-date material on recent medical discoveries, pertinent legislation and medical news, both state and national. Scientific articles are contributed by state and out-of-state physicians or others working in a medical field. Departments include: Original Scientific Articles, Editorials, News Section, Literature, Personals, Socio-Economics, and Special Feature Articles.
**Readers:** Primarily Mississippi physicians.
**Deadline:** story-15th of prior mo.; news-15th of prior mo.; photo-15th of prior mo.; ads-15th of prior mo.

---

**JOURNAL OF THE NATIONAL MEDICAL ASSOCIATION**                               23862

1012 10th St., N.W.
Washington, DC 20001
Telephone: (202) 347-1895
FAX: (202) 842-3293
Year Established: 1908
Pub. Frequency: m.
Page Size: standard
Subscrip. Rate: $50/yr. individuals; $60/yr. institutions
Circulation: 25,000
Circulation Type: controlled
**Owner(s):**
Slack, Inc.
6900 Grove Rd.
Thorofare, NJ 08086
Telephone: (609) 848-1000
Ownership %: 100
**Management:**
Richard Roash ........................Publisher
**Editorial:**
Calvin C. Sampson, M.D. ...................Editor
Mary Jerrell .........................Managing Editor
Alyce Gullattee, M.D. ...............Assistant Editor
Axel Hansen .........................Assistant Editor
Leslie Alexander, M.D. ............Assistant Editor
George H. Rawls, M.D. ............Assistant Editor
Walter W. Shervington, M.D. .....Assistant Editor

**Desc.:** Covers original scientific papers in any medical field, editorials relating to scientific subjects or public issues with medical aspects, briefs relating to noteworthy occurrences and developments in medicine, personal news related to members of the Association and its constituent societies, announcements and book reviews. Departments include: Original Communications, President's Column, Editorials, Integration Battle Front; Talent Recruitment; Professional News; Legal Counsel Column; Clinico-Pathological Diagnostic Problems; N.M.A. Authors, N.M.A. Activities; Medical History; Announcements; Women's Auxiliary; Book Reviews.

**Materials Accepted/Included:** 01-Business news 02-By-line articles 03-Fashion news 04-Food news 05-Freelance copy 06-Letters to editor 07-Real estate news 08-Sports news 09-Travel news 10-Book rev. 11-Movie rev. 12-Music rev. 13-TV rev. 14-Theater rev. 15-Coming events 16-Obituaries 17-Question & answer 18-Social announcements 19-Artwork 20-Cartoons 21-Photos 22-TV listings 23-Audio rec. 24-Video rec. 25-Books 26-Films/film clips 27-Personnel news 28-Press releases 29-New product news/photos 30-Trade lit. 31-Contracts awarded 32-Display adv. 33-Classified adv.

4-241

**Readers:** Mostly general practitioners, cross section.

### JOURNAL OF THE OKLAHOMA STATE MEDICAL ASSOCIATION
23869

601 N.W. Expressway
Oklahoma City, OK 73118
Telephone: (405) 843-9571
Year Established: 1908
Pub. Frequency: m.
Page Size: standard
Subscrip. Rate: $30/yr.
Freelance Pay: negotiable
Circulation: 4,200
Circulation Type: paid
**Owner(s):**
Oklahoma State Medical Association
601 NW Expressway
Oklahoma City, OK 73118
Telephone: (405) 843-9571
Ownership %: 100
**Management:**
Susan Records .................Advertising Manager
**Editorial:**
Ray V. McIntyre, M.D. .................Editor in Chief
Robert L. Scott, M.D. ...............................Editor
Susan Records ........................Managing Editor
Harris D. Riley, Jr. ...........Book Review Editor M.D.
**Desc.:** The types of articles used in the Journal are mostly scientific. An editorial page written by Dr. McIntyre, scientific articles submitted by different doctors and the news stories cover important events that have happened over the state, of interest to the physicians.
**Readers:** Physicians, hospitals, medical library staff.

### JOURNAL OF THE SOUTH CAROLINA MEDICAL ASSOCIATION
23875

3210 Fernandina Rd.
Columbia, SC 29210
Telephone: (803) 798-6207
FAX: (803) 772-6783
Mailing Address:
   P.O. Box 11188
   Columbia, SC 29211
Year Established: 1905
Pub. Frequency: m.
Page Size: standard
Subscrip. Rate: $15/yr. members; $25/yr. non-members
Materials: 06,32,33
Print Process: offset
Circulation: 4,500
Circulation Type: controlled
**Owner(s):**
South Carolina Medical Association
P.O. Box 11188
Columbia, SC 29211
Telephone: (803) 798-6207
Ownership %: 100
**Management:**
J. Chris Hawk, M.D. .............................President
William F. Mahon .......Executive Vice President
Joy G. Drennen .................Advertising Manager
**Editorial:**
Charles S. Bryan, M.D. ...........................Editor
Joy G. Drennen ....................Managing Editor
O. Marion Burton, M.D. ...........................C.E.O.
Edward E. Kimbrough, M.D. ....Editor Emeritus
Joy G. Drennen ........................Technical Editor
**Desc.:** Scientific news, editorials, announcements.
**Readers:** Members of the Medical Association.

### JOURNAL OF THE TENNESSEE MEDICAL ASSOCIATION
23877

2301 21st Ave., S.
Nashville, TN 37212-0909
Telephone: (615) 385-2100
FAX: (615) 383-5918
Mailing Address:
   P.O. Box 120909
   Nashville, TN 37212-0909
Year Established: 1902
Pub. Frequency: m.
Page Size: standard
Subscrip. Rate: $20/yr.
Circulation: 6,700
Circulation Type: paid
**Owner(s):**
Tennessee Medical Association
P.O. Box 120909
Nashville, TN 37212-0909
Telephone: (615) 385-2100
Ownership %: 100
**Management:**
Donald A. Alexander ............Executive Director
**Editorial:**
John B. Thomison, M.D. ...........................Editor
Jean Wishnick .......................Managing Editor
L.H. Williams .................Chief Executive Officer
**Desc.:** Editorial policy calls for promotion of better health and medical care. Articles cover such subjects as new drugs, new surgical techniques, voluntary health insurance, medical legislation, and socio-economic problems related to the practice of medicine.
**Readers:** Doctors of medicine in Tennessee.

### JOURNAL OF THORACIC & CARDIOVASCULAR SURGERY, THE
23878

11830 Westline Industrial Dr.
St. Louis, MO 63146
Telephone: (314) 872-8370
FAX: (314) 432-1380
Year Established: 1931
Pub. Frequency: m.
Page Size: standard
Subscrip. Rate: $112/yr. individuals; $192/yr. institutions; $51/yr. students
Circulation: 10,644
Circulation Type: free & paid
**Owner(s):**
Mosby-Year Book, Inc.
11830 Westline Industrial Dr.
St. Louis, MO 63146
Telephone: (314) 872-8370
Ownership %: 100
**Management:**
Carol Trumbold ...............................Publisher
Kathy Preston ..................Advertising Manager
**Editorial:**
John W. Kirklin, M.D. ...............................Editor
Kathy Keller ......................Production Director
**Desc.:** Published for surgeons specializing in diseases of the chest, heart, lungs and great vessels where surgical intervention is indicated.
**Readers:** Thoracic surgeons, general surgeons. Official publication of The American Association for Thoracic Surgery and The Western Thoracic Surgical Association.

### JOURNAL OF TRAUMA, THE
23879

428 E. Preston St.
Baltimore, MD 21202
Telephone: (410) 528-4000
FAX: (410) 528-4312
Year Established: 1961
Pub. Frequency: m.

Page Size: standard
Subscrip. Rate: $89/yr. individuals; $123/yr. institutions
Circulation: 6,200
Circulation Type: paid
**Owner(s):**
Williams & Wilkins Co.
428 E. Preston St.
Baltimore, MD 21202
Telephone: (301) 528-4000
Ownership %: 100
**Management:**
Gayle Miller ......................Advertising Manager
**Editorial:**
John H. Davis, M.D. ...............................Editor
Bridget Mason ........................Advertising Editor
Larry Floersch ...........................Assistant Editor
**Desc.:** Papers promoting the effective management of serious injury, prevention of traumas, and critical analysis of innovative surgical procedures.
**Readers:** Subscribers, including members of the American Association for the Surgery of Trauma, orthopaedic surgeons, plastic surgeons, and general surgeons.

### JOURNAL OF UROLOGY, THE
23880

1120 N. Charles St.
Baltimore, MD 21201
Telephone: (301) 539-8138
Mailing Address:
   428 E. Preston St.
   Baltimore, MD 21202
Year Established: 1917
Pub. Frequency: m.
Page Size: 4 color photos/art
Subscrip. Rate: $193/yr. individuals; $215/yr. institutions
Circulation: 17,300
Circulation Type: paid
**Owner(s):**
Williams & Wilkins Co.
428 E. Preston St.
Baltimore, MD 21202
Telephone: (410) 528-4000
Ownership %: 100
**Management:**
Alma Wills ........................................President
Roland Keve ....................Advertising Manager
**Editorial:**
Jay Gillenwater ...................................Editor
**Desc.:** Devoted to those interested in urology. Covers the whole field of urology in all its aspects from surgery to the development of new cystoscopic instruments. Incorporates urological survey and investigative urology.
**Readers:** Internists, surgeons, management of researchers, pediatricians and paraurologics. urology, general practice, general surgery, pediatrics, nephrology.

### JOURNAL OF VASCULAR NURSING
70398

11830 Westline Industrial Dr.
St. Louis, MO 63146
Telephone: (314) 872-8370
FAX: (314) 872-9164
Year Established: 1982
Pub. Frequency: q.
Subscrip. Rate: $8/copy; $45/yr. individual; $65/yr. institutional
Circulation: 1,100
Circulation Type: controlled
**Owner(s):**
Mosby-Year Book, Inc.
11830 Westline Industrial Dr.
St. Louis, MO 63146
Telephone: (314) 872-8370
FAX: (314) 872-9146
Ownership %: 100

**Desc.:** As the official publication for the Society for Vascular Nursing, it presents original, peer-reviewed articles detailing the etiologies, diagnostic procedures, treatment options, and nursing implications of vascular system disorders.
**Readers:** Vascular nurses practicing in a variety of settings and specialties, including outpatient care, medical/surgical, critical care, operating/recovery room, diagnostic vascular laboratory, angiography, community health, gerontology, and academcis.

### JOURNAL OF VASCULAR SURGERY
56416

11830 Westline Industrial Dr.
St. Louis, MO 63146
Telephone: (314) 872-8370
FAX: (314) 432-1380
Year Established: 1984
Pub. Frequency: m.
Page Size: standard
Subscrip. Rate: $98/yr. individuals; $181/yr. institutions; $43/yr. students
Circulation: 7,635
Circulation Type: free & paid
**Owner(s):**
Society for Vascular Surgery
13 Elm St.
Manchester, MA 01944
Telephone: (508) 526-8330
Ownership %: 100
**Management:**
Carol Trumbold ...............................Publisher
Kathy Preston ..................Advertising Manager
**Editorial:**
Calvin B. Ernst, MD ...............................Editor
James C. Stanley, MD ...............................Editor
Kathy Keller ......................Production Director
**Desc.:** A comprehensive forum for the latest advances in knowledge of the peripheral vascular system, especially as it relates to the theory and practice of vascular surgery. It provides stimulating, original articles on all aspects of disease and injury to the arterial and venous systems, as well as certain associated blood disturbances.
**Readers:** General surgeons, cardiovascular surgeons. Official publication of the Society for Vascular Surgery, International Society for Cardiovascular Surgery, North American Chapter.

### JOURNAL OF VESTIBULAR RESEARCH
66484

660 White Plains Rd.
Tarrytown, NY 10591-5153
Telephone: (914) 333-2444
Pub. Frequency: q.
Subscrip. Rate: $115/yr. institutions
Circulation: 1,500
Circulation Type: paid
**Owner(s):**
Pergamon Press, Inc.
660 White Plains Rd.
Tarrytown, NY 10591-5153
Telephone: (914) 524-9200
Ownership %: 100
**Management:**
Susan Rosenthal ......................Sales Manager

### JOURNALS OF GERONTOLOGY
23846

1275 K St., N.W. Ste. 250
Washington, DC 20052-4006
Telephone: (202) 842-1275
FAX: (202) 842-1150
Year Established: 1945
Pub. Frequency: bi-m.

Page Size: standard
Subscrip. Rate: $157/yr.; $240/yr. instn.;
  $177/yr. foreign; $260/yr. foreign instn.
Freelance Pay: none
Circulation: 9,400
Circulation Type: controlled
**Owner(s):**
Gerontological Society of America
1275 K St., N.W.
Ste. 350
Washington, DC 20052-4006
Ownership %: 100
**Management:**
Elizabeth L. Borgen ..........Advertising Manager
**Editorial:**
Edward J. Masaro, Ph.D. .........................Editor
Kenneth L. Minaker, M.D. ......................Editor
Richard Schulz, Ph.D. ...........................Editor
David J. Ekert, Ph.D. .............................Editor
Bettie L. Donley .................Publication Director
**Desc.:** Original research papers dealing
with or bearing on the problems of aging
as related to the fields of biology,
medicine, psychology & social sciences.
Carries review articles and book reviews.
Preference given to manuscripts
containing observational data. In two
volumes: Biological Sciences and
Medical Sciences, and Psychological
Sciences and Social Sciences.
**Readers:** Physicians, scientists,
researchers, educators and other
professionals in the field of aging.

23854
**KANSAS MEDICINE**
623 W. Tenth Ave.
Topeka, KS 66612-1627
Telephone: (913) 235-2383
Year Established: 1901
Pub. Frequency: m.
Page Size: standard
Subscrip. Rate: $45/yr. US; $50/yr. foreign
Print Process: offset
Circulation: 3,700
Circulation Type: paid
**Owner(s):**
Kansas Medical Society
623 W. Tenth Ave.
Topeka, KS 66612-1627
Telephone: (913) 235-2383
Ownership %: 100
**Management:**
Jeremy Slaughter ...............Business Manager
**Editorial:**
Susan Ward ............................Production Editor
**Desc.:** All scientific material is contributed
for approval of Editorial Board. Most
contributors are members of the Kansas
Medical Society, but
occasionally physicians from other
states contribute. Editorials are prepared
by members of the Kansas Medical
Society and Journal staffs. Feature and
news stories usually concern activities of
medical profession within the state, and
are also prepared by the staff.
Photographs are used with articles.
**Readers:** Primarily members of medical
profession in Kansas.
**Deadline:** ads-10th of mo. prior to pub.
date

23881
**LABORATORY INVESTIGATION**
Thomas Jefferson Univ.
1020 Locust St.
Philadelphia, PA 19107
Telephone: (215) 955-4847
Year Established: 1952
Pub. Frequency: m.
Page Size: standard
Subscrip. Rate: $84-$278/yr.
Materials: 06
Circulation: 6,000
Circulation Type: paid

**Owner(s):**
Williams & Wilkins Co.
428 E. Preston St.
Baltimore, MD 21202
Telephone: (301) 528-4000
Ownership %: 100
**Management:**
G. James Gallagher ............................President
Don Nichols .......................Advertising Manager
**Editorial:**
Emanuel Rubin ..............................................Editor
Beth Missett ......................Marketing Director
**Desc.:** Journal of experimental methods
and pathology. Devoted to the
publication of original investigations,
experimental techniques, and
observations in the basic medical
sciences. Presents specifically, papers
dealing with experimental and anatomic
pathology, histochemistry, cytological
and histological methods, tissue culture,
electromicroscopy, radioactive tracer
methods, cardiac anomalies, and
comparative pathology.
**Readers:** Pathologists, V.A. and
government hospitals.

23882
**LABORATORY MEDICINE**
2100 W. Harrison St.
Chicago, IL 60612
Telephone: (312) 738-1336
FAX: (312) 738-0101
Year Established: 1970
Pub. Frequency: m.
Page Size: standard
Subscrip. Rate: $50/yr.
Materials: 01,15,27,28,29,32,33
Print Process: web
Circulation: 166,000
Circulation Type: paid
**Owner(s):**
American Soc. of Clinical Pathologists
2100 W. Harrison St.
Chicago, IL 60612-1336
Telephone: (312) 738-4860
Ownership %: 100
**Management:**
Joe Dingee .......................Advertising Manager
**Editorial:**
Paul Phillip Sher, M.D. ............................Editor
Lynn Schneidhorst Olson .......Managing Editor
**Desc.:** Articles and editorial items to inform
medical technologists and pathologists,
etc. about current thought, opinion,
concepts, developments, techniques,
products, and educational events in the
field of laboratory medicine.
**Readers:** Medical technologists,
pathologists, and clinical chemists.
**Deadline:** news-1st of mo., 2 mos. prior to
pub. date; photo-1st of mo., 1 mo. prior;
ads-7th of mo., 1 mo. prior

23884
**LACMA PHYSICIAN**
1925 Wilshire Blvd.
Los Angeles, CA 90057
Telephone: (213) 483-1581
Mailing Address:
  P.O. Box 3465
  Los Angeles, CA 90051
Year Established: 1871
Pub. Frequency: 20/yr.
Page Size: standard
Subscrip. Rate: $15/yr. members; $30/yr.
  others
Freelance Pay: negotiable
Circulation: 10,000
Circulation Type: paid
**Owner(s):**
Los Angeles County Medical Association
P.O. Box 3465
Los Angeles, CA 90051
Telephone: (310) 483-1581
Ownership %: 100

**Management:**
Chele Graham ..................Advertising Manager
**Editorial:**
Janice Nagano ......................Managing Editor
**Desc.:** Contains staff articles, coming
events, letters to the editor,
socioeconomic, legislative and
legal news in area of medicine.
**Readers:** Physician members of the Los
Angeles County Medical Assn.

23885
**LARYNGOSCOPE, THE**
10 S. Broadway, Ste. 1401
St. Louis, MO 63102
Telephone: (314) 621-6550
FAX: (314) 621-6688
Year Established: 1896
Pub. Frequency: m.
Page Size: standard
Subscrip. Rate: $110/yr. individuals;
  $135/yr. foreign; $150/yr. institutions;
  $175/yr. foreign
Materials: 06,32
Print Process: offset
Circulation: 7,800
Circulation Type: paid
**Owner(s):**
Triological Society, Inc., The
10 S. Broadway, Ste. 1401
St. Louis, MO 63102
Telephone: (314) 621-6550
FAX: (314) 621-6688
Ownership %: 100
**Management:**
Victoria L. Harrison ...........Advertising Manager
Donna Lewis .........................Business Manager
Curtis Hayes ......................Circulation Manager
**Editorial:**
J. Gershon Spector, M.D. .......................Editor
Ronald Brockman ........................Copy Director
Michael McConnell .......Production Coordinator
**Desc.:** Carries papers on diseases of the
ear, nose, and throat. Reviews books. Is
the official publication of the American
Laryngological, Rhinological,
and Otological Society, Inc.
**Readers:** Otolaryngologists, specialists,
audiologists, hospital personnel.

66486
**MAGNETIC RESONANCE IMAGING**
Pergamon Press Inc.
660 White Plains Rd.
Tarrytown, NY 10591-5153
Telephone: (914) 524-9200
Pub. Frequency: 6/yr.
Page Size: standard
Subscrip. Rate: $42/yr. individual; $301/yr.
  institution
Circulation: 5,200
Circulation Type: paid
**Owner(s):**
Pergamon Press, Inc.
660 White Plains Rd.
Tarrytown, NY 10591-5153
Telephone: (914) 524-9200
**Management:**
Roger A. Dunn ...................................President
**Editorial:**
Tina Bonanno .........................Managing Editor
Susan Rosenthal ..............................Advertising
**Desc.:** Provides peer-reviewed, timely
articles covering clinical, physical and
life science investigations relating to the
development and use of magnetic
resonance methods and instrumentation
including both imaging and
spectroscopic techniques and their
applications.

48844
**MALPRACTICE REPORTER, THE**
332 Bleeker St.
New York, NY 10014
Telephone: (212) 989-8303
FAX: (212) 406-9855

Year Established: 1981
Pub. Frequency: m.
Page Size: standard
Subscrip. Rate: $128/yr.
Circulation: 1,000
Circulation Type: paid
**Owner(s):**
Public Reporting Services, Inc.
332 Bleeker St.
New York, NY 10014
Telephone: (212) 989-8303
FAX: (212) 406-9855
Ownership %: 100
**Editorial:**
Neil Fabricant ....................Book Review Editor
**Desc.:** Covers recent developments in
medical malpractice for the medical,
legal, health services and insurance
communities including recent
claims against hospitals and physicians
and settlements and awards. Feature
articles on medical malpractice are
supplemented by regular
columns including "Drugs and Devices",
"In the Courts" and "News and
Analysis".
**Readers:** Doctors, lawyers, libraries,
medical law schools, insurance
companies.

68976
**MANAGED CARE**
301 Oxford Valley Rd., Ste. 603
Yardley, PA 19067
Telephone: (215) 321-6663
FAX: (215) 321-6670
Year Established: 1992
Pub. Frequency: m.
Page Size: standard
Subscrip. Rate: $72/yr.
Circulation: 76,000
Circulation Type: controlled
**Owner(s):**
Stezzi Communications, Inc.
301 Oxford Valley Rd.
Ste. 603B
Yardley, PA 19067
Telephone: (215) 321-6663
Ownership %: 100
**Editorial:**
Carroll V. Dowden .....................................Editor
**Desc.:** Advises physicians in managed
care on the conduct of their careers.
Informs them of their rapidly changing
options and opportunities.

69304
**MANAGED CARE QUARTERLY**
200 Orchard Ridge Dr.
Gaithersburg, MD 00008
Telephone: (301) 417-7500
FAX: (301) 417-7550
Year Established: 1993
Pub. Frequency: q.
Page Size: standard
Subscrip. Rate: $94/yr.; $112/yr. foreign
Materials: 06,10,15,32
Print Process: DTP
Circulation: 2,200
Circulation Type: paid
**Owner(s):**
Aspen Publishers, Inc.
200 Orchard Ridge Dr.
Gaithersburg, MD 20878
Telephone: (301) 417-7500
Ownership %: 100
**Management:**
Michael B. Brown .......................Vice President
Nina Kasari ........................Production Manager
**Editorial:**
Lenda P. Hill ...........................Managing Editor
Jack Bruggeman ......................Editorial Director
Amy Martin ...............................Assistant Editor
Ernest V. Manzella .........Senior Vice President

**Materials Accepted/Included:** 01-Business news 02-By-line articles 03-Fashion news 04-Food news 05-Freelance copy 06-Letters to editor 07-Real estate news 08-Sports news 09-Travel news 10-Book rev. 11-Movie rev. 12-Music rev. 13-TV rev. 14-Theater rev. 15-Coming events 16-Obituaries 17-Question & answer 18-Social announcements 19-Artwork 20-Cartoons 21-Photos 22-TV listings 23-Audio rec. 24-Video rec. 25-Books 26-Films/film clips 27-Personnel news 28-Press releases 29-New product news/photos 30-Trade lit. 31-Contracts awarded 32-Display adv. 33-Classified adv.

4-243

**Desc.:** Provides current information to health care executives who require in-depth material on specific managed care issues.

### MARYLAND MEDICAL JOURNAL
23888

1211 Cathedral St.
Baltimore, MD 21201-5585
Telephone: (410) 539-0872
FAX: (410) 547-0915
Year Established: 1839
Pub. Frequency: m.
Page Size: standard
Subscrip. Rate: $45/yr. US; $57/yr. foreign
Materials: 02,06,10,15,16,25,27,32,33
Print Process: web offset
Circulation: 7,600
Circulation Type: controlled & paid
**Owner(s):**
Medical & Chirurgical Faculty of MD
1211 Cathedral St.
Baltimore, MD 21201-5585
Telephone: (410) 539-0872
FAX: (410) 547-0915
Ownership %: 100
**Management:**
Rebecca Cook ..................Advertising Manager
**Editorial:**
Victor R. Hrehorovich, M.D. .....................Editor
Janet Campbell .......................Managing Editor
Henry P. Laughlin, M.D. ..........Associate Editor
**Desc.:** Carries mainly scientific articles and contributions from member organizations. Also includes material on physician practice issues, member information, medical book reviews, and updates on a medical-related legislation.
**Readers:** Doctors primarily, and some press & government personnel.
**Deadline:** story-4 mo. prior to pub. date; news-4 mo. prior; photo-2 mo. prior; ads-2 mo. prior

### MAYO CLINIC PROCEEDINGS
23889

Mayo Foundation
200 First St., S.W.
Rochester, MN 55905
Telephone: (507) 284-2154
FAX: (507) 284-0252
Mailing Address:
Siebens Bldg., Rm. 660
Rochester, MN 55905
Year Established: 1926
Pub. Frequency: m.
Page Size: standard
Subscrip. Rate: $72/yr. individuals & institutions
Circulation: 100,000
Circulation Type: controlled & paid
**Owner(s):**
Mayo Foundation
200 First St., S.W.
Rochester, MN 55905
Telephone: (507) 284-2154
Ownership %: 100
**Management:**
Tony DiBiase ....................Advertising Manager
**Desc.:** A peer-reviewed journal, publishes original articles dealing with clinical and laboratory medicine, clinical research, basic science research, animal studies, and clinical epidemiology. The primary goal of the journal is to serve as an educational instrument to enhance the practice of medicine.
**Readers:** MD.'s, DO.'s, and medical students

### MEDICAL CARE
23892

227 E. Washington Sq.
Philadelphia, PA 19106
Telephone: (215) 238-4273
Year Established: 1963
Pub. Frequency: m.

Page Size: 4 color photos/art
Subscrip. Rate: $115/yr. US; $128/yr. out of country
Circulation: 2,411
Circulation Type: paid
**Owner(s):**
J.B. Lippincott Co.
227 E. Washington Sq.
Philadelphia, PA 19106
Telephone: (215) 238-4273
Ownership %: 100
**Management:**
Monica Brent .....................Advertising Manager
**Editorial:**
Duncan Neuhauser, Ph.D. .........................Editor
**Desc.:** Original articles describing significant current developments in the field of medical care (documenting progress in the research, planning, organization, financing, provision and evaluation of health services). Official journal of the medical care section of the American Public Health Association.
**Readers:** Physicians.

### MEDICAL CARE PRODUCTS
61292

100 S. Main St., Ste. 208
Sayville, NY 11782
Telephone: (516) 244-7396
FAX: (516) 244-7397
Year Established: 1982
Pub. Frequency: 7/yr.
Page Size: tabloid
Subscrip. Rate: $14/yr.
Circulation: 87,600
Circulation Type: paid
**Owner(s):**
Gordon Publications, Inc.
22 N. Tyson Ave.
Floral Park, NY 11001
Telephone: (516) 326-8350
Ownership %: 100
**Management:**
Jack Martin ................................Publisher
Noreen Costelloe ...............Associate Publisher
**Editorial:**
Sue Ludlum ................................Editor
**Desc.:** Medical Care Products provides its readers with information on new patient care technology.
**Readers:** Nurse managers, administration, purchasing & physician managers in hospitals, nursing homes, & clinics.

### MEDICAL DEVICE TECHNOLOGY
66324

7500 Old Oak Blvd.
Cleveland, OH 44130
Telephone: (216) 826-2839
FAX: (216) 891-2726
Year Established: 1990
Pub. Frequency: 9/yr.
Page Size: standard
Subscrip. Rate: $117/yr. European medical professionals
Circulation: 20,000
Circulation Type: paid
**Owner(s):**
Advanstar Communications, Inc.
7500 Old Oak Blvd.
Cleveland, OH 44130
Telephone: (216) 826-2839
Ownership %: 100
**Editorial:**
Annie Ellerton ................................Editor

### MEDICAL DOSIMETRY
66488

660 White Plains Rd.
Tarrytown, NY 10591-5153
Telephone: (914) 524-9200
FAX: (914) 333-2444
Year Established: 1974
Pub. Frequency: q.
Page Size: standard
Subscrip. Rate: $145/yr. institution

Circulation: 1,500
Circulation Type: paid
**Owner(s):**
Pergamon Press, Inc.
660 White Plains Rd.
Tarrytown, NY 10591-5153
Telephone: (914) 524-9200
Ownership %: 100
**Editorial:**
Ray Garcia ........................Editor in Chief

### MEDICAL ECONOMICS
23896

Five Paragon Dr.
Montvale, NJ 07645-1742
Telephone: (201) 358-7200
FAX: (201) 573-0867
Year Established: 1923
Pub. Frequency: bi-w.
Page Size: standard
Subscrip. Rate: $94/yr.; $148/yr. foreign
Materials: 01,02,06,20
Freelance Pay: negotiable
Circulation: 174,000
Circulation Type: paid
**Owner(s):**
Medical Economics Publishing Co., Inc.
Five Paragon Dr.
Montvale, NJ 07645-1742
Ownership %: 100
**Management:**
James J. Pfister .............................President
Richard F. Kiernan ..........................Publisher
Robert Preston ..........................Sales Manager
**Editorial:**
James D. Hendricks .................Executive Editor
Stephen K. Murata .............................Editor
Larry Frederick .........................Managing Editor
**Desc.:** Editorial approach is to cover all nonclinical aspects of medical practice-the handling of patients as human beings, the hiring of help, personnel policies, medical office management, fee setting and collecting, health insurance, hospital practice, health-care reform, professional liability-plus such financial subjects as insurance, investments, tax and estate planning. The scope extends to medical ethics, medical humor, medical family life, and virtually all topics of direct interest to a physician except diagnosis and treatment. Style is both tutorial and reportorial. Articles should be 1,000 words or more. Departments include: Professional Briefs, Letters to the Editors, Financial Briefs, Practice Management, Money Management, What's Ahead.
**Readers:** Self employed physicians-i.e. MDs and DOs.

### MEDICAL ELECTRONICS & EQUIPMENT NEWS
23898

532 Busse Hwy.
Park Ridge, IL 60068
Telephone: (312) 693-3773
FAX: (708) 696-0946
Year Established: 1961
Pub. Frequency: bi-m.
Page Size: tabloid
Subscrip. Rate: $45/yr.
Materials: 28,29,32,33
Circulation: 60,000
Circulation Type: free
**Owner(s):**
Reilly Publishing Co.
532 Busse Hwy.
Park Ridge, IL 60068
Telephone: (312) 693-3773
FAX: (708) 696-0946
Ownership %: 100

**Bureau(s):**
Sean P. Reilly & Associates
22 San Mateo
Rancho Santa M., CA 92688
Telephone: (714) 459-0770
Contact: Sean Reilly, Sales

Carol Mackie & Associates
6 Broadacre Dr.
St. Laurel, NJ 08054
Telephone: (609) 778-4180

George D. Mooney & Associates
419 S. Ojibwa Trail
Mt. Prospect, IL 60056
Telephone: (708) 364-1060
Contact: George Mooney, Sales
**Management:**
John Reilly ..................................President
Kevin J. Kridle ...............................Publisher
Rudi Hein ........................Circulation Manager
Patti Podboy ..................Production Manager
**Editorial:**
Paula Krapf ................................Editor
Maryjane Antonov ........Administrative Assistant
**Desc.:** Charts availability of in-vivo instrumentation, electronic and electro-mechanical devices, materials and accessories used in clinical applications, diagnoses, therapy, radiology, surgery, analyses, research and more.
**Readers:** AMA identified specialists, hospital department supervisors, university medical school research directors, deans, department heads & instrument manufacturers.
**Deadline:** news-1 mo. prior to pub. date; ads-1 mo. prior

### MEDICAL ELECTRONICS / MEDICAL ELECTRONIC PRODUCTS
23897

2994 W. Liberty Ave.
Pittsburgh, PA 15216
Telephone: (412) 343-9666
FAX: (412) 343-9685
Year Established: 1970
Pub. Frequency: bi-m.
Page Size: standard
Subscrip. Rate: $22/yr.
Materials: 01,10,15,28,29,32,33
Circulation: 70,000
Circulation Type: controlled & paid
**Owner(s):**
M&D Corporation
2994 W. Liberty Ave.
Pittsburgh, PA 15216
Telephone: (412) 343-9666
FAX: (412) 343-9685
Ownership %: 100
**Management:**
M. Aronson ..................................Publisher
Deborah Ervin ...................Advertising Manager
Nancy Gordon ..................Production Manager
**Editorial:**
Gina Romary ................................Editor
H. Saluja ..........................Managing Editor
Steve McLane ..........................Articles Editor
Kristin Raup .......................New Products Editor
**Desc.:** Edited for physicians, technicians and healthcare professionals who use and purchase medical equipment. Focuses on the fields of cardiology, radiology, pulmonary, respiratory , general instrumentation and safety equipment.
**Readers:** Physicians, radiologists, cardiologists, pulmonary and anesthesiologists, RN's, biomedical engineers, and hospital administrators.

**Materials Accepted/Included:** 01-Business news 02-By-line articles 03-Fashion news 04-Food news 05-Freelance copy 06-Letters to editor 07-Real estate news 08-Sports news 09-Travel news 10-Book rev. 11-Movie rev. 12-Music rev. 13-TV rev. 14-Theater rev. 15-Coming events 16-Obituaries 17-Question & answer 18-Social announcements 19-Artwork 20-Cartoons 21-Photos 22-TV listings 23-Audio rec. 24-Video rec. 25-Books 26-Films/film clips 27-Personnel news 28-Press releases 29-New product news/photos 30-Trade lit. 31-Contracts awarded 32-Display adv. 33-Classified adv.

## MEDICAL ETHICS ADVISOR
61289

3525 Piedmont Rd.,N.E.
Bldg. 6 #400
Atlanta, GA 30305
Telephone: (404) 262-7436
Pub. Frequency: m.
Subscrip. Rate: $299/yr.
**Owner(s):**
American Health Consultants
3525 Piedmont Rd.,N.E.,
Bldg. 6 #400
Atlanta, GA 30305
Telephone: (404) 262-7436
Ownership %: 100
**Editorial:**
Terry Hartnett ............................................Editor
Cheli Brown ..............................Managing Editor
**Desc.:** Reports, case studies, policy &
guidelines on hospital ethics issues.
**Readers:** Hospital ethics committee
members, bioethicists & other health
care executives.

## MEDICAL GROUP MANAGEMENT JOURNAL
23367

104 Inverness Terr., E.
Englewood, CO 80112
Telephone: (303) 799-1111
FAX: (303) 799-1683
Year Established: 1953
Pub. Frequency: bi-m.
Page Size: 4 color photos/art
Subscrip. Rate: $45/yr.
Materials: 02,32
Print Process: offset
Circulation: 20,000
Circulation Type: controlled & paid
**Owner(s):**
Medical Group Management Association
104 Inverness Terr., E.
Englewood, CO 80112
Telephone: (303) 799-1111
Ownership %: 100
**Management:**
Frederick J. Wenzel, ...........Executive Director
FACMPE
**Editorial:**
Fred E. Graham, II, Ph.D., ........Editor in Chief
FAC
Dennis Barnhardt, APR ...........Executive Editor
Chris Lawrence ........................Managing Editor
Eileen Barker .................................Advertising
Barbara U. Hamilton ..........Book Review Editor
Deborah V. Kennington ........Editorial Associate
**Desc.:** Consists of articles and special
reports on current and pertinent
information on medical group practice
management.
**Readers:** Medical group administrators,
chief medical administrators, physicians,
and professional personnel in the
administration of medical
group practices.

## MEDICAL INTERFACE
65461

66 Palmer Ave., #49
Bronxville, NY 10708
Telephone: (914) 337-7878
Year Established: 1988
Pub. Frequency: m.
Page Size: standard
Subscrip. Rate: $65/yr. US; $85/yr. foreign
Circulation: 25,686
Circulation Type: controlled
**Owner(s):**
Medicom International, Inc.
66 Palmer Ave., Ste. 49
Bronxville, NY 10708
Telephone: (914) 337-7878
**Management:**
Raymond B. Hargreaves ....................President
Jane Armstrong ..........................Vice President

**Editorial:**
Stanton R. Mehr ..............................Editor
**Desc.:** The facilities communication among
the various groups in the medical fields.
An open forum for those involved in
managed care
**Readers:** Key managed care executives,
HNOS, PPOS, APAS, administrators,
physicans, pharmaceutical company
personnel and corporate benefits
administrators.

## MEDICAL LABORATORY OBSERVER
61291

5 Paragon Dr.
Montvale, NJ 07645-1742
Telephone: (201) 358-7200
FAX: (201) 573-1045
Year Established: 1969
Pub. Frequency: m.
Page Size: standard
Subscrip. Rate: $65/yr.
Materials: 06,17,32,33
Print Process: web offset
Circulation: 58,000
Circulation Type: controlled
**Owner(s):**
International Thomson Organization
245 Park Ave.
New York, NY 10167
Telephone: (212) 557-9333
Ownership %: 100
**Management:**
Hal Avery .......................................Publisher
**Editorial:**
Robert Fitzgibbon .................................Editor
Lisa Maher ..........................Managing Editor
**Desc.:** Business editorial for clinical lab
management personnels.
**Readers:** Managerial level lab employees,
including pathologists, lab directors and
lab managers.

## MEDICAL LETTER ON DRUGS & THERAPEUTICS, THE
61246

1000 Main St.
New Rochelle, NY 10801
Telephone: (914) 235-0500
Year Established: 1959
Pub. Frequency: bi-w.
Page Size: standard
Subscrip. Rate: $37.50/yr.; $61/2 yrs.;
$83.50/3 yrs.
Circulation: 150,000
Circulation Type: paid
**Owner(s):**
Medical Letter, Inc., The
1000 Main St.
New Rochelle, NY 10801-7537
Telephone: (914) 235-0500
Ownership %: 100
**Editorial:**
Mark Abramowicz, M.D. ...........................Editor
**Desc.:** An independent non-profit
publication providing unbiased critical
evaluations of drugs with regard to their
effectiveness, adverse effects and
possible alternative medications. It
carries no advertising and is supported
entirely by subscription fees.
**Readers:** Physicians & pharmacists.

## MEDICAL PRODUCT MANUFACTURING NEWS
61293

3340 Ocean Park Blvd., Ste. 1000
Santa Monica, CA 90405
Telephone: (310) 392-5509
FAX: (310) 392-4920
Year Established: 1985
Pub. Frequency: 10/yr.
Page Size: tabloid
Subscrip. Rate: free
Circulation: 30,000
Circulation Type: controlled

**Owner(s):**
Canon Communications, Inc.
3340 Ocean Park Blvd. Ste 1000
Santa Monica, CA 90405
Telephone: (310) 392-5509
Ownership %: 100
**Management:**
Linda Madore ....................Promotion Manager
**Editorial:**
John Bethune ................................Editor
**Desc.:** Equipment, material, component
and service news for medical device and
medical electronics manufacturers.
Specifically OEMS, not end-users.
**Readers:** Medical device manufacturers,
diagnostic test kit manufacturers,
medical electronics.

## MEDICAL PRODUCTS SALES
23904

Two Northfield Plaza
Ste. 300
Northfield, IL 60093
Telephone: (708) 441-3700
FAX: (708) 441-3701
Year Established: 1970
Pub. Frequency: m.
Page Size: tabloid
Subscrip. Rate: $5/issue; $49.95/yr.;
$55.95/yr. Canada; $69.95/yr. foreign
Materials: 01,27,28,29,32,33
Print Process: web offset
Circulation: 23,800
Circulation Type: controlled
**Owner(s):**
McKnight Medical Communications
Two Northfield Plaza
Ste. 300
Northfield, IL 60093
Telephone: (708) 441-3700
Ownership %: 100
**Management:**
Christopher J. Bale ............................Publisher
Merrilly Nicolazzi ................Business Manager
Gregg Haunroth ................Circulation Manager
Deborah Tobiaski ..............Production Manager
Gena Grant ...............................Sales Manager
Nick Kosan ...............................Sales Manager
**Editorial:**
William Briggs .................................Editor
John Andrews .........................Associate Editor
Constance Heard ................Production Director
**Desc.:** Serves individuals and companies
who distribute medical products for
home health care, institutional and
physician office market, as well as other
health care facilities.
**Readers:** Suppliers and dealers of medical
products.
**Deadline:** story-2 mos. prior to pub. date;
news-2 mos. prior; photo-2 mos. prior;
ads-1 mo. prior

## MEDICAL STAFF LEADER
61294

737 N. Michigan Ave., Ste. 700
Chicago, IL 60611
Telephone: (312) 440-6800
FAX: (312) 951-8491
Year Established: 1978
Pub. Frequency: m.
Page Size: standard
Subscrip. Rate: $22/yr. US; $35/yr. foreign
Circulation: 14,000
Circulation Type: paid
**Owner(s):**
American Hospital Association
737 N. Michigan Ave.
Chicago, IL 60611
Telephone: (312) 440-6800
Ownership %: 100
**Editorial:**
Mary T. Koska .........................Managing Editor
Mary Grayson ......................Editorial Director
John McCormack ................Editorial Assistant

**Readers:** Medical staff, physicians,
hospital CEO.

## MEDICAL TRIBUNE
23363

257 Park Ave., S.
New York, NY 10010
Telephone: (212) 674-8500
FAX: (212) 529-8490
Year Established: 1960
Pub. Frequency: bi-w.
Page Size: tabloid
Subscrip. Rate: $26/yr.
Freelance Pay: negotiable
Circulation: 130,000
Circulation Type: controlled
**Owner(s):**
Medical Tribune, Inc.
257 Park Ave., S.
New York, NY 10010
Telephone: (212) 674-8500
Ownership %: 100
**Desc.:** News and features of clinical or
general interest to physicians. Special
emphasis on effects of government
policies, major clinical advances, new
concepts of health care delivery.
Departments include: In Consultation,
Current Opinion, Law and Medicine,
Handling the Alcoholic Clinical
Perfection, Doctors Debate, Sports
Medicine.
**Readers:** 160,000 MD's in private practice.

## MEDICAL WORLD NEWS
23910

257 Park Ave., S., 19th Fl.
New York, NY 10010
Telephone: (212) 674-8500
FAX: (212) 529-8490
Year Established: 1936
Pub. Frequency: m.
Page Size: standard
Subscrip. Rate: $55/yr.; free to qualified
physicians
Freelance Pay: $90/col.
Circulation: 130,000
Circulation Type: paid
**Owner(s):**
Medical Tribune, Inc.
257 Park Ave., S.
New York, NY 10010
Ownership %: 100
**Bureau(s):**
MWN Washington Bureau
1431 21st St., N.W., Rm. 101
Washington, DC 20036
Telephone: (202) 737-1078
Contact: Fran Pollner, Bureau Chief
**Management:**
Vicki Brentnall ............................Sales Manager
**Editorial:**
Nick Zittell ..................................Editor in Chief
**Desc.:** News items of current important
issues for primary care physicians.
**Readers:** Physicians.

## MEDICINAL RESEARCH REVIEWS
65620

605 Third Ave.
New York, NY 10158
Telephone: (212) 850-6289
Year Established: 1981
Pub. Frequency: bi-m.
Subscrip. Rate: $332/yr.; $404.50/yr.
foreign
Circulation: 700
Circulation Type: paid
**Owner(s):**
John Wiley & Sons, Inc.
605 Third Ave.
New York, NY 10158
Ownership %: 100
**Editorial:**
George de Stevens ..............................Editor

---

**Materials Accepted/Included:** 01-Business news 02-By-line articles 03-Fashion news 04-Food news 05-Freelance copy 06-Letters to editor 07-Real estate news 08-Sports news 09-Travel news 10-Book rev. 11-Movie rev. 12-Music rev. 13-TV rev. 14-Theater rev. 15-Coming events 16-Obituaries 17-Question & answer 18-Social announcements 19-Artwork 20-Cartoons 21-Photos 22-TV listings 23-Audio rec. 24-Video rec. 25-Books 26-Films/film clips 27-Personnel news 28-Press releases 29-New product news/photos 30-Trade lit. 31-Contracts awarded 32-Display adv. 33-Classified adv.

4-245

**Desc.:** Embraces all aspects of research addressing the study of disease and the consequent development of therapeutic agents.

55914

## MEDICINE
428 E. Preston St.
Baltimore, MD 21202
Telephone: (410) 528-4000
FAX: (410) 528-4312
Year Established: 1954
Pub. Frequency: bi-m.
Page Size: standard
Subscrip. Rate: $72/yr. individuals;
  $132/yr. institutions
Circulation: 5,100
Circulation Type: paid
**Owner(s):**
Williams & Wilkins Co.
428 E. Preston St.
Baltimore, MD 21202
Telephone: (410) 528-4000
Ownership %: 100
**Editorial:**
Dr. Victor A. McKusick .............................Editor
**Desc.:** The only general medicine review journal to cover areas of interest to the internist including literature review and follow-up studies.
**Readers:** Subscribers, nearly all internists.

24238

## MEMBER NEWS OF THE NATIONAL SOCIETY TO PREVENT BLINDNESS
500 E. Remington Rd.
Schaumburg, IL 60173
Telephone: (708) 843-2020
FAX: (708) 843-8458
Year Established: 1951
Pub. Frequency: q.
Page Size: tabloid
Subscrip. Rate: free
Circulation: 25,000
Circulation Type: controlled
**Owner(s):**
National Society to Prevent Blindness
500 E. Remington Rd.
Schaumburg, IL 60173
Telephone: (708) 843-2020
Ownership %: 100
**Editorial:**
Patricia Kaar ................................Editor in Chief
Debra Wheeling ................Production Assistant
**Desc.:** Professional journal for health professionals concerned with or interested in the prevention of blindness in all its aspects. Articles and features cover the major eye health problems in America and the ways they are being studied, prevented, or treated in various disciplines (medical, paramedical, behavioral and social sciences). Departments include: Early Detection, Eye Defects and Diseases, Research, Legislation and Public Regulatory Aspects, Health Education, Eye Safety, Financial, Organizational, and Manpower Approaches to Blindness Prevention.
**Readers:** Eye-care professionals, family physicians, pediatricians, orthoptists, public health workers; Those in occupational medicine, volunteer programs, social workers, teachers, nurses, engineers.

23913

## MICHIGAN MEDICINE, JOURNAL OF MICHIGAN STATE MEDICAL SOCIETY
120 W. Saginaw St.
East Lansing, MI 48823
Telephone: (517) 337-1351
FAX: (517) 337-2490

Mailing Address:
  P. O. Box 950
  East Lansing, MI 48823
Year Established: 1902
Pub. Frequency: m.
Page Size: standard
Subscrip. Rate: $100/yr.
Freelance Pay: varies
Circulation: 11,000
Circulation Type: paid
**Owner(s):**
Michigan State Medical Society
120 W. Saginaw St.
East Lansing, MI 48823
Telephone: (517) 337-1351
Ownership %: 100
**Management:**
Betty J. McNerney .............Advertising Manager
**Editorial:**
Betty J. McNerney ................................Editor
**Desc.:** News, socio-economic and opinion articles of interest to members of Michigan State Medical Society, no original scientific papers. Paid advertising of pharmaceutical firms.
**Readers:** Members of the Michigan State Medical Society.

23915

## MILITARY MEDICINE
9320 Old Georgetown Rd.
Bethesda, MD 20814
Telephone: (301) 897-8800
FAX: (301) 530-5446
Year Established: 1891
Pub. Frequency: m.
Page Size: standard
Subscrip. Rate: $35/yr. US; $40/yr. foreign
Circulation: 16,755
Circulation Type: paid
**Owner(s):**
Assn. of Military Surgeons of the US
9320 Old Georgetown Rd.
Bethesda, MD 20814
Telephone: (301) 897-8800
Ownership %: 100
**Editorial:**
Lt. Gen. Max B. Bralliar ...........Executive Editor
R. Adm. John C. Duffy, M.D. .....................Editor
Maggie Hatten ..........................Managing Editor
**Desc.:** Supports knowledge concerning medical activities of the Federal Medical Services, including developments in medical technology, education, management and research.

23916

## MINNESOTA MEDICINE
3433 Broadway St. N.E.
Ste. 300
Minneapolis, MN 55413-1761
Telephone: (612) 378-1875
FAX: (612) 378-3875
Year Established: 1918
Pub. Frequency: m.
Page Size: standard
Subscrip. Rate: $3 newsstand; $36/yr. US;
  $60/yr. foreign
Materials: 02,05,06,10,19,21,25,27,28,29,
  32,33
Freelance Pay: $600/2,500 wds.
Circulation: 9,000
Circulation Type: paid
**Owner(s):**
Minnesota Medical Association
3433 Broadway St. N.E.
#300
Minneapolis, MN 55413-1761
Telephone: (612) 378-1875
FAX: (612) 378-3875
Ownership %: 100
**Management:**
Michael Soucheray ...........Advertising Manager
**Editorial:**
Charles Meyer, M.D. ...............................Editor
Meredith McNab ......................Managing Editor

**Desc.:** Journal of clinical and health affairs, offering a blend of socio-economic, medical-legal, and scientific material. The scientific section presents original papers, case reports, reviews of medical literature, abstracts, and special medical articles. The non-scientific content includes feature stories and covers book reviews, organizational news, reports and announcements of medical meetings, public health reports, medical and socio-economics, reports of the state board of medical examiners and essays.
**Readers:** Medical field, primary physicians.
**Deadline:** ads-1st of mo. prior to mo. of pub. date

23917

## MISSOURI MEDICINE
113 Madison
Jefferson City, MO 65102
Telephone: (314) 636-5151
FAX: (314) 636-8552
Mailing Address:
  P.O. Box 1028
  Jefferson City, MO 65102
Year Established: 1904
Pub. Frequency: m.
Page Size: standard
Subscrip. Rate: $20/yr.
Circulation: 7,000
Circulation Type: controlled & paid
**Owner(s):**
Missouri State Medical Association
113 Madison
Jefferson City, MO 65101
Telephone: (314) 636-5151
Ownership %: 100
**Management:**
Royal O. Cooper ........................Vice President
**Editorial:**
J. Regan Thomas ................................Editor
Dennis Weiser ........................Managing Editor
Angie Allen ............................Editorial Assistant
**Desc.:** Contains scientific section, editorial section, practice management section, organization news, general news and information concerning the field of medicine and the physicians in the state of Missouri. It is published primarily for the members of the Missouri State Medical Association.
**Readers:** Physicians in all specialty fields.

23918

## MLO/MEDICAL LABORATORY OBSERVER
Five Paragon Dr.
Montvale, NJ 07645-1742
Telephone: (201) 358-7200
FAX: (201) 573-0344
Year Established: 1969
Pub. Frequency: m.
Page Size: standard
Subscrip. Rate: $65/yr. US; $75/yr. foreign
Materials: 02,06,17,19,21,28,29,32,33
Print Process: web offset
Circulation: 59,000
Circulation Type: controlled
**Owner(s):**
Medical Economics Publishing Co., Inc.
Five Paragon Dr.
Montvale, NJ 07645-1742
Telephone: (201) 358-7200
Ownership %: 100
**Management:**
James J. Pfister ................................President
Hal Avery ................................Publisher
Sheryl Urangst ...................Circulation Manager
Russell Johns ..............Classified Adv. Manager
**Editorial:**
Robert J. Fitzgibbon ................................Editor
Lisa A. Maher ........................Managing Editor
Robin Sodaro ................................Art Editor
Alvin Ira Bronstein ...........Production Director

**Desc.:** Improves the management skills of clinical laboratory supervisors. Trained in medicine and science, these readers have a great need to acquire management expertise, and MLO is the only laboratory journal devoted exclusively to filling that need. Practical, informative articles probe management problems confronting laboratory supervisors and provide useful solutions and advice based on in-lab experience. Regular departments carry pertinent information on technical, regulatory, management topics related to efficient laboratory operation. Departments include: Tips on Technology, Management Q & A, Washington Report, Viewpoint, Letters to the Editor, Computer Dialog, Technology Update.
**Readers:** Pathologists and clinical laboratory directors, managers, supervisors and department heads in hospital and independent clinical laboratories.
**Deadline:** ads-1st of mo. prior to pub. date

68973

## MODERN MEDICINE
7500 Old Oak Blvd.
Cleveland, OH 44130-3343
Telephone: (216) 243-8100
FAX: (216) 891-2735
Year Established: 1932
Pub. Frequency: m.
Page Size: standard
Subscrip. Rate: $46/yr.
Materials: 05,06,19,21,28,29,32,33
Freelance Pay: standard
Print Process: web offset
Circulation: 120,000
Circulation Type: controlled
**Owner(s):**
Advanstar Communications, Inc.
7500 Old Oak Blvd.
Cleveland, OH 44130-3343
Telephone: (216) 243-8100
FAX: (216) 891-2735
Ownership %: 100
**Editorial:**
Martin M. Stevenson ................................Editor
**Desc.:** Covers medical news, diagnosis and therapy, clinical techniques, and medical meetings.
**Deadline:** ads-1st of mo. prior to pub. date

65663

## MOLECULAR & CELLULAR BIOLOGY
1325 Massachusetts Ave., N.W.
Washington, DC 20005-4171
Telephone: (202) 737-3600
Year Established: 1981
Pub. Frequency: m.
Page Size: standard
Subscrip. Rate: $379/yr.
Materials: 02,32
Print Process: web offset
Circulation: 6,000
Circulation Type: paid
**Owner(s):**
American Society for Microbiology
1325 Massachusetts Ave., N.W.
Washington, DC 20005-4171
Telephone: (202) 737-3600
Ownership %: 100
**Editorial:**
Alan M. Weiner ...........................Editor in Chief
Linda M. Illig ................................Director

**Materials Accepted/Included:** 01-Business news 02-By-line articles 03-Fashion news 04-Food news 05-Freelance copy 06-Letters to editor 07-Real estate news 08-Sports news 09-Travel news 10-Book rev. 11-Movie rev. 12-Music rev. 13-TV rev. 14-Theater rev. 15-Coming events 16-Obituaries 17-Question & answer 18-Social announcements 19-Artwork 20-Cartoons 21-Photos 22-TV listings 23-Audio rec. 24-Video rec. 25-Books 26-Films/film clips 27-Personnel news 28-Press releases 29-New product news/photos 30-Trade lit. 31-Contracts awarded 32-Display adv. 33-Classified adv.

**Desc.:** Publishes articles on the molecular biology of eukaryotic cells, of both microbial and higher organisms. The scope includes cellular morphology and function, genome organization, regulation of expression, morphogenesis, and somatic cell genetic expression, morphogensis, and somatic cell genetics. In addition, articles also cover plasmid vector and virus-infected cells, such that the emphasis is clearly on the cell.
**Readers:** Molecular and cellular biologists, cancer researchers, virologists and immunologists.

58931
**MOLECULAR ENDOCRINOLOGY**
428 E. Preston St.
Baltimore, MD 21202
Telephone: (410) 528-4000
FAX: (410) 528-4312
Year Established: 1987
Pub. Frequency: m.
Subscrip. Rate: $110/yr. individual;
   $170/yr. institution
Circulation: 1,900
Circulation Type: paid
**Owner(s):**
Endocrine Society, The
9650 Rockville Pk.
Bethesda, MD 20814
Telephone: (301) 530-9660
Ownership %: 100
**Management:**
Don Pfarr ...........................Advertising Manager
Ken Startt ............................................Manager
**Editorial:**
E. Brad Thompson, M.D. ........................Editor
John Ewers ...........................Marketing Director

61628
**NEBRASKA MEDICAL JOURNAL**
233 S. 13th St., Ste. 1512
Lincoln, NE 68508
Telephone: (402) 474-4472
FAX: (402) 474-2198
Year Established: 1916
Pub. Frequency: m.
Page Size: standard
Subscrip. Rate: $23/yr. US; $25/yr. foreign
Print Process: offset
Circulation: 2,100
Circulation Type: controlled
**Owner(s):**
Nebraska Medical Association
233 S. 13th St., Ste. 1512
Lincoln, NE 68508
Telephone: (404) 474-4472
Ownership %: 100
**Editorial:**
Dr. Benjamin Gelber ..............................Editor
**Desc.:** Scientific medical journal.
**Readers:** Members of the Nebraska Medical Assoc. plus subscribers.

66489
**NEURAL NETWORKS**
660 White Plains Rd.
Tarrytown, NY 10591-5153
Telephone: (914) 524-9200
FAX: (914) 333-2444
Year Established: 1988
Pub. Frequency: 8/yr.
Subscrip. Rate: $267/yr.
Circulation: 3,000
Circulation Type: paid
**Owner(s):**
Pergamon Press, Ltd.
Journals Division
660 White Plains Rd.
Tarrytown, NY 10591-5153
Telephone: (914) 524-9200
Ownership %: 100
**Management:**
Michael Boswood ......................Vice President

**Editorial:**
Rosemarie Fazzolari .........................Advertising
**Desc.:** Publishes research concerning the modeling of brain and behavioral processes and the application of these models to computer, and related technologies. This research is also precipitating a fundamental shift in computer science and artificial intelligence. Scientists and engineers are now using Neural Network models to help solve key technological problems. Interest in implementing these models in real-time hardware is, therefore, very high.

23921
**NEUROSURGERY**
1200 N. State St., Ste. 5046
Los Angeles, CA 90033
Telephone: (213) 224-2200
FAX: (213) 224-2201
Year Established: 1977
Pub. Frequency: m.
Page Size: standard
Subscrip. Rate: $135/yr. individual;
   $190/yr. institutional
Circulation: 8,500
Circulation Type: paid
**Owner(s):**
Congress of Neurological Surgeons, Inc.
428 E. Preston St.
Baltimore, MD 21202
Ownership %: 100
**Editorial:**
Michael L.J. Puzzo, M.D. ........................Editor
Stephen Lenier ........................Managing Editor
**Desc.:** The official publication of the Congress of Neurological Surgeons, Inc. established by the Congress to maintain high standards of neurosurgical practice, to promote the education of younger neurosurgeons around the world, to disseminate scientific knowledge, to encourage research in neurosurgery and related fields, and to promote fellowship among neurosurgeons.
**Readers:** Neurosurgeons world-wide, including members of the Congress of Neurological Surgeons.

61282
**NEW ENGLAND JOURNAL OF MEDICINE**
10 Shattuck St.
Boston, MA 02115
Telephone: (617) 734-9800
Year Established: 1812
Pub. Frequency: w.
Page Size: standard
Subscrip. Rate: $96/yr.
Circulation: 228,000
Circulation Type: paid
**Owner(s):**
Massachusetts Medical Society
10 Shattuck St.
Boston, MA 02115
Telephone: (617) 734-9800
Ownership %: 100
**Editorial:**
Jerome Kassirer ........................Editor in Chief
**Desc.:** Presents original articles and interpretive reviews of a variety of developments in the major aspects of medicine, its science, its art and practice and its position in today's society.

23860
**NEW JERSEY MEDICINE**
2 Princess Rd.
Lawrenceville, NJ 08648
Telephone: (609) 896-1766
FAX: (609) 896-1368
Year Established: 1904
Pub. Frequency: m.
Page Size: standard
Subscrip. Rate: $35/yr.

Circulation: 10,018
Circulation Type: paid
**Owner(s):**
Medical Society of New Jersey
2 Princess Rd.
Lawrenceville, NJ 08648
Telephone: (609) 896-1766
Ownership %: 100
**Management:**
Elizabeth Cookson ............Advertising Manager
**Editorial:**
Geraldine R. Hutner .................Executive Editor
Howard D. Slobodien, M.D. ....................Editor
Nancy M. Propsner ...................Assistant Editor
**Desc.:** Carries original articles by physicians dealing with research, therapy, case studies. Departments include: Editorials, Original Articles, State Society Activities, Clinical Notes, Obituaries, Commentary, Personal Items, Letters, and Book Reviews, CME Calendar.
**Readers:** Physicians, government agencies, hospital personnel, students, affiliated agencies.

23923
**NEW PHYSICIAN, THE**
1890 Preston White Dr.
Reston, VA 22091
Telephone: (703) 620-6600
FAX: (703) 620-5873
Year Established: 1952
Pub. Frequency: 9/yr.
Page Size: standard
Subscrip. Rate: $3 newsstand; $22/yr. non-members
Materials: 02,04,05,06,10,20,25,28,29,32,33
Print Process: web offset
Circulation: 30,000
Circulation Type: paid
**Owner(s):**
American Medical Student Association
1890 Preston White Dr.
Reston, VA 22091
Telephone: (703) 620-6600
FAX: (703) 620-5873
Ownership %: 100
**Management:**
Paul Wright ......................................Publisher
**Editorial:**
Laura Milani ........................................Editor
Lisa Adams ....................................Advertising
Steve George .........................Associate Editor
Amy Magaro .............................Associate Editor
Christine Bixler .....................Editorial Assistant
Ruth Lipson ..........................Production Editor
**Desc.:** Articles on social, economic, political issues in medicine. Articles on medical problems include those on diagnosis, therapy, introduction to specialties, research, etc. Investigative articles on medical politics, policy making, student and housestaff issues, due process cases. Those on socioeconomic aspects include health care for the poor, national health insurance, women in medicine, access to records, financing medical education.
**Readers:** Medical students, interns and residents, allied health professionals.
**Deadline:** ads-6 wks.

23926
**NORTH CAROLINA MEDICAL JOURNAL**
P.O. Box 3910
Duke University Medical Center
Durham, NC 27710
Telephone: (919) 286-6410
FAX: (919) 286-9219
Year Established: 1940
Pub. Frequency: m.

Page Size: standard
Subscrip. Rate: $17/yr.
Materials: 06,10,25,32,33
Print Process: web offset
Circulation: 8,500
Circulation Type: controlled & free
**Owner(s):**
North Carolina Medical Society
P.O. Box 27167
Raleigh, NC 27611
Telephone: (919) 833-3836
FAX: (919) 833-2023
Ownership %: 100
**Management:**
Donald R. Wall ....................Business Manager
**Editorial:**
Francis A. Neelon, M.D. ..........................Editor
Jeanne C. Yohn ......................Managing Editor
**Desc.:** For North Carolina doctors and their patients. Papers devoted to medical/scientific topics therapeutic procedures in medical field. Departments include: Continuing Medical Education, Classified Ads, Letters to the Editor. Photos and illustrations used only with professional articles.
**Readers:** Professional.

53967
**OB-GYN NEWS**
12230 Wilkins Ave.
Rockville, MD 20852
Telephone: (301) 816-8700
Year Established: 1966
Pub. Frequency: s-m.
Page Size: tabloid
Subscrip. Rate: $96/yr.
Freelance Pay: negotiable
Circulation: 30,150
Circulation Type: controlled
**Owner(s):**
Capital Cities Communications, Inc.
24 E. 51st St.
New York, NY 10022
Ownership %: 100
**Management:**
Tom Fowler ........................................Publisher
**Editorial:**
Jo Weekley .........................................Editor
Michele Robinson ....................Managing Editor
**Desc.:** Provides comprehensive reporting of information of specific or general interest to the obstetrician/gynecologist. Concentrates primarily on first person coverage of clinical meetings, symposia and conventions.
**Readers:** Obstetricians/gynecologists.

23928
**OBSTETRICAL & GYNECOLOGICAL SURVEY**
428 E. Preston St.
Baltimore, MD 21202
Telephone: (410) 528-4000
FAX: (410) 528-4312
Year Established: 1946
Pub. Frequency: m.
Page Size: standard
Subscrip. Rate: $93/yr. individuals;
   $130/yr. institutions
Circulation: 10,100
Circulation Type: paid
**Owner(s):**
Williams & Wilkins Co.
428 E. Preston St.
Baltimore, MD 21202
Telephone: (410) 528-4000
Ownership %: 100
**Management:**
Gary Walchli ....................Advertising Manager
Leslie Kendrick ....................................Manager
Annette Grayson ..............Production Manager
**Editorial:**
Robert C. Cefalo, M.D. ..........................Editor
Howard W. Jones, III ..............................Editor
Robert B. Jaffe, M.D. ............................Editor

**Materials Accepted/Included:** 01-Business news 02-By-line articles 03-Fashion news 04-Food news 05-Freelance copy 06-Letters to editor 07-Real estate news 08-Sports news 09-Travel news 10-Book rev. 11-Movie rev. 12-Music rev. 13-TV rev. 14-Theater rev. 15-Coming events 16-Obituaries 17-Question & answer 18-Social announcements 19-Artwork 20-Cartoons 21-Photos 22-TV listings 23-Audio rec. 24-Video rec. 25-Books 26-Films/film clips 27-Personnel news 28-Press releases 29-New product news/photos 30-Trade lit. 31-Contracts awarded 32-Display adv. 33-Classified adv.

4-247

Watson A. Bowes, Jr., M.D. ..............Editor
**Desc.:** Reviews papers appearing in the world literature summarizing the current status of topics of interest to obstetricians and gynecologists. Articles are condensed in such a manner that reader does not have to refer back to the original article. As an added bonus, a member of the editorial board gives a pertinent evaluation of the information presented.
**Readers:** Obstetricians, gynecologists, general practitioners.

23929

## OBSTETRICS & GYNECOLOGY

655 Ave. of the Americas
New York, NY 10010
Telephone: (212) 989-5800
FAX: (212) 633-3977
Year Established: 1953
Pub. Frequency: m.
Page Size: standard
Subscrip. Rate: $115/yr. individual; $182/yr. institution
Circulation: 37,291
Circulation Type: paid
**Owner(s):**
American College of Obstetricians & Gynecologists
409 12th St., S.W.
Washington, DC 20024
Ownership %: 100
**Management:**
Susan Tagliaferro ..............Advertising Manager
Paula Gantz ......................Manager
**Editorial:**
Roy M. Pitkin, MD. ..............Editor in Chief
Janet D. Bailey ..............Associate Publisher
**Desc.:** Research articles and clinical reports related to the practice of Ob/Gyn.
**Readers:** Board certified obstetricians and gynecologists.

23930

## OCCUPATIONAL HEALTH & SAFETY

225 N. New Rd.
Waco, TX 76710
Telephone: (817) 776-9000
FAX: (817) 776-9018
Mailing Address:
P.O. Box 2573
Waco, TX 76702
Year Established: 1932
Pub. Frequency: m.
Page Size: standard
Subscrip. Rate: $114/yr. US; $148/yr. Canada
Materials: 01,05,06,21,28,29,32,33
Freelance Pay: negotiable
Print Process: web offset
Circulation: 165,047
Circulation Type: free & paid
**Owner(s):**
Medical Publications, Inc.
P.O. Box 2573
Waco, TX 76702
Telephone: (817) 776-9000
Ownership %: 100
**Management:**
Craig S. Stevens ..................President
Russell Lindsay ..............Vice President
Russell Lindsay ..................Publisher
Stan Terry ......................Sales Manager
**Editorial:**
Blake Smith ......................Senior Editor
Roy Sanders & Teri Lyn ........Managing Editor
Eisma
Mark Hartley ..............Editorial Director
Connie Reinke ..................Advertising
Chris Weatherly ..................Advertising
Barbara Blake ..................Advertising
Paula Ryan ......................Advertising

**Desc.:** Objective is to report on news about occupational health and safety from around the world.
**Readers:** Occupational physicians, safety engineers, occupational health nurses, industrial hygienists and professionals concerned with biomedical safety.

61635

## OCULAR SURGERY NEWS

6900 Grove Rd.
Thorofare, NJ 08086-9447
Telephone: (609) 848-1000
FAX: (609) 853-5991
Year Established: 1982
Pub. Frequency: s-m.
Page Size: tabloid
Subscrip. Rate: $185/yr.
Materials: 01,02,05,06,10,15,17,20,21,23, 24,25,28,29,30,32,33
Freelance Pay: negotiable; $.30/wd. max.
Print Process: web
Circulation: 20,000
Circulation Type: controlled & paid
**Owner(s):**
Slack, Inc.
6900 Grove Rd.
Thorofare, NJ 08086-9447
Telephone: (609) 848-1000
FAX: (609) 853-5991
Ownership %: 100
**Editorial:**
Keith J. Croes ..................Executive Editor
Donald Sanders, M.D., Ph.D. ..................Editor
**Desc.:** News for ophthalmologists, with emphasis on the anterior segment. Editions include: OCULAR SUGERY NEWS INTERNATIONAL EDITION
**Readers:** U.S. ophthalmologists.

69472

## OHIO FAMILY PHYSICIAN NEWS

4075 N. High St.
Columbus, OH 43214
Telephone: (614) 267-7867
Year Established: 1955
Pub. Frequency: m.
Page Size: pocket
Subscrip. Rate: $2/yr.
Circulation: 3,800
Circulation Type: controlled
**Owner(s):**
Ohio Academy of Family Physicians
4075 N. High St.
Columbus, OH 43214
Telephone: (614) 267-7867
Ownership %: 100
**Editorial:**
Dr. Robert D. Gillette ..................Editor

66476

## ONCOLOGY RESEARCH

660 White Plains Rd.
Tarrytown, NY 10591-5153
Telephone: (914) 524-9200
FAX: (914) 333-2444
Pub. Frequency: m.
Subscrip. Rate: $265/yr.
**Owner(s):**
Pergamon Press, Inc.
Journals Division
660 White Plains Rd.
Tarrytown, NY 10591-5153
Telephone: (914) 524-9200
Ownership %: 100
**Management:**
Michael Boswood ..................President
**Editorial:**
A.C. Sartorelli ..................Editor
Rosomarie Fazzolari ..................Advertising
**Desc.:** Rapid dissemination journal for full research papers and short communications contributing to the understanding of cancer in areas of molecular biology, cell biology, biochemistry, biophysics, genetics, virology, endocrinology and immunology.

61569

## OPHTHALMIC SURGERY

6900 Grove Rd.
Thorofare, NJ 08086
Telephone: (609) 848-1000
Year Established: 1969
Pub. Frequency: m.
Page Size: standard
Subscrip. Rate: $49/yr.
Materials: 06,10,15,25,28,29,30,32,33
Circulation: 3,000
Circulation Type: paid
**Owner(s):**
Slack, Inc.
6900 Grove Rd.
Thorofare, NJ 08086
Telephone: (609) 848-1000
Ownership %: 100
**Management:**
Peter Slack ..................President
Richard Roash ..................Publisher
Donna Carpenter ..................Associate Publisher
Wayne McCourt ..................Associate Publisher
Les Robeson ..................Circulation Manager
**Editorial:**
George L. Spaeth, M.D. ..................Editor
Patricia A. Perry ..................Managing Editor
**Desc.:** Dedicated to advancing the clinical knowledge of ophthalmic surgeons. Presents original peer-reviewed articles on glaucoma, cataract surgery, IOL implantation, trabeculectomy, and more.
**Readers:** Ophthalmic surgeons.

59483

## OPHTHALMOLOGY

E. Washington Sq.
Philadelphia, PA 19106
Telephone: (215) 238-4200
Year Established: 1907
Pub. Frequency: m.
Subscrip. Rate: $95/yr. individual; $130/yr. institution
Circulation: 22,654
Circulation Type: paid
**Owner(s):**
J.B. Lippincott Co.
E. Washington Sq.
Philadelphia, PA 19106
Telephone: (215) 238-4200
Ownership %: 100
**Management:**
Joseph W. Lippincott III ..................Publisher
Earl Gerhardt ..................Manager
Joe Baiocco ..................Production Manager
**Editorial:**
Paul R. Lichter, M.D. ..................Editor
Virginia Kelly ..................Marketing Director
**Desc.:** The journal publishes original articles of practical value for the clinician and reflects the best in state of the art. Material includes presentations given at the annual meeting of the American Academy of Ophthalmology.
**Readers:** American Association of Ophthalmology members, non-member physicians, institutions and residents.

61563

## OPHTHALMOLOGY TIMES

7500 Old Oak Blvd.
Cleveland, OH 44130
Telephone: (216) 243-8100
Year Established: 1976
Pub. Frequency: bi-w.
Page Size: tabloid
Subscrip. Rate: $100/yr.
Freelance Pay: $125/news story
Circulation: 15,695
Circulation Type: controlled
**Owner(s):**
Edgell Communications, Inc.
7500 Old Oak Blvd.
Cleveland, OH 44130
Telephone: (216) 243-8100
Ownership %: 100

**Bureau(s):**
Edgell Communications, Inc.
7500 Old Oak Blvd.
Cleveland, OH 44130
Telephone: (216) 243-8100
Contact: Dean Celia, Editor in Chief
**Management:**
Bern Rogers ..................President
Bern Rogers ..................Publisher
**Editorial:**
Dean Celia ..................Editor in Chief
Bruce Millar ..................Exec. Editor
Roger Soderman ..................Associate Publisher
Jack Dodick ..................Medical Editor
**Desc.:** A scientific specialty tabloid providing fast, accurate news of ophthalmology.
**Readers:** Physicians & residents whose primary specialty is ophthalmology.

23933

## ORTHOPAEDIC REVIEW

105 Raider Blvd.
Belle Mead, NJ 08502
Telephone: (908) 874-8550
FAX: (908) 874-0707
Year Established: 1972
Pub. Frequency: m.
Page Size: standard
Subscrip. Rate: $75/yr. US; $94/yr. foreign
Circulation: 28,000
Circulation Type: controlled
**Owner(s):**
Reed Elsevier Medical Publishers, USA
Core Publishing Division
105 Raider Blvd.
Belle Mead, NJ 08502
Telephone: (908) 874-8550
Ownership %: 100
**Management:**
Linda Nelson Fox ..................Publisher
Susan Levey ..................Sales Manager
**Editorial:**
Glenn Williams ..................Editor
Helena Kravitz ..................Administrative Assistant
Steve Claps ..................Group Publisher
**Desc.:** Orthopaedic Review is a professional surgical journal. Our articles are clinical and surgical articles for the practicing orthopaedist. We are committed to the continuing education of the orthopaedic surgeon. All of our articles are prepared by leading orthopaedic surgeons in the country and overseas, and must be cleared by our editorial board before publication. We do not accept publicity material or releases of any sort, other than clinical books for review, and brief items about continuing education courses, scientific meetings, new products of specific interest to the orthopaedic surgeon. Departments include: Comment & Response, New Products, Imaging Rounds, Tips of the Trade, and Controversies in Orthopaedics.
**Readers:** Specialists in orthopaedic surgery, traumatic surgery, rheumatology, physical medicine and rehabilitation, hand surgery, and head and neck surgery.

23934

## ORTHOPEDICS

6900 Grove Rd.
Thorofare, NJ 08086
Telephone: (609) 848-1000
FAX: (609) 853-5991
Year Established: 1978
Pub. Frequency: m.
Page Size: standard
Subscrip. Rate: $130/yr.
Materials: 02,06,15,29,32,33
Print Process: web offset
Circulation: 26,000
Circulation Type: controlled

**Materials Accepted/Included:** 01-Business news 02-By-line articles 03-Fashion news 04-Food news 05-Freelance copy 06-Letters to editor 07-Real estate news 08-Sports news 09-Travel news 10-Book rev. 11-Movie rev. 12-Music rev. 13-TV rev. 14-Theater rev. 15-Coming events 16-Obituaries 17-Question & answer 18-Social announcements 19-Artwork 20-Cartoons 21-Photos 22-TV listings 23-Audio rec. 24-Video rec. 25-Books 26-Films/film clips 27-Personnel news 28-Press releases 29-New product news/photos 30-Trade lit. 31-Contracts awarded 32-Display adv. 33-Classified adv.

4-248

**Owner(s):**
Slack, Inc.
6900 Grove Rd.
Thorofare, NJ 08086
Telephone: (609) 848-1000
Ownership %: 100
**Management:**
Peter Slack .................................President
Richard N. Roash ........................Publisher
**Editorial:**
Jennifer A. Kilpatrick ...........Executive Editor
Robert D'Ambrosia, M.D. .....................Editor
Donna Carpenter ...............Publishing Director
Betsy Kelton ...................................Sales
**Desc.:** Original and review articles dealing with the following topics in the field of orthopedics: trauma, adult reconstructive, pediatric and rehabilitative. Special features include: Radiologic Case Study, Answer Please, Sports Medicine, Health Policy and Legislation, Trauma Update, Orthopedic Grand Rounds, Arthroplasty Rounds, Letters to the Editor, Calendar of Events, and New Products.
**Readers:** Orthopedic surgeons.

56417
## OTOLARYNGOLOGY-HEAD AND NECK SURGERY
11830 Westline Industrial Dr.
St. Louis, MO 63146
Telephone: (314) 872-8370
FAX: (314) 432-1380
Year Established: 1896
Pub. Frequency: m.
Page Size: standard
Subscrip. Rate: $102/yr. individuals;
    $168/yr. institutions
Circulation: 9,268
Circulation Type: paid
**Owner(s):**
American Academy of Otolaryngology Head & Neck Surgery Foundation
1101 Vermont Ave., N.W.
Washington, DC 20005
Telephone: (202) 289-4607
Ownership %: 100
**Management:**
Carol Trumbold ............................Publisher
Kathy Preston ................Advertising Manager
**Editorial:**
J. Gail Neely, MD ...........................Editor
Kathy Keller ...................Production Director
**Desc.:** Serves the clinical and continuing education needs of specialists in otolaryngology - head and neck surgery.
**Readers:** Otolaryngologists. Official publication of the American Academy of Otolaryngology, Head and Neck Surgery Foundation; the American Academy of Otolaryngic Allergy; and the American Neurotology Society.

25702
## PARAPLEGIA NEWS
2111 E. Highland Ave., Ste. 180
Phoenix, AZ 85016-4702
Telephone: (602) 224-0500
FAX: (602) 224-0507
Year Established: 1947
Pub. Frequency: m.
Page Size: standard
Subscrip. Rate: $15/yr. US; $22/yr. foreign
Freelance Pay: negotiable
Circulation: 27,000
Circulation Type: paid
**Owner(s):**
Paralyzed Veterans Of America, Inc.
801 18th St., N.W., 10th Fl.
Washington, DC 20006
Telephone: (202) 872-1300
Ownership %: 100
**Management:**
Cliff Crase ..................................Publisher
Sherri Shea ...................Advertising Manager

Brenda Davis ...............Circulation Manager
**Editorial:**
Cliff Crase .......................................Editor
Susan Robbins .......................Assistant Editor
Meryl Poticha ...............Production Coordinator
**Desc.:** Published in the interest of disseminating important and useful information to spinal cord injured, and other disabled, and their families and medical professionals. Official organ of the Paralyzed Veterans of America, Inc.

23937
## PATIENT CARE
5 Paragon Dr.
Montvale, NJ 07645-1742
Telephone: (201) 358-7300
FAX: (201) 573-4625
Year Established: 1967
Pub. Frequency: 20/yr.
Page Size: standard
Subscrip. Rate: $79/yr. US; $115/yr. foreign
Materials: 32,33
Print Process: web offset
Circulation: 115,000
Circulation Type: controlled
**Owner(s):**
Medical Economics Publishing Co., Inc.
5 Paragon Dr.
Montvale, NJ 07645
Telephone: (201) 358-7300
Ownership %: 100
**Management:**
David M. Mjolsness ......................Publisher
Julie Betlejewski .............Circulation Manager
Kathy Walker ...............Production Manager
**Editorial:**
Jeffrey H. Forster ...........................Editor
**Desc.:** Helps the primary care physician provide more effective care for his patients in day-to-day practice and on a continuing basis. Covers patient management, problems, symptoms & diseases, as well as improved systems for delivering patient care. Most articles staff written from interviews with several authorities in different regions to ensure objectivity and completeness.
**Readers:** Primary care physicians (GPS, FPS, IMS, DOS, CARDS, and geriatricians).
**Deadline:** ads-1 mo. prior to pub. date

23939
## PEDIATRIC ANNALS
6900 Grove Rd.
Thorofare, NJ 08086
Telephone: (609) 848-1000
Year Established: 1972
Pub. Frequency: m.
Page Size: standard
Subscrip. Rate: $98/yr.
Materials: 15,32,33
Circulation: 32,000
Circulation Type: controlled
**Owner(s):**
Slack, Inc.
6900 Grove Rd.
Thorofare, NJ 08086
Telephone: (609) 848-1000
Ownership %: 100
**Management:**
Peter Slack .................................President
Richard N. Roash ........................Publisher
Les Robeson ...................Circulation Manager
**Editorial:**
Mary L. Jerrell ...............................Editor
Kelly Cusack ..........................Advertising

**Desc.:** Dedicated to the continuing education of the practicing pediatrician and practices in every area of pediatrics. Each issue deals with one subject and covers the physical and clinical treatment of a specific topic. Provides postgraduate information in a symposium-type format, with recognized experts as guest-editors. All articles are original. Departments include: Editorial Director's Page, CME Quiz, classified advertising, index to advertisers, Listed in Index Medicus.

55911
## PEDIATRIC EMERGENCY CARE
428 E. Preston St.
Baltimore, MD 21202
Telephone: (410) 528-4000
FAX: (410) 528-4312
Year Established: 1985
Pub. Frequency: q.
Page Size: standard
Subscrip. Rate: $77/yr. individuals;
    $123/yr. institutions
Circulation: 2,650
Circulation Type: paid
**Owner(s):**
Williams & Wilkins Co.
428 E. Preston St.
Baltimore, MD 21202
Telephone: (410) 528-4312
**Editorial:**
Gary Fleisher ..................................Editor
Stephen Ludwig ...............................Editor
**Desc.:** Valuable clinical information for emergency physicians and pediatricians who care for acutely ill or injured children and adolescents.
**Readers:** Subscribers, including hospital-based pediatricians (70%) and emergency physicians (30%).

66723
## PEDIATRIC MANAGEMENT
110 Summit Ave.
Montvale, NJ 07645
Telephone: (201) 391-9100
FAX: (201) 391-2778
Year Established: 1990
Pub. Frequency: m.
Page Size: standard
Subscrip. Rate: $65/yr. US; $80/yr. foreign non-physicians
Freelance Pay: $800-$1000/2000 wd. article
Circulation: 35,000
Circulation Type: controlled
**Owner(s):**
Dowden Publishing Co.
Ownership %: 100
**Editorial:**
Mark Dowden ...................Editor in Chief
Tom Garry .....................Executive Editor
**Desc.:** Provides pediatricians with specialty-specific information and advice to enable them to better manage their practices, their professional lives, and their delivery of patient care. When discussing delivery of care, the magazine overlays clinical information with nonclinical, helping pediatricians make clinical decisions that take into account socioeconomic factors such as cost, time, patient wishes, potential liability, and personal expertise. The magazine's editors place considerable emphasis on interpreting for readers the newest tends in patient management, payment mechanisms, practice patterns, legislation, and regulation. In so doing, Pediatric Management aims to help pediatricians thrive personally and professionally.
**Readers:** The nation's pediatricians.

53968
## PEDIATRIC NEWS
12230 Wilkins Ave.
Rockville, MD 20852
Telephone: (301) 816-8772
Year Established: 1967
Pub. Frequency: m.
Page Size: tabloid
Subscrip. Rate: $60/yr.
Materials: 06,16,20,28,29
Freelance Pay: varies
Circulation: 35,000
Circulation Type: controlled
**Owner(s):**
International Medical News Group
12230 Wilkins Ave.
Rockville, MD 20852
Telephone: (301) 816-8700
Ownership %: 100
**Management:**
Tom Fowler ................................Publisher
**Editorial:**
Phyllis Schaeffer ..............................Editor
**Desc.:** Provides the practicing pediatrician with timely and relevant news and commentary about clinical developments in the field and about the impact of health care policy on the specialty and the physician's practice.
**Readers:** Pediatricians, pediatric allergists, pediatric cardiologists.
**Deadline:** story-2 mos. prior to pub. date; news-2 mos. prior; photo-2 mos. prior

55904
## PEDIATRIC RESEARCH
428 E. Preston St.
Baltimore, MD 21202
Telephone: (410) 528-4000
FAX: (410) 528-4312
Year Established: 1971
Pub. Frequency: m.
Subscrip. Rate: $105/yr. individuals;
    $180/yr. institutions
Circulation: 2,965
Circulation Type: paid
**Owner(s):**
International Pediatric Research Foundation
**Editorial:**
Dr. Dennis M. Bier ...........................Editor
**Desc.:** Covers the latest advances in the understanding and management of pediatric pulmonary, endocrinological, gastroenterological, and nutrition disorders.
**Readers:** Subscribers, including members of The International Pediatric Research Foundation.

23940
## PEDIATRICS
141 Northwest Point Blvd.
Elk Grove Village, IL 60009-0927
Telephone: (708) 228-5005
FAX: (708) 288-5088
Mailing Address:
    P.O. Box 927
    Elk Grove Village, IL 60007
Year Established: 1948
Pub. Frequency: m.
Page Size: standard
Subscrip. Rate: $95/yr. individuals;
    $160/yr. institutions
Circulation: 54,000
Circulation Type: paid
**Owner(s):**
American Academy of Pediatrics
141 Northwest Point Blvd.
Elk Grove Village, IL 60009-0927
Telephone: (708) 228-5005
Ownership %: 100
**Management:**
Kim Kleinberg ...............Advertising Manager
**Editorial:**
Jerold F. Luccy, M.D. ........................Editor
Joe Largent ..........................Managing Editor

**Materials Accepted/Included:** 01-Business news 02-By-line articles 03-Fashion news 04-Food news 05-Freelance copy 06-Letters to editor 07-Real estate news 08-Sports news 09-Travel news 10-Book rev. 11-Movie rev. 12-Music rev. 13-TV rev. 14-Theater rev. 15-Coming events 16-Obituaries 17-Question & answer 18-Social announcements 19-Artwork 20-Cartoons 21-Photos 22-TV listings 23-Audio rec. 24-Video rec. 25-Books 26-Films/film clips 27-Personnel news 28-Press releases 29-New product news/photos 30-Trade lit. 31-Contracts awarded 32-Display adv. 33-Classified adv.

4-249

Ralph Feigin, M.D. ..................Associate Editor
**Desc.:** Professional publication edited for the pediatrician and those concerned with child care and development. Each issue contains papers on original research and special feature or review articles in the field of pediatrics as broadly defined.
**Readers:** Pediatricians, general practitioners, hospitals, medical libraries, residents, interns & medical students.

66490

## PEPTIDES
660 White Plains Rd.
Tarrytown, NY 10591-5153
Telephone: (914) 524-9200
FAX: (914) 333-2444
Year Established: 1980
Pub. Frequency: bi-m.
Subscrip. Rate: $520/yr.
**Owner(s):**
Pergamon Press, Inc.
Journals Division
660 White Plains Rd.
Tarrytown, NY 10591-5153
Telephone: (914) 524-9200
Ownership %: 100
**Management:**
Rosemarie Fazzolari ................Sales Manager
**Editorial:**
Abba J. Kastin ..........................Editor in Chief
**Desc.:** Original contributions on the chemistry, biochemistry, endocrinology, gastroenterology, physiology and pharmacology of peptides and their neurological, psychological and behavioral effects.

64711

## PERSPECTIVES IN BIOLOGY & MEDICINE
5720 S. Woodlawn Ave.
Chicago, IL 60637
Telephone: (312) 753-3347
FAX: (312) 753-0811
Year Established: 1957
Pub. Frequency: q.
Subscrip. Rate: $35/yr. individuals; $55/yr. institutions; $15/yr. students
Circulation: 2,900
Circulation Type: paid
**Owner(s):**
University of Chicago Press
5720 S. Woodlawn Ave.
Chicago, IL 60637
Telephone: (312) 753-3347
Ownership %: 100
**Editorial:**
Richard L. Landau ....................Editor

23943

## PHILADELPHIA MEDICINE
2100 Spring Garden St.
Philadelphia, PA 19130
Telephone: (215) 564-3059
FAX: (215) 563-3627
Year Established: 1905
Pub. Frequency: m.
Page Size: standard
Subscrip. Rate: $15/yr.
Materials: 32,33
Print Process: offset
Circulation: 4,500
Circulation Type: paid
**Owner(s):**
Philadelphia County Medical Society
2100 Spring Garden St.
Philadelphia, PA 19130
Telephone: (215) 564-3059
FAX: (215) 563-3627
Ownership %: 100
**Editorial:**
William Weiss, M.D. ....................Editor
Anne Hlywiak ..........................Assistant Editor

**Desc.:** Primary purpose is to disseminate medical news of a local nature to the members of the society and to publish contributed articles of an authoritative nature on medical subjects. Departments include: Editorials, Picture Section, News, Announcements of Grants, Gifts, and Awards, and Appointments.
**Readers:** Members of the Philadelphia County Medical Society and subscribers.
**Deadline:** 1 wk. prior to 1st of previous mo.

23944

## PHYSICIAN & SPORTSMEDICINE, THE
4530 W. 77th St., Ste. 350
Minneapolis, MN 55435
Telephone: (612) 835-3222
Year Established: 1973
Pub. Frequency: m.
Page Size: standard
Subscrip. Rate: $46/yr. US; $61/yr. Canada; $100/yr. elsewhere; free to qualified personnel
Freelance Pay: $400-$750
Circulation: 104,000
Circulation Type: paid
**Owner(s):**
McGraw-Hill, Inc.
1221 Ave. of the Americas
New York, NY 10020
Telephone: (212) 512-2000
Ownership %: 100
**Bureau(s):**
Physician & Sportsmedicine, The
4530 W. 77th St.
Edina, MN 55435
Telephone: (612) 835-3222
Contact: Daniel M. Kelley, Vice President
**Management:**
Daniel M. Kelley ..........................Vice President
Bradley J. Moore ..................Business Manager
Marilyn Larson ..................Circulation Manager
**Editorial:**
Richard H. Strauss, MD .............Editor in Chief
Terry Monahan ........................Managing Editor
Glen Griffin, MD .....................Editorial Director
Tina Adamek .....................................Art Director
William Faust ....................Associate Publisher
Stephen Rose .....................Marketing Director
Suzanne Johnson ...............Production Director
**Desc.:** Publishes scientific articles by physicians and others in the field of sports medicine. These generally deal with the problems of identifying (diagnostics) and treating or preventing sports - related illness and injury. In addition, we use staff-written and free-lance-written features, often by-lined, of personalities and situations in which the medical aspects of sports are always prominent; lengths vary from the very brief to 1000 words or more. Publicity material may occasionally stimulate or form the basis for a staff-written article. Departments include: Scientific and News.
**Readers:** Physicians, family and general practitioners internists and osteopathic physicians, allergists, cardiologists, dermatologists, general and orthopedic surgeons, obstetricians and gynecologists, and pediatricians, in patient care, office and hospital based.

23946

## PHYSICIAN'S MANAGEMENT
7500 Old Oak Blvd.
Cleveland, OH 44130
Telephone: (216) 243-8100
FAX: (216) 891-2726
Year Established: 1961
Pub. Frequency: m.
Page Size: standard
Subscrip. Rate: $46/yr.

Circulation: 121,500
Circulation Type: controlled
**Owner(s):**
Advanstar Communications, Inc.
7500 Old Oak Blvd.
Cleveland, OH 44130
Telephone: (216) 826-2839
Ownership %: 100
**Management:**
Bernard J. Rogers ........................President
Ed O'Donnell ..............................Publisher
Debbie Donald ..................Circulation Manager
**Editorial:**
Bruce Millar ......................Executive Editor
Robert Feigenbaum ......................Editor
Bonnie Ling ..................Production Director
Susan Panetta ...............................Sales
Francis Ring ...................................Sales
Karen Horner ..................................Sales
**Desc.:** A business management information service edited to assist the physician with the problems involved in the management of his practice, his personal financial affairs, his relationships with other professionals, and with his community. It includes the latest in management techniques, developments, and philosophies. Articles are prepared by authorities in each particular subject area. Editorial style and graphic presentation are intended to help the physician absorb a maximum amount of information in a minimum amount of reading time.

70366

## PHYSICIAN'S OFFICE LABORATORIES ADVISOR
5 Paragon Dr.
Montvale, NJ 07645-1742
Telephone: (204) 358-7200
FAX: (201) 573-1045
Year Established: 1993
Pub. Frequency: m.
Page Size: tabloid
Circulation: 35,000
**Owner(s):**
Medical Economics Publishing Co., Inc.
5 Paragon Dr.
Montvale, NJ 07645-1742
Telephone: (201) 358-7200
FAX: (201) 573-1045
Ownership %: 100

71255

## PHYSICIAN'S PRACTICE DIGEST
100 S. Charles St.
Baltimore, MD 21201
Telephone: (410) 539-3100
FAX: (410) 539-3188
Pub. Frequency: q.
Page Size: standard
Subscrip. Rate: $32/yr.
Print Process: offset
Circulation: 30,000
Circulation Type: paid
**Owner(s):**
Gerry Hartung & Scott Weber
100 S. Charles St., 13th Fl.
Baltimore, MD 21201
Telephone: (410) 539-3100
Ownership %: 100
**Management:**
Scott Weber ..............................Publisher
**Editorial:**
Bruce Goldfarb ...............................Editor
Jeffrey Furniss ..................Marketing Director

23945

## PHYSICIAN ASSISTANT
105 Raider Blvd.
Belle Mead, NJ 08502
Telephone: (908) 874-8550
FAX: (908) 874-0707
Year Established: 1977
Pub. Frequency: m.

Page Size: standard
Subscrip. Rate: $60/yr.
Freelance Pay: varies
Circulation: 21,000
Circulation Type: controlled
**Owner(s):**
Reed Elsevier Medical Publishers, USA
Core Publishing Division
105 Raider Blvd.
Belle Mead, NJ 08502
Telephone: (908) 874-8550
Ownership %: 100
**Management:**
Robert J. Frattaroli ........................President
David Mittman ...........................Publisher
**Editorial:**
Diana VerNooy ..................Senior Editor
Dave MacDougall ...............................Editor
Susan Lusty ..........................Advertising
**Desc.:** This magazine is the first and oldest in its field to provide clinical material and feature articles of particular interest to the physician assistant.
**Readers:** 18,000 PA's; includes 2,000 students; 85% - primary care, 15% - specialty PA's, surgery, emergency medical, occupational disease.

23948

## PLASTIC & RECONSTRUCTIVE SURGERY
233 N. Michigan Ave., Ste. 1900
Chicago, IL 60601
Telephone: (312) 856-1818
Mailing Address:
   428 E. Preston St.
   Baltimore, MD 21202
Year Established: 1946
Pub. Frequency: 14/yr.
Page Size: standard
Subscrip. Rate: $159/yr. individuals; $189/yr. institutions
Circulation: 13,400
Circulation Type: paid
**Owner(s):**
Amer Soc of Plastic & Reconstructive Surgeons, Inc
233 N. Michigan Ave., Ste.1900
Chicago, IL 60601
Telephone: (312) 856-1818
Ownership %: 100
**Management:**
Don Pfarr ..........................Advertising Manager
**Editorial:**
Robert M. Goldwyn, M.D. ......................Editor
**Desc.:** Any phase of plastic surgery, operative procedures, clinical or laboratory research. Case reports of special import, comprehensive abstract section, and a book review section.
**Readers:** Plastic, general, head & neck, hand & foot surgeons, research institutions.

24513

## PMA
20 N. Wacker Dr., Ste. 1575
Chicago, IL 60606-2903
Telephone: (312) 899-1500
FAX: (312) 899-1259
Year Established: 1957
Pub. Frequency: bi-m.
Page Size: standard
Subscrip. Rate: $30/yr.
Materials: 02,06,10,28,32
Circulation: 17,250
Circulation Type: paid
**Owner(s):**
American Association of Medical Assistants
20 N. Wacker Dr., Ste. 1575
Chicago, IL 60606-2903
Telephone: (312) 899-1500
FAX: (312) 899-1259

**Materials Accepted/Included:** 01-Business news 02-By-line articles 03-Fashion news 04-Food news 05-Freelance copy 06-Letters to editor 07-Real estate news 08-Sports news 09-Travel news 10-Book rev. 11-Movie rev. 12-Music rev. 13-TV rev. 14-Theater rev. 15-Coming events 16-Obituaries 17-Question & answer 18-Social announcements 19-Artwork 20-Cartoons 21-Photos 22-TV listings 23-Audio rec. 24-Video rec. 25-Books 26-Films/film clips 27-Personnel news 28-Press releases 29-New product news/photos 30-Trade lit. 31-Contracts awarded 32-Display adv. 33-Classified adv.

4-250

**Management:**
Donald A. Balasa ..................Executive Director
Lisa McCollum, CMA ..........Circulation Manager
**Editorial:**
Jean M. Lynch ...............................Editor
James Gillespie ....................Editorial Assistant
**Desc.:** Articles and material of interest
to administrative and clinical medical
assistants and other allied health
personnel.
**Readers:** Medical assistants and other
allied health personnel.

## POSTGRADUATE MEDICINE
23949
4530 W. 77th St.
Minneapolis, MN 55435
Telephone: (612) 835-3222
FAX: (612) 835-3460
Year Established: 1947
Pub. Frequency: 16/yr.
Page Size: standard
Subscrip. Rate: $6/issue; $54/yr.
Materials: 06,32
Circulation: 137,800
Circulation Type: controlled
**Owner(s):**
McGraw-Hill, Inc.
1221 Ave. of the Americas
New York, NY 10020
Telephone: (212) 512-4636
Ownership %: 100
**Management:**
Harold W. McGraw, III ........................President
Daniel M. Kelley .....................Vice President
M. James Dougherty ...................Vice President
M. James Dougherty ...........................Publisher
Cindy Waggoner ................Circulation Manager
**Editorial:**
Janet Storhoff ...............................Senior Editor
Mary Hoff .......................................Senior Editor
Patricia Flynn ...........................Managing Editor
Martha Heiberg ......Associate Managing Editor
Glen C. Griffin, M.D. ..............Editorial Director
Bradley J. Moore ...............Dir. of Fin. & Opers.
Tina Adamek .........................Exec. Art Director
Stephen J. Rose ...................Marketing Director
Suzanne Johnson ...............Production Director
**Desc.:** Clinical articles presenting
information that can be applied in daily
practice by physicians in primary care.
**Readers:** Coverage of FP, GP, IM, DO,
CD, GE, EM under age 65, in patient
care, office and hospital based.
**Deadline:** story-1 mo. prior to pub. date

## PRACTICAL GASTROENTEROLOGY
23950
32 Mill Rd.
Westhampton Beach, NY 11978
Telephone: (516) 288-4404
FAX: (516) 288-4435
Year Established: 1977
Pub. Frequency: 12/yr.
Page Size: standard
Subscrip. Rate: $115/yr. US; $160/yr.
foreign
Freelance Pay: negotiable
Circulation: 32,000
Circulation Type: controlled
**Owner(s):**
Shugar Publishing, Inc.
32 Mill Rd.
Westhampton Beach, NY 11978
Telephone: (516) 288-4404
Ownership %: 100
**Management:**
Gerald R. Shugar ...............................President
Gerald R. Shugar ...............................Publisher
**Editorial:**
Andrew Kiburis ........................Managing Editor

**Desc.:** Professional clinical journal
concerned with the diagnosis, therapy,
and management of digestive disorders.
Each issue consists of original
contributions and continuing series on
topics that the practitioner encounters in
daily practice.
**Readers:** Gastroenterologists, colon and
rectal surgeons, internists.

## PRIVATE PRACTICE
23951
10005 S. Pennsylvania, Ste. A
Oklahoma City, OK 73159
Telephone: (405) 696-4466
FAX: (405) 692-4446
Mailing Address:
P.O. Box 890547
Oklahoma City, OK 73189
Year Established: 1968
Pub. Frequency: m.
Page Size: standard
Subscrip. Rate: $36/yr.
Materials: 02,05,06,20,28,32
Freelance Pay: $100-$400
Print Process: web
Circulation: 140,000
Circulation Type: controlled
**Owner(s):**
CCMS Publishing Co., Inc.
P.O. Box 890547
Oklahoma City, OK 73189
Telephone: (405) 692-4466
Ownership %: 100
**Management:**
Francis A. Davis ...............................Publisher
Debra J. Griffith ................Advertising Manager
**Editorial:**
Brian Sherman ....................................Editor
Rocky C. Hails ...............................Art Director
**Desc.:** Journal of political, economic and
social medicine.
**Readers:** Physicians.
**Deadline:** ads-10th of previous mo.

## PROGRESS IN CARDIOVASCULAR DISEASES
23953
Curtis Center
Independence Sq., W.
Philadelphia, PA 19106
Telephone: (215) 238-7807
FAX: (215) 238-6445
Year Established: 1958
Pub. Frequency: bi-m.
Page Size: standard
Subscrip. Rate: $38/issue; $99/yr.
individuals; $158/yr. institutions;
$199/yr. foreign; $47/yr. students, fellow
& residents
Circulation: 3,914
Circulation Type: paid
**Owner(s):**
W.B. Saunders Co.
Curtis Center.
Independence Sq., W.
Philadelphia, PA 19106
Telephone: (215) 238-7800
Ownership %: 100
**Management:**
Steve Gray .........................Circulation Manager
**Editorial:**
Edmund Sonnenblick, M.D. .....................Editor
Mrvica Associates .............................Advertising
Michael Lesch, M.D. .................Associate Editor
Denise Schubert ................Production Director
**Desc.:** Original article relating to
cardiovascular diseases. Each issue is
devoted to one topic and all papers are
by invitation only.
**Readers:** Cardiologists and internists.

## RADIOLOGIC TECHNOLOGY
23955
15000 Central Ave., S. E.
Albuquerque, NM 87123-3917
Telephone: (505) 298-4500
FAX: (505) 298-5063
Year Established: 1927
Pub. Frequency: bi-m.
Page Size: standard
Subscrip. Rate: $29.50/yr. student; $49/yr.
Materials: 01,06,10,25,28,29,30,32,33
Print Process: heat-set web
Circulation: 30,000
Circulation Type: paid
**Owner(s):**
American Society of Radiologic
Technologists
15000 Central Ave., S. E.
Albuquerque, NM 87123-3917
Telephone: (505) 298-4500
FAX: (505) 298-5063
Ownership %: 100
**Management:**
Peggy Green ....................Advertising Manager
**Editorial:**
Ceela McElveny .....................Managing Editor
Nora Tuggle .........................Publication Director
**Desc.:** A technical and organizational
publication aimed at radiologic
technologists. The scientific articles are
usually written by members of the
profession. Stories of new developments
in the field are used in general news
section, and the balance of the journal
is taken up with organizational matters.
**Readers:** Radiologic technologists,
basically members of the American
Society of Radiologic Technologists.
**Deadline:** story-2 mo. prior to pub. date;
news-2 mo.; photo-2 mo.; ads-6 wks.
prior to pub. date

## RADIOLOGY
23956
2021 Spring Rd., Ste. 600
Oak Brook, IL 60521
Telephone: (708) 571-7819
FAX: (708) 571-7837
Year Established: 1918
Pub. Frequency: m.
Page Size: standard
Subscrip. Rate: $195/yr. US; $235/yr.
Canada & Mexico; $240/yr. foreign
Materials: 32,33
Circulation: 36,451
Circulation Type: paid
**Owner(s):**
Radiological Society of North America, Inc.
2021 Spring Rd., Ste. 600
Oak Brook, IL 60521
Telephone: (708) 574-2670
Ownership %: 100
**Management:**
Tom Shimala .....................Advertising Manager
**Editorial:**
Stanley S. Siegelman, M.D. ......................Editor
Harry J. Griffiths ................Book Review Editor
David A. Bluemke, M.D. ...............Deputy Editor
Donna Magid, M.D. ....................Deputy Editor
Andrew J. Dwyer, M.D. ...............Deputy Editor
Del Stauffer ....................................Director
**Desc.:** Professional publication devoted to
clinical radiology and allied sciences.
Carries society news, book reviews,
abstracts of current literature as well as
professional papers and state-of-the-art
reviews.
**Readers:** Clinical radiologists and
physicists.
**Deadline:** ads-20th of mo., 2 mos. prior to
pub. date

## RADIOLOGY & IMAGING LETTER
54058
1351 Titan Way
Brea, CA 92621
Telephone: (714) 738-6400

Year Established: 1981
Pub. Frequency: s-m.
Page Size: standard
Subscrip. Rate: $204/yr. US, Mexico,
Canada; $242/yr. airmail
**Owner(s):**
Quest Publishing Co.
1351 Titan Way
Brea, CA 92621
Telephone: (714) 738-6400
Ownership %: 100
**Management:**
Allan F. Pacela .....................................Publisher
**Editorial:**
Sheldon M. Stern ...........................Senior Editor
Gregory F. Nighswonger ..........Managing Editor
**Desc.:** This newsletter details the latest
and most significant developments in
the fields of radiology, diagnostic
imaging, ultrasound, nuclear medicine
and radiation therapy. Periodic
supplements provide detailed coverage
of significant issues. Information
contacts listed with most articles permit
the reader to delve further into subjects
of particular interest.
**Readers:** Medical imaging professionals,
from physicians to technologists; also
those involved in nuclear medicine,
ultrasound, and radiation therapy.
Manufacturers, investors, and others
interested in high technology.

## REGIONAL ANESTHESIA
61832
227 E. Washington Sq.
Philadelphia, PA 19106
Telephone: (215) 238-4200
Year Established: 1975
Pub. Frequency: bi-m.
Page Size: standard
Subscrip. Rate: $90/yr. individuals;
$117/yr. foreign; $120/yr. institutions;
$147/yr. foreign
Circulation: 8,388
Circulation Type: paid
**Owner(s):**
J.P. Lippincott Co.
227 E. Washington Sq.
Philadelphia, PA 19106
Telephone: (215) 238-4200
Ownership %: 100
**Management:**
J. W. Lippincott ...................................Manager
**Editorial:**
Gerard Ostheimer, M.D. .............Editor in Chief
Jennifer Bass-Gropper ....................Advertising

## REGIONAL IMMUNOLOGY
65618
605 Third Ave.
New York, NY 10158
Telephone: (212) 850-6645
FAX: (212) 850-6088
Pub. Frequency: bi-m.
Page Size: standard
Subscrip. Rate: $260/yr.
Circulation: 2,400
Circulation Type: paid
**Owner(s):**
John Wiley & Sons, Inc.
605 Third Ave.
New York, NY 10158
Ownership %: 100
**Management:**
Susan Heaney .....................................Manager
**Editorial:**
J. Wayne Streilein ......................Editor in Chief

## REPRODUCTIVE TOXICOLOGY
66491
660 White Plains Rd.
Tarrytown, NY 10591-5153
Telephone: (914) 524-9200
FAX: (914) 333-2444
Year Established: 1988

**Materials Accepted/Included:** 01-Business news 02-By-line articles 03-Fashion news 04-Food news 05-Freelance copy 06-Letters to editor 07-Real estate news 08-Sports news 09-Travel news 10-Book rev. 11-Movie rev. 12-Music rev. 13-TV rev. 14-Theater rev. 15-Coming events 16-Obituaries 17-Question & answer 18-Social announcements 19-Artwork 20-Cartoons 21-Photos 22-TV listings 23-Audio rec. 24-Video rec. 25-Books 26-Films/film clips 27-Personnel news 28-Press releases 29-New product news/photos 30-Trade lit. 31-Contracts awarded 32-Display adv. 33-Classified adv.

4-251

Pub. Frequency: bi-m.
Subscrip. Rate: $263/yr.
**Owner(s):**
Pergamon Press, Inc.
Journals Division
660 White Plains Rd.
Tarrytown, NY 10591-5153
Telephone: (914) 524-9200
Ownership %: 100
**Editorial:**
Dr. Anthony R. Scialli ...............................Editor
**Desc.:** Publishes original research on the
   influence of chemical and physical
   agents on reproduction, focusing on the
   application of in vitro, animal and clinical
   research to the practice of clinical
   medicine.

23959
### RESIDENT & STAFF PHYSICIAN
80 Shore Rd.
Port Washington, NY 11050
Telephone: (516) 883-6350
FAX: (516) 883-6609
Year Established: 1955
Pub. Frequency: m.
Page Size: standard
Subscrip. Rate: $55/yr.
Freelance Pay: varies
Circulation: 102,000
Circulation Type: controlled
**Owner(s):**
Romaine Pierson Publishers, Inc.
80 Shore Road
Port Washington, NY 11050
Telephone: (516) 883-6350
Ownership %: 100
**Management:**
William F. Morando ...............................President
Carl Roselle ......................................Publisher
Carl Roselle ...............................Sales Manager
**Editorial:**
Alfred Jay Bollet ......................Editor in Chief
Anne Mattarella .......................Executive Editor
Isabel Tavio ................................Art Director
Ann Hussey ........................Production Director
**Desc.:** Editorial material consists of original
   articles diagnosis and treatment that will
   be of interest to hospital - based
   physicians and residents. Departments
   include: New Products, Editorials, Self -
   Assessment, Quizzes from the Nation's
   Leading Medical Centers, Hospital
   Techniques.
**Readers:** Hospital - based physicians &
   residents Controlled circulation.

23962
### RHODE ISLAND MEDICINE
106 Francis St.
Providence, RI 02903
Telephone: (401) 331-3207
Year Established: 1917
Pub. Frequency: m.
Page Size: standard
Subscrip. Rate: $4/issue; $40/yr.
Freelance Pay: no pay
Circulation: 1,700
Circulation Type: paid
**Owner(s):**
Rhode Island Medical Society
106 Francis St.
Providence, RI 02903
Telephone: (401) 331-3207
Ownership %: 100
**Editorial:**
Stanley M. Aronson, M.D. ..........Editor in Chief
John Sulima ...........................Managing Editor
**Desc.:** Medical articles, news of interest to
   physicians.
**Readers:** Medical Profession of Rhode
   Island, Trustees, Etc., Of Hospitals and
   Specialized Etc. State Medical Societies,
   Libraries/Hospitals in U.S. & Overseas.

23967
### SEXUALLY TRANSMITTED DISEASES
227 E. Washington Sq.
Philadelphia, PA 19106
Telephone: (215) 238-4200
Year Established: 1974
Pub. Frequency: bi-m.
Page Size: standard
Subscrip. Rate: $57/yr. student; $125/yr.
   individual; $173/yr. institution
Circulation: 1,995
Circulation Type: paid
**Owner(s):**
J.B. Lippincott Co.
Telephone: (215) 238-4200

American Venereal Disease Association
2194 Creek Park Rd.
Decatur, GA 30033
Telephone: (215) 238-4200
**Management:**
Marcia Serepy ................................Publisher
Susan Eidson ....................Advertising Manager
Beverly Dietrich ...............Circulation Manager
Joe Baiocco ......................Production Manager
**Editorial:**
Lulius Schachter ...............................Editor
Jill Cameron ........................Marketing Director
Suzann Graff ...........Senior Marketing Manager
**Desc.:** Original articles and brief reports on
   all aspects of the sexually transmitted
   conditions including clinical, diagnostic,
   epidemiologic, therapeutic and sociologic
   aspects. Review articles, editorial
   comment, and news
   and announcements of the AVDA and
   other relevant organizations. Official
   journal of the American Venereal
   Disease Association.

23968
### SKIN & ALLERGY NEWS
12230 Wilkins Ave.
Rockville, MD 20852
Telephone: (301) 816-8700
Year Established: 1970
Pub. Frequency: m.
Page Size: tabloid
Subscrip. Rate: $70/yr.
Materials: 06,15,16,20,21,29,32,33
Freelance Pay: negotiable
Print Process: web offset
Circulation: 17,500
Circulation Type: controlled
**Owner(s):**
Capital Cities-ABC, Inc.
77 W. 66th St.
New York, NY 10023
Ownership %: 100
**Bureau(s):**
International Medical News Group
51 John F. Kennedy Pkwy.
Short Hills, NJ 07078
Telephone: (201) 379-8777
Contact: Thomas A. Fowler, Publisher
**Management:**
Thomas A. Fowler ...............................Publisher
Lorraine Dowd ....................Advertising Manager
**Editorial:**
Richard Camer ...............................Editor
**Desc.:** Provides fast, accurate reports of
   current news, trends, and developments
   in dermatology, allergy and pediatric
   allergy. Signed feature articles by
   recognized leaders covering new
   concepts and techniques in research,
   diagnosis and treatment in the field.
**Readers:** To dermatologists, allergists, and
   pediatric allergists in patient care, and
   residents. Also to office-based GP's and
   FP's who qualify as high prescribers of
   related drug categories and who request
   the publication.

23969
### SOUTH DAKOTA JOURNAL OF MEDICINE
1323 S. Minnesota Ave.
Sioux Falls, SD 57105
Telephone: (605) 336-1965
FAX: (605) 336-0270
Year Established: 1948
Pub. Frequency: m.
Page Size: standard
Subscrip. Rate: $15/yr.
Materials: 06,32,33
Print Process: offset
Circulation: 1,400
Circulation Type: controlled
**Owner(s):**
South Dakota Medical Association
1323 S. Minnesota Ave.
Sioux Falls, SD 57105
Telephone: (605) 336-1965
Ownership %: 100
**Management:**
Robert D. Johnson ...............Business Manager
**Editorial:**
John F. Barlow, M.D. ...........................Editor
Jerome W. Freeman, M.D. .......................Editor
Jeri Spars ...........................Managing Editor
**Desc.:** Contains medical articles on
   research, literature reviews, case
   reports, and feature articles on medical
   economics, and medical honors. Also
   covers local news of interest to
   physicians.
**Readers:** Physicians.
**Deadline:** story-1 mo.; news-1 mo.; photo-
   1 mo.; ads-1 mo.

23970
### SOUTHERN MEDICAL JOURNAL
35 Lakeshore Dr.
Birmingham, AL 35209
Telephone: (205) 945-1840
FAX: (205) 945-1548
Mailing Address:
   P.O. Box 190088
   Birmingham, AL 35219
Year Established: 1906
Pub. Frequency: m.
Page Size: standard
Subscrip. Rate: $4/yr. members; $55/yr.
   nonmembers
Materials: 06,32,33
Print Process: web offset
Circulation: 31,000
Circulation Type: controlled
**Owner(s):**
Southern Medical Association
P.O. Box 190088
Birmingham, AL 35219
Telephone: (205) 945-1840
Ownership %: 100
**Management:**
Anfus M. McBryde, Jr., MD ................President
William J. Ranieri .......Executive Vice President
Cathy Galloway ...................Editorial Production
                                           Manager
**Editorial:**
Rose Marie Hughes Morgan ........Senior Editor
J. Graham Smith, Jr., MD ........................Editor
Wendy Ried ...............................Advertising
Bruce J. Bellande, Ph.D. ........................Director
**Desc.:** Published for members of the
   Southern Medical Association.
   Containing articles such as original
   clinical papers, review articles, medical
   and surgical grand rounds, current
   concepts in diagnosis and therapy and
   case reports.
**Readers:** Physicians and surgeons.
**Deadline:** ads-1st of mo. prior to pub. date

61790
### SPINE
227 E. Washington Sq.
Philadelphia, PA 19106
Telephone: (215) 238-4200
FAX: (215) 238-4227
Year Established: 1976
Pub. Frequency: 16/yr.
Page Size: standard
Subscrip. Rate: $238/yr. individual US;
   $393/yr. individual foreign; $402/yr.
   institution US
Circulation: 10,059
Circulation Type: paid
**Owner(s):**
J.B. Lippincott Co.
227 E. Washington Sq.
Philadelphia, PA 19106
Telephone: (215) 238-4200
Ownership %: 100
**Management:**
Marcia E. Serepy ...............................Publisher
Jennifer Bass-Gropper .....................Advertising
                                           Manager
**Editorial:**
James N. Weinstein ...................Editor in Chief
Suzann Graff ..........Senior Marketing Manager

70431
### STRENGTH & CONDITIONING: THE PROFESSIONAL JOURNAL OF THE NATIONAL STRENGTH & CONDITIONING ASSOCIATION (S&C)
1607 N. Market St.
Champaign, IL 61820
Telephone: (217) 351-5076
FAX: (217) 351-2674
Year Established: 1994
Pub. Frequency: 6/yr.
Page Size: standard
Subscrip. Rate: $72/yr. institutions
Materials: 25,29
Print Process: offset
Circulation: 8,000
Circulation Type: paid
**Owner(s):**
National Strength & Conditioning
   Association
530 Communications Circle
Ste. 204
Colorado Springs, CO 80905
Telephone: (719) 632-6722
FAX: (719) 632-6367
Ownership %: 100
**Management:**
Rainer Martens ...............................Publisher
Peg Goyette ...............................Manager
**Editorial:**
Harvey Newton ...............................Editor
Linda A. Bump ........................Journal Director
**Desc.:** Professional journal devoted to the
   practical application of both research
   findings and experiential knowledge in
   strength and conditioning.
**Readers:** strength and conditioning
   coaches, personal trainers, physical
   educators, athletic trainers, physical
   therapists

67655
### SUBSTANCE ABUSE REPORT
817 Broadway
New York, NY 10003
Telephone: (212) 673-4700
FAX: (212) 475-1790
Year Established: 1970
Pub. Frequency: s-m.
Page Size: standard
Subscrip. Rate: $245/yr.
**Owner(s):**
Business Research Publications, Inc.
817 Broadway,
New York, NY 10003
Telephone: (212) 673-4700
Ownership %: 100

**Materials Accepted/Included:** 01-Business news 02-By-line articles 03-Fashion news 04-Food news 05-Freelance copy 06-Letters to editor 07-Real estate news 08-Sports news 09-Travel news 10-Book rev. 11-Movie rev. 12-Music rev. 13-TV rev. 14-Theater rev. 15-Coming events 16-Obituaries 17-Question & answer 18-Social announcements 19-Artwork 20-Cartoons 21-Photos 22-TV listings 23-Audio rec. 24-Video rec. 25-Books 26-Films/film clips 27-Personnel news 28-Press releases 29-New product news/photos 30-Trade lit. 31-Contracts awarded 32-Display adv. 33-Classified adv.

**Management:**
John Roche ..........................Publisher
**Editorial:**
Alison Knopf ..........................Editor
**Desc.:** Analysis of current developments in the substance abuse treatment field. Contains news and information on treatment programs, medical research and laboratory breakthroughs written for a professional audience.
**Readers:** Professionals in medicine.

56413
**SURGERY**
11830 Westline Industrial Dr.
St. Louis, MO 63146
Telephone: (314) 872-8370
FAX: (314) 432-1380
Year Established: 1937
Pub. Frequency: m.
Page Size: standard
Subscrip. Rate: $89/yr. individual; $175/yr. institution
Circulation: 8,500
Circulation Type: paid
**Owner(s):**
Mosby-Year Book, Inc.
11830 Westline Industrial Dr.
St. Louis, MO 63146
Telephone: (314) 872-8370
Ownership %: 100
**Management:**
Carol Trumbold ..........................Publisher
Kathy Preston ..................Advertising Manager
**Editorial:**
Walter F. Ballinger, M.D. ..........................Editor
George D. Zuidema, M.D. ..........................Editor
Kathy Keller ..........................Production Director
**Desc.:** Edited for practicing surgeons, including those physicians holding positions of authority as department heads or professor in their hospitals and surgical community.
**Readers:** Surgeons, general surgeons and physicians, department heads and professors in hospitals. Official publication of the Society of University Surgeons, Central Surgical Association and American Association of Endocrine Surgeons.

24516
**SURGICAL TECHNOLOGIST, THE**
7108-C S. Alton Way
Englewood, CO 80112-2106
Telephone: (303) 694-9130
Year Established: 1969
Pub. Frequency: m.
Page Size: standard
Subscrip. Rate: $4/copy; $36/yr.
Materials: 01,02,05,06,10,21,23,24,25,28, 29,30,32,33
Freelance Pay: varies
Circulation: 16,600
Circulation Type: paid
**Owner(s):**
Assn. of Surgical Technologists
7108-C S. Alton Way
Englewood, CO 80112
Telephone: (303) 694-9130
Ownership %: 100
**Management:**
Bill Teutsch ..........................Executive Director
**Editorial:**
Sharon Pellowe ..........................Editor
Michelle Armstrong ..................Communications Manager
**Desc.:** Educational features concentrating on the operating room: procedures, supplies, and equipment, and aseptic technique. Also legal/legislative issues affecting the medical profession, professional and association development.

**Readers:** Surgical technologists, instructors, nurses.
**Deadline:** story-15th of mo. 2 mos. prior to pub. date; news-15th of mo. 2 mos. prior; photo-15th of mo. 2 mos. prior; ads-23rd of mo. 2 mos. prior

23974
**SURVEY OF ANESTHESIOLOGY**
428 E. Preston St.
Baltimore, MD 21202
Telephone: (410) 528-4000
FAX: (410) 528-4312
Year Established: 1957
Pub. Frequency: bi-m.
Page Size: standard
Subscrip. Rate: $73/yr. individuals; $95/yr. institutions
Circulation: 3,550
**Owner(s):**
Williams & Wilkins Co.
428 E. Preston St.
Baltimore, MD 21202
Telephone: (301) 528-4000
Ownership %: 100
**Management:**
Gary Walchli ..................Advertising Manager
**Editorial:**
Burnell R. Brown, Jr., M.D.,PhD. ..........Editor
Alma Wills ..........................Director
**Desc.:** Reports the latest developments in the anesthesiology relating to physiology, pharmacology, metabolic work and biochemistry.
**Readers:** Anesthesiologists, nurses, technicians.

24240
**SURVEY OF OPHTHALMOLOGY**
7 Kent St., Ste. 4
Brookline, MA 02146
Telephone: (617) 566-2138
FAX: (617) 566-4019
Year Established: 1956
Pub. Frequency: bi-m.
Page Size: standard
Subscrip. Rate: $60/yr. US; $70/yr. Canada; $100/yr. elsewhere
Circulation: 10,500
Circulation Type: paid
**Owner(s):**
Survey of Ophthalmology, Inc.
7 Kent St., Ste. 4
Brookline, MA 02146
Telephone: (617) 566-2138
Ownership %: 100
**Management:**
Bernard Schwarts ..........................Owner
Ina Orenstein ..................Advertising Manager
David Newcombe ..............Circulation Manager
Dorothy Bell ..................Circulation Manager
**Editorial:**
Bernard Schwartz ..................Editor in Chief
Susan Erickson ..................Managing Editor
Ina Orenstein ..........Associate Managing Editor
**Desc.:** Publishes in-depth reviews in both the clinical and basic sciences of ophthalmology, and succinct abstracts of current international ophthalmic literature accompanied by critical comments. Editorial features include: Current Ophthalmology, Clinical Pathological Reviews, Medicolegalities, Perspectives in Refraction, Therapeutic Reviews, History of Ophthalmology, The Present Scene, Viewpoints, Book Reviews, Editorials.
**Readers:** Ophthalmologists, optometrists and other eye care professionals.

67229
**TEAMREHAB REPORT**
P.O. Box 3640
Culver City, CA 90231-3640
Telephone: (310) 337-9717
FAX: (310) 337-1041
Year Established: 1978

Pub. Frequency: m.
Page Size: standard
Subscrip. Rate: $24/yr.
Materials: 01,02,06,10,28,29,32,33
Circulation: 12,500
Circulation Type: controlled
**Owner(s):**
Miramar Publishing Co.
P.O. Box 3640
Culver City, CA 90231-7881
Telephone: (310) 337-9717
FAX: (310) 337-1041
Ownership %: 100
**Management:**
Andria Segedy ..........................Publisher
Jody Rich ..................Advertising Manager
**Editorial:**
Andria Segedy ..........................Editor
**Readers:** Rehab professionals who work with assistive technology and service delivery for clients who are permanently disabled.
**Deadline:** story-3 mos. prior to pub. date; news-2 mos. prior; photo-3 mos. prior; ads-15th of mo. 2 mos. prior

58798
**TECHNIQUES IN ORTHOPAEDICS**
1185 Ave. of the Americas
New York, NY 10036
Telephone: (212) 930-9500
Year Established: 1986
Pub. Frequency: q.
Page Size: standard
Subscrip. Rate: $115/yr.; $55/yr. for residents
Circulation: 2,200
Circulation Type: paid
**Owner(s):**
Raven Press
1185 Ave. of the Americas
New York, NY 10036
Ownership %: 100
**Editorial:**
Maxine Langwell ..................Managing Editor
**Desc.:** Provides information on the latest orthopaedic procedures as they are devised and used by top orthopaedic surgeons. The approach is technique-oriented, covering operations, manipulations, and instruments being developed and applied in such areas as arthroscopy, arthroplasty, and trauma.
**Readers:** Orthopaedic surgeons.

23975
**TEXAS MEDICINE**
401 W. 15th St.
Austin, TX 78701
Telephone: (512) 370-1300
Year Established: 1905
Pub. Frequency: m.
Page Size: standard
Subscrip. Rate: $20/yr. members; $40/yr. non-members
Circulation: 31,000
**Owner(s):**
Texas Medical Association
401 W. 15th St.
Austin, TX 78701
Telephone: (512) 370-1300
Ownership %: 100
**Management:**
Laurie Reece ..................Advertising Manager
**Editorial:**
Kathryn Trombatore ..................Exec. Editor

**Desc.:** Two chief purposes of journal: (1) Medium of communication for association activities and policies. (2) Educational by publication of scientific and medical articles, list of continuing education courses/meetings for physicians. With few exceptions articles and editorials are written by m.d.'s and staff. News stories and features on topics of medical interest will be considered; No products, new buildings or business reports. Pictures submitted are not generally used. Departments include: Legislative and Legal Columns, Practice Management, Public Health, Science, Medical Economics.
**Readers:** Texas physicians.

58598
**TOPICS IN EMERGENCY MEDICINE**
200 Orchard Ridge Dr.
Gaithersburg, MD 20878
Telephone: (301) 417-7500
FAX: (301) 417-7550
Year Established: 1979
Pub. Frequency: q.
Page Size: standard
Subscrip. Rate: $77/yr. US; $92/yr. foreign
Materials: 06,10,15,32
Print Process: DTP
Circulation: 3,400
Circulation Type: paid
**Owner(s):**
Aspen Publishers, Inc.
200 Orchard Ridge Dr.
Gaithersburg, MD 20878
Telephone: (301) 417-7500
Ownership %: 100
**Management:**
Michael Brown ..........................President
Jane Garwood ..........................Publisher
**Editorial:**
Lenda Hill ..........................Acquist Editor
**Desc.:** Peer-reviewed journal that provides practical, authoritative, clinical information that while medically oriented, encompasses the coordinated responsibilities of emergency physicians, nurses and paramedics.
**Readers:** Emergency physicians, nurses, paramedics

58599
**TOPICS IN GERIATRIC REHABILITATION**
7201 McKinney Cir.
Frederick, MD 21701
Telephone: (301) 698-7100
Mailing Address:
200 Orchard Ridge Dr.
Gaithersburg, MD 20878
Year Established: 1985
Pub. Frequency: q.
Page Size: standard
Subscrip. Rate: $63/yr. US; $76/yr. foreign
Materials: 06,10,32
Print Process: DTP
Circulation: 2,581
Circulation Type: paid
**Owner(s):**
Aspen Publishers, Inc.
200 Orchard Ridge Dr.
Gaithersburg, MD 20878
Telephone: (301) 417-7500
Ownership %: 100
**Management:**
Michael B. Brown ..................Vice President
Michael B. Brown ..........................Publisher
**Editorial:**
Lenda Hill ..................Managing Editor
Stephen M. Zollo ..................Editorial Director
Janis Treacy ..................Marketing Manager
A. Maria R. ..................Production Coordinator
Ernest V. Manzella ........Senior Vice President, Publishing Services

**Materials Accepted/Included:** 01-Business news 02-By-line articles 03-Fashion news 04-Food news 05-Freelance copy 06-Letters to editor 07-Real estate news 08-Sports news 09-Travel news 10-Book rev. 11-Movie rev. 12-Music rev. 13-TV rev. 14-Theater rev. 15-Coming events 16-Obituaries 17-Question & answer 18-Social announcements 19-Artwork 20-Cartoons 21-Photos 22-TV listings 23-Audio rec. 24-Video rec. 25-Books 26-Films/film clips 27-Personnel news 28-Press releases 29-New product news/photos 30-Trade lit. 31-Contracts awarded 32-Display adv. 33-Classified adv.

4-253

Kenneth E. Lawrence ............Vice President, Development
Cynthia Smith ...........Vice President, Marketing
**Desc.:** We are a peer-reviewed journal that presents clinical, basic, and applied research, as well as theoretical information, consolidated into a clinically relevant form and provides a resource for the health care professional practicing in the area of geriatric rehabilitation.
**Readers:** Physical therapists, occupational therapists, rehabilitation nurses, gerontologists.

**TOPICS IN LANGUAGE DISORDERS** 58795
200 Orchard Ridge Dr.
Gaithersburg, MD 20878
Telephone: (301) 417-7500
FAX: (301) 417-7550
Year Established: 1980
Pub. Frequency: q.
Page Size: standard
Subscrip. Rate: $63/yr. US; $76/yr. foreign
Materials: 06,10,15,32
Print Process: DTP
Circulation: 4,550
Circulation Type: paid
**Owner(s):**
Aspen Publishers, Inc.
200 Orchard Ridge Dr.
Gaithersburg, MD 20878
Telephone: (301) 417-7500
Ownership %: 100
**Management:**
Michael B. Brown ........................Vice President
Michael B. Brown ........................Publisher
**Editorial:**
Lenda P. Hill ..........................Managing Editor
Janis Treacy ........................Marketing Manager
A. Maria R. ..................Production Coordinator
Loretta J. Stock .............Senior Developmental Editor
Ernest V. Manzella ........Senior Vice President, Publishing Services
Kenneth E. Lawrence ................Vice President, Development
Cynthia Smith ...........Vice President, Marketing
**Readers:** Professionals who have a clinical interest in language and its disorders.

**TRANSFUSION** 23977
8101 Glenbrook Rd.
Bethesda, MD 20814-2749
Telephone: (301) 907-6977
FAX: (301) 907-6895
Year Established: 1961
Pub. Frequency: 11/yr.
Page Size: standard
Subscrip. Rate: $135/yr. US.; $195/yr. foreign; $335/yr. institutions
Materials: 06,10,15,32,33
Print Process: web
Circulation: 15,375
Circulation Type: controlled & paid
**Owner(s):**
American Assn. of Blood Banks
8101 Glenbrook Rd.
Bethesda, MD 20814-2749
Telephone: (301) 907-6977
FAX: (301) 907-6895
Ownership %: 100
**Management:**
Betsy Colgan ...................Production Manager
**Editorial:**
Jeffrey McCullough, M.D. .........................Editor
Laurel Munk ...................Publication Director
**Desc.:** Pertaining to all fields relating to clinical transfusion, blood storage, etc.
**Readers:** Blood bank and transfusion service persons.

**TRANSPLANTATION** 58592
428 E. Preston St.
Baltimore, MD 21202
Telephone: (410) 528-4000
FAX: (410) 528-4312
Year Established: 1963
Pub. Frequency: m.
Page Size: standard
Subscrip. Rate: $178/yr. individuals; $286/yr. institutions
Circulation: 3,700
Circulation Type: paid
**Owner(s):**
Transplantation Society, The
Ownership %: 100
**Management:**
Don Pfarr ........................Advertising Manager
Alma Wills ........................Manager
**Editorial:**
A. P. Monaco, M.D. ..................Editor
Nancy Collins ......................Marketing Director

**TRANSPLANTATION PROCEEDINGS** 65609
25 Van Zant St.
Norwalk, CT 06855
Telephone: (203) 838-4400
Pub. Frequency: bi-m.
Page Size: standard
Subscrip. Rate: $172/yr. US individual; $225/yr. institutions; $198/yr. Canada; $243/yr. institutions
Circulation: 2,400
Circulation Type: paid
**Owner(s):**
Felix Rapaport, MD
Health Sciences Ctr.
SUNY at Stony Brook
Stony Brook, NY 11793-8192
Telephone: (516) 444-2209
Ownership %: 100
**Management:**
Marketta Pehway ...................Customer Service Manager
Patricia Fogle ....................Production Manager
**Editorial:**
Felix Rapaport, MD ........................Editor
Louise Whelan ........................Managing Editor
Nancy Graves ........................Advertising
Dorthea L. Robinson ..........Circulation Coordinator
Peg Cameron ......................Copy Editor
**Desc.:** Reviews and original reports by experts in current problems in transplantation biology and medicine. It is specifically designed for all those directly or indirectly concerned with this dynamic and expanding field. Has been recognized as the world's most complete reference source for transplantation.
**Readers:** Physicians involved in transplantation including immunologists, nephrologists, surgeons, cardiologists, and pathologists.

**TRAUMA QUARTERLY** 58614
1185 Ave. of the Americas
New York, NY 10036
Telephone: (212) 930-9500
FAX: (212) 869-3495
Year Established: 1984
Pub. Frequency: q.
Page Size: standard
Subscrip. Rate: $89/yr.
Circulation: 2,100
Circulation Type: paid
**Owner(s):**
Wolters Kluwer NV
Netherlands
Ownership %: 100
**Editorial:**
Robert F. Buckman, Jr. ........................Editor

**Readers:** Trauma surgeons and teams.

**ULTRASOUND IN MEDICINE & BIOLOGY** 66492
660 White Plains Rd.
Tarrytown, NY 10591-5153
Telephone: (914) 527-9200
FAX: (914) 333-2444
Year Established: 1974
Pub. Frequency: 9/yr.
Page Size: standard
Subscrip. Rate: $315/yr.
Circulation: 2,000
Circulation Type: paid
**Owner(s):**
Pergamon Press, Inc.
660 White Plains Rd.
Tarrytown, NY 10591-5153
Telephone: (914) 524-9200
Ownership %: 100
**Editorial:**
Denis N. White ........................Editor

**UNIQUE OPPORTUNITIES** 68977
455 S. Fourth Ave., Ste. 817
Louisville, KY 40202
Telephone: (502) 589-8250
FAX: (502) 587-0848
Year Established: 1991
Pub. Frequency: bi-m.
Page Size: standard
Subscrip. Rate: $30/yr.
Materials: 02,05,06,28,32
Freelance Pay: $.50/wd.
Circulation: 80,000
Circulation Type: controlled
**Owner(s):**
UO, Inc.
455 S. Fourth Ave., Ste. 817
Louisville, KY 40202
Telephone: (502) 589-5280
FAX: (502) 587-0848
Ownership %: 100
**Editorial:**
Mollie Vento Hudson ........................Editor
Bett Coffman ........................Assistant Editor
Mel Weinberger ...............Publisher/Advertising
Barbara Barry ...............Publisher/Art Director
**Readers:** Physicians
**Deadline:** ads-30 days prior to pub. date

**UROLOGIC NURSING** 70390
11830 Westline Industrial Dr.
St. Louis, MO 63146
Telephone: (314) 872-8370
FAX: (314) 872-9164
Year Established: 1980
Pub. Frequency: q.
Subscrip. Rate: $8/copy; $33/yr. individuals; $51/yr. institutions
Circulation: 27,520
Circulation Type: free & paid
**Owner(s):**
Mosby-Year Book, Inc.
11830 Westline Industrial Dr.
St. Louis, MO 63146
Telephone: (314) 872-8370
FAX: (314) 872-9164
Ownership %: 100
**Desc.:** Each quarterly issue publishes original, peer-reviewed articles covering clinical, educational, and research topics relevant to the care of patients with urologic problems.
**Readers:** Nurses, technicians, and allied health care professionals in a variety of clinical settings--hospitals, clinics, urology offices, extended- care facilities, and surgical units.

**UROLOGY** 23980
249 W. 17th St.
New York, NY 10011
Telephone: (212) 463-6705
FAX: (212) 463-6700
Year Established: 1973
Pub. Frequency: m.
Page Size: standard
Subscrip. Rate: $75/yr. individuals; $110/yr. institutions
Circulation: 7,300
Circulation Type: paid
**Owner(s):**
Reed Elsevier Medical Publishers, USA
249 W. 17th St.
New York, NY 10011
Telephone: (212) 463-6705
Ownership %: 100
**Management:**
Barry J. Murphy ........................Publisher
Dominic Barone ...............Advertising Manager
**Editorial:**
P. A. Morales ........................Editor
Mary Politano ........................Managing Editor
**Desc.:** Contains contributed original scientific articles and reviews of current interest, preliminary communications, letters to the editor, guest editorials, and book reviews. Aims to provide a forum for recording the pulse beat of clinical urology.
**Readers:** Primarily urologists, residents, hospitals, libraries, and nephrologists.

**UROLOGY TIMES** 23981
7500 Old Oak Blvd.
Cleveland, OH 44130
Telephone: (216) 243-8100
FAX: (216) 891-2726
Year Established: 1973
Pub. Frequency: m.
Page Size: tabloid
Subscrip. Rate: $75/yr. US; $125/yr. Canada; $140/yr. elsewhere
Freelance Pay: $125/news story
Circulation: 9,152
Circulation Type: controlled
**Owner(s):**
Advanstar Communications, Inc.
7500 Old Oak Blvd.
Cleveland, OH 44130
Telephone: (216) 243-8100
Ownership %: 100
**Management:**
Kevin Conlan ........................President
Roger Soderman ........................Publisher
**Editorial:**
Michael Malley ........................Editor in Chief
Nancy Weyhe ........................Managing Editor
Dean Celia ........................Group Editor
A Richard Kendall ........................Medical Editor
**Desc.:** Provides timely, reliable news of urology.
**Readers:** All urologists in patient care and all osteopathic urologists in patient care.

**U.S. MEDICINE** 23982
1155 21st St. N.W., Ste. 505
Washington, DC 20036
Telephone: (202) 463-6000
Year Established: 1964
Pub. Frequency: m.
Page Size: tabloid
Subscrip. Rate: $125/yr.
Materials: 06,15,28,32,33
Freelance Pay: art only
Print Process: web
Circulation: 33,509
Circulation Type: controlled & paid

**Owner(s):**
U.S. Medicine, Inc.
1155 21St. St., NW
Suite 505
Washington, DC 20036
Telephone: (202) 463-6000
Ownership %: 100
**Management:**
Frank M. Best .............................President
Frank M. Best .............................Publisher
William J. Brugeman ........Advertising Manager
George Young ...................Advertising Manager
Ann O. Cannon Finch ..........Business Manager
**Editorial:**
Nancy Tomich ...............................Editor
Ann O. Cannon Finch ..........Circulation Director
**Desc.:** Contains medical news for federal, state and local medical officers (physicians), pharmacists and medical administrators and those in managed care organizations. Contains primarily staff written articles and features, plus signed articles by medical authorities.
**Readers:** Full time physicians, pharmacists and medical administrators employed by government or managed care organizations.

## VA PRACTITIONER
65997
249 W. 17th St.
New York, NY 10011
Telephone: (212) 463-6522
FAX: (212) 463-6404
Year Established: 1884
Pub. Frequency: m.
Subscrip. Rate: $44.95/yr. US; $89.95/yr. foreign
Circulation: 25,854
Circulation Type: paid
**Owner(s):**
Reed Elsevier Medical Publishers, USA
249 W. 17th St.
New York, NY 10011
Telephone: (212) 463-6522
Ownership %: 100
**Editorial:**
Nina Tobier ...............................Editor

## VASCULAR SURGERY
64925
1044 Northern Blvd., Ste. 103
Roslyn, NY 11576
Telephone: (516) 484-6882
FAX: (516) 625-1174
Mailing Address:
708 Glen Cove Ave.
Glen Cove, NY 11545
Year Established: 1967
Pub. Frequency: 9/yr.
Page Size: standard
Subscrip. Rate: $115/yr.
Print Process: offset
Circulation: 3,100
Circulation Type: paid
**Owner(s):**
Westminster Publications, Inc.
708 Glen Cove Ave.
Glen Cove, NY 11545
Telephone: (516) 759-0025
FAX: (516) 759-5524
Ownership %: 100
**Editorial:**
Lawrence Gould, MD ....................Editor
T.R. McLaughlin ...............Production Editor
T.R. McLaughlin ..............Public Affairs Director
**Desc.:** Editorial coverage of original papers relating to any phase of vascular diseases, operative procedures, clinical or laboratory research and case reports. Reports of medical meetings and continuing medical education symposia.

**Readers:** General surgeons, cardivascular surgeons, neurosurgeons, thoracic surgeons, peripheral vascular surgeonss, radiologists, nuclear medicine, cardiologists, medical libraries, hospitals, clinics, research institutions, clinical investigators.

## WESTERN JOURNAL OF MEDICINE
23743
221 Main St.
San Francisco, CA 94105
Telephone: (415) 882-5179
FAX: (415) 882-5116
Year Established: 1902
Pub. Frequency: m.
Page Size: tabloid
Subscrip. Rate: $40/yr.
Materials: 32,33
Freelance Pay: negotiable
Circulation: 45,000
Circulation Type: paid
**Owner(s):**
California Medical Association
221 Main St.
San Francisco, CA 94105
Telephone: (415) 882-5179
Ownership %: 100
**Editorial:**
Dr. Linda Hawes Clever ...................Editor
Diana McAninch ...................Managing Editor
**Desc.:** Contains socioeconomic articles, scientific information, medical education seminars. Future medical meetings and various items of general interest to the medical profession.
**Readers:** Members of the California Medical Association, subscribers other than members. Community Leaders and media representatives.

## WISCONSIN MEDICAL JOURNAL
23985
330 E. Lakeside St.
Madison, WI 53715
Telephone: (608) 257-6781
Mailing Address:
P.O. Box 1109
Madison, WI 53701
Year Established: 1903
Pub. Frequency: m.
Page Size: standard
Subscrip. Rate: $35/yr.
Circulation: 8,000
Circulation Type: controlled
**Owner(s):**
State Medical Society of Wisconsin
P.O. Box 1109
Madison, WI 53701
Telephone: (608) 257-6781
Ownership %: 100
**Management:**
James Paxton ...........................Publisher
Russell King ...................Advertising Manager
Russell King ...................Business Manager
Lynne Bjorgo ...................Circulation Manager
Russell King ...................General Manager
**Editorial:**
R. D. Sautter, M.D. ......................Editor
Russell K. King ..........................Editor
Vicki Meyer ...............Administrative Assistant
Lynne Bjorgo ...............Administrative Assistant
Shari Hamilton ...............Assistant Editor
Russell K. King ........Government Affairs Editor
Lynne Bjorgo ............................Librarian
Thomas L. Adams, ...........Publication Director
CAE

**Desc.:** Primarily scientific articles on all phases of medicine and public health. Most articles in this area are unsolicited. Departments include: Organizational Reports; Personals and News Notes of Wisconsin Physicians; Book Reviews; Organizational News; Medical Meeting Announcements; Socio-Economic/Medicolegal Legislative Articles.
**Readers:** Physicians, medical students, clinic managers, hospitals, governmental agencies, and other professionals.

## WOUND REPAIR & REGENERATION
70391
11830 Westline Industrial Dr.
St. Louis, MO 63146
Telephone: (314) 872-8370
FAX: (314) 872-9164
Year Established: 1993
Pub. Frequency: q.
Subscrip. Rate: $13 newsstand; $25/yr. student; $50/yr. individual; $75/yr. institutional
Circulation: 2,000
Circulation Type: paid
**Owner(s):**
Mosby-Year Book, Inc.
11830 Westline Industrial Dr.
St. Louis, MO 63146
Telephone: (314) 872-8370
FAX: (314) 872-9164
**Desc.:** Current scientific knowledge in wound healing. This international forum offers peer-reviewed scientific and clinical studies covering advances in tissue repair and the clinical management of wounds.
**Deadline:** story-1 mo. prior to pub. date; news-1 mo. prior

## Group 160-Military

## AIR FORCE JOURNAL OF LOGISTICS
69621
501 Ward St., Bldg. 205
Maxwell AFB, AL 36114-3236
Telephone: (205) 416-4087
FAX: (205) 416-4638
Year Established: 1976
Pub. Frequency: q.
Page Size: standard
Subscrip. Rate: $7.50/yr.
Materials: 06,10
Print Process: offset
Circulation: 18,900
Circulation Type: free & paid
**Owner(s):**
US Air Force Logistics Management Agency
501 Ward St., Bldg. 205
Maxwell AFB, Gunter Annex, AL 36114-3236
Telephone: (205) 416-4087
FAX: (205) 416-4638
Ownership %: 100
**Editorial:**
Lt. Col. Bruce A. Newell ...................Editor
**Desc.:** Provides an open forum for the presentation of issues, ideas, research and information of concern to logisticians who plan, acquire, maintain, supply, transport and provide supporting engineering and services for military aerospace forces.
**Deadline:** story-1st mo. of quarter; photo-1st mo. of quarter

## AIR FORCE MAGAZINE
24043
1501 Lee Hwy.
Arlington, VA 22209
Telephone: (703) 247-5800

Year Established: 1942
Pub. Frequency: m.
Page Size: standard
Subscrip. Rate: $25/yr.
Freelance Pay: negotiable
Circulation: 200,000
Circulation Type: paid
**Owner(s):**
Air Force Association
1501 Lee Hwy.
Arlington, VA 22209
Telephone: (703) 247-5800
Ownership %: 100
**Management:**
Monroe W. Hatch Jr. ...................Publisher
**Editorial:**
John T. Correll ...................Editor in Chief
Robert S. Dudney ...................Executive Editor
James W. Canan ...................Senior Editor
Francine Krasowska ...................Managing Editor
Daniel M. Sheehan ...........Assistant Managing Editor
Guy Aceto ...........................Art Director
Shevryl Coombs ...............Associate Art Director
Frank Oliveri ...................Associate Editor
Tamar Mehuron ...................Associate Editor
Monroe W. Hatch Jr. ...........Executive Director
Robert T. Shaughness ........Production Director
**Desc.:** By-line articles covering various phases of Air Force life and operations, technical developments, doctrines, policies and Air Force history, etc. Departments include Aerospace World, Washington Watch and Capitol Hill.
**Readers:** For members of the Air Force, Air Force Association, AFROTC Cadets, Air Force Academy Cadets, and members of the Air Force Reserve and the Air National Guard.

## AIR FORCE TIMES
24044
6883 Commercial Dr.
Springfield, VA 22159-0240
Telephone: (703) 750-8646
FAX: (703) 750-8622
Year Established: 1947
Pub. Frequency: w.
Page Size: tabloid
Subscrip. Rate: $48/yr.
Circulation: 93,000
Circulation Type: paid
**Owner(s):**
Army Times Publishing Co.
6883 Commercial Dr.
Springfield, VA 22159
Telephone: (703) 750-8646
Ownership %: 100
**Management:**
Henry Belber ...........................President
Nat Kornfeld ...................Advertising Manager
**Editorial:**
Tom Breen ...............................Editor
Barbara Harrison ...................Managing Editor
**Desc.:** Covers news of interest to Air Force members and their families.
**Readers:** Active duty, retired, and reserve members.

## AIRPOWER JOURNAL
24045
401 Chennault Circle
Maxwell Air Force Base
Montgomery, AL 36112-6428
Telephone: (205) 953-5322
FAX: (205) 953-6739
Year Established: 1947
Pub. Frequency: q.
Page Size: tabloid
Subscrip. Rate: $13/yr. US; $16.25/yr. foreign
Materials: 02,06,10,19,21
Freelance Pay: up to $500
Circulation: 20,000
Circulation Type: controlled

**Materials Accepted/Included:** 01-Business news 02-By-line articles 03-Fashion news 04-Food news 05-Freelance copy 06-Letters to editor 07-Real estate news 08-Sports news 09-Travel news 10-Book rev. 11-Movie rev. 12-Music rev. 13-TV rev. 14-Theater rev. 15-Coming events 16-Obituaries 17-Question & answer 18-Social announcements 19-Artwork 20-Cartoons 21-Photos 22-TV listings 23-Audio rec. 24-Video rec. 25-Books 26-Films/film clips 27-Personnel news 28-Press releases 29-New product news/photos 30-Trade lit. 31-Contracts awarded 32-Display adv. 33-Classified adv.

4-255

**Owner(s):**
U.S. Air Force
Ownership %: 100
**Editorial:**
Lt. Col. Richard B. Clark ............Editor in Chief
Al B. Lopes ..........................................Editor
Michael A. Gunter ................................Editor
Steven C. Garst ...........................Art Editor
Maj Gwendolyn Fayne .............Associate Editor
Dorothy M. McCluskie ...........Production Editor
**Desc.:** Official U.S. Air Force professional journal of thought and opinion on the application of aerospace power at the operational-level of war. Quarterly editions in Spanish and Portuguese available.
**Readers:** Mostly U.S. & foreign Air Force officers, U.S. government executives, & scholars.

---

**ARMED FORCES JOURNAL INTERNATIONAL**                    24046
2000 L St., N.W., Ste. 520
Washington, DC 20036
Telephone: (202) 296-0450
FAX: (202) 296-5727
Year Established: 1863
Pub. Frequency: m.
Page Size: standard
Subscrip. Rate: $24/yr. US; $85/yr. foreign
Freelance Pay: $100/pg.
Circulation: 50,000
Circulation Type: free
**Owner(s):**
Army and Navy Journal
1414 22nd St., N.W., Ste. 104
Washington, DC 20037
Telephone: (202) 296-0450
Ownership %: 100
**Management:**
Don Fruehling ...............................President
Judy Jaicks McCoy ...............Vice President
Don Fruehling ...............................Publisher
**Editorial:**
John Roos ........................................Editor
Judy Jaicks McCoy ...........Associate Publisher
Benjamin F. Schemmer .................Secretary & Treasurer

**Desc.:** Covers defense legislation, organization, concepts, doctrine, strategy, personnel matters, weapon systems procurement, research and development, and news of the Services in general. Contending points of view on official matters written with professional insight.
**Readers:** Mainly at the lieutenant colonel level and above, all generals & admirals, defense department and military departments, members of Congress, defense industry.

---

**ARMOR**                                                24048
U.S. Army Armor Center
Fort Knox, KY 40121
Telephone: (502) 624-2249
FAX: (502) 942-6219
Mailing Address:
   ATSB - AM
   Fort Knox, KY 40121
Year Established: 1888
Pub. Frequency: bi-m.
Page Size: standard
Subscrip. Rate: $16/yr. members; $20 non-members
Materials: 06,10
Freelance Pay: none
Circulation: 15,000
Circulation Type: free & paid

---

**Owner(s):**
U.S. Army Armor School ATSB - AM
Bldg. 4401
Fort Knox, KY 40121
Telephone: (502) 624-2249
Ownership %: 100
**Editorial:**
Maj. Patrick J. Cooney ...........Editor in Chief
Jon Clemens .........................Managing Editor
**Desc.:** Illustrated professional military journal covering current and future developments, operational techniques, training and management in the field of mobile warfare and its means to include vehicles, tanks, helicopters, weapons, communications, and control systems. Analyzes historical developments. Departments include: Books, Letters, Personnel Note, Bustle Rack.
**Readers:** Armed Forces personnel including active duty, reserve, and retirees; operations research personnel, and historians.

---

**ARMY**                                                 24049
2425 Wilson Blvd.
Arlington, VA 22201
Telephone: (703) 841-4300
FAX: (703) 525-9039
Mailing Address:
   P.O. Box 1560
   Arlington, VA 22201
Year Established: 1904
Pub. Frequency: m.
Page Size: standard
Subscrip. Rate: $25/yr.
Freelance Pay: $.12-.18/wd.
Circulation: 121,000
Circulation Type: paid

**Owner(s):**
Association of the U.S. Army
2425 Wilson Blvd.
Arlington, VA 22201
Telephone: (703) 841-4300
Ownership %: 100

**Editorial:**
Karen Herrel ....................................Editor
Mary Blake French ................Managing Editor
Bruce Hermit ...................Advertising Director
Patty Zukerowski ......................Art Director
Paul W. Bartels .................................Artist
Catherine O'keefe .................Assistant Editor
Eric C. Ludvigsen ................Associate Editor
Charles E. Kirkpatrick .......Book Review Editor
Martin Blumenson .............Contributing Editor
Susan Voliva ......................Editorial Assistant
Connie Nelson ..........................Miscellaneous
Dennis Steele ............................Staff Writer
Eric C. Ludvigsen ..................Technical Editor
**Desc.:** Monthly professional military journal published for members of The Association of the U.S. Army. Covers new developments in weapons, equipment, tactics, techniques, strategy, national and world defense policy, personnel policies, and news of the Army. An unofficial publication serving as a springboard for military discussion.
**Readers:** Officers, non - commissioned officers, enlisted personnel, reservists, civilians, retired military, foreign military, government officials.

---

**ARMY AVIATION**                                        24050
49 Richmondville Ave.
Westport, CT 06880
Telephone: (203) 226-8184
FAX: (203) 222-9863
Year Established: 1953
Pub. Frequency: 10/yr.
Page Size: pocket
Subscrip. Rate: $25/yr.
Circulation: 16,100
Circulation Type: paid
**Owner(s):**
Army Aviation Publications, Inc.
49 Richmondville Ave.
Westport, CT 06880
Telephone: (203) 226-8184
Ownership %: 100
**Management:**
Lynn Coakley ..............................Publisher
Barbara Ross ................Production Manager
**Editorial:**
William R. Harris ..............................Editor
Terrence M. Coakley .........Associate Publisher
Steve Moore ........................Editorial Assistant
Steve Moore ....................Production Assistant
**Desc.:** Operations, logistics, procurements, and personnel in U.S. Army aviation.
**Readers:** Military industry.

---

**ARMY TIMES**                                           24051
6883 Commercial Dr.
Springfield, VA 22159
Telephone: (703) 750-8699
FAX: (703) 750-8622
Year Established: 1940
Pub. Frequency: w.
Page Size: tabloid
Subscrip. Rate: $2/copy; $48/yr.
Circulation: 134,000
Circulation Type: paid
**Owner(s):**
Army Times Publishing Co.
6883 Commercial Dr.
Springfield, VA 22159
Telephone: (703) 750-8699
Ownership %: 100
**Management:**
James Doyle ........................Vice President
William Donnelly .........................Publisher
**Editorial:**
Donna Peterson .................................Editor
Evamarie Socha ...................Managing Editor
Kate Patterson ...................................Photo
**Desc.:** Principal news coverage can be divided into following main groups: Capitol Hill/reports on Congressional activities that affect the serviceman; Pentagon reports and interprets developments in Army promotion, retirement and training policies. Special features on United States weapons are developed regularly. Officer transfers listed weekly; US Posts-information, news from military posts throughout the world. Departments include: Defense, Feature Section, Editorial.
**Readers:** Active, reserve and retired army officers and enlisted, their families.

---

**DEFENSE & FOREIGN AFFAIRS STRATEGIC POLICY**            55919
P.O. Box 19289
Alexandria, VA 22320
Telephone: (703) 684-8455
FAX: (703) 684-7476
Year Established: 1972
Pub. Frequency: m.
Page Size: 4 color photos/art
Subscrip. Rate: $120/yr.
Materials: 01,06,10,19,21,25,27,28,29,31,32
Freelance Pay: $350/major feature
Print Process: offset

---

Circulation: 4,953
Circulation Type: paid
**Owner(s):**
International Media Corp.
P.O. Box 19289
Alexandria, VA 22320
Telephone: (703) 684-8455
FAX: (703) 684-7476
Ownership %: 100
**Management:**
Pamela von Gruber ..........................Publisher
**Editorial:**
Gregory R. Copley .....................Editor in Chief
**Desc.:** Global coverage and analysis of strategic and political-military issues.
**Readers:** Senior government defense and defense industry officals worldwide.
**Deadline:** story-15th of mo. prior to pub. date; news-15th of mo. prior; photo-15th of mo. prior; ads-15th of mo. prior

---

**EXCHANGE & COMMISSARY NEWS**                            24057
825 Old Country Rd.
Westbury, NY 11590
Telephone: (516) 334-3030
FAX: (516) 334-3059
Mailing Address:
   P.O. Box 1500
   Westbury, NY 11590
Year Established: 1962
Pub. Frequency: m.
Page Size: tabloid
Subscrip. Rate: $8/copy; $85/yr.; $40/yr. convention/workshop/directory
Circulation: 11,500
Circulation Type: controlled
**Owner(s):**
Executive Business Media, Inc.
Telephone: (516) 334-3030
Ownership %: 100
**Bureau(s):**
Exchange Commission News
3453 Warner Rd.
Richmond, VA 23225
Telephone: (804) 272-4437
Contact: Pete Allen, Director

German Bureau
Fuersten Berger Strasse 2
6000 Frankfurt a.M. Germany
Telephone: 69-59-5751
Contact: Hazel Guild, Director
**Management:**
Murry Greenwald ...........................President
Fred Schaen .........................Vice President
Joe Haik ...............................Vice President
Helen Scheller .......................Vice President
**Editorial:**
Robert Moran .........................Executive Editor
Bob Platts ...................................Art Director
Thom McMenemy ......................Feature Editor
Janet Patterson ................Production Director
Carol Lamb ........................Production Editor
**Desc.:** Covers in depth the activities of the military resale systems of all five armed services, particularly the exchange and commissary store systems, as well as State Department resale facilities and Veterans' Canteens. The market involves billions of dollars per year, and coverage ranges from Congressional actions which affect the market to Defense Department and industry decisions.
**Readers:** Exchange, commissary store and other government resale officials and military representatives (civilian businessman). Also the Congress and other top government departments.

---

## INTERNATIONAL DEFENSE REVIEW
24059

1340 Braddock Pl., #300
Alexandria, VA 22314
Telephone: (703) 683-3700
FAX: (703) 836-5328
Year Established: 1968
Pub. Frequency: m.
Page Size: standard
Subscrip. Rate: $171/yr.
Freelance Pay: variable
**Owner(s):**
Jane's Information Group
1340 Braddock Pl., #300
Alexandria, VA 22314
Telephone: (703) 683-3700
Ownership %: 100
**Bureau(s):**
Jane's Information Group
17310 Red Hill Ave., Ste. 370
Irvine, CA 92714
Telephone: (714) 724-0868

Jane's Information Group
Sentinel House
163 Brighton Rd., Coulsdon
Surrey CR3 2NX, United Kingdom
Contact: Gowri Sundaram, Editor
**Management:**
Alfred Rolington ...............................President
**Editorial:**
Rupert Pengelley .......................................Editor
**Desc.:** Covers latest worldwide military developments and trends with particular emphasis on significant military equipment advances and procurement requirements of individual military services. Departments include: Weapons/Vehicles/Equipment; International Defense Digest. IDR is available in English, German, French, Spanish.
**Readers:** Ranking officers, executives, armed forces and defense industries of world.

## INTERSERVICE
24075

1133 15th St., N.W., Ste. 640
Washington, DC 20005
Telephone: (202) 466-2520
FAX: (202) 296-4419
Year Established: 1980
Pub. Frequency: q.
Page Size: standard
Subscrip. Rate: $20/yr. institutions & libraries; $25/yr. foreign
Freelance Pay: $250-$1,000
Circulation: 10,000
Circulation Type: controlled
**Owner(s):**
American Logistics Assn.
1133 15th St., N.W., Ste. 640
Washington, DC 20005
Telephone: (202) 466-2520
Ownership %: 100
**Management:**
Richard Murray .......................................President
Lisa Strauss .......................Advertising Manager
**Editorial:**
Herman Marshall ......................................Editor
**Desc.:** Communicates sales & marketing trends, developments and opportunities in military resale market comprising commissaries, exchanges, clubs, other nonappropriated fund activities and military subsistence programs worldwide.
**Readers:** Military resale/troop subsistence professionals, officials and government/industry supply/ military and civilian logisticians, congress, DOD distribution specialists.

## JOURNAL OF MILITARY HISTORY
68992

c/o Marshall Library, Virginia Military Institute
Lexington, VA 24450
Telephone: (703) 464-7468
FAX: (703) 464-5229
Year Established: 1937
Pub. Frequency: q.
Page Size: 6X9
Subscrip. Rate: $25/yr. individuals; $45/yr. institutions
Circulation: 1,800
Circulation Type: paid
**Owner(s):**
Society for Military History
c/o Charles R. Shrader, Exec.
910 Forbes Rd
Carlisle, PA 17013
Telephone: (703) 464-7468
Ownership %: 100
**Editorial:**
Henry S. Bausum ...........................Editor
**Desc.:** Contains scholarly articles and reviews on all aspects of military history.
**Readers:** Historians - Academic, Government - Persons with strong interest in history.

## LEATHERNECK-MAGAZINE OF THE MARINES
24060

Marine Corps Assn., Bldg. 715
PO Box 1775
Quantico, VA 22134-0775
Telephone: (800) 336-0291
FAX: (703) 640-0823
Mailing Address:
Marine Corps Assn. Box 1775
Quantico, VA 22134
Year Established: 1917
Pub. Frequency: m.
Page Size: standard
Subscrip. Rate: $3/yr.; $18.75/yr.
Freelance Pay: negotiable
Circulation: 95,439
Circulation Type: paid
**Owner(s):**
Marine Corps Association
Box 1775
Quantico, VA 22134-0775
Telephone: (703) 640-6161
Ownership %: 100
**Management:**
Walter E. Boomer .............................President
LGen A. Lukeman ..............................Publisher
Gen. A. Lukeman ................Executive Director
Col. W. V. H. White .........Advertising Manager
USMC (Ret.
Terry Traywick .....................Business Manager
Candy M. Kaufman ...........Circulation Manager
Charlene Gibbs ......Customer Service Manager
**Editorial:**
W.V.H. White, USMC (Ret.) .....................Editor
T. P. Bartlett ........................Managing Editor
Judy Brunkow .................................Accountant
Jack Christian .................Advertising Coorinator
Jon Dodd .......................................Art Director
Jason Monroe ........................................Artist
Jason Mohroe ....................Assistant Art Director
Renaldo R. Keen, USMC ........Associate Editor
Donna J. Boots ...........................Book Service
Veronica Vanden Bout ..........Contributing Editor
Guy Anslmo, Jr., USNR ......Contributing Editor
Eric Hammel ........................Contributing Editor
LtCol. Jack Lewis ................Contributing Editor
Mary Ann Preston ..........................Copy Editor
Patricia Everett ....................Editorial Assistant
Ron Lunn ..................................Graphics Editor
Richard E. Stillson ..................Insurance Editor
W.V.H. White ..........................Manuscript Editor
Teri Elie .................................................Photo
Charli Jackson ........................................Photo
Tina Dodd ..............................................Photo
Lura Sdao ...............................................Photo
Cheryl Sherman ......................................Photo

Ron Lunn ...............................Photographer
Ron Lunn ......................Photography Editor
**Desc.:** Designed to educate, inform and entertain, with editorial content consisting of articles with photographs concerning the U.S. Marine Corps. past, present or future. Focus is on history, tradition, schools, training, professionalism, personalities physical fitness, weapons and equipment. Most material is staff produced, but queries from free-lancers are encouraged. Buys first rights, cartoons, poetry are also purchased.
**Readers:** Active duty and former Marines of all ranks. Marine families, friends of the Corps, a large high school, college and library readership. Newsstand distribution monthly. Published in 1917, it is by far the most widely read Marine-Oriented magazine, with a paid circulation three times the size of the next largest.

## MARINE CORPS GAZETTE
24062

715 Broadway St.
Quantico, VA 22134
Telephone: (703) 640-6161
FAX: (703) 640-0823
Mailing Address:
P.O. Box 1775
Quantico, VA 22134
Year Established: 1916
Pub. Frequency: m.
Page Size: standard
Subscrip. Rate: $3 newsstand; $18/yr.; $33.75/2 yrs.; $50/3 yrs.
Materials: 06,10,25,28
Freelance Pay: $200-$400/feature; $50-$100/short article
Print Process: web offset
Circulation: 37,863
Circulation Type: paid
**Owner(s):**
Marine Corps Association
P.O. Box 1775
Quantico, VA 22134
Telephone: (703) 640-6161
Ownership %: 100
**Bureau(s):**
Marine Corps Association
Box 1775
Quantico, VA 22134
Telephone: (703) 640-6161
Contact: Lt. Gen. Anthony Lukeman, Director
**Management:**
Lt. Gen. Anthony Lukeman, ...............Publisher
USMC
**Editorial:**
Col John E Greenwood, USMC Ret ........Editor
Lt. Col Steven M. .................Managing Editor
Crittenden
Robbert T. Foley .......................Assistant Editor
Matthew T. Robinson .............Associate Editor
Richard H. Westbrook ...........Graphic Designer
**Desc.:** Editorial material is restricted to articles of professional value for Marine Corps officers and staff non-commissioned officers. Carries book reviews, information on new products, which can be applied to the national defense effort by the Marine Corps.
**Readers:** Personnel, active and reserve of Marine Corps., primarily officers and noncoms.
**Deadline:** ads-20th of mo. prior to pub. date

## MHQ: THE QUARTERLY JOURNAL OF MILITARY HISTORY
68993

29 W. 38th St.
New York, NY 10018
Telephone: (212) 398-1550
FAX: (212) 840-6790
Year Established: 1988
Pub. Frequency: q.
Subscrip. Rate: $20 newsstand; $60/yr.
US; $70/yr. foreign
Materials: 02,06,10,11,15,19,24,25,28,29
Print Process: web offset
Circulation: 20,000
Circulation Type: paid
**Owner(s):**
American Historical Publications, Inc.
29 W. 38th St.
New York, NY 10018
Telephone: (212) 398-1550
FAX: (212) 840-6790
Ownership %: 100
**Management:**
Byron Hollinshead ...............................Publisher
**Editorial:**
Robert Cowley .............................................Editor
**Desc.:** Examines all aspects of military history from the past to the present.

## MILITARY CHAPLAIN, THE
24063

P.O. Box 42660
Washington, DC 20015
Telephone: (717) 642-6792
FAX: (717) 642-6792
Year Established: 1925
Pub. Frequency: bi-m.
Page Size: standard
Subscrip. Rate: $10/yr.; $25/3 yrs.
Materials: 05,06,10,16,21,32
Freelance Pay: varies
Print Process: offset lithography
Circulation: 1,900
Circulation Type: controlled
**Owner(s):**
Military Chaplains Association
P.O. Box 42660
Washington, DC 20015
Telephone: (717) 642-6792
Ownership %: 100
**Management:**
Lorraine Potter .....................................President
Chaplain G. William .............Executive Director
Dando
Chaplain G. William .........Advertising Manager
Dando
**Editorial:**
Chaplain G. William Dando .....................Editor
**Desc.:** Covers the religious activities in all branches of the armed forces and all religious faiths and related national affairs, includes news of Veterans Administration Chaplain Service.
**Readers:** Chaplains, former chaplains & donors, libraries in the USA & foreign countries, endorsing agencies (Churches).
**Deadline:** story-15th of even # mos. prior to pub. date; news-15th of even # mos. prior; photo-15th of even # mos. prior; ads-15th of even # mos. prior

## MILITARY LIFESTYLE
68994

4800 Montgomery Ln., 7th Fl.
Bethesda, MD 20814-5341
Telephone: (301) 718-7600
FAX: (301) 718-7652
Year Established: 1969
Pub. Frequency: m.
Page Size: 10 7/8 X 8 1/4
Subscrip. Rate: $2.50 newsstand; $18/yr.
Materials: 02,03,04,05,06,07,08,09,21,25, 28,29,32,33
Freelance Pay: varies
Print Process: web offset

Circulation: 100,000
Circulation Type: controlled & paid
**Owner(s):**
Downey Communications, Inc.
4800 Montgomery Ln., 7th Fl.
Bethesda, MD 20814-5341
Telephone: (301) 718-7600
FAX: (301) 718-7652
Ownership %: 100
**Editorial:**
Hope M. Daniels ..............................Editor
**Desc.:** Publishes articles on parenting, health, travel, fashion, food, finances, second careers, real estate, investing and general military interest for active-daty and retired military families.
**Readers:** Active-duty and retired military families aged 25-50. Families are more financially set than younger service members, purchasing homes, traveling, paying college tuitions, planning second careers. They are fitness and health-oriented and involved in leisure and cultural activities.
**Deadline:** story-3-6 mos. prior to pub. date; news-3 mos. prior; photo-1-2 mos. prior; ads-2 mos. prior

**MILITARY MARKET MAGAZINE** 24064
6883 Commercial Dr.
Springfield, VA 22159
Telephone: (703) 750-8676
Year Established: 1950
Pub. Frequency: m.
Page Size: standard
Subscrip. Rate: $60/yr.
Circulation: 12,500
Circulation Type: controlled
**Owner(s):**
Army Times Publishing Co.
6883 Commercial Dr.
Springfield, VA 22159
Telephone: (703) 750-2000
Ownership %: 100
**Management:**
Henry Belber ..................................President
Chana Schlosselberg .......Advertising Manager
**Editorial:**
Larry Moffi ........................................Editor
David Craig ........................Managing Editor
Cathy Riddle ......................Associate Editor
Minda Morgan Caesar ..........Associate Editor
David Craig ....................New Products Editor
**Desc.:** Devoted to buyers and sellers of consumer goods for retail sales in post exchanges and for the buyer and marketer for commissaries, which are the military equivalent of supermarkets. Contains news, financial data, and demographics featuring this market.
**Readers:** Buyers for post exchanges, commissaries, and for their suppliers.

**MILITARY REVIEW** 24065
Truesdell Hall
Ft. Leavenworth, KS 66027-6910
Telephone: (913) 684-5642
FAX: (913) 684-2448
Mailing Address:
USACGSC
Ft. Leavenworth, KS 66027-6910
Year Established: 1922
Pub. Frequency: m.
Page Size: tabloid
Subscrip. Rate: $4 newsstand; $24/yr.
Materials: 06,10
Freelance Pay: $50-$300
Print Process: web
Circulation: 27,000
Circulation Type: controlled & paid

**Owner(s):**
U.S. Army Command & General Staff
College
Bell Hall
Ft. Leavenworth, KS 66027
Telephone: (913) 684-5642
Ownership %: 100
**Editorial:**
John W. Reitz ......................Editor in Chief
Ronald N. Mazzia ................Managing Editor
**Desc.:** Covers a variety of subject areas including strategy, organization, logistics, special warfare, weapons and equipment, communist forces, leadership, professional development and other subjects related to military affairs of current interest and significance.
**Readers:** Military officers and non-commissioned officers, both active duty and retired. Other professionals interested in military affairs worldwide.
**Deadline:** story-6 mos. prior to pub. date; news-6 mos. prior; photo-6 mos. prior

**NATIONAL DEFENSE** 24066
2101 Wilson Blvd., Ste. 400
Arlington, VA 22201
Telephone: (703) 522-1820
Year Established: 1920
Pub. Frequency: 10/yr.
Page Size: 4 color photos/art
Subscrip. Rate: $35/yr.
Freelance Pay: negotiable
Circulation: 35,000
Circulation Type: controlled
**Owner(s):**
American Defense Preparedness Assn.
2101 Wilson Blvd., Ste. 400
Arlington, VA 22201
Telephone: (703) 522-1820
Ownership %: 100
**Management:**
Lawrence F. Skibbie ..........................Publisher
Judi Block ........................Advertising Manager
James McInerny, Jr. ..........Circulation Manager
**Editorial:**
F. Clifton Berry, Jr. ............................Editor
Vincent P. Grimes ................Managing Editor
Steven M. Blackwood ..............Art Director
Julie L. Houk ........................Assistant Editor
Julie L. Houk ....................Book Review Editor
Clinton N. ......................Graphics Coordinator
Julie L. Houk ................New Products Editor
Sandra Meadows ................Production Editor
**Desc.:** National Defense focuses on all facts of the North American industrial base - both military and civil. Every issue contains a mix of features and receiving departments examining and reporting on trends & people in the defense field.
**Readers:** Military Personnel, Industry & Government Officials

**NATIONAL GUARD MAGAZINE** 24067
1 Massachusetts Ave., N.W.
Washington, DC 20001
Telephone: (202) 789-0031
FAX: (202) 782-9358
Year Established: 1947
Pub. Frequency: m.
Page Size: standard
Subscrip. Rate: $20/yr.
Freelance Pay: $300-$500
Circulation: 62,000
Circulation Type: paid
**Owner(s):**
The National Guard Assn. of the United States
1 Massachusetts Ave., N.W.
Washington, DC 20001
Telephone: (202) 789-0031
Ownership %: 100

**Management:**
General John L. Matthews ................President
General Robert S. Enslen ................Publisher
Glenn Ross ....................Advertising Manager
**Editorial:**
Pamela Kane ..................................Editor
**Desc.:** Primarily military subject matter, focused upon Army and Air Force with an Army or Air National Guard frame of reference. Departments include: Posting the Guard (unit activities-supplied by units), Washington Report (Congressional and Pentagon activities of interest to Army National Guard and Air National Guard). People (informative blurbs about Army and Air Guardsmen and their accomplishments). All material is distinctly relevant to military affairs.
**Readers:** Officers and noncommissioned officers of the National Guard.

**NAVAL AFFAIRS MAGAZINE** 24068
125 N. West Street
Alexandria, VA 22314
Telephone: (703) 683-1400
FAX: (703) 549-6610
Year Established: 1924
Pub. Frequency: m.
Page Size: standard
Subscrip. Rate: free to members; $7/yr. to non-members
Circulation: 165,000
Circulation Type: free
**Owner(s):**
Fleet Reserve Association
125 N. West Street
Alexandria, VA 22314
Telephone: (703) 683-1400
Ownership %: 100
**Editorial:**
Patricia J. Williamson ..........................Editor
**Desc.:** Naval Affairs is published for the interests and benefits of the membership of the Fleet Reserve Association and their dependents. Contents cover legislation enacted by Congress; rules, orders, and regulations issued by the Navy, Marine Corps, and Coast Guard departments; benefits extended to veterans and widows of deceased veterans, and items of interest published by other governmental departments affecting active duty personnel and veterans.
**Readers:** Retired, reserve active duty members and their families.

**NAVAL AVIATION NEWS** 24069
901 M St., S.E.
Washington, DC 20374
Telephone: (202) 433-4407
FAX: (202) 433-2343
Mailing Address:
Washington, Navy Yd., Bldg. 157-1
Washington, DC 20374
Year Established: 1917
Pub. Frequency: bi-m.
Page Size: standard
Subscrip. Rate: $7.50/yr.
Circulation: 30,000
Circulation Type: controlled
**Owner(s):**
U.S. Navy Government Publication
Naval Historical Ctr. Bldg. 57
Washington, DC 20374
Telephone: (202) 433-4407
Ownership %: 100
**Editorial:**
Cdr. Russell Jowers ..........................Editor
Sandy Russell ........................Managing Editor
Charles C. Cooney ..................Art Director
JOCS (AW) T.L. Dunn ............Assistant Editor
J01 (SW) Eric S. Sesit ............Assistant Editor
Cdr. Peter Mersky, ......... Book Review Editor
USNR-R

Capt. R. Rausa, USNR .......Contributing Editor
(Ret.)
Harold Andrews ........................Technical Editor

**Desc.:** All stories must deal with naval aviation, regardless of whether it is a feature or just a filler. Uses nothing but naval aviation news dealing with latest developments in aviation, historical material, or human interest stories involving naval aviation personnel.
**Readers:** Navy and Marine Corps personnel and aviation community at large, both military and civilian, educational institutions, government agencies, members of Congress, foreign embassies, NATO staffs, aerospace industry, etc. Also, readers worldwide who subscribe through Superintendent of Documents, GPO.

**NAVAL ENGINEERS JOURNAL** 24070
1452 Duke St.
Alexandria, VA 22314
Telephone: (703) 836-6727
FAX: (703) 836-7491
Year Established: 1889
Pub. Frequency: bi-m.
Page Size: standard
Subscrip. Rate: $65/yr.
Circulation: 90,000
Circulation Type: paid
**Owner(s):**
Amer. Soc. of Naval Eng., Inc.
1452 Duke St.
Alexandria, VA 22314
Telephone: (703) 836-6727
Ownership %: 100
**Management:**
Radm. Lowell J. Holloway, USN ........President
Patrick Sweeney ................Advertising Manager
**Editorial:**
Peter M. Edmondo ..............................Editor
Patrick Sweeney ........................Assistant Editor
Capt. Charles J. Smith, ......Executive Director
USN
Capt. J. E. Grabb, ..............Technical Director
USCG

**Desc.:** Publishes carefully screened original, and preferably previously unpublished, technical papers on naval engineering subjects. Reports developments and technical aspects of new designs, materials and systems used in the naval ship building industry worldwide. Editorial content covers: supporting naval engineers in enhancing the position of their profession, the U.S. Navy, the U.S. Coast Guard, the U.S. Merchant Marine to concern itself with the most pressing and challenging problems of naval engineering both present and future.
**Readers:** Persons whose primary interest is the design operation and maintenance of naval ships and their installed systems.

**NAVY NEWS** 24047
2429 Bowland Pkwy., Ste. 118
Virginia Beach, VA 23454
Telephone: (804) 486-8000
Mailing Address:
P.O. Box 8918
Virginia Beach, VA 23450
Year Established: 1927
Pub. Frequency: w.
Page Size: tabloid
Subscrip. Rate: $29.95/yr.
Circulation: 46,000
Circulation Type: free

**Materials Accepted/Included:** 01-Business news 02-By-line articles 03-Fashion news 04-Food news 05-Freelance copy 06-Letters to editor 07-Real estate news 08-Sports news 09-Travel news 10-Book rev. 11-Movie rev. 12-Music rev. 13-TV rev. 14-Theater rev. 15-Coming events 16-Obituaries 17-Question & answer 18-Social announcements 19-Artwork 20-Cartoons 21-Photos 22-TV listings 23-Audio rec. 24-Video rec. 25-Books 26-Films/film clips 27-Personnel news 28-Press releases 29-New product news/photos 30-Trade lit. 31-Contracts awarded 32-Display adv. 33-Classified adv.

4-258

**Owner(s):**
AD Crafters of Virginia
P.O. Box 8918
Virginia Beach, VA 23450
Telephone: (804) 486-8000
Ownership %: 100
**Management:**
Brian Clark ...........................President
Brian Clark ...........................Publisher
**Editorial:**
Nicole Ain ...............................Editor
Nancy Hoeflaak ...............General Manager
**Desc.:** To serve the best interests of all
service personnel and their families, and
to provide a medium of education for
the better understanding between the
service and civilian communities that we
serve. News of the Armed Services.
Editions: Navy News, Veterans News-
Armed Forces.
**Readers:** Service personnel, their families
and dependents.

24072
## NAVY TIMES
6883 Commercial Dr.
Springfield, VA 22159-0170
Telephone: (703) 750-8636
Year Established: 1951
Pub. Frequency: w.
Page Size: tabloid
Subscrip. Rate: $48/yr.
Materials: 05,06,16,20,21,23,24,25,27,28,
32,33
Freelance Pay: varies
Circulation: 90,000
Circulation Type: paid
**Owner(s):**
Army Times Journal Co.
Springfield, VA 22159-0170
Telephone: (703) 750-8636
Ownership %: 100
**Management:**
Henry Belber ..............................President
Wm. Donnelly ...........Chairman Editorial Board
Nat Kornfeld ...............Advertising Manager
**Editorial:**
Tobias Naegele .............................Editor
Jean Reid Norman ..............Managing Editor
James Doyle ...............Editorial Director
Kate Patterson ...............Photography Editor
**Desc.:** Covers Navy and Congressional
activities that affect servicemen, and
Pentagon news explaining developments
in sea services promotion, retirement
and training policies. Also contains
defense trends reports on weapons
development, strategy and tactics.
**Readers:** Active, reserve and retired
officers and enlisted of Navy, Marines
and Coast Guard and their families.

24073
## OFFICER, THE
One Constitution Ave., N.E.
Washington, DC 20002
Telephone: (202) 479-2200
FAX: (202) 479-0416
Year Established: 1924
Pub. Frequency: m.
Page Size: standard
Subscrip. Rate: $1.15/copy; $12/yr.
Circulation: 115,000
Circulation Type: controlled
**Owner(s):**
Reserve Officers Assn. of the U.S.
One Constitution Ave., N.E.
Washington, DC 20002
Telephone: (202) 479-2200
Ownership %: 100
**Bureau(s):**
Graphic Concepts, Inc. - Advertising Rep.
6110 Executive Blvd., Ste. 810
Rockville, MD 20852
Telephone: (301) 984-7333
Contact: Mr. Robert Silverstein, Advertising

**Management:**
Maj. Gen. Roger Sandler ...................Publisher
**Editorial:**
Col. Norman S Burzynski, USAFR ...........Editor
Carol T. Wilson .........................Assistant Editor
**Desc.:** Contributed articles deal with
national security, training, etc. Reports
on association developments, carries
news items of interest to members.
Edited for those in the military services
both Reserve and Regular. Emphasis
upon legislation & policy affecting the
Reserve Forces of the military services.
News articles, editorials, analytical
pieces treat trends of military. Magazine
also reports substance of association
activities in 55 departments & 1,
000 chapters. Editorial content
includes: legislative reports (40%);
military policy analysis (20%); ROA
activities (30%); other topics (10%).
**Readers:** The President of the U.S., ROA
members, Army, Navy, Marine Corps,
Coast Guard, Congress, Air Force.

68995
## PRE-VUE ENTERTAINMENT MAGAZINE
7825 Fay Ave.
La Jolla, CA 92037
Telephone: (619) 456-5577
FAX: (619) 542-0114
Year Established: 1991
Pub. Frequency: m.
Page Size: 5 5/16 x 8 5/16
Subscrip. Rate: free
Circulation: 300,000
Circulation Type: controlled
**Owner(s):**
National Pre-Vue Network
7825 Fay Ave.
La Jolla, CA 92037
Telephone: (619) 456-5577
Ownership %: 100
**Desc.:** Highlights new music and movies.
**Readers:** Military personnel.

24074
## RETIRED OFFICER MAGAZINE
201 N. Washington St.
Alexandria, VA 22314-2539
Telephone: (703) 549-2311
FAX: (703) 838-8179
Year Established: 1945
Pub. Frequency: m.
Page Size: 8 1/8" X 10 7/8"
Subscrip. Rate: $2/issue; $20/yr.
Materials: 05,06,09,10,16,17,19,21,32,33
Freelance Pay: $75-$1000
Print Process: web offset
Circulation: 410,000
Circulation Type: paid
**Owner(s):**
Retired Officers Association
201 N. Washington St.
Alexandria, VA 22314-2539
Telephone: (703) 838-8179
Ownership %: 100
**Management:**
VADM Thomas J. Kilcline ...................President
L. Col. Brian Hacker .........Advertising Manager
L. Col. Brian Hacker ............Business Manager
**Editorial:**
Col. Charles D. Cooper ...........................Editor
Julia Leigh ...............Managing Editor
Lynne Woychik ...............Art Director
Pam Reed .................Assistant Art Director
Lisa Frantz ...............Assistant Editor
Kris Hagle ...............Associate Editor
Julia Leigh ...............Book Review Editor

**Desc.:** Reports on current events, and
news of legislation and other
developments in military retirement
matters, officers' rights and benefits and
veterans' affairs. Contents also cater to
readers' interest in history and in cultural
business and economic activities,
coverage of business and career
opportunities included. Articles include:
Travel, Home Handicrafts, Recreation,
Woman's Features, Military History,
Current Events, and Financial Planning.
**Readers:** Active, retired and former
officers of the seven uniformed services
and their spouses.

24076
## SEA POWER
2300 Wilson Blvd.
Arlington, VA 22201-3306
Telephone: (703) 528-1775
FAX: (703) 528-2333
Year Established: 1957
Pub. Frequency: m.
Page Size: standard
Subscrip. Rate: $25/yr.
Freelance Pay: $100-$600
Circulation: 75,000
Circulation Type: paid
**Owner(s):**
Navy League of the United States
2300 Wilson Blvd.
Arlington, VA 22201-3308
Telephone: (703) 528-1775
Ownership %: 100
**Management:**
Evan S. Baker .............................President
Evan S. Baker .............................Publisher
A. Wiley Loughran ...........Advertising Manager
Kenneth E. Cornell ...............Business Manager
**Editorial:**
James D. Hessman ...............Editor in Chief
Mary Nolan ...............Managing Editor
A. Wiley Loughran ...............Advertising
John Kaljee ...............Art Director
John Dalrymple ...............Associate Publisher
Patricia L. Howard ...............Production Editor
**Desc.:** Covers issues of national security
and defense from a primarily sea-service
perspective. Also covers present and
future programs and other defense
issues of general national importance,
rather than those of a more historical
nature. It is the strategic approach to
national issues rather than tactical views
that we seek. Articles should look at
subjects of interest to the layman
interested in the U.S. sea services and
national maritime strength: Navy, Marine
Corps, Coast Guard, Merchant Marine,
and Oceanography.
**Readers:** More than 70,000 prominent,
representative U.S. citizens plus senior
civilians and military personnels of Navy
and other sea services, members of
Congress and staff personnels, scholars,
columnists, students, and foreign
circulation among government, military
and industry.

24077
## SHIPMATE
Alumni House
Annapolis, MD 21402
Telephone: (301) 263-4448
FAX: (301) 269-0151
Year Established: 1938
Pub. Frequency: 10/yr.
Page Size: standard
Subscrip. Rate: $25/yr.
Circulation: 30,000

**Owner(s):**
U.S. Naval Academy Alumni Association,
Inc.
Alumni House
Annapolis, MD 21402
Telephone: (301) 263-4469
Ownership %: 100
**Management:**
Admril J. Lung USN-Ret ...................President
Paul Gilbert ...............Advertising Manager
Cordelia Richards ........Classified Adv. Manager
**Editorial:**
Col. J. W. Hammond Jr., USMC ...........Editor
Paul Gilbert ...............Advertising
John F. Coleman ...............Assistant Editor
Cordelia Richards ...............Editorial Assistant
Capt. W. S. Busik ...............Publication Director
Daniel M. Truax ...............Secretary & Treasurer
**Desc.:** All published material is oriented to
the Naval Academy, the Sea Services,
and Naval Academy alumni. Articles are
historical, of current developments,
philosophical or anecdotal. Authors are
by-lined except when staff written, most
are unsolicited but a good many are
commissioned. Usual length is 1,500-4,
000 words. Photos are used extensively,
occasionally as photo essay spreads.
Periodically publish articles on activities
or policies of the Alumni Association.
Departments include: Regular Sections
of Naval Academy Sports, Legislation
Affecting the Navy, General News Items,
A Midshipman's Page, and On Our Tour
Programs.
**Readers:** Officers of the Armed Services.

24081
## TRANSLOG MAGAZINE
5611 Columbia Pike
Falls Church, VA 22041
Telephone: (703) 756-1242
FAX: (703) 756-0492
Year Established: 1968
Pub. Frequency: q.
Page Size: standard
Subscrip. Rate: $5/yr.
Circulation: 26,000
Circulation Type: controlled & paid
**Owner(s):**
Military Traffic Management Command
5611 Columbia Pike
Falls Church, VA 22041
Telephone: (703) 756-1242
Ownership %: 100
**Editorial:**
Corenthia Libby ...........................Editor
**Desc.:** Provides information on policies,
plans, operations and technical
developments in the Department
of Defense transportation field, as well
as in the civilian transportation industry
and federal agencies which impact on
transportation. Publicity material,
including half-tone black and white
photographs, about transportation
services, developments, trends,
products, etc., is frequently used in a
news review section.
**Readers:** Army, Navy, Air Force, Marine,
Coast Guard, transportation personnel
members of the civilian transportation
community and other federal agencies.

24082
## U.S. NAVAL INSTITUTE PROCEEDINGS
U.S. Naval Institute
Annapolis, MD 21402
Telephone: (410) 268-6110
FAX: (410) 269-7940
Mailing Address:
118 Maryland Ave.
Annapolis, MD 21402
Year Established: 1873
Pub. Frequency: m.

---

Materials Accepted/Included: 01-Business news 02-By-line articles 03-Fashion news 04-Food news 05-Freelance copy 06-Letters to editor 07-Real estate news 08-Sports news 09-Travel news 10-Book rev. 11-Movie rev. 12-Music rev. 13-TV rev. 14-Theater rev. 15-Coming events 16-Obituaries 17-Question & answer 18-Social announcements 19-Artwork 20-Cartoons 21-Photos 22-TV listings 23-Audio rec. 24-Video rec. 25-Books 26-Films/film clips 27-Personnel news 28-Press releases 29-New product news/photos 30-Trade lit. 31-Contracts awarded 32-Display adv. 33-Classified adv.

Page Size: standard
Subscrip. Rate: $30/yr. members; $33/yr.
   non-members
Freelance Pay: varies
Circulation: 111,000
Circulation Type: paid
Owner(s):
U.S. Naval Institute
Naval Institute
Annapolis, MD 21402
Telephone: (410) 268-6110
Ownership %: 100
Management:
Capt. James Barber, USN Ret. ..........Publisher
James Burke ....................Advertising Manager
Editorial:
Fred Rainbow ...........................Editor in Chief
John Miller ...........................Managing Editor
Julie Olver ...............................Associate Editor
Fred Schultz ............................Associate Editor
Mac Greeley ............................Associate Editor
Scott Belliveau ........................Associate Editor
Norman Polmar ..............................Columnist
Desc.: Non-technical monthly magazine
   devoted to articles by naval officers,
   distinguished civilians (both American
   and foreign), on naval, maritime, and
   national defense subjects.
Readers: Navy, Marine, Coast Guard and
   other armed civilian executives, foreign
   civilians and officers.

## Group 162-Mining & Minerals
69000
### AMERICAN MINERALOGIST
1130 17th St. N.W., Ste. 330
Washington, DC 02006
Telephone: (202) 775-4344
FAX: (202) 775-0018
Year Established: 1916
Pub. Frequency: bi-m.
Subscrip. Rate: $225/yr. US; $235/yr.
   foreign
Circulation: 4,000
Circulation Type: paid
Owner(s):
Mineralogical Society of America
1130 17th St., N.W. Ste. 330
Washington, DC 20036
Telephone: (202) 775-4344
Ownership %: 100
Editorial:
Steven Bohlen ...................................Editor
Donald Peacor ...................................Editor
Desc.: Publishes the results of original
   scientific research in the general fields
   of mineralogy, crystallography, and
   petrology.

24097
### AMERICAN MINING CONGRESS
   JOURNAL
1920 N St. N.W., Ste. 300
Washington, DC 20036-1662
Telephone: (202) 861-2800
FAX: (202) 861-7535
Year Established: 1915
Pub. Frequency: m.
Page Size: 4 color photos/art
Subscrip. Rate: $40/yr. US
Materials: 01,06,15,16,27,28,29,32
Print Process: web
Circulation: 8,000
Circulation Type: controlled
Owner(s):
American Mining Congress
1920 N Street, N.W. Ste. 300
Washington, DC 20036-1662
Telephone: (202) 861-2800
Ownership %: 100
Management:
John A. Knebel ...................................Publisher
Editorial:
Carol Sheppard .........................Senior Editor
Bob Webster ............................Senior Editor

Joyce Morgan ...................................Editor
Michelle McNichol ..........................Art Director
Erin Doherty ...................................Proofreader
Desc.: A check-list of what's happening
   and what's ahead in Congress and the
   Executive Branch for decision makers in
   the mining industry. Discusses
   related AMC policy and activities as well
   as industry news. Uses personals, new
   equipment and new literature relating to
   industry.
Readers: Operating Company
   Management, Executives, Legislators,
   Regulators
Deadline: story-2nd Fri.; news-3rd Fri.;
   photo-2nd Wed.; ads-1 mo. prior to pub.
   date

24089
### COAL
29 N. Wacker Dr.
Chicago, IL 60606
Telephone: (312) 726-2802
Year Established: 1911
Pub. Frequency: m.
Page Size: standard
Subscrip. Rate: $62.50/yr.
Freelance Pay: negotiable
Circulation: 22,000
Circulation Type: controlled
Owner(s):
Maclean Hunter Publishing Co.
29 N. Wacker Dr.
Chicago, IL 60606
Telephone: (312) 726-2802
Ownership %: 100
Management:
M. Dan Sember ...............................President
Robert Dimond ...............................Publisher
Editorial:
Authur Sanda ...................................Editor
Steve Fiscor ...........................Associate Editor
Patricia A. Olsen ...............Editorial Assistant
Russell Carter ...........................Field Editor
Desc.: Directed to managers and
   engineers at North American coal mines.
   Feature articles cover
   underground mining, surface mining and
   coal processing. Departments include
   news articles written by contributors and
   staff to describe the impact of recent
   events, new regulations and industry
   trends.
Readers: Managers, supervisors and
   engineers of coal producing and
   processing companies in North
   American.

24093
### COAL JOURNAL
P.O. Box 3068
Pikeville, KY 41501
Telephone: (606) 432-0206
FAX: (606) 432-2162
Year Established: 1975
Pub. Frequency: m.
Page Size: tabloid
Subscrip. Rate: $18/yr.; $36/2 yrs.; $45/3
   yrs.
Freelance Pay: $50 up
Circulation: 24,500
Circulation Type: controlled
Owner(s):
Kentucky Coal Journal, Inc.
P.O. Box 3068
Pikeville, KY 41501
Telephone: (606) 432-0206
Ownership %: 100
Management:
Terry May ...................................Publisher
Mary Alice Sosby ..............Circulation Manager
Editorial:
Terry May ...................................Editor
Mike Billiter ...................Account Executive

Desc.: Published for the coal producers of
   Kentucky. It is dedicated to the progress
   and protection of Kentucky's coal
   industry. It concentrates on factors that
   affect the industry at the county, state
   and national levels; technological
   developments that would enhance the
   need for coal, and conversely, laws and
   regulations that would inhibit production;
   coal markets; and the proper use of
   taxes levied on the coal industry. In
   addition, feature articles concern
   technological advances in methods and
   equipment.
Readers: Coal operators, owners,
   engineers, lawyers, etc.
Deadline: news-10th of each mo. prior to
   pub. date; photo-non-camera ready, 10th
   of each mo.; camera ready, 15th of
   each mo.

68996
### COAL PREPARATION
270 Eighth Ave.
New York, NY 10011
Telephone: (212) 206-8900
FAX: (212) 645-2459
Pub. Frequency: 12/yr.
Owner(s):
Gordon & Breach Science Publishers
270 Eight Ave.
New York, NY 10011
Telephone: (212) 206-8900
Ownership %: 100
Editorial:
J. Laskowski ...................................Editor

66785
### COAL WEEK
1221 Ave. of the Americas, 36th Fl.
New York, NY 10020
Telephone: (212) 512-6410
Year Established: 1975
Pub. Frequency: w.
Page Size: standard
Subscrip. Rate: $847/yr. US; $880/yr.
   foreign
Owner(s):
McGraw-Hill, Inc.
1221 Ave. of the Americas
36th Fl.
New York, NY 10020
Ownership %: 100
Editorial:
John K. Higgins ...................................Editor

66710
### COAL WEEK INTERNATIONAL
1221 Ave. of the Americas
New York, NY 10020
Telephone: (212) 512-6410
Year Established: 1979
Pub. Frequency: w.
Subscrip. Rate: $1,056/yr.
Owner(s):
McGraw-Hill, Inc., Energy & Business
   Newsletters
1221 Ave. of the Americas
New York, NY 10020
Telephone: (212) 512-6410
Editorial:
John K. Higgins ...............Chief Editor

24091
### ENGINEERING & MINING
   JOURNAL
29 N. Wacker
Chicago, IL 60606
Telephone: (312) 726-2802
Year Established: 1866
Pub. Frequency: m.
Page Size: standard
Subscrip. Rate: $90/yr.; $135/yr. air mail
Materials: 01,02,06,15,19,21,25,27,28,29,
   30,32,33
Print Process: web offset
Circulation: 24,721

Circulation Type: controlled
Owner(s):
Maclean Hunter Publishing Co.
29 N. Wacker
Chicago, IL 60606
Telephone: (312) 726-2802
Ownership %: 100
Management:
Robert Dimond ...................................Publisher
Editorial:
Robert J. M. Wyllie ...............................Editor
Dick Phelps ...........................Managing Editor
Desc.: E & MJ'S editorial content provides
   operating, technical, and business
   information needed by the executive and
   operations management responsible for
   metal and non-metallic ores and
   minerals production, engineering,
   processing, safety, and maintenance
   world-wide. Articles cover such topics as
   production, exploration, concentrating,
   smelting, refining, and other process
   treatments, and provide updates on
   industry developments and trends,
   technological advances, mineral
   markets, and prices and demand.
Readers: World-wide mineral mining and
   processing. Executive and operations
   management.

24092
### GEOTIMES
4220 King St.
Alexandria, VA 22302-1507
Telephone: (703) 379-2480
FAX: (703) 379-7563
Year Established: 1956
Pub. Frequency: m.
Page Size: standard
Subscrip. Rate: $24.95/yr.
Circulation: 10,000
Circulation Type: paid
Owner(s):
American Geological Institute
4220 King St.
Alexandria, VA 22302
Telephone: (703) 379-2480
Ownership %: 100
Management:
Todd McLaughlin ...............Advertising Manager
Sharon Cisco ...................Circulation Manager
Editorial:
Julie A. Jackson ...................................Editor
Johanna Wertz ............Administrative Assistant
Darcie Simpson ...................Assistant Editor
Lisa Rossbacher ...........................Columnist
Christina Tecson ..................Editorial Assistant
A. Christina Tecson ..............Editorial Assistant
Desc.: News magazine for geologists,
   geophysicists, and other earth scientists.
   It gives accounts of geologic events,
   research projects, scientific meetings,
   developments in education, government
   policies and activities and technical
   publications.
Readers: Geoscientists in industry,
   academics, government; earth science
   educators, and government and industry
   decision makers.

24086
### INTERNATIONAL CALIFORNIA
   MINING JOURNAL
9011 Soquel Dr.
Aptos, CA 95003
Telephone: (408) 662-2899
FAX: (408) 662-3014
Mailing Address:
   P.O. Box 2260
   Aptos, CA 95001
Year Established: 1931
Pub. Frequency: m.
Page Size: standard
Subscrip. Rate: $21.95/yr.
Freelance Pay: $75-$100/3,000 wds.
Circulation: 13,000

Materials Accepted/Included: 01-Business news 02-By-line articles 03-Fashion news 04-Food news 05-Freelance copy 06-Letters to editor 07-Real estate news 08-Sports news 09-Travel news
10-Book rev. 11-Movie rev. 12-Music rev. 13-TV rev. 14-Theater rev. 15-Coming events 16-Obituaries 17-Question & answer 18-Social announcements 19-Artwork 20-Cartoons 21-Photos 22-TV listings
23-Audio rec. 24-Video rec. 25-Books 26-Films/film clips 27-Personnel news 28-Press releases 29-New product news/photos 30-Trade lit. 31-Contracts awarded 32-Display adv. 33-Classified adv.

4-260

Circulation Type: paid
**Owner(s):**
Kenneth & Kathleen Harn
P.O. Box 2260
Aptos, CA 95001
Telephone: (408) 662-2899
Ownership %: 100
**Management:**
Kenneth L. Harn .............................President
Kenneth L. Harn .............................Publisher
Diane Craig .......................Advertising Manager
**Editorial:**
Kenneth L. Harn .............................Editor
**Desc.:** Mining news and features. Articles
on mining methods, technology &
equipment. A financial section on
precious metals and mining
stocks. Current information on laws and
regulations affecting mining. A large
advertising section for the mining
industry.
**Readers:** Miners, prospectors, government
agencies, mining schools and other
related interests.

---

24095

## MINE & QUARRY TRADER
7355 N. Woodland Dr.
Indianapolis, IN 46278
Telephone: (317) 297-5500
FAX: (317) 299-1356
Mailing Address:
P.O. Box 603
Indianapolis, IN 46206-0603
Year Established: 1976
Pub. Frequency: m.
Page Size: standard
Subscrip. Rate: free in US; $60/yr. foreign
or 1st class
Materials: 28,29,30,32,33
Print Process: web
Circulation: 38,203
Circulation Type: controlled & free
**Owner(s):**
Southam Business Communications, Inc.
P.O. Box 603
Indianapolis, IN 46206
Telephone: (317) 297-5500
FAX: (317) 299-1356
Ownership %: 100
**Management:**
Justina Faulkner ...........................Manager
**Desc.:** Editorial content is limited to
federal/state regulation changes, market
statistics, pertinent corporate personnel
changes, and services available to the
mine and quarry industry from outside
sources.
**Readers:** To the US mines and quarry
operations and heavy construction
industry.
**Deadline:** ads-20th of mo. prior to pub.
date

---

68997

## MINERALS & METALLURGICAL PROCESSING
P.O. Box 625002
Littleton, CO 80162-5002
Telephone: (303) 973-9550
FAX: (303) 973-3845
Year Established: 1984
Pub. Frequency: q.
Subscrip. Rate: $70/yr.
Circulation: 900
Circulation Type: paid
**Owner(s):**
Society for Mining, Metallurgy &
Exploration
P.O. Box 625002
Littleton, CO 80162-5002
Telephone: (303) 973-9550
Ownership %: 100
**Management:**
R.L. White .............................Publisher

**Editorial:**
Roshan B. Bhappu .............................Editor

---

69626

## MINERALS ENGINEERING
660 White Plains Rd.
Tarrytown, NY 10591-5153
Telephone: (914) 524-9200
FAX: (914) 333-2444
Year Established: 1988
Pub. Frequency: 12/yr.
**Owner(s):**
Pergamon Press, Inc.
660 White Plains Rd.
Tarrytown, NY 10295-5153
Telephone: (914) 524-9200
Ownership %: 100
**Editorial:**
B.A. Wills .............................Editor
**Desc.:** Reports developments in mineral
processing technology and applications.

---

68998

## MINERIA PAN-AMERICANA
9500 S. Dadeland Blvd., Ste. 950
Miami, FL 33156-2819
Telephone: (305) 670-4818
FAX: (305) 670-4820
Year Established: 1987
Pub. Frequency: q.
Page Size: standard
Subscrip. Rate: $30/yr.
Circulation: 7,239
Circulation Type: paid
**Owner(s):**
Mineria Pan-Americana, Inc.
9300 S. Dadeland Blvd., # 103
Miami, FL 33156
Telephone: (305) 670-4818
Ownership %: 100
**Editorial:**
Juan Escalante .............................Editor
**Desc.:** Covers mining equipment and new
products, international trade fairs,
methods of mining exploration and
production, minerals processing and
transport. Written in Spanish.

---

24098

## MINING ENGINEERING
8307 Shaffer Pkwy.
Littleton, CO 80127
Telephone: (303) 973-9550
FAX: (303) 973-3845
Mailing Address:
P.O. Box 625002
Littleton, CO 80162
Year Established: 1949
Pub. Frequency: m.
Page Size: standard
Subscrip. Rate: $100/yr.
Circulation: 22,000
**Owner(s):**
Soc. for Mining Metallurgy and
Explorations, Inc.
P.O. Box 625002
Littleton, CO 80162
Telephone: (303) 973-9550
Ownership %: 100
**Management:**
Robert Freas .............................President
Lane White .............................Publisher
**Editorial:**
R.L. White .............................Editor
Tim O'Neil .............................Managing Editor
Steve Kral .............................Associate Editor
Gary Howell .............................Executive Director
Robert Young .............................Production Director
**Desc.:** Covers field of mining (metal and
coal), geology, geophysics, and mineral
benefication. By-line feature articles and
pictures deal with all phases
of operating and construction.
Departments include: News, Products,
New Literature and Books, Professional
News, Personals and Mine and Mill
Maintenance.

---

**Readers:** Mining companies & officers,
mine and plant superintendents and
operating staff, engineers, school &
colleges, government agencies.

---

24100

## MINING JOURNAL
151 Railroad Ave.
Greenwich, CT 06830
Telephone: (203) 629-3400
FAX: (203) 629-3755
Year Established: 1835
Pub. Frequency: w.
Page Size: standard
Subscrip. Rate: $340/yr.
Circulation: 5,863
Circulation Type: paid
**Owner(s):**
Mining Journal Ltd.
151 Railroad Ave.
Greenwich, CT 06830
Telephone: (203) 629-3400
Ownership %: 100
**Management:**
Michael West .............................Chairman of Board
Lawrence Williams .............................Vice President
Lawrence Williams .............................Publisher
Michael Bellenger .............................Advertising Manager
Lawrence Williams .............................Business Manager
John U. Farley, Jr. .............................Manager
**Editorial:**
Roger Ellis .............................Editor
Chris Hinde .............................Editorial Director
John Chadwick .............................Editorial Director
Michael Bellenger .............................Advertising
Nathalie Rosin .............................Assistant Editor
Geoff Pearse .............................Consulting Editor
Lawrence Williams .............................Marketing Director
Greg Cosens .............................Production Director
Mike Smith .............................Technical Editor
**Desc.:** A news weekly edited for senior
minerals industry management around
the world.
**Readers:** Senior mining industry
management, worldwide.

---

24101

## MINING MAGAZINE
151 Railroad Ave.
Greenwich, CT 06830
Telephone: (203) 629-3400
FAX: (203) 629-3755
Year Established: 1909
Pub. Frequency: m.
Page Size: standard
Subscrip. Rate: $40/yr. surface; $90/yr.
airmail
Freelance Pay: negotiable
Circulation: 12,601
Circulation Type: paid
**Owner(s):**
Mining Journal Ltd.
151 Railroad Ave.
Greenwich, CT 06830
Telephone: (203) 629-3400
Ownership %: 100
**Management:**
Michael West .............................Chairman of Board
Michael Bellenger .............................Advertising Manager
Lawrence Williams .............................Managing Director
**Editorial:**
Tony Brewis .............................Editor
Alan Kennedy .............................Managing Editor
John Chadwick .............................Editorial Director
Chris Hinde .............................Associate Editor
Nathalie Rosin .............................Associate Editor
Roger Ellis .............................Associate Editor
Geoff Pearse .............................Consulting Editor
John Spooner .............................Director
Lawrence Williams .............................Director
Susan Roberts .............................Production Editor
Mike Smith .............................Technical Editor

---

**Desc.:** Edited for senior mining
management around the world. Handles
longer technical articles, abstracts, and
less urgent news items than the weekly
Mining Journal.
**Readers:** Senior mining technical
management, worldwide.

---

24102

## MINING RECORD
5350 S. Roslyn St., Ste. 390
Englewood, CO 80111
Telephone: (303) 770-6791
Mailing Address:
P.O. Box 37510
Denver, CO 80237
Year Established: 1889
Pub. Frequency: w.
Page Size: tabloid
Subscrip. Rate: $39/yr.
Circulation: 6,000
Circulation Type: paid
**Owner(s):**
The Mining Record Co.
P.O. Box 37510
Denver, CO 80237
Telephone: (303) 770-6791
Ownership %: 100
**Management:**
Don E. Howell .............................President
Howell Publishing Co. .............................Publisher
Nina Morrone .............................Advertising Manager
**Editorial:**
Don E. Howell .............................Executive Editor
**Desc.:** Articles covering mining industry in
the western U.S. and Canada. Uses
news of mining operations, new finds,
leases, meetings, financial news.
**Readers:** Mining company executives,
mine managers, suppliers, government
officials, mining associations, geologists,
engineers & investors.

---

24104

## PAY DIRT
Copper Queen Plaza
Bisbee, AZ 85603
Telephone: (602) 432-2244
FAX: (602) 432-2247
Mailing Address:
P.O. Drawer 48
Bisbee, AZ 85603
Year Established: 1938
Pub. Frequency: m.
Page Size: standard
Subscrip. Rate: $25/yr.
Circulation: 5,000
Circulation Type: paid
**Owner(s):**
Copper Queen Publishing Co.
P.O. Drawer 48
Bisbee, AZ 85603
Telephone: (602) 432-2244
Ownership %: 100
**Management:**
William C. Epler .............................President
William C. Epler .............................Publisher
Caryl Larkins .............................Advertising Manager
Caryl Larkins .............................Circulation Manager
**Editorial:**
William C. Epler .............................Editor
**Desc.:** Informs readers on current mining
developments, changes in policies by
state and federal agencies affecting
mining.
**Readers:** Management and technical
people in the hard rock mining industry.

---

68999

## STONE REVIEW
1415 Elliot Pl., N.W.
Washington, DC 20007-2506
Telephone: (202) 342-1100
FAX: (202) 342-0702
Year Established: 1985
Pub. Frequency: bi-m.

---

Materials Accepted/Included: 01-Business news 02-By-line articles 03-Fashion news 04-Food news 05-Freelance copy 06-Letters to editor 07-Real estate news 08-Sports news 09-Travel news 10-Book rev. 11-Movie rev. 12-Music rev. 13-TV rev. 14-Theater rev. 15-Coming events 16-Obituaries 17-Question & answer 18-Social announcements 19-Artwork 20-Cartoons 21-Photos 22-TV listings 23-Audio rec. 24-Video rec. 25-Books 26-Films/film clips 27-Personnel news 28-Press releases 29-New product news/photos 30-Trade lit. 31-Contracts awarded 32-Display adv. 33-Classified adv.

Page Size: standard
Subscrip. Rate: $48/yr.
Materials: 02,05,06,32
Print Process: offset
Circulation: 4,000
Circulation Type: paid
**Owner(s):**
National Stone Association
1415 Elliot Pl., N.W.
Washington, DC 20007-2506
Telephone: (202) 345-1100
FAX: (202) 342-0702
Ownership %: 100
**Editorial:**
Frank E. Atlee .............................Editor
**Desc.:** Provides a communication forum for
the crushed stone industry and to
facilitate the exchange of information on
industry technology, trends,
developments, and concerns. Opinions
expressed within by authors other than
the staff do not necessarily reflect the
official positions or policies of the
association.
**Readers:** Mid-upper management at
member companies (stone produceers
and equipment/service providers);
industry-related federal and state
agencies and officials.

24106

**UNITED MINE WORKERS
JOURNAL**
900 15th St. N.W.
Washington, DC 20005
Telephone: (202) 842-7200
FAX: (202) 842-7227
Pub. Frequency: m.
Page Size: pg: 47 picas x 62 picas; col: 15
picas; photo: yes
Subscrip. Rate: $10/yr. non-members;
$25/yr. institution; $100/yr. corporations
Circulation: 200,000
**Owner(s):**
United Mine Workers Journal
Washington, DC 20005
Ownership %: 100
**Editorial:**
Tom Johnson ...........................Managing Editor
Holly Syrrakos .........................Art Director
Dorothy Hinnah .......................Miscellaneous
Thelma Blount ...................Research Assistant
**Desc.:** Stories on coal miners, coal mining,
mine health and safety, Appalachian as
a region, labor unions and their fight for
social progress, governmental agencies
affecting miners such as Bureau of
Mines, Appalachian Regional
Commission.
**Readers:** Coal miners, union officials,
media people and libraries.

## Group 164-Motorcycles & Bicycles

24117

**AMERICAN BICYCLIST**
400 Skokie Blvd., Ste. 400
Northbrook, IL 60062
Telephone: (708) 291-1117
FAX: (708) 559-4444
Year Established: 1879
Pub. Frequency: m.
Page Size: standard
Subscrip. Rate: $40/yr.
Circulation: 11,025
Circulation Type: controlled
**Owner(s):**
Willow Publishing Company
400 Skokie Blvd., Ste. 395
Northbrook, IL 60062
Telephone: (708) 298-1117
FAX: (708) 559-4444
Ownership %: 100
**Management:**
John William Roberts ...........................Publisher

**Editorial:**
Ed McKinley .............................Editor
**Desc.:** Features include stories on
successful deals, product orientated
stories, trends and industry movements.
Departments include: product reviews,
retailing operations, industry news,
historical pieces, literature reviews and
calendar of events.
**Readers:** Bicycle wholesale distributors,
retailers, manufacturers, importers,
buyers for chains.

24119

**BICYCLE BUSINESS JOURNAL**
1904 Wenneca
Ft. Worth, TX 76102
Telephone: (817) 870-0341
FAX: (817) 332-1619
Mailing Address:
P.O. Box 1570
Ft. Worth, TX 76101
Year Established: 1947
Pub. Frequency: m.
Page Size: standard
Subscrip. Rate: $14/yr.
Freelance Pay: $37.50/article
Circulation: 10,000
Circulation Type: controlled
**Owner(s):**
Quinn Publications
P.O. Box 1570
Ft. Worth, TX 76101
Telephone: (817) 870-0341
Ownership %: 100
**Management:**
Bill Quinn ...........................Publisher
Rix Quinn ...........................Publisher
**Editorial:**
Rix Quinn ...........................Editor
Lynn Quinn ...................Associate Editor
**Desc.:** Stories dealing with a single
outstanding feature of sales or service
of an independently owned store that
services what it sells. 250-300 words
sufficient. Only one photo desired, must
be vertical, to feature subject matter of
story.
**Readers:** Dealers who service what they
sell, bike distributors and manufacturers.

61583

**BICYCLE U.S.A.**
190 W. Ostend St., Ste. 120
Baltimore, MD 21230-3755
Telephone: (410) 539-3399
FAX: (410) 539-3496
Year Established: 1965
Pub. Frequency: 8/yr.
Page Size: standard
Subscrip. Rate: $25/yr. (League of
American Wheelmen membership)
Freelance Pay: membership
Circulation: 27,762
Circulation Type: paid
**Owner(s):**
League of American Bicyclists
190 W. Ostend St., Ste. 120
Baltimore, MD 21230-3755
Telephone: (410) 539-3399
Ownership %: 100
**Editorial:**
John W. Duvall ...........................Editor
**Desc.:** Published by the League of
American Bicyclists, founded in 1880 as
the League of American Wheelmen, the
National Organization of Bicyclists.
Membership magazine serving the
needs of today's bicyclist. It focuses on
advocacy, eduation, fitness, and the
enjoyment of bicycling.
**Readers:** Recreational bicyclists, advocacy
oriented cyclists.

24123

**DEALERNEWS**
201 E. Sendpointe Ave.
Ste. 600
Santa Ana, CA 72707-5761
Telephone: (714) 513-8400
FAX: (714) 513-8414
Year Established: 1965
Pub. Frequency: 14/yr.
Page Size: standard
Subscrip. Rate: $25/yr. US; $70/yr. foreign
Freelance Pay: negotiable
Circulation: 15,000
Circulation Type: controlled
**Owner(s):**
Advanstar Communications, Inc.
201 E. Sandpointe Ave.
Ste. 600
Santa Ana, CA 92707-5761
Telephone: (714) 513-8400
FAX: (714) 513-8414
Ownership %: 100
**Management:**
John F. Murphy, Jr. ...........................Publisher
Kristina Adamek ...............Production Manager
John McCarthy ...........................Sales Manager
**Editorial:**
Mr. Robin Hartfiel ...........................Editor
Wendy F. Black .......................Associate Editor
**Desc.:** Articles on merchandising, finance,
business procedures, tax advice,
legislation, advertising, M/C industry
news, and other subjects of interest to
M/C dealers are used. All articles
should be between 500-1,500 words,
and sent on speculation. Photos are
always asked for. Departments include:
R. L. Polk Registration Statistics,
Motorcycle Industry News, New Product
Showcase, Dealer Profile Interviews,
Regional Reports, Dealer Management
Techniques, Reviews, and others.
**Readers:** Motorcycle and aftermarket
dealers, distributors, manufacturers and
allied trades, and government officials.

61595

**MOTORCYCLE INDUSTRY
MAGAZINE**
31194 La Baya, Ste. 200
Thousand Oaks, CA 91362
Telephone: (818) 991-2070
FAX: (818) 991-9427
Mailing Address:
P.O. Box 2087
Thousand Oaks, CA 91358
Year Established: 1980
Pub. Frequency: m.
Page Size: tabloid
Subscrip. Rate: free US; $120/yr foreign
Materials: 01,02,06,10,11,15,21,27,28,29,
32,33
Freelance Pay: negotiable
Print Process: web offset
Circulation: 15,000
Circulation Type: controlled
**Owner(s):**
Industry Shopper Publ., Inc.
**Management:**
Rick Campbell ...........................Publisher
**Editorial:**
Loren Orr ...........................Associate Editor
**Readers:** Retailers, wholesalers and
manufactures of after market motorcycle
and related products and services.
**Deadline:** story-Last Fri. of 2nd mo. prior
to pub. date; news-Last Fri. of 2nd mo.
prior; photo-Last Fri. of 2nd mo. prior;
ads-1st Fri. of mo. prior to pub. date

24124

**MOTORCYCLE PRODUCT NEWS**
6633 Odessa Ave.
Van Nuys, CA 91406
Telephone: (818) 997-0644
FAX: (818) 997-1058

Mailing Address:
P.O. Box 2338
Van Nuys, CA 91404
Year Established: 1974
Pub. Frequency: m.
Page Size: standard
Subscrip. Rate: $18/yr.
Freelance Pay: varies
Circulation: 12,951
Circulation Type: controlled
**Owner(s):**
MH West, Inc.
6633 Odessa Ave.
Van Nuys, CA 91406
Telephone: (818) 997-0644
Ownership %: 100
**Management:**
Timothy Jenkins ...........................Publisher
**Editorial:**
Bob Jackson ...........................Editor
**Desc.:** Monthly product & information
magazine edited exclusively for the
wholesale motorcycle trade &
motorcycle dealers. Plus the annual
Product News Trade Directory, available
each January.
**Readers:** Motorcycle industry dealers and
retailers, distributors, manufacturers,
importers & exporters and related
insurance, finance & governmental
offices.

## Group 168-Music & Music Trades

58548

**AMERICAN MUSIC**
54 E. Gregory Dr.
Champaign, IL 61820
Telephone: (217) 333-8935
Year Established: 1983
Pub. Frequency: q.
Subscrip. Rate: $30/yr. individual US;
$42/yr. insitution; $37/yr. individual
foreign; $49/yr. institution
Circulation: 1,650
Circulation Type: paid
**Owner(s):**
University of Illinois Press
54 E. Gregory Dr.
Champaign, IL 61820
Telephone: (217) 333-0950
**Management:**
Carole S. Appel ...........................Manager
**Editorial:**
Wayne Shirley ...........................Editor
Samuel Brylowski ...............Editorial Associate
Gail Sonnemann ...................Editorial Associate
**Desc.:** American Music is the only
publication devoted exclusively to all
aspects of American music and music in
America. Published in cooperation with
the Sonneck Society, it presents articles
on composers, performers, publishers,
institutions, events and the music
industry as well as book and record
reviews.
**Readers:** Scholars and laypersons
interested in music and music history.

24126

**AMERICAN MUSIC TEACHER, THE**
441 Vine St.
Ste. 505
Cincinnati, OH 45202-2814
Telephone: (513) 421-1420
FAX: (513) 421-2503
Year Established: 1951
Pub. Frequency: 6/yr.
Page Size: standard
Subscrip. Rate: $16/yr.
Materials: 10,12,24,25,28,29,32
Print Process: web
Circulation: 25,000
Circulation Type: paid

**Owner(s):**
Music Teachers National Association
441 Vine St.
Ste. 505
Cincinnati, OH 45202-2814
Telephone: (513) 421-1420
Ownership %: 100
**Management:**
Shirley A. Raut ............................Publisher
Stacy Clark ..................Advertising Manager
**Editorial:**
Michael Oxley ................................Editor
**Desc.:** Publishes articles of musical
interest in research, performance,
practice and pedagogy.
**Readers:** Musicians in teaching, research,
administrations.

## AMERICAN ORGANIST, THE
24127
475 Riverside Dr., Ste. 1260
New York, NY 10115
Telephone: (212) 870-2310
FAX: (212) 870-2163
Year Established: 1967
Pub. Frequency: m.
Page Size: standard
Subscrip. Rate: $42/yr.
Circulation: 25,000
Circulation Type: controlled
**Owner(s):**
American Guild of Organists
475 Riverside Dr., Ste. 1260
New York, NY 10115
Telephone: (212) 870-2310
Ownership %: 100
**Management:**
Margaret Kekmper ........................President
Daniel N. Colburn, II ..........Executive Director
Anthony Baglivi ................Advertising Manager
**Editorial:**
Anthony Baglivi ............................Editor
Robert Price ................Administrative Assistant
John Wattai ......................Art Department
**Desc.:** Advertising and marketing, staff and
by-lined articles, book reviews, coming
events, and trade literature.
**Readers:** Organists, singers, teachers,
performers, harpsichordists and organ
builders.

## BILLBOARD
24128
1515 Broadway
New York, NY 10036
Telephone: (212) 764-7300
FAX: (212) 944-1719
Year Established: 1894
Pub. Frequency: w.
Page Size: tabloid
Subscrip. Rate: $4.95/issue; $209/yr.
Freelance Pay: negotiable
Circulation: 46,833
Circulation Type: paid
**Owner(s):**
Billboard Publications, Inc.
1515 Broadway
New York, NY 10036
Telephone: (212) 764-7300
Ownership %: 100
**Bureau(s):**
Billboard Publications
9107 Wilshire Blvd.
Beverly Hills, CA 90210
Telephone: (310) 273-7040
Contact: Lee Zhito

Billboard Publications
49 Music Square, W.
Nashville, TN 37203
Telephone: (615) 748-8100
Contact: Gerry Wood, Bureau Chief
**Management:**
Gerald S. Hobbs ..........................President
Howard Lander ............................Publisher
Gene Smith ......................Associate Publsiher

**Editorial:**
Ken Schlager ..........................Managing Editor
**Desc.:** International music & home
entertainment newsweekly covers music
record and video fields; talent, radio-TV,
home electronics, computer software.
**Readers:** Retailers of music, video &
computer software; programmers of
radio - TV; manufacturers of music,
video & computer software products;
talent agencies & venues.

## CASH BOX
24129
51 E. Eighth St., Ste. 155
New York, NY 10003-6494
Telephone: (212) 245-4224
Page Size: pg.: 10 x 13 1/2; col.: 2 1/8 x
12 1/2; photo: yes
Subscrip. Rate: $180/yr. US; $225/yr.
foreign
Circulation: 5,200
**Owner(s):**
Cash Box Pub. Co.
6464 Sunset Blvd.
Los Angeles, CA 90028
Ownership %: 100
**Editorial:**
Lee Neejeske ..............................Editor
**Desc.:** General music news; singles,
albums, talent, charts, coin machine
and international music news.
**Readers:** General music and coin-machine
industries

## CLAVIER
24130
200 Northfield Rd.
Northfield, IL 60093
Telephone: (708) 446-5000
FAX: (704) 446-6363
Year Established: 1962
Pub. Frequency: 10/yr.
Page Size: standard
Subscrip. Rate: $18/yr.
Freelance Pay: varies
Circulation: 19,000
Circulation Type: paid
**Owner(s):**
The Instrumentalist Co.
200 Northfield Rd.
Northfield, IL 60093
Telephone: (708) 446-5000
Ownership %: 100
**Management:**
James Rohner ............................Publisher
Will Garvey ......................Advertising Manager
**Desc.:** Major emphasis on piano,
secondary on organ covered. Practical
articles, emphasizing how to teach, how
to improve playing,
personality interviews, and scholarly
articles, new music reviews, records,
books, new products and news of music
contests.
**Readers:** Teachers and serious students
of keyboard.

## COLLEGE MEDIA JOURNAL NEW MUSIC REPORT
69016
11 Middle Neck Rd., Suite 400
Great Neck, NY 11021-3308
Telephone: (516) 466-6000
FAX: (516) 466-7159
Year Established: 1978
Pub. Frequency: w.
Page Size: 9X12
Subscrip. Rate: $295/yr.
Materials: 12,23,24,32
Circulation: 3,000
Circulation Type: paid

**Owner(s):**
College Media, Inc.
11 Middle Neck Rd. Suite 400
Great Neck, NY 11021-3308
Telephone: (516) 466-6000
Ownership %: 100
**Editorial:**
Robert Haber ..............................Editor

## DIAPASON, THE
24131
380 E. Northwest Hwy.
Des Plaines, IL 60016-2282
Telephone: (708) 298-6622
FAX: (708) 390-0408
Year Established: 1909
Pub. Frequency: m.
Page Size: oversize
Subscrip. Rate: $18/yr.
Materials: 01,02,06,10,12,15,16,21,23,25,
27,28,29,32,33
Freelance Pay: none
Circulation: 6,000
Circulation Type: controlled
**Owner(s):**
Scranton Gillette Communications, Inc.
380 E. Northwest Hwy.
Des Plaines, IL 60016-2282
Telephone: (708) 298-6622
FAX: (708) 390-0408
Ownership %: 100
**Management:**
S. E. Gruenstein ..........................Founder
Halbert S. Gillette ............................Owner
Halbert S. Gillette ..........................President
Linda Lambdin ................Circulation Manager
**Editorial:**
Jerome Butera ............................Editor
Wesley Vos ......................Assistant Editor
Jerome Butera ......................Music Editor
James Hartman ........................Staff Writer
James McCray ........................Staff Writer
Herbert Huestis ......................Staff Writer
Larry Palmer ........................Staff Writer
**Desc.:** Devoted to organists, church
musicians, harpsichordists, and
carillonneurs. Contains news of events,
descriptions of new instruments, reviews
of performances and new publications.
**Readers:** Organists, choir directors, organ
builders, carillonneurs, harpsichordists,
teachers.
**Deadline:** story-2 mo. prior to pub. date;
news-6 wks. prior to pub. date; photo-6
wks. prior to pub. date; ads-1 mo. prior
to pub. date

## DOWN BEAT
24132
180 W. Park
Elmhurst, IL 60126
Telephone: (708) 941-2030
FAX: (708) 941-3210
Year Established: 1934
Pub. Frequency: m.
Page Size: standard
Subscrip. Rate: $1.75 newsstand; $18/yr.
Freelance Pay: $20-$300/article
Circulation: 96,314
Circulation Type: paid
**Owner(s):**
Maher Publications
180 W. Park
Elmhurst, IL 60126
Telephone: (708) 941-2030
Ownership %: 100
**Management:**
Jack Maher ..............................President
Selia Polido ......................Circulation Manager
**Editorial:**
Bill Beuttler ......................Associate Editor
Bill Beuttler ......................Education Editor

**Desc.:** Covers all phases of music
business with emphasis on
contemporary music (Jazz/Rock/Blues)
and news of the professional and school
musicians and educators. Departments
include: Record Reviews, Caught in the
Act, Music Arrangements, Music
Instruction, Methods, Electronics,
Improvisations, Artist Interviews &
Profiles, Concert and Festival
Apperances, Book Reviews, Humor
Auditions.
**Readers:** 93 percent male, average 23.6
years; med.average reader interested in
music as amateur or professional.

## GEORGIA MUSIC NEWS
69619
University of Georgia, School of Music
Athens, GA 30602
Year Established: 1940
Pub. Frequency: q.
Subscrip. Rate: $4/yr.
Materials: 02,06,10,15,21,29,32
Circulation: 2,472
Circulation Type: controlled
**Owner(s):**
Georgia Music Educators Association
Ownership %: 100
**Editorial:**
Mary Leglar ..............................Editor

## HARMONIZER, THE
24135
6315 Third Ave.
Kenosha, WI 53143
Telephone: (414) 653-8440
Year Established: 1943
Pub. Frequency: bi-m.
Page Size: standard
Subscrip. Rate: $3/issue; $18/yr.
Materials: 32
Circulation: 38,000
Circulation Type: controlled
**Owner(s):**
SPEBSQSA, Inc.
6315 Third Ave.
Kenosha, WI 53143
Telephone: (414) 653-8440
Ownership %: 100
**Editorial:**
Dan Daily ..............................Editor
**Desc.:** All material prepared by and for
members of our organization. Articles
deal with technical aspects of singing
Barbershop Harmony, administrative
procedures, general news items of
chapter and district activities, plus
features dealing with various aspects of
being in a quartet.
**Readers:** All members or prospective
members SPEBSQSA.

## INSTRUMENTALIST, THE
24139
200 Northfield Rd.
Northfield, IL 60093
Telephone: (708) 446-5000
FAX: (708) 446-6263
Year Established: 1946
Pub. Frequency: m.
Page Size: standard
Subscrip. Rate: $22/yr.
Freelance Pay: $25-$40/pg.
Circulation: 19,200
Circulation Type: paid
**Owner(s):**
The Instrumentalist Co.
Telephone: (708) 446-5000
Ownership %: 100
**Management:**
James T. Rohner ..........................Publisher
William H. Garvey ..........Advertising Manager
**Editorial:**
Catherine Sell ..........................Senior Editor
Katherine L. Olsen ..........Assistant Publisher

**Materials Accepted/Included:** 01-Business news 02-By-line articles 03-Fashion news 04-Food news 05-Freelance copy 06-Letters to editor 07-Real estate news 08-Sports news 09-Travel news
10-Book rev. 11-Movie rev. 12-Music rev. 13-TV rev. 14-Theater rev. 15-Coming events 16-Obituaries 17-Question & answer 18-Social announcements 19-Artwork 20-Cartoons 21-Photos 22-TV listings
23-Audio rec. 24-Video rec. 25-Books 26-Films/film clips 27-Personnel news 28-Press releases 29-New product news/photos 30-Trade lit. 31-Contracts awarded 32-Display adv. 33-Classified adv.

4-263

**Desc.:** Emphasis on school band and orchestra directors and teachers of instrumental music. How to play the instruments, how to organize and motivate the programs, new music reviews, records, etc.

**Readers:** School band and orchestra directors, all members of NBA (National Band Association) and NSOA (National School Orchestra Association).

24140

## INTERNATIONAL MUSICIAN
1501 Broadway, Ste. 600
Paramount Bldg.
New York, NY 10036
Telephone: (212) 869-1330
FAX: (212) 302-4374
Year Established: 1898
Pub. Frequency: m.
Page Size: tabloid
Subscrip. Rate: $20/yr. in US; $25/yr. Canada; $30/yr. foreign
Freelance Pay: negotiable
Circulation: 155,000
Circulation Type: paid
**Owner(s):**
American Fed. of Musicians
1501 Broadway, #600
Paramount Bldg.
New York, NY 10036
Telephone: (212) 869-1330
Ownership %: 100
**Management:**
Stephen R. Sprague ............................Publisher
Jim Rubbone .....................Advertising Manager
**Editorial:**
Stephen R. Sprague ...................................Editor
Jessica Roe ............................Managing Editor
**Desc.:** Nonfiction articles on prominent instrumental musicians (classical, jazz, country, rock).
**Readers:** Professional musicians.

69646

## JOURNAL OF ORGANBUILDING
P.O. Box 130982
Houston, TX 77219-0982
Telephone: (713) 529-2212
Year Established: 1986
Pub. Frequency: q.
Subscrip. Rate: $12/yr. US; $16/yr. foreign
Materials: 01,02,06,10,15,16,17,27,28,29, 30,32,33
Freelance Pay: $50-$100
Circulation: 600
Circulation Type: paid
**Owner(s):**
American Institute of Organbuilders
P.O. Box 130982
Houston, TX 77219-0982
Telephone: (713) 529-2212
**Editorial:**
Howard Maple ........................................Editor
**Desc.:** Includes technical articles and product reviews.
**Readers:** Pipe organ builders and tuning and maintenance technicians.

24142

## LATIN AMERICAN MUSIC REVIEW
Univ. of Texas Press
P.O. Box 7819
Austin, TX 78713-7819
Telephone: (512) 471-4531
FAX: (512) 320-0668
Year Established: 1980
Pub. Frequency: s-a.
Page Size: standard
Subscrip. Rate: $20/yr. individual; $35/yr. institution
Materials: 12,15,24,32
Freelance Pay: $1.25-$1.90/pg.
Circulation: 500
Circulation Type: paid

**Owner(s):**
Univ. of Texas Press, Journals Dept.
P.O. Box 7819
Austin, TX 78713
Telephone: (512) 471-4531
FAX: (512) 320-0668
Ownership %: 100
**Management:**
Leah Dixon ........................Promotion Manager
**Editorial:**
Gerard Behague ......................Executive Editor
Gerard Behague ...................................Editor
Madeleine Vernezze ..............Managing Editor
Gerad Behague ................Book Review Editor
**Desc.:** Concentrates on Latin America's varied oral and written traditions, with diverse theoretical and methodological approaches in historical, folkloric and musicological studies of one or our most highly structured expressive behaviors. Book reviews and announcements of self performance and organizational achievers.
**Readers:** Scholars in musicological and folkloric areas.
**Deadline:** ads-Apr. & Oct. 15

69635

## LOS ANGELES SONGWRITERS SHOWCASE MUSEPAPER
P.O. Box 93759
Hollywood, CA 90093
Telephone: (213) 467-7823
Year Established: 1986
Pub. Frequency: m.
Subscrip. Rate: $19/yr.
Circulation: 20,000
**Owner(s):**
Music & Arts Foundation of America, Los Angeles
P.O. Box 93759
Hollywood, CA 90093
Telephone: (213) 467-7823
Ownership %: 100
**Editorial:**
John Braheny ...................................Editor

61691

## MUSIC & MEDIA
1515 Broadway
New York, NY 10036
Telephone: (212) 764-7300
FAX: (212) 536-5236
Year Established: 1980
Pub. Frequency: w.
Subscrip. Rate: $270/yr.
Circulation: 5,000
Circulation Type: paid
**Owner(s):**
BPI Communications, Inc.
1515 Broadway
New York, NY 10036
Telephone: (212) 764-7300
Ownership %: 100
**Management:**
Edwin Loupias ...................................Controller
Theo Roos ...........................................Publisher
Ron Betist ......................................Sales Manager
**Editorial:**
Jeff Green ......................................Editor in Chief
Machgiel Bakker ..........................Senior Editor
Jeff Green ..........................Associate Publisher
Ron Betist ..........................Associate Publisher
Annette Knijnenber ..............Marketing Director
**Desc.:** Europe's leading music radio weekly.
**Readers:** Radio programmers, music industry personnel.

24587

## MUSICAL MERCHANDISE REVIEW
100 Wells Ave.
Newton Center, MA 02159
Telephone: (617) 964-5100
FAX: (617) 964-2752
Year Established: 1878
Pub. Frequency: m.

Page Size: standard
Subscrip. Rate: $27/yr.
Circulation: 12,000
Circulation Type: controlled
**Owner(s):**
Larkin Publications, Inc.
100 Wells Ave.
Newton Center, MA 02159
Telephone: (617) 964-5100
Ownership %: 100
**Management:**
Sidney Davis ...................................Publisher
Elayne Selig ......................Circulation Manager
**Editorial:**
Don Johnson ...................................Editor
Joanna Drew ...................................Art Director
Jerry Kaplow ......................Production Director
**Desc.:** Covers merchandising market trends, sales for dealers, manufacturers and wholesalers. Carries news briefs, new appointments, news and notes of manufacturers and distributors, new products.
**Readers:** Music dealers, retailers, wholesalers, manufacturers of all types of musical instruments and related electronic sound equipment, general music aids.

24143

## MUSIC EDUCATORS JOURNAL
1806 Robert Fulton Dr.
Reston, VA 22091-4348
Telephone: (703) 860-4000
FAX: (703) 860-4826
Year Established: 1914
Pub. Frequency: m.
Page Size: standard
Subscrip. Rate: $20/yr. members; $60/yr.
Materials: 24,32,33
Circulation: 62,000
Circulation Type: paid
**Owner(s):**
Music Educators National Conference
1806 Robert Fulton Dr.
Reston, VA 22091-4348
Telephone: (703) 860-1531
Ownership %: 100
**Management:**
Helen Crowley ...................Advertising Manager
**Editorial:**
Michael Blakeslee ...................................Editor
Helen Crowley ...........................Advertising
Jeanne Spaeth ...........................Articles Editor
Ella Wilcox ...........................Book Review Editor
Evonne Nolan ...................New Products Editor
Neal Snyder ...............................News Editor
Adriane Darvishian ..............Production Director
Margaret A. Senko ..............Publication Director
**Desc.:** Articles discuss problems and developments in the fields of music and music education. Material pertains to techniques, experiences, results in field of music teaching and schools, colleges, community centers, research. Departments include: Bulletin Board (news of current events, curricula, developments and premieres), Book Reviews, Technology for Teaching (technological innovations for the classroom), and the Market Space (covering new teaching materials, instruments, and equipment). Official publication of the Music Educators National Conference, and 61 federated and auxiliary state and national organizations.
**Readers:** Teachers, educators, musicians, administrators.

69013

## MUSIC PAPER
P.O. Box 304
Manhassett, NY 11030
Telephone: (516) 883-8898
FAX: (516) 883-2577

Year Established: 1979
Pub. Frequency: m.
Subscrip. Rate: $1.95/issue; $12/yr.
Materials: 01,02,05,06,10,12,16,17,19,21, 23,24,25,27,28,29,30,32,33
Circulation: 70,000
Circulation Type: paid
**Owner(s):**
Sound Resources
P.O. Box 304
Manhassett, NY 11030
Telephone: (516) 883-8898
Ownership %: 100
**Editorial:**
Karen A. Cavill ...................................Editor
**Desc.:** Contemporary music coverage geared towards musicians, including reviews (live and product), interviews, profiles, instruction columns, industry news, new product information, and new technology information.
**Readers:** Musicians and music lovers, all styles, all ages.

69638

## MUSIC QUARTERLY
200 Madison Ave.
New York, NY 10016
Telephone: (212) 679-7300
FAX: (212) 689-5312
Year Established: 1915
Pub. Frequency: q.
Subscrip. Rate: $34/yr. individuals; $48/yr. institutions
Circulation: 3,500
**Owner(s):**
Oxford University Press
200 Madison Ave.
New York, NY 10016
Telephone: (212) 679-7300
Ownership %: 100
**Editorial:**
Leon Botstein ...................................Editor
**Desc.:** Contains original articles covering the entire range of musical composition and performance, from early music to the Classical- Romantic tradition to twentieth-century jazz and pop to the latest developments in theory and practice.

66758

## MUSIC RETAILING
70 Rte. 202 N.
Peterborough, NH 03458
Telephone: (603) 924-0058
FAX: (603) 924-8613
Year Established: 1990
Pub. Frequency: bi-w.
Page Size: tabloid
Subscrip. Rate: $95/yr.
Circulation: 9,000
Circulation Type: controlled
**Owner(s):**
Out to Launch, Inc.
Forest Rd.
Hancock, NH 03449
Telephone: (603) 525-4201
Ownership %: 100
**Editorial:**
Don Fluckinger ...................................Editor
Jim Kendrick ......................Associate Publisher
**Desc.:** Publishes news, ideas, and information for sellers of prerecorded music.
**Readers:** Record store owners, managers, and buyers.

24146

## MUSIC TRADES
80 West St.
Englewood, NJ 07631
Telephone: (201) 871-1965
FAX: (201) 871-0455
Mailing Address:
P.O. Box 432
Englewood, NJ 07631

Year Established: 1890
Pub. Frequency: m.
Page Size: standard
Subscrip. Rate: $14/yr.; $20/2 yrs.
Circulation: 7,350
Circulation Type: paid
**Owner(s):**
Music Trades Corp.
Telephone: (201) 871-1965
Ownership %: 100
**Management:**
Paul A. Majeski .......................Publisher
**Editorial:**
Brian T. Majeski ...........................Editor
**Desc.:** News magazine covering the
business side of the music industry,
including industry news and activities,
awards, promotions, advertising, outlook.
Departments include: New Products,
Musical Merchandise, New Stores,
Sheet Music, Pianos, Organs,
Dealer News, Accordions, Band
Instruments, Drums, Small Goods and
Piano Tuning.
**Readers:** Music dealers serving all industry
branch wholesalers, importers,
exporters, etc.

24148
**NOTES, QUARTERLY JOURNAL
OF THE MUSIC LIBRARY
ASSOCIATION**
Conservatory Library, Oberlin College
Oberlin, OH 44074
Telephone: (216) 775-8280
Year Established: 1934
Pub. Frequency: q.
Page Size: pg.: 6 x 9; col.: 27 x 41 picas;
Subscrip. Rate: $60/yr. individuals; $65/yr.
institutions
Materials: 02,06,10,12,32
Circulation: 2,625
Circulation Type: paid
**Owner(s):**
Music Library Association
P.O. Box 487
Canton, MA 02021
Telephone: (617) 828-8450
Ownership %: 100
**Editorial:**
Daniel Zager ...............................Editor
Susan Dearborn ..............Advertising Editor
David Hunter ...............Book Review Editor
Frances Barulich .................Music Editor
**Desc.:** Renders as comprehensive a report
on new music materials as possible,
articles on music history, music
bibliography, music libraries. Other
regular features are lists and reviews of
published books and music, periodicals,
music software, music publishers;
catalogs, index to music obituaries, &
index to CD and record reviews.
**Readers:** Librarians, musicologists,
libraries with music divisions, college
and university libraries, music trade and
individuals interested in music
publications.

70449
**OPERA QUARTERLY**
905 W. Main Ste., 18-B
Duke Universtiy Press
Durham, NC 27701
Telephone: (919) 687-3636
FAX: (919) 688-4574
Mailing Address:
  P.O. Box 90660
  Durham, NC 27708-0660
Year Established: 1983
Pub. Frequency: q.
Page Size: standard
Subscrip. Rate: $36/yr. individuals; $60/yr.
institutions
Materials: 32
Circulation: 5,000

Circulation Type: controlled & paid
**Owner(s):**
Duke University Press
P.O. Box 90660
Durham, NC 27708-0660
Telephone: (919) 687-3600
FAX: (919) 688-4574
Ownership %: 100
**Management:**
Patricia Thomas .......................Manager
**Editorial:**
William Ashbrook .......................Editor

24149
**PIANO TECHNICIANS JOURNAL,
THE**
3930 Washington St.
Kansas City, MO 64111-2963
Telephone: (816) 753-7747
FAX: (816) 531-0070
Year Established: 1958
Pub. Frequency: m.
Page Size: standard
Subscrip. Rate: $10/issue; $85/yr.
Circulation: 4,000
Circulation Type: paid
**Owner(s):**
Piano Technicians Guild, Inc.
3930 Washington St.
Kansas City, MO 64111-2963
Telephone: (816) 753-7747
FAX: (816) 531-0070
Ownership %: 100
**Editorial:**
Larry Goldsmith .................Executive Editor
**Desc.:** A technical journal for piano tuner-
technicians and the allied trades.
Features a Technical Forum and other
technical articles. Reprints
from magazines and newspapers of
interest to technicians with credit to
publication and writer. Only publication
devoted to the technical and economic
interests of persons engaged in piano
service, both independent
and employed. Read by manufacturers,
suppliers and dealers. Appears in
numerous school and technical libraries.
Distributed all over the world. Taped for
the blind.
**Readers:** Tuner-technicians, dealers,
manufacturers.

24153
**SOUTHWESTERN MUSICIAN-
TEXAS MUSIC EDUCATOR**
4507 North I-35
Austin, TX 78722
Telephone: (512) 452-0710
FAX: (512) 451-9213
Mailing Address:
  P.O. Box 49469
  Austin, TX 78765
Year Established: 1932
Pub. Frequency: 10/yr.
Page Size: standard
Subscrip. Rate: $15/yr.; $30/2 yrs.; $45/3
yrs.
Freelance Pay: $50-$100
Print Process: offset
Circulation: 9,524
Circulation Type: paid
**Owner(s):**
Texas Music Educators Association
4507 North I-35
Austin, TX 78722
Telephone: (512) 452-0710
Ownership %: 100
**Management:**
Tesa Kelly .................Advertising Manager
**Editorial:**
Robert Floyd ...............Executive Editor

**Desc.:** Serves the music educators in
Texas as a means of communication
among the membership, report on
significant research in music education,
band, choral and orchestral publications
and new books on music are reviewed
regularly.
**Readers:** Practicing and prospective music
teachers.

69015
**STRINGS**
P.O. Box 767
San Anselmo, CA 94979-0767
Telephone: (415) 485-6946
FAX: (415) 485-0831
Year Established: 1986
Pub. Frequency: bi-m.
Page Size: standard
Subscrip. Rate: $4.95 newsstand; $36/yr.
  US; $43.50/yr. Canada; $51/yr.
  elsewhere
Materials: 06,10,12,15,16,21,23,24,25,26,
  28,29,30,32,33
Print Process: web
Circulation: 10,000
Circulation Type: paid
**Owner(s):**
String Letter Press, Inc.
P.O. Box 767
San Anselmo, CA 94979-0767
Telephone: (415) 485-6946
Ownership %: 100
**Editorial:**
Mary VanClay ...........................Editor
**Readers:** Practicing and performing
musicians.

## Group 170-Nuclear Science

69066
**ANNALS OF NUCLEAR ENERGY**
660 White Plains Rd.
Tarrytown, NY 10591-5153
Telephone: (914) 524-9200
FAX: (914) 333-2444
Year Established: 1974
Pub. Frequency: m.
Circulation: 1,100
Circulation Type: paid
**Owner(s):**
Pergamon Press, Inc.
660 White Plains Rd.
Tarrytown, NY 10591-5153
Telephone: (914) 524-9200
Ownership %: 100
**Editorial:**
M.M.R. Williams ...........................Editor
L.E. Weaver ...........................Editor
**Desc.:** Provides an international medium
for the communication of original
research in all areas of the field of
nuclear science and
technology. Provides an international
medium for the communication of
original research in all areas of the field
of nuclear science and technology.
Written in English, French and German.

52641
**ANS NEWS**
555 N. Kensington Ave.
La Grange, IL 60525
Telephone: (708) 352-6611
FAX: (708) 352-0499
Year Established: 1983
Pub. Frequency: m.
Page Size: tabloid
Subscrip. Rate: $82/yr. US; $89/yr. foreign
Circulation: 16,000
Circulation Type: paid
**Owner(s):**
American Nuclear Society, Inc.
555 N. Kensington Ave.
La Grange, IL 60525
Telephone: (708) 352-6611
Ownership %: 100

**Management:**
Edward D. Fuller ...........................President
Edward O. Fuller ...................Vice President
James G. Toscas ...........Executive Director
**Editorial:**
Lloyd A. Wright ...........................Treasurer
**Desc.:** ANS News contains society &
member news, PI-Education information
and articles, news on ANS committees,
divisions, local sections, plant branches
and student branches, ANS journal
contents, important dates and deadlines,
new members, a president's letter and
guest editors.
**Readers:** ANS membership and library
subscribers.

52684
**FUSION TECHNOLOGY**
555 N. Kensington Ave.
La Grange, IL 60525
Telephone: (708) 352-6611
Year Established: 1981
Pub. Frequency: 8/yr. plus 4 supplements
Page Size: standard
Subscrip. Rate: $485/yr.
Print Process: offset
Circulation: 950
Circulation Type: controlled
**Owner(s):**
American Nuclear Society, Inc.
555 N. Kensington Ave.
La Grange, IL 60525
Telephone: (708) 352-6611
Ownership %: 100
**Management:**
Edward Fuller ...........................President
Rod Clemmons ..............Business Manager
Mary Beth Gardner ...................Manager
**Editorial:**
George W. Miley ...........................Editor
Loyd Wright ...........................Treasurer
**Desc.:** Keeps subscribers up-to-date on all
aspects of applied fusion energy.
**Readers:** Nuclear engineers, physicists,
and mathematicians.

69067
**JOURNAL OF FUSION ENERGY**
233 Spring St.
New York, NY 10013-1578
Telephone: (212) 620-8000
FAX: (212) 463-0742
Year Established: 1981
Pub. Frequency: q.
Page Size: 14
Subscrip. Rate: $285/yr. US; $335/yr.
  foreign
**Owner(s):**
Plenum Publishing Corp.
233 Spring St.
New York, NY 10013-1578
Telephone: (212) 620-8000
Ownership %: 100
**Editorial:**
Daniel Cohn ...........................Editor

49916
**NUCLEAR FUEL**
1200 G St., N.W., Ste. 1100
Washington, DC 20005-3802
Telephone: (202) 383-2167
FAX: (202) 383-2125
Year Established: 1976
Pub. Frequency: bi-w.
Page Size: standard
Subscrip. Rate: $1510/yr. US; $1605/yr.
  foreign
**Owner(s):**
McGraw-Hill, Inc.
1221 Ave. of the Americas
New York, NY 10020
Ownership %: 100
**Management:**
John E. Slater ...........................Publisher
**Editorial:**
Michael Knapik ...................Chief Editor

**Materials Accepted/Included:** 01-Business news 02-By-line articles 03-Fashion news 04-Food news 05-Freelance copy 06-Letters to editor 07-Real estate news 08-Sports news 09-Travel news
10-Book rev. 11-Movie rev. 12-Music rev. 13-TV rev. 14-Theater rev. 15-Coming events 16-Obituaries 17-Question & answer 18-Social announcements 19-Artwork 20-Cartoons 21-Photos 22-TV listings
23-Audio rec. 24-Video rec. 25-Books 26-Films/film clips 27-Personnel news 28-Press releases 29-New product news/photos 30-Trade lit. 31-Contracts awarded 32-Display adv. 33-Classified adv.

4-265

**Desc.:** Industry newsletter reporting news of nuclear/uranium industries and government agencies.
**Readers:** Nuclear, uranium corporations, and utilities government offices.

## NUCLEAR MONITOR
69071

1424 16th St., N.W., Ste. 601
Washington, DC 20036
Telephone: (202) 328-0002
FAX: (202) 462-2183
Year Established: 1985
Pub. Frequency: bi-w.
Subscrip. Rate: $250/yr.
Circulation: 1,200
Circulation Type: paid
**Owner(s):**
Nuclear Information & Resource Service
1424 16th St., N.W., Ste. 601
Washington, DC 20036
Telephone: (202) 328-0002
Ownership %: 100
**Editorial:**
Michael Mariotte ..............................Editor
**Desc.:** Covers nuclear power, radioactive waste and sustainable energy news.
**Readers:** Investment bankers, state and local officials, media and environmental activists.

## NUCLEAR NEWS
24179

555 N. Kensington
La Grange Park, IL 60525
Telephone: (708) 579-8242
FAX: (708) 352-6464
Year Established: 1959
Pub. Frequency: 15/yr.
Page Size: standard
Subscrip. Rate: $200/yr.
Circulation: 15,787
Circulation Type: controlled
**Owner(s):**
American Nuclear Society, Inc.
555 N. Kensington Ave.
La Grange Park, IL 60525
Telephone: (708) 352-6611
Ownership %: 100
**Management:**
Edward D. Fuller ..........................President
John Payne ................................Publisher
Gregg M. Taylor ............Advertising Manager
**Editorial:**
Nancy Zacha ..................................Editor
Allen Zeyher ......................Associate Editor
Richard Michal ..................Associate Editor
Laurel P. Gallagher ............Associate Editor
Simon Rippon ......................European Editor
Elizabeth S. Tompkins ..........Senior Associate Editor
Loyd Wright ..............................Treasurer
**Desc.:** Devoted entirely to topics concerning nuclear energy/including licensing, plant operation, fuel, transport, waste management, safeguards. Departments include: Power, Fuel, International, Operations, Education, Nuclear Industry, New Publications, Meetings, People, New Equipment Materials, Services and Literature from Suppliers.
**Readers:** Consists of management, supervisors, engineers, scientists, physicists, chemists, technicians at government agencies, construction, engineering and consulting firms, national laboratories, utilities and manufacturers.

## NUCLEAR NEWS BUYERS GUIDE
52642

555 N. Kensington Ave.
La Grange Park, IL 60525
Telephone: (708) 579-8242
FAX: (708) 352-6464
Year Established: 1969

Pub. Frequency: a.
Page Size: standard
Subscrip. Rate: $65/yr. (free with Nuclear News)
Circulation: 15,000
Circulation Type: controlled
**Owner(s):**
American Nuclear Society, Inc.
555 N. Kensington Ave.
La Grange, IL 60525
Telephone: (708) 352-6611
Ownership %: 100
**Management:**
Edward D. Fuller ..........................President
Jon Payne ................................Publisher
James G. Toscas ................Executive Director
**Editorial:**
Nancy Zacha ..................................Editor
Gregg M. Taylor ............Adv. Sales Manager
Loyd Wright ..............................Treasurer
**Desc.:** More than 2000 manufacturers and the products, material and services they market are incorporated in this international directory. The comprehensive listing contains more than 500 categories representing nuclear components and services available today. The Guide offers three alphabetized directories: an index to categories; nuclear products, materials and services directory; and a directory of suppliers.
**Readers:** Managers, engineers, operators and other personnel employed at utilities, architect and engineering firms, consulting companies, service and maintenance organizations, and private and government research establishments.

## NUCLEAR PLANT JOURNAL
53956

799 Roosevelt Rd.
Bldg. 6, Ste. 208
Glen Ellyn, IL 60137-5925
Telephone: (708) 858-6161
FAX: (708) 858-8787
Year Established: 1982
Pub. Frequency: 7/yr.
Page Size: standard
Subscrip. Rate: $102/yr. US non-qualified
Materials: 28,29,30,31,32,33
Print Process: web offset
Circulation: 22,000
Circulation Type: controlled
**Owner(s):**
EQES, Inc.
799 Roosevelt Rd.
Bldg. 6, Ste. 208
Glen Ellyn, IL 60137-2925
Telephone: (708) 858-6161
Ownership %: 100
**Management:**
Anu Agnihotri ............................Publisher
**Editorial:**
Newal Agnihotri ......................Senior Editor
**Desc.:** Provides updates on efforts being pursued during maintenance, operation, design and construction of nuclear power plants in U.S.A. and abroad. Includes technical papers, informative articles, and departments aimed at developing better products and services in the nuclear power industry. Nuclear Plant Journal is a tool for information exchange among utilities, architect engineers, manufacturers, educational institutions, research organizations, Nuclear Regulatory Commission, and other private and governmental organizations.
**Readers:** Managers, supervisors & engineers in nuclear energy related industries including utilities.

## NUCLEAR SCIENCE & ENGINEERING
24887

555 N. Kensington Ave.
La Grange, IL 60525
Telephone: (708) 352-6611
Year Established: 1956
Pub. Frequency: m.
Page Size: standard
Subscrip. Rate: $405/yr.
Print Process: offset
Circulation: 1,800
Circulation Type: controlled
**Owner(s):**
American Nuclear Society, Inc.
555 N. Kensington Ave.
La Grange, IL 60525
Telephone: (708) 352-6611
Ownership %: 100
**Management:**
Edward Fuller ............................President
James G. Tosras ................Executive Director
Rod Clemmons ..................Business Manager
Mary Beth Gardner ........................Manager
**Editorial:**
Dan G. Cacuci ..............................Editor
Gunther Kessler ..................Associate Editor
Loyd Wright ..............................Treasurer
**Desc.:** Presents unreported fundamental research in the nuclear sciences and engineering. Technical papers describe original work or scientific investigation in all areas of the nuclear field and related disciplines.
**Readers:** Nuclear science-engineers whose work deals with research and development.

## NUCLEAR TECHNOLOGY
24180

555 N. Kensington Ave.
La Grange, IL 60525
Telephone: (708) 352-6611
Year Established: 1965
Pub. Frequency: m.
Page Size: standard
Subscrip. Rate: $440/yr.
Print Process: offset
Circulation: 1,900
Circulation Type: controlled
**Owner(s):**
American Nuclear Society, Inc.
555 N. Kensington Ave.
La Grange, IL 60525
Telephone: (708) 352-6611
Ownership %: 100
**Management:**
Edward Fuller ............................President
James G. Toscas ................Executive Director
Rod Clemmons ..................Business Manager
Mary Beth Gardner ........................Manager
**Editorial:**
Wm. F. Vogelsang ..........................Editor
M. M. El-Wakil ..................Associate Editor
Gunther Kessler ..................Associate Editor
Noboyuki Suzuki ..................Associate Editor
Loyd Wright ..............................Treasurer

**Desc.:** A journal of established international stature covering the broad spectrum of applications of nuclear science and engineering, as well as related technologies. Publishes review papers and unreported work in all areas of fundamental research applied anywhere in the nuclear field from radioisotope uses in industry and medicine to civil explosion application; but especially in the rapidly expanding aspects of nuclear reactor technology development - reactor engineering, nuclear materials, instrumentation, nuclear fuels and the fuel cycle. Also published are book reviews, critical reviews, NT letters, letters to the editor and technical notes reporting preliminary results and extensions of previously reported work. Indexes are part of each of the four volumes published annually.
**Readers:** Nuclear scientists, physicists, educators.

## NUCLEONICS WEEK
23457

1200 G St., N.W., Ste. 1100
Washington, DC 20005
Telephone: (202) 383-2170
Year Established: 1960
Pub. Frequency: w.
Page Size: standard
Subscrip. Rate: $1360/yr. US & Canada; $1460/yr. elsewhere
**Owner(s):**
McGraw-Hill, Inc.
1221 Ave. of the Americas
New York, NY 10020
Telephone: (212) 512-3194
Ownership %: 100
**Management:**
John E. Slater ............................Publisher
**Editorial:**
Margaret Ryan ......................Editor in Chief
**Desc.:** A weekly 10-18 page international newsletter for nuclear power utility executives, suppliers of equipment, fuel, etc., architect-engineers, consultants and government officials.

## PROCEEDINGS OF THE CONFERENCE ON REMOTE SYSTEMS TECHNOLOGY
52689

555 N. Kensington Ave.
La Grange, IL 60525
Telephone: (708) 352-6611
Year Established: 1960
Pub. Frequency: a.
Page Size: standard
Subscrip. Rate: $45/yr.
Print Process: offset
Circulation: 400
Circulation Type: controlled
**Owner(s):**
American Nuclear Society, Inc.
555 N. Kensington Ave.
La Grange, IL 60525
Telephone: (708) 352-6611
Ownership %: 100
**Management:**
Edward Fuller ............................President
Rod Clemmons ..................Business Manager
**Editorial:**
Irene Macke ..................................Editor
Mary Beth Gardner ............Publication Director
Loyd Wright ..............................Treasurer
**Desc.:** Contains complete papers presented at the meetings of the Remote Systems Technology Division of the American Nuclear Society, addressing handling of materials in high radiation, through remotely controlled devices of manipulators.
**Readers:** Nuclear scientists, educators and technicians.

Materials Accepted/Included: 01-Business news 02-By-line articles 03-Fashion news 04-Food news 05-Freelance copy 06-Letters to editor 07-Real estate news 08-Sports news 09-Travel news 10-Book rev. 11-Movie rev. 12-Music rev. 13-TV rev. 14-Theater rev. 15-Coming events 16-Obituaries 17-Question & answer 18-Social announcements 19-Artwork 20-Cartoons 21-Photos 22-TV listings 23-Audio rec. 24-Video rec. 25-Books 26-Films/film clips 27-Personnel news 28-Press releases 29-New product news/photos 30-Trade lit. 31-Contracts awarded 32-Display adv. 33-Classified adv.

4-266

## PROGRESS IN NUCLEAR ENERGY
69068

660 White Plains Rd.
Tarrytown, NY 10591-5153
Telephone: (914) 524-9200
FAX: (914) 333-2444
Year Established: 1977
Pub. Frequency: q.
**Owner(s):**
Pergamon Press, Inc.
660 White Plains Rd.
Tarrytown, NY 10591-5153
Telephone: (914) 524-9200
Ownership %: 100
**Editorial:**
T.D. Benyon ................................Editor
Bal Raj Sehgal ............................Editor
**Desc.:** Covers developments in nuclear
physics and engineering, as well as
related issues including safety, siting,
environmental problems, economics and
fuel management.

## RE-ACTIONS
54041

555 N. Kensington Ave.
La Grange, IL 60525
Telephone: (708) 579-8232
Year Established: 1985
Pub. Frequency: 5/yr.
Page Size: standard
Subscrip. Rate: free to practicing teachers
Circulation: 18,000
Circulation Type: free
**Owner(s):**
American Nuclear Society, Inc.
555 N. Kensington Ave.
La Grange, IL 60525
Telephone: (708) 579-8261
Ownership %: 100
**Management:**
A. David Rossin ..........................President
Edward D. Fuller ...................Vice President
Rod Clemmons ............Business Manager
**Editorial:**
Paul Vlajcic ...............................Editor
Julie Jennings ...............Editorial Assistant
Wayne Witek ...............Production Director
Nancy Zacha ...............Publication Director
**Desc.:** Provides information to educators
interested in learning and teaching about
the various peaceful uses of nuclear
science and technology.
**Readers:** Primarily, teachers at elementary
and high school levels.

## TRANSACTIONS OF THE AMERICAN NUCLEAR SOCIETY
52638

555 N. Kensington Ave.
La Grange, IL 60525
Telephone: (708) 352-6611
Year Established: 1958
Pub. Frequency: bi-a.
Page Size: standard
Subscrip. Rate: $340/yr. 3 vols. plus 1
supplement
Print Process: offset
Circulation: 1,300
Circulation Type: controlled
**Owner(s):**
American Nuclear Society, Inc.
555 N. Kensington Ave.
La Grange, IL 60525
Telephone: (708) 352-6611
Ownership %: 100
**Management:**
Edward Fuller .............................President
James G. Toscas ...........Executive Director
Rod Clemmons ............Business Manager
Mary Beth Gardner ......................Manager
**Editorial:**
Irene Macke ................................Editor
Lloyd Wright ............................Treasurer

**Desc.:** Bi-annual publication containing
450-900 word summaries of all papers
presented at the annual and winter ANS
meetings, believed to contribute to the
advancement of nuclear science and
technology. Summaries of papers
presented at some National Topical
Meetings devoted to one area of nuclear
technology are printed in supplements to
transactions.
**Readers:** Nuclear scientists, educators,
technicians and those involved in
nuclear power for utilities.

## Group 172-Nursing

## AANA JOURNAL
24495

222 S. Prospect Ave.
Park Ridge, IL 60068-4001
Telephone: (708) 692-7050
FAX: (708) 692-6968
Year Established: 1933
Pub. Frequency: bi-m.
Page Size: standard
Subscrip. Rate: $24/yr.
Circulation: 27,000
Circulation Type: controlled & paid
**Owner(s):**
AANA Publishing, Inc.
222 S. Prospect Ave.
Park Ridge, IL 60068-4001
Telephone: (708) 692-7050
Ownership %: 100
**Bureau(s):**
Slack, Inc., Adv. Reps.
6900 Grove Rd.
Thorofare, NJ 08086
Telephone: (609) 848-1000
Contact: Getsy Kelton, Sales Manager
**Management:**
John F. Garde ...............Executive Director
Getsy Kelton ...............Advertising Manager
**Editorial:**
Betty Colitti-Stuffers ............Managing Editor
Sally Aquino ...............Associate Editor
Chuck Biddle ...............Science Editor
**Desc.:** Published for members of AANA
and others interested in the theory and
practice of anesthesiology. Clinical
articles pertaining to anesthesia and
allied subjects comprise the bulk of the
book.
**Readers:** Nurse anesthetists and others in
the health care field.

## AAOHN JOURNAL
24507

6900 Grove Rd.
Thorofare, NJ 08086-9447
Telephone: (609) 848-1000
FAX: (609) 853-5991
Year Established: 1949
Pub. Frequency: m.
Page Size: standard
Subscrip. Rate: $12/issue; $46/yr.
Materials: 02,06,10,15,25,29,32
Print Process: web offset
Circulation: 14,500
Circulation Type: paid
**Owner(s):**
American Assn. Occup. Health Nurses, Inc.
50 Lenox Pointe
Atlanta, GA 30324
Telephone: (404) 262-1162
Ownership %: 100
**Management:**
Richard N. Roash ........................Publisher
Les Robeson ...............Circulation Manager
**Editorial:**
Geraldine C. Williamson ...........Editor in Chief
Jennifer Kilpatrick ...............Executive Editor
Theresa Duscio ...............Assistant Editor
Susan Walker ...............Publishing
Donna O. ...............Publishing Director/Editorial
Carpenter

Kelly Cusack ................................Sales
**Desc.:** Edited primarily for the registered
nurse employed in commerce or industry
and others who are concerned with the
health of employees; physicians,
industrial hygienists, safety
professionals, members of management,
public health officials, schools, hospitals,
and universities. Contains original
articles of interest to all members of the
occupational health team.
**Readers:** National

## ADVANCES IN NURSING SCIENCE
58707

200 Orchard Ridge Dr.
Gaithersburg, MD 20878
Telephone: (301) 417-7500
FAX: (301) 417-7550
Year Established: 1978
Pub. Frequency: q.
Page Size: standard
Subscrip. Rate: $39/yr. student rate;
$64/yr.; $77/yr. foreign
Materials: 06,10,32
Print Process: DTP
Circulation: 4,395
Circulation Type: paid
**Owner(s):**
Aspen Publishers, Inc.
200 Orchard Ridge Dr.
Gaithersburg, MD 20878
Telephone: (301) 417-7500
Ownership %: 100
**Management:**
Michael B. Brown ...............Vice President
Michael B. Brown ...............Publisher
**Editorial:**
Lenda Hill ...............Managing Editor
Jane Garwood ...............Acquisitions Editor
Sandra L. Lunsford ...............Associate Editor
Janis Treacy ...............Marketing Manager
A. Maria R. ...............Production Coordinator
Ernest V. Manzella .......Senior V.P., Publishing
Services
Cynthia Smith ...........Vice President, Marketing
**Desc.:** Peer reviewed journal that provides
contribution to the development of
nursing science and promotes the
application of emerging theories and
research findings to practice.
**Readers:** Nurses interested in the
development of nursing science.

## AMERICAN JOURNAL OF CRITICAL CARE
68989

101 Columbia
Aliso Viejo, CA 92656
Telephone: (714) 362-2000
FAX: (714) 362-2020
Year Established: 1992
Pub. Frequency: bi-m.
Page Size: standard
Subscrip. Rate: $10 newsstand; $45/yr.
US; $52/yr. Canada & Mexico
Materials: 32,33
Print Process: web
Circulation: 78,000
Circulation Type: paid
**Owner(s):**
American Association of Critical Care
Nurses
101 Columbia
Aliso Viejo, CA 92656
Telephone: (714) 362-2000
Ownership %: 100
**Management:**
Bonnie Horrigan ........................Publisher
Scott Schmidt ...............Advertising Manager
**Editorial:**
Kathleen Dracup ...............Editor in Chief
Christopher Bryan-Brown ...........Editor in Chief
Michael Villaire ...............Managing Editor

**Desc.:** Communicates important advances
in clinical science and research in
critical care.

## AMERICAN JOURNAL OF MATERNAL CHILD NURSING, THE
58621

555 W. 57th St.
New York, NY 10019
Telephone: (212) 582-8820
Year Established: 1976
Pub. Frequency: bi-m.
Subscrip. Rate: $23/yr.
Circulation: 32,127
Circulation Type: paid
**Owner(s):**
American Journal of Nursing Co
555 W. 57th St.
New York, NY 10019
Telephone: (212) 582-8820
**Management:**
Barbara Severs ........................Manager
**Editorial:**
Barbara E. Bishop, R.N. ...............Editor

## AMERICAN JOURNAL OF NURSING
24475

555 W. 57th St.
New York, NY 10019
Telephone: (212) 582-8820
FAX: (212) 586-5462
Year Established: 1900
Pub. Frequency: m.
Page Size: standard
Subscrip. Rate: $35/yr. individual; $45/yr.
institution
Circulation: 233,000
Circulation Type: paid
**Owner(s):**
American Journal of Nursing Co.
555 W. 57th St.
New York, NY 10019
Telephone: (212) 582-8820
Ownership %: 100
**Management:**
Howard Clutterbach ....................President
Thelma M. Schorr ......................Publisher
Robert D'Angelo ...............Advertising Manager
Karen Zuckerman .............Circulation Manager
**Editorial:**
Martin diCarlantonio ...............Editor in Chief
**Desc.:** Contributed articles cover clinical
and technical subjects, nursing service,
nursing education, student interest,
general information. Carries news, new
books, audiovisuals including videotapes
and computer software reviews.
**Readers:** Nurses, head nurses,
administrators, nurse practitioners, public
health nurses, nursing educators,
nursing students.

## AMERICAN NURSE, THE
68987

600 Maryland Ave., S.W., Ste. 100
Washington, DC 20024-2571
Telephone: (202) 554-4444
FAX: (202) 554-2262
Year Established: 1969
Pub. Frequency: 10/yr.
Subscrip. Rate: $20/yr.
Circulation: 200,000
Circulation Type: paid
**Owner(s):**
American Nurses Association
600 Maryland Ave. S.W., #100
Washington, DC 20024-2571
Telephone: (202) 554-4444
Ownership %: 100
**Editorial:**
Mandy Mikulencak ......................Editor

## AORN JOURNAL
61318

2170 S. Parker Rd.
Denver, CO 80231-5711
Telephone: (303) 755-6300
Year Established: 1960
Pub. Frequency: m.
Subscrip. Rate: $50/yr.
Materials: 06,28,29,32,33
Print Process: web
Circulation: 52,000
Circulation Type: paid
**Owner(s):**
Association of Operating Room Nurses,
Inc.
2170 S. Parker Rd.
Denver, CO 80231-5711
Telephone: (303) 755-6300
**Editorial:**
Beverly Giordano .........................................Editor
Joyce Merriman ...........................................Editor
**Readers:** Operating rooms nurses.
**Deadline:** ads-1st. of mo. prior to pub.
date

## CALIFORNIA NURSE
24479

1145 Market St., Ste. 1100
San Francisco, CA 94103
Telephone: (415) 864-4141
FAX: (415) 431-1011
Year Established: 1905
Pub. Frequency: 10/yr.
Page Size: tabloid
Subscrip. Rate: $30/yr. in US; $35/yr.
foreign
Materials: 32,33
Circulation: 26,000
Circulation Type: controlled
**Owner(s):**
California Nurses' Association
1145 Market St., Ste. 1100
San Francisco, CA 94103
Telephone: (415) 864-4141
Ownership %: 100
**Desc.:** Written by staff and free lance
writers. Provides features on all areas of
interest to California nurses.
**Readers:** Registered nurses, various
universities, colleges, schools and
libraries within and outside California.
**Deadline:** ads-10th of mo. prior to pub.
date

## CANCER NURSING
69611

1185 Ave. of the Americas
New York, NY 10036
Telephone: (212) 930-9500
FAX: (212) 869-3495
Year Established: 1978
Pub. Frequency: bi-m.
Subscrip. Rate: $40/yr. individuals; $69/yr.
institutions
Circulation: 7,300
Circulation Type: paid
**Owner(s):**
Raven Press
1185 Ave. of the Americas
New York, NY 10036
Telephone: (212) 930-9500
Ownership %: 100
**Editorial:**
Carol Reed-Ash ..........................................Editor
**Desc.:** Covers problems arising in the care
of cancer patients.

## CLINICAL NURSE SPECIALIST
59041

428 E. Preston St.
Baltimore, MD 21202
Telephone: (410) 528-4000
FAX: (410) 528-4312
Year Established: 1986
Pub. Frequency: bi-m.

Page Size: standard
Subscrip. Rate: $67/yr. individual; $90/yr.
institution
Circulation: 3,300
Circulation Type: paid
**Owner(s):**
Williams & Wilkins Co.
428 E. Preston St.
Baltimore, MD 21202
Telephone: (410) 528-4000
Ownership %: 100
**Management:**
Don Pfarr ...........................Advertising Manager
Alma Wills .........................................Manager
**Editorial:**
Pauline C. Beecroft ....................................Editor
Nancy Collins ......................Marketing Director
**Desc.:** Information for the clinician,
consultant, executive, peer, and patient
educator.
**Readers:** Clinical nurse specialist, nurse
administrators and educators in all
disciplines.

## COMPUTERS IN NURSING
61834

E. Washington Sq.
Philadelphia, PA 19106
Telephone: (215) 238-4200
FAX: (205) 985-2018
Year Established: 1983
Pub. Frequency: bi-m.
Page Size: standard
Subscrip. Rate: $42/yr. individuals US;
$64/yr. foreign; $90/yr. US institutions;
$120/yr. foreign
Circulation: 3,801
Circulation Type: paid
**Owner(s):**
Wolters Kluwer U.S. Corporation
E. Washington Sq.
Philadelphia, PA 19106
Telephone: (215) 238-4200
**Management:**
Linda Krumpholz ...................................Manager
**Editorial:**
Gary D. Hales ............................................Editor
**Readers:** Nurses in education and
practice.

## CRITICAL CARE NURSE
68985

101 Columbia
Aliso Viejo, CA 92656
Telephone: (714) 362-2000
Year Established: 1980
Pub. Frequency: 6/yr.
Subscrip. Rate: $8 newsstand; $27/yr.
individuals; $45/yr. institutions
Materials: 06,10,17,25,32,33
Print Process: web
Circulation: 95,000
Circulation Type: paid
**Owner(s):**
American Association of Critical Care
Nurses
101 Columbia
Aliso Viejo, CA 92656
Telephone: (714) 362-2000
FAX: (714) 362-2020
Ownership %: 100
**Editorial:**
Joann Grif Alspach ....................................Editor
**Desc.:** Provides current information and
perspectives on a wide range of topics
in critical care nursing. The magazine is
dedicated to clinical topics which will
help critical care nurses deliver better
patient care.
**Readers:** Critical care nurses.

## DERMATOLOGY NURSING
67204

N. Woodbury Rd.
P.O. Box 56
Pitman, NJ 08071
Telephone: (609) 589-2319
FAX: (609) 589-7463
Year Established: 1989
Pub. Frequency: bi-m.
Page Size: standard
Subscrip. Rate: $28/yr.
Circulation: 6,000
Circulation Type: paid
**Owner(s):**
Jannetti Publications, Inc.
N. Woodbury Rd.
P.O. Box 56
Pitman, NJ 08071
Telephone: (609) 589-2319
Ownership %: 100
**Management:**
Michael Cunningham ........Advertising Manager
**Editorial:**
Marcia Hill .................................................Editor
**Desc.:** Official journal of the Dermatology
Nurses Association strives to develop
and foster the highest standards of
dermatology nursing care through
education and research.
**Readers:** Dermatology nurses, wound care
nurses.

## HEART & LUNG-JOURNAL OF
## CRITICAL CARE
24484

11830 Westline Ind. Dr.
St. Louis, MO 63146
Telephone: (314) 872-8370
FAX: (312) 432-1380
Year Established: 1972
Pub. Frequency: bi-m.
Page Size: standard
Subscrip. Rate: $36/yr. individual
Circulation: 15,000
Circulation Type: paid
**Owner(s):**
Mosby-Year Book, Inc.
11830 Westline Industrial Dr.
St. Louis, MO 63146
Telephone: (314) 872-8370
Ownership %: 100
**Management:**
Carol Trumbold ......................................Publisher
Kathy Preston ..................Advertising Manager
**Editorial:**
Kathleen A. Stone .....................................Editor
Kathy Keller .......................Production Director
**Desc.:** Recognizes the nurses role and
responsibility in the care and
management of cardiovascular
and pulmonary conditions in critically ill
patients.
**Readers:** Nurses, M.D.'s, cardiopulmonary
technicians. Official publication of the
American Association of Critical-Care
Nurses.

## HOLISTIC NURSING PRACTICE
58708

7201 McKinney Cir.
Frederick, MD 21701
Telephone: (301) 698-7100
Mailing Address:
200 Orchard Ridge Dr.
Gaithersburg, MD 20878
Year Established: 1979
Pub. Frequency: q.
Page Size: standard
Subscrip. Rate: $71/yr. US; $85/yr. foreign
Materials: 06,10,32
Print Process: DTP
Circulation: 3,000
Circulation Type: paid

**Owner(s):**
Aspen Publishers, Inc.
200 Orchard Ridge Dr
Gaithersburg, MD 20878
Telephone: (301) 417-7500
**Editorial:**
Jane Garwood .....................Acquisitions Editor
Sandra Lunsford ....................Associate Editor
**Desc.:** HNP is a peer-reviewed journal that
provides nurse clinicians and educators
with information on holistic approaches
to nursing practice in clinical settings.
**Readers:** Nurses in all specialties
interested in the holistic perspective.

## HOME HEALTHCARE NURSE
65606

210 E. Washington Sq.
Philadelphia, PA 19100
Telephone: (215) 238-4206
Pub. Frequency: bi-m.
Subscrip. Rate: $25/yr. individuals; $40/yr.
institutions
Circulation: 10,000
Circulation Type: paid
**Owner(s):**
Lippincot
210 E. Washington Sq.
Philadelphia, PA 19106
Ownership %: 100
**Desc.:** Original editorial geared to the
practicing professional nurse in the
home health, community health, and
public health areas. The articles keep
readers abreast of new developments
and procedures in such important areas
as preventive medicine, quality
assurance, managed health care, and
family care.
**Readers:** Professional nurses working for
VNA'S, home health agencies
(independent and hospital based), and
discharge planners.

## IMAGE: JOURNAL OF NURSING
## SCHOLARSHIP
68990

550 W. North St.
Indianapolis, IN 46202
Telephone: (317) 634-8171
FAX: (317) 634-8188
Year Established: 1967
Pub. Frequency: q.
Page Size: 8 1/2 X 11
Subscrip. Rate: $25/yr. US; $35/yr. foreign
Materials: 32,33
Print Process: web offset
Circulation: 101,500
Circulation Type: controlled & paid
**Owner(s):**
Sigma Theta Tau International Honor
Society
550 W. North St.
Indianapolis, IN 46202
Telephone: (317) 634-8171
Ownership %: 100
**Editorial:**
Beverly Henry ............................................Editor

## IMPRINT
24485

555 W. 57th St.
Ste. 1327
New York, NY 10019
Telephone: (212) 581-2211
FAX: (212) 581-2368
Year Established: 1968
Pub. Frequency: 5/yr.
Page Size: standard
Subscrip. Rate: $15/yr.
Circulation: 38,000
Circulation Type:

**Owner(s):**
National Student Nurses Association Inc.
555 W. 57th St.
New York, NY 10019
Telephone: (212) 581-2211
Ownership %: 100
**Management:**
Mike Cunningham ..............Advertising Manager
**Editorial:**
Caroline Jaffe ..........................Managing Editor
**Desc.:** The publication carries news and
articles of student opinion on current
issues or trends in nursing and nursing
education.
**Readers:** Student nurses, others in nursing
profession.

## INTERNATIONAL NURSING INDEX
58686
555 W. 57th St.
New York, NY 10019
Telephone: (212) 582-8820
Year Established: 1966
Pub. Frequency: q.
Subscrip. Rate: $250/yr.
Circulation: 2,000
Circulation Type: paid
**Owner(s):**
American Journal of Nursing Co.
555 W. 57th St.
New York, NY 10019
Telephone: (212) 582-8820
**Management:**
Janet Dyer ...............................................Manager
**Editorial:**
Frederick W. Pattison ...............................Editor
**Desc.:** Abstracting coverage of more than
270 international journals in the field of
nursing.

## JOURNAL OF CARDIOVASCULAR NURSING, THE
58603
200 Orchard Ridge Dr.
Gaithersburg, MD 20878
Telephone: (301) 417-1700
FAX: (301) 417-7550
Year Established: 1986
Pub. Frequency: q.
Page Size: standard
Materials: 06,10,15,32
Circulation: 3,300
Circulation Type: paid
**Owner(s):**
Aspen Publishers, Inc.
200 Orchard Ridge Dr.
Gaithersburg, MD 20878
Telephone: (301) 417-7500
Ownership %: 100
**Management:**
Jack Bruggeman ................................Publisher
Frances Ray ......................Advertising Manager
**Editorial:**
Lenda P. Hill ...........................Managing Editor
Jane Garwoo ...........................Associate Editor
**Desc.:** JCN is a peer-reviewed journal that
provides nurses and allied health care
professionals with information to foster
expert clinical practice in cardiovascular
nursing, and to increase their ability to
meet the physiologic, psychologic, and
social responses of cardiovascular
patients and their families in a variety of
environments.
**Readers:** Nurses & allied health
professionals

## JOURNAL OF EMERGENCY NURSING
24488
216 Higgins Rd.
Park Ridge, IL 60068
Telephone: (708) 698-9400
FAX: (708) 698-9406
Year Established: 1975
Pub. Frequency: bi-m.

Page Size: standard
Subscrip. Rate: $44/yr.
Materials: 02,06,10,15,32,33
Print Process: offset lithography
Circulation: 27,000
Circulation Type: controlled & paid
**Owner(s):**
Emergency Nurses Association
216 Higgins Rd.
Park Ridge, IL 60068
Telephone: (708) 698-9400
FAX: (708) 698-9406
Ownership %: 100
**Editorial:**
Gail Pisarcik Lenehan ..............................Editor
Karen E. Halm ..........................Managing Editor
**Desc.:** Published for nurses and other
professionals working in emergency
departments, offering new techniques
and procedures for improving the
emergency health care of patients.
**Readers:** Emergency nurses and other
health care professionals.

## JOURNAL OF ET NURSING
70395
11830 Westline Industrial Dr.
St. Louis, MO 63146
Year Established: 1974
Pub. Frequency: bi-m.
Subscrip. Rate: $8/copy; $26/yr. student;
$44/yr. individual; $107/yr. institution
Print Process: offset
Circulation: 4,139
Circulation Type: free & paid
**Desc.:** Journal articles cover the entire
scope of enterostomal therapy practice
as defined by professionals active in the
field. Topics include the specialized care
and management of persons with
abdominal stomas, fistulas, wounds,
incontinence, pressure ulcers, and
vascular ulcers.

## JOURNAL OF GERONTOLOGICAL NURSING
24489
6900 Grove Rd.
Thorofare, NJ 08086
Telephone: (609) 848-1000
FAX: (609) 853-5991
Year Established: 1975
Pub. Frequency: m.
Page Size: standard
Subscrip. Rate: $36/yr. individuals; $48/yr.
institutions
Circulation: 11,000
Circulation Type: paid
**Owner(s):**
Slack, Inc.
6900 Grove Rd.
Thorofare, NJ 08086
Telephone: (609) 848-1000
Ownership %: 100
**Management:**
Richard Roash ....................................Publisher
Theresa Demtsey .............Advertising Manager
**Editorial:**
Edna Stilwell ..........................................Editor
**Desc.:** This journal is dedicated to the
continuing education of gerontological
nurses.
**Readers:** Gerontological Nurses

## JOURNAL OF INTRAVENOUS NURSING
23925
227 E. Washington Sq.
Philadelphia, PA 19106
Telephone: (215) 238-4200
Year Established: 1978
Pub. Frequency: bi-m.
Page Size: standard
Subscrip. Rate: $18/issue; $60/yr. US;
$75/yr. foreign
Circulation: 10,107
Circulation Type: paid

**Owner(s):**
J.B. Lippincott Co.
227 E. Washington Sq.
Philadelphia, PA 19106
Telephone: (215) 238-4273

Intravenous Nurses Society
Two Brighton St.
Belmont, MA 02178
**Management:**
Beverly Dietrich .................Circulation Manager
Joe Baiocco .......................Production Manager
**Editorial:**
Mary Larkin, R.N. ....................................Editor
Virginia Martin ......................................Director
Susan Graff .............Senior Marketing Manager
**Desc.:** I.V. related articles, studies, reports,
and reviews for the continuing education
of the professionals involved in I.V.
therapy correspondence, book reviews
and an employment placement service
are included as well as news of and for
association members through a special
INS News section.
**Readers:** INS membership, I.V.
Supervisors, pharmacy services in
hospitals of 100 beds or more.

## JOURNAL OF NURSING ADMINISTRATION, THE
61796
227 E. Washington Square
Philadelphia, PA 19105
Telephone: (215) 238-4200
Year Established: 1971
Pub. Frequency: 11/yr.
Page Size: standard
Subscrip. Rate: $15/issue; $56/yr.
individuals; $89/yr. foreign; $140/yr.
institutions; $178/yr. foreign
Materials: 33
Circulation: 11,607
Circulation Type: paid
**Owner(s):**
J.B. Lippincott Co.
E. Washington Sq.
Philadelphia, PA 19106
Telephone: (215) 238-4200
Ownership %: 100
**Bureau(s):**
JONA Editorial Office
4301 32nd St., W., Ste. C-12
Bradenton, FL 34205
Telephone: (813) 753-5662
Contact: Suzanne Smith Blancett, Editor in
Chief
**Management:**
Kathleen Phelan ..............Advertising Manager
Lisa Marshall ..........................................Manager
**Editorial:**
Suzanne Smith Blancett ..........................Editor
Karyn Crislip ...........................Managing Editor
**Desc.:** JONA is the authorative source of
information on developments and
advances in nursing administration and
management. Content is
aimed specifically at upper level nurse
executives in both hospital and
community health agencies.
**Readers:** Nursing executives, including
VPs, directors of nursing, associate and
assistant directors of nursing and
nursing managers.

## JOURNAL OF NURSING CARE QUALITY
58605
200 Orchard Ridge Dr.
Gaithersburg, MD 20878
Telephone: (301) 417-7500
FAX: (301) 417-7550
Year Established: 1986
Pub. Frequency: q.
Page Size: standard
Subscrip. Rate: $75/yr.
Circulation: 4,300
Circulation Type: paid

**Owner(s):**
Aspen Publishers, Inc.
200 Orchard Ridge Dr.
Gaithersburg, MD 20878
Telephone: (301) 417-7623
Ownership %: 100
**Desc.:** Peer-reviewed journal that provides
practicing nurses as well as nurses who
have leadership roles in nursing quality
assurance (QA) programs with useful
information regarding the application of
QA principles and concepts in the
practice setting. The journal offers a
forum for the scholarly discussion of
"real world" implementation of QA
activities.
**Readers:** Practicing nurses, nurse
administrators

## JOURNAL OF NURSING EDUCATION
24490
6900 Grove Rd.
Thorofare, NJ 08086
Telephone: (609) 848-1000
FAX: (609) 853-5991
Year Established: 1961
Pub. Frequency: 9/yr.
Page Size: standard
Subscrip. Rate: $44/yr. individual; $59 inst.
Circulation: 4,000
Circulation Type: paid
**Owner(s):**
Slack, Inc.
6900 Grove Rd.
Thorofare, NJ 08086
Telephone: (609) 848-1000
Ownership %: 100
**Management:**
Richard N. Roash ................................Publisher
Wayne McCourt ................Advertising Manager
**Editorial:**
Dawn Duperre ..........................Managing Editor
Peter Sensp ......................................Advertising
**Desc.:** Contains original articles and new
ideas for nursing educators in various
types and levels of nursing programs,
with the aim of enhancing the teaching-
learning process, promoting curriculum
development, and stimulating creative
innovation and research in nursing
education.

## JOURNAL OF NURSING STAFF DEVELOPMENT
61786
227 E. Washington Sq.
Philadelphia, PA 19106
Telephone: (215) 238-4200
Year Established: 1985
Pub. Frequency: bi-m.
Subscrip. Rate: $44/yr. individuals; $99/yr.
institutions
Circulation: 3,850
Circulation Type: paid
**Owner(s):**
J.B. Lippincott Co.
227 E. Washington Sq.
Philadelphia, PA 19106
Telephone: (215) 238-4200
**Management:**
Earl Gerhardt ........................................Manager
**Editorial:**
Belinda E. Puetz ....................................Editor

## JOURNAL OF OBSTETRIC, GYNECOLOGIC & NEONATAL NURSING
24491
700 14th St.
Ste. 600
Washington, DC 20005-2019
Telephone: (202) 662-1632
FAX: (202) 737-0575

**Materials Accepted/Included:** 01-Business news 02-By-line articles 03-Fashion news 04-Food news 05-Freelance copy 06-Letters to editor 07-Real estate news 08-Sports news 09-Travel news
10-Book rev. 11-Movie rev. 12-Music rev. 13-TV rev. 14-Theater rev. 15-Coming events 16-Obituaries 17-Question & answer 18-Social announcements 19-Artwork 20-Cartoons 21-Photos 22-TV listings
23-Audio rec. 24-Video rec. 25-Books 26-Films/film clips 27-Personnel news 28-Press releases 29-New product news/photos 30-Trade lit. 31-Contracts awarded 32-Display adv. 33-Classified adv.

4-269

Mailing Address:
227 E. Washington Sq.
Philadelphia, PA 19105
Year Established: 1972
Pub. Frequency: 9/yr.
Page Size: standard
Subscrip. Rate: $55/yr.
Materials: 06,10
Circulation: 27,000
Circulation Type: paid
**Owner(s):**
Association of Women's Health, Obstetric, & Neonatal Nursing
700 14th St., Ste. 600
Washington, DC 20005-2019
Telephone: (202) 662-1600
FAX: (202) 737-0525
Ownership %: 100
**Management:**
J.B. Lippincott Co. ...............................Publisher
**Editorial:**
Karen Haller ..............................................Editor
**Desc.:** This journal is edited for nurses who have specific responsibilities in the area of obstetric, gynecological and neonatal nursing. It offers a forum to publish research, new practices and current policies.
**Readers:** Nurses in the areas of obstetric, gynecologic and neonatal nursing.

24492
## JOURNAL OF PRACTICAL NURSING, THE
1400 Spring St.
Ste. 310
Silver Spring, MD 20910
Telephone: (301) 588-2491
FAX: (301) 588-2839
Year Established: 1951
Pub. Frequency: 4/yr.
Page Size: standard
Subscrip. Rate: $15/yr. US; $23/yr. foreign
Freelance Pay: $25-$150/submission
Circulation: 7,000
Circulation Type: controlled & paid
**Owner(s):**
Nat'l Assn. for Practical Nurse
1400 Spring St., #310
Silver Spring, MD 20910
Telephone: (301) 588-2491
Ownership %: 100
**Bureau(s):**
Bashian Publishing, Inc.
1501 Euclid Ave.
Cleveland, OH 44115
Telephone: (216) 621-2858
Contact: Charles Bashian, President
**Editorial:**
Mathew Green ..........................................Editor
John Word ...........................Executive Director
**Desc.:** Devoted to the field of practical nursing. Uses articles, features and photos of nursing interest. Welcome releases and articles. Departments include: New Drugs, Association News, Books, Legislation and Medical News of Interest to Nurses, Calendar of Meetings, Products, Nutrition.
**Readers:** Licensed practical/vocational nurses, RN's, hospital and nursing home administrators.

24493
## JOURNAL OF PSYCHOSOCIAL NURSING
6900 Grove Rd.
Thorofare, NJ 08086
Telephone: (609) 848-1000
Year Established: 1962
Pub. Frequency: m.
Page Size: standard
Subscrip. Rate: $48/yr.
Circulation: 14,500
Circulation Type: paid

**Owner(s):**
Slack, Inc.
6900 Grove Rd.
Thorofare, NJ 08086
Telephone: (609) 848-1000
Ownership %: 100
**Management:**
Peter Slack ..........................................President
Richard N. Roash ...............................Publisher
Les Robeson ...................Circulation Manager
**Editorial:**
Shirley Smoyak, RN, Ph D .........Editor in Chief
Mary Jo Krey ...........................Managing Editor
Michelle Tordoff ..................................Advertising
Amy Slugg Moore ....................Assistant Editor
Donna Carpenter ..............Associate Publisher
Matthew McDaniel ...............Manuscript Editor
**Desc.:** Directed to the professional registered nurses and other members who are concerned with the issues and trends surrounding the prevention and treatment of mental health disorders.
**Readers:** Psychiatric nursing personnel, psychiatric allied services.

56419
## JOURNAL OF WOUND, OSTOMY, & CONTINENCE NURSING
11830 Westline Industrial Dr.
St. Louis, MO 63146
Telephone: (314) 872-8370
FAX: (314) 432-1380
Year Established: 1974
Pub. Frequency: bi-m
Page Size: standard
Subscrip. Rate: $40/yr. individual
Circulation: 3,172
Circulation Type: paid
**Owner(s):**
The Wound, Ostomy and Continence Nurses Society
2755 Briston St.
Ste. 110
Costa Mesa, CA 92626
Telephone: (714) 476-0268
Ownership %: 100
**Management:**
Carol Trumbold ....................................Publisher
Kathy Preston ..................Advertising Manager
**Editorial:**
Mikel Gray, Ph.D., CURN, CCCN .............Editor
Kathy Keller .........................Production Director
**Desc.:** Serves an international network of enterostomal therapy practitioners and provides data related to the care of persons with ostomies, draining wounds, fistulae, and pressure ulcers. Researchers, educators, and practitioners contribute originally submitted peer - reviewed clinical studies in each issue.
**Readers:** Enterostomal nurses. Official publication of the International Association for Enterostomal Therapy (IAET).

61833
## NURSE EDUCATOR
227 E. Washington Sq.
Philadelphia, PA 19106
Telephone: (215) 238-4200
Pub. Frequency: bi-m.
Subscrip. Rate: $43/yr. individuals; $77/yr. institutions
Circulation: 3,625
Circulation Type: paid
**Owner(s):**
J.P. Lippincott Co.
227 E. Washington Sq.
Philadelphia, PA 19106
Telephone: (215) 238-4200
**Management:**
Lisa Marshall ......................................Publisher
**Editorial:**
Susan Eidson .........................Advertising Sales
Randy Hendrickson ....................Design Editor

Dionne Henderson ................Production Editor

68988
## NURSEWEEK
1156 Aster Ave., Ste. C
Sunnyvale, CA 94086-6801
Telephone: (408) 249-5877
FAX: (408) 249-8204
Year Established: 1986
Pub. Frequency: bi-m.
Subscrip. Rate: $40/yr.
Circulation: 190,000
Circulation Type: paid
**Owner(s):**
Nurseweek
1156 Aster Ave., Ste. C
Sunnyvale, CA 94086-6801
Telephone: (408) 249-5877
Ownership %: 100
**Editorial:**
Clarice Hutchinson .....................................Editor
**Readers:** Experienced, career-oriented nurses in hospitals and other California health care facilties.

24505
## NURSING '95
1111 Bethlehem Pike
Spring House, PA 19477
Telephone: (215) 646-8700
FAX: (215) 646-4399
Year Established: 1971
Pub. Frequency: m.
Page Size: standard
Subscrip. Rate: $38/yr.
Materials: 32,33
Print Process: web offset
Circulation: 442,626
Circulation Type: paid
**Owner(s):**
Reed Elsevier Medical Publishing, Inc.
6 Chesterfield Gardens
London W1A 1EJ, United Kingdom
Telephone: 44-71-4918212
Ownership %: 100
**Management:**
Kevin M. Hurley ...............................President
Maryanne Wagner ....................Vice President
Melissa J. Warner .....................Vice President
**Editorial:**
Jane Benner ........................Managing Editor
Joan Cassin .........................Assistant Editor
K. Carey .............................Associate Editor
Patricia Nornhold, RN, ....................Director
Jerry Locke ........................Personnel Manager
**Desc.:** A skill-enrichment journal for practicing nurses. Contains how-to articles dealing with clinical nursing. Articles written on assignment by nurses and health professionals chosen for expert knowledge. Manuscripts are previewed and pretested for accuracy and usability by members of the 44-member editorial and advisory boards.
**Readers:** Clinical nurses interested in patient care.

58601
## NURSING ADMINISTRATION QUARTERLY
7201 McKinney Cir.
Frederick, MD 21701
Telephone: (301) 251-5449
FAX: (301) 695-7931
Year Established: 1976
Pub. Frequency: q.
Page Size: standard
Subscrip. Rate: $92/yr. US; $110/yr. foreign
Materials: 06,10,32
Print Process: offset
Circulation: 4,300
Circulation Type: free & paid

**Owner(s):**
Aspen Publishers, Inc.
200 Orchard Ridge Dr.
Gaithersburg, MD 20878
Telephone: (301) 417-7500
Ownership %: 100
**Management:**
Michael B. Brown ..............................Publisher
Jack Bruggeman ................Associate Publisher
Nin Kasari ...........................Production Manager
**Editorial:**
Lenda P. Hill ........................Managing Editor
Sandra L. Lunsford ............Associate Editor
**Desc.:** A peer-reviewed journal that provides nursing administrators with practical up-to-date information on the effective management of nursing services in modern health care facilities.
**Readers:** Nursing administrators.

69595
## NURSING CONNECTIONS
110 Irving St., N.W.
Washington, DC 20010
Telephone: (202) 877-3048
FAX: (202) 877-3078
Year Established: 1988
Pub. Frequency: q.
Page Size: standard
Subscrip. Rate: $55/yr. individuals; $69/yr. libraries
Materials: 06,32
Circulation: 1,040
Circulation Type: free & paid
**Owner(s):**
Washington Hospital Center, Div. of Nursing
110 Irving St., N.W.
Washington, DC 20010
Telephone: (202) 877-3048
Ownership %: 100
**Management:**
Joyce Johnson .......................................Publisher
**Editorial:**
Molly Billingsley ..........................Editor in Chief
**Desc.:** Describes collaborative projects between practice, research, administration and education to solve health care problems.
**Readers:** Nursing leaders, deans and hospital administrators.

24501
## NURSING FORUM
1211 Locust St.
Philadelphia, PA 19107
Telephone: (215) 545-7222
Year Established: 1961
Pub. Frequency: q.
Page Size: standard
Subscrip. Rate: $40/yr. individual; $52/yr. instn.
Circulation: 1770
Circulation Type: paid
**Owner(s):**
Nursecom, Inc.
1211 Locust St.
Philadelphia, PA 19107
Telephone: (215) 545-7222
Ownership %: 100
**Management:**
Alice R. Clarke ....................................Publisher
Kelly Collins ......................Circulation Manager
**Editorial:**
Lynda Carpenito .........................................Editor
**Desc.:** Professional nursing journal presenting innovative ideas and emerging issues in nursing.

24515
## NURSING MANAGEMENT
103 N. Second St., Ste. 200
Dundee, IL 60118
Telephone: (708) 426-6100
FAX: (708) 426-6146
Year Established: 1970
Pub. Frequency: m.

**Materials Accepted/Included:** 01-Business news 02-By-line articles 03-Fashion news 04-Food news 05-Freelance copy 06-Letters to editor 07-Real estate news 08-Sports news 09-Travel news 10-Book rev. 11-Movie rev. 12-Music rev. 13-TV rev. 14-Theater rev. 15-Coming events 16-Obituaries 17-Question & answer 18-Social announcements 19-Artwork 20-Cartoons 21-Photos 22-TV listings 23-Audio rec. 24-Video rec. 25-Books 26-Films/film clips 27-Personnel news 28-Press releases 29-New product news/photos 30-Trade lit. 31-Contracts awarded 32-Display adv. 33-Classified adv.

Page Size: standard
Subscrip. Rate: $25/yr.; $32/yr. Canada;
    $45/yr. elsewhere
Freelance Pay: negotiable
Circulation: 135,000
Circulation Type: paid
**Owner(s):**
S-N Publications
103 N. Second St., Ste. 200
Dundee, IL 60118
Telephone: (708) 426-6100
Ownership %: 100
**Management:**
John Harling .............................Publisher
**Editorial:**
Leah L. Curtin ....................Executive Editor
Andrew Miller ..........................Managing Editor
Paula Gonzalez ....................Assistant Editor
Leah L. Curtin ............................Photo
Carolina Zurlage ..........................Photo
**Desc.:** Professional articles in nursing
management (personnel, budgeting,
staffing, unit management, federal
legislation of health care). Departments
include: Book Reviews, Legal Column,
Technology; Nursing The System,
Legislative Effects: What's Next?, Ethics:
The Dynamics of Decision, Financial
Management, Continuing Education,
Perspectives on Nursing, New Products,
Demographic Editions: Critical Care,
Surgical Care, Full Run.
**Readers:** Directors of nursing service,
supervisors, head nurses, graduate
students in nursing and health
administration.

**NURSING OUTLOOK**                    24503
11830 Westline Industrial Dr.
Saint Louis, MO 63146
Telephone: (314) 872-8370
FAX: (314) 432-1380
Year Established: 1953
Pub. Frequency: bi-m.
Page Size: standard
Subscrip. Rate: $29/yr. individuals; $39/yr.
    institutions; $19/yr. students
Circulation: 10,588
Circulation Type: paid
**Owner(s):**
Mosby-Year Book, Inc.
11830 Westline Industrial Dr.
St. Louis, MO 63146
Telephone: (314) 872-8370
**Management:**
Carol Trumbold .......................Publisher
Kathy Preston ...................Advertising Manager
Kate Carter .......................Circulation Manager
**Editorial:**
Carole Anderson, Ph.D., RN ...................Editor
**Desc.:** Primary editorial emphasis is on
advanced nursing concepts, trends and
practices for leaders in nursing, including
education. Editorial content consists of
original articles solicited from
recognized authorities in their respective
fields plus news of organizations and
individuals. News includes continuing
education and meetings, calls for
papers, new programs, grants and
appointments. N.O. is the official journal
of the American Academy of Nursing.
**Readers:** Professional nurses who for the
most part are educators, clinical
specialists, and nurse executives.

**NURSING RESEARCH**                    24504
555 W. 57th St.
New York, NY 10019
Telephone: (212) 582-8820
FAX: (212) 586-5462
Year Established: 1952
Pub. Frequency: bi-m.

Page Size: standard
Subscrip. Rate: $7/copy; $90/yr.
    institutions; $40/yr. individuals; $30/yr.
    students
Materials: 06,25,28,32,33
Print Process: web offset
Circulation: 12,000
Circulation Type: paid
**Owner(s):**
American Journal of Nursing Co.
555 W. 57th St.
New York, NY 10019
Telephone: (212) 582-8820
FAX: (212) 586-5462
Ownership %: 100
**Management:**
Howard Clutterbuck .....................President
James Clements .........................Publisher
Robert D'Angelo ............Advertising Manager
**Editorial:**
Florence S. Downs .......................Editor
Astrid Dadourian ................Managing Editor
**Readers:** Nursing profession, hospital
administration.
**Deadline:** ads-15th. of mo. prior to pub.
date

**NURSING SCIENCE QUARTERLY**          69599
P.O. Box 22492
Pittsburgh, PA 15222
Telephone: (412) 391-8585
FAX: (412) 391-8458
Year Established: 1988
Pub. Frequency: q.
Page Size: standard
Subscrip. Rate: $25/yr. students; $50/yr.
    individuals; $70/yr. institutions
Materials: 06,18,27,28,32,33
Print Process: offset lithography
Circulation: 2,800
Circulation Type: free & paid
**Owner(s):**
Chestnut House Publications
P.O. Box 22492
Pittsburgh, PA 15222
Telephone: (412) 391-8585
FAX: (412) 391-8458
Ownership %: 100
**Editorial:**
Rosemarie Rizzo Parse .....................Editor
**Desc.:** Covers key aspects of nursing
science, such as theoretical dilemmas,
research issues, and practice
applications.
**Deadline:** news-60 days; ads-60 days

**NURSINGWORLD JOURNAL**               24502
470 Boston Post Rd.
Weston, MA 02193
Telephone: (617) 899-2702
FAX: (617) 899-4900
Year Established: 1974
Pub. Frequency: m.
Page Size: tabloid
Subscrip. Rate: $37.50/yr.
Freelance Pay: varies
Circulation: 35,000
Circulation Type: paid
**Owner(s):**
Prime National Publishing Corp.
470 Boston Post Rd.
Weston, MA 02193
Telephone: (617) 899-2702
Ownership %: 100
**Management:**
E. F. DeVito ..........................President
R. A. DeVito ..........................Publisher
Peg Moreland ................Advertising Manager
**Editorial:**
Eileen DeVito ....................Editor in Chief
Randy Gates ..................Managing Editor

**Desc.:** Contains news and features about
nursing; reviews of major healthcare
articles as they apply to nursing;
information on nursing employment
opportunities.
**Readers:** Nurses and nursing students,
highly mobil.

**REVOLUTION: THE JOURNAL OF**          67210
**NURSING EMPOWERMENT**
56 McArthur Ave.
Staten Island, NY 10312
Telephone: (800) 331-6534
FAX: (718) 317-0858
Year Established: 1991
Pub. Frequency: q.
Page Size: standard
Subscrip. Rate: $19.95/yr.
Circulation: 50,000
Circulation Type: paid
**Owner(s):**
A.D. Von Publishers, Inc.
56 McArthur Ave.
Staten Island, NY 10312
Telephone: (800) 331-6534
Ownership %: 100
**Management:**
Laura Gaspanis Vonfrolio .............Publisher
Susan Peck .................Advertising Manager
**Editorial:**
Joan Swirsky .............................Editor
**Desc.:** Provides articles that empower
nurses.
**Readers:** Registered nurses.

**RN, NATIONAL MAGAZINE FOR**           24514
**REGISTERED NURSES**
Five Paragon Dr.
Montvale, NJ 07645
Telephone: (201) 358-7200
FAX: (201) 573-8979
Year Established: 1937
Pub. Frequency: m.
Page Size: standard
Subscrip. Rate: $35/yr.; $50/yr. foreign
Freelance Pay: negotiable
Circulation: 295,284
Circulation Type: paid
**Owner(s):**
Medical Economics Co., Inc.
Five Paragon Dr.
Montvale, NJ 07645
Telephone: (201) 358-7200
Ownership %: 100
**Management:**
Alex Davidson .........................Publisher
Mindy Meldrim .................Advertising Manager
**Editorial:**
Marianne Dekker Mattera ...................Editor
Helen Lippman ................Managing Editor
**Desc.:** Clinical magazine for registered
nurses. Covers all items that would be
of interest to registered nurses and the
nursing profession.
**Readers:** Registered nurses, nursing
students.

**TAR HEEL NURSE**                      69601
P.O. Box 12025
Raleigh, NC 27605
Telephone: (919) 821-4250
FAX: (919) 829-5807
Year Established: 1939
Pub. Frequency: bi-m.
Page Size: standard
Subscrip. Rate: $25/yr. US; $50/yr. foreign
Circulation: 3,500
Circulation Type: paid
**Owner(s):**
North Carolina Nurses Association
P.O. Box 12025
Raleigh, NC 27605
Telephone: (919) 821-4250
Ownership %: 100

**WASHINGTON NURSE**                    69605
2505 Second Ave., Ste. 500
Seattle, WA 98121-1460
Telephone: (206) 433-9762
FAX: (206) 728-2074
Year Established: 1977
Pub. Frequency: 6/yr.
Page Size: standard
Subscrip. Rate: $3.35 newsstand; $26/yr.
    US; $28/yr. Canada & Mexico; $35/yr.
    elsewhere
Materials: 06,16,32,33
Print Process: web
Circulation: 7,300
Circulation Type: paid
**Owner(s):**
Washington State Nurses Association
2505 Second Ave., Ste. 500
Seattle, WA 98121-1460
Telephone: (206) 433-9762
FAX: (206) 728-2074
Ownership %: 100
**Editorial:**
Dennis Burnside .........................Editor
**Deadline:** story-1 mo. prior to pub. date;
news-1 mo. prior to pub. date; photo-1
mo. prior; ads-1 mo. prior

**WESTERN JOURNAL OF NURSING**          65061
**RESEARCH**
2455 Teller Rd.
Thousand Oaks, CA 91320
Telephone: (805) 499-0721
FAX: (805) 499-0871
Year Established: 1979
Pub. Frequency: bi-m.
Page Size: standard
Subscrip. Rate: $66/yr. individuals;
    $172/yr. institutions
Circulation: 1,950
Circulation Type: paid
**Owner(s):**
Sage Publications, Inc.
2455 Teller Rd.
Thousand Oaks, CA 91320
Telephone: (805) 499-0721
Ownership %: 100
**Editorial:**
Pamela J. Brink, U. of Alberta .................Editor
**Desc.:** An innovative forum for scholarly
debate, as well as for research and
theoretical papers. Clinical studies have
commentaries and rebuttals.
Departments deal with current issues in
nursing research.

## Group 174-Nutrition

**AMERICAN JOURNAL OF**                 24474
**CLINICAL NUTRITION**
9650 Rockville Pike, Rm. 3404
Bethesda, MD 20814-3998
Telephone: (301) 530-7110
FAX: (301) 571-8303
Mailing Address:
    Morgan Hall, Room 119
    University of California
    Berkeley, CA 94712
Year Established: 1952
Pub. Frequency: m.
Page Size: standard
Subscrip. Rate: $90/yr. US; $110 foreign;
    $135/yr. institutions
Circulation: 8,000
Circulation Type: controlled
**Owner(s):**
American Society for Clinical Nutrition, Inc.
9650 Rockville Pike, Rm. 3404
Bethesda, MD 20814-3998
Telephone: (301) 530-7110
Ownership %: 100
**Editorial:**
Norman Kretchmer .........................Editor

**Materials Accepted/Included:** 01-Business news 02-By-line articles 03-Fashion news 04-Food news 05-Freelance copy 06-Letters to editor 07-Real estate news 08-Sports news 09-Travel news 10-Book rev. 11-Movie rev. 12-Music rev. 13-TV rev. 14-Theater rev. 15-Coming events 16-Obituaries 17-Question & answer 18-Social announcements 19-Artwork 20-Cartoons 21-Photos 22-TV listings 23-Audio rec. 24-Video rec. 25-Books 26-Films/film clips 27-Personnel news 28-Press releases 29-New product news/photos 30-Trade lit. 31-Contracts awarded 32-Display adv. 33-Classified adv.

4-271

David Schnakenberg ...............Managing Editor
**Desc.:** Contains topics of concern in the field of clinical nutrition.
**Readers:** Personnel involved in the field of clinical nutrition, hospitals, nursing homes, dietitians, teaching, medicine.

## JOURNAL OF APPLIED NUTRITION

24487

3913 Medical Pkwy., Ste. #101
Austin, TX 78756-4016
Telephone: (512) 453-4051
FAX: (512) 453-7174
Year Established: 1947
Pub. Frequency: 4/yr.
Page Size: standard
Subscrip. Rate: $60/yr. US; $75/yr. foreign
Materials: 02,05,06,16,32
Circulation: 1,100
Circulation Type: paid
**Owner(s):**
Int'l. Academy of Nutrition & Preventive Medicine
P.O. Box 18433
Asheville, NC 28814
Telephone: (704) 258-3243
Ownership %: 100
**Editorial:**
James Heffley, PhD ....................Editor in Chief
**Desc.:** Publishes refereed scientific reports and reviews, case studies, commentaries, editorials, book reviews, abstracts, and correspondence that stress the practical, human applications of nutritional knowledge and preventive medicine. It is a multidisciplinary journal of primary interest to physicians, dentists, nutritionists, psychologists, biochemists, veterinarians, and agronomists. In the broadest sense the science of nutrition includes all factors affecting the production and distribution of food as well as factors influencing the health of humans and animals consuming such food.
**Readers:** Professionals, lay persons, libraries.

## JOURNAL OF NUTRITIONAL BIOCHEMISTRY

69019

80 Montvale Ave.
Stoneham, MA 02180
Telephone: (617) 438-8464
FAX: (617) 438-6112
Year Established: 1970
Pub. Frequency: m.
Page Size: standard
Subscrip. Rate: $110/yr. US individuals; $140/yr. foreign; $360/yr. US institutions; $415/yr. foreign
**Owner(s):**
Butterworth-Heinemann
80 Montvale Ave.
Stoneham, MA 02180
Telephone: (617) 438-8464
Ownership %: 100
**Editorial:**
Dr. Steven H. Zeisel .....................Editor
**Desc.:** Forum on advances and issues in nutrition, nutritional biochemistry, and food sciences and experimental nutrition as it interfaces with biochemistry, physiology, pharmacology and toxicology.

## JOURNAL OF NUTRITION, THE

23867

9650 Rockville Pike
Bethesda, MD 20814
Telephone: (301) 530-7027
FAX: (301) 571-1892
Year Established: 1928
Pub. Frequency: m.

Page Size: standard
Subscrip. Rate: $90/yr. non-members; $45/yr. members; $175/yr. institutions; $25/yr. students
Circulation: 4,430
Circulation Type: paid
**Owner(s):**
American Institute of Nutrition
9650 Rockville Pike
Bethesda, MD 20814
Telephone: (301) 530-7050
Ownership %: 100
**Management:**
Linda Acuff .........................Advertising Manager
George T. Wingate, Jr. ........Business Manager
**Editorial:**
Robert J. Cousins ....................Associate Editor
Reynaldo Martorell ...................Associate Editor
Peter J. Reeds ........................Associate Editor
L.H. Allen ...............................Associate Editor
John W. Suttie .........................Associate Editor
J.L. Lipton ..............................Associate Editor
A.H. Merrill Jr. .........................Associate Editor
Richard G. Allison ...................Executive Officer
**Desc.:** Edited for nutrition scientists and related research workers engaged in experimental nutrition. Contains concise reports of original research bearing on the nature of food nutrients and function in a variety of organisms and articles which report the development of new nutritional concepts and interrelationships of importance in human and animal nutrition. Also included periodically within the regular text pages or as supplements are more intensive reports of research, proceedings of symposia, and information on the activities of the American Institute of Nutrition.
**Readers:** Members of the American Institute of Nutrition and other nutrition scientists, libraries and academic departments in the life sciences.

## JOURNAL OF OPTIMAL NUTRITION

69020

2552 Regis Dr.
Davis, CA 95616
Telephone: (916) 756-3311
FAX: (916) 758-7444
Year Established: 1992
Pub. Frequency: q.
Subscrip. Rate: $75/yr. US; $90/yr. foreign; $50/yr. US students; $60/yr. foreign
Materials: 06,10
**Owner(s):**
Institute for the Study of Optimal Nutrition
2552 Regis Dr.
Davis, CA 95616
Telephone: (916) 756-3311
FAX: (916) 758-7444
Ownership %: 100
**Editorial:**
Brian Leibovitz, Ph.D. ..................Editor in Chief
Jennifer Mueller ......................Managing Editor
**Desc.:** Focuses on elucidating the optimal levels of macronutrients and micronutrients for the prevention and treatment of disease as well as for the maintenance of optimal health.

## JOURNAL OF PARENTERAL & ENTERAL NUTRITION

69021

8630 Fenton St., Ste. 412
Silver Spring, MD 20910-3805
Telephone: (301) 587-6315
FAX: (301) 587-3323
Year Established: 1979
Pub. Frequency: bi-m.
Subscrip. Rate: $75/yr. individuals; $100/yr. institutions
Materials: 06,10,25,28,29,32,33

Circulation: 10,453
Circulation Type: paid
**Owner(s):**
Amer. Society for Parenteral & Enteral Nutrition
8630 Fenton St., Ste. 412
Silver Spring, MD 20910-3805
Telephone: (301) 587-6315
Ownership %: 100
**Management:**
Cindy Joy-Rodgers ...........Advertising Manager
**Editorial:**
Dr. John L. Rombeau ......................Editor
Robin Bodisbough ........................Director
Robin Bodishbaugh ..............Marketing Director
**Desc.:** Contains research on nutritional deficiency and its treatment, including administration, risks and complications.

## JOURNAL OF THE AMERICAN COLLEGE OF NUTRITION

65622

4802 Tenth Ave.
Brooklyn, NY 11219
Telephone: (718) 283-5226
FAX: (718) 283-5226
Pub. Frequency: bi-m.
Page Size: standard
Subscrip. Rate: $150/yr.
Materials: 02,06,10,29
Circulation: 2,200
Circulation Type: paid
**Owner(s):**
American College of Nutrition, Inc.
c/o Hospital for Joint Disease
301 E. 17th St.
New York, NY 10003
Telephone: (212) 777-1037
Ownership %: 100
**Editorial:**
Dr. Fima Lifshitz ..........................Editor
Corinne Mimouni ......................Managing Editor

## JOURNAL OF THE AMERICAN DIETETIC ASSOCIATION

23048

216 W. Jackson, Ste. 800
Chicago, IL 60606-6995
Telephone: (312) 899-0040
FAX: (312) 899-1757
Year Established: 1923
Pub. Frequency: m.
Page Size: standard
Subscrip. Rate: $9.75/copy; $98/yr. US; $119/yr. Canada; $164/yr. elsewhere
Materials: 06,10,15,16,29,32,33
Print Process: web offset
Circulation: 64,825
Circulation Type: paid
**Owner(s):**
The American Dietetic Association
216 W. Jackson, Ste. 800
Chicago, IL 60606
Telephone: (312) 899-0040
Ownership %: 100
**Management:**
Vicki Guinta ......................Advertising Manager
**Editorial:**
Elaine R. Monsen, Ph.D., R.D. ..................Editor
Elisabeth Crist ..........................Managing Editor
**Desc.:** Articles are professional contributions on scientific research in nutrition, large-scale food administration, professional education. Not interested in notices of appointments to new jobs. Are interested in new product announcements and new, worthwhile literature.
**Readers:** Professional dietitians, and related areas of nutrition.

## NUTRITION IN CLINICAL PRACTICE

59039

8630 Fenton St., 412
Silver Spring, MD 20910
Telephone: (301) 587-6315
FAX: (301) 587-3323
Year Established: 1985
Pub. Frequency: bi-m.
Page Size: standard
Subscrip. Rate: $35/yr.
Materials: 06,28,29,32,33
Circulation: 8,500
Circulation Type: free
**Owner(s):**
Amer. Society for Parenteral & Enteral Nutrition
8630 Fenton St., 412
Silver Spring, MD 20910
Telephone: (301) 587-6315
Ownership %: 100
**Management:**
Barney Sellers ......................Executive Director
Cindy Joy-Rodgers ...........Advertising Manager
**Editorial:**
Robin Bodishbaugh ...........Publication Director
**Readers:** MD, RD, RN, RP, HD

## NUTRITION RESEARCH

69023

660 White Plains Rd.
Tarrytown, NY 10591-5153
Telephone: (914) 524-8200
FAX: (914) 333-2444
Year Established: 1981
Pub. Frequency: 12/yr.
**Owner(s):**
Pergamon Press, Inc.
660 White Plains Rd.
Tarrytown, NY 10591-5153
Telephone: (914) 524-9200
Ownership %: 100
**Editorial:**
Ranjit K. Chandra .....................................Editor
**Desc.:** Reports on basic and applied research on all aspects of the nutritional sciences, including concerns of the social sciences.

## NUTRITION REVIEWS

24506

P.O. Box 1897
Lawerence, KS 66044-8897
Telephone: (800) 627-0629
Year Established: 1942
Pub. Frequency: m.
Page Size: pocket
Subscrip. Rate: $46/yr. for individuals; $75/yr. instn.
Circulation: 4,000
Circulation Type: paid
**Owner(s):**
International Life Sciences Institute
P.O. Box 1897
Lawerence, KS 66044-8897
Telephone: (800) 627-0629
Ownership %: 100
**Editorial:**
Erwin Rosenberg ......................................Editor
Jill Schuman ......................Managing Editor
Dr. Robert Russell ....................Associate Editor
Dr. Richard Wood ....................Associate Editor
**Desc.:** Reviews current research literature in the sSpecial articles written by a recognized authority. Reviews cover clinical nutrition, experimental nut
**Readers:** Medical profession, researchers and other

## NUTRITION TODAY

59040

428 E. Preston St.
Baltimore, MD 21202
Telephone: (410) 528-4000
FAX: (410) 528-4312
Year Established: 1966

Pub. Frequency: bi-m.
Subscrip. Rate: $29.50/yr. individuals;
$72/yr. institutions
Circulation: 5,850
Circulation Type: paid
**Owner(s):**
Williams & Wilkins Co.
428 E. Preston St.
Baltimore, MD 21202
Telephone: (410) 528-4000
Ownership %: 100
**Management:**
Don Pfarr ........................Advertising Manager
Maria Reid ........................Circulation Manager
Alma Wills ........................Manager
**Editorial:**
Helen A. Guthrie, Ph. D. ...................Editor
**Desc.:** Articles on new developments in
nutrition for dieticians, nutritionists and
physicians.

### PROGRESS IN FOOD & NUTRITION SCIENCE
69024

660 White Plains Rd.
Tarrytown, NY 10591-5153
Telephone: (914) 524-9200
FAX: (914) 333-2444
Year Established: 1975
Pub. Frequency: q.
**Owner(s):**
Pergamon Press, Inc.
660 White Plains Rd.
Tarrytown, NY 10591-5153
Telephone: (914) 524-9200
Ownership %: 100
**Editorial:**
Ranjit K. Chandra ........................Editor
**Desc.:** Contains critical reviews of topical
subjects within the general area of food
and nutrition science.

### TOPICS IN CLINICAL NUTRITION
58577

7201 McKinney Cir.
Frederick, MD 21701
Telephone: (301) 698-7100
Mailing Address:
200 Orchard Ridge Dr.
Gaithersburg, MD 20878
Year Established: 1986
Pub. Frequency: q.
Page Size: standard
Subscrip. Rate: $66/yr. US; $79/yr. foreign
Circulation: 2,425
Circulation Type: paid
**Owner(s):**
Aspen Publishers, Inc.
200 Orchard Ridge Dr.
Gaithersburg, MD 20878
Telephone: (301) 417-7500
Ownership %: 100
**Management:**
Michael B. Brown ........................Vice President
Michael Brown ........................Publisher
Nina Kasari ........................Production Manager
**Editorial:**
Lenda P. Hill ........................Managing Editor
Janis Treacy ........................Marketing Manager
Ernest V. Manzella ........Senior VP, Publishing
Service
Kenneth E. Lawrence ................Vice President,
Development
Cynthia Smith ............Vice President, Marketing
**Desc.:** Designed as a resource for the
continuing education and clinical
practice of dietitians and nutritionists.
Each issue addresses current topics, of
interest primarily to dietitians and
nutritionists, but also to other health
care professionals involved in the
nutrition care of patients.

**Readers:** Hospitals-based and private;
practice dietitians and nutritionists.

## Group 176-Office Equipment & Supplies

### BUSINESS FORMS, LABELS & SYSTEMS
24183

401 N. Broad St.
Philadelphia, PA 19108
Telephone: (215) 238-5300
FAX: (215) 238-5457
Year Established: 1963
Pub. Frequency: s-m.
Page Size: standard
Subscrip. Rate: $49/yr.
Freelance Pay: negotiable
Circulation: 6,007
Circulation Type: paid
**Owner(s):**
North American Publishing Co.
401 N. Broad St.
Philadelphia, PA 19108
Telephone: (215) 238-5300
Ownership %: 100
**Bureau(s):**
Business Forms, Labels & Systems
2415 Summerhill Dr.
Encinitas, CA 92024
Telephone: (619) 436-4174
Contact: Elliot King
**Management:**
Judith Cavaliere ........................Publisher
**Editorial:**
Gar Raines ........................Exec. Editor
William Drennan ........................Editor
Laura Johnston ........................Assistant Editor
Lori Valentino ........................Associate Publisher
**Desc.:** Contains staff articles, by-lined
articles, covers coming events, finance,
general news, new product news,
personnel news, and trade literature.
**Readers:** Forms manufacturers &
distributors, forms equipment
manufacturers.

### BUSINESS MACHINE DEALER
68962

14 W. South St.
Corry, PA 16407
Telephone: (814) 664-8624
FAX: (814) 664-7781
Pub. Frequency: m.
Circulation: 30,000
Circulation Type: paid
**Owner(s):**
North American Publishing Co.
14 W. South St.
Corry, PA 16407
Telephone: (814) 664-8624
Ownership %: 100
**Editorial:**
Terry Peterson ........................Editor

### HOTLINE
68963

12411 Wornall Rd.
Kansas City, MO 64145
Telephone: (816) 941-3100
Year Established: 1968
Pub. Frequency: s-m.
Circulation: 25000
Circulation Type: paid
**Owner(s):**
National Office Machine Dealers
Association
12411 Wornall Rd.
Kansas City, MO 64145
Telephone: (816) 941-3100
Ownership %: 100
**Editorial:**
Brent Hoskins ........................Editor
**Desc.:** Features industry news, association
news and information on new products.

### OFFICE EQUIPMENT EXPORTER
24189

Managing Office Technology
1100 Superior Ave.
Cleveland, OH 44114
Telephone: (216) 696-7000
FAX: (216) 696-7648
Pub. Frequency: a.
Page Size: pocket
Subscrip. Rate: free
Circulation: 17,090
Circulation Type: controlled & free
**Owner(s):**
Penton Publishing
1100 Superior Ave.
Cleveland, OH 44114
Telephone: (216) 696-7000
Ownership %: 100
**Management:**
John DiPaola ........................Publisher
**Editorial:**
Lura Romei ........................Editor
**Desc.:** Covers dealers, distributors,
importers, agents for business machines
and equipment in all countries outside
the Iron Curtain, except the Spanish-
speaking countries.
**Readers:** Dealers, stationers, distributors
and agents

### OFFICE WORLD NEWS
24205

1905 Swarthmore Ave.
Lakewood, NJ 08701
Telephone: (908) 363-0708
FAX: (908) 367-2426
Year Established: 1972
Pub. Frequency: m.
Page Size: tabloid
Subscrip. Rate: $50/yr.; free to qualified
subscribers
Materials: 01,06,15,21,27,28,29,30,31,32,33
Freelance Pay: negotiable
Circulation: 31,500
Circulation Type: controlled
**Owner(s):**
BUS Publishing Group
1905 Swarthmore Ave.
Lakewood, NJ 08701
Telephone: (908) 363-0708
Ownership %: 100
**Management:**
William P. Urban ........................President
William P. Urban ........................Publisher
**Editorial:**
Kim Chandlee McCabe ..............Editor in Chief
Jan Stafford ........................Exec. Editor
Rosemary Massa ........................Art Director
**Desc.:** Office World News is the only
national news tabloid covering the full
range of business systems and supplies
for the dealers, wholesalers,
manufacturers and sales representatives
who make up the distribution chain.
**Readers:** Office equipment supplies and
systems dealers, value added dealers,
wholesalers, distributors and
manufacturers.

### OFICINA, LA
24187

Managing Office Technology
1100 Superior Ave.
Cleveland, OH 44114
Telephone: (216) 696-7000
FAX: (216) 696-7648
Pub. Frequency: s-a.
Page Size: pocket
Subscrip. Rate: free
Circulation: 15,140
Circulation Type: controlled & free
**Owner(s):**
Penton Publishing
1100 Superior Ave.
Cleveland, OH 44114
Telephone: (216) 696-7000
Ownership %: 100

**Management:**
John DiPaola ........................Publisher
Gina McKenna ..................Advertising Manager
Jodi Svenson ..................Circulation Manager
**Editorial:**
Lura Romei ........................Editor
**Desc.:** Covers market for office machines
and equipment.
**Readers:** Office executives, dealers and
distributors.

### SCHOOL & HOME OFFICE PRODUCTS
68964

6151 Powers Ferry Rd., N.W.
Atlanta, GA 30339-2941
Telephone: (404) 955-2500
FAX: (404) 955-0400
Year Established: 1992
Pub. Frequency: 6/yr.
Page Size: 11 x 14 1/2
Subscrip. Rate: $42/yr. US; $62/yr. foreign
Circulation: 10000
Circulation Type: paid
**Owner(s):**
Communication Channels, Inc.
6151 Powers Ferry Rd., N.W.
Atlanta, GA 30339-2941
Telephone: (404) 955-2500
Ownership %: 100
**Editorial:**
Ben Johnson ........................Editor
**Readers:** Buying executives in
superstores, chain stores, discount drug
chain stores, office product warehouses
and warehouse clubs.

## Group 178-Office Management & Methods

### IMC JOURNAL
24306

1650 38th St.
Boulder, CO 80301-2638
Telephone: (303) 440-7085
FAX: (303) 440-7234
Year Established: 1967
Pub. Frequency: bi-m.
Page Size: standard
Subscrip. Rate: $90/yr.
Materials: 01,02,05,06,21,28,29,30,32
Print Process: web
Circulation: 30,000
Circulation Type: paid
**Owner(s):**
International Information Management
Congress
1650 38th St.
Boulder, CO 80301-2623
Telephone: (303) 440-7085
FAX: (303) 440-7234
Ownership %: 100
**Management:**
John Lacy ........................Chairman of Board
Warren A. Cole ................Advertising Manager
**Editorial:**
Joel Sloss ........................Editor
**Desc.:** Most editorial material comes from
people in the Document Based
Information Systems field. Information in
these stories includes: application
stories, reports, technical articles, book
reviews in the field of information
management. This magazine
is specifically published for the
International Information Management
Congress. Editions are available in
English and German.
**Readers:** Members of The International
Information Management Congress,
Association for Information & Image
Management, Association of Records
Managers and Administrators, Society of
Office Automation Professionals.

---

**Materials Accepted/Included:** 01-Business news 02-By-line articles 03-Fashion news 04-Food news 05-Freelance copy 06-Letters to editor 07-Real estate news 08-Sports news 09-Travel news
10-Book rev. 11-Movie rev. 12-Music rev. 13-TV rev. 14-Theater rev. 15-Coming events 16-Obituaries 17-Question & answer 18-Social announcements 19-Artwork 20-Cartoons 21-Photos 22-TV listings
23-Audio rec. 24-Video rec. 25-Books 26-Films/film clips 27-Personnel news 28-Press releases 29-New product news/photos 30-Trade lit. 31-Contracts awarded 32-Display adv. 33-Classified adv.

24202

**MANAGING OFFICE TECHNOLOGY**
1100 Superior Ave.
Cleveland, OH 44114
Telephone: (216) 696-7000
FAX: (216) 696-7658
Year Established: 1956
Pub. Frequency: m.
Page Size: standard
Subscrip. Rate: $45./yr.
Circulation: 150,000
Circulation Type: controlled
**Owner(s):**
Penton Publishing, Div. of Pittway Corp.
1100 Superior Ave.
Cleveland, OH 44114
Telephone: (216) 696-7000
Ownership %: 100
**Management:**
Jerry Burns ...............................Publisher
**Editorial:**
Patricia Panchak ...........Senior Editor
Lura K. Romei .................................Editor
Catherine Radwan ...............Assistant Editor
Mary S. Malik ................Associate Editor
John B. Dykeman ........Associate Publisher
H. Holtzman ...........Contributing Editor
Belden Menkus ................Contributing Editor
Gina Runyon .................Production Editor
**Desc.:** Provides management with the
information that will enable them to
integrate technology and human
resources in the workplace to improve
productivity. This information will help
them to better evaluate, specify, and
manage today's information and office
equipment, products, furniture, systems,
and services.

67263

**MOBILE OFFICE**
21800 Oxnard Ave., Ste. 250
Woodland Hills, CA 91367
Telephone: (818) 593-6100
FAX: (818) 593-6153
Year Established: 1990
Pub. Frequency: m.
Page Size: standard
Subscrip. Rate: $23.90/yr.
Materials: 05,06,32,33
Circulation: 107,000
Circulation Type: paid
**Owner(s):**
Cowles Business Media
21800 Oxnard St., Ste. 250
Woodland Hills, CA 91367
Telephone: (818) 593-6100
Ownership %: 100
**Management:**
Susan Curtis ...............................Publisher
Ms. Dale Stone ................Advertising Manager
**Editorial:**
Doug Garr ...................Editor in Chief

61637

**OFFICE GUIDE TO ORLANDO**
P.O. Box 915077
Longwood, FL 32791-5077
Telephone: (407) 426-9446
FAX: (407) 426-9276
Year Established: 1981
Pub. Frequency: q.
Page Size: standard
Subscrip. Rate: $30/yr.
Freelance Pay: $.10/wd.
Circulation: 10,000
Circulation Type: controlled
**Owner(s):**
LKZ Management, Inc.
701 E. Washington
Orlando, FL 32801
Ownership %: 20

Zink Media Group, Ltd.
701 E. Washington
Orlando, FL 32801
Telephone: (407) 426-9446
Ownership %: 80
**Management:**
Dennis Zink ...............................President
**Editorial:**
Sherry Valle ...............................Editor
Michele L. Davis ...........Associate Publisher
**Desc.:** Office Guide to Orlando is the
complete guide to office and industrial
space, products, and services for the
greater Orlando area.
**Readers:** Company presidents and
commercial real estate directors.

58555

**OFFICEMATION PRODUCT REPORTS**
401 E. Rt. 70
Cherry Hill, NJ 08034
Telephone: (609) 428-1020
FAX: (609) 428-1683
Year Established: 1980
Pub. Frequency: m.
Page Size: standard
Subscrip. Rate: $721/yr.
**Owner(s):**
Management Information Group
401 E. Rt. 70
Cherry Hill, NJ 08034
Telephone: (609) 428-1020
Ownership %: 100
**Editorial:**
Mark Kostic ...............................Managing Editor
**Desc.:** Office Products Reports integrates
data processing and office requirements.
Includes evaluations of word processing
systems, professional work stations,
office automation equipment and
software available worldwide. Each
month new products are evaluated and
major office automation issues are
discussed. Service includes 2 volumes
plus monthly reports.
**Readers:** MIS, vendors, government
officials.

61640

**OFFICE SYSTEMS '95**
941 Danbury Rd.
Georgetown, CT 06829
Telephone: (203) 544-9526
FAX: (203) 544-8465
Year Established: 1984
Pub. Frequency: m.
Page Size: standard
Subscrip. Rate: $36/yr.
Freelance Pay: $200-$300
Circulation: 100,000
Circulation Type: controlled & paid
**Owner(s):**
Springhouse Corp.
1111 Bethlehem Pike
Spring House, PA 19477
Telephone: (215) 646-8700
Ownership %: 100
**Editorial:**
Scott Cullen ...............................Editor
Rosemary Fleiss ...........Associate Editor
**Desc.:** Office Systems magazine covers all
aspects of office automation with an
emphasis on the concerns of the small
to midsize company. Features include
articles on telecommunications,
micrographics, filing,
computers/computer supplies, office
machines, office supplies, mailroom
technology, and furniture. There is also
a new products section.
**Readers:** Executives in small to midsize
companies.

24204

**OFFICE, THE**
Managing Office Technology
1100 Superior Ave.
Cleveland, OH 44114
Telephone: (216) 696-7000
Year Established: 1935
Pub. Frequency: m.
Page Size: standard
Subscrip. Rate: $40/yr.
Circulation: 152,000
**Owner(s):**
Penton Publishing
1100 Superior Ave.
Cleveland, OH 44114
Telephone: (216) 696-7000
Ownership %: 100
**Management:**
William Schulhof ...............................President
William Schulhof ...............................Publisher
Dick Flanagan ...........Advertising Manager
Ken Kiernan ...............Circulation Manager
**Editorial:**
William Schulhof ...............................Editor
Al Masson ...............Managing Editor
Fred Nevin ...............Associate Editor
Scott Cullen ...............Associate Editor
**Desc.:** Articles discuss office management,
office automation, personnel relations,
equipment applications methods in
actual use by business organizations.
Departments include: New Books, New
Products (for office use), News of the
Office (news of meetings, companies),
News of the Industry (dealers,
manufacturers), Software Development,
Data Processing.
**Readers:** Administrative management
executives, data processing/word
processing executives, office managers,
MIS executives.

24207

**SECRETARY, THE**
2800 Shirlington Rd., Ste. 706
Arlington, VA 22206
Telephone: (703) 998-2534
FAX: (703) 379-4561
Year Established: 1942
Pub. Frequency: 9/yr.
Page Size: standard
Subscrip. Rate: $3/copy; $19/yr. US
Materials: 01,02,03,04,05,06,10,17,19,21,
25,28,29,30,32
Freelance Pay: $350-$1000
Print Process: web offset
Circulation: 45,000
Circulation Type: paid
**Owner(s):**
Professional Secretaries International
10502 N.W. Ambassador Dr.
Kansas City, MO 64153
Telephone: (816) 891-6600
Ownership %: 100
**Editorial:**
Debra J. Stratton ...............................Editor
Robin Perry Allen ...............Managing Editor
Tracy Fellin Savidge ...........Feature Editor
**Desc.:** Articles on professional and career
development for secretaries, new office
products/services, new trends in office
procedures, and office technology.
Departments include: Random Input, PSI
News, Office Ethics, Working Smart,
Product News, Bookends, Word
Watching. The official publication of
Professional Secretaries International.
**Readers:** Professional secretaries in all 50
states, and internationally.
**Deadline:** story-1st of mo., 2 mos. prior to
pub. date; ads-1st of mo. prior

61638

**SOUTH FLORIDA OFFICE GUIDE**
5201 Ravenswood Rd.
Ste. 121
Ft. Lauderdale, FL 33312-6007

Year Established: 1983
Pub. Frequency: q.
Subscrip. Rate: $31.80/yr.; $53/2 yrs.;
$63.60/3 yrs.
Circulation: 19,000
Circulation Type: paid
**Owner(s):**
Dennis Zink
800 N. Magnolia Ave., #1200
Orlando, FL 32803
Telephone: (407) 839-6100
Ownership %: 100

## Group 180-Optometry

24219

**AMERICAN OPTICIAN**
10341 Democracy Ln.
Fairfax, VA 22030
Telephone: (703) 691-8355
FAX: (703) 691-3929
Year Established: 1950
Pub. Frequency: bi-m.
Page Size: standard
Subscrip. Rate: free with membership
Circulation: 8,500
Circulation Type: controlled
**Owner(s):**
Opticians Association of America
10341 Democracy Ln.
Fairfax, VA 22030
Telephone: (703) 691-8355
Ownership %: 100
**Management:**
Jacqueline E. ...........Advertising Manager
Fairbarns
**Editorial:**
Jacqueline E. Fairbarns ...........Editor
**Desc.:** Covers news of legislation,
governmental actions, products,
meetings, association activities and
programs of interest to dispensing
opticians and contact lens fitters. Also
covers business management issues,
such as financial control, marketing,
and merchandise.
**Readers:** Managers and owners of optical
stores, and firms as well as individual
dispensers.

24214

**AMERICAN OPTOMETRIC ASSOCIATION NEWS**
243 N. Lindbergh Blvd.
St. Louis, MO 63141
Telephone: (314) 991-4100
FAX: (314) 991-4101
Year Established: 1962
Pub. Frequency: s-m.
Page Size: tabloid
Subscrip. Rate: $12/yr. members; $35/yr.
non-members
Circulation: 29,173
Circulation Type: controlled
**Owner(s):**
American Optometric Association
243 N. Lindbergh Blvd.
St. Louis, MO 63141
Telephone: (314) 991-4100
Ownership %: 100
**Management:**
Joel Raeber ...............Advertising Manager
**Desc.:** Contains news of affiliated state
optometric associations, government,
colleges of optometry, and ophthalmic
trade.
**Readers:** A.O.A. members, optometrists
and optometry students.

24216

**CALIFORNIA OPTOMETRY**
801 12th St., Ste. 2020
Sacramento, CA 95814-2930
Telephone: (916) 441-3990

**Materials Accepted/Included:** 01-Business news 02-By-line articles 03-Fashion news 04-Food news 05-Freelance copy 06-Letters to editor 07-Real estate news 08-Sports news 09-Travel news 10-Book rev. 11-Movie rev. 12-Music rev. 13-TV rev. 14-Theater rev. 15-Coming events 16-Obituaries 17-Question & answer 18-Social announcements 19-Artwork 20-Cartoons 21-Photos 22-TV listings 23-Audio rec. 24-Video rec. 25-Books 26-Films/film clips 27-Personnel news 28-Press releases 29-New product news/photos 30-Trade lit. 31-Contracts awarded 32-Display adv. 33-Classified adv.

Mailing Address:
P.O. Box 2591
Sacramento, CA 95812
Year Established: 1932
Pub. Frequency: bi-m.
Page Size: standard
Subscrip. Rate: $35/yr.
Freelance Pay: $35-$100/artwork
Circulation: 3,900
**Owner(s):**
California Optometric Association
801 12th St., Ste. 2020
Sacramento, CA 95814-2930
Telephone: (916) 441-3990
Ownership %: 100
**Management:**
Tim Mar ..............................Advertising Manager
**Editorial:**
Margaret Clausen ......................................Editor
**Desc.:** Developments in the field of optometry, including features on optometrists in California, research results, new product news, public service vision programs involving California O.D.S. Special emphasis on legislative and legal matters affecting California optometry. Almost entirely staff written (exceptions are opinion pieces and occasionally, research reports). Special section each month covers continuing optometric education opportunities on the West Coast.
**Readers:** Members of the California Optometric Association, their staff & spouses; optometry students in California (approx. 650), government officials, state legislators; approx. 200 O.D.'S who are not members of the association.

## CONTACT LENS SPECTRUM
24217
50 Washington St.
Norwalk, CT 06854
Telephone: (203) 838-9100
FAX: (203) 838-2550
Year Established: 1986
Pub. Frequency: m.
Page Size: standard
Subscrip. Rate: $40/yr.
Circulation: 32,000
Circulation Type: paid
**Owner(s):**
Cardinal Business Media
50 Washington St.
Norwalk, CT 06854
Telephone: (203) 838-9100
**Management:**
Ron Walker ..................................Publisher
Tom Meinert ....................Advertising Manager
**Editorial:**
Dr. Joseph Barr ..............................Editor
Selene Craig ............................Managing Editor
**Readers:** Ophthalmologists and optometrists.

## CONTACTO
24218
910 Skokie Blvd., Ste. 207a
Northbrook, IL 60062
Telephone: (708) 564-4652
FAX: (708) 764-0807
Year Established: 1957
Pub. Frequency: q.
Page Size: standard
Subscrip. Rate: $80/yr.
Circulation: 500
Circulation Type: free & paid
**Owner(s):**
National Eye Research Foundation
910 Skokie Blvd.
Northbrook, IL 60062
Telephone: (708) 564-4652
Ownership %: 100

**Management:**
Newton K. Wesley, ............Chairman of Board
O.D., M.D.
Roy K. A. Wesley ................................President
**Editorial:**
Roy K. A. Wesley ................................Editor
**Desc.:** The purpose is to correlate the various aspects of the eye and health care field, including the contact lens field, and to bring about closer communication among the practitioners. Articles detailing various research reports, case histories, fitting techniques, manufacturing techniques, and applications of methodologies from other fields.
**Readers:** The readers consist of eye care practitioners as well as those in other related branches of science.

## FRAMES
24220
2 Park Plz., Ste. 900
Irvine, CA 92714
Telephone: (714) 756-2218
FAX: (714) 756-5322
Year Established: 1968
Pub. Frequency: q.
Page Size: standard
Subscrip. Rate: $245/yr.
Circulation: 22,000
Circulation Type: paid
**Owner(s):**
Frames Data
2 Park Plz., Ste. 900
Irvine, CA 92714
Telephone: (714) 956-2218
Ownership %: 100
**Management:**
Skip Johnson ................................Publisher
**Editorial:**
Cindy Thomas ................................Editor
**Desc.:** Anything about eyeglass frames could be used. Non-staff material by assignment.
**Readers:** Optometrists, ophthalmologists, opticians and manufacturers.

## GLAUCOMA
69614
59 Oakwood Dr.
Madison, CT 06443-1823
Year Established: 1979
Pub. Frequency: bi-m.
Subscrip. Rate: $55/yr. individuals; $65/yr. libraries & institutions
Circulation: 15,000
Circulation Type: paid
**Owner(s):**
Altier & Maynard Communications, Inc.
6 Farmingville Rd.
Ridgefield, CT 06877
Ownership %: 100
**Editorial:**
Dr. John G. Bellows ................................Editor
**Desc.:** Edited by the American Society of Contemporary Ophthalmology and the International Glaucoma Congress.

## INTERNATIONAL CONTACT LENS CLINIC
24221
225 Wildwood Ave.
Unit B
Woburn, MA 01801
Telephone: (800) 366-2665
FAX: (617) 438-1479
Year Established: 1974
Pub. Frequency: bi-m.
Page Size: standard
Subscrip. Rate: $125/yr. US; $150/yr. foreign
Circulation: 893
Circulation Type: paid

**Owner(s):**
Elsevier Science, Inc.
655 Avenue of the Americas
New York, NY 10010
Telephone: (212) 633-3740
Ownership %: 100
**Management:**
William N. Topaz ................................President
William N. Topaz ................................Publisher

## JOURNAL OF THE AMERICAN OPTOMETRIC ASSOCIATION
24222
243 N. Lindbergh Blvd.
St. Louis, MO 63141
Telephone: (314) 991-4100
FAX: (314) 991-4101
Year Established: 1928
Pub. Frequency: m.
Page Size: standard
Subscrip. Rate: $50/yr. non-member; $25/yr. member
Circulation: 29,500
Circulation Type: controlled
**Owner(s):**
American Optometric Association
243 N. Lindbergh Blvd.
St. Louis, MO 63141
Telephone: (314) 991-4100
Ownership %: 100
**Management:**
Joel Raeber ....................Advertising Manager
**Editorial:**
John Potter ..............................Executive Editor
Mary Horner ............................Managing Editor
**Desc.:** This is a non-profit publication of a national association. Technical articles within the field of vision are contributed by recognized men and women in related fields. Departments include: Book Reviews, Abstracts, Professional Office, P.R. Notes, New Products, State Projects, and Items of Interest.
**Readers:** The official publication of the American Optometric Association. Readership includes Doctors of Optometry (ODs), optometric students and others allied to the field including industry representatives, academians, libraries and government.

## MICHIGAN OPTOMETRIST, THE
24226
530 W. Ionia St., Ste. A
Lansing, MI 48933-1062
Telephone: (517) 482-0616
FAX: (517) 482-1611
Year Established: 1921
Pub. Frequency: m.
Page Size: standard
Subscrip. Rate: $13/yr.
Materials: 01,02,06,15,16,21,27,28,30,32,33
Print Process: offset
Circulation: 850
Circulation Type: controlled
**Owner(s):**
Michigan Optometric Association
530 W. Ionia St., Ste. A
Lansing, MI 48933
Telephone: (517) 482-0616
FAX: (517) 482-1611
Ownership %: 100
**Management:**
William D. Dansby ................................Publisher
William D. Dansby ............Advertising Manager
**Editorial:**
William D. Dansby ....................Executive Editor
William D. Dansby ..............New Product Editor
William D. Dansby ............................News Editor
William D. Dansby ................................Photo

**Desc.:** Contains news for and about optometrists, the optometric profession, and related fields. Most articles are 1,000 to 2,000 words. The publication emphasizes good visuals and is heavy on photos and other visuals. Very seldom are handouts from commercial firms utilized in the publication. By-lines are given for original articles.
**Readers:** Optometrists, optometric students, school subscribers.
**Deadline:** story-20th of mo. prior to mo. prior to pub. date; news-20th of mo. prior to mo. prior; photo-20th of mo. prior to mo. prior; ads-20th of mo. prior to mo. prior

## NEW ENGLAND JOURNAL OF OPTOMETRY
24227
101 Tremont St.
Ste. 401
Boston, MA 02108
Telephone: (617) 542-1233
Year Established: 1949
Pub. Frequency: q.
Page Size: standard
Subscrip. Rate: $35/yr. non-members
Circulation: 1,900
Circulation Type: controlled
**Owner(s):**
New England Council of Optometrists
101 Tremont St.
Boston, MA 02108
Telephone: (617) 542-1233
Ownership %: 100
**Editorial:**
Roger Wilson, O. D. ....................Editor in Chief
Frances Flynn ............................Managing Editor
**Desc.:** Original scientific papers relating to vision and optical science plus news items concerning vision.
**Readers:** Optometrists and other health professionals interested in vision.

## OPTOMETRIC ECONOMICS
67023
243 N. Lindbergh Blvd.
St. Louis, MO 63141
Telephone: (314) 991-4100
FAX: (314) 991-4101
Year Established: 1991
Pub. Frequency: m.
Page Size: standard
Subscrip. Rate: free to members; $30/yr. non-members; foreign $60/yr.
Circulation: 30,095
Circulation Type: controlled & paid
**Owner(s):**
American Optometric Association
243 N. Lindbergh Blvd.
St. Louis, MO 63141
Telephone: (314) 991-4100
Ownership %: 100
**Management:**
Reynold Malmer ................................Publisher
Joel Raeber ....................Advertising Manager
**Editorial:**
Jack Runninger ................................Editor
**Desc.:** Non-clinical journal for optometrists in private practice. Oriented towards management.

## OPTOMETRIC MANAGEMENT
24230
656 E. Swedesford Rd.
Radnor, PA 19087
Telephone: (215) 964-8801
Mailing Address:
1515 Broadway, 34th Fl.
New York, NY 10036
Pub. Frequency: m.
Page Size: standard
Subscrip. Rate: $28/yr.

**Materials Accepted/Included:** 01-Business news 02-By-line articles 03-Fashion news 04-Food news 05-Freelance copy 06-Letters to editor 07-Real estate news 08-Sports news 09-Travel news 10-Book rev. 11-Movie rev. 12-Music rev. 13-TV rev. 14-Theater rev. 15-Coming events 16-Obituaries 17-Question & answer 18-Social announcements 19-Artwork 20-Cartoons 21-Photos 22-TV listings 23-Audio rec. 24-Video rec. 25-Books 26-Films/film clips 27-Personnel news 28-Press releases 29-New product news/photos 30-Trade lit. 31-Contracts awarded 32-Display adv. 33-Classified adv.

**Owner(s):**
Viscom Publications
50 Washington St.
Norwalk, CT 06856
Telephone: (205) 838-9100
Ownership %: 100
**Management:**
Tom Gangenni ..................Advertising Manager
**Editorial:**
Stan Herrin ....................................Editor
**Desc.:** Articles on practice management, financial investments and social and political problems affecting the profession of optometry. Departments include News Briefs, Practice Management Suggestions, and New Products.
**Readers:** Opticians.

## OPTOMETRY & VISION SCIENCE
55910
428 E. Preston St.
Baltimore, MD 21202
Telephone: (410) 528-4000
FAX: (410) 528-4312
Year Established: 1976
Pub. Frequency: m.
Page Size: standard
Subscrip. Rate: $75/yr. individuals; $98/yr. institutions
Circulation: 3,950
Circulation Type: paid
**Owner(s):**
American Academy of Optometry
**Editorial:**
Dr. William M. Lyle ........................Editor
**Desc.:** Articles document research and clinical findings in optometry, plus case reports and instrument and technique reviews.
**Readers:** Subscribers include optometrists in practice and research. For member list, contact the American Academy of Optometry.

## REVIEW OF OPTOMETRY
24237
1 Chilton Way
Radnor, PA 19087
Telephone: (215) 964-4370
FAX: (610) 964-2959
Year Established: 1891
Pub. Frequency: m.
Page Size: standard
Subscrip. Rate: $38/yr.
Circulation: 33,491
Circulation Type: controlled
**Owner(s):**
Chilton Company
One Chilton Way
Radnor, PA 19087
Telephone: (215) 964-4000
Ownership %: 100
**Management:**
Richard D. Bay ........................Publisher
Suzanne Merola ................Production Manager
**Editorial:**
Richard M. Kirkner ..............................Editor
**Desc.:** Covers news of optometric interest-courses, meetings, association elections, personnel changes, new lines, feature articles on issues and events in the field, and contributed articles from O.D.'s.
**Readers:** Optometrists, dispensing opticians.

## SOUTHERN JOURNAL OF OPTOMETRY
24239
4661 N. Shallowford Rd.
Dunwoody, GA 30338
Telephone: (404) 451-8206
Year Established: 1959
Pub. Frequency: q.
Page Size: standard
Subscrip. Rate: $12/yr.; $30/3 yrs.

Circulation: 5,500
Circulation Type: paid
**Owner(s):**
Southern Council of Optometrists, Inc.
4661 N. Shallowford Rd.
Dunwoody, GA 30338
Telephone: (404) 451-8206
Ownership %: 100
**Management:**
Sam J. Galloway, Jr. ............Business Manager
**Editorial:**
Lyman Norden, O.D. ...................Editor
Lee Porter ....................Production Coordinator
**Desc.:** It publishes original referred papers and is used as an instrument for keeping the recipients informed of current developments in the ophthalmic field. The editorial policy reflects current thinking concerning courses of action for the profession of optometry's future development. Special sections are provided for reviews of optometric literature, reports on new products, and a calendar of coming events.
**Readers:** Optometrists, students, optometric assist/paraoptometrics.

## TEXAS OPTOMETRY, JOURNAL OF TEXAS OPTOMETRIC ASSN.
24241
1503 Sl. Hwy. 35
Austin, TX 78741
Telephone: (512) 707-2020
FAX: (512) 326-8504
Mailing Address:
    P.O. Box 1434
    Round Rock, TX 78680
Year Established: 1944
Pub. Frequency: bi-m.
Page Size: standard
Subscrip. Rate: $12/yr.
Circulation: 1,600
Circulation Type: paid
**Owner(s):**
Texas Optometric Assn.
1503 S.I. Hwy. 35
Austin, TX 78741
Telephone: (512) 707-2020
Ownership %: 100
**Management:**
Allen Connally ..................Advertising Manager
**Editorial:**
Dr. Beverly Wiatrek ..................................Editor
**Desc.:** For past 35 years, it has been devoted to improving the optometry profession; a professional journal.
**Readers:** Members of professional association.

## 20/20
24242
100 Ave. of the Americas
New York, NY 10013-1678
Telephone: (212) 274-7062
FAX: (212) 431-0500
Year Established: 1974
Pub. Frequency: m.
Page Size: tabloid
Subscrip. Rate: $85/yr.
Freelance Pay: negotiable
Circulation: 50,000
Circulation Type: controlled
**Owner(s):**
Jobson Publishing Corp.
100 Ave. of the Americas
New York, NY 10013
Telephone: (212) 274-7000
Ownership %: 100
**Management:**
Marc Ferrara ..........................................Publisher
**Editorial:**
Marge Axelrod ........................Editorial Director
**Desc.:** Marketing, merchandising and product information for eyecare professionals.

**Readers:** Dispensers and retailers of eyewear products.

## 20/20 EUROPE
66470
100 Ave. of the Americas
New York, NY 10013
Telephone: (212) 274-7000
FAX: (212) 431-0500
Year Established: 1989
Pub. Frequency: m.
Page Size: standard
Subscrip. Rate: $275/yr.
Circulation: 23,000
Circulation Type: controlled
**Owner(s):**
Jobson Publishing Corp.
100 Ave. of the Americas
New York, NY 10013-1678
Telephone: (212) 274-7000
Ownership %: 100
**Editorial:**
Barry Winbolt .............................................Editor

## Group 182-Osteopathy

## AAO JOURNAL
69208
3500 DePauw Blvd., Ste. 1080
Indianapolis, IN 46268-1136
Telephone: (317) 879-1881
FAX: (317) 879-0563
Year Established: 1991
Pub. Frequency: q.
Page Size: standard
Subscrip. Rate: $25/yr.
Materials: 32
Circulation: 3,300
Circulation Type: paid
**Owner(s):**
American Academy of Osteopathy
3500 DePauw Blvd., Ste. 1080
Indianapolis, IN 46268-1136
Telephone: (317) 879-1881
Ownership %: 100
**Editorial:**
Raymond J. Hruby ......................................Editor
**Desc.:** Includes clinically related articles that illustrate the art and science of osteopathic practice.
**Deadline:** story-45 days prior to pub. date

## D.O., THE
24244
142 E. Ontario St.
Chicago, IL 60611
Telephone: (312) 280-5800
Year Established: 1960
Pub. Frequency: m.
Page Size: standard
Subscrip. Rate: $40/yr.
Freelance Pay: negotiable
Circulation: 38,500
Circulation Type: controlled
**Owner(s):**
American Osteopathic Association
142 E. Ontario St.
Chicago, IL 60611
Telephone: (312) 280-5800
Ownership %: 100
**Management:**
Sandra Williamson ...............................Manager
**Editorial:**
Thomas W. Allen, D.O. ..............Editor in Chief
Mike Fitzgerald ..................Associate Editor
**Desc.:** Staff-written articles of news and developments within the profession; state organizations; legislation; hospital and college development; news of specialty, auxiliary and other groups; obituaries; marketing; practice management.
**Readers:** Osteopathic physicians and osteopathic students.

## JOURNAL OF THE AMERICAN OSTEOPATHIC ASSOCIATION
24245
142 E. Ontario St.
Chicago, IL 60611
Telephone: (312) 280-5800
FAX: (312) 280-5893
Year Established: 1901
Pub. Frequency: m.
Page Size: standard
Subscrip. Rate: $50/yr.
Materials: 02,06,10,25,29,32
Print Process: web
Circulation: 41,500
Circulation Type: controlled
**Owner(s):**
American Osteopathic Association
142 E. Ontario St.
Chicago, IL 60611
Telephone: (312) 280-5800
Ownership %: 100
**Management:**
Sandra M. Williamson ........................Publisher
**Editorial:**
Thomas W. Allen, D.O. ..............Editor in Chief
Andrea Dzik ..............................Associate Editor
**Desc.:** Contributed professional articles (formal scientific papers, short clinical material). Carries Editorial, Forum and Letters for reader participation, current medical literature.
**Readers:** Osteopathic physicians and students.

## TEXAS D.O.
68969
1717 IH-35, Ste. 100
Round Rock, TX 78664-2901
Telephone: (512) 388-9400
FAX: (512) 388-5957
Year Established: 1945
Pub. Frequency: m.
Subscrip. Rate: $50/yr.
Circulation: 2,650
Circulation Type: paid
**Owner(s):**
Texas Osteopathic Medical Association
1717 IH-35, Ste. 100
Round Rock, TX 78664-2901
Telephone: (512) 388-9400
FAX: (512) 388-5957
Ownership %: 100
**Editorial:**
Terry R. Boucher ......................................Editor

## Group 184-Packaging

## BOXBOARD CONTAINERS
24249
29 N. Wacker Dr.
Chicago, IL 60606
Telephone: (312) 726-2802
FAX: (312) 726-2574
Year Established: 1892
Pub. Frequency: m.
Page Size: standard
Subscrip. Rate: $28/yr. US; $37/yr. Can. & foreign
Materials: 01,02,06,15,27,28,29,30,32,33
Freelance Pay: project basis
Print Process: web offset
Circulation: 14,212
Circulation Type: controlled & paid
**Owner(s):**
MacLean-Hunter Publishing Co.
29 N. Wacker Dr.
Chicago, IL 60606
Telephone: (312) 726-2802
FAX: (201) 947-2271
Ownership %: 100

**Materials Accepted/Included:** 01-Business news 02-By-line articles 03-Fashion news 04-Food news 05-Freelance copy 06-Letters to editor 07-Real estate news 08-Sports news 09-Travel news 10-Book rev. 11-Movie rev. 12-Music rev. 13-TV rev. 14-Theater rev. 15-Coming events 16-Obituaries 17-Question & answer 18-Social announcements 19-Artwork 20-Cartoons 21-Photos 22-TV listings 23-Audio rec. 24-Video rec. 25-Books 26-Films/film clips 27-Personnel news 28-Press releases 29-New product news/photos 30-Trade lit. 31-Contracts awarded 32-Display adv. 33-Classified adv.

**Bureau(s):**
Boxboard Containers
2400 Lemoine Ave.
Fort Lee, NJ 07024
Telephone: (201) 947-2300
Contact: Edmond K. Matta, Associate
Publisher
**Management:**
John Skeels .............................President
Michael C. Del Galdo ..................Publisher
Michael C. Del Galdo .......Advertising Manager
Lee A. Carlson ...............Circulation Manager
**Editorial:**
Charles J. Huck ..............Executive Editor
Greg Kishbaugh .........................Editor
Richard Pedraza ...............Managing Editor
Lyn Bollmeyer ........................Art Director
John W. Enders ...............Economics Editor
Robert O. Forrest ...............Marketing Editor
Anita Sljivar .................Production Assistant
Gill Gavin ..................Production Director
Pamela Martin ...............Research Director
**Desc.:** By means of on-the-spot reports
and interviews, Boxboard Containers
brings its readers information on what
progressive box and carton makers are
doing in the development and use of
new ideas that can lead to greater
productivity & profitability. Upper &
middle management executives.
**Readers:** Senior management &
production executives in corrugated,
folding cartons, rigid paper boxes & fibre
cans, tubes & drum markets.

69029

## CONVERSION Y EMPAQUE
1680 S.W. Bayshore Blvd.
Port St. Lucie, FL 34984-3598
Telephone: (407) 879-6666
FAX: (407) 879-7388
Year Established: 1992
Pub. Frequency: bi-m.
Page Size: standard
Subscrip. Rate: $40/yr.
Materials: 06,27,28,29,30,32,33
Print Process: web offset
Circulation: 15,000
Circulation Type: controlled
**Owner(s):**
Coast Publishing, Inc.
1680 S.W. Bayshore Blvd.
Port St. Lucie, FL 34984-3598
Telephone: (407) 879-6666
FAX: (407) 879-7388
Ownership %:  50

Carvajal International
901 Ponce de Leon
Ste. 901
Coral Gables, FL 33134
Telephone: (305) 448-6875
FAX: (305) 448-9942
Ownership %:  50
**Editorial:**
Miguel Garzon ...............................Editor
Robert Schweiger .......................Director
Francisco Piedrahita .....................Director
Cyndi Schulman .........................Director
David Ashe ...............................Director
Juan Carlos Gayoso ...........International Sales
Director
**Desc.:** Written in Spanish. A joint venture
between US and Colombia.
**Readers:** Paper, film and foil converters
and package printing professionals
throughout Latin America.

56375

## CONVERTING MAGAZINE
455 N. Cityfront Plaza Dr.
Chicago, IL 60611
Telephone: (312) 222-2000
FAX: (312) 222-2026
Year Established: 1983
Pub. Frequency: m.

Page Size: standard
Subscrip. Rate: free to qualified personnel
Materials: 01,06,15,17,23,24,25,27,28,29,
30,32,33
Freelance Pay: varies
Print Process: web offset
Circulation: 47,223
Circulation Type: controlled
**Owner(s):**
Reed Publishing (USA) Inc.
275 Washington St.
Newton, MA 02158
Telephone: (617) 964-3030
Ownership %: 100
**Management:**
Stephen D. Bowers .....................Publisher
Christina Barbosa ..........Production Manager
**Editorial:**
Yolanda Simonsis ...............Editor in Chief
Deborah Donberg ...............Managing Editor
Elizabeth Coleman ..........Advertising Contracts
Coordinator
**Desc.:** Converting Magazine presents
industry and product news and reviews
developments in machinery, equipment,
and materials and process technology
for manufacturers involved in converting
paper, paperboard, plastic, film & foil
into packaging and other products.
Editorial coverage is directed to the
informational needs of a full range of
converting industry managers.
**Readers:** The full range of converting
industry managers; administrative,
production, engineering, R&D, design,
technical, purchasing and marketing.
**Deadline:** story-3 mo. prior to pub. date;
news-15th of mo. prior to pub. date;
ads-15th of mo. prior to pub. date

24258

## GOOD PACKAGING MAGAZINE
1315 E. Julian St.
San Jose, CA 95116-1094
Telephone: (408) 286-1661
FAX: (408) 275-8071
Year Established: 1940
Pub. Frequency: m.
Page Size: standard
Subscrip. Rate: $30/yr. US & Canada;
$80/yr. elsewhere
Materials: 04,19,29,
Print Process: offset lithography
Circulation: 9,700
Circulation Type: paid
**Owner(s):**
Pacific Trade Journals
1315 E. Julian St.
San Jose, CA 95116-1094
Telephone: (408) 286-1661
FAX: (408) 275-8071
**Management:**
Jerry E. Erich .........................Publisher
Kenneth O. Dean ...........Advertising Manager
Audrey A. Clark ...............Circulation Manager
**Editorial:**
Manuel J. Fernandez ..........Production Director
**Desc.:** Articles dealing with improvements
in packaging and innovations in use of
packaging materials and machinery.
Carries company news, new machinery
and products section, literature on the
packaging industry. Serving the needs of
the Western Packaging Professional for
more than four decades -- keeping all
abreast of new developments, new
technologies, new advancements in
electronic design, microprocessor and
computer aided techniques, new
services -- anything and everything
affecting the packaging industry.

**Readers:** Food processors, industrial,
candy, beverage packagers, distillery
and winery packagers, machinery
manufacturers, container suppliers,
designers, consultants, advertising
agencies, florists, lithographers/printers.
**Deadline:** story-10th of mo. prior to pub.
date

69031

## MARI-BOARD CONVERTING NEWS ESPANOL
43 Main St.
Avon By Sea, NJ 07717
Telephone: (908) 502-0500
FAX: (908) 502-9606
Pub. Frequency: bi-m.
Page Size: standard
Subscrip. Rate: $45/yr.
Materials: 01,02,06,16
Circulation: 4,100
Circulation Type: controlled & paid
**Owner(s):**
NV Business Publishers Corp.
43 Main St.
Avon By Sea, NJ 07717
Telephone: (908) 502-0500
Ownership %:  49
**Editorial:**
Ted Vilardi ...............................Editor
**Deadline:** story-1 mo. prior to pub. date;
news-1 mo. prior; photo-1 mo. prior; ads-
1 mo. prior

24259

## PACKAGING
1350 E. Touhy Ave.
Des Plaines, IL 60018
Telephone: (708) 635-8800
FAX: (708) 635-6856
Mailing Address:
P.O. Box 5080
Des Plaines, IL 60017-5080
Pub. Frequency: 13/yr.
Page Size: standard
Subscrip. Rate: $84.95/yr. US; $149.95/yr.
foreign
Freelance Pay: negotiable
Circulation: 116,300
Circulation Type: controlled & paid
**Owner(s):**
Cahners Publishing Co.
1350 E. Touhy Ave.
Des Plaines, IL 60018
Telephone: (708) 635-8800
Ownership %: 100
**Management:**
John Blatnik .............................Publisher
**Editorial:**
Greg Erickson ...........................Editor
**Desc.:** Feature material must be written
from viewpoint of package user, not
supplier. Department open to suppliers
for new product announcements. Staff-
written and contributed articles cover
design, technical problems, use of
materials, equipment.
**Readers:** Manufacturers, packagers,
suppliers.

24253

## PACKAGING DIGEST
455 N. Cityfront Plaza Dr., 24th Fl.
Chicago, IL 60611
Telephone: (312) 222-2000
FAX: (312) 222-2026
Year Established: 1963
Pub. Frequency: m.
Page Size: tabloid
Subscrip. Rate: free to qualified personnel;
$75/yr.
Circulation: 114,391
Circulation Type: controlled

**Owner(s):**
Reed-Elsevier Business Press
301 Gilbrater Dr.
Morris Plains, NJ 07950
Telephone: (201) 292-5900
Ownership %: 100
**Management:**
Diane Jacobs ...............Vice President
John Kimler .............................Publisher
Lisa Hess ..................Advertising Manager
**Editorial:**
Robert W. Heitzman ......................Editor
Curt Snider ........................Art Director
**Desc.:** Edited for those in the packaging
industry responsible for industrial and
consumer packaging evaluation,
specification, purchase, design,
engineering, R&D, and line production.
Reports on new and improved products,
developments in packaging machinery
and equipment; paper, plastic, glass,
wood, metal, paperboard and flexible
packaging, adhesives, labels, tape, inks,
etc.
**Readers:** Circulation is directed at the
packaging industry, including
wholesalers and consultants. Packaging
Digest is edited for and distributed to
decision-making occupational functions,
SIC's 20 through 39, and other selected
classifications, and the makers and
prime users of packaging.

61681

## PACKAGING STRATEGIES
122 S. Church St.
West Chester, PA 19382
Telephone: (215) 436-4220
FAX: (215) 436-6277
Year Established: 1983
Pub. Frequency: s-m.
Page Size: standard
Subscrip. Rate: $377/yr. & $42/yr.
overseas postage
Materials: 01,04,28,29
Circulation: 1,300
Circulation Type: paid
**Owner(s):**
Packaging Strategies, Inc.
122 S. Church St.
West Chester, PA 19382
Telephone: (215) 436-4220
Ownership %: 100
**Bureau(s):**
Ben Miyares
31408 Narragansett Ln.
Cleveland, OH 44140
Telephone: (216) 892-7908
**Editorial:**
William LeMaire ...........................Editor
**Desc.:** An exclusive intelligence service on
critical trends and new developments in
packaging materials, containers, and
machinery.
**Readers:** Users and suppliers of the
packaging industry.

69033

## PACKER-SHIPPER
2809-A Fruitvale Blvd.
Yakima, WA 98907
Telephone: (509) 248-2452
FAX: (509) 248-4056
Mailing Address:
P.O. Box 1467
Yakima, WA 98907-1467
Year Established: 1993
Pub. Frequency: 6/yr.
Page Size: standard
Subscrip. Rate: $15/yr. US; $30/yr.
Canada & Mexico; $45/yr. elsewhere
Materials: 01,02,04,05,06,15,16,20,21,28,
29,30,32,33
Freelance Pay: $100-$150
Print Process: web
Circulation: 8,508

**Materials Accepted/Included:** 01-Business news 02-By-line articles 03-Fashion news 04-Food news 05-Freelance copy 06-Letters to editor 07-Real estate news 08-Sports news 09-Travel news
10-Book rev. 11-Movie rev. 12-Music rev. 13-TV rev. 14-Theater rev. 15-Coming events 16-Obituaries 17-Question & answer 18-Social announcements 19-Artwork 20-Cartoons 21-Photos 22-TV listings
23-Audio rec. 24-Video rec. 25-Books 26-Films/film clips 27-Personnel news 28-Press releases 29-New product news/photos 30-Trade lit. 31-Contracts awarded 32-Display adv. 33-Classified adv.

4-277

Circulation Type: controlled
**Owner(s):**
D. Brent Clement
681 Ames Rd.
Selah, WA 98942
Telephone: (509) 697-3070
Ownership %: 50

J. Mike Stoker
4705 W. Powerhouse Rd.
Yakima, WA 98908
Telephone: (509) 966-7731
Ownership %: 50
**Management:**
J. Mike Stoker ...........................Publisher
**Editorial:**
Ken Hodge ...................................Editor
Steve Call ...............................Advertising
Lynn Schucharda ..........Advertising Editor
Kathy Noble ...............................Producer
**Desc.:** Packer-Shipper is being mailed to
    every known fruit and vegetable packer
    and shipper in the U.S. Editorial goal is
    to update the target audience on the
    latest in equipment, materials, supplies
    and service options available, thus
    helping them remain more competitive.
**Deadline:** story-60 days prior to pub. date;
    news-60 days; photo-60 days; ads-30
    days

24256
## PAPERBOARD PACKAGING
7500 Old Oak Blvd.
Cleveland, OH 44130
Telephone: (216) 891-2730
FAX: (216) 891-2675
Year Established: 1916
Pub. Frequency: m.
Page Size: standard
Subscrip. Rate: $30/yr.
Materials: 01,02,06,15,17,21,27,28,29,30,
    32,33
Freelance Pay: negotiable
Print Process: web offset
Circulation: 14,055
Circulation Type: controlled
**Owner(s):**
Advanstar Communications, Inc.
7500 Old Oak Blvd.
Cleveland, OH 44130
Telephone: (800) 225-4569
Ownership %: 100
**Management:**
Robyn H. Smith ...........................Publisher
**Editorial:**
Jackie Schultz .....................Editor in Chief
Tricia Hyland .......................Managing Editor
Robin Daugherty ...................Assistant Editor
Linda O'Hara ...............Production Director
**Desc.:** Attention is paid to management
    policy, marketing, technical, production,
    industry statistics, economics, etc. Uses
    features that give manufacturers useful
    data, help save them money, and
    provide new techniques. Profitability
    stories, products used in box plants,
    supplier stories.
**Readers:** Plant managers of every known
    board converting plant throughout the
    world. This includes corrugated, folding,
    carton & rigid box plants.
**Deadline:** ads-1 mo.

## Group 186-Paints & Painting

24263
## AMERICAN PAINT & COATINGS JOURNAL
2911 Washington Ave.
St. Louis, MO 63103-1372
Telephone: (314) 534-0301
FAX: (314) 534-4458
Year Established: 1906
Pub. Frequency: bi-m.

Page Size: pocket
Subscrip. Rate: $25/yr.
Freelance Pay: negotiable
Circulation: 7,300
Circulation Type: paid
**Owner(s):**
American Paint Journal Co.
Telephone: (314) 534-0301
Ownership %: 100
**Management:**
W. Clark Voss ...........................President
**Editorial:**
Joe Maty .....................................Editor
David O'Neill ........................Assistant Editor
Paul Stoecklein ...................Associate Editor
Abel Banov ...............................Co-Publisher
**Desc.:** News, features, technical articles,
    etc., of interest to the paint, varnish and
    lacquer manufacturing industry. Covers
    raw material firms supplying industry,
    plant superintendents, paint chemists.
**Readers:** Executives, chemists, production
    superintendents, suppliers in the paint,
    varnish and lacquer manufacturing
    industry.

24265
## AMERICAN PAINTING CONTRACTOR
2911 Washington Ave.
Saint Louis, MO 63103
Telephone: (314) 534-0301
Year Established: 1924
Pub. Frequency: m.
Page Size: pocket
Subscrip. Rate: $2.50/copy; $24/yr.;
    special contractor's rate-$12/yr.
Circulation: 24,000
Circulation Type: controlled
**Owner(s):**
American Paint Journal Co.
2911 Washington Ave.
Saint Louis, MO 63103
Telephone: (314) 534-0301
Ownership %: 100
**Management:**
A. F. Voss, Jr. ...........................Publisher
Patricia Workes .............Advertising Manager
**Editorial:**
Paul Stoecklein ...........................Editor
Maria Minowitz ...................Assistant Editor
W. Clark Voss ...................Associate Editor
Abel Banov ......................Associate Editor
Chuck Reitter ...................Associate Editor
Kelley Devine ...............Production Coordinator
**Desc.:** Use technical articles on coatings
    as a corrosion preventive in industry,
    new types of coatings, interior and
    exterior decoration, unusual or big paint
    jobs. Departments include: New
    Products, Industry News, Classified,
    Questions and Answers, Monthly
    Editorials.
**Readers:** Professional painting and
    decorating contractors, architects,
    specifications writers, engineers.

24267
## JCT: JOURNAL OF COATINGS TECHNOLOGY
492 Norristown Rd.
Blue Bell, PA 19422-2307
Telephone: (215) 940-0777
FAX: (215) 940-0292
Year Established: 1922
Pub. Frequency: m.
Page Size: standard
Subscrip. Rate: $30/yr.
Circulation: 10,000
Circulation Type: paid
**Owner(s):**
Federation of Societies for Coatings
    Technology
Telephone: (215) 545-1506
Ownership %: 100

**Management:**
Robert F. Ziegler .........................Publisher
Lorraine Ledford .............Advertising Manager
**Editorial:**
Daniel Sandoval ...........................Editor
Patricia D. Viola ...................Managing Editor
Samuel Amicone ...................Associate Editor
Thomas A. Kocis ...................Contributing Editor
Thomas J. Miranda ...................Technical Editor
**Desc.:** Contributed technical papers
    dealing with the latest developments
    and trends in the paint, varnish, lacquer
    and allied industries, plus trade industry
    and association news. The Federation is
    comprised of 22 constituent societies in
    the United States, two in Canada, one in
    England, and one in Mexico.
**Readers:** Chemists, chief chemists, and
    production managers employed in more
    than 1,200 plants engaged in related
    protective and decorative coatings.

69028
## JOURNAL OF PROTECTIVE COATINGS & LININGS
2100 Wharton St., Ste. 31
Pittsburgh, PA 15203
Telephone: (412) 431-8300
FAX: (412) 431-5428
Year Established: 1984
Pub. Frequency: m.
Page Size: standard
Subscrip. Rate: $45/yr.
Materials: 01,02,06,10,15,16,17,25,27,28,
    29,32,33
Print Process: web
Circulation: 15,000
Circulation Type: controlled & paid
**Owner(s):**
Technology Publishing Co.
2100 Wharton St., Ste. 31
Pittsburgh, PA 15203
Telephone: (412) 431-8300
FAX: (412) 431-5428
Ownership %: 100
**Management:**
Harold E. Hower .........................Publisher
Toni Watkins ...................Circulation Manager
**Editorial:**
Karen Kapsanis ...................Managing Editor
Bret Thomas ...................Ad Sales Manager
Karen Kapsanis ...................Editor-in-Chief
**Desc.:** Provides technical and regulatory
    information about the use of heavy-duty
    corrosion protective coating for
    maintaining steel and concrete industrial
    structures.
**Readers:** Persons who specify, purchase,
    formulate, or apply protective paints and
    coatings for industrial structures.
**Deadline:** story-3 mo. prior to pub. date;
    news-3 mo. prior to pub. date; photo-3
    mo. prior to pub. date; ads-2 mo. prior to
    pub. date

24268
## MODERN PAINT & COATINGS
6151 Powers Ferry N.W.
Atlanta, GA 30339-2941
Telephone: (404) 955-2500
FAX: (404) 955-0400
Year Established: 1910
Pub. Frequency: m.
Page Size: standard
Subscrip. Rate: $49/yr.
Circulation: 15,500
Circulation Type: paid
**Owner(s):**
Argus Business
6151 Powers Ferry N.W.
Atlanta, GA 30339-2941
Telephone: (404) 955-2500
Ownership %: 100
**Management:**
J.M. Palmer ...........................Publisher

**Editorial:**
Larry Anderson ...........................Editor
David Greenfield ...................Associate Editor
**Desc.:** Uses technical articles dealing with
    formulation of paints and coatings.
    Covers general industrial news, financial
    news, personnel changes, new
    equipment, new materials, new literature,
    market news.
**Readers:** Administration, research &
    development, production & engineering
    personnel.

69034
## PAINT DEALER
10097 Manchester Rd.
Ste. 208
St. Louis, MO 63122
Telephone: (314) 984-0800
FAX: (314) 984-0866
Year Established: 1992
Pub. Frequency: 10/yr.
Page Size: standard
Subscrip. Rate: $25/yr.
Circulation: 21,000
Circulation Type: controlled
**Owner(s):**
Paint Dealer
10097 Manchester Rd.
Ste. 208
St. Louis, MO 63122
Telephone: (314) 256-3214
Ownership %: 100
**Management:**
Chris Mugler ...........................President
Chris Mugler ...........................Publisher
**Editorial:**
Mike Matthews ...........................Editor
Jerrold Rabushka ...................Associate Editor
Chris Pierce ...................Circulation Director
**Desc.:** Covers product innovations,
    merchandising ideas, store management
    and industry news.

24270
## PAINTING & WALLCOVERING CONTRACTOR
8730 Big Bend Blvd.
St. Louis, MO 63119
Telephone: (314) 961-6644
FAX: (314) 961-4809
Mailing Address:
    2800 NE 41st St.
    Pompano Beach, FL 33064
Year Established: 1938
Pub. Frequency: bi-m.
Page Size: standard
Subscrip. Rate: $19.95/yr.
Freelance Pay: $150-$300
Circulation: 37,000
Circulation Type: controlled
**Owner(s):**
Painting & Wallcovering Contractor
7223 Lee Hwy.
Falls Church, VA 22046
Telephone: (703) 534-1201
Ownership %: 100
**Bureau(s):**
PWC Magazine Sls Mktg New Prd
2800 N.E. 1st St.
Pompano Beach , FL 33064
Telephone: (305) 781-5609
Contact: Kathy Lambla-Goodman, Vice
    President
**Management:**
Tom Finan ...........................Publisher
Kathy Gardner ...................Advertising Manager
**Editorial:**
Jeff Beckner ...................Executive Editor
Jeff Beckner ...................New Products Editor

**Materials Accepted/Included:** 01-Business news 02-By-line articles 03-Fashion news 04-Food news 05-Freelance copy 06-Letters to editor 07-Real estate news 08-Sports news 09-Travel news 10-Book rev. 11-Movie rev. 12-Music rev. 13-TV rev. 14-Theater rev. 15-Coming events 16-Obituaries 17-Question & answer 18-Social announcements 19-Artwork 20-Cartoons 21-Photos 22-TV listings 23-Audio rec. 24-Video rec. 25-Books 26-Films/film clips 27-Personnel news 28-Press releases 29-New product news/photos 30-Trade lit. 31-Contracts awarded 32-Display adv. 33-Classified adv.

**Desc.:** Covers all phases of the painting, decorating and wallcovering industry. Technical articles are furnished by members and research departments of the various paint industry manufacturers. Also, our Legal Counsel supplies a monthly article on various legal decisions affecting the painting contractor. The annual national convention activities are widely publicized. Outstanding jobs performed by contractors are spotlighted.
**Readers:** Painting and decorating contractors.

## Group 188-Paper & Paper Products

### AMERICAN PAPERMAKER MAGAZINE
24282
57 Executive Park S., Ste. 310
Atlanta, GA 30329
Telephone: (404) 325-9153
FAX: (404) 325-9581
Year Established: 1938
Pub. Frequency: m.
Page Size: standard
Subscrip. Rate: $45/yr.
Circulation: 30,500
Circulation Type: controlled
**Owner(s):**
MacLean Hunter Publishing Co.
777 Bay St.
Toronto ON, M5W 1A7, Canada CN
Telephone: (416) 596-5000
Ownership %: 100
**Editorial:**
Jerry Komcel .................................Editor
Chuck Swann ...............................Editor
Jackie Cox ..................................Editor
Lesa Welch .................................Editor
**Desc.:** Articles cover pulpwood procurement; manufacture of pulp, paper and paperboard; converting of pulp, paper or paperboard into bags, containers, boxes, etc. Departments include: New Developments, Personnel News, Industry Meetings, General News, On The Job. Full coverage given to industry and trade news as well as to new products. Publishes annual review number with mill and personnel directory section on October 1st.
**Readers:** Officials, management, production, engineers.

### ENVIRONMENTALLY SOUND PAPER NEWS
69035
10 Lombard St., Ste. 250
San Francisco, CA 94111
Telephone: (415) 433-1000
FAX: (415) 391-7890
Pub. Frequency: bi-m.
Subscrip. Rate: $59/yr.
Circulation: 25,000
Circulation Type: paid
**Owner(s):**
Conservatree Paper Co.
10 Lombard St., Ste. 250
San Francisco, CA 94111
Telephone: (415) 433-1000
Ownership %: 100
**Editorial:**
David Assmann .............................Editor
**Desc.:** Discusses environmentally sound paper issues including recycled paper and chlorine-free paper issues.

### FIBRE MARKET NEWS
24273
4012 Bridge Ave.
Cleveland, OH 44113
Telephone: (216) 961-4130
FAX: (216) 961-0364

Year Established: 1963
Pub. Frequency: w.
Page Size: standard
Subscrip. Rate: $118/yr.
Materials: 01,06,27,28,29,30,31,32,33
Freelance Pay: $300
Circulation: 2,700
Circulation Type: paid
**Owner(s):**
GIE, Inc.
4012 Bridge Ave.
Cleveland, OH 44113
Telephone: (216) 961-4130
Ownership %: 100
**Management:**
Richard J. W. Foster ....................Publisher
Rosalie Slusher ..............Circulation Manager
Madaline Gladstone ...............Sales Manager
**Editorial:**
Daniel Sandoval ...........................Editor
Jami Childs .....................Production Director
**Desc.:** Includes daily markets, quotations and trade news in the paper recycling industries. Also recycling industries, particularly paper, and municipal and state recycling programs.
**Readers:** Paper stock dealers, public recycling officials, government officials, mill officials, private companies.

### INTERNATIONAL PAPER BOARD INDUSTRY
69030
43 Main St.
Avon By Sea, NJ 07717
Telephone: (908) 502-0500
FAX: (908) 502-9606
Year Established: 1956
Pub. Frequency: m.
Page Size: standard
Subscrip. Rate: $55/yr.
Materials: 01,02,06,16,32,33
Circulation: 10,200
Circulation Type: free & paid
**Owner(s):**
NV Business Publishers Corp.
43 Main St.
Avon By Sea, NJ 07717
Telephone: (908) 502-0500
Ownership %: 100
**Editorial:**
Michael Brunton ...........................Editor
Ted Vilardi ..................................Editor
**Deadline:** story-1 mo. prior to pub. date; news-1 mo. prior to pub. date; photo-1 mo. prior to pub. date; ads-1 mo. prior to pub. date

### NPTA MANAGEMENT NEWS
69036
111 Great Neck Rd., Ste. 418
Great Neck, NY 11021
Telephone: (516) 829-3070
FAX: (516) 829-3074
Year Established: 1959
Pub. Frequency: m.
Page Size: standard
Subscrip. Rate: $20/yr.
Circulation: 21,000
Circulation Type: paid
**Owner(s):**
National Paper Trade Association, Inc.
111 Great Neck Rd., Ste. 418
Great Neck, NY 11021
Telephone: (516) 829-3070
Ownership %: 100
**Editorial:**
Edward D. Pasternack .....................Editor

### OFFICIAL BOARD MARKETS
24274
233 N. Michigan Ave., 24th Fl.
Chicago, IL 60601
Telephone: (312) 938-2345
Year Established: 1914
Pub. Frequency: 52/yr.
Subscrip. Rate: $130/yr.

Circulation: 5,500
Circulation Type: paid
**Owner(s):**
Advanstar Communications, Inc.
233 N. Michigan Ave., 24th Fl.
Chicago, IL 60601
Telephone: (312) 938-2345
Ownership %: 100
**Editorial:**
Mark Arzoumanian ........................Editor
**Desc.:** Covers paperboard, converted paperboard products, pulp, wastepaper, prices and all related news from the paperboard field.
**Readers:** Paperboard mills, paperboard converters, purchasers of paperboard.

### PAPER AGE
24275
400 Old Hook Rd., Ste. G-6
Westwood, NJ 07675
Telephone: (201) 666-2262
FAX: (201) 666-9046
Year Established: 1884
Pub. Frequency: m.
Page Size: tabloid
Subscrip. Rate: $50/yr. US; $75/yr. foreign
Freelance Pay: $110/5,000 wds.
Circulation: 32,000
Circulation Type: controlled
**Owner(s):**
Global Publications
400 Old Hook Rd., Ste. G-6
Westwood, NJ 07675
Telephone: (201) 666-2262
Ownership %: 100
**Management:**
J. F. O'Brien ..............................President
J. F. O'Brien ..............................Publisher
A. Schuermann ....................Office Manager
**Editorial:**
Mark McCready ............................Editor
Linda Cohen ......................Managing Editor
Kathy Burack ...........................Art Director
**Desc.:** Monthly news tabloid for pulp and paper industry. Carries some articles dealing with trends in paper usage; pulp and paper manufacture; converting/finishing; wood fiber processing; developments opening new avenues for sales (technological, such as new coatings enabling entry into new packaging fields), convention reports. Features new equipment.
**Readers:** Pulp and paper manufacturers and converters.

### PAPER INDUSTRY
61687
225 Hanrick St.
Montgomery, AL 36104
Telephone: (205) 834-1170
Mailing Address:
    P.O. Box 2268
    Montgomery, AL 36102
Year Established: 1984
Pub. Frequency: bi-m.
Page Size: tabloid
Subscrip. Rate: $12/yr. non-member
Circulation: 19,120
Circulation Type: controlled
**Owner(s):**
Hatton-Brown Publishers, Inc.
225 Hanrick St.
Montgomery, AL 36104
Telephone: (205) 834-1170
Ownership %: 100
**Management:**
David Knight ..............................Publisher
Dianne C. Sullivan ...............General Manager
**Editorial:**
David Knight ..........................Editor in Chief
Rich Donnell .....................Editorial Director
Tim Shaddick ...........................Advertising
Kay Oldham ..............................Advertising
Alan Brett .................................Advertising

John Hibbard ...........Advertising Sales Manager
Patti Campbell ...................Media Coordinator
**Readers:** Pulp, paper and paperboard manufacturers

### PAPER INDUSTRY MANAGEMENT ASSOCIATION (PIMA) MAGAZINE
24277
2400 E. Oakton St.
Arlington Heights, IL 60005-4898
Telephone: (708) 956-0250
FAX: (708) 956-0520
Year Established: 1919
Pub. Frequency: m.
Page Size: standard
Subscrip. Rate: $75/yr.
Materials: 01,02,05,06,10,16,19,21,25,27, 28,29,30,32,33
Print Process: web offset
Circulation: 22,000
Circulation Type: controlled
**Owner(s):**
PIMA
2400 E. Oakton St.
Arlington Heights, IL 60005-4898
Telephone: (708) 956-0250
FAX: (708) 956-0520
Ownership %: 100
**Management:**
E. Lindsay Beddingfield ..................Publisher
Judy A. Burke ...................Circulation Manager
**Editorial:**
Alan Rooks ...........................Editor in Chief
Jan Bottiglieri .......................Managing Editor
Victoria Higgins ....................Assistant Editor
Alan Rooks ...............Communications Director
**Desc.:** Staff written and contributed by-line articles covering paper management techniques, management development, review of new processes and equipment, developments, practical paper making and practical problem solving. Departments include: Economic Trends, Industry News, New Products and Equipment, New Literature, Industry Personnel.
**Readers:** Top management, superintendents, engineers, mill managers

### PULP & PAPER
24281
600 Harrison St.
San Francisco, CA 94107
Telephone: (415) 905-2200
FAX: (415) 905-2240
Year Established: 1927
Pub. Frequency: m.
Page Size: standard
Subscrip. Rate: $105/yr.
Materials: 01,02,06
Print Process: web offset
Circulation: 49,000
Circulation Type: controlled
**Owner(s):**
United Newspapers PLC
Ownership %: 100
**Bureaus:**
Miller Freeman Publications
2000 Powers Ferry Center 450
Marietta, GA 30067
Telephone: (404) 952-1303
Contact: Ken Patrick, Editor in Chief

Miller Freeman Publications
370 Lexington Ave.
New York, NY 10017
Telephone: (212) 683-9294
Contact: Noel DeKing, Associate Editor

Miller Freeman Publications
35 E. Wacker Dr.
Chicago, IL 60601
Telephone: (312) 372-6238
Contact: Roberts Burton, Sales Manager

---

**Materials Accepted/Included:** 01-Business news 02-By-line articles 03-Fashion news 04-Food news 05-Freelance copy 06-Letters to editor 07-Real estate news 08-Sports news 09-Travel news 10-Book rev. 11-Movie rev. 12-Music rev. 13-TV rev. 14-Theater rev. 15-Coming events 16-Obituaries 17-Question & answer 18-Social announcements 19-Artwork 20-Cartoons 21-Photos 22-TV listings 23-Audio rec. 24-Video rec. 25-Books 26-Films/film clips 27-Personnel news 28-Press releases 29-New product news/photos 30-Trade lit. 31-Contracts awarded 32-Display adv. 33-Classified adv.

**Management:**

Clifford D. Jakes ................Chairman of Board
Marshall W. Freeman ..........................President
Leigh M. Freeman ...............................Publisher

**Editorial:**

Ken L. Patrick ...........................Editor in Chief
Will E. Mies .............................Executive Editor
Debra A. Garcia ...........................Senior Editor
Kelly H. Ferguson ...................................Editor
Virginia C. Stefan .....................................Editor
Kurt F. Duecker ..........................Managing Editor
Carl P. Espe ......................................News Editor
Rob Galin ..........................................News Editor
Noel DeKing .....................................News Editor
Jim Young .....................................Technical Editor
Andy Harrison .............................Technical Editor

**Desc.:** Staff-written and contributed features and articles cover papermaking, converting, chemistry and chemical use in mills, pulping, environmental improvement, new equipment and technology, pulp and paper industry personalities, industry statistical & marketing news, news of suppliers, trends, and pulpwood/forestry.

**Readers:** Pulp and paper management, executives, engineering, production, technical.

**Deadline:** story-1st of mo. prior to pub. date; news-1st of mo. prior; photo-1st of mo. prior

24283

**TAPPI JOURNAL**
15 Technology Pkwy. S.
Norcross, GA 30092
Telephone: (404) 446-1400
FAX: (404) 446-6947
Year Established: 1949
Pub. Frequency: 12/yr.
Page Size: standard
Subscrip. Rate: $75/yr.
Materials: 01,02,05,06,27,28,29,32,33
Freelance Pay: negotiable
Circulation: 48,000
Circulation Type: controlled & paid

**Owner(s):**
TAPPI
P.O. Box 105113
Atlanta, GA 30348
Telephone: (404) 446-1400
Ownership %: 100

**Management:**
R.B. Estridge ....................................President
M.J. Coleman ...................................Publisher
W.L. Cullison ..........................Executive Director
L.S. Puckett .......Assistant Advertising Manager
M.B. Bennett .........................Business Manager

**Editorial:**
D.G. Meadows ........................................Editor
L.S. Bisges ......................Advertising Assistant
B.R. Puett ..........................Advertising Director
S.M. Clites .............................Associate Editor
M.K. Cooper .......................Editorial Assistant
D.E. Swann .................Production Coordinator
R.C. DeFreitas .....Traffic Production Assistant

**Desc.:** Serves domestic and international manufacturers of pulp, paper, paperboard, packaging, and converted products and producers of chemicals, equipment, parts, components, and other materials used to manufacture these products. It is edited for engineering, technical, scientific, and supervisory personnel and their managers. Editorial features cover advances in technology, engineering, and research that can be actually applied to the development and design of new products in industry. Special features report on management practices, process design and control, product research and Development, and original research. Also presented are special departments on Business and Technology, TAPPI Conference Updates, New Products, New Literature, Industry News, reviews of the other TAPPI technical publications, and reports of current TAPPI technical committee projects and activities.

**Readers:** Engineering, technical, scientific, and management personnel employed by domestic and international manufacturers of pulp, paper, paperboard, packaging, and converted products and producers of chemicals, equipment, parts components, and other materials used in the manufacture of these products.

## Group 190-Parks

69145

**JOURNAL OF PARK & RECREATION ADMINISTRATION**
302 W. Hill St.
P.O. Box 647
Champaign, IL 61824-0647
Telephone: (217) 359-5940
FAX: (217) 359-5979
Year Established: 1986
Pub. Frequency: q.
Subscrip. Rate: $35/yr. individuals; $40/yr. institutions; $45/yr. foreign
Circulation: 720
Circulation Type: controlled

**Owner(s):**
Sagamore Publishing, Inc.
302 W. Hill St.
P.O. Box 647
Champaign, IL 61824-0647
Telephone: (217) 359-5940
Ownership %: 100

**Desc.:** Scholarly articles on planning, finance, organizational practice, personnel evaluation, programming, and marketing and promotion.

23076

**NATIONAL PARKS**
1776 Massachusetts Ave., N.W.
Washington, DC 20036
Telephone: (202) 223-6722
FAX: (202) 659-0650
Year Established: 1919
Pub. Frequency: bi-m.
Page Size: standard
Subscrip. Rate: $25/yr.
Freelance Pay: $75 - $800
Circulation: 300,000
Circulation Type: paid

**Owner(s):**
National Parks and Conservation Association
1776 Massachusetts Ave., N.W.
Washington, DC 20036
Telephone: (202) 223-6722
Ownership %: 100

**Bureau(s):**
National Parks Advertising Office
1776 Massachusetts Ave., NW
Washington, DC 20036
Telephone: (202) 223-6722
Contact: Carol Cummins, Advertising Manager

**Management:**
Paul C. Pritchard ...............................President

**Editorial:**
Sue Dodge ............................................Editor
Linda Rancourt ........................Associate Editor
Katherine Heinrich ................Editorial Assistant
Kim O'Connell ..............................News Editor

**Desc.:** We consider articles about national parks and monuments, stressing threats confronting them or their particularly unique or significant floral, faunal, geological, or historical features; human interest and wildlife features related to national parks; and travel articles about national parks. Articles are welcome. We suggest a thorough treatment of a limited subject. Like queries; SASE 1,500-2,000 word articles w/B&W color & pix, drawings OK; no mentions, quotes xp; include one-time photo rights with story. Report 4-6 weeks.

**Readers:** Enlightened, interested in nature, outdoors, well educated.

24286

**PARK & GROUNDS MANAGEMENT**
730 W. Frances St.
Appleton, WI 54914
Telephone: (414) 733-2301
Mailing Address:
P.O. Box 1936
Appleton, WI 54913
Year Established: 1948
Pub. Frequency: 10/yr.
Page Size: standard
Subscrip. Rate: $22/yr.
Circulation: 12,000
Circulation Type: controlled

**Owner(s):**
Madison Publishing Div.
P.O. Box 1936
Appleton, WI 54913
Telephone: (414) 733-2301
Ownership %: 100

**Management:**
Erik L. Madisen, Jr. ...........................Publisher
Hooper Jones ...................Advertising Manager
Janis Willems .....................Circulation Manager

**Editorial:**
Erik L. Madisen, Jr. ..................................Editor
Barbara Walters .......................Managing Editor
Monica Molnar ...................Production Director

**Desc.:** By-line articles deal with the practical side of park, golf course, campus and recreation facilities maintenance. News material must be of interest to buyers and users of machinery, chemicals, seeds, etc., in those fields. Departments include: Publications Received, Industry News, Sports Turf Management.

**Readers:** Superintendents of parks, golf courses, college campuses and school districts.

24287

**PARKS & RECREATION MAGAZINE**
2775 S. Quincy St.
Arlington, VA 22206
Telephone: (703) 820-4940
FAX: (703) 671-6772
Year Established: 1903
Pub. Frequency: m.
Page Size: standard
Subscrip. Rate: $25/yr.
Circulation: 20,000
Circulation Type: paid

**Owner(s):**
National Recreation and Park Assn.
3101 Park Center Dr.
Alexandria, VA 22302
Telephone: (703) 820-4940
Ownership %: 100

**Management:**
R. Dean Tice ......................................President

**Editorial:**
Pamela Leigh ........................................Editor
Jennifer Ford ...............................Advertising
Annabel Markle ..............................Art Director

**Desc.:** Serves the administrative and supervisory executives in the National, State, Regional, County, Metropolitan, Municipal park and recreation field who develop and maintain park and recreation areas and facilities, including governmental and private parks.

**Readers:** Municipal park superintendents, recreation/park administrators, executives, park and recreation board members, superintendents, zoological park directors, and interested lay persons.

## Group 192-Personnel Management

22286

**COMPENSATION & BENEFITS REVIEW**
135 W. 50th St.
New York, NY 10020-1201
Telephone: (212) 586-8100
Year Established: 1969
Pub. Frequency: bi-m.
Page Size: standard
Subscrip. Rate: $80.10/yr. members; $89/yr. non-members
Materials: 02,10
Circulation: 6,000
Circulation Type: paid

**Owner(s):**
American Management Associations
135 W. 50th St.
New York, NY 10020
Telephone: (212) 586-8100
Ownership %: 100

**Editorial:**
Hermine Zagat Levine ................Editor in Chief

**Desc.:** Technical articles for specialists in the broad field of compensation and benefit plan development and administration. Departments include: Compensation Currents, Selected Readings, In Brief, Compensation Management In Practice, and Features.

**Readers:** Individuals responsible for the development of compensation benefits and pension plans in a variety of institutional settings.

69496

**EAP DIGEST**
1863 Technology Dr.
Troy, MI 48083-4244
Telephone: (313) 588-7733
FAX: (313) 588-6633
Year Established: 1980
Pub. Frequency: bi-m.
Page Size: standard
Subscrip. Rate: $46/yr.
Print Process: web offset
Circulation: 20,000
Circulation Type: controlled & paid

**Owner(s):**
Performance Resource Press, Inc.
1863 Technology Dr.
Troy, MI 48083-4244
Telephone: (313) 588-7733
Ownership %: 100

**Editorial:**
George Watkins .......................................Editor

**Materials Accepted/Included:** 01-Business news 02-By-line articles 03-Fashion news 04-Food news 05-Freelance copy 06-Letters to editor 07-Real estate news 08-Sports news 09-Travel news 10-Book rev. 11-Movie rev. 12-Music rev. 13-TV rev. 14-Theater rev. 15-Coming events 16-Obituaries 17-Question & answer 18-Social announcements 19-Artwork 20-Cartoons 21-Photos 22-TV listings 23-Audio rec. 24-Video rec. 25-Books 26-Films/film clips 27-Personnel news 28-Press releases 29-New product news/photos 30-Trade lit. 31-Contracts awarded 32-Display adv. 33-Classified adv.

## EEO REVIEW
58689

22 W. 21st St.
New York, NY 10010
Telephone: (212) 645-7880
FAX: (212) 645-1160
Year Established: 1968
Pub. Frequency: m.
Page Size: standard
Subscrip. Rate: $159/yr.
**Owner(s):**
Executive Enterprises Publications Co., Inc.
22 W. 21st St.
New York, NY 10010
Telephone: (212) 645-7880
Ownership %: 100
**Editorial:**
Sarah Magee ................................................Editor
Jean Stephenson ....................Managing Editor
**Desc.:** Explains to personnel managers
  and supervisors how to handle their
  EEO and other personnel policy
  responsibilities in such areas as drugs
  and alcohol, AIDS, firing, hiring,
  promotion, discipline, counseling,
  performance appraisal, and career
  counseling.
**Readers:** Supervisors and personnel
  specialists.

## EMPLOYEE BENEFIT PLAN REVIEW
22311

250 S. Wacker Dr., Ste. 600
Chicago, IL 60606-5834
Telephone: (312) 993-7900
FAX: (312) 993-7910
Year Established: 1946
Pub. Frequency: m.
Page Size: standard
Subscrip. Rate: $56/yr.
Materials: 01,06,10,27,28,29,30,32,34
Print Process: offset
Circulation: 30,000
Circulation Type: controlled & paid
**Owner(s):**
Charles D. Spencer & Associates, Inc.
250 S. Wacker Dr., Ste. 600
Chicago, IL 60606
Telephone: (312) 993-7900
Ownership %: 100
**Bureau(s):**
Mary Papa
2000 L St., N.W.
Washington, DC 20036
Telephone: (202) 659-1763
FAX: (202) 833-3843
Contact: Mary Papa, Senior Editor
**Management:**
Bruce F. Spencer .................................Publisher
Barbara Williams ...............Advertising Manager
James Williams ....................Business Manager
**Editorial:**
Seymour LaRock ....................Executive Editor
Bruce F. Spencer ......................................Editor
Stephen Huth ..........................Managing Editor
Susan Burzawa ........................Product Manager
**Desc.:** Articles describing health, Sec.
  401(K), profit-sharing, pension and other
  benefit plans; contract negotiations
  relating to these areas; introduction of
  plans, and plan design; new laws,
  regulations, and legal developments
  relating to employee benefits, trends and
  survey data relating to employee
  benefits.
**Readers:** Corporate benefit and human
  resource managers, consultants,
  insurance companies, third-party
  administrators.
**Deadline:** story-2 mos.; news-2 mos.; ads-
  1 mo.

## EMPLOYEE RELATIONS LAW JOURNAL
58691

22 W. 21st St.
New York, NY 10010
Telephone: (212) 645-7880
FAX: (212) 645-1160
Year Established: 1974
Pub. Frequency: q.
Page Size: standard
Subscrip. Rate: $198/yr.
**Owner(s):**
Executive Enterprises Publications Co., Inc.
22 W. 21st St.
New York, NY 10010
Telephone: (212) 645-7880
Ownership %: 100
**Editorial:**
William J. Kilberg ......................Editor in Chief
Diane Scent ...............................................Editor
Jean Stephenson ....................Managing Editor
**Desc.:** A quarterly journal providing in-
  depth analysis of legal issues in equal
  employment opportunity, occupational
  health & safety, labor-management
  relations, and employee benefits.
**Readers:** Attorneys, personnel executives.

## EMPLOYEE SERVICES MANAGEMENT
22391

2211 York Rd., Ste 207
Oak Brook, IL 60521-2371
Telephone: (708) 368-1280
FAX: (708) 368-1286
Year Established: 1958
Pub. Frequency: 10/yr.
Page Size: standard
Subscrip. Rate: $4/issue; $37/yr.
Freelance Pay: varies
Circulation: 6,500
Circulation Type: paid
**Owner(s):**
National Employee Services & Recreation
  Assn.
2211 York Rd.
Oak Brook, IL 60521-2371
Telephone: (708) 386-1280
Ownership %: 100
**Management:**
Patrick B. Stinson ...............................Publisher
Charles A. Bashian ...........Advertising Manager
Cynthia M. Helson ....................Public Relations
  Manager
**Editorial:**
Cynthia M. Helson ...................Executive Editor
**Desc.:** Edited for managers responsible for
  business and industry's broad scope of
  employee services and recreation
  programs, including fitness, pre-
  retirement planning, discount, travel,
  sports, employee assistance and
  dependent care program, company
  picnics and hobby clubs. Interested in
  news which is pertinent to the fields of
  recreation and human resources
  management and describes new and
  useful products or services. Departments
  include: News in Brief, Health Promotion
  Update, Employee Store Candid Corner.
**Readers:** Recreation managers, human
  resource managers

## EMPLOYMENT RELATIONS TODAY
58690

22 W. 21st St.
New York, NY 10010-6990
Telephone: (212) 645-7880
FAX: (212) 645-1160
Year Established: 1973
Pub. Frequency: q.
Page Size: standard
Subscrip. Rate: $175/yr.

**Owner(s):**
Executive Enterprises Publications Co., Inc.
22 W. 21st St.
New York, NY 10010
Telephone: (212) 645-7880
Ownership %: 100
**Editorial:**
Carol Di Paolo ..........................................Editor
Jane G. Bensahel ..............Director, Business
  Publications
**Desc.:** For senior human resources
  managers, it covers significant changes
  in the workforce; the work environment,
  the way people work, and the way they
  think about work.
**Readers:** Senior human resources and
  personnel executives.

## EQUAL OPPORTUNITY
22313

150 Motor Pkwy. #420
Hauppauge, NY 11788-5108
Telephone: (516) 273-0066
FAX: (516) 273-8936
Year Established: 1970
Pub. Frequency: 3/yr.
Page Size: standard
Subscrip. Rate: $4.50/copy; $13/yr.; $25/2
  yrs.; $36/3 yrs.
Freelance Pay: $.10/wd.
Circulation: 15,000
Circulation Type: paid
**Owner(s):**
Equal Opportunity Publications, Inc.
44 Broadway
Greenlawn, NY 11740
Telephone: (516) 261-8899
Ownership %: 100
**Bureau(s):**
Equal Opportunity Publications, Inc.
44 Broadway
Greenlawn, NY 11740
Telephone: (516) 261-8899
Contact: John R. Miller, III, President
**Management:**
John R. Miller, III ................................Publisher
Barbara A. O'Connor .........Circulation Manager
**Editorial:**
James F. Schneider ................Executive Editor
Anne Kelly ...............................Senior Editor
Greg Crescas .....................................Advertising
Eileen Nester .........................Associate Editor
Kay Z. Miller ................................VP-Marketing
**Desc.:** An affirmative action career
  magazine published for minority students
  and graduates. A multi-ethnic, "tell it like
  it is" magazine whose purpose is to
  close the communications gap between
  college minorities (blacks, Hispanics,
  Asian & Native Americans) and
  companies who are sincere in seeking
  minority talent for meaningful career
  positions in the business world. Articles
  are written about prominent minorities
  and business people, minority
  employees on their way up, and college
  students. The magazine offers a variety
  of career opportunities from industry,
  government, schools, and hospitals.
  It contains articles on job hunting,
  interviews, resumes, and pertinent
  information procedures for seeking
  employment as well as role models.
**Readers:** Minority students & graduates.

## HR FOCUS
24951

135 W. 50th St.
New York, NY 10020
Telephone: (212) 586-8100
Year Established: 1922
Pub. Frequency: m.

Page Size: standard
Subscrip. Rate: $46.75/yr. US members;
  $51.75/yr. non-members; $56.75/yr.
  foreign members, $61.75/yr. non-
  members
Circulation: 18,000
Circulation Type: controlled
**Owner(s):**
American Management Association
135 W. 50 St.
New York, NY 10020
Telephone: (212) 586-8100
Ownership %: 100
**Editorial:**
Bob Smith ................................................Editor
William Wagel ..........................Managing Editor
**Desc.:** Contributed by-line articles by
  personnel executives, social scientists
  and educators dealing with personnel
  administration and industrial
  relations. Covers human relations,
  personnel techniques, labor-
  management relations, compensation
  and benefits, developments and trends,
  research.
**Readers:** Personnel and industrial-relations
  executives.

## HUMAN RESOURCE DEVELOPMENT QUARTERLY
68965

350 Sansome St., 5th Fl.
San Francisco, CA 94104
Telephone: (415) 433-1767
FAX: (415) 433-0499
Year Established: 1990
Pub. Frequency: q.
Page Size: pocket
Subscrip. Rate: $47/yr. individuals; $76/yr.
  institutions
Circulation: 2,000
Circulation Type: paid
**Owner(s):**
American Society for Training and
  Development

Jossey-Bass Inc., Publishers
350 Sansome St., 5th Fl.
San Francisco, CA 94104
Telephone: (415) 433-1767
Ownership %: 100
**Editorial:**
Gary N. McLean .......................................Editor
**Desc.:** Draws together the work of
  scholars and practitioners in a range of
  related areas: training, management,
  industrial psychology, organizational
  behavior and adult education.
**Deadline:** story-3 mos. prior to pub. date

## HUMAN RESOURCE PLANNING
68966

41 E. 42nd St., Ste. 1509
New York, NY 10017-5200
Telephone: (212) 490-6387
FAX: (212) 682-6851
Year Established: 1978
Pub. Frequency: q.
Subscrip. Rate: $80/yr. US; $94/yr. foreign
Circulation: 2200
Circulation Type: paid
**Owner(s):**
Human Resource Planning Society
41 E. 42nd St., Ste. 1509
New York, NY 10017-5200
Telephone: (212) 490-6387
Ownership %: 100
**Editorial:**
Charles H. Fay ..........................................Editor

## HUMAN RESOURCES ABSTRACTS
64991

2455 Teller Rd.
Thousand Oaks, CA 91320
Telephone: (805) 499-0721
FAX: (805) 499-0871

**Materials Accepted/Included:** 01-Business news 02-By-line articles 03-Fashion news 04-Food news 05-Freelance copy 06-Letters to editor 07-Real estate news 08-Sports news 09-Travel news
10-Book rev. 11-Movie rev. 12-Music rev. 13-TV rev. 14-Theater rev. 15-Coming events 16-Obituaries 17-Question & answer 18-Social announcements 19-Artwork 20-Cartoons 21-Photos 22-TV listings
23-Audio rec. 24-Video rec. 25-Books 26-Films/film clips 27-Personnel news 28-Press releases 29-New product news/photos 30-Trade lit. 31-Contracts awarded 32-Display adv. 33-Classified adv.

4-281

Year Established: 1965
Pub. Frequency: q.
Page Size: standard
Subscrip. Rate: $93/yr. individuals;
  $273/yr. institutions
Circulation: 800
Circulation Type: paid
**Owner(s):**
Sage Publications, Inc.
2455 Teller Rd.
Thousand Oaks, CA 91320
Telephone: (805) 499-0721
Ownership %: 100
**Editorial:**
Paul McDowell .............................Editor
**Desc.:** Contains abstracts of the most
important recent literature for the
professional who needs easy reference
to current and changing ideas in the
diverse area of manpower and human
resources development, and related
social/governmental policy questions.
**Readers:** Professionals who deal with
social, and government policies.

22330

**IAPES NEWS**
1801 Louisville Rd.
Frankfort, KY 40601
Telephone: (502) 223-4459
FAX: (502) 223-4127
Year Established: 1941
Pub. Frequency: bi-m.
Page Size: tabloid
Subscrip. Rate: $25/yr.
Freelance Pay: negotiable
Circulation: 25,000
Circulation Type: paid
**Owner(s):**
Intl. Assn. of Personnel in Employment
  Security
1801 Louisville Rd.
Frankfort, KY 40601
Telephone: (502) 223-4459
Ownership %: 100
**Editorial:**
Michael R. Stone .........................Editor
**Desc.:** A technical-trade journal and
association house organ combination.
Covers general association news of
national headquarters and state and
provincial chapters in U.S., Canada and
other countries. Feature and technical
articles dealing in operations, methods,
techniques, etc., of personnel
administration, job placement,
unemployment compensation; disability
insurance, vocational counseling, labor
market and manpower utilization;
research and analysis, disabled job
placement services and other broad or
specifically related fields in socioeconomic areas of interest including
psychology, industrial, public and human
relations, management, research and
statistics, occupational analysis.
**Readers:** Salaried government workers,
state & federal, in job service and
unemployment compensation or related
fields.

69439

**JOURNAL OF HUMAN
  RESOURCES**
Social Sciences Bldg.
1180 Observatory Dr.
Madison, WI 53706
Telephone: (608) 262-4867
FAX: (608) 265-3119
Year Established: 1966
Pub. Frequency: q.
Page Size: 36X54
Subscrip. Rate: $35/yr. individuals; $75/yr.
  institutions
Circulation: 2,500
Circulation Type: paid

**Owner(s):**
University of Wisconsin Press
114 N. Murray St.
Madison, WI 53715
Telephone: (608) 262-4952
Ownership %: 100
**Editorial:**
C. Manski ..................................Editor
Jan Levine Thal ...............Managing Editor
**Desc.:** An academic journal that uses
state-of-the-art empirical methods in
economics and related fields. Peer
reviewed through blend-blend refering
process.

65004

**MANAGEMENT COMMUNICATION
  QUARTERLY**
2455 Teller Rd.
Thousand Oaks, CA 91320
Telephone: (805) 499-0721
FAX: (805) 499-0871
Year Established: 1974
Pub. Frequency: q.
Page Size: standard
Subscrip. Rate: $46/yr. individuals;
  $134/yr. insitutions
Circulation: 1,200
Circulation Type: paid
**Owner(s):**
Sage Publications, Inc.
2455 Teller Rd.
Thousand Oaks, CA 91320
Telephone: (803) 499-0721
Ownership %: 100
**Editorial:**
Katherine I. Miller .......................Editor
Larry Smeltzer ...........................Editor
**Desc.:** Brings together communication
research from a wide variety of fields,
with a focus on managerial and
organizational effectiveness. Includes
book previews and notes from
preofessional in the field.
**Readers:** Academic communities.

24953

**PERSONNEL JOURNAL**
245 Fischer Ave., B2
Costa Mesa, CA 92626
Telephone: (714) 751-1883
FAX: (714) 751-4106
Mailing Address:
  P.O. Box 2440
  Costa Mesa, CA 92628
Year Established: 1922
Pub. Frequency: m.
Page Size: standard
Subscrip. Rate: $62/yr.
Materials: 01,02,05,06,32,33
Freelance Pay: $800-$2,000
Print Process: web
Circulation: 30,000
Circulation Type: paid
**Owner(s):**
ACC Communications, Inc.
245 Fischer Ave., B2
Costa Mesa, CA 92626
Telephone: (714) 751-1883
FAX: (714) 751-4106
Ownership %: 100
**Management:**
Betty Hartzell ...............Chairman of Board
Margaret Magnus ....................President
Elizabeth Hartzell ................Vice President
Kate MacIntyre ......................Publisher
Kim Henderson .............Circulation Manager
Susan Villareal ..........Classified Adv. Manager
Stephanie Lawrence .........Production Manager
**Editorial:**
Brenda Paik Sunoo ...............Senior Editor
Allan Halcrow ..........................Editor
Steve Stewart ......................Art Director
Margaret Magnus ..........Secretary & Treasurer

**Desc.:** Contributed by-lined articles on
labor relations, personnel management,
training, recruitment, compensation and
benefits, future employment trends,
office automation, robots, relocation,
awards/incentive programs, diversity,
legalities connected with human
resources and employment law.
**Readers:** Human resources executives,
personnel directors, industrial/labor
relations, training, safety, security.
**Deadline:** story-90 days prior to pub. date;
ads-25th of mo. 2 mos. prior

68967

**PUBLIC PERSONNEL
MANAGEMENT**
1617 Duke St.
Alexandria, VA 22314
Telephone: (703) 549-7100
FAX: (703) 684-0948
Year Established: 1940
Pub. Frequency: q.
Subscrip. Rate: $50/yr.
Materials: 32
Print Process: offset
Circulation: 10,000
Circulation Type: paid
**Owner(s):**
International Personnel Management
  Association
1617 Duke St.
Alexandria, VA 22314
Telephone: (703) 549-7100
Ownership %: 100
**Editorial:**
Sarah A. I. Shiffert .....................Editor
**Desc.:** Articles on labor relations,
assessment issues, comparative
personnel policies, governmental
reform and other areas of concern to
personnel managers in the public sector.

22411

**SUPERVISORY MANAGEMENT**
135 West 50th St.
New York, NY 10020-1201
Telephone: (212) 586-8100
Year Established: 1955
Pub. Frequency: m.
Page Size: standard
Subscrip. Rate: $38/yr.
Materials: 01,02,05
Freelance Pay: $20/hr.
Circulation: 14,000
Circulation Type: paid
**Owner(s):**
American Management Assn.
135 W. 50th St.
New York, NY 10020
Telephone: (212) 586-8100
Ownership %: 100
**Management:**
John Doerr .............................President
Rosemary Carlough .................Publisher
**Editorial:**
Florence Stone .........................Editor
Seval Newton .....................Art Director
**Desc.:** Feature articles are directed to first-
line and middle managers in the public
and private sectors. Most of the articles
are contributed by people who have had
practical experience in management.
Interested in articles in the following
areas: broad principles of management
(planning, control, motivation, etc.);
special aspects of management
(automated office, work measurement,
etc.); human relations and
communications; labor relations.
Average article length 650 words.
Departments include: Your Personal
Management; Cases; Arbitration; Cost
Cutting/Profit Making Ideas
**Readers:** Supervisors and managers.

68968

**TECHNICAL & SKILLS TRAINING**
1640 King St.
Alexandria, VA 22313
Telephone: (703) 683-8129
FAX: (703) 683-8103
Year Established: 1990
Pub. Frequency: 8/yr.
Page Size: standard
Subscrip. Rate: $59/yr. US; $84/yr. foreign
Circulation: 20,000
Circulation Type: paid
**Owner(s):**
American Society for Training &
  Development
1640 King St.
P.O. Box 1443
Alexandria, VA 22313
Telephone: (703) 683-8129
Ownership %: 100
**Editorial:**
Ellen S. Carnevale .......................Editor
**Desc.:** Reports news and trends affecting
the field, includes products available and
articles on companies and techniques.

58641

**TODAY'S SUPERVISOR**
1121 Spring Lake Dr.
Itasca, IL 60143
Telephone: (708) 285-1121
FAX: (708) 775-2285
Pub. Frequency: m.
Page Size: 5 1/2" X 8 1/2"
Subscrip. Rate: $23/yr.
Materials: 02,05,06,19
Freelance Pay: negotiable
Circulation: 130,000
Circulation Type: paid
**Owner(s):**
National Safety Council
1121 Spring Lake Dr.
Itasca, IL 60143-3201
Telephone: (708) 285-1121
Ownership %: 100
**Management:**
Kevin H. Axe ..........................Publisher
**Editorial:**
Kathy Henderson .......................Editor
**Desc.:** Addresses the everyday safety,
health and environmental problems &
issues of the first-line supervisor
including accident prevention,
occupational health management,
principles and human relations.
**Readers:** Managers and supervisors.

24208

**TRAINING**
Lakewood Bldg. 50 S. Ninth St.
Minneapolis, MN 55402
Telephone: (612) 333-0471
FAX: (612) 333-6526
Year Established: 1964
Pub. Frequency: m.
Page Size: standard
Subscrip. Rate: $68/yr. US; $78/yr. Can.;
  $89/yr. foreign
Materials: 01,02,06,11,15,20,21,24,25,28,
  29,30,32,33
Print Process: web offset
Circulation: 55,000
Circulation Type: paid
**Owner(s):**
Lakewood Publ., Inc., a MacLean Hunter
  Publ. Co.
Lakewood Bldg., 50 S. 9th St.
Minneapolis, MN 55402
Telephone: (612) 333-0471
FAX: (612) 333-6526
Ownership %: 100

**Materials Accepted/Included:** 01-Business news 02-By-line articles 03-Fashion news 04-Food news 05-Freelance copy 06-Letters to editor 07-Real estate news 08-Sports news 09-Travel news 10-Book rev. 11-Movie rev. 12-Music rev. 13-TV rev. 14-Theater rev. 15-Coming events 16-Obituaries 17-Question & answer 18-Social announcements 19-Artwork 20-Cartoons 21-Photos 22-TV listings 23-Audio rec. 24-Video rec. 25-Books 26-Films/film clips 27-Personnel news 28-Press releases 29-New product news/photos 30-Trade lit. 31-Contracts awarded 32-Display adv. 33-Classified adv.

**Bureau(s):**
Lakewood Publications, Inc.
761 Lighthouse Ave.
Ste. D
Monterey, CA 93940
Telephone: (408) 649-8042
FAX: (408) 649-8207
Contact: Judi Leidiger

Lakewood Publications, Inc.
P.O. Box 271
Rindge, NH 03461
Telephone: (603) 899-3010
Contact: Richard J. Alden

Lakewood Publications, Inc.
1761 Great Trail
Smyrna, GA 30080
Telephone: (404) 438-2523
Contact: Doug Lewis
**Management:**
James P. Secord ............................President
Jerry C. Noack ..........................Vice President
Nancy Swanson ...............Circulation Manager
Pat Grawert ......................Production Manager
**Editorial:**
Jack Gordon ................................Editor
Chris Lee ................................Managing Editor
Cory Goddard ...........................Acct. Manager
Marc Hequet ...........................Associate Editor
Jerry C. Noack .........................Group Publisher
Elizabeth K. Fellman ........Marketing Manager/
Publication Director
Michele Picard ...................New Products Editor
Maureen Fletcher ...........Senior Acct. Manager
Beverly Geber ..................Spicial Projects Editor
Bob Filipczak ................................Staff Editor
**Desc.:** Business publication focusing on
"The Human Side of Business" - human
performance and productivity in the
workplace. Articles tackle the challenges
shaping today's business environment,
the role training plays in helping
companies achieve excellence, and the
support areas critical to successful
human resources development programs
- from AV products to productive and
effective meeting environments.
**Readers:** Subscribers range from
corporate officers, training directors,
trainers and personnel directors to sales
and marketing executives, audiovisual
directors, hospital-based education
managers and government officials. It is
written and edited for anyone who
manages the training and development
of others--applying adult learning
motivation and performance to making
people more productive.
**Deadline:** ads-25th of mo., 2 mo. prior to
pub. date

24683
## TRAINING & DEVELOPMENT
1640 King St.
Alexandria, VA 22314
Telephone: (703) 683-8100
FAX: (703) 683-8103
Mailing Address:
P.O. Box 1443
Alexandria, VA 22313-2043
Year Established: 1947
Pub. Frequency: m.
Page Size: standard
Subscrip. Rate: $7.50/copy; $75/yr.
Materials: 01,02,06,10,25,28,29,30,32,33
Print Process: web offset
Circulation: 35,311
Circulation Type: paid
**Owner(s):**
American Soc. for Training and
Development
P.O. Box 1443
Alexandria, VA 22313-2403
Telephone: (703) 683-8100
FAX: (703) 683-8103
Ownership %: 100

**Editorial:**
Patricia Galagan ......................Executive Editor
Cathy Petrini ............................Managing Editor
Michael DiSanto ......................Advertising
Leigh Caruso ............................Art Director
Theresa Minton/Eversole .......Associate Editor
Haidee Allerton .......................Associate Editor
Cynthia Mitchell .....................Editorial Assistant
Callie Norton ..................Production Coordinator
Donna Ferrier .......................Publication Editor
**Desc.:** Basic and advanced subjects in
manpower training and development in
business, industry, government and
service organizations. Techniques,
philosophy, surveys, typical programs,
new developments ranging from
apprenticeship to executive training.
Departments include: Feature Articles,
Training 101, In Practice, New Training
Tools, Research Capsules, Techtalk,
FaxForum, Classified Ads, Letters to the
Editor, Book Reviews.
**Readers:** Training professionals and
others interested in current training &
human resources practices in business,
industry, government, academic, and
consulting industries.
**Deadline:** story-5-6 mos. prior to pub.
date; news-4 mos. prior; ads-3 mos.
prior

## Group 194-Pets

24295
## AMERICAN PIGEON JOURNAL
P.O. Box 278
Warrenton, MO 63383
Telephone: (314) 456-2122
Year Established: 1912
Pub. Frequency: m.
Page Size: standard
Subscrip. Rate: $18/yr.; $22/yr. foreign
Circulation: 8,000
Circulation Type: paid
**Owner(s):**
American Pigeon Journal Co.
P.O. Box 278
Warrenton, MO 63383
Telephone: (314) 456-2122
Ownership %: 100
**Management:**
William L. Worley ..............................Publisher
**Editorial:**
William L. Worley ...................Executive Editor
**Desc.:** Pigeon and squab raising industry,
fanciers of racing pigeons and persons
who raise pigeons as a hobby.
**Readers:** All pigeon fanciers and squab
breeders, racing fanciers.

24294
## BIRD BREEDER
P.O. Box 420235
Palm Coast, FL 32142-0235
Telephone: (904) 445-4608
FAX: (904) 445-4608
Year Established: 1928
Pub. Frequency: m.
Page Size: pocket
Subscrip. Rate: $21.95/yr.
Freelance Pay: $25-$75 for one time use
Circulation: 56,000
Circulation Type: paid
**Owner(s):**
Fancy Publications
Telephone: (714) 855-8822
Ownership %: 100
**Management:**
Arthur Freud ...............................President
Arthur Freud ...............................Publisher
Anne Frizzell ...................Advertising Manager
Joan Mulcahy .................Production Manager
**Editorial:**
Arthur Freud ................................Editor
Peggy Shy ................................Art Director
Edith Wilson ..........................Associate Editor

Jean Tremel ..........................Circulation Editor
Ken Granville ..................Production Coordinator
**Desc.:** Articles discuss care and breeding
of cage and aviary birds.
**Readers:** Breeders, veterinarians, pet
shops, bird fanciers, and hobbyists.

24296
## CAT WORLD INTERNATIONAL
19219 N. 109th Ave.
Sun City, AZ 85015
Telephone: (602) 995-1822
FAX: (602) 246-4840
Mailing Address:
P.O. Box 35635
Phoenix, AZ 85069
Year Established: 1973
Pub. Frequency: bi-m
Page Size: standard
Subscrip. Rate: $17/yr.
Circulation: 8000
Circulation Type: paid
**Owner(s):**
Cat World International Magazine
P.O. Box 35635
Phoenix, AZ 85069
Telephone: (602) 995-1822
Ownership %: 100
**Management:**
Tom Corn ...............................Publisher
Naomi Corn ...............................Publisher
**Editorial:**
Tom Corn ................................Editor
**Desc.:** Articles are written by well-known
judges and experienced cat breeders
from different countries by invitation.
Subjects include in-depth breed studies,
veterinary colum, genetics, pictorial
worldwide show results, showguide,
how-to's, display advertising.
**Readers:** Breeders and exhibitors of
registered show cats, in U.S., Canada,
U.K., South Africa, Japan, European
Continent countries, Australia, N.Z.,
Middle East, Asia.

54040
## GROOM & BOARD
20 E. Jackson Blvd., Ste. 200
Chicago, IL 60604-2383
Telephone: (312) 663-4040
FAX: (312) 663-5676
Year Established: 1980
Pub. Frequency: 9/yr.
Page Size: standard
Subscrip. Rate: free to qualified; $25/yr.
others
Materials: 01,02,05,06,15,16,17,19,21
Freelance Pay: varies
Circulation: 18,261
Circulation Type: controlled
**Owner(s):**
H.H. Backer Associates, Inc.
20 E. Jackson Blvd., Ste. 200
Chicago, IL 60604
Telephone: (312) 663-4040
FAX: (312) 663-5676
Ownership %: 100
**Management:**
Ginger Norton ...............................Publisher
**Editorial:**
Karen Long MacLeod .......................Editor
Mary Dempsey .......................Associate Editor
Michele Claney ..................Production Director
**Desc.:** The only national trade magazine
specifically for pet-care professionals,
including groomers, kennel operators,
and service-oriented veterinarians.
Editorial features emphasize professional
development, including progressive
business management, animal handling
procedures, emerging business
opportunities, profiles of successful pet-
care operations, etc. Departments cover
industry events, products, etc.

**Readers:** Grooming operations, boarding
kennels, veterinary clinics, pet shops
and boarding kennels with grooming
services, pet supply distributors and their
salespersons.
**Deadline:** story-3-6 mos.; news-1 mo.;
photo-2 mos.

24297
## PET AGE
20 E. Jackson Ave., Ste. 200
Chicago, IL 60604
Telephone: (312) 663-4040
FAX: (312) 663-5676
Year Established: 1971
Pub. Frequency: m.
Page Size: standard
Subscrip. Rate: free to qualified
subscribers; $25/yr. others in US
Materials: 01,02,05,06,15,16,17,19,20,21
Freelance Pay: negotiable
Print Process: web
Circulation: 19,422
Circulation Type: controlled
**Owner(s):**
H.H. Backer Associates, Inc.
20 E. Jackson Blvd., Ste. 200
Chicago, IL 60604
Telephone: (312) 663-4040
FAX: (312) 663-5676
Ownership %: 100
**Management:**
Sue Busch ...............................Publisher
Ginger Norton ...............................Publisher
**Editorial:**
Karen Long MacLeod ...........................Editor
Mary Dempsey .......................Associate Editor
Michele Claney ..................Production Director
**Desc.:** Pet Age, the magazine for the
professional retailer, features first-rate
articles and departments designed to
help readers improve their businesses
and increase profits. Departments
include: News Beat, The Human Side,
Selling Successfully, Product Buylines,
Trade Dates, Capital Capsules, Letters.
**Readers:** Owners and managers of retail
pet outlets; groomers, kennel operators,
pet supply wholesalers, distributors,
manufacturers in the pet industry.
**Deadline:** story-3-6 mos.; news-1st of 2nd
mo. prior to pub. date; ads-15th of 2nd
mo. prior to pub. date

24298
## PET BUSINESS
5400 N.W. 84th Ave.
Miami, FL 33166-3333
Telephone: (305) 592-9890
FAX: (305) 592-9726
Mailing Address:
P.O. Box 2300
Miami, FL 33243
Year Established: 1973
Pub. Frequency: m.
Page Size: standard
Subscrip. Rate: $24/yr.
Freelance Pay: up to $200/pg.
Circulation: 14,500
Circulation Type: controlled
**Owner(s):**
Pet Business of Florida
7330 N.W. 66th St.
Miami, FL 33166
Telephone: (317) 846-5253
Ownership %: 100
**Bureau(s):**
Geri Mitchell
10741 Moor Park St., #8
N Hollywood, CA 91602
Telephone: (818) 763-3215
**Management:**
Dr. Bern Levine ...............................President
Mike Hammond ...............................Publisher
Mike Hammond ..................Advertising Manager

**Materials Accepted/Included:** 01-Business news 02-By-line articles 03-Fashion news 04-Food news 05-Freelance copy 06-Letters to editor 07-Real estate news 08-Sports news 09-Travel news 10-Book rev. 11-Movie rev. 12-Music rev. 13-TV rev. 14-Theater rev. 15-Coming events 16-Obituaries 17-Question & answer 18-Social announcements 19-Artwork 20-Cartoons 21-Photos 22-TV listings 23-Audio rec. 24-Video rec. 25-Books 26-Films/film clips 27-Personnel news 28-Press releases 29-New product news/photos 30-Trade lit. 31-Contracts awarded 32-Display adv. 33-Classified adv.

4-283

**Editorial:**
Elizabeth McKey .............................................Editor
**Desc.:** Editorial matter is designed for retailer, distributor, fish farmer, full line pet suppliers and manufacturers within the aquarium industry. Includes interviews, "success" stories, how-to information, sales aids and similar data, legislative appraisals and reports, show reports, news from industry and public areas, product news, new publications and books, lists of coming events, evaluations of fish and news of sources for them. Departments include: Marine (salt water), Fresh Water, Retail, Distributors, Manufacturers.
**Readers:** Controlled circulation to manufacturers, tion is carefully controlled with request cards.

24299
**PET DEALER, THE**
567 Morris Ave.
Elizabeth, NJ 07208
Telephone: (908) 353-7373
FAX: (908) 353-8221
Year Established: 1952
Pub. Frequency: m.
Page Size: standard
Subscrip. Rate: $25/yr.
Materials: 01,02,06,10,15,25,28,29,32,33
Circulation: 17,000
Circulation Type: controlled & paid
**Owner(s):**
PTN Publishing Co.
445 Broad Hollow Rd.
Nelville, NY 11747
Telephone: (516) 845-2700
Ownership %: 100
**Management:**
Howard Wasserman ............................Publisher
**Editorial:**
Gina Geslewitz ....................................Editor
Bob Sinnott .............Advertising Sales Manager
**Desc.:** The business monthly for pet shop owners/managers covering merchandising, news, operations, products.
**Readers:** Independent pet shop owners and managers.

24300
**PETFOOD INDUSTRY**
122 S. Wesley Ave.
Mt. Morris, IL 61054
Telephone: (815) 734-4171
FAX: (815) 734-4201
Year Established: 1959
Pub. Frequency: bi-m.
Page Size: standard
Subscrip. Rate: $8/copy; $48/yr.
Materials: 01,06,30,32,33
Print Process: web offset
Circulation: 6,000
Circulation Type: controlled
**Owner(s):**
Watt Publishing Co.
122 S. Wesley Ave.
Maywood, IL 60154
Telephone: (815) 734-4171
Ownership %: 100
**Bureau(s):**
(European Office) Watt Publishing Co.
Runnenburg 36, 3981 AZ.
Telephone: (034) 041-7414
Contact: David Gale, Sales Manager
**Management:**
James W. Watt ......................................President
Clay Schreiber ......................................Publisher
Marty Wittig .................................Sales Manager
**Editorial:**
Tim Phillips, DVM .................................Editor
Clayton Gill .............................Editorial Director
Laurance Laskos ..............Art Department

**Desc.:** For worldwide pet food manufacturing and marketing industry. Edited for management, marketing and technical personnel of pet food manufacturing companies around the world producing foods for dogs and cats. Editorial content includes in-plant features, marketing data, reports on advances in pet food technology and nutrition, state and federal regulations. Special features include an annual Yearbook/Buyers' Guide, Directory of Private Label Manufacturers, Industry News, Retailer's Corner and Product News.
**Readers:** Manufacturers, merchandisers, brokers, chain store buyers, and others with a direct interest in pet food manufacture and sales.

69048
**PET PRODUCT NEWS & PET SUPPLIES MARKETING**
P.O. Box 6050
Mission Viejo, CA 92690
Telephone: (714) 855-8822
FAX: (714) 855-3045
Year Established: 1993
Pub. Frequency: m.
Subscrip. Rate: free
**Owner(s):**
Fancy Publications, Inc.
P.O. Box 6050
Mission Viejo, CA 92690
Telephone: (714) 855-8822
Ownership %: 100
**Editorial:**
John Chadwell ......................................Editor
Andy Lamedman ..........................Advertising
**Desc.:** Covers industry news, including trade shows, legal issues, corporate takeovers and personnel changes, with emphasis on new products.
**Readers:** Pet store operators.

69049
**RETRIEVER FIELD TRIAL NEWS**
4213 S. Howell Ave.
Milwaukee, WI 53207
Telephone: (414) 481-2760
FAX: (414) 481-2743
Year Established: 1964
Pub. Frequency: 10/yr.
Page Size: tabloid
Subscrip. Rate: $35/yr.
Materials: 02,06,16,17,19,21,32
Print Process: offset
Circulation: 3,900
Circulation Type: paid
**Owner(s):**
National Retriever Club
4213 S. Howell Ave.
Milwaukee, WI 53207
Telephone: (414) 481-2760
Ownership %: 50

National Amateur Retriever Club
4213 S. Howell Ave.
Milwaukee, WI 53207
Telephone: (414) 481-2760
Ownership %: 50
**Editorial:**
Mary C. Knapp ....................................Editor
**Desc.:** Provides results of trials, tests and other matters of interest to the owners, breeders and trainers of retrievers.
**Deadline:** story-1st of mo. prior to pub. date; news-1st of mo. prior; photo-1st of mo. prior; ads-1st of mo. prior

## Group 196-Photography

24304
**AMERICAN CINEMATOGRAPHER**
1782 N. Orange Dr.
Los Angeles, CA 90028
Telephone: (310) 876-5080

Mailing Address:
P.O. Box 2230
Los Angeles, CA 90078
Year Established: 1919
Pub. Frequency: m.
Page Size: standard
Subscrip. Rate: $4 newsstand; $24/yr.
Freelance Pay: negotiable
Circulation: 32,000
Circulation Type: paid
**Owner(s):**
ASC Holding Corp.
1782 N. Orange Dr.
Los Angeles, CA 90028
Telephone: (310) 876-5080
Ownership %: 100
**Management:**
Patricia Armacost ..............Circulation Manager
**Editorial:**
David Heuring .......................................Editor
Angie Gollmann ..............................Advertising
Steve Pizzello ...........................Associate Editor
**Desc.:** Interested in factual articles dealing with professional motion picture photography in all fields-theatrical, TV film, industrial, research, etc. Departments include: Book Reviews, New Products, Camera, Video, Special Effects, Sound.
**Readers:** Motion picture directors of photography, cameramen, producers, directors, production personnel, television personnel, students.

61599
**DARKROOM & CREATIVE CAMERA TECHNIQUES**
7800 Merrimac Ave.
Niles, IL 60714
Telephone: (708) 965-0566
FAX: (708) 965-7639
Mailing Address:
P.O. Box 48312
Niles, IL 60714
Year Established: 1979
Pub. Frequency: bi-m.
Page Size: standard
Subscrip. Rate: $17.95/yr.
Freelance Pay: $100/pg.; $300/cover photo
Circulation: 45,000
Circulation Type: paid
**Owner(s):**
Seaton Preston
7800 Merrimac Ave., Box 48312
Niles, IL 60714
Telephone: (708) 965-0566
Ownership %: 100
**Management:**
David Jay ..............................................Manager
**Editorial:**
David Jay ..............................................Editor
**Desc.:** For those who take photography seriously, from the dedicated amateur to the experienced professional including anyone who wishes to fully understand the photographic process. The unique approach provides an abundance of technical information found in no other photographic or darkroom magazine.
**Readers:** Serious amateur and professional photographers.

24307
**INDUSTRIAL PHOTOGRAPHY**
445 Broadhollow Rd., Ste. 21
Melville, NY 11747-4722
Telephone: (516) 845-2700
FAX: (516) 845-7109
Year Established: 1962
Pub. Frequency: m.
Page Size: standard
Subscrip. Rate: $60/yr.
Freelance Pay: open
Circulation: 45,000
Circulation Type: controlled

**Owner(s):**
PTN Publishing Co.
445 Broadhollow Rd., Ste. 21
Melville, NY 11747
Telephone: (516) 845-2700
Ownership %: 100
**Management:**
Tom Martin ...........................................Publisher
Ira Golden .........................Advertising Manager
**Editorial:**
Steve Shaw ..........................................Editor
**Desc.:** Contains feature material on professional photographic techniques, ideas, new approaches and applications, motion pictures, audio-visuals, TV, photo-instrumentation and problem solving, management problems and department administration, photography portfolios, industry news, electronic imaging.
**Readers:** Industrial photographers, audio-visual and videography specialists, scientists & engineers.

24309
**INFORM**
1100 Wayne Ave., Ste. 1100
Silver Spring, MD 20910
Telephone: (301) 587-8202
Year Established: 1967
Pub. Frequency: m.
Page Size: standard
Subscrip. Rate: $85/yr. US; $105/yr. foreign
Materials: 01,02,05,06,10,21,28,32,33
Freelance Pay: varies, up to $1,000/article
Circulation: 40,000
Circulation Type: free & paid
**Owner(s):**
Association for Information & Image Management
1100 Wayne Ave., Ste. 1100
Silver Spring, MD 20910
Telephone: (301) 587-8202
Ownership %: 100
**Editorial:**
John Harney ..........................................Editor
Atwood Group, The .........................Advertising
Katharine J. Brophy ...................Assistant Editor
Gregory E. Kaebnick ........Book Review Editor
Yvonne M. Kidd ..................................Columnist
James E. Breuer .................................Director
Gregory E. Kaebnick ................................Photo
**Desc.:** Feature articles on document management applications, technology and products, letters to the editor, book reviews on request. Each article carries author's name, title and biography. Brief (50-word) abstract is required of each article. Articles should be approximately 1,000-2,000 words in length, with available illustrations. Illustrations should be color transparencies, black and white photographs, line drawings, graphs. Departments include: New Product Announcements, Events, Columns, Book Reviews.
**Readers:** Members of the Association for Information and Image Management including information professionals, users, consultants, libraries, systems designers as well as the 30,000 attendees of our annual trade show.
**Deadline:** story-3 mo. prior to pub. date; news-3 mo.; photo-3 mo.; ads-3 mo.

69059
**INTERNATIONAL PHOTOGRAPHER**
7715 Sunset Blvd., Ste. 300
Hollywood, CA 90046
Telephone: (213) 876-0160
FAX: (213) 876-6383
Year Established: 1929
Pub. Frequency: m.
Subscrip. Rate: $20/yr.
Circulation: 11,500

---

**Materials Accepted/Included:** 01-Business news 02-By-line articles 03-Fashion news 04-Food news 05-Freelance copy 06-Letters to editor 07-Real estate news 08-Sports news 09-Travel news 10-Book rev. 11-Movie rev. 12-Music rev. 13-TV rev. 14-Theater rev. 15-Coming events 16-Obituaries 17-Question & answer 18-Social announcements 19-Artwork 20-Cartoons 21-Photos 22-TV listings 23-Audio rec. 24-Video rec. 25-Books 26-Films/film clips 27-Personnel news 28-Press releases 29-New product news/photos 30-Trade lit. 31-Contracts awarded 32-Display adv. 33-Classified adv.

Circulation Type: paid
**Owner(s):**
Intl. Alliance of Moving Machine Picture
  Operators
c/o Local 659
7715 Sunset Blvd., Ste. 300
Hollywood, CA 90046
Telephone: (213) 876-0160
Ownership %: 100
**Editorial:**
George J. Toscas .....................Editor
**Desc.:** Covers cinematography and video
  techniques.

24310
## JOURNAL OF BIOLOGICAL PHOTOGRAPHY
115 Stoneridge Dr.
Chapel Hill, NC 27514
Telephone: (919) 967-8247
FAX: (919) 967-8246
Year Established: 1932
Pub. Frequency: q.
Page Size: 4 color photos/art
Subscrip. Rate: $65/yr. US; $75/yr. foreign
Circulation: 2,000
Circulation Type: paid
**Owner(s):**
Biological Photographic Association, Inc.
115 Stoneridge Dr.
Chapel Hill, NC 27514
Telephone: (919) 967-8247
Ownership %: 100
**Management:**
Raymond Lund .....................President
**Editorial:**
Joe Ogrodnick .....................Editor
Tom Hurtgen, FBPA .........Executive Director
Keith Bullis .................New Products Editor
**Desc.:** Short and long articles on the
  techniques and applications of digital
  imaging and photography in biological
  and natural sciences, medicine, botany,
  anatomy and other sciences concerned
  with living and/or dead matter.
  Departments include: New Products
  (photographic equipment, materials,
  processes for technical photographers),
  Book Reviews (books in optics,
  microscopy, photography and laboratory
  methods).
**Readers:** Scientific photographers, medical
  photographers, biophotographers,
  medical doctors, science teachers,
  laboratories, hospitals & research
  institutes, other scientific workers.

24320
## JOURNAL OF IMAGING SCIENCE & TECHNOLOGY
7003 Kilworth La.
Springfield, VA 22151
Telephone: (703) 642-9090
FAX: (703) 642-9094
Year Established: 1947
Pub. Frequency: bi-m.
Page Size: standard
Subscrip. Rate: $120/yr. US; $135/yr.
  foreign
Circulation: 10,000
**Owner(s):**
IS&T: Society for Imaging Science &
  Technology
7003 Kilworth La.
Springfield, VA 22151
Telephone: (703) 642-9090
Ownership %: 100
**Editorial:**
Vivian K. Walworth .....................Editor
Gary Thompson .................Managing Editor
Jonathan S. Arney .................Associate Editor
Allen E. Ames .................Associate Editor
**Desc.:** Provides the imaging community
  documentation of a broad range of
  research, development, and applications
  in imaging.

**Readers:** Imaging engineers and
  scientists.

69063
## MINI LAB FOCUS
3000 Picture Pl.
Jackson, MI 49201
Telephone: (517) 788-8100
FAX: (517) 788-8371
Pub. Frequency: m.
Subscrip. Rate: membership
Circulation: 3,800
Circulation Type: paid
**Owner(s):**
Photo Marketing Association International
3000 Picture Pl.
Jackson, MI 49201
Telephone: (517) 788-8100
Ownership %: 100
**Editorial:**
Gary Pageau .....................Editor

24312
## NEWS PHOTOGRAPHER
1446 Conneaut Ave.
Bowling Green, OH 43402-2145
Telephone: (419) 352-8175
FAX: (419) 354-5435
Mailing Address:
  P.O. Box 1107
  Bowling Green, OH 43402-1107
Year Established: 1946
Pub. Frequency: m.
Page Size: standard
Subscrip. Rate: $28/yr.
Materials: 01,02,05,06,10,16,21,25,27,28,
  29,32,33
Freelance Pay: $200/article
Print Process: web offset
Circulation: 10,500
Circulation Type: paid
**Owner(s):**
National Press Photographers Association
3200 Croasdaile Dr., Ste. 306
Durham, NC 27705
Telephone: (919) 383-7246
Ownership %: 100
**Management:**
James R. Gordon .............Advertising Manager
**Editorial:**
James R. Gordon .....................Editor
**Desc.:** News photography and all related
  fields such as newspaper, magazine,
  and television. Contains new items,
  technical features, trade news, new
  products, book reviews, and letters.
**Readers:** News photographers,
  management photographers, TV news
  photographers, general photographic
  field.
**Deadline:** story-5th of mo., 2 mos. prior;
  news-5th of mo., 2 mos. prior; photo-5th
  of mo., 2 mos. prior; ads-5th of mo., 2
  mos. prior

61572
## OUTDOOR PHOTOGRAPHER
12121 Ventura Blvd., Ste. 1220
Los Angeles, CA 90025-1175
Telephone: (310) 820-1500
FAX: (310) 826-5008
Year Established: 1985
Pub. Frequency: 10/yr.
Page Size: standard
Subscrip. Rate: $21.95/yr.
Freelance Pay: $.15-$.20/wd.; $75-
  $300/photo
Circulation: 175,000
Circulation Type: paid
**Owner(s):**
Werner Publishing Corp.
12121 Ventura Blvd., Ste. 1220
Los Angeles, CA 90025-1175
Telephone: (310) 820-1500
Ownership %: 100
**Management:**
Don Werner .....................President

Steve Werner .....................Publisher
**Editorial:**
Steve Werner .....................Editor
Mike McMann .................Associate Publisher
**Desc.:** The photo magazine for scenic
  travel, sport and wildlife enthusiasts.
**Readers:** Photographers who enjoy the
  outdoors.

64889
## PHOTO DISTRICT NEWS & PHOTO/DESIGN
1515 Broadway
New York, NY 10036
Telephone: (212) 536-5322
FAX: (212) 536-5351
Year Established: 1980
Pub. Frequency: m.
Page Size: oversize
Subscrip. Rate: $36/yr.
Freelance Pay: $500
Circulation: 20,000
Circulation Type: paid
**Owner(s):**
BPI
1515 Broadway
New York, NY 10036
Telephone: (212) 536-5322
Ownership %: 100
**Management:**
Scott Luksch .................Advertising Manager
Maureen O'Brien .............Circulation Manager
**Editorial:**
Elizabeth Forst .....................Editor in Chief
Nancy Madlin .....................Editor
**Desc.:** PDN covers all aspects of
  commercial photography produced for
  advertising, magazines, newspapers, and
  graphic design.
**Readers:** Professional photographers of all
  types, photo editors, and photo buyers
  of commercial photography.

24315
## PHOTO ELECTRONIC IMAGING
57 Forsyth St., N.W.
Ste. 1600
Atlanta, GA 30303
Telephone: (404) 522-8600
FAX: (404) 614-6405
Year Established: 1958
Pub. Frequency: m.
Page Size: standard
Subscrip. Rate: $18/yr.
Circulation: 45,000
Circulation Type: paid
**Owner(s):**
Professional Photographers of America
  Asst.
1090 Executive Way
Des Plaines, IL 60018
Telephone: (708) 299-8161
Ownership %: 100
**Management:**
Margo Fuller .................Circulation Manager
**Editorial:**
Kim Brady .....................Editor
**Desc.:** Methods and techniques for
  working photographers in industry,
  government, military, major educational
  institutions and science.
  Imaging methods include still
  photography as well as motion picture,
  video, micro graphics, computer graphics
  animation & instrumentation.
**Readers:** Photographers, technicians and
  scientists, av managers, free-lance and
  those who use photography as a tool.

24317
## PHOTOGRAMMETRIC ENGINEERING & REMOTE SENSING
5410 Grosvenor Ln., Ste. 210
Bethesda, MD 20814
Telephone: (301) 493-0290
FAX: (301) 493-0208

Year Established: 1934
Pub. Frequency: m.
Page Size: 8 3/8 X 10 7/8
Subscrip. Rate: $120/yr.
Materials: 06,16,27,28,29,31,32,33
Print Process: web offset
Circulation: 11,500
Circulation Type: paid
**Owner(s):**
Amer. Society for Photogrammetry &
  Remote Sensing
5410 Grosvenor Ln., Ste. 210
Bethesda, MD 20814
Telephone: (301) 493-0290
FAX: (301) 493-0208
Ownership %: 100
**Management:**
William D. French .................Executive Director
**Editorial:**
Dr. James B. Case .................Editor in Chief
Joann Treadwell .....................Editor
**Desc.:** PE & RS is produced for those
  engaged in the acquisition, mensuration,
  interpretation, and application of (aerial)
  photographs, remote sensing, and
  geographic information systems.
  Departments include: Technical Articles,
  Book Reviews, Discussion Articles,
  Forthcoming Articles, articles in other
  Photogrammetric Journals, News
  Columns, and a Calendar of Events.
**Readers:** Those engaged in the
  application of Photogrammetry, Remote
  Sensing, and Geographic Information
  Systems.

24318
## PHOTOGRAPHER'S MARKET
1507 Dana Ave.
Cincinnati, OH 45207
Telephone: (513) 531-2690
FAX: (513) 531-4744
Year Established: 1978
Pub. Frequency: a.: Sep.
Page Size: standard
Subscrip. Rate: $3/copy; $22.95/yr.
Materials: 21
Freelance Pay: $50/photo
Circulation: 36,000
Circulation Type: paid
**Owner(s):**
Writer's Digest Books
Telephone: (513) 531-2222
Ownership %: 100
**Management:**
Richard Rosenthal .....................President
Richard Rosenthal .....................Publisher
**Editorial:**
Michael Willins .....................Editor
**Desc.:** An annual directory listing names,
  addresses, and photography
  requirements of buyers of photography,
  film and video tapes.
  Departments include: Advertising
  Agencies, PR Firms, Audiovisual
  Companies, Business & Organizations,
  Competitions, Magazine and Book
  Publishers, Newspapers, Newsletters,
  Greeting Card Firms, Stock Photo
  Agencies, Galleries, etc.
**Readers:** Photographers, filmmakers,
  videographers, and various types of
  photobuyers
**Deadline:** photo-Feb. 28

24319
## PHOTOGRAPHIC PROCESSING
445 Broad Hollow Rd.
Melville, NY 11747
Telephone: (516) 845-2700
Year Established: 1965
Pub. Frequency: m.
Page Size: standard
Subscrip. Rate: $35/yr.; $50/2 yrs.
Materials: 01,02,10,27,28,29,32,33
Freelance Pay: negotiable

---

**Materials Accepted/Included:** 01-Business news 02-By-line articles  03-Fashion news  04-Food news  05-Freelance copy  06-Letters to editor  07-Real estate news  08-Sports news 09-Travel news
10-Book rev. 11-Movie rev. 12-Music rev. 13-TV rev. 14-Theater rev. 15-Coming events 16-Obituaries 17-Question & answer 18-Social announcements 19-Artwork 20-Cartoons 21-Photos 22-TV listings
23-Audio rec. 24-Video rec. 25-Books  26-Films/film clips 27-Personnel news  28-Press releases  29-New product news/photos 30-Trade lit. 31-Contracts awarded 32-Display adv. 33-Classified adv.

4-285

Circulation: 19,000
Circulation Type: paid
**Owner(s):**
PTN Publishing Co.
445 Broad Hollow Rd.
Melville, NY 11747
Telephone: (516) 845-2700
Ownership %: 100
**Management:**
Kathy Collester ........................Publisher
**Editorial:**
Bill Schiffner ...............................Editor
**Desc.:** Articles dealing with photo finishing
   minilabs, digital imaging and color labs
   equipment. Also contains quality control,
   merchandising, and promotion articles,
   environmental issues, and government
   articles regarding legislation affecting the
   industry. By-lines used. Length
   insignificant. Departments include:
   People, New Products, and For Your
   Information.
**Readers:** Photofinishers, electronic
   imaging, mini and color lab personnel.

24323

## PHOTOGRAPHIC TRADE NEWS
445 Broadhollow Rd., Ste. 21
Melville, NY 11747
Telephone: (516) 845-2700
FAX: (516) 845-7109
Year Established: 1938
Pub. Frequency: 24/yr.
Page Size: standard
Subscrip. Rate: $25/yr.
Circulation: 14,000
Circulation Type: paid
**Owner(s):**
PTN Publishing Co.
445 Broad Hollow Rd., Ste. 21
Melville, NY 11747-4722
Telephone: (516) 845-2700
Ownership %: 100
**Bureau(s):**
Norman Schindler & Assoc.
7050 Owensmouth Ave., 209
Canoga Park, CA 91303
Telephone: (818) 999-1414
Contact: Matt Askanas, Advertising

Pattis Group, The
4761 W. Touhy Ave.
Chicago, IL 60646
Telephone: (312) 679-1100
Contact: Robert Pattis, Advertising
**Management:**
Stanley Sills ...........................President
George Schaub .......................Publisher
**Editorial:**
Bill Schiffner ...............................Editor
**Desc.:** Directory to photographic trades,
   listing all products manufactured for and
   used by all types of photography.
**Readers:** Retailers, both management and
   sales.

69064

## PHOTO LAB MANAGEMENT
1312 Lincoln Blvd.
Santa Monica, CA 90406
Telephone: (310) 451-1344
FAX: (310) 395-9058
Year Established: 1979
Pub. Frequency: m.
Subscrip. Rate: $15/yr.
Materials: 01,02,05,06,17,27,28,29,32,33,34
Circulation: 18,150
Circulation Type: paid
**Owner(s):**
PLM Publishing
1312 Lincoln Blvd.
P.O. Box 1700
Santa Monica, CA 90406
Telephone: (310) 451-1344
Ownership %: 100
**Editorial:**
Carolyn Ryan ...............................Editor

**Readers:** Photo lab owners and managers;
   mini lab owners; digital imaging service
   bureaus.

61690

## PHOTOLETTER
Pine Lake Farm
Osceola, WI 54020
Telephone: (715) 248-3800
FAX: (715) 248-7394
Year Established: 1976
Pub. Frequency: m.
Page Size: standard
Subscrip. Rate: $9/mo.; $110/yr.
Freelance Pay: $20-$100
Circulation: 1,232
Circulation Type: paid
**Owner(s):**
Photosource International
Pine Lake Farm
Osceola, WI 54020
Telephone: (715) 248-3800
Ownership %: 100
**Editorial:**
Lynette Layer ...............................Editor
Lori Johnson .................................Editor
**Desc.:** Lists photo needs, deadline,
   photobuyer address and phone.
**Readers:** A photo marketing newsletter
   which pairs picture buyers with
   photographers.

24314

## PHOTO MARKETING
3000 Picture Pl.
Jackson, MI 49201
Telephone: (517) 788-8100
FAX: (517) 788-8371
Year Established: 1924
Pub. Frequency: bi-m.
Page Size: standard
Subscrip. Rate: $30/yr. US; $35/2 yrs.;
   $35/yr. Canada; $55/2 yrs.; $50/yr.
   foreign; $70/2 yrs.
Materials: 02,05,06,27,28,29,32,33
Freelance Pay: negotiable
Print Process: web offset
Circulation: 22,000
Circulation Type: controlled
**Owner(s):**
Photo Marketing Association International
3000 Picture Pl.
Jackson, MI 49201
Telephone: (517) 788-8100
Ownership %: 100
**Bureau(s):**
The Lewin Group
2177 Ventura Blvd., Ste. 254
Woodland Hills, CA 91364
Telephone: (818) 248-5288
Contact: Jay Lewin, Sales

The Lewin Group
1 Crosby Ct.
Peekskill, NY 10566
Telephone: (914) 736-6218
Contact: Mario Grande, Sales
**Management:**
Roy S. Pung ...........................Publisher
**Editorial:**
Chuck Davenport ................Senior Editor
Margaret Hooks ................Managing Editor
Terri Cameron ..............Advertising Director
Bruce Aldrich ............Associate Publisher
Gary T. Pageau ..............Contributing Editor
Cathy Haldame ..........Production Coordinator
**Desc.:** Interested only in material having a
   direct or indirect interest to the
   photographic, imaging, and video trade,
   particularly camera shop dealers and
   photo finishers. Departments include:
   News of the Photo Market, Product
   News, Promotion Ideas, Ideas for Better
   Photographic Business, Sound
   Marketing, People, Anonymous
   Consumer.

**Readers:** Camera shop dealers, photofinishers, mini-labs, photographic
   manufacturers, distributors and retailers,
   video retailers, photo & video repair
   firms, professional labs,
   wholesale/amateur finishers.
**Deadline:** story-2 mos. prior to pub. date;
   news-2 mos. prior; photo-2 mos. prior;
   ads-1 mo. prior

69061

## PHOTO MARKETING NEWSLINE
3000 Picture Pl.
Jackson, MI 49201
Telephone: (517) 788-8100
FAX: (517) 788-8371
Year Established: 1969
Pub. Frequency: m.
Subscrip. Rate: membership
Circulation: 13,400
Circulation Type: controlled & paid
**Owner(s):**
Photo Marketing Association International
3000 Picture Pl.
Jackson, MI 49201
Telephone: (517) 788-8100
Ownership %: 100
**Editorial:**
Margaret Hooks ...........................Editor

24322

## PROFESSIONAL PHOTOGRAPHER
57 Forsyth St. NW
Ste. 1600
Atlanta, GA 30303-2206
Telephone: (404) 522-8600
FAX: (404) 614-6405
Year Established: 1907
Pub. Frequency: m.
Page Size: standard
Subscrip. Rate: $25/yr.
Materials: 27,28,29,30,31,32,33,
Freelance Pay: to $100
Print Process: web offset
Circulation: 30,000
Circulation Type: paid
**Owner(s):**
PPA Publications & Events, Inc.
57 Forsyth St., N.W.
Ste. 1600
Atlanta, GA 30303
Telephone: (404) 522-8600
Ownership %: 100
**Management:**
Andrew N. Foster, Jr. ..................Publisher
Diane Durham ............Advertising Manager
Margo Fuller .............Circulation Manager
Stacey Isenhour .........Classified Adv. Manager
**Editorial:**
Elmo Sapwater ...............Executive Editor
Lorna Gentry ................Managing Editor
Kimberly Brady ............Editorial Director
Debbie Todd ...................Art Director
Cynthia Ryals ............New Products Editor
Donna McMahon ............................Sales
**Desc.:** Primarily interested in material
   which will help the professional
   photographer operate more efficiently
   and successfully. By-lined, contributed
   articles deal with photographic
   techniques, business operation,
   marketing methods. Departments
   include: News, New Products, Books,
   Letters.
**Readers:** Limited to professional
   photographers.

24324

## RANGEFINDER, THE
1312 Lincoln Blvd.
Santa Monica, CA 90401-1703
Telephone: (310) 451-8506
FAX: (310) 395-9058
Mailing Address:
   P.O. Box 1703
   Santa Monica, CA 90401-1703
Year Established: 1951

Pub. Frequency: m.
Page Size: standard
Subscrip. Rate: $18/yr.
Materials: 01,02,05,17,27,28,29,30,32,33
Freelance Pay: $60/editorial pg.
Print Process: web offset
Circulation: 50,000
Circulation Type: controlled
**Owner(s):**
Rangefinder Publishing Co., Inc.
1312 Lincoln Blvd.
Santa Monica, CA 90401
Telephone: (310) 451-8506
Ownership %: 100
**Management:**
Steve Sheanin .........................President
Steve Sheanin .........................Publisher
Gerald Goldstein ............Advertising Manager
Michelle Michon-Perkins ..................Circulation
                                          Manager
Sandi Salina Messana ...............Classified Adv.
                                          Manager
**Editorial:**
Arthur C. Stern ...............................Editor
Gennie Kiuchi ..................Art Department
Jacqueline C. Bruno ......................Artist
Sandi Salina Messana .............Assistant Editor
Carolyn Ryan .................Associate Editor
Jacqueline C. Bruno ..........Production Director
**Desc.:** Dedicated to the advancement of
   professional photography. Features
   encompass all phases of professional
   photo practices, handling assignments,
   equipment test reviews, and future
   trends.
**Readers:** Professional photographers.

69065

## SPECIALTY LAB UPDATE
3000 Picture Pl.
Jackson, MI 49201
Telephone: (517) 788-8100
FAX: (517) 788-8371
Pub. Frequency: m.
Subscrip. Rate: membership
Circulation: 2,300
Circulation Type: paid
**Owner(s):**
Photo Marketing Association International
3000 Picture Pl.
Jackson, MI 49201
Telephone: (517) 788-8100
Ownership %: 100
**Editorial:**
Linda Tien ...............................Editor
**Readers:** Commercial, private and in-
   house photographic lab personnel.

24326

## STUDIO PHOTOGRAPHY
445 Broad Hollow Rd., Ste. 21
Melville, NY 11747-4722
Telephone: (516) 845-2700
FAX: (516) 845-7109
Year Established: 1964
Pub. Frequency: m.
Page Size: standard
Subscrip. Rate: $40/yr.
Freelance Pay: $75/pg.
Circulation: 50,050
Circulation Type: paid
**Owner(s):**
PTN Publishing Co.
445 Broad Hollow Rd., Ste. 21
Melville, NY 11747-4722
Telephone: (516) 845-2700
Ownership %: 100
**Management:**
Marvin Walter ...........................Publisher
**Editorial:**
G. Faye Guercio ...............................Editor
Kathie Collester ..........Production Coordinator

**Materials Accepted/Included:** 01-Business news 02-By-line articles 03-Fashion news 04-Food news 05-Freelance copy 06-Letters to editor 07-Real estate news 08-Sports news 09-Travel news 10-Book rev. 11-Movie rev. 12-Music rev. 13-TV rev. 14-Theater rev. 15-Coming events 16-Obituaries 17-Question & answer 18-Social announcements 19-Artwork 20-Cartoons 21-Photos 22-TV listings 23-Audio rec. 24-Video rec. 25-Books 26-Films/film clips 27-Personnel news 28-Press releases 29-New product news/photos 30-Trade lit. 31-Contracts awarded 32-Display adv. 33-Classified adv.

**Desc.:** Studio Photography is the business magazine of professional photography providing the commercial, corporate and wedding photographer with the information he or she needs to operate a profitable, successful studio.

69382

**WEDDING PHOTOGRAPHER, THE**
1312 Lincoln Blvd.
P.O. Box 2003
Santa Monica, CA 90406
Telephone: (310) 451-0090
FAX: (310) 395-9058
Year Established: 1978
Pub. Frequency: m.
Subscrip. Rate: free to members; $75/yr.
Materials: 01,02,05,06,10,15,16,17,20,21, 25,28,29
Freelance Pay: $50-$150/article
Circulation: 3,000
**Owner(s):**
Rangefinder Publishing Co., Inc.
1312 Lincoln Blvd.
P.O. Box 2003
Santa Monica, CA 90406
Telephone: (310) 451-0090
**Editorial:**
Sandi Salina Messana ...............................Editor
**Desc.:** Provides information to association members of WPI on running a wedding photography studio, how- to techniques, business management, continuing education. Also publishes print competition winners, new products, seminar listings.
**Readers:** Wedding & portrait studio photographers; also, some bridal consultants.
**Deadline:** story-2 mos. prior to pub. date; news-2 mos. prior; photo-2 mos. prior

## Group 198-Plastics

65625

**ADVANCES IN POLYMER TECHNOLOGY**
605 Third Ave.
New York, NY 10158
Telephone: (212) 850-6289
Pub. Frequency: q.
Subscrip. Rate: $306/yr. US; $361/yr. foreign
Circulation: 300
Circulation Type: paid
**Owner(s):**
John Wiley & Sons, Inc.
Ownership %: 100
**Editorial:**
Marino Xanthos ........................................Editor
**Desc.:** Features articles, technical papers and the latest news on plastics technology, processing, and physics. Focuses on materials developments, new processing techniques, and materials and processes involving new fields such as plastics in solar energy.

65624

**BIOPOLYMERS**
605 Third Ave.
New York, NY 10158
Telephone: (212) 850-6289
Pub. Frequency: m.
Page Size: standard
Subscrip. Rate: $1,530/yr. US; $1,695/yr. foreign
Circulation: 900
Circulation Type: paid
**Owner(s):**
John Wiley & Sons, Inc.
**Editorial:**
Murray Goodman ......................................Editor

**Desc.:** Covers organic and physical chemistry, experimental and theoretical research, static and dynamic aspects on structure. Includes an examination of the broad aspects of biospectroscopy.

69704

**CARD MANUFACTURING**
34-C Washington Rd.
Princeton Junction, NJ 08550
Telephone: (609) 799-4900
FAX: (609) 799-7032
Year Established: 1990
Pub. Frequency: bi-m.
Page Size: standard
Subscrip. Rate: $55/yr.
Materials: 02,27,28,29,30,32
Circulation: 1,000
Circulation Type: paid
**Owner(s):**
Creative Marketing Alliance, Inc.
34-C Washington Rd.
Princeton Junction, NJ 08550
Telephone: (609) 799-4900
Ownership %: 100
**Editorial:**
Mary Kay Metcalf ....................Managing Editor
Natalie Heringes .........Publications Coordinator
**Desc.:** Official publication of the International Card Manufacturers Association. Supports, promotes and encourages the success and growth of companies and organizations that participate in the plastic card industry.
**Readers:** Manufacturers, industry suppliers and service providers.

68822

**GMP HORIZONS**
608 E. Baltimore Pike
Media, PA 19063
Telephone: (215) 565-5051
Year Established: 1982
Pub. Frequency: m.
Page Size: standard
Subscrip. Rate: free
Circulation: 85,000
Circulation Type: controlled
**Owner(s):**
Glass, Pottery, Plastics & Allied Workers
Ownership %: 100
**Editorial:**
Richard Kline .............................................Editor

24329

**JOURNAL OF CELLULAR PLASTICS**
851 New Holland Ave., Box 3535
Lancaster, PA 17601
Telephone: (717) 291-5609
FAX: (717) 295-4538
Year Established: 1964
Pub. Frequency: bi-m.
Page Size: pocket
Subscrip. Rate: $175/yr.; $340/2 yrs.; $505/3 yrs.
Circulation: 650
Circulation Type: paid
**Owner(s):**
Technomic Publishing Co., Inc.
851 New Holland Ave., Box 3535
Lancaster, PA 17601
Telephone: (717) 291-5609
Ownership %: 100
**Bureau(s):**
Technomic Publishing AG
Missionsstrasse 44
CH-4055 Basel Switzerland
Contact: Frank Versaci, Director
**Editorial:**
Dr. Sidney H. Metzger, Jr. ......................Editor

**Desc.:** This is the only periodical devoted exclusively to the rapidly growing foamed plastics field. The latest technical information is provided on all types of foams. Applications and marketing of foams are reported in every field in which foams are or can be used. Also publishes digests of patents and articles from other periodicals, industry news, reports from the SPI cellular plastics division.

58739

**JOURNAL OF PLASTIC FILM & SHEETING**
851 New Holland Ave., Box 3535
Lancaster, PA 17601
Telephone: (717) 291-5609
FAX: (717) 295-4538
Year Established: 1985
Pub. Frequency: q.
Subscrip. Rate: $265/yr.; $520/2 yrs.; $775/3 yrs.
Circulation: 350
Circulation Type: paid
**Owner(s):**
Melvyn A. Kohudic
851 New Holland Ave., Box 3535
Lancaster, PA 17601
Telephone: (717) 291-5609
**Bureau(s):**
Technomic Publishing AG
Missionsstrasse 44
CH-4055 Basel Switzerland
Contact: Frank Versaci, Director
**Editorial:**
James Harrington ......................................Editor
**Desc.:** New developments in polymer science and plastics technology as they relate to films and sheeting.

58741

**JOURNAL OF REINFORCED PLASTICS & COMPOSITES**
851 New Holland Ave., Box 3535
Lancaster, PA 17601
Telephone: (717) 291-5609
FAX: (717) 295-4538
Year Established: 1981
Pub. Frequency: m.
Subscrip. Rate: $670/yr.; $1330/2 yrs.; $1990/3 yrs.
Circulation: 400
Circulation Type: paid
**Owner(s):**
Melvyn A. Kohudic
851 New Holland Ave., Box 3535
Lancaster, PA 17601
Telephone: (717) 291-5609
**Bureau(s):**
Technomic Publishing AG
Missionsstrasse 44
CH-4055 Basel Switzerland
**Editorial:**
George S. Springer ..................................Editor
**Desc.:** Original research papers on the technology of reinforced plastics and composites.

65152

**JOURNAL OF THERMOPLASTIC COMPOSITE MATERIALS**
851 New Holland Ave., Box 3535
Lancaster, PA 17601
Telephone: (717) 291-5609
FAX: (717) 295-4538
Year Established: 1988
Pub. Frequency: q.
Subscrip. Rate: $57/issue; $225/yr.; $440/2 yrs.; $655/3 yrs.
Circulation: 300
Circulation Type: paid
**Owner(s):**
Melvyn A. Kohudic
851 New Holland Ave., Box 3535
Lancaster, PA 17601
Telephone: (717) 291-5609

**Bureau(s):**
Technomic Publishing AG
Missionsstrasse 44
CH-4055 Basel Switzerland
**Editorial:**
Selcuk I. Guceri ........................................Editor
Jean Rhoads ....................Marketing Assistant
**Desc.:** Original research papers on the technology of thermoplastic composite materials, covering materials, properties and performance, design, characterization and analysis, and computer software assistance.

24330

**MODERN PLASTICS**
1221 Ave. of the Americas
New York, NY 10020
Telephone: (212) 512-6241
FAX: (212) 512-6111
Year Established: 1924
Pub. Frequency: m.
Page Size: standard
Subscrip. Rate: $41.75/yr.
Circulation: 62,000
Circulation Type: controlled & paid
**Owner(s):**
McGraw-Hill, Inc.
1221 Ave. of the Americas
New York, NY 10020
Telephone: (212) 512-2000
**Management:**
Thomas Britton ......................................Publisher
Maurice Persiani ...............Circulation Manager
Viveca Yrisarry ...................Promotion Manager
**Editorial:**
Robert Leaversuch ..................Senior Editor
Robert Burns .............................................Editor
Joseph Innace ...........................................Editor
Karen F. Lindsay ....................Managing Editor
Patrick A. Toensmeier .............Managing Editor
Bob Barravecchia ........................Art Director
Jean Corvington ....................Assistant Editor
Keith R. Kreisher ....................Associate Editor
Jack K. Rogers .....................Associate Editor
Maria Varvaro ................Editorial Assistant
Gordon Graff ...................Encyclopedia Editor
William Graham ...............Production Director
Cynthia Miele ....................Production Manager
Dr. Gordon M. Kline .................Technical Editor
**Desc.:** Specifically edited for processors and users of plastics to provide them with the latest news on end products, materials, market developments, methods, machine and equipment, and processing techniques. Articles cover new applications, engineering and technical developments, general industry news.
**Readers:** Key purchasing decision makers in all aspects of the plastics industry.

69072

**PLASTICS COMPOUNDING**
1753 Hemlock Farms
Hawley, PA 18428
Telephone: (717) 775-6017
FAX: (717) 775-6746
Year Established: 1978
Pub. Frequency: bi-m.
Page Size: standard
Subscrip. Rate: $48/yr.
Materials: 01,02,05,06,10,15,20,21,23,24, 25,28,29,30
Circulation: 16,500
Circulation Type: controlled
**Owner(s):**
Advanstar Communications, Inc.
7500 Old Oak Blvd.
Cleveland, OH 44130
Telephone: (216) 826-2839
Ownership %: 100
**Editorial:**
Mary C. McMurrer ....................................Editor

Materials Accepted/Included: 01-Business news 02-By-line articles 03-Fashion news 04-Food news 05-Freelance copy 06-Letters to editor 07-Real estate news 08-Sports news 09-Travel news 10-Book rev. 11-Movie rev. 12-Music rev. 13-TV rev. 14-Theater rev. 15-Coming events 16-Obituaries 17-Question & answer 18-Social announcements 19-Artwork 20-Cartoons 21-Photos 22-TV listings 23-Audio rec. 24-Video rec. 25-Books 26-Films/film clips 27-Personnel news 28-Press releases 29-New product news/photos 30-Trade lit. 31-Contracts awarded 32-Display adv. 33-Classified adv.

4-287

**Desc.:** Discusses resin production, compounding and formulating techniques, compounding equipment, addlines and applications.

## PLASTICS DESIGN FORUM
69073

859 Willamette St.
Eugene, OR 97401
Telephone: (503) 343-1200
FAX: (503) 344-3514
Year Established: 1976
Pub. Frequency: 10/yr.
Page Size: standard
Subscrip. Rate: $40/yr.
Materials: 06,15,28,29,30
Circulation: 47,800
Circulation Type: controlled
**Owner(s):**
Advanstar Communications, Inc.
859 Willamette St.
Eugene, OR 97401
Telephone: (503) 343-1200
FAX: (503) 344-3514
Ownership %: 100
**Editorial:**
Joanne Wolfe .............................................Editor
**Desc.:** Information on plastics as a material of design: performance properties, design techniques, applications.

## PLASTICS DISTRIBUTOR & FABRICATOR MAGAZINE
69074

2701 N. Pulaski Rd.
Chicago, IL 60639-2119
Telephone: (312) 235-3800
FAX: (312) 235-7204
Year Established: 1980
Pub. Frequency: bi-m.
Page Size: 8 1/2 X 14
Subscrip. Rate: $50/yr.
Materials: 01,02,05,06,10,15,16,19,21,27,
    28,29,30,31,32,33
Circulation: 18,100
Circulation Type: controlled
**Owner(s):**
PMD Publishing, Inc.
2701 N. Pulaski Rd.
Chicago, IL 60639-2119
Telephone: (312) 235-3800
Ownership %: 100
**Editorial:**
Harry Greenwald .........................................Editor

## PLASTICS ENGINEERING
24333

14 Fairfield Dr.
Brookfield, CT 06804-0403
Telephone: (203) 775-0471
FAX: (203) 775-8490
Mailing Address:
    P.O. Box 403
    Brookfield, CT 06804-0403
Year Established: 1944
Pub. Frequency: m.
Page Size: standard
Subscrip. Rate: $50/yr.
Materials: 01,02,05,06,24,25,28,29,30,32,33
Freelance Pay: accept gratis articles only
Print Process: web
Circulation: 39,000
Circulation Type: paid
**Owner(s):**
Society of Plastics Engineers, Inc.
14 Fairfield Dr.
Brookfield, CT 06804
Telephone: (203) 775-0471
FAX: (203) 775-8490
Ownership %: 100
**Management:**
Eugene DeMichele ...........................Publisher
Richard F. Mulligan ..........Advertising Manager
**Editorial:**
Roger M. Ferris .........................................Editor
Donald J. Domoff ....................Managing Editor

Michele Correia ................................Production
**Desc.:** Articles on chemistry, manufacture, molding, extrusion, design, testing, and other phases of the plastics industry including machinery operations. News of society activities on both international and local levels. Columns on processing and design. Departments include: Articles, Society News, Industry News, Book Reviews, Legal, New Products, Manufacturing Literature, Plastics Issues, New Materials Comment.
**Readers:** Members of The Society of Plastics Engineers and nonmember subscribers.
**Deadline:** story-3 mos. prior to pub. date; news-2 mos. prior; ads-1 mo. prior

## PLASTICS IN BUILDING/CONSTRUCTION
58738

851 New Holland Ave., Box 3535
Lancaster, PA 17601
Telephone: (717) 291-5609
FAX: (717) 295-4538
Year Established: 1976
Pub. Frequency: m.
Page Size: standard
Subscrip. Rate: $185/yr.; $360/2 yrs.;
    $535/3 yrs.
Circulation: 180
Circulation Type: paid
**Owner(s):**
Melvyn A. Kohudic
851 New Holland Ave., Box 3535
Lancaster, PA 17601
Telephone: (717) 291-5609
Ownership %: 100
**Bureau(s):**
Technomic Publishing AG
Missionsstrasse 44
CH-4055 Basel Switzerland
**Editorial:**
Joseph Eckenrode ....................................Editor
**Desc.:** Monthly report on the plastics and plastic products used in building, construction, and civil engineering today.

## PLASTICS, MACHINERY & EQUIPMENT
67672

859 Willamette St.
Eugene, OR 97401
Telephone: (503) 343-1200
FAX: (503) 343-3514
Year Established: 1972
Pub. Frequency: 12/yr.
Page Size: tabloid
Subscrip. Rate: $48/yr. US; $59/yr.
    Canada, Mexico; $75/yr. foreign
Materials: 01,02,05,06,15,19,21,24,25,27,
    28,29,30,31,32,33
Freelance Pay: varies
Circulation: 28,739
Circulation Type: controlled & paid
**Owner(s):**
Advanstar Communications, Inc.
7500 Old Oak Blvd.
Cleveland, OH 44130
Telephone: (216) 243-8100
Ownership %: 100
**Bureau(s):**
Sales Office: Advanstar Communications
195 Main St.
Metuchen, NJ 08840
Telephone: (908) 549-3000
FAX: (908) 549-0113
Contact: Bob Joudanin, Publisher
**Management:**
Robert Joudanin ...................................Publisher
**Editorial:**
Jane Ganter ..............................................Editor
Art Rosenberg ......................Group Publisher

**Desc.:** Publishes feature articles and columns that offer practical information on plastics processing (injection molding, extrusion, thermoforming, and other methods) with an emphasis on how to get the most from the tooling, machinery, and equipment they use to create plastic products. Publishes developments in machinery and equipment and provides other information on the state of the industry as it affects the readers' professional lives. Regular columns and departments: Injection Notes, Extrusion Notes, Quality Matters, Product Showcase, Product Literature, Library, Datebook.
**Readers:** Production and manufacturing managers
**Deadline:** story-10-12 wks. prior to pub. date; news-4 wks. prior to pub. date; photo-4 wks.; ads-4 wks.

## PLASTICS NEWS
69076

1725 Merriman Rd.
Akron, OH 44313-2322
Telephone: (216) 836-9180
FAX: (216) 836-1005
Year Established: 1989
Pub. Frequency: w.
Subscrip. Rate: $1.75/issue; $50/yr.
Materials: 01,06,15,16,21,27,28,29,30,31,
    32,33
Circulation: 60,000
Circulation Type: paid
**Owner(s):**
Crain Communications, Inc.
1725 Merriman Rd.
Akron, OH 44313-3185
Telephone: (216) 836-9180
FAX: (216) 836-1005
Ownership %: 100
**Editorial:**
Robert Grace .............................................Editor
Ron Shinn ..............................Managing Editor
**Desc.:** Covers financial moves, plant closings, acquisitions, process developments, new machinery and raw materials pricing.

## PLASTICS TECHNOLOGY
24336

355 Park Ave., S.
New York, NY 10010-1789
Telephone: (212) 592-6570
FAX: (212) 592-6579
Year Established: 1955
Pub. Frequency: 13/yr.
Page Size: standard
Subscrip. Rate: $65/yr.
Circulation: 47000
Circulation Type: controlled & paid
**Owner(s):**
Bill Communications, Inc.
355 Park Ave., S.
New York, NY 10010-1789
Telephone: (212) 592-6200
Ownership %: 100
**Management:**
Gary Rekstad .......................................Publisher
**Editorial:**
Matthew Naitove .......................................Editor
Sherri Fuchs .............................Managing Editor
Therese Hoarty ...................Production Director

**Desc.:** Provides news and trend interpretation on materials, equipment, and methods to help maximize productivity for engineers and managers involved in plastics processing and fabricating. Departments include: technology news, industry news, materials pricing update, additives pricing, regulatory update, manufacturing activity index, molders' hourly rate survey, literature/books/software, letters to the editor, calendar of coming events, and editorial.
**Readers:** Engineers and managers in manufacturing firms that convert raw materials into plastic products.

## PLASTICS WORLD
24337

445 Broad Hollow Rd.
Ste. 21
Melville, NY 11747
Telephone: (516) 845-2700
FAX: (516) 845-7109
Year Established: 1942
Pub. Frequency: m.
Page Size: Standard
Subscrip. Rate: $74.95/yr.
Circulation: 51,400
Circulation Type: controlled & paid
**Owner(s):**
PTN Publishing Co.
445 Broad Hollow Rd.
Melville, NY 11747
Telephone: (516) 845-2700
FAX: (516) 845-7109
Ownership %: 100
**Management:**
Robert Moran ......................................Publisher
**Editorial:**
James Callari .............................................Editor
Michael McEnaney .................Managing Editor
**Desc.:** Plastics World is the magazine for managers and engineers who are buyers of plastics processing equipment and machinery, resins, additives, and services used in the manufacture or design of plastic products. It provides editorial for the entire buying team: General management, manufacturing and design. Editorial is aimed at helping readers perform their jobs more effectively. This is done by examining leading edge technologies, new products, business strategies that boost productivity and profitability, as well as how-to articles on process trouble-shooting, design-integrated manufacturing and other topics that generate high readership and inquiry response. Plastics World editorial is aimed both at what-to-expect and day-to-day decision making for the new and experienced plastics professional.
**Readers:** Technical managers and engineers who specify and buy materials and equipment used in the design and manufacture of plastic products.

## POLYMER ENGINEERING & SCIENCE
22622

14 Fairfield Dr.
Brookfield, CT 06804
Telephone: (203) 775-0471
FAX: (203) 775-8490
Mailing Address:
    P.O. Box 0403
    Brookfield, CT 06804-0403
Year Established: 1961
Pub. Frequency: s-m.
Page Size: standard
Subscrip. Rate: $135/yr. for members;
    $190/yr. non-members; $450/yr. corp.,
    libraries, and inst.
Circulation: 1,800

**Materials Accepted/Included:** 01-Business news 02-By-line articles 03-Fashion news 04-Food news 05-Freelance copy 06-Letters to editor 07-Real estate news 08-Sports news 09-Travel news 10-Book rev. 11-Movie rev. 12-Music rev. 13-TV rev. 14-Theater rev. 15-Coming events 16-Obituaries 17-Question & answer 18-Social announcements 19-Artwork 20-Cartoons 21-Photos 22-TV listings 23-Audio rec. 24-Video rec. 25-Books 26-Films/film clips 27-Personnel news 28-Press releases 29-New product news/photos 30-Trade lit. 31-Contracts awarded 32-Display adv. 33-Classified adv.

4-288

Circulation Type: paid
**Owner(s):**
Society of Plastics Engineers
P.O. Box 0403
Brookfield, CT 06804-0403
Telephone: (203) 775-0471
Ownership %: 100
**Management:**
Michael R. Cappelletti .......Circulation Manager
**Editorial:**
Roger S. Porter ........................Editor
Daniel J. Domoff ..................Managing Editor
Dr. Richard E. Ball ..................Associate Editor
Dr. Robert A. Weiss ...............Associate Editor
Dava Johnson ...................Production Director
**Desc.:** Reporting the results of
  fundamental research in plastics and
  polymers, such as structure-property
  relationships, polymer synthesis and
  physics, design predictions, processing
  techniques.
**Readers:** Polymer scientists and
  engineers, institutions and libraries.

69569
## RESOURCE RECYCLING'S BOTTLE/CAN RECYCLING UPDATE
P.O. Box 10540
Portland, OR 97210-0540
Telephone: (503) 227-1319
FAX: (503) 227-6135
Year Established: 1990
Pub. Frequency: m.
Page Size: standard
Subscrip. Rate: $85/yr.
Materials: 01,15,28,29,30,31,32
Circulation: 1,000
Circulation Type: paid
**Owner(s):**
Resource Recycling, Inc.
P.O. Box 10540
Portland, OR 97210-0540
Telephone: (503) 227-1319
FAX: (503) 227-6135
Ownership %: 100
**Editorial:**
Jerry Powell ...............................Editor
**Desc.:** Covers all aspects of the recycling
  of plastic, glass, aluminium, tin and bi-
  metal containers, including markets,
  legislation, technology and economic
  issues.

## Group 199-Pollutants & Pollution Control

65291
## ASBESTOS ABATEMENT REPORT
951 Pershing Dr.
Silver Spring, MD 20910-4464
Telephone: (301) 587-6300
FAX: (301) 587-1081
Year Established: 1987
Pub. Frequency: 26/yr.
Page Size: standard
Subscrip. Rate: $484.54/yr.
**Owner(s):**
Business Publishers, Inc.
951 Pershing Dr.
Silver Spring, MD 20910-4464
Telephone: (301) 587-6300
Ownership %: 100
**Management:**
Martha Mattare ..................Operations Manager
**Editorial:**
Liz Lohr ........................................Editor
**Desc.:** Covers areas of control techniques,
  worksite health and safety, new federal
  standards, medical research efforts,
  state and local regulations, waste
  disposal, insurance, documentation,
  financing, contract management,
  analysis technology, and certification
  rules.

23202
## BIO CYCLE-JOURNAL OF WASTE RECYCLING
419 State Ave.
Emmaus, PA 18049
Telephone: (215) 967-4135
Year Established: 1960
Pub. Frequency: m.
Page Size: standard
Subscrip. Rate: $63/yr. US; $85/yr.
  Canada; $90/yr. foreign
Circulation: 14,500
Circulation Type: paid
**Owner(s):**
J.G. Press, Inc.
419 State Ave., #2
Emmaus, PA 18049
Telephone: (215) 967-4135
Ownership %: 100
**Management:**
Jerome Goldstein ...............................President
Jerome Goldstein ...............................Publisher
**Editorial:**
Nora Clark ...............................Executive Editor
Jerome Goldstein ........................................Editor
Ann Miller ...............................New Products Editor
**Desc.:** Journal of waste recycling. Reports
  on entire field of land application,
  composting, and recycling of organic
  solid wastes; industrial & municipal.
**Readers:** Professionals in waste
  management, government and industry,
  researchers, planners, public officials,
  investors and entrepreneurs.

25241
## CLEARWATERS
90 Presidential Plz., Ste. 122
Syracuse, NY 13202
Telephone: (315) 422-7811
Year Established: 1929
Pub. Frequency: q.
Page Size: standard
Subscrip. Rate: $6/yr. for non-members
Freelance Pay: negotiable
Circulation: 3,000
Circulation Type: controlled
**Owner(s):**
New York Environmental Association
90 Presidential Plz.
Syracuse, NY 13202
Telephone: (315) 422-7811
Ownership %: 100
**Editorial:**
Leah Fleckenstein ...............................Editor
R. D. Hennigan ...............Secretary & Treasurer
**Desc.:** Feature-length articles that deal
  with all aspects of water quality
  management as well as related
  environmental issues, with the focus on
  New York State. Approx. 1,000-3,000
  words, photos and other illustrations
  requested. Departments include: People
  and Places, Newsnotes, On the Market,
  Briefly.
**Readers:** Consulting engineers, waste
  water treatment and others
  professionally involved in water pollution,
  universities, libraries, environmental
  groups, government agencies.

25242
## CWPCA BULLETIN
3050 Citrus Cir., Ste. 225
Walnut Creek, CA 94598
Telephone: (510) 938-0182
Year Established: 1951
Pub. Frequency: q.
Page Size: standard
Subscrip. Rate: $20/yr.
Circulation: 7,000
Circulation Type: controlled

**Owner(s):**
California Water Pollution Control Assn.
3050 Citrus Cir., Ste. 225
Walnut Creek, CA 94598-2628
Telephone: (510) 938-0182
Ownership %: 100
**Management:**
Linda Brewer ...............................Publisher
Linda Brewer ...................Advertising Manager
**Editorial:**
Linda Brewer ...............................Editor
**Desc.:** Serves technical, professional
  advancement, and semi-social interests
  of Association Members. Editorial
  content concerns: design, construction,
  operation and managements of pollution
  control facilities (sewers, sewage
  treatment plants, labs, disposal pipes or
  reclamation systems), both public and
  industrial; manufacturing for the trade;
  and related disciplines.
**Readers:** Association members.

68714
## ECON: THE ENVIRONMENTAL MAGAZINE
455 Broad Hollow Rd., Ste. 21
Melville, NY 11747-4722
Telephone: (516) 845-2700
FAX: (516) 845-7109
Year Established: 1986
Pub. Frequency: m.
Subscrip. Rate: $45/yr.
Circulation: 25,050
Circulation Type: controlled & paid
**Owner(s):**
PTN Publishing Co.
445 Broad Hollow Rd., Ste. 21
Melville, NY 11747-4722
Telephone: (516) 845-2700
Ownership %: 100
**Editorial:**
Judith Hogan ...............................Editor
**Desc.:** Covers the removal of asbestos
  and other hazardous wastes.

65409
## ENVIRONMENTAL CLAIMS JOURNAL
22 W. 21st St.
New York, NY 10010-6990
Telephone: (212) 645-7880
FAX: (212) 645-1160
Year Established: 1988
Pub. Frequency: q.
Page Size: standard
Subscrip. Rate: $189/yr.
Materials: 02,06,32
Circulation: 1,000
Circulation Type: paid
**Owner(s):**
Executive Enterprises Publications Co., Inc.
22 W. 21st St.
New York, NY 10010
Telephone: (212) 645-7880
Ownership %: 100
**Editorial:**
Lynne M. Miller ...........................Editor in Chief
Nancy Hale .......................................Editor
Deborah Wenger ...........................Managing Editor
**Desc.:** Provides useful, authoritative and
  innovative information on the prevention
  and litigation of environmental claims,
  including risk assessment and
  management, trial tactics and strategies,
  insurance, complex cases, settlements
  and negotiations, claims investigation
  and management and technical
  management.
**Readers:** Insurers, attorneys, business
  owners, consultants and advisors,
  technical specialists and managers.

23243
## ENVIRONMENTAL MANAGEMENT
4350 DiPaolo Center
Ste. C
Glenview, IL 60825
Telephone: (708) 699-6362
FAX: (708) 699-1703
Year Established: 1969
Pub. Frequency: q.
Page Size: standard
Subscrip. Rate: free to members
Circulation: 6,500
Circulation Type: controlled
**Owner(s):**
Environmental Management Association
Ownership %: 100
**Management:**
Dianna Rampy ...............................Publisher
Dianna Rampy ...................Advertising Manager
Dianna Rampy ...................Circulation Manager
**Editorial:**
Dianna Rampy ...............................Editor
Eugene Ueler ...........................Associate Editor
**Desc.:** Editorial emphasis on new
  technical, instructive, beneficial and
  informative material to assist
  its professional audience in both specific
  and general areas of facilities
  management, maintenance and
  industrial sanitation include: Facilities
  Planning & Design, Internal Systems,
  Service & Management, Waste
  Management & Recycling
  Product/Service Profiles, Career
  Opportunities, Issues & Events-
  Association News EMA Mail.
**Readers:** Facilities managers and
  industrial sanitarians.

22474
## ENVIRONMENTAL SCIENCE & TECHNOLOGY
1155 16th St., N.W.
Washington, DC 20036
Telephone: (800) 333-9511
FAX: (202) 872-6060
Year Established: 1967
Pub. Frequency: m.
Page Size: 4 color photos/art
Subscrip. Rate: $89/yr. non-members;
  $43/yr. members
Circulation: 12,400
Circulation Type: paid
**Owner(s):**
American Chemical Society
1155 16th St., N.W.
Washington, DC 20036
Telephone: (202) 872-4581
Ownership %: 100
**Management:**
American Chemical Society ...............Publisher
Bruce Poorman ...................Advertising Manager
**Editorial:**
Dr. William H. Glaze ...............................Editor
Stanton S. Miller ...................Managing Editor
Alan Newman ...........................Associate Editor
Julian Josephson ...............Book Review Editor
**Desc.:** Contains research and technology
  in water, air, and waste chemistry,
  provides news and reports on the
  political and industrial aspects of the
  management of the environment-of-
  interest to governmental, university and
  industrial officials.
**Readers:** Scientists, engineers,
  consultants, industries.

67662
## ENVIRONMENTAL WATCH
875 N. Michigan Ave., 2400
Chicago, IL 60611-1980
Telephone: (312) 335-4100
FAX: (312) 335-4400
Year Established: 1988
Pub. Frequency: q.

**Materials Accepted/Included:** 01-Business news 02-By-line articles 03-Fashion news 04-Food news 05-Freelance copy 06-Letters to editor 07-Real estate news 08-Sports news 09-Travel news 10-Book rev. 11-Movie rev. 12-Music rev. 13-TV rev. 14-Theater rev. 15-Coming events 16-Obituaries 17-Question & answer 18-Social announcements 19-Artwork 20-Cartoons 21-Photos 22-TV listings 23-Audio rec. 24-Video rec. 25-Books 26-Films/film clips 27-Personnel news 28-Press releases 29-New product news/photos 30-Trade lit. 31-Contracts awarded 32-Display adv. 33-Classified adv.

4-289

Page Size: standard
Subscrip. Rate: $40/yr. nonmembers
Materials: 01,02,07,10,15,25,28,30
Circulation: 14,000
Circulation Type: controlled & paid
**Owner(s):**
Appraisal Institute
875 N. Michigan Ave., 2400
Chicago, IL 60611
Telephone: (312) 335-4100
Ownership %: 100
**Editorial:**
Joy M. White .................................Editor
**Readers:** Real estate and finance
    professionals

68715
## ENVIRONMENT INTERNATIONAL
660 White Plains Rd.
Tarrytown, NY 10591-5153
Telephone: (914) 524-9200
FAX: (914) 333-2444
Year Established: 1978
Pub. Frequency: bi-m.
Circulation: 1978
Circulation Type: controlled & paid
**Owner(s):**
Pergamon Press, Inc.
660 White Plains Rd.
Tarrytown, NY 10591-5153
Telephone: (914) 524-9200
Ownership %: 100
**Editorial:**
Alan Moghissi .............................Editor
Barbara Moghissi .........................Editor
**Desc.:** Contains original literature on
    causes of pollution, methods for
    protection, and data.

23205
## ENVIRONMENT MAGAZINE
1319 18th St., NW
Washington, DC 20036-1802
Telephone: (202) 296-6267
FAX: (202) 296-5149
Year Established: 1958
Pub. Frequency: 10/yr.
Page Size: standard
Subscrip. Rate: $33/yr. individual; $66/yr.
    institutions; add $14/outside US
Freelance Pay: varies
Circulation: 10,216
Circulation Type: paid
**Owner(s):**
Heldref Publications
1319 18th St., N.W.
Washington, DC 20036-1802
Telephone: (202) 296-6267
Ownership %: 100
**Management:**
Walter Beach ...........................Publisher
Raymond M. Rallo ...........Advertising Manager
Cathy Welker ...............Circulation Manager
Kerri P. Kilbane ...............Promotion Manager
**Editorial:**
Barbara Richman ...............Managing Editor
**Desc.:** Presents today's most critical
    environmental issues put in perspective
    by the world's foremost scientists and
    policymakers. Regular features include
    news briefs of current issues, critical
    reviews of major government and
    institutional reports, listings of notable
    books, and commentaries that provide
    differing points of view on the articles.
**Readers:** Environmental professionals,
    college & university professors and
    students as well as public & academic
    libraries.

66100
## FEDERAL FACILITIES ENVIRONMENTAL JOURNAL
22 W. 21st St.
New York, NY 10010
Telephone: (212) 645-7880
FAX: (212) 645-1160

Year Established: 1990
Pub. Frequency: q.
Page Size: standard
Subscrip. Rate: $175/yr.
Materials: 02,06,32
Circulation: 1,000
Circulation Type: paid
**Owner(s):**
Executive Enterprises Publications Co., Inc.
22 W. 21st St.
New York, NY 10010
Telephone: (212) 645-7880
Ownership %: 100
**Editorial:**
John T. Willig ............................Editor
Deborah Wenger ...............Managing Editor
**Desc.:** Seeks to provide the most
    authoritative information available on
    environmental issues at federal facilities,
    combining the analytical & the
    practical in one journal.
**Readers:** Environmental managers,
    consultants, and attorneys who work at
    or deal with federal facilities.

49910
## JOURNAL OF ENVIRONMENTAL QUALITY
677 S. Segoe Rd.
Madison, WI 53711
Telephone: (608) 273-8080
FAX: (608) 273-2021
Year Established: 1972
Pub. Frequency: q.
Page Size: standard
Subscrip. Rate: $45/yr.
Materials: 32
Circulation: 3,850
Circulation Type: paid
**Owner(s):**
American Society of Agronomy
677 S. Segoe Rd.
Madison, WI 53711
Telephone: (608) 273-8080
Ownership %: 100
**Management:**
Robert F Barnes .......Executive Vice President
K.R. Schlesinger ...............Advertising Manager
Roger Watkins ...................Circulation Manager
David M. Kral ...................Operations Manager
**Editorial:**
R. J. Wagenet ..........................Editor
Susan Ernst ...................Managing Editor
K.R. Schlesinger ...............Marketing Manager
**Desc.:** Provides an outlet for technical
    reports and brief reviews that are
    concerned with the protection and
    improvement of environmental quality in
    natural and agricultural ecosystems.
**Readers:** People interested in agriculture
    and the environment.

68721
## JOURNAL OF ENVIRONMENTAL SYSTEMS
26 Austin Ave.
Amityville, NY 11701
Telephone: (516) 691-1270
FAX: (516) 691-1170
Mailing Address:
    P.O. Box 337
    Amityville, NY 11701
Year Established: 1971
Pub. Frequency: q.
Subscrip. Rate: $112/yr. institutions
**Owner(s):**
Baywood Publishing Co., Inc.
26 Austin Ave.
P.O. Box 337
Amityville, NY 11701
Telephone: (516) 691-1270
FAX: (516) 691-1770
Ownership %: 100
**Management:**
Stuart Cohen ...........................President
Stuart Cohen ...........................Publisher

**Editorial:**
Sheldon Reaven .........................Editor
**Desc.:** Deals with the analysis of and
    solutions to problems which relate to the
    system-complexes which make up our
    total societal-environment.

23217
## JOURNAL OF THE AIR & WASTE MANAGEMENT ASSOCIATION
P.O. Box 2861
Pittsburgh, PA 15230
Telephone: (412) 232-3444
FAX: (412) 232-3450
Year Established: 1951
Pub. Frequency: m.
Page Size: standard
Subscrip. Rate: $90/yr. non-professional;
    $200/yr. others
Circulation: 15,000
Circulation Type: paid
**Owner(s):**
Air & Waste Management Association
P.O. Box 2861
Pittsburgh, PA 15230
Telephone: (412) 232-3444
Ownership %: 100
**Management:**
Steve Stasko .........................Publisher
Bill Tony .................Advertising Manager
James D. Morton .............Production Manager
**Editorial:**
Bill Tony .................................Editor
Gretchen Watson .......................Advertising
Maureen Brown .......................Assistant Editor
Debbie Reichert .................Editorial Assistant
**Desc.:** The journal of the Air & Wash
    Management Association carries peer-
    reviewed technical papers on a variety
    of environmental topics. According to
    the Library of Congress, it is one of the
    most frequently cited scientific journals
    in the world. The journal also includes
    feature articles, news, departments
    and columns that professionals in the
    environmental field look to each month.

69260
## MARINE POLLUTION BULLETIN
660 White Plains Rd.
Tarrytown, NY 10591-5153
Telephone: (914) 524-9200
FAX: (914) 333-2444
Year Established: 1970
Pub. Frequency: 24/yr.
Page Size: standard
Circulation: 2,000
Circulation Type: paid
**Owner(s):**
Pergamon Press, Inc.
660 White Plains Rd.
Tarrytown, NY 10591-5153
Telephone: (914) 524-9200
Ownership %: 100
**Editorial:**
C. Sheppard ............................Editor
**Desc.:** Concerned with the rational use of
    maritime and marine resources in
    estuaries, seas and oceans.
**Readers:** Marine envrionmentalists,
    scientists, engineers, administrators,
    politicians, and lawyers.

24671
## OCCUPATIONAL HAZARDS
1100 Superior Ave.
Cleveland, OH 44114-2543
*see Service,Trade,Professional
    Magazines, Safety*

61815
## OPERATIONS FORUM, THE
601 Wythe St.
Alexandria, VA 22314
Telephone: (703) 684-2400
Year Established: 1985
Pub. Frequency: m.

Page Size: standard
Subscrip. Rate: $50/yr.
Materials: 06,07,28,29,30,32,33
Circulation: 17,000
Circulation Type: free & paid
**Owner(s):**
Water Environment Federation
601 Wythe St.
Alexandria, VA 22314
Telephone: (703) 684-2400
FAX: (703) 684-2492
Ownership %: 100
**Editorial:**
Lisa Preston ............................Editor
**Desc.:** Provides technical, applicable
    information on the day to day workings
    of wastewater treatment systems.
**Readers:** Superintendents, managers and
    operators of wastewater treatment
    facilities.
**Deadline:** story-4 mos.; news-4 mos.;
    photo-4 mos.; ads-1st of mo.

23239
## POLLUTION ABSTRACTS
7200 Wisconsin Ave., 6th Fl.
Bethesda, MD 20814
Telephone: (301) 961-6750
FAX: (301) 961-6720
Year Established: 1970
Pub. Frequency: m.
Page Size: standard
Subscrip. Rate: $885/yr. US; $995/yr.
    foreign
**Owner(s):**
Cambridge Scientific Abstracts
7200 Wisconsin Ave., 6th Fl.
Bethesda, MD 20814
Telephone: (301) 961-6750
Ownership %: 100
**Bureau(s):**
Cambridge Scientific Abstracts
7200 Wisconsin Ave.
Bethesda, MD 20814
Telephone: (301) 961-6750
Contact: Roberta Gorinson, Editor
**Management:**
Robert Snyder ...........................President
Philip Hixon ...........................Publisher
**Editorial:**
Evelyn Beck ............................Editor
**Desc.:** Pollution abstracts cites, abstracts,
    and indexes international technical
    literature on pollution. It is available as a
    bimonthly journal, as an on-line data
    base, or through magnetic tape lease.
    Scope includes environmental pollution
    including marine and freshwater
    pollution, sewage and waste water
    treatment, waste management, land
    pollution, toxicology and health, and
    environmental action.
**Readers:** Serious researchers in the
    pollution/environmental fields.

23240
## POLLUTION ENGINEERING
1350 E. Touhy Ave.
Des Plaines, IL 60018
Telephone: (708) 635-8800
FAX: (708) 390-2636
Year Established: 1969
Pub. Frequency: s-m.; 1 issue Jul., Aug.,
    Sep.
Page Size: standard
Subscrip. Rate: controlled
Circulation: 60,000
Circulation Type: controlled
**Owner(s):**
Cahners Publishing Co.
1350 E. Touhy Ave.
Des Plaines, IL 60018
Telephone: (708) 498-9840
Ownership %: 100
**Management:**
Richard Young ..........................Publisher

Materials Accepted/Included: 01-Business news 02-By-line articles 03-Fashion news 04-Food news 05-Freelance copy 06-Letters to editor 07-Real estate news 08-Sports news 09-Travel news 10-Book rev. 11-Movie rev. 12-Music rev. 13-TV rev. 14-Theater rev. 15-Coming events 16-Obituaries 17-Question & answer 18-Social announcements 19-Artwork 20-Cartoons 21-Photos 22-TV listings 23-Audio rec. 24-Video rec. 25-Books 26-Films/film clips 27-Personnel news 28-Press releases 29-New product news/photos 30-Trade lit. 31-Contracts awarded 32-Display adv. 33-Classified adv.

4-290

**Editorial:**
Diane Pirocanac ..............................Chief Editor

**Desc.:** Features articles covering subjects of air, water, noise pollution, solid waste disposal, hazardous and toxic materials. They must carry by-line of engineer or technical manager responsible for environmental or energy control. Feature articles on practical solutions to specific energy and environmental engineering problems. Departments include: Case Histories, Industrial and Governmental News, Editorial Comment, Handy reference file pages, Book Reviews, New Products, New Trade Literature, News of Manufacturers.

**Readers:** Environmental managers and engineers employed in all manufacturing industries, government and consulting firms.

### POLLUTION EQUIPMENT NEWS
23241
8650 Babcock Blvd.
Pittsburgh, PA 15237-5821
Telephone: (412) 364-5366
Year Established: 1968
Pub. Frequency: 8/yr.
Page Size: tabloid
Subscrip. Rate: free to qualified personnel
Materials: 01,25,29,30,32,33
Circulation: 92,200
Circulation Type: controlled
**Owner(s):**
Rimbach Publishing, Inc.
8650 Babcock Blvd.
Pittsburgh, PA 15237
Telephone: (412) 364-5366
Ownership %: 100
**Management:**
Norberta Rimbach ..........................Publisher
**Editorial:**
David C. Lavender ..............................Editor
**Desc.:** Serves the pollution control market. It is edited for those responsible for the specification, installation and maintenance of pollution equipment and products. Contains staff-written new product items and new literature reviews; news from the field; industrial activity, etc. Departments include: News, New Products, New Literature, Calendar, Book Reviews.
**Readers:** Individuals responsible for the purchase, specification and installation of pollution abatement products.
**Deadline:** story-2 mos.; news-2 mos.; photo-2 mos.; ads-1st of mo.

### RECYCLING TIMES
67232
1730 Rhode Island Ave., N.W.
Ste. 1000
Washington, DC 20036
Telephone: (202) 861-0708
FAX: (202) 659-0925
Year Established: 1989
Pub. Frequency: bi-w.
Page Size: standard
Subscrip. Rate: $95/yr.
Freelance Pay: $100-$500
Circulation: 5,000
Circulation Type: paid
**Owner(s):**
National Solid Wastes Management
1730 Rhode Island Ave., N.W.
Washington, DC 20036
Telephone: (202) 861-0708
Ownership %: 100
**Management:**
John T. Aquino ..............................Publisher
**Editorial:**
Kathleen White ........................Senior Editor
**Readers:** Recycling coordinators, municipal and federal employees, industry and environmentalists.

### RECYCLING TODAY
23465
4012 Bridge Ave.
Cleveland, OH 44113
Telephone: (216) 961-4130
FAX: (216) 961-0364
Year Established: 1963
Pub. Frequency: m.
Page Size: standard
Subscrip. Rate: $30/yr.
Freelance Pay: $200-$300
Circulation: 15,000
Circulation Type: paid
**Owner(s):**
GIE
4012 Bridge Ave.
Cleveland, OH 44113
Telephone: (216) 961-4130
**Management:**
Richard J.W. Foster ........................President
Richard J.W. Foster ........................Publisher
Rosalie Slusher ...............Circulation Manager
Jim Keefe ..............................Sales Manager
**Editorial:**
John Bruening ..................................Editor
Jami Childs ......................Production Director
**Desc.:** Concerns itself with the collection, processing, and recycling of post-consumer materials by public and private sector organizations. Special sections include Commodities News, Government News, International News, Letters, Calendar, Guest Columns, Products, People, etc.
**Readers:** Municipal, state & federal elected officials and government employees involved in solid-waste management and recycling.

### REUSE/RECYCLE
22501
851 New Holland Ave.
Lancaster, PA 17601
Telephone: (717) 291-5609
FAX: (717) 295-4538
Mailing Address:
Box 3535
Lancaster, PA 17604
Year Established: 1970
Pub. Frequency: m.
Page Size: standard
Subscrip. Rate: $195/yr.
Circulation: 200
Circulation Type: paid
**Owner(s):**
Technomic Publishing Co., Inc.
851 New Holland Ave.
Lancaster, PA 17604
Telephone: (717) 291-5609
Ownership %: 100
**Management:**
Michael J. Margotta ........................Publisher
**Editorial:**
Jack Milgram ..................................Editor
Teresa Wiegand ......................Assistant Editor
**Desc.:** Provides information on the new and emerging processes for economical, often profitable, recycling of wastes. Recycling processes for all types of industrial, municipal, and agricultural wastes are explored-solid, liquid, and gas. Development in both the U.S. and abroad are covered. Special Washington report on pending legislation and its effects included monthly.

### WASTE AGE
25238
1730 Rhode Island Ave., N.W., Ste. 1000
Washington, DC 20036
Telephone: (202) 861-0708
FAX: (202) 659-0925
Year Established: 1971
Pub. Frequency: m.
Page Size: standard
Subscrip. Rate: $48/yr.
Freelance Pay: $300/story

Circulation: 37,000
Circulation Type: controlled
**Owner(s):**
National Solid Wastes Management Association
1730 Rhode Island Ave., N.W.
Washington, DC 20036
Telephone: (202) 655-4613
Ownership %: 100
**Management:**
John T. Aquino ..............................Publisher
Jerry Schwartz ...............Advertising Manager
**Editorial:**
John T. Aquino ..................................Editor
Cheryl McAdams ...................Managing Editor
Randy Woods ......................Associate Editor
Kathleen Sheehan ........................News Editor
**Desc.:** Waste Age reports problems and solutions for private and public sector professionals concerned with the control, management, transport and disposal of solid, hazardous, infectious, and liquid wastes. Features report on collecting, handling, hauling, transferring, incinerating, burying, recycling, and otherwise managing society's wastes. News items report current political, economic, social, and technological developments and successful applications of existing technologies. Industrial, institutional, commercial, private, municipal, county, and state problems and solutions are reported. Special features include resource recovery, sanitary landfills, street sweeping and components and parts developments for the specified refuse truck. Buyers guides appear annually on topics ranging from truck bodies and chassis to tank trucks, containers, landfill equipment, carts, sweepers and incinerators.
**Readers:** Solid waste and refuse management professionals.

### WORLD WASTES SPECIFICATION CATALOG
24918
6151 Powers Ferry Rd.
Atlanta, GA 30339-2941
Telephone: (404) 955-2500
Year Established: 1960
Pub. Frequency: a.
Page Size: standard
Subscrip. Rate: $38.95/yr.
Circulation: 36,500
Circulation Type: controlled
**Owner(s):**
Argus Business, Inc.
6151 Powers Ferry Rd.
Atlanta, GA 30339-2941
Telephone: (404) 955-2500
Ownership %: 100
**Management:**
Jerry France ..............................President
William Wolpin ..............................Publisher
George Brennan ...............Advertising Manager
**Editorial:**
Barbara Katinsky ..............................Editor
Ann Benson ......................Associate Editor
**Desc.:** Specifications for various solid waste management and truck equipment.

**Readers:** Private refuse removal contractor, municipal wastes contractors, and plant, chain store and other wastes managers, wastes generators.

## Group 200-Power & Power Plants

### DIESEL PROGRESS ENGINES AND DRIVES
24379
13555 Bishop's Ct.
Brookfield, WI 53005
Telephone: (414) 784-9177
FAX: (414) 784-8133
Year Established: 1935
Pub. Frequency: m.
Page Size: standard
Subscrip. Rate: $6/copy; $60/yr.
Freelance Pay: negotiable
Circulation: 30,000
Circulation Type: controlled
**Owner(s):**
Diesel Engines, Inc.
13555 Bishop's Ct.
Brookfield, WI 53005
Telephone: (414) 771-4562
Ownership %: 100
**Management:**
R.A. Wilson ..............................President
R.A. Wilson ..............................Publisher
P. M. May ...................Advertising Manager
Faye Edwards ...............Circulation Manager
Chris Martin ......................Production Manager
**Editorial:**
Michael J. Osenga ....................Editor in Chief
Mike Brezonick ...................Managing Editor
Dave Bode ..............................Feature Editor
Mark McNeely ..............................News Editor
**Desc.:** Published for those concerned with the design, distribution and service of equipment powered by diesel, gasoline, or natural gas engines including all types of mobile on and off highway equipment and stationary equipment. Markets covered include: construction, mining, forestry agricultural and turf maintenance equipment; trucks and buses; pleasure boats; and generator pump and compressor sets. Editorial focus is on new products and technology with particular attention paid to engine, powertrain and hydraulic developments.
**Readers:** Manufacturers of stationary, on-road, off-road, marine, etc.

### ELECTRIC UTILITY WEEK
22864
1221 Ave. of the Americas
New York, NY 10020
Telephone: (212) 512-2905
FAX: (212) 512-2723
Year Established: 1970
Pub. Frequency: 51/yr.
Page Size: newsletter
Subscrip. Rate: $1,275/yr. in US/Canada; $1,295/yr. foreign
Materials: 01,28,31
Freelance Pay: $17-$20/col. in.
**Owner(s):**
McGraw-Hill, Inc.
1221 Ave. of the Americas
New York, NY 10020
Telephone: (212) 512-2904
Ownership %: 100
**Bureau(s):**
Washington, D.C.
1120 Vermont Ave., N.W., 1200
Washington, DC 20005
Telephone: (202) 463-1655
Contact: Brian Jordan, Bureau Chief
**Editorial:**
Brian Jordan ..............................Bureau Chief
Daniel Tanz ..............................Chief Editor
Paul Carlsen ..............................Senior Editor
Kathy Carolin Larsen ...................Senior Editor

**Materials Accepted/Included:** 01-Business news 02-By-line articles 03-Fashion news 04-Food news 05-Freelance copy 06-Letters to editor 07-Real estate news 08-Sports news 09-Travel news 10-Book rev. 11-Movie rev. 12-Music rev. 13-TV rev. 14-Theater rev. 15-Coming events 16-Obituaries 17-Question & answer 18-Social announcements 19-Artwork 20-Cartoons 21-Photos 22-TV listings 23-Audio rec. 24-Video rec. 25-Books 26-Films/film clips 27-Personnel news 28-Press releases 29-New product news/photos 30-Trade lit. 31-Contracts awarded 32-Display adv. 33-Classified adv.

4-291

Richard Schwartz ......................Associate Editor
Robert Ingraham ......................Associate Editor
Ron Dionne ..............................Associate Editor
Kim Pyko ..................................Associate Editor
Chris Holley ..............................Associate Editor
Kim Martin ................................Associate Editor
Peter Maloney ..........................Associate Editor
**Desc.:** News of electric utility industry
    management, finance, legislation,
    regulation, and court cases.
**Readers:** Utility Executives and
    consultants, executives of supplier
    companies, and government officials.

**ENERGY EFFICIENCY JOURNAL**     69701
34-C Washington Rd.
Princeton Junction, NJ 08550
Telephone: (609) 799-4900
FAX: (609) 799-7032
Year Established: 1993
Pub. Frequency: bi-m.
Page Size: standard
Materials: 02,06,27,28,29,30,32
Circulation: 500
Circulation Type: paid
**Owner(s):**
Creative Marketing Alliance, Inc.
34-C Washington Rd.
Princeton Junction, NJ 08550
Telephone: (609) 799-4900
Ownership %: 100
**Editorial:**
Terry Singer ................................Executive Editor
Mary Kay Metcalf ......................Managing Editor
Diane Knott ................................Art Director
Natalie Heringes ..........Publications Coordinator
**Desc.:** Official publication of the National
    Association of Energy Service
    Companies. Acts as a forum for the
    evolving energy efficiency industry to
    discuss such issues as finance,
    technology- applications, marketing,
    business management and legal and
    legislative issues.
**Readers:** Energy service companies and
    allied electric and gas utilities and other
    organizations.
**Deadline:** story-1 mo. prior to pub. date

**ENERGY MAGAZINE**     64943
25 Van Zant St.
Norwalk, CT 06855
Telephone: (203) 853-4266
FAX: (203) 853-0348
Pub. Frequency: 5/yr.
Page Size: standard
Subscrip. Rate: $185/yr.
Circulation: 500
Circulation Type: paid
**Owner(s):**
Louis Naturman
25 Van Zant St.
Norwalk, CT 06855
Telephone: (203) 853-4266
Ownership %: 100
**Management:**
Robert Butler ..............................Manager
**Editorial:**
Eve Greenberg ..........................Editor
**Desc.:** Energy Magazine serves the hybrid
    functions of an important journal of
    records and an interdisciplinary
    magazine that reports and analyzes
    major energy developments as they
    occur. Energy Magazine subscribers
    need the invaluable and unique
    complication of energy thinking and
    analysis found in each issue. Energy
    Magazine editors examine the energy
    scene to offer a carefully gathered blend
    of energy-related news and commentary
    that represents the events and concerns
    of the time.

**Readers:** Energy analysts, engineers,
    librarians in petrochemical, coal, gas,
    utility and other energy and related
    industries.

**ENERGY TODAY**     55874
1079 National Press Bldg.
Washington, DC 20045
Telephone: (202) 393-0031
FAX: (202) 393-1732
Year Established: 1973
Pub. Frequency: m.
Page Size: standard
Subscrip. Rate: $795/yr.
Materials: 10,15,23,24,28
**Owner(s):**
Trends Publishing, Inc.
1079 National Press Bldg.
Washington, DC 20045
Telephone: (202) 393-0031
Ownership %: 100
**Editorial:**
A. Kranish ..................................Editor
**Readers:** Business and professional
    people in the energy field.

**GAS TURBINE WORLD**     24381
P.O. Box 447
Southport, CT 06490
Telephone: (203) 259-1812
Year Established: 1971
Pub. Frequency: bi-m.
Page Size: standard
Subscrip. Rate: $60/yr.
Circulation: 8,561
Circulation Type: paid
**Owner(s):**
Pequot Publishing, Inc.
P.O. Box 447
Southport, CT 06490
Telephone: (203) 259-1812
Ownership %: 100
**Management:**
Victor de Biasi ..........................Publisher
Jim Janson ................................Advertising Manager
**Editorial:**
Robert Farmer ..........................Executive Editor
**Readers:** Technical management among
    industry users.

**INSIDE ENERGY WITH FEDERAL
LANDS**     66712
1200 G St. N.W., Ste. 1100
Washington, DC 20005-3802
Telephone: (202) 383-2240
FAX: (202) 383-2125
Year Established: 1977
Pub. Frequency: w.
Page Size: standard
Subscrip. Rate: $1,065/yr. US & Canada;
    $1,090/yr. elsewhere
Materials: 01,28,29,31
Freelance Pay: negotiable
**Owner(s):**
McGraw-Hill, Inc.
1200 G St., N.W., Ste. 1100
Washington, DC 20005-3802
Ownership %: 100
**Editorial:**
William Loveless ........................Editor
Jeff Barber ................................Managing Editor
David Kramer ............................Associate Editor
Sheryl Morris ............................Associate Editor
Lira Behrens ..............................Associate Editor
**Desc.:** Covers Department of Energy and
    energy/minerals programs at
    Department of Interior.
**Readers:** Energy and government
    executives.

**INTERNATIONAL OPERATING
ENGINEER, THE**     24382
1125 17th St., N.W.
Washington, DC 20036
Telephone: (202) 429-9100
FAX: (202) 429-0316
Year Established: 1896
Pub. Frequency: bi-m.
Page Size: standard
Subscrip. Rate: $5/yr.
Circulation: 300,000
**Owner(s):**
International Union of Operating Engineers
1125 17th St., N.W.
Washington, DC 20036
Telephone: (202) 347-8560
Ownership %: 100
**Management:**
Frank Hamley ............................President
**Editorial:**
N. Budd Coutts ..........................Editor
**Desc.:** In addition to union news, carries
    articles on energy, environment and
    government.
**Readers:** Members of union.

**INTERNATIONAL SOLAR ENERGY
INTELLIGENCE REPORT**     65021
951 Pershing Dr.
Silver Spring, MD 20910
Telephone: (301) 587-6300
FAX: (301) 587-1081
Pub. Frequency: bi-w.
Page Size: standard
Subscrip. Rate: $371.54/yr.
**Owner(s):**
Business Publishers, Inc.
951 Pershing Dr.
Silver Spring, MD 20910
Telephone: (301) 587-6300
Ownership %: 100
**Management:**
Leonard A. Eiser ......................Publisher
**Editorial:**
Leonard A. Eiser ......................Editor
Patricia A. Nugman ..............Marketing Manager

**LAND USE LAW REPORT**     65022
951 Pershing Dr.
Silver Spring, MD 20910-4464
Telephone: (301) 587-6300
FAX: (301) 585-9075
Year Established: 1973
Pub. Frequency: bi-w.
Subscrip. Rate: $273/yr.
**Owner(s):**
Business Publishers, Inc.
951 Pershing Dr.
Silver Spring, MD 20910-4464
Telephone: (301) 587-6300
**Editorial:**
James Lawlor ............................Editor
**Desc.:** Presents rulings on land use,
    especially as related to US and state
    environmental regulations; lender liability
    emphasized.

**NATIONAL ENGINEER MAGAZINE**     24383
1 Springfield St.
Chicopee, MA 01013-2624
Telephone: (413) 592-6273
FAX: (413) 592-1998
Year Established: 1897
Pub. Frequency: m.
Page Size: standard
Subscrip. Rate: $23.40/yr.
Circulation: 7,000
Circulation Type: paid

**Owner(s):**
National Association of Power Engineers
1 Springfield St.
Chicopee, MA 01013-2624
Telephone: (413) 592-6273
Ownership %: 100
**Management:**
D. Chabak ................................Office Manager
**Editorial:**
W.F. Judd ..................................Editor
**Desc.:** Steam and power generation,
    heating, air conditioning, refrigeration,
    water supply, compressed air, and all
    related utility services in all industries,
    buildings (hotels, hospitals, schools,
    etc.), public utilities and municipalities.
**Readers:** Men and women in charge of
    the operations and maintenance of
    buildings, including building supervisors,
    plant engineers, and consulting
    engineers.

**POWER**     24384
11 W. 19th St.
2nd Fl.
New York, NY 10011
Telephone: (212) 337-4061
FAX: (212) 627-3811
Year Established: 1882
Pub. Frequency: m.
Page Size: standard
Subscrip. Rate: $55/yr.
Circulation: 61,349
Circulation Type: paid
**Owner(s):**
McGraw-Hill, Inc.
1221 Ave. of the Americas
New York, NY 10020
Telephone: (212) 512-2000
Ownership %: 100
**Management:**
J. E. Slater ..............................Publisher
**Editorial:**
Jason Makansi ..........................Editor
Robert Schwieger ....................Editorial Director
Loretta Applegate ..............Circulation Editor
**Desc.:** Specifically covers power
    generation and plant energy systems.
    Deals with modern technology basic to
    the function of producing and applying
    energy as well as the equipment and
    techniques required.
**Readers:** Engineers in manufacturing
    industries, electric utilities, process
    industries and consulting engineering
    firms.

**POWER ENGINEERING**     24385
1421 S. Sheridan
Tulsa, OK 74112
Telephone: (708) 382-2450
FAX: (918) 831-9834
Year Established: 1896
Pub. Frequency: m.
Page Size: standard
Subscrip. Rate: $45/yr. US; $55/yr.
    Canada
Freelance Pay: negotiable
Circulation: 59,500
Circulation Type: controlled & paid
**Owner(s):**
Penn Well Publishing Co.
1421 S. Sheridan
Tulsa, OK 74112
Telephone: (708) 382-2450
Ownership %: 100
**Management:**
Joseph A. Wolking ....................President
John Kovacs ..............................Publisher
**Editorial:**
Bob Smock ................................Chief Editor
Larry Spiker ..............................Production Director

**Materials Accepted/Included:** 01-Business news 02-By-line articles 03-Fashion news 04-Food news 05-Freelance copy 06-Letters to editor 07-Real estate news 08-Sports news 09-Travel news 10-Book rev. 11-Movie rev. 12-Music rev. 13-TV rev. 14-Theater rev. 15-Coming events 16-Obituaries 17-Question & answer 18-Social announcements 19-Artwork 20-Cartoons 21-Photos 22-TV listings 23-Audio rec. 24-Video rec. 25-Books 26-Films/film clips 27-Personnel news 28-Press releases 29-New product news/photos 30-Trade lit. 31-Contracts awarded 32-Display adv. 33-Classified adv.

4-292

**Desc.:** Covers power generation and power plant construction, retrofit and maintenance in electric utilities and heavy industry. Departments include: Literature File, New Equipment, News, Nuclear Power Engineering, Generation in Focus, Washington Energy Report, Environmentally Speaking, Letters, Field Notes, Contracts, People.
**Readers:** Power engineers in the electric utilities and heavy industry, and consultants/constructors in the US and Canada

## PUBLIC POWER
2301 M St., N.W.
Washington, DC 20037
Telephone: (202) 467-2948
FAX: (202) 467-2910
Year Established: 1942
Pub. Frequency: bi-m.
Page Size: standard
Subscrip. Rate: $50/yr.
Freelance Pay: negotiable
Circulation: 12,000
Circulation Type: controlled
**Owner(s):**
American Public Power Association
2301 M St., N.W.
Washington, DC 20037
Telephone: (202) 467-2900
Ownership %: 100
**Management:**
Jeanne Wickline LaBella ..................Publisher
**Editorial:**
Jeanne Wickline LaBella ..........................Editor
Mary Kate Wallace ....................Managing Editor
Nancy Petersen ................................Advertising
Sue Partyke ........................................Advertising
Mitchell Petersen ............................Advertising
**Desc.:** Covers local consumer-owned electric utilities/municipal electric systems, public power districts, public utility districts, rural electric cooperatives and other entities providing nonprofit electric service. It is designed especially for operating and policy making officials of publicly owned electric systems.
**Readers:** Operating and policy-making officials of electric power systems, government officials and financial community.

## PUBLIC UTILITIES FORTNIGHTLY
2111 Wilson Blvd., Ste. 200
Arlington, VA 22201
Telephone: (800) 368-5001
FAX: (703) 527-5829
Year Established: 1929
Pub. Frequency: 22/yr.
Page Size: standard
Subscrip. Rate: $99/yr.
Freelance Pay: negotiable
Circulation: 6,700
Circulation Type: paid
**Owner(s):**
Public Utilities Reports, Inc.
2111 Wilson Blvd., Ste. 200
Arlington, VA 22201
Telephone: (800) 368-5001
FAX: (703) 527-5829
Ownership %: 100
**Management:**
Randall F. Spencer ..............................President
Bruce Radford ..............................Vice President
**Editorial:**
Bruce W. Radford ....................Editor in Chief
David Wagman ....................................Editor
Emily Aitken ............................Managing Editor
Al Liedel ..........................................Advertising
Danielle Pearson ..............Production Director

**Desc.:** Feature articles deal with topics of importance to public utility executives, with primary emphasis on national problems and regulation. An open forum is provided in the manner of a professional journal for the exchange of ideas on matters affecting public utilities, supplemented by news column and editorial developments.

## TRANSMISSION & DISTRIBUTION
9800 Metcalf
Shawnee Mission, KS 66212-2215
Telephone: (913) 341-1300
FAX: (913) 967-1898
Year Established: 1949
Pub. Frequency: m.
Page Size: standard
Subscrip. Rate: $32/yr.; $50/2 yrs. US; $54/yr.; $74/2 yrs. foreign
Materials: 01,02,05,06,15,19,21,28,29,30, 32,33
Freelance Pay: negotiable
Print Process: web offset
Circulation: 35,000
Circulation Type: controlled
**Owner(s):**
Intertec Publishing Corp.
9800 Metcalf
Shawnee Mission, KS 66212
Telephone: (913) 341-1300
Ownership %: 100
**Management:**
Barry H. LeCerf ................................Publisher
Elgin G. Enabnit, Jr. ..........Associate Publsiher
Carin Freas ................Classified Adv. Manager
**Editorial:**
Pam Kufahl ................................Exec. Editor
Earl Hazan ............................................Editor
John T. Tyner ......................................Editor
Elgin G. Enabnit, Jr. ............Editorial Director
**Desc.:** Covers all phases of the design, construction, operation and maintenance of and purchasing for transmission lines, substations, distribution lines, and street and highway lighting systems.
**Deadline:** story-4 mo. prior to pub. date; news-2 mo. prior to pub. date; photo-4 mo. prior to pub. date; ads-1 mo. prior to pub. date

## TURBOMACHINERY INTERNATIONAL
50 Day St.
Norwalk, CT 06854
Telephone: (203) 853-6015
FAX: (203) 852-8175
Mailing Address:
P.O. Box 5550
Norwalk, CT 06856
Year Established: 1959
Pub. Frequency: 7/yr.
Page Size: standard
Subscrip. Rate: $49/yr.
Circulation: 11,500
Circulation Type: controlled & paid
**Owner(s):**
Business Journals, Inc.
50 Day St.
Norwalk, CT 06854
Telephone: (203) 853-6015
Ownership %: 100
**Management:**
G. Renfrew Brighton ..........Chairman of Board
Skip Ruch ........................................Publisher
Arthur Heilman ................Circulation Manager
**Editorial:**
Tom Barker ..........................................Editor
Frances Salamon ................Production Director

**Desc.:** Serves energy conversion managers and engineers, covering turbines, compressors and related rotating equipment and accessories used for power generation, mechanical drive, co-generation and power recovery, including overhaul, maintenance and repair.
**Readers:** Top management and engineers in oil and gas, electric utilities, chemical and other turbomachinery user industries.

## UTILITY CONSTRUCTION & MAINTENANCE
321 Cary Point Dr.
Cary, IL 60013
Telephone: (708) 639-2200
FAX: (708) 639-9542
Mailing Address:
P.O. Box 183
Cary, IL 60013
Year Established: 1990
Pub. Frequency: 4/yr.
Page Size: standard
Subscrip. Rate: $11/yr.
Freelance Pay: $50/page
Circulation: 25,500
Circulation Type: controlled
**Owner(s):**
Practical Communications, Inc.
321 Cary Point Dr.
Cary, IL 60013
Telephone: (708) 639-2200
Ownership %: 100
**Management:**
Judy Chance ........................................President
Bob Lanham ........................................Publisher
Jim Queenan ....................Circulation Manager
**Editorial:**
Alan Richter ............................Editor in Chief
**Desc.:** On-the-job type articles, case histories, trends, technical data, product introduction, tutorials, buyers guides, tips and advice.
**Readers:** Construction, maintenance and equipment buyers and specifiers employed by the nation's largest electric, gas and water utilities, cable TV operators, public works departments, municipalities and related contractors.

## Group 202-Printing & Graphic Arts

## AMERICAN INK MAKER
445 Broad Hollow Rd., 21
Melville, NY 11747
Telephone: (516) 845-2700
FAX: (516) 845-7109
Year Established: 1923
Pub. Frequency: m.
Page Size: standard
Subscrip. Rate: $60/yr.; $90/2 yrs.
Materials: 01,02,06,15,16,17,27,28,29,30, 32,33
Freelance Pay: varies
Circulation: 5,000
Circulation Type: paid
**Owner(s):**
American Ink Maker
Ownership %: 100
**Management:**
Stanley Sills ........................................President
Dale Pritchett ....................Advertising Manager
**Editorial:**
Suzanne Christiansen ..........................Editor
**Desc.:** Contributed articles cover ink manufacture testing, industry progress, business management. Departments cover technical notes, company news, raw materials, association news, industry news, bulletins, etc.

**Readers:** Printing ink makers, dry and flushed color producers, carbon paper, writing, duplicating and color specialty manufacturing firms.
**Deadline:** story-1st of the mo.; news-1st of the mo.; photo-1st of the mo.; ads-15th of the mo.

## AMERICAN PRINTER
29 N. Wacker Dr.
Chicago, IL 60606
Telephone: (312) 726-2802
Year Established: 1883
Pub. Frequency: m.
Page Size: standard
Subscrip. Rate: $5/copy; $50/yr. US
Circulation: 94,105
Circulation Type: controlled
**Owner(s):**
MacLean-Hunter Publishing Co.
29 N. Wacker Dr.
Chicago, IL 60606
Telephone: (312) 726-2802
Ownership %: 100
**Management:**
M. Dan Sember ..................................President
John Favat, Jr. ....................................Publisher
Grace Bellino ....................Circulation Manager
Pam Janousek ....................Promotion Manager
**Editorial:**
Jill Roth ................................................Editor
Mark Smith ............................Managing Editor
J. Smuda ............................Assistant Publisher
Werner Rebsamen ............................Columnist
Michael Bruno ....................................Columnist
Vincent Mallardi ................................Columnist
Don Merit ............................................Columnist
Dennis Frantsve ................................Columnist
John C. Behrens ................................Columnist
Terry Scarlett ......................................Columnist
Gill Gavin ............................Production Director
**Desc.:** American Printer is edited for members of the printing, publishing and graphic arts industry in managing and operating efficiently. Feature articles contain subjects ranging from industry/technology trends to management and production techniques. In addition to regular features the publication's specialized departments include: Prepress Imaging, Newspaper Operations, Pressroom Electronics, Production Management, Selling and Salesmanship, Direct Mail/Promotion, In-plant/Corporate Publishing Operations, New Equipment, Books/Tapes, and Washington Outlook.
**Readers:** Managers and supervisory personnel, owners, executives, superintendents, production personnel, (color separators, platemaking, trade shops, bindery plants). Commercial printers, newspaper, non-commercial printers and specialty operations.

## ART & DESIGN NEWS
5783 Park Plaza Ct.
Indianapolis, IN 46220
Telephone: (317) 849-6110
FAX: (317) 576-5859
Mailing Address:
P.O. Box 501100
Indianapolis, IN 46250
Year Established: 1977
Pub. Frequency: bi-m.
Page Size: tabloid
Subscrip. Rate: $15/yr.
Materials: 02,06,19,21,29,32,33
Print Process: web offset
Circulation: 51,404
Circulation Type: controlled & paid

**Materials Accepted/Included:** 01-Business news 02-By-line articles 03-Fashion news 04-Food news 05-Freelance copy 06-Letters to editor 07-Real estate news 08-Sports news 09-Travel news 10-Book rev. 11-Movie rev. 12-Music rev. 13-TV rev. 14-Theater rev. 15-Coming events 16-Obituaries 17-Question & answer 18-Social announcements 19-Artwork 20-Cartoons 21-Photos 22-TV listings 23-Audio rec. 24-Video rec. 25-Books 26-Films/film clips 27-Personnel news 28-Press releases 29-New product news/photos 30-Trade lit. 31-Contracts awarded 32-Display adv. 33-Classified adv.

4-293

**Owner(s):**
Boyd Publishing Co.
5783 Park Plaza Ct.
Indianapolis, IN 46220
Telephone: (317) 849-6110
FAX: (317) 576-5859
Ownership %: 100
**Management:**
Richard A. Boyd .............................President
Jeanne A. Pulliam ...........................Publisher
Jeanne Pulliam ...............Advertising Manager
Pamela Keller ................Circulation Manager
**Editorial:**
Paul Schmidt ...................................Editor
**Desc.:** Product and service information.
During the course of a year editorial
coverage includes: new and existing
product features (75%), services (10%),
technique articles (10%), and other
information (5%).
**Readers:** Artists and designers in
agencies, corporations and studios
throughout the United States.

24590
**BAR CODE REPORTER**
100 Daingerfield Rd., 4th Fl.
Alexandria, VA 22314-2888
Telephone: (703) 519-8160
FAX: (703) 548-2867
Year Established: 1987
Pub. Frequency: q.
Page Size: standard
Subscrip. Rate: $55/yr. members; $95/yr.-
others
Circulation: 200
Circulation Type: free & paid
**Owner(s):**
Graphic Communications Association
100 Daingerfield, Rd., 4th Fl.
Alexandria, VA 22314-2888
Telephone: (703) 519-8160
Ownership %: 100
**Editorial:**
Alan Kotok ......................................Editor
Vivian Sanchez ......................Managing Editor
**Desc.:** Quarterly journal on bar codes and
EDI in the printing & publishing industry
reporting on new standards activities in
the US and overseas. Shows how
companies are using these
technologies to control inventories, track
job progress & reduce overhead.
**Readers:** GCA Members, MIS Managers,
Inventory Supervisors.

24391
**COMMUNICATION ARTS**
410 Sherman Ave.
Palo Alto, CA 94306
Telephone: (415) 326-6040
FAX: (415) 326-1648
Mailing Address:
P.O. Box 10300
Palo Alto, CA 94303
Year Established: 1959
Pub. Frequency: 8/yr.
Page Size: standard
Subscrip. Rate: $98/yr.
Materials: 06,25,27,28,29,30,32
Print Process: web offset
Circulation: 60,120
Circulation Type: paid
**Owner(s):**
Patrick Coyne
410 Sherman Ave.
Palo Alto, CA 94306
Telephone: (415) 326-6040
Ownership %: 33

Martha Coyne
410 Sherman Ave.
Palo Alto, CA 94306
Telephone: (415) 326-6040
Ownership %: 33

Eric Coyne
410 Sherman Ave.
Palo Alto, CA 94306
Telephone: (415) 326-6040
Ownership %: 33
**Management:**
Mike Krigel .................Advertising Manager
Scott Perry .................Production Manager
Lisa Marie Perez ..............Traffic Manager
**Editorial:**
Jean A. Coyne .................Executive Editor
Patrick Coyne ..............................Editor
Anne Telford .................New Products Editor
Patrick Coyne ...........................News Editor
Jason Jackson ..............Subscription Manager
**Desc.:** Articles on graphic design and
illustrated studies of outstanding people
and studios in the field. Also articles on
photographers, illustrators and
advertising agencies. Covers corporate
design; individual pieces of work;
information on production, color,
typography and printing. Departments
include: Editor's Column, Books, Club
News, Materials, Literature and
Technology Reviews.
**Readers:** Art directors, graphic designers,
photographers, illustrators.
**Deadline:** ads-2 mos. prior to pub. date

69395
**CONFETTI**
1425 Lunt Ave.
Elk Grove Village, IL 60007
Telephone: (708) 437-6604
FAX: (708) 437-6618
Mailing Address:
P.O. Box 1426
Elk Grove Village, IL 60009
Year Established: 1988
Pub. Frequency: bi-m.
Subscrip. Rate: $35/yr.
Circulation: 15,000
Circulation Type: paid
**Owner(s):**
Randall Publishing, Inc.
1425 Lunt Ave.
Elk Grove Village, IL 60007
Telephone: (708) 437-6604
**Editorial:**
Peg Carmack Short ...........................Editor
**Desc.:** Covers all aspects of
communication arts, with emphasis on
print.
**Readers:** Visual and verbal communication
professionals.

69077
**DEALER COMMUNICATOR**
777 S. State Rd. 7
Margate, FL 33068
Telephone: (800) 327-8999
FAX: (305) 971-4362
Year Established: 1980
Pub. Frequency: m.
Page Size: tabloid
Subscrip. Rate: $30/yr.
Materials: 27,28,29,30,32
Print Process: web offset
Circulation: 9,110
Circulation Type: controlled
**Owner(s):**
Fichera Publications
777 S. State. Rd. 7
Margate, FL 33068
Telephone: (800) 327-8999
Ownership %: 100
**Management:**
Orazio "O. Mike" Fichera .................President
Orazio "O. Mike" Fichera .................Publisher
Rick Kelly .................Advertising Manager
Marcy Sellard .................Circulation Manager
**Editorial:**
Paul Mc Elroy .................Managing Editor
Patricia Leavitt .................Associate Publisher
Paul Mc Elroy .................Editor-in-Chief

**Desc.:** Presents news about products and
graphic arts dealers.
**Deadline:** story-1 mo. prior to pub. date;
news-1 mo. prior; photo-1 mo. prior; ads-
1 mo. prior

24420
**ELECTRONIC PUBLISHING &
TYPEWORLD**
10 Tara Blvd.
5th Fl.
Nashua, NH 03062-2801
Telephone: (603) 891-9157
FAX: (603) 891-0539
Year Established: 1977
Pub. Frequency: 18/yr.
Page Size: tabloid
Subscrip. Rate: $2.95 newsstand US;
$3.95 Canada; $30/yr. US; $165/yr.
foreign
Materials: 01,02,06,10,15,19,21,25,28,29,
30,32,33
Circulation: 50,000
Circulation Type: controlled
**Owner(s):**
Penn Well Publishing Co.
10 Tara Blvd.
5th Fl.
Nashua, NH 03062-2801
Telephone: (603) 891-9157
FAX: (603) 891-0539
Ownership %: 100
**Management:**
Robert Holton .................................Publisher
Paul McPherson ...............Advertising Manager
**Editorial:**
Keith Hevenor .........................Managing Editor
**Desc.:** Covers all the latest news and
related developments from the fields of
electronic prepress, printing, desktop
publishing, design and typography. A
one stop source for digital publishing
professionals. Provides extensive
coverage of industry announcements
and introductions; brings insightful
articles on technology trends and
historical retrospectives.
**Readers:** Publishers, printers, prepress
professionals, desktop publishers,
designers and those involved in any
aspect of electronic publishing.

69351
**EMIGRE**
4475 D St.
Sacramento, CA 95819
Telephone: (916) 451-4344
FAX: (916) 451-4351
Year Established: 1982
Pub. Frequency: q.
Subscrip. Rate: $28/yr. US; $35/yr.
Canada; $58/yr. elsewhere
Circulation: 7,000
**Owner(s):**
Emigre Graphics
4475 D St.
Sacramento, CA 95819
Telephone: (916) 451-4344
Ownership %: 100
**Editorial:**
Rudy Vander Lans .............................Editor
**Desc.:** Features both established and
emerging graphic design talents from
around the world. Focuses on a specific
design topic and showcases works,
often experimental in nature.

24394
**GRAPHIC ARTS MONTHLY**
249 W. 17th St.
New York, NY 10011
Telephone: (212) 463-6834
FAX: (212) 463-6733
Year Established: 1929
Pub. Frequency: m.

Page Size: standard
Subscrip. Rate: $84.95/yr. US; $164.95/yr.
Canada
Freelance Pay: $.10/wd.
Circulation: 94,000
Circulation Type: controlled
**Owner(s):**
Cahners Publishing Company, Inc.
249 W. 17th St.
New York, NY 10011
Telephone: (212) 463-6834
Ownership %: 100
**Management:**
Terry McDermott .............................President
Ronald C. Andriani .........................Publisher
Gerry Arotsky .................Business Manager
**Editorial:**
Roger Ynostroza ..............................Editor
Michael Karol .................Managing Editor
Debbi Toth .................Associate Editor
Earl Wilken .................Associate Editor
Lisa Cross .................Associate Editor
Bridgett Riusella .................Associate Editor
Lisa Cross .................Associate Editor
Bridgett Riusella .................Associate Editor
**Desc.:** National business magazine for
printing and allied industries, including
corporate electronic publishing,
documentation, logistics and training.
Departments include: Selling, Estimation,
Composing Room Operations,
Platemaking, Presswork, Binding, Paper,
Materials Handling, New Products, Free
Literature, News about People,
Companies and Associations.
**Readers:** Management, supervisory and
production.

69392
**GRAPHIC COMMUNICATIONS
WORLD**
P.O. Box 727
Hartsdale, NY 10530-0727
Telephone: (914) 472-3051
FAX: (914) 472-3880
Year Established: 1968
Pub. Frequency: bi-w.
Subscrip. Rate: $247/yr. individuals;
$172/yr. educational institutions
Materials: 28,29,30,31
Print Process: offset lithography
Circulation: 4,000
Circulation Type: paid
**Owner(s):**
Green Sheet Communications, Inc.
P.O. Box 727
Hartsdale, NY 10530-0727
Telephone: (914) 472-3051
FAX: (914) 472-3880
Ownership %: 100
**Editorial:**
John R. Werner ................................Editor
**Desc.:** Covers new technology and
management trends for senior
management in the printing and
publishing industry.

21762
**GRAPHIC DESIGN: USA**
1556 Third Ave.
New York, NY 10128
Telephone: (212) 534-5500
FAX: (212) 534-4415
Year Established: 1965
Pub. Frequency: m.
Page Size: standard
Subscrip. Rate: $60/yr.
Circulation: 30,000
Circulation Type: controlled
**Owner(s):**
Kaye Publishing Corp.
1556 Third Ave.
New York, NY 10128
Telephone: (212) 534-5500
Ownership %: 100

**Management:**
Gordon Kaye ..........................President
Gordon Kaye ..........................Publisher
**Editorial:**
Laura Roth ..................Circulation Director
**Desc.:** Provides news, ideas, information
on various subjects that affect the
livelihood of people in the graphic
design field. News of design trends,
costs, people, events, logos, change,
opportunity.
**Readers:** Art directors, designers and
other graphic communicators who buy
and specify graphic products & services.

## GRAPHIC NETWORK
69078

729 Washington Rd.
Pittsburgh, PA 15228
Telephone: (412) 341-3722
FAX: (412) 341-6344
Year Established: 1984
Pub. Frequency: m.
Page Size: standard
Subscrip. Rate: $45/yr.
Materials: 01,06,15,32,33
Circulation: 30,000
Circulation Type: paid
**Owner(s):**
Graphic Network
729 Washington Rd.
Pittsburgh, PA 15228
Telephone: (412) 341-3722
Ownership %: 100
**Editorial:**
Jack Grove ..........................Editor
**Readers:** Graphics consumers and
producers in the Mid-Atlantic area.

## GRAPHICOMMUNICATOR
24423

1900 L Street, N.W.
Washington, DC 20036-5076
Telephone: (202) 462-1400
FAX: (202) 331-9516
Year Established: 1983
Pub. Frequency: 8/yr.
Page Size: tabloid
Subscrip. Rate: $12/yr. US & Canada;
$15/yr. elsewhere
Materials: 01,28,29,30
Freelance Pay: negotiable
Print Process: web offset
Circulation: 155,000
Circulation Type: controlled & paid
**Owner(s):**
Graphic Communications International
Union
1900 L St., N.W.
Washington, DC 20036
Telephone: (202) 462-1400
Ownership %: 100
**Editorial:**
James J. Norton ..........................Editor in Chief
Herald Grandstaff ..................Managing Editor
**Desc.:** Used as a technical and news
publication of the graphic
communications/printing industry. This
tabloid-sized newspaper is mainly for
and about GCIU members and their
union. Its major circulation is to
craftspeople (bookbinders lithographers,
rotogravure, letterpress, flexography,
newspapers, and photoengravers) in the
printing/publishing industry. It also has a
high percentage of readers who are in
the executive side of the industry, as
well as libraries and technical societies.
Departments include: news of Graphic
communications/printing industry, news
for the suppliers, technical trade articles,
safety and health news, AFL-CIO and
general labor news reports, articles on
political action.

**Readers:** Highly skilled graphic arts
craftspeople, fairly well educated, having
served apprenticeship must continuously
read technical material to keep abreast
of new technology.

## HIGH VOLUME PRINTING
22090

425 Huehl Rd., Bldg. 11 B
Northbrook, IL 60062
Telephone: (708) 564-5940
FAX: (708) 564-8361
Mailing Address:
P.O. Box 368
Northbrook, IL 60065
Year Established: 1982
Pub. Frequency: bi-m.
Page Size: standard
Subscrip. Rate: $45/yr.; $75/2yrs.
Materials: 01,02,06,27,28,29,30,32,33
Freelance Pay: $300
Print Process: web offset
Circulation: 41,000
Circulation Type: controlled
**Owner(s):**
Innes Publishing Co.
P.O. Box 368
Northbrook, IL 60065
Telephone: (708) 564-5940
FAX: (708) 564-8361
Ownership %: 100
**Management:**
Edward M. Innes ..........................President
Steve Austin ..........................Publisher
**Editorial:**
Catherine M. Stanulis ..........................Editor
**Desc.:** Includes reports on the application
of new equipment, management and
production methods and
materials/supplies (including paper and
ink).
**Readers:** Top management, sales
managers, production managers in large
and medium-sized printing companies
and related services.
**Deadline:** news-1st of mo. prior to pub.
mo.; photo-1st of mo. prior; ads-1st of
mo. prior

## IN-PLANT PRINTER INCLUDING CORPORATE IMAGING
24396

425 Huehl Rd., Bldg. 11
Northbrook, IL 60062
Telephone: (708) 564-5940
FAX: (708) 564-8361
Mailing Address:
P.O. Box 368
Northbrook, IL 60062
Year Established: 1966
Pub. Frequency: bi-m.
Page Size: standard
Subscrip. Rate: $45/yr.
Freelance Pay: $100-$500
Circulation: 42,000
Circulation Type: controlled
**Owner(s):**
Innes Publishing Co.
P.O. Box 368
Northbrook, IL 60062
Telephone: (708) 564-5940
Ownership %: 100
**Management:**
Edward M. Innes ..........................President
**Editorial:**
Anne Marie Mohan ..........................Editor
**Desc.:** Edited exclusively for in-plant
printers and documentation
professionals dealing with typesetting,
make-up, platemaking, printing, copying
and duplicating services. Electronic text
and graphics, page layout, proofing and
reproduction methods are also covered.
**Readers:** Educators, operators, managers
and supervisors of printing and graphic
composition facilities.

## IN-PLANT REPRODUCTIONS
24415

401 N. Broad St.
Philadelphia, PA 19108
Telephone: (215) 238-5300
FAX: (215) 238-5452
Year Established: 1951
Pub. Frequency: m.
Page Size: standard
Subscrip. Rate: free
Freelance Pay: $150/article
Circulation: 42,000
Circulation Type: controlled
**Owner(s):**
North American Publishing Co.
401 N. Broad St.
Philadelphia, PA 19108
Telephone: (215) 238-5300
Ownership %: 100
**Management:**
Jeff Okon ..........................Publisher
**Editorial:**
Judy Bocklage ..........................Editor
**Desc.:** Articles are published by authorities
on both technical and management
subjects, statistical and interpretive
studies and interviews are made by the
editors. There are special-interest
departments. Departments include:
Prepress Clinic, Letters to the Editor,
News Review, Calendar of Events, Q&A,
Electronic Publishing Systems,
Electronic Prepress, New Products,
Management Tips.
**Readers:** Managers of in-house printing,
electronic publishing, typesetting and
graphic arts departments.

## LETTERHEADS
69346

10 E. 39th St.
New York, NY 10016
Telephone: (212) 889-6500
FAX: (212) 889-6504
Year Established: 1977
Pub. Frequency: a.
Subscrip. Rate: $59.95/yr.
Circulation: 6,200
Circulation Type: paid
**Owner(s):**
Art Direction Book Co.
10 E. 39th St.
New York, NY 10016
Telephone: (212) 889-6500
**Editorial:**
David E. Carter ..........................Editor
**Desc.:** International annual of letterhead
design.

## PACKAGE PRINTING AND CONVERTING
24402

401 N. Broad St.
Philadelphia, PA 19108
Telephone: (215) 238-5356
FAX: (215) 238-5356
Year Established: 1955
Pub. Frequency: m.
Page Size: 4 color photos/art
Subscrip. Rate: $49/yr.
Freelance Pay: $100/pg.
Circulation: 24,000
Circulation Type: controlled & paid
**Owner(s):**
North American Publishing Co.
401 N. Broad St.
Philadelphia, PA 19108
Telephone: (215) 238-5300
Ownership %: 100
**Bureau(s):**
North American Publ. Co.
201 E. Ogden Ave., Ste. 226
Hinsdale, IL 60521
Telephone: (708) 325-9555
Contact: Brian Ludwick, Publisher

**Management:**
Ned Borowsky ..........................President
Brian Ludwick ..........................Publisher
**Editorial:**
David Luttenberger ..........................Editor
William Knight ..........................Art Director
**Desc.:** Technical and management-
oriented articles on the flexographic,
gravure, offset, letterpress and
lithographic printing industries in the
production of printed packages (flexible
packaging, folding cartons, boxboard
containers, tags and labels, etc.). Also
covers die-making/die-cutting markets.
**Readers:** Owners, executives &
supervisory plant personnel who
produce flexible packaging, folding
cartons, corrugated containers, tags &
labels.

## PREPRESS BULLETIN, THE
24404

552 W. 167th St.
South Holland, IL 60473
Telephone: (708) 596-5110
FAX: (708) 596-5112
Year Established: 1911
Pub. Frequency: bi-m.
Page Size: standard
Subscrip. Rate: $15/yr. US; $17/yr. foreign
Circulation: 2,000
Circulation Type: paid
**Owner(s):**
International Prepress Association
552 W. 167th St.
South Holland, IL 60473
Telephone: (708) 596-5110
Ownership %: 100
**Editorial:**
Bessie Halfacre ..........................Editor
**Readers:** The Prepress Bulletin is edited
for management of those companies
which produce color separations, film,
and other prepress preparatory materials
for the graphic arts industry.

## PRINT-EQUIP NEWS
24406

215 Allen St.
Glendale, CA 91201
Telephone: (818) 954-9495
FAX: (818) 954-0452
Mailing Address:
P.O. Box 5540
Glendale, CA 91221
Year Established: 1964
Pub. Frequency: m.
Page Size: tabloid
Subscrip. Rate: $24/yr.
Materials: 01,02,28,29,30,32,33
Print Process: web offset
Circulation: 25,000
Circulation Type: controlled
**Owner(s):**
P-EN Publications, Inc.
P.O. Box 5540
Glendale, CA 91221
Telephone: (818) 954-9495
Ownership %: 100
**Management:**
Richard E. Jutras ..........................Publisher
Jeff Jutras ..........................Advertising Manager
Elaine Centeno ..........................Classified Adv. Manager
**Editorial:**
Paul B. Kissel ..........................Editor
**Desc.:** Publishes news stories on new
products and services in every phase of
the printing field. Encourages convention
listings, stories to do with the schools
and colleges which train graphic arts
students. Emphasis is on Graphic Arts
activities and developments in 19
Western states.
**Readers:** Largely to owners/managers of
print shops, department manager,
printing equipment dealers.

---

**Materials Accepted/Included:** 01-Business news 02-By-line articles 03-Fashion news 04-Food news 05-Freelance copy 06-Letters to editor 07-Real estate news 08-Sports news 09-Travel news 10-Book rev. 11-Movie rev. 12-Music rev. 13-TV rev. 14-Theater rev. 15-Coming events 16-Obituaries 17-Question & answer 18-Social announcements 19-Artwork 20-Cartoons 21-Photos 22-TV listings 23-Audio rec. 24-Video rec. 25-Books 26-Films/film clips 27-Personnel news 28-Press releases 29-New product news/photos 30-Trade lit. 31-Contracts awarded 32-Display adv. 33-Classified adv.

## PRINT BUSINESS REGISTER

59140

800 W. Huron, Ste. 4S
Chicago, IL 60622-5973
Telephone: (312) 226-5600
FAX: (312) 226-4640
Year Established: 1986
Pub. Frequency: 24/yr.
Page Size: standard
Subscrip. Rate: $297/yr.
Materials: 01,07,27,28,29,30,31
Print Process: offset
Circulation: 650
Circulation Type: paid
**Owner(s):**
Quoin Publishing, Inc.
800 W. Huron, Ste. 4S
Chicago, IL 60622-5973
Telephone: (312) 226-5600
Ownership %: 100
**Management:**
Rod Piechowski ...................................Publisher
**Editorial:**
Rod Piechowski .......................................Editor
**Desc.:** Follows activities in the commercial
printing industry, including mergers and
acquisitions, major contracts,
installations, bankruptcies, trends,
and legal proceedings of note.
**Readers:** Top printer management,
financial industry.

## PRINTING IMPRESSIONS

24409

401 N. Broad St.
Philadelphia, PA 19108
Telephone: (215) 238-5300
Year Established: 1958
Pub. Frequency: s-m.
Page Size: tabloid
Subscrip. Rate: $75/yr.
Materials: 01,06,17,28,29,30,31,32,33
Freelance Pay: negotiable
Circulation: 94,500
Circulation Type: controlled
**Owner(s):**
North American Publishing Co.
401 N. Broad St.
Philadelphia, PA 19108
Telephone: (215) 238-5300
Ownership %: 100
**Management:**
Ned Borowsky ....................................President
Carl W. Lock .......................................Publisher
Sara Bodison ....................Production Manager
**Editorial:**
Mark Michelson ......................................Editor
Josephine Kukuka .............Production Director
**Desc.:** Uses news and feature material on
management, marketing, and technical
aspects of printing and publishing
operations. Departments include: New
Products, Equipment and Supply
Review, People in the News, Supplier
News, Industry News, Calendar, etc.
**Readers:** Executives and production
managers of the leading commercial
printing plants, newspaper, and in-plant
operations.

## PRINTING JOURNAL

24410

1432 Duke St.
Alexandria, VA 22314-3436
Telephone: (703) 683-8800
FAX: (703) 683-8801
Year Established: 1974
Pub. Frequency: m.
Page Size: tabloid
Subscrip. Rate: $39/yr. US.; $82/yr.
foreign; free qualified subscribers
Freelance Pay: negotiable
Circulation: 19,000
Circulation Type: controlled

**Owner(s):**
East-West Communications
1432 Duke St.
Alexandria, VA 22314
Telephone: (703) 683-8800
Ownership %: 100
**Management:**
Geoffrey G. Lindsay ...............................Owner
Geoffrey G. Lindsay ...........................Publisher
**Editorial:**
Carole Turner ........................................Editor
**Desc.:** Use printing/printing related
editorial up to 1,000 words. Accept free
lance submissions: send SASE if
manuscript to be returned. Uses
industry-related factual news releases on
equipment, personnel, materials, events,
occasional speeches and applicable
book reviews. Photos as material/space
dictates. Technical articles welcome.
**Readers:** Printing industry, graphic
designers, typesetters, print buyers in
western states.

## PRINTING NEWS-EAST

24411

445 Broad Hollow Rd.
Melville, NY 11747
Telephone: (516) 845-2700
FAX: (512) 845-7109
Year Established: 1928
Pub. Frequency: 51/yr.
Page Size: tabloid
Subscrip. Rate: $24.95/yr.
Freelance Pay: $300-$550
Circulation: 9,000
Circulation Type: paid
**Owner(s):**
PTN Publishing Co.
445 Broad Hollow Rd.
Melville, NY 11747
Telephone: (516) 845-2700
Ownership %: 100
**Management:**
Bill Lewis ...........................................Publisher
Jacqueline Serra ...............Circulation Manager
Suzanne Noguere .......Classified Adv. Manager
Evelyn Krejci .....................Production Manager
**Editorial:**
Heidi Tolliver .........................................Editor
Richard Snyder ...................Display Advertizing
Manager
**Desc.:** Devoted primarily to the marketing
area of the greater metropolitan area, as
well as New York, New Jersey and
Connecticut.
**Readers:** Printing executives, managers,
technical, all those associated with the
graphic arts industries.

## PRINT MAGAZINE

24407

104 Fifth Ave., 19th Fl.
New York, NY 10011
Telephone: (212) 463-0600
FAX: (212) 989-9891
Year Established: 1940
Pub. Frequency: bi-m.
Page Size: 4 color photos/art
Subscrip. Rate: $7.50/yr., $53/yr.
Freelance Pay: varies
Circulation: 55,000
Circulation Type: paid
**Owner(s):**
R C Publications, Inc.
104 Fifth Ave.
New York, NY 10011
Telephone: (212) 463-0600
Ownership %: 100
**Management:**
Howard Cadel ....................................Publisher
Elayne Recupero ..............Advertising Manager
**Editorial:**
Carol Stevens .............................Executive Editor
Martin Fox ...............................................Editor
Julie Lasky ................................Managing Editor

Andrew Kner .................................Art Director
Tod Lippy ..............................Associate Editor
**Desc.:** Devoted to all areas of graphic
design and visual communications, print
design, typography, advertising design,
environmental graphics, computer-aided
design, television and film design.
**Readers:** Art directors, graphic designers,
illustrators, graphic artists,
photographers, printers, animators,
filmmakers, visual-minded executives.

## QUICK PRINTING

24414

1680 S.W. Bayshore Blvd.
Port St. Lucie, FL 34984
Telephone: (407) 879-6666
FAX: (407) 879-7388
Mailing Address:
1680 S.W. Bayshore Blvd.
Port St. Lucie, FL 34984
Year Established: 1977
Pub. Frequency: m.
Page Size: standard
Subscrip. Rate: $25/yr.
Freelance Pay: $75-$250
Circulation: 62,000
Circulation Type: controlled
**Owner(s):**
Coast Publishing, Inc.
1680 S.W. Bayshore Blvd.
Port St. Lucie, FL 34984
Telephone: (407) 879-6666
Ownership %: 100
**Management:**
Robert Schweiger ...........................President
K.J. Moran ........................................Publisher
Bonnie DeCuba .................Circulation Manager
**Editorial:**
Tara Marini ...........................................Editor
Rosalye Sapiro .................................Advertising
Randi Meyer ....................................Advertising
Kelley Holmes .................................Advertising
Jann Levesque .................................Advertising
Robin Moran ...................................Advertising
Betsy Eichelberger ...............Marketing Director
Jeff Macharyas ....................Production Director
Karen Seymour ........................Sales Director
**Desc.:** Devoted to needs and interests of
commercial quick printing and copyshop
industry owners, particularly ideas for
improving profit of a business, quality of
products printed, methods for improving
shop efficiency and techniques for self-
promotion. Methods of marketing and
producing specific products and
application of various machines in
unique ways are also covered.
Departments include: Industry News,
Product News, Interview, Profile,
Calendar, Copier Review, Management,
Marketing, and Features.
**Readers:** Most are college educated, age
varies from mid 20's to 60's, business
owners with $225,000 gross average.

## SCREEN PRINTING

24417

407 Gilbert Ave.
Cincinnati, OH 45202
Telephone: (513) 421-2050
FAX: (513) 421-5144
Year Established: 1953
Pub. Frequency: 13/yr.
Page Size: standard
Subscrip. Rate: $39/yr.
Materials: 01,02,05,06,15,19,20,21,28,29,
30,32,33
Freelance Pay: $50-$500/article
Print Process: offset
Circulation: 15,000
Circulation Type: paid

**Owner(s):**
S.T. Publishing, Inc.
407 Gilbert Ave.
Cincinnati, OH 45202
Telephone: (513) 421-2050
Ownership %: 100
**Management:**
David R. Swormstedt, ........Chairman of Board
Jr.
Jerry R. Swormstedt .........................President
**Editorial:**
Steve Ducilli .........................................Editor
Jo Ellen Duennes .................Managing Editor
Emily Schneider .............................Art Director
Tom Frecska ....................Associate Editor
R. T. Jordan ...........................Group Publisher
Pam Hines ....................Production Coordinator
**Desc.:** The editorial content reflects "the
state of the art" of the entire screen
printing industry. The magazine is a
source book for "on hand" technology,
business know-how and general
information on screen printing not to be
found in any other publication. New
product releases, industrial and
association news deal with subjects and
events relevant to all areas of
specialization. Also serves as a forum
for new ideas and as a connecting link
between the many specialized
applications within the industry.
**Readers:** They are primarily commercial
and special captive shops, specialists,
such as textile, decal, electronic,
manufacturers and suppliers to the
screen printing industry in the U.S. and
Canada.
**Deadline:** story-3 mos.; news-3 mos.;
photo-3 mos.; ads-3 mos.

## SOUTHERN GRAPHICS

24395

1680 S.W. Bayshore Blvd.
Port St. Lucie, FL 34984
Telephone: (407) 879-6666
FAX: (407) 879-7388
Year Established: 1924
Pub. Frequency: m.
Page Size: standard
Subscrip. Rate: $9.75/yr., $17.50/2 yrs.
Materials: 01,02,05,28,29,30
Freelance Pay: negotiable
Print Process: offset
Circulation: 22,000
Circulation Type: controlled
**Owner(s):**
Coast Publishing, Inc.
1680 S.W. Bayshore Blvd.
Port St Lucie, FL 34984
Telephone: (407) 879-6666
Ownership %: 100
**Management:**
Robert Schweiger ................Chairman of Board
Cyndi Schulman .........................Vice President
K.J. Moran ........................................Publisher
Bonnie deCuba .................Circulation Manager
**Editorial:**
Cathy Donohue ......................................Editor
Jeff Macharyas ...........................Art Department
**Desc.:** A monthly magazine for the graphic
arts industry in 14 southern states. Our
editorial focuses on showing our readers
ways to improve efficiency and increase
sales and profits. It is the oldest, largest,
and most universally-acclaimed
magazine for the graphic arts industry in
the southern United States.
**Readers:** Printing plant executives,
supervisors.
**Deadline:** news-1-1/2 mos.; photo-1-1/2
mos.; ads-1 mo.

**Materials Accepted/Included:** 01-Business news 02-By-line articles 03-Fashion news 04-Food news 05-Freelance copy 06-Letters to editor 07-Real estate news 08-Sports news 09-Travel news 10-Book rev. 11-Movie rev. 12-Music rev. 13-TV rev. 14-Theater rev. 15-Coming events 16-Obituaries 17-Question & answer 18-Social announcements 19-Artwork 20-Cartoons 21-Photos 22-TV listings 23-Audio rec. 24-Video rec. 25-Books 26-Films/film clips 27-Personnel news 28-Press releases 29-New product news/photos 30-Trade lit. 31-Contracts awarded 32-Display adv. 33-Classified adv.

## STEP-BY-STEP GRAPHICS
69080

6000 N. Forest Park Dr.
Peoria, IL 61614-3592
Telephone: (309) 668-2300
FAX: (309) 688-8515
Year Established: 1985
Pub. Frequency: bi-m.
Subscrip. Rate: $42/yr.
Materials: 01,02,05,06,10,15,19,25,28,30,32
Freelance Pay: varies
Print Process: offset
Circulation: 46,000
Circulation Type: paid
**Owner(s):**
Step-by-Step Publishing
6000 N. Forest Park Dr.
Peoria, IL 61614-3592
Telephone: (309) 688-2300
FAX: (309) 688-2300
Ownership %: 100
**Editorial:**
Nancy Aldrich-Ruenzel ...........................Editor
**Desc.:** How-to magazine for graphic
designers, illustrators, art directors, etc.,
working traditionally or electronically.
Provides technical, artistic, and business
information.
**Readers:** Professional graphic designers
and illustrators.
**Deadline:** news-2 mo. prior to pub. date

## TECHNIQUE, THE HOW-TO GUIDE TO SUCCESSFUL COMMUNICATIONS
69734

10 Post Office Sq., Ste. 600S
Boston, MA 02109-4616
Telephone: (617) 422-8640
FAX: (617) 423-4426
Year Established: 1994
Pub. Frequency: bi-m.
Subscrip. Rate: $19.95/yr.
Materials: 02,05,06,10,17,20,28,30,32,33
Print Process: web
Circulation: 125,000
Circulation Type: paid
**Owner(s):**
In Print Publishing, Inc.
10 Post Office Sq.
Ste. 600S
Boston, MA 02109-4616
Telephone: (617) 422-8640
FAX: (617) 423-4426
Ownership %: 100
**Management:**
Susan D. Sigel ...........................Publisher
Pamela D'Amico ...................Sales Manager
**Editorial:**
Jill Robbins Israel ...............Editor in Chief
Alex Asmanis Candelas ...........Design Director
Jennifer Paul ...................Editorial Assistant
Leigh Ann Teague ............Marketing Assistant
Amy Hensiek ..................Marketing Consultant
Anne Farbman .................Marketing Director
**Desc.:** Covers desktop publishing. Helps
readers create good-looking documents
and presentations. Focuses on projects,
with step-by-step instructions,
photos and illustrations.
**Readers:** Personal computer users who
are producing documents and
presentations, both in the work place
and the home office.

## TEXAS PRINTER
65466

120 St. Louis
Fort Worth, TX 76104
Telephone: (817) 332-6306
FAX: (817) 332-4990
Year Established: 1988
Pub. Frequency: q.
Page Size: standard
Subscrip. Rate: varies
Circulation: 4,000

Circulation Type: paid
**Owner(s):**
Branch-Smith, Inc.
120 St. Louis
Fort Worth, TX 76104
Ownership %: 100
**Editorial:**
Nolan Moore ...............................Editor
**Desc.:** Addresses major issues facing
printers.
**Readers:** Serves Texas printers.

## U & LC: UPPER & LOWERCASE
24422

866 Second Ave.
New York, NY 10017
Telephone: (212) 371-0699
FAX: (212) 752-4752
Year Established: 1974
Pub. Frequency: q.
Page Size: tabloid
Subscrip. Rate: $30/3 yrs.
Freelance Pay: varies
Circulation: 180,000
Circulation Type: controlled
**Owner(s):**
International Typeface Corporation
866 Second Ave.
New York, NY 10017
Telephone: (212) 371-0699
Ownership %: 100
**Management:**
Charles M. Wilhelm ...........................Publisher
**Editorial:**
Margaret Richardson ...............................Editor
Joyce Rutter Kaye ...................Managing Editor
Jane DiBucci ............Creative Services Director
**Desc.:** Articles on graphic and
communications art, typography and
design, and general interest features
interesting to a visually
sophisticated readership. some features
on new communications technologies.
some major trade news.
**Readers:** Graphic designers, art directors,
type directors, editors, graphic arts
educators and students.

## Group 204-Produce

## FRESH CUT
70367

2809-A Fruitvale Blvd.
Yakima, WA 98907
Telephone: (509) 248-2452
FAX: (509) 248-4056
Mailing Address:
  P.O. Box 1467
  Yakima, WA 98907-1467
Year Established: 1993
Pub. Frequency: 6/yr.
Page Size: standard
Subscrip. Rate: $15/yr. US; $30/yr.
Canada & Mexico; $45/yr. elsewhere
Materials: 01,02,05,06,15,16,20,21,28,29,
30,32,33
Print Process: web
Circulation: 5,984
Circulation Type: controlled
**Owner(s):**
D. Brent Clement
681 Ames Rd.
Selah, WA 98942
Telephone: (509) 697-3070
Ownership %: 50

J. Mike Stoker
4705 W. Power House Rd.
Yakima, WA 98908
Telephone: (509) 966-7731
Ownership %: 50
**Management:**
J. Mike Stoker ...........................Publisher
**Editorial:**
Ken Hodge ...............................Editor
Steve Call ............................Advertising

Lynn Schuchardt ...........................Advertising
Kathy Noble ...............................Production
**Desc.:** Fresh Cut magazine is targeted at
the $4 billion fresh-cut produce industry,
whose growth today is described as
"explosive." Published six times per
year, Fresh Cut is both a forum for the
industry and an educational tool, helping
end-users understand how to profit from
fresh-cut products.
**Deadline:** story-2 mos. prior to pub. date;
news-2 mos. prior; photo-2 mos. prior;
ads-1 mo. prior

## PACKER, THE
24430

7950 College Blvd.
Shawnee Msn, KS 66210
Telephone: (913) 451-2200
Mailing Address:
  P.O. Box 2939
  Shawnee Msn, KS 66201
Year Established: 1893
Pub. Frequency: w.
Page Size: broadsheet
Subscrip. Rate: $49/yr.
Circulation: 15,000
Circulation Type: paid
**Owner(s):**
Vance Publishing Corp.
P.O. Box 400
Lincolnshire, IL 60069
Telephone: (708) 634-2600
Ownership %: 100
**Management:**
James J. Staudt ...........................President
W. E. Coon ...........................Vice President
**Editorial:**
Bill O'Neill ...............................Editor
Gordon Billingsley ...................Managing Editor
Bill O'Neill ...................Associate Publisher
W. E. Coon ...................Publication Director
**Desc.:** Covers news of commercial
growers, packers, shippers, receivers,
distributors and retailers of fruits,
vegetables,
**Readers:** Vertical Produce Industry and
Allied Trades.

## PRODUCE NEWS, THE
24431

2185 Lemoine Ave.
Fort Lee, NJ 07024
Telephone: (201) 592-9100
FAX: (201) 592-0809
Year Established: 1897
Pub. Frequency: w.
Page Size: tabloid
Subscrip. Rate: $49/yr.
Circulation: 10,000
Circulation Type: paid
**Owner(s):**
ZIM-MER Trade Publications, Inc.
2185 Lemoine Ave.
Fort Lee, NJ 07024
Telephone: (201) 592-9100
Ownership %: 100
**Management:**
Jack Bricker ...........................Publisher
Harilyn Zimmerman ..........Advertising Manager
Dorothy McDermott ..........Circulation Manager
**Editorial:**
Gordon Hochberg ...........................Editor
**Desc.:** Weekly trade paper covering
growing, shipping, distributing & retailing
of fresh fruits and vegetables.
Departments include: In The Good Old
Days, Florida Citrus, Texas Trade
Topics, Western Perspective, Fresh
Marketing Trends, Calendar of Events,
In the News, The Retail View, Import
Update.
**Readers:** Dealers, shippers, packers,
growers, chain store buyers, terminal
market personnel, wholesalers, retailers.

## WESTERN GROWER & SHIPPER
24432

17620 Fitch St.
Irvine, CA 92714
Telephone: (714) 863-1000
FAX: (714) 863-9028
Mailing Address:
  P.O. Box 2130
  Newport Beach, CA 92658
Year Established: 1929
Pub. Frequency: m.
Page Size: standard
Subscrip. Rate: $18/yr.
Freelance Pay: $100-$400
Circulation: 6,000
Circulation Type: controlled
**Owner(s):**
Western Grower Service Corp.
P.O. Box 2130
Newport Beach, CA 92658
Telephone: (714) 863-1000
Ownership %: 100
**Editorial:**
Heather Flower ...........................Editor
**Desc.:** Business publication for the
Western Fresh Produce Industry. Carries
articles on prepackaging, crop outlook,
new developments, government
regulations. Material should be of
specialized interest to growers, packers,
shippers and handlers of fresh produce,
especially vegetables, melons and
strawberries, and fresh fruit and citrus.
Departments include: People &
Products, Western Growers Association
Activities, Fresh From the West (feature
story on various vegetable producing
districts), and Labor Column.
**Readers:** Growers, packers, shippers of
fresh fruits, citrus and vegetables, plus
food brokers and allied industries.

## Group 206-Product Design & Engineering

## BEST PRACTICES REPORT
61561

1050 Commonwealth Ave.
Boston, MA 02215
Telephone: (617) 232-8080
Year Established: 1989
Pub. Frequency: m.
Page Size: standard
Subscrip. Rate: $197/yr.
Materials: 01,02,05,17
**Owner(s):**
Stewart Maws of Management Round
  Table
824 Boylston St.
Chestnut Hill, MA 02167
Telephone: (617) 282-8080
Ownership %: 100
**Management:**
Jacquelin Cooper ...........................Manager
**Editorial:**
Bruce Hoard Editor ...............................Editor
**Readers:** Engineers

## CHILD DEVELOPMENT
64726

5720 S. Woodlawn Ave.
Chicago, IL 60637
Telephone: (312) 753-3347
FAX: (312) 753-0811
Year Established: 1930
Pub. Frequency: bi-m.
Subscrip. Rate: $126/yr.
Circulation: 8,600
Circulation Type: paid
**Owner(s):**
Society Research in Child Development,
  Inc.
5720 S. Woodlawn Ave.
Chicago, IL 60637
Telephone: (312) 702-7470

**Materials Accepted/Included:** 01-Business news 02-By-line articles 03-Fashion news 04-Food news 05-Freelance copy 06-Letters to editor 07-Real estate news 08-Sports news 09-Travel news
10-Book rev. 11-Movie rev. 12-Music rev. 13-TV rev. 14-Theater rev. 15-Coming events 16-Obituaries 17-Question & answer 18-Social announcements 19-Artwork 20-Cartoons 21-Photos 22-TV listings
23-Audio rec. 24-Video rec. 25-Books 26-Films/film clips 27-Personnel news 28-Press releases 29-New product news/photos 30-Trade lit. 31-Contracts awarded 32-Display adv. 33-Classified adv.

4-297

**Editorial:**
Susan C. Somerville ..................Editor
**Desc.:** Child Development is a publication outlet for reports of empirical research, theoretical articles and reviews that have theoretical implications for developmental research. As a publication of an interdisciplinary organization, contributions from all disciplines concerned with developmental processes are welcome.
**Readers:** Scientists & Researchers in the Developmental Field.

24436

**DESIGNFAX**
29100 Aurora Rd., Ste. 200
Solon, OH 44139
Telephone: (216) 248-1125
FAX: (216) 686-0214
Year Established: 1979
Pub. Frequency: m.
Page Size: oversize
Subscrip. Rate: $54/yr.
Freelance Pay: negotiable
Circulation: 110,000
Circulation Type: controlled
**Owner(s):**
Huebcore Communications, Inc.
29100 Aurura Rd., Ste. 200
Solon, OH 44139
Telephone: (216) 248-1125
Ownership %: 100
**Management:**
Thomas J. Corcoran ..................President
Thomas J. Corcoran ..................Publisher
Dick Benson ..................Circulation Manager
Fred C. Rodgers ..................Sales Manager
**Editorial:**
Mike Malley ..................Editor in Chief
Mario Cavlovicak ..................Art Director
Georgene Retych ..................Production Director
**Desc.:** Written for design engineers, engineering management and research and development personnel in the original equipment market. Editorial ranges across the total design field and includes coverage of developments in mechanical power transmission, electronics, computers, CAD/CAM, fluid power and materials. Balanced editorial package includes feature articles, news and other magazine departments that provide the latest information on design and management practices as well as new product developments.

23996

**DESIGN NEWS**
275 Washington St.
Newton, MA 02158-1630
Telephone: (617) 964-3030
FAX: (617) 558-4402
Year Established: 1946
Pub. Frequency: s-m.
Page Size: standard
Subscrip. Rate: $94.95/yr. US; $149.75/yr. Canada; $139.95/yr. Mexico; $179.95/yr. elsewhere
Print Process: offset
Circulation: 170,193
Circulation Type: controlled
**Owner(s):**
Cahners Publishing Co.
275 Washington St.
Newton, MA 02158-1630
Telephone: (617) 964-3030
Ownership %: 100
**Bureau(s):**
Design News
1350 E. Touhy Ave.
Des Plaines, IL 60018
Telephone: (708) 635-8800
Contact: Brian J. Hogan, Editor

Design News
429 Fourth Ave.
Pittsburgh, PA 15219
Telephone: (412) 281-8828
Contact: E. J. Stefanides, Editor

Design News
1101 W. Lake St., Ste. 306
Oak Park, IL 60301
Telephone: (708) 386-2777
Contact: Brian Hogan, Editor

Design News
12233 W. Olympic Blvd.
Los Angeles, CA 90064
Telephone: (310) 826-5818
Contact: Joseph K. Corrado

Design News
205 E. 42nd St.
New York, NY 10017
Telephone: (212) 949-4400
Contact: Frank Yeaple, Editor

Design News
3031 Tisch Way
San Jose, CA 95128
Telephone: (408) 243-8838
Contact: Joseph K. Corrado, Editor
**Management:**
Saul Goldweitz ..................President
Steve A. Thompson ..................Publisher
**Editorial:**
Gary Chamberlain ..................Senior Editor
David J. Bak ..................Editor
Lawrence D. Maloney ..................Editor
L. G. Soderholm ..................Editorial Director
F. William Tortolane ..................Associate Editor
**Desc.:** World-wide coverage of design development for product and machinery designers in all branches of American industries. Editorial coverage includes: Engineering News (news of design developments and processes), Usable Design Ideas for Design Engineers in OEM Industries, Special Reports (feature reports on new methods and components, processes and design methods and procedures), New Product Announcements.
**Readers:** Engineers in design and development in the original equipment market.
**Deadline:** story-2 mos. prior to pub. date

56424

**EXPERIMENTAL TECHNIQUES**
7 School St.
Bethel, CT 06801
Telephone: (203) 790-6373
Year Established: 1980
Pub. Frequency: bi-m.
Page Size: standard
Subscrip. Rate: $88/yr. US; $100/yr. foreign
Materials: 29,32
Print Process: offset
Circulation: 4,000
Circulation Type: controlled & paid
**Owner(s):**
Society for Experimental Mech.
7 School St.
Bethel, CT 06801
Telephone: (203) 790-6373
Ownership %: 100
**Management:**
G.L. Cloud ..................President
K.A. Galione ..................Publisher
Joni Jones ..................Advertising Manager
**Editorial:**
Patricia K. Brothers ..................Editor
**Desc.:** Experimental techniques publishes how to do it articles on obtaining valid results in experimental mechanics, as well as new- product announcements, book reviews, and abstract index.

**Readers:** Scientists and mechanical engineers working in experimental mechanics.

65629

**FENESTRATION**
310 Madison Ave.
New York, NY 10017
Telephone: (212) 682-7681
FAX: (212) 697-8331
Year Established: 1987
Pub. Frequency: 7/yr.
Page Size: standard
Subscrip. Rate: $15/yr.
Circulation: 11,000
Circulation Type: controlled & paid
**Owner(s):**
Ashlee Publishing Co., Inc.
310 Madison Ave.
New York, NY 10017
Telephone: (212) 682-7681
Ownership %: 100
**Management:**
B. Lee ..................Chairman of Board
S.J. Berardino ..................President
Oscar S. Glasberg ..................Vice President
Charles E. Keil ..................Publisher
Frida Garcia ..................Circulation Manager
Regina Gelman ..................Office Manager
Hazel Cristan ..................Sales Manager
**Editorial:**
John G. Swanson ..................Editor
Charles B. Cumpston ..................Editorial Director
Bill Maciolek ..................Art Director
Lowell E. Perrine ..................Associate Editor
R. Gelman ..................Secretary & Treasurer
**Desc.:** Serves top management and manufacturing management of companies producing and distributing windows, doors, entrance ways, skylights, greenhouses, solar/sunroofs, and other related products.
**Readers:** Presidents, vice presidents, sales managers, controlling executives, plant manufacturing executives, and supervisors in the construction/remodeling industry.

24438

**INTERNATIONAL DESIGN**
440 Park Ave., S., 14th Fl.
New York, NY 10016
Telephone: (212) 447-1400
FAX: (212) 447-5231
Year Established: 1954
Pub. Frequency: bi-m.
Page Size: standard
Subscrip. Rate: $40/yr.
Freelance Pay: $25-$600/article
Circulation: 19,500
Circulation Type: paid
**Owner(s):**
Design Magazines, Ltd.
440 Park Ave. S., 14th Fl.
New York, NY 10016
Ownership %: 100
**Management:**
Suzanne Haber ..................Advertising Manager
Erin O'Mara ..................Circulation Manager
**Editorial:**
Chee Pearlman ..................Editor
**Desc.:** Every issue includes features on materials, design management, new technologies and components, case studies on product development, design trends, and aesthetics. Also includes a product portfolio, new sources, news of people and events, book reviews.
**Readers:** Industrial designers, architects, graphic designers, artists, exhibit & environmental designers.

24439

**MACHINE DESIGN**
1100 Superior Ave.
Cleveland, OH 44114
Telephone: (216) 696-7000
FAX: (216) 621-8469
Year Established: 1929
Pub. Frequency: bi-w.
Page Size: standard
Subscrip. Rate: $100/yr. US; $160/yr. foreign
Materials: 02,06,27,28,29,30,31,32,33
Freelance Pay: varies
Print Process: web offset
Circulation: 191,000
Circulation Type: controlled & paid
**Owner(s):**
Penton Publishing Co.
1100 Superior Ave.
Cleveland, OH 44114
Telephone: (216) 696-7000
Ownership %: 100
**Management:**
Joseph DiFranco ..................Publisher
Bonnie Velikonya ..................Advertising Manager
**Editorial:**
Leland E. Teschler ..................Executive Editor
Ronald Khol ..................Editor
Randall Rubenking ..................Art Editor
Ann Halligan ..................Art Editor
**Desc.:** Technical articles written for design engineers. Covers product design, materials specification, design analysis, machine components, engineering management. Departments include: Scanning the Field For Ideas, Computer Center, Design International, Helpful Literature, New Parts and Materials, Engineering News.
**Readers:** Engineers responsible for product design.

67186

**MOBILE PRODUCT NEWS**
7811 Montrose Rd.
Potomac, MD 20854
Telephone: (301) 340-2100
FAX: (301) 340-0542
Year Established: 1984
Pub. Frequency: m.
Page Size: tabloid
Subscrip. Rate: free to qualified personnel
Circulation: 23,000
Circulation Type: controlled
**Owner(s):**
Phillips Publishing, Inc.
7811 Montrose Rd.
Potomac, MD 20854
Telephone: (301) 340-2100
**Management:**
Tom Phillips ..................President
David Durham ..................Publisher
Tony Carlson ..................Assistant Manager
**Editorial:**
Lisa Portner ..................Editor
Barbara Bink ..................Managing Editor
Betsy Bosnell ..................Marketing Director
**Desc.:** Includes new products for the cellular, paging and two-way radio industries.
**Readers:** Top and senior-level management.

56423

**MODAL ANALYSIS: THE INTERNATIONAL JOURNAL OF ANALYTICAL & EXPERIMENTAL MODAL ANALYSIS**
7 School St.
Bethel, CT 06801-9001
Telephone: (203) 790-6373
FAX: (203) 790-4472
Year Established: 1986
Pub. Frequency: q.

Page Size: standard
Subscrip. Rate: $75/yr.
Print Process: offset
Circulation: 600
Circulation Type: paid
**Owner(s)**
Society for Experimental Mechanics
7 School St.
Bethel, CT 06801
Telephone: (203) 790-6373
Ownership %: 100
**Management:**
Kenneth A. Galione ...........................Publisher
Kristin L. MacDonald .........Associate Publisher
**Editorial:**
Patricia K. Brothers ...............................Editor
**Desc.:** Publishes original peer-reviewed papers documenting the latest developments in vibrations and dynamic research.

24443

## PRODUCT DESIGN & DEVELOPMENT
201 King of Prussia Rd.
Radnor, PA 19089
Telephone: (215) 964-4350
FAX: (215) 964-4947
Mailing Address:
  Chilton Way
  Radnor, PA 19087
Year Established: 1946
Pub. Frequency: m.
Page Size: tabloid
Subscrip. Rate: $35/yr.; $65/2 yrs.
Materials: 28,29,32,33
Print Process: web offset
Circulation: 162,078
Circulation Type: controlled
**Owner(s):**
Chilton Publications, Inc.
Chilton Way
Radnor, PA 19087
Telephone: (215) 964-4000
Ownership %: 100
**Management:**
Lee Hufnagel ...............................President
Scott R. Sward .............................Publisher
Jerry Clark .....................Circulation Manager
Arlene Falcone .................Production Manager
John Wintersteen ......................Sales Manager
**Editorial:**
Robert R. Bierwirth .............................Editor
Lisa Arrigo ............................Associate Editor
Barbara Hahn .....................Editorial Assistant
Kathleen M. Raum .................Marketing Director
**Desc.:** Covers news of new components and materials, new research and design equipment.
**Readers:** Designers, development engineers, executives.

## Group 208-Psychiatry & Psychology

58922

## AMERICAN ACADEMY OF CHILD & ADOLESCENT PSYCHIATRY
428 E. Preston St.
Baltimore, MD 21202
Telephone: (410) 528-4000
FAX: (410) 528-4312
Year Established: 1962
Pub. Frequency: bi-m.
Subscrip. Rate: $90/yr. individual; $165/yr. institution
Circulation: 7,450
Circulation Type: paid
**Owner(s):**
American Academy of Child Psychiatry
3615 Wisconsin Ave., N.W.
Washington, DC 20016
Ownership %: 100
**Management:**
Don Pfarr ...........................Advertising Manager

Alma Wills ...................................Manager
**Editorial:**
Melvin Lewis, M.D. .............................Editor
Claudia Brookes ..................Marketing Director

64998

## AMERICAN BEHAVIORAL SCIENTIST
2455 Teller Rd.
Thousand Oaks, CA 91320
Telephone: (805) 499-0721
FAX: (805) 499-0871
Year Established: 1957
Pub. Frequency: bi-m.
Page Size: standard
Subscrip. Rate: $60/yr. individual; $200/yr. institution
Circulation: 1,800
Circulation Type: paid
**Owner(s):**
Sage Publications, Inc.
2455 Teller Rd.
Thousand Oaks, CA 91320
**Desc.:** Contains writings by guest editors on emerging cross-disciplinary interests, research and problems in social sciences.
**Readers:** Academic communities.

24453

## AMERICAN JOURNAL OF PSYCHIATRY
1400 K St., N.W.
Washington, DC 20005
Telephone: (202) 682-6020
FAX: (202) 682-6016
Year Established: 1844
Pub. Frequency: m.
Page Size: standard
Subscrip. Rate: $60/yr. US; $90/yr. foreign; $80/yr. institutions
Circulation: 44,687
Circulation Type: paid
**Owner(s):**
American Psychiatric Association
1400 K St., N.W.
Washington, DC 20005
Telephone: (202) 682-6020
Ownership %: 100
**Management:**
Nancy Frey ......................Advertising Manager
**Editorial:**
Nancy C. Andreasen ...............................Editor
Sandra L. Patterson ................Managing Editor
**Desc.:** Publish articles on various aspects of mental health field, e.g., drug therapy, psychotherapy, diagnosis, forensic issues, economic issues, etc.
**Readers:** Psychiatrists, other mental health professionals.

24454

## AMERICAN JOURNAL OF PSYCHOLOGY
1325 S. Oak St., Rm. 124
Champaign, IL 61820-6903
Telephone: (217) 244-4682
FAX: (217) 244-8082
Mailing Address:
  603 E. Daniel St.
  Champaign, IL 61820
Year Established: 1887
Pub. Frequency: q.
Page Size: standard
Subscrip. Rate: $54/yr. institutions; $26/yr. individuals
Materials: 02,10,16,21,25,32
Circulation: 3,000
Circulation Type: paid
**Owner(s):**
University of Illinois Press
1325 S. Oak St.
Champaign, IL 61820-6903
Telephone: (217) 244-4682
FAX: (217) 244-8082
Ownership %: 100

**Management:**
Cat Warren ......................Advertising Manager
**Editorial:**
Donelson E. Dulany ....................Editor in Chief
Rand B. Evans ...................................Editor
Hilda M. Banks .......................Assistant Editor
Dominic W Massaro, ........Book Review Editor
Santa Cruz
Ann Lowry .............................Journals Manager
**Desc.:** Professional journal serving the field of psychology generally and experimental psychology in particular. The journal has 4 departments: Articles, AJP Forum, Book Reviews, Obituaries and History of Psychology.
**Readers:** Teaching and experimental psychologists.

24455

## AMERICAN PSYCHOLOGIST
750 First St., N.E.
Washington, DC 20002-4242
Telephone: (202) 336-5600
FAX: (202) 336-5568
Year Established: 1945
Pub. Frequency: m.
Page Size: standard
Subscrip. Rate: $131/yr. individuals; $262/yr. institutions
Circulation: 105,128
Circulation Type: paid
**Owner(s):**
American Psychological Association
750 First St., N.E.
Washington, DC 20002
Telephone: (202) 336-5600
Ownership %: 100
**Management:**
Jodi Ashcraft .....................Advertising Manager
**Editorial:**
Raymond Fowler ...............................Editor
Mary R. Dworkin ....................Chief Copy Editor
Lois Czapiewski ..................Production Director
Timothy Bentler ....................Production Editor
**Desc.:** Official journal of the American Psychological Association. Publishes articles on current issues in psychology as well as empirical, theoretical, and practical articles on broad aspects of psychology. Includes official papers and business proceedings of the APA, listings of officers, boards and committees, calendars of professional meetings, and announcements concerning the APA convention.
**Readers:** All members of the Association, educators and other individuals concerned with the behavioral aspects of psychology.

23735

## ARCHIVES OF GENERAL PSYCHIATRY
515 N. State St.
Chicago, IL 60610
Telephone: (312) 464-5000
FAX: (312) 464-2580
Year Established: 1919
Pub. Frequency: m.
Page Size: standard
Subscrip. Rate: $85/yr. in US; $120/yr. foreign
Circulation: 33,000
Circulation Type: controlled
**Owner(s):**
American Medical Association
515 N. State St.
Chicago, IL 60610
Ownership %: 100
**Management:**
Robert L. Kennett ...............................Publisher
John P. Cahill ....................Advertising Manager
**Editorial:**
Jack D. Barchas, M.D. ...........................Editor
Michael D. Springer ..........Associate Publisher

**Desc.:** Publishes clinically relevant peer-reviewed original articles dealing with psychiatry, focusing in particular on the biological origin of mental disorders and pharmaceutical therapy. The journal is well known for its publication of long-term, multicenter studies.
**Readers:** Psychiatrists and other physicians.

66473

## ARTS IN PSYCHOTHERAPY, THE
660 White Plains Rd.
Tarrytown, NY 10591-5153
Telephone: (914) 592-7700
FAX: (914) 333-2444
Year Established: 1973
Pub. Frequency: 5/yr.
Subscrip. Rate: $140/yr.
**Owner(s):**
Pergamon Press, Inc.
Journals Division
660 White Plains Rd.
Tarytown, NY 10591-5153
Telephone: (914) 524-9200
Ownership %: 100
**Editorial:**
Robert J. Landy ...............................Editor
**Desc.:** Innovative research in artistic inquiry and expression and its use in the treatment of mental disorders.

24456

## BEHAVIORAL & BRAIN SCIENCES
20 Nassau St.
Princeton, NJ 08542
Telephone: (609) 921-7771
FAX: (609) 921-7293
Year Established: 1978
Pub. Frequency: q.
Page Size: standard
Subscrip. Rate: $80/yr. individuals; $196/yr. institution
Materials: 02,10,32
Circulation: 3,000
Circulation Type: paid
**Owner(s):**
Cambridge University Press
40 W. 20th St.
New York, NY 10011
Telephone: (212) 924-3900
Ownership %: 100
**Management:**
James Alexander ..............Advertising Manager
**Editorial:**
Stevan Harnad ...............................Editor
Nancy Simon .........................Managing Editor
**Desc.:** An unusual quarterly journal providing critical interdisciplinary peer review and commentary on submitted articles in all areas of psychology, neuroscience, behavioral biology and cognitive science.
**Readers:** Individuals doing research in phychology, behavioral science and related subjects; university and college libraries.

54084

## BEHAVIORAL MEDICINE
1319 18th St., N.W.
Washington, DC 20036-1802
Telephone: (202) 296-6267
FAX: (202) 296-5149
Year Established: 1975
Pub. Frequency: q.
Page Size: standard
Subscrip. Rate: $45/yr. individuls US; $84/yr. institutions US; $94/yr. institutions foreign
Circulation: 735
Circulation Type: paid

**Materials Accepted/Included:** 01-Business news 02-By-line articles 03-Fashion news 04-Food news 05-Freelance copy 06-Letters to editor 07-Real estate news 08-Sports news 09-Travel news 10-Book rev. 11-Movie rev. 12-Music rev. 13-TV rev. 14-Theater rev. 15-Coming events 16-Obituaries 17-Question & answer 18-Social announcements 19-Artwork 20-Cartoons 21-Photos 22-TV listings 23-Audio rec. 24-Video rec. 25-Books 26-Films/film clips 27-Personnel news 28-Press releases 29-New product news/photos 30-Trade lit. 31-Contracts awarded 32-Display adv. 33-Classified adv.

4-299

**Owner(s):**
Heldref Publications
1319 18th St., N.W.
Washington, DC 20036-1802
Telephone: (202) 296-6267
Ownership %: 100
**Management:**
Walter E. Beach ....................Publisher
**Editorial:**
Martha Wedeman ........................Editor
Raymond M. Rallo ............Advertising Director
Catherine Welker ................Circulation Director
Kerri P. Kilbane ................Promotion Director
**Desc.:** Behavioral Medicine is an
interdisciplinary journal of particular
interest to physicians, psychologists,
nurses, educators, and all who are
concerned with behavioral and social
influences on mental and physical
health.
**Readers:** Physicians, Educators,
Psychologists, and Nurses

64936
**BEHAVIOR MODIFICATION**
2455 Teller Rd.
Thousand Oaks, CA 91320
Telephone: (805) 499-0721
FAX: (805) 499-0871
Year Established: 1976
Pub. Frequency: q.
Page Size: standard
Subscrip. Rate: $53/yr. individuals;
$155/yr. institutions
Circulation: 1,500
Circulation Type: paid
**Owner(s):**
Sage Publications, Inc.
2455 Teller Rd.
Thousand Oaks, CA 91320
Telephone: (805) 499-0721
Ownership %: 100
**Management:**
Cris Anderson ....................Circulation Manager
**Editorial:**
Michel Hersen ........................Editor
Alan S. Bellack ........................Editor
**Desc.:** Describes assessment and
modification techniques for problems in
psychiatric, clinical, educational, and
rehabilitational settings.
**Readers:** Academics

69577
**BIOLOGICAL PSYCHIATRY**
655 Ave. of the Americas
New York, NY 10010
Telephone: (212) 989-5800
FAX: (212) 633-3990
Year Established: 1969
Pub. Frequency: s-m.
Subscrip. Rate: $790/yr. institutions US;
$875/yr. foreign
**Owner(s):**
Elsevier Science Publishing Co., Inc.
655 Ave. of the Americas
New York, NY 10010
Telephone: (212) 989-5800
Ownership %: 100
**Desc.:** Covers the whole range of
psychiatric research interest. Edited by
the Society of Biological Psychiatry.

69083
**CALIFORNIA THERAPIST, THE**
7901 Raytheon Rd.
San Diego, CA 92111-1606
Telephone: (619) 292-2638
FAX: (619) 292-2666
Year Established: 1989
Pub. Frequency: bi-m.
Page Size: standard
Subscrip. Rate: $24/yr.
Materials: 06,10
Circulation: 25,000
Circulation Type: paid

**Owner(s):**
California Assn. of Marriage & Family
Therapists
3465 Camino del Rio S., #350
San Diego, CA 92108
Telephone: (619) 280-0505
Ownership %: 100
**Editorial:**
Mary Riemersma ........................Editor
**Readers:** Licensed marriage, family and
child counselors in California.
**Deadline:** story-10th of mo. prior to pub.
date; news-10th of mo. prior; photo-10th
of mo. prior; ads-10th of mo. prior

24457
**CLINICAL PSYCHIATRY NEWS**
12230 Wilkins Ave.
Rockville, MD 20852
Telephone: (301) 816-8772
Year Established: 1973
Pub. Frequency: m.
Page Size: tabloid
Subscrip. Rate: $60/yr.
Circulation: 31,200
Circulation Type: controlled
**Owner(s):**
Capital Cities Communications, Inc.
7 E. 12th St.
New York, NY 10003
Ownership %: 100
**Management:**
Tom Fowler ........................Publisher
**Editorial:**
Richard Camer ........................Editor
**Desc.:** A specialty tabloid newspaper
bringing psychiatrists the latest clinical
developments and research findings via
coverage of medical meetings and
interviews with researchers. We also
cover socioeconomic news as it relates
to the psychiatrist's practice, and
provide opinion and commentary.
**Readers:** Psychiatrists, child psychiatrists
in patient care, and residents in those
specialties.

69084
**CLINICAL PSYCHOLOGIST**
Yeshiwa University, Mazer Bldg.
1300 Morris Ave.
Bronx, NY 10461
Year Established: 1946
Pub. Frequency: 4/yr.
Subscrip. Rate: membership
Circulation: 6,000
Circulation Type: paid
**Owner(s):**
American Psychological Association
P.O. Box 22727
Oklahoma City, OK 73123-1727
Telephone: (405) 721-2792
Ownership %: 100
**Editorial:**
Ron Blount ........................Editor

24458
**CONTEMPORARY PSYCHOLOGY:
A JOURNAL OF REVIEWS**
205 Spence Laboratories
Iowa City, IA 52242
Mailing Address:
P.O. Box 91700
Washington, DC 20090-1700
Year Established: 1955
Pub. Frequency: m.
Page Size: standard
Subscrip. Rate: $50/yr. US; $59/yr. foreign
Circulation: 7,994
Circulation Type: controlled
**Owner(s):**
American Psychological Association
750 First St., N.E.
Washington, DC 20002
Telephone: (202) 336-5500
Ownership %: 100

**Management:**
Lancaster Press ........................Publisher
Jodi Ashcroft ........................Advertising Manager
Jodi Ashcroft ........................Promotion Manager
**Editorial:**
Dr. John Harvey ........................Editor
Elizabeth Altmaier ........................Associate Editor
Peter Nathan ........................Associate Editor
Betsy Showalter ........................Production Editor
**Desc.:** A journal devoted primarily to
reviews of psychological books, films,
and other media, and a letters-to-the-
editor department.
**Readers:** Psychology faculty, professional
psychologists.

64980
**COUNSELING PSYCHOLOGIST,
THE**
2455 Teller Rd.
Thousand Oaks, CA 91320
Telephone: (805) 499-0721
FAX: (805) 499-0871
Year Established: 1972
Pub. Frequency: q.
Page Size: pocket
Subscrip. Rate: $48/yr. individuals;
$142/yr. institutions
Circulation: 5,400
Circulation Type: paid
**Owner(s):**
Sage Publications, Inc.
2455 Teller Rd.
Thousand Oaks, CA 91320
Telephone: (805) 499-0721
Ownership %: 100
**Editorial:**
Gerald L. Stone ........................Editor
**Desc.:** Presents timely coverage especially
in new or developing areas of practice
and research, which are of immediate
interest to counseling
psychologists. Defines the field and
communicates that identity to the
profession as well as to those in other
disciplines.
**Readers:** Counseling psychologists and
professionals of related disciplines.

65060
**CRIMINAL JUSTICE & BEHAVIOR**
2455 Teller Rd.
Thousand Oaks, CA 91320
Telephone: (805) 499-0721
FAX: (805) 499-0871
Year Established: 1973
Pub. Frequency: q.
Page Size: standard
Subscrip. Rate: $47/yr. individual; $140/yr.
institution
Circulation: 1,950
Circulation Type: paid
**Owner(s):**
Sage Publications, Inc.
2455 Teller Rd.
Thousand Oaks, CA 91320
Telephone: (805) 499-0721
Ownership %: 100
**Editorial:**
Allen K. Hess ........................Editor
Cris Anderson ............Circulation Administrator
**Desc.:** Official publication of the AACP.
Provides a means of communication
among mental health professionals,
behavioral scientists, researchers, and
practitioners in the area of criminal
justice.

67668
**DEVELOPMENT PSYCHOLOGY**
750 First St., N.E.
Washington, DC 20002
Telephone: (202) 336-5500
Year Established: 1969
Pub. Frequency: bi-m.

Page Size: standard
Subscrip. Rate: $110/yr. nonmembers;
$45/yr. members; $258/yr. foreign;
$222/yr. institutions
Circulation: 4,800
Circulation Type: paid
**Owner(s):**
American Psychological Association
750 First St., N.E.
Washington, DC 20002
Telephone: (202) 336-5500
Ownership %: 100
**Management:**
Jodi Ashcraft ....................Advertising Manager
**Editorial:**
Carolyn Zahn-Waxler ........................Editor
**Desc.:** Empirical contributions that
advance knowledge and theory about
human psychological growth and
development from infancy to old age.

69547
**GENERAL HOSPITAL PSYCHIATRY**
655 Ave. of the Americas
New York, NY 10010
Telephone: (212) 989-5800
FAX: (212) 633-3990
Year Established: 1979
Pub. Frequency: 6/yr.
Subscrip. Rate: $234/yr. institutions US;
$264/yr. foreign
**Owner(s):**
Elsevier Science Publishing Co., Inc.
655 Ave. of the Americas
New York, NY 10010
Telephone: (212) 989-5800
Ownership %: 100
**Editorial:**
Don R. Lipsitt ........................Editor
**Desc.:** Emphasizes a biopsychosocial
approach to illness and health, and
provides a forum for
communication among professionals
with clinical, academic and research
interests in psychiatry.

54088
**GENETIC, SOCIAL & GENERAL
PSYCHOLOGY MONOGRAPHS**
1319 18th St., N.W.
Washington, DC 20036-1802
Telephone: (202) 296-6267
FAX: (202) 296-5149
Year Established: 1891
Pub. Frequency: q.
Page Size: pocket
Subscrip. Rate: $92/yr. US; $102/yr.
foreign
Circulation: 528
Circulation Type: paid
**Owner(s):**
Heldref Publications
1319 Eighteenth St., N.W.
Washington, DC 20036-1802
Telephone: (202) 296-6267
**Management:**
Walter E. Beach ........................Publisher
Raymond M. Rallo ............Advertising Manager
Catherine Welker ............Circulation Manager
Kerri P. Kilbane ................Promotion Manager
**Editorial:**
Doris Chalfin ........................Editor
**Desc.:** Publishes articles of monograph
length that make an outstanding
contribution to the field of psychology.

69591
**INTERNATIONAL JOURNAL OF
PSYCHIATRY IN MEDICINE**
26 Austin Ave.
Amityville, NY 11701
Telephone: (516) 691-1270
FAX: (516) 691-1770
Mailing Address:
P.O. Box 337
Amityville, NY 11701
Year Established: 1970

Pub. Frequency: q.
Subscrip. Rate: $40/yr. individuals;
$112/yr. institutions
**Owner(s):**
Baywood Publishing Co., Inc.
26 Austin Ave.
Amityville, NY 11701
Telephone: (516) 691-1270
FAX: (516) 691-1770
Ownership %: 100
**Management:**
Stuart Cohen ...........................President
Stuart Cohen ...........................Publisher
**Editorial:**
Dr. Daniel S.P. Schubert .........................Editor
**Desc.:** Contains articles that apply the
methods of psychiatry and psychology to
the further understanding of psychiatric
disorders.

57282

## JOURNAL OF APPLIED GERONTOLOGY
2455 Teller Rd.
Thousand Oaks, CA 91320
Telephone: (805) 499-0721
FAX: (805) 499-0871
Year Established: 1982
Pub. Frequency: q.
Page Size: standard
Subscrip. Rate: $49/yr. individuals;
$134/yr. institutions
Circulation: 1,650
Circulation Type: paid
**Owner(s):**
Sage Publications, Inc.
2455 Teller Rd.
Thousand Oaks, CA 91320
Telephone: (805) 499-0721
Ownership %: 100
**Editorial:**
William J. McAuley ...........................Editor
**Desc.:** A comprehensive forum devoted to
practice and policy research in the field
of aging. International in scope.
**Readers:** Academics, practitioners,
students, professionals.

67667

## JOURNAL OF APPLIED PSYCHOLOGY
750 First St., N.E.
Washington, DC 20002-4242
Telephone: (202) 336-5500
FAX: (202) 336-5568
Year Established: 1917
Pub. Frequency: bi-m.
Page Size: standard
Subscrip. Rate: $111/yr. non-members;
$45/yr. members; $222/yr. institutions
Circulation: 5,500
Circulation Type: paid
**Owner(s):**
American Psychological Association
750 First St., N.E.
Washington, DC 20002-4242
Telephone: (202) 336-5500
Ownership %: 100
**Management:**
Jodi Ashcraft ...................Advertising Manager
**Editorial:**
Neal Schmitt ...........................Editor
**Desc.:** Research on applications of
psychology in work settings such as
industry, correction systems,
government, and educational institutions.

23840

## JOURNAL OF CLINICAL PSYCHIATRY, THE
785 Crossover Ln., Ste. 209
Memphis, TN 38117
Telephone: (901) 682-1001
FAX: (901) 682-6992
Mailing Address:
P.O. Box 240008
Memphis, TN 38124

Year Established: 1940
Pub. Frequency: m.
Page Size: standard
Subscrip. Rate: $66/yr. US; $110/yr.
foreign; $40/yr. student
Circulation: 32,000
Circulation Type: controlled
**Owner(s):**
Physicians Postgraduate Press, Inc.
P.O. Box 240008
Memphis, TN 38124
Telephone: (901) 682-1001
Ownership %: 100
**Management:**
John Shelton, MD ...........................President
John S. Shelton ...............Advertising Manager
**Editorial:**
Alan J. Gelenberg, MD ...............Editor in Chief
**Desc.:** Medical journal
**Readers:** Psychiatrists and neurologists.

64993

## JOURNAL OF CONFLICT RESOLUTION
2455 Teller Rd.
Thousand Oaks, CA 91320
Telephone: (805) 499-0721
FAX: (805) 499-0871
Year Established: 1957
Pub. Frequency: q.
Page Size: standard
Subscrip. Rate: $56/yr. individuals;
$172/yr. institutions
Circulation: 2,350
Circulation Type: paid
**Owner(s):**
Sage Publications, Inc.
2455 Teller Rd.
Thousand Oaks, CA 91320
Telephone: (805) 499-0721
Ownership %: 100
**Editorial:**
Bruce M. Russett ...........................Editor
**Desc.:** Draws from interdisciplinary sources
in its focus on the analysis of causes,
prevention, and solution of international,
domestic, and interpersonal conflicts.
**Readers:** Academics.

66554

## JOURNAL OF CONSULTING & CLINICAL PSYCHOLOGY
750 First St., N.E.
Washington, DC 20002
Telephone: (202) 336-5500
FAX: (202) 336-5568
Year Established: 1968
Pub. Frequency: bi-m.
Page Size: standard
Subscrip. Rate: $50/yr. members; $125/yr.
non-members; $143/yr. foreign
Print Process: offset
Circulation: 10,300
Circulation Type: paid
**Owner(s):**
American Psychological Association
750 First St., N.E.
Washington, DC 20002
Telephone: (202) 336-5500
Ownership %: 100
**Management:**
Jodi Ashcraft ...................Advertising Manager
Juanita Broadie ...............Circulation Manager
**Editorial:**
Larry Beutler ...........................Editor
**Desc.:** Research on techniques of
diagnosis & treatment in disordered
behavior as well as studies of
populations of clinical interests.

69085

## JOURNAL OF COUNSELING PSYCHOLOGY
750 First St., N.E.
Washington, DC 20002
Telephone: (202) 336-5600
FAX: (202) 336-5568

Year Established: 1954
Pub. Frequency: q.
Subscrip. Rate: $65/yr. non-members;
$26/yr. members; $130/yr. institutions
Circulation: 7100
Circulation Type: paid
**Owner(s):**
American Psychological Association
750 First St., N.E.
Washington, DC 20002-4242
Telephone: (202) 336-5600
Ownership %: 100
**Editorial:**
Lenore W. Harmon ...........................Editor
**Desc.:** Empirical studies about counseling
processes and interventions, theoretical
articles about counseling, and studies
dealing with evaluation of counseling
applications and programs.

64995

## JOURNAL OF CROSS-CULTURAL PSYCHOLOGY
2455 Teller Rd.
Thousand Oaks, CA 91320
Telephone: (805) 499-0721
FAX: (805) 499-0871
Year Established: 1970
Pub. Frequency: q.
Page Size: standard
Subscrip. Rate: $50/yr. individuals;
$142/yr. institutions
Circulation: 2,350
Circulation Type: paid
**Owner(s):**
Sage Publications, Inc.
2455 Teller Rd.
Thousand Oaks, CA 91320
Telephone: (805) 499-0721
**Editorial:**
Walter J. Lonner ...........................Senior Editor
**Desc.:** Presents behavioral and social
research concentrating on psychological
phenomena as differentially conditioned
by culture, and on the individual as
a member of the cultural group.
**Readers:** Academic communities.

64997

## JOURNAL OF FAMILY PSYCHOLOGY
750 First St., N.E.
Washington, DC 20002-4242
Telephone: (202) 336-5600
FAX: (202) 336-5568
Year Established: 1987
Pub. Frequency: q.
Page Size: standard
Subscrip. Rate: $40/yr. individuals; $80/yr.
institutions
Circulation: 2,000
Circulation Type: paid
**Owner(s):**
American Psychological Association
750 First St., N.E.
Washington, DC 20002-4242
Telephone: (202) 336-5600
Ownership %: 100
**Editorial:**
Ronald F. Levant, EdD ...........................Editor
**Desc.:** Enhances theory, research, and
clinical practice in family psychology and
deals with: family and marital theory and
concepts; research and evaluation;
therapeutic frame works and methods;
training supervision; policies and legal
matters concerning the family and
marriage.
**Readers:** Academics.

53935

## JOURNAL OF GENERAL PSYCHOLOGY, THE
1319 18th St., N.W.
Washington, DC 20036-1802
Telephone: (202) 296-6267
FAX: (202) 296-5149

Year Established: 1927
Pub. Frequency: q.
Page Size: pocket
Subscrip. Rate: $86/yr. US; $96/yr. foreign
Circulation: 1,181
Circulation Type: paid
**Owner(s):**
Heldref Publications
1319 18th St., N.W.
Washington, DC 20036-1802
Telephone: (202) 296-6267
Ownership %: 100
**Management:**
Walter E. Beach ...........................Publisher
Raymond M. Rallo ...............Advertising Manager
Catherine Welker ...............Circulation Manager
Kerri P. Kilbane ...............Promotion Manager
**Editorial:**
Laura Zaner ...........................Editor
George Geeva-ratne ...........................Editor
**Desc.:** Devoted to experimental,
physiological, and comparative
psychology. It publishes articles that
establish functional relationships, involve
a series of integrated studies, or further
the development of new theoretical
insights; replications, refinements, and
comments in brief are also published.
**Readers:** Professionals in the fields of
experimental physiological and
comparative psychology.

53937

## JOURNAL OF GENETIC PSYCHOLOGY, THE
1319 18th St., N.W.
Washington, DC 20036-1802
Telephone: (202) 296-6267
FAX: (202) 296-5149
Year Established: 1891
Pub. Frequency: q.
Page Size: pocket
Subscrip. Rate: $88/yr. US; $98/yr. foreign
Circulation: 1,122
Circulation Type: paid
**Owner(s):**
Heldref Publications
1319 18th St., N.W.
Washington, DC 20036-1802
Telephone: (202) 296-6267
Ownership %: 100
**Management:**
Walter E. Beach ...........................Publisher
Raymond M. Rallo ...........Advertising Manager
Catherine Welker ...............Advertising Manager
Kerri P. Kilbane ...............Promotion Manager
**Editorial:**
Elizabeth Bruce ...........................Editor
George Geeva-Ratne ...........................Editor
**Desc.:** Devoted to research and theory in
developmental and clinical psychology.
Articles deal with the biological as well
as the behavioral and social aspects of
those fields.
**Readers:** Professionals in the fields of
developmental and clinical psychology.

53938

## JOURNAL OF GROUP PSYCHOTHERAPY, PSYCHODRAMA & SOCIOMETRY
1319 18th St., N.W.
Washington, DC 20036-1802
Telephone: (202) 296-6267
FAX: (202) 296-5149
Year Established: 1947
Pub. Frequency: q.
Page Size: standard
Subscrip. Rate: $40/yr. individuals US;
$64/yr. institutions US; $74/yr.
institutions foreign
Circulation: 430
Circulation Type: paid

**Materials Accepted/Included:** 01-Business news 02-By-line articles 03-Fashion news 04-Food news 05-Freelance copy 06-Letters to editor 07-Real estate news 08-Sports news 09-Travel news
10-Book rev. 11-Movie rev. 12-Music rev. 13-TV rev. 14-Theater rev. 15-Coming events 16-Obituaries 17-Question & answer 18-Social announcements 19-Artwork 20-Cartoons 21-Photos 22-TV listings
23-Audio rec. 24-Video rec. 25-Books 26-Films/film clips 27-Personnel news 28-Press releases 29-New product news/photos 30-Trade lit. 31-Contracts awarded 32-Display adv. 33-Classified adv.

4-301

**Owner(s):**
Heldref Publications
1319 Eighteenth St., N.W.
Washington, DC 20036-1802
Telephone: (202) 296-6267
**Management:**
Walter E. Beach .........................Publisher
Raymond M. Rallo .............Advertising Manager
Martha Wedeman ...........Advertising Manager
Catherine Welker ...............Circulation Manager
Kerri P. Kilbane .................Promotion Manager
**Editorial:**
Helen Kress ...............................................Editor
**Desc.:** Published in cooperation with the
American Society of Group
Psychotherapy and Psychodrama, this
journal features articles on the
application of action methods to the
fields of psychotherapy, counseling and
education.
**Readers:** Professionals in the fields of
psychotherapy counseling and
education.

### JOURNAL OF HUMANISTIC PSYCHOLOGY
24460

2455 Teller Rd.
Thousand Oaks, CA 91320
Telephone: (805) 499-0721
FAX: (805) 499-0871
Year Established: 1961
Pub. Frequency: q.
Page Size: standard
Subscrip. Rate: $46/yr. individuals;
$136/yr. institutions
Materials: 32
Circulation: 3,000
Circulation Type: paid
**Owner(s):**
Association for Humanistic Psychology
325 Ninth St.
San Francisco, CA 94103
Telephone: (415) 626-2375
Ownership %: 100
**Editorial:**
Thomas Greening ................................Editor
**Desc.:** Official quarterly publication of the
Association for Humanistic Psychology
presents a wide range of articles of
interest to lay persons as well as
professionals in the fields of psychology,
philosophy, education, sociology, social
science, parapsychology and others.
Contains experiential reports, theoretical
papers and research studies all applying
humanistic psychology to contemporary
society. Topics range from self
actualization, the search for meaning,
psychosynthesis, to politics and
humanism, and group encounter. Photos
are only used as part of the biographical
description of authors. No publicity is
used but advertising is.
**Readers:** Primarily professionals in fields
of psychology.

### JOURNAL OF INTERPERSONAL VIOLENCE
64999

2455 Teller Rd.
Thousand Oaks, CA 91320
Telephone: (805) 499-0721
FAX: (805) 499-0871
Year Established: 1986
Pub. Frequency: q.
Page Size: standard
Subscrip. Rate: $45/yr. individuals;
$118/yr. institutions
Circulation: 6,250
Circulation Type: paid

**Owner(s):**
Sage Publications, Inc.
2455 Teller Rd.
Thousand Oaks, CA 91320
Telephone: (805) 499-0721
Ownership %: 100
**Editorial:**
Jon R. Conte .................................Editor
**Desc.:** Provides a forum for discussion of
the concerns and activities of
professionals and researchers working in
domestic violence, child sexual abuse,
rape and sexual assault, physical child
abuse, and violent crime.

### JOURNAL OF MOTOR BEHAVIOR
54080

1319 Eighteenth St., N.W.
Washington, DC 20036-1802
Telephone: (202) 296-6267
FAX: (202) 296-5149
Year Established: 1969
Pub. Frequency: q.
Page Size: standard
Subscrip. Rate: $45/yr. individuals US;
$86/yr. institutions US; $55/yr.
individuals foreign
Circulation: 1,113
Circulation Type: paid
**Owner(s):**
Heldref Publications
1319 Eighteenth St., N.W.
Washington, DC 20036-1802
Telephone: (202) 296-6267
**Management:**
Walter E. Beach .......................Publisher
**Editorial:**
Betty Adelman ............................Editor
Raymond M. Rallo .............Advertising Director
Catherine Welker ...............Circulation Director
Kerri P. Kilbane .................Promotion Director
**Desc.:** Devoted to an understanding of
motor behavior as it is most broadly
defined, this journal presents papers
from various perspectives and differing
levels of analysis. It encompasses all
areas of motor behavior including
psychology, kinesiology, neurophysiology
& biomechanics.
**Readers:** Professionals in the areas of
psychology, kinesiology, neurophysiology
& biomechanics.

### JOURNAL OF NERVOUS & MENTAL DISEASE, THE
24461

428 E. Preston St.
Baltimore, MD 21202
Telephone: (410) 528-4000
FAX: (410) 528-4312
Mailing Address:
70 Olmsted Green
Baltimore, MD 21210
Year Established: 1874
Pub. Frequency: m.
Page Size: standard
Subscrip. Rate: $98/yr. US;
$175/yr. institutions
Circulation: 2,250
Circulation Type: paid
**Owner(s):**
Williams & Wilkins Co
428 E. Preston St.
Baltimore, MD 21202
Telephone: (410) 528-4000
Ownership %: 100
**Editorial:**
Eugene M. Brody, M.D. ...........................Editor
**Desc.:** New ideas and equipment as well
as new drugs for those in the fields of
mental diseases.
**Readers:** Neurologists and psychiatrists.

### JOURNAL OF PARAPSYCHOLOGY
24462

402 N. Buchanan Blvd.
Durham, NC 27701
Telephone: (919) 688-8241
FAX: (919) 683-4338
Year Established: 1937
Pub. Frequency: q.
Page Size: standard
Subscrip. Rate: $30/yr. individuals; $45/yr.
institutions
Circulation: 900
Circulation Type: paid
**Owner(s):**
Parapsychology Press
402 N. Buchanan Blvd.
Durham, NC 27701
Telephone: (919) 688-8241
Ownership %: 100
**Management:**
Libby Blackley ......................Business Manager
**Editorial:**
K. R. Rao ......................................Editor
Phil A. Worthington .................Managing Editor
Patricia M. Spivey ...................Assistant Editor
Douglas Stokes ....................Consulting Editor
John Palmer ..........................Consulting Editor
Dorothy H. Pope ....................Editorial Advisor
Donald S. Burdick ...................Statistical Editor
**Desc.:** Papers deal with research in
extrasensory perception (clairvoyance,
telepathy, precognition) and
psychokinesis (the influence of mind
over matter). Departments include Book
Reviews, Correspondence, News,
Comments, and Abstracts of Related
Literature.
**Readers:** Research workers, students,
laymen, academics (professors,
lecturers, etc.)

### JOURNAL OF PERSONALITY
61003

Bright Leaf Sq., Ste. 18-B
805 W. Main St.
Durham, NC 27701
Telephone: (919) 687-3636
FAX: (919) 688-4574
Mailing Address:
P.O. Box 90660
Durham, NC 27708
Year Established: 1932
Pub. Frequency: q.
Page Size: standard
Subscrip. Rate: $44/yr. individuals; $88/yr.
institutions
Materials: 32
Circulation: 2,000
Circulation Type: paid
**Owner(s):**
Duke University Press
P.O. Box 90660
Durham, NC 27708
Telephone: (919) 687-3600
FAX: (919) 688-4574
Ownership %: 100
**Management:**
Patricia Thomas .................................Manager
**Editorial:**
Howard Tennen .........................................Editor

### JOURNAL OF PERSONALITY & SOCIAL PSYCHOLOGY
24463

750 First St., N.E.
Washington, DC 20002-4242
Telephone: (202) 336-5600
FAX: (202) 336-5568
Year Established: 1965
Pub. Frequency: m.
Page Size: standard
Subscrip. Rate: $249/yr. individuals;
$499/yr. institutions
Circulation: 5,748
Circulation Type: paid

**Owner(s):**
American Psychological Association
750 First St., N.E.
Washington, DC 20002-4242
Telephone: (202) 336-5600
Ownership %: 100
**Editorial:**
Abraham Tesser ...............................Editor
Norman Miller ...................................Editor
Russell Geen ....................................Editor
Susan Knapp ..........................Managing Editor
Keith Cooke ....................Production Director
**Desc.:** Main emphasis is scientific rather
than clinical and is concerned with basic
research and theory of man as a social
creature including the structure of
personality; psychodynamic processes in
normal populations; attitudes; motivation
and learning; social cognition;
interpersonal & group processes; and
personality.
**Readers:** Psychologists, sociologists.

### JOURNAL OF PSYCHOHISTORY, THE
24464

140 Riverside Dr.
New York, NY 10024-2605
Telephone: (212) 799-2294
Year Established: 1973
Pub. Frequency: q.
Page Size: standard
Subscrip. Rate: $48/yr. individual; $99/yr.
institution
Circulation: 6,000
Circulation Type: paid
**Owner(s):**
Association for Psychohistory, Inc.
140 Riverside Dr.
New York, NY 10024-2605
Telephone: (212) 799-2294
Ownership %: 100
**Management:**
Lloyd deMause ...............................Publisher
**Editorial:**
Lloyd deMause ....................................Editor
**Desc.:** Scholarly articles on childhood,
development, personalities and history
treated in a psychohistorical context,
book reviews and state of the art.
**Readers:** Psychologists, historians,
psychiatrists, scientists and others
concerned with the field.

### JOURNAL OF PSYCHOLOGY, THE
53939

1319 18th St., N.W.
Washington, DC 20036-1802
Telephone: (202) 296-6267
FAX: (202) 296-5149
Year Established: 1935
Pub. Frequency: bi-m.
Page Size: pocket
Subscrip. Rate: $95/yr. US; $107/yr.
foreign
Circulation: 1,454
Circulation Type: paid
**Owner(s):**
Heldref Publications
1319 18th St., N.W.
Washington, DC 20036
Telephone: (202) 296-6267
Ownership %: 100
**Editorial:**
Doris Chalfin ......................................Editor
**Desc.:** Publishes a variety of research and
theoretical articles in the field of
psychology, with emphasis on articles
that integrate divergent data and
theories, explore new avenues for
thinking and research or present
outrageous criticisms of the present
status of behavioral disciplines.
**Readers:** Professionals in the field of
psychology.

**Materials Accepted/Included:** 01-Business news 02-By-line articles 03-Fashion news 04-Food news 05-Freelance copy 06-Letters to editor 07-Real estate news 08-Sports news 09-Travel news 10-Book rev. 11-Movie rev. 12-Music rev. 13-TV rev. 14-Theater rev. 15-Coming events 16-Obituaries 17-Question & answer 18-Social announcements 19-Artwork 20-Cartoons 21-Photos 22-TV listings 23-Audio rec. 24-Video rec. 25-Books 26-Films/film clips 27-Personnel news 28-Press releases 29-New product news/photos 30-Trade lit. 31-Contracts awarded 32-Display adv. 33-Classified adv.

## JOURNAL OF SOCIAL PSYCHOLOGY, THE
53940

1319 18th St., N.W.
Washington, DC 20036-1802
Telephone: (202) 296-6267
FAX: (202) 296-5149
Year Established: 1929
Pub. Frequency: bi-m.
Page Size: pocket
Subscrip. Rate: $102/yr. US; $114/yr. foreign
Circulation: 2,115
Circulation Type: paid
**Owner(s):**
Heldref Publications
1319 18th St., N.W.
Washington, DC 20036-1802
Telephone: (202) 296-6267
Ownership %: 100
**Management:**
Walter E. Beach ........................Publisher
Raymond M. Rallo ............Advertising Manager
Catherine Welker ................Circulation Manager
Kerri P. Kilbane ................Promotion Manager
**Editorial:**
Marcie Kanakis .................................Editor
George Geeva-Ratne ..............................Editor
**Desc.:** Publishes experimental, empirical, and field studies of groups, cultural effects, cross-national problems, language, and ethnicity. It also publishes cross-cultural notes and briefly reported replications and refinements.
**Readers:** Professionals in the researching, experimental, empirical and field studies of groups, cultural effects and ethnicity.

## JOURNAL OF SPORT & EXERCISE PSYCHOLOGY (JSEP)
58612

1607 N. Market St.
Champaign, IL 61820
Telephone: (217) 351-5076
FAX: (217) 351-2674
Mailing Address:
   P.O. Box 5076
   Champaign, IL 61825
Year Established: 1979
Pub. Frequency: q.
Page Size: standard
Subscrip. Rate: $24/yr. students; $36/yr. individuals; $88/yr. institutions
Materials: 10,25,29
Print Process: offset
Circulation: 1,979
Circulation Type: paid
**Owner(s):**
Human Kinetics Publishers, Inc.
1607 N. Market St.
Champaign, IL 61820
Telephone: (217) 351-5076
FAX: (217) 351-2674
Ownership %: 100
**Management:**
Rainer Martens ..................................Publisher
Thomas Moone ..................................Manager
**Editorial:**
W. Jack Rejeski .................................Editor
Linda A. Bump ......................Journals Director
**Desc.:** The journal is designed to stimulate and communicate research and theory in all areas of sport and exercise psychology. Various psychological perspectives include personality, clinical, social, cognitive, motivational, and development psychology.
**Readers:** Members of the North American Society for the Psychology of Sport and Physical Activity; individual subscribers.

## JOURNAL OF SUBSTANCE ABUSE TREATMENT
66483

660 White Plains Rd.
Tarrytown, NY 10591-5153
Telephone: (914) 524-9200
FAX: (914) 333-2444
Year Established: 1984
Pub. Frequency: bi-m.
Page Size: standard
Subscrip. Rate: $110/yr. professionals; $235/yr. institutions
**Owner(s):**
Elsevier Science, Ltd.
The Boulevard, Langford Lane
Kidlington
 Oxford OX5 1GB, United Kingdom
Telephone: 44-865-843000
FAX:44-865-843010
Ownership %: 100
**Bureau(s):**
John Imhof, Ph.D.
North Shore Univ. Hospital
Cornell University Medical College
Manhasset, NY 11030
**Editorial:**
John Imhof ........................Editor in Chief
Christine Giaccone ......Senior Publishing Editor

## JOURNAL OF THE AMERICAN ACADEMY OF CHILD & ADOLESCENT PSYCHIATRY
55897

428 E. Preston St.
Baltimore, MD 21202
Telephone: (410) 528-4000
FAX: (410) 528-4312
Year Established: 1982
Pub. Frequency: bi-m.
Subscrip. Rate: $90/yr. individuals; $165 institutions
Circulation: 5,900
Circulation Type: paid
**Owner(s):**
American Academy of Child & Adolescent Psychiatry
**Editorial:**
John F. McDermott, Jr. .........................Editor
**Desc.:** Leading journal in child psychiatry publishes high quality original papers in psychiatric research and treatment of the child and adolescent.
**Readers:** Subscribers are child psychiatrists, including all members of the American Academy of Child & Adolescent Psychiatry.

## KNOWLEDGE: CREATION, DIFFUSION, UTILIZATION
65002

2455 Teller Rd.
Thousand Oaks, CA 91320
Telephone: (805) 499-0721
FAX: (805) 499-0871
Year Established: 1979
Pub. Frequency: q.
Page Size: standard
Subscrip. Rate: $51/yr. individual; $141/yr. institution
Circulation: 900
Circulation Type: paid
**Owner(s):**
Sage Publications, Inc.
2455 Teller Rd.
Thousand Oaks, CA 91320
Ownership %: 100
**Editorial:**
Prof. Marcel LaFollette ...........................Editor
**Desc.:** Provides a forum for researchers, policymakers, R & D managers, and practitioners engaged in the process of knowledge development, which includes processes of creation, diffusion, and utilization.
**Readers:** Academic communities.

## MERRILL-PALMER QUARTERLY: JOURNAL OF DEVELOPMENTAL PSYCHOLOGY
58748

5959 Woodward Ave.
Detroit, MI 48202
Telephone: (313) 577-6120
FAX: (313) 577-6131
Mailing Address:
   Dept. of Psychology
   71 W. Warren Ave.
   Detroit, MI 48202
Year Established: 1954
Pub. Frequency: q.
Page Size: standard
Subscrip. Rate: $38/yr. individuals; $72/yr. institutions; $24/yr. students
Materials: 10,32
Print Process: offset
Circulation: 1,300
Circulation Type: paid
**Owner(s):**
Wayne State University Press
5959 Woodward Ave.
Detroit, MI 48202
Telephone: (313) 577-6120
FAX: (313) 577-6131
Ownership %: 100
**Editorial:**
Carolyn Shantz .................................Editor
Keith Stanovich ........................Associate Editor
Nancy Eisengberg ....................Associate Editor
Edith Niemark ....................Book Review Editor
**Desc.:** One of the early important journals publishing empirical and theoretical papers in the areas of human development and family-child relationships.

## NEW IDEAS IN PSYCHOLOGY
58736

660 White Plains Rd.
Tarrytown, NY 10591-5153
Telephone: (914) 524-9200
FAX: (914) 333-2444
Year Established: 1983
Pub. Frequency: 3/yr.
Circulation: 1,500
Circulation Type: paid
**Owner(s):**
Pergamon Press, Inc.
660 White Plains Rd.
Tarrytown, NY 10591-5153
Telephone: (914) 524-9200
Ownership %: 100
**Management:**
Roger A. Dunn .................................President
Rosemarie Fazzolari .........Advertising Manager
**Editorial:**
Dr. J. M. Broughton .............................Editor
Pierre Moessinger .............................Editor
Richard Kitchener .............................Editor
**Desc.:** Provides a forum for theorizers striving to integrate the fragmented ideas and theories currently found in theoretical psychology.

## PERSONALITY & SOCIAL PSYCHOLOGY BULLETIN
65006

2455 Teller Rd.
Thousand Oaks, CA 91320
Telephone: (805) 499-0721
FAX: (805) 499-0871
Year Established: 1975
Pub. Frequency: q.
Page Size: standard
Subscrip. Rate: $64/yr. individuals; $230/yr. institutions
Circulation: 4,250
Circulation Type: paid

**Owner(s):**
Sage Publications, Inc.
2455 Teller Rd.
Thousand Oaks, CA 91320
Telephone: (805) 499-0721
Ownership %: 100
**Editorial:**
Arie Kruglanski ..................................Editor
**Desc.:** Publishes theoretical articles and empirical reports of research in all areas of personality and social psychology.
**Readers:** Academics

## PERSPECTIVES IN PSYCHIATRIC CARE
24511

1211 Locust St.
Philadelphia, PA 19107
Telephone: (215) 545-7222
Year Established: 1963
Pub. Frequency: q.
Page Size: standard
Subscrip. Rate: $40/yr. individuals; $52/yr. institutions
Circulation: 2,580
Circulation Type: paid
**Owner(s):**
Nursecom, Inc.
1211 Locust St.
Philadelphia, PA 19107
Telephone: (215) 545-7222
Ownership %: 100
**Management:**
Alice R. Clarke ..................................Publisher
Kelly Collins ......................Circulation Manager
**Editorial:**
Norine Kerr ......................................Editor
**Desc.:** Focuses on research, clinical practice, trends, and innovations in psychiatric and mental-health nursing.
**Readers:** Professionals involved in the psychiatric profession.

## PROFESSIONAL PSYCHOLOGY; RESEARCH & PRACTICE
69086

750 First St., N.E.
Washington, DC 20002-4242
Telephone: (202) 336-5600
FAX: (202) 336-5568
Year Established: 1969
Pub. Frequency: q.
Subscrip. Rate: $67/yr. nonmembers; $27/yr. members; $133/yr. institutions
Circulation: 5000
Circulation Type: paid
**Owner(s):**
American Psychological Association
750 First St., N.E.
Washington, DC 20002-4242
Telephone: (202) 336-5600
Ownership %: 100
**Editorial:**
Ursula Delworth ..................................Editor
**Desc.:** Articles on techniques and practices used in the application of psychology, including applications of research, standards of practice, interprofessional relations, delivery of services, and training.

## PSYCHIATRIC ANNALS
24466

6900 Grove Rd.
Thorofare, NJ 08086
Telephone: (609) 848-1000
FAX: (609) 853-5991
Year Established: 1971
Pub. Frequency: m.
Page Size: standard
Subscrip. Rate: $98/yr. individuals; $108/yr. institutions
Circulation: 30,000
Circulation Type: controlled

**Materials Accepted/Included:** 01-Business news 02-By-line articles 03-Fashion news 04-Food news 05-Freelance copy 06-Letters to editor 07-Real estate news 08-Sports news 09-Travel news 10-Book rev. 11-Movie rev. 12-Music rev. 13-TV rev. 14-Theater rev. 15-Coming events 16-Obituaries 17-Question & answer 18-Social announcements 19-Artwork 20-Cartoons 21-Photos 22-TV listings 23-Audio rec. 24-Video rec. 25-Books 26-Films/film clips 27-Personnel news 28-Press releases 29-New product news/photos 30-Trade lit. 31-Contracts awarded 32-Display adv. 33-Classified adv.

4-303

**Owner(s):**
Slack, Inc.
6900 Grove Rd.
Thorofare, NJ 08086
Telephone: (609) 848-1000
Ownership %: 100
**Management:**
Richard N. Roash .......................Publisher
Andrea Magdo ..................Advertising Manager
**Editorial:**
Dawn Duperre ......................Managing Editor
**Desc.:** Fills the need for a regular, balanced, and comprehensive analysis of the concepts and practices in every area of psychiatry. Presents the expertise of the leaders in American psychiatry as well as drawing on physicians of international reknown. The mode of presenting psychiatry in depth varies. Primarily, a vital aspect of psychiatry is treated intensively in a single symposium issue. A recognized expert, commissioned to function as guest editor, prepares the main paper, and other authors in the particular discipline contribute supplementary papers. A few issues during each year analyze various salient aspects of psychiatry in a series of articles.
**Readers:** Psychiatrists, child psychiatrists, neurologists, psychoanalysts.

69562

## PSYCHIATRIC FORUM
P.O. Box 202
Columbia, SC 29202
Telephone: (803) 734-7154
FAX: (803) 734-0791
Year Established: 1969
Pub. Frequency: s-a.
Subscrip. Rate: free
Circulation: 4,000
Circulation Type: controlled
**Owner(s):**
SC Dept. of Mental Health
Hall Psychiatric Institution
P.O. Box 202
Columbia, SC 29202
Telephone: (803) 734-7154
Ownership %: 100
**Editorial:**
Dr. Lucius C. Pressley ..............................Editor
**Desc.:** Original articles related to mental health.

24467

## PSYCHIATRIC NEWS
1400 K St., N.W.
Washington, DC 20005
Telephone: (202) 682-6210
FAX: (202) 682-6114
Year Established: 1966
Pub. Frequency: s-m.
Page Size: tabloid
Subscrip. Rate: $40/yr. US.; $52/yr. foreign
Freelance Pay: negotiable
Circulation: 38,000
Circulation Type: controlled
**Owner(s):**
American Psychiatric Association
1400 K St., N.W.
Washington, DC 20005
Telephone: (202) 682-6000
Ownership %: 100
**Bureau(s):**
American Psychiatric Assn.
2444 Morris Ave.
Union, NJ 07083
Telephone: (201) 964-3100
Contact: Ray Purkis, Advertising
**Management:**
Nancy Frey .......................Advertising Manager
**Editorial:**
Robert J. Campbell, M.D. ...........Editor in Chief
Herbert M. Gant .......................Exec. Editor

B. Alma Herndon .....................Assistant Editor
Richard Karel .........................Assistant Editor
Patrick Cody ..........................Assistant Editor
Kenneth Hausman ....................Assistant Editor
Herbert M. Gant .........................News Editor
Cathy Brown .........................Production Editor
**Desc.:** The newspaper of the American Psychiatric Association. Publishes news and features on all subjects of interest to psychiatrists, including, but not limited to, drug research and therapy, patient treatment methods, judicial and legislative activities affecting psychiatry and medicine, psychiatric politics, and the mental health field in general. Most articles are staff-written. By-lined news and features are accepted from freelance writers after query and approval by the editor. All material must be professionally oriented to MD's. Departments include: Book Reviews, Letters to the Editor, Briefly Noted (short takes on topics of interest), and Appointments and Awards.
**Readers:** 95% of readers are psychiatrists; remainder of subscribers are health professionals, libraries, hospitals, etc.

69567

## PSYCHIATRIC QUARTERLY
233 Spring St.
New York, NY 10013-1578
Telephone: (212) 620-8000
FAX: (212) 463-0742
Year Established: 1927
Pub. Frequency: q.
Subscrip. Rate: $195/yr. US; $230/yr. foreign
**Owner(s):**
Human Sciences Press, Inc.
233 Spring St.
New York, NY 10013-1578
Telephone: (212) 620-8000
Ownership %: 100
**Editorial:**
Dr. Stephen Rachlin ..............................Editor
**Desc.:** Includes articles on the social, clinical, administrative, legal, political and ethical aspects of mental illness care. Presents pertinent scientific and delivery system data.

68983

## PSYCHIATRIC TIMES
1924 E. Deere Ave.
Santa Ana, CA 92705-5723
Telephone: (800) 447-4474
FAX: (714) 250-0445
Year Established: 1985
Pub. Frequency: m.
Subscrip. Rate: $108/yr. US; $200/yr. foreign
Circulation: 39,545
Circulation Type: controlled
**Owner(s):**
CME, Inc.
1924 E. Deere Ave.
Santa Ana, CA 92705-5723
Telephone: (800) 447-4474
Ownership %: 100
**Editorial:**
Dr. John L. Schwartz ..............................Editor

24468

## PSYCHOANALYTIC QUARTERLY
175 Fifth Ave.
New York, NY 10010
Telephone: (212) 982-9358
Year Established: 1932
Pub. Frequency: q.
Page Size: standard
Subscrip. Rate: $22 newsstand; $75/yr.
Circulation: 3,300
Circulation Type: paid

**Owner(s):**
Psychoanalytic Quarterly, Inc.
175 Fifth Ave.
New York, NY 10010-7799
Telephone: (212) 982-9358
Ownership %: 100
**Editorial:**
Owen Renik, M.D. .........................Editor
Josephine Shapiro ..................Managing Editor
Martin A. Silverman, .........Book Review Editor
M.D.
**Desc.:** Original contributions in the field of theoretical, clinical, and applied psychoanalysis. Departments include: Book Reviews, Abstracts, Notes.
**Readers:** Psychoanalysts, psychiatrists, psychologists & public.

24469

## PSYCHOLOGICAL BULLETIN
750 First St., N.E.
Washington, DC 20002-4242
Telephone: (202) 336-5600
FAX: (202) 336-5568
Year Established: 1904
Pub. Frequency: bi-m.
Page Size: standard
Subscrip. Rate: $126/yr. individuals; $251/yr. institutions
Circulation: 7,469
**Owner(s):**
American Psychological Association
750 First St., N.E.
Washington, DC 20002-4242
Telephone: (202) 336-5600
Ownership %: 100
**Bureau(s):**
APA
1400 N. Uhle St.
Arlington, VA 22201
Telephone: (202) 833-3560
Contact: Virginia O'Leary, Assistant
Advertising Manager
**Management:**
Barny Strickland ..............................President
Jodi Asheraft ..................Advertising Manager
**Editorial:**
John C. Masters .........................Editor
Robert Sternberg .........................Editor
Ann Mahoney ..........................Managing Editor
Jennie Ruby ..........................Technical Editor
**Desc.:** Contains evaluative and integrative reviews and interpretations of substantive and methodological issues in scientific psychology. Reports of original research or original theoretical articles not accepted.
**Readers:** College and university libraries, members in Psychological Association.

69087

## PSYCHOLOGICAL PERSPECTIVES
10349 W. Pico Blvd.
Los Angeles, CA 09004-2694
Telephone: (310) 556-2290
FAX: (310) 556-1193
Year Established: 1970
Pub. Frequency: s-a.
Subscrip. Rate: $15/copy; $22/yr. US; $26/yr. foreign
Materials: 10,11,12,13,14,19,21
Circulation: 18000
Circulation Type: paid
**Owner(s):**
C.G. Jung Institute of Los Angeles
10349 W. Pico Blvd.
Los Angeles, CA 90064-2694
Telephone: (310) 556-1193
FAX: (310) 556-2290
Ownership %: 100
**Editorial:**
Ernest L. Rossi ..............................Editor
**Desc.:** Journal of Jungian thought featuring articles, interviews, poetry and fiction.

24470

## PSYCHOLOGICAL REVIEW
750 First St., N.E.
Washington, DC 20002-4242
Telephone: (202) 336-5600
FAX: (202) 336-5568
Year Established: 1894
Pub. Frequency: q.
Page Size: standard
Subscrip. Rate: $73/yr. individuals; $145/yr. institutions
Circulation: 6,969
Circulation Type: paid
**Owner(s):**
American Psychological Association
750 First St., N.E.
Washington, DC 20002-4242
Telephone: (202) 336-5600
Ownership %: 100
**Editorial:**
Walter Kintsch ..............................Editor
**Desc.:** Professional journal containing theoretical papers in the area of psychology.
**Readers:** Psychologists, staff of universities.

24472

## PSYCHOSOMATICS
1400 K St., N.W.
Washington, DC 20005
Telephone: (202) 682-6130
FAX: (202) 789-2648
Year Established: 1960
Pub. Frequency: bi-m.
Page Size: standard
Subscrip. Rate: $99/yr. individual; $149/yr. institutions
Materials: 32
Circulation: 2,500
Circulation Type: paid
**Owner(s):**
American Psychiatric Press, Inc.
1400 K St., N.W.
Washington, DC 20005
Telephone: (202) 682-6130
Ownership %: 100
**Management:**
Elizabeth Flynn ..................Advertising Manager
Richard Bardes ....................Business Manager
Beth Prester .....................Circulation Manager
Jacqueline C. Young .........Circulation Manager
Ronald E. McMillen ...............General Manager
**Editorial:**
John McDuffie ..........................Managing Editor
Claire Reinburg .........................Editorial Director
Jane Hoover Davenport .....Production Director

**Desc.:** Concerns itself with the interaction of the mind and body in disease, with emphasis on the role of psychiatry in the daily pratice of comprehensive medicine. Features timely, practical, peer-reviewed articles written by physicians and encompassing management of psychosomatic problems encountered in medical and psychiatric practice. Departments include: Review Articles, Original Research Reports, Perspectives, Book Reviews, Case Reports, Editorials, Letters to the Editor.
**Readers:** Psychiatrists and other physicians with an interest in medical psychiatry.

68986

## READINGS
330 W. Seventh Ave., 18th Fl.
New York, NY 10001
Telephone: (212) 564-5930
FAX: (212) 564-6180
Year Established: 1986
Pub. Frequency: q.
Subscrip. Rate: $25/yr. individuals; $35/yr. institutions
Materials: 10,32
Circulation: 11,000

Materials Accepted/Included: 01-Business news 02-By-line articles 03-Fashion news 04-Food news 05-Freelance copy 06-Letters to editor 07-Real estate news 08-Sports news 09-Travel news 10-Book rev. 11-Movie rev. 12-Music rev. 13-TV rev. 14-Theater rev. 15-Coming events 16-Obituaries 17-Question & answer 18-Social announcements 19-Artwork 20-Cartoons 21-Photos 22-TV listings 23-Audio rec. 24-Video rec. 25-Books 26-Films/film clips 27-Personnel news 28-Press releases 29-New product news/photos 30-Trade lit. 31-Contracts awarded 32-Display adv. 33-Classified adv.

4-304

Circulation Type: paid
**Owner(s):**
American Orthopsychiatric Association, Inc.
330 Seventh Ave., 18th Fl.
New York, NY 10001
Telephone: (212) 564-5930
Ownership %: 100
**Editorial:**
Ernest Herman ...........................Editor
**Desc.:** Contains four to six essay reviews and 30-40 brief reviews of books of interest to the mental health professional.
**Readers:** Association members, individual subscribers and libraries.

65015
## SMALL GROUP RESEARCH
2455 Teller Rd.
Thousand Oaks, CA 91320
Telephone: (805) 499-0721
FAX: (805) 499-0871
Year Established: 1970
Pub. Frequency: q.
Page Size: standard
Subscrip. Rate: $52/yr. individuals; $147/yr. institutions
Circulation: 1,300
Circulation Type: paid
**Owner(s):**
Sage Publications, Inc.
2455 Teller Rd.
Thousand Oaks, CA 91320
Telephone: (805) 499-0721
Ownership %: 100
**Editorial:**
Richard Brian Polley ...................Editor
Charles Garvin ...........................Editor
**Desc.:** Small Group Research is an international journal of therapy counseling and training.
**Readers:** Academic communities.

## Group 210-Public Health

69587
## ANNUAL REVIEW OF PUBLIC HEALTH
4139 El Camino Way
Palo Alto, CA 94303-0139
Telephone: (415) 493-4400
FAX: (415) 855-9815
Mailing Address:
P.O. Box 10139
Palo Alto, CA 94303-0139
Year Established: 1980
Pub. Frequency: a.
Page Size: standard
Subscrip. Rate: $52/yr. US; $57/yr. foreign
**Owner(s):**
Annual Reviews, Inc.
4139 El Camino Way
Box 10139
Palo Alto, CA 94303-0139
Telephone: (415) 493-4400
FAX: (415) 855-9815
Ownership %: 100
**Editorial:**
Gilbert S. Omenn .......................Editor
**Desc.:** Original reviews of critical literature and current developments in public health.

69463
## APPLIED OCCUPATIONAL & ENVIRONMENTAL HYGIENE
1330 Kemper Meadow Dr., Ste. 600
Cincinnati, OH 45240-1634
Telephone: (513) 742-2020
FAX: (513) 742-3355
Year Established: 1986
Pub. Frequency: m.

Page Size: standard
Subscrip. Rate: $95/yr. individuals; $155/yr. institutions
Materials: 32,33
Print Process: offset
Circulation: 6,500
Circulation Type: paid
**Owner(s):**
Applied Industrial Hygiene, Inc.
1330 Kemper Meadow Dr., Ste. 6
Cincinnati, OH 45240-1634
Telephone: (513) 742-2020
FAX: (513) 742-3355
Ownership %: 100
**Editorial:**
J.M. Dement ...................Editor in Chief
**Desc.:** For occupational and environmental health and safety professionals.

68878
## EPIDEMIOLOGY
428 E. Preston St.
Baltimore, MD 21202
Telephone: (410) 528-4000
FAX: (410) 528-4312
Year Established: 1990
Pub. Frequency: 6/yr.
Subscrip. Rate: $93/yr. individuals; $130/yr. institutions
Circulation: 1580
Circulation Type: paid
**Owner(s):**
Williams & Wilkins Co.
428 E. Preston St.
Baltimore, MD 21202
Telephone: (410) 528-4000
Ownership %: 100
**Editorial:**
Kenneth J. Rothman ...................Editor
Stacey Fernandez .............Advertising
**Desc.:** Scientific discussion on priciples and methods in data analysis.

56410
## FAMILY LIFE EDUCATOR
4 Carbonero Way
Santa Cruz, CA 95066
Telephone: (408) 438-4060
Mailing Address:
P.O. Box 1830
Santa Cruz, CA 95061
Year Established: 1981
Pub. Frequency: q.
Page Size: standard
Subscrip. Rate: $35/yr. individuals; $55/yr. institutions
Freelance Pay: negotiable
Circulation: 2,200
Circulation Type: paid
**Owner(s):**
E.T.R. Associates
P.O. Box 1830
Santa Cruz, CA 95061
Telephone: (408) 438-4060
Ownership %: 100
**Management:**
Janice Valdivia ...........Circulation Manager
**Editorial:**
Kay Clark ...................................Editor
Ann Smiley ...................Design Director
Steven Bignell ...........Marketing Director
**Desc.:** Devoted to providing practical up-to-date information to educators and professionals. Each issue contains background articles on relevant issues, update reports on research, legislation, training, resources, and reproducible teaching activities with student worksheets.
**Readers:** Family life educators in schools, private counselors and consultants, Professionals in the fields of sexuality education, family life, and family health.

24481
## FDA CONSUMER
5600 Fishers Ln.
Rockville, MD 20857
Telephone: (301) 443-3220
Year Established: 1967
Pub. Frequency: 10/yr.
Page Size: standard
Subscrip. Rate: $15/yr.
Materials: 02,06,20
Freelance Pay: $800-$1200/article
Circulation: 28,000
Circulation Type: paid
**Owner(s):**
U.S. Food & Drug Admininistration
5600 Fishers Ln.
Rockville, MD 20857
Telephone: (301) 443-3220
Ownership %: 100
**Editorial:**
Judith Levine Willis ...................Editor
Patricia Edwards ...............Art Director
Carol Ballentine ...............Copy Chief
Michael Herndon ...........Production Director
**Desc.:** Offical magazine of the U.S. Food and Drug Administration and is not copyrighted. It reports on FDA programs, policies, and decisions and on FDA's view of the safety and effectiveness of the products regulated by FDA. Most articles are written by FDA employees familiar with the technical background of policies and decisions. Occasionally, a freelancer is assigned to work with a technical expert on an article.
**Readers:** General public with interest in health issues.

69593
## INTERNATIONAL QUARTERLY OF COMMUNITY HEALTH EDUCATION
26 Austin Ave.
Amityville, NY 11701
Telephone: (516) 691-1270
FAX: (516) 691-1770
Mailing Address:
P.O. Box 337
Amityville, NY 11701
Year Established: 1981
Pub. Frequency: q.
Subscrip. Rate: $36/yr. individuals; $112/yr. institutions
**Owner(s):**
Baywood Publishing Co., Inc.
26 Austin Ave.
Box 337
Amityville, NY 11701
Telephone: (516) 691-1270
FAX: (516) 691-1770
**Management:**
Stuart Cohen ...........................President
Stuart Cohen ...........................Publisher
**Editorial:**
Dr. George P. Cernada ...........Editor
**Desc.:** Focuses on the systematic application of social science and health education theory and methodology to public health problems. Applies consumer-directed approaches to control preventive and curative health services.

24496
## JOURNAL OF AMERICAN COLLEGE HEALTH
1319 18th St., N.W.
Washington, DC 20036-1802
Telephone: (202) 296-6267
FAX: (202) 296-5149
Year Established: 1952
Pub. Frequency: bi-m.
Page Size: standard
Subscrip. Rate: $46/yr. individuals US; $79/yr. institutions US; $91/yr. institutions foreign

Circulation: 641
Circulation Type: paid
**Owner(s):**
Heldref Publications
1319 Eighteenth St., NW
Washington, DC 20036-1802
Telephone: (202) 296-6267
**Management:**
Walter E. Beach ...........................Publisher
Raymond M. Rallo ...........Advertising Manager
Catherine Welker ...............Circulation Manager
Kerri P. Kilbane ...............Promotion Manager
**Editorial:**
Martha Wedeman ...........................Editor
**Desc.:** The Journal of American College Health is the only publication devoted entirely to the health of college students. It covers developments and research in this broad field, including clinical and preventive medicine, health promotion and education, administration, mental health, nursing, and sports medicine.
**Readers:** Physicians, psychologists, nurses, and other professionals concerned with adolescent and young adult health issues.

24922
## JOURNAL OF ENVIRONMENTAL HEALTH
720 S. Colorado Blvd., Ste. 970, S. Tower
Denver, CO 80222
*see Service,Trade,Professional Magazines, Pollutants & Pollution Control*

25364
## JOURNAL OF FOOD PROTECTION
6200 Aurora Ave., Ste. 200W
Des Moines, IA 50322
*see Service,Trade,Professional Magazines, Foods & Food Processing*

68865
## JOURNAL OF PUBLIC HEALTH POLICY
208 Meadowood Dr.
S. Burlington, VT 05403
Telephone: (802) 658-0136
FAX: (802) 862-4011
Year Established: 1980
Pub. Frequency: q.
Subscrip. Rate: $110/yr. US; $120/yr. foreign
Circulation: 1800
Circulation Type: paid
**Owner(s):**
Journal of Public Health Policy, Inc.
208 Meadowood Dr.
S. Burlington, VT 05403
Telephone: (802) 658-0136
Ownership %: 100
**Editorial:**
Dr. Milton Terris ...........................Editor

24494
## JOURNAL OF SCHOOL HEALTH, THE
7263 State Rte. 43
Kent, OH 44240
Telephone: (216) 678-1601
FAX: (216) 678-4526
Mailing Address:
P.O. Box 708
Kent, OH 44240
Year Established: 1930
Pub. Frequency: 10/yr.
Page Size: standard
Subscrip. Rate: $85/yr.
Circulation: 7,000
Circulation Type: controlled & paid

**Materials Accepted/Included:** 01-Business news 02-By-line articles 03-Fashion news 04-Food news 05-Freelance copy 06-Letters to editor 07-Real estate news 08-Sports news 09-Travel news 10-Book rev. 11-Movie rev. 12-Music rev. 13-TV rev. 14-Theater rev. 15-Coming events 16-Obituaries 17-Question & answer 18-Social announcements 19-Artwork 20-Cartoons 21-Photos 22-TV listings 23-Audio rec. 24-Video rec. 25-Books 26-Films/film clips 27-Personnel news 28-Press releases 29-New product news/photos 30-Trade lit. 31-Contracts awarded 32-Display adv. 33-Classified adv.

4-305

**Owner(s):**
American School Health Association
P.O. Box 708
Kent, OH 44240
Telephone: (216) 678-1601
Ownership %: 100
**Management:**
Sally White .........................Circulation Manager
**Editorial:**
R. Morgan Pigg, Jr., HSD, MPH ...............Editor
Tom Reed ..........................Managing Editor
**Desc.:** Provides timely articles on current
trends, research and developments for
professionals concerned about the
physical and mental health of school-
age children. Includes practical articles
on resources for classroom instruction,
programs for disease control and sex
education, the administration and
development of health education
programs, reports of existing health and
dental education programs, alcohol,
smoking and drug education, and
special issues devoted to relevant
concerns in the field. Special columns,
book reviews, news briefs,
workshop and convention
announcements and status reports of
health legislation are also included.
**Readers:** School nurses, health educators,
school physicians, and others interested
in promoting health in the schools.

24498

**NATION'S HEALTH, THE**
1015 15th St., N.W.
Washington, DC 20005
Telephone: (202) 789-5600
FAX: (202) 789-5661
Year Established: 1971
Pub. Frequency: 11/yr.
Page Size: tabloid
Subscrip. Rate: $15/yr. in US & Canada;
$18/yr. foreign
Freelance Pay: $100-500/article
Circulation: 32,000
Circulation Type: paid
**Owner(s):**
American Public Health Assn.
1015 15th St., N.W.
Washington, DC 20005
Telephone: (202) 789-5664
Ownership %: 100
**Management:**
Fernando Trevino .................................Publisher
**Editorial:**
Fernando Trevino ....................Executive Editor
Joan Murphy ......................................Editor
**Desc.:** Current issues in health, including
legislative, political, new developments,
current events, professional news,
meetings, books. Departments include:
What to Write For, Members on the
Move, Notes, State Health Reports.
**Readers:** Physicians, nurses, public health
professionals, health administrators,
public health educators,
environmentalists.

68879

**SEARCHLINES**
201 N. Link Ln.
Fort Collins, CO 80524-2712
Telephone: (303) 224-9101
FAX: (303) 226-0907
Year Established: 1979
Pub. Frequency: bi-m.
Page Size: standard
Subscrip. Rate: $25/yr.
Materials: 01,02,06,10,15,17,21,23,24,25,
26,27,28,29,30,32
Print Process: offset
Circulation: 2,575
Circulation Type: free & paid

**Owner(s):**
Intl. Association of Dive Rescue Specialists
201 N. Link Ln.
Fort Collins, CO 80524-2712
Telephone: (303) 224-9101
FAX: (303) 226-0907
Ownership %: 100
**Editorial:**
Steven J. Linton ...............................Editor
**Desc.:** Covers techniques, equipment, and
experiences pertinent to the job of
public safety diver.

## Group 212-Public Relations

52644

**CRITICAL STUDIES IN MASS
COMMUNICATION**
5105 Backlick Rd., Bldg. E
Annandale, VA 22003
Telephone: (703) 750-0533
Year Established: 1984
Pub. Frequency: q.
Page Size: standard
Subscrip. Rate: $50/yr. member US;
$53/yr. member foreign
Circulation: 3,000
Circulation Type: paid
**Owner(s):**
Speech Communication Association
5105 Backlick Rd., Bldg. E
Annandale, VA 22003
Telephone: (703) 750-0533
Ownership %: 100
**Management:**
Norma Geiger ....................Advertising Manager
**Editorial:**
Sari Thomas ......................................Editor
**Desc.:** Provides a forum for cross-
disciplinary research and welcomes a
wide range of theoretical orientations
and methodological approaches.
Includes the evolution, organization,
control, economics, administration, and
technological innovations of mass
communication systems. Manuscripts
may contribute original research, provide
an analysis, or advance new arguments.
**Readers:** Scholars, teachers, students,
researchers in mass communication.

66618

**IDENTITY**
407 Gilbert Ave.
Cincinnati, OH 45202
Telephone: (513) 421-2050
Year Established: 1988
Pub. Frequency: q.
Page Size: standard
Subscrip. Rate: $48/yr. US; $60/yr. foreign
airmail
Freelance Pay: $300-$500/article
Circulation: 13,800
Circulation Type: controlled
**Owner(s):**
ST Publications, Inc.
407 Gilbert Ave.
Cincinnati, OH 45202
Telephone: (513) 421-2050
Ownership %: 100
**Management:**
Robert T. Jordan ........................Vice President
Joseph E. Cuzzort ......................Vice President
Jerry Swormstedt ..........................Publisher
**Editorial:**
Lynn Baxter ......................................Editor
W.S. Moore, III ........................Associate Editor
David Williamson ................Associate Publisher

**Desc.:** Serves corporate identity and
environmental graphic design firms and
their corporate clients who administer
identify signage programs, including:
developers, retail establishments, food
and lodging firms, financial institutions,
health facilities, transportation facilities,
manufacturers and distributors,
advertising agencies, community and
educational institutions, sign companies
and others allied to the field concerned
with corporate identity, signage, and
logo programs.
**Readers:** Presidents, CEO's, owners, vice-
presidents, creative directors, design
directors, marketing managers, planners,
architects, art directors, purchasing
agents, consultants, students,
educators and others interested in
corporate identity, signage and logo
programs.

65480

**O'DWYER'S PR SERVICES
REPORT**
271 Madison Ave., Ste. 600
New York, NY 10016
Telephone: (212) 679-2471
Year Established: 1987
Pub. Frequency: m.
Page Size: standard
Subscrip. Rate: $40/yr.
Circulation: 5,000
**Owner(s):**
J.R. O'Dwyer Co., Inc.
271 Madison Ave., Ste. 600
New York, NY 10016
Telephone: (212) 679-2471
Ownership %: 100
**Management:**
Jack O'Dwyer ...........................Publisher
**Editorial:**
Jack O'Dwyer ................................Editor
**Desc.:** Features financial management,
legal matters, hiring, and case histories
of PR campaigns.
**Readers:** Serves public relations
executives, executive recruiters,
research firms, and computer software
firms.

24521

**PUBLIC RELATIONS JOURNAL**
33 Irving Pl.
New York, NY 10003
Telephone: (212) 460-1413
FAX: (212) 995-0757
Year Established: 1945
Pub. Frequency: m.
Page Size: standard
Subscrip. Rate: $49/yr.; $93/2 yrs.;
$137/3 yrs.
Materials: 01,02,03,04,05,06,07,08,09,10,
15,19,21,22,25,28,29,30,31,32,33
Freelance Pay: $150-$1200
Print Process: web offset
Circulation: 20,185
Circulation Type: paid
**Owner(s):**
Public Relations Society of America
33 Irving Pl.
New York, NY 10003
Telephone: (212) 995-2230
Ownership %: 100
**Management:**
Harland W. Warner ..........................President
Anne Fetsch ....................Advertising Manager
Alex Ortiz ..........................Circulation Manager
Teta Gorgani .............Classified Adv. Manager
**Editorial:**
Judy A. Gordon ........................Exec. Editor
Susan Fry Bovet ..............................Editor
Susan Yip ..................................Art Director
Jay Weiser .........................Production Director

**Desc.:** Articles should be addressed to
public relations practitioners and
educators. They should be issue
oriented and relate to those concerns
that affect America's businesses and
institutions.
**Readers:** Members of CPRS and PRSSA.

24523

**PUBLIC RELATIONS QUARTERLY,
THE**
44 W. Market St.
Rhinebeck, NY 12572-0311
Telephone: (914) 876-2081
FAX: (914) 876-2561
Mailing Address:
P.O. Box 311
Rhinebeck, NY 12572-0311
Year Established: 1955
Pub. Frequency: q.
Page Size: standard
Subscrip. Rate: $40/yr.
Materials: 02,06,10,23,24,25,28,32,33
Print Process: offset
Circulation: 5,000
Circulation Type: paid
**Owner(s):**
Public Relations Quarterly
44 W. Market St.
P.O. Box 311
Rhinebeck, NY 12572-0311
Telephone: (914) 876-2081
FAX: (914) 876-2561
Ownership %: 100
**Management:**
Howard Penn Hudson .........................Publisher
**Editorial:**
Howard Penn Hudson .................Editor in Chief
Paul Swift ......................................Editor
Edward L. Bernays ..........................Columnist
E.W. Brody ..................................Columnist
**Desc.:** Professional magazine devoted
exclusively to public relations.
Departments include: Books, Research,
and Education.
**Readers:** Public relations practitioners and
educators.

## Group 214-Public Transportation

69153

**BUS INDUSTRY MAGAZINE**
195 Lancelot Dr.
Manchester, NH 03104-1420
Telephone: (603) 669-7160
Year Established: 1963
Pub. Frequency: q.
Subscrip. Rate: $20/yr. US; $25/yr.
Canada
Circulation: 400
Circulation Type: paid
**Owner(s):**
Bus History Association, Inc.
195 Lancelot Dr.
Manchester, NH 03104-1420
Telephone: (603) 669-7160
Ownership %: 100
**Editorial:**
Loring M. Lawrence ...............................Editor
**Desc.:** News and articles pertaining to city
and intercity historical and contemporary
bus operations.

69154

**BUS OPERATOR**
1210 Eighth Ave., S.
Nashville, TN 37203
Telephone: (615) 242-7747
Year Established: 1985
Pub. Frequency: bi-m.
Page Size: standard
Circulation: 7,000
Circulation Type: paid

**Materials Accepted/Included:** 01-Business news 02-By-line articles 03-Fashion news 04-Food news 05-Freelance copy 06-Letters to editor 07-Real estate news 08-Sports news 09-Travel news 10-Book rev. 11-Movie rev. 12-Music rev. 13-TV rev. 14-Theater rev. 15-Coming events 16-Obituaries 17-Question & answer 18-Social announcements 19-Artwork 20-Cartoons 21-Photos 22-TV listings 23-Audio rec. 24-Video rec. 25-Books 26-Films/film clips 27-Personnel news 28-Press releases 29-New product news/photos 30-Trade lit. 31-Contracts awarded 32-Display adv. 33-Classified adv.

**Owner(s):**
Tom Jackson & Associates, Inc.
1210 Eighth Ave., S.
Nashville, TN 37203
Telephone: (615) 242-7747
Ownership %: 100
**Editorial:**
Berlinda Yandell .........................Editor
**Desc.:** Provides technical and
management information and regulatory
and legislative news.
**Readers:** Intercity bus operations
professionals.

69694
## DARTLINES
1401 Pacific Ave.
Dallas, TX 75266
Telephone: (214) 748-3278
Pub. Frequency: bi-m.
Page Size: standard
Subscrip. Rate: free
Circulation: 15,000
Circulation Type: free
**Owner(s):**
Dallas Area Rapid Transit
Ownership %: 100
**Editorial:**
Don Gililland ...............................Editor

69693
## ENTERPRISE
1401 Pacific Ave.
Dallas, TX 75266
Telephone: (214) 748-3278
Pub. Frequency: q.
Page Size: standard
Subscrip. Rate: free
**Owner(s):**
Dallas Area Rapid Transit
Ownership %: 100
**Editorial:**
Tony Salters ...............................Editor

25100
## MASS TRANSIT
445 Broadhollow Rd.
Melville, NY 11747
Telephone: (516) 845-2700
Year Established: 1974
Pub. Frequency: m.
Page Size: standard
Subscrip. Rate: $40/yr. US; $65/yr. foreign
Materials: 01,02,32,33
Freelance Pay: varies
Circulation: 18,000
Circulation Type: paid
**Owner(s):**
PTN Publishing
445 Broadhollow Rd.
Melville, NY 11747
Telephone: (516) 845-2700
**Management:**
Stanley S. Sills ........................Publisher
Judy Cecchini ...................Advertising Manager
**Editorial:**
Faye Guercio ............................Editor
John A. Pomeroy .................Assistant Editor
**Desc.:** Four-color publication covering
mass transportation in cities worldwide.
**Readers:** In over 90 countries - audited by
BPA.
**Deadline:** ads-1 mo. prior to pub. date

25101
## METRO MAGAZINE
2512 Artesia Blvd.
Redondo Beach, CA 90278
Telephone: (310) 376-8788
FAX: (310) 376-9043
Year Established: 1904
Pub. Frequency: 7/yr.
Page Size: standard
Subscrip. Rate: $25/yr.; $34/2 yrs.; $25 for
Annual Fact Book
Materials: 01,02,05,06,15,16,19,20,21,27,
28,29,30,31,32,33
Print Process: offset lithography

Circulation: 18,000
Circulation Type: controlled
**Owner(s):**
Bobit Publishing Co.
2512 Artesia Blvd.
Redondo Beach, CA 90278
Telephone: (310) 376-8788
Ownership %: 100
**Management:**
Edward J. Bobit ...............Chairman of Board
Ty Bobit ...............................President
Frank DiGiacomo ......................Publisher
**Editorial:**
Jody Bush ..........................Senior Editor
Cliff Henke ..............................Editor
Lenny Levine .....................Managing Editor
**Desc.:** Management-level articles on mass
transportation, including bus and rail
public transit activities and privately
owned intercity tour and charter
bus transportation companies.
**Readers:** Professional staffs of publicly
owned transit agencies and privately
owned intercity-, charter- tour bus
companies, government officials in the
field  of mass transportation, transit
industry consultants, and transit
commissions and boards.

61596
## NATIONAL BUS TRADER
9698 W. Judson Rd.
Polo, IL 61064
Telephone: (815) 946-2341
FAX: (815) 946-2347
Year Established: 1977
Pub. Frequency: m.
Page Size: standard
Subscrip. Rate: $20/yr.
Circulation: 5,400
Circulation Type: paid
**Owner(s):**
National Bus Trader, Inc.
9698 W. Judson Rd.
Polo, IL 61064
Telephone: (815) 946-2341
**Editorial:**
Larry Plachno ...........................Editor
Jackie Plachno ......................Advertising
Linda Faivre ........................Subscriptions
**Desc.:** Definitive magazine on intercity
motor coaches with emphasis on
equipment and components.
**Readers:** Motor coach owners and
dealers.

22431
## PASSENGER TRANSPORT
1201 New York Ave., N.W., Ste. 400
Washington, DC 20005
Telephone: (202) 898-4000
FAX: (202) 898-4095
Year Established: 1943
Pub. Frequency: w.
Page Size: tabloid
Subscrip. Rate: $2/copy; $65/yr.
Materials: 02,06,15,27,28,29,31,32,33
Print Process: offset
Circulation: 4,073
Circulation Type: paid
**Owner(s):**
American Public Transit Association
1201 New York Ave., N.W.
Washington, DC 20005
Telephone: (202) 898-4000
Ownership %: 100
**Management:**
Cecilia May .......................Advertising Manager
**Editorial:**
Dennis Kouba ...........................Editor
Rhonda Goldberg .................Managing Editor
Susan Berlin ......................Associate Editor

**Desc.:** Published for bus and rail transit
systems, their managers, government
officials and manufacturers, and
suppliers in related industry. Coverage
includes federal and state actions
affecting transit, with emphasis on FTA,
Congress, national transportation
policies, and public interest groups'
positions on transit issues.
**Readers:** Transit executives, transit
systems, state and federal Departments
of Transportation, businesses serving
transit providers.
**Deadline:** story-2 wks. prior to pub. date;
news-2 wks. prior; photo-2 wks. prior;
ads-1 wk. prior

22432
## SCHOOL BUS FLEET
2512 Artesia Blvd.
Redondo Beach, CA 90278
Telephone: (310) 376-8788
FAX: (310) 376-9043
Year Established: 1956
Pub. Frequency: 9/yr.
Page Size: standard
Subscrip. Rate: $25/yr.; $34/2 yrs.
Materials: 01,05,06,21,28,29,30,31,32,33
Circulation: 17,500
Circulation Type: controlled
**Owner(s):**
Bobit Publishing Co.
2512 Artesia Blvd.
Redondo Beach, CA 90278
Telephone: (310) 376-8788
Ownership %: 100
**Management:**
Frank Di Giacomo ......................Publisher
**Editorial:**
Jody Bush ...........................Exec. Editor
Lenny Levine .......................Senior Editor
Clifford D. Henke ......................Editor
Y. Bobit ........................Group Publisher
**Desc.:** Articles cover operation and
maintenance of school buses, discussing
equipment selection, schedules, routing,
driver selection and training, safety, and
kindred subjects. Also features
alternative fuels and new products.
**Readers:** School bus fleet purchasing
agents, transportation directors, and
maintenance supervisors in school (all
levels and categories)  and privately
owned school bus contract operators
serving the pupil transportation market.

69156
## SCHOOL TRANSPORTATION
NEWS
700 Torrance Blvd., Ste. C
Redondo Beach, CA 90277-3493
Telephone: (310) 792-2226
FAX: (310) 792-2231
Year Established: 1991
Pub. Frequency: m.
Page Size: tabloid
Subscrip. Rate: $24/yr.
Materials: 01,02,06,15,20,28,31,32,33
Print Process: web offset
Circulation: 15,300
Circulation Type: controlled & paid
**Owner(s):**
William E. Paul, Inc.
700 Torrance Blvd., Ste. C
Redondo Beach, CA 90277
Telephone: (310) 792-2226
Ownership %: 100
**Management:**
William E. Paul ........................Publisher
**Editorial:**
John Wyman .......................Associate Editor
**Desc.:** Focuses on new developments in
school transportation at all academic
levels.
**Deadline:** ads-10th of preceding mo.

22433
## TAXICAB & LIVERY
MANAGEMENT
3849 Farragut Ave.
Kensington, MD 20895-2004
Telephone: (301) 946-5701
FAX: (301) 946-4641
Year Established: 1966
Pub. Frequency: q.
Page Size: standard
Subscrip. Rate: $16/yr.
Materials: 01,02,05,06,15,21,27,28,29,30,32
Freelance Pay: negotiable
Print Process: sheetfed
Circulation: 5,800
**Owner(s):**
International Taxicab & Livery Association
3849 Farragut Ave.
Kensington, MD 20895-2004
Telephone: (301) 946-5701
Ownership %: 100
**Management:**
Murray Rosenberg ......................President
Craig Bates ......................Vice President
Alfred B. LaGasse, III .................Publisher
**Editorial:**
Irene R. Kiebuzinski .....................Editor
**Desc.:** Provides valuable business
information on maintenance, government
affairs, public relations, marketing,
research, and contracting. The main
thrust is to provide mix of hard and soft
news to assist owners of fleets to
provide better service and reduce costs.
Features articles that alert readers to
legislative changes, trends in the
industry, and ways to improve service
and reduce costs. Examples of articles
include those on maintenance,
insurance, obtaining good PR, what's
available in communications equipment.
**Readers:** Owners and managers of taxi,
limousine, livery, van and minibus fleets
in U.S., Canada, Australia, U.K., and all
over the world; suppliers of products for
the industry; government officials.
**Deadline:** story-6 wks. prior to pub. date;
news-6 wks. prior; photo-6 wks. prior

## Group 216-Publishing,
## Journalism & Writing

22088
## AB BOOKMAN'S WEEKLY
P.O. Box AB
Clifton, NJ 07015
Telephone: (201) 772-0020
FAX: (201) 772-9281
Year Established: 1948
Pub. Frequency: w.
Page Size: standard
Subscrip. Rate: $10/copy; $80/yr. mailed
3rd class; $125/yr. mailed 1st class
Materials: 32,33
Circulation: 9,000
Circulation Type: paid
**Owner(s):**
AB Bookman Publications, Inc.
P.O. Box AB
Clifton, NJ 07015
Telephone: (201) 772-0020
Ownership %: 100
**Editorial:**
Jacob L. Chernofsky .....................Editor
**Desc.:** Front of book carries book news,
book reviews, notes and antiquarian
book notes. Also features on book
history, printing, publishing, bookselling,
etc. Remainder of magazine devoted to
"books wanted" and "for sale" listings.
**Readers:** Book buyers, dealers, collectors
and libraries.

---

**Materials Accepted/Included:** 01-Business news 02-By-line articles 03-Fashion news 04-Food news 05-Freelance copy 06-Letters to editor 07-Real estate news 08-Sports news 09-Travel news 10-Book rev. 11-Movie rev. 12-Music rev. 13-TV rev. 14-Theater rev. 15-Coming events 16-Obituaries 17-Question & answer 18-Social announcements 19-Artwork 20-Cartoons 21-Photos 22-TV listings 23-Audio rec. 24-Video rec. 25-Books 26-Films/film clips 27-Personnel news 28-Press releases 29-New product news/photos 30-Trade lit. 31-Contracts awarded 32-Display adv. 33-Classified adv.

69529

**AMERICA'S CENSORED NEWSLETTER**
P.O. Box 310
Cotati, CA 94911
Year Established: 1992
Pub. Frequency: m
Subscrip. Rate: $20/yr.
**Owner(s):**
Censored Publications
**Editorial:**
Carl Jensen .................................Editor
**Desc.:** Offers information and encouragement.
**Readers:** Would-be writers.

68741

**AMERICAN BOOKSELLER**
828 S. Broadway
Tarrytown, NY 10591-5112
Telephone: (800) 637-0037
FAX: (914) 591-2717
Year Established: 1977
Pub. Frequency: m.
Subscrip. Rate: $49.99/yr.
Materials: 01,06,29,30,32,33
Circulation: 10,416
Circulation Type: paid
**Owner(s):**
American Booksellers Association
828 S. Broadway
Tarrytown, NY 10591-5112
Telephone: (800) 637-0037
FAX: (914) 591-2717
Ownership %: 100
**Editorial:**
Dan Cullen .................................Editor

58749

**AMERICAN IMAGO: STUDIES IN PSYCHOANALYSIS & CULTURE**
2715 N. Charles St.
Baltimore, MD 21218
Telephone: (410) 516-6985
Year Established: 1939
Pub. Frequency: q.
Page Size: standard
Subscrip. Rate: $8 newsstand; $32/yr. individuals; $47/yr. institutions
Circulation: 1,000
Circulation Type: paid
**Owner(s):**
Johns Hopkins University Press
2715 N. Charles St.
Baltimore, MD 21218
Telephone: (410) 516-6985
Ownership %: 100
**Editorial:**
Martin Gliserman .................................Editor
**Desc.:** Journal of the Association for Applied Psychoanalysis.
**Readers:** Academics and Psychoanalysts interested in cultural issues.

68943

**AMERICAN JOURNALISM REVIEW**
8701 Adelphia Rd.
Adelphi, MD 20783-1716
Telephone: (301) 512-0001
FAX: (301) 441-9495
Year Established: 1977
Pub. Frequency: 10/yr.
Page Size: standard
Subscrip. Rate: $2.95 newsstand; $24/yr.
Materials: 06,10,25,27,32
Freelance Pay: negotiable
Print Process: offset
Circulation: 27,200
Circulation Type: controlled & paid
**Owner(s):**
University of Maryland, College of Journalism
8701 Adelphi Rd., Ste. 310
Adelphi, MD 20783
Telephone: (301) 431-4771
Ownership %: 100

**Editorial:**
Rem Rieder .................................Editor
Rem Rieder .................Senior Vice President
**Desc.:** Covers issues relating to print and broadcast journalism.
**Readers:** Publishers, Editors, Reporters, elected Officials, CEOs, Commentators, News Directors, Producers, Artists, Professionals.

69481

**AUTHORSHIP**
1450 S. Havana, Ste. 620
Aurora, CO 80012
Telephone: (303) 751-7844
FAX: (303) 751-8593
Year Established: 1943
Pub. Frequency: bi-m.
Subscrip. Rate: $18/yr.
Circulation: 4,000
Circulation Type: paid
**Owner(s):**
National Writers Club
1450 S. Havana, Ste. 424
Aurora, CO 80012
Telephone: (303) 751-7844
Ownership %: 100
**Editorial:**
Sandy Whelchel .................................Editor
**Desc.:** Discusses creative and compositional techniques.

64942

**A VIEW FROM THE LOFT**
66 Malcom, S.E.
Minneapolis, MN 55414
Telephone: (612) 379-8999
Pub. Frequency: m. except Jul.
Subscrip. Rate: $35/yr.; $18/yr. low income
Materials: 05,06,20,32,33
Freelance Pay: $65/article
Circulation: 2,700
Circulation Type: paid
**Owner(s):**
Loft, The
**Editorial:**
Ellen Hawley .................................Editor
**Desc.:** Provides a forum for the exchange of opinions and information about writing. Accepts unsolicited articles about writing.
**Readers:** Writers and people interested in literature.

68742

**BOOK DEALERS WORLD**
P.O. Box 606
Cottage Grove, OR 97424
Telephone: (503) 942-7455
Year Established: 1980
Pub. Frequency: q.
Page Size: standard
Subscrip. Rate: $30/yr.
Materials: 10,15,21,23,24,25,28,32,33,34
Print Process: web offset
Circulation: 20,000
Circulation Type: free & paid
**Owner(s):**
North American Book Dealers Exchange
P.O. Box 606
Cottage Grove, OR 97424
Telephone: (503) 942-7455
Ownership %: 100
**Editorial:**
Al Galasso .................................Editor
**Readers:** Book dealers, independent publishers, direct marketers, book buyers, catalog firms, business opportunity seekers.

68743

**BOOK PAGE**
2501 21st Ave., S., No. 5
Nashville, TN 37212-5626
Telephone: (615) 292-8926
Year Established: 1988

Pub. Frequency: m.
Subscrip. Rate: $18/yr.
Circulation: 550,000
Circulation Type: paid
**Owner(s):**
ProMotion, Inc.
2501 21st Ave., S., No. 5
Nashville, TN 37212-5626
Telephone: (615) 292-8926
Ownership %: 100
**Editorial:**
Ann Meador Shayne .................................Editor
**Desc.:** Features book reviews, author interviews and news of the world of books.

61610

**BOOK REPORT, THE**
480 E. Wilson Bridge Rd., Ste. L
Worthington, OH 43085
Telephone: (614) 436-7107
FAX: (614) 436-9490
Year Established: 1982
Pub. Frequency: bi-m.
Page Size: standard
Subscrip. Rate: $39/yr.
Circulation: 11,000
Circulation Type: paid
**Owner(s):**
Marlene Woo-Lun
5701 N. High St., 1
Worthington, OH 43085
Telephone: (614) 436-7107
Ownership %: 100
**Management:**
Jennifer Wilson .................Advertising Manager
**Editorial:**
Carolyn Hamilton .................................Editor
Annette Thorson .................Assistant Editor
**Desc.:** Provides articles, tips, and ideas for day-to-day school library management, as well as reviews of audio visuals and software, all written by school librarians.

22091

**BOOKSTORE JOURNAL**
2620 Venetucci Blvd.
Colorado Springs, CO 80906
Telephone: (719) 576-7880
FAX: (719) 576-0795
Mailing Address:
P.O. Box 200
Colorado Spring, CO 80906
Year Established: 1968
Pub. Frequency: 12/yr.
Page Size: standard
Subscrip. Rate: $45/yr.
Materials: 01,02,05,06,10,12,15,16,17,19, 20,21,24,27,28,29,30,31,32,33
Freelance Pay: $120/pg.
Print Process: offset
Circulation: 6,500
Circulation Type: paid
**Owner(s):**
CBA Service Corp.
P.O. Box 200
Colorado Springs, CO 80901
Telephone: (719) 576-7880
Ownership %: 100
**Management:**
Dorothy Gore .................................Publisher
Leota Pacquette .................Advertising Manager
Mike Royal .................Production Manager
**Editorial:**
Todd Hafer .................................Editor
Linda Vixie .................Book Review Editor
**Desc.:** Contains how-to articles about Christian bookstore management, marketing, sales, advertising, staff training, inventory control, budgeting, store location, store appearance, and other related subjects.

**Readers:** Owners and managers and staff of Christian bookstores. Manufacturers and distributors of religious goods.
**Deadline:** story-2 mos.; news-2 mos.; photo-2 mos.; ads-2 mos.

61622

**BP REPORT**
213 Dunbury Rd.
Wilton, CT 06897
Telephone: (203) 834-0033
FAX: (203) 834-1771
Mailing Address:
P.O. Box 7430
Wilton, CT 06897
Year Established: 1977
Pub. Frequency: w.
Page Size: standard
Subscrip. Rate: $415/yr.
**Owner(s):**
Simba Information, Inc.
213 Danbury Rd.
Wilton, CT 06897
Telephone: (203) 834-0033
**Management:**
Alan Brigish .................................Publisher
Marsha Nierenberg ..........Advertising Manager
**Editorial:**
Jim Milliot .................................Editor
**Desc.:** Covers the business of book publishing.
**Readers:** Book publishing executives

69546

**BYLINE**
P.O. Box 130596
Edmond, OK 73013-0001
Telephone: (405) 348-5591
Year Established: 1981
Pub. Frequency: m.
Subscrip. Rate: 3.50 newsstand; $20/yr.; $36/2 yrs.
Materials: 02,32,33
Freelance Pay: $5-10/poem; $50/short article
Print Process: offset
Circulation: 3,000
Circulation Type: paid
**Owner(s):**
Marcia Preston
Box 130596
Edmond, OK 73013-0001
Telephone: (405) 348-5591
Ownership %: 100
**Management:**
Marcia Preston .................................Publisher
**Editorial:**
Marcia Preston .................................Editor
Kathryn Fanning .................Managing Editor
**Desc.:** Targets all writers, especially those new to the business.
**Deadline:** story-continuous; ads-2 mo. prior to pub. date

22093

**CALIFORNIA PUBLISHER**
1225 Eighth St., Ste. 260
Sacramento, CA 95814-4809
Telephone: (916) 443-5991
FAX: (916) 443-6447
Year Established: 1918
Pub. Frequency: bi-m.
Page Size: tabloid
Subscrip. Rate: $15/yr.
Materials: 01,02,06,15,16,17,19,20,21,27, 28,29,30,32
Freelance Pay: $25-30/article
Print Process: offset
Circulation: 1,700
Circulation Type: controlled

Materials Accepted/Included: 01-Business news 02-By-line articles 03-Fashion news 04-Food news 05-Freelance copy 06-Letters to editor 07-Real estate news 08-Sports news 09-Travel news 10-Book rev. 11-Movie rev. 12-Music rev. 13-TV rev. 14-Theater rev. 15-Coming events 16-Obituaries 17-Question & answer 18-Social announcements 19-Artwork 20-Cartoons 21-Photos 22-TV listings 23-Audio rec. 24-Video rec. 25-Books 26-Films/film clips 27-Personnel news 28-Press releases 29-New product news/photos 30-Trade lit. 31-Contracts awarded 32-Display adv. 33-Classified adv.

4-308

**Owner(s):**
California Newspaper Publishers
   Association (CNPA)
1225 Eighth St., Ste. 260
Sacramento, CA 95814-4809
Telephone: (916) 443-5991
FAX: (916) 443-6447
Ownership %: 100
**Management:**
Brien Manning .........................................President
David Sams .......................Advertising Manager
**Editorial:**
Diane Donohue ........................Executive Editor
Jodie Morris .................................................Editor
**Readers:** California publishers, editors, and
   newspaper department heads.
**Deadline:** story-10th of mo.

23552

**COLORADO EDITOR**
1336 Glenarm Pl.
Denver, CO 80204
Telephone: (303) 571-5117
Year Established: 1924
Pub. Frequency: m.
Page Size: tabloid
Subscrip. Rate: $5/yr.
Circulation: 1,050
Circulation Type: paid
**Owner(s):**
Colorado Press Association
1336 Glenarm Pl.
Denver, CO 80204
Telephone: (303) 571-5117
Ownership %: 100
**Management:**
Mark Thomas .......................................Publisher
**Editorial:**
Marge Easton ..............................................Editor
**Desc.:** Activities, news developments in
   newspaper and printing industry with
   emphasis on Colorado. Uses personals,
   newspaper news, new equipment news.
**Readers:** Working press in Colorado.

68744

**COLOR PUBLISHING**
10 Tara Blvd., 5th Fl.
Nashua, NH 03062-2801
Telephone: (603) 891-9166
FAX: (603) 891-0539
Year Established: 1991
Pub. Frequency: bi-m.
Page Size: standard
Subscrip. Rate: $4.95 newsstand;
   $19.90/yr.
Materials: 02,05,06,10,28,29,32
Freelance Pay: varies
Print Process: web offset
Circulation: 24,000
Circulation Type: controlled
**Owner(s):**
PennWell Publishing Co.
10 Tara Blvd., 5th Fl.
Nashuard, NH 03062
Telephone: (603) 891-9166
FAX: (603) 891-0539
Ownership %: 100
**Editorial:**
Tom McMillan ..............................................Editor
**Desc.:** Covers developments in color
   publishing technology for the technical
   professional.

23553

**COLUMBIA JOURNALISM REVIEW**
700 Journalism Bldg.
Columbia University
New York, NY 10027
Telephone: (212) 854-1881
FAX: (212) 854-8580
Year Established: 1961
Pub. Frequency: bi-m.
Page Size: standard
Subscrip. Rate: $19.95/yr.
Freelance Pay: $.20/word
Circulation: 31,000

Circulation Type: paid
**Owner(s):**
Trustees of Columbia University
Telephone: (212) 854-2716
Ownership %: 100
**Management:**
Joan Konner .......................................Publisher
Louisa D. Kearney .............Advertising Manager
**Editorial:**
Roger Rosenblatt .......................Editor in Chief
Suzanne Braun Levine ...........................Editor
Gloria Cooper ........................Managing Editor
Dennis F. Giza ...................Associate Publisher
**Desc.:** Analyzes and comments on the
   journalistic performance of newspapers,
   magazines, television, and radio.
**Readers:** Primarily working journalists and
   others involved in communications.

64938

**COMMUNICATION ABSTRACTS**
2455 Teller Rd.
Thousand Oaks, CA 91320
Telephone: (805) 499-0721
FAX: (805) 499-0871
Year Established: 1977
Pub. Frequency: bi-m.
Page Size: standard
Subscrip. Rate: $125/yr. individuals;
   $380/yr. institutions
Circulation: 1,250
Circulation Type: paid
**Owner(s):**
Sage Publications, Inc.
2455 Teller Rd.
Thousand Oaks, CA 91320
Ownership %: 100
**Editorial:**
Thomas F. Gordon .....................................Editor
**Desc.:** Provides coverage of recent
   literature in all areas of communication
   studies (both mass and interpersonal).
   Includes expanded coverage of new
   communications technologies.

58610

**COMMUNICATIONS PRODUCT
REPORTS**
401 E. Rte. 70
Cherry Hill, NJ 08034
Telephone: (609) 428-1020
FAX: (609) 428-1683
Mailing Address:
   P.O. Box 5062
   Cherry Hill, NJ 08034
Year Established: 1981
Pub. Frequency: m.
Page Size: standard
Subscrip. Rate: $821/yr.
**Owner(s):**
Lawrence Feidelman
Management Info. Corp. (MIC)
401 E. Rt. 70
Cherry Hill, NJ 08034
Telephone: (609) 428-1020
Ownership %: 100
**Management:**
Lawrence Feidelman ...........................Publisher
Carol Bell .........................Circulation Manager
**Editorial:**
Don Stuart ...................................................Editor
**Desc.:** Provides evaluations of major data
   communications products. Includes
   overviews and product evaluations
   relating to 13 areas, such as local area
   networks, modems, and data
   communication carriers. Service includes
   two volumes plus monthly reports.
**Readers:** Data communications managers,
   government officials, and vendors.

22297

**CONTACTS**
35-20 Broadway
Astoria, NY 11106
Telephone: (718) 721-0508
Year Established: 1971

Pub. Frequency: w.
Page Size: standard
Subscrip. Rate: $287/yr.
Circulation: 5,000
Circulation Type: paid
**Owner(s):**
CA Communications Associates, Ltd.
35-20 Broadway
Astoria, NY 11106
Telephone: (212) 721-0508
Ownership %: 100
**Management:**
Michael M. Smith ................................President
Michael M. Smith ................................Publisher
**Editorial:**
Madeleine Gillis ........................................Editor
**Desc.:** Weekly service that keeps PR
   people up-to-date on the types of
   information that editors and producers
   want to receive from them. Covers the
   business press, consumer press,
   newspapers, wire services, syndicates,
   the trade press, TV & radio. Reports on
   new columns and departments, new
   publications and provides a weekly in-
   depth interview and/or survey.
**Readers:** Public relations practitioners at
   corporate associations, PR companies,
   government agencies, other
   organizations.

22095

**CUMULATIVE BOOK INDEX**
950 University Ave.
Bronx, NY 10452
Telephone: (718) 588-8400
FAX: (718) 590-1617
Year Established: 1898
Pub. Frequency: m. exc. Aug.
Page Size: standard
Subscrip. Rate: depends on quantity
   ordered
**Owner(s):**
H.W. Wilson Co.
950 University Ave.
Bronx, NY 10452
Telephone: (718) 588-8400
Ownership %: 100
**Management:**
Leo M. Weins .......................................President
Leo M. Weins .......................................Publisher
**Editorial:**
Nancy C. Wong .........................................Editor
Donald Cannon ........................Associate Editor
Ann Case ................Indexing Services Director
**Desc.:** An author, title, and subject index
   to current books in the English language
   published in all countries. Government
   publications, pamphlets, self-published
   works, subsidy-press publications, and
   ephemera are excluded.
**Readers:** Librarians and patrons of
   libraries.

61253

**DIGITAL IMAGING REPORT**
21150 Hawthorne Blvd., Ste. 104
Torrance, CA 90503
Telephone: (310) 371-5787
FAX: (310) 542-0849
Year Established: 1984
Pub. Frequency: m.
Page Size: standard
Subscrip. Rate: $295/yr.
Materials: 02,06,15,27,28,29,32,33
Print Process: offset
**Owner(s):**
James Cavuoto, Pub. & Ed.
21150 Hawthorne Blvd, Ste. 104
Torrance, CA 90503
Telephone: (310) 371-5787
Ownership %: 100
**Editorial:**
James Cavuoto ...........................................Editor
Stephen Beale .........................Managing Editor
David Pope .............................Consulting Editor

Karen Nickelson ...................Editorial Assistant
**Desc.:** Provides detailed analysis of market
   and industry trends, vendor profiles,
   show reports, personnel, and financial
   briefs.
**Readers:** Uses of Graphic Services.

23554

**EDITOR & PUBLISHER - THE
FOURTH ESTATE**
11 W. 19th St.
New York, NY 10011
Telephone: (212) 675-4380
FAX: (212) 929-1259
Year Established: 1884
Pub. Frequency: w.
Page Size: standard
Subscrip. Rate: $1.75/issue; $55/yr.
Circulation: 24,584
Circulation Type: paid
**Owner(s):**
Editor & Publisher Co., Inc., The
11 W. 19th St.
New York, NY 10011
Telephone: (212) 675-4380
Ownership %: 100
**Bureau(s):**
Editor & Publisher Co.
8 S. Michigan Ave.
Chicago, IL 60603
Telephone: (312) 641-0041
Contact: Mark Fitzgerald, Editor

Editor & Publisher Co.
1128 National Press Bldg.
Washington, DC 20045
Telephone: (202) 662-7234
Contact: Debra Gersh, Editor
**Management:**
Robert U. Brown ...............................President
Ferdinand C. Teubner .........................Publisher
Steven A. Townsley .........Advertising Manager
**Editorial:**
Robert U. Brown .........................................Editor
John P. Consoli ........................Managing Editor
Hiley Ward ............................Book Review Editor
**Desc.:** Carries news of newspaper industry
   and allied fields, as well as advertising,
   syndicates, wire services, newspaper
   printing, and production.
**Readers:** Daily and weekly newspaper
   executives and employees, journalism
   schools, libraries, advertising agencies,
   advertisers, news services and feature
   syndicates, PR firms, government,
   graphic arts and printing services, and
   other news organizations.

23555

**FOLIO: THE MAGAZINE FOR
MAGAZINE MANAGEMENT**
470 Park Ave., S.
New York, NY 10016
Telephone: (212) 683-3540
FAX: (212) 683-3986
Year Established: 1972
Pub. Frequency: s-m.
Page Size: standard
Subscrip. Rate: $96/yr. US; $124/yr.
   Canada & Mexico
Materials: 01,06,15,17,27,29,30,32,33
Freelance Pay: negotiable
Print Process: web offset
Circulation: 10,500
Circulation Type: paid
**Owner(s):**
Conles Business Media
911 Hope St.
Stamford, CT 06907
Telephone: (203) 358-9900
Ownership %: 100
**Bureau(s):**
Los Angeles Bureau
1060 Calle Cordillera, Ste. 10
San Clemente, CA 92673
Telephone: (714) 366-0442
Contact: Erica Isler, Bureaus Editor

---

**Materials Accepted/Included:** 01-Business news 02-By-line articles 03-Fashion news 04-Food news 05-Freelance copy 06-Letters to editor 07-Real estate news 08-Sports news 09-Travel news 10-Book rev. 11-Movie rev. 12-Music rev. 13-TV rev. 14-Theater rev. 15-Coming events 16-Obituaries 17-Question & answer 18-Social announcements 19-Artwork 20-Cartoons 21-Photos 22-TV listings 23-Audio rec. 24-Video rec. 25-Books 26-Films/film clips 27-Personnel news 28-Press releases 29-New product news/photos 30-Trade lit. 31-Contracts awarded 32-Display adv. 33-Classified adv.

**Management:**
David Cox ............................Chairman of Board
Hershel Sarbin ........................................President
William D. Holiber ................................Publisher
**Editorial:**
Anne Russell ..............................................Editor
**Desc.:** Serves the magazine publishing
  industry. Contains how-to features,
  industry news, money-, labor-, and time-
  saving tips; and departments devoted to
  management, editing, circulation,
  production, sales, and art direction.
**Readers:** Magazine publishers, editors,
  sales managers, art directors,
  presidents, and other personnel.

**GA PRESS BULLETIN**                            24392
3066 Mercer University Dr., Ste. 200
Atlanta, GA 30304-4137
Telephone: (404) 454-6776
FAX: (404) 454-6778
Year Established: 1887
Pub. Frequency: m.
Page Size: tabloid
Subscrip. Rate: $20/yr.
Circulation: 730
Circulation Type: free
**Owner(s):**
Georgia Press Association
3066 Mercer University Dr., St
Atlanta, GA 30304-4137
Telephone: (404) 454-6776
Ownership %: 100
**Editorial:**
Sue Rodman ................................................Editor
**Desc.:** Material relating to newspapers.
**Readers:** Newspaper editors, publishers,
  staffers, association executives,
  business leaders.

**ILLINOIS PUBLISHER, THE**                      69580
1701 S. Grand Ave., W.
Springfield, IL 62704
Telephone: (217) 523-5092
FAX: (217) 523-5103
Year Established: 1917
Pub. Frequency: q.
Subscrip. Rate: $12/yr.
Circulation: 2,000
Circulation Type: paid
**Owner(s):**
Illinois Press Association, Inc.
1701 S. Grand Ave., W.
Springfield, IL 62704
Ownership %: 100
**Editorial:**
David Porter ................................................Editor

**INPRINT**                                      69588
206 W. State St.
Trenton, NJ 08608-1095
Telephone: (609) 695-3366
FAX: (609) 695-8729
Year Established: 1934
Pub. Frequency: m.
Page Size: tabloid
Subscrip. Rate: $12/yr.; $8/yr. to students
Materials: 01,02,06,10,17,18,21,28,30,32,33
Print Process: offset
Circulation: 1,200
Circulation Type: controlled
**Owner(s):**
New Jersey Press Association
206 W. State St.
Trenton, NJ 08608-1095
Telephone: (609) 695-3366
FAX: (609) 695-8729
Ownership %: 100
**Management:**
John O'Brien ........................................Publisher
Elisabeth Hagen ........................Sales Manager
**Editorial:**
Elisabeth Hagen ..................Editor in Chief

**Desc.:** Covers events, issues, and
  personalities in the New Jersey
  newspaper industry.
**Readers:** Publishers and heads of
  departments and staffers at New Jersey
  paid circulation and free distribution
  newspapers.

**JOURNAL-NEWSLETTER OF THE**       69576
**AMERICAN ASSOCIATION OF**
**DENTAL EDITORS**
1100 Lake St., Ste. 24D
Oak Park, IL 60301
Telephone: (708) 445-0322
FAX: (708) 445-0321
Year Established: 1973
Pub. Frequency: q.
Page Size: standard
Subscrip. Rate: $25/yr. US; $40/yr. foreign
Print Process: offset
Circulation: 325
Circulation Type: controlled
**Owner(s):**
American Association of Dental Editors
1100 Lake St., Ste. 24D
Oak Park, IL 60301
Telephone: (708) 445-0322
FAX: (708) 445-0321
**Editorial:**
Joanna Carey ..............................................Editor

**JQ: JOURNALISM QUARTERLY**        68944
1621 College St.
University of South Carolina
Columbia, SC 29208-0251
Telephone: (803) 777-2005
Year Established: 1924
Pub. Frequency: q.
Subscrip. Rate: $30/yr. individuals; $40/yr.
  foreign
Circulation: 4,100
Circulation Type: controlled & paid
**Owner(s):**
Assn. for Education in Journalism and
  Mass Comm.
1621 College St.
University of South Carolina
Columbia, SC 29208-0251
Telephone: (803) 777-2005
Ownership %: 100
**Editorial:**
Jean Folkerts ..............................................Editor

**LOCUS: THE NEWSPAPER OF THE**     69062
**SCIENCE FICTION FIELD**
34 Ridgewood Ln.
Oakland, CA 94611
Telephone: (510) 339-9196
FAX: (510) 339-8144
Mailing Address:
  P.O. Box 13305
  Oakland, CA 94661
Year Established: 1968
Pub. Frequency: m
Page Size: standard
Subscrip. Rate: $3.95 newsstand; $38/yr.
Materials: 01,16,21,23,24,25,26,27,28,29,
  30,31,32,33
Print Process: web offset
Circulation: 9,000
Circulation Type: paid
**Owner(s):**
Locus Publications
34 Ridgewood Ln.
Oakland, CA 94611
Telephone: (510) 339-9196
FAX: (510) 339-8144
Ownership %: 100
**Management:**
Charles N. Brown ................................Publisher
**Editorial:**
Charles N. Brown ....................................Editor
Marianne S. Jablon ..............Assistant Editor
Carolyn F. Cushman ............Assistant Editor

Faren C. Miller ........................Associate Editor
**Desc.:** News of the science fiction
  publishing world, including author
  interviews, news of industry personnel,
  forthcoming books, reports from the
  electronic frontier, and extensive book
  reviews.
**Readers:** Professional and interested
  readers.

**MAGAZINE & BOOKSELLER**           22098
322 Eighth Ave.
New York, NY 10001
Telephone: (212) 620-7330
FAX: (212) 620-7335
Year Established: 1937
Pub. Frequency: 8/yr.
Page Size: standard
Subscrip. Rate: $49/yr.
Freelance Pay: $150-$500/article
Circulation: 20,000
Circulation Type: controlled
**Owner(s):**
North American Publishing Co.
401 N. Broad St.
Philadelphia, PA 19108
Telephone: (215) 238-5300
Ownership %: 100
**Management:**
Ned Borowsky ..............................President
**Editorial:**
Patricia McMcarthy ........................Senior Editor
**Desc.:** The trade magazine of mass
  periodical and paperback distribution for
  wholesalers and retailers. Departments
  include: Display, Store Arrangement,
  Point of Sale Material, Previews of
  Publications, Magazine Directory,
  Computer Publications, Book
  Review Capsules, Advance Buying
  Guide, New Magazines on the
  Newsstand, ABC Directories and
  Retailer Success Stories.
**Readers:** Retailers at supermarkets,
  convenience stores, independent outlets,
  magazine and book wholesalers, drug
  chains, bookstores, college stores and
  national distributors, and publishers.

**MAGAZINE ISSUES**                 52680
P.O. Box 23010
Knoxville, TN 37933
Telephone: (615) 584-1918
Year Established: 1982
Pub. Frequency: bi-m.
Page Size: standard
Subscrip. Rate: $20/yr.
Freelance Pay: varies
Circulation: 13,000
Circulation Type: controlled
**Owner(s):**
Feredonna Communications
P.O. Box 23010
Knoxville, TN 37933
Telephone: (615) 584-1918
Ownership %: 100
**Management:**
Michael Ward ........................................Publisher
Nita Moyers ........................Circulation Manager
**Desc.:** A magazine specifically designed
  for trade, consumer, and non-profit
  publications. The purpose of it is to
  increase the sales and the profitability of
  its subscriber publications. Features and
  reports are aimed to assist readers in
  managing the business side of their
  publishing companies. Each issue
  includes feature articles, monthly
  columns and departments in "how-to"
  format covering the various aspects of
  publishing as well as products, services
  and trends.

**Readers:** Publishers, editors, production,
  advertising & circulation managers for
  publications with circulations under
  500,000.

**MAGAZINEWEEK**                    64916
233 W. Central St.
Natick, MA 01760
Telephone: (508) 650-1001
FAX: (508) 650-4648
Pub. Frequency: w.
Page Size: tabloid
Subscrip. Rate: $98/yr.
Circulation: 45,000
Circulation Type: paid
**Owner(s):**
Lighthouse Communications Group, Inc.
233 W. Central St.
Natick, MA 01760
Telephone: (508) 650-1001
Ownership %: 100
**Management:**
Jack Berkowitz ..........Executive Vice President
Kenneth L. Fadner ................................Publisher
Jowa Coffey ......................Circulation Manager
**Editorial:**
Stanley Mieses ......................Executive Editor
Richard Thau ................................Senior Editor
Milton Glaser ................................Senior Editor
Stanley Mieses ..............................................Editor
Sharlene Breakey ......................Managing Editor
Gary Hoenig ............................Editorial Director
Ann Terrell ....................................Art Director
Marc Boisclair ..........................Associate Editor
Paul McDougall ........................Associate Editor
Michael C. Roberts ............Associate Publisher
**Desc.:** Weekly record of important news,
  trends and ideas in magazine publishing.
**Readers:** Magazine publishers and
  management personnel.

**MASTHEAD**                        69597
6223 Executive Blvd.
Rockville, MD 20852
Telephone: (301) 984-3015
FAX: (301) 231-0026
Year Established: 1948
Pub. Frequency: q.
Subscrip. Rate: $25/yr.
Circulation: 1,000
Circulation Type: paid
**Owner(s):**
National Conference of Editorial Writers
6223 Executive Blvd.
Rockville, MD 20852
Telephone: (301) 984-3015
**Editorial:**
Sue Ryon ..............................................Editor
**Desc.:** Devoted to all aspects of producing
  editorials in all media, from determining
  editorial policy to writing, design and
  presentation.

**MICRO PUBLISHING NEWS**           70456
21150 Hawthorne Blvd., Ste. 104
Torrance, CA 90503
Telephone: (310) 371-5787
FAX: (310) 542-0849
Year Established: 1986
Pub. Frequency: m.
Page Size: tabloid
Subscrip. Rate: free in state; $24.95/yr.
  out of state
Materials: 02,06,16,27,28,29,32,33
Print Process: offset
**Owner(s):**
James Cavuoto
21150 Hawthorne Blvd., Ste. 10
Torrance, CA 90503
Telephone: (310) 371-5787
Ownership %: 100
**Management:**
James Cavuoto ........................................Publisher

**Materials Accepted/Included:** 01-Business news 02-By-line articles 03-Fashion news 04-Food news 05-Freelance copy 06-Letters to editor 07-Real estate news 08-Sports news 09-Travel news 10-Book rev. 11-Movie rev. 12-Music rev. 13-TV rev. 14-Theater rev. 15-Coming events 16-Obituaries 17-Question & answer 18-Social announcements 19-Artwork 20-Cartoons 21-Photos 22-TV listings 23-Audio rec. 24-Video rec. 25-Books 26-Films/film clips 27-Personnel news 28-Press releases 29-New product news/photos 30-Trade lit. 31-Contracts awarded 32-Display adv. 33-Classified adv.

**Editorial:**
James Cavuoto .................................Editor
Stephen Beale ....................Managing Editor
David Pope ......................Consulting Editor
Karen Nickelson ..............Editorial Assistant
**Desc.:** Consists of micro-computer publishing product reviews, news & trend analysis and product announcement.
**Readers:** Electronic designers & publishers.

## MISSOURI PRESS NEWS
23558

802 Locust St.
Columbia, MO 65201
Telephone: (314) 449-4167
FAX: (314) 874-5894
Year Established: 1938
Pub. Frequency: m.
Page Size: standard
Subscrip. Rate: $7.50/yr.
Freelance Pay: varies
Circulation: 1,100
Circulation Type: paid
**Owner(s):**
Missouri Press Association
802 Locust St.
Columbia, MO 65201
Telephone: (314) 449-4167
Ownership %: 100
**Management:**
Mike Sell ..........................Advertising Manager
Doug Crews ......................Business Manager
**Editorial:**
Kent M. Ford ..............................Editor
**Desc.:** Content for newspaper, advertising, printing industry. Departments include: printing, advertising news, features on newspapers, trade tricks, new methods.
**Readers:** Newspaper personnel, advertising agencies.

## MLQ (MODERN LANGUAGE QUARTERLY)
70448

905 W. Main St., Ste. 18-B
Duke University Press
Durham, NC 27701
Telephone: (919) 687-3636
FAX: (919) 688-4574
Mailing Address:
  P.O. Box 90660
  Durham, NC 27708-0660
Year Established: 1940
Pub. Frequency: q.
Page Size: standard
Subscrip. Rate: $20/yr. students; $40/yr. institutions
Materials: 32
Circulation: 1,800
Circulation Type: controlled & paid
**Owner(s):**
Duke University Press
P.O. Box 90660
Durham, NC 27708-0660
Telephone: (919) 687-3600
FAX: (919) 688-4574
Ownership %: 100
**Management:**
Patricia Thomas ............................Manager
**Editorial:**
Marshall Brown ..............................Editor
John C. Coldeway ..........................Editor

## NETWORK
69615

P.O. Box 810 Gracie Sta.
New York, NY 10028
Telephone: (212) 737-7536
Year Established: 1980
Pub. Frequency: bi-m.
Page Size: standard
Subscrip. Rate: $35/yr. US; $45/yr. foreign
Materials: 06,15,21,32,33
Print Process: offset

Circulation: 3,000
Circulation Type: paid
**Owner(s):**
International Women's Writing Guild
P.O. Box 810 Gracie Sta.
New York, NY 10028
Telephone: (212) 737-7536
FAX: (212) 737-7469
Ownership %: 100
**Editorial:**
Tatiana Stounen ..............................Editor
**Desc.:** News of and by women writers.

## NEWSPAPERS & TECHNOLOGY
66595

4800 Wadsworth Blvd., Ste. 309
Wheat Ridge, CO 80033-1053
Telephone: (303) 456-4880
FAX: (303) 456-4870
Year Established: 1988
Pub. Frequency: m.
Page Size: tabloid
Subscrip. Rate: free
Freelance Pay: $150-$200/article
Print Process: web offset
Circulation: 18,000
Circulation Type: controlled
**Owner(s):**
Citizen Publishing
805 Park Ave.
Beaver Dam, WI 53916
Telephone: (414) 887-0321
Ownership %: 100
**Management:**
Mary Van Meter ..........................Publisher
**Editorial:**
Brad Moritz ..............................Editor
**Desc.:** Covers new technologies, and their applications to the newspaper industry.
**Readers:** Newspaper publishers, production directors, editors & technology directors.

## OKLAHOMA PUBLISHER
23560

3601 N. Lincoln
Oklahoma City, OK 73105-5499
Telephone: (405) 524-4421
FAX: (405) 524-2201
Year Established: 1924
Pub. Frequency: m.
Page Size: tabloid
Subscrip. Rate: $5/yr.
Circulation: 1,200
Circulation Type: paid
**Owner(s):**
Oklahoma Press Association
3601 N. Lincoln
Oklahoma City, OK 73105
Telephone: (405) 524-4421
Ownership %: 100
**Management:**
Bob Stacy ..........................Advertising Manager
Ben Blackstock ..........................Manager
**Editorial:**
Ben Blackstock ..............................Editor
Jennifer Gilliland ..................Managing Editor
**Desc.:** Concerns the activities of the Oklahoma Press Association and news about Oklahoma newspapers and their personnel.
**Readers:** All employees of Oklahoma newspapers.

## PNPA PRESS
23561

2717 N. Front St.
Harrisburg, PA 17110
Telephone: (717) 234-4067
FAX: (717) 734-0746
Year Established: 1929
Pub. Frequency: m.
Page Size: tabloid
Subscrip. Rate: $17.75/yr.
Materials: 30,32,33
Print Process: web
Circulation: 900

Circulation Type: paid
**Owner(s):**
Pennsylvania Newspaper Publishers Association
2717 N. Front St.
Harrisburg, PA 17110
Telephone: (717) 234-4067
Ownership %: 100
**Management:**
Timothy M. Williams ..........................Publisher
**Editorial:**
Amy H. Smith ..............................Editor
**Desc.:** News and developments of general interest to the newspaper publishing and general printing fields; emphasis on material concerning Pennsylvania. By-line features by newspaper executives in the state present case histories, discuss new equipment, comment on developments. Departments include: Freedom of Information Material, Personnel Post, News & Views.
**Readers:** Publishers, editors, business managers, general managers, advertising & classified managers, and other top executives of newspapers.
**Deadline:** story-10th of mo.; news-10th of mo.; photo-10th of mo.; ads-10th of mo.

## POETICS TODAY
65672

Brightleaf Sq., Ste. 18-B
805 W. Main St.
Durham, NC 27701
Telephone: (919) 687-3636
FAX: (919) 688-4574
Mailing Address:
  P.O. Box 90660
  Durham, NC 27708
Year Established: 1979
Pub. Frequency: q.: Feb., May, Aug., Nov.
Page Size: standard
Subscrip. Rate: $72/yr. institutions; $32/yr. individual; $16/yr. students
Materials: 32
Circulation: 1,000
Circulation Type: paid
**Owner(s):**
Duke University Press
P.O. Box 90660
Durham, NC 27708
Ownership %: 100
**Management:**
Patricia Thomas ............................Manager
**Editorial:**
Itamar Even-Zohar ..............................Editor
Janet Pursell ..................Journals Marketing Schipporeit
**Desc.:** The leading international journal in the theory and analysis of literature and communication. Each issue features book reviews and the valuable "New Books at a Glance" section.

## PRESS WOMAN
69606

1105 Main St., Box 99
Blue Springs, MO 64013
Telephone: (816) 229-1666
Year Established: 1937
Pub. Frequency: bi-m
Page Size: standard
Subscrip. Rate: $20/yr.
Circulation: 4,000
Circulation Type: paid
**Owner(s):**
National Federation of Press Women, Inc.
c/o Lois Lauer Wolfe
1105 Main St., Box 99
Blue Springs, MO 64013
Telephone: (816) 229-1666
Ownership %: 100
**Editorial:**
Lois Lauer Wolfe ..............................Editor

## PUBLISH!
64920

501 Second St., Ste. 310
San Francisco, CA 94107
Telephone: (415) 978-3280
FAX: (415) 495-2354
Year Established: 1986
Pub. Frequency: m.
Page Size: standard
Subscrip. Rate: $23.95/yr.
Freelance Pay: negotiable
Circulation: 100,000
Circulation Type: paid
**Owner(s):**
PCW Communications, Inc.
501 Second St., Ste. 310
San Francisco, CA 94107
Telephone: (415) 978-3280
Ownership %: 100
**Management:**
Gordon Haight ..............................President
Bruce Gray ..............................Publisher
Michael Goldstein ..........................Manager
**Editorial:**
Jake Widman ..................Editor in Chief
Neil Versen ..................Advertising Director
Bobbie Long ..........................Art Director
Jayne Boyer ..................Production Director
**Desc.:** The how-to magazine of desktop publishing.
**Readers:** All manner of desktop publishers.

## PUBLISHERS' AUXILIARY
23562

1525 Wilson Blvd., Ste. 550
Arlington, VA 22209
Telephone: (703) 907-7900
FAX: (703) 907-7901
Year Established: 1865
Pub. Frequency: bi-w.
Page Size: tabloid
Subscrip. Rate: $55/yr.
Freelance Pay: $50/article
Circulation: 7,500
Circulation Type: paid
**Owner(s):**
National Newspaper Association
1627 K St., NW
Washington, DC 20006
Telephone: (202) 466-7200
Ownership %: 100
**Management:**
David C. Simonson ..............................Publisher
Sharon E. ........Assistant Advertising Manager
McFarland
**Editorial:**
Edward C. Holahan ..............................Editor
Stanley Schwartz ..................Associate Editor
Harry Heath ..................Book Review Editor
**Desc.:** Contains material of interest to the newspaper industry-general news items, stories on advertising, circulation, all phases of newspaper publishing, new products descriptions. No publicity material is used that is not direct interest to readers. Editorial departments include General News Section, Mechanical Products Section, Advertising, Circulation, Promotion Section, Management, Washington Report, Business and Finance.
**Readers:** Publishers, general managers, production, ad managers, circulation managers, etc.

## PUBLISHERS WEEKLY
22102

249 W. 17th St.
New York, NY 10011
Telephone: (212) 463-6758
FAX: (212) 463-6631
Year Established: 1872
Pub. Frequency: w.
Page Size: standard
Subscrip. Rate: $129/yr.
Freelance Pay: $200/printed page

---

Materials Accepted/Included: 01-Business news 02-By-line articles 03-Fashion news 04-Food news 05-Freelance copy 06-Letters to editor 07-Real estate news 08-Sports news 09-Travel news 10-Book rev. 11-Movie rev. 12-Music rev. 13-TV rev. 14-Theater rev. 15-Coming events 16-Obituaries 17-Question & answer 18-Social announcements 19-Artwork 20-Cartoons 21-Photos 22-TV listings 23-Audio rec. 24-Video rec. 25-Books 26-Films/film clips 27-Personnel news 28-Press releases 29-New product news/photos 30-Trade lit. 31-Contracts awarded 32-Display adv. 33-Classified adv.

Circulation: 38,349
Circulation Type: paid
**Owner(s):**
Reed Publishing (USA)
249 W. 17th St.
New York, NY 10011
Telephone: (212) 463-6758
Ownership %: 100
**Management:**
Terry McDermott .............................President
John F. Baker ...........................Vice President
Fred Ciporen .............................Publisher
**Editorial:**
Nora Rawlinson ..........................Editor in Chief
Daisy Maryles ...........................Executive Editor
John Mutter ............................Executive Editor
Sybil S. Steinberg ......................Senior Editor
Michael Coffey .........................Managing Editor
Robin Lenz ..............Associate Managing Editor
Karen E. Jones ..........................Art Director
Genevieve Stuttaford .........Book Review Editor
Jim Borth ...............................Circulation Director
Herbert R. Lottman (Int'l) ...........Foreign Editor
**Desc.:** News and by-line articles about
book publishing, bookselling, and
bookmaking.
**Readers:** Booksellers, librarians,
publishers, book reviewers, motion
picture producers, agents,
manufacturers, and suppliers.

65296
**PUBLISHING & PRODUCTION
EXECUTIVE**
401 N. Broad St.
Philadelphia, PA 19108
Telephone: (215) 238-5300
FAX: (215) 238-5457
Year Established: 1987
Pub. Frequency: m.
Page Size: standard
Subscrip. Rate: free to qualified
subscribers
Materials: 02,06,20,21,28,29
Print Process: web offset
Circulation: 33,000
Circulation Type: controlled
**Owner(s):**
North American Publishing Co.
401 N. Broad St.
Philadelphia, PA 19108
Telephone: (215) 238-5300
Ownership %: 100
**Management:**
Irvin Borowsky ...............Chairman of Board
Ned Borowsky ...........................President
Mark Hertzog ...........................Publisher
**Editorial:**
Rose Blessing ...........................Editor
**Desc.:** Publishes cases studies and
technical tutorials relating to leading-
edge trends of the publishing industry.
**Readers:** Buyers of printing, prepress,
paper, and publishing systems for
magazines, catalogs, books, agencies,
and corporate communications.

23564
**QUILL & SCROLL**
University of Iowa
Iowa City, IA 52242-1590
Telephone: (319) 335-5795
FAX: (319) 335-5210
Year Established: 1926
Pub. Frequency: q.
Page Size: standard
Subscrip. Rate: $3.25/copy; $12/yr.
Circulation: 13,500
Circulation Type: paid
**Owner(s):**
Quill & Scroll Society
School of Jour. & Mass Comm.
Iowa City, IA 52242-1590
Telephone: (319) 335-5795
Ownership %: 100

**Editorial:**
Richard P. Johns ........................Editor
Mary Arnold ...........................Assistant Editor
Roland E. Wolseley ..........Book Review Editor
**Desc.:** Devoted exclusively to the field of
high school publications-filled with
articles, pictures, news items and helpful
hints for students and advisers. Carries
up-to-date and authoritative information
about careers in journalism and
developments in the field of journalism
teaching and advising.
**Readers:** High school students and
publication advisors.

58695
**QUILL, THE**
16 S. Jackson St.
Greencastle, IN 46135
Telephone: (317) 653-3333
Mailing Address:
P.O. Box 77
Greencastle, IN 46135
Year Established: 1909
Pub. Frequency: 10/yr.
Page Size: standard
Subscrip. Rate: $3 newsstand; $29/yr. US;
$39/yr. foreign
Materials: 01,05,10,28,30,32,33
Freelance Pay: $250-$750/article
Print Process: web offset
Circulation: 22,000
Circulation Type: paid
**Owner(s):**
Society of Professional Journalists
16 S. Jackson
P.O. Box 77
Greencastle, IN 46135
Telephone: (317) 653-3333
FAX: (317) 653-4631
Ownership %: 100
**Management:**
Greg Christopher ...............Advertising Manager
**Editorial:**
Brian Steffens ...........................Editor
Kelli Patrick ...........................Associate Editor
**Desc.:** National magazine for professional
journalists as well as students and
teachers of journalism. Examines
contemporary issues and problems in
journalism, including 1st Amendment
and Freedom of Information Act.
Includes a section of Society News of
interest to members.
**Readers:** Members of the Soc. of
Professional Journalists.

69616
**REGISTERED WRITER'S
COMMUNIQUE-CONTACTS &
ASSIGNMENTS**
P.O. Pox 600927
N. Miami Beach, FL 33160
Year Established: 1986
Pub. Frequency: m.
Page Size: standard
Subscrip. Rate: $18/yr.
**Owner(s):**
Gibbs Publishing Co.
Box 600927
N. Miami Beach, FL 33160
Ownership %: 100
**Editorial:**
James Calvin Gibbs ........................Editor
**Readers:** Directed to professional
freelance writers.

59136
**SCITECH BOOK NEWS**
5600 N.E. Hassalo St.
Portland, OR 97213
Telephone: (503) 281-9230
FAX: (503) 284-8859
Year Established: 1977
Pub. Frequency: m.

Page Size: standard
Subscrip. Rate: $45/yr. individuals; $65/yr.
institutions
Freelance Pay: $.03/wd.
Circulation: 2,400
Circulation Type: paid
**Owner(s):**
Book News, Inc.
5600 N.E. Hassalo St.
Portland, OR 97213
Telephone: (503) 281-9230
Ownership %: 100
**Management:**
Fred Gullette ...........................Publisher
**Editorial:**
Jane Erskine ...........................Editor
**Desc.:** Concise reviews of high-level books
in science, technology, medicine,
engineering and agriculture.
**Readers:** Librarians, faculty and non-
academic specialists having a need to
know of important recent sci-tech
books.

69579
**SFWA BULLETIN**
P.O. Box 1277
Eugene, OR 97440
Telephone: (503) 935-6322
FAX: (503) 935-6324
Year Established: 1965
Pub. Frequency: q.
Page Size: standard
Subscrip. Rate: $15/yr.
Circulation: 1,500
Circulation Type: controlled
**Owner(s):**
Science-Fiction & Fantasy Writers of
America
**Editorial:**
Dan Hatch ...........................Editor

59134
**SMALL PRESS BOOK REVIEW,
THE**
P.O. Box 176
Southport, CT 06490
Telephone: (203) 332-7629
Year Established: 1985
Pub. Frequency: bi-m.
Page Size: standard
Subscrip. Rate: $40/yr.
Materials: 25,28,30
Freelance Pay: 2 copies of issue
Print Process: electronic publishing for
database
Circulation: 3,000
Circulation Type: paid
**Owner(s):**
Greenfield Press
P.O. Box 176
Southport, CT 06490
Telephone: (203) 332-7629
Ownership %: 100
**Bureau(s):**
The Library Corp.
Research Park
Inwood, WV 25428-9733
**Editorial:**
Henry Berry ...........................Editor
David Parks ...........................Editor
Laurie Hiller ...........................Editorial Assistant
**Desc.:** Contains brief descriptive, critical
reviews of all types of books published
by independent presses. Includes a
children's book section and news notes.
**Readers:** Librarians, booksellers, and
general public.

23565
**ST. LOUIS JOURNALISM REVIEW**
8380 Olive Blvd.
St. Louis, MO 63132
Telephone: (314) 991-1699
FAX: (314) 997-1898
Year Established: 1970
Pub. Frequency: m.

Page Size: tabloid
Subscrip. Rate: $25/yr.; $42/2 yrs.; $51/3
yrs.
Freelance Pay: varies
Print Process: web offset
Circulation: 5,000
Circulation Type: paid
**Owner(s):**
St. Louis Journalism Review
8380 Olive Blvd.
St. Louis, MO 63132
Telephone: (314) 991-1699
Ownership %: 100
**Management:**
Charles L. Klotzer ...........................Publisher
Rose F. Klotzer .................Associate Publisher
**Editorial:**
Charles L Klotzer ...........................Editor
**Desc.:** A critique of primarily St. Louis, MO,
metropolitan affairs and print and
broadcast media but also national media
by working journalists in the St. Louis
area. Also covers news and
developments not covered by the mass
media. Critique of media: press,
broadcasting, TV, cable, advertising, PR,
communications. Independent,
investigative journal evaluating local,
regional, and national presentation of
news. Content of direct interest to both
the general public and the media
community.
**Readers:** Highly educated, middle and
upper income, professional, business,
academic and community leaders in
general and communications industry.

22103
**TECHNICAL COMMUNICATIONS**
901 N. Stuart St., Ste. 904
Arlington, VA 22203
Telephone: (703) 522-4114
FAX: (703) 522-2075
Year Established: 1953
Pub. Frequency: q.
Page Size: standard
Subscrip. Rate: $50/yr.
Circulation: 19,000
Circulation Type: controlled
**Owner(s):**
Society for Technical Communication
901 N. Stuart St., Ste. 904
Arlington, VA 22203-1854
Telephone: (703) 522-4114
Ownership %: 100
**Management:**
William C. Stolgitis ...............Executive Director
**Editorial:**
Dr. Frank R. Smith ...........................Editor
Susan Dressell ...................Book Review Editor
**Desc.:** Articles on new techniques of
technical writing, editing, illustrating, and
document production. Tutorial features.
Articles on professional growth
opportunities. Features on
novel equipment or publications.
Departments include: Correspondence,
Books, Status of Tech
Manual Specs/STDS, Recent and
Relevant (article abstracts).
**Readers:** Technical communicators and
writers, editors, professors,
administrators, and managers.

23567
**VIRGINIA'S PRESS**
202 Lakeridge Pkwy.
Ashland, VA 23005
Telephone: (804) 550-2361
Mailing Address:
P.O. Box 85613
Richmond, VA 23285-5613
Year Established: 1915
Pub. Frequency: s-w.
Page Size: tabloid
Subscrip. Rate: $15/yr. US; $20/yr. foreign

**Materials Accepted/Included:** 01-Business news 02-By-line articles 03-Fashion news 04-Food news 05-Freelance copy 06-Letters to editor 07-Real estate news 08-Sports news 09-Travel news 10-Book rev. 11-Movie rev. 12-Music rev. 13-TV rev. 14-Theater rev. 15-Coming events 16-Obituaries 17-Question & answer 18-Social announcements 19-Artwork 20-Cartoons 21-Photos 22-TV listings 23-Audio rec. 24-Video rec. 25-Books 26-Films/film clips 27-Personnel news 28-Press releases 29-New product news/photos 30-Trade lit. 31-Contracts awarded 32-Display adv. 33-Classified adv.

Circulation: 1,000
Circulation Type: controlled
**Owner(s):**
Virginia Press Association, Inc.
202 Lakeridge Pkwy.
Richmond, VA 23227
Telephone: (804) 550-2361
Ownership %: 100
**Management:**
Forrest M. Landon ...............................President
Ginger Stanley ...................................Publisher
Judy Lovelace ...................Advertising Manager
**Editorial:**
Ginger Stanley .........................Executive Editor
Ray Hall ...................................................Editor
R.S. Hall .................................Publications Editor
**Desc.:** A newsletter of news and events of
the Virginia Press Assn., publishers,
editors, and staff members of Virginia
daily and weekly newspapers.
**Readers:** Key personnel of Virginia's daily
and weekly newspapers.

**VISIBLE LANGUAGE**　58720
4807 S. Greenwood Ave., Ste. 2
Chicago, IL 60615-1913
Telephone: (716) 381-1552
FAX: (716) 223-8202
Year Established: 1967
Pub. Frequency: q.
Page Size: pocket
Subscrip. Rate: $35/yr. individuals; $55/yr.
institutions
Circulation: 1,000
Circulation Type: paid
**Owner(s):**
Sharon Poggenpohl
6 Hidden Bridge
Pittsford, NY 14534
Ownership %: 100
**Editorial:**
Sharon Poggenpohl ...............................Editor
**Desc.:** Concerned with research and ideas
that define the unique role and
properties of written language on the
basis of the premise that writing and
reading form an autonomous system of
language expression, which must be
defined and developed on its own terms.
**Readers:** Scholars, teachers, language
and design practitioners.

**WORDSWORTH CIRCLE, THE**　59641
Department of English
Temple University
Philadelphia, PA 19147
Telephone: (215) 787-4716
Year Established: 1970
Pub. Frequency: q.
Page Size: standard
Subscrip. Rate: $20/yr.
Circulation: 1,200
Circulation Type: paid
**Owner(s):**
Marilyn Gaull
Department of English
Temple University
Philadelphia, PA 19122
Telephone: (215) 787-4716
Ownership %: 100
**Editorial:**
Dr. Marilyn Gaull ...................................Editor
**Desc.:** Is an international quarterly learned
journal founded in 1970 to improve
communication among colleagues
interested in the lives, works, and times
of the English Romantic writers. Covers
the writers and artists who lived during
the Romantic Era (1760-1859).
**Readers:** College professors and scholars.

**WORLD LITERATURE TODAY**　22105
University of Oklahoma
630 Parrington Oval, Rm. 110
Norman, OK 73019-0375
Telephone: (405) 325-4531
FAX: (405) 325-7495
Year Established: 1927
Pub. Frequency: q.
Page Size: standard
Subscrip. Rate: $9 newsstand; $30/yr.
Materials: 02,10,25,28,30,32
Circulation: 2,000
Circulation Type: free & paid
**Owner(s):**
University of Oklahoma
630 Parrington Oval, Rm. 110
Norman, OK 73019
Telephone: (405) 325-4531
FAX: (405) 325-7495
Ownership %: 100
**Management:**
Victoria Vaughn ...................Circulation Manager
**Editorial:**
Dr. Djclal Kadir .......................................Editor
David D. Clark .........................Assistant Editor
Dr. William Riggan ..................Associate Editor
Marla Chess ...........................Editorial Assistant
**Desc.:** Specializes in the review of and
comment on recently published books in
all languages, in the field of literature
and the humanities. Article sections
featuring studies of living writers and
contemporary literary movements.
Departments include: Article Section,
Commentaries, World Literature in
Review, French, Spanish, Italian, other
Romance Languages, German, English,
other Germanic languages, Russian,
other Slavic languages, Finno-Ugric and
Baltic, Greek, other European and
American, Africa, Near East, Asia and
Pacific, Comparative Studies.
**Readers:** One-third of the subscribers are
foreign. Two-thirds of all subscribers are
institutional.

**WRITER'S DIGEST**　23569
1507 Dana Ave.
Cincinnati, OH 45207
Telephone: (513) 531-2222
Year Established: 1920
Pub. Frequency: m.
Page Size: standard
Subscrip. Rate: $21/yr.
Freelance Pay: $.10-$.20/wd.
Circulation: 230,000
Circulation Type: paid
**Owner(s):**
F & W Publications, Inc.
1507 Dana Ave.
Cincinnati, OH 45207
Telephone: (513) 531-2222
FAX: (513) 531-1843
Ownership %: 100
**Management:**
Richard Rosenthal ..............................President
Jeff Lapin ..........................................Publisher
David Lee .........................Circulation Manager
Colleen Cannon ........Public Relations Manager
**Editorial:**
Thomas Clark ............................Senior Editor
Bruce Woods .........................................Editor
Peter Blocksom .......................Managing Editor
Dan Pessell .................................Art Department
David Lee .................................Marketing Director
Angela Terez .........................Submissions Editor
**Desc.:** Contributed articles on writing
techniques, markets, success stories,
and profiles and interviews of authors.
Covers nonfiction, fiction, poetry,
playwriting, TV, radio, photography, and
word processing.
**Readers:** Freelance writers.

**WRITER'S YEARBOOK**　23570
1507 Dana Ave.
Cincinnati, OH 45207
Telephone: (513) 531-2222
Year Established: 1930
Pub. Frequency: a.
Page Size: standard
Subscrip. Rate: $4.95/yr.
Freelance Pay: $0.25/wd.
Circulation: 225,000
Circulation Type: paid
**Owner(s):**
F & W Publications, Inc.
1507 Dana Ave.
Cincinnati, OH 45207
Telephone: (513) 531-2222
FAX: (513) 531-1843
Ownership %: 100
**Management:**
Jeffry M. Lapin ...................................Publisher
David Lee .........................Circulation Manager
**Editorial:**
Thomas Clark ............................Senior Editor
Bruce Woods .........................................Editor
Peter Blocksom .......................Managing Editor
Carri Bostian ........................Editorial Assistant
Angela Terez .........................Submissions Editor
**Desc.:** For freelance writers who want to
earn while they write. Features
interviews, lively and timely departments,
and clearheaded advice on writing short
stories, novels, articles, plays, and TV
and movie scripts. Covers trends in
writing fields and, occasionally, features
articles on specialized writing, such as
audiovisual writing, greeting cards, and
songwriting. Also covers the marketing
of what is written; the how-to-sell aspect
of the writing game. The marketing
coverage and reporting is the most
exhaustive in the field. Writers can read
the yearbook to refuel and reflect on the
writing life.
**Readers:** Freelance writers and
professional writers interested in creative
writing of all kinds.

**WRITER, THE**　23568
120 Boylston St.
Boston, MA 02116
Telephone: (617) 423-3157
Year Established: 1887
Pub. Frequency: m.
Page Size: standard
Subscrip. Rate: $2.25 newsstand; $27/yr.;
$50/2 yrs.
Materials: 05,06,25,28,32
Freelance Pay: varied
Print Process: web offset
Circulation: 54,550
Circulation Type: controlled & paid
**Owner(s):**
The Writer, Inc.
120 Boylston St.
Boston, MA 02116
Telephone: (617) 423-3157
Ownership %: 100
**Management:**
Sylvia K. Burack ...................................Owner
Sylvia K. Burack .................................Publisher
Ann-Margaret Calhoun .......Promotion Manager
**Editorial:**
Anne Drowns ............................Senior Editor
Sylvia K. Burack .....................................Editor
Elizabeth Preston ....................Managing Editor
Virginia McDonough ................Associate Editor
Linda Burtt .............................Circulation Editor
Monica Mahoney ...................Circulation Editor
Miriam G. Madfis .....................................Sales
Sylvia K. Burack .................................Treasurer

**Desc.:** Magazine for aspiring and
professional writers. Each issue features
articles by experts in the publishing and
writing field, up-to-date market
information, and tips on manuscript
submission.
**Readers:** Freelance writers, professors of
English, students.

**WRITTEN COMMUNICATION**　65063
2455 Teller Rd.
Thousand Oaks, CA 91320
Telephone: (805) 499-0721
FAX: (805) 499-0871
Year Established: 1984
Pub. Frequency: q.
Page Size: standard
Subscrip. Rate: $50/yr. individuals;
$144/yr. institutions
Circulation: 1,350
Circulation Type: paid
**Owner(s):**
Sage Publications, Inc.
2455 Teller Rd.
Thousand Oaks, CA 91320
Telephone: (805) 499-0721
Ownership %: 100
**Editorial:**
Deborah Brandt ......................................Editor
Martin Nystrand ......................................Editor
Stephen P. Witte ....................................Editor
**Desc.:** Provides a forum for the free
exchange of ideas, theoretical
viewpoints, and methodological
approaches that better define and
further develop thought and practice in
the exciting study of the written word.

## Group 218-Purchasing

**BUSINESS DOCUMENTS**　65453
401 N. Broad St.
Philadelphia, PA 19108
Telephone: (215) 238-5300
Year Established: 1988
Pub. Frequency: q.
Page Size: standard
Subscrip. Rate: $36/yr. US; $56/yr. foreign
Circulation: 15,000
Circulation Type: controlled
**Owner(s):**
North American Publishing Co.
401 N. Broad St.
Philadelphia, PA 19108
Telephone: (215) 238-5300
**Management:**
Judy Cavaliere ...................................Publisher
**Editorial:**
William Drennan .....................................Editor
Jennifer Mariano ...................Managing Editor
**Desc.:** Focus on forms design, purchasing,
and management for designers, buyers
in business and government and on
electronic document systems.
**Readers:** Targets designers and buyers in
business and government.

**CHICAGO PURCHASOR, THE**　24530
201 N. Wells St.
Chicago, IL 60606
Telephone: (312) 782-1940
FAX: (312) 782-9732
Year Established: 1920
Pub. Frequency: bi-m.
Page Size: standard
Subscrip. Rate: $15/yr.
Circulation: 5,000
Circulation Type: controlled & paid

**Materials Accepted/Included:** 01-Business news 02-By-line articles 03-Fashion news 04-Food news 05-Freelance copy 06-Letters to editor 07-Real estate news 08-Sports news 09-Travel news
10-Book rev. 11-Movie rev. 12-Music rev. 13-TV rev. 14-Theater rev. 15-Coming events 16-Obituaries 17-Question & answer 18-Social announcements 19-Artwork 20-Cartoons 21-Photos 22-TV listings
23-Audio rec. 24-Video rec. 25-Books 26-Films/film clips 27-Personnel news 28-Press releases 29-New product news/photos 30-Trade lit. 31-Contracts awarded 32-Display adv. 33-Classified adv.

4-313

**Owner(s):**
Purchasing Management Association of Chicago
201 N. Wells St.
Chicago, IL 60606
Telephone: (312) 782-1940
Ownership %: 100
**Management:**
Jackie Stinson ....................Advertising Manager
**Editorial:**
John T. Pressley .........................................Editor
**Desc.:** Covers purchasing subjects and problem-solving techniques for puchasing executives.
**Readers:** 98 percent purchasing executives.

65993

## GLOBAL DESIGN NEWS
275 Washington St.
Newton, MA 02158
Telephone: (617) 558-4761
FAX: (617) 558-4512
Year Established: 1993
Pub. Frequency: bi-m.
Page Size: standard
Subscrip. Rate: $75/yr.
Print Process: web offset
Circulation: 35,000
Circulation Type: free
**Owner(s):**
Cahners Publishing Co.
275 Washington St.
Newton, MA 02158
Telephone: (617) 964-3030
**Editorial:**
Kevin R. Fitzgerald .......................Editor
Diana Kessler ........................Managing Editor
**Desc.:** Serves OEM design engineers in 20 European countries.

24537

## HOOSIER PURCHASOR
6213 LaPas Trail
Bldg. 3, Ste. 100
Indianapolis, IN 46268
Telephone: (317) 298-3831
FAX: (317) 298-6375
Year Established: 1951
Pub. Frequency: m.
Page Size: standard
Subscrip. Rate: $24/yr. non-members
Freelance Pay: negotiable
Circulation: 5,500
Circulation Type: controlled
**Owner(s):**
Rex Eagon
6213 LaPas Trail
Bldg. 3, Ste. 100
Indianapolis, IN 46268
Telephone: (317) 298-3831
Ownership %: 100
**Editorial:**
Maleah Schreiner .......................................Editor
**Desc.:** The bulk of publication is devoted to association developments, news, and other subjects of interest to purchasing executives in Indiana, Michigan, and areas in the states contiguous to Indiana. Carries feature articles covering subjects of general interest to decision making executives and purchasing agents, for example, an article on the laws relating to price discrimination. Departments include: President's Page (message from the association president); Commodity Reports; Local, State, and Natl. Business Surveys; Industrial Material Developments (new items, materials, chemicals); New Firms; and Firm Changes. Pictures are of all pertinent information and subject matter.
**Readers:** Purchasing agents, engineers, middle to upper executives.

24538

## INDUSTRIAL PURCHASING AGENT
21 Russell Woods Rd.
Great Neck, NY 11021
Telephone: (516) 487-0990
FAX: (516) 487-0809
Year Established: 1956
Pub. Frequency: m.
Page Size: tabloid
Subscrip. Rate: $25/yr.
Materials: 01,02,12,19,21,23,24,25,27,28, 29,30,32
Print Process: offset
Circulation: 25,000
Circulation Type: controlled
**Owner(s):**
Publications for Industry
21 Russell Woods Rd.
Great Neck, NY 11021
Telephone: (516) 487-0990
FAX: (516) 487-0809
Ownership %: 100
**Management:**
Jack S. Panes ...............................President
Jack S. Panes ...............................Publisher
B. Grillo ..........................Advertising Manager
**Editorial:**
Pearl Shaine Panes ...............................Editor
**Desc.:** Specializes in reporting on new product releases concerning all aspects of the manufacturing field. Contains special section on new literature, such as brochures and catalogs. Special section on general industrial news subjects such as plant expansion and new plant construction. Publicity releases with photos accepted. Special feature story presented each issue of general interest to industrial purchasing agents.
**Readers:** Industrial purchasing agents of the top manufacturing companies in SIC 19-39 employ 100 or more and responsible for 75 percent of the nations industrial business.
**Deadline:** story-1st of mo.; news-1st of mo.; photo-1st of mo.; ads-1st of mo.

67052

## KANSAS CITY COMMERCE
P.O. Box 28830
St. Louis, MO 63123
Telephone: (314) 638-4050
FAX: (314) 476-1616
Year Established: 1990
Pub. Frequency: m.
Page Size: standard
Subscrip. Rate: $20/yr.
Circulation: 5,583
Circulation Type: paid
**Owner(s):**
ADmore, Inc.
P.O. Box 28830
St. Louis, MO 63123
Telephone: (314) 638-4050
Ownership %: 100
**Management:**
Tony Nolan ...............................Publisher
Janine Tate .....................Advertising Manager
**Editorial:**
Mary Wulford ...............................Editor
**Desc.:** Presents features covering purchasing disciplines.

24539

## KENTUCKIANA PURCHASOR
c/o Prestige Magazine Co.
6213 La Pas Trail, Bldg. 3 - Ste. 100
Indianapolis, IN 46268
Telephone: (317) 298-3831
FAX: (317) 298-3839
Year Established: 1946
Pub. Frequency: bi-m.
Page Size: standard
Materials: 02,05,15,19,28,29,30,32,33

**Owner(s):**
Purchasing Management Association of Louisville
P.O. Box 35428
Louisville, KY 40232
Telephone: (502) 454-4636
Ownership %: 100
**Editorial:**
Maleah Schreiner .....................Managing Editor
**Desc.:** Deals with anything of interest to purchasing managers, plant engineers and management personnel. Mostly staff written, it also acts as organ for Purchasing Management Association of Louisville. Departments include: Question of Month, How is Business, Business Briefs. Special issues include: Roster, Buyers' Guide, Metals, Conference, Office Products.
**Readers:** Mostly purchasing and business industrial personnel.
**Deadline:** story-1 mo. prior to pub. date

24544

## NEW ENGLAND PURCHASER
200 Baker Ave., Ste. 306
Concord, MA 01742
Telephone: (617) 371-2522
Year Established: 1921
Pub. Frequency: q.
Page Size: standard
Circulation: 2,000
Circulation Type: controlled
**Owner(s):**
Purchasing Management Association of Boston
200 Baker St., Ste. 306
Concord, MA 01742
Telephone: (617) 371-2522
Ownership %: 100
**Desc.:** Provides association news and articles relevant to purchasing, materials management and logistics professionals.
**Readers:** Members of the association representing companies in the Greater Boston, MA, area.

65242

## P-O-P TIMES
2000 N. Racine Ave.
Chicago, IL 60614
Telephone: (312) 281-3400
FAX: (312) 281-8369
Year Established: 1988
Pub. Frequency: 9/yr.
Page Size: tabloid
Subscrip. Rate: $22/yr.
Circulation: 18,500
Circulation Type: paid
**Owner(s):**
Hoyt Publishing
2000 N. Racine Ave.
Chicago, IL 60614
Telephone: (312) 281-3400
Ownership %: 100
**Management:**
Peter W. Hoyt ...............................Publisher
Thomas Hoyt .....................General Manager
**Editorial:**
Rex Davenport .....................Managing Editor
**Desc.:** Reports on corporate development point-of-purchase campaigns, research, and new technologies.
**Readers:** Personnel to consumer marketers who use point-of-purchase ads and displays.

24547

## PACIFIC PURCHASOR
819 S. Main St.
Burbank, CA 91506
Telephone: (818) 841-4712
Year Established: 1918
Pub. Frequency: m.
Page Size: standard
Subscrip. Rate: $18/yr.
Freelance Pay: negotiable

Circulation: 15,000
Circulation Type: controlled
**Owner(s):**
Purchasing Management Assn. of Northern California
1727 M.L. King Way, Ste. 217
Oakland, CA 94612
Telephone: (510) 272-0944
Ownership %: 100
**Editorial:**
Bert Johnson ...............................Editor
Jeanne Vlazny ...............................Advertising
Bill Murowski ...............................Art Director
Scott Reese ...............................Associate Editor
**Desc.:** Articles on projects, techniques, law, management, performance, and negotiations as they apply to the purchasing profession. Also purchasing management association and people news from the States of California, Colorado, Arizona, Nevada, Utah, Washington, and Oregon.
**Readers:** Purchasing managers, assistant purchasing managersand buyers.

24549

## PURCHASING
275 Washington St.
Newton, MA 02158
Telephone: (617) 964-3030
FAX: (617) 558-4327
Year Established: 1915
Pub. Frequency: 18/yr.
Page Size: standard
Subscrip. Rate: free to professionals; $89.95/yr. others; $152.95/yr. Canada & Mexico; $124.95/yr. elsewhere
Materials: 01,02,05,06,28,29,30,31,32,33
Print Process: web offset
Circulation: 95,386
Circulation Type: controlled & paid
**Owner(s):**
Cahners Publishing Co.
275 Washington St.
Newton, MA 02158
Telephone: (617) 964-3030
Ownership %: 100
**Management:**
John F. O'Connor .....................Vice President
John F. O'Connor ...............................Publisher
Kathy Doyle .....................Business Manager
**Editorial:**
James P. Morgan .....................Editor in Chief
Ernest Raia ...............................Editor
Kate Evans-Correia ...............................Editor
Peter Bradley ...............................Editor
Wendy Skillings DelCampo ............Art Director
Susan Avery ...............Associate New Products Editor
Anne Millen Porter ...............Economics Editor
Tom Stundza ...............................Market Editor
Peter Bradley .....................Transportation Editor
**Desc.:** Articles by professionals with heavy experience in the practical aspects of purchasing. Covers material, products, processes, and equipment; purchasing systems and methods; purchasing policies and ethics; legal decisions affecting procurement; economic factors affecting purchasing; internal and external public relations; value analysis and cost-reduction techniques. Departments include: Inside Purchasing, Negotiation Perspective, Washington Perspective, Transportation News, Metals Outlook, Office Products, Business and Computer Systems, Leadtimes, and Forecasts.
**Readers:** Serves purchasing personnel in industry.

---

**Materials Accepted/Included:** 01-Business news 02-By-line articles 03-Fashion news 04-Food news 05-Freelance copy 06-Letters to editor 07-Real estate news 08-Sports news 09-Travel news 10-Book rev. 11-Movie rev. 12-Music rev. 13-TV rev. 14-Theater rev. 15-Coming events 16-Obituaries 17-Question & answer 18-Social announcements 19-Artwork 20-Cartoons 21-Photos 22-TV listings 23-Audio rec. 24-Video rec. 25-Books 26-Films/film clips 27-Personnel news 28-Press releases 29-New product news/photos 30-Trade lit. 31-Contracts awarded 32-Display adv. 33-Classified adv.

## PURCHASING MAGAZINES BUYING STRATEGY FORECAST

65994

275 Washington St.
Newton, MA 02158
Telephone: (617) 964-3030
Mailing Address:
   P.O. Box 447
   New Town Branch
   Boston, MA 02258
Year Established: 1975
Pub. Frequency: bi-w.
Page Size: standard
Subscrip. Rate: $238/yr. US; $310/yr.
   foreign
Circulation: 1,000
Circulation Type: paid
Owner(s):
Cahners Publishing Co.
275 Washington St.
Newton, MA 02158
Telephone: (617) 964-3030
Ownership %: 100
Management:
Kim Dempsey ......................Business Manager
Editorial:
Tom Stundza ...............................Editor
Desc.: The Buying Strategy Forecast
   provides eight pages of insider market
   information, economic analysis, and
   forecasts especially written for
   purchasing professionals.
Readers: Purchasing professionals.

## SOUTHERN PURCHASER, THE

24555

5601 Roanne Way, Ste.312
Greensboro, NC 27409-2915
Telephone: (910) 292-9228
FAX: (910) 292-8415
Year Established: 1970
Pub. Frequency: bi-m.
Page Size: 4 color photos/art
Subscrip. Rate: free
Circulation: 8,000
Circulation Type: controlled & free
Owner(s):
NAPM of Carolinas-Virginia, Inc.
5601 Roanne Way, Ste. 312
Greensboro, NC 27409-2915
Telephone: (910) 292-9228
FAX: (910) 292-8415
Ownership %: 100
Management:
V. Gilbert Snyder, Jr. ...........................Publisher
Editorial:
V. Gilbert Snyder, Jr. ...........................Editor
Desc.: Designed to interest a multiplied
   readership in the fields of purchasing
   and general management. Articles are
   on purchasing and allied subjects,
   management, economic conditions,
   markets and news from suppliers.
Readers: Purchasing and general business
   management.

## Group 220-Radio & Television

## BROADCAST ENGINEERING

24568

9800 Metcalf
Overland Park, KS 66212-2215
Telephone: (913) 967-1898
FAX: (913) 967-1898
Mailing Address:
   P.O. Box 12901
   Shawnee Mission, KS 66282-2901
Year Established: 1959
Pub. Frequency: 13/yr.
Page Size: standard
Subscrip. Rate: $50/yr. US; $60/yr.
   foreign; $115/yr. air mail
Materials: 01,02,27,28,29,31,32,33
Freelance Pay: $100-$200
Print Process: web offset

Circulation: 35,000
Circulation Type: controlled
Owner(s):
K-III Communications Corp.
717 5th Ave., 22nd Fl.
New York, NY 10022
Telephone: (212) 745-0100
Ownership %: 100
Bureau(s):
Intertec Publishing
888 Seventh Ave., 38th Fl.
New York, NY 10106
Telephone: (212) 332-0628
FAX: (212) 332-0663
Contact: Joanne Melton, Marketing
   Manager

MC2
501 Santa Monica Blvd.
Ste. 401
Santa Monica, CA 90401
Telephone: (310) 393-9987
FAX: (310) 393-2381
Contact: Jason Perlman, Owner

Intertec Publishing
55 E. Jackson, Ste. 1100
Chicago, IL 60604
Telephone: (312) 435-2301
FAX: (312) 922-1408
Contact: Vytas Urbonas, Marketing
   Manager

Gordon & Associates
210 President St., #4
Brooklyn, NY 11231
Telephone: (718) 802-0488
Contact: Josh Gordon, Owner

Intertec Publishing
Unit 3, Farm Business Centre
Clifton Rd.
OX15 4TP Oxford United Kingdom
Telephone: (44) 0869-38799
FAX: (44) 0869-38040
Contact: Richard Wooley

Oriet Echo
1101 Grand Maison
Shimomiyabi-Cho 2-18
 Shinjuku-Ku, Tokyo 162 Japan
Telephone: (3) 3235-5961
FAX: (3) 3235-5852
Contact: Mastly Yoshikawa
Management:
Romona E. Maloney ...........................President
Cameron Bishop ........................Vice President
Don Soetaert ...............................Controller
Dennis Triola ...............................Publisher
Mary Birnbaum ................Advertising Manager
Kathryn Buckley ................Promotion Manager
Editorial:
Brad Dick ...............................Editor
Tom Cook ......................Managing Editor
Deanna Rood ........................Associate Editor
Tom Brick ..........................Marketing Director
Dawn Hightower ..........Senior Associate Editor
Steve Epstein ........................Technical Editor
Skip Pizzi ........................Technical Editor
Desc.: Edited for corporate, engineering,
   and operations management personnel
   responsible for the selection, purchase,
   installation, and operation of broadcast
   equipment and consultants.
Readers: Broadcast cable, teleproduction,
   and nonbroadcast TV technical
   management personnel, general, and
   operations management
Deadline: story-90 days; news-1 mo.;
   photo-90 days; ads-1 mo.

## BROADCASTING & CABLE

24569

1705 De Sales St., N.W.
Washington, DC 20036-5300
Telephone: (202) 659-2340
FAX: (202) 429-0651

Mailing Address:
   245 W. 17th St.
   New York, NY 10011
Year Established: 1931
Pub. Frequency: Mon.
Page Size: standard
Subscrip. Rate: $3.95 newsstand; $117/yr.
Materials: 06,16,21,25,27,28,29,30,31,32,33
Print Process: offset
Circulation: 34,290
Circulation Type: controlled & paid
Owner(s):
Cahners Publishing Co.
475 Park Ave., S.
New York, NY 10016
Telephone: (212) 340-9860
Ownership %: 100
Bureau(s):
New York
245 W. 17th St.
New York, NY 10011
Telephone: (212) 645-0067
FAX: (212) 337-7028
Contact: Geoffrey Foise, Bureau Chief

Los Angeles
5700 Wilshire Blvd.
Ste. 120
Los Angeles, CA 90036
Telephone: (213) 549-4100
FAX: (213) 937-4240
Contact: Steve Coe, Bureau Chief
Management:
Robert L. Krakoff .................Chairman of Board
John J. Beni ........................Vice President
Donald West ........................Vice President
Peggy Conlon ...............................Publisher
Editorial:
Donald West ...............................Editor
Lawrence W. Oliver ........................Advertising
Richard Vitale ..........VP-Operations & Planning
Desc.: All-inclusive business newsweekly
   of broadcasting (i.e., radio, television,
   and cable TV), staff written and edited
   to serve broadcasters, national and
   regional broadcast advertisers, and
   allied businesses. Publishes
   broadcasting index and broadcasting
   yearbook annually.
Readers: Ad Agency Executives, Radio,
   TV and Cable Executives, & Allied
   Businesses.
Deadline: news-Wed.; photo-Wed.; ads-10
   days prior to pub. date

## CABLEVISION

24573

825 Seventh Ave., 6th Fl.
New York, NY 10019
Telephone: (212) 887-8400
FAX: (212) 887-8585
Year Established: 1975
Pub. Frequency: bi-w.
Page Size: standard
Subscrip. Rate: $55/yr.
Freelance Pay: varies
Circulation: 16,000
Circulation Type: controlled & paid
Owner(s):
Capital Cities-ABC, Inc.
825 Seventh Ave.
6th Fl.
New York, NY 10019
Telephone: (212) 887-8400
Ownership %: 100
Bureau(s):
Washington Bureau, CableVision Magazine
P.O. Box 33578
Washington, DC 20033
Telephone: (703) 521-4187
Contact: Howard Fields, Bureau Chief

New York Bureau
432 Park Ave., S., Ste. 1109
New York, NY 10016
Telephone: (212) 213-3110
Contact: Len Scaffidi, Associate Publisher

West Coast Bureau
101 N. Robertson Blvd., Ste.20
Beverly Hills, CA 90211
Telephone: (310) 659-3965
Contact: Eric Taub, Bureau Chief

CableVision Magazine, Denver Bureau
600 S. Cherry St., Ste. 400
Denver, CO 80222
Telephone: (303) 393-7449
Contact: Chuck Moozakis, Bureau Chief

Management:
William McGorry ........................Vice President
Editorial:
Simon Applebaum ........................Senior Editor
Craig Leddy ...............................Editor
Laurel Gross ...........................Managing Editor
Richard Petralia .................Associate Publisher
Desc.: Management and technical
   coverage of the cable TV industry.
   Published for cable television system
   and MSO managers. Focuses on cable
   industry management, marketing,
   legislation, technology, programming,
   and finance. It reports and interprets
   industry events and related
   developments for system management
   personnel and suppliers. Provides a
   comprehensive look at industry progress
   through a series of charts in its
   CableStats section. These charts feature
   information on subscriber penetration,
   system and MSO subcounts, film and
   PPV product comparisons, satellite
   lineups, cable advertising,
   system transactions, and industry stock
   activity; it also features classified
   advertising.
Readers: MSO and cable system
   management personnel.

## CES DAILY NEWS

24562

211 E. 43rd St.
New York, NY 10017
Telephone: (212) 682-7320
FAX: (212) 949-9051
Year Established: 1973
Pub. Frequency: 8/yr.
Page Size: tabloid
Subscrip. Rate: free
Circulation: 100,000
Circulation Type: controlled & free
Owner(s):
Hampton International Communications
211 E. 43rd St.
New York, NY 10017
Telephone: (212) 682-7320
FAX: (212) 949-9051
Ownership %: 100
Management:
Lee M. Oser ...............................Publisher
Editorial:
Lee M. Oser ...............................Editor in Chief
Desc.: Trade magazine directed to
   retail management.
Readers: Attendees at CES Shows

## COMMUNICATIONS ENGINEERING & DESIGN (CED)

24577

600 S. Cherry St., Ste. 400
Denver, CO 80222
Telephone: (303) 393-7449
FAX: (303) 393-6654
Year Established: 1975
Pub. Frequency: m.
Page Size: standard
Subscrip. Rate: free to qualified personnel;
   $48/yr. others
Materials: 01,02,05,06,15,21,28,29,31,32,33

Materials Accepted/Included: 01-Business news 02-By-line articles 03-Fashion news 04-Food news 05-Freelance copy 06-Letters to editor 07-Real estate news 08-Sports news 09-Travel news
10-Book rev. 11-Movie rev. 12-Music rev. 13-TV rev. 14-Theater rev. 15-Coming events 16-Obituaries 17-Question & answer 18-Social announcements 19-Artwork 20-Cartoons 21-Photos 22-TV listings
23-Audio rec. 24-Video rec. 25-Books 26-Films/film clips 27-Personnel news 28-Press releases 29-New product news/photos 30-Trade lit. 31-Contracts awarded 32-Display adv. 33-Classified adv.

4-315

Freelance Pay: varies
Circulation: 18,000
Circulation Type: controlled
**Owner(s):**
Capital Cities/ABC, Inc.
600 S. Cherry, Ste. 400
Denver, CO 80222
Telephone: (303) 393-7449
Ownership %: 100
**Management:**
Robert Stuehrk ..............................Publisher
Cathy Wilson ....................Advertising Manager
**Editorial:**
Roger Brown ....................................Editor
Leslie Ellis ..............................Managing Editor
Elaine Callahan ...................Production Director
**Desc.:** Management and technical
coverage of the cable TV industry; also
news and features on broadband (CATV
- type) local area networks.
**Readers:** Engineers, industry executives,
systems personnel, telecommunications
managers.
**Deadline:** story-1st of mo., prior to pub.
date; news-1st of mo.; photo-1st of mo.;
ads-1st of mo.

69474

**COMMUNITY TELEVISION REVIEW**
666 11th St., N.W., Ste. 806
Washington, DC 20001-4542
Telephone: (202) 393-2560
FAX: (202) 393-2653
Year Established: 1977
Pub. Frequency: 6/yr.
Subscrip. Rate: $25/yr.
Circulation: 8,500
**Owner(s):**
Alliance for Community Media
666 11th St., N.W., Ste. 806
Washington, DC 20001-4542
Telephone: (202) 393-2560

22880

**ELECTRONIC SERVICING & TECHNOLOGY**
76 N. Broadway
Hicksville, NY 11801
Telephone: (516) 681-2922
FAX: (516) 681-2926
Year Established: 1951
Pub. Frequency: m.
Page Size: standard
Subscrip. Rate: $24.75/yr.
Freelance Pay: negotiable
Circulation: 30,000
Circulation Type: paid
**Owner(s):**
CQ Communications, Inc.
76 N. Broadway
Hicksville, NY 11801
Telephone: (516) 681-2922
Ownership %: 100
**Management:**
Richard Ross ..............................President
Richard Ross ..............................Publisher
**Editorial:**
Conrad Persson ....................................Editor
Diane Klusner ....................Advertising Director
**Desc.:** Tailored for the professional whose
livelihood is centered on the consumer
electronics industry.
**Readers:** Radio, industrial electronic, and
commercial communication service
organizations and their service
personnel.

24595

**ELECTRONICS NOW**
500-B Bi-County Blvd.
Farmingdale, NY 11735
Telephone: (516) 293-3000
FAX: (516) 293-3115
Year Established: 1929
Pub. Frequency: m.

Page Size: standard
Subscrip. Rate: $3.50 newsstand US;
$3.95 newsstand Canada; $19.97/yr.
Materials: 01,02,05,06,10,15,20,25,28,29,30
Freelance Pay: $100-$500/article
Circulation: 151,303
Circulation Type: paid
**Owner(s):**
Gernsback Publications, Inc.
500-B Bi-County Blvd.
Farmingdale, NY 11735
Telephone: (516) 293-3000
Ownership %: 100
**Bureau(s):**
Ralph Bergen
One Northfield Plz., Ste. 300
Northfield, IL 60093-1214
Telephone: (708) 446-1444
FAX: (708) 559-0562
Contact: Ralph Bergan, Sales Manager

Pacific Advertising
1800 N. Highland Ave., Ste. 71
Hollywood, CA 90028
Telephone: (213) 462-2700
FAX: (213) 463-0544
Contact: Blake Murphey

Stan Levitan Co.
One Overlook Dr.
Great Neck, NY 11021
Telephone: (516) 487-9357
FAX: (516) 487-8402
Contact: Stan Levitan, Sales Manager

Electronic Shopper
P.O. Box 169
Idyllwild, CA 92549
Telephone: (909) 659-9743
FAX: (909) 659-2469
Contact: Joe Shere
**Management:**
Larry Steckler ..............................President
Larry Steckler ..............................Publisher
**Editorial:**
Brian Fenton ....................................Editor
Arline Fishman ..................Advertising Director
Neil Sclater ..............................Associate Editor
Marc Spiwak ..............................Associate Editor
Jackie Cheesboro ..............Circulation Director
David Lachenbruch ..............Contributing Editor
Teri E. Scaduto ....................Contributing Editor
Don Lancaster ....................Contributing Editor
Bob Grossblatt ....................Contributing Editor
Larry Klein ..............................Contributing Editor
Ruby Yee ..........................Production Director
**Desc.:** Reports on microcomputers, the
electronics industry, technology, and
service. Coverage includes feature
articles, building projects, products
reviews.
**Readers:** Radio-television technicians,
industrial, electronics engineers,
technical students.
**Deadline:** story-3 mos. prior to pub. date;
news-3 mos. prior; photo-3 mos. prior

69254

**ENTERTAINMENT RETAILING INDUSTRY**
2455 E. Sunrise Blvd., 9th Fl.
Ft. Lauderdale, FL 33304-3118
Telephone: (305) 561-3505
FAX: (305) 561-4129
Year Established: 1986
Pub. Frequency: m.
Page Size: standard
Subscrip. Rate: $15/yr.
Materials: 01,06,10,11,12,13,14,15,16,23,
24,25,26,27,28,29,30,32,33
Circulation: 31,878
Circulation Type: paid

**Owner(s):**
AFI Communications Group, Inc.
2455 E. Sunrise Blvd., 9th Fl.
Ft. Lauderdale, FL 33304-3118
Telephone: (305) 561-3505
Ownership %: 100
**Editorial:**
Robert Lesmeister ....................................Editor
**Desc.:** Business to business publication
from the Video Retailers Assn.
**Readers:** Video retailers.

69257

**GMV: GOVERNMENT & MILITARY VIDEO**
2 Park Ave., 18th Fl.
New York, NY 10016
Telephone: (212) 213-3444
FAX: (212) 213-3484
Year Established: 1989
Pub. Frequency: m.
Page Size: standard
Subscrip. Rate: $30/yr.
Circulation: 8,335
Circulation Type: paid
**Owner(s):**
PSN Publications
2 Park Ave., 18th Fl.
New York, NY 10016
Telephone: (212) 213-3444
Ownership %: 100
**Editorial:**
Ron Merrell ....................................Editor
**Readers:** Video professionals in federal,
state, and city government and the
military.

24584

**INTERNATIONAL TELEVISION & VIDEO ALMANAC**
159 W. 53rd St.
New York, NY 10019
Telephone: (212) 247-3100
FAX: (212) 489-0871
Year Established: 1956
Pub. Frequency: a.
Page Size: standard
Subscrip. Rate: $88.50/yr.
**Owner(s):**
Quigley Publishing Co., Inc.
159 W. 53rd St.
New York, NY 10019
Telephone: (212) 247-1300
Ownership %: 100
**Management:**
Martin Quigley ..............................President
Martin Quigley ..............................Publisher
Jim Moser ..............................Business Manager
**Editorial:**
Barry Monush ....................................Editor
William Pay ....................................Editor
**Desc.:** Comprehensive facts about TV and
home video industries, noteworthy
persons, producers, distributors, station
data, equipment supplies, major retail
stores, awards, and statistics.
**Readers:** Amusement industry executives.

21668

**MEDIA NEWS KEYS**
40-29 27th St., 2nd Fl.
Long Island City, NY 11101
Telephone: (718) 937-3990
Year Established: 1950
Pub. Frequency: q.
Page Size: standard
Subscrip. Rate: $125/yr.
Circulation: 1,000
Circulation Type: paid
**Owner(s):**
Television Index, Inc.
40-29 27th St., 2nd Fl.
Long Island City, NY 11101
Telephone: (718) 937-3990
Ownership %: 100
**Management:**
Timothy Hunter ..............................Publisher

**Editorial:**
Timothy Hunter ....................................Editor
**Desc.:** Service paper listing network and
local radio and TV talk and news
programs, discussing staffs and
information needs of major consumer
and business magazines; describes the
types of guests required by programs
and who to contact.
**Readers:** Publicists and public relations
counsels.

49852

**MOBILE RADIO TECHNOLOGY**
9800 Metcalf
Overland Park, KS 66212-2215
Telephone: (913) 341-1300
FAX: (913) 967-1898
Year Established: 1983
Pub. Frequency: m.
Page Size: standard
Subscrip. Rate: free to qualified personnel;
$30/yr. others
Freelance Pay: negotiable
Circulation: 24,213
Circulation Type: controlled
**Owner(s):**
Intertec Publishing Corp.
9800 Metcalf
Overland Park, KS 66212-2215
Telephone: (913) 341-1300
Ownership %: 100
**Management:**
Mercy Contreras ..............................Publisher
Sandra Stewart ...................Circulation Manager
**Editorial:**
Don Bishop ....................................Editor
Jane Bryant ....................................Editor
**Desc.:** Mobile Radio Technology provides
technical information to dealers,
community repeater operators,
specialized mobile radio operators,
mobile radio equipment manufacturers,
manufacturers' representatives,
distributors, engineering, consulting
firms, national governments, and others
allied to the field.

69271

**M STREET JOURNAL**
304 Park Ave. S., 7th Fl.
New York, NY 10010
Telephone: (212) 473-4668
FAX: (212) 473-4626
Year Established: 1984
Pub. Frequency: w.
Page Size: newsletter
Subscrip. Rate: $115/yr.
Materials: 01,10,12,15,23,27,28,29,30,32
Print Process: offset
Circulation: 700
Circulation Type: paid
**Owner(s):**
M Street Corp.
304 Park Ave. S., 7th Fl.
New York, NY 10010
Telephone: (212) 473-4668
FAX: (212) 473-4626
Ownership %: 100
**Editorial:**
Robert Unmacht ....................................Editor
**Desc.:** Reports on AM and FM stations'
format, technical, call letter and
ownership changes; major decisions and
actions taken by the FCC regarding
radio broadcasting each week.
**Deadline:** story-Tue.; news-Tue.; photo-
Tue.; ads-Tue.

52674

**MULTICHANNEL NEWS**
825 Seventh Ave., 6th Fl.
New York, NY 10019
Telephone: (212) 887-8400
Year Established: 1980
Pub. Frequency: w.

---

Page Size: tabloid
Subscrip. Rate: $78/yr.
Materials: 01,06,32,33
Freelance Pay: $5/in.
Circulation: 16,000
Circulation Type: controlled
**Owner(s):**
Capital Cities/ABC, Inc.
825 Seventh Ave., 6th Fl.
New York, NY 10019
Telephone: (212) 887-8400
FAX: (212) 887-8384
Ownership %: 100
**Bureau(s):**
New York Office
825 Seventh Ave.
New York, NY 10019
Telephone: (212) 887-8400
FAX: (212) 887-8384
Contact: Andy Grossman, News Editor

D.C.
601 13th St. N.W.
Ste. 520 S.
Washington DC, 20005
Telephone: (202) 639-6934
FAX: (202) 639-2080
Contact: Ted Hearn, Bureau Chief

Denver
600 Cherry St.
Denver, CO 80222
Telephone: (303) 393-7449
FAX: (303) 393-7139
Contact: Peter Lambert, Editor

London
56 Kingsway
London United Kingdom
Contact: Bill Mahoney, Editor
**Management:**
Joel A. Berger .......................................Publisher
Paul Audino ................................Sales Manager
**Editorial:**
Marianne Paskowski ....................................Editor
**Desc.:** Hard news for the electronic media
including cable TV, broadcast TV, pay
TV, STV, MDS, DBS, CPTV, MMDS,
teletext, videotext, PPV, etc.
**Readers:** Executives in the new electronic
media.

69124
**PRO SOUND NEWS**
2 Park Ave., 18th Fl.
New York, NY 10016
Telephone: (212) 213-3444
FAX: (212) 213-3484
Year Established: 1979
Pub. Frequency: m.
Page Size: tabloid
Subscrip. Rate: $30/yr.
Circulation: 19,877
Circulation Type: paid
**Owner(s):**
United Newspapers Publications Ltd.
2 Park Ave., 18th Fl.
New York, NY 10016
Telephone: (212) 213-3444
Ownership %: 100
**Editorial:**
Debra A. Pagan ........................................Editor

48194
**RADIO & RECORDS**
1930 Century Park W.
Los Angeles, CA 90067
Telephone: (213) 553-4330
FAX: (310) 203-8727
Year Established: 1972
Pub. Frequency: w.
Page Size: tabloid
Subscrip. Rate: $275/yr.
Freelance Pay: varies
Circulation: 8,300
Circulation Type: paid

**Owner(s):**
Radio & Records, Inc.
1930 Century Park W.
Los Angeles, CA 90067
Telephone: (213) 553-4330
Ownership %: 100
**Bureau(s):**
Radio & Records
1610 16th Ave., S.
Nashville, TN 37212
Telephone: (615) 292-8982
Contact: Lon Helton, Bureau Chief
**Management:**
Dick Krizman ...............................Vice President
Bob Wilson ....................................Publisher
**Editorial:**
Ken Barnes ....................................Senior Editor
Michael Atkinson .................Marketing Director

21676
**RADIO CAMPAIGNS**
200 N. Fourth St.
Burlington, IA 52601
Telephone: (319) 752-5415
Mailing Address:
  P.O. Box 1
  Burlington, IA 52601
Pub. Frequency: m.
Page Size: standard
Subscrip. Rate: $54/mo.
Circulation: 259
Circulation Type: paid
**Owner(s):**
National Research Bureau
200 N. Fourth St.
Burlington, IA 52601
Telephone: (319) 752-5415
Ownership %: 100
**Management:**
Michael S. Darnall ...............................Publisher
**Editorial:**
Teresa Levinson ....................................Editor
**Desc.:** Service is divided into three
separate sections: Station Managers
Section contains sales tips, successful
program case histories and management
ideas. Continuity section contains 50
pages of outline commercials. Disc
Jockey Section contains material for
wide variety of programs. Departments
include: Programs, Sales, Promotion,
Continuity, Station Management.
**Readers:** Station managers, sales
managers, continuity and promotional
directors.

69273
**RADIO RESOURCE
INTERNATIONAL**
P.O. Box 4635
Englewood, CO 80155-4635
Telephone: (303) 792-2390
FAX: (303) 792-2391
Year Established: 1987
Pub. Frequency: 3/yr.
Page Size: standard
Subscrip. Rate: free
Materials: 01,02
**Owner(s):**
Pandata Corp.
P.O. Box 4635
Englewood, CO 80155-4635
Telephone: (303) 792-2390
FAX: (303) 792-2391
Ownership %: 100
**Editorial:**
Rikki T. Lee ........................................Editor
**Desc.:** Covers the international mobile
communications market.

25024
**RADIO WORLD**
5827 Columbia Pk., Ste. 310
Falls Church, VA 22041
Telephone: (703) 998-7600
FAX: (703) 998-2966

Mailing Address:
  P.O. Box 1214
  Falls Church, VA 22041
Year Established: 1977
Pub. Frequency: bi-w.
Page Size: tabloid
Subscrip. Rate: free to qualified personnel
Freelance Pay: varies
Circulation: 22,000
Circulation Type: controlled
**Owner(s):**
Industrial Marketing Advisory Services, Inc.
5827 Columbia Pk., Ste. 310
Falls Church, VA 22041
Telephone: (703) 998-7600
Ownership %: 100
**Bureau(s):**
Radio World
7576 Community Dr.
Citrus Heights, CA 95610-4402
Telephone: (916) 721-3410
FAX: (916) 729-0810
Contact: Dale Tucker, Sales Manager
**Management:**
Stevan B. Dana ...............................President
Stevan B. Dana ...............................Publisher
Carmel King .....................Associate Publisher
Rebecca Seaborg .............Circulation Manager
Kim Lowe ......................Production Manager
**Editorial:**
Lucia Cobo ........................................Editor
Randy Sukow ....................Managing Editor
Skip Tash ........................................Advertising
Charles Taylor ....................Associate Editor
Alan Carter ....................International Editor
John Gatski ........................News Editor
**Desc.:** Edited for engineering and technical
management personnel in the U.S. and
international radio broadcasting industry.
Topics of interest to recording studio
engineers are covered. Features include
technical news stories. Regular monthly
in-depth technical columns, the
Broadcast Equipment Exchange
classified section, and the Buyer's Guide
product-review section.
**Readers:** Chief engineers and managers
of radio stations and networks, radio
station consultants, TV stations and
recording studios in the US.

56275
**RELIGIOUS BROADCASTING**
7839 Ashton Ave.
Manassas, VA 22110-2883
*see Service,Trade,Professional
Magazines, Religious*

68797
**SATELLITE RETAILER**
1300 S. DeKalb St.
Shelby, NC 28152
Telephone: (704) 482-9673
FAX: (704) 484-8558
Mailing Address:
  P.O. Box 2384
  Shelby, NC 28152
Year Established: 1985
Pub. Frequency: m.
Page Size: standard
Subscrip. Rate: $29/yr.
Materials: 01,02,06,15,17,19,20,21,28,29,
30,32
Print Process: web offset
Circulation: 10,700
Circulation Type: controlled & paid
**Owner(s):**
Triple D Publishing, Inc.
P.O. Box 2384
Shelby, NC 28151-2384
Telephone: (704) 482-9673
FAX: (704) 484-8558
Ownership %: 100
**Editorial:**
David Melton ........................................Editor

**Desc.:** Marketing, sales, technology
articles related to the satellite TV
industry. Each month features a product
review, new products, calendar of
events, and industry insight.
**Readers:** Satellite professionals from
executives to installers.
**Deadline:** story-7 wks. prior to pub. date;
news-6 wks. prior; photo-6 wks. prior;
ads-6 wks. prior

49832
**SATELLITE WEEK**
2115 Ward Ct.
Washington, DC 20037
Telephone: (202) 872-9200
FAX: (202) 293-3435
Year Established: 1979
Pub. Frequency: w.
Page Size: standard
Subscrip. Rate: $773/yr.
**Owner(s):**
Warren Publishing, Inc.
2115 Ward Ct.
Washington, DC 20037
Telephone: (202) 872-9200
Ownership %: 100
**Management:**
Roy W. Easley, III ...............................Controller
Albert Warren ...............................Publisher
Gene Edwards .................Advertising Manager
Betty Alvine ....................Circulation Manager
**Editorial:**
Dawson B. Nail ....................Executive Editor
Paul Warren ....................Senior Editor
Daniel Warren ....................Senior Editor
Art Brodsky ....................Senior Editor
Albert Warren ........................................Editor
Michael French ....................Managing Editor
David Lachenbruch ............Editorial Director
Lori Keesey ....................Contributing Editor
Gary Madderom ............Marketing Director
**Desc.:** Covers latest developments in
satellite broadcasting,
telecommunications, Earth observation,
and space industrialization.
**Readers:** Executives and policy-makers in
foregoing fields.

25579
**SHOOT**
1515 Broadway
New York, NY 10036
Telephone: (212) 764-7300
FAX: (212) 536-5321
Year Established: 1960
Pub. Frequency: w.
Page Size: tabloid
Subscrip. Rate: $2/issue; $60/yr.
Freelance Pay: negotiable
Circulation: 20,000
Circulation Type: controlled & paid
**Owner(s):**
Billboard Publications, Inc.
1515 Broadway
New York, NY 10036
Ownership %: 100
**Bureau(s):**
Back Stage West
5150 Wilshire Blvd.
Los Angeles, CA 90036
Telephone: (310) 936-5200
Contact: Bob Goldrich, Director

Back Stage New England
P.O. Box 102
Bridgton, ME 04009
Telephone: (207) 647-2552
Contact: Elizabeth Creamer

Back Stage Midwest
841 N. Addison Ave.
Elmhurst, IL 60126
Telephone: (708) 834-7533
Contact: Candice Hadley
**Management:**
Roberta Griefer ...............................Publisher

**Materials Accepted/Included:** 01-Business news 02-By-line articles 03-Fashion news 04-Food news 05-Freelance copy 06-Letters to editor 07-Real estate news 08-Sports news 09-Travel news
10-Book rev. 11-Movie rev. 12-Music rev. 13-TV rev. 14-Theater rev. 15-Coming events 16-Obituaries 17-Question & answer 18-Social announcements 19-Artwork 20-Cartoons 21-Photos 22-TV listings
23-Audio rec. 24-Video rec. 25-Books 26-Films/film clips 27-Personnel news 28-Press releases 29-New product news/photos 30-Trade lit. 31-Contracts awarded 32-Display adv. 33-Classified adv.

4-317

Neal Greenberg ...............Advertising Manager
**Editorial:**
Peter Caranicas .................................Editor
**Desc.:** Covers TV and industrial films,
commercials and advertising agencies,
general news in entertainment field. TV
stations and series. Prefer pictures.
**Readers:** Producers of TV commercials,
suppliers & services, advertising
agencies, TV programs and feature
films, general public.

68807

**TELEVISION BROADCAST**
2 Park Ave., 18th Fl.
New York, NY 10016
Telephone: (212) 213-3444
FAX: (212) 213-3484
Year Established: 1978
Pub. Frequency: m.
Subscrip. Rate: $38/yr.
Circulation: 30,653
Circulation Type: controlled
**Owner(s):**
PSN Publications
2 Park Ave., 18th Fl.
New York, NY 10016
Telephone: (212) 213-3444
Ownership %: 100
**Editorial:**
Ed Rosenthal ...................................Editor

24601

**TELEVISION DIGEST WITH
    CONSUMER ELECTRONICS**
2115 Ward Ct., N.W.
Washington, DC 20037
Telephone: (202) 872-9200
FAX: (202) 293-3435
Year Established: 1945
Pub. Frequency: w.
Page Size: tabloid
Subscrip. Rate: $730/yr.
**Owner(s):**
Warren Publishing, Inc.
2115 Ward Ct., N.W.
Washington, DC 20037
Telephone: (202) 872-9200
Ownership %: 100
**Bureau(s):**
Warren Publishing, Inc.
475 Fifth Ave.
New York, NY 10017
Telephone: (212) 686-5410
Contact: David Lachenbruch, Editorial
    Director
**Management:**
Albert Warren ...........................Publisher
Betty Alvine ....................Circulation Manager
**Editorial:**
Dawson B. Nail ...................Executive Editor
Albert Warren .................................Editor
Dan Warren .....................Managing Editor
David Lachenbruch .................Editorial Director
Gene Edwards .........................Advertising
Paul Warren ...........................Associate Editor
Gary Madderom ...................Marketing Director
**Desc.:** News covering TV, radio, cable,
consumer electronics, and related fields.
**Readers:** Executives in foregoing fields.

68808

**TRANSPONDER**
4250 N. State St.
Center St. Ext.
Salamanca, NY 14779
Telephone: (716) 945-3488
FAX: (716) 945-5238
Year Established: 1986
Pub. Frequency: m.
Page Size: tabloid
Materials: 01,02,05,06,17,21,27,28,29,30,
    31,32,33
Circulation: 14,500
Circulation Type: controlled

**Owner(s):**
Terra Publishing, Inc.
4250 N. State St.
Salamanca, NY 14779
Telephone: (716) 945-3488
FAX: (716) 945-5238
Ownership %: 100
**Editorial:**
Timothy L. Jackson .......................Editor
**Desc.:** Covers the satellite television
industry.
**Deadline:** story-15th of mo. prior to pub.
    date; news-15th of mo. prior; photo-15th
    of mo. prior; ads-15th of mo. prior

24589

**WORD, THE**
4621 N. Kedzie Ave.
Chicago, IL 60625
Telephone: (312) 463-2499
Year Established: 1950
Pub. Frequency: m.
Page Size: standard
Subscrip. Rate: $2 newsstand; $12/yr.
Materials: 01,02,06,10,15,23,24,25,27,28,
    29,30,31,32,33
Circulation: 3,000
Circulation Type: controlled
**Owner(s):**
Electronic Service Dealers Association
4621 N. Kedzie Ave.
Chicago, IL 60625
Telephone: (312) 463-2499
Ownership %: 100
**Management:**
George J. Weiss .........................Publisher
George J. Weiss ...............Advertising Manager
George J. Weiss ..................Business Manager
**Editorial:**
George J. Weiss ...................Executive Editor
**Desc.:** Contains articles pertaining to
business practices in the electronics
service industry, including ethics,
technological change, and general news
of interest to electronics people.
**Readers:** Owners and/or operators of
retail consumer electronics service
businesses.
**Deadline:** story-15th of previous mo.;
    news-15th of previous mo.; photo-15th
    of previous mo.

68809

**WORLD BROADCAST NEWS**
9800 Metcalf
Overland Park, KS 66212-2215
Telephone: (913) 341-1300
FAX: (913) 967-1898
Pub. Frequency: m.
Subscrip. Rate: free
Circulation: 11,212
Circulation Type: controlled
**Owner(s):**
Intertec Publishing Corp.
9800 Metcalf
Overland Park, KS 66212-2215
Telephone: (913) 341-1300
Ownership %: 100
**Editorial:**
Gerlad Walker ...............................Editor

**Group 222-Railroads**

25095

**BROTHERHOOD OF
    MAINTENANCE OF WAY
    EMPLOYEES (RAILWAY)**
26555 Evergreen Rd., Ste. 200
Southfield, MI 48076-4225
Telephone: (313) 948-1010
FAX: (313) 948-7150
Year Established: 1892
Pub. Frequency: 10/yr.
Page Size: tabloid
Subscrip. Rate: $16/yr.
Circulation: 70,000

Circulation Type: paid
**Owner(s):**
Brotherhood of Maintenance of Way
    Employes
26555 Evergreen Rd., Ste. 200
Southfield, MI 48076-4225
Telephone: (313) 948-1010
Ownership %: 100
**Management:**
Mac A. Fleming ...........................President
**Editorial:**
Charles Fountain ...................Associate Editor
**Desc.:** The trade union that represents
workers who build, repair, and maintain
the tracks, buildings, and bridges on the
railroads of the U.S. and Canada.
**Readers:** Members, industry leaders,
regulatory agency's staff, transportation
congressional members.

69169

**FREIGHT CARS JOURNAL**
P.O. Box 2480
Monrovia, CA 91017-6480
Year Established: 1983
Pub. Frequency: q.
Page Size: standard
Subscrip. Rate: $20/yr. US; $35/yr. foreign
Circulation: 1,000
Circulation Type: paid
**Owner(s):**
Society of Freight Car Historians
P.O. Box 2480
Monrovia, CA 91017
Ownership %: 100
**Editorial:**
David G. Casdorph ..........................Editor
**Desc.:** Original articles on the history and
development of American railway freight
cars and related subjects.

24610

**INTERNATIONAL RAILWAY
    JOURNAL**
345 Hudson St.
New York, NY 10014
Telephone: (212) 620-7200
FAX: (212) 633-1165
Year Established: 1960
Pub. Frequency: m.
Page Size: standard
Subscrip. Rate: $35/yr.; $60/2 yrs.
Materials: 01,05,06,21,32,33
Freelance Pay: negotiable
Print Process: web offset
Circulation: 9,425
Circulation Type: controlled
**Owner(s):**
Simmons-Boardman Publishing Corp.
345 Hudson St.
New York, NY 10014
Telephone: (212) 620-7200
Ownership %: 100
**Bureau(s):**
International Railway Journal
4-A Berkeley Ct., Kiligrew St.
 Falmouth, Cornwall United Kingdom
Telephone: 011-44-326-313945
Contact: M. Knutton, Editor in Chief
**Management:**
A.J. McGinnis, Jr. .........................President
R.G. Lewis .....................Advertising Manager
**Editorial:**
Mike Knutton .....................Managing Editor
David Briginshaw ...................Assistant Editor
Steve Bennett .........................News Editor
R.G. Lewis ...................Publication Director

**Desc.:** The international magazine in the
Railway Age group of magazines serving
the railway, rapid transit, and railway
supply industries. Its circulation is
worldwide and it is devoted to covering
news and developments in these fields
all over the world. The orientation is
toward business and engineering, rather
than enthusiast. Major articles are
accompanied by summaries in French,
German, and Spanish. Departments
include: Feature Section of Articles,
World Report, World Market, Products,
The World in Transit, This Month
(opinion page).
**Readers:** Senior railway managers and
engineers; department  heads; railway
and rail transit officials; and supply
industry leaders.
**Deadline:** ads-7th of prior mo. to pub. date

69170

**NEW ELECTRIC RAILWAY
    JOURNAL**
717 Second St., N.E.
Washington, DC 20002
Telephone: (202) 546-3000
FAX: (202) 544-2819
Mailing Address:
    6305 N. Kenmore #1
    Chicago, IL 60660
Year Established: 1988
Pub. Frequency: q.
Page Size: standard
Subscrip. Rate: $6.95 newsstand; $25/yr.
    US; $32.50/yr. foreign
Materials: 15,21,29,32
Circulation: 11,000
Circulation Type: controlled & paid
**Owner(s):**
Free Congress Foundation
717 Second St., N.E.
Washington, DC 20002
Telephone: (202) 546-3000
Ownership %: 100
**Editorial:**
Richard Kunz ................................Editor

24614

**PASSENGER TRAIN JOURNAL**
923 Friedman Dr.
Waukesha, WI 53186
Telephone: (414) 542-4900
Mailing Address:
    P.O. Box 379
    Waukesha, WI 53187
Year Established: 1968
Pub. Frequency: m.
Page Size: standard
Subscrip. Rate: $3.50/copy; $30/yr.
Freelance Pay: $2-$3/col. in.
Print Process: web offset
Circulation: 13,100
Circulation Type: paid
**Owner(s):**
Pentrex
P.O. Box 94911
Pasadena, CA 91109
Telephone: (818) 793-3400
FAX: (818) 793-3797
Ownership %: 100
**Management:**
Michael Clayton ...........................Publisher
**Editorial:**
Carl Swanson ...............................Editor
**Desc.:** News and features on current and
historic rail passenger service here and
abroad. Departments include: news,
features, and travel.
**Readers:** Railroad enthusiasts and people
in the rail and mass transit industry.

**Materials Accepted/Included:** 01-Business news 02-By-line articles 03-Fashion news 04-Food news 05-Freelance copy 06-Letters to editor 07-Real estate news 08-Sports news 09-Travel news 10-Book rev. 11-Movie rev. 12-Music rev. 13-TV rev. 14-Theater rev. 15-Coming events 16-Obituaries 17-Question & answer 18-Social announcements 19-Artwork 20-Cartoons 21-Photos 22-TV listings 23-Audio rec. 24-Video rec. 25-Books 26-Films/film clips 27-Personnel news 28-Press releases 29-New product news/photos 30-Trade lit. 31-Contracts awarded 32-Display adv. 33-Classified adv.

## PROGRESSIVE RAILROADING
24615

230 W. Monroe, Ste. 2210
Chicago, IL 60606
Telephone: (312) 629-1200
FAX: (312) 629-1304
Year Established: 1957
Pub. Frequency: m.
Page Size: standard
Subscrip. Rate: $45/yr. U.S.; $50/yr.
   Canada; $75/yr. foreign
Materials: 32,33
Print Process: offset
Circulation: 20,000
Circulation Type: controlled
**Owner(s):**
Murphy-Richter Publishing Co.
230 W. Monroe, Ste. 2210
Chicago, IL 60606
Telephone: (312) 629-1200
Ownership %: 100
**Management:**
Ron Mitchell ...........................President
Richard J. Zemencik ...................Vice President
**Editorial:**
Thomas Judge ...........................Editor
Margaret L. McEnery ..........Production Director
**Desc.:** Serves railroads, rail transit
   companies, and others allied to the field.
   It covers the problems and advances in
   technology relating to those areas.
**Readers:** Railroad industry.

## RAILWAY AGE
24617

345 Hudson St.
New York, NY 10014
Telephone: (212) 620-7200
FAX: (212) 633-1165
Year Established: 1856
Pub. Frequency: m.
Page Size: standard
Subscrip. Rate: $45/yr.
Circulation: 18,127
Circulation Type: controlled
**Owner(s):**
Simmons-Boardman Publishing Corp.
345 Hudson St.
New York, NY 10014
Telephone: (212) 620-7200
Ownership %: 100
**Management:**
A.J. McGinnis, Jr. ...........................President
A.J. McGinnis, Jr. ...........................Publisher
**Editorial:**
Gus Welty ...........................Senior Editor
Luther S. Miller ...........................Editor
Mike Knutton ...........................Editor
Paul P. Gerbino ...........Associate Publisher
Tom Shedd ...........................Consulting Editor
John H. Armstrong ...........Consulting Editor
William D. Middleton ...........Consulting Editor
Robert Roberts ...........Consulting Editor
Joseph Asher ...........................Consulting Editor
Wanda Welty ...........................Editorial Assistant
Robert Tuzik ...........................Engineering Editor
Anthony D. Kruglinski ...........Financial Editor
Mickey Mates ...........................Graphics Editor
Robert G. Lewis ...........Publication Director
**Desc.:** Articles are directed to railway, rail
   transit, and traffic management. Keeps
   the busy executive informed about the
   full range of industry and government
   developments with appealing format and
   full-color graphics.
**Readers:** Railroad and rail transit
   personnel at top management and
   supervisory levels.

## RAILWAY TRACK & STRUCTURES
24618

175 W. Jackson Blvd., Ste. A1927
Chicago, IL 60604
Telephone: (312) 427-2729
FAX: (312) 427-3014
Year Established: 1905
Pub. Frequency: m.

Page Size: standard
Subscrip. Rate: $16/yr.
Materials: 01,02,05,25,28,29,30,32,33
Print Process: web offset
Circulation: 7,629
Circulation Type: paid
**Owner(s):**
Simmons-Boardman Publishing Co.
345 Hudson St.
New York, NY 10014
Telephone: (212) 620-7200
**Management:**
Arthur J. Mc Ginnis, Jr. ...........President
Arthur J. Mc Ginnis, Jr. ...........Publisher
**Editorial:**
Jerome V. Kramer ...........Executive Editor
Robert Tuzik ...........................Editor
Allan M. Zarembski ...........Consulting Editor
Tom Shedd ...........................Consulting Editor
**Desc.:** Reports on construction,
   maintenance, materials, methods,
   devices used in construction and
   maintenance of railroads, news of
   particular roads, and supply trade news.
**Readers:** Mainly supervisory officers in
   charge of railroad maintenance of way
   and structures.

## SIGNALMAN'S JOURNAL, THE
24619

601 West Golf Rd.
Mt Prospect, IL 60056
Telephone: (708) 439-3732
FAX: (708) 439-3743
Mailing Address:
   P.O. Box U
   Mt Prospect, IL 60056
Year Established: 1920
Pub. Frequency: bi-m.
Page Size: standard
Subscrip. Rate: $2/issue; $10/yr.
Circulation: 15,500
Circulation Type: controlled & paid
**Owner(s):**
Brotherhood of Railroad Signalmen
P.O. Box U
Mt Prospect, IL 60056
Telephone: (708) 439-3732
Ownership %: 100
**Editorial:**
J.L. Mattingly ...........................Editor
**Desc.:** Contributed technical articles; new
   installation news. Uses new product
   stories only with apparatus or devices
   used by railway signal departments.
   Must be Union made.
**Readers:** Railroad signal department
   employees who install and maintain
   signal systems. Congressmen, Senators,
   Railroad officials, Government Officials,
   Railroad Retirees.

## SPEEDLINES
69171

206 Valley Ct., Ste. 800
Pittsburgh, PA 15237
Telephone: (412) 364-9306
FAX: (412) 364-1353
Year Established: 1984
Pub. Frequency: m.
Subscrip. Rate: membership
Materials: 01,06,21
Print Process: offset lithography
Circulation: 20,000
Circulation Type: free & paid
**Owner(s):**
High Speed Rail/Maglev Association
206 Valley Ct., Ste. 800
Pittsburgh, PA 15237
Telephone: (412) 364-9306
FAX: (412) 364-1353
Ownership %: 100
**Editorial:**
Robert J. Casey ...........................Editor

**Desc.:** News about the new transportation
   mode and industry of high-speed rail.

## TRACK YEARBOOK
69172

230 W. Monroe, Ste. 2210
Chicago, IL 60606
Telephone: (312) 629-1200
Year Established: 1982
Pub. Frequency: a.
Page Size: standard
Subscrip. Rate: $50/copy
Circulation: 6,200
Circulation Type: controlled & paid
**Owner(s):**
Murphy-Richter Publishing Co.
230 W. Monroe, Ste. 2210
Chicago, IL 60606
Telephone: (312) 629-1200
Ownership %: 100
**Editorial:**
Tom Morgan ...........................Editor

## UTU NEWS
24621

14600 Detroit Ave.
Cleveland, OH 44107-4250
Telephone: (216) 228-9400
FAX: (216) 228-5755
Year Established: 1969
Pub. Frequency: 12/yr.
Page Size: tabloid
Subscrip. Rate: membership
Print Process: web
Circulation: 131,000
Circulation Type: controlled
**Owner(s):**
United Transportation Union
14600 Detroit Ave.
Cleveland, OH 44107
Telephone: (216) 228-9400
Ownership %: 100
**Editorial:**
G. T. DuBose ...........................Editor
Eric J. Eakin ...........................P.R. Director
**Desc.:** Covers railroad and bus industry
   and its economic and labor problems.
   Also carries educational, explanatory
   matter of economic, social and political
   issues and facts about transportation,
   and news of general interest to the labor
   movement in the United States.
**Readers:** Mainly railroad and bus workers
   in union, and public officials, libraries,
   and colleges.

## WAYBILL
69173

P.O. Box 486
Hyde Park, MA 02136-0486
Telephone: (617) 361-4445
Year Established: 1970
Pub. Frequency: q.
Page Size: tabloid
Subscrip. Rate: $4/yr.
Circulation: 14,000
Circulation Type: paid
**Owner(s):**
Mystic Valley Railway Society
P.O. Box 486
Hyde Park, MA 02136-0486
Telephone: (617) 361-4445
Ownership %: 100
**Editorial:**
W. Russell Rylko ...........................Editor
**Desc.:** Provides education in the field of
   railroad transportation.

# Group 224-Religious

## BLACK SACRED MUSIC
70443

905 W. Main St., Ste.18-B
Duke University Press
Durham, NC 27701
*see Service,Trade,Professional*
*Magazines, Music & Music Trades*

## CATHOLIC HISTORICAL REVIEW
25042

620 Michigan Ave., N.E.
Washington, DC 20064
Telephone: (202) 319-5079
FAX: (202) 319-5802
Year Established: 1915
Pub. Frequency: q.
Page Size: standard
Subscrip. Rate: $30/yr.
Circulation: 1,956
Circulation Type: paid
**Owner(s):**
Catholic University of America Press
620 Michigan Ave., N.E.
Washington, DC 20064
Telephone: (202) 319-5052
Ownership %: 100
**Management:**
Marian E. Goode ...........Advertising Manager
**Editorial:**
Rev. Robert Trisco ...........................Editor
Maryann Urbanski ........Administrative Assistant
Joseph N. Moody ...........Associate Editor
Mary Homan ...........................Miscellaneous
**Desc.:** Contains articles dealing with the
   history of the Catholic church in this
   country and abroad, book reviews, brief
   notices, and lists of periodical literature
   pertaining to church history in general
   and news of interest to historians of
   Christianity. Articles are limited to 30
   typed pages, double-spaced, including
   footnotes.
**Readers:** Members of the American
   Catholic Historical Association, teachers,
   and students of history, especially
   ecclesiastical history.

## CHRISTIAN MINISTRY, THE
26203

407 S. Dearborn St.
Chicago, IL 60605-1150
Telephone: (312) 427-5380
FAX: (312) 427-1302
Year Established: 1929
Pub. Frequency: bi-m.
Page Size: standard
Subscrip. Rate: $2.50 newsstand; $14/yr.
Materials: 06,10,19,20,21,25,32
Freelance Pay: varies
Print Process: web offset
Circulation: 12,000
Circulation Type: paid
**Owner(s):**
The Christian Century Foundation
407 S. Dearborn
Chicago, IL 60605
Telephone: (312) 427-5380
Ownership %: 100
**Management:**
Ann James ...........................Advertising Manager
**Editorial:**
Rev. James M. Wall ...........................Editor
Victoria Rebeck ...........................Managing Editor
Eugene Roehlkepartain ...........Miscellaneous
**Desc.:** Geared primarily to Protestant
   clergy. Includes articles related to
   church life; book reviews; sermons.
   Each issue is based upon a
   specific theme.
**Readers:** 90 percent Protestant ministers.
**Deadline:** story-3 mo. prior to pub. date;
   news-3 mo. prior; photo-3 mo. prior; ads-
   2 mo. prior

## CLERGY JOURNAL
25044

2450 Stratford Dr.
Austin, TX 78746
Telephone: (512) 327-8501
Mailing Address:
   P.O. Box 162527
   Austin, TX 78716
Year Established: 1924
Pub. Frequency: 10/yr.

Materials Accepted/Included: 01-Business news 02-By-line articles 03-Fashion news 04-Food news 05-Freelance copy 06-Letters to editor 07-Real estate news 08-Sports news 09-Travel news 10-Book rev. 11-Movie rev. 12-Music rev. 13-TV rev. 14-Theater rev. 15-Coming events 16-Obituaries 17-Question & answer 18-Social announcements 19-Artwork 20-Cartoons 21-Photos 22-TV listings 23-Audio rec. 24-Video rec. 25-Books 26-Films/film clips 27-Personnel news 28-Press releases 29-New product news/photos 30-Trade lit. 31-Contracts awarded 32-Display adv. 33-Classified adv.

4-319

Page Size: standard
Subscrip. Rate: $27/yr.
Freelance Pay: $20-$30/article
Circulation: 73,000
Circulation Type: paid
**Owner(s):**
Church Management, Inc.
P.O. Box 162527
Austin, TX 78716
Telephone: (512) 327-8501
Ownership %: 100
**Management:**
Manfred Holck, Jr. ...................Publisher
**Editorial:**
Manfred Holck, Jr. ...........Executive Editor
**Desc.:** Professional magazine for
Protestant, Catholic, and Jewish
clergymen interested in the business
side of the church rather than theology.
By-line articles cover law, architecture,
building, worship, religious education,
ministers' personal lives, and church
finance.
**Readers:** Protestant, Catholic, and Jewish
clergymen.

**EVANGELICAL MISSIONS QUARTERLY**
25 W. 560 Geneva Rd.
Carol Stream, IL 60188
Telephone: (708) 653-2158
Mailing Address:
P.O. Box 794
Carol Stream, IL 60188
Year Established: 1964
Pub. Frequency: q.
Page Size: standard
Subscrip. Rate: $19.95/yr.
Freelance Pay: varies
Circulation: 8,000
Circulation Type: paid
**Owner(s):**
EMIS
P.O. Box 794
Wheaton, IL 60189
Telephone: (708) 653-2158
Ownership %: 100
**Management:**
Jean Warren ...............Advertising Manager
Karen Rummel ...............Circulation Manager
Dona Diehl ...............Production Manager
**Editorial:**
James W. Reapsome ...............Editor
Jean Warren ...............Assistant Editor
Stanley Guthrie ...............Associate Editor
**Desc.:** Professional journal for missionaries
emphasizing Evangelical missionary life,
thought & practice
**Readers:** Protestant missionaries

**HAWAIIAN CHURCH CHRONICLE**
229 Queen Emma Square
Honolulu, HI 96813-2304
Telephone: (808) 536-7776
FAX: (808) 536-2099
Year Established: 1910
Pub. Frequency: 9/yr.
Page Size: tabloid
Subscrip. Rate: free
**Owner(s):**
Episcopal Church of Hawaii
Ownership %: 100
**Management:**
Bishop Donald P. Hart ...............Publisher
**Editorial:**
Rev. John Paul Engelcke ...........Editor in Chief

**HISTORY OF RELIGIONS**
5720 S. Woodlawn Ave.
Chicago, IL 60637
Telephone: (312) 753-3347
FAX: (312) 753-0811
Year Established: 1961
Pub. Frequency: q.

Page Size: standard
Subscrip. Rate: $29/yr. individuals; $60/yr.
institutions; students $20/yr.
Circulation: 1,800
Circulation Type: paid
**Owner(s):**
University of Chicago Press
5720 S. Woodlawn Ave.
Chicago, IL 60637
Telephone: (312) 753-3347
**Editorial:**
Joseph M. Kitagawa ...............Editor
Frank E. Reynolds ...............Editor
Wendy Doniger ...............Editor
Gary L. Ebersole ...............Editor
Charles Long ...............Editorial Advisor
Lawrence Sullivan ...............Editorial Advisor
**Readers:** Academic

**HOMILETIC & PASTORAL REVIEW, THE**
86 Riverside Dr.
New York, NY 10024
Telephone: (212) 799-2600
FAX: (212) 787-0351
Year Established: 1900
Pub. Frequency: m.
Page Size: standard
Subscrip. Rate: $24/yr.
Materials: 06,10,17,19,32
Print Process: web offset
Circulation: 15,000
Circulation Type: paid
**Owner(s):**
Catholic Polls, Inc.
86 Riverside Dr.
New York, NY 10024
Telephone: (212) 799-2600
FAX: (212) 787-0351
Ownership %: 100
**Management:**
Elizabeth Schmitz ...........Advertising Manager
Bernard Belson ...............General Manager
**Editorial:**
Rev. Kenneth Baker ...............Editor
**Desc.:** Published for Catholic priests and
lay people concerned with current issues
of dogmatic and moral nature of
practical concern to the priest.
**Readers:** 95 percent Catholic clergy.

**INTERPRETATION**
3401 Brook Rd.
Richmond, VA 23227
Telephone: (804) 355-0671
FAX: (804) 355-3919
Year Established: 1947
Pub. Frequency: q.
Subscrip. Rate: $15.50/yr.
Circulation: 10,500
Circulation Type: paid
**Owner(s):**
Union Theological Seminary in Virginia
3401 Brook Rd.
Richmond, VA 23227
Telephone: (804) 355-0671
Ownership %: 100
**Editorial:**
Jack D. Kingsbury ...............Editor
**Desc.:** Publishes articles and essays of
biblical and theological interpretation for
scholars, clergy, and laity of all
denominations.

**LEADERSHIP**
465 Gunderson Dr.
Carol Stream, IL 60188
Telephone: (708) 260-6200
Year Established: 1980
Pub. Frequency: 4/yr.
Subscrip. Rate: $22/yr.
Circulation: 63,000
Circulation Type: paid

**Owner(s):**
Christianity Today, Inc.
465 Gundersen Dr.
Carol Stream, IL 60188
Telephone: (708) 260-6200
Ownership %: 100
**Editorial:**
Kevin A. Miller ...............Editor

**LITURGY 90**
1800 N. Hermitage Ave.
Chicago, IL 60622-1101
Telephone: (312) 486-8970
FAX: (312) 496-7094
Year Established: 1970
Pub. Frequency: 8/yr.
Subscrip. Rate: $18/yr.
Circulation: 6,120
Circulation Type: paid
**Owner(s):**
Liturgy Training Publications
1800 N. Hermitage Ave.
Chicago, IL 60622-1101
Telephone: (312) 486-8970
Ownership %: 100
**Editorial:**
Elizabeth Hoffman ...............Editor

**MODERN LITURGY**
160 E. Virginia St., #290
San Jose, CA 95112
Telephone: (408) 286-8505
FAX: (408) 287-8748
Year Established: 1973
Pub. Frequency: 10/yr.
Page Size: 4 color photos/art
Subscrip. Rate: $4 newsstand; $40/yr.
Freelance Pay: varies
Circulation: 15,000
Circulation Type: controlled
**Owner(s):**
William & Susan Burns
6244 Rainbow Dr.
San Jose, CA 95129
Telephone: (408) 253-0574
Ownership %: 100
**Management:**
William Burns ...............President
Mary J. Dent ...............Business Manager
**Editorial:**
Tom Musbach ...............Managing Editor
Kenneth Guentert ...............Editorial Director
Kimberly Chernock ...............Advertising
George Collopy ...............Art Director
Charles Poeck ...............Marketing Director
**Desc.:** Provides practical and creative
resource ideas for people who are
involved in planning and/or leading
religious worship services or preparing
any art form for use in a worship
service.
**Readers:** Church leaders who look for
ideas and examples that will help them
in planning and executing their own
liturgical prayer services and enhance
the environment in their worship space.

**MOMENTUM**
1077 30th St., N.W., Ste. 100
Washington, DC 20007
Telephone: (202) 337-6232
FAX: (202) 333-6706
Year Established: 1970
Pub. Frequency: q.
Page Size: standard
Subscrip. Rate: $20/yr.
Circulation: 25,000
Circulation Type: paid
**Owner(s):**
National Catholic Educational Association
1077 30th St., N.W., Ste. 100
Washington, DC 20007
Telephone: (202) 337-6232

**Editorial:**
Patricia Feistritzer ...............Editor
**Readers:** Catholic educators-all levels.

**PARISH LITURGY**
16160 S. Seton Dr.
S. Holland, IL 60473-1863
Telephone: (708) 331-5485
Year Established: 1978
Pub. Frequency: q.
Subscrip. Rate: $10/yr.
Materials: 02,06,10,12,19,20,25
Circulation: 1,500
Circulation Type: free & paid
**Owner(s):**
American Catholic Press
16160 S. Seton Dr.
S. Holland, IL 60473
Telephone: (708) 331-5485
Ownership %: 100
**Editorial:**
Michael Gilligan ...............Editor
**Readers:** Roman Catholic parish
personnel.

**PREACHING**
409 Godfrey Ave.
Louisville, KY 40206
Telephone: (502) 899-3119
FAX: (502) 893-5069
Mailing Address:
P.O. Box 7728
Louisville, KY 40257-0728
Year Established: 1985
Pub. Frequency: bi-m.
Page Size: standard
Subscrip. Rate: $24.95/yr.
Materials: 02,28,30,32
Print Process: offset
Circulation: 10,000
Circulation Type: paid
**Owner(s):**
Preaching Resources, Inc.
1529 Cesery Blvd.
Jacksonville, FL 32211
Telephone: (904) 743-5994
Ownership %: 100
**Editorial:**
Michael Duduit ...............Editor
**Desc.:** Practical articles on preaching,
sermon manuscripts, and homiletic
helps.
**Readers:** Interdenominational, primarily
pastors.
**Deadline:** ads-6 wks. prior to pub. date

**PRIEST, THE**
200 Noll Plz.
Huntington, IN 46750
Telephone: (219) 356-8400
FAX: (219) 356-8472
Mailing Address:
P.O. Box 920
Huntington, IN 46750
Year Established: 1945
Pub. Frequency: m.
Page Size: standard
Subscrip. Rate: $30/yr.; $58/2 yrs.; $84/3
yrs.
Freelance Pay: $175-$250/article
Circulation: 10,500
Circulation Type: paid
**Owner(s):**
Our Sunday Visitor, Inc.
200 Noll Plz.
Huntington, IN 46750
Telephone: (219) 356-8400
Ownership %: 100
**Management:**
Robert Lockwood ...............Publisher
**Editorial:**
Owen F. Campion ...............Editor
Peter Schownir ...............Advertising
Robert A. Willems ...............Associate Editor

Joseph Isca ...................................Miscellaneous
**Desc.:** Devoted to the priestly life and ministry. Seeks articles or features that will benefit priests and seminarians in the areas of priestly spirituality, contemporary theology, liturgy, apostolate and ministry, pastoral notes, and scripture. Manuscripts should be no less than 20 double-spaced, typed pages. Black-and-white photos used with some features. By-lines accompany all items. Departments include: Letters to Editor, Priesttalk (short precis of news and notes for clergy), The Homily (liturgy for Sundays of the following month), Viewpoints (guest articles), About Books, Questions and Answers.
**Readers:** Reaches 12,000 Catholic priests and brothers primarily in the U.S.

**PULPIT DIGEST**   25048
1160 Battery St.
San Francisco, CA 94111
Telephone: (415) 477-4400
FAX: (415) 421-5865
Year Established: 1936
Pub. Frequency: bi-m.
Page Size: pocket
Subscrip. Rate: $24.95/yr.; $45.95/2 yrs.; $64.95/3 yrs.
Circulation: 10,000
Circulation Type: paid
**Owner(s):**
Harper San Francisco, Div. of Harper-Collins
1160 Battery St.
San Francisco, CA 94111
Telephone: (415) 477-4400
Ownership %: 100
**Management:**
Clayton E. Carlson ...............................Publisher
Thomas R. Artz .................Circulation Manager
**Editorial:**
Dr. David A. Farmer .................Executive Editor
Kandace Hawkinson ...................................Editor
Steve Anderson ....................Editorial Assistant
**Desc.:** An ecumenical preaching journal designed to enhance the preacher's creativity. Contains at least 12 original sermons in each issue.
**Readers:** Largely Protestant ministers with some Catholic priests and Jewish rabbis.

**THIS PEOPLE**   71250
2898 Oakhurst Dr.
Salt Lake City, UT 84110
Telephone: (801) 581-0881
Mailing Address:
P.O. Box 2250
Salt Lake City, UT 84110
Pub. Frequency: q.
Page Size: standard
Subscrip. Rate: $3.25/copy; $11.95/yr. US; $16.95/yr. Canada
**Owner(s):**
Utah Alliance Publishing, Inc.
2898 Oakhurst Dr.
Salt Lake City, UT 84110
**Editorial:**
Maurine Jensen Proctor ...........................Editor
Scot Facer Proctor ...................................Editor
Robert E. Passey ...........................Art Director
Cheri Loveless ....................Associate Editor
Linda Nimori ...............................Copy Director
**Desc.:** Exploring issues and personalities for church members.

**YEARS AHEAD, THE**   52605
2401 Cedar Spring
Dallas, TX 75204
Telephone: (214) 720-0511
FAX: (214) 720-4784
Year Established: 1954
Pub. Frequency: 3/yr.

Page Size: standard
Subscrip. Rate: free
Freelance Pay: $100-$500/article
Circulation: 75,000
Circulation Type: controlled
**Owner(s):**
Annuity Board of Southern Baptist Convention
2401 Cedar Spring
Dallas, TX 75204
Telephone: (214) 720-0511
FAX: (214) 720-4784
Ownership %: 100
**Editorial:**
Tim Tune ...................................Editor
Ray Furr ................Communications Director
**Readers:** Southern Baptist Ministers & church lay leadership.

**YOUR CHURCH**   25050
465 Gundersen Dr.
Carol Stream, IL 60188
Telephone: (708) 260-6200
FAX: (708) 260-0114
Year Established: 1955
Pub. Frequency: bi-m.
Page Size: standard
Subscrip. Rate: $15/yr.
Freelance Pay: $.10/wd.
Print Process: web offset
Circulation: 150,000
Circulation Type: controlled
**Owner(s):**
Christianity Today, Inc.
465 Gundersen Dr.
Carol Stream, IL 60188
Telephone: (708) 260-6200
Ownership %: 100
**Management:**
Chrisitanity Today, Inc. ...................Publisher
John Grey ................Advertising Manager
**Editorial:**
James D. Berkley ...................................Editor
**Desc.:** Articles pertain solely to charch business administration matters, not general religious topics.
**Readers:** Pastors of all denominations.

## Group 226-Rental & Leasing

**APARTMENT AGE**   52686
621 S. Westmoreland Ave.
Los Angeles, CA 90005
Telephone: (310) 384-4131
Year Established: 1967
Pub. Frequency: m.
Page Size: standard
Subscrip. Rate: $48/yr.
Freelance Pay: $.10-$.25/wd.
Circulation: 40,000
Circulation Type: controlled
**Owner(s):**
Apartment Association of Greater Los Angeles
621 S. Westmoreland Ave.
Los Angeles, CA 90005
Telephone: (310) 384-4131
Ownership %: 100
**Management:**
Charles A. Isham ...............................Publisher
Catherine C. ................Advertising Manager
Campbell
**Editorial:**
Kevin B. Postema ...................................Editor
**Desc.:** Known as the voice of the industry. Keeps apartment owners, and operators abreast of the rapidly changing political, legal, management, and operating developments and techniques in the industry.
**Readers:** Apartment owners and managers primarily in Los Angeles County, CA.

**MONITOR**   65219
4 Stamford Forum
Stamford, CT 06901-3202
Telephone: (203) 325-3500
Year Established: 1970
Pub. Frequency: 6/yr.
Page Size: standard
Subscrip. Rate: $45/yr. US; $50/yr. Canada; $58/yr. elsewhere
Circulation: 33,000
Circulation Type: paid
**Owner(s):**
Maclean Hunter Media
4 Stamford Forum
Stamford, CT 06901-3202
Telephone: (203) 325-3500
**Editorial:**
Robert E. O'Neill ...................................Editor
**Desc.:** Data, studies, and information on the shopping center and chain retail store market.

**RENTAL EQUIPMENT REGISTER**   23467
6133 Bristol Pkwy.
Culver City, CA 90230
Telephone: (310) 337-9717
Mailing Address:
P.O. Box 3640
Culver City, CA 90230
Year Established: 1957
Pub. Frequency: m.
Page Size: standard
Subscrip. Rate: free
Freelance Pay: varies
Circulation: 15,000
Circulation Type: free
**Owner(s):**
Miramar Publishing Co.
Telephone: (310) 477-1033
**Management:**
Tim Novoselski ...............................Publisher
Aaron Smith ...........................Sales Manager
**Editorial:**
Michael Roth ...................................Editor
**Desc.:** Publish articles describing various particular aspects of rental service yards and stores across the country, including promotional methods, store layouts, inventory processing, employee relations, etc. Ideas on how to do things that will help our readers, and information on trends in the rental industry. Departments include: News, Briefly Noted, Viewpoint, New Products, Product Spotlight, Calendar, Toll Free Numbers, Rentopics, Sotcher on Safety, Lewis' Dollars & Sense, Rer on the Road, Classifieds, Rep Directory, The Personnel File, Risk Manager, Promo Power, Tech Session, Equipment Focus.
**Readers:** Owners and operators of rental stores and they rent all kinds of equipment.

**RENTAL MANAGEMENT**   23466
1900 19th St.
Moline, IL 61265
Telephone: (309) 764-2475
FAX: (309) 764-1533
Year Established: 1970
Pub. Frequency: m.
Page Size: standard
Subscrip. Rate: $2/issue; $24/yr.
Freelance Pay: negotiated
Circulation: 13,500
Circulation Type: paid
**Owner(s):**
American Rental Association, Inc.
1900 19th St.
Moline, IL 61265
Telephone: (309) 764-2475
Ownership %: 100
**Management:**
Fred Anderson ...................................Publisher

**Editorial:**
Robert Buttgen ...................................Editor
Tammy Dawson ...................Managing Editor
Susan Stapleton ...................Associate Editor
**Desc.:** Magazine's intent to 1) cover all pertinent subjects pertaining to the rental business, including safety, legislation, employee hiring and training, equipment maintenance, store and service image, inventory control, advertising, etc.; and 2) cover activities of the American Rental Association such as national convention, corporate meetings, regional conferences, new membership services, activities of members, etc. Rental Age appeals to the general rental operator (all types of goods) with photo spreads, in-depth feature news coverage, "how-to" articles, opinion, federal review, filler, etc. Tries to maintain serious tone but uses visuals for interest. Departments include: Letters to the Editor, Manufacturers News, Bulletin Board, Editorial Page, Local & State Assn. News, Up Front (news), News You Can Use.
**Readers:** Members of the American Rental Association, other rental businesses, manufacturers and suppliers.

**RENTAL PRODUCT NEWS**   23468
1233 Janesville Ave.
Fort Atkinson, WI 53538
Telephone: (414) 563-6388
FAX: (414) 563-1701
Year Established: 1978
Pub. Frequency: 9/yr.
Page Size: tabloid
Subscrip. Rate: $40/yr. US; $55/yr. in Canada & Mexico; $120/yr. foreign
Freelance Pay: varies
Circulation: 20,000
Circulation Type: controlled
**Owner(s):**
Johnson Hill Press, Inc.
1233 Janesville Ave.
Fort Atkinson, WI 53538
Telephone: (414) 563-6388
Ownership %: 100
**Management:**
Jonathan Pellegrin ...........Chairman of Board
Richard Moeller ...........................President
**Editorial:**
Jeff Ignaszak ...................................Editor
Cyndi Ehrke ...................Associate Editor
Richard Reiff ...........................Group Publisher
Amy Romans ...............Production Coordinator
Pat Boyer ...................................Sales
**Desc.:** Provides and editorial curriculum that assists rental operators and retailers who have diversified into the rental business to more effectively select and profitably rent products.
**Readers:** Owners, managers and suppliers for the nation.

**RYDER RESOURCE**   69707
3600 N.W. 82nd Ave.
Miami, FL 33166
Telephone: (305) 593-3210
FAX: (305) 593-3203
Mailing Address:
P.O. Box 020816
Miami, FL 33102-0816
Pub. Frequency: 3/yr.
Page Size: 24 pg.; 8 1/2 x 11, 4-color
Subscrip. Rate: Free to customers
**Owner(s):**
Ryder System, Inc.
3600 N.W. 82nd Ave.
Miami, FL
Telephone: (305) 593-3210
Ownership %: 100

**Materials Accepted/Included:** 01-Business news 02-By-line articles 03-Fashion news 04-Food news 05-Freelance copy 06-Letters to editor 07-Real estate news 08-Sports news 09-Travel news 10-Book rev. 11-Movie rev. 12-Music rev. 13-TV rev. 14-Theater rev. 15-Coming events 16-Obituaries 17-Question & answer 18-Social announcements 19-Artwork 20-Cartoons 21-Photos 22-TV listings 23-Audio rec. 24-Video rec. 25-Books 26-Films/film clips 27-Personnel news 28-Press releases 29-New product news/photos 30-Trade lit. 31-Contracts awarded 32-Display adv. 33-Classified adv.

4-321

**Desc.:** Objective is to inform prospects and customers of services available through the Ryder System.

## Group 228-Restaurants & Food Service

24623

**AIRLINE, SHIP & CATERING ONBOARD SERVICES MAGAZINE**
665 La Villa Dr.
Miami Springs, FL 33166
Telephone: (305) 887-1700
FAX: (305) 885-1923
Year Established: 1968
Pub. Frequency: 9/yr.
Page Size: tabloid
Subscrip. Rate: $25/yr. US; $65/yr. foreign
Freelance Pay: $75-$150/story
Circulation: 9,000
Circulation Type: paid
**Owner(s):**
International Publishing Co. of America
665 La Villa Dr.
Miami Springs, FL 33166
Telephone: (305) 887-1700
Ownership %: 100
**Management:**
Alexander Morton ..............................Publisher
Charlene Gardener ...........Circulation Manager
George Mazola ....................Managing Director
**Editorial:**
Raymond G. Feldman ..............................Editor
Alex Morton ......................Managing Editor
Hector Ruz ............................Art Director
**Desc.:** Contains current news articles about transportation food service companies, their personnel, and news dealing with industry innovations, new products, and government regulations. Regular features include points of interest in airline, cruise ship, railroad, duty-free, catering, onboard entertainment, and ship supplier industries.
**Readers:** Persons involved in food service and onboard entertainment. Management of airline, ship and railroad industries; catering executives; managers of duty-free stores; and suppliers to the travel industry.

69642

**ART CULINAIRE**
P.O. Box 9268
Morristown, NJ 07963-9268
Telephone: (201) 993-5500
FAX: (201) 993-8779
Year Established: 1986
Pub. Frequency: q.
Subscrip. Rate: $59/yr. US; $75/yr. foreign
Circulation: 7,538
**Owner(s):**
Franz Mitterer
P.O. Box 9268
Morristown, NJ 07960
Telephone: (201) 993-5500
Ownership %: 100
**Editorial:**
Mitchell Davis ....................................Editor

24624

**CHEF MAGAZINE**
20 N. Wacker Dr., Ste. 3230
Chicago, IL 60606
Telephone: (800) 229-1967
FAX: (312) 849-2184
Year Established: 1956
Pub. Frequency: 9/yr.
Page Size: standard
Subscrip. Rate: $20/yr.; $35/2 yrs.
Materials: 01,04,06
Circulation: 43,300
Circulation Type: controlled & paid

**Owner(s):**
Talcott Communications Co.
20 N. Wacker Rd.
Chicago, IL 60606
Telephone: (800) 229-1967
Ownership %: 100
**Management:**
Daniel Von Rabenau ..........................Publisher
**Editorial:**
Paul Clark ..................................................Editor
**Desc.:** Anything of interest to executive chefs and food service directors.
**Readers:** Professional chefs

24627

**COOKING FOR PROFIT**
104 S. Main St., 7th Fl.
Fond du Lac, WI 54935
Telephone: (414) 923-3700
FAX: (414) 923-6805
Mailing Address:
P.O. Box 267
Fond du Lac, WI 54936-0267
Year Established: 1932
Pub. Frequency: m.
Page Size: standard
Subscrip. Rate: $24/yr.
Materials: 01,04,10,25
Freelance Pay: varies
Circulation: 50,000
Circulation Type: paid
**Owner(s):**
C.P. Publishing, Inc.
104 S. Main St., 7th Fl.
Fond du Lac, WI 54935
Telephone: (414) 923-3700
FAX: (414) 923-6805
Ownership %: 100
**Management:**
Colleen Phalen ..................................Publisher
**Editorial:**
Colleen Phalen ..........................Editor in Chief
Thomas Remo ........................................Artist
Kristin Deutsch ........................Assistant Editor
Walt Sinisi ......................................Food Editor
Thomas Remo ..........................Graphics Editor
Mary Campbell ..............................Office Clerk
**Desc.:** Editorially concerned with operations management, especially energy topics and gas equipment usage in food-service establishments. In-depth profiles of successful food-service operations, along with a focus on current food trends. Specializing in recipes.
**Readers:** Owners and managers of commercial and noncommercial food-service operations and institutions.

68921

**CULINARY TRENDS**
6285 Spring St., Ste. 107
Long Beach, CA 90808
Telephone: (310) 496-2558
FAX: (310) 982-1432
Year Established: 1990
Pub. Frequency: q.
Page Size: standard
Subscrip. Rate: $5.95 newsstand; $21.60/yr.
Materials: 04,10,29
Circulation: 5,000
Circulation Type: paid
**Owner(s):**
Culinary Trends Publications
6285 Spring St., Ste. 107
Long Beach, CA 90808
Telephone: (310) 496-2558
Ownership %: 100
**Editorial:**
Fred Mensings ........................................Editor
**Readers:** Executives and working chefs, food and beverage directors, propietors, and general managers of hotels, resorts, private clubs, high-end catering establishments, and fine restaurants.

24625

**FOOD & SERVICE**
1400 Lavaca
Austin, TX 78701
Telephone: (512) 472-3666
FAX: (512) 472-2777
Mailing Address:
P.O. Box 1429
Austin, TX 78767-1429
Year Established: 1940
Pub. Frequency: 11/yr.
Page Size: 4 color photos/art
Subscrip. Rate: membership in TRA
Freelance Pay: negotiable
Circulation: 6,200
Circulation Type: controlled & paid
**Owner(s):**
Texas Restaurant Association
1400 Lavaca
Austin, TX 78767
Telephone: (512) 472-3666
Ownership %: 100
**Management:**
Richie Jackson ..................................Publisher
**Editorial:**
Julie Stephen Sherrier ............Managing Editor
Neil Ferguson ..............................Art Director
Julie Stephen Sherrier ..................New Products Editor
**Desc.:** Provides business solutions to restaurateurs. Carries new equipment, industry news, association activities, government regulations, the industry, and other developments affecting the Texas-Southwest hospitality (i.e., food, drink, and lodging).
**Readers:** Members of foodservice operators and suppliers.

65471

**FOOD ARTS**
387 Park Ave. S.
New York, NY 10016
Telephone: (212) 371-1333
Year Established: 1988
Pub. Frequency: 10/yr.
Page Size: standard
Subscrip. Rate: $30/yr.
Circulation: 53,000
Circulation Type: paid
**Owner(s):**
Quatro Group, The
387 Park Ave., S.
New York, NY 10016
Telephone: (212) 371-1333
Ownership %: 100
**Management:**
Michael Batterbury ..............................Publisher
Arianne Batterbury ..............................Publisher
**Desc.:** Covers trends in the area of upscale restaurants on an international and national scale.
**Readers:** Professionals in the restaurant business.

24632

**FOOD MANAGEMENT**
122 E. 42nd St., Ste. 900
New York, NY 10168
Telephone: (212) 309-7620
FAX: (212) 808-4189
Year Established: 1972
Pub. Frequency: m.
Page Size: oversize
Subscrip. Rate: $45/yr.
Freelance Pay: negotiable
Circulation: 53,000
Circulation Type: controlled
**Owner(s):**
Penton Publishing
1100 Superior Ave.
Cleveland, OH 44114
Telephone: (216) 696-7000
Ownership %: 100
**Management:**
Sal Marino ....................Chairman of Board
Dan Ramella ..............................President

Gerald White ................................Publisher
**Editorial:**
Donna L. Boss ....................Editor in Chief
Debbie Kearney ..................Editorial Assistant
**Desc.:** Timely articles written for management professionals in food service who want to know how to do their jobs better.
**Readers:** 62,000 food-service directors and dietitians in schools, hospitals, nursing homes, colleges, business and industry, airlines, prisons, government institutions, and independently run food services.

65251

**FOOD SERVICE DIRECTOR**
355 Park Ave. S.
New York, NY 10010-1789
Telephone: (212) 592-6542
FAX: (212) 592-6539
Year Established: 1988
Pub. Frequency: m.
Page Size: tabloid
Subscrip. Rate: members only
Materials: 01,04,06,15,20,27,28,29,30,32,33
Freelance Pay: up to $400/pg.
Print Process: web offset
Circulation: 45,000
Circulation Type: controlled
**Owner(s):**
Bill Communications, Inc.
355 Park Ave. S.
New York, NY 10010-1789
Telephone: (212) 593-6542
Ownership %: 100
**Management:**
Jess Grossberg ..................................Publisher
**Editorial:**
Walter Schruntek ....................................Editor
**Desc.:** Mission is to be the first-read news publication of the non-commercial food-service field.
**Readers:** Professionals at schools, colleges, hospitals, nursing homes, airlines, penal institutions, and other noncommercial contract management corporations and organizations.
**Deadline:** story-45 days prior to pub. date; news-30 days; photo-45 days; ads-30 days

23389

**FOODSERVICE EAST**
76 Summer St., Ste. 5C
Boston, MA 02110-1225
Telephone: (617) 695-9080
Year Established: 1925
Pub. Frequency: 7/yr.
Page Size: tabloid
Subscrip. Rate: $20/yr.
Materials: 01,07,32,33
Print Process: web
Circulation: 25,000
Circulation Type: controlled & paid
**Owner(s):**
Newbury St. Group, Inc., The
76 Summer St., Ste. 5C
Boston, MA 02110-1225
Telephone: (617) 695-9080
Ownership %: 100
**Management:**
Susan G. Holaday ..............................President
Richard E. Dolby ..............................Publisher
**Editorial:**
Susan G. Holaday ....................................Editor
**Desc.:** Contains news articles, surveys, and features reporting on growth and expansion plans, marketing programs, promotional and operational techniques, economic trends, association activities, governmental legislation, and personnel changes in or affecting the lodging and food-service industry. Special features include allied news and new products and services.

---

**Materials Accepted/Included:** 01-Business news 02-By-line articles 03-Fashion news 04-Food news 05-Freelance copy 06-Letters to editor 07-Real estate news 08-Sports news 09-Travel news 10-Book rev. 11-Movie rev. 12-Music rev. 13-TV rev. 14-Theater rev. 15-Coming events 16-Obituaries 17-Question & answer 18-Social announcements 19-Artwork 20-Cartoons 21-Photos 22-TV listings 23-Audio rec. 24-Video rec. 25-Books 26-Films/film clips 27-Personnel news 28-Press releases 29-New product news/photos 30-Trade lit. 31-Contracts awarded 32-Display adv. 33-Classified adv.

**Readers:** Food-service and lodging personnel responsible for buying, specifying for, and managing restaurants, hotels, motor hotels, schools, colleges, hospitals, nursing homes, caterers, clubs, chains, and & multiple-unit headquarters.

## FOOD SERVICE EQUIPMENT & SUPPLIES SPECIALIST
24635

1350 E. Touhy Ave.
Des Plaines, IL 60018
Telephone: (708) 635-8800
Mailing Address:
  P.O. Box 5080
  Des Plaines, IL 60017
Year Established: 1948
Pub. Frequency: m.
Page Size: standard
Subscrip. Rate: $69.95/yr. US; $107.95/yr. Mexico; $114.95/yr. Canada; $129.95/yr. elsewhere
Freelance Pay: negotiable
Circulation: 22,125
Circulation Type: controlled
**Owner(s):**
Cahners Publishing Co.
1350 Touhy Ave.
Des Plaines, IL 60018
Telephone: (708) 635-8800
Ownership %: 100
**Management:**
Lisa Ullman ..................New Products Manager
**Editorial:**
Gregory B. Richards ...................Editor
Brian Ward ...............................Managing Editor
**Desc.:** Articles cover market trends in the food-service equipment industry. Departments include: Industry News, Reviews of Equipment, Layout and Design (of food-service facilities), Dealer Sales Index, Product Focus, New Products & Literature.
**Readers:** Food service equipment dealers & distributors, food service design consultants, restaurant chain equipment buyers, independent equipment service agencies, independent sales representatives.

## FOODSERVICE PRODUCT NEWS
24630

1101 Richmond Ave., Ste. 201
Pt. Pleasant Beach, NJ 08742-3049
Telephone: (908) 295-5959
FAX: (908) 295-5979
Year Established: 1967
Pub. Frequency: 9/yr.
Page Size: Tabloid
Subscrip. Rate: free
Circulation: 132,000
Circulation Type: controlled & free
**Owner(s):**
Young/Conway Publications, Inc.
1101 Richmond Ave., Ste. 201
Pt. Pleasant Beach, NJ 08742-3049
Ownership %: 100
**Management:**
Art Conway ...............................President
Mark Conway ...........................Publisher
Mark Conway ...........................Sales Manager
**Editorial:**
Judy Ann Young ......................Editor
Steve Cutler .............................Associate Editor
Judy Ann Young ................New Product Editor
**Desc.:** A product news tabloid, our editorial consists solely of new product news or literature or improvements of existing products of interest to the institutional food service industry.
**Readers:** Restaurant operators, schools, colleges, feeding operations, clubs, etc. and distributors,

## ID MAGAZINE
23488

355 Park Ave. S., 3rd Fl.
New York, NY 10010-1706
Telephone: (212) 592-6200
Year Established: 1965
Page Size: standard
Subscrip. Rate: $80/yr.
Freelance Pay: open
Circulation: 47,000
Circulation Type: controlled
**Owner(s):**
Bill Communications, Inc.
633 Third Ave.
New York, NY 10017
Telephone: (212) 592-6200
Ownership %: 100
**Management:**
John Wickersham ....................President
Niles Crum ..............................Publisher
**Editorial:**
Richard Petreycik ..........Senior Editor
Caroline Perkins .........................Editor
Lisa Bocchino ..............Managing Editor
Katherine Allen ..................Art Director
Michele McCoy .........Assistant Editor
Jeffrey P. Berlind .........Vice President & Group Pub.
**Desc.:** Heavy use of photos. Most material is staff written, success stories on sales techniques in our industry. Features rarely more than seven or eight pages. Departments include: News, New Products, Equipt., Supplies and Food Product Knowledge (called Market Savvy). Pro Buyer Sales Talk.
**Readers:** Foodservice distribution industry, foodservice distributor executives & their sales reps.

## IOWA APPETIZER
23029

606 Merle Hay Tower
Des Moines, IA 50310
Telephone: (515) 276-1454
FAX: (515) 276-3660
Year Established: 1933
Pub. Frequency: m.
Page Size: standard
Subscrip. Rate: $2/ea.; $20/yr.
Materials: 01,04,09,20,29,30,32,33
Print Process: web offset
Circulation: 1,100
Circulation Type: controlled
**Owner(s):**
Iowa Restaurant and Beverage Association
606 Merle Hay Tower
Des Moines, IA 50310
Telephone: (515) 276-1454
FAX: (515) 276-1454
Ownership %: 100
**Management:**
Iowa Restaurant Assn. ........................Publisher
Lester R. Davis ................Advertising Manager
**Editorial:**
Lester R. Davis ..........................Editor
Lester R. Davis ...........Executive Director
**Desc.:** Stories related to food service industry; new products; new developments.
**Readers:** Restaurant & bar owners, managers, and proprietors.
**Deadline:** story-15th of mo.; news-20th of mo.; photo-15th of mo.; ads-15th of mo.

## JOBSON'S CHEERS
66671

100 Ave. of the Americas
New York, NY 10013-1678
Telephone: (212) 274-7000
FAX: (212) 431-0500
Year Established: 1990
Pub. Frequency: bi-m.
Page Size: standard
Subscrip. Rate: $24/yr.
Materials: 01,02,04,06,28,29,30,32,33

Freelance Pay: varies
Print Process: offset
Circulation: 100,000
Circulation Type: controlled
**Owner(s):**
Jobson Publishing Corp.
100 Ave. of The Americas
New York, NY 10013
Telephone: (212) 274-7000
Ownership %: 100
**Management:**
Seymour L. Leikind ..............Publisher
**Editorial:**
Robert Keane ...............................Editor
**Readers:** Owner/operators of high volume food service (commercial) establishments.

## KANSAS RESTAURANT, THE
24637

359 S. Hydraulic
Wichita, KS 67211
Telephone: (316) 267-8383
Mailing Address:
  P.O. Box 235
  Wichita, KS 67211
Year Established: 1933
Pub. Frequency: 4/yr.
Page Size: 4 color photos/art
Subscrip. Rate: $24/yr. members
Freelance Pay: None
Circulation: 900
Circulation Type: controlled
**Owner(s):**
Kansas Restaurant Assn.
359 S. Hydraulic
Wichita, KS 67211
Telephone: (316) 267-8383
Ownership %: 100
**Management:**
George Puckett ...........................Publisher
**Editorial:**
Trish Phelps ...............................Editor
**Desc.:** News, news features report on association activities, promotion programs, innovations within the industry. Prints news of food industry suppliers, question and answer page for operators lists each new Kansas operations.
**Readers:** Management of restaurants, hotels, clubs.

## MICHIGAN RESTAURATEUR
68928

225 W. Washtenaw
Lansing, MI 48933-3037
Telephone: (517) 482-5244
Year Established: 1935
Pub. Frequency: bi-m.
Page Size: standard
Subscrip. Rate: $24/yr.
Materials: 04,10,15,20,21,32,33
Circulation: 3,500
Circulation Type: paid
**Owner(s):**
Michigan Restaurant Association
225 W. Washtenaw
Lansing, MI 48933-3037
Telephone: (517) 482-5244
Ownership %: 100
**Editorial:**
Kim Ohlemacher ...............................Editor
**Readers:** Estimated 11,000 readership throughout Michigan.
**Deadline:** story-1 mo. prior to pub. date

## MIDSOUTHWEST RESTAURANT MAGAZINE
24640

3800 N. Portland
Oklahoma City, OK 73112
Telephone: (405) 942-8181
Year Established: 1937
Pub. Frequency: bi-m.

Page Size: standard
Subscrip. Rate: $25/yr.
Materials: 04,32,33
Print Process: offset
Circulation: 2,200
Circulation Type: controlled & paid
**Owner(s):**
Oklahoma Restaurant Association
3800 N. Portland
Oklahoma City, OK 73112
Telephone: (405) 942-8181
Ownership %: 100
**Management:**
Robert T. Clift .........................Publisher
Cheryl Walker ...............Advertising Manager
**Editorial:**
Cheryl Walker ..........................News Editor
Cheryl Walker ..........................Photo
**Desc.:** Magazine of the Oklahoma Restaurant Association featuring members, industry trends, and management principles.
**Readers:** Restaurant, food service operators, and hospitality managers.

## MIDWEST HOSPITALITY
61647

4049 Pennsylvania, Ste. 201
Kansas City, MO 64111
Telephone: (816) 753-5222
FAX: (816) 753-6993
Mailing Address:
  P.O. Box 10277
  Kansas City, MO 64111
Year Established: 1916
Pub. Frequency: 10/yr.
Page Size: standard
Subscrip. Rate: $15/yr.
Materials: 01,02,04,05,06,15,17,19,20,21, 27,28,29,30,32,33
Freelance Pay: varies
Print Process: offset
Circulation: 3,400
Circulation Type: controlled
**Owner(s):**
Missouri Restaurant Association
4049 Pennsylvania, Ste. 201
Kansas City, MO 64111
Telephone: (816) 753-5222
FAX: (816) 753-6993
Ownership %: 100
**Editorial:**
Michelle A. Holden ...............................Editor
**Desc.:** Regional trade publication serving food service owners, operators and suppliers in the three-state region of Missouri, Eastern Kansas and Western Illinois. Articles focus on trends, industry news, profiles and issues that affect the food service industry.
**Readers:** Foodservice owners, management and suppliers.
**Deadline:** story-15th of mo., prior to pub. date; news-15th of mo.; photo-15th of mo.; ads-1st of mo.

## MILITARY CLUB & HOSPITALITY
23376

825 Old Country Rd.
Westbury, NY 11590
Telephone: (516) 334-3030
FAX: (516) 334-3059
Mailing Address:
  P.O. Box 1500
  Westbury, NY 11590
Year Established: 1967
Pub. Frequency: 8/yr.
Page Size: standard
Subscrip. Rate: $35/yr.
Circulation: 10,000
Circulation Type: controlled

---

**Materials Accepted/Included:** 01-Business news 02-By-line articles 03-Fashion news 04-Food news 05-Freelance copy 06-Letters to editor 07-Real estate news 08-Sports news 09-Travel news 10-Book rev. 11-Movie rev. 12-Music rev. 13-TV rev. 14-Theater rev. 15-Coming events 16-Obituaries 17-Question & answer 18-Social announcements 19-Artwork 20-Cartoons 21-Photos 22-TV listings 23-Audio rec. 24-Video rec. 25-Books 26-Films/film clips 27-Personnel news 28-Press releases 29-New product news/photos 30-Trade lit. 31-Contracts awarded 32-Display adv. 33-Classified adv.

4-323

**Owner(s):**
Executive Business Media, Inc.
825 Old Country Road
P.O. Box 1500
Westbury, NY 11590
Telephone: (516) 334-3030
Ownership %: 100
**Management:**
Murry H. Greenwald .............................President
Jerry Thornton ...................Advertising Manager
**Editorial:**
Robert Moran ...........................Executive Editor
James Pond .............................Managing Editor
Carol Angrisani .......................Associate Editor
Janet Patterson ..................Production Director
Helen Scheller ...............Vice President, Finance
Fred Schaen .............Vice President, Marketing
**Desc.:** In a lively, up-to-date style, this journal contains news and feature articles pertaining to all areas of club, lodging, recreation, and food-service management. Edited for buyers, managers, and executives of Armed Forces officers; non-commissioned officers and enlisted men's clubs in the U.S. and overseas; managers of Armed Forces retail liquor stores; owners of guest houses; managers of billeting facilities; and directors of recreation and fitness centers. Also geared toward managers of the 5,000 Armed Forces food-service outlets, including troop and ship dining halls, snack bars, restaurants. Editorial emphasis is on news, activities, and features of the decentralized military club and food-service system, as well as policy and practice affecting it. Uses many photos. Departments include: Opinion, Top Priority, European Front, Trade Topics, Product Report, Letters to Editor, Reader Service, Classified.
**Readers:** Managers of Armed Forces clubs, lodges, recreation facilites, and food-service and liquor store facilities.

### NATION'S RESTAURANT NEWS
24642
425 Park Ave.
New York, NY 10022
Telephone: (212) 756-5000
Year Established: 1967
Pub. Frequency: 50/yr.
Page Size: tabloid
Subscrip. Rate: $34.50/yr. for restaurants
Circulation: 95,000
Circulation Type: paid
**Owner(s):**
Lebhar-Friedman, Inc.
425 Park Ave.
New York, NY 10022
Telephone: (212) 756-5000
Ownership %: 100
**Management:**
James Doherty .................................Publisher
Mira Charlton .............................Sales Manager
**Editorial:**
Rick Van Warner .....................................Editor
Paul Frumkin ...............................National Editor
Dan Mills .........................................Treasurer
**Desc.:** A newspaper for restaurant operators who are executives and managers of food-service chains, single-unit restaurants, and food-service management companies. A national news gathering network to report changes in today's food-service industry. Regular features include Washington outlook, labor outlook, and new technological developments in food-service equipment and food products.
**Readers:** Multiple-unit food-service executives, independents, and food-service management leaders.

### NIGHT CLUB & BAR MAGAZINE
68924
307 W. Jackson Ave.
Oxford, MS 38655-2154
Telephone: (601) 236-5510
FAX: (601) 236-5541
Year Established: 1984
Pub. Frequency: m.
Page Size: standard
Subscrip. Rate: $25/yr.
Materials: 01,02,04,05,06,08,23,24,25,26, 28,29,30,32,33
Circulation: 20,000
Circulation Type: paid
**Owner(s):**
Oxford Publishing
307 W. Jackson Ave.
Oxford, MS 38655-2154
Telephone: (601) 236-5510
Ownership %: 100
**Editorial:**
Rick Hynum .........................................Editor

### RESTAURANT BUSINESS
24643
355 Park Ave., S., 3rd Fl.
New York, NY 10010-1789
Telephone: (212) 592-6200
FAX: (212) 592-6509
Year Established: 1902
Pub. Frequency: 18/yr.
Page Size: standard
Subscrip. Rate: $79/yr.
Freelance Pay: $300-$750
Circulation: 130,000
Circulation Type: controlled
**Owner(s):**
Restaurant Business, Inc.
355 Park Ave., S.
New York, NY 10010-6509
Telephone: (212) 592-6505
Ownership %: 100
**Management:**
Jeffrey Berlind .................................President
Jeffrey Berlind .................................Publisher
**Editorial:**
Scott Allmendinger ...................................Editor
Ralph Raffio ...........................................Editor
Tom Strenk ...........................Managing Editor
**Desc.:** Concentrates on ways and means of exploiting growth opportunities and increasing productivity through the better use of management's basic resources, manpower, materials, machines, methods, money, and markets.
**Readers:** Owners, managers, and executives.

### RESTAURANT HOSPITALITY
23381
1100 Superior Ave.
Cleveland, OH 44114-2543
Telephone: (216) 696-7000
Year Established: 1919
Pub. Frequency: m.
Page Size: 9" X 12"
Subscrip. Rate: $5.25/copy; $60/yr.
Materials: 01,02,04,05,06,07,10,15,17,21, 29,32
Freelance Pay: negotiable
Print Process: web offset
Circulation: 123,000
Circulation Type: controlled
**Owner(s):**
Penton Publishing
1100 Superior Ave.
Cleveland, OH 44114
Telephone: (216) 696-7000
Ownership %: 100
**Management:**
Rob Dorfmeyer ...............................Publisher
Kathy Lamovec .................Promotion Manager
**Editorial:**
Gail Bellamy ................................Senior Editor
Michael DeLuca ...................................Editor
Michael Sanson ......................Managing Editor
John Soeder .........................Associate Editor

David Farkas ............................Feature Editor
Cecile Lamalle ............................Food Editor
Katie Smith ......................New Products Editor
Sue Apple .........................Production Director
**Desc.:** Covers all phases of management in commercial food service operations.
**Readers:** Company officers, food service management, operations management, chefs, kitchen managers and owners.
**Deadline:** story-60 days prior to pub. date; news-60 days prior; photo-60 days prior; ads-30 days prior

### RESTAURANT MANAGEMENT INSIDER
65746
1541 Morris Ave.
Bronx, NY 10457
Telephone: (212) 583-8060
Year Established: 1972
Pub. Frequency: bi-w.
Page Size: standard
Subscrip. Rate: $225/yr.
Circulation: 536
Circulation Type: paid
**Owner(s):**
Walker Communications, Inc.
1541 Morris Ave.
Bronx, NY 10457
Telephone: (718) 583-8060
FAX: (718) 583-8258
Ownership %: 100
**Management:**
Beverley Walker ...............................Publisher
**Editorial:**
Michael Schau .......................................Editor
**Readers:** Owners and managers of restaurants and food-service establishments.

### RESTAURANTS & INSTITUTIONS
23490
1350 E. Touhy Ave.
Des Plaines, IL 60017-5080
Telephone: (708) 635-8800
FAX: (708) 299-8622
Year Established: 1937
Pub. Frequency: m.
Page Size: standard
Subscrip. Rate: $104.95/yr. US; $179.95/yr. Mexico; $192.55/yr. Canada; $234.95/yr. elsewhere
Materials: 01,04,06,15,19,20,25,27,29,32,33
Circulation: 162,000
Circulation Type: controlled
**Owner(s):**
Reed Publishing (USA) Inc.
275 Washington St.
Newton, MA 02158
Ownership %: 100
**Management:**
Jane Wallace .................................Publisher
Jacqueline Rance .............Production Manager
**Editorial:**
Michael Bartlett ..........................Editor in Chief
Lisa Bertagnoli .......................Managing Editor
Tony Pronoitis ........................Art Department
Queenie Burns .........................Art Director
Nancy Ryan ......................Book Review Editor
Erin Nicholas .......................Chief Copy Editor
Jeff Weinstein ........................Education Editor
Beth Lorenzini ...........................Feature Editor
Nancy DeRoin Ryan ...................Feature Editor
Karen Straus ............................Food Editor
Nancy Ryan ...............................Food Editor
Jeff Weinstein ..........Government Affairs Editor
Susie Stephenson ........................Institutions
Jeff Weinstein .............................Labor Editor
Jacqueline Rance ...................Production Editor
Molly Ingram ..........................Products Editor
**Desc.:** For the food-service and lodging industies, ideas from the most successful restaurants and institutional food-service operations around the U.S.

**Readers:** Management of restaurants, fast-food stores, hotels, motels, clubs, hospitals and dealers, wholesalers, and architects.
**Deadline:** story-8-10 wks. prior to pub. date; news-8-10 wks.; photo-8-10 wks.; ads-8-10 wks.

### RESTAURANTS USA
24641
1200 17th St., N.W.
Washington, DC 20036
Telephone: (202) 331-5900
Year Established: 1981
Pub. Frequency: 11/yr.
Page Size: standard
Subscrip. Rate: $125/yr. non-members
Freelance Pay: $250-$850/article
Circulation: 30,000
Circulation Type: paid
**Owner(s):**
National Restaurant Association
1200 17th St., N.W.
Washington, DC 20036
Telephone: (202) 331-5900
Ownership %: 100
**Editorial:**
Jennifer Batty ........................................Editor
Melanie Crosby ......................Managing Editor
Jeffrey Prince ......................................Director
**Desc.:** Business-oriented material pertaining to the food-service industry. Specifically, trends and operations information. Reports of association programs, projects, and activities. Many how-to business articles.
**Readers:** Food-service and lodging owners and managers.

### SCHOOL FOODSERVICE & NUTRITION
24649
1600 Duke St.
Alexandria, VA 22314-3436
Telephone: (703) 739-3900
FAX: (703) 739-3915
Year Established: 1947
Pub. Frequency: 11/yr.
Page Size: standard
Subscrip. Rate: $125/yr.
Materials: 01,02,04,06,15,28,29,32
Print Process: web
Circulation: 65,000
Circulation Type: paid
**Owner(s):**
American School Food Service Association
1600 Duke St.
Alexandria, VA 22314-3436
Telephone: (703) 739-3900
Ownership %: 100
**Bureau(s):**
Advertising Media Sales
15W 700 W. Frontage Rd.
Hinsdale, IL 60521
Telephone: (708) 887-9503
Contact: Shawn Lamberson

Tubridy Associates, Inc.
3 Glenwood Rd.
Weston, CT 06883
Telephone: (203) 222-7004
Contact: Martin Tubridy
**Management:**
Tina Logsdon ...................Advertising Manager
**Editorial:**
Adrienne Gall Tufts ...................................Editor
**Desc.:** Editorial includes new developments, legislative happenings, industry trend-setters, professional development, product advances, and the latest in recipes and ideas in the school food-service industry.
**Readers:** School food-service professionals nationwide.
**Deadline:** ads-25th of mo., 2 mo. prior to pub. date

---

Materials Accepted/Included: 01-Business news 02-By-line articles 03-Fashion news 04-Food news 05-Freelance copy 06-Letters to editor 07-Real estate news 08-Sports news 09-Travel news 10-Book rev. 11-Movie rev. 12-Music rev. 13-TV rev. 14-Theater rev. 15-Coming events 16-Obituaries 17-Question & answer 18-Social announcements 19-Artwork 20-Cartoons 21-Photos 22-TV listings 23-Audio rec. 24-Video rec. 25-Books 26-Films/film clips 27-Personnel news 28-Press releases 29-New product news/photos 30-Trade lit. 31-Contracts awarded 32-Display adv. 33-Classified adv.

## SOUTHEAST FOOD SERVICE NEWS
23323

3678 A-1 Steward Rd.
Doraville, GA 30340
Telephone: (404) 452-1807
FAX: (404) 457-3829
Mailing Address:
P.O. Box 47719
Atlanta, GA 30362
Year Established: 1977
Pub. Frequency: m.
Page Size: tabloid
Subscrip. Rate: $28/yr.
Materials: 01,02,04,06,21,29
Freelance Pay: negotiable
Print Process: web offset
Circulation: 19,100
Circulation Type: controlled & paid
**Owner(s):**
Southeast Publishing Co., Inc.
P.O. Box 47719
Atlanta, GA 30362
Telephone: (404) 452-1807
Ownership %: 100
**Management:**
R. Dal Rasmussen .............................Publisher
**Editorial:**
John P. Hayward ..................................Editor
Elliott Fischer ...................New Products Editor
R. Dal Rasmussen .........................News Editor
**Desc.:** Edited for the food service industry in the states of Georgia, Florida, North Carolina, South Carolina, Alabama, Tennessee, Louisiana, Mississippi, and Virginia. Contains features on personalities and on companies within industry. Also covers trade functions and trade shows and new products.
**Readers:** Food-service distributors and food brokers, as well as food-service managers at school systems, colleges and universities, manufacturers, airline kitchens, fast-food chains, restaurants, hotels and motels.

## VIVA ITALIA
68926

303 N. Second St.
Holland, IN 47541
Telephone: (812) 536-4762
FAX: (812) 536-3110
Year Established: 1992
Pub. Frequency: 12/yr.
Page Size: standard
Subscrip. Rate: free to qualified recipients
Materials: 01,02,04,05,06,20,21,27,28,29, 30,32,33
Print Process: web offset
Circulation: 42,169
Circulation Type: controlled
**Owner(s):**
Amazon Enterprises, Inc.
303 N. Second St.
Holland, IN 47541
Telephone: (812) 536-4762
FAX: (812) 536-3110
Ownership %: 100
**Management:**
Theresa Acles Cole ...........................President
Theresa Acles Cole ...........................Publisher
Karla Beier .........................Advertising Manager
Janie Morton ......................Circulation Manager
Nancy Libbert ........................General Manager
**Editorial:**
Amy Lorton ................................Editor in Chief
Elaine Dill ...........................Mail Order Division
**Desc.:** For the pizza, pasta and Italian restaurant industry.
**Readers:** Owners and managers of pizza, pasta and Italian food service operations including franchises, chains, independent, institutional and distribution.
**Deadline:** story-2 mos.; news-2 mos.; photo-2 mos.; ads-1 mo.

## WISCONSIN RESTAURATEUR
24652

31 S. Henry
Ste. 300
Madison, WI 53703-0110
Telephone: (608) 251-3663
FAX: (608) 251-3666
Year Established: 1933
Pub. Frequency: bi-m.
Page Size: standard
Subscrip. Rate: $17.50/yr. members; $48/yr. non-members
Materials: 02,04,05,06,20,28,29,32,33
Freelance Pay: $5-$50
Circulation: 4,000
Circulation Type: paid
**Owner(s):**
Wisconsin Restaurant Association
31 S. Henry
Ste. 300
Madison, WI 53703
Telephone: (608) 251-3663
FAX: (608) 251-3663
Ownership %: 100
**Management:**
Ron Heuser ......................................President
Ed Lump ...................Executive Vice President
Wis Restaurant Assoc. .......................Publisher
Kerry Koppen ....................Advertising Manager
Dennis Hartman ................Circulation Manager
Kerry Koppen ..............................Sales Manager
**Editorial:**
Sonya Knecht Bicea ...............Executive Editor
Bob Goldman .................................Columnist
Pamela Rowe .......................Contributing Writer
Sally Scott ...............................Education Editor
Jan LaRue .....................................News Editor
**Desc.:** Articles on the Wisconsin food service industry, national trends, humor, specialty foods, equipment, restaurant real estate, energy (for restaurants), dairy, sanitation, merchandising, etc.
**Readers:** Owners, managers and purchasing agents of resorts, clubs, schools, hospitals, catering firms, restaurants, food service students, dieticians, home economics teachers, vocational school, university instructors, health officers.
**Deadline:** story-10th of mo. prior to pub. date; news-10th of mo. prior; photo-10th of mo. prior; ads-10th of mo. prior

## YANKEE FOOD SERVICE
68929

1099 Hingham St.
Rockland, MA 02370
Telephone: (617) 878-5300
FAX: (617) 871-4721
Year Established: 1979
Pub. Frequency: m.
Page Size: tabloid
Subscrip. Rate: $35/yr.
Circulation: 21,000
Circulation Type: paid
**Owner(s):**
Griffin Publishing Co., Inc.
1099 Hingham St.
Rockland, MA 02370
Telephone: (617) 878-5300
Ownership %: 100

## Group 230-Retail Trade

## ANSOM
23159

567 Morris Ave.
Elizabeth, NJ 07208
Telephone: (908) 353-7373
FAX: (908) 353-8221
Year Established: 1946
Pub. Frequency: m.
Page Size: tabloid
Subscrip. Rate: $25/yr.
Materials: 01,02,06,15,28,29,32,33
Circulation: 10,200

Circulation Type: controlled & paid
**Owner(s):**
PTN Publishing Co.
445 Broad Hollow Rd.
Melville, NY 11747
Telephone: (516) 845-2700
Ownership %: 100
**Management:**
Howard Wasserman ...........................Publisher
Noble Salem ....................Advertising Manager
**Editorial:**
Paul Bubny .........................................Editor
**Desc.:** News and features designed to inform, assist, entertain retailers in this amorphous field. Mostly staff-written with some freelance features and a few by-lined articles by authorities in a given area. News and new product publicity must relate to stores in the field; B & W glossies needed. All press releases re-written. Feature stories must be exclusive to us. Departments include: News, Features, New Products, Columnists.
**Readers:** Owners/managers of Army/Navy-type stores and wholesalers and manufacturers of camping, hunting, workingman's clothing.

## CHAIN STORE AGE EXECUTIVE WITH SHOPPING CENTER AGE
22450

425 Park Ave.
New York, NY 10022
Telephone: (212) 756-5000
Year Established: 1925
Pub. Frequency: m.
Page Size: standard
Subscrip. Rate: $79/yr.
Circulation: 23,000
Circulation Type: paid
**Owner(s):**
Lebhar-Friedman, Inc.
425 Park Ave.
New York, NY 10022
Telephone: (212) 371-9400
Ownership %: 100
**Bureau(s):**
New England
One Gateway Center
Newton, MA 02158
Telephone: (617) 527-6394
Contact: Robert Perry, Vice President


West Coast
606 N. Larchmont Blvd.
Los Angeles, CA 90004
Telephone: (310) 464-8321
Contact: John Donoghue, Manager


Midwest
444 N. Michigan Ave.
Chicago, IL 60611
Contact: James de Graffenreid, Vice President
**Management:**
J. Roger Friedman ...........................President
John Rapuzzi ...................................Publisher
John Rapuzzi ...................Advertising Manager
Laura Wegehaugh ...........Circulation Manager
**Editorial:**
Rick Gallagher ......................Executive Editor
Deborah Hazel ...........................Senior Editor
Murray Forseter ...................................Editor
Mary Alice Elmer ......................Managing Editor
Milt Berwin ..................................Art Director

**Desc.:** Staff-written features on financial operations, advertising and promotion, store operations, backroom technology, warehousing, transportation, store planning and construction, modernization, real estate, shopping centers. Departments include: Retail Technology, Shopping Center Age, New Equipment, New and Remodeled Stores, Shopping Centers, Washington Commentary, Accounting News & Views, Realtor Services, Classified, MIS & EDP.
**Readers:** Chain store and shopping center headquarters executives.

## COLLEGE STORE EXECUTIVE
22836

825 Old Country Rd.
Westbury, NY 11590
Telephone: (516) 334-3030
FAX: (516) 334-3059
Mailing Address:
P.O. Box 1500
Westbury, NY 11590
Year Established: 1970
Pub. Frequency: 10/yr.
Page Size: tabloid
Freelance Pay: $2/col. in.
Circulation: 85,000
Circulation Type: controlled
**Owner(s):**
Executive Business Media
Telephone: (516) 334-3030
**Bureau(s):**
Executive Business Media
333 N. Michigan Ave. Suite 630
Chicago, IL 60601
Telephone: (312) 368-1660
Contact: Steven Caming, Advertising Manager
**Management:**
Murry Greenwald ...........................President
Murry Greenwald ...........................Publisher
Rick Freund ......................Advertising Manager
Diana Lee .........................Circulation Manager
Catherine Youssis .......Classified Adv. Manager
Fred Schaen ......................Promotion Manager
**Desc.:** Specifically for college store managers and buyers. Geared primarily toward merchandising aspects, i.e., display, stocking, inventory control, EDP in novations, discounting promotions, college store profiles, etc. Departments include: New Products, Industry Briefs, Regional News.
**Readers:** College store managers and buyers.

## COLLEGE STORE JOURNAL, THE
24184

500 E. Lorain St.
Oberlin, OH 44074-1298
Telephone: (216) 775-7777
FAX: (216) 775-4769
Year Established: 1933
Pub. Frequency: a.
Page Size: standard
Subscrip. Rate: $54/yr. members; $64/yr. non-members
Freelance Pay: $50/article
Circulation: 6,600
Circulation Type: paid
**Owner(s):**
National Association of College Stores, Inc.
500 E. Lorain St.
Oberlin, OH 44074-1298
Telephone: (216) 775-7777
Ownership %: 100
**Management:**
Karen Moran-Germ ...........................Publisher
Chip Wigton ....................Advertising Manager
**Editorial:**
Ron Stevens ........................Executive Editor
Barbara Brucker .............................Art Director

---

Materials Accepted/Included: 01-Business news 02-By-line articles 03-Fashion news 04-Food news 05-Freelance copy 06-Letters to editor 07-Real estate news 08-Sports news 09-Travel news 10-Book rev. 11-Movie rev. 12-Music rev. 13-TV rev. 14-Theater rev. 15-Coming events 16-Obituaries 17-Question & answer 18-Social announcements 19-Artwork 20-Cartoons 21-Photos 22-TV listings 23-Audio rec. 24-Video rec. 25-Books 26-Films/film clips 27-Personnel news 28-Press releases 29-New product news/photos 30-Trade lit. 31-Contracts awarded 32-Display adv. 33-Classified adv.

Ben Ryba ......................Production Coordinator
**Desc.:** Articles cover all phases of college store operation and administration, merchandising, modernization, personnel, and ideas.
**Readers:** College store managers, buyers, and personnel of manufacturers.

64906
## DOLLARS & CENTS OF SHOPPING CENTERS
625 Indiana Ave., N.W., Ste. 400
Washington, DC 20004-2930
Telephone: (202) 624-7000
FAX: (202) 624-7140
Year Established: 1960
Pub. Frequency: biennial
Page Size: standard
Subscrip. Rate: $199.95/yr. members;
$249.95/yr. non-members
**Owner(s):**
The ULI-Urban Land Institute
625 Indiana Ave., N.W., Ste.40
Washington, DC 20004-2930
Telephone: (204) 624-7000
Ownership %: 100
**Management:**
Frank H. Spink, Jr. ......................Vice President
**Editorial:**
Michael Beyard ..............................Editor
**Desc.:** A biennial study of shopping centers operations in the U.S. and Canada including centerwide data and detailed tenant data on 132 categories of tenants.
**Readers:** Developers, owners and managers of shopping centers, tenant groups, appraisers, and others.

22375
## HEARTLAND RETAILER
10310 Ellison Circle
Omaha, NE 68134
Telephone: (402) 496-0717
FAX: (402) 496-0678
Year Established: 1974
Pub. Frequency: m.
Page Size: tabloid
Subscrip. Rate: $10/yr.
Materials: 01,02,06,15
Print Process: web offset
Circulation: 15,000
Circulation Type: controlled
**Owner(s):**
Eugene J. Podany
10310 Ellison Circle
Omaha, NE 68134
Telephone: (402) 496-0717
FAX: (402) 496-0678
Ownership %: 100
**Management:**
Fred C. Hess ..............................Founder
Eugene Podany ..........................Publisher
Eugene Podany ................Advertising Manager
**Editorial:**
Eugene Podany ..............................Editor
**Desc.:** A free distribution, dealer and builder oriented publication. We provide an efficient and economical way to bring advertising messages, product information, and news directly to the attention of the dealer and his employees. The news content is product and people oriented and the high news to advertising ratio assures superior readability.
**Readers:** Major and minor appliances, home entertainment, hardware and housewares, lumber & building materials, and home furnishings, plumbing and heating, air conditioning, stores, electrical contractors, kitchen specialists and service technicians.

66023
## MMR: MASS MARKET RETAILERS
220 Fifth Ave.
New York, NY 10001
Telephone: (212) 213-6000
FAX: (212) 213-6106
Pub. Frequency: bi-w.
Page Size: tabloid
Subscrip. Rate: $99/yr.
Circulation: 26,915
Circulation Type: controlled
**Owner(s):**
Racher Press, Inc.
220 Fifth Ave.
New York, NY 10001
Telephone: (212) 213-6000
**Editorial:**
David Pinto ..............................Editor
Jeff Woldf ........................Managing Editor
**Readers:** Headquarter personnels at mass market retail business.

69534
## NEW AGE RETAILER
1300 N. State St., Ste. 105
Bellingham, WA 98225
Telephone: (206) 676-0789
FAX: (206) 676-0932
Year Established: 1987
Pub. Frequency: bi-m.
Page Size: standard
Subscrip. Rate: $25/yr.
Materials: 01,02,05,06,10,12,20,23,24,25, 29,30,32,33
Print Process: web
Circulation: 5,800
Circulation Type: controlled
**Owner(s):**
Continuity Publishing, Inc.
1300 N. State St., Ste. 105
Bellingham, WA 98225
Telephone: (206) 676-0789
FAX: (206) 676-0932
Ownership %: 100
**Management:**
Duane Sweeney ......................Publisher
Judith Sult ....................Advertising Manager
**Editorial:**
Dwight Lucky ..............................Editor
Betty Berens ..............................Editor
**Desc.:** Articles and news of interest to retailers of quality Metaphysical, Personal Growth and New Age books, music, videos, and sidelines.
**Readers:** Store owners and inventory purchasers of New Age and Metaphysical book and gift stores.

23169
## NON-FOODS MERCHANDISING
298 Fifth Ave., 7th Fl.
New York, NY 10001-4522
Telephone: (212) 563-5301
FAX: (212) 967-4662
Year Established: 1958
Pub. Frequency: m.
Page Size: tabloid
Subscrip. Rate: $85/yr.
Freelance Pay: $250-$350/article
Circulation: 22,000
Circulation Type: controlled
**Owner(s):**
Cardinal Business Media
Ownership %: 100
**Management:**
Jordan Rosenstrach ......................Publisher
**Editorial:**
Al Heller ..............................Editor
**Desc.:** Stories must deal with the merchandising and displaying of non-foods in supermarkets. Non-foods are classified as: health and beauty aids; hardware; housewares; garden supplies; toys; stationery and school supplies; notions; records; soft goods; pet supplies; appliances.

**Readers:** Executives, buyers, and merchandisers concerned with general merchandise and H & BA in supermarkets and convenience stores plus the wholesalers and service merchandisers servicing them.

61686
## PARTY & PAPER RETAILER
70 New Canaan Ave.
Norwalk, CT 06850
Telephone: (203) 845-8020
FAX: (203) 845-8022
Year Established: 1986
Pub. Frequency: m.
Page Size: standard
Subscrip. Rate: $5.80/copy; $33/yr. US; $43/yr. Canada
Materials: 01,06,17,28,30,32,33
Freelance Pay: varies
Circulation: 22,000
Circulation Type: paid
**Owner(s):**
4 Ward Corporation
70 New Canaan Ave.
Norwalk, CT 06850
Telephone: (203) 845-8020
Ownership %: 100
**Management:**
Russell Ward ..............................Publisher
**Editorial:**
Trisha McMahon Drain ......................Editor
**Desc.:** Four-color publication devoted entirely to party and fine stationery supplies, featuring helpful articles for store owners on improving all facets of their businesses.
**Readers:** Retailers of party goods.

53959
## SHOPPING CENTER DIGEST
7 S. Myrtle Ave.
Spring Valley, NY 10977
Telephone: (914) 426-0040
Mailing Address:
P.O. Box 1708
Spring Valley, NY 10977
Year Established: 1973
Pub. Frequency: s-m.
Page Size: standard
Subscrip. Rate: $164/yr. US; $179/yr. foreign
**Owner(s):**
Murray Shor
P.O. Box 1708
Spring Valley, NY 10977
Telephone: (914) 426-0040
**Bureau(s):**
Jomurpa Publishing, Inc.
430 Mallard Dr.
Santa Rosa, CA 95401
Telephone: (707) 528-3631
Contact: Paul Stolmaker, Advertising Manager
**Management:**
Murray Shor ..............................Publisher
**Editorial:**
Murray Shor ..............................Editor
Tama J. Shor ....................Managing Editor

**Desc.:** Presents information on new and expanding shopping centers, shopping centers with lease space available, and the expansion needs of retail tenants. The Directory of Major Malls is published annually each January and provides in-depth information on existing and planned shopping centers of more than 250,000 sq. ft. of gross leasable area in the U.S. and Canada. Data includes complete portfolios of existing and planned malls of major developers, names and addresses of top retailers, maps of leading metro areas pinpointing the regional malls within those markets, and - for existing and planned major malls - such specifics as size, location, population and sales figures, tenant lists broken down according to category, names and addresses of owners, leasing agents, managers, marketing and promotion directors, and the like.
**Readers:** Real estate, leasing professionals with owners and developers, managers of shopping centers, retail chains, consultants, financing institutions, investors, marketing and promotional personnel, and those serving the shopping center and retail chain industries in the U.S. and Canada.

22402
## SHOPPING CENTER WORLD
6151 Powers Ferry Rd., N.W.
Atlanta, GA 30339-2941
Telephone: (404) 955-2500
FAX: (404) 955-0400
Year Established: 1972
Pub. Frequency: m.
Page Size: standard
Subscrip. Rate: $60/yr.; $96/2 yrs.
Freelance Pay: varies
Circulation: 36,000
Circulation Type: controlled
**Owner(s):**
Argus Business
6151 Powers Ferry Rd., N.W.
Atlanta, GA 30339-2941
Telephone: (404) 955-2500
Ownership %: 100
**Management:**
Jerrold France ..............................President
Jerrold France ..............................Publisher
Laura Patterson ................Production Manager
**Editorial:**
Teresa DeFranks ..............................Editor
Allyson H. Sicard ....................Managing Editor
Leslie Messmer ......................Art Director
Geoffrey Richards ....................Associate Editor
Richard DiFiore ....................Associate Publisher
Maria Bennett ................Managing Circ. Director
Martin Greene ................Production Director
**Desc.:** Provides total coverage of the shopping center industry and chain retailing, stresses latest news, trends, in-depth reports from some 80 correspondents and by-lined articles from knowledgeable professionals in the industries. Departments include: People & Places; New Products & Services; New Shopping Center Locations and Openings; Trends in Financing; Leasing; Marketing and Promotion; Management; Sales, Leases and Financing; Retailers Seeking Space; Centers for Sale; Surplus Property. Columns on retailing, finance, legislation, leases, construction and maintenance.
**Readers:** Developers and owners, leasing agents, chain-store executives, shopping center managers, promotion directors, contractors, mortgage bankers, lenders, and architects.

**Materials Accepted/Included:** 01-Business news 02-By-line articles 03-Fashion news 04-Food news 05-Freelance copy 06-Letters to editor 07-Real estate news 08-Sports news 09-Travel news 10-Book rev. 11-Movie rev. 12-Music rev. 13-TV rev. 14-Theater rev. 15-Coming events 16-Obituaries 17-Question & answer 18-Social announcements 19-Artwork 20-Cartoons 21-Photos 22-TV listings 23-Audio rec. 24-Video rec. 25-Books 26-Films/film clips 27-Personnel news 28-Press releases 29-New product news/photos 30-Trade lit. 31-Contracts awarded 32-Display adv. 33-Classified adv.

**STORES** 22840

325 Seventh St., N.W.
Ste. 1000
Washington, DC 20004-2802
Telephone: (202) 783-7971
FAX: (202) 737-2849
Year Established: 1912
Pub. Frequency: m.
Page Size: standard
Subscrip. Rate: $49/yr. US; $80/2 yrs.;
　$79/yr. other countries; $150/2 yrs.
Freelance Pay: $15/wd.
Circulation: 35,000
Circulation Type: paid
**Owner(s):**
National Retail Federation
3215 Seventh St. N.W.
Ste. 1000
Washington, DC 20004-2802
Telephone: (202) 783-7971
Ownership %: 100
**Management:**
Tracy Mullin .............................President
Rick Gallagher .........................Publisher
Jim Oot ...................Advertising Manager
**Editorial:**
Rick Gallagher ...............................Editor
**Desc.:** Articles to specific assignment only,
　on the various facets of department and
　specialty store field, including public
　relations, sales promotion,
　merchandising, credit, traffic and other
　topics of interest to top
　management retailers.
**Readers:** NRMA membership plus other
　senior management executives in the
　general merchandise retail industry.

**TELEMARKETING** 58670

One Technology Plz.
Norwalk, CT 06854
Telephone: (203) 852-6800
FAX: (203) 853-2845
Year Established: 1982
Pub. Frequency: m.
Page Size: standard
Subscrip. Rate: $49/yr.
Freelance Pay: varies
Circulation: 28,000
Circulation Type: paid
**Owner(s):**
Nadji Tehrani
One Technology Plz.
Norwalk, CT 06854
Telephone: (203) 852-6800
Ownership %: 100
**Management:**
Nadji Tehrani ...........................Publisher
**Editorial:**
Linda Driscoll ..................................Editor
Sheila Baker .....................Assistant Editor
**Desc.:** Edited for business executives,
　sales and marketing professionals, and
　those responsible for purchasing
　telecommunications equipment, related
　hardware and software, and marketing
　services. Editorial focuses on
　telemarketing techniques, examines
　trends and innovations affecting the use
　of telecommunications for business-to-
　business and retail marketing, and
　demonstrates how telemarketing can
　interrelate effectively with other
　marketing functions, such as advertising,
　sales promotion, direct mail,
　merchandising, and customer service.
**Readers:** Mid-to upper-level management.

**UFCW ACTION** 23329

1775 K St., N.W.
Washington, DC 20006
Telephone: (202) 223-3111
FAX: (202) 466-1562
Year Established: 1979

Pub. Frequency: bi-m.
Page Size: standard
Subscrip. Rate: free to members; $5/yr.
　non-members
Circulation: 1,300,000
Circulation Type: controlled
**Owner(s):**
United Food and Commercial Workers Int'l
　Union
1775 K St. N.W.
Washington, DC 20006
Telephone: (202) 223-3111
Ownership %: 100
**Management:**
Douglas H. Dority .......................President
**Editorial:**
Douglas H. Dority ............................Editor
Susan L. Phillips .........Publication Director
**Desc.:** Labor union publication for the 1.3
　million members of the United Food &
　Commercial Workers International Union.
　Articles are of interest to workers in
　retailing, manufacturing and processing
　foods, packaging, barber and
　cosmetology, insurance, finance and
　health care, and related industries.
**Readers:** Members of UFCW locals.

**VALUE RETAIL NEWS** 64888

P.O. Box 17209
Clearwater, FL 34622-0129
Telephone: (813) 536-4047
FAX: (813) 536-4389
Year Established: 1982
Pub. Frequency: m.
Page Size: tabloid
Subscrip. Rate: $144/yr.
Freelance Pay: open
Circulation: 5,000
Circulation Type: paid
**Owner(s):**
Robert T. Dunham
Ownership %: 100
**Management:**
Terry Dunham ............................Publisher
Janice Kilpatrick ...............Advertising Manager
Sue Mavris ...........Customer Service Manager
Gary Muller ......................General Manager
**Editorial:**
Tom Kirwan ...........................Editor in Chief
Dan Cochran ......................Marketing Director
Cher Russell ......................Research Director
**Desc.:** Serves the specialized information
　needs of outlet, off-price and other
　value-oriented retailers, and shopping
　center developers throughout the U.S. It
　reports on news and trends affecting the
　industry and on activities of retail and
　development firms.

**VISUAL MERCHANDISING &** 22786
**STORE DESIGN**

407 Gilbert Ave.
Cincinnati, OH 45202-2285
Telephone: (513) 421-2050
FAX: (513) 421-5144
Year Established: 1922
Pub. Frequency: m.
Page Size: standard
Subscrip. Rate: $39/yr.
Materials: 01,02,03,06,10,16,24,25,27,28,
　29,30,31,32,33
Freelance Pay: $300-$400/copy; $50/slide
Print Process: web offset
Circulation: 18,000
Circulation Type: controlled & paid
**Owner(s):**
ST Publications
407 Gilbert Ave.
Cincinnati, OH 45202
Telephone: (513) 421-2050
FAX: (513) 421-5144
Ownership %: 100

**Management:**
Joseph E. Cuzzort .......................Publisher
**Editorial:**
Janet Groeber ...............................Editor
**Desc.:** Directed to merchandisers in retail
　marketing and store designers.
　Examines display approaches used in
　stores throughout the country, in
　addition to products used for
　merchandise presentation.
**Readers:** Primarily visual merchandisers,
　store designers, architects, and retail
　management. Also caters to designers
　and producers of displays and exhibits.
**Deadline:** story-3 mos. prior to pub date;
　news-3 mos. prior; photo-3 mos. prior;
　ads-6 wk. prior

## Group 232-Roads & Streets

**BETTER ROADS MAGAZINE** 24655

6333 E. Mockingbird Ln., Ste. 147
Dallas, TX 75214
Telephone: (708) 693-7710
FAX: (708) 696-3445
Mailing Address:
　P.O. Box 558
　Park Ridge, IL 60068
Year Established: 1931
Pub. Frequency: m.
Page Size: standard
Subscrip. Rate: $20/yr.
Materials: 02,23,24,25,29,30,32,33
Freelance Pay: minimal
Circulation: 42,000
Circulation Type: controlled
**Owner(s):**
William O. Dannhausen
P.O. Box 558
Park Ridge, IL 60068
Telephone: (708) 693-7710
Ownership %: 100
**Management:**
W.O. Dannhausen ......................Publisher
**Editorial:**
Ruth Stidger ..........................Editor in Chief
W.O. Dannhausen ..................Editorial Director
Carol Miller ..........................Assistant Editor
Ruth Stidger ......................Associate Publisher
A.R. Pagan P.E. ...............................Engineer
Joel B. Johnson ....................Technical Editor
**Desc.:** A magazine of current information
　relating to road and street department
　management engineers; elected officials
　and operations of governmental roads;
　streets and bridges; traffic control and
　safety; questions and answers on
　current problems and solutions; highway
　and street legislation; highway, bridges,
　street and airport construction and
　maintenance; improvements; recycling;
　rehabilitation; traffic control; work zone
　safety; new products; and all other news
　of interest to management, engineering
　construction maintenance operations,
　and state prequalified road contractors
　working on current projects.
**Readers:** Governmental road, street,
　bridge, and traffic engineers;
　supervisors; managers; federal, state,
　county, and municipal officials;
　consultants; licensed contractors; and
　transportation commissions.
**Deadline:** story-60-90 days prior to pub.
　date; news-60-90 days; photo-60-90
　days; ads-1st day of mo. prior to pub.
　date

**MAINE TRAILS** 24658

146 State
Augusta, ME 04330
Telephone: (207) 622-0526
FAX: (207) 623-2928
Year Established: 1939

Pub. Frequency: bi-m.
Page Size: standard
Subscrip. Rate: $12/yr.
Circulation: 1,200
Circulation Type: controlled
**Owner(s):**
Maine Better Transportation Association
146 State St.
Augusta, ME 04330
Telephone: (207) 622-0526
Ownership %: 100
**Management:**
Maria Fuentes ...................Advertising Manager
**Editorial:**
Maria Fuentes .........................Managing Editor
**Desc.:** Covers the transportation
　construction industry; trends in
　engineering, financial side of
　business. All aspects of transportation at
　the state and local level.
**Readers:** Highway and bridge contractors,
　town and city managers, land managers,
　pulp and paper companies, and county
　and state officials.

**ROADS & BRIDGES MAGAZINE** 24660

380 Northwest Hwy.
Des Plaines, IL 60016
Telephone: (708) 298-6622
FAX: (708) 390-0408
Year Established: 1940
Pub. Frequency: m.
Page Size: standard
Subscrip. Rate: $15/yr.
Materials: 01,06,27,29,30,32,33
Freelance Pay: varies
Print Process: web offset
Circulation: 65,000
Circulation Type: controlled
**Owner(s):**
Scranton Gillette Communications, Inc.
380 Northwest Hwy.
Des Plaines, IL 60016
Telephone: (708) 298-6622
FAX: (708) 390-0408
Ownership %: 100
**Management:**
C. R. Gillette ....................Chairman of Board
Hal Gillette .......................Chairman of Board
Halbert S. Gillette ...............Chairman of Board
Don Hogan .................................President
W. D. Shoup ...........................Vice President
Anne Gillette ...............................Controller
W. D. Shoup ...............................Publisher
Shirley Marcinko ...............Advertising Manager
**Editorial:**
Tom Kuennen .................................Editor
Judy Schmueser ................Production Director
**Desc.:** Articles of interest to public
　officials, engineers, and contractors
　engaged in the administration,
　management, engineering, and contract
　execution on construction and
　maintenance of highways, roads,
　bridges, tunnels, and airport pavements
　throughout the U.S., including their
　rehabilitation, restoration, renovation,
　and reconstruction.

---

**Materials Accepted/Included:** 01-Business news 02-By-line articles 03-Fashion news 04-Food news 05-Freelance copy 06-Letters to editor 07-Real estate news 08-Sports news 09-Travel news 10-Book rev. 11-Movie rev. 12-Music rev. 13-TV rev. 14-Theater rev. 15-Coming events 16-Obituaries 17-Question & answer 18-Social announcements 19-Artwork 20-Cartoons 21-Photos 22-TV listings 23-Audio rec. 24-Video rec. 25-Books 26-Films/film clips 27-Personnel news 28-Press releases 29-New product news/photos 30-Trade lit. 31-Contracts awarded 32-Display adv. 33-Classified adv.

4-327

**Readers:** Serves officials, engineers, consulting engineers, and independent contractors engaged in planning, engineering, construction, improvements (including recycling and rehabilitation), maintenance and administration of public roads, highways, interstate highways, bridges, tunnels, viaducts, and airport paving in state, county, city, township, municipal, federal, and special road districts.
**Deadline:** story-60 days prior to pub. date; news-60 days; photo-60 days; ads-4th of mo., prior to pub. date

## Group 234-Rubber

**RUBBER & PLASTICS NEWS**
24664
1725 Merriman Rd., Ste. 300
Akron, OH 44313-5251
Telephone: (216) 836-9180
FAX: (216) 836-1005
Year Established: 1971
Pub. Frequency: 26/yr.
Page Size: tabloid
Subscrip. Rate: $60/yr.
Freelance Pay: $8/inch
Circulation: 15,300
Circulation Type: controlled
**Owner(s):**
Crain Communications, Inc.
1400 Woodbridge Ave.
Detroit, MI 48207
Telephone: (313) 446-6000
Ownership %: 100
**Bureau(s):**
Rubber & Plastic News-Washington
814 National Press Bldg (1253)
Washington, DC 20045
Telephone: (202) 662-7200
Contact: Miles Moore, Writer

Rubber & Plastics News
34 N. Hawkins Ave.
Akron, OH 44313

Rubber & Plastics News
220 E. 42nd St.
New York, NY 10017
**Management:**
Keith Crain ........................................President
Robert Simmons ..............................Publisher
**Editorial:**
Allan Gerlat ............................Managing Editor
**Desc.:** Emphasis is on news in the rubber industry covering tires, inner tubes, mechanical and industrial rubber goods, synthetics and plastic products, and so forth manufactured by rubber companies. New articles cover development and technical aspects of new materials, processes, engineering, equipment, machinery, and general news of the industry.
**Readers:** Manufacturers of rubber products.

**RUBBER WORLD**
24665
1867 W. Market St.
Akron, OH 44313
Telephone: (216) 864-2122
Mailing Address:
P.O. Box 5451
Akron, OH 44334
Year Established: 1889
Pub. Frequency: 16/yr.
Page Size: tabloid
Subscrip. Rate: $29/yr.
Materials: 01,02,06,10,16,27,28,29,30,31, 32,33
Print Process: web offset
Circulation: 11,400
Circulation Type: controlled

**Owner(s):**
Lippincott & Peto, Inc.
1867 W. Market St.
Akron, OH 44313
Telephone: (216) 864-2122
FAX: (216) 864-5298
Ownership %: 100
**Management:**
Job H. Lippincott ...............................President
Job H. Lippincott ..............................Publisher
Sally Dowling ........................Assistant Manager
Barbara Gordon ................Production Manager
**Editorial:**
Don R. Smith .........................................Editor
Jill Wrigley ............................Managing Editor
Deanne Dodd ......................Editorial Assistant
Dennis Kennelly .....................................Sales
**Desc.:** Articles encompassing activities in the rubber industry (technical, business, and individual). Departments include: Meeting and Reports; News; New Products, Materials & Equipment; Publications; International Developments; Market & Financial Developments; Statistics, Prices and Relevant Legislative Events.
**Readers:** Chemists, engineers, and process managers of rubber product manufacturing.
**Deadline:** ads-10th of mo. prior to pub. date

## Group 236-Safety

**FAMILY SAFETY & HEALTH**
58634
1121 Spring Lake Dr.
Itasca, IL 60143
Telephone: (708) 285-1121
FAX: (708) 285-0797
Mailing Address:
P.O. Box 558
Itasca, IL 60143-0558
Year Established: 1961
Pub. Frequency: q.
Page Size: standard
Subscrip. Rate: $15/yr. members; $19/yr. non-members
Freelance Pay: $500
Circulation: 2,000,000
Circulation Type: paid
**Owner(s):**
National Safety Council
1121 Spring Lake Dr.
Itasca, IL 60143
Telephone: (708) 285-1121
FAX: (708) 285-0797
Ownership %: 100
**Management:**
Kevin H. Axe .....................................Publisher
**Editorial:**
Laura Coyne .........................................Editor
**Desc.:** A publication for the prevention of home injuries and the promotion of health and fitness.
**Readers:** Consumer

**INDUSTRIAL HYGIENE NEWS**
24920
8650 Babcock Blvd.
Pittsburgh, PA 15237-5821
Telephone: (412) 364-5366
Year Established: 1978
Pub. Frequency: bi-m.
Page Size: tabloid
Subscrip. Rate: free to qualified personnel
Materials: 01,29,30,32,33
Print Process: web offset
Circulation: 62,000
Circulation Type: controlled
**Owner(s):**
Rimbach Publishing, Inc.
8650 Babcock Blvd.
Pittsburgh, PA 15237
Telephone: (412) 364-5366
Ownership %: 100

**Management:**
Norberta Rimbach ..............................Publisher
**Editorial:**
David C. Lavender ..................................Editor
**Desc.:** Provides new product information for the occupational health and safety professional. Departments include: New Products, New Literature, Events, Product Briefs.
**Readers:** Persons responsible for the industrial hygiene function, nurses and physicians, management, insurance executives, industrial hygienists, safety director and plant engineer.
**Deadline:** story-2 mo. prior to pub. date; news-2 mo. prior to pub. date; photo-2 mo. prior to pub. date; ads-1st of mo. prior to pub. date

**INTERNATIONAL LABOR & WORKING CLASS**
58546
54 E. Gregory Dr.
Champaign, IL 61820
Telephone: (217) 244-0626
FAX: (217) 244-8082
Pub. Frequency: s-a.
Page Size: standard
Subscrip. Rate: $16/yr. individulas; $22/yr. foreign; $26/yr. institutions; $32/yr. foreign institutions
Circulation: 700
Circulation Type: paid
**Owner(s):**
Cambridge University Press
40 West 20
New York, NY 10011
Telephone: (212) 924-3900
Ownership %: 100
**Bureau(s):**
New School for Social Research
64 University Pl.
New York, NY 10003
Telephone: (212) 864-6323
Contact: Prof. Ira Katznelson, Editor
**Management:**
James Alexander ................................Manager
**Editorial:**
Ira Katznelson ......................................Editor
**Desc.:** Linking labor and social historians throughout the world, Presents new scholarship on some of the most vital issues and controversies in their fields. Each issue features in-depth review essays, reports on international and regional conferences, and original research.
**Readers:** History and labor history scholars.

**PROFESSIONAL SAFETY**
24672
1800 E. Oakton St.
Des Plaines, IL 60018-2187
Telephone: (708) 692-4121
FAX: (708) 296-3769
Year Established: 1956
Pub. Frequency: m.
Page Size: standard
Subscrip. Rate: $60/yr.
Materials: 01,02,06,10,15,19,21,28,29,32,33
Print Process: web offset
Circulation: 27,000
Circulation Type: paid
**Owner(s):**
American Society of Safety Engineers
Telephone: (708) 692-4121
FAX: (708) 296-3769
Ownership %: 100
**Management:**
Judy T. Neel ........................Executive Director
**Editorial:**
Neal Lorenzi ........................................Editor
Roxanne Bernauer ................Editorial Assistant
Ken Hatter ............................Marketing Director
Roxanne Bernauer ...........New Products Editor

**Desc.:** Written and edited for the professional safety engineering industry, and related disciplines. Articles provide technical, scientific, and informational assistance to readers on safety, program implementation, fire protection, industrial hygiene, ergonomics, system safety theory, standards, research, and development. Departments include: Safety Literature, New Product Reviews, Safety Digest, Regulatory News, Upfront, Personnel Center, Readers Pulse, Book Review.
**Readers:** Mostly members of the society; see editorial statement.

**TRAFFIC SAFETY**
24675
1121 Spring Lake Dr.
Itasca, IL 60143
Telephone: (708) 285-1121
Year Established: 1957
Pub. Frequency: bi-m.
Page Size: standard
Subscrip. Rate: $4.75/copy; $30/yr.
Freelance Pay: negotiable
Circulation: 20,000
Circulation Type: paid
**Owner(s):**
National Safety Council
1121 Spring Lake Dr.
Itasca, IL 60143-3201
Telephone: (708) 285-1121
Ownership %: 100
**Management:**
T. C. Gilchrest ...................................President
Sr. Irvin B. Etter .........Executive Vice President
Kevin H. Axe ....................................Publisher
Joel Wakitsch ...................Advertising Manager
**Editorial:**
Carrie Smith Fearn ...................Executive Editor
John P. Jackson ......................Managing Editor
Bruce Swart ..................................Art Director
Frederic D. Rine ..........Assistant Vice President
Robert E. Krawisz .......Assistant Vice President
John Kaplafka ........................Marketing Director
Michael A. Meersman ........................Treasurer
**Desc.:** Outside professional writers contribute articles that cover traffic; commercial vehicle safety; and driver education, alcohol and driving, restraint use. Departments Include: Today's Traffic, Coming Events, New Products, Statistics.
**Readers:** Municipal safety officers, traffic engineers, state and national governments, and governmental schools, boards of education, driver education teachers, company safety directors, fleets, transit utility companies, and highway officials.

## Group 238-Schools & Education

**AAUW OUTLOOK**
24752
1111 16th St., N.W.
Washington, DC 20036
Telephone: (202) 785-7774
FAX: (202) 872-1425
Year Established: 1989
Pub. Frequency: q.
Page Size: standard
Subscrip. Rate: $15/yr.
Materials: 10,32,33
Circulation: 135,000
Circulation Type: free & paid
**Owner(s):**
American Association of University Women
1111 16th St., N.W.
Washington, DC 20036
Telephone: (202) 785-7728
Ownership %: 100
**Editorial:**
Ellie Horwitz ..........................................Editor

Patricia Vieira ..........Advertising Representative
Judith Markoe ........Director of Communications
**Desc.:** Concentration on woman-related
  issues, as well as economy, families
  facing change, and managing resources.
**Readers:** Women with at least a
  bachelor's degree.

## ACADEME
56235

1012 14th St., N.W., Ste. 500
Washington, DC 20005
Telephone: (202) 737-5900
FAX: (202) 737-5526
Year Established: 1915
Pub. Frequency: bi-m.
Page Size: standard
Subscrip. Rate: $47/yr.
Circulation: 47,000
Circulation Type: paid
**Owner(s):**
American Association of University
  Professors
1012 14th St., N.W., Ste. 500
Washington, DC 20005
Telephone: (202) 737-5900
Ownership %: 100
**Editorial:**
Eugene Arden ..............................Editor
Julia Ridgely ..........................Managing Editor
Bruce Herzig ..........................Assistant Editor
**Desc.:** A magazine of higher education.
**Readers:** College and university professors
  nationwide.

## ACTION LINE
24687

344 N. Charles St.
Baltimore, MD 21201
Telephone: (410) 727-7676
FAX: (410) 783-0585
Year Established: 1865
Pub. Frequency: 8/yr.
Page Size: Tabloid
Subscrip. Rate: Free to members
Freelance Pay: None
Circulation: 45,000
Circulation Type: controlled
**Owner(s):**
Maryland State Teachers Assn.
344 N. Charles St.
Baltimore, MD 21201
Telephone: (410) 727-7676
Ownership %: 100
**Editorial:**
Roger Kuhn ..............................Editor
**Desc.:** Most articles have to do with
  teacher problems, instructional
  procedures, new ideas, subjects
  of interest to teachers, editorial
  comment on current legislative or
  controversial matters of direct interest to
  the profession. Departments include
  Professional Aids (book reviews),
  News and Views.
**Readers:** Teachers, principals, supervisors,
  superintendents, etc.

## ADAPTED PHYSICAL ACTIVITY QUARTERLY (APAQ)
58658

1607 N. Market St.
Champaign, IL 61820
Telephone: (217) 351-5076
FAX: (217) 351-2674
Mailing Address:
  P.O. Box 5076
  Champaign, IL 61825
Year Established: 1984
Pub. Frequency: q.
Page Size: standard
Subscrip. Rate: $24/yr. students; $36/yr.
  individuals; $80/yr. institutions
Materials: 10,25,29
Print Process: offset
Circulation: 895
Circulation Type: paid

**Owner(s):**
Human Kinetics
P.O. Box 5076
Champaign, IL 61825
Telephone: (217) 351-5076
FAX: (217) 351-2674
Ownership %: 100
**Management:**
Rainer Martens ..............................Publisher
Julie Anderson ..............................Manager
**Editorial:**
Greg Reid ..............................Editor
Linda A. Bump ..............................Journals Director
**Desc.:** A multidisciplinary journal providing
  information about physical activity for
  special populations from the
  perspectives of therapy, health care,
  physical education, recreation, and
  rehabilitation.
**Readers:** Specialists in adapted physical
  education, recreation, and rehabilitation.

## ADULT LEARNING
24783

1101 Connecticut Ave., N.W., Ste. 700
Arlington, VA 20036
Telephone: (703) 522-2234
Year Established: 1960
Pub. Frequency: 8/yr.
Page Size: standard
Subscrip. Rate: $37/yr. US; $45/yr. foreign
Circulation: 6,000
Circulation Type: controlled
**Owner(s):**
American Assn. for Adult & Continuing
  Education
1112 16th St., N.W., Ste. 420
Washington, DC 20036
Telephone: (202) 822-7866
Ownership %: 100
**Editorial:**
Jeanette Smith ..............................Editor
**Readers:** Educators, administrators,
  directors, and continuing education
  students.

## ADVOCATE
61307

316 W. 12th St.
Austin, TX 78701
Telephone: (512) 476-5355
FAX: (512) 469-0766
Pub. Frequency: 7/yr.
Page Size: tabloid
Subscrip. Rate: free to members
Circulation: 95000
Circulation Type: controlled & free
**Owner(s):**
Texas State Teachers Assoc.
316 W. 12th St.
Austin, TX 78701
Telephone: (512) 476-5355
Ownership %: 100
**Editorial:**
Deborah Mohondro ..............................Editor

## AEA ADVOCATE
24702

2102 W. Indian School Rd.
Phoenix, AZ 85015-4999
Telephone: (602) 264-1774
Pub. Frequency: 7/yr.
Page Size: tabloid
Subscrip. Rate: membership
Circulation: 30,000
Circulation Type: controlled
**Owner(s):**
Arizona Education Association
2102 W. Indian School Rd.
Phoenix, AZ 85015
Telephone: (602) 264-1774
Ownership %: 100
**Management:**
Kay Lybeck ..............................President
Cheryl Anderson ..............................Program Manager

**Desc.:** Covers current issues in public
  education, trends, practices, professional
  events and objectives, legislation, and
  labor relations.
**Readers:** Education professionals, and
  members of AEA and NEA.

## AGRI-NATURALIST
24712

Ohio State Univ., 203 Ag. Admin. Bldg.
2120 Fyffe
Columbus, OH 43210-1067
Telephone: (614) 292-0202
FAX: (614) 292-7007
Year Established: 1895
Pub. Frequency: 3/yr.
Page Size: standard
Subscrip. Rate: $10/yr.
Circulation: 3,000
Circulation Type: paid
**Owner(s):**
Ohio State University
2120 Fyffe
Columbus, OH 43210
Telephone: (614) 422-5341
Ownership %: 100
**Editorial:**
Robert Agunga ..............................Editorial Advisor
**Desc.:** By, for, and about the students in
  the Ohio State College of Agriculture
  and Home Economics and School of
  Natural Resources. Features articles on
  people, departments, and happenings in
  the college and on new developments in
  agriculture, home economics, and
  natural resources.
**Readers:** Students, faculty, and staff in the
  College of Agriculture and interested
  others including alumni.

## AGRICULTURAL EDUCATION MAGAZINE
24689

124 Mumford Hall
Urbana, IL 61801
Telephone: (217) 333-3166
FAX: (217) 333-1952
Year Established: 1927
Pub. Frequency: m.
Page Size: standard
Subscrip. Rate: $10/yr.; $4/yr. students
Circulation: 4,500
Circulation Type: paid
**Owner(s):**
Agricultural Education Magazine, Inc.
2441 Suzanne Dr.
Mechanicsville, VA 23111-4028
Telephone: (804) 746-3538
Ownership %: 100
**Management:**
Stacey Gartin ..............................Chairman of Board
David Doerfert ..............................Vice Chairman
**Editorial:**
Glenn Anderson ..............................Editor
Phillip Zurbvick ..............................Consulting Editor
**Desc.:** Covers the professional field of
  agricultural education. Carries staff and
  by-lined articles and personnel news.
**Readers:** Teachers of Agriculture in
  secondary & post secondary schools.

## AGRICULTURE EDUCATORS DIRECTORY
24690

Maple Ave. at Tunnel St.
Greensburg, PA 15601
Telephone: (412) 834-7600
FAX: (412) 836-7759
Mailing Address:
  P.O. Box 68
  Greensburg, PA 15601-0068
Year Established: 1952
Pub. Frequency: a.
Page Size: pocket
Subscrip. Rate: free to agricultural
  education personnel
Circulation: 12,200

Circulation Type: free
**Owner(s):**
Charles M. Henry Printing Co.
P.O. Box 68
Greensburg, PA 15601-0068
Telephone: (412) 834-7600
Ownership %: 100
**Management:**
Charles E. Henry ..............................President
Jim Guilinger ..............................Advertising Manager
Lawrence W. Jones ..............................Production Manager
**Editorial:**
Sarah L. Henry ..............................Editor
**Desc.:** Features 1, 2, & 3 page articles for
  teachers, teacher educators about
  careers in agribusiness and teaching
  materials, strictly for
  agricultural education; advertising,
  agricultural and vocational agricultural
  books, references, teaching materials.
  Directory of all agricultural education
  personnel, nationwide.
  Publication supported entirely by
  advertising, rates available upon request.
**Readers:** All agricultural education
  personnel in universities, high schools,
  colleges.

## AMERICAN ANNALS OF THE DEAF
24692

KDES PAS 6
800 Florida Ave., N.E.
Washington, DC 20002-3695
Telephone: (202) 651-5340
FAX: (202) 651-5708
Year Established: 1847
Pub. Frequency: 5/yr.: Mar.,Apr.,Jul.,Oct.,
  Dec.
Page Size: standard
Subscrip. Rate: $50/yr.
Materials: 06,28,29,32,33
Freelance Pay: varies
Circulation: 4,000
Circulation Type: controlled & paid
**Owner(s):**
Convention of American Instructors of the
  Deaf
Michael Finneran, Pres.
Calif. School for the Deaf, 39350 Gallaudet
  Dr.
Fremont, CA 94538
Ownership %: 50

Conference of Ed. Administrators Serving
  the Deaf
Dr. William Johnson, Pres.
Iowa School for the Deaf, 1600 S. Hwy.
  275
Council Bluffs, IA 51503
Ownership %: 50
**Editorial:**
Donald F. Moores ..............................Editor
Constance Toliver ..............................Managing Editor
**Desc.:** Articles by educators dealing with
  the education of the deaf and the hard
  of hearing. Covers teaching techniques,
  rehabilitation, associations, books, films,
  etc. The Reference (April) Issue
  contains information on schools and
  classes for the deaf in the U.S. and
  Canada, listings for teacher training
  programs and other services for the
  deaf, as well as up-to-date reports on
  research in the field of deafness.
**Readers:** Teachers of the deaf,
  administrators in speech & hearing
  clinics, rehabilitation personnel, special
  education departments & parents of
  deaf.
**Deadline:** ads-1st of mo. prior to pub. date

## AMERICAN BIOLOGY TEACHER
24693

11250 Roger Bacon Dr., Ste. 19
Reston, VA 22090-5202
Telephone: (703) 471-1134
FAX: (703) 435-5582

**Materials Accepted/Included:** 01-Business news 02-By-line articles 03-Fashion news 04-Food news 05-Freelance copy 06-Letters to editor 07-Real estate news 08-Sports news 09-Travel news 10-Book rev. 11-Movie rev. 12-Music rev. 13-TV rev. 14-Theater rev. 15-Coming events 16-Obituaries 17-Question & answer 18-Social announcements 19-Artwork 20-Cartoons 21-Photos 22-TV listings 23-Audio rec. 24-Video rec. 25-Books 26-Films/film clips 27-Personnel news 28-Press releases 29-New product news/photos 30-Trade lit. 31-Contracts awarded 32-Display adv. 33-Classified adv.

4-329

Year Established: 1938
Pub. Frequency: 8/yr. (Sep.-May)
Page Size: standard
Subscrip. Rate: $50/yr. US; $65/yr. foreign
Circulation: 11,000
Circulation Type: paid
**Owner(s):**
National Association of Biology Teachers
11250 Roger Bacon Dr., Ste. 19
Reston, VA 22090-5202
Telephone: (703) 471-1134
FAX: (703) 435-5582
Ownership %: 100
**Management:**
Ivo Lindaeur ...............................................President
Patricia McWethy ...................................Publisher
**Editorial:**
Randy Moore ...............................................Editor
Michele D. Bedsaul ..............Managing Editor
Rachel Hays .........................A V Review Editor
Dan Wivagg ...........................Associate Editor
Christine Chantry ..................Associate Editor
Michael Emsley .................Book Review Editor
Richard Duhrkopf ..................Computer Editor
Maura C. Flannery ...............Department Editor
**Desc.:** Journal of professional society with
articles and reviews on biology
curriculum, laboratory equipment,
teaching and laboratory techniques,
social implications of biology.
**Readers:** Teachers of biology in
elementary, middle and secondary
schools, community colleges, and
universities.

53969
**AMERICAN EDUCATOR**
555 New Jersey Ave., N.W.
Washington, DC 20001
Telephone: (202) 879-4400
Year Established: 1977
Pub. Frequency: q.
Subscrip. Rate: $8/yr.
Circulation: 700,000
**Owner(s):**
American Federation of Teachers
555 New Jersey Ave., N.W.
Washington, DC 20001
Telephone: (202) 879-4400
Ownership %: 100
**Editorial:**
Liz McPike ...................................................Editor

24695
**AMERICAN JOURNAL OF
EDUCATION**
5835 Kimbark Ave.
University of Chicago
Chicago, IL 60637
Telephone: (312) 702-1555
FAX: (312) 702-0248
Year Established: 1893
Pub. Frequency: q.
Page Size: standard
Subscrip. Rate: $28/yr.
Circulation: 3,000
Circulation Type: paid
**Owner(s):**
University of Chicago Press, Journals
Department
5720 Woodlawn Ave.
Chicago, IL 60637
Telephone: (312) 702-0694
Ownership %: 100
**Editorial:**
Philip W. Jackson ......................................Editor
Robert Dreeben .......................Assistant Editor
John E. Craig .........................Associate Editor
Susan Stodolsky ....................Associate Editor
Zalman Usiskin .......................Associate Editor

**Desc.:** Centers attention on specific
questions of educational policy and
practice and on fundamental,
philosophical, and theoretical issues in
all sectors of the educational enterprise.
Welcomes articles that argue for or
against a position on one of
these questions or issues or report or
evaluate research in education and
related disciplines.
**Readers:** Teachers, administrators,
researchers and students of education.

24696
**AMERICAN JOURNAL OF PHYSICS**
One Physics Ellipse
College Park, MD 20740-3845
Telephone: (301) 209-3300
FAX: (301) 209-0845
Year Established: 1933
Pub. Frequency: m.
Page Size: standard
Subscrip. Rate: $215/yr.
Materials: 06,25,32
Print Process: web
Circulation: 8,000
**Owner(s):**
American Association of Physics Teachers
One Physics Ellipse
College Park, MD 20740-3845
Telephone: (301) 209-3300
Ownership %: 100
**Editorial:**
Robert H. Romer ........................................Editor
Karla Keyes .................Administrative Assistant
Linda Sigmon ...............Advertising Coordinator
Don S. Lemons ........................Assistant Editor
Ralph Baierlein ...................Book Review Editor
**Desc.:** Publishes discussions of new ideas,
techniques, and equipment used in the
teaching of physics. Emphasizes the
publication of review articles intended to
clarify and summarize recent and
important research about which
information is widely scattered in the
literature. Departments include: Notes
and Discussion (brief articles), Book
Reviews, Letters to the Editor,
Apparatus Notes.
**Readers:** Members of the American Assn.
of Physics Teachers in the U.S. and
abroad and other college and university
physics professors.
**Deadline:** ads-15th of mo., 6 wks. prior to
pub. date

24697
**AMERICAN MATHEMATICAL
MONTHLY, THE**
1529 18th St., N.W.
Washington, DC 20036
Telephone: (202) 387-5200
FAX: (202) 265-2384
Year Established: 1896
Pub. Frequency: 10/yr.
Page Size: standard
Subscrip. Rate: $100/yr.
Circulation: 15,000
Circulation Type: paid
**Owner(s):**
The Mathematical Association of America,
Inc.
1529 18th St., N.W.
Washington, DC 20036
Telephone: (202) 387-5200
Ownership %: 100
**Management:**
Elaine Pedreira ..................Advertising Manager
**Editorial:**
John Ewing ...........................Editor in Chief
Harry Waldman ....................Editorial Director
**Desc.:** Publishes major expository and
survey articles, as well as book reviews
addressed to those who have an
interest in collegiate and early graduate
mathematics.

58580
**AMERICAN PHILOSOPHICAL
QUARTERLY**
Philosophy Documentation Center
Bowling Green State University
Bowling Green, OH 43402
Telephone: (419) 372-2419
FAX: (419) 372-6987
Pub. Frequency: q.
Subscrip. Rate: $34/yr. individual; $135/yr.
institution
Circulation: 1,546
Circulation Type: paid
**Owner(s):**
North American Philosophical Publications,
Inc.
1021 Cathedral of Learning
Pittsburgh, PA 15260
Telephone: (412) 624-5950
Ownership %: 100
**Management:**
Cindy Richards .....................Business Manager
**Editorial:**
Nicholas Rescher .......................................Editor
Richard H. Lineback ...............................Director
**Desc.:** One of the principal English
language vehicles for the publication of
scholarly work in philosophy. Each issue
contains articles and a listing of
new philosophy books received. Only
self-sufficient papers are published.

24698
**AMERICAN SCHOOL &
UNIVERSITY**
401 N. Broad St.
Philadelphia, PA 19108
Telephone: (215) 238-5300
Year Established: 1928
Pub. Frequency: m.
Page Size: standard
Subscrip. Rate: $65/yr.
Circulation: 48,640
Circulation Type: controlled
**Owner(s):**
North American Publishing Co.
401 N. Broad St.
Philadelphia, PA 19108
Telephone: (215) 238-5300
Ownership %: 100
**Management:**
Michael E. Spring ...............................Publisher
**Editorial:**
Joe Agron ...................................................Editor
Diane Rotondo .........................Associate Editor
**Desc.:** Aims to help educational
administrators with the task of solving
problems related to their management
and business interests and to the
design, construction, furnishing,
equipping, operation and maintenance of
their facilities. To develop case history
and how-to materials illustrating good
practices that might be emulated by
school and college administrators. The
publication serves to bring its readers a
wide range of new ideas and techniques
that are of immediate or long-range
importance.
**Readers:** Chief administrators, chief
business officers, directors of buildings
& grounds, facility planners, school
architects, management & data
processing officials, transportation,
administrators in all significant school
districts and private schools, colleges,
and universities in the U.S.

24699
**AMERICAN SCHOOL BOARD
JOURNAL, THE**
1680 Duke St.
Alexandria, VA 22314
Telephone: (703) 838-6722
FAX: (703) 683-7590
Year Established: 1891

Pub. Frequency: m.
Page Size: standard
Subscrip. Rate: $48/yr.
Materials: 02,05,06,10,19,25,32,33
Freelance Pay: $100-$500
Circulation: 42,000
Circulation Type: paid
**Owner(s):**
National School Boards Association
1680 Duke St.
Alexandria, VA 22314
Telephone: (703) 838-6722
Ownership %: 100
**Management:**
E. Harold Fisher ...................................President
Don B. Blom ............................................Publisher
Thomas A. Shannon .........................Publisher
Mike DiSanto ...............Advertising Manager
Susan Jedrey .................Circulation Manager
**Editorial:**
Gregg Downey ......................Editor in Chief
Marilee Rist .................................Senior Editor
Donna Harrington - Lueker ...........Senior Editor
Sally Zakariya .......................Managing Editor
Andrew Trotter .........................Assistant Editor
JoAnna Natale .........................Assistant Editor
Lars Kongshelm ...................Editorial Assistant
Bonnie Becker .......................Production Director
**Desc.:** Covers administration of public
schools in cities, towns, rural areas.
Departments include School Finance
and Taxation, School Architecture,
School Furnishings and Equipment,
General Business Management, School
Law, Salaries, Personnel, Audiovisual
Education, School Lunch, School Plant
Maintenance.
**Readers:** School boards, superintendents,
supervisors.

24700
**AMERICAN TEACHER**
555 New Jersey Ave., N.W.
Washington, DC 20001
Telephone: (202) 879-4400
Year Established: 1916
Pub. Frequency: 8/yr.
Page Size: tabloid
Subscrip. Rate: $12/yr.
Materials: 25,29,32
Freelance Pay: varies
Print Process: web
Circulation: 680,000
Circulation Type: controlled
**Owner(s):**
American Federation of Teachers
555 New Jersey Ave., N.W.
Washington, DC 20001
Telephone: (202) 879-4430
Ownership %: 100
**Management:**
Albert Shanker ......................................President
American Fed. Of Teachers ...............Publisher
**Editorial:**
Trish Gorman ...............................................Editor
**Desc.:** AFT national, local, and state news
is supplemented by news of recent
developments in education, international
relations, and economics, as they
pertain to teacher unions and education
in general. Some material carried on
teacher aids, new books, and
conferences scheduled.
**Readers:** Mostly teachers, some
administrators.

24701
**ARITHMETIC TEACHER**
1906 Association Dr.
Reston, VA 22091-1593
Telephone: (703) 620-9840
FAX: (703) 476-2970
Year Established: 1954
Pub. Frequency: m., Sep.-May

**Materials Accepted/Included:** 01-Business news 02-By-line articles 03-Fashion news 04-Food news 05-Freelance copy 06-Letters to editor 07-Real estate news 08-Sports news 09-Travel news
10-Book rev. 11-Movie rev. 12-Music rev. 13-TV rev. 14-Theater rev. 15-Coming events 16-Obituaries 17-Question & answer 18-Social announcements 19-Artwork 20-Cartoons 21-Photos 22-TV listings
23-Audio rec. 24-Video rec. 25-Books 26-Films/film clips 27-Personnel news 28-Press releases 29-New product news/photos 30-Trade lit. 31-Contracts awarded 32-Display adv. 33-Classified adv.

4-330

Page Size: standard
Subscrip. Rate: $45/yr.
Materials: 06,32,33
Print Process: web
Circulation: 68,000
Circulation Type: paid
**Owner(s):**
National Council of Teachers of
Mathematics
1906 Association Dr.
Reston, VA 22091
Telephone: (703) 620-9840
FAX: (703) 476-2970
Ownership %: 100
**Management:**
Jack Price ........................................President
James D. Gates ....................Executive Director
Rowena G. Martelino ........Advertising Manager
Cynthia C. Rosso .................Business Manager
Robert Chandler .................Circulation Manager
**Editorial:**
Andy Reeve .............................Editorial Director
Ann Butterfield ......................Editorial Assistant
Harry B. Tunis ....................Publication Director
**Desc.:** Concerned with the teaching of
mathematics in kindergarten through
eighth grade. Features teaching and
curriculum problems, computer materials,
classroom ideas, and teaching aids.
**Readers:** Teachers, mathematics
supervisors, mathematics education
personnel, others.

### ARKANSAS EDUCATOR
24703
1500 W. Fourth St.
Little Rock, AR 72201
Telephone: (501) 375-4611
FAX: (501) 375-4620
Year Established: 1975
Pub. Frequency: 10/yr.
Page Size: tabloid
Subscrip. Rate: $4/yr. non-members
Circulation: 18,672
Circulation Type: controlled
**Owner(s):**
Arkansas Education Association
1500 W. Fourth St.
Little Rock, AR 72201
Telephone: (501) 375-4611
Ownership %: 100
**Management:**
Grainger Ledbetter ..............................President
Betty Moore ......................Advertising Manager
**Editorial:**
Pat Jones .........................Publication Director
**Desc.:** Serves as the official publication of
the Arkansas Education Association,
reporting AEA business and activities.
**Readers:** Members of the Arkansas
Education Association.

### ART EDUCATION
24704
1916 Association Dr.
Reston, VA 22091-1590
Telephone: (703) 860-8000
FAX: (703) 860-2960
Year Established: 1947
Pub. Frequency: bi-m.
Page Size: standard
Subscrip. Rate: $50/yr.
Print Process: web
Circulation: 16,000
Circulation Type: controlled
**Owner(s):**
The National Art Education Association
1916 Association Dr.
Reston, VA 22091
Telephone: (703) 860-8000
FAX: (703) 860-2960
Ownership %: 100
**Management:**
Mark Hansen ....................................President
Thomas A. Hatfield ................Executive Director
Beverly Jeanne Davis .......Advertising Manager

Cam Luccarelli .................Business Manager
Cam Luccarelli .................Circulation Manager
**Editorial:**
Thomas A. Hatfield ...............Executive Editor
Ronald MacGregor ................................Editor
Beverly Jeanne Davis ..............Managing Editor
**Desc.:** Directed to the profession of art
teaching at every level of the education
program-elementary, secondary, college,
and adult. Articles on teaching
techniques, methods, materials, up-to-
date articles, philosophy, and practices.
**Readers:** Education directors, supervisors,
art students, & art teachers.

### ARTS & ACTIVITIES
24705
591 Camino de la Reina, Ste. 200
San Diego, CA 92108-3192
Telephone: (619) 297-8520
FAX: (619) 297-5353
Year Established: 1932
Pub. Frequency: m.: 10/yr.
Page Size: standard
Subscrip. Rate: $24.95/yr. Sep.-Jun.
Materials: 02,05,06,10,15,19,24,25,28,29,32
Freelance Pay: $35-$150
Print Process: web offset
Circulation: 23,996
Circulation Type: paid
**Owner(s):**
Publishers' Development Corporation
591 Camino de la Reina, Ste. 2
San Diego, CA 92108
Telephone: (619) 297-5350
Ownership %: 100
**Management:**
George E. von Rosen .........................Publisher
Steve Polite ......................Advertising Manager
**Editorial:**
Maryellen Bridge ...................................Editor
Niki Ackermann ...............Graphics Coordinator
**Desc.:** Articles deal with creative art,
photography, graphic, industrial arts,
computer artwork, and craft projects for
elementary and high school
teachers. Emphasis is on helping
teachers carry on creative art programs.
Shop Talk column covers new art
and craft materials, visual aids.
**Readers:** Classroom teachers, art
teachers, supervisors, kindergarten
through senior high school. Also used as
text in teacher colleges.
**Deadline:** story-120 days prior to pub.
date; news-120 days; photo-120 days;
ads-2 mo. prior to pub. date

### ARTS EDUCATION POLICY REVIEW
24733
1319 18th St., N.W.
Washington, DC 20036-1802
Telephone: (202) 296-6267
FAX: (202) 296-5149
Year Established: 1899
Pub. Frequency: bi-m.
Page Size: standard
Subscrip. Rate: $34/yr. individual; $59/yr.
institution; $12 postage outside US
Circulation: 1,528
Circulation Type: paid
**Owner(s):**
Heldref Publications
1319 18th St., N.W.
Washington, DC 20036-1802
Telephone: (202) 296-6267
Ownership %: 100
**Management:**
Walter E. Beach ................................Publisher
Raymond M. Rallo ............Advertising Manager
Catherine Welker ...............Circulation Manager
Kerri P. Kilbane ...................Promotion Manager
**Editorial:**
Sheila Barrows ......................................Editor
Karen Luzader Eskew .....................Art Director

**Desc.:** Discusses major policy issues
concerning K-12 education in the
various arts. Presents a variety of views
rather than taking sides. Emphasizes
analytical exploration. Aims to produce
the most insightful, comprehensive, and
rigorous exchange of ideas ever
available on arts education.
**Readers:** Arts educators, administrators,
policy analysts, arts advocacy groups,
and parents.

### ASEE PRISM
24744
11 Dupont Cir., Ste. 200
Washington, DC 20036
Telephone: (202) 293-7080
FAX: (202) 265-8504
Year Established: 1910
Pub. Frequency: 10/yr.
Page Size: standard
Subscrip. Rate: $36/yr.; $46/yr. overseas
**Owner(s):**
American Society for Engineering
Education
Telephone: (202) 293-7080
Ownership %: 100
**Management:**
Dr. Thomas ......................Advertising Manager
**Editorial:**
Patricia W. Samaras .................Managing Editor
**Desc.:** Publishes papers by members and
nonmembers. Areas of interest include:
effective teaching, college
administration, curricula and degree
programs, ethics, philosophy of
education, research in engineering,
teaching methods and aids, and news of
events and products.
**Readers:** Engineering and technical
institute faculty technical librarians,
training and personnel staff in industry &
gov't. Considerable foreign circulation.

### ATHLETIC MANAGEMENT
68827
438 W. State St.
Ithaca, NY 14850-5220
Telephone: (607) 272-0265
FAX: (607) 273-0701
Pub. Frequency: 6/yr.
Page Size: standard
Subscrip. Rate: free
Circulation: 25,973
Circulation Type: controlled
**Owner(s):**
College Athletic Administrator, Inc.
438 W. State St.
Ithaca, NY 14850-5220
Telephone: (607) 272-0265
Ownership %: 100

### BENT OF TAU BETA PI, THE
24709
508 Dougherty Engineering Bldg.
Knoxville, TN 37996
Telephone: (615) 546-4578
FAX: (615) 546-4579
Mailing Address:
P.O. Box 8840
Knoxville, TN 37996
Year Established: 1906
Pub. Frequency: q.
Page Size: standard
Subscrip. Rate: $10/yr.; $50/life
Circulation: 93,000
Circulation Type: paid
**Owner(s):**
The Tau Beta Pi Association, Inc.
P.O. Box 8840
Knoxville, TN 37996
Telephone: (615) 546-4578
Ownership %: 100
**Editorial:**
James D. Froula ......................................Editor
Roger E. Hawks ...............................Advertising
Judith A. Stewart ................Editorial Assistant

James D. Froula ............Secretary & Treasurer
**Desc.:** Official publication of the Tau Beta
Pi Association, Inc., national engineering
honor society. Concerned with
membership, current issues involving
excellence in engineering, education,
and liberal culture. Solicits features from
members. Runs engineering recruitment
advertising only.
**Readers:** 93,000 engineering graduates &
undergraduate juniors and seniors from
210 collegiate chapters, at 210 colleges
and universities.

### BOUNDARY 2
70444
905 W. Main St., Ste. 18-B
Duke University Press
Durham, NC 27701
Telephone: (919) 687-3636
FAX: (919) 688-4574
Mailing Address:
P.O. Box 90660
Durham, NC 27708-0660
Year Established: 1972
Pub. Frequency: 3/yr.
Page Size: standard
Subscrip. Rate: $24/yr. individuals; $54/yr.
institutions
Materials: 32
Circulation: 800
Circulation Type: controlled & paid
**Owner(s):**
Duke University Press
P.O. Box 90660
Durham, NC 27708-0660
Telephone: (919) 687-3600
FAX: (919) 688-4574
Ownership %: 100
**Management:**
Patricia Thomas .................................Manager
**Editorial:**
Paul A. Bove .........................................Editor

### BULLETIN OF THE CENTER FOR CHILDREN'S BOOKS, THE
64721
1512 N. Fremont, Ste. 105
Chicago, IL 60622
Telephone: (312) 944-5253
FAX: (312) 944-0629
Year Established: 1947
Pub. Frequency: m. exc. Aug.
Subscrip. Rate: $29/yr.
Circulation: 7,500
Circulation Type: paid
**Owner(s):**
University of Illinois, Graduate School of
Library
410 David Kinley Hall
1407 W. Gregory Dr.
Urbana, IL 61801-3680
Ownership %: 100
**Editorial:**
Betsy Hearne ...........................Editor in Chief
Roger Sutton ...........................Executive Editor
Deborah Stevenson ................Assistant Editor
**Desc.:** Reviews and evaluates more than
900 new childrens books each year.
**Readers:** Librarians, teachers, parents.

### BUSINESS EDUCATION FORUM
24714
1914 Association Dr.
Reston, VA 22091
Telephone: (703) 860-8300
FAX: (703) 620-4483
Year Established: 1947
Pub. Frequency: q.
Page Size: standard
Subscrip. Rate: $60/yr.
Materials: 02
Print Process: web
Circulation: 15,300
Circulation Type: paid

---

**Materials Accepted/Included:** 01-Business news 02-By-line articles 03-Fashion news 04-Food news 05-Freelance copy 06-Letters to editor 07-Real estate news 08-Sports news 09-Travel news 10-Book rev. 11-Movie rev. 12-Music rev. 13-TV rev. 14-Theater rev. 15-Coming events 16-Obituaries 17-Question & answer 18-Social announcements 19-Artwork 20-Cartoons 21-Photos 22-TV listings 23-Audio rec. 24-Video rec. 25-Books 26-Films/film clips 27-Personnel news 28-Press releases 29-New product news/photos 30-Trade lit. 31-Contracts awarded 32-Display adv. 33-Classified adv.

**Owner(s):**
National Business Education Association
1914 Association Dr.
Reston, VA 22091
Telephone: (703) 860-8300
Ownership %: 100
**Editorial:**
Regina McDowell .....................................Editor
Julie Fintel .....................................Assistant Editor
Helen C. Sellman .....................Consulting Editor
**Readers:** Business teachers, supervisors, and administrators from junior high schools through graduate schools of business and education.

24715
**BUSINESS EDUCATION WORLD**
1221 Ave. of the Americas
New York, NY 10020
Telephone: (212) 512-2845
Year Established: 1919
Pub. Frequency: 2/yr.
Page Size: standard
Subscrip. Rate: free
Freelance Pay: artists-$12/hr.
**Owner(s):**
Glencoe/McGraw - Hill
1221 Ave. of the Americas
New York, NY 10020
Telephone: (212) 512-6905
Ownership %: 100
**Management:**
Peter F. Sayeski .................................Publisher
**Editorial:**
Katharine H. Glynn ...............................Editor
**Desc.:** Innovative application of teaching methods, educational theories, trends in business and office education. Business education subjects - typing, shorthand, secretarial office procedures, accounting, data processing, consumer education, career education. Departments include: Professional News, The Gregg Outline, Accounting Update, Classroom Capsules and Conversations With...
**Readers:** Business education teachers, educators and administrators.

69543
**BUSINESS OFFICER**
One Dupont Circle, Ste. 500
Washington, DC 20036-1178
Telephone: (202) 861-2500
FAX: (202) 861-2583
Year Established: 1967
Pub. Frequency: m.
Subscrip. Rate: membership
Circulation: 17,500
**Owner(s):**
Natl. Assn. of College & University Bus. Officers
One Dupont Circle, Ste. 500
Washington, DC 20036-1178
Telephone: (202) 861-2500
Ownership %: 100
**Editorial:**
Donna Klinger .........................................Editor

22436
**CAMPING MAGAZINE**
5000 State Rd., 67, N.
Martinsville, IN 46151
Telephone: (317) 342-8456
FAX: (317) 342-2065
Year Established: 1926
Pub. Frequency: 6/yr.
Page Size: standard
Subscrip. Rate: $23.95/yr.
Materials: 02,05,06,10,15,27,28,29,30,32,33
Print Process: offset
Circulation: 7,000
Circulation Type: paid

**Owner(s):**
American Camping Association, Inc.
5000 State Rd., 67, N.
Martinsville, IN 46151
Telephone: (317) 342-8456
Ownership %: 100
**Management:**
John Miller .................Executive Vice President
American Camping Assn., Inc. ...........Publisher
Bill Willems .........................Advertising Manager
**Editorial:**
Nancy L. Gordon ......................Managing Editor
Bill Willems ...........................New Products Editor
**Desc.:** Publishes material for professionals working with youth and adult camps and outdoor programming. Includes articles on programming, marketing, staff, operations; regular columns on legislation, risk management, camper development, new products and services.
**Readers:** Organized-camp owners, directors, executives, college/university professors, summer staff and other outdoor education leaders.
**Deadline:** story-2 mo. prior to pub. date; news-2 mo. prior to pub. date; photo-2 mo. prior to pub. date; ads-2 mo. prior to pub. date

68795
**CAMPUS ACTIVITIES TODAY**
917 Calhoun St.
Columbia, SC 29201
Telephone: (803) 771-8966
FAX: (803) 254-5798
Year Established: 1992
Pub. Frequency: 8/yr.
Page Size: standard
Subscrip. Rate: $18/yr.
Circulation: 4,874
Circulation Type: paid
**Owner(s):**
Cameo Publishing Group
917 Calhoun St.
Columbia, SC 29201
Telephone: (803) 771-8966
Ownership %: 100
**Desc.:** Provides information on entertainment, films, music and special events for student activities directors.

24725
**CAREER WOMAN**
150 Motor Pkwy., Ste. 420
Hauppauge, NY 11788-5145
Telephone: (516) 273-0066
FAX: (516) 273-8936
Pub. Frequency: a.
Page Size: standard
Subscrip. Rate: $5/copy
Circulation: 10,000
Circulation Type: paid
**Owner(s):**
Equal Opportunity Publications, Inc.
150 Motor Pkwy., Ste. 420
Hauppauge, NY 11788-5145
Ownership %: 100
**Management:**
John Miller, III .....................................President
Kay Zollar Miller ...............................Publisher
John Muller ........................Advertising Manager
Christine Desmond ..............Business Manager
Barbara O'Connor ..............Circulation Manager
Pat Plattner ..................................Office Manager
**Editorial:**
Eileen Nester ........................................Editor

**Desc.:** An affirmative-action career magazine that addresses itself to the professional and personal growth opportunities facing woman career seekers upon graduation. Articles are written by college students, recent graduates, young professionals, placement directors, and campus recruiters. Articles are about career directions in engineering, health care, computers, banking, insurance, and other segments of industry and government.
**Readers:** College students and graduate women seeking careers.

24718
**CHANGE MAGAZINE**
1319 18th St., N.W.
Washington, DC 20036-1802
Telephone: (202) 296-6267
FAX: (202) 296-5149
Year Established: 1969
Pub. Frequency: bi-m.
Page Size: standard
Subscrip. Rate: $34/yr., individuals; $65/yr. institutions; add $12 outside of US
Circulation: 4,482
Circulation Type: paid
**Owner(s):**
Heldref Publications
1319 18th St., N.W.
Washington, DC 20036
Telephone: (202) 296-6267
Ownership %: 100
**Management:**
Walter E. Beach .................................Publisher
Raymond M. Rallo ...........Advertising Manager
Catherine Welker ..............Circulation Manager
Kerri P. Kilbane .................Promotion Manager
**Editorial:**
Nanette Wiese ......................................Editor
**Desc.:** Well-known and respected as an opinion magazine dealing with contemporary issues in higher learning, the award-winning CHANGE spotlights trends, provides new insights, and analyzes the implications of educational programs.
**Readers:** Faculty members, administrators, trustees, local, state and federal officials, and corporate and foundation officers.

64720
**CHILD DEVELOPMENT ABSTRACTS & BIBLIOGRAPHY**
University of Kansas-Bailey Hall
Lawrence, KS 66045
Telephone: (913) 864-4526
Year Established: 1927
Pub. Frequency: 3/yr.
Page Size: standard
Subscrip. Rate: $65/yr.
Circulation: 10,000
Circulation Type: paid
**Owner(s):**
Society for Research in Child Development
University of Michigan
Ann Arbor, MI 48109
Ownership %: 100
**Editorial:**
Neil Salkind ...........................................Editor

24719
**CHILDHOOD EDUCATION**
11501 Georgia Ave., Ste. 315
Silver Spring, MD 20902
Telephone: (301) 942-2443
FAX: (301) 942-3012
Year Established: 1924
Pub. Frequency: 5/yr.
Page Size: standard
Subscrip. Rate: $45/yr. membership
Circulation: 14,000
Circulation Type: paid

**Owner(s):**
Association for Childhood Education International
11501 Georgia Ave., Ste. 315
Silver Spring, MD 20902
Telephone: (301) 942-2443
Ownership %: 100
**Management:**
Carol Vukelich ....................................President
Bruce Herzig ......................Advertising Manager
**Editorial:**
Anne Watson Bauer ...............................Editor
Gerald C. Odland .................Executive Director
Marilyn Gardner ...................Marketing Director
**Desc.:** Professional publications dealing with teaching problems, teaching techniques, child growth and development, research, family life, child care and related disciplines. Departments include: Books for Children, Books for Adults, Among the Magazines, Films, ERIC/EECE, Teaching Strategies and Educational Media Reviews (including software).
**Readers:** Members, teachers, students of education, parents, education institutions.

24720
**CHRONICLE OF HIGHER EDUCATION, THE**
1255 23rd St., N.W., Ste. 700
Washington, DC 20037
Telephone: (202) 466-1000
FAX: (202) 296-2691
Year Established: 1966
Pub. Frequency: w.
Page Size: tabloid
Subscrip. Rate: $40.50/6 mo.; $75/yr.
Freelance Pay: $25-$500
Circulation: 100,000
Circulation Type: paid
**Owner(s):**
Chronicle of Higher Education, The
1255 23rd St., N.W.
Washington, DC 20037
Telephone: (202) 466-1080
Ownership %: 100
**Management:**
Roibinette D. Ross ...............................Publisher
**Editorial:**
Corbin Gwaltney .....................................Editor
Malcolm Scully ........................Managing Editor
Edward R. Weidlein .................Associate Editor
Robin Wilson .......................................News Editor
**Desc.:** A professional news source and forum for decision-making professors and administrators at colleges and universities in the US and Canada, as well as other professionals concerned with higher education.
**Readers:** 16% senior administrative officers; 32.5% other business officers; 24.1% academic officers; 32.9% faculty members; 12.9% others in higher education; 15% not in higher education.

24721
**CLASSICAL JOURNAL**
Dept. of Classics, 144 New Cabell Hall
University of Virginia
Charlottesville, VA 22903
Telephone: (804) 924-6538
FAX: (804) 982-2002
Year Established: 1905
Pub. Frequency: q.
Page Size: pocket
Subscrip. Rate: $30/yr.
Circulation: 2,900
Circulation Type: paid

**Materials Accepted/Included:** 01-Business news 02-By-line articles 03-Fashion news 04-Food news 05-Freelance copy 06-Letters to editor 07-Real estate news 08-Sports news 09-Travel news 10-Book rev. 11-Movie rev. 12-Music rev. 13-TV rev. 14-Theater rev. 15-Coming events 16-Obituaries 17-Question & answer 18-Social announcements 19-Artwork 20-Cartoons 21-Photos 22-TV listings 23-Audio rec. 24-Video rec. 25-Books 26-Films/film clips 27-Personnel news 28-Press releases 29-New product news/photos 30-Trade lit. 31-Contracts awarded 32-Display adv. 33-Classified adv.

**Owner(s):**
Classical Assn. of the Middle West and
South, Inc.
c/o John F. Hall
118 KMB, Brigham Young University
Provo, UT 84602
Ownership %: 100
**Editorial:**
John F. Miller ...............................Editor in Chief
Jenny Strauss Clay ............Book Review Editor
**Desc.:** Papers, either scholarly or
pedagogical on topics in the history,
literature and linguistics of the classical
world.
**Readers:** Professors of Greek, Latin, and
other subjects relating to the classics,
high school teachers, and interested
nonacademics.

54075
## CLEARING HOUSE, THE
1319 18th St., N.W.
Washington, DC 20036
Telephone: (202) 296-6267
FAX: (202) 296-5149
Year Established: 1925
Pub. Frequency: bi-m.
Page Size: standard
Subscrip. Rate: $29/yr. individuals; $51/yr.
institutions; add $12 outside of US
Circulation: 2,860
Circulation Type: paid
**Owner(s):**
Heldref Publications
1319 18th St., N.W.
Washington, DC 20036-1802
Telephone: (202) 296-6267
Ownership %: 100
**Management:**
Walter E. Beach ..................................Publisher
Kerri P. Kilbane .................Promotion Manager
**Editorial:**
Judy Cusick .........................................Editor
Raymond M. Rallo ..............Advertising Director
Catherine Welker ................Circulation Director
**Desc.:** Each issue has a variety of articles
for teachers and administrators of
middle schools & junior/senior high
schools. It includes experiments, trends,
and accomplishments in courses,
teaching methods, administrative
procedures, & school programs.
**Readers:** Teachers and administrators of
middle schools and junior/senior high
schools

24723
## COLLEGE COMPOSITION & COMMUNICATION
1111 W. Kenyon Rd.
Urbana, IL 61801-1096
Telephone: (217) 328-3870
FAX: (217) 328-0977
Year Established: 1949
Pub. Frequency: q.
Page Size: standard
Subscrip. Rate: $12/yr. members
Materials: 02,06,10,15,32
Print Process: web offset
Circulation: 12,000
Circulation Type: paid
**Owner(s):**
National Council of Teachers of English
1111 W. Kenyon Rd.
Urbana, IL 61801-1096
Telephone: (217) 328-3870
Ownership %: 100
**Editorial:**
Joseph Harris ...............................................Editor

**Desc.:** Published by the Conference on
College Composition and
Communication of the National Council
of Teachers of English. A forum for
teachers of writing in two- and four-year
colleges. It presents articles on error
analysis, invention, the composing
process, writer's block, the teaching of
basic writing, and language studies, and
it includes book reviews and a staffroom
interchange section.
**Readers:** Teachers of writing in two- and
four-year colleges.
**Deadline:** ads-2 mo prior to pub. date

56242
## COLLEGE ENGLISH
1111 W. Kenyon Rd.
Urbana, IL 61801-1096
Telephone: (217) 328-3870
FAX: (217) 328-9645
Year Established: 1938
Pub. Frequency: 8/yr.
Page Size: standard
Subscrip. Rate: $40/yr. (incl. with NCTE
membership)
Freelance Pay: 2 free copies
Circulation: 19,000
Circulation Type: paid
**Owner(s):**
National Council of Teachers of English
1111 W. Kenyon Rd.
Urbana, IL 61801-1096
Telephone: (217) 328-3870
Ownership %: 100
**Editorial:**
Louise Smith .......................................Editor
**Desc.:** Contains articles on the working
concepts of criticism, the nature of
critical and scholary reasoning,
pedagogy and education theory, issues
of concern to college English teachers,
contemporary poetry, reviews of recent
books, and comment and response
section.
**Readers:** English teachers at the college
level.

24724
## COLLEGE STUDENT JOURNAL
P.O. Box 8508, Spring Hill Sta.
Mobile, AL 36689
Telephone: (205) 343-1878
Year Established: 1963
Pub. Frequency: q.
Page Size: standard
Subscrip. Rate: $15/yr. individuals; $20/yr.
institutions
Circulation: 1,000
Circulation Type: paid
**Owner(s):**
Project Innovation of Mobile
P.O. Box 8508
Mobile, AL 36689
Telephone: (205) 343-1878
Ownership %: 100
**Bureau(s):**
Project Innovation
1362 Santa Cruz Crt.
Chula Vista, CA 91910
Telephone: (619) 421-9377
Contact: Dr. Russell N. Cassel, Editor
**Management:**
Dr. George Uhlig .................Business Manager
**Editorial:**
George Uhlig ...........................Managing Editor
Mary Ann Gillis ..................Book Review Editor
**Desc.:** Original investigations and
theoretical papers dealing with college
student values, attitudes, opinions, and
learning. This includes the graduate and
professional students as well.
**Readers:** College, university professors,
college students in general.

54076
## COLLEGE TEACHING
1319 18th St., N.W.
Washington, DC 20036
Telephone: (202) 296-6267
FAX: (202) 296-5149
Year Established: 1953
Pub. Frequency: q.
Page Size: standard
Subscrip. Rate: $29/yr. individuals; $53/yr.
institutions; add $10 outside of US
Circulation: 2,175
Circulation Type: paid
**Owner(s):**
Heldref Publications
1319 18th St., N.W.
Washington, DC 20036-1802
Telephone: (202) 296-6267
Ownership %: 100
**Management:**
Walter E. Beach ..................................Publisher
Kerri P. Kilbane .................Promotion Manager
**Editorial:**
Cherie Bottum .......................................Editor
Raymond M. Rallo ..............Advertising Director
Catherine Welker ................Circulation Director
**Desc.:** College Teaching is the unique,
interdisciplinary journal that supports
faculty members in their often-
overlooked role as teachers. It is also a
journal with practical ideas, successful
methods, and new program for faculty
development.
**Readers:** Teachers and administrators

24726
## COLORADO SCHOOL JOURNAL
3131 S. Vaughn Way, Ste. 500
Aurora, CO 80014
Telephone: (303) 695-4300
FAX: (303) 696-1797
Year Established: 1885
Pub. Frequency: 5/yr.
Page Size: tabloid
Subscrip. Rate: $12/yr. non-members
Circulation: 29,000
Circulation Type: controlled
**Owner(s):**
Colorado Education Association
3131 W. Vaughn Way, Ste. 500
Aurora, CO 80014
Telephone: (303) 695-4300
Ownership %: 100
**Editorial:**
Jeanne L. Beyer .......................................Editor
**Desc.:** Most stories written by educators;
within the State of Colorado. Features
articles about teaching and teaching
techniques, association news political &
social issues of interest to educators.
**Readers:** Members of Colo. Ed. Assn.
including teachers.

24938
## COMMUNICATION EDUCATION
5105 Backlick Rd., Bldg. E
Annandale, VA 22003
Telephone: (703) 750-0533
Year Established: 1952
Pub. Frequency: q.
Page Size: standard
Subscrip. Rate: $96/yr. in US; $102/yr.
foreign
Circulation: 4,400
Circulation Type: paid
**Owner(s):**
Speech Communication Association
5105 Backlick Rd., Bldg. E
Annandale, VA 22003
Telephone: (703) 750-0533
Ownership %: 100
**Editorial:**
Douglas M. Trank ...............................Editor
Isa Engleberg ....................Book Review Editor

**Desc.:** Deals with all aspects of speech
communication education, verbal and
nonverbal language development,
interpersonal & small group
communication, speech correction,
drama, and oral interpretation. Stresses
teaching research at all levels of
education.
**Readers:** Teachers, students, and lay
people.

24727
## COMMUNITY COLLEGE JOURNAL
One Dupont Cir., N.W., Ste. 410
Washington, DC 20036
Telephone: (202) 728-0200
FAX: (202) 223-9390
Year Established: 1930
Pub. Frequency: bi-m.
Page Size: standard
Subscrip. Rate: $22/yr.
Circulation: 24,000
Circulation Type: paid
**Owner(s):**
American Association of Community
Colleges
One Dupont Circle, N.W.
Washington, DC 20036
Telephone: (202) 728-0200
Ownership %: 100
**Management:**
Ken Silverstein .................Advertising Manager
**Editorial:**
Ronald Stanley .........................Managing Editor
**Desc.:** Covers the latest trends,
innovations, & research affecting two-
year colleges. Features exemplary
programs, practices, & policies.
**Readers:** Administrators, faculty, and
CEO's of two-year colleges.

64715
## COMPARATIVE EDUCATION REVIEW
1712 Neil Ave.
Columbus, OH 43210
Telephone: (614) 292-9660
Year Established: 1956
Pub. Frequency: q.
Page Size: standard
Subscrip. Rate: $31/yr.
Circulation: 2,400
Circulation Type: paid
**Owner(s):**
Comparative Education Review
Ownership %: 100
**Editorial:**
Erwin H. Epstein ...............................Editor
**Desc.:** Features social science applications
to international issues of education.
**Readers:** Social scientists, educators,
policymakers, development planners.

69516
## CONTEMPORARY EDUCATION
Statesman Towers, Rm. 1005
Terre Haute, IN 47809
Telephone: (812) 237-2970
FAX: (812) 237-4348
Year Established: 1929
Pub. Frequency: q.
Subscrip. Rate: $12/yr.
Materials: 06,10,20
Circulation: 1,500
Circulation Type: free & paid
**Owner(s):**
Indiana State University
School of Education
Statesman Towers, Rm. 1005
Terre Haute, IN 47809
Telephone: (812) 237-2970
**Editorial:**
David A. Gilman ...............................Editor
**Readers:** Education and University
Libraries.

**Materials Accepted/Included:** 01-Business news 02-By-line articles 03-Fashion news 04-Food news 05-Freelance copy 06-Letters to editor 07-Real estate news 08-Sports news 09-Travel news
10-Book rev. 11-Movie rev. 12-Music rev. 13-TV rev. 14-Theater rev. 15-Coming events 16-Obituaries 17-Question & answer 18-Social announcements 19-Artwork 20-Cartoons 21-Photos 22-TV listings
23-Audio rec. 24-Video rec. 25-Books 26-Films/film clips 27-Personnel news 28-Press releases 29-New product news/photos 30-Trade lit. 31-Contracts awarded 32-Display adv. 33-Classified adv.

4-333

## COUNSELING NEWS
24753

5999 Stevenson Ave.
Alexandria, VA 22304
Telephone: (703) 823-9800
FAX: (703) 823-0252
Year Established: 1959
Pub. Frequency: m.
Page Size: tabloid
Subscrip. Rate: $30/yr.
Materials: 02,06,10,16
Print Process: web offset
Circulation: 60,000
Circulation Type: controlled
**Owner(s):**
American Counseling Association
5999 Stevenson Ave.
Alexandria, VA 22304
Telephone: (703) 823-9800
Ownership %: 100
**Editorial:**
Jennifer L. Sacks ........................Editor
Libby Blaker ...........................Advertising
**Desc.:** Carries news and features about
counseling and guidance and related
topics. This includes news of federal,
state and local legislation; education;
work attitudes; leisure activities;
psychology; family relations; alcohol and
drug abuse; juveniles; minorities; women;
disabilities; elderly; veterans; association
activities and publications. Books are
briefly reviewed. Carries classified and
display advertising for products or
services of professional interest to
members of the association. This
includes employment ads, seminars,
books, movies.
**Readers:** Counselors: In schools, colleges
and universities, mental health agencies,
rehabilitation and corrections facilities,
employment services, government and
industry.
**Deadline:** story-3 wks. prior to pub. date;
news-3 wks. prior; photo-3 wks. prior;
ads-10 days prior

## CRITICISM
59658

5959 Woodward Ave.
Detroit, MI 48202
Telephone: (313) 577-6120
FAX: (313) 577-6131
Year Established: 1959
Pub. Frequency: q.
Subscrip. Rate: $28/yr., $52/2 yrs., $78/3
yrs. individuals; $50/yr., $90/2 yrs.,
$142/3 yrs. institutions
Circulation: 1,200
Circulation Type: paid
**Owner(s):**
Wayne State University Press
5959 Woodward Ave.
Detroit, MI 48202
Telephone: (313) 577-4606
**Editorial:**
Arthur Marotti ...............................Editor
**Desc.:** Deals with artists, art, and literature
from all periods, either individually or in
their interrelationships. Emphasizes on
poststructuralist critical approaches,
feminist, and new historian
interpretation.
**Readers:** Scholars and academical people
in the field of literature and arts.

## CURATOR
22301

79th & Central Park W.
New York, NY 10024
Telephone: (212) 769-5450
FAX: (212) 769-5426
Year Established: 1958
Pub. Frequency: q.

Page Size: standard
Subscrip. Rate: $22/yr. students; $30/yr.
individuals; $54/2yrs.; $85/yr.
institutions; $99/2yrs.;
Materials: 02,06,10
Circulation: 1,200
Circulation Type: paid
**Owner(s):**
American Museum of Natural History
Central Park W. at 79th St.
New York, NY 10024
Telephone: (212) 769-5000
Ownership %: 100
**Management:**
L. Thomas Kelly .........................Publisher
Edward R. Buller .................Business Manager
**Editorial:**
Samuel M. Taylor ...........................Editor
William Moynihan ...........................Editor
Stanley Freed ...............................Editor
Nancy Creshkoff ..................Assistant Editor
Mark Abraham ..............Production Coordinator
**Desc.:** Technical and non-technical articles
for all museum professionals. Articles
can include B&W pictures. Must be
pertinent to museum.
**Readers:** Museum professionals, university
professors, archaeologists,
anthropologists, historians, curators, art
historians, exhibit designers, museum
studies students.

## CURRENT HEALTH 1 & 2
26648

245 Long Hill Rd.
Middletown, CT 06457
Telephone: (800) 446-3355
Year Established: 1974
Pub. Frequency: 9/yr.
Page Size: standard
Subscrip. Rate: $7.95/yr.
Circulation: 404,000
Circulation Type: paid
**Owner(s):**
Weekly Reader Corporation
245 Long Hill Rd.
Middletown, CT 06457
Telephone: (800) 446-3355
Ownership %: 100
**Editorial:**
Sandra Maccarone ...........................Editor
**Desc.:** Educational publications for
classroom use in health and related
curricula, presenting factual, up-to-date
information in the field of health. Current
Health 1 covers grades 4-7; Current
Health 2 covers grades 7-12.
**Readers:** 1,250,000 students.

## CURRENT SCIENCE
26649

245 Long Hill Rd.
Middletown, CT 06457
Telephone: (203) 638-2400
Year Established: 1927
Pub. Frequency: bi-w.
Page Size: standard
Subscrip. Rate: $5.50/yr.
Freelance Pay: staff only
Circulation: 400,000
Circulation Type: paid
**Owner(s):**
Weekly Reader Corporation
Telephone: (203) 638-2400
Ownership %: 100
**Management:**
Richard BeBrasseur ........................President
**Editorial:**
Vincent Marteka ..................Managing Editor
Nancy Webb ....................Editorial Director
Hugh Westrup ..................Associate Editor
Ingrid Wickelgren ...............Associate Editor

**Desc.:** Presents the latest advances in
science, health and technology in
popular style. Each issue includes two
major feature stories, three to four
pages of news briefs, four shorter
features, a photo spread, and an activity
page.
**Readers:** Middle schools and junior high
schools.

## CURRICULUM PRODUCT NEWS
24730

992 High Ridge Rd.
Stamford, CT 06905
Telephone: (203) 322-1300
FAX: (203) 329-9177
Year Established: 1972
Pub. Frequency: 10/yr.
Page Size: standard
Subscrip. Rate: free-controlled
Circulation: 53,000
Circulation Type: controlled
**Owner(s):**
Educational Media, Inc.
992 High Ridge Rd.
Stamford, CT 06905
Telephone: (203) 322-1300
FAX: (203) 329-9177
Ownership %: 100
**Management:**
Howard A. Reed ...........................Publisher
**Editorial:**
Jane Woodward ...............................Editor
Joseph Kantorski .......................Art Director
Jeffrey Horton ..................Associate Publisher
Terry Wilson ...........................Miscellaneous
Suzi LaHines ...........................Miscellaneous
Ellen McCormick ........................Miscellaneous
Susan Leach ...........................Miscellaneous
Margot Jahnke ........................Miscellaneous
**Desc.:** Published ten times a year,
September through June. Each issue
contains brief, non-evaluative reviews of
new curriculum materials for K - 12
classrooms, including textbooks and
other print materials, audiovisual
materials, school equipment, micro-
computer hardware and software, kits,
games, and catalogs. Regular
departments are: Computer-Aided
Instruction; Early Childhood Materials;
Library/Media Center Materials;
Administration/ Professional
Development; Home/Industrial/
Business Education; Reading &
Language Arts; School Equipment;
Mathematics; Science; Social Studies;
Special Education; The Arts; Testing/
Guidance/Career Education; and ESL. A
Special Focus section each month
highlights one curriculum area.
**Readers:** Curriculum planners at the
district level.

## DAY CARE & EARLY EDUCATION
24731

351 Peasant St., Ste. 330
Northampton, MA 01060
Year Established: 1973
Pub. Frequency: q.
Page Size: standard
Subscrip. Rate: $19/yr. individuals; $53/yr.
institutions
Freelance Pay: varies
Circulation: 3,500
Circulation Type: paid
**Owner(s):**
Human Sciences Press, Inc.
233 Spring St.
New York, NY 10013
Telephone: (212) 620-8000
Ownership %: 100
**Management:**
Sophia Guyers ..................Advertising Manager

**Editorial:**
Randa Roen Nachbar ........................Editor
Bill Jobson ...........................Art Director
**Desc.:** Publishes articles on methods and
materials, child development trends,
funding and administrative issues, the
politics of day care, parental
participation, personnel development,
and standards.
**Readers:** Administrators, teachers,
parents, students, day care workers,
early education professionals.

## DEAF AMERICAN
24732

814 Thayer Ave.
Silver Spring, MD 20910-4500
Telephone: (301) 587-1788
FAX: (301) 587-1791
Year Established: 1948
Pub. Frequency: a.
Page Size: standard
Subscrip. Rate: $20/yr.
Circulation: 6,600
Circulation Type: paid
**Owner(s):**
National Association of the Deaf
814 Thayer Ave.
Silver Spring, MD 20910
Telephone: (301) 587-1788
Ownership %: 100
**Editorial:**
Merv Garretson ...............................Editor
**Desc.:** Articles, opinion letters and essays
about topics important to deaf and hard
of hearing persons.
**Readers:** The deaf and parents of deaf
children, professionals.

## DECA DIMENSIONS
24794

1908 Association Dr.
Reston, VA 22091
Telephone: (703) 860-5000
FAX: (703) 860-4013
Year Established: 1947
Pub. Frequency: 4/yr.
Page Size: standard
Subscrip. Rate: $5/yr.
Materials: 01,02,03,05,10,17,20,28,29,32
Freelance Pay: $100-$125
Print Process: offset
Circulation: 155,000
Circulation Type: paid
**Owner(s):**
National DECA
1908 Association Dr.
Reston, VA 22091
Telephone: (703) 860-5000
Ownership %: 100
**Editorial:**
Carol Lund .................................Editor
**Desc.:** Contributed articles by educators,
students, business on topics relating to
business, careers, leadership,
professional development.
**Readers:** High school and postsecondary
students, public school teachers, training
(cadet teachers).

## DIRECTORY OF AMERICAN PHILOSOPHERS
58667

Philosophy Documentation Ctr.
Bowling Green State Univ.
Bowling Green, OH 43403-0189
Telephone: (419) 372-2419
FAX: (419) 372-6987
Year Established: 1962
Pub. Frequency: bi-a.
Subscrip. Rate: $36/yr. individuals; $96/yr.
institutions
Circulation: 950
Circulation Type: paid

Materials Accepted/Included: 01-Business news 02-By-line articles 03-Fashion news 04-Food news 05-Freelance copy 06-Letters to editor 07-Real estate news 08-Sports news 09-Travel news 10-Book rev. 11-Movie rev. 12-Music rev. 13-TV rev. 14-Theater rev. 15-Coming events 16-Obituaries 17-Question & answer 18-Social announcements 19-Artwork 20-Cartoons 21-Photos 22-TV listings 23-Audio rec. 24-Video rec. 25-Books 26-Films/film clips 27-Personnel news 28-Press releases 29-New product news/photos 30-Trade lit. 31-Contracts awarded 32-Display adv. 33-Classified adv.

4-334

**Owner(s):**
Philosophy Documentation Center
Bowling Green State University
Bowling Green, OH 43402
Telephone: (419) 372-2419
Ownership %: 100
**Management:**
Cindy Richards ....................Business Manager
**Editorial:**
Archie J. Bahm ..........................................Editor
Kathleen Tweney .........Administrative Assistant
Richard H. Lineback ..............................Director
**Desc.:** Covers philosophy in the United
States and Canada. Provides information
on colleges and universities, centers and
institutes, societies, journals
and publishers. Includes addresses and
phone numbers of philosophy
departments as well as department
chairs, philosophy faculty, and degrees,
rank.

23911
## DRUGS & DRUG ABUSE EDUCATION
P.O. Box 20754
Seattle, WA 98102
FAX: (206) 322-8387
Year Established: 1971
Pub. Frequency: m.
Page Size: standard
Subscrip. Rate: $89/yr.; $104/yr. foreign
**Owner(s):**
Editorial Resources, Inc./Substance Abuse
News Svc
1060-A National Press Bldg.
Washington, DC 20045
Telephone: (202) 783-2929
Ownership %: 100
**Management:**
David L. Howell ................................Publisher
D.D. Hancock ....................................Manager
**Editorial:**
David L. Howell ......................................Editor
**Desc.:** Covers all aspects of the drug
abuse and alcoholism treatment and
prevention scene. This includes research
developments, educational techniques,
legislation, law enforcement trends,
treatment methods, prevention news.
Also includes calendar of events and
book reviews.
**Readers:** Treatment professionals (public,
private, military), school administrators,
guidance personnel, law enforcement
personnel.

59573
## DUKE MATHEMATICAL JOURNAL
Brightleaf Sq., Ste. 18B
805 W. Main St.
Durham, NC 27701
Telephone: (919) 684-5636
FAX: (919) 688-4574
Mailing Address:
P.O Box 90660
Durham, NC 27708-0660
Year Established: 1935
Pub. Frequency: m.
Page Size: standard
Subscrip. Rate: $288/yr. individuals;
$576/yr. institutions
Circulation: 1,200
Circulation Type: paid
**Owner(s):**
Duke University Press
P.O. Box 90660
Durham, NC 27708-0660
Telephone: (919) 684-2173
FAX: (919) 688-4574
Ownership %: 100
**Management:**
Patricia Thomas ..................................Manager
**Editorial:**
Morris Weisfeld ......................................Editor

**Desc.:** Publishes 2,000 pages per year of
original research in all areas of
mathematics and its applications.

24736
## EDUCATION
1362 Santa Cruz Ct.
Chula Vista, CA 91910-7114
Telephone: (619) 421-9377
Year Established: 1880
Pub. Frequency: q.
Page Size: standard
Subscrip. Rate: $20/yr. individual; $26/yr.
institution
Materials: 02,29
Circulation: 3,500
Circulation Type: paid
**Owner(s):**
Project Innovation
1362 Santa Cruz Ct.
Chula Vista, CA 91910
Telephone: (619) 421-9377
Ownership %: 100
**Editorial:**
Russell N. Cassel ....................................Editor
Lan Cassel ............................Managing Editor
Lan Cassel ........................Book Review Editor
**Desc.:** Articles on curriculum, instructional
procedures, practices, trends,
philosophy, and literature of education.
Reviews professional and children's
books.
**Readers:** College and university
professors.

24737
## EDUCATION & TRAINING IN MENTAL RETARDATION
1920 Association Dr.
Reston, VA 22091
Telephone: (703) 620-3660
Year Established: 1966
Pub. Frequency: q.
Page Size: standard
Subscrip. Rate: $30/yr. individual; $55/yr.
institution
Circulation: 9,800
Circulation Type: controlled
**Owner(s):**
Council for Exceptional Children
1920 Association Dr.
Reston, VA 22091
Telephone: (703) 620-3660
Ownership %: 100
**Editorial:**
Stanley H. Zucker ....................................Editor
**Desc.:** Material that is of interest and value
to persons working with children and
young adults with mental retardation or
developmental disabilities.
**Readers:** Primarily, teachers, and
education professionals.

64982
## EDUCATION & URBAN SOCIETY
2455 Teller Rd.
Thousand Oaks, CA 91320
Telephone: (805) 499-0721
FAX: (805) 499-0871
Pub. Frequency: q.
Page Size: standard
Subscrip. Rate: $45/yr. individual; $135/yr.
institution
Circulation: 1,100
Circulation Type: paid
**Owner(s):**
Sage Publications, Inc.
2455 Teller Rd.
Thousand Oaks, CA 91320
Telephone: (805) 499-0721
Ownership %: 100
**Management:**
Cris Anderson ....................Circulation Manager

**Desc.:** Education & Urban Society provides
through theme-organized issues
prepared under guest editors, a forum
for social scientific research on
education as a social institutions within
urban environments, the politics of
educations, and educational institutions
and processes as agents of social
change.

64984
## EDUCATIONAL ADMINISTRATION ABSTRACTS
2455 Teller Rd.
Thousand Oaks, CA 91320
Telephone: (805) 499-0721
FAX: (805) 499-0871
Pub. Frequency: q.
Page Size: standard
Subscrip. Rate: $79/yr. individual; $250/yr.
institution
Circulation: 1,000
Circulation Type: paid
**Owner(s):**
Sage Publications, Inc.
2455 Teller Rd.
Thousand Oaks, CA 91320
Telephone: (805) 499-0721
Ownership %: 100
**Editorial:**
Paul V. McDowell ....................................Editor
**Desc.:** Educational Administration
Abstracts provides abstracts drawn from
more than 140 professional journals
relating to educational administration.
**Readers:** Academic communities.

64983
## EDUCATIONAL ADMINISTRATION QUARTERLY
2455 Teller Rd.
Thousand Oaks, CA 91320
Telephone: (805) 499-0721
FAX: (805) 499-0871
Pub. Frequency: q.
Page Size: standard
Subscrip. Rate: $45/yr. individual; $130/yr.
institution
Circulation: 2,100
Circulation Type: paid
**Owner(s):**
Sage Publications, Inc.
2455 Teller Rd.
Thousand Oaks, CA 91320
Telephone: (805) 499-0721
Ownership %: 100
**Editorial:**
James G. Cibulka ....................................Editor
**Desc.:** Published in cooperation with the
University Council for Educational
Administration. It seeks to stimulate
critical thought and to disseminate the
latest knowledge about research and
practice in educational administration.
**Readers:** Academic communities

68830
## EDUCATIONAL FORUM, THE
1601 W. State St.
West Lafayette, IN 47906-0576
Telephone: (317) 743-1705
FAX: (317) 743-2202
Year Established: 1936
Pub. Frequency: 4/yr.
Page Size: standard
Subscrip. Rate: $16/yr. US; $18/yr. foreign
Materials: 06,10,32
Print Process: web
Circulation: 3,600
Circulation Type: free

**Owner(s):**
Kappa Delta Pi International Honor Society
in Ed.
P.O. Box A
West Lafayette, IN 47906-0576
Telephone: (317) 743-1705
FAX: (317) 743-2202
Ownership %: 100
**Editorial:**
Carol Bloom ..........................................Editor
**Desc.:** Presents scholarly inquiries that
generate new knowledge and insights
on issues of great importance in the
improvement of education, presenting
culturally and intellectually diverse
viewpoints for learned discussion of
these issues.
**Readers:** university professors of
education, education graduate students,
educational leaders, classroom teachers.

24739
## EDUCATIONAL LEADERSHIP
1250 N. Pitt St.
Alexandria, VA 22314
Telephone: (703) 549-9110
FAX: (703) 549-3891
Year Established: 1943
Pub. Frequency: 8/yr.
Page Size: standard
Subscrip. Rate: $36/yr.
Freelance Pay: negotiable
Circulation: 178,000
Circulation Type: paid
**Owner(s):**
Assn. for Supervision & Curriculum
Development
1250 N. Pitt St.
Alexandria, VA 22314
Telephone: (703) 549-9110
Ownership %: 100
**Management:**
Gene R. Carter ....................Executive Director
Teola T. Jones ..................Advertising Manager
**Editorial:**
Ronald S. Brandt ....................Executive Editor
Marge Scherer ......................Managing Editor
Becky DeRigge ...........Administrative Assistant
Gary Bloom ..................................Art Director
JoAnn Irick Jones ....................Associate Editor
Mary Walker ............................Associate Editor
Mary Beth Nielson ................Editorial Assistant
Stephanie Kenworthy ......................Production
Nancy Modrak ....................Publication Editor
**Desc.:** Official journal of association for
supervision and curriculum development.
Its focus is in the curriculum area; its
main object is the general improvement
of instruction and supervision. Most
issues develop a theme.
**Readers:** Read principally by those
interested in elementary and secondary
schools. Professional classifications
include elementary and secondary
principals, supervisors, curriculum
directors, assistant superintendents,
professors in education,
superintendents, directors of and private
schools, and libraries.

24740
## EDUCATIONAL RESEARCHER
1230 17th St., N.W.
Washington, DC 20036-3078
Telephone: (202) 223-9485
FAX: (202) 775-1824
Year Established: 1972
Pub. Frequency: 9/yr.
Page Size: standard
Subscrip. Rate: $39/yr. individuals; $51/yr.
institutions
Circulation: 19,000
Circulation Type: controlled

---

**Materials Accepted/Included:** 01-Business news 02-By-line articles 03-Fashion news 04-Food news 05-Freelance copy 06-Letters to editor 07-Real estate news 08-Sports news 09-Travel news 10-Book rev. 11-Movie rev. 12-Music rev. 13-TV rev. 14-Theater rev. 15-Coming events 16-Obituaries 17-Question & answer 18-Social announcements 19-Artwork 20-Cartoons 21-Photos 22-TV listings 23-Audio rec. 24-Video rec. 25-Books 26-Films/film clips 27-Personnel news 28-Press releases 29-New product news/photos 30-Trade lit. 31-Contracts awarded 32-Display adv. 33-Classified adv.

**Owner(s):**
American Educational Research
　Association
1230 17th St., N.W.
Washington, DC 20036
Telephone: (202) 223-9485
Ownership %: 100
**Management:**
William Russell ....................Executive Director
**Editorial:**
Robert E. Floden ..........................................Editor
Lauren Sosniak ..................Book Review Editor
Susan L. Wantland ..........Publication Director
**Desc.:** News and commentary on events in
　the field of educational research; articles
　which synthesize or analyze in a
　scholarly fashion matters of general
　significance to research in
　education. Special features include
　interviews with prominent individuals in
　the field and review essays on
　significant publications. The ER
　news section reports events and
　developments of specialized interest to
　the educational research community.
　Departments include: Editorials, Letters,
　Brief Notes, Meetings,
　Professional Activities.
**Readers:** University faculty in educational
　research.

### EDUCATIONAL TECHNOLOGY
24741
700 Palisade Ave.
Englewood Cliffs, NJ 07632
Telephone: (201) 871-4007
FAX: (201) 871-4009
Year Established: 1961
Pub. Frequency: m.
Page Size: standard
Subscrip. Rate: $119/yr.
Materials: 01,02,06,28,29,30,32
Print Process: offset
**Owner(s):**
Educational Technology Publications, Inc.
700 Palisade Ave.
Englewood Cliffs, NJ 07632
Telephone: (201) 871-4007
FAX: (201) 871-4009
Ownership %: 100
**Management:**
L. Lipsitz ...............................................President
L. Lipsitz ...............................................Publisher
**Editorial:**
L. Lipsitz ...................................Executive Editor
**Desc.:** Developments in computer-aided
　learning, educational television,
　corporate training, media news,
　computer news, new products reviews.
　Departments include: news, new
　equipment and materials, research, book
　reviews, interactive video, and other new
　optical technologies.
**Readers:** School administrators, trainers,
　professors, teachers, instructional
　designers, software developers, media
　personnel
**Deadline:** story-1st of mo.

### EDUCATIONAL THEORY
69518
1310 S. Sixth St.
Champaign, IL 61820
Telephone: (217) 333-3003
FAX: (217) 244-7064
Year Established: 1951
Pub. Frequency: q.
Subscrip. Rate: $20/yr. US individuals;
　$30/yr. US institutions; $22/yr. foreign
　individuals; $32/yr. foreign institutions
Circulation: 2,200
Circulation Type: paid

**Owner(s):**
University of Illinois at Urbana-Champaign
College of Education
1310 S. Sixth St.
Champaign, IL 61820
Telephone: (217) 333-3003
Ownership %: 100
**Editorial:**
Nicholas C. Barbules .................................Editor

### EDUCATION DIGEST, THE
24738
275 Metty Dr., Ste. 1
Ann Arbor, MI 48103
Telephone: (313) 769-1211
FAX: (313) 769-8383
Mailing Address:
　P.O. Box 8623
　Ann Arbor, MI 48107-8623
Year Established: 1934
Pub. Frequency: m.: Sep.-May
Page Size: digest
Subscrip. Rate: $36/yr.
Materials: 06,10,15,20,25,28,29,32,33
Freelance Pay: negotiable
Print Process: web offset
Circulation: 23,000
Circulation Type: paid
**Owner(s):**
Prakken Publications, Inc.
275 Metty Dr., Ste. 1
Ann Arbor, MI 48105
Telephone: (313) 769-1211
FAX: (313) 769-8383
Ownership %: 100
**Management:**
George F. Kennedy .............................Publisher
Alice B. Augustus .............Advertising Manager
Janice Knope ...........................Business Manager
Turalee Barlow ...................Circulation Manager
**Editorial:**
Kenneth Schroeder .................Managing Editor
Terence N. Tice .......................Editorial Advisor
Vicki Hubert .........................Marketing Manager
**Desc.:** Carries condensations of articles
　dealing with education, public and
　private schools, preschool through
　higher education. No original articles.
　Reports on Washington trends affecting
　the profession; educational news
　items/new educational materials/books,
　literature, audio-visual material. Also,
　columns on tips for teachers, research
　review, and peacekeeping for educators.
**Readers:** Broad educational readership,
　including superintendents, high school
　and elementary principals, school media
　centers, teachers, teacher educators
　and parents.
**Deadline:** story-1st of 2nd mo. prior to
　pub. date; news-1st of mo. prior; photo-
　1st of 2nd mo. prior; ads-25th of 2nd
　mo. prior

### EDUCATION WEEK
57263
4301 Connecticut Ave., N.W., Ste. 250
Washington, DC 20008
Telephone: (202) 364-4114
Year Established: 1981
Pub. Frequency: 40/yr.
Page Size: tabloid
Subscrip. Rate: $59.94/yr.
Print Process: web offset
Circulation: 50,000
Circulation Type: paid
**Owner(s):**
Editorial Projects in Education
4301 Connecticut Ave., N.W., S
Washington, DC 20008
Telephone: (202) 364-4114
Ownership %: 100
**Management:**
Ronald A. Wolk ...................................Publisher
Michael P. McKenna ........Advertising Manager

**Editorial:**
Virginia Edwards ........................Exec. Editor
Ronald A. Wolk ...................................Editor
Karen Creedon ....................Marketing Director
**Desc.:** A national, independent, weekly
　newspaper of record on elementary and
　secondary education, public and private.
　It is published by Editorial Projects in
　Education, Inc., the nonprofit, tax-
　exempt organization that founded the
　Chronicle of Higher Education.
**Readers:** Some 87.9% of readers are
　principals, teachers, administrators,
　superintendents, or professors.

### EDUCATORS' ADVOCATE
24742
411 E. Capitol
Pierre, SD 57501
Telephone: (605) 224-9263
FAX: (605) 224-5810
Year Established: 1958
Pub. Frequency: Aug.-May
Page Size: standard
Subscrip. Rate: $5/yr.
Materials: 32
Print Process: offset
Circulation: 8,400
Circulation Type: controlled
**Owner(s):**
SDEA/NEA
411 E. Capitol
Pierre, SD 57501
Telephone: (605) 224-9263
Ownership %: 100
**Editorial:**
Bob Stevens ...........Communications Specialist
**Desc.:** Both house news and in depth
　treatment of educational topics.
**Readers:** Educators, college students in
　education

### ELEMENTARY SCHOOL JOURNAL
24743
5720 S. Woodlawn Ave.
Chicago, IL 60637
Mailing Address:
　1507 E Broadway Hillcrest Hall
　Columbia, MO 65211
Year Established: 1900
Pub. Frequency: 5/yr. May-Sep.
Page Size: oversize
Subscrip. Rate: $19.50/yr. students;
　$29.50/yr. individuals; $56 institutions
Circulation: 5,500
Circulation Type: paid
**Owner(s):**
Dept. of Ed. and Un. of Chicago Press
Telephone: (708) 753-3332
**Management:**
Sally Merar .........................Advertising Manager
**Editorial:**
Thomas L. Good .......................................Editor
Gail M. Hinkel ..........................Managing Editor
**Desc.:** Features articles of general interest
　to teachers and administrators of
　elementary schools. Reports of
　significant research in the field of
　elementary education. It also contains
　articles of interest and concern to those
　who prepare elementary school
　teachers.
**Readers:** Elementary school principals,
　school superintendents, school teachers,
　professors of educations, education
　researchers.

### ENGLISH JOURNAL
68821
1111 W. Kenyon Rd.
Urbana, IL 61801-1096
Telephone: (217) 328-3870
Year Established: 1912
Pub. Frequency: 8/yr.
Subscrip. Rate: $40/yr. individual; $50/yr.
　institutional
Circulation: 57,500

Circulation Type: paid
**Owner(s):**
National Council of Teachers of English
1111 W. Kenyon Rd.
Urbana, IL 61801-1096
Telephone: (217) 328-3870
Ownership %: 100
**Editorial:**
Ben Nelms ...............................................Editor

### ETHNOHISTORY
59567
Brightleaf Sq., Ste. 18-B
Durham, NC 27701
Telephone: (919) 687-3636
FAX: (919) 688-4574
Mailing Address:
　P.O. Box 90660
　Durham, NC 27708
Pub. Frequency: q.
Page Size: standard
Subscrip. Rate: $24/yr. individuals; $38/yr.
　institutions
Circulation: 1,300
Circulation Type: paid
**Owner(s):**
American Society for Ethnohistory
Newberry Library
c/o  W. O. Autry
Chicago, IL 60610
Ownership %: 100
**Management:**
Patricia Thomas ...................................Manager
**Editorial:**
Ross Hassig .............................................Editor
**Desc.:** It has established a strong
　reputation for its studies of native
　peoples in the Americas and has
　recently opened its pages to encourage
　the combination of approaches and
　materials from history and anthropology
　in the study of social and cultural
　processes.

### ETR&D: EDUCATIONAL TECHNOLOGY RESEARCH & DEVELOPMENT
24734
1025 Vermont Ave., N.W., Ste. 820
Washington, DC 20005-3516
Telephone: (202) 347-7834
FAX: (202) 347-7839
Year Established: 1953
Pub. Frequency: 4/yr.
Page Size: 6 3/4 x 9 3/4
Subscrip. Rate: $45/yr. US; $53/yr. foreign
Circulation: 5,000
Circulation Type: paid
**Owner(s):**
Assn. for Educational Communications &
　Technology
1025 Vermont Ave., N.W., Ste.8
Washington, DC 20005-3516
Telephone: (202) 347-7834
Ownership %: 100
**Management:**
Kent Gustafson ....................................President
Stan Zenor .............................Executive Director
**Editorial:**
Steve Ross ...............................................Editor
Norman Higgins ........................................Editor
Robert Braden ....................Book Review Editor
**Desc.:** All articles have by-lines; coverage
　is devoted to the research, theory, and
　comment of all phases of educational
　technology and communications.
　Departments include: Book Reviews,
　Research Abstracts, and International
　Letters.
**Readers:** Leaders in instructional
　technology.

---

**Materials Accepted/Included:** 01-Business news 02-By-line articles 03-Fashion news 04-Food news 05-Freelance copy 06-Letters to editor 07-Real estate news 08-Sports news 09-Travel news 10-Book rev. 11-Movie rev. 12-Music rev. 13-TV rev. 14-Theater rev. 15-Coming events 16-Obituaries 17-Question & answer 18-Social announcements 19-Artwork 20-Cartoons 21-Photos 22-TV listings 23-Audio rec. 24-Video rec. 25-Books 26-Films/film clips 27-Personnel news 28-Press releases 29-New product news/photos 30-Trade lit. 31-Contracts awarded 32-Display adv. 33-Classified adv.

## EXCEPTIONAL CHILD EDUCATION RESOURCES
24746
1920 Association Dr.
Reston, VA 22091
Telephone: (703) 620-3660
Year Established: 1968
Pub. Frequency: q.
Page Size: standard
Subscrip. Rate: $20/copy; $75/yr.
Circulation: 1,000
Circulation Type: paid
**Owner(s):**
The Council for Exceptional Children
1920 Association Dr.
Reston, VA 22091
Telephone: (703) 620-3660
Ownership %: 100
**Editorial:**
Kathleen McLane ........................................Editor
Janet Drill ........................Coordinating Editor
**Desc.:** Publication contains abstracts of published literature in special education covering the education and development of gifted individuals and persons with handicaps.
**Readers:** Colleges and universities; libraries, individual researchers.

## EXCEPTIONAL CHILDREN
24747
1920 Association Dr.
Reston, VA 22091
Telephone: (703) 620-3660
FAX: (703) 264-9454
Year Established: 1934
Pub. Frequency: bi-m.
Page Size: standard
Subscrip. Rate: $45/yr.
Circulation: 57,525
Circulation Type: paid
**Owner(s):**
The Council for Exceptional Children
1920 Association Dr.
Reston, VA 22091
Telephone: (703) 620-3660
Ownership %: 100
**Management:**
James Casamento ............Advertising Manager
**Editorial:**
Naomi Zigmond ..........................Editor in Chief
Cathy Mack ..........................Production Editor
**Desc.:** Research, trend and issues in special education.
**Readers:** Administrators, researchers, college faculty, college students, district level supervisors, psychologists and consultants.

## EXECUTIVE EDUCATOR
69551
1680 Duke St.
Alexandria, VA 22314
Telephone: (703) 838-6722
FAX: (703) 683-7590
Year Established: 1979
Pub. Frequency: m.
Page Size: standard
Subscrip. Rate: $53/yr.
Materials: 02,05,06,10,19,25,32,33
Circulation: 18,000
**Owner(s):**
National School Boards Association
1680 Duke St.
Alexandria, VA 22314
Telephone: (703) 838-6722
Ownership %: 100
**Editorial:**
Gregg Downey, Editor ................................Editor

## FLORIDA MUSIC DIRECTOR
24748
207 Office Plaza Dr.
Tallahassee, FL 32301
Telephone: (904) 878-6845
FAX: (904) 942-1793
Year Established: 1947
Pub. Frequency: 10/yr.
Page Size: standard
Subscrip. Rate: $10/yr. for members
Materials: 01,02,06,15,19,27,29,30,32
Print Process: offset
Circulation: 4,400
Circulation Type: paid
**Owner(s):**
Florida Music Educators Association
207 Office Plaza Dr.
Tallahassee, FL 32301
Telephone: (904) 878-6845
Ownership %: 100
**Management:**
Vicki Miazga ........................Advertising Manager
**Editorial:**
Charles R. Hoffer ........................................Editor
Vicki Miazga ..............Communications Director
**Desc.:** Carries material of interest to music educators and school administrators. Official magazine of Florida Music Educators Association and Florida State Music Teachers Association.
**Readers:** School and college administrators, music educators and education students.
**Deadline:** story-45 days prior to pub. date; news-45 days prior; photo-45 days prior; ads-1 mo. prior

## FOCUS ON AUTISTIC BEHAVIOR
70468
8700 Shoal Creek Blvd.
Austin, TX 78757-6897
Telephone: (512) 451-3246
FAX: (512) 451-8542
Year Established: 1986
Pub. Frequency: bi-m.
Page Size: standard
Subscrip. Rate: $20/yr. individual; $40/yr. institutions
Materials: 15,32,33
Circulation: 1,249
Circulation Type: free & paid
**Owner(s):**
Pro-Ed Journals
8700 Shoal Creek Blvd.
Austin, TX 78757-6897
Telephone: (512) 451-3246
FAX: (512) 451-8542
Ownership %: 100
**Management:**
Donald D. Hammill ................................Publisher
**Editorial:**
Richard Simpson ........................Editor in Chief
Lisa Tippett ........................Managing Editor
**Desc.:** Practical elements of management, treatment, planning and education for persons with autism and pervasive developmental disorders.
**Readers:** Educators, psychologists, clinicians and other professionals interested in autism and pervasive developmental disorders.

## FORECAST FOR THE HOME ECONOMIST
24750
730 Broadway
New York, NY 10003
Telephone: (212) 343-6100
Year Established: 1954
Pub. Frequency: 8/yr. includes double issue
Page Size: standard
Subscrip. Rate: $19.95/yr.
Circulation: 50,000
Circulation Type: paid
**Owner(s):**
Scholastic, Inc.
740 Broadway
New York, NY 10003
Telephone: (212) 505-3000
Ownership %: 100
**Management:**
M. Richard Robinson ..........Chairman of Board
Stephen Bernard ........................Vice President
Robert Mitchell ........................Business Manager
Richard Walsh ................Editorial Production Manager
**Editorial:**
Victoria Chapman ................Editorial Director
Margaret Massa ........................................Art Editor
Cathy Carr ................................Assistant Editor
Barbara Sullivan ........................Miscellaneous
Jeanne Josephson ..............Research Director
**Desc.:** A professional journal for home economists, with reports on the latest developments, ideas, and products in the field.
**Readers:** Home economics teachers and professional home economists in business.

## FOREST & CONSERVATION HISTORY
59566
701 Vickers Ave.
Durham, NC 27701-3147
Telephone: (919) 682-9319
Year Established: 1957
Pub. Frequency: q.
Page Size: oversize
Subscrip. Rate: $30/yr. individual; $50/yr. institution
Materials: 32
Print Process: offset
Circulation: 2,200
Circulation Type: paid
**Owner(s):**
Forest History Society
701 Vickers Ave.
Durham, NC 27701-3147
Telephone: (919) 682-9319
Ownership %: 100
**Editorial:**
Kevin Foy ................................................Editor
Alice Poffinberger ....................Assistant Editor
**Desc.:** Research articles pertaining to the conservation, management, commercial use, history, environment, and artistic depiction of natural resources and landscapes, especially forests throughout the United States and the world.
**Readers:** Historians, forecasters, natural scientists.

## FORUM
24844
118 N. Monroe St.
Tallahassee, FL 32301
Telephone: (904) 224-1161
FAX: (904) 681-2905
Year Established: 1980
Pub. Frequency: q.
Page Size: standard
Subscrip. Rate: $10/yr.
Freelance Pay: negotiable
Circulation: 57,000
Circulation Type: controlled
**Owner(s):**
Florida Education Assn.-United
118 N. Monroe St.
Tallahassee, FL 32301
Telephone: (904) 224-1161
Ownership %: 100
**Management:**
Pat L. Tornillo, Jr. ................................President
Sam W. Lewis ........................Vice President
Laura Lamb ....................Advertising Manager
**Editorial:**
April Herrle ............................Managing Editor
Ron Sachs ................Communications Director
Carey Mcnamara ................Graphics Coordinator
Robert F. Lee ................Secretary & Treasurer
**Desc.:** Covers news and issues of interest to teachers, education employees, faculty and union members.
**Readers:** Teachers, public employees, university faculty, general education system employees, legislators, state press.

## FRENCH HISTORICAL STUDIES
70445
905 W. Main St., Ste. 18-B
Durham University Press
Durham, NC 27701
Telephone: (919) 687-3636
FAX: (919) 688-4574
Mailing Address:
 P.O. Box 90660
 Durham, NC 27708
Year Established: 1958
Pub. Frequency: s-a.
Page Size: standard
Subscrip. Rate: $20/yr. individuals; $30/yr. institutions
Materials: 32
Circulation: 1,200
Circulation Type: controlled & paid
**Owner(s):**
Duke University Press
P.O. Box 90660
Durham, NC 27708-0660
Telephone: (919) 687-3600
FAX: (919) 688-4574
Ownership %: 100
**Management:**
Patricia Thomas ................................Manager
**Editorial:**
James R. Farr ............................................Editor
John J. Contreni ........................................Editor

## FRENCH REVIEW, THE
24751
57 E. Armory Ave.
Champaign, IL 61820
Telephone: (217) 333-2842
FAX: (217) 333-2842
Year Established: 1927
Pub. Frequency: 6/yr.
Page Size: standard
Subscrip. Rate: $35/yr. US; $38/yr. foreign
Circulation: 12,000
Circulation Type: paid
**Owner(s):**
American Assn. of Teachers of French
57 E. Armory Ave.
Champaign, IL 61820
Telephone: (217) 333-2842
FAX: (217) 333-2842
Ownership %: 100
**Management:**
Rebecca Valette ................................President
Edwards Bros ........................................Publisher
W. O. Goode ....................Advertising Manager
**Editorial:**
Ronald W. Tobin ........................................Editor
Leona LeBlanc ........................Managing Editor
**Desc.:** Articles on literary history (French), pedagogical articles (teaching of French, language, literature, culture), materials for teaching French: books, records, tapes, maps, charts, gadgets, films, TV, and anything that might interest teachers of French. Departments include literary, pedagogical, civilization, elementary schools, and review sections dealing with scholarly books, original literary works, textbooks, books about France.
**Readers:** Teachers of French at all levels.

## GERMANIC REVIEW, THE
54089
1319 18th St., N.W.
Washington, DC 20036-1802
Telephone: (202) 296-6267
FAX: (202) 296-5149
Year Established: 1926
Pub. Frequency: q.
Page Size: standard
Subscrip. Rate: $32/yr. individuals; $64/yr. institutions; add $10 outside of US
Circulation: 841

**Materials Accepted/Included:** 01-Business news 02-By-line articles 03-Fashion news 04-Food news 05-Freelance copy 06-Letters to editor 07-Real estate news 08-Sports news 09-Travel news 10-Book rev. 11-Movie rev. 12-Music rev. 13-TV rev. 14-Theater rev. 15-Coming events 16-Obituaries 17-Question & answer 18-Social announcements 19-Artwork 20-Cartoons 21-Photos 22-TV listings 23-Audio rec. 24-Video rec. 25-Books 26-Films/film clips 27-Personnel news 28-Press releases 29-New product news/photos 30-Trade lit. 31-Contracts awarded 32-Display adv. 33-Classified adv.

4-337

Circulation Type: paid
**Owner(s):**
Heldref Publications
1319 18th St., N.W.
Washington, DC 20036-1802
Telephone: (202) 296-6267
Ownership %: 100
**Management:**
Walter E. Beach .....................Publisher
Raymond M. Rallo ...........Advertising Manager
Catherine Welker ..............Circulation Manager
Kerri P. Kilbane .................Promotion Manager
**Editorial:**
Heidi Whitesell .....................................Editor
**Desc.:** A highly respected, timely journal of
Germanic languages and literatures.
Each issue delivers to its readers
thoroughly documented, clear, and
concise analysis of prose and poetry
from German literature and thoughtful
reviews of the newest books in the field.
**Readers:** College & university scholars
worldwide, as well as non-academicians
with an interest in germanic languages &
literature.

55923
## HARVARD BUSINESS SCHOOL BULLETIN
Ludcke Center, Soldiers Field
Boston, MA 02163
Telephone: (617) 495-6554
FAX: (617) 496-8180
Pub. Frequency: bi-m.
Page Size: 4 color photos/art
Subscrip. Rate: free to alumni; $35/yr. US.;
$50/yr. foreign
Circulation: 57,000
Circulation Type: free & paid
**Owner(s):**
Harvard University
Boston, MA 02163
Ownership %: 100
**Editorial:**
Deborah Balgg ...............................Editor

69514
## HARVARD EDUCATIONAL REVIEW
6 Appian Way, Ste. 349
Cambridge, MA 02138
Telephone: (617) 495-3432
Year Established: 1931
Pub. Frequency: q.
Subscrip. Rate: $39/yr. individuals; $76/yr.
institutions
Materials: 06,10,32
Print Process: offset
Circulation: 9,750
Circulation Type: free & paid
**Owner(s):**
Harvard University, Graduate School of
Education
Gutman Library
6 Appian Way, Ste. 349
Cambridge, MA 02138
Telephone: (617) 495-3432
**Management:**
Karen Maloney ......................................Publisher
Joan Gorman ..................Advertising Manager
Karen Maloney ..................Circulation Manager
**Editorial:**
Dody Riggs .............................Managing Editor
**Desc.:** Scholarly quarterly in education.
**Readers:** Education Administrators and
higher education faculty, teachers.

24755
## HISPANIA
Georgetown University
Spanish Department
Washington, DC 20057-0989
Telephone: (202) 687-6124
Year Established: 1917
Pub. Frequency: q.
Page Size: standard
Subscrip. Rate: $30/yr.; $15/yr. students
Materials: 32

Freelance Pay: none
Circulation: 13,000
Circulation Type: paid
**Owner(s):**
American Assn. of Teachers of Spanish &
Portuguese
106 Gunter Hall
Univ. of Northern Colorado
Greeley, CO 80639
Ownership %: 100
**Management:**
Prof. Walter C. Oliver .......Advertising Manager
**Editorial:**
Prof. Estelle Irizarry ....................Editor in Chief
**Desc.:** Articles by members of American
Association of Teachers of Spanish and
Portuguese only, discussing literature,
language, and pedagogy, in relation
to Spanish and Portuguese.
Departments include: professional news,
linguistics, chapter news, book reviews,
The Hispanic World (news items of
social and educational significance,
obituaries, etc.). Multimedia, pedagogy.
**Readers:** Teachers and professors of
Spanish and Portuguese in U.S., also in
Canada, Europe, Latin America, and
Australia.

59570
## HISPANIC AMERICAN HISTORICAL REVIEW
Brightleaf Square, Ste. 18-B
805 Main St.
Durham, NC 27701
Telephone: (919) 687-3636
FAX: (919) 688-4574
Mailing Address:
P.O. Box 90660
Durham, NC 27708
Pub. Frequency: q.
Page Size: standard
Subscrip. Rate: $40/individual; $80/yr.
institution; $20/yr. students with current
ID
Circulation: 2,400
Circulation Type: paid
**Owner(s):**
Duke University Press
P.O. Box 90660
Durham, NC 27708-0660
Telephone: (919) 687-3600
FAX: (919) 688-4574
Ownership %: 100
**Management:**
Patricia Thomas ................................Manager
**Editorial:**
Mark Szuchman ..................................Editor

58579
## HISTORY OF PHILOSOPHY QUARTERLY
Philosophy Docum. Center
Bowling Green State Univ.
Bowling Green, OH 43403-0189
Telephone: (419) 372-2419
FAX: (419) 372-6987
Year Established: 1984
Pub. Frequency: q.
Subscrip. Rate: $34/yr. individuals;
$135/yr. institutions
Circulation: 437
Circulation Type: paid
**Owner(s):**
North American Philosophical Publications,
Inc.
1201 Cathedral of Learning
Pittsburgh, PA 15260
Telephone: (412) 624-5950
Ownership %: 100
**Management:**
Cindy Richards ...................Business Manager
**Editorial:**
Nicholas Rescher ...............................Editor
Richard H. Lineback ..........................Director

**Desc.:** A scholarly journal that is devoted
to general surveys on particular topics
concerned with the history of
philosophy. It is particularly interested in
papers that cultivate philosophical
history in the spirit of "philosophia
perennis". The journal specializes in
papers that manifest a strong interaction
between contemporary and historical
concerns.

59572
## HISTORY OF POLITICAL ECONOMY
Brightleaf Sq.
805 W. Main St.
Durham, NC 27701
Telephone: (919) 687-3636
FAX: (919) 688-4574
Year Established: 1969
Pub. Frequency: q.
Page Size: standard
Subscrip. Rate: $55/yr. individual; $110/yr.
institutions; $28/yr. students with current
ID
Materials: 32
Circulation: 1,600
Circulation Type: paid
**Owner(s):**
Duke University Press
P.O. Box 90660
Durham, NC 27708-0660
Telephone: (919) 687-3600
FAX: (919) 688-4574
Ownership %: 100
**Management:**
Patricia Thomas ..................................Manager
**Editorial:**
Craufurd D. W. Goodwin ..........................Editor
**Desc.:** Widely acknowledged as a major
force in the development of this field of
study and remains its foremost means of
communication; a book review section is
included in each issue.

24758
## ILLINOIS SCHOOL BOARD JOURNAL
430 East Vine St.
Springfield, IL 62703-2236
Telephone: (217) 528-9688
FAX: (217) 528-2831
Year Established: 1934
Pub. Frequency: bi-m.
Page Size: standard
Subscrip. Rate: $12/yr.
Materials: 02,06,10,20,21,32
Print Process: offset
Circulation: 8,100
Circulation Type: paid
**Owner(s):**
Illinois Association of School Boards
430 East Vine St.
Springfield, IL 62703-2236
Telephone: (217) 528-9688
Ownership %: 100
**Management:**
Diane Cape .......................Advertising Manager
**Editorial:**
Gerald R. Glaub ...............................Editor
Jessica C. Billings ....................Managing Editor
Gary Adkins ..............................Assistant Editor
**Desc.:** Focuses on current issues that
affect school board policies and school
management. Twenty-five per cent of
copy written by staff, remainder
generally comes from Illinois educators
and others. Departments include:
Current Events, Public Relations, Humor
and Editorial Opinion.
**Readers:** Members of Illinois Association
of School Boards and other state and
local school officials.

24759
## INDEPENDENT SCHOOL
1620 L St., N.W.
Washington, DC 20036-5605
Telephone: (202) 973-9700
Year Established: 1940
Pub. Frequency: 3/yr.
Subscrip. Rate: $17.50/yr.
Circulation: 7,500
Circulation Type: paid
**Owner(s):**
National Assn. of Independent Schools
1620 L St., N.W.
Washington, DC 20036-5605
Telephone: (202) 973-9700
Ownership %: 100
**Management:**
Dr. Peter Relic ....................................President
**Editorial:**
Catherine O'neill ...............................Editor
Publisher Services Inc. ...................Advertising
**Desc.:** An open forum for exchange of
information and opinion about secondary
and elementary education in general,
and independent education in particular.
**Readers:** Teachers, administrators,
trustees, parents.

24760
## INDUSTRIAL EDUCATION
6557 Forest Park Dr.
Troy, MI 48098-1954
Telephone: (313) 358-4900
Year Established: 1911
Pub. Frequency: 10/yr.
Page Size: 4 color photos/art
Subscrip. Rate: $20/yr.
Freelance Pay: $25+/pg.
Circulation: 46,500
Circulation Type: controlled
**Owner(s):**
Cummins Publishing Co., Inc.
6557 Forest Park Dr.
Troy, MI 48098-1954
Telephone: (313) 358-4900
Ownership %: 100
**Management:**
Andrew Cummins ................................Publisher
**Editorial:**
Andrew Cummins ....................Executive Editor
Sue Becker ..........................................Editor
**Desc.:** This magazine thoroughly covers
the fields of industrial arts and
vocational and technical education as
they are being carried on in senior high
schools, teacher training schools,
colleges, universities, vocational schools
and technical schools. Its editorial
coverage embraces administration,
operation, organization, and teaching of
subjects in the field.

66698
## INSTRUCTOR
411 Lafayette St., 4th Fl.
New York, NY 10003
Telephone: (212) 505-4900
FAX: (212) 260-8595
Year Established: 1891
Pub. Frequency: 9/yr.
Page Size: standard
Subscrip. Rate: $14.95/yr. US; $27.95/yr.
foreign
Circulation: 254,361
Circulation Type: paid
**Owner(s):**
Scholastic Magazines, Inc.
730 Broadway
New York, NY 10003
Telephone: (212) 505-3000
Ownership %: 100
**Editorial:**
Debra Martorelli ...................Executive Editor
Lauren Leon ......................Managing Editor

---

**Materials Accepted/Included:** 01-Business news 02-By-line articles 03-Fashion news 04-Food news 05-Freelance copy 06-Letters to editor 07-Real estate news 08-Sports news 09-Travel news
10-Book rev. 11-Movie rev. 12-Music rev. 13-TV rev. 14-Theater rev. 15-Coming events 16-Obituaries 17-Question & answer 18-Social announcements 19-Artwork 20-Cartoons 21-Photos 22-TV listings
23-Audio rec. 24-Video rec. 25-Books 26-Films/film clips 27-Personnel news 28-Press releases 29-New product news/photos 30-Trade lit. 31-Contracts awarded 32-Display adv. 33-Classified adv.

**Desc.:** Features articles on a variety of topics of interest to elementary school teachers. Includes articles on computer applications for teaching techniques, educational software reviews and children's fiction book reviews.

58806

## INTERNATIONAL DIRECTORY OF PHILOSOPHY & PHILOSOPHERS

Philosophy Docum. Center
Bowling Green State Univ.
Bowling Green, OH 43402
Telephone: (419) 372-2419
FAX: (419) 372-6987
Pub. Frequency: every 4 yrs.
Page Size: standard
Subscrip. Rate: $89/yr. institutions
Circulation: 650
Circulation Type: paid
**Owner(s):**
Philosophy Documentation Ctr.
Bowling Green State University
Bowling Green, OH 43403-0189
Telephone: (419) 372-2419
Ownership %: 100
**Management:**
Cindy Richards ...................Business Manager
**Editorial:**
R. Cormier & R. H. Lineback ...................Editor
Kathleen Tweeny .........Administrative Assistant

69730

## INTERNATIONAL JOURNAL OF EDUCATIONAL REFORM

851 New Holland Ave.
Lancaster, PA 17604
Telephone: (717) 291-5609
FAX: (717) 295-4538
Mailing Address:
   P.O. Box 3535
   Lancaster, PA 17604
Year Established: 1992
Pub. Frequency: q.
Page Size: standard
Subscrip. Rate: $65/yr.; $120/2 yrs.;
   $175/3 yrs.
Circulation: 220
Circulation Type: paid
**Owner(s):**
Technomic Publishing Co., Inc.
851 New Holland Ave.
Lancaster, PA 17604
Telephone: (717) 291-5609
Ownership %: 100
**Editorial:**
Fenwick W. English ...................Editor
Betty E. Steffy ...................Editor
**Desc.:** Features the lastest strategies and tactics in education reform.

70446

## INTERNATIONAL MATHEMATICS RESEARCH NOTES

905 W. Main St., Ste. 18-B
Duke University Press
Durham, NC 27701
Telephone: (919) 687-3636
FAX: (919) 688-4574
Mailing Address:
   P.O. Box 90660
   Durham, NC 27708-0660
Year Established: 1993
Pub. Frequency: irregular
Page Size: standard
Subscrip. Rate: $300/yr. individuals;
   $600/yr. institutions
Materials: 32
**Owner(s):**
Duke University Press
P.O. Box 90660
Durham, NC 27701
Telephone: (919) 687-3636
FAX: (919) 688-4574
Ownership %: 100
**Management:**
Patricia Thomas ...................Manager

**Editorial:**
Morris Weisfeld ...................Editor

24686

## INTERVENTION IN SCHOOL & CLINIC

8700 Shoal Creek Blvd.
Austin, TX 78757-6897
Telephone: (512) 451-3246
FAX: (512) 451-8542
Year Established: 1965
Pub. Frequency: 5/yr.
Page Size: standard
Subscrip. Rate: $35/yr. individuals; $80/yr.
   institutions; $105/yr. foreign
Materials: 10,32,33
Print Process: offset
Circulation: 4,500
Circulation Type: paid
**Owner(s):**
Pro Ed Publications
8700 Shoal Creek Blvd.
Austin, TX 78757-6897
Telephone: (512) 451-3246
Ownership %: 100
**Editorial:**
Gerald Wallace ...................Editor
Lisa Tippett ...................Managing Editor
Judy Voress ...................Periodicals Director
**Desc.:** An interdisciplinary journal directed to an international audience involved in the field of learning, reading, and communication disabilities. The purpose is to make available a wide spectrum of methods for identification, diagnosis, and remediation of these disabilities.
**Readers:** Parents, educators, other professionals.
**Deadline:** story-2-3 mo. prior to pub. date; news-2-3 mo. prior to pub. date; photo-2-3 mo. prior to pub. date; ads-2-3 mo. prior to pub. date

24833

## ISTA ADVOCATE

150 W. Market St.
Indianapolis, IN 46204
Telephone: (317) 634-1515
FAX: (317) 237-6128
Pub. Frequency: 5/yr.
Page Size: tabloid
Subscrip. Rate: $6/yr.
Circulation: 52,000
Circulation Type: controlled
**Owner(s):**
Indiana State Teachers Association
150 W. Market St.
Indianapolis, IN 46204
Telephone: (317) 634-1515
Ownership %: 100
**Management:**
Garrett Harbron ...................President
Kathleen A. Berry ...................Advertising Manager
**Editorial:**
Warren L. Williams ...................Executive Editor
Kathleen A. Berry ...................Editor
**Desc.:** Educational Community
**Readers:** Teachers, superintendents, principals.

24763

## JOURNAL FOR RESEARCH IN MATHEMATICS EDUCATION

1906 Association Dr.
Reston, VA 22091
Telephone: (703) 620-9840
Year Established: 1970
Pub. Frequency: 5/yr.
Page Size: standard
Subscrip. Rate: $45/yr.
Circulation: 11,676
Circulation Type: paid

**Owner(s):**
National Council of Teachers of Mathematics
1906 Association Dr.
Reston, VA 22091
Telephone: (703) 620-9840
Ownership %: 100
**Management:**
Jack Price ...................President
James D. Gates ...................Executive Director
Rowena G. Martelino ...................Advertising Manager
Cynthia C. Rosso ...................Business Manager
Anthony Fragnito ...................Circulation Manager
**Editorial:**
Jean Armistead ...................Editor
Jean Carpenter ...................Editorial Associate
Harry Tunis ...................Publication Director
**Desc.:** Concerned with research into significant problems in mathematics education, elementary school through college. Includes reports of studies, articles about current research.
**Readers:** Math teachers, supervisors.

24764

## JOURNAL OF ADVENTIST EDUCATION

12501 Old Columbia Pike
Silver Spring, MD 20904-6600
Telephone: (301) 680-5075
FAX: (301) 622-9627
Year Established: 1939
Pub. Frequency: 5/yr.
Page Size: standard
Subscrip. Rate: $15.75/yr.
Freelance Pay: Up to $100
Circulation: 7,600
Circulation Type: controlled
**Owner(s):**
Dept. of Ed., Gen. Conf. of Seventh-Day Adventist
12501 Old Columbia Pike
Silver Spring, MD 20904
Telephone: (301) 680-5061
Ownership %: 100
**Editorial:**
Beverly J. Rumble ...................Editor
Clarence Dunbebin ...................Book Review Editor
L. Herbert Fletcher ...................Consulting Editor
A. C. Segovia ...................Consulting Editor
Roberto de Azevedo ...................Consulting Editor
K. Jesuratnam ...................Consulting Editor
Robert G. Pierson ...................Consulting Editor
Lester Devine ...................Consulting Editor
Shozo Tabuchi ...................Consulting Editor
Orville Woolford ...................Consulting Editor
V. S. Wakaba ...................Consulting Editor
Ronald Strasdowsky ...................Consulting Editor
Svein Johansen ...................Consulting Editor
Hudson Kibuuka ...................Consulting Editor
Gordon Madgwick ...................Consulting Editor
Gilbert Plubell ...................Consulting Editor
Harry Mayden ...................Consulting Editor
Enrique Becerra ...................Consulting Editor
T. S. Geraty ...................Editor Emeritus
G. J. Millet ...................Editor Emeritus
Jerome D. Thayer ...................Research Editor
**Desc.:** Deals with the procedures, philosophy, and subject matter of Christian education; is the official professional organ of the Department of Education covering elementary, secondary, and higher education for all Seventh-Day Adventist educational personnel, also official organ of the Association of Seventh-Day Adventist Educators.
**Readers:** Primarily school administrators and teachers.

58545

## JOURNAL OF AESTHETIC EDUCATION

54 E. Gregory Dr.
Champaign, IL 61820
Telephone: (217) 333-0950
FAX: (217) 244-8082
Year Established: 1966
Pub. Frequency: q.
Subscrip. Rate: $22/yr. individuals; $35/yr.
   institutions US; $29/yr. individuals;
   $42/yr. institutions foreign
Circulation: 1,050
Circulation Type: paid
**Owner(s):**
University of Illinois Press
54 E. Gregory Dr.
Champaign, IL 61820
Telephone: (217) 333-0950
Ownership %: 100
**Editorial:**
Ralph A. Smith ...................Editor
Karen A. Buckner ...................Journals Assistant
**Desc.:** An educational response to perennial challenges to improve the quality and style of our civilization. The major purpose of the journal is to clarify the issues of aesthetic education understood in its most extensive meaning, including not only the problems of formal institutions in the arts and the humanities at all levels of schooling, but also the aesthetic problems of the larger society created by twentieth century existence.
**Readers:** Scholars and teachers in arts education and philosophy of education.

22342

## JOURNAL OF CAREER PLANNING & EMPLOYMENT

62 Highland Ave.
Bethlehem, PA 18017
Telephone: (215) 868-1421
FAX: (215) 868-0208
Year Established: 1940
Pub. Frequency: q.
Page Size: standard
Subscrip. Rate: $72/yr.
Freelance Pay: $200-$400/article upon
   acceptance
Circulation: 4,200
Circulation Type: paid
**Owner(s):**
College Placement Council, Inc.
62 Highland Ave.
Bethlehem, PA 18017
Telephone: (215) 868-1421
Ownership %: 100
**Management:**
Michael Forrest ...................Publisher
Michael Forrest ...................Executive Director
Joan M. Bowser ...................Advertising Manager
**Editorial:**
Mimi Collins ...................Editor
Paula Ziegler ...................Art Director
William Beebe ...................Associate Editor
Claudia Allen ...................Associate Editor
Sarita E. Hunter ...................Circulation Editor
Kathleen E. Katchur ...................Circulation Editor
Valerie Patterson ...................Production Assistant
**Desc.:** The professional magazine of college career planning and placement directors and representatives of employers who hire college graduates. It features articles on career opportunities; original surveys; new and unusual employment; techniques employed to interest and retain graduates. Articles usually limited to a maximum of 12 double-spaced pages. Departments include: Career Media, New Resources, Dialogue, How Others Do It, Perceptions, Your Turn, Legal Questions and Answers.

**Materials Accepted/Included:** 01-Business news 02-By-line articles 03-Fashion news 04-Food news 05-Freelance copy 06-Letters to editor 07-Real estate news 08-Sports news 09-Travel news 10-Book rev. 11-Movie rev. 12-Music rev. 13-TV rev. 14-Theater rev. 15-Coming events 16-Obituaries 17-Question & answer 18-Social announcements 19-Artwork 20-Cartoons 21-Photos 22-TV listings 23-Audio rec. 24-Video rec. 25-Books 26-Films/film clips 27-Personnel news 28-Press releases 29-New product news/photos 30-Trade lit. 31-Contracts awarded 32-Display adv. 33-Classified adv.

4-339

**Readers:** Career planning and placement directors of four-year and two-year colleges and universities in the United States as well as personnel directors and recruiters of employers hiring college graduates.

24766
### JOURNAL OF COLLEGE SCIENCE TEACHING
3140 N. Washington Blvd.
Arlington, VA 22201
Telephone: (703) 243-7100
FAX: (703) 243-7177
Mailing Address:
  1840 Wilson Blvd.
  Arlington, VA 22201
Year Established: 1971
Pub. Frequency: 6/yr.
Page Size: standard
Subscrip. Rate: $52/yr.
Materials: 01,06,10,20,21,25,28,32
Print Process: offset
Circulation: 5,000
Circulation Type: free & paid
**Owner(s):**
National Science Teachers Association
1840 Wilson Blvd.
Arlington, VA 22201
Telephone: (703) 243-7100
FAX: (703) 243-7177
Ownership %: 100
**Management:**
Paul Kuntzler ....................Advertising Manager
**Editorial:**
Lester G. Paldy ..........................................Editor
Michael A. Byrnes ...................Managing Editor
Fred Rosenberg ................Book Review Editor
**Desc.:** Devoted to the teaching of science at the college level, principally in the introductory courses and courses for nonscience majors. Articles on philosophy and methods of teaching and practical how-to articles. Manuscript preparation guide offers full information.
**Readers:** College & university professors, some advanced level high school teachers (grades 11 & 12), science associations.
**Deadline:** story-2 mo. prior to pub. date; news-2 mo. prior; photo-2 mo. prior; ads-2 wks. prior

24952
### JOURNAL OF COUNSELING & DEVELOPMENT
5999 Stevenson Ave.
Alexandria, VA 22304
Telephone: (703) 823-9800
FAX: (703) 823-0252
Year Established: 1921
Pub. Frequency: bi-m.
Page Size: standard
Subscrip. Rate: $40/yr. individuals; $65/yr. institutions
Circulation: 60,000
Circulation Type: paid
**Owner(s):**
American Counseling Association
5999 Stevenson Ave.
Alexandria, VA 22304
Telephone: (703) 823-9800
Ownership %: 100
**Management:**
Libby B. Laker ...................Advertising Manager
Terry Ackerman ....................Production Manager
**Editorial:**
Dr. Edwin L. Herr ......................................Editor
Terry Ackerman ......................Managing Editor
Jennifer Sacks ..........Communications Director

**Desc.:** Contributed articles cover current professional and scientific issues, research reports of unusual significance to practitioners, critical integration of published research, new techniques or innovative practices and programs, and AACD as an organization and its role in society. Departments include: Letters and Comments.
**Readers:** Distributed nationally to AACD members and subscribers to the journal. Readership includes 48,000 professional counselors, counselor educators, and related human development specialists.

53934
### JOURNAL OF ECONOMIC EDUCATION, THE
1319 18th St., N.W.
Washington, DC 20036-1802
Telephone: (202) 296-6267
Year Established: 1969
Pub. Frequency: q.
Page Size: pocket
Subscrip. Rate: $33/yr. individual; $65/yr. institutions; add $10/yr. foreign
Circulation: 1,174
Circulation Type: paid
**Owner(s):**
Heldref Publications
1319 18th St., N.W.
Washington, DC 20036-1802
Telephone: (202) 296-6267
Ownership %: 100
**Management:**
Walter E. Beach ................................Publisher
Raymond M. Rallo ............Advertising Manager
Catherine Welker ...............Circulation Manager
Kerri P. Kilbane ..................Promotion Manager
**Editorial:**
Rosalind Springsteen .............................Editor
**Desc.:** Offers original articles on innovations in and evaluations of teaching techniques, materials, and programs in economics.
**Readers:** Instructors of introductory through graduate level economics.

24767
### JOURNAL OF EDUCATIONAL RESEARCH, THE
1319 18th St., N.W.
Washington, DC 20036-1802
Telephone: (202) 296-6267
FAX: (202) 296-5149
Year Established: 1935
Pub. Frequency: bi-m.
Page Size: standard
Subscrip. Rate: $35/yr. individudals; $70/yr. indstitutions; add $12 outside of US
Circulation: 3,114
Circulation Type: paid
**Owner(s):**
Heldref Publications
1319 18th St., N.W.
Washington, DC 20036
Telephone: (202) 296-6267
Ownership %: 100
**Management:**
Walter E. Beach ................................Publisher
Raymond M. Rallo ............Advertising Manager
Catherine Welker ...............Circulation Manager
Kerri P. Kilbane ..................Promotion Manager
**Editorial:**
Jeanne Bebo .............................................Editor
**Desc.:** Since 1920 has contributed to the advancement of educational practice in elementary and secondary schools. Authors experiment with new procedures, evaluate traditional practices, replicate previous research for validation, and perform other work central to understanding and improving the education of today's students and teachers.

**Readers:** Teachers, counselors, supervisors, administrators, planners, and educational researchers.

24765
### JOURNAL OF EDUCATION FOR BUSINESS
1319 18th St., N.W.
Washington, DC 20036-1802
Telephone: (202) 296-6267
FAX: (202) 296-5149
Year Established: 1924
Pub. Frequency: bi-m.
Page Size: standard
Subscrip. Rate: $31/yr. individuals; $52/yr. institutions; add $12 outside of US
Circulation: 1,767
Circulation Type: paid
**Owner(s):**
Heldref Publications
1319 Eighteenth St., NW
Washington, DC 20036-1802
Telephone: (202) 296-6267
Ownership %: 100
**Management:**
Walter E. Beach ................................Publisher
Raymond M. Rallo ............Advertising Manager
Catherine Welker ...............Circulation Manager
Kerri P. Kilbane ..................Promotion Manager
**Editorial:**
Isabella Owen ..........................................Editor
**Desc.:** Features basic and applied research-based articles on business fundamentals, career education, consumer economics, distributive education, management, and trends in communications, information systems and knowledge systems for business.
**Readers:** Instructors, supervisors, administrators at secondary, post secondary, and collegiate levels.

70471
### JOURNAL OF EMOTIONAL & BEHAVIORAL DISORDERS
8700 Shoal Creek Blvd.
Austin, TX 78757
Telephone: (512) 451-3246
FAX: (512) 451-8542
Year Established: 1993
Pub. Frequency: q.
Page Size: 8 3/8 x 10 7/8
Subscrip. Rate: $35/yr. individuals; $70/yr. institutions
Materials: 32,33
Circulation: 1,876
Circulation Type: free & paid
**Owner(s):**
Pro-Ed Journals
8700 Shoal Creek Blvd.
Austin, TX 78757-6897
Telephone: (512) 451-3246
FAX: (512) 451-8542
Ownership %: 100
**Management:**
Donald D. Hammill ...........................Publisher
**Editorial:**
Michael Epstein ...........................Editor in Chief
Douglas Cullinen .....................................Editor
Lisa Tippett ...............................Managing Editor
**Desc.:** Articles in research, practice and theory related to individuals with emotional & behavioral disorders, topics of interest to individuals from a wide range of disciplines.
**Readers:** Professionals in corrections, psychology, psychiatry, mental health, counseling and rehabilitation.

54046
### JOURNAL OF ENVIRONMENTAL EDUCATION, THE
1319 18th St., N.W.
Washington, DC 20036-1802
Telephone: (202) 296-6267
FAX: (202) 296-5149
Year Established: 1969

Pub. Frequency: q.
Page Size: standard
Subscrip. Rate: $33/yr. individual; $63/yr. institutions; add $10/yr. foreign
Circulation: 1,395
Circulation Type: paid
**Owner(s):**
Heldref Publications
1319 18th St., N.W.
Washington, DC 20036
Telephone: (202) 296-6267
Ownership %: 100
**Management:**
Walter E. Beach ................................Publisher
Raymond M. Rallo ...........Advertising Manager
Catherine Welker ...............Circulation Manager
Kerri P. Kilbane ..................Promotion Manager
**Editorial:**
Marla Fogelman ......................................Editor
**Desc.:** A vital research journal for anyone teaching about the environment. Each issue features case studies of relevant projects, evaluation of new research, and discussion of public policy and philosophy in the area of environmental education.
**Readers:** Department chairmans/directors: programs in outdoor education.

54078
### JOURNAL OF EXPERIMENTAL EDUCATION, THE
1319 18th St., N.W.
Washington, DC 20036-1802
Telephone: (202) 296-6267
FAX: (202) 296-5149
Year Established: 1932
Pub. Frequency: q.
Page Size: pocket
Subscrip. Rate: $31/yr. US individual; $62/yr. US institutions; add $10/yr. foreign
Circulation: 1,282
Circulation Type: paid
**Owner(s):**
Heldref Publications
1319 18th St., N.W.
Washington, DC 20036-1802
Telephone: (202) 296-6267
Ownership %: 100
**Management:**
Walter E. Beach ................................Publisher
Raymond M. Rallo ...........Advertising Manager
Catherine Welker ...............Circulation Manager
Kerri P. Kilbane ..................Promotion Manager
**Editorial:**
Paige Jackson .........................................Editor
**Desc.:** Aims to improve educational practice by publishing basic and applied research studies and employing the range of quantitative and qualitative methodologies found in the behavioral, cognitive, and social sciences.
**Readers:** Researchers & practitioners interested in the advancement of educational research.

24769
### JOURNAL OF GENERAL EDUCATION
Ste. C, Barbara Bldg.
University Park, PA 16802
Telephone: (814) 865-1327
FAX: (814) 863-1408
Year Established: 1946
Pub. Frequency: q.
Page Size: pocket
Subscrip. Rate: $20/vol. individuals; $30/vol. institutions
Circulation: 841
Circulation Type: paid

**Owner(s):**
Pennslyvania State University Press
Ste. C, Barbara Bldg.
University Park, PA 16802
Telephone: (814) 865-1327
Ownership %: 100
**Bureau(s):**
CSHE - Penn State University
403 S. Allen St., Ste. 104
University Park, PA 16802-5252
Telephone: (814) 865-6347
Contact: Sally Kelly, Editorial Assistant
**Editorial:**
James Ratcliff .................................................Editor
Gary Ratcliff ..................................Assistant Editor
Elizabeth Jones ........................Associate Editor
Susan Twombly .......................Associate Editor
**Desc.:** Provides stimulating reading for school, college and university faculty, academic leaders, administrators and policy makers. Presents critical essays and analyses, contemporary research, profiles of exemplary practices and reviews of new books and monographs. Tackles the current thinking and significant issues under debate in the field of general education.
**Readers:** Faculty in colleges and universities.

## JOURNAL OF GEOGRAPHY, THE
24770

16A Leonard Hall, IUP
Indiana, PA 15701
Telephone: (412) 357-6290
Year Established: 1917
Pub. Frequency: 6/yr.
Page Size: standard
Subscrip. Rate: $60/yr.
Materials: 06,10,15,25,28,29,32
Circulation: 4,500
Circulation Type: paid
**Owner(s):**
National Council for Geographic Education
16A Leonard Hall, IUP
Indiana, PA 15701
Telephone: (412) 357-6290
Ownership %: 100
**Management:**
Ruth I. Shirey .......................Executive Director
Robert Bednarz ....................Business Manager
**Editorial:**
Robert Bednarz .........................................Editor
**Desc.:** Contributed articles by educators discuss geographic education, teaching aids, economic development of geographical areas, field work for classes, etc. Departments include: Geographers' Forum, Films, Media Review, Book Reviews, Material Received, National Council at Work, News From Geographical Societies, Entrepot, Panorama, Regional Geography, Remote Sensing.
**Readers:** Educational (in the field of geography).

## JOURNAL OF HEALTH POLITICS, POLICY & LAW
59571

Bright Leaf Sq., Ste. 18-B
805 W. Main St.
Durham, NC 27701
Telephone: (919) 687-3636
FAX: (919) 688-4574
Mailing Address:
P.O. Box 90660
Durham, NC 27708
Year Established: 1976
Pub. Frequency: q.
Page Size: standard
Subscrip. Rate: $44/yr. individuals; $88/yr. institutions; $22/yr. students
Materials: 32
Circulation: 2,400
Circulation Type: paid

**Owner(s):**
Duke University Press
P.O. Box 90660
Durham, NC 27708
Telephone: (919) 687-3600
FAX: (919) 688-4574
Ownership %: 100
**Management:**
Patricia Thomas ....................................Manager
**Editorial:**
Mark A. Peterson .......................................Editor

## JOURNAL OF HIGHER EDUCATION
24771

1070 Carmack Rd.
Columbus, OH 43210-1002
Telephone: (614) 292-6930
Year Established: 1930
Pub. Frequency: bi-m.
Page Size: standard
Subscrip. Rate: $30/yr. individuals; $55/yr. institutions
Circulation: 5,000
Circulation Type: paid
**Owner(s):**
Ohio State University Press
1070 Carmack Rd.
Columbus, OH 43210-1002
Telephone: (614) 292-6930
Ownership %: 100
**Editorial:**
Robert J. Silverman ..................................Editor
Margaret Starbuck ...................Managing Editor
Margaret Starbuck ................Journals Manager
Bertina Povenmire ...........Production Director
**Desc.:** Interpretive articles deal with various phases of higher education and social forces which influence higher education. Published in affiliation with the American Association for Higher Education. Reviews new books.
**Readers:** Higher education faculty and administrators.

## JOURNAL OF INSTRUCTIONAL PSYCHOLOGY
24772

P.O. Box 8826, Spring Hill Station
Mobile, AL 36689
Telephone: (205) 460-6277
Year Established: 1974
Pub. Frequency: q.
Page Size: standard
Subscrip. Rate: $25/yr.; $45/2 yrs.; $65/3 yrs.
Circulation: 500
Circulation Type: paid
**Owner(s):**
Dr. George Uhlig
**Editorial:**
George E. Uhlig ..........................Editor in Chief
**Desc.:** Articles on theory and research pertaining to innovations in the guidance of learning activity and the science of instruction. Reviews books in education and psychology. Reviews microcomputer software & hardware.
**Readers:** College, university professors, teachers, teaching and instruction in general.

## JOURNAL OF INSTRUCTION DELIVERY SYSTEMS
69487

50 Culpeper St.
Warrenton, VA 22186
Telephone: (703) 347-0055
FAX: (703) 349-3169
Year Established: 1987
Pub. Frequency: q.
Subscrip. Rate: $60/yr.
Materials: 02,05,06,15
Print Process: offset
Circulation: 900
Circulation Type: paid

**Owner(s):**
Learning Technology Institute
50 Culpeper St.
Warrenton, VA 22186
Telephone: (703) 347-0055
Ownership %: 100
**Editorial:**
Barbara J. Clinton, Ed.D. .........................Editor
**Desc.:** Articles, news items, commentary and interviews addressing the enhancement of production in education and job training through interactive multimedia technology.
**Deadline:** story-Jan. 1, Apr. 1, Jul. 1, Oct. I

## JOURNAL OF LEARNING DISABILITIES
69557

8700 Shoal Creek Blvd.
Austin, TX 78757-6897
Telephone: (512) 451-3246
FAX: (512) 451-8542
Year Established: 1968
Pub. Frequency: 10/yr.
Page Size: standard
Subscrip. Rate: $45/yr. individual; $90/yr. institution; $115/yr. foreign
Materials: 06,32,33
Print Process: offset
Circulation: 8,824
Circulation Type: free & paid
**Owner(s):**
Pro-Ed, Inc.
8700 Shoal Creek Blvd.
Austin, TX 78757-6897
Telephone: (512) 451-3246
Ownership %: 100
**Management:**
Donald D. Hammill .............................Publisher
**Editorial:**
J. Lee Wiederholt ........................Editor in Chief
**Desc.:** Contains articles on practice, research, and theory related to learning disabilities.
**Readers:** Professionals; including educators, psychologists, physicians, optometrists, opthomologists and attorneys.
**Deadline:** story-15th of mo., 4 mos. prior to pub. date; news-15th of mo., 4 mos. prior; photo-15th of mo., 4 mos. prior; ads-15th of mo., 4 mos. prior

## JOURNAL OF PHILOSOPHICAL RESEARCH
58669

Philosophy Documentation Ctr.
Bowling Green State Univ.
Bowling Green, OH 43402
Telephone: (419) 372-2419
FAX: (419) 372-6987
Pub. Frequency: a.
Subscrip. Rate: $24/yr. individuals; $58/yr. institutions
Circulation: 183
Circulation Type: paid
**Owner(s):**
Philosophy Documentation Ctr.
Bowling Green State University
Bowling Green, OH 43403-0189
Telephone: (419) 372-2419
Ownership %: 100
**Management:**
Cindy Richards ....................Business Manager
**Editorial:**
Panayot Butchvarov ...................................Editor
Richard H. Lineback .................................Director
**Desc.:** Features articles on any topic in philosophy. Articles in French as well as English are welcome. With an outstanding group of 350 referees, the journal welcomes articles that reflect enlightening philosophical perspectives.

## JOURNAL OF PHYSICAL EDUCATION, RECREATION & DANCE
24774

1900 Association Dr.
Reston, VA 22091
Telephone: (703) 476-3400
Year Established: 1885
Pub. Frequency: 9/yr.
Page Size: standard
Subscrip. Rate: $85/yr.
Materials: 08
Print Process: web
Circulation: 30,000
Circulation Type: paid
**Owner(s):**
American Alliance for Health, Physical Education
1900 Association Dr.
Reston, VA 22091
Telephone: (703) 476-3400
Ownership %: 100
**Management:**
A. Gilson Brown .........................Vice President
Tim Burton ................Advertising Manager
**Editorial:**
Frances Rowan .......................Managing Editor
Nancy Jones ........................Book Review Editor
**Desc.:** Official association publication carrying by-line articles and short features on all aspects of physical education, recreation, dance, athletics, safety education as taught in schools and colleges. Covers administration, curriculum methods, equipment. Also carries new books, products, and audio-visual aids. Field material for regular features should be submitted to the editor.
**Readers:** Physical education, recreation, health & other personnel regularly at the college and secondary school level.

## JOURNAL OF READING
24775

800 Barksdale Rd.
Newark, DE 19711
Telephone: (302) 731-1600
Mailing Address:
P.O. Box 8139
Newark, DE 19714
Year Established: 1957
Pub. Frequency: 8/yr., Sep.-May
Page Size: standard
Subscrip. Rate: $38/yr.; $41/yr. institutions
Circulation: 19,000
Circulation Type: paid
**Owner(s):**
International Reading Association
800 Barksdale Rd.
Newark, DE 19711
Telephone: (302) 731-1600
FAX: (302) 731-1057
Ownership %: 100
**Management:**
Linda Hunter .....................Advertising Manager
**Editorial:**
Janet Ramage Binkley .............................Editor
June Hollins ................................Assistant Editor
Susan Reinhardt ........................Assistant Editor
Kate Tyler Wall ........................Associate Editor
Wayne Otto ...........................................Columnist
Jeanne Schumm ...................................Columnist
Noreen McAloon ...................................Columnist
Teri Lesesne ...........................................Columnist
Joseph Sanacore ...................................Columnist
**Desc.:** Published by the International Reading Association as a service to its members and other interested persons. It provides a forum for the exchange of information and opinion on theory, research, and practice on reading at the adolescent and adult levels.
**Readers:** Primarily educators.

---

**Materials Accepted/Included:** 01-Business news 02-By-line articles 03-Fashion news 04-Food news 05-Freelance copy 06-Letters to editor 07-Real estate news 08-Sports news 09-Travel news 10-Book rev. 11-Movie rev. 12-Music rev. 13-TV rev. 14-Theater rev. 15-Coming events 16-Obituaries 17-Question & answer 18-Social announcements 19-Artwork 20-Cartoons 21-Photos 22-TV listings 23-Audio rec. 24-Video rec. 25-Books 26-Films/film clips 27-Personnel news 28-Press releases 29-New product news/photos 30-Trade lit. 31-Contracts awarded 32-Display adv. 33-Classified adv.

4-341

## JOURNAL OF SCHOOL LEADERSHIP
66621

851 New Holland Ave.
Lancaster, PA 17601
Telephone: (717) 291-5609
FAX: (717) 295-4538
Mailing Address:
P.O. Box 3535
Lancaster, PA 17601
Year Established: 1991
Pub. Frequency: bi-m
Subscrip. Rate: $95/yr.; $180/2 yrs.;
$265/3 yrs.
Circulation: 375
Circulation Type: paid
**Owner(s):**
Melvyn A. Kohudic
851 New Holland Ave.
Lancaster, PA 17601
Telephone: (717) 291-5609
**Bureau(s):**
Technomic Publishing AG
Missionsstrasse 44
Basel CH-4055, Switzerland
Contact: Frank Versaci, Director
**Editorial:**
Paula Short ...................................Editor

## JOURNAL OF SPECIAL EDUCATION
70472

8700 Shoal Creek Blvd.
Austin, TX 78754-6897
Telephone: (512) 451-3246
FAX: (512) 451-8542
Year Established: 1966
Pub. Frequency: q.
Page Size: 7" X 10"
Subscrip. Rate: $35/yr. individuals; $70/yr.
institutions
Materials: 15,32,33
Circulation: 3,376
Circulation Type: free & paid
**Owner(s):**
Pro- Ed Journals
8700 Shoal Creek Blvd.
Austin, TX 78757-6897
Telephone: (512) 451-3246
FAX: (512) 451-8542
Ownership %: 100
**Management:**
Donald D. Hammill ...............................Publisher
**Editorial:**
Lyn D. Douglas Fuchs ...............Editor in Chief
Lisa Tippett .........................Managing Editor
**Desc.:** Research articles and scholarly
reviews in all sub-specialties of special
education articles on families, transition,
technology, general-special education
interface legislation and litigation.
**Readers:** Educators, psychologists and
other professionals.

## KEA NEWS
24779

401 Capitol Ave.
Frankfort, KY 40601
Telephone: (502) 875-2889
FAX: (502) 227-8062
Year Established: 1964
Pub. Frequency: 10/yr. (Aug.-May)
Page Size: tabloid
Subscrip. Rate: $5/yr.
Circulation: 36,000
Circulation Type: paid
**Owner(s):**
Kentucky Education Association
401 Capitol Ave.
Frankfort, KY 40601
Telephone: (502) 875-2889
Ownership %: 100
**Editorial:**
Mary Ann Blankenship ..................Editor
Jamie Morton ...............................Editor

**Desc.:** Uses news articles that would
interest teachers and administrators at
all phases of education, methods of
teaching, new materials. Departments
include: Editorials, Articles on Education,
Educational Features, News Columns for
Various Reader Groups.
**Readers:** Classroom teachers, city and
county school support personnel.

## LAE NEWS
24781

P.O. Box 479
Baton Rouge, LA 70821
Telephone: (504) 343-9243
Year Established: 1978
Pub. Frequency: 8/yr.
Page Size: tabloid
Subscrip. Rate: $3/yr. members; $25/yr.
non-members
Print Process: web
Circulation: 23,000
Circulation Type: paid
**Owner(s):**
Louisiana Association of Educators
P.O. Box 479
Baton Rouge, LA 70821
Telephone: (504) 343-9243
Ownership %: 100
**Management:**
Mike Deshotels ...............Executive Director
**Editorial:**
Dr. Jeff Simon ...............................Editor
**Desc.:** Carries articles of general or
specialized interest to members on all
phases of education, usually written by
professional educators of national or
state reputation, or by LAE staff.
**Readers:** Teachers, supervisors and
administrators, institutions of higher
education and special education.

## LANGUAGE ARTS
56243

1111 W. Kenyon Rd.
Urbana, IL 61801-1096
Telephone: (217) 328-3870
FAX: (217) 328-0977
Year Established: 1924
Pub. Frequency: m.: Sep.-Apr.
Page Size: standard
Subscrip. Rate: $40/yr. membership
Materials: 02,06,10,15,32
Freelance Pay: none
Print Process: web offset
Circulation: 26,500
Circulation Type: paid
**Owner(s):**
National Council of Teachers of English
1111 W. Kenyon Rd.
Urbana, IL 61801-1096
Telephone: (217) 328-3870
Ownership %: 100
**Management:**
Miles Myers ...................Executive Director
Katherine Hope ...............Business Manager
**Editorial:**
Bill Teale ...................................Editor
**Desc.:** Publishes original contributions on
all facets of language arts teaching and
learning. It is of primary interest to
teachers and teacher educators
of children in the preschool through
middle school years. It is the policy of
NCTE in its journals and other
publications to provide a forum for the
open discussion of ideas concerning the
content and the teaching of English and
Language Arts. Publicity accorded to any
particular point of view does not imply
endorsement by the Executive
Committee, the Board of Directors, or
the membership at large, except as
specified.

**Readers:** Teacher educators and
elementary classroom teachers.
**Deadline:** story-13 mo. prior to pub. date;
news-4 mo. prior to pub. date; ads-2 mo.
prior to pub. date

## LEARNING & INSTRUCTION
69523

660 White Plains Rd.
Tarrytown, NY 10591-5153
Telephone: (914) 524-9200
FAX: (914) 524-9200
Year Established: 1991
Pub. Frequency: 4/yr.
**Owner(s):**
Pergamon Press, Inc.
660 White Plains Rd.
Tarrytown, NY 10591-5153
Telephone: (914) 524-9200
**Editorial:**
Erik DeCorte ...............................Editor
**Desc.:** Presents papers and review articles
on the processes of learning,
development, instruction, and teaching
representing a variety of theoretical
perspectives and different
methodological approaches.

## LEARNING 95
24782

1111 Bethlehem Pike
Springhouse, PA 19477
Telephone: (215) 646-8700
FAX: (215) 646-0908
Mailing Address:
P.O. Box 908
Springhouse, PA 19477-0908
Year Established: 1971
Pub. Frequency: 8/yr., Aug.-May
Page Size: standard
Subscrip. Rate: $20/yr.
Materials: 02,05,29,32,33
Freelance Pay: $75-$350 features; $10-
$200 depts.
Circulation: 285,000
Circulation Type: paid
**Owner(s):**
Elsevier US Holdings, Inc.
4520 East-West Hwy.
Bethesda, MD 20814
Ownership %: 100
**Management:**
Eugene W. Jackson ............Chairman of Board
Kevin Hurley ...............................President
**Editorial:**
Charlene Gaynor ...........................Editor
Mary Wardlaw ...............................Advertising
Jon Kirk ...............................Design Director
**Desc.:** Creative ideas and insights for
teachers. Learning is an innovative
education magazine aimed primarily at
K-8 teachers, administrators and
professors of education. It focuses on
trends and controversies, new practice
and philosophies and critical
assessments of innovations and
materials, as well as providing teachers
with a wealth of classroom-tested
teaching ideas.
**Readers:** Elementary and junior high
school teachers, senior high school
teachers, computer specialists, parents,
curriculum specialists, and
administrators, professors of education.
**Deadline:** story-4 mo. prior to pub. date;
ads-1 mo. prior to pub. date

## LINGUA FRANCA
67185

172 E. Boston Post Rd.
Mamaroneck, NY 10543
Telephone: (914) 698-9427
FAX: (914) 698-9488
Year Established: 1990
Pub. Frequency: bi-m.
Page Size: standard
Subscrip. Rate: $19.95/yr.

Circulation: 21,000
Circulation Type: paid
**Owner(s):**
Lingua Franca, Inc.
712 E. Boston Post Rd.
Mamaroneck, NY 10543
Telephone: (914) 698-9427
Ownership %: 100
**Management:**
Jeffrey Kittay ...............................Publisher
Barbara Kimmel ...............Advertising Manager
**Editorial:**
Judy Shuleitz ...............................Senior Editor
Jeffrey Kittay ...............................Editor
Henry Lincoln ...............................Associate Editor
**Desc.:** Covers hiring and tenurings,
publishing, research topics, financial
issues including retirement, academic
computing, and the impact of political
and social issues on academic careers.
**Readers:** For university professors,
administrators, and graduate students in
the humanities and social sciences.

## MATHEMATICS & COMPUTER EDUCATION
24787

P.O. Box 158
Old Bethpage, NY 11804
Telephone: (516) 822-5475
Year Established: 1967
Pub. Frequency: 3/yr.
Page Size: standard
Subscrip. Rate: $62/yr.
Materials: 02,06,10,25
Freelance Pay: varies
Print Process: offset
Circulation: 1,200
Circulation Type: paid
**Owner(s):**
The MATYC Journal, Inc.
Plainview, NY 11803
Telephone: (516) 822-5475
Ownership %: 100
**Management:**
George M. Miller ...............................Publisher
**Editorial:**
George M. Miller ...............................Editor
**Desc.:** A journal of mathematics and
computer education for college teachers.
types of features: articles on math and
computer teaching techniques, book and
software reviews, calculator and
computer articles, applications and
problem solving.
**Readers:** Mathematics and computer
educators, college and upper division
high school.
**Deadline:** story-6 mo. prior to pub. date

## MATHEMATICS TEACHER
24786

1906 Association Dr.
Reston, VA 22091-1593
Telephone: (703) 620-9840
FAX: (703) 476-2970
Year Established: 1921
Pub. Frequency: 9/yr.
Page Size: standard
Subscrip. Rate: $45/yr.
Materials: 06,32,33
Print Process: web
Circulation: 65,000
Circulation Type: paid
**Owner(s):**
National Council of Teachers of
Mathematics
1906 Association Dr.
Reston, VA 22091-1593
Telephone: (703) 620-9840
FAX: (703) 476-2970
Ownership %: 100
**Management:**
Jack Price ...............................President
James D. Gates ...............Executive Director
Rowena G. Martelino ........Advertising Manager

**Materials Accepted/Included:** 01-Business news 02-By-line articles 03-Fashion news 04-Food news 05-Freelance copy 06-Letters to editor 07-Real estate news 08-Sports news 09-Travel news 10-Book rev. 11-Movie rev. 12-Music rev. 13-TV rev. 14-Theater rev. 15-Coming events 16-Obituaries 17-Question & answer 18-Social announcements 19-Artwork 20-Cartoons 21-Photos 22-TV listings 23-Audio rec. 24-Video rec. 25-Books 26-Films/film clips 27-Personnel news 28-Press releases 29-New product news/photos 30-Trade lit. 31-Contracts awarded 32-Display adv. 33-Classified adv.

Cynthia C. Rosso ................Business Manager
Robert Chandler ................Circulation Manager
**Editorial:**
Joan Armistead ......................Editorial Director
Ann Butterfield ....................Editorial Assistant
Harry B. Tunis ....................Publication Director
**Desc.:** Concerned with the junior high school, secondary and two-year college levels; contains by-line articles on mathematics and the teaching of the subject as well as the role of mathematics in our society. Includes reviews of computer materials and practical ways to teach mathematics.
**Readers:** Teachers, mathematics supervisors, mathematics education personnel, others.

24788
## MEA TODAY
1232 E. Sixth Ave.
Helena, MT 59601-3927
Telephone: (406) 442-4250
FAX: (406) 443-5081
Pub. Frequency: 10/yr.
Page Size: standard
Subscrip. Rate: $30.75/yr. membership
Circulation: 10,000
**Owner(s):**
Montana Education Association
Telephone: (406) 442-4250
Ownership %: 100
**Management:**
Eric Feaver .............................................Publisher
**Editorial:**
Nancy Robbins .........................................Editor
David Smith .................Administrative Assistant
**Desc.:** Official publication of the Montana Education Association. The editorial content is slanted to the memberships. Covers teacher welfare, teaching methods and educational welfare of the state's youngsters.
**Readers:** Teachers and other education professionals in Montana.

24835
## MEA VOICE
1216 Kendale Blvd.
East Lansing, MI 48823
Telephone: (517) 332-6551
Mailing Address:
P.O. Box 2573
East Lansing, MI 48826-2573
Year Established: 1923
Pub. Frequency: m.
Page Size: tabloid
Subscrip. Rate: $15/yr.
Materials: 06,20,21,30,32,33
Print Process: web
Circulation: 126,000
Circulation Type: paid
**Owner(s):**
Michigan Education Association
P.O. Box 2573
East Lansing, MI 48826
Telephone: (517) 332-6551
Ownership %: 100
**Management:**
Michigan Education Association .........Publisher
**Editorial:**
Dennis Keenon .......................Managing Editor
Gertie Buren .........................Editorial Assistant
**Desc.:** Articles and features on topics pertaining to education, employee bargaining and relations, How-To-Do-It, etc. Features usually cover accomplishments of educational groups, individuals, and school systems. Departments include: Letters, Important Dates.

**Readers:** Education personnels of K through higher education, both instructional and support staff.
**Deadline:** story-3 wks. prior to pub. date; news-3 wks. prior; photo-3 wks. prior; ads-2 wks. prior

24789
## MEDIA & METHODS
1429 Walnut St.
Philadelphia, PA 19102
Telephone: (215) 563-3501
FAX: (215) 563-1588
Year Established: 1964
Pub. Frequency: 5/yr.
Page Size: standard
Subscrip. Rate: $29/yr. US; $47/yr. foreign
Freelance Pay: $75-$100
Circulation: 42,000
Circulation Type: paid
**Owner(s):**
American Society of Educators
1429 Walnut St.
Philadelphia, PA 19102
Telephone: (215) 563-3501
Ownership %: 100
**Management:**
Michelle Sokoloff ................................President
Michelle Sokoloff ................................Publisher
Michelle Sokoloff ..............Advertising Manager
**Editorial:**
Michelle Sokoloff ....................Managing Editor
Ann Gebhard ......................Book Review Editor
Andrea Epstein .............................Design Editor
**Desc.:** Provides a link between contemporary teaching technologies and practical classroom application.
**Readers:** Educators, media specialists, AV directors, librarians & administrators, computer education directory, curriculum planners, department heads & teachers committed to the use of teaching media.

70447
## MEDITERRANEAN QUARTERLY
905 W. Main St., Ste. 18-B
Duke University Press
Durham, NC 27701
Telephone: (919) 687-3636
FAX: (919) 688-4574
Mailing Address:
P.O. Box 90660
Durham, NC 27708-0660
Year Established: 1989
Pub. Frequency: q.
Page Size: standard
Subscrip. Rate: $12/yr. students; $24/yr. individuals; $44/yr. institutions
Materials: 32
**Owner(s):**
Duke University Press
P.O. Box 90660
Durham, NC 27708-0660
Telephone: (919) 687-3600
FAX: (919) 688-4574
Ownership %: 100
**Management:**
Patricia Thomas ...................................Manager
**Editorial:**
Nikolaos A. Stavrou ..................................Editor

24785
## MTA TODAY
20 Ashburton Pl.
Boston, MA 02108-2727
Telephone: (617) 742-7950
FAX: (617) 742-7046
Pub. Frequency: m.
Page Size: tabloid
Subscrip. Rate: membership
Freelance Pay: $0-$500
Circulation: 70,000
Circulation Type: controlled

**Owner(s):**
Massachusetts Teachers Association
20 Ashburton Pl.
Boston, MA 02108-2727
Telephone: (617) 742-7950
**Management:**
Ruth Kaplan ......................Advertising Manager
**Editorial:**
Andrew D. Linebaugh ..............................Editor
Claire Ross .....................................Miscellaneous
Maria Plati ......................................Miscellaneous
**Desc.:** Includes articles pertinent to Massachusetts education.
**Readers:** MTA affiliates.

24883
## MUSEUM NEWS
1225 Eye St., N.W., Ste. 200
Washington, DC 20005
Telephone: (202) 289-1818
FAX: (202) 289-6578
Year Established: 1924
Pub. Frequency: bi-m.
Page Size: standard
Subscrip. Rate: $38/yr.
Materials: 25,28,29,32
Circulation: 12,500
Circulation Type: paid
**Owner(s):**
American Association of Museums
1225 Eye St., N.W., Ste. 200
Washington, DC 20005
Telephone: (202) 289-1818
Ownership %: 100
**Management:**
Jeff Menett ......................Advertising Manager
**Editorial:**
Donald Garfield .............................Senior Editor
John Strand ...............................................Editor
Polly Sexton .........................Managing Editor
Catharine Hall ..................Advertising Assistant
Susannah Cassidy ...................Associate Editor
**Desc.:** Entirely devoted to issues of concern to the museum community, including illustrated feature articles, departments (reviews, editorials, media) special theme issues, in all fields such as art, science, history, children's museums, industrial museums, historic houses and preservation projects.
**Readers:** Museum professionals, trustees, volunteers, and others with professional interest in museums.

24791
## NASSP BULLETIN
1904 Association Dr.
Reston, VA 22091
Telephone: (703) 860-0200
Year Established: 1916
Pub. Frequency: m.
Page Size: standard
Subscrip. Rate: $125/yr. members
Circulation: 40,000
Circulation Type: paid
**Owner(s):**
National Association of Secondary School
1904 Association Dr.
Reston, VA 22091
Telephone: (703) 860-0200
Ownership %: 100
**Editorial:**
Robert Mahaffey ......................................Editor
Carol Bruce ................................Associate Editor
Patricia Lucas George ........Book Review Editor
Arlene Locke ...............................Miscellaneous
Eugenia Cooper Potter ............Technical Editor
**Desc.:** A professional journal that publishes from 10 to 20 articles each month. Most articles are unsolicited and average from 7 to 10 pages each. The subjects of articles are those that interest educators generally and administrators specifically.

**Readers:** Secondary school principals, assistant principals, superintendents, teachers, professors, librarians.

24795
## NEW YORK TEACHER, THE
159 Wolf Rd.
Albany, NY 12205
Telephone: (212) 254-7660
Year Established: 1917
Pub. Frequency: bi-w. (Sep.-June)
Subscrip. Rate: $8/yr.
Circulation: 326,000
Circulation Type: paid
**Owner(s):**
New York State United Teachers
159 Wolf Rd.
Albany, NY 12205
Ownership %: 100
**Bureau(s):**
New York State United Teachers
260 Park Ave. S.
New York, NY 10010
Telephone: (212) 254-7660
**Management:**
Mildred Diaz ......................Advertising Manager
**Editorial:**
Ted Bleecker ...............................Editor in Chief
Edna Valle ..................Administrative Assistant
Rickie Flanders .........................Assistant Editor
Antonio Ramirez .......................Assistant Editor
Charles Michaelson ..................Associate Editor
Renee Dorsa .................................Miscellaneous
Bob Fritzpatrick ...............New Products Editor
Matthew Doherty ..........................News Editor
**Desc.:** For teaching personnel. News and features cover organizations' developments at local, state and national levels, innovations, accounts of individual schools, teachers and school system personnel.

24797
## NJEA REVIEW
180 W. State St.
Trenton, NJ 08608
Telephone: (609) 599-4561
FAX: (609) 392-6321
Mailing Address:
P.O. Box 1211
Trenton, NJ 08607-1211
Year Established: 1927
Pub. Frequency: 9/yr. (Sep.-May)
Page Size: standard
Subscrip. Rate: $25/yr.
Materials: 02,20,21,23,24,25,32
Circulation: 143,000
Circulation Type: controlled
**Owner(s):**
N.J. Education Association
180 W. State St.
Trenton, NJ 08608
Telephone: (609) 599-4561
Ownership %: 100
**Editorial:**
Martha O. DeBlieu ...................................Editor
Teresa A. Jacobson ..........................Advertising
**Desc.:** Covers all phases of educational activities in public schools and colleges of New Jersey. Journal contains teaching methods and materials, educational administration problems, and general items of interest to New Jersey active and retired public school employees as a professional group (ex.: study, scholar achievements, grants). Departments include: Morning Post (letters); People in News; Nature in the Classroom; Dateline (meetings and special events in N.J.); President's Message; Capital Outlook (national and state news); Sussex to Cape May (miscellaneous local news); Editorial, Booktalk (reviews).

**Readers:** Public school elementary and secondary teachers, principals, and supervisors; college instructors and administrators; all public school employees; all college employees; retired public school employees; student teachers-to-be.
**Deadline:** story-1 mo. prior to pub. date; ads-1 mo. prior to pub. date

### NORTH CAROLINA EDUCATION
24798

700 S. Salisbury St.
Raleigh, NC 27611-7347
Telephone: (919) 832-3000
FAX: (919) 829-1626
Mailing Address:
  P.O. Box 27347
  Raleigh, NC 27611-7347
Year Established: 1908
Pub. Frequency: a.
Page Size: standard
Subscrip. Rate: $2/yr.
Circulation: 56,000
Circulation Type: paid
Owner(s):
North Carolina Association of Educators
P.O. Box 27347
Raleigh, NC 27611
Telephone: (919) 832-3000
Ownership %: 100
Management:
Virginia Dumont .................Advertising Manager
Editorial:
Jacqueline Vaughn ......................................Editor
Virginia Dumont ..................Book Review Editor
**Desc.:** Professional articles designed to inform, instruct, and inspire teachers of North Carolina children and administrators in North Carolina public schools. New items concerning education in general and activities of the North Carolina Association of Educators in particular.
**Readers:** K-12 public school personnel.

### NORTH DAKOTA EDUCATIONS NEWS
24799

P.O. Box 5005
Bismarck, ND 58502
Telephone: (701) 223-0450
FAX: (701) 224-8535
Year Established: 1887
Pub. Frequency: 9/yr.
Page Size: tabloid
Subscrip. Rate: $15/yr. membership
Materials: 32
Circulation: 6,500
Circulation Type: controlled
Owner(s):
North Dakota Education Association
P.O. Box 5005
Bismarck, ND 58502
Telephone: (701) 223-0450
Ownership %: 100
Management:
Bill Lipp .............................................President
Editorial:
Linda Harsche ...........................................Editor
Joseph Westby ...................Executive Director
**Desc.:** Departments include: Instruction and Professional Development Ideas, News Around The State.
**Readers:** Teachers.
**Deadline:** story-1st of ea. mo.; news-1st of ea. mo.; photo-1st of ea. mo.

### NOVA DIGEST
61831

3602 S.W. College Ave.
Ft Lauderdale, FL 33314
Pub. Frequency: 1-2/yr.
Page Size: tabloid
Subscrip. Rate: free
Circulation: 8,000
Circulation Type: controlled

Owner(s):
Broward County School Board
**Desc.:** It is published by high school students once or twice a year with news of the research and development activities.
**Readers:** Teachers in Broward County and Parents of Children In The Nova Schools.

### OHIO SCHOOLS
24801

225 E. Broad St.
Columbus, OH 43215
Telephone: (614) 228-4526
FAX: (614) 228-8771
Mailing Address:
  P.O. BOX 2550
  Columbus, OH 43216
Year Established: 1852
Pub. Frequency: m.
Page Size: standard
Subscrip. Rate: $18/yr.
Materials: 32,33
Circulation: 109,083
Circulation Type: controlled & paid
Owner(s):
Ohio Education Association
225 E. Broad St.
Columbus, OH 43215
Telephone: (614) 228-4526
Ownership %: 100
Management:
Maxine Flynn ....................Advertising Manager
Editorial:
Richard J. Baker .......................................Editor
**Desc.:** Magazine is a combination of articles and news stories relative to education employees. Contains copy chosen to serve as a medium of exchange of ideas or techniques originating in Ohio classrooms. Aims to promote the professional and personal welfare and growth of education employees, and to keep education employees informed on organized professional activities and current educational news.
**Readers:** Public education employees of Ohio.

### OREGON EDUCATION
24804

6900 S.W. Haines St.
Tigard, OR 97223-8598
Telephone: (503) 684-3300
FAX: (503) 684-8063
Year Established: 1954
Pub. Frequency: 9/yr. (Sep.-June)
Page Size: tabloid
Subscrip. Rate: $10/yr.
Materials: 28,29,30
Freelance Pay: none
Circulation: 39,445
Circulation Type: controlled & paid
Owner(s):
Oregon Education Association
6900 S.W. Haines Rd.
Tigard, OR 97223
Telephone: (503) 684-3300
FAX: (503) 684-8063
Ownership %: 100
Management:
Bruce Adams ......................................President
Kris Gray ...........................Circulation Manager
Editorial:
Shari Forbes Thomas ...............................Editor
Shari Forbes Thomas ........Book Review Editor
Shari Forbes Thomas .......................Columnist
**Desc.:** All educational articles.
**Readers:** Teachers, members, publishing houses, legislators.

### PERSPECTIVES ON POLITICAL SCIENCE
54081

1319 18th St., N.W.
Washington, DC 20036-1802
Telephone: (202) 296-6267
FAX: (202) 296-5149
Year Established: 1973
Pub. Frequency: 4/yr.
Page Size: standard
Subscrip. Rate: $88/yr. institutions; $44/yr. individuals; add $10 outside US
Circulation: 529
Circulation Type: paid
Owner(s):
Heldref Publications
1319 18th St., N.W.
Washington, DC 20036-1802
Telephone: (202) 296-6267
FAX: (202) 296-5149
Ownership %: 100
Management:
Walter E. Beach ..............................Publisher
Editorial:
Lisa Culp Neikirk ......................................Editor
Catherine Welker ...............Circulation Director
Kerri P. Kilbane ...................Promotion Director
**Desc.:** Each issue contains reviews of new books in the ever-changing fields of government, politics, international affairs, and political thought. These books are reviewed by outstanding specialists one to twelve months after publication. Also included are major articles covering ideas and theories concerning politics.
**Readers:** Educators, students, researchers

### PHI DELTA KAPPA
24807

Eighth & Union St.
Bloomington, IN 47402
Telephone: (812) 339-1156
Mailing Address:
  P.O. Box 789
  Bloomington, IN 47402
Year Established: 1906
Pub. Frequency: 10/yr.
Page Size: 4 color photos/art
Subscrip. Rate: $4.50/issue; $35/yr.
Freelance Pay: $250-$750
Circulation: 150,000
Circulation Type: controlled & paid
Owner(s):
Phi Delta Kappa, Inc.
Eighth & Union St.
Bloomington, IN 47402
Telephone: (812) 339-1156
Ownership %: 100
Management:
Carol Bucheri ....................Advertising Manager
Editorial:
Pauline B. Gough ......................................Editor
Bruce M. Smith ...................Managing Editor
Carol Bucheri ..........................................Photo
**Desc.:** Articles range from scholarly, research-oriented pieces to feature stories on breaking education events, balanced approach preferred. Length preferred: 2,000-5,000 words. By-lines used for all articles. Staff writes occasional articles. Photos used. Little, if any, publicity material used. Departments include: De Jure, In Europe, In Canada, Washington Commentary, Research, Backtalk, Prototypes, and Stateline.
**Readers:** 25% K-12 grade administrators; 25% college professors; 25% classroom teachers; 10% state & federal; 10% graduate students; 5% other.

### PHILOSOPHER'S INDEX, THE
58668

Philosophy Documentation Ctr.
Bowling Green State University
Bowling Green, OH 43403-0189
Telephone: (419) 372-2419
FAX: (419) 372-6987
Year Established: 1967
Pub. Frequency: q.
Page Size: standard
Subscrip. Rate: $49/yr. individuals; $165/yr. institutions
Circulation: 2,156
Circulation Type: paid
Owner(s):
Richard H. Lineback, Pres.
317 Knollwood
Bowling Green, OH 43402
Telephone: (419) 372-2419
Ownership %: 100
Management:
Cindy Richards ....................Business Manager
Editorial:
Richard H. Lineback ..............................Editor
Richard H. Lineback ..........................Director
**Desc.:** A subject and author index to philosophy articles, books, contributions in anthologies, and the anthologies themselves. The Index provides up-to-date and comprehensive coverage of scholarly work in philosophy.

### PHYSICS TEACHER, THE
24808

One Physics Ellipse
College Park, MD 20740-3845
Telephone: (301) 209-3300
FAX: (301) 209-0845
Year Established: 1963
Pub. Frequency: 9/yr.
Page Size: standard
Subscrip. Rate: $127/yr.
Materials: 06,24,25,26,32,33
Print Process: web
Circulation: 10,000
Circulation Type: paid
Owner(s):
American Assn. of Physics Teachers
One Physics Ellipse
College Park, MD 20740-3845
Telephone: (301) 209-3300
Ownership %: 100
Editorial:
Clifford E. Swartz ......................................Editor
**Desc.:** Manuscripts should contribute to the strengthening of the teaching of introductory physics at any level. Articles should not be more than 5,000 words in length. Notes should not be more than 1,000 words. Photographs, drawings, charts, tables, and graphs are recommended and must be furnished by the author.
**Readers:** High school, college, & university teaching physicists concerned with the creative teaching of introductory physics.
**Deadline:** ads-15th of mo., 6 wks. prior to pub. date

### PMLA, PUBLICATIONS OF THE MODERN LANGUAGE ASSN.
24809

10 Astor Pl.
New York, NY 10003-6981
Telephone: (212) 475-9500
FAX: (212) 477-9863
Year Established: 1884
Pub. Frequency: 6/yr.
Page Size: standard
Subscrip. Rate: $108/yr. institutions; members free
Materials: 32
Circulation: 35,000
Circulation Type: paid

---

**Materials Accepted/Included:** 01-Business news 02-By-line articles 03-Fashion news 04-Food news 05-Freelance copy 06-Letters to editor 07-Real estate news 08-Sports news 09-Travel news 10-Book rev. 11-Movie rev. 12-Music rev. 13-TV rev. 14-Theater rev. 15-Coming events 16-Obituaries 17-Question & answer 18-Social announcements 19-Artwork 20-Cartoons 21-Photos 22-TV listings 23-Audio rec. 24-Video rec. 25-Books 26-Films/film clips 27-Personnel news 28-Press releases 29-New product news/photos 30-Trade lit. 31-Contracts awarded 32-Display adv. 33-Classified adv.

**Owner(s):**
Modern Language Association of America
10 Astor Pl.
New York, NY 10003-6981
Telephone: (212) 475-9500
Ownership %: 100
**Management:**
Cynthia R. Port ..................Advertising Manager
**Editorial:**
Domna C. Stanton .......................Editor
Judy Goulding ........................Managing Editor
**Desc.:** Contains essays of interest to those concerned with the study of language and literature. Only members of the association may submit articles to PMLA.
**Readers:** Scholars of language and literature.

### POSITIONS
70450
905 W. Main St., Ste. 18-B
Duke University Press
Durham, NC 27701
Telephone: (919) 687-3636
FAX: (919) 688-4574
Mailing Address:
P.O. Box 90660
Durham, NC 27709-0660
Year Established: 1993
Pub. Frequency: 3/yr.
Page Size: standard
Subscrip. Rate: $20/yr. individuals; $40/yr. institutions
Materials: 32
Circulation: 650
Circulation Type: controlled & paid
**Owner(s):**
Duke University Press
P.O. Box 90660
Durham, NC 27708-0660
Telephone: (919) 687-3600
FAX: (919) 688-4574
Ownership %: 100
**Management:**
Patricia Thomas .......................Manager
**Editorial:**
Tani E. Barlow .........................Editor

### PREVENTING SCHOOL FAILURE
54083
1319 18th St., N.W.
Washington, DC 20036-1802
Telephone: (202) 296-6267
FAX: (202) 296-5149
Year Established: 1976
Pub. Frequency: q.
Page Size: standard
Subscrip. Rate: $36/yr. individuals; $67/yr. institutions; add $10 outside US
Circulation: 685
Circulation Type: paid
**Owner(s):**
Heldref Publications
1319 18th St., N.W.
Washington, DC 20036-1802
Telephone: (202) 296-6267
FAX: (202) 296-5149
Ownership %: 100
**Management:**
Walter E. Beach ......................Publisher
**Editorial:**
Isabella Owen ...........................Editor
Raymond M. Rallo ...........Advertising Director
Catherine Welker ................Circulation Director
Kerri P. Kilbane ...................Promotion Director
**Desc.:** The journal for educators and parents seeking strategies for promoting the success of students with learning and behavioral problems. Articles are written by teachers, teacher educators, and parents.
**Readers:** Educators & parents of students with special needs.

### PRINCIPAL
24792
1615 Duke St.
Alexandria, VA 22314
Telephone: (703) 684-3345
FAX: (703) 548-6021
Year Established: 1921
Pub. Frequency: 5/yr.
Page Size: standard
Subscrip. Rate: $155/yr. membership
Materials: 02,20,21,32
Print Process: web
Circulation: 29,000
Circulation Type: controlled & paid
**Owner(s):**
National Assn. of Elementary School Principals
1615 Duke St.
Alexandria, VA 22314
Telephone: (703) 684-3345
Ownership %: 100
**Management:**
Louanne Wheeler ............Advertising Manager
Doris A. Belfield ...................Business Manager
**Editorial:**
Leon E. Greene ........................Editor
**Desc.:** Provides a forum for both practitioners and theorists in elementary and middle school education, to keep them informed about contemporary issues in education and educational administration, curriculum, educational reform, and social issues affecting education.
**Readers:** Elementary and middle school principals, administrators and others concerned with elementary and middle school education.

### PSBA BULLETIN
24713
774 Limekiln Rd.
New Cumberlnd, PA 17070-2398
Telephone: (717) 774-2331
FAX: (717) 774-0718
Year Established: 1937
Pub. Frequency: bi-m.
Page Size: standard
Subscrip. Rate: $25/yr. members; $50/yr. non-members
Materials: 32
Print Process: offset
Circulation: 11,300
Circulation Type: controlled
**Owner(s):**
PSBA, Inc.
774 Limekiln Rd.
New Cumberland, PA 17070-2398
Telephone: (717) 774-2331
FAX: (717) 774-0718
Ownership %: 100
**Management:**
Fritzi Schreffler ..................Advertising Manager
**Editorial:**
Lynn H. Manion ..........................Editor
Lynn H. Manion ..................Assistant Executive Director
Fritzi Schreffler .......................Associate Editor
**Desc.:** Covers all phases of school administration and supervision; particularly as applicable to Pennsylvania schools.
**Readers:** School board members, school administration, solicitors, etc. Readers interested in research in education, legislative issues, education trends, school law, etc.

### PUBLIC AFFAIRS QUARTERLY
58581
Philosophy Docum. Center
Bowling Green State Univ.
Bowling Green, OH 43403-0189
Telephone: (419) 372-2419
FAX: (419) 372-6987
Year Established: 1987
Pub. Frequency: q.

Page Size: standard
Subscrip. Rate: $32/yr. individuals; $90/yr. institutions
Circulation: 85
Circulation Type: paid
**Owner(s):**
North American Philosophical Publications, Inc.
1021 Cathedral of Learning
Pittsburgh, PA 15260
Telephone: (412) 624-5950
Ownership %: 100
**Management:**
Cindy Richards ....................Business Manager
**Editorial:**
Nicholas Rescher ........................Editor
Richard H. Lineback ......................Director
**Desc.:** Specializes in the philosophical study of public policy issues. The journal takes no sides, but instead provides a forum for the open discussion of such issues.

### RE: VIEW
54077
1319 18th St., N.W.
Washington, DC 20036-1802
Telephone: (202) 296-6267
FAX: (202) 296-5149
Year Established: 1951
Pub. Frequency: q.
Page Size: pocket
Subscrip. Rate: $27/yr. individual; $53/yr. institution; add $10/yr. foreign
Circulation: 584
Circulation Type: paid
**Owner(s):**
Heldref Publications
1319 Eighteenth St., N.W.
Washington, DC 20036-1802
Telephone: (202) 296-6267
Ownership %: 100
**Management:**
Walter E. Beach ......................Publisher
Raymond M. Rallo .............Advertising Manager
Catherine Welker ..............Circulation Manager
Kerri P. Kilbane ..................Promotion Manager
**Editorial:**
Helen Strang ...........................Editor
**Desc.:** Review interests of educators, researchers, parents, and others concerned with visually handicapped children, youth, and young adults, including multihandicapped and deaf-blind.
**Readers:** Educators, researchers, parents and others concerned with the development of the visually handicapped.

### READING IMPROVEMENT
24812
P.O. Box 8508
Mobile, AL 36689
Telephone: (205) 343-1878
Year Established: 1962
Pub. Frequency: q.
Page Size: standard
Subscrip. Rate: $15/yr. individuals; $20/yr. institutions
Circulation: 2,000
Circulation Type: paid
**Owner(s):**
Project Innovation, Inc.
P.O. Box 8508
Mobile, AL 36689
Telephone: (205) 343-1878
Ownership %: 50

Phillip Feldman
P.O. Box 8508
Mobile, AL 36689
Telephone: (205) 343-1878
Ownership %: 50
**Editorial:**
Phillip Feldman ..........................Editor

**Desc.:** Articles on theory and research pertaining to reading instruction and reading improvement at every level of development and in every area of instruction.
**Readers:** College, university professors, K-12 schools, public libraries, government agencies and individuals.

### READING RESEARCH QUARTERLY
69532
800 Barksdale Rd.
Newark, DE 19714-8139
Telephone: (302) 731-1600
FAX: (302) 731-1057
Mailing Address:
P.O. Box 8139
Newark, DE 19714
Year Established: 1965
Pub. Frequency: 4/yr.
Page Size: standard
Subscrip. Rate: $10/copy; $38/yr. individuals; $41/yr. institutions
Circulation: 10,000
Circulation Type: paid
**Owner(s):**
International Reading Association, Inc.
800 Barksdale Rd.
Newark, DE 19714-8139
Telephone: (302) 731-1600
FAX: (302) 731-1057
Ownership %: 100
**Editorial:**
Michael Kamil ...........................Editor

### READING TEACHER, THE
24813
800 Barksdale Rd.
Newark, DE 19711-8139
Telephone: (302) 731-1600
FAX: (302) 731-1057
Mailing Address:
414 White Hall
Kent State Univ.
Kent, OH 44242-0001
Year Established: 1948
Pub. Frequency: 8/yr.; Sep.-May
Page Size: standard
Subscrip. Rate: $6/issue; $38/yr.
Materials: 32
Circulation: 65,000
Circulation Type: paid
**Owner(s):**
International Reading Association
800 Barksdale
Newark, DE 19711
Telephone: (302) 731-1600
Ownership %: 100
**Management:**
Linda Hunter .....................Advertising Manager
**Editorial:**
Nancy D. Paduk .........................Editor
Timothy V. Rasinski ......................Editor
Janet R. Binkley ...................Managing Editor
**Desc.:** Published as a service to members of IRA and to all others who are concerned with reading, especially as it is practiced and encouraged through instruction and supervision in preschool and elementary schools.
**Readers:** Reading teachers, school system reading coordinators, clinicians, professors.

### REMEDIAL & SPECIAL EDUCATION
70470
8700 Shoal Creek Blvd.
Austin, TX 78757-0007
Telephone: (512) 451-3246
FAX: (512) 854-2000
Year Established: 1984
Pub. Frequency: bi-m.
Page Size: 8 3/8 x 10 7/8
Subscrip. Rate: $35/yr. individual; $80/yr. institutions
Materials: 15

---

**Materials Accepted/Included:** 01-Business news 02-By-line articles 03-Fashion news 04-Food news 05-Freelance copy 06-Letters to editor 07-Real estate news 08-Sports news 09-Travel news 10-Book rev. 11-Movie rev. 12-Music rev. 13-TV rev. 14-Theater rev. 15-Coming events 16-Obituaries 17-Question & answer 18-Social announcements 19-Artwork 20-Cartoons 21-Photos 22-TV listings 23-Audio rec. 24-Video rec. 25-Books 26-Films/film clips 27-Personnel news 28-Press releases 29-New product news/photos 30-Trade lit. 31-Contracts awarded 32-Display adv. 33-Classified adv.

4-345

Circulation: 2,800
Circulation Type: free & paid
**Owner(s):**
Pro-Ed Journals
8700 Shoal Creek Blvd.
Austin, TX 78757-6897
Telephone: (512) 451-3246
FAX: (512) 451-8542
Ownership %: 100
**Management:**
Donald D. Hamill .....................Publisher
**Editorial:**
Lorna Idol ......................Editor in Chief
Lisa Tippett ................Managing Editor
**Desc.:** Interpretation of research literature
and recommendations for practice of
remedial and special
education. Interpretation of research
literature and recommendations for
practice of remedial and special
education.
**Readers:** Educators, psychologists,
clinicians and other professionals
interested in the education of students
requiring remedial and special education.

66599
**SCHOLASTIC DYNAMATH**
555 Broadway
New York, NY 10012-3999
Telephone: (212) 343-6461
FAX: (212) 343-6484
Year Established: 1982
Pub. Frequency: 8/yr.
Page Size: standard
Subscrip. Rate: $6.50/yr.
Materials: 01,02,03,04,05,08,09,10,11,12,
13,15,19,20,21,28,29
Freelance Pay: $50-$350
Circulation: 352,000
Circulation Type: free & paid
**Owner(s):**
Scholastic Magazines, Inc.
555 Broadway
New York, NY 10012-3999
Telephone: (212) 343-6461
FAX: (212) 343-6484
Ownership %: 100
**Editorial:**
Joe D'Agnese .....................Senior Editor
Jackie Glasthal .........................Editor
Bob Hugel .....................Associate Editor
Cecilia Dinio-Durkin .......Associate Editor
Jack Silbert ................Associate Editor
**Desc.:** Aims to make math fun and
relevant by talking about the math
people do on their jobs as well as
consumer math. It also contains fun
math activities and puzzles.
**Readers:** 5th and 6th graders.
**Deadline:** story-3 mo. prior to pub. date;
news-3 mo.; photo-3 mo.; ads-3 mo.

66602
**SCHOLASTIC MATH MAGAZINE**
555 Broadway
New York, NY 10012-3999
Telephone: (212) 343-6435
FAX: (212) 343-6484
Year Established: 1980
Pub. Frequency: 10/yr.
Page Size: standard
Subscrip. Rate: $6.95/yr.
Circulation: 245,000
Circulation Type: paid
**Owner(s):**
Scholastic Magazines, Inc.
555 Broadway
New York, NY 10012-3949
Telephone: (212) 343-6100
Ownership %: 100
**Editorial:**
Tracey Randinelli ........................Editor

**Desc.:** Classroom magazine for junior
high/middle school math students.
Activities and features focusing
on consumer math, math on the job,
computation to problem solving practice.
**Readers:** Junior high/middle school math
students.

24796
**SCHOLASTIC NEWS**
555 Broadway
New York, NY 10012
Telephone: (212) 343-6100
Year Established: 1922
Pub. Frequency: w.
Page Size: tabloid
Subscrip. Rate: $2.95/school yr.
Freelance Pay: $100/pg. publ.
Circulation: 3,500,000
Circulation Type: paid
**Owner(s):**
Scholastic Magazines, Inc.
555 Broadway
New York, NY 10012
Telephone: (212) 343-6100
Ownership %: 100
**Management:**
Dick Robinson .....................Publisher
**Editorial:**
Shelley Bedik .........................Editor
Jill Safro .........................Editor
Catherine Vanderhoof .........Editorial Director
Bob Lascaro .....................Art Director
Grace Howe ...............Photography Editor
**Desc.:** Carrier news, features, quizzes,
hobbies, interviews, science, arts, sports,
political developments and governmental
coverage, literature supplement, photo
essay.
**Readers:** Average 1-6th grade boy or girl.

26660
**SCHOLASTIC NEWS: NEWSTIME**
555 Broadway
New York, NY 10012
Telephone: (212) 343-6100
FAX: (212) 343-6484
Year Established: 1965
Pub. Frequency: 26/yr. (Sep.-May)
Page Size: tabloid
Subscrip. Rate: $10/yr. group of 10
Circulation: 3,500,000
Circulation Type: paid
**Owner(s):**
Scholastic Magazines, Inc.
555 Broadway
New York, NY 10012
Telephone: (212) 343-6100
Ownership %: 100
**Management:**
Richard Robinson .....................President
Ernest Fleishman .....................Publisher
**Editorial:**
Jan Van Raay .........................Editor
Patarick Daley ...............Editorial Director
**Desc.:** National classroom magazine.
**Readers:** 5th and 6th grade students.

24820
**SCHOLASTIC SCOPE**
555 Broadway
3rd Floor
New York, NY 10012
Telephone: (212) 343-6100
FAX: (212) 343-6333
Year Established: 1964
Pub. Frequency: 20/yr
Page Size: standard
Subscrip. Rate: $6.95/yr.
Circulation: 600,000
Circulation Type: paid
**Owner(s):**
Scholastic Magazines, Inc.
555 Broadway
New York, NY 10012
Telephone: (212) 343-6100
Ownership %: 100

**Management:**
M. Richard Robinson .....................Publisher
G. Estabrook Kindred .......Advertising Manager
**Editorial:**
Deborah Sussman .....................Senior Editor
John Rearick .........................Editor
Joy Makon .....................Art Director
Leigh Brower .........................Artist
Adrienne Su .....................Assistant Editor
Ken Jones .....................Associate Editor
Lucy Evankow .........................Librarian
Michael Nolan .................Marketing Manager
**Desc.:** Reading level 4th-6th grade -
maturity level 7th-12th grade. Covers
reading development, language skills,
fiction, plays, articles on human behavior
and decision making situations.
**Readers:** Uninterested or reluctant readers
in junior & senior high school who need
easy-to-read, yet mature reading
material.

57276
**SCHOLASTIC UPDATE**
555 Broadway
New York, NY 10012-3999
Telephone: (212) 343-6271
FAX: (212) 343-6333
Year Established: 1983
Pub. Frequency: 14/yr. (bi-w. during school
yr.)
Page Size: standard
Subscrip. Rate: $20/yr. single sub.;
$5.95/yr. bulk rate (10 or more)
Materials: 02,05,19,20,21,23,26,28,32
Freelance Pay: $150-$300/page
Print Process: offset
Circulation: 297,029
Circulation Type: free & paid
**Owner(s):**
Scholastic Magazines, Inc.
555 Broadway
New York, NY 10012
Telephone: (212) 343-3100
**Management:**
Richard Robinson .....................Publisher
**Editorial:**
Steven Manning .........................Editor
Phil Sudo ...............Managing Editor
Norbert Buchsbaum .................Senior Writer
**Desc.:** Current affairs magazine for high
school students, designed for use in
social studies classrooms. It examines
14 topics a year, one per issue, from the
perspectives of the five major social
studies curriculum areas. Aims to
provide a context, within the the social
studies, for understanding the day's
major public concerns.
**Readers:** Students in grades 8-12,
primarily in grades 11 & 12.

24825
**SCHOOL & COLLEGE**
1100 Superior Ave.
Cleveland, OH 44114-2543
Telephone: (216) 696-1777
FAX: (216) 696-1606
Year Established: 1962
Pub. Frequency: m.
Page Size: standard
Subscrip. Rate: $30/yr.
Materials: 01,06,15,25,28,29,30,32,33
Freelance Pay: varies
Print Process: offset
Circulation: 55,000
Circulation Type: controlled
**Owner(s):**
Peter Li, Inc.
330 Progress Rd.
Dayton, OH 45449
Telephone: (513) 847-5900
Ownership %: 100
**Management:**
Peter J. Li .....................Publisher

**Editorial:**
Roger Morton .........................Editor
Marge Smith ...............Production Coordinator
**Desc.:** Covers products to build, operate,
and maintain schools and colleges.
Departments include: Product News,
Literature and Catalogs, Book Reviews,
Audiovisual Software.
**Readers:** Administrative-level personnel.

24821
**SCHOOL & COMMUNITY**
407 S. Sixth St.
Columbia, MO 65201
Telephone: (314) 442-3127
FAX: (314) 443-5079
Mailing Address:
P.O. Box 458
Columbia, MO 65205
Year Established: 1915
Pub. Frequency: q.
Page Size: standard
Subscrip. Rate: $10/yr.
Circulation: 30,000
Circulation Type: paid
**Owner(s):**
Missouri State Teachers Association
P.O. Box 458
Columbia, MO 65205
Telephone: (314) 442-3127
Ownership %: 100
**Editorial:**
Bruce Moe .........Communications Director
Letha Albright .........Publication Editor
**Desc.:** Articles about school projects,
activities, association activities affecting
the Missouri school systems and
teachers.
**Readers:** Missouri educators and libraries.
Also superintendents & school board
members.

24822
**SCHOOLARTS**
50 Portland
Worcester, MA 01608
Telephone: (508) 754-7201
FAX: (508) 753-3834
Year Established: 1901
Pub. Frequency: 9/yr.
Page Size: standard
Subscrip. Rate: $4/issue; $23/yr.
Materials: 05,06,15,19,24,25,28,29,30,32
Print Process: web offset
Circulation: 25,000
Circulation Type: controlled & paid
**Owner(s):**
Davis Publications, Inc.
50 Portland St.
Worcester, MA 01608
Telephone: (508) 754-7201
Ownership %: 100
**Management:**
Wyatt Wade .........................Publisher
Allison Hughes .................Advertising Manager
Gerald J. Stashak .................General Manager
**Editorial:**
Eldon Katter .........................Editor
Holly Hanson .................Production Editor
**Desc.:** Art and craft teaching - educational.
Used for teaching and reference by art,
craft and classroom teachers in public
schools from elementary through high
school. Used as text in teachers
colleges, and for reference in libraries of
public and private schools and colleges.
**Readers:** Art supervisors, art teachers,
classroom teachers, superintendents,
principals and boards of education in
elementary, junior high and high schools
- public, parochial and private, college
and university art educators and
museums.

**Materials Accepted/Included:** 01-Business news 02-By-line articles  03-Fashion news 04-Food news 05-Freelance copy  06-Letters to editor  07-Real estate news  08-Sports news 09-Travel news 10-Book rev. 11-Movie rev. 12-Music rev. 13-TV rev. 14-Theater rev. 15-Coming events 16-Obituaries 17-Question & answer 18-Social announcements 19-Artwork 20-Cartoons 21-Photos 22-TV listings 23-Audio rec. 24-Video rec. 25-Books 26-Films/film clips 27-Personnel news 28-Press releases 29-New product news/photos 30-Trade lit. 31-Contracts awarded 32-Display adv. 33-Classified adv.

## SCHOOL BUSINESS AFFAIRS
24823

11401 N. Shore Dr.
Reston, VA 22090
Telephone: (703) 478-0405
FAX: (703) 478-0205
Year Established: 1936
Pub. Frequency: m.
Page Size: standard
Subscrip. Rate: $68/yr. to non-members
Materials: 02,10,28,29,30,32
Freelance Pay: none
Print Process: web
Circulation: 6,000
Circulation Type: paid
**Owner(s):**
Association of School Business Officials
11401 N. Shore Dr.
Reston, VA 22090
Telephone: (703) 478-0405
Ownership %: 100
**Management:**
Peg D. Kirkpatrick .............................Publisher
**Editorial:**
Peg D. Kirkpatrick .............................Editor
Robert Gluck .........................Assistant Editor
Don Tharpe .....................Executive Director
Peggy Gartner .................Production Editor
**Desc.:** Articles pertain to the field of
school business management.
**Readers:** School Business Officials
Charged With All Operational Aspects of
Schools.

## SCHOOLDAYS
68829

23740 Hawthorn Blvd.
Torrance, CA 90505
Telephone: (213) 378-1133
FAX: (213) 375-5090
Year Established: 1982
Pub. Frequency: q.
Subscrip. Rate: $18/yr.
Freelance Pay: per page a specific to
complexity of project
Circulation: 84,000
Circulation Type: paid
**Owner(s):**
Frank Schaffer Publications, Inc.
23740 Hawthorne Blvd.
Torrance, CA 90505
Telephone: (213) 378-1133
Ownership %: 100
**Editorial:**
Marsha Elyn Wright ...........................Editor
**Desc.:** Contains reproducible worksheets,
activities and ideas for the elementary
classroom and early childhood
curriculum.
**Readers:** Teachers of grades K-3;
teachers of early childhood.

## SCIENCE & CHILDREN
24827

1840 Wilson Blvd.
Arlington, VA 22201
Telephone: (703) 243-7100
FAX: (703) 243-7177
Year Established: 1963
Pub. Frequency: 8/yr.
Page Size: standard
Subscrip. Rate: $50/yr.
Circulation: 23,500
Circulation Type: paid
**Owner(s):**
N.S.T.A.
1840 Wilson Blvd.
Arlington, VA 22201
Telephone: (703) 243-7100
Ownership %: 100
**Management:**
Paul Kuntzler .....................Advertising Manager
**Editorial:**
Phyllis Marcuccio ...........................Editor
Mary Loleta Gwynn .................Managing Editor
Monica Locke .....................Associate Editor
Sebastian C. Hayman ..........Editorial Assistant

**Desc.:** A professional journal for
elementary and middle school science
teachers.
**Readers:** Elementary and middle school
teachers, science consultants, science
department heads, junior high teachers.

## SCIENCE ACTIVITIES
24897

1319 18th St., N.W.
Washington, DC 20036-1802
Telephone: (202) 296-6267
FAX: (202) 296-5149
Year Established: 1964
Pub. Frequency: q.
Page Size: standard
Subscrip. Rate: $30/yr. individual; $54/yr.
institution
Circulation: 1,110
Circulation Type: paid
**Owner(s):**
Heldref Publications
1319 18th St., N.W.
Washington, DC 20036-1802
Telephone: (202) 296-6267
Ownership %: 100
**Management:**
Walter E. Beach .............................Publisher
Raymond M. Rallo ..........Advertising Manager
Cathy Welker .....................Circulation Manager
Kerri P. Kilbane .................Promotion Manager
**Editorial:**
Claire Wilson .........................Managing Editor
**Desc.:** Science Activities is a storehouse
of up-to-date, creative science projects
for the K-12 classroom teacher. A one-
step source of experiments, explorations
and projects in the biological, physical
and behavioral sciences, its ideas have
been teacher-tested, providing the best
of actual classroom experiences.
**Readers:** Teachers in grades K-12.

## SCIENCE TEACHER, THE
24828

1840 Wilson Blvd.
Arlington, VA 22201
Telephone: (703) 243-7100
FAX: (703) 243-7177
Year Established: 1943
Pub. Frequency: 9/yr.
Page Size: standard
Subscrip. Rate: $50/yr.
Freelance Pay: negotiable
Circulation: 27,000
Circulation Type: paid
**Owner(s):**
National Science Teachers Association
1742 Connecticut Ave., N.W.
Washington, DC 20009
Telephone: (202) 328-5600
Ownership %: 100
**Management:**
Paul Kuntzler .....................Advertising Manager
**Editorial:**
Juliana Texley .............................Editor
Shelley Carey .........................Managing Editor
**Desc.:** Articles by instructors discuss
scientific topics (all scientific disciplines),
teaching techniques, use of experiments
and demonstrations, professional
approach, etc. To the teaching of
science on the junior high and high
school levels.
**Readers:** Junior and senior high school
science teachers.

## SCIENCE WORLD
24901

730 Broadway
New York, NY 10003
Telephone: (212) 343-6100
Year Established: 1958
Pub. Frequency: 14/yr.
Page Size: standard
Subscrip. Rate: $6.95/yr.
Circulation: 550,000

Circulation Type: paid
**Owner(s):**
Scholastic Magazines, Inc.
730 Broadway
New York, NY 10003
Telephone: (212) 505-3072
Ownership %: 100
**Management:**
Richard Robinson .............................Publisher
Michelle Magazine ..........Advertising Manager
**Editorial:**
Karen McNulty .............................Editor
**Desc.:** Covers recent developments in
general science, nature study, earth and
space science, biology, chemistry, and
physics for students in 7 through 10
grades for classroom use and
supplementary reading.
**Readers:** Junior and senior high school
science teachers.

## SOCIAL EDUCATION
24830

3501 Newark St., N.W.
Washington, DC 20016
Telephone: (202) 966-7840
Year Established: 1937
Pub. Frequency: 7/yr.
Page Size: standard
Subscrip. Rate: $50/yr.
Circulation: 26,000
Circulation Type: paid
**Owner(s):**
National Council for the Social Studies
3501 Newark St., N.W.
Washington, DC 20016
Telephone: (202) 966-7840
Ownership %: 100
**Management:**
Susan Grifin .....................Advertising Manager
**Editorial:**
Salvatore J. Natoli .............................Editor
Pamela Hollar .........................Associate Editor
John Haas .........................Book Review Editor
Dorothy Skeel .....................Education Editor
Kathryn Scott .........................Research Editor
**Desc.:** Publishes articles on such topics as
creative ways of strengthening social
studies education, innovative materials
and methods directly related to social
studies instruction.
**Readers:** Members of the National Council
for the Social Studies - teachers,
chairpersons, supervisors, and research
scholars.

## SOCIALIST REVIEW
70451

905 W. Main St., Ste. 18-B
Duke University Press
Durham, NC 27701
Telephone: (919) 687-3636
FAX: (919) 688-4574
Mailing Address:
P.O. Box 90660
Durham, NC 27708-0660
Year Established: 1970
Pub. Frequency: q.
Page Size: standard
Subscrip. Rate: $28/yr. individuals; $65/yr.
institutions
Materials: 32
Circulation: 2,500
Circulation Type: controlled & paid
**Owner(s):**
Duke University Press
P.O. Box 90660
Durham, NC 27708-0660
Telephone: (919) 687-3600
FAX: (919) 688-4574
Ownership %: 100
**Management:**
Patricia Thomas .............................Manager
**Editorial:**
David Trend .............................Editor

## SOCIAL SCIENCE COMPUTER REVIEW
59568

Brightleaf Sq., Ste. 18-B
Durham, NC 27701
Telephone: (919) 687-3636
FAX: (919) 688-4574
Year Established: 1982
Pub. Frequency: q.
Page Size: standard
Subscrip. Rate: $48/yr. individuals; $88/yr.
institutions; $24/yr. students with ID
Materials: 32
Circulation: 1,000
Circulation Type: paid
**Owner(s):**
Duke University Press
P.O. Box 90660
Durham, NC 27708-0660
Telephone: (919) 687-3600
FAX: (919) 688-4574
Ownership %: 100
**Management:**
Patricia Thomas .............................Manager
**Editorial:**
G. David Garson .............................Editor
**Desc.:** SSCR provides a unique forum for
social scientists to acquire and share
information on the research and
teaching applications of microcomputing.
**Readers:** Social Scientists

## SOCIAL SCIENCE HISTORY
59569

Brightleaf Sq., Ste. 18-B
805 Main St.
Durham, NC 27701
Telephone: (919) 687-3636
FAX: (919) 688-4574
Year Established: 1976
Pub. Frequency: q.
Page Size: standard
Subscrip. Rate: $30/yr. individuals; $65/yr.
institutions; $12/yr. students
Materials: 32
Circulation: 1,000
Circulation Type: paid
**Owner(s):**
Social Science History Association
c/o H. W. Allen, History Dept.
Carbondale, IL 62901
Ownership %: 100
**Management:**
Patricia Thomas .............................Manager
**Editorial:**
Ron Aminzade .............................Editor
Mary Jo Maynes .............................Editor
Russell R. Menard .............................Editor
Steven Ruggles .............................Editor

## SOCIOLOGY OF EDUCATION
24831

1722 N Street, N.W.
Washington, DC 20036
Telephone: (202) 833-3410
Year Established: 1963
Pub. Frequency: q.
Page Size: standard
Subscrip. Rate: $36/yr. individual; $66/yr.
add; $6-postage out US
Circulation: 3,000
Circulation Type: paid
**Owner(s):**
The American Sociological Association
1722 N Street, NW
Washington, DC 20036
Telephone: (202) 833-3410
Ownership %: 100
**Management:**
Karen G. Edwards ..........Advertising Manager
**Editorial:**
Julia Wrigley .............................Editor

---

**Materials Accepted/Included:** 01-Business news 02-By-line articles 03-Fashion news 04-Food news 05-Freelance copy 06-Letters to editor 07-Real estate news 08-Sports news 09-Travel news 10-Book rev. 11-Movie rev. 12-Music rev. 13-TV rev. 14-Theater rev. 15-Coming events 16-Obituaries 17-Question & answer 18-Social announcements 19-Artwork 20-Cartoons 21-Photos 22-TV listings 23-Audio rec. 24-Video rec. 25-Books 26-Films/film clips 27-Personnel news 28-Press releases 29-New product news/photos 30-Trade lit. 31-Contracts awarded 32-Display adv. 33-Classified adv.

**Desc.:** Provides a forum for studies of education by scholars in all the social sciences from all parts of the world. Theoretical perspectives of anthropology, economics, history, political science, psychology and sociology for the task of analyzing educational institutions.
**Readers:** Largely educators and social scientists.

59565

**SOUTH ATLANTIC QUARTERLY, THE**
Brightleaf Sq., Ste. 18-B
805 Main St.
Durham, NC 27701
Telephone: (919) 687-3636
FAX: (919) 688-4574
Year Established: 1902
Pub. Frequency: q.
Page Size: standard
Subscrip. Rate: $24/yr. individual; $54/yr. institutions
Materials: 32
Circulation: 1,800
Circulation Type: paid
**Owner(s):**
Duke University Press
P.O. Box 90660
Durham, NC 27701
Telephone: (919) 687-3600
FAX: (919) 688-4574
Ownership %: 100
**Management:**
Patricia Thomas ...........................Manager
**Editorial:**
Fredric Jameson ..............................Editor

70453

**SOUTHERN CULTURES**
905 W. Main St., Ste. 18-B
Duke University Press
Durham, NC 27701
Telephone: (919) 687-3636
FAX: (919) 688-4574
Mailing Address:
    P.O. Box 90660
    Durham, NC 27708-0660
Year Established: 1993
Pub. Frequency: q.
Page Size: standard
Subscrip. Rate: $24/yr. individuals
Materials: 32
**Owner(s):**
Duke University Press
P.O. Box 90660
Durham, NC 27708-0660
Telephone: (919) 687-3600
FAX: (919) 688-4574
Ownership %: 100
**Management:**
Patricia Thomas ...........................Manager
**Editorial:**
John Shelton Reed ...........................Editor
Harry L. Watson ..............................Editor

58804

**STATE EDUCATION LEADER**
707 17th St., Ste 2700
Denver, CO 80202-3427
Telephone: (303) 299-3626
FAX: (303) 296-8332
Year Established: 1985
Pub. Frequency: 3/yr.
Page Size: tabloid
Subscrip. Rate: $15/yr.
Freelance Pay: up to $200
Print Process: offset
Circulation: 5,000
Circulation Type: free & paid
**Owner(s):**
Education Commission of the States
707 17th St., Ste 2700
Denver, CO 80202-3427
Telephone: (303) 299-3626
Ownership %: 100

**Editorial:**
Sherry F. Walker ..............................Editor
**Desc.:** Focus on issues, trends & events affecting education policy decisions.
**Readers:** Education policy makers.

69299

**TEACHING & LEARNING WITH CHILDREN & YOUNG ADULTS**
39 Pearl St.
Brandon, VT 05733
Telephone: (802) 247-8312
Mailing Address:
    P.O. Box 328
    Brandon, VT 05733-0328
Year Established: 1993
Pub. Frequency: 5/yr.
Page Size: standard
Subscrip. Rate: $29/yr.
Circulation: 150
Circulation Type: paid
**Owner(s):**
Psychology Press - Holistic Education Press
39 Pearl St.
Brandon, VT 05733
Telephone: (802) 247-8312
Ownership %: 100
**Management:**
Charles S. Jakiela ...........................President
**Editorial:**
Sid S. Glassner .........................Editor in Chief
**Readers:** Educators and parents interested in helping children experience high quality children's literature. Teachers, professors, curriculum developers, reading specialists.

66585

**TEACHING ELEMENTARY PHYSICAL EDUCATION (TEPE)**
1607 N. Market St.
Champaign, IL 61820
Telephone: (217) 351-5076
FAX: (217) 351-2674
Mailing Address:
    P.O. Box 5076
    Champaign, IL 61825
Year Established: 1990
Pub. Frequency: 6/yr.
Page Size: standard
Subscrip. Rate: $12/yr. students; $18/yr. individuals; $36/yr. institutions
Print Process: offset
Circulation: 4,000
Circulation Type: paid
**Owner(s):**
Human Kinetics Publishers, Inc
1607 N. Market St.
Champaign, IL 61820
Telephone: (217) 351-5076
FAX: (217) 351-2674
Ownership %: 100
**Management:**
Rainer Martens ...........................Publisher
**Editorial:**
Christine Hopple ...........................Editor
Scott Wikgren ..............................Director
**Desc.:** The newsletter for specialists, teachers and administrators that effectively bridges the gap between theory and the demands of the real world in children's physical education. It contains practical ideas for instruction, a listing of resources and events, news, professional issues, profiles, and more.
**Readers:** Physical education specialists, physical education teachers and professors, education administrators.

24836

**TEACHING EXCEPTIONAL CHILDREN**
1920 Association Dr.
Reston, VA 22091
Telephone: (703) 620-3660
FAX: (703) 264-9494

Year Established: 1968
Pub. Frequency: q.
Page Size: standard
Subscrip. Rate: $30/yr. to non-members
Circulation: 55,367
Circulation Type: paid
**Owner(s):**
Council for Exceptional Children
1920 Association Dr.
Reston, VA 22091
Telephone: (703) 620-3660
Ownership %: 100
**Management:**
James Casamento ...........Advertising Manager
**Editorial:**
H. William Heller ...................Associate Editor
Fred Spooner ........................Associate Editor
Cathy Mack ..........................Production Editor
**Desc.:** Practical articles about teaching exceptional children (all exceptionalities, all ages).
**Readers:** Special education teachers, administrators, directors, principals, teacher educators, supervisors, student teachers, reading specialists, therapists (physical, speech & occupational), social workers, and counselors.

24735

**TEACHING K-8**
40 Richards Ave.
Norwalk, CT 06854-2309
Telephone: (203) 855-2650
FAX: (203) 855-2656
Year Established: 1970
Pub. Frequency: 8/yr. (Sep.-May)
Page Size: standard
Subscrip. Rate: $19.77/yr.
Materials: 05,06,20,32
Freelance Pay: varies
Circulation: 142,000
Circulation Type: paid
**Owner(s):**
Highlights for Children, Inc.
Box 269
Columbus, OH 43216
Telephone: (614) 486-0631
Ownership %: 100
**Management:**
Allen Raymond ..........................Publisher
Lisa Hershey ...................Advertising Manager
**Editorial:**
Patricia Broderick ...........................Editor
Carol Hurst ....................Book Review Editor
**Desc.:** A professional magazine for teachers, pre-school through grade 8.
**Readers:** Elementary school teachers.

58805

**TEACHING PHILOSOPHY**
Philosophy Documentation Center
Bowling Green State University
Bowling Green, OH 43403-0189
Telephone: (419) 372-2419
FAX: (419) 372-6987
Pub. Frequency: q.
Page Size: standard
Subscrip. Rate: $57.50/yr.; $23.50/yr. individuals
Circulation: 950
Circulation Type: paid
**Owner(s):**
Philosophy Documentation Center
Bowling Green State Univ.
Bowling Green, OH 43402
Telephone: (419) 372-2419
Ownership %: 100
**Management:**
Cindy Richards ...................Business Manager
**Editorial:**
Arnold Wilson ...........................Editor
**Desc.:** Provides an open forum for the exchange and evaluation of ideas, information, and materials concerned with the teaching of philosophy.

24826

**TECH DIRECTIONS**
275 Metty Dr., Ste. 1
Ann Arbor, MI 48103
Telephone: (313) 769-1211
FAX: (313) 769-8383
Mailing Address:
    P.O. Box 8623
    Ann Arbor, MI 48107-8623
Year Established: 1941
Pub. Frequency: m.: Aug.-May
Page Size: standard
Subscrip. Rate: $25/yr.
Materials: 01,02,05,06,15,19,20,21,25,28, 29,30,32,33
Freelance Pay: $25-$200
Print Process: web offset
Circulation: 44,000
Circulation Type: controlled
**Owner(s):**
Prakken Publications, Inc.
P.O. Box 8623
Ann Arbor, MI 48107-8623
Telephone: (313) 769-1211
FAX: (313) 769-8383
Ownership %: 100
**Management:**
George F. Kennedy ...........................Publisher
Alice B. Augustus ............Advertising Manager
Turalee Barlow ..................Circulation Manager
**Editorial:**
Susanne Peckham ...........................Editor
Paul Bamford ...............................Editor
Sharon K. Miller ...............................Art Director
Vicki Hubert ....................Marketing Manager
**Desc.:** Articles by teachers and teacher educators in vocational/technical and technology education, covering projects, practices, and programs in the field. Uses short news releases on new products for these fields. Departments include: News (items of interest to teachers and administrators), News from Industry (new products and teaching aids), Instructional Resources (books, pamphlets, audio-visual materials), From Washington, Technology's Past, On Tools.
**Readers:** School shop teachers, administrators and teacher educators in all phases of industrial, vocational, and technical education.
**Deadline:** story-1st of mo. prior to pub. date; news-10th of mo. prior; photo-1st of mo. prior; ads-1st of mo. prior

24784

**TECHNOLOGY TEACHER, THE**
1914 Association Dr.
Reston, VA 22091
Telephone: (703) 860-2100
Year Established: 1939
Pub. Frequency: 8/yr.
Page Size: standard
Subscrip. Rate: $55/yr. US; $60/yr. foreign
Materials: 25,28,29,32
Print Process: offset
Circulation: 8,000
Circulation Type: paid
**Owner(s):**
International Technology Education Assn.
1914 Association Dr.
Reston, VA 22091
Telephone: (703) 860-2100
Ownership %: 100
**Management:**
Jane Day ...........................Advertising Manager
**Editorial:**
Kendall N. Starkweather ...........Editor in Chief
Judy Miller ...............................Editor

**Materials Accepted/Included:** 01-Business news 02-By-line articles 03-Fashion news 04-Food news 05-Freelance copy 06-Letters to editor 07-Real estate news 08-Sports news 09-Travel news 10-Book rev. 11-Movie rev. 12-Music rev. 13-TV rev. 14-Theater rev. 15-Coming events 16-Obituaries 17-Question & answer 18-Social announcements 19-Artwork 20-Cartoons 21-Photos 22-TV listings 23-Audio rec. 24-Video rec. 25-Books 26-Films/film clips 27-Personnel news 28-Press releases 29-New product news/photos 30-Trade lit. 31-Contracts awarded 32-Display adv. 33-Classified adv.

**Desc.:** Articles of fact and opinion on new developments in technology education, education, philosophy and practical application: Information of interest to teachers of technology/research, workshops, problems, trends, etc. Book reviews, product reviews, researchers application.
**Readers:** Teachers of technology education, supervisors, administrators; libraries.
**Deadline:** ads-1st of mo. prior to pub. date

**TECHTRENDS**   24565
1025 Vermont Ave., N.W.
Ste. 820
Washington, DC 20005
Telephone: (202) 347-7834
FAX: (202) 347-7839
Year Established: 1955
Pub. Frequency: 6/yr.
Page Size: standard
Subscrip. Rate: $36/yr.
Circulation: 10000
Circulation Type: paid
**Owner(s):**
Assn. for Educational Communications & Tech.
1025 Vermont Ave. N.W.
Ste. 820
Washington, DC 20005
Telephone: (202) 347-7834
Ownership %: 100
**Management:**
Stan Zenor ..........................Publisher
**Editorial:**
Mary Cavaliere ..........................Editor
**Desc.:** Covers the field of instructional technology and the uses of new technology including computers, interactive video, film, and so forth. Also includes articles on legislation affecting education, instructional materials centers & other developments affecting education and training. Departments include: The Leading Edge, Instructional Resources, New Products, The Copyright Column, School Learning Resources.
**Readers:** Educational technologists at all levels of education and industry, professors, directors of learning centers, media specialists, audiovisual specialists.

**TEXAS HISTORIAN**   24838
Richardson Hall 2-306
University Sta.
Austin, TX 78712
Telephone: (512) 471-1525
Year Established: 1940
Pub. Frequency: 5/yr.
Page Size: standard
Subscrip. Rate: $6/yr.
Circulation: 2,500
Circulation Type: paid
**Owner(s):**
Texas State Historical Association
Sid Richardson Hall 2-306
University Sta.
Austin, TX 78712
Telephone: (512) 471-1525
Ownership %: 100
**Editorial:**
Ron Tyler ..........................Editor
**Desc.:** A magazine of Texas history written by and for young historians. Articles cover communities, art, local industry, personalities, settling of the state, etc. Writers are junior and senior high school students.
**Readers:** Professional historians, others interested. History buffs, students, etc.

**T.H.E. JOURNAL:**   24832
**TECHNOLOGICAL HORIZONS IN EDUCATION**
150 El Camino Real, Ste. 112
Tustin, CA 92680
Telephone: (714) 730-4011
Year Established: 1973
Pub. Frequency: 11/yr. plus 4 special issues
Page Size: standard
Subscrip. Rate: $29/yr. non-qualified subscribers US.
Circulation: 141,500
Circulation Type: controlled
**Owner(s):**
T.H.E. Journal
150 El Camino Real, Ste. 112
Tustin, CA 92680
Telephone: (714) 730-4011
Ownership %: 100
**Management:**
Edward W. Warnshuis ..........President
Wendy LaDuke ..........Vice President
Edward W. Warnshuis ..........Publisher
**Editorial:**
Dr. Sylvia Charp ..........Editor in Chief
Dr. John Hamblen ..........Editor
Dr. Phil Lewis ..........Editor
Dr. Bernard Luskin ..........Editor
Terian Tyre ..........Managing Editor
Barbara Calvert ..........Director
Cheri Edwards ..........Director
Tom Creevy ..........Director
Wendy LaDuke ..........Director
**Desc.:** Application of technology to education. A forum for educators sharing techniques to improve the education process in public school, higher education and industry training through use of technology products and services.
**Readers:** Administrative and instructional managers in public schools, higher education and industry training.

**TODAY'S CATHOLIC TEACHER**   24840
330 Progress Rd.
Dayton, OH 45449
Telephone: (513) 847-5900
FAX: (513) 847-5910
Year Established: 1968
Pub. Frequency: 8/yr.
Page Size: standard
Subscrip. Rate: $14.95/yr.
Freelance Pay: varies
Circulation: 50,000
Circulation Type: paid
**Owner(s):**
Peter Li, Inc.
330 Progress Rd.
Dayton, OH 45449
Telephone: (513) 847-5900
Ownership %: 100
**Management:**
Peter J. Li ..........Publisher
Rosemary E. Walker ..........Circulation Manager
**Editorial:**
Ruth A. Matheny ..........Executive Editor
Stephen Brittan ..........Editor
Ann Tomsic ..........Advertising
Anthony Malone ..........Art Director
Stewart Halface ..........Design
**Desc.:** Contains articles, columns and announcements on Catholic education in school and at home, for parents, teachers, and administrators. Departments include: Special Columns, General Features, New Products, News to Use, Computers in Education, On Development.
**Readers:** Teachers and administrators in Catholic and other private education, parents, pastors, boards of education.

**TOPICS IN EARLY CHILDHOOD EDUCATION**   70469
8700 Shoal Creek Blvd.
Austin, TX 78757-6897
Telephone: (512) 451-3246
FAX: (512) 451-8542
Year Established: 1981
Pub. Frequency: q.
Page Size: 6" x 9"
Subscrip. Rate: $35/yr. institutions; $70/yr. institutions
Circulation: 2,615
Circulation Type: controlled & paid
**Owner(s):**
Pro-Ed Journals
8700 Shoal Creek Blvd.
Austin, TX 78757-6897
Telephone: (512) 451-3246
FAX: (512) 451-8542
Ownership %: 100
**Management:**
Donald D. Hammill ..........Publisher
**Editorial:**
Mark Wolery ..........Editor
Lisa Tippett ..........Managing Editor
**Desc.:** Multi-disciplinary focus on the status, issues, research in early childhood special education.
**Readers:** Educators, psychologists, clinicians and other specialists.

**TRENDS IN HIGH SCHOOL & COLLEGE MEDIA**   24818
620 Rarig Ctr., 330 21st Ave., S., U of Minn.
Minneapolis, MN 55455
Telephone: (612) 625-8335
FAX: (612) 625-0720
Year Established: 1921
Pub. Frequency: 3/yr.
Page Size: tabloid
Subscrip. Rate: $20/yr.
Freelance Pay: negotiable
Circulation: 4,000
Circulation Type: paid
**Owner(s):**
National Scholastic Press
620 Rarig Ctr./U. of Minnesota
Minneapolis, MN 55455
Telephone: (612) 625-8335
Ownership %: 100
**Management:**
Tom Keekly ..........Advertising Manager
Don Reedes ..........Business Manager
Annie Witta ..........Circulation Manager
**Editorial:**
Tom E. Rolnicki ..........Editor
Tom Keekly ..........Managing Editor
Don Reeder ..........Assistant Editor
Tom E. Rolnicki ..........Director
Don Reeder ..........New Products Editor
Tom Keekly ..........Production Director
**Desc.:** Covers all phases of student publications (yearbook, newspaper, magazine), how-to-do-it suggestions, new ideas and developments in the field, production, editorial and business problems, advisers' news and suggestions; facts and figures from the field in general; for 63 years has led the field of student publications. Official organ of national scholastic press association. Departments include: Technology Watch, Book Update, Memories on Video, Today's Photographer, Desktop Repartee.
**Readers:** Advisers and staffs of high school and college publications (newspaper, yearbook, feature-literary magazines) in all states and interested in student publications.

**UEA ACTION**   24842
875 E. 5180 S.
Salt Lake Cty, UT 84107
Telephone: (801) 266-4461
FAX: (801) 265-2249
Year Established: 1969
Pub. Frequency: m. exc. Jun. & Aug.
Page Size: tabloid
Subscrip. Rate: $4/yr.
Materials: 06,28
Freelance Pay: N/A
Print Process: web offset
Circulation: 16,700
Circulation Type: paid
**Owner(s):**
Utah Education Association
875 E. 5180 S.
Salt Lake Cty, UT 84107
Telephone: (801) 266-4461
FAX: (801) 265-2249
Ownership %: 100
**Editorial:**
Steve Hale ..........Editor
**Desc.:** Covers national, state and local association activities, and the professional aspects of teaching.
**Readers:** Principally classroom teachers, counselors.

**UNIVERSITY GAZETTE**   58661
210 Pittsboro St.
CB #6205
Chapel Hill, NC 27599-6205
Telephone: (919) 962-7124
Pub. Frequency: s-m., exc. Dec.
Page Size: tabloid
Subscrip. Rate: membership
Print Process: web
Circulation: 9,000
Circulation Type: controlled & free
**Owner(s):**
UNC-Chapel Hill
210 Pittsboro St.
Chapel Hill, NC 27516
Telephone: (919) 962-7124
Ownership %: 100
**Editorial:**
Margaret Plumb Balcom ..........Editor
**Desc.:** Faculty/Staff newspaper for UNC at Chapel Hill.
**Readers:** Faculty and staff University of North Carolina at Chapel Hill.

**URBAN EDUCATION**   65059
2455 Teller Rd.
Thousand Oaks, CA 91320
Telephone: (805) 499-0721
FAX: (805) 499-0871
Year Established: 1966
Pub. Frequency: q.
Page Size: standard
Subscrip. Rate: $45/yr. individual; $145/yr. institution
Circulation: 780
Circulation Type: paid
**Owner(s):**
Sage Publications, Inc.
2455 Teller Rd.
Thousand Oaks, CA 91320
Telephone: (805) 499-0721
Ownership %: 100
**Editorial:**
Kofl Nomotey ..........Editor
Cris Anderson ..........Circulation Administrator
**Desc.:** Aims to improve the quality of urban education by making the results of relevant empirical and scholarly inquiry from a variety of fields more widely available.
**Readers:** Academic communities.

Materials Accepted/Included: 01-Business news 02-By-line articles 03-Fashion news 04-Food news 05-Freelance copy 06-Letters to editor 07-Real estate news 08-Sports news 09-Travel news 10-Book rev. 11-Movie rev. 12-Music rev. 13-TV rev. 14-Theater rev. 15-Coming events 16-Obituaries 17-Question & answer 18-Social announcements 19-Artwork 20-Cartoons 21-Photos 22-TV listings 23-Audio rec. 24-Video rec. 25-Books 26-Films/film clips 27-Personnel news 28-Press releases 29-New product news/photos 30-Trade lit. 31-Contracts awarded 32-Display adv. 33-Classified adv.
4-349

**USA TODAY**　24843
99 Hawthorne Ave Ste. 518
Valley Stream, NY 11580
Telephone: (516) 568-9191
Year Established: 1915
Pub. Frequency: m.
Page Size: standard
Subscrip. Rate: $2.25/issue; $24/1 yr.;
　$39.95/2 yrs.; $54/3 yrs.
Materials: 01,02,04,06,09,10,11,24,25,28,
　29,32
Freelance Pay: varies
Print Process: web offset
Circulation: 251,000
Circulation Type: paid
**Owner(s):**
Society for the Advancement of Education
99 W. Hawthorne Ave
Valley Stream, NY 11580
Telephone: (516) 568-9191
Ownership %: 100
**Management:**
Stanley Lehrer .................................Publisher
Robert S. Rothenberg .......Advertising Manager
**Editorial:**
Robert S. Rothenberg .............Managing Editor
**Desc.:** Covers 19 areas of universal
　interest: national affairs, international
　affairs, social affairs, education,
　economics, psychology, law and justice,
　medicine and health, philosophy,
　religion, business and finance, history,
　mass media, literature, art, theater,
　science and technology, ecology, books
　and geography.
**Readers:** Americans leaders and general
　public.
**Deadline:** story-10 wks. prior to pub. date;
　news-6 wks. prior; ads-4 wks. prior

**VIRGINIA JOURNAL OF**　24845
　**EDUCATION**
116 S. Third St.
Richmond, VA 23219
Telephone: (804) 648-5801
Year Established: 1903
Pub. Frequency: m.
Page Size: standard
Subscrip. Rate: $10/yr.
Circulation: 50,500
Circulation Type: paid
**Owner(s):**
Virginia Education Association
116 S. Third St.
Richmond, VA 23219
Telephone: (804) 648-5801
Ownership %: 100
**Editorial:**
Joseph W. Bland .................Executive Editor
Tom Allen ...........................................Editor
Yolanda Morris ...........................Advertising
Rosemarie Studer .............Contributing Editor
Yolanda Morris .....................Editorial Assistant
**Desc.:** Contributed and staff-written articles
　on current educational issues, research
　with direct application to the classroom,
　inspirational as well as tried and true
　practices in the classroom, trends in
　education, and "how-to-do-it" articles
　from Kindergarten through grade 12.
**Readers:** Teachers, principals,
　administrators, counselors, other school
　employees, central office staff, state
　department of education, general
　assembly members.

**VOCATIONAL EDUCATION**　24847
　**JOURNAL**
1410 King St.
Alexandria, VA 22314
Telephone: (703) 683-3111
FAX: (703) 683-7424
Year Established: 1925

Pub. Frequency: 8/yr.
Page Size: standard
Subscrip. Rate: $32/yr. US.; $64/yr.
　foreign
Materials: 06,10,15,24,25,29,32,33
Print Process: web offset
Circulation: 45,000
Circulation Type: paid
**Owner(s):**
American Vocational Association
1410 King St.
Alexandria, VA 22314
Telephone: (703) 683-3111
**Management:**
Charles Buzzell ..................Executive Director
Fred Kurst ........................Advertising Manager
**Editorial:**
Paul Plawin ........................................Editor
Kathy Leftwich ........................Managing Editor
**Desc.:** Covers current and emerging issues
　pertaining to education for work,
　examines and discusses professional
　issues related to vocational education,
　presents promising practices, programs
　and products.
**Readers:** Vocational, technical educators,
　teachers.
**Deadline:** story-3 mo. prior to pub. datee;
　news-3 mo. prior; ads-15th of mo. prior
　to pub. date

**VOLTA REVIEW, THE**　24848
3417 Volta Place, N.W.
Washington, DC 20007-2778
Telephone: (202) 337-5220
FAX: (202) 337-8314
Year Established: 1899
Pub. Frequency: 5/yr.
Page Size: standard
Subscrip. Rate: $42/yr.
Materials: 06,10
Circulation: 5,700
Circulation Type: paid
**Owner(s):**
Alexander Graham Bell Assn. for the Deaf,
Inc.
3417 Volta Place, N.W.
Washington, DC 20007-2778
Telephone: (202) 337-5220
Ownership %: 100
**Management:**
Patrick Stone ..................................President
Elizabeth Quigley .............Advertising Manager
**Editorial:**
David F. Conway ................................Editor
K. Brooke Rigler ....................Managing Editor
Nola Kende ...........Associate Managing Editor
Nancy McGarr ........................Associate Editor
Christine Yoshinaga-Itano .......Associate Editor
John Vaughan .......................Associate Editor
Carol Kagel ..........................Associate Editor
Agnes Phillips .......................Associate Editor
Jean-Pierre Gagne ................Associate Editor
**Desc.:** Covers deaf oralism, speech
　therapy, mainstream education of the
　hearing impaired.
**Readers:** Teachers, parents & others
　working with the hearing impaired, deaf
　adults; researchers, speech & language
　pathologists, audiologists, and
　psychologists.

**WEA NEWS**　24854
115 E. 22nd St.
Cheyenne, WY 82001
Telephone: (307) 634-7991
FAX: (307) 778-8161
Year Established: 1949
Pub. Frequency: 5/yr.
Page Size: standard
Subscrip. Rate: $10/yr.
Materials: 28,32
Print Process: offset

Circulation: 7,050
Circulation Type: paid
**Owner(s):**
Wyoming Education Association
115 E. 22nd St.
Cheyenne, WY 82001
Telephone: (307) 634-7991
Ownership %: 100
**Editorial:**
Ron Sniffin ..............................Editor in Chief
Ron Sniffin ................................News Editor
**Desc.:** Carries articles by teachers and
　educators dealing with teaching
　developments and news of state,
　national and international interest.
**Readers:** Teachers, superintendents,
　school boards, other school personnel
　and legislators.

**WORLD NEWSMAP OF THE**　48335
　**WEEK-HEADLINE FOCUS**
245 Long Hill Rd.
Middletown, CT 06457
Telephone: (800) 446-3355
Year Established: 1938
Pub. Frequency: 27/yr.
Page Size: poster format
Subscrip. Rate: $79.95/yr.
Circulation: 12,663
Circulation Type: paid
**Owner(s):**
Weekly Reader Corporation
245 Long Hill Rd.
Middletown, CT 06457
Telephone: (800) 466-3355
Ownership %: 100
**Editorial:**
Sandra Maccarone ...................................Editor
**Desc.:** Every issue includes a world map
　projection with international news. One
　news story is presented in detail in a
　Nation-in-the-News focus article.
**Readers:** Middle school and high school
　students enrolled in geography, current
　events and history courses.

## Group 240-Science, General

**ABSTRACTS OF PAPERS**　58718
**PRESENTED TO THE AMERICAN**
**MATHEMATICAL SOCIETY**
201 Charles St.
Providence, RI 02904
Telephone: (401) 455-4000
FAX: (401) 331-3842
Year Established: 1979
Pub. Frequency: bi-m.
Page Size: standard
Subscrip. Rate: $68/yr.
**Owner(s):**
American Mathematical Society
P.O. Box 6248
Providence, RI 02940
Telephone: (401) 272-9500
Ownership %: 100
**Management:**
Robert M. Fossum .............Chairman of Board
**Editorial:**
Joseph A. Cima ...................................Editor
W. Wistar Comfort ...............................Editor
Andy Roy Magid ..................................Editor
Lance W. Small ...................................Editor
**Desc.:** Contains abstracts of contributed &
　invited talks presented at AMS
　meetings. In addition to abstracts of
　invited hour addresses, papers
　presented in special sessions or in
　sessions for contributed papers, there is
　a section of abstracts of papers
　presented to the society by title.
**Readers:** Professional mathematicians and
　mathematical researchers in government
　industry & academics.

**AMERICAN BIRDS**　59052
700 Broadway
New York, NY 10003
Telephone: (212) 979-3000
Year Established: 1947
Pub. Frequency: 5/yr.
Page Size: standard
Subscrip. Rate: $30/yr. individual; $32/yr.
　institution
Circulation: 14,500
Circulation Type: paid
**Owner(s):**
National Audubon Society
700 Broadway
New York, NY 10003
Telephone: (212) 979-3000
Ownership %: 100
**Editorial:**
Susan Roney Drennan .............................Editor
Geoff LeBaron ...................................Editor
Victoria Leidner ......................Managing Editor
Kenn Kaufman ........................Associate Editor
**Desc.:** Devoted to bird life of North
　America.
**Readers:** American Birds subscribers are a
　select group whose lifelong commitment
　to birds makes them an extraordinarily
　dedicated and faithful audience.

**AMERICAN INDUSTRIAL HYGIENE**　23702
　**ASSOCIATION JOURNAL**
2700 Prosperity Ave., Ste. 250
Fairfax, VA 22031
Telephone: (703) 849-8888
FAX: (703) 207-3561
Year Established: 1940
Pub. Frequency: m.
Page Size: standard
Subscrip. Rate: $110/yr. US; $135/yr. CN
　& MX; $175/yr. elsewhere
Circulation: 11,000
Circulation Type: paid
**Owner(s):**
American Industrial Hygiene Association
2700 Prosperity Ave., Ste. 250
Fairfax, VA 22031
Telephone: (703) 849-8888
Ownership %: 100
**Management:**
Fagthe Beuson ....................................Manager
**Editorial:**
Howard Cohen ..........................Editor in Chief
Rona Bagart ..................................Advertising
Linda Marsicano ..................Editorial Assistant
Georgiann DeDenzo ..........Marketing Director
**Desc.:** Peer reviewed articles dealing with
　detection, identification, evaluation,
　control and correction of environmental
　hazards in industry and prevention of
　control of occupational injuries. Regular
　features include: meetings, new
　products, Letters to the Editor, book
　reviews, industrial hygiene summary
　reports, and IH Forum.
**Readers:** Industrial hygienists,
　environmental health administrators,
　safety and health professionals,
　industrial physicians, and toxicologists.

**AMERICAN SCIENTIST**　24859
99 Alexander Dr.
Research Triangle Park, NC 27709
Telephone: (919) 549-0097
FAX: (919) 549-0090
Mailing Address:
　P.O. Box 13975
　Durham, NC 27709
Year Established: 1913
Pub. Frequency: bi-m.
Page Size: standard
Subscrip. Rate: $28/yr.
Materials: 02,06,10,19,20,21,25,32
Circulation: 125,000

**Materials Accepted/Included:** 01-Business news 02-By-line articles 03-Fashion news 04-Food news 05-Freelance copy 06-Letters to editor 07-Real estate news 08-Sports news 09-Travel news 10-Book rev. 11-Movie rev. 12-Music rev. 13-TV rev. 14-Theater rev. 15-Coming events 16-Obituaries 17-Question & answer 18-Social announcements 19-Artwork 20-Cartoons 21-Photos 22-TV listings 23-Audio rec. 24-Video rec. 25-Books 26-Films/film clips 27-Personnel news 28-Press releases 29-New product news/photos 30-Trade lit. 31-Contracts awarded 32-Display adv. 33-Classified adv.

4-350

Circulation Type: controlled & paid
**Owner(s):**
Sigma Xi, The Scientific Research Society,
Inc.
P.O. Box 13975
Durham, NC 27709
Telephone: (919) 549-0097
Ownership %: 100
**Editorial:**
Rosalind Reid .............................Editor
David Scheonmaker ...............Managing Editor
Linda Huff ................................Art Director
Michelle Hoffman ...................Associate Editor
Mike May .................................Associate Editor
Michael Szpir ..........................Associate Editor
Hannah W. Andrews .........Book Review Editor
Kelly B. Fuller ....................Marketing Manager
**Desc.:** Professional journal covering the
entire field of scientific research,
including biological, physical, behavioral,
and engineering sciences. Carries news
about Sigma Xi and matters of concern
to scientists, and a large book review
section.
**Readers:** Scientists in all disciplines.

## ANNALS OF THE ASSOCIATION
## OF AMERICAN GEOGRAPHERS
24861
1710 16th St., N.W.
Washington, DC 20009
Telephone: (202) 234-1450
Year Established: 1911
Pub. Frequency: q.
Page Size: standard
Subscrip. Rate: $100.50/yr. US;
$115.50/yr. foreign
Materials: 32
Circulation: 7,700
Circulation Type: paid
**Owner(s):**
Association of American Geographers
1710 16th St., N.W.
Washington, DC 20009
Telephone: (202) 234-1450
Ownership %: 100
**Bureau(s):**
Blackwell Publishers
238 Main St.
Cambridge, MA 02142
Telephone: (617) 547-7110
Contact: Anne M. Jones, Executive Editor
**Management:**
David Forrester .................Advertising Manager
**Editorial:**
Stanley D. Brunn ........................Editor
William L. Graf .......................Associate Editor
John R. Jensen ......................Associate Editor
Richard Morrill .......................Associate Editor
Judy M. Olson ......................Associate Editor
Karl B. Raitz ....................Book Review Editor
**Desc.:** Articles by professional
geographers deal with studies of rural
and urban settlements, cartographical
analysis, population shifts and trends,
economic effects of various
migrations physical & environmental
features of the landscape and other
phases of geographic study.
**Readers:** Primarily association members,
faculty & students of geography, and
university libraries.

## APPLIED OPTICS
24215
2010 Massachusetts Ave., N.W.
Washington, DC 20036-1023
Telephone: (202) 416-1905
FAX: (202) 416-6120
Year Established: 1962
Pub. Frequency: 3/m.
Page Size: standard
Subscrip. Rate: $1090/yr.
Circulation: 7,000
Circulation Type: paid

**Owner(s):**
Optical Society of America
2010 Massachusetts Ave., N.W.
Washington, DC 20036-1023
Telephone: (202) 223-8130
Ownership %: 100
**Management:**
Kathleen Lyons .................Advertising Manager
**Editorial:**
William T. Rhodes .....................Editor
E. Kleiber ...........................Managing Editor
**Desc.:** A scientific journal providing those
in optical science and engineering with
the best, most significant new work in
experimental, theoretical, and Applied
research. AO reports on optical
instrumentation and the practical
aspects of modern optics in such areas
as atmospheric optics, optical
communications, fiber optics,
holography, infrared and ultraviolet
techniques, interferometry, information
processing, laser technology, solar
energy, spectroscopy, and more.
**Readers:** Applied physicists; space
scientists and astronomers; information
processing scientists; optical, electrical
and mechanical engineers.

## APPLIED SPECTROSCOPY
24863
198 TJ Dr. S-2
Frederick, MD 21702-4317
Telephone: (301) 694-8122
FAX: (301) 694-6860
Year Established: 1957
Pub. Frequency: 12/yr.
Page Size: standard
Subscrip. Rate: $200/yr.
Materials: 06,10,16,29
Circulation: 7,000
Circulation Type: paid
**Owner(s):**
Society for Applied Spectroscopy
198 TJ Dr. S-2
Frederick, MD 21702-4317
Telephone: (301) 694-8122
FAX: (301) 694-6860
Ownership %: 100
**Bureau(s):**
Allen Press
1041 New Hampshire
Lawrence, KS 66044
Telephone: (913) 843-1235
Contact: Karen Breen, Advertising
**Management:**
Karen Breen ...................Advertising Manager
JoAnn Brown .....................Business Manager
**Editorial:**
J.A. Holcombe ........................Editor
D. Bruce Chase .................Associate Editor
Sandy O'Neil ......................Miscellaneous
Deborah Bradshaw ...................News Editor
**Readers:** Scientific consumers.

## ASTRONOMY QUARTERLY, THE
66474
660 White Plains Rd.
Tarrytown, NY 10591-5153
Telephone: (914) 524-9200
FAX: (914) 333-2444
Pub. Frequency: q.
Subscrip. Rate: $250/yr.
**Owner(s):**
Pergamon Press, Inc.
Journals Division
660 White Plains Rd.
Tarrytown, NY 10591-5153
Telephone: (914) 524-9200
Ownership %: 100
**Management:**
Arnold Kranzler .........................Sales Manager
**Editorial:**
R.E. White ........................Editor in Chief

## ASTROPHYSICAL JOURNAL
24864
Kitt Peak National Observatory
Box 26732
Tucson, AZ 85726
Telephone: (602) 325-9214
FAX: (602) 323-4183
Mailing Address:
P.O. Box 26732
Tucson, AZ 85726-6732
Year Established: 1895
Pub. Frequency: 3/mo.
Page Size: standard
Subscrip. Rate: $740/yr.
Materials: 02,06
Freelance Pay: $125/pg.(charge)
Print Process: offset
Circulation: 2,900
Circulation Type: paid
**Owner(s):**
American Astronomical Society
2000 Florida Ave., N.W., #300
Washington, DC 20009
Telephone: (202) 328-2010
FAX: (202) 234-2560
Ownership %: 100
**Editorial:**
Dr. Helmut A. Abt .................Managing Editor
Dr. A. Dalgarno .....................Letters Editor
Tulie O'Connor ...................Production Director
**Desc.:** Carries professional papers
describing research, observation.
**Readers:** Astronomers, scientists.

## BIOMEDICAL PRODUCTS
23754
301 Gibraltar Dr.
Box 650
Morris Plains, NJ 07950-0650
Telephone: (201) 292-5100
FAX: (201) 898-9281
Year Established: 1976
Pub. Frequency: m.
Page Size: tabloid
Subscrip. Rate: $12/yr.
Materials: 02,21,28,29,30,32
Print Process: offset
Circulation: 75,000
Circulation Type: controlled
**Owner(s):**
Gordon Publications, Inc.
Div. of Cahners Publishing Co.
301 Gibraltar Dr.
Morris Plains, NJ 07950
Telephone: (201) 292-5100
Ownership %: 100
**Management:**
William R. Rakay ..........................President
Cheryl Hackos ...........................Publisher
Steve Koppleman .............Circulation Manager
Carol Cmielewski ...................Customer Service
Manager
**Editorial:**
Steve Ernst .............................Editor
Helen Robinson ...................Editorial Manager
Laurie Taylor ...................Production Director
**Desc.:** Contains product information about
instruments supplies and apparatus of
interest to the scientific community
involved in life science,
biotechnology research.
**Readers:** Life science researchers.
**Deadline:** story-1st of mo., 1 mo. prior to
pub. date; news-1st of mo.; photo-1st of
mo.; ads-1st of mo.

## BIONICS
65678
917 S. Park St.
Owosso, MI 48867-4422
Telephone: (517) 485-7800
Year Established: 1988
Pub. Frequency: q.
Page Size: standard
Subscrip. Rate: $20/yr.
Freelance Pay: $.05/wd.
Circulation: 4,000

Circulation Type: paid
**Owner(s):**
Ben Campbell
**Editorial:**
Ben Campbell ...........................Editor
**Desc.:** Reports on the latest technological
breakthroughs in the bionics industry.
Describes who is researching and
developing what. Describes the different
uses of bionics in industry and the
military. Discloses the identities of
individuals interested in investing in
bionic inventions. Reports on
stockmarket activities of bionic
companies. BIONICS is the only news
media that reports on the bionics
industry.
**Readers:** primarily employed or interested
people in the bionics industry. Includes
bionic researchers, scientists, inventors,
executives, military commanders,
investors.

## BIOTECHNOLOGY NEWSWATCH
66600
1221 Ave. of the Americas, 36th Fl.
New York, NY 10020
Telephone: (212) 512-6140
FAX: (212) 512-2723
Year Established: 1981
Pub. Frequency: s-m.
Page Size: standard
Subscrip. Rate: $737/yr.
Materials: 01,05,10,15,16,25,27,28,29,30,31
**Owner(s):**
McGraw-Hill, Inc.
1221 Ave. of the Americas
New York, NY 10020
Telephone: (212) 512-2000
Ownership %: 100
**Editorial:**
Mara Bovsun ...........................Editor

## BULLETIN OF THE AMERICAN
## MATHEMATICAL SOCIETY
24868
201 Charles St.
Providence, RI 02904
Telephone: (401) 455-4000
FAX: (401) 331-3842
Mailing Address:
P.O. Box 6248
Providence, RI 02940
Year Established: 1979
Pub. Frequency: bi-m.
Page Size: standard
Subscrip. Rate: $202/yr.
Circulation: 23,000
Circulation Type: paid
**Owner(s):**
American Mathematical Society
P.O. Box 6248
Providence, RI 02940
Telephone: (401) 272-9500
Ownership %: 100
**Management:**
Frank S. Quinn ...................Chairman of Board
**Editorial:**
Richard S. Palais .........................Editor
Murray H. Protter ...........................Editor
**Desc.:** Contains expository articles, book
reviews, and research announcements.
**Readers:** Professional mathematicians
including colleges, government research
and industrial laboratories.

## CANCER & GENETICS REPORT
70353
1221 Ave. of the Americas
36th Fl.
New York, NY 10020
Telephone: (212) 512-6140
FAX: (212) 512-2723
Year Established: 1993
Pub. Frequency: m.
Page Size: standard
Subscrip. Rate: $395/yr.

**Materials Accepted/Included:** 01-Business news 02-By-line articles 03-Fashion news 04-Food news 05-Freelance copy 06-Letters to editor 07-Real estate news 08-Sports news 09-Travel news 10-Book rev. 11-Movie rev. 12-Music rev. 13-TV rev. 14-Theater rev. 15-Coming events 16-Obituaries 17-Question & answer 18-Social announcements 19-Artwork 20-Cartoons 21-Photos 22-TV listings 23-Audio rec. 24-Video rec. 25-Books 26-Films/film clips 27-Personnel news 28-Press releases 29-New product news/photos 30-Trade lit. 31-Contracts awarded 32-Display adv. 33-Classified adv.

4-351

**Owner(s):**
McGraw-Hill, Inc.
1221 Ave. of the Americas
New York, NY 10020
Telephone: (212) 512-2000
Ownership %: 100

## CARIBBEAN JOURNAL OF SCIENCE
69724

P.O. Box 5000
Mayaguez, PR 00681-0500
Year Established: 1961
Pub. Frequency: s-a
Subscrip. Rate: $20/yr. to individuals;
$35/yr. to institutions; $13/yr. to students
Circulation: 700
Circulation Type: paid
**Owner(s):**
University of Puerto Rico, Dept. Arts & Sciences
P.O. Box 5000
Mayaguez, PR 00681-5000
Ownership %: 100
**Editorial:**
Allen R. Lewis .....................................Editor

## CREATION/EVOLUTION
69109

P.O. Box 9477
Berkeley, CA 94709-0477
Telephone: (510) 526-1674
Year Established: 1980
Pub. Frequency: 2/yr.
Subscrip. Rate: $20/yr. US; $25/yr. foreign
Circulation: 3,000
Circulation Type: paid
**Owner(s):**
National Center for Science Education
2530 San Pablo Ave., Ste. D
Berkeley, CA 94702-2013
Telephone: (510) 843-3393
Ownership %: 100
**Editorial:**
John R. Cole .......................................Editor
**Desc.:** Promotes the understanding of evolutionary science, with articles addressing creationist claims about dinosaurs and other anti-evolutionist arguments, and analyzing the creationist phenomena.

## CURRENT MATHEMATICAL PUBLICATIONS
58717

P.O. Box 8604
Ann Arbor, MI 48107
Telephone: (313) 996-5250
Mailing Address:
P.O. Box 6248
Providence, RI 02940
Year Established: 1968
Pub. Frequency: 17/yr.
Page Size: standard
Subscrip. Rate: $359/yr.
**Owner(s):**
American Mathematical Society
P.O. Box 6248
Providence, RI 02940
Telephone: (401) 272-9500
Ownership %: 100
**Editorial:**
Don Babbit ...........................Executive Editor
J. E. Kister ...........Associate Executive Editor
**Desc.:** A subject index of recent and forthcoming mathematical publications which have been classified by the editors of mathematical reviews.
**Readers:** Libraries, professional mathematicians in government, industry and academic research.

## ECONOMIC GEOLOGY & BULLETIN OF THE SOCIETY OF ECONOMIC GEOLOGISTS
24869

91-A Yale Station
Yale University
New Haven, CT 06515
Telephone: (203) 432-3166
Year Established: 1905
Pub. Frequency: 8/yr.
Page Size: oversize
Subscrip. Rate: $65/yr.
Circulation: 7,000
Circulation Type: paid
**Owner(s):**
Economic Geology Publishing Co.
101 Vowell Hall
University of Texas
El Paso, TX 79968
Telephone: (915) 544-7416
Ownership %: 100
**Management:**
Kenneth F. Clark ...............Advertising Manager
Kenneth F. Clark .................Business Manager
**Editorial:**
Brian J. Skinner ...............................Editor
Nancy A. Ahlstrom ..................Managing Editor
Mabel J. Peterson ....................Assistant Editor
Jack Murphy ...............................News Editor
**Desc.:** Articles deal with all phases of economic and applied geology. Covers mineral and petroleum deposits, land formations, methods, research, and developments.
**Readers:** Scientists, libraries, engineers, geologists.

## EMPLOYMENT INFORMATION IN THE MATHEMATICAL SCIENCE
58694

201 Charles St.
Providence, RI 02904
Telephone: (401) 455-4000
FAX: (401) 331-3842
Mailing Address:
P.O. Box 6248
Providence, RI 02940
Year Established: 1973
Pub. Frequency: 6/yr. Nov.-Aug.
Page Size: standard
Subscrip. Rate: $155/yr.
**Owner(s):**
American Mathematical Society
P.O. Box 6248
Providence, RI 02940
Telephone: (401) 272-9500
Ownership %: 100
**Desc.:** Provides information on the available positions in the mathematical sciences.
**Readers:** Professional mathematicians and those seeking employment in mathematics and related positions in universities, government and industry.

## ENDEAVOUR
24870

395 Saw Mill River Rd.
Elmsford, NY 10523
Telephone: (914) 592-7700
Year Established: 1977
Pub. Frequency: q.
Page Size: standard
Subscrip. Rate: $65/yr. institution
Circulation: 100,000
Circulation Type: paid
**Owner(s):**
Pergamon Press, Inc.
Headington Hill Hall
Oxford OX3-0BW, United Kingdom
Ownership %: 100
**Management:**
Roger A. Dunn ...................................President
Rosemarie Fazzolari .........Advertising Manager
**Editorial:**
Dr. Trevor I. Williams ..............Executive Editor

**Desc.:** Records the progress of science and technology in the service of mankind, in terms understandable not only by the practicing scientist and engineer but by the interested general reader.

## ENTOMOLOGICAL REVIEW
65637

605 Third Ave.
New York, NY 10158
Telephone: (212) 850-6289
Pub. Frequency: 9/yr.
Page Size: standard
Subscrip. Rate: $996/yr. US; $1086/yr. CN & MX; $1119/yr. elsewhere
Circulation: 996
Circulation Type: paid
**Owner(s):**
John Wiley & Sons, Inc.
605 Third Ave.
New York, NY 10158
Telephone: (212) 692-6000
Ownership %: 100
**Editorial:**
George C. Steyskal .............................Editor
**Desc.:** Covers all aspects of entomology: systematics, faunistics, ecology, morphology, physiology and biochemistry of insects, as well as biological and chemical control of insect pests.

## EURASIAN SOIL SCIENCE
65621

605 Third Ave.
New York, NY 10158
Telephone: (212) 850-6000
Year Established: 1969
Pub. Frequency: m.
Page Size: standard
Subscrip. Rate: $997/yr.
**Owner(s):**
John Wiley & Sons, Inc.
605 Third Ave.
New York, NY 10158
Telephone: (212) 850-6000
Ownership %: 100
**Editorial:**
G. V. Dobrovolski .....................Editor in Chief
N. N. Pelnikof ..........................Editor in Chief
Andrew P. Mazurak ..................Editor Emeritus

## FASEB JOURNAL
23801

9650 Rockville Pike
Bethesda, MD 20814-3998
Telephone: (301) 530-7100
FAX: (301) 571-1855
Year Established: 1987
Pub. Frequency: m.
Page Size: standard
Subscrip. Rate: $95/yr. non-members;
$275/yr. institutions; $39/yr. students & members
Materials: 06,29,32,33
Circulation: 10,000
Circulation Type: paid
**Owner(s):**
Federation of Amer. Soc./Experimental Biology
9650 Rockville Pike
Bethesda, MD 20814
Telephone: (301) 530-7100
Ownership %: 100
**Management:**
Michael J. Jackson ...............Executive Director
**Editorial:**
William J. Whelan ......................Editor in Chief
Lewis I. Gidez ..........................Executive Editor
Linda Acuff ...........................Marketing Director

**Desc.:** Designed to report on rapidly changing developments in biological sciences, we publish brief, definitive, original research communications and state-of-the-art reviews in disciplines of anatomy, biochemistry, biophysics, cell biology, development biology genetics, immunology, neurobiology, nutrition, pathology, pharmacology, physiology. The journal includes editorials, letters, a book list, news items, calendar, employment opportunities and public affairs. Additional issues contain abstracts of papers to be presented at the annual meeting with author and subject indexes.
**Readers:** Biological scientists in the fields of physiology, biochemistry, pharmacology, pathology nutrition, immunology, cell biology, genetics, molecular biology, neurobiology, biophysics and anatomy.
**Deadline:** ads-1st of mo. prior to pub. date

## GEMS & GEMOLOGY
24872

1660 Stewart St.
Santa Monica, CA 90404
Telephone: (310) 829-2991
Mailing Address:
P.O. Box 2110
Santa Monica, CA 90407
Year Established: 1934
Pub. Frequency: q.
Page Size: standard
Subscrip. Rate: $54.95/yr.
Materials: 06,10,19,21,29
Print Process: offset
Circulation: 10,000
Circulation Type: paid
**Owner(s):**
Gemological Institute of America
1660 Stewart St.
Santa Monica, CA 90404
Telephone: (310) 829-2991
Ownership %: 100
**Management:**
Jin Lim ...............................Circulation Manager
**Editorial:**
Richard T. Liddicoat ...................Editor in Chief
Alice S. Keller .......................................Editor
Irv Dierdorff ...........................Assistant Editor
William Boyajian .......................Associate Editor
D. Vincent Manson ....................Associate Editor
John Sinkankas .......................Associate Editor
Chuck Fryer .........................Contributing Editor
John I. Koivula ......................Contributing Editor
Robert C. Kammerling .........Contributing Editor
**Desc.:** Articles of interest to jewelers, gemstone collectors and hobbyists, mineralogists, and gemologists. Covers all phases of gemology, from antique jades to modern gems and jewelry. Interested in technical material dealing with gemstones, science of gemology, current news on gemological developments and discoveries, short reports of scientific research in field.
**Readers:** Gemologists, geologists, jewelers, hobbyists, mineral collectors.

## GEOGRAPHICAL REVIEW
24873

156 Fifth Ave., Ste. 600
New York, NY 10010
Telephone: (212) 242-0214
Year Established: 1916
Pub. Frequency: q.
Page Size: tabloid
Subscrip. Rate: $46/yr. individuals; $65/yr. institutions

**Materials Accepted/Included:** 01-Business news 02-By-line articles 03-Fashion news 04-Food news 05-Freelance copy 06-Letters to editor 07-Real estate news 08-Sports news 09-Travel news 10-Book rev. 11-Movie rev. 12-Music rev. 13-TV rev. 14-Theater rev. 15-Coming events 16-Obituaries 17-Question & answer 18-Social announcements 19-Artwork 20-Cartoons 21-Photos 22-TV listings 23-Audio rec. 24-Video rec. 25-Books 26-Films/film clips 27-Personnel news 28-Press releases 29-New product news/photos 30-Trade lit. 31-Contracts awarded 32-Display adv. 33-Classified adv.

4-352

**Owner(s):**
American Geographical Society
156 Fifth Ave., Ste. 600
New York, NY 10010
Telephone: (212) 242-0214
Ownership %: 100
**Editorial:**
Douglas R. McManis .............................Editor
**Desc.:** Contributed articles by professional geographers and other scientists. Covers all fields of geography. Departments include: Book Reviews, Geographical Record Notes.
**Readers:** Members of the American Geographical Society, academics, governmental officials, professionals.

58547
## ILLINOIS JOURNAL OF MATHEMATICS
54 E. Gregory Dr.
Champaign, IL 61820
Telephone: (217) 333-8935
FAX: (217) 244-8082
Year Established: 1957
Pub. Frequency: q.
Page Size: standard
Subscrip. Rate: $98/yr.
Circulation: 1,000
Circulation Type: paid
**Owner(s):**
University of Illinois Press
54 E. Gregory Dr.
Champaign, IL 61820
Telephone: (217) 333-0950
Ownership %: 100
**Editorial:**
Prof. Philippe Tondeur ...........................Editor
**Desc.:** Publishes original research papers in pure and applied mathematics.
**Readers:** Mathematicians in US and abroad.

70428
## IMPULSE: THE INTERNATIONAL JOURNAL OF DANCE SCIENCE, MEDICINE, & EDUCATION
1607 N. Market St.
Champaign, IL 61820
Telephone: (217) 351-5076
FAX: (217) 351-2674
Year Established: 1993
Pub. Frequency: q.
Page Size: standard
Subscrip. Rate: $24/yr. students; $40/yr. individuals; $90/yr. institutions
Materials: 10,25,29
Print Process: offset
Circulation: 350
Circulation Type: paid
**Owner(s):**
Human Kinetics
1607 N. Market St.
Champaign, IL 61820
Telephone: (217) 351-5076
FAX: (217) 351-2674
Ownership %: 100
**Management:**
Rainer Martens ....................................Publisher
Peg Goyette ...........................................Manager
**Editorial:**
Luke Kahlich ............................................Editor
Linda A. Bump ........................Journal Director
**Desc.:** Includes original research articles and scholarly review articles on dance and dance-related issues.
**Readers:** Dancers, dance educators, dance medicine specialists, dance scientists

25814
## INDEPENDENT ENERGY MAGAZINE
620 Central Ave., N.
Milaca, MN 56353-1788
Telephone: (612) 983-6892
FAX: (612) 983-6893
Year Established: 1971
Pub. Frequency: 10/yr.
Subscrip. Rate: $81/yr.; $135/2 yrs.; $107/yr. foreign; $185/2 yrs. foreign
Materials: 01,02,06,15,21,27,28,30,31,32
Freelance Pay: negotiable
Print Process: sheetfed
Circulation: 10,500
Circulation Type: controlled & paid
**Owner(s):**
Marier Communications, Inc.
620 Central Ave., N.
Milaca, MN 56353-1788
Telephone: (612) 983-6892
FAX: (612) 983-6893
Ownership %: 100
**Management:**
Rick Huntzicker .................Advertising Manager
Linda Day .........................Circulation Manager
Shelly Stanek ....................Production Manager
**Editorial:**
Donald Marier .........................Executive Editor
John Anderson ....................................Editor
Peter Douglass ...................Marketing Director
Abby Marier ...........Vice President, Adv. & Mktg.
**Desc.:** Provides senior executives at companies that develop, own and operate independent power production facilities worldwide with news and critical insights that help them better manage their growing businesses.
**Readers:** Executives involved in the independent power industry.
**Deadline:** story-8 wks. prior to pub. date; news-8 wks.; photo-8 wks.; ads-5 wks.

65639
## INTERNATIONAL JOURNAL OF IMAGING SYSTEMS & TECHNOLOGY
605 Third Ave.
New York, NY 10158
Telephone: (212) 850-6000
Year Established: 1989
Pub. Frequency: q.
Page Size: standard
Subscrip. Rate: $185/yr.
Circulation: 350
Circulation Type: paid
**Owner(s):**
John Wiley & Sons, Inc.
Ownership %: 100
**Editorial:**
Glen Wade ...............................................Editor
Enders A. Robinson ................................Editor

23442
## INTERNATIONAL LABORATORY
30 Controls Dr.
Shelton, CT 06484
Telephone: (203) 926-9300
FAX: (203) 926-9310
Mailing Address:
P.O. Box 870
Shelton, CT 06484
Year Established: 1971
Pub. Frequency: 9/yr.
Page Size: standard
Subscrip. Rate: $135/yr. Europe; $140/yr. elsewhere
Circulation: 70,000
Circulation Type: controlled
**Owner(s):**
International Scientific Comm. Inc.
30 Controls Dr.
Shelton, CT 06484
Telephone: (203) 926-9300
Ownership %: 100

**Bureau(s):**
International Scientific Communications
Progress Business Centre
Contact: Paul Mills, Manager

International Scientific Communications
123A Chaussee de Charleroi, #5
Contact: Gisela Saarmann, Assistant Manager

International Scientific Communications, Inc.
No. 15-1 Nishihara 2 - Chome
Contact: Hidemasa Takeda
**Management:**
William N. Wham .................................Publisher
Helene Zaleski ..................Business Manager
Audrey L. Bajoros ..............Circulation Manager
**Editorial:**
Dr. Brian Howard ........................Editor in Chief
Nancy Santossio ...................Managing Editor
Lynn McCorvie ........Assistant Managing Editor
Laurence Lustig ...............................Art Director
Norma Celia Kane ................Marketing Director
Linda Basheer ....................New Product Editor
Maureen Jezierny ............Production Assistant
Maureen Magner .................Production Director
Carol Tenedine ..................Publication Director
**Desc.:** Applications of modern laboratory instrumentation and related products. With articles written by leading experts in the field, the editorial covers recent developments in various types of laboratory instrumentation.
**Readers:** Chemists and biologists employed research laboratories.

69110
## ISIS
5720 S. Woodlawn Ave.
Chicago, IL 60637
Telephone: (312) 753-3347
FAX: (312) 753-0811
Year Established: 1912
Pub. Frequency: q.
Subscrip. Rate: $49/yr. individuals; $125/yr. institutions; $26/yr. students
Circulation: 4,400
Circulation Type: paid
**Owner(s):**
History of Science Society, Inc.

University of Chicago Press
5720 S. Woodlawn Ave.
Chicago, IL 60637
Telephone: (312) 753-3347
Ownership %: 100
**Editorial:**
Ronald Numbers ....................................Editor
**Desc.:** International review devoted to the history of science and its cultural influences.

66729
## ISPNEWS
498 Concord St.
Framingham, MA 01701
Telephone: (508) 879-9792
FAX: (508) 872-1153
Year Established: 1990
Pub. Frequency: bi-m.
Page Size: standard
Subscrip. Rate: $36/yr.
Circulation: 25,000
Circulation Type: controlled
**Owner(s):**
MIS Training Institute Press, Inc.
Framingham, MA 01701
Ownership %: 100
**Editorial:**
Michael Alexander ..................Editor in Chief
Russell Kay ............................................Editor
Tim Garon .............................Managing Editor

69111
## ISSUES IN SCIENCE & TECHNOLOGY
2101 Constitution Ave. N.W.
Washington, DC 20418
Year Established: 1984
Pub. Frequency: q.
Subscrip. Rate: $36/yr. individuals; $65/yr. institutions
Circulation: 18,500
Circulation Type: paid
**Owner(s):**
National Academy of Sciences
2101 Constitution Ave., N.W.
Washington, DC 20418
Telephone: (202) 334-3305
Ownership %: 100
**Editorial:**
Kevin Finneran ....................................Editor
**Desc.:** Explores the policy implications of new developments in science, technology and health.

67028
## JOURNAL OF APPLIED PHYSICS
335 E. 45th St.
New York, NY 10017
Telephone: (212) 661-9404
FAX: (516) 349-9704
Year Established: 1931
Pub. Frequency: s-m.
Page Size: standard
Subscrip. Rate: $1240/yr.; $1430/yr. foreign
Circulation: 5,000
Circulation Type: paid
**Owner(s):**
American Institute of Physics
335 E. 45th St.
New York, NY 10017
Telephone: (212) 661-9404
Ownership %: 100
**Management:**
Edward Greeley ................Advertising Manager
**Editorial:**
Steven Rothman ....................................Editor

65634
## JOURNAL OF APPLIED POLYMER SCIENCE
605 Third Ave.
New York, NY 10158
Telephone: (212) 850-6000
Pub. Frequency: bi-w.
Page Size: standard
Subscrip. Rate: $3530/yr.
**Owner(s):**
John Wiley & Sons, Inc.
605 Third Ave.
New York, NY 10158
Ownership %: 100
**Editorial:**
Eric Baer ....................................................Editor

65615
## JOURNAL OF AUTOMATION INFORMATION SCIENCES
605 Third Ave.
New York, NY 10158
Telephone: (212) 850-6000
Year Established: 1968
Pub. Frequency: bi-m.
Page Size: standard
Subscrip. Rate: $675/yr.
Circulation: 200
Circulation Type: paid
**Owner(s):**
John Wiley & Sons, Inc.
605 Third Ave.
New York, NY 10158
Telephone: (212) 850-6000
Ownership %: 100
**Editorial:**
V. Avtomatika ...........................Editor in Chief
M. Kuntsevich ..........................Editor in Chief
Robert N. McDonough ..............................Editor

**Materials Accepted/Included:** 01-Business news 02-By-line articles 03-Fashion news 04-Food news 05-Freelance copy 06-Letters to editor 07-Real estate news 08-Sports news 09-Travel news 10-Book rev. 11-Movie rev. 12-Music rev. 13-TV rev. 14-Theater rev. 15-Coming events 16-Obituaries 17-Question & answer 18-Social announcements 19-Artwork 20-Cartoons 21-Photos 22-TV listings 23-Audio rec. 24-Video rec. 25-Books 26-Films/film clips 27-Personnel news 28-Press releases 29-New product news/photos 30-Trade lit. 31-Contracts awarded 32-Display adv. 33-Classified adv.

4-353

**JOURNAL OF COMPOSITE MATERIALS** 23443
851 New Holland Ave., Box 3535
Lancaster, PA 17601
Telephone: (717) 291-5609
FAX: (717) 295-4538
Year Established: 1966
Pub. Frequency: 18/yr.
Page Size: tabloid
Subscrip. Rate: $795/yr.; $1580/2 yrs.; $2365/3 yrs.
Circulation: 1,225
Circulation Type: paid
**Owner(s):**
Technomic Publishing Co., Inc.
Telephone: (717) 291-5609
Ownership %: 100
**Bureau(s):**
Technomic Publishing AG
Missionsstrasse 44
CH-4055 Basel Switzerland
Contact: Frank Versaci, Director
**Management:**
Melvyn A. Kohudic .................Publisher
**Editorial:**
Dr. Stephen W. Tsai ..................Editor
**Desc.:** Over 150 pages of new information on the technology of multiphase materials in each issue. As they relate to composites, these areas are covered: Polymer Science, Metallurgy, Chemical Engineering, Ceramics Science, Applied Mechanics Chemistry, Physics, and others.

**JOURNAL OF GEOLOGY** 24876
5720 S. Woodlawn Ave.
Chicago, IL 60637
Telephone: (312) 702-7600
FAX: (312) 753-0811
Year Established: 1893
Pub. Frequency: bi-m.
Page Size: tabloid
Subscrip. Rate: $33/yr. individuals
Circulation: 2,800
Circulation Type: paid
**Owner(s):**
University of Chicago Dept. of Geophysical Science
5734 S. Ellis Ave.
Chicago, IL 60637
Telephone: (312) 702-8103
Ownership %: 100
**Management:**
Sandra Waistler ................Advertising Manager
**Editorial:**
A. T. Anderson, Jr ....................Editor
R. C. Newton ..........................Editor
Barbara J. Sivertsen ...............Managing Editor
**Desc.:** Contributed scientific articles on results of basic research in geology, geochemistry and geophysics. Departments include: Reviews (contributed book reviews), Geological Notes, Discussion & Reply.
**Readers:** Petroleum and mining geologists, research personnel, professors and students of geology & geophysics.

**JOURNAL OF GEOPHYSICAL RESEARCH** 24877
2000 Florida Ave., N.W.
Washington, DC 20009
Telephone: (202) 462-6900
FAX: (202) 328-0566
Year Established: 1896
Pub. Frequency: w.
Page Size: standard
Subscrip. Rate: $3065/yr. non-members
Print Process: offset

**Owner(s):**
American Geophysical Union
2000 Florida Ave., N.W.
Washington, DC 20009
Telephone: (202) 462-6900
FAX: (202) 328-0566
Ownership %: 100
**Editorial:**
Tamas Gombosi ........................Editor
William J. Hinze .......................Editor
Julian P. McCreary ...................Editor
Guy Brasseur ..........................Editor
Clark R. Chapman ....................Editor
**Desc.:** Original contributions on the physics and chemistry of the earth and solid planets; their oceans and atmospheres; and space physics. Issued 5 times per month in five disciplinary sections. It is one of the most widely cited journals in the earth sciences. Approximately 26400 pages in Volume 98 will be published.
**Readers:** Students, scientists, and libraries with interests in the earth sciences.

**JOURNAL OF INTELLIGENT MATERIAL SYSTEMS & STRUCTURES** 65696
851 New Holland Ave., Box 3535
Lancaster, PA 17601
Telephone: (717) 291-5609
FAX: (717) 295-4538
Year Established: 1990
Pub. Frequency: bi-m.
Subscrip. Rate: $395/yr.; $780/2 yrs.; $1165/3 yrs.
Circulation: 300
Circulation Type: paid
**Owner(s):**
Melvyn A. Kohudic
851 New Holland Ave., Box 3535
Lancaster, PA 17601
Telephone: (717) 291-5609
**Bureau(s):**
Technomic Publishing AG
Missionstrasse 44
CH-4055 Basel Switzerland
Contact: Frank Versaci, Director
**Editorial:**
Craig A. Rogers ........................Editor
**Desc.:** Creates higher forms of material systems and structures by providing sensing, actuation, control, and intelligence to composite materials and structures.

**JOURNAL OF RECEPTOR RESEARCH** 70386
270 Madison Ave.
New York, NY 10016
Telephone: (212) 696-9000
FAX: (212) 685-4540
Year Established: 1980
Pub. Frequency: 8/yr.
Page Size: standard
Subscrip. Rate: $272/yr. individuals; $545/yr. institutions
**Owner(s):**
Marcel Dekker, Inc.
270 Madison Ave.
New York, NY 10016
Telephone: (212) 696-9000
FAX: (212) 685-4540
Ownership %: 100
**Editorial:**
Ross B. Mikkelsen .....................Editor
Vladimir K. Pliska .....................Editor

**Desc.:** This publication accommodates all aspect of cell surface, cytoplasmatic, and nuclear receptors for drugs, hormones, immunologically active ligands, growth factors, toxins, lectins, viruses, protozoans, and other cells, the properties of the receptors, and their interactions and normal responses. The field of receptor pathobiology and the role of receptors in diagnosis and therapy of disease are also included.
**Readers:** Endocrinologists, immunologists, pharmacologists, toxicologists, students in endocrinology and immunology courses.

**JOURNAL OF RESEARCH IN SCIENCE TEACHING** 65592
605 Third Ave.
New York, NY 10158
Telephone: (212) 850-6000
Pub. Frequency: 10/yr.
Page Size: standard
Subscrip. Rate: $295/yr. US; $395/yr. CN & MX, $432.50/yr. foreign
Circulation: 2,500
Circulation Type: paid
**Owner(s):**
John Wiley & Sons, Inc.
605 Third Ave.
New York, NY 10158
Telephone: (212) 850-6000
**Editorial:**
William C. Kyle, Jr. ....................Editor

**JOURNAL OF THE AMERICAN MATHEMATICAL SOCIETY** 64922
201 Charles St.
Providence, RI 02904
Telephone: (401) 455-4000
FAX: (401) 351-3842
Mailing Address:
P.O. Box 6248
Providence, RI 02940
Year Established: 1988
Pub. Frequency: 4/yr.
Page Size: standard
Subscrip. Rate: $136/yr.
**Owner(s):**
American Mathematical Society
P.O. Box 6248
Providence, RI 02940
Telephone: (401) 455-4000
Ownership %: 100
**Editorial:**
Andrew Odlyzko ........................Editor
H. Blaine Lawson, Jr. .................Editor
Richard Melrose ........................Editor
Robert D. MacPherson ...............Editor
Wilfried Schmid .........................Editor
**Desc.:** Contains research articles of the highest quality in all areas of pure and applied mathematics.
**Readers:** Libraries, professional mathematicians in government, industry and academia.

**JOURNAL OF THE OPTICAL SOCIETY OF AMERICA PART A** 24223
2010 Massachusetts Ave., N.W.
Washington, DC 20036-1023
Telephone: (202) 223-8130
FAX: (202) 223-1096
Year Established: 1917
Pub. Frequency: m.
Page Size: standard
Subscrip. Rate: $610/yr.
Materials: 02
Print Process: web offset
Circulation: 9,782
Circulation Type: paid

**Owner(s):**
Optical Society of America
2010 Massachusetts Ave., N.W.
Washington, DC 20036
Telephone: (202) 223-8130
Ownership %: 100
**Editorial:**
Baha Saleh ..............................Editor
Joanne Sprehe ..........................Design Editor
**Desc.:** Presents basic research on optical phenomena. Includes atmospheric, physiological and statistical optics; image processing; scattering and coherence theory, machine and color vision; design and diffraction.
**Readers:** Optical scientists, engineers and designers.

**JOURNAL OF THE OPTICAL SOCIETY OF AMERICA PART B** 68660
2010 Massachusetts Ave., N.W.
Washington, DC 20036
Telephone: (202) 223-8130
Year Established: 1917
Pub. Frequency: m.
Subscrip. Rate: $530/yr.
Circulation: 9,782
Circulation Type: paid
**Owner(s):**
Optical Society of America
2010 Massachusetts Ave., N.W.
Washington, DC 20036
Telephone: (202) 223-8130
Ownership %: 100
**Editorial:**
Paul Liao .................................Editor
JoAnne Sprehe ..........................Design Editor

**JOURNAL OF THERMOPHYSICS & HEAT TRANSFER** 64919
370 L'Enfant Promenade, S.W.
Washington, DC 20024-2518
Telephone: (202) 646-7400
Year Established: 1987
Pub. Frequency: q.
Page Size: standard
Subscrip. Rate: $190/yr. non-members; $230/yr. foreign; $32/yr. members; $52/yr. foreign
Circulation: 1,000
Circulation Type: paid
**Owner(s):**
AIAA
370 L'Enfant Promenade, S.W.
Washington, DC 20024-2518
Telephone: (202) 646-7400
Ownership %: 100
**Management:**
John Newbauer .........................Publisher
**Editorial:**
Alfred L. Crosbie .......................Editor in Chief
William O'Connor ......................Managing Editor
Norma Brennan .................Publication Director
**Desc.:** Covers new technical knowledge and exploratory developments and applications in the revitalized field of thermophysics and heat transfer. Subjects include: properties and mechanisms involved in thermal energy transfer and storage in gases, liquids, and solids or combinations therof; nonintrusive diagnostics; aerothermodynamics; thermal control; radiative heat transfer; conduction-phase change; thermophysical properties; convective and numerical heat transfer.
**Readers:** Engineers involved in thermophysics.

**LABORATORY EQUIPMENT** 22496
301 Gibraltar Dr.
Morris Plains, NJ 07950
Telephone: (201) 292-5100
FAX: (201) 539-3471

**Materials Accepted/Included:** 01-Business news 02-By-line articles 03-Fashion news 04-Food news 05-Freelance copy 06-Letters to editor 07-Real estate news 08-Sports news 09-Travel news 10-Book rev. 11-Movie rev. 12-Music rev. 13-TV rev. 14-Theater rev. 15-Coming events 16-Obituaries 17-Question & answer 18-Social announcements 19-Artwork 20-Cartoons 21-Photos 22-TV listings 23-Audio rec. 24-Video rec. 25-Books 26-Films/film clips 27-Personnel news 28-Press releases 29-New product news/photos 30-Trade lit. 31-Contracts awarded 32-Display adv. 33-Classified adv.

4-354

Mailing Address:
P.O. Box 650
Morris Plains, NJ 07950
Year Established: 1963
Pub. Frequency: m.
Page Size: tabloid
Subscrip. Rate: free to qualified members;
$33/yr. US; $49/yr. foreign
Circulation: 120,050
Circulation Type: controlled
**Owner(s):**
Gordon Publications, Inc.
P.O. Box 650
Morris Plains, NJ 07950
Telephone: (201) 292-5100
Ownership %: 100
**Management:**
John J. McDevitt ...............Publisher
**Editorial:**
Helen Robinson ..................Editor
Wayne Curtis ..........National Sales Manager
**Desc.:** Brief new product and new
literature descriptions covering
instruments, chemicals, books,
apparatus and materials of interest to
the laboratory research team.
Departments include: New Laboratory
Chemicals; New Literature, Technical
Books.
**Readers:** Research scientists, engineers.

## LC-GC (MAGAZINE OF LIQUID & GAS CHROMATOGRAPHY)
859 Willamette St.
Eugene, OR 97401-6806
Telephone: (503) 343-1200
FAX: (503) 344-3514
Year Established: 1983
Pub. Frequency: m.
Page Size: standard
Subscrip. Rate: $12 newsstand; $59/yr. in
US.; $79/yr.Can.; $117/yr. foreign
Materials: 06,10,15,25,28,29,32,33
Print Process: web offset
Circulation: 55,721
Circulation Type: controlled
**Owner(s):**
Advanstar Communications, Inc.
7500 Old Oak Blvd.
Cleveland, OH 44130
Telephone: (216) 243-8100
Ownership %: 100
**Management:**
Ed Aster ..................President
**Editorial:**
Jeff Schier ..................Editor
Janaya Reitz ..........Assistant Editor
Lisa McAdam ..........Associate Editor
Steve Brown ..........Technical Editor
**Desc.:** LC-GC publishes peer-reviewed
articles describing research and
applications of separation science -
Liquid, gas, and planar chromatography;
supercritical fluid and solid-phase
extraction; capillary electrophoresis; and
preparative-scale chromatography.
Regular columns provide practical tips
on instrument repair and maintenance,
data handling, and sample preparation,
while New Products and New Literature
departments present a wide range of
equipment and services of specific
interest to chromatographers.
**Readers:** Analytical chemists using
chromatography.
**Deadline:** ads-1st of mo. prior to pub. date

## MATERIALS EVALUATION
1711 Arlingate Ln.
P.O. Box 28518
Columbus, OH 43228-0518
Telephone: (614) 274-6003
FAX: (614) 274-6899

Mailing Address:
P.O. Box 28518
Columbus, OH 43228-0518
Year Established: 1942
Pub. Frequency: m.
Page Size: standard
Subscrip. Rate: $95/yr.domestic; $165/yr.
international
Materials: 01,06,10,25,27,28,29,30,31,32
**Owner(s):**
American Society for Nondestructive
Testing, Inc.
1711 Arlingate Ln.
P.O. Box 28518
Columbus, OH 43228
Telephone: (614) 274-6003
FAX: (614) 274-6899
Ownership %: 100
**Management:**
Sotirios J. Vahaviolos ..........Chairman of Board
Vicki E. Panhuise ..................President
Timothy B. Strawn ..................Publisher
Larry Trask ..................Advertising Manager
Tim Jones ..................Production Manager
**Editorial:**
Charles Lopez ..................Editor
Terry Fogle ..................Librarian
Charles Lopez ..................New Products Editor
Elizabeth McKinney ..................News Editor
Tim Jones ..................Photo
Paul McIntire ..................Publication Director
Emmanuel Papadakis ..........Technical Editor
**Desc.:** Contains articles, reports and
technical papers on nondestructive test
methods, including x-rays eddy current,
ultrasonics, etc. Also contains releases
on new products, literature and services,
and upcoming meetings and courses.
**Readers:** Nondestructive testing
inspectors, researchers, managers,
engineers

## MATHEMATICAL REVIEWS
416 Fourth St.
Ann Arbor, MI 48103
Telephone: (313) 764-7228
Mailing Address:
P.O. Box 6248
Providence, RI 02940
Year Established: 1940
Pub. Frequency: m.
Page Size: oversize
Subscrip. Rate: $4591/yr.
Circulation: 2,547
Circulation Type: paid
**Owner(s):**
American Mathematical Society
P.O. Box 6248
Providence, RI 02940
Telephone: (401) 455-4000
Ownership %: 100
**Bureau(s):**
Mathematical Reviews
416 Fourth St.
Ann Arbor, MI 48103
Telephone: (313) 764-7228
Contact: Don Babbitt, Executive Editor
**Editorial:**
Don Babbitt ..................Executive Editor
Jane Kister ..................Associate Editor
**Desc.:** Reviewing journal for current
mathematical literature around the world
in all areas of pure and applied
mathematics.
**Readers:** Professional mathematicians,
researchers, and government, industry &
university libraries.

## MEMOIRS OF THE AMERICAN MATHEMATICAL SOCIETY
P.O. Box 6248
Providence, RI 02940-6248
Telephone: (401) 455-4183
FAX: (401) 331-3842

Year Established: 1950
Pub. Frequency: 6/yr.
Page Size: tabloid
Subscrip. Rate: $282/yr. member; $353/yr.
non-member
**Owner(s):**
American Mathematical Society
P.O. Box 6248
Providence, RI 02940-6248
Telephone: (401) 455-4000
FAX: (401) 331-3842
Ownership %: 100
**Editorial:**
Victoria Ancona ..................Supervisor
**Desc.:** A journal devoted to research in
pure and applied mathematics.
**Readers:** Professional mathematicians,
researchers in mathematics in
government, industry, and academics.

## NORTHWEST SCIENCE
Washington State University
Pullman, WA 99164-5910
Telephone: (509) 335-3518
Year Established: 1923
Pub. Frequency: q.
Page Size: standard
Subscrip. Rate: $20/yr. individuals; $40/yr.
institutions; $10/yr. students
Circulation: 900
Circulation Type: paid
**Owner(s):**
Northwest Scientific Association
c/o Washington State Univ. Pre
Pullman, WA 99164-5910
Telephone: (509) 335-3518
Ownership %: 100
**Management:**
Thomas H. Sanders ..................Publisher
**Editorial:**
David L. Peterson ..................Editor
Nancy J. Grunewald ..........Managing Editor
**Desc.:** Research articles in the field of
botany, chemistry, engineering, forestry,
geology, geography, mathematics,
physics, social sciences, soils,
aquatic sciences, wildlife and fisheries,
and zoology are published. Open to
scientists in the basic and applied
sciences wherein original or fundamental
research is presented.
**Readers:** Scientists, college teachers,
college libraries, science teachers.

## NOTICES OF THE AMERICAN MATHEMATICAL SOCIETY
201 Charles St.
Providence, RI 02904
Telephone: (401) 455-4000
FAX: (401) 455-4004
Mailing Address:
P.O. Box 6248
Providence, RI 02940
Year Established: 1954
Pub. Frequency: 9/yr.
Page Size: standard
Subscrip. Rate: free/members; $153/yr.
Circulation: 21,289
Circulation Type: free & paid
**Owner(s):**
American Mathematical Society
P.O. Box 6248
Providence, RI 02940
Telephone: (401) 272-9500
Ownership %: 100
**Management:**
Robert Fossum ..........Chairman Editorial Board
**Editorial:**
Eric Soderberg ..................Marketing Manager

**Desc.:** One of most widely read periodicals
in the world dealing with matters of
interest to the mathematical community.
Announces mathematical meetings
throughout the world. Contains
news items of interest to mathematical
scientists, articles outlining current
trends and developments, reports on
federal funding levels, informational
items, software and book reviews, news
products published by the Society.
**Readers:** Professional mathematicians
including college professors in
government, and research industrial
laboratories and mathematicians.

## NUCLEAR STANDARDS NEWS
555 N. Kensington Ave.
La Grange Park, IL 60525
Telephone: (708) 579-8268
FAX: (708) 352-6464
Year Established: 1971
Pub. Frequency: m.
Page Size: standard
Subscrip. Rate: $260/yr.
Circulation: 170
Circulation Type: free & paid
**Owner(s):**
American Nuclear Society, Inc.
555 Kensington Ave.
La Grange Park, IL 60525
Telephone: (708) 579-8268
Ownership %: 100
**Editorial:**
Marilyn Weber ..................Editor

## OHIO JOURNAL OF SCIENCE
1500 W. Third Ave., Ste. 223
Columbus, OH 43212-2817
Telephone: (614) 488-2228
FAX: (614) 488-2228
Year Established: 1900
Pub. Frequency: 5/yr.
Page Size: standard
Subscrip. Rate: $50/yr. US; $55/yr. foreign
Materials: 10,32
Freelance Pay: none
Print Process: offset
Circulation: 2,500
Circulation Type: paid
**Owner(s):**
Ohio Academy of Science
1500 W. Third Ave., Ste. 223
Columbus, OH 43212
Telephone: (614) 488-2228
FAX: (614) 488-2228
Ownership %: 100
**Management:**
Lynn Elfner ..................Advertising Manager
**Editorial:**
Lee Meserve ..................Editor in Chief
Lee Meserve ..................Executive Editor
**Desc.:** Articles cover all branches of
scientific research. Also publishes
symposia on subjects of general
scientific interest. Book notices section
reviews current works on a wide variety
of scientific subjects such as physical
geography, minerology, botany, biology,
biomed services, biochemistry, etc.
**Readers:** Scientists throughout the world.
**Deadline:** story-1 mo. prior to pub. date;
news-1 mo. prior; photo-1 mo. prior; ads-
1 mo. prior

## OPTICS & PHOTONICS NEWS
2010 Massachusetts Ave., N.W.
Washington, DC 20036
Telephone: (202) 223-8130
FAX: (202) 223-1096
Year Established: 1975
Pub. Frequency: m.
Page Size: standard
Subscrip. Rate: $99/yr.; free to members

Freelance Pay: negotiable
Circulation: 22,000
Circulation Type: free & paid
**Owner(s):**
Optical Society of America
2010 Massachusetts Ave., N.W.
Washington, DC 20036
Telephone: (202) 223-8130
Ownership %: 100
**Management:**
David W. Hennate ...............................Publisher
Kathleen Lyons .................Advertising Manager
**Editorial:**
Susan Reiss ...........................................Editor
Susan Reiss ......................Book Review Editor
**Desc.:** Monthly news magazine of interest
  to engineers and scientists working in all
  areas of optics and photonics. Special
  features on technical meetings
  of interest to optical workers. Overview
  and tutorial articles written by experts in
  their fields and aimed at general
  readership with science or engineering
  background. Departments include:
  Scatterings, Around OSA, Capital Eye,
  Books in Review, New Members, Optics
  & Photonics Calendar, Employment
  Marketplace, Journal Contents. Other
  Departments: Engineering, Education,
  Electronic Information.
**Readers:** Entire membership of the Optical
  Society.

### OPTICS LETTERS
24232
2010 Massachusetts Ave., N.W.
Washington, DC 20036
Telephone: (202) 223-8130
Year Established: 1977
Pub. Frequency: s-m.
Page Size: standard
Subscrip. Rate: $625/yr.
Materials: 02
Freelance Pay: none
Print Process: web offset
Circulation: 4,000
Circulation Type: paid
**Owner(s):**
Optical Society Of America
2010 Massachusetts Ave., N.W.
Washington, DC 20036
Telephone: (202) 223-8130
FAX: (202) 223-1096
Ownership %: 100
**Editorial:**
P.W.E. Smith ........................................Editor
Joanne B. Sprehe ...................Managing Editor
**Desc.:** Nnew, important results in all
  branches of optics. Consists entirely of
  letters describing new research results
  in optics.
**Readers:** Scientists and engineers working
  in all branches of optics.

### PACIFIC DISCOVERY
59644
Golden Gate Pk.
San Francisco, CA 94118
Telephone: (415) 750-7116
Mailing Address:
  CA Academy of Sciences
  San Francisco, CA 94118
Year Established: 1948
Pub. Frequency: q.
Page Size: standard
Subscrip. Rate: $13/yr. individuals; $11/yr.
  institutions
Freelance Pay: $.25/wd.
Circulation: 30,000
Circulation Type: paid
**Owner(s):**
California Academy of Sciences
Golden Gate Pk.
San Francisco, CA 94118
Telephone: (415) 221-5100
Ownership %: 100

**Editorial:**
Keith Howell ..........................................Editor
Susan Schneider ...........................Art Director
**Desc.:** Explores the world of nature and
  human culture. Compelling stories and
  beautiful photography serve as a bridge
  between new insights about the
  natural world and the threats to its
  welfare.
**Readers:** Members of the California
  Academy of Sciences, and subscribers.

### PACIFIC SCIENCE
69106
2840 Kolowalu St.
Honolulu, HI 96822
Telephone: (808) 956-8833
FAX: (808) 988-6052
Year Established: 1947
Pub. Frequency: q.
Page Size: 7" X 10"
Subscrip. Rate: $30/yr. individuals; $45/yr.
  institutions
Materials: 32
Print Process: offset lithography
Circulation: 600
Circulation Type: paid
**Owner(s):**
University of Hawaii Press
2840 Kolowalu St.
Honolulu, HI 96822
Telephone: (808) 956-8833
Ownership %: 100
**Editorial:**
E. Alison Kay .......................................Editor
**Desc.:** Presents international and
  multidisciplinary reports on biological
  and physical sciences of the Pacific
  region.
**Readers:** Scholars/academic

### PEDIATRIC EXERCISE SCIENCE
### (PES)
66583
1607 N. Market St.
Champaign, IL 61820
Telephone: (217) 351-5076
FAX: (217) 351-2674
Mailing Address:
  P.O. Box 5076
  Champaign, IL 61825
Year Established: 1989
Pub. Frequency: q.
Page Size: standard
Subscrip. Rate: $40/yr. individuals; $90/yr.
  institutions
Materials: 10,25,29
Print Process: offset
Circulation: 523
Circulation Type: paid
**Owner(s):**
Human Kinetics Publishers, Inc.
1607 N. Market St.
Champaign, IL 61820
Telephone: (217) 351-5076
FAX: (217) 351-3674
Ownership %: 100
**Management:**
Rainer Martens ...................................Publisher
Thomas Moore .....................................Manager
**Editorial:**
Thomas W. Roland ...............................Editor
Linda A. Bump ......................Journals Director
**Desc.:** Devoted to enriching the scientific
  knowledge of exercise during childhood.
  Stimulates better understanding and
  greater awareness of the importance of
  childhood exercise to scientists, health-
  care providers, and physical educators.
**Readers:** Bio-mechanists, physiologists,
  pediatricians, other health-care
  providers, physical educators.

### PHOTONICS SPECTRA
24231
Berkshire Common
Pittsfield, MA 01201
Telephone: (413) 499-0514
FAX: (413) 442-3180
Mailing Address:
  P.O. Box 4949
  Pittsfield, MA 01202
Year Established: 1967
Pub. Frequency: m.
Page Size: standard
Subscrip. Rate: $98/yr.
Materials: 01,06,28,29,30,31,32,33
Freelance Pay: varies
Circulation: 85,000
Circulation Type: controlled
**Owner(s):**
Laurin Publishing Co., Inc., Teddi C. Laurin
Berkshire Common
Pittsfield, MA 01201
Telephone: (413) 449-0514
Ownership %: 100
**Management:**
Francis T. Laurin ...............................President
Thomas F. Laurin ........................Vice President
Frank Boisvere ...................................Controller
Teddi C. Laurin ..................................Publisher
**Editorial:**
Charles Troy ..........................................Editor
**Desc.:** Technology, business, R & D and
  personnel news; economic trends;
  technology trends; a designer's
  handbook; and fiber optic section.
**Readers:** Scientists, engineers, technicians
  & management personnel involved with
  optics, electro - optics, lasers, fiber
  optics, imaging & related fields.
**Deadline:** story-2 mos. prior; ads-1 mo.
  prior

### PHYSICS TODAY
24890
One Physics Ellipse
College Park, MD 20740-3843
Telephone: (301) 209-3040
Year Established: 1948
Pub. Frequency: m.
Page Size: standard
Subscrip. Rate: $40/yr. members; $50/yr.
  non-members; $147/yr. institutions
Materials: 02,06,10,15,16,19,20,21,25,28,
  29,32,33
Print Process: offset
Circulation: 120,000
Circulation Type: controlled
**Owner(s):**
American Institute of Physics
500 Sunnyside Blvd.
Woodbury, NY 11797
Telephone: (516) 576-2478
Ownership %: 100
**Management:**
Charles Harris ...................................Publisher
Richard Kobel ...................Advertising Manager
**Editorial:**
Gloria B. Lubkin ......................Editor in Chief
Ken McNaughton ...................Managing Editor
Elliot Plotkin ....................................Art Director
Steven Benka ...........................Associate Editor
Denis Cioffi .............................Associate Editor
Warren Kornberg ...............Book Review Editor
Ray Ladbury ......................New Products Editor
**Desc.:** Technical articles and news about
  physics and physicists. Non-technical,
  news items, meetings, people, etc.
**Readers:** All members of the American
  Institute of Physics as well as other
  scientists & engineers involved in
  various disciplines of physics.

### PROFESSIONAL GEOGRAPHER, THE
24893
1710 16th St., N.W.
Washington, DC 20009
Telephone: (202) 234-1450
FAX: (202) 234-2744
Year Established: 1949
Pub. Frequency: q.
Page Size: standard
Subscrip. Rate: $85.50/yr. US; $101.50/yr.
  elsewhere
Materials: 10,32
Circulation: 7,100
Circulation Type: paid
**Owner(s):**
Association of American Geographers
1710 16th St., N.W.
Washington, DC 20009
Telephone: (202) 234-1450
Ownership %: 100
**Bureau(s):**
Blackwell Publishers
238 Main St.
Cambridge, MA 02142
Telephone: (617) 547-7110
Contact: Anne M. Jones, Executive Editor
**Management:**
David A. Forrester ............Advertising Manager
**Editorial:**
J. Dennis Lord .....................................Editor
Elizabeth K. Burns ...................Associate Editor
Robert G. Cromley ...................Associate Editor
Roger M. McCoy ................Book Review Editor
**Desc.:** Articles on research techniques,
  methods, views and opinions, status of
  geography, new developments,
  philosophy, and institutional functions,
  facilities and programs. Reports on
  conferences, book reviews, and
  contents of other North American
  geography journals.
**Readers:** Assn. members, university
  faculty and students, & research
  libraries.

### QUALITY
23463
191 S. Gary Ave.
Carol Stream, IL 60188
Telephone: (708) 665-1000
Year Established: 1963
Pub. Frequency: m.
Page Size: standard
Subscrip. Rate: $70/yr. US; $85/yr.
  Canada & Mexico
Freelance Pay: $50-$500
Circulation: 92,000
Circulation Type: controlled
**Owner(s):**
Chilton Publications, Inc.
One Chilton Way
Radner, PA 19089
Telephone: (215) 964-4000
Ownership %: 100
**Management:**
Leon Hutnagel ....................................President
Richard A. Templeton .........................Publisher
Carol Valha ......................Advertising Manager
**Editorial:**
Chester Placek ........................Editor in Chief
John Kendrick ...............................Senior Editor
Gail Stout .....................................Senior Editor
Jerry Wolak ...............................Managing Editor
Jean McNamara .............................Art Director
Marjory Gonzales ..................Editorial Assistant
Toni Spalding ........................Marketing Director
Karen Panvino ...............Production Coordinator
Dolores Yehling ...................Production Editor

---

**Materials Accepted/Included:** 01-Business news 02-By-line articles 03-Fashion news 04-Food news 05-Freelance copy 06-Letters to editor 07-Real estate news 08-Sports news 09-Travel news 10-Book rev. 11-Movie rev. 12-Music rev. 13-TV rev. 14-Theater rev. 15-Coming events 16-Obituaries 17-Question & answer 18-Social announcements 19-Artwork 20-Cartoons 21-Photos 22-TV listings 23-Audio rec. 24-Video rec. 25-Books 26-Films/film clips 27-Personnel news 28-Press releases 29-New product news/photos 30-Trade lit. 31-Contracts awarded 32-Display adv. 33-Classified adv.

**Desc.:** Covers all facets of the quality discipline including management, test systems and procedures; destructive and nondestructive testing; dimensional gaging; electronic, environmental and material testing. Departments include: Quality Reports, Calendar, Quality and the Law, Management Viewpoint, On the Quality Scene, New Products, Literature, Basic Training Review, and Instrumentation Scouting Report, Automated Testing, Electronic and other Quality Watch, Software Directory, Annual July Buyers Guide.
**Readers:** Managers and engineers responsible for product assurance and reliability. Implementation of quality equipment and systems for test programs, inspection, metrology, data analysis and education.

23433

## RESEARCH & DEVELOPMENT
1350 E. Touhy Ave.
Des Plaines, IL 60018
Telephone: (708) 635-8800
Mailing Address:
P.O. Box 5080
Des Plaines, IL 60017-5080
Year Established: 1959
Pub. Frequency: m.
Page Size: standard
Subscrip. Rate: $75/yr. US.; $128/yr. Canada; $112/yr. Mexico; $134.95 elsewhere
Materials: 01,28,29,30
Freelance Pay: varies
Circulation: 101,610
Circulation Type: controlled
**Owner(s):**
Cahners Publishing Co.
Div. Reed Publishing USA, Inc.
1350 E. Touhy Ave.
Des Plaines, IL 60018
Telephone: (708) 635-8800
Ownership %: 100
**Management:**
Don Knapp ...............................Publisher
**Editorial:**
Tim Studt .....................Executive Editor
Howard Goldner ...............Senior Editor
Robert Cassidy ...............................Editor
Vic Comello ...................Managing Editor
John Morkes ...........Assistant Managing Editor
**Desc.:** Technical review of applied research and development with scientific data from all industrial areas.
**Readers:** Corporate officers, R & D executives, project management, and professional staff members in industrial, government, university, and independent research laboratories.

22393

## RESEARCH TECHNOLOGY MANAGEMENT
1550 M. St., N.W.
Washington, DC 20005-1708
Telephone: (202) 872-6350
FAX: (202) 872-6356
Year Established: 1958
Pub. Frequency: bi-m.
Page Size: standard
Subscrip. Rate: $50/yr. individual; $90/yr. institutions
Materials: 01,02,05,15
Freelance Pay: negotiable
Print Process: offset
Circulation: 4,200
Circulation Type: paid
**Owner(s):**
Industrial Research Institute, Inc.
1550 M. St., N.W.
Washington, DC 20005
Telephone: (202) 872-6350
Ownership %: 100

**Management:**
C.F. Larson ...............................Publisher
**Editorial:**
M. F. Wolff .................................Editor
**Desc.:** Covers the management and administration of research, development, science and engineering. Major topics and subject areas are: research management operations, personnel, finances, methodology, and techniques. By-lined articles by research managers and others constitute 80 percent of each issue. A board of editors reviews all submitted articles. Departments include: News Perspectives, Information Resources.
**Readers:** Managers of research, development, science and technology.

24895

## REVIEWS OF GEOPHYSICS
2000 Florida Ave., N.W.
Washington, DC 20009
Telephone: (202) 462-6900
FAX: (202) 328-0566
Year Established: 1963
Pub. Frequency: q.
Page Size: standard
Subscrip. Rate: $25/yr. members; $220 libraries
Print Process: offset
**Owner(s):**
American Geophysical Union
2000 Florida Ave., N.W.
Washington, DC 20009
Telephone: (202) 462-6900
FAX: (202) 328-0566
Ownership %: 100
**Editorial:**
Alan D. Chave ...................Editor in Chief
**Desc.:** Contains review essays covering the full spectrum of geophysics. Provides up to date summaries of research in all earth sciences enabling readers to be kept informed of subjects outside their own specialties.
**Readers:** Members of AGU including students and scientists. Also goes to institution libraries.

65591

## SCIENCE EDUCATION
605 Third Ave.
New York, NY 10158
Telephone: (212) 850-6000
FAX: (212) 850-6088
Year Established: 1930
Pub. Frequency: 6/yr.
Page Size: standard
Subscrip. Rate: $205/yr.
Circulation: 2,000
Circulation Type: paid
**Owner(s):**
John Wiley & Sons, Inc.
605 Third Ave.
New York, NY 10158
Telephone: (212) 850-6000
Ownership %: 100
**Editorial:**
Richard Duscho .............................Editor
Diane Gern ...............Associate Editor

24902

## SCIENCES, THE
2 E. 63 St.
New York, NY 10021
Telephone: (212) 838-0230
FAX: (212) 260-1356
Year Established: 1961
Pub. Frequency: 6/yr.
Page Size: standard
Subscrip. Rate: $18/yr.
Materials: 06,28,29,32
Circulation: 50,000
Circulation Type: paid

**Owner(s):**
New York Academy Of Sciences
2 E. 63rd St.
New York, NY 10021
Telephone: (212) 838-0230
Ownership %: 100
**Editorial:**
Peter G. Brown ...................Chief Editor
Robert Coontz, Jr. ...........Senior Editor
Richrad Jerome ...............Senior Editor
Patricia Bontinen ...............Managing Editor
Laurence Marschall ...................Columnist
Wendy Marston ...........Editorial Assistant
Steven Diamond ...........Photography Editor
Matthew Katz ...............Program Director
**Desc.:** At least 8 major by-lined articles per issue by leading scientists, engineers, and physicians on research developments, topics in science policy and cultural affairs. Authors from outside science also contribute on topics of interest to scientists and the wider community. Dramatically illustrated articles are written at the level of the intelligent nonscientist. Publicity materials are used for the magazine's news brief column called "Quanta". Departments include: Letters, Quanta, Field Notes, Essays & Comment, Book Reviews, Anecdotal Evidence, Works in Progress and Physika.
**Readers:** Physicians, scientists, engineers.

24900

## SCIENCE TRENDS
National Press Bldg.
Washington, DC 20045
Telephone: (202) 393-0031
FAX: (202) 393-1732
Year Established: 1958
Pub. Frequency: s-m.
Page Size: standard
Subscrip. Rate: $650/yr.
Materials: 10,15,23,24,28
**Owner(s):**
Trends Publishing, Inc.
Natl. Press Bldg.
Washington, DC 20045
Telephone: (202) 393-0031
Ownership %: 100
**Management:**
A. Kranish ...............................President
A. Kranish ...............................Publisher
**Editorial:**
A. Kranish .................................Editor
**Desc.:** Detailed weekly report on research and development, science and technology policies, new books, publications and resource materials.
**Readers:** Management of science and technology programs.

58588

## SPECTROSCOPY
195 Main St.
Metuchen, NJ 08840-2737
Year Established: 1985
Pub. Frequency: 9/yr.
Page Size: standard
Subscrip. Rate: $59/yr. US; $117/yr. foreign; free to qualified personnel
Circulation: 30,000
Circulation Type: controlled
**Owner(s):**
Advanstar Communications, Inc.
7500 Old Oak Blvd.
Cleveland, OH 44130
Telephone: (216) 826-2839
Ownership %: 100
**Editorial:**
Linda Crabtree ...............................Editor
Deb Johnson ...............Associate Editor

**Desc.:** Publishers concise research and applications articles of immediate interest to all types of spectroscopists. The editorial combines practical information with principles of modern science. Areas covered include UV/VIS, IR, FT - IR, laser, NMR, mass, AA, ICP, fluorescence, X-ray, and raman spectroscopies.
**Readers:** Practicing spectroscopists in academia & industry.

65695

## SUGAKU EXPOSITIONS
201 Charles St.
Providence, RI 02904
Telephone: (401) 455-4000
FAX: (401) 331-3842
Mailing Address:
P.O. Box 6248
Providence, RI 02940
Year Established: 1988
Pub. Frequency: 2/yr.
Page Size: standard
Subscrip. Rate: $100/yr.
**Owner(s):**
American Mathematical Society
P.O. Box 6248
Providence, RI 02940
Telephone: (401) 455-4000
Ownership %: 100
**Desc.:** Contains translations into English of expository articles from the Japanese journal Sugaku. Each issue contains articles which provide highly informative accounts of a variety of current areas of mathematical research.
**Readers:** Professional mathematicians in academia, government research and industry.

65449

## SUPERCONDUCTOR INDUSTRY
17 S. Franklin Tnpk.
Ramsey, NJ 07446
Telephone: (201) 825-2552
Mailing Address:
P.O. Box 555
Ramsey, NJ 07446
Year Established: 1988
Pub. Frequency: q.
Page Size: standard
Subscrip. Rate: $17/yr.; $32/2 yrs.
Circulation: 6,300
Circulation Type: controlled
**Owner(s):**
Rodman Publishing Co.
P.O. Box 555
Ramsey, NJ 07446
Telephone: (201) 825-2552
Ownership %: 100
**Management:**
Rodman J. Zilenziger ...........Publisher
**Editorial:**
Chris Gillespie ...............................Editor
**Desc.:** Reports on patent technology, equipment and machinery, research & development, marketing, legal and government issues.
**Readers:** Industry academic & government personnels.

58556

## TECHNOLOGY IN SOCIETY
660 White Plains Rd.
Tarrytown, NY 10591-5153
Telephone: (914) 524-9200
FAX: (914) 333-2444
Year Established: 1979
Pub. Frequency: q.
Page Size: standard
Subscrip. Rate: $360/yr

**Materials Accepted/Included:** 01-Business news 02-By-line articles 03-Fashion news 04-Food news 05-Freelance copy 06-Letters to editor 07-Real estate news 08-Sports news 09-Travel news 10-Book rev. 11-Movie rev. 12-Music rev. 13-TV rev. 14-Theater rev. 15-Coming events 16-Obituaries 17-Question & answer 18-Social announcements 19-Artwork 20-Cartoons 21-Photos 22-TV listings 23-Audio rec. 24-Video rec. 25-Books 26-Films/film clips 27-Personnel news 28-Press releases 29-New product news/photos 30-Trade lit. 31-Contracts awarded 32-Display adv. 33-Classified adv.

4-357

**Owner(s):**
Pergamen Press, Inc.
660 White Plains Rd.
Tarrytown, NY 10591-5153
Telephone: (914) 524-9200
Ownership %: 100
**Editorial:**
Dr. George Bugliarello ..............................Editor
A. George Schillinger ..............................Editor
**Desc.:** An international journal devoted to interdisciplinary research on the economic, social, political and cultural impact of technology and the uses of technology.

49890

**TECHNOLOGY NY REPORT**
1223 Peoples Ave.
Troy, NY 12180
Telephone: (518) 276-8769
Mailing Address:
  P.O. Box 535
  Troy, NY 12181
Year Established: 1983
Pub. Frequency: m.
Page Size: standard
Subscrip. Rate: $150/yr.
Materials: 01
Freelance Pay: varies
Circulation: 15,000
Circulation Type: paid
**Owner(s):**
Technolgy, NY
RPI Incubator Ctr.
Troy, NY 12180
Telephone: (518) 276-8769
Ownership %: 100
**Management:**
John C. Wallner ..............................Publisher
**Editorial:**
Olga K. Anderson ..............................Editor
**Desc.:** Covers the business and politics of technology development in New York State. News covered includes new companies and products in N.Y., legislation relating to technology, academic developments at N.Y. institutions as they impact on high tech businesses, and sources, of venture capital and other financing for high technology business development.
**Readers:** Leaders in government, business and academia nationwide.
**Deadline:** news-1 mo. prior to pub. date

24908

**TECHNOLOGY REVIEW**
201 Vassar St.
Cambridge, MA 02139
Telephone: (617) 253-8250
Mailing Address:
  MIT W59-200
  Cambridge, MA 02139
Year Established: 1899
Pub. Frequency: 8/yr.
Page Size: standard
Subscrip. Rate: $30/yr.; $48/2 yrs.
Freelance Pay: varies
Circulation: 93,000
Circulation Type: paid
**Owner(s):**
Association of Alumni and Alumae of MIT, The
77 Mass. Ave., Rm 10-110
Cambridge, MA 02139
Telephone: (617) 253-8200
Ownership %: 100
**Management:**
William J. Hecht ..............................Publisher
Peter Gellatly ..............................Business Manager
Beth Barovick ..............................Circulation Manager
**Editorial:**
Steven J. Marcus ..............................Editor in Chief
Phil LoPiccolo ..............................Senior Editor
Susan Lewis ..............................Senior Editor
Herbert Brody ..............................Senior Editor

Sandra Knight ..............................Senior Editor
Laura van Dam ..............................Senior Editor
Sandra Hackman ..............................Managing Editor
Faith Hruby ..............................Associate Editor
David Brittan ..............................Associate Editor
Beth Horning ..............................Associate Editor
Peter Gellatly ..............................Associate Publisher
Kathleen Sayre ..............................Design Director
Nancy Cahners ..............................Design Editor
**Desc.:** Science and technology and their relation to current affairs. Departments include: trend of affairs, books, letters, columns.
**Readers:** General readership.

24909

**TEST ENGINEERING & MANAGEMENT**
3756 Grand Ave., Ste. 205
Oakland, CA 94610
Telephone: (510) 839-0909
FAX: (510) 839-2950
Year Established: 1959
Pub. Frequency: bi-m.
Page Size: 4 color photos/art
Subscrip. Rate: $35/yr.
Freelance Pay: $50/pg.
Circulation: 10,000
Circulation Type: controlled
**Owner(s):**
Mattingley Publishing Co., Inc., The
3756 Grand Ave., Ste. 205
Oakland, CA 94610
Telephone: (510) 839-0909
Ownership %: 100
**Management:**
Eve Mattingley-Hannigan ..............................Publisher
**Editorial:**
Eve Mattingley-Hannigan ..............................Editor
**Desc.:** Industrial and personal news about people working in the field of reliability testing (environmental quality control; non-destructive testing; materials testing; etc.) Also technical features written by engineers and dealing with the technology of reliability testing and the state-of-the-art in testing equipment.
**Readers:** Engineers, scientists, top & technical managers.

58727

**TRANSACTIONS OF AMERICAN MATH SOCIETY**
201 Charles St.
Providence, RI 02904
Telephone: (401) 455-4000
FAX: (401) 331-3842
Mailing Address:
  P.O. Box 6248
  Providence, RI 02940
Year Established: 1900
Pub. Frequency: m.
Page Size: standard
Subscrip. Rate: $893/yr.
**Owner(s):**
American Mathematical Society
P.O. Box 6248
Providence, RI 02940
Telephone: (401) 455-4000
Ownership %: 100
**Editorial:**
Philip J. Hanlon ..............................Editor
Ralph L. Cohen ..............................Editor
Robert Bryant ..............................Editor
Judith Sally ..............................Editor
Avner D. Ash ..............................Editor
James E. Baumgartner ..............................Editor
Wen-Ching Winnie Li ..............................Editor
Sun-Yung A. Chang ..............................Editor
Richard Durrett ..............................Editor
David Jerison ..............................Editor
Masamichi Takesaki ..............................Editor
John J. Mallet-Paret ..............................Editor
Peter Shalen ..............................Managing Editor

**Desc.:** Devoted entirely to research in pure and applied mathematics. Annual index in December issue.
**Readers:** Professional mathematicians and mathematical researchers in government, industry and academia.

65720

**WONDERSCIENCE**
1155 16th St., N.W.
Washington, DC 20036
Telephone: (202) 452-2113
Pub. Frequency: m.: Oct.-May
Circulation: 15,000
Circulation Type: paid
**Owner(s):**
American Chemical Society
1155 16th St., N.W.
Washington, DC 20036
Telephone: (202) 452-2113
Ownership %: 100
**Editorial:**
James Kessler ..............................Editor

58558

**WORLD DEVELOPMENT**
660 White Plains Rd.
Tarrytown, NY 10591-5153
Telephone: (914) 524-9200
FAX: (914) 333-2444
Year Established: 1978
Pub. Frequency: 12/yr.
Subscrip. Rate: $750/yr
**Owner(s):**
Pergamon Press, Inc.
660 White Plains Rd.
Tarrytown, NY 10591-5153
Telephone: (914) 524-9200
Ownership %: 100
**Editorial:**
Paul Streeten ..............................Editor
Janet Craswell ..............................Managing Editor
**Desc.:** Encourages the publication of original articles and review papers which will help to stimulate and improve the development and application of appropriate science & technology in developing countries.
**Readers:** Academic scholars.

24181

**YALE SCIENTIFIC**
305 Crown St.
New Haven, CT 06511
Telephone: (203) 432-2374
Mailing Address:
  244A Yale Station
  New Haven, CT 06515
Year Established: 1894
Pub. Frequency: q.
Page Size: standard
Subscrip. Rate: $15/yr.
Circulation: 7,500
Circulation Type: paid
**Owner(s):**
Yale Scientific Publications, Inc.
244 - A Yale Sta.
New Haven, CT 06515
Telephone: (203) 432-2374
Ownership %: 100
**Management:**
Hubert H. Chuany ..............................Publisher
Julien Martinez ..............................Advertising Manager
Todd Wyche ..............................Business Manager
Brian Prakash ..............................Circulation Manager
**Editorial:**
Gautam Prakash ..............................Editor
Christopher Gumper ..............................Managing Editor
**Desc.:** Articles on every scientific topic, (engineering, natural and social sciences) written for specialists, non - specialists, and laymen.

**Readers:** Scientists, Engineers, Faculty, And Students (Including All Yale Undergrads). Also Yale Alumni.

## Group 242-Security

22317

**ACCESS CONTROL**
6151 Powers Ferry Rd., N.W.
Atlanta, GA 30339
Telephone: (404) 955-2500
FAX: (404) 955-0400
Year Established: 1958
Pub. Frequency: m.
Page Size: tabloid
Subscrip. Rate: $48/yr.
Materials: 01,02,05,06,21,27,28,29,30,31, 32,33
Freelance Pay: $.20/wd., $10/photo
Circulation: 28,000
Circulation Type: controlled
**Owner(s):**
Argus Press Holdings Co., Inc.
Ownership %: 100
**Bureau(s):**
New York Office
390 5th Ave.
New York, NY 10018
Telephone: (212) 613-9700
Contact: Jill Aronson, Sales

Dallas (Mesquite) Bureau
18601 LBJ Freeway, Ste. 240
Mesquite, TX 75150
Telephone: (214) 270-6651
Contact: Tim Clary

Atlanta Office
6151 Powers Ferry Rd. N.W.
Atlanta, GA 30339
Telephone: (404) 955-2500
FAX: (404) 955-0400

White & Assoc.
1424 4th St., Ste 231
Santa Monica, CA 90401
Telephone: (213) 451-5655
Contact: Kent Beaver, Sales

Chicago Office
307 N. Michigan Ave.
Chicago, IL 60601
Telephone: (312) 451-5655
Contact: Tad Sieck, Sales
**Management:**
Jerry France ..............................President
Wm. B. Manning ..............................Publisher
Wm. B. Manning ..............................Advertising Manager
Libby Purvis ..............................Circulation Manager
Valerie Ambrozevitch ..............................Classified Adv. Manager
Shirly Hartman ..............................Production Manager
Jamie Hood ..............................Promotion Manager
**Editorial:**
Gregg Echols ..............................Editor
David Alden ..............................Art Director
Jonna Jefferis ..............................New Products Editor
Jonna Jefferis ..............................News Editor
Martin Green ..............................Production Director
**Desc.:** Provide users of access control equipment with information about the installation, specifications and features of such products. Emphasizes installation case histories, which will provide a step-by-step description of a particular project accompanied by a full complement of photographs, diagrams and charts. Also features technical stories on perimeter fencing, gates and operator systems, card and door entry, sensors, CCTV technology, and comprehensive product overviews.

Materials Accepted/Included: 01-Business news 02-By-line articles 03-Fashion news 04-Food news 05-Freelance copy 06-Letters to editor 07-Real estate news 08-Sports news 09-Travel news 10-Book rev. 11-Movie rev. 12-Music rev. 13-TV rev. 14-Theater rev. 15-Coming events 16-Obituaries 17-Question & answer 18-Social announcements 19-Artwork 20-Cartoons 21-Photos 22-TV listings 23-Audio rec. 24-Video rec. 25-Books 26-Films/film clips 27-Personnel news 28-Press releases 29-New product news/photos 30-Trade lit. 31-Contracts awarded 32-Display adv. 33-Classified adv.

4-358

**Readers:** Access control and security end users, architectural specifiers, building and security managers, technical consultants, dod and doe end users, military security designers.

**Deadline:** story-1 1/2 mo. prior to pub. date; news-1 1/2 mo. prior; photo-1 1/2 mo. prior; ads-1 1/2 mo. prior

23473

## AMERICAN SOCIETY FOR INDUSTRIAL SECURITY
1655 N. Ft. Myer Dr., Ste. 1200
Arlington, VA 22209
Telephone: (703) 522-5800
FAX: (703) 522-5226
Year Established: 1957
Pub. Frequency: m.
Page Size: standard
Subscrip. Rate: $48/yr. in US, Canada & Mexico
Materials: 01,02,05,10,15,19,27,28,29,30,31
Freelance Pay: negotiable
Print Process: web
Circulation: 25,000
Circulation Type: paid
**Owner(s):**
American Society for Industrial Security
1655 N. Ft. Myer Dr.
Arlington, VA 22209
Telephone: (703) 522-5800
Ownership %: 100
**Management:**
Mary Alice Crawford .....................Publisher
Sandra Wade ..................Advertising Manager
Paul D'Addario ...................Circulation Manager
Melissa Sprott ...................Production Manager
**Editorial:**
Sherry Harowitz .......................................Editor
Lisa Arbetter .............................Assistant Editor
Joan Murphy .............................Associate Editor
Lisa Arbetter .........................Book Review Editor
Joan Murphy ...................New Products Editor
Teri Anderson ...................................News Editor
Roy Comisky .........................................Photo
Mary Alice Crawford ...........Publication Director
**Desc.:** Official publication of American Society for Industrial Security. Monthly features focus on expert opinion, studies in depth, monograms, and analysis of plant protection, disaster control and prevention, industrial and commercial investigations, safeguarding sensitive defense and proprietary data, physical and personal security, and allied subjects. Goes to executives of security and loss prevention programs in all types of organizations. Departments include: Industry News (Company & People News); Marketplace (New products), Reviews, Pentagon Corner (information on managing DOD security); ASIS In Action (news about The American Society for Industrial Security); Legal Reporter (legislation in Congress and judicial decisions); Letters, Security Spotlight (short news items).
**Readers:** Key executives, administrative and supervisory personnel responsible for security function in organizations.
**Deadline:** story-1st of mo., 3 mo. prior to pub. date; news-1st of mo.; photo-1st of mo.; ads-1st of mo., 1 mo. prior to pub. date

23413

## BULLETIN OF THE ATOMIC SCIENTISTS
6042 S. Kimbark Ave.
Chicago, IL 60637
Telephone: (312) 702-2555
FAX: (312) 702-0725
Year Established: 1945
Pub. Frequency: 10/yr.

Page Size: standard
Subscrip. Rate: $5 newsstand; $30/yr.
Materials: 02,05,06,10,15,19,20,21,32
Freelance Pay: varies
Circulation: 28,400
Circulation Type: paid
**Owner(s):**
Educational Foundation for Nuclear Science
6042 S. Kimbark Ave.
Chicago, IL 60637
Telephone: (312) 702-2555
FAX: (312) 702-0725
Ownership %: 100
**Management:**
Cheree Dillon ..................Advertising Manager
Scott Ziegler ......................Circulation Manager
Nancy Watson ......................General Manager
**Editorial:**
Mike Moore ..........................................Editor
Linda Rothstein ........................Managing Editor
Sarah Johanson ........................Assistant Editor
**Desc.:** Publishes non-technical articles on science and international security for a general audience. The central concern is the prevention of nuclear war. Departments include reader comment, book reviews, reports.
**Readers:** Scientists, political leaders, journalists, concerned citizens, teachers and students.

23372

## NATIONAL LOCKSMITH, THE
1533 Burgundy Pkwy.
Streamwood, IL 60107
Telephone: (708) 837-2044
FAX: (708) 837-1210
Year Established: 1929
Pub. Frequency: m.
Page Size: standard
Subscrip. Rate: $36/yr.
Freelance Pay: varies
Circulation: 17,500
Circulation Type: paid
**Owner(s):**
National Publishing Co.
1533 Burgundy Pkwy.
Streamwood, IL 60107
Telephone: (708) 837-2044
Ownership %: 100
**Management:**
Marc Goldberg .................................Publisher
Jeff Adair ..........................Advertising Manager
Nancy Town .......................Circulation Manager
**Editorial:**
Marc Goldberg .......................................Editor
Tom Seroogi .............................Managing Editor
Debbie Schertzing ............Adv. Sales Assistant
Jack Roberts .......................Book Review Editor
Jake Jakubuwski .........................Technical Editor
**Desc.:** Informs on technical breakdowns of locks and related items, as well as the news of the industry. Articles dealing with all phases of physical security welcomed, as well as industry-related publicity. Departments include: Techniips (tips from our readers), the Association Report (news from localities across the U.S.), Exploded Views (diagrams of locks).
**Readers:** Locksmiths and individuals involved in physical security.

66003

## SDM SECURITY DISTRIBUTING & MARKETING
1350 E. Touhy Ave.
Des Plaines, IL 60018
Telephone: (708) 635-8800
Year Established: 1971
Pub. Frequency: m.
Page Size: standard
Materials: 01,06,15,23,24,27,28,29,30,31,32,33
Circulation: 28,000

Circulation Type: paid
**Owner(s):**
Cahners Publishing Co.
1350 E. Touhy Ave.
Des Plaines, IL 60018
Telephone: (708) 635-8800
Ownership %: 100
**Editorial:**
Gary Parr ............................................Editor
**Desc.:** Provides technology, applications, and installation information on the electronic security industry, as well as information on marketing and management of security-installing companies. Features cover equipment applications, business decision-making, installation techniques, market trends, and industry developments. Also presented are industry and association news, research reports, industry statistics, product field test reports, and new product information.
**Readers:** Dealers who sell, install and service electronic security systems.

23474

## SECURITY
Cahners Plz., 1350 E. Touhy Ave.
Des Plaines, IL 60018
Telephone: (708) 635-8800
FAX: (708) 635-9950
Mailing Address:
   P.O. Box 5080
   Des Plaines, IL 60017
Year Established: 1964
Pub. Frequency: 12/yr.
Page Size: standard
Subscrip. Rate: $70/yr.; free to qualified readers
Materials: 01,21,23,24,25,26,27,28,29,30,31,32,33
Circulation: 40,000
Circulation Type: controlled
**Owner(s):**
Cahners Publishing Co.
Cahners Plz.
1350 E. Touhy Ave.
Des Plaines, IL 60018
Telephone: (708) 635-8800
FAX: (708) 635-9950
Ownership %: 100
**Management:**
Robert Krakoff ...................................President
Michael Boyle ..................................Publisher
**Editorial:**
Bill Zalud ..............................................Editor
Tim Russow ..........................Production Editor
**Desc.:** Magazine for security decision makers, provides buying decision-making information in 3 general areas: News, views, and ideas for loss prevention and asset protection; features on emerging issues and challenges and problem-solving analyses; and information on the products and services needed to implement an effective security program.
**Readers:** Individuals responsible for loss prevention/ security including executives/financial management & security titled personnel.
**Deadline:** story-2 mos.; news-2 mos.; photo-2 mos.; ads-2 mos.

23472

## SECURITY DEALER
445 Broad Hollow Rd.
Melville, NY 11747
Telephone: (516) 845-2700
FAX: (516) 845-7109
Year Established: 1972
Pub. Frequency: m.
Page Size: standard
Subscrip. Rate: $25/yr.
Materials: 01,02,06,15,17,19,21,27,28,29,30,31,32,33

Freelance Pay: negotiable
Print Process: offset
Circulation: 24,000
Circulation Type: controlled
**Owner(s):**
PTN Acquisition Corp.
445 Broad Hollow Rd.
Melville, NY 11747
Telephone: (516) 845-2700
Ownership %: 100
**Management:**
Arnold Blumenthal ..............................Publisher
**Editorial:**
Susan A. Brady ...................................Editor
Thomas S. Kapinos, CPP .......Editorial Director
**Desc.:** Articles on security equipment applications and installations. Management issues. Departments include: New Products, Burglar Alarm Systems, Notebook, CCTV, Installation Tips, News, Access Control, Home Automation, Power & Lighting, Sound & Communications, Dealer Services and Business Briefs.
**Readers:** Security alarm dealers and installers.
**Deadline:** story-1st of mo. prior to pub. date; news-1st of mo. prior; photo-1st of mo. prior; ads-5th of mo. prior

23471

## SECURITY DISTRIBUTING & MARKETING
1350 E. Touhy Ave.
Des Plaines, IL 60017
Telephone: (708) 635-8800
Mailing Address:
   P.O. Box 5080
   Des Plaines, IL 60017
Year Established: 1971
Pub. Frequency: m.
Page Size: standard
Subscrip. Rate: $69.95/yr.
Circulation: 28,000
Circulation Type: controlled
**Owner(s):**
Cahners Publishing Co.
1350 E. Touhy Ave.
Des Plaines, IL 60017
Telephone: (708) 635-8800
Ownership %: 100
**Management:**
Susan A. Whitehurst ..........................Publisher
**Editorial:**
Gary Parr ............................................Editor
**Desc.:** Concerns the profitable and effective management of the protection equipment business for sales and service.
**Readers:** Serves decision makers at companies that sell and/or install security products and systems for the nation's homes, businesses and institutions. Recipients may be managers, installers or service technicians at these companies.

## Group 244-Selling

22251

## AGENCY SALES MAGAZINE
P.O. Box 3467
Laguna Hills, CA 92654-3467
Telephone: (714) 859-4040
FAX: (714) 855-2973
Year Established: 1949
Pub. Frequency: m.
Page Size: standard
Subscrip. Rate: $37.50/yr.
Circulation: 15,000
Circulation Type: paid

Materials Accepted/Included: 01-Business news 02-By-line articles 03-Fashion news 04-Food news 05-Freelance copy 06-Letters to editor 07-Real estate news 08-Sports news 09-Travel news 10-Book rev. 11-Movie rev. 12-Music rev. 13-TV rev. 14-Theater rev. 15-Coming events 16-Obituaries 17-Question & answer 18-Social announcements 19-Artwork 20-Cartoons 21-Photos 22-TV listings 23-Audio rec. 24-Video rec. 25-Books 26-Films/film clips 27-Personnel news 28-Press releases 29-New product news/photos 30-Trade lit. 31-Contracts awarded 32-Display adv. 33-Classified adv.

4-359

**Owner(s):**
Manufacturers' Agents National Assn.
P.O. Box 3467
Laguna Hills, CA 92654
Telephone: (714) 859-4040
Ownership %: 100
**Management:**
Jane Holm ..........................Advertising Manager
**Editorial:**
Bert Holtje .................................................Editor
**Desc.:** Articles on agent-manufacturer and agent-customer relations; daily operating situations of agents including employees, taxes, record keeping, agency contracts, commissions. News of agent appointments by manufacturers; sales and achievement awards; new agencies and offices. Departments include: Feature Articles, Letters, News, Coming Events of Major Trade Shows.
**Readers:** Manufacturers' agents.

### AMERICAN SALESMAN, THE

24677

200 N. Fourth St.
Burlington, IA 52601-0001
Telephone: (319) 752-5415
FAX: (319) 752-3421
Mailing Address:
  P.O. Box 1
  Burlington, IA 52601
Year Established: 1955
Pub. Frequency: m.
Page Size: standard
Subscrip. Rate: $40.35/yr.
Materials: 02,05,10
Freelance Pay: $.03/wd.
Print Process: offset
Circulation: 1,500
Circulation Type: paid
**Owner(s):**
National Research Bureau
200 N. Fourth St.
P.O. Box 1
Burlington, IA 52601
Telephone: (319) 752-5415
FAX: (319) 752-3421
Ownership %: 100
**Management:**
Michael S. Darnall ..............................Publisher
**Editorial:**
Barbara Boeding ........................................Editor
**Desc.:** Articles provide concrete, down-to-earth, practical ways to help salespeople solve day-to-day problems, improve selling techniques, stimulate creative ideas for increasing sales, analyze customer motivations, develop personality, gain confidence, etc. Includes examples and illustrations of top notch know-how that show how salespeople may adapt these methods to increase their potential.
**Readers:** Salespeople in every field of business.

### BUREAU NEWS

24680

1801 Peachtree St., N.E., Ste. 200
Atlanta, GA 30309
Telephone: (404) 351-7355
Year Established: 1946
Pub. Frequency: m.
Page Size: tabloid
Subscrip. Rate: $10/yr.
Materials: 01,02,03,06,10,16,19,20,21,23, 24,25,27,28,30,32
Circulation: 17,000
Circulation Type: paid
**Owner(s):**
Bureau of Wholesale Sales Reps' News
1819 Peachtree St. NE Ste. 210
Atlanta, GA 30309
Telephone: (404) 351-7355
Ownership %: 100

**Management:**
Kathy Bruno ......................Advertising Manager
**Editorial:**
Jill Bunch .....................................................Editor
Michael E. Blackman ........................Director of
**Desc.:** News, features of interest to apparel salesmen/fashion trends, economic trends, general interest. By-lines on material outside house.
**Readers:** Apparel salespersons (wholesale).
**Deadline:** story-8th of mo. prior to pub.; news-8th of mo. prior; photo-8th of mo. prior; ads-8th of mo. prior

### OPPORTUNITY & INCOME PLUS

65724

73 Spring St., Ste. 303
New York, NY 10012
Telephone: (212) 925-3180
FAX: (212) 925-3612
Year Established: 1923
Pub. Frequency: m.
Page Size: standard
Subscrip. Rate: $15.89/yr.
Materials: 01,02,05,17,28,29,32,33
Freelance Pay: $20-$40/manuscript
Circulation: 250,000
Circulation Type: controlled
**Owner(s):**
Opportunity Associates
73 Spring St., Ste. 303
New York, NY 10012
Telephone: (212) 725-3180
Ownership %: 100
**Management:**
Greg Rapport ....................Advertising Manager
**Editorial:**
Donna Ruffini ...............................................Editor
Lillian Finnerty ..............Merchandising Director
**Desc.:** Instructional, inspirational, describing how to start a small business or make extra money on the side. Articles cover direct selling, franchising and unique business opportunities. Highlights new lines and items for profitable selling.
**Readers:** Direct salespeople.
**Deadline:** story-3 mos. prior to pub. date; news-3 mos. prior; photo-3 mos. prior; ads-3 mos. prior

## Group 246-Shoes, Boots & Leather Goods

### AMERICAN SHOEMAKING

23576

P.O. Box 198
Cambridge, MA 02140
Telephone: (617) 648-8160
Year Established: 1901
Pub. Frequency: m.
Page Size: standard
Subscrip. Rate: $37/yr.
Materials: 01,02,03,06,27,28,29,32,33
Print Process: offset
**Owner(s):**
Shoe Trades Publishing Co.
61 Massachusetts Ave.
Arlington, MA 02174
Telephone: (617) 648-8160
FAX: (617) 492-0126
Ownership %: 100
**Management:**
J. J. Moynihan .....................................Publisher
John J. Moynihan .............Advertising Manager
**Editorial:**
James D. Sutton ........................................Editor
**Desc.:** Technical articles on shoe manufacturing, telling the shoe manufacturer how to make better shoes. Departments include: News Section, Technical Section, Leather and Hide Markets, Trade Centers, Washington Report.

**Readers:** Shoe manufacturers, superintendents, foreman.

### EXECUTIVE DIGEST OF THE FOOTWEAR INDUSTRIES OF AMERICA

69115

1420 K St., N.W., Ste. 600
Washington, DC 20005
Pub. Frequency: m.
Subscrip. Rate: $60/yr. non-members
Circulation: 900
Circulation Type: paid
**Owner(s):**
Footwear Industries of America
1420 K St., N.W. Ste. 600
Washington, DC 20005
Telephone: (202) 789-1420
Ownership %: 100
**Editorial:**
Barbara Singer ............................................Editor
**Desc.:** Covers the technology, marketing, statistics and legislation of the footwear industry.

### FOOTWEAR MANUAL

69114

1420 K St. N.W., Ste. 600
Washington, DC 20005
Telephone: (202) 789-1420
FAX: (202) 789-4058
Year Established: 1975
Pub. Frequency: a.
Subscrip. Rate: $130/yr. members; $295/yr. non-members; $200/yr. libraries
Circulation: 300
Circulation Type: paid
**Owner(s):**
Footwear Industries of America
1420 K St., N.W., Ste. 600
Washington, DC 20005
Ownership %: 100
**Editorial:**
John Stebbins ............................................Editor
**Desc.:** Analysis of today's industry including marketing, manufacturing, international trade, finance and raw materials.

### FOOTWEAR NEWS

23577

Seven W. 34th St.
New York, NY 10001
Telephone: (212) 630-3800
FAX: (212) 630-3796
Year Established: 1945
Pub. Frequency: w.
Page Size: tabloid
Subscrip. Rate: $51/yr.
Materials: 01,06,16,23,24,27,28,29,32,33
Circulation: 23,000
Circulation Type: paid
**Owner(s):**
Fairchild Fashion & Merchandising Group
7 W. 34th St.
New York, NY 10001
Telephone: (212) 630-4199
Ownership %: 100
**Management:**
Phil Meek ...............................................President
Mark Sullivan .......................................Publisher
Jack Powers ......................Advertising Manager
**Editorial:**
Dick Silverman ........................Executive Editor
Valerie Seckler ........................Managing Editor
Vivian Infantino ........................Fashion Director
**Desc.:** Covers new developments, fashion trends, retailing, design and business news of the international footwear industry.
**Readers:** Men's, women's and children's footwear retailers.

### FOOTWEAR PLUS

66471

225 W. 34th St., Ste. 1212
New York, NY 10122
Telephone: (212) 563-2742
FAX: (212) 629-3249
Year Established: 1990
Pub. Frequency: 10/yr.
Page Size: tabloid
Subscrip. Rate: $36/yr.
Circulation: 20,000
Circulation Type: controlled
**Owner(s):**
Earnshaw Publications, Inc.
225 W. 34th St., Ste. 1212
New York, NY 10122
Telephone: (212) 563-2742
Ownership %: 100
**Bureau(s):**
Earnshaw Publications
475 Fire Island Ave.
Babylon, NY 11702
Telephone: (516) 661-4637
**Management:**
Michael Atmore ..................Associate Publisher
**Editorial:**
Michael Atmore ...........................................Editor
**Desc.:** A fashion and business magazine for the footwear industry.
**Readers:** Footwear retailers and manufacturers.

### LEATHER MANUFACTURER, THE

23578

61 Massachusetts Ave.
Arlington, MA 02174
Telephone: (617) 648-8160
Mailing Address:
  P.O. Box 198
  Cambridge, MA 02140
Year Established: 1883
Pub. Frequency: m.
Page Size: standard
Subscrip. Rate: $43/yr.
Materials: 01,03,05,06,10,15,16,20,21,25, 27,28,29,30,31,32,33
Print Process: offset
Circulation: 2,200
Circulation Type: controlled
**Owner(s):**
Shoe Trades Publishing Co.
Telephone: (617) 648-8160
Ownership %: 100
**Management:**
John J. Moynihan ..............................President
John J. Moynihan ..............................Publisher
John J. Moynihan .............Advertising Manager
**Editorial:**
J. D. Sutton ................................................Editor
**Desc.:** News magazine dealing with the tanning, finishing, and processing of hides and leather. Reports on association news, meetings, markets, company news. Articles discuss tanning methods and research activities.
**Readers:** Tanners, finishers, suppliers.

### QUARTERLY REPORT OF THE FOOTWEAR INDUSTRIES OF AMERICA

69113

1420 K St., N.W., Ste. 600
Washington, DC 20005
Telephone: (202) 789-1420
FAX: (202) 789-4058
Pub. Frequency: q.
Subscrip. Rate: $100/yr.
**Owner(s):**
Footwear Industries of America
1420 K St., N.W., Ste. 600
Washington, DC 20005
Ownership %: 100
**Desc.:** Provides data on production, foreign trade, marketing, labor prices, consumer expenditures and quarterly trends in the footwear industry.

**Materials Accepted/Included:** 01-Business news 02-By-line articles 03-Fashion news 04-Food news 05-Freelance copy 06-Letters to editor 07-Real estate news 08-Sports news 09-Travel news 10-Book rev. 11-Movie rev. 12-Music rev. 13-TV rev. 14-Theater rev. 15-Coming events 16-Obituaries 17-Question & answer 18-Social announcements 19-Artwork 20-Cartoons 21-Photos 22-TV listings 23-Audio rec. 24-Video rec. 25-Books 26-Films/film clips 27-Personnel news 28-Press releases 29-New product news/photos 30-Trade lit. 31-Contracts awarded 32-Display adv. 33-Classified adv.

## SHOE RETAILING TODAY
69116

9861 Broken Land Pkwy., Ste. 255
Columbia, MD 21046-1151
Telephone: (410) 381-8582
FAX: (410) 381-1167
Pub. Frequency: bi-m.
Subscrip. Rate: $20/yr. non-members
**Owner(s):**
National Shoe Retailers Association
9861 Broken Land Pkwy., Ste. 2
Columbia, MD 21046-1151
Telephone: (410) 381-8282
Ownership %: 100
**Editorial:**
Carol Blank ................................Editor
**Desc.:** Covers trends in the industry.

## SHOE SERVICE
23580

5024-R Campbell Blvd.
Baltimore, MD 21236
Telephone: (410) 931-8100
FAX: (410) 931-8111
Year Established: 1920
Pub. Frequency: m.
Page Size: standard
Subscrip. Rate: $18/yr.; $26/2 yrs.; $33/3 yrs.
Freelance Pay: $.05/wd.
Circulation: 17,000
Circulation Type: paid
**Owner(s):**
SSIA Service Corp.
5024-R Campbell Blvd.
Baltimore, MD 21236
Telephone: (410) 931-8100
Ownership %: 100
**Management:**
Mitchell Lebovic ................Circulation Manager
**Editorial:**
Mitchell Lebovic ........................Editor
Mitchell Lebovic ................Publication Director
**Desc.:** Contains articles of interest to shoe service shop owners, managers, and employee personnel. Payment on acceptance and publication only. Cartoons, photos, articles, outlines considered.
**Readers:** Shoe servicers, manufacturers & wholesalers of products related to the industry.

## SHOWCASE MAGAZINE
23585

350 Fifth Ave., Ste. 2624
New York, NY 10118
Telephone: (212) 695-2340
FAX: (212) 643-8021
Year Established: 1975
Pub. Frequency: bi-m.
Page Size: standard
Subscrip. Rate: $35/yr.
Materials: 01,06,15,16,21,27,28,29,32,33
Freelance Pay: negotiable
Print Process: web
Circulation: 11,394
Circulation Type: free & paid
**Owner(s):**
Luggage & Leather Goods Mfgrs. of
America, Inc.
350 Fifth Ave., Ste. 2624
New York, NY 10118
Telephone: (212) 695-2340
FAX: (212) 643-8021
Ownership %: 100
**Management:**
Jay Weiner ................................President
Robert K. Ermatinger ................Publisher
John J. Murray ................Advertising Manager
John Misiano ................Production Manager
**Editorial:**
Michele M. Pittenger ................Editor

**Desc.:** Contains articles edited for retailers, dealers, manufacturers, and suppliers about luggage, business cases, personal leather goods, handbags, and accessories. Special articles report on trends in fashion, promotions, selling and marketing techniques. Industry statistics and other educational and promotional features for industry improvement and advancement. Editorial comment is included as well as reports of industry happenings and news about industry personalities.
**Readers:** Retailers, dealers, manufacturers and suppliers of luggage, business cases, personal leather goods, and related accessories.
**Deadline:** story-1 mo.; ads-1 mo.

## SHOW REPORTER
23581

335 Boylston St.
Newton Center, MA 02159
Telephone: (617) 965-4577
Year Established: 1968
Pub. Frequency: 3/yr.
Page Size: tabloid
Subscrip. Rate: free
Circulation: 5,000
Circulation Type: free
**Owner(s):**
Show Reporter Publ. Co., Inc.
Ownership %: 100
**Management:**
Irv Roberts ................................Publisher
H. Winslow Davenport ......Advertising Manager
**Editorial:**
Irv Roberts ................................Editor
Wm. Davenport ................................Artist
Peter Silowan ................................Photographer
Wm. Davenport ................Production Director
**Desc.:** Publish features, general news, news fashions.
**Readers:** Executives in Shoe and Leather Industry.

## TRAVELWARE
23584

50 Day St.
Norwalk, CT 06854
Telephone: (203) 853-6015
FAX: (203) 852-8175
Mailing Address:
P.O. Box 5550
Norwalk, CT 06856
Year Established: 1898
Pub. Frequency: 9/yr.
Page Size: standard
Subscrip. Rate: $32/yr.
Materials: 27,28,29,30,32,33
Freelance Pay: negotiable
Circulation: 12,700
Circulation Type: controlled & paid
**Owner(s):**
Business Journals, Inc.
50 Day St.
Norwalk, CT 06854
Telephone: (203) 853-6015
FAX: (203) 852-8175
Ownership %: 100
**Bureau(s):**
Travelware
60 Madison Ave.
New York, NY 10010
Telephone: (212) 947-9190
**Management:**
G. Renfrew Brighton ..........Chairman of Board
James E. Jones ................................President
Woody Winfree ................................Publisher
**Editorial:**
Villia Morgan ................................Editor
Annette Dexter ................Assistant Editor
Mary Sullivan ................Associate Publisher

**Desc.:** Product photo features in fashion-oriented, lifestyle settings, market reports, and merchandising articles. Manufacturer and retailer profiles and interviews. Statistical analysis. Industry news. Trade show announcements, reviews and calendar.
**Readers:** Store presidents, luggage buyers, small leather goods buyers, department managers, sales people, manufacturers, retail buying offices, specialty stores.

## WORLD LEATHER
68953

61 Massachusetts
Arlington, MA 02174
Telephone: (617) 648-8160
FAX: (617) 492-0126
Year Established: 1987
Pub. Frequency: 6/yr.
Page Size: standard
Subscrip. Rate: $55/yr.
Materials: 01,02,03,05,06,10,15,16,19,20,
21,25,27,28,29,30,31,32,33
Circulation: 5,000
Circulation Type: paid
**Owner(s):**
World Leather
61 Massachusetts
Arlington, MA 02174
Telephone: (617) 648-8160
Ownership %: 100
**Editorial:**
Iain Howie ................................Editor
**Desc.:** Covers the leather tanning industry worldwide.

# Group 248-Social Sciences

## ADMINISTRATION & SOCIETY
64933

2455 Telles Rd.
Thousand Oaks, CA 91320
Telephone: (805) 499-0721
FAX: (805) 499-0871
Year Established: 1978
Pub. Frequency: q.
Page Size: standard
Subscrip. Rate: $55/yr. individual; $157/yr. institution
Circulation: 1,300
Circulation Type: paid
**Owner(s):**
Sage Publications, Inc.
2455 Teller Rd.
Thousand Oaks, CA 91320
Ownership %: 100
**Editorial:**
Gary L. Wamsley ................................Editor
Cris Anderson ............Circulation Administrator
**Desc.:** Deals with administration, bureaucracy, public policies, and their impact on our society.
**Readers:** Academic communities.

## AFFILIA JOURNAL OF WOMEN & SOCIAL WORK
64935

2455 Teller Rd.
Thousand Oaks, CA 91320
Telephone: (805) 499-0721
FAX: (805) 499-0871
Year Established: 1985
Pub. Frequency: q.
Page Size: standard
Subscrip. Rate: $41/yr. individual; $113/yr. institutions
Circulation: 1,250
Circulation Type: paid
**Owner(s):**
Sage Publications, Inc.
2455 Teller Rd.
Thousand Oaks, CA 91320
Ownership %: 100

**Editorial:**
Carol H. Meyer ................................Editor
**Desc.:** For and about women social workers and their clients. Its intent is to bring insight and knowledge to the field of social work from a feminist persepctive and tools necessary to make significant changes and improvements in the delivery of social services.
**Readers:** Academic Communities

## AMERICAN HISTORICAL REVIEW
24932

914 Atwater
Indiana Univ.
Bloomington, IN 47405
Telephone: (812) 855-7609
Year Established: 1895
Pub. Frequency: 5/yr.
Page Size: 5 1/2″ X 8″
Subscrip. Rate: sliding scale by income; institutions $52/yr.
Materials: 02,06,10,11,19,21,32
Print Process: web
Circulation: 18,000
Circulation Type: paid
**Owner(s):**
American Historical Association
400 A Street, S.E.
Washington, DC 20003
Telephone: (202) 544-2422
Ownership %: 100
**Bureau(s):**
American Historical Association
400 A Street, S.E.
Washington, DC 20003
Telephone: (202) 544-2422
Contact: Sharon K. Tune
**Management:**
Shannon Kahler ................Office Manager
**Editorial:**
David L. Ransel ................................Editor
Allyn Roberts ................Assistant Editor
William V. Bishel ................Assistant Editor
Augusta Davis ................Production Assistant
**Desc.:** Scholarly articles, review essays, film reviews and book reviews concerning all fields of history.
**Readers:** Academic persons, professors, scholars.

## AMERICAN JOURNAL OF ISLAMIC SOCIAL SCIENCES
69339

555 Grove St.
Herndon, VA 22070
Telephone: (703) 471-1133
FAX: (703) 471-3922
Mailing Address:
P.O. Box 669
Herndon, VA 22070
Year Established: 1984
Pub. Frequency: q.
Subscrip. Rate: $30/yr. individuals; $45 institutions
Circulation: 3,000
Circulation Type: paid
**Owner(s):**
International Institute of Islamic Thought
P.O. Box 669
Herndon, VA 22070
Telephone: (703) 471-1133
**Editorial:**
Sayyid M. Syeed ................Editor in Chief
Jay Willoughby ................Managing Editor
Mumtaz Ahmad ................Associate Editor
Akhtar H. Siddiqi ................Book Review Editor
Anas al Shaikh Ali ................Book Review Editor
**Desc.:** Publishes original refereed research articles on issues relating to Islamic social sciences and human studies.
**Readers:** Scholarly audience, including members of the Association of Muslim Social Scientists.

**Materials Accepted/Included:** 01-Business news 02-By-line articles 03-Fashion news 04-Food news 05-Freelance copy 06-Letters to editor 07-Real estate news 08-Sports news 09-Travel news 10-Book rev. 11-Movie rev. 12-Music rev. 13-TV rev. 14-Theater rev. 15-Coming events 16-Obituaries 17-Question & answer 18-Social announcements 19-Artwork 20-Cartoons 21-Photos 22-TV listings 23-Audio rec. 24-Video rec. 25-Books 26-Films/film clips 27-Personnel news 28-Press releases 29-New product news/photos 30-Trade lit. 31-Contracts awarded 32-Display adv. 33-Classified adv.

4-361

## AMERICAN LITERATURE
24933

905 W. Main St., Ste. 18-B
Duke University Press
Durham, NC 27708-0020
Telephone: (919) 687-3630
FAX: (919) 688-4574
Mailing Address:
P.O. Box 90660
Durham, NC 27708-0660
Year Established: 1929
Pub. Frequency: q.
Page Size: standard
Subscrip. Rate: $14/yr. students; $28/yr.
individuals & secondary schools; $56/yr.
institutions
Materials: 32
Circulation: 5,500
Circulation Type: paid
**Owner(s):**
Duke University Press
P.O. Box 6697
Durham, NC 27708
Telephone: (919) 684-2173
Ownership %: 100
**Management:**
Patricia Thomas ...................................Manager
**Editorial:**
Cathy N. Davidson ...................................Editor
**Desc.:** Contains articles dealing with
American literary history, criticism and
bibliography, not original verse or fiction.
Also reviews important books in this
field.
**Readers:** Scholars, teachers, students of
literature.

## AMERICAN POLITICS QUARTERLY
64934

2455 Teller Rd.
Thousand Oaks, CA 91320
Telephone: (805) 499-0721
FAX: (805) 499-0871
Year Established: 1972
Pub. Frequency: q.
Page Size: standard
Subscrip. Rate: $48/yr. individual; $140
institution
Circulation: 1,250
Circulation Type: paid
**Owner(s):**
Sage Publications, Inc.
2455 Teller Rd.
Thousand Oaks, CA 91320
**Editorial:**
James C. Garand ...................................Editor
Cris Anderson .............Circulation Administrator
**Desc.:** Promotes basic research in all
areas of American political behavors,
including urban, state, and national
politics, as well as pressing social
problems requiring political solutions.
**Readers:** Academic communities.

## AMERICAN SOCIOLOGICAL REVIEW
24934

1722 N Street, N.W.
Washington, DC 20036
Telephone: (202) 833-3410
Pub. Frequency: bi-m.
Page Size: standard
Subscrip. Rate: $50/yr. indiv.; $105/yr.
inst.; add $10 postage out of US
Materials: 32
Print Process: offset
Circulation: 12,500
Circulation Type: paid
**Owner(s):**
American Sociological Association
1722 N Street N.W.
Washington, DC 20036
Telephone: (202) 833-3410
Ownership %: 100
**Management:**
Karen G. Edwards .............Advertising Manager

**Editorial:**
Gerald Marwell ...................................Editor
**Desc.:** Publishes studies, research material
dealing with sociological problems.
**Readers:** Sociologists, students of
sociology.

## ANNALS OF THE AMERICAN ACADEMY OF POLITICAL & SOCIAL SCIENCE
24935

2455 Teller Rd.
Thousand Oaks, CA 91320
Telephone: (805) 499-0721
FAX: (805) 499-0871
Year Established: 1889
Pub. Frequency: bi-m.
Page Size: standard
Subscrip. Rate: individual $45/yr. paper,
$65/yr. cloth; institution $145/yr. paper,
$172/yr. cloth
Circulation: 4,850
Circulation Type: paid
**Owner(s):**
American Academy of Political and Social
Science
3937 Chestnut St.
Philadelphia, PA 19104
Telephone: (215) 386-4594
Ownership %: 100
**Bureau(s):**
American Academy of Political and Social
Science
3937 Chestnut St.
Philadelphia, PA 19104
Telephone: (215) 386-4594
**Management:**
Dr. Richard Lambert ...........................President
Mary E. Harris ....................Business Manager
**Editorial:**
Dr. Richard D. Lambert ...........................Editor
Erica Ginsburg ........................Assistant Editor
Dr. Alan W. Heston .................Associate Editor
Dr. Thorsten Sellin ...................Editor Emeritus
**Desc.:** Each issue is devoted to a single
topic in political or social sciences, or
economics, both national and
international. A specialist on the subject
covered acts as editor of each volume.
Specialists review 50 books in each
issue.
**Readers:** Professionals, laypersons,
businessmen, who take seriously the
world's social, political and economic
responsibilities.

## ASIAN AFFAIRS: AN AMERICAN REVIEW
54086

1319 18th St., N.W.
Washington, DC 20036-1802
Telephone: (202) 296-6267
FAX: (202) 296-5149
Year Established: 1973
Pub. Frequency: q.
Page Size: pocket
Subscrip. Rate: $34/yr. individuals; $66/yr.
institutions; add $9/outside US
Circulation: 354
Circulation Type: paid
**Owner(s):**
Heldref Publications
1319 18th St., N.W.
Washington, DC 20036
Telephone: (202) 296-6267
Ownership %: 100
**Management:**
Walter E. Beach ...........................Publisher
Raymond M. Rallo ...........Advertising Manager
Catherine Welker ............Circulation Manager
Kerri P. Kilbane .................Promotion Manager
**Editorial:**
John Neikirk ...................................Editor

**Desc.:** Focuses on US policy in Asia, and
on domestic politics, economics, and
international relations of the Asian
countries. Written primarily for readers
who need information about a part of
the world that is of vital importance to
American interests, it is also a valuable
resource for teachers, political analysts,
and those involved in international
business.
**Readers:** Teachers, political analysts,
journalists, current affair groups &
international business communities.

## BLACK SCHOLAR, THE
25715

485 65th St.
Oakland, CA 94609
Telephone: (510) 547-6633
FAX: (510) 547-6679
Mailing Address:
P.O. Box 2869
Oakland, CA 94609
Year Established: 1969
Pub. Frequency: q.
Page Size: standard
Subscrip. Rate: $30/yr. individual; $50/yr.
institutions
Materials: 02,05,10,25,33
Print Process: web
Circulation: 10,000
Circulation Type: paid
**Owner(s):**
The Black World Foundation
P.O. Box 2869
Oakland, CA 94609
Telephone: (510) 547-6633
Ownership %: 100
**Management:**
Robert Chrisman ...........................Publisher
**Editorial:**
Robert L. Allen ...................Senior Editor
Robert Chrisman ...........................Editor
JoNina M. Abron .......................Associate Editor
**Desc.:** The leading journal of black cultural
and political thought of this country.
**Readers:** 2/3 educators, executives and
social service, 1/3 college-level
students.

## CHILD WELFARE
24937

440 First St., N.W., Ste. 310
Washington, DC 20001
Telephone: (202) 638-2952
FAX: (202) 638-4004
Year Established: 1929
Pub. Frequency: bi-m.
Page Size: standard
Subscrip. Rate: $61/yr. US individual,
$77/yr. institution; $39/yr. students
Circulation: 12,000
Circulation Type: paid
**Owner(s):**
Transaction Publications
Dept. 3092
Rutgers University
New Brunswick, NJ 08903
Telephone: (908) 932-2280
Ownership %: 100
**Bureau(s):**
CWLA
440 First St., N.W.
Washington, DC 20001
Telephone: (202) 638-2952
Contact: David Liederman, Executive
Director
**Management:**
Kathy Thomas ..................Advertising Manager
Kathy Thomas .......Customer Service Manager
**Editorial:**
Carl Schoenberg ...........................Senior Editor
Eve Malakoff-Klein .................Managing Editor
Susan J. Brite .................Publication Director

**Desc.:** Covers all aspects of child welfare
or related service, including
administration, supervision, casework,
group work, community organization,
teaching, and research.
**Readers:** Practitioners and professionals in
voluntary and public agencies,
administrators, child care workers, and
board members.

## CLASSICAL PHILOLOGY
64959

1010 E. 59th St.
Chicago, IL 60637
Mailing Address:
P.O. Box 1, Faculty Exchange
University of Chicago
Chicago, IL 60637-1497
Year Established: 1906
Pub. Frequency: q.
Page Size: standard
Subscrip. Rate: $32/yr.
Circulation: 1,550
Circulation Type: paid
**Owner(s):**
University of Chicago Press
5720 S. Woodlawn
Chicago, IL 60637
Telephone: (312) 702-7600
Ownership %: 100
**Editorial:**
Richard P. Saller ...................................Editor
Bruce King ..............................Managing Editor
**Desc.:** Languages, literatures, art,
philosophy, religion, history and social
life of Greek and Roman antiquity;
original contribution to the understanding
of the subject.
**Readers:** Students and teachers of
classical languages and literatures

## COMPARATIVE POLITICAL STUDIES
64939

2455 Teller Rd.
Thousand Oaks, CA 91320
Telephone: (805) 499-0721
FAX: (805) 499-0871
Year Established: 1968
Pub. Frequency: q.
Page Size: standard
Subscrip. Rate: $47/yr. individual; $146/yr.
institition
Circulation: 1,750
Circulation Type: paid
**Owner(s):**
Sage Publications, Inc.
2455 Teller Rd.
Thousand Oaks, CA 91320
Ownership %: 100
**Editorial:**
James A. Caporaso ...................................Editor
**Desc.:** Publishes theoretical and empirical
research articles by scholars engaged in
cross-national studies. Also includes
research notes and review essays.
**Readers:** Academics

## CONTRIBUTIONS TO INDIAN SOCIOLOGY
57281

2455 Teller Rd.
Thousand Oaks, CA 91320
Telephone: (805) 499-0721
FAX: (805) 499-0871
Year Established: 1969
Pub. Frequency: s-a
Page Size: standard
Subscrip. Rate: $30/yr. individual; $67/yr.
institution
**Owner(s):**
Sage Publications, Inc.
P.O. Box 4215
110048 New Delhi
Ownership %: 100

Materials Accepted/Included: 01-Business news 02-By-line articles 03-Fashion news 04-Food news 05-Freelance copy 06-Letters to editor 07-Real estate news 08-Sports news 09-Travel news 10-Book rev. 11-Movie rev. 12-Music rev. 13-TV rev. 14-Theater rev. 15-Coming events 16-Obituaries 17-Question & answer 18-Social announcements 19-Artwork 20-Cartoons 21-Photos 22-TV listings 23-Audio rec. 24-Video rec. 25-Books 26-Films/film clips 27-Personnel news 28-Press releases 29-New product news/photos 30-Trade lit. 31-Contracts awarded 32-Display adv. 33-Classified adv.

**Bureau(s):**
India Prt., Ltd.
Contact: Tejeshwar Singh, Managing Director
**Editorial:**
Veena Das ...................................Editor
Ramachandra Guha .....................Editor
Dipankar Gupta ...........................Editor
Patricia Uberoi ...........................Editor
**Desc.:** Presents research studies on South Asian societies and cultures. Discusses different approaches to their studies.
**Readers:** Scholars and university students.

54087

**CURRENT**
1319 18th St., N.W.
Washington, DC 20036-1802
Telephone: (202) 296-6267
FAX: (202) 296-5149
Year Established: 1960
Pub. Frequency: 10/yr.
Page Size: standard
Subscrip. Rate: $32 individuals; $56/yr. institutions
Circulation: 3,047
Circulation Type: paid
**Owner(s):**
Heldref Publications
1319 18th St., N.W.
Washington, DC 20036-1802
Telephone: (202) 296-6267
Ownership %: 100
**Management:**
Walter E. Beach ......................Publisher
Raymond M. Rallo ...........Advertising Manager
Catherine Welker ..........Circulation Manager
Kerri P. Kilbane ..............Promotion Manager
**Editorial:**
Joyce Horn ...................................Editor
**Desc.:** Significant ideas on a wide range of topics including education, politics, and other social issues.
**Readers:** Professionals and readers interested in current topics and issues.

23625

**CURRENT BIOGRAPHY**
950 University Ave.
Bronx, NY 10452
Telephone: (800) 367-6770
FAX: (718) 590-1617
Year Established: 1940
Pub. Frequency: m. exc. Dec.
Page Size: Pg: 7 x 10; col: 16 picas
Subscrip. Rate: $60/yr. US & Canada; $70 elsewhere
Freelance Pay: $300-500/article
Circulation: 20,000
Circulation Type: paid
**Owner(s):**
H.W. Wilson Co.
950 University Ave.
Bronx, NY 10452
Telephone: (800) 367-6770
Ownership %: 100
**Editorial:**
Judith Graham ............................Editor
**Desc.:** Presents articles on people who are prominent in the news, in national and international affairs, the sciences, the arts, labor and industry.
**Readers:** Libraries.

64716

**ECONOMIC DEVELOPMENT & CULTURAL CHANGE**
5720 S. Woodlawn Ave.
Chicago, IL 60637
Telephone: (312) 753-3347
FAX: (312) 753-0811
Year Established: 1952
Pub. Frequency: q.
Page Size: standard
Subscrip. Rate: $34/yr. individuals; $70/yr. institutions; $27/yr. students
Circulation: 3,100

Circulation Type: paid
**Owner(s):**
University of Chicago Press
5720 S. Woodlawn Ave.
Chicago, IL 60637
Telephone: (312) 753-3347
Ownership %: 100
**Editorial:**
D. Gale Johnson ..........................Editor
**Readers:** Social Scientists, Academic.

64981

**ECONOMIC DEVELOPMENT QUARTERLY**
2455 Teller Rd.
Thousand Oaks, CA 91320
Telephone: (805) 499-0721
FAX: (805) 499-0871
Year Established: 1986
Pub. Frequency: q.
Page Size: standard
Subscrip. Rate: $53/yr. individual; $148/yr. institution
Circulation: 1,300
Circulation Type: paid
**Owner(s):**
Sage Publications, Inc.
2455 Teller Rd.
Thousand Oaks, CA 91320
Telephone: (805) 499-0721
Ownership %: 100
**Editorial:**
Richard D. Bingham ....................Editor
Sammis B. White .........................Editor
Gail Garfield Schwartz .................Editor
**Desc.:** Disseminates information on the latest research, programs, policies, and trends in the field of economic development. EDQ is unique in its concern for all areas of development; large cities, small towns, rural areas, and overseas trade and expansion.

64985

**ENVIRONMENT & BEHAVIOR**
2455 Teller Rd.
Thousand Oaks, CA 91320
Telephone: (805) 499-0721
FAX: (805) 499-0871
Year Established: 1968
Pub. Frequency: bi-m.
Page Size: standard
Subscrip. Rate: $64/yr. indiv.; $183/yr. inst.
Circulation: 1,600
Circulation Type: paid
**Owner(s):**
Sage Publications, Inc.
2455 Teller Rd.
Thousand Oaks, CA 91320
Telephone: (805) 499-0721
Ownership %: 100
**Editorial:**
Robert B. Bechtel .......................Editor
**Desc.:** Reports rigorous experimental and theoretical work on the study, design, and control of the physical environment and its interaction with human behavioral systems.

69410

**ETHICS & POLICY**
2400 Ridge Rd.
Berkeley, CA 94709
Telephone: (510) 848-1674
FAX: (510) 848-0626
Year Established: 1974
Pub. Frequency: q.
Page Size: standard
Subscrip. Rate: $35
Circulation: 6,000
Circulation Type: paid

Circulation Type: paid
**Owner(s):**
Center for Ethics & Social Policy
2400 Ridge Rd.
Berkeley, CA 94709
Telephone: (510) 848-1674
Ownership %: 100
**Desc.:** Discusses issues relating to ethics in social policy and business ethics.

64987

**EVALUATION REVIEW**
2455 Teller Rd.
Thousand Oaks, CA 91320
Telephone: (805) 499-0721
FAX: (805) 499-0871
Year Established: 1976
Pub. Frequency: bi-m.
Page Size: standard
Subscrip. Rate: $63/yr. indiv.; $183/yr. inst.
Circulation: 1,600
Circulation Type: paid
**Owner(s):**
Sage Publications, Inc.
2455 Teller Rd.
Thousand Oaks, CA 91320
Telephone: (805) 499-0721
Ownership %: 100
**Editorial:**
Richard A. Berk ..........................Editor
Howard E. Freeman ....................Editor
**Desc.:** A forum for researchers, planners, and policy makers engaged in the development, implementation, and utilization of evaluation studies. Reflects a wide range of methodological and conceptual approaches to evaluation and its many applications.

69118

**FAMILY RELATIONS**
3989 Central Ave. N.E., Ste. 550
Minneapolis, MN 55421-3921
Telephone: (612) 781-9331
FAX: (612) 781-9348
Year Established: 1952
Pub. Frequency: q.
Subscrip. Rate: $45/yr. individuals; $75/yr. institutions & libraries
Materials: 32
Circulation: 5,200
Circulation Type: paid
**Owner(s):**
National Council on Family Relations
3989 Central Ave., N.E. #550
Minneapolis, MN 55421-3921
Telephone: (612) 781-9331
Ownership %: 100
**Editorial:**
Mark Fine ...................................Editor
**Desc.:** Covers applied scholarly articles with emphasis on family relationships across the life cycle with implications for intervention, education and public policy.

69276

**FEMINIST STUDIES**
c/o Women's Studies Program
Univ. of Maryland
College Park, MD 20742
Telephone: (301) 405-7415
FAX: (301) 314-9190
Year Established: 1972
Pub. Frequency: 3/yr.
Page Size: standard
Subscrip. Rate: $28/yr. individuals; $60/yr. institutions
Materials: 10,15,19,21,32
Print Process: offset
Circulation: 8,000
Circulation Type: paid

**Owner(s):**
Feminist Studies, Inc.
c/o Women's Studies Program
Univ. of Maryland
College Park, MD 20742
Telephone: (301) 405-7415
FAX: (301) 314-9190
Ownership %: 100
**Editorial:**
Claire Moses ..............................Editor
**Desc.:** Presents scholarly research, essays, art, book reviews, poetry, fiction and creative narrative pertaining to the feminist experience in the social sciences, history, politics, and literature.
**Readers:** Individuals and institutions.

64988

**GENDER & SOCIETY**
2455 Teller Rd.
Thousand Oaks, CA 91320
Telephone: (805) 499-0721
FAX: (805) 499-0871
Year Established: 1986
Pub. Frequency: q.
Page Size: standard
Subscrip. Rate: $44/yr. individuals; $117/yr. institutions
Circulation: 2,650
Circulation Type: paid
**Owner(s):**
Sage Publications, Inc.
2455 Teller Rd.
Thousand Oaks, CA 91320
Ownership %: 100
**Editorial:**
Margaret Anderson .....................Editor
**Desc.:** Focuses on the social and structural study of gender as a primary social category. Emphasizing theory and research, G&S aims to advance both the study of gender and feminist scholarship.
**Readers:** Academic communities.

24940

**GERONTOLOGIST, THE**
1275 K St., N.W., Ste. 350
Washington, DC 20005
Telephone: (202) 842-1275
FAX: (202) 842-1150
Year Established: 1961
Pub. Frequency: bi-m.
Page Size: standard
Subscrip. Rate: $20/copy; $60/yr.; $94/yr. instn.; $70/yr. foreign; $104/yr. foreign instn.
Freelance Pay: none
Circulation: 10,500
Circulation Type: paid
**Owner(s):**
Gerontological Society of America
1275 K St., N.W., Ste. 350
Washington, DC 20005
Telephone: (202) 842-1275
Ownership %: 100
**Editorial:**
Rose C. Gibson Ph.D. ...........Editor in Chief
Elizabeth Borgen ............Advertising Director
Andrea Nevins ..................Audiovisual Editor
Robert Binstock, Ph.D. .......Book Review Editor
Nancy Wilson ...........Practice Concepts Editor
**Desc.:** Presents and interprets results of research and innovative practices and applies it to practice and policy development. A multidisciplinary journal for practitioners in the field of aging, it also includes practice concepts; books and audio-visual reviews; and editorials. Only peer reviewed professional articles accepted.
**Readers:** Researchers, educators, & professionals interested in the field of aging.
**Deadline:** ads-1st of mo. preceeding pub. date

**Materials Accepted/Included:** 01-Business news 02-By-line articles 03-Fashion news 04-Food news 05-Freelance copy 06-Letters to editor 07-Real estate news 08-Sports news 09-Travel news 10-Book rev. 11-Movie rev. 12-Music rev. 13-TV rev. 14-Theater rev. 15-Coming events 16-Obituaries 17-Question & answer 18-Social announcements 19-Artwork 20-Cartoons 21-Photos 22-TV listings 23-Audio rec. 24-Video rec. 25-Books 26-Films/film clips 27-Personnel news 28-Press releases 29-New product news/photos 30-Trade lit. 31-Contracts awarded 32-Display adv. 33-Classified adv.

4-363

## GROUP & ORGANIZATION MANAGEMENT

64989

2455 Teller Rd.
Thousand Oaks, CA 91320
Telephone: (805) 499-0721
FAX: (805) 499-0871
Year Established: 1975
Pub. Frequency: q.
Page Size: standard
Subscrip. Rate: $55/yr. individuals;
$145/yr. institutions
Circulation: 1,550
Circulation Type: paid
**Owner(s):**
Sage Publications, Inc.
2455 Teller Rd.
Thousand Oaks, CA 91320
Ownership %: 100
**Editorial:**
Michael J. Kavanagh ...............................Editor
**Desc.:** Bridges the gap between research
and practice for psychologists, group
facilitators, educators, and consultants
who are involved in the broad field of
human relations training.
**Readers:** Academics.

## HEALTH & SOCIAL WORK

24941

750 First St., N.E., Ste. 700
Washington, DC 20002-4241
Telephone: (800) 638-8799
Year Established: 1976
Pub. Frequency: q.
Page Size: standard
Subscrip. Rate: $60/yr. individual; $76/yr.
institution
Circulation: 6,000
Circulation Type: paid
**Owner(s):**
National Association of Social Workers
750 First St., NE, Ste. 700
Washington, DC 20002-4241
Telephone: (202) 408-8600
Ownership %: 100
**Management:**
Barbara W. White ...............................President
**Editorial:**
Judith W. Ross ...........................Editor in Chief
Nancy Winchester ....................Managing Editor
Linda Beebe .................Director of Publications
Sheldon R. Goldstein ...........Executive Director
**Desc.:** Articles deal with types of practice,
methods of training, and emerging areas
of patient care. Specifically written for
social workers in the health and mental
health fields. Departments include:
Letters, Book Reviews, National Health
Line. Professional articles are selected
by an anonymous peer review process.
**Readers:** Primarily social workers & other
helping professionals, libraries, medical
schools, hospitals.

## HISTORICAL METHODS

54090

1319 18th St., N.W.
Washington, DC 20036-1802
Telephone: (202) 296-6267
FAX: (202) 296-5149
Year Established: 1967
Pub. Frequency: q.
Page Size: standard
Subscrip. Rate: $32/yr. individuals; $79/yr.
institutions; add $10 outside of US
Circulation: 491
Circulation Type: paid
**Owner(s):**
Heldref Publications
1319 18th St., N.W.
Washington, DC 20036-1802
Telephone: (202) 296-6267
Ownership %: 100
**Management:**
Walter E. Beach ...............................Publisher

Raymond M. Rollo ............Advertising Manager
Catherine Welker ...............Circulation Manager
Kerri P. Kilbane ..................Promotion Manager
**Editorial:**
Barbara Kahn ...............................................Editor
**Desc.:** Historians and social scientists who
are concerned with interdisciplinary
approaches to the study of the past look
to historical methods as the leading
source of information about new data
sources, new approaches to older
sources, and theoretical and practical
discussions of data collection, sampling
prodecures, and statistical analyses.
**Readers:** Historians & social scientists

## HISTORY: REVIEWS OF NEW BOOKS

53931

1319 18th St., N.W.
Washington, DC 20036-1802
Telephone: (202) 296-6267
FAX: (202) 296-5149
Year Established: 1972
Pub. Frequency: q.
Page Size: standard
Subscrip. Rate: $43.50/yr. individual;
$83/yr. institute; add $10 postage out of
US.
Circulation: 432
Circulation Type: paid
**Owner(s):**
Heldref Publications
1319 18th St., N.W.
Washington, DC 20036-1802
Telephone: (202) 296-6267
Ownership %: 100
**Management:**
Walter E. Beach ...............................Publisher
Raymond M. Rallo .............Advertising Manager
Catherine Welker ...............Circulation Manager
Kerri P. Kilbane ..................Promotion Manager
**Editorial:**
John Neikirk ...............................................Editor
**Desc.:** History provides informative,
authoritative evaluations of books 1-12
months after their publication. Reviews
describe the contents of each book,
its major strengths and weaknesses, the
authors credentials, and the intended
audience.
**Readers:** Educators, Authors, Publishers,
Historians

## HUMAN COMMUNICATION RESEARCH

64990

2455 Teller Rd.
Thousand Oaks, CA 91320
Telephone: (805) 499-0721
FAX: (805) 499-0871
Year Established: 1973
Pub. Frequency: q.
Page Size: standard
Subscrip. Rate: $54/yr. individual; $142/yr.
institute
Circulation: 3,850
Circulation Type: paid
**Owner(s):**
Sage Publications, Inc.
2455 Teller Rd.
Thousand Oaks, CA 91320
Telephone: (805) 499-0721
Ownership %: 100
**Editorial:**
Howard Giles ...............................................Editor
**Desc.:** Important research and high- quality
reports that contribute to the expanding
body of knowledge about human
communication.
**Readers:** Academic Communities

## HUMAN RIGHTS QUARTERLY

69119

701 W. 40th St., Ste. 275
Baltimore, MD 21211
Telephone: (410) 516-6987
FAX: (410) 516-6998
Year Established: 1979
Pub. Frequency: q.
Subscrip. Rate: $26/yr. individuals; $69/yr.
institutions
Circulation: 11560
Circulation Type: paid
**Owner(s):**
Johns Hopkins University Press
701 W. 40th St., Ste. 275
Baltimore, MD 21211
Telephone: (410) 516-6987
**Editorial:**
Bert B. Lockwood, Jr. ..............................Editor
**Desc.:** Presents current work in rights
research and policy analysis, and
philosophical essays probing the
fundamental nature of human rights as
defined by the Universal Declaration of
Human Rights.

## INDIAN ECONOMIC & SOCIAL HISTORY REVIEW

55869

2455 Teller Rd.
Thousand Oaks, CA 91320
Telephone: (805) 499-0721
FAX: (805) 499-0871
Pub. Frequency: q.
Page Size: standard
Subscrip. Rate: $86/yr. inst.; $41/yr. indiv.
Circulation: 400
Circulation Type: paid
**Owner(s):**
Sage Publications, Inc.
P.O. Box 4215
New Delhi India
Ownership %: 100
**Editorial:**
Dharma M. Kumar ...............................Editor
**Desc.:** Welcomes contributions from
historians, economists, social
anthropologists, and other social
scientists interested in the social
and economic history of India and its
subcontinents.
**Readers:** Academicians & students in any
of the above fields.

## INTERNATIONAL JOURNAL OF AMERICAN LINGUISTICS

64727

5720 S. Woodlawn Ave.
Chicago, IL 60637
Telephone: (312) 702-7600
Year Established: 1917
Pub. Frequency: q.
Page Size: standard
Subscrip. Rate: $37/yr. indiv.; $80/yr.
instit.
Circulation: 1,750
Circulation Type: paid
**Owner(s):**
University of Chicago Press
5720 S. Woodlawn Ave.
Chicago, IL 60637
Telephone: (312) 702-7600
Ownership %: 100
**Management:**
Univ. of Chicago Press ........................Publisher
**Editorial:**
David S. Rood ...........................................Editor
Patricia Scarry .......Assistant Journals Manager
**Desc.:** A scholarly journal devoted to the
study of the indigenous languages of the
Americas. Manuscripts are subject to
peer review.
**Readers:** Academic/Scholarly students of
native American languages.

## INTERNATIONAL MIGRATION REVIEW

69274

209 Flagg Pl.
Staten Island, NY 10304-1199
Telephone: (718) 351-8800
FAX: (718) 667-4598
Year Established: 1966
Pub. Frequency: q.
Page Size: standard
Subscrip. Rate: $27.50/yr. individuals;
$54/yr. institutions
Materials: 06,10,25,32
Circulation: 3,900
Circulation Type: controlled & paid
**Owner(s):**
Center for Migration Studies
209 Flagg Pl.
Staten Island, NY 10304-1199
Telephone: (718) 351-8800
Ownership %: 100
**Editorial:**
Silvano M. Tomasi ...............................Editor
**Desc.:** Articles and research notes on
migration and refugee issues.
Conference reports, book reviews,
review of reviews, International
Newsletter on Migration (ISA), books
received, ads.

## INTERNATIONAL ORGANIZATION

24942

Center for International Studies
Los Angeles, CA 90089-0035
Telephone: (310) 740-4299
FAX: (213) 742-0281
Year Established: 1946
Pub. Frequency: q.
Page Size: standard
Subscrip. Rate: $35/yr. indiv.; $85/yr. inst.
Materials: 02,06,10,32
Circulation: 3,000
Circulation Type: paid
**Owner(s):**
MIT Press Journals
55 Hayward St.
Cambridge, MA 02142
Telephone: (617) 253-2889

IO Foundation
Center for International Studi
University of So. California
Los Angeles, CA 90089-0035
Telephone: (213) 740-4299
**Management:**
Miles Kahler ........................Chairman of Board
Rebecca McLeod .............Advertising Manager
**Editorial:**
John S. Odell ...........................................Editor
Candyce Kornblum Anger ........Managing Editor
**Desc.:** Articles on the various aspects of
international and regional organizations,
international politics, and economics.
**Readers:** Specialists in international affairs
in governments, corporations,
universities and colleges.

## INTERNATIONAL STUDIES

55871

2455 Teller Rd.
Thousand Oaks, CA 91320
Telephone: (805) 499-0721
Pub. Frequency: q.
Page Size: standard
Subscrip. Rate: $41/yr. individuals; $86/yr.
institutions
**Owner(s):**
Sage Publications, Inc.
P.O. Box 4215
110048 New Delhi
Ownership %: 100
**Bureau(s):**
India
**Editorial:**
R. Naryanan ...............................................Editor

**Materials Accepted/Included:** 01-Business news 02-By-line articles 03-Fashion news 04-Food news 05-Freelance copy 06-Letters to editor 07-Real estate news 08-Sports news 09-Travel news 10-Book rev. 11-Movie rev. 12-Music rev. 13-TV rev. 14-Theater rev. 15-Coming events 16-Obituaries 17-Question & answer 18-Social announcements 19-Artwork 20-Cartoons 21-Photos 22-TV listings 23-Audio rec. 24-Video rec. 25-Books 26-Films/film clips 27-Personnel news 28-Press releases 29-New product news/photos 30-Trade lit. 31-Contracts awarded 32-Display adv. 33-Classified adv.

**Desc.:** The most outstanding Indian research journal in the field of international affairs and area studies,- international politics & organization, political geography, international law, defense and strategy.
**Readers:** Academicians & students in international affairs.

## JOURNAL OF BLACK STUDIES
64992
2455 Teller Rd.
Thousand Oaks, CA 91320
Telephone: (805) 499-0721
FAX: (805) 499-0871
Year Established: 1970
Pub. Frequency: q.
Page Size: standard
Subscrip. Rate: $50/yr. individuals;
  $138/yr. institutions
Circulation: 1,800
Circulation Type: paid
**Owner(s):**
Sage Publications, Inc.
2455 Teller Rd.
Thousand Oaks, CA 91320
Telephone: (805) 499-0721
Ownership %: 100
**Editorial:**
Molefi Asante ..............................Editor
**Desc.:** Sustains full analytical discussion of economic, political, sociological, historical, literary, and philosophical issues related to persons of African descent.
**Readers:** Academic.

## JOURNAL OF BRITISH STUDIES
64718
Duke Univ.
204 Carr Bldg.
Durham, NC 27708
Telephone: (919) 684-2264
FAX: (919) 681-7890
Year Established: 1961
Pub. Frequency: q.
Page Size: standard
Subscrip. Rate: $43/yr. non-members;
  $70/yr. institutions
Materials: 10,25,32
Circulation: 1,850
Circulation Type: paid
**Owner(s):**
North American Conference on British Studies
Ownership %: 100
**Editorial:**
Cynthia Herrup ............................Editor
Amy Froide ..................Assistant Editor
**Readers:** Academic - humanities, social science.

## JOURNAL OF CONTEMPORARY ETHNOGRAPHY
64994
2455 Teller Rd.
Thousand Oaks, CA 91320
Telephone: (805) 499-0721
FAX: (805) 499-0871
Year Established: 1972
Pub. Frequency: q.
Page Size: standard
Subscrip. Rate: $50/yr. individuals;
  $153/yr. institutions
Circulation: 1,300
Circulation Type: paid
**Owner(s):**
Sage Publications, Inc.
2455 Teller Rd.
Thousand Oaks, CA 91320
Telephone: (805) 499-0721
Ownership %: 100
**Editorial:**
Patricia Adler ..............................Editor
Peter Adler ..................................Editor

**Desc.:** Dedicated to ethnography and qualitative research in general. Advances sociological knowledge through intensive, in-depth studies of human behavior in natural settings.
**Readers:** Academic communities.

## JOURNAL OF FAMILY ISSUES
64996
2455 Teller Rd.
Thousand Oaks, CA 91320
Telephone: (805) 499-0721
FAX: (805) 499-0871
Year Established: 1980
Pub. Frequency: q.
Page Size: standard
Subscrip. Rate: $50/yr. individuals;
  $146/yr. institutions
Circulation: 1,700
Circulation Type: paid
**Owner(s):**
Sage Publications, Inc.
2455 Teller Rd.
Thousand Oaks, CA 91320
Telephone: (805) 499-0721
Ownership %: 100
**Editorial:**
Patricia Voydanoff ......................Editor
**Desc.:** Sponsored by the National Council on Family Relations. Devoted to contemporary social issues and social problems related to marriage and family and family life, and to theoretical and professional issues of current interest to those who work with and study families.
**Readers:** Academics.

## JOURNAL OF HEALTH & SOCIAL BEHAVIOR
23848
1722 N St., N.W.
Washington, DC 20036
Telephone: (202) 833-3410
Year Established: 1967
Pub. Frequency: q.
Page Size: standard
Subscrip. Rate: $40/yr. individuals; $80/yr. institutions
Materials: 32
Print Process: web
Circulation: 3,500
Circulation Type: paid
**Owner(s):**
American Sociological Association
1722 N St. N.W.
Washington, DC 20036
Telephone: (202) 833-3410
Ownership %: 100
**Management:**
American Sociological Assoc. ............Publisher
Karen G. Edwards ............Advertising Manager
**Editorial:**
Ronald Angel ..............................Editor
**Desc.:** Papers using sociology as the central approach in defining and analyzing problems of human welfare, emphasis on the analysis of those aspects of social life bearing on human health and welfare, and the institutions and occupations devoted to diagnosing and managing them.
**Readers:** Medical and social scientists.

## JOURNAL OF MARRIAGE & THE FAMILY
24943
3989 Central Ave., N.E., Ste. 550
Minneapolis, MN 55421
Telephone: (612) 781-9331
Year Established: 1938
Pub. Frequency: q.
Page Size: 6 3/4 x 10
Subscrip. Rate: $50/yr.
Materials: 32
Circulation: 8,000
Circulation Type: paid

**Owner(s):**
National Council on Family Relations
3989 Central Ave., N.E., #550
Minneapolis, MN 55421
Telephone: (612) 781-9331
Ownership %: 100
**Management:**
Pat Knaub ..............................President
Graphic Publishing Co. ........................Publisher
Mary Jo Czaplewski .........Advertising Manager
**Editorial:**
Marilyn Coleman ....................Executive Editor
Lawrence Ganong .............Book Review Editor
Tonda March ...........................Miscellaneous
Roylene Laswell ........................Miscellaneous
**Desc.:** Professional publication; a medium for the presentation of original theory, research interpretation, and critical discussion of materials that have to do with marriage and the family. Book reviews included.
**Readers:** Family life educators, home economists, physicians, sociologists and psychologists, social workers, family studies experts.

## JOURNAL OF MEDIEVAL & RENAISSANCE STUDIES
61024
Bright Leaf Sq., Ste. 18-B
805 W. Main St.
Durham, NC 27701
Telephone: (919) 687-3636
FAX: (919) 688-4574
Mailing Address:
  P.O. Box 90660
  Durham, NC 27708
Pub. Frequency: 3/yr.
Page Size: standard
Subscrip. Rate: $32/yr. individuals; $72/yr. institutions
Materials: 32
Circulation: 900
Circulation Type: paid
**Owner(s):**
Duke University Press
P.O. Box 90660
Durham, NC 27708
Telephone: (919) 687-3636
FAX: (919) 688-4574
Ownership %: 100
**Management:**
Patricia Thomas ......................Manager
**Editorial:**
Marcel Tetel ...............................Editor
Annabel Patterson .......................Editor
**Desc.:** Focusing on late medieval and renaissance society.

## JOURNAL OF MODERN HISTORY, THE
64714
5720 S. Woodlawn Ave.
Chicago, IL 60637
Telephone: (312) 753-3347
FAX: (312) 753-0811
Year Established: 1929
Pub. Frequency: q.
Page Size: Pocket
Subscrip. Rate: $30/yr. individuals; $61/yr. institutions; $23/yr.students
Circulation: 4,300
Circulation Type: paid
**Owner(s):**
University of Chicago Press
5720 S. Woodlawn Ave.
Chicago, IL 60637
Telephone: (312) 753-3347
**Editorial:**
John W. Boyer ..............................Editor
Julius Kirshner ............................Editor
Mary Van Steenbergh .........Managing Editor

**Desc.:** Covers the history of the European continent since the Renaissance, studies intellectual, and cultural history of events and movements in specific countries as well as broader questions.
**Readers:** Academic historians and political scientists.

## JOURNAL OF NEAR EASTERN STUDIES
64713
1155 E. 58th St.
Chicago, IL 60637
Telephone: (312) 702-9540
Year Established: 1884
Pub. Frequency: q.
Page Size: standard
Subscrip. Rate: $35/yr.indiv.; $73/yr.instit.
Materials: 02,10
Circulation: 2,100
Circulation Type: paid
**Owner(s):**
University of Chicago Press
5801 Ellis Ave.
Chicago, IL 60637
Telephone: (312) 702-7700
Ownership %: 100
**Editorial:**
Robert D. Biggs ..............................Editor
L. Paula Woods ...............Managing Editor
**Desc.:** Articles pertaining to the history and literature of the ancient and premodern Near East.
**Readers:** An academic journal appealing mainly to scholars and specialists.

## JOURNAL OF POLICY HISTORY
69309
Barbara Bldg., Ste. C
820 N. University Dr.
University Park, PA 16802-1003
Telephone: (814) 865-1327
FAX: (814) 863-1408
Year Established: 1989
Pub. Frequency: q.
Page Size: 6 x 9
Subscrip. Rate: $27.50/yr. individuals US;
  $32.50/yr. foreign; $40/yr. institutions
  US; $45/yr. foreign
Materials: 10
Circulation: 366
Circulation Type: paid
**Owner(s):**
The Pennsylvania State University
USB - 1C
University Park, PA 16802-1003
Telephone: (814) 865-1327
FAX: (814) 863-1408
Ownership %: 100
**Editorial:**
Donald C. Critchlow ......................Editor
**Desc.:** Offers a new approach to policy analysis that is both historical and innovative. Provides a forum for scholars concerned with enriching our understanding of public policies and their development through historical inquiry and interpretation. Encourages interdisciplinary research into the origins and development of public policy in the United States and in other countries as well.

## JOURNAL OF RESEARCH IN CRIME & DELIQUENCY
65000
2455 Teller Rd.
Thousand Oaks, CA 91320
Telephone: (805) 499-0721
FAX: (805) 499-0871
Year Established: 1963
Pub. Frequency: q.

**Materials Accepted/Included:** 01-Business news 02-By-line articles 03-Fashion news 04-Food news 05-Freelance copy 06-Letters to editor 07-Real estate news 08-Sports news 09-Travel news 10-Book rev. 11-Movie rev. 12-Music rev. 13-TV rev. 14-Theater rev. 15-Coming events 16-Obituaries 17-Question & answer 18-Social announcements 19-Artwork 20-Cartoons 21-Photos 22-TV listings 23-Audio rec. 24-Video rec. 25-Books 26-Films/film clips 27-Personnel news 28-Press releases 29-New product news/photos 30-Trade lit. 31-Contracts awarded 32-Display adv. 33-Classified adv.

4-365

Page Size: standard
Subscrip. Rate: $51/yr. individuals;
  $144/yr. institutions
Circulation: 1,650
Circulation Type: paid
**Owner(s):**
Sage Publications, Inc.
2455 Teller Rd.
Thousand Oaks, CA 91320
Telephone: (805) 499-0721
Ownership %: 100
**Editorial:**
Jeffrey Fagan ...............................Editor
Susan Cornett .................Managing Editor
**Desc.:** Reports on original research in
  crime and delinquency, new theory, and
  the critical analyses of theories and
  concepts especially pertinent to
  research development in this field.
**Readers:** Academic communities.

69122
**JOURNAL OF SOCIAL WORK
EDUCATION**
1600 Duke St.
Alexandria, VA 02234-3421
Telephone: (703) 683-8080
FAX: (703) 683-8099
Year Established: 1965
Pub. Frequency: 3/yr.
Page Size: 7X10
Subscrip. Rate: membership
Materials: 06,10,32,33
Print Process: offset
Circulation: 3800
Circulation Type: paid
**Owner(s):**
Council on Social Work Education
1600 Duke St.
Alexandria, VA 22314-3421
Telephone: (703) 683-8080
Ownership %: 100
**Editorial:**
Nancy E. Barr ..........................Managing Editor
**Desc.:** Contains research articles on
  education in the fields of social work
  knowledge and social welfare, focusing
  on developments, innovations and
  problems pertaining to social work
  education at the undergraduate,
  master's and postgraduate levels.

24777
**JOURNAL OF THE HISTORY OF
IDEAS**
Rutgers Univ., 88 College Ave.
New Brunswick, NJ 08903
Telephone: (908) 932-1227
FAX: (908) 932-8708
Year Established: 1940
Pub. Frequency: q.
Page Size: PG: 7 1/4 x 10 1/4; COL: 28
  picas
Subscrip. Rate: $20/yr.; $35/2 yrs.
Materials: 25
Circulation: 2,900
Circulation Type: paid
**Owner(s):**
Journal of the History of Ideas, Inc.
  Editorial
Rutgers Univ., 88 College Ave.
New Brunswick, NJ 08903
Telephone: (908) 932-1227
Ownership %: 100
**Bureau(s):**
Journal of The History of Ideas, Inc.,
  Business
Temple University
748 Anderson Hall
Philadelphia
Contact: Dr. Kee S. Shin, Managing Editor

Journals Div., The Johns Hopkins
  University Press
2715 N. Charles St.
Baltimore, MD 21218-4319
Telephone: (410) 516-6981
Contact: Marie Hansen
**Management:**
J. B. Schneewind .............................President
John F. Callahan .....................Vice President
John Yolton ...........................Vice President
Tara Dorai-Berry ...............Advertising Manager
**Editorial:**
Donald R. Kelley ...................Executive Editor
Marie Hansen ........................Managing Editor
Donald R. Kelley ...............Book Review Editor
William Connell ..............Secretary & Treasurer
Sidney Axinn ...............................Treasurer
**Desc.:** Articles on the history of literature
  and arts, science, philosophy, social and
  political thought.
**Readers:** Scholars, teachers, graduate
  students.

69718
**JOURNAL OF THE VIRGIN
ISLANDS ARCHAEOLOGICAL
SOCIETY**
P.O. Box 368
Frederiksted, St. Croix, VI 00841
Year Established: 1974
Pub. Frequency: s-a.
Subscrip. Rate: $25/yr.
Circulation: 350
Circulation Type: paid
**Owner(s):**
Virgin Islands Archaeological Society
P.O. Box 368
Frederiksted, St. Croix, VI 00841
Ownership %: 100

65001
**JOURNAL OF URBAN HISTORY**
2455 Teller Rd.
Thousand Oaks, CA 91320
Telephone: (805) 499-0721
FAX: (805) 499-0871
Year Established: 1974
Pub. Frequency: q.
Page Size: 5 1/2  x 8 1/2
Subscrip. Rate: $48/yr. individuals;
  $151/yr. institutions
Circulation: 1,400
Circulation Type: paid
**Owner(s):**
Sage Publications, Inc.
2455 Teller Rd.
Thousand Oaks, CA 91320
**Editorial:**
David Goldfield ...............................Editor
**Desc.:** Studies the history of cities and
  urban societies in all periods of human
  history and in all geographical areas of
  the world.

69120
**JOURNAL OF VOLUNTEER
ADMINISTRATION**
P.O. Box 4584
Boulder, CO 80306
Telephone: (303) 541-0238
Year Established: 1982
Pub. Frequency: q.
Subscrip. Rate: $29/yr. US; $32/yr.
  Canada & Mexico; $40/yr. elsewhere
Circulation: 2000
Circulation Type: paid
**Owner(s):**
Association for Volunteer Administration
P.O. Box 4584
Boulder, CO 80306
Telephone: (303) 541-0238
Ownership %: 100
**Editorial:**
Barbara Gilfillen ...............................Editor

**Desc.:** Contains articles on program
  management, model projects and tested
  techniques for successful volunteer
  involvement.

24946
**LANGUAGE**
Dept. of Linguistics, University of
  Pittsburgh
Pittsburgh, PA 15260
Telephone: (412) 624-1354
Mailing Address:
  University of Pittsburgh
  Dept. of Linguistics
  Pittsburgh, PA 15260
Year Established: 1924
Pub. Frequency: q.
Page Size: standard
Subscrip. Rate: $55/yr. individual; $75/yr.
  institution; $25/yr. student
**Owner(s):**
Linguistic Society of America
1325 18th St., N.W., Ste. 211
Washington, DC 20036
Telephone: (202) 835-1714
Ownership %: 100
**Management:**
Arnold Zwicky .............................President
Margaret Reynolds ...........Advertising Manager
Margaret Reynolds ...............Business Manager
**Editorial:**
Sarah Grey Thomason .........................Editor
Frederick Newmeyer ......Secretary & Treasurer
**Desc.:** Articles and reviews bearing on
  field of linguistic science. Departments
  include: Publications Received (quarterly
  listing of books received for review),
  Book Notices (brief reviews), Review
  Articles & Book Reviews, & Editor's
  Department (commentary, letters).
**Readers:** Scholars and scientists in the
  field of linguistics.

65003
**LATIN AMERICAN PERSPECTIVES**
2455 Teller Rd.
Thousand Oaks, CA 91320
Telephone: (805) 499-0721
FAX: (805) 499-0871
Year Established: 1974
Pub. Frequency: q.
Page Size: standard
Subscrip. Rate: $44/yr. individual; $137/yr.
  institution
Circulation: 1,500
Circulation Type: paid
**Owner(s):**
Sage Publications, Inc.
2455 Teller Rd.
Thousand Oaks, CA 91320
Ownership %: 100
**Editorial:**
Ronald H. Chilcote .................Managing Editor
**Desc.:** Discusses and debates critical
  issues relating to capitalism, imperialism,
  and socialism as they affect individuals,
  societies, and nations throughout the
  Americas.
**Readers:** Academic communities.

65005
**MODERN CHINA**
2455 Teller Rd.
Thousand Oaks, CA 91320
Telephone: (805) 499-0721
FAX: (803) 499-0871
Year Established: 1975
Pub. Frequency: q.
Page Size: standard
Subscrip. Rate: $54/yr. individual; $152/yr.
  institute
Circulation: 1,250
Circulation Type: paid

**Owner(s):**
Sage Publications, Inc.
2455 Teller Rd.
Thousand Oaks, CA 91320
Ownership %: 100
**Editorial:**
Philip C. C. Huang .............................Editor
**Desc.:** Encourages a new interdisciplinary
  scholarship and dialogue on China's
  ongoing revolutionary experience.
**Readers:** Academic communities.

64712
**MODERN PHILOLOGY**
1050 E. 59th St.
Chicago, IL 60637
Telephone: (312) 702-8497
Year Established: 1903
Pub. Frequency: q.
Page Size: standard
Subscrip. Rate: $18/yr. student; $28/yr.
  individual; $54/yr. institution
Circulation: 2,200
Circulation Type: paid
**Owner(s):**
University of Chicago Press, The
  Journals Division
P.O. Box 37005
Chicago, IL 60637
Telephone: (312) 702-7600
Ownership %: 100
**Bureau(s):**
Modern Philology
1050 E. 59th St.
Chicago, IL 60637
Telephone: (312) 702-8497
Contact: Janel Mueller, Editor
**Editorial:**
Janel Mueller ...............................Editor
Anne Myles ...........................Editorial Assistant
**Desc.:** Emphasizes English and American
  literature. Also covers Continental,
  Eastern, and Latin American subjects.
**Readers:** Individuals interested in literary
  criticism, literary history, bibliography,
  and theory.

24947
**MONTANA: THE MAGAZINE OF
WESTERN HISTORY**
225 N. Roberts
Helena, MT 59620-1201
Telephone: (406) 444-4708
FAX: (406) 444-2696
Mailing Address:
  P.O. Box 201201
  Helena, MT 59620-1201
Year Established: 1951
Pub. Frequency: q.
Page Size: standard
Subscrip. Rate: $6.50/newsstand; $20/yr.;
  $38/2 yrs.
Materials: 02,06,10,11,13,32,33
Freelance Pay: no pay
Print Process: offset
Circulation: 10,000
Circulation Type: paid
**Owner(s):**
Montana Historical Society
225 N. Roberts St.
Helena, MT 59601
Telephone: (406) 444-4708
FAX: (406) 444-2696
Ownership %: 100
**Management:**
Tammy L. Ryan .................Circulation Manager
Richard Boyd ...............................Manager
**Editorial:**
Charles E. Rankin .........................Exec. Editor
Marilyn Grant .......................Managing Editor
Charles E. Rankin ...............Book Review Editor
Vivian A. Paladin .......................Editor Emeritus
William L. Lang .......................Editor Emeritus
Pam Otto .........................Editorial Assistant
Glenda Bradshaw .............................Photo

**Materials Accepted/Included:** 01-Business news 02-By-line articles 03-Fashion news 04-Food news 05-Freelance copy 06-Letters to editor 07-Real estate news 08-Sports news 09-Travel news
10-Book rev. 11-Movie rev. 12-Music rev. 13-TV rev. 14-Theater rev. 15-Coming events 16-Obituaries 17-Question & answer 18-Social announcements 19-Artwork 20-Cartoons 21-Photos 22-TV listings
23-Audio rec. 24-Video rec. 25-Books 26-Films/film clips 27-Personnel news 28-Press releases 29-New product news/photos 30-Trade lit. 31-Contracts awarded 32-Display adv. 33-Classified adv.

**Desc.:** Authentic, documented and strictly factual articles about the history of the Western states

**Readers:** People interested in Western history. 50% in Montana and 50% in other states and foreign countries. Readership includes members of the Western History Association, Montana Historical Society, and lay readers throughout the world.

## NASW NEWS
24948

750 First St., N.E.
Washington, DC 20002-4241
Telephone: (202) 408-8600
FAX: (202) 336-8310
Year Established: 1956
Pub. Frequency: 10/yr.
Page Size: tabloid
Subscrip. Rate: $25/yr.
Materials: 06,28,32,33
Freelance Pay: negotiable
Circulation: 137,000
**Owner(s):**
National Association of Social Workers
750 First St., N.E.
Washington, DC 20002
Telephone: (202) 408-8600
Ownership %: 100
**Management:**
Natl. Assoc. of Social Workers ..........Publisher
Sheldon R. Goldstein ..........Executive Director
**Editorial:**
Linda Beebe .................Editor in Chief
Susan Landers ..........................Editor
M. Scott Moss .........................Managing Editor
Lyn Carter ...............................Advertising
Jon Hiratsuka .............................Writer
**Desc.:** Contains current information for social workers about NASW, NASW members, the social work profession, and social issues and legislation/regulations. Material concerning jobs, salaries, and personnel matters of interest; help wanted ads; product and conference ads.
**Readers:** Social workers, agency administrators, educators, mental health professionals, policy makers.

## NEBRASKA HISTORY
24949

1500 R St.
Lincoln, NE 68508
Telephone: (402) 471-3270
Mailing Address:
  P.O. Box 82554
  Lincoln, NE 68501
Year Established: 1918
Pub. Frequency: q.
Page Size: standard
Subscrip. Rate: $20/yr. membership fee
Materials: 02,10
Circulation: 4,800
Circulation Type: controlled
**Owner(s):**
Nebraska State Historical Society
P.O. Box 82554
Lincoln, NE 68501
Telephone: (402) 471-3270
Ownership %: 100
**Editorial:**
James E. Potter ..........................Editor
**Desc.:** Contributed by-line articles on colonization, politics, economic development, archeology of Nebraska and surrounding states. Departments include: Book Reviews, Along the Trail (descriptive roundup of historical articles), Book Notes.
**Readers:** Members of the Nebraska State Historical.

## NEW ENGLAND HISTORICAL & GENEALOGICAL REGISTER
24950

101 Newbury St.
Boston, MA 02116
Telephone: (617) 536-5740
FAX: (617) 536-7307
Year Established: 1847
Pub. Frequency: q.
Page Size: standard
Subscrip. Rate: $35/yr.
Circulation: 14,000
Circulation Type: controlled & paid
**Owner(s):**
New England Historic Genealogical Society
101 Newbury St.
Boston, MA 02116
Telephone: (617) 536-5740
Ownership %: 100
**Editorial:**
Jane Fletcher Fiske .......................Editor
**Desc.:** Articles on genealogical, historical, heraldic subjects. Includes listing of recent books, book reviews, editor's notes and comments.
**Readers:** Members of the New England Historic Genealogical Society, historians, genealogists, antiquarians.

## PALACIO, EL
24939

113 Lincoln Ave.
Santa Fe, NM 87501
Telephone: (505) 827-6451
FAX: (505) 827-6427
Mailing Address:
  P.O. Box 2087
  Santa Fe, NM 87504-2087
Year Established: 1913
Pub. Frequency: q.
Page Size: standard
Subscrip. Rate: $12/yr.
Materials: 02,05,06,10,32
Freelance Pay: negotiable
Circulation: 10,000
**Owner(s):**
Museum of New Mexico
P.O. Box 2087
Santa Fe, NM 87504
Telephone: (505) 827-6451
FAX: (505) 827-6427
Ownership %: 100
**Management:**
Museum of New Mexico .....................Publisher
**Editorial:**
Beverly Becker ...........................Editor
Cheryle Mitchell .....................Managing Editor
Mary Sweitzer .............................Design
**Desc.:** Study of the Southwest, Archaeology, Anthropology, Art, History, Natural Science, and Related Arts and Sciences in the Southwest. Reviews Books.
**Readers:** General Public, Scholars, Libraries, UnivLovers of the Southwest.

## POLITICAL THEORY
65008

2455 Teller Rd.
Thousand Oaks, CA 91320
Telephone: (805) 499-0721
FAX: (805) 499-0871
Year Established: 1973
Pub. Frequency: q.
Page Size: standard
Subscrip. Rate: $52/yr. individuals;
  $155/yr. institutions
Circulation: 2,300
Circulation Type: paid
**Owner(s):**
Sage Publications, Inc.
2455 Teller Rd.
Thousand Oaks, CA 91320
Telephone: (805) 499-0721
Ownership %: 100

**Editorial:**
Tracy B. Strong, U.C.S.D. ...............Editor
**Desc.:** Forum for the diverse orientations in the study of political ideas, including the history of political thought, modern theory, conceptual analysis, and polemic argumentation.

## POPULATION & DEVELOPMENT REVIEW
69385

1 Dag Hammarskjold Plaza
New York, NY 10017
Telephone: (212) 339-0500
FAX: (212) 755-6052
Year Established: 1975
Pub. Frequency: q
Subscrip. Rate: $32/yr.
Circulation: 5,000
Circulation Type: paid
**Owner(s):**
Population Council
1 Dag Hammarskjold Plaza
New York, NY 10017
Telephone: (212) 339-0500
Ownership %: 100
**Editorial:**
Paul Demeny .............................Editor

## POPULATION BULLETIN
69278

1875 Connecticut Ave., N.W., Ste. 520
Washington, DC 20009
Telephone: (202) 483-1100
FAX: (202) 328-3937
Year Established: 1945
Pub. Frequency: 4/yr.
Page Size: standard
Subscrip. Rate: $7 newsstand; $45/yr.
Print Process: offset
Circulation: 6,000
Circulation Type: paid
**Owner(s):**
Population Reference Bureau, Inc.
1875 Connecticut Ave., N.W.
Ste. 520
Washington, DC 20009
Telephone: (202) 483-1100
Ownership %: 100
**Editorial:**
Mary Kent ...............................Editor
**Desc.:** Focuses on national and world issues in the field by recognized authorities.

## PUBLIC OPINION QUARTERLY
64710

University of Maryland
College Park, MD 20742
Telephone: (301) 314-7776
Year Established: 1937
Pub. Frequency: q.
Page Size: standard
Subscrip. Rate: $20/yr.
Circulation: 4,950
Circulation Type: paid
**Owner(s):**
Public Opinion Quarterly
**Editorial:**
Howard Schuman ........................Editor

## QUARTERLY JOURNAL OF SPEECH
24954

5105 Backlick Rd., Bldg. E
Annandale, VA 22003
Telephone: (703) 750-0533
Year Established: 1914
Pub. Frequency: q.
Page Size: standard
Subscrip. Rate: $96/yr.; $102/yr. foreign
Circulation: 4,696
Circulation Type: paid

**Owner(s):**
Speech Communication Association
5105 Backlick Rd., Bldg. E
Annandale, VA 22003
Telephone: (703) 750-0533
Ownership %: 100
**Management:**
Sharon Helbert ...............Advertising Manager
**Editorial:**
Robert L. Ivy ............................Editor
Martin Medhurst ................Book Review Editor
James Gaudino ...........................Director
**Desc.:** Contributed articles by authorities in the field of speech on such subjects as rhetoric, drama, theater history, interpretation; history of public address, dramatics, public speaking, debating, radio and television, semantics, phonetics, homiletics, speech pathology, etc.
**Readers:** Lecturers, teachers but primarily college and university teachers.

## RURAL SOCIOLOGY
24955

Dept. of Sociology
Ames, IA 50011-1070
Telephone: (515) 294-8337
FAX: (515) 294-2303
Year Established: 1936
Pub. Frequency: q.
Page Size: standard
Subscrip. Rate: $40/yr.
Circulation: 3,000
Circulation Type: controlled
**Owner(s):**
Allen Press
Telephone: (713) 845-2135
Ownership %: 100
**Editorial:**
Willis Goudy .............................Editor
**Desc.:** Reports on research studies and theoretical developments in field. Also publishes by-line papers on general sociology and other sciences. Review books pertinent to rural sociology.
**Readers:** Teachers, professors, government agency.

## SAGE FAMILY STUDIES ABSTRACTS
65010

2455 Teller Rd.
Thousand Oaks, CA 91320
Telephone: (805) 499-0721
FAX: (805) 499-0871
Year Established: 1979
Pub. Frequency: q.
Page Size: standard
Subscrip. Rate: $87/yr. individual; $267/yr.
  institution
Circulation: 750
Circulation Type: paid
**Owner(s):**
Sage Publications, Inc.
2455 Teller Rd.
Thousand Oaks, CA 91320
Telephone: (805) 499-0721
Ownership %: 100
**Editorial:**
Paul V. McDowell ........................Editor
**Desc.:** Abstracts major articles, reports, books and other materials on policy, theory, and research relating to the family, traditional and alternative lifestyles, and therapy and counseling.
**Readers:** Academics.

## SAGE PUBLIC ADMINISTRATION ABSTRACTS
65011

2455 Teller Rd.
Thousand Oaks, CA 91320
Telephone: (805) 499-0721
FAX: (805) 499-0871
Year Established: 1974
Pub. Frequency: q.

**Materials Accepted/Included:** 01-Business news 02-By-line articles 03-Fashion news 04-Food news 05-Freelance copy 06-Letters to editor 07-Real estate news 08-Sports news 09-Travel news 10-Book rev. 11-Movie rev. 12-Music rev. 13-TV rev. 14-Theater rev. 15-Coming events 16-Obituaries 17-Question & answer 18-Social announcements 19-Artwork 20-Cartoons 21-Photos 22-TV listings 23-Audio rec. 24-Video rec. 25-Books 26-Films/film clips 27-Personnel news 28-Press releases 29-New product news/photos 30-Trade lit. 31-Contracts awarded 32-Display adv. 33-Classified adv.

4-367

Page Size: standard
Subscrip. Rate: $90/yr. individual; $269/yr.
   institution
Circulation: 750
Circulation Type: paid
**Owner(s):**
Sage Publications, Inc.
2455 Teller Rd.
Thousand Oaks, CA 91320
Telephone: (805) 499-0721
Ownership %: 100
**Editorial:**
Paul V. McDowell ..........................Editor
**Desc.:** Publishes cross-indexed abstracts
   covering recent literature (plus related
   citations) on all aspects of public
   administration. Entries are drawn
   from books, articles, pamphlets,
   government publications, significant
   speeches, legislative research studies,
   and other fugitive material.

65012
**SAGE URBAN STUDIES**
   **ABSTRACTS**
2455 Teller Rd.
Thousand Oaks, CA 91320
Telephone: (805) 499-0721
FAX: (805) 499-0871
Year Established: 1973
Pub. Frequency: q.
Page Size: standard
Subscrip. Rate: $87/yr. individual; $267/yr.
   institution
Circulation: 750
Circulation Type: paid
**Owner(s):**
Sage Publications, Inc.
2455 Teller Rd.
Thousand Oaks, CA 91320
Telephone: (805) 499-0721
Ownership %: 100
**Editorial:**
Paul V. McDowell ..........................Editor
**Desc.:** Publishes cross-indexed abstracts
   of important recent literature (plus
   related citations) on all aspects of urban
   studies: government and administration
   policy, transportation, spatial analysis,
   planning, social analysis, community
   studies, education, finance and
   economics, law, management,
   environment, and comparative urban
   analysis.
**Readers:** Academic communities.

69277
**SIGNS: JOURNAL OF WOMEN IN**
   **CULTURE & SOCIETY**
5720 S. Woodlawn Ave.
Chicago, IL 60637
Telephone: (312) 753-3347
FAX: (312) 753-0811
Year Established: 1975
Pub. Frequency: q.
Subscrip. Rate: $32.50/yr. individuals;
   $74/yr. institutions; $23/yr. students
Circulation: 6,100
Circulation Type: paid
**Owner(s):**
University of Chicago Press
5720 S. Woodlawn Ave.
Chicago, IL 60637
Telephone: (312) 753-3347
Ownership %: 100
**Editorial:**
Barbara Laslett ..........................Editor
Ruth-Ellen Botcher Joeres ..............Editor
**Desc.:** Examines theories and
   methodologies from a variety of
   disciplines and provides important links
   between feminist theory and the realities
   of women's lives.

65014
**SIMULATION & GAMING**
2455 Teller Rd.
Thousand Oaks, CA 91320
Telephone: (805) 499-0721
FAX: (805) 499-0871
Year Established: 1970
Pub. Frequency: q.
Page Size: standard
Subscrip. Rate: $50/yr. individual; $157/yr.
   institutions
Circulation: 1,800
Circulation Type: paid
**Owner(s):**
Sage Publications, Inc.
2455 Teller Rd.
Thousand Oaks, CA 91320
Telephone: (805) 499-0721
Ownership %: 100
**Editorial:**
David Crookall ..........................Editor
**Desc.:** Theoretical and empirical papers
   related to man and man-machine
   simulations of social processes.
   Featured are theoretical papers about
   simulations in research and teaching,
   empirical studies, and technical papers
   on new gaming techniques.
**Readers:** Academicians.

24956
**SOCIAL PSYCHOLOGY**
   **QUARTERLY**
1722 N St., N.W.
Washington, DC 20036
Telephone: (202) 833-3410
Year Established: 1956
Pub. Frequency: q.
Page Size: standard
Subscrip. Rate: $40/yr. individual; $80/yr.
   institution; add $10 postage outside US
Print Process: web
Circulation: 3,500
Circulation Type: paid
**Owner(s):**
American Sociological Association
1722 N St., N.W.
Washington, DC 20036
Telephone: (202) 833-3410
Ownership %: 100
**Management:**
Karen G. Edwards ............Advertising Manager
**Editorial:**
Edward J. Lawter ..........................Editor
**Desc.:** Publishes studies, research material
   dealing with the behavioral sciences.
   Scientific manuscripts only.
**Readers:** Sociologists, psychologists.

64708
**SOCIAL SERVICE REVIEW**
969 E. 60th St.
Chicago, IL 60637
Telephone: (312) 702-1165
FAX: (312) 702-0874
Mailing Address:
   969 E. 60th St.
   Chicago, IL 60637
Year Established: 1927
Pub. Frequency: q.
Subscrip. Rate: $30/yr. individual; $21/yr.
   students & alumni
Freelance Pay: N/A
Circulation: 2,800
Circulation Type: paid
**Owner(s):**
University of Chicago
5720 Woodlawn
Chicago, IL 60637
Ownership %: 100
**Editorial:**
John R. Schuerman ..........................Editor
Barbara Ray ..........................Managing Editor
**Desc.:** Devoted to the wide-ranging
   scientific interests of all those
   concerned with social welfare issues.

**Readers:** Academic, and social work
   practitioners.

54085
**SOCIAL STUDIES, THE**
1319 Eighteenth St., N.W.
Washington, DC 20036-1802
Telephone: (202) 296-6267
FAX: (202) 296-5149
Year Established: 1908
Pub. Frequency: bi-m.
Page Size: Standard
Subscrip. Rate: $31/yr. individual; $51/yr.
   institution
Circulation: 2,118
Circulation Type: paid
**Owner(s):**
Heldref Publications
1319 Eighteenth St., N.W.
Washington, DC 20036
Telephone: (202) 296-6267
**Management:**
Walter E. Beach ..........................Publisher
Raymond M. Rallo ..........Advertising Manager
Catherine Welker ..............Circulation Manager
Kerri P. Kilbane ................Promotion Manager
**Editorial:**
Helen Kress ..........................Editor
**Desc.:** This journal presents teachers'
   practical methods and classroom-tested
   suggestions for teaching social studies,
   history, political science, economics,
   geography, and future studies.
**Readers:** Classroom teachers, teacher
   educators, curriculum administrators.

70452
**SOCIAL TEXT**
905 W. Main St., Ste. 18-B
Durham, NC 27701
Telephone: (919) 687-3636
FAX: (919) 688-4574
Mailing Address:
   P.O. Box 90660
   Durham, NC 27708-0660
Year Established: 1979
Pub. Frequency: q.
Page Size: standard
Subscrip. Rate: $16/yr. students; $24/yr.
   individuals; $60/yr. institutions
Materials: 32
Circulation: 1,500
Circulation Type: controlled & paid
**Owner(s):**
Duke University Press
P.O. Box 90660
Durham, NC 27708-0660
Telephone: (919) 687-3600
FAX: (919) 688-4574
Ownership %: 100
**Management:**
Patricia Thomas ..........................Manager
**Editorial:**
Bruce Robbins ..........................Editor
Andrew Ross ..........................Editor

24957
**SOCIAL WORK**
750 First St., N.E., Ste. 700
Washington, DC 20002-4241
Telephone: (202) 408-8600
Mailing Address:
   750 First St., NE, Ste. 700
   Washington, DC 20002-4241
Year Established: 1956
Pub. Frequency: bi-m.
Page Size: standard
Subscrip. Rate: $61/yr. individual; $85/yr.
   institution
Circulation: 145,000
Circulation Type: paid
**Owner(s):**
National Association of Social Workers
750 First St., NE, Ste. 700
Washington, DC 20002-4241
Telephone: (202) 408-8600

**Management:**
Barbara White ..........................President
NASW Press ..........................Publisher
**Editorial:**
Linda Beebe ........Associate Executive Director
Sheldon R. Goldstein ..........Executive Director
Amy Eades ..........................Marketing Director
**Desc.:** Covers new insights into
   established practices, new techniques
   and research, and current problems.
   Departments include: book reviews,
   points and viewpoints, comments on
   currents. Professional articles are
   selected by an anonymous peer review
   process.
**Readers:** Social workers, agencies,
   libraries, faculty, corporations

69121
**SOCIAL WORK IN EDUCATION**
750 First St., N.E. Ste. 700
Washington, DC 20002-4241
Telephone: (202) 408-8600
FAX: (202) 336-8312
Year Established: 1978
Pub. Frequency: q.
Subscrip. Rate: $53/yr. non-members;
   $74/yr. institutions
Circulation: 3700
Circulation Type: paid
**Owner(s):**
National Association of Social Workers
750 First St., N.E. Ste. 700
Washington, DC 20002-4241
Telephone: (202) 408-8600
Ownership %: 100
**Editorial:**
Paula Allen-Meares ..........................Editor
**Readers:** School social workers and their
   colleagues.

24958
**SOCIETY**
Rutgers-The State University
New Brunswick, NJ 08903
Telephone: (908) 932-2280
FAX: (908) 932-3138
Year Established: 1963
Pub. Frequency: s-a.
Page Size: standard
Subscrip. Rate: $40/76/108/yr. individual;
   $102/192/270/yr. institution
Materials: 10,32
Freelance Pay: no free lancers
Circulation: 30,000
Circulation Type: paid
**Owner(s):**
Transaction Publishers
Rutgers University
New Brunswick, NJ 08903
Telephone: (908) 932-2280
Ownership %: 100
**Bureau(s):**
Swets Publishing Services
Heere Weq 347
Contact: Henrik Lang, Managing Director
**Management:**
Daniel Yankelovich ..............Chairman of Board
Irving Louis Horowitz ..........................President
Scott B. Bramson ..........................Vice President
Mary E. Curtis ..........................Vice President
Alicja Garbie ..................Advertising Manager
**Editorial:**
Irving Louis Horowitz ..................Editor in Chief
Nathaniel J. Pallone ..................Senior Editor
Aaron Wildavsky ..................Senior Editor
Brigitte M. Goldstein ..............Managing Editor
David K. Hart ..................Book Review Editor
**Desc.:** The general periodical of record in
   the social sciences. It is the magazine
   that stimulates as well as records
   changes and developments in our
   society.

**Materials Accepted/Included:** 01-Business news 02-By-line articles 03-Fashion news 04-Food news 05-Freelance copy 06-Letters to editor 07-Real estate news 08-Sports news 09-Travel news 10-Book rev. 11-Movie rev. 12-Music rev. 13-TV rev. 14-Theater rev. 15-Coming events 16-Obituaries 17-Question & answer 18-Social announcements 19-Artwork 20-Cartoons 21-Photos 22-TV listings 23-Audio rec. 24-Video rec. 25-Books 26-Films/film clips 27-Personnel news 28-Press releases 29-New product news/photos 30-Trade lit. 31-Contracts awarded 32-Display adv. 33-Classified adv.

**Readers:** Policy makers, social researchers, social science teachers, and others interested in social and political change.

65016

## SOCIOLOGICAL METHODS & RESEARCH
2455 Teller Rd.
Thousand Oaks, CA 91320
Telephone: (805) 499-0721
FAX: (805) 499-0871
Year Established: 1972
Pub. Frequency: q.
Page Size: standard
Subscrip. Rate: $57/yr. individual; $159/yr. institution
Circulation: 1,550
Circulation Type: paid
**Owner(s):**
Sage Publications, Inc.
2455 Teller Rd.
Thousand Oaks, CA 91320
Telephone: (805) 499-0721
Ownership %: 100
**Editorial:**
J. Scott Long ........................................Editor
**Desc.:** A leading journal of quantitative research and methodology in the social sciences.
**Readers:** Academic professionals.

69117

## SOCIOLOGICAL QUARTERLY
Dept. of Sociology
Southern Illinois University.
Carbondale, IL 62901-4524
Telephone: (618) 453-2494
FAX: (618) 453-3253
Year Established: 1960
Pub. Frequency: q.
Page Size: standard
Subscrip. Rate: $30/yr. members; $55/yr. non-members; $110/yr. institutions
Materials: 32
Print Process: web offset
Circulation: 1,500
Circulation Type: paid
**Owner(s):**
Midwest Sociological Society
Dept. of Sociology,
Southern Illinois University
Carbondale, IL 62901
Telephone: (618) 453-2494
FAX: (618) 453-3253
Ownership %: 100
**Editorial:**
Thomas G. Eynon ...................................Editor
**Desc.:** Current research on sociological topics.
**Readers:** Professional Sociologists.

24960

## SOUTHWESTERN HISTORICAL QUARTERLY
2-306 Richardson Hall, University Station
Austin, TX 78712
Telephone: (512) 471-1525
Year Established: 1897
Pub. Frequency: q.
Page Size: pocket
Subscrip. Rate: $25/yr.
Materials: 10
Print Process: offset
**Owner(s):**
Texas State Historical Association
2-306 Richardsn Hall
University Station
Austin, TX 78712
Telephone: (512) 471-1525
Ownership %: 100
**Management:**
Texas State Historical Assn. ...............Publisher
**Editorial:**
Ron Tyler ..............................................Editor
George B. Ward .....................Managing Editor
Janice M. Pinney ...................Assistant Editor

Martin Kohout ..........................Associate Editor
Dr. Norman Brown .............Book Review Editor
**Desc.:** Contributed by-line historical articles on people and events in American Southwest, especially Texas, contiguous states, and Northern Mexico, South as Texas forms a part of Southern history, Spanish Southwest. Spanish Southwest (or "Old Southwest") includes Florida Panhandle, Alabama, Mississippi, Louisiana.
**Readers:** Professional historians.

69387

## STUDIES IN FAMILY PLANNING
1 Dag Hammarskjold Plz.
New York, NY 10017
Telephone: (212) 339-0500
FAX: (212) 755-6052
Year Established: 1963
Pub. Frequency: bi-m.
Page Size: standard
Subscrip. Rate: $4/issue; $24/yr.; $40/2 yrs.
Circulation: 5,500
Circulation Type: free & paid
**Owner(s):**
Population Council
1 Dag Hammarskjold Plz.
New York, NY 10017
Telephone: (212) 339-0500
FAX: (212) 755-6052
Ownership %: 100
**Editorial:**
Julie Reich ...........................................Editor
**Desc.:** Bi-monthly peer-reviewed journal concerned wtih all aspects of reproductive health, fertility regulation, and family planning programs, and their relation to health and development in both developed and developing countries.
**Readers:** Researchers, policy makers, family planning program people.

55872

## STUDIES IN HISTORY
2455 Teller Rd.
Thousand Oaks, CA 91320
Telephone: (805) 499-0721
FAX: (805) 499-0871
Year Established: 1985
Pub. Frequency: bi-a.
Page Size: standard
Subscrip. Rate: $33/yr. individual; $65/yr. institutional
**Owner(s):**
Sage Publications, Inc.
P.O. Box 4215
110 048 New Delhi
Ownership %: 100
**Bureau(s):**
India
**Editorial:**
S. Gopal ...............................................Editor
**Desc.:** Reflects the considerable expansion and diversification that has occurred in historical research in India in recent years - social, economic, and cultural history.
**Readers:** Academicians in history and Third World studies.

64957

## TECHNOLOGY & CULTURE
5720 S. Woodlawn Ave.
Chicago, IL 60637
Telephone: (312) 753-3347
FAX: (312) 753-0811
Year Established: 1960
Pub. Frequency: q.
Subscrip. Rate: $29/yr. individuals; $63/yr. institutions; $20/yr. students; $24 emeritus
Circulation: 2,600
Circulation Type: paid

**Owner(s):**
Society for the History of Technolgy
Michigan Technical Univ.
Haughton, MI
Telephone: (906) 487-2459
Ownership %: 100
**Editorial:**
Robert C. Post .........................Editor in Chief
Joan Mentzer ..........................Managing Editor
**Readers:** College professors and museum curators.

24115

## THANATOS, JOURNAL ON DYING, DEATH & BEREAVEMENT
502 E. Jefferson St.
Tallahassee, FL 32301
Telephone: (904) 224-1969
Mailing Address:
P.O. Box 6009
Tallahassee, FL 32314
Year Established: 1975
Pub. Frequency: q.
Page Size: standard
Subscrip. Rate: $15/yr.
Circulation: 8,000
Circulation Type: paid
**Owner(s):**
Florida Funeral Directors Services, Inc.
502 E. Jefferson St.
Tallahassee, FL 32301
Telephone: (904) 224-1969
Ownership %: 100
**Management:**
M. Ed Wilder ........................................President
**Editorial:**
Jan Scheff ............................................Editor
Alana Schwermer ...............Book Review Editor
**Desc.:** Objective: to enhance the quality of life through an understanding of dying, death and bereavement. Profiles of organizations, stories about personal experience.
**Readers:** Nurses, doctors, clergy, funeral directors, teachers, organizations, consumer related groups, libraries, hospitals, self - help groups, & the enlightened public.

65019

## URBAN AFFAIRS QUARTERLY
2455 Teller Rd.
Thousand Oaks, CA 91320
Telephone: (805) 499-0721
Year Established: 1965
Pub. Frequency: q.
Page Size: standard
Subscrip. Rate: $50/yr. individual; $150/yr. institution
Circulation: 2,000
Circulation Type: paid
**Owner(s):**
Sage Publications, Inc.
2455 Teller Rd.
Thousand Oaks, CA 91320
Telephone: (805) 499-0721
Ownership %: 100
**Editorial:**
Dennis R. Judd .....................................Editor
Donald Phares ......................................Editor
Cris Anderson .............Circulation Administrator
**Desc.:** Emphasizes state-of-art research and scholarly analysis on urban themes: urban life, metropolitan systems, urban economic development, and urban policy. Historical and cross-cultural perspectives are added to its interdisciplinary features.
**Readers:** Academic

64960

## WINTERTHUR PORTFOLIO
Henry Francis du Pont Winterthur Museum
Winterthur, DE 19735
Telephone: (302) 888-4803
FAX: (302) 888-4950

Year Established: 1964
Pub. Frequency: 3/yr.
Page Size: standard
Subscrip. Rate: $30/yr. individual; $64/yr. institution
Materials: 02,10
Freelance Pay: $12-$15/hr.
Circulation: 1,900
Circulation Type: paid
**Owner(s):**
Winterthur Portfolio
Ownership %: 100
**Editorial:**
Catherine E. Hutchins ...............................Editor
Onie Rollins, Lisa .............Book Review Editor
Lock
Susan Randolph ....................Production Editor
**Desc.:** Winterthur Portfolio is an interdisciplinary journal committed to fostering knowledge of the American past by publishing articles on the arts in America and the context in which they developed. Arts is used in its broadest sense to include all products of human ingenuity that satisfy functional, aesthetic, or symbolic needs. Preference is given to articles that are analytical rather than descriptive and to studies that integrate artifacts into their cultural framework.
**Readers:** Academics in American art, history, and American studies; museum curators and educators; collectors and dealers; other Americanists.

65062

## WORK & OCCUPATIONS
2455 Teller Rd.
Thousand Oaks, CA 91320
Telephone: (805) 499-0721
FAX: (805) 499-0871
Year Established: 1974
Pub. Frequency: q.
Page Size: standard
Subscrip. Rate: $48/yr. individual; $133/yr. institution
Circulation: 1,250
Circulation Type: paid
**Owner(s):**
Sage Publications, Inc.
2455 Teller Rd.
Newbury Park, CA 91320
Telephone: (805) 499-0721
Ownership %: 100
**Editorial:**
Andrew Abbott, U. of Chicago .................Editor
**Desc.:** An international forum for sociological research and theory in the substantive areas of work, occupations, leisure - their structures and interrelationships.
**Readers:** Academic communities.

53936

## WORLD AFFAIRS
1319 Eighteenth St., N.W.
Washington, DC 20036-1802
Telephone: (202) 296-6267
FAX: (202) 296-5149
Year Established: 1834
Pub. Frequency: q.
Page Size: standard
Subscrip. Rate: $35/yr. individual; $54/yr. institutions; add $10/yr. foreign
Circulation: 602
Circulation Type: paid
**Owner(s):**
Heldref Publications
1319 Eighteenth St., N.W.
Washington, DC 20036-1802
Telephone: (202) 296-6267
Ownership %: 100
**Management:**
Walter E. Beach ...................................Publisher
Raymond M. Rallo ............Advertising Manager
Catherine Welker ..............Circulation Manager

**Materials Accepted/Included:** 01-Business news 02-By-line articles 03-Fashion news 04-Food news 05-Freelance copy 06-Letters to editor 07-Real estate news 08-Sports news 09-Travel news 10-Book rev. 11-Movie rev. 12-Music rev. 13-TV rev. 14-Theater rev. 15-Coming events 16-Obituaries 17-Question & answer 18-Social announcements 19-Artwork 20-Cartoons 21-Photos 22-TV listings 23-Audio rec. 24-Video rec. 25-Books 26-Films/film clips 27-Personnel news 28-Press releases 29-New product news/photos 30-Trade lit. 31-Contracts awarded 32-Display adv. 33-Classified adv.

4-369

Kerri P. Kilbane .................Promotion Manager
**Editorial:**
Joyce Horn .........................................Editor
**Desc.:** Published by the American Peace Society since 1834, World Affairs is the oldest journal of international affairs in the United States.
**Readers:** Educators, historians, political scientists and researchers.

64937

### CHINA REPORT: JOURNAL OF EAST ASIAN STUDIES
2455 Teller Rd.
Thousand Oaks, CA 91320
Telephone: (805) 499-0721
FAX: (805) 499-0871
Year Established: 1973
Pub. Frequency: q.
Page Size: standard
Subscrip. Rate: $38/yr. individuals; $74/yr. institutions
Circulation: 100
Circulation Type: paid
**Owner(s):**
Sage Publications, Inc.
2455 Teller Rd.
Thousand Oaks, CA 91320
Telephone: (805) 499-0721
Ownership %: 100
**Editorial:**
Manoran Jan Mohanty .............................Editor
**Desc.:** Eencourages the increased understanding of contemporary China and its East Asian neighbors, their cultures and ways of development, and their impact on India and other South Asian countries.
**Readers:** Academic communities

65064

### YOUTH & SOCIETY
2455 Teller Rd.
Thousand Oaks, CA 91320
Telephone: (805) 499-0721
FAX: (805) 499-0871
Year Established: 1969
Pub. Frequency: q.
Page Size: standard
Subscrip. Rate: $48/yr. individuals; $143/yr. institutions
Circulation: 1,300
Circulation Type: paid
**Owner(s):**
Sage Publications, Inc.
2455 Teller Rd.
Thousand Oaks, CA 91320
Telephone: (805) 499-0721
Ownership %: 100
**Editorial:**
Margaret LeCompte ................................Editor
Kathryn G. Herr ....................................Editor
**Desc.:** Brings together interdisciplinary empirical studies and theoretical papers on the broad social and political implications and development; concentration is primarily on the age span from mid- adolescence through young adulthood.
**Readers:** Academic communities.

## Group 250-Sports & Sporting Goods

24964

### AMERICAN FIREARMS INDUSTRY
2455 E. Sunrise, 916
Ft. Lauderdale, FL 33304
Telephone: (305) 561-3505
FAX: (305) 561-4129
Year Established: 1972
Pub. Frequency: m.
Page Size: standard
Subscrip. Rate: $25/yr.
Materials: 01,06,10,15,16,27,28,29,30,31,32
Freelance Pay: $200-$250

Circulation: 27,000
Circulation Type: controlled
**Owner(s):**
AFI Communications Group, Inc.
2455 E. Sunrise Blvd., 916
Ft Lauderdale, FL 33304
Telephone: (305) 561-3505
Ownership %: 100
**Management:**
A. Molchan ....................................President
A. Molchan ....................................Publisher
Jim Hatfield ....................Advertising Manager
**Editorial:**
Don Shumar ......................................Editor
R. A. Lesmeister ......................Managing Editor
R. A. Lesmeister ................Book Review Editor
Tracey Attlee .......................Marketing Editor
R. A. Lesrneister ................New Product Editor
A. Molchan .................................News Editor
R. A. Lesmeister ......................Political Editor
Mike Gruber ........................Technical Director
**Desc.:** An industrial book for the firearms industry.
**Readers:** Firearms dealers, merchandisers, distributors.

24987

### AMERICAN HOCKEY MAGAZINE
1022 W. 80th St.
Bloomington, MN 55420
Telephone: (612) 881-3183
FAX: (612) 881-2172
Year Established: 1980
Pub. Frequency: 8/yr.
Page Size: tabloid
Subscrip. Rate: $13/yr.; free to registered members
Freelance Pay: $50-$100
Circulation: 275,000
Circulation Type: controlled
**Owner(s):**
USA Hockey, Publishing Group
1022 W. 80th St.
Bloomington, MN 55420
Telephone: (612) 881-3183
FAX: (612) 881-2172
Ownership %: 100
**Bureau(s):**
David Ogrean
4965 N. 30th St.
Colorado Springs, CO 80919
Telephone: (719) 599-5500
**Editorial:**
Darryl Seibel .....................................Editor
David Jensen ................................Advertising
Wade Martin ........................Production Editor
**Desc.:** Covers hockey rules, profiles, referees and rink management.
**Readers:** Rink & arena managers; university, college & amateur hockey coaches, team representatives, referees, officials, players & fans.

66609

### ARCHERY BUSINESS
601 Lakeshore Pkwy., Ste. 600
Minnetonka, MN 55305-5215
Telephone: (612) 476-2200
Year Established: 1975
Pub. Frequency: bi-m.
Page Size: standard
Materials: 01,28,29,32
Freelance Pay: $40-$350
Circulation: 14,100
Circulation Type: controlled
**Owner(s):**
Ehlert Publishing Group, Inc.
601 Lakeshore Pkwy., Ste. 600
Minnetonka, MN 55305-5215
Telephone: (612) 476-2200
FAX: (612) 476-8065
Ownership %: 100
**Editorial:**
Mike Strandlund ..................................Editor
Tom Kacheroski ......................Managing Editor
Stacey Marmolejo ...........Associate Publisher

**Desc.:** The premier trade magazine serving the industry. Written primarily for dealers, it also is required reading for reps, manufacturers and distributors.

24707

### ATHLETIC BUSINESS
1846 Hoffman St.
Madison, WI 53704
Telephone: (608) 249-0186
FAX: (608) 249-1153
Year Established: 1976
Pub. Frequency: m.
Page Size: standard
Subscrip. Rate: $5/copy; $36/yr.
Freelance Pay: none
Circulation: 40,666
Circulation Type: controlled
**Owner(s):**
Athletic Business
1846 Hoffman St.
Madison, WI 53704
Telephone: (608) 249-0186
Ownership %: 100
**Management:**
Gretchen Kelsey Brown .......................Publisher
Peter Brown ..................................Publisher
Bonnie Madison .................Production Manager
Brad Zaugg ...............................Sales Manager
**Editorial:**
Sue Schmid ........................................Editor
Rick Berg .............................Editorial Director
Diane Ebner ........................Advertising Director
Paul Graff .............................Art Director
**Desc.:** A business magazine for athletic administrators and purchasers. Articles report on business aspects of running-athletic-recreation-fitness programs, on purchasing of athletic supplies and equipment, and on financing, planning, constructing & operating athletic facilities. Departments include: Coming Events, Current News, New Products, Letters to the Editor, Industry Briefings, Liability/Sports, Sports Marketing, Recreation Management, High School Sports, Sports Law.
**Readers:** Athletic Business goes exclusively to administrators of sports/recreation/fitness programs and facilities.

66584

### CANADIAN JOURNAL OF APPLIED PHYSIOLOGY
1607 N. Market St.
Champaign, IL 61820
Telephone: (217) 351-5076
FAX: (217) 351-2674
Mailing Address:
P.O. Box 5076
Champaign, IL 61825
Year Established: 1976
Pub. Frequency: q.
Page Size: standard
Subscrip. Rate: $24/yr. students; $40/yr. individuals; $88/yr. others
Materials: 06,10,25,29
Print Process: offset
Circulation: 1,000
Circulation Type: paid
**Owner(s):**
Canadian Society for Exercise Physiology
James Naismith Dr.
1600 Prom.
Gloucester ON, Canada CN
Telephone: (613) 748-5768
FAX: (613) 748-5763
Ownership %: 100
**Management:**
Rainer Martens ................................Publisher
Peg Goyette ...................................Manager
**Editorial:**
David Cunningham ...............................Editor
Linda Bump ...........................Journals Director

**Desc.:** Publishes articles that focus on the relationship between the biological sciences and physical activity, fitness and health.
**Readers:** Members of the Canadian Society for Exercise Physiology; individual subscribers.

69452

### CLUB BUSINESS INTERNATIONAL
253 Summer St.
Boston, MA 02210-1114
Telephone: (617) 951-0055
FAX: (617) 951-0056
Year Established: 1982
Pub. Frequency: m.
Subscrip. Rate: $27/yr. membership
Circulation: 7,000
Circulation Type: controlled
**Owner(s):**
IRSA, the Assn. of Quality Clubs
253 Summer St.
Boston, MA 02210-1114
Telephone: (617) 951-0055
Ownership %: 100
**Desc.:** Covers management and profitability issues for racquet and fitness clubs. Includes club profiles, practical advice, and new product information.

65463

### DIVING WORLD
7628 Densmore Ave.
Van Nuys, CA 91406
Telephone: (818) 782-7328
Pub. Frequency: m.
Page Size: standard
Subscrip. Rate: $15/yr.
Circulation: 11,000
Circulation Type: controlled
**Owner(s):**
Creative Age Publications, Inc.
Ownership %: 100
**Management:**
Carol Summer ...................................Publisher
Deborah Carner ..............................Publisher
**Editorial:**
Marie Nordberg ...................................Editor
Barbara Feiner ......................Managing Editor
**Desc.:** How-to articles, equipment reviews, and selling strategies for the diving industry.
**Readers:** Managers, owners and instructors of diving stores as well as diving enthusiasts.

67189

### EYE, THE
501 W. 11th St.
Wilmington, DE 19801
Telephone: (302) 571-6975
FAX: (302) 656-5035
Year Established: 1985
Pub. Frequency: m.: Oct.-May
Page Size: oversize
Subscrip. Rate: free
Circulation: 20,000
Circulation Type: free
**Owner(s):**
YMCA Of Delaware
501 W. 11th St.
Wilmington, DE 19801
Telephone: (302) 571-6975
Ownership %: 100
**Management:**
Doris Bolt ......................................Publisher

23007

### FISHING TACKLE TRADE NEWS
6918 E. Fourth Plain Blvd.
Vancouver, WA 98661
Telephone: (206) 693-4721
FAX: (206) 693-3997
Mailing Address:
P.O. Box 2669
Vancouver, WA 98668
Year Established: 1952
Pub. Frequency: m.

Page Size: standard
Subscrip. Rate: $45/yr. US & CN; $70/yr.
  foreign; $135/yr. foreign airmail
Freelance Pay: negotiable
Circulation: 24,000
Circulation Type: controlled
**Owner(s):**
Vickers Communications Corp.
P.O. Box 2669
Vancouver, WA 98668
Telephone: (206) 693-4721
Ownership %: 100
**Management:**
Bob Vickers .................................Publisher
**Editorial:**
John Kirk .............................................Editor
Nancy Smith ...........................Art Director
Jean Farmer ...........Assistant to the Publisher
Bob Vickers ......................Marketing Director
Scott Ansley .........................................Sales
John Valente .........................................Sales
**Desc.:** Tells how to merchandise & sell
  fishing equipment & the various products
  fishermen use. Emphasis placed on
  selling quality goods at a profit. Buyers
  from various types of retail & wholesale
  firms are interviewed on successful
  merchandising technique & their
  expertise is shared with readers.
  Features cover industry issues &
  problems, like fisheries management,
  pollution control, fishing regulations &
  other subjects that will help buyers and
  retail sales clerks sell from a broad base
  of knowledge. Other editorial includes
  news of the industry, new product
  announcements, shows & important
  events, statistical reports on market
  trends, retailer & wholesaler surveys.
  Also, in-store management products and
  techniques.
**Readers:** Distributed to retailers,
  wholesalers, & salesmen of sportfishing and related products.

### GOLF COURSE MANAGEMENT
23187

1421 Research Park Dr.
Lawrence, KS 66049-3859
Telephone: (913) 832-4490
FAX: (913) 832-4433
Year Established: 1927
Pub. Frequency: m.
Page Size: standard
Subscrip. Rate: $30/yr. US; $42/yr. foreign
Materials: 01,02,05,08,09,19,20,21,23,24,
  25,28,29,32,33
Freelance Pay: $100-$350
Print Process: offset
Circulation: 24,000
Circulation Type: controlled
**Owner(s):**
Golf Course Supt. Assn. of America
1421 Research Park Dr.
Lawrence, KS 66049
Telephone: (913) 832-4490
Ownership %: 100
**Management:**
Steve Mona .................Executive Director
Robert Shively ...............Advertising Manager
**Editorial:**
Clay Loyd ...........................................Editor
Chris Caldwell ...................Managing Editor
**Desc.:** Practical and academic material
  related to the field of turf-grass
  maintenance and golf course
  management. News items pertinent to
  membership of The Golf Course
  Superintendents Association of
  America and the golf turf industry.
**Readers:** Golf course superintendents,
  agronomists, golf club officials, golf pros,
  green committee chairmen,  club
  managers, landscapers, sports editors,
  golf club members.

### GOLF PRO MAGAZINE
65255

7 W. 34th St.
New York, NY 10001
Telephone: (212) 630-4000
Year Established: 1988
Pub. Frequency: 8/yr.
Page Size: standard
Subscrip. Rate: free
Circulation: 12,000
Circulation Type: controlled & free
**Owner(s):**
Fairchild Publications
7 W. 34th St.
New York, NY 10001
Telephone: (212) 630-4000
Ownership %: 100
**Management:**
Mark Sullivan ...........................Vice President
Ken Cohen ...................................Publisher
**Editorial:**
Ken Cohen ...........................................Editor
**Desc.:** Focuses on buying and selling
  equipment, clothing, and footwear.
**Readers:** Golf-pro managers and sporting
  goods store.

### GOLF SCENE MAGAZINE
67053

9701 Gravois Ave.
St. Louis, MO 63123
Telephone: (314) 638-4050
FAX: (314) 638-3880
Year Established: 1985
Pub. Frequency: 4/yr.
Page Size: standard
Subscrip. Rate: $9.95/yr.
Circulation: 20,000
Circulation Type: paid
**Owner(s):**
Admore Publishing Co., Inc.
9701 Gravois Ave.
Saint Louis, MO 63123
Telephone: (314) 638-4050
Ownership %: 100
**Management:**
Ed Lang ..............................................Publisher
Ron Gilmore ...............Advertising Manager
**Editorial:**
Dan Reardon .......................................Editor

### GOLF SHOP OPERATIONS
24971

5520 Park Ave.
Trumbull, CT 06611-0395
Telephone: (203) 373-7048
Mailing Address:
  P.O. Box 395
  Trumbull, CT 06611-0395
Year Established: 1963
Pub. Frequency: 10/yr.
Page Size: tabloid
Subscrip. Rate: $72/yr.
Materials: 01,02,03,05,06,08,15,16,19,20,
  21,27,28,29
Freelance Pay: $200-$650
Circulation: 16,787
Circulation Type: controlled
**Owner(s):**
New York Times Company Magazine
  Group
5520 Park Ave.
Trumbull, CT 06611-0395
Telephone: (203) 373-7000
Ownership %: 100
**Management:**
Jay FitzGerald .................................President
Roger J. Casl ....................................Publisher
Diana O'Donnell .............Circulation Manager
Stu Schneider ...........Public Relations Manager
**Editorial:**
Mark Godich .......................................Editor
Mark Godich .......................Managing Editor
Susan Discipio ...........................Advertising
Gloria Melfi ...................................Art Director
Steve Donahue ...................Associate Editor
Eileen Rafferty Broderick .........Fashion Editor

Amy Lee ...............................Feature Editor
Mary Jane McGirr ......................Librarian
Dom Furore ...........................Photographer
Christine Huebener .......Production Coordinator
Joe Mossa .......................Production Director
Hugh White ...........................Research Director
**Desc.:** Emphasizes features and profiles of
  successful operations at specific golf
  shops.
**Readers:** Golf professionals, owners and
  operators at golf courses & golf retail
  stores.

### INTERNATIONAL JOURNAL OF SPORT NUTRITION
66582

1607 N. Market St.
Champaign, IL 61820
Telephone: (217) 351-5076
FAX: (217) 351-2674
Mailing Address:
  P.O. Box 5076
  Champaign, IL 61825
Year Established: 1991
Pub. Frequency: q.
Page Size: standard
Subscrip. Rate: $24/yr. students; $36/yr.
  individuals; $80/yr. institutions
Materials: 10,25,29
Print Process: offset
Circulation: 913
Circulation Type: paid
**Owner(s):**
Human Kinetics Publishers, Inc.
P.O. Box 5076
Champaign, IL 61825-5076
Telephone: (217) 351-5076
FAX: (217) 351-2674
Ownership %: 100
**Management:**
Rainer Martens .................................Publisher
Julie Anderson .................................Manager
**Editorial:**
Priscilla Clarkson ...............................Editor
Linda A. Bump .......................Journals Director
**Desc.:** Advances the understanding of the
  nutritional aspects of human physical
  and athletic performance. It includes
  experimental and experiential evidence
  on all aspects of athletic ability, levels of
  fitness, or health status of the
  participants.
**Readers:** Nutrition researchers, clinical
  nutritionists, nutrition consultants,
  physiologists

### INTERNATIONAL SADDLERY & APPAREL JOURNAL
56406

1130 Guynn Rd.
Paint Lick, KY 40461-9727
Telephone: (606) 986-3044
Mailing Address:
  P.O. Box 3039
  Berea, KY 40403-3039
Year Established: 1992
Pub. Frequency: m.
Page Size: tabloid
Subscrip. Rate: free to qualified retailers;
  $48/yr. others
Materials: 01,03,05,06,08,19,20,21,28,29,
  30,32,33
Freelance Pay: varies
Circulation: 8,057
Circulation Type: controlled
**Owner(s):**
EEMG, Inc.
Box 3039
Berea, KY 40403
Telephone: (606) 986-4644
Ownership %: 100
**Management:**
Bill Buell ............................................Publisher
Janice Zuccaro ...............Advertising Manager
Anne Manzella ...............Circulation Manager

**Editorial:**
Janet Buell ..........................................Editor
**Desc.:** Serves the business and marketing
  needs of the equine trade industry.
  Feature departments present articles
  which address the current business and
  marketing issues, trends, and practices
  in the equestrian and equine goods
  industries. Monthly news and products
  sections are also included.
**Readers:** Retailers, distributors,
  manufacturers of horse related products
  - both national & international.
**Deadline:** story-10th of mo. prior pub.
  date; news-10th of mo. prior; photo-10th
  of mo. prior; ads-10th of mo. prior

### JOURNAL OF PHILOSOPHY OF SPORT (JPS)
58673

1607 N. Market St.
Champaign, IL 61820
Telephone: (217) 351-5076
FAX: (217) 351-2674
Mailing Address:
  P.O. Box 5076
  Champaign, IL 61825
Year Established: 1974
Pub. Frequency: a.
Page Size: standard
Subscrip. Rate: $12/yr. students; $19/yr.
  individuals; $30/yr. institutions
Materials: 25
Print Process: offset
Circulation: 524
Circulation Type: paid
**Owner(s):**
Philosophic Society for the Study of Sport
Kean College of New Jersey
Union, NJ 07083-9982
Telephone: (908) 527-2101
Ownership %: 100
**Management:**
Rainer Martens .................................Publisher
Julie Anderson .................................Manager
**Editorial:**
Klaus V. Meier ...................................Editor
Linda A. Bump .......................Journals Director
**Desc.:** The journal contains stimulating
  articles, critical reviews of work
  completed, and discussions about the
  philosophy of sport. It is the primary
  resource for communicating
  contemporary philosophy with regard to
  sport.
**Readers:** Members of the Philosophic
  Society for the Study of Sport; individual
  subscribers.

### JOURNAL OF SPORT MANAGEMENT (JSM)
58675

1607 N. Market St.
Champaign, IL 61820
Telephone: (217) 351-5076
FAX: (217) 351-2674
Mailing Address:
  P.O. Box 5076
  Champaign, IL 61825
Year Established: 1987
Pub. Frequency: 3/yr.
Page Size: standard
Subscrip. Rate: $18/yr. students; $30/yr.
  individuals; $64/yr. institutions
Materials: 10,25,29
Print Process: offset
Circulation: 850
Circulation Type: paid
**Owner(s):**
Human Kinetics Publishers, Inc.
P.O. Box 5076
Champaign, IL 61825-5076
Telephone: (217) 351-5076
FAX: (217) 351-2674
Ownership %: 100

---

**Materials Accepted/Included:** 01-Business news 02-By-line articles 03-Fashion news 04-Food news 05-Freelance copy 06-Letters to editor 07-Real estate news 08-Sports news 09-Travel news 10-Book rev. 11-Movie rev. 12-Music rev. 13-TV rev. 14-Theater rev. 15-Coming events 16-Obituaries 17-Question & answer 18-Social announcements 19-Artwork 20-Cartoons 21-Photos 22-TV listings 23-Audio rec. 24-Video rec. 25-Books  26-Films/film clips 27-Personnel news 28-Press releases 29-New product news/photos 30-Trade lit. 31-Contracts awarded 32-Display adv. 33-Classified adv.

**Management:**
Rainer Martens .............................Publisher
Julie Anderson .............................Manager
**Editorial:**
Joy DeSensi .............................Editor
Linda A. Bump .............................Journals Director
**Desc.:** This journal publishes theoretical and applied articles pertaining to all areas of sport management including athletic administration, recreation and leisure.
**Readers:** Members of the North American Society for Sport Management, individual subscribers.

66586
**JOURNAL OF SPORT REHABILITATION (JSR)**
1607 N. Market St.
Champaign, IL 61820
Telephone: (217) 351-5076
FAX: (217) 351-2674
Mailing Address:
   P.O. Box 5076
   Champaign, IL 61825
Year Established: 1992
Pub. Frequency: q.
Page Size: 6 x 9
Subscrip. Rate: $24/yr. students; $36/yr. individuals; $80/yr. institutions
Materials: 10,25,29
Print Process: offset
Circulation: 567
Circulation Type: paid
**Owner(s):**
Human Kinetics Publishers, Inc
1607 N. Market St.
Champaign, IL 61820
Telephone: (217) 351-5076
FAX: (217) 351-2674
Ownership %: 100
**Management:**
Rainer Martens .............................Publisher
Julie Anderson .............................Manager
**Editorial:**
David H. Perrin .............................Editor
Linda A. Bump .............................Journals Director
**Desc.:** Committed to advancing the understanding of all aspects of rehabilitation process for sports injuries. The journal will publish original research reports, scholarly reviews, case studies, and clinical applications articles that pertain directly to rehabilitation of injuries incurred in sport and exercise setting.
**Readers:** All members of the sports medicine team: athletic trainers, team physicians, sport physical therapists, sport podiatrists, sport nutritionists, exercise physiologists, sport bio mechanics, sport psychologists, and strength and conditioning coaches.

69308
**JOURNAL OF STRENGTH & CONDITIONING RESEARCH**
1607 N. Market St.
Champaign, IL 61820
Telephone: (217) 351-5076
FAX: (217) 351-2674
Mailing Address:
   P.O. Box 5076
   Champaign, IL 61820
Year Established: 1987
Pub. Frequency: q.
Page Size: standard
Subscrip. Rate: $20/yr. students; $32/yr. individuals; $64/yr. institutions
Materials: 25,29
Print Process: offset
Circulation: 8,100
Circulation Type: paid

**Owner(s):**
National Strength & Conditioning Association
530 Communications Circle
Ste. 204
Colorado Springs, CO 80905
Telephone: (719) 632-6722
FAX: (719) 632-6367
Ownership %: 100
**Management:**
Rainer Martens .............................Publisher
**Editorial:**
William J. Kraemer .............................Editor
Peg Goyette .............................Managing Editor
Linda A. Bump .............................Director
**Desc.:** Source for the newest information about strength and conditioning in sport and exercise. Includes current research accompanied by recommendations for application, selected symposia, reviews of literature and notes, comments and methods discussions.
**Readers:** Sport scientists, exercise physiologists.

58674
**JOURNAL OF TEACHING IN PHYSICAL EDUCATION (JPE)**
1607 N. Market St.
Champaign, IL 61820
Telephone: (217) 351-5076
FAX: (217) 351-2674
Mailing Address:
   P.O. Box 5076
   Champaign, IL 61825
Year Established: 1981
Pub. Frequency: q.
Page Size: standard
Subscrip. Rate: $24/yr. students; $36/yr. individuals; $80/yr. institutions
Materials: 10,25,29
Print Process: offset
Circulation: 1,005
Circulation Type: paid
**Owner(s):**
Human Kinetics
1607 N. Market St.
Champaign, IL 61820
Telephone: (217) 351-5076
FAX: (217) 351-2674
Ownership %: 100
**Management:**
Rainer Martens .............................Publisher
Thomas Moone .............................Manager
**Editorial:**
Mary O'Sullivan .............................Editor
Stephen Silverman .............................Editor
Linda A. Bump .............................Journals Director
**Desc.:** Serves as a forum for research and topical discussion articles concerned with teacher education. It contains theoretical and applied articles drawn from studies in the classroom as well as the laboratory.
**Readers:** Teachers, teacher educators, students, and administrators in physical education.

69131
**LEGENDS SPORTS MEMORABILIA**
2044 1st Ave.
Ste. 300
San Diego, CA 92101-2089
Telephone: (619) 460-9219
FAX: (619) 460-4919
Pub. Frequency: bi-m.
Subscrip. Rate: $27/yr.
Circulation: 155,470
Circulation Type: paid
**Owner(s):**
Legends Sports Memorabilia
9950 Campo Rd., #202
Spring Valley, CA 91977
Telephone: (619) 460-9219
Ownership %: 100

**Editorial:**
Michael Godfrey .............................Editor
James Thompson .............................Advertising
**Desc.:** Offers articles and price guides relating to collecting sports memorabilia, and sports athlete features by nationally-recognized writers. Includes sportscard and postcard insert sheets.

24972
**NATIONAL SPEED SPORT NEWS**
79 Chestnut St.
Ridgewood, NJ 07450
Telephone: (201) 445-3117
FAX: (201) 445-7677
Mailing Address:
   P.O. Box 608
   Ridgewood, NJ 07451
Year Established: 1934
Pub. Frequency: w.
Page Size: tabloid
Subscrip. Rate: $1 newsstand; $32.50/yr.
Materials: 01,02,06,24,25,27,28,29,30,31, 32,33
Circulation: 75,000
Circulation Type: paid
**Owner(s):**
Kay Publishing Co., Inc.
79 Chestnut St.
P.O. Box 608
Ridgewood, NJ 07451
Telephone: (201) 445-3117
Ownership %: 100
**Management:**
Chris Economaki .............................President
Corinne Economaki .............................Publisher
Wayne Cloth .............................Advertising Manager
**Editorial:**
Chris Economaki .............................Executive Editor
Ron Lemasters .............................Editor
Chris Economaki .............................Managing Editor
Keith Waltz .............................News Editor
Mike Kerchner .............................Photo
**Desc.:** Covers auto racing in all of its phases: oval track and road racing, stock car, Indianapolis car, sports car, etc. News, weekly results of events, point standings, business stories, sponsors purse arrangements, photos of events, tech photos of new developments in cars and tracks.
**Readers:** Predominantly male, young and auto and sports oriented.
**Deadline:** story-Mon., 12:00 pm; news-Mon., 12:00 pm; photo-Mon., 12:00 pm; ads-Mon., 12:00 pm

24975
**NSGA RETAIL FOCUS**
1699 Wall St.
Mt Prospect, IL 60056
Telephone: (708) 439-4000
Year Established: 1947
Pub. Frequency: m.: Jan.-Nov.
Page Size: tabloid
Subscrip. Rate: $50/yr.; $75/yr. foreign; members only
Freelance Pay: negotiable
Circulation: 9,000
Circulation Type: paid
**Owner(s):**
National Sporting Goods Association
1699 Wall St.
Mt Prospect, IL 60056
Telephone: (708) 439-4000
Ownership %: 100
**Management:**
Thomas G. Drake .............................Publisher
Larry Weindruch .............................Associate Publisher
Robert K. Nieman .............................Circulation Manager
**Editorial:**
Robert K. Nieman .............................Editor
Dana Parker .............................Contributing Writer
Chris Ferguson .............................Design Coordinator

**Desc.:** Primarily a magazine for sporting goods retailers, although it is also read by sales reps. and manufacturers. Articles designed to help the sporting goods retailer sell more goods at a profit by improving all phases of his operations; marketing, merchandising, management, articles about legislation affecting the retailer; and articles of other organizations in the industry (trade shows, conventions, etc.).
**Readers:** Retailers of sporting goods, sales representatives, manufacturers.

23189
**PGA MAGAZINE**
888 W. Big Beaver
Ste. 600
Troy, MI 48084
Telephone: (810) 362-7400
FAX: (810) 362-7425
Year Established: 1920
Pub. Frequency: m.
Page Size: standard
Subscrip. Rate: $36/yr.
Freelance Pay: approx. $300
Circulation: 50,000
Circulation Type: paid
**Owner(s):**
Professional Golfers' Assn. of America
P.O. Box 109601
West Palm Beach, FL 33410
Telephone: (407) 626-3600
Ownership %: 100
**Management:**
Robert S. Vincent .............................Publisher
**Editorial:**
Kelly Elbin .............................Editor
Julie Barth .............................Associate Editor
**Desc.:** Features dealing with various aspects of professional golf, teaching, promotion, club management, PGA Tour, etc. News and features covering major golf events, personalities, history, architecture, instruction of golf, industry leaders, photographic essays.
**Readers:** PGA membership, amateur golfers (club members, collegiate players etc.), members of the press.

26445
**PRORODEO SPORTS NEWS**
101 Pro Rodeo Dr.
Colorado Springs, CO 80919
Telephone: (719) 593-8840
FAX: (719) 548-4899
Year Established: 1952
Pub. Frequency: bi-w.: Wed.
Page Size: tabloid
Subscrip. Rate: $24/yr.
Freelance Pay: varies
Circulation: 34,000
Circulation Type: paid
**Owner(s):**
PRCA Properties
101 Pro Rodeo Dr.
Colorado Springs, CO 80919
Telephone: (719) 593-8840
Ownership %: 100
**Management:**
Lewis Cryer .............................President
Steve Fleming .............................Publisher
**Editorial:**
Kendra Santos .............................Editor in Chief
D.D. Deleo .............................Advertising
**Desc.:** Official publication of the Association of Professional Rodeo Cowboys. Publishes all official business of PRCA, lists upcoming rodeos and results of past rodeos, news and feature stories, action photos.
**Readers:** Fans of professional rodeo, PRCA members.

## QUEST
64879

1607 N. Market
Champaign, IL 61820
Telephone: (217) 351-5076
FAX: (217) 351-2674
Mailing Address:
　P.O. Box 5076
　Champaign, IL 61825-5076
Year Established: 1949
Pub. Frequency: q.
Page Size: standard
Subscrip. Rate: $36/yr. individuals; $80/yr.
　institutions; $24/yr. students
Print Process: offset
Circulation: 1,440
Circulation Type: paid
**Owner(s):**
National Assn. for Physical Educ. in Higher
　Educ.
c/o G. Evans, Dept. of Hum.Per
San Jose State University
San Jose, CA 95192-0054
Telephone: (408) 924-3029
Ownership %: 100
**Management:**
Rainer Martens ...................................Publisher
Jackie Hoyt ........................Circulation Manager
Thomas Moore .................................Manager
**Editorial:**
Amelia Lee ...............................................Editor
Linda A. Bump ........................Journal Director
**Desc.:** Publishes articles with issues critical
　to physical education in higher eduction.
**Readers:** Members of the National
　Association for Physical Education in
　Higher Education; academicians,
　teachers and administrators.

## RODEO NEWS
26457

721 N. Cedar
Pauls Valley, OK 73075
Telephone: (405) 238-3310
FAX: (405) 238-3725
Mailing Address:
　P.O. Box 598
　Pauls Valley, OK 73075
Year Established: 1961
Pub. Frequency: 11/yr.
Page Size: standard
Subscrip. Rate: $2.50/newsstand; $20/yr.
Materials: 02,03,05,06,10,11,12,16,20,21,
　23,24,25,28,29,30,32,33
Freelance Pay: $.05-$.07/wd.
Circulation: 10,500
Circulation Type: paid
**Owner(s):**
Rodeo News, Inc.
721 N. Cedar
P.O. Box 598
Pauls Valley, OK 73075
Telephone: (405) 238-3310
Ownership %: 100
**Management:**
Janet Smith ...........................................President
Janet Smith ...........................................Publisher
Londa Beck ........................Circulation Manager
**Editorial:**
Johnna Crevens .......................................Editor
Pat Seeley ..........................................Copy Chief
Gaylen Guinn ........................Production Director
Tom Vienske ........................Production Director

**Desc.:** Edited for rodeo fans, cowboy and
cowgirl contestants, contrast act
performers, sponsors, stock contractors,
producers, and managers, covering the
industry as a sport, entertainment, and
business at all levels of competition
from Little Britches to professional.
Feature articles deal with rodeo, rodeo
personalities, bucking stock, Western
fashions, livestock and equipment.
Regular monthly departments include
rodeo management ideas, reviews of
Western/rodeo oriented books and
records, tips for the rookie contestant,
upcoming rodeos sanctioned by the
International Professional Rodeo
Association, rodeo results, current world
championship point standings.
**Readers:** 65,000 plus readers in all 50
states & 19 foreign countries; 77% are
horse owners & over 52% own cattle
also.
**Deadline:** story-1st of mo. prior to pub.
date; news-1st of mo.; photo-1st of mo.;
ads-1st of mo.

## SCHOLASTIC COACH
24817

730 Broadway
New York, NY 10003
Telephone: (212) 505-3418
FAX: (212) 505-3199
Year Established: 1931
Pub. Frequency: m. exc. Jun. & Jul.
Page Size: standard
Subscrip. Rate: $23.95/yr.
Freelance Pay: varies
Circulation: 42,000
Circulation Type: paid
**Owner(s):**
Scholastic Magazines, Inc.
730 Broadway
New York, NY 10003
Telephone: (212) 505-3000
Ownership %: 100
**Management:**
Richard Robinson ...........................President
Bruce Weber ..................................Publisher
Terry Wm. Perkins ............Circulation Manager
**Editorial:**
Herman L. Masin .................................Editor
Dwight Hunting ..........................Advertising
Robert Harrison ..................Advertising Director
Francis Klaess .............................Art Director
Herman L. Masin ...............Book Review Editor
Herman L. Masin ...............New Product Editor
Dominique Fleurima ............Production Director
**Desc.:** Technical (how-to) articles on
college and high school sports, written
primarily by coaches. Practically no
news stories or publicity releases are
used except new items of sports
equipments. Departments include:
Editorial Page, Humor Page, Book
Reviews, New Equipment, Administration
Column, Strength Training Page, Feature
Interviews, Sports Technology Column.
**Readers:** College and high school
coaches, athletic directors, municipal
and corporate recreation directors,
athletic trainers, equipment managers.

## SHOOTING INDUSTRY
24976

591 Camino de la Reina, Ste. 200
San Diego, CA 92108
Telephone: (619) 297-8520
FAX: (619) 297-5353
Year Established: 1956
Pub. Frequency: m.
Page Size: standard
Subscrip. Rate: $25/Yr.
Circulation: 27,164
Circulation Type: controlled

**Owner(s):**
Publishers Development Corp.
591 Camino De La Reina, #200
San Diego, CA 92108
Telephone: (619) 297-5350
Ownership %: 100
**Management:**
Tom von Rosen ....................................President
Thomas Hollander .......................Vice President
Geo. von Rosen ..................................Publisher
Anita Carson ..................Advertising Manager
**Editorial:**
Russ Thurman ...........................................Editor
**Desc.:** Want articles designed to tell gun
dealers how to sell more guns and more
shooting-hunting equipment (including
clothing, camping gear, etc.), how and
where to advertise; salesman selection
and articles for and
about manufacturers.
**Readers:** Gun dealers, industry executives,
military material in this field.

## SKI AREA MANAGEMENT
24977

45 Main St., N.
Woodbury, CT 06798
Telephone: (203) 263-0888
FAX: (203) 266-0452
Mailing Address:
　P.O. Box 644
　Woodbury, CT 06798
Year Established: 1962
Pub. Frequency: bi-m.
Page Size: standard
Subscrip. Rate: $26/yr.
Materials: 01,02,05,06,10,21,27,28,30,32,33
Freelance Pay: $175 - $500
Print Process: offset
Circulation: 4,045
Circulation Type: paid
**Owner(s):**
Beardsley Publishing Corp.
P.O. Box 644
Woodbury, CT 06798
Telephone: (203) 263-0888
Ownership %: 100
**Management:**
David Rowan ......................................President
David Rowan ......................................Publisher
Jennifer Rowan .................Advertising Manager
**Editorial:**
Janet Nelson ......................Executive Editor
David Rowan .........................................Editor
Ann Hasper ...........................Managing Editor
Nils Ericksen ..........................Technical Editor
**Desc.:** Covers new equipment for ski
areas, equipment for maintenance,
cafeteria, lighting, office, summer
recreation, ski area design and planning,
and marketing.
**Readers:** Managers and other managerial
and supervisory personnel at ski areas
in U.S. and Canada.
**Deadline:** story-6 wks. prior to pub. date;
news-6 wks. prior to pub. date; photo-6
wks. prior to pub. date; ads-6 wks. prior
to pub. date

## SKI PATROL MAGAZINE
69128

Ski Patrol Bldg., Ste. 100
133 S. Van Gordon St.
Lakewood, CO 80228
Telephone: (303) 988-1111
FAX: (303) 988-3005
Year Established: 1984
Pub. Frequency: q.
Page Size: standard
Subscrip. Rate: $20/yr. US; $30/yr. foreign
Materials: 01,02,05,06,08,10,15,16,19,21,
　32,33
Freelance Pay: $100/magazine pge.
Print Process: web offset
Circulation: 30,000
Circulation Type: controlled & paid

**Owner(s):**
National Ski Patrol System, Inc.
Ski Patrol Bldg., Ste. 100
133 S. Van Gordon St.
Lakewood, CO 80228
Telephone: (303) 988-1111
Ownership %: 100
**Editorial:**
Rebecca W. Ayers ...............................Editor
**Desc.:** Discusses avalanche mitigation and
rescue, ski mountaineering, equipment,
winter emergency care, ski safety,
fitness, and risk management. Includes
ski area profiles.

## SKI RACING INTERNATIONAL
24979

Rt. 100, P.O. Box 1125
Waitsfield, VT 05673
Telephone: (802) 496-7700
FAX: (802) 496-7704
Year Established: 1968
Pub. Frequency: 20/yr.
Page Size: tabloid
Subscrip. Rate: $1.95/issue; $19.95/yr.
Materials: 06,32,33
Freelance Pay: negotiable
Circulation: 25,000
Circulation Type: paid
**Owner(s):**
Ski Racing International
Rt. 100 Box 1125
Waitsfield, VT 05673
Telephone: (802) 496-7700
Ownership %: 100
**Management:**
Gary Black, Jr. ...................................President
Gary Black, Jr. ...................................Publisher
Sandy Seymour ................Circulation Manager
**Editorial:**
Andy Bigford ........................................Editor
Perkins Miller .......................................Editor
Mary McKahn ......................................Editor
Julie Hall ..............................................Editor
Richard M. Basoco .......Chief Operating Officer
Josie Ritter .........................Production Director
Hank McKee ...................................Reporter
Tim Etchells .........................V.P. of Editorial
**Desc.:** Offers year-round coverage of ski
competition and national ski news.
Articles on technique, equipment, races,
racer profiles, training, and other
subjects of interest to racers are used.
Also travel information for skiers, ski
academies, summer ski camp issues,
special Winter Olympic Games
coverage.
**Readers:** Competition members of US. Ski
Assn., amateur and professional racers,
coaches, ski industry, consumers.

## SKI TECH
69144

P.O. Box 1125
Waitsfield, VT 05673-1125
Telephone: (802) 496-7700
FAX: (802) 496-7704
Year Established: 1986
Pub. Frequency: 5/yr.
Page Size: standard
Subscrip. Rate: $16/yr.
Materials: 03,06,32,33
Circulation: 19000
Circulation Type: controlled & free
**Owner(s):**
Ski Racing International
P.O. Box 1125
Waitsfield, VT 05673-1125
Telephone: (802) 496-7700
FAX: (802) 496-7704
Ownership %: 100
**Management:**
Gary Black, Jr. ...................................Publisher
Phil Knaub .......................Advertising Manager
Sandy Seymour ................Circulation Manager
Josie Ritter .........................Production Manager

**Materials Accepted/Included:** 01-Business news 02-By-line articles 03-Fashion news 04-Food news 05-Freelance copy 06-Letters to editor 07-Real estate news 08-Sports news 09-Travel news
10-Book rev. 11-Movie rev. 12-Music rev. 13-TV rev. 14-Theater rev. 15-Coming events 16-Obituaries 17-Question & answer 18-Social announcements 19-Artwork 20-Cartoons 21-Photos 22-TV listings
23-Audio rec. 24-Video rec. 25-Books 26-Films/film clips 27-Personnel news 28-Press releases 29-New product news/photos 30-Trade lit. 31-Contracts awarded 32-Display adv. 33-Classified adv.

4-373

**Editorial:**
Andy Bigford ...............................Editor in Chief
Susan Fresolo ...........Ad Production Manager
Kathryn Friedland .........Administrative Services
Victoria Chapman .......................Art Director
Gary Black, Jr. ...........Chief Executive Officer
Richard M. Basoco .......Chief Operating Officer
Julie K. Hall ...............................Fashion Editor
Bill Abbott-Koch ....................Financial Services
Mary McKhann ..............................Staff Writer
Tim Etchells ...............................VP Publications
**Desc.:** Provides product information on ski
equipment, ski wear and accessories
with a comprehensive alpine ski listing, a
user- friendly guide to fiber & fabric, in-
depth trends in skis, boots, bindings &
poles.
**Readers:** Owners, managers, buyers, sales
and service personnel of ski shops,
instructors, coaches, industry suppliers
and their sales reps, the ski press, and
consumers who buy, repair & service
their own equipment.

24978
**SNOW COUNTRY BUSINESS**
5520 Park Ave.
Trumbull, CT 06611
Telephone: (203) 373-7059
FAX: (203) 371-2127
Year Established: 1961
Pub. Frequency: bi-m.
Page Size: tabloid
Subscrip. Rate: 30/yr. US; 35/yr. Canada;
$65/yr. foreign
Freelance Pay: $100-$400/500-1,500 wds.
Circulation: 12,888
Circulation Type: controlled
**Owner(s):**
N.Y. Times Magazine Group
Trumbull, CT
Telephone: (203) 373-7059
Ownership %: 100
**Management:**
Rip Warendorf .......................................Publisher
**Editorial:**
Irwin Curtin ...............................................Editor
John Fry .............................................Group Editor
**Desc.:** Serves the ski industry, ski area
executives and instructors.
**Readers:** Operators of ski specialty shops,
department store ski shops.

64877
**SOCIOLOGY OF SPORT JOURNAL
(SSJ)**
1607 N. Market
Champaign, IL 61820
Telephone: (217) 351-5076
FAX: (217) 351-2674
Mailing Address:
P.O. Box 5076
Champaign, IL 61825
Year Established: 1984
Pub. Frequency: q.
Page Size: standard
Subscrip. Rate: $24/yr. students; $36/yr.
individual; $80/yr. institution
Materials: 10,25,29
Print Process: offset
Circulation: 983
Circulation Type: paid
**Owner(s):**
Human Kinetics Publishers, Inc.
Box 5076
Champaign, IL 61825-5076
Telephone: (217) 351-5076
FAX: (217) 351-2674
Ownership %: 100
**Management:**
Rainer Martens .....................................Publisher
Julie Anderson .........................................Manager
**Editorial:**
Peter Donnelly ..........................................Editor
Linda A. Bump .........................Journal Director

**Desc.:** Focuses on the relationship
between sport society, and social
institutions from the perspectives
of social psychology, sociology, and
anthropology.
**Readers:** Members of The North American
Society for The Sociology Of Sport;
individual subscribers.

24981
**SPORTING GOODS BUSINESS**
1515 Broadway
New York, NY 10036
Telephone: (212) 869-1300
FAX: (212) 921-0838
Year Established: 1968
Pub. Frequency: m.
Page Size: tabloid
Subscrip. Rate: free to qualified individuals
Materials: 01,03,06,08,15,21,28,29,30,32,33
Freelance Pay: $100-$450
Circulation: 28,000
Circulation Type: controlled
**Owner(s):**
Miller Freeman, Inc.
1515 Broadway
New York, NY 10036
Telephone: (212) 869-1300
Ownership %: 100
**Management:**
Doug Cheney .......................................Publisher
Mark Cooper ....................Advertising Manager
**Editorial:**
Andrew Gaffney ..........................................Editor
Greg Posky ...........................Managing Editor
Pat Doran .....................................Fashion Editor
Alyssa Lustigmann ......................Feature Editor
Greg Pesky ........................New Products Editor
**Desc.:** Magazine aimed primarily at
sporting goods stores or sporting goods
buyers of department stores, mass
merchandisers and other chains.
**Readers:** Retailers, wholesalers, sales
agents, manufacturers.

24982
**SPORTING GOODS DEALER**
1212 N. Lindbergh Blvd.
St. Louis, MO 63132
Telephone: (314) 997-7111
Year Established: 1899
Pub. Frequency: m.
Page Size: standard
Subscrip. Rate: $100/yr.
Materials: 32,33
Circulation: 30,000
Circulation Type: free & paid
**Owner(s):**
Times Mirror Co.
Times Mirror Sq.
Los Angeles, CA 90053
Telephone: (314) 997-7111
Ownership %: 100
**Management:**
Nick Niles .............................................Publisher
**Editorial:**
Mike Jacobsen ..........................................Editor
Dave Sparrow ........................Managing Editor
Nancy Puskuldjian ............................Advertising
Ron Gabriel ...........................................Art Director
**Desc.:** Articles present case histories of
successful sale and merchandising of
sporting goods. Deals with management
and industry news. Monthly columns on
Advertising/Promotions, Planning/
Inventory and Personnel Management.
**Readers:** Retailers, wholesalers,
manufacturers.

64878
**SPORT PSYCHOLOGIST, THE
(TSP)**
1607 N. Market
Champaign, IL 61820
Telephone: (217) 351-5076
FAX: (217) 351-2674

Mailing Address:
P.O. Box 5076
Champaign, IL 61825
Year Established: 1987
Pub. Frequency: q.
Page Size: standard
Subscrip. Rate: $24/yr. students; $36/yr.
individuals; $80/yr. institutions
Materials: 10,25,29
Print Process: offset
Circulation: 1,125
Circulation Type: paid
**Owner(s):**
Human Kinetics Publishers, Inc.
P.O. Box 5076
Champaign, IL 61825-5076
Telephone: (217) 351-5076
FAX: (217) 351-2674
Ownership %: 100
**Management:**
Rainer Martens .....................................Publisher
Thomas Moore .....................................Manager
**Editorial:**
Robin S. Vealey ........................................Editor
Linda A. Bump .........................Journal Director
**Desc.:** This journal focuses on applied
research and the application of research
in the delivery of psychological services
to coaches and athletes.
**Readers:** Members of International Society
of Sport Psychology; individual
subscribers.

69307
**SPORT SCIENCE REVIEW (SSR)**
1607 N. Market St.
Champaign, IL 61820
Telephone: (217) 351-5076
FAX: (217) 351-2674
Year Established: 1992
Pub. Frequency: s-a.
Page Size: standard
Subscrip. Rate: $26/yr. individuals; $52/yr.
institutions
Print Process: offset
Circulation: 550
Circulation Type: paid
**Owner(s):**
Human Kinetics Publishers, Inc.
P.O. Box 5076
Champaign, IL 61825-5076
Telephone: (217) 351-5076
FAX: (217) 351-2674
Ownership %: 100
**Management:**
Rainer Martens .....................................Publisher
**Editorial:**
Peg Goyette ...........................Managing Editor
Linda A. Bump ..........................................Director
**Desc.:** Provides 2 major international
reviews each year of important
achievements in the sport sciences.
Each issue is devoted to one of the
following themes: sport physiology, sport
psychology, sport sociology, coaching
science, motor learning and control,
sports medicine, sport philosophy, sport
biomechanics, sport pedagogy and sport
history.
**Readers:** Members of the International
Council of Sport Science and Physical
Education: sport scientists.

24983
**SPORTS TREND MAGAZINE**
6255 Barfield Rd., Ste. 200
Atlanta, GA 30328-4300
Telephone: (404) 252-8831
FAX: (404) 252-4436
Year Established: 1967
Pub. Frequency: m.
Page Size: tabloid
Subscrip. Rate: free; $64/yr.
Freelance Pay: varies
Circulation: 28,500
Circulation Type: controlled & free

**Owner(s):**
Shore Communications, Inc.
6255 Bairfield Rd., Ste. 200
Atlanta, GA 30328-4300
Telephone: (404) 252-8831
Ownership %: 100
**Management:**
Angelo Varrone ....................................President
**Editorial:**
Marcy O'Koon ...........................Senior Editor
Tim Darnell ...............................................Editor
Jeffrey Atkinson ............................Co-Publisher
Arthur Bernstein ............................Co-Publisher
**Desc.:** Editorial style integrates coverage
of all products related to each and every
sport, providing a complete picture of
emerging trends and buying habits.
Extensive interviews with top executives
in both retailing and manufacturing
provide the basis for special pre-buying,
buying and selling season reports.
Regular departments include:
Newstrends, a major retail and
manufacturer interview, financial trends,
product news, coming events, products,
literature, merchandising aids, outdoor
market and footwear reports.
**Readers:** Retailers and wholesalers of
sporting goods and allied lines, including
independent sporting goods retailers,
mass merchandisers, department stores,
chains, catalog stores plus
manufacturers and others allied to the
trade.

69134
**SPORTSTURF**
68-860 Perez Rd., Rm. J
Cathedral City, CA 92234-7248
Telephone: (818) 781-8300
Year Established: 1985
Pub. Frequency: m.
Subscrip. Rate: $33/yr.
Circulation: 21,371
Circulation Type: paid
**Owner(s):**
Gold Trade Publications, Inc.
P.O. Box 8420
Van Nuys, CA 91409
Telephone: (818) 781-8300
Ownership %: 100
**Editorial:**
Matthew Trulio ...........................................Editor

24984
**TACK 'N TOGS MERCHANDISING**
12400 Whitewater Dr., Ste. 160
Hopkins, MN 55343
Telephone: (612) 931-0211
Mailing Address:
P.O. Box 2400
Hopkins, MN 55343
Year Established: 1970
Pub. Frequency: m.
Page Size: standard
Subscrip. Rate: $25/yr.
Circulation: 20,000
Circulation Type: controlled
**Owner(s):**
Miller Publishing Co.
P.O. Box 2400
Hopkins, MN 55343
Telephone: (612) 931-0211
Ownership %: 100
**Management:**
Bob Clarity .........................Advertising Manager
**Editorial:**
Dan DeWeese ..........................................Editor
Bill Poehler ...........................Managing Editor
**Desc.:** Accepts free-lance articles dealing
with the buying, selling and
merchandising of products.
**Readers:** Those involved in the marketing
of products, services for the horse and
rider.

**TENNISPRO**                    69135
P.O. Box 4739
Hilton Head Island, SC 29938
Telephone: (803) 785-7244
FAX: (803) 686-2033
Year Established: 1988
Pub. Frequency: 6/yr.
Subscrip. Rate: free to membership
Materials: 02,06,08,19,20,21,23,24,25,27,
  28,29,30,32
Print Process: offset
Circulation: 9,600
Circulation Type: free
Owner(s):
US Professional Tennis Registry
P.O. Box 4739
Hilton Head Island, SC 29938
Telephone: (803) 785-7244
Ownership %: 100
Editorial:
Jeff Dalpiaz ................................................Editor
Desc.: Includes sports science,
  programming, sports medicine, new drills
  and product reviews.
Readers: Tennis teachers and coaches.
Deadline: story-6 wks. prior to pub. date;
  news-6 wks. prior; photo-6 wks. prior;
  ads-4 wks. prior

**USA GYMNASTICS**                    55980
Pan American Plz. Ste. 300
201 S. Capitol Ave.
Indianapolis, IN 46225
Telephone: (317) 237-5050
FAX: (317) 237-5069
Year Established: 1973
Pub. Frequency: 6/yr.
Page Size: standard
Subscrip. Rate: $15/yr. US; $32/yr. foreign
Freelance Pay: varies
Circulation: 63000
Owner(s):
United States Gymnastics Federation
201 S. Capitol Dr., #300
Indianapolis, IN 46225
Telephone: (317) 237-5050
Ownership %: 100
Editorial:
Luan Peszek ................................................Editor
Desc.: Covers gymnastics news, trends,
  events in USA and Europe. Also
  interested in human interest features
  and personalities involved in the sport.
Readers: 50% girls 8-16 years of age;
  30% boys (teens); 20% adults (parents,
  coaches, fans), of upper middle class
  families.

**WATER SCOOTER BUSINESS**            66737
601 Lakeshore Pkwy., Ste. 600
Minnetonka, MN 55305-5215
Telephone: (612) 476-2200
FAX: (612) 476-8065
Year Established: 1990
Pub. Frequency: bi-m.
Page Size: standard
Subscrip. Rate: free to qualified personnel
Circulation: 5,000
Circulation Type: controlled
Owner(s):
Ehlert Publishing Group, Inc.
601 Lakeshore Pkwy., Ste. 600
Minnetonka, MN 55305-5215
Telephone: (612) 476-2200
Ownership %: 100
Management:
John A. Ehlert ................................Publisher
Skip Johnson ..................Associate Publsiher
Editorial:
Joel Johnson ................................................Editor

**WEEKLY TRACK TOPICS**               68913
P O. Box 931
Far Hills, NJ 07931-0931
Telephone: (201) 000-0000
FAX: (201) 000-0000
Year Established: 1963
Pub. Frequency: bi-w.
Circulation: 2,000
Circulation Type: paid
Owner(s):
Harness Tracks of America, Inc.
35 Airport Rd.
Morristown, NJ 07960
Telephone: (201) 285-9090
Ownership %: 100
Editorial:
Stanley F. Bergstein ................................Editor
Desc.: Covers topics of interest to
  management of race tracks and racing
  associations.

**WOODALL'S CAMPGROUND**             22439
**  MANAGEMENT**
28167 N. Keith Dr.
Lake Forest, IL 60045-5000
Telephone: (708) 362-6700
FAX: (708) 362-8776
Mailing Address:
  P.O. Box 5000
  Lake Forest, IL 60045-5000
Year Established: 1970
Pub. Frequency: m.
Page Size: tabloid
Subscrip. Rate: $24.95/yr.
Materials: 01,02,05,06,07,15,25,28,29,30,
  32,33
Freelance Pay: $50-$20/article
Print Process: web offset
Circulation: 10,000
Circulation Type: controlled
Owner(s):
Woodall Publishing Co.
28167 N. Keith Dr.
Lake Forest, IL 60045-5000
Telephone: (708) 362-6700
Ownership %: 100
Management:
Linda L. Profaizer ................................President
Mary Saraglino ..................Advertising Manager
Cis Tossi ............................Circulation Manager
Editorial:
Mike Byrnes ................................................Editor
Rollin Cooper ................................Columnist
Desc.: News and features on trends and
  developments in the campground
  industry, how-to information on all
  phases of campground operation and
  management (business, promotion,
  repair, remodeling, expansion, etc.) news
  or features on individual campgrounds,
  profitable services, rentals and sales
  operations.
Readers: Owners, operators and
  managers of private campgrounds,
  public recreation and camping officials
  and agencies.
Deadline: story-60 days; news-30 days;
  photo-30 days; ads-30 days

## Group 252-Sugar

**SUGARBEET GROWER, THE**            25000
503 Broadway
Fargo, ND 58102
Telephone: (701) 237-5747
Year Established: 1962
Pub. Frequency: bi-m.
Page Size: standard
Subscrip. Rate: $6.75/yr. US; $15/yr.
  foreign
Freelance Pay: $150/article; $50/cover
  photo (color)
Circulation: 1,230

Circulation Type: controlled
Owner(s):
Sugar Publications
503 Broadway
Fargo, ND 58102
Telephone: (701) 237-5747
Ownership %: 100
Management:
Don Lilleboe ..................Advertising Manager
Editorial:
Don Lilleboe ................................................Editor
Desc.: Contains articles and advertising
  about the sugarbeet industry and its
  related fields and interests in the U.S.
  and foreign countries.
Readers: Mainly U.S. growers; some trade
  personnel.

**SUGAR BULLETIN**                    24997
206 E. Bayou Rd.
Thibodaux, LA 70301
Telephone: (504) 448-3707
Mailing Address:
  P.O. Drawer 938
  Thibodaux, LA 70302
Year Established: 1922
Pub. Frequency: m.
Page Size: standard
Subscrip. Rate: $10/yr.
Circulation: 1,600
Circulation Type: paid
Owner(s):
American Sugar Cane League of the
  U.S.A.
206 E. Bayou Rd.
Thibodaux, LA 70301
Telephone: (504) 448-3707
Ownership %: 100
Editorial:
Charles Melancon ................................Editor
Charles Melancon ..................Managing Editor
Dr. Charley Richard ........................Field Editor
Windell Jackson ........................Miscellaneous
Desc.: Staff-written articles dealing with
  production developments, legislation,
  research reports as well as items of
  current interest to the sugar industry.
Readers: Top-level management engaged
  in sugar production.

**SUGAR JOURNAL**                     24998
129 S. Cortez St.
New Orleans, LA 70119
Telephone: (504) 482-3914
FAX: (504) 482-4205
Year Established: 1938
Pub. Frequency: m.
Page Size: standard
Subscrip. Rate: $33/yr.
Circulation: 3,300
Circulation Type: controlled & paid
Owner(s):
Kriedt Enterprises, Ltd.
129 S. Cortez St.
New Orleans, LA 70119
Telephone: (504) 482-3914
Ownership %: 100
Management:
Romney Kriedt ................................Publisher
Desc.: Staff-written and contributed
  features discuss technical problems and
  procedures in world-wide cane and beet
  sugar factory and field operations.
  Carries industry news as well as a
  monthly column by recognized experts.
Readers: Processor and producer
  executives and management, factory
  and field superintendents, consultants,
  sugar traders, technical libraries.

**SUGAR PRODUCER, THE**               25550
520 Park Ave.
Idaho Falls, ID 83402
Telephone: (208) 524-7000
FAX: (208) 522-5241
Year Established: 1974
Pub. Frequency: 6/yr.
Page Size: standard
Subscrip. Rate: $8/yr.
Materials: 01,15,27,28,29,32
Freelance Pay: $.10 per word
Circulation: 19,000
Circulation Type: controlled
Owner(s):
Harris Publishing Co., Inc.
520 Park Ave.
Idaho Falls, ID 83402
Telephone: (208) 524-7000
FAX: (208) 522-5241
Ownership %: 100
Management:
Darryl Harris ................................Publisher
Mel Erickson ..................Advertising Manager
Editorial:
Steve Janes ........................Editor in Chief
Gary Rawlings ................................................Editor
Lane Lindstrom ........................Assistant Editor
Janet Chase ........................Production Editor
Richard Holley ................................................Sales
Desc.: Editorial coverage includes all
  phases of growing, planting, fertilizing,
  frost protection, insect and disease
  control, weed control, thinning,
  harvesting, etc., as well as personal
  stories of beet growers, research
  programs, world trends, and
  other material relating to the farm
  picture.
Readers: Sugar beet growers and related
  industry.
Deadline: story-45 days prior to pub. date;
  news-45 days prior; photo-45 days prior;
  ads-1st day of mo. prior

**SUGAR Y AZUCAR**                    24999
452 Hudson Terr.
Englewood Cliffs, NJ 07632
Telephone: (201) 871-9200
FAX: (201) 871-9639
Year Established: 1916
Pub. Frequency: m.
Page Size: standard
Subscrip. Rate: $30/yr. qualified; $75/yr.
  non-qualified
Freelance Pay: negotiable
Circulation: 5,800
Circulation Type: controlled
Owner(s):
Ruspan Communications, Inc.
452 Hudson Terr.
Englewood Cliffs, NJ 07632
Telephone: (201) 871-9200
Ownership %: 100
Management:
R.E. Slimermeyer ................................Publisher
R.E. Slimermeyer ..................Advertising Manager
R.L. Sylander ..................Circulation Manager
Editorial:
Raichard B. Miller ................................................Editor
Desc.: Bi-lingual, English and Spanish
  articles on outlook, developments
  affecting production of sugar industry.
Readers: Sugar Growers, Processors,
  Users

## Group 254-Swimming Pools

**AQUATICS INTERNATIONAL**           65470
6151 Powers Ferry Rd.
Atlanta, GA 30339
Telephone: (404) 925-2500
FAX: (404) 925-0400
Year Established: 1989

Materials Accepted/Included: 01-Business news 02-By-line articles 03-Fashion news 04-Food news 05-Freelance copy 06-Letters to editor 07-Real estate news 08-Sports news 09-Travel news
10-Book rev. 11-Movie rev. 12-Music rev. 13-TV rev. 14-Theater rev. 15-Coming events 16-Obituaries 17-Question & answer 18-Social announcements 19-Artwork 20-Cartoons 21-Photos 22-TV listings
23-Audio rec. 24-Video rec. 25-Books 26-Films/film clips 27-Personnel news 28-Press releases 29-New product news/photos 30-Trade lit. 31-Contracts awarded 32-Display adv. 33-Classified adv.

4-375

Pub. Frequency: bi-m.
Page Size: standard
Subscrip. Rate: $39/yr.; $62/2 yrs.
Materials: 02,05,06,10,16,17,21,28,29,31,
32,33
Freelance Pay: $125/pg.
Print Process: web offset
Circulation: 30,000
Circulation Type: controlled
**Owner(s):**
Argus, Inc.
6151 Powers Ferry Rd.
Atlanta, GA 30330-2941
Ownership %: 100
**Bureau(s):**
Steve Liput
35 E. Wacker Dr., Ste. 700
Chicago, IL 60601-2198
Telephone: (312) 726-7277
FAX: (312) 726-0241

Lisa Scott
White Associates
1424 Fourth St., Ste. 231
Santa Monica, CA 90401
Telephone: (310) 451-5655
FAX: (310) 451-4228
**Management:**
Michael Grossman .............Associate Publisher
Jeannie Morton ..........Classified Adv. Manager
Penny Capps .....................Production Manager
**Editorial:**
Terri Simmons ...............................................Editor
Eden Jackson ...........................Associate Editor
**Desc.:** Features cover operational
information for commerical-type aquatic
facilities, including those at colleges and
schools, municipal county and state,
hotel and resorts, fitness clubs, rehab
centers and waterparks.
**Readers:** Public and semi-public pool
owners, operators and managers.
**Deadline:** story-4 mos.; news-2 mos.; ads-
6 wks.

26440
### POOL & SPA NEWS
3923 W. 6th St.
Los Angeles, CA 90020
Telephone: (213) 385-3926
FAX: (213) 383-1152
Year Established: 1961
Pub. Frequency: s-m.
Page Size: standard
Subscrip. Rate: $16.50/yr.
Freelance Pay: $.10-$.14/wd.
Circulation: 16,000
Circulation Type: paid
**Owner(s):**
Leisure Publications
Telephone: (213) 385-2209
Ownership %: 100
**Management:**
Jules Field .....................................................Publisher
**Editorial:**
Jim McCloskey .............................................Editor
**Desc.:** Articles relating to swimming pools
& spas, or news of these products or
the companies that produce them.
**Readers:** Swimming pool trade and spa
trade.

22006
### SWIMMING POOL-SPA AGE
6151 Powers Ferry Rd., N.W.
Atlanta, GA 30339-2914
Telephone: (404) 955-2500
FAX: (404) 618-0343
Year Established: 1926
Pub. Frequency: 12/yr.
Page Size: tabloid
Subscrip. Rate: $39/yr.
Materials: 01,02,05,06,15,16,17,21,27,28,
29,32,33
Freelance Pay: $.10/word
Print Process: web offset
Circulation: 17,621

Circulation Type: controlled & paid
**Owner(s):**
Argus Business, A Div. of Argus Inc.
6151 Powers Ferry Rd., N.W.
Atlanta, GA 30339
Telephone: (404) 955-2500
FAX: (404) 955-0400
Ownership %: 100
**Bureau(s):**
Argus Business
35 E. Wacker Dr., Ste. 700
Chicago, IL 60601
Telephone: (312) 726-7277
Contact: Steve Liput, Sales
**Management:**
Jerold France ...................................President
Shawn Demario ...............Circulation Manager
**Editorial:**
Brian Buxton .................................Art Director
Terri Simmons ...................Associate Publisher
Michael Grossman .............Associate Publisher
Ted Lotz .............................................Group Publisher
Buford Bryant ...........Secretary & Treasurer
**Desc.:** Covers all segments of the
swimming pool industry - retail,
construction, service, and distribution.
Provides product and marketing
information. Will accept contributed
feature articles & photos (B&W and 4-
color). Departments include: new
products; letters to the editor; calendar
of events; news of the industry; people;
merchandising; perspective; sounding
board; successful selling; management.
**Readers:** Contractors, suppliers, builders,
dealers, and service, distribution,
manufacturing personnel.
**Deadline:** story-3-6 mos. prior to pub.
date; news-15th of 2nd. mo. prior;
photo-15th of 2nd. mo. prior; ads-25th of
2nd mo. prior

69146
### SWIMMING POOLS TODAY
1213 Ridgecrest Circle
Denton, TX 76205
Year Established: 1985
Pub. Frequency: q.
Subscrip. Rate: $5/yr.
Circulation: 100,000
Circulation Type: paid
**Owner(s):**
National Swimming Pool Owner's
Association
1213 Ridgecrest Circle
Denton, TX 76205
Ownership %: 100
**Editorial:**
Tom A. Doron ..............................................Editor
**Desc.:** Featuring swimming pool safety,
chemistry, cleaning, repair and new
products. Covers swimming for fitness
and health, and poolside entertainment.

### Group 256-
### Telecommunications
### (Telephone & Telegraph)

22715
### AMERICA'S NETWORK
7500 Old Oak Blvd.
Cleveland, OH 44130
Telephone: (216) 826-2839
FAX: (216) 891-2726
Year Established: 1909
Pub. Frequency: s-m.
Page Size: standard
Subscrip. Rate: $36/yr.
Freelance Pay: negotiable
Circulation: 44,597
Circulation Type: controlled

**Owner(s):**
Advanstar Communications, Inc.
7500 Old Oak Blvd.
Cleveland, OH 44130
Telephone: (216) 826-2839
Ownership %: 100
**Management:**
Ray H. Smith .................................Publisher
Francis Heid ...................Circulation Manager
**Editorial:**
Robert Stoffels ...............................................Editor
Mary Walter ...................Managing Editor
Vincent Vittore ...........................Assistant Editor
**Desc.:** Staff-written management and
engineering articles directed at members
of the tele-communications industry to
help them better serve the
communication needs of their
communities. Carriers news briefs, new
products. Departments include:
Plant/Engineering, Washington Reports,
News, Management Notes,
Observations, Party Line, Supervisor,
New Products, New Literature,
International News, International Scene,
Forum.
**Readers:** Managers and executives of
telephone companies, other
telecommunications carriers,
interconnect contractors, and others
allied to telecommunications industry.

68812
### BUSINESS COMMUNICATIONS
### REVIEW
950 York Rd.
Hinsdale, IL 60521-2939
Telephone: (312) 986-1432
Year Established: 1971
Pub. Frequency: m.
Subscrip. Rate: $45/yr.
Materials: 01,02,05,28,29,30
Print Process: offset
Circulation: 13,759
Circulation Type: free & paid
**Owner(s):**
BCR Enterprises, Inc.
950 York Rd.
Hinsdale, IL 60521-2939
Telephone: (312) 986-1432
Ownership %: 100
**Editorial:**
Fred S. Knight ...............................................Editor
Steve Makey ...........................Managing Editor
Sandra Borthick ...................Assistant Editor
Jane Lipp ...................................Assistant Editor
**Desc.:** Analysis of issues, trends, new
products and services affecting
telecommunications management.
**Deadline:** story-30 days prior to pub. date;
news-45 days; photo-30 days; ads-30
days

57266
### BUSINESS RADIO
1501 Duke St.
Alexandria, VA 22314
Telephone: (703) 739-0300
FAX: (703) 836-1608
Year Established: 1965
Pub. Frequency: 10/yr. (combined
Jul./Aug., Jan./Feb.)
Page Size: standard
Subscrip. Rate: $6.50/newsstand; $45/yr.
members; $65/yr. non-members; $75/yr.
foreign
Materials: 01,02,05,06,10,21,28,29,30,32,33
Freelance Pay: $100-$350/article
Print Process: offset
Circulation: 3,000
Circulation Type: paid

**Owner(s):**
National Assn. of Business & Educational
Radio
1501 Duke St.
Alexandria, VA 22314
Telephone: (703) 739-0300
Ownership %: 100
**Editorial:**
A.E. Goetz ...................................................Editor
Terry Banks ...........................Managing Editor
Robin E. Little ...................Advertising Executive
Shannon Brooks ...............Editorial/Production
Coordinator
**Readers:** Users, dealers, private carrier
paging and specialized mobile radio
service operator & technicians

68813
### CELLULAR & MOBILE
### INTERNATIONAL
9800 Metcalf
Overland Park, KS 66212-2215
Telephone: (913) 341-1300
FAX: (913) 967-1898
Year Established: 1991
Pub. Frequency: q.
Page Size: standard
Subscrip. Rate: $5/copy
Circulation: 10,000
Circulation Type: paid
**Owner(s):**
Intertec Publishing Corp.
9800 Metcalf
Overland Park, KS 66212-2215
Telephone: (913) 341-1300
Ownership %: 100
**Editorial:**
Rhonda Hickman ...............................................Editor
Don Bishop ...................................................Editor

22709
### COMMUNICATIONS NEWS
2405 N. Tamiami Trail
Nokomis, FL 34275
Telephone: (813) 966-9521
FAX: (813) 966-2590
Year Established: 1964
Pub. Frequency: m.
Page Size: standard
Subscrip. Rate: $50/yr.
Materials: 01,02,06,10,17,18,19,28,29,30,
32,33
Print Process: web offset
Circulation: 70,031
Circulation Type: controlled
**Owner(s):**
Nelson Publishing
2405 N. Tamiami Trl.
Nokomis, FL 34275
Telephone: (813) 966-9521
Ownership %: 100
**Management:**
Jim Russell ...................................................Publisher
Jim Russell ...................Advertising Manager
**Editorial:**
Curt Harler ...................................................Editor
Morris Edwards ...................Associate Editor
Kevin Tanzillo ...................Associate Editor
Roger Underwood ...............Contributing Editor
Paul Kirvan ...................Contributing Editor
**Desc.:** Contains news and newsworthy
items in voice, video and data
communication; new products, new
techniques, case histories of
applications of new communications
equipment in all segments of activity.
**Readers:** Communications, network, and
information systems management
people involved in all areas of voice,
data, video networking
**Deadline:** ads-1st of mo. prior to pub. date

**Materials Accepted/Included:** 01-Business news 02-By-line articles 03-Fashion news 04-Food news 05-Freelance copy 06-Letters to editor 07-Real estate news 08-Sports news 09-Travel news 10-Book rev. 11-Movie rev. 12-Music rev. 13-TV rev. 14-Theater rev. 15-Coming events 16-Obituaries 17-Question & answer 18-Social announcements 19-Artwork 20-Cartoons 21-Photos 22-TV listings 23-Audio rec. 24-Video rec. 25-Books 26-Films/film clips 27-Personnel news 28-Press releases 29-New product news/photos 30-Trade lit. 31-Contracts awarded 32-Display adv. 33-Classified adv.

## COMMUNICATIONS WEEK INTERNATIONAL
65448

600 Community Dr.
Manhasset, NY 11030
Telephone: (516) 562-5000
Year Established: 1988
Pub. Frequency: bi-w.
Page Size: tabloid
Subscrip. Rate: $150/yr.
Materials: 01,05,06,19,21,24,27,28,29,30, 31,32,33
Freelance Pay: varies; $.50/wd.
Print Process: web offset
Circulation: 30,000
Circulation Type: controlled & paid
**Owner(s):**
CMP Publications
600 Community Dr.
Manhasset, NY 11030
Telephone: (516) 562-5000
FAX: (516) 562-5718
Ownership %: 100
**Bureau(s):**
Paris International HQ
14 Rue De Bassano
75116 Paris France
Telephone: +33 1 495233 00
FAX: +33 1 472367 07
Contact: Malcolm Laws, Editor

London
66-68 Margaret St.
WIN7FL London United Kingdom
Telephone: +44 71 636 3303
FAX: +44 71 414 8106
Contact: Dawn Hayes, Bureau Chief

Washington DC
529 14th St. NW
Ste.1222
Washington, DC 20045
Telephone: (202) 383-4796
FAX: (202) 737-0980
Contact: Karen Lynch, Editor

Dusseldorf, Germany
Lietenstrasse 51
D-40476
 Dusseldorf
Telephone: +49 211 444431
FAX: +49 211 482663
Contact: John Blau, Editor
**Editorial:**
Malcolm Laws .......................................Editor
Wendy Byrne .....................Associate Publisher
Denis Gilhooly .....................Publishing Director
**Desc.:** Covers latebreaking news, trends and events for management in voice and data communications, corporate communications, and financial communications.
**Readers:** Senior managers in organizations that buy communications products and services.
**Deadline:** story-2 wks. prior to pub. date; news-1 wk.; photo-1-2 wks.; ads-2 wks.

## NEWMEDIA AGE
66753

901 Mariners Island Blvd.
Ste. 365
San Mateo, CA 94404
Telephone: (415) 573-5170
FAX: (408) 773-8309
Year Established: 1991
Pub. Frequency: bi-w.
Page Size: standard
Subscrip. Rate: $24/yr.
Circulation: 40,000
Circulation Type: controlled
**Owner(s):**
Hypermedia Communications, Inc.
Mariners Island, Ste. 365
San Mateo, CA 94404
Telephone: (415) 573-5170
Ownership %: 100

**Management:**
Robert J. Lydon .................................Publisher
**Editorial:**
Ben Calica .............................................Editor
Gillian Newson .........................Associate Editor

## ON THE LINE
69512

P.O. Box 1787
Olympia, WA 98507-1787
Telephone: (206) 754-0470
FAX: (206) 754-0470
Year Established: 1985
Pub. Frequency: bi-m.
Subscrip. Rate: $25/yr.
Materials: 01,02,06,17,20,21,28,29,32,33
Print Process: offset
Circulation: 5,000
Circulation Type: free & paid
**Owner(s):**
California Payphone Association
P.O. Box 1787
Olympia, WA 98507
Telephone: (206) 754-0470
Ownership %: 100
**Management:**
CA. Payphone Association ..................Publisher
Mary Lougheed .................Advertising Manager
**Editorial:**
Rebecca Carter ........................Managing Editor
Tom Keane ........................Associate President
**Desc.:** Covers regulatory and legislative issues, new products and privately-owned pay telephones.
**Readers:** Members of the private payphone industry.

## PCIA JOURNAL
24603

1019 19th St., N.W.
Ste. 1100
Washington, DC 20036
Telephone: (202) 467-4770
FAX: (202) 467-6987
Year Established: 1977
Pub. Frequency: 11/yr.
Page Size: standard
Subscrip. Rate: $60/yr.
Freelance Pay: Up to $600
Circulation: 3000
Circulation Type: paid
**Owner(s):**
Personal Communications Industry Assoc.
1019 19th St., N.W.
Ste. 1100
Washington, DC 20036
Telephone: (202) 467-4770
Ownership %: 100
**Bureau(s):**
Telocator
2000 M St., N.W., Ste. 230
Washington, DC 20036
Telephone: (202) 467-4770
Contact: David Easter, Exec. Editor
**Editorial:**
Lindsay Smith ........................................Editor
**Desc.:** News articles report on the development and technical aspects of new equipment, federal regulation, legal considerations and member profiles. Departments include: Letters to The Editor, New Products, Late Reports, Professional Directory Classifieds, Guest Contributor Technical Report.
**Readers:** Those in the cellular telephone and radio paging industries.

## PROCOMM ENTERPRISES MAGAZINE
68814

P.O. Box 886
San Anselmo, CA 94979-0886
Telephone: (415) 459-4669
FAX: (415) 459-4591
Year Established: 1987
Pub. Frequency: m.
Subscrip. Rate: $39/yr.

Circulation: 28,200
Circulation Type: paid
**Owner(s):**
Procomm Enterprises
P.O. Box 886
San Anselmo, CA 94979-0886
Telephone: (415) 459-4669
Ownership %: 100
**Editorial:**
Jason Bray .............................................Editor
**Readers:** Professional data and voice communications managers and consultants.

## PUBLIC COMMUNICATIONS MAGAZINE
68815

10700 Richmond Ave., Ste. 147
Houston, TX 77040
Telephone: (713) 783-8999
Year Established: 1984
Pub. Frequency: m.
Subscrip. Rate: $33/yr.
Circulation: 12,000
Circulation Type: paid
**Owner(s):**
Multimedia Publishing Corp.
10700 Richmond Ave., Ste. 147
Houston, TX 77042
Telephone: (713) 783-8999
Ownership %: 100

## RURAL TELECOMMUNICATIONS
69508

2626 Pennsylvania Ave., N.W.
Washington, DC 20037-1695
Telephone: (202) 298-2300
FAX: (202) 298-2320
Year Established: 1963
Pub. Frequency: bi-m.
Page Size: standard
Subscrip. Rate: $30/yr.
Materials: 01,02,05,06,17,19,21,29,32
Circulation: 5,000
Circulation Type: controlled & paid
**Owner(s):**
National Telephone Cooperative Association
2626 Pennsylvania Ave., N.W.
Washington, DC 20037-1695
Telephone: (202) 298-2300
Ownership %: 100
**Editorial:**
Lisa Westbrook ........................Managing Editor

## SATELLITE COMMUNICATIONS MAGAZINE
24598

6300 S. Syracuse Way
Ste. 650
Englewood, CO 80111
Telephone: (303) 220-0600
FAX: (303) 721-7227
Year Established: 1977
Pub. Frequency: m.
Page Size: standard
Subscrip. Rate: $27/yr.
Freelance Pay: negotiable
Circulation: 11,500
Circulation Type: controlled & paid
**Owner(s):**
Argus Inc.
6151 Powers Ferry Rd., N.W.
Atlanta, GA 30393-2491
Telephone: (404) 955-2500
FAX: (404) 955-0400
Ownership %: 100
**Bureau(s):**
Washington Bureau
214 Massachusetts Ave NG 360
Washington, DC 20002
Telephone: (202) 544-4043
Contact: Lou Manuta, Bureau Chief
**Editorial:**
Carolyn Horowitz ....................................Editor

**Desc.:** The magazine covers news, business, people, products & offers in-depth features in satellite communications in the commercial arena.
**Readers:** Engineers & upper management in the satellite communications industry. Also government & upper management in retail, computers, oil, trucking - any industry using satellite communications.

## SOUND & COMMUNICATIONS
22930

25 Willowdale Ave.
Port Washington, NY 11050
Telephone: (516) 767-2500
FAX: (516) 767-9335
Year Established: 1955
Pub. Frequency: m.
Page Size: standard
Subscrip. Rate: $5/issue; $15/yr.
Circulation: 12,800
Circulation Type: paid
**Owner(s):**
Testa Communications
25 Willowdale Ave.
Port Washington, NY 11050
Telephone: (516) 767-2500
Ownership %: 100
**Management:**
Vincent P. Testa ................................President
Vincent P. Testa .................................Publisher
Judith Morrison ...................Associate Publsiher
John Carr ...........................Advertising Manager
**Editorial:**
Judith Morrison .......................................Editor
Andrew Elias .....................................Art Director
Ted Uzzle ................................Book Review Editor
Chris Foreman ......................Consulting Editor
Jerome Brookman ................Consulting Editor
Gary Davis .........................Contributing Editor
Jesse Klapholz .......................Technical Editor
**Desc.:** We cover the world of private technical communication utilizing audio and telephone and radio circuits within the 4 walls of an establishment, and interconnected to the national telephone network and radio circuit outside as 1-way paging. Our articles cover semi-technically all 3 circuits plus security systems; plus economics, sales and leases, and government actions under FCC regulations.
**Readers:** Contractors & distributors of brand products/systems; also sub-assemblers of systems.

## TE & M'S TELECOM ASIA
66343

7500 Old Oak Blvd.
Cleveland, OH 44130
Telephone: (216) 826-2839
FAX: (216) 891-2726
Year Established: 1989
Pub. Frequency: q.
Subscrip. Rate: $30/yr.
Circulation: 12,000
Circulation Type: controlled
**Owner(s):**
Advanstar Communications, Inc.
7500 Old Oak Blvd.
Cleveland, OH 44130
Telephone: (216) 826-2839
Ownership %: 100
**Editorial:**
Bob Stoffels ...........................................Editor
**Desc.:** Covers technical topics of interest to managers of the national postal, telephone and telegraph authorities.

## TELECOMMUNICATIONS
22714

685 Canton St.
Norwood, MA 02062
Telephone: (617) 769-9750
FAX: (617) 762-9071
Year Established: 1967

**Materials Accepted/Included:** 01-Business news 02-By-line articles 03-Fashion news 04-Food news 05-Freelance copy 06-Letters to editor 07-Real estate news 08-Sports news 09-Travel news 10-Book rev. 11-Movie rev. 12-Music rev. 13-TV rev. 14-Theater rev. 15-Coming events 16-Obituaries 17-Question & answer 18-Social announcements 19-Artwork 20-Cartoons 21-Photos 22-TV listings 23-Audio rec. 24-Video rec. 25-Books 26-Films/film clips 27-Personnel news 28-Press releases 29-New product news/photos 30-Trade lit. 31-Contracts awarded 32-Display adv. 33-Classified adv.

4-377

Pub. Frequency: m.
Page Size: standard
Subscrip. Rate: $67/yr.; $120/yr. foreign
Materials: 01,06,15,28,29,30,32,33
Circulation: 80,000
Circulation Type: controlled
**Owner(s):**
Horizon House Publications, Inc.
685 Canton St.
Norwood, MA 02062
Telephone: (617) 769-9750
Ownership %: 100
**Bureau(s):**
Telecommunications
48 Lyford Drive
Ste. 4
Tiburon, CA 94920
Telephone: (415) 435-9722
FAX: (415) 435-8065
Contact: T.D. Clark, Sales Manager

Telecommunications
P.O. Box 2608
130 N. 21st St.
Purcellville, VA 22132
Telephone: (703) 338-5665
FAX: (703) 338-5163
Contact: Jeremy Kendall, Sales Manager

Telecommunications
260 Mockingbird Lane
South Pasadena, CA 91030
Telephone: (818) 799-2704
FAX: (818) 799-3924
Contact: Rob Walby, Sales Manager
**Management:**
William Bazzy .......................Chairman of Board
William M. Bazzy ................................President
George Davis ......................................Publisher
Thomas Raleigh ................Circulation Manager
**Editorial:**
James N. Budwey ..................................Editor
Melissa Urann ........................Managing Editor
Ed Kiessling ......................................Advertising
Mark Gabrenya ................................Art Director
Robert Bass .........................Production Director
**Desc.:** Comprehensive treatment of the
multifaceted communications field from
an applied technology point of view.
Concern is focused on technical,
economic, regulatory, social and
commercial aspects. Each issue is
balanced with feature articles, case
studies, industry news, product and
service information.
**Readers:** Management and technical
personnel working in the total spectrum
of communications worldwide.
**Deadline:** story-6-8 wks. prior to pub. date;
news-6-8 wks.; photo-6-8 wks.; ads-5th
of mo. prior to pub. date

65616
**TELECOMMUNICATIONS & RADIO
ENGINEERING**
605 Third Ave.
New York, NY 10158
Telephone: (212) 850-6289
Pub. Frequency: m.
Page Size: standard
Subscrip. Rate: $785/yr. US; $897/yr.
foreign
Circulation: 228
Circulation Type: paid
**Owner(s):**
John Wiley & Sons, Inc.
605 Third Ave.
New York, NY 10158
Ownership %: 100
**Editorial:**
Reuben C. Glass ..................................Editor

**Desc.:** Covers digital and analog wire,
radio, video and optical communications,
facsimile, micro and millimeter wave
communications, switching and coding
theory, signal processing, voice and
pattern recognition, antennae and
waveguides.

67657
**TELECOMMUNICATIONS REPORTS**
1333 H. St., N.W. 11th Fl. W.
Washington, DC 20005
Telephone: (202) 842-3006
FAX: (202) 842-3047
Year Established: 1934
Pub. Frequency: w.
Page Size: standard
Subscrip. Rate: $895/yr. US.; $645/yr.
gov't & non-profit enterprise; $970/yr.
out of N. Amer.
Materials: 01,10,15,27,28,29,30,31
**Owner(s):**
Business Research Publications, Inc.
1333 H. St., N.W. 11th Flr. W
Washington, DC 20005
Telephone: (202) 842-3006
Ownership %: 100
**Management:**
Andrew Jacobson ...............................Publisher
**Editorial:**
Victoria Mason ......................................Editor
**Desc.:** Follows domestic and international
regulatory/policy events in the
telecommunications field. Also covers
new telecom technology and business
developments. 50 pages per week.
**Readers:** Policy-makers, executives in the
business and government.

67656
**TELECOMMUNICATIONS WEEK**
1333 H St., N.W., Second Fl.
Washington, DC 20005
Telephone: (202) 842-0520
FAX: (202) 475-1790
Year Established: 1985
Pub. Frequency: w.
Page Size: standard
Subscrip. Rate: $395/yr. US.
**Owner(s):**
Business Research Publications, Inc.
1333 H. St., N.W., Second Fl.
Washington, DC 20005
Telephone: (202) 842-0520
Ownership %: 100
**Management:**
Andrew Jacobson ...............................Publisher
**Editorial:**
Karen Kinard ......................................Editor
**Desc.:** Covers current events in all aspects
of the domestic communications
industry.

58737
**TELEMATICS & INFORMATICS**
660 White Plains Rd.
Tarrytown, NY 10591-5153
Telephone: (914) 524-9200
FAX: (914) 333-2444
Year Established: 1984
Pub. Frequency: q.
Page Size: standard
Circulation: 3,000
Circulation Type: paid
**Owner(s):**
Pergamon Press, Inc.
660 White Plains Rd.
Tarrytown, NY 10591-5153
Telephone: (914) 524-9200
Ownership %: 100
**Management:**
Michael Boswood ................................President
Paul Titcombe ...................Advertising Manager
**Editorial:**
Dr. Indu B. Singh ..................................Editor

**Desc.:** Telematics and informatics is an
international journal that publishes
research and review articles in applied
telecommunications and information
sciences in business, industry,
government, and educational
establishments.
**Readers:** Academics and researchers.

22716
**TELEPHONY**
55 E. Jackson, Ste. 1100
Chicago, IL 60604
Telephone: (312) 922-2435
FAX: (312) 922-1408
Year Established: 1901
Pub. Frequency: w.
Page Size: standard
Subscrip. Rate: $45/yr.; $80/yr. foreign
Materials: 01,06,15,27,28,31,32,33
Freelance Pay: $50/pg. published;
freelance fees negotiable
Circulation: 48,307
Circulation Type: controlled
**Owner(s):**
Telephony Publishing Corp.
9800 Metcalf
Overland Park, KS 66212-2215
Telephone: (913) 341-1300
Ownership %: 100
**Management:**
Larry Lannon ......................................Publisher
**Editorial:**
Carol Wilson ......................................Editor
Mark Hickey ...........................Associate Publisher
Richard Karpinski ...................Technical Editor
**Desc.:** Covers all phases of the public
telecommunications industry, including
telephone companies, wireless and
cellular companies and CATV
companies. The focus is on network
technology. Departements include: In
the Nation's Capital, The Plant Man's
Notebook, New Products, Helpful
Literature, Book Reviews, News of
Industry, Letters to the Editor.
**Readers:** Executives and employees of
telephone companies, cellular service
producers, CATV companies, alternative
access providers, public service
commissions, communications
departments, foreign telecom executives
and employees.

66538
**UTILITY & TELEPHONE FLEETS**
321 Cary Point Dr.
Cary, IL 60013
Telephone: (708) 639-2200
FAX: (708) 639-9542
Mailing Address:
P.O. Box 183
Cary, IL 60013
Year Established: 1987
Pub. Frequency: 8/yr.
Page Size: standard
Subscrip. Rate: $20/yr.
Materials: 01,02,05,06,15,24,25,27,28,29,
30,31,32,33
Freelance Pay: open
Print Process: offset
Circulation: 18,000
Circulation Type: controlled
**Owner(s):**
Practical Communications, Inc. -J. Chance
321 Cary Point Dr.
Cary, IL 60013
Telephone: (708) 639-2200
**Management:**
J. Chance .............................................President
N. Rose ..........................................Vice President
James T. Queenan ................................Publisher
L. Jack Stober ......................................Publisher
**Editorial:**
Alan Richter ............................Group Publisher
Bob Lanham .....................Marketing Director

**Desc.:** Contains on-the-job type feature
articles, case histories, tutorials, buyers
guides, tips & advice covering the
operation, maintenance, purchasing &
specifying of passenger cars, vans,
trucks, trailers, cranes, aerial lifts,
digger/derricks, as well as other related
tools & construction equipments.
**Readers:** Fleet superintendents,
managers, supervisors & administrators
and related specifiers & buyers
employed by the nation's largest electric
gas & water utilities, telephone
companies, cable TV operators, public
works departments, municipalities &
interconnect companies & industry
contractors.

69306
**VOICE PROCESSING MAGAZINE**
201 E. Sandpointe Ave
Rm. 600
Santa Ana, CA 92707-5761
Telephone: (714) 513-8400
FAX: (714) 513-8482
Year Established: 1989
Pub. Frequency: m.
Page Size: standard
Subscrip. Rate: $24/yr.
Materials: 01,02,06,28,29,30,32,33
Print Process: web offset
Circulation: 50,000
Circulation Type: controlled & paid
**Owner(s):**
Advanstar Communications, Inc.
7500 Old Oak Blvd.
Cleveland, OH 44130
Telephone: (216) 826-2839
Ownership %: 100
**Editorial:**
Peter Meade ......................................Editor
**Desc.:** Covers products, service
applications, benefits of voice mail and
messaging, networking, service bureaus
and transaction processing. Computer
tTelephone product & service.
**Readers:** Technical end users, vars, vads,
systems integrators & consultants.
**Deadline:** story-1st of mo. prior to pub.
date; ads-2 mo. prior

## Group 258-Textiles

25005
**AMERICA'S TEXTILES
INTERNATIONAL**
2100 Powers Ferry Rd., Ste. 125
Atlanta, GA 30339
Telephone: (404) 955-5656
Year Established: 1887
Pub. Frequency: m.
Page Size: standard
Subscrip. Rate: $43/yr. US; $53/yr.
Canada; $115/yr. elsewhere
Circulation: 32,368
Circulation Type: controlled & paid
**Owner(s):**
Billian Publishing Co.
2100 Powers Ferry Rd., Ste.125
Atlanta, GA 30358
Telephone: (404) 256-1555
Ownership %: 100
**Management:**
Stephen C. Croft ................................President
J. Randolph Taylor ...............................Publisher
Ralph Benoy ...................Advertising Manager
**Editorial:**
Samuel J. Warlick ...............Editor in Chief
Monte G. Plott ......................................Editor
W.W. Newcomb ...............Associate Editor
Lucy Reep .........................Associate Editor
Samuel J. Warlick ...........Associate Publisher

**Materials Accepted/Included:** 01-Business news 02-By-line articles 03-Fashion news 04-Food news 05-Freelance copy 06-Letters to editor 07-Real estate news 08-Sports news 09-Travel news 10-Book rev. 11-Movie rev. 12-Music rev. 13-TV rev. 14-Theater rev. 15-Coming events 16-Obituaries 17-Question & answer 18-Social announcements 19-Artwork 20-Cartoons 21-Photos 22-TV listings 23-Audio rec. 24-Video rec. 25-Books 26-Films/film clips 27-Personnel news 28-Press releases 29-New product news/photos 30-Trade lit. 31-Contracts awarded 32-Display adv. 33-Classified adv.

**Desc.:** Articles deal with spinning, weaving and wet finishing processes and techniques. Editorial sections include: Opening, Picking, Carding and Spinning, Warp Preparation and Weaving, Bleaching, Dyeing and Finishing, Maintenance, Engineering and Handling. Departments include: Personal News, Mill News, For the Textile Industry's Use (equipment, supplies, services, literature), Serving the Textile Industry (supplier news).
**Readers:** Executives, designers, master mechanics.

25002
**AMERICAN DYESTUFF REPORTER**
Harmon Cove Towers, Prom. A, Ste. 2
Secaucus, NJ 07094
Telephone: (201) 867-9230
FAX: (201) 867-4545
Year Established: 1917
Pub. Frequency: m.
Page Size: standard
Subscrip. Rate: $30/yr.
Circulation: 12,000
Circulation Type: controlled & paid
**Owner(s):**
SAF International Publications, Inc.
Harmon Cove Towers, Prom.A, 2
Secaucus, NJ 07094
Telephone: (201) 867-9230
Ownership %: 100
**Management:**
Herbert A. Stauderman ........................President
Herbert A. Stauderman ........................Publisher
**Editorial:**
Edward Fox ..............................................Editor
Dr. J. Edward Lynn ................Editorial Director
**Desc.:** Contributed technical articles cover textile bleaching, dyeing, printing, finishing. Covers new supplies and equipment, literature, company news, staff-written articles, in-plant stories. Departments include: Abstracts, News, Names in the News (promotions, appointments), New Products and Developments, Technical Literature.
**Readers:** Technically trained and management personnel in textile wet-processing.

25006
**CARPET & RUG INDUSTRY**
17 S. Franklin Tpk.
Ramsey, NJ 07446
Telephone: (201) 825-2552
Mailing Address:
  P.O. Box 555
  Ramsey, NJ 07446
Year Established: 1973
Pub. Frequency: m.
Page Size: standard
Subscrip. Rate: $42/yr.
Circulation: 6,000
Circulation Type: controlled
**Owner(s):**
Rodman Publishing Co.
17 S. Franklin Tpke.
Ramsey, NJ 07446
Telephone: (201) 825-2552
Ownership %: 100
**Management:**
Rodman J. Zilenziger ..........................Publisher
**Editorial:**
Janet Herlihy ...........................................Editor
Janet Kirby .........................................Columnist
**Desc.:** Covers new equipment, chemicals, dyes, yarns, fibers and related industry.
**Readers:** Manufacturers & distributors of carpets.

58752
**DAVISON'S TEXTILE BLUE BOOK**
295 Godwin Ave.
Midland Park, NJ 07432
Telephone: (201) 445-3135
FAX: (201) 445-4397
Mailing Address:
  P.O. Box 477
  Ridgewood, NJ 07451
Year Established: 1866
Pub. Frequency: a.
Page Size: standard
Subscrip. Rate: $120/yr.
Materials: 27,28,29,30
Circulation: 5,000
Circulation Type: paid
**Owner(s):**
Davison Publishing Co., Inc., Bruce Nealy, Owner
P.O. Box 477
Ridgewood, NJ 07451
Telephone: (201) 445-3135
Ownership %: 50

Davison Publishing Co., Inc., Carol Nealy, Owner
P.O. Box 477
Ridgewood, NJ 07451
Telephone: (201) 445-3135
Ownership %: 50
**Bureau(s):**
Davison Publishing Co., Inc.
5403 Tory Hill Dr.
Greensboro, NC 27410
Telephone: (910) 288-5284
Contact: Fred McCausland

Davison Publishing Co., Inc.
6720 Fairway Point Dr.
Charlotte, NC 28269
Telephone: (704) 875-8201
Contact: William Nealy
**Management:**
Carol Nealy ....................Advertising Manager
**Editorial:**
Bruce Nealy ............................................Editor
**Desc.:** Most comprehensive listing of US, Canadian and Mexican textile companies available anywhere. Contains names of almost every yarn and fabric forming company as well as weaving, knitting and non-woven mills.
**Readers:** Textile industry.
**Deadline:** ads-Nov. 15

23167
**FABRICNEWS**
80 Park Ave.
New York, NY 10016
Telephone: (212) 697-5780
FAX: (212) 697-5143
Pub. Frequency: q.
Page Size: tabloid
Subscrip. Rate: free
Circulation: 10,000
Circulation Type: controlled & free
**Owner(s):**
Arthur Imparato
80 Park Ave.
New York, NY 10016
Telephone: (212) 697-5780
Ownership %: 100
**Management:**
Arthur Imparato .....................................Publisher
**Editorial:**
Arthur Imparato .........................................Editor
Shirley Douglas Jones .........Assistant Publisher

54021
**HOME FASHIONS MAGAZINE**
Seven W. 34th St.
New York, NY 10001
Telephone: (212) 630-3708
FAX: (212) 630-3475
Pub. Frequency: m.
Page Size: standard
Subscrip. Rate: $30/yr.
Circulation: 12,000

Circulation Type: controlled
**Owner(s):**
Capital Cities Communications, Inc.
24 E. 51st St.
New York, NY 10022
Telephone: (212) 421-9595
Ownership %: 100
**Editorial:**
Laurie Kahle ...........................................Editor

69148
**HOME TEXTILES TODAY**
245 W. 17th St.
New York, NY 10011
Telephone: (212) 337-6900
FAX: (212) 337-6922
Year Established: 1979
Pub. Frequency: w.
Page Size: tabloid
Subscrip. Rate: $5 newsstand; $89.97/yr.
Materials: 06,15,16,25,27,28,29,30,32,33
Print Process: web offset
Circulation: 12,069
Circulation Type: controlled & paid
**Owner(s):**
Cahners Business Newspapers
200 S. Main St.
P.O. Box 2754
High Point, NC 27261
Telephone: (212) 337-6900
FAX: (212) 337-6922
Ownership %: 100
**Editorial:**
Warren Shoulberg ..................................Editor
Jeff Malester ..........................Managing Editor
**Desc.:** Marketing, merchandising and retailing of home textile products.

25010
**INDUSTRIAL FABRIC PRODUCTS REVIEW**
345 Cedar St., Ste. 800
St. Paul, MN 55101
Telephone: (612) 222-2508
Year Established: 1912
Pub. Frequency: m.
Page Size: standard
Subscrip. Rate: $34/yr.
Freelance Pay: $250-$400
Circulation: 10,000
Circulation Type: controlled
**Owner(s):**
Industrial Fabrics Association International
345 Cedar Bldg., Ste. 800
St. Paul, MN 55101
Telephone: (612) 222-2508
Ownership %: 100
**Management:**
Frank McGinty ......................................Publisher
Mary Hennessy .................Advertising Manager
**Editorial:**
Sue Hagen ...............................................Editor
**Desc.:** The editorial objectives are (1) to provide authoritative information on current management practices in the industry, (2) to report new concepts and ideas for management's use, (3) to provide statistics, information, new trends as they relate to the industry, (4) to provide news of the programs and activities of the industrial fabrics association international.
Regular departments include: News of New Products and Services, News of Personnel and Ownership Changes, Association News, Calendar of Coming Events.
**Readers:** Manufacturers of canvas and industrial fabric products and their suppliers.

69150
**INTERNATIONAL FIBER JOURNAL**
2919 Spalding Dr.
Atlanta, GA 30350-4628
Telephone: (404) 394-6098
FAX: (404) 393-0161

Year Established: 1986
Pub. Frequency: bi-m.
Page Size: standard
Subscrip. Rate: $20/yr.
Materials: 01,02,05,06,10,15,16,21,27,28, 29,30,31,32,33
Freelance Pay: $100/set page
Print Process: offset
Circulation: 9,000
Circulation Type: controlled & paid
**Owner(s):**
McMickle Publications, Inc.
2919 Spalding Dr.
Atlanta, GA 30350-4628
Telephone: (404) 394-6098
Ownership %: 100
**Editorial:**
Anne H. Snider .........................................Editor
**Readers:** Upper and middle management in polymerizers, fiber producers, texturers, nonwovens, and yarn spinning.
**Deadline:** story-15th of mo., 2 mo. prior to pub. date; news-15th of mo., 2 mo. prior; photo-15th of mo., 2 mo. prior; ads-1st of mo., 1 mo. prior

23573
**KNITTING TIMES**
386 Park Ave., S.
New York, NY 10016
Telephone: (212) 683-7520
FAX: (212) 532-0766
Year Established: 1933
Pub. Frequency: m.
Page Size: standard
Subscrip. Rate: $35/yr.
Freelance Pay: varies
Circulation: 7,500
Circulation Type: paid
**Owner(s):**
National Knitwear Sportswear Association
386 Park Ave., S.
New York, NY 10016
Telephone: (212) 683-7520
Ownership %: 100
**Bureau(s):**
NKSA
1859 Interstate 85, S.
Charlotte, NC 28208
Telephone: (704) 391-9537
Contact: Eric Hertz, Publication Director
**Editorial:**
David Gross ..............................................Editor
Eric Hertz ..............................................Director
**Desc.:** News, new lines, new production methods, association developments, seasonal lines, industry outlook, allied fields, economic future, new developments in natural and synthetic fibers, knitting yarns (spun and textured) and knitting machinery, warp and weft. Covers sweaters, swim suits, infants' wear, knit fabrics, polo shirts, gloves, headwear, all areas of cut-and-sewn apparel manufacture. Reports on new developments in equipment, materials, fashions, industry news, new books.
**Readers:** Manufacturers, distributors, sales executives, fabric & garment knitters, textile executives, retailers, home furnishings, executives.

69149
**MARINE TEXTILES**
Twelve Oaks Center, Ste. 922
Wayzata, MN 55391
Telephone: (612) 473-5088
FAX: (612) 473-7068
Year Established: 1986
Pub. Frequency: 9/yr.
Page Size: standard
Subscrip. Rate: $30/yr.
Circulation: 5,500
Circulation Type: paid

**Materials Accepted/Included:** 01-Business news 02-By-line articles 03-Fashion news 04-Food news 05-Freelance copy 06-Letters to editor 07-Real estate news 08-Sports news 09-Travel news 10-Book rev. 11-Movie rev. 12-Music rev. 13-TV rev. 14-Theater rev. 15-Coming events 16-Obituaries 17-Question & answer 18-Social announcements 19-Artwork 20-Cartoons 21-Photos 22-TV listings 23-Audio rec. 24-Video rec. 25-Books 26-Films/film clips 27-Personnel news 28-Press releases 29-New product news/photos 30-Trade lit. 31-Contracts awarded 32-Display adv. 33-Classified adv.

4-379

**Owner(s):**
RCM Enterprises, Inc.
12 Oaks Ctr., Ste. 922
Wayzata, MN 55391
Telephone: (612) 473-5088
Ownership %: 100
**Management:**
Robert C. Mead ...........................Publisher
**Editorial:**
Sue Klemond .................................Editor
**Desc.:** Covers fabric products and furnishings used in boating.
**Readers:** Companies in the boating industry that use textiles.

### NONWOVENS INDUSTRY
23663

17 S. Franklin Tpke.
Ramsey, NJ 07446
Telephone: (201) 825-2552
FAX: (201) 825-0553
Mailing Address:
  P.O. Box 555
  Ramsey, NJ 07446
Year Established: 1970
Pub. Frequency: m.
Page Size: standard
Subscrip. Rate: $52/yr. US; $60/yr.
  Canada & Mexico
Circulation: 11,000
Circulation Type: paid
**Owner(s):**
Rodman Publishing Co.
17 S. Franklin Turnpike
Ramsey, NJ 07446
Telephone: (201) 825-2552
Ownership %: 100
**Management:**
Rodman J. Zilenziger, Jr. ...............President
Rodman J. Zilenziger, Jr. ...............Publisher
Mathew Montgomery ........Advertising Manager
Mary Zocco ................Circulation Manager
**Editorial:**
Ellen Noonan ................................Editor
Scott Sullivan ...........................Associate Editor
Sharon Messner .................Production Director
**Desc.:** Want feature articles concerning manufacturing, marketing and new techniques in roll goods manufacturing and converting of nonwovens. Feature material also includes articles on conversion and marketing of durable nonwovens and disposable soft goods. By-lines used. About half of feature material is staff-written. Also interested in surveys of various aspects of the industry. Article length 1,000 words or more.
**Readers:** Manufacturers of nonwoven fabrics, suppliers and finishers of nonwovens, and distributors.

### PRINTWEAR MAGAZINE
65269

1008 Depot Hill
Broomfield, CO 80038
Telephone: (303) 469-0424
FAX: (303) 469-5730
Mailing Address:
  P.O. Box 1416
  Broomfield, CO 80020
Year Established: 1987
Pub. Frequency: m.
Page Size: standard
Subscrip. Rate: $26/yr.
Materials: 01,02,03,05,06,15,16,17,19,21,
  25,27,28,29,30,32,33
Print Process: web offset
Circulation: 22,000
Circulation Type: controlled

**Owner(s):**
National Business Media, Inc.
P.O. Box 1416
Broomfield, CO 80020
Telephone: (303) 469-0424
FAX: (303) 469-5730
Ownership %: 100
**Management:**
Scott Owen ...........................Publisher
**Editorial:**
Mark Buchanan ...........................Editor
**Desc.:** Covers screen printing, embroidery, business tips, and product reviews.
**Readers:** Targets screen printers of imprinted sportswear, wholesalers, and manufacturers.

### SOUTHERN TEXTILE NEWS
25013

4900 Wallace Neal Rd.
Charlotte, NC 28208
Telephone: (704) 394-5111
FAX: (704) 394-5114
Mailing Address:
  P.O. Box 668926
  Charlotte, NC 28266
Year Established: 1945
Pub. Frequency: w.
Page Size: tabloid
Subscrip. Rate: $25/yr.; $37.50/2 yrs.;
  $50/3 yrs.
Circulation: 7,800
Circulation Type: paid
**Owner(s):**
Mullen Publications
P.O. Box 668926
Charlotte, NC 28266
Telephone: (704) 394-5111
Ownership %: 100
**Bureau(s):**
Southern Textile News
P.O. Box 5805
Columbus, GA 31906
Telephone: (706) 327-5016
Contact: Marjorie Richardson
**Management:**
Mason W. Smith, III ...........................President
David O'Neal ...........................Manager
Mason W. Smith, III ..........Operations Manager
**Editorial:**
Marjorie T. Richardson ...........................Editor
**Desc.:** Articles and features on the textile field and allied industries. Editorial policy is the present management's interests in the industry.
**Readers:** Top level management.

### TEXTILE CHEMIST & COLORIST
25014

One Davis Dr.
Research Triangle Park, NC 27709-2215
Telephone: (919) 549-8141
FAX: (919) 549-8933
Mailing Address:
  P.O. Box 12215
  Research Triangle Park, NC 27709-2215
Year Established: 1969
Pub. Frequency: m.
Page Size: standard
Subscrip. Rate: $30/yr. U.S. & Canada;
  $40/yr. elsewhere
Materials: 01,03,15,16,27,29,32,33
Circulation: 10,500
Circulation Type: paid
**Owner(s):**
American Assn. of Textile Chemists & Colorists
P.O. Box 12215
Research Tringle Park, NC 27709
Telephone: (919) 549-8141
Ownership %: 100
**Management:**
William B. Davis ................Advertising Manager
**Editorial:**
Susan H. Keesee ...........................Editor
Patricia Calomeris ...............Production Director

**Desc.:** Publish all nonpromotional news of interest to the textile wet processing industry and its suppliers. Departments include: Trade News, People, Products-Literature.
**Readers:** Range from High School level to Ph.D.
**Deadline:** ads-1st of mo. preceding mo. of pub. date

### TEXTILE MANUFACTURING
66340

12 Perimeter Park Dr., Ste. 102
Chamblee, GA 30341
Telephone: (404) 451-4990
Year Established: 1988
Pub. Frequency: bi-m.
Page Size: standard
Subscrip. Rate: $30/yr.
Circulation: 20,000
Circulation Type: controlled
**Owner(s):**
Merit Publications, Inc.
12 Perimeter Park Dr., Ste 102
Chamblee, GA 30341
Telephone: (404) 451-4990
Ownership %: 100
**Management:**
James L. Prendergast ...........................Publisher
**Editorial:**
Earl G. Whited ...........................Editor

### TEXTILE RESEARCH JOURNAL
25018

601 Prospect Ave.
Princeton, NJ 08540
Telephone: (609) 924-3150
Mailing Address:
  P.O. Box 625
  Princeton, NJ 08542
Year Established: 1930
Pub. Frequency: m.
Page Size: 8 x 10 3/4
Subscrip. Rate: $140/yr.
Circulation: 2,200
Circulation Type: paid
**Owner(s):**
Textile Research Institute
601 Prospect Ave.
Princeton, NJ 08542
Telephone: (609) 924-3150
Ownership %: 100
**Management:**
Gary A. Zarrilli ...................Business Manager
**Editorial:**
Richard K. Toner ...........................Editor
Marilee Nissen ...................Production Editor
Harriet Heilweil ...................Technical Editor
**Desc.:** Articles deal with all phases of fundamental and applied research and developments in the textiles and allied industries.
**Readers:** Researchers, and scientists.

### TEXTILES PANAMERICANOS
25019

2100 Powers Ferry Rd.
Atlanta, GA 30339
Telephone: (404) 955-5656
FAX: (404) 952-0669
Year Established: 1941
Pub. Frequency: q.
Page Size: standard
Subscrip. Rate: free/qualified personnel;
  $40/yr.; $70/2yrs.
Circulation: 12,000
Circulation Type: controlled
**Owner(s):**
Billian Publishing Co.
2100 Powers Ferry Rd.
Atlanta, GA 30339
Ownership %: 100
**Management:**
Stephen C. Croft ...........................Publisher
**Editorial:**
James A. Woodroffe ...............Editorial Director

**Desc.:** Publicity and news items must deal with products of interest to textile manufacturers. Available for use by mills in the Latin-American countries.
**Readers:** Textile and apparel manufacturers in Latin-America.

## Group 260-Tobacco

### RETAIL TOBACCONIST
69152

9607 Gayton Rd., Ste. 201
Richmond, VA 23233
Telephone: (804) 741-6704
FAX: (804) 750-2399
Pub. Frequency: 6/yr.
Subscrip. Rate: $45/yr. US; $75/yr.
  Canada & Mexico; $95/yr. elsewhere
**Owner(s):**
Leo Douglas, Inc.
9607 Gayton Rd., Ste. 201
Richmond, VA 23233
Telephone: (804) 741-6704
Ownership %: 100

### SMOKESHOP
25056

Seven Penn Plz.
New York, NY 10001
Telephone: (212) 594-4120
FAX: (212) 714-0514
Year Established: 1974
Pub. Frequency: bi-m.
Page Size: standard
Subscrip. Rate: $36/yr.
Freelance Pay: $3/in.
Circulation: 4,172
Circulation Type: controlled
**Owner(s):**
T/SF Communications
2407 E. Skelly Dr.
Tulsa, OK 74105
Telephone: (918) 747-2600
Ownership %: 100
**Bureau(s):**
BMT Publications, Inc.
221 Mountain View Ave.
Scotch Plains, NJ 07076
Telephone: (908) 889-2376
Contact: Betsy McQuade, Executive
    Director
**Management:**
Hedy Halpert ...........................President
Paul Dworin ...........................Publisher
Bruce Smith ...........................Publisher
Daniel Petrocelli ...................General Manager
**Editorial:**
Betsy Mcquade ...................Account Executive
Paul Dworin ...................Editorial Advisor
Bruce Smith ...........................Sales
**Desc.:** Editorial emphasis is on retail tobacco shop management and merchandising, including store design, fixturing, interior and window display, promotion and advertising for special events, occasions and seasons.
**Readers:** Owners and operators of high-grade tobacco stores.

### TOBACCO AND NEW PRODUCTS WORLD
65292

P.O. Box 1107
Santa Monica, CA 90406
Telephone: (310) 397-4217
Year Established: 1960
Pub. Frequency: 3/yr.
Page Size: tabloid
Subscrip. Rate: $6/copy; $18/yr.
Materials: 01,04,06,15,27,28,29,30,32,33
Print Process: web
Circulation: 2,000
Circulation Type: controlled

---

**Materials Accepted/Included:** 01-Business news 02-By-line articles 03-Fashion news 04-Food news 05-Freelance copy 06-Letters to editor 07-Real estate news 08-Sports news 09-Travel news 10-Book rev. 11-Movie rev. 12-Music rev. 13-TV rev. 14-Theater rev. 15-Coming events 16-Obituaries 17-Question & answer 18-Social announcements 19-Artwork 20-Cartoons 21-Photos 22-TV listings 23-Audio rec. 24-Video rec. 25-Books 26-Films/film clips 27-Personnel news 28-Press releases 29-New product news/photos 30-Trade lit. 31-Contracts awarded 32-Display adv. 33-Classified adv.

4-380

**Owner(s):**
Lott Publishing Co.
13222-B Admiral Ave.
Marina del Rey, CA 90292
Telephone: (310) 397-4217
Ownership %: 100
**Editorial:**
Dave Lott ...................................Editor

25059
## TOBACCO REPORTER
3000 Highwoods Blvd., Ste. 300
Raleigh, NC 27604
Telephone: (919) 872-5040
FAX: (919) 876-6531
Mailing Address:
  P.O. Box 95075
  Raleigh, NC 27625
Year Established: 1873
Pub. Frequency: m.
Page Size: standard
Subscrip. Rate: $30/yr. US; $65/yr. foreign
Freelance Pay: $.10-$.15/wd.
Circulation: 5,500
Circulation Type: controlled
**Owner(s):**
Specialized Agricultural Publications, Inc.
3000 Highwoods Blvd., Ste. 300
Raleigh, NC 27604
Telephone: (919) 872-5040
Ownership %: 100
**Management:**
Dayton H. Matlick ...............................Publisher
Sue Burleson .....................Circulation Manager
**Editorial:**
Colleen Zimmerman ..................................Editor
Ann Jeffries ..........................................Advertising
Vicki Gardner .......................Production Director
**Desc.:** International monthly business
  publication for all involved in production,
  manufacture and trade of tobacco and
  tobacco products. Distributed in 140
  countries worldwide.
**Readers:** Manufacturers of tobacco
  products, processors and exporters of
  tobacco leaf. All related equipment and
  service suppliers.

## Group 262-Toys, Crafts & Hobbies

25062
## AMERICAN CRAFT
72 Spring St.
New York, NY 10012
Telephone: (212) 274-0630
FAX: (212) 274-0650
Year Established: 1941
Pub. Frequency: bi-m.
Page Size: standard
Subscrip. Rate: $5.00 newsstand; $40/yr.
Materials: 06,10,15,32,33
Freelance Pay: $100 & up
Print Process: offset
Circulation: 35,000
Circulation Type: free & paid
**Owner(s):**
American Craft Council
72 Spring St.
New York, NY 10012
Telephone: (212) 274-0630
Ownership %: 100
**Management:**
Don Zanone ......................Advertising Manager
**Editorial:**
Lois Moran ....................................Editor in Chief
Patricia Dandignac ........................Senior Editor
Joyce Lovelace .........................Associate Editor
Beverly Sanders .......................Associate Editor
Kiyoshi Kanai .............................Design Director

**Desc.:** Especially interested in the craft
  arts field, including metal, clay, wood,
  glass and fiber. Interested in the work of
  nation's and foreign top artists -
  craftsmen. Departments include:
  Calendar, Gallery Exhibitions,
  Commissions, Books, Craft World
  (news).
**Readers:** Professional and vocational
  craftsmen, teachers, designers,
  architects, collectors, administrators,
  retailers.

25063
## CRAFT & NEEDLEWORK AGE
225 Gordons Corner Rd.
Englishtown, NJ 07726-9928
Telephone: (908) 446-4900
Mailing Address:
  P.O. Box 420
  Englishtown, NJ 07726-9928
Year Established: 1946
Pub. Frequency: m.
Page Size: standard
Subscrip. Rate: $20/yr.
Materials: 01,10,15,32,33
Freelance Pay: $200-$300
Print Process: web
Circulation: 34,000
Circulation Type: controlled
**Owner(s):**
Hobby Publications, Inc.
P.O. Box 420
Englishtown, NJ 07726
Telephone: (908) 446-4900
Ownership %: 100
**Management:**
David Gherman ...................................President
Paul Confrey ........................................Publisher
Tammy Keck ....................Advertising Manager
**Editorial:**
Karen Ancona .........................................Editor
**Desc.:** Specifically retail merchandising
  articles are carried. Use all
  merchandising or success stories if they
  are specifically pointed to our field. Case
  histories of successful hobby dealers
  are especially wanted, with special
  reference to how their use of window
  and counter display, or some other
  special merchandising technique, gave
  them profit.
**Readers:** A business merchandising
  magazine serving the craft & needlework
  industry at all levels, but primarily at the
  retailer & jobber levels.
**Deadline:** story-2 mo. prior to pub. date;
  news-2 mo. prior; photo-2 mo. prior; ads-
  1st of mo. prior to pub. date

69241
## CRAFT MARKETING NEWS
P.O. Box 1541
Clifton, NJ 07015-1541
Year Established: 1984
Pub. Frequency: m.
Page Size: standard
Subscrip. Rate: $25.90/yr.
Materials: 10,28,29
Print Process: offset
Circulation: 500
Circulation Type: paid
**Owner(s):**
Front Room Publishers
P.O. Box 1541
Clifton, NJ 07015-1541
Ownership %: 100
**Editorial:**
Adele Patti .............................................Editor
**Desc.:** Contains information on crafts
  marketing: wholesale sales to shops and
  galleries.
**Deadline:** story-3 mos. prior to pub. date;
  news-3 mos. prior

53944
## CRAFTS REPORT, THE
300 Water St.
Wilmington, DE 19801
Telephone: (302) 656-2209
FAX: (302) 656-4894
Mailing Address:
  P.O. Box 1992
  Wilmington, DE 19801
Year Established: 1974
Pub. Frequency: m.
Page Size: tabloid
Subscrip. Rate: $3.95 newsstand;
  $24.95/yr
Materials: 01,05,06,10
Freelance Pay: varied
Print Process: web
Circulation: 20,000
Circulation Type: free & paid
**Owner(s):**
Crafts Report Publishing Co., Inc.
300 Water St.
Wilmington, DE 19801
Telephone: (302) 656-2209
Ownership %: 100
**Management:**
Lammot Copeland, Jr. ......................Publisher
Deborah L. Copeland ......................Publisher
**Editorial:**
Marilyn Stevens .......................................Editor
**Desc.:** To provide business news and
  information to professional craftspeople,
  especially in the areas of marketing and
  management.
**Readers:** Professional Craftspeople and
  crafts retailers.
**Deadline:** story-3 mos.; news-3 mos.;
  photo-3 mos.; ads-2 mos.

23178
## DECOR MAGAZINE
330 N. Fourth St.
St. Louis, MO 63102-2041
Telephone: (314) 421-5445
FAX: (314) 421-1070
Year Established: 1880
Pub. Frequency: m.
Page Size: standard
Subscrip. Rate: $20/yr.; $44/3 yrs.
Materials: 01,06,10,25,27,29,30,32,33
Freelance Pay: negotiable
Print Process: web offset
Circulation: 24,000
Circulation Type: paid
**Owner(s):**
Commerce Publications, Inc.
330 N. Fourth St.
St. Louis, MO 63102-2036
Telephone: (314) 421-5445
FAX: (314) 421-1070
Ownership %: 100
**Management:**
David A. Baetz .................................President
Gary S. Goldman ...............................Publisher
D. Severino .......................Advertising Manager
**Editorial:**
Sharon Shinn ..............................Senior Editor
Gary S. Goldman ...................................Editor
Alice Gibson ...................New Products Editor
Alice Gibson ...........................Technical Editor
**Desc.:** By-line articles, merchandising,
  store location, selection developments
  and other factors affecting the industry.
  Reports on new promotions, trends, new
  items, markets, people in the news, new
  books.
**Readers:** Art galleries, buyers for picture
  departments, and picture framers.
**Deadline:** news-1st of mo., 2 mo. prior to
  pub. date; photo-1st of mo., 1 mo. prior
  to pub. date

59138
## DOLL CRAFTER
30595 Eight Mile Rd.
Livonia, MI 48152
Telephone: (313) 477-6650
FAX: (313) 477-6795
Year Established: 1983
Pub. Frequency: 12/yr.
Page Size: standard
Subscrip. Rate: $29.95/yr. US; $41.95/yr.
  foreign
Circulation: 115,000
Circulation Type: paid
**Owner(s):**
Scott Advertising & Publishing Co.
30595 Eight Mile Rd.
Livonia, MI 48152
Telephone: (313) 477-6650
Ownership %: 100
**Management:**
Bill Thompson .............................Vice President
R.H. Keessen ......................................Publisher
**Editorial:**
Barbara Campbell ....................................Editor
Annette Malis ..........................Editorial Director
Bill Latocki ...............................Creative Director
Jeanette Foxe ...................Distribution Manager
Vern Schafer ......................Production Director
**Desc.:** How-to magazine for creating
  porcelain antique reproductions and
  modern dolls; also other types of dolls -
  created for the dollmakers and
  collectors. Each issue includes at least 6
  doll projects in full color, easy step-by-
  step instructions, and a full size doll
  dress pattern, plus personality profiles.
**Readers:** Hobbyists, professional
  dollmakers, collectors.

69581
## JOURNAL OF SPORTS PHILATELY
322 Riverside Dr.
Huron, OH 44839
Telephone: (216) 433-5315
Year Established: 1962
Pub. Frequency: bi-m.
Subscrip. Rate: $10/yr. US; $15/yr. foreign
Circulation: 500
Circulation Type: controlled
**Owner(s):**
Sports Philatelists International
322 Riverside Dr.
Huron, OH 44839
Telephone: (216) 433-5315
Ownership %: 100
**Editorial:**
John La Porta ..........................................Editor

22367
## MINIATURES DEALER
21027 Crossroads Cir.
Waukesha, WI 53186
Telephone: (414) 273-6332
FAX: (414) 796-0126
Mailing Address:
  P.O. Box 1612
  Waukesha, WI 53187
Year Established: 1978
Pub. Frequency: m.
Page Size: standard
Subscrip. Rate: $24/yr.
Freelance Pay: $.10/wd.
Circulation: 1,180
Circulation Type: paid
**Owner(s):**
Kalmbach Publishing Co.
P.O. Box 1612
Waukesha, WI 53187
Telephone: (414) 796-8776
Ownership %: 100
**Management:**
Robert Hayden ...................................Publisher
Saro Benz .......................Advertising Manager
**Editorial:**
Geraldine Willems ..................................Editor

Materials Accepted/Included: 01-Business news 02-By-line articles 03-Fashion news 04-Food news 05-Freelance copy 06-Letters to editor 07-Real estate news 08-Sports news 09-Travel news 10-Book rev. 11-Movie rev. 12-Music rev. 13-TV rev. 14-Theater rev. 15-Coming events 16-Obituaries 17-Question & answer 18-Social announcements 19-Artwork 20-Cartoons 21-Photos 22-TV listings 23-Audio rec. 24-Video rec. 25-Books 26-Films/film clips 27-Personnel news 28-Press releases 29-New product news/photos 30-Trade lit. 31-Contracts awarded 32-Display adv. 33-Classified adv.

4-381

**Desc.:** Edited for the dollhouse miniatures wholesaler dealing in dollhouses, miniature furniture, accessories, building supplies, tools, patterns, and books. It contains articles involving the many facets of miniatures, with emphasis placed on the problems of merchandising these products. Features include interviews with leading retailers, new products, trade show coverage, and industry trends. Departments include: Trade Calendar, Business Articles, Miniatures Update, New Products.
**Readers:** Read by retailers in U.S. and Canada.

25068

**MODEL RETAILER**
14121 Parke Long Ct., Ste. 112
Chantilly, VA 22021-1645
Telephone: (703) 263-0900
FAX: (703) 263-0905
Year Established: 1975
Pub. Frequency: m.
Page Size: standard
Subscrip. Rate: $35/yr. trade; $80/yr. non-trade
Materials: 01,02,06,10,15,21,24,25,27,28,29,30,32,33
Freelance Pay: $.10+/wd.
Print Process: offset
Circulation: 6,900
Circulation Type: controlled
**Owner(s):**
Kalmbach Publishing Co.
21027 Crossroads Cir.
Waukesha, WI 53186
Telephone: (414) 796-8776
Ownership %: 100
**Bureau(s):**
Model Retailer
14121 Parke Long Ct., Ste. 112
Chantilly, VA 22021-1645
Telephone: (703) 263-0900
Contact: Carl Smith, Contributing Editor
**Management:**
Walt Mundschau ..............................President
Geoff Wheeler ...................................Publisher
George Zombakis ..............Advertising Manager
**Editorial:**
Carl Smith ...........................................Editor
Carol Collier ........................................Editor
**Desc.:** Business magazine edited for the hobby and model industry, specializing in model airplanes, model railroading, adventure and adult games, plastic kit models, assorted static display models, books, videos, wearable, memorabilia and computer software.
**Readers:** Hobby store owners, hobby distributors, manufacturers and publishers. 92% of circulation is to retailers and distributors.
**Deadline:** story-70 days prior to pub. date; news-45 days prior; photo-45 days prior; ads-30 days prior

25070

**PROFITABLE CRAFT MERCHANDISING**
Two News Plaza
Peoria, IL 61614
Telephone: (309) 682-6626
FAX: (309) 682-7394
Mailing Address:
P.O. Box 1790
Peoria, IL 61656
Year Established: 1965
Pub. Frequency: 12/yr.
Page Size: standard
Subscrip. Rate: $30/yr.
Materials: 01,10,24,25,27,28,29,30,32,33
Freelance Pay: $200-$500
Circulation: 37,000
Circulation Type: controlled

**Owner(s):**
PJS Publications, Inc.
Two News Plaza
P.O. Box 1790
Peoria, IL 61656
Telephone: (309) 682-6626
FAX: (309) 682-7394
Ownership %: 100
**Management:**
Jerry Constantino ..............................President
Del Rusher ........................................Publisher
Mike Irish ........................Advertising Manager
**Editorial:**
Miriam Olson ........................................Editor
**Desc.:** Designed for craft supply, needlework supply, and sewing supply manufacturers, wholesalers and retailers. All articles are written with one theme in mind: Will the material help the readers either make or save money? Feature articles deal with product trends, trade show coverage, industry news, and store management. Also used are new product, new book, and new catalog information. Articles are used in depth. Articles are as long as necessary to tell the story.
**Readers:** Retailers, manufacturers, wholesalers, and publishers.
**Deadline:** news-1 1/2 mos. prior to pub. date; ads-21st of mo., 2 mos. prior

22673

**SMALL WORLD**
225 W. 34th St.
New York, NY 10122
Telephone: (212) 563-2742
Year Established: 1950
Pub. Frequency: m.
Page Size: standard
Subscrip. Rate: $18/yr.
Freelance Pay: negotiable
Circulation: 8,000
Circulation Type: controlled
**Owner(s):**
Earnshaw Publications, Inc.
225 W. 34th St.
New York, NY 10122
Telephone: (212) 563-2742
Ownership %: 100
**Bureau(s):**
Earnshaw Publications, Inc.
110 E. 97th St.
Los Angeles, CA 90003
Telephone: (310) 624-1083
Contact: Patricia Schumann, Advertising Manager
**Management:**
Thomas W. Hudson ..........................President
Thomas W. Hudson ............................Publisher
**Editorial:**
Maryann LoRusso ...............................Editor
Caroline Bournos ...........................Advertising
Debby Albenda .............................Art Director
**Desc.:** Covers nursery furniture, wheel goods, infant apparel, toys and accessories at the retailers level. By-line features as well as staff-written. Carries store news, shows, promotions, case histories, new product news and other helpful material for the retailer.
**Readers:** Nursery furniture dealers, department stores, accessory buyers and manufacturers of nursery furniture, and mass merchants furniture stores that sell juvenile furniture.

25072

**TOY & HOBBY WORLD**
41 Madison Ave., 5th Fl.
New York, NY 10010
Telephone: (212) 685-0404
FAX: (212) 685-0483
Year Established: 1963
Pub. Frequency: m.

Page Size: standard
Subscrip. Rate: $50/yr.
Freelance Pay: $.20-$.50/wd.
Circulation: 18,700
Circulation Type: controlled
**Owner(s):**
Toy & Hobby World
New York, NY 10010
Ownership %: 100
**Management:**
Ted Schoenhaus ...............................Publisher
**Editorial:**
Robert McCoy .......................................Editor
**Desc.:** A monthly tabloid magazine, with emphasis on news of the industry. Feature material includes merchandising features, particularly those aimed at mass merchandisers, toys and hobbies.
**Readers:** Retail and wholesale buyers of toys. Companies in toy, hobby and craft industries.

## Group 264-Trailers & Accessories

25081

**MANUFACTURED HOME MERCHANDISER**
203 N. Wabash, Ste. 800
Chicago, IL 60601
Telephone: (312) 236-3528
Year Established: 1952
Pub. Frequency: m.
Page Size: standard
Subscrip. Rate: $36/yr.
Materials: 01,02,05,15,32,33
Print Process: offset
Circulation: 16,000
Circulation Type: controlled
**Owner(s):**
RLD Group, Inc.
203 N. Wabash, Ste. 800
Chicago, IL 60601
Telephone: (312) 236-3528
Ownership %: 100
**Management:**
Herbert E. Tieder ..............................President
Herbert E. Tieder ................................Publisher
**Desc.:** Merchandising, sales promotion, advertising, public relations, selling, and business articles on phases of manufactured homes, sales techniques, promotion, merchandising, business management, service, community and public relations, cost accounting, inventory control, display, advertising and market development. Departments include: New Products, Editorial, Advertising Index, New Models, New Literature, Industry Statistics.
**Readers:** Those actively engaged in building, and retailing of manufactured housing.

25083

**RV BUSINESS**
3601 Calle Tecate
Camarillo, CA 93012
Telephone: (805) 389-0300
FAX: (805) 389-0378
Year Established: 1949
Pub. Frequency: s-m.
Page Size: standard
Subscrip. Rate: $48/yr.; free to trade
Freelance Pay: varies
Circulation: 21,000
Circulation Type: controlled
**Owner(s):**
TL Enterprises, Inc.
3601 Calle Tecate
Camarillo, CA 93012
Telephone: (805) 389-0300

**Bureau(s):**
TL Enterprises Midwest Office
2300 Middlebury St.
Elkhart, IN 46516
Telephone: (219) 295-7820
Contact: Sherman Goldenberg, Bureau Chief
**Management:**
Joe McAdams .....................................President
Michael Schneider .............................Publisher
Brenda Hutchinson ..........Production Manager
**Editorial:**
Sherman Goldenberg ....................Bureau Chief
Katherine Sharma ................................Editor
Ellen Siegel Koller ......................Art Director
Carol Henry ....................Associate Art Director
Bill Estes .............Director Technical Services
Janet Van Bibber .........National Sales Director
Robert Helms .....................Production Director
Stephen Boilon ...................Sr. Managing Editor
**Desc.:** Published for the recreational vehicle industry: manufacturers, suppliers, dealers and related industries such as automotive, financial, insurance, camping and tourism. Covers industry news, economic trends and forecasts. Feature articles probe techniques and methods for marketing, servicing/repairing, manufacturing, business management. Departments include: Letters, Columns, RV People/Promotions/Awards, (Show) Calendar, Profitmakers (new products) and associations.
**Readers:** Personnel; management and non-management of RV manufacturing firms, dealerships, campgrounds, supplier firms, distributors, financial corporations, legislators, anyone connected with the RV industry.

25086

**RV NEWS**
6125 S. Ash Ave.
Ste. 8
Tempe, AZ 85283
Telephone: (602) 839-8130
FAX: (602) 820-0934
Year Established: 1975
Pub. Frequency: m.
Page Size: standard
Subscrip. Rate: $36/yr.
Freelance Pay: varies
Circulation: 11,971
Circulation Type: controlled & paid
**Owner(s):**
J. Daniel Holt
6125 S. Ash Ave.
Ste. 8
Tempe, AZ 85283
Telephone: (602) 839-8130
Ownership %: 100
**Management:**
J. Daniel Holt ....................................Publisher
Carmel F. Holt ...................Circulation Manager
**Editorial:**
Don Magary ............................Executive Editor
**Desc.:** Reports all news affecting the recreational vehicle industry. Feature articles include spotlights on RV manufacturers, suppliers, distributors, associations, and new products. Our prime consideration for using any material is its news value and potential reader interest.

**Materials Accepted/Included:** 01-Business news 02-By-line articles 03-Fashion news 04-Food news 05-Freelance copy 06-Letters to editor 07-Real estate news 08-Sports news 09-Travel news 10-Book rev. 11-Movie rev. 12-Music rev. 13-TV rev. 14-Theater rev. 15-Coming events 16-Obituaries 17-Question & answer 18-Social announcements 19-Artwork 20-Cartoons 21-Photos 22-TV listings 23-Audio rec. 24-Video rec. 25-Books 26-Films/film clips 27-Personnel news 28-Press releases 29-New product news/photos 30-Trade lit. 31-Contracts awarded 32-Display adv. 33-Classified adv.

**Readers:** Recreational vehicle manufacturers, supplier/component manufacturers, warehouse distributors, RV dealers, aftermarket dealers, service centers, hitch installers, air conditioning specialists, campground owners, van and mini-truck converters and parts and accessory retailers, marine parts distributors, manufacturer's agents, RV associations, legislators, universities, and bankers.

## Group 266-Travel

### ARIZONA BUSINESS MAGAZINE
61639

3111 N. Central Ave., Ste. 230
Phoenix, AZ 85012
Telephone: (602) 277-6045
FAX: (602) 277-6046
Year Established: 1985
Pub. Frequency: q.
Page Size: standard
Subscrip. Rate: $30/yr.
Circulation: 16,500
Circulation Type: paid
**Owner(s):**
Michael Atkinson
3111 N. Central Ave., Ste. 230
Phoenix, AZ 85012-2650
Telephone: (602) 277-6045
Ownership %: 100
**Management:**
Michael Arkinson ..................Publisher
**Editorial:**
Paul Beakley ..........................Editor
**Desc.:** Focuses on virtually every facet of the business community; from development and construction to the environment, building management and architecture.

### BUSINESS TRAVEL MANAGEMENT
67201

488 Madison Ave.
New York, NY 10022-5772
Telephone: (212) 888-1500
FAX: (212) 888-8008
Year Established: 1989
Pub. Frequency: m.
Page Size: standard
Subscrip. Rate: $75/yr.
Circulation: 45,000
Circulation Type: controlled
**Owner(s):**
Coastal Communications Corp.
488 Madison Ave.
New York, NY 10022
Telephone: (212) 888-1500
Ownership %: 100
**Management:**
Harvey Grotsky ....................President
Harvey Grotsky ....................Publisher
Joseph Volte ............Advertising Manager
**Editorial:**
Margot Owens ..........................Editor
**Desc.:** For corporate executives, business travel managers, and travel professionals servicing commercial accounts.

### BUS TOURS MAGAZINE
64866

9698 W. Judson Rd.
Polo, IL 61064
Telephone: (815) 946-2341
FAX: (815) 946-2347
Year Established: 1979
Pub. Frequency: bi-m.
Page Size: standard
Subscrip. Rate: $10/yr.
Materials: 27,28,32
Freelance Pay: varies
Print Process: offset lithography
Circulation: 11,000
Circulation Type: controlled

**Owner(s):**
National Bus Trader, Inc.
9698 W. Judson Rd.
Polo, IL 61064
Telephone: (815) 946-2341
FAX: (815) 946-2347
Ownership %: 100
**Management:**
Jackie Plachno ..................Advertising Manager
Joe Plachno ..................Production Manager
**Editorial:**
Larry Plachno ..........................Editor
Karen Ball ..........................Editor
Linda Faivre ................Administrative Assistant
**Desc.:** Provides information for individuals who plan motor coach tours.
**Readers:** Circulates to individuals that plan motor coach tours.

### CORPORATE & INCENTIVE TRAVEL
69174

488 Madison Ave.
New York, NY 10022-5772
Telephone: (212) 888-1500
FAX: (212) 888-8008
Year Established: 1983
Pub. Frequency: m.
Subscrip. Rate: $55/yr.
Circulation: 54,835
Circulation Type: paid
**Owner(s):**
Coastal Communications Corp.
488 Madison Ave.
New York, NY 10022
Telephone: (212) 888-1500
Ownership %: 100
**Editorial:**
Harvey Grotsky ..........................Editor
**Desc.:** Covers corporate meeting and incentive travel planning.

### CRUISE & VACATION VIEWS
69175

60 E. 42nd St., Ste. 924
New York, NY 10165-0905
Telephone: (212) 867-7470
FAX: (212) 682-4437
Year Established: 1987
Pub. Frequency: bi-m.
Page Size: standard
Subscrip. Rate: $20/yr.
Materials: 01,02,05,06,09,17,28,30,32
Circulation: 35000
Circulation Type: controlled
**Owner(s):**
Orban Communications, Inc.
60 E. 42nd St., Ste. 924
New York, NY 10165-0905
Telephone: (212) 867-7470
Ownership %: 100
**Editorial:**
Michael Brown ..........................Editor

### FREQUENT FLYER
66782

1775 Broadway, 19th Fl.
New York, NY 10019
Telephone: (212) 237-3000
Year Established: 1980
Pub. Frequency: m.
Page Size: standard
Subscrip. Rate: $24/yr.
Circulation: 275,000
Circulation Type: paid
**Owner(s):**
Official Airline Guides, Inc.
1775 Broadway, 19th Fl.
New York, NY 10019
Telephone: (212) 237-3000
Ownership %: 100
**Management:**
Martin Deutsch ..........................Publisher
**Editorial:**
Joe Brancatelli ..........................Editor
**Desc.:** Provides travel tips for business people who must travel frequently.

### JAX FAX TRAVEL MARKETING MAGAZINE
25131

397 Post Rd.
Darien, CT 06820
Telephone: (203) 655-8746
FAX: (203) 655-6257
Mailing Address:
  P.O. Box 4013
  Darien, CT 06820
Year Established: 1973
Pub. Frequency: m.
Page Size: standard
Subscrip. Rate: $12/yr.
Materials: 01,02,05,09,10,32
Freelance Pay: negotiable
Circulation: 27,000
Circulation Type: controlled & paid
**Owner(s):**
Jet Airtransport Exchange, Inc., C.N. Cooke
397 Post Rd.
Darien, CT 06820
Telephone: (203) 655-8746
Ownership %: 100
**Management:**
Clifton N. Cooke ..................President
Jody Brennan ..................Vice President
Clifton N. Cooke ..................Publisher
Nancy Adcox ..................Business Manager
Laura Canestrini ..................Circulation Manager
Nancy Adcox ..................Operations Manager
Rhoda Cunningham ........Production Manager
**Editorial:**
Julie Barton ..........................Editor
Jody Brennan ..................Art Director
Donna Attra ..................Associate Editor
Randi White ..................Marketing Director
Kathy Belluzzi ..................Marketing Director
Gwen Marguerite ..................Marketing Director
**Desc.:** Covers airline news, profiles of ground operators, destination & transportation services. Displays over 3, 000 specific listings of inclusive tours and 'air only' scheduled and charter flights.
**Readers:** Retail travel agents (86%), tour operators, wholesalers, and the travel industry such as: airline executives and group organizers, tourist boards, travel wholesalers.

### MATURE GROUP TRAVELER
69431

100 Prospect St.
1st Fl.
Stamford, CT 06901-1640
Telephone: (203) 975-1416
FAX: (203) 975-7594
Year Established: 1991
Pub. Frequency: q.
Page Size: standard
Subscrip. Rate: $15/yr.
Materials: 09,15,21,28,32
Print Process: offset
Circulation: 12,130
Circulation Type: controlled
**Owner(s):**
Meetings Info-Resources, Inc.
100 Prospect St.
1st Fl.
Stamford, CT 06901
Telephone: (203) 975-1416
FAX: (203) 975-7594
Ownership %: 100
**Editorial:**
George Lowden ..........................Editor
Lori Defelice ..........................Advertising
**Desc.:** Covers travel services, destinations and other information of interest to tour leaders and others in senior group-travel market.
**Deadline:** story-30 days prior to pub. date; news-30 days; photo-30 days; ads-5th of mo. prior to pub. date

### MEXICO UPDATE
69178

5838 Edison Pl., Ste. 100
Carlsbad, CA 92008
Telephone: (619) 929-0707
FAX: (619) 929-0714
Year Established: 1992
Pub. Frequency: a.
Page Size: 8 3/8 x 1 7/8
Circulation: 40000
Circulation Type: controlled
**Owner(s):**
Travel Mexico Magazine Group
5838 Edison Pl., Ste. 100
Carlsbad, CA 92008
Telephone: (619) 929-0707
Ownership %: 100
**Desc.:** Covers Mexico travel issues for the US and Canadian travel industry.

### OAG DESKTOP FLIGHT GUIDE
25141

2000 Clearwater Dr.
Hinsdale, IL 60521
Telephone: (708) 574-6000
FAX: (708) 574-6565
Mailing Address:
  P.O. Box 51703
  Boulder, CO 80322
Year Established: 1964
Pub. Frequency: m.
Page Size: oversize
Subscrip. Rate: $346/yr.
Circulation: 41,000
Circulation Type: controlled & paid
**Owner(s):**
Official Airline Guides, Inc.
2000 Clearwater Dr.
Oak Brook, IL 60521
Telephone: (708) 574-6091
Ownership %: 100
**Management:**
Richard Nelson ..........................Publisher
**Desc.:** Reference guide to international direct and connecting air services for all scheduled airlines worldwide. Does not include air services within and between the U.S., Canada, Mexico and Caribbean.
**Readers:** Travel agents, international business travelers, and airlines.

### OFFICIAL RAILWAY GUIDE, NORTH AMERICAN TRAVEL EDITION
24613

424 W. 33rd St.
New York, NY 10001
Telephone: (212) 714-3100
FAX: (212) 695-5025
Year Established: 1868
Pub. Frequency: 6/yr.
Page Size: standard
Subscrip. Rate: $172/yr.
Circulation: 85000
Circulation Type: paid
**Owner(s):**
K-III Directory Corp.
424 W. 33rd St.
New York, NY 10001
Telephone: (212) 714-3100
Ownership %: 100
**Bureau(s):**
Int'l Thomson Transport Press
424 W. 33rd St.
New York, NY 10001
Telephone: (212) 714-3154
Contact: H. Alfred Solomon, Vice President
**Management:**
Alan Glass ..........................Publisher
**Editorial:**
Frank Coyle ..........................Editor
Alan Basis ..........................Advertising
**Readers:** Travel agents, corporate & other travel professionals, individual rail travelers.

**Materials Accepted/Included:** 01-Business news 02-By-line articles 03-Fashion news 04-Food news 05-Freelance copy 06-Letters to editor 07-Real estate news 08-Sports news 09-Travel news 10-Book rev. 11-Movie rev. 12-Music rev. 13-TV rev. 14-Theater rev. 15-Coming events 16-Obituaries 17-Question & answer 18-Social announcements 19-Artwork 20-Cartoons 21-Photos 22-TV listings 23-Audio rec. 24-Video rec. 25-Books 26-Films/film clips 27-Personnel news 28-Press releases 29-New product news/photos 30-Trade lit. 31-Contracts awarded 32-Display adv. 33-Classified adv.

4-383

## PHYSICIANS' TRAVEL & MEETING GUIDE

69181

105 Raider Blvd.
Belle Mead, NJ 08502
Telephone: (908) 281-3729
FAX: (908) 874-6096
Year Established: 1982
Pub. Frequency: m.
Page Size: standard
Subscrip. Rate: $65/yr.
Materials: 05,09,10,15,32,33
Circulation: 154,900
Circulation Type: controlled & paid
**Owner(s):**
Reed Elsevier Medical Publishers, USA
105 Raider Blvd.
Belle Mead, NJ 08502
Telephone: (908) 281-3729
Ownership %: 100
**Editorial:**
Bea Riemschneider .............Editor in Chief
Susann Tepperberg ...........Managing Editor
**Desc.:** Helps physicians plan their
attendance at medical meetings and
their personal and business travel.

## RELAX

69184

7500 Old Oak Blvd.
Cleveland, OH 44130
Telephone: (216) 826-2839
FAX: (216) 891-2726
Year Established: 1984
Pub. Frequency: m.
Subscrip. Rate: $60/yr.
Circulation: 115,174
Circulation Type: paid
**Owner(s):**
Advanstar Communications, Inc.
7500 Old Oak Blvd.
Cleveland, OH 44130
Telephone: (216) 826-2839
Ownership %: 100
**Editorial:**
Mary Kay Stray ..............................Editor

## TOUR & TRAVEL NEWS

65986

600 Community Dr.
Manhasset, NY 11030
Telephone: (516) 562-5000
FAX: (516) 562-5465
Year Established: 1985
Pub. Frequency: w.
Page Size: tabloid
Subscrip. Rate: $40/yr.
Circulation: 48,000
Circulation Type: controlled
**Owner(s):**
CMP Publications, Inc.
600 Community Dr.
Manhasset, NY 11030
Telephone: (516) 562-5000
Ownership %: 100
**Editorial:**
Linda Bull ..................................Editor
Jeff Barrington ..............Managing Editor
**Desc.:** Tour & Travel News, the newspaper
for the retail travel industry, delivers the
latest news and information of the
industry. Each issue is separated into
easy to locate departments and
destinations, with special features and
supplements through-out the year with a
focus on the role of travel retailers and
the many travel products they sell and
recommend.
**Readers:** Over 53,000 Readers, with a
pass-along of 220,000 travel agents,
tour operators, and wholesalers
specializing in retail travel.

## TRAVELAGE MIDAMERICA

25154

320 N. Michigan Ave., Ste. 601
Chicago, IL 60601
Telephone: (312) 346-4952
Year Established: 1975
Pub. Frequency: w.
Page Size: standard
Subscrip. Rate: $28/yr.
Freelance Pay: $2/in.
Circulation: 19,000
Circulation Type: controlled
**Owner(s):**
Official Airlines Guides, Inc.
Telephone: (708) 574-6000
Ownership %: 100
**Management:**
Martin B. Deutsch ...................Publisher
**Editorial:**
Martin B. Deutsch ......................Editor
Karen Goodwin ...............Managing Editor
**Desc.:** Directed to travel agency sales
counselors in 17 mid-American states
plus Ontario and Manitoba. News,
destination stories, features and
standing columns are all designed to aid
the sales counselor in his job of selling
travel. Unlike consumer
travel publications, this magazine
includes details (prices, commissions,
who the tour operator is, what the
facilities are like, etc.) rather than mood
travel features. Departments Include:
Seminars For Travel Agents, Changing
Faces (Personnel Shifts), Agencies and
Tourist Offices Changing Addresses.
Phone Numbers, Adding WATS Lines,
Industry News, Marketing Features,
Destination Updates, Hotel News and
New Product Announcements.
**Readers:** Travel agency sales counselors
in 19 mid-American states, Ontario &
Manitoba.

## TRAVEL AGENT

25149

801 Second Ave.
New York, NY 10017
Telephone: (212) 370-5050
FAX: (212) 370-4491
Year Established: 1933
Pub. Frequency: w.
Page Size: standard
Subscrip. Rate: $79/yr. US.; $149/yr.
foreign
Freelance Pay: varies
Circulation: 52,000
Circulation Type: paid
**Owner(s):**
Universal Media, Inc.
801 2nd Ave.
New York, NY 10017
Telephone: (212) 370-5050
Ownership %: 100
**Bureau(s):**
Washington Bureau
529 14th St., N.W.
Washington, DC 20045
Telephone: (202) 393-6280
Contact: Roland Leiser, Bureau Chief

Florida Bureau
6100 Hollywood Blvd.
Hollywood, FL 33024
Telephone: (305) 966-2400
Contact: Lene Stackel, Editor
**Management:**
Richard P. Friese ....................Publisher
Mark Beaven ...............Business Manager
Yvette Walker ............Circulation Manager
**Editorial:**
Eric Friedheim ...............Editor in Chief
Mikki Dorsey ...........................Editor
David Moseder ..............Managing Editor
John Ballantyne ..........Associate Publisher
Marilyn Hiris ...........Production Director

**Desc.:** Covers all phases of the travel
industry; travel agents, transportation
companies, government, state, and local
tourist information and promotion
bureaus, hotels, hotel representatives,
sightseeing companies and attractions,
tour operators. Publishes news, features,
statistical data, photographs, Business
Travel Report.
**Readers:** Travel agents; tour operators, air
and shiplines, railroads, government
and local tourist offices, sales and
executive personnel, hoteliers, hotel
representatives, tourist information and
agencies interested in travel.

## TRAVELAGE WEST

25156

49 Stevenson, No. 460
San Francisco, CA 94105
Telephone: (415) 905-1155
FAX: (415) 905-1145
Year Established: 1969
Pub. Frequency: w.
Page Size: standard
Subscrip. Rate: free to qualified readers;
$20/yr. others
Materials: 09,28,32,33
Freelance Pay: $4/col. in.
Circulation: 32,000
Circulation Type: controlled
**Owner(s):**
Reed Travel Group
500 Plaza Dr.
Secaucus, NJ 07096
Telephone: (201) 902-2000
Ownership %: 100
**Bureau(s):**
Travel Age Magazines
2999 Overland Ave.
Los Angeles, CA 90064
Telephone: (310) 204-1184
Contact: Mimi Kmet, Bureau Chief

Travel Management Daily
500 Plaza Dr.
Secaucus, NJ 07096
Telephone: (201) 902-1775
Contact: Steve Ballinger, Managing Editor
**Management:**
Bill Scott .........................Vice President
Martin Deutsch (NYC) ...............Publisher
Katie Tom ...............Circulation Manager
Ellen Walker .........Classified Adv. Manager
**Editorial:**
Robert Carlsen ...............Managing Editor
Marilyn Doswell .....................Advertising
Ginny Graves .................Associate Editor
Doug Oakley .................Associate Editor
Lyn Hikida ......................Associate Editor
Lori Tenny ......................Associate Editor
Richard Neal ...............Associate Publisher
**Desc.:** Covers the sales and business side
of the travel agency business.
Circulation is west of the Rocky
Mountains. Covers any news which will
help the travel agency employee work or
sell more effectively. Much information
from publicity releases but heavily
edited. Always need specifics: prices,
times, contact addresses for the
product. Departments include: Discount
Counter (reduced-rate travel for agents);
Destination Report (staff-written articles
on spots around the West and the
world); Sales Rack (new films,
brochures, guides, sales aids), Business
Travel Report, The Automated Agent.
**Readers:** Sales employees of every travel
agency, Colorado West in U.S.; in
Canada; British Columbia, Alberta and
Saskatchewan.

## TRAVEL TRADE

25151

15 W. 44th St.
6th Fl.
New York, NY 10036
Telephone: (212) 883-1110
FAX: (212) 730-7137
Year Established: 1929
Pub. Frequency: w.
Page Size: PG: 10 1/2 x 15; COL: 1 5/8;
PHOTO: Yes; MAT: No;
Subscrip. Rate: $10/yr.
Circulation: 42,500
Circulation Type: paid
**Owner(s):**
Travel Trade Publications, Inc.
15 W. 44th St.
6th Fl.
New York, NY 10036
Telephone: (212) 883-1110
Ownership %: 100
**Bureau(s):**
Travel Trade
3611 39th St. N.W., E 329
Washington, DC 20016
Telephone: (202) 363-7314
Contact: Don Knoles
**Management:**
Joel M. Abels .......................Publisher
**Editorial:**
Patricia Collins ...............Executive Editor
Joel M. Abels ..........................Editor
David Spinelli .................Managing Editor
**Desc.:** Editorial news and feature coverage
of the travel industry for the travel trade.
**Readers:** Primarily travel agents, tour
operators and foreign government tourist
office personnel.

## TRAVEL WEEKLY

25152

500 Plaza Dr.
Secaucus, NJ 07094
Telephone: (201) 902-1500
Year Established: 1958
Pub. Frequency: s-w.
Page Size: tabloid
Subscrip. Rate: $26/yr.; travel agent
$19.50/yr.
Circulation: 50,000
Circulation Type: paid
**Owner(s):**
Reed Travel Group
500 Plaza Dr.
Secaucus, NJ 07094
Telephone: (201) 902-1500
Ownership %: 100
**Management:**
William D. Scott II ....................Publisher
**Editorial:**
Alan Fredericks ..........................Editor
**Readers:** Travel retailers & wholesalers,
corporate travel department, travel
promotion officials.

## VACATION INDUSTRY REVIEW

69185

6262 Sunset Dr., Penthouse 1
S. Miami, FL 33143
Telephone: (305) 666-1861
FAX: (305) 665-2546
Year Established: 1984
Pub. Frequency: q.
Page Size: 8 1/2 x 11
Subscrip. Rate: free
Materials: 01,02,05,06,07,09,10,15,21,27,
28,29,30,32
Freelance Pay: $.20/wd.; negotiable
Print Process: offset
Circulation: 12000
Circulation Type: controlled & free
**Owner(s):**
Worldex Corp.
626 Sunset Dr., Penthouse 1
S. Miami, FL 33143
Telephone: (305) 666-1861
Ownership %: 100

**Materials Accepted/Included:** 01-Business news 02-By-line articles 03-Fashion news 04-Food news 05-Freelance copy 06-Letters to editor 07-Real estate news 08-Sports news 09-Travel news 10-Book rev. 11-Movie rev. 12-Music rev. 13-TV rev. 14-Theater rev. 15-Coming events 16-Obituaries 17-Question & answer 18-Social announcements 19-Artwork 20-Cartoons 21-Photos 22-TV listings 23-Audio rec. 24-Video rec. 25-Books 26-Films/film clips 27-Personnel news 28-Press releases 29-New product news/photos 30-Trade lit. 31-Contracts awarded 32-Display adv. 33-Classified adv.

**Editorial:**
George Leposky ..............................Editor
Cheryl Clarke ........................Advertising
**Desc.:** Covers development, finance, marketing and management of timeshare resorts and mixed-use projects such as hotels, resorts and second- home communities with a vacation-ownership component.
**Readers:** People who develop, market, sell, finance, and manage timeshare resorts and other vacation-ownership properties, and suppliers to this industry.
**Deadline:** story-1st of 2nd mo. of each calendar quarter; news-1st of 2nd mo.; photo-1st of 2nd mo.; ads-15th of 2nd mo.

## Group 268-Trucks & Trucking

58678

### ALLEGHENY TRUCKER
7355 N. Woodland Dr.
Indianapolis, IN 46278
Telephone: (317) 297-5500
Mailing Address:
P.O. Box 603
Indianapolis, IN 46206
Year Established: 1978
Pub. Frequency: m.
Page Size: standard
Subscrip. Rate: $18/yr.
Circulation: 39,405
Circulation Type: paid
**Owner(s):**
Allied Publications
P.O. Box 603
Indianapolis, IN 46206
Telephone: (317) 297-5500
Ownership %: 100
**Bureau(s):**
Allied Publications
7355 N. Woodland Dr.
Indianapolis, IN 46278
Telephone: (317) 297-5500
Contact: Leslie Rogers, Office Manager
**Management:**
Jim Bellin ..................................Manager
**Desc.:** Contains display & trailer, classified advertising for new & used trucks, equipment, supplies, financing, and other services related to the trucking industry. Provides a medium for advertisers to market their products and services to a specific and narrowly defined readership.
**Readers:** Owner/operators and fleet owners of over 26000 GVW trucks.

25660

### AMCA TRUCKING REPORT
501 Woodlane St., Ste. 107
Little Rock, AR 72201
Telephone: (501) 372-3462
FAX: (501) 376-1810
Year Established: 1992
Pub. Frequency: bi-m.
Page Size: standard
Subscrip. Rate: free to members
Materials: 21,32,33
Print Process: offset
Circulation: 300
Circulation Type: controlled & free
**Owner(s):**
Arkansas Motor Carriers Association, Inc.
P.O. Box 2798
Little Rock, AR 72203
Telephone: (501) 372-3462
FAX: (501) 376-1810
Ownership %: 100
**Editorial:**
Shelly Hartnedy ..............................Editor
**Desc.:** Incorporates items and articles of interest for members of the trucking. Stress is placed on safety, regulatory compliance, and trucking issues.

**Readers:** Members of trucking and bus industry.

58802

### AMERICAN MOTOR CARRIER DIRECTORY
424 W. 33rd St.
New York, NY 10001
Telephone: (212) 714-3100
FAX: (212) 695-5025
Year Established: 1943
Pub. Frequency: s-a.
Page Size: standard
Subscrip. Rate: $286/yr.
Circulation: 5,000
Circulation Type: paid
**Owner(s):**
K-III Directory Corp.
424 W. 33rd St.
New York, NY 10001
Telephone: (212) 714-3100
Ownership %: 100
**Editorial:**
Diane Oatis ..................................Editor
**Desc.:** Single source reference to LTL motor freight routings between all points in North America.
**Readers:** Purchasers/users of LTL general commodity motor freight.

25166

### AMERICAN TRUCKER (BUCKEYE EDITION)
7355 N. Woodland Dr.
Indianapolis, IN 46278
Telephone: (317) 297-5500
FAX: (317) 299-1356
Mailing Address:
P.O. Box 603
Indianapolis, IN 46206
Year Established: 1976
Pub. Frequency: m.
Page Size: standard
Subscrip. Rate: $18/yr.
Circulation: 26,000
Circulation Type: controlled & paid
**Owner(s):**
Southam Business Communications
P.O. Box 603
Indianapolis, IN 46206
Telephone: (317) 297-5500
Ownership %: 100
**Management:**
Jim Bellin ..................................President
Leslie Rogers ....................Office Manager
**Desc.:** Contains display and classifed advertising for new and used trucks, trailers, equipment, supplies, financing, and other services related to the trucking industry. A publication providing a medium for advertisers to market their products and services to a specific and narrowly defined readership.
**Readers:** Owner/operators and fleet owners of over 26000 GVW trucks.

58682

### BADGER TRUCKER
7355 N. Woodland Dr.
Indianapolis, IN 46278
Telephone: (317) 297-5500
Mailing Address:
P.O. Box 603
Indianapolis, IN 46206
Year Established: 1977
Pub. Frequency: m.
Page Size: standard
Subscrip. Rate: $18/yr.
Circulation: 20,000
**Owner(s):**
Allied Publications
P.O. Box 603
Indianapolis, IN 46206
Telephone: (317) 297-5500
Ownership %: 100
**Management:**
Jim Bellin ..................................Manager

Leslie Rogers ....................Office Manager
**Desc.:** Contains display, trailers, & classified advertising for new & used trucks, equipment, supplies, financing, and other services related to the trucking industry. A publication providing a medium for advertisers to market their products & services to a specific & narrowly defined readership.
**Readers:** Owner/operators and fleet owners of over 26,000 GVW trucks.

58681

### CALIFORNIA TRUCKER
7355 N. Woodland Dr.
Indianapolis, IN 46278
Telephone: (317) 297-5500
Mailing Address:
P.O. Box 603
Indianapolis, IN 46206
Year Established: 1979
Pub. Frequency: m.
Page Size: standard
Subscrip. Rate: $18/yr.
Circulation: 25,000
**Owner(s):**
Allied Publications
P.O. Box 603
Indianapolis, IN 46206
Telephone: (317) 297-5500
Ownership %: 100
**Management:**
Jim Bellin ..................................Manager
**Desc.:** Contains display and trailers, classified advertising for new and used trucks, equipment, supplies, financing and other services related to the trucking industry. A publication providing a medium for advertisers to market their products and services to a specific and narrowly defined readership.
**Readers:** Merchandising guides to owner/operators and fleet owners of over 26,000 GVW trucks.

58784

### CASCADE TRUCKER
7355 N. Woodland Dr.
Indianapolis, IN 46278
Telephone: (317) 297-5500
Mailing Address:
P.O. Box 603
Indianapolis, IN 46206
Year Established: 1980
Pub. Frequency: m.
Page Size: standard
Subscrip. Rate: $18/yr.
Circulation: 20,000
**Owner(s):**
Allied Publications
P.O. Box 603
Indianapolis, IN 46206
Telephone: (317) 297-5500
Ownership %: 100
**Management:**
Jim Bellin ..................................Manager
**Desc.:** Contains displays and trailers, classified advertising for new and used trucks, equipment, supplies, financing and other services related to the trucking industry. A publication providing a medium for advertisers to market their products and services to a specific and narrowly defined readership.
**Readers:** Owner/operators and fleet owners of over 26000 GVW trucks.

58783

### CENTRAL STATES TRUCKER
7355 N. Woodland Dr.
Indianapolis, IN 46278
Telephone: (317) 297-5500
Mailing Address:
P.O. Box 603
Indianapolis, IN 46206
Year Established: 1980
Pub. Frequency: m.

Page Size: standard
Subscrip. Rate: $18/yr.
Circulation: 20,000
**Owner(s):**
Allied Publications
P.O. Box 603
Indianapolis, IN 46206
Telephone: (317) 297-5500
Ownership %: 100
**Management:**
Jim Bellin ..................................Manager
**Desc.:** Contains displays and trailers, classified advertising for new and used trucks, equipment, supplies, financing and other services related to the trucking industry. A publication providing a medium for advertisers to market their products and services to a specific and narrowly defined readership.
**Readers:** Owners/operators and fleet owners of over 26000 GVW trucks.

25167

### COMMERCIAL CARRIER JOURNAL
Chilton Way
Radnor, PA 19089
Telephone: (610) 964-4511
FAX: (610) 964-4512
Year Established: 1911
Pub. Frequency: m.
Page Size: standard
Subscrip. Rate: $45/yr.
Materials: 01,06,27,28,29,30,31,32,33
Freelance Pay: negotiable
Print Process: web offset
Circulation: 85,520
Circulation Type: controlled
**Owner(s):**
Chilton Co. (Div. of ABC Publishing)
Chilton Way
Radnor, PA 19087
Telephone: (215) 964-4000
Ownership %: 100
**Management:**
Sarah Frankson ....................Vice President
Gregory S. Sheremet ................Publisher
Holly Wange ..............Business Manager
Sofia Pables ..............Circulation Manager
Liam Collins ........Classified Adv. Manager
Sue Corialos ..............Production Manager
Haig Dagdigian ..............Sales Manager
**Editorial:**
Gerald Standley ..............Editor in Chief
Parry Desmond ..............Executive Editor
Carole Smith ..............Managing Editor
Michael Trinsey ..............Art Director
Carol Hope Heavens ..........Associate Editor
Eileen Cleaves ..............Products Editor
Richard Cross ..............Technical Editor
Paul Richards ..............Technical Editor
**Desc.:** News, features, columns and technical articles slanted to truck and bus fleet management, maintenance, safety and operation, and purchasing. Presents personnel changes, new products and literature, etc.
**Readers:** Professional fleet managers

24378

### DES (DIESEL EQUIPMENT SUPERINTENDENT)
50 Day St.
Norwalk, CT 06854
Telephone: (203) 853-6015
Mailing Address:
P.O. Box 5550
Norwalk, CT 06856
Year Established: 1923
Pub. Frequency: m.
Page Size: standard
Subscrip. Rate: $35/yr.
Circulation: 25,000
Circulation Type: controlled

**Materials Accepted/Included:** 01-Business news 02-By-line articles 03-Fashion news 04-Food news 05-Freelance copy 06-Letters to editor 07-Real estate news 08-Sports news 09-Travel news 10-Book rev. 11-Movie rev. 12-Music rev. 13-TV rev. 14-Theater rev. 15-Coming events 16-Obituaries 17-Question & answer 18-Social announcements 19-Artwork 20-Cartoons 21-Photos 22-TV listings 23-Audio rec. 24-Video rec. 25-Books 26-Films/film clips 27-Personnel news 28-Press releases 29-New product news/photos 30-Trade lit. 31-Contracts awarded 32-Display adv. 33-Classified adv.

4-385

**Owner(s):**
Diesel Publications, Inc.
P.O. Box 5550
Norwalk, CT 06856
Telephone: (203) 853-6015
Ownership %: 100
**Management:**
James E. Jones .........................Publisher
**Editorial:**
Seth Skydel .......................Executive Editor
James E. Jones ...............................Editor
Philip Rumba .....................Managing Editor
Peter Reid ........................Assistant Editor
**Desc.:** Articles cover maintenance,
utilization and design of diesel trucks
and truck trailers and related vehicles.
Carries trade news, new products and
literature, industry and company news.
Departments include: News Section,
Monthly Feature (profile of outstanding
equipment executive), New Products,
New Literature, Maintenance Meeting
(covers activities of maintenance
associations).
**Readers:** Truck equipment executives,
manufacturers, engine sales
representatives, distributors, and
dealers.

**FLEET EQUIPMENT**    25170
134 W. Slade St.
Palatine, IL 60067-5031
Telephone: (708) 359-6100
Year Established: 1974
Pub. Frequency: m.
Page Size: standard
Subscrip. Rate: $82/yr.
Materials: 01,02,27,28,29,30,32,33,34
Freelance Pay: negotiable
Print Process: offset
Circulation: 65,000
Circulation Type: controlled
**Owner(s):**
Maple Publishing
134 W. Slade St.
Palatine, IL 60067
Telephone: (708) 359-6100
Ownership %: 100
**Management:**
Robert Dorn .............................President
Tom Gelinas .....................Vice President
Robert Dorn .............................Publisher
Pat Hopps .................Production Manager
**Editorial:**
Carol Birkland ...................Senior Editor
Tom Gelinas ...............................Editor
Joe Bowlby ..........................Art Director
Paula Golubski ................Associate Editor
Bob Deierlein ...................Research Editor
**Desc.:** Feature length covering
specification purchase, & maintenance
of the equipment used in the heavy
truck & bus industry. News, products, &
equipment covered in departments. Four
color format used in features.
Departments include: News, New
Products, New Equipment, Literature.

**FLEET OWNER**    25171
707 Westchester Ave., Ste. 101
White Plains, NY 10604-3102
Telephone: (914) 949-8500
FAX: (914) 287-6752
Year Established: 1928
Pub. Frequency: m.
Page Size: standard
Subscrip. Rate: $40/yr. US; $50/yr.
Canada; $70/yr. elsewhere
Materials: 01,06,15,19,21,27,28,29,30,32,33
Print Process: offset
Circulation: 100,000
Circulation Type: controlled

**Owner(s):**
Intertec Publishing Corp.
707 Westchester Ave., Ste. 101
White Plains, NY 10604-3102
Telephone: (914) 949-8500
FAX: (914) 287-6752
Ownership %: 100
**Management:**
Paul B. Kisseberth ....................Publisher
**Editorial:**
Jim Miele ...........................Senior Editor
Jack Dwyer ........................Senior Editor
Dave Cullen .......................Senior Editor
Stewart Siegel ...................Senior Editor
Thomas Duncan ...........................Editor
Marilyn Wilson .................Managing Editor
Peggy Navarre ....................Art Director
Daniel Zeis .............Associate Art Director
Bill Cassidy ...........................News Editor
John Dwyer, Jr. .........Special Projects Editor
Robert Saxton .................................Sports
**Desc.:** Carries articles on fleet operation,
industry problems, personnel problems,
maintenance, government regulations,
as well as industry news and new
products.
**Readers:** Top executives in trucking
companies and private fleets.
**Deadline:** story-1st of mo. prior to pub.
date; news-1st of mo. prior; photo-1st of
mo. prior; ads-5th of mo. prior

**FLORIDA TRUCK NEWS**    25173
350 E. College Ave.
Tallahassee, FL 32301
Telephone: (904) 222-9900
FAX: (904) 222-9363
Year Established: 1936
Pub. Frequency: m.
Page Size: standard
Subscrip. Rate: $14/yr. plus 7% sales tax
Materials: 01,02,10,15,27,29,32,33
Print Process: offset
Circulation: 2,300
Circulation Type: controlled
**Owner(s):**
Florida Trucking Association, Inc.
350 E. College Ave.
Tallahassee, FL 32301
Telephone: (904) 222-9900
FAX: (904) 222-9363
Ownership %: 100
**Management:**
A.E. Pooser ..............Advertising Manager
Bonnie White ...............Circulation Manager
**Editorial:**
Tom B. Webb, Jr. ...........................Editor
Kathy S. Barber ...............Managing Editor
**Desc.:** This is a trucking industry related
publication covering state and federal
legislation; safety events and
information; ICC news from other states;
new product information and personnel
and industry briefs.
**Readers:** Trucking & industry-related
executives and management.
**Deadline:** story-1st of mo. prior to pub.
date; news-1st of mo. prior; photo-1st of
mo. prior; ads-1st of mo. prior

**GO WEST**    25174
11344 Coloma Rd., Ste. 445
Gold River, CA 95670
Telephone: (916) 852-5700
FAX: (916) 852-7705
Year Established: 1941
Pub. Frequency: m.
Page Size: standard
Subscrip. Rate: $30/yr.
Materials: 01,02,05,06,15,28,29,32,33
Freelance Pay: $100-$500
Print Process: web offset
Circulation: 50,000
Circulation Type: controlled

**Owner(s):**
Motor Transport Publishers, Inc.
11344 Coloma Rd., Ste. 445
Gold River, CA 95670
Telephone: (916) 852-5700
Ownership %: 100
**Management:**
Tom Schumacher .......................Publisher
Marc Associates ...............Circulation Manager
**Editorial:**
Bill Fitzgerald ......................Editor in Chief
Jim Beach .......................................Editor
Laura Ulach ...........................Art Director
Steve Traut .......................Associate Editor
Bob Titus .....................Associate Publisher
Carole Sabo ................Production Director
**Desc.:** Serves individuals, companies, or
other entities who are involved in the
operation of diesel powered trucks,
truck-tractors, tractor-trailer
combinations, buses or off-road
equipment throughout the western,
southwestern and central US. As the
manager's for Trucking Management,
GO's editorial purpose is to help truck
operators whether they are responsible
for one truck or a thousand, make their
investment in truck transportation more
profitable. Each issue has important
information about regulatory changes,
new equipment and services,
maintenance management, safety, news
of western trucking, tax information, and
outlook for the industry. The annual GO
Official Update of Highway Vehicle Size
& Weight Limits is an industry standard.
Each year, GO Magazine is the official
magazine of the International Trucking
Show. Feature articles are written to
explore new avenues to increase
efficiency in truck transportation.
**Readers:** Trucking company owners,
managers, operators, lessors, corporate
officers, maintenance and operations
personnel.
**Deadline:** story-45 days prior to pub. date;
news-45 days prior; photo-45 days prior;
ads-30 days prior

**HEAVY DUTY TRUCKING**    25177
38 Executive Pk., Ste. 300
Irvine, CA 92714
Telephone: (714) 261-1636
FAX: (714) 261-2904
Year Established: 1968
Pub. Frequency: m.
Page Size: standard
Subscrip. Rate: $4/issue; $45/yr.
Materials: 01,05,06,15,24,28,29,30,32,33
Print Process: web offset
Circulation: 100,000
Circulation Type: controlled
**Owner(s):**
HIC Corp.
38 Executive Pk., Ste. 300
Irvine, CA 92714
Telephone: (714) 261-1636
**Management:**
Kent Powell .............................President
George Jacovides .......................Publisher
**Editorial:**
Andrew Ryder .................................Editor
Deborah Whistler ...............Managing Editor
**Desc.:** Primarily staff-written articles cover
new equipment and design, safety, and
cost-cutting in fleet operation.
**Readers:** Medium and heavy truck fleets
**Deadline:** story-1st of mo. prior to pub.
date

**ILLINOIS TRUCKER**    58785
7355 N. Woodland Dr.
Indianapolis, IN 46278
Telephone: (317) 297-5500
FAX: (317) 299-1356
Mailing Address:
   P.O. Box 603
   Indianapolis, IN 46206-0603
Year Established: 1977
Pub. Frequency: m.
Page Size: standard
Subscrip. Rate: $18/yr.
Circulation: 20,000
**Owner(s):**
Allied Publications
P.O. Box 603
Indianapolis, IN 46206-0603
Telephone: (317) 297-5500
Ownership %: 100
**Management:**
Jim Bellin ...................................Manager
**Desc.:** Contains display and trailers, and
classified advertising for new and used
trucks, equipment, supplies, financing
and other services related to the
trucking industry. A publication providing
a medium for advertisers to market their
products and services to a specific and
narrowly defined readership.
**Readers:** Owners/operators and fleet
owners of over 26000 GVW trucks.

**ILLINOIS TRUCK NEWS**    25178
2000 Fifth Ave.
River Grove, IL 60171
Telephone: (708) 452-3500
FAX: (708) 452-3508
Year Established: 1954
Pub. Frequency: q.
Subscrip. Rate: free
Circulation: 5,500
Circulation Type: free
**Owner(s):**
Illinois Transportation Assns.
2000 Fifth Ave.
River Grove, IL 60171
Telephone: (708) 452-3500
Ownership %: 100
**Editorial:**
Kin Cherry ......................................Editor
**Desc.:** Trucking industry management,
allied industry & legislators.
**Readers:** Trucking Co.'s, Allied Industries,
Senator's, Mayor's, Libraries.

**INDIANA TRUCKER**    58677
7355 N. Woodland Dr.
Indianapolis, IN 46278
Telephone: (317) 297-5500
Mailing Address:
   P.O. Box 603
   Indianapolis, IN 46206
Year Established: 1975
Pub. Frequency: m.
Page Size: standard
Subscrip. Rate: $18/yr.
Circulation: 20,000
**Owner(s):**
Allied Publications
P.O. Box 603
Indianapolis, IN 46206
Telephone: (317) 297-5500
Ownership %: 100
**Management:**
Jim Bellin ...................................Manager
**Desc.:** Contains display and trailers, and
classified advertising for new and used
trucks, equipment, supplies, financing
and other services related to the
trucking industry. A publication providing
a medium for advertisers to market their
products and services to a specific and
narrowly defined readership.

**Materials Accepted/Included:** 01-Business news 02-By-line articles 03-Fashion news 04-Food news 05-Freelance copy 06-Letters to editor 07-Real estate news 08-Sports news 09-Travel news 10-Book rev. 11-Movie rev. 12-Music rev. 13-TV rev. 14-Theater rev. 15-Coming events 16-Obituaries 17-Question & answer 18-Social announcements 19-Artwork 20-Cartoons 21-Photos 22-TV listings 23-Audio rec. 24-Video rec. 25-Books 26-Films/film clips 27-Personnel news 28-Press releases 29-New product news/photos 30-Trade lit. 31-Contracts awarded 32-Display adv. 33-Classified adv.

4-386

## IOWA TRUCKING LIFELINER
25181

600 E. Ct.
Des Moines, IA 50309
Telephone: (515) 244-5193
Year Established: 1943
Pub. Frequency: bi-m.
Page Size: standard
Subscrip. Rate: $4/yr.
Circulation: 3,500
Circulation Type: controlled & paid
**Owner(s):**
Iowa Motor Truck Association
600 E. Ct., Ste. D
Des Moines, IA 50309
Ownership %: 100
**Management:**
Scott Weisor .........................................Publisher
**Editorial:**
Brenda Neville .......................................Editor
**Desc.:** Use news releases of interest to
motor carriers on a national level and
especially news from around the state of
Iowa. Official publication of the Iowa
Motor Truck Association.
**Readers:** Iowa Motor Truck Association
members, for hire, allied industries,
private carriers & managers.

## KEYSTONE/JERSEY TRUCK EXCHANGE
58679

7355 N. Woodland Dr.
Indianapolis, IN 46278
Telephone: (317) 297-5500
Mailing Address:
P.O. Box 603
Indianapolis, IN 46206
Year Established: 1980
Pub. Frequency: m.
Page Size: standard
Subscrip. Rate: $18/yr.
Circulation: 21,000
**Owner(s):**
Allied Publications
P.O. Box 603
Indianapolis, IN 46206
Telephone: (317) 297-5500
**Management:**
Jim Bellin .........................................Manager
**Desc.:** Contains display & classified
advertising for new & used trucks &
trailers, equipment, supplies, financing
and other services related to the
trucking industry. A publication providing
a medium for advertisers to market their
products and services to a specific and
narrowly defined readership.

## LAND-LINE
22347

311 R.D. Mize Rd.
Grain Valley, MO 64029
Telephone: (816) 229-5791
FAX: (816) 229-0518
Year Established: 1975
Pub. Frequency: bi-m.
Page Size: standard
Subscrip. Rate: $14/yr.; $24/2 yrs.
Materials: 01,02,05,06,19,20,21,32,33
Freelance Pay: negotiable
Circulation: 82,000
Circulation Type: controlled
**Owner(s):**
Owner-Operator Ind. Drivers Assn., Inc.
311 R.D. Mize Rd.
Grain Valley, MO 64029
Telephone: (816) 229-5791
Ownership %: 100
**Management:**
Todd Spencer ...................................Publisher
Roseanne Patow ..............Circulation Manager
**Editorial:**
Todd Spencer .....................................Editor
Sandi Laxson ...........................Managing Editor
Ray Gurney ..................................Advertising

Jim Johnston ...............................Columnist
Anne Cartegena ...........................Columnist
**Desc.:** Strives to keep the owner-0perator
current on the industry and legislation as
it affects his business and to keep the
industry and government posted on how
the owner-operator views happenings
from their side of the business. Articles
must be current and to the point. By-line
credits will be given. Publicity articles, as
such, are not accepted. New products
articles and pictures are welcomed,
subject to editing. Acceptance of
advertising material is at the discretion
of the editor. Editorial encompasses
maintenance, new product reviews,
money management.
**Readers:** Owners & operators of heavy
trucks involved in interstate
transportation & drivers of
such equipment.
**Deadline:** story-11th of month; news-11th
of month; photo-13th of month; ads-5th
of the month

## LIFTING & TRANSPORTATION INTERNATIONAL
25206

9607 Gayton Rd., Ste. 201
Richmond, VA 23233
Telephone: (804) 741-6704
FAX: (804) 750-2399
Year Established: 1953
Pub. Frequency: 10/yr.
Page Size: standard
Subscrip. Rate: $65/yr.
Materials: 01,02,05,15,16,21,23,24,25,26,
27,28,29,30,31,32,33
Circulation: 18,036
Circulation Type: controlled
**Owner(s):**
Leo Douglas, Inc.
9607 Gayton Rd., Ste. 201
Richmond, VA 23233
Telephone: (804) 750-2399
Ownership %: 100
**Management:**
Carolyn Ward ...................Advertising Manager
Dorothy Edgar ..................Production Manager
**Editorial:**
Carole Sewell .......................................Editor
**Desc.:** Magazine carries stories and
information of interest to heavy
specialized carriers, rigging contractors,
crane contractors and heavy
construction contractors.
**Readers:** Owners and executive personnel
segments of rigging and heavy hauling
industry.

## MAINE MOTOR TRANSPORT NEWS
25135

524 Western Ave.
Augusta, ME 04330
Telephone: (207) 623-4128
Year Established: 1946
Pub. Frequency: 10/yr.
Page Size: 4 color photos/art
Subscrip. Rate: $25/yr. memeber; $35/yr.
non-member
Materials: 06,15,21,27,30,32,33
Print Process: offset
Circulation: 4,700
Circulation Type: controlled
**Owner(s):**
Maine Motor Transport Association
524 Western Ave.
Augusta, ME 04330
Telephone: (207) 623-4128
Ownership %: 100
**Management:**
Mark Hutchins .....................................President
Gayle Baber ....................Advertising Manager
**Editorial:**
Richard C. Jones .................Executive Editor

**Desc.:** A spokesman of Maine industry.
Contains features from the president's
desk and articles on trucking safety, and
legislation affecting the trucking industry.
Wide use of photos of the trucking
industry.
**Readers:** Professionals, legislators,
industrial executives.
**Deadline:** story-10th

## MICHIGAN TRUCK EXCHANGE
66102

7355 N. Woodland Dr.
Indianapolis, IN 46278
Telephone: (317) 297-5500
Mailing Address:
P.O. Box 603
Indianapolis, IN 46206
Year Established: 1989
Pub. Frequency: s-m.
Page Size: standard
Subscrip. Rate: $18/yr.
Circulation: 2,500
Circulation Type: controlled & paid
**Owner(s):**
Allied Publications
P.O. Box 603
Indianapolis, IN 46206
Telephone: (317) 297-5500
Ownership %: 100
**Management:**
Jim Bellin ......................Sales Manager
**Desc.:** Contains display and classified
advertising for new and used trucks,
trailers, equipment, supplies, financing
and other services related to the
trucking industry. A publication providing
a medium for advertisers to market their
products and services to a specific and
narrowly defined readership.
**Readers:** Owner/operators and fleet
owners of over 26,000 GVW trucks.

## MID-AMERICA TRANSPORTER, THE
25098

2900 S. Topeka Blvd.
Topeka, KS 66611
Telephone: (913) 267-1641
Mailing Address:
P.O. Box 1673
Topeka, KS 66601-1673
Year Established: 1946
Pub. Frequency: m.
Page Size: standard
Subscrip. Rate: $12/yr.
Materials: 01,06,16,27,28,29,30,32,33
Print Process: offset
Circulation: 4,100
Circulation Type: controlled & paid
**Owner(s):**
The Kansas Motor Carriers Assoc.
2900 S. Topeka
P.O. Box 1673
Topeka, KS 66601-1673
Telephone: (913) 267-1641
Ownership %: 100
**Management:**
Carl Hill ...........................Advertising Manager
**Editorial:**
Carl Hill .............................................Editor
Darcy Wall ...........................Associate Editor
**Desc.:** News stories concern personalities
of the industry, management changes,
new equipment developments,
application of new business procedures
and related subjects. The magazine
carries reports on legislative matters,
safety, regulatory directives and profiles
of government agencies and individuals
concerned with motor carrier operations.
Departments include: Editorial Notes,
LTL (short news items).

**Readers:** Carriers operating motor truck
vehicles in Kansas and Missouri. The
circulation list is kept up-to-date.
Contract carrier operating in or through
the mid-America region.
**Deadline:** story-15th of mo. prior to pub.
date; ads-10th of mo. prior to pub. date

## MILK & LIQUID FOOD TRANSPORTER
25367

N80 W12878 Fond du Lac Ave.
Menomonee Falls, WI 53051
Telephone: (414) 255-0108
Mailing Address:
P.O. Box 878
Menomonee Falls, WI 53052-0878
Year Established: 1960
Pub. Frequency: m.
Page Size: standard
Subscrip. Rate: $12/yr.
Circulation: 3,000
Circulation Type: controlled
**Owner(s):**
Karl F. Ohm, Sr., The Brady Company
P.O. Box 878
Menomonee Falls, WI 53052-0878
Ownership %: 100
**Management:**
Karl F. Ohm, III ..................................Publisher
Linda Mittag ....................Business Manager
**Editorial:**
Linda Mittag .......................................Editor
**Desc.:** Monthly magazine for owners,
operators, trucking firms and
management people involved in
transporting bulk milk and other liquid
food products in the United States and
Canada. We do interpretative reporting
and feature stories on timely issues
affecting the business of transporting
milk and other liquid food products such
as vegetable oils, corn sweeteners,
liquid sugars and apple juice. Regular
columns include: New Products,
Upcoming Meetings, New Publications,
and People.
**Readers:** Farm-to-plant and plant-to-plant
milk haulers, major intrastate and
interstate liquid food transporters,
transportation managers and top
management personnel of dairy plants,
dairy cooperatives, cheese factories, and
liquid food manufacturing firms, food-
grade tank manufacturers and repair
firms.

## MINNESOTA-DAKOTA TRUCK MERCHANDISER
65988

7355 N. Woodland Dr.
Indianapolis, IN 46278
Telephone: (317) 297-5500
Mailing Address:
P.O. Box 603
Indianapolis, IN 46206
Year Established: 1975
Pub. Frequency: m.
Page Size: standard
Subscrip. Rate: $18/yr.
Circulation: 19,558
**Owner(s):**
Allied Publications
P.O. Box 603
Indianapolis, IN 46206
Telephone: (317) 297-5500
Ownership %: 100
**Management:**
Jim Bellin ......................Sales Manager

**Materials Accepted/Included:** 01-Business news 02-By-line articles 03-Fashion news 04-Food news 05-Freelance copy 06-Letters to editor 07-Real estate news 08-Sports news 09-Travel news 10-Book rev. 11-Movie rev. 12-Music rev. 13-TV rev. 14-Theater rev. 15-Coming events 16-Obituaries 17-Question & answer 18-Social announcements 19-Artwork 20-Cartoons 21-Photos 22-TV listings 23-Audio rec. 24-Video rec. 25-Books 26-Films/film clips 27-Personnel news 28-Press releases 29-New product news/photos 30-Trade lit. 31-Contracts awarded 32-Display adv. 33-Classified adv.

4-387

**Desc.:** Contains display and classified advertising for new and used trucks, trailers, equipment, supplies, financing and other services related to the trucking industry. A publication providing a medium for advertisers to market their products and services to specific and narrowly defined readership.

**Readers:** Owners/operators and fleet owners of over 26,000 GVW trucks.

25187

## MODERN BULK TRANSPORTER
4200 S. Sheperd
Houston, TX 77098
Telephone: (713) 523-8124
Mailing Address:
 P.O. Box 66010
 Houston, TX 77266
Year Established: 1938
Pub. Frequency: m.
Page Size: standard
Subscrip. Rate: free
Freelance Pay: varies
Circulation: 15,000
Circulation Type: controlled
**Owner(s):**
Tunnell Publications, Inc., Tunnell Family
P.O. Box 66010
Houston, TX 77266
Telephone: (713) 523-8124
Ownership %: 100
**Management:**
Wanda Tunnell ...........................Vice President
**Editorial:**
Charles Wilson ................................Editor
Paul Schenck ....................Editorial Director
Robin Anderson .................................Advertising
Raymond T. Anderson ....................Advertising
**Desc.:** Success stories on companies, news of direct and generally exclusive (in relation to the trucking industry) interest to tank truck operators. We use company personnel by-lines. Articles range 1,000-3,000 words with 0-10 pix depending on subject. Departments include: New Products, People in the News, Coming Events, News, Features.

58680

## MOUNTAIN AMERICA TRUCK TRADER
7355 N. Woodland Dr.
Indianapolis, IN 46278
Telephone: (317) 297-5500
Mailing Address:
 P.O. Box 603
 Indianapolis, IN 46206
Year Established: 1978
Pub. Frequency: m.
Page Size: standard
Subscrip. Rate: $18/yr.
Circulation: 18,000
**Owner(s):**
Allied Publications
P.O. Box 603
Indianapolis, IN 46206
Telephone: (317) 292-5500
Ownership %: 100
**Management:**
Jim Bellin ..........................................Manager
**Desc.:** Contains display and classified advertising for new and used trucks, trailers, equipment, supplies, financing and other services related to the trucking industry. A publication providing a medium for advertisers to market their products and services to a specific and narrowly defined readership.

65112

## MY LITTLE SALESMAN TRUCK CATALOG
2895 Chad Dr.
Eugene, OR 97401
Telephone: (503) 324-1201
FAX: (503) 342-3307

Mailing Address:
 P.O. Box 70208
 Eugene, OR 97401
Year Established: 1958
Pub. Frequency: m.
Page Size: pocket
Subscrip. Rate: $18/yr.
Materials: 29
Circulation: 60,000
Circulation Type: controlled & paid
**Owner(s):**
My Little Salesman, Inc.
Ownership %: 100
**Management:**
Rod Womack ...........................Sales Manager
**Editorial:**
Peter Pawell ............National Marketing Diretor
**Desc.:** Consists primarily of advertising by dealers and distributors of new and used heavy trucks and trailers. Includes some editorial information of interest to those in the marketplace. Readership consists solely of those actively interested in the buying and selling trucks and trailers.
**Readers:** Buyers of new and used trucks and trailers.

25189

## NEBRASKA TRUCKER
1701 K St.
Lincoln, NE 68508
Telephone: (402) 476-7822
FAX: (402) 476-0579
Mailing Address:
 P.O. Box 81010
 Lincoln, NE 68501
Year Established: 1940
Pub. Frequency: m.
Page Size: standard
Subscrip. Rate: $16/yr.
Materials: 05,06,20,28,29,30,32,33
Freelance Pay: negotiable
Print Process: offset
Circulation: 3,361
Circulation Type: controlled
**Owner(s):**
Nebraska Motor Carriers' Association
1701 K St.
Lincoln, NE 68508
Telephone: (402) 476-8504
Ownership %: 100
**Management:**
Charlie Bacon ................................President
Sue Wilson ...................Advertising Manager
**Editorial:**
Nance Kirk ...........................................Editor
Sandy Heather ....................Associate Editor
**Desc.:** Current news and features of interest to Nebraska based trucking companies and allied industries.
**Readers:** Truck company owners, operators, industry.
**Deadline:** ads-1 mo.

58676

## NEW ENGLAND TRUCK EXCHANGE
7355 N. Woodland Dr.
Indianapolis, IN 46278
Telephone: (317) 297-5500
Mailing Address:
 P.O. Box 603
 Indianapolis, IN 46206
Year Established: 1981
Pub. Frequency: m.
Subscrip. Rate: $18/yr.
Circulation: 21,000
**Owner(s):**
Allied Publications
P.O. Box 603
Indianapolis, IN 46206
Telephone: (317) 297-5500
**Management:**
Jim Bellin ..........................................Manager

**Desc.:** Contains display and classified advertising for new and used trucks, trailers, equipment, supplies, financing and other services related to the trucking industry. A publication providing a medium for advertisers to market their products and services to a specific and narrowly defined readership.

25190

## NEW JERSEY MOTOR TRUCK ASSOCIATION BULLETIN
160 Tices Ln.
E. Brunswick, NJ 08816
Telephone: (908) 254-5000
FAX: (908) 613-1745
Year Established: 1914
Pub. Frequency: m.
Page Size: 4 color photos/art
Subscrip. Rate: $45/yr.
Materials: 01,02,06,10,25,27,28,29,30,32,33
Circulation: 2,100
Circulation Type: controlled
**Owner(s):**
New Jersey Motor Truck Association
160 Tices Ln.
E. Brunswick, NJ 08816
Telephone: (908) 254-5000
Ownership %: 100
**Editorial:**
Anthony Buccino ..........................................Editor
**Desc.:** Covers news and other aspects of trucking industry.
**Readers:** Fleet owners and parts suppliers.
**Deadline:** story-1st of mo.; news-1st of mo.; photo-1st of mo.

58781

## NEW YORK TRUCK EXCHANGE
7355 N. Woodland Dr.
Indianapolis, IN 46278
Telephone: (317) 297-5500
Mailing Address:
 P.O. Box 603
 Indianapolis, IN 46206
Year Established: 1978
Pub. Frequency: m.
Page Size: standard
Subscrip. Rate: $18/yr.
Circulation: 20,000
**Owner(s):**
Allied Publications
P.O. Box 603
Indianapolis, IN 46206
Telephone: (317) 297-5500
Ownership %: 100
**Management:**
Jim Bellin ..........................................Manager
**Desc.:** Contains display and classified advertising for new and used trucks, trailers, equipment, supplies, financing and other services related to the trucking industry. A publication providing a medium for advertisers to market their products and services to a specific and narrowly defined readership.

25102

## OFFICIAL MOTOR FREIGHT/SHIPPERS GUIDE
1700 W. Cortland
Chicago, IL 60622
Telephone: (312) 278-2454
FAX: (312) 489-0482
Year Established: 1872
Pub. Frequency: s-a.
Page Size: standard
Subscrip. Rate: $45/yr.
Circulation: 13,357
Circulation Type: paid
**Owner(s):**
Official Motor Freight Guide, Inc.
1700 W. Cortland St.
Chicago, IL 60622
Telephone: (312) 278-2454
Ownership %: 100

**Management:**
Charles J. Vojta ...........................President
Charles J. Vojta ...........................Publisher
Deborah Jarosz ...........Circulation Manager
**Editorial:**
E. Eric Robison ......................Executive Editor
Edward Koch ...........................................Editor
Hugh Morgan .........Advertising Sales Manager
**Desc.:** Motor freight routing guide. Does not contain editorial matter other than listings of cities served by truck lines and air freight routings. Publishing a total of 16 Motor Freight/Shippers Guides and the Official Motor Carrier Directory.
**Readers:** Traffic managers of leading industrial companies.

25193

## OKLAHOMA MOTOR CARRIER
7201 N. Classen, Ste. 106
Oklahoma City, OK 73116
Telephone: (405) 843-9488
FAX: (405) 843-7310
Mailing Address:
 P.O. Box 14620
 Oklahoma City, OK 73113
Year Established: 1932
Pub. Frequency: q.
Page Size: standard
Subscrip. Rate: $1/copy; $4/yr.
Materials: 01,02,05,06,15,17,27,28,30,32
Freelance Pay: negotiable
Print Process: offset
Circulation: 3,500
Circulation Type: controlled
**Owner(s):**
Associated Motor Carriers of Oklahoma
7201 N. Classen, Ste. 106
Oklahoma City, OK 73116
Telephone: (405) 843-9488
FAX: (405) 843-7310
Ownership %: 100
**Management:**
Jalynn Marsee ...................Advertising Manager
**Editorial:**
Jalynn Marsee .........................Executive Editor
Jalynn Marsee .........................Associate Editor
**Desc.:** General industry news including legislative and regulatory information, personnel news, photos of awards, new facilities, etc. Also economic and safety related news.
**Readers:** Trucking industry management.

25195

## OVERDRIVE MAGAZINE
3200 Rice Mine Rd., N.E.
Tuscaloosa, AL 35406
Telephone: (205) 349-2990
FAX: (205) 758-6945
Mailing Address:
 P.O. Box 3187
 Tuscaloosa, AL 35403
Year Established: 1961
Pub. Frequency: m.
Page Size: standard
Subscrip. Rate: $2.95 newsstand; $23.97/yr.
Materials: 01,05,06,28,29
Freelance Pay: negotiable
Circulation: 92,000
Circulation Type: controlled
**Owner(s):**
Randall Publishing Co.
P.O. Box 3187
Tuscaloosa, AL 35403
Telephone: (205) 349-2990
Ownership %: 100
**Management:**
Pettus Randall ....................Chairman of Board
Mike Reilly ...........................................President
**Editorial:**
G.C. Skipper ....................Editor in Chief
Deborah Lockridge .................Managing Editor
Jeffrey Mason ....................Associate Publisher

---

**Materials Accepted/Included:** 01-Business news 02-By-line articles 03-Fashion news 04-Food news 05-Freelance copy 06-Letters to editor 07-Real estate news 08-Sports news 09-Travel news 10-Book rev. 11-Movie rev. 12-Music rev. 13-TV rev. 14-Theater rev. 15-Coming events 16-Obituaries 17-Question & answer 18-Social announcements 19-Artwork 20-Cartoons 21-Photos 22-TV listings 23-Audio rec. 24-Video rec. 25-Books 26-Films/film clips 27-Personnel news 28-Press releases 29-New product news/photos 30-Trade lit. 31-Contracts awarded 32-Display adv. 33-Classified adv.

**Desc.:** Written and edited for long haul class 8 truck owner/operators and small fleet owners of 1-30 trucks. Features on maintenance, new products, business management and industry issues.

**Readers:** Over-the-road truckers, independent truckers, owner/operators and small fleet managers.

**Deadline:** story-1st of mo. prior to pub. date; news-1st of mo. prior; photo-1st of mo. prior; ads-1st of mo. prior

25196

## OWNER OPERATOR
One Chilton Way
Radnor, PA 19089
Telephone: (610) 964-4264
Year Established: 1970
Pub. Frequency: 9/yr.
Page Size: standard
Subscrip. Rate: $16/yr.
Materials: 01,02,06,28,29,30,32,33
Freelance Pay: negotiable
Print Process: offset
Circulation: 96,000
Circulation Type: controlled & paid
**Owner(s):**
Chilton Co., Inc.
201 King of Prussia Rd.
Wayne, PA 19089

American Broadcasting Co.
Radio City Music Hall
New York, NY 10020

Capital Cities Communications, Inc.
**Management:**
Gregory Shereuet ...............................Publisher
**Editorial:**
Leon Witconis .........................Editor in Chief
Frank Conte ...........................................Editor
Carole Smith ...........................Copy Director
John Baxter .......................New Products Editor
Sue Corialos ................Production Coordinator
**Desc.:** Covers vehicle selection, new equipment specification, reports on new vehicle and components developments, vehicle operation, industry news, safe driving, maintenance, new products, legislation, pollution, record keeping, cost reduction. Every phase of activity that will help make the truck owner conduct a more successful and profitable business.
**Readers:** For the independent trucker and small fleet operator who leases his truck, tractor or complete rig to major carriers, private fleets, or engages in broker operations.
**Deadline:** story-2 mos. prior to pub. date; news-2 mos. prior; photo-2 mos. prior; ads-2 mos. prior

25197

## PENNTRUX
910 Linda Ln.
Camp Hill, PA 17011-6401
Telephone: (717) 761-7122
Year Established: 1933
Pub. Frequency: m.
Page Size: standard
Subscrip. Rate: membership only
Circulation: 2,600
Circulation Type: controlled
**Owner(s):**
Pennsylvania Motor Truck Association
P.O. Box 128
Camp Hill, PA 17001
Telephone: (717) 761-7122
Ownership %: 100
**Management:**
William E. Yocum ...............................President
William F. Sperry ..............Advertising Manager
**Editorial:**
Charles A. Schulz ...............................Editor
William F. Sperry ...........................News Editor

William F. Sperry ............................................Photo
**Desc.:** Official monthly publication of the Pennsylvania Motor Truck Association designed to furnish pertinent information to its members. Paid advertising is accepted.
**Readers:** Owners & leading officers of trucking companies in Pennsylvania.

25105

## PRIVATE CARRIER
66 Canal Center Plz., Ste. 600
Alexandria, VA 22314
Telephone: (703) 683-1300
FAX: (703) 683-1217
Year Established: 1964
Pub. Frequency: m.
Page Size: standard
Subscrip. Rate: controlled
Freelance Pay: $250/article
Circulation: 12,000
Circulation Type: controlled
**Owner(s):**
Private Carrier Conference, Inc.
66 Canal Center Plz., Ste. 600
Alexandria, VA 22314
Telephone: (703) 683-1300
Ownership %: 100
**Management:**
Gene S. Bergoffen ...............................Publisher
Elaine Robinson ................Advertising Manager
**Editorial:**
Donald Tepper .........................................Editor
**Desc.:** Articles report on legal, technological, and governmental developments in the field of private carriage. Regular editorial features include: Legal Developments, Industry News, Executive Vice President's Report, Legal Column, Job Clearinghouse.
**Readers:** Companies operating private trucks.

25148

## ROADWISE
501 N. Sanders
Helena, MT 59601
Telephone: (406) 442-6600
Mailing Address:
P.O. Box 1714
Helena, MT 59624
Year Established: 1949
Pub. Frequency: s-a.
Page Size: standard
Subscrip. Rate: $12.50/yr.
Freelance Pay: negotiable
Circulation: 1,000
Circulation Type: controlled
**Owner(s):**
Montana Motor Carriers Association, Inc.
P.O. Box 1714
Helena, MT 59624
Telephone: (406) 442-6600
Ownership %: 100
**Editorial:**
B.G. Havdahl ...........................................Director
**Desc.:** All material concerning all phases of the motor carrier industry.
**Readers:** Motor carrier executives, employees, city officials and municipal employees.

61604

## SCTA HI-LIGHTS
2425 Devine St.
Columbia, SC 29205-0166
Telephone: (803) 799-4306
FAX: (803) 254-7148
Mailing Address:
P.O. Box 50166
Columbia, SC 29250-0166
Year Established: 1937
Pub. Frequency: m.
Page Size: tabloid
Subscrip. Rate: $5/yr.
Circulation: 2,500

Circulation Type: controlled
**Owner(s):**
South Carolina Trucking Association
**Management:**
Harriette Derrick .......................Office Manager
**Editorial:**
J. Richards Todd .......................................Editor
**Readers:** SCTA members, truck operators, fleet owners.

25201

## SOUTHERN MOTOR CARGO MAGAZINE
1509 Madison
Memphis, TN 38104
Telephone: (901) 276-5424
FAX: (901) 276-5400
Mailing Address:
P.O. Box 40169
Memphis, TN 38174
Year Established: 1945
Pub. Frequency: m.
Page Size: standard
Subscrip. Rate: free to fleet; $25/yr.
Freelance Pay: $.08/Word
Circulation: 50,000
Circulation Type: controlled
**Owner(s):**
Southern Motor Cargo
1509 Madison Ave.
Memphis, TN 38104
Telephone: (901) 276-5424
Ownership %: 100
**Management:**
Wallace Witmer .....................................Publisher
Wallace Witmer ................Advertising Manager
Alicia Leslie .........................Circulation Manager
**Editorial:**
Randy Duke ..............................................Editor
Pierce Hammond .......................Assistant Editor
**Desc.:** Slanted to fleet operators - anyone who maintains a fleet of 1 or more trucks, such as bakeries, dairies, common carriers, etc. Prefers material about new trucks, trucking equipment, laws, facts, maintenance, etc.
**Readers:** Fleet operators.

25108

## TARHEEL WHEELS
219 W. Martin St.
Raleigh, NC 27601
Telephone: (919) 834-0387
FAX: (919) 832-0390
Mailing Address:
P.O. Box 2977
Raleigh, NC 27602
Year Established: 1954
Pub. Frequency: q.
Page Size: standard
Subscrip. Rate: $3.15/yr.
Circulation: 4,500
Circulation Type: paid
**Owner(s):**
N.C. Trucking Association
219 W. Martin
Raleigh, NC 27601
Telephone: (919) 834-0387
Ownership %: 100
**Management:**
Gene H. Humphries ..........Circulation Manager
**Editorial:**
E.L. Peters ...............................Executive Editor
Holi G. Hassinger .......................Assistant Editor
Holi G. Hassinger ............New Products Editor
Holi G. Hassinger ...........................News Editor
**Desc.:** Staff written articles featuring coming events, entertainment, letters to the editor and personnel news, industry news in transportation (motor), topical features of North Carolina interest.
**Readers:** General interest.

25204

## TENNESSEE TRUCKING NEWS
530 Church St., Ste. 700
Nashville, TN 37219
Telephone: (615) 255-0558
FAX: (615) 244-0495
Mailing Address:
P.O. Box 190538
Nashville, TN 37219-0538
Year Established: 1972
Pub. Frequency: bi-m.
Page Size: standard
Subscrip. Rate: free
Materials: 01,15,29,32
Print Process: offset
Circulation: 1,000
Circulation Type: free
**Owner(s):**
Tennessee Trucking Association, Inc.
530 Church St., Ste. 700
Nashville, TN 37219
Telephone: (615) 255-0558
FAX: (615) 244-0495
Ownership %: 100
**Management:**
Ron Gant ...............................................President
**Editorial:**
Ron Gant ....................................................Editor
**Desc.:** News highlights on products sold by allied members, promotion, innovations, expansion of members facilities, legislative activities relating to trucking industry. Departments include: From the President's Desk, Capitol Digest, Industry News.
**Readers:** Allied industry personnel and membership second.
**Deadline:** story-1st mo. previous mo. of pub. date.

58782

## TEXAS/LOUISIANA TRUCKER
7355 N. Woodland Dr.
Indianapolis, IN 46278
Telephone: (317) 297-5500
FAX: (317) 299-1356
Mailing Address:
P.O. Box 603
Indianapolis, IN 46206-0603
Year Established: 1975
Pub. Frequency: m.
Page Size: standard
Subscrip. Rate: $18/yr.
Circulation: 25,000
**Owner(s):**
Allied Publications
P.O. Box 603
Indianapolis, IN 46206-0603
Telephone: (317) 297-5500
Ownership %: 100
**Management:**
Jim Bellin .................................................Manager
**Desc.:** Contains display and classified advertising for new and used trucks, trailers, equipment, supplies, financing and other services related to the trucking industry. Provides a medium for advertisers to market their products and services to a specific and narrowly defined readership.
**Readers:** Merchandising guides to new and used trucks, equipment, supplies, financing and other services geared to the trucking industry.

25203

## TRAILER/BODY BUILDERS
4200 S. Shepherd St.
Houston, TX 77098
Telephone: (713) 523-8124
FAX: (713) 523-8384
Mailing Address:
P.O. Box 66010
Houston, TX 77266
Year Established: 1959
Pub. Frequency: m.

---

Materials Accepted/Included: 01-Business news 02-By-line articles 03-Fashion news 04-Food news 05-Freelance copy 06-Letters to editor 07-Real estate news 08-Sports news 09-Travel news 10-Book rev. 11-Movie rev. 12-Music rev. 13-TV rev. 14-Theater rev. 15-Coming events 16-Obituaries 17-Question & answer 18-Social announcements 19-Artwork 20-Cartoons 21-Photos 22-TV listings 23-Audio rec. 24-Video rec. 25-Books 26-Films/film clips 27-Personnel news 28-Press releases 29-New product news/photos 30-Trade lit. 31-Contracts awarded 32-Display adv. 33-Classified adv.

Page Size: standard
Subscrip. Rate: free to members
Freelance Pay: $5/in.
Circulation: 14,000
Circulation Type: controlled
**Owner(s):**
Tunnell Publications, Inc.
P.O. Box 66010
Houston, TX 77266
Telephone: (713) 523-8124
Ownership %: 100
**Management:**
W.L. Tunnell ............................Publisher
Ray Anderson .................Advertising Manager
**Editorial:**
Paul Schenck ..............................Editor
Bruce Sauer ......................Managing Editor
Charles Wilson ................Associate Editor
**Desc.:** Factual stories on production,
sales, and management from the
manufacturers or distributors of truck
bodies, truck trailers, bus bodies, tank
transports, and van containers. Stories
on new products and new types of truck
bodies or truck trailers, giving complete
specifications and how manufactured
(gauge materials, alloys used, beam type
and thickness, etc.).
**Readers:** Management of truck body and
truck trailer manufacturing plants and
their sales distributors and service
shops.

**TRANSPORT TOPICS**                      25205
2200 Mill Rd.
Alexandria, VA 22314
Telephone: (703) 838-1781
Year Established: 1933
Pub. Frequency: w.
Page Size: tabloid
Subscrip. Rate: $69/yr.
Materials: 01,05,06,28,29,30,32,33
Freelance Pay: negotiable
Circulation: 31,900
Circulation Type: paid
**Owner(s):**
American Trucking Association
2200 Mill Rd.
Alexandria, VA 22314
Telephone: (703) 838-1874
Ownership %: 100
**Bureau(s):**
Transport Topics
5 Rue Mirabeeau
75016 Paris France
Telephone: 145 24 3869
Contact: John G. Parker
**Management:**
Charles Duttweiler ........................President
Charles Duttweiler ........................Publisher
Lori Roddy .......................Circulation Manager
**Editorial:**
Patricia Cavanaugh ..................Senior Editor
Oliver B. Patton ............................Editor
**Desc.:** Covers trucking and competitive
fields, national newspaper for motor
freight carriers; editorial interests are
financial, economic, political,
transportation in interstate commerce;
truck fleet operation/I.C.C. regulations
accounting, safety, claims, maintenance
and repair of vehicles; new vehicles;
mechanical developments, etc.
**Readers:** Trucking industry owners,
managers and other employees;
suppliers; customers and others who
follow trucking affairs.

**TRUCK PARTS & SERVICE**                25176
707 Lake Cook Rd.
Deerfield, IL 60015
Telephone: (708) 498-3180
FAX: (708) 498-3197
Year Established: 1966

Pub. Frequency: 12/yr.
Page Size: standard
Subscrip. Rate: $50/yr. US; $60/yr.
   Canada & foreign
Materials: 01,02,05,06,15,21,27,28,29,30,
   32,33
Freelance Pay: negotiable
Print Process: web offset
Circulation: 17,378
Circulation Type: controlled
**Owner(s):**
Kona Communications, Inc.
707 Lake Cook Rd.
Deerfield, IL 60015
Telephone: (708) 498-3180
Ownership %: 100
**Management:**
James D. Moss ...........................President
James D. Moss ...........................Publisher
**Editorial:**
David Zaritz ...........................Executive Editor
**Desc.:** Serves the independent truck
service and repair trade, the
independent truck parts distribution
market and the parts and service
departments of heavy-duty truck
dealerships.
**Readers:** Owners, partners, managers &
executives of truck specialists, truck,
trailer, bus dealers, and heavy duty parts
distributors.
**Deadline:** story-2 mos. prior to pub. date;
news-2 mos. prior; photo-2 mos. prior;
ads-1st of mo. prior

**TRUCKSTOP WORLD**                      65475
38 Executive Pk., Ste. 300
Irvine, CA 92705
Telephone: (916) 786-3030
Year Established: 1987
Pub. Frequency: q.
Page Size: standard
Subscrip. Rate: $18/yr.
Freelance Pay: $350-$400/pg.
Circulation: 12,000
Circulation Type: controlled
**Owner(s):**
Newport Publications
Ownership %: 100
**Management:**
Thomas Stanford. ........................Publisher
**Desc.:** Addresses the concerns of owners,
general managers, and department
managers of truckstop areas. Articles
include "How-To" and What's New.
**Readers:** Operations of truck and auto
service centers, truck lubing and
maintenance centers and owners of
truckstops along the highways.

**TRUX**                                 25212
500 Piedmont Ave., N.E.
Atlanta, GA 30308
Telephone: (404) 876-4313
FAX: (404) 874-9765
Year Established: 1949
Pub. Frequency: q.
Page Size: standard
Subscrip. Rate: $10/yr.
Circulation: 4,000
Circulation Type: free & paid
**Owner(s):**
Georgia Motor Trucking Association
500 Piedmont Ave.
Atlanta, GA 30308
Telephone: (404) 876-4313
Ownership %: 100
**Management:**
Ernest Quickel ..................Advertising Manager
**Editorial:**
Ernest Quickel ..............................Editor

**Desc.:** Concentration is on information for
and about southeastern truckers and
shippers. Includes "how-to-do-it"
articles, general interest (sales,
personnel, public relations), features
unusual "personalities" in the trucking or
shipping world. Use publicity material
that will interest readers, without being
unduly "biased" toward advertisers.
Major portion of stories are staff-
covered, but also carry contributions
(with by-lines) by important figures.
**Readers:** Truck owners, operators, and
shippers.

**WYOMING TRUCKER**                       25215
555 N. Poplar
Casper, WY 82601
Telephone: (307) 234-1579
FAX: (307) 234-7082
Mailing Address:
   P.O. Box 1909
   Casper, WY 82602
Year Established: 1945
Pub. Frequency: bi-m.
Page Size: standard
Subscrip. Rate: free
Circulation: 4,200
Circulation Type: free
**Owner(s):**
Wyoming Trucking Association, Inc.
Box 1909
Casper, WY 82602
Telephone: (307) 234-1579
Ownership %: 100
**Management:**
Sheila D. Foertsch ............Advertising Manager
**Editorial:**
Sharon D. Nichols ....................Executive Editor
**Desc.:** Geared to trucking industry in
Wyoming. Reflects viewpoint of
organized industry and publicity
favorable thereto. Covers news,
legislation and regulations of interest to
truckers.
**Readers:** Truckers, suppliers, law
enforcement people, government
personnel, general public, new media.

## Group 270-Veterinary

**AGRI-PRACTICE**                          52566
7 Ashley Ave., S.
Santa Barbara, CA 93103
Telephone: (805) 965-1028
FAX: (805) 965-0722
Mailing Address:
   P.O. Box 4457
   Santa Barbara, CA 93140-4457
Year Established: 1979
Pub. Frequency: 10/yr.
Page Size: standard
Subscrip. Rate: $36/yr.
Materials: 06,10,15,21,28,29,32
Freelance Pay: $10/printed page
Circulation: 5,500
Circulation Type: controlled
**Owner(s):**
Veterinary Practice Publishing Co.
P.O. Box 4457
Santa Barbara, CA 93140-4457
Telephone: (805) 965-1028
Ownership %: 100
**Management:**
Nancy Bull ................................Publisher
Rebecca Mendoza ............Circulation Manager
**Editorial:**
Nancy Bull ......................Marketing Director
Nancy Becker ......................Staff Editor

**Desc.:** Published for veterinarians in food
animal practice. Authors are DVMs in
private practice, in university research
and teaching, or in commercial R&D
work. Articles are chosen specifically for
their usefulness to the veterinarian in
everyday practice. Research reports are
generally regarded as being too far
removed from practice and, although
given consideration, are rarely used.
Departments include: Book Reviews,
New Products, Dialog (letters to the
editor), Clinical Forum (questions &
answers), Practice Bulletin.
**Readers:** Doctors of veterinary medicine,
veterinary students, scholars,
pharmaceutical companies.

**AMERICAN JOURNAL OF
VETERINARY RESEARCH**                    25217
1931 N. Meacham Rd., Ste. 100
Schaumburg, IL 60173-4360
Telephone: (708) 925-8070
FAX: (708) 925-1329
Pop. Served: 1,940
Year Established: 1940
Pub. Frequency: m.
Page Size: standard
Subscrip. Rate: $150/yr.
Materials: 02,06,32,33
Print Process: web offset
Circulation: 7,000
Circulation Type: paid
**Owner(s):**
American Veterinary Medical Association
1931 N. Meacham Rd., Ste. 100
Schaumburg, IL 60173
Telephone: (708) 925-8070
FAX: (708) 925-1329
Ownership %: 100
**Management:**
B.G. Clune ......................Production Manager
**Editorial:**
A.J. Koltveit ....................Editor in Chief
J.H. Audin ..............................Editor
L. Daristotle ....................Assistant Editor
C. Lundin ....................Assistant Editor
K.J. Matushek ....................Assistant Editor
C.A. Smith ....................Assistant Editor
N.W. Leveque ....................Associate Editor
**Desc.:** Devoted almost exclusively to
reports of research in veterinary
medicine or related fields. The length of
article or number of photographs is
not limited. Each manuscript is accepted
or rejected solely on its merit.
Manuscripts are reviewed by a specialist
in the field before being accepted for
publication.
**Readers:** Domestic/foreign veterinarians
and others in biomedical research.
**Deadline:** ads-40 days prior to pub. date

**CALIFORNIA VETERINARIAN**               25218
5231 Madison Ave.
Sacramento, CA 95841
Telephone: (916) 344-4985
Year Established: 1947
Pub. Frequency: bi-m.
Page Size: standard
Subscrip. Rate: $35/yr.
Circulation: 7,000
Circulation Type: paid
**Owner(s):**
California Veterinary Medical Association
5231 Madison Ave.
Sacramento, CA 95841
Telephone: (916) 344-4985
Ownership %: 100
**Editorial:**
Rosanne VanCleve ..................Editor in Chief

**Materials Accepted/Included:** 01-Business news 02-By-line articles 03-Fashion news 04-Food news 05-Freelance copy 06-Letters to editor 07-Real estate news 08-Sports news 09-Travel news 10-Book rev. 11-Movie rev. 12-Music rev. 13-TV rev. 14-Theater rev. 15-Coming events 16-Obituaries 17-Question & answer 18-Social announcements 19-Artwork 20-Cartoons 21-Photos 22-TV listings 23-Audio rec. 24-Video rec. 25-Books 26-Films/film clips 27-Personnel news 28-Press releases 29-New product news/photos 30-Trade lit. 31-Contracts awarded 32-Display adv. 33-Classified adv.

**Desc.:** Carries news of interest to doctors of veterinary medicine. Featuring scientific articles, new discoveries in the field of veterinary medicine, business related articles.

**Readers:** Doctors of veterinary medicine.

---

**CANINE PRACTICE** — 25219

7 Ashley Ave., S.
Santa Barbara, CA 93103
Telephone: (805) 965-1028
Mailing Address:
    P.O. Box 4457
    Santa Barbara, CA 93140
Year Established: 1970
Pub. Frequency: bi-m.
Page Size: standard
Subscrip. Rate: $28/yr.
Materials: 10,15,21,28,29,32
Freelance Pay: $10/pg.
Circulation: 6,500
Circulation Type: paid
**Owner(s):**
Veterinary Practice Publishing Co.
P.O. Box 4457
Santa Barbara, CA 93140
Telephone: (805) 965-1028
Ownership %: 100
**Management:**
Nancy A. Bull .........................Publisher
Rebecca Mendoza ...........Circulation Manager
**Editorial:**
Joseph Alexander ..........................Editor
Fran Setbacken ...............Graphics Coordinator
**Desc.:** Published for veterinarians in small animal practice. Contains practical articles on canine health. Departments include: Book Reviews, New Products, Dialog (letters to the editor), Clinical Forum (questions & answers), Practice Bulletin.
**Readers:** Doctors of veterinary medicine, veterinary students, scholars, pharmaceutical companies.

---

**DVM, THE NEWSMAGAZINE OF VETERINARY MEDICINE** — 25221

195 Main St. Bldg.
Metuchen, NJ 03340-2737
Telephone: (216) 826-2829
FAX: (216) 891-2675
Year Established: 1970
Pub. Frequency: 12/yr.
Page Size: tabloid
Subscrip. Rate: $39/yr.
Materials: 01,02,06,15,21,28,32,33
Freelance Pay: negotiable
Circulation: 43,236
Circulation Type: controlled
**Owner(s):**
Advanstar Communications, Inc.
7500 Old Oak Blvd.
Cleveland, OH 44130
Telephone: (216) 826-2829
Ownership %: 100
**Management:**
Raymond C. Lender, Jr. ..................Publisher
Rosy Bradley ....................Production Manager
**Editorial:**
Maureen Hrehocik .......................Editor
Dan Verdon ...........................Managing Editor
**Desc.:** Serves all veterinarians in private practice with news, new products, issues and new clinical information. Provides articles on practice management, fee-setting, and business building. Exclusive features include round-table discussions with profession leaders, feature reports on emerging areas of importance and complete coverage of FDA & USDA activities.

---

**Readers:** Reaches all veterinarians in private practice as well as animal health technicians, hospital managers and veterinary supply distributors.

**Deadline:** story-1st of mo. prior to pub. date; news-1st of mo. prior; photo-1st of mo. prior; ads-1st of mo. prior

---

**EQUINE PRACTICE** — 52563

7 Ashley Ave., S.
Santa Barbara, CA 93103
Telephone: (805) 965-1028
FAX: (805) 965-0722
Mailing Address:
    P.O. Box 4457
    Santa Barbara, CA 93140-4457
Year Established: 1979
Pub. Frequency: 10/yr.
Page Size: standard
Subscrip. Rate: $36/yr.
Materials: 06,10,15,21,28,29,32
Freelance Pay: $10/printed page
Circulation: 5,000
Circulation Type: controlled
**Owner(s):**
Veterinary Practice Publishing Co.
P.O. Box 4457
Santa Barbara, CA 93140
Telephone: (805) 965-1028
Ownership %: 100
**Management:**
Nancy A. Bull .........................Publisher
Rebecca Mendoza ...........Circulation Manager
**Editorial:**
Dr. Charles Vail ...........................Editor
Fran Setbacken ...............Graphics Coordinator
**Desc.:** Published for veterinarians in equine practice. Authors are DVMs in private practice, in university research and teaching, or in commercial R&D work. Research reports are generally regarded as being too far removed from practice and, although given consideration, are rarely used. Departments include: Book Reviews, New Products, Dialog (letters to the editor), Clinical Forum (questions & answers), Practice Bulletin.
**Readers:** Doctors of veterinary medicine, veterinary students, scholars, pharmaceutical companies.

---

**FELINE PRACTICE** — 25222

7 Ashley Ave., S.
Santa Barbara, CA 93103
Telephone: (805) 965-1028
Mailing Address:
    P.O. Box 4457
    Santa Barbara, CA 93140
Year Established: 1971
Pub. Frequency: bi-m.
Page Size: 4 color photos/art
Subscrip. Rate: $28/yr.
Materials: 10,15,21,28,29,32
Circulation: 6,500
Circulation Type: paid
**Owner(s):**
Veterinary Practice Publishing Co.
P.O. Box 4457
Santa Barbara, CA 93140
Telephone: (805) 965-1028
Ownership %: 100
**Management:**
Nancy A. Bull .........................Publisher
Nancy Bull ......................Advertising Manager
**Editorial:**
Nancy A. Bull .........................Managing Editor

---

**JOURNAL OF THE AMERICAN VETERINARY MEDICAL ASSOCIATION** — 25224

1931 N. Meacham Rd., Ste. 100
Schaumburg, IL 60173-4360
Telephone: (708) 925-8070
Year Established: 1877
Pub. Frequency: s-m.
Page Size: standard
Subscrip. Rate: $6 newsstand; $100/yr.
Materials: 01,06,10,15,16,17,27,32,33
Print Process: web offset
Circulation: 54,000
Circulation Type: paid
**Owner(s):**
American Veterinary Medical Association
1931 N. Meacham Rd., Ste. 100
Schaumburg, IL 60173
Telephone: (708) 925-8070
FAX: (708) 925-1329
Ownership %: 100
**Management:**
B.G. Clune .........................Production Manager
**Editorial:**
A.J. Koltveit ...................Editor in Chief
J.H. Audin ...............................Editor
L. Daristotle .......................Assistant Editor
C. Lundin ...........................Assistant Editor
K.M. Matushek ...................Assistant Editor
C.A. Smith ...........................Assistant Editor
N.W. Leveque ...................Associate Editor
S. Kahler ...............................News Editor
**Desc.:** To educate, inform, serve as symbol of veterinary profession, provide forum for exchange of ideas, authenticated scientific material, and historical record of the profession.
**Readers:** Veterinarians and others in biomedicine.
**Deadline:** ads-40 days

---

**JOURNAL OF VETERINARY INTERNAL MEDICINE** — 61798

227 E. Washington Sq.
Philadelphia, PA 19106
Telephone: (215) 238-4200
Year Established: 1987
Pub. Frequency: bi-m.
Subscrip. Rate: $42/yr. individuals;
    $62.50/yr. institutions
Circulation: 1,000
Circulation Type: paid
**Owner(s):**
J.B. Lippincott Co.
227 E. Washington Sq.
Philadelphia, PA 19105
Telephone: (215) 238-4273
**Management:**
Randi Hendrickson .........................Manager
**Editorial:**
Alfred M. Legendre .........................Editor

---

**JOURNAL OF VETERINARY MEDICAL EDUCATION** — 69190

VA-MD Reg. College of Veterinary Medicine
Va. Polytech Inst. & State Univ.
Blacksburg, VA 24061
Telephone: (703) 552-4701
FAX: (703) 552-8143
Year Established: 1974
Pub. Frequency: 2/yr.
Page Size: standard
Subscrip. Rate: $20/yr. individuals; $30/yr. institutions & foreign
Circulation: 3,400
Circulation Type: paid

---

**Owner(s):**
Assoc. of American Veterinary Medical Colleges
VA-MD Reg. Col. of Vet. Med.
VA Polytech Inst. & State Univ.
Blacksburg, VA 24061
Telephone: (703) 552-4701
Ownership %: 100
**Editorial:**
Richard B. Talbot .........................Editor

---

**LAB ANIMAL** — 25225

65 Bleecker St.
New York, NY 10012
Telephone: (212) 477-9600
Year Established: 1972
Pub. Frequency: 11/yr.
Page Size: standard
Subscrip. Rate: $70/yr.
Materials: 29,32,33
Circulation: 10,000
Circulation Type: controlled
**Owner(s):**
Nature Publishing Co.
65 Bleecker St.
New York, NY 10012
Telephone: (212) 477-9600
Ownership %: 100
**Management:**
Nicholas Byam Shaw ..........Chairman of Board
James Skowrenski ...........................President
James Skowrenski ...........................Publisher
**Editorial:**
Julia Schulhof .........................Managing Editor
Barbara Nasto .........................Assistant Editor
**Desc.:** Provides users of laboratory animals with review articles on the following subjects: new animal models, breeds or breeding practices, and in vitro or computer alternatives to animal use; lab animal care and nutrition; new ideas or techniques in psychological or biomedical research involving animals; short notes on research in progress; personnel and facility management; facility design and computerization; education and training on all levels; diagnostic activities; toxicology, genetics and embryology as they relate to the animal research field.
**Readers:** Users of laboratory animals in biomedical research, and animal care facility personnel.
**Deadline:** ads-mid-month

---

**LABORATORY ANIMAL SCIENCE** — 25226

70 Timber Creek Dr.
Ste. 5
Cordova, TN 38018
Telephone: (901) 754-8620
Year Established: 1950
Pub. Frequency: bi-m.
Page Size: standard
Subscrip. Rate: $70/yr.
Circulation: 4,100
Circulation Type: paid
**Owner(s):**
American Assn. for Laboratory Animal Science
Telephone: (901) 754-8620
Ownership %: 100
**Management:**
Donald W. Keene .........................Publisher
Donald W. Keene .............Advertising Manager
**Desc.:** Articles submitted in field of laboratory animal science, reviewed by experts, and accepted or rejected on basis of reviewers' recommendations.
**Readers:** Professional and technical people employed in this field of biomedical resources.

---

## LARGE ANIMAL VETERINARIAN
23261

122 S. Wesley Ave.
Mt. Morris, IL 61054
Telephone: (815) 734-4171
Year Established: 1945
Pub. Frequency: bi-m.
Page Size: standard
Subscrip. Rate: $7/issue; $36/yr.
Circulation: 21,000
Circulation Type: controlled
**Owner(s):**
Watt Publishing Company
122 S. Wesley Ave
Mt. Morris, IL 61054
Telephone: (815) 734-4171
Ownership %: 100
**Management:**
Clay Schreiber .......................Publisher
**Editorial:**
Tim Phillips .............................Editor
Clayton Gill .............................Editorial Director
Theresa Stukenberg .......................Art Director
**Desc.:** Provides quick-to-read information for improving veterinary clients' overall herd profitability. It covers: health, nutrition, animal environment, new products and technology, government regulatory policies, and overall herd economics for the large animal veterinarian. Qualified recipients are large and mixed practice veterinarians.
**Readers:** Food animal veterinarians, nutritionists, industrial veterinarians; manufacturers/distributors/brokers of veterinary drug products, animal health, feed ingredients, or feed additives; extension livestock specialists, farm advisors, county agents; experiment stations; college, university, government and regulatory personnel; consultants, veterinary students, trade associations, and financial advisors.

## SWINE PRACTITIONER
65314

7950 College Blvd.
Shawnee Msn, KS 66210
Telephone: (913) 451-2200
Year Established: 1988
Pub. Frequency: 8/yr.
Page Size: standard
Subscrip. Rate: $20/yr. US
Freelance Pay: varies
Circulation: 4,000
Circulation Type: controlled
**Owner(s):**
Vance Publishing Corp.
Ownership %: 100
**Management:**
William Newham .......................Publisher
**Editorial:**
Thomas Quaife .........................Editor
**Desc.:** Deals with business practices and marketing.
**Readers:** Serves veterinarians working with swine herds.

## VETERINARY CLINICAL PATHOLOGY
52562

7 Ashley Ave., S.
Santa Barbara, CA 93103
Telephone: (805) 965-1028
Mailing Address:
P.O. Box 4457
Santa Barbara, CA 93140-4457
Year Established: 1977
Pub. Frequency: q.
Page Size: standard
Subscrip. Rate: $28/yr.
Circulation: 1,500
Circulation Type: paid

**Owner(s):**
Veterinary Practice Publishing Co.
P.O. Box 4457
Santa Barbara, CA 93140-4457
Telephone: (805) 965-1028
Ownership %: 100
**Management:**
Nancy A. Bull .........................Publisher
**Editorial:**
Dr. Alan Rebar .........................Editor in Chief
**Desc.:** Authors are DVMs in private practice, in university research and teaching, or in commercial R&D work. Provides current, in-depth technical information on subjects relevant to veterinary clinical pathology. Includes technical papers, analyses of instrumentation, reviews, answers to questions and courses in continuing education. Official publication of the American Society for Veterinary Clinical pathology.
**Readers:** Doctors of veterinary medicine, clinical pathologists, scholars, students, pharmaceutical companies.

## VETERINARY ECONOMICS
25230

9073 Lenexa Dr.
Lenexa, KS 66215
Telephone: (913) 492-4300
FAX: (913) 492-4157
Year Established: 1960
Pub. Frequency: m.
Page Size: standard
Subscrip. Rate: $35/yr.
Freelance Pay: negotiable
Circulation: 38,000
Circulation Type: controlled
**Owner(s):**
Medical Economics Publishing Co., Inc.
Northvale, NJ 07647
Telephone: (201) 358-7000
Ownership %: 100
**Management:**
Ray Glick, DVM .......................Publisher
Doug Catt .........................Advertising Manager
**Editorial:**
Rebecca R. Turner .......................Editor
**Desc.:** Specifically covers the business phase of veterinary practice. Articles deals with business management, and personal finance, etc. Departments include: Forecasts, Letters to the Editor, Client Relations, Management Strategy, Practice Finances, Hospital Design, Personal Finances.
**Readers:** Doctors of veterinary medicine.

## VETERINARY FORUM
69188

1610-A Frederica Rd.
St. Simons Island, GA 31522-2509
Telephone: (912) 638-4848
FAX: (912) 634-0768
Year Established: 1982
Pub. Frequency: m.
Subscrip. Rate: $35/yr.
Circulation: 45,000
Circulation Type: controlled
**Owner(s):**
Forum Publications, Inc.
1610-A Frederica Rd.
St. Simons Island, GA 31522-2509
Telephone: (912) 638-4848
Ownership %: 100
**Editorial:**
Michael D. Sollars .......................Editor
**Desc.:** Educates readers on the various ways they can offer more services and products to their clients. Serves as a ready reference in medical and practical management.

## VETERINARY MEDICINE
25231

9073 Lenexa Dr.
Lenexa, KS 66215
Telephone: (913) 492-4300
FAX: (913) 492-4157
Year Established: 1905
Pub. Frequency: m.
Page Size: standard
Subscrip. Rate: $49/yr.
Circulation: 25,000
Circulation Type: paid
**Owner(s):**
Veterinary Medicine Publ.Co.Div.of
Med.Economics
9073 Lenexa Dr.
Lenexa, KS 66215
Telephone: (913) 492-4300
Ownership %: 100
**Management:**
P. Ray Glick .........................President
P. Ray Glick .........................Publisher
**Editorial:**
Margaret Rampey .......................Managing Editor
Peggy Shandy .........................Senior Associate Editor
**Desc.:** Professional papers dealing with livestock and pet animal health. Carries news items of interest to the profession, abstracts, meetings, etc.
**Readers:** Professionals.

## VETERINARY PRACTICE STAFF
69189

7 Ashley Ave. S.
Santa Barbara, CA 93103-9989
Telephone: (805) 965-1028
FAX: (805) 965-0722
Year Established: 1989
Pub. Frequency: bi-m.
Page Size: standard
Subscrip. Rate: $28/yr.
Materials: 06,10,15,21,28,29,32
Circulation: 16,000
Circulation Type: paid
**Owner(s):**
Veterinary Practice Publishing Co.
7 Ashley Ave. S.
Santa Barbara, CA 93103-9989
Telephone: (805) 965-1028
Ownership %: 100
**Editorial:**
Dr. Donald Applegate .......................Editor
**Readers:** Employees of the veterinary clinic: technicians, assistants, office personnel, and receptionists.

## Group 272-Water Supply

## FLORIDA WATER RESOURCES JOURNAL
25250

5200 N.W. 43rd St., Ste. 102-301
Gainesville, FL 32606
Telephone: (904) 374-4946
Mailing Address:
P.O. Box 147050
Gainesville, FL 32614
Year Established: 1949
Pub. Frequency: m.
Page Size: standard
Subscrip. Rate: $24/yr. or membership
Materials: 01,02,06,27,29,32,33
Print Process: web
Circulation: 8,000
Circulation Type: controlled
**Owner(s):**
Florida Water Resources Journal, Inc.
5200 N.W. 43rd St., Ste. 102-3
Gainesville, FL 32606
Telephone: (904) 374-4946
Ownership %: 50

American Water Works Association, FL
Section
Telephone: (904) 374-4946
Ownership %: 25

Florida Pollution Control Association
Telephone: (904) 374-4946
Ownership %: 25
**Management:**
John D. Crane .......................Advertising Manager
**Editorial:**
John D. Crane .......................Managing Editor
**Desc.:** Aimed at persons engaged in water, wastewater and pollution control activities in Florida.
**Readers:** Members of Florida Water & Pollution Control Operators Association, American Water Association-Florida Section, and Florida Pollution Control Associaton.
**Deadline:** story-60 days prior; news-60 days prior; photo-60 days prior; ads-30 days prior

## GROUND WATER AGE
25243

13 Century Hill
Latham, NY 12110
Telephone: (518) 783-1281
FAX: (518) 783-1386
Year Established: 1967
Pub. Frequency: m.
Page Size: standard
Subscrip. Rate: $39/yr.
Materials: 01,02,06,28,29,32,33
Print Process: offset
Circulation: 15,000
Circulation Type: controlled
**Owner(s):**
National Trade Publications, Inc.
13 Century Hill
Latham, NY 12110
Telephone: (518) 783-1281
FAX: (518) 783-1386
Ownership %: 100
**Management:**
Alice J. Savino .......................Publisher
Mary Ann Ryan .......................Business Manager
Jean Sullivan .......................Circulation Manager
**Editorial:**
Rosyln Dahl .......................Editor
Charlotte Prior .......................Advertising
Ellen Lam .......................Production Director
**Desc.:** Edited for water well contractors, water systems specialists and others engaged in the design, sale, installation and servicing of private and public ground water supply systems. Editorial emphasis is on technical marketing and business management information designed to be helpful to the healthy growth of the water well industry. The publication also serves as a spokesman for the ground water industry in its dealings with government officials and others. In addition to major features, editorial content includes legislative reports, product and literature developments, industry news and editorial comment. Departments include: News-general, Products Development, literature pertaining to the industry, other information pertaining to the industry.
**Readers:** Water well drillers, pump specialists.
**Deadline:** story-8 wks. prior to pub. date; news-6 wks. prior; ads-6 wks. prior

## HYDROBIOLOGICAL JOURNAL
65647

605 Third Ave.
New York, NY 10158
Telephone: (212) 850-6000
Year Established: 1980
Pub. Frequency: 7/yr.
Subscrip. Rate: $695/yr.
Circulation: 275
Circulation Type: paid

Materials Accepted/Included: 01-Business news 02-By-line articles 03-Fashion news 04-Food news 05-Freelance copy 06-Letters to editor 07-Real estate news 08-Sports news 09-Travel news 10-Book rev. 11-Movie rev. 12-Music rev. 13-TV rev. 14-Theater rev. 15-Coming events 16-Obituaries 17-Question & answer 18-Social announcements 19-Artwork 20-Cartoons 21-Photos 22-TV listings 23-Audio rec. 24-Video rec. 25-Books 26-Films/film clips 27-Personnel news 28-Press releases 29-New product news/photos 30-Trade lit. 31-Contracts awarded 32-Display adv. 33-Classified adv.

4-392

**Owner(s):**
John Wiley & Sons, Inc.
605 Third Ave.
New York, NY 10158
Telephone: (212) 850-6000
Ownership %: 100
**Editorial:**
Robert J. Behnke ..................................Editor

69193

**INDUSTRIAL WASTEWATER**
601 Wythe St.
Alexandria, VA 22314
Telephone: (703) 684-2400
FAX: (703) 684-2492
Year Established: 1993
Pub. Frequency: bi-m.
Page Size: 8 3/16 x 11
Circulation: 20,000
Circulation Type: paid
**Owner(s):**
Water Environment Federation
601 Wythe St.
Alexandria, VA 22314
Telephone: (703) 684-2400
Ownership %: 100
**Editorial:**
Kimberly Roy ..................................Editor

69191

**INTERNATIONAL DESALINATION
& WATER REUSE QUARTERLY**
10842 Pine Bark Ln.
Boca Raton, FL 33428
Telephone: (407) 451-9429
FAX: (407) 451-9435
Year Established: 1991
Pub. Frequency: q.
Page Size: standard
Subscrip. Rate: $40/yr.
Materials: 01,06,28,29,30,32,33
Circulation: 8,200
Circulation Type: controlled
**Owner(s):**
Lineal Publishing Co.
10842 Pine Bark Ln.
Boca Raton, FL 33428
Telephone: (407) 451-9429
FAX: (407) 451-9435
Ownership %: 100
**Management:**
Irv Lineal ..................................Publisher
Paul Green ..................................Publisher
**Editorial:**
Floyd H. Meller ..................................Editor
**Desc.:** This journal of the International
Desalination Association contains a mix
of technical articles on current practices
and advancements in technology, case
studies, approaches to project financing,
and history of the industry; as well as
environmental issues and the service
the desalination industry's technologies
can supply in this area. In addition,
editorials address needs for expanded
education and training.

46859

**INTERNATIONAL WATER REPORT**
1099 18th St., Ste. 2150
Denver, CO 80202
Telephone: (303) 391-8799
Year Established: 1978
Pub. Frequency: q.
Page Size: standard
Subscrip. Rate: $47/yr. US; $57/yr.
   overseas
**Owner(s):**
Water Information Center, Inc.
1099 18th St.
Ste. 2150
Denver, CO 80202
Telephone: (303) 391-8799
Ownership %: 100
**Management:**
David W. Miller ..................................President
Fred L. Troise ..................................Publisher

Michelle Hankins ..................................Manager
**Editorial:**
Judith Schoeck ..................................Editor
Janet Sterling ..................................Associate Editor
**Desc.:** Provides the manager, scientist,
technician, educator and legislator with
up-to-date developments in the water
field throughout the world. Subscribers
are provided with recent knowledge of
water development, supply and
treatment; treaties and legislation and
news-on pollution control from around
the world. Pertinent meetings are
announced and reviews are included for
new publications and products.
**Readers:** Technical personnel in water
field.

58758

**JOURNAL OF THE AMERICAN
WATER WORKS ASSOCIATION**
6666 W. Quincy Ave.
Denver, CO 80235
Telephone: (303) 794-7711
Year Established: 1914
Pub. Frequency: m.
Page Size: 4 color photos/art
Subscrip. Rate: $50/yr. US; $75/yr. foreign
Circulation: 40,000
Circulation Type: paid
**Owner(s):**
American Water Works Association
6666 W. Quincy Ave.
Denver, CO 80235
Telephone: (303) 794-7711
Ownership %: 100
**Editorial:**
Nancy M. Zeilig ..................................Editor
Marcia Lacey ..................................Managing Editor
Diane Managan ..................................Art Director
Linda Bevard ..................................Associate Editor
Norman Udevtz ..................................Publication Director
**Readers:** Water industry operators,
   managers, scientists, professionals.

25247

**JOURNAL OF THE MAINE WATER
UTILITIES ASSOCIATION**
P.O. Box 120
Readfield, ME 04355
Year Established: 1925
Pub. Frequency: 4/yr.
Page Size: pocket
Subscrip. Rate: membership
Circulation: 550
Circulation Type: controlled
**Owner(s):**
Maine Water Utilities Association
P.O. Box 120
Readfield, ME 04355
Telephone: (207) 685-4334
Ownership %: 100
**Editorial:**
Jeff Jenks ..................................Editor
**Desc.:** Reports proceedings of association
conferences including reviews of
technical papers and discussions.
Devoted to field of water supply in New
England in general and Maine in
particular. Articles cover systems and
equipment, supply, health measures,
defense precautions. Carries personal
and news notes from advertisers. Also
carries a directory of manufacturers and
jobbers, listing various products with
name and Maine representatives.
**Readers:** New England water system
personnel, key personnel, officials,
libraries of colleges and universities.

25248

**JOURNAL OF THE NEW ENGLAND
WATER WORKS ASSOCIATION**
42A Dilla St.
Milford, MA 01757
Telephone: (508) 478-6996
FAX: (508) 634-8643

Mailing Address:
   35 Old Coach Cir.
   Ludlow, MA 01056
Year Established: 1886
Pub. Frequency: q.
Page Size: 7 1/4 x 10
Subscrip. Rate: $20/yr. US & US
   possessions; $28/yr. elsewhere
Materials: 06,10,16,21,30,32
Print Process: offset
Circulation: 2,900
Circulation Type: paid
**Owner(s):**
New England Water Works Association
42A Dilla St.
Milford, MA 01757
Telephone: (508) 478-6996
Ownership %: 100
**Management:**
Bridget Foley ..................................Advertising Manager
**Editorial:**
Peter C. Karalekas, Jr. ..................................Executive Editor
Robert P. Grady ..................................Assistant Editor
James J. Matera ..................................Editor Emeritus
**Desc.:** Technical publication covering the
water works profession. Technical
papers from members and non-members
considered for publication, although
most papers are presented at a meeting
of the Association.
**Readers:** Water utility managers, chemists,
   engineers, public, educators,
   manufacturers and suppliers, students.

24911

**NATIONAL WATERLINE**
3800 N. Fairfax Dr., Ste. 4
Arlington, VA 22203
Telephone: (703) 524-1544
Year Established: 1932
Pub. Frequency: m.
Page Size: standard
Subscrip. Rate: $150/yr.
Circulation: 3,500
Circulation Type: paid
**Owner(s):**
National Water Resources Association
3800 N. Fairfax Dr., Ste. 4
Arlington, VA 22203
Telephone: (703) 524-1544
FAX: (703) 524-1548
Ownership %: 100
**Management:**
Thomas F. Donnelly ..................................Executive Vice
                                          President
**Editorial:**
Gratia P. Bone ..................................Editor
**Desc.:** National Waterline reports on
developments in water resources
development with major emphasis on
Congressional activities and policy
decisions of the administration relative
to water policy.
**Readers:** Members of Congress &
Congressional staffs, administration
officials, state & local officials with
responsibilities for water supply,
agribusinessmen, lawyers and irrigators.

68836

**OPFLOW**
6666 W. Quincy Ave.
Denver, CO 80235
Telephone: (303) 794-7711
Year Established: 1975
Pub. Frequency: m.
Subscrip. Rate: $10.50/yr. non-members;
   $16/yr. foreign non-members
Circulation: 40,000
Circulation Type: controlled & paid
**Owner(s):**
American Water Works Association
6666 W. Quincy Ave.
Denver, CO 80235
Telephone: (303) 794-7711
Ownership %: 100

**Editorial:**
Constance Hardesty ..................................Editor

69194

**TEXAS WATER UTILITIES
JOURNAL**
1106 Clayton Ave., Ste. 101 E.
Austin, TX 78723-3124
Telephone: (512) 459-3124
FAX: (512) 459-7124
Year Established: 1990
Pub. Frequency: m.
Subscrip. Rate: $15/yr. US; $20/yr. foreign
Circulation: 9,200
Circulation Type: paid
**Owner(s):**
Texas Water Utilities Association
1106 Clayton Ave., Ste. 101 E.
Austin, TX 78723-3124
Telephone: (512) 459-3124
Ownership %: 100
**Editorial:**
Christine Loven ..................................Editor
**Desc.:** Covers essential information for all
individuals working within the water
utilities industry in Texas, including rules
and regulations, certification, education,
and communication.

25253

**WATER & WASTES DIGEST**
380 Northwest Hwy.
Des Plaines, IL 60016
Telephone: (708) 298-6622
FAX: (708) 392-0408
Year Established: 1961
Pub. Frequency: bi-m.
Page Size: tabloid
Subscrip. Rate: $35/yr. US; $55/yr. foreign
Circulation: 100,000
Circulation Type: controlled
**Owner(s):**
Scranton Gillette Communications, Inc.
380 E. Northwest Hwy.
Des Plaines, IL 60016-2282
Telephone: (708) 298-6622
Ownership %: 100
**Management:**
Sheldon Schultz ..................................Publisher
Linda Lambdin ..................................Circulation Manager
**Editorial:**
Dan Miller ..................................Editor
**Desc.:** For sanitary and civil engineers,
public works superintendents, city
engineers and systems plant
superintendents. Covers new products,
processes, techniques and applications
related to the design, construction,
operation and maintenance of water
and wastewater systems, industrial
wastes.
**Readers:** Management, system planning,
collection, and maintenance personnel in
the water and sewage industry.

25255

**WATER CONDITIONING &
PURIFICATION MAGAZINE**
2800 E. Ft. Lowell Rd.
Tucson, AZ 85716
Telephone: (602) 323-6144
FAX: (602) 323-7412
Year Established: 1959
Pub. Frequency: m.
Page Size: standard
Subscrip. Rate: $39/yr. US & Canada;
   $89/yr. foreign
Freelance Pay: by agreement
Circulation: 17,606
Circulation Type: controlled
**Owner(s):**
Publicom, Inc.
5635 N. Espina
Tucson, AZ 85718
Telephone: (602) 299-2893
Ownership %: 85

---

**Management:**
Jerome Peterson .....................Publisher
Sharon Peterson .....................Publisher
Patricia Steiner ..................Circulation Manager
**Editorial:**
Darlene J. Scheel .........................Editor
Kurt C. Peterson .............Advertising Director
James Turner ..............................Assistant Editor
**Desc.:** Serves domestic and commercial-industrial water treatment markets for working water and drinking water.
**Readers:** Marketers of commercial and industrial water conditioning and purification water treatment equipment and chemicals.

### WATER ENGINEERING & MANAGEMENT
25252

380 E. Northwest Hwy.
Des Plaines, IL 60016
Telephone: (708) 298-6622
FAX: (708) 392-0408
Year Established: 1882
Pub. Frequency: m.
Page Size: standard
Subscrip. Rate: $25/yr. US; $45/yr. foreign
Circulation: 41,000
Circulation Type: paid
**Owner(s):**
Scranton Gillette Communications, Inc.
380 Northwest Hwy.
Des Plaines, IL 60016
Telephone: (708) 298-6622
Ownership %: 100
**Management:**
Sheldon Schultz ..........................Publisher
Linda Lambdin ..................Circulation Manager
**Editorial:**
Dan Miller ..................................Editor
Judy Schmueser .................Production Director
**Desc.:** Dedicated to the advancement of technology and the transfer of information in the field of municipal county and regional water supply and water pollution control.
**Readers:** Consulting engineers and managers of water & wastewater facilities.

### WATER RESEARCH
69192

660 White Plains Rd.
Tarrytown, NY 10591-5153
Telephone: (914) 524-9200
FAX: (914) 333-2444
Year Established: 1967
Pub. Frequency: 12/yr.
Circulation: 3,800
Circulation Type: paid
**Owner(s):**
Pergamon Press, Inc.
660 White Plains Rd.
Tarrytown, NY 10591-5153
Telephone: (914) 524-9200
Ownership %: 100
**Editorial:**
K.J. Ives .......................................Editor
**Desc.:** Covers all aspects of the pollution of ground water, marine and fresh water, and the management of water resources and water quality.

### WATER TECHNOLOGY
69195

13 Century Hill Dr.
Latham, NY 12110-2197
Telephone: (518) 783-1281
FAX: (518) 783-1386
Year Established: 1978
Pub. Frequency: m.
Page Size: standard
Subscrip. Rate: $39/yr.
Materials: 01,06,10,15,25,27,28,29,30,32,33
Print Process: web
Circulation: 17,715
Circulation Type: controlled

**Owner(s):**
National Trade Publications, Inc.
13 Century Hill
Latham, NY 12110-2197
Telephone: (518) 783-1281
FAX: (518) 783-1386
Ownership %: 100
**Editorial:**
Greg Norton ................................Editor
Charlotte Prior ........................Advertising
**Readers:** Water treatment professionals.

### WATER WELL JOURNAL
25257

6375 Riverside Dr.
Dublin, OH 43017
Telephone: (614) 761-3222
FAX: (614) 761-3446
Year Established: 1946
Pub. Frequency: m.
Page Size: standard
Subscrip. Rate: $24/yr.
Freelance Pay: $50/printed page
Print Process: offset
Circulation: 32,000
Circulation Type: controlled & paid
**Owner(s):**
Ground Water Publishing Co.
6375 Riverside Dr.
Dublin, OH 43017
Telephone: (614) 761-3222
Ownership %: 100
**Management:**
Anita Stanley ..........................Publisher
**Editorial:**
Gloria Swanson ......................Senior Editor
Anita Stanley ..............................Editor
Joni Jouer ..............................Products Editor
**Desc.:** Articles aimed at water well contractors, pump dealers, others concerned with groundwater supply. Carries new trade literature, personnel changes, association news, new products news.
**Readers:** 75% water well contractors.

## Group 274-Welding & Brazing

### GASES & WELDING DISTRIBUTOR
25260

1100 Superior Ave.
Cleveland, OH 44114
Telephone: (216) 696-7000
FAX: (216) 696-7658
Year Established: 1957
Pub. Frequency: bi-m.
Page Size: standard
Subscrip. Rate: $30/yr.
Materials: 01,02,06,16,21,27,28,29,30,31,32,33
Freelance Pay: $65/printed pg.
Print Process: web offset
Circulation: 11,000
Circulation Type: controlled & paid
**Owner(s):**
Penton Publishing
1100 Superior Ave.
Cleveland, OH 44114
Telephone: (216) 696-7000
FAX: (216) 696-7658
Ownership %: 100
**Editorial:**
Mike Vasilakes ..........................Editor
Ronald Welter ......................Associate Editor
Patricia Smith .................Editorial Assistant
Ann Reiss .......................Production Editor
**Desc.:** Marketing, technology, business operations and regulations management for distributors of welding supplies and industrial, medical and safety gases.
**Readers:** Welding supply distributors, gas distributors, mill supply houses, air conditioning supply, safety supply, manufacturers, sales and owners.

### WELDING DESIGN & FABRICATION
25259

1100 Superior Ave.
Cleveland, OH 44114
Telephone: (216) 696-7000
FAX: (216) 696-7658
Year Established: 1917
Pub. Frequency: m.
Page Size: standard
Subscrip. Rate: $45/yr.
Materials: 02,05,06,15,17,25,27,28,29,30,31,32,33
Freelance Pay: $75/printed page
Circulation: 42,000
Circulation Type: controlled
**Owner(s):**
Penton Publishing
1100 Superior Ave.
Cleveland, OH 44114
Telephone: (216) 696-7000
Ownership %: 100
**Management:**
Sal F. Marino .....................Chairman of Board
Daniel Ramella ...........................President
Rosalie Brosilow ..........................Publisher
Lynne McLaughlin .......Classified Adv. Manager
**Editorial:**
Rosalie Brosilow ..........................Editor
Larry Davis ..........................Art Department
**Desc.:** Material must be of interest to manufacturers of fabricated-metal products, and users of fabricating and inspection processes. Describes economical use of best types of materials, equipment, accessories, tools, etc. for best quality fabrication by welding, cutting and forming. Departments Include: Products, Industry News, Applications, Safety & Health, Research, People, Literature, Headlines, Welding Date Sheet, Library, Events, Education.
**Readers:** Engineers, designers, purchasing agents, production and maintenance managers.

### WELDING JOURNAL
25261

550 N.W. LeJeune Rd.
Miami, FL 33126
Telephone: (305) 443-9353
FAX: (305) 442-7451
Year Established: 1919
Pub. Frequency: m.
Page Size: standard
Subscrip. Rate: $90/yr. non-members; free to members of A.W.S.
Materials: 01,02,06,15,16,27,29,30,32,33
Print Process: web offset
Circulation: 46,000
Circulation Type: paid
**Owner(s):**
American Welding Society
550 N.W. Le Jeune Rd.
Miami, FL 33126
Telephone: (305) 443-9353
Ownership %: 100
**Management:**
Jeff Weber ...............................Publisher
Rob Saltzstein ...................Advertising Manager
**Editorial:**
Andrew Cullison .......................Senior Editor
Jeff Weber ..................................Editor
Linda Hart ...........................Managing Editor

**Desc.:** Editorial material divided into following sections: Feature Articles; Practical Welder; Society and Related Events; Welding Research Supplement. Illustrated technical articles written by experts in the field. Departments include: News of the Industry, New Products, New Literature, Safety & Health, Personnel, Contracts, Coming Events, Classified Ads, Press-Time News, Metalworking Press Notes, Editorial, Society News, Section News.
**Readers:** Executives, engineers, metallurgists, contractors and operators.

## Group 276-Wire

### WIRE JOURNAL INTERNATIONAL
22935

1570 Boston Post Rd.
Guilford, CT 06437
Telephone: (203) 453-2777
FAX: (203) 453-8384
Mailing Address:
P.O. Box H
Guilford, CT 06437
Year Established: 1968
Pub. Frequency: m.
Page Size: standard
Subscrip. Rate: $60/yr. US; $70/yr. Canada; $80/yr. foreign; $25/add for airmail
Materials: 01,06,27,28
Freelance Pay: negotiable
Print Process: web
Circulation: 35,670
Circulation Type: controlled & paid
**Owner(s):**
Wire Association International
1570 Boston Post Rd.
Guilford, CT 06437
Telephone: (203) 453-2777
FAX: (203) 453-8384
Ownership %: 100
**Management:**
Paul R. Casteran ..........................Publisher
Jan Valois ..........................Circulation Manager
**Editorial:**
Lee Bayusik ..............................Editor
Adam Barrett ...........................Art Director
Anita Oliva ...................Director of Publications
John S. Slater ...................Marketing Director
**Desc.:** Staff and by-lined articles on methods and developments relating to drawing, extruding, rolling, forming and processing wire for the wire and cable manufacturing industry. Official publication of Wire Association International.
**Readers:** Operational and technical engineers and managers in the manufacturing of ferrous, nonferrous and electrical wire and cable and fabricators who use wire to produce wire end products, including fiber optics. General and administrative, sales and marketing personnel.

### WIRE TECHNOLOGY INTERNATIONAL MAGAZINE
23481

3869 Darrow Rd., Ste. 101
Cuyahoga Falls, OH 44224
Telephone: (216) 686-9544
FAX: (216) 686-9563
Year Established: 1973
Pub. Frequency: bi-m.
Page Size: standard
Subscrip. Rate: $30/yr. US & Canada; $60/yr. foreign
Circulation: 10,725
Circulation Type: controlled

**Materials Accepted/Included:** 01-Business news 02-By-line articles 03-Fashion news 04-Food news 05-Freelance copy 06-Letters to editor 07-Real estate news 08-Sports news 09-Travel news 10-Book rev. 11-Movie rev. 12-Music rev. 13-TV rev. 14-Theater rev. 15-Coming events 16-Obituaries 17-Question & answer 18-Social announcements 19-Artwork 20-Cartoons 21-Photos 22-TV listings 23-Audio rec. 24-Video rec. 25-Books 26-Films/film clips 27-Personnel news 28-Press releases 29-New product news/photos 30-Trade lit. 31-Contracts awarded 32-Display adv. 33-Classified adv.

**Owner(s):**
Initial Publications, Inc.
3869 Darrow Rd., Ste. 101
Cuyahoga Falls, OH 44224
Telephone: (216) 686-9544
FAX: (216) 686-9563
Ownership %: 100
**Management:**
John L. Jones ..............................President
John L. Jones ..............................Publisher
**Editorial:**
Thomas H. Dreher ........................Editor
James C. Keebler ...........Technical Director
**Desc.:** Wire Technology magazine is a
vertical technical publication devoted to
the manufacture of ferrous and
nonferrous bare and insulated wire, and
to users of equipment whose end
products are made with or from wire,
rod, bar, and metal tubing. Job studies,
forecasts and survey articles are
included. Departments include: Coming
Events, New Products, Free Literature,
Industry News, Fiber Optic News, Fiber
Optic Products, and Fiber Optic
Literature.
**Readers:** Technical articles, economic and
management reports, and all articles of
interest to people in the wire and cable
industry. Jobs studies and area focus
are two outstanding features published.
Coverage of meetings and profiles of
upcoming exhibitions. Departments
include: Industry News, Wiremen, New
Equipment, New Literature, Innovations,
Translations, New Products - all to do
with the wire industry.

## Group 278-Woodworking & Plywood

65458
### CABINETMAKER
455 N. Cityfront Plaza Dr.
Chicago, IL 60611
Telephone: (312) 222-2000
Year Established: 1987
Pub. Frequency: bi-m.
Page Size: standard
Subscrip. Rate: $25/yr.
Materials: 28,29,30,32,33
Circulation: 30,000
Circulation Type: paid
**Owner(s):**
Delta Communications, Inc.
455 N. Cityfront Plaza Dr.
Chicago, IL 60611
Telephone: (312) 222-2000
Ownership %: 100
**Management:**
S. L. Berliner ..............................Publisher
**Editorial:**
Bruce Plantz ..............................Editor
**Desc.:** Features American and European
cabinet design, construction and
finishing.
**Readers:** Kitchen cabinetmakers are the
main audience.

68754
### CREATIVE WOODWORK & CRAFTS
243 Newton-Sparta Rd.
Newton, NJ 07860
Telephone: (201) 383-8080
FAX: (201) 383-8133
Pub. Frequency: bi-m.

**Owner(s):**
MSC Publishing, Inc.
243 Newton-Sparta Rd.
Newton, NJ 07860
Telephone: (201) 383-8080
Ownership %: 100
**Editorial:**
Robert Becker ..............................Editor

66739
### HARDWOOD EXPRESSIONS
400 Penn Center Blvd,. Ste. 530
Pittsburgh, PA 15235
Telephone: (412) 829-0770
FAX: (412) 829-0844
Year Established: 1990
Pub. Frequency: q.
Page Size: 4 color photos/art
Subscrip. Rate: free
Circulation: 25,000
Circulation Type: controlled
**Owner(s):**
Hardwood Manufacturers Association
Ownership %: 100
**Management:**
Laurie L. Cochran .............Operations Manager
**Editorial:**
Susan Regan ...........................Executive Editor

65244
### HARDWOOD FLOORS
1846 Hoffman St.
Madison, WI 53704
Telephone: (608) 249-0186
FAX: (608) 249-1153
Year Established: 1987
Pub. Frequency: bi-m.
Subscrip. Rate: $36/yr.
Circulation: 24,000
Circulation Type: controlled & paid
**Owner(s):**
Athletic Business Publications, Inc.
1846 Hoffman St.
Madison, WI 53704
Telephone: (608) 249-0186
Ownership %: 100
**Management:**
Gretchen Kelsey Brown ...............Publisher
**Editorial:**
Rick Berg ......................Editorial Director
**Desc.:** Covers design applications,
association news and major issues.
**Readers:** Floor covering retailers, builders
and interior designers.

25265
### MODERN WOODWORKING
167 E. Hwy. 72
Collierville, TN 38017
Telephone: (901) 853-7478
FAX: (901) 853-6437
Mailing Address:
P.O. Box 640
Collierville, TN 38017
Year Established: 1954
Pub. Frequency: 12/yr.
Page Size: tabloid
Subscrip. Rate: $24/yr.
Circulation: 53,300
Circulation Type: free
**Owner(s):**
Associations Publications, Inc.
P.O. Box 640
Collierville, TN 38017
Telephone: (901) 853-7478
Ownership %: 100
**Management:**
James D. Powell ..............................Publisher
Zea Knight ...........................Circulation Manager
**Editorial:**
Joyce Powell ......................Managing Editor
Michael W. Powell .......Administrative Assistant

Raymond A. Helmers ...............Technical Editor
**Readers:** Furniture and cabinet
manufacturers.

25267
### NATIONAL HARDWOOD MAGAZINE
1235 Sycamore View Rd.
Memphis, TN 38184
Telephone: (901) 372-8280
FAX: (901) 373-6180
Mailing Address:
P.O. Box 34908
N. Memphis, TN 38184
Year Established: 1927
Pub. Frequency: m.
Page Size: standard
Subscrip. Rate: $35/yr.
Materials: 32,33
Circulation: 5,000
Circulation Type: controlled & paid
**Owner(s):**
Miller Publishing, Inc.
P.O. Box 34908
Memphis, TN 38184
Telephone: (901) 372-8280
Ownership %: 100
**Management:**
Paul J. Miller, Sr. ..............................Publisher
**Editorial:**
Gary Miller ..............................Editor
**Readers:** Plant management, purchasing
executives.
**Deadline:** story-60 days; ads-60 days

25268
### PANEL WORLD
225 Hanrick St.
Montgomery, AL 36104
Telephone: (205) 834-1170
FAX: (205) 834-4525
Mailing Address:
P.O. Box 2268
Montgomery, AL 36102
Year Established: 1960
Pub. Frequency: bi-m.
Page Size: standard
Subscrip. Rate: $12/yr. US; $20/yr.
Canada; $25/yr. foreign; $35/yr. airmail
Circulation: 11,000
Circulation Type: controlled
**Owner(s):**
Panel World, Inc.
P.O. Box 2268
Montgomery, AL 36102
Telephone: (205) 834-1170
Ownership %: 100
**Management:**
David Ramsey ..............................Publisher
David Knight ..............................Publisher
Dianne C. Sullivan ...............Business Manager
**Editorial:**
David Knight ......................Executive Editor
Rich Donnell ......................Editorial Director
Kay Oldham ..............................Advertising
Tim Shaddick ..............................Advertising
Alan Brett ..............................Advertising
John Hibbard .........Advertising Sales Manager
Patti Campbell ...........Production Coordinator
**Desc.:** News concerning plywood, veneer,
panel, and particleboard manufacturing
firms and officials, distributors, and
dealers of such. Features articles on
plywood-veneer and particleboard sales
techniques and manufacturing methods.
Much of this material is staff-written,
based on field contact. Articles are up to
1,500 words. Publicity material used only
if newsworthy and not commercially
slanted, with photos credited.

**Readers:** Industrial buyers and fabricators
of plywood, composite wood panels, and
veneer manufacturers.

25269
### WOOD & WOOD PRODUCTS
400 Knightsbridge Pkwy.
Lincolnshire, IL 60069
Telephone: (708) 634-2600
FAX: (708) 634-4379
Mailing Address:
P.O. Box 1400
Lincolnshire, IL 60069
Year Established: 1896
Pub. Frequency: 13/yr.
Page Size: standard
Subscrip. Rate: $45/yr.
Freelance Pay: $150-$250
Circulation: 51,466
Circulation Type: controlled
**Owner(s):**
Vance Publishing Corp.
P.O. Box 400
Lincolnshire, IL 60069
Telephone: (708) 634-2600
Ownership %: 100
**Management:**
William Vance ...............Chairman of Board
Harry Urban ..............................Publisher
Donna Tribble .............Classified Adv. Manager
**Editorial:**
Rich Christianson ..............................Editor
**Desc.:** Covers all phases of the furniture,
cabinet and wood products industry.
Contributed articles deal with all phases
of furniture and plant operations, both
basic materials and furniture and wood
product manufacturing and use
of machinery plus production methods.
Generally run from 1,000 to 1,500 words
with illustrations. Departments include:
New Products, Production Ideas, Trends
and News.
**Readers:** Manufacturers of all types of
furniture, cabinets, & wood products.

65478
### WOOD DIGEST
445 Broadhollow Rd., Ste. 21
Melville, NY 11747-3601
Telephone: (212) 845-2700
Year Established: 1969
Pub. Frequency: q.
Page Size: tabloid
Subscrip. Rate: free
Materials: 01,02,05,06,10,15,16,17,19,20,
21,23,24,25,27,28,29,30,32,33
Freelance Pay: varies
Print Process: web offset
Circulation: 55,000
Circulation Type: controlled
**Owner(s):**
PTN Publishingt Co.
445 Broad Hollow Rd.
Melville, NY 11747
Telephone: (212) 845-2700
FAX: (212) 845-7109
Ownership %: 100
**Management:**
John Aufderhaar ..............................Publisher
**Editorial:**
Alan Richman ..............................Editor
Chris Palermo ...........................Managing Editor
Eliot Sefrin ......................Editorial Director
**Desc.:** productivity solutions for
manufacturers of furniture, cabinets,
millwork and specialty wood products.
**Readers:** Manufacturers of furniture,
cabinets, store fixtures and casegoods
panel laminators, millwork specialists,
architects, distributors and product
representatives.

---

**Materials Accepted/Included:** 01-Business news 02-By-line articles 03-Fashion news 04-Food news 05-Freelance copy 06-Letters to editor 07-Real estate news 08-Sports news 09-Travel news
10-Book rev. 11-Movie rev. 12-Music rev. 13-TV rev. 14-Theater rev. 15-Coming events 16-Obituaries 17-Question & answer 18-Social announcements 19-Artwork 20-Cartoons 21-Photos 22-TV listings
23-Audio rec. 24-Video rec. 25-Books 26-Films/film clips 27-Personnel news 28-Press releases 29-New product news/photos 30-Trade lit. 31-Contracts awarded 32-Display adv. 33-Classified adv.

4-395

# Section 5
# FARM & AGRICULTURAL MAGAZINES

This section contains complete listing for magazines that are farm or agriculturally oriented. The magazines are listed alphabetically within each subject group. Subject groups follow numerical order according to group number.

A subject listing is provided with a page reference to where each group heading may be found within the main listings.

Please refer to the Alphabetical Cross Index in Section 3 to locate related subject publications within the Farm and Agricultural Magazine section or related subject categories/listings in the Service, Trade, Professional, Industrial or Consumer Magazine or Newsletter section.

For materials accepted/included, refer to the coded list at the bottom of each page.

## SUBJECT GROUPS INCLUDED

## Group 502-Beekeeping

**AMERICAN BEE JOURNAL**　25272
51 S. Second St.
Hamilton, IL 62341
Telephone: (217) 847-3324
FAX: (217) 847-3660
Year Established: 1861
Pub. Frequency: m.
Page Size: standard
Subscrip. Rate: $16.20/yr.
Freelance Pay: $.75/col. in.
Circulation: 13,000
Circulation Type: paid
**Owner(s):**
Dadant & Sons
51 S. Second St.
Hamilton, IL 62341
Telephone: (217) 847-3324
Ownership %: 100
**Management:**
Charles Dadant .......................President
Marta Menn .......................Advertising Manager
**Editorial:**
Joe M. Graham ...........................Editor
**Desc.:** Articles on all phases of
beekeeping and honey production.
**Readers:** Beekeepers.

**BEE CULTURE**　25273
623 W. Liberty St.
Medina, OH 44256
Telephone: (216) 725-6677
FAX: (216) 725-5624
Mailing Address:
P.O. Box 706
Medina, OH 44258
Year Established: 1873
Pub. Frequency: m.
Page Size: standard
Subscrip. Rate: $16.50/yr.
Materials: 05,06,10,15,20,25,28,29,30,32,33
Freelance Pay: negotiable
Circulation: 12,000
Circulation Type: paid
**Owner(s):**
A. I. Root Co.
P.O. Box 706
Medina, OH 44258
Telephone: (216) 725-6677
FAX: (216) 725-5624
Ownership %: 100
**Management:**
Dawn Brotherton ...............Advertising Manager
**Editorial:**
Kim Flottum .............................Editor
Dr. Richard Taylor ...............Contributing Editor
Dr. Mark Winston ...............Contributing Editor
Ann Harmon ...................Contributing Editor
Richard Bonney ...................Contributing Editor
Dr. Roger Morse ....................Research Editor
**Desc.:** Provides beekeeping information for
the beginner, sideliner and commercial
beekeeper. Also, we have articles on
honey plants, gardening and other
peripheral areas of this pastime.
**Readers:** Beekeepers and those interested
in environmental issues.
**Deadline:** story-1st of mo. prior to pub.
date; news-1st of mo. prior; photo-1st of
mo. prior; ads-1st of mo. prior

**SPEEDY BEE**　68818
P.O. Box 998
Jesup, GA 31545-0998
Telephone: (912) 427-4018
FAX: (912) 427-8447
Year Established: 1972
Pub. Frequency: m.

Page Size: tabloid
Subscrip. Rate: $1.75 newsstand;
$17.75/yr.
Materials: 02,06,10,15,16,19,20,21,25,28,
29,30,32,33
Print Process: offset
Circulation: 5,000
Circulation Type: paid
**Owner(s):**
Fore's Honey Farms, Inc.
P.O. Box 998
Jesup, GA 31545-0998
Telephone: (912) 427-4018
FAX: (912) 427-8447
Ownership %: 100
**Management:**
Donna G. Poythress ..........Advertising Manager
**Editorial:**
Troy H. Fore, Jr. ..............................Editor
**Desc.:** Covers the beekeeping and honey
industry.
**Readers:** Covers all aspects of
beekeeping, from hobbyist to
commercial beekeepers, research
scientists, supply dealers, etc.
**Deadline:** story-20th of mo. prior to date of
issue; news-20th of mo.; photo-20th of
mo.; ads-20th of mo.

## Group 504-Farm Organizations & Cooperatives

**AG ALERT**　25404
1601 Exposition Blvd. - FB 9
Sacramento, CA 95815
Telephone: (916) 924-4140
FAX: (916) 929-1680
Year Established: 1974
Pub. Frequency: w.
Page Size: tabloid
Subscrip. Rate: membership
Materials: 01,05,06,15,28,30,32,33
Freelance Pay: negotiable
Print Process: web offset
Circulation: 45,000
Circulation Type: controlled
**Owner(s):**
California Farm Bureau Federation
1601 Exposition Blvd., FB9
Sacramento, CA 95815
Telephone: (916) 924-4140
FAX: (916) 929-1680
Ownership %: 100
**Management:**
Clark Biggs .............................Publisher
Jim Taylor .........................Advertising Manager
Margaret Rodriguez ..........Operations Manager
**Editorial:**
Steve Adler .............................Editor
Don Myrick ...........................Managing Editor
**Desc.:** Covers all phases of agriculture in
California. Primarily staff-written; uses
little outside material.
**Readers:** Members of the California Farm
Bureau Federation.
**Deadline:** story-16 days prior to pub. date;
news-16 days; photo-16 days; ads-16
days

**AG FOCUS**　25406
420 E. Main St.
Batavia, NY 14020
Telephone: (716) 343-2244
FAX: (716) 343-1275
Year Established: 1974
Pub. Frequency: m.
Page Size: standard
Subscrip. Rate: $30/yr.
Materials: 33
Freelance Pay: no paid articles
Print Process: offset
Circulation: 1,500

Circulation Type: paid
**Owner(s):**
Cooperative Extension
420 East Main St.
Batavia, NY 14020
Telephone: (716) 343-3040
Ownership %: 100
**Management:**
Cooperative Extension ........................Publisher
Judi Best ..........................Advertising Manager
**Editorial:**
Nathan Herendeen ................Executive Editor
Nathan Herendeen ................Managing Editor
Nathan Herendeen .......................News Editor
Nathan Herendeen .............................Photo
Nathan Herendeen ....................Technical Editor
**Desc.:** Educational information for
agricultural producers in the counties of
Niagara, Orleans, Genesee and Monroe
in New York State. Departments include:
Dairy, Field Crops, Vegetable Crops,
Horticultural Crops, Land Use, Beef,
Sheep and Swine, and Farm
Business Management.
**Readers:** Farmers and agri-business.

**ALFA NEWS**　25408
2108 E. South Blvd.
Montgomery, AL 36116
Telephone: (205) 288-3900
FAX: (205) 284-3957
Mailing Address:
P.O. Box 11000
Montgomery, AL 36111
Year Established: 1924
Pub. Frequency: q.
Page Size: Standard
Subscrip. Rate: included in membership
dues
Materials: 32,33
Freelance Pay: assignment only
Print Process: offset
Circulation: 269,000
Circulation Type: controlled
**Owner(s):**
Alabama Farmers Federation
P.O. Box 11000
Montgomery, AL 36111
Telephone: (205) 288-3900
Ownership %: 100
**Management:**
Ronnie McKinney ..............Advertising Manager
**Editorial:**
Mark Morrison ..............................Editor
**Desc.:** Pertains to consumer information,
especially as it relates to Farmer
Federation policyholders. New slant
toward health & fitness including
exercise, nutrition, etc.
**Readers:** Associate members of Alabama
Farmers Federation.

**ARIZONA FARM BUREAU NEWS**　25411
3401 E. Elwood St.
Phoenix, AZ 85040-1626
Telephone: (602) 470-0088
FAX: (602) 470-0178
Year Established: 1948
Pub. Frequency: s-m.
Page Size: tabloid
Subscrip. Rate: $25/yr.
Materials: 01,02,04,05,06,17,24,25,28,29,
30,32
Print Process: offset lithography
Circulation: 4,500
Circulation Type: controlled & paid
**Owner(s):**
Arizona Farm Bureau Federation
Telephone: (602) 470-0088
Ownership %: 100
**Management:**
Andy Kurtz ...............................Publisher

**Desc.:** Generally promotional material is
used in ads. Information related to
agriculture is featured.
**Readers:** Farmers and ranchers (members
of Arizona Farm Bureau).
**Deadline:** story-2 wks. prior to pub. date;
news-2 wks. prior; photo-2 wks. prior;
ads-2 wks. prior

**FARM NEWS & VIEWS**　25488
6200 N.W. 2nd St.
Oklahoma City, OK 73127
Telephone: (405) 789-5666
FAX: (405) 491-1599
Mailing Address:
P.O. Box 24000
Oklahoma City, OK 73124
Year Established: 1920
Pub. Frequency: m.
Page Size: tabloid
Subscrip. Rate: free with membership;
$11/yr.
Circulation: 110,000
Circulation Type: free & paid
**Owner(s):**
Okla. Farmers Union
P.O. Box 24000
Oklahoma City, OK 73124
Telephone: (405) 789-5666
Ownership %: 100
**Editorial:**
Phillip Klutts ................................Editor
H. Lee Streetman ...................Managing Editor
**Desc.:** News, pictures and features mostly
about members of the organization, local
and county organizations, state
organizations, and their projects.
Considerable space devoted to
legislation before Congress and the
Oklahoma Legislature. Departments
include: "The president reports to the
membership". Devoted to preservation
of the Family Farm System of
Agriculture in the United States.
**Readers:** Members, News Media,
Members of State Legislature, Ag
Officials.
**Deadline:** news-20th of mo.; ads-15th of
mo.

**FARM NEWS OF ERIE & WYOMING COUNTIES**　25436
21 S. Grove St.
East Aurora, NY 14052
Telephone: (716) 652-5401
FAX: (716) 652-5073
Year Established: 1914
Pub. Frequency: m.
Page Size: pg.: 7 13/16 x 10; col.: 1 7/8
Subscrip. Rate: $15/yr.
Circulation: 1,600
Circulation Type: paid
**Owner(s):**
Cooperative Extension Association of Erie
County
21 S. Grove St.
East Aurora, NY 14052
Telephone: (716) 652-5401
Ownership %: 100
**Editorial:**
David Weaver .................................Editor
**Desc.:** Strictly an agricultural publication,
consisting primarily of local articles of
interest to readers in county.
**Readers:** Agricultural people.

**FLORIDAGRICULTURE**　25453
5700 S.W. 34th St.
Gainesville, FL 32608
Telephone: (904) 374-1523
FAX: (904) 374-1501
Mailing Address:
P.O. Box 147030
Gainesville, FL 32614

**Materials Accepted/Included:** 01-Business news 02-By-line articles 03-Fashion news 04-Food news 05-Freelance copy 06-Letters to editor 07-Real estate news 08-Sports news 09-Travel news 10-Book rev. 11-Movie rev. 12-Music rev. 13-TV rev. 14-Theater rev. 15-Coming events 16-Obituaries 17-Question & answer 18-Social announcements 19-Artwork 20-Cartoons 21-Photos 22-TV listings 23-Audio rec. 24-Video rec. 25-Books 26-Films/film clips 27-Personnel news 28-Press releases 29-New product news/photos 30-Trade lit. 31-Contracts awarded 32-Display adv. 33-Classified adv.

Year Established: 1943
Pub. Frequency: m.
Page Size: tabloid
Subscrip. Rate: members only
Materials: 04,05,06,15,21,27,30,32,33
Freelance Pay: varies
Print Process: offset
Circulation: 96,500
Circulation Type: free & paid
**Owner(s):**
Florida Farm Bureau Fed.
P.O. Box 147030
Gainesville, FL 32614
Telephone: (904) 378-1321
Ownership %: 100
**Management:**
Larry Ewing ...........................Executive Director
Mary Griffis ..............Classified Adv. Manager
**Editorial:**
Rick Bush ........................................Editor
Mary Ward ..............................Assistant Editor
Rod Hemphill ......................Contributing Editor
Osmara Salas ..............Production Coordinator
Tom Lampert ...........................................Sales
**Desc.:** Material concerns topics affecting agriculture in general and Florida Farm Bureau Federation news.
**Readers:** Florida agricultural producers, related agri-businesses, and all FFB members.
**Deadline:** ads-1st of mo. prior to pub. date

69317

**FMRA NEWS**
950 S. Cherry St., Ste. 508
Denver, CO 80222-2662
Telephone: (303) 758-3513
FAX: (303) 758-0190
Year Established: 1937
Pub. Frequency: a.
Page Size: 8 1/2 X 11
Subscrip. Rate: $20/yr.
Materials: 01,02,15,18
Circulation: 4,000
Circulation Type: paid
**Owner(s):**
American Soc. of Farm Managers & Rural Appraisers
950 S. Cherry St., Ste. 508
Denver, CO 80222
Telephone: (303) 758-3513
FAX: (303) 758-0190
Ownership %: 100
**Editorial:**
Alan L. Yoder ........................................Editor
**Readers:** Agri-business professionals involved in farm management and rural appraisal. Includes information on the organization's activities as well as articles covering current issues.

25455

**GEORGIA FARM BUREAU NEWS**
1620 Bass Rd.
Macon, GA 31210
Telephone: (912) 474-8411
Mailing Address:
P.O. Box 7068
Macon, GA 31298
Year Established: 1938
Pub. Frequency: m.
Page Size: tabloid
Subscrip. Rate: $9/yr.
Materials: 32,33
Circulation: 218,000
Circulation Type: paid
**Owner(s):**
Georgia Farm Bureau Federation
P.O. Box 7068
Macon, GA 31298
Telephone: (912) 474-8411
Ownership %: 100
**Management:**
Camille Smith ....................Advertising Manager
Paul Beliveau ....................Circulation Manager

**Editorial:**
Cecil Yancy .................................................Editor
**Desc.:** Covers the various aspects of agricultural events, legislation, activities of various Farm Bureaus, etc. Primary emphasis is on interpretation of events, policies and legislation affecting the industry rather than technical farm data.
**Readers:** Georgia Farm Bureau Federation membership.

25384

**GRANGE ADVOCATE FOR RURAL PENNSYLVANIA**
1604 N. Second St.
Harrisburg, PA 17102
Telephone: (717) 234-5001
Year Established: 1979
Pub. Frequency: 3/wk.
Page Size: tabloid
Subscrip. Rate: free with membership
Materials: 02,06,16,19,20,21,28,32
Circulation: 35,000
Circulation Type: controlled
**Owner(s):**
Pennslyvania State Grange
1604 N. Second St.
Harrisburg, PA 17102
Telephone: (717) 234-5001
Ownership %: 100
**Editorial:**
James C. Mentzer ..........................Editor
Gordon Hiller ..........................Managing Editor
**Desc.:** Staff-written publication dealing with general news and personnel of farming industry with an emphasis on rural issues.
**Readers:** Pennsylvania farm families, rural Pennsylvania.

25460

**IOWA FARM BUREAU SPOKESMAN**
5400 University
West Des Moines, IA 50266
Telephone: (515) 225-5532
Year Established: 1934
Pub. Frequency: 48/yr.
Page Size: tabloid
Subscrip. Rate: members only
Materials: 04,06
Freelance Pay: negotiated
Print Process: web offset
Circulation: 102,000
Circulation Type: paid
**Owner(s):**
Iowa Farm Bureau
5400 University
West Des Moines, IA 50265
Telephone: (515) 225-5532
Ownership %: 100
**Management:**
John Doak ........................Advertising Manager
**Editorial:**
Darryl Jahn ........................................Editor
Dale Johnson ..........................Managing Editor
**Desc.:** Stories dealing with agricultural policies, programs, production and rural living.
**Readers:** Iowa family farmers.

25472

**MICHIGAN FARM NEWS RURAL LIVING**
P.O. Box 30690
Lansing, MI 48909
Telephone: (517) 323-7000
FAX: (517) 323-6793
Year Established: 1923
Pub. Frequency: q.
Page Size: standard
Subscrip. Rate: membership
Freelance Pay: $50-$150
Circulation: 45,640
Circulation Type: controlled

**Owner(s):**
Michigan Farm Bureau
7373 W. Saginaw Hwy.
Box 30690
Lansing, MI 48917
Telephone: (517) 323-7000
Ownership %: 100
**Management:**
Connie Turbin ....................Advertising Manager
**Editorial:**
Denis Rudat ........................................Editor
Donna Wilber ....................Contributing Editor
**Desc.:** Publication of Michigan Farm Bureau. Devoted to the advancement and improvement of the agricultural interests of Michigan and the nation, educationally, legislatively, and economically.
**Readers:** Farm and rural families in Michigan.

25389

**MISSISSIPPI FARM BUREAU NEWS**
6310 I-55 N.
Jackson, MS 39211
Telephone: (601) 957-3200
Mailing Address:
P.O. Box 1972
Jackson, MS 39215
Year Established: 1922
Pub. Frequency: 6/yr.
Page Size: tabloid
Subscrip. Rate: $2/yr.
Circulation: 185,000
Circulation Type: controlled
**Owner(s):**
Mississippi Farm Bureau Federation, Jackson
6310 I-55 N.
Jackson, MS 39211
Telephone: (601) 957-3200
Ownership %: 100
**Management:**
Glynda Phillips ..................Advertising Manager
**Editorial:**
Glynda Phillips ........................................Editor
**Desc.:** Wide use of photos because of offset printing. Covers news of general interest to farmers (legislation and organization affairs). Articles usually should be one column in length or shorter.
**Readers:** Farm families in all 82 counties of the state.

25475

**MONTANA FARM BUREAU SPOKESMAN**
502 S. 19th Ave., Ste. 4
Bozeman, MT 59715
Telephone: (406) 587-3153
FAX: (406) 587-0319
Year Established: 1919
Pub. Frequency: m. (exc. Mar. & Apr.)
Page Size: tabloid
Subscrip. Rate: $4/yr. members; $25/yr. non-members
Circulation: 5,600
Circulation Type: controlled
**Owner(s):**
Montana Farm Bureau Federation
502 S. 19th Ave., Ste. 4
Bozeman, MT 59715
Telephone: (406) 587-3153
Ownership %: 100
**Editorial:**
Lorna Frank ........................................Editor
J.T. (Jake) Cummins, Jr. ..........Managing Editor
**Desc.:** Features the various meetings held by Montana Farm Bureau, the policies adopted by the state organization and the American Farm Bureau Federation and the political activities of both organizations. Discusses farm problems, both social and economic, from the standpoint of farmers and ranchers.

**Readers:** Practically all Montana farmers and ranchers.

25478

**NEBRASKA FARM BUREAU NEWS**
5225 S. 16th St.
Lincoln, NE 68512
Telephone: (402) 421-4405
FAX: (402) 421-4432
Mailing Address:
P.O. Box 80299
Lincoln, NE 68501
Year Established: 1983
Pub. Frequency: 11/yr.
Page Size: tabloid
Subscrip. Rate: $.50 members
Freelance Pay: varies
Circulation: 45,000
Circulation Type: controlled & paid
**Owner(s):**
Nebraska Farm Bureau Fed.
P.O. Box 80299
Lincoln, NE 68501
Telephone: (402) 421-4405
Ownership %: 100
**Management:**
Cheryl Stubbendieck .........Advertising Manager
**Editorial:**
Cheryl Stubbendieck ..............................Editor
Kim Rogers ....................................Staff Writer
**Desc.:** A publication which goes to the membership of the Nebraska Farm Bureau Federation. Editorial scope is hard news and features relating to farm policy, public relations for agriculture and news of what local organizations are doing.
Some information on production and marketing methods. Publication seeks advertising account placements, subject to guidelines of its Operating Policies.
**Readers:** Nebraska farm families in 88 counties of the state and others who are members of Farm Bureau. These families represent a potential readership of 70,000 persons.
**Deadline:** 1 wk. prior to pub. date

25391

**NEBRASKA UNION FARMER**
1305 Plum St.
Lincoln, NE 68502
Telephone: (402) 476-8815
FAX: (402) 476-8859
Mailing Address:
P.O. Box 22667
Lincoln, NE 68502
Year Established: 1914
Pub. Frequency: m.
Page Size: tabloid
Subscrip. Rate: $10/yr.
Circulation: 4,300
Circulation Type: free
**Owner(s):**
Nebraska Farmers Union
1305 Plum
Lincoln, NE 68502
Telephone: (402) 476-8815
Ownership %: 100
**Editorial:**
Jeff Kirkpatrick ..................Managing Editor
**Desc.:** Midwest agricultural, livestock and crops.
**Readers:** Members of Nebraska Farmers Union.

25481

**NEVADA FARM BUREAU AGRICULTURE & LIVESTOCK JOURNAL**
1300 Marietta Way
Sparks, NV 89431
Telephone: (702) 358-3276
FAX: (702) 358-2107
Year Established: 1931
Pub. Frequency: m.

---

**Materials Accepted/Included:** 01-Business news 02-By-line articles 03-Fashion news 04-Food news 05-Freelance copy 06-Letters to editor 07-Real estate news 08-Sports news 09-Travel news 10-Book rev. 11-Movie rev. 12-Music rev. 13-TV rev. 14-Theater rev. 15-Coming events 16-Obituaries 17-Question & answer 18-Social announcements 19-Artwork 20-Cartoons 21-Photos 22-TV listings 23-Audio rec. 24-Video rec. 25-Books 26-Films/film clips 27-Personnel news 28-Press releases 29-New product news/photos 30-Trade lit. 31-Contracts awarded 32-Display adv. 33-Classified adv.

Page Size: tabloid
Subscrip. Rate: $1/yr.
Materials: 04,06,28,32,33
Print Process: web offset
Circulation: 7,400
Circulation Type: free & paid
**Owner(s):**
Nevada Farm Bureau Federation
1300 Marietta Way
Sparks, NV 89431
Telephone: (702) 358-7737
Ownership %: 100
**Management:**
Norm Cardoza ..................Advertising Manager
**Editorial:**
Norm Cardoza .............................................Editor
**Desc.:** The official publication for the
Nevada Farm Bureau Federation. Most
of the material is agricultural oriented
and use only material that would be
relevant to Nevada agriculture. Use a
few articles on national issues, but try to
tie them in with Nevada agriculture or a
national Farm Bureau issue. Interested
in articles, papers, photos re: rangeland,
cattle culture, potato, alfalfa, onion,
garlic farming, arid region land
management and use.
**Readers:** Mostly ranchers and farmers in
rural Nevada. Many suburbanites in
Reno and Las Vegas.
**Deadline:** story-1 mo.; news-1 mo.; photo-
1 mo.; ads-1 mo.

25392

**OHIO GRANGER**
1031 E. Broad St.
Columbus, OH 43205
Telephone: (614) 258-9569
FAX: (614) 258-3232
Year Established: 1983
Pub. Frequency: bi-m.
Page Size: standard
Subscrip. Rate: $2/yr.
Circulation: 14,500
Circulation Type: controlled
**Owner(s):**
Ohio State Grange
1031 E. Broad St.
Columbus, OH 43205
Telephone: (614) 258-9569
Ownership %: 100
**Management:**
Barbara McKenzie ............Advertising Manager
**Editorial:**
Bernard Shoemaker .................Executive Editor
Barbara McKenzie ..................Assistant Editor
**Desc.:** Features articles of citizenship,
community.
**Readers:** Rural or small town members of
Ohio Granger.

25486

**OKLAHOMA FARM BUREAU
JOURNAL**
2501 N. Stiles
Oklahoma City, OK 73105
Telephone: (405) 523-2300
FAX: (405) 523-2362
Year Established: 1949
Pub. Frequency: m.
Page Size: tabloid
Subscrip. Rate: $5/yr. non-members
Materials: 28,29,30,32,33
Print Process: web offset
Circulation: 102,447
Circulation Type: controlled & paid
**Owner(s):**
Oklahoma Farm Bureau
2501 N. Stiles
Oklahoma City, OK 73105
Telephone: (405) 523-2300
FAX: (405) 523-2362
Ownership %: 100
**Management:**
Mike Nichols ..................Advertising Manager

**Editorial:**
Mike Nichols ..........................Executive Editor
Mike Nichols ....................................Photo
**Desc.:** Almost entirely devoted to news of
the Oklahoma Farm Bureau.
**Readers:** Members of the Oklahoma Farm
Bureau.
**Deadline:** story-1st of mo.; news-1st of
mo.; photo-1st of mo.; ads-last day of
mo.

25393

**OREGON GRANGE BULLETIN**
1125 S.E. Madison, Ste. 102
Portland, OR 97214-3681
Telephone: (503) 236-1118
FAX: (503) 236-4018
Year Established: 1900
Pub. Frequency: m.
Page Size: tabloid
Subscrip. Rate: $10/yr. or membership
Materials: 01,06,28,29,32,33
Print Process: web
Circulation: 17,500
Circulation Type: free & paid
**Owner(s):**
Oregon State Grange
1125 S.E. Madison, Ste. 102
Portland, OR 97214
Telephone: (503) 236-1118
Ownership %: 100
**Management:**
Oregon State Grange ..........................Publisher
Edward Luttrell ...................Advertising Manager
**Editorial:**
Edward Luttrell ............................................Editor
**Desc.:** Grange and community news,
agricultural, public interest, and human
interest stories concerning rural areas
primarily. Features are family farm,
public power and community service
oriented.
**Readers:** Oregon farm and suburban
people.
**Deadline:** story-20th of mo. prior to pub.
date; news-20th of mo. prior; photo-20th
of mo. prior; ads-20th of mo. prior

25399

**TENNESSEE FARM BUREAU
NEWS**
Hwy. 412 E.
Columbia, TN 38402
Telephone: (615) 388-7872
Mailing Address:
P.O. Box 313
Columbia, TN 38402-0313
Year Established: 1922
Pub. Frequency: 10/yr.
Page Size: tabloid
Subscrip. Rate: $5/yr.
Circulation: 422,000
Circulation Type: paid
**Owner(s):**
Tennessee Farm Bureau Federation
P.O. Box 313
Columbia, TN 38402
Telephone: (615) 388-7872
Ownership %: 100
**Editorial:**
Murray Miles ...........................................Editor
**Desc.:** Covers general farm organization
news.
**Readers:** Members of Tennessee Farm
Bureau Federation.

25401

**TEXAS AGRICULTURE**
7420 Fish Pond Rd.
Waco, TX 76710
Telephone: (817) 772-3030
FAX: (817) 772-3628
Mailing Address:
P.O. Box 2689
Waco, TX 76702
Year Established: 1935
Pub. Frequency: s-m.

Page Size: tabloid
Subscrip. Rate: $5/yr.
Materials: 01,06,07,10,11,12,20,21,23,24,
25,26,28,29,30,32,33
Print Process: offset
Circulation: 132,228
Circulation Type: paid
**Owner(s):**
Texas Farm Bureau
P.O. Box 2689
Waco, TX 76702
Telephone: (817) 772-3030
Ownership %: 100
**Management:**
James Gholke ..................Advertising Manager
**Editorial:**
Mike Barnett ............................................Editor
Cathy Krall ..........................................Art Director
**Desc.:** Publication of Texas Farm Bureau
for commercial farmers and ranchers.
**Readers:** Farm, ranch and rural.

54014

**TEXAS NEIGHBORS**
7420 Fish Pond Rd.
Waco, TX 76710
Telephone: (817) 772-3030
FAX: (817) 772-1766
Mailing Address:
P.O. Box 2689
Waco, TX 76702
Year Established: 1985
Pub. Frequency: q.
Page Size: tabloid
Subscrip. Rate: free to members
Freelance Pay: negotiable
Circulation: 318,050
Circulation Type: controlled
**Owner(s):**
Texas Farm Bureau
P.O. Box 2689
Waco, TX 76702
Telephone: (817) 772-3030
Ownership %: 100
**Management:**
Gene Hall .............................................Publisher
**Editorial:**
Mike Barnett ............................................Editor
Larry Binz ...........................................Field Editor
**Desc.:** Features articles on programs,
activities and services of the Texas
Farm Bureau. Emphasizes articles on
rural family living.
**Readers:** Member families of the Texas
Farm Bureau.

25508

**VIRGINIA FARM BUREAU NEWS**
P.O. Box 27552
Richmond, VA 23261
Telephone: (804) 225-7520
FAX: (804) 225-7668
Year Established: 1941
Pub. Frequency: 10/yr. (Sep.-Oct. & Dec.-
Jan. combined)
Page Size: tabloid
Subscrip. Rate: free to members
Freelance Pay: $25/article
Circulation: 109,000
Circulation Type: paid
**Owner(s):**
Virginia Farm Bureau Federation
P.O. Box 27552
Richmond, VA 23261
Telephone: (804) 788-1234
Ownership %: 100
**Editorial:**
Kathy Dixon ............................................Editor
Linda Brown .......................................Advertising
Barbara Zeidman .......Special Services Director
**Desc.:** Covers farm news plus state and
national legislation news concerning
farm people in Virginia. Also includes
articles of interest to our non-farming
members, who read paper for consumer
and voter information and features.

**Readers:** Virginia farmers and others
interested in rural Virginia.

25385

**WASHINGTON STATE GRANGE
NEWS**
924 Capitol Way, S.
Olympia, WA 98501
Telephone: (206) 943-9911
FAX: (206) 357-3548
Year Established: 1912
Pub. Frequency: m.
Page Size: tabloid
Subscrip. Rate: $4.75/yr.; $8.50/2 yrs.
Materials: 10,21,32,33
Print Process: web offset
Circulation: 49,000
Circulation Type: paid
**Owner(s):**
Washington State Grange
P.O. Box 1186
Olympia, WA 98507-1186
Telephone: (206) 943-9911
FAX: (206) 357-3548
Ownership %: 100
**Management:**
Barbara Martino ...................Business Manager
**Editorial:**
Patricia Nikula ..........................Associate Editor
**Desc.:** Devoted to practical agriculture and
grange. Carries articles on homemaking,
cooking, rural life, gardening, travel, and
money.
**Readers:** Every Grange family in state of
Washington, non-members interested in
farm news.
**Deadline:** story-1st Mon. of each mo. prior
to pub. date; news-1st Mon. of each mo.
prior; photo-1st Mon. of each mo. prior;
ads-1st Mon. of each mo. prior

## Group 506-Field Crops

61675

**BETTER CROPS WITH PLANT
FOOD**
655 Engineering Dr., Ste. 110
Norcross, GA 30092-2821
Telephone: (404) 447-0335
FAX: (404) 448-0439
Year Established: 1923
Pub. Frequency: q.
Page Size: pocket
Subscrip. Rate: $8/yr.; free to qualified
subscribers
Circulation: 20,000
Circulation Type: controlled
**Owner(s):**
Potash & Phosphate Institute
655 Engineering Dr., Ste. 110
Norcross, GA 30092-2821
Telephone: (404) 447-0335
Ownership %: 100
**Editorial:**
Don Armstrong ...........................................Editor

25517

**COTTON FARMING**
6263 Poplar Ave.
Ste. 540
Memphis, TN 38119
Telephone: (901) 767-4020
Year Established: 1957
Pub. Frequency: 15/yr.
Page Size: 4 color photos/art
Subscrip. Rate: $12/yr.
Freelance Pay: $150-$300
Circulation: 55,000
Circulation Type: controlled & paid
**Owner(s):**
Little Publications, Inc.
6263 Poplar Ave.
Ste. 540
Memphis, TN 38119
Telephone: (901) 767-4020
Ownership %: 100

**Materials Accepted/Included:** 01-Business news 02-By-line articles 03-Fashion news 04-Food news 05-Freelance copy 06-Letters to editor 07-Real estate news 08-Sports news 09-Travel news 10-Book rev. 11-Movie rev. 12-Music rev. 13-TV rev. 14-Theater rev. 15-Coming events 16-Obituaries 17-Question & answer 18-Social announcements 19-Artwork 20-Cartoons 21-Photos 22-TV listings 23-Audio rec. 24-Video rec. 25-Books 26-Films/film clips 27-Personnel news 28-Press releases 29-New product news/photos 30-Trade lit. 31-Contracts awarded 32-Display adv. 33-Classified adv.

5-4

**Management:**
Walter Little ..............................President
**Editorial:**
Carroll Headley ..............................Editor
**Desc.:** Articles on production of cotton/things farmers do or can do to produce more and better cotton, cut costs, improve operation.
**Readers:** Highly technical, chemical farmers, crop farmers.
**Deadline:** 10th of mo. prior to pub. date

48966

**COTTON GROWER**
8001 Centerview Pkwy., Ste. 212
Cordova, TN 38018
Telephone: (901) 756-8822
FAX: (901) 756-8879
Year Established: 1901
Pub. Frequency: 10/yr.
Page Size: standard
Subscrip. Rate: $14/yr.
Print Process: web offset
Circulation: 58,619
Circulation Type: controlled
**Owner(s):**
Meister Publishing Co.
37733 Euclid Ave.
Willoughby, OH 44094-5992
Telephone: (216) 942-2000
FAX: (216) 975-3447
Ownership %: 100
**Editorial:**
William Spencer ..............................Editor
Alan C. Strohmaier ...........Advertising Director
Chris Demaske ..............Associate Editor
Alan C. Strohmaier .........Associate Publisher
John Graveno ..............Production Director
**Desc.:** Articles include: (1) information pertaining to new chemicals and machinery for cotton and soybeans and for innovative cultural, harvesting and ginning practices to increase efficiency and reduce costs, and (2) analyses of cotton markets, marketing trends and the changing cotton economy. The Southeast and Mid-South editions contain special Southern Soybean Marketing Section. Editorial is 60% on farming practices and 40% on markets and the cotton economy.
**Readers:** Cotton Grower serves the growing, ginning and marketing factions of the cotton industry. For growers of 50 acres or more throughout the cotton belt, with the exception of Texas-Oklahoma where the floor of eligibility is 100 acres.

48962

**COTTON INTERNATIONAL**
8001 Centerview Pkwy., Ste. 212
Cordova, TN 38018-7928
Telephone: (901) 756-8822
FAX: (901) 756-8879
Year Established: 1933
Pub. Frequency: a.
Page Size: standard
Subscrip. Rate: $15/yr. US; $8/yr. foreign
Print Process: web offset
**Owner(s):**
Meister Publishing Co.
37733 Euclid Ave.
Willoughby, OH 44094-5992
Telephone: (216) 942-2000
FAX: (216) 975-3447
Ownership %: 100
**Editorial:**
William Spencer ..............................Editor
Alan C. Strohmaier ...........Advertising Director
David Jones ..............Associate Editor
Alan C. Strohmaier .........Associate Publisher

**Desc.:** Produced for the cotton community throughout the world. This includes large cotton growers, textile manufacturers, brokers and distributors, divided into departments for each producing country in the world and for each country manufacturing cotton textiles. Maintains editorial agents in each country of the world and these people provide worldwide editorial coverage of the cotton and textile industries.
**Readers:** Importers and exporters, as well as merchants, brokers, agents, distributors and mills. Also importers, buyers, distributors and purchasing groups of textile goods. Includes some banks, forwarders, insurers, controllers, and government agencies.

22979

**CROP SCIENCE**
677 S. Segoe Rd.
Madison, WI 53711
Telephone: (608) 273-8080
FAX: (608) 273-2021
Year Established: 1961
Pub. Frequency: bi-m.
Page Size: standard
Subscrip. Rate: $92/yr.
Materials: 32
Circulation: 7,230
Circulation Type: paid
**Owner(s):**
Crop Science Society of America
677 South Segoe Rd.
Madison, WI 53711
Telephone: (608) 273-8080
Ownership %: 100
**Management:**
Robert F. Barnes .......Executive Vice President
Keith R. Schlesinger ........Advertising Manager
Roger Watkins ..............Circulation Manager
David M. Kral ..............Operations Manager
**Editorial:**
Elizabeth L. Klepper ..............................Editor
William R. Luellen ..............Managing Editor
Nicholas Rhodehamel ..............Assistant Editor
**Desc.:** Publication medium for reports of scientific research in crop breeding, genetics, cytology, metabolism, ecology, physiology, biology and molecular genetics.
**Readers:** 90 percent of the readership consists of research scientists in universities, colleges, experiment stations and other public/private research organizations.

25520

**FLUE CURED TOBACCO FARMER**
3000 Highwoods Blvd.
Ste. 300
Raleigh, NC 27604-1029
Telephone: (919) 872-5040
FAX: (919) 876-6531
Year Established: 1964
Pub. Frequency: 9/yr.
Page Size: standard
Subscrip. Rate: $10/yr.; $24/3 yrs.
Materials: 01,02,05,06,10,27,28,29,30,32
Freelance Pay: negotiable
Print Process: web offset
Circulation: 22,963
Circulation Type: controlled
**Owner(s):**
Specialized Agricultural Publications, Inc.
P.O. Box 95075
Raleigh, NC 27625
Telephone: (919) 872-5040
Ownership %: 100
**Management:**
Dayton Matlick ..............................Publisher
Sue Burleson ..............Circulation Manager
Dorothy Kuffler ..............Sales Manager
**Editorial:**
Dayton Matlik ..............................Editor

Mary Evans ..............Managing Editor
Victoria Gardner ..............Production Director
**Desc.:** Feature articles deal with the research-backed production, harvesting and marketing aspects of flue cured tobacco. Included monthly are interviews of farmers, connected businessmen, and research and extension personnel; releases; political aspects relating to tobacco and world news. Semi-technical articles covering every phase of the industry are presented.
**Readers:** Tobacco producers and connected businessmen.
**Deadline:** story-2 mos.; news-2 mos.; photo-2 mos.

68707

**HAY & FORAGE GROWER**
7900 International Dr.
Minneapolis, MN 55425
Telephone: (612) 851-4677
FAX: (612) 851-4601
Year Established: 1986
Pub. Frequency: 3/yr.
Subscrip. Rate: $5/issue; $9.95/yr.
Circulation: 89,900
Circulation Type: paid
**Owner(s):**
Intertec Publishing Corp.
7900 International Dr.
Minneapolis, MN 55425
Telephone: (612) 851-4677
Ownership %: 100
**Management:**
Ron Sorensen ..............................Publisher
**Editorial:**
Neil Tietz ..............................Editor

61565

**OREGON WHEAT**
P.O. Box 400
Pendleton, OR 97801
Telephone: (503) 276-7330
FAX: (503) 276-1723
Year Established: 1954
Pub. Frequency: m.
Page Size: 4 color photos/art
Subscrip. Rate: $1.50/issue; $15/yr.
Circulation: 8,800
Circulation Type: controlled
**Owner(s):**
Oregon Wheat Growers League
Box 400
Pendleton, OR 97801
Telephone: (503) 276-7330
Ownership %: 100
**Bureau(s):**
J A Publishing Corp. dba Master Printers
206 S.E. Court Ave.
Pendleton, OR 97801
Telephone: (503) 276-7845
Contact: Virgil Rupp/Jim Eardley, Associate Editor
**Editorial:**
Scott Hutchinson ..............................Editor
Virgil Rupp ..............Associate Editor
**Desc.:** Official publication of the Oregon Wheat Growers League. Featured articles deal with planting, fertilizers, selection of varieties, weed and disease warnings control techniques, storage, marketing and transportation of all grains is dealt with specifically when new developments or changes emerge. Agricultural policy issues including environmental issues are reported.
**Readers:** Members of Oregon Wheat League and others connected with wheat production and marketing.

25525

**RICE FARMING**
6263 Poplar Ave.
Ste. 540
Memphis, TN 38119
Telephone: (901) 767-4020

Year Established: 1967
Pub. Frequency: 6/yr.
Page Size: standard
Subscrip. Rate: $9/yr.
Freelance Pay: $300-400
**Owner(s):**
Little Publications, Inc.
6263 Poplar Ave.
Ste. 540
Memphis, TN 38119
Telephone: (901) 767-4020
Ownership %: 100
**Management:**
Walter Little ..............................President
**Editorial:**
Carroll Headley ..............................Editor
**Desc.:** Articles on the production of rice, and things farmers do or can do to produce more and better rice, cut costs and improve operation.
**Readers:** Highly technical, chemical farmers, largescale crops.
**Deadline:** 10th of mo. prior to pub. date

25526

**RICE JOURNAL, THE**
3000 Highwoods Blvd., Ste. 300
Raleigh, NC 27604-1029
Telephone: (919) 872-5040
FAX: (919) 876-6531
Year Established: 1897
Pub. Frequency: 6/yr.
Page Size: standard
Subscrip. Rate: $10/yr.; $24/3 yrs.
Materials: 01,02,05
Freelance Pay: negotiable
Print Process: offset sheetfed
Circulation: 13,000
Circulation Type: controlled & paid
**Owner(s):**
Specialized Agricultural Publications
3000 Highwoods Blvd., Ste. 300
Raleigh, NC 27604
Telephone: (919) 872-5040
Ownership %: 100
**Management:**
Dayton Matlick ..............................Publisher
Sue Burleson ..............Circulation Manager
**Editorial:**
Mary Evans ..............................Design Editor
Victoria Gardner ..............Production Director
**Desc.:** Directed toward the many phases of the rice industry: rice farmers, millers, processors, exporters, shippers, and government leaders.
**Readers:** Rice farmers, processors, brokers, and shippers.
**Deadline:** story-2 mo. prior to 1st of pub. mo.; ads-1st of mo. prior to pub. date

68679

**SEED & CROPS INDUSTRY**
2302 W. First St.
Cedar Falls, IA 50613
Telephone: (319) 277-3599
FAX: (319) 277-3783
Mailing Address:
P.O. Box 7
Cedar Falls, IA 06130
Year Established: 1950
Pub. Frequency: 10/yr.
Page Size: standard
Subscrip. Rate: $30/yr.
Circulation: 5,000
Circulation Type: paid
**Owner(s):**
Freiberg Publishing Co.
2302 W. First St.
Cedar Falls, IA 50613-2282
Telephone: (319) 277-3599
Ownership %: 100
**Editorial:**
Bill Freiberg ..............................Editor

**Materials Accepted/Included:** 01-Business news 02-By-line articles 03-Fashion news 04-Food news 05-Freelance copy 06-Letters to editor 07-Real estate news 08-Sports news 09-Travel news 10-Book rev. 11-Movie rev. 12-Music rev. 13-TV rev. 14-Theater rev. 15-Coming events 16-Obituaries 17-Question & answer 18-Social announcements 19-Artwork 20-Cartoons 21-Photos 22-TV listings 23-Audio rec. 24-Video rec. 25-Books 26-Films/film clips 27-Personnel news 28-Press releases 29-New product news/photos 30-Trade lit. 31-Contracts awarded 32-Display adv. 33-Classified adv.

5-5

## SEED TRADE BUYER'S GUIDE
68681

380 E. Northwest Hwy.
Des Plaines, IL 60016-2282
Telephone: (708) 298-6622
FAX: (708) 390-0408
Year Established: 1917
Pub. Frequency: a.: Apr.
Page Size: standard
Subscrip. Rate: $20/yr.
Materials: 32
Print Process: offset
Circulation: 5,000
Circulation Type: paid
**Owner(s):**
Scranton Gillette Communications, Inc.
380 E. Northwest Hwy.
Des Plaines, IL 60016-2282
Telephone: (708) 298-6622
Ownership %: 100
**Management:**
Gene H. McCormick ...........................Publisher
Doug O'Gorden ........................Sales Manager
**Editorial:**
Lynn Whitmore Grooms ....................Editor
**Desc.:** Contains a compilation of revised
state-by-state seed laws, as well as
company and supplier listings.
**Deadline:** ads-Feb. 14

## WHEAT LIFE
25530

109 E. First Ave.
Ritzville, WA 99169
Telephone: (509) 659-0610
FAX: (509) 659-4302
Year Established: 1956
Pub. Frequency: m.
Page Size: standard
Subscrip. Rate: $1 newsstand; $12/yr.
Circulation: 14,700
Circulation Type: paid
**Owner(s):**
Washington Assn. of Wheat Growers
109 E. First Ave.
Ritzville, WA 99169
Telephone: (509) 659-0610
Ownership %: 100
**Management:**
David Andersen ...................................Publisher
**Desc.:** Published for commercial growers
of wheat and barley and wheat and
barley land owners. Contains wheat
industry news, marketing information,
industry advertising,
production information, and editorials.
Emphasis on efforts of Wash. Assn. of
Wheat Growers, regional wheat
research, legislation and
export developments.
**Readers:** 90% Washington state wheat
growers & landlords, 5% out of state
growers, 5% agri - businesses, schools,
media.
**Deadline:** 1st of mo. prior to pub. date

## Group 508-Fruits, Nuts &
## Vegetables

## AMERICAN FRUIT GROWER
48969

37733 Euclid Ave.
Willoughby, OH 44094-5992
Telephone: (216) 942-2000
FAX: (216) 975-3447
Year Established: 1880
Pub. Frequency: m.
Page Size: standard
Subscrip. Rate: $14/yr.
Print Process: web offset
Circulation: 56,499
Circulation Type: controlled

**Owner(s):**
Meister Publishing Co.
37733 Euclid Ave.
Willoughby, OH 44094-5592
Telephone: (216) 942-2000
FAX: (216) 975-3447
Ownership %: 100
**Editorial:**
Gary Acuff ...............................................Editor
Carol J. Schram ...............Advertising Director
Carol J. Schram ...............Associate Publisher
Denise Derrer ........................Editorial Assistant
**Desc.:** Covers all phases of growing,
shipping, packaging, variety selection
planting, fertilizing, frost protection,
insect and disease control, pruning,
mechanical harvesting, storage and
marketing. Monthly features are included
on new equipment, state grower news,
grower labor and special departments
covering apples, berries, grapes, citrus,
stone fruits, pears and nuts. Grower
marketing efforts, including market
research and advertising to the ultimate
consumer, along with coverage of
pesticides and spraying equipment are
incorporated.
**Readers:** Commercial fruit growers,
orchard managers, orchard supply
dealers & jobbers, fruit associations &
grower-owned co-ops, shippers, packers,
canners & fruit processors, state &
national horticultural & pomological
societies, agricultural schools &
colleges, students and professional
horticulturists.

## AMERICAN POTATO JOURNAL
25535

University Of Maine
Orono, ME 04469
Telephone: (207) 581-3160
FAX: (207) 581-1636
Mailing Address:
241 Main St.
Orono, ME 04473
Year Established: 1923
Pub. Frequency: m.
Page Size: standard
Subscrip. Rate: $40/yr. individual; $65/yr.
institution; $15/yr. student
Freelance Pay: none
Circulation: 1,500
Circulation Type: paid
**Owner(s):**
Potato Association of America
241 Main St.
Orono, ME 04473
Telephone: (207) 866-4793
Ownership %: 100
**Management:**
Joseph Sieczka ...............................President
Ronald Knight ...................Advertising Manager
**Editorial:**
Hugu J. Murphy ...................Editor in Chief
**Desc.:** Devoted to publication of research
workers, handlers or processors. Also
uses articles of a less technical nature
with special interests to growers,
reviews of exceptional books on the
potato industry, foreign publications and
bulletins.
**Readers:** Research personnels in
universities, state institutions, growers,
handlers, processors of potatoes.

## AMERICAN VEGETABLE GROWER
48968

37733 Euclid Ave.
Willoughby, OH 44094-5992
Telephone: (216) 942-2000
FAX: (216) 942-0662
Year Established: 1953
Pub. Frequency: m.

Page Size: standard
Subscrip. Rate: $14/yr.
Print Process: web offset
Circulation: 37,352
Circulation Type: controlled
**Owner(s):**
Meister Publishing Co.
37733 Euclid Ave.
Willoughby, OH 44094-5992
Telephone: (216) 942-2000
FAX: (216) 975-3447
Ownership %: 100
**Editorial:**
Gary Acuff ...............................................Editor
Laurie Moses ........................Managing Editor
Carol J. Schram ...............Advertising Director
Lisa C. Heacox ........................Associate Editor
Carol J. Schram ...............Associate Publisher
Jean D. Aylsworth ........................Staff Writer
**Desc.:** Covers all phases of growing,
shipping and packaging of commercial
vegetables. Feature articles relating to
cultural methods, variety selections,
processing, packaging and marketing
are incorporated. Mechanization
programs for packing house and infield
machinery are included. Monthly
features are marketing, packages and
packaging equipment, bedding plants,
greenhouses and greenhouse crops,
grower news, processing and new
equipment. Grower marketing efforts,
including market research and
advertising to the ultimate consumer,
along with complete coverage of
pesticides and spraying equipment
are incorporated.
**Readers:** Commercial vegetable & potato
industries including processing and fresh
market growers, bedding plant &
greenhouse vegetable growers, packers,
canners, processors, merchandisers,
and retailers.

## CALIFORNIA & WESTERN STATES
## GRAPE GROWER
25539

4974 E. Clinton Way, Ste. 214
Fresno, CA 93727
Telephone: (209) 252-7000
FAX: (209) 252-7387
Year Established: 1969
Pub. Frequency: m.
Page Size: standard
Subscrip. Rate: $19.95/yr.; $26.95/2 yrs.;
$31.95/3 yrs.
Freelance Pay: varies
Print Process: web offset
Circulation: 15,000
Circulation Type: controlled & paid
**Owner(s):**
Western Agricultural Publishing Co., Inc.
Telephone: (209) 252-7000
Ownership %: 100
**Management:**
Paul Baltimore ...............................Publisher
Vicki Rabbiosi ...................Advertising Manager
**Editorial:**
Patrick Cavanaugh ...............................Editor
**Desc.:** About growers for growers.
Provides the latest techniques used by
farmers in producing profitable crops.
**Readers:** Majority are growers.

## CALIFORNIA GROWER
25537

4915 Carpinteria Ave.
Ste. K
Carpinteria, CA 93013
Telephone: (805) 684-6581
FAX: (805) 684-1535
Mailing Address:
P.O. Box 370
Carpinteria, CA 93014
Pub. Frequency: m.

Page Size: standard
Subscrip. Rate: $3.95 newsstand; $22/yr.
US; $47/yr. foreign
Materials: 02,05,06,15,17,19,21,28,30,32,33
Freelance Pay: open
Print Process: offset
Circulation: 5,000
Circulation Type: controlled & paid
**Owner(s):**
Rincon Information Management Corp.
P.O. Box 370
Carpinteria, CA 93014
Telephone: (805) 684-6581
FAX: (805) 684-1535
Ownership %: 100
**Management:**
Willard Thompson ...............................President
Willard Thompson ...............................Publisher
Ken Spencer ...................Advertising Manager
Dawn Gendron ...................Circulation Manager
**Editorial:**
Willard Thompson ...............................Editor
**Desc.:** The primary information source for
the California avocado, citrus, apple and
subtropical fruit industries. Circulation is
international. Articles, news and
information on any aspect of the tree
fruit and vine fruit industries considered
for publication. Extensive use of freelance writers, especially experts in
certain areas of above-mentioned
industries, by-lines given for every
published article. Magazine is 48 page
average using full color in advertising
and editorial. Publicity material accepted.
No limit on photo spread use,
dependent on quality of photo.
Departments include: Letters to Editor,
Research, Meeting Reports, Cultural
Methods, Political Issue (of industry),
Market Analysis.
**Readers:** Primarily avocado, citrus apple
and subtropical fruit trees & vines
growers: average yearly income
$102, 000.

## CITROGRAPH
25540

4974 E. Clinton Way, 214
Fresno, CA 93727
Telephone: (209) 252-7000
Year Established: 1915
Pub. Frequency: m.
Page Size: standard
Subscrip. Rate: $15/yr.; $23/2 yrs.; $31/3
yrs.
Print Process: web offset
Circulation: 130,000
Circulation Type: controlled & paid
**Owner(s):**
California Citrograph Publishing Co., Ltd.
Telephone: (310) 225-0608
Ownership %: 100
**Management:**
Paul Baltimore ...............................Publisher
Vicki Rabbiosi ...................Advertising Manager
Wendy Forstiere ...............Circulation Manager
**Editorial:**
Lewis Robison ...............................................Editor
**Desc.:** Contributed articles discuss cultural
aspect analyses soil treatment, use of
wind machines, etc. Departments
include: Texas Citrus Exchange (TCX)
editorial feature.
**Readers:** California/Arizona citrus growers
and packers.

## CITRUS & VEGETABLE MAGAZINE
25542

400 Knightsbridge Pkwy.
Lincolnshire, IL 60069
Telephone: (312) 634-2600
Mailing Address:
4902 Eisenhower Blvd.
P.O. Box 291
Tampa, FL 33634

**Materials Accepted/Included:** 01-Business news 02-By-line articles 03-Fashion news 04-Food news 05-Freelance copy 06-Letters to editor 07-Real estate news 08-Sports news 09-Travel news 10-Book rev. 11-Movie rev. 12-Music rev. 13-TV rev. 14-Theater rev. 15-Coming events 16-Obituaries 17-Question & answer 18-Social announcements 19-Artwork 20-Cartoons 21-Photos 22-TV listings 23-Audio rec. 24-Video rec. 25-Books 26-Films/film clips 27-Personnel news 28-Press releases 29-New product news/photos 30-Trade lit. 31-Contracts awarded 32-Display adv. 33-Classified adv.

Year Established: 1938
Pub. Frequency: m.
Page Size: standard
Subscrip. Rate: $20/yr. US; $55/yr. foreign
Materials: 01,02,05,06,10,15,21,27,28,29, 30,32,33
Freelance Pay: varies
Circulation: 12,500
Circulation Type: controlled
**Owner(s):**
Vance Publishing Corp.
400 Knightsbridge Pkwy.
Lincolnshire, IL 60069
Telephone: (312) 634-2600
Ownership %: 100
**Editorial:**
Gordon Smith ................................Editor
Scott Emerson ...............Associate Editor
Sonia Tighe ...........Publication Director
**Desc.:** A magazine published exclusively for the industry. Covers articles of interest to the citrus and vegetable industry in Florida.
**Readers:** Commercial citrus and vegetable growers in Florida, packers, processors, shippers, citrus grove caretakers, farm managers, county agricultural agents, extension personnel and researchers.

25541
**CITRUS INDUSTRY, THE**
495 E. Summerlin St.
Bartow, FL 33830
Telephone: (813) 533-4114
FAX: (813) 534-1758
Mailing Address:
P.O. Box 89
Bartow, FL 33831
Year Established: 1919
Pub. Frequency: m.
Page Size: standard
Subscrip. Rate: $16/yr.
Circulation: 10,000
Circulation Type: controlled & paid
**Owner(s):**
Associated Publications Corp.
495 E. Summerlin St.
Bartow, FL 33830
Telephone: (813) 533-4114
FAX: (813) 534-1758
Ownership %: 100
**Management:**
Mariann Holland ....................Publisher
Sheree Vickers ...............Office Manager
**Editorial:**
Mariann Holland ...............................Editor
**Desc.:** Covers the various phases of citrus growing, shipping, processing, packing, etc. Deals with equipment and methods, marketing, conditions, research, etc.
**Readers:** Citrus growers and members of allied industry.
**Deadline:** 5th of mo. prior to pub. date

25543
**CRANBERRIES**
Cranberry Rd.
South Carver, MA 02366-0858
Telephone: (508) 866-5055
FAX: (508) 866-2970
Mailing Address:
P.O. Box 858
South Carver, MA 02366-0858
Year Established: 1936
Pub. Frequency: 11/yr.
Page Size: standard
Subscrip. Rate: $20/yr. US; $30/yr. foreign
Materials: 01,02,04,05,06,10,16,20,28,32
Freelance Pay: $40-$80
Print Process: offset
Circulation: 800
Circulation Type: paid
**Owner(s):**
Cranberries
**Management:**
Carolyn Gilmore ........................Publisher

**Desc.:** The only general publication devoted to the growing of cranberries throughout the USA. Departments include: Cranberry Recipe Page, New Products, Weather, Regional Notes, Technical Articles.
**Readers:** Cranberry growers, chemical personnel, research personnel, handlers.
**Deadline:** story-6 wks.; news-6 wks.; photo-6 wks.; ads-6 wks.

25545
**GOOD FRUIT GROWER**
1005 Tieton Dr.
Yakima, WA 98902
Telephone: (509) 575-2315
FAX: (509) 453-4880
Mailing Address:
P.O. Box 9219
Yakima, WA 98909
Year Established: 1946
Pub. Frequency: s-m.
Page Size: tabloid
Subscrip. Rate: $30/yr.
Circulation: 12,560
Circulation Type: paid
**Owner(s):**
Washington State Fruit Comm.
1005 Tieton Drive
Yakima, WA 98902
Telephone: (509) 575-2315
Ownership %: 100
**Management:**
Randy Morrison .............Advertising Manager
Nancy Born ...................Circulation Manager
Eve Glidewell ..........Classified Adv. Manager
**Editorial:**
Jim Black ......................Managing Editor
Geraldine Warner ...............Associate Editor
**Desc.:** The only magazine covering the Northwest fruit industry solely and entirely, it concentrates on tree fruits only...information relative to apples, pears, peaches, prunes, apricots, cherries. Goes to every commercial tree fruit grower on record in Washington State as well as to growers in important fruit producing districts of Oregon, Idaho, Utah, Colorado, British Columbia. Official publication of Washington Fruit Commission, Apple Commission, Purple Plum Assn., Idaho, Colorado and Utah Horticultural Societies.
**Readers:** Made up wholly and exclusively of commercial fruitgrowers, marketers, shippers, handlers, grape producers and processors in Pacific Northwest & nation.

25546
**GREAT LAKES FRUIT GROWERS NEWS**
343 S. Union St.
Sparta, MI 49345
Telephone: (616) 887-8615
FAX: (616) 887-2666
Mailing Address:
P.O. Box 128
Sparta, MI 49345
Year Established: 1961
Pub. Frequency: m.
Page Size: tabloid
Subscrip. Rate: $6/yr.; $15/3 yrs.
Circulation: 11,515
Circulation Type: paid
**Owner(s):**
Barry D. Brand
343 S. Union St.
Sparta, MI 49345
Telephone: (616) 887-8615
Ownership %: 100

**Bureau(s):**
Great Lakes Publishing Co.
343 S. Union St., P.O. Box 128
Sparta, MI 49345
Telephone: (616) 887-9008
Contact: Ronald L. Gaskill, Manager
**Management:**
Barry D. Brand ........................Publisher
**Editorial:**
Barry D. Brand ...............................Editor
Dee Rau .......................................Advertising
**Desc.:** The Great Lakes Fruit Growers News strives to keep fruit growers (including grape, blueberry, strawberry and bramble), handlers, roadside market operators, processors and shippers up to date on new developments, meetings and events in the fruit industry.
**Readers:** Fruit associations and societies pay for their membership-also individual subscribers.
**Deadline:** news-2nd wk., the mo. of pub. date; ads-1st wk., the mo. of pub. date

25547
**GREAT LAKES VEGETABLE GROWERS NEWS**
343 S. Union St.
Sparta, MI 49345
Telephone: (616) 887-8615
FAX: (616) 887-2666
Mailing Address:
P.O. Box 128
Sparta, MI 49345
Year Established: 1966
Pub. Frequency: m.
Page Size: tabloid
Subscrip. Rate: $6/yr.; $15/3 yrs.
Circulation: 13,322
Circulation Type: paid
**Owner(s):**
Barry D. Brand
343 S. Union St.
Sparta, MI 49345
Telephone: (616) 887-8615
Ownership %: 100
**Bureau(s):**
Great Lakes Publishing Co.
343 S. Union St., P.O. Box 128
Sparta, MI 49345
Telephone: (616) 887-9008
Contact: Ronald L. Gaskill, Manager
**Management:**
Barry D. Brand ........................Publisher
**Editorial:**
Barry D. Brand ...............................Editor
Dee Rau .......................................Advertising
**Desc.:** Edited with the idea of maintaining a flow of information to vegetable and potato growers, bedding plant and greenhouse growers and roadside market operators about events, meetings and new developments in the vegetable industry.
**Readers:** Vegetable growers, roadside market operators, greenhouse and bedding plant producers.
**Deadline:** news-1st wk., mo. of pub. date; ads-1st wk., mo. of pub. date

25536
**GREENHOUSE GROWER**
37733 Euclid Ave.
Willoughby, OH 44094-5992
Telephone: (216) 942-2000
FAX: (216) 975-3447
Year Established: 1983
Pub. Frequency: m.
Page Size: standard
Subscrip. Rate: $25/yr.
Print Process: web offset
Circulation: 21,537
Circulation Type: controlled

**Owner(s):**
Meister Publishing Co.
37733 Euclid Ave.
Willoughby, OH 44094-5992
Telephone: (216) 942-2000
Ownership %: 100
**Editorial:**
Robyn Dill ........................................Editor
Carol J. Schram ...............Advertising Director
William Carlson .................Associate Editor
Katherine McCann ...............Associate Editor
Carol J. Schram ...............Associate Publisher
John Graveno ...............Production Director
Jean D. Aylsworth .....................Staff Writer
**Desc.:** Offers articles and columns examining the expanding technology of greenhouse production with regular interviews of successful growers and their operations in the U.S. and abroad. Editorial material focuses on varieties, equipment and machinery, chemicals, growth media, cultural practices and their application to specific greenhouse crops and growing conditions. Special emphasis is placed on the business management aspect of a greenhouse operation with regular reviews of production, marketing and financial topics.
**Readers:** Readers include growers of vegetable and flowering bedding plants, potted plants, cut flowers, ornamentals, etc. Covers all crops grown under glass or plastic.

61799
**MICHIGAN DRY BEAN DIGEST**
P.O. Box 6008
Saginaw, MI 48608-6008
Telephone: (517) 790-3010
FAX: (517) 790-3747
Year Established: 1976
Pub. Frequency: 4/yr.
Page Size: standard
Subscrip. Rate: $25/yr. US; $35/yr. foreign; free to MI. grower & dealer members
Materials: 01,15
Circulation: 5,326
Circulation Type: free & paid
**Owner(s):**
Michigan Bean Shippers Association
P.O. Box 6008
Saginaw, MI 48608
Telephone: (517) 790-3010
FAX: (517) 790-3747
Ownership %: 100
**Editorial:**
John A. McGill, Jr. ..............................Editor

25516
**NUT GROWER**
4974 E. Clinton Way, Ste. 214
Fresno, CA 93727
Telephone: (209) 252-7000
FAX: (209) 252-7387
Year Established: 1982
Pub. Frequency: 10/yr.
Page Size: standard
Subscrip. Rate: $19.95/yr.
Circulation: 10,000
Circulation Type: controlled & paid
**Owner(s):**
Western Agricultural Publishing Co., Inc.
4974 E. Clinton, Ste. 214
Fresno, CA 93727
Telephone: (209) 252-7000
Ownership %: 100
**Management:**
Paul Baltimore ........................Publisher
Vicki Rabbiosi ...............Advertising Manager
**Editorial:**
Patrick Cavanaugh ...............................Editor
**Desc.:** About growers for growers. Provides the latest techniques used by farmers in producing profitable crops.

**Materials Accepted/Included:** 01-Business news 02-By-line articles 03-Fashion news 04-Food news 05-Freelance copy 06-Letters to editor 07-Real estate news 08-Sports news 09-Travel news 10-Book rev. 11-Movie rev. 12-Music rev. 13-TV rev. 14-Theater rev. 15-Coming events 16-Obituaries 17-Question & answer 18-Social announcements 19-Artwork 20-Cartoons 21-Photos 22-TV listings 23-Audio rec. 24-Video rec. 25-Books 26-Films/film clips 27-Personnel news 28-Press releases 29-New product news/photos 30-Trade lit. 31-Contracts awarded 32-Display adv. 33-Classified adv.

5-7

**Readers:** Majority are growers.

### PACIFIC FRUIT NEWS
69640

P.O. Box 460
Copperopolis, CA 95228
Telephone: (209) 785-3377
Year Established: 1888
Pub. Frequency: w.: Sat.
Page Size: standard
Subscrip. Rate: $40/yr. US; $42/yr. foreign
Materials: 04,30,32,33
Print Process: offset
Circulation: 1,000
Circulation Type: paid
**Owner(s):**
Frank Crawford
P.O. Box 460
Copperopolis, CA 95228
Telephone: (209) 785-3377
Ownership %: 100
**Editorial:**
Frank Crawford ..............................Editor
**Desc.:** Covers events and market
quotations in the processed fruit,
vegetable, dried fruit and tree nut
industries on the West Coast.
**Readers:** Growers, packers, canners,
freezers, brokers, institutional buyers,
trade associations, processing
equipment buyers/sellers.
**Deadline:** story-1 wk.; ads-10 days

### PEANUT FARMER, THE
25523

3000 Highwoods Blvd., Ste. 300
Raleigh, NC 27604-1029
Telephone: (919) 872-5040
FAX: (919) 876-6531
Year Established: 1965
Pub. Frequency: 8/yr.: Jan.-Jul., plus one
spec. issue
Page Size: standard
Subscrip. Rate: $10/yr.; $24/3 yrs.
Materials: 01,02,05,06,15,21,27,28,29,30,32
Freelance Pay: negotiable
Print Process: web offset
Circulation: 20,121
Circulation Type: controlled
**Owner(s):**
Specialized Agricultural Publications, Inc.
3000 Highwoods Blvd., Ste. 300
Raleigh, NC 27604
Telephone: (919) 872-5040
Ownership %: 100
**Management:**
Dayton Matlick ..........................Publisher
Sue Burleson ....................Circulation Manager
Dorothy Kuffler ..........................Sales Manager
**Editorial:**
Dayton Matlick ..............................Editor
Mary Evans ....................Managing Editor
Victoria Gardner ..................Production Director
**Desc.:** Feature articles deal with research-
backed production, harvesting and
marketing aspects of peanuts. Included
monthly are interviews of farmers,
connected businessmen, and research
and extension personnel; reviews of
industry products/"how to use"; label
clearance releases; political aspects
relating to peanuts and world news.
**Readers:** Commercial peanut producers.

### PEANUT GROWER
67021

P.O. Box 83
Tifton, GA 31793
Telephone: (912) 386-8591
FAX: (912) 386-9772
Year Established: 1989
Pub. Frequency: 7/yr.: Jan.-Jul.
Page Size: standard
Subscrip. Rate: $12/yr. US; $42/yr. foreign
Circulation: 28,000
Circulation Type: controlled

**Owner(s):**
Vance Publishing Corp.
400 Knights Bridge
Lincolnshire, IL 60069
Telephone: (708) 634-2600
Ownership %: 100
**Management:**
James Staudt ..........................President
Sonia Tighe ..............................Publisher
Alicia Fremont ..................Advertising Manager
**Editorial:**
Catherine Andrews ..........................Editor
**Readers:** Peanut farmers.

### PECAN SOUTH
25524

4348 Carter Creek, #101
Bryan, TX 77802
Telephone: (409) 846-3285
FAX: (409) 846-1752
Mailing Address:
P.O. Drawer CC
College Station, TX 77841
Year Established: 1967
Pub. Frequency: 12/yr.
Page Size: tabloid
Subscrip. Rate: $15/yr.; $27/2 yrs.
Circulation: 5,400
Circulation Type: paid
**Owner(s):**
Texas Pecan Growers Association
P.O. Drawer CC
College Station, TX 77841
Telephone: (409) 846-3285
Ownership %: 100
**Management:**
Cindy Loggins Wise ..................Executive Vice
President
**Desc.:** For commercial pecan growers in
the Southeastern and Southwestern
United States. Information is related to
production, marketing, and other news
items of interest to the industry.
**Readers:** Commercial pecan growers of
the United States.

### POTATO GROWER OF IDAHO
25549

520 Park Ave.
Idaho Falls, ID 83402
Telephone: (208) 524-7000
FAX: (208) 522-5241
Year Established: 1972
Pub. Frequency: m.
Page Size: standard
Subscrip. Rate: $19/yr.
Materials: 01,15,27,28,29,32
Freelance Pay: $.10/wd.
Circulation: 16,000
Circulation Type: controlled
**Owner(s):**
Harris Publishing Co., Inc.
520 Park Ave.
Idaho Falls, ID 83402
Telephone: (208) 524-7000
FAX: (208) 524-7000
Ownership %: 100
**Management:**
Darryl W. Harris ..........................Publisher
Melvin L. Erickson ..........Advertising Manager
**Editorial:**
Seve Janes ..................Editor in Chief
Gary Rawlings ..............................Editor
Lane Lindstrom ..................Assistant Editor
Janet Chase ..................Production Director
Richard Holley ..............................Sales
**Desc.:** Editorial coverage includes all
phases of growing, shipping, packaging,
planting, fertilizing, frost protection,
insect and disease control, weed
control, harvesting, storage,
and marketing methods.

**Readers:** Potato growers, packers,
shippers, buyers.
**Deadline:** story-45 days prior to pub. date;
news-45 days prior; photo-45 days prior;
ads-1st of mo. prior

### SOUTHEASTERN PEANUT FARMER
25527

110 E. 4th St.
Tifton, GA 31794
Telephone: (912) 386-3470
FAX: (912) 386-3501
Mailing Address:
P.O. Box 706
Tifton, GA 31793
Year Established: 1962
Pub. Frequency: m. exc. Oct. & Dec.
Page Size: tabloid
Subscrip. Rate: $5/yr. US; $20/yr. foreign
Materials: 02,21,28,29,32,33
Print Process: offset
Circulation: 13,000
Circulation Type: paid
**Owner(s):**
Georgia Peanut Commission
P.O. Box 967
Tifton, GA 31793
Telephone: (912) 386-3470
FAX: (912) 386-3501
Ownership %: 100
**Management:**
Don Koehler ..............................Publisher
Joan S. Underwood ..........Advertising Manager
**Editorial:**
Jocelyn Richburg ..................Associate Editor
**Desc.:** General coverage of peanut
production farm and new products.
**Readers:** Peanut growers of the
Southeast.
**Deadline:** story-1 mo. prior to pub. date;
ads-10th of mo. prior

### SUN-DIAMOND GROWER
69644

P.O. Box 1727
Stockton, CA 95201
Telephone: (209) 467-6219
FAX: (209) 467-6714
Year Established: 1969
Pub. Frequency: q.
Subscrip. Rate: free
Circulation: 12,000
Circulation Type: free
**Owner(s):**
Sun-Diamond Growers of California
P.O. Box 1727
Stockton, CA 95201
Telephone: (209) 467-6219
Ownership %: 100
**Editorial:**
Sandra McBride ..............................Editor
**Desc.:** Contains information for dried fruit,
grape and nut growers about production
techniques and industry affairs.

### VALLEY POTATO GROWER
68680

420 Business Hwy. 2
E. Grand Forks, MN 56721
Telephone: (218) 773-3633
FAX: (218) 773-6227
Mailing Address:
P.O. Box 301
E. Grand Forks, MN 56721
Year Established: 1946
Pub. Frequency: m.
Page Size: standard
Materials: 04,19,20,27,28,29,32,33
Print Process: web
Circulation: 11,773
Circulation Type: controlled & paid

**Owner(s):**
Red River Valley Potato Growers
Association
P.O. Box 301
420 Business Hwy. 2
E. Grand Forks, MN 56721
Telephone: (218) 773-3633
FAX: (218) 773-6227
Ownership %: 100
**Editorial:**
Christle Johnson ..............................Editor
**Desc.:** Covers current events, innovations,
industry problems and solutions,
marketing and production information,
research results, safety and
governmental issues, and pest-weed
control.
**Readers:** Potato growers throughout the
U.S., parts of Canada plus a few in
other countries, and potato industry
officials throughout the U.S., and few
retailers of produce and processing
company officials.
**Deadline:** story-1st of mo. prior to pub.
date; news-1st of mo. prior; photo-1st of
mo. prior; ads-5th of mo. prior

### WESTERN FRUIT GROWER
48970

3509 Coffee Rd., D-18
Modesto, CA 95355-8740
Telephone: (209) 577-0602
FAX: (209) 577-2737
Year Established: 1947
Pub. Frequency: m.
Page Size: standard
Subscrip. Rate: $14/yr.
Print Process: web offset
Circulation: 28,827
Circulation Type: controlled
**Owner(s):**
Meister Publishing Co.
37733 Euclid Ave.
Willoughby, OH 44094-5992
Telephone: (216) 942-2000
FAX: (216) 975-3447
Ownership %: 100
**Editorial:**
Gary Acuff ..............................Editor
Carol J. Schram ..........................Advertising
Carol J. Schram ..................Associate Publisher
Denise Derrer ..................Editorial Assistant
Jim Moore ..............................Field Editor
Jean D. Aylsworth ..........................Staff Writer
**Desc.:** Edited for the commercial fruit, nut
and grape producer in the 13 western
states.
**Readers:** Commercial fruit growers,
orchard managers, orchard supply
dealers and jobbers, fruit associations
and grower-owned co-ops; shippers,
packers, canners and fruit processors;
state and national horticultural and
pomological societies, agricultural
schools and colleges, students and
professional horticulturists.

## Group 510-General Agriculture & Farming

### AG CONSULTANT
48965

37733 Euclid Ave.
Willoughby, OH 44094-5992
Telephone: (216) 942-2000
FAX: (216) 975-3447
Year Established: 1945
Pub. Frequency: 9/yr.
Page Size: standard
Subscrip. Rate: $14/yr.
Print Process: web offset
Circulation: 22,158
Circulation Type: controlled

---

**Materials Accepted/Included:** 01-Business news 02-By-line articles 03-Fashion news 04-Food news 05-Freelance copy 06-Letters to editor 07-Real estate news 08-Sports news 09-Travel news 10-Book rev. 11-Movie rev. 12-Music rev. 13-TV rev. 14-Theater rev. 15-Coming events 16-Obituaries 17-Question & answer 18-Social announcements 19-Artwork 20-Cartoons 21-Photos 22-TV listings 23-Audio rec. 24-Video rec. 25-Books 26-Films/film clips 27-Personnel news 28-Press releases 29-New product news/photos 30-Trade lit. 31-Contracts awarded 32-Display adv. 33-Classified adv.

**Owner(s):**
Meister Publishing Co.
37733 Euclid Ave.
Willoughby, OH 44094-5992
Telephone: (216) 942-2000
FAX: (216) 975-3447
Ownership %: 100
**Editorial:**
Judy Ferguson ...................................Editor
Alan C. Strohmaier ...........Advertising Director
Alan C. Strohmaier .............Associate Publisher
Gina LaVecchia .....................Editorial Assistant
**Desc.:** Seeks to improve agriculture and
profits through informed agri-fieldmen,
thus to increase production within the
framework of environmental and
governmental restrictions and to
publicize new legislation and product
information. Articles cover the use of
pesticides, fertilizers, animal health
products and farm equipment.
**Readers:** For crop consultants who own or
are employed by private consulting
firms; licensed pest control advisors;
technical fieldmen employed solely by
food processors and large scale farms;
technical fieldmen for distributors,
dealers, manufacturers, ground and
aerial applicators; county agricultural
agents, farm advisors, specialists in
weed science, entomology, horticulture,
agronomy and plant pathology.

25407
**AGRIBUSINESS FIELDMAN**
4974 E. Clinton Way, Ste. 214
Fresno, CA 93727-1520
Telephone: (209) 252-7000
FAX: (209) 252-7387
Year Established: 1971
Pub. Frequency: 12/yr.
Page Size: standard
Subscrip. Rate: $19.95/yr.
Materials: 32,33
Freelance Pay: $550-$250
Print Process: web offset
Circulation: 5,391
Circulation Type: paid
**Owner(s):**
Agribusiness Publications
4974 E. Clinton Way, Ste. 214
Fresno, CA 93727
Telephone: (209) 486-8990
Ownership %: 100
**Management:**
Paul Baltimore ...................................Publisher
Leo Nist ............................................Publisher
**Editorial:**
Mark Arcamonte ..................................Editor
Theresa Keenan ...........................Advertising
Marni Katz ...........................Assistant Editor
Judy Drake .........................Production Director
**Desc.:** Contains how-to farming articles,
mostly about vegetables and field crops.
Also covers chemicals, equipment
developments, and new applications,
and provides financial and legislative
advice for agribusinessmen.
**Readers:** Commercial farmers and
agribusinessmen.

25513
**AGRIBUSINESS WORLDWIDE**
150 Great Neck Rd.
Great Neck, NY 11021
Telephone: (516) 829-9210
FAX: (516) 829-5414
Year Established: 1980
Pub. Frequency: bi-m.
Page Size: standard
Subscrip. Rate: $42/yr.
Materials: 01,02,05,28,29,30,31,32,33
Print Process: offset
Circulation: 25,000
Circulation Type: controlled

**Owner(s):**
Keller International Publishing Co.
150 Great Neck Rd.
Great Neck, NY 11021
Telephone: (516) 829-9210
FAX: (516) 829-5414
Ownership %: 100
**Management:**
Robert Herlihy ...................General Manager
Orlando Llerandi ................Promotion Manager
**Editorial:**
Jane Mahoney ..................Publication Director
**Desc.:** Agribusiness Worldwide serves
those responsible for agricultural &
livestock development in Asia, the
Middle East, Africa & Latin America.
Articles cover agricultural production,
financing, marketing, storage, handling &
processing. Includes translation of
editorial in Spanish.
**Readers:** Agricultural producers,
processors, government ministries of
agriculture, development bankers,
agricultural researchers & technicians.

25409
**AMERICAN AGRICULTURIST**
2333 N. Triphammer Rd., Ste. 202
Ithaca, NY 14850
Telephone: (607) 257-8670
FAX: (607) 257-8238
Year Established: 1842
Pub. Frequency: m.
Page Size: standard
Subscrip. Rate: $14.98/yr.; $34.94/yr.
Materials: 32,33
Circulation: 39,000
Circulation Type: paid
**Owner(s):**
Farm Progress Companies
191 S. Gary Ave.
Carol Stream, IL 60188
Telephone: (708) 690-5600
Ownership %: 100
**Management:**
Allan Johnson ...................................President
Thomas Budd ...................................Publisher
Richard Wright ..................Advertising Manager
Charles Wiegold ................Circulation Manager
Jerry Lucht ...................................Sales Manager
**Editorial:**
Eleanor Jacobs ...................................Editor
**Desc.:** Devoted to diversified farming in
the Northeast. Covers all phases of
dairy, poultry, fruit, potatoes and
vegetable farming. Features deal with
personal stories about farm families,
recommendations of colleges and
experiment stations, entertainment bits,
etc. Prefers articles of 1,000 words;
maximum 2,000 words. Uses single
pictures with 50 - 100 word
outlines covering farm handy items,
farmers, farmwives, and rural
youngsters. Departments include: What's
New, Farmer's Dollar Guide, Livestock
and Poultry, and Home Department
(recipes, patterns, decorations, etc.).
News items chiefly staff - written.
**Readers:** Primarily farmers of New York,
New Jersey, New England.

25412
**ARIZONA FARMER**
Review Tower, 999 W. Riverside Ave.
Spokane, WA 99210
Telephone: (509) 459-5377
Mailing Address:
  P.O. Box 2160
  Spokane, WA 99210
Year Established: 1922
Pub. Frequency: m.
Page Size: tabloid
Subscrip. Rate: $18/yr.
Materials: 32,33
Print Process: web offset

Circulation: 1,649
Circulation Type: paid
**Owner(s):**
Cowles Publishing Co.
999 W. Riverside Ave.
Spokane, WA 99201
Telephone: (509) 459-5377
**Management:**
William Stacey Cowles ...............Publisher
Michael R. Craigen ...............General Manager
**Editorial:**
E.W.Ramsey ...........................Managing Editor
**Desc.:** General farm magazine.
**Readers:** Farmers and agriculturally -
oriented businesses.

25417
**BUSINESS FARMER**
1617 Ave. A
Scottsbluff, NE 69361
Telephone: (308) 635-2045
FAX: (308) 635-2348
Mailing Address:
  P.O. Box 770
  Scottsbluff, NE 69363
Year Established: 1925
Pub. Frequency: Fri.
Page Size: broadsheet
Subscrip. Rate: $18-$24/yr.
Circulation: 3,600
Circulation Type: paid
**Owner(s):**
Business Farmer Printing Co.
1617 Ave. A
Scottsbluff, NE 69361
Telephone: (308) 635-2045
Ownership %: 100
**Management:**
Penny Yekel ...................................Publisher
Doug Fitzgerald ...............Advertising Manager
Ann Henderson ..............Editorial Production
                       Manager
**Editorial:**
Penny Yekel ...................................Editor
**Desc.:** Farm newspaper with primarily local
interests devoted to general agriculture
and farm living. All technical and
research information applied by
State University and local experiment
station. Features and other articles
cover general news of some phase of
rural homemaking. Women's page
devoted to young people and mothers,
housekeeping, landscaping, etc. Chief
function is to keep subscribers informed
of general farm happenings, crop
forecasts, and other items of interest to
coverage area only, with editorial
emphasis on farm management and
business aspects of farming. Uses by-
lines and little outside publicity.
**Readers:** Farmers and rural dwellers.

25418
**CALIFORNIA FARMER**
2300 Clayton Rd., Ste. 1360
Concord, CA 94520
Telephone: (510) 687-1662
FAX: (510) 687-4945
Year Established: 1854
Pub. Frequency: 15/yr.
Page Size: standard
Subscrip. Rate: $14.98/yr.; $34.94/3 yrs. in
  CA, AZ, & NV
Materials: 32,33
Circulation: 52,000
Circulation Type: paid
**Owner(s):**
Farm Progress Companies
191 S. Gary Ave.
Carol Stream, IL 60188
Telephone: (708) 690-5600
Ownership %: 100
**Management:**
Allan Johnson ...................................President
Thomas Budd ...................................Publisher

Charles Wiegold ................Circulation Manager
Dennis Duncan ...........................Sales Manager
**Editorial:**
Len Richardson ...................................Editor
David Woltman ...........................Associate Editor
Kevin Thompson ...........................Associate Editor
**Desc.:** Commercial farm magazine for
California.
**Readers:** Commercial farmers, ranchers
and growers.

25419
**CALIFORNIA GRANGE NEWS**
2101 Stockton Blvd.
Sacramento, CA 95817
Telephone: (916) 454-5805
FAX: (916) 739-8189
Year Established: 1931
Pub. Frequency: m.
Page Size: tabloid
Subscrip. Rate: $6.50/yr.
Materials: 01,02,04,28,29,30,32,33
Print Process: web offset
Circulation: 35,754
Circulation Type: paid
**Owner(s):**
California State Grange
2101 Stockton Blvd.
Sacramento, CA 95817
Telephone: (916) 454-5805
FAX: (916) 739-8189
Ownership %: 100
**Management:**
Bob Clouse ...................................Publisher
Bob Clouse ...........................Advertising Manager
Bob Clouse ...........................Business Manager
J.D. Hartz ..........Editorial Production Manager
**Editorial:**
J.D. Hartz ...................................Editor
J.D. Hartz ...................................Farm Editor
J.D. Hartz ...........................Livestock Editor
J.D. Hartz ...................................News Editor
Katherine Foster ...........................Youth Editor
**Desc.:** Publishes agricultural news, rural
living news, information about activities
of the state, national and local granges,
news of legislative and governmental
developments affecting agriculture,
general agricultural and educational
features. Extensively illustrated. Use
news photos of new products related to
agriculture.
**Readers:** Primarily California grange.
**Deadline:** story-1st Mon. of mo.; news-1st
Mon.; photo-1st Mon.; ads-1st Mon.

25301
**COLORADO RANCHER & FARMER**
4155 E. Jewell Ave.
Ste. 901
Denver, CO 80222
Telephone: (303) 756-1526
Year Established: 1947
Pub. Frequency: m.
Page Size: standard
Subscrip. Rate: $14.98/yr.; $25/yr.
  elsewhere
Freelance Pay: negotiable
Circulation: 14,417
Circulation Type: paid
**Owner(s):**
Farm Progress Co.
Carol Stream, IL
Ownership %: 100
**Management:**
Allen Johnson ...................................President
Chuck Weigold ...................Circulation Manager
**Editorial:**
Sally Schuff ...................................Editor
Tom Budd ...........................Editorial Director
Darlene Bottum ...........Regional Sales Manager

**Materials Accepted/Included:** 01-Business news 02-By-line articles 03-Fashion news 04-Food news 05-Freelance copy 06-Letters to editor 07-Real estate news 08-Sports news 09-Travel news
10-Book rev. 11-Movie rev. 12-Music rev. 13-TV rev. 14-Theater rev. 15-Coming events 16-Obituaries 17-Question & answer 18-Social announcements 19-Artwork 20-Cartoons 21-Photos 22-TV listings
23-Audio rec. 24-Video rec. 25-Books 26-Films/film clips 27-Personnel news 28-Press releases 29-New product news/photos 30-Trade lit. 31-Contracts awarded 32-Display adv. 33-Classified adv.

5-9

**Desc.:** By-line articles cover all phases of farming, ranching, and dairying. Deals with methods, equipment, management, research progress, marketing, transportation, and the various aspects of farm living; social, economic, and health. Principal field crops covered are winter wheat, potatoes, corn, small grain, sorghum, hay and alfalfa. Space given to new farm equipment, things for the farm home, etc. Reviews new products and services for ranchers and farmers. Departments include: Colorado Comment (general opinion), Capitol Comment (Washington activities), What's New (new equipment), Livestock (sheep, beef, cattle, dairy cattle, swine, etc.), Market Briefs, Livestock Events, and Women's Section (dealing with fashions and patterns, recipes, etc.), Agri - Business (news about people and companies serving Colorado ranchers and farmers). Profusely illustrated.
**Readers:** Primarily ranchers and farmers in Colorado.
**Deadline:** story-10th of mo. prior; news-10th of mo. prior; photo-10th of mo. prior; ads-10th of mo. prior

**COLUMBIA BASIN FARMER, THE** 25424
P.O. Drawer O
Othello, WA 99344
Telephone: (509) 488-3342
FAX: (509) 488-3345
Year Established: 1956
Pub. Frequency: m.
Page Size: oversize
Subscrip. Rate: $5/yr.
Materials: 32
Freelance Pay: copies & by-line
Circulation: 9,000
Circulation Type: paid
**Owner(s):**
Basin Publishing Co.
P.O. Drawer O
Othello, WA 99344
Telephone: (509) 488-3342
Ownership %: 100
**Management:**
Dan Leary ..................................Publisher
**Editorial:**
Dan Leary ..........................Executive Editor
**Desc.:** Features on local growers, agricultural technology, new farming methods, crops, prices and legislative news.
**Readers:** Farmers in Washington's Columbia Basin.

**COUNTRY CHRONICLE, THE** 25483
138 Main St.
Denmark, WI 54208
Telephone: (414) 863-2154
FAX: (414) 863-6102
Mailing Address:
  P.O. Box 610
  Denmark, WI 54208
Year Established: 1939
Pub. Frequency: w.
Page Size: tabloid
Subscrip. Rate: $12/yr.
Circulation: 15,000
Circulation Type: paid
**Owner(s):**
Metropolitan Newspaper Corp.
P.O. Box 2467
Green Bay, WI 54306
Telephone: (414) 432-2941
Ownership %: 100
**Management:**
Frank Wood ..................................Publisher
Jeff Kralovetz ................General Manager
Jeff Kralovetz ....................Sales Manager

**Editorial:**
Cindy Thompson ..............................Editor
**Desc.:** Coveres current news, local, state and national, from the farm and economic standpoint. Touches occasionally on technical or how-to aspects of farming except for occasional authorative report on new developments. Deals with sales, trends and financial news and such phases of general agriculture as soil conservation, diseases, insect control, new machinery, building problems, etc. Reports government action affecting farms and any other pertinent changes and developments that might be considered news to readers. Considerable space devoted to farm-family-items. Departments include: Women's and Food Pages (recipes, household hints, patterns, decoration, etc.). National and local sports columns, television log. Uses few by-lines.
**Readers:** Primarily active farmers.

**COUNTRY JOURNAL** 25428
6405 Flank Dr.
Harrisburg, PA 17112
Telephone: (717) 657-9555
Mailing Address:
  P.O. Box 8200
  Harrisburg, PA 17112
Year Established: 1974
Pub. Frequency: bi-m.
Page Size: oversize
Subscrip. Rate: $2.95/issue; $24/yr.
Freelance Pay: varies
Circulation: 200,000
Circulation Type: paid
**Owner(s):**
Cowles Magazines, Inc.
P.O. Box 8200
Harrisburg, PA 17105
Telephone: (717) 657-9555
Ownership %: 100
**Management:**
Bruce Barnet ..............................President
**Editorial:**
Peter V. Fossel ..............................Editor
Lisa Bishop ........................Managing Editor
**Desc.:** Pragmatic, useful information for rural living.
**Readers:** People who live in the country or wish they did.

**COUNTRYSIDE & SMALL STOCK JOURNAL** 25429
N2601 Winter Sports Rd.
Withee, WI 54498
Telephone: (715) 785-7979
FAX: (715) 785-7414
Year Established: 1917
Pub. Frequency: bi-m.
Page Size: standard
Subscrip. Rate: $3/newsstand; $18/yr.
Materials: 06,10,15,17,32,33
Print Process: web offset
Circulation: 50,000
Circulation Type: paid
**Owner(s):**
Countryside Publications, Ltd.
N2601 Winter Sports Rd.
Withee, WI 54498
Telephone: (715) 785-7979
FAX: (715) 785-7414
Ownership %: 100
**Management:**
J.D. Belanger ..............................Publisher
**Editorial:**
J.D. Belanger ..................................Editor

**Desc.:** This magazine is about country living at its best. Designed for people interested in country living and self-reliance. Strong emphasis is placed on detailed, authoritative, illustrated information on livestock management, especially small stock such as goats, rabbits, bees, and poultry. Regular features cover, in general, small farm or homestead management and in particular, gardening, country cooking and food storage, rural skills and crafts, ecology, veterinary problems, and visits with country neighbors.
**Readers:** People with city jobs who have an interest in (and the affluence to) pursue a country lifestyle.
**Deadline:** story-2 mo. prior to pub. date; news-2 mo.; photo-2 mo.; ads-2 mo.

**DELTA FARM PRESS** 25432
14920 Hwy. 61
Clarksdale, MS 38614
Telephone: (601) 624-8503
FAX: (601) 627-1977
Mailing Address:
  P.O. Box 1420
  Clarksdale, MS 38614
Year Established: 1944
Pub. Frequency: w.
Page Size: tabloid
Subscrip. Rate: $25/yr.
Materials: 32,33
Circulation: 28,000
Circulation Type: controlled
**Owner(s):**
Argus Press Group
4151 Powers Ferry Rd., N.W.
Ste. 400
Atlanta, GA 30339-2941
Telephone: (404) 955-1116
Ownership %: 100
**Management:**
John Montandon ..............................Publisher
Darrah Parker ................Production Manager
**Editorial:**
Ben Pryor ........................Managing Editor
Ken Dean ........................Advertising
**Desc.:** Serves the needs of farmers and agribusinessmen in 5 states across the southern US - Mississippi, Louisiana, Arkansas, Missouri Bootheel, Western Tennessee.
**Readers:** Farmers & agri-businessmen.

**FARM & DAIRY** 25437
185-205 E. State St.
Salem, OH 44460
Telephone: (216) 337-3419
FAX: (216) 337-9550
Mailing Address:
  P.O. Box 38
  Salem, OH 44460
Year Established: 1914
Pub. Frequency: w.
Page Size: tabloid
Subscrip. Rate: $19/yr.
Materials: 32,33
Freelance Pay: upon application
Circulation: 25,000
Circulation Type: paid
**Owner(s):**
The Lyle Printing & Publishing Co.
P.O. Box 38
Salem, OH 44460
Telephone: (216) 337-3419
Ownership %: 100
**Management:**
W. T. Darling ..............................Publisher
Scot M. Darling ................Advertising Manager
**Editorial:**
Susan Crowell ..............................Editor
Marcy Todd ................Women's Interest Editor

**Desc.:** Briefs of research reports from experiment stations in agriculture; success stories concerning farmers of the tri-state area (Ohio, Pennsylvania, W. Virginia); sale and livestock market reports; homemakers' recipes and ideas; farm sales and antique sales and columns. Separate antique section.
**Readers:** Primarily farmers and farm managers; rural families in Ohio, West Virginia and Pennsylvania. Also public sale attenders.

**FARM & RANCH LIVING** 68664
5400 S. 60th St.
Greendale, WI 53129
Telephone: (414) 423-0100
FAX: (414) 423-8463
Year Established: 1979
Pub. Frequency: bi-m.
Subscrip. Rate: $16.95/yr.
Circulation: 400,000
Circulation Type: paid
**Owner(s):**
Reiman Publications, Inc.
5400 S. 60th St.
Greendale, WI 53129
Telephone: (414) 423-0100
Ownership %: 100
**Editorial:**
Bob Ottum ..................................Editor

**FARMER'S DIGEST** 25449
P.O. Box 624
Brookfield, WI 53008
Telephone: (414) 782-4480
FAX: (414) 782-1252
Mailing Address:
  P.O. Box 624
  Brookfield, WI 53008
Year Established: 1936
Pub. Frequency: m.: Oct.-May
Page Size: pocket
Subscrip. Rate: $2/copy, $15/yr.
Materials: 06,10,17,24,25,28,29,33
Circulation: 18,000
Circulation Type: paid
**Owner(s):**
Lessiter Publications, Inc.
P.O. Box 624
Brookfield, WI 53008
Telephone: (414) 782-4480
Ownership %: 100
**Management:**
Frank Lessiter ..............................Publisher
Sue Ramstack ................Circulation Manager
**Editorial:**
Frank Lessiter ..............................Editor
**Desc.:** A digest of best published information about agriculture. Editors select and digest articles from 300 current national and foreign farm magazines each month.
**Readers:** Subscribers are 90% male.

**FARMER'S EXCHANGE** 25450
19401 Industrial Dr.
New Paris, IN 46553
Telephone: (219) 831-2138
FAX: (219) 831-2131
Mailing Address:
  P.O. Box 45
  New Paris, IN 46553
Year Established: 1926
Pub. Frequency: w.
Page Size: tabloid
Subscrip. Rate: $16/yr.
Print Process: web offset
Circulation: 14,000
Circulation Type: paid
**Owner(s):**
Exchange Publishing Corp.
Telephone: (219) 831-2138
Ownership %: 100

**Materials Accepted/Included:** 01-Business news 02-By-line articles 03-Fashion news 04-Food news 05-Freelance copy 06-Letters to editor 07-Real estate news 08-Sports news 09-Travel news 10-Book rev. 11-Movie rev. 12-Music rev. 13-TV rev. 14-Theater rev. 15-Coming events 16-Obituaries 17-Question & answer 18-Social announcements 19-Artwork 20-Cartoons 21-Photos 22-TV listings 23-Audio rec. 24-Video rec. 25-Books 26-Films/film clips 27-Personnel news 28-Press releases 29-New product news/photos 30-Trade lit. 31-Contracts awarded 32-Display adv. 33-Classified adv.

5-10

**Management:**
S. E. Yeater ..............................Publisher
**Editorial:**
Paul Hershberger ..........................Editor
**Desc.:** Farm newspaper covering Northern
Indiana, and Southern Michigan
counties. Carries by-lines. Primarily
devoted to pictures, stories and feature
articles of and about farm families in
area served. Makes little use of general
information material. Departments staff-
written or syndicated. Covers general
agriculture, poultry, and livestock from
the news and trend standpoint rather
than technical or scientific.
**Readers:** Primarily farm families in
Northern Indiana.

68662
## FARMERS & CONSUMERS
## MARKET BULLETIN
19 Martin Luther King Dr., Rm. 226
Capitol Sq.
Atlanta, GA 30334
Telephone: (404) 656-3722
FAX: (404) 651-7957
Year Established: 1917
Pub. Frequency: w.: Wed.
Subscrip. Rate: free in state; $10/yr. out of
state
Circulation: 250,000
Circulation Type: free & paid
**Owner(s):**
Challenge Publications, Inc.
7950 Deering Ave.
Canoga Park, CA 91324
Telephone: (818) 887-0550
Ownership %: 100
**Editorial:**
Carlton B. Moore ..........................Editor
Pat Glenn ............................Circulation Director

25440
## FARM INDUSTRY NEWS
7900 International Dr.
Ste. 300
Minneapolis, MN 55425
Telephone: (612) 851-4680
Year Established: 1967
Pub. Frequency: m.
Page Size: standard
Subscrip. Rate: $12.95/yr.
Materials: 01,02,05,06,10,19,21,25,28,29,
32,33
Freelance Pay: negotiable
Circulation: 252,000
Circulation Type: controlled
**Owner(s):**
Webb Division, Intertec Publishing Corp.
7900 International Dr.
Ste. 300
Minneapolis, MN 55425
Telephone: (612) 851-9329
FAX: (612) 851-4600
Ownership %: 100
**Management:**
Ron Sorenson ..............................Publisher
Deb Weinhold ....................Personnel Manager
Kim Zilverberg ..............Promotion Manager
**Editorial:**
Joseph Degnan ..........................Editor
Peg Zenk ..........................Managing Editor
Pat Arthur ........................Associate Editor
Kristi Lee Johnson ..............Associate Editor
Roxanne Furlong ..............Editorial Assistant
Lynn Varpness ....................Graphics Editor
Cindy Kramer ..........................Miscellaneous
Laurie Peterson ............Production Coordinator

**Desc.:** The only farm publication dealing
exclusively with product news. Its
purpose is to help buyers of farm
implements, and high volume users of
seeds, chemicals, fertilizers, equipment
feed and animal health products,
evaluated new and improved products.
Departments include: Machinery, Shop,
Crops, Livestock, Around the Farm,
Information, Chemicals, Agriculture
business Letters, and Electronics.
**Readers:** Farmers (predominantly class I &
IA) in Illinois, Indiana, Iowa, Kansas,
Michigan, Minnesota, Missouri,
Nebraska, North Dakota, Ohio, South
Dakota and Wisconsin.

25443
## FARM JOURNAL
230 W. Washington Sq.
Philadelphia, PA 19106
Telephone: (215) 829-4830
Year Established: 1877
Pub. Frequency: 13/yr.
Page Size: standard
Subscrip. Rate: $14/yr.
Freelance Pay: $50-$500
Circulation: 800,000
Circulation Type: paid
**Owner(s):**
Farm Journal, Inc.
230 W. Washington Sq.
Philadelphia, PA 19106
Telephone: (215) 574-1200
Ownership %: 100
**Management:**
Dale Smith ..........................President
Roger Randall ..........................Publisher
**Editorial:**
Earl Ainsworth ..........................Editor
Karen Freiburg ..............Managing Editor
Dick Braun ..........................Miscellaneous
Clair Urbain ....................New Products Editor
**Desc.:** National farm monthly published in
several regional editions. Publishes news
and feature material dealing with all
aspects of farming, farm living, farm-
management, etc., as well as general
information of interest to farm families.
Helpful, entertaining reading for the
entire farm family. Profusely illustrated.
Practically unlimited in scope and
coverage.
**Readers:** Families who own or operate
farms.

25383
## FARMLAND NEWS
P.O. Box 240
Archbold, OH 43502-0240
Telephone: (419) 445-9456
Year Established: 1933
Pub. Frequency: w.
Page Size: tabloid
Subscrip. Rate: $18/yr.
Freelance Pay: $15-$150
Circulation: 7,522
Circulation Type: controlled
**Owner(s):**
O. Roger Taylor
309 Murbach St.
Archbold, OH 43502
Telephone: (419) 445-5411
Ownership %: 100
**Management:**
Doug Nutter ..............Advertising Manager
Jed Wegner Grisez ............Business Manager
Larkin Chappuis ..............Circulation Manager
**Editorial:**
Jeremy Rohrs ..........................Editor
**Desc.:** Deals with farm news, rural living
and farm management. By-line features
and articles are general. Also covers
legislative actions affecting farms.
Primary coverage area mainly staff-
covered.

**Readers:** Primarily farmers in Northwest
Ohio and Southeast Michigan.
**Deadline:** story-Thu.; news-Thu.; photo-
Thu.; ads-12:00 pm, Fri.

25445
## FARM SHOW
20088 Kenwood Trail
Lakeville, MN 55044
Telephone: (612) 469-5572
FAX: (612) 469-5575
Mailing Address:
P.O. Box 1029
Lakeville, MN 55044
Year Established: 1977
Pub. Frequency: bi-m.
Page Size: tabloid
Subscrip. Rate: $13.95/yr.
Print Process: web
Circulation: 170,000
Circulation Type: paid
**Owner(s):**
Farm Show Publishing, Inc.
2008 Kenwood Trail
Lakeville, MN 55044
Telephone: (612) 469-5572
FAX: (612) 469-5575
Ownership %: 100
**Management:**
Harold M. Johnson ..............................Publisher
Joan C. Johnson ....................Office Manager
**Editorial:**
Mark Newhall ..........................Editor
Bill Gergen ........................Associate Editor
**Desc.:** Focuses exclusively on latest new
products of interest to high volume
farmers, ranchers throughout the U.S.
Name, address, phone listed with each
new product report so interested readers
can contact the company direct for more
information. Each issue carries section
devoted to new products of interest to
farm wives, and a section in which
randomly selected readers discuss their
best and worst buys.
**Readers:** Primarily high volume farmers
and ranchers.

25435
## FARMWEEK
27 N. Jefferson St.
Knightstown, IN 46148
Telephone: (317) 345-5133
Mailing Address:
P.O. Box 90
Knightstown, IN 46148
Year Established: 1955
Pub. Frequency: w.
Page Size: tabloid
Subscrip. Rate: $17.95/yr. in area;
$26.95/yr. out of area
Materials: 32,33
Freelance Pay: $2/in. news; $50/feature
Print Process: offset
Circulation: 31,808
Circulation Type: paid
**Owner(s):**
Mayhill Publications Inc.
P.O. Box 90
Chesterfield, IN 46017
Telephone: (317) 345-5133
Ownership %: 100
**Management:**
R.T. Mayhill ..........................Publisher
Dane Parish ..............Advertising Manager
**Editorial:**
Nancy Searfoss ..........................Editor
Amy J. Butt ........................Associate Editor
Nancy Searfoss ..........................News Editor
Nancy Searfoss ..........................Photo

**Desc.:** Condensed stories covering 80
counties in Indiana plus most counties in
Kentucky and Western Ohio. 4-H news,
anything of interest to the farmer,
such as new products, national & state
show winners, state fairs, also national
ag news all on a local basis are used.
Carries many sale bills, others besides
farm sales are covered.
**Readers:** Farm oriented.

25477
## FFA NEW HORIZONS
5632 Mt. Vernon Memorial Hwy.
Alexandria, VA 22309
Telephone: (703) 360-3600
FAX: (703) 360-5524
Mailing Address:
P.O. Box 15160
Alexandria, VA 22309
Year Established: 1952
Pub. Frequency: bi-m.
Page Size: standard
Subscrip. Rate: $3.50/yr.
Freelance Pay: $20/b&w photo
Circulation: 456,856
Circulation Type: paid
**Owner(s):**
National FFA Organization
P.O. Box 15160
Alexandria, VA 22309
Telephone: (703) 360-3600
Ownership %: 100
**Management:**
Dottie M. Hinkle ................Circulation Manager
**Editorial:**
Andrew Markwart ..........................Editor
Glenn Luedke ................Advertising Director
Linda Flint ..........................Art Director
Lawinna McGary ................Associate Editor
Jack Pitzer ........................Contributing Editor
Phillis Macintosh ..............Publishing Assistant
**Desc.:** Activities on the FFA, new and
improved methods in agriculture &
managing a business, hobbies, and
sports stories for youth 14-21 years of
age. By-line and photo credits are given.
Some publicity material used. Feature
article length of 1,000 or less words
desired, with photos if possible.
**Readers:** Teen-age rural & some urban
youths, (average age 17), agriculture
education, and their families.
**Deadline:** story-20th of the mo.; 2 mos.
prior to pub. date

25452
## FLORIDA FUTURE FARMER
## MAGAZINE
325 Gaines St., Ste. 1224
Tallahassee, FL 32399
Telephone: (904) 487-1594
Year Established: 1928
Pub. Frequency: a.
Page Size: tabloid
Subscrip. Rate: free-membership
**Owner(s):**
Dept. Of Education-Knott Building
325 W. Gaines St.
Tallahassee, FL 32399
Telephone: (904) 487-1544
Ownership %: 100
**Editorial:**
Danny Bartlett ..........................Editor
**Desc.:** Covers activities of Future Farmers
of America in Florida and developments
in agriculture which affects them.
Reports on conventions, fairs, sales,
exhibitions, etc. Emphasis is on the
part of youth in agriculture of tomorrow
and in practical, informative articles
indicating trends and techniques of the
future. Gives by-lines.
**Readers:** Members of F.F.A., friends,
parents and leaders in agriculture.

**Materials Accepted/Included:** 01-Business news 02-By-line articles 03-Fashion news 04-Food news 05-Freelance copy 06-Letters to editor 07-Real estate news 08-Sports news 09-Travel news 10-Book rev. 11-Movie rev. 12-Music rev. 13-TV rev. 14-Theater rev. 15-Coming events 16-Obituaries 17-Question & answer 18-Social announcements 19-Artwork 20-Cartoons 21-Photos 22-TV listings 23-Audio rec. 24-Video rec. 25-Books 26-Films/film clips 27-Personnel news 28-Press releases 29-New product news/photos 30-Trade lit. 31-Contracts awarded 32-Display adv. 33-Classified adv.

5-11

## HIGH PLAINS JOURNAL
25456

1500 E. Wyatt Earp Blvd.
Dodge City, KS 67801
Telephone: (316) 227-7171
FAX: (316) 227-7173
Mailing Address:
  P.O. Box 760
  Dodge City, KS 67801-0760
Year Established: 1882
Pub. Frequency: Mon.
Page Size: tabloid
Subscrip. Rate: $56/yr.
Freelance Pay: $1/in.; $10/b&w photo
Print Process: web offset
Circulation: 57,765
Circulation Type: paid
**Owner(s):**
High Plains Publishers, Inc.
P.O. Box 760
Dodge City, KS 67801-0760
Telephone: (316) 227-7171
FAX: (316) 227-7173
Ownership %: 100
**Bureau(s):**
High Plains Journal
P.O. Box 9
Lawrence, KS 66044
Telephone: (913) 749-5304
Contact: Doug Rich, Associate Editor
**Management:**
Duane Ross ........................President
Duane Ross ........................Publisher
Tom Taylor ...............Advertising Manager
**Editorial:**
Galen Hubbs .............................Editor
Larry Dreiling ...............Associate Editor
Doug Rich ....................Associate Editor
Diane James .................Associate Editor
Tim Mc Alavy ................Associate Editor
**Desc.:** Farm publication in five editions:
  Western Kansas; Eastern Kansas,
  Missouri; Colorado, Wyoming,
  New Mexico; Nebraska; Oklahoma and
  Texas. All features and articles keyed to
  its local edition area-wheat, milo, corn
  livestock are primary farming activities.
  By-lines on contributed material. Most
  material staff-written. Publicity must key
  to area interests. Photo for illustration.
  Uses high plains history and book
  reviews. Special interest columns for
  farm youth.
**Readers:** Farmers, ranchers, rural families
  in high plains states.

## HRI BUYERS GUIDE
61013

182 Queens Blvd.
Bayville, NJ 08721
Telephone: (908) 240-5330
FAX: (908) 341-0891
Mailing Address:
  P.O. Box 389
  Toms River, NJ 08754
Year Established: 1971
Pub. Frequency: Fri.
Page Size: tabloid
Subscrip. Rate: $70/yr.
Circulation: 150
Circulation Type: paid
**Owner(s):**
Urner Barry Publications, Inc.
P.O. Box 389
Toms River, NJ 08754
Telephone: (908) 240-5330
Ownership %: 100
**Management:**
Lisa Sharkus ..............Advertising Manager
**Editorial:**
Michael E. O'Shaughnessy .................Editor

## IDAHO FARMER
25458

Review Tower, 999 W. Riverside Ave.
Spokane, WA 99210
Telephone: (509) 459-5361

Mailing Address:
  P.O. Box 2160
  Spokane, WA 99210
Year Established: 1895
Pub. Frequency: 11/yr.
Page Size: standard
Subscrip. Rate: $18/yr.
Materials: 32,33
Print Process: web offset
Circulation: 13,819
Circulation Type: paid
**Owner(s):**
Cowles Publishing Co.
P.O. Box 2160
Spokane, WA 99210-1615
Telephone: (509) 459-5361
**Management:**
W.H. Cowles ..........................Publisher
Micahel R. Craigen ...........General Manager
**Editorial:**
E.W. Ramsey ...................Managing Editor
**Desc.:** General farm magazine.
**Readers:** Farmers, ranchers.

## ILLINOIS AGRI-NEWS
65995

420 Second St.
La Salle, IL 61301
Telephone: (815) 223-2558
FAX: (815) 223-5997
Year Established: 1977
Pub. Frequency: w.
Page Size: broadsheet
Subscrip. Rate: $17/yr.
Materials: 01,04,06,07,15,27,28,29,31,32,33
Freelance Pay: negotiable
Print Process: web offset
Circulation: 52,000
Circulation Type: paid
**Owner(s):**
Agri-News Publications
420 Second St.
La Salle, IL 61301
Telephone: (815) 223-2558
FAX: (815) 223-5997
Ownership %: 100
**Management:**
Lynn Barker ...................Vice President
Lou Lesniak .........................Publisher
**Editorial:**
W. Pufahl ..............................Editor
**Desc.:** Illinois Agri-news serves working
  farmers in the state of Illinois. Local
  news and events make up 50% of the
  publication's content. Features include
  news of national and state political
  trends as they affect the state of Illinois.
  Regular features include commodity
  market reports, women's features and
  articles written by specialists.
**Readers:** Working farm families.
**Deadline:** story-Fri. prior to pub. date;
  news-Fri.; photo-Fri.; ads-Fri.

## INDIANA PRAIRIE FARMER
25494

2346 S. Lynhurst, #304
Indianapolis, IN 46241-8602
Telephone: (317) 248-0681
Mailing Address:
  P.O. Box 421309
  Indianapolis, IN 46242-1309
Year Established: 1841
Pub. Frequency: 1st & 3rd Sat. in Jan.-
  Mar.; 1st Wed. in Apr.-Dec.
Page Size: standard
Subscrip. Rate: $2 newsstand; $14.98/yr.;
  $34.94/3 yrs.
Materials: 05,06,20,29,32,33
Freelance Pay: variable
Print Process: web offset
Circulation: 49,850
Circulation Type: controlled & paid

**Owner(s):**
Prairie Farmer Publishing Co.
191 S. Gary Ave.
Carol Stream, IL 60188-2089
Telephone: (708) 690-5600
Ownership %: 100
**Management:**
Allan R. Johnson ......................President
Thomas Budd ......................Vice President
Charles Roth .....................Vice President
Steve Joss .......................Vice President
Thomas Budd ...........................Publisher
Charles Wiegold .........Circulation Manager
Allan R. Johnson .............General Manager
Jerry Lucht .......................Sales Manager
**Editorial:**
Paul Queck ...............................Editor
Thomas Budd ...............Editorial Director
Charles Roth .......................Advertising
Thomas Bechman ...............Associate Editor
Sevie Kenyon ......................Dairy Editor
John Otte ......................Economics Editor
Jeanine Berry ......................Family Editor
Sara Wyant ...............National Affairs Editor
Judy Sturm ...................Production Director
Michael Morgan ............Production Editor
James Rieck ..................Research Director
JoAnn Alumbaugh .................Swine Editor
Trenna Grabowski .....................Tax Editor
**Desc.:** By-line articles cover all phases of
  farming and news of interest to the
  Indiana farmer. Carries wide variety of
  material on planting, crop selection,
  cultivation, equipment, marketing trends,
  insecticides, animal science, harvesting,
  storage, production, safety features, etc.
  Also uses news of industry and items of
  interest to family such as
  home entertainment, hobbies, etc.
  Women's section deals with all aspects
  of rural housekeeping: canning,
  preserving, recipes, home decoration,
  sewing, fashion, etc. Material submitted
  should include at least one good picture.
  Departments include: Letters, Home and
  Family (women's section). Farm
  Management Questions and Answers,
  weather.
**Readers:** Farmers and farm suppliers in
  Indiana.
**Deadline:** story-1 mo. prior to pub. date;
  news-1 mo. prior; photo-1 mo. prior; ads-
  1 mo. prior

## INLAND FARMER
71247

Review Tower, 999 Riverside Ave.
Spokane, WA 99210
Telephone: (509) 459-5377
FAX: (509) 459-5102
Mailing Address:
  P.O. Box 2160
  Spokane, WA 99210
Year Established: 1992
Pub. Frequency: m.; twice in Feb. & Mar.
Subscrip. Rate: $18/yr.
Materials: 32,33
Print Process: web offset
Circulation: 15639
Circulation Type: paid
**Owner(s):**
Cowles Publishing Co.
P.O. Box 2160
Spokane, WA 99210
Telephone: (509) 459-5377
FAX: (509) 459-5102
Ownership %: 100
**Management:**
Barry Roach ..............Advertising Manager
Michael Craigen ...............General Manager
**Editorial:**
E.W. Ramsey ...................Managing Editor
Michael Wohld ......................Field Editor
**Deadline:** mo. prior to pub. date

## JOURNAL OF RANGE MANAGEMENT
25310

1839 York St.
Denver, CO 80206
Telephone: (303) 355-7070
FAX: (303) 355-5059
Year Established: 1949
Pub. Frequency: bi-m.
Page Size: standard
Subscrip. Rate: $56/yr. or membership
Materials: 32
Circulation: 6,000
Circulation Type: paid
**Owner(s):**
Society for Range Management
1839 York St.
Denver, CO 80206
Telephone: (303) 355-7070
Ownership %: 100
**Editorial:**
Patty Perez ...............................Editor
**Desc.:** Publishes research reports,
  technical notes, and general articles
  related to rangeland resource use and
  management worldwide.
**Readers:** Ranchers, researchers, teachers,
  land managers.

## KANSAS FARMER
25465

3310 S.W. Harrison St.
Topeka, KS 66611
Telephone: (913) 232-3276
Year Established: 1863
Pub. Frequency: 12/yr.
Page Size: standard
Subscrip. Rate: $12/yr.; $24/3 yrs.
Freelance Pay: negotiable
Circulation: 54,100
Circulation Type: paid
**Owner(s):**
Farm Progress Companies
191 S. Gary Ave.
Carol Stream, IL 60188
Telephone: (708) 690-5600
Ownership %: 100
**Management:**
Allan Johnson ........................President
Thomas Budd ...........................Publisher
Terry Butzirus ...............Advertising Manager
Charles Wiegold .........Circulation Manager
**Editorial:**
Hank Ernst ..............................Editor
Joe Link .......................Editorial Director
**Desc.:** General farm magazine exclusive to
  Kansas. Most editorial material is
  obtained by staff members and field
  editors. Special assignments go
  to agricultural college scientists and
  other specialists in all phases of
  agriculture.
**Readers:** Farmers, ranchers, rural
  Kansans & agribusinessmen

## KENTUCKY FARMER
25466

7701 Six Forks Rd., Ste. 132
Raleigh, NC 27624
Telephone: (919) 676-3276
FAX: (919) 676-9803
Mailing Address:
  P.O. Box 150001
  Raleigh, NC 27624
Year Established: 1865
Pub. Frequency: m.
Page Size: tabloid
Subscrip. Rate: $12/yr.
Materials: 32,33
Circulation: 21,000
Circulation Type: paid

**Materials Accepted/Included:** 01-Business news 02-By-line articles 03-Fashion news 04-Food news 05-Freelance copy 06-Letters to editor 07-Real estate news 08-Sports news 09-Travel news 10-Book rev. 11-Movie rev. 12-Music rev. 13-TV rev. 14-Theater rev. 15-Coming events 16-Obituaries 17-Question & answer 18-Social announcements 19-Artwork 20-Cartoons 21-Photos 22-TV listings 23-Audio rec. 24-Video rec. 25-Books 26-Films/film clips 27-Personnel news 28-Press releases 29-New product news/photos 30-Trade lit. 31-Contracts awarded 32-Display adv. 33-Classified adv.

**Owner(s):**
Rural Press USA
7701 Six Forks Rd.
Raleigh, NC 27615
Telephone: (919) 676-3276
Ownership %: 100
**Management:**
Allan Williams .........................Publisher
Blake Lewis, Jr. ..............Advertising Manager
**Editorial:**
Wayne Harr ....................................Editor
**Desc.:** Covers all phases of general
farming, including livestock, in Kentucky.
Articles deal with new programs and
methods, markets, improvements, etc.
Departments include: Women's
Department, Livestock and Tobacco.
**Readers:** Primarily Kentucky farmers.

### KENTUCKY PRAIRIE FARMER
67022

10303 Vantage Rd.
Jeffersontown, KY 40299
Telephone: (502) 266-5263
Year Established: 1841
Pub. Frequency: w.: 1st & 3rd Sat./Jan.-
Mar.; m.: 1st Wed./Apr.-Dec.
Page Size: standard
Subscrip. Rate: free to qualified persons;
$2/newsstand; $25/yr.
Materials: 05,06,20,29,32,33
Freelance Pay: variable
Print Process: web offset
Circulation: 10,582
Circulation Type: controlled
**Owner(s):**
Farm Progress Co., Inc.
191 S. Gary Ave.
Carol Stream, IL 60188-2089
Telephone: (708) 690-5600
Ownership %: 100
**Management:**
Allan Johnson ............................President
Steve Joss ............................Vice President
Tom Budd ............................Vice President
Tom Budd ...............................Publisher
Charles Roth ................Advertising Manager
Chuck Wiegold ...............Circulation Manager
**Editorial:**
Paul Queck ....................Executive Editor
John Otte ....................Economics Editor
Jeanine Berry ......................Family Editor
Sara Wyant .......................National Editor
Jim Rieck ...................Research Director
JoAnn Alumbaugh ..................Swine Editor
Trenna R. Grabowski ...............Tax Editor
**Desc.:** By-line articles cover all phases of
farming and news of interest to the
Kentucky farmer, to include corn,
soybean, tobacco, wheat, forage, and
livestock production and marketing
features. Carries wide variety of material
on planting, crop selection, cultivation,
equipment, marketing trends,
insecticides, animal science, harvesting,
storage, production, safety features, etc.
Also uses news of industry and items of
interest to family such as
home entertainment, hobbies, etc.
Women's section deals with all aspects
of rural housekeeping: canning,
preserving, recipes, home decoration,
sewing, fashion, etc. Material submitted
should include at least one good picture.
Departments include: Letters, Home and
Family, Farm Management Questions
and Answers, weather.
**Deadline:** story-1 mo. prior to pub. date;
news-1 mo.; ads-1 mo.

### LANCASTER FARMING
25467

1 E. Main St.
Ephrata, PA 17522
Telephone: (717) 626-1164
FAX: (717) 733-6058

Mailing Address:
P.O. Box 609
Ephrata, PA 17522
Year Established: 1955
Pub. Frequency: w.
Page Size: tabloid
Subscrip. Rate: $19/yr; $36/2 yrs.
Materials: 01,04,05,06
Freelance Pay: negotiable
Print Process: web offset
Circulation: 49,768
Circulation Type: paid
**Owner(s):**
Lancaster County Weeklies, Inc.
Ownership %: 100
**Management:**
Gary Meyer ................Advertising Manager
Robert G. Campbell ...............General Manager
**Editorial:**
Everett Newswanger ..............................Editor
**Desc.:** Its editorial philosophy is to inform
and report, and to stimulate thinking on
technological, political and social
developments which may affect farmers
economically. Area farm news and
activities are covered in depth; articles
featuring local rural youth and business
farmers are used regularly. Each issue
contains the latest egg, poultry and
livestock market reports available.
Distribution blankets
"highly/agriculturalized" PA and extends
into surrounding states.

### LAND, THE
25468

418 S. Second St.
Mankato, MN 56002
Telephone: (507) 345-4523
Mailing Address:
P.O. Box 3169
Mankato, MN 56002
Year Established: 1973
Pub. Frequency: bi-w.
Page Size: tabloid
Subscrip. Rate: free; $5/yr. in 5 cys.;
$12/yr. out of state
Materials: 32,33
Freelance Pay: $25-$45
Print Process: web
Circulation: 40,000
Circulation Type: free & paid
**Owner(s):**
Free Press Co.
418 S. Second St.
Mankato, MN 56001
Telephone: (507) 625-4451
Ownership %: 100
**Bureau(s):**
J.L. Farmakis, Inc.
P.O. Box 1004
New Canaan, CT 06840
Telephone: (203) 966-1746
Contact: Jack Farmakis
**Management:**
Kathy Weinstein ...............General Manager
**Editorial:**
Randy Frahm ..............................Editor
**Desc.:** Local and regional agricultural news
and features: rural people and the
activities and involvements, including
profiles. Also carries columns by
area people, market projections, and a
Washington report, via correspondent.
**Readers:** Farmers and agri-business
people only. Circulation in 55 county
areas in Minnesota.

### MISSOURI RURALIST
25474

1007 N. College Ave.
Ste. 3
Columbia, MO 65201
Telephone: (314) 875-5445
Year Established: 1856
Pub. Frequency: 15/yr.

Page Size: standard
Subscrip. Rate: $14.98/yr. in state; $25/yr.
outside of state
Materials: 32,33
Freelance Pay: negotiable
Circulation: 59,900
Circulation Type: paid
**Owner(s):**
Farm Progress Companies
191 S. Gary Ave.
Carol Stream, IL 60188
Telephone: (708) 690-5600
Ownership %: 100
**Management:**
Allan Johnson ............................President
Thomas Budd ............................Publisher
Leon Kincaid ...............Advertising Manager
Charles Wiegold ...............Circulation Manager
**Editorial:**
Larry S. Harper ..............................Editor
Steve Fairchild .....................Field Editor
**Desc.:** General farming magazine, covers
all phases of agriculture. Virtually all
material obtained by staff members, field
men with special assignments to
scientists and specialists in various
fields of agriculture.
**Readers:** Farmers and ranchers in
Missouri, agribusiness people.

### MONTANA FARMER
25476

Review Tower, 999 W. Riverside Ave.
Spokane, WA 99210
Telephone: (509) 459-5361
Mailing Address:
P.O. Box 2160
Spokane, WA 99210
Year Established: 1913
Pub. Frequency: m.
Page Size: pg. 9 1/6 x 13 9/16; col. 12
ems
Subscrip. Rate: $18/yr.
Materials: 21,32,33
Circulation: 17,250
Circulation Type: paid
**Owner(s):**
Cowles Publishing Co.
Spokane, WA
Telephone: (509) 459-5361
Ownership %: 100
**Management:**
Stacey Cowles ............................Publisher
Michael R. Craigen ...............General Manager
**Editorial:**
E.W. Ramsey ...............Managing Editor
Clint Peck .....................Field Editor
**Desc.:** General farm magazine.
**Readers:** Farmers and agriculturally-
oriented business people.

### NEBRASKA FARMER
25479

5625 O St.
Ste. 5
Lincoln, NE 68510
Telephone: (402) 489-9331
FAX: (402) 489-9335
Mailing Address:
P.O. Box 5467
Lincoln, NE 68505
Year Established: 1859
Pub. Frequency: 21/yr.
Page Size: standard
Subscrip. Rate: $14.98/yr.; $34.94/3 yr.;
$25/yr. out of NE; $60/3 yr. out of NE
Circulation: 53,062
Circulation Type: paid
**Owner(s):**
Farm Progress Companies
191 S. Gary Ave.
Carol Stream, IL 60188
Telephone: (708) 462-2892
Ownership %: 100
**Management:**
Tom Budd ............................Publisher

Terry Butzirus ...............Advertising Manager
**Editorial:**
Dave Howe ..............................Editor
Don McCabe ...............Managing Editor
Becky Ohlde ...............Assistant Editor
**Desc.:** All aspects of the business of
farming in Nebraska.
**Readers:** Farmers and ranchers of
Nebraska.
**Deadline:** ads-30 days prior to pub. date

### NEBRASKA FERTILIZER & AG-CHEMICAL DIGEST
23270

1111 Lincoln Mall, Ste. 308
Lincoln, NE 68508
*see Service, Trade, Professional
Magazines, Fertilizer*

### NEIGHBORS
25480

2108 E. South Blvd.
Montgomery, AL 36116
Telephone: (205) 288-3900
FAX: (205) 284-3957
Mailing Address:
P.O. Box 11000
Montgomery, AL 36191-0001
Year Established: 1976
Pub. Frequency: m.
Page Size: standard
Subscrip. Rate: free for members;
$.80/issue for non-members
Circulation: 100,000
Circulation Type: controlled & paid
**Owner(s):**
Alabama Farmer's Federation
2108 E. South Blvd.
Montgomery, AL 36116
Telephone: (205) 288-3900
FAX: (205) 284-3957
Ownership %: 100
**Editorial:**
Mark Morrison ..............................Editor
**Desc.:** Written for Alabama farming and
rural community with slant toward
Agricultural information and insight into
the state's rural sector
**Readers:** Rural and agricultural Alabama
audience.
**Deadline:** 1st of mo. prior to pub. date

### NEVADA RANCHER, THE
25321

680 Greenbrae Dr., Ste. 223
Sparks, NV 89431
Telephone: (702) 358-2681
FAX: (702) 358-2686
Mailing Address:
P.O. Box 1465
Sparks, NV 89432
Year Established: 1970
Pub. Frequency: m.
Page Size: tabloid
Subscrip. Rate: $7.50/yr.
Materials: 32,33
Freelance Pay: $1/in.
Circulation: 2,500
Circulation Type: paid
**Owner(s):**
Nevada Rancher
P.O. Box 1465
Sparks, NV 89432
Telephone: (702) 358-2681
Ownership %: 100
**Management:**
Carolyn Hansen ............................Publisher
Carolyn Hansen ...............Advertising Manager
**Editorial:**
Joan Curry .......................Advertising
**Desc.:** Organization publication devoted
primarily to cattle and agricultural news.
**Readers:** People interested in agriculture
and ranching, horse activities, 4-H and
FFA.

**Materials Accepted/Included:** 01-Business news 02-By-line articles 03-Fashion news 04-Food news 05-Freelance copy 06-Letters to editor 07-Real estate news 08-Sports news 09-Travel news 10-Book rev. 11-Movie rev. 12-Music rev. 13-TV rev. 14-Theater rev. 15-Coming events 16-Obituaries 17-Question & answer 18-Social announcements 19-Artwork 20-Cartoons 21-Photos 22-TV listings 23-Audio rec. 24-Video rec. 25-Books 26-Films/film clips 27-Personnel news 28-Press releases 29-New product news/photos 30-Trade lit. 31-Contracts awarded 32-Display adv. 33-Classified adv.

5-13

## NEW ENGLAND FARMER
61672

50 Bay St.
St. Johnsbury, VT 05819-1902
Telephone: (802) 748-1373
FAX: (802) 748-5547
Year Established: 1822
Pub. Frequency: m.
Page Size: tabloid
Subscrip. Rate: $12/yr. in US; $25/yr.
    foreign
Materials: 32,33
Circulation: 20,000
Circulation Type: paid
**Owner(s):**
Rural Press USA
P.O. Box 4187
St. Johnsbury, VT 05819
Telephone: (802) 748-1373
**Management:**
Allen Williams .........................Publisher
**Editorial:**
Gus Howe ...................................Editor
**Desc.:** Agricultural journal with fresh
    editorial copy for all aspects of farming.
    Includes a bi-monthly supplement, Grow,
    for the fruit & vegetable industry and a
    pull-out supplement for the maple
    sugaring industry called The
    Sugarmaker.
**Readers:** Dairy farmers, vegetable & fruit
    growers, maple sugar producers, sheep,
    beef & Xmas tree producers.
**Deadline:** ads-10th of mo. prior to pub.
    date

## NEW FARM, THE
25482

222 Main St.
Emmaus, PA 18098
Telephone: (610) 967-8405
FAX: (610) 967-8959
Year Established: 1979
Pub. Frequency: 7/yr.
Page Size: standard
Subscrip. Rate: $2.75 newsstand;
    $14.97/yr.
Materials: 06,25,28,30,32,33
Freelance Pay: negotiable
Circulation: 50,000
Circulation Type: paid
**Owner(s):**
Rodale Institute
222 Main St.
Emmaus, PA 18098
Telephone: (215) 967-8405
Ownership %: 100
**Management:**
Ardath Rodale ...............Chairman of Board
John Haberern ........................President
Mike Brusko ...........................Publisher
Teri Sorg-McManamon ...............Advertising
                                    Manager
**Editorial:**
Craig Cramer ...............Editorial Director
Denise Shade ...................Art Department
Debra Protchko ...............Marketing Director
Tom Gettings ...........................Photo
**Desc.:** Dedicated to putting people, profit
    and biological permanence back into
    farming. Major themes include slashing
    farmer's production costs while
    conserving/improving soil & water, non-
    chemical weed control, developing
    biological fertility, new farming/marketing
    systems. Departments include:
    Questions and Answers, Rural Delivery
    (letters to editor), With The Editor,
    Research Update, Parting Shots.
**Readers:** Commercial farmers throughout
    U.S. & Canada, extension agents, public
    & private agricultural researchers, and
    other agricultural professionals.

## NEW MEXICO FARM & RANCH
25322

421 N. Water St.
Las Cruces, NM 88001
Telephone: (505) 526-5521
FAX: (505) 525-0858
Year Established: 1944
Pub. Frequency: m.
Page Size: tabloid
Subscrip. Rate: $9/yr.
Materials: 32,33
Freelance Pay: $1.25/col. in.
Print Process: web
Circulation: 11,010
Circulation Type: paid
**Owner(s):**
New Mexico Farm and Ranch, Inc.
421 N. Water
Las Cruces, NM 88001
Telephone: (505) 526-5521
Ownership %: 100
**Editorial:**
B. J. Porter ...........................Editor
Erik Ness ......................Managing Editor
Eric Ness ...........................Advertising
Christine Nordstrom .............Circulation Editor
Erik Ness .........................News Editor
**Desc.:** Welcomes releases, photos,
    features, etc. on new trends in New
    Mexico farming and ranching.
    Invites receipt of possible cover photos
    of scenes of New Mexico agriculture.
    Focuses primarily on general
    developments on New Mexico farm-
    ranch scene.
**Readers:** Farmers and ranchers within
    New Mexico, others in ag-related
    businesses, i.e. feeds, seeds, tractors.

## NEW MEXICO STOCKMAN
25323

P.O. Box 7127
Albuquerque, NM 87194
Telephone: (505) 243-9515
FAX: (505) 243-9598
Year Established: 1935
Pub. Frequency: m.
Page Size: standard
Subscrip. Rate: $9/yr.; $15/2 yrs.
Freelance Pay: $.06/wd.
Circulation: 11,000
Circulation Type: paid
**Owner(s):**
Livestock Publications, Inc.
P.O. Box 7127
Albuquerque, NM 87194
Telephone: (505) 243-9515
Ownership %: 100
**Management:**
Charles Stocks ........................Publisher
Mae Lopez ........................Business Manager
**Editorial:**
Charles Stocks .........................Editor
**Desc.:** Covers farm and livestock
    production in New Mexico and bordering
    areas. News items cover ranches and
    ranchers, sales, shows, markets, etc.
    Features deal with various phases of
    livestock breeding, raising, feeding,
    health, trends, transportation and
    marketing problems, governmental
    actions, etc. Carries veterinary reports
    on disease, control, drugs, etc.
    Publishes an occasional by-line feature
    on some topic of interest to field. A
    typical title of this type might be: New
    Animal Disease Test Developed;
    describing new research for early
    detection of certain diseases in
    livestock. Departments include: Farm
    News, Notes of Interest to
    Southwestern Livestock Growers and
    Farmers, and Obituaries. Interested in 4-
    H club activities and rodeo news.

**Readers:** Farmers, livestock growers and
    business in New Mexico and bordering
    areas of Arizona.

## NEWS & FARMER
25484

117 N. Main St.
Federalsburg, MD 21632
Telephone: (410) 754-3331
FAX: (410) 754-3340
Mailing Address:
    P.O. Box 459
    Preston, MD 21655
Year Established: 1866
Pub. Frequency: w.
Page Size: tabloid
Subscrip. Rate: $10.50/yr.
Circulation: 5,000
Circulation Type: paid
**Owner(s):**
Shore News, Inc.
P.O. Box 459
Preston, MD 21655
Telephone: (410) 754-3331
FAX: (410) 754-3340
Ownership %: 100
**Management:**
Carl Thornton .........................Publisher
Pat McNeal ...................Advertising Manager
**Editorial:**
Craig McGinnes .........................Editor
**Desc.:** This publication enjoys a sound
    high-buying-power circulation in the
    heart of the Chesapeake Bay country
    and the Delmarva Peninsula, famous
    for agriculture food processing, poultry
    production, small industry, seafood/sport
    fishing. In the heart of the Eastern shore
    of Maryland/land of pleasant living.
**Readers:** Subscribed to by farm, business
    and seafood. Talbot, Wicomico,
    Somerset, Kent & Caroline, Dorchester,
    Queen Anne's.
**Deadline:** story-5:00 pm. Fri. prior to pub.
    date

## NO-TILL FARMER
61673

P.O. Box 624
Brookfield, WI 53008
Telephone: (414) 782-4480
Year Established: 1972
Pub. Frequency: 17/yr.
Page Size: standard
Subscrip. Rate: $29.95/yr.
Materials: 02,06,10,15,17,19,21,24,25,27,
    28,29,30,32,33
Freelance Pay: $175-$250
Circulation: 10,000
Circulation Type: paid
**Owner(s):**
Lessitea Publications, Inc.
P.O. Box 624
Brookfield, WI 53008
Telephone: (414) 782-0604
Ownership %: 100
**Management:**
Frank Lessiter .........................Publisher
Sue Ramstack ...................Circulation Manager
**Editorial:**
Frank Lessiter .........................Editor
**Desc.:** Presents the latest information
    dealing with reduced tillage.

## OHIO FARMER
25485

1350 W. Fifth Ave.
Ste. 124
Columbus, OH 43212
Telephone: (614) 486-9637
FAX: (614) 486-4789
Year Established: 1848
Pub. Frequency: 15/yr.
Page Size: standard
Subscrip. Rate: $12.98/yr.; $29.94/3 yrs.
Freelance Pay: negotiable
Circulation: 66,000

Circulation Type: paid
**Owner(s):**
Farm Progress Companies
191 S. Gary Ave.
Carol Stream, IL 60188
Telephone: (708) 462-2892
Ownership %: 100
**Management:**
Tom Budd ...........................Publisher
Marti Smith ...................Advertising Manager
**Editorial:**
Tim White .............................Editor
**Desc.:** Family farm journal covering all
    aspects of farming in Ohio. Deals with
    technical farm problems, labor,
    equipment, seeding, crop rotation,
    marketing, trends, etc. Also
    covers dairying, animal husbandry,
    breeding, poultry, etc. Primarily
    interested in articles about Ohio farm
    families describing new farm practices
    and how they aid Ohio farmers to be
    more efficient. Departments include:
    Over the Back Fence (farm chatter),
    Letters From Readers, Women's
    Page (anything of interest to a farm wife,
    Patterns, Recipes, Upholstery, etc.).
    Helps for the Homemaker (helpful hints
    to the farm wife on new Household
    Equipment, Ideas, etc.), 4H Club News.
    Prefers articles of four or five
    pages. Materials should be accompanied
    by good action photographs.
**Readers:** Farmers in Ohio, agribusinesses.

## OKLAHOMA FARMER-STOCKMAN, THE
61590

7301 N. Broadway, Ste. 230
Oklahoma City, OK 73116
Telephone: (405) 848-2805
Year Established: 1911
Pub. Frequency: m.
Page Size: standard
Subscrip. Rate: $12/yr. qualified personnel
Circulation: 43,000
Circulation Type: paid
**Owner(s):**
Farm Progress Co., Inc.
191 S. Gary Ave.
Carol Stream, IL 60188
Telephone: (708) 462-2892
Ownership %: 100
**Editorial:**
Dan Crummett ..........................Editor

## ORNAMENTAL OUTLOOK
25519

1331 N. Mills Ave.
Orlando, FL 32803
Telephone: (407) 894-6522
FAX: (407) 894-6511
Year Established: 1907
Pub. Frequency: m.
Page Size: standard
Subscrip. Rate: $35/yr. in FL; $45/yr.
    elsewhere
Circulation: 12,500
Circulation Type: controlled & paid
**Owner(s):**
FGR, Inc.
1331 N. Mills Ave.
Orlando, FL 32803
Telephone: (407) 894-6522
FAX: (407) 894-6511
Ownership %: 100
**Management:**
Sondra G. Abrahamson ...............Publisher
Sharon L. Butler .................Business Manager
**Editorial:**
Rhonda Hunsinger .......................Editor
**Deadline:** 1st of mo. prior to pub. date

Materials Accepted/Included: 01-Business news 02-By-line articles 03-Fashion news 04-Food news 05-Freelance copy 06-Letters to editor 07-Real estate news 08-Sports news 09-Travel news 10-Book rev. 11-Movie rev. 12-Music rev. 13-TV rev. 14-Theater rev. 15-Coming events 16-Obituaries 17-Question & answer 18-Social announcements 19-Artwork 20-Cartoons 21-Photos 22-TV listings 23-Audio rec. 24-Video rec. 25-Books 26-Films/film clips 27-Personnel news 28-Press releases 29-New product news/photos 30-Trade lit. 31-Contracts awarded 32-Display adv. 33-Classified adv.

## PACIFIC FARMER

71248

Review Tower, 999 W. Riverside Ave.
Spokane, WA 99210
Telephone: (509) 459-5377
FAX: (509) 459-5102
Mailing Address:
  P.O. Box 2160
  Spokane, WA 99210
Year Established: 1992
Pub. Frequency: m.; twice Feb. & Mar.
Subscrip. Rate: $18/yr.
Materials: 32, 33
Print Process: web offset
Circulation: 13689
Circulation Type: paid
**Owner(s):**
Cowles Publishing Co.
P.O. Box 2160
Spokane, WA 99210
Telephone: (509) 459-5377
FAX: (509) 459-5102
Ownership %: 100
**Management:**
Barry Roach ..................Advertising Manager
Michael Craigen ..................General Manager
**Editorial:**
E.W. Ramsey ..................Managing Editor
Richard Yost ..................Field Editor
Norman Herdrich ..................Production Editor
**Deadline:** mo. prior to pub. date

## PENNSYLVANIA FARMER

25492

704 Lisburn Rd.
Camp Hill, PA 17011
Telephone: (717) 761-6050
FAX: (717) 761-4517
Year Established: 1877
Pub. Frequency: m.
Page Size: standard
Subscrip. Rate: $14.98/yr.
Freelance Pay: negotiable
Circulation: 46,000
Circulation Type: paid
**Owner(s):**
Farmer Progress Companies
191 S. Gary Ave.
Carol Stream, IL 60188
Telephone: (708) 462-2892
Ownership %: 100
**Management:**
Alan R. Johnson ..................President
Tom Budd ..................Publisher
Joyce Barone ..................Advertising Manager
Charles Wiegold ..................Circulation Manager
**Editorial:**
John Vogel ..................Editor
**Desc.:** Farm magazine carrying primarily
staff - written material relating primarily
to production agriculture in
Pennsylvania, Maryland, Delaware, New
Jersey and West Virginia. Farm Home
section deals with farm wives, their
business and their families, interior
decorating and furnishings, patterns,
children, history, etc. Departments
include: Market Trends, Farm Update,
Livestock, Dairy, Animal Health, Crops,
Agricultural Engineering, New in
Equipment, Poultry, News Notes. Free
lance material accepted with query
approval and formula - writing.
**Readers:** Farmers in Pennsylvania, New
Jersey, Delaware, Maryland and West
Virginia.

## POTATO COUNTRY

56343

2809-A Fruitvale Blvd.
Yakima, WA 98902
Telephone: (509) 248-2452
Mailing Address:
  P.O. Box 1467
  Yakima, WA 98907
Year Established: 1985
Pub. Frequency: 9/yr.

Page Size: standard
Subscrip. Rate: $15/yr. US; $30/yr.
  Canada & Mexico; $45/yr. foreign
Materials: 01,02,04,05,06,15,16,20,21,28,
  29,30,32,33
Freelance Pay: depends on length/quality;
  most articles $125
Print Process: web
Circulation: 7,317
Circulation Type: controlled
**Owner(s):**
D. Brent Clement
681 Ames Rd.
Selah, WA 98942
Telephone: (509) 697-3070
Ownership %: 50

J. Mike Stoker
1407 W. Powerhouse Rd.
Yakima, WA 98908
Telephone: (509) 966-7731
Ownership %: 50
**Management:**
Beverly Stoker ..................Circulation Manager
J. Mike Stoker ..................Manager
**Editorial:**
D. Brent Clement ..................Editor
J. Mike Stoker ..................Advertising
Lynn Schuchardt ..................Advertising
Kathy Noble ..................Production Director
**Desc.:** Edited for potato growers, shippers,
and allied industry people in 11 western
states: WA, OR, MT, ID, CO, CA, NM,
WY, NV, UT, & AZ. Content includes
grower and industry articles on
production and marketing, product
information, and general potato news.
**Readers:** Potato growers in the 11
western states of Washington, Oregon,
Idaho, Colorado, California, Montana,
Utah, Arizona, New Mexico, Nevada and
Wyoming.
**Deadline:** story-2 mos. prior to pub. date;
news-2 mos. prior; photo-2 mos. prior;
ads-1 mo. prior

## PRAIRIE FARMER

25493

191 S. Gary Ave.
Carol Stream, IL 60188
Telephone: (708) 690-5600
FAX: (708) 462-2892
Year Established: 1841
Pub. Frequency: 15/yr.
Page Size: standard
Subscrip. Rate: $14.98/yr.
Materials: 05,20
Freelance Pay: $150-$500/article
Circulation: 83,500
Circulation Type: controlled & paid
**Owner(s):**
Capitol Cities-American Broadcasting Co.,
Inc.
77 W. 66th St.
New York, NY 10023
Telephone: (212) 456-7777
Ownership %: 100
**Bureau(s):**
Prairie Farmer-Illinois
P.O. Box 3217
Decatur, IL 62524
Telephone: (217) 877-9070
FAX: (217) 877-9695
Contact: Michael Wilson, Editor

Prairie Farmer-Indiana
Indianapolis, IN 46241
Telephone: (317) 248-0681
Contact: Paul Queck, Editor

Prairie Farmer-Kentucky
10303 Vantage Rd.
Jeffersontown , KY 40299
Telephone: (502) 266-5263
Contact: Timothy Sickman, Editor
**Management:**
Thomas Budd ..................Publisher

Charles Roth ..................Advertising Manager
**Editorial:**
Carl Eiche ..................Senior Editor
Paul Queck, Indiana ..................Editor
Tom Bechman ..................Associate Editor
John Otte ..................Economics Editor
John Pocock ..................Field Editor
Cheri Stout ..................Field Editor
Sara Wyant ..................National Affairs Editor
Trenna Grabowski ..................Tax Editor
**Desc.:** By-line articles cover all phases of
farming and news of interest to the
cornbelt farmer. Carries wide variety of
material on planting, crop selection,
cultivation, equipment, marketing, trends,
animal science, insecticides, harvesting,
storage, production, safety features, etc.
Women's section deals with all aspects
of rural housekeeping: recipes, home
decoration, sewing, fashion, etc.
Departments include: Letters, Letter
from a Farmer's Wife, Home and Family
(women's section), Farm
Management Questions and Answers,
Washington Farm Report. Material
submitted should include at least one
decent picture.
**Readers:** Farmers and farm suppliers in
Illinois, Indiana, and Kentucky.
**Deadline:** story-1 mo.; news-1 mo.; photo-
1 mo.; ads-1 mo.

## PROGRESSIVE FARMER

25495

2100 Lake Shore Dr.
Birmingham, AL 35209
Telephone: (205) 877-6000
FAX: (205) 877-6450
Mailing Address:
  P.O. Box 2581
  Birmingham, AL 35202
Year Established: 1886
Pub. Frequency: m.
Page Size: standard
Subscrip. Rate: $14.95/yr.
Circulation: 415,000
Circulation Type: paid
**Owner(s):**
Southern Progressive Co.
2100 Lake Shore Dr.
Birmingham, AL 35209
Telephone: (205) 877-6000
Ownership %: 100
**Management:**
Jim Nelson ..................President
Ed Dickinson ..................Publisher
**Editorial:**
Jack Odle ..................Editor in Chief
**Desc.:** General agriculture and country
living.

## PROGRESSIVE FARMER (TX-OK-NM-AZ-KS EDITION)

25496

9020-I, Capital of Texas Hwy. N.
Ste. 345
Austin, TX 78759
Telephone: (512) 346-6500
FAX: (512) 346-7319
Year Established: 1886
Pub. Frequency: m.
Page Size: standard
Subscrip. Rate: $14.95/yr.; $24.95/2 yrs.;
  $32.95/3 yrs.
Freelance Pay: varies
Circulation: 240,000
Circulation Type: paid
**Owner(s):**
Southern Progress Corp. (subsidiary of
Time, Inc.)
P.O. Box 2581
Birmingham, AL 35202
Telephone: (205) 877-6000
Ownership %: 100
**Management:**
Ed Dickinson ..................Publisher

**Editorial:**
Jack Odle ..................Editor
Eugene Butler ..................Editor Emeritus
Kim Allen ..................New Products Editor
Karl Wolfshohl ..................Southwest Editor
Kim Allen ..................Western Editor
**Desc.:** General farm publication edited for
farm & ranch readers.
**Readers:** Farmers, ranchers, agribusiness
leaders.

## ROCKY MOUNTAIN UNION FARMER

69319

10800 E. Bethany Dr.
4th Floor
Aurora, CO 80014-2632
Telephone: (303) 752-5800
FAX: (303) 752-5810
Year Established: 1912
Pub. Frequency: bi-m.
Page Size: tabloid
Subscrip. Rate: $7/yr.
Circulation: 8000
Circulation Type: paid
**Owner(s):**
Rocky Mountain Farmers Union
10800 E. Bethany Dr., #450
Aurora, CO 80014-2632
Telephone: (303) 752-5800
Ownership %: 100
**Editorial:**
Melissa Elliott ..................Editor

## SMALL FARM TODAY

61674

3903 W. Ridge Trail Rd.
Clark, MO 65243-9525
Telephone: (314) 687-3525
FAX: (314) 687-3148
Year Established: 1984
Pub. Frequency: bi-m.
Page Size: standard
Subscrip. Rate: $4 newsstand; $21/yr.;
  $39/2 yrs.; $54/3 yrs.
Materials: 05,06,15,19,20,25,28,29,30,32,33
Freelance Pay: $1.50/col. in.
Print Process: web
Circulation: 12,000
Circulation Type: paid
**Owner(s):**
Missouri Farm Publishing, Inc.
3903 W. Ridge Trail Rd.
Clark, MO 65243
Telephone: (314) 687-3525
**Editorial:**
Ron Macher ..................Editor
Paul Berg ..................Managing Editor
**Desc.:** Small Farm Today was founded
and is dedicated to the preservation and
promotion of small farming and rural
living. It accomplishes this goal with
how-to articles on agricultural
alternatives for the new family farm,
including specialty crops and livestock
and direct marketing. Other articles
cover successful small farmers and
various aspects of rural living.
**Readers:** Small farmers and others
interested in agricultural alternatives.

## SOUTHEAST FARM PRESS

25500

14920 U.S. Hwy. 61
Clarksdale, MS 38614
Telephone: (601) 624-8503
FAX: (601) 627-1977
Mailing Address:
  P.O. Box 1420
  Clarksdale, MS 38614
Year Established: 1974
Pub. Frequency: s-m.
Page Size: tabloid
Subscrip. Rate: $3.50 newsstand; $25/yr.
Circulation: 54,000
Circulation Type: paid

**Materials Accepted/Included:** 01-Business news 02-By-line articles 03-Fashion news 04-Food news 05-Freelance copy 06-Letters to editor 07-Real estate news 08-Sports news 09-Travel news 10-Book rev. 11-Movie rev. 12-Music rev. 13-TV rev. 14-Theater rev. 15-Coming events 16-Obituaries 17-Question & answer 18-Social announcements 19-Artwork 20-Cartoons 21-Photos 22-TV listings 23-Audio rec. 24-Video rec. 25-Books 26-Films/film clips 27-Personnel news 28-Press releases 29-New product news/photos 30-Trade lit. 31-Contracts awarded 32-Display adv. 33-Classified adv.

5-15

**Owner(s):**
Argus Press Group, D.E.T. Publishing Co.
54-62 Regent St.
Ownership %: 100
**Management:**
John Montandon ..............................President
Dave Whaley ....................General Manager
Darrah Parker ..............Production Manager
**Editorial:**
James Hudson ...................................Editor
Hembree Brandon ..............Editorial Director
**Desc.:** Each provides readers with
pertinent up to date information covering
farming production, marketing and
legislation for the local area.
**Readers:** Farmers, planters and related
fields in southeastern states.
**Deadline:** 2 weeks prior to pub. date

68667

**SOUTHWEST FARM PRESS**
P.O. Box 1420
Clarksdale, MS 38614
Telephone: (601) 624-8503
FAX: (601) 627-1977
Year Established: 1974
Pub. Frequency: s-m.
Page Size: tabloid
Subscrip. Rate: $25/yr.
Circulation: 45,000
Circulation Type: paid
**Owner(s):**
Argus, Inc.
Atlanta, GA
Ownership %: 100
**Management:**
Ken Dean ...........................Advertising Manager
Darrah Parker ..................Production Manager
**Editorial:**
Glenn Rutz ........................Managing Editor

25501

**SUCCESSFUL FARMING**
17 16 Locust St.
Des Moines, IA 50309-3023
Telephone: (515) 284-2139
FAX: (515) 284-3563
Year Established: 1902
Pub. Frequency: m.
Page Size: standard
Subscrip. Rate: $14/yr.
Freelance Pay: $200-$500
Circulation: 485,000
Circulation Type: paid
**Owner(s):**
Meredith Corp.
17 16 Locust St.
Des Moines, IA 50309-3023
Telephone: (515) 284-3000
FAX: (515) 284-3563
Ownership %: 100
**Management:**
Jim Cornick ...............................Publisher
Gil Spears ...................Advertising Manager
**Editorial:**
Loren Kruse ...................................Editor
Gene Johnston .................Managing Editor
**Desc.:** Covers all phases of farming and
livestock, crops and soils, machinery,
buildings, economics and management.
Both contributed (technical) and staff-
written. Departments include: All Around
the Farm, Land, Money, Marketing,
Womens Interest, Machinery,
Technology, Great Outdoors, and
Livestock.
**Readers:** Average subscriber lives on
farm. Circulation 485000, 1990 Rate
Base, Includes 91% of US.

25502

**TENNESSEE FARMER**
7701 Six Forks Rd.
Ste. 132
Raleigh, NC 27615
Telephone: (919) 676-3276
FAX: (919) 676-9803

**Mailing Address:**
P.O. Box 150001
Raleigh, NC 27624
Year Established: 1954
Pub. Frequency: m.
Page Size: tabloid
Subscrip. Rate: $12/yr.
Circulation: 20,200
Circulation Type: paid
**Owner(s):**
Rural Press USA
7701 Six Forks Rd.
Ste. 132
Raleigh, NC 27615
Telephone: (919) 676-3276
Ownership %: 100
**Management:**
Blake Lewis ...................Advertising Manager
**Editorial:**
Jeff Tennant ........................Editor in Chief
Wayne Harr ...................................Editor
Kris Wheeler .......................Managing Editor
**Desc.:** Covers subjects within the borders
of the state of Tennessee or Tennessee
adaptions of national or regional
happenings. Concentrates on subjects
related to agriculture. Emphasis on hay,
pasture, corn, wheat, cotton, soybeans,
tobacco, beef, dairy, and hogs. Stories
run on one-half page, and full page.
Include general agriculture pertaining to
Tennessee and nation.
**Readers:** Farmers within the state of
Tennessee.

64923

**TEXAS FARMER STOCKMAN**
200 Chisholm Pl.
Ste. 106
Plano, TX 75075
Telephone: (214) 881-2677
FAX: (214) 881-2675
Pub. Frequency: m.
Page Size: standard
Subscrip. Rate: $14.98/yr.
Circulation: 72,822
Circulation Type: paid
**Owner(s):**
Farm Progess Companies
Carol Stream, IL
Ownership %: 100
**Management:**
Tom Budd ...................................Publisher
**Editorial:**
Charles Taylor ...............................Editor

25504

**TEXAS FFA MAGAZINE**
1701 N. Congress Ave.
Austin, TX 78701
Telephone: (512) 463-9687
FAX: (512) 475-3575
**Mailing Address:**
P.O. Box 13064
Austin, TX 78711
Year Established: 1929
Pub. Frequency: 6/yr.
Page Size: 8 1/2 x 11; 14 picas
Subscrip. Rate: $1/yr.
Materials: 21
Circulation: 47,000
Circulation Type: controlled & paid
**Owner(s):**
Texas FFA Association
P.O. Box 13064
Austin, TX 78711
Telephone: (512) 463-9687
Ownership %: 100
**Editorial:**
Rebecca L. McClinton ........................Editor
Rebecca L. McClinton ..............Managing Editor

**Desc.:** An association publication for
teenage boys and girls who belong to
the Texas Association of Future Farmers
of America. Most material pertains to
activities in the various FFA chapters,
but use some feature material,
particularly during the fall months. This
material should consist of information
and pictures helpful or interesting to
future agriculturists. Do not give by-lines,
but do give recoginition to companies or
or organizations whose material is used.
Publish one magazine for every three
members in the FFA in Texas.
**Readers:** 60,000 Texas Future Farmers,
ages 14-21; industrialists.

25505

**TODAY'S FARMER**
615 Locust St.
Columbia, MO 65201
Telephone: (314) 876-5252
Year Established: 1908
Pub. Frequency: 10/yr.
Page Size: standard
Subscrip. Rate: $1/issue; $5/yr.
Freelance Pay: $50-$400
Circulation: 42,000
Circulation Type: paid
**Owner(s):**
MFA, Inc.
615 Locust St.
Columbia, MO 65201
Telephone: (314) 876-5252
Ownership %: 100
**Editorial:**
Chuck Lay .....................................Editor
Janice Spears ...............................Advertising
Tom Montgomery ......Communications Director
**Desc.:** Places strong emphasis on photo
layouts to tell its story. Covers livestock
production and management, crop
production, machinery operation and
maintenance, crop harvesting,
conservation, school and farm safety,
etc. All stories must have a Midwest
angle or locale. Primarily staff-written.
Main purchase of free lance material is
agricultural production. By-lines given.
**Readers:** Rural Missourians and
surrounding states.

61018

**URNER BARRY'S PRICE-
CURRENT. WEST COAST
EDITION**
182 Queens Blvd.
Bayville, NJ 08721
Telephone: (908) 240-5330
FAX: (908) 341-0891
**Mailing Address:**
P.O. Box 389
Toms River, NJ 08754
Year Established: 1978
Pub. Frequency: s-w.: Tue. & Thu.
Page Size: tabloid
Subscrip. Rate: $116/yr.
Circulation: 110
Circulation Type: paid
**Owner(s):**
Urner Barry Publications, Inc.
182 Queens Blvd.
Bayville, NJ 08721
Telephone: (908) 240-5330
Ownership %: 100
**Management:**
Lisa Sharkus ...................Advertising Manager
**Editorial:**
Richard A. Brown .............................Editor

25507

**UTAH FARMER**
Review Tower, 999W Riverside Ave.
Spokane, WA 99210
Telephone: (509) 459-5377
FAX: (509) 459-5102

**Mailing Address:**
P.O. Box 2160
Spokane, WA 99210
Pub. Frequency: m.
Page Size: 13 9/16 x 9 1/6
Subscrip. Rate: $18/yr.
Materials: 21
Circulation: 5,716
Circulation Type: paid
**Owner(s):**
Cowles Publishing Co.
P.O. Box 2160
Spokane, WA 99210
Telephone: (509) 459-5377
Ownership %: 100
**Management:**
Barry Roach ...................Advertising Manager
**Editorial:**
E. W. Ramsey ..................Managing Editor
Mike Wohld ...................Associate Editor
Richard Yost ...........................Field Editor
Norman Herdrich ..............Production Editor
**Desc.:** General farm magazine.
**Readers:** Farmers and ranchers.

25506

**UTAH SCIENCE**
Utah State University
Logan, UT 84322-4845
Telephone: (801) 750-2189
FAX: (801) 750-3321
Year Established: 1940
Pub. Frequency: q.
Page Size: standard
Subscrip. Rate: free on request
Freelance Pay: none
Circulation: 4,000
Circulation Type: free
**Owner(s):**
Utah Agricultural Experiment Station
Utah State University
Logan, UT 84322
Telephone: (801) 750-2206
Ownership %: 100
**Editorial:**
Kurt W. Gutknecht ...........................Editor
**Desc.:** Articles deal primarily with research
and findings of the Utah Agricultural
Experimental Station. Covers plant and
animal science, soils and irrigation,
agricultural economics, natural
resources, and rural and urban life,
nutrition and food sciences, sociology
and forestry.
**Readers:** Farmers, ranchers, county
agents, professional, lay public.

25509

**WALLACES FARMER**
6900 Aurora Ave., Ste. 609E
Urbandale, IA 50322-2838
Telephone: (515) 278-7781
FAX: (515) 278-7797
Year Established: 1856
Pub. Frequency: 15/yr.
Page Size: standard
Subscrip. Rate: $14.98/yr. in state; $25/yr.
out of state
Freelance Pay: varies
Circulation: 85,000
Circulation Type: paid
**Owner(s):**
American Broadcasting Companies, Inc.
1330 Ave. of the Americas
New York, NY 10019
Telephone: (212) 887-7777
Ownership %: 100
**Bureau(s):**
Farm Progress Companies
191 S. Gary
Carol Stream, IL 60188
Telephone: (708) 690-5600
Contact: Tom Budd, Publisher
**Management:**
Tom Budd ...................................Publisher
Editorial Production

**Materials Accepted/Included:** 01-Business news 02-By-line articles 03-Fashion news 04-Food news 05-Freelance copy 06-Letters to editor 07-Real estate news 08-Sports news 09-Travel news 10-Book rev. 11-Movie rev. 12-Music rev. 13-TV rev. 14-Theater rev. 15-Coming events 16-Obituaries 17-Question & answer 18-Social announcements 19-Artwork 20-Cartoons 21-Photos 22-TV listings 23-Audio rec. 24-Video rec. 25-Books 26-Films/film clips 27-Personnel news 28-Press releases 29-New product news/photos 30-Trade lit. 31-Contracts awarded 32-Display adv. 33-Classified adv.

Kathryn VanZee .................
Manager
Dick Kuhn .....................Sales Manager
**Editorial:**
Monte Sesker ...........................Editor
Frank Holdmeyer ......................Managing Editor
Rod Swoboda .....................Associate Editor
John Otte ....................Economics Editor
JoAnn Alumbaugh ......................Producer
Mick Kreidler .........................Producer
Carole L. Flanders ......................Producer
Trenna Grabowski .....................Tax Editor
**Desc.:** A farm magazine covering all phases of crop and livestock farming in Iowa and adjacent territory. Publishes widely varied material concerning crops and crop conditions, markets and prices, research (fertilizers, vaccines, new products, etc.), safety, national and state legislation, trends in buildings, etc. Departments include: Beef Business, Dairy Business, Sheep Business, Agri - Business, Farm Machinery and Equipment, Farm Chemicals, What's Ahead (outlook information), Taxes. Also carries news of livestock sales and shows.
**Readers:** Primarily farmers in Iowa.

48963
## WEED CONTROL MANUAL
37733 Euclid Ave.
Willoughby, OH 44094
Telephone: (216) 942-2000
FAX: (216) 975-3447
Year Established: 1962
Pub. Frequency: a.
Page Size: standard
Subscrip. Rate: $30/yr.
Print Process: web offset
**Owner(s):**
Meister Publishing Co.
37733 Euclid Ave.
Willoughby, OH 44094
Telephone: (216) 942-2000
Ownership %: 100
**Editorial:**
Diane Chinchar ...........................Editor
Charlotte Sine ....................Editorial Director
Alan C. Strohmaier .....................Advertising
Alan C. Strohmaier .............Associate Publisher
Glenn Schwaller ........................Director
**Desc.:** Reference book on herbicides which describes and explains the uses of herbicides. Herbicides are listed by crops and information includes recommended rates, weeds controlled, suggestions on mixing, applications and other data. It covers major and minor crops, as well as non-cropland and aquatic. It includes indexes on herbicides, weeds, crops, a list of manufacturers with addresses, and a section of color illustrations of important weeds to aid in identification.

25511
## WISCONSIN AGRICULTURIST
2976 Triverton Pike
Madison, WI 53711
Telephone: (608) 274-9400
FAX: (608) 274-2006
Year Established: 1849
Pub. Frequency: 15/yr.
Page Size: standard
Subscrip. Rate: $14.98/yr.
Circulation: 49,500
Circulation Type: paid
**Owner(s):**
Farm Progress Companies
191 S. Gary Ave.
Carol Stream, IL 60188
Telephone: (708) 690-5600
Ownership %: 100

**Bureau(s):**
Farm Progress Publications
191 S. Gary Ave.
Carol Stream, IL 60188
Telephone: (708) 690-5600
Contact: Tom Budd, Publisher
**Management:**
Tom Budd ...........................Publisher
**Editorial:**
Al Morrow ...............................Editor
**Desc.:** Covers farm management and technology for Wisconsin farmers (mostly dairymen). Most articles are staff-written, averaging 750-1,000 words. Departments include: What's New (new farm equipment); What's Ahead (economic outlook); Farm Business (new farm products).
**Readers:** Primarily Wisconsin farmers.
**Deadline:** 2 mo. prior to pub. date

25351
## WYOMING STOCKMAN-FARMER
702 W. Lincolnway
Cheyenne, WY 82001
Telephone: (307) 634-7964
FAX: (307) 778-7163
Year Established: 1894
Pub. Frequency: m.
Page Size: tabloid
Subscrip. Rate: $12/yr.
Circulation: 6,000
Circulation Type: paid
**Owner(s):**
Cheyenne Newspapers, Inc.
702 W. Lincolnway
Cheyenne, WY 82001
Telephone: (307) 634-7964
Ownership %: 100
**Management:**
Karen Scheid .....................Advertising Manager
Karen Scheid .....................Circulation Manager
Janet Henry .................Classified Adv. Manager
**Editorial:**
Janet Jedrzejewski .................Executive Editor
**Desc.:** Advertising and marketing news, personnel news, and general farm and stock news.
**Readers:** Diversified agriculture.

## Group 512-Irrigation, Conservation, Land and Soil Management

22587
## IRRIGATION JOURNAL
68-860 Perez Rd., Ste. J
Cathedral City, CA 92234
Telephone: (619) 770-4370
FAX: (619) 770-8019
Year Established: 1950
Pub. Frequency: bi-m.
Page Size: standard
Subscrip. Rate: $25/yr. US; $55/yr. foreign
Materials: 01,02,10,15,27,28,29,30,32,33
Freelance Pay: negotiable
Print Process: web
Circulation: 15,000
Circulation Type: controlled
**Owner(s):**
Gold Trade Publications, Inc.
68-860 Perez Rd., Ste. J
Cathedral City, CA 92234
Telephone: (619) 770-4370
FAX: (619) 770-8019
Ownership %: 100
**Management:**
Mark Adams ...........................Publisher
**Editorial:**
Bruce Shank ...........................Editor
Bruce Shank .....................Associate Publisher

**Desc.:** Geared to reach agriculture and irrigation professionals. Features articles on new technological advances in drip and mist systems, low volume, mini sprinklers and water conservation. Also includes conventional irrigation systems, devoted to irrigation as it pertains to agriculture only. Departments include: From the Publisher, Calendar of Events, Business Outlook, and Products on Parade.
**Readers:** Irrigation engineers and designers, installers, dealers, consultants, distributors, manufacturers, irrigation specialists, service and corporate farmers. Irrigation district and water company management.

23072
## JOURNAL OF SOIL & WATER CONSERVATION
7515 N.E. Ankeny Rd.
Ankeny, IA 50021
Telephone: (515) 289-2331
FAX: (515) 289-1227
Year Established: 1946
Pub. Frequency: bi-m.
Page Size: standard
Subscrip. Rate: $39/yr. US-Canada; $45/yr. elsewhere
Freelance Pay: varies
Circulation: 11,500
Circulation Type: paid
**Owner(s):**
Soil and Water Conservation Society
7515 N.E. Ankeny Rd.
Ankeny, IA 50021
Telephone: (515) 289-2331
Ownership %: 100
**Editorial:**
Paula Porter ...........................Editor
Doug Snyder .....................Assistant Editor
Anne Harness .................Production Assistant
**Desc.:** Any manuscripts relating to land and water resources management will be considered. Articles should not exceed 15 pages (60 character type line) typescript. Departments include: By-lined feature articles; Research Reports; Personal News; Book Reviews; Current Literature Briefs; Field Notes in Land Use & Natural Resources Management, Commentary.
**Readers:** Administrators, researchers, land and water managers and educators.

22987
## SOIL SCIENCE
Rutgers University, Cook College
Dept. of Environmental Science
New Brunswick, NJ 08903
Telephone: (908) 932-9800
FAX: (908) 932-8644
Year Established: 1916
Pub. Frequency: m.
Page Size: standard
Subscrip. Rate: $72/yr.; $128/yr. institutional
Circulation: 3,000
Circulation Type: paid
**Owner(s):**
Williams & Wilkins Co.
428 E. Preston St.
Baltimore, MD 21202
Telephone: (410) 528-4000
Ownership %: 100
**Editorial:**
Dr. Robert Tate ...........................Editor
Dr. Robert Tate .................Book Review Editor
Maryann Rossano .................Editorial Assistant
**Desc.:** Professional papers dealing with soils and with plants in relation thereto. Carries book reviews, notes.
**Readers:** Soil and plant scientists, environmental scientists.

49912
## SOIL SCIENCE SOCIETY OF AMERICA JOURNAL
677 S. Segoe Rd.
Madison, WI 53711
Telephone: (608) 273-8080
FAX: (608) 273-2021
Year Established: 1936
Pub. Frequency: 6/yr.
Page Size: standard
Subscrip. Rate: $92/yr.
Materials: 32
Circulation: 8,290
Circulation Type: paid
**Owner(s):**
Soil Science Society of America
677 S. Segoe Rd.
Madison, WI 53711
Telephone: (608) 273-8080
Ownership %: 100
**Management:**
Robert F Barnes ........Executive Vice President
Keith R. Schlesinger ........Advertising Manager
Roger Watkins .................Circulation Manager
David M. Kral .................Operations Manager
**Editorial:**
Robert J. Luxmoore ...........................Editor
William R. Luellen .................Managing Editor
Pamm Kasper .....................Assistant Editor
**Desc.:** This journal covers the entire field of modern soil science - physics, chemistry, mineralogy, microbiology, biochemistry, plant nutrition, fertility and genesis, morphology, classification, management and conservation, forest and range soils, and fertilizer technology and use.
**Readers:** Professional soil scientists.

## Group 514-Livestock - Beef

25284
## ALABAMA CATTLEMAN
600 Adams Ave.
Montgomery, AL 36104
Telephone: (205) 265-1867
FAX: (205) 269-1927
Mailing Address:
P.O. Box 2499
Montgomery, AL 36102
Year Established: 1958
Pub. Frequency: m.
Page Size: standard
Subscrip. Rate: $20/yr.
Circulation: 17,000
Circulation Type: controlled
**Owner(s):**
Alabama Cattlemen's Assoc.
**Management:**
Wm. E. Powell ...........................Publisher
**Editorial:**
Wm. E. Powell ...........................Editor
**Desc.:** Covers beef cattle production, marketing and research.
**Readers:** Members of Alabama Cattlemen's Association and agribusiness leaders.

25286
## AMERICAN HEREFORD JOURNAL
1501 Wyandotte
Kansas City, MO 64108
Telephone: (816) 842-8878
FAX: (816) 842-6931
Year Established: 1910
Pub. Frequency: m.
Page Size: trim 50 x 67 picas; col: 13 x 60 picas
Subscrip. Rate: $15/yr.
Freelance Pay: varies
Circulation: 7,500
Circulation Type: paid

**Materials Accepted/Included:** 01-Business news 02-By-line articles 03-Fashion news 04-Food news 05-Freelance copy 06-Letters to editor 07-Real estate news 08-Sports news 09-Travel news 10-Book rev. 11-Movie rev. 12-Music rev. 13-TV rev. 14-Theater rev. 15-Coming events 16-Obituaries 17-Question & answer 18-Social announcements 19-Artwork 20-Cartoons 21-Photos 22-TV listings 23-Audio rec. 24-Video rec. 25-Books 26-Films/film clips 27-Personnel news 28-Press releases 29-New product news/photos 30-Trade lit. 31-Contracts awarded 32-Display adv. 33-Classified adv.

5-17

**Owner(s):**
Hereford Publications, Inc.
P.O. Box 014059
Kansas City, MO 64101
Telephone: (816) 842-3757
Ownership %: 100
**Management:**
Sue Jenkins ......................Advertising Manager
**Editorial:**
Lovell Kuykendall ...............................Editor
Bob McCaffrey ...................Production Director
**Desc.:** Trade paper of the Hereford beef
cattle industry. Emphasis on news
relevant to this field. Also carries articles
dealing with breed's performance and
efficiency, marketing, etc. Other
articles pertain to specific ranches, with
details on operations, management
procedures, animal health, etc. Use staff
coverage for news, with feature material
welcome from outside
sources. Occasional photo spreads
used. Departments include: News and
Feature.
**Readers:** Breeders of registered and
commercial Hereford cattle.

**AMERICAN RED ANGUS**                                    69322
4201 I-35 North
Denton, TX 76207-3415
Telephone: (817) 387-3502
FAX: (817) 383-4036
Year Established: 1954
Pub. Frequency: m. (exc. June-July)
Page Size: standard
Subscrip. Rate: $15/yr.
Materials: 01,02,15,18,19,20,21,28,29,30,
32,33
Freelance Pay: none
Print Process: sheet
Circulation: 6,000
Circulation Type: controlled
**Owner(s):**
Red Angus Association of America
4201 I-35 North
Denton, TX 76207
Telephone: (817) 387-3502
Ownership %: 100
**Editorial:**
Dora Hilburn .................................Editor
**Deadline:** news-1 mo. prior to pub. date;
photo-1 mo. prior; ads-1 mo. prior

**ANGUS**                                                69320
P.O. Box 613
Fair Oaks, CA 95628-0613
Telephone: (916) 965-6122
FAX: (916) 965-1128
Year Established: 1987
Pub. Frequency: m.
Subscrip. Rate: $15/yr.
Circulation: 4,000
Circulation Type: paid
**Owner(s):**
James Danekas Association, Inc.
P.O. Box 613
Fair Oaks, CA 95628
Telephone: (916) 965-6122
Ownership %: 100
**Editorial:**
James A. Danekas ..........................Editor

**ANGUS JOURNAL**                                        25276
3201 Frederick
St. Joseph, MO 64506
Telephone: (816) 233-0508
Year Established: 1919
Pub. Frequency: m.
Page Size: standard
Subscrip. Rate: $20/yr.
Circulation: 19,500
Circulation Type: paid

**Owner(s):**
American Angus Association
3201 Frederick
St. Joseph, MO 64506
Telephone: (816) 233-3101
Ownership %: 100
**Management:**
Cheryl Oxley ....................Advertising Manager
Terry Cotton ...........................General Manager
**Editorial:**
Jerilyn Johnson ................................Editor
Cheryl Oxley ...................Production Director
**Desc.:** Official publication for the American
Angus Breeders' Association. Contains
features and pictures related to breeding
Angus cattle, ranching, herd
management, and reports on association
activities, registrations, and researches.
**Deadline:** story-25th of mo., 1 mo. prior

**ARKANSAS CATTLE BUSINESS**                             25288
310 Executive Ct.
Little Rock, AR 72205
Telephone: (501) 224-2114
FAX: (501) 224-5377
Year Established: 1965
Pub. Frequency: m.
Page Size: standard
Subscrip. Rate: $20/yr.
Circulation: 8,900
Circulation Type: paid
**Owner(s):**
Arkansas Cattlemen's Association
310 Executive Ct.
Little Rock, AR 72205
Telephone: (501) 224-2114
Ownership %: 100
**Management:**
Mark Cowan ...........................Publisher
Sandi Walker ...................Business Manager
Jodi Shull ....................Production Manager
**Editorial:**
Mark Cowan .................................Editor
Sandi Walker ....................Advertising Director
**Desc.:** Magazine is devoted to beef cattle
industry in Arkansas. Livestock
magazine services purebred &
commercial beef cattle producers,
horsemen, and range livestock
producers in particular.
**Readers:** Beef cattle producers in
Arkansas, and all surrounding states to
some degree.

**BEEF**                                                 25289
7900 International Dr., Ste. 300
Minneapolis, MN 55425
Telephone: (612) 851-9329
Year Established: 1964
Pub. Frequency: m.
Page Size: standard
Subscrip. Rate: $17.95/yr. US; $25/yr.
foreign
Circulation: 105,000
Circulation Type: controlled
**Owner(s):**
K-III
Ownership %: 100
**Management:**
Robert Moraozewski ...................Vice President
Wayne Bollum .............................Publisher
**Editorial:**
Joe Roybal .................................Editor
Greg Lamp .......................Managing Editor
Shawna Hermel ....................Associate Editor
Warren Kester .......................Feature Editor
**Desc.:** Contains feature stories about
successful feeding operations of cow-
calf operators, backgrounders, stocker &
growers and preconditioners, as well as
reports on college research in the field.
**Readers:** Cattle feeders, cow & calf
operators, backgrounders,
preconditioners, stocker-growers.

**BEEF BUSINESS BULLETIN**                               68708
5420 S. Quebec St.
Englewood, CO 80111
Telephone: (303) 694-0305
FAX: (303) 694-2851
Mailing Address:
   P.O. Box 3469
   Englewood, CO 80155-3469
Year Established: 1977
Pub. Frequency: Fri.
Subscrip. Rate: free to members
Circulation: 38,000
Circulation Type: controlled & paid
**Owner(s):**
National Cattlemen's Association
5420 S. Quebec St.
Englewood, CO 80111
Telephone: (303) 694-0305
Ownership %: 100
**Management:**
Brett Erickson ...................Advertising Manager
**Editorial:**
Kendal Frazier ...............................Editor
**Desc.:** Focuses on the cattle breeding
industry.

**BEEFMASTER COWMAN**                                    69323
11201 Morning Ct.
San Antonio, TX 78213
Telephone: (210) 344-8300
FAX: (210) 344-4258
Year Established: 1979
Pub. Frequency: m.
Page Size: standard
Subscrip. Rate: $20/yr.
Materials: 05,06,15,16,21,29,32
Print Process: offset
Circulation: 8,191
Circulation Type: paid
**Owner(s):**
Gulf Coast Publishing Corp.
11201 Morning Ct.
San Antonio, TX 78213
Telephone: (210) 344-8300
FAX: (210) 344-8300
Ownership %: 100
**Management:**
E.C. Larkin, Jr. .............................Publisher
**Editorial:**
Gretchen Reuwer ...........................Editor
Stefan Marchman ...............Advertising Director
**Desc.:** Focuses on the Beefmaster cattle
breeding industry.
**Deadline:** story-5th of mo.; ads-5th of mo.

**BEEF TODAY**                                           68709
230 W. Washington Sq.
Philadelphia, PA 19104
Telephone: (215) 829-4700
Year Established: 1985
Pub. Frequency: m.
Subscrip. Rate: free
Circulation: 224,840
Circulation Type: paid
**Owner(s):**
Farm Journal, Inc.
230 W. Washington Sq.
Philadelphia, PA 19105
Telephone: (215) 829-4700
Ownership %: 100
**Management:**
Roger Randall ...................Advertising Manager
E.J. Rittersbach ...............Circulation Manager
**Editorial:**
Bill Miller .................................Editor
**Desc.:** Focuses on the cattle breeding
industry.

**CALF NEWS CATTLE FEEDER**                              25294
P.O. Box 88312
Colorado Springs, CO 80908-8312
Telephone: (719) 495-0303
Year Established: 1963

Pub. Frequency: m.
Page Size: standard
Subscrip. Rate: $26/yr.
Freelance Pay: $150/article; $10/photo
Circulation: 4,300
Circulation Type: controlled
**Owner(s):**
California News Magazine, Ltd.
P.O. Box 88312
Colorado Springs, CO 80908
Telephone: (719) 495-0303
Ownership %: 100
**Management:**
Steve Dittmer ...........................Publisher
Deb Dittmer ....................Advertising Manager
**Editorial:**
Steve Dittmer .............................Editor
**Desc.:** Covers commercial feeding industry
trends for over thirty years, economic
outlook & analysis, business
management, feedlot visits, computer
management, as well as animal health
and nutrition, marketing, new products.
**Readers:** Large commercial cattle feedlots
nationwide (1,000 head and over) &
large private feeders.

**CALIFORNIA CATTLEMAN**                                 25295
P.O. Box 613
Fair Oaks, CA 95628
Telephone: (916) 444-0845
FAX: (916) 965-1128
Year Established: 1917
Pub. Frequency: m.
Page Size: standard
Subscrip. Rate: $20/yr.
Circulation: 4,836
Circulation Type: controlled
**Owner(s):**
California Cattlemen's Association
P.O. Box 613
Fair Oaks, CA 95628-0613
Telephone: (916) 965-6122
Ownership %: 100
**Management:**
James A. Danekas ...............Business Manager
**Editorial:**
Kimberly Bradley ....................Executive Editor
James A. Danekas .........................Advertising
Steve Van Dyke ...........................Art Director
Sheila Massey ..................Contributing Editor
**Desc.:** Covers association activities,
policies and legislation, both state and
national, that affect the California beef
industry and ranching industry.
**Readers:** Commercial and purebred cattle
producers.

**CATTLE BUSINESS**                                      25297
1202 Mississippi St.
Jackson, MS 39202
Telephone: (601) 354-8951
Year Established: 1960
Pub. Frequency: m.
Page Size: standard
Subscrip. Rate: membership
Circulation: 6,000
**Owner(s):**
Mississippi Cattlemen's Association
121 N. Jefferson
Jackson, MS 39201
Telephone: (601) 354-8951
Ownership %: 100
**Editorial:**
Jim Newsome .................................Editor
**Desc.:** Cattle production and market
oriented articles.
**Readers:** Cattle producers.

**CATTLE GUARD**                                         25298
8833 Ralston Road
Arvada, CO 80002
Telephone: (303) 431-6422
FAX: (303) 431-6446

**Materials Accepted/Included:** 01-Business news 02-By-line articles 03-Fashion news 04-Food news 05-Freelance copy 06-Letters to editor 07-Real estate news 08-Sports news 09-Travel news 10-Book rev. 11-Movie rev. 12-Music rev. 13-TV rev. 14-Theater rev. 15-Coming events 16-Obituaries 17-Question & answer 18-Social announcements 19-Artwork 20-Cartoons 21-Photos 22-TV listings 23-Audio rec. 24-Video rec. 25-Books 26-Films/film clips 27-Personnel news 28-Press releases 29-New product news/photos 30-Trade lit. 31-Contracts awarded 32-Display adv. 33-Classified adv.

# FARM AND AGRICULTURAL

**Group 514-Livestock - Beef**

Year Established: 1955
Pub. Frequency: m.
Page Size: standard
Subscrip. Rate: $20/yr.
Freelance Pay: variable
Circulation: 3,500
Circulation Type: paid
**Owner(s):**
CO Cattlemen's Assn./Cattlemen's
Communications
8833 Ralston Rd.
Arvada, CO 80002
Telephone: (303) 431-6422
Ownership %: 100
**Management:**
Steve Dittmer ..................Advertising Manager
**Editorial:**
Steve Dittmer ..............................Editor
Todd Inglee .................Assistant News Director
**Desc.:** Published and edited for the beef
cattle producers in Colorado. Editorial
materials deals with beef cattle
production and management, dry - lot
feeding, animal health, processing,
promotion, marketing, taxation, state and
national legislation, and any other
activities directly relating to the Colorado
Cattlemen's Association.
**Readers:** Membership of Colorado
Cattlemen's Association.

**COW COUNTRY**                                    25302
113 E. 20th
Cheyenne, WY 82001
Telephone: (307) 638-3942
FAX: (307) 635-2524
Mailing Address:
P.O. Box 206
Cheyenne, WY 82003
Year Established: 1951
Pub. Frequency: 11/yr.
Page Size: standard
Subscrip. Rate: $20/yr.
Freelance Pay: varies
Circulation: 1,600
Circulation Type: paid
**Owner(s):**
Wyoming Stock Growers Association
P.O. Box 206
Cheyenne, WY 82003
Telephone: (307) 638-3942
Ownership %: 100
**Editorial:**
Cindy Garretson-Weibel ......................Editor
**Desc.:** We deal with news that relates to
our association's activities and try to
inform Wyoming cattle producers what is
going on in the industry; both nationally
and at the state level.
**Readers:** Primarily Wyoming cattle
producers who make their living with
cattle.

**DROVERS JOURNAL**                               25434
P.O. Box 2939
Shawnee Mission, KS 66201
Telephone: (913) 451-2200
FAX: (913) 451-5821
Year Established: 1873
Pub. Frequency: m.
Page Size: standard
Subscrip. Rate: $25/yr.
Circulation: 82,441
Circulation Type: controlled
**Owner(s):**
Vance Publishing Corp.
400 Knightsbridge Pkwy.
Lincolnshire, IL 60069
Telephone: (708) 634-2600
Ownership %: 100
**Management:**
Warren E. Morse ..................Publisher
Angela Pishny ..................Publisher

**Editorial:**
Greg Henderson ..................Publication Director
**Desc.:** Serves high volume cattle
producers with current production and
marketing news.
**Readers:** Beef cattle producers.

**GULF COAST CATTLEMAN &**                         25306
**LOUISIANA CATTLEMAN &**
**STOCKMAN**
11201 Morning Ct.
San Antonio, TX 78213-1300
Telephone: (210) 344-8300
Year Established: 1935
Pub. Frequency: m.
Page Size: standard
Subscrip. Rate: $15/yr.
Freelance Pay: negotiable
Circulation: 14,110
Circulation Type: controlled
**Owner(s):**
Gulf Coast Publishing Corp.
11201 Morning Ct.
San Antonio, TX 78213
Telephone: (210) 344-8300
Ownership %: 100
**Management:**
Ralph S. Cooper ..................Founder
E. C. Larkin, Jr. ..................Publisher
Stefan Marchman ..........Advertising Manager
**Editorial:**
E. C. Larkin, Jr. ..................Executive Editor
**Desc.:** Devoted to improvement of
breeding, feeding, and marketing of
livestock in southern states. Concerned
primarily with commercial beef cattle
production in the Gulf Coast states.
Stories deal with feeding, breeding, care,
pastures, insect control, disease,
equipment, markets, etc. News articles
primarily cover registered cattle sales,
shows, field days, association doings,
fairs, expositions, etc. Departments
include: Field Findings, Ranch
Library (Book Reviews), Buying and
Selling, Bull (humor), Livestock
Calendar.
**Readers:** Cattle producers living in the gulf
coast states.

**KANSAS STOCKMAN**                                25311
6031 S.W. 37th
Topeka, KS 66614
Telephone: (913) 273-5115
Year Established: 1916
Pub. Frequency: 10/yr.
Page Size: standard
Subscrip. Rate: $100/yr.
Freelance Pay: negotiable
Circulation: 7,060
Circulation Type: paid
**Owner(s):**
Kansas Livestock Association
6013 S.W. 37th
Topeka, KS 66614
Telephone: (913) 273-5115
Ownership %: 100
**Management:**
Tammy Jauken ..................Advertising Manager
**Editorial:**
Todd Domer ..................Editor
Amber Pike ..................Editorial Assistant
**Desc.:** Contains articles pertaining to
producing or feeding cattle in Kansas.
**Readers:** 7,000 members of Kansas
Livestock Association.
**Deadline:** ads-5th of mo., mo. prior to pub.

**KETCH PEN, THE**                                 25346
1720 Canyon Rd.
Ellensburg, WA 98926
Telephone: (509) 925-9871
FAX: (509) 925-3004

Mailing Address:
P.O. Box 96
Ellensburg, WA 98926
Year Established: 1983
Pub. Frequency: 9/yr.
Page Size: standard
Subscrip. Rate: $65/yr. members
Materials: 32
Print Process: web
Circulation: 1,800
Circulation Type: controlled
**Owner(s):**
Washington Cattlemen's Association
P.O. Box 96
Ellensburg, WA 98926
Telephone: (509) 925-9871
Ownership %: 100
**Editorial:**
Kent Lebsach ..................Editor
**Readers:** Beef cattle producers and
members of Washington Catlmen's
Association.

**LIVESTOCK MARKET DIGEST**                        25314
P.O. Box 7458
Albuquerque, NM 87194
Telephone: (505) 243-9515
Year Established: 1953
Pub. Frequency: w.
Page Size: tabloid
Subscrip. Rate: $20/yr.; $30/2 yrs.
Circulation: 48,500
Circulation Type: paid
**Owner(s):**
Livestock Publications
P.O. Box 7458
Albuquerque, NM 87194
Telephone: (505) 243-9515
Ownership %: 100
**Bureau(s):**
Livestock Market Digest, Inc.
301 E. Armour Blvd., Ste. 500
Kansas City, MO 64111
Telephone: (816) 531-2235
Contact: Joyce Mayfield, Managing
Director
**Management:**
Chuck Stocks ..................Publisher
Mae Lopez ..................Business Manager
**Editorial:**
Lee Pitts ..................Managing Editor
Ron Archer ..................Advertising
**Desc.:** Features current marketing news
and articles of interest to livestock
producers and related industry groups in
numerous business editions located in
the western U.S.
**Readers:** Cow - calf operators, feed lots,
feeder and stocker operations,
registered breeders and related
industries.

**MISSOURI BEEF CATTLEMAN**                        25315
3520 W. 75th, Ste. 204
Shawnee Mission, KS 66208
Telephone: (913) 384-1918
FAX: (913) 384-2455
Mailing Address:
Box 16050
Kansas City, MO 64112
Year Established: 1971
Pub. Frequency: m.
Page Size: standard
Subscrip. Rate: $37/yr. membership
Materials: 32,33
Print Process: offset
Circulation: 6,300
Circulation Type: controlled
**Owner(s):**
Larry Atzenweiler
3520 W. 75th, St. 204
Shawnee Mission, KS 66208
Telephone: (913) 384-1918

**Management:**
Larry Atzenweiler ..................Publisher
**Editorial:**
Larry Atzenweiler ..................Editor
**Desc.:** Official publication of Missouri
Cattlemen's Association.
**Readers:** Members of Missouri
Cattlemen's Association and related
industry people.

**MONTANA STOCKGROWER, THE**                       25316
420 N. California
Helena, MT 59601
Telephone: (406) 442-3420
FAX: (404) 449-5105
Mailing Address:
P.O. Box 1679
Helena, MT 59624
Year Established: 1929
Pub. Frequency: 6/yr.
Page Size: standard
Subscrip. Rate: membership
Circulation: 3,000
**Owner(s):**
Montana Stockgrowers Association
P.O. Box 1679
Helena, MT 59624
Telephone: (406) 442-3420
Ownership %: 100
**Editorial:**
Joyce Lancey ..................Editor
**Desc.:** Beef cattle industry information, of
all forms, including advertising. Activities
of the association and related interests.
Short time articles preferred catering to
the limited reading time of busy
ranchers. Illustrations and subheads
needed. Related photos on
specific subject matter.
**Readers:** Cattle producers located in all
counties financial institutions and ranch
service organizations.

**NATIONAL CATTLEMEN**                             68710
5420 S. Quebec St.
Englewood, CO 80111
Telephone: (303) 694-0305
FAX: (303) 694-2851
Mailing Address:
P.O. Box 3469
Englewood, CO 80155-3469
Year Established: 1985
Pub. Frequency: m.
Subscrip. Rate: free to members
Circulation: 38,000
Circulation Type: controlled & paid
**Owner(s):**
National Cattlemen's Association
5420 S. Quebec St.
Englewood, CO 80111
Telephone: (303) 694-0305
Ownership %: 100
**Management:**
Brett Erickson ..................Advertising Manager
**Editorial:**
Kendal Frazier ..................Editor

**NEBRASKA CATTLEMAN, THE**                        25320
521 S. 14th, Ste. 101
Lincoln, NE 68508
Telephone: (402) 475-2333
Year Established: 1944
Pub. Frequency: 11/yr.
Page Size: standard
Subscrip. Rate: $7.50/yr.
Freelance Pay: negotiable
Circulation: 9,500
Circulation Type: paid
**Owner(s):**
Nebraska Cattlemen
521 S. 14th, Ste. 101
Lincoln, NE 68508
Telephone: (402) 475-2333
Ownership %: 100

**Materials Accepted/Included:** 01-Business news 02-By-line articles 03-Fashion news 04-Food news 05-Freelance copy 06-Letters to editor 07-Real estate news 08-Sports news 09-Travel news 10-Book rev. 11-Movie rev. 12-Music rev. 13-TV rev. 14-Theater rev. 15-Coming events 16-Obituaries 17-Question & answer 18-Social announcements 19-Artwork 20-Cartoons 21-Photos 22-TV listings 23-Audio rec. 24-Video rec. 25-Books 26-Films/film clips 27-Personnel news 28-Press releases 29-New product news/photos 30-Trade lit. 31-Contracts awarded 32-Display adv. 33-Classified adv.

5-19

**Editorial:**
Mike Fitzgerald ..........Communications Director
**Desc.:** Published and edited for Nebraska beef cattle raisers. Most of the editorial is information about the cattle industry, designed to be of use and interest to the publisher's membership. Included are accounts of cattle industry legislation; cattle theft losses; regular articles on types of training offered by the State College of Agriculture and home economics; articles on livestock health problems and range management; an occasional article on a pioneer family; "In Memoriam"; purebred sale reports. Also contains activities of the Nebraska Cattlemen and its auxiliaries - The Nebraska Cattlewomen and junior cattlemen.
**Readers:** Cattlemen - Members of Nebraska Cattlemen.
**Deadline:** story-25th of mo.; news-25th of mo.; photo-25th of mo.; ads-25th of mo.

25325
**NORTH DAKOTA STOCKMAN, THE**
407 S. Second
Bismarck, ND 58504
Telephone: (701) 223-2522
Year Established: 1953
Pub. Frequency: m.
Page Size: standard
Subscrip. Rate: $30/yr.
Circulation: 3,000
Circulation Type: paid
**Owner(s):**
North Dakota Stockman
407 S. Second
Bismarck, ND 58504
Telephone: (701) 223-2522
**Editorial:**
Janell Feiring ...................................Editor
**Desc.:** News and information of interest to state and county cattlemen, feeders and livestock leaders.
**Deadline:** story-20th of mo.; ads-20th of mo.

25327
**OKLAHOMA COWMAN, THE**
2500 Exchange Ave.
Oklahoma City, OK 73108
Telephone: (405) 235-4391
FAX: (405) 235-3608
Mailing Address:
P.O. Box 82395
Oklahoma City, OK 73148
Year Established: 1958
Pub. Frequency: m.
Page Size: standard
Subscrip. Rate: $50/yr. membership
Freelance Pay: recognition only
Circulation: 5,600
Circulation Type: paid
**Owner(s):**
Oklahoma Cattlemen's Association
2500 Exchange
Oklahoma City, OK 73108
Telephone: (405) 235-4391
Ownership %: 100
**Management:**
Rhonda Rhines .................Advertising Manager
**Editorial:**
A.J. Smith ....................................Editor
**Desc.:** Publish material considered of value to beef cattle producers in Oklahoma, specifically OCA members. Departments include: Historical, Success Stories of Cattlemen, and Management Practices, Cattlewomen (Cattlemen's Association Auxiliary), News, News Stories on OCA Members.
**Readers:** Members of OCA.

25328
**OREGON BEEF PRODUCER**
729 N.E. Oregon St., Ste. 190
Portland, OR 97232
Telephone: (503) 731-3200
FAX: (503) 731-3233
Year Established: 1952
Pub. Frequency: m.
Page Size: standard
Subscrip. Rate: membership
Circulation: 2,500
Circulation Type: controlled
**Owner(s):**
Oregon Cattlemen's Association
729 N.E. Oregon St., Ste. 190
Portland, OR 97232
Telephone: (503) 731-3200
Ownership %: 100
**Editorial:**
Polly Owen ..........................Managing Editor
**Desc.:** Published by and for members of Oregon Cattlemen's Association. Articles of interest to cattlemen include market news, production stories, new methods of operation, new feeding methods, forage production, taxes and freight rates, promotion of beef and cattle industry. Due to limited time ranchers have for reading, all articles are kept short and to the point.

25331
**POLLED HEREFORD WORLD**
11020 N.W. Ambassador Dr.
Kansas City, MO 64153
Telephone: (816) 891-8400
FAX: (816) 891-8811
Year Established: 1947
Pub. Frequency: m.
Page Size: standard
Subscrip. Rate: $20/yr.
Circulation: 10,000
Circulation Type: paid
**Owner(s):**
American Polled Hereford Publications
11020 N.W. Ambassador Dr.
Kansas City, MO 64153
Telephone: (816) 891-8400
Ownership %: 100
**Editorial:**
C. Edward Bible ...........................Editor
**Desc.:** A national livestock breed publication. Publishes news concerning the industry as a whole; Reports of the shows and sales in which polled Herefords have a part; Feature material on breeding, feeding, and management of interest to the breeder of Polled Herefords.
**Readers:** People who are engaged, either directly or indirectly in production of polled Hereford beef cattle.

25333
**RECORD STOCKMAN, THE**
4800 Wadsworth Blvd., Ste. 200
Wheat Ridge, CO 80033
Telephone: (303) 425-5777
FAX: (303) 431-8911
Mailing Address:
P.O. Box 1209
Wheat Ridge, CO 80034
Year Established: 1889
Pub. Frequency: w.
Page Size: tabloid
Subscrip. Rate: $35/yr.; $70/3 yrs.
Materials: 01,02,05,29,32
Print Process: offset
Circulation: 30,000
Circulation Type: paid
**Owner(s):**
Harry Green, Jr. & Daniel E. Green
P.O. Box 1209
Wheat Ridge, CO 80034
Telephone: (303) 573-7223
Ownership %: 100

**Management:**
Harry Green, Jr. ........................Publisher
**Editorial:**
Daniel Green ..............................Editor
**Desc.:** Weekly business publication for those engaged in livestock business, concentrating on market reporting and news coverage of business from ranch to retailing. Regional readership in Colorado, Wyoming, Montana, Utah, Nebraska, Kansas, New Mexico, Texas, Washington, Oregon, Oklahoma, Idaho, Arizona, Dakotas, Nevada, California, Saskatchewan, Alberta, Iowa and Minnesota. Consider any articles dealing with livestock industry. By-lines given staff and paid contributors. Publicity material judged on news value. Prefer news stories 408" or under, features for annual magazine section to 1,500 words. Departments Include: new and usable products. Special editions include: Feeder Magazine in May, Livestock Directory and Buyers Guide in June, Federadition (tabloid) in August, annual edition (magazine supplement) in December, and National Western Stock Show edition in January.

25281
**RED POLL BEEF JOURNAL**
3123 Preston Hwy.
Louisville, KY 40213
Telephone: (502) 635-6540
Mailing Address:
P.O. Box 35519
Louisville, KY 40232
Year Established: 1937
Pub. Frequency: 4/yr.
Page Size: standard
Subscrip. Rate: $8/yr.
Circulation: 3,500
Circulation Type: paid
**Owner(s):**
America Red Poll Association
P.O. Box 35519
Louisville, KY 40232
Telephone: (502) 635-6540
Ownership %: 100
**Management:**
Carrie H. Schueler ...........Advertising Manager
**Editorial:**
Carrie H. Schueler ...................Executive Editor
**Desc.:** Staff-written and contributed articles devoted to promotion and betterment of purebred Red Poll cattle. News features cover some phase of the Red Poll breed such as breeding, sales, shows, trends, feeding, care and equipment, success stories, birth weight, weaning weight, yearling weight, weaning gain, carcass merit, etc. Prefers 2000 to 3000 words. Extensive use of photos, charts and graphs. Few by-lines.
**Readers:** Breeders of Red Poll cattle.

25339
**SOUTH DAKOTA STOCK GROWER**
426 St. Joseph St.
Rapid City, SD 57701
Telephone: (605) 342-0429
Year Established: 1940
Pub. Frequency: m.
Page Size: standard
Subscrip. Rate: $1 copy; $7.50/yr.
Materials: 32
Print Process: offset
Circulation: 8,000
Circulation Type: controlled
**Owner(s):**
South Dakota Stock Grower Association
426 St. Joseph St.
Rapid City, SD 57701
Telephone: (605) 342-0429
Ownership %: 100

**Management:**
Fenske Printing ..........................Publisher
Darlene Huett .......................Executive Director
**Editorial:**
Marilyn Hanson ...........Administrative Secretary
**Desc.:** Promote livestock industry of South Dakota.

68712
**WESTERN BEEF PRODUCER**
W. 999 Riverside Ave.
Spokane, WA 99201
Telephone: (509) 459-5361
FAX: (509) 459-5102
Year Established: 1993
Pub. Frequency: 16/yr.
Page Size: tabloid
Subscrip. Rate: $25/yr.
Materials: 01,02,04,06,15,17,21,24,25,27, 28,29,30
Print Process: web offset
Circulation: 28,500
Circulation Type: controlled & free
**Owner(s):**
Wester Farmer-Stockman Magazines
W. 999 Riverside Ave.
Spokane, WA 99201
Telephone: (509) 459-5361
Ownership %: 100
**Management:**
Henry McKeown ................Circulation Manager
Richard Brantly ..........................Sales Manager
**Editorial:**
EW Ramsey .............................Managing Editor
Bary Roach .........................Advertising Director
**Deadline:** story-1 mo. prior to pub. date; news-1 mo. prior; photo-1 mo. prior

## Group 516-Livestock - Dairy

25374
**AGRI-MARK JOURNAL**
100 Milk St.
Office Park
Methuen, MA 01844
Telephone: (508) 689-4442
Mailing Address:
P.O. Box 5800
Lawrence, MA 01842
Year Established: 1980
Pub. Frequency: 4/yr.
Page Size: standard
Subscrip. Rate: $15/yr.
Materials: 32
Freelance Pay: $0-$300/dairy industry articles
Circulation: 4,800
Circulation Type: controlled
**Owner(s):**
Agri-Mark, Inc.
P.O. Box 5800
Lawrence, MA 01842
Telephone: (508) 689-4442
Ownership %: 100
**Editorial:**
Douglas J. DiMento ......................Editor
**Desc.:** Stories and articles on dairy farming, espcially those that apply to the Northeastern U.S. Emphasis on the milk producer, especially our own cooperative members.
**Readers:** Dairy farmer members of Agri-MARK, Inc., throughout New England and New York State.

25329
**ATLANTIC COMMUNICATOR**
1225 Industrial Hwy.
Southampton, PA 18966-0127
Telephone: (215) 322-0200
FAX: (215) 322-8790
Mailing Address:
P.O. Box 127
Southampton, PA 18966
Year Established: 1987
Pub. Frequency: bi-m.

**Materials Accepted/Included:** 01-Business news 02-By-line articles 03-Fashion news 04-Food news 05-Freelance copy 06-Letters to editor 07-Real estate news 08-Sports news 09-Travel news 10-Book rev. 11-Movie rev. 12-Music rev. 13-TV rev. 14-Theater rev. 15-Coming events 16-Obituaries 17-Question & answer 18-Social announcements 19-Artwork 20-Cartoons 21-Photos 22-TV listings 23-Audio rec. 24-Video rec. 25-Books 26-Films/film clips 27-Personnel news 28-Press releases 29-New product news/photos 30-Trade lit. 31-Contracts awarded 32-Display adv. 33-Classified adv.

Page Size: standard
Subscrip. Rate: $3/yr.
Circulation: 5,000
Circulation Type: controlled & free
**Owner(s):**
Atlantic Dairy Cooperative
1225 Industrial Hwy.
Southampton, PA 18966-0127
Telephone: (215) 322-0200
FAX: (215) 322-8790
Ownership %: 100
**Editorial:**
Laura E. England ........................Editor
**Desc.:** Published in the interest of dairy
   farmers. Advertising not accepted.
**Readers:** Dairy farmers, primarily in Mid-
   Atlantic region.

## BROWN SWISS BULLETIN
25355

800 Pleasant St.
Beloit, WI 53511
Telephone: (608) 365-4474
FAX: (608) 365-5577
Mailing Address:
   P.O. Box 1038
   Beloit, WI 53512-1038
Year Established: 1922
Pub. Frequency: m.
Page Size: standard
Subscrip. Rate: $15/yr. US; $30/yr. foreign
Materials: 15,17,32
Print Process: web
Circulation: 3,000
Circulation Type: paid
**Owner(s):**
Brown Swiss Cattle Breeders' Association
P.O. Box 1038
Beloit, WI 53512
Telephone: (608) 365-4474
Ownership %: 100
**Editorial:**
Jane Crull ........................................Editor
**Desc.:** Covers all phases of Brown Swiss
   breeders activities, meetings, shows,
   fairs, tours, picnics, field days, type
   classification, production testing, coming
   events, sales, spotlight on the breeders,
   etc. Roundtable discussions.
**Readers:** Breeders of registered Brown
   Swiss cattle, anyone interested in the
   breed.

## CHEESE MARKET NEWS
68670

71818 Big Sky Dr.
Madison, WI 53719
Telephone: (608) 833-2020
FAX: (608) 833-2988
Mailing Address:
   P.O. Box 620244
   Middleton, WI 53562-0244
Year Established: 1981
Pub. Frequency: w.
Page Size: tabloid
Subscrip. Rate: $3.50 newsstand; $70/yr.
Materials: 01,04,06,15,16,27,28,29,32,33
Print Process: web offset
Circulation: 2,495
Circulation Type: paid
**Owner(s):**
Cahners Publishing
455 N. Cityfront Plaza Dr.
Chicago, IL 60611-5503
Telephone: (312) 222-2000
FAX: (312) 222-2026
Ownership %: 100
**Editorial:**
Anne Salinas ...................................Editor

**Desc.:** Reports news and issues affecting
   the cheese market, including market
   trends, legislation and regulatory
   happenings, new processing techniques,
   new products and equipment, emerging
   opportunities, plant expansions, mergers
   and acquisitions, personnel changes,
   industry events, personality and
   company profiles as well as innovative
   processors and marketers--all in a
   concise, professional, easy-to-read
   format.
**Readers:** Cheese makers/marketers; dairy
   processors/miscellaneous; suppliers to
   cheese manufacturers;
   brokers/distributors; retailers,
   foodservice, ingredient buyers and
   others(including government agencies,
   academia, associations, consultants,
   libraries and trade journals).
**Deadline:** story-1 wk. prior to pub. date;
   news-1 wk. prior; photo-1 wk. prior; ads-
   2 wks. prior to pub. date

## DAIRY FOODS
52577

455 N. Cityfront Plz. Dr.
Chicago, IL 60611
Telephone: (312) 222-2000
FAX: (312) 222-2026
Year Established: 1900
Pub. Frequency: m.
Page Size: standard
Subscrip. Rate: $82/yr.; $145/yr. foreign
Materials: 32,33
Print Process: web offset
Circulation: 20,284
Circulation Type: controlled
**Owner(s):**
Cahners Publishing Co.
455 N. Cityfront Plz. Dr.
Chicago, IL 60611
Telephone: (312) 222-2000
Ownership %: 100
**Management:**
Chuck Moodhe ........................President
Roy G. Hlavacek ..............Vice President
Carolyn Dress ........................Publisher
Jay Sandler ..............Associate Publisher
Brana O'Bradovich ..........Advertising Manager
**Editorial:**
Jeff Reiter ........................Senior Editor
Ellen Dexheimer ........................Editor
Paul Rogers ..............Managing Editor
Lisa Mierzwa ........................Art Director
Jerry Dryer ..............Market Analyst
Marty Friedman ..............New Products Editor
Jack Mans ..............Plant Operations Editor
Phyllis Pontikis ..............Production Editor
Gail Rosenbaum ..............Senior News Editor
Paul Rogers ..............Special Projects Director
Claudia Dziuk ..............Technology Director
O'Donnel
Donna Gorski ..............Technology Editor

**Desc.:** Serves the dairy products industry -
   the companies that process and
   distribute fluid products (fluid milk,
   flavored milk, buttermilk,
   evaporated/condensed, juices, drinks
   (non - carbonated) water process and
   distribute ice cream & dessert products,
   novelties (stick/stick-less); process and
   distribute milk products including
   cheese, butter and/or margarine,
   cultured and dried products (American
   and Italian type cheese, other natural
   cheese, processed cheese, cold pack,
   cottage cheese, yogurt, dips and sour
   cream (dairy and non - dairy), cream
   cheese, dried whole milk, non - fat dried
   milk, dried buttermilk, dried whey, dried
   cheese, condensed whey, whey protein
   concentrate, lactose). Also served are:
   distributors, jobbers, dealers, brokers,
   manufacturers/suppliers of equipment,
   ingredients & supplies, cooperatives &
   consultants, testing labs, universities,
   associations, and others allied to the
   field.
**Readers:** Qualified recipients are
   presidents, owners, vice presidents,
   general managers, plant managers,
   production managers, chief engineers,
   quality control managers, research &
   development managers, purchasing
   agents, marketing managers, sales
   managers, distribution managers & traffic
   managers.

## DAIRY GOAT JOURNAL
25356

2997 W. Market Rd.
Helenville, WI 53137
Telephone: (414) 593-8385
FAX: (414) 593-8384
Year Established: 1916
Pub. Frequency: m.
Page Size: standard
Subscrip. Rate: $18/yr. US; $30/yr. foreign
Materials: 02,05,06,17,32,33
Freelance Pay: $1/col. in.
Circulation: 7,000
Circulation Type: paid
**Owner(s):**
Kane Communications, Inc.
Ownership %: 100
**Management:**
Scott C. Borowsky ..............Publisher
**Editorial:**
Dave Thompson ........................Editor
Harvey Considine ..............Staff Writer
Dr. Nancy E. East ..............Staff Writer
**Desc.:** Contributed and staff-written articles
   cover all phases of dairy goat industry.
   Interested in material concerning
   nutrition, breeding, care and health,
   equipment, milk production, goat farm
   operation, etc. Articles are practical and
   helpful. Anything of a promotional or
   betterment nature in the field is
   acceptable. Departments include:
   Bleatings, New Products, "Something
   New Has Been Added", Strippings
   (news of shows, people, fairs, etc.),
   Worry Corner (question and answer
   column), Veterinary (breeding and health
   problems), Goat Club Doings. Seldom
   uses articles of over 1,500 words.
**Readers:** Commercial goat dairymen, milk
   processors, hobbyists. Subscribers range
   from small herd owners to commercial
   owners.

## DAIRY HERD MANAGEMENT
25357

7950 College Blvd.
Overland Park, KS 66210
Telephone: (913) 451-2200
FAX: (913) 451-5821

Mailing Address:
   P.O. Box 2939
   Shawnee Mission, KS 66201
Year Established: 1965
Pub. Frequency: m.
Page Size: standard
Subscrip. Rate: $25/yr.
Materials: 01,17,29,32
Circulation: 106,300
Circulation Type: paid
**Owner(s):**
Vance Publishing Corp.
7950 College Blvd.
Overland Park, KS 66210
Telephone: (913) 451-2200
Ownership %: 100
**Management:**
Warren Morris ........................Publisher
**Editorial:**
Tom Quaife ........................................Editor
Susan Mantey ..............Assistant Editor
Rhonda Franck ..............Assistant Editor
Mike Smith ..............Contributing Editor
Ken Bailey ..............Contributing Editor
**Desc.:** All materials accepted must appeal
   to the management interests of
   commercial milk producers in the areas
   of breeding, feeding, milking, housing,
   milk handling, storage, marketing,
   legislation. Departments include: New
   Science, Business Report, New
   Products, Health, Questions And
   Answers.
**Readers:** It is read by the top (minimum of
   30 cows) dairy farmers.

## DAIRYMAN, THE
25358

14970 Chandler Ave.
Corona, CA 91720
Telephone: (909) 735-2730
FAX: (909) 735-2460
Mailing Address:
   P.O. Box 819
   Corona, CA 91718
Year Established: 1922
Pub. Frequency: m.
Page Size: standard
Subscrip. Rate: $29/yr.
Materials: 02,30,32,33
Freelance Pay: $100/article
Circulation: 19,000
Circulation Type: controlled
**Owner(s):**
Holstein-Friesian World, Inc.
P.O. Box 120417
New Brighton, MN 55112
Ownership %: 100
**Bureau(s):**
Holstein-Friesian World, Inc.
P.O. Box 120417
New Brighton, MN 55112
Telephone: (612) 636-2117
Contact: Stanley E. Bird, Executive Vice
   President
**Management:**
Stanley E. Bird ..........Executive Vice President
Stanley E. Bird ..............Publisher
Dan Woodbury ..............Circulation Manager
Lisa Aguirre ..............Sales Manager
Kim Hawthorne ..............Sales Manager
**Editorial:**
Dennis Halladay ........................Editor
Maria Bise ..............Production Director

**Materials Accepted/Included:** 01-Business news 02-By-line articles 03-Fashion news 04-Food news 05-Freelance copy 06-Letters to editor 07-Real estate news 08-Sports news 09-Travel news 10-Book rev. 11-Movie rev. 12-Music rev. 13-TV rev. 14-Theater rev. 15-Coming events 16-Obituaries 17-Question & answer 18-Social announcements 19-Artwork 20-Cartoons 21-Photos 22-TV listings 23-Audio rec. 24-Video rec. 25-Books 26-Films/film clips 27-Personnel news 28-Press releases 29-New product news/photos 30-Trade lit. 31-Contracts awarded 32-Display adv. 33-Classified adv.

5-21

**Desc.:** Devoted to the interests of large-herd commercial dairy producers, processors, dairy product manufacturers and distributors in the western US. Primarily interested in major dairy operations in California, Arizona, Texas, Utah, Idaho, Nevada, Colorado, Washington, Oregon, New Mexico, Texas, Oklahoma, Wyoming, Hawaii. Uses national dairy news. By-line articles, deal with all phases of dairying such as feeding, milk production, market trends and predictions, diseases and new drugs, legislation, breeding, etc.
**Readers:** Primarily producing dairymen.

**DAIRYMEN'S DIGEST**                                    25359
116 N. Main St.
Shawano, WI 54166
Telephone: (715) 526-2131
FAX: (715) 526-6440
Mailing Address:
   P.O. Box 397
   Shawano, WI 54166
Year Established: 1970
Pub. Frequency: 10/yr.
Page Size: standard
Subscrip. Rate: $2/yr. members; $3/yr. non-members
Freelance Pay: negotiable
Print Process: offset
Circulation: 15,000
**Owner(s):**
Associated Milk Producers
116 N. Main St.
Shawano, WI 54166
Telephone: (715) 526-2131
Ownership %: 100
**Editorial:**
JoDee Sattler ............................................Editor
**Desc.:** Contains material pertaining to the dairy business.
**Readers:** Dairy farmers in eight midwest states.

**DAIRY TODAY**                                          68669
230 W. Washington Sq.
Philadelphia, PA 19105
Telephone: (215) 829-4700
Year Established: 1985
Pub. Frequency: m.
Subscrip. Rate: free
Circulation: 128,000
Circulation Type: paid
**Owner(s):**
Farm Journal, Inc.
230 W. Washington Sq.
Philadelphia, PA 19105
Telephone: (215) 829-4700
Ownership %: 100
**Management:**
Roger Randall ...................Advertising Manager
E.J. Rittersbach .................Circulation Manager
**Editorial:**
Jim Dickrell ...............................................Editor
**Desc.:** Contains information on changes in federal regulations, marketing data and insight related to the industry.

**DAIRY WORLD**                                          25361
19 River St.
Millbury, MA 01527
Telephone: (508) 865-2507
Year Established: 1967
Pub. Frequency: bi-m.
Page Size: standard
Subscrip. Rate: $2/issue; $12/yr.
Freelance Pay: varies
Circulation: 42,000
Circulation Type: paid

**Owner(s):**
IBA Inc.
27 Providence Road
Millbury, MA 01527
Telephone: (617) 865-2507
Ownership %: 100
**Management:**
Peter Bianca ....................Advertising Manager
Beth Auclair .....................Circulation Manager
**Editorial:**
Joseph Scolaro ......................Executive Editor
Peter Bianca ...........................Managing Editor
**Desc.:** Published for those on or related to the dairy farm. Provides the reader with updated information including the results of original research on such subjects as animal health, milk production and marketing, sanitation, government regulations and activities, equipment and supplies. We have several writers who write on a regular basis, but we are always looking for news as long as it applies to dairying. Length not to exceed 3 typewritten pages. The more photos the better. Departments include: Herd Health column, New Products column, Classified Ads, Common Sense Cooking, Bits N' Pieces, The Udder Side (Humor).
**Readers:** Dairy farmers, sanitarians, veterinarians, and herd health personnel, related industry personnel, etc.

**GUERNSEY BREEDERS' JOURNAL**                           25278
7614 Slate Ridge Blvd.
Reynoldsburg, OH 43068
Telephone: (614) 864-2409
Mailing Address:
   P.O. Box 666
   Reynoldsburg, OH 43068
Year Established: 1910
Pub. Frequency: 10/yr.
Page Size: standard
Subscrip. Rate: $15/yr.
Freelance Pay: $25-$100/article
Circulation: 1,900
Circulation Type: paid
**Owner(s):**
American Guernsey Association
P.O. Box 666
Reynoldsburg, OH 43068
Telephone: (614) 864-2409
FAX: (614) 864-5614
Ownership %: 100
**Management:**
Ida Albert .........................Circulation Manager
**Editorial:**
Becky Goodwin ..........................................Editor
Sheri Spelman ............................................Editor
**Desc.:** Covers breeding, dairy management, disease control, milk marketing, and other issues relating to Guernsey dairy cattle.
**Readers:** Guernsey breeders, commercial dairymen.

**HOARD'S DAIRYMAN**                                     25362
28 Milwaukee Ave., W.
Fort Atkinson, WI 53538
Telephone: (414) 563-5551
FAX: (414) 563-7298
Year Established: 1885
Pub. Frequency: s-m.
Page Size: tabloid
Subscrip. Rate: $12/yr.; $24/3 yrs.
Print Process: web offset
Circulation: 129,000
Circulation Type: paid
**Owner(s):**
W.D. Hoard & Sons
28 Milwaukee Ave., W.
Fort Atkinson, WI 53538
Telephone: (414) 563-5551
Ownership %: 100

**Management:**
W. D. Knox .................................Publisher
Gary L. Vorpahl .................Advertising Manager
W. D. Knox .............................General Manager
**Editorial:**
W. D. Knox ..................................................Editor
E.H. Row ...................................Managing Editor
S. A. Larson ............................Associate Editor
Christina Vilter .......................Associate Editor
**Desc.:** Staff-written and contributed articles deal with dairy farm management, family projects, co-op relations, science, etc. Short articles deal with specific farm items/farm sales, breeding, etc. Departments include Washington Dairygrams, Farm Flashes, Dairy Farm Home, Young Dairyman, Veterinary.
**Readers:** Dairy farmers.

**HOLSTEIN WORLD**                                       25363
8036 Lake St.
Sandy Creek, NY 13145
Telephone: (315) 387-3441
FAX: (315) 387-3655
Mailing Address:
   P.O. Box 299
   Sandy Creek, NY 13145
Year Established: 1904
Pub. Frequency: m.
Page Size: standard
Subscrip. Rate: $27.50/yr.
Materials: 01,15,21,29,32
Circulation: 23,000
Circulation Type: paid
**Owner(s):**
Joel P. Hastings
P.O. Box 299
Sandy Creek, NY 13145
Telephone: (315) 387-3441
Ownership %: 100
**Management:**
Stanley Bird ..............................Vice President
Joel Hastings ....................................Publisher
Robert McKown ................Advertising Manager
Jeannie Gove .......................................Manager
**Editorial:**
Daniel Bernick ..........................................Editor
Jean Annexstad .......................Associate Editor
Janice Barrett ..........................Associate Editor
Carol Moyer .................Production Coordinator
**Desc.:** Carries news of fairs, meetings, breeders, 4-h activities, etc. Profusely illustrated with pictures of Holstein cattle. News of the Trade reports new legislation, new medical compounds, milk promotion campaigns, other items of interest.
**Readers:** Holstein breeders, dairy farmers.

**JERSEY JOURNAL**                                       25309
6486 E. Main St.
Reynoldsburg, OH 43068-2362
Telephone: (614) 861-3636
FAX: (614) 861-8040
Year Established: 1953
Pub. Frequency: m.
Page Size: standard
Subscrip. Rate: $15/yr.
Materials: 01,02,05,06,16,21,32
Print Process: offset
Circulation: 4,300
Circulation Type: paid
**Owner(s):**
American Jersey Cattle Club
6486 E. Main St.
Reynoldsburg, OH 43068-2362
Telephone: (614) 861-3636
FAX: (614) 861-8040
Ownership %: 100
**Management:**
Floella G. Taylor ..............Circulation Manager
**Editorial:**
Lynn G. Bell ...............................................Editor
Kimberly A. Billman ................Associate Editor

Sara L. Gaetz ..........................Associate Editor
**Desc.:** Covers Jersey dairy farms, sales, outstanding production records.
**Readers:** Jersey breeders, and other dairy industry representatives.
**Deadline:** story-1 mo.; news-1 mo.; photo-1 mo.; ads-1 mo.

**MILKING SHORTHORN JOURNAL**                            25365
800 Pleasant St.
Beloit, WI 53511
Telephone: (608) 365-3332
FAX: (608) 365-5577
Mailing Address:
   P.O. Box 449
   Beloit, WI 53512-0449
Year Established: 1919
Pub. Frequency: bi-m.
Page Size: standard
Subscrip. Rate: $10/yr. US; $15/yr. foreign
Materials: 15,21,28,29,32
Circulation: 1,200
Circulation Type: paid
**Owner(s):**
American Milking Shorthorn Society
800 Pleasant
Beloit, WI 53511
Telephone: (608) 365-3332
Ownership %: 100
**Editorial:**
Jayne Krull .................................................Editor
Betsy Bierdek ...................Executive Secretary
**Desc.:** Covers all phases of the breeding and raising of registered Milking Shorthorn cattle and Illawarra cattle. Interested in any material which would contribute to the advancement of the breed, news of state fairs and other exhibitions, sales, methods and equipment, milk production, sires, herd building, care and feeding, etc. Departments include: From the Secretary's Desk (Society news in general), Field Notes, Letters, News of the Trade, Junior Page. Also gives news of 4-H Club activities as applied to field, breeder's calendar, etc. Profusely illustrated.
**Readers:** Breeders, buyers.

**NEW YORK HOLSTEIN NEWS**                               25324
957 Mitchell
Ithaca, NY 14851
Telephone: (607) 273-7591
Mailing Address:
   P.O. Box 190
   Ithaca, NY 14851
Year Established: 1950
Pub. Frequency: m.
Page Size: standard
Subscrip. Rate: $15/yr.
Materials: 01,15,16,17,18,28,32,33
Circulation: 4,200
Circulation Type: controlled
**Owner(s):**
New York Holstein Association
957 Mitchell
Ithaca, NY 14851
Telephone: (607) 273-7591
Ownership %: 100
**Management:**
William Fought .................................Publisher
Jenny Kelly ............................General Manager
**Editorial:**
Jenny Kelly ...............................................Editor
**Desc.:** Holstein herd stories, show and sale reports, includes publicity material if possible; articles need to be brief, limited use of photos.
**Readers:** Breeders of registered Holstein-Friesian cattle.
**Deadline:** story-30 days; news-30 days; photo-30 days; ads-30 days.

**Materials Accepted/Included:** 01-Business news 02-By-line articles 03-Fashion news 04-Food news 05-Freelance copy 06-Letters to editor 07-Real estate news 08-Sports news 09-Travel news 10-Book rev. 11-Movie rev. 12-Music rev. 13-TV rev. 14-Theater rev. 15-Coming events 16-Obituaries 17-Question & answer 18-Social announcements 19-Artwork 20-Cartoons 21-Photos 22-TV listings 23-Audio rec. 24-Video rec. 25-Books 26-Films/film clips 27-Personnel news 28-Press releases 29-New product news/photos 30-Trade lit. 31-Contracts awarded 32-Display adv. 33-Classified adv.

**OHIO JERSEY NEWS**                25370
804 E. Water St.
Prospect, OH 43342
Telephone: (614) 494-2312
Mailing Address:
   P.O. Box 532
   Prospect, OH 43342
Year Established: 1936
Pub. Frequency: m.
Page Size: standard
Subscrip. Rate: $10/yr.; $13/yr. Canada
Materials: 01,02,15,18,21,28
Circulation: 1,900
Circulation Type: paid
**Owner(s):**
Ohio Jersey Breeders Association
P.O. Box 532
Prospect, OH 43342
Telephone: (614) 494-2312
Ownership %: 100
**Management:**
Jane Miller ...............................Office Manager
**Editorial:**
Linda Billman .......................................Editor
**Desc.:** Material includes dairy articles, farm
   stories, show (dairy) reports, and items
   of general interest to Jersey breeders,
   dairymen and rural people.

## Group 518-Livestock - Horses

**AMERICAN FARRIERS JOURNAL**        68914
P.O. Box 624
Brookfield, WI 53008
Telephone: (414) 782-4480
FAX: (414) 782-1252
Pub. Frequency: 7/yr.
Subscrip. Rate: $42.95/yr.
Materials: 02,05,06,10,17,19,21,24,25,27,
   28,29,30,32,33
Print Process: web
Circulation: 7000
Circulation Type: paid
**Owner(s):**
Lessiter Publications, Inc.
P.O. Box 624
Brookfield, WI 53008
Telephone: (414) 782-4480
Ownership %: 100
**Desc.:** Articles on horse anatomy and
   physiology, leg pathology and therapy,
   shoeing, blacksmithing and horse
   handling.

**APPALOOSA JOURNAL**                25722
P.O. Box 8403
Moscow, ID 83843
Telephone: (208) 882-5578
FAX: (208) 882-8150
Year Established: 1946
Pub. Frequency: m.
Page Size: 4 color photos/art
Subscrip. Rate: $3 newsstand; $20/yr.
   non-members
Materials: 02,05,06,15,16,21,23,24,25,28,
   29,30,32,33
Freelance Pay: negotiable
Print Process: web offset
Circulation: 14,000
Circulation Type: paid
**Owner(s):**
Appaloosa Horse Club, Inc.
P.O. Box 8403
Moscow, ID 83843
Telephone: (208) 882-5578
FAX: (208) 882-8150
Ownership %: 100
**Management:**
Gretchen Naccarato .........Advertising Manager
**Editorial:**
Debbie Pitner Moors ..............................Editor
A.J. Mangum .........................Assistant Editor

Deborah Smith ......................Assistant Editor
**Desc.:** Anything of interest to Appaloosa
   horse owners - technical, veterinary,
   events, tips on showing, racing, distance
   riding.
**Readers:** Appaloosa horse owners and
   breeders.
**Deadline:** story-15th of 2nd mo. prior to
   pub. date; news-15th of 2nd mo. prior;
   photo-15th of 2nd mo. prior; ads-15th of
   2nd mo. prior

**ARABIAN HORSE EXPRESS**            68908
512 Green Bay Rd.
Kenilworth, IL 60043-1073
Year Established: 1976
Pub. Frequency: m.
Page Size: standard
Subscrip. Rate: $25/yr.
Materials: 01,02,05,06,08,09,10,15,16,19,
   21,24,25,28,29,30,32,33
Freelance Pay: $50-$250
Circulation: 3,500
Circulation Type: free & paid
**Owner(s):**
Arabian Horse Express
512 Greenbay Rd.
Kenilworth, IL 60043
Telephone: (708) 256-0021
FAX: (708) 256-5898
Ownership %: 100
**Editorial:**
Kathleen Gallagher ...................Executive Editor
Mitch Kruczek ..........................Managing Editor

**ARABIAN HORSE WORLD**              25723
824 San Antonio Ave.
Palo Alto, CA 94303
Telephone: (415) 856-0500
FAX: (415) 856-2831
Year Established: 1959
Pub. Frequency: m.
Page Size: standard
Subscrip. Rate: $36/yr.
Materials: 21
Freelance Pay: $250-$2500
Circulation: 12,000
Circulation Type: paid
**Owner(s):**
Nat Gorham
824 San Antonio Ave.
Palo Alto, CA 94303
Telephone: (415) 856-0500
Ownership %: 50

Jan Shuler
824 San Antonio Ave.
Palo Alto, CA 94303
Ownership %: 50
**Management:**
Nat Gorham ...................................Publisher
Jan Schuler ...................................Publisher
Liane Streb ....................Advertising Manager
**Editorial:**
Jan Shuler .........................................Editor
Denise Hearst ....................................Editor
Cathy DeRosa ..............................Art Director
Jon Card .............................Production Director
**Desc.:** Any editorial feature dealing with
   the promotion of the Arabian horse is
   welcome. Fees are negotiable and a by-
   line is always given. Articles are
   accompanied by color photos. 500 to
   2000 word articles is the range. Field
   writers cover most events.
**Readers:** Those who are owners,
   breeders.

**BACKSTRETCH, THE**                 25724
19899 W. Nine Mile Rd.
Southfield, MI 48075
Telephone: (810) 354-3232
FAX: (810) 354-3157
Year Established: 1962

Pub. Frequency: bi-m.
Page Size: standard
Subscrip. Rate: $3 newsstand; $14/yr.
Materials: 05,06,08,10,15,19,21,25,28,29,
   30,32,33
Freelance Pay: negotiable
Print Process: offset
Circulation: 12,000
Circulation Type: paid
**Owner(s):**
United Thoroughbred Trainers of America,
   Inc.
19899 W. Nine Mile Rd.
Southfield, MI 48075
Telephone: (810) 354-3232
FAX: (810) 354-3157
Ownership %: 100
**Management:**
Shelia L. Eck .....................Advertising Manager
Ed Frederick ........................Business Manager
**Editorial:**
Harriet Dalley .....................................Editor
Harriet Dalley ....................Book Review Editor
**Desc.:** Slanted to the interest of persons
   involved with and interested in
   thoroughbred racing. All of the material
   and stories have to do with
   thoroughbred horsemen, jockeys,
   trainers, horses, tracks, veterinarian
   articles, breeding stories and facts. One
   of the most important features of
   distribution is via bulk shipments to the
   racing secretaries at every thoroughbred
   track in sufficient quantity to provide
   copies for all the trainers on the
   grounds.
**Readers:** Persons involved in one or more
   facets of thoroughbred racing; owners,
   trainers, track management personnel,
   jockeys, agents, grooms, racing fans,
   farm owners & managers, etc.
**Deadline:** story-1st of mo. prior to pub.
   date; ads-15th of mo. prior

**BLOOD-HORSE, THE**                 25293
1736 Alexandria Dr.
Lexington, KY 40504
Telephone: (606) 278-2361
Mailing Address:
   P.O. Box 4038
   Lexington, KY 40544
Year Established: 1916
Pub. Frequency: w.
Page Size: standard
Subscrip. Rate: $3.50; $79.95/yr.
Freelance Pay: $200-$500
Circulation: 22,170
Circulation Type: paid
**Owner(s):**
The Blood-Horse, Inc.
1736 Alexandria Dr.
Lexington, KY 40504
Telephone: (606) 278-2361
Ownership %: 100
**Management:**
Stacy V. Bearse ...............................Publisher
**Editorial:**
Ray Paulick ............................Editor in Chief
Dan Mearns ..........................Managing Editor
Greg Medley .................................Advertising
Charles B. Dowdy, III .........Associate Publisher
Debbie Tipton ..........................Research Editor
**Desc.:** A Weekly Publication of the
   Thoroughbred Owners and Breeders
   Association.

**BRAYER**                           68909
2901 N. Elm St.
Denton, TX 76207-7631
Telephone: (817) 382-6845
Year Established: 1968
Pub. Frequency: q.
Subscrip. Rate: $18/yr.
Circulation: 5,000

Circulation Type: paid
**Owner(s):**
American Donkey & Mule Society, Inc.
2901 N. Elm St.
Denton, TX 76207-7631
Telephone: (817) 382-6845
Ownership %: 100
**Editorial:**
Betsy Hutchins .......................................Editor
**Desc.:** Provides information on donkeys
   and mules.

**DRAFT HORSE JOURNAL**              68713
P.O. Box 670
Waverly, IA 50677
Telephone: (319) 352-4046
Year Established: 1964
Pub. Frequency: q.
Page Size: standard
Subscrip. Rate: $20/yr.; $36/2 yrs.
Materials: 02,05,06
Freelance Pay: variable
Print Process: web
Circulation: 24,100
Circulation Type: controlled & paid
**Owner(s):**
Draft Horse Journal, Inc.
P.O. Box 670
Waverly, IA 50677
Telephone: (319) 352-4046
Ownership %: 100
**Editorial:**
Jeannine Telleen .....................................Editor
Maurice Telleen .....................................Editor
**Desc.:** Covers the draft horse industry,
   including all heavy horse breeds and
   draft mules.

**HOOF BEATS**                       25740
750 Michigan Ave.
Columbus, OH 43215
Telephone: (614) 224-2291
FAX: (614) 224-4575
Year Established: 1933
Pub. Frequency: m.
Page Size: standard
Subscrip. Rate: $3.50 issue; $30/yr.
Materials: 32,33
Freelance Pay: negotiable
Circulation: 22,000
Circulation Type: paid
**Owner(s):**
U.S. Trotting Assn.
750 Michigan Ave.
Columbus, OH 43215
Telephone: (614) 224-2291
Ownership %: 100
**Management:**
Richard Dakin ...................Advertising Manager
**Editorial:**
Dean A. Hoffman ....................Executive Editor
Jenny L. Gilbert ...................................Design
**Desc.:** The world's largest standardbred
   magazine, featuring articles about
   harness racing. It is edited for
   participants and spectators
   alike. Regular monthly features deal with
   trotting and pacing horse owners,
   trainers, drivers, horses, race track
   officials and executives,
   pedigree analysis, nutrition & shoeing.
**Readers:** Available to members of the
   U.S. Trotting and interested subscribers.
**Deadline:** ads-11th of mo. prior to pub.
   date

**HORSE & HORSEMAN**                 25741
34249 Camino Capistrano
Capistrano Beach, CA 92624
Telephone: (714) 493-2101
Mailing Address:
   P.O. Box HH
   Capistrano Beach, CA 92624
Year Established: 1972

**Materials Accepted/Included:** 01-Business news 02-By-line articles 03-Fashion news 04-Food news 05-Freelance copy 06-Letters to editor 07-Real estate news 08-Sports news 09-Travel news 10-Book rev. 11-Movie rev. 12-Music rev. 13-TV rev. 14-Theater rev. 15-Coming events 16-Obituaries 17-Question & answer 18-Social announcements 19-Artwork 20-Cartoons 21-Photos 22-TV listings 23-Audio rec. 24-Video rec. 25-Books 26-Films/film clips 27-Personnel news 28-Press releases 29-New product news/photos 30-Trade lit. 31-Contracts awarded 32-Display adv. 33-Classified adv.

5-23

Pub. Frequency: m.
Page Size: standard
Subscrip. Rate: $14/yr.; $25/2 yrs.
Materials: 03,05,06,19,20,21,25,28,29,32
Freelance Pay: $300
Print Process: offset
Circulation: 92,000
Circulation Type: paid
**Owner(s):**
Gallant/Charger Publications, Inc.
P.O. Box 2429
Capistrano Beach, CA 92624
Telephone: (714) 493-2101
Ownership %: 100
**Management:**
Jack Lewis .............................Publisher
Nadine Symons ...............Advertising Manager
**Editorial:**
Jack Lewis .............................Editor
Claudia Dane ....................Editorial Director
Gary Duck ..........................Art Director
**Desc.:** We present material of interest to
pleasure horse owners for the most part.
We do, however, cover the rest of the
equine world, from rodeo to play-days,
on a somewhat lesser scale. Training
tips, do-it-yourself pieces, grooming and
feeding, stable management, tack
maintenance, sports, personalities and
general features of horse-related nature
are sought. Departments include: Sage
Remarks (letters), Bridle Fashions,
Veterinary Notebook, Tack Talk (new
products), Horse Happenings (press
clippings), What's Your Problem
(question & answer).
**Readers:** Mostly female, 15-40 yrs., taking
pleasure in horses or showings.

25742
### HORSE & RIDER
1060 Calle Cordillera, Ste. 103
San Clemente, CA 92673
Telephone: (714) 361-1955
FAX: (714) 361-0333
Year Established: 1967
Pub. Frequency: m.
Page Size: standard
Subscrip. Rate: $2.95 newsstand;
$19.95/yr.
Materials: 02,03,05,06,10,17,18,21,28,29
Freelance Pay: varies
Circulation: 157,000
Circulation Type: paid
**Owner(s):**
Cowles Magazines, Inc.
6405 Flank Dr.
Harrisburg, PA 17112
Telephone: (717) 657-9555
Ownership %: 100
**Bureau(s):**
Cowles Equine Publications
45 E. 58th Ave., Ste. 4780
Denver, CO 80216
Telephone: (303) 293-0222
Contact: Pat Eskew, Associate Publisher
**Management:**
Harry Myers ...........................Publisher
Pat Eskew .....................Advertising Manager
Barbara Bradley ...............Circulation Manager
**Editorial:**
Juli S. Thorson ..........................Editor
Sue M. Copeland ...............Managing Editor
Lisa Wrigley ...........................Art Director
Lee Nudo ..........................Associate Editor
Rene E. Riley .....................Associate Editor
**Desc.:** Western performance horse
owners, trainers, and breeders wishing
to improve knowledge and horse skills.
**Readers:** Western riders.

25747
### HORSEMAN & FAIR WORLD
904 N. Broadway
Lexington, KY 40505
Telephone: (606) 254-4026
FAX: (606) 231-0656
Mailing Address:
P.O. Box 11688
Lexington, KY 40577
Year Established: 1877
Pub. Frequency: Wed.
Page Size: standard
Subscrip. Rate: $60/yr.
Materials: 32,33
Circulation: 7,000
Circulation Type: paid
**Owner(s):**
Horseman Publ. Co., Inc.
904 N. Broadway
Lexington, KY 40505
Telephone: (606) 254-4026
Ownership %: 100
**Management:**
Katherine N. Sautter ....................President
Greg Schuler ...............Advertising Manager
**Editorial:**
Chip Diehl ..............................Editor
**Desc.:** Devoted to the racing, training,
raising and breeding of standardbred
harness horses.
**Readers:** Owners, trainers and breeders of
standardbred horses.
**Deadline:** ads-Fri., 1 wk. prior to pub. date

25749
### HORSEPLAY
11 Park Ave.
Gaithersburg, MD 20884
Telephone: (301) 840-1866
FAX: (301) 840-5722
Mailing Address:
P.O. Box 130
Gaithersburg, MD 20884
Year Established: 1975
Pub. Frequency: m.
Page Size: standard
Subscrip. Rate: $3/issue; $23.97/yr.
Materials: 32,33
Freelance Pay: $35-$200
Circulation: 46,000
Circulation Type: paid
**Owner(s):**
HP Partnership
Telephone: (301) 840-1866
Ownership %: 100
**Management:**
John M. Raaf ...........................Publisher
Carol Shiro ..................Advertising Manager
**Editorial:**
Lisa Kiser ......................Managing Editor
**Desc.:** Edited for the English riding
enthusiast and competitor. Contains
how-to and photo stories and covers
fox-hunting, combined training, dressage
and show jumping on a regular basis.
Also contains profiles of famous riders
and trainers.
**Readers:** Active horsepersons, English
riding.
**Deadline:** ads-15th of mo., 2 mo. prior to
pub. date

25751
### HORSETRADER, THE
8398 Bundysburg Rd.
Middlefield, OH 44062-0728
Telephone: (216) 632-5266
FAX: (216) 632-5631
Mailing Address:
P.O. Box 728
Middlefield, OH 44062-0728
Year Established: 1960
Pub. Frequency: m.
Page Size: tabloid
Subscrip. Rate: $2 copy; $15/yr.
Freelance Pay: none
Circulation: 34,948

Circulation Type: controlled
**Owner(s):**
Horsetrader, Inc., The
P.O. Box 728
Middlefield, OH 44062
Telephone: (216) 632-5266
Ownership %: 100
**Management:**
Jerome Goldberg ........................President
Jerome Goldberg ........................Publisher
**Desc.:** An all breed publication comprised
entirely of classified and display
advertisements, dealing with the buying
and selling of horses, equipment, sales,
shows, auctions, clinics and rodeos.
**Readers:** People interested in the horse
business and all breed horse owners
and others in all related fields of horse
industry.

25745
### HORSE WORLD
730 Madison St.
Shelbyville, TN 37160
Telephone: (615) 684-8123
FAX: (615) 684-8196
Mailing Address:
P.O. Box 1007
Shelbyville, TN 37160
Year Established: 1943
Pub. Frequency: m.
Page Size: standard
Subscrip. Rate: $3 issue; $35/yr.; $60/2
yrs.; $87.50/3 yrs.
Freelance Pay: varies
Circulation: 6,000
Circulation Type: paid
**Owner(s):**
Dabora, Inc.
P.O. Box 1007
Shelbyville, TN 37160
Telephone: (615) 684-8123
**Management:**
David L. Howard ........................President
David L. Howard ........................Publisher
Nancy Edwards ....................General Manager
**Editorial:**
Mary Jane Cochran ..............Managing Editor
**Desc.:** Devoted to the saddle horse &
morgan horse industry, with editorial
articles on care of horse, feeding,
training, shoeing, show reports of major
horse shows throughout the U.S., with
accompanying pictures. Length
determined by our editorial department,
as well as photos too.

68912
### LONE STAR HORSE REPORT
5129 E. Belknap
Fort Worth, TX 76117
Telephone: (817) 838-8642
FAX: (817) 838-6410
Mailing Address:
P.O. Box 14767
Fort Worth, TX 76117
Year Established: 1983
Pub. Frequency: m.
Subscrip. Rate: $10/yr.
Materials: 01,02,05,10,15,16,21,23,24,25,
27,28,29,30,32,33
Print Process: web offset
Circulation: 8,000
Circulation Type: paid
**Owner(s):**
Lone Star Horse Report
5129 E. Belknap
Fort Worth, TX 76117
Telephone: (817) 838-8642
FAX: (817) 838-6410
Ownership %: 100
**Editorial:**
Henry L. King .............................Editor

**Desc.:** Dedicated to the distribution of
information about horses, horsemen,
events and places in the
North Texas/Southern Oklahoma horse
market.
**Deadline:** story-15th of mo., prior to pub.
date; news-15th of mo.; photo-15th of
mo.; ads-15th of mo.

61685
### PAINT HORSE JOURNAL
P.O. Box 961023
Fort Worth, TX 76161-0023
Telephone: (817) 439-3412
FAX: (817) 439-1509
Year Established: 1962
Pub. Frequency: m.
Page Size: 4 color photos/art
Subscrip. Rate: $23/yr.
Freelance Pay: $100-$500
Print Process: web offset
Circulation: 16,321
Circulation Type: paid
**Owner(s):**
American Paint Horse Association
P.O. Box 961023
Fort Worth, TX 76161-0023
Telephone: (817) 439-3400
FAX: (817) 439-3484
Ownership %: 100
**Editorial:**
Darrell Dodds .............................Editor
Jackie McGinnis ......................Advertising
Darrell Dodds ...........................Art Director
Dan Streeter .....................Associate Editor
**Desc.:** The Paint Horse Journal is directed
to owners of American Paint Horses.
Editorial content is intended to help
those persons gain greater use,
pleasure and enjoyment from their
horses.
**Readers:** Members of the American Paint
Horse Association, plus owners and
breeders of Paint Horses.

25757
### PALOMINO HORSES
15253 E. Skelly Dr.
Tulsa, OK 74116
Telephone: (918) 438-1234
FAX: (918) 438-1232
Year Established: 1941
Pub. Frequency: m.
Page Size: standard
Subscrip. Rate: $17.50/yr. US; $27.50/yr.
foreign
Materials: 32,33
Circulation: 5,500
Circulation Type: controlled
**Owner(s):**
Palomino Horse Breeders of America
15253 E. Skelly Dr.
Tulsa, OK 74116
Telephone: (918) 438-1234
Ownership %: 100
**Bureau(s):**
Southern Publishing Co.
P.O. Box 71
Meridian, MS 39302
Telephone: (800) 647-6672
Contact: Pete Willis, Advertising Manager
**Management:**
Thelma Thompson .......................Publisher
Pete Willis ...................Advertising Manager
Tracy Thompson ...................General Manager
**Editorial:**
Thelma Thompson ................Managing Editor

**Materials Accepted/Included:** 01-Business news 02-By-line articles 03-Fashion news 04-Food news 05-Freelance copy 06-Letters to editor 07-Real estate news 08-Sports news 09-Travel news 10-Book rev. 11-Movie rev. 12-Music rev. 13-TV rev. 14-Theater rev. 15-Coming events 16-Obituaries 17-Question & answer 18-Social announcements 19-Artwork 20-Cartoons 21-Photos 22-TV listings 23-Audio rec. 24-Video rec. 25-Books 26-Films/film clips 27-Personnel news 28-Press releases 29-New product news/photos 30-Trade lit. 31-Contracts awarded 32-Display adv. 33-Classified adv.

**Desc.:** Devoted exclusively to palomino horses. Articles cover breeding, distinctive bloodlines, stables, facilities, etc. Primarily interested in shows, fairs and other competitions featuring the Palomino strain. Features concern Palominos or Palomino fanciers. Departments include State Association News, trading and sale column, markets page. Profusely illustrated.
**Readers:** Palomino owners, breeders, fanciers, etc.
**Deadline:** ads-1st of mo., 2 mo. prior to pub. date

25760

## PRACTICAL HORSEMAN
P.O. Box 589
Unionville, PA 19375
Telephone: (215) 380-8977
FAX: (215) 380-8304
Year Established: 1973
Pub. Frequency: m.
Page Size: standard
Subscrip. Rate: $2.95/issue; $24.95/yr.
Freelance Pay: $200
Circulation: 82,000
Circulation Type: paid
**Owner(s):**
Cowles Publishing
329 Portland Ave.
Minneapolis, MN 55415
Telephone: (215) 380-8977
Ownership %: 100
**Management:**
Lua Southard .........................Publisher
Lori Lampert .............Advertising Manager
Kathy Rhodes ...............Circulation Manager
**Editorial:**
Mandy Lorraine ...............................Editor
**Desc.:** Consists of how-to-do-it interviews with top professional horsemen in the hunter/jumper and dressage fields (breeders, riders, trainers, etc.), interviews with veterinarians on research and/or horse management, and stable management articles, as they relate to the hunter/jumper horseman. Articles have no set length, like them to cover the topic as needed. Prefer a query, and, if accepted, a list of proposed questions to be presented to the subject of the interview. By-lines are given for all features not written by staff members. Photos are borrowed, some staff, some free lance.
**Readers:** Knowledgeable horsemen interested in showing jumpers, dressage, or combined training. Most readers are female, and compete in above activities.

25762

## QUARTER HORSE JOURNAL, THE
2701 I-40 E.
Amarillo, TX 79168
Telephone: (806) 376-4888
FAX: (806) 376-8364
Mailing Address:
P.O. Box 32470
Amarillo, TX 79120
Year Established: 1948
Pub. Frequency: m.
Page Size: standard
Subscrip. Rate: $19/yr. US; $45/yr. foreign
Materials: 01,06,15,25,29,32,33
Freelance Pay: $.05-$.07/word
Print Process: web offset
Circulation: 73,000
Circulation Type: paid
**Owner(s):**
American Quarter Horse Association
2701 I-40 E.
Amarillo, TX 79168
Telephone: (806) 376-4888
Ownership %: 100

**Management:**
Doug Hayes .............Advertising Manager
Karen Green ...............Circulation Manager
**Editorial:**
Jim Jennings .......................Editor in Chief
Audie Rackley .......................Executive Editor
**Desc.:** Non-fictional, containing factual articles of interest to those who own, train, breed, exhibit and race AQHA registered quarter horses. Lead articles may be concerned with individuals, either human or equine, associated with the breed. Articles on training practices, veterinary advances, equine research reports or breeding farm procedures. Various departments are devoted to youth activities and sale reports. Dates of future shows and sales, AQHA update informs readers of official actions and rulings of the American Quarter Horse Association.
**Readers:** Breeders, owners, exhibitors of quarter horses.
**Deadline:** story-25th of 2nd mo. prior to pub. date; news-25th of 2nd mo. prior; photo-25th of 2nd mo. prior; ads-25th of 2nd mo. prior

25763

## QUARTER HORSE TRACK
P.O. Box 9648
Fort Worth, TX 76107
Telephone: (817) 870-1990
FAX: (817) 870-2087
Year Established: 1975
Pub. Frequency: m.
Page Size: standard
Subscrip. Rate: $20/yr.
Circulation: 8,611
Circulation Type: paid
**Owner(s):**
Quarter Horse Track Publishers, Inc.
Box 9648
Fort Worth, TX 76147
Telephone: (817) 332-3801
Ownership %: 100
**Management:**
Terri Isbell ...............Circulation Manager
**Editorial:**
Ben Hudson ...............Associate Editor
Jerry McAdams ...............Associate Editor
**Desc.:** Offers fresh and realistic reporting on Quarter Horse racing in the United States. Each monthly issue contains news and feature articles on topics pertinent to the horse business-racing news, articles on breeding and training techniques, and marketing reports. Deals objectively with controversial issues in the Quarter racing business and reports race results from major Quarter Horse tracks across the country, along with schedules of upcoming events. First published in September 1975, we have established a solid reputation for professional journalism. Emphasis on concise, informative and entertaining articles has made it the most quoted magazine in the Quarter Horse racing market.
**Readers:** Active people in the horse business today.

69584

## ROCKY MOUNTAIN QUARTER HORSE MAGAZINE
318 Livestock Exchange Bldg.
Denver, CO 80216
Telephone: (303) 296-1143
Year Established: 1963
Pub. Frequency: m.
Subscrip. Rate: $20/yr.
Circulation: 1,500
Circulation Type: paid

**Owner(s):**
Rocky Mountain Quarter Horse Association
318 Livestock Exchange Bldg.
Denver, CO 80216
Telephone: (303) 296-1143
Ownership %: 100
**Editorial:**
Darlene Goodwin .............................Editor
Ann McLarty .............................Editor

25767

## SADDLE & BRIDLE
375 N. Jackson Ave.
St. Louis, MO 63130-4243
Telephone: (314) 725-9115
FAX: (314) 725-9115
Year Established: 1927
Pub. Frequency: 12/yr.
Page Size: standard
Subscrip. Rate: $5 newsstand; $38/yr.
Materials: 02,06,08,16,17,18,20,28,29,30, 32,33
Freelance Pay: $50-$250/article
Print Process: web offset
Circulation: 5,600
Circulation Type: controlled & paid
**Owner(s):**
Jeffrey Thompson
375 N. Jackson Ave.
St. Louis, MO 63130
Telephone: (314) 725-9115
FAX: (314) 725-6440
Ownership %: 50

Chris Thompson
375 N. Jackson Ave.
St. Louis, MO 63130
Telephone: (314) 725-9115
FAX: (314) 725-6440
Ownership %: 50
**Management:**
Christopher Thompson .............Publisher
Jeffrey Thompson .............Publisher
Christopher Thompson .............Advertising Manager
**Editorial:**
Jeffrey Thompson .............................Editor
Carol Hinkamp .............Managing Editor
**Desc.:** Features deal with horse shows, horses and all activities concerned with the showing of the American saddle horse, hackneys, ponies, horses, road horses and morgan horses. Articles are obtained from show managers, owners and correspondents.
**Readers:** Owners, exhibitors, professional horsepersons and all others interested in horses.
**Deadline:** story-10th of mo.; news-10th of mo.; photo-10th of mo.; ads-10th of mo.

54013

## SADDLE HORSE REPORT
730 Madison St.
Shelbyville, TN 37160
Telephone: (615) 684-8123
FAX: (615) 684-8196
Mailing Address:
P.O. Box 1007
Shelbyville, TN 37160
Year Established: 1976
Pub. Frequency: Mon.
Page Size: tabloid
Subscrip. Rate: $2 issue; $50/yr.
Freelance Pay: open
Circulation: 4,500
Circulation Type: paid
**Owner(s):**
Dabora, Inc.
730 Madison St.
Shelbyville, TN 37160
Telephone: (615) 684-8123
**Management:**
David L. Howard .............................President
David L. Howard .............................Publisher
**Editorial:**
Richard Hudgins .............Managing Editor

**Desc.:** Devoted to the saddle horse industry, with editorial articles on care of horse, feeding training, shoeing, show reports of major horse shows throughout the U.S., with accompanying pictures. Length determined by our editorial department, as well as photos too.

25768

## SPUR
725 Broad St.
Augusta, GA 30901
Telephone: (703) 687-6314
FAX: (703) 724-3873
Year Established: 1965
Pub. Frequency: bi-m.
Page Size: standard
Subscrip. Rate: $5/issue; $24/yr. US; $51/yr. foreign
Freelance Pay: $50-$200/col.
Circulation: 30,000
Circulation Type: paid
**Owner(s):**
Morris Communications
Augusta, GA 30901
Ownership %: 100
**Management:**
John M. Heckler .............Chairman of Board
Sheryl Bills Heckler .............................President
Sheryl Bills Heckler .............................Publisher
William S. Morris, III .............................Publisher
Lea Cockerham .............Advertising Manager
Gianna Nelson .............Circulation Manager
**Editorial:**
Cathy W. Laws .............................Editor
**Desc.:** Quality international publication, edited for the owners, breeders, trainers and enthusiasts of thoroughbred horses and sports.
**Readers:** Very high socio - economic group of throughbred owners breeders, trainers and enthusiasts.

25282

## THOROUGHBRED OF CALIFORNIA, THE
201 Colorado Pl.
Arcadia, CA 91007
Telephone: (818) 445-7800
FAX: (818) 574-0852
Mailing Address:
P.O. Box 60018
Arcadia, CA 91066-0018
Year Established: 1941
Pub. Frequency: m.
Page Size: standard
Subscrip. Rate: $42/yr.
Materials: 02,05,06,10,16,28,32,33
Freelance Pay: $100-$200/article
Print Process: offset
Circulation: 5,000
Circulation Type: paid
**Owner(s):**
California Thoroughbred Breeders Assn.
201 Colorado Pl.
Arcadia, CA 91007
Telephone: (818) 445-7800
FAX: (818) 574-0852
Ownership %: 100
**Management:**
Ed Wilson .............Advertising Manager
**Editorial:**
Nathaniel B. Wess .............................Editor
Tracy Gantz .............Managing Editor

**Materials Accepted/Included:** 01-Business news 02-By-line articles 03-Fashion news 04-Food news 05-Freelance copy 06-Letters to editor 07-Real estate news 08-Sports news 09-Travel news 10-Book rev. 11-Movie rev. 12-Music rev. 13-TV rev. 14-Theater rev. 15-Coming events 16-Obituaries 17-Question & answer 18-Social announcements 19-Artwork 20-Cartoons 21-Photos 22-TV listings 23-Audio rec. 24-Video rec. 25-Books 26-Films/film clips 27-Personnel news 28-Press releases 29-New product news/photos 30-Trade lit. 31-Contracts awarded 32-Display adv. 33-Classified adv.

5-25

**Desc.:** Publishes articles to do with all phases of the Thoroughbred horse/from breeding and animal husbandry at the farm level to complete coverage of the racing scene in California. We also run a great deal of historical information concerning the Thoroughbred in California. Photo spreads are extensive. Editorial comment is constructive and analytical, covering all Thoroughbred breeding and racing operations. By-lines given for feature articles. Articles vary in length. Staff and feature writers do most of coverage.

**Readers:** Persons in the Thoroughbred breeding and racing operations.

**Deadline:** story-4 wks. prior to pub. date; ads-6 wks. prior

54016

**WALKING HORSE REPORT**
730 Madison St.
Shelbyville, TN 37160
Telephone: (615) 684-8123
FAX: (615) 684-8196
Mailing Address:
P.O. Box 1007
Shelbyville, TN 37160
Year Established: 1971
Pub. Frequency: Mon.
Page Size: tabloid
Subscrip. Rate: $2/issue; $50/yr.
Freelance Pay: varies
Circulation: 6,000
Circulation Type: paid
**Owner(s):**
Dabora, Inc.
730 Madison St.
Shelbyville, TN 37160
Telephone: (615) 684-8123
Ownership %: 100
**Management:**
David L. Howard ........................President
David L. Howard .......................Publisher
**Editorial:**
Janie Hugh ....................................Editor
**Desc.:** Devoted to the walking horse industry, with editorial articles on care, feeding, training, shoeing; show reports of major horse shows throughout the US, with accompanying pictures. Article length and photos determined by our editorial departments.
**Readers:** Horse enthusiasts.

25771

**WESTERN HORSEMAN**
3850 N. Nevada Ave.
Colorado Springs, CO 80907
Telephone: (719) 633-5524
FAX: (719) 633-1392
Mailing Address:
P.O. Box 7980
Colorado Springs, CO 80933
Year Established: 1936
Pub. Frequency: m.
Page Size: standard
Subscrip. Rate: $2.50/issue; $18/yr.
Freelance Pay: $85-$400
Circulation: 235,000
Circulation Type: paid
**Owner(s):**
Western Horseman, Inc. (employee owned)
P.O. Box 7980
Colorado Springs, CO 80933
Telephone: (719) 633-5524
Ownership %: 100
**Management:**
Randy Witte ..............................Publisher
Corliss Palmer ..............Advertising Manager
**Editorial:**
Pat Close .....................................Editor
Gary Vorhes ....................Managing Editor
Kathy Kadash ..................Associate Editor
Butch Morgan ...............Marketing Director

**Desc.:** General interest horse magazine, but the emphasis is on western riding and western lifestyles involving horses. Topics include ranching; rodeo; profiles of individual horses, owners and trainers; various horse training techniques; equine health care; horse gear and western apparel; and western historical stories that have a strong horse angle. Most issues also include some cowboy poetry, humor, and trail riding stories.
**Readers:** Ranchers, businessmen, riding club members, professional trainers, veterinarians, rodeo hands, western artists, cowboys, western lifestyle advocates.

## Group 520-Livestock - General

25285

**AMERICAN HAMPSHIRE HERDSMAN**
1769 U.S. 52 W.
West Lafayette, IN 47906-0007
Telephone: (317) 497-4123
FAX: (317) 497-2959
Mailing Address:
P.O. Box 2807
West Lafayette, IN 47906-0007
Year Established: 1920
Pub. Frequency: m.
Page Size: standard
Subscrip. Rate: $15/yr.
Circulation: 4,000
Circulation Type: paid
**Owner(s):**
Hampshire Swine Registry
1769 U.S. 52 W.
West Lafayette, IN 47906-0007
Telephone: (317) 497-4123
FAX: (317) 497-2959
Ownership %: 100
**Editorial:**
Rex Smith ....................................Editor
Eunice Perry ....................Associate Editor
**Desc.:** A hogman's magazine, featuring advertising of purebred Hampshire Breeders, news about swine industry, feeding, management, shows, performance testing.
**Readers:** Hog producers, breeders, college instructors.

25303

**DUROC NEWS**
1769 U.S. W. 52
West Lafayette, IN 47906-0007
Telephone: (317) 497-4084
FAX: (317) 497-2959
Mailing Address:
P.O. Box 2397
West Lafayette, IN 47906-0007
Year Established: 1926
Pub. Frequency: m.
Page Size: standard
Subscrip. Rate: $15/yr.
Freelance Pay: negotiable
Circulation: 5,000
Circulation Type: paid
**Owner(s):**
United Duroc Swine Registery
1769 U.S. W. 52
West Layfayette, IN 47906-0007
Telephone: (317) 497-4084
FAX: (317) 497-2959
Ownership %: 100
**Editorial:**
Gary E. Huffington .........................Editor
Wayne Whipps ..................Managing Editor
Eunice Perry ....................Associate Editor

**Desc.:** Devoted to promotion and betterment of purebred Duroc swine. Staff-written articles cover various aspects of breeding and raising the Duroc breed, shows and competitions, pedigree records, sales, notable improvements in the strain, etc. Also carries personal notes and news of association members and their families, obituaries, etc. Departments include: Duroc News & Views (general information column), Listening In (letters to the editors), Production Registry News (new litter registration, etc.), Regional Field Notes, Fieldmen's Page (reports from field editors), and sales dates. Address all material to managing editor.
**Readers:** Purebred and commercial hog breeders, industry related personnel.

25305

**FLORIDA CATTLEMAN & LIVESTOCK JOURNAL**
P.O. Box 421403
Kissimmee, FL 34742-1403
Telephone: (407) 846-8025
FAX: (407) 933-8209
Year Established: 1936
Pub. Frequency: m.
Page Size: standard
Subscrip. Rate: $25.50/yr. for member
Materials: 01,02,06,21,32,33
Circulation: 7,231
Circulation Type: paid
**Owner(s):**
Florida Cattlemen's Association
P.O. Box 1929
Kissimmee, FL 32742
Telephone: (407) 846-2800
Ownership %: 100
**Editorial:**
Rick Hickenbottom .........................Editor
Rita Wilson .............................Advertising
Barbara Starcher ..........Production Coordinator
**Desc.:** Concerned with Florida and Floridians elsewhere. News and news features cover pastures, beef and dairy cattle and swine, personal notes, etc. All Florida livestock events given full staff coverage. Special numbers include Animal Health, Continental Breeds, Brahman, American Breeds, Marketing, Better Bulls, Angus, Hereford, Pastures.
**Readers:** Florida livestock raisers.
**Deadline:** story-1st of mo. prior to pub. date; news-1st of mo. prior; photo-1st of mo. prior; ads-5th of mo. prior

25317

**MONTANA WOOLGROWER**
7 Edwards St.
Helena, MT 59601
Telephone: (406) 442-1330
Mailing Address:
P.O. Box 1693
Helena, MT 59624
Year Established: 1928
Pub. Frequency: bi-m.
Page Size: standard
Subscrip. Rate: $35/yr.
Freelance Pay: negotiable
Circulation: 2,550
Circulation Type: free & paid
**Owner(s):**
Montana Wool Growers Association
P.O. Box 1693
Helena, MT 59624
Telephone: (406) 442-1330
Ownership %: 100
**Management:**
Robert N. Gilbert ..........................Publisher
Robert N. Gilbert ...............Advertising Manager
**Editorial:**
Laura Schwenk ..................Executive Editor
Robert N. Gilbert ................Managing Editor

**Desc.:** We use anything pertaining to the sheep industry.
**Readers:** 95% sheep producers.

25318

**NATIONAL HOG FARMER**
7900 International Dr., Ste. 300
Minneapolis, MN 55425
Telephone: (612) 851-9329
FAX: (612) 851-4600
Year Established: 1956
Pub. Frequency: m.
Page Size: standard
Subscrip. Rate: free to qualified producers; $25/yr.
Materials: 01,02,05,06,15,29,32,33,34
Print Process: web offset
Circulation: 95,540
Circulation Type: controlled
**Owner(s):**
Intertec Publishing Corp.
9800 Metcalf
Overland Park, KS 66212
Telephone: (913) 341-1300


Webb Division, Intertec Publishing Corp.
7900 International Dr., Ste. 3
Minneapolis, MN 55425
Telephone: (612) 851-4710
**Management:**
Robert Moraczewski ..................Vice President
Wayne Bollum .........................Publisher
**Editorial:**
Dale Miller ....................................Editor
Karen McMahon ..................Managing Editor
Lora Durbury-Berg ..................Associate Editor
Eric Meester ..................Production Director
Joe Vansickle ..............Senior Associate Editor
**Desc.:** Staff-written news magazine dealing with swine. Editorial covers the entire pork production industry, from on-farm hog production to the marketing, processing and retailing of pork.
**Readers:** Hog producers who market over 200 head of hogs/pigs, annually.

25319

**NATIONAL LAMB & WOOL GROWER**
6911 S. Yosemite St.
Englewood, CO 80112-1414
Telephone: (303) 771-3500
FAX: (303) 771-8200
Year Established: 1911
Pub. Frequency: m.
Page Size: standard
Subscrip. Rate: $25/yr. US; $35/yr. foreign
Circulation: 22,500
Circulation Type: controlled
**Owner(s):**
American Sheep Industry Association
6911 S. Yosemite St.
Englewood, CO 80112
Telephone: (303) 771-3500
Ownership %: 100
**Bureau(s):**
ASI Washington Office, Meyers & Associates
412 First St., S.W. #100
Washington, DC 20003
Telephone: (202) 484-2778
Contact: Larry or Rick Meyers
**Management:**
Kay Ann Tshmad ..............Advertising Manager
Lisa Hawker .....................Circulation Manager
**Editorial:**
Janice Grauberger ..................Managing Editor

**Materials Accepted/Included:** 01-Business news 02-By-line articles 03-Fashion news 04-Food news 05-Freelance copy 06-Letters to editor 07-Real estate news 08-Sports news 09-Travel news 10-Book rev. 11-Movie rev. 12-Music rev. 13-TV rev. 14-Theater rev. 15-Coming events 16-Obituaries 17-Question & answer 18-Social announcements 19-Artwork 20-Cartoons 21-Photos 22-TV listings 23-Audio rec. 24-Video rec. 25-Books 26-Films/film clips 27-Personnel news 28-Press releases 29-New product news/photos 30-Trade lit. 31-Contracts awarded 32-Display adv. 33-Classified adv.

**Desc.:** Articles cover all phases of sheep industry, including breeding, marketing, research and developments in feeding and housing, government plans and actions, regional and national sales of sheep, association news, comparative price reports, butchering and merchandising, tariff regulations, and reports. Regular departments include: DC Report, From the President, Industry News, Farm Policy, People, Marketing, Technology and Show/Sale.
**Readers:** Members of the American Sheep Industry Association.

**PIG INTERNATIONAL** 25330
122 S. Wesley Ave.
Mount Morris, IL 61054
Telephone: (815) 734-4171
FAX: (815) 734-4201
Year Established: 1971
Pub. Frequency: m.
Page Size: standard
Subscrip. Rate: $48/yr.
Freelance Pay: varies
Circulation: 21,000
Circulation Type: controlled
**Owner(s):**
Watt Publishing Co.
122 S. Wesley Ave.
Mount Morris, IL 61054
Telephone: (815) 734-4171
Ownership %: 100
**Management:**
James W. Watt ...................Chairman of Board
James W. Watt ...................................President
Clay Schreiber ...................................Publisher
**Editorial:**
Peter Best .............................................Editor
Clayton Gill .............................Editorial Director
**Desc.:** Aimed at commercial pig businessmen in Europe, Asia-Pacific, Africa. Emphasis is placed on basic production, animal health, husbandry, management and marketing.
**Readers:** Pig breeders, pig finishers/producers, pig feed manufacturers/dealers, servicemen, veterinarians, nutritionists.

**PORK 1995** 25307
7950 College Blvd.
Overland Park, KS 66210
Telephone: (913) 451-2200
FAX: (913) 951-5821
Year Established: 1981
Pub. Frequency: m.
Page Size: standard
Subscrip. Rate: $25/yr.
Circulation: 80,805
Circulation Type: paid
**Owner(s):**
Vance Publishing, Inc.
7950 College Blvd.
Overland Park, KS 66210
Ownership %: 100
**Management:**
Al Fagin ...............................Circulation Manager
**Editorial:**
Marlys Miller .........................................Editor
**Desc.:** Editorial content is aimed at serving the management side of production, with emphasis on profit making techniques and ideas. Welcome items on new equipment, usually handled in our "products" section. Departments include: News Briefs, Industry Bulletins, Products, A Program for Health, Swine Research Review.
**Readers:** Producers who market 1000 hogs per year.

**RANCH & RURAL LIVING MAGAZINE** 25332
P.O. Box 2678
San Angelo, TX 76902
Telephone: (915) 655-4434
FAX: (915) 658-8250
Year Established: 1920
Pub. Frequency: m.
Page Size: standard
Subscrip. Rate: $20/yr. US; $30/yr. foreign
Materials: 30,32,33
Freelance Pay: negotiable
Circulation: 7,000
Circulation Type: paid
**Owner(s):**
Scott Campbell
P.O. Box 2678
San Angelo, TX 76902
Telephone: (915) 655-7388
Ownership %: 100
**Management:**
Scott Campbell .....................................Publisher
Kelley Taylor ....................Circulation Manager
DeAnna Campbell ..................General Manager
**Editorial:**
Gary Cutrer .......................................Advertising
D'Lyn Lloyd ......................................Advertising
**Desc.:** Covers all phases of ranching as it applies to sheep, angora goats & cattle, cashmere and beer goats, exotics. Also deals with several aspects of ranching in general. Primary interests are feeding, breeding, showing, and marketing. By-line feature articles deal with some phase of ranching such as water supply, disease control, pasture, equipment, research. Departments include: Editorials, Last Minute Report on Livestock Markets, (current news of governmental actions and Department of Agricultural releases), Breeder's Directory, (fashions, wool notes, etc.). Extensive use of pictures. Specializing a different cattle breed each month, as well as regular articles on sheep & goats.
**Readers:** Livestock producers.
**Deadline:** story-10th of mo.; ads-10th of mo.

**SHEEP BREEDER & SHEEPMAN** 25335
1120 Wilkes Blvd.
Columbia, MO 65201
Telephone: (314) 442-8257
Mailing Address:
P.O. Box 796
Columbia, MO 65205
Year Established: 1880
Pub. Frequency: 10/yr.
Page Size: standard
Subscrip. Rate: $18/yr.
Materials: 01,15,29,32
Print Process: web offset
Circulation: 5,000
Circulation Type: paid
**Owner(s):**
Mead Livestock Services, Inc.
1120 Wilkes Blvd.
Columbia, MO 65201
Telephone: (314) 442-8257
Ownership %: 100
**Management:**
Larry E. Mead .....................................Publisher
Janet Glascock ................Advertising Manager
Bud Mead ...........................Business Manager
Nola Jacobson ..................Circulation Manager
**Editorial:**
Larry E. Mead .......................................Editor
Bill Shultz .............................Assistant Editor
**Desc.:** General news, new product news, advertising, marketing and coming events of interest to the sheep producers and small flock owners.
**Readers:** Purebred sheep producers.

**SHEPHERD, THE** 25336
5696 Johnston Rd.
New Washington, OH 44854
Telephone: (419) 492-2364
Mailing Address:
P.O. Box 97
Cardington, OH 43315
Year Established: 1956
Pub. Frequency: m.
Page Size: standard
Subscrip. Rate: $18/yr. US; $32/2 yrs. US; $24/yr. Canada
Freelance Pay: varies
Circulation: 8,500
Circulation Type: paid
**Owner(s):**
Sheep & Farm Life, Inc.
5696 Johnston Rd.
New Washington, OH 44854
Telephone: (419) 492-2364
Ownership %: 100
**Management:**
Ken Kark ..........................Advertising Manager
Kathy Kark ...........................Business Manager
**Editorial:**
Guy Flora .............................................Editor
Pat Flora ...............................................Editor
**Desc.:** An informative monthly publication devoted to all aspects of the sheep industry. Produced on a sheep farm by a staff having over 100 years experience in sheep raising and farm life.
**Readers:** Sheep farmers and ranchers, wool handcraft, schools, colleges, and libraries.

**WEEKLY LIVESTOCK REPORTER, THE** 25347
120 N. Rayner St.
Fort Worth, TX 76111
Telephone: (817) 831-3147
FAX: (817) 831-3117
Mailing Address:
P.O. Box 7655
Fort Worth, TX 76111
Year Established: 1897
Pub. Frequency: w.
Page Size: tabloid
Subscrip. Rate: $15/yr.; $23/2 yrs.; $24/3 yrs.
Materials: 32,33
Print Process: offset
Circulation: 13,000
Circulation Type: paid
**Owner(s):**
Livestock Service, Inc.
P.O. Box 7655
Fort Worth, TX 76111
Telephone: (817) 831-3147
Ownership %: 100
**Management:**
Tommy Brown ...................................Publisher
Donna Hamby ...................Circulation Manager
Edna Downey ...........Classified Adv. Manager
Rosemary Gouldy ................General Manager
**Editorial:**
Rosemary Gouldy ...................................Editor
Bryan Davis .....................................Field Editor
Phil Stoll .........................................Field Editor
**Desc.:** Livestock and farming publication, with general and household news used to some degree. News features of practically all types are used, especially those which deal with improved livestock or farm production, planning, living, homemaking. Offers field service to livestock advertisers. Includes articles for each member of the farm or ranch family. Departments include Livestock Markets, Registered Cattle Sales and Results, Editorials.
**Readers:** For farmers, ranchers and those interested in farm or ranch pursuits or marketing endeavors.

**WESTERN LIVESTOCK JOURNAL WEEKLY** 25348
650 S. Lipan St.
Denver, CO 80223
Telephone: (303) 722-7600
FAX: (303) 722-0155
Mailing Address:
P.O. Drawer 17F
Denver, CO 80217
Year Established: 1945
Pub. Frequency: w.
Page Size: tabloid
Subscrip. Rate: $27/yr.; $54/3 yrs.
Materials: 32
Print Process: offset
Circulation: 22,000
Circulation Type: paid
**Owner(s):**
Crow Publications, Inc.
650 S. Lipan
Denver, CO 80223
Telephone: (303) 623-2800
**Management:**
Dick Crow ..........................................President
Don Engel ..........................................Controller
Dick Crow ...........................................Publisher
Pete Crow ........................Advertising Manager
**Editorial:**
Fred Wortham, Jr. ....................Executive Editor
**Desc.:** Devoted to management news and features about the business operations of the modern cattle and sheep ranching industry. Extensive photo coverage including sales and events of interest to the industry.
**Readers:** Cattle ranchers & commercial producers.

**WESTERN LIVESTOCK REPORTER** 25349
18th & Minnesota
Billings, MT 59107
Telephone: (406) 259-4589
Year Established: 1940
Pub. Frequency: w.: Fri.
Page Size: tabloid
Subscrip. Rate: $23/yr.
Materials: 02,05,06,15,16,27,28,30,32,33
Freelance Pay: $25-$200/article
Print Process: offset
Circulation: 12,000
Circulation Type: paid
**Owner(s):**
Western Livestock Reporter, Inc. Publications
P.O. Box 30758
Billings, MT 59107
Telephone: (406) 259-4589
Ownership %: 100
**Management:**
Patrick K. Goggins .............................Publisher
Bonnie Zieske .................Advertising Manager
Clarice Swan ......................Circulation Manager
**Editorial:**
Marcia Krings .......................................Editor
Jerry Abbie .....................................Art Director

**Materials Accepted/Included:** 01-Business news 02-By-line articles 03-Fashion news 04-Food news 05-Freelance copy 06-Letters to editor 07-Real estate news 08-Sports news 09-Travel news 10-Book rev. 11-Movie rev. 12-Music rev. 13-TV rev. 14-Theater rev. 15-Coming events 16-Obituaries 17-Question & answer 18-Social announcements 19-Artwork 20-Cartoons 21-Photos 22-TV listings 23-Audio rec. 24-Video rec. 25-Books 26-Films/film clips 27-Personnel news 28-Press releases 29-New product news/photos 30-Trade lit. 31-Contracts awarded 32-Display adv. 33-Classified adv.

5-27

**Desc.:** Rancher's business paper covering ten Northwest states and Western Canadian provinces. Carries news of market trends, sales, shows, trading, ranch real estate, breeding, etc., and other items of interest to raisers of registered and commercial cattle, sheep, hogs, and horses. Essentially a business publication for the livestock industry of the Northwest. Departments include: As I See It (notes and observations from the field), Coming Shows and Sales, Animal Health, and Columns covering various state and regional activity, etc. Publishes an annual supplementary magazine (WLR Breeder Edition) listing livestock breeders and feeders, as well as commercial firms interested in ranch and livestock activity in the Northwest, and carrying features designed to be of help and interest to readership. Sales results, weekly interviews on national issues affecting the livestock industry.
**Readers:** Primarily livestock raisers in North Dakota, South Dakota, Nebraska, Western Colorado, Montana, Wyoming, Washington, Oregon, Idaho.

25350

## WOOL SACK, THE
315 Fifth St.
Brookings, SD 57006
Telephone: (605) 692-2324
FAX: (605) 692-8182
Mailing Address:
  P.O. Box 328
  Brookings, SD 57006
Year Established: 1931
Pub. Frequency: s-a.
Page Size: tabloid
Subscrip. Rate: free
Print Process: web offset
Circulation: 18,000
Circulation Type: free
**Owner(s):**
Mid-states Wool Growers Cooperative
3900 Grooves Rd.
Columbus, OH 43232-0461
Telephone: (614) 861-2533
FAX: (614) 861-7531
Ownership %: 100
**Management:**
Ronald W. Seeley ............Advertising Manager
**Editorial:**
Dick Boniface ...................................Editor
**Desc.:** The magazine features full information on sheep raising, wool preparation and handling, and lamb and wool markets. It is down-to-earth, how-to-do-it stuff. The publication is closely read, for it is the voice of seven state wool growers associations who have made money for years for their members through proper handling and marketing of wool. Departments include: Bottom of the Bag, Your Sheep Business, Sheep and Lamb Markets, National Column.
**Readers:** Every reader is a sheep grower.

## Group 522-Poultry

25554

## BROILER INDUSTRY
513 Fifth St., S.W.
Cullman, AL 35055
Telephone: (205) 734-6800
FAX: (205) 739-6945
Mailing Address:
  P.O. Box 947
  Cullman, AL 35056
Year Established: 1937
Pub. Frequency: m.
Page Size: standard
Subscrip. Rate: $48/yr.

Freelance Pay: $200+
Circulation: 16,000
Circulation Type: controlled
**Owner(s):**
Watt Publishing Co.
Sandstone Bldg.
Mount Morris, IL 61054
Telephone: (815) 734-4171
Ownership %: 100
**Management:**
James Watt ...............................President
Charles Olentine ........................Publisher
John Todd .................Advertising Manager
**Editorial:**
Gary Thornton ..............................Editor
Amanda Parker ........................Art Director
Jeffrey Swanson ............Production Director
**Desc.:** Editorial coverage pertaining to broiler growing, processing, distribution, and marketing operations in US and Canada. It is addressed to middle and upper management levels of the broiler industry and their customers, including key retail and institutional buyers.
**Readers:** Primarily integrated broiler companies, further poultry processors, distributors, and key institutional, food service, and retail buyers.

25562

## EGG INDUSTRY
122 S. Wesley Ave.
Mt. Morris, IL 61054
Telephone: (815) 734-4171
FAX: (815) 734-4201
Year Established: 1894
Pub. Frequency: bi-m.
Page Size: standard
Subscrip. Rate: $24/yr.
Materials: 01,04,06
Freelance Pay: negotiable
Circulation: 8,000
Circulation Type: controlled
**Owner(s):**
Watt Publishing Co.
122 S. Wesley Ave.
Mt. Morris, IL 61054
Telephone: (815) 734-4171
Ownership %: 100
**Management:**
Charles G. Olentine, Jr. .............Vice President
Charles G. Olentine, Jr. ...............Publisher
John Todd .................Advertising Manager
**Editorial:**
Virginia Lazar ...............................Editor
**Desc.:** Editorial material is developed for egg industry managers to help in both their day-to-day management and long-range planning.
**Readers:** Egg producers, processors, marketing firms.

25555

## GOBBLES
2380 Wycliff St.
St. Paul, MN 55114
Telephone: (612) 646-4553
FAX: (612) 646-4554
Year Established: 1947
Pub. Frequency: m.
Page Size: standard
Subscrip. Rate: $25/yr.
Materials: 01,02,05,06,30,32,33
Circulation: 1,025
Circulation Type: paid
**Owner(s):**
Minnesota Turkey Growers Association
2380 Wycliff St.
Saint Paul, MN 55114
Telephone: (612) 646-4553
FAX: (612) 646-4554
Ownership %: 100
**Editorial:**
Kristine Claussen ...........................Editor

**Desc.:** Features must capture the interest of turkey growers and persons in allied industries. Most editorial material must be directed to growers. Articles, except those of scientific nature, deal with Minnesota and surrounding states.
**Readers:** Turkey growers, processors, hatchery personnel, feed dealers, & other poultry industry people.

25556

## INDUSTRIA AVICOLA
122 S. Wesley Ave.
Mt. Morris, IL 61054
Telephone: (815) 734-4171
FAX: (815) 734-4201
Year Established: 1952
Pub. Frequency: m.
Page Size: standard
Subscrip. Rate: $48/yr. in Pan-American countries
Materials: 32
Circulation: 15,000
Circulation Type: controlled
**Owner(s):**
Watt Publishing Co.
122 S. Wesley Ave.
Mt. Morris, IL 61054
Telephone: (815) 734-4171
Ownership %: 100
**Management:**
Dr. Charles Olentine, Jr. .....................Publisher
**Editorial:**
Robert T. Tuten ..............................Editor
**Desc.:** For the commercial poultry industry in Latin America; covers all aspects of growing, processing and marketing of poultry and eggs.

24373

## POULTRY & EGG MARKETING
345 Green St., N.W.
Gainesville, GA 30501
Telephone: (404) 536-2476
FAX: (404) 532-4894
Mailing Address:
  P.O. Box 1338
  Gainesville, GA 30503
Year Established: 1926
Pub. Frequency: bi-m.
Page Size: tabloid
Subscrip. Rate: $12/yr.; $33/3 yrs.; free to qualified subscribers
Materials: 01,04,05,06,21,27,28,29,30,32
Freelance Pay: negotiable
Circulation: 10,423
Circulation Type: controlled
**Owner(s):**
Poultry And Egg News (Gannett Co., Inc.)
P.O. Box 1338
Gainesville, GA 30503
Telephone: (404) 536-2476
Ownership %: 100
**Management:**
Peggy Clements .................Circulation Manager
Randall Smallwood .................General Manager
**Editorial:**
Jim Mathis ..................................Editor
Charles McEachern .......................Advertising
Kelly Hulsey ..............................News Editor
**Desc.:** Covers processing, marketing and merchandising of poultry and eggs. Covers new industry equipment supplies, and trade activities.
**Readers:** Processors, wholesalers, distributors, retail/food service buyers of eggs and poultry.

25557

## POULTRY DIGEST
P.O. Box 947
Cullman, AL 35056
Telephone: (205) 734-6800
Year Established: 1939

Page Size: standard
Subscrip. Rate: $6/mo.; $48/yr.
Materials: 01,02,06,10,15,21,28,29,30,32,33
Freelance Pay: $250
Circulation: 19,000
Circulation Type: controlled
**Owner(s):**
Watt Publishing Co.
Mount Morris, IL 61054
Telephone: (815) 734-4171
Ownership %: 100
**Management:**
Charles Olentine .........................Publisher
**Editorial:**
Charles Perry ................................Editor
Roland C. Hartman ..............Contributing Editor
**Desc.:** Provides production technology for the broiler, egg, and turkey industries. Total emphasis is on poultry husbandry information that contributes to performance of layers, broilers, and turkeys. Includes poultry health, nutrition, housing and environment, hatching, and flock management. Departments cover recent research, new products, etc.
**Readers:** Poultry servicemen and service managers, poultry diagnostic laboratories, veterinarians, others related to the industry.
**Deadline:** story-15th of mo.; news-2 mos. prior

25558

## POULTRY INTERNATIONAL
122 S. Wesley Ave.
Mt. Morris, IL 61054
Telephone: (815) 734-4171
FAX: (815) 734-4201
Year Established: 1962
Pub. Frequency: m.
Page Size: standard
Subscrip. Rate: $6/issue; $56/yr.
Materials: 32
Circulation: 22,000
Circulation Type: controlled
**Owner(s):**
Watt Publishing Co.
122 S. Wesley Ave.
Mount Morris, IL 61054
Telephone: (815) 734-4171
Ownership %: 100
**Management:**
James W. Watt ...............................President
Dr. Charles Olentine, Jr. ...................Publisher
Nico G. Toonen ........................Sales Manager
John Todd ................................Sales Manager
**Editorial:**
Terry Evans ..................................Editor
**Desc.:** Serves commercial poultry operations at the management level in Europe, Middle East/Africa, Asia/Pacific, and Caribbean regions. Stresses business management information. Departments include: Features, New Products, Research Reports, World News, Market Information.
**Readers:** Producers, Importers, Distributors, and Dealers. Serves this audience worldwide in Europe, Middle East/Africa, Asia & Pacific and Caribbean.

25559

## POULTRY PRESS
P.O. Box 542
Connersville, IN 47331-0542
Telephone: (317) 827-0932
Year Established: 1914
Pub. Frequency: m.
Page Size: tabloid
Subscrip. Rate: $12/yr.
Materials: 02,21
Circulation: 6,400
Circulation Type: paid

**Materials Accepted/Included:** 01-Business news 02-By-line articles 03-Fashion news 04-Food news 05-Freelance copy 06-Letters to editor 07-Real estate news 08-Sports news 09-Travel news 10-Book rev. 11-Movie rev. 12-Music rev. 13-TV rev. 14-Theater rev. 15-Coming events 16-Obituaries 17-Question & answer 18-Social announcements 19-Artwork 20-Cartoons 21-Photos 22-TV listings 23-Audio rec. 24-Video rec. 25-Books 26-Films/film clips 27-Personnel news 28-Press releases 29-New product news/photos 30-Trade lit. 31-Contracts awarded 32-Display adv. 33-Classified adv.

**Owner(s):**
Poultry Press
P.O. Box 542
Connersville, IN 47331-0542
Telephone: (317) 827-0932
Ownership %: 100
**Management:**
William F. Wulff .................................Publisher
**Editorial:**
William F. Wulff ....................................Editor
**Desc.:** Paper devoted to poultry, including
waterfowl, and the bantam industry.
Features cover news and views of
industry. Primarily interested in reports of
exhibitions and shows throughout the
country. Uses little technical information.
By-lines given for both pictures and
articles. Material should be limited to
one column; pictures to three (two
preferred).
**Readers:** Breeders of poultry, waterfowl,
bantams.

**POULTRY PROCESSING**     68711
122 S. Wesley Ave.
Mount Morris, IL 60154-1497
Telephone: (815) 734-4171
FAX: (815) 734-4201
Year Established: 1986
Pub. Frequency: bi-m.
Subscrip. Rate: $24/yr.
Circulation: 10,100
Circulation Type: paid
**Owner(s):**
Watt Publishing Co.
122 S. Wesley Ave.
Mount Morris, IL 60154-1497
Telephone: (815) 734-4171
Ownership %: 100
**Management:**
Dr. Charles Olentine, Jr. .....................Publisher
**Editorial:**
Virginia Lazar .........................................Editor
**Desc.:** Contains news for the industry.
Covers slaughtering, cutting up,
processing, marketing, distributing and
retailing.

**POULTRY SCIENCE**     25560
309 W. Clark St.
Champaign, IL 61820
Telephone: (217) 356-3182
FAX: (217) 398-4119
Year Established: 1921
Pub. Frequency: m.
Page Size: standard
Subscrip. Rate: $60/yr.
Materials: 32,33
Print Process: offset
Circulation: 3,500
Circulation Type: paid
**Owner(s):**
Poultry Science Association, Inc.
309 W. Clark St.
Champaign, IL 61820
Telephone: (217) 356-3182
Ownership %: 100
**Management:**
Carl Johnson .....................Advertising Manager
**Editorial:**
J.A. Renden ...........................Executive Editor
Carl Parsons ...........................Associate Editor
D.N. Foster ............................Associate Editor
L.D. Bacon .............................Associate Editor
J.R. Smyth, Jr. .......................Associate Editor
William E. Huff .......................Associate Editor
W.B. Roush ...........................Associate Editor
Jerry L. Sell ...........................Associate Editor
J. McMurtry ...........................Associate Editor
Alan Sams .............................Associate Editor
Phillip E. Plumart ..........................Index Editor
Louis C. Arrington ........................News Editor
Ann M. Mester .......................Technical Editor

**Desc.:** Scientific papers dealing with all
aspects of poultry science, including
anatomy, behavior, biochemistry,
economics, embryology, engineering,
environment, genetics, histology,
marketing, microbiology, pathology,
physics, physiology and processing.
Departments include: Book Reviews,
News and Notes.
**Readers:** Poultry scientists.

**POULTRY TIMES**     25563
345 Green St.
Gainesville, GA 30501
Telephone: (404) 536-2476
FAX: (404) 532-4894
Mailing Address:
   P.O. Box 1338
   Gainesville, GA 30503
Year Established: 1954
Pub. Frequency: 26/yr.
Page Size: tabloid
Subscrip. Rate: $9/yr. US; $18/yr. foreign
Materials: 01,02,04,05,06,15,16,27,28,29,
32,33
Freelance Pay: negotiable
Circulation: 12,997
Circulation Type: paid
**Owner(s):**
Poultry & Egg News Inc. Div. of Gannett
Co. Inc.
P.O. Box 1338
Gainesville, GA 30503
Telephone: (404) 536-2476
Ownership %: 100
**Management:**
Randall Smallwood .................General Manager
**Editorial:**
Jim Mathis ..............................................Editor
Jennifer Englano ...............................Advertising
Charles McEachen ............Advertising Director
Chris Counts .................................News Editor
**Desc.:** We are a poultry and egg trade
paper principally covering all states.
Editorial directed to the production of
poultry, eggs, and turkeys. Contains
current market report as well as stock
information.
**Readers:** Broiler, commercial eggs, turkey,
breeder people, bankers, feed mill
operators, processors, and brokers.

**TURKEY WORLD**     24374
122 S. Wesley Ave.
Mount Morris, IL 61054
Telephone: (815) 734-4171
Year Established: 1926
Pub. Frequency: 9/yr.
Page Size: standard
Subscrip. Rate: $36/yr.
Circulation: 10,000
Circulation Type: controlled
**Owner(s):**
Watt Publishing Co.
122 S. Wesley Ave.
Mount Morris, IL 61054
Telephone: (815) 734-4171
Ownership %: 100
**Management:**
Charles Olentine ...............................Publisher
Walter Stephens ...............Circulation Manager
**Editorial:**
Bernard E. Heffernan ...............................Editor
**Desc.:** Articles cover all phases of the
turkey industry. Features are on industry
problems, trends, production
management, marketing, diseases, etc.
**Readers:** People involved in the
production, processes and marketing of
turkeys.

**URNER BARRY'S MEAT &**     61021
**POULTRY DIRECTORY**
182 Queens Blvd.
Bayville, NJ 08721
Telephone: (908) 240-5330
FAX: (908) 341-0891
Mailing Address:
   P.O. Box 389
   Toms River, NJ 08754
Year Established: 1984
Pub. Frequency: a.
Page Size: oversize
Subscrip. Rate: $95/yr.
Circulation: 2,500
Circulation Type: paid
**Owner(s):**
Urner Barry Publications, Inc.
P.O. Box 389
Bayville, NJ 08754
Telephone: (908) 240-5330
Ownership %: 100
**Management:**
Lisa Sharkus .....................Advertising Manager
**Editorial:**
Paul B. Brown, Jr. .....................................Editor
Joseph T. Soja ..........................Associate Editor
**Readers:** People in the meat & poultry
business.

**WEEKLY INSIDERS TURKEY**     61016
**LETTER & HATCH REPORT**
182 Queens Blvd.
Bayville, NJ 08721
Telephone: (908) 240-5330
Mailing Address:
   P.O. Box 389
   Toms River, NJ 08754
Pub. Frequency: Wed.
Subscrip. Rate: $142/yr.
Circulation: 275
Circulation Type: paid
**Owner(s):**
Urner Barry Publications, Inc.
P.O. Box 389
Toms River, NJ 08754
Telephone: (908) 240-5330
Ownership %: 100
**Management:**
Lisa Sharkus .....................Advertising Manager
**Editorial:**
Paul B. Brown ..........................................Editor

**WEEKLY TURKEY LETTER &**     61011
**WEEKLY POULTRY REPORT**
182 Queens Blvd.
Bayville, NJ 08721
Telephone: (908) 240-5330
FAX: (908) 341-0891
Mailing Address:
   P.O. Box 389
   Toms River, NJ 08754
Year Established: 1947
Pub. Frequency: Wed.
Page Size: tabloid
Subscrip. Rate: $10/issue; $278/yr.
Circulation: 125
Circulation Type: paid
**Owner(s):**
Urner Barry Publications, Inc.
P.O. Box 389
Toms River, NJ 08754
Telephone: (908) 240-5330
Ownership %: 100
**Management:**
Paul B. Brown ....................................President
Lisa Sharkus .....................Advertising Manager

**Editorial:**
Michael E. O'Shaughnessy ......................Editor

## Group 524-Rural Electricity

**COLORADO COUNTRY LIFE**     25423
1313 W. 46th Ave.
Denver, CO 80211
Telephone: (303) 455-2700
FAX: (303) 455-2807
Year Established: 1953
Pub. Frequency: m.
Page Size: standard
Subscrip. Rate: $12/yr.
Materials: 02,15,32,33
Print Process: web offset
Circulation: 103,500
Circulation Type: paid
**Owner(s):**
Colorado Rural Electricity Association
1313 W. 46th Ave.
Denver, CO 80211
Telephone: (303) 455-2700
Ownership %: 100
**Management:**
Frank McCrea .....................................Publisher
Kimber McCrea .................Advertising Manager
**Editorial:**
Frank McCrea ...........................Executive Editor
Carolyn Alvarez .....................Production Editor
**Desc.:** Features on rural, small town and
city populations and the use and
benefits of electricity. Features also on
topics related to Colorado, its history,
people, natural phenomena, wildlife and
geography. Regular columns include:
gardening, cooking and people.
**Readers:** 36% professional managerial,
30% own their business, 30% lg. farms
& ranches
**Deadline:** ads-1st of mo., prior to pub.
date

**ELECTRIC CONSUMER**     25459
720 N. High School Rd.
Indianapolis, IN 46214
Telephone: (317) 248-9453
FAX: (317) 247-5220
Mailing Address:
   P.O. Box 24517
   Indianapolis, IN 46224
Year Established: 1951
Pub. Frequency: m.
Page Size: tabloid
Subscrip. Rate: $4/yr.
Materials: 04,05,06,09,15,17,19,21,28,29,32
Freelance Pay: negotiable
Print Process: offset
Circulation: 269,070
Circulation Type: controlled
**Owner(s):**
Indiana Statewide REC, Inc.
P.O. Box 24517
Indianapolis, IN 46224
Telephone: (317) 248-9453
Ownership %: 100
**Editorial:**
Emily Born .................................................Editor
Maury Boyd .......................................Advertising
Richard Biever ...........................Associate Editor
**Desc.:** Educates members of cooperatives
on the principles of cooperation, and
encourages participation. If material can
be given a local flavor, or slant, we will
make use of special articles.
Departments include: Food Pages,
Classified Section, Agricultural
Highlights, Product News, Poets Corner,
Genealogy, Gardening.
**Readers:** Rural & urban homeowners.

---

**Materials Accepted/Included:** 01-Business news 02-By-line articles 03-Fashion news 04-Food news 05-Freelance copy 06-Letters to editor 07-Real estate news 08-Sports news 09-Travel news
10-Book rev. 11-Movie rev. 12-Music rev. 13-TV rev. 14-Theater rev. 15-Coming events 16-Obituaries 17-Question & answer 18-Social announcements 19-Artwork 20-Cartoons 21-Photos 22-TV listings
23-Audio rec. 24-Video rec. 25-Books 26-Films/film clips 27-Personnel news 28-Press releases 29-New product news/photos 30-Trade lit. 31-Contracts awarded 32-Display adv. 33-Classified adv.

## ENCHANTMENT
22887

614 Don Gaspar Ave.
Santa Fe, NM 87501
Telephone: (505) 982-4671
FAX: (505) 982-0153
Year Established: 1960
Pub. Frequency: m.
Page Size: tabloid
Subscrip. Rate: $4/yr.
Materials: 01,02,05,06,15,21,28,32,33
Freelance Pay: varies
Print Process: web
Circulation: 100,000
Circulation Type: controlled
**Owner(s):**
N.M.R.E.C.A.
614 Dongaspan
Santa Fe, NM 87501
Telephone: (505) 982-4671
FAX: (505) 982-0153
Ownership %: 100
**Editorial:**
John Whitcomb ...........................Editor
**Desc.:** Covers subjects on rural lifestyles &
issues, etc. Written to interest the
average rural, small town reader.
**Deadline:** ads-15th of mo. prior to pub.
date

## GEORGIA MAGAZINE
25396

2100 E. Exchange Pl.
Tucker, GA 30084
Telephone: (404) 270-6950
FAX: (404) 270-6995
Mailing Address:
P.O. Box 1707
Tucker, GA 30085
Year Established: 1945
Pub. Frequency: m.
Page Size: standard
Subscrip. Rate: $9.95/yr.
Materials: 01,15,29
Freelance Pay: $50-$250/article
Circulation: 280,000
Circulation Type: controlled
**Owner(s):**
Georgia Electric Membership Corp.
2100 E. Exchange Pl.
Tucker, GA 30085
Telephone: (404) 270-6950
Ownership %: 100
**Management:**
Laurel Garrett George .......Advertising Manager
**Editorial:**
Ann Elstad ...............................Editor
Jane Walk ...............................Associate Editor
Terri Brown ...........................Editorial Assistant
**Desc.:** News items, features and other
material relating to the rural
electrification program in Georgia and
the 42 electric cooperatives in Georgia,
and matters of interest to the member
consumers of the cooperatives.
Contents include: News Features,
Foods, Electrical Uses, Energy
Conservation, Gardening, Profiles and
Features on Georgia people, places
& events.
**Readers:** The member-consumers of
electric cooperatives in GA.

## KANSAS COUNTRY LIVING
25386

7332 S.W. 21st St.
Topeka, KS 66615-0267
Telephone: (913) 478-4554
FAX: (913) 478-4852
Mailing Address:
P.O. Box 4267
Topeka, KS 66604
Year Established: 1951
Pub. Frequency: m.

Page Size: standard
Subscrip. Rate: $8.40/yr.
Materials: 06,15,32,33
Print Process: web offset
Circulation: 80,561
Circulation Type: paid
**Owner(s):**
Kansas Electric Cooperatives, Inc.
7332 S.W. 21st St.
Topeka, KS 66615
Telephone: (913) 478-4554
Ownership %: 100
**Management:**
Larry Freeze ......................Advertising Manager
**Editorial:**
Larry Freeze ...............................Managing Editor
Bob Jennings ........................Editorial Assistant
Larry Freeze ...............................Photo
**Desc.:** The underlying purpose of the
publication is to bring factual stories of
electrical power use on the farm and
home to the readers. Features cover
all phases of rural use, both on the farm
and in the home, also in youth club
activities, mainly FFA and 4-H, although
many other types of organizations are
touched upon. News stories will cover
the same type of information as do the
feature stories. Photographs are widely
used. Outright publicity material
occasionally used editorially.
Departments include: Women's Page,
Manager's Column, Food Page,
Consumer Corner, Poetry, and Classified
Advertising.
**Readers:** Farmers and suburbanites within
the state comprise the bulk of
readership.
**Deadline:** story-1st of mo., 1 mo. prior to
pub. date

## KENTUCKY LIVING
25498

4515 Bishop Lane
Louisville, KY 40218
Telephone: (502) 451-2430
FAX: (502) 459-3209
Mailing Address:
P.O. Box 32170
Louisville, KY 40232
Year Established: 1948
Pub. Frequency: m.
Page Size: standard
Subscrip. Rate: $1.50 newsstand; $9/yr.
Materials: 02,05,15,20,32
Freelance Pay: $75-$350
Print Process: web offset
Circulation: 385,000
Circulation Type: paid
**Owner(s):**
Kentucky Association of Electric
Cooperatives
P.O. Box 32170
Louisville, KY 40232
Telephone: (502) 451-2430
FAX: (502) 459-3209
Ownership %: 100
**Management:**
Joyce Clark ......................Advertising Manager
**Editorial:**
Gary W. Luhr ...............................Editor
**Desc.:** General feature magazine
specializing in Kentucky-related profiles
(people, places or events), history,
biography, recreation, travel, leisure or
lifestyle articles or book excerpts;
articles on contemporary subjects of
general public interest and general
consumer-related features including
service pieces. Publishes some
humorous and first-person articles of
exceptional quality and opinion
pieces from qualified authorities. No
fiction, poetry or general nostalgia.

**Readers:** Rural and suburban dwellers and
their families.
**Deadline:** story-6 mo. prior to pub. date;
ads-1st of mo., 1 mo. prior to pub. date

## LIVING IN SOUTH CAROLINA
22902

808 Knox Abbott Dr.
Cayce, SC 29033
Telephone: (803) 796-6060
FAX: (803) 796-6064
Year Established: 1950
Pub. Frequency: m.
Page Size: 4 color photos/art
Subscrip. Rate: $2/yr.
Materials: 04,10,15,32
Print Process: web offset
Circulation: 392,000
Circulation Type: paid
**Owner(s):**
S.C. Electric Cooperative Association, Inc.
808 Knox Abbott Dr.
Cayce, SC 29033
Telephone: (803) 796-6060
FAX: (803) 796-6064
Ownership %: 100
**Bureau(s):**
Papert Co., The
960 Hartford Bldg.
Dallas, TX 75201
**Management:**
Larry Cribb ......................Advertising Manager
**Editorial:**
Larry Cribb ...............................Editor
**Desc.:** General rural and suburban
publication, with emphasis on modern
living and rural area development in all
phases. Liberal use of photos. Prefer
brief stories with S.C. angle. Not
interested in personnel changes unless
definite rural and S.C. angle. Emphasis
on improving life and culture for rural
and suburban readers.
**Readers:** Members of Rural Electric
Cooperatives about 90% of the time are
not full-time farmers, but live near cities.
There is a trend from strictly farm
material to state equipment.
**Deadline:** story-1 mo. prior to pub. date

## LOUISIANA COUNTRY
25397

10725 Airline Hwy.
Baton Rouge, LA 70816
Telephone: (504) 293-3450
Year Established: 1950
Pub. Frequency: m.
Page Size: tabloid
Subscrip. Rate: $2.40/yr. members; $5/yr.
non-members
Materials: 02,29
Circulation: 130,000
Circulation Type: paid
**Owner(s):**
Assn. of Louisiana Electric Cooperatives,
Inc.
10725 Airline Hwy.
Baton Rouge, LA 70816
Telephone: (504) 293-3450
Ownership %: 100
**Editorial:**
Whitney L. Belanger ...............................Editor
Rick Shinabery ........................Associate Editor
Carlos Harkness ..........Senior Managing Editor
**Desc.:** A 16-page magazine distributed to
members of Rural Electric Cooperatives.
News and features deal primarily with
homemaking and farming with specific
emphasis on the role of electricity on
the farm and in the house. Much
emphasis is also placed on energy and
energy-related matters.
**Readers:** Suburban and rural residents,
farmers, and business people.

## NORTH DAKOTA REC/RTC
MAGAZINE
22917

3201 Nygren Dr., N.W.
Mandan, ND 58554
Telephone: (701) 663-6501
Mailing Address:
P.O. Box 727
Mandan, ND 58554
Year Established: 1954
Pub. Frequency: m.
Page Size: standard
Subscrip. Rate: $12/yr.; $24/yr. Canada
Freelance Pay: $35-$250
Circulation: 75,000
Circulation Type: paid
**Owner(s):**
N.D. Association of Rural Electric Co-ops.
P.O. Box 727
Mandan, ND 58554-0727
Telephone: (701) 663-6501
Ownership %: 100
**Management:**
Gerald Oberg ...............................President
Dan Holzer ........................Advertising Manager
**Editorial:**
Dennis Hill ...............................Editor in Chief
Karl Karlgaard ...............................Editor
Vicki Russell ...............................Editor
Kent Brick ...............................Editor
Jo Ann Winistorfer ...................Managing Editor
**Desc.:** Devoted to assisting with
information and features the use of
electricity by rural and urban families.
However, much other information is
included, i.e. news for homemakers,
general farm and ranch news,
government agricultural news, plus
entertainment columns, cartoons and
features, livestock news and sales
reports, photo and people features.
**Readers:** Approximately 50% each rural
and urban families.

## OKLAHOMA LIVING
25487

2325 N.E. I44 Service Rd.
Oklahoma City, OK 73111
Telephone: (405) 478-1455
FAX: (405) 478-0246
Mailing Address:
P.O. Box 54309
Oklahoma City, OK 73154-1309
Year Established: 1948
Pub. Frequency: m.
Page Size: Tabloid
Subscrip. Rate: $5/yr.
Freelance Pay: $60-$125
Circulation: 233,000
Circulation Type: paid
**Owner(s):**
Oklahoma Assn. of Electric Cooperatives
P.O. Box 54309
Oklahoma City, OK 73154-1309
Telephone: (405) 478-1455
Ownership %: 100
**Management:**
Fred Albert ........................Advertising Manager
Larry Watkins ........................General Manager
**Editorial:**
Mary Logan ...............................Editor
**Desc.:** General material that is of interest
to people, both urban and rural, will be
considered. Use features on new
electrical appliances, new uses of
electricity, new developments in farm,
home making, small industry.
Departments include: Agriculture, Power
Use, Women's Editorial.
**Readers:** Rural people, both farm and
non-farm.
**Deadline:** 15th of mo.

---

Materials Accepted/Included: 01-Business news 02-By-line articles 03-Fashion news 04-Food news 05-Freelance copy 06-Letters to editor 07-Real estate news 08-Sports news 09-Travel news 10-Book rev. 11-Movie rev. 12-Music rev. 13-TV rev. 14-Theater rev. 15-Coming events 16-Obituaries 17-Question & answer 18-Social announcements 19-Artwork 20-Cartoons 21-Photos 22-TV listings 23-Audio rec. 24-Video rec. 25-Books 26-Films/film clips 27-Personnel news 28-Press releases 29-New product news/photos 30-Trade lit. 31-Contracts awarded 32-Display adv. 33-Classified adv.

## RURAL ARKANSAS
25394

8000 Scot Hamilton Dr.
Little Rock, AR 72209
Telephone: (501) 570-2200
FAX: (501) 570-2205
Mailing Address:
  P.O. Box 510
  Little Rock, AR 72203
Year Established: 1946
Pub. Frequency: m.
Page Size: standard
Subscrip. Rate: $4/yr.
Circulation: 256,000
Circulation Type: paid
**Owner(s):**
Arkansas Electric Co-ops.
8000 Scot Hamilton Dr.
Little Rock, AR 72209
Telephone: (501) 570-2200
FAX: (501) 570-2205
Ownership %: 100
**Editorial:**
Ouida H. Cox ............................Editor
**Readers:** Electric cooperative members.

## RURAL ELECTRIC NEBRASKAN
25395

800 S. 13th
Lincoln, NE 68508
Telephone: (402) 475-4988
Mailing Address:
  P.O. Box 82048
  Lincoln, NE 68501
Year Established: 1946
Pub. Frequency: m.
Page Size: standard
Subscrip. Rate: $7/yr.
Freelance Pay: $75/printed page
Print Process: offset
Circulation: 58,000
Circulation Type: controlled
**Owner(s):**
Nebraska Rural Electric Association
Telephone: (402) 475-4988
Ownership %: 100
**Management:**
Dirk Maley .........................Advertising Manager
**Editorial:**
Jack Merritt ..................................Editor
**Desc.:** How-to articles show how electricity can be used efficiently. Home pages cover interior decoration trends, use of electricity in the home, parties, cooking, etc. Departments include: Homemakers Section.
**Readers:** Rural electric users in Nebraska.

## RURAL ELECTRIFICATION MAGAZINE
22925

1800 Massachusetts Ave., N.W.
Washington, DC 20036
Telephone: (202) 857-9500
FAX: (202) 857-9791
Year Established: 1948
Pub. Frequency: m.
Page Size: standard
Subscrip. Rate: $5/copy; $18/yr.
Freelance Pay: negotiable
Circulation: 36,754
Circulation Type: paid
**Owner(s):**
National Rural Electric Cooperative Assn.
1800 Massachusetts Ave., NW
Washington, DC 20036
Telephone: (202) 857-9500
Ownership %: 100
**Bureau(s):**
National Advertising Sales Office
6110 Executive Blvd.
Rockville, MD 20852
Telephone: (301) 984-7333
Contact: Janice Starrs, Manager
**Management:**
Andrea Smith ....................Advertising Manager

Lisa Guttman .....................Production Manager
**Editorial:**
Frank Gallant ..............................Editor
Jean Rosenberg ...........Business Development
Jennifer Rothwell ....................Columnist
Arlene Dookwha .......................Miscellaneous
Paul Wesslund ........................Miscellaneous
Al Birbaum ........................Technical Advisor
John Vanvig ...............................Writer
Jill Kunka ..................................Writer
John Lowery ..............................Writer
**Desc.:** Articles, features, news items deal with more efficient operation and management of rural electric systems. Technical articles should not require extensive technical knowledge for comprehension. Editorial content divided into special features, legislation and law, trends and technical; association items; state and local (news meetings). Editorial departments include: Book Reviews, Manufacturers' News, New Products, including Personnel Changes and Publications.
**Readers:** Managers, employees and directors of all rural electric cooperatives in the United States.

## RURALITE
25499

2040 A St.
Forest Grove, OR 97116
Telephone: (503) 357-2105
FAX: (503) 357-8615
Mailing Address:
  P.O. Box 558
  Forest Grove, OR 97116
Year Established: 1954
Pub. Frequency: m.
Page Size: standard
Subscrip. Rate: $6/yr.
Materials: 02,05,21,32
Freelance Pay: $50-$400
Print Process: web offset
Circulation: 260,000
Circulation Type: paid
**Owner(s):**
Ruralite Services, Inc.
P.O. Box 558
Forest Grove, OR 97116
Telephone: (503) 357-2105
FAX: (503) 357-8615
Ownership %: 100
**Management:**
Bob Gallucci ............................President
John Hillman .............................Publisher
Pat Evey ..................Production Manager
**Editorial:**
Curtis Condon .............................Editor
Mike Teagarden ........................Assistant Editor
Walter Wentz ....................Associate Editor
Janis Corrieri ..................Production Assistant
**Desc.:** General interest consumer publication with rural, small town & urban audience, in Alaska, Oregon, Idaho, Nevada and Northern California. Departments include: food, financial, how-to, homemaker, kids, adult pen pals, classifieds, energy, people, features, general interest. 4-8 pages relate to local editions (52 total) for various public utilities; remainder of 32 pages are regional.
**Readers:** Split small-town (20%) urban (20%) & rural, users of rural electric consumer-owned utilities.

## RURAL MISSOURI
22924

2722 E. McCarty
Jefferson City, MO 65101
Telephone: (314) 635-6857
Year Established: 1948
Pub. Frequency:

Page Size: tabloid
Subscrip. Rate: $4.25/yr. non-member;
  $11.25/3 yrs.
Freelance Pay: varies
Circulation: 364,000
Circulation Type: paid
**Owner(s):**
Assn. of Missouri Electric Cooperatives, Inc.
2722 E. McCarty
Jefferson City, MO 65101
Telephone: (314) 635-6857
Ownership %: 100
**Management:**
Mary Davis ......................Advertising Manager
**Editorial:**
Jim McCarty ...............................Editor
Jeff Joiner ..........................Managing Editor
Heather Berry .......................Assistant Editor
Heather Berry .......................Editorial Assistant
Bob McEowen .............................Field Editor
**Desc.:** Majority of editorial material consists of farm and home features, including those where electricity is involved. Departments include: New Electrical Products; bulletins in electric power field (including legislation); home features of all kinds, do-it-yourself articles, human interest features, humorous articles based on rural or suburban life. Specialize in strong photo packages in b&w and color.
**Readers:** Rural families.
**Deadline:** ads-1st mo., 1 mo. prior

## RURAL MONTANA
22911

501 Bay Dr.
Great Falls, MT 59404
Telephone: (406) 761-8333
FAX: (406) 761-8339
Mailing Address:
  P.O. Box 1641
  Great Falls, MT 59403
Year Established: 1952
Pub. Frequency: m.
Page Size: standard
Subscrip. Rate: $6/yr.
Freelance Pay: varies
Circulation: 70,000
Circulation Type: paid
**Owner(s):**
Montana Electric Cooperatives' Association
P.O. Box 1306
Great Falls, MT 59403
Telephone: (406) 454-1521
**Management:**
Jay Downen ...............Executive Vice President
Mack McConnell ...............Advertising Manager
**Editorial:**
Mack McConnell ...........................Editor
Mack McConnell ...............Publication Director
**Desc.:** Published in the interests of better rural urban understanding/not only for the benefits of cooperative electrification, but in most every area of human relations. Edited to provide broad coverage of farm and home information and entertainment features. Written as straight news or features and photos to interest average farmer, rancher and family on rural electric lines. Editorial departments include: News, Features, Photos, Teenage and Women's News.
**Readers:** Farm, ranch, suburban families.
**Deadline:** story-1st of mo. prior to pub.; news-1st of mo.; photo-1st of mo.; ads-1st of mo.

## TODAY IN MISSISSIPPI
22910

2805 Greenway Dr.
Jackson, MS 39204
Telephone: (601) 922-2341
FAX: (601) 933-7897

Mailing Address:
  P.O. Box 7897
  Jackson, MS 39284-7897
Year Established: 1948
Pub. Frequency: m.
Page Size: tabloid
Subscrip. Rate: $.25/copy; $2.50/yr.
Print Process: web offset
Circulation: 324,635
Circulation Type: paid
**Owner(s):**
Electric Power Association of Mississippi
P.O. Box 7897
Jackson, MS 39284
Telephone: (601) 922-2341
Ownership %: 100
**Editorial:**
Hobson Waits ..............................Editor
Floyd Mobley ........................Managing Editor
Debra Stringer ..............Special Features Editor
**Desc.:** Designed specifically for rural electric consumers in Mississippi. Includes features relating to rural electric developments on a local and national basis, outstanding contributions and events by members of a rural electric system, and historical people, places, and things on rural lines. Use some non-technical general articles on electrical development, ladies page, recipes, and household hints. Includes features relating to industries such as dairying, poultry and other agricultural and non-agricultural industries.
**Readers:** Rural.
**Deadline:** story-1st of mo. prior to pub. date; news-1st of mo. prior; photo-1st of mo. prior; ads-1st of mo. prior

## WYOMING RURAL ELECTRIC NEWS
22936

340 W. B St.
Casper, WY 82601
Telephone: (307) 234-6152
FAX: (307) 234-4115
Mailing Address:
  P.O. Box 380
  Casper, WY 82602
Year Established: 1954
Pub. Frequency: 11/yr.
Page Size: standard
Subscrip. Rate: $4.50/yr.
Freelance Pay: $40 cover photo; $20-$45 essays & articles
Circulation: 30,000
Circulation Type: paid
**Owner(s):**
Wyoming Rural Electric Association
P.O. Box 380
Casper, WY 82602
Telephone: (307) 234-6152
Ownership %: 100
**Management:**
Judy Eastman ....................Executive Director
**Editorial:**
Mary England ..................Finance Administrator
**Desc.:** Main emphasis on subjects of interest to rural people, i.e.: agriculture, mining, timbering, history local, politics, conservation, rural health, energy, Western Wyoming fiction & non-fiction. Material on rural electricification and rural economic development. Attempts to educate and inform. Wyoming's largest monthly publication.
**Readers:** Country home owners, rural families, farm and ranch families, legislators, libraries.
**Deadline:** story-20th of mo., 1 mo. prior; news-20th of mo., 1 mo. prior; photo-20th of mo., 1 mo. prior; ads-20th of mo., 1 mo. prior

**Materials Accepted/Included:** 01-Business news 02-By-line articles 03-Fashion news 04-Food news 05-Freelance copy 06-Letters to editor 07-Real estate news 08-Sports news 09-Travel news 10-Book rev. 11-Movie rev. 12-Music rev. 13-TV rev. 14-Theater rev. 15-Coming events 16-Obituaries 17-Question & answer 18-Social announcements 19-Artwork 20-Cartoons 21-Photos 22-TV listings 23-Audio rec. 24-Video rec. 25-Books 26-Films/film clips 27-Personnel news 28-Press releases 29-New product news/photos 30-Trade lit. 31-Contracts awarded 32-Display adv. 33-Classified adv.

5-31

# Section 6
# CONSUMER MAGAZINES

This section contains complete listings for magazines that are directed toward the consumer audience. The magazines are listed alphabetically within each subject group. Subject groups follow numerical order according to group number.

A subject listing is provided with a page reference to where each group heading may be found within the main listings.

Please refer to the Alphabetical Cross Index in Section 3 to locate related subject publications within the Consumer Magazine section or related subject categories/listings in the Service, Trade, Professional, Industrial or Farm and Agricultural Magazine or Newsletter sections.

For materials accepted/included, refer to the coded list at the bottom of each page.

## SUBJECT GROUPS INCLUDED

## Group 602-Adult

**CHIC**                                                    26108
9171 Wilshire Blvd.
Ste. 300
Beverly Hills, CA 90210
Telephone: (310) 858-7100
FAX: (310) 275-3857
Year Established: 1976
Pub. Frequency: 13/yr.
Page Size: standard
Subscrip. Rate: $4.99 newsstand;
   $39.95/yr.
Materials: 02,19,32
Freelance Pay: varies
Circulation: 50,000
Circulation Type: paid
**Owner(s):**
HG Publications
9171 Wilshire Blvd.
Ste. 300
Beverly Hills, CA 90210
Telephone: (310) 858-7100
FAX: (310) 275-3857
Ownership %: 100
**Management:**
Larry Flynt .............................Publisher
Paul Lesser ...............Advertising Manager
**Desc.:** Sex-oriented articles and erotic
   fiction that appeal to a male reading
   audience. Includes interviews with
   nonmainstream personalities and
   readers' sexual experiences.
**Readers:** Ages 18-35, fairly affluent,
   middle-class, nonpreppie, unpretentious,
   liberal-minded.

**CLUB**                                                    26109
P.O. Box 200
Sandy Hook, CT 06482
Telephone: (203) 426-6533
Year Established: 1975
Pub. Frequency: 13/yr.
Page Size: standard
Subscrip. Rate: $39/yr.
Circulation: 700,000
Circulation Type: paid
**Owner(s):**
Paragon Publ.
P.O. Box 200
Sandy Hook, CT 06482
Telephone: (203) 426-6533
Ownership %: 100
**Bureau(s):**
Fiona Press, Inc.
P.O. Box 1379
Norwalk, CT 06856
Telephone: (203) 838-5484
**Management:**
John Montanaro ...............................Publisher
Susan Freeman ...............Advertising Manager
Steve Kolitz ...................Circulation Manager
**Editorial:**
Nigel Franks .............................Editor
**Desc.:** Club devotes itself to the subjects
   of sex, lifestyles and humor. It includes
   interviews, tasteful pictorials, fiction,
   cartoons, automobiles, video reviews,
   and readers letters and advice.
**Readers:** 18-34 year old males.

**FUTURE SEX**                                              69550
60 Federal St., Ste. 502
San Francisco, CA 94107
Telephone: (415) 541-7725
FAX: (415) 541-9860
Year Established: 1992
Pub. Frequency: q.
Page Size: standard
Subscrip. Rate: $4.95/copy; $18/yr.
Materials: 02,05,06,10,11,12,19,20,21,27,
   28,32

**Owner(s):**
Kundalini Publishing, Inc.
60 Federal St., Ste. 502
San Francisco, CA 94107
Telephone: (415) 541-7725
FAX: (415) 541-9860
Ownership %: 100
**Editorial:**
Lisa Palac ...............................Editor
Brett Beutel ...........................Advertising

**GALLERY**                                                 26113
401 Park Ave., S.
3rd Fl.
New York, NY 10016
Telephone: (212) 779-8900
FAX: (212) 725-7215
Year Established: 1975
Pub. Frequency: m.
Page Size: standard
Subscrip. Rate: $25/yr.
Freelance Pay: varies
Circulation: 500,000
Circulation Type: paid
**Owner(s):**
Montcalm Publishing Corp.
401 Park Ave., S.
3rd Fl.
New York, NY 10016
Telephone: (212) 779-8900
Ownership %: 100
**Management:**
Russell Orenstein ...............................Publisher
**Editorial:**
Barry Janoff ...............Editor in Chief
Judy Linden ...................Senior Editor
**Desc.:** Men's life-style and entertainment
   magazine. Departments include: Film,
   Books, News, Features, Interviews,
   Environmental, Health, Investigative
   Reports, and Entertainment.
**Readers:** Male 18-34, college educated.

**HEAVY METAL**                                             69266
584 Broadway, Ste. 608
New York, NY 10012
Telephone: (212) 274-8462
FAX: (212) 274-8969
Year Established: 1977
Pub. Frequency: bi-m.
Page Size: standard
Subscrip. Rate: $3.95; $12.95/yr.
Materials: 20,30
Print Process: web offset
Circulation: 140,000
Circulation Type: paid
**Owner(s):**
Metal Mammoth
584 Broadway, Ste. 608
New York, NY 10012
Telephone: (212) 274-8462
Ownership %: 100
**Editorial:**
Debra Rabas ...............Managing Editor
Howard Jurofsky ..........Advertising & Exec. Dir.
**Desc.:** Adult illustrated fantasy magazine.

**HUSTLER MAGAZINE**                                        26115
9171 Wilshire Blvd., Ste. 300
Beverly Hills, CA 90210
Telephone: (310) 858-7100
FAX: (310) 275-3857
Year Established: 1974
Pub. Frequency: m.
Page Size: standard
Subscrip. Rate: $4.95/issue; $39.95/yr.
Freelance Pay: $1,500/article; illus., varies;
   $1,000/fiction
Circulation: 1,200,000
Circulation Type: paid

**Owner(s):**
L.F.P., Inc.
9171 Wilshire Blvd., Ste. 300
Beverly Hills, CA 90210
Telephone: (310) 858-7100
Ownership %: 100
**Management:**
Larry Flynt ...............................Publisher
Perry Taryson ...................Advertising Manager
**Editorial:**
Allan MacDonell ...................Executive Editor
John Thompson ...............Art Director
James Baes ...........................Photo
**Desc.:** The second-largest men's
   magazine. Uses hard-hitting expose
   articles (4,000- 5,000 words), interviews
   (5,000 words), and personality profiles
   (4,000-5,000 words). No public-relations
   pieces. All are by-lined. Also use news
   stories on unusual happenings, reviews
   of new and/or unusual sex-related
   products or activities. Photo features
   include four nude photo spreads, movie
   features and parodies. Monthly features
   include: X-rated video reviews, humor
   and cartoons, reader's stories, and
   letters to the editor. Writing submitted
   should be in simple, straightforward
   style, the tone irreverent. Departments
   include: Art, Photo, General Editorial.
**Readers:** Males 25-40, variety of
   professional backgrounds,  income
   levels.

**PENTHOUSE**                                               26119
1965 Broadway
New York, NY 10023
Telephone: (212) 496-6100
FAX: (212) 580-3693
Year Established: 1969
Pub. Frequency: m.
Page Size: Four-color photos and art
Subscrip. Rate: $36/yr.
Circulation: 1,254,207
Circulation Type: paid
**Owner(s):**
General Media Publishing Group
1965 Broadway
New York, NY 10023-5965
Telephone: (212) 496-6100
**Management:**
Bob Guccione ...............................Publisher
Audrey Arnold ...................Advertising Manager
**Editorial:**
Bob Guccione ...................Executive Editor
Peter Bloch ...............................Editor
Heidi Handman ...................Managing Editor
Catherine Koatz ..........Administrative Assistant
Kathy Keeton ...............................CEO
**Desc.:** The full range of sophisticated male
   entertainment news, features, from
   outspoken contemporary comment to
   photographic essays of some of the
   world's most beautiful women.
   Departments include Interviews, Articles,
   Fiction, Reviews, Fashion, Food and
   Drink.
**Readers:** High percentage of college-
   educated.

**PENTHOUSE FORUM**                                         69244
1965 Broadway
New York, NY 10023
Telephone: (212) 496-6100
FAX: (212) 580-3693
Year Established: 1976
Pub. Frequency: m.
Page Size: pocket
Subscrip. Rate: $27/yr.
Circulation: 400,000
Circulation Type: paid

**Owner(s):**
General Media Publishing Group
1965 Broadway
New York, NY 10023
Telephone: (212) 496-6100
Ownership %: 100
**Editorial:**
V.K. McCarty ...............................Editor
**Desc.:** Allows men and women to share
   experiences and fantasies. Provides
   data and entertainment concerning sex
   and sexuality.

**PENTHOUSE LETTERS**                                       49803
1965 Broadway
New York, NY 10023-4965
Telephone: (212) 496-6100
FAX: (212) 580-3693
Year Established: 1981
Pub. Frequency: 13/yr.
Page Size: standard
Subscrip. Rate: $5.50 newsstand; $28/yr.
Materials: 32,33
Freelance Pay: negotiable
Circulation: 550,000
Circulation Type: paid
**Owner(s):**
General Media Publishing Group
1965 Broadway
New York, NY 10023-4965
Telephone: (212) 496-6100
Ownership %: 100
**Management:**
Don Myrus ...............................Publisher
**Editorial:**
John Borelli ...............Managing Editor
James B. Mortise ...............Circulation Director
**Desc.:** A magazine of sexual marvels
   devoted to revealing all the fun involved
   in the pursuit and attainment of happy
   sex.

**PENTHOUSE VARIATIONS**                                    69245
1965 Broadway
New York, NY 10023
Telephone: (212) 496-6100
FAX: (212) 580-3693
Year Established: 1978
Pub. Frequency: m.
Page Size: digest
Subscrip. Rate: $3.98/issue; $27/yr.
Materials: 05,06
Circulation: 425,000
Circulation Type: paid
**Owner(s):**
General Media Publishing Group
1965 Broadway
New York, NY 10023-4965
Telephone: (212) 496-6100
Ownership %: 100
**Editorial:**
V.K. McCarty ...............................Editor
**Desc.:** Provides interpersonal portraits of
   America's couples. Offers sexual fact
   and fiction for entertainment and
   education.

**PLAYBOY**                                                 26120
680 N. Lake Shore Dr.
Chicago, IL 60611
Telephone: (312) 751-8000
FAX: (312) 751-2818
Year Established: 1953
Pub. Frequency: m.
Page Size: standard
Subscrip. Rate: $29.97/yr.
Freelance Pay: $2,000-$3,000
Circulation: 3,400,000
Circulation Type: paid

Materials Accepted/Included: 01-Business news 02-By-line articles 03-Fashion news 04-Food news 05-Freelance copy 06-Letters to editor 07-Real estate news 08-Sports news 09-Travel news 10-Book rev. 11-Movie rev. 12-Music rev. 13-TV rev. 14-Theater rev. 15-Coming events 16-Obituaries 17-Question & answer 18-Social announcements 19-Artwork 20-Cartoons 21-Photos 22-TV listings 23-Audio rec. 24-Video rec. 25-Books 26-Films/film clips 27-Personnel news 28-Press releases 29-New product news/photos 30-Trade lit. 31-Contracts awarded 32-Display adv. 33-Classified adv.

**Owner(s):**
Playboy Enterprises, Inc.
680 N. Lake Shore Dr.
Chicago, IL 60611
Telephone: (312) 751-8000
Ownership %: 100
**Bureau(s):**
Playboy Magazine, West Coast
8560 Sunset Blvd.
Los Angeles, CA 90069
Telephone: (310) 659-4080
Contact: Stephen Randall, Editor

Playboy Magazine, New York Office
747 Third Ave.
New York, NY 10017
Telephone: (212) 688-3030
Contact: Alice K. Tumerz, Fiction Editor
**Management:**
Christie Hefner ...........................President
Michael Perlis ............................Publisher
**Editorial:**
Arthur Kretchmer ...............Editorial Director
Tom Staebter .......................Art Director
John Rezek ........................Articles Editor
James Span Fellen ..........Assistant Publisher
Barbara Nellis ................Book Review Editor
Alice K. Turner .......................Fiction Editor
David Stevens ..................New Product Editor
Gary Cole ...................................Photo
**Desc.:** Regularly features politics, music, topical humor, personality profiles, sex and relationships, business and finance, science and technology, sports, and other topics that have some bearing on our readers' life-styles.

### PLAYERS MAGAZINE
26121
8060 Melrose Ave.
Los Angeles, CA 90046
Telephone: (213) 653-8060
FAX: (213) 655-9452
Year Established: 1972
Pub. Frequency: m.
Page Size: standard
Subscrip. Rate: $4.95/copy; $45/yr.
Materials: 02,03,05,06,08,09,10,11,12,13, 14,19,20,21,23,24,25,26,27,28,29,32
Freelance Pay: $150-$500
Print Process: web offset
Circulation: 175,000
Circulation Type: paid
**Owner(s):**
Players International Pub.
8060 Melrose Ave.
Los Angeles, CA 90046
Telephone: (310) 653-8060
FAX: (213) 655-9452
Ownership %: 100
**Editorial:**
Lesil D. Wells ...............................Editor
**Desc.:** Informative as well as entertaining articles approach all subjects from a black perspective that are of current interest to the young black male. Sports, Music, Politics, History, Entertainment, Fiction, Interviews, Business, Economics, Etc.
**Readers:** 18-35 yr. old black males.

### Group 604-Almanacs

25568
### BLUM'S FARMERS & PLANTERS ALMANAC & TURNER'S CAROLINA
3301 Healy Dr., S.W.
Winston-Salem, NC 27103
Telephone: (910) 765-5811
FAX: (910) 659-1252
Year Established: 1828
Pub. Frequency: a.
Page Size: standard
Subscrip. Rate: $2.25/yr.
Circulation: 600,000

Circulation Type: paid
**Owner(s):**
Blum's Almanac Co.
3301 Healy Dr., S.W.
Winston-Salem, NC 27103
Telephone: (919) 765-5811
Ownership %: 100
**Editorial:**
Allen S. Goslen ...........................Editor
Mark A. Goslen ...............Production Director
**Desc.:** A family almanac written for those desiring useful information on gardening, weather, zodiac signs, moon's phases and fishing. Featuring articles on agriculture, jokes and stories, helpful household hints, and articles of general interest.

25569
### GRIER'S ALMANAC
5123 Charmant Pl.
Atlanta, GA 30360-1405
Telephone: (404) 395-6381
FAX: (404) 395-6381
Year Established: 1807
Pub. Frequency: a.
Page Size: pocket
Subscrip. Rate: free
Circulation: 3,000,000
Circulation Type: controlled
**Owner(s):**
Grier's Almanac Publishing Co.
5123 Charmant Pl.
Atlanta, GA 30360
Telephone: (404) 395-6381
Ownership %: 100
**Management:**
Bryan Bachler ...........................President
Leslie G. Bachler ................General Manager
**Editorial:**
Robert L. Garges .................Consulting Editor
Bryan Bachler .......................Technical Editor

25570
### J. GRUBER'S HAGERSTOWN TOWN & COUNTRY ALMANACK
1120 Professional Ct.
Hagerstown, MD 21740
Telephone: (301) 733-2530
FAX: (301) 791-1478
Mailing Address:
    P.O. Box 609
    Hagerstown, MD 21741
Year Established: 1797
Pub. Frequency: a.
Page Size: pg: 5 1/4" x 8 3/8"; col: 4"
Subscrip. Rate: $1.95/yr.
Circulation: 175,000
Circulation Type: controlled
**Owner(s):**
Gruber Almanack Company
1120 Professional Ct.
Hagerstown, MD 21740
Telephone: (301) 733-2530
Ownership %: 100
**Management:**
Gerald W. Spessard ..........Advertising Manager
F. S. Leiter ......................Sales Manager
**Editorial:**
Charles W. Fisher ...........................Editor

58566
### NATIONAL GUARD ALMANAC
6231 Leesburg Pike, #L-2
Falls Church, VA 22044
Telephone: (703) 532-1631
FAX: (703) 532-1635
Mailing Address:
    P.O. Box 4144
    Falls Church, VA 22044
Year Established: 1975
Pub. Frequency: a.
Page Size: pocket
Subscrip. Rate: $6.95/yr.
Materials: 10,28
Print Process: web offset
Circulation: 35,000

Circulation Type: paid
**Owner(s):**
Uniformed Services Almanac, Inc.
6231 Leesburg Pike, #L-2
Falls Church, VA 22044
Telephone: (703) 532-1631
FAX: (703) 532-1635
Ownership %: 100
**Management:**
Sol Gordon ...............................Manager
**Editorial:**
Sol Gordon ...................................Editor
**Desc.:** US Military Forces: pay & benefits information for members of the Army and Air National Guard and their families.
**Readers:** National Guard Members, Military Leaders, Members of Congress

25572
### OLD FARMER'S ALMANAC, THE
Main St.
Dublin, NH 03444
Telephone: (603) 563-8111
FAX: (603) 563-8252
Mailing Address:
    P.O. Box 520
    Dublin, NH 03444
Year Established: 1792
Pub. Frequency: a.
Page Size: pocket
Subscrip. Rate: $2.95/yr.
Circulation: 4,400,000
Circulation Type: paid
**Owner(s):**
Yankee Publishing, Inc.
Main St.
Dublin, NH 03444
Telephone: (603) 563-8111
Ownership %: 100
**Management:**
John Pierce ...............................Publisher
Kevin Scully ...............Advertising Manager
**Editorial:**
Jud Hale ...................................Editor
**Desc.:** The Old Farmer's Almanac is a resource book for country life, including astronomical, astrological and meterological information plus entertaining and informative articles.
**Readers:** National, varied.

58568
### RESERVE FORCES ALMANAC
6231 Leesburg Pike, #L-2
Falls Church, VA 22044
Telephone: (703) 532-1631
FAX: (703) 532-1635
Mailing Address:
    P.O. Box 4144
    Falls Church, VA 22044
Year Established: 1975
Pub. Frequency: a.
Page Size: pocket
Subscrip. Rate: $6.95/yr.
Materials: 10,28
Print Process: web offset
Circulation: 45,000
Circulation Type: paid
**Owner(s):**
Uniformed Services Almanac, Inc.
6231 Leesburg Pike, #L-2
Falls Church, VA 22044
Telephone: (703) 532-1631
FAX: (703) 532-1635
Ownership %: 100
**Management:**
Sol Gordon ...............................Manager
**Editorial:**
Sol Gordon ...................................Editor
**Desc.:** US Military Forces: pay and benefits information for members of the Army, Navy, Air Force, Marine Corps, and Coast Guard Reserves and their families.

**Readers:** Members of the reserve forces, researchers, military leaders and members of congress.

58567
### RETIRED MILITARY ALMANAC
6231 Leesburg Pike, #L-2
Falls Church, VA 22044
Telephone: (703) 532-1631
FAX: (703) 532-1635
Mailing Address:
    P.O. Box 4144
    Falls Church, VA 22044
Year Established: 1979
Pub. Frequency: a.
Page Size: pocket
Subscrip. Rate: $6.95/yr.
Materials: 10,28
Print Process: web offset
Circulation: 45,000
Circulation Type: paid
**Owner(s):**
Uniformed Services Almanac, Inc.
6231 Leesburg Pike, #L-2
Falls Church, VA 22044
Telephone: (703) 532-1631
Ownership %: 100
**Management:**
Sol Gordon ...............................Manager
**Editorial:**
Sol Gordon ...................................Editor
**Desc.:** Provides important information on retired pay and benefits, health care, survivor benefits, listings and other valuable information for military retirees.
**Readers:** Retired military personnel and families, researchers, military leaders and members of congress.

25571
### SINGLES ALMANAC
38 Kellogg St.
Jersey City, NJ 07305
Telephone: (201) 433-8644
FAX: (201) 433-0847
Year Established: 1968
Pub. Frequency: m.
Page Size: standard
Subscrip. Rate: $2 newsstand; $24/yr.
Materials: 03,04,05,09,10,11,12,14,15,18, 28,32,33
Print Process: web
Circulation: 15,000
Circulation Type: paid
**Owner(s):**
Almanac Publications
38 Kellogg St.
Jersey City, NJ 07305
Telephone: (201) 433-8644
FAX: (201) 433-0847
Ownership %: 100
**Management:**
Michael Brandon ...........................Publisher
**Editorial:**
Michael Brandon ...........................Editor
**Desc.:** A calendar of community and cultural events serving New York City and the suburbs. Many of these events are free, one-time happenings, that are listed day-by-day, Friday through Thursday. Events are single, single-oriented or single-related. Also contains personals, profiles and classifieds.
**Readers:** Mostly single adults, 20-50 years of age.
**Deadline:** story-20th of mo.; news-20th of mo.; photo-20th of mo.; ads-20th of mo.

58569
### UNIFORMED SERVICES ALMANAC
6231 Leesburg Pike, #L - 2
Falls Church, VA 22044
Telephone: (703) 532-1631
FAX: (703) 532-1635
Mailing Address:
    P.O. Box 4144
    Falls Church, VA 22044

---

**Materials Accepted/Included:** 01-Business news 02-By-line articles 03-Fashion news 04-Food news 05-Freelance copy 06-Letters to editor 07-Real estate news 08-Sports news 09-Travel news 10-Book rev. 11-Movie rev. 12-Music rev. 13-TV rev. 14-Theater rev. 15-Coming events 16-Obituaries 17-Question & answer 18-Social announcements 19-Artwork 20-Cartoons 21-Photos 22-TV listings 23-Audio rec. 24-Video rec. 25-Books 26-Films/film clips 27-Personnel news 28-Press releases 29-New product news/photos 30-Trade lit. 31-Contracts awarded 32-Display adv. 33-Classified adv.

Year Established: 1959
Pub. Frequency: a.
Page Size: standard
Subscrip. Rate: $6.95/yr.
Materials: 10,28
Print Process: web offset
Circulation: 50,000
Circulation Type: paid
**Owner(s):**
Uniformed Services Almanac, Inc.
6231 Leesburg Pike, #L - 2
Falls Church, VA 22044
Telephone: (703) 532-1631
FAX: (709) 532-1635
Ownership %: 100
**Management:**
Sol Gordon ...........................................Publisher
Sol Gordon ...........................................Manager
**Editorial:**
Sol Gordon ...........................................Editor
**Desc.:** Military - Active Duty Pay &
　Benefits and other valuable information
　including health care, survivor benefits,
　taxes, social security and many other
　subjects of interest and importance to
　military personnel and their families.
**Readers:** Active duty military and families,
　researchers, military leaders and
　members of congress.

## Group 606-Art & Antiques

68731
## AMERICAN INDIAN ART MAGAZINE
7314 E. Osborn Dr.
Scottsdale, AZ 85251
Telephone: (602) 994-5445
Year Established: 1975
Pub. Frequency: q.
Page Size: standard
Subscrip. Rate: $5 newsstand; $20/yr.
Materials: 05,10,15,25,28,30,32
Freelance Pay: $150-300/article
Print Process: offset lithography
Circulation: 23000
Circulation Type: paid
**Owner(s):**
American Indian Art, Inc.
7314 E. Osborn Dr.
Scottsdale, AZ 85251
Telephone: (602) 994-5445
Ownership %: 100
**Editorial:**
Roanne P. Goldfein ...........................Editor
**Desc.:** Devoted to prehistoric, historic, and
　contemporary American Indian arts.

25607
## ANTIQUE AUTOMOBILE
501 W. Governor Rd.
Hershey, PA 17033
Telephone: (717) 534-1910
Mailing Address:
　P.O. Box 417
　Hershey, PA 17033
Year Established: 1935
Pub. Frequency: bi-m.
Page Size: standard
Subscrip. Rate: $20/yr. members
**Owner(s):**
Antique Automobile Club of America
501 W. Governor Rd.
P.O. Box 417
Hershey, PA 17033
Telephone: (717) 534-1910
Ownership %: 100
**Editorial:**
William H. Smith ...............................Editor
Jeanne H. Brandt ...............Associate Editor
Keith Marvin ...............Book Review Editor

**Desc.:** Official publication of the oldest and
　largest automotive historical society, the
　Antique Automobile Club of America.
　Automotive historical articles, present
　day tour accounts of antique cars,
　technical articles on how to restore,
　maintain, club activities, and
　national and international news
　concerning antique automobiles.
**Readers:** Antique car collectors.

21728
## ANTIQUES & AUCTION NEWS
Route 230, W., P.O. Box 500
Mount Joy, PA 17552
Telephone: (717) 653-1833
Year Established: 1967
Pub. Frequency: w.
Page Size: tabloid
Subscrip. Rate: $15/yr. 3rd class
Materials: 28,32,33
Freelance Pay: $5 - $20
Circulation: 30,000
Circulation Type: free
**Owner(s):**
Engle Publishing Company
Rt. 230, W., P.O. Box 500
Mount Joy, PA 17552
Telephone: (717) 653-1833
**Editorial:**
Doris Ann Johnson ...........................Editor
**Readers:** Antiques collectors, antiques &
　collectibles dealers, auctioneers, history
　buffs, collectors, shop owners, museum
　curators.

68883
## ANTIQUES & COLLECTIBLES MAGAZINE
P.O. Box 33
Westbury, NY 11590
Telephone: (516) 334-9650
FAX: (516) 334-5740
Year Established: 1980
Pub. Frequency: m.
Subscrip. Rate: $15/yr.
Materials: 09,10,29,32
Print Process: web offset
Circulation: 5,000
Circulation Type: paid
**Owner(s):**
Antiques & Collectibles, Inc.
P.O. Box 33
Westbury, NY 11590
Telephone: (516) 334-9650
FAX: (516) 334-5740
Ownership %: 100
**Editorial:**
Rich Branciforte ...............................Editor
**Readers:** Dealers and serious collectors.
**Deadline:** story-2 wks. prior to pub. date;
　ads-1 wk. prior to pub. date

25609
## ANTIQUE TRADER WEEKLY, THE
100 Bryant St.
Dubuque, IA 52003
Telephone: (319) 588-2073
Mailing Address:
　P.O. Box 1050
　Dubuque, IA 52004
Year Established: 1957
Pub. Frequency: w.
Page Size: tabloid
Subscrip. Rate: $28/yr.
Circulation: 60,000
Circulation Type: paid
**Owner(s):**
Landmark Community Newspapers
P.O. Box 1050
Dubuque, IA 52004
Telephone: (319) 588-2073
Ownership %: 100
**Management:**
Ted Jones ...........................................Publisher
Marvin Willenbring ...........Advertising Manager

**Editorial:**
Kyle D. Husfloen ...............................Editor
Jimmie O'Donley ...............Advertising Sales
　　　　　　　　　　　　　　　　　Manager
Kyle D. Husfloen ...............Book Review Editor
Kyle D. Husfloen ...............................News Editor
**Desc.:** Articles on all types of antiques and
　collector's items.
**Readers:** Mainly antique and limited-
　edition collectors and dealers.

25614
## ART & ANTIQUES
2100 Powers Ferry Rd.
Ste. 300
Atlanta, GA 30339
Telephone: (404) 955-5656
FAX: (404) 952-0669
Year Established: 1978
Pub. Frequency: 10/yr.
Page Size: standard
Subscrip. Rate: $4.95/issue; $35/yr. US;
　$50/yr. Canada; $55/yr. foreign
Freelance Pay: $350/article
Circulation: 150,000
Circulation Type: paid
**Owner(s):**
Trans World Publishing, Inc.
2100 Powers Ferry Rd., Ste.300
Atlanta, GA 30339
Telephone: (404) 955-5656
Ownership %: 100
**Management:**
Douglas C. Billian ...............................President
Douglas C. Billian ...............................Publisher
Robin R. Domeniconi ...........Associate Publisher
Pamela K. Daniels ...........Advertising Manager
Elvira Lopez ...................Circulation Manager
**Editorial:**
Mark S. Mayfield ...............................Editor
Susan Colgan ...................Managing Editor
Jerry Demoney ...................Art Director
M. J. Madigan ...............Book Review Editor
Ruth Johnston ...................Production Director
Dion Birney ...................Production Editor
**Desc.:** Edited for collectors of the fine and
　decorative arts. Emphasizes American
　painting to 1940 and pre-1940
　decorative arts of all cultures.
**Readers:** Collectors, dealers, museum
　curators.

25618
## ARTFORUM INTERNATIONAL MAGAZINE
65 Bleecker St.
New York, NY 10012
Telephone: (212) 475-4000
FAX: (212) 529-1257
Year Established: 1962
Pub. Frequency: 10/yr.
Page Size: oversize
Subscrip. Rate: $7/yr.; $46/yr.
Freelance Pay: varies
Circulation: 30,000
Circulation Type: paid
**Owner(s):**
Artforum International Magazine
65 Bleecker St.
New York, NY 10012
Telephone: (212) 475-4000
Ownership %: 100
**Management:**
Anthony Korner ...............................Publisher
Knight Landesman ...........Advertising Manager
**Editorial:**
Jack Bankowsky ...............................Editor
Timothy Mennell ...................Managing Editor
Charles Guarino ...................Associate Publisher
**Desc.:** Commentary on and criticism of
　contemporary and avant-garde art.
**Readers:** Artists, art students, teachers,
　libraries, museums, gallery curators, the
　art-buying public, collectors.

25620
## ARTNEWS
48 W. 38th St.
New York, NY 10018
Telephone: (212) 398-1690
FAX: (212) 819-0394
Year Established: 1902
Pub. Frequency: 10/yr.
Page Size: standard
Subscrip. Rate: $6 newsstand; $32.95/yr.
　US; $52.95/yr. Canada; $67.95/yr.
　foreign
Circulation: 74,000
Circulation Type: paid
**Owner(s):**
ARTnews Associates
Ownership %: 100
**Management:**
Milton Esterow ...............................President
Milton Esterow ...............................Publisher
Arnold Obler ...................Advertising Manager
**Editorial:**
Steven Henry Madoff ...............Executive Editor
Milton Esterow ...............................Editor
Deidre Stein ...................Managing Editor
Ron De Feo ...................Book Review Editor
**Desc.:** The art world's only complete news
　magazine. It provides news, reviews &
　essays on the art world, profiles &
　interviews, articles on topical issues.
**Readers:** Collectors, museum directors,
　curators, art dealers, artists, art
　historians, architects and designers.

25621
## ART NOW GALLERY GUIDE
97 Grayrock Rd.
Clinton, NJ 08809
Telephone: (908) 638-5255
FAX: (908) 638-8737
Mailing Address:
　P.O. Box 5541
　Clinton, NJ 08809
Year Established: 1970
Pub. Frequency: 11/yr.
Page Size: pocket
Subscrip. Rate: $4.95 newsstand; $35/yr.
Circulation: 100,000
Circulation Type: paid
**Owner(s):**
Art Now, Inc.
P.O. Box 219
Scotch Plains, NJ 07076
Telephone: (201) 322-8333
Ownership %: 100
**Management:**
Roger M. Peskin ...............................Publisher
**Editorial:**
Susan Housewent ...............................Editor
Lia Kudless ...............................Editor
Ellen Gwynn ...............................Editor
Valerie Frasca ...............................Editor
Bridget Daley ...............................Editor
Laurie Carroll ...............................Editor
Bernice Shor ...................Managing Editor
Minnie Carbo ...............Administrative Assistant
Ed Cole ...................Production Editor
Mary Ann Kuzinitz ...............................Treasurer
**Desc.:** A listing directory for galleries and
　museums of their exhibitions. All listings
　are paid advertising. Nine editions are
　published: International (includes all 8
　regions), New York, Europe,
　Boston/New England, Southeast
　Chicago/ Midwest, Southwest,
　Philadelphia, West Coast.
**Readers:** Persons interested in art,
　collecting andand museums.

65423
## ART OF THE WEST
15612 Hwy. 7, #235
Minnetonka, MN 55345
Telephone: (612) 935-5850
FAX: (612) 935-6546

**Materials Accepted/Included:** 01-Business news 02-By-line articles 03-Fashion news 04-Food news 05-Freelance copy 06-Letters to editor 07-Real estate news 08-Sports news 09-Travel news 10-Book rev. 11-Movie rev. 12-Music rev. 13-TV rev. 14-Theater rev. 15-Coming events 16-Obituaries 17-Question & answer 18-Social announcements 19-Artwork 20-Cartoons 21-Photos 22-TV listings 23-Audio rec. 24-Video rec. 25-Books 26-Films/film clips 27-Personnel news 28-Press releases 29-New product news/photos 30-Trade lit. 31-Contracts awarded 32-Display adv. 33-Classified adv.

6-4

Mailing Address:
P.O. Box 1702
Minnetonka, MN 55345-9900
Year Established: 1987
Pub. Frequency: bi-m.
Page Size: four-color photos/art
Subscrip. Rate: $4.50 newsstand US; $6
Canada; $21/yr.; $37/2 yrs.
Materials: 06,19,32
Print Process: web
Circulation: 25,000
Circulation Type: paid
**Owner(s):**
Thomas F. Tierney
15612 Hwy. 7, 235
Minnetonka, MN 55345
Telephone: (612) 935-5850
FAX: (612) 935-6546
Ownership %: 50

Allan J. Duerr
15612 Hwy. 7, 235
Minnetonka, MN 55345
Telephone: (612) 935-5850
FAX: (612) 935-6546
Ownership %: 50
**Management:**
Allan J. Duerr .........................................Publisher
Thomas F. Tierney ...............................Publisher
**Editorial:**
Vicki Stavig .................................................Editor
**Desc.:** Features new and established
artists who will bring the beauty,
excitement, and deep roots of your
heritage through a wide variety of
western art subject matter. Covers
landscape and seascapes, Native
American art, mountain men art, and
cowboy art, from the old Wild West days
to the working cowboy of today.
**Readers:** Art gallery owners, collectors
and admirers of western paintings,
sculptures, pottery, cast papers, prints
and crafts.
**Deadline:** ads-45 days prior to pub. date

68733
## ARTS INDIANA
47 S. Pennsylvania, Ste. 701
Indianapolis, IN 46204-3620
Telephone: (317) 632-7894
FAX: (317) 632-7966
Year Established: 1979
Pub. Frequency: 10/yr.
Page Size: oversize
Subscrip. Rate: $3.50 newsstand; $22/yr.
Materials: 05,06,10,12,14,19,20
Freelance Pay: varies
Circulation: 12,000
Circulation Type: paid
**Owner(s):**
Arts Indiana, Inc.
47 S. Pennsylvania, Ste. 701
Indianapolis, IN 46204
Telephone: (317) 632-7894
Ownership %: 100
**Editorial:**
Richard J. Roberts ......................................Editor
**Desc.:** Devoted to statewide coverage of
the visual, literary and performing arts in
Indiana.
**Deadline:** story-3 mo. prior to pub. date;
news-70 days prior to pub. date; photo-
70-90 days prior to pub. date

69774
## COUNTRY FOLK ART MAGAZINE
8393 E. Holly Rd.
Holly, MI 48442
Telephone: (313) 634-9675
FAX: (313) 634-0301
Year Established: 1988
Pub. Frequency: bi-m.
Subscrip. Rate: $4.95/issue

**Owner(s):**
Long Publications, Inc.
8393 E. Holly Rd.
Holly, MI 48442
Telephone: (313) 634-9675
Ownership %: 100
**Editorial:**
Tanya Lane ...............................Managing Editor

68734
## NEW ART EXAMINER
1255 S. Wabash Ave., 4th Fl.
Chicago, IL 60605-2427
Telephone: (312) 786-0200
FAX: (312) 786-1565
Year Established: 1973
Pub. Frequency: 10/yr.
Page Size: standard
Subscrip. Rate: $4.75 newsstand; $35/yr.
Materials: 06,27,28,32,33
Freelance Pay: $40-$300/article
Circulation: 20,000
Circulation Type: paid
**Owner(s):**
Chicago New Art Association
1255 S. Wabash Ave., 4th Fl.
Chicago, IL 60605-2427
Telephone: (312) 786-0200
Ownership %: 100
**Editorial:**
Ann Wiens ...................................................Editor
**Desc.:** Contains commentary on and
analysis of the exhibition and making of
the visual arts.

67247
## RUG HOOKING
500 Vaughn St.
Harrisburg, PA 17110-2220
Telephone: (717) 234-5091
FAX: (717) 234-1359
Year Established: 1989
Pub. Frequency: bi-m.
Page Size: standard
Subscrip. Rate: $6.95 newsstand;
$24.95/yr.
Circulation: 10,869
Circulation Type: paid
**Owner(s):**
Stackpole Books
5067 Ritter Rd.
Mechanicsburg, PA 17055
Telephone: (717) 234-5091
Ownership %: 100
**Management:**
David Detweiler ......................................President
David Detweiler ......................................Publisher
Diana Marcum ..................Advertising Manager
**Editorial:**
MacDonald Kennedy .................................Editor

69781
## SOUTHWEST ART
5444 Westheimer, Ste. 1440
Houston, TX 77056-0535
Telephone: (713) 850-0990
FAX: (713) 850-1314
Mailing Address:
P.O. Box 460535
Houston, TX 77056-0535
Year Established: 1971
Pub. Frequency: m.
Page Size: standard
Subscrip. Rate: $4.95/copy; $32/yr.
Materials: 02,05,06,15,16,17,19,21,25,28
Freelance Pay: $400
Print Process: web
Circulation: 70,698
**Owner(s):**
CBH Publishing, Inc.
P.O. Box 460535
Houston, TX 77256-0535
Telephone: (713) 850-0990
FAX: (713) 850-1314
Ownership %: 100
**Management:**
Clay B. Hall ............................................President

John Fair ................................................Controller
Robert Phillips III ..................................Publisher
**Editorial:**
Susan Hallsten McGarry ...........................Editor
Mary Mizwa .......................Circulation Director
Janet Meyer ......................Production Director
**Desc.:** Artists, events and trends in the
representational fine arts west of the
Mississippi River. Feature articles and
columns entertain and inform, building
reader appreciation of fine arts as well as
consumer confidence in making art-
buying decisions.
**Readers:** SWA readers are male (43%)
and female (57%) art buyers (average
age 58) who purchase much of their art
out of town (9 trips/yr.). They are
college educated with an annual income
of $125,499. They spend 3 hours with
each issue and 98% claim to have
taken action based on reading SWA.
**Deadline:** story-4 mos. prior to pub. date;
news-3 mos. prior; photo-3 mos. prior;
ads-1 1/2 mos. prior

65370
## TREASURE CHEST
2112 Broadway - #414
New York, NY 10023
Telephone: (212) 496-2234
Year Established: 1988
Pub. Frequency: m.
Page Size: tabloid
Subscrip. Rate: $25/yr.; $40/2 yrs.; $55/3
yrs.
Materials: 02,05,10,15,19,20,25,28,30,32,33
Freelance Pay: negotiable
Circulation: 50,000
Circulation Type: free & paid
**Owner(s):**
Venture Publsihing Co.
2112 Broadway - #414
New York, NY 10023
Telephone: (212) 496-2234
Ownership %: 100
**Management:**
Howard E. Fischer ................................Publisher
**Desc.:** The information source &
marketplace for collectors & dealers of
antiques & collectibles-calendar of
events, feature articles, cartoons &
illustrations, advertising-display &
classified, freelancers encouraged.
**Readers:** Collectors, dealers & others
interested in antiques & collectibles.
**Deadline:** ads-20th of mo. prior to pub.
date

69347
## WILDLIFE ART NEWS
4725 Highway 7
St. Louis Park, MN 55416-0246
Telephone: (612) 927-9056
FAX: (612) 927-9353
Mailing Address:
P.O. Box 16246
St. Louis Park, MN 55416
Year Established: 1982
Pub. Frequency: bi-m.
Subscrip. Rate: $29.95/yr.
Circulation: 55,000
Circulation Type: paid
**Owner(s):**
Pothole Publications, Inc.
P.O. Box 16246
St. Louis Park, MN 55416-0246
Telephone: (612) 927-9056
Ownership %: 100
**Desc.:** Contains interviews with artists, a
calendar of events, and business news.

**Readers:** For wildlife art collectors.

## Group 608-Automobiles and Accessories

65699
## AAA DELAWARE MOTORIST
875 AAA Blvd.
Newark, DE 19713
Telephone: (215) 864-5455
FAX: (215) 568-1153
Year Established: 1966
Pub. Frequency: 6/yr.
Page Size: tabloid
Subscrip. Rate: $1/yr. AAA members
Circulation: 55,600
Circulation Type: controlled
**Owner(s):**
AAA Mid-Atlantic, Inc.
2040 Market St.
Philadelphia, PA 19103
Telephone: (215) 864-5455
Ownership %: 100
**Management:**
Edward L. Jones, Jr. ...........Chairman of Board
Robert R. Rugel ...................................President
**Editorial:**
John C. Moyer ...........................................Editor
Birchard T. Clothier .......Secretary & Treasurer
William J. Clarke ....................................Treasurer
**Desc.:** Automotive and travel interest.
Paper is tailored to a membership
consisting of motorists and travelers.
Departments include: Automotive,
Travel, Government Regulations, RVs,
Camping Attractions, Leisure-Time
Activities.
**Readers:** Circulation exclusively among
automobile club members.

65700
## AAA SHORE MOTORIST
2040 Market St.
Philadelphia, PA 19103
Telephone: (215) 864-5455
FAX: (215) 568-1153
Year Established: 1970
Pub. Frequency: 6/yr.
Page Size: tabloid
Subscrip. Rate: $1/yr. AAA members
Circulation: 29,000
Circulation Type: controlled
**Owner(s):**
AAA Mid-Atlantic, Inc.
2040 Market St.
Philadelphia, PA 19103
Telephone: (215) 864-5455
Ownership %: 100
**Management:**
Edward L. Jones, Jr. ...........Chairman of Board
Robert R. Rugel ...................................President
**Editorial:**
John C. Moyer ...........................................Editor
Birchard T. Clothier .......Secretary & Treasurer
**Desc.:** Material must be of automotive or
travel interest; paper is tailored to a
membership consisting of motorists and
travelers. Departments include:
Automotive, Travel, Government
Regulations, Camping Attractions,
Leisure-Time Activities.
**Readers:** Circulation exclusively among
automobile club members.

69157
## AMERICAN RODDER
28210 Dorothy Dr.
Agoura Hills, CA 91301
Telephone: (818) 889-8740
FAX: (818) 889-4726
Mailing Address:
P.O. Box 3075
Agoura Hills, CA 91301
Year Established: 1987
Pub. Frequency: m.

**Materials Accepted/Included:** 01-Business news 02-By-line articles 03-Fashion news 04-Food news 05-Freelance copy 06-Letters to editor 07-Real estate news 08-Sports news 09-Travel news
10-Book rev. 11-Movie rev. 12-Music rev. 13-TV rev. 14-Theater rev. 15-Coming events 16-Obituaries 17-Question & answer 18-Social announcements 19-Artwork 20-Cartoons 21-Photos 22-TV listings
23-Audio rec. 24-Video rec. 25-Books 26-Films/film clips 27-Personnel news 28-Press releases 29-New product news/photos 30-Trade lit. 31-Contracts awarded 32-Display adv. 33-Classified adv.

6-5

Page Size: standard
Subscrip. Rate: $3.50 newsstand;
　$29.95/yr.; $46/2 yrs.
Materials: 32
Print Process: offset
Circulation: 59,119
Circulation Type: paid
**Owner(s):**
Paisano Publications, Inc.
28210 Dorothy Dr.
Agoura Hills, CA 91301
Telephone: (818) 889-8740
Ownership %: 100
**Management:**
Lizette Hotinger .................Advertising Manager
Lisa Lennard ....................Circulation Manager
**Editorial:**
Joe Kress ...............................................Editor

25638
## AREA AUTO RACING NEWS
2829-31 S. Broad St.
Trenton, NJ 08610
Telephone: (609) 888-3618
FAX: (609) 888-2538
Mailing Address:
　P.O. Box 8547
　Trenton, NJ 08650-0547
Year Established: 1963
Pub. Frequency: w.
Page Size: tabloid
Subscrip. Rate: $1.50 newsstand; $33/yr.
Materials: 01,02,06,08,13,15,16,17,21,22,
　24,25,26,27,28,29,30,32,33
Print Process: web offset
Circulation: 72,000
Circulation Type: paid
**Owner(s):**
Area Auto Racing News, Inc.
Ownership %: 100
**Management:**
Lenny H. Sammons ...........................President
Lenny H. Sammons ...........................Publisher
**Editorial:**
Lenny H. Sammons ...............................Editor
Joe Pratt ......................................Advertising
**Desc.:** Any or all types of automobile
　racing articles are covered. All features,
　news stories, new products, are of
　interest to the auto racing fan.
**Readers:** Anyone interested in auto racing.
**Deadline:** story-Mon., 12:00 pm prior to
　pub. date; news-Mon., 12:00 pm prior;
　photo-Mon., 12:00 pm prior; ads-Mon.,
　12:00 pm prior

61662
## AUTOMOBILE
200 Madison Ave.
New York, NY 10016
Telephone: (212) 447-4778
Year Established: 1986
Pub. Frequency: m.
Page Size: standard
Subscrip. Rate: $18/yr.; $26/yr. foreign
Circulation: 575,000
Circulation Type: controlled
**Owner(s):**
K-III Magazines
200 Madison Ave.
New York, NY 10016
Telephone: (212) 447-4700
Ownership %: 100
**Bureau(s):**
Michigan Bureau
120 E. Liberty
Ann Arbor, MI 48104
Telephone: (313) 994-3500
**Management:**
Terrance Russell ...............................Publisher
**Editorial:**
David E. Davis, Jr. .................................Editor
Jean Lindamood .......................Deputy Editor
David E. Davis, Jr. .............Publication Director

**Desc.:** Seeks to entertain as much as to
　inform; it is filled with pictures of great
　cars in beautiful surroundings; and it
　defines great cars as those that are fast,
　fun to drive, unique in their technical
　specifications, or important in a historic
　or classic sense. It is an automotive
　magazine created by writers, artists,
　designers, and editors, not mechanical
　engineers.
**Readers:** Sophisticated young car
　enthusiasts who do not take themselves
　or the world too seriously.

26365
## AUTOWEEK
1400 Woodbridge Ave.
Detroit, MI 48207-3187
Telephone: (313) 446-6000
FAX: (313) 446-1650
Year Established: 1958
Pub. Frequency: w.
Page Size: standard
Subscrip. Rate: $28/yr.
Circulation: 268,595
Circulation Type: paid
**Owner(s):**
Crain Communications, Inc.
1400 Woodbridge Ave.
Detroit, MI 48207
Telephone: (313) 446-6000
Ownership %: 100
**Management:**
Leon Mandel ......................................Publisher
Jay Mc Kenzie .................Advertising Manager
**Editorial:**
Matt De Lorenzo ...........................Senior Editor
James D. Sawyer ...................Managing Editor
Keith Crain ........................Editorial Director
Charles Krasner ...............................Art Director
Kevin A. Wilson ...............................News Editor
Larry Edsall ..............................................Sports
**Desc.:** Consumer newsmagazine
　concerned with motoring. Departments
　include competition and competitive
　motorsports; world news (consumer and
　product information); Yesterday
　(nostalgia and collector's cars); Driving
　Impressions, and Travel.
**Readers:** Automotive enthusiasts.

66613
## BRASS LAMP, THE
8868 Rock Forest Dr.
St. Louis, MO 63123-1116
Telephone: (314) 849-5249
Year Established: 1944
Pub. Frequency: m.
Page Size: standard
Subscrip. Rate: includes yearly
　membership to Horseless Carriage Club
Materials: 01,10,21,24
Print Process: offset
Circulation: 1,000
Circulation Type: controlled
**Owner(s):**
Horseless Carriage Club of Missouri, Inc.
8868 Rock Forest Dr.
St. Louis, MO 63123-1116
Telephone: (314) 849-5249
Ownership %: 100
**Editorial:**
Gerald Perschbacher ..............Managing Editor
**Desc.:** Interested in receiving press
　material (photos and releases) on
　current new vehicles in the USA
　and overseas; similar material re: history
　of automobiles. Purpose: to educate and
　inform the readership (membership) on
　current and past trends regarding the
　history of motorized vehicles. Antique
　auto material accepted. Reviews on
　books and videos included in
　publication.

**Readers:** Mainly St. Louis area, but also
　includes readers in Illinois and Missouri
　leaders in business & society.
**Deadline:** story-1st of mo. prior to pub.
　date

26379
## CAR & DRIVER
2002 Hogback Rd.
Ann Arbor, MI 48105
Telephone: (313) 971-3600
FAX: (313) 971-9188
Year Established: 1955
Pub. Frequency: m.
Page Size: standard
Subscrip. Rate: $35.40/yr.
Circulation: 1,000,000
Circulation Type: paid
**Owner(s):**
Hachette Filipacchi Magazines, Inc.
New York, NY
Telephone: (212) 767-4500
Ownership %: 100
**Management:**
William Jeanes ...............................Publisher
**Editorial:**
Csaba Csere .........................................Editor
**Desc.:** Latest news, features and reports
　on new cars both imported and
　domestic are treated in depth.
　Road tests are conducted by an expert
　full-time staff. Other features are
　handled by name authors and writers in
　the field. Photography is both technical
　and artistic in nature and is of top
　quality; all features must be extensively
　illustrated. Standards are high but so are
　the rates of payment to satisfy one of
　the largest car readerships in the world.
**Readers:** Well educated, well-heeled men
　and women around the world interested
　in up-to-date opinion and information on
　automotive subjects. This publication is
　also a source of entertainment because
　all material is prepared in a witty and
　thought-provoking style.

65347
## CAR AUDIO & ELECTRONICS
21700 Oxnard St., Ste. 1600
Woodland Hills, CA 91367
Telephone: (818) 593-3900
FAX: (818) 593-2274
Year Established: 1988
Pub. Frequency: m.
Page Size: standard
Subscrip. Rate: $21.95/yr.
Materials: 02,05,06,15,19,21,23,28,29,32
Freelance Pay: varies
Circulation: 128,000
Circulation Type: paid
**Owner(s):**
Car Audio And Electronics
**Bureau(s):**
New York
237 Park Ave., 21st Fl.
New York, NY 10017
Telephone: (212) 551-3516
Contact: Myles Fuchs, Advertising Manager
**Management:**
Jeannie Kane ...................................Publisher
**Editorial:**
William Neill .........................................Editor
**Desc.:** Emphasizes audio equipment, radar
　detectors, security systems soundoffs,
　along with product test reports.
**Readers:** Teenagers and young urban
　professionals.

21795
## CAR CRAFT MAGAZINE
6420 Wilshire Blvd.
Los Angeles, CA 90048
Telephone: (213) 782-2000
FAX: (310) 854-2263
Year Established: 1953
Pub. Frequency: m.

Page Size: standard
Subscrip. Rate: $19.94/yr.
Freelance Pay: $750 & up/feature
Circulation: 441,448
Circulation Type: paid
**Owner(s):**
Petersen Publishing Co.
8490 Sunset Blvd.
Los Angeles, CA 90069
Telephone: (310) 854-2222
Ownership %: 100
**Management:**
Robert E. Petersen .................................Owner
Robert E. Petersen ...........Chairman of Board
Fred Waingrow ...............................President
Peter Clancey ...........................Vice President
Bruce Bakke ......................................Publisher
Leonard Emanuelson .........................Publisher
**Editorial:**
Marlan Davis .............................Senior Editor
John Baechtel ......................................Editor
Bennie Clark Allen ..................Managing Editor
Tim McGowan .....................Editorial Director
Deborah Woodworth .................Administrative
　　　　　　　　　　　　　　　　　　Assistant
Alan Huber ......................................Art Director
Pennie French ....................Assistant Publisher
J. P. Huffman ..........................Associate Editor
Jon Asher ...........................Contributing Editor
Brian Kaya ............................Editorial Assistant
Michael Johnson .......Special Projects Director
**Desc.:** A street machine magazine dealing
　with 1955 and later vehicles.
**Readers:** For 18-34 males, who are do-it-
　yourself enthusiasts, whose interests lie
　in later model personalized street
　machines, drag- racing, superior
　handling, performance and appearance.

65129
## CAR STEREO REVIEW
1633 Broadway, 45th Fl.
New York, NY 10019
Telephone: (212) 767-6020
FAX: (212) 767-5615
Year Established: 1987
Pub. Frequency: bi-m.
Page Size: standard
Subscrip. Rate: $3.50 newsstand;
　$16.98/yr.
Materials: 01,02,05,06,12,15,16,19,20,21,
　23,24,25,28,29,30,32
Freelance Pay: $700/article, $300/column
Circulation: 110,000
Circulation Type: paid
**Owner(s):**
Hachette Filipacchi Magazines, Inc.
1633 Broadway
New York, NY 10019
Telephone: (212) 767-6010
Ownership %: 100
**Management:**
Tom Witschi .....................................Publisher
**Editorial:**
Marc Horowitz .........................Senior Editor
Bill Wolfe ...........................................Editor
Mike Mettler ..........................Managing Editor
Laura Sutcliffe ...............................Art Director
Peter Barry, Michael ............Associate Editors
Gelfand
Jose Garcia .................Database Coordinator
Barbara Aiken ......................Project Coordinator
**Desc.:** Dedicated to providing the latest
　(and last) word on buying, installing, and
　using car stereo and mobile electronics
　equipment.
**Readers:** Consumer enthusiasts
**Deadline:** story-1st of mo. prior to pub.
　date; news-1st of mo. prior; photo-1st of
　mo. prior; ads-1st of mo. prior

## CHEVY HIGH PERFORMANCE
66702

6420 Wilshire Blvd.
Los Angeles, CA 90048
Telephone: (213) 782-2000
FAX: (213) 782-2263
Year Established: 1985
Pub. Frequency: bi-m.
Subscrip. Rate: $3.95 newsstand;
$13.95/yr.
Circulation: 103,160
Circulation Type: paid
**Owner(s):**
Petersen Publishing Co.
6420 Wilshire Blvd.
Los Angeles, CA 90048
Telephone: (213) 854-2222
FAX: (213) 782-2263
Ownership %: 100
**Management:**
John Dianna .....................Vice President
**Editorial:**
Mike Magda .................................Editor
Don Evans .....................Editorial Director
Rochelle Kanott ...............Design Editor

## DRIVE!
69515

3470 Buskirt Ave.
Pleasant Hill, CA 94523
Telephone: (510) 934-3700
FAX: (510) 934-3958
Year Established: 1986
Pub. Frequency: m.
Page Size: oversize
Subscrip. Rate: free newsstand; $32/yr.
1st class; $18/yr. 3rd class
Circulation: 100,000
Circulation Type: paid
**Owner(s):**
Bam Publications, Inc.
3470 Buskirk Ave.
Pleasant Hill, CA 94523
Telephone: (510) 934-3700
Ownership %: 100
**Editorial:**
Pete Biro .....................................Editor
**Readers:** California car and truck
enthusiasts.

## DRIVING
25126

One Hanover Rd.
Florham Park, NJ 07932-1888
Telephone: (201) 377-7200
Year Established: 1969
Pub. Frequency: bi-m.
Page Size: tabloid
Subscrip. Rate: $4/yr.
Materials: 09,10,21,32
Circulation: 165,000
Circulation Type: controlled
**Owner(s):**
N.J. Automobile Club (AAA)
One Hanover Rd.
Florham Park, NJ 07932
Telephone: (201) 377-7200
Ownership %: 100
**Management:**
Frederick L. Gruel ...................Publisher
**Editorial:**
Betsy Adey ...............Executive Editor
Pam Fischer ..............................Editor
**Desc.:** Offers travel information - tips,
discounts & advice for membership - car
care, insurance & safety information &
legislative updates of importance to the
traveling/motoring public.
**Readers:** Club members - N.J. Automobile
Club (AAA).
**Deadline:** story-2 mo. prior to pub. date;
news-2 mo. prior to pub. date; photo-2
mo. prior; ads-2 mo. prior

## DUNE BUGGIES & HOT VW'S
25647

2950 Airway A7
Costa Mesa, CA 92626
Telephone: (714) 979-2560
FAX: (714) 979-3998
Mailing Address:
P.O. Box 2260
Costa Mesa, CA 92628
Year Established: 1967
Pub. Frequency: m.
Page Size: standard
Subscrip. Rate: $19.97/yr.
Freelance Pay: $75/pg.
Circulation: 101,000
Circulation Type: paid
**Owner(s):**
Wright Publishing Co., Inc.
2950 Airway A7
Costa Mesa, CA 92626
Telephone: (714) 979-2560
Ownership %: 100
**Management:**
Judy Wright .............................President
Judy Wright ..............................Publisher
Linda Dill .................Advertising Manager
Tom Chambers ...............General Manager
**Editorial:**
Bruce Simurda ...........................Editor
John Pilcher ......................Art Director
Dean Kirsten ................................Photo
**Desc.:** Coverage includes new car
features, races, technical, how-to-build,
new products, technical question and
answer column, personalities, club news.
Features generally 2-4 pages, use some
photospread features.
**Readers:** Single males-early 20's.

## EUROPEAN CAR
67082

12100 Wilshire Blvd., 250
Los Angeles, CA 90025
Telephone: (310) 820-3601
FAX: (310) 207-9388
Mailing Address:
P.O. Box 49659
Los Angeles, CA 90049
Year Established: 1971
Pub. Frequency: 12/yr.
Page Size: standard
Subscrip. Rate: $18.80/yr.
Materials: 05,24,25,28,29
Freelance Pay: $100/pg.
Circulation: 84,000
Circulation Type: paid
**Owner(s):**
Argus Publishers Corporation
12100 Wilshire Blvd., 250
Los Angeles, CA 90025
Telephone: (310) 820-3601
FAX: (310) 207-9388
Ownership %: 100
**Management:**
Jeff Morton .................Advertising Manager
**Editorial:**
Greg Brown ...............................Editor
Stephanie Wolfe .............Managing Editor
**Desc.:** Covers European marques,
aftermarket products, replacement parts,
restorations, and how-to-do-it, where-to-
get-it articles.

## EXCELLENCE
67282

42 Digital Dr. #5
Novato, CA 94949
Telephone: (415) 382-0580
FAX: (415) 382-0587
Mailing Address:
P.O. Box 1529
Ross, CA 94957
Year Established: 1987
Pub. Frequency: 8/yr.
Page Size: standard
Subscrip. Rate: $20/yr.
Circulation: 40,000

Circulation Type: paid
**Owner(s):**
Ross Periodicals, Inc.
P.O. Box 1529
Ross, CA 94957
Telephone: (415) 382-0580
Ownership %: 100
**Management:**
Stan Michelman ...............Advertising Manager
**Editorial:**
Thomas Toldrian .........................Editor
**Readers:** Porsche fanatics

## FAMILY MOTOR COACHING
25077

8291 Clough Pike
Cincinnati, OH 45244
Telephone: (513) 474-3622
FAX: (513) 474-2332
Mailing Address:
P.O. Box 44209
Cincinnati, OH 45244
Year Established: 1963
Pub. Frequency: m.
Page Size: standard
Subscrip. Rate: $2.95 newsstand; $24/yr.
Materials: 32,33
Freelance Pay: negotiable
Print Process: offset
Circulation: 96,000
Circulation Type: controlled
**Owner(s):**
Family Motor Coach Association
P.O. Box 44209
Cincinnati, OH 45244
Telephone: (513) 474-3622
Ownership %: 100
**Management:**
Virginia Bauman .......................Publisher
Virginia Bauman ...............Advertising Manager
**Editorial:**
Pamela Kay ...............................Editor
Candy Johnson ......................Art Director
Catherine Crowley .........Production Coordinator
**Desc.:** Featured are articles on travel and
recreation, association news, meetings,
activities, and conventions plus articles
on facets of motorhome life and new
products.
**Readers:** Members and prospective
members of the Family Motor Coach
Association considering the purchase of
recreational vehicles of the motor home
state.

## FOUR WHEELER MAGAZINE
25649

6728 Eton Ave.
Canoga Park, CA 91303
Telephone: (818) 992-4777
FAX: (818) 992-4979
Year Established: 1962
Pub. Frequency: m.
Page Size: standard
Subscrip. Rate: $2.95/issue; $17.87/yr.
Freelance Pay: $100/page
Circulation: 323,731
**Owner(s):**
General Media Internatioal
Ownership %: 100
**Management:**
Patrick Gavin ...........................President
**Editorial:**
John Stewart ...............................Editor
Doug McCollach .............Managing Editor
Christopher Ballard ............Advertising Director
Willie Worthy .............................Columnist
Peter MacGillivray ...............Feature Editor
Ken Von Helmolt ...............Technical Editor
Greg Whale ...............................Writer
Jill Bohna ...................................Writer
Jimmy Nylund ...............................Writer

**Desc.:** Content includes some of the
following each month - 4 x 4 road tests,
competition events, technical how-to
stories, and features which include
travel stories, specific vehicles, and
tests on other equipment used by four
wheelers. Use both color transparencies,
and black & white (8 x 10 glossy
photos). Articles run from 1-6 pages, the
average being 2-3. Have staff coverage
and buy-outs. Columns: Backcountry.
Departments: Letters - reader feedback,
Keep on Truckin - industry news,
Readers' Rigs - custom showcase,
Getting There, Tech Line - for the
greasy fingernail set, What's New - new
products, Off - Road Calendar - coming
events, Rear View - reader's photo.
**Readers:** 97% male, median age: 28-53
years; median income $33,430.

## HEMMINGS MOTOR NEWS
69773

P.O. Box 256
Bennington, VT 05201
Telephone: (802) 442-3101
FAX: (802) 447-1561
Year Established: 1954
Pub. Frequency: m.
Subscrip. Rate: $23.95/yr.
Circulation: 265,000
Circulation Type: controlled & paid
**Owner(s):**
Watering, Inc.
P.O. Box 256
Bennington, VT 05201
Telephone: (800) 227-4373
Ownership %: 100
**Editorial:**
Terry Ehrich ...............................Editor

## HOT ROD
26412

6420 Wilshire Blvd.
Los Angeles, CA 90048
Telephone: (213) 782-2000
FAX: (213) 782-2223
Year Established: 1948
Pub. Frequency: m.
Page Size: standard
Subscrip. Rate: $19.94/yr.
Freelance Pay: varies
Circulation: 800,000
Circulation Type: paid
**Owner(s):**
Petersen Publishing Co.
6420 Wilshire Blvd.
Los Angeles, CA 90048
Telephone: (213) 782-2000
**Management:**
Fred Waingrow ...........................President
John Dianna .....................Vice President
Jim Savas .................................Publisher
Nancy Schwartz ...............Editorial Production
Manager
**Editorial:**
Jeff Smith ...............Executive Editor
Gray Baskerville ............Senior Editor
Drew Hardin ...............................Editor
Cecily Chittick ...............Managing Editor
Donald R. Evans ...............Editorial Director
Peter Clancey ...............................Advertising
Joe Pettitt ...............Feature Editor
Marlan Davis ...............Technical Editor
**Readers:** Readers are from 18 to 34, high-
performance aftermarket automotive
enthusiasts interested in the hands-on
approach to hot rodding.

## MIDWEST RACING NEWS
26419

6646 W. Fairview Ave.
Milwaukee, WI 53213
Telephone: (414) 778-4700
FAX: (414) 778-4688
Year Established: 1959

**Materials Accepted/Included:** 01-Business news 02-By-line articles 03-Fashion news 04-Food news 05-Freelance copy 06-Letters to editor 07-Real estate news 08-Sports news 09-Travel news 10-Book rev. 11-Movie rev. 12-Music rev. 13-TV rev. 14-Theater rev. 15-Coming events 16-Obituaries 17-Question & answer 18-Social announcements 19-Artwork 20-Cartoons 21-Photos 22-TV listings 23-Audio rec. 24-Video rec. 25-Books 26-Films/film clips 27-Personnel news 28-Press releases 29-New product news/photos 30-Trade lit. 31-Contracts awarded 32-Display adv. 33-Classified adv.

6-7

Pub. Frequency: w. (Apr.-Sep.); m. (Oct.-Mar.)
Page Size: tabloid
Subscrip. Rate: $1 newsstand; $30/yr.; $36/2 yrs.
Materials: 01,02,05,06,08,09,10,11,13,15, 16,17,19,20,22,28,29,32,33
Freelance Pay: none
Print Process: web
Circulation: 12,000
Circulation Type: controlled & paid
**Owner(s):**
Midwest Racing News, Inc.
6646 W. Fairview Ave.
Milwaukee, WI 53213
Telephone: (414) 778-4700
FAX: (414) 778-4688
Ownership %: 100
**Management:**
Wanda Wilson ...................Circulation Manager
**Editorial:**
Dave Haberkorn ..............................Editor
James Wehner ........................Managing Editor
Dean Strom ......................................Advertising
Gerry Belsha ...........................Associate Editor
Mary Champion .....................................Layout
Jennifer Moeller .......................Miscellaneous
Miscell Staff ..................................Staff Writer
**Desc.:** Stories or features pertaining to news concerning the sport of automobile or motor racing. By-lined articles accepted if material meets requirements and is of general interest to the race-minded public.
**Readers:** Auto racing fans, drivers, mechanics, etc.
**Deadline:** story-Mon., 12:00 pm prior to pub. date; news-Mon., 12:00 pm prior; photo-Mon., 12:00 pm prior; ads-Mon., 12:00 pm prior

**MOTORHOME**                                      25082
3601 Calle Tecate
Camarillo, CA 93012
Telephone: (805) 389-0300
FAX: (805) 389-0484
Mailing Address:
    P.O. Box 6060
    Camarillo, CA 93011
Year Established: 1963
Pub. Frequency: m.
Page Size: standard
Subscrip. Rate: $2.95 newsstand; $26/yr.
Materials: 02,05,09,17,21,29,30,32,33
Freelance Pay: $150-$800/article
Circulation: 148,000
Circulation Type: paid
**Owner(s):**
T.L. Enterprises, Inc.
3601 Calle Tecate
Camarillo, CA 93012
Telephone: (805) 389-0300
Ownership %: 100
**Bureau(s):**
T.L. Enterprises
2300 Middlebury St.
Elkhart, IN 46516
Telephone: (219) 295-7820
Contact: Janet VanBibber, Sales Manager

Thomas E. Strong
18530 Mack Ave., Ste. 317
Detroit, MI 48236
Telephone: (313) 885-0241
Contact: Thomas E. Strong, Advertising Manager
**Management:**
Bill Estes ...................................Publisher
**Editorial:**
Jim Brightly .........................Managing Editor
Barbara Leonard .....................Editorial Director
Barbara Gerbe ....................Circulation Director
Olga Markowitz ................Publication Director

**Desc.:** Feature stories show all phases of motorhome recreation, including travel, maintenance, accessories, custom-builts, rental adventures, reader opinion. Travel features and major personality features are especially encouraged. All feature stories submitted should include both black and white photos and four-color transparencies. Departments include: Guest Editorial, Motorhome Maintenance, Travel Features, Motorhome News, Hotline, From the Road, Product Previews.
**Readers:** Owners and enthusiasts of top-line motorhomes.

**MOTOR TREND MAGAZINE**                     21817
6420 Wilshire Blvd.
Los Angeles, CA 90048
Telephone: (213) 782-2000
FAX: (310) 854-2355
Year Established: 1949
Pub. Frequency: m.
Page Size: standard
Subscrip. Rate: $19.94/yr.
Freelance Pay: negotiable
Circulation: 900,000
Circulation Type: paid
**Owner(s):**
Petersen Publishing Co.
Ownership %: 100
**Management:**
Robert E. Petersen .............Chairman of Board
Fredrick R. Waingrow ........................President
Miles T. Killoch .........................Vice President
Terry Shiver .....................................Publisher
Nigel Heaton ....................Circulation Manager
**Editorial:**
Bob Nagy ..........................Executive Editor
Jeff Karr ..............................................Editor
Jacqueline Manfredi ..............Managing Editor
Susan Perrault ........Associate Managing Editor
Terry Shiver ..................Advertising Director
William Claxton ..........................Art Director
Lonie Mysior ........................Assistant Publisher
Nancy Anderson ............Associate Art Director
Cheryl Bennett ....................Editorial Assistant
Ron Grable ........................Engineering Editor
Lee Kelley ........................Executive Publisher
Jeff Karr ..................................Feature Editor
James Krenek ...................Production Director
Sally Parisi ........................Production Director
Leo D. LaRew .................................Treasurer
**Desc.:** Editorial features average 1,000-2,000 words in length. Subjects covered include news, trends and tests of automotive field/both domestic and foreign. Can use good general-interest pieces on motor sports, automotive and racing personalities (preferably on current scene); photo stories on unusual custom and classic cars. Can consider releases on new automotive products for editorial listing (photo of product appreciated). Most materials staff written or assigned, but welcome submissions.
**Readers:** Motor Trend readership comprises mostly men between the ages of 16-40 who have interests in automobiles, purchasing and/or selling an automobile, and maintenance of their automobiles.

**MOTOR WORLD**                                   69159
951 S. Oxford, No. 109
Los Angeles, CA 90006
Telephone: (213) 732-3477
FAX: (213) 732-9123
Year Established: 1991

Pub. Frequency: q.
Subscrip. Rate: $29.99/yr.
Materials: 01,02,03,04,05,06,07,08,09,10, 11,12,13,14,15,16,17,18,19,20,21,22,23, 24,25,26,27,28,29,30,31,32,33
Freelance Pay: $.20-$.50
Print Process: web
Circulation: 120,000
Circulation Type: controlled & paid
**Owner(s):**
Publishing & Business Consultants
951 S. Oxford, No. 109
Los Angeles, CA 90006
Telephone: (213) 732-3477
FAX: (213) 732-9123
Ownership %: 100
**Editorial:**
Andeson Napoleon Atia ...........................Editor
**Desc.:** Covers automotive maintenance with news of industry trends.
**Deadline:** story-2 wks. prior to pub. date; news-2 wks. prior; photo-2 wks. prior; ads-90 days prior

**MUSCLECARS**                                     69517
299 Market St.
Saddle Brook, NJ 07662
Telephone: (201) 712-9300
FAX: (201) 712-9899
Mailing Address:
    P.O. Box 1010
    Denville, NJ 07834
Year Established: 1983
Pub. Frequency: bi-m.
Page Size: standard
Subscrip. Rate: $3.25 newsstand; $16/yr.
Print Process: offset
Circulation: 40,000
Circulation Type: paid
**Owner(s):**
CSK Publishing Co., Inc.
299 Market St.
Sanddle Brook, NJ 07662
Telephone: (201) 712-9300
Ownership %: 100
**Management:**
Ralph Monti ...................................Publisher
**Editorial:**
Richard Lentinello ...............................Editor
Peter Eston ........................Managing Editor
**Desc.:** For car lovers of the late fifties, sixties and early seventies (1958-1972). Features all musclecars such as GTO, Hemi, Mustang, Chevelle, Camaro.

**MUSTANG & FORDS**                               68889
6420 Wilshire Blvd.
Los Angeles, CA 90048
Telephone: (213) 782-2000
FAX: (213) 782-2263
Year Established: 1980
Pub. Frequency: bi-m.
Page Size: standard
Subscrip. Rate: $3.25 newsstand; $15.95/yr. US; $20.90/yr. foreign
Materials: 32,33
Circulation: 121,000
Circulation Type: paid
**Owner(s):**
Peterson Publishing Co.
6420 Wilshire Blvd.
Los Angeles, CA 90048
Telephone: (213) 782-2000
Ownership %: 100
**Management:**
W. Jeff Young .................................Publisher
Andrea Higgins ................Advertising Manager
**Editorial:**
Jim Smart ........................................Editor

**NATIONAL DRAGSTER**                            26428
2035 Financial Way
Glendora, CA 91740
Telephone: (818) 963-7695
FAX: (818) 335-6651
Mailing Address:
    P.O. Box 5555
    Glendora, CA 91740
Year Established: 1960
Pub. Frequency: 48/yr.
Page Size: tabloid
Subscrip. Rate: $52/yr.
Materials: 06,32,33
Freelance Pay: negotiable
Print Process: web offset
Circulation: 80,000
Circulation Type: paid
**Owner(s):**
National Hot Rod Association
2035 Financial Way
Glendora, CA 91740
Telephone: (818) 963-7695
FAX: (818) 335-6651
Ownership %: 100
**Management:**
Neil Britt ..........................................Publisher
Sandy Wasserbeck ..........Advertising Manager
Maria G. Aguilar ...............Assistant Advertising Manager
Adriane Pierson ..................Business Manager
Robert Jaramillo .........Classified Adv. Manager
Joni Elmslie .................Classified Adv. Manager
Linda Robertson ...................Credit Manager
Paula Alt .......................Production Manager
**Editorial:**
Chris Martin .............................Senior Editor
Phil Burgess ........................................Editor
Vicky Walker .........................Managing Editor
Chuck Hanson .................................Advertising
Jill Flores ......................................Art Director
Billie Petty ......................Circulation Director
Leslie Lovett ..................Photography Editor
**Desc.:** Contains race results from championship drag racing events and reports submitted by dragstrips, and photos on racing. Feature material includes racer personalities, new technical developments, publicity material in drag racing.
**Readers:** Motorsport enthusiasts-85% in 18-34-year-old male age group, drivers, mechanics, high-erformance industry managers & executives.
**Deadline:** ads-15 days prior to pub. date

**OFF-ROAD MAGAZINE**                            25650
12100 Wilshire Blvd., Ste. 250
Los Angeles, CA 90025
Telephone: (310) 820-3601
FAX: (310) 207-9388
Year Established: 1969
Pub. Frequency: m.
Page Size: standard
Subscrip. Rate: $2.95/issue; $14.98/yr.
Freelance Pay: $75-100/page
Circulation: 68,889
Circulation Type: paid
**Owner(s):**
Gordon H. Behn
12301 Wilshire Blvd.
Los Angeles, CA 90025
Telephone: (310) 820-3601
Ownership %: 50

Don Werner
12301 Wilshire Blvd.
Los Angeles, CA 90025
Telephone: (310) 820-3601
Ownership %: 50
**Management:**
Don Werner .....................................President
**Editorial:**
Duane Elliot .....................................Editor

**Desc.:** Editorial slant is directed toward the two and four-wheel-drive genuine recreational vehicle enthusiast. Feature articles deal with new vehicle testing, modification for the do-it-yourselfer, special equipment and accessories. Coverage of major off-road events with action pictures and behind the scenes reports from car owners and drivers give the racing enthusiast tips toward what they might anticipate with their own vehicle. Camping, travel hints, and up to date club information round off the editorial package.
**Readers:** Age 24.1, income $27,838.00.

## OLD CARS NEWS & MARKETPLACE
21825

700 E. State St.
Iola, WI 54990
Telephone: (715) 445-2214
Year Established: 1972
Pub. Frequency: w.
Page Size: tabloid
Subscrip. Rate: $29.95/yr.
Materials: 05,06,10,32,33
Freelance Pay: $.03-$.05/wd.
Circulation: 80,000
Circulation Type: paid
**Owner(s):**
Krause Publications, Inc.
700 E. State St.
Iola, WI 54990
Telephone: (715) 445-2214
Ownership %: 100
**Management:**
Roger Case ............................President
Cliff Mischler ..........................President
John Gunnell ..........................Publisher
Richard Hare ..............Advertising Manager
Suzanne Olkowski ..........Circulation Manager
Steve Rapp ..................Promotion Manager
**Editorial:**
Brad Bowling ..............................Editor
Cindy Biadez ..........................Advertising
Barbara Lane ..........................Advertising
Paul Katzke ............................Advertising
Ron Kowalke ......................Associate Editor
Giles Aever ..................Secretary & Treasurer
**Desc.:** Edited for antique and vintage auto enthusiasts and collectors nationwide. It features rapid, newspaper-style coverage of hobby activities as well as feature articles on cars and personalities within the hobby. Regular columns include tips on restoration work, Questions 'N Answers. Special emphasis on market conditions through reports of vintage car auctions throughout the country.
**Readers:** Anyone interested in collecting and/or restoring cars.

## OLD CARS PRICE GUIDE
58561

700 E. State St.
Iola, WI 54990-0001
Telephone: (715) 445-2214
FAX: (715) 445-4087
Year Established: 1978
Pub. Frequency: bi-m.
Page Size: standard
Subscrip. Rate: $3.98 newsstand;
   $16.95/yr.
Materials: 32,33
Freelance Pay: $.03/wd.; $5/photo
Print Process: web offset
Circulation: 50,000
Circulation Type: paid

**Owner(s):**
Krause Publications, Inc.
700 E. State St.
Iola, WI 54990-0001
Telephone: (715) 445-2214
FAX: (715) 445-4087
Ownership %: 100
**Management:**
Greg Smith ..............................Publisher
**Editorial:**
James T. Lenzke ....................Senior Editor
Kenneth Buttolph ..........................Editor
**Desc.:** Estimated prices for collectible vehicles in six different states of condition, 1901-1987.
**Readers:** Collectors, dealers, hobbyists, investors, appraisers, insurers.

## OPEN WHEEL
66726

47 S. Main
Ipswich, MA 01938
Telephone: (508) 356-7030
FAX: (508) 356-2492
Year Established: 1980
Pub. Frequency: m.
Page Size: standard
Subscrip. Rate: $18.95/yr.
Materials: 01,02,05,06,08,10,20,21,27,28, 29,30,32
Freelance Pay: up to $400/story
Circulation: 60,000
Circulation Type: paid
**Owner(s):**
General Media Publishing Group
1965 Broadway
New York, NY 10023
Telephone: (212) 496-6100
Ownership %: 100
**Editorial:**
Dick Berggren ..............................Editor
**Desc.:** Covers all forms of American open wheel auto racing.
**Deadline:** story-1st of mo.; news-1st of mo.; photo-1st of mo.; ads-1st of mo.

## PETERSEN'S 4 WHEEL & OFF-ROAD
66701

6420 Wilshire Blvd.
Los Angeles, CA 90048
Telephone: (213) 782-2000
FAX: (213) 782-2263
Year Established: 1978
Pub. Frequency: m.
Subscrip. Rate: $3.95 newsstand;
   $19.94/yr.
Circulation: 300,000
Circulation Type: paid
**Owner(s):**
Petersen Publishing Co.
6420 Wilshire Blvd.
Los Angeles, CA 90069
Telephone: (213) 782-2000
FAX: (213) 782-2263
Ownership %: 100
**Editorial:**
Drew Hardin ..............................Editor
Cecily Chittick ........................Design Editor

## POPULAR HOT RODDING
26441

12100 Wilshire Blvd., Ste. 250
Los Angeles, CA 90025
Telephone: (310) 820-3601
FAX: (310) 207-9388
Mailing Address:
   P.O. Box 49659
   Los Angeles, CA 90049
Year Established: 1962
Pub. Frequency: m.
Page Size: standard
Subscrip. Rate: $16.94/yr.
Freelance Pay: $75-$100/pg.
Circulation: 248,210
Circulation Type: paid

**Owner(s):**
Gordon H. Behn
12301 Wilshire Blvd., #316
Los Angeles, CA 90025
Telephone: (310) 820-3601
Ownership %: 50

Don Werner
12301 Wilshire Blvd., #316
Los Angeles, CA 90025
Ownership %: 50
**Management:**
Don Werner ..............................President
George Elliott ..........................Publisher
Bill Lloyd ..................Advertising Manager
**Editorial:**
C. Van Tune ......................Executive Editor
Doug Marion ..............................Editor
George Elliott ..................Editorial Director
Chris Hemer ..........................Feature Editor
Steve Reyes ..............................Photo
Kevin Boales ......................Technical Editor
**Desc.:** Includes staff and by-lined articles on coming events, new products news, trade literature, letters to the editors and questions and answers.

## ROAD & TRACK
26455

1499 Monrovia Ave.
Newport Beach, CA 92663
Telephone: (714) 720-5300
FAX: (714) 631-2757
Mailing Address:
   P.O. Box 1757
   Newport Beach, CA 92658
Year Established: 1947
Pub. Frequency: m.
Page Size: standard
Subscrip. Rate: $2.95 newsstand US;
   $3.95 Canada; $19.94/yr.
Freelance Pay: varies
Print Process: web offset
Circulation: 740,000
Circulation Type: paid
**Owner(s):**
Hachette Filipacchi Magazines, Inc.
1633 Broadway
New York, NY 10019
Telephone: (212) 767-6000
Ownership %: 100
**Management:**
David J. Pecker ..........................President
**Editorial:**
Rich Homan ......................Executive Editor
Joe Rusz ..........................Senior Editor
Thos L. Bryant ..............................Editor
Ellida Maki ........................Managing Editor
Richard Baron ..........................Art Director
Henry Thomas ..............Associate Art Director
Lorraine Keeton ......................Copy Director
Dennis Simanaitis ................Engineering Editor
Andrew Bornhop ......................Feature Editor
Jill Carter ..........................Marketing Manager
**Desc.:** Use feature articles up to 2,000 words on automotive subjects with special emphasis on the enthusiast cars; use coverage of major sports car and Grand Prix racing events throughout the world; use articles on classic cars and their restoration as well as technical articles on home-built sports car specials. All editorial material should be accompanied by appropriate illustrations and must be submitted on a speculative basis unless prior assignments are made. Query preferred by-lines and photo credit are given. Departments include: Letters to the Editor, Miscellaneous Ramblings, Technical Correspondence, People & Places, Years Ago, Road Test Summary, Reviews, Time & Place, About the Sport, Ampersand, PS, European Newsletters, Marketplace.
**Readers:** Motor enthusiasts.

## ROD & CUSTOM MAGAZINE
69163

6420 Wilshire Blvd.
Los Angeles, CA 90048
Telephone: (213) 782-2000
FAX: (213) 782-2263
Year Established: 1989
Pub. Frequency: m.
Page Size: standard
Subscrip. Rate: $2.95 newstand US; $2.10 UK; $3.75 Canada
Materials: 32
Freelance Pay: varies
Circulation: 100,000
Circulation Type: paid
**Owner(s):**
Petersen Publishing Co.
8490 Sunset Blvd.
Los Angeles, CA 90069
Telephone: (213) 854-2222
Ownership %: 100
**Management:**
DeEtte Crow ..............................Publisher
**Editorial:**
Jeff Tann ..............................Editor
Anna Rigopoulos ................Advertising Director
Pamela King ..............................Sales
**Desc.:** Focuses on aspects of contemporary street rodding, including trends, racing and techniques.

## SOUTHERN MOTORACING
26482

1049 Northwest Blvd.
Winston Salem, NC 27101
Telephone: (910) 723-5227
FAX: (919) 722-3757
Mailing Address:
   P.O. Box 500
   Winston Salem, NC 27102
Year Established: 1964
Pub. Frequency: bi-w.
Page Size: tabloid
Subscrip. Rate: $.75 newsstand; $15/yr. US; $17/yr. Canada
Freelance Pay: varies
Circulation: 18,000
Circulation Type: paid
**Owner(s):**
Universal Services, Inc.
1049 Northwest Blvd.
Winston Salem, NC 27101
Telephone: (919) 723-5227
Ownership %: 100
**Management:**
Hank Schoolfield ..........................Publisher
**Editorial:**
Hank Schoolfield ..........................Editor
Greer Smith ......................Assistant Editor
**Desc.:** Devoted to the motor racing fan, with emphasis on news and personality stories and a small and general treatment of technical material. Most of the material is supplied by staff members, stringers, and speedway publicists, with little market for the freelance writer. Most of the content is aimed at the motor racing fan of the Southeastern U.S., with brief coverage of national and international motor racing.
**Readers:** 90 percent Southeastern U.S. motor racing fans.

## SPECIALTY CAR
66704

8490 Sunset Blvd.
Los Angeles, CA 90069
Telephone: (213) 782-2000
Year Established: 1984
Pub. Frequency: m.
Subscrip. Rate: $15.95/yr.
Circulation: 80,000
Circulation Type: paid

---

**Materials Accepted/Included:** 01-Business news 02-By-line articles 03-Fashion news 04-Food news 05-Freelance copy 06-Letters to editor 07-Real estate news 08-Sports news 09-Travel news 10-Book rev. 11-Movie rev. 12-Music rev. 13-TV rev. 14-Theater rev. 15-Coming events 16-Obituaries 17-Question & answer 18-Social announcements 19-Artwork 20-Cartoons 21-Photos 22-TV listings 23-Audio rec. 24-Video rec. 25-Books 26-Films/film clips 27-Personnel news 28-Press releases 29-New product news/photos 30-Trade lit. 31-Contracts awarded 32-Display adv. 33-Classified adv.

**Owner(s):**
Petersen Publishing Co.
8490 Sunset Blvd.
Los Angeles, CA 90069
Telephone: (213) 782-2000
Ownership %: 100
**Editorial:**
Steve Temple ....................................Editor
Bari Dennison ........................Design Editor

26492

## SPORTS CAR
1371 E. Warner Ave.
Ste. E
Tustin, CA 92680
Telephone: (714) 259-8240
FAX: (714) 259-9377
Year Established: 1944
Pub. Frequency: m.
Page Size: standard
Subscrip. Rate: free to members; $18/yr.
   non-members
Freelance Pay: variable per assignment
Circulation: 53,000
Circulation Type: controlled & paid
**Owner(s):**
Pfanner Communications, Inc.
1371 E. Warner Ave.
Ste. E
Tustin, CA 92680
Telephone: (714) 259-8240
Ownership %: 100
**Management:**
Bill Sparks ................................Publisher
**Editorial:**
Elyse Barrett ........................Assistant Editor
R. A. McCormack ............Marketing Director
**Desc.:** A general-interest motor sports
   publication offering news and analysis of
   SCCA competition events. There is
   comprehensive coverage of SCCA
   professional and amateur road racing,
   including showroom stock endurance
   events as well as autocross and rallying.
   Emphasis is on event reportage and
   news. The magazine is also the official
   source for point standings, schedules
   and regulation updates.
**Readers:** Members of the Sports Car Club
   of America.

69522

## SPORTS CAR INTERNATIONAL
42 Digital Dr., #5
Novato, CA 94949
Telephone: (415) 382-0580
FAX: (415) 382-0587
Year Established: 1985
Pub. Frequency: m.
Page Size: standard
Subscrip. Rate: $2.95 newsstand;
   $17.95/yr.
Print Process: web offset
Circulation: 90,000
Circulation Type: paid
**Owner(s):**
SCI Publishing, Inc.
42 Digital Dr., #5
Novato, CA 94949
Telephone: (415) 382-0580
Ownership %: 100
**Management:**
Tom Toldrian ..............................Publisher
**Editorial:**
John Lamm ..................................Editor
**Readers:** Performance car enthusiasts and
   those traditionalists who define cars as
   entertainment.

66703

## SPORT TRUCK
8490 Sunset Blvd.
Los Angeles, CA 90069
Telephone: (213) 782-2000
Year Established: 1988
Pub. Frequency: m.

Page Size: standard
Subscrip. Rate: $19.94/yr.
Circulation: 131,000
Circulation Type: paid
**Owner(s):**
Petersen Publishing Co.
8490 Sunset Blvd.
Los Angeles, CA 90069
Telephone: (213) 782-2000
Ownership %: 100
**Editorial:**
Hoyt Vanderberg ........................Editor
Barri Denison ........................Design Editor
**Desc.:** Presents a forum for information on
   the entire range of light-duty trucks, with
   an emphasis on performance.

26494

## STOCK CAR RACING MAGAZINE
47 S. Main St.
Ipswich, MA 01938
Telephone: (508) 356-7030
FAX: (508) 356-2492
Mailing Address:
   P.O. Box 715
   Ipswich, MA 01938
Year Established: 1966
Pub. Frequency: m.
Page Size: standard
Subscrip. Rate: $3.50 newsstand;
   $18.95/yr.
Freelance Pay: up to $400/feature
Circulation: 196,000
Circulation Type: paid
**Owner(s):**
General Media International
1965 Broadway
New York, NY 10023-4965
Telephone: (212) 496-6100
Ownership %: 100
**Management:**
Bob Guccione ..........................President
Chris Ballard ..............Advertising Manager
**Editorial:**
Dick Berggren ..............................Editor
Robin Hartford ..................Associate Editor
Tammy Francover ........................Photo
Doug Gore ....................Technical Editor
**Desc.:** Includes anything that has
   something to do with stock car racing.
   We are the largest publication in the
   world devoted exclusively to stock car
   racing.
**Readers:** Auto racing fans, officials,
   owners, drivers, pit people.

69164

## STREET ROD ACTION
7950 Deering Ave.
Canoga Park, CA 91304
Telephone: (818) 887-0550
FAX: (818) 883-1343
Year Established: 1972
Pub. Frequency: m.
Page Size: standard
Subscrip. Rate: $3.95 newsstand;
   $19.95/yr.
Materials: 32
Circulation: 95,000
Circulation Type: paid
**Owner(s):**
Challenge Publications, Inc.
7950 Deering Ave.
Canoga Park, CA 91304
Telephone: (818) 887-0550
Ownership %: 100
**Editorial:**
Eric Pierce ..................................Editor
**Desc.:** Covers auto rebuilding and
   restoration.

25658

## SUPER CHEVY
12100 Wilshire Blvd., Ste. 250
Los Angeles, CA 90025
Telephone: (310) 820-3601
FAX: (310) 207-9388

Year Established: 1972
Pub. Frequency: m.
Page Size: standard
Subscrip. Rate: $16.94/yr.
Freelance Pay: $70-$100/pg.
Circulation: 161,586
Circulation Type: paid
**Owner(s):**
Gordon H. Behn
Telephone: (310) 820-3601
Ownership %: 50
Don Werner
Ownership %: 50
**Management:**
Don Werner ..............................President
George Elliott ..........................Publisher
Jeff Morton ................Advertising Manager
**Editorial:**
Bruce Hampson ........................Editor
Steve Reyes ..............................Photo
**Desc.:** High-performance Chevrolet
   enthusiasts publication. Technical how-to
   articles, events, meets, race coverage,
   vehicle features about Chevys of all
   types. Usual column fillers.
**Readers:** Males-average age, 25 yrs;
   average income, $24,106.

25659

## SUPER STOCK & DRAG
## ILLUSTRATED
6728 Eaton Ave.
Canoga Park, CA 91303
Telephone: (818) 992-4777
FAX: (818) 992-4979
Year Established: 1964
Pub. Frequency: m.
Page Size: standard
Subscrip. Rate: $2.95 newsstand;
   $17.95/yr.; $35.90/2 yrs.
Materials: 05,06,10,15,21,24,25,28,29,30
Freelance Pay: $150-$200/pg. pub.
Circulation: 44,022
Circulation Type: paid
**Owner(s):**
General Media Publishing Group
1965 Broadway
New York, NY 10023-4965
Telephone: (212) 496-6100
Ownership %: 100
**Management:**
Patrick Gavin ..................Vice President
John Stewart ..............................Publisher
**Editorial:**
Steve Collison ............................Editor
Lisa Mingus ....................Assistant Editor
**Desc.:** Automobile drag racing.
**Readers:** Hands-on drag racing
   enthusiasts and drag racing fans.

25087

## TRAILER LIFE
3601 Calle Tecate
Camarillo, CA 93012
Telephone: (805) 386-2000
FAX: (818) 597-2403
Year Established: 1941
Pub. Frequency: m.
Page Size: standard
Subscrip. Rate: $2.95 newsstand; $22/yr.
Materials: 02,05,09,17,21,29,30,32,33
Freelance Pay: $50-$550/article
Circulation: 300,073
Circulation Type: paid
**Owner(s):**
T.L. Enterprises, Inc.
3601 Calle Tecate
Camarillo, CA 93012
Telephone: (805) 386-2000
Ownership %: 100
**Management:**
Bill Estes ..................................Publisher
**Editorial:**
Sherry McBride ..................Managing Editor
Barbara Leonard ................Editorial Director
Michael Schneider ..............Consulting Editor

Olga Markowitz ..............Publication Director
**Desc.:** Uses articles dealing with all
   aspects of trailer, motorhome, and
   pickup camper traveling and technical
   how-to-do's, travel, RV, test reports. All
   travel stories should contain data on
   road conditions, trailer accommodations
   and other information of specific interest
   to trailerists. Also use trailer-slanted
   fillers and photographs, and human
   interest stories as they pertain to trailer
   people. Article length from 750 to 1,800
   words, fillers to 500 words. By-lines
   given. Picture stories on trailers and
   camper clubs often used. New product
   and news releases given special
   consideration. Departments include: Club
   News Section, 10-Minute-Tech, Travel
   Section.
**Readers:** Owners and enthusiasts of
   recreational vehicles.

25662

## TRUCKIN'
774 S. Placentia Ave.
Placentia, CA 92670
Telephone: (714) 572-2255
FAX: (714) 533-9879
Year Established: 1974
Pub. Frequency: m.
Page Size: standard
Subscrip. Rate: $23.95/yr.
Circulation: 220,000
Circulation Type: paid
**Owner(s):**
McMullen and Yee Publishing
774 S. Placentia Ave.
Placentia, CA 92670
Telephone: (714) 572-2255
Tom McMullen
Ownership %: 50
Ken Yee
Ownership %: 50
**Management:**
Bill Porter ................................President
Tom McMullen ..........................Publisher
John Nething ............Advertising Manager
**Editorial:**
Steve Stillwell ............................Editor
Brian McCormick ..............Managing Editor
Tim Foss ..............................Advertising
Tracey Douglas ..............Editorial Assistant
**Desc.:** Coverage of custom full-size
   trucks and mini-trucks.
**Readers:** Younger to older generations.

3743

## WESTERN AUTO SUPPLY CO.
2107 Grand Ave.
Kansas City, MO 64108
Telephone: (816) 346-4495
Pub. Frequency: n/a
**Owner(s):**
Western Auto

26571

## WESTERN PENNSYLVANIA
## MOTORIST
5900 Baum Blvd.
Pittsburgh, PA 15206
Telephone: (412) 365-7243
FAX: (412) 362-0926
Year Established: 1930
Pub. Frequency: m.
Page Size: tabloid
Subscrip. Rate: $2/yr.; $1 for members
Circulation: 510,000
Circulation Type: paid
**Owner(s):**
AAA West Penn/West VA
5900 Baum Blvd.
Pittsburgh, PA 15206
Telephone: (412) 365-7243
Ownership %: 100
**Management:**
Richard S. Hamilton ..................Publisher

**Materials Accepted/Included:** 01-Business news 02-By-line articles 03-Fashion news 04-Food news 05-Freelance copy 06-Letters to editor 07-Real estate news 08-Sports news 09-Travel news 10-Book rev. 11-Movie rev. 12-Music rev. 13-TV rev. 14-Theater rev. 15-Coming events 16-Obituaries 17-Question & answer 18-Social announcements 19-Artwork 20-Cartoons 21-Photos 22-TV listings 23-Audio rec. 24-Video rec. 25-Books 26-Films/film clips 27-Personnel news 28-Press releases 29-New product news/photos 30-Trade lit. 31-Contracts awarded 32-Display adv. 33-Classified adv.

**Editorial:**
Ann Reed Rose .....................Managing Editor
**Desc.:** News of interest to motorists and travelers-legislation, AAA policies, safety and travel.
**Readers:** Members of AAA motor club.
**Deadline:** 6 wks. prior to pub. date

## Group 610-Boating

**BOAT - US REPORTS**                    69412
880 S. Pickett St.
Alexandria, VA 22304
Telephone: (703) 823-9550
FAX: (703) 461-2845
Year Established: 1966
Pub. Frequency: bi-m.
Subscrip. Rate: $12.50/yr.
Circulation: 500,000
Circulation Type: controlled
**Owner(s):**
Boat Owners Association of the United States
880 S. Pickett St.
Alexandria, VA 22304
Telephone: (703) 823-9550
Ownership %: 100
**Editorial:**
Michael Sciulla ..............................Editor
**Desc.:** Covers legislative, regulatory and consumer issues of interest to recreational boat owners.

**BOAT BUILDER**                         67648
75 Holly Hill Ln.
Greenwich, CT 06830-2910
Telephone: (203) 661-6111
FAX: (203) 661-4802
Year Established: 1982
Pub. Frequency: bi-m.
Page Size: standard
Subscrip. Rate: $5 newsstand; $22.97/yr.
Circulation: 16,950
Circulation Type: paid
**Owner(s):**
Belvoir Publications, Inc.
P.O. Box 2626
Greenwich, CT 06836
Telephone: (203) 661-6111
Ownership %: 100
**Management:**
Robert Englander .......................President
Keith Lawrence ..........................Publisher
**Editorial:**
Keith Lawrence ..............................Editor

**BOATING**                              22070
1633 Broadway
New York, NY 10019
Telephone: (212) 767-5525
FAX: (212) 767-5618
Year Established: 1957
Pub. Frequency: m.
Page Size: pocket
Subscrip. Rate: $3.50 newsstand; $26/yr.
Circulation: 195,445
Circulation Type: paid
**Owner(s):**
Hachette Filipacchi Magazines, Inc.
1633 Broadway
New York, NY 10019
Telephone: (212) 767-6000
Ownership %: 100
**Management:**
Daniel Filipacchi .......................President
Richard Amann ..........................Publisher
**Editorial:**
John Owens ..................................Editor

**Desc.:** Editorial gives comprehensive, practical information on powerboats of all types: motor yachts, cruisers, performance boats, sportboats, and sportfishing boats; marine engines and motors; and marine electronics and products. Features include powerboat and equipment tests; authoritative guides to products for boatmen; articles on engines, electronics, boat handling/ seamanship, sportfishing, and cruising areas; plus boat maintenance and troubleshootings tips.
**Readers:** Power boat owners and enthusiasts.

**BOATING WORLD**                        68704
2100 Powers Ferry Rd.
Atlanta, GA 30339
Telephone: (404) 955-5656
FAX: (404) 952-0669
Year Established: 1979
Pub. Frequency: 9/yr.
Page Size: standard
Subscrip. Rate: $2.95 newsstand US; $3.95 Canada; $18/yr. US; $27/yr. foreign
Materials: 01,02,05,06,15,17,19,20,21,27, 28,29,30,31,32,33
Freelance Pay: $.30/word
Print Process: web
Circulation: 134,500
Circulation Type: controlled & paid
**Owner(s):**
Trans World Publishing, Inc.
2100 Powers Ferry Rd.
Atlanta, GA 30339
Telephone: (404) 955-5656
Ownership %: 100
**Editorial:**
Richard M. Lebovitz .......................Editor
**Desc.:** Provides information on equipment selection, maintenance and boating enjoyment.

**CLASSIC BOATING**                      68706
280 Lac la Belle Dr.
Oconomowoc, WI 53066-1648
Telephone: (414) 567-4800
Year Established: 1984
Pub. Frequency: bi-m.
Page Size: standard
Subscrip. Rate: $20/yr. US.; $27/yr. foreign
Materials: 32,33
Freelance Pay: $75-300
Print Process: offset
Circulation: 8,500
Circulation Type: paid
**Owner(s):**
Jim Wangard, Ed. & Pub.
280 Lac la Belle Dr.
Oconomowoc, WI 53066-1648
Telephone: (414) 567-4800
Ownership %: 100
**Management:**
Jim Wangard ..............................Publisher
**Editorial:**
Jim Wangard ..................................Editor
**Deadline:** ads-1 1/2 mo. prior to pub. date

**CRUISING WORLD**                       26387
5 John Clarke Rd.
Newport, RI 02840
Telephone: (401) 847-1588
FAX: (401) 848-5048
Year Established: 1973
Pub. Frequency: m.
Page Size: standard
Subscrip. Rate: $2.95 newsstand; $24/yr.; $40/2 yrs.
Freelance Pay: $25-$500
Circulation: 143,000
Circulation Type: paid

**Owner(s):**
New York Times Co., The
229 W. 43rd St.
New York, NY 10036
Telephone: (212) 556-1234
Ownership %: 100
**Management:**
James FitzGerald .......................President
James FitzGerald .......................Publisher
**Editorial:**
Bernadette Brennan .........................Editor
Lynda Morris Childress ..........Managing Editor
Nim Marsh ........................Associate Editor
Quentin Warren ..................Associate Editor
William Roche ....................Design Director
**Desc.:** Feature articles with accompanying illustrations about cruises under sail, people involved in cruising, and subjects of interest to seafarers. Short articles of 50 to 300 words, and illustrations, for the column Shoreline on subjects ranging from incidents on the water to 200' schooners, what's under the water, and people. Technical articles on all aspects of cruising under sail. Color photographs (sliced 35-mm or 2 1/4 square) suitable for the cover or photo essays. B&W photographs that capture the atmosphere of cruising. Cruising gear and ideas. Poetry, art, and humorous drawings.
**Readers:** Sailors and people in North America and internationally.

**EMBASSY'S MARINE MARKETPLACE**         68719
142 Ferry Rd., Ste. 16
Saybrook, CT 06475
Telephone: (203) 395-0188
FAX: (203) 395-0410
Year Established: 1992
Pub. Frequency: 6/yr.
Page Size: 8 1/4" X 10 3/4"
Subscrip. Rate: $2/newsstand; $15/yr.
Materials: 32,33
Print Process: web
Circulation: 15000
Circulation Type: paid
**Owner(s):**
Embassy Imprint, Inc.
142 Ferry Rd., Ste. 16
Old Saybrook, CT 06475
Telephone: (203) 395-0188
Ownership %: 100
**Management:**
Mark Borton .............................President
Mark Borton .............................Publisher
Laura Bloom ...................Advertising Manager
Irene Roy ......................Circulation Manager
Dibben Joy ......................Sales Manager
**Editorial:**
Ian Quarier ....................Editor in Chief
Donna Caruso ...................Managing Editor

**HEARTLAND BOATING**                    67273
Route 1 Box 145
Martin, TN 38237
Telephone: (901) 587-6791
FAX: (901) 587-6893
Mailing Address:
    P.O. Box 1067
    Martin, TN 38237
Year Established: 1988
Pub. Frequency: 7/yr.
Page Size: standard
Subscrip. Rate: $2.95 newsstand; $15.95/yr.; $27.95/2 yrs.; $39.95/3 yrs.
Materials: 04,05,06,10,15,20,21,25,28,29, 30,32,33
Freelance Pay: varies
Print Process: offset
Circulation: 75,000
Circulation Type: paid

**Owner(s):**
Inland Publications
P.O. Box 1067
Martin, TN 38237
Telephone: (901) 587-6791
FAX: (901) 587-6893
Ownership %: 100
**Management:**
Douglas Blom ...........................Publisher
Douglas Blom ...................Advertising Manager
**Editorial:**
Molly Lightfoot-Blom ........................Editor
**Desc.:** Freshwater inland rivers and lake of mid-America. Recreation and pleasure boating discussed.
**Readers:** Houseboaters, cruisers, sailors on inland lakes and rivers are most interested.
**Deadline:** ads-6 wks. prior to pub. date

**LAKELAND BOATING**                     22075
1560 Sherman Ave., Ste. 1220
Evanston, IL 60201
Telephone: (708) 869-5400
FAX: (708) 869-5989
Year Established: 1946
Pub. Frequency: 11/yr.
Page Size: standard
Subscrip. Rate: $2.95 newsstand US; $3.50 Canada; $18.94/yr.
Circulation: 50,000
Circulation Type: controlled
**Owner(s):**
O'Meara-Brown Publications, Inc.
1560 Sherman Ave., Ste. 1220
Evanston, IL 60201
Telephone: (708) 869-5400
Ownership %: 100
**Management:**
Walter B. O'Meara .......................President
Walter B. O'Meara .......................Publisher
Douglas Leik ...................Advertising Manager
**Editorial:**
John Wooldridge ............................Editor
Ed Crosby ......................Art Department
Liz Crosby ......................News Producer
**Desc.:** The only publication serving the sport in the Great Lakes and Inland Waterways. Covers boats of all types, outboard, inboard, power, and sail. Also contains news of racing, fishing, and cruise.

**MOTOR BOATING & SAILING**              22077
250 W. 55th St., 4th Fl.
New York, NY 10019
Telephone: (212) 649-4099
FAX: (212) 489-9258
Year Established: 1907
Pub. Frequency: m.
Page Size: standard
Subscrip. Rate: $3 newsstand; $15.97/yr.
Materials: 02,05,06,09,17,19,21,27,28,29, 32,33
Print Process: web offset
Circulation: 141,186
Circulation Type: paid
**Owner(s):**
Hearst Corp.
250 W. 55th St., 4th Fl.
New York, NY 10019
Telephone: (212) 649-4300
Ownership %: 100
**Management:**
Peter A. Janssen .......................Publisher
Tom Herber ...................Business Manager
**Editorial:**
Daniel C. Fales .......................Executive Editor
John Clemans .......................Senior Editor
Polly Whittell .......................Senior Editor
Peter A. Janssen ..........................Editor
Louisa Rudeen ...................Managing Editor
Erin Becker ......................Art Director
John Hearst, Jr. ...................Associate Editor

**Materials Accepted/Included:** 01-Business news 02-By-line articles 03-Fashion news 04-Food news 05-Freelance copy 06-Letters to editor 07-Real estate news 08-Sports news 09-Travel news 10-Book rev. 11-Movie rev. 12-Music rev. 13-TV rev. 14-Theater rev. 15-Coming events 16-Obituaries 17-Question & answer 18-Social announcements 19-Artwork 20-Cartoons 21-Photos 22-TV listings 23-Audio rec. 24-Video rec. 25-Books 26-Films/film clips 27-Personnel news 28-Press releases 29-New product news/photos 30-Trade lit. 31-Contracts awarded 32-Display adv. 33-Classified adv.

Michael Perrella ...............Marketing Director
John Oberg ................National Sales Manager
Michael Verdon ................New Products Editor
Lori Rubin ...............................Production Editor
**Desc.:** By-line articles covering all phases of boating.
**Readers:** Owners of all sizes of sail and motor boats, heavy participation in the boating sport.

69420

## MULTIHULLS
421 Hancock St.
N. Quincy, MA 02171
Telephone: (617) 328-8181
FAX: (617) 471-0118
Year Established: 1975
Pub. Frequency: bi-m.
Page Size: standard
Subscrip. Rate: $3.95 newsstand; $21/yr.
Materials: 02,05,06,08,19,20,21,32,33
Print Process: offset
Circulation: 39,800
Circulation Type: free & paid
**Owner(s):**
Chiodi Advertising & Publishing, Inc.
421 Hancock St.
N. Quincy, MA 02171
Telephone: (617) 328-8181
FAX: (617) 471-0118
Ownership %: 100
**Editorial:**
Charles Chiodi .............................................Editor

69429

## NOR'WESTING
6044 Seaview Ave. N.W.
Seattle, WA 98107
Telephone: (206) 783-8939
FAX: (206) 783-9011
Year Established: 1965
Pub. Frequency: m.
Page Size: standard
Subscrip. Rate: $15/yr. US; $17.50/yr.
   Canada; $20/yr. foreign
Circulation: 10,600
Circulation Type: paid
**Owner(s):**
Nor'westing, Inc.
6044 Seaview Ave. N.W.
Seattle, WA 98107
Telephone: (206) 783-8939
FAX: (206) 783-9011
Ownership %: 100
**Editorial:**
Thomas Kincaid ...........................Editor in Chief
Gloria Kruzner ..........................................Editor
**Desc.:** Covers recreational boating in the Pacific Northwest, British Columbia, and Alaska.

70387

## POWER & MOTORYACHT
475 Park Ave. S.
New York, NY 10016-6901
Telephone: (212) 340-9880
FAX: (212) 340-9877
Year Established: 1985
Pub. Frequency: m.
Page Size: standard
Subscrip. Rate: $3.95 newsstand; $29.95/yr.
Materials: 02,05,09,17,19,21,32,33
Freelance Pay: $500-1000
Print Process: offset
Circulation: 156,391
Circulation Type: controlled
**Owner(s):**
Power & Motoryacht
**Editorial:**
Richard Thiel ...............................................Editor
**Desc.:** Reviews boats, engines, and accessories for owners of powerboats 24 feet and longer, with special emphasis on the 35-foot-plus market. PMY also reports on chartering, cruising, sportfishing, and the environment.

**Readers:** PMY is for owners of powerboats who consider boating to be more than a hobby - it's a lifestyle. Readers have an average of 28 years' experience on the water, and enjoy reading about do-it- yourself maintenance, cruising destinations, and other issues that affect their enjoyment of boating.
**Deadline:** story-4-6 mo. prior to pub. date; news-4-6 mo. prior; photo-4-6 mo. prior

69434

## POWERBOAT REPORTS
P.O. Box 2626
Greenwich, CT 06836-2626
Telephone: (203) 661-6111
FAX: (203) 661-4802
Year Established: 1988
Pub. Frequency: s-m.
Subscrip. Rate: $68/yr. US; $80/yr. foreign
**Owner(s):**
Belvoir Publications, Inc.
P.O. Box 2626
Greenwich, CT 06836-2626
Telephone: (203) 661-6111
Ownership %: 100
**Editorial:**
Timothy Cole ............................................Editor

22080

## SAIL
275 Washington St.
Newton, MA 02158
Telephone: (617) 964-3030
FAX: (617) 964-8948
Year Established: 1970
Pub. Frequency: 12/yr.
Page Size: standard
Subscrip. Rate: $2.95/newsstand; $23.94/yr.
Materials: 32,33
Freelance Pay: $300-$600
Print Process: web offset
Circulation: 183,468
Circulation Type: controlled & paid
**Owner(s):**
Cahners Publishing Co.
275 Washington Street
Newton, MA 02158
Telephone: (617) 964-3030
Ownership %: 100
**Management:**
Donald A. Macaulay ...........................Publisher
Kip Winchester ..............Circulation Manager
Sarah Day ...........Editorial Production Manager
**Editorial:**
Charles E. Mason III ..............Executive Editor
Gail Anderson ..............................Senior Editor
Freeman Pittman ..........................Senior Editor
Patience Wales .......................................Editor
Amy Ullrich ...........................Managing Editor
Betsy Harkins ......................Assoc. Advertising
                                                      Production
                                                      Manager
Richard Devlin ....................Associate Publisher
Robert Johnson ........................Design Director
Linda Klockner .....................Marketing Director
**Desc.:** Departments include: Techniques, Features, Technical, Just Launched, Book Reviews, News and Side Features. Written and edited for sailors at all levels, both racers and cruisers, from serious novices to experts, all actively involved in the development of their sailing skills.
**Readers:** Specialized readership interested in cruising, one-design events, racing, plus learning to sail.

22081

## SAILING MAGAZINE
125 E. Main St.
Port Washington, WI 53074
Telephone: (414) 284-3494
FAX: (414) 284-7764

Mailing Address:
   P.O. Box 249
   Port Washington, WI 53074
Year Established: 1966
Pub. Frequency: m.
Page Size: oversize
Subscrip. Rate: $3.50 newsstand; $24.75/yr.
Freelance Pay: varies
Circulation: 39,000
Circulation Type: paid
**Owner(s):**
Port Publications, Inc.
125 E. Main St.
Port Washington, WI 53074
Telephone: (414) 284-3494
Ownership %: 100
**Management:**
Wm. F. Schanen, III .........................Publisher
Kenneth R. Quant ...........Advertising Manager
**Editorial:**
Wm. F. Schanen, III ...............................Editor
Micca L. Hutchins ..................................Editor
Kenneth R. Quant .................Advertising Sales
Carolyn Seuss .......................Advertising Sales
Greta Reichelsdorfer .................Assistant Editor
Doris L. Stuht .....................................Circulation
Jane M. Farnham .........Production Coordinator
Robert H. Perry ....................Technical Editor
**Desc.:** Sailing pictorial slant is augmented by monthly written features including columns, reviews, news.
**Readers:** Boat owners, cruisers, day sailors, racers, yacht owners.

22084

## SAILING WORLD
5 John Clarke Rd.
Newport, RI 02840
Telephone: (401) 847-1588
FAX: (401) 848-5048
Year Established: 1962
Pub. Frequency: m.
Page Size: oversize
Subscrip. Rate: $2.50 newsstand; $24/yr.
Freelance Pay: $250/pg.
Circulation: 61,000
Circulation Type: paid
**Owner(s):**
New York Times
110 Fifth Ave.
New York, NY 10011
Telephone: (212) 146-1000
Ownership %: 100
**Management:**
James FitzGerald ................................Publisher
**Editorial:**
John Burnham .........................................Editor
Kris McClintock .......................Managing Editor
Joy Scott ............................Production Director
**Desc.:** Carries results and descriptions of all major regional, national, and international sailboat racing events. Also contains regular features on all technical aspects of sailboat racing and performance sailing.
**Readers:** Skippers and crewmen of racing and performance sailboats.

26461

## SAIL 1995 SAILBOAT BUYERS GUIDE
275 Washington St.
Newton, MA 02158-1630
Telephone: (617) 964-3030
FAX: (617) 964-8948
Year Established: 1967
Pub. Frequency: a.
Page Size: standard
Subscrip. Rate: $4.95 newsstand; $6.95/copy mailed
Materials: 19,21,28,29,32,34
Print Process: web
Circulation: 85,000
Circulation Type: paid

**Owner(s):**
Cahners Publishing Company, Inc.
275 Washington Street
Newton, MA 02158
Telephone: (617) 964-3030
FAX: (617) 964-8948
Ownership %: 100
**Management:**
Donald A. Macaulay ...........................Publisher
Sarah Day .............................................Manager
**Editorial:**
Patience Wales .......................................Editor
Dick Devlin ......................Associate Publisher
Sarah Day ...........................Production Editor
Jay E. Paris ............................Technical Editor
**Desc.:** Complete reference guide to buying and equipping your sailboat. Includes specs, boat plans and photographs of hundreds of daysailers, one-designs, multihulls, cruisers. Thousands of gear and accessory listings with photographs as well as special editorial features.
**Readers:** Sailing enthusiasts interested in purchasing boats and/or gear.
**Deadline:** news-July 1; ads-Sep. 1

26464

## SEA
17782 Cowan, Ste. C
Irvine, CA 92714
Telephone: (714) 660-6150
FAX: (714) 660-6172
Year Established: 1908
Pub. Frequency: m.
Page Size: standard
Subscrip. Rate: $15.94/yr.
Freelance Pay: $.20/wd.
Circulation: 60,000
Circulation Type: paid
**Owner(s):**
Duncan McIntosh Co., Inc.
17782 Cowan, Ste. C
Irvine, CA 92714
Telephone: (714) 660-6150
Ownership %: 100
**Bureau(s):**
Sea Magazine, Northwest Sales Office
22727 Highway 99, Ste. 107
Edmonds, WA 98026
Telephone: (206) 670-0285
Contact: Melinda Ybarra
**Management:**
Duncan McIntosh .................................Publisher
**Editorial:**
Eston Ellis ..................................Senior Editor
John Vigor .............................Managing Editor
Jeffrey Fleming ...................Associate Publisher
Christa Chavez ....................Editorial Assistant
**Desc.:** Technical, cruising, and competition articles covering both power and sail boat activities of interest to the recreational boat owner in the 13 western states. Articles include both staff-written material and articles purchased from freelance sources.
**Readers:** Recreational boaters in 13 western states, British Columbia and Mexico.

69442

## SEA KAYAKER
7001 Seaview Ave., N.W., Ste. 135
Seattle, WA 98117-6059
Telephone: (206) 789-1326
FAX: (206) 781-1141
Mailing Address:
   P.O. Box 17170
   Seattle, WA 98107-0870
Year Established: 1984
Pub. Frequency: bi-m.
Page Size: standard
Subscrip. Rate: $3.95 newsstand; $21/yr.
Materials: 08,09,19,20,21,29,30,32,33
Print Process: web
Circulation: 18,000
Circulation Type: paid

**Owner(s):**
Sea Kayaker, Inc.
7001 Seaview Ave., N.W.
Ste. 135
Seattle, WA 98117-6059
Telephone: (206) 789-1326
Ownership %: 100
**Editorial:**
Chris Cunningham ........................Editor
**Desc.:** Explores kayak touring on sea and
lakes, safety techniques, health,
destinations, history, and much more.

22079

## SEA MAGAZINE
17782 Cowan
Irvine, CA 92714
Telephone: (714) 660-6150
FAX: (714) 660-6172
Year Established: 1908
Pub. Frequency: m.
Page Size: standard
Subscrip. Rate: $2.95 newsstand;
$19.94/yr.; $27.94/yr. Canada;
$29.94/yr. foreign
Freelance Pay: up to $300
Circulation: 70,000
Circulation Type: paid
**Owner(s):**
Duncan McIntosh Co., Inc.
17782 Cowan
Irvine, CA 92714
Telephone: (714) 660-6150
Ownership %: 100
**Bureau(s):**
Sea Magazine - Northwest Sales Office
1818 Westlake Ave., N., 429
Seattle, WA 98109
Telephone: (206) 285-7783
Contact: Melinda Ybarra, Advertising
**Management:**
Duncan McIntosh, Jr. ...............Publisher
Teresa Ybarra ...........................Publisher
Kimberly Burke .............Advertising Manager
**Editorial:**
Eston Ellis ...................Executive Editor
Duncan McIntosh, Jr. ...................Editor
Jeffrey Fleming ............Associate Publisher
**Desc.:** Recreational Boating on West
Coast; Covers Pleasureboating in The
13 Western United States And British
Columbia; Powerboating; Also Covers
Sportfishing (Offshore)
**Readers:** Boat Owners in The Western
U.S.

25937

## SOUNDINGS
35 Pratt St.
Essex, CT 06426-1122
Telephone: (203) 767-3200
FAX: (203) 767-1048
Year Established: 1963
Pub. Frequency: m.
Page Size: tabloid
Subscrip. Rate: $18.97/yr.
Circulation: 90,000
Circulation Type: controlled
**Owner(s):**
Soundings Publications, Inc.
35 Pratt St.
Essex, CT 06426
Telephone: (203) 767-3200
Ownership %: 100
**Bureau(s):**
Jim Flannery
2170 S.E. 17th St.
Ft Lauderdale , FL 33316
Telephone: (305) 523-6419

Liz Schensted
2505 West Coast Hwy., #203
Newport Beach , CA 92663
Telephone: (714) 646-6727

Esme Neely
222 Severn Ave.
P.O. Box 4966
Annapolis, MD 21403
Telephone: (301) 263-2386
**Management:**
John P. Turner ........................President
John P. Turner ........................Publisher
Russ Lennon ...............Advertising Manager
**Editorial:**
William Sisson ..................Senior Editor
Marleah Ross ............................Editor
John Woods ...............Marketing Director
Esme Neely ............................Reporter
**Desc.:** A monthly newspaper covering
boating for recreational mariners and
others interested in boats, the water and
the waterfront in the U.S. Covers local,
state, and national legislative news,
fishing news as it effects the
recreational boatman, ecology and the
environment, the Coast Guard, DNR,
and other policy making and enforcing
agencies.

22082

## SOUTHERN BOATING
1766 Bay Rd.
Miami Beach, FL 33139
Telephone: (305) 538-0700
Year Established: 1972
Pub. Frequency: m.
Page Size: standard
Subscrip. Rate: $15/yr.
Materials: 06,08,09,15,21,28,29,32,33
Freelance Pay: $75/average, includes
photos
Circulation: 29,000
Circulation Type: controlled & paid
**Owner(s):**
Southern Boating & Yachting, Inc.
1766 Bay Rd.
Miami Beach, FL 33139
Telephone: (305) 538-0700
Ownership %: 100
**Management:**
Skip Allen ...........................Publisher
Richard Allen ...............Business Manager
Cathryn Allen-Zubi ...........Circulation Manager
**Editorial:**
Skip Allen ............................Editor
Andree Conrad ..................Managing Editor
Richard Allen ........................Advertising
Lissie Allen ........................Art Director
Debbie Reznik ................Creative Director
**Desc.:** Edited for boatowners who cruise
and sail the waters from Texas to
Florida, the Bahamas, and the
Caribbean. Feature articles focus on
cruising, racing, sailing, fishing, marine-
related regional color and history.
Departments include: Boating Log,
Fishing Tip, Words From Readers,
Racing Roundup, Boat Shopper,
Designers Choice, Yacht Brokerage,
Trade-A-Boat, Who's Who.

22083

## TRAILER BOATS
20700 Belshaw Ave.
Carson, CA 90746-3510
Telephone: (310) 537-6322
FAX: (310) 537-8735
Year Established: 1971
Pub. Frequency: 11/yr.
Page Size: standard
Subscrip. Rate: $19.97/yr.
Materials: 02,05,10,21,32,33
Freelance Pay: varies
Circulation: 87,000
Circulation Type: paid

**Owner(s):**
Poole Publications, Inc.
20700 Belshaw Ave.
Carson, CA 90746-3510
Telephone: (310) 537-6322
Ownership %: 100
**Bureau(s):**
Poole Publications
13180 N. Cleveland Ave., # 137
N. Ft. Myers, FL 33903
Telephone: (813) 656-4199
Contact: Joan Key, Advertising

Poole Publications
708 N. First St., Ste. 235B
Minneapolis, MN 55401
Telephone: (612) 375-1073
Contact: Jim Bryant, Advertising
**Management:**
Ralph Poole ...........................President
Wiley Poole ...........................Publisher
Joan Key ...............Advertising Manager
Carlotta Poole ..............Business Manager
**Editorial:**
Randy Scott ............................Editor
Bob Kovacik ...............Automotive Editor
Gordon West ........................Miscellaneous
Patti Higginbotham ...............Miscellaneous
Larry Carpenter .....................Miscellaneous
Brandy Schaffels ...........New Products Editor
Jim Barron ...................Technical Editor
**Desc.:** Reports and evaluations of
products useful to trailer boatmen,
including boat test on current
model cruisers, runabout, fishing, ski,
and houseboats are part of every issue.
Also articles on proper towing, launching
and loading procedures; how-to features,
camping, and travel stories attractive to
trailer boaters, as are true adventures
involving small boats.
**Readers:** Trailer boaters and prospective
purchasers of trailerable-size boats.

68738

## WOODENBOAT
P.O. Box 78
Brooklin, ME 04616
Telephone: (207) 359-4651
FAX: (207) 359-8920
Year Established: 1974
Pub. Frequency: bi-m.
Subscrip. Rate: $4.95 newsstand;
$24.95/yr.
Circulation: 120,000
Circulation Type: paid
**Owner(s):**
Woodenboat Publications, Inc.
P.O. Box 78
Brooklin, ME 04616
Telephone: (207) 359-4651
Ownership %: 100
**Management:**
Carl Cramer ...........................Publisher
**Editorial:**
Jonathan A. Wilson ....................Editor

22085

## YACHTING
Two Park Ave.
New York, NY 10016
Telephone: (212) 779-5300
FAX: (212) 725-1035
Year Established: 1907
Pub. Frequency: m.
Page Size: standard
Subscrip. Rate: $3/copy; $19.98/yr.
Freelance Pay: $300-$1000
Circulation: 132,000
Circulation Type: paid
**Owner(s):**
Times Mirror Magazines, Inc.
Two Park Ave.
New York, NY 10016
Ownership %: 100
**Management:**
Oliver Moore, III ...................Publisher

**Editorial:**
Charles Barthold ...................Executive Editor
Tessie Quioque ...................Managing Editor
Frank Rothmann ........................Art Director
Dennis Caprio ........................How-To Editor
Dennis Caprio ...............New Products Editor
Kenny Wooton ........................Sail Editor
**Desc.:** Contributed and staff-written articles
cover all phases of recreational boating
and allied interests: design, navigation,
cruises, etc. Interested in new
equipment having marine application.
**Readers:** Boat owners, yachtsmen, the
marine trader.

69458

## 48 DEGREES NORTH
6327 Seaview Ave., N.W.
Seattle, WA 98107
Telephone: (206) 789-7350
FAX: (206) 789-6392
Year Established: 1981
Pub. Frequency: m.
Page Size: standard
Subscrip. Rate: $15/yr.
Materials: 01,02,05,06,08,09,10,11,15,19,
20,21,24,25,28,29,32,33
Print Process: web offset
Circulation: 22,000
Circulation Type: free & paid
**Owner(s):**
Boundless Enterprises, Inc.
6327 Seaview Ave., N.W.
Seattle, WA 98107
Telephone: (206) 789-7350
Ownership %: 100
**Management:**
Charles Streatch ...........................President
Charles Streatch ...........................Publisher
Michael Collins ...............Advertising Manager
Jane Larson ...................Circulation Manager
Michael Collins ...................Sales Manager
**Editorial:**
Rich Hazelton ...................Editor in Chief
Karen Higginson ........................News Editor
**Desc.:** Reports on boating activities and
racing for the Northwest.
**Deadline:** story-1st of mo.; news-10th of
mo.; photo-10th of mo.; ads-10th of mo

## Group 612-Business

61660

## AAII JOURNAL
625 N. Michigan Ave., 1900
Chicago, IL 60611
Telephone: (312) 280-0170
FAX: (312) 280-6125
Year Established: 1979
Pub. Frequency: m.
Subscrip. Rate: $49/yr.
Materials: 01,02,05,06,17,28,29,30
Circulation: 110,000
Circulation Type: paid
**Owner(s):**
A.A.I.I.
625 N. Michigan Ave.
Suite 1900
Chicago, IL 60611
Telephone: (312) 280-0170
FAX: (312) 280-1625
Ownership %: 100
**Editorial:**
Maria Crawford Scott .....................Editor
**Desc.:** The AAII Journal provides
information and how-to articles that help
individual investors to learn investment
fundamentals. The Journal does not
promote a specific viewpoint
or encourage specific investments and
does not accept advertising.
**Readers:** 110,000 serious individual
investors.

**Materials Accepted/Included:** 01-Business news 02-By-line articles 03-Fashion news 04-Food news 05-Freelance copy 06-Letters to editor 07-Real estate news 08-Sports news 09-Travel news 10-Book rev. 11-Movie rev. 12-Music rev. 13-TV rev. 14-Theater rev. 15-Coming events 16-Obituaries 17-Question & answer 18-Social announcements 19-Artwork 20-Cartoons 21-Photos 22-TV listings 23-Audio rec. 24-Video rec. 25-Books 26-Films/film clips 27-Personnel news 28-Press releases 29-New product news/photos 30-Trade lit. 31-Contracts awarded 32-Display adv. 33-Classified adv.

6-13

## ACROSS THE BOARD
25665

845 Third Ave.
New York, NY 10022
Telephone: (212) 759-0900
FAX: (212) 980-7014
Year Established: 1973
Pub. Frequency: 10/yr.
Page Size: standard
Subscrip. Rate: $4 newsstand; $40/yr.
Materials: 01,02,05,06,10,19,21,25,28,32
Freelance Pay: varies
Print Process: offset
Circulation: 30,000
Circulation Type: controlled & paid
**Owner(s):**
Conference Board, Inc.
845 Third Ave.
New York, NY 10022
Telephone: (212) 759-0900
Ownership %: 100
**Management:**
Preston Townley ..............................President
Roberta Stern ...................Advertising Manager
**Editorial:**
A. J. Vogl ...............................................Editor
**Desc.:** Across the Board offers new angles
   and lively debate on managing people
   and organizations. It also roams widely
   covering public-policy issues, life-style
   changes, developments in science,
   technology and education - any and all
   trends that can eventually affect
   business.
**Readers:** Business executives, universities,
   government CEO's, senior management
   of Fortune 500.

## BETTER INVESTING
22265

711 W. Thirteen Mile Rd.
Madison Heights, MI 48071
Telephone: (810) 583-6242
FAX: (810) 583-4880
Year Established: 1951
Pub. Frequency: m.
Page Size: standard
Subscrip. Rate: $20/yr.
Freelance Pay: negotiable
Circulation: 140,000
Circulation Type: paid
**Owner(s):**
National Association of Investors
   Corporation
711 W. Thrirteen Mile Rd.
Madison Heights, MI 48071
Telephone: (810) 583-6242
FAX: (810) 583-4880
Ownership %: 100
**Management:**
T. E. O'Hara ........................Chairman of Board
K. S. Janke, Sr. ...............................Publisher
Martha F. Stephens ..........Advertising Manager
**Editorial:**
Donald E. Danko ....................Executive Editor
Rosemary A. Nicholson ................Layout Editor
**Desc.:** Articles on individual securities,
   stock market trends, industry reviews
   and investment news. Editor reviews
   articles for publication. Majority of
   articles written by investment
   professionals, do-it-yourself investors
   and editorial staff. Covers people
   involved in investing-highlighting their
   personality, investment philosophy, and
   goals.
**Readers:** All investors, average income -
   $62,665. 42.6 % are 50 years old or
   younger, 35.5% are over 60.

## BOISE BUSINESS TODAY
65390

P.O. Box 2368
Boise, ID 83701
Telephone: (208) 344-5515
FAX: (208) 344-5849
Year Established: 1974

Pub. Frequency: m.
Page Size: standard
Subscrip. Rate: free with membership
Circulation: 3,200
Circulation Type: controlled
**Owner(s):**
Boise Area Chamber of Commerce
P.O. Box 2638
Boise, ID 83701
Telephone: (208) 344-5515
Ownership %: 100
**Editorial:**
Kathy O'Neill ...........................................Editor

## BUSINESS PHILADELPHIA
67292

260 S. Broad St.
Philadelphia, PA 19102
Telephone: (215) 735-6969
FAX: (215) 735-6965
Year Established: 1990
Pub. Frequency: m.
Page Size: standard
Subscrip. Rate: $2.50 newsstand;
   $32.50/yr.
Materials: 01,02,05,06,07,08,27,28,29
Print Process: web offset
Circulation: 25,150
Circulation Type: paid
**Owner(s):**
Geographic Business Publishers, Inc.
260 S. Broad St.
Philadelphia, PA 19102
Telephone: (215) 735-6969
FAX: (215) 735-6965
Ownership %: 100
**Management:**
Gil Wetzel ............................................President
Maury Z. Levy ......................................Publisher
Annie Batchelder ................Associate Publisher
Lauren Stevenson ...........Advertising Manager
Yacina
**Editorial:**
Maury Z. Levy ........................................Editor
**Desc.:** Features personality profiles, with
   information about the business,
   community and recreational lives of the
   city's business leaders.
**Deadline:** ads-45 days

## BUSINESS START-UPS
65362

2392 Morse Ave.
Irvine, CA 92714
Telephone: (714) 261-2325
FAX: (714) 755-4211
Year Established: 1989
Pub. Frequency: m.
Page Size: standard
Subscrip. Rate: $9.97/yr.
Freelance Pay: $300
Circulation: 210,000
Circulation Type: paid
**Owner(s):**
Entrepreneur Media, Inc.
2392 Morse Ave.
Irvine, CA 92714
Telephone: (714) 261-2325
Ownership %: 100
**Management:**
Lee Jones .............................................Publisher
**Editorial:**
Rieva Lesonsky ...........................Editor in Chief
Maria Anton .............................Managing Editor
**Desc.:** Giving advice to those hoping to
   start their own business.
**Readers:** Persons starting their own
   business.

## BUSINESS TRAVELLER INTERNATIONAL
65356

51 E. 42nd St., Ste. 1806
New York, NY 10017-5404
Telephone: (212) 697-1700
FAX: (212) 697-1005
Pub. Frequency: m.

Page Size: standard
Subscrip. Rate: $3 newsstand; $29.37/yr.
Circulation: 45,000
Circulation Type: paid
**Owner(s):**
Perry Publications, Inc.
51 E. 42nd St., Ste. 1806
New York, NY 10017-5404
Telephone: (212) 697-1700
Ownership %: 100
**Management:**
Francis X. Gallagher ..........................Publisher
**Editorial:**
Kate Rice ...............................................Editor
**Desc.:** Overviews of business climates and
   descriptions of the most comfortable,
   efficient, travel services available,
   includes current tariff information and
   best air fares, hotel and car rental rates.
**Readers:** Overseas business travelers.

## CREDIT & FINANCE
68757

951 S. Oxford, No. 109
Los Angeles, CA 90006
Telephone: (213) 732-3477
FAX: (213) 732-9123
Mailing Address:
   P.O. Box 75392
   Los Angeles, CA 90075
Year Established: 1991
Pub. Frequency: q.
Subscrip. Rate: $29/yr.
Materials: 01,02,03,04,05,06,07,08,09,10,
   11,12,13,14,15,16,17,18,19,20,21,22,23,
   24,25,26,27,28,29,30,31,32,33
Print Process: web
Circulation: 120,000
Circulation Type: controlled & paid
**Owner(s):**
Publishing & Business Consultants
951 S. Oxford, No. 109
Los Angeles, CA 90006
Telephone: (213) 732-3477
FAX: (213) 732-3477
Ownership %: 100
**Editorial:**
Andeson Napoleon Atia ...........................Editor
**Desc.:** Covers consumer related credit
   card issues.
**Deadline:** story-2 wks. prior to pub. date;
   news-2 wks. prior; photo-2 wks. prior;
   ads-90 days prior

## CURRENT EMPLOYMENT
69279

951 S. Oxford, No. 109
Los Angeles, CA 90006
Telephone: (213) 732-3477
FAX: (213) 732-3477
Year Established: 1991
Pub. Frequency: q.
Subscrip. Rate: $29.99/yr.
Materials: 01,02,03,04,05,06,07,08,09,10,
   11,12,13,14,15,16,17,18,19,20,21,23,24,
   25,26,27,28,29,30,32,33
Freelance Pay: $.20-.50/word
Print Process: web
Circulation: 120,000
Circulation Type: controlled & paid
**Owner(s):**
Publishing & Business Consultants
951 S. Oxford, No. 109
Los Angeles, CA 90006
Telephone: (213) 732-3477
FAX: (213) 732-3477
Ownership %: 100
**Editorial:**
Andeson Napoleon Atia ...........................Editor
**Desc.:** Provides updated information on
   government jobs, with employment
   trends and forecasts.
**Deadline:** story-2 wks. prior to pub. date;
   news-2 wks. prior to pub. date; photo-2
   wks. prior to pub. date; ads-90 days
   prior to pub. date

## DIABLO
64747

2520 Camino Dieblo
Ste. 200
Walnut Creek, CA 94596
Telephone: (510) 943-1111
FAX: (510) 943-1045
Year Established: 1978
Pub. Frequency: m.
Page Size: standard
Subscrip. Rate: $2 newsstand; $18/yr. in
   state
Freelance Pay: $50-$650 (Approx.
   $.25/wd.)
Circulation: 60,000
Circulation Type: paid
**Owner(s):**
Diablo Publications
2520 Camino Dieblo
Ste. 200
Walnut Creek, CA 94596
Ownership %: 100
**Management:**
Steve Riveria ......................................Publisher
Carol Vogl ...................................Office Manager
Bob Rivera ...................................Sales Manager
**Editorial:**
Umberto Tosi .........................................Editor

## DOLLAR$ENSE
68685

401 Shatto Pl., Ste. 105
Los Angeles, CA 90020
Telephone: (213) 386-2111
FAX: (213) 386-6470
Year Established: 1977
Pub. Frequency: q.
Page Size: standard
Subscrip. Rate: $12/yr. to qualified
   personnel
Materials: 02,05,10,17
Print Process: web offset
Circulation: 800,000
Circulation Type: controlled
**Owner(s):**
E.F. Baumer & Co.
401 Shatto Pl., Ste. 105
Los Angeles, CA 90020
Telephone: (213) 386-2111
Ownership %: 100
**Editorial:**
Richard Baumer .......................................Editor
**Desc.:** Covers personal finance, estate
   and retirement planning.
**Readers:** Top customers of client financial
   institutions; officers of client financial
   institutions.

## ENTREPRENEUR
59560

2392 Morse Ave.
Irvine, CA 92714
Telephone: (714) 261-2325
FAX: (714) 755-4211
Year Established: 1973
Pub. Frequency: m.
Page Size: standard
Subscrip. Rate: $3 newsstand; $19.97/yr.
Materials: 01,06,25,28,29,32,33
Freelance Pay: varies
Circulation: 385,000
Circulation Type: paid
**Owner(s):**
Entrepreneur Media, Inc.
2392 Morse Ave.
Irvine, CA 92714
Telephone: (714) 261-2325
Ownership %: 100
**Management:**
Lee Jones .............................................Publisher
Don Cron ...........................Circulation Manager
**Editorial:**
Rieva Lesonsky ........................................Editor
Steve Olson ....................................Advertising
**Desc.:** Provides information on running a
   small business.

**Materials Accepted/Included:** 01-Business news 02-By-line articles 03-Fashion news 04-Food news 05-Freelance copy 06-Letters to editor 07-Real estate news 08-Sports news 09-Travel news 10-Book rev. 11-Movie rev. 12-Music rev. 13-TV rev. 14-Theater rev. 15-Coming events 16-Obituaries 17-Question & answer 18-Social announcements 19-Artwork 20-Cartoons 21-Photos 22-TV listings 23-Audio rec. 24-Video rec. 25-Books 26-Films/film clips 27-Personnel news 28-Press releases 29-New product news/photos 30-Trade lit. 31-Contracts awarded 32-Display adv. 33-Classified adv.

**Readers:** Small business owners.
**Deadline:** story-6 mos. prior to pub. date; ads-25th of mo. 3 mos. prior to pub. date

### FAIRFIELD COUNTY BUSINESS JOURNAL

65627

22 Sawmill River Rd.
Hawthorne, NY 10532
Telephone: (914) 347-5200
FAX: (914) 347-5576
Year Established: 1968
Pub. Frequency: w.
Page Size: tabloid
Subscrip. Rate: $1.25 newsstand; $48/yr.; $75/2 yrs.
Materials: 01,02,05,06,07,20,21,28,29,30, 31,32,33
Freelance Pay: negotiable
Print Process: web offset
Circulation: 12,000
Circulation Type: controlled
**Owner(s):**
West Fair Communications, Inc.
22 Saw Mill River Rd.
Hawthorne, NY 10532
Telephone: (914) 347-5200
FAX: (914) 347-5576
Ownership %: 100
**Management:**
Dee DelBello ............................Publisher
**Editorial:**
Mills Korte ....................................Editor
**Desc.:** A recent survey revealed that 82.9% of the Journal's readers are top executives with an average annual family income of $148,000. They consider the Journal their primary source of local business news. Popular features include: business lists, newsmaker profiles, focus sections, tradetips, industry supplements and records of incorporations, deeds, etc.
**Readers:** Decision-makers in corporations and businesses, executives, professionals and managers, business owners.
**Deadline:** story-1 wk. prior to pub. date; news-5 days prior; photo-1 wk. prior; ads-10 days prior

### FLORIDA OUTLOOK, THE

59053

University of Florida
P.O. Box 117140
Gainesville, FL 32611-7140
Telephone: (904) 392-0171
FAX: (904) 392-4739
Year Established: 1977
Pub. Frequency: q.
Page Size: standard
Subscrip. Rate: $200/yr.
Circulation: 350
Circulation Type: paid
**Owner(s):**
Bureau of Economic & Business Research
University of Florida
221 Matherly Hall
Gainesville, FL 32611-2017
Telephone: (904) 392-0171
Ownership %: 100
**Editorial:**
Dr. Carol A. Taylor West ..........................Editor
Ann C. Pierce ......................Managing Editor
**Desc.:** Quarterly forecasts of the economy of Florida and its 20 metro areas, including population, personal income, housing starts, tourists, employment, sales.
**Readers:** Business community, local governments, planners, researchers interested in the Florida economy.

### GUAM BUSINESS NEWS

69719

P.O. Box 3191
Agana, GU 96910
Telephone: (671) 472-7606
FAX: (671) 472-2163
Year Established: 1983
Pub. Frequency: m.
Page Size: standard
Subscrip. Rate: $3 newsstand; $60/yr. US; $130/yr. foreign
Materials: 01,06,07,10,32
Print Process: offset
**Owner(s):**
Glimpses of Guam, Inc.
P.O. Box 3191
Agana, GU 96910
Telephone: (671) 472-7606
Ownership %: 100
**Management:**
Stephen V. Nygard ............................Publisher
**Editorial:**
Alison Russell ....................................Editor
**Desc.:** Guam Business News is the premier source for an analytical look at business in Guam, Micronesia and surrounding Asian neighbors.

### HUDSON VALLEY BUSINESS JOURNAL

65626

County Rt. 1
Pine Island, NY 10969-0339
Telephone: (914) 258-4008
FAX: (914) 258-4111
Mailing Address:
P.O. Box 339
Pine Island, NY 10969-0339
Year Established: 1987
Pub. Frequency: bi-w.
Page Size: tabloid
Subscrip. Rate: $.75 issue; $20/yr.; $35/2 yrs.
Materials: 01,32,33
Freelance Pay: $50/article
Circulation: 15,000
Circulation Type: paid
**Owner(s):**
County Business Journals Publications
P.O. Box 339
Pine Island, NY 10969-0339
Telephone: (914) 258-4008
Ownership %: 100
**Management:**
Edward Klein ............................Publisher
**Editorial:**
Carol Betley ....................................Editor
**Desc.:** Serves Orange & Rock Island counties in 2 split editions.
**Readers:** Businesses & executives

### INCOME OPPORTUNITIES

22333

1500 Broadway
New York, NY 10036
Telephone: (212) 642-0600
FAX: (212) 302-8269
Year Established: 1956
Pub. Frequency: m.
Page Size: standard
Subscrip. Rate: $2.50 copy; $17.89/yr.
Materials: 01,02,04,05,06,09,10,27,28,29, 30,32,33
Freelance Pay: $.20/wd.
Circulation: 425,000
Circulation Type: paid
**Owner(s):**
IO Publications, Inc.
1500 Broadway
New York, NY 10036
Telephone: (212) 642-0600
Ownership %: 100
**Management:**
Edward Lewis ............................Publisher
Armie Dandre ..................Advertising Manager

**Editorial:**
Stephen Wagner ..........................Editor
Arthur Blougouras ....................Managing Editor
**Desc.:** Articles report on franchises, independent businesses, mail order & spare-time opportunities giving investment & earning potential. selling articles, directed to various types of salesmen, are intended to improve sales techniques and increase sales; management improvement enterprise. Departments include: Mail Order Pipeline, Franchising Today, Your Home Business, New Products, Business Hotline, Successful Selling & Letters to the Editor.
**Readers:** People desiring to own a business.

### INDIVIDUAL INVESTOR

67268

333 7th Ave., 5th Fl.
New York, NY 10001
Telephone: (212) 689-2777
FAX: (212) 843-2777
Year Established: 1981
Pub. Frequency: m.
Page Size: oversize
Subscrip. Rate: $29.95/yr.
Circulation: 160,000
Circulation Type: paid
**Owner(s):**
Individual Investor Group
333 7th Ave., 5th Fl.
New York, NY 10001
Telephone: (212) 689-2777
Ownership %: 100
**Management:**
Scot Rosenblum ............................Publisher
Harvey Lichtman ..............Advertising Manager
**Editorial:**
Jonathan Steinberg ..................Editor in Chief
Gordon G. Anderson ..................Senior Editor
**Desc.:** Investor's guide to value and growth among America's small companies. Features in-depth stories on dynamic and undervalued stocks; reviews the best performing mutual funds.

### INTERNATIONAL ROUND TABLE, THE

65304

P.O. Box 1056
Seffner, FL 33584
Telephone: (813) 681-3105
FAX: (813) 684-1076
Year Established: 1974
Pub. Frequency: m.
Page Size: standard
Subscrip. Rate: $25/yr.; $40/2 yrs.
Circulation: 8,500
Circulation Type: paid
**Owner(s):**
C.W. Thomae, Inc.
P.O. Box 1056
Seffner, FL 33584
Telephone: (813) 681-3105
Ownership %: 100
**Editorial:**
Vicki J. Thomae ............................Editor
**Desc.:** Publication is geared to new to export and small export firms.
**Readers:** Exporters, Potential Exporters

### JOURNAL OF MATERIALS PROCESSING & MANUFACTURING SCIENCE

69729

851 New Holland Ave.
Lancaster, PA 17604
Telephone: (717) 291-5609
FAX: (717) 295-4538
Mailing Address:
P.O. Box 3535
Lancaster, PA 17604
Year Established: 1992

Pub. Frequency: q.
Page Size: standard
Subscrip. Rate: $195/yr.; $380/2 yrs.; $565/3 yrs.
Circulation: 100
Circulation Type: paid
**Owner(s):**
Technomic Publishing Co., Inc.
851 New Holland Ave.
Box 3535
Lancaster, PA 17604
Telephone: (717) 291-5609
Ownership %: 100
**Editorial:**
Selcuk Guceri ............................Editor
**Desc.:** Forum for research in materials processing and manufacturing. Provides new developments in processing metals, polymers and composites, ceramics, powders and specialty materials.

### KIPLINGER'S PERSONAL FINANCE MAGAZINE

22279

1729 H St., N.W.
Washington, DC 20006
Telephone: (202) 887-6400
FAX: (202) 331-1206
Year Established: 1947
Pub. Frequency: m.
Page Size: standard
Subscrip. Rate: $18/yr.; $32/2 yrs.; $44/3 yrs.
Circulation: 1,350,000
Circulation Type: paid
**Owner(s):**
Kiplinger Washington Editors, Inc.
1729 H St., NW
Washington, DC 20006
Telephone: (202) 887-6400
Ownership %: 100
**Management:**
Knight Kiplinger ............................Publisher
Carol LePere ....................Circulation Manager
**Editorial:**
Knight A. Kiplinger ......................Editor in Chief
Theodore Miller ............................Editor
Mark Solheim ....................Managing Editor
Carol LePere ....................Associate Publisher
Don Fragale ....................Production Director
**Desc.:** Covers family and personal economics, life and other insurance, autos, education, careers, home buying, budgets, civic affairs, children, health, buying, investments, savings.
**Readers:** General.

### MONEY

25882

Time & Life Bldg., Rockefeller Ctr.
1271 Ave. of the Americas
New York, NY 10020
Telephone: (212) 522-1212
FAX: (212) 522-0332
Year Established: 1972
Pub. Frequency: m.
Page Size: standard
Subscrip. Rate: $3.95/issue; $35.95/yr.
Freelance Pay: varies
Circulation: 2,077,000
Circulation Type: paid
**Owner(s):**
Time Warner, Inc.
Time & Life Bldg., Rm. 33-17
New York, NY 10020
Telephone: (212) 522-1212
Ownership %: 100
**Management:**
Betsy Martin ............................Publisher
**Editorial:**
Jason McManus ..........................Editor in Chief
Frank Lalli ....................Managing Editor
Traci Churchill ....................Art Director
Deborah Pierce ....................Picture Editor

---

Materials Accepted/Included: 01-Business news 02-By-line articles 03-Fashion news 04-Food news 05-Freelance copy 06-Letters to editor 07-Real estate news 08-Sports news 09-Travel news 10-Book rev. 11-Movie rev. 12-Music rev. 13-TV rev. 14-Theater rev. 15-Coming events 16-Obituaries 17-Question & answer 18-Social announcements 19-Artwork 20-Cartoons 21-Photos 22-TV listings 23-Audio rec. 24-Video rec. 25-Books 26-Films/film clips 27-Personnel news 28-Press releases 29-New product news/photos 30-Trade lit. 31-Contracts awarded 32-Display adv. 33-Classified adv.

**Desc.:** Departments include: Money Helps, Washington Letter, Wall Street Letter, Current Accounts, Moneymakers, Top Deals, Savings Roundup, Fund Watch, Love & Money, Money Profile.
**Readers:** Affluent men & women gaining maximum return on investments, increasing earning power, saving wisely, obtaining quality and values in key purchases.

22370

**MONEY MAKING OPPORTUNITIES**
11071 Ventura Blvd.
Studio City, CA 91604
Telephone: (818) 980-9166
Pub. Frequency: 8/yr.
Subscrip. Rate: $8/yr.
Circulation: 220,000
Circulation Type: paid
**Owner(s):**
Success Publishing International
11071 Ventura Blvd.
Studio City, CA 91604
Telephone: (818) 980-9166
**Management:**
Donald H. Perry ............................Publisher
Donald H. Perry ...............Advertising Manager
**Editorial:**
Donald H. Perry ................................Editor
William Davis ....................Business Editor
**Desc.:** Direct selling, opportunity.
**Readers:** People looking for direct selling and money - making opportunities.

69280

**NATIONAL BUSINESS EMPLOYMENT WEEKLY**
P.O. Box 300
Princeton, NJ 08543-0003
Telephone: (609) 520-4305
Year Established: 1980
Pub. Frequency: w.
Page Size: tabloid
Subscrip. Rate: $3.95 newsstand
Materials: 02,05,06,15,20,28,32,33
Circulation: 35,000
Circulation Type: paid
**Owner(s):**
Dow Jones & Co., Inc.
P.O. Box 300
Princeton, NJ 08543-0300
Telephone: (609) 520-4305
Ownership %: 100
**Editorial:**
Tony Lee .......................................Editor
**Desc.:** Provides career guidance and job-hunting ideas.
**Readers:** Wall Street Journal readers.

25668

**PENTON EXECUTIVE NETWORK**
1100 Superior Ave.
Cleveland, OH 44114
Telephone: (216) 696-7000
Year Established: 1970
Pub. Frequency: m.
Page Size: standard
Circulation: 2,251,513
Circulation Type: controlled
**Owner(s):**
Penton Publishing
1100 Superior Ave.
Cleveland, OH 44114
Telephone: (216) 696-7000
Ownership %: 100
**Management:**
Rusty Piersons ..........................Publisher
Scott Beech ..................Production Manager
**Editorial:**
Christine Ravas ...............Advertising Services Manager
Grace Heese ..................Marketing Manager

**Desc.:** Edited for professional/managerial subscribers. Each month, it provides editorials on technical and managerial subjects critical to the business interests of the Network's specialized readers.
**Deadline:** ads-6 wks. prior to pub. date

66515

**PROSALES**
One Thomas Cir., Ste. 600
Washington, DC 20005
Telephone: (202) 452-0800
Year Established: 1989
Pub. Frequency: q.
Page Size: standard
Subscrip. Rate: $3.95/copy
Materials: 01,02,05,28,29,32,33
Circulation: 40,000
Circulation Type: controlled
**Owner(s):**
Hanley-Wood, Inc.
One Thomas Cir., Ste. 600
Washington, DC 20005
Telephone: (202) 452-0800
Ownership %: 100
**Management:**
Michael J. Tucker ........................Publisher
**Editorial:**
Boyce Thompson ..........................Editor
**Desc.:** Helps building product dealers, distributors, and wholesalers better understand the needs of their professional customers, home builders and remodeling contractors.

25655

**ROAD KING**
3100 West End Ave.
Ste. 200
Nashville, TN 37203-1349
Telephone: (615) 783-2600
FAX: (615) 385-1788
Year Established: 1963
Pub. Frequency: bi-m.
Page Size: pocket
Subscrip. Rate: $12/yr.
Freelance Pay: $50-$400
Circulation: 220,000
Circulation Type: controlled
**Owner(s):**
National Auto/Truckstops, Inc.
1650 E. Golf Rd.
Schaumburg, IL 60173
Telephone: (708) 330-5310
Ownership %: 100
**Management:**
Rial Greenman ..........................Publisher
**Editorial:**
William A. Coop ...............Executive Editor
George Friend ..............................Editor
Rich Vurva ..................................Editor
Mary Beth Burns ..................Art Director
Dick Hanrahan ............................Sales
Wil Robey ...................................Sales
**Desc.:** A leisure reading publication edited specifically for the long- haul, over-the-road truck driver.
**Readers:** Fleet drivers and independent truckers, both exempt haulers and independents under contract or lease.

68684

**SMARTMONEY**
1790 Broadway
New York, NY 10019
Telephone: (212) 649-2000
Year Established: 1992
Pub. Frequency: m.
Subscrip. Rate: $2.50 newsstand; $24/yr.
Circulation: 550,000
Circulation Type: paid
**Owner(s):**
Hearst Magazine Division, The
1790 Broadway
New York, NY 10019
Telephone: (212) 649-2000
Ownership %: 100

**Editorial:**
Steven Swartz ............................Editor
**Desc.:** Covers a variety of personal finance topics for upscale readers.

22407

**SPARE TIME MAGAZINE**
5810 W. Oklahoma Ave.
Milwaukee, WI 53219-4384
Telephone: (414) 543-8110
FAX: (414) 543-9767
Year Established: 1955
Pub. Frequency: 9/yr.
Page Size: standard
Subscrip. Rate: $2.50 newsstand; $15/yr.
Materials: 02,05,10,28,29,32,33
Freelance Pay: $.10/wd.
Print Process: web offset
Circulation: 301,750
Circulation Type: paid
**Owner(s):**
Kipen Publishing Corp.
5810 W. Oklahoma Ave.
Milwaukee, WI 53219-4384
Telephone: (414) 543-8110
FAX: (414) 543-9767
Ownership %: 100
**Management:**
Dennis Wilk ............................Publisher
Barbara Gautz-Zach .........Advertising Manager
Julie Partenheimer ...............Classified Adv. Manager
**Editorial:**
Stan Holden ..............................Editor
Deborah Roan ..................Circulation Director
**Desc.:** Money making opportunities and ideas, spare or full time.
**Readers:** Men and women looking for opportunities of small independent business and new trades or training.
**Deadline:** ads-45 days

25669

**SUCCESS MAGAZINE**
230 Park Ave., 7th Fl.
New York, NY 10169-0014
Telephone: (212) 551-9500
FAX: (212) 922-2919
Year Established: 1954
Pub. Frequency: m.
Page Size: standard
Subscrip. Rate: $19.97/yr. US; $29.97/yr. foreign
Circulation: 475,000
Circulation Type: paid
**Owner(s):**
Lang Communications, Inc.
230 Park Ave., 7th Fl.
New York, NY 10169
Telephone: (212) 551-9500
Ownership %: 100
**Management:**
Dale Lang ..............................President
Scott DeGarmo ........................Publisher
**Editorial:**
Scott DeGarmo ............................Editor
Cathy Brower ..................Managing Editor
David Bayer ..........................Art Director
Rose Sullivan ..................Production Director
**Desc.:** Features self-help and motivational material profiles of successful persons, money management and investment materials. Average feature is 2,500 words. Anything helping our readers to achieve success in their business and personal lives.
**Readers:** Professional and management, college graduate.

65303

**TAMPA BAY BUSINESS JOURNAL**
405 N. Reo St.
Ste. 210
Tampa, FL 33609
Telephone: (813) 289-8225
FAX: (813) 289-4518
Year Established: 1981

Pub. Frequency: w.
Page Size: tabloid
Subscrip. Rate: $1 newsstand; $48/yr. mailed
Freelance Pay: varies
Circulation: 13,000
Circulation Type: paid
**Owner(s):**
American City Business Journals
128 S. Tyson St.
Ste. 2200
Charlotte, NC 28202
Telephone: (704) 375-7404
Ownership %: 100
**Management:**
John Beddow ............................Publisher
Debbie McCaw ..................Advertising Manager
Angie Joseph ..................Circulation Manager
**Editorial:**
Allen Greenberg ..........................Editor
**Readers:** Business Executives, Owners, Etc.; Business Practices

65302

**TAMPA BAY MAGAZINE**
2531 Landmark Dr.
Ste. 101
Clearwater, FL 34621
Telephone: (813) 791-4800
FAX: (813) 796-0527
Year Established: 1986
Pub. Frequency: bi-m.
Page Size: standard
Subscrip. Rate: $2.95 newsstand; $12/yr.
Print Process: web offset
Circulation: 25,000
Circulation Type: paid
**Owner(s):**
Tampa Bay Publications, Inc.
2531 Landmark Dr.
Ste. 101
Clearwater, FL 34621
Telephone: (813) 791-4800
Ownership %: 100
**Management:**
Aaron Fodiman ..........................Publisher
Mike Stovekem ..................Advertising Manager
**Editorial:**
Aaron Fodiman ............................Editor
Sherry Babbitt ..................Associate Editor
**Readers:** Upscale, affluent

67065

**TREASURY & RISK MANAGEMENT**
253 Summer St.
Boston, MA 02210
Telephone: (617) 345-9700
Mailing Address:
    111 W. 57th St.
    New York, NY 10019
Year Established: 1991
Pub. Frequency: 6/yr.
Page Size: standard
Subscrip. Rate: $60/yr.
Materials: 01,05,06,28,29,32
Freelance Pay: $.75-$1/wd.
Circulation: 46,000
Circulation Type: controlled
**Owner(s):**
Economist Group, The
253 Summer St.
Boston, MA 02210
Telephone: (617) 345-9700
Ownership %: 100
**Management:**
David Laird ............................Publisher
Lissa Short ..................Advertising Manager
**Editorial:**
Maile Hulihan ............................Editor
**Desc.:** We aim to inform, educate and entertain our readership with leading-edge articles about corporate finance, pension management foreign exchange, cash management, and risk strategies.

---

**Readers:** CFO's, treasurers and VP's of finance of large corporations.

## Group 614-Children & Youth Magazines

### AMERICAN GIRL
68782
8400 Fairway Pl.
Madison, WI 53562
Telephone: (608) 836-4848
FAX: (608) 831-7089
Year Established: 1992
Pub. Frequency: bi-m.
Subscrip. Rate: $19.95/yr.
Circulation: 350,000
Circulation Type: paid
**Owner(s):**
Pleasant Company
8400 Fairway Pl.
Madison, WI 53562
Telephone: (608) 836-4848
Ownership %: 100
**Management:**
Margo Clark ............................Publisher
**Editorial:**
Judy Woodburn ........................Editor
Jennifer Gross ............Circulation Director
**Desc.:** Features articles on American girls, past and present, stories by noted children's authors, paper dolls and cut-out clothes, games and entertainment.
**Readers:** Girls ages 7-12.

### BIG BOPPER, THE
65405
3500 W. Olive Ave., #850
Burbank, CA 91505
Telephone: (818) 953-7999
Year Established: 1983
Pub. Frequency: m.
Page Size: standard
Subscrip. Rate: $21.95/yr.
Materials: 21,23,24,26,28
**Owner(s):**
Laufer Publishing Co.
3500 W. Olive Ave., #850
Burbank, CA 91505
Telephone: (818) 953-7999
Ownership %: 100
**Editorial:**
Rick Rodgers ............................Editor

### BOYS' LIFE
25674
P.O. Box 152079
Irving, TX 75015-2079
Telephone: (214) 580-2366
FAX: (214) 580-2079
Year Established: 1911
Pub. Frequency: m.
Page Size: standard
Subscrip. Rate: $2.50/issue, $15.60/yr.
Freelance Pay: $250-$1,500
Circulation: 1,400,000
Circulation Type: paid
**Owner(s):**
Boy Scouts of America
1325 Walnut Hill Ln.
Irving, TX 75038
Telephone: (214) 580-2360
Ownership %: 100
**Management:**
J. Warren Young ......................Publisher
**Editorial:**
Scott Stuckey ..........................Editor
Beth Hardaway-Morgan ......Art Director
Douglass K. Daniel ..........Articles Editor
Joseph P. Connolly ..........Design Director
Kathy DaGroomes ............Fiction Editor
Brian Payne ............................Photo
William E. Butterworth, IV ....Senior Writer

**Desc.:** Material must be consistent with Scouting objectives, character building and citizenship training, palpably presented. Some of the subjects suggested are adventure, mystery, nature and the out-of-doors, sports, athletics, school life, sea and boats, history, science-fiction, animals, humor, aviation, Scouting and many others.
**Readers:** Boys 8-18.

### CAMPUS LIFE
26641
465 Gundersen Dr.
Carol Stream, IL 60188
Telephone: (708) 260-6200
FAX: (708) 260-0114
Year Established: 1942
Pub. Frequency: m.
Page Size: standard
Subscrip. Rate: $14.95/yr.
Circulation: 120,000
Circulation Type: paid
**Owner(s):**
Christianity Today, Inc.
465 Gundersen Dr.
Carol Stream, IL 60188
Telephone: (708) 260-6200
Ownership %: 100
**Management:**
Harold L. Myra ......................President
Paul D. Robbins ..............Vice President
**Editorial:**
Chris Lutes ........................Senior Editor
Harold Smith ..........................Editor
Linda Schaumbach ..............Advertising
Melodie DeVel ......................Advertising
Dan Poorman ........................Advertising
Harold L. Myra ........Chief Executive Officer
Paul D. Robbins ......Chief Operating Officer
Tim Stafford ..................Consulting Editor
Diane Eble ................Contributing Editor
Rob Wilkins ..............Contributing Editor
**Desc.:** Unique new products, unique activities of teenagers. Contemporary magazine directed to young people of discriminating tastes.
**Readers:** Young people of high school and college age.

### CAREER WORLD
26642
245 Long Hill Rd.
Middletown, CT 06457
Telephone: (800) 446-3355
Mailing Address:
3001 Cindel Dr.
Delran, NJ 08370
Year Established: 1969
Pub. Frequency: 7/yr.
Page Size: standard
Subscrip. Rate: $8.25/yr.
Circulation: 120,000
Circulation Type: paid
**Owner(s):**
Weekly Reader Corporation
245 Long Hill Rd.
Middletown, CT 06457
Telephone: (800) 446-3355
Ownership %: 100
**Management:**
Richard Lebrasser ..................President
Richard Lebrasser ..................Publisher
**Editorial:**
Joyce Lain Kennedy ........Executive Editor
Sandra Maccarone ....................Editor
Jill Lewis ......................Managing Editor
Shelley Sherman ............Assistant Editor
Lois S. Mandel ..............Assistant Editor
Cecily Rosenwald ....................Photo
Donna Powell ............Production Director

**Desc.:** Career education periodical for junior, senior high school students. Published monthly during the school year. Career World features current information on career exploration for guidance programs and reading classes.
**Readers:** Over 1,000,000 junior, senior high school students.

### CHILD LIFE
26643
1100 Waterway Blvd.
Indianapolis, IN 46206-0567
Telephone: (317) 636-8881
FAX: (317) 684-8094
Mailing Address:
P.O. Box 567
Indianapolis, IN 46206-0567
Year Established: 1922
Pub. Frequency: 8/yr.
Page Size: 6 1/8″ X 9 1/2″
Subscrip. Rate: $14.95/yr.
Materials: 02,05,08,09,15,19,20,21,23,24,
25,26,27,28,29,30,32
Freelance Pay: negotiable
Print Process: offset
Circulation: 80,000
Circulation Type: paid
**Owner(s):**
Children's Better Health Institute
P.O. Box 567
Indianapolis, IN 46206
Telephone: (317) 636-8881
Ownership %: 100
**Bureau(s):**
L. R. Barnhart Associates
211 E. Sycamore
Independence, KS 67301
Telephone: (316) 331-1233
Contact: Barny Barnhart, Advertising
**Editorial:**
Elizabeth A. Rinck ............Executive Editor
Lise Hoffman ..........................Editor
Janet Moir ........................Art Director
Betsy Terry ......................Health Editor
**Desc.:** Entertainment plus sports, fitness, and health education for children approximately 9-11 years old. Stories, articles, poems, art, make-and-do projects are featured. The oldest independent children's magazine published in the country, now in its 73rd year. Emphasis is placed on good health, exercise, nutrition and safety.
**Readers:** Children 9 to 11 years old.
**Deadline:** story-8 mos. prior to pub. date; news-8 mos. prior; photo-8 mos. prior

### CHILDREN'S DIGEST
26644
1100 Waterway Blvd.
Indianapolis, IN 46202
Telephone: (317) 636-8881
FAX: (317) 637-0126
Mailing Address:
P.O. Box 567
Indianapolis, IN 46206
Year Established: 1950
Pub. Frequency: 8/yr.
Page Size: 4 color photos/art
Subscrip. Rate: $1.75/issue, $13.95/yr.
Materials: 05,32
Freelance Pay: negotiable
Circulation: 130,000
Circulation Type: paid
**Owner(s):**
Benjamin Franklin Literary & Medical Society, Inc.
P.O. Box 567
Indianapolis, IN 46206
Telephone: (317) 636-8881
**Management:**
Eric Servaas ..........................Publisher
**Editorial:**
Elizabeth Rinck ..................Exec. Editor

Sandy Grieshop ........................Editor
Janet Moir ........................Art Director
Greg Joray ..................Marketing Director
**Desc.:** Features adventure stories, science articles, crafts, word games, poetry, humor and much more to delight and to stimulate young minds and imagination. Emphasis is placed on good health, exercise, nutrition and safety. Length should not exceed 1,500 words.
**Readers:** Children; ages 10-13.

### CHILDREN'S PLAYMATE
68783
1100 Waterway Blvd.
Indianapolis, IN 46202
Telephone: (317) 636-8881
FAX: (317) 637-0126
Mailing Address:
P.O. Box 567
Indianapolis, IN 46202
Year Established: 1929
Pub. Frequency: 8/yr.
Page Size: 6″ x 9″
Subscrip. Rate: $13.95/yr.
Materials: 05,10,19,32
Circulation: 142,000
Circulation Type: paid
**Owner(s):**
Benjamin Franklin Literary & Medical Society, Inc.
P.O. Box 567
1100 Waterway Blvd.
Indianapolis, IN 46202
Telephone: (317) 636-8881
Ownership %: 100
**Editorial:**
Janet Flynn Hoover ....................Editor
Elizabeth Rinck ............Editorial Director
Marty Jones ......................Art Director
**Readers:** Children ages 6-8.
**Deadline:** story-8 mos. prior to pub. date; ads-3 mos. prior to pub. date

### CLUBHOUSE
69409
464 W. Ferry
Berrien Springs, MI 49103
Telephone: (616) 471-9009
FAX: (616) 471-4661
Year Established: 1951
Pub. Frequency: bi-m.
Subscrip. Rate: $5/yr.
Materials: 05,20
Freelance Pay: $25-35 for 1,000-2,000 word story
Circulation: 10,000
Circulation Type: paid
**Owner(s):**
Your Story Hour, Inc.
464 W. Ferry
Berrien Springs, MI 49103
Telephone: (616) 471-9009
**Editorial:**
Elaine Trumbo ..........................Editor
**Desc.:** Adventure, true and historical stories, puzzles, advice columns, all with a religious overtone.
**Readers:** Ages 8-14
**Deadline:** story-Mar. & Apr.

### CREATIVE KIDS
68784
P.O. Box 8813
Waco, TX 76714-8813
Telephone: (817) 756-3337
FAX: (817) 756-3339
Year Established: 1980
Pub. Frequency: q.
Page Size: standard
Subscrip. Rate: $19.95/q.
Materials: 06,10,19,20,21,32
Circulation: 2,000
Circulation Type: paid

**Materials Accepted/Included:** 01-Business news 02-By-line articles 03-Fashion news 04-Food news 05-Freelance copy 06-Letters to editor 07-Real estate news 08-Sports news 09-Travel news 10-Book rev. 11-Movie rev. 12-Music rev. 13-TV rev. 14-Theater rev. 15-Coming events 16-Obituaries 17-Question & answer 18-Social announcements 19-Artwork 20-Cartoons 21-Photos 22-TV listings 23-Audio rec. 24-Video rec. 25-Books 26-Films/film clips 27-Personnel news 28-Press releases 29-New product news/photos 30-Trade lit. 31-Contracts awarded 32-Display adv. 33-Classified adv.

6-17

**Owner(s):**
Prufrock Press
P.O. Box 8813
Waco, TX 76714-8813
Telephone: (817) 756-3337
FAX: (817) 756-3339
Ownership %: 100
**Editorial:**
Andrea Harrington ..................Managing Editor
Stephanie Stout ........................Editorial Director
**Desc.:** Contains stories, poems, art, music, and more, submitted by children for others to enjoy. Motivates children's creativity.

26646
## CRICKET, (AGES 9-14)
315 Fifth St.
Peru, IL 61354
Telephone: (815) 223-2520
FAX: (815) 224-6675
Mailing Address:
P.O. Box 300
Peru, IL 61354
Year Established: 1973
Pub. Frequency: m.
Page Size: standard
Subscrip. Rate: $29.97/yr.
Freelance Pay: up to $.25/wd.
Circulation: 100,000
Circulation Type: paid
**Owner(s):**
Carus Publishing Co.
P.O. Box 315
Peru, IL 61354
Telephone: (815) 223-2520
Ownership %: 100
**Management:**
Milton Blouke Carus ...........................President
Robert W. Harper ........................Vice President
Robert W. Harper ................................Publisher
John Toraason ..................Production Manager
**Editorial:**
Marianne Carus .............................Chief Editor
Lynn Gutknecht ........................Executive Editor
Deborah Vetter ...............................Senior Editor
Ron McCutchan ...............................Art Director
Lee Franklin .........................Fulfillment Director
**Desc.:** An award-winning literary magazine for children. Outstanding stories and illustrations for 9 to 14-year-olds by top authors and artists.
**Readers:** Children between the ages of 9 and 14.

66775
## DISNEY ADVENTURES
3800 W. Alameda Ave., Ste. 100
Burbank, CA 91505
Telephone: (818) 973-4333
FAX: (818) 563-9344
Mailing Address:
500 S. Buena Vista St.
Burbank, CA 91521
Year Established: 1990
Pub. Frequency: m.
Page Size: pocket
Subscrip. Rate: $19.95/yr. US; $29.95/yr. Canada
Circulation: 950,000
Circulation Type: paid
**Owner(s):**
Walt Disney Publications
500 S. Bueana Vista
Burbank, CA 91521
Ownership %: 100
**Management:**
Lynn Lehmkuhl ...................................Publisher
**Editorial:**
Tommi Lewis .............................................Editor
Suzanne Harper ........................Managing Editor

**Desc.:** Disney Adventures is the general-interest magazine for kids ages 7-14, available at checkout stands and newsstands nationwide as well as through subscription. Covers science, sports, entertainment, fiction, games & puzzles, comics, with an overall theme of adventure.
**Readers:** Kids ages 7-14.

26650
## EXPLORING
1325 W. Walnut Hill Lane
Irving, TX 75038
Telephone: (214) 580-2365
FAX: (214) 580-2079
Mailing Address:
P.O. Box 152079
Irving, TX 75015-2079
Year Established: 1970
Pub. Frequency: q.
Page Size: standard
Subscrip. Rate: members only
Materials: 02,03,05,09,10,11,12,13,15,19, 21,23,24,28,29,32
Freelance Pay: varies
Print Process: offset
Circulation: 350,000
Circulation Type: controlled
**Owner(s):**
Boy Scouts of America
P.O. Box 152079
Irving, TX 75015
Telephone: (214) 580-2000
Ownership %: 100
**Management:**
J. Warren Young .................................Publisher
Chuck Carroll ...................Advertising Manager
**Editorial:**
Ernest Doclar .............................Editor in Chief
Scott Daniels .........................Executive Editor
Joe Connolly .............................Design Director
Brian Payne ...............................................Photo
**Desc.:** Features include colleges, schools, travel, food, cars, entertainment, entertainers, careers, music, contemporary youth activities, sports, interviews, profiles, outdoor activities. Departments include: Sports, Careers, Profiles, Entertainment (music, books, etc.), Careers Education, Outdoors, Autocare/Repair.
**Readers:** Coeds; ages 14-20.

67284
## FAITH 'N STUFF: THE MAGAZINE FOR KIDS
39 Seminary Hill Rd.
Carmel, NY 10512
Telephone: (914) 225-3681
Year Established: 1989
Pub. Frequency: bi-m.
Page Size: 4 color photos/art
Subscrip. Rate: $15.95/yr.
Materials: 05,19,21
Circulation: 150,000
Circulation Type: paid
**Owner(s):**
Guideposts Associates, Inc.
39 Seminary Hill Rd.
Carmel, NY 10512
Telephone: (914) 225-3681
Ownership %: 100
**Management:**
John Temple ........................................President
**Editorial:**
Mary Lou Carney ......................................Editor
**Desc.:** A Bible-based value-centered magazine that is fun to read.
**Readers:** Kids 7-12 yrs. old.

26652
## FOR SENIORS ONLY
339 N. Main St.
Georgetown Office Plaza
New City, NY 10956
Telephone: (914) 638-0333

Mailing Address:
P.O. Box 367
New City, NY 10956
Year Established: 1970
Pub. Frequency: s-a.
Page Size: 5 1/2 X 8 3/8
Subscrip. Rate: free
Materials: 01,02,09,10,11,12,13,14,19,20, 21,22,23,24,25,27,28,29,30,32
Freelance Pay: varies
Print Process: web offset
Circulation: 350,000
Circulation Type: controlled & free
**Owner(s):**
Campus Communications, Inc.
339 N. Main St.
Georgetown Office Plaza
New City, NY 10956
Telephone: (914) 638-0333
Ownership %: 100
**Management:**
Darryl G. Elberg ..................................President
Darryl G. Elberg ..................................Publisher
Charlene Blaze .................Advertising Manager
**Editorial:**
Judi Oliff .....................................Editor in Chief
Meredith Fahn ........................Executive Editor
Shana Alyse .............................Managing Editor
David Burns ......................................Art Director
Randi Wendelkin ..............................Art Director
Paul Dodd ...............................................Columnist
Michael Bratten ...............................News Editor
Sam Davids ...............................................Photo
**Desc.:** Objective is to provide information on the post-high school opportunities available to graduates in four general categories: college, technical and specialized schools, the military and job opportunities. Also general articles are presented on clothing, autos, and consumer products of interest to this age group. For Seniors Only also is published in a single-sponsor format with tailored editorial and distribution to fit a clients needs. N.E. and S.E. editions.
**Readers:** High school juniors and seniors, male and female.
**Deadline:** story-Fall-8/1; Spring-11/1; news-Fall-8/1; Spring-11/1; photo-Fall-8/1; Spring-11/1; ads-Fall-9/1; Spring-1/1

26653
## HIGHLIGHTS FOR CHILDREN
803 Church St.
Honesdale, PA 18431
Telephone: (717) 253-1080
FAX: (717) 253-0179
Year Established: 1946
Pub. Frequency: 12/yr.
Page Size: standard
Subscrip. Rate: $23.64/yr.
Materials: 02,05,06,19,20,21
Freelance Pay: varied
Print Process: web offset
Circulation: 3,000,000
Circulation Type: paid
**Owner(s):**
Highlights For Children, Inc.
803 Church St.
Honesdale, PA 18431
Telephone: (717) 253-1080
FAX: (717) 253-0179
Ownership %: 100
**Bureau(s):**
Highlights For Children
2300 W. Fifth
Columbus, OH 43215
Telephone: (800) 848-8922
FAX: (614) 487-2700
Contact: Elmer Meider, President
**Management:**
Elmer Meider ....................................President
**Editorial:**
Tom White ...................................Senior Editor
Kent L. Brown, Jr. ...................................Editor

Rosanne Guararra ............................Art Director
Christine French Clark ............Associate Editor
Marileta Robinson ....................Associate Editor
Rich Wallace ...................Coordinating Editor
Marileta Robinson ........................Fiction Editor
Dr. Jack Myers ...............................Science Editor
**Desc.:** Unusual wholesome stories that depart from the beaten path; stories full of action and word pictures. Departments include: Editor, Editorial Assistants, Artists, Advisory Board.
**Readers:** Children from ages 2-12 yrs.

69403
## HOPSCOTCH
P.O. Box 164
Bluffton, OH 45817-0164
Telephone: (419) 358-6410
FAX: (419) 358-5027
Year Established: 1989
Pub. Frequency: bi-m.
Page Size: standard
Subscrip. Rate: $15/yr.; $27.50/2 yrs.
Circulation: 9,000
Circulation Type: paid
**Owner(s):**
Bluffton News Printing and Publishing Co.
P.O. Box 164
Bluffton, OH 45817-0164
Telephone: (419) 358-6410
**Editorial:**
Marilyn Edwards ......................................Editor
**Desc.:** Covers pets, nature, hobbies, crafts, science, games , sports, short stories, and photography.
**Readers:** Girls ages 6 to 12.

26654
## HUMPTY DUMPTY'S MAGAZINE
1100 Waterway Blvd.
Indianapolis, IN 46202
Telephone: (317) 636-8881
Mailing Address:
P.O. Box 567
Indianapolis, IN 46206
Year Established: 1952
Pub. Frequency: 8/yr.
Page Size: 4 color photos/art
Subscrip. Rate: $1.75/issue; $13.95/yr.
Freelance Pay: $.10/wd.
Circulation: 350,000
Circulation Type: paid
**Owner(s):**
Benjamin Franklin Literary & Medical Society, Inc.
P.O. Box 567
Indianapolis, IN 46206
Telephone: (317) 636-8881
Ownership %: 100
**Bureau(s):**
L. R. Barnhart Associates
211 E. Sycamore
Independence, KS 67301
Telephone: (316) 331-1233
Contact: Barny Barnhart, Advertising
**Management:**
Eric Servaas ........................................Publisher
**Editorial:**
Janet F. Hoover ......................................Editor
Larry Simmons ...............................Art Director
Sandra Grieshop ......................Assistant Editor
Greg Joray .........................Marketing Director
**Desc.:** Market is the 4 to 6-year-old child, and much of the material deals with reading and the language arts and numbers. Stories run from 500 to 800 words in length and are easy to read for beginning readers. Puzzles and identification pages feature reading readiness and vocabulary development, while other activities promote following instructions, finger dexterity and working with numbers. Stories and poems are accepted on a freelance basis. Emphasis on health, nutrition, exercise, and safety.

---

**Materials Accepted/Included:** 01-Business news 02-By-line articles 03-Fashion news 04-Food news 05-Freelance copy 06-Letters to editor 07-Real estate news 08-Sports news 09-Travel news 10-Book rev. 11-Movie rev. 12-Music rev. 13-TV rev. 14-Theater rev. 15-Coming events 16-Obituaries 17-Question & answer 18-Social announcements 19-Artwork 20-Cartoons 21-Photos 22-TV listings 23-Audio rec. 24-Video rec. 25-Books 26-Films/film clips 27-Personnel news 28-Press releases 29-New product news/photos 30-Trade lit. 31-Contracts awarded 32-Display adv. 33-Classified adv.

Readers: Children ages 4-6

## JACK & JILL
26655

1100 Waterway Blvd.
Indianapolis, IN 46202
Telephone: (317) 636-8881
FAX: (317) 684-8094
Mailing Address:
P.O. Box 567
Indianapolis, IN 46206
Year Established: 1938
Pub. Frequency: 8/yr.
Page Size: 4 color photos/art
Subscrip. Rate: $14.95/yr.
Materials: 04,05,06,08,23,24,25,28,29,32
Freelance Pay: negotiable
Circulation: 327,000
Circulation Type: paid
Owner(s):
Benjamin Franklin Literary & Medical
Society, Inc.
1100 Waterway Blvd.
Indianapolis, IN 46202
Telephone: (317) 636-8881
Ownership %: 100
Bureau(s):
L. R. Barnhart Associates, Inc.
211 E. Sycamore
Independence, KS 67301
Telephone: (316) 331-1233
Contact: Barny Barnhart, Advertising
Manager
Management:
Cory SerVaas, M.D. ............................Publisher
Editorial:
Elizabeth Rinck .........................Executive Editor
Steve Charles .................................................Editor
Ed Cortese ...........................................Art Director
Desc.: Entertainment plus education for
children. Humorous and adventure
stories, poems, make and do projects,
pages on famous people, nature and
science. Emphasis on health, nutrition,
exercise, and safety.
Readers: Children

## JUNIOR SCHOLASTIC
24778

555 Broadway
New York, NY 10012
Telephone: (212) 343-6295
FAX: (212) 343-6333
Year Established: 1937
Pub. Frequency: 18/yr. Sep.-May
Page Size: standard
Subscrip. Rate: $7.25/yr.
Materials: 02,05,06,15,19,20,21,24,25,26,32
Freelance Pay: $.35/wd.
Circulation: 600,000
Circulation Type: paid
Owner(s):
Scholastic, Inc.
730 Broadway
New York, NY 10003
Telephone: (212) 343-6100
Ownership %: 100
Management:
Richard Robinson ................................President
Michelle Magazine .............Advertising Manager
Editorial:
Lee Baier ..........................................................Editor
Sean Price ...............................Associate Editor
Sean McCollum .......................Associate Editor
Kathy Wilmore ...............................Senior Writer
Desc.: Carries pertinent US and world
news items and articles of interest to
social studies students (ages 11-14).
Readers: Pupils in grades 6-8.
Deadline: story-6 wks. prior to pub. date;
news-6 wks. prior; photo-6 wks. prior;
ads-8 wks. prior

## LADYBUG, THE MAGAZINE FOR YOUNG CHILDREN
66615

315 Fifth St.
Peru, IL 61354
Telephone: (815) 223-2520
Mailing Address:
P.O. Box 300
Peru, IL 61354
Year Established: 1990
Pub. Frequency: m.
Page Size: 4 color photos/art
Subscrip. Rate: $29.97/yr.
Materials: 05,06,19,23,25
Freelance Pay: varies
Circulation: 135,421
Circulation Type: paid
Owner(s):
Carus Publishing/The Cricket Magazine
Group
P.O. Box 300
Peru, IL 61354
Telephone: (815) 223-2520
Ownership %: 100
Management:
Milton Blouke Carus ..........................President
Robert W. Harper .......................Vice President
Milton Blouke Carus ..........................Publisher
Editorial:
Marianne Carus .............................................Editor
Ron McCuthon ...............................Art Director
Paula Morrow .........................Assistant Editor
Lee Franklin ...........................................Director
Desc.: Outstanding stories and illustrations
for 2-6 year-olds by top authors and
artists.
Readers: Children ages 2-6 years.

## MAGAZINE FOR CHRISTIAN YOUTH, THE
26651

201 Eighth Ave., S.
Nashville, TN 37203
Telephone: (615) 749-6000
FAX: (615) 749-6079
Mailing Address:
P.O. Box 801
Nashville, TN 37202-0801
Year Established: 1985
Pub. Frequency: m.
Page Size: 4 color photos/art
Subscrip. Rate: $2/issue; $18/yr.
Materials: 05,32
Freelance Pay: $.05/wd.
Circulation: 30,000
Circulation Type: paid
Owner(s):
United Methodist Publishing House
201 Eighth Ave., S.
Nashville, TN 37203
Telephone: (615) 749-6000
Ownership %: 100
Editorial:
Anthony E. Peterson ...............................Editor
John J. Rudin, III .......................Assistant Editor
Marc Lewis ...........................Marketing Director
Desc.: Poetry and prose that speaks to
teenagers' concerns about their faith,
purpose in life, personal relationships,
goals, and feelings. Helps teenagers
develop Christian identity and live the
Christian faith in their contemporary
culture.
Readers: Teenagers.

## NOISE, THE
66719

443 E. Irving Dr.
Burbank, CA 91504
Telephone: (818) 846-0400
FAX: (818) 841-4964
Year Established: 1990
Pub. Frequency: m.
Page Size: tabloid
Subscrip. Rate: $12/yr.
Freelance Pay: $100-$130/feature

Circulation: 50,000
Circulation Type: controlled
Owner(s):
Wingate Enterprises, Inc.
443 E. Irving Dr.
Burbank, CA 91504
Telephone: (818) 846-0400
Ownership %: 100
Management:
Carey Bierman ...............................Publisher
Editorial:
Norbert Sparrow .........................Editor in Chief
Jack Bierman .........................Executive Editor
Desc.: Reflects the teen life-styles in the
LA area, from academic enrichment to
entertainment.
Readers: Sophisticated teens & high
school students.

## ODYSSEY
46864

Seven School St.
Peterborough, NH 03458
Telephone: (603) 924-7209
FAX: (603) 924-7380
Year Established: 1979
Pub. Frequency: 10/yr.
Page Size: 7 x 9
Subscrip. Rate: $22.95/yr.
Materials: 02,05,15,19,21,23,24,25
Print Process: offset
Circulation: 35,000
Circulation Type: paid
Owner(s):
Cobblestone Publishing, Inc.
Seven School St.
Peterborough, NH 03458
Telephone: (603) 924-9209
FAX: (603) 924-7380
Ownership %: 100
Management:
Lyell C. Dawes ...............................Publisher
Manula Meier .....................Promotion Manager
Editorial:
Elizabeth Lindstrom ...............................Editor
Desc.: Odyssey is theme-related
astronomy and outer space magazine
for young people. The magazine
explores many aspects of astronomy
and space science, from observational
astronomy to the Space Shuttle
program.
Readers: Young people 8-14.

## OF CABBAGES & KINGS
68785

121 Chanlon Rd.
New Providence, NJ 07974
Telephone: (800) 521-8110
FAX: (908) 665-6688
Year Established: 1991
Pub. Frequency: a.
Subscrip. Rate: $29.95/yr.
Owner(s):
R.R. Bowker, Reed Reference Publishing
121 Chanlon Rd.
New Providence, NJ 07974
Telephone: (800) 521-8110
Ownership %: 100
Editorial:
Kimberly Olson Fakih ...............................Editor
Desc.: Selects the year's best magazine
writings for children.

## P3
66301

P.O. Box 52
Montgomery, VT 05470
Telephone: (802) 326-4669
Mailing Address:
P.O. Box 52
Montgomery, VT 05470
Year Established: 1990
Pub. Frequency: 5/yr.
Page Size: standard
Subscrip. Rate: $14/yr.
Circulation: 22,000

Circulation Type: paid
Owner(s):
The Fun Group, Inc.
P.O. Box 52
Montgomery, VT 05470
Telephone: (802) 326-4669
Editorial:
Randi Hacker ...............................Editor in Chief
Jackie Kaufman ...........................................Editor
Veronica Elkins ...........................Assistant Editor
Desc.: Teaches children environmental
consciousness
Readers: Elementary - School Age
Children

## RANGER RICK
68787

1400 16th St., N.W.
Washington, DC 20036-2266
Telephone: (202) 797-6800
FAX: (202) 442-7332
Year Established: 1967
Pub. Frequency: m.
Subscrip. Rate: $15/yr.
Materials: 06,17,19,20,21
Freelance Pay: $100-$2000
Print Process: offset
Circulation: 850,000
Circulation Type: paid
Owner(s):
National Wildlife Federation
1400 16th St., N.W.
Washington, DC 20036-2266
Telephone: (202) 797-6800
FAX: (703) 442-7332
Ownership %: 100
Editorial:
Gerry Bishop ...........................................Editor
Desc.: Contains articles and photos about
wildlife and children in the outdoors.
Advocates the conservation of natural
resources and protection of the
environment.

## READ
26658

245 Long Hill Rd.
Middletown, CT 06457
Telephone: (203) 638-2400
FAX: (203) 346-5826
Year Established: 1951
Pub. Frequency: 18/yr.
Page Size: pocket
Subscrip. Rate: $7.95/yr.
Freelance Pay: $100-$500
Circulation: 380,750
Circulation Type: paid
Owner(s):
Weekly Reader Corporation
245 Long Hill Rd.
Middletown, CT 06457
Telephone: (203) 638-2400
Ownership %: 100
Editorial:
Sandra Maccarone ...............................Editor
Desc.: Language arts magazine-for English
and reading for junior high school and
middle school children.
Readers: Grades 6 and up-reading level
5.5-7 yrs.

## RIGHT ON
26659

355 Lexington Ave., 13th Fl.
New York, NY 10017
Telephone: (212) 973-3200
FAX: (212) 986-5926
Mailing Address:
233 Park Ave. South, Sixth Fl.
New York, NY 10003
Year Established: 1971
Pub. Frequency: m.
Page Size: standard
Subscrip. Rate: $14.95/yr.
Materials: 02,03,06,10,11,23,24,25,26,32,33
Freelance Pay: varies
Print Process: offset

Materials Accepted/Included: 01-Business news 02-By-line articles 03-Fashion news 04-Food news 05-Freelance copy 06-Letters to editor 07-Real estate news 08-Sports news 09-Travel news 10-Book rev. 11-Movie rev. 12-Music rev. 13-TV rev. 14-Theater rev. 15-Coming events 16-Obituaries 17-Question & answer 18-Social announcements 19-Artwork 20-Cartoons 21-Photos 22-TV listings 23-Audio rec. 24-Video rec. 25-Books 26-Films/film clips 27-Personnel news 28-Press releases 29-New product news/photos 30-Trade lit. 31-Contracts awarded 32-Display adv. 33-Classified adv.

6-19

Circulation: 200,800
Circulation Type: paid
**Owner(s):**
Sterling/MacFadden Partnership
233 Park Ave. South
New York, NY 10003
Telephone: (212) 780-3500
FAX: (212) 780-3555
Ownership %: 100
**Management:**
John Plunkett .............................Publisher
Allen Tuller .................Advertising Manager
John Moore .................Advertising Manager
**Editorial:**
Cynthia M. Horner ..............Executive Editor
Joanne Madhere ...................Assistant Editor
**Desc.:** Features are about well known
celebrities. A monthly teen/young adult
oriented publication featuring black
celebrities.
**Readers:** Teenage women median age 12-
17. Some male median age 12-17.
**Deadline:** story-3 mos. prior to pub. date;
news-3 mos. prior; photo-3 mos. prior;
ads-3 mos. prior

24722
**SCHOLASTIC CHOICES**
55 Broadway
New York, NY 10012
Telephone: (212) 343-6100
FAX: (212) 343-6333
Year Established: 1956
Pub. Frequency: m.: Sep.-May.
Page Size: standard
Subscrip. Rate: $11.50/yr. individual;
$7.45/yr. for 10 or more
Print Process: offset
Circulation: 180,000
Circulation Type: paid
**Owner(s):**
Scholastic Magazines, Inc.
730 Broadway
New York, NY 10003
Telephone: (212) 505-3000
Ownership %: 100
**Management:**
M. Richard Robinson, Jr. ............President
M. Richard Robinson, Jr. ............Publisher
Diane Lombardi ...............Advertising Manager
**Editorial:**
Lauren Tarshis ..................................Editor
Cecelia Seupel .................Editorial Director
**Desc.:** Includes articles on foods, nutrition,
clothing, grooming, personal
development, home management, and
family living. Offers guidance on
personal problems, interviews with home
economics, profiles of teenagers in other
countries, short fiction.
**Readers:** Pupils in junior high and high
school home economics classes.

69413
**SCIENCELAND**
501 Fifth Ave.
New York, NY 10017
Telephone: (212) 490-2180
FAX: (212) 490-2187
Year Established: 1977
Pub. Frequency: 8/yr.
Page Size: standard
Subscrip. Rate: $42/yr.
Circulation: 16,000
Circulation Type: paid
**Owner(s):**
Scienceland, Inc.
501 Fifth Ave.
New York, NY 10017
Telephone: (212) 490-2180
FAX: (212) 490-2187
Ownership %: 100
**Editorial:**
A.H. Matano ......................................Editor

**Desc.:** A reading picture book in magazine
format on natural and physical sciences
for ages 5-10 yr. to nurture scientific
thinking.
**Readers:** Schools, school libraries, public
libraries, teachers, parents,
grandparents, special schools, home
schools, etc.

69745
**SESAME STREET**
One Lincoln Plaza
New York, NY 10023
Telephone: (212) 595-3456
Year Established: 1971
Pub. Frequency: 10/yr.
Subscrip. Rate: $19.90/yr.
Circulation: 1,200,000
Circulation Type: paid
**Owner(s):**
Children's Television Workshop
One Lincoln Plaza
New York, NY 10023
Telephone: (212) 595-3456
Ownership %: 100
**Editorial:**
Ira Wolfman .........................................Editor

26661
**SEVENTEEN**
850 Third Ave.
New York, NY 10022
Telephone: (212) 407-9700
FAX: (212) 935-4237
Year Established: 1944
Pub. Frequency: m.
Page Size: standard
Subscrip. Rate: $15.95/yr.
Freelance Pay: $850-$2,000/article
Circulation: 1,900,000
Circulation Type: paid
**Owner(s):**
K-111 Communications Corp.
717 Fifth Ave.
New York, NY 10022
Telephone: (212) 745-0100
Ownership %: 100
**Bureau(s):**
Seventeen Magazine
5670 Wilshire Blvd.
Los Angeles, CA 90036
Telephone: (213) 938-3873
Contact: Kim Hynes, Editor
**Management:**
Janice Grossman ...........................Publisher
**Editorial:**
Caroline Miller ................Editor in Chief
Catherine Cavender ..............Executive Editor
Shem Law ...............................Art Editor
Eileen Livers ......................Articles Editor
Elizabeth Brovs ........................Beauty Editor
Nancy Hessel Weber ..............Creative Director
Sasha Charnin Morrison ...........Fashion Editor
Susan Swimmer ...........Fitness & Food Editor
**Desc.:** Service publication for women 24 &
under. Aims to entertain, educate,
enlighten, and advise the readers.
Provide information on relationships,
fashion, sex, careers, school, books,
social problems, personal problems,
health, entertainment, money and the
world. Also provide fashion and beauty
information that emphasizes personal
expression over prescribed style, and
tips that make fashion and beauty
affordable and accessible. Departments
are staff-written. Articles and photos are
freelance. Interested in article ideas
and fiction stories that meet the needs
of our readers. Must be intelligent, fresh.
Departments include: Movie, Record,
Book Review in addition to those listed
above.
**Readers:** Young women 12 to 24.

69415
**SHOFAR**
43 Northcote Dr.
Melville, NY 11747
Telephone: (516) 643-4598
FAX: (516) 643-4598
Year Established: 1984
Pub. Frequency: m.; Oct.-May; double
issues Dec./Jan.; Apr./May
Page Size: standard
Subscrip. Rate: $3.00 newsstand;
$14.95/yr. US; $18.95 foreign
Freelance Pay: varied
Circulation: 16,000
Circulation Type: paid
**Owner(s):**
Shofar
**Management:**
Gerald Grayson .............................Publisher
**Editorial:**
Kerry Olitzky ..............Executive Editor
Gerald Grayson ................................Editor
Debra Klein .................................Art Director
Alan Kay .........................Editor Emeritus
Judi Oliff ..............Production Coordinator
**Desc.:** Presents a forum intended to
enhance the Jewish child's identity by
featuring profiles of high-profile Jewish
celebrities, poetry, nonfiction, fiction,
photos, puzzles, games, cartoons.

69490
**SOCCER JR.**
27 Unquowa Rd.
Fairfield, CT 06430
Telephone: (203) 259-5766
Year Established: 1992
Pub. Frequency: bi-m.
Subscrip. Rate: $16.97/yr.
Print Process: web
Circulation: 60,000
Circulation Type: paid
**Owner(s):**
Triplepoint, Inc.
27 Unquowa Rd.
Fairfield, CT 06430
Telephone: (203) 259-5766
Ownership %: 100
**Editorial:**
Joe Povey ...........................................Editor
**Desc.:** Contains profiles of soccer stars to
provide kids with role models. Also
contains teaching skills and tactics for
use at practice and in games.
**Readers:** Soccer-playing kids 8-16 years
old & their parents.

70369
**SPIDER, THE MAGAZINE FOR
CHILDREN (AGES 6-9)**
315 Fifth St.
Peru, IL 61354
Telephone: (815) 223-2520
FAX: (815) 224-6675
Mailing Address:
P.O. Box 300
Peru, IL 61354
Year Established: 1994
Pub. Frequency: m.
Page Size: standard
Subscrip. Rate: $29.97/yr.
Circulation: 54,000
Circulation Type: paid
**Owner(s):**
Carus Publishing Co.
315 Fifth St.
Peru, IL 61354
Telephone: (815) 223-2520
FAX: (815) 224-6675
Ownership %: 100
**Management:**
Milton Blouke ...............................President
Robert W. Harper ............................Publisher
John Toraason .................Production Manager
**Editorial:**
Marianne Carus ...................Editor in Chief

Lynn Gutknecht .....................Executive Editor
Ron McCutchan ............................Art Director
**Desc.:** Stories, poems, puzzles, games and
contests.
**Readers:** Children between the ages of six
and nine.

26662
**TEEN**
6420 Wilshire Blvd.
Los Angeles, CA 90048
Telephone: (213) 782-2000
FAX: (213) 782-2660
Year Established: 1957
Pub. Frequency: m.
Page Size: standard
Subscrip. Rate: $2.50/copy; $15.95/yr.
Materials: 03,05,06,27,28,29,30,32,33
Freelance Pay: varies
Circulation: 1,100,000
Circulation Type: paid
**Owner(s):**
Petersen Publishing Co.
6420 Wilshire Blvd.
Los Angeles, CA 90048
Telephone: (213) 782-2000
Ownership %: 100
**Management:**
Fred Waingrow .............................President
Jay N. Cole .................................Publisher
George McGuire ..............Advertising Manager
Gustavo Alonzo ...........Circulation Manager
Karle Dickerson .................Operations Manager
**Editorial:**
Roxanne Camron ..............................Editor
Robert F. MacLeod .............Editorial Director
Kelly Higgins ...........................News Editor
Lori Moore ...........................Promotion Director
**Desc.:** Designed to serve the total needs
girls ages 12-19. Provides a wide
spectrum of contemporary information to
help young girls as they progress
through the crucial teen years. Focus is
on self-improvement in areas of
grooming and physical and intellectual
development.
**Readers:** Teenagers; female, 12-19 years
of age.

26663
**TEEN BEAT**
233 Park Ave., S.
New York, NY 10003
Telephone: (212) 979-4800
Mailing Address:
233 Park Ave. South
New York, NY 10003-1606
Year Established: 1976
Pub. Frequency: m.
Page Size: standard
Subscrip. Rate: $2.50 newsstand US;
$2.75 Canada; $19.95/yr.
Freelance Pay: $50/story; $35/photo
Circulation: 150,000
Circulation Type: paid
**Owner(s):**
Sterling/MacFadden Partnership
233 Park Ave., S.
New York, NY 10003-1606
Telephone: (212) 780-3500
FAX: (212) 780-3555
Ownership %: 100
**Management:**
Michael J. Boylan .............................President
Allen Tuller .................Advertising Manager
**Editorial:**
Karen L. Williams ..............................Editor
Ellen Faraci ...........................Managing Editor
Dana Carr .................................Art Director
Jane Checkett .................Associate Editor
Arthur Deitsch .................Production Director

**Materials Accepted/Included:** 01-Business news 02-By-line articles 03-Fashion news 04-Food news 05-Freelance copy 06-Letters to editor 07-Real estate news 08-Sports news 09-Travel news 10-Book rev. 11-Movie rev. 12-Music rev. 13-TV rev. 14-Theater rev. 15-Coming events 16-Obituaries 17-Question & answer 18-Social announcements 19-Artwork 20-Cartoons 21-Photos 22-TV listings 23-Audio rec. 24-Video rec. 25-Books 26-Films/film clips 27-Personnel news 28-Press releases 29-New product news/photos 30-Trade lit. 31-Contracts awarded 32-Display adv. 33-Classified adv.

**Desc.:** Feature articles dealing with music, TV and film personalities with an emphasis on personal interviews and photo stories, news, puzzles, contests and a service department with advice, beauty, fashion, food, diet and dating column.
**Readers:** Young teens, mainly female.

69419

### TQ; TEEN QUEST
2845 W. Airport Fwy. #137
Irving, TX 75062
Telephone: (214) 570-7599
FAX: (214) 257-0632
Year Established: 1946
Pub. Frequency: 11/yr.
Page Size: standard
Subscrip. Rate: $2.25 newsstand; $14.50/yr.
Materials: 02,05,06,10,12,17,19,20,21,23, 24,25,28,29,32
Freelance Pay: $.10-$.15/wd.
Circulation: 35,000
Circulation Type: free & paid
**Owner(s):**
Shepherd Ministries
2845 W. Airport Fwy. #137
Irving, TX 75062
Telephone: (214) 570-7599
FAX: (214) 257-0632
Ownership %: 100
**Editorial:**
Chris Lyon ..................................Editor
**Desc.:** Magazine for Bible-believing Christian students seeking contemporary Christian fiction, challenging articles on teen issues and the latest on Christian music.

68786

### TURTLE
1100 Waterway Blvd.
Indianapolis, IN 46202
Telephone: (317) 636-8881
FAX: (317) 684-8094
Mailing Address:
P.O. Box 567
Indianapolis, IN 46206
Year Established: 1979
Pub. Frequency: 8/yr.
Page Size: 6" X 9"
Subscrip. Rate: $13.95/yr.
Materials: 05,19,25,32
Circulation: 420,000
Circulation Type: paid
**Owner(s):**
Benjamin Franklin Literary & Medical Society, Inc.
1100 Waterway Blvd.
Indianapolis, IN 46202
Telephone: (317) 636-8881
Ownership %: 100
**Editorial:**
Elizabeth A. Rinck ..................................Editor
**Readers:** Children ages 2-5.
**Deadline:** story-8 mos. prior to pub. date; ads-3 mos. prior

65337

### U.S. KIDS
1100 Waterway Blvd.
Indianapolis, IN 46202
Telephone: (317) 636-8881
FAX: (317) 684-8094
Mailing Address:
P.O. Box 567
Indianapolis, IN 46202
Year Established: 1987
Pub. Frequency: 8/yr.
Page Size: standard
Subscrip. Rate: $2.95 newsstand; $20.95/yr.
Circulation: 225,000
Circulation Type: paid

**Owner(s):**
Children's Better Health Institute
1100 Waterway Blvd.
Indianapolis, IN 46202
Telephone: (317) 636-8881
Ownership %: 100
**Management:**
Cory Servaas, MD ..................................President
Cory Servaas, MD ..................................Publisher
Karen Neilgh ..................................Production Manager
**Editorial:**
Steve Charles ..................................Editor
Todd Seifferline ..................................Marketing Director
**Desc.:** U.S. news interpreted for children. A 44-page magazine with a real world focus. Helps children understand the world around them, interest them in learning, and develop creativity and imagination. Includes: science and nature stories, fun activities, and fiction.
**Readers:** Children, ages 5 to 10 years.

26666

### VICA JOURNAL
14001 James Monroe Hwy.
Leesburg, VA 22075-0300
Telephone: (703) 777-8810
FAX: (703) 777-8999
Mailing Address:
P.O. Box 3000
Leesburg, VA 22075-0300
Year Established: 1965
Pub. Frequency: 4/yr.
Page Size: tabloid
Subscrip. Rate: $1/newsstand; $8/yr. nonmembers
Materials: 06,19,21,29,30,32
Print Process: web
Circulation: 250,000
Circulation Type: paid
**Owner(s):**
Vocational Industrial Clubs of America, Inc.
P.O. Box 3000
Leesburg, VA 22075
Telephone: (703) 777-8810
FAX: (703) 777-8999
Ownership %: 100
**Management:**
Doonald D. Conham ..................................Advertising Manager
**Editorial:**
E. Thomas Hall ..................................Editor
Stephen Denby ..................................Executive Director
**Desc.:** Feature articles and photos about organization members (VICA is national organization for students in trade, industrial, technical and health occupations programs), their career interests, achievements, hobbies. Staff writes most articles or rewrites information submitted by chapters, teachers, and contacted authors.
**Readers:** Students, teachers, administrators, industry leaders & representatives.

69509

### WARP
353 Airport Rd.
Oceanside, CA 92054-1203
Telephone: (619) 722-7777
Mailing Address:
P.O. Box 469006
Escondido, CA 92046
Year Established: 1992
Pub. Frequency: q.
Subscrip. Rate: $25.95/yr.
**Owner(s):**
TransWorld Publications, Inc.
353 Airport Rd.
Oceanside, CA 92054
Telephone: (619) 722-7777
Ownership %: 100
**Desc.:** Combines surfing, skateboarding, and snowboarding, rounded out with progressive music.

**Readers:** Action-lifestyle magazine for young males.

69407

### YOUNG ADULT PRESS
P.O. Box 21
Mound, MN 55364
Telephone: (612) 472-0809
FAX: (612) 472-0842
Year Established: 1991
Pub. Frequency: 10/yr.
Page Size: tabloid
Subscrip. Rate: $10/yr.
Materials: 02,03,05,06,08,09,10,11,12,13, 14,15,17,19,20,21,28,32,33
Print Process: web
Circulation: 30,000
Circulation Type: paid
**Owner(s):**
Young Adult Press
3227 N.W. 62nd St.
Maple Lake, MN 55358
Telephone: (612) 472-0809
FAX: (612) 472-0842
Ownership %: 100
**Editorial:**
Tamara Cree ..................................Editor
**Desc.:** Articles, letters, essays, short stories, poems, art work, and cartoons.
**Readers:** Young people ages 13 through 20.
**Deadline:** story-18th of mo. prior to pub. date; ads-24th of mo. prior

67287

### ZILLIONS
101 Truman Ave.
Yonkers, NY 10703
Telephone: (914) 378-2550
FAX: (914) 378-2904
Year Established: 1990
Pub. Frequency: bi-m.
Page Size: standard
Subscrip. Rate: $2.75 newsstand US; $2.95 Canada; $16/yr.
Circulation: 250,000
Circulation Type: paid
**Owner(s):**
Consumers Union
101 Truman Ave.
Yonkers, NY 10703
Telephone: (914) 378-2550
Ownership %: 100
**Management:**
Rhoda Karpatkin ..................................Executive Director
**Editorial:**
Charlotte Baecher ..................................Editor

## Group 616-Clubs, Fraternal & Service Organizations, Etc.

26105

### AMERICAN LEGION MAGAZINE
700 N. Pennsylvania St.
Indianapolis, IN 46204
Telephone: (317) 630-1200
FAX: (317) 630-1280
Mailing Address:
P.O. Box 1055
Indianapolis, IN 46204
Year Established: 1919
Pub. Frequency: m.
Page Size: standard
Subscrip. Rate: $12/yr.
Materials: 02,05,06,19,20,32,33
Freelance Pay: $500-$1,000 and up
Print Process: web offset
Circulation: 2,900,000
Circulation Type: paid
**Owner(s):**
The American Legion
P.O. Box 1055
Indianapolis, IN 46206
Telephone: (317) 630-1200
Ownership %: 100

**Management:**
Daniel S. Wheeler ..................................Publisher
Donald B. Thomson ..................................Advertising Manager
William L. Poff ..................................Production Manager
**Editorial:**
Daniel S. Wheeler ..................................Editor in Chief
John E. Greenwald ..................................Editor
Miles Z. Epstein ..................................Managing Editor
Simon Smith ..................................Art Editor
**Desc.:** Edited primarily as a general-interest consumer magazine. Major articles deal with the background of events and trends in the world today with subjects of broad consumer interest. Monthly departments include: Opposite Views on major issues by members of Congress, Editorials bearing on Current Events. Organizational material, and news of veterans affairs are contained in a staff written section.
**Readers:** Members of the American Legion.
**Deadline:** ads-1st day of 2nd mo. prior to pub. date

25675

### CAA TODAY
12 S. Michigan Ave.
Chicago, IL 60603
Telephone: (312) 236-7500
FAX: (312) 236-7537
Year Established: 1894
Pub. Frequency: m.
Page Size: standard
Subscrip. Rate: free to members
Circulation: 2,100
Circulation Type: free
**Owner(s):**
Chicago Athletic Association
Telephone: (312) 236-7500
Ownership %: 100
**Editorial:**
Tom Caruso ..................................Editor
**Desc.:** Official publication of the Chicago Athletic Association, which includes features about members, club news, travel, business, and other related information.
**Readers:** Presidents or owners of corporations, top supervisors, managers and other leading professionals.

25677

### CAC JOURNAL
1118 Euclid Ave.
Cleveland, OH 44115
Telephone: (216) 621-8900
FAX: (216) 621-3864
Year Established: 1909
Pub. Frequency: 10/yr.
Page Size: standard
Subscrip. Rate: $2 newsstand; $22/yr.
Circulation: 2,200
Circulation Type: controlled
**Owner(s):**
CAC Journal
1118 Euclid Ave.
Cleveland, OH 44115
Telephone: (216) 621-8900
Ownership %: 100
**Management:**
John Rolf ..................................General Manager
**Editorial:**
Robert W. Gibb ..................................Editor
**Desc.:** Published for members of the Cleveland Athletic Club and provides news about its members, social events, entertainment, elections, sports, officers, directors and committee personnel, and other member activities. Also carries articles and other features on members and staff.
**Readers:** Corporate officers, managers, executives and professionals.

**Materials Accepted/Included:** 01-Business news 02-By-line articles 03-Fashion news 04-Food news 05-Freelance copy 06-Letters to editor 07-Real estate news 08-Sports news 09-Travel news 10-Book rev. 11-Movie rev. 12-Music rev. 13-TV rev. 14-Theater rev. 15-Coming events 16-Obituaries 17-Question & answer 18-Social announcements 19-Artwork 20-Cartoons 21-Photos 22-TV listings 23-Audio rec. 24-Video rec. 25-Books 26-Films/film clips 27-Personnel news 28-Press releases 29-New product news/photos 30-Trade lit. 31-Contracts awarded 32-Display adv. 33-Classified adv.

6-21

**CLUB DIRECTOR**
68793
3050 K St., N.W., Ste. 330
Washington, DC 20007-5108
Telephone: (202) 625-2080
FAX: (202) 625-9044
Year Established: 1983
Pub. Frequency: 6/yr.
Page Size: standard
Subscrip. Rate: $15/yr.
Materials: 02,06,10,16,21,25,28,29,32
Print Process: offset
Circulation: 9,500
Circulation Type: controlled
**Owner(s):**
National Club Association
3050 K St., N.W., Ste. 330
Washington, DC 20007-5108
Telephone: (202) 625-2080
FAX: (202) 625-9044
Ownership %: 100
**Editorial:**
Mary Barnes Embody ............................Editor
**Desc.:** Covers strategic planning, policies
and procedures, taxation and capital
improvements, industry trends, and
financial and personnel management.
**Readers:** Officers, directors and managers
of private clubs.
**Deadline:** photo-4 wks. prior to pub. date;
ads-4 wks. prior to pub. date

**DAC JOURNAL**
25680
19 West St.
New York, NY 10004
Telephone: (212) 425-7000
FAX: (212) 269-4547
Pub. Frequency: s-a.: Jul. & Dec.
Page Size: standard
Subscrip. Rate: $20/yr.
Circulation: 4,000
Circulation Type: paid
**Owner(s):**
Downtown Athletic Club
19 West St.
New York, NY 10004
Telephone: (212) 425-7000
Ownership %: 100
**Management:**
C. Peter Lambos .......................President
John DiSomma .................Advertising Manager
Raymond C. Mott ...................General Manager
**Editorial:**
Margaret B. Koenig ....................Miscellaneous
**Desc.:** Departments include: Club News,
Entertainment, Food, Club Sports,
Fitness.
**Readers:** Upper income level executives in
New York.

**D.A.C. NEWS**
25681
241 Madison Ave.
Detroit, MI 48226
Telephone: (313) 963-5993
FAX: (313) 963-8891
Year Established: 1916
Pub. Frequency: 9/yr.
Page Size: standard
Subscrip. Rate: $36/yr.
Freelance Pay: $50-$250/mo.
Circulation: 4,500
Circulation Type: paid
**Owner(s):**
Detroit Athletic Club
241 Madison Ave.
Detroit, MI 48226
Telephone: (313) 963-5993
Ownership %: 100
**Management:**
Bruce Walker ..............................Publisher
Albert C. Cochrane ...........Advertising Manager
**Editorial:**
Bruce Walker ..............................Editor
Nancy Kleinsmith ....................Managing Editor

**Desc.:** Articles on entertainment, business,
humor, sport, drama, travel, automotive
industry and cosmopolitan living.
Features about Detroit and its activities.
Features and pictures about D.A.C.
members and their social activities.
**Readers:** Business executives and
families.

**EAGLE MAGAZINE**
25683
12660 W. Capitol Dr.
Brookfield, WI 53005
Telephone: (414) 781-7585
FAX: (414) 781-5046
Mailing Address:
P.O. Box 25916
Milwaukee, WI 53225-0916
Year Established: 1913
Pub. Frequency: q.
Page Size: standard
Subscrip. Rate: $1/yr.
Freelance Pay: negotiable
Circulation: 685,971
Circulation Type: paid
**Owner(s):**
Fraternal Order of Eagles
12660 W. Capitol Dr.
Brookfield, WI 53005
Telephone: (414) 781-7585
Ownership %: 100
**Editorial:**
Robert W. Hansen ..........................Editor
Fran Ehrmann ....................Managing Editor
**Desc.:** Official publication of the Fraternal
Order of Eagles with emphasis on
reporting Eagle programs and activities
at local and national levels, special
features on home, personalities, humor,
travel and the outdoors. Regular
features are sports, entertainment and
social security information.
**Readers:** All members of the Fraternal
Order of Eagles.

**ELKS MAGAZINE, THE**
25685
425 W. Diversey Pkwy.
Chicago, IL 60614-6196
Telephone: (312) 528-4500
Year Established: 1922
Pub. Frequency: 10/yr.
Page Size: standard
Subscrip. Rate: $3.50/yr. members.; $5/yr.
non-members.
Freelance Pay: varies
Circulation: 1,400,000
Circulation Type: paid
**Owner(s):**
Benevolent & Protective Order of Elks of
the U.S.
Telephone: (312) 528-4500
Ownership %: 100
**Management:**
Rita Kenny .......................Advertising Manager
William Paliotte ....................Business Manager
**Editorial:**
Fred D. Oakes ..............................Editor
Judith L. Keogh ....................Managing Editor
Jim O'Kelley ........................Associate Editor
Bettina E. Lee ....................Editorial Assistant
Fred D. Oakes ...................Marketing Director
**Desc.:** Business, travel, current events,
retirement, more for your money,
general interest articles, humor, medical
advances, national and international
affairs are some of the topics treated
editorially along with fraternal news.
**Readers:** Members of the order and their
families

**EXCHANGITE, THE**
25686
3050 Central Ave.
Toledo, OH 43606
Telephone: (419) 535-3232
FAX: (419) 535-1989

Year Established: 1921
Pub. Frequency: 8/yr.
Page Size: standard
Subscrip. Rate: $6/yr.
Circulation: 38,000
Circulation Type: paid
**Owner(s):**
The National Exchange Club
3050 Central Ave.
Toledo, OH 43606
Telephone: (419) 535-3232
Ownership %: 100
**Editorial:**
James R. Lazette ..........................Editor
Ellen L. Williams .................Editorial Specialist
**Desc.:** By-lined articles. Topics covered
are America, American citizenship,
patriotism, crime prevention, national
defense, traffic safety, education, youth,
aviation, agriculture, fire prevention,
community service, child abuse
prevention & networking.
**Readers:** Exchangites in exchange
(service) clubs. Business and
professional men & women.

**GFWC CLUBWOMAN**
26582
1734 N St., N.W.
Washington, DC 20036-2990
Telephone: (202) 347-3168
FAX: (202) 835-0246
Year Established: 1917
Pub. Frequency: 6/yr.
Page Size: standard
Subscrip. Rate: $6/yr. members
Materials: 32
Print Process: web offset
Circulation: 17,000
Circulation Type: controlled
**Owner(s):**
General Federation of Women's Clubs
1734 N St., N.W.
Washington, DC 20036-2990
Telephone: (202) 347-3168
FAX: (202) 835-0246
Ownership %: 100
**Management:**
Ann L. Holland .............................President
**Desc.:** The quarterly magazine of the
General Federation of Women's Clubs
(GFWC), which is the largest volunteer
women's service organization in the
world. The magazine features GFWC's
official programs and projects dealing
with the arts, conservation, education,
home life, international affairs and
public affairs. In addition, the magazine
carries news from local GFWC clubs
across the country and articles on
current issues that are of interest to
today's clubwoman.
**Readers:** GFWC clubwomen (community
volunteers).

**GIRL SCOUT LEADER**
26590
420 Fifth Ave.
New York, NY 10018-2702
Telephone: (212) 852-8000
FAX: (212) 852-6511
Year Established: 1923
Pub. Frequency: 4/yr.
Page Size: standard
Subscrip. Rate: $5/yr. US; $7.50/yr.
foreign
Print Process: web offset
Circulation: 800,000
Circulation Type: paid
**Owner(s):**
Girl Scouts of the U.S.A.
420 Fifth Ave.
New York, NY 10018-2702
Telephone: (212) 852-8000
Ownership %: 100

**Editorial:**
Carolyn Caggine ..........................Editor
**Desc.:** Communicator of current programs
& philosophies including news, events,
Girl Scout programs, training,
management, leadership, and health,
safety & home & family relations.
**Readers:** All adults in Girl Scouting-
volunteers (including leaders) and staff.

**JUNIOR LEAGUE REVIEW**
25672
660 First Ave.
New York, NY 10016
Telephone: (212) 683-1515
FAX: (212) 481-7196
Year Established: 1911
Pub. Frequency: s-a.
Page Size: standard
Subscrip. Rate: $10/yr. non-members
Circulation: 190,000
Circulation Type: paid
**Owner(s):**
Association of Jr. Leagues International,
Inc.
660 First Ave.
New York, NY 10016
Telephone: (212) 683-1515
Ownership %: 100
**Editorial:**
Betsey Steeger ..........................Editor
**Desc.:** Carries in-depth articles on issues
of general interest to women as well as
reports on activities of the association
and information on trends affecting the
voluntary sector.
**Readers:** Junior Leagues, other nonprofit
organizations, leaders in government,
business, and the media.

**KIWANIS**
25690
3636 Woodview Trace
Indianapolis, IN 46268
Telephone: (317) 875-8755
FAX: (317) 879-0204
Year Established: 1915
Pub. Frequency: m.
Page Size: standard
Subscrip. Rate: $6.50/yr. members;
$7.50/yr. non-members
Materials: 01,02,05,06,19,20,21,32,33
Freelance Pay: $600-$1,000
Circulation: 280,000
Circulation Type: paid
**Owner(s):**
Kiwanis International
Telephone: (317) 875-8755
Ownership %: 100
**Management:**
A.G. Terry Shaffer ..............................Publisher
Patrick Hatcher .................Advertising Manager
Elizabeth Alexander ..........Circulation Manager
**Editorial:**
Chuck Jonak ....................Managing Editor
Jim Patterson ..........................Art Director
Jack Brockley ....................Associate Editor
Diane Bartley ...................Production Director
**Desc.:** Interested in thoroughly researched,
analytical, objectively written articles for
small business and professional
persons. Areas of interest are business,
the community, youth, the family,
national and international concerns and
general interest topics.
**Readers:** Business and professional men
and women interested in community
service.
**Deadline:** news-3 mo. prior to pub. date;
ads-10th of mo., 1 mo. prior to pub. date

**LION MAGAZINE, THE**
25691
300 22nd St.
Oak Brook, IL 60521
Telephone: (708) 571-5466
FAX: (708) 571-8890

---

**Materials Accepted/Included:** 01-Business news 02-By-line articles 03-Fashion news 04-Food news 05-Freelance copy 06-Letters to editor 07-Real estate news 08-Sports news 09-Travel news 10-Book rev. 11-Movie rev. 12-Music rev. 13-TV rev. 14-Theater rev. 15-Coming events 16-Obituaries 17-Question & answer 18-Social announcements 19-Artwork 20-Cartoons 21-Photos 22-TV listings 23-Audio rec. 24-Video rec. 25-Books 26-Films/film clips 27-Personnel news 28-Press releases 29-New product news/photos 30-Trade lit. 31-Contracts awarded 32-Display adv. 33-Classified adv.

6-22

Year Established: 1918
Pub. Frequency: m.
Page Size: standard
Subscrip. Rate: $.75 issue; $6/yr.
Materials: 02,05,06,20,21,32
Freelance Pay: $100-$700
Print Process: web offset
Circulation: 600,000
Circulation Type: controlled
**Owner(s):**
Lions Clubs International
300 22nd St.
Oak Brook, IL 60521
Telephone: (708) 571-5466
Ownership %: 100
**Management:**
James T. Coffey ...................................President
Mary Kay Rietz ............Advertising Manager
**Editorial:**
Mark Lukas ...................................Editor in Chief
Robert Kleinfelder ........................Senior Editor
Patrick Cannon .........................Managing Editor
Lisa Champelli ...........................Assistant Editor
Pamela Mohr ............................Associate Editor
James Jebavy .................Graphics Coordinator
**Desc.:** Official publication, Lions Clubs
    International, a worldwide association of
    Lions Clubs. Contents include reports of
    club activities, general interest articles,
    cartoons and photos appealing primarily
    to people in the fields of community
    betterment and self-improvement.
**Readers:** Business and community
    leaders, bulk of readers in US and
    Canada. Also publishes editions in
    Spanish, French, German, Korean,
    Portuguese, Dutch, Chinese, Danish,
    Japanese, Swedish, Italian, Finnish,
    Icelandic, Greek, Flemish, Turkish, Thai,
    and Hindi.
**Deadline:** story-3 mo. prior to pub. date;
    news-3 mo.; photo-3 mo.; ads-2 1/2 mo.

25692
**M.A.C. GOPHER MAGAZINE**
615 Second Ave. S.
Minneapolis, MN 55402
Telephone: (612) 339-3655
FAX: (612) 339-7923
Year Established: 1915
Pub. Frequency: m.
Page Size: standard
Subscrip. Rate: $25/yr.
Circulation: 4,000
Circulation Type: paid
**Owner(s):**
Minneapolis Athletic Club
615 Second Ave. S.
Minneapolis, MN 55402
Telephone: (612) 339-3655
Ownership %: 100
**Management:**
Marilyn A. Siebert ...............................Publisher
Jan Wiggs ....................Advertising Manager
**Editorial:**
Marilyn A. Siebert .................................Editor
**Desc.:** Primarily for members of the
    Minneapolis Athletic Club, so most of
    the editorial material has some sort of
    club angle. Reports on the various
    activities of the club members, articles
    on travel, food, and business. Generally,
    all news must involve in some way, a
    club member. Also includes news of a
    member's promotion or of his or her
    business. The same policy applies to
    photos.
**Readers:** Members of the Minneapolis
    Athletic Club.

25696
**MOOSE MAGAZINE**
Supreme Lodge Bldg.
Mooseheart, IL 60539-1174
Telephone: (708) 859-2000
FAX: (708) 859-6620

Year Established: 1910
Pub. Frequency: bi-m.
Page Size: standard
Subscrip. Rate: $2/yr.
Materials: 20
Freelance Pay: negotiable
Circulation: 1,300,000
**Owner(s):**
Moose International, Inc.
Supreme Lodge Bldg.
Mooseheart, IL 60539
Telephone: (708) 859-2000
Ownership %: 100
**Management:**
Frank A. Sarnecki ...............................Publisher
**Editorial:**
Kurt N. Wehrmeister ...............Managing Editor
Joseph Tiffany ..........................Associate Editor
**Desc.:** Entire editorial content mostly
    confined to Moose organization
    activities.

25697
**NATIONAL FRATERNAL CLUB
NEWS**
43 E. Ohio
Chicago, IL 60611
Telephone: (312) 527-0580
Pub. Frequency: a.
Subscrip. Rate: $12/yr.
Circulation: 75,000
Circulation Type: paid
**Owner(s):**
National Fraternal Club News
**Management:**
Leonard Winer .....................................President
Janice Greening .........................Office Manager

68794
**PRIVATE CLUBS**
3030 LBJ Freeway, Ste. 600
Dallas, TX 75234-7703
Telephone: (214) 888-7547
FAX: (214) 888-7338
Year Established: 1986
Pub. Frequency: bi-m.
Subscrip. Rate: $12/yr.
Circulation: 212,100
Circulation Type: paid
**Owner(s):**
Associate Clubs Publications, Inc.
3030 LBJ Freeway, Ste. 600
Dallas, TX 75234-7703
Telephone: (214) 888-7547
Ownership %: 100
**Management:**
George Gretser ..................................Publisher
**Editorial:**
Julie Bain ...............................................Editor
Bunny Pool .......................Advertising Director
Rita Atkins .........................Circulation Director

25704
**ROTARIAN, THE**
One Rotary Center
1560 Sherman Ave.
Evanston, IL 60201
Telephone: (708) 866-3000
FAX: (708) 328-8554
Year Established: 1905
Pub. Frequency: m.
Page Size: standard
Subscrip. Rate: $1/copy; $12/yr.
Freelance Pay: varies
Circulation: 521,000
Circulation Type: paid
**Owner(s):**
Rotary International
One Rotary Center
1560 Sherman Ave.
Evanston, IL 60201
Telephone: (708) 866-3000
Ownership %: 100
**Management:**
Bill Huntley ........................................President
Ed Schimmelpfennig .........Advertising Manager

**Editorial:**
Willmon L. White ...................................Editor
Charles W. Pratt ....................Managing Editor
Andrew Sohn ...............................Advertising
Pelayia Limbos .................................Art Editor
Joseph T. Agnew ....................Assistant Editor
Cary Silver ...............................Assistant Editor
David Dee ................................Assistant Editor
Joaquin Mejia ..........................Assistant Editor
Jo Nugent ...............................Associate Editor
Judy Lee ...............................................Photo
Beth Pearson ............Special Services Director
**Desc.:** Articles to improve communities
    and standards of businesses and
    professions and to advance international
    understanding, as well as Rotary news.
    Maximum length 2,000 words. Use by-
    lines of free lancers, staff and others.
    Prefer article queries rather than
    manuscripts. Departments include: By
    the Way (editor's column), Stripped
    Gears (humor page), Your Letters, This
    Rotary World (news about activities and
    achievements of Rotary Clubs and
    individual Rotary members), Manager's
    Memo (business column), Trends
    column, Book Review, Rotary Authors,
    Fellowship Forum, Earth Diary, Executive
    Health/Lifestyle, Emporium /Classified.
**Readers:** Business and professional
    people in Rotary Clubs, their families
    and children, many readers in reading
    rooms of schools and libraries.

26625
**ROYAL NEIGHBOR, THE**
230 16th St.
Rock Island, IL 61201
Telephone: (309) 788-4561
FAX: (309) 788-9234
Year Established: 1900
Pub. Frequency: m.
Page Size: standard
Subscrip. Rate: membership only
Circulation: 175,000
Circulation Type: controlled & free
**Owner(s):**
Royal Neighbors of America
230 16th St.
Rock Island, IL 61201
Telephone: (309) 788-4561
Ownership %: 100
**Management:**
Priscilla Ann Curtis ............................Publisher
**Editorial:**
Priscilla Ann Curtis ................................Editor
Barbara Keller .........................Assistant Editor
**Desc.:** Features activities of the home and
    of the society which has more than 211,
    000 members, including 32,000 junior
    members. Features are Recipes,
    Fraternal, Home and junior activities.
**Readers:** Mostly women from typical
    American families.

25699
**SCOTTISH RITE JOURNAL, THE**
1733 16th St., N.W.
Washington, DC 20009-3199
Telephone: (202) 232-3579
FAX: (202) 387-1843
Year Established: 1904
Pub. Frequency: m.
Page Size: standard
Subscrip. Rate: $4/yr.
Materials: 06,10
Freelance Pay: voluntary
Print Process: web
Circulation: 515,000
**Owner(s):**
Supreme Council, 33 Degrees
1715 16th St., N.W.
Washington, DC 20009-3199
Telephone: (202) 232-3579
Ownership %: 100

**Editorial:**
C. Fred Kleinknecht ..............Editor in Chief
Dr. John W. Boettjer ..............Managing Editor
**Readers:** Almost entirely Masons and their
    families.

25705
**SCOUTING MAGAZINE**
1325 W. Walnut Hill Ln.
Irving, TX 75015-2079
Telephone: (214) 580-2355
Mailing Address:
    P.O. Box 152079
    Irving, TX 75015-2079
Year Established: 1913
Pub. Frequency: 6/yr.
Page Size: standard
Subscrip. Rate: membership
Materials: 06,17,20,24,25
Freelance Pay: $400-$600
Print Process: web offset
Circulation: 1,000,000
Circulation Type: paid
**Owner(s):**
Boy Scouts of America
1325 W. Walnut Hill Ln.
Irving, TX 75015-2079
Telephone: (214) 580-2355
Ownership %: 100
**Management:**
J. Warren Young ...............................Publisher
Chuck Carroll ....................Advertising Manager
**Editorial:**
Jon Halter ...............................Executive Editor
Ernest Doclar ..........................................Editor
Brian Payne ............................................Photo
**Desc.:** Few unsolicited articles. Most
    articles are assigned to experienced
    professional writers, photographers,
    illustrators. Most material describes
    actual experiences of adult leaders in
    Scouting or descriptive articles to help
    them become successful in Scouting.
**Readers:** Volunteer adult leaders in the
    BSA.

22415
**TOASTMASTER, THE**
23182 Arroyo Vista
Rancho Santa Margarita, CA 92688
Telephone: (714) 858-8255
FAX: (714) 858-1207
Mailing Address:
    P.O. Box 9052
    Mission Viejo, CA 92690
Year Established: 1934
Pub. Frequency: m.
Page Size: Four-color photos/art
Subscrip. Rate: n/a
Materials: 02,05,06
Freelance Pay: $100-$250
Circulation: 180,000
Circulation Type: controlled
**Owner(s):**
Toastmasters International
23182 Arroyo Vista
Rancho Santa Margarita, CA 92688
Telephone: (714) 858-8255
FAX: (714) 858-1207
Ownership %: 100
**Editorial:**
Terrence J. McCann ...............Executive Editor
Suzanne Frey ..........................................Editor
Paul Haven Design .........................Art Director
Kathy O'Connell ......................Associate Editor

**Materials Accepted/Included:** 01-Business news 02-By-line articles 03-Fashion news 04-Food news 05-Freelance copy 06-Letters to editor 07-Real estate news 08-Sports news 09-Travel news 10-Book rev. 11-Movie rev. 12-Music rev. 13-TV rev. 14-Theater rev. 15-Coming events 16-Obituaries 17-Question & answer 18-Social announcements 19-Artwork 20-Cartoons 21-Photos 22-TV listings 23-Audio rec. 24-Video rec. 25-Books 26-Films/film clips 27-Personnel news 28-Press releases 29-New product news/photos 30-Trade lit. 31-Contracts awarded 32-Display adv. 33-Classified adv.

6-23

**Desc.:** How-to improve speaking, listening, thinking skills, leadership, and other topics, with realistic examples, humor (on leadership, communications or management techniques), interviews (with communications or management experts which members can directly apply to their self-improvement efforts; should contain how-to information). Prepared and impromptu speaking, speech evaluation, conducting meetings leadership, Parliamentary Procedure: Listening; Audiovisual Techniques; Debates; Humor.
**Readers:** Members and public.

25709
**VFW MAGAZINE**
405 W. 34th St.
Kansas City, MO 64111
Telephone: (816) 756-3390
FAX: (816) 968-1169
Year Established: 1914
Pub. Frequency: 11/yr.
Page Size: standard
Subscrip. Rate: $10/yr.
Materials: 05,06,19,21,25,32,33
Freelance Pay: $400
Print Process: web offset
Circulation: 2,020,000
Circulation Type: controlled
**Owner(s):**
Veterans of Foreign Wars of the United States
406 W. 34th St.
Kansas City, MO 64111
Telephone: (816) 756-3390
Ownership %: 100
**Management:**
Richard K. Kolb .................Publisher
Bob Greene ....................Circulation Manager
**Editorial:**
Richard K. Kolb ...................Editor
Gary L. Bloomfield ...............Managing Editor
Bob Widener .....................Art Director
**Desc.:** Timely and factual articles on subjects of national interest and concern, especially with a veterans slant. Factual accounts of military actions.
**Readers:** American veterans of overseas wartime service.
**Deadline:** story-6 mo. prior to pub. date

25679
**WISCONSIN WEST MAGAZINE**
2645 Harlem St., Ste. 1C
Eau Claire, WI 54701-4506
Telephone: (715) 835-3800
Year Established: 1987
Pub. Frequency: bi-m.
Page Size: standard
Subscrip. Rate: $2.50 newsstand; $14/yr.
Materials: 04,05,06,08,09,15,32
Freelance Pay: negotiable
Print Process: offset
Circulation: 30,000
Circulation Type: controlled
**Owner(s):**
Modern Communications, Inc.
2645 Harlem St., Ste. 1C
Eau Claire, WI 54701-4506
Telephone: (715) 835-3800
Ownership %: 100
**Editorial:**
Wayne Turnquist ...................Editor
**Desc.:** Regional magazine featuring interesting and provocative articles about western Wisconsin's rich heritage and uniqueness.
**Readers:** Head of households earning $35,000 or more per year.

65595
**WOMAN ENGINEER**
150 Motor Pkwy., Ste. 420
Hauppauge, NY 11788-5145
Telephone: (516) 273-0066
FAX: (516) 273-8936
Year Established: 1968
Pub. Frequency: 4/yr.
Page Size: standard
Subscrip. Rate: $17/yr.
Circulation: 16,013
Circulation Type: free
**Owner(s):**
EOP, Inc.
150 Motor Pkwy., Ste. 420
Hauppauge, NY 11788-5145
Telephone: (516) 273-0066
Ownership %: 100
**Management:**
John R. Miller, III ...................President
Kay Zollar Miller ...................Publisher
Christine Desmond .............Business Manager
Barbara O'Connor .............Circulation Manager
**Editorial:**
James Schneider ...................Exec. Editor
Anne Kelly ...................Editor
James Schneider ...............Production Director
**Desc.:** An affirmative action recruitment magazine for women college students, graduates and professional engineers. Articles about women engineers, career guidance, career news, surveys, salaries, conventions and how-to-succeed. Free resume service. Engineering career opportunities in industry, government and the military.
**Readers:** Women engineers - college level and graduates.

25712
**WOODMEN**
1700 Farnam St.
Omaha, NE 68102
Telephone: (402) 342-1890
FAX: (402) 271-7269
Year Established: 1890
Pub. Frequency: bi-m.
Page Size: standard
Subscrip. Rate: $.50/copy; $3/yr.
Materials: 16,20,21
Print Process: web offset
Circulation: 500,000
Circulation Type: controlled
**Owner(s):**
Woodmen of the World Life Insurance Society
1700 Farnam St.
Omaha, NE 68102
Telephone: (402) 342-1890
FAX: (402) 271-7269
Ownership %: 100
**Editorial:**
Scott J. Darling ...................Editor
Billie Jo Foust ...................Assistant Editor
**Desc.:** Content includes news stories about Woodmen, lodges and members of the Society, stories about the Society's operations, general interest articles.
**Readers:** Persons in all walks of life.
**Deadline:** photo-2 mos. prior to pub. date

## Group 618-College & Alumni

25012
**ALUMNI UPDATE**
School House Ln. & Henry Ave.
Philadelphia, PA 19144
Telephone: (215) 951-2700
FAX: (215) 951-2615
Year Established: 1990
Pub. Frequency: 4/yr.
Page Size: standard
Subscrip. Rate: free to alumni
Materials: 32
Circulation: 14,000

Circulation Type: controlled
**Owner(s):**
Philadelphia College of Textiles and Science
School House Ln. & Henry Ave.
Philadelphia, PA 19144
Telephone: (215) 951-2700
Ownership %: 100
**Editorial:**
James McDevitt ...................Art Director
Pat Laws ...................Director
Lynda Irwin ...................Editorial Assistant
Roslyn Levine ...................Editorial Assistant
**Desc.:** Contents keep alumni posted on happenings at the College, and news about themselves.
**Readers:** Alumni, Parents and Friends

68798
**ALUMNUS**
1008 S. Elizabeth
So. Illinois Univ. Student Center
Carbondale, IL 62901-6522
Telephone: (618) 536-7531
FAX: (618) 453-2000
Year Established: 1940
Pub. Frequency: q.
Page Size: standard
Subscrip. Rate: $30/yr.
Materials: 06,10,16,25,27,28
Print Process: web offset
Circulation: 100,000
Circulation Type: controlled & paid
**Owner(s):**
University Print Communications
1008 S. Elizabeth
Carbondale, IL 62901-6522
Telephone: (618) 536-7531
Ownership %: 100
**Editorial:**
Laraine Wright ...................Editor

24710
**BLACK COLLEGIAN, THE**
1240 S. Broad St.
New Orleans, LA 70125
Telephone: (504) 821-5694
FAX: (504) 821-5713
Year Established: 1970
Pub. Frequency: bi-m.
Page Size: standard
Subscrip. Rate: $12/yr.
Materials: 06,10,11,21,23,24,25,28,29,30,31
Freelance Pay: $25-$400
Circulation: 109,637
Circulation Type: controlled
**Owner(s):**
Black Collegiate Services, Inc.
1240 S. Broad St.
New Orleans, LA 70125
Telephone: (504) 821-5694
FAX: (504) 821-5713
Ownership %: 100
**Management:**
Preston J. Edwards, Sr. .......Chairman of Board
Melba Lemieux-Nevills ...................Vice President
Preston J. Edwards, Sr. ...................Publisher
Edmond Patterson .............Circulation Manager
C.C. Campbell-Rock ...................Public Relations Manager
**Editorial:**
Kuumba Kazi ...................Editor
Kuumba Kazi ...................Production Director
**Desc.:** Material oriented to the black college student and young professional careers, entertainment, black history, current events and politics. Black art, sports, bulletin board and lifestyle.
**Readers:** Black college students & young professionals.
**Deadline:** story-20th of mo. prior to pub. date; ads-1st of mo. prior

55927
**BROWN ALUMNI MONTHLY**
71 George St.
Providence, RI 02906
Telephone: (401) 863-2873
FAX: (401) 751-9255
Mailing Address:
P.O. Box 1854
Providence, RI 02912
Pub. Frequency: m.: 9/yr.
Page Size: 4 color photos/art
Subscrip. Rate: $30/yr.
Circulation: 69,000
Circulation Type: controlled
**Owner(s):**
Brown University
71 George St.
Providence, RI 29060
Telephone: (401) 863-2873
Ownership %: 100
**Editorial:**
Anne Diffily ...................Editor
**Desc.:** Edited for alumni bound together by an active interest in Brown University.
**Readers:** Alumni, students, faculty, friends and interested observers.

25717
**CAMPUS VOICE**
333 Main Ave.
Knoxville, TN 37902
Telephone: (615) 595-5000
FAX: (615) 595-5390
Year Established: 1969
Pub. Frequency: 9/yr.
Page Size: oversize
Subscrip. Rate: free to college students
Freelance Pay: $.30-$1/wd.
Circulation: 1,200,000
Circulation Type: free
**Owner(s):**
Whittle Communications L.P.
333 Main Ave.
Knoxville, TN 37902
Telephone: (615) 595-5000
Ownership %: 100
**Management:**
Chris Whittle ...................Chairman of Board
Nicholas Glover ...................President
John Glascott ...................Advertising Manager
**Editorial:**
Keith Bellows ...................Exec. Editor
Sheila De La Rosa ...................Senior Editor
Su Poganey ...................Art Director
Ken Smith ...................Design Director
**Desc.:** A biweekly feature publication for the college community, primarily college students ages 18 to 22.
**Readers:** College students.

58648
**CAROLINA ALUMNI REVIEW**
Stadium Dr.
Chapel Hill, NC 27514
Telephone: (919) 962-1208
FAX: (919) 962-0010
Mailing Address:
P.O. Box 660
Chapel Hill, NC 27514
Year Established: 1912
Pub. Frequency: q.
Page Size: standard
Subscrip. Rate: $25/yr.
Freelance Pay: $300+
Circulation: 51,000
Circulation Type: paid
**Owner(s):**
UNC-General Alumni Association
P.O. Box 660
Chapel Hill, NC 27514
Telephone: (919) 962-1208
Ownership %: 100
**Management:**
Doug Dibbert ...................Publisher
**Editorial:**
F. Weston Fenhagen ...................Editor
Diana Palmer ...................Managing Editor

**Materials Accepted/Included:** 01-Business news 02-By-line articles 03-Fashion news 04-Food news 05-Freelance copy 06-Letters to editor 07-Real estate news 08-Sports news 09-Travel news 10-Book rev. 11-Movie rev. 12-Music rev. 13-TV rev. 14-Theater rev. 15-Coming events 16-Obituaries 17-Question & answer 18-Social announcements 19-Artwork 20-Cartoons 21-Photos 22-TV listings 23-Audio rec. 24-Video rec. 25-Books 26-Films/film clips 27-Personnel news 28-Press releases 29-New product news/photos 30-Trade lit. 31-Contracts awarded 32-Display adv. 33-Classified adv.

6-24

Karen Wertman .................Advertising Director
Cornelia Lee .........................Associate Editor
**Readers:** 51,000 alumni, University faculty, staff and friends.
**Deadline:** story-6-8 wks.; photo-6-8 wks.; ads-6-8 wks.

## COLUMBIA COLLEGE TODAY
55926

475 Riverside Dr.
Columbia University
New York, NY 10115
Telephone: (212) 870-2752
FAX: (212) 870-2747
Pub. Frequency: 3/yr.
Page Size: standard
Subscrip. Rate: complimentary; $15/yr.
Circulation: 45,000
Circulation Type: controlled
**Owner(s):**
Trustees of Columbia University
New York, NY 10027
Ownership %: 100
**Editorial:**
James C. Katz ................................Editor
**Desc.:** Edited for an audience bound together by an active interest in today's universities.
**Readers:** Readership includes alumni, students, faculty, friends and interest observers.

## CORNELL MAGAZINE
55925

55 Brown Rd.
Ithaca, NY 14850
Telephone: (607) 257-5133
FAX: (607) 257-1782
Year Established: 1899
Pub. Frequency: 10/yr.
Page Size: standard
Subscrip. Rate: $3.25 newsstand; $29/yr.; $32.50/yr. newsstand price
Print Process: web offset
Circulation: 40,000
Circulation Type: paid
**Owner(s):**
Cornell Alumni Federation
Ownership %: 100
**Management:**
Jack Krieger ...............................Publisher
Stephen Madden ..............Associate Publisher
**Editorial:**
Stephen Madden ................................Editor
Andrew Wallenstein .......Business Ad Systems Manager

## DARTMOUTH ALUMNI MAGAZINE
55924

38 N. Main St.
Hanover, NH 03755
Telephone: (603) 646-2256
FAX: (603) 646-1209
Year Established: 1908
Pub. Frequency: 9/yr.
Page Size: standard
Subscrip. Rate: $3 newsstand; $21.50/yr.
Materials: 02,05,06,16,19,20,21,23,24,25, 27,28,29,30,32,33
Print Process: web
Circulation: 45,000
Circulation Type: paid
**Owner(s):**
Dartmouth College
Ownership %: 100
**Bureau(s):**
Ivy League Magazine Network
305 Madison Ave., Ste. 1436
New York, NY 10165
Telephone: (212) 972-2559
Contact: John Donoghue, Advertising
**Editorial:**
Jay Heinrichs ................................Editor
**Deadline:** story-varies; news-varies; photo-varies; ads-1 mo. prior to pub. date

## DELTA COLLEGIATE
22452

Delta College
University Center
Bay City, MI 48710
Telephone: (517) 686-9337
FAX: (517) 686-8736
Year Established: 1961
Pub. Frequency: w.
Page Size: tabloid
Subscrip. Rate: free
Freelance Pay: $.25/col. in.
Circulation: 3,500
Circulation Type: free
**Owner(s):**
Delta Collegiate
Delta College
Bay City, MI 48710
Telephone: (517) 686-9337
Ownership %: 100
**Management:**
Joan Ramm ...............................President
Matt Moorman ...............Advertising Manager
**Editorial:**
Melinda Matthews .............................Editor
**Desc.:** The Collegiate is a weekly publication by and for the Delta College Community. All opinion and commentary articles published in this paper are the sole opinions of the editors and/or the writers of the Collegiate, not necessarily those of the administration, faculty or student-body of this college. The Collegiate welcomes and encourages all student input.
**Readers:** Student body, faculty, staff and community.

## HARVARD MAGAZINE
25863

7 Ware St.
Cambridge, MA 02138
Telephone: (617) 495-5746
FAX: (617) 495-0324
Year Established: 1898
Pub. Frequency: bi-m.
Page Size: standard
Subscrip. Rate: $4.95; $30/yr.
Freelance Pay: $.10/wd.
Circulation: 220,000
Circulation Type: controlled
**Owner(s):**
Harvard Magazine, Inc.
7 Ware St.
Cambridge, MA 02138
Telephone: (617) 495-5746
**Management:**
David Ives ...............................President
Laura Freid ...............................Publisher
**Editorial:**
John T. Bethell ................................Editor
Christopher Reed ...................Managing Editor
Jean Martin .............Associate Managing Editor
Gretchen Friesingerd ...............Associate Editor
Janet Hawkins ......................Associate Editor
Craig Lambert ........................Associate Editor
Richard Marius ....................Contributing Editor
Liam Rector ...........................Poetry Editor
**Desc.:** A general interest, national magazine devoted to continuing education. Articles deal with all subjects likely to be found in a college curriculum. written by faculty members of Harvard or other institutions, or by free-lance writers, or by staff members. Articles vary in length from a few hundred to 5,000 words. A strong emphasis is placed on graphics, with top-quality four-color reproduction. Departments include: science, humanism, books, travel, recordings, questions answered.
**Readers:** Extremely upscale, well educated, affluent.

## LA SALLE
4714

1900 W. Olney Ave.
Philadelphia, PA 19141
Telephone: (215) 951-1080
FAX: (215) 951-1066
Pub. Frequency: q.
Page Size: standard
Print Process: offset
Circulation: 39,000
Circulation Type: free
**Owner(s):**
La Salle University
1900 W. Olney Ave.
Philadelphia, PA 19141
Telephone: (215) 951-1080
Ownership %: 100
**Editorial:**
Robert S. Lyons, Jr. ................................Editor
**Desc.:** Feature articles and news items of interest to La Salle alumni.

## LEADERSHIP FOR STUDENT ACTIVITIES
58625

1904 Association Dr.
Reston, VA 22091
Telephone: (703) 860-0200
FAX: (703) 476-5432
Year Established: 1974
Pub. Frequency: m.: Sep.-May
Page Size: standard
Subscrip. Rate: $10/yr. membership
Circulation: 25,000
Circulation Type: paid
**Owner(s):**
Natl. Assn. for School Principals
1904 Association Dr.
Reston, VA 22091
Telephone: (703) 860-0200
Ownership %: 100
**Management:**
Thomas F. Koerner ........................Manager
**Editorial:**
Jackie Rough ................................Editor
**Desc.:** Emphasis is on leadership activities for students in middle schools as well as high schools.
**Readers:** Student Leaders and School Activities Directors.

## LOYOLA MAGAZINE
69461

1 E. Deleware St.
Chicago, IL 60611
Telephone: (312) 915-6157
FAX: (312) 915-6215
Year Established: 1971
Pub. Frequency: 3/yr.
Subscrip. Rate: free to alumni
Circulation: 93,000
Circulation Type: controlled & free
**Owner(s):**
Loyola University Chicago
Office of Public Relations
1 E. Deleware St.
Chicago, IL 60611
Telephone: (312) 915-6157
Ownership %: 100
**Editorial:**
Mary Nowesnick ................................Editor
**Desc.:** News and features of interest to Loyola alumni and benefactors.
**Readers:** Loyola alumni and benefactors.

## MAGAZINE OF SIGMA CHI, THE
25693

1714 Hinman Ave.
Evanston, IL 60201
Telephone: (708) 869-3655
Mailing Address:
P.O. Box 469
Evanston, IL 60204
Year Established: 1881
Pub. Frequency: q.

Page Size: standard
Subscrip. Rate: $25/yr. membership
Materials: 01,02,06,08,10,16,19,20,21,25, 27,28,32
Freelance Pay: negotiable
Print Process: web
Circulation: 50,000
Circulation Type: paid
**Owner(s):**
The Sigma Chi Fraternity
1714 Hinman Ave.
Evanston, IL 60201
Telephone: (708) 869-3655
Ownership %: 100
**Editorial:**
Walter Hutchens ......................Executive Editor
**Desc.:** Articles about the Fraternity and its chapters and their activities and plans, and also stories about successful and interesting members. We also include articles about the college campus scene or general information likely to be of interest to college students and college alumni. We avoid "publicity" material unless it is of specific pertinence to our members as Sigma Chis, but welcome news about members.
**Readers:** College students and their parents, alumni members and college officials.

## MINORITY ENGINEER
65593

150 Motor Pkwy., Ste. 420
Hauppauge, NY 11788-5145
Telephone: (516) 273-0066
FAX: (516) 273-8936
Year Established: 1979
Pub. Frequency: q.
Page Size: standard
Subscrip. Rate: $17/yr.
Materials: 01,02,05,17,19,21,28,32,33
Print Process: web
Circulation: 16,000
Circulation Type: free
**Owner(s):**
Equal Opportunity Publications, Inc.
John R. Miller, III, Owner
150 Motor Pkwy., Ste. 420
Hauppauge, NY 11788-5145
Telephone: (516) 273-0066
FAX: (516) 273-8936
Ownership %: 100
**Management:**
John R. Miller, III ...........................President
John R. Miller, III ...........................Publisher
Christine Desmond .............Business Manager
Barbara O'Connor .............Circulation Manager
**Editorial:**
James Schneider ................................Editor
Anne Kelly ......................Associate Editor
James Schneider ...............Production Director
**Desc.:** Affirmative action recruitment magazine for minorities including Black, Hispanic, Asian American and Native American college students, graduates and professional engineers. Articles on minority engineers, career news, affirmative action news and techniques in the job-hunting field. Free resume service, career opporopportunities in business, industry, government and the military.
**Readers:** Minority engineering students and graduates

## MISSOURI ALUMNUS
68800

407 D.W. Renolds Alumni & Visitor Ctr.
Columbia, MO 65211
Telephone: (314) 882-7357
FAX: (314) 882-7290
Year Established: 1912
Pub. Frequency: q.
Page Size: standard
Subscrip. Rate: $25/yr.

**Materials Accepted/Included:** 01-Business news 02-By-line articles 03-Fashion news 04-Food news 05-Freelance copy 06-Letters to editor 07-Real estate news 08-Sports news 09-Travel news 10-Book rev. 11-Movie rev. 12-Music rev. 13-TV rev. 14-Theater rev. 15-Coming events 16-Obituaries 17-Question & answer 18-Social announcements 19-Artwork 20-Cartoons 21-Photos 22-TV listings 23-Audio rec. 24-Video rec. 25-Books 26-Films/film clips 27-Personnel news 28-Press releases 29-New product news/photos 30-Trade lit. 31-Contracts awarded 32-Display adv. 33-Classified adv.

Circulation: 115,000
Circulation Type: controlled
**Owner(s):**
Publications & Alumni Communication
407 D.W. Renolds Alumni Ctr.
Columbia, MO 65211
Telephone: (314) 882-7357
Ownership %: 100
**Desc.:** Covers happenings at the university. Includes articles on student life, teaching, research and educational issues.

4272

**NORTH CAROLINA STATE UNIVERSITY ALUMNI ASSOCIATION**
P.O. Box 7503
Raleigh, NC 27695
Telephone: (919) 515-3375
FAX: (919) 515-7386
Pub. Frequency: a.
**Owner(s):**
North Carolina State University Alumni Association

68801

**NORTHEASTERN UNIVERSITY MAGAZINE**
271 Huntington Ave., Ste. 220
Boston, MA 02115
Telephone: (617) 373-5433
FAX: (617) 373-5430
Year Established: 1975
Pub. Frequency: bi-m.
Page Size: standard
Print Process: web
Circulation: 120,000
Circulation Type: controlled
**Owner(s):**
Northeastern University
Office of Communications
271 Huntington Ave., Ste. 220
Boston, MA 02115
Telephone: (617) 373-5433
FAX: (617) 373-5430
Ownership %: 100
**Editorial:**
David J. Gibson ....................................Editor

69466

**NORTHWESTERN PERSPECTIVE**
555 Clark St.
2nd Fl.
Evanston, IL 60208-1230
Telephone: (708) 491-5000
FAX: (708) 491-2376
Year Established: 1988
Pub. Frequency: q.
Subscrip. Rate: free to alumni
Circulation: 95,624
Circulation Type: controlled & free
**Owner(s):**
Northwestern University
555 Clark St.
Evanston, IL 60208-1230
Telephone: (708) 491-5000
Ownership %: 100
**Editorial:**
Kenneth J. Wildes ..............................Editor
Stephanie Russell ....................Assistant Editor

69469

**OREGON QUARTERLY**
13001 Chapman Hall
5228 University of Oregon
Eugene, OR 97403-5228
Telephone: (503) 346-5047
FAX: (503) 346-5047
Year Established: 1919
Pub. Frequency: q.
Subscrip. Rate: $2 newsstand; $10/yr.
Materials: 32
Print Process: web offset
Circulation: 95,000
Circulation Type: controlled

**Owner(s):**
University of Oregon
130 Chapman Hall
5228 University of Oregon
Eugene, OR 97403-5228
Telephone: (503) 346-5047
FAX: (503) 346-2220
Ownership %: 100
**Editorial:**
Tom Hager ........................................Editor
Mike Lee ...............................Managing Editor
**Desc.:** Covers Northwest regional issues using the expertise of alumni and faculty of the University of Oregon.

24805

**PEABODY REFLECTOR, THE**
1202 18th Ave.
Nashville, TN 37212
Telephone: (615) 322-2601
Mailing Address:
Peabody Sta., P.O. Box 161
Nashville, TN 37203
Year Established: 1927
Pub. Frequency: 2/yr.
Page Size: standard
Subscrip. Rate: free to alumni
Circulation: 26,000
Circulation Type: controlled & free
**Owner(s):**
George Peabody College for Teachers Alumni Assn.
P.O. Box 161
Nashville, TN 37203
Telephone: (615) 322-2601
Ownership %: 100
**Editorial:**
O. Nelson Bryan ................................Editor
Gillian Murray ...............................Design Editor
**Desc.:** Features informative articles of educators and current educational trends.
**Readers:** Alumni of Peabody College of Vanderbilt University.

68802

**PENN STATER**
105 Old Main
University Park, PA 16802-1559
Telephone: (814) 865-2709
FAX: (814) 865-3325
Year Established: 1913
Pub. Frequency: bi-m.
Page Size: standard
Subscrip. Rate: $25/yr.
Materials: 02,05,06,08,16,19,20,21,28,32
Print Process: web
Circulation: 120,000
Circulation Type: paid
**Owner(s):**
Penn State Alumni Association
105 Old Main
University Park, PA 16802
Telephone: (814) 865-2709
FAX: (814) 865-3325
Ownership %: 100
**Editorial:**
Debbie Williams Ream ...........................Editor
April Scimio ..................................Art Director
Judy Hazel .........................Class News Editor
Scott Elmquist ...............................Staff Writer
Felicia Thibeault Mulley .................Staff Writer
**Desc.:** Contains information on Penn State, alumni and the association.

55922

**PENNSYLVANIA GAZETTE, THE**
3533 Locust Walk, Alumni Ctr.
Philadelphia, PA 19104
Telephone: (215) 898-5555
Pub. Frequency: 8/yr.
Page Size: standard
Subscrip. Rate: varies
Circulation: 90,000
Circulation Type: controlled

**Owner(s):**
General Alumni Society of University of PA.
3533 Locust Walk, Alumni Ctr.
Philadelphia, PA 19104
Telephone: (215) 898-5555
Ownership %: 100
**Bureau(s):**
Ivy League Magazines
626 Thurston Ave.
Ithaca, NY 14850
Telephone: (607) 255-4121
Contact: John Marcham, Chairman of Board

55921

**PRINCETON ALUMNI WEEKLY**
194 Nassau St.
Princeton, NJ 08542
Telephone: (609) 258-4885
FAX: (609) 258-2247
Year Established: 1900
Pub. Frequency: 17/yr. (Sep.-July)
Page Size: 4 color photos/art
Subscrip. Rate: $19.50/yr. US; $24.50 foreign
Circulation: 58,000
Circulation Type: controlled
**Owner(s):**
Princeton Alumni Publications
194 Nassau St.
Princeton, NJ 08542
Telephone: (609) 258-4885
Ownership %: 100
**Bureau(s):**
Ivy League Magazine Network
305 Madison Ave., Ste. 1436
New York, NY 10165
Telephone: (212) 972-2559
Contact: John Donoghue, Advertising
**Management:**
Nancy S. MacMillan .............Business Manager
R.T. Howell .......................Production Manager
**Editorial:**
J.I. Merritt .......................................Editor
Andrew C. Mytelka ..................Managing Editor
Lolly O'Brien ....................Advertising Director
Stacy M. Wszola .............................Art Director
Paul Hager ...............................Associate Editor
**Desc.:** Independent non-profit alumni magazine recording news of Princeton alumni, and providing an impartial review of the achievements and problems of the administration, faculty and students of Princeton University.
**Readers:** Alumni and alumnae and their families, and friends of Princeton University.

69471

**RADCLIFFE QUARTERLY**
10 Garden St.
Cambridge, MA 02138
Telephone: (617) 495-8608
FAX: (617) 496-0255
Year Established: 1916
Pub. Frequency: q.
Subscrip. Rate: free
Circulation: 33,000
Circulation Type: controlled & free
**Owner(s):**
Radcliffe College
10 Garden St.
Cambridge, MA 02138
Telephone: (617) 495-8608
Ownership %: 100
**Editorial:**
Diane Sherlock ..................................Editor
Joan Urdang ...........................Managing Editor
**Desc.:** Covers issues of interest to educated women.
**Readers:** Students and alumni.

68796

**STUDENT LEADER**
738 N.W. 23rd St.
Gainesville, FL 32609
Telephone: (904) 373-6907
FAX: (904) 373-8120
Mailing Address:
P.O. Box 14081
Gainesville, FL 32604-2081
Year Established: 1993
Pub. Frequency: s-a.
Subscrip. Rate: $10/copy
Materials: 05,06,10,19,20,21,28,32,33
Print Process: web offset
Circulation: 130,000
Circulation Type: controlled & paid
**Owner(s):**
Oxendine Publishing, Inc.
738 N.W. 23rd St.
Gainesville, FL 32609
Telephone: (904) 373-8120
Ownership %: 100
**Editorial:**
W.H. Oxendine, Jr. ..............................Editor
**Desc.:** Gives tips and suggestions on how to improve leadership skills and enhance their effectiveness.

65332

**U. THE NATIONAL COLLEGE MAGAZINE**
1800 Century Park E., 820
Los Angeles, CA 90067
Telephone: (310) 551-1381
FAX: (310) 551-1659
Year Established: 1988
Pub. Frequency: 9/yr.
Page Size: tabloid
Subscrip. Rate: $1.80/issue; $18/yr.
Materials: 02,03,05,06,08,09,10,11,12,13, 17,19,20,21,23,24,25,26,28,29,32,33
Freelance Pay: $25-$100
Print Process: web offset
Circulation: 1,530,000
Circulation Type: free
**Owner(s):**
American Collegiate Network, Inc.
1800 Century Park E., 820
Los Angeles, CA 90067
Telephone: (310) 551-1381
FAX: (310) 551-1659
Ownership %: 100
**Bureau(s):**
American Collegiate Network, Inc.
1800 Century Park E., 820
Los Angeles, CA 90067
Telephone: (310) 551-1381
FAX: (310) 551-1659
Contact: Tracy Matthews-Holbert, Circulation Manager
**Management:**
Gayle Morris Sweetland ....................President
Gayle Morris Sweetland ....................Publisher
**Desc.:** Written by college newspaper journalists from 430 leading colleges and universities, which are members of the American Collegiate Network. Editorial is comprised of most relevant journalism, photography, graphics, and cartoons from the member newspapers and selected by former editors of college newspapers on fellowship.
**Readers:** U. The National College Magazine serves young adults, primarily students attending four-year colleges and universities.

55920

**YALE ALUMNI MAGAZINE**
149 York St.
New Haven, CT 06511
Telephone: (203) 432-0645
FAX: (203) 432-0651
Mailing Address:
P.O. Box 1905
New Haven, CT 06509

**Materials Accepted/Included:** 01-Business news 02-By-line articles 03-Fashion news 04-Food news 05-Freelance copy 06-Letters to editor 07-Real estate news 08-Sports news 09-Travel news 10-Book rev. 11-Movie rev. 12-Music rev. 13-TV rev. 14-Theater rev. 15-Coming events 16-Obituaries 17-Question & answer 18-Social announcements 19-Artwork 20-Cartoons 21-Photos 22-TV listings 23-Audio rec. 24-Video rec. 25-Books 26-Films/film clips 27-Personnel news 28-Press releases 29-New product news/photos 30-Trade lit. 31-Contracts awarded 32-Display adv. 33-Classified adv.

Year Established: 1937
Pub. Frequency: 8/yr.
Page Size: 4 color photos/art
Subscrip. Rate: $18.50/yr.
Circulation: 73,000
Circulation Type: paid
**Owner(s):**
Yale Alumni Publications, Inc.
149 York St.
New Haven, CT 06511
Telephone: (203) 432-0645
Ownership %: 100
**Editorial:**
Carter Wiseman ............................Editor

## Group 620-Consumer Electronics

66757

### AMIGAWORLD
80 Elm St.
Peterborough, NH 03458
Telephone: (603) 924-0100
FAX: (603) 924-4066
Year Established: 1985
Pub. Frequency: m.
Page Size: standard
Subscrip. Rate: $29.97/yr.
Circulation: 90,000
Circulation Type: paid
**Owner(s):**
IDG Communications, Inc.
One Exeter Plz., 15th Fl.
Boston, MA 02116
Telephone: (617) 534-1200
Ownership %: 100
**Management:**
Dale Strang ...........................Publisher
Karen Peterson ................Operations Manager
**Editorial:**
Tim Walsh ...........................Senior Editor
Dan Sullivan ...............................Editor
Howard Happ ...........................Art Director
Wendie Marro ...............Marketing Director
**Desc.:** Contains product reviews, new
product information, tutorials, industry
news and much more.
**Readers:** Commodore Amiga users.

25973

### C&E HOBBY HANDBOOKS
220 Carol Jean Way
Somerville, NJ 08876
Telephone: (908) 231-1518
FAX: (908) 231-1518
Mailing Address:
P.O. Box 5148
North Branch, NJ 08876
Year Established: 1986
Pub. Frequency: s-a.
Page Size: standard
Subscrip. Rate: $15/4 issues; $18/yr. in
Canada & Mexico
Materials: 05,06,10,28,29,32,33
Circulation: 100,000
Circulation Type: paid
**Owner(s):**
C & E Hobby Handbooks
220 Carol Jean Way
Somerville, NJ 08876
Telephone: (908) 231-1518
Ownership %: 100
**Management:**
Don Gabree ...........................Publisher
**Editorial:**
Ivan Rodenko ...............................Editor
Bill Whittier ...............................Editor
E. V. Stockwell, III ...........Book Review Editor
Gordon Hanaford ..............New Products Editor
Bill Axsen ...................Technical Editor
**Desc.:** Material related to electronic project
construction, new developments and
projects connected with
communications, related projects and
theory involving electronics and radio for
the active hobbyists and experimenters.

**Readers:** Active hobbyists in electronics.

69230

### CALIFORNIA COMPUTER NEWS
9719 Lincoln Village Dr., Ste. 500
Sacramento, CA 95827
Telephone: (916) 363-5000
FAX: (916) 363-5197
Year Established: 1983
Pub. Frequency: m.
Page Size: standard
Subscrip. Rate: free
Materials: 32,33
Circulation: 51,000
Circulation Type: paid
**Owner(s):**
GMW Communication, Inc.
9719 Lincoln Village Dr., Ste. 500
Sacramento, CA 95827
Telephone: (916) 363-5000
Ownership %: 100
**Management:**
Dennis McKenna ...........................Publisher
Craig Miller ...............Advertising Manager
Kelli Ottavi ...............Circulation Manager
**Editorial:**
Michelle Gamble-Risley ...........................Editor
**Desc.:** Covers local and regional
computer-related topics, new hardware
and software products and industry
news.

52614

### COMPUTE
324 W. Wendover Ave., No. 200
Greensboro, NC 27408
Telephone: (910) 275-9809
FAX: (910) 275-9837
Year Established: 1979
Pub. Frequency: m.
Page Size: standard
Subscrip. Rate: $12.97/yr.
Materials: 28,29,32,33
Freelance Pay: $50-$600/article
Circulation: 275,000
Circulation Type: paid
**Owner(s):**
General Media Publishing Group
1965 Broadway
New York, NY 10023
Telephone: (212) 496-6100
Ownership %: 100
**Management:**
Kathy Keeton ...........................President
William Tynan ..........Executive Vice President
**Editorial:**
Clifton Karnes ...............Editor in Chief
David English ...............Managing Editor
**Desc.:** Each monthly issue contains
feature articles, product reviews,
programming tips, and columns for users
of IBM, Tandy, and MS - DOS
compatible computers. Emphasis is on
the at - home, small business, and
educational users of personal
computers.
**Readers:** Home computer owners and
users.

66779

### COMPUTER SHOPPER
One Park Ave.
New York, NY 10016
Telephone: (800) 999-7467
FAX: (212) 503-3999
Year Established: 1979
Pub. Frequency: m.
Page Size: oversize
Subscrip. Rate: $29.97/yr.
Freelance Pay: $.60/wd.
Circulation: 458,418
Circulation Type: paid
**Owner(s):**
Coastal Associates Publishing, L. P.
One Park Ave.
New York, NY 10016
Ownership %: 100

**Editorial:**
John Blackford ...............................Editor
Anne Seltz ...............Marketing Director
**Desc.:** For individuals and companies
interested in buying, re-selling and using
computer hardware, software and
peripherals. Articles offer information on
popular models of computers, software,
new products, club news, network news
and magazine reviews.

24571

### CQ, THE RADIO AMATEURS' JOURNAL
76 N. Broadway
Hicksville, NY 11801
Telephone: (516) 681-2922
FAX: (516) 681-2926
Year Established: 1945
Pub. Frequency: m.
Page Size: standard
Subscrip. Rate: $24.50/yr.; $27/yr. Canada
& Mexico
Materials: 32
Freelance Pay: $35/pg.
Circulation: 113,309
Circulation Type: paid
**Owner(s):**
CQ Communications, Inc.
76 N. Broadway
Hicksville, NY 11801
Telephone: (516) 681-2922
Ownership %: 100
**Management:**
Richard A. Ross ...........................President
Richard A. Ross ...........................Publisher
Arnold Sposato ...............Advertising Manager
**Editorial:**
Alan M. Dorhoffer ...............................Editor
Gail Schieber ...............Associate Editor
**Desc.:** Wide interest in amateur radio field.
Every issue devoted to construction
projects of amateur interest and state of
the communication art. Special monthly
sections devoted to contests, awards,
equipment, propagation forecasts, new
products, DX, antennas, novice.
**Readers:** Amateur radio operators,
engineers.

66288

### EQ
2 Park Ave., Ste. 1820
New York, NY 10016
Telephone: (212) 213-3444
Year Established: 1991
Pub. Frequency: bi-m.
Subscrip. Rate: $19.97/yr.
Circulation: 49,350
Circulation Type: paid
**Owner(s):**
PSN Publications
2 Park Ave., Ste. 1820
New York, NY 10016
Telephone: (212) 213-3444
**Management:**
Paul Gallo ...........................Publisher
Hector Latorre ...............Executive Director
**Editorial:**
Martin Porter ...............Executive Editor
**Desc.:** Covers projects recording and
sound studio techniques for the
professional audio market.
**Readers:** Professional audio market.

69125

### HIGH PERFORMANCE REVIEW
P.O. Box 346
Woodbury, CT 06798
Telephone: (203) 266-0084
FAX: (203) 263-4730
Year Established: 1981
Pub. Frequency: q.

Page Size: standard
Subscrip. Rate: $3.95 newsstand; $4.95
Can.; $15/yr.; $25/2yrs.; $35/3yrs.
Materials: 01,02,05,06,10,11,12,14,16,17,
19,21,23,24,25,27,28,29,30,32,33
Freelance Pay: varies
Circulation: 18,000
Circulation Type: paid
**Owner(s):**
High Performance Review Publishing
P.O. Box 346
Woodbury, CT 06798
Telephone: (203) 266-0084
FAX: (203) 263-4730
Ownership %: 100
**Editorial:**
Steve Saunders ...............................Editor
Henry Ruppel ...............Advertising Director
**Desc.:** Lab test and listening reviews of
new audio hi-fi stereo equipment and
home theater. Reviews of over 100
classical, pop and jazz recording
releases. Interviews with major
composers and performers.
**Readers:** Mean age: 44 Median income:
$55,000 % with college degree: 64 %
with advanced degree: 33
**Deadline:** story-1 mo. prior to pub. date;
news-1 mo. prior; photo-1 mo. prior; ads-
1 mo. prior

65350

### HOME & STUDIO RECORDING
7318 Topanga Canyon Blvd., Ste. 200
Canoga Park, CA 91303
Telephone: (818) 346-3404
FAX: (818) 346-3597
Year Established: 1987
Pub. Frequency: m.
Page Size: standard
Subscrip. Rate: $2.95 newsstand; $20/yr.
Materials: 05,06,12,17,19,21,23,24,25,28,
29,32,33
Print Process: web
Circulation: 24,500
Circulation Type: paid
**Owner(s):**
Music Maker Publication
Ownership %: 100
**Management:**
Tom Hawley ...........................Publisher
**Editorial:**
Nick Batzdorf ...............................Editor
Steve Dickinson ...............Advertising Director
Trevor Gilchrist ...........................Art Director
**Desc.:** Products, techniques of recording
for home or studio.
**Readers:** People involved in recording
music at home or smaller studios, and
songwriters.

49838

### HOME OFFICE COMPUTING
411 Lafayette St.
New York, NY 10003
Telephone: (212) 505-4220
FAX: (212) 505-4260
Year Established: 1983
Pub. Frequency: m.
Page Size: standard
Subscrip. Rate: $2.95 newsstand;
$19.97/yr.
Materials: 32,33
Freelance Pay: varies
Circulation: 4,400,000
Circulation Type: paid
**Owner(s):**
Scholastic Magazines, Inc.
555 Broadway
New York, NY 10003
Telephone: (212) 505-3000
Ownership %: 100
**Management:**
Hugh Roome ...........................Publisher
**Editorial:**
Nick Sullivan ...............Senior Editor

**Materials Accepted/Included:** 01-Business news 02-By-line articles 03-Fashion news 04-Food news 05-Freelance copy 06-Letters to editor 07-Real estate news 08-Sports news 09-Travel news 10-Book rev. 11-Movie rev. 12-Music rev. 13-TV rev. 14-Theater rev. 15-Coming events 16-Obituaries 17-Question & answer 18-Social announcements 19-Artwork 20-Cartoons 21-Photos 22-TV listings 23-Audio rec. 24-Video rec. 25-Books 26-Films/film clips 27-Personnel news 28-Press releases 29-New product news/photos 30-Trade lit. 31-Contracts awarded 32-Display adv. 33-Classified adv.

6-27

David Hallerman ......................Senior Editor
Bernadette Grey .............................Editor
Cathy Brower ...............Managing Editor
George Elmeger ...........Advertising Director
Judy Kamiliar .........................Art Director
**Desc.:** Directs editorial coverage to the
needs of people who use computers
and related technology to conduct part
or all of their income-producing work at
home, primarily those who run small
businesses, telecommute, or bring work
home from corporate offices, and to the
needs of the families who coexist with
these home offices.

61657

**MACWORLD**
501 Second St., Ste. 500
San Francisco, CA 94107
Telephone: (415) 243-0505
Year Established: 1984
Pub. Frequency: m.
Page Size: standard
Subscrip. Rate: $30/yr.
Freelance Pay: negotiable
Circulation: 550,000
Circulation Type: paid
**Owner(s):**
Macworld Communications
501 Second St.
San Francisco, CA 94107
Telephone: (415) 243-0505
Ownership %: 100
**Management:**
Jim E. Martin ..............................President
**Editorial:**
Adrian Mello ...................Editor in Chief
Debra Branscum ...............Executive Editor
Charles Barrett ...............Managing Editor
Dennis McLeod ...............Design Director
**Desc.:** Features articles on applications
and hardwares. Regular columns include
new products, questions and answers,
hardware and software reviews.
**Readers:** For Macintosh personal
computer user.

52621

**PC WORLD**
501 Second St.
San Francisco, CA 94107
Telephone: (415) 243-0500
FAX: (415) 442-1891
Year Established: 1982
Pub. Frequency: m.
Page Size: standard
Subscrip. Rate: $29.90/yr.
Materials: 28
Freelance Pay: $150-$3,000/article
Circulation: 916,000
Circulation Type: paid
**Owner(s):**
IDG Communications, Inc.
One Exeter Plz.
Boston, MA 02116
Telephone: (617) 534-1200
Ownership %: 100
**Bureau(s):**
PC WORLD Communications, Inc.
77 Franklin St.
Boston, MA 02111
Telephone: (617) 482-8470
Contact: Evie Bender, Executive Editor
**Management:**
Rich Marino ..............................Publisher
**Editorial:**
Phil Lemmons ...................Editor in Chief
Russell Glitman ...............Executive Editor
Cathryn Baskin ...............Managing Editor
Robert Kanes ...........................Art Director

**Desc.:** A full-service PC publication, we
deliver timely coverage of new products
and industry news along with in-depth
features, detailed how-to articles, and
rigorous product reviews backed by one
of the industry's most respected test
centers. In its selection, analysis and
presentation of topical subjects, we
apply a lively mixture of enthusiasm and
consumer advocacy for a readership
averaging over 6 yrs. of experience.
**Readers:** 80% professional, 96% college
educated, medium-upper income
bracket.
**Deadline:** story-90 days prior to pub. date;
news-90 days prior; photo-90 days prior

24593

**QST**
225 Main St.
Newington, CT 06111
Telephone: (203) 666-1541
FAX: (203) 665-7531
Year Established: 1915
Pub. Frequency: m.
Page Size: standard
Subscrip. Rate: $30/yr. membership
Materials: 32
Freelance Pay: $50/pg.
Circulation: 160,000
Circulation Type: controlled & paid
**Owner(s):**
American Radio Relay League, Inc.
225 Main St.
Newington, CT 06111
Telephone: (203) 666-1541
Ownership %: 100
**Management:**
David Sumnern .........................Publisher
Brad Thomas ...............Advertising Manager
**Editorial:**
David Sumner .............................Editor
Albert Brogdon ...............Managing Editor
Joel Kleinman ...............Technical Editor
**Desc.:** Devoted entirely to amateur radio.
Most articles written by staff or
submitted by technical
people. Welcomes publicity and news
products material dealing with the
radio/electronics industry, but will only
publish new product notes and photos
on new developments affecting radio
amateurs.
**Readers:** Amateur radio operators.

66339

**SOFTWARE**
1900 W. Park Dr.
Westborough, MA 01581
Telephone: (508) 366-2031
Year Established: 1981
Pub. Frequency: m.
Page Size: standard
Subscrip. Rate: free to qualified personnel;
$65/yr. in US; $75/yr. in Canada;
$125/yr. elsewhere
Materials: 01,02,05,06,17,19,21,27,28,29,
30,31,32,33
Freelance Pay: varies
Circulation: 100,000
Circulation Type: controlled
**Owner(s):**
Sentry Publishing Co., Inc.
1900 W. Park Dr.
Westborough, MA 01581
Telephone: (508) 366-2031
Ownership %: 100
**Bureau(s):**
West Coast
105 S. Avenida De Le Estrella
San Clemente, CA 92672
Telephone: (714) 498-1400
FAX: (714) 498-5941
Contact: Elizabeth V. Harding
**Editorial:**
Michael Bucken ..............................Editor

Jack Vaughan ......................News Editor
**Desc.:** Feature articles offer timely
information on software applications and
industry developments. Also contains
news briefs and new software package
announcements for mainframe, mini and
microcomputers.
**Readers:** For business and professional
users.
**Deadline:** story-2 mos.; news-6 wks.;
photo-6 wks.

24154

**STEREO REVIEW**
1633 Broadway
New York, NY 10019
Telephone: (212) 767-6000
Year Established: 1958
Pub. Frequency: m.
Page Size: standard
Subscrip. Rate: $15.94/yr.
Freelance Pay: varies
Circulation: 500,000
Circulation Type: paid
**Owner(s):**
Hachette Filipacchi Magazines, Inc.
1633 Broadway
New York, NY 10019
Telephone: (212) 767-6000
Ownership %: 100
**Editorial:**
Louise Boundas ...................Editor in Chief
Michael Riggs ...................Exec. Editor
Bob Ankosko ...................Senior Editor
Steve Simels ...................Music Editor
**Desc.:** Focuses on consumer audio
equipment and recordings. Includes
equipment test reports, new products,
and articles on how to buy and how to
use stereo components as well as
reviews of recordings and performer
profiles. Also touches on technological
developments, audio/video systems, and
car stereo.
**Readers:** Audio enthusiasts, record
collectors.

67644

**TWICE: THIS WEEK IN CONSUMER
ELECTRONICS**
245 W. 17th St.
New York, NY 10011
Telephone: (212) 337-6980
FAX: (212) 337-7066
Year Established: 1986
Pub. Frequency: bi-w.
Page Size: tabloid
Subscrip. Rate: $85/yr.
Circulation: 31,000
Circulation Type: controlled
**Owner(s):**
Cahners Publishing Company, Inc.
249 W. 17th St.
New York, NY 10011
Telephone: (212) 337-6980
Ownership %: 100
**Management:**
Marcia Grand ..............................Publisher
Sheila Rice ...............Advertising Manager
**Editorial:**
Bob Gerson ...................Editor in Chief
George Hundley ...............Executive Editor

65360

**VIDEO GAMES**
9171 Wilshire Blvd., Ste. 300
Beverly Hills, CA 90210
Telephone: (310) 858-7155
FAX: (310) 247-1708
Year Established: 1988
Pub. Frequency: m.
Page Size: standard
Subscrip. Rate: $19.95/yr.
Materials: 06,24,26,28,32,33
Freelance Pay: varies
Circulation: 120,000
Circulation Type: paid

**Owner(s):**
Larry Flint Publications
9171 Wilshire Blvd., Ste. 300
Beverly Hills, CA 90210
Telephone: (310) 858-7100
FAX: (310) 275-3857
Ownership %: 100
**Editorial:**
Chris Bienier ...................Executive Editor
Nikos Constant ...............Associate Editor
**Desc.:** Covers news, features and product
information on popular home video
games systems. Also, VG covers coin-
operated game machines and
developments in electronic
entertainment.
**Readers:** Targets home users of video
games.

67075

**VIDEO MAGAZINE**
460 W. 34th St.
New York, NY 10001
Telephone: (212) 947-6500
FAX: (212) 947-6727
Year Established: 1991
Pub. Frequency: bi-m.
Page Size: standard
Subscrip. Rate: $2.95 newsstand
Circulation: 50,000
Circulation Type: paid
**Owner(s):**
Reese Communications, Inc.
460 W. 34th St.
New York, NY 10001
Telephone: (212) 947-6500
Ownership %: 100
**Management:**
Eric Schwartz ..............................Publisher
Kristin Barbieri ...............Advertising Manager
**Editorial:**
Stan Pinkwas .............................Editor
Marshall Mosley ...........................Art Director
**Desc.:** For professionals and hobbyists
purchasing video recorders, cameras
and related equipment.

69776

**WALL STREET & TECHNOLOGY**
1515 Broadway
New York, NY 10036
Telephone: (212) 869-1300
Year Established: 1983
Pub. Frequency: m.
Subscrip. Rate: $49/yr.
Circulation: 25,305
Circulation Type: controlled & paid
**Owner(s):**
Miller Freeman, Inc.
1515 Broadway
New York, NY 10036
Telephone: (212) 869-1300
Ownership %: 100
**Editorial:**
Pavan Sahgal ..............................Editor

69232

**WIRED**
544 Second St.
San Francisco, CA 94107
Telephone: (415) 904-0660
FAX: (415) 904-0669
Year Established: 1993
Pub. Frequency: m.
Page Size: standard
Subscrip. Rate: $4.95 newsstand;
$39.95/yr.
Materials: 05,06,10,12,19,21,23,25,29
Circulation: 155,000
Circulation Type: paid
**Owner(s):**
Wired Ventures, Ltd.
544 Second St.
San Francisco, CA 94107
Telephone: (415) 904-0660
FAX: (415) 904-0669
Ownership %: 100

---

**Materials Accepted/Included:** 01-Business news 02-By-line articles 03-Fashion news 04-Food news 05-Freelance copy 06-Letters to editor 07-Real estate news 08-Sports news 09-Travel news 10-Book rev. 11-Movie rev. 12-Music rev. 13-TV rev. 14-Theater rev. 15-Coming events 16-Obituaries 17-Question & answer 18-Social announcements 19-Artwork 20-Cartoons 21-Photos 22-TV listings 23-Audio rec. 24-Video rec. 25-Books 26-Films/film clips 27-Personnel news 28-Press releases 29-New product news/photos 30-Trade lit. 31-Contracts awarded 32-Display adv. 33-Classified adv.

**Management:**
Jane Metcalfe ...................................President
**Editorial:**
John Battelle ............................Managing Editor
Kathleen Lyman .................................Advertising
Louis Rossett .....................Editor & Publisher
**Desc.:** Covers the digital revolution and
related advances in computers,
communications and lifestyles.

22713

## 73 AMATEUR RADIO TODAY
70 Rte. 202 N.
Peterborough, NH 03458
Telephone: (603) 924-0058
FAX: (603) 924-9327
Year Established: 1960
Pub. Frequency: m.
Page Size: standard
Subscrip. Rate: $2.95 newsstand;
$19.97/yr.
Materials: 05,06,28,29,30,32,33
Freelance Pay: varies
Print Process: web offset
Circulation: 65,000
Circulation Type: paid
**Owner(s):**
Wayne Green, Inc.
Ownership %: 100
**Management:**
Wayne Green ...................................President
David Cassidy ....................Associate Publsiher
**Editorial:**
Dan Harper .....................................Advertising
**Desc.:** An educational, technical and
instructional publication directed toward
radio amateurs and others having an
interest in communications and
electronics.
**Readers:** Amateur radio enthusiasts,
electronic engineers, hobbyists, builders,
equipment modifiers.

## Group 622-Cooking, Dining & Food

26035

## BETTER HOMES & GARDENS HOLIDAY COOKING
1716 Locust St.
Des Moines, IA 50309
Telephone: (515) 284-3000
FAX: (515) 284-3697
Year Established: 1969
Pub. Frequency: a.
Page Size: standard
Subscrip. Rate: $3.50 newsstand
Circulation: 625,000
Circulation Type: paid
**Owner(s):**
Meredith Corp.
1716 Locust St.
Des Moines, IA 50309
Telephone: (515) 284-3000
Ownership %: 100
**Management:**
Steve Levinson ...................................Publisher
Pat Tomlinson ...................Advertising Manager
**Editorial:**
Willam Yates ..............................Editor in Chief
Janet Figg .........................................Editor

52618

## BON APPETIT MAGAZINE
6300 Wilshire Blvd., 10th Fl.
Los Angeles, CA 90048
Telephone: (213) 965-3600
FAX: (213) 930-2369
Year Established: 1975
Pub. Frequency: m.

Page Size: standard
Subscrip. Rate: $2.95 newsstand; $18/yr.
Materials: 32
Freelance Pay: varies
Circulation: 1,300,000
Circulation Type: paid
**Owner(s):**
The Conde Nast Publications, Inc.
350 Madison Ave.
New York, NY 10007
Ownership %: 100
**Bureau(s):**
Bon Appetit
360 Madison Ave.
New York, NY 10007
Contact: Lynn Heiler, Publisher
**Management:**
Lynn Heiler ......................................Publisher
**Editorial:**
William J. Garry .........................Editor in Chief
Barbara Fairchild ......................Executive Editor
Campion Primm .............................Art Director
**Desc.:** America's leading food monthly, is
written for the growing number of food
enthusiasts who want information on all
aspects of creative cooking and
entertaining, food trends, restaurants,
products and recipes. Included in each
issue are features devoted to these
subjects, written in informal style and
illustrated with photographs of finished
dishes and step-by-step recipe
techniques. The recipes are easy to
follow whether they are geared for the
talented amateur or food professional.
**Readers:** Male - 25.4%; Female - 74.6%;
Median Age - 39.8% Median Household
Income - $44,418; Attended/Graduated
College - 60.5%.

69630

## COOK'S ILLUSTRATED
17 Station St.
Brookline, MA 02147
Telephone: (617) 232-1000
FAX: (617) 532-1572
Year Established: 1980
Pub. Frequency: 6/yr.
Page Size: standard
Subscrip. Rate: $4 newsstand; $24.95/yr.
Circulation: 160,000
Circulation Type: paid
**Owner(s):**
Natural Health Limited Partners
17 Station St.
Brookline, MA 02147
Telephone: (617) 232-1000
Ownership %: 100
**Management:**
Chris Kimball ...................................Publisher
**Editorial:**
Chris Kimball .......................................Editor
**Desc.:** Discusses practical home cooking
techniques.

71266

## COOKBOOK DIGEST
950 Third Ave., 16th Fl.
New York, NY 10022
Telephone: (212) 888-1855
FAX: (212) 838-8420
Year Established: 1985
Pub. Frequency: bi-m.
Page Size: standard
Subscrip. Rate: $3.50 newsstand; $21/yr.
Materials: 32
Circulation: 325,000
Circulation Type: paid
**Owner(s):**
Grass Roots Publishing Co., Inc.
950 Third Ave., 16th Fl.
New York, NY 10022
Telephone: (212) 888-1855
Ownership %: 100
**Management:**
Suzann Hochman ...........................Publisher

Robert Miller ......................Advertising Manager
**Editorial:**
Andre DiNoto ......................................Editor
Renee Cajigal-Delgodo .......Marketing Manager

68907

## COOKING CONNECTION
12125 16th Ave., S.
Burnville, MN 55337
Telephone: (612) 890-6655
FAX: (612) 890-6033
Mailing Address:
P.O. Box 1271
Burnville, MN 00007
Year Established: 1975
Pub. Frequency: bi-m.
Page Size: standard
Subscrip. Rate: $2.25 newsstand;
$11.95/yr.
Materials: 32,33
Circulation: 15,000
Circulation Type: paid
**Owner(s):**
Recipes Unlimited, Inc.
P.O. Box 1271
Burnville, MN 55337
Telephone: (612) 890-6655
Ownership %: 100
**Management:**
Janet Sadlack ..................................Publisher
**Editorial:**
Janet Sadlack ......................................Editor
**Desc.:** Recipes and hints for microwave
cooking.

66030

## COOKING LIGHT
2100 Lakeshore Dr.
Birmingham, AL 35209-9558
Telephone: (205) 877-6000
FAX: (205) 877-6700
Year Established: 1987
Pub. Frequency: 7/yr.
Subscrip. Rate: $15/yr.
Circulation: 1,026,000
Circulation Type: paid
**Owner(s):**
Southern Progress Corp.
2100 Lakeshore Dr.
Birmingham, AL 35209-9558
Telephone: (205) 877-6000
Ownership %: 100
**Editorial:**
Katherine M. Eakin ...............................Editor
B. Ellen Templeton ................Managing Editor
H. Johnson ..........................V.P. of Circulation
**Desc.:** Contains articles on food, nutrition,
and exercise implementing a positive
approach to a healthier lifestyle.

65752

## FOOD & WINE
1120 Ave. of the Americas
New York, NY 10036
Telephone: (212) 382-5600
FAX: (212) 768-1573
Year Established: 1978
Pub. Frequency: m.
Page Size: standard
Subscrip. Rate: $1.25 newsstand; $26/yr.
Circulation: 718,195
Circulation Type: paid
**Owner(s):**
American Express Publishing
1120 Ave. of the Americas
New York, NY 10036
Telephone: (212) 382-5600
Ownership %: 100
**Editorial:**
Mary Simons .......................................Editor

68922

## FOOD PAPER, THE
555 Fulton St., Ste. 215
San Francisco, CA 94102
Telephone: (415) 552-4664
Year Established: 1991
Pub. Frequency: q

Page Size: standard
Subscrip. Rate: $12/yr.
Materials: 04,05,09,10,15,18
Print Process: offset
Circulation: 200,000
Circulation Type: paid
**Owner(s):**
Gault Millau, Inc.
5900 Wilshire Blvd., #1820
Los Angeles, CA 90036
Telephone: (213) 965-3593
FAX: (213) 936-2883
Ownership %: 100
**Editorial:**
Andre Gayot .......................................Editor
**Desc.:** Contains articles on food and wine,
restaurants & recipes, etc. in two
editions for the Los Angeles and San
Francisco areas.

25859

## GOURMET
560 Lexington Ave.
New York, NY 10022
Telephone: (212) 371-1330
Year Established: 1941
Pub. Frequency: m.
Page Size: standard
Subscrip. Rate: $2.95 newsstand; $20/yr.
Freelance Pay: varies
Circulation: 818,000
Circulation Type: paid
**Owner(s):**
Gourmet, Inc./Conde Nast Publications
Telephone: (212) 371-1330
Ownership %: 100
**Bureau(s):**
Sperling & Jones, Inc.
847 Sansome St.
San Francisco , CA 94111
Telephone: (415) 434-2675
Contact: Barbara Steinmetz, Advertising

Midwest
875 N. Michigan Ave.
Chicago, IL 60611
Telephone: (312) 943-2710
Contact: Rebecca Snave, Advertising

South
2500 S. Dixie Hwy.
Miami, FL 33133
Telephone: (305) 856-8326
Contact: Joel Meltzer, Advertising

Detroit
3250 W. Big Beaver Rd.
Troy, MI 48084
Telephone: (313) 643-0540
Contact: Larry Wallace, Advertising

Sperling & Jones, Inc.
4311 Wilshire Blvd.
Los Angeles, CA 90010
Telephone: (310) 934-6600
Contact: Karen Kanter, Advertising
**Management:**
Peter King Hunsinger ..........................Publisher
Betty Caldwell ...............Editorial Production
Manager
**Editorial:**
Gail Zweigenthal ...................Executive Editor
Irwin Glusker ..................................Art Director
Fred Feretti ........................................Columnist
Zanne Zakroff ...............................Food Editor
Dave Kupiec ....................Marketing Director
**Desc.:** Articles, recipes, restaurant, food
and wine reviews and shopping tips.
Covers ethnic and gourmet cuisines, and
food-related travel ideas.
**Readers:** Educated, upper-income men
and woman who travel, entertain and
live well.

**Materials Accepted/Included:** 01-Business news 02-By-line articles 03-Fashion news 04-Food news 05-Freelance copy 06-Letters to editor 07-Real estate news 08-Sports news 09-Travel news 10-Book rev. 11-Movie rev. 12-Music rev. 13-TV rev. 14-Theater rev. 15-Coming events 16-Obituaries 17-Question & answer 18-Social announcements 19-Artwork 20-Cartoons 21-Photos 22-TV listings 23-Audio rec. 24-Video rec. 25-Books 26-Films/film clips 27-Personnel news 28-Press releases 29-New product news/photos 30-Trade lit. 31-Contracts awarded 32-Display adv. 33-Classified adv.

6-29

## MISSOURI WINE COUNTRY JOURNAL
67301
514 Wein St.
Hermann, MO 65041
Telephone: (314) 486-5522
FAX: (314) 486-3126
Year Established: 1990
Pub. Frequency: s-a.
Page Size: standard
Subscrip. Rate: $10.95/yr.
Circulation: 10,000
Circulation Type: paid
**Owner(s):**
Wein Press
514 Wein St.
Hermann, MO 65041
Telephone: (314) 486-5522
Ownership %: 100
**Management:**
Sandy Barks ..............................President
Sandy Barks ..............................Publisher
**Editorial:**
Sandy Barks ..............................Editor
**Desc.:** Magazine of Missouri wine, food
and travel.

## QUICK 'N EASY COUNTRY COOKIN'
68906
P.O. Box 66
Davis, SD 57021
Telephone: (605) 238-5704
FAX: (605) 238-5339
Year Established: 1986
Pub. Frequency: bi-m.
Subscrip. Rate: $2.95 newsstand;
$12.95/yr.
Materials: 04,05,20,21,32
Freelance Pay: $10/manuscript pub.
Print Process: web offset
Circulation: 29000
Circulation Type: paid
**Owner(s):**
Parkside Publishing
P.O. Box 66
Davis, SD 57021
Telephone: (605) 238-5704
Ownership %: 100
**Editorial:**
Pam Schrag ..............................Editor
**Desc.:** Articles on quick and easy cooking.
Includes craft and sewing ideas, poetry,
low cholesterol and diabetic recipes.
Humorous and human interest stories.
**Deadline:** story-15th of mo. 4 mos. prior;
photo-15th of mo. 4 mos. prior; ads-15th
of mo. 4 mos. prior

## RESTAURANT ROW MAGAZINE
68925
P.O. Box 13109
Long Beach, CA 90803-8109
Telephone: (213) 438-6565
Year Established: 1983
Pub. Frequency: m.
Page Size: tabloid
Subscrip. Rate: $24/yr.
Materials: 04,09,28
Print Process: web offset
Circulation: 56,000
Circulation Type: paid
**Owner(s):**
Restaurant Row, Inc.
P.O. Box 13109
Long Beach, CA 90803-8109
Telephone: (213) 438-6565
Ownership %: 100
**Editorial:**
Ron Hodges ..............................Editor in Chief
**Desc.:** Covers the Los Angeles and
Orange County markets with articles on
restaurant dining, food, wines and spirits,
and hotels and resorts.

## WOMAN'S DAY GREAT HOLIDAY BAKING
56393
1633 Broadway, 45th Fl.
New York, NY 10019
Telephone: (212) 767-6000
Year Established: 1977
Pub. Frequency: a.
Page Size: standard
Subscrip. Rate: $2.95 newsstand
Freelance Pay: varies
Circulation: 750,000
Circulation Type: paid
**Owner(s):**
Hachette Magazines, Inc.
1633 Broadway, 45th Fl.
New York, NY 10019
Telephone: (212) 767-6000
Ownership %: 100
**Management:**
Susan Buckley ..............................Publisher
**Editorial:**
Carolyn Gatto ..............................Editor in Chief
Rowann Gilman ..............................Editor
**Desc.:** A magazine of beautiful tempting
old-fashioned desserts, and quickly
prepared Christmas spectaculars and
gifts from the kitchen which includes
recipes for all food shown.
**Readers:** Women - subject of magazine
dictates reader profile.

## WOMAN'S DAY LIGHT MEALS IN MINUTES
56400
1633 Broadway, 45th Fl.
New York, NY 10019
Telephone: (212) 767-6000
Year Established: 4977
Pub. Frequency: a.
Page Size: standard
Subscrip. Rate: $2.95 newsstand
Freelance Pay: varies
Circulation: 450,000
Circulation Type: paid
**Owner(s):**
Hachette Magazines, Inc.
1633 Broadway
New York, NY 10019
Telephone: (212) 767-6000
Ownership %: 100
**Management:**
Susan Buckley ..............................Publisher
**Editorial:**
Carolyn Gatto ..............................Editor in Chief
Rowann Gilman ..............................Editor
**Desc.:** Easily prepared recipes for busy
people with a focus on lightness and
good quality food. All recipes are
oriented toward time-saving.
**Readers:** Working women. Profile varies
depending on subject of magazine.

## WOMAN'S DAY LOW FAT MEALS
68858
1633 Broadway, 45th Fl.
New York, NY 10019
Telephone: (212) 767-6745
FAX: (212) 767-5612
Year Established: 1992
Pub. Frequency: s-a.
Subscrip. Rate: $2.95 copy
Circulation: 450000
Circulation Type: paid

**Owner(s):**
Hachette Filipacchi Magazines, Inc.
1633 Broadway, 45th Fl.
New York, NY 10019
Telephone: (212) 767-6745
Ownership %: 100

# Group 624-Entertainment

## ACTION PURSUIT GAMES MAGAZINE
67074
4201 Vanowen Pl.
Burbank, CA 91505-1139
Telephone: (818) 845-2656
FAX: (818) 845-7761
Year Established: 1987
Pub. Frequency: m.
Page Size: standard
Subscrip. Rate: 2.95 newsstand; $24.50/yr.
Materials: 05,06,15,32,33
Print Process: web offset
Circulation: 65,000
Circulation Type: controlled & paid
**Owner(s):**
CFW Enterprises, Inc.
4201 Vanowen Pl.
Burbank, CA 91505
Telephone: (818) 845-7761
Ownership %: 100
**Management:**
Mark Komuro ..............................Publisher
Eric Sutter ..............................Advertising Manager
William J.N. Porter ..............................General Manager
**Editorial:**
Randy Kamiya ..............................Editor
Jessica Sparks ..............................Field Editor
**Desc.:** Action Pursuit Games is the leading
nationally distributed newsstand
magazine dedicated to the sport of
paintball. The goal is to continue to be
the forum and information source that
will help focus and expand the game's
entertainment value, competitive skills
and exhilarating action across
America and around the world.
**Readers:** Paintball players, both beginners
and advanced.
**Deadline:** story-2 mo. prior to pub. date;
news-2 mo.; photo-2 mo.; ads-50 days
prior to pub. date

## AMERICAN SQUAREDANCE
25959
661 Middlefield Rd.
Salinas, CA 93906
Telephone: (408) 443-0761
FAX: (408) 443-6402
Year Established: 1945
Pub. Frequency: m.
Page Size: standard
Subscrip. Rate: $20/yr.; $35/2 yrs.
Freelance Pay: $5-$10/photo
Circulation: 20,000
Circulation Type: paid
**Owner(s):**
Sanborn Enterprises
661 Middlefield Rd.
Salinas, CA 93906
Telephone: (408) 443-0761
Ownership %: 50

Susan Sanborn
661 Middlefield Rd.
Salinas, CA 93906
Telephone: (408) 443-0761
Ownership %: 50
**Management:**
Jon Sanborn ..............................Publisher
**Editorial:**
Jon Sanborn ..............................Executive Editor
**Readers:** Square and round dancers and
callers.

## CABLE GUIDE
69736
309 Lakeside Dr.
Horsham, PA 19044
Telephone: (215) 443-9300
FAX: (215) 443-8647
Year Established: 1982
Pub. Frequency: m.
Subscrip. Rate: $14/yr.
**Owner(s):**
TVSM
309 Lakeside Dr.
Horsham, PA 19044
Telephone: (215) 443-9300
Ownership %: 100
**Editorial:**
Allan Wragg ..............................Editor

## CINEASTE
69628
200 Park Ave., S.
New York, NY 10003-1503
Telephone: (212) 982-1241
Year Established: 1967
Pub. Frequency: q.
Subscrip. Rate: $5 newsstand; $16/yr.
individuals; $33/yr. institutions
Materials: 10,11,24,25,26,32
Circulation: 9,000
Circulation Type: paid
**Owner(s):**
Cineaste Publishers, Inc.
200 Park Ave. S.
New York, NY 10003-1503
Telephone: (212) 982-1241
Ownership %: 100
**Desc.:** Features contributions from many
of America's most articulate and
outspoken writers, critics, and scholars.
Focuses on both the art and politics of
the cinema.

## CINEMA JOURNAL
58571
Comal St.
Austin, TX 78713
Telephone: (512) 471-7233
FAX: (512) 320-0668
Mailing Address:
P.O. Box 7819
Austin, TX 78713
Year Established: 1961
Pub. Frequency: q.
Page Size: standard
Subscrip. Rate: $25/yr. individuals; $40/yr.
institutions
Circulation: 1,600
Circulation Type: paid
**Owner(s):**
University of Texas Press
Comal St.
P.O. Box 7819
Austin, TX 78713
Telephone: (512) 471-7233
Ownership %: 100
**Bureau(s):**
Prof. David Desser
2111 Foreign Language Bldg.
707 S. Matthews
Urbana, IL 61801
Telephone: (217) 333-3356
Contact: Prof. David Desser, Editor
**Management:**
Carole S. Appel ..............................Manager
**Editorial:**
David Desser ..............................Editor
Sarah Martin ..............................Circulation Assistant

**Materials Accepted/Included:** 01-Business news 02-By-line articles 03-Fashion news 04-Food news 05-Freelance copy 06-Letters to editor 07-Real estate news 08-Sports news 09-Travel news 10-Book rev. 11-Movie rev. 12-Music rev. 13-TV rev. 14-Theater rev. 15-Coming events 16-Obituaries 17-Question & answer 18-Social announcements 19-Artwork 20-Cartoons 21-Photos 22-TV listings 23-Audio rec. 24-Video rec. 25-Books 26-Films/film clips 27-Personnel news 28-Press releases 29-New product news/photos 30-Trade lit. 31-Contracts awarded 32-Display adv. 33-Classified adv.

**Desc.:** An essential forum and guide for scholars, fans, students, and teachers; contains the best in both new and traditional film scholarship including historical, feminist, Marxist, psychoanalytic and structuralist approaches. Leading film scholars contribute lively articles on film and television criticism, aesthetics, history, theory, acting, writing, production, economics, and teaching.
**Readers:** Film and TV scholars and enthusiasts.

**CIRCUS MAGAZINE** 26645
6 W. 18th St., 2nd Fl.
New York, NY 10011
Telephone: (212) 242-4902
FAX: (212) 242-5734
Year Established: 1969
Pub. Frequency: m.
Page Size: standard
Subscrip. Rate: $22/yr.; $42/2 yrs. US; $28/yr. foreign
Materials: 05,21,32
Freelance Pay: varies
Circulation: 100,000
Circulation Type: paid
**Owner(s):**
Circus Enterprises Corp.
6 W. 18th St., 2nd Fl.
New York, NY 10011
Telephone: (212) 242-4902
FAX: (212) 242-5734
Ownership %: 100
**Bureau(s):**
Eisenberg Communications Group, Inc.
10920 Wilshire Blvd., #600
Los Angeles, CA 90024
Telephone: (310) 824-5297
Contact: Jon Yoffie, Advertising Manager
**Management:**
Gerald Rothberg .................................Publisher
Art Ford ...............................Associate Publisher
Irwin E. Billman .................Circulation Manager
Lani Zarief .........................Production Manager
**Editorial:**
Gerald Rothberg ...........................Editor in Chief
Luca Rensi ...................................Executive Editor
Mordechai Kleidermacher .......Managing Editor
Michael Renchiwich ..........................Art Director
Jeff Hogan ...............................Editorial Associate
Michael D. Beinner ..............................Publicity
Renee Ford ..................Special Projects Director
Bobby Lynn ...................Transcription Editor
Corey Levitan .........................West Coast Editor
Paul Gallotta .......................................Writer
Jeff Kitts ............................................Writer
Moira McCormick .................................Writer
James K. Willcox ................................Writer
**Desc.:** America's Rock Magazine. Monthly music magazine aimed at youth; males and females 16-26.
**Readers:** High school, college and graduate school.

**DAYTIME TV** 25583
233 Park Ave. S.
New York, NY 10003
Telephone: (212) 780-3500
FAX: (212) 780-3555
Year Established: 1969
Pub. Frequency: m.
Page Size: standard
Subscrip. Rate: $20/yr. US; $25/yr. Canada
Circulation: 120,000
Circulation Type: paid
**Owner(s):**
Morton Tuller
Ownership %: 100
**Management:**
Morton Tuller ......................................Publisher

**Editorial:**
Lucille Giordano .................................Editor

**DESTINATION DISCOVERY** 68803
7700 Wisconsin Ave., 7th Fl.
Bethesda, MD 20814
Telephone: (301) 986-0444
FAX: (301) 986-4628
Year Established: 1985
Pub. Frequency: m.
Subscrip. Rate: $19.95/yr.
Circulation: 200,000
Circulation Type: paid
**Owner(s):**
Discovery Publishing
7700 Wisconsin Ave., 7th Fl.
Bethesda, MD 20814
Telephone: (301) 986-0444
Ownership %: 100

**ELEVEN** 65439
5400 N. St. Louis Ave.
Chicago, IL 60625
Telephone: (312) 583-5000
FAX: (312) 583-3046
Year Established: 1987
Pub. Frequency: 10/yr.
Page Size: standard
Subscrip. Rate: $40/yr.
Circulation: 180,000
Circulation Type: controlled
**Owner(s):**
WTTW/Chicago
5400 N. St. Louis Ave.
Chicago, IL 60625
Ownership %: 100
**Editorial:**
Elizabeth Altick McCarthy .......................Editor
Jenny Epstein ...........................Managing Editor
**Desc.:** Covers programs on WTTW.
**Readers:** Viewers of WTTW.

**ENTERTAINMENT WEEKLY** 65677
1675 Broadway
New York, NY 10019
Telephone: (212) 522-5600
FAX: (212) 522-0074
Year Established: 1990
Pub. Frequency: w.
Subscrip. Rate: $2.50/copy; $51.48/yr.
Print Process: web offset
Circulation: 1,075,000
Circulation Type: paid
**Owner(s):**
Time, Inc.
1675 Broadway
New York, NY 10019
Telephone: (212) 522-5600
Ownership %: 100
**Bureau(s):**
Cable Nevhaus
11766 Wilshire Blvd., Ste. 170
Los Angeles, CA 90025-6542
Telephone: (310) 268-7200
FAX: (310) 268-7610
**Editorial:**
Jason McManus .........................Editor in Chief
James Seymore ...........................Managing Editor
Mark Michaelson ..............................Art Director
Robert Newman ........................Design Director
Mary Dunn ........................Photography Director
**Desc.:** Reviews and reports on what is new and noteworthy in TV, movies, video, music, books, and kids' entertainment.

**FACETS FEATURES** 69636
1517 W. Fullerton Ave.
Chicago, IL 60614
Telephone: (312) 281-9075
FAX: (312) 929-5437
Year Established: 1975
Pub. Frequency: bi-m.

Page Size: standard
Subscrip. Rate: $12/yr.
Circulation: 50,000
Circulation Type: paid
**Owner(s):**
Facets Multimedia, Inc.
1517 W. Fullerton Ave.
Chicago, IL 60614
Telephone: (312) 281-9075
Ownership %: 100
**Editorial:**
Milos Stehlik ...................................Editor
**Desc.:** Covers the world of international films and video. Includes a catalog of new foreign, independent and classic releases.

**FILM BILL** 69002
250 W. 54 St.
New York, NY 10019
Telephone: (212) 977-4140
FAX: (212) 977-4404
Year Established: 1970
Pub. Frequency: m.
Page Size: 6 X 9
Materials: 01,02,03,10,11,12,14,15,21,24, 25,26,27,28,29,32
Print Process: offset
Circulation: 500,000
Circulation Type: controlled
**Owner(s):**
Film Bill, Inc.
250 W. 54th St.
New York, NY 10019
Telephone: (212) 977-4140
Ownership %: 100

**FILM COMMENT** 25585
70 Lincoln Ctr. Plz.
New York, NY 10023
Telephone: (212) 875-5610
FAX: (212) 875-5636
Year Established: 1962
Pub. Frequency: bi-m.
Page Size: standard
Subscrip. Rate: $24.95/yr.
Materials: 02,06,10,11,13,21,24,25,26,28,32
Freelance Pay: $200-400/pg.
Circulation: 45,000
Circulation Type: paid
**Owner(s):**
Film Society of Lincoln Ctr., The
70 Lincoln Ctr. Plz.
New York, NY 10023
Telephone: (212) 875-5610
FAX: (212) 875-5636
Ownership %: 100
**Management:**
Tony Impavido .................Advertising Manager
Doris Fellerman ...................Business Manager
**Editorial:**
Richard T. Jameson ...............................Editor
**Desc.:** Fact-filled articles, lavishly illustrated, covering the world via films, film-makers and film-making, theory, and criticism.
**Readers:** Industry professionals, film-makers, academics/students, and literate culture consumers.

**FILMS IN REVIEW** 25586
P.O. Box 589
New York, NY 10021
Telephone: (212) 628-1594
Year Established: 1950
Pub. Frequency: bi-m.
Page Size: pocket
Subscrip. Rate: $18/yr.
Circulation: 45,000
Circulation Type: paid
**Owner(s):**
National Board of Review of Motion Pictures, Inc.
Telephone: (212) 535-2528

**Management:**
Zoe Ray ...............................Circulation Manager
**Editorial:**
Robin Little .......................................Editor
**Desc.:** Carries by-line articles on the various aspects of the motion picture/cultural, educational, commercial, technical, financial. Reviews current films, current books on the industry, films shown on TV, VCR.
**Readers:** People interested in the motion pictures.

**FILM THREAT** 69003
9171 Wilshire Blvd., Ste. 300
Beverly Hills, CA 90210
Telephone: (310) 858-7155
FAX: (310) 274-7985
Year Established: 1985
Pub. Frequency: 6/yr.
Page Size: standard
Subscrip. Rate: $4.99 newsstand; $11.85/yr.
Materials: 23,24,25,26,28,29
Circulation: 125,000
Circulation Type: paid
**Owner(s):**
LFP, Publishing Inc.
9171 Wilshire Blvd., Ste. 300
Beverly Hills, CA 90210
Telephone: (310) 858-7155
FAX: (310) 247-1708
Ownership %: 100
**Editorial:**
Paul Zimmerman .....................Executive Editor
Christian Gore .....................................Editor
**Desc.:** Features celebrities and coverage from big studio releases to independent films.
**Readers:** Targeting the "Twentysomething" generation.

**FREETHINKER FORUM** 66344
8945 Renken Rd.
Staunton, IL 62088
Telephone: (618) 637-2202
FAX: (618) 637-2666
Mailing Address:
P.O. Box 14447
St. Louis, MO 63178
Year Established: 1993
Pub. Frequency: m.
Page Size: standard
Subscrip. Rate: $25/yr.
Freelance Pay: negotiable
Circulation: 10,000
Circulation Type: controlled
**Owner(s):**
Duncan Publications
8945 Renken Rd.
Staunton, IL 62088
Telephone: (618) 637-2202
Ownership %: 100
**Management:**
Paul Scott .....................................Vice President
Susan Duncan .....................................Publisher
**Editorial:**
Susan Duncan .....................................Editor
**Desc.:** Designed to enhance and celebrate the single lifestyle as a legitimate choice, with an emphasis on the positive aspects of single living.
**Readers:** Single females 25 and older.

**GAMES MAGAZINE** 25978
19 W. 21st St.
New York, NY 10010
Telephone: (212) 727-7100
FAX: (212) 727-7661
Year Established: 1977
Pub. Frequency: bi-m.
Page Size: standard
Subscrip. Rate: $17.97/yr.
Circulation: 700,000

---

**Materials Accepted/Included:** 01-Business news 02-By-line articles 03-Fashion news 04-Food news 05-Freelance copy 06-Letters to editor 07-Real estate news 08-Sports news 09-Travel news 10-Book rev. 11-Movie rev. 12-Music rev. 13-TV rev. 14-Theater rev. 15-Coming events 16-Obituaries 17-Question & answer 18-Social announcements 19-Artwork 20-Cartoons 21-Photos 22-TV listings 23-Audio rec. 24-Video rec. 25-Books 26-Films/film clips 27-Personnel news 28-Press releases 29-New product news/photos 30-Trade lit. 31-Contracts awarded 32-Display adv. 33-Classified adv.

Circulation Type: paid
**Owner(s):**
B & P Publishing Co., Inc.
575 Boylston St.
Boston, MA 02116
**Management:**
Alan Segal .........................Publisher
**Editorial:**
Will Shortz ....................Senior Editor
**Desc.:** Puzzles, games, contests, and
feature articles. Departments include:
News Notes, Chess, Bridge,
Backgammon, Book & Game Reviews,
Trivia and Photo Identification Quizzes,
Map Quizzes, Crossword and Other
Puzzles, Original Games, etc.
**Readers:** Dual audience, 34 yrs., well
educated, Prof/Mgr.

**INTERVIEW**     25820
575 Broadway, 5th Fl.
New York, NY 10012
Telephone: (212) 941-2900
Year Established: 1969
Pub. Frequency: m.
Page Size: tabloid
Subscrip. Rate: $20/yr.
Circulation: 137,071
Circulation Type: paid
**Owner(s):**
Brant Publications, Inc.
575 Broadway, 5th Fl.
New York, NY 10012
Telephone: (212) 941-2900
Ownership %: 100
**Bureau(s):**
Interview/West Coast
1728 1/2 N. Whitley Ave.
Los Angeles, CA 90028
Telephone: (310) 463-8400
Contact: Marci Voss, Manager
**Management:**
Bill Fine .........................Vice President
Sandy Brant ............................Publisher
**Editorial:**
Ingrid Sischy .................Editor in Chief
Paige Powell ......................Advertising
**Desc.:** Features exclusive conversations
with interesting and glamorous people.
Interview presents the names and faces
that are well known or soon to be,
and reports on ideas, new dances, the
night scene, gallery openings, fashion
shows. Also features original fiction and
regular columns devoted to music,
humor, and movies. Departments
include: Art, Entertainment, Fashion,
Society.
**Readers:** Affluent trendsetters who spend
money.

**JUST FOR LAUGHS**     69151
22 Miller Ave.
Mill Valley, CA 94941
Telephone: (415) 383-4746
FAX: (415) 383-0142
Year Established: 1983
Pub. Frequency: 4/yr.
Page Size: standard
Subscrip. Rate: $1 newsstand; $18/yr.
Materials: 32,33
Circulation: 50,000
Circulation Type: paid
**Owner(s):**
JFL Communications, Inc.
22 Miller Ave.
Mill Valley, CA 94941
Telephone: (415) 383-4746
Ownership %: 100
**Management:**
John Fox .............................Publisher
**Editorial:**
John Fox ..................................Editor

**Desc.:** Chronicles stand-up comedy.
Profiles performers, lists locations and
schedules, provides stories and gossip.

**LOUISVILLE MAGAZINE**     22351
1 Riverfront Plz., #604
Louisville, KY 40202
Telephone: (502) 625-0100
FAX: (502) 625-0109
Year Established: 1950
Pub. Frequency: m.
Page Size: standard
Subscrip. Rate: $2.50 issue; $15/yr.
Freelance Pay: $40-$300
Circulation: 30,000
Circulation Type: paid
**Owner(s):**
Louisville Magazine, Inc.
1 Riverfront Plz., #604
Louisville, KY 40202
Telephone: (502) 625-0100
Ownership %: 100
**Editorial:**
John Filiatreau ............................Editor
Cammie Cox ...............Managing Editor
**Desc.:** News and features covering
Louisville area people, events and
issues.
**Readers:** The general community.

**MEGA PLAY**     67262
1920 Highland Ave. Ste. 222
Lombard, IL 60148
Telephone: (708) 916-7222
FAX: (708) 916-7227
Year Established: 1990
Pub. Frequency: bi-m.
Page Size: Standard
Subscrip. Rate: $3.95 newsstand;
$14.95/yr.
Circulation: 60000
Circulation Type: paid
**Owner(s):**
Eisenberg Communications
2121 Avenue of The Stars
Ste. 630
Los Angeles, CA 90067
Telephone: (310) 551-6587
Ownership %: 100
**Management:**
Steve Harris ...........................Publisher
Dave Marshall ........Circulation Manager
**Editorial:**
Ed Semrad ................................Editor

**METAL EDGE-TV PICTURE LIFE**     25602
233 Park Ave. S.
New York, NY 10003
Telephone: (212) 780-3500
FAX: (212) 780-3555
Pub. Frequency: m.
Page Size: standard
Subscrip. Rate: $24/yr.; $45/2 yrs.
Circulation: 250,000
Circulation Type: paid
**Owner(s):**
Sterling's Magazines, Inc.
233 Park Ave. S.
New York, NY 10003
Telephone: (212) 780-3500
FAX: (212) 780-3555
Ownership %: 100
**Management:**
Sanford Schwarz ....................Publisher
**Editorial:**
Gerry Miller .................................Editor
Frank Rusco ........................Art Director
Susan Rohall ..........Assistant Art Director
Robert Schartoff ............Creative Director

**MODERN SCREEN'S COUNTRY MUSIC SPECIAL**     25588
233 Park Ave. S.
New York, NY 10003
Telephone: (212) 780-3500
FAX: (212) 780-3555
Pub. Frequency: m.
Page Size: standard
Subscrip. Rate: $24/yr.
Circulation: 200,000
**Owner(s):**
Sterlings Magazines
233 Park Ave. S.
New York, NY 10003
Telephone: (212) 780-3500
Ownership %: 100
**Editorial:**
Mike Greenblatt .........................Editor
**Desc.:** Illustrated articles describe the
country music stars' lives, doings,
romances, etc. Departments include:
Movie Reviews, Record Reviews.
**Readers:** Country fans

**MOVIE MARKETPLACE**     67300
990 Grove St.
Evanston, IL 60201
Telephone: (708) 491-6440
Year Established: 1987
Pub. Frequency: bi-m.
Page Size: pocket
Subscrip. Rate: $3.75 newsstand; $9.97/yr.
Freelance Pay: $150/350-800 wds. with
photos
Circulation: 150,000
Circulation Type: paid
**Owner(s):**
World Publishing Co.
990 Grove St.
Evanston, IL 60201
Telephone: (708) 491-6440
Ownership %: 100
**Management:**
Norman Jacobs ........................President
Norman Jacobs ........................Publisher
Norman Jacobs ............Advertising Manager
**Editorial:**
Robert Meyers ...............Editor in Chief

**MOVIE MIRROR**     25591
233 Park Ave. S.
New York, NY 10003
Telephone: (212) 780-3500
FAX: (212) 780-3555
Pub. Frequency: bi-m.
Page Size: standard
Subscrip. Rate: $10/yr.
Circulation: 70,000
Circulation Type: paid
**Owner(s):**
Sterling's Magazines, Inc.
233 Park Ave. S.
New York, NY 10003
Telephone: (212) 780-3500
Ownership %: 100
**Management:**
Sanford Schwarz ....................Publisher
**Editorial:**
Kathleen Ludwig ..........................Editor
Frank Rasco ........................Art Director
Carmen Correa ...........Assistant Art Director
Bob Schantoff ..............Creative Director
Roger Glazer ............Photography Editor

**MUSE, THE**     65127
842 Commonwealth Ave.
Boston, MA 02215
Telephone: (617) 232-6841
FAX: (617) 232-0592
Year Established: 1981
Pub. Frequency: w.: Thu.

Page Size: standard
Subscrip. Rate: $85/yr.
Materials: 02,03,10,11,12,14,15,21,23,24,
25,26,32
Circulation: 21,000
Circulation Type: free & paid
**Owner(s):**
Back Bay Publishing Co., Inc.
842 Commonwealth Ave.
Boston, MA 02215
Telephone: (617) 232-6841
**Management:**
Jason Madoux .........................President
Todd Hanna ..............Advertising Manager
**Editorial:**
Aimee Bartol ...............................Editor

**NATIONAL LAMPOON**     25889
10850 Wilshire Blvd., Ste. 100
Los Angeles, CA 90024
Telephone: (310) 474-5252
FAX: (310) 474-1219
Year Established: 1970
Pub. Frequency: bi-m.
Page Size: standard
Subscrip. Rate: $3.95/issue; $22/yr.
Freelance Pay: $.40/wd.
Circulation: 250,000
Circulation Type: paid
**Owner(s):**
J-2 Communication
10850 Wilshire Blvd., Ste. 100
Los Angeles, CA 90024
Telephone: (310) 474-5280
Ownership %: 100
**Management:**
Jim Jimuro ...........................President
Chet Cooper ..........................Publisher
**Editorial:**
David Garrett .................Senior Editor
Jason Ward ..............................Editor
Terry Whitley .....................Art Director
**Desc.:** A humor magazine, 100%, and only
interested in humorous pieces.
**Readers:** Ages 18-35.

**ONSAT-AMERICA'S WEEKLY SATELLITE GUIDE**     68804
1300 S. DeKalb St.
Shelby, NC 28152
Telephone: (704) 482-9673
FAX: (704) 484-8558
Mailing Address:
P.O. Box 167
Selby, NC 28151-0167
Year Established: 1984
Pub. Frequency: w.
Page Size: standard
Subscrip. Rate: $49.97/yr.
Materials: 02,06,08,11,13,15,21,22,24,26,
28,29,32
Freelance Pay: varies
Print Process: web
Circulation: 383,927
Circulation Type: paid
**Owner(s):**
Triple D Publishing, Inc.
1300 S. DeKalb St.
Shelby, NC 28151
Telephone: (704) 482-9673
Ownership %: 100
**Editorial:**
Jim H. Cothran ...........................Editor
**Desc.:** Includes listings and articles
concerning satellite TV programming.
**Deadline:** story-4 wks. prior to pub. date;
news-3-4 wks. prior; photo-3-4 wks.
prior; ads-3 wks. prior

Materials Accepted/Included: 01-Business news 02-By-line articles 03-Fashion news 04-Food news 05-Freelance copy 06-Letters to editor 07-Real estate news 08-Sports news 09-Travel news 10-Book rev. 11-Movie rev. 12-Music rev. 13-TV rev. 14-Theater rev. 15-Coming events 16-Obituaries 17-Question & answer 18-Social announcements 19-Artwork 20-Cartoons 21-Photos 22-TV listings 23-Audio rec. 24-Video rec. 25-Books 26-Films/film clips 27-Personnel news 28-Press releases 29-New product news/photos 30-Trade lit. 31-Contracts awarded 32-Display adv. 33-Classified adv.

6-32

## PASSPORT TO WORLD BAND RADIO
69272

825 Cherry Ln.
P.O. Box 300
Penn's Park, PA 18943-0300
Telephone: (215) 794-3410
FAX: (215) 794-3396
Year Established: 1984
Pub. Frequency: a.
Page Size: 7 X 9 3/16
Subscrip. Rate: $19.90 copy
Materials: 02,19,21,27,28,29,30,32
Freelance Pay: $100 & up
Circulation: 80,000
Circulation Type: paid
**Owner(s):**
International Broadcasting Services, Ltd.
825 Cherry Ln.
P.O. Box 300
Penn's Park, PA 18943-0300
Telephone: (215) 794-3410
FAX: (215) 598-3794
Ownership %: 100
**Bureau(s):**
Latin America (IBS Paraguay)
Casilla 1844
 Asuncion Paraguay
Telephone: 595-21-440-788
FAX: 595-21-446-373
Contact: Tony Jonss, Bureau Chief
**Management:**
Jane Brinkler .......................Associate Publisher
**Editorial:**
Lawrence Magne ...............................Editor
Mary Kroszner ...............................Advertising
**Desc.:** Reference to news, sports and
entertainment shortwave broadcasts
available from around the world.
**Deadline:** story-May; news-July; photo-
June; ads-May

## PERFORMING ARTS MAGAZINE
25633

3539 Motor Ave.
Los Angeles, CA 90034-4800
Telephone: (310) 839-8000
FAX: (310) 839-5651
Year Established: 1967
Pub. Frequency: m.
Page Size: standard
Subscrip. Rate: free
Circulation: 700,000
Circulation Type: controlled
**Owner(s):**
Gilman Kraft
3539 Motor Ave.
Los Angeles, CA 90034-4800
Telephone: (310) 839-8000
Ownership %: 100
**Bureau(s):**
Performing Arts Magazine
3680 Fifth Ave.
San Diego, CA 92103
Telephone: (619) 297-6430
Contact: M. B. Merrymen, Vice President
**Management:**
Charles Schmuck ...............................Publisher
**Editorial:**
Dana Kitaj ...............................Editor
**Desc.:** Covers music, film, theatre, audio-
video, travel and real estate. Provides
synopses, cast biographies and
background information on plays and
concerts.
**Readers:** Informed, educated, high-income
theatergoers; Los Angeles, San
Francisco, San Diego and Orange
County.

## PLAYBILL
25911

52 Vanderbilt Ave.
New York, NY 10017
Telephone: (212) 557-5757
Year Established: 1884

Pub. Frequency: m.
Page Size: pocket
Subscrip. Rate: $2.50 newsstand; $24/yr.
Freelance Pay: $600/full length articles
Circulation: 1,553,000
Circulation Type: controlled
**Owner(s):**
Arthur T. Birsh
52 Vanderbilt Ave.
New York, NY 10017
Telephone: (212) 557-5757
Ownership %: 100
**Management:**
Arthur T. Birsh ...............................President
Philip Birsh ...............................Publisher
Robert Charles ...............Advertising Manager
**Editorial:**
June Samelson ...............Editor in Chief
Louis Botto ...............................Senior Editor
Andrew Gans ...............................Associate Editor
**Desc.:** Features include theatre related
articles concerning background of
performances and performers, as well
as fashion, travel, food, beauty; all
written by contributing editors, assigned
authors, or professionals in the theatre
from whom material is requested. Free
lance material bought. Departments
include: Fashion (Women's), Beauty,
Entertainment.
**Readers:** Theatre goers, distributed in all
New York Theatres & by subscription
and newsstand nationally.

## PREMIERE MAGAZINE
69004

2 Park Ave., 11th Fl.
New York, NY 10016
Telephone: (212) 545-3500
FAX: (212) 725-3442
Year Established: 1987
Pub. Frequency: m.
Page Size: standard
Subscrip. Rate: $2.95 newsstand;
$19.98/yr.
Materials: 32
Circulation: 600,000
Circulation Type: paid
**Owner(s):**
K-III Magazines
2 Park Ave., 11th Fl.
New York, NY 10016
Telephone: (212) 545-3500
FAX: (212) 725-3442
Ownership %: 100
**Management:**
Terry Russell ...............................Publisher
**Editorial:**
Susan Lyne ...............................Editor
Mark Furlong ...............Advertising Director
**Desc.:** Contains interviews, investigative
reports, profiles of new and old
releases, and behind-the-camera looks
at film production.

## PROMENADE
25596

20 E. 49th St., 6th Fl.
New York, NY 10017
Telephone: (212) 888-3500
FAX: (212) 888-3602
Year Established: 1934
Pub. Frequency: s-a.
Page Size: oversize
Subscrip. Rate: $5 issue
Circulation: 2,000,000
Circulation Type: paid
**Owner(s):**
Promenade Magazines,Inc.
20 E. 49th St., 6th Fl.
New York, NY 10017
Telephone: (212) 888-3500
Ownership %: 100
**Management:**
Christopher C. Ifejika ...............Controller
James M. White ...............................Publisher

**Editorial:**
James M. White ...............Editor in Chief
Victoria Kohl ...............................Editor
Melissa White ...............Advertising Director
Shelly Wolson ...............Editorial Assistant
Barbara Whitney ...........Senior Vice President
**Readers:** Guests of 56 leading New York
hotels. Also 50,000 luxury co-op and
condo residents.

## SATELLITE ORBIT
57265

8330 Boone Blvd.
Vienna, VA 22182
Telephone: (703) 827-0511
FAX: (703) 356-6179
Year Established: 1979
Pub. Frequency: m.
Page Size: standard
Subscrip. Rate: $52/yr.
Freelance Pay: $300/750 wd., 1 pg. article
Circulation: 400,000
Circulation Type: paid
**Owner(s):**
Commtek Publishing Co., Inc.
8330 Boone Blvd.
Vienna, VA 22182
Telephone: (703) 827-0511
Ownership %: 100
**Editorial:**
Phil Swan ...............................Editor
Linda Ramsey ...............Managing Editor
Laura Fries ...............Entertainment Editor
Jay Hylsky ...............Information Director
**Desc.:** A monthly listings and features
magazine for home satellite TV viewers.
Features and departments provide
coverage of programming, technology,
personalities, and political issues. The
Birdwatcher Programming Guide
contains listings for more than 75
satellite TV channels.
**Readers:** Owners of home satellite TV
systems.

## SATELLITE TV WEEK
68805

P.O. Box 308
Fortuna, CA 95540
Telephone: (707) 725-6951
FAX: (707) 725-4311
Year Established: 1981
Pub. Frequency: w.
Subscrip. Rate: $2.50 newsstand; $52/yr.
Circulation: 400,000
Circulation Type: paid
**Owner(s):**
Fortuna Communications Corp.
P.O. Box 308
Fortuna, CA 95540
Telephone: (707) 725-6951
Ownership %: 100
**Management:**
Patrick O'Dell ...............................Publisher
Patrick Sharpe ...............Circulation Manager
**Editorial:**
James E. Scott ...............................Editor
**Desc.:** Reports TV program listings for
satellite channels. Includes editorial
coverage of issues affecting the satellite
industry, as well as entertainment
features, sports coverage, consumer
electronics and personality interviews.

## SCARLET STREET
69264

P.O. Box 604
Glen Rock, NJ 07452
Telephone: (201) 836-1113
Year Established: 1991
Pub. Frequency: q.
Page Size: standard
Subscrip. Rate: $5.95 newsstand; $20/yr.
Materials: 06,10,11,12,13,14,15,21,22,23,
24,25,26,28,32,33
Circulation: 26,000
Circulation Type: paid

**Owner(s):**
Scarlet Street, Inc.
P.O. Box 604
Glen Rock, NJ 07452
Telephone: (201) 836-1113
Ownership %: 100
**Editorial:**
Richard Valley ...............................Editor
**Desc.:** Magazine of mystery and horror in
literature, movies, tv, comics and radio.

## SCENE: AT THE MOVIES
69005

240 E. 79th St., Ste. 10D
New York, NY 10021
Telephone: (212) 737-8100
FAX: (212) 237-8884
Year Established: 1990
Pub. Frequency: m.
Page Size: pocket
Subscrip. Rate: free
Circulation: 1,500,000
Circulation Type: free
**Owner(s):**
Scene
240 E. 79th St., Ste. 10D
New York, NY 10021
Telephone: (212) 737-8100
Ownership %: 100
**Management:**
Ann Fell ...............................Publisher
**Editorial:**
James Grant ...............................Editor
**Desc.:** Covers new movies, actors and
actresses, producers and directors.

## SOAP OPERA DIGEST
26628

888 7th Ave.
New York, NY 10106
Telephone: (212) 332-0255
FAX: (212) 332-0252
Year Established: 1975
Pub. Frequency: 26/yr.
Page Size: pocket
Subscrip. Rate: $2.49 newsstand;
$47.91/yr.
Circulation: 1,396,346
Circulation Type: paid
**Owner(s):**
K-III Magazines
200 Madison Ave.
New York, NY 10016
Telephone: (212) 332-0255
Ownership %: 100
**Management:**
Harry McQillen ...............................President
Linda Vaughan ...............................Publisher
**Editorial:**
Lynn Leahey ...............Editor in Chief
Jason Bondadeoff ...............Managing Editor
**Desc.:** A news and entertainment
magazine dealing with all aspects of
daytime and nighttime television "Soap
Operas".

## SOAP OPERA MAGAZINE
69478

600 S. East Coast Ave.
Lantana, FL 33462
Telephone: (407) 586-1111
FAX: (407) 582-1008
Pub. Frequency: w.
Subscrip. Rate: $1.39 newsstand;
$39.84/yr.
Circulation: 325,000
Circulation Type: paid
**Owner(s):**
SOM Publishing, Inc.
600 S. East Coast Ave.
Lantana, FL 33462
Telephone: (407) 586-1111
Ownership %: 100
**Editorial:**
Joseph J. Policy ...............................Editor
David Minter ...............Managing Editor
Cynthia Rigg ...............Assistant Editor

**Materials Accepted/Included:** 01-Business news 02-By-line articles 03-Fashion news 04-Food news 05-Freelance copy 06-Letters to editor 07-Real estate news 08-Sports news 09-Travel news 10-Book rev. 11-Movie rev. 12-Music rev. 13-TV rev. 14-Theater rev. 15-Coming events 16-Obituaries 17-Question & answer 18-Social announcements 19-Artwork 20-Cartoons 21-Photos 22-TV listings 23-Audio rec. 24-Video rec. 25-Books 26-Films/film clips 27-Personnel news 28-Press releases 29-New product news/photos 30-Trade lit. 31-Contracts awarded 32-Display adv. 33-Classified adv.

6-33

**Desc.:** A weekly record of daily television soap operas, featuring interviews with stars, previews and behind the scenes gossip.

65352

**SOAP OPERA UPDATE**
270 Sylvan Ave.
Englewood Cliffs, NJ 07632-2513
Telephone: (201) 569-6699
FAX: (201) 569-2510
Year Established: 1988
Pub. Frequency: bi-w.
Page Size: standard
Subscrip. Rate: $59/yr.
Circulation: 200,000
Circulation Type: paid
**Owner(s):**
Soap Opera Update Magazine, Inc.
270 Sylvan Ave.
Englewood Cliffs, NJ 07632-2513
Ownership %: 100
**Management:**
Angela Shapiro ..............................Publisher
Jerome Shapiro ..............................Publisher
Lynette Perillo ..................Circulation Manager
**Editorial:**
Angela Shapiro ......................Editor in Chief
Dawn Mazurco ........................Executive Editor
Richard Spencer ......................Executive Editor
Bill Lieberman ........................Managing Editor
**Desc.:** Program synopses, celebrity profiles, issues from the stars perspective. Along with recipes from restaurants portrayed in the soaps.
**Readers:** Daytime and nightime television soap opera viewers.

69500

**SOAP OPERA WEEKLY**
41 W. 25th St.
8th Fl.
New York, NY 10010
Telephone: (212) 447-4700
FAX: (212) 447-4778
Pub. Frequency: w.
Subscrip. Rate: $1.29 newsstand; $56.68/yr.
Circulation: 50,000
Circulation Type: paid
**Owner(s):**
K-III Magazines
717 5th Ave.
New York, NY 10022
Telephone: (212) 447-4700
Ownership %: 100
**Editorial:**
Mimi Torchin ..............................Editor
**Desc.:** News magazine devoted to the plots and personalities of TV dramas, with interviews and a variety of feature columns.

66297

**SOUND & IMAGE**
1633 Broadway, 45th Fl.
New York, NY 10019
Telephone: (212) 767-6020
FAX: (212) 767-5615
Year Established: 1990
Pub. Frequency: q.
Page Size: standard
Subscrip. Rate: $3.95 newsstand; $14.97/yr.
Materials: 01,02,05,06,08,10,11,12,13,15, 19,20,21,23,24,25,26,28,29,32
Freelance Pay: $200-$2000/article
Circulation: 40,000
Circulation Type: paid
**Owner(s):**
Hachette Filipacchi Magazines, Inc.
1633 Broadway
New York, NY 10019
Telephone: (212) 767-6000
Ownership %: 100
**Management:**
Thomas Witschi ..............................Publisher

**Editorial:**
Bill Wolfe ..............................Editor in Chief
Marc Horowitz ..............................Senior Editor
Peter Barry ..............................Senior Editor
Mike Mettler ..............................Managing Editor
Michael Gelfand ..............................Associate Editor
Tony Catalano ..................Associate Publisher
**Desc.:** Reports on the changing nature of electronic home entertainment, focusing on home theater, computers, on-line services, home automation, and more.
**Readers:** Upscale buyers of home entertainment systems.
**Deadline:** story-Feb. 1; May 1; Aug. 1; Nov. 1; ads-Jan. 1; Mar. 1; June 1; Sep. 1

25942

**STAR MAGAZINE**
660 White Plains Rd.
Tarrytown, NY 10591
Telephone: (914) 332-5000
FAX: (914) 332-5043
Year Established: 1974
Pub. Frequency: w.
Page Size: tabloid
Subscrip. Rate: $37.44/yr. US; $58.44/yr. foreign
Freelance Pay: $35/article
Circulation: 2,957,925
Circulation Type: paid
**Owner(s):**
Enquirer-Star, Inc.
600 South East Coast Ave.
Lantana, FL 33464
Ownership %: 100
**Bureau(s):**
Star Magazine
625 Smallwood Rd.
Rockville, MD 20850
Telephone: (301) 762-2560
Contact: Norma Langley

Star
280 S. Beverly Dr., Ste. 507
Beverly Hills , CA 90212
Telephone: (310) 858-1591
Contact: Robert Smith, Bureau Chief
**Management:**
Roger Wood ..............................President
Cheryl Corbett ..............................Controller
Barbara Hannah Grufferman ..............Publisher
Katherine Jose ..................Advertising Manager
**Editorial:**
Stephen LeGrice ..............................Executive Editor
Richard Kaplan ..............................Editor
Stephen LeGrice ..............................Managing Editor
Kevin Corbett ..............................Art Director
Barbara DeGarmo ..............................Associate Editor
Lynne Dorsey ..............................Associate Editor
Philip Wilkinson ..............................Feature Editor
Dick Belsky ..............................News Editor
Alistair Duncan ..............................Photography Editor
William Trevor ..............................Production Editor
**Desc.:** A blend of topical news, stories behind the news, personalities, fashion, politics, entertainment, and informative advice particularly in medical, health and consumer fields.
**Readers:** America's younger families and young singles.

68810

**STAR TREK: THE OFFICIAL FAN CLUB MAGAZINE**
P.O. Box 111000
Aurora, CO 80042
Telephone: (303) 341-1813
FAX: (303) 341-1401
Year Established: 1980
Pub. Frequency: bi-m.
Subscrip. Rate: $14.95/yr.
Materials: 06,10,11,13,15,17,19,20,21,28, 29,32,33
Print Process: web offset
Circulation: 110,000
Circulation Type: paid

**Owner(s):**
Official Star Trek Fan Club
P.O. Box 111000
Aurora, CO 80011
Telephone: (303) 341-1813
Ownership %: 100
**Editorial:**
Dan Madsen ..............................Editor
**Desc.:** Covers anything and everything pertaining to Star Trek: movies, TV and fandom.

25627

**TDR, THE DRAMA REVIEW**
721 Broadway, Sixth Fl.
New York, NY 10003
Telephone: (212) 998-1626
FAX: (212) 995-4060
Year Established: 1955
Pub. Frequency: q.
Page Size: oversize
Subscrip. Rate: $8 newsstand; $32/yr. individual; $80/yr. institution
Freelance Pay: $.02/wd.
Circulation: 5,000
Circulation Type: paid
**Owner(s):**
New York University, Tisch School Of The Arts
721 Broadway, 6th Fl.
New York, NY 10003
Telephone: (212) 598-2407
Ownership %: 50

MIT Press Journals
55 Hayward St.
Cambridge, MA 02142
Telephone: (617) 253-2864
Ownership %: 50
**Management:**
Rebecca McLeod ..............Advertising Manager
**Editorial:**
Richard Schechner ..............................Editor
Anna Bean ..............................Managing Editor
Pamela Brown ..............................Assistant Editor
Barbara Harrington ..............................Assistant Editor
Mariellen R. Sandford ..............Associate Editor
**Desc.:** America's most prestigious theatre magazine, publishing continuously for over 25 years. Basically a scholarly journal devoted to avant-garde performance. We document theatre, dance and art performances in the U.S. and abroad. Our goal is to get TDR into the hands of people in many fields: the arts, the social sciences, critical theory, history. We feel that live performances-- from ritual and sports to dance and theatre--are ways of thinking as well as entertainments, art forms, and worship. Our intention is to make a journal that relates these various kinds of performative behaviors--a journal indispensable to artists and thinkers whose work, thought, and play can no longer be boundaried.
**Readers:** Theatre scholars, professors, students, performing arts, the general theatre-going public.

68806

**TELEGUIA USA**
1241 Soto St., Ste. 203-M
Los Angeles, CA 90023
Telephone: (213) 881-6515
FAX: (213) 881-6524
Year Established: 1985
Pub. Frequency: Tue.
Page Size: standard
Subscrip. Rate: free
Materials: 01,03,04,06,07,08,09,11,12,13, 14,15,16,17,18,19,20,21,22
Print Process: web
Circulation: 170,000
Circulation Type: controlled & free

**Owner(s):**
Four Star Productions
1241 Soto St., Ste. 203-M
Los Angeles, CA 90023
Telephone: (213) 881-6515
FAX: (213) 881-6524
Ownership %: 100
**Editorial:**
Angel Morales ..............................Editorial Director
John DiCarlo ..............................Advertising
**Desc.:** Guide to TV broadcasts. Includes coverage of sports, food entertainment, automobiles, health and beauty. Written in Spanish.
**Deadline:** story-Wed., 4:00 pm; news- Wed., 4:00 pm; photo-Wed., 4:00 pm; ads-Wed., 4:00 pm

25601

**TV & MOVIE SCREEN**
233 Park Ave. S.
New York, NY 10003
Telephone: (212) 780-3500
FAX: (212) 780-3555
Pub. Frequency: bi-m.
Page Size: standard
Subscrip. Rate: $12/yr.
Circulation: 250,000
**Owner(s):**
Sterling's Magazines, Inc.
233 Park Ave. S.
New York, NY 10003
Telephone: (212) 780-3500
Ownership %: 100
**Management:**
Frank Rasco ..............................Vice President
Sanford Schwarz ..............................Publisher
**Editorial:**
Louise B. Barile ..............................Editor
Frank Rasco ..............................Art Director
Robert Schartoff ..............................Creative Director
Roger Glazer ..............................Photography Editor
**Desc.:** News features on showbiz personalities and columns.

26186

**TV GUIDE**
4 Radnor Corporate Ctr.
100 Matsonford Rd.
Radnor, PA 19088
Telephone: (215) 293-8500
FAX: (215) 688-3285
Mailing Address:
P.O. Box 500
Radnor, PA 19088
Year Established: 1953
Pub. Frequency: w.
Page Size: pocket
Subscrip. Rate: $.89 newsstand; $45.24/yr.
Freelance Pay: $1/wd.
Circulation: 15,800,000
Circulation Type: paid
**Owner(s):**
News America Publications, Inc.
4 Radnor Corporate Ctr.
Radnor, PA 19087
Telephone: (215) 293-8500
Ownership %: 100
**Bureau(s):**
TV Guide-New York
1290 Ave. of the Americas
New York, NY 10104
Telephone: (212) 484-9900
Contact: Neil Hickey, Bureau Chief

TV Guide-Hollywood
9000 Sunset Blvd.
Los Angeles, CA 90069
Telephone: (310) 276-0676
Contact: Steve Gelman, Chief Dir.

TV Guide-Wasington
818 18th St., N.W.
Washington, DC 20006
Telephone: (202) 822-8632
Contact: John Weisman, Chief Dir.

---

**Materials Accepted/Included:** 01-Business news 02-By-line articles 03-Fashion news 04-Food news 05-Freelance copy 06-Letters to editor 07-Real estate news 08-Sports news 09-Travel news 10-Book rev. 11-Movie rev. 12-Music rev. 13-TV rev. 14-Theater rev. 15-Coming events 16-Obituaries 17-Question & answer 18-Social announcements 19-Artwork 20-Cartoons 21-Photos 22-TV listings 23-Audio rec. 24-Video rec. 25-Books 26-Films/film clips 27-Personnel news 28-Press releases 29-New product news/photos 30-Trade lit. 31-Contracts awarded 32-Display adv. 33-Classified adv.

**Management:**
Joseph Barletta ................Chairman of Board
Jackie Gordetsky ............Advertising Manager
**Editorial:**
Barry Golson .......................Executive Editor
Myles Callum .........................Senior Editor
Anthea Disney ..............................Editor
Jack Curry ..........................Managing Editor
Andrew Mills ..........Assistant Managing Editor
**Desc.:** Uses feature stories about all aspects of television: not only network news and entertainment shows and personalities, but developments in cable, home video and technology as well. Many of these stories are staff written, but the magazine is open to contributions. These should be brief, fresh, and of general interest. Free lancers, in submitting ideas about TV personalities, should first consider that all these people are constantly under the scrutiny of staff editors and writers. The writer should therefore have a fresh angle on performers, or submit more general television themes, preferably from the point of view of the TV viewer.
**Readers:** The television viewers of America.

25605
## WHERE MAGAZINE
600 Third Ave., 15th Fl.
New York, NY 10016
Telephone: (212) 687-4646
Year Established: 1936
Pub. Frequency: m.
Page Size: standard
Subscrip. Rate: free to hotel visitors
Circulation: 500,000
Circulation Type: free
**Owner(s):**
KPCL Publishing Co., Ltd.
59 Front St., E.
New York, NY 10004
Telephone: (416) 846-3333
Ownership %: 100
**Management:**
Merrie Davis .............................Publisher
**Editorial:**
Kelly Tucker .......................Executive Editor
**Desc.:** Pertains to coming events, entertainment, films and other items of interest for travelers and the general public.
**Readers:** Travelers and tourists in the U.S. (domestic and international).

25856
## WIN
16760 Stagg St., Ste. 213
Van Nuys, CA 91406
Telephone: (818) 781-9355
FAX: (818) 781-3125
Year Established: 1977
Pub. Frequency: m.
Page Size: standard
Subscrip. Rate: $44/yr.
Freelance Pay: $50-$150/article
Circulation: 50,000
Circulation Type: paid
**Owner(s):**
Gambling Times, Inc.
16760 Stagg St., #213
Van Nuys, CA 91406
Telephone: (818) 781-9355
Ownership %: 100
**Management:**
Stanley R. Sludikoff .........................President
Stanley R. Sludikoff .........................Publisher
**Editorial:**
Cecil Suzuki .........................Senior Editor
Stanley R. Sludikoff .........................Editor
Stan Roberts .........................Miscellaneous
Mort Olshan .........................Miscellaneous
Mark Cramer .........................Miscellaneous

**Desc.:** The player's guide and gambling newsmagazine. Covers all gambling activities: casino games, horse and dog racing, card games, jai alai, sports betting, etc. Articles include: betting and handicapping systems, computer analysis of wagering propositions, personal experiences, profiles of major gambling and sports personalities, travel features on gambling abroad, developments in the gaming industry. Reports on major events such as the World Series of poker and offers consumer- oriented information on casino industry regulations, house rules, best games. Most byline articles purchased from freelancers; 1,000-3,000 words, $75-150, paid on publication. Freelance photos of gambling subjects: $5-$50/print, paid on acceptance. Occasional illustrations on assignment.
**Readers:** Business and professional people who gamble, casino and racing executives.

56284
## WINNING POKER
16760 Stagg St., Ste. 213
Van Nuys, CA 91406
Telephone: (818) 781-9355
Year Established: 1982
Pub. Frequency: m.
Page Size: standard
Subscrip. Rate: $48/yr.
Freelance Pay: $50
Circulation: 20,000
Circulation Type: paid
**Owner(s):**
Gambling Times, Inc.
16760 Stagg St., Ste. 213
Van Nuys, CA 91406
Telephone: (818) 781-9355
Ownership %: 100
**Management:**
Stan Sludikoff .........................Publisher
**Editorial:**
Dwight Chuman .........................Associate Editor
**Desc.:** Devoted to improving player's skills and winnings at the various poker games-Hold 'em, 7 Stud, Draw, Lo Ball, Razz, Hi-Low Split, etc. Educates player on above, provides money management techniques, and demonstrates how to play on all games.
**Readers:** 85% male, avid poker players in public card rooms.

## Group 626-Environment

69259
## AIR CURRENTS
939 Ellis St.
San Francisco, CA 94109
Telephone: (415) 749-4900
FAX: (415) 928-8560
Year Established: 1959
Pub. Frequency: m.
Page Size: tabloid
Subscrip. Rate: free
Print Process: offset
Circulation: 3,000
Circulation Type: free
**Owner(s):**
Bay Area Air Quality Management District
939 Ellis St.
San Francisco, CA 94109
Telephone: (415) 749-4900
Ownership %: 100
**Editorial:**
Will Taylor .........................Editor
**Desc.:** Keeps readers alert of air quality issues, new regulations, clean-air legislation and other matters affecting the Bay area.

23062
## ALABAMA CONSERVATION
Administration Bldg., 64 N. Union St.
Montgomery, AL 36130
Telephone: (205) 242-3151
Year Established: 1929
Pub. Frequency: bi-m.
Page Size: standard
Subscrip. Rate: $8/yr.; $14/2 yrs.; $20/3 yrs.
Circulation: 12,000
Circulation Type: paid
**Owner(s):**
Alabama Dept. of Conservation & Natural Resources
64 N. Union St.
Montgomery, AL 36130
Telephone: (205) 242-3151
Ownership %: 100
**Management:**
Cindy Thompson .........................Circulation Manager
**Editorial:**
Bettina Wood .........................Editor
Bettina Wood .........................Information Director
**Desc.:** By-line features, news about the Alabama conservation program. Staff-written articles cover hunting season, fishing, farm fish pond management, wildlife, state parks, marine resources and marine police. Will use outside material if there is a logical tie in with state program. Outside contributions accepted on: General interest photos & features on hunting & fishing, outdoor recreation, boating, hiking, and camping. Technical or popular features on wildlife, wildflowers, Alabama state parks, Seafood recipes, Freshwater fish recipes, Game recipes, Children's features relating to conservation & environment.
**Readers:** Organizations, individuals interested in conservation in Alabama. Hunters, fishermen, photographers, campers, park visitors, wildflower/wildlife enthusiasts, recreational boaters, marine fishermen.

65365
## ANIMALS' VOICE MAGAZINE
6433 Topanga Canyon Blvd.
Ste. 405
Canoga Park, CA 91303
Telephone: (818) 883-3722
FAX: (818) 883-3729
Pub. Frequency: q.
Page Size: standard
Subscrip. Rate: $23/yr.
Circulation: 35,000
Circulation Type: paid
**Owner(s):**
The Animal's Voice
6433 Topanga Canyon Blvd.
Ste. 405
Canoga Park, CA 91303-8830
Telephone: (818) 883-3722
Ownership %: 100
**Management:**
Jeri Lerner .........................Publisher
**Editorial:**
Laura A. Moretti .........................Editor
**Desc.:** Dedicated to animal defense issues for the protection and rights of animals.
**Readers:** Animal rights activists.

23065
## AUDUBON
700 Broadway
New York, NY 10003
Telephone: (212) 979-3126
FAX: (212) 353-0508
Year Established: 1899
Pub. Frequency: bi-m.
Page Size: standard
Subscrip. Rate: $30/yr.
Materials: 02,05,06,10,21,32
Circulation: 500,000

Circulation Type: paid
**Owner(s):**
National Audubon Society
700 Broadway
New York, NY 10003
Telephone: (212) 979-3000
Ownership %: 100
**Management:**
Peter A. A. Berle .........................President
Peter A. A. Berle .........................Publisher
John S. Gourley .........................Advertising Manager
**Editorial:**
Gary Soucie .........................Executive Editor
Michael W. Robbins .........................Editor
Mary Powel Thomas .........................Managing Editor
Frank Graham .........................Field Editor
Peter Howe .........................Photography Editor
**Desc.:** By-line articles deal with natural history as well as current conservation and environmental problems. Story lengths vary greatly; current conservation news and comment sections in book largely staff-written. Generous use of high quality color photos. Departments include: Letters, Editorials, current conservation issues reported in columns.
**Readers:** Members and affiliates of National Audubon Society; schools and libraries.

65363
## BUZZWORM'S EARTH JOURNAL
1033 Walnut St., Ste. 304
Boulder, CO 80302-5138
Telephone: (303) 442-1969
FAX: (303) 442-4875
Year Established: 1988
Pub. Frequency: q.
Page Size: standard
Subscrip. Rate: $4.95 issue US; $5.95 issue Canada; $17.97/yr. US
Materials: 02,05,06,09,15,23,24,25,26,28, 29,30,32,33
Print Process: web offset
Circulation: 100,000
Circulation Type: paid
**Owner(s):**
Buzzworm, Inc.
1033 Walnut St., Ste. 304
Boulder, CO 80302
Telephone: (303) 442-1969
FAX: (303) 442-4875
Ownership %: 100
**Editorial:**
Joseph E. Daniel .........................Editor
**Desc.:** An independent look at environmental culture.
**Readers:** Persons interested in environmental issues nationwide.

68717
## COMMUNITY SPIRIT MAGAZINE
P.O. Box 4628
Carmel, CA 93921
Telephone: (408) 625-1557
FAX: (408) 625-3424
Year Established: 1981
Pub. Frequency: m.
Page Size: tabloid
Subscrip. Rate: $15/yr.
Materials: 02,04,05,06,09,10,12,19,20,21, 23,24,25,28,29,32
Print Process: web offset
Circulation: 65,000
Circulation Type: paid
**Owner(s):**
Community Spirit Publications
P.O. Box 4628
Carmel, CA 93921
Telephone: (408) 625-1557
FAX: (408) 625-3424
Ownership %: 100
**Management:**
Stewart Long .........................Publisher

**Materials Accepted/Included:** 01-Business news 02-By-line articles 03-Fashion news 04-Food news 05-Freelance copy 06-Letters to editor 07-Real estate news 08-Sports news 09-Travel news 10-Book rev. 11-Movie rev. 12-Music rev. 13-TV rev. 14-Theater rev. 15-Coming events 16-Obituaries 17-Question & answer 18-Social announcements 19-Artwork 20-Cartoons 21-Photos 22-TV listings 23-Audio rec. 24-Video rec. 25-Books 26-Films/film clips 27-Personnel news 28-Press releases 29-New product news/photos 30-Trade lit. 31-Contracts awarded 32-Display adv. 33-Classified adv.

6-35

**Editorial:**
Jonathan C. Drake ...................Editor
**Desc.:** environmental issues, eco-tourism, new adult contemporary media products, books, CD's, tapes, etc.
**Deadline:** story-2 mo. prior to pub. date; news-2 mo. prior; photo-2 mo. prior; ads-2 mo. prior

68720

## CONSCIOUS CONSUMER & COMPANY
P.O. Box 51
Wauconda, IL 60084
Telephone: (708) 526-0522
Year Established: 1990
Pub. Frequency: q.
Page Size: 8 1/2 X 11
Subscrip. Rate: $19.95/yr.
Materials: 01
**Owner(s):**
New Consumer Institute, Inc.
P.O. Box 51
Wauconda, IL 60084
Telephone: (708) 526-0522
Ownership %: 100
**Editorial:**
John F. Wasik ...................Editor
**Desc.:** Provides socially responsible and environmentally sound product information.

25780

## DUCKS UNLIMITED
One Waterfowl Way
Memphis, TN 38120
Telephone: (901) 758-3825
FAX: (901) 758-3909
Year Established: 1937
Pub. Frequency: bi-m.
Page Size: standard
Subscrip. Rate: $20/yr. members
Materials: 32,33
Freelance Pay: $50-$250/photo; $500 photoessay
Circulation: 500,000
Circulation Type: paid
**Owner(s):**
Ducks Unlimited, Inc.
One Waterfowl Way
Memphis, TN 38120
Telephone: (901) 758-3825
Ownership %: 100
**Management:**
Beth Bryan ...................Advertising Manager
**Editorial:**
Lee Salber ...................Editor in Chief
Chris Dorsey ...................Exec. Editor
Chuck Pitrie ...................Senior Editor
Michael Di Frisco ...................Creative Director
Diane Harvey ...................Production Coordinator
Matt Young ...................Staff Writer
**Desc.:** A private non-profit membership organization dedicated to the conservation and propagation of North America's waterfowl as a valuable natural resource.
**Readers:** Waterfowlers and other conservationists.

67044

## EARTH
21027 Crossroads Circle
Waukesha, WI 53187
Telephone: (414) 796-8776
FAX: (414) 769-1142
Mailing Address:
P.O. Box 1612
Waukesha, WI 53187
Year Established: 1991
Pub. Frequency: bi-m.
Page Size: standard
Subscrip. Rate: $3.95 newsstand; $19.95/yr.
Circulation: 90,000
Circulation Type: paid

**Owner(s):**
Kalmbach Publishing Co.
21027 Crossroads Cir.
Waukesha, WI 53186
Telephone: (414) 796-8776
Ownership %: 100
**Management:**
Russell Larson ...................Publisher
Daniel R. Lance ...................Advertising Manager
**Editorial:**
Tom Yulsman ...................Editor
**Desc.:** Covers different earth sciences topics for a general audience, including geology, planetology, oceanography, meteorology and mineralogy, as well as travel and exploration.
**Readers:** For the general audience.

65424

## E MAGAZINE
28 Knight St.
Norwalk, CT 06851
Telephone: (203) 854-5559
FAX: (203) 866-0602
Mailing Address:
P.O. Box 5098
Westport, CT 06881
Year Established: 1990
Pub. Frequency: bi-m.
Page Size: standard
Subscrip. Rate: $3.95 newsstand; $20/yr.
Freelance Pay: negotiable
Circulation: 50,000
Circulation Type: paid
**Owner(s):**
Earth Action Network
P.O. Box 5098
Westport, CT 06881
Telephone: (203) 854-5559
Ownership %: 100
**Management:**
Doug Moss ...................Publisher
**Editorial:**
Doug Moss ...................Editor
Deborah Kamlani ...................Associate Publisher
**Desc.:** Covers enviornmental issues.

69330

## ENVIRONMENTAL ACTION
6930 Carroll Ave., Ste. 600
Takoma Park, MD 20912
Telephone: (301) 891-1100
FAX: (301) 891-2218
Year Established: 1970
Pub. Frequency: q.
Subscrip. Rate: $25/yr. individuals; $35/yr. institutions
Materials: 06,10,21,25,32,33
Print Process: web offset
Circulation: 14,000
Circulation Type: free & paid
**Owner(s):**
Environmental Action, Inc.
6930 Carroll Ave., Ste. 600
Takoma Park, MD 20912
Telephone: (301) 891-1100
Ownership %: 100
**Editorial:**
Barbara Ruben ...................Editor
David Lapp ...................Editor
**Desc.:** Quarterly magazine of non-profit environmental organization with lively articles and in-depth investigations on environmental policy & politics and grassroots activism.

58628

## ENVIRONMENTAL PROGRESS
345 E. 47th St.
New York, NY 10017
Telephone: (212) 705-7327
FAX: (212) 752-3294
Year Established: 1982
Pub. Frequency: q.
Page Size: standard
Subscrip. Rate: $150/yr. non-members
Circulation: 5,000

Circulation Type: paid
**Owner(s):**
American Institute of Chemical Engineers
345 E. 47th St.
New York, NY 10017
Telephone: (212) 705-7330
**Management:**
Stephen R. Smith ...................Publisher
**Editorial:**
Gary F. Bennett ...................Editor
Maura Mullen ...................Managing Editor

58624

## ENVIRONMENT REPORT
National Press Building, Ste. 1079
Washington, DC 20045
Telephone: (202) 393-0031
FAX: (202) 393-1732
Year Established: 1969
Pub. Frequency: bi-w.
Page Size: standard
Subscrip. Rate: $650/yr.
Materials: 01,10,15
Print Process: offset
**Owner(s):**
Trends Publishing, Inc.
1079 National Press Building
Washington, DC 20045
Telephone: (202) 393-0031
Ownership %: 100
**Editorial:**
Arthur Kranish ...................Editor

67190

## ENVIRONMENT TODAY
1483 Chain Bridge Rd.
Ste. 202
Mc Lean, VA 22101
Telephone: (703) 448-0322
FAX: (703) 448-0270
Year Established: 1989
Pub. Frequency: m.
Page Size: tabloid
Subscrip. Rate: $56/yr.
Circulation: 56,000
Circulation Type: controlled & paid
**Owner(s):**
Enterprise Communications
1483 Chain Bridge Rd
Ste. 202
Mc Lean, VA 22101
Telephone: (703) 448-0322
Ownership %: 100
**Management:**
Douglas Field ...................President
Robert Hickoxs ...................Publisher
**Editorial:**
Paul Harris ...................Editor

67271

## GARBAGE: THE INDEPENDENT ENVIRONMENTAL QUARTERLY
2 Main St.
Gloucester, MA 01930
Telephone: (508) 283-3200
FAX: (508) 283-4629
Year Established: 1989
Pub. Frequency: q.
Page Size: standard
Subscrip. Rate: $9.95 newsstand; $39/yr.
Materials: 01,02,06,10,17,19,20,25,28,30
Circulation: 50,000
Circulation Type: paid
**Owner(s):**
Dovetale Publishers
2 Main St.
Gloucester, MA 01930
Telephone: (508) 283-3200
Ownership %: 100
**Management:**
Patricia Poore ...................President
Patricia Poore ...................Publisher
Ellen Higgins ...................Circulation Manager
**Editorial:**
Bill Breen ...................Managing Editor

**Desc.:** Covers diverse environmental topics, offering science, corporate environmentalism, news features. Often irreverent and contrary to conventional environmental thinking.

25792

## IDAHO WILDLIFE
600 S. Walnut St.
Boise, ID 83712-0025
Telephone: (208) 334-3746
FAX: (208) 334-2148
Mailing Address:
P.O. Box 25
Boise, ID 83707-0025
Year Established: 1978
Pub. Frequency: bi-m.
Page Size: 4 color photos/art
Subscrip. Rate: $12.95/yr.; $24.95/2 yrs.
Materials: 06,10,21
Freelance Pay: varies
Circulation: 24,000
Circulation Type: paid
**Owner(s):**
State Wildlife Agency, Idaho Dept. Fish and Game
P.O. Box 25
Boise, ID 83707-0025
Telephone: (208) 334-3700
Ownership %: 100
**Management:**
Linn French ...................Circulation Manager
**Editorial:**
Diane M. Ronayne ...................Editor
Diane M. Ronayne ...................Art Director
**Desc.:** Wildlife and ecology articles of interest to general public.
**Readers:** State and federal wildlife employees & general public, 1/2 readers out-of-state.

23069

## ILLINOIS WILDLIFE FEDERATION
123 S. Chicago St.
Rossville, IL 60963
Telephone: (217) 748-6365
FAX: (217) 748-6040
Year Established: 1936
Pub. Frequency: s-m.
Page Size: tabloid
Subscrip. Rate: $10/yr.
Print Process: web offset
Circulation: 17,000
Circulation Type: paid
**Owner(s):**
Illinois Wildlife Federation
123 S. Chicago St.
Rossville, IL 60963
Telephone: (217) 748-6365
Ownership %: 100
**Management:**
John Skinner ...................President
**Editorial:**
Thomas Mills ...................Editor
**Desc.:** Deals with conserving our national resources, legislation dealing with conservation. It's the voice of outdoor Illinois sportsmen and conservationists.
**Readers:** Associate, contributing and sportsmen conservationists.

23070

## IOWA CONSERVATIONIST
Wallace State Office Bldg.
Des Moines, IA 50319-0034
Telephone: (515) 281-6159
FAX: (515) 281-8895
Year Established: 1942
Pub. Frequency: bi-m.
Page Size: standard
Subscrip. Rate: $9.97/yr.; $14.97/2 yrs.; $19.97/3 yrs.
Circulation: 60,000
Circulation Type: paid
**Owner(s):**
State of Iowa, Dept. of Natural Resources
Ownership %: 100

**Management:**
Beth Chip ....................Circulation Manager
**Editorial:**
Julie Sparks ......................Executive Editor
Tami Foster ........................Managing Editor
**Desc.:** Features, articles and news concerning wildlife conservation, outdoor activities and environmental issues. Article length varies greatly.
**Readers:** Fishermen, hunters, campers, school children, vacationers, i.e. camping, traveling, picnicking; people interested in the outdoors and environmental issues.

69340

**KOKOPELLI NOTES**
P.O. Box 8186
Asheville, NC 28814
Telephone: (704) 683-4844
Year Established: 1990
Pub. Frequency: 4/yr.
Page Size: standard
Subscrip. Rate: $16/yr.
Materials: 02,06,10,15,19,20,21,23,28,32,33
Print Process: offset
Circulation: 800
Circulation Type: paid
**Owner(s):**
Kokopelli Council, Inc.
P.O. Box 8186
Asheville, NC 28814
Telephone: (704) 683-4844
Ownership %: 100
**Editorial:**
Patrick Clark ..................................Editor
Linai Deyo ..........................Associate Editor

69321

**NEW CRUCIBLE**
RR 1 Box 76
Stark, KS 66775-9802
Year Established: 1964
Pub. Frequency: irreg.
Page Size: standard
Subscrip. Rate: $24/yr.
Materials: 02,05,06,10,19,20,21,32,33
Circulation: 2,500
Circulation Type: paid
**Owner(s):**
De Young Press
RR 1 Box 76
Stark, KS 66775-9802
Ownership %: 100
**Editorial:**
Garry De Young ...............................Editor
**Desc.:** Deals with the total human environment including all ecological factors impacting upon man such as political, psychological, religious, and physical.

66676

**NORTHWEST PARKS & WILDLIFE**
1525 12th St.
Florence, OR 97439-0130
Telephone: (503) 997-8401
FAX: (503) 997-1124
Mailing Address:
P.O. Box 18000
Florence, OR 97439-0130
Year Established: 1991
Pub. Frequency: bi-m.
Page Size: standard
Subscrip. Rate: $2.95 newsstand;
$16.95/yr.
Materials: 02,05,06,10,15,21,25,28
Freelance Pay: $75-$350/article
Circulation: 25,000
Circulation Type: paid
**Owner(s):**
Educational Publications Foundation
P.O. Box 18000
Florence, OR 97439-0130
Telephone: (503) 997-8401
FAX: (503) 997-1124
Ownership %: 100

**Management:**
Robert Spooner ..............................Publisher
Alicia Spooner ................................Publisher
**Editorial:**
Dave Peden ......................................Editor
Judy Fleagle .....................Managing Editor
Alicia Spooner ..............Creative Director
**Desc.:** Primarily devoted to stories about parks, wilderness areas, backroads, museums, flora and people of the Pacific Northwest.
**Readers:** 40's and up, middle class and higher, well educated, like to travel and are interested in the environment.
**Deadline:** story-3-1/2 mos.

25795

**OUTDOOR AMERICA**
1401 Wilson Blvd., Level B
Arlington, VA 22209
Telephone: (703) 528-1818
FAX: (703) 528-1836
Year Established: 1922
Pub. Frequency: q.
Page Size: standard
Subscrip. Rate: $20/yr.
Materials: 02,05,06,20,21,32,33
Freelance Pay: $.20/wd.
Print Process: web offset
Circulation: 58,000
Circulation Type: paid
**Owner(s):**
Izaak Walton League of America, Inc.
1401 Wilson Blvd., Level B
Arlington, VA 22209
Telephone: (703) 528-1818
Ownership %: 100
**Editorial:**
Michael E. Diegel ............................Editor
**Desc.:** Edited for members of the Izaak Walton League of America and those interested and active in environmental issues, the out of doors and the conservation of our natural resources.
**Readers:** Outdoor enthusiasts, sportsmen and conservationists.

25706

**SIERRA**
730 Polk St.
San Francisco, CA 94109
Telephone: (415) 923-5656
Year Established: 1893
Pub. Frequency: bi-m.
Page Size: standard
Subscrip. Rate: $15/yr.; $26/2 yrs.
Materials: 32,33
Freelance Pay: $500-$2500
Circulation: 500,000
Circulation Type: controlled
**Owner(s):**
Sierra Club
730 Polk St.
San Francisco, CA 94109
Telephone: (415) 776-2211
Ownership %: 100
**Management:**
Philip Berry ...................................President
Carole Pisarczyk ...........................Publisher
**Editorial:**
Jonathan F. King ................Editor in Chief
Joan Hamilton .......................Senior Editor
Reed McManus ....................Senior Editor
Marc Lecard .......................Managing Editor
Martha Geering ......................Art Director
Paul Rander ......................Associate Editor
Mark Mardon ....................Associate Editor
Annie Stine ...........................Deputy Editor
Lacey Tuttle ..................Production Director

**Desc.:** Published for members and friends of the Sierra Club, which works in the United States and in other countries to restore the quality of the natural environment and to maintain the integrity of ecosystems. Includes book reviews of about 1,000 to 3,000 words. Manuscripts and photos are purchased from freelance writers and photographers as needed. Publicity materials are not used. Departments include: Features, News, Commentary, books, club news, letters.
**Readers:** Members of the Sierra Club plus subscribers.

26506

**TEXAS PARKS & WILDLIFE**
4200 Smith School Rd.
Austin, TX 78744
Telephone: (512) 707-1833
FAX: (512) 707-1913
Year Established: 1944
Pub. Frequency: m.
Page Size: tabloid
Subscrip. Rate: $12.95/yr.
Circulation: 200,000
Circulation Type: paid
**Owner(s):**
Texas Parks and Wildlife Department
4200 Smith School Rd.
Austin, TX 78744
Telephone: (512) 389-4800
**Editorial:**
Andy Samson .....................Executive Editor
David Baxter ...................................Editor
Mary-Love Bigony .............Associate Editor
**Desc.:** By-line articles on conservation, game, and endangered wildlife species. No fiction. Must be informative and focus on Texas. Articles run from 300-3,250 words. Articles use pictures that tie in with copy. Photo spreads run up to 6 pages.
**Readers:** Over 90 percent in Texas.

58563

**URBAN LAND**
625 Indiana Ave., N.W.
Washington, DC 20004-2930
Telephone: (202) 624-7000
FAX: (202) 624-7140
Year Established: 1941
Pub. Frequency: m.
Page Size: standard
Subscrip. Rate: membership
Materials: 02,06,07
Freelance Pay: $500-$1500/article
Print Process: web offset
Circulation: 14,000
Circulation Type: controlled
**Owner(s):**
ULI-Urban Land Institute, The
625 Indiana Ave., N.W.
Washington, DC 20004
Telephone: (204) 624-7000
Ownership %: 100
**Management:**
Karen Shaar ..................................Manager
Christine Schuyler .........................Manager
**Editorial:**
Libby Howland ................................Editor
Julie Stern ........................Associate Editor
**Desc.:** Provides members of Urban Land Institute with information on current trends. Also carries pictures in land use and development.
**Readers:** Members & associates of the Urban Land Institute.

67068

**WILDLIFE CONSERVATION**
2300 Southern Blvd.
Bronx, NY 10460
Telephone: (718) 220-5121
FAX: (718) 584-2625
Year Established: 1895
Pub. Frequency: bi-m.

Page Size: standard
Subscrip. Rate: $2.95 newsstand;
$13.95/yr.; $24.50/2 yrs.
Circulation: 178,319
Circulation Type: paid
**Owner(s):**
Wildlife Conservation
2300 Southern Blvd.
Bronx, NY 10460
Telephone: (718) 220-5121
Ownership %: 100
**Editorial:**
Joan Downs .............................Editor in Chief

67238

**ZOO LIFE**
4676 Admiralty Way, Ste. 300
Marina Del Rey, CA 90292
Telephone: (310) 574-5325
FAX: (310) 574-5326
Year Established: 1989
Pub. Frequency: bi-m.
Page Size: standard
Subscrip. Rate: $3.95 newsstand;
$19.95/yr.
Freelance Pay: $.50/wd. for editorial
Print Process: web offset
Circulation: 250,000
Circulation Type: free & paid
**Owner(s):**
Baio & Company Publishing N.A., Inc.
4676 Admiralty Way
Marina Del Rey, CA 90202
Telephone: (310) 574-5325
FAX: (310) 574-5326
Ownership %: 100
**Management:**
Louis Baio, Sr. ...............................Publisher
Bob Heck ......................Managing Director
**Editorial:**
Mary Batten ....................................Editor
**Desc.:** Informs, entertains and educates readers about national and international efforts of zoos, aquariums and wild animal parks to preserve the world's wildlife, especially threatened and endangered species.

## Group 627-Ethnic

26164

**EBONY**
820 S. Michigan Ave.
Chicago, IL 60605
Telephone: (312) 322-9200
FAX: (312) 322-9375
Year Established: 1945
Pub. Frequency: m.
Page Size: standard
Subscrip. Rate: $16/yr.
Freelance Pay: negotiable
Circulation: 1,992,000
Circulation Type: paid
**Owner(s):**
Johnson Publishing Co.
820 S. Michigan Ave.
Chicago, IL 60605
Telephone: (312) 322-9200
Ownership %: 100
**Bureau(s):**
Johnson Publishing Co. (Washington Bureau)
1750 Pennsylvania Ave., N.W.
Washington, DC 20006
Telephone: (202) 393-5860
Contact: Simeon Booker, Bureau Chief

Johnson Publishing Co. (New York Bureau)
1270 Ave. of The Americas
New York, NY 10020
Telephone: (212) 586-2911
Contact: Jeff Burns

**Materials Accepted/Included:** 01-Business news 02-By-line articles 03-Fashion news 04-Food news 05-Freelance copy 06-Letters to editor 07-Real estate news 08-Sports news 09-Travel news 10-Book rev. 11-Movie rev. 12-Music rev. 13-TV rev. 14-Theater rev. 15-Coming events 16-Obituaries 17-Question & answer 18-Social announcements 19-Artwork 20-Cartoons 21-Photos 22-TV listings 23-Audio rec. 24-Video rec. 25-Books 26-Films/film clips 27-Personnel news 28-Press releases 29-New product news/photos 30-Trade lit. 31-Contracts awarded 32-Display adv. 33-Classified adv.

6-37

Johnson Publishing Co. (Los Angeles
  Bureau)
3600 Wilshire Blvd.
Los Angeles, CA 90010
Telephone: (310) 386-5200
Contact: Aldore Collier, Editor
**Management:**
John H. Johnson ..............................Publisher
Dennis Boston ..................Advertising Manager
**Editorial:**
Lerone Bennett, Jr. ..................Executive Editor
John H. Johnson ..................................Editor
Hans J. Massaquoi ..................Managing Editor
Basil Phillips ........................Photography Editor
**Desc.:** Black-oriented picture magazine
  covering features of general interest.
**Readers:** A cross section of the U.S.

66234

**HISPANIC USA**
230 N. Michigan Ave.
Suite 300
Chicago, IL 60601
Telephone: (312) 977-1975
Year Established: 1984
Pub. Frequency: m.
Page Size: standard
Subscrip. Rate: $24/yr.
Materials: 01,10,32,33
Print Process: web offset
Circulation: 119,000
Circulation Type: controlled & paid
**Owner(s):**
Jack Terrazas
230 N. Michigan Ave.
Chicago, IL 60601
Telephone: (312) 977-1975
FAX: (312) 977-0097
Ownership %: 100
**Management:**
Joe Martin ...............................................Manager
**Editorial:**
Diane Martinez .........................................Editor
**Readers:** Hispanic business personnel.

69674

**INDIA CURRENTS**
P.O. Box 21285
San Jose, CA 95151
Telephone: (408) 274-6966
FAX: (408) 274-2733
Year Established: 1987
Pub. Frequency: m.
Subscrip. Rate: $19.95/yr.
Materials: 01,06,09,10,11,12,15,20,21,32,33
Circulation: 30,000
Circulation Type: paid
**Owner(s):**
India Currents
P.O. Box 21285
San Jose, CA 95151
Telephone: (408) 274-6966
Ownership %: 100
**Management:**
Ashok Jethanandani ...........................Publisher
Vandana Kumar .................Circulation Manager
**Editorial:**
Arvind Kumar .........................................Editor
**Desc.:** Informs the public of the FDA's
  activities on behalf of
  consumers. Covers Indian events, films,
  music, books, and travel.
**Deadline:** story-1st of mo.; news-1st of
  mo.; photo-1st of mo.; ads-20th of mo.

69675

**INTERRACE PUBLICATIONS**
P.O. Box 12048
Atlanta, GA 30355-2048
Telephone: (404) 364-9690
FAX: (404) 365-9965
Year Established: 1989
Pub. Frequency: bi-m.
Page Size: standard
Subscrip. Rate: $3.50/issue; $24/yr.
Materials: 02,05,06,08,10,11,12,13,14,15,
  16,17,19,20,21,25,27,28,2932,33

Freelance Pay: $10-75
Print Process: web
Circulation: 25,000
Circulation Type: paid
**Owner(s):**
Interrace
P.O. Box 12048
Atlanta, GA 30355
Telephone: (404) 364-9690
FAX: (404) 364-9965
Ownership %: 100
**Editorial:**
Candy Mills ...............................................Editor
**Desc.:** Covers interracial couples and
  families, biracial and multiracial people,
  transracial adoption, and race relations.
**Readers:** All ethnicities and races - black,
  white, Asian, Latins, Native Americans

69676

**LIFESTYLE/USA**
126 Library Ln.
Mamaroneck, NY 10543
Telephone: (914) 381-4740
Year Established: 1991
Pub. Frequency: q.
Page Size: standard
Subscrip. Rate: $2.95 newsstand;
  $14.97/yr.
Circulation: 50,000
Circulation Type: paid
**Owner(s):**
Meadow Publications, Inc.
126 Library Ln.
Mamaroneck, NY 10543
Telephone: (914) 381-4740
Ownership %: 100
**Management:**
Susan Meadow .....................................Publisher
Janet Fonte ........................Associate Publisher
**Editorial:**
Aiko Masazumi .........................Editor in Chief
Eric Meadow ......................Advertising Director
**Desc.:** Written in Japanese, covers
  fashion, travel, American lifestyles and
  culture for Japanese residents in the
  greater New York metropolitan area.

52581

**MIAMI MENSUAL**
104 S. Crandon Blvd. #424
Key Biscayne, FL 33149
Telephone: (305) 444-5678
FAX: (305) 854-2065
Year Established: 1980
Pub. Frequency: m.
Page Size: standard
Subscrip. Rate: $16/yr.
Materials: 02,03,04,05,06,07,08,09,10,11,
  12,13,18,32
Circulation: 25,000
Circulation Type: controlled & paid
**Owner(s):**
Frank & Ana Soler
104 S. Crandon Blvd.
Ste. 424
Key Biscayne, FL 33149
Telephone: (305) 444-5678
FAX: (305) 361-9707
Ownership %: 100
**Management:**
Frank Soler ..........................................Publisher
Ana Soler ...............................General Manager
**Editorial:**
Frank Soler ...............................Editor in Chief
**Desc.:** The Spanish-language monthly for
  upscale, sophisticated Hispanics in
  South Florida.
**Readers:** Upscale.
**Deadline:** story-8 wks. prior to pub. date;
  ads-6 wks. prior to pub. date

69677

**NOVEDADES**
1271 Soto St., Ste. 203-M
Los Angeles, CA 90023
Telephone: (213) 881-6515
FAX: (213) 881-6524
Year Established: 1992
Pub. Frequency: Thu.
Page Size: tabloid
Subscrip. Rate: free
Materials: 01,03,04,06,07,08,09,11,12,13,
  14,15,16,17,18,19,20,21,22,23,24,25,26,
  27,28,29,30,31,32,33
Print Process: web
Circulation: 100,000
Circulation Type: controlled & free
**Owner(s):**
Four Star Productions
1241 Soto St., Ste. 203-M
Los Angeles, CA 90023
Telephone: (213) 881-6515
FAX: (213) 881-6524
Ownership %: 100
**Management:**
John Di Carlo ......................................Publisher
**Editorial:**
Angel Morales .........................................Editor
**Desc.:** Written in Spanish, covers current
  events, food, automobiles,
  entertainment, celebrities, health and
  beauty, sports and more.
**Deadline:** story-Tue., 4:00 pm; news-Tue.,
  4:00 pm; photo-Tue., 4:00 pm; ads-Tue.,
  4:00 pm

69678

**OCA IMAGE**
1001 Connecticut Ave., N.W. Ste. 707
Washington, DC 20036
Telephone: (202) 223-5500
FAX: (202) 296-0540
Year Established: 1980
Pub. Frequency: q.
Page Size: standard
Subscrip. Rate: membership; $25/yr.
Circulation: 5,000
Circulation Type: controlled
**Owner(s):**
Organization of Chinese Americans
1001 Connecticut Ave., N.W.
Ste. 707
Washington, DC 20036
Telephone: (202) 223-5500
Ownership %: 100
**Editorial:**
Daphne Kwok ...........................................Editor

69679

**SERB WORLD U.S.A.**
415 E. Mabel
Tucson, AZ 85705
Telephone: (602) 624-4887
Year Established: 1979
Pub. Frequency: bi-m.
Page Size: 8 1/2 x 11
Subscrip. Rate: $19.50/yr.
Materials: 01,02,05,06,08,10,11,12,18,32,33
Print Process: offset
Circulation: 4,000
Circulation Type: paid
**Owner(s):**
Serb World USA, Inc.
415 E. Mabel
Tucson, AZ 85705
Telephone: (602) 624-4887
Ownership %: 100
**Editorial:**
Mary Nicklanovich Hart ...........................Editor
**Desc.:** Covers Serbian-American cultural
  and historical interests.
**Deadline:** story-2 wks. prior to pub. date;
  news-2 wks.; photo-2 wks.; ads-2 wks.

69681

**UPSCALE**
594 Fielding Ln.
Atlanta, GA 30310
Telephone: (404) 758-7467
FAX: (404) 752-7655
Year Established: 1989
Pub. Frequency: 9/yr.
Page Size: standard
Subscrip. Rate: $9.95/yr.
Print Process: offset
Circulation: 237,720
Circulation Type: paid
**Owner(s):**
Upscale Communications, Inc.
594 Fielding Ln.
Atlanta, GA 30310
Telephone: (800) 877-2253
Ownership %: 100
**Management:**
Bernard Bronner ...............................Publisher
**Editorial:**
Sheila Bronner ...........................Editor in Chief

68952

**US IMMIGRATION**
951 S. Oxford, No. 109
Los Angeles, CA 90006
Telephone: (213) 732-3477
FAX: (213) 732-3477
Year Established: 1991
Pub. Frequency: q.
Page Size: 8 1/2" X 10 1/4"
Subscrip. Rate: $29.99/yr.
Materials: 01,02,03,04,05,06,07,08,09,10,
  11,12,13,14,15,16,17,18,19,20,21,22,23,
  24,25,26,27,28,29,30,31,32,33
Freelance Pay: $.20-$.50
Print Process: web
Circulation: 120,000
Circulation Type: controlled & paid
**Owner(s):**
Publishing & Business Consultants
951 S. Oxford, No. 109
Los Angeles, CA 90006
Telephone: (213) 732-3477
Ownership %: 100
**Editorial:**
Andeson Napoleon Atia ...........................Editor
**Desc.:** Provides general information on
  visas and other immigration topics
  affecting foreign nationals in the US.
**Deadline:** story-2 wks. prior to pub. date;
  news-2 wks. prior; photo-2 wks. prior;
  ads-90 days prior

**Group 628-Fiction -
Adventure, Mystery
Romance, Science Fiction**

69262

**ABORIGINAL SCIENCE FICTION**
P.O. Box 2449
Woburn, MA 01888-0849
Year Established: 1986
Pub. Frequency: q.
Subscrip. Rate: $18/yr. US; $21/yr. foreign
Circulation: 12,000
Circulation Type: paid
**Owner(s):**
Second Rennaisance Foundation, Inc.
P.O. Box 2449
Woburn, MA 01888-0849
Ownership %: 100
**Editorial:**
Charles C. Ryan .......................................Editor
Mary Ryan ........................................Advertising
**Desc.:** Publishes original science fiction
  short stories and poetry, developments
  in science, and news of the science
  fiction film industry, including
  forthcoming films.

**Materials Accepted/Included:** 01-Business news 02-By-line articles 03-Fashion news 04-Food news 05-Freelance copy 06-Letters to editor 07-Real estate news 08-Sports news 09-Travel news 10-Book rev. 11-Movie rev. 12-Music rev. 13-TV rev. 14-Theater rev. 15-Coming events 16-Obituaries 17-Question & answer 18-Social announcements 19-Artwork 20-Cartoons 21-Photos 22-TV listings 23-Audio rec. 24-Video rec. 25-Books 26-Films/film clips 27-Personnel news 28-Press releases 29-New product news/photos 30-Trade lit. 31-Contracts awarded 32-Display adv. 33-Classified adv.

## AFFAIRE DE COEUR
68832
3996 Oak Hill Rd.
Oakland, CA 94605-4931
Telephone: (510) 569-5675
FAX: (510) 632-8868
Year Established: 1979
Pub. Frequency: m.
Page Size: 01,02,05,06,09,10,16,18,19,21,
   30,32,33
Subscrip. Rate: $2.75 newsstand; $30/yr.
Circulation: 117,000
Circulation Type: paid
**Owner(s):**
Keenan-Shead, Inc.
3996 Oak Hill Rd.
Oakland, CA 94605-4931
Telephone: (510) 569-5675
FAX: (510) 632-8868
Ownership %: 100
**Editorial:**
Louise Snead ..........................................Editor
**Desc.:** Features articles on romance and
   mystery, including fiction and some non-
   fiction.

## ANALOG SCIENCE FICTION & FACT
26096
1540 Broadway
New York, NY 10036
Telephone: (212) 354-6500
Year Established: 1930
Pub. Frequency: 13/yr.
Page Size: pocket
Subscrip. Rate: 2.95 newsstand;
   $34.95/yr.
Materials: 05,06,32,33
Freelance Pay: $.05-$.08/wd.
Circulation: 83,000
Circulation Type: paid
**Owner(s):**
Dell Magazines Fiction Group
1540 Broadway
New York, NY 10036
Telephone: (212) 354-6500
Ownership %: 100
**Management:**
Chris Haas-Heye ..........................President
Chris Haas-Heye ..........................Publisher
Fred Sabloff ......................Advertising Manager
**Editorial:**
Stanley Schmidt ..............................Editor
Tina Lee ................................Managing Editor
Terri Czeczko ............................Art Director
Tom Easton ..................Book Review Editor
**Desc.:** Science fiction and science fact.
**Readers:** Ages from 10 to 90, upper-level
   intelligence.

## ASIMOV'S SCIENCE FICTION
69265
1540 Broadway
New York, NY 10036
Telephone: (212) 782-8532
Year Established: 1977
Pub. Frequency: 13/yr.
Subscrip. Rate: $34.97/yr.; $2.95
   newsstand U.S.; $3.75 Can.
Materials: 05,06,20,25,28,29,30,
Freelance Pay: $.05-.08/word
Circulation: 90,000
Circulation Type: paid
**Owner(s):**
Dell Magazines
1540 Broadway
New York, NY 10036
Telephone: (212) 782-8532
Ownership %: 100
**Editorial:**
Gardner Dozois ..........................Editor

## FICTION INTERNATIONAL
69497
San Diego University
San Diego, CA 92182
Telephone: (619) 594-6220

Year Established: 1973
Pub. Frequency: s-a.
Page Size: standard
Subscrip. Rate: $14/yr. individuals; $28/yr.
   institutions
Materials: 32
Circulation: 1,000
Circulation Type: paid
**Owner(s):**
San Diego State University Press
San Diego State University
San Diego, CA 92182
Telephone: (619) 594-6220
Ownership %: 100
**Editorial:**
Harold Jaffe ................................Editor
Harry Polkinhorn ..................Managing Editor
**Desc.:** Postmodern fiction, includes a
   thematic focus in each issue.
**Deadline:** ads-Dec. 1 for spring; May 1 for
   fall

## MAGAZINE OF FANTASY & SCIENCE FICTION, THE
25878
143 Cream Hill Rd.
West Cornwall, CT 06796
Telephone: (203) 672-6376
FAX: (203) 672-2643
Year Established: 1949
Pub. Frequency: m.
Page Size: digest
Subscrip. Rate: $2.75 newsstand; $26/yr.
Freelance Pay: negotiable
Circulation: 63,500
Circulation Type: paid
**Owner(s):**
Mercury Press, Inc.
143 Cream Hill Rd.
West Cornwall, CT 06796
Telephone: (203) 672-6376
FAX: (203) 672-2643
Ownership %: 100
**Bureau(s):**
Editorial Office
P.O. Box 11526
Eugene, OR 97440
Telephone: (503) 935-0335
Contact: Kristine K. Rusch
**Management:**
Edward L. Ferman ..........................Publisher
**Editorial:**
Kristine K. Rusch ..........................Editor
Audrey Ferman ..................Assistant Publisher
O. S. Card ......................Book Review Editor
Bruce Sterling ..............................Columnist
Gregory Benford ..........................Columnist
Harlan Ellison ..............................Film Editor
**Desc.:** High quality fantasy and science
   fiction short stories and novelettes.
   Departments include: Book Reviews,
   Film Reviews, Science Column.
**Readers:** Males-67%; females-33%; 86%
   college educated.

## MYSTERY READERS JOURNAL
69263
P.O. Box 8116
Berkeley, CA 94707-8116
Telephone: (510) 339-2800
FAX: (510) 339-8309
Year Established: 1985
Pub. Frequency: q.
Subscrip. Rate: $22.50/yr. individuals;
   $35/yr. libraries
Materials: 06,10,15,16
Print Process: offset
Circulation: 1,500
Circulation Type: paid
**Owner(s):**
Mystery Readers International
P.O. Box 8116
Berkeley, CA 94707-8116
Telephone: (510) 339-2800
Ownership %: 100

**Editorial:**
Janet A. Rudolph ..........................Editor
**Desc.:** Each issue contains articles,
   interviews, and reviews on a specific
   theme, as well as special columns, a
   calendar of events and other mystery-
   related material.

## PULPHOUSE-A FICTION MAGAZINE
69268
P.O. Box 1227
Eugene, OR 97440-1227
Year Established: 1991
Pub. Frequency: m.
Page Size: standard
Subscrip. Rate: $3.95 newsstand; $39/yr.
Materials: 06,10,20,21,25,32
Print Process: web offset
Circulation: 10,000
Circulation Type: paid
**Owner(s):**
Pulphouse Publishing, Inc.
P.O. Box 1227
Eugene, OR 97440
Telephone: (503) 935-3247
FAX: (503) 935-0335
Ownership %: 100
**Management:**
Dean Smith ..............................Publisher
**Editorial:**
Jonathan Bond ..........................Editor
**Desc.:** Publishes original science fiction,
   fantasy and horror, mystery,
   mainstream with nonfiction and
   critical articles.

## SCIENCE FICTION EYE
69267
P.O. Box 18539
Asheville, NC 28814
Year Established: 1987
Pub. Frequency: 3/yr.
Page Size: 8" X 10 1/2"
Subscrip. Rate: $5 copy; $12.50/3 issues
   US & Canada; $25/3 issues foreign
Materials: 02,06,10,19,21
Freelance Pay: payment in copies
Print Process: offset
Circulation: 3,000
Circulation Type: free
**Owner(s):**
SF Eye
P.O. Box 18539
Asheville, NC 28814
Telephone: (704) 684-5779
Ownership %: 100
**Editorial:**
Stephen P. Brown ..........................Editor
**Desc.:** Critical articles, commentary and
   interviews in the science fiction field.

## TRUE CONFESSIONS
26630
233 Park Ave., S.
New York, NY 10003
Telephone: (212) 979-4800
FAX: (212) 979-7507
Year Established: 1922
Pub. Frequency: m.
Page Size: standard
Subscrip. Rate: $14.95/yr.
Freelance Pay: $.05/wd.
Circulation: 200,000
Circulation Type: paid
**Owner(s):**
Sterling MacFadden Partnership
233 Park Ave., S.
New York, NY 10003
Telephone: (212) 979-4800
Ownership %: 100
**Management:**
Michael Boylan ..........................President
Barbara H. Marks ..........................Publisher
**Editorial:**
Peter Callahan ..................Editor in Chief
Patricia Vitucci ..........................Editor

Frances M. Adrian ..........................Art Director
Kim Fryer ................................Associate Editor
Janet Tanke ..................New Products Editor
Constance Brukin ..........................Photo
**Readers:** Young (median age 32 years)
   Middle-American married women.

## TRUE DETECTIVE
25946
460 W. 34th St.
New York, NY 10001
Telephone: (212) 947-6500
FAX: (212) 947-6727
Year Established: 1924
Pub. Frequency: 7/yr.
Page Size: standard
Subscrip. Rate: $12/yr.
Freelance Pay: $250/15-30 pgs.
Circulation: 250,000
Circulation Type: paid
**Owner(s):**
RGH Publishing Corp.
460 W. 34th St.
New York, NY 10001
Telephone: (212) 947-6500
Ownership %: 100
**Management:**
J. Rosenfield ..............................President
J. Rosenfield ..............................Publisher
J. Burriesci ..................Advertising Manager
**Editorial:**
Rose Mandelsberg ..................Editor in Chief
Christofer Pierson ..................Managing Editor
Ben Harvey ................................Art Editor
Julia Lawrence ..................Editorial Assistant
**Desc.:** Covers current crime cases which
   have strong elements of police action or
   investigation. Stories written from police
   or investigator's view point preferred, but
   occasional offtrail treatment permitted
   upon query. Writers advised to query
   first, promptly upon discovery of crime,
   giving facts as known and probable
   course of events to come. All stories
   must be thoroughly documented with
   newsclips or other authorative sources.

## TRUE STORY
26631
233 Park Ave., S.
New York, NY 10003
Telephone: (212) 979-4800
FAX: (212) 979-7342
Year Established: 1919
Pub. Frequency: m.
Page Size: standard
Subscrip. Rate: $14.95/yr.
Freelance Pay: $.05/wd. & up
Circulation: 750,000
Circulation Type: paid
**Owner(s):**
Sterling MacFadden Partnership
233 Park Ave., S.
New York, NY 10003
Telephone: (212) 979-4800
Ownership %: 100
**Bureau(s):**
MacFadden Holding, Inc.
233 Park Ave., S.
New York, NY 10003
Telephone: (212) 979-4800
Contact: Sue Weiner, Editor in Chief
**Management:**
Peter Callahan ..........................Owner
Barbara Grufferman ..........................Publisher
**Editorial:**
Lisa Rabidoux ..........................Editor
Nancy Mack ................................Art Director
Rose Bernstein ..................Associate Editor
Constance Brukin ..........................Photo

**Materials Accepted/Included:** 01-Business news 02-By-line articles 03-Fashion news 04-Food news 05-Freelance copy 06-Letters to editor 07-Real estate news 08-Sports news 09-Travel news
10-Book rev. 11-Movie rev. 12-Music rev. 13-TV rev. 14-Theater rev. 15-Coming events 16-Obituaries 17-Question & answer 18-Social announcements 19-Artwork 20-Cartoons 21-Photos 22-TV listings
23-Audio rec. 24-Video rec. 25-Books 26-Films/film clips 27-Personnel news 28-Press releases 29-New product news/photos 30-Trade lit. 31-Contracts awarded 32-Display adv. 33-Classified adv.

6-39

**Desc.:** Stories should deal with the problems that most vitally interest young, Middle-American women. Should be written simply and movingly, told in the first person. Stories range from short-shorts, 1500-2000 words to longer pieces averaging 3000-8000 words.
**Readers:** Mostly young housewives; median age 31.

**WOOD** 69756
1716 Locust St.
Des Moines, IA 50336
Telephone: (515) 284-3000
Year Established: 1984
Pub. Frequency: 8/yr.
Subscrip. Rate: $4.95 issue; $22/yr.
Circulation: 650,000
Circulation Type: paid
**Owner(s):**
Meredith Corp.
1716 Locust St.
Des Moines, IA 50336
Telephone: (515) 284-3000
Ownership %: 100
**Management:**
Bill Reed .........................Publisher
**Editorial:**
Larry Clayton .........................Editor

## Group 630-Fishing & Hunting

**ALASKA OUTDOORS** 48203
200 Albrecht
Palmer, AK 99645
Telephone: (907) 746-3324
FAX: (907) 746-3324
Mailing Address:
P.O. Box 443
Palmer, AK 99645
Year Established: 1978
Pub. Frequency: m.
Page Size: standard
Subscrip. Rate: $2.95 newsstand; $23.95/yr.
Materials: 05,06,09,10,11,15,17,19,21,28, 29,32,33
Freelance Pay: $250
Print Process: offset
Circulation: 4,000
Circulation Type: paid
**Owner(s):**
Alaska Outdoor Development Corp.
P.O. Box 443
Palmer, AK 99695
Telephone: (907) 746-3324
FAX: (907) 743-3327
Ownership %: 100
**Management:**
Evan E. Swensen .........................Publisher
**Editorial:**
Evan Swensen .........................Editor

**Desc.:** The average American's desire to experience the "ultimate" in outdoor recreation has skyrocketed over the past several years. Overcrowded fishing and hunting areas, anti-hunting sentiments, and low stocks of fish and game have sportsmen looking for that "outdoor Nirvana," a place where the outdoors can be experienced in its purest form. ALASKA OUTDOORS MAGAZINE fulfills this desire by entertaining as well as informing the reader to the myriad possibilities of outdoor adventures available in the 49th state. Not only do we publish where-to-go and how-to articles dealing with fishing and hunting in the Last Frontier, but also run features on backpacking, camping, boating, whitewater rafting, gold panning, and other outdoor interests complemented by outstanding photography. Our columns solve the questions most people have concerning outdoor sports in Alaska, gear which has been tested under Alaska conditions, tips on how to solve a variety of wilderness problems, and local issues affecting both residents and non-residents alike. ALASKA OUTDOORS contains interesting and useful information, for those planning a trip to Alaska for the first time or those planning a return adventure. Our advertisers benefit from regional effectiveness as well as national exposure with the same ad. If it's in the outdoors and in Alaska, it's in ALASKA OUTDOORS!
**Readers:** An active, outdoor recreation-minded audience.

**AMERICAN FIELD** 25773
542 S. Dearborn St.
Chicago, IL 60605
Telephone: (312) 663-9797
FAX: (312) 663-5557
Year Established: 1874
Pub. Frequency: w.
Page Size: tabloid
Subscrip. Rate: $30/yr.
Circulation: 13,000
Circulation Type: paid
**Owner(s):**
American Field Publishing Co.
222 W. Adams St.
Chicago, IL 60606
Telephone: (312) 372-1383
Ownership %: 100
**Management:**
V. E. Brown .........................Publisher
Ronald Betley .........................Advertising Manager
S. H. Bysiek .........................Circulation Manager
**Editorial:**
Bernard J. Matthys .........................Managing Editor
Marie Murphy .........................Associate Editor
Bernard J. Matthys .........................New Product Editor
Bernard J. Matthys .........................News Editor
Bernard J. Matthys .........................Photo
**Desc.:** Uses factual articles about the breeding, rearing, development and training of hunting dogs, principally pointing breeds. Practical stories of upland game hunting, particularly quail, pheasant, ruffed grouse and prairie chicken. Departments include: Game and Shooting, Fish and Fishing, Kennel, Natural History, Field Dog Stud Book.
**Readers:** Practical sportsmen devoted to bird dogs.

**AMERICAN HUNTER** 25774
11250 Waples Mill Rd.
Fairfax, VA 22030-7400
Telephone: (703) 267-1300
Year Established: 1973
Pub. Frequency: m.
Page Size: standard
Subscrip. Rate: $2 issue; $25/yr.
Materials: 06,21,29,33
Freelance Pay: up to $400
Circulation: 1,300,000
Circulation Type: paid
**Owner(s):**
National Rifle Association
11250 Waples Mill Rd.
Fairfax, VA 22030
Telephone: (703) 267-1000
Ownership %: 100
**Management:**
E.G. "Red" Bell, Jr. .........................Publisher
David Crosby .........................Advertising Manager
**Editorial:**
Tom Fulgham .........................Editor
John Zent .........................Managing Editor
Diane Senesac .........................Advertising
**Desc.:** Interested in all aspects of sport hunting. Preferred article length 1,800-2,000 words.

**BASSIN'** 52628
15115 S. 76th E. Ave.
Bixby, OK 74008
Telephone: (918) 366-4441
FAX: (918) 366-4439
Year Established: 1976
Pub. Frequency: 8/yr.
Page Size: standard
Subscrip. Rate: $2.50, $2.95 newsstand, $23.95/12 issues
Materials: 02,06,09,17,20,21,23,24,25,28, 29,30,32,33
Freelance Pay: $275-$400
Print Process: web offset
Circulation: 250,000
Circulation Type: paid
**Owner(s):**
NatCom, Inc.
15115 S. 76th E. Ave.
Bixby, OK 74008
Telephone: (918) 366-4441
Ownership %: 100
**Editorial:**
Simon McCaffery .........................Managing Editor
**Desc.:** Editorial features include how-to on bass fishing: large mouth (emphasized), smallmouth, spotted, striped, and white.
**Readers:** 95% male, ages 35-49

**BASSMASTER MAGAZINE** 25777
5845 Carmichael Rd.
Montgomery, AL 36117
Telephone: (205) 272-9530
FAX: (205) 279-7148
Mailing Address:
P.O. Box 17900
Montgomery, AL 36141
Year Established: 1967
Pub. Frequency: 10/yr.
Page Size: standard
Subscrip. Rate: $16/yr.
Circulation: 535,720
Circulation Type: paid
**Owner(s):**
B.A.S.S., Inc.
5845 Carmichael Rd.
Montgomery, AL 36117
Telephone: (205) 272-9530
Ownership %: 100
**Management:**
Helen Sevier .........................Publisher
Ken Woodard .........................Advertising Manager
Martha Thornburgh .........................Circulation Manager
**Editorial:**
Dave Precht .........................Editor

Wayne Goble .........................Advertising Promotional Director
Scott Hughes .........................Associate Art Director
Anita Capouano .........................Marketing Manager
Gerald Crawford .........................Photographer
Bill Holmes .........................Production Director
Janeen Coker .........................Promotions Coordinator
Wayne Goble .........................Research Director
**Desc.:** Delivers quality editorial readers want in a full-color format. "How-to", "Where-to" and information on the latest bass tackle, boats and other fishing equipment are included in every issue to help keep subscribers up-to-date.

**BOW & ARROW HUNTING** 26375
34249 Camino Capistrano
Capistrano Beach, CA 92624
Telephone: (714) 493-2101
Mailing Address:
P.O. Box 2429
Capistrano Beach, CA 92624
Year Established: 1963
Pub. Frequency: bi-m.
Page Size: standard
Subscrip. Rate: $15/yr.
Freelance Pay: up to $300
Circulation: 98,000
Circulation Type: paid
**Owner(s):**
Gallant/Charger Publishing Co., Inc.
34249 Camino Capistrano
Capistrano Beach, CA 92624
Telephone: (714) 493-2101
Ownership %: 100
**Management:**
Jack Lewis .........................Publisher
Charles Rowe .........................Advertising Manager
**Editorial:**
Jack Lewis .........................Editor
Roger Combs .........................Editorial Director
Bob Arsenault .........................Director
Jim Dougherty .........................Field Editor
Emery J. Loiselle .........................Technical Editor
**Desc.:** Covers all phases of archery, bowhunting, news and new products. Departments include: Equipment News and Tips, Hunting Hints and New Products.
**Readers:** Archery enthusiasts, bowhunters.

**BOWHUNTER** 52607
6405 Flank Dr.
Harrisburg, PA 17112
Telephone: (717) 657-9555
FAX: (717) 657-9526
Mailing Address:
P.O. Box 8200
Harrisburg, PA 17105-8200
Year Established: 1971
Pub. Frequency: bi-m.
Page Size: standard
Subscrip. Rate: $24/yr.
Freelance Pay: $50-$500
Circulation: 184,203
Circulation Type: paid
**Owner(s):**
Cowles Magazines, Inc.
6405 Flank Drive
Harrisburg, PA 17112
Telephone: (717) 657-9555
Ownership %: 100
**Management:**
Dave Canfield .........................Publisher
Fred Wallace .........................Advertising Manager
David Kefford .........................General Manager
Don Clark .........................Public Relations Manager
**Editorial:**
M. R. James .........................Editor
Richard Cochran .........................Managing Editor
Lisa Wayand .........................Art Director
Jeffrey Waring .........................Associate Editor
**Desc.:** The magazine for, by and about the hunting archer.

**Materials Accepted/Included:** 01-Business news 02-By-line articles 03-Fashion news 04-Food news 05-Freelance copy 06-Letters to editor 07-Real estate news 08-Sports news 09-Travel news 10-Book rev. 11-Movie rev. 12-Music rev. 13-TV rev. 14-Theater rev. 15-Coming events 16-Obituaries 17-Question & answer 18-Social announcements 19-Artwork 20-Cartoons 21-Photos 22-TV listings 23-Audio rec. 24-Video rec. 25-Books 26-Films/film clips 27-Personnel news 28-Press releases 29-New product news/photos 30-Trade lit. 31-Contracts awarded 32-Display adv. 33-Classified adv.

Readers: Outdoorsmen.

**BOWHUNTING**                                        69137
6420 Wilshire Blvd.
Los Angeles, CA 90048-5515
Telephone: (213) 782-5515
FAX: (213) 782-2867
Pub. Frequency: 8/yr.
Subscrip. Rate: $3.25 copy; $13.95/yr.
Freelance Pay: $300-$400/feature
Circulation: 115000
Circulation Type: paid
Owner(s):
Petersen Publishing Co.
6420 Wilshire Blvd.
Los Angeles, CA 90048-5515
Telephone: (213) 854-2222
Ownership %: 100
Editorial:
Greg Tinsley ................................Editor

**BOWHUNTING WORLD**                          26363
601 Lakeshore Pkwy., Ste. 600
Minnetonka, MN 55305-5215
Telephone: (612) 476-2200
FAX: (612) 476-8065
Year Established: 1937
Pub. Frequency: 8/yr.
Page Size: standard
Subscrip. Rate: $2.95/copy US;
   $3.95/copy Canada; $20/yr.
Materials: 01,05,06,28,29,32,33
Freelance Pay: varies
Circulation: 200,000
Circulation Type: paid
Owner(s):
Ehlert Publishing Group, Inc.
601 Lakeshore Pkwy., Ste. 600
Minnetonka, MN 55305-5215
Telephone: (612) 476-2200
FAX: (612) 476-8065
Ownership %: 100
Editorial:
Mike Strandlund ............................Editor
Tom Kacheroski ....................Managing Editor
Stacey Marmolejo ..............Associate Publisher
Readers: All-season bowhunting
   sportsmen.

**CHASE, THE (A FULL CRY OF**          25728
   **HUNTING)**
1150 Industry Rd.
Lexington, KY 40505-3812
Telephone: (606) 254-4262
Mailing Address:
   P.O. Box 55090
   Lexington, KY 40555-5090
Year Established: 1920
Pub. Frequency: 11/yr.
Page Size: standard
Subscrip. Rate: $20/yr.
Materials: 06,15,16,27,32,33
Print Process: web offset
Circulation: 3,000
Circulation Type: paid
Owner(s):
The Chase
P.O. Box 5090
Lexington, KY 40505
Telephone: (606) 254-4262
Ownership %: 100
Editorial:
JoAnn Stone ........................News Editor
JoAnn Stone ..............................Photo
Desc.: Magazine is of interest to fox
   hunters.
Readers: Fox hunters.
Deadline: story-13th preceeding Mon. prior
   to pub. date; news-13th preceeding
   Mon.; ads-10th preceeding Mon.

**COONHOUND BLOODLINES**          25731
100 E. Kilgore Rd.
Kalamazoo, MI 49001
Telephone: (616) 343-9020
FAX: (616) 343-7037
Year Established: 1974
Pub. Frequency: m.
Page Size: standard
Subscrip. Rate: $2.50/copy; $14/yr. US;
   $25/yr. foreign
Freelance Pay: approx. $100 per sub.
Circulation: 23,000
Circulation Type: paid
Owner(s):
United Kennel Club, Inc.
100 E. Kilgore Rd.
Kalamazoo, MI 49001
Telephone: (616) 343-9020
Ownership %: 100
Management:
Fred T. Miller ........................President
Cindy Ftickley ..............Advertising Manager
Sondra McGee ................Editorial Production
                                   Manager
Sondra McGee ..........................Manager
Steve Fielder ................New Products Manager
Editorial:
Kerry Knudsen ............................Editor
Steve Fielder ............................Columnist
Lisa Watson ..............Production Assistant
Vicki Rand ................Special Features Editor
Desc.: Columns and stories on the six
   breeds of U.K.C. recognized
   coonhounds with news
   concerning coonhounds, product
   reviews, health and veterinary
   information, hunting experiences, etc.
   Stories on famous hounds,
   outstanding houndsmen, histories of
   breeds, etc. Reports from various
   coonhunter clubs and breed
   associations all over the U.S.
   and Canada with news of dog shows,
   hunts, club activities, etc. All contributors
   are given a by - line. A list of all
   upcoming U.K.C. licensed activities
   appears in each issue. Can and do use
   articles featuring information on puppy
   and dog care, training, showing,
   breeding, and other pertinent material
   concerning dogs. Feature Writers
   welcome.
Readers: Dog fanciers, owners, breeders,
   and hunters.

**FIELD & STREAM**                          26398
2 Park Ave.
New York, NY 10016
Telephone: (212) 779-5000
FAX: (212) 725-3836
Year Established: 1895
Pub. Frequency: m.
Page Size: standard
Subscrip. Rate: $2.50 newsstand;
   $15.94/yr.
Freelance Pay: $500/article
Circulation: 2,000,000
Circulation Type: paid
Owner(s):
Times Mirror Magazines, Inc.
2 Park Ave.
New York, NY 10016
Telephone: (212) 779-5000
Ownership %: 100
Management:
Michael Rooney ........................Publisher
Editorial:
David Petzal ....................Executive Editor
Duncan Barnes ............................Editor

Desc.: While hunting and fishing is the
   core of the editorial coverage, each
   issue features articles and departments
   devoted to conservation, fish and game
   recipes, camping, boating, gun dogs,
   vehicles, humor, and new products.
   Each issue also includes a locally edited
   section specifically tailored to the needs
   of outdoorsmen in each of five
   geographic regions.
Readers: Sportsmen.

**FISHERMAN, NEW ENGLAND**          25793
   **EDITION**
P.O. Box 211
Mystic, CT 06355
Telephone: (203) 572-0564
FAX: (203) 536-1581
Year Established: 1974
Pub. Frequency: w.
Page Size: pocket
Subscrip. Rate: $23/yr.
Materials: 32,33
Circulation: 25,000
Circulation Type: paid
Owner(s):
Long Island Fisherman
14 Ramsey Pl.
Shirley, NY 11967
Telephone: (516) 345-5200
Ownership %: 100
Management:
Rich Reina ............................Publisher
Editorial:
Tim Coleman ....................Executive Editor
Desc.: Strongest regional, total fishing
   magazine in the country today,
   dedicated to just one pursuit, fishing.
   Each weekly edition is edited for the
   specific area and local experts report
   with the emphasis on the how-to aspect
   of the sport, conservation, local fishing
   areas, seasonal information,
   fishing tackle and boats.
Readers: Active salt and fresh water
   fishermen.

**FISHERMAN, THE**                          25783
14 Ramsey Rd.
Shirley, NY 11967
Telephone: (516) 345-5200
Year Established: 1966
Pub. Frequency: 50 wks/yr.
Page Size: standard
Subscrip. Rate: $20/yr.
Materials: 32,33
Freelance Pay: $100-$150/full feature
Circulation: 85,000
Circulation Type: paid
Owner(s):
LIF Publ. Corp.
14 Ramsey Rd.
Shirley, NY 11967
Telephone: (516) 725-4200
Ownership %: 100
Management:
Rich Reina ............................President
Rich Reina ............................Publisher
Gary Caputi ................Advertising Manager
Editorial:
Pete Barrett ....................Senior Editor
Fred Golofaro ............................Editor
Stu Miller ..............Advertising Editor
Fred Golofaro ................Book Review Editor
Carl Safina ................Conservation Editor
Fred Golofaro ................New Products Editor
Fred Golofaro ............................News Editor
Fred Golofaro ............................Photo
Fred Golofaro ................Technical Editor

Desc.: A hard hitting regional weekly,
   saltwater oriented. 6 - 8 articles per
   issue guts info, e.g. how to, where to,
   etc. Detailed weekly fishing reports.
   Articles written by staff and contributing
   writers. Federal, State and County
   legislation watched and reported
   upon when fishing and ecology of region
   effected. We are The Bible in our region.
   Departments include: Conservation
   Comments, Beach Talk, Product Profile,
   Tackle Doctor, Casting Around, Pass It
   On (news), Short Casts (letters to
   editor).
Readers: Avid salt water fishermen from
   pro to nov. SPORT FISHERMEN.

**FISHING & HUNTING NEWS**          25784
511 Eastlake Ave. E.
Seattle, WA 98109
Telephone: (206) 624-3845
FAX: (206) 340-9816
Mailing Address:
   P.O. Box 19000
   Seattle, WA 98109
Year Established: 1954
Pub. Frequency: bi-w.
Page Size: tabloid
Subscrip. Rate: $49.95/yr.
Freelance Pay: negotiable
Circulation: 120,000
Circulation Type: paid
Owner(s):
Fishing & Hunting News
Telephone: (206) 624-3845
Ownership %: 100
Management:
Bill Hofer ............................President
Bill Farden ............................Publisher
Dick Openshaw ................Associate Publsiher
Terry McCormick ................Associate Publsiher
Editorial:
Patrick McGann ....................Managing Editor
Brian Thurston ........Vice President-Advertising
Ric Farren ............Vice President-Circulation &
                                   Marketing
Desc.: Features localized outdoor news
   coverage and major regional information
   in 13 states.
Readers: Sportsmen of the West.

**FISHING FACTS**                          25785
312 E. Buffalo St.
Milwaukee, WI 53202
Telephone: (414) 287-4333
Year Established: 1966
Pub. Frequency: 7/yr.
Page Size: standard
Subscrip. Rate: $14.97/yr.
Freelance Pay: $300-$500/story
Circulation: 125,000
Circulation Type: paid
Owner(s):
Fishing Facts, Inc.
312 E. Buffalo St.
Milwaukee, WI 53202
Telephone: (414) 287-4333
Ownership %: 100
Management:
Betty Quadrachi ........................President
Betty Quadrachi ........................Publisher
Editorial:
Betty Quadrachi ............................Editor
Carl Malz ....................Managing Editor
Spencer Petros ....................Managing Editor
Desc.: Methods and techniques for
   successful freshwater sport fishing.
Readers: Upscale, married males.

**FISHING IN MARYLAND**          25786
P.O. Box 201
Phoenix, MD 21131
Telephone: (410) 561-3720
Year Established: 1953

Materials Accepted/Included: 01-Business news 02-By-line articles 03-Fashion news 04-Food news 05-Freelance copy 06-Letters to editor 07-Real estate news 08-Sports news 09-Travel news 10-Book rev. 11-Movie rev. 12-Music rev. 13-TV rev. 14-Theater rev. 15-Coming events 16-Obituaries 17-Question & answer 18-Social announcements 19-Artwork 20-Cartoons 21-Photos 22-TV listings 23-Audio rec. 24-Video rec. 25-Books 26-Films/film clips 27-Personnel news 28-Press releases 29-New product news/photos 30-Trade lit. 31-Contracts awarded 32-Display adv. 33-Classified adv.

6-41

Pub. Frequency: a.
Page Size: 4 color photos/art
Subscrip. Rate: $6.95/yr.
Materials: 32
Freelance Pay: negotiable
Circulation: 28,000
Circulation Type: paid
**Owner(s):**
W. Cary DeRussy
10 Shanney Brook Ct.
Phoenix, MD 21131
Telephone: (410) 561-3720
Ownership %: 100
**Management:**
W. Cary de Russy .........................President
W. Cary de Russy ..........................Publisher
W. Cary de Russy ............Advertising Manager
**Editorial:**
Bill Burton ...........................................Editor
**Desc.:** Annual publication dedicated to the
encouragement of and assistance to salt
and fresh water fisherman who frequent
the states of Maryland, Delaware, and
Virginia. Made up of informative articles,
maps, tide tables, forecasts, where to go
and how to do. It renders full service to
all fisherman and boat owners, and
stimulates fishing interest through its
awards and citations programs.
**Readers:** Fishermen & boat owners.

**FISHING WORLD**                                      26399
700 W. 47th St., Ste. 310
Kansas City, MO 64112
Telephone: (816) 531-5730
FAX: (816) 531-3873
Year Established: 1955
Pub. Frequency: bi-m.
Page Size: 4 color photos/art
Subscrip. Rate: $2.95 newsstand;
$12.95/yr.
Freelance Pay: $500 and under
Circulation: 400,000
Circulation Type: paid
**Owner(s):**
K. C. Publishing
700 W. 47th St., Ste. 310
Kansas City, MO 64112
Telephone: (816) 531-5730
FAX: (816) 531-3873
Ownership %: 100
**Management:**
John Prebich .............................President
John Prebich ..............................Publisher
Connie Moss ..................Advertising Manager
Beth Dawson .................Circulation Manager
**Editorial:**
David Richey ........................................Editor
**Desc.:** Methods and tackle, how-to-do-it
information. Best fishing waters, boating
and other aspects of the sport. Must be
factual. Regular columns cover
new tackle, boats, and every aspect of
fresh and saltwater fishing.
**Readers:** Sports fishermen and their
families.

**FLY FISHERMAN MAGAZINE**                25787
6405 Flank Dr.
Harrisburg, PA 17105-8200
Telephone: (717) 657-9555
Mailing Address:
P.O. Box 8200
Harrisburg, PA 17105
Year Established: 1969
Pub. Frequency: 6/yr.
Page Size: standard
Subscrip. Rate: $24/yr.
Materials: 02,06,10,21,32,33
Freelance Pay: $35-$750
Circulation: 130,000
Circulation Type: paid

**Owner(s):**
Cowles Magazines, Inc.
6405 Flank Dr.
Harrisburg, PA 17112
Telephone: (717) 657-9555
FAX: (717) 657-9526
Ownership %: 100
**Management:**
Donald D. Zahner .............................Founder
Bruce Barnet ...............................President
Linda Walter ...................Advertising Manager
**Editorial:**
John D. Randolph .................................Editor
Philip Hanyok ......................Managing Editor
Jeff King .......................................Art Director
Deb Skonezney ...........Production Coordinator
**Desc.:** Edited for those anglers who fish
primarily with a fly rod, and for other
anglers who would like to learn more
about fly fishing. Articles cover
both fresh and salt-water fly rodding, fly-
tying, angling tradition and history, rod-
making and tackle-fussing, where-to-go
features and regular, extensive coverage
of new products of interest to fly
fishermen.
**Readers:** 79% are college-educated, 99%
are male and have sizeable income.

**FLY ROD & REEL**                                   70425
Rt. 1, Roxmont
Rockport, ME 04856
Telephone: (207) 594-9544
FAX: (207) 594-7215
Mailing Address:
P.O. Box 370
Camden, ME 04843
Year Established: 1979
Pub. Frequency: 6/yr.
Page Size: standard
Subscrip. Rate: $2.95 newsstand;
$14.97/yr.
Materials: 02,03,04,05,06,08,09,10,11,15,
17,19,20,21,28,29,30,32,33
Print Process: web offset
Circulation: 38,000
Circulation Type: free & paid
**Owner(s):**
Down East Enterprise
P.O. Box 1357
Camden, ME 04843
Ownership %: 100
**Management:**
H. Allen Fernald ...............................President
H. Allen Fernald ...............................Publisher
Bill Anderson ...................Advertising Manager
Deb Dodge .....................Circulation Manager
**Editorial:**
Silvio Calabi .............................Editor in Chief
James Butler ......................Managing Editor
**Desc.:** This publication brings you
intriguing and informative stories of fly-
fishing at its best. Each issue has: tackle
comparisons, fly tying and casting
instruction from the experts.
**Readers:** male-affluent-married.

**FULL CRY (TREE HOUNDS)**                25736
P.O. Box 10
Boody, IL 62514
Telephone: (217) 865-2332
FAX: (217) 865-2334
Year Established: 1939
Pub. Frequency: m.
Page Size: standard
Subscrip. Rate: $15/yr.; $27/2 yrs.
Materials: 01,06,08,10,25,27,28,29,32,33
Freelance Pay: none
Print Process: offset
Circulation: 25,800
Circulation Type: paid

**Owner(s):**
Gault Publications, Inc.
P.O. Box 10
Boody, IL 62514
Telephone: (217) 865-2332
Ownership %: 100
**Management:**
Seth R. Gault ...............................President
**Editorial:**
Seth R. Gault ...................................Editor
Seth R. Gault ....................Entertainment Editor
**Desc.:** A hunting magazine; tree hounds,
big game and coon hounds.
**Readers:** National & international hunters.

**FUR-FISH-GAME (HARDING'S**           25788
**MAGAZINE)**
2878 E. Main St.
Columbus, OH 43209
Telephone: (614) 231-9585
Year Established: 1925
Pub. Frequency: m.
Page Size: standard
Subscrip. Rate: $2.50 newsstand; $16/yr.;
$30/2 yrs.
Materials: 17,20,21,24,25,28,29,30,32,33
Freelance Pay: $35-$150
Circulation: 120,000
Circulation Type: paid
**Owner(s):**
A. R. Harding Publishing Co.
2878 E. Main St.
Columbus, OH 43209
Telephone: (614) 231-9585
Ownership %: 100
**Management:**
Jeff Kirn .......................................President
Jeff Kirn .......................................Publisher
Eric Schweinhagen ...........Advertising Manager
**Editorial:**
Mitch Cox ........................................Editor
Kurt Herrmann ....................Advertising Director
Mitch Cox ....................New Products Editor
**Desc.:** We use true stories only in our
publication covering such subjects as
hunting, fishing, boating, dogs, camping
and trapping. We prefer the stories
to have a locale in United States or
Canada. We prefer that the articles be
accompanied by good
glossy photographs, and caption
information. The length of the article can
be from 1,500 to 3,000 words.
Departments include: Fishing, Guns and
Ammunition, Fish & Tackle, The Gun
Rack, Gun Dogs, The Trapline &
Trappers' Alert, Trapping and Camping.
**Readers:** Primarily males interested in
outdoor activities.

**GUN DOG**                                             49846
1901 Bell Ave., #4
Des Moines, IA 50315
Telephone: (515) 243-2472
FAX: (515) 243-0233
Year Established: 1981
Pub. Frequency: bi-m.
Page Size: standard
Subscrip. Rate: $19.97/yr.; $33.97/2 yr.
Materials: 05,21,28,29,32,33
Freelance Pay: varies
Print Process: web offset
Circulation: 60,000
Circulation Type: paid
**Owner(s):**
Roger D. Stover
1901 Bell Ave. #4
Des Moines, IA 50315
Telephone: (515) 243-2472
Ownership %: 100
**Management:**
Roger D. Stover ...............................Owner
Carrell E. Bunn ...............................President
Carrell E. Bunn ...............................Publisher

**Editorial:**
Bob Wilbanks ...................................Editor
**Desc.:** Edited for serious upland bird &
waterfowl hunters.
**Readers:** Affluent "gentlemen-sportsmen";
98% men, $64,700 average income,
42.7 years average age; hunters who
own dogs, an average of 3 each.

**GUNS & AMMO MAGAZINE**                25790
6420 Wilshire Blvd.
Los Angeles, CA 90048
Telephone: (310) 854-2222
FAX: (310) 854-2477
Year Established: 1958
Pub. Frequency: m.
Page Size: standard
Subscrip. Rate: $2.95 copy; $21.94/yr.
Freelance Pay: varies
Circulation: 650,000
Circulation Type: paid
**Owner(s):**
Petersen Publishing Co.
6420 Wilshire Blvd.
Los Angeles, CA 90048
Telephone: (310) 854-2222
Ownership %: 100
**Management:**
Thomas J. Siatos ..................Vice President
Doug Hamlin ..............................Publisher
Peter F. Clancey ..............Advertising Manager
**Editorial:**
Tom Siatos ..........................Executive Editor
Red Bell, Jr. ...................................Editor
Christine Potvin ...................Managing Editor
Carol Winet ................................Art Director
Kevin Steele ......................Associate Editor
Phil Spagenberger ..................Feature Editor
Bob Milek ..............................Field Editor
**Desc.:** Semi-technical vertical hobby
magazine.
**Readers:** Shooting sports enthusiasts, gun
collectors and hunters.

**HOUNDS & HUNTING**                         25752
554 Derrick Rd.
Bradford, PA 16701
Telephone: (814) 368-6154
FAX: (814) 368-3522
Mailing Address:
P. O. Box 372
Bradford, PA 16701
Year Established: 1903
Pub. Frequency: m.
Page Size: standard
Subscrip. Rate: $14/yr.
Materials: 32,33
Circulation: 14,500
Circulation Type: paid
**Owner(s):**
Hounds & Hunting
554 Derrick Rd.
Bradford, PA
Telephone: (814) 368-6154
Ownership %: 100
**Management:**
Dorothy M. Wilson ..........Advertising Manager
Robert Slike .....................Business Manager
R. F. Slike ...........................General Manager
**Editorial:**
R. F. Slike ...........................Executive Editor
**Desc.:** Beagle field trial and gundog trials
and related articles on hunting.

**HUNTER'S HORN**                              25791
20 W. Second, Rm. 202
Sand Springs, OK 74063
Telephone: (918) 245-9571
Mailing Address:
P.O. Box 426
Sand Springs, OK 74063
Year Established: 1924
Pub. Frequency: m.

Page Size: standard
Subscrip. Rate: $14/yr.
Materials: 02,05,06,08,15,16,21,32,33
Freelance Pay: none
Circulation: 10,541
Circulation Type: paid
**Owner(s):**
Hunters Horn, Inc.
P.O. Box 707
Sesser, IL 62884
Telephone: (618) 625-2711
FAX: (618) 625-6221
Ownership %: 100
**Management:**
George Slankard ......................Publisher
**Editorial:**
George Slankard ..........................Editor
**Desc.:** Devoted to fox and wolf hunting.
Coverage restricted largely to news and
features on hounds and sport. Items on
hound history and breeding welcome.
Pictures are mostly of hounds.
Departments include: Breeders'
Information, Obituaries, Reports of Field
Trials and Bench Shows, and regional
news columns.
**Readers:** Hound owners concentrated in
rural areas. Circulation is mostly East of
the Rockies.
**Deadline:** story-end of mo.; news-end of
mo.; photo-end of mo.; ads-end of mo.

71275
## HUNTING
6420 Wilshire Blvd.
Los Angeles, CA 90048
Telephone: (213) 782-2000
FAX: (213) 782-2263
Year Established: 1980
Pub. Frequency: m.
Page Size: standard
Subscrip. Rate: $3.95 newsstand
Materials: 32
Circulation: 110,000
Circulation Type: paid
**Owner(s):**
Petersen Publishing Co.
6420 Wilshire Blvd.
Los Angeles, CA 90048
Telephone: (213) 782-2000
FAX: (213) 782-2263
Ownership %: 100
**Management:**
W. Jeff Young ......................Publisher
**Editorial:**
Todd Smith ..........................Editor

69139
## HUNTING ANNUAL
6420 Wilshire Blvd.
Los Angeles, CA 90048
Telephone: (213) 782-2000
FAX: (213) 782-2263
Year Established: 1980
Pub. Frequency: a.
Page Size: standard
Subscrip. Rate: $6.95/copy
Materials: 32
Circulation: 110,000
Circulation Type: paid
**Owner(s):**
Petersen Publishing Co.
6420 Wilshire Blvd.
Los Angeles, CA 90048
Telephone: (213) 782-2000
Ownership %: 100
**Management:**
W. Jeff Young ......................Publisher
Andrea Higgins ................Advertising Manager
**Editorial:**
Gerry Lee ..........................Editor

69140
## IN-FISHERMAN
2 In-Fisherman Dr.
Brainerd, MN 56401-0999
Telephone: (218) 829-1648
FAX: (218) 829-3091
Mailing Address:
P.O. Box 999
Brainerd, MN 56401
Year Established: 1975
Pub. Frequency: 7/yr.
Page Size: standard
Subscrip. Rate: $2.95 newsstand US;
$3.95 newsstand Canada; $16/yr. US
Materials: 32
Circulation: 321,000
Circulation Type: paid
**Owner(s):**
In-Fisherman Communications Network
1 In-Fisherman Dr.
Brainerd, MN 56401-0999
Telephone: (218) 829-1648
Ownership %: 100
**Management:**
Al Lindner ..........................President
Stu Legaard ..........................Publisher
Chuck Nelson ....................Circulation Manager
**Editorial:**
Doug Stange ..........................Editor
Joann Phipps ....................Managing Editor
Stu Legaard ....................Advertising Director

69141
## INTERNATIONAL BOWHUNTER
P.O. Box 67
Pillager, MN 56473-0067
Telephone: (218) 746-3333
FAX: (218) 746-3307
Year Established: 1983
Pub. Frequency: 6/yr.
Page Size: standard
Subscrip. Rate: $12/yr. US; $19/yr.
Canada & Mexico; $29/yr. elsewhere
Materials: 01,02,03,04,06,08,09,10,15,20,
21,24,27,28,29,30
Print Process: sheet fed
Circulation: 32,000
Circulation Type: free & paid
**Owner(s):**
International Bowhunting Organization
P.O. Box 67
Pillager, MN 56473-0067
Telephone: (218) 746-3333
Ownership %: 100
**Editorial:**
Johnny E. Boatner ..........................Editor
**Desc.:** Official newsletter of the
International Bowhunting Organization.
**Deadline:** story-3 mos.; news-3 mos.;
photo-3 mos.; ads-3 mos.

26417
## MICHIGAN OUT-OF-DOORS
P.O. Box 30235
Lansing, MI 48909
Telephone: (517) 371-1041
FAX: (517) 371-1505
Year Established: 1947
Pub. Frequency: m.
Page Size: standard
Subscrip. Rate: $25/yr.
Freelance Pay: $200/features
Circulation: 133,000
Circulation Type: paid
**Owner(s):**
Michigan United Conservation Clubs
P.O. Box 30235
Lansing, MI 48909
Telephone: (517) 371-1041
Ownership %: 100
**Management:**
Thomas L. Washington ..................Publisher
William Donahue ..............Advertising Manager
Michael Soczek ..............Circulation Manager
A. Mark Battaglia ........Classified Adv. Manager
**Editorial:**
Kenneth S. Lowe ..............Executive Editor

Christie Bleck ..........................Associate Editor
**Desc.:** Use outdoor news stories,
especially factual items concerning
hunting and fishing. Cover national
conservation laws, regulations,
legislation affecting conservation, state
laws, and many other outdoor subjects.
Also carry news of organized
sportsmen and what they are doing to
further conservation of our natural
resources.
**Readers:** A wide range of readers, most
are hunters or fishermen members,
dedicated conservationists, and ordinary
outdoor recreation enthusiasts.

25789
## NEW GUN WEEK, THE
267 Linwood Ave.
Buffalo, NY 14209
Telephone: (716) 885-6408
Mailing Address:
P.O. Box 488, Station C
Buffalo, NY 14209-0488
Year Established: 1966
Pub. Frequency: w.
Page Size: tabloid
Subscrip. Rate: $2/copy; $32/yr. in US;
$40/yr. foreign
Materials: 01,02,06,08,10,20,21,29,32,33
Freelance Pay: negotiable
Print Process: web offset
Circulation: 21,000
Circulation Type: paid
**Owner(s):**
Second Amendment Foundation
12500 N.E. Tenth Pl.
Bellevue, WA 98005
Telephone: (206) 454-7012
Ownership %: 100
**Bureau(s):**
CCRKBA
600 Pennsylvania Ave, SE, #205
Washington, DC 20003
Telephone: (202) 543-3363
Contact: John M. Snyder, Editor
**Management:**
Alan M. Gottlieb ..................Publisher
Peggy Tartano ..................Advertising Manager
**Editorial:**
Joseph P. Tartaro ..........................Editor
Sheila Link ..........................Associate Editor
Bill Hughes ..........................Field Editor
Glen Voorhees ..........................Field Editor
Phil Johnston ..........................Gun Editor
Robert Housman ..........................Industry Editor
James C. Schneider ..........Legislative Director
Gene B. Crum ..........................Technical Editor
**Desc.:** Nationally circulated paper reporting
firearms and hunting legistation,
regulation, court cases, competition
results, new products, collectibles, also
prints feature articles on all
firearm/airgun subjects/opinion.
**Readers:** Firearms activists, gun group
leaders.
**Deadline:** story-3 wks. prior to cover date;
news-3 wks. prior; ads-3 wks. prior

65996
## NORTH AMERICAN FISHERMAN
12301 Whitewater Dr, Ste. 260
Hopkins, MN 55343
Telephone: (612) 936-0555
FAX: (612) 936-9755
Mailing Address:
P.O. Box 3404
Hopkins, MN 55343
Year Established: 1988
Pub. Frequency: bi-m.
Page Size: standard
Subscrip. Rate: $18/yr.
Freelance Pay: $200-500
Circulation: 480,000
Circulation Type: paid

**Owner(s):**
North American Outdoor Group, Inc.
**Management:**
Steven F. Burke ..........................President
Mark LaBarbera ..................Vice President
Cliff Thom ..........................Controller
Mark LaBarbera ..........................Publisher
Russell M. Nolan ..........Advertising Manager
**Desc.:** Official publication of the North
American Fishing Club is an in-depth
magazine for the avid anglers both fresh
and saltwater. Appeals to affluent
sportsmen who can afford to travel.
**Readers:** Traveling, Avid Sportsmen.

52635
## NORTH AMERICAN HUNTER
12301 Whitewater Dr.
Minnetonka, MN 55343
Telephone: (612) 936-9333
FAX: (612) 936-9755
Mailing Address:
P.O. Box 3401
Hopkins, MN 55343
Year Established: 1979
Pub. Frequency: bi-m.
Page Size: standard
Subscrip. Rate: $18/yr.
Materials: 32,33
Freelance Pay: $200-$325/article
Circulation: 225,000
Circulation Type: paid
**Owner(s):**
North American Outdoor Group, Inc.
12301 Whitewater Dr.
Minnetonka, MN 55343
Ownership %: 100
**Management:**
Steven F. Burke ..........................President
Cliff Thom ..........................Controller
Mark LaBarbera ..........................Publisher
Russell M. Nolan ..........Advertising Manager
**Editorial:**
Bill Miller ..........................Editor
Gregg Gutschow ..................Associate Editor
**Desc.:** Official publication of the North
American Hunting Club, is an in-depth
magazine written for the serious hunter
of game birds and animals. Covers rifles
shotguns, bows, handguns &
muzzleloaders.
**Readers:** Wingshot, riflemen, bowhunters
& muzzleloaders.

25796
## OUTDOOR PRESS, THE
N. 2012 Ruby St.
Spokane, WA 99207
Telephone: (509) 328-9392
FAX: (509) 327-9861
Year Established: 1966
Pub. Frequency: w.
Page Size: tabloid
Subscrip. Rate: $30/yr.
Circulation: 6,000
Circulation Type: paid
**Owner(s):**
The Outdoor Press
2012 Ruby St.
Spokane, WA 99207
Telephone: (509) 327-9861
Ownership %: 100
**Management:**
Doris Polegay ..........................President
F. L. Peterson ..........................Publisher
G. B. Peterson ..................Advertising Manager
Doris Polegay ..........................General Manager
**Editorial:**
F. C. Peterson II ..........Executive Editor
Dick Lee ..........................Columnist
Dennis Clay ..........................Columnist
Bob Vierling ..........................Miscellaneous
Everett Caryl ..........................Miscellaneous
Chris Carges ..........................Reporter
Ray Lebsack ..........................Reporter

**Materials Accepted/Included:** 01-Business news 02-By-line articles 03-Fashion news 04-Food news 05-Freelance copy 06-Letters to editor 07-Real estate news 08-Sports news 09-Travel news
10-Book rev. 11-Movie rev. 12-Music rev. 13-TV rev. 14-Theater rev. 15-Coming events 16-Obituaries 17-Question & answer 18-Social announcements 19-Artwork 20-Cartoons 21-Photos 22-TV listings
23-Audio rec. 24-Video rec. 25-Books 26-Films/film clips 27-Personnel news 28-Press releases 29-New product news/photos 30-Trade lit. 31-Contracts awarded 32-Display adv. 33-Classified adv.

6-43

**Desc.:** Fishing and hunting reports of the Northwest only. Mostly staff produced outdoor weekly tabloid. Ad rates on request. New readership profile available on request with SASE.
**Readers:** Sportsmen, RV owners, boat owners.

25797

## PENNSYLVANIA ANGLER
3532 Walnut St.
Harrisburg, PA 17109
Telephone: (717) 657-4520
Mailing Address:
　P.O. Box 6700
　Harrisburg, PA 17105-7000
Year Established: 1931
Pub. Frequency: m.
Page Size: 4 color photos/art
Subscrip. Rate: $1.50 copy; $9/yr.
Circulation: 48,000
Circulation Type: paid
**Owner(s):**
Pennsylvania Fish & Boat Commission
P.O. Box 1673
Harrisburg, PA 17105
Telephone: (717) 657-4520
Ownership %: 100
**Editorial:**
Art Michaels ...................................Editor
**Desc.:** Articles and stories about fishing and boating in Pennsylvania. Conservation subjects related to water.
**Readers:** Outdoorsmen and their families.

25799

## PETERSEN'S HUNTING MAGAZINE
6420 Wilshire Blvd.
Los Angeles, CA 90048
Telephone: (310) 854-2222
Year Established: 1973
Pub. Frequency: m.
Page Size: standard
Subscrip. Rate: $19.94/yr.
Freelance Pay: varies
Circulation: 325,000
Circulation Type: paid
**Owner(s):**
Petersen Publishing Co.
6420 Wilshire Blvd.
Los Angeles, CA 90048
Telephone: (310) 854-2222
Ownership %: 100
**Management:**
W. Jeff Young ...........................Publisher
**Editorial:**
Craig Boddington .........................Editor
Denise LaSalle ...............Managing Editor
**Desc.:** Devoted exclusively to the sport of recreational hunting with appeal to all hunters. It offers only the finest, up-to-date information and mirrors the intense interest and involvement of the true hunter. Guidelines for authors and photographers available upon request with SASE articles on big game, small game, upland game, waterfowl, varmints, and exotics each month. Departments include: Industry News, Legislation, New Products, Gun Dogs, Equipment, Handloading, Guns and Loads, Automotive, Bowhunting, and Optics.
**Readers:** The American hunting enthusiast.

25800

## SAFARI
4800 W. Gates Pass Rd.
Tucson, AZ 85745
Telephone: (602) 620-1220
Year Established: 1971
Pub. Frequency: bi-m.
Page Size: standard
Subscrip. Rate: $4 issue; $30/yr.
Freelance Pay: $200/story
Circulation: 19,500
Circulation Type: paid

**Owner(s):**
Safari Club International
4800 W. Gates Pass Rd.
Tucson, AZ 85745
Telephone: (602) 620-1220
Ownership %: 100
**Management:**
Safari Club International ..............Publisher
Eric Hubbell ..............Advertising Manager
**Editorial:**
William R. Quimby ........................Editor
Elaine Cummings .......Publications Coordinator
**Desc.:** Consists of stories of big game hunting from all over the world, and wildlife conservation material pertinent to big game enthusiasts.
**Readers:** Big game hunters (wildlife professionals, hunting guides and outfitters, taxidermist - all).

25801

## SALT WATER SPORTSMAN
77 Franklin St.
Boston, MA 02210-1510
Telephone: (617) 439-9977
FAX: (617) 439-9357
Year Established: 1939
Pub. Frequency: m.
Page Size: standard
Subscrip. Rate: $3 newsstand; $24.95/yr.
Materials: 06,08,21,28,29,32,33
Freelance Pay: $.10-$.30/wd.
Circulation: 150,000
Circulation Type: paid
**Owner(s):**
Times-Mirror, Inc.
380 Madison Ave.
New York, NY 10017
Ownership %: 100
**Management:**
Edward F. Andresen ...................Publisher
Jaye McAuliffe .................Advertising Manager
**Editorial:**
Frank Woolner ...................Senior Editor
Barry Gibson ..............................Editor
Margaret Earley .................Production Director
**Desc.:** Covers salt water sport fishing on the Atlantic, Gulf, and Pacific Coasts. Uses little news other than that supplied by regular coastal correspondents. Features and photos with a slant towards salt water sport fishing in the areas named above desired. This is a specialized market and general fishing releases are not of interest to us. Good action photos of salt water sport fishing always in demand. Articles should be between 1000 and 1500 words. Departments include: Boating, Tactics & Tackle, New Angles, Sportsman's Workbench, Electronics Aboard, New Boats, New Electronics.
**Readers:** Salt water sport fishing enthusiasts of the Atlantic, Pacific and Gulf coasts.

70426

## SHOOTING SPORTSMAN
Rt. 1 Roxmont
Rockport, ME 04856
Telephone: (207) 594-9544
FAX: (207) 594-7215
Mailing Address:
　P.O. Box 1357
　Camden, ME 04843
Year Established: 1986
Pub. Frequency: bi-m.
Page Size: standard
Subscrip. Rate: $4.95 newsstand;
　$24.95/yr.
Materials: 04,05,06,09,10,11,19,20,21,25,
　28,29,32,33
Print Process: web offset
Circulation: 11,000
Circulation Type: paid

**Owner(s):**
Down East Enterprise,
P.O. Box 679
Camden, ME 04843
Ownership %: 100
**Management:**
H. Allen Fernald ..........................President
H. Allen Fernald ..........................Publisher
Bill Anderson ..............Advertising Manager
Deb Dodge ....................Circulation Manager
**Editorial:**
Silvio Calabi ..........................Editor in Chief
Ralph Stuart ....................Managing Editor
**Desc.:** Publication brings its readers the best in wing shooting and fine shotguns. From upland gunning and waterfowling to sporting clays, the magazine cover the traditions of the sport.
**Readers:** Male, affluent, hunters.

25808

## TROUT
1500 Wilson Blvd., #310
Arlington, VA 22209-2310
Telephone: (703) 522-0200
FAX: (703) 284-9400
Year Established: 1959
Pub. Frequency: q.
Page Size: standard
Subscrip. Rate: $25/yr. membership;
　$10/yr. libraries
Materials: 05,06,10,15,19,20,21,27,29,32,33
Freelance Pay: negotiable
Print Process: web offset
Circulation: 70,000
Circulation Type: paid
**Owner(s):**
Trout Unlimited, Inc.
1500 Wilson Blvd., #310
Arlington, VA 22209-2310
Telephone: (703) 522-0200
FAX: (703) 284-9400
Ownership %: 100
**Editorial:**
Peter Rafle ..............................Editor
**Desc.:** Official publication of Trout Unlimited, a nonprofit conservation organization dedicated to the protection and restoration of America's cold water fisheries.
**Readers:** Members and supporters of Trout Unlimited and other conservation groups.

58565

## WHO'S WHO IN THE FISH INDUSTRY
182 Queens Blvd.
Bayville, NJ 08721
Telephone: (908) 240-5330
FAX: (908) 341-0891
Mailing Address:
　P.O. Box 389
　Toms River, NJ 08754
Year Established: 1980
Pub. Frequency: a.
Page Size: oversize
Subscrip. Rate: $95/yr.
Circulation: 2,500
Circulation Type: paid
**Owner(s):**
Urner Barry Publications, Inc.
P.O. Box 389
Toms River, NJ 08754
Telephone: (908) 240-5330
Ownership %: 100
**Management:**
Lisa Sharkus ..............Advertising Manager
**Editorial:**
Paul B. Brown, Jr. .........................Editor
Joseph T. Soja ...............Associate Editor

3116

## WILDLIFE HARVEST
P.O. Box 96
Goose Lake, IA 52750
Telephone: (319) 242-3046

Pub. Frequency: m.
Page Size: pocket
Subscrip. Rate: $3 newsstand; $25/yr.
Materials: 01,02,04,15,17,19,20,21,28,29,
　30,32,33
Print Process: offset
**Owner(s):**
Wildlife Harvest Publications
P.O. Box 96
Goose Lake, IA 52750
Ownership %: 100
**Management:**
John M. Mullin ..........................Publisher
**Editorial:**
Peggy Mullin Boehmer ...........Associate Editor
**Desc.:** Magazine for gamebird production and improved hunting. Readers are involved in operating hunting resorts, sportsmen's clubs, dog kennels and in gamebird propagation.
**Deadline:** ads-1st day of mo.

25809

## WISCONSIN SPORTSMAN
2250 Newmarket Pkwy., Ste. 110
Marietta, GA 30067
Telephone: (404) 953-9222
FAX: (404) 933-9510
Mailing Address:
　P.O. Box 741
　Marietta, GA 30061-0741
Year Established: 1972
Pub. Frequency: m.
Page Size: standard
Subscrip. Rate: $14.95/yr.
Materials: 02,05,06,21,25,28,29
Freelance Pay: manuscripts $125-$300
Circulation: 33,000
Circulation Type: paid
**Owner(s):**
Game & Fish Publications, Inc.
2250 Newmarket Pkwy., Ste. 110
Marietta, GA 30067
Telephone: (404) 953-9222
Ownership %: 100
**Management:**
Steven W. Vaughn ..............................President
Steven W. Vaughn ..............................Publisher
Terri March ...................Advertising Manager
**Editorial:**
Dennis Schmidt ..............................Editor
Ken Dunwoody ....................Editorial Director
**Desc.:** Editorial coverage dedicated exclusively to Wisconsin fishing, hunting and outdoor life. Emphasis on where-to.
**Readers:** 51 percent college educated, 40.7 percent take more than 20 hunting trips per year within their own State, Wisconsin.

## Group 631-Gay & Lesbian

25812

## ADVOCATE, THE
6922 Hollywood Blvd., 10th Fl.
Los Angeles, CA 90028
Telephone: (213) 871-1225
FAX: (213) 467-6805
Mailing Address:
　P.O. Box 4371
　Los Angeles, CA 90078
Year Established: 1967
Pub. Frequency: bi-w.
Page Size: standard
Subscrip. Rate: $3.95 newsstand;
　$39.95/yr.
Materials: 01,03,05,06,09,10,11,12,14,16,
　21,23,24,25,26,27,28,29,30,32,33
Freelance Pay: $100-$1500
Circulation: 80,000
Circulation Type: paid

**Materials Accepted/Included:** 01-Business news 02-By-line articles 03-Fashion news 04-Food news 05-Freelance copy 06-Letters to editor 07-Real estate news 08-Sports news 09-Travel news 10-Book rev. 11-Movie rev. 12-Music rev. 13-TV rev. 14-Theater rev. 15-Coming events 16-Obituaries 17-Question & answer 18-Social announcements 19-Artwork 20-Cartoons 21-Photos 22-TV listings 23-Audio rec. 24-Video rec. 25-Books 26-Films/film clips 27-Personnel news 28-Press releases 29-New product news/photos 30-Trade lit. 31-Contracts awarded 32-Display adv. 33-Classified adv.

**Owner(s):**
Liberation Publications, Inc.
P.O. Box 4371
Los Angeles, CA 90078
Telephone: (213) 871-1225
FAX: (213) 467-0173
Ownership %: 100
**Bureau(s):**
Washington Bureau
P.O. Box 73725
Washington, DC 20056-3725
FAX: (202) 588-5159
Contact: Chris Bull, Bureau Chief

San Francisco Bureau
3315 Sacramento St.
Ste. 502
San Francisco , CA 94118
FAX: (415) 386-6640
Contact: John Gallagher, Bureau Chief
**Management:**
Sam Watters ................................President
Stephanie K. Blackwood ...........Vice President
Sam Watters ................................Publisher
**Editorial:**
Jeff Yarbrough ............................Editor in Chief
Jim Schroeder ............................Senior Editor
Mark Thompson ............................Senior Editor
Gerry Kroll ................................Editor
Ronald Goins ................................Art Director
Don Tuthill ...................Associate Publisher
Stephanie K. Blackwood ...............Director of
Don Tuthill .......Director of National Advertising
**Desc.:** The national gay & lesbian news -
  magazine. Covers newest features of
  national & international interest to the
  gay and lesbian reader.
**Readers:** Upwardly mobile, young (25-40),
  college educated.

69662

**BLK**
P.O. Box 83912
Los Angeles, CA 90083-0912
Telephone: (310) 410-0808
FAX: (310) 410-9250
Year Established: 1988
Pub. Frequency: m.
Page Size: standard
Subscrip. Rate: $18/yr. US; $29/yr. foreign
Materials: 02,03,05,06,09,10,11,12,13,14,
  16,18,20,21,23,24,25,26,28,32,33
Print Process: web offset
Circulation: 37,000
Circulation Type: paid
**Owner(s):**
Blk Publishing Co.
P.O. Box 83912
Los Angeles, CA 90083-0912
Telephone: (310) 410-0808
FAX: (310) 410-9250
Ownership %: 100
**Bureau(s):**
New York Bureau
P.O. Box 2412
Long Island City, NY 11102-2412
Telephone: (212) 663-5890
FAX: (212) 663-0853
Contact: Eric Washington
**Editorial:**
Don Thomas ................................Editor
**Desc.:** Includes news, feature stories, a
  media column, calendar of events,
  cartoons and resource listing.
**Readers:** Black lesbians and gay men.

69661

**CRUISE ENTERTAINMENT
  MAGAZINE**
660 Livernois Ave.
Ferndale, MI 48220
Telephone: (810) 545-9040
FAX: (810) 545-1073
Year Established: 1979
Pub. Frequency: w.

Page Size: pocket
Subscrip. Rate: $60/yr.
Materials: 01,02,03,05,08,09,10,11,12,13,
  14,15,16,20,21,23,24,25,28,32,33
Print Process: offset lithography
Circulation: 5,000
Circulation Type: free & paid
**Owner(s):**
Tony Rome Enterprises, Inc.
P.O. Box 398
Royal Oak, MI 48068
Telephone: (810) 545-9040
FAX: (810) 545-1073
Ownership %: 100
**Editorial:**
Philip O'Jibway ................................Editor
**Desc.:** Contains information on activities in
  the Michigan-Ohio and Windsor, Ontario
  area.
**Deadline:** story-Fri.; news-Fri.; photo-Fri.;
  ads-Fri.

69670

**DENEUVE**
2336 Market St.
No. 15
San Francisco, CA 94114
Telephone: (415) 863-6538
FAX: (415) 863-1609
Year Established: 1991
Pub. Frequency: bi-m.
Subscrip. Rate: $4 newsstand; $22/yr.
Materials: 01,02,03,04,05,06,07,08,09,10,
  11,12,13,14,15,18,19,20,21,25,28,29,30,
  32,33, personals
Circulation: 42,000
Circulation Type: paid
**Owner(s):**
FRS Enterprises
2336 Market St., No. 15
San Francisco, CA 94114
Telephone: (415) 863-6538
FAX: (415) 863-1609
Ownership %: 100
**Editorial:**
Frances Stevens ................................Editor
**Desc.:** Covers a wide variety of topics.
**Readers:** Lesbian community.

69663

**GUIDE: GAY TRAVEL,
  ENTERTAINMENT, POLITICS &
  SEX**
P.O. Box 593
Boston, MA 02199
Telephone: (617) 266-8557
FAX: (617) 266-1125
Year Established: 1980
Pub. Frequency: m.
Page Size: tabloid
Subscrip. Rate: $2.95 newsstand; $40/yr.
  1st class; $25/yr. 3rd. class
Print Process: web
Circulation: 30,000
Circulation Type: paid
**Owner(s):**
Fidelity Publishing
P.O. Box 593
Boston, MA 02199
Telephone: (617) 266-8557
Ownership %: 100
**Management:**
Edward Houghen ................................Publisher
**Editorial:**
French Wall ................................Editor
**Desc.:** Information and entertainment on
  travel, politics, sexuality, and gay history.

69664

**LAMBDA BOOK REPORT**
1625 Connecticut Ave., N.W.
Washington, DC 20009
Telephone: (202) 462-7924
FAX: (202) 462-7257
Year Established: 1987
Pub. Frequency: bi-m.

Page Size: standard
Subscrip. Rate: $3.95 newsstand;
  $19.95/yr.
Materials: 02,05,06,10,16,19,20,21,28,32,33
Print Process: offset
Circulation: 11,000
Circulation Type: paid
**Owner(s):**
Lambda Rising, Inc.
1625 Connecticut Ave., N.W.
Washington, DC 20009-1013
Telephone: (202) 462-7924
Ownership %: 100
**Editorial:**
Jim Marks ................................Editor
**Desc.:** Reviews all gay and lesbian books
  published nationally. Includes author
  interviews, essays, trade news and best-
  seller lists.

69665

**LESBIAN NEWS**
P.O. Box 1430
Twentynine Palms, CA 92277
Telephone: (213) 848-4469
FAX: (619) 367-3386
Year Established: 1975
Pub. Frequency: m.
Subscrip. Rate: $35/yr.
Materials: 012,05,06,19,20,21,25,28,30,32,
  33
Print Process: web offset
Circulation: 32,000
Circulation Type: free & paid
**Owner(s):**
Deborah Bergman
P.O. Box 1430
Twentynine Palms, CA 92277
Telephone: (213) 658-0258
Ownership %: 100
**Desc.:** Features and news stories on
  lesbian issues and trends.
**Deadline:** ads-15th of mo. prior to pub.
  date

69666

**OPTIONS**
P.O. Box 470
Port Chester, NY 10573
Year Established: 1981
Pub. Frequency: 10/yr.
Page Size: 5 3/8 x 8 1/4
Subscrip. Rate: $3.50 newsstand;
  $19.90/yr.
Materials: 05,06,11,15,17,18,19,20,21
Freelance Pay: $75-$200
Circulation: 75,000
Circulation Type: paid
**Owner(s):**
AJA Publishing Corp.
P.O. Box 470
Port Chester, NY 10573
Ownership %: 100
**Editorial:**
Don Stone ................................Editor
**Desc.:** Emphasizes safe, loving
  relationships. Covers sexual interactions
  between homosexuals, bisexuals, and
  lesbians.
**Deadline:** story-5-6 mos. prior to pub.
  date; ads-4 mos. prior

67249

**OUR WORLD**
1104 N. Nova Rd., Ste. 251
Daytona Beach, FL 32117
Telephone: (904) 441-5367
FAX: (904) 441-5604
Year Established: 1989
Pub. Frequency: 10/yr.
Page Size: standard
Subscrip. Rate: $4.95 newsstand; $35/10
  issues
Materials: 06,09,10,32,33
Print Process: web
Circulation: 20,000
Circulation Type: paid

**Owner(s):**
Our World Publishing Corp.
1104 N. Nova Rd., Ste. 251
Daytona Beach, FL 32117
Telephone: (904) 441-5367
Ownership %: 100
**Management:**
Richard Valdmanis ...................Vice President
Wayne Whiston ...................Publisher
**Editorial:**
Wayne Whiston ................................Editor
**Desc.:** Travel magazine for gays and
  lesbians featuring inns, resorts, hotels,
  tours, trips and cruises throughout the
  world.
**Readers:** Gay and lesbian travelers.
**Deadline:** story-1st of mo. prior to pub.
  date; news-1st of mo. prior; photo-1st of
  mo. prior; ads-15th of mo. prior

69668

**OUT**
110 Greene St.
Ste. 800
New York, NY 10012-3836
Telephone: (212) 334-9119
FAX: (212) 334-9227
Year Established: 1992
Pub. Frequency: 10/yr.
Page Size: standard
Subscrip. Rate: $24.95/yr.
Materials: 01,03,04,05,06,09,10,11,12,13,
  14,15,19,21,22,23,24,25,29,32,33
Freelance Pay: $.50-$.75/wd.
Print Process: web offset
Circulation: 100,000
Circulation Type: controlled & paid
**Owner(s):**
Out Publishing, Inc.
110 Greene St., Apt. 800
New York, NY 10012-3836
Telephone: (212) 334-9119
Ownership %: 100
**Management:**
Michael Goff ................................President
George Slowik ................................Publisher
**Editorial:**
Michael Goff ................................Editor
Harry Taylor ................................Advertising
**Desc.:** National, general interest magazine
  for gay men & lesbians. Quality
  contributions from the mainstream media
  and the highest production values.
  Serious journalism, cutting edge
  consumer and fashion editorial as well
  as directed service and broad
  entertainment coverage.
**Readers:** Upscale gay and lesbian
  community.

69669

**10 PERCENT**
54 Mint St., Ste. 200
San Francisco, CA 94103
Telephone: (415) 905-8590
FAX: (415) 227-0463
Year Established: 1992
Pub. Frequency: bi-m.
Page Size: standard
Subscrip. Rate: $3 newsstand; $17.95/yr.
Print Process: web offset
Circulation: 70,000
Circulation Type: paid
**Owner(s):**
Browning-Grace Communications
54 Mint St., Ste. 200
San Francisco, CA 94103
Telephone: (415) 905-8590
Ownership %: 100

---

**Materials Accepted/Included:** 01-Business news 02-By-line articles 03-Fashion news 04-Food news 05-Freelance copy 06-Letters to editor 07-Real estate news 08-Sports news 09-Travel news
10-Book rev. 11-Movie rev. 12-Music rev. 13-TV rev. 14-Theater rev. 15-Coming events 16-Obituaries 17-Question & answer 18-Social announcements 19-Artwork 20-Cartoons 21-Photos 22-TV listings
23-Audio rec. 24-Video rec. 25-Books 26-Films/film clips 27-Personnel news 28-Press releases 29-New product news/photos 30-Trade lit. 31-Contracts awarded 32-Display adv. 33-Classified adv.

**Readers:** Lesbian and gay professionals.

## Group 632-General Interest

### AMERICAN SURVIVAL GUIDE
66700
774 S. Placentia Ave.
Placentia, CA 92670-6832
Telephone: (714) 572-2255
FAX: (714) 572-1864
Year Established: 1979
Pub. Frequency: m.
Page Size: standard
Subscrip. Rate: $3.50 newsstand;
 $26.95/yr.; $44.95/2 yrs.
Materials: 02,04,05,06,10,28,29,30,32,33
Freelance Pay: $200-$300/article
Circulation: 72,000
Circulation Type: paid
**Owner(s):**
McMullen And Yee Publishing, Inc.
774 S. Placentia Ave.
Placentia, CA 92656
Telephone: (714) 572-2255
FAX: (714) 572-1864
Ownership %: 100
**Editorial:**
Jim Benson .................................Editor
Bob Clark ...............................Editorial Director
Scott Stoddard ........................Associate Editor
**Desc.:** Dedicated to people concerned
 with protection of life and property and
 with independent, self-reliant living.
**Readers:** Average age is late 30's; mostly
 military and law enforcement
 personnels.

### ARCHAEOLOGY
25960
135 William St.
New York, NY 10038
Telephone: (212) 732-5154
FAX: (212) 732-5707
Year Established: 1948
Pub. Frequency: bi-m
Page Size: standard
Subscrip. Rate: $19.97/yr.
Print Process: web offset
Circulation: 160,000
Circulation Type: paid
**Owner(s):**
Archaeological Institute of America
675 Commonwealth Ave.
Boston, MA 02215
Telephone: (617) 353-9361
FAX: (617) 353-9330
Ownership %: 100
**Management:**
Phyllis P. Katz ...........................Publisher
Charlene Sugihara ............Advertising Manager
Amy Lubelski .....................Production Manager
**Editorial:**
Peter A. Young ....................Editor in Chief
Mark Rose ..........................Managing Editor
Spencer P.M. Harrington ........Associate Editor
Angela M.H. Schuster ..............Associate Editor
Fran Kane ...........................Circulation Editor
Elinor J. Pettit .......................Design Director
Peter S. Allen .........................Film Editor
**Desc.:** Contributed articles written by
 archaeologists and edited for the
 general public, deal with
 various disciplines. Emphasis placed on
 techniques and their applications, recent
 finds, special studies of ancient cultures.
 Reviews of books on archaeology or
 related subjects.
**Readers:** Archaeology enthusiasts.
**Deadline:** ads-10th of 2nd mo. prior to
 issue date

### BOYCOTT QUARTERLY
69672
P.O. Box 64
Olympia, WA 98507-0064
Telephone: (206) 357-4705
Year Established: 1993

Pub. Frequency: q.
Page Size: standard
Subscrip. Rate: $4.95/copy US; $5.95
 Canada; $20/yr. US; $27/yr. Canada &
 Mexico; $40/yr. elsewhere
Materials: 02,06,20,28
Print Process: web offset
Circulation: 4,600
Circulation Type: paid
**Owner(s):**
Boycott Quarterly
**Editorial:**
Zachary D. Lyons ..........................Editor
**Desc.:** Provides lists and descriptions of
 active consumer boycotts. Provides
 boycott news & updates, in-depth
 boycott coverage, and coverage of a
 wide variety of other Economic
 Democracy topics.
**Deadline:** story-Mar. 1, Jun. 1, Sep. 1,
 Dec. 1; news-Mar. 1, Jun. 1, Sep. 1,
 Dec. 1; photo-Apr. 1, Jul. 1, Oct. 1, Jan.
 1

### CITY COUNTY MAGAZINE
70417
223 E. Davis
Burlington, NC 27215
Telephone: (910) 226-8436
FAX: (910) 226-8437
Mailing Address:
 P.O. Box 517
 Burlington, NC 27215
Year Established: 1976
Pub. Frequency: m.
Page Size: 8 x 11
Subscrip. Rate: $1.50 newsstand; $12/yr.
Freelance Pay: varies
Print Process: offset
Circulation: 5,000
Circulation Type: paid
**Owner(s):**
P.N. Thompson Printing Co., Inc.
P.O. Box 517
Burlington, NC 27216
Telephone: (910) 226-8436
Ownership %: 100
**Management:**
Dean Thompson ...........................President
Vicky Hunley .............................Publisher
**Editorial:**
Jennifer Atkins Brwon ......................Editor
**Desc.:** General interest-local.

### CONSUMER INFO NEWS
70483
275 Bay 37th St.
Brooklyn, NY 11214
Telephone: (718) 996-5406
FAX: (718) 373-1352
Pub. Frequency: w.: Mon.
Page Size: standard
Subscrip. Rate: $2.95 newsstand; $40/yr.
Circulation: 127,000
Circulation Type: paid
**Owner(s):**
Kenneth Brown, Sr.
275 Bay 37th St.
Brooklyn, NY 11214
Telephone: (718) 996-5406
FAX: (718) 373-1352
Ownership %: 100
**Management:**
Kenneth Brown, Sr. .........................Publisher
Adrienne Knoll ..................Advertising Manager
**Desc.:** General interest magazine.

### CONSUMER REPORTS
25840
101 Truman Ave.
Yonkers, NY 10703-1057
Telephone: (914) 378-2000
FAX: (914) 378-2900
Mailing Address:
 P.O. Box 53029
 Yonkers, NY 10703
Year Established: 1936

Pub. Frequency: m.
Page Size: standard
Subscrip. Rate: $2.95/copy; $22/yr.
Materials: 32,33
Circulation: 5,000,000
Circulation Type: paid
**Owner(s):**
Consumers Union of United States, Inc.
101 Truman Ave.
Yonkers, NY 10703-1057
Telephone: (914) 378-2000
Ownership %: 100
**Editorial:**
Irwin Landau ..............................Editor
Eileen Denver .......................Managing Editor
Flora S. H. Ling .....................Associate Editor
**Desc.:** Features objective comparative
 evaluations, ratings and tests of
 consumer items from small household
 appliances to automobiles.

### CONSUMERS' RESEARCH MAGAZINE
22296
800 Maryland Ave., N.E.
Washington, DC 20002
Telephone: (202) 546-1713
Year Established: 1927
Pub. Frequency: m.
Page Size: standard
Subscrip. Rate: $2.50 newsstand; $24/yr.;
 $42/2 yrs.
Materials: 01,02,04,05,06,07,08,09,11,17,
 19,21
Freelance Pay: $100/pg.
Print Process: web
Circulation: 12,000
Circulation Type: paid
**Owner(s):**
Consumers' Research, Inc.
800 Maryland Ave., N.E.
Washington, DC 20002
Telephone: (202) 546-1713
Ownership %: 100
**Management:**
F. J. Schlink ...............................Founder
M. Stanton Evans .............Chairman of Board
M. Stanton Evans ...........................President
M. Stanton Evans ...........................Publisher
Mary Jo Buckland ...............Business Manager
Christina Sobran ..............Circulation Manager
**Editorial:**
Peter Spencer ......................Executive Editor
Guy Murdoch .........................Managing Editor
Michael Chapman ...................Associate Editor
**Desc.:** To provide the public with scientific
 technical and educational information on
 topics of consumer interest.
**Readers:** Consumers at large, US and
 abroad.

### CONSUMERS DIGEST
25841
5705 N. Lincoln Ave.
Chicago, IL 60659
Telephone: (312) 275-3590
Year Established: 1959
Pub. Frequency: bi-m.
Page Size: standard
Subscrip. Rate: $15.97/yr.
Freelance Pay: negotiable
Circulation: 1,000,000
Circulation Type: paid
**Owner(s):**
Consumers Digest, Inc.
5705 N. Lincoln Ave.
Chicago, IL 60659
Telephone: (312) 275-3590
Ownership %: 100
**Management:**
Arthur Weber ...........................President
Randy Weber ...........................Publisher
Nancy Friend ....................Business Manager
Charles Michell ..............Circulation Manager
**Editorial:**
John Manos .........................Editor in Chief

Elliott McCleary ......................Executive Editor
Jim Gorzelany .........................Senior Editor
John Wasik ...............................Editor
Howard Plissner ...............Advertising Director
George Kenton ..........................Art Director
Mary Butler ........................Assistant Editor
Robert Miller ........................Services Director
**Desc.:** Consumer guide to best values in
 products & services.

### COUNTRY
69201
5400 S. 60th St.
Greendale, WI 53129
Telephone: (414) 423-0100
Year Established: 1987
Pub. Frequency: bi-m.
Subscrip. Rate: $16.98/yr.
Circulation: 2,100,000
Circulation Type: paid
**Owner(s):**
Reiman Publications, Inc.
5400 S. 60th St.
Greendale, WI 53129
Telephone: (414) 423-0100
Ownership %: 100
**Editorial:**
Roy J. Reiman ...............................Editor

### COUNTRY SAMPLER
66770
707 Kautz Rd.
St. Charles, IL 60174
Telephone: (708) 377-8000
FAX: (708) 377-8194
Year Established: 1984
Pub. Frequency: bi-m.
Page Size: standard
Subscrip. Rate: $19.96/yr.
Circulation: 533,000
Circulation Type: paid
**Owner(s):**
Sampler Publications
707 Kautz Rd.
St. Charles, IL 60174
Telephone: (708) 377-8000
Ownership %: 100
**Management:**
Mark Nickel ...............................Owner
Margaret Kernan ...........................Publisher
**Editorial:**
Cheryl Schaefer ....................Managing Editor
**Desc.:** Contains information about country
 home accessories and crafts.

### DOCTOR'S LIFE, THE
26585
325 E. 41st St.
New York, NY 10017
Telephone: (212) 986-2177
Year Established: 1980
Pub. Frequency: 4/yr.
Page Size: standard
Subscrip. Rate: $5/yr.
Materials: 04,09,15,25,29
Circulation: 180,000
Circulation Type: controlled
**Owner(s):**
Doctor's Life, Inc.
325 E. 41st St.
New York, NY 10017
Telephone: (212) 986-2177
Ownership %: 100
**Management:**
Alice Towsley ...........................Publisher
**Editorial:**
Alice Towsley .......................Executive Editor
Anita Gerard ...............................Editor
Charles Allen .......................Associate Editor

**Desc.:** A consumer type publication, directed to interest, entertain, and inform about the doctor's life. All material must have a specific appeal and relate to this particular audience. It is non-medical, other than special material relating to life in social, home, and professional aspects, such as theater, records, movies, art, radio-TV, sports and all areas of the entertainment field, travel, beauty, finance, home and office decorating, fashion, new products, human-interest stories.
**Readers:** Doctors & families.

26138

## FEATURE
P.O. Box 1708
Cheyenne, WY 82003-1708
Telephone: (307) 777-4375
Pub. Frequency: m.
Page Size: standard
Subscrip. Rate: members only
**Owner(s):**
Wyoming Transportation Dept.
P.O. Box 1708
Cheyenne, WY 82003-1708
Ownership %: 100
**Management:**
Alfred E. Knobler ..................................President
Rick Bard .............................................Publisher
**Editorial:**
Peter Knobler ...........................................Editor
Tony Petrella .................................Art Director

69671

## FREEBIES
1135 Eugenia Pl.
Carpinteria, CA 93013
Telephone: (805) 566-1225
FAX: (805) 566-0305
Year Established: 1977
Pub. Frequency: 5/yr.
Subscrip. Rate: $8.95/yr.
Print Process: web
Circulation: 400,000
Circulation Type: paid
**Owner(s):**
Freebies Publishing Co.
1135 Eugenia Pl.
Carpinteria, CA 93013
Telephone: (805) 566-1225
Ownership %: 100
**Editorial:**
Linda Cook ...................................................Editor

69739

## GLOBE
5401 N.W. Broken Sound Blvd.
Boca Raton, FL 33487
Telephone: (407) 997-7733
Year Established: 1954
Pub. Frequency: w.
Subscrip. Rate: $29.75/yr.
Circulation: 1,300,000
Circulation Type: paid
**Owner(s):**
Globe Communications Corp.
5401 N.W. Broken Sound Blvd.
Boca Raton, FL 33487
Telephone: (407) 997-7733
Ownership %: 100
**Editorial:**
Phil Bunton .................................................Editor

52610

## GRAY PANTHER NETWORK
2025 Pennsylvania Ave., N.W., Ste. 821
Washington, DC 20006
Telephone: (202) 466-3132
FAX: (202) 466-3133
Year Established: 1972
Pub. Frequency: q.
Page Size: tabloid
Subscrip. Rate: $20/yr. individuals; $35/yr. institutions; $40/yr. foreign
Materials: 06,20,21
Circulation: 30,000

Circulation Type: paid
**Owner(s):**
Gray Panthers Project Fund
2025 Pennsylvania Ave., N.W.
Ste. 821
Washington, DC 20006
Telephone: (202) 466-3132
Ownership %: 100
**Desc.:** Chronicles the activities of the dynamic network of Panther activists, as well as the many issues - ageism, health care, employment, environmental preservation, housing and peace - that Gray Panthers work on toward improving all of society.
**Readers:** Activists of all ages, majority 50 years old or older.

26170

## GRIT
1503 S.W. 42nd St.
Topeka, KS 66609
Telephone: (913) 274-4300
FAX: (913) 274-4305
Year Established: 1882
Pub. Frequency: bi-w.
Page Size: tabloid
Subscrip. Rate: $1.50/copy; $26.95/yr.
Freelance Pay: $.12/wd.-2nd rights
Circulation: 400,000
Circulation Type: paid
**Owner(s):**
Stauffer Communications, Inc.
616 Jefferson
Topeka, KS 66607
Telephone: (913) 295-1111
Ownership %: 100
**Management:**
Donald R. Keating ....................Vice President
E. Van Anderson ..............Advertising Manager
Donald R. Keating .................General Manager
**Editorial:**
Roberta Peterson ....................................Editor
Nancy Peterson .....................Associate Editor
Dave Wood .........................................Columnist
Rochelle Lyon ...................................Columnist
Carl Larsen ........................................Columnist
Betsy Miller ......................................Food Editor
John Maddox ..........................Marketing Editor
**Desc.:** Carries small town stories, stories on families making an important contribution to their community or the American way of life, stories on religion, jobs, recreation, families, necessities (how people cope), first-person articles in which readers talk about their funniest moments, turning points in their lives; food pages, romance, mystery and western serials, sports, readers/forum, readers letters.
**Readers:** C & D size counties throughout the United States.

55970

## HEALTH MASTER
P.O. Box 9
Drain, OR 97435
Telephone: (503) 836-2358
FAX: (503) 836-2358
Year Established: 1978
Pub. Frequency: s-a.
Page Size: standard
Subscrip. Rate: free
Circulation: 80,000
Circulation Type: free
**Owner(s):**
Conscious Living Foundation
P.O. Box 9
Drain, OR 97435
Telephone: (503) 836-2358
Ownership %: 100
**Editorial:**
Dr. Tim Lowenstein ...............................Editor
**Readers:** People interested in self-improvement and stress management. Individuals and professionals.

69753

## HEMISPHERES
1301 Carolina St.
Greensboro, NC 27401
Telephone: (910) 378-6065
FAX: (910) 275-2864
Year Established: 1957
Pub. Frequency: m.
Page Size: standard
Subscrip. Rate: $28/yr.
Materials: 01,02,03,06,08,09,10,15,19,20, 21,25,26,32
Print Process: web offset
Circulation: 500,000
Circulation Type: controlled & paid
**Owner(s):**
Pace Communications, Inc.
1301 Carolina St.
Greensboro, NC 27401
Telephone: (919) 378-6065
Ownership %: 100
**Editorial:**
Kate Greer ...............................................Editor
John Ballantyne ..............VP Sales & Marketing
**Desc.:** Inflight magazine for United Airlines.
**Deadline:** story-3 mo. prior to pub. date; news-3 mo. prior to pub. date; photo-3 mo. prior to pub. date; ads-1 1/2 mo. prior to pub. date

68938

## IDEAS FOR BETTER LIVING
3380 Tremont Rd.
Columbus, OH 43221-2112
Telephone: (614) 451-6548
FAX: (614) 451-6554
Mailing Address:
P.O. Box 12098
Columbus, OH 43212
Year Established: 1945
Pub. Frequency: m.
Page Size: 7 1/2" X 10 1/2"
Subscrip. Rate: free
Print Process: web offset
Circulation: 250,000
Circulation Type: controlled
**Owner(s):**
Boulevard Publications, Inc.
3380 Tremont Rd.
Columbus, OH 43221-2112
Telephone: (614) 451-6548
Ownership %: 100
**Editorial:**
Steve Bulkley ...........................................Editor
**Desc.:** Includes home decorating articles, as well as articles on health, pets, good money sense, travel, interesting hobbies, gardening, and nearly all general-interest subjects.
**Readers:** Adult, mature audience, 40, up to full-retired; middle to lower-upper income brackets.

52623

## IN TOUCH
10 Woodward Hall, URI
Kingston, RI 02881-0804
Telephone: (401) 792-2465
Year Established: 1978
Pub. Frequency: bi-m.
Page Size: tabloid
Subscrip. Rate: free
Materials: 04,19,20,21
Circulation: 24,000
Circulation Type: controlled & free
**Owner(s):**
Univ. of RI, College Resource Development
Woodward Hall
Kingston, RI 02881
Telephone: (401) 792-2474
Ownership %: 100
**Editorial:**
Jacqueline McGrath ................................Editor

**Desc.:** A free public service. Its editorial content provides information to consumers, gardeners, conservationists and those interested in nutrition and health.
**Readers:** General audience.
**Deadline:** ads-6 wks. prior to pub. date

25873

## KNOWLEDGE MAGAZINE
3863 S.W. Loop 820, Ste. 100
Fort Worth, TX 76116
Telephone: (817) 292-4272
Year Established: 1976
Pub. Frequency: q.
Page Size: pocket
Subscrip. Rate: $6/issue; $30/yr.
Freelance Pay: $50 and up
Circulation: 2,500
Circulation Type: paid
**Owner(s):**
Knowledge, Inc.
3863 S.W. Loop 820, Ste. 100
Fort Worth, TX 76133-2063
Telephone: (817) 292-4272
Ownership %: 100
**Management:**
O. A. Battista ........................................Publisher
**Editorial:**
O. A. Battista .................................Editor in Chief
Naomi L. Matous .....................Managing Editor
Lou Benner .........................Book Review Editor
Nita B. Griffin .................................Miscellaneous
O. A. Battista ...........................Technical Editor
**Desc.:** Dedicated to informing the world of new knowledge, spreading knowledge to support truths, developing people's minds, and creating World Olympiads Of Knowledge. Official publication of World Olympiads of Knowledge.
**Readers:** All classes, lay and professional.

26175

## LIFE
Time & Life Bldg.
1271 Ave. of the Americas
New York, NY 10020
Telephone: (212) 522-1212
Year Established: 1978
Pub. Frequency: m.
Page Size: oversize
Subscrip. Rate: $2.95 newsstand; $32/yr.
Freelance Pay: varies
Circulation: 1,500,000
Circulation Type: paid
**Owner(s):**
Time Warner, Inc.
Time & Life Bldg.
New York, NY 10020
Telephone: (212) 522-1212
Ownership %: 100
**Management:**
Reginald K. Brach, Jr. .........Chairman of Board
Ed McCarrick .......................................Publisher
**Editorial:**
Daniel Okrent .......................Managing Editor
Bill Kupper .............................................Advertising
Mark Hintsa .........................Marketing Director
**Desc.:** A monthly magazine of photojournalism from around the world, featuring pictures and articles of general interest.
**Readers:** Affluent, college educated adults.

49871

## MAKING IT! CAREERS NEWSMAGAZINE
5 Rose Ave.
Great Neck, NY 11021
Telephone: (516) 829-8829
Year Established: 1982
Pub. Frequency: q.
Page Size: 4 color photos/art
Subscrip. Rate: $10/yr.
Circulation: 50,000
Circulation Type: paid

---

**Materials Accepted/Included:** 01-Business news 02-By-line articles 03-Fashion news 04-Food news 05-Freelance copy 06-Letters to editor 07-Real estate news 08-Sports news 09-Travel news 10-Book rev. 11-Movie rev. 12-Music rev. 13-TV rev. 14-Theater rev. 15-Coming events 16-Obituaries 17-Question & answer 18-Social announcements 19-Artwork 20-Cartoons 21-Photos 22-TV listings 23-Audio rec. 24-Video rec. 25-Books 26-Films/film clips 27-Personnel news 28-Press releases 29-New product news/photos 30-Trade lit. 31-Contracts awarded 32-Display adv. 33-Classified adv.

6-47

**Owner(s):**
Workstyles, Inc.
5 Rose Ave.
Great Neck, NY 11021
Telephone: (516) 829-8829
Ownership %: 100
**Management:**
Karen Rubin .............................Publisher
**Editorial:**
Karen Rubin .................................Editor
Neil Leiberman ..............Marketing Manager
**Desc.:** Edited to help graduating students, people returning to the workforce and those changing careers, locate and land positions as professionals and managers. Focuses on specific companies and industries--what they are, where they are headed and what they offer the prospective employee--in order to help people make more informed decisions leading to fulfilling careers.
**Readers:** College and graduate school students, people returning to workforce and those changing careers.

66681

**MANCHESTER**
100 Main St.
Nashua, NH 03060
Telephone: (603) 883-3150
Year Established: 1991
Pub. Frequency: m.
Subscrip. Rate: $20/yr.
Circulation: 6,500
Circulation Type: paid
**Owner(s):**
Connections Network, Inc.
100 Main St.
Nashua, NH 03060
Telephone: (603) 883-3150
FAX: (603) 889-5557
Ownership %: 100
**Management:**
David Gregg ...............................President
Patricia Gregg ............................Publisher
**Editorial:**
Richard Broussard ........................Editor

25880

**MASTER DETECTIVE**
460 W. 34th St., 20th Fl.
New York, NY 10001
Telephone: (212) 947-6500
FAX: (212) 947-6272
Year Established: 1930
Pub. Frequency: 7/yr.
Page Size: standard
Freelance Pay: $250/5,000-6,000 wds.;
   $500-dbl. length
Circulation: 175,000
Circulation Type: controlled
**Owner(s):**
Div. of Reese Communications
460 W 34th St., 20th Fl.
New York, NY 10001
Telephone: (212) 947-6500
**Management:**
J. Rosenfield ..............................President
J. Rosenfield ..............................Publisher
J. Burriesci ...............Advertising Manager
**Editorial:**
Rose Mandelsberg ..............Editor in Chief
Ben Harvey ............................Art Director
**Desc.:** Covers current and classic accounts of police action or investigative work. Manuscripts, 5,000-6,000 words each, should combine strict attention to factual detail with a lively, dramatic narrative style. Stories written from police viewpoint preferreed. Query in advance of submission is required. Photos used to illustrate all full length pieces.

25884

**MOTHER EARTH NEWS, THE**
24 E. 23rd St.
New York, NY 10010
Telephone: (212) 260-7210
FAX: (212) 267-7445
Year Established: 1970
Pub. Frequency: bi-m.
Page Size: standard
Subscrip. Rate: $3.00 newsstand; $18/yr.
Circulation: 400,000
Circulation Type: paid
**Owner(s):**
Sussex Publishers, Inc.
24 E. 23rd St., 5th Fl.
New York, NY 10010
Telephone: (212) 260-7210
Ownership %: 100
**Management:**
John Brink .................................Publisher
**Editorial:**
Matt Scanlon ................................Editor
Pat Stone ........................Assistant Editor
S. Pacher ......................Associate Editor
**Desc.:** Presents ideas and ideals for independent living and provides information on gardening, using alternative energy resources, designing and constructing energy efficient homes and retrofitting. Encourages conservation of natural resources and presents articles on money-saving do-it-yourself skills and projects, crafts for fun and profit, entrepreneurs and home businesses, new product reviews, ways to improve and maintain personal health and enjoy good health through recreation. The focus is on developing personal and material resources to improve standards of living and to create a richer, more fulfilling way of life.

66682

**NASHUA**
100 Main St.
Nashua, NH 03060
Telephone: (603) 883-3150
FAX: (603) 889-5557
Year Established: 1988
Pub. Frequency: m.
Subscrip. Rate: $20/yr.
Circulation: 6,500
Circulation Type: paid
**Owner(s):**
Connections Network, Inc.
100 Main St.
Nashua, NH 03060
Telephone: (603) 883-3150
FAX: (603) 889-5557
Ownership %: 100
**Management:**
David Gregg ...............................President
Patricia Gregg ............................Publisher
**Editorial:**
Richar Broussard .........................Editor

25887

**NATIONAL GEOGRAPHIC**
1145 17th St.
Washington, DC 20036
Telephone: (202) 857-7000
Year Established: 1888
Pub. Frequency: m.
Page Size: standard
Subscrip. Rate: $21/yr.
Freelance Pay: $6000
Circulation: 9,300,000
Circulation Type: paid
**Owner(s):**
National Geographic Society
17th & M. Sts., N.W.
Washington, DC 20036
Telephone: (202) 857-7000
Ownership %: 100
**Management:**
Gilbert M. Grosvenor ....................President

**Editorial:**
William Graves ..............................Editor
Thomas R. Kennedy .........................Photo
Robert B. Sims ..........Senior Vice President
**Desc.:** Extensively illustrated first-person narratives cover travel, people, wildlife, folklore, commodities, meteorology, the sea, scientific research, industry, etc. Articles are written for the layman, but are factual and authentic. Interested in color transparencies 35mm or larger and manuscripts bearing on geography in the broadest sense of the word. Typical titles are Kyoto and Nara: Keepers of Japan's Past; Bad Days For The Brown Pelican; Irish Ways Live On In Dingle; Sea Gypsies Of The Philippines. Articles written from first-hand experience. Query first concerning interest.
**Readers:** Families in the United States and abroad.

65369

**NATIONAL GREYHOUND UPDATE**
21684 Granada Ave.
Cupertino, CA 95014
Telephone: (408) 446-0551
FAX: (408) 824-8436
Year Established: 1986
Pub. Frequency: 7/yr.
Page Size: standard
Subscrip. Rate: $3.95 newsstand;
   $19.90/yr.; $34.90/2 yrs.
Circulation: 20,000
Circulation Type: paid
**Owner(s):**
Hobson Publishing
21684 Granada Ave.
Cupertino, CA 95014
Telephone: (408) 446-0551
Ownership %: 100
**Management:**
David Hobson ...........................Publisher
**Editorial:**
Pres Hobson .................................Editor

25908

**PEOPLE WEEKLY**
Time & Life Bldg., Rockefeller Ctr.
1271 Ave. of the Americas
New York, NY 10020-1393
Telephone: (212) 522-4461
Year Established: 1974
Pub. Frequency: Mon.
Page Size: standard
Subscrip. Rate: $2.39 newsstand;
   $82.68/yr.
Circulation: 3,150,000
Circulation Type: paid
**Owner(s):**
Time, Inc.
1271 Ave. of the Americas
New York, NY 10020-1393
Telephone: (212) 522-1212
Ownership %: 100
**Management:**
Ann Moore ...............................President
Ann Jackson ..............................Publisher
**Editorial:**
Landon Y. Jones Jr. ...........Managing Editor

65425

**QUEST, THE**
P.O. Box 270
Wheaton, IL 60189
Telephone: (708) 668-1571
FAX: (708) 668-4976
Year Established: 1988
Pub. Frequency: q.
Page Size: standard
Subscrip. Rate: $4.95 newsstand;
   $15.97/yr.
Freelance Pay: up to $300/article
Circulation: 25,000
Circulation Type: controlled & paid

**Owner(s):**
Theosophical Society in America
1926 N. Main St.
Wheaton, IL 60187
Telephone: (708) 668-1571
Ownership %: 100
**Management:**
Joyce Knutsen ...............Production Manager
**Editorial:**
William Metzger .............................Editor
Ray Grasse ..............................Advertising
Pat Coleman ..........................Art Director
Ray Grasse ......................Assistant Editor
**Desc.:** Comparative study of philosophy, science, religion, and the arts.
**Readers:** General public and members of Theosophical Society in America.

25921

**READER'S DIGEST**
Pleasantville, NY 10570
Telephone: (914) 238-1000
FAX: (914) 244-2505
Year Established: 1922
Pub. Frequency: m.
Page Size: pocket
Subscrip. Rate: $2.25 newsstand;
   $22.46/yr.
Circulation: 15,000,000
Circulation Type: paid
**Owner(s):**
Reader's Digest Association, Inc.
Pleasantville, NY 10570
Telephone: (914) 238-1000
Ownership %: 100
**Management:**
DeWitt Wallace ............................Founder
George V. Grune ..............Chairman of Board
Gregory G. Coleman ......................Publisher
Martha Molnar ..........Public Relations Manager
**Editorial:**
Kenneth Y. Tomlinson ...........Editor in Chief
**Desc.:** A digest of leading articles and books that have appeared in other publications, plus original articles developed by staff writers and others.
**Readers:** General public.

59653

**RUSSELL REGISTER**
2873 Mercedes
Odessa, TX 79764
Telephone: (915) 381-1047
Year Established: 1978
Pub. Frequency: q.
Page Size: standard
Subscrip. Rate: $20/yr.
Materials: 06
Circulation: 200
Circulation Type: paid
**Owner(s):**
Shirley Shumate
2873 Mercedes
Odessa, TX 79764
Telephone: (915) 381-1047
Ownership %: 100
**Management:**
Shirley Shumate ..........................Publisher
Shirley Shumate ............................Manager
**Editorial:**
Shirley Shumate ............................Editor
**Readers:** Genealogy.

25927

**SATURDAY EVENING POST, THE**
1100 Waterway Blvd.
Indianapolis, IN 46202
Telephone: (317) 636-8881
FAX: (317) 636-0126
Mailing Address:
   P.O. Box 1144
   Indianapolis, IN 46206
Year Established: 1728
Pub. Frequency: bi-m.
Page Size: standard
Subscrip. Rate: $2.90/issue; $13.97/yr.
Circulation: 520,000

**Materials Accepted/Included:** 01-Business news 02-By-line articles 03-Fashion news 04-Food news 05-Freelance copy 06-Letters to editor 07-Real estate news 08-Sports news 09-Travel news 10-Book rev. 11-Movie rev. 12-Music rev. 13-TV rev. 14-Theater rev. 15-Coming events 16-Obituaries 17-Question & answer 18-Social announcements 19-Artwork 20-Cartoons 21-Photos 22-TV listings 23-Audio rec. 24-Video rec. 25-Books 26-Films/film clips 27-Personnel news 28-Press releases 29-New product news/photos 30-Trade lit. 31-Contracts awarded 32-Display adv. 33-Classified adv.

Circulation Type: paid
**Owner(s):**
Benjamin Franklin Literary & Medical
  Society, Inc.
P.O. Box 1144
Indianapolis, IN 46202
Telephone: (317) 636-8881
Ownership %: 100
**Management:**
Robert Silvers .....................Vice President
Dr. Cory SerVaas ...........................Publisher
Don Sutton ....................Advertising Manager
Georgia Ratliff .................Circulation Manager
**Editorial:**
Dr. Cory SerVaas ...............Executive Editor
Ted Krieter .............................Senior Editor
Dr. Cory SerVaas ...............................Editor
Chris Wilhoite ...........................Art Director
Steve Pettinga ...............................Librarian
Karen Smith ....................New Products Editor
Pat Perry ......................................Photo
Dwight Lamb ...................Production Director
Byron Estes ....................Research Director
Dwight Lamb ....................Technical Editor
**Desc.:** A general interest magazine
  directed at readers who believe in
  values rapidly disappearing in today's
  society; family life, clean humor,
  thoughtful fiction, self-reliance and in-
  depth examinations of current political
  trends.
**Readers:** 45.2% men, 54.8% women;
  median age: 44.4, median HHI: $33,686.

---

65690

**SILVER CIRCLE**
4900 Rivergrade Rd.
Baldwin Park, CA 91706
Telephone: (818) 814-7282
Year Established: 1973
Pub. Frequency: q.
Page Size: 4 color photos/art
Subscrip. Rate: $6/yr.
Freelance Pay: $200-$1,200
Circulation: 575,000
Circulation Type: paid
**Owner(s):**
Home Savings of America
4900 Rivergrade Rd.
Baldwin Park, CA 91706
Ownership %: 100
**Management:**
Caren Roberson ...........................Publisher
**Editorial:**
Jay Binkley ...................................Editor
**Desc.:** Provides practical information on
  personal finance, home ownership,
  travel, health and medical, recreation,
  hobbies, self-improvement, food and
  lifestyle.
**Readers:** Despite the magazine's name,
  it's not a senior publication. Rather, we
  target the dynamic and active, middle to
  upper income 40 years old and up
  group.

---

25936

**SMITHSONIAN**
Arts & Industries Bldg.
900 Jefferson Dr., S.W.
Washington, DC 20560
Telephone: (202) 786-2900
FAX: (202) 786-2564
Year Established: 1970
Pub. Frequency: m.
Page Size: standard
Subscrip. Rate: $22/yr.
Materials: 02,06,10,19,20,21,32
Freelance Pay: $1,000-$3,000
Print Process: web offset
Circulation: 2,300,000
Circulation Type: paid

**Owner(s):**
Smithsonian Institution
Arts & Industries Bldg.
900 Jefferson Dr., S.W.
Washington, DC 20560
Telephone: (202) 357-2600
Ownership %: 100
**Management:**
Ron Walker ...............................Publisher
Dave Cator .....................Advertising Manager
**Editorial:**
Don Moser ...................................Editor
Kathleen Burke ..............Book Review Editor
Marlane A. Liddell .....................Miscellaneous
Caroline Despard .......................Picture Editor
**Desc.:** Material relates to history, museum
  objects, science, artworks, nature,
  ethnology, air-space, personalities, book
  reviews, ecology.
**Readers:** People with above average
  income, some college.
**Deadline:** story-2 mos. prior to issue date
  on 20th; news-2 mos.; photo-2 mos.;
  ads-2 mos.

---

26335

**SOUTHWESTERN LORE**
P.O. Box 1004
Boulder, CO 80306-1004
Telephone: (303) 449-2852
Year Established: 1935
Pub. Frequency: q.
Page Size: standard
Subscrip. Rate: $12.50/yr. single; $15/yr.
  family; $25/yr. library/institution
Freelance Pay: free
Circulation: 1,000
Circulation Type: paid
**Owner(s):**
Colorado Archaeological Society
Executive Board of Directors
920 Balsam St.
Cortez, CO 81321
Telephone: (303) 565-6454
Ownership %: 100
**Management:**
Robert Brooks ...........................President
Larry Riggs ....................Business Manager
**Editorial:**
Gordon Tucker ...............Executive Editor
Gordon Tucker ...............................Editor
Frederic J. .................Administrative Assistant
Athearn
Marilyn Martorono ....................Assistant Editor
Payson D. Sheets, ...........Book Review Editor
PhD
Larry Riggs .....................Executive Secretary
Donald C. Tucker ...........................Membership
Elizabeth Bacon .......................Treasurer
**Desc.:** Articles deal with any phase of
  Southwestern Rocky Mountain and High
  Plains archaeology, anthropology,
  biology, geology, paleontology, history,
  or related subjects.
**Readers:** Members of the Colorado
  Archaeological Society and
  archaeologists.

---

25943

**TOWN & COUNTRY**
1700 Broadway
New York, NY 10019
Telephone: (212) 903-5000
Year Established: 1846
Pub. Frequency: m.
Page Size: standard
Subscrip. Rate: $12/yr.
Circulation: 500,000
Circulation Type: paid
**Owner(s):**
Hearst Corp.
959 Eighth Ave.
New York, NY 10019
Telephone: (212) 262-5700
Ownership %: 100

**Management:**
Molly Schaefer ...........................Publisher
**Editorial:**
Pamela Fiori ...............................Editor
Susan Bleeker .....................Managing Editor
Margot Frankel ...........................Art Director
**Deadline:** story-4 mos.

---

69742

**US**
1290 Ave. of the Americas
New York, NY 10104
Telephone: (212) 484-1616
FAX: (212) 767-8204
Year Established: 1977
Pub. Frequency: m.
Subscrip. Rate: $2.95 newsstand;
  $14.97/yr.
**Owner(s):**
Wenner Media
1290 Ave. of the Americas
New York, NY 10104
Telephone: (212) 484-1616
Ownership %: 100
**Management:**
Paul Rothkopf ...................Advertising Manager
**Editorial:**
Jim Meigs ...................................Editor

---

69772

**UTNE READER**
1624 Harmon Pl., Ste. 330
Minneapolis, MN 55403
Telephone: (612) 338-5040
Year Established: 1984
Pub. Frequency: bi-m.
Page Size: 7 1/2 X 10
Subscrip. Rate: $4.95 newsstand; $18/yr.
Materials: 06,10,20,23,24,25,32,33
Freelance Pay: $100
Print Process: web offset
Circulation: 305,000
Circulation Type: controlled & paid
**Owner(s):**
Lens Publishing Co., Inc.
1624 Harmon Pl., Ste. 330
Minneapolis, MN 44503
Telephone: (612) 338-5040
Ownership %: 100
**Editorial:**
Jay Walljusper ...............................Editor
**Deadline:** ads-2 mo. prior to pub.date

---

66694

**WORLD & I, THE**
3400 New York Ave., N.E.
Washington, DC 20002
Telephone: (202) 636-3369
FAX: (202) 526-3497
Year Established: 1986
Pub. Frequency: m.
Page Size: standard
Subscrip. Rate: $90/yr.
Materials: 06,10,32
Freelance Pay: negotiable
Print Process: offset
Circulation: 45,000
Circulation Type: controlled & paid
**Owner(s):**
News World Communications, Inc.
3600 New York Ave., N.E.
Washington, DC 20002
Telephone: (202) 636-3000
Ownership %: 100
**Management:**
Francis Buckingham .........Advertising Manager
**Editorial:**
Michael Marshall ....................Executive Editor
Morton A. Kaplan ...............................Editor
Dong Moor Joo .....................Associate Editor
**Desc.:** Articles provide complete and
  balanced coverage of cultural, political
  and social issues, including science and
  the arts. Also publishes fiction and
  poetry.

**Readers:** Mature (median 47), financially
  comfortable (median $80K), well
  educated (50% have masters).
**Deadline:** ads-6 wks. prior to 1st of mo. of
  pub. date

---

25953

**YALE REVIEW, THE**
53 Wall St.
New Haven, CT 06511
Telephone: (203) 432-0499
FAX: (203) 432-0510
Mailing Address:
  Yale University
  P.O. Box 208243
  New Haven, CT 06520-8243
Year Established: 1911
Pub. Frequency: q.
Page Size: standard
Subscrip. Rate: $22/yr. individuals; $46/yr.
  institutions
Materials: 10,12,25,32
Freelance Pay: $100-$300/article
Circulation: 6,000
Circulation Type: paid
**Owner(s):**
Yale University
Telephone: (203) 432-0499
**Editorial:**
J.D. McClatchy ...........................Editor
Susan Bianconi .......................Managing Editor
**Desc.:** Articles on foreign and domestic
  affairs, literature, arts, society; some
  fiction and poetry. Length of articles 2,
  500 to 4,000 words.
**Readers:** Cultured men and women
  interested in a broad range of issues
  and in fiction and poetry.

---

## Group 634-Health & Nutrition

---

24931

**ACCENT ON LIVING**
P.O. Box 700
Bloomington, IL 61702-0700
Telephone: (309) 378-2961
FAX: (309) 378-4420
Year Established: 1956
Pub. Frequency: q.
Page Size: 5" X 7"
Subscrip. Rate: $3/copy; $10/yr.
Materials: 06,08,09,15,17,20,21,28,29,32,33
Freelance Pay: $.10/wd.
Print Process: offset
Circulation: 20,000
Circulation Type: paid
**Owner(s):**
Cheever Publishing, Inc.
P.O. Box 700
Bloomington, IL 61702
Telephone: (309) 378-2961
FAX: (309) 378-4420
Ownership %: 100
**Management:**
R. C. Cheever ...........................President
R. C. Cheever ...........................Publisher
Nancy Kiel .....................Advertising Manager
Robert E. Mosser ...................General Manager
**Editorial:**
R. C. Cheever ...........................Editor in Chief
Betty Garee ...............................Editor
Grace C. Cheever ...................Associate Editor
Betty Garee .......................New Product Editor

---

**Materials Accepted/Included:** 01-Business news 02-By-line articles 03-Fashion news 04-Food news 05-Freelance copy 06-Letters to editor 07-Real estate news 08-Sports news 09-Travel news
10-Book rev. 11-Movie rev. 12-Music rev. 13-TV rev. 14-Theater rev. 15-Coming events 16-Obituaries 17-Question & answer 18-Social announcements 19-Artwork 20-Cartoons 21-Photos 22-TV listings
23-Audio rec. 24-Video rec. 25-Books 26-Films/film clips 27-Personnel news 28-Press releases 29-New product news/photos 30-Trade lit. 31-Contracts awarded 32-Display adv. 33-Classified adv.

6-49

**Desc.:** Emphasis on success stories of seriously handicapped persons; work at home and businesses where the handicapped person makes average or above income from business; new ideas, innovations and techniques used by handicapped people; new developments such as assistive devices; new products to enable people with limited physical strength to do a job and new medical and surgical techniques resulting in improvement in a physical disability. Departments include: New Products and Services, Accent on the News, Travel-Thumbs Up, Thumbs Down.
**Readers:** Principally handicapped people. Also leading medical rehabilitation specialists, counselors, therapists, etc.
**Deadline:** ads-Feb. 1, May 1, Aug. 1, Nov. 1

**AMERICAN HEALTH**                    69751
28 W. 23rd St.
New York, NY 10010
Telephone: (212) 366-8900
FAX: (212) 366-8999
Year Established: 1982
Pub. Frequency: 10/yr.
Subscrip. Rate: $17.97/yr.
Circulation: 1,000,000
Circulation Type: paid
**Owner(s):**
Reader's Digest Association, Inc.
28 W. 23rd St.
New York, NY 10010
Telephone: (212) 366-8900
Ownership %: 100
**Editorial:**
Joel Gurin ......................................Editor

**BETTER NUTRITION FOR**              24478
**TODAY'S LIVING**
6151 Powers Ferry Rd.
Atlanta, GA 30339-0001
Telephone: (404) 613-9700
FAX: (404) 613-9740
Mailing Address:
    5 Penn Plz., 13th Fl.
    New York, NY 10001
Year Established: 1938
Pub. Frequency: m.
Page Size: standard
Subscrip. Rate: $22/yr.; $82/yr. foreign
Materials: 04,06,17,28,29,30,32
Freelance Pay: $200-$300/1200 wds.
Print Process: web offset
Circulation: 475,000
Circulation Type: paid
**Owner(s):**
Argus Business
5 Penn Plz., 13th Fl.
New York, NY 10001
Telephone: (212) 613-9700
FAX: (212) 613-9749
Ownership %: 100
**Management:**
Bill Manning .............................Publisher
**Editorial:**
Frank Murray ...............................Editor
Donna Guest .................Associate Editor
**Desc.:** Our primary interests are products sold in health food stores: vitamins, minerals, organic produce.
**Readers:** Consumers who shop in health food stores.

**BODY MIND & SPIRIT MAGAZINE**      66622
255 Hope St.
Providence, RI 02906
Telephone: (401) 351-4320
FAX: (401) 272-5767

Mailing Address:
    P.O. Box 701
    Providence, RI 02901
Year Established: 1982
Pub. Frequency: 6/yr.
Page Size: standard
Subscrip. Rate: $3.95/copy; $21/yr.
Materials: 02,04,05,06,09,10,11,12,13,15,
    16,19,20,21,23,24,25,26,27,28,29,30,31,
    32,33
Freelance Pay: $100-$400
Print Process: web
Circulation: 150,000
Circulation Type: paid
**Owner(s):**
Paul Zuromski
255 Hope St.
Providence, RI 02906
Telephone: (401) 351-4320
Ownership %: 100
**Management:**
Paul Zuromski ..........................Publisher
Jim Vallier .................Advertising Manager
Deborah Zuromski .............Circulation Manager
**Editorial:**
Rochelle Gordon ..........................Editor
Richard Marthers ....................Art Director
**Desc.:** A natural living, metaphysical, personal improvement information resource. We provide practical, creative tools to improve and enrich the body, mind and spirit.
**Readers:** Well educated, upscale Americans who practice a spiritually-minded alternative lifestyle.
**Deadline:** story-3 mos.; news-3 mos.; photo-3 mos.; ads-3 mos.

**BODYWISE**                          66506
4151 Knob Dr.
Ste. 200
St. Paul, MN 55122
Telephone: (612) 452-0571
FAX: (612) 454-5791
Year Established: 1991
Pub. Frequency: bi-m.
Page Size: pocket
Subscrip. Rate: $2.95 newsstand;
    $24.78/yr.
Materials: 02,03,04,,05,09,15,17,19,20,21,
    24,28,29,30,32,33
Freelance Pay: $200-$300/600-1,500 wds.
Print Process: offset
Circulation: 200,000
Circulation Type: paid
**Owner(s):**
Russ Moore & Associates, Inc.
4151 Knob Dr.
Ste. 200
St. Paul, MN 55122
Telephone: (612) 452-0571
FAX: (612) 454-5791
Ownership %: 100
**Management:**
Russ Moore ..............................Publisher
John Kramer .............Advertising Manager
Sue Nielsen ...............Production Manager
**Editorial:**
Carla Waldmar ................Executive Editor
Kathy Shaw ..........................Art Director
Lucinda Spencer ..........Circulation Director
Kathy Bauwens ..................Design Director
Danny Harp ................Vice President, Sales
**Desc.:** A magazine of fitness, diet, and preventive medicine for the nineties. Features popular topics such as: medicine, psychology, eating for longevity, and teen health issues.
**Readers:** Women ages 20-45.
**Deadline:** story-10th of mo. prior to pub. date

**BUENA SALUD**                       69721
1700 Fernandez Juncos Ave., Stop 25
San Juan, PR 00909-2999
Telephone: (809) 728-3000
FAX: (809) 728-7325
Year Established: 1987
Pub. Frequency: m.
Page Size: standard
Subscrip. Rate: $2.25 newsstand; $17/yr.
Materials: 04,15,17,19,21,25,28,29
Circulation: 70,000
Circulation Type: paid
**Owner(s):**
Casiano Communications, Inc.
1700 Fernandez Juncos Ave.
San Juan, PR 00909-2999
Telephone: (809) 728-3000
Ownership %: 100
**Editorial:**
Ivonne Longueira ..........................Editor
**Desc.:** Covers health and fitness for families and individuals in Puerto Rico.

**CREATIVE LIVING**                   26534
400 Plaza Dr.
Secaucus, NJ 07094
Telephone: (201) 865-7500
FAX: (201) 865-0753
Mailing Address:
    P.O. Box 1505
    Secaucus, NJ 07094
Year Established: 1972
Pub. Frequency: q.
Page Size: standard
Subscrip. Rate: $2.50/issue; $8/yr.; $15/2 yrs.
Freelance Pay: varies
Circulation: 315000
Circulation Type: paid
**Owner(s):**
Northwestern Mutual Life Insurance Co.
720 E. Wisconsin Ave.
Milwaukee, WI 53202
Telephone: (414) 271-1444
Ownership %: 100
**Management:**
Santo Saliture ..........................Publisher
**Editorial:**
Robert H. Spencer .........................Editor
Alice Degenhardt ....................Art Director
**Desc.:** Aims to help reader achieve self fulfillment
**Readers:** Intelligent, active, self-improving audience. Upscale: more than 40% of audience has had postgraduate college education.

**DIABETES FORECAST**                 59555
1660 Duke St.
Alexandria, VA 22314
Telephone: (703) 549-1500
FAX: (703) 836-7439
Year Established: 1948
Pub. Frequency: m.
Page Size: standard
Subscrip. Rate: $24/yr. US; $39/yr.
    Canada & Mexico; $49/yr. elsewhere
Circulation: 280,000
Circulation Type: paid
**Owner(s):**
American Diabetes Assn., Inc.
1660 Duke St.
Alexandria, VA 22314
Telephone: (703) 549-1500
Ownership %: 100
**Management:**
Susan Koughlin ..........................Publisher
**Editorial:**
Andrew Keegan ................Managing Editor
Peter Banks ..................Editorial Director

**Desc.:** Provides factual information to patients on the causes, treatment, and care of diabetes. The aim is to help readers achieve a better understanding and acceptance of diabetes and to present readers with news of the latest research developments aimed at better control and ultimately, a cure.
**Readers:** People with diabetes and their families.

**EATING WELL**                       67279
Ferry Rd.
Charlotte, VT 05445
Telephone: (802) 425-3961
FAX: (802) 425-3307
Mailing Address:
    P.O. Box 1000
    Charlotte, VT 05445
Year Established: 1989
Pub. Frequency: bi-m.
Page Size: standard
Subscrip. Rate: $2.95/copy; $12.97/yr.
Circulation: 525,000
Circulation Type: paid
**Owner(s):**
Telemedia Communications
Ferry Rd.
Charlotte, VT 05445
Telephone: (802) 425-3961
Ownership %: 100
**Management:**
Francois de Gaspe Beaubien .............Publisher
**Editorial:**
Scott Mowbray ..........................Editor
**Desc.:** Devoted to all aspects of healthy cooking, including nutritional journalism, travel, recipes, and wine recommendations.

**EXERCISE FOR MEN ONLY**             69575
Empire State Bldg.
350 Fifth Ave.
New York, NY 10118
Telephone: (212) 947-4322
FAX: (212) 563-4774
Pub. Frequency: bi-m.
Page Size: standard
Subscrip. Rate: $4.95 newsstand; $33.15/2 yrs.
Print Process: web
**Owner(s):**
Chelo Publishing, Inc.
Empire State Bldg.
350 Fifth Ave.
New York, NY 10118
Telephone: (212) 847-4322
Ownership %: 100
**Management:**
Cheh N. Lowe ..........................Publisher
**Editorial:**
Steve Downs ..............................Editor

**FITNESS PLUS**                      66278
28 W. 25th St., 7th Fl.
New York, NY 10010
Telephone: (212) 647-0222
FAX: (212) 647-0236
Year Established: 1990
Pub. Frequency: q.
Page Size: standard
Subscrip. Rate: $19.95/yr.
Circulation: 250,000
Circulation Type: paid
**Owner(s):**
Scott Magazine Distribution Corp.
28 W. 25th St., 7th Fl.
New York, NY 10010
Telephone: (212) 647-0222
FAX: (212) 647-0236
Ownership %: 100
**Management:**
Henry Mcqueeney ..........................Publisher
John Wilson ................Associate Publsiher

**Materials Accepted/Included:** 01-Business news 02-By-line articles 03-Fashion news 04-Food news 05-Freelance copy 06-Letters to editor 07-Real estate news 08-Sports news 09-Travel news 10-Book rev. 11-Movie rev. 12-Music rev. 13-TV rev. 14-Theater rev. 15-Coming events 16-Obituaries 17-Question & answer 18-Social announcements 19-Artwork 20-Cartoons 21-Photos 22-TV listings 23-Audio rec. 24-Video rec. 25-Books 26-Films/film clips 27-Personnel news 28-Press releases 29-New product news/photos 30-Trade lit. 31-Contracts awarded 32-Display adv. 33-Classified adv.

**Editorial:**
Russ Oliver ......................Editor in Chief
**Desc.:** Covers fashions, exercise, nutrition, dieting and other fitness related news.

**HEALTH** 26589
301 Howard St., 18th Fl.
San Francisco, CA 94105
Telephone: (415) 512-9100
FAX: (415) 512-9600
Year Established: 1987
Pub. Frequency: 7/yr.
Page Size: standard
Subscrip. Rate: $2.95 newsstand; $18/yr.
Circulation: 900,000
Circulation Type: paid
**Owner(s):**
Time Publishing Ventures, Inc.
301 Howard St., 18th Fl.
San Francisco, CA 94105
Telephone: (415) 512-9100
Ownership %: 100
**Management:**
William P. Kupper ....................Publisher
**Editorial:**
Eric Schrier ................................Editor
**Desc.:** Covers health-related issues, including fitness, food and nutrition, medicine and the life sciences, problems of aging, prenatal and childhood care, new therapies and practical self-help.
**Readers:** Characteristics of our readers: 78% female; median age of 46; 76% attended or graduated from college; 55% are professional or managerial.

**HEALTH & YOU** 61658
One Executive Dr.
Moorestown, NJ 08057
Telephone: (609) 778-0011
Year Established: 1984
Pub. Frequency: q.
Page Size: digest
Subscrip. Rate: membership
Freelance Pay: $300-$500
Print Process: offset
Circulation: 750,000, bulk
Circulation Type: paid
**Owner(s):**
Health Ink, Inc.
One Executive Dr.
Moorestown, NJ 08057
Telephone: (609) 778-0011
Ownership %: 100
**Editorial:**
Gerry Williams ..........................Executive Editor
**Desc.:** Health magazine and 16 newsletters on health, wellness, health insurance.

**HEALTH DIET & NUTRITION** 69025
951 S. Oxford, No. 109
Los Angeles, CA 90006
Telephone: (213) 732-3477
FAX: (213) 732-9123
Year Established: 1991
Pub. Frequency: q.
Page Size: standard
Subscrip. Rate: $29.99/yr.
Materials: 01,02,03,04,05,06,0,08,09,10,11, 12,13,14,15,16,17,18,19,20,21,22,23,24, 25,26,27,28,29,30,31,32,33
Freelance Pay: $.20-.50/wd.
Print Process: web
Circulation: 120,000
Circulation Type: controlled & paid
**Owner(s):**
Publishing & Business Consultants
951 S. Oxford, No. 109
Los Angeles, CA 90006
Telephone: (213) 732-3477
FAX: (213) 732-9123
Ownership %: 100

**Editorial:**
Andeson Napoleon Atia ..........................Editor
**Desc.:** Covers basic nutrition information, dietary habits and personal health care.
**Deadline:** story-2 wks. prior to pub. date; news-2 wks.; photo-2 wks.; ads-90 days prior to pub. date

**HEALTH EXPRESS** 65339
6225 U.S. Hwy. 290 E.
Austin, TX 78761
Telephone: (512) 465-1000
FAX: (512) 465-1090
Pub. Frequency: m.
Page Size: standard
Subscrip. Rate: $26/yr. member; $36/yr. non-member
Materials: 01,02,06,32,33
Circulation: 6,500
Circulation Type: paid
**Owner(s):**
Texas Hospital Association
6225 U.S. Hwy. 290 E.
Austin, TX 78761
Telephone: (512) 465-1000
Ownership %: 100
**Editorial:**
Cindy Rachicano ........Subscription Coordinator
**Desc.:** HTX provides information on current trends in integrated delivery systems and operational issues, analysis of new regulations and legislation that affect Texas hospitals and advice from leaders in healthcare.
**Readers:** Serves the health conscious population.

**HEALTH NEWS AND REVIEW** 54000
27 Pine St.
New Canaan, CT 06840
Telephone: (203) 966-8721
Mailing Address:
P.O. Box 876
New Canaan, CT 06840
Year Established: 1982
Pub. Frequency: bi-m.
Page Size: tabloid
Subscrip. Rate: $9.95/yr.(4 issues); $15.95/yr. (8 issues)
Circulation: 135,000
Circulation Type: controlled & paid
**Owner(s):**
Keats Publishing, Inc.
27 Pine St.
New Canaan, CT 06840
Telephone: (203) 966-8721
Ownership %: 100
**Desc.:** Devoted to preventive Health Care developments, views, news fitness and sports.
**Readers:** Distributed nationally and abroad. 30-40 years of age/women/married with families. To doctors and their patients, as well as many students.

**HOLISTIC EDUCATION REVIEW** 65414
39 Pearl St.
Brandon, VT 05733-1007
Telephone: (802) 247-8312
FAX: (802) 247-8312
Mailing Address:
P.O. Box 328
Brandon, VT 05733-0328
Year Established: 1988
Pub. Frequency: q.
Page Size: standard
Subscrip. Rate: $35/yr. individuals; $65/yr. library
Materials: 06,10,32,33
Print Process: offset
Circulation: 1,300
Circulation Type: paid

**Owner(s):**
Psychology Press
39 Pearl St.
Brandon, VT 05733
Telephone: (802) 247-8312
Ownership %: 100
**Management:**
Charles Jakiela ....................Publisher
**Editorial:**
Jeffrey Kane ................................Editor
**Desc.:** The premier journal of leading-edge thinking in progressive, holistic educational theory and practice.
**Readers:** Educators, scholars, parents, interested in educational alternatives.

**HOMECARE** 66717
6133 Bristol Pkwy.
Culver City, CA 90230
Telephone: (310) 337-9717
FAX: (310) 337-1041
Mailing Address:
P.O. Box 3640
Culver City, CA 90231-3640
Year Established: 1978
Pub. Frequency: m.
Page Size: standard
Subscrip. Rate: $48/yr.; free to qualified personnel
Circulation: 16,000
Circulation Type: controlled
**Owner(s):**
Miramar Publishing Co.
P.O. Box 3640
Culver City, CA 90231-3640
Telephone: (310) 337-9717
Ownership %: 100
**Management:**
Denise Novoselski ....................Publisher
**Editorial:**
Janis Samaripa ................................Editor
Ken Bruce ......................Associate Publisher
**Desc.:** Business news magazine serving the home health industry.

**JOE WEIDER'S MUSCLE & FITNESS** 54006
21100 Erwin St.
Woodland Hills, CA 91367
Telephone: (818) 884-6800
FAX: (818) 704-5734
Year Established: 1940
Pub. Frequency: m.
Page Size: standard
Subscrip. Rate: $3.95 newsstand US; $4.95 newsstand Canada; $35/yr.
Materials: 04,06,20,28,29,33
Freelance Pay: negotiable
Circulation: 624,000
Circulation Type: paid
**Owner(s):**
Weider Health and Fitness
21100 Erwin St.
Woodland Hills, CA 91367
Telephone: (818) 884-6800
Ownership %: 100
**Management:**
Joseph Weider ....................Publisher
Bob Washburn ..........Advertising Manager
**Editorial:**
Tom Deters ..........................Editor in Chief
Mary Ann Mucica ..........Executive Editor
Jim Wright, Ph.D. ..........................Editor
Jim Chada ..........................Art Director
Tom Deters ..........Associate Publisher
Lisa Clark ..........Photography Editor

**Desc.:** Presents the nation's new consciousness of physical fitness to the serious exercise and athletic training enthusiast. Readers are both men and women-active participants in sports and exercise programs who are interested in health and nutrition.
**Readers:** Men and women, 18 - 34 years old.

**LET'S LIVE MAGAZINE** 25874
320 N. Larchmont Blvd.
Los Angeles, CA 90004
Telephone: (213) 469-8379
Mailing Address:
P.O. Box 74908
Los Angeles, CA 90004
Year Established: 1933
Pub. Frequency: m.
Page Size: standard
Subscrip. Rate: $14.95/yr.
Freelance Pay: $150/article
Circulation: 800,000
**Owner(s):**
Hilltopper Publications, Inc.
320 N. Larchmont Blvd.
Los Angeles, CA 90004
Telephone: (310) 469-3901
Ownership %: 100
**Management:**
T. K. Vodrey ..........................President
Judith Vodrey ..........................Publisher
**Editorial:**
Patty Padilla-Gallagher ..........................Editor
Dick Wieland ..........................Advertising
Patty Padilla-Gallagher ..........News Editor
**Desc.:** Edited for people interested in information on natural living/nutrition, diet, the outdoors, physical fitness, organic gardening, environmental protection, and preventive medicine. Monthly articles also keep readers up-to-date on the latest scientific research on vitamins and minerals. Regular features include: Columns on Medical Questions and Answers, Natural Beauty, Book Reviews, Exercise, Preventive Medicine, Q&A Preventive Dentistry, Pets, Recipes, Homeopathy, Herbs. Sold by subscription and in health food stores only.
**Readers:** General readership interested in nutrition.

**LONGEVITY** 65374
1965 Broadway
New York, NY 10023
Telephone: (212) 496-6100
Year Established: 1989
Pub. Frequency: m.
Page Size: standard
Subscrip. Rate: $2.95/issue; $17.97/yr.
Materials: 04,05,09,17,23,24,25,26,28,29, 32,33
Freelance Pay: $1/wd.
Circulation: 375,000
Circulation Type: paid
**Owner(s):**
General Media Publishing Group
1965 Broadway
New York, NY 10023-4965
Telephone: (212) 496-6100
Ownership %: 100
**Management:**
Susan E. Meskil ....................Publisher
**Editorial:**
Susan Millar Perry ..........Editor in Chief
Penelope Weiss ..........Managing Editor
Carveth Kramer ..........................Art Director
Karyn Repinski ..........................Beauty Editor
Margaret Pierpont ..........Deputy Editor of Travel/Fitness

---

Materials Accepted/Included: 01-Business news 02-By-line articles 03-Fashion news 04-Food news 05-Freelance copy 06-Letters to editor 07-Real estate news 08-Sports news 09-Travel news 10-Book rev. 11-Movie rev. 12-Music rev. 13-TV rev. 14-Theater rev. 15-Coming events 16-Obituaries 17-Question & answer 18-Social announcements 19-Artwork 20-Cartoons 21-Photos 22-TV listings 23-Audio rec. 24-Video rec. 25-Books 26-Films/film clips 27-Personnel news 28-Press releases 29-New product news/photos 30-Trade lit. 31-Contracts awarded 32-Display adv. 33-Classified adv.

**Desc.:** Health/lifestyle book for baby-boomers looking to stay young and healthy. Coverage includes fitness, beauty, nutrition, science breakthroughs and celebrity profiles.
**Readers:** Male/female, mid 30's-50's.

66774

## LOOKING FIT
4141 N. Scottsdale Rd., Ste. 316
Scottsdale, AZ 85251
Telephone: (602) 990-1101
FAX: (602) 990-0819
Mailing Address:
P.O. Box 5400
Scottsdale, AZ 85261
Year Established: 1987
Pub. Frequency: m.
Page Size: Standard
Subscrip. Rate: $45/yr.
Circulation: 20,000
Circulation Type: controlled & paid
Owner(s):
Virgo Publishing Co
4141 N. Scottsdale Rd.
Scottsdale, AZ 85251
Telephone: (602) 483-0014
Ownership %: 100
Management:
Jennifer Lutener .....................Publisher
Editorial:
Nancy S. Bercaw .........................Editor
Judy Gaillard ...............................Editor
**Desc.:** Edited for indoor tanning salons. Articles cover tanning and related services.

69506

## LOTUS: THE JOURNAL OF PERSONAL TRANSFORMATION
4421 W. Okmulgee, Ste. 157
Muskogee, OK 74401
Telephone: (918) 683-4560
FAX: (918) 683-2466
Mailing Address:
P.O. Box 2271
Muskogee, OK 74402
Year Established: 1991
Pub. Frequency: 5/yr.
Page Size: 4 color photos/art
Subscrip. Rate: $4.95 newsstand; $19.50/yr.
Circulation: 29,000
Circulation Type: paid
Owner(s):
Lotus, Inc.
4032 S. Lamar Blvd.
No. 500-137
Austin, TX 78704-7900
Telephone: (512) 441-9111
Ownership %: 100
Management:
Mary Ann Vavalette ..........Advertising Manager
Editorial:
Mary Nurrie Stearns ....................Editor
**Desc.:** Covers a variety of personal growth issues and strategies.

69285

## MAINSTREAM
2973 Beech St.
San Diego, CA 92102
FAX: (619) 234-3138
Year Established: 1975
Pub. Frequency: 10/yr.
Page Size: standard
Subscrip. Rate: $4 newsstand; $24/yr. US; $46/yr. foreign
Circulation: 18,200
Circulation Type: paid
Owner(s):
Exploding Myths, Inc.
2973 Beech St.
San Diego, CA 92102
Ownership %: 100
Management:
Cyndi Jones ...........................Publisher

**Desc.:** Serves the interests of active, disabled consumers by examining the current thought and politics directly affecting them. Looks at the marketing devices used by manufacturers to facilitate their independent lifestyle.

69578

## MEN'S EXERCISE
350 Fifth Ave., Ste. 8216
New York, NY 10118
Telephone: (212) 947-4322
Year Established: 1990
Pub. Frequency: bi-m.
Page Size: standard
Subscrip. Rate: $3.95/issue; $17.75/yr.
Print Process: web
Owner(s):
Pumpkin Press, Inc.
350 Fifth Ave., Ste. 8216
New York, NY 10118
Telephone: (212) 947-4322
Management:
Cheh N. Low .........................Publisher
Editorial:
Steve Downs ...............................Editor

54005

## MEN'S FITNESS
21100 Erwin St.
Woodland Hills, CA 91367
Telephone: (818) 884-6800
FAX: (818) 704-5734
Year Established: 1985
Pub. Frequency: m.
Page Size: standard
Subscrip. Rate: $3.50/copy,; $21.97/yr.
Materials: 04,06,08,09,10,25,28,29
Freelance Pay: negotiable
Circulation: 240,000
Circulation Type: paid
Owner(s):
Weider Health & Fitness
21100 Erwin St.
Woodland Hills, CA 91367
Telephone: (818) 884-6800
Ownership %: 100
Management:
Joseph Weider .........................Publisher
Peter Miller ....................Advertising Manager
Editorial:
Peter Sikowitz ...............Editor in Chief
Jim Rosenthal .....................Executive Editor
Jeff Lucia .................Managing Editor
Patti Ratchford .........................Art Director
Mike Powers .................Assistant Art Director
Matthew Segal .................Associate Editor
Sharon Cohen ...............Co-Executive Editor
Ted Rand ...............................Health Editor
**Desc.:** A fitness lifestyle geared to the active male, whether he's a serious athlete or a recreational enthusiast. A broad range of health and fitness-related topics, including weight-training, sports, psychology, nutrition, sexuality and men's issues.
**Readers:** Men 18-49 years old.

68873

## MUSCULAR DEVELOPMENT FITNESS & HEALTH
2120 Smithtown Ave.
Ronkonkoma, NY 11779
Telephone: (516) 467-2042
FAX: (516) 467-1241
Year Established: 1964
Pub. Frequency: m.
Page Size: standard
Subscrip. Rate: $3.95 newsstand; $29.95/yr.
Materials: 05,06
Print Process: web
Circulation: 242,000
Circulation Type: paid

Owner(s):
Advanced Research Press, Inc.
2120 Smithtown Ave.
Ronkonkoma, NY 11779
Telephone: (516) 467-2042
FAX: (516) 467-1241
Ownership %: 100
Management:
Roy Ulin ...............Business Manager
Editorial:
Alan Paul .................................Editor
**Desc.:** Comprehensive coverage of bodybuilding, sports nutrition, muscular development and strength training.

25846

## NATURAL HEALTH
17 Station St.
Brookline, MA 02146
Telephone: (617) 232-1000
Mailing Address:
P.O. Box 1200
Brookline, MA 02147
Year Established: 1971
Pub. Frequency: bi-m.
Page Size: standard
Subscrip. Rate: $24/yr.
Freelance Pay: $.10-$.20/wd.
Circulation: 250,000
Circulation Type: paid
Owner(s):
Natural Health L.P.
17 Station St.
Brookline, MA 02146
Telephone: (617) 232-1000
Ownership %: 100
Editorial:
Mark Bittman ...........................Editor
Margaret Hanshaw .................Managing Editor
Ann D'Alasandro .................Advertising Director
Lisa Puccio ...............................Art Director
Ellen Grimm ...............Associate Editor
Amy Klee ...............................Design
**Desc.:** Covers all aspects of natural foods, natural health and self care, including naturopathy, holistic health and alternative health care and prevention options. Cooking, gardening, energy, healing, books columns every issue. Departments include: Cooking Articles, New Events, Camping, Alternative businesses, etc.
**Readers:** Average age is 30-35 years, college educated.

25899

## NUTRITION HEALTH REVIEW
171 Madison Ave.
New York, NY 10016
Telephone: (212) 679-3590
FAX: (212) 679-3597
Mailing Address:
27 Turnbridge Rd.
Haverford, PA 19041
Year Established: 1976
Pub. Frequency: q.
Page Size: tabloid
Subscrip. Rate: $2 newsstand
Materials: 04,10,17,20,21,25,26,28,30
Print Process: offset
Circulation: 310,000
Circulation Type: paid
Owner(s):
Vegetus Publications
171 Madison
New York, NY 10016
Telephone: (212) 679-3590
Ownership %: 100
Management:
Frank Ray Rifkin .........................Publisher
Noreen Curtin .................Circulation Manager
Editorial:
Andrew Rifkin ...............Executive Editor
William Renaurd ...........................Editor
Michael Lee ...............................Photo

**Desc.:** Devoted to health, psychiatry, nutrition, and medical information.
**Readers:** Health oriented persons.

69026

## OUTPOST EXCHANGE
102 E. Capitol Dr.
Milwaukee, WI 53212
Telephone: (414) 964-7789
FAX: (414) 961-1961
Year Established: 1971
Pub. Frequency: m.
Page Size: standard
Subscrip. Rate: free; $12/yr.
Materials: 32
Circulation: 26,000
Circulation Type: paid
Owner(s):
Outpost Natural Foods Corp.
100 E. Capitol Dr.
Milwaukee, WI 53212
Ownership %: 100
Management:
Anu Skinner .................Production Manager
Editorial:
Malcolm McDowell Woods .................Editor
Dianne Lynne Schieffer .................Advertising
Marie Greenfield .................Marketing Manager

66507

## PERSONAL FITNESS & WEIGHT LOSS
4151 Knob Dr., Ste. 200
Saint Paul, MN 55122
Telephone: (612) 452-0571
FAX: (612) 454-5791
Year Established: 1988
Pub. Frequency: bi-m.
Subscrip. Rate: $12/yr.
Circulation: 100,000
Circulation Type: paid
Owner(s):
Russ Moore & Assoicates, Inc.
4151 Knob Dr., Ste. 200
St. Paul, MN 55122
Telephone: (612) 452-0571
FAX: (612) 454-5791
Ownership %: 100
Management:
Russ Moore ...........................Publisher
Editorial:
Diane Steen ...............Executive Editor
Carla Anderson ...............Art Director

25917

## PREVENTION
33 E. Minor St.
Emmaus, PA 18098-0099
Telephone: (610) 967-5171
FAX: (610) 967-7723
Year Established: 1950
Pub. Frequency: m.
Page Size: pocket
Subscrip. Rate: $1.95 newsstand; $19.97/yr.
Materials: 02,04,05,06,20,21,28,29,32,33
Freelance Pay: $200-$500
Print Process: offset
Circulation: 6,560,000
Circulation Type: controlled & paid
Owner(s):
Rodale Press, Inc.
33 E. Minor St.
Emmaus, PA 18098-0099
Telephone: (610) 967-5171
Ownership %: 100
Management:
Kenneth Wallace .........................Publisher
Editorial:
Emrika Padus ...............Executive Editor
Mark Bricklin ...........................Editor
Lewis Vaugn ...............Managing Editor
Karyn Barczewski ..........Mail Order Advertising Manager
Steve Giannetti ...............National Advertising Director

**Desc.:** America's family health coach; edited for readers who take an active role in achieving and maintaining good health and fitness for themselves and their families. Stresses disease prevention and health promotion.
**Readers:** Persons interested in maintaining a healthy lifestyle.
**Deadline:** ads-2 1/2 mos.

## PSYCHOLOGY TODAY
49 E. 21st St., 11th Fl.
New York, NY 10010
Telephone: (212) 260-7210
FAX: (212) 260-7445
Year Established: 1967
Pub. Frequency: bi-m.
Page Size: standard
Subscrip. Rate: $3 newsstand; $18/yr.
Circulation: 325,000
Circulation Type: paid
**Owner(s):**
Sussex Publishers, Inc.
24 E. 23rd St., 5th Fl.
New York, NY 10010
Telephone: (212) 260-7210
Ownership %: 100
**Management:**
John Colman .............................Publisher
Sheryl Sue Sober .............Advertising Manager
**Editorial:**
Owen Lipstein .....................Editor in Chief
Hara Marano ..................................Editor
Clare Conway ...................Managing Editor
**Desc.:** Lifestyle magazine providing information on human behavior relating to all aspects of life. Articles encompass such contemporary issues as health, family, career, stress, nutrition, and personal relationships.
**Readers:** College educated, young, upscale, professional/managerial audience, 60% female, 40% male; median HHI $53,000 (52% above the U.S. average); source (1992 SMRB)

## REHABILITATION GAZETTE
5100 Oakland Ave., Ste. 206
St. Louis, MO 63110-1406
Telephone: (314) 534-0475
FAX: (314) 534-5070
Year Established: 1958
Pub. Frequency: s-a.
Subscrip. Rate: $12/yr. individuals; $20/yr. institutions & health professionals
Circulation: 7,000
Circulation Type: paid
**Owner(s):**
Gazette International Networking Institute
5100 Oakland Ave., Ste. 206
St. Louis, MO 63110-1406
Telephone: (314) 534-0475
Ownership %: 100
**Editorial:**
Joan Headley ..................................Editor
**Desc.:** News, features, and profiles pertaining to persons with disabilities, focusing on technologies for assuming independent living and pursuing careers and social opportunities.

## REMEDY
120 Post Rd., W.
Westport, CT 06880
Telephone: (203) 221-4910
Pub. Frequency: bi-m.
Page Size: standard
Subscrip. Rate: $2/copy; $12/yr.
**Owner(s):**
Rx Remedy, Inc.
120 Post Rd., W.
Westport, CT 06880
Telephone: (203) 221-4910
Ownership %: 100

**Management:**
Robert P. Mountain, Jr. .......................Publisher
**Editorial:**
Val Griffith Weaver ......................Editor in Chief
Richard W. Warner ..........................Art Director
**Desc.:** Articles are meant to increase reader awareness of developments in the health field. Its contents should not be construed as medical advice or instruction on individual health matters, which should be obtained directly from a health professional.

## SELF
350 Madison Ave.
New York, NY 10017
Telephone: (800) 274-6111
FAX: (212) 880-8110
Year Established: 1979
Pub. Frequency: m.
Subscrip. Rate: $15/yr.
Circulation: 1,408,975
Circulation Type: paid
**Owner(s):**
Conde Nast Publications, Inc.
350 Madison Ave.
New York, NY 10017
Telephone: (800) 274-6111
Ownership %: 100
**Editorial:**
Alexandra Penney .....................Editor

## TOTAL HEALTH MAGAZINE
6001 Topanga Canyon Bldg., Ste. 300
Woodland Hills, CA 91367
Telephone: (818) 887-6484
FAX: (818) 887-7960
Year Established: 1979
Pub. Frequency: bi-m.
Page Size: standard
Subscrip. Rate: $2.50 copy; $13/yr.
Materials: 02,03,04,32,33
Freelance Pay: varies
Circulation: 100,000
Circulation Type: paid
**Owner(s):**
Trio Publications
6001 Topanga Canyon Bldg., Ste
Woodland Hills, CA 91367
Telephone: (818) 887-6484
Ownership %: 100
**Management:**
Robert L. Smith ...........................President
Robert L. Smith ...........................Publisher
Erica Groten ....................Circulation Manager
**Editorial:**
Robert L. Smith ..............................Editor
Jeffery Ward ...................Managing Editor
Ruth McKinney ........................Art Director
Rosemary Hofer ..............................Photo
Robert L. Smith .....................Travel Editor
**Desc.:** Focuses on total health for the whole person. Content is integrated into three areas; physical, mental, and spiritual. It is a publication for the family with articles and columns on nutrition, diet, fitness, exercise, mental and emotional well-being and wholeness. Departments feature: Doctor's Columns on Preventative Health Care, Nutritionists Dept., Food and Recipes, Family Fitness Book Reviews, Mental Health Q & A, Skin and Body Care, and Sports Fashion Layouts.
**Readers:** Mid-life; ages 25-55 yrs.
**Deadline:** story-2 mo. prior to pub. date; news-2 mo. prior; ads-45 days prior to pub. date

## TUFTS UNIVERSITY DIET & NUTRITION LETTER
53 Park Pl., 8th Fl.
New York, NY 10007
Telephone: (212) 608-6515
FAX: (212) 608-5317
Year Established: 1983
Pub. Frequency: m.
Subscrip. Rate: $20/yr.
Circulation: 280,000
Circulation Type: paid
**Owner(s):**
Tufts University
School of Nutrition
Medford, MA 02155
Telephone: (212) 608-6515
Ownership %: 100
**Editorial:**
Stanley N. Gershoff .....................Editor

## VEGETARIAN JOURNAL
P.O. Box 1463
Baltimore, MD 21203-1463
Telephone: (410) 366-8343
Year Established: 1982
Pub. Frequency: bi-m.
Page Size: standard
Subscrip. Rate: $20/yr.
Materials: 02,04,05,06,09,10,19,20,25,28,29
Print Process: offset lithography
Circulation: 15,000
Circulation Type: paid
**Owner(s):**
Vegetarian Resource Group
P.O. Box 1463
Baltimore, MD 21203
Telephone: (410) 366-8343
Ownership %: 100
**Editorial:**
Charles Stahler ..............................Editor
Debra Wasserman ..........................Editor
**Desc.:** Covers various aspects of vegetarianism including health, recipes, ethics, ecology, world hunger and animal rights.

## VEGETARIAN TIMES
1140 W. Lake St.
Oak Park, IL 60301
Telephone: (708) 848-8100
FAX: (708) 848-8175
Mailing Address:
P.O. Box 570
Oak Park, IL 60303
Year Established: 1974
Pub. Frequency: m.
Page Size: standard
Subscrip. Rate: $2.95 newsstand; $24.95/yr.
Materials: 01,02,04,06,08,09,10,15,17,19, 20,21,32,33
Freelance Pay: $.10-$.25/wd.
Print Process: web
Circulation: 311,000
Circulation Type: paid
**Owner(s):**
Vegetarian Life & Times, Inc.
P.O. Box 570
Oak Park, IL 60303
Telephone: (708) 848-8100
FAX: (708) 848-8175

Subsidiary of Cowles Magazines
P.O. Box 8200
Harrisburg, PA 17105
Telephone: (717) 657-9555
**Management:**
Bruce Barnett .............................President
Marianne Harkness .......................Publisher
Rob Riordan ....................Circulation Manager
**Editorial:**
Joe Vlatowski ........................Art Director
Joni Apgar ..............................Food Editor

**Desc.:** The national publication for vegetarians. Health meatless food, and other items of interest to vegetarians. Many cooking articles. Use black & white & color photos. Also uses many interviews & profiles of prominent or interesting Vegetarians. Primarily a service magazine.
**Readers:** Health & cooking.

## VEGGIE LIFE
1041 Shary Circle
Concord, CA 94518
Telephone: (510) 671-9852
FAX: (510) 671-0692
Year Established: 1993
Pub. Frequency: 6/yr.
Page Size: standard
Subscrip. Rate: $17/yr.; $30/2 yrs.
Freelance Pay: $100/pg.
Circulation: 25,000
Circulation Type: paid
**Owner(s):**
EGW Publishing Co.
1041 Shary Circle
Concord, CA 94518
Telephone: (510) 671-9852
Ownership %: 100
**Management:**
Wayne Lin ..............................President
John Dixon .....................Advertising Manager
Diana Sharp .....................Circulation Manager
John Dixon .....................Operations Manager
**Editorial:**
Phil Fischer ..................Executive Editor
David Camp .................Editorial Director
Ginny Westland .................Art Department
**Readers:** People interested in growing, eating and cooking green.

## VIBRANT LIFE
55 W. Oak Ridge Dr.
Hagerstown, MD 21740
Telephone: (301) 791-7000
FAX: (301) 790-9716
Year Established: 1885
Pub. Frequency: bi-m.
Page Size: 4 color photos/art
Subscrip. Rate: $8.97/yr.
Materials: 04
Freelance Pay: $80-$250
Circulation: 50,000
Circulation Type: paid
**Owner(s):**
Review & Herald Publishing Assn.
55 W. Oak Ridge Dr.
Hagerstown, MD 21740
Telephone: (301) 791-7000
Ownership %: 100
**Management:**
Mark Thomas ...................Advertising Manager
**Editorial:**
Melynie Tooley .................Advertising Sales
**Desc.:** Publishes articles that promote better health, a happier family, and a more complete marriage. It emphasizes prevention topics, and does not want articles discussing certain diseases or articles focusing primarily on people over 50 years of age. As a Christian publication, it seeks material written from a Christian perspective - inspirational pieces, human interest stories, etc. Nutrition topics are presented from an Ovolactovegetarian viewpoint.
**Readers:** Lay readers, man-in-the-street, Christian background woman-in-the-street.

## VIEW
521 Wall St.
Seattle, WA 98121
Telephone: (206) 448-5999
FAX: (206) 448-4271

---

Materials Accepted/Included: 01-Business news 02-By-line articles 03-Fashion news 04-Food news 05-Freelance copy 06-Letters to editor 07-Real estate news 08-Sports news 09-Travel news 10-Book rev. 11-Movie rev. 12-Music rev. 13-TV rev. 14-Theater rev. 15-Coming events 16-Obituaries 17-Question & answer 18-Social announcements 19-Artwork 20-Cartoons 21-Photos 22-TV listings 23-Audio rec. 24-Video rec. 25-Books 26-Films/film clips 27-Personnel news 28-Press releases 29-New product news/photos 30-Trade lit. 31-Contracts 32-Display adv. 33-Classified adv.

6-53

Year Established: 1957
Pub. Frequency: bi-m.
Page Size: standard
Subscrip. Rate: $12/yr.
Circulation: 187,622
Circulation Type: paid
**Owner(s):**
Group Health Cooperative
521 Wall St.
Seattle, WA 98121
Telephone: (206) 448-5999
Ownership %: 100
**Editorial:**
Jan Short .................................Editor
**Desc.:** Covers health and fitness lifestyles for the Greater Seattle area.

### WEIGHT WATCHERS MAGAZINE
26634
360 Lexington Ave.
New York, NY 10017
Telephone: (212) 370-0644
FAX: (212) 687-4398
Year Established: 1968
Pub. Frequency: m.
Page Size: standard
Subscrip. Rate: $15.97/yr.
Freelance Pay: $500-$1,000
Circulation: 1,000,000
Circulation Type: paid
**Owner(s):**
W/W Twentyfirst Corp.
360 Lexington Ave.
New York, NY 10017
Telephone: (212) 370-0644
Ownership %: 100
**Bureau(s):**
Weight Watchers Magazine
625 N. Michigan Ave., Ste. 500
Chicago, IL 60611
Telephone: (312) 951-6069
Contact: Kathleen Cianchetti, Manager
**Management:**
Kathleen H. Parmenter ...............Vice President
Kent Q. Kreh ...........................Publisher
Anne Finn-Nelson ...............Circulation Manager
**Editorial:**
Lee Haiken ...................Editor in Chief
Nancy Gagliardi ...............Managing Editor
Kathleen H. Parmenter ...................Advertising
Shelly Stansfield ...................Art Director
Jeri Anne Sennessey ...............Beauty Editor
Cathrine Censor ...................Feature Editor
Manuel Tome ...................Finance Director
**Desc.:** The personal choice of women committed to self improvement and a healthy lifestyle. A complete and focused editorial package about Health, Nutrition, Fitness, Fashion, Beauty, and Food.
**Readers:** Women.

### Group 636-History, Public Affairs, Political & Social Concerns

### ADOLESCENT MAGAZINE
66190
8577 154th Ave., N.E.
Redmond, WA 98052
Telephone: (800) 851-9100
FAX: (206) 881-5247
Year Established: 1988
Pub. Frequency: bi-m.
Page Size: 4 color photos/art
Subscrip. Rate: $26/yr.
Freelance Pay: negotiable
Circulation: 26,000
Circulation Type: paid
**Owner(s):**
A & D Publications Corp.
8577 154th Ave., N.E.
Redmond, WA 98052
Telephone: (206) 867-5024
Ownership %: 100

**Management:**
Ed Hearn ...........................Publisher
**Editorial:**
Susan J. Carr ...........................Editor

### AFRICA REPORT
26158
833 United Nations Plz.
New York, NY 10017
Telephone: (212) 949-5666
FAX: (212) 682-6174
Year Established: 1956
Pub. Frequency: bi-m.
Page Size: standard
Subscrip. Rate: $30/yr. individuals; $37/yr. institutions
Materials: 02,06,21,32
Freelance Pay: $100-$250
Circulation: 14,000
Circulation Type: paid
**Owner(s):**
African-American Institute
833 United Nations Plz.
New York, NY 10017
Telephone: (212) 949-5666
Ownership %: 100
**Management:**
Frank E. Ferrari ...................Publisher
**Editorial:**
Margaret A. Novicki ...................Editor
Russell Geekie ...................Assistant Editor
Joseph Margolis ...................Production Editor
**Desc.:** Economic, political news; analysis of events in and relating to Africa, especially as they affect or interest Americans. Anxious to receive releases on new investments and commerce with Africa angles. Departments include: Book Reviews, In Washington (review of Africa-related news), African Update (review of African political & economic developments.)
**Readers:** Leaders of government, business, academic interest in Africa.

### AMERICAN ATHEIST
25815
7215 Cameron Rd.
Austin, TX 78752
Telephone: (512) 458-1244
Mailing Address:
P.O. Box 140195
Austin, TX 78714
Year Established: 1958
Pub. Frequency: q.
Page Size: standard
Subscrip. Rate: $25/yr.
Circulation: 40,000
Circulation Type: free & paid
**Owner(s):**
American Atheist Press
P.O. Box 140195
Austin, TX 78714
Telephone: (512) 458-1244
Ownership %: 100
**Bureau(s):**
Northern Illinois, Office
P.O. Box 2263
Chicago, IL 60690
Telephone: (312) 870-0700
Contact: Rob Sherman
**Management:**
Robin Murray-O'Hair ...................President
**Editorial:**
Robin Murray-O'Hair ...................Executive Editor
Jon G. Murray ...................Managing Editor
Madalyn O'Hair ...................Book Review Editor
Jon G. Murray ...................Columnist
Frank Zindler ...................Columnist

**Desc.:** Articles on atheism, agnosticism, humanism, secularism, rationalism, iconoclasm, objectivism, and church/state separation are our main fare. Also use interviews, reviews, humor, history, exposes, and personal experience pieces which fit into the themes above. Emphasis on well researched, intelligently written pieces, not emotional outbursts. Length is open, but prefer to use articles between 1,000 and 6,000 words. Departments include: News, Cartoons, Letters to the Editor, Guest Editorials, fillers, Quotes, Features, "Ask A.A.", Historical Notes, Talking Back.
**Readers:** Our readers are 83% male, 43% married, 46% have a bachelor's degree or beyond.

### AMERICAN ENTERPRISE, THE
23246
1150 17th St., N.W.
Washington, DC 20036
Telephone: (202) 862-5800
FAX: (202) 862-7178
Year Established: 1990
Pub. Frequency: bi-m.
Page Size: standard
Subscrip. Rate: $49/yr. inst.; $28/yr. ind.
Circulation: 15,000
Circulation Type: paid
**Owner(s):**
American Enterprise Institute
1150 17th Street, N.W.
Washington, DC 20036
Telephone: (202) 862-5800
Ownership %: 100
**Management:**
Christopher C. DeMuth ...................Publisher
**Editorial:**
Everett Carll Ladd ...................Senior Editor
Ben J. Wattenberg ...................Senior Editor
Carolyn L. Weaver ...................Senior Editor
Karlyn H. Bowman ...................Senior Editor
Christine Doane ...................Managing Editor
Paula C. Duggan ...................Art Director
Jennifer Baggette ...................Assistant Editor
Paul J. Vizza ...................Business Editor
Seymour M. Lipset ...................Miscellaneous
Ben J. Wattenberg ...................Miscellaneous
**Desc.:** Articles on economic, foreign and domestic policies, and public opinion. Non-technical material aimed at broad, educated audience. Articles commissioned by editors. The magazine is now accepting advertising.
**Readers:** Businessmen, Journalists, Academics, Researchers, Government Audience, Students of Public Opinion.

### AMERICAN GENEALOGIST
69282
P.O. Box 398
Demorest, GA 30535-0398
Telephone: (206) 865-6440
Year Established: 1922
Pub. Frequency: q.
Page Size: standard
Subscrip. Rate: $20/yr.
Materials: 02,05
Print Process: offset lithography
Circulation: 1,700
Circulation Type: paid
**Owner(s):**
David L. Greene
P.O. Box 398
Demorest, GA 30535-0398
Telephone: (206) 865-6440
Ownership %: 100
**Management:**
David L. Greene ...................President
David L. Greene ...................Publisher
Robert C. Anderson ...................Publisher
**Editorial:**
A. Jane McFerrin ...................Editor in Chief

**Desc.:** Documented analysis of genealogical problems. Includes short compiled genealogies.

### AMERICAN HERITAGE
69761
60 Fifth Ave.
New York, NY 10011
Telephone: (212) 206-5500
FAX: (212) 620-2332
Year Established: 1954
Pub. Frequency: 8/yr.
Page Size: standard
Subscrip. Rate: $4.95/copy; $32/yr.
Materials: 02,06,09,10,11,12,13,23,24,25, 32,33
Print Process: web offset
Circulation: 300,000
**Owner(s):**
Forbes, Inc.
60 Fifth Ave.
New York, NY 10011
Telephone: (212) 206-5500
Ownership %: 100
**Editorial:**
Richard Snow ...................Editor

### AMERICAN HISTORY ILLUSTRATED
25816
6405 Flank Dr.
Harrisburg, PA 17112-8200
Telephone: (717) 657-9555
Mailing Address:
P.O. Box 8200
Harrisburg, PA 17105-8200
Year Established: 1966
Pub. Frequency: bi-m.
Page Size: 4 color photos/art
Subscrip. Rate: $3.75 newsstand; $20/yr.
Materials: 02,06,10,19,21,32,33
Freelance Pay: $.10-$.15/wd.
Circulation: 160,000
Circulation Type: paid
**Owner(s):**
Cowles Media Co.
329 Portland Ave.
Minneapolis, MN 55415
Telephone: (612) 375-7000
Ownership %: 100
**Management:**
Bruce Barnet ...................President
Diane Myers ...................Advertising Manager
**Editorial:**
Ed Holm ...................Editor
Deborah Skonezney ...................Production Director
**Desc.:** Published for a general audience interested in history and the advancement of historical writing. Non-fiction only: US history, prehistoric to 1960's, biography, military, social, cultural, political. Also US in relation to rest of the world, as in WWI, WWII, diplomacy. Style should be readable and entertaining, but not glib or casual. Taboos: shallow research, extensive quotation. 2,500 to 6,000 words. Pays $200-$1,000. Photos: Buy only occasionally with mss; 8 x 10 glossies preferred. Departments include: 5-7 feature per issue, readers letters, history today, book and tape reviews, and major art exhibitions relating to american history. No unsolicited mss. Require prior query: Send for guidelines prior to submission and include LSASE. Sample copies $4.25.
**Readers:** General audience ranges from high school students to professional historians.
**Deadline:** story-4-6 mo. prior to pub. date; ads-3 mo. prior

## AMERICAN INDEPENDENT, THE
58617
8158 Palm St.
Lemon Grove, CA 91945
Telephone: (619) 460-4484
Year Established: 1974
Pub. Frequency: m.
Subscrip. Rate: $15/yr.
Circulation: 2,500
Circulation Type: paid
**Owner(s):**
W.K. Shearer
8158 Palm St.
Lemon Grove, CA 91945
Telephone: (619) 460-4484
**Management:**
W.K. Shearer ..............................Publisher
**Editorial:**
W.K. Shearer ..............................Editor
**Desc.:** Covers activities of California's American Independent Party.
**Readers:** American Independent Party leadership & other interested subscribers.

## AMERICAN SCHOLAR
25819
1811 Q St., N.W.
Washington, DC 20009
Telephone: (202) 265-3808
Year Established: 1932
Pub. Frequency: q.
Page Size: standard
Subscrip. Rate: $23/yr.
Freelance Pay: $500/article
Circulation: 26,000
Circulation Type: paid
**Owner(s):**
Phi Beta Kappa Society
1811 Q St., N.W.
Washington, DC 20009
Telephone: (202) 265-3808
Ownership %: 100
**Management:**
Claire Iseli ....................Advertising Manager
Claire Iseli ....................Promotion Manager
**Editorial:**
Joseph Epstein ..............................Editor
Jean Stipicevic ..................Managing Editor
Sandra Costich ..................Associate Editor
Thomas Nieman ..................Editorial Assistant
**Desc.:** Primarily interested in articles by scholars and thinkers which are written for a general audience. Range of interests is wide - philosophical concepts, literature, international politics, etc. Scholarly articles written in specialized language for specialists are not wanted. Articles run from 3,500 to 5,000 words and must be approved by at least two members of the editorial board in addition to the editor before acceptance.
**Readers:** General intelligent audience.

## BRITISH HERITAGE
25829
6405 Flank Dr.
Harrisburg, PA 17112
Telephone: (717) 657-9555
FAX: (717) 657-9526
Mailing Address:
P.O. Box 8200
Harrisburg, PA 17105-8200
Year Established: 1974
Pub. Frequency: bi-m.
Page Size: 4 color photos/art
Subscrip. Rate: $30/yr.
Freelance Pay: $200/1,000 wds.
Circulation: 100,000
Circulation Type: paid
**Owner(s):**
Cowles Magazines, Inc.
P.O. Box 8200
Harrisburg, PA 17105
Telephone: (717) 657-9555

Cowles Media Co.
329 Portland Ave.
Minneapolis, MN 55415
Telephone: (612) 375-7000
Ownership %: 100
**Bureau(s):**
Cowles Magazines, Inc.
2245 Kohn Rd.
Harrisburg, PA 17110
Telephone: (717) 657-9555
Contact: Ruth Karabcievschy, Personnel Manager
**Management:**
Suzanne Kradel ................Advertising Manager
**Editorial:**
Gail Huganir ..............................Editor
Bruce Heydt ....................Managing Editor
Gail Huganir ..................Book Review Editor
**Desc.:** Covers the history and culture of Britain including current and former members of the British Commonwealth and British Empire. Nonfiction only: Biographical, military, travel & history, social, cultural and political articles, 1,000 to 2,000 words. Pays $100 per 1,000 words. Suggestions for illustrations needed. Style should be readable and entertaining but not glib or casual. Avoid shallow research, extensive quotation. Departments include: Readers' Correspondence, Book Reviews, Update, Chronicle of Events. Please query with samples of work and request author guidelines (SAE).
**Readers:** Professional, well-educated people with great interest in Britain: travel, food, culture and history.

## CALIFORNIA STATESMAN
58619
8158 Palm St.
Lemon Grove, CA 91945
Telephone: (619) 460-4484
Year Established: 1962
Pub. Frequency: m.
Page Size: standard
Subscrip. Rate: $15/yr. (includes 4 newsletters)
Circulation: 800
Circulation Type: free & paid
**Owner(s):**
W.K. Shearer
8158 Palm St.
Lemon Grove, CA 91945
Telephone: (619) 460-4484
**Management:**
W.K. Shearer ..............................Manager
**Editorial:**
W.K. Shearer ..............................Editor
**Desc.:** Covers political subjects.
**Readers:** American Independent Party and U.S. taxpayers party leadership; other subscribers.

## CAREERS & THE DISABLED
65594
150 Motor Pkwy., Ste. 420
Hauppauge, NY 11788-5145
Telephone: (516) 273-0066
FAX: (516) 273-8936
Year Established: 1986
Pub. Frequency: 3/yr.
Page Size: standard
Subscrip. Rate: $10/yr.
Circulation: 10,000
Circulation Type: paid
**Owner(s):**
Equal Opportunity Publications, Inc.
150 Motor Pkwy., Ste. 420
Hauppauge, NY 11788-5145
Telephone: (516) 273-0066
Ownership %: 100
**Management:**
John R. Miller, III ..............................President
John R. Miller, III ..............................Publisher
Christine Desmond ................Business Manager

Barbara O'Connor ............Circulation Manager
**Editorial:**
James Schneider ..............................Editor
Anne Kelly ....................Associate Editor
James Schneider ..................Production Director
**Desc.:** A career magazine for professional career counsellors of the disabled and for the disabled. Profiles disabled people who have achieved successful careers. Features a career section in Braille, career guidance, career news, affirmative action news. Free resume service. Career opportunities in industry, business, schools, hospitals, service utilities and government.
**Readers:** Career-oriented disabled individuals.

## CHRONICLE OF PHILANTHROPY, THE
65429
1255 23rd St., N.W.
Washington, DC 20037
Telephone: (202) 466-1200
FAX: (202) 466-2078
Year Established: 1988
Pub. Frequency: bi-w.
Page Size: tabloid
Subscrip. Rate: $4 newsstand; $67.50/yr.
Materials: 02,06,10,15,20,21,23,24,25,27, 28,30,32,33
Print Process: web offset
Circulation: 30,906
Circulation Type: paid
**Owner(s):**
The Chronicle of Higher Education, Inc.
1255 23rd St., N.W.
Washington, DC 20037
Telephone: (202) 466-1000
Ownership %: 100
**Management:**
Corbin Gwaltney ..............................Publisher
**Editorial:**
Philip Semas ..............................Editor
Stacy Palmer ....................Managing Editor
Robin Ross ....................Associate Publisher
Joyce Guisto ....................Associate Publisher
William C. Criger ..................Associate Publisher
**Desc.:** Provides news and information about the activities of foundations, corporate grant makers, and non-profit organizations. Also offers lists of recent grants, fund-raising ideas, statistics, updates on state and federal regulations, reports on tax and court rulings, summaries of books, and calendar of events.
**Readers:** Fund raisers, executives at non-profit organizations and corporate foundations, and government grant makers.

## CIVIL WAR
66323
P.O. Box 770
Berryville, VA 22611
Telephone: (703) 955-1176
Year Established: 1983
Pub. Frequency: bi-m.
Page Size: standard
Subscrip. Rate: $3.95/copy; $19.97/yr.
Materials: 05,06,10,15,21,28,32,33
Print Process: web
Circulation: 20,000
Circulation Type: paid
**Owner(s):**
Outlook, Inc.
P.O. Box 770
Berryville, VA 22611
Telephone: (703) 955-3621
FAX: (703) 955-2321
Ownership %: 100
**Management:**
Christopher Curran ..............................Publisher

**Editorial:**
William Miller ..............................Editor

## CIVIL WAR TIMES ILLUSTRATED
25837
6405 Flank Dr.
Harrisburg, PA 17112
Telephone: (717) 657-9555
FAX: (717) 657-9526
Mailing Address:
P.O. Box 8200
Harrisburg, PA 17105-8200
Year Established: 1962
Pub. Frequency: bi-m.
Page Size: standard
Subscrip. Rate: $21/yr.
Freelance Pay: $50-$450
Circulation: 174,054
**Owner(s):**
Cowles Magazines, Inc.
2245 Kohn Rd.
Harrisburg, PA 17105-8200
Telephone: (717) 657-9555
Ownership %: 100
**Management:**
Robert H. Fowler ..............................Founder
Christopher Little ..............................President
Diane Myers ....................Advertising Manager
**Editorial:**
John Stanchak ..............................Editor
Douglas Shirk ..............................Art Director
Carl Zebrowski ..................Associate Editor
Andrea E.A. Ebeling ............Editorial Assistant
Tyrone Dickey ..............Production Coordinator
**Desc.:** Covers the events, personalities, leaders, and battles of the Civil War period. Readers share the thoughts and emotions of men at war through eye witness accounts and stories illuminated by priceless paintings, photographs, and detailed maps. Nonfiction only: The Civil War, military, biography, technological, social, diplomatic, political. Style should be readable and entertaining, but not glib or casual. Taboos: shallow research, extensive quotation. 2,500 to 5,000 words. Pays $50 to $450. Welcome suggestions for illustrations; buy photos only occasionally with mss; 8 X 10 glossies preferred. Departments include: The War in Words, The Gates Report (current publications and happenings re: Civil War), Readers Letters, Book Reviews.
**Readers:** For persons interested in American history, particularly Civil War enthusiasts.

## COMMENTARY
26163
165 E. 56th St.
New York, NY 10022
Telephone: (212) 751-4000
FAX: (212) 751-1174
Year Established: 1945
Pub. Frequency: m.
Page Size: standard
Subscrip. Rate: $3.75 newsstand; $39/yr.
Circulation: 25,000
Circulation Type: paid
**Owner(s):**
American Jewish Committee
165 E. 56th St.
New York, NY 10022
Telephone: (212) 751-4000
Ownership %: 100
**Management:**
Sarah Stern ....................Advertising Manager
**Editorial:**
Norman Podhoretz ..................Editor in Chief
Neal Kozodoy ..............................Editor
Brenda Brown ....................Managing Editor

**Materials Accepted/Included:** 01-Business news 02-By-line articles 03-Fashion news 04-Food news 05-Freelance copy 06-Letters to editor 07-Real estate news 08-Sports news 09-Travel news 10-Book rev. 11-Movie rev. 12-Music rev. 13-TV rev. 14-Theater rev. 15-Coming events 16-Obituaries 17-Question & answer 18-Social announcements 19-Artwork 20-Cartoons 21-Photos 22-TV listings 23-Audio rec. 24-Video rec. 25-Books 26-Films/film clips 27-Personnel news 28-Press releases 29-New product news/photos 30-Trade lit. 31-Contracts awarded 32-Display adv. 33-Classified adv.

6-55

**Desc.:** An independent, intellectual monthly dealing with culture, the social sciences, religion, politics and literature. Departments include: Observations, In the Community, Letters from Readers, Books in Review, Fiction, Theater, Movies, Music.
**Readers:** Leaders in business, industry and the professions.

25842
**CRISIS, THE**
4805 Mount Hope Dr.
Baltimore, MD 21215
Telephone: (410) 358-8900
Year Established: 1910
Pub. Frequency: 8/yr.
Page Size: standard
Subscrip. Rate: $2/issue; $15/yr.
Circulation: 400,000
Circulation Type: paid
**Owner(s):**
Crisis Publishing Co., Inc.
4805 Mount Hope Dr.
Baltimore, MD 21215
Telephone: (301) 358-8900
Ownership %: 100
**Management:**
Gentry Trotter .........................Publisher
**Editorial:**
Denise Crittendon ........................Editor
Judith Hill .............National Marketing Manager
**Desc.:** Founded 1910 by W.E.B. Du Bois, this is the nation's oldest black magazine. Official organ of NAACP.
**Readers:** All persons interested in human and minority rights.
**Deadline:** story-10th of mo. prior to pub.

58618
**FOREIGN POLICY REVIEW**
8158 Palm St.
Lemon Grove, CA 91945
Telephone: (619) 460-4484
Year Established: 1972
Pub. Frequency: m.
Page Size: standard
Subscrip. Rate: $15/yr.
Circulation: 800
Circulation Type: free & paid
**Owner(s):**
W.K. Shearer
8158 Palm St.
Lemon Grove, CA 91945
Telephone: (619) 460-4484
Ownership %: 100
**Management:**
W. K. Shearer ..........................Manager
**Editorial:**
W. K. Shearer ............................Editor
**Desc.:** Foreign policy issues. Supports non-interventionist foreign policy.
**Readers:** American Independent Party leadership; other subscribers.

69287
**FRANCE TODAY**
1051 Divisadero
San Francisco, CA 94115
Telephone: (415) 921-5100
Pub. Frequency: 10/yr.
Page Size: standard
Materials: 04,05,06,09,10,11,21,28,29,32,33
Freelance Pay: query for details
Circulation: 10,000
Circulation Type: paid
**Owner(s):**
France Press, Inc.
1051 Divisadero
San Francisco, CA 94115
Telephone: (415) 921-5100
Ownership %: 100
**Management:**
Marie Galanti .........................Publisher
Allyn Kaufmann ................Advertising Manager
**Desc.:** Material related to France.

26169
**FREEMAN, THE**
30 S. Broadway
Irvington, NY 10533
Telephone: (914) 591-7230
Year Established: 1950
Pub. Frequency: m.
Page Size: standard
Subscrip. Rate: free in US; $40/yr. foreign
Freelance Pay: $.10/wd.
Circulation: 25,000
Circulation Type: controlled
**Owner(s):**
The Foundation for Economic Education
30 S. Broadway
Irvington, NY 10533
Telephone: (914) 591-7230
FAX: (914) 591-8910
Ownership %: 100
**Editorial:**
Beth A. Hoffman ...................Managing Editor
**Desc.:** A monthly journal of ideas on liberty, presenting the libertarian philosophy of limited government, free market economics and individual freedom. Views expressed in articles are consistent with the belief that in a free society each individual can best discover his potentialities and develop them to the fullest. Manuscripts from the libertarian viewpoint are invited for consideration by the editor. All articles appear with by-line; articles run from 1,000 to 4,000 words. Writings by various senior Foundation staff members appear monthly in The Freeman.

69283
**HERITAGE QUEST MAGAZINE**
P.O. Box 329
Bountiful, UT 84011-0329
Telephone: (801) 298-5358
FAX: (801) 298-5468
Year Established: 1985
Pub. Frequency: bi-m.
Page Size: standard
Subscrip. Rate: $28/yr.
Materials: 02,05,10,15,17,21
Print Process: web offset
Circulation: 10,000
Circulation Type: paid
**Owner(s):**
Heritage Quest Magazine
P.O. Box 329
Bountiful, UT 84011-0329
Telephone: (801) 298-5358
Ownership %: 100
**Management:**
Bradley W. Steuart ....................Publisher
**Editorial:**
Leland K. Meitzler ........................Editor
Evan L. Whipple ........Administration/Marketing
**Desc.:** Includes articles on how to find and record genealogical data; international in scope.
**Readers:** Readers are of age 45+.
**Deadline:** story-45 days prior to pub. date; photo-45 days prior to pub. date

25864
**HIGH TIMES**
235 Ave. S., 5th Fl.
New York, NY 10003-1405
Telephone: (212) 387-0500
FAX: (212) 475-7684
Year Established: 1974
Pub. Frequency: m.
Page Size: 4 color photos/art
Subscrip. Rate: $29.95/yr. US; $37.95/yr. foreign
Materials: 03,05,06,09,10,11,12,16,17,19,20,21
Freelance Pay: $50-$350
Circulation: 250,000
Circulation Type: paid

**Owner(s):**
Trans-High Corp.
235 Park Ave. S., 5th Fl.
New York, NY 10003-1405
Telephone: (212) 387-0500
Ownership %: 100
**Management:**
John Holmstrom ........................Publisher
Harry Crossfield, Jr. ..........Advertising Manager
**Editorial:**
Steven Hager ......................Editor in Chief
Erik-Loren Council .......................Art Editor
**Desc.:** Monthly culture and politics journal, devoted to the counter culture.
**Readers:** 18-35 years old, median income $22,000.

58627
**HISTORIC PRESERVATION**
1785 Massachusetts Ave., N.W.
Washington, DC 20036
Telephone: (202) 673-4000
Year Established: 1949
Pub. Frequency: bi-m.
Page Size: 4 color photos/art
Subscrip. Rate: $15/yr. individual; $24/yr. family
Freelance Pay: $500-850/assigned manuscripts
Circulation: 211,813
Circulation Type: paid
**Owner(s):**
Natl. Trust-Historic Preservation
1785 Massachusetts Ave., N.W.
Washington, DC 20036
Telephone: (202) 673-4000
Ownership %: 100
**Editorial:**
T.J. Colin ...............................Editor
Bob Barron .........................Advertising Editor
**Desc.:** Publishes lively, full-color features about efforts to preserve America's architectural heritage. The focus is on the people who are restoring old houses, interiors and gardens, and putting historic commercial structures back to work. Articles cover landmarks, antiques, travel, collecting, and how-to.
**Readers:** Readers are mature (median age 50), well educated (93% attended college), financially secure (median HHI $65,000) and urban (over 40% reside in CA, NY, MD, IL, FL).

59559
**ISLANDER**
P. O. Box 5950
Hilton Head, SC 29938
Telephone: (803) 785-3613
FAX: (803) 785-4345
Pub. Frequency: m.
Subscrip. Rate: $28.50/yr.
Circulation: 10,000
Circulation Type: paid
**Owner(s):**
Islander
Ownership %: 100
**Management:**
Mark Wargan ....................Advertising Manager
**Editorial:**
Lois Claus ..............................Editor

65042
**JEWISH FRONTIER**
275 Seventh Ave., Rm. 17R
New York, NY 10001-6776
Telephone: (212) 229-2280
Year Established: 1934
Pub. Frequency: bi-m.
Page Size: standard
Subscrip. Rate: $15/yr.
Freelance Pay: $.05/word
Circulation: 5000
Circulation Type: paid

**Owner(s):**
Labor Zionist Letters, Inc.
33 E. 67th St.
New York, NY 10021
Telephone: (212) 988-7339
**Editorial:**
Nahum Guttman ..........................Editor
**Desc.:** A Labor Zionist Journal. Reporting on Jewish culture, Israel, North American Jews. Zionism and labor concerns. Art, film, book reviews, essays and editorials.
**Readers:** Leading Intellectuals, Libraries, Politicians, Rabbis, Jewish Leaders

26174
**JOURNAL OF INTERNATIONAL AFFAIRS**
420 W. 118th
Columbia University
New York, NY 10027
Telephone: (212) 854-4775
Mailing Address:
P.O. Box 4 - Intl. Affairs Bldg.
Columbia University
New York, NY 10027
Year Established: 1948
Pub. Frequency: s-a.
Page Size: standard
Subscrip. Rate: $16/yr. individuals; $32/yr. institutions
Circulation: 1700
Circulation Type: paid
**Owner(s):**
School of Intl. & Public Affairs, Columbia Univ.
420 W. 118th St.
New York, NY 10027
Telephone: (212) 280-5406
Ownership %: 100
**Management:**
Sophia Lewisohn ..................Business Manager
**Editorial:**
M. Kathleen Tedesco .....................Editor
Timothy Clark .......................Managing Editor
Susan Vecsey .......................Circulation Editor
Joanne Lee .........................Marketing Editor
**Desc.:** Publishes scholarly articles in the social sciences relevant to international relations. Articles in each issue are devoted to a single topic.
**Readers:** Scholars, libraries, institutions, and private individuals.

69384
**MIDDLE EAST POLICY**
1730 M St., N.W., Ste. 512
Washington, DC 20036-4505
Telephone: (202) 296-6767
FAX: (202) 296-5791
Year Established: 1982
Pub. Frequency: q.
Subscrip. Rate: $35/yr.
Print Process: web
Circulation: 7,000
Circulation Type: controlled & paid
**Owner(s):**
Middle East Policy Council
1730 M St., N.W., Ste. 512
Washington, DC 20036
Telephone: (202) 296-6767
FAX: (202) 296-5791
Ownership %: 100
**Editorial:**
Anne Joyce ..............................Editor
**Desc.:** Provides viewpoints on recent developments that affect US-Middle East policies.

66333
**MILITARY HISTORY**
602 S. King St., Ste. 300
Leesburg, VA 22075
Telephone: (703) 771-9400
FAX: (703) 777-4627
Year Established: 1984

**Materials Accepted/Included:** 01-Business news 02-By-line articles 03-Fashion news 04-Food news 05-Freelance copy 06-Letters to editor 07-Real estate news 08-Sports news 09-Travel news 10-Book rev. 11-Movie rev. 12-Music rev. 13-TV rev. 14-Theater rev. 15-Coming events 16-Obituaries 17-Question & answer 18-Social announcements 19-Artwork 20-Cartoons 21-Photos 22-TV listings 23-Audio rec. 24-Video rec. 25-Books 26-Films/film clips 27-Personnel news 28-Press releases 29-New product news/photos 30-Trade lit. 31-Contracts awarded 32-Display adv. 33-Classified adv.

6-56

Pub. Frequency: bi-m.
Subscrip. Rate: $16/yr.
Freelance Pay: Varies
Circulation: 200,000
Circulation Type: paid
**Owner(s):**
Cowles History Group
602 S. King St., Ste. 300
Leesburg, VA 22075
Telephone: (703) 771-9400
**Management:**
Gregg Oehler ............................Publisher
**Editorial:**
Brian Kelly ..................................Editor

25885

## MOTHER JONES
731 Market St., #600
San Francisco, CA 94103
Telephone: (415) 665-6637
FAX: (415) 665-6696
Year Established: 1976
Pub. Frequency: 6/yr.
Page Size: standard
Subscrip. Rate: $2.95 newsstand; $18/yr.
    US; $28/yr. foreign
Materials: 06
Freelance Pay: $.75/wd.
Circulation: 120,000
Circulation Type: paid
**Owner(s):**
Foundation for National Progress
731 Market St.
San Francisco, CA 94103
Telephone: (415) 665-6637
Ownership %: 100
**Management:**
Jay Harris ..................................Publisher
Dan Cawley ..................Business Manager
Suzanne McCloskey ..........Circulation Manager
**Editorial:**
Katharine Fong ..................Managing Editor
Kerry Tremain ......................Art Director
Chris Orr ..............................Articles Editor
Deborah Schmidt ..................Associate Editor
Doug Foster ..................Book Review Editor
Jeffrey Klein ..................Editor-in-Chief
**Desc.:** A general-interest magazine of
politics, investigative reporting, and
popular culture.
**Readers:** Young, professional, educated,
civic minded, direct response oriented.
**Deadline:** story-3 mo. prior to pub. date;
photo-3 mo. prior; ads-2 mo. prior

69284

## NATIONAL GENEALOGICAL
## SOCIETY QUARTERLY
4527 17th St. N.
Arlington, VA 22207
Telephone: (703) 525-0050
Mailing Address:
    1732 Ridgedale Dr.
    Tuscaloosa, AL 35406
Year Established: 1912
Pub. Frequency: q.
Page Size: standard
Subscrip. Rate: $35/yr.
Materials: 02,10,32
Circulation: 13,000
Circulation Type: paid
**Owner(s):**
National Genealogical Society Quarterly
4527 17th St. N.
Arlington, VA 22207-2399
Telephone: (703) 525-0050
Ownership %: 100
**Editorial:**
Elizabeth Shown Mills ..................Editor
Gary Bernard Mills ......................Editor

26177

## NATIONAL JOURNAL
1501 M St., N.W., 3rd Fl.
Washington, DC 20005
Telephone: (202) 739-8400
Year Established: 1969

Pub. Frequency: w.
Page Size: standard
Subscrip. Rate: $883/yr.
Circulation: 6,000
Circulation Type: paid
**Owner(s):**
Times Mirror
Times Mirror Square
Los Angeles, CA 90053
Ownership %: 100
**Management:**
John Fox Sullivan ......................President
John Fox Sullivan ......................Publisher
**Editorial:**
Michael Wright ......................Exec. Editor
Richard S. Frank ......................Editor
Bill Hogan ......................Managing Editor
Steve Hull ..................Associate Publisher
**Desc.:** A weekly magazine reporting in
depth and detail on federal policy
issues. Factual, nonpartisan reports
examine the pressures, the people,
institutions, and interests, both private
and public/ that shape national
decisions. Binders and indexes are
available.
**Readers:** Corporate and government
executives, White House, Congressional
committe staffs, law firms, business
lobby groups, associations, media.

26178

## NATIONAL REVIEW
150 E. 35th St.
New York, NY 10016
Telephone: (212) 679-7330
FAX: (212) 696-0309
Year Established: 1955
Pub. Frequency: bi-w.
Page Size: standard
Subscrip. Rate: $57/yr.
Freelance Pay: $100/article
Circulation: 270,000
Circulation Type: paid
**Owner(s):**
National Review, Inc.
150 E. 35th St.
New York, NY 10016
Telephone: (212) 679-7330
Ownership %: 100
**Management:**
Thomas L. Rhodes ......................President
Edward A. Capano ......................Publisher
Scott Budd ..................Advertising Manager
**Editorial:**
John O'Sullivan ......................Editor
Linda Bridges ......................Managing Editor
Jack Fowler ..................Assistant Publisher
**Desc.:** A bi-weekly journal of conservative
news and opinions. Reports and
analyzes what both liberals and
conservatives throughout the country are
thinking, doing, writing, saying.
Departments include: Books, Arts and
Manners, For The Record, and The
Week, On the Right, and On the Scene.

26176

## NATION, THE
72 Fifth Ave.
New York, NY 10011
Telephone: (212) 242-8400
FAX: (212) 463-9712
Year Established: 1865
Pub. Frequency: w.
Page Size: standard
Subscrip. Rate: $48/yr.
Freelance Pay: $100-$250
Circulation: 98,000
Circulation Type: paid
**Owner(s):**
Nation Company, Inc.
72 Fifth Ave.
New York, NY 10011
Telephone: (212) 242-8400
Ownership %: 100

**Management:**
Neil Black ..................................President
Arthur L. Carter ..................Publisher
Peter Millard ..................Advertising Manager
**Editorial:**
Richard Lingeman ..................Executive Editor
Victor Navasky ......................Editor
Micah Sifry ..................Assistant Editor
Elsa Dixler ..................Book Review Editor
Grace Schulman ......................Poetry Editor
**Desc.:** The nation focuses on American
politics, foreign policy, social issues,
education and civil liberties; an average
one-third of each issue is devoted to
literature and the arts.
**Readers:** Highly educated, intelligent,
liberal, middle-upper income
professionals in government, business,
academic, communications and public
interest organizations.
**Deadline:** story-2 weeks prior to pub. date;
ads-2 weeks prior

65354

## NATIVE PEOPLES
5333 N. Seventh St., Ste. C-224
Phoenix, AZ 85014
Telephone: (602) 252-2236
FAX: (602) 265-3113
Year Established: 1987
Pub. Frequency: q.
Page Size: standard
Subscrip. Rate: $4.75 newsstand; $18/yr.
Materials: 04,05,06,10,12,19,21,23,24,25,32
Freelance Pay: $.25/wd.
Circulation: 110,000
Circulation Type: paid
**Owner(s):**
Media Concept Group, Inc.
Ownership %: 100
**Management:**
Janell Sixkiller ..................Advertising Manager
**Editorial:**
Gary Avey ......................Editor
Rebecca Withers ..................Editorial Director
Virginia Rayner ..................Administrative Manager
Rush Scott ..................Education Program
Alan Tack ..................Publication Reviewer
Jerome Bess ......................Treasurer
**Desc.:** Personal stories of native American
individuals and families. Dedicated to the
sensitive portrayal of the arts and
lifeways of native peoples of the
Americas.
**Readers:** Upper demographic, affiliated
with nine institutions, including National
Museum of the American Indian, and
Smithsonian Institution.

65431

## NAVAL HISTORY
U.S. Naval Institute, 118 Maryland Ave.
Annapolis, MD 21402
Telephone: (410) 268-6110
FAX: (410) 269-7940
Year Established: 1987
Pub. Frequency: bi-m.
Page Size: standard
Subscrip. Rate: $20/yr. non-members;
    $18/yr. members
Freelance Pay: $28-$350
Circulation: 27,038
Circulation Type: paid
**Owner(s):**
U.S. Naval Institute
118 Maryland Ave.
Annapolis, MD 21402
Telephone: (410) 268-6110
Ownership %: 100
**Management:**
Jim Barber ..................................Publisher
**Editorial:**
Fred Schultz ..................................Editor

**Desc.:** Covers naval history for different
countries, eras as well as covering
Marine Corps, Merchant Marine and U.S.
Coast Guard.
**Readers:** Enthusiasts of naval history and
scholars.

25817

## NEW AMERICAN, THE
770 Westhill Blvd.
Appleton, WI 54915
Telephone: (414) 749-3784
FAX: (414) 749-3785
Mailing Address:
    P.O. Box 54913
    Appleton, WI 54913
Year Established: 1985
Pub. Frequency: bi-w.
Page Size: standard
Subscrip. Rate: $39/yr.
Freelance Pay: $100/page
Circulation: 30,000
Circulation Type: paid
**Owner(s):**
Review of The News, Inc., The
P.O. Box 54913
Appleton, WI 54913
Telephone: (414) 749-3784
Ownership %: 100
**Management:**
John Mcmanus ......................Publisher
Julie DuFranc ..................Advertising Manager
Julie DuFranc ..................Circulation Manager
**Editorial:**
Gary Benoit ......................Editor
David Bohon ..................Managing Editor
Scott Alberts ......................Art Director
Thomas Bedlum ..................Research Director
Steve DuBord ......................Typesetter
**Desc.:** Conservative journal of news and
commentary on the world, the nation
and our cultural heritage.
**Readers:** Conservatives, economic
libertarians.

26180

## NEW REPUBLIC, THE
1220 19th St., N.W., Ste. 600
Washington, DC 20036
Telephone: (202) 331-7494
FAX: (202) 331-0275
Year Established: 1914
Pub. Frequency: w.
Page Size: standard
Subscrip. Rate: $2.95 newsstand;
    $69.97/yr.
Freelance Pay: $.20/wd.
Circulation: 100,000
Circulation Type: paid
**Owner(s):**
Martin Peretz
1220 19th St., N.W.
Washington, DC 20036
Telephone: (202) 331-7494
Ownership %: 100
**Management:**
Martin Peretz ..................Chairman of Board
Jeffrey Dearth ......................President
Joan Stapleton ......................Publisher
Jim McCabe ..................Associate Publisher
Cecilia Stephens ..................Circulation Manager
**Editorial:**
Martin Peretz ..................Editor in Chief
Andrew Sullivan ......................Editor
Dorothy Wickenden ..................Managing Editor
Jennifer Barrett ......................Advertising
Leon Wieseltier ..................Book Review Editor
**Desc.:** Unsigned news pieces, foreign
communications, articles on political and
social topics, essays and reviews on
books and the arts, poems.
**Readers:** Educated, intelligent, cultured
middle-upper class, politically active,
upscale consumers.

Materials Accepted/Included: 01-Business news 02-By-line articles 03-Fashion news 04-Food news 05-Freelance copy 06-Letters to editor 07-Real estate news 08-Sports news 09-Travel news
10-Book rev. 11-Movie rev. 12-Music rev. 13-TV rev. 14-Theater rev. 15-Coming events 16-Obituaries 17-Question & answer 18-Social announcements 19-Artwork 20-Cartoons 21-Photos 22-TV listings
23-Audio rec. 24-Video rec. 25-Books 26-Films/film clips 27-Personnel news 28-Press releases 29-New product news/photos 30-Trade lit. 31-Contracts awarded 32-Display adv. 33-Classified adv.

6-57

**OFFICIAL DETECTIVE**                    25900
460 W. 34th St., 20th Fl.
New York, NY 10001
Telephone: (212) 947-6500
FAX: (212) 947-6727
Year Established: 1930
Pub. Frequency: 7/yr.
Page Size: standard
Subscrip. Rate: $2.50 newsstand; $15/yr.;
   $28/2 yrs.
Materials: 21,24,25
Freelance Pay: $250/standard-length
   article
Circulation: 122,500
Circulation Type: paid
**Owner(s):**
RGH Publishing Corp.
460 W. 34th St., 20th Fl.
New York, NY 10001
Telephone: (212) 947-6500
FAX: (212) 947-6727
Ownership %: 100
**Management:**
J. Rosenfield .............................President
J. Rosenfield .............................Publisher
J. Burriesci ..................Advertising Manager
**Editorial:**
Rose Mandelsberg ...............Editor in Chief
Christofer Pierson ...............Managing Editor
Mark Edwards ........................Art Director
**Desc.:** Factual reporting of actual crimes
   for an audience of middle-aged arm
   chair crime buffs.
**Readers:** Middle-aged crime buffs, arm
   chair detectives.

**OLD WEST**                    25902
205 W. Seventh, Ste. 202
Stillwater, OK 74074
Telephone: (405) 743-3370
FAX: (405) 743-3374
Mailing Address:
   P.O. Box 2107
   Stillwater, OK 74076
Year Established: 1964
Pub. Frequency: q.
Page Size: standard
Subscrip. Rate: $10.95/6 issues
Freelance Pay: $.03-$.06/wd.
Circulation: 30,000
Circulation Type: paid
**Owner(s):**
Western Periodicals, Inc.
P.O. Box 2107
Stillwater, OK 74076
Ownership %: 100
**Management:**
Steve Gragert .............................Publisher
Steve Gragert ...................Advertising Manager
**Editorial:**
John Joerschke ...............................Editor
**Desc.:** Carries articles and stories on
   badmen, range wars, Indian fights, ghost
   towns, lost mines, outlaws, trail drives,
   cowboys, ranch life, and pioneers of the
   Old West. Consists of true incidents
   occuring west of the Mississippi roughly
   between 1840-1910.
**Readers:** Persons interested in western
   history.

**PRESIDENTS & PRIME MINISTERS**                    70370
799 Roosevelt Rd., #6/208
Glen Ellyn, IL 60137-5925
Telephone: (708) 858-6161
FAX: (708) 858-8787
Year Established: 1992
Pub. Frequency: bi-m.
Subscrip. Rate: $5.75 newsstand; $27/yr.;
   $42/2 yr.; $63/3 yr.
Materials: 01,02,21,28,32,33
Print Process: web offset

**Owner(s):**
EQES, Inc.
799 Roosevelt Rd., #6/208
Glen Ellyn, IL 60137-5925
Telephone: (708) 858-6161
FAX: (708) 858-8787
Ownership %: 100
**Management:**
N.K. Agnihotri .............................Publisher
Ann Agnihotri ...............Advertising Manager
Kimberly Graba .................Sales Manager
**Editorial:**
N.K. Agnihotri ...............................Editor
Linda H. Thompson ...............Managing Editor
**Deadline:** story-3rd Fri.-even mos.; news-
   3rd Fri.-even mos.; photo-3rd Fri-even
   mos.; ads-1st Fri.-odd mo.

**PROFESSIONAL COUNSELOR**
   **MAGAZINE**                    66189
3201 S.W. 15 St.
Deerfield, FL 33442-8190
Telephone: (305) 360-0909
FAX: (305) 360-0034
Year Established: 1986
Pub. Frequency: bi-m.
Page Size: 4 color photos/art
Subscrip. Rate: $26/yr.
Materials: 10,33
Freelance Pay: negotiable
Circulation: 23,000
Circulation Type: paid
**Owner(s):**
A & D Publications Corp.
8577 154th Ave., N.E.
Redmond, WA 98052
Telephone: (206) 867-5024
Ownership %: 100
**Management:**
Ed Hearn .............................Publisher
**Editorial:**
Cliff Creager ...............................Editor

**PROGRESSIVE, THE**                    25919
409 E. Main St.
Madison, WI 53703
Telephone: (608) 257-4626
FAX: (608) 257-3373
Year Established: 1909
Pub. Frequency: m.
Page Size: standard
Subscrip. Rate: $3/copy; $36/yr.
Freelance Pay: $100-$300/article
Circulation: 40,000
Circulation Type: paid
**Owner(s):**
The Progressive, Inc.
409 E. Main St.
Madison, WI 53703
Telephone: (608) 257-4626
Ownership %: 100
**Management:**
Matthew Rothschild .............................Publisher
**Editorial:**
Erwin Knoll ...............................Editor
Linda Rocawich ...............Managing Editor
Pat Flynn ........................Art Director
Linda Rocawich ...............Book Review Editor
**Desc.:** Reports, analysis, and commentary
   on political, social and economic
   developments in the US. and abroad.

**REASON**                    25922
3415 S. Sepulveda Blvd., Ste. 400
Los Angeles, CA 90034
Telephone: (310) 391-2245
Year Established: 1968
Pub. Frequency: m.
Page Size: standard
Subscrip. Rate: $24/yr.
Materials: 06
Freelance Pay: varies
Print Process: web
Circulation: 45,000

Circulation Type: paid
**Owner(s):**
Reason Foundation
3415 S. Sepulveda Blvd., Ste.
Los Angeles, CA 90034
Telephone: (310) 391-2245
Ownership %: 100
**Management:**
Robert W. Poole, Jr. .............................President
Elizabeth Larson ...............Production Manager
**Editorial:**
Virginia I. Postrel ...............................Editor
Jacob Sullum ...............Managing Editor
Barbara Burch ........................Art Director
Nicholas Gillespie ...............Assistant Editor
Bryan Snyder ...............Associate Publisher
Alyssa Garey ...............Circulation Director
Rick Henderson ...............Washington Editor
**Desc.:** Covers political and cultural issues
   from a free market individualist
   perspective. Includes investigative
   journalism, public policy analysis,
   interviews and profiles, focused think
   pieces and lively cultural essays. Article
   length: 500- 5,000 words.
**Readers:** Median age 40, average
   household income $61,143, 60%
   married, 78% with college degree.

**REVIEW OF POLITICS, THE**                    25924
P.O. Box B
Notre Dame, IN 46556
Telephone: (219) 631-6623
Year Established: 1938
Pub. Frequency: q.
Page Size: standard
Subscrip. Rate: $25/yr. individuals; $30/yr.
   institutions
Circulation: 1,700
Circulation Type: paid
**Owner(s):**
University of Notre Dame
Notre Dame, IN 46556
Telephone: (219) 631-6623
Ownership %: 100
**Editorial:**
Donald P. Kommers ...............................Editor
Dennis Moran ...............Managing Editor
Walter Nicgorski ...............Book Review Editor
**Desc.:** By-line articles cover various
   aspects of the international politics,
   trends, developments, theories, etc.
   Primarily interested in the philosophical
   and historical approach to political
   science although institutions and
   techniques are also covered. Typical
   features might be a discussion of the
   fundamentals of democracy, an analysis
   of the influence of prominent
   personalities on their countries
   international affairs, etc. Extensive book
   review sections, report on and
   publications dealing with political
   subjects.
**Readers:** International relations, political
   circle colleges, and universities.

**SOCIETY PAGE**                    61002
270 Bryn Mawr Ave.
Bryn Mawr, PA 19010
Telephone: (215) 526-2500
Year Established: 1961
Pub. Frequency: bi-m.
Page Size: standard
Subscrip. Rate: membership
Print Process: web
Circulation: 36,000
Circulation Type: free
**Owner(s):**
American Society of CLU & CHFC
270 Bryn Mawr Ave.
Bryn Mawr, PA 19010
Telephone: (215) 526-2500
Ownership %: 100

**Editorial:**
Carl L. Hall ...............................Editor

**SPOTLIGHT, THE**                    25941
300 Independence Ave., S.E.
Washington, DC 20003
Telephone: (202) 544-1794
Year Established: 1975
Pub. Frequency: w.
Page Size: tabloid
Subscrip. Rate: $.85 newsstand; $38/yr.;
   $70/2 yrs.
Freelance Pay: negotiated on acceptance
Circulation: 100,000
Circulation Type: paid
**Owner(s):**
Liberty Lobby, Inc.
**Management:**
James M. Wolfington ........Advertising Manager
**Editorial:**
Paul Croke ...............................Editor
Fred Blahut ...............Managing Editor
Pat Garvey ...............Production Director
**Desc.:** Specializes in stories that are
   suppressed, ignored, minimized or
   written, presented from an unbalanced
   perspective by the mass media. Interest
   is limited to public affairs and financial
   issues involving America's self-interest in
   the world. Strongly nationalistic and
   patriotic.
**Readers:** Middle-class, strongly patriotic.

**TIMELINE**                    69107
1982 Velma Ave.
Columbus, OH 43211-2497
Telephone: (614) 297-2332
Year Established: 1984
Pub. Frequency: bi-m.
Subscrip. Rate: $22.50/yr.
Materials: 05
Print Process: offset lithography
Circulation: 16,900
Circulation Type: free & paid
**Owner(s):**
Ohio Historical Society
1982 Velma Ave.
Columbus, OH 43211-2497
Telephone: (614) 297-2332
Ownership %: 100
**Editorial:**
Christopher S. Duckworth ...............Editor
**Desc.:** Covers the fields of history,
   prehistory and the natural sciences.

**TRUE WEST**                    26124
205 W. Seventh, #202
Stillwater, OK 74074
Telephone: (405) 743-3370
FAX: (405) 743-3374
Year Established: 1953
Pub. Frequency: m.
Page Size: standard
Subscrip. Rate: $19.95/yr.; $37/2 yrs.
Freelance Pay: $.03-$.06/wd.
Circulation: 30,000
Circulation Type: paid
**Owner(s):**
Western Publications
P.O. Box 2107
Stillwater, OK 74076
Telephone: (405) 743-3370
Ownership %: 100
**Management:**
Steve Gragert .............................Publisher
**Editorial:**
John Joerschke ...............................Editor
**Desc.:** A magazine that carries factual
   accounts of the Old West, 1840-1910.
   Departments include: Truly Western,
   Book Reviews, Trails Grown Dim, and
   Editorial, and Western Roundup, Answer
   Man, Great Western Gunfights.

**Materials Accepted/Included:** 01-Business news 02-By-line articles 03-Fashion news 04-Food news 05-Freelance copy 06-Letters to editor 07-Real estate news 08-Sports news 09-Travel news 10-Book rev. 11-Movie rev. 12-Music rev. 13-TV rev. 14-Theater rev. 15-Coming events 16-Obituaries 17-Question & answer 18-Social announcements 19-Artwork 20-Cartoons 21-Photos 22-TV listings 23-Audio rec. 24-Video rec. 25-Books 26-Films/film clips 27-Personnel news 28-Press releases 29-New product news/photos 30-Trade lit. 31-Contracts awarded 32-Display adv. 33-Classified adv.

**Readers:** Persons interested in western history.

## VANITY FAIR
53996

350 Madison Ave.
New York, NY 10017
Telephone: (212) 880-8800
FAX: (212) 880-8289
Year Established: 1983
Pub. Frequency: m.
Page Size: 4 color photos/art
Subscrip. Rate: $15/yr.
Freelance Pay: varies
Circulation: 1,013,761
Circulation Type: paid
**Owner(s):**
Conde Nast Publications, Inc.
350 Madison Ave.
New York, NY 10017
Telephone: (212) 880-8800
Ownership %: 100
**Bureau(s):**
Conde Nast
6300 Wilshire Blvd.
Los Angeles, CA 90048
Telephone: (213) 965-3594
Contact: Krista Margo Smith, Editor
**Management:**
Kathy Neisloss Leventhal ..................Publisher
**Editorial:**
E. Graydon Carter ..................Editor in Chief
Chris Garrett ..........................Managing Editor
**Readers:** Smart, spirited, inquisitive and acquisitive, people with up- to-the-minute ideas.

## VIETNAM
66334

602 S. King St., Ste. 300
Leesburg, VA 22075
Telephone: (703) 771-9400
Year Established: 1988
Pub. Frequency: bi-m.
Page Size: standard
Subscrip. Rate: $2.95 newsstand US;
$3.50 Canada; $14.95/yr.
Materials: 02,10,25,28,32
Circulation: 160,000
Circulation Type: paid
**Owner(s):**
Cowles History Group
602 S. King St., Ste. 300
Leesburg, VA 22075
Telephone: (703) 771-9400
Ownership %: 100
**Management:**
Thomas O'Keefe ......................Publisher
**Editorial:**
Col. Harry Summers, Jr. ..................Editor

## WORLD WAR II
66332

602 S. King St., Ste. 300
Leesburg, VA 22075
Telephone: (703) 771-9400
FAX: (703) 777-4627
Year Established: 1936
Pub. Frequency: bi-m.
Subscrip. Rate: $16/yr.
Freelance Pay: Varies
Circulation: 190,000
Circulation Type: controlled
**Owner(s):**
Cowles History Group
602 S. King St., Ste. 300
Leesburg, VA 22075
Telephone: (703) 771-9400
**Management:**
Gregg Oehler ..........................Publisher

**Editorial:**
Mike Haskew ..............................Editor

## Group 638-Hobbies & Crafts

## AMERICAN PHILATELIST
65398

100 Oakwood Ave.
State College, PA 16803
Telephone: (814) 237-3803
Mailing Address:
P.O. Box 8000
State College, PA 16803
Year Established: 1887
Pub. Frequency: m.
Page Size: standard
Subscrip. Rate: $2.25/copy
Materials: 01,02,05,06,10,15,16,27,28,29,
30,32,33
Freelance Pay: $50/article
Print Process: web offset
Circulation: 57,000
Circulation Type: paid
**Owner(s):**
American Philatelic Society
P.O. Box 800
State College, PA 16803
Telephone: (814) 237-3803
FAX: (814) 237-6128
Ownership %: 100
**Editorial:**
Bill Welch ..............................Editor
**Readers:** Members of the American Philatelic Society, the nation's largest organization for stamp collectors.
**Deadline:** story-1 yr. prior to pub. date; news-2 mo. prior; ads-1st of mo. prior

## AMERICAN REVENUER
69574

P.O. Box 56
Rockford, IA 50468-0056
Telephone: (515) 756-3542
Year Established: 1947
Pub. Frequency: 10/yr.
Page Size: standard
Subscrip. Rate: $18/yr.
Materials: 06,10
Print Process: offset lithography
Circulation: 1,350
Circulation Type: paid
**Owner(s):**
American Revenue Association
P.O. Box 56
Rockford, IA 50468
Telephone: (515) 756-3542
Ownership %: 100
**Editorial:**
Kenneth Trettin ..............................Editor
**Desc.:** Contains articles about and catalogue listings of tax stamps of the U.S. and the world.

## AMERICAN WOODWORKER
66696

33 E. Minor St.
Emmaus, PA 18098
Telephone: (215) 967-5171
FAX: (215) 967-8956
Year Established: 1985
Pub. Frequency: 7/yr.
Page Size: standard
Subscrip. Rate: $3.25 newsstand; $27/yr.
Materials: 02,05,06,32,33
Freelance Pay: $150/published page
Circulation: 300,000
Circulation Type: paid
**Owner(s):**
Rodale Press, Inc.
33 E. Minor St.
Emmaus, PA 18098
Telephone: (215) 967-5171
Ownership %: 100
**Management:**
David Sloan ..........................Publisher
**Editorial:**
David Sloan ..............................Editor

Kevin Ireland ..........................Managing Editor
Catherine Pierce Mace ..................Art Director
Dave Sellers ..........................New Products Editor
**Desc.:** A how-to magazine edited for the woodworking enthusiast looking to improve his/her skills.
**Readers:** Amateur woodworking enthusiasts & small-shop professionals

## BANK NOTE REPORTER
22704

700 E. State St.
Iola, WI 54990
Telephone: (715) 445-2214
FAX: (715) 445-4087
Year Established: 1967
Pub. Frequency: m.
Page Size: tabloid
Subscrip. Rate: $2.95 newsstand;
$29.95/yr.
Freelance Pay: negotiable
Circulation: 6,000
Circulation Type: paid
**Owner(s):**
Krause Publications, Inc.
700 E. State St.
Iola, WI 54990
Telephone: (715) 445-2214
Ownership %: 100
**Management:**
Clifford Mishler ..........................President
Rick Groth ..........................Publisher
Joel Edler ..........................Advertising Manager
Suzanne Olkowski ..........................Circulation Manager
**Editorial:**
Dave Harper ..............................Editor
**Desc.:** Contains news and marketplace information for collectors of US & foreign paper money, notes, checks, and related fiscal paper. It provides current prices for bank notes of the US and world as well as an active buy/sell marketplace.
**Readers:** Geared toward collectors of US and foreign paper money, checks, stocks, and bonds.

## BECKETT BASEBALL CARD MONTHLY
68904

15850 Dallas Pkwy.
Dallas, TX 75248
Telephone: (214) 991-6657
FAX: (214) 991-8930
Year Established: 1984
Pub. Frequency: m.
Page Size: standard
Subscrip. Rate: $2.95 newsstand;
$19.95/yr.
Materials: 02,05,06,08,19,20,21,28,29,30
Freelance Pay: $200-300
Circulation: 757,766
Circulation Type: paid
**Owner(s):**
Dr. James Beckett, III
15850 Dallas Parkway
Dallas, TX 75248
Telephone: (214) 991-6657
FAX: (214) 991-8930
Ownership %: 100
**Management:**
Dr. James Beckett, III ..........................Publisher
**Editorial:**
Dr. James Beckett, III ..............................Editor
Van Johnson ..........................Managing Editor
Pepper Hastings ..........................Editorial Director
**Desc.:** Baseball card and sports memorabilia collecting.

## BECKETT BASKETBALL MONTHLY
70473

15850 Dallas Pkwy.
Dallas, TX 75248
Telephone: (214) 991-6657
FAX: (214) 991-8930
Year Established: 1990

Pub. Frequency: m
Page Size: standard
Subscrip. Rate: $2.95 newsstand;
$19.95/yr.
Materials: 02,05,06,08,19,20,21,28,29,30,32
Freelance Pay: $200-300
Print Process: web offset
Circulation: 306,277
Circulation Type: paid
**Owner(s):**
Dr. James Beckett, III
15850 Dallas Parkway
Dallas, TX 75248
Telephone: (214) 991-8930
**Management:**
Dr. James Beckett, III ..........................Publisher
**Editorial:**
Dr. James Beckett, III ..............................Editor
Jay Johnson ..........................Managing Editor
**Desc.:** Basketball card and sports memorabilia collecting

## BECKETT FOCUS ON FUTURE STARS
70476

15850 Dallas Pkwy.
Dallas, TX 75248
Telephone: (214) 991-6657
FAX: (214) 991-8930
Year Established: 1991
Pub. Frequency: m.
Page Size: standard
Subscrip. Rate: $2.95 newsstand;
$19.95/yr.
Materials: 02,05,06,08,19,20,21,28,29,30,32
Freelance Pay: $200-300
Print Process: web offset
Circulation: 81,327
Circulation Type: paid
**Owner(s):**
Dr. James Beckett, III
15850 Dallas Parkway
Dallas, TX 75248
Ownership %: 100
**Management:**
Dr. James Beckett, III ..........................Publisher
**Editorial:**
Dr. James Beckett, III ..............................Editor
Jay Johnson ..........................Managing Editor
Pepper Hastings ..........................Editorial Director
**Desc.:** Superstar coverage of young, outstanding players in baseball (professional & college), basketball and football with an emphasis on collecting sports cards and memorabilia

## BECKETT HOCKEY MONTHLY
70478

15850 Dallas Pkwy.
Dallas, TX 75248
Telephone: (214) 991-6657
FAX: (214) 991-8930
Year Established: 1990
Pub. Frequency: m.
Page Size: standard
Subscrip. Rate: $2.95 newsstand;
$19.95/yr.
Materials: 02,05,06,08,19,20,21,
Freelance Pay: $200-300
Print Process: web offset
Circulation: 185,800
Circulation Type: paid
**Owner(s):**
Dr. James Beckett, III
15850 Dallas Pkwy.
Dallas, TX 75248
Telephone: (214) 991-6657
FAX: (214) 991-8930
**Management:**
Dr. James Beckett, III ..........................Publisher
**Editorial:**
Dr. James Beckett, III ..............................Editor
Jay Johnson ..........................Managing Editor
Pepper Hastings ..........................Editorial Director
**Desc.:** Hockey card and sports memorabilia collecting

**Materials Accepted/Included:** 01-Business news 02-By-line articles 03-Fashion news 04-Food news 05-Freelance copy 06-Letters to editor 07-Real estate news 08-Sports news 09-Travel news 10-Book rev. 11-Movie rev. 12-Music rev. 13-TV rev. 14-Theater rev. 15-Coming events 16-Obituaries 17-Question & answer 18-Social announcements 19-Artwork 20-Cartoons 21-Photos 22-TV listings 23-Audio rec. 24-Video rec. 25-Books 26-Films/film clips 27-Personnel news 28-Press releases 29-New product news/photos 30-Trade lit. 31-Contracts awarded 32-Display adv. 33-Classified adv.

6-59

## BETTER HOMES & GARDENS HOLIDAY CRAFTS
25961

1716 Locust St.
Des Moines, IA 50336
Telephone: (515) 284-3009
Year Established: 1974
Pub. Frequency: a.
Page Size: standard
Subscrip. Rate: $3.50 newsstand; $4.50 Canada
Circulation: 700,000
Circulation Type: paid
**Owner(s):**
Meredith Corp.
1716 Locust St.
Des Moines, IA 50336
Telephone: (515) 284-3000
Ownership %: 100
**Management:**
Stephen B. Levinson ...........................Publisher
**Editorial:**
Michael Senior ...................Circulation Director
Jerry Ward ...............V.P. Publications Director
**Desc.:** Twenty-two Special Interest titles for 1990. They offer something for everyone - from building projects & decorating to crafts, cooking & gardening.

## BRIDAL CRAFTS
67252

701 Lee St., Ste. 1000
Des Plaines, IL 60016
Telephone: (708) 297-7400
FAX: (708) 297-8328
Year Established: 1991
Pub. Frequency: a.
Page Size: standard
Circulation: 110,000
Circulation Type: paid
**Owner(s):**
Clapper Communications Co.
701 Lee St., Ste. 1000
Des Plaines, IL 60016
Telephone: (708) 297-7400
Ownership %: 100
**Management:**
Lyle Clapper ...........................................President
Marie Clapper .......................................Publisher
Stuart Hochwert ..............Advertising Manager
**Editorial:**
Julie Stephani .............................................Editor

## CARD COLLECTOR'S PRICE GUIDE
67303

155 E. Ames Ct.
Plainview, NY 11803
Telephone: (516) 349-9494
FAX: (516) 349-9516
Year Established: 1992
Pub. Frequency: m.
Page Size: standard
Subscrip. Rate: $3.95 newsstand; $17.95/yr.
Circulation: 75,000
Circulation Type: paid
**Owner(s):**
Century Publishing Co.
990 Grove St.
Evanston, IL 60201-4370
Telephone: (708) 491-6440
Ownership %: 100
**Management:**
Norman Jacobs ....................................Publisher
Doug Ingram .....................Advertising Manager
Marty Michalek ..................Circulation Manager
**Editorial:**
Douglas Kale .............................Editor in Chief
David Karp ...................................................Editor
**Desc.:** Comprehensive coverage of sports and non-sports cards for collectors, including auto racing, golf, soccer, entertainment, television, history and music cards.

## CELATOR, THE
68897

P.O. Box 123
Lodi, WI 53555
Telephone: (608) 592-4684
FAX: (608) 592-4684
Year Established: 1987
Pub. Frequency: m.
Page Size: standard
Subscrip. Rate: $3.50 newsstand; $27/yr. US; $30/yr. Canada; $48/yr. elsewhere
Materials: 10,15,20,21,28,32,33
Circulation: 2,000
Circulation Type: paid
**Owner(s):**
Celator, Inc.
P.O. Box 123
Lodi, WI 53555
Telephone: (608) 592-4684
Ownership %: 100
**Editorial:**
Wayne G. Sayles .......................................Editor
**Deadline:** story-1st of mo. prior to pub. date; news-1st of mo. prior; photo-1st of mo. prior; ads-1st of mo. prior

## CERAMIC ARTS & CRAFTS
22511

30595 Eight Mile Rd.
Livonia, MI 48152-1798
Telephone: (313) 477-6650
FAX: (810) 477-6795
Year Established: 1955
Pub. Frequency: m.
Page Size: standard
Subscrip. Rate: $2.25 newsstand; $19.60/yr. US; $26.60/yr. foreign
Freelance Pay: $25/article
Circulation: 50,000
Circulation Type: paid
**Owner(s):**
Scott Advertising & Publishing Co.
30595 Eight Mile Rd.
Livonia, MI 48152
Telephone: (313) 477-6650
Ownership %: 100
**Management:**
Bill Thompson .............................Vice President
R. H. Keessen .....................................Publisher
Jeanette Foxe ...................Circulation Manager
Verno Schafer ...................Production Manager
**Editorial:**
Bill Thompson ..............................................Editor
Barbara Campbell ................Managing Editor
Anette Malis ........................Assistant Publisher
William A. Latocki .....................Creative Director
Peggy Austen .......................Editorial Assistant
Carmela Gurizzian ..............Editorial Associate
Tom Grimes .........................Marketing Director
**Desc.:** Edited and published by ceramists for ceramists. Editorial consists of step-by-step projects on hobby ceramics, china painting, porcelain, non-firing stains, claywork, applied decoration, etc. All projects are accompanied by full-color photos. Credit is given to manufacturers in the Editor's Note at the end of each article. All authors contributing to editorial material are given by-lines. Departments include: Free listings of shows coming, New Products, News in the Industry, Book Reviews, Pattern Section, A Special Studio Listing, (studios handling 24 or more counter copies of our magazine), Santa's Workshop, series of interest to our readers.
**Readers:** Hobby ceramists, china painters, manufacturers.

## CERAMICS MONTHLY
25963

1609 Northwest Blvd.
Columbus, OH 43212
Telephone: (614) 488-8236
FAX: (614) 488-4561
Year Established: 1953
Pub. Frequency: m.: Sep.-June
Page Size: standard
Subscrip. Rate: $3.50 newsstand; $22/yr.
Circulation: 38,000
Circulation Type: paid
**Owner(s):**
Professional Publications, Inc.
P.O. Box 12448
Columbus, OH 43212
Telephone: (614) 488-8236
Ownership %: 100
**Management:**
Spencer L. Davis .................................President
Spencer Davis .......................................Publisher
Connie Belcher ................Advertising Manager
**Editorial:**
William C. Hunt ...........................................Editor
Ruth Butler ...............................Associate Editor
**Desc.:** Covers all aspects of ceramic art and crafts.
**Readers:** Potters both amateur and professional, collectors, art/craft dealers, galleries, craft historians, art teachers and professors, ceramic sculptors.

## COINAGE
25967

4880 Market St.
Ventura, CA 93003
Telephone: (805) 643-3664
FAX: (805) 644-3875
Year Established: 1964
Pub. Frequency: m.
Page Size: standard
Subscrip. Rate: $2.95; $23/yr.
Circulation: 150,000
Circulation Type: paid
**Owner(s):**
Miller Magazines, Inc.
4880 Market St.
Ventura, CA 93003
**Management:**
James Miller .........................................President
James Miller .........................................Publisher
Mike Gumpel .....................Advertising Manager
**Editorial:**
Karey Miller .........................Managing Editor
**Desc.:** Coin collecting, plus investing in gold & silver.
**Readers:** Readers: Interested in numismatics

## COIN PRICES
25965

700 E. State St.
Iola, WI 54990
Telephone: (715) 445-2214
Year Established: 1967
Pub. Frequency: bi-m.
Page Size: standard
Subscrip. Rate: $16.95/yr.; $31.95/2 yrs.
Materials: 32,33
Circulation: 90,000
Circulation Type: paid
**Owner(s):**
Krause Publications, Inc.
700 E. State St.
Iola, WI 54990
Telephone: (715) 445-2214
Ownership %: 100
**Management:**
Clifford Mishler .....................................President
Albert "Bo" Smith ...............................Publisher
Joel Edler .........................Advertising Manager
**Editorial:**
Robert E. Wilhite .......................................Editor
**Desc.:** Provides comprehensive, up-to-date valuations on all U.S. coins from 1792 to date. Valuations provided in up to four grades of preservation. All types and major varieties illustrated. Full mintage figures incorporated. U.S. paper money, Canadian and Mexican coins, mint errors incorporated periodically.
**Readers:** Average reader is male, 25-55 years of age.

## COINS
25968

700 E. State St.
Iola, WI 54990-0001
Telephone: (715) 445-2214
FAX: (715) 445-4087
Year Established: 1955
Pub. Frequency: m.
Page Size: standard
Subscrip. Rate: $2.95; $22.95/yr.
Freelance Pay: $.03/wd. and up
Circulation: 63,000
Circulation Type: paid
**Owner(s):**
Krause Publications, Inc.
700 E. State St.
Iola, WI 54990-0001
Telephone: (715) 445-2214
Ownership %: 100
**Management:**
Clifford Mishler .....................................President
Rick Groth ...........................................Publisher
Joel Edler .........................Advertising Manager
**Editorial:**
Alan Herbert .............................................Editor
**Desc.:** Provides in-depth features on US coins accompanied by crisp full-color photographs, helpful collector columns, and US and world coin hobby news. Updated, easy-to-use US coin price guide covers most popular US coins. Perfect hobby guide for novice or casual and advanced collectors.
**Readers:** Written for the coin hobbyist. It deals with the "how to" aspects of coin collecting: cataloguing, selecting, grading, storing and displaying.

## COIN WORLD
25966

911 Vandemark Rd.
Sidney, OH 45365
Telephone: (513) 498-2111
FAX: (513) 498-0812
Mailing Address:
  P.O. Box 150
  Sidney, OH 45365
Year Established: 1960
Pub. Frequency: Mon.
Page Size: tabloid
Subscrip. Rate: $1.95/issue; $28/yr.
Freelance Pay: $.08/wd.
Circulation: 65,000
Circulation Type: paid
**Owner(s):**
Amos Press, Inc.
911 Vandemark Road
Sidney, OH 45367
Telephone: (513) 498-2111
Ownership %: 100
**Management:**
Bruce Boyd ...........................................President
Ann Marie Aldrich ...............................Publisher
Bill Hampton .....................Advertising Manager
**Editorial:**
Beth Deisher ...............................................Editor
**Desc.:** Weekly newspaper covering field on numismatics (all phases of coin collecting). Coin collecting from novice to scholar also readers who are investments oriented, precious metals investors.

## COMIC BUYERS GUIDE
58626

700 E. State St.
Iola, WI 54990
Telephone: (715) 445-2214
Year Established: 1971
Pub. Frequency: w.
Page Size: tabloid
Subscrip. Rate: $2.50 newsstand; $34.95/yr.
Materials: 02,05,06,20,32,33
Freelance Pay: varies
Print Process: offset
Circulation: 19,000

---

**Materials Accepted/Included:** 01-Business news 02-By-line articles 03-Fashion news 04-Food news 05-Freelance copy 06-Letters to editor 07-Real estate news 08-Sports news 09-Travel news 10-Book rev. 11-Movie rev. 12-Music rev. 13-TV rev. 14-Theater rev. 15-Coming events 16-Obituaries 17-Question & answer 18-Social announcements 19-Artwork 20-Cartoons 21-Photos 22-TV listings 23-Audio rec. 24-Video rec. 25-Books 26-Films/film clips 27-Personnel news 28-Press releases 29-New product news/photos 30-Trade lit. 31-Contracts awarded 32-Display adv. 33-Classified adv.

Circulation Type: paid
**Owner(s):**
Krause Publications, Inc.
700 E. State St.
Iola, WI 54990
Telephone: (715) 445-2214
FAX: (715) 445-4087
Ownership %: 100
**Management:**
Greg Loescher ............................Publisher
Jim Felhoper ......................Advertising Manager
**Editorial:**
Don & Maggie Thompson ........................Editor
Donald R. Johnson ..........Vice President, Sales
**Desc.:** Comics buyers guide is edited for people who collect comic books, as well as for those involved in the comics industry itself. Each issue includes feature articles on people who create comics, a comic convention calendar and a list of new comic books by all publishers.
**Readers:** Primarily male; average age is 32 yrs. old.
**Deadline:** ads-Tue., 5:00 pm prior to pub. date

66754

**CONTEMPORARY DOLL MAGAZINE**
30595 Eight Mile Rd.
Livonia, MI 48152
Telephone: (313) 477-6650
FAX: (810) 477-6795
Year Established: 1990
Pub. Frequency: bi-m.
Page Size: oversize
Subscrip. Rate: $19.90/yr.
Circulation: 55,000
Circulation Type: paid
**Owner(s):**
Scott Publications
30595 Eight Mile Rd.
Livonia, MI 48152
Telephone: (313) 477-6650
Ownership %: 100
**Management:**
Robert Keessen ............................Publisher
**Editorial:**
Barbara Campbell ....................Managing Editor
Anna Galli ................................Associate Editor
William Latocki ........................Creative Director
**Desc.:** Presents dolls as fine art collectibles.
**Readers:** Directed to makers and collectors of fine-art dolls.

69236

**COUNTRY HANDCRAFTS**
5400 S. 60th St.
Greendale, WI 53129
Telephone: (414) 423-0100
FAX: (414) 423-1143
Year Established: 1983
Pub. Frequency: bi-m.
Page Size: standard
Subscrip. Rate: $2.95 newsstand; $16.98/yr.
Materials: 05,06,15,29
Circulation: 700,000
Circulation Type: paid
**Owner(s):**
Reiman Publications, Inc.
5400 S. 60th St.
Greendale, WI 53129
Telephone: (414) 423-0100
Ownership %: 100
**Editorial:**
Kathleen Zimmer ............................Editor

69396

**CRAFT & HOME PRODUCTS**
950 Third Ave., 16th Fl.
New York, NY 10022
Telephone: (212) 888-1855
FAX: (212) 838-8420
Year Established: 1987

Pub. Frequency: bi-m.
Page Size: standard
Subscrip. Rate: $3.50 newsstand; $21/yr.
Materials: 04,10,15
Freelance Pay: varies
Circulation: 390,000
Circulation Type: paid
**Owner(s):**
Women's Publishing Co.
1950 Third Ave.
New York, NY 10022
Telephone: (212) 888-1855
Ownership %: 100
**Management:**
Suzann Hochman ............................Publisher
Robert Miller ......................Advertising Manager
**Editorial:**
Christine Burns Roth ............................Editor
Renee Cajigal-Delgodo .......Marketing Manager
**Desc.:** Focuses on craft and home projects.
**Deadline:** story-4 mo. prior to pub. date; news-4 mo. prior; photo-4 mo. prior

69237

**CRAFTS**
P.O. Box 1790
Peoria, IL 61656
Telephone: (309) 682-6626
FAX: (309) 682-7394
Year Established: 1978
Pub. Frequency: m.
Page Size: standard
Subscrip. Rate: $3.95 newsstand; $17.95/yr.
Materials: 32
Circulation: 400,000
Circulation Type: paid
**Owner(s):**
Veronis Suhler Associates, Inc.
350 Park Ave.
New York, NY 10022
Ownership %: 100
**Management:**
Art Setterlund ....................Advertising Manager
Chuck Boysen ....................Circulation Manager
**Editorial:**
Judith Brassart ............................Editor
**Desc.:** Includes needlecrafts, tile painting, doll making, kids crafts, and gift giving crafts.

25970

**CRAFTS 'N THINGS**
701 Lee St., Ste. 1000
Des Plaines, IL 60016
Telephone: (708) 297-7400
FAX: (708) 297-8328
Year Established: 1975
Pub. Frequency: 10/yr.
Page Size: standard
Subscrip. Rate: $14.97/yr.
Circulation: 300,000
Circulation Type: paid
**Owner(s):**
Clapper Communications Companies
701 Lee St., Ste. 1000
Des Plaines, IL 60016
Telephone: (708) 297-7400
Ownership %: 100
**Management:**
Lyle Clapper ............................President
Marie Petersen ......................Publisher
Paul Withington ................Advertising Manager
**Editorial:**
Julie Stephani ............................Editor
Irene Zimmer ............................Advertising
Mary Ellen Boyd ............................Advertising
Stuart Hochwert ............................Advertising

**Desc.:** A craft instruction magazine written and edited to involve those with an interest in one or two crafts and in trying more and more new ideas and techniques. Success oriented, step-by-step instructions bring every craft imaginable - needlecraft, macrame, leathercraft, calligraphy, decoupage, etc. - within the creative reach of begineer and enthusiast. Many articles are written and designed by guest experts in their fields. For those who like to make nice things for fun or fund raising. Departments include: Just Between Us, Write Here, Taylor Tacks, The Meeting Place, Crafter's Notebook, The Bookshelf, Basic Embroidery Stitches, Pattern Section, The Marketplace (classified), Crafter's Showcase, One Last Thought, Source of Supplies.
**Readers:** Mostly women who have an interest in crafting.

69238

**CRAFTWORKS FOR THE HOME**
243 Newton-Sparta Rd.
Newton, NJ 07860-2748
Telephone: (201) 383-8080
Year Established: 1985
Pub. Frequency: m.
Page Size: standard
Subscrip. Rate: $2.94 newsstand US; $3.50 Canada; $35.40/yr. US
Materials: 32
Circulation: 325,000
Circulation Type: paid
**Owner(s):**
All American Crafts, Inc.
243 Newton-Sparta Rd.
Newton, NJ 07860-2748
Telephone: (201) 383-8080
Ownership %: 100
**Management:**
Jerry Cohen ............................Publisher
Barbara Smith ....................Advertising Manager
Marie Claire MacDonald ....Circulation Manager
**Editorial:**
Matthew Jones ............................Editor
**Desc.:** Features original craft projects, designs, instructions, and diagrams for all skill levels.

66764

**CROSSWORD**
P.O. Box 909
Bellmore, NY 11710
Telephone: (516) 679-8608
Year Established: 1990
Pub. Frequency: bi-m.
Page Size: standard
Subscrip. Rate: $3.95 issue; $18/yr.
Materials: 02,06,23,25,32,33
Freelance Pay: negotiable
Circulation: 5,000
Circulation Type: paid
**Owner(s):**
Megalo Media, Inc.
P.O. Box 678
Syosset, NY 11791
Ownership %: 100
**Management:**
J. Baxter Newgate ............................Publisher
**Editorial:**
J. Baxter Newgate ............................Editor
Fred Piscop ......................Design Editor
**Desc.:** crossword puzzles

66767

**DOLL READER**
6405 Flank Dr.
Harrisburg, PA 17112-0003
Telephone: (717) 540-6656
Year Established: 1972
Pub. Frequency: 9/yr.

Page Size: standard
Subscrip. Rate: $26.95/yr. US; $35.95/yr. Canada
Materials: 01,05,06,17,21,28,29,32,33
Freelance Pay: $65/published pg.
Circulation: 97,700
Circulation Type: paid
**Owner(s):**
Cowles Magazines, Inc.
6405 Flank Dr.
Harrsburg, PA 17112
Telephone: (717) 657-9555
FAX: (717) 540-6169
Ownership %: 100
**Management:**
Steve Norton ............................Publisher
**Editorial:**
Deborah Thompson ............................Editor
Pam Lefkowitz ......................Design Editor
**Readers:** Adult doll collectors.

65394

**DOLLS**
170 Fifth Ave.
New York, NY 10010
Telephone: (212) 989-8700
FAX: (212) 645-8976
Year Established: 1982
Pub. Frequency: 10/yr.
Page Size: standard
Subscrip. Rate: $4.50 newsstand; $39.95/yr.
Materials: 02,06,15,25,28,29,32,33
Freelance Pay: $150-$350
Circulation: 120,000
Circulation Type: paid
**Owner(s):**
Collector Communications, Corp.
170 Fifth Ave.
New York, NY 10010
Telephone: (212) 989-8700
FAX: (212) 645-8976
Ownership %: 100
**Management:**
Robert Bowe ............................Publisher
**Editorial:**
Joan M. Pursley ............................Editorial
Diane Kane ............Vice President, Advertising
Edward Michel ............Vice President, Finance
John Bleho ............Vice President, Production
**Desc.:** Dolls is geared to serious collectors. Covers antique dolls and contemporary one of a kind and limited edition dolls and the artist's and companies who design and make them.
**Readers:** Doll collectors.

25976

**FIRST DAYS**
P.O. Box 5295
Fairlawn, OH 44333
Telephone: (216) 657-2238
Year Established: 1955
Pub. Frequency: 8/yr.
Page Size: pocket
Subscrip. Rate: $15/yr.
Circulation: 3,900
Circulation Type: paid
**Owner(s):**
American First Day Cover Society
P.O. Box 5295
Fairlawn, OH 44333
Telephone: (216) 657-2238
Ownership %: 100
**Management:**
Doug Kelsey ......................Advertising Manager
**Editorial:**
Barry Newton ............................Editor
**Desc.:** Covers news and research articles on first day covers. Philatelic orientation. Aspects of the U.S. and foreign countries.
**Readers:** Philatelists, collectors of first day covers.

**Materials Accepted/Included:** 01-Business news 02-By-line articles 03-Fashion news 04-Food news 05-Freelance copy 06-Letters to editor 07-Real estate news 08-Sports news 09-Travel news 10-Book rev. 11-Movie rev. 12-Music rev. 13-TV rev. 14-Theater rev. 15-Coming events 16-Obituaries 17-Question & answer 18-Social announcements 19-Artwork 20-Cartoons 21-Photos 22-TV listings 23-Audio rec. 24-Video rec. 25-Books 26-Films/film clips 27-Personnel news 28-Press releases 29-New product news/photos 30-Trade lit. 31-Contracts awarded 32-Display adv. 33-Classified adv.

6-61

## FLYING MODELS
25977

Fredon-Springdale Rd., Fredon Township
Newton, NJ 07860
Telephone: (201) 383-3355
FAX: (201) 383-4064
Mailing Address:
  P.O. Box 700
  Newton, NJ 07860
Year Established: 1928
Pub. Frequency: m.
Page Size: standard
Subscrip. Rate: $23/yr. US; $29/yr.
  Canada; $27/yr. foreign
Materials: 32,33
Circulation: 33,710
Circulation Type: paid
**Owner(s):**
Carstens Publications, Inc.
P.O. Box 700
Newton, NJ 07860
Telephone: (201) 383-3355
Ownership %: 100
**Management:**
Harold H. Carstens .............................President
Harold H. Carstens .............................Publisher
John Earley ........................Advertising Manager
Pieter Uptegrove ................Advertising Manager
Henry R. Carstens .............Circulation Manager
**Editorial:**
Bob Hunt ...............................................Editor
John Earley .........................Advertising Director
Frank Fannelli ...........................Associate Editor
Robert Cosgrove .................Marketing Director
**Desc.:** Devoted exclusively to modelers in
  model aviation and radio control with
  emphasis on how-to articles on plane
  construction and flying. Also full scale
  aviation features of special interest to
  modelers. Also carries discussion-type
  articles by model builders on subjects of
  current interest to readers. Runs
  photographs of model builders and their
  planes, including full information on
  wingspan, length, weight, engine used,
  etc. Departments include: Air Mail
  (letters from readers), Flying Report
  (industry news), Trade Winds (new
  products reviews), FM Clinic (questions
  and answers), FS Timetable (coming
  events). Special Radio Control Boating
  and Cov. section in every issue.

## GAMEPRO
66705

951 Mariners Island Blvd., Ste. 700
San Mateo, CA 94404-1561
Telephone: (415) 349-4300
FAX: (415) 349-7482
Year Established: 1989
Pub. Frequency: m.
Subscrip. Rate: $19.97/yr.
Circulation: 325,000
Circulation Type: paid
**Owner(s):**
GamePro Custom Publishing Inc.
951 Mariners Island Blvd.
San Mateo, CA 94404-1561
Telephone: (415) 349-4300
Ownership %: 100
**Management:**
Patrick Farrell ...................................Publisher
**Editorial:**
LeeAnne McDermott ...............................Editor
Wes Nihei .......................................Design Editor
**Desc.:** Provides information for young
  video game players on the newest
  games and the best tips for playing, with
  emphasis on Nintendo, Sega and Atari.
**Readers:** Video game players.

## GLASS COLLECTOR'S DIGEST
68779

201 Acme St.
Marietta, OH 45750
Telephone: (614) 373-9959
FAX: (614) 373-5530

Mailing Address:
  P.O. Box 553
  Marietta, OH 45750-0553
Year Established: 1987
Pub. Frequency: bi-m.
Subscrip. Rate: $19/yr.
Circulation: 7,000
Circulation Type: paid
**Owner(s):**
Antique Publications
201 Acme St.
P.O. Box 553
Marietta, OH 45750
Telephone: (614) 373-9959
Ownership %: 100
**Editorial:**
D. Thomas O'Connor ...............................Editor

## KITPLANES
52632

2401 Beverly Blvd.
Los Angeles, CA 90057
Telephone: (213) 385-2222
FAX: (213) 855-3045
Mailing Address:
  P.O. Box 6050
  Mission Viejo, CA 92690
Year Established: 1984
Pub. Frequency: m.
Page Size: standard
Subscrip. Rate: $3.95 newsstand;
  $26.97/yr.
Materials: 05,32
Freelance Pay: $60-$70/pg.
Circulation: 70,000
Circulation Type: paid
**Owner(s):**
Fancy Publications, Inc.
P.O. Box 57900
Los Angeles, CA 90057
Telephone: (213) 385-2222
Ownership %: 100
**Management:**
Norman Ridker ...................................Publisher
Cindy Pedersen ................Advertising Manager
Vera Geuther ....................Circulation Manager
**Editorial:**
Dave Martin ...........................................Editor
**Desc.:** Provide readers with the latest
  developments in the homebuilt aircraft
  industry. Features and departments will
  focus on construction details, pilot
  reports, and general news of interest to
  kitplane enthusiasts. Outstanding
  designers, craftsmen, and pilots of
  homebuilt aircraft will be profiled, as will
  new designs, materials and techniques
  and product directories of who the
  manufacturers of kits, accessories and
  avionics are and where they can be
  located.
**Readers:** Home-crafts people, both pilots
  and non-pilots, interested in building
  their own aircrafts.

## LAPIDARY JOURNAL
25987

60 Chestnut Ave., Ste. 201
Devon, PA 19333
Telephone: (610) 293-1112
FAX: (610) 293-1717
Year Established: 1947
Pub. Frequency: m.
Page Size: standard
Subscrip. Rate: $3/issue; $6.50/Apr. issue;
  $24/yr.
Freelance Pay: $.75/col. in.
Circulation: 40,000
Circulation Type: paid
**Owner(s):**
Lapidary Journal, Inc.
60 Chestnut Ave., Ste. 201
Devon, PA 19333
Telephone: (610) 293-1112
Ownership %: 100

**Management:**
Sonia Gilbert ..........................................Owner
Leif Owen Klein ..................................Publisher
Paul Salotto ...............................Sales Manager
**Editorial:**
Merle Berk ..............................Editor in Chief
Adam Samson ...................Associate Publisher
Moscow
Cindi Willcox ......................Circulation Director
**Desc.:** Carries bead and jewelry making
  workshops, field trip articles, how-to-do-it
  articles, articles on gemology, as well as
  minerals and fossils.
**Readers:** Gem cutters, gem collectors and
  jewelers. Bead and jewelry makers.
  Rock, gem and jewelry enthusiasts.

## LEATHER CRAFTERS JOURNAL, THE
25065

4307 Oak Dr.
Rhinelander, WI 54501-9717
Telephone: (715) 362-5393
FAX: (715) 362-5393
Year Established: 1956
Pub. Frequency: bi-m.
Page Size: standard
Subscrip. Rate: $32/yr.; $26/yr. Canada;
  $48/yr. foreign
Materials: 01,06,15,29,30,32,33
Freelance Pay: $50-$200
Circulation: 10,000
Circulation Type: paid
**Owner(s):**
The Leather Crafters & Saddlers Journal
4307 Oak Dr.
Rhinelander, WI 54501-9717
Telephone: (715) 362-5393
Ownership %: 100
**Management:**
Dorothea Reis ...................Advertising Manager
Charil Reis ........................Circulation Manager
**Editorial:**
W. R. (Bill) Reis ......................Executive Editor
**Desc.:** Leathercraft functions of state,
  regional, national or international nature.
  Some staff-written material, limited staff
  coverage outside. Free lance and
  craftsmen main contributors of How-To,
  Step-By-Step material. Departments
  include: Tips & Hints, New Products,
  Coming Events-Guild News, and Profiles.
**Readers:** Teachers, students, beginners,
  occupational craftsmen, saddle & boot
  makers and leather artists.

## LINN'S STAMP NEWS
25990

911 Vandemark Rd.
Sidney, OH 45365
Telephone: (513) 498-0801
Mailing Address:
  P.O. Box 29
  Sidney, OH 45365
Year Established: 1928
Pub. Frequency: w.
Page Size: tabloid
Subscrip. Rate: $34/yr.
Freelance Pay: $10-$60/feature
Circulation: 70,000
Circulation Type: paid
**Owner(s):**
Amos Press, Inc.
911 Vandemark Rd.
Sidney, OH 45365
Telephone: (513) 498-2111
Ownership %: 100
**Management:**
Michael Laurence ...............................Publisher
**Editorial:**
Michael Laurence ...................................Editor
Elaine Boughner ......................Managing Editor
Fred Baumann ...........................Associate Editor
Denise Hatton ...........................Associate Editor
Michael Baadke ........................Associate Editor
Michael Schreiber .....................Associate Editor

Donna O'Keefe ...........................Miscellaneous
**Desc.:** Devoted to news, pictures and
  articles of interest to stamp collectors.
  New issues and discoveries are reported
  on regularly. Provides coverage of
  trends, values and personalities
  concerned with the hobby. Philatelic
  articles range from basic ones with
  suggestions for beginning collectors, to
  highly specialized scholarly articles.
**Readers:** Worldwide, although mostly in
  the U.S.

## MODEL AIRPLANE NEWS
25067

251 Danbury Rd.
Wilton, CT 06897
Telephone: (203) 834-2900
FAX: (203) 762-9803
Year Established: 1929
Pub. Frequency: m.
Page Size: standard
Subscrip. Rate: $2.95/issue; $22.95/yr.
Materials: 32,33
Freelance Pay: varies
Circulation: 80,000
Circulation Type: paid
**Owner(s):**
Air Age, Inc.
251 Danbury Rd.
Wilton, CT 06897
Telephone: (203) 834-2900
Ownership %: 100
**Management:**
Louis DeFrancesco, Sr., DDS .............Publisher
Sharon Warner ...................Advertising Manager
**Editorial:**
Tom Atwood ..............................Editor in Chief
Alan Palermo ...............................Art Director
Louis DeFrancesco, Jr. .....Associate Publisher
Yvonne Micik ....................Associate Publisher
**Desc.:** This is the oldest, continuously
  published magazine in the radio-
  controlled model aircraft field. The
  magazine also includes R/C cars and
  boats. Articles and monthly columns
  present technical and general
  information on construction, equipment,
  engines, flying techniques, major
  competition events, modeling
  personalities and products. "How To"
  articles, product evaluations and
  construction plans are featured in every
  issue.
**Readers:** Average age, 37 yrs. in all
  professions.

## MODEL AVIATION
68899

5151 E. Memorial Dr.
Muncie, IN 47302
Telephone: (317) 288-4899
Year Established: 1975
Pub. Frequency: m.
Page Size: standard
Subscrip. Rate: $2.50 newsstand; $18/yr.
Materials: 32
Circulation: 170,000
Circulation Type: paid
**Owner(s):**
Academy of Model Aeronautics
5151 E. Memorial Dr.
Muncie, IA 47302
Telephone: (317) 287-1256
Ownership %: 100
**Editorial:**
Jim Haught ...........................................Editor

## MODEL BUILDER
68900

34249 Camino Capistrano
Capistrano Beach, CA 92624-1156
Telephone: (714) 496-5411
FAX: (714) 496-5427
Mailing Address:
  P.O. Box 2459
  Capistrano Beach, CA 92624

Year Established: 1971
Pub. Frequency: m.
Page Size: standard
Subscrip. Rate: $2.95 newsstand; $25/yr.
Materials: 32,33
Circulation: 95,000
Circulation Type: paid
**Owner(s):**
Gallant Models, Inc.
34249 Camino Capistrano
Capistrano Beach, CA 92624-1156
Telephone: (714) 496-5411
Ownership %: 100
**Management:**
Marc Thiffault ........................................Publisher
Don Kremers .....................Advertising Manager
**Editorial:**
Mark Thiffault ....................................Editor
Phil Bernhardt ...........................Managing Editor

25994

## MODEL RAILROADER
21027 Crossroads Circle
Waukesha, WI 53187
Telephone: (414) 796-8776
FAX: (414) 796-0126
Mailing Address:
    P.O. Box 1612
    Waukesha, WI 53187
Year Established: 1934
Pub. Frequency: m.
Page Size: standard
Subscrip. Rate: $3.50 newsstand;
    $34.95/yr.
Freelance Pay: $66/pg.
Circulation: 230,000
Circulation Type: paid
**Owner(s):**
Kalmbach Publishing Co.
21027 Crossroads Circle
Waukesha, WI 53187
Telephone: (414) 796-8776
Ownership %: 100
**Management:**
Walter Mundschau ..............................President
Russel Larson ..................................Publisher
Frederick J. Hamilton ........Advertising Manager
**Editorial:**
Russell G. Larson ....................................Editor
Andy Sperondeo ....................Managing Editor
Dick Christianson ................Assistant Publisher
Andy Sperandeo ....................Associate Editor
Keith Thompson ....................Associate Editor
Bob Thorson ........................Production Director
**Desc.:** Devoted to scale model railroading.
    Articles discuss layouts, planning,
    operation, maintenance, scale model
    construction. Also reviews of new
    products and literature in the field.
**Readers:** Scale model railroad enthusiasts.

65445

## MOVIE COLLECTOR'S WORLD
P.O. Box 309
Fraser, MI 48026
Telephone: (313) 774-4311
FAX: (313) 774-5450
Year Established: 1976
Pub. Frequency: bi-w.
Page Size: standard
Subscrip. Rate: $35/26 issues
Materials: 01,05,06,10,11,13,14,15,16,17,
    24,25,26,29,32,33
Freelance Pay: $.03/wd.
Print Process: web offset
Circulation: 5,000
Circulation Type: paid
**Owner(s):**
Arena Publishing
P.O. Box 309
Fraser, MI 48026
Telephone: (313) 774-4311
Ownership %: 100
**Management:**
Brian A. Bukantis ..................................Publisher

**Editorial:**
Brian A. Bukantis .........................Editor
**Desc.:** Covers all aspects of collecting
    movie memorabilia.
**Readers:** Movie buffs, collectors of 16mm
    film, posters, books and any movie
    memoribilia.

25999

## NUMISMATIC NEWS
700 E. State St.
Iola, WI 54990
Telephone: (715) 445-2214
Year Established: 1952
Pub. Frequency: w.
Page Size: standard
Subscrip. Rate: $27.95/yr.
Freelance Pay: $.03/wd. & up
Print Process: web
Circulation: 40,000
Circulation Type: paid
**Owner(s):**
Krause Publications, Inc.
700 E. State
Iola, WI 54990
Telephone: (715) 445-2214
Ownership %: 100
**Bureau(s):**
Krause Publications-Washington Bureau
632 A St., S.E.
Washington, DC 20003
Telephone: (202) 543-6745
Contact: Burnett Anderson
**Management:**
Clifford Mishler ....................................President
Albert "Bo" Smith ..............................Publisher
**Editorial:**
Bob Wilhite ....................................Editor
**Desc.:** Weekly guide to the news and
    advertising of the U.S. coin collecting
    field, featuring comprehensive guides to
    U.S. coin values.
**Readers:** Coin collectors and others
    interested in coins and coin collections.

22702

## NUMISMATIST, THE
818 N. Cascade Ave.
Colorado Springs, CO 80903
Telephone: (719) 632-2646
FAX: (719) 634-4085
Year Established: 1888
Pub. Frequency: m.
Page Size: pocket
Subscrip. Rate: $26/yr. membership;
    $28/yr. foreign
Materials: 01,06,10,16,24,25,28,32,33
Freelance Pay: $2.75/in.; $2.50-$5/ill.
Print Process: web
Circulation: 28,000
Circulation Type: controlled
**Owner(s):**
American Numismatic Association
818 N. Cascade Ave.
Colorado Springs, CO 80903-3279
Telephone: (719) 632-2646
FAX: (719) 634-4085
Ownership %: 100
**Management:**
David L. Ganz ....................................President
Barbara J. Gregory ..............................Publisher
Ed Marcus ........................Advertising Manager
Nawana Britenriker ...........Production Manager
**Editorial:**
Barbara J. Gregory ....................................Editor
Marilyn Reback ....................Associate Editor

**Desc.:** Official publication of the American
    Numismatic Association, dealing with the
    science of numismatics-coins, medals,
    tokens and paper money from ancient
    times to present. Articles from 200
    words to long serials on general or
    specialized topics. Uses news items
    concerning current domestic and
    foreign coinages, paper money, new
    issues of coins, tokens, medals. Notes
    on individual numismatists. Reports
    international, national, regional and state
    numismatic convention and coin club
    affairs. Quarterly supplement for
    beginning collectors.
**Readers:** People of all ages interested in
    numismatics.

66351

## PAINTCHECK
67 High Point Cir.
Newburgh, NY 12550-7236
Telephone: (914) 923-3543
Year Established: 1989
Pub. Frequency: m.
Page Size: standard
Subscrip. Rate: $24/yr.; $45/2 yrs.
Freelance Pay: $100-$300
Circulation: 55,000
Circulation Type: paid
**Owner(s):**
CB Publications, Inc.
67 High Point Cir.
Newburgh, NY 12550-7236
Ownership %: 100
**Management:**
Claudia Welitison ..................................Publisher
**Editorial:**
Len Canter ....................................Editor
**Desc.:** Covers all information for and about
    paintball enthusiasts.
**Readers:** Paintball Enthusiasts

22520

## POPULAR CERAMICS
N7450 Aanstad Rd.
Iola, WI 54945
Telephone: (715) 445-5000
FAX: (715) 445-4053
Year Established: 1949
Pub. Frequency: m.
Page Size: standard
Subscrip. Rate: $2.25 newsstand;
    $21.95/yr.
Materials: 02,06,10,17,32,33
Print Process: web offset
Circulation: 20,000
Circulation Type: controlled & paid
**Owner(s):**
Jones Publishing, Inc.
N7450 Aanstad Rd.
Iola, WI 54945
Telephone: (715) 445-5000
FAX: (715) 445-4053
Ownership %: 100
**Management:**
Scott Kolpien ....................................Publisher
Joan Grawvunder ..............Advertising Manager
Barbara Beyersdorf ...........Circulation Manager
**Editorial:**
Barb Case ....................................Editor
**Desc.:** Edited to teach the ceramic
    hobbyist to create functional and
    decorative ceramic objects. Its readers
    have interests in raw materials and
    accessories to make and decorate their
    projects. Feature articles are illustrated
    in full-color, presented step-by-step by
    experienced teachers and hobbyists.
    Pullout pattern section also included in
    each issue.
**Readers:** Ceramists in hobby field.

58562

## POSTCARD COLLECTOR
N7450 Aanstad Rd.
Iola, WI 54945
Telephone: (715) 445-5000
FAX: (715) 445-4053
Mailing Address:
    P.O. Box 5000
    Iola, WI 54945
Year Established: 1983
Pub. Frequency: m.
Page Size: standard
Subscrip. Rate: $23.95/yr.
Materials: 01,02,05,06,15,17,28,29,32,33
Freelance Pay: $.03-$.05/wd.
Print Process: web
Circulation: 6,500
Circulation Type: paid
**Owner(s):**
Jones Publishing, Inc.
P.O. Box 5000
Iola, WI 54945
Telephone: (715) 445-5000
Ownership %: 100
**Management:**
Joe Jones ....................................Publisher
**Editorial:**
Deborah Lengkeek ....................................Editor
**Desc.:** Editorial & advertising focus on
    postcards from 1870 to the present.
**Readers:** Postcard enthusiasts &
    collectors, investors, dealers.
**Deadline:** story-1st of mo. prior to pub.
    date

71263

## R/C MODELER MAGAZINE
144 W. Sierra Madre Blvd.
Sierra Madre, CA 91024
Telephone: (818) 355-1476
FAX: (818) 355-6415
Mailing Address:
    P.O. Box 487
    Sierra Madre, CA 91025
Year Established: 1981
Pub. Frequency: m.
Page Size: standard
Subscrip. Rate: $3.25 newsstand US;
    $4.25 newsstand Canada; $24.47/yr.
    US; $32/yr. foreign
Materials: 32,33
Circulation: 200,000
Circulation Type: paid
**Owner(s):**
RC Publications Corp.
144 W. Sierra Madre Blvd.
Sierra Madre, CA 91025
Telephone: (818) 355-1476
Ownership %: 100
**Management:**
Don Dewey ....................................Publisher
Kathy Acton ....................Advertising Manager
**Editorial:**
Patricia Crews ....................................Editor
David Vaughn ....................................Art Director
Jim Pearson ....................Assistant Editor
Dick Kidd ....................Technical Editor

71251

## RADIO CONTROL BOAT MODELER
251 Danbury Rd.
Wilton, CT 06897
Telephone: (203) 834-2900
FAX: (203) 762-9803
Pub. Frequency: bi-m.
Page Size: standard
Subscrip. Rate: $2.95 newsstand
Materials: 32
Print Process: offset
Circulation: 50,000
Circulation Type: paid
**Owner(s):**
Air Age, Inc.
251 Danbury Rd.
Wilton, CT 06897
Telephone: (203) 834-2900
Ownership %: 100

**Materials Accepted/Included:** 01-Business news 02-By-line articles 03-Fashion news 04-Food news 05-Freelance copy 06-Letters to editor 07-Real estate news 08-Sports news 09-Travel news 10-Book rev. 11-Movie rev. 12-Music rev. 13-TV rev. 14-Theater rev. 15-Coming events 16-Obituaries 17-Question & answer 18-Social announcements 19-Artwork 20-Cartoons 21-Photos 22-TV listings 23-Audio rec. 24-Video rec. 25-Books 26-Films/film clips 27-Personnel news 28-Press releases 29-New product news/photos 30-Trade lit. 31-Contracts awarded 32-Display adv. 33-Classified adv.

6-63

**Management:**
Louis DeFrancesco, Sr., DDS .............Publisher
Sharon Warner ..................Advertising Manager
**Editorial:**
Tom Atwood .........................Editor in Chief
Alan Palermo .............................Art Director
Louis DeFrancesco, Jr. ......Associate Publisher
Yvonne Micik .................Associate Publisher

68902
### RADIO CONTROL MODEL CARS & TRUCKS
34249 Camino Capistrano
Capistrano Beach, CA 92624
Telephone: (714) 496-5411
FAX: (714) 496-5427
Mailing Address:
    P.O. Box 2459
    Capistrano Beach, CA 92624
Year Established: 1985
Pub. Frequency: m.
Page Size: standard
Subscrip. Rate: $2.95 newsstand; $25/yr.
Materials: 32,33
Circulation: 72,000
Circulation Type: paid
**Owner(s):**
Gallant Models, Inc.
34249 Camino Capistrano
Capistrano Beach, CA 92624
Telephone: (714) 496-5411
Ownership %: 100
**Management:**
Mark Thiffault ...........................Publisher
Don Kremers ...................Advertising Manager
**Editorial:**
Mark Thiffault ...............................Editor
Richard Dowdy ........................Managing Editor
**Desc.:** Covers r.c. car and truck building
    and racing.

68901
### RADIO CONTROL NEWS
P.O. Box 6246
Woodland, CA 91365
Telephone: (818) 340-5750
FAX: (818) 348-4648
Year Established: 1982
Pub. Frequency: m.
Page Size: standard
Subscrip. Rate: $3 newsstand; $30/yr.
Circulation: 175,000
Circulation Type: paid
**Owner(s):**
Alta Publishing, Inc.
P.O. Box 6246
Woodland, CA 91365
Telephone: (818) 340-5750
Ownership %: 100
**Management:**
Loni Peralta ......................Advertising Manager
**Editorial:**
Lori Peralta ...............................Editor
**Desc.:** Covers all areas of radio controlled
    cars, racing and related industry matters.

24616
### RAILFAN & RAILROAD
Fredon-Springdale Rd., Fredon Twp.
Newton, NJ 07860-0700
Telephone: (201) 383-3355
FAX: (201) 383-4064
Mailing Address:
    P.O. Box 700
    Newton, NJ 07860
Year Established: 1906
Pub. Frequency: m.
Page Size: standard
Subscrip. Rate: $2.95 copy; $25/yr.;
    $31/yr. Canada; $33/yr. foreign
Materials: 32,33
Circulation: 50,000
Circulation Type: paid
**Owner(s):**
Carstens Publications, Inc.
Telephone: (201) 383-3355
Ownership %: 100

**Management:**
Harold H. Carstens ..........................President
Harold H. Carstens ..........................Publisher
John Earley ....................Advertising Manager
Henry R. Carstens .............Circulation Manager
**Editorial:**
James A. Boyd ...............................Editor
Pieter Uptegrove ...........................Advertising
**Desc.:** All articles deal with railroading:
    real railroads, museum railroads, railroad
    photography, plus railroad collectibles.
**Readers:** Those interested in railroading or
    railroads.

25071
### RAILROAD MODEL CRAFTSMAN
Fredon Springdale Rd., Fredon Twnship.
Newton, NJ 07860-0700
Telephone: (201) 383-3355
FAX: (201) 383-4064
Mailing Address:
    P.O. Box 700
    Newton, NJ 07860-0700
Year Established: 1933
Pub. Frequency: m.
Page Size: standard
Subscrip. Rate: $25/yr.; $31/yr. Canada;
    $33/yr. foreign
Circulation: 94,000
Circulation Type: paid
**Owner(s):**
Carstens Publications, Inc.
P.O. Box 700
Newton, NJ 07860
Telephone: (201) 383-3355
Ownership %: 100
**Management:**
Harold H. Carstens ...........................Owner
Harold H. Carstens ..........................President
Harold H. Carstens ..........................Publisher
John Earley ...................Advertising Manager
Henry R. Carstens .............Circulation Manager
Henry R. Carstens .............Circulation Manager
**Editorial:**
William Schaumburg ...........................Editor
Robert O. Cosgrove ........................Advertising
James Ancrom ......................Associate Editor
Chris D'Amato ......................Associate Editor
**Desc.:** All articles deal with scale model
    railroading or are applicable to model
    railroading. Strong on How-To-Do
    articles of model railroads, and related
    items, including stories of how modelers
    have built their own scale model layouts,
    as well as photos of scale model
    railroads and top notch railroad cars,
    structures, etc. Some material is staff
    written, including departments. Rely on
    freelancers for such material. Essential
    that freelancers be actual model
    railroaders. Not interested in
    personalities but rather in the hobby
    itself. Credit line given on all editorial
    matter, rarely on news handouts unless
    of feature calibre. Also use prototype
    railroad material when of interest to
    model railroaders. Departments include:
    Safety Valve (letters from readers);
    Dispatchers Report (news and
    comments on the model railroad and
    railroad industries and the model railroad
    hobby in general); Trouble Shooting
    (answering technical problems of
    readers); Test Track (testing and review
    of samples sent in for that purpose);
    Book Reviews (only on railroads); Model
    Railroad Books. News releases are
    often mentioned in Dispatcher Column
    but not in Test Track where every item
    is staff tested.

26006
### ROCK & GEM
4880 Market St..
Ventura, CA 93003-7783
Telephone: (805) 644-3824
FAX: (805) 644-3875
Year Established: 1971
Pub. Frequency: m.
Page Size: standard
Subscrip. Rate: $2.95 newsstand; $23/yr.;
    $36/2 yrs.; $49/3 yrs.
Materials: 01,02,05,06,09,10,15,20,21,23,
    24,25,28,29,30,32,33
Freelance Pay: $150-300/article
Circulation: 65,000
Circulation Type: paid
**Owner(s):**
Miller Magazines, Inc.
4880 Market St.
Ventura, CA 93003
Telephone: (805) 644-3824
FAX: (805) 644-3875
Ownership %: 100
**Management:**
James L. Miller ............................Publisher
Marlene Collier ...............Advertising Manager
**Editorial:**
Susan Haverland .....................Managing Editor
Bill Reid ..................................Art Director
Kari Stone ..........................Associate Editor
Susan Haverland .................Book Review Editor
Mike Pangburn .......................Design Editor
**Desc.:** Rockhounding, lapidary, gold
    prospecting, geology, field trips, and
    crafts for the hobbyist.

69541
### SCALE AUTO ENTHUSIAST
N. 50 W. 13605 Overview Dr.
Menomonee Falls, WI 53051
Telephone: (414) 783-7740
FAX: (414) 783-7710
Mailing Address:
    P.O. Box 10167
    Milwaukee, WI 53210
Year Established: 1979
Pub. Frequency: bi-m.
Page Size: standard
Subscrip. Rate: $3.95 newsstand; $16/yr.
Materials: 02,05,06,10,11,13,15,17,19,20,
    21,25,28,29,32,33
Print Process: web offset
Circulation: 62,000
Circulation Type: paid
**Owner(s):**
Highland Productions, Inc.
N. 50 W. 13605 Overview Dr.
Menomonee Falls, WI 53051
Telephone: (414) 783-7740
FAX: (414) 783-7710
Ownership %: 100
**Editorial:**
Gary Schmidt ...............................Editor
**Desc.:** Devoted to building and collecting
    static models of automobiles, trucks,
    motorcycles, and racecars.

68898
### SCOTT STAMP MONTHLY
911 Vandemark Rd.
Sidney, OH 45365
Telephone: (513) 498-0802
FAX: (513) 498-0808
Mailing Address:
    P.O. Box 828
    Sidney, OH 45365
Year Established: 1920
Pub. Frequency: m.
Page Size: standard
Subscrip. Rate: $2.75 newsstand;
    $16.95/yr.
Materials: 32,33
Circulation: 21,000
Circulation Type: paid

26006
### ROCK & GEM

**Owner(s):**
Scott Publishing Co.
911 Vandemark Rd.
Sidney, OH 45365
Telephone: (513) 498-0802
Ownership %: 100
**Management:**
S. Morrissey ............................Publisher
David Lodge ...................Advertising Manager
Tim Wagner .................Circulation Manager
**Editorial:**
Wayne Youngblood ..........................Editor

26007
### S GAUGIAN
7236 W. Madison St.
Forest Park, IL 60130
Telephone: (708) 366-1973
Year Established: 1962
Pub. Frequency: bi-m.
Page Size: standard
Subscrip. Rate: $26/yr.; $32/yr. foreign
Circulation: 5,000
Circulation Type: paid
**Owner(s):**
Heimburger House Publishing Co.
7236 W. Madison
Forest Park, IL 60130
Telephone: (708) 366-1973
Ownership %: 100
**Management:**
Donald Heimburger .........................President
Donald Heimburger ..........................Publisher
Donald Heimburger ..........Advertising Manager
**Editorial:**
Donald Heimburger ............Executive Editor
R. Brooks Stover ............................Artist
Roger Shimon ...............................Artist
Jim Gonyier ................................Artist
Susan O'Brien ......................Assistant Editor
Tom Jarcho ........................Contributing Editor
Paul C. Nelson ...................Contributing Editor
Robert Jones ....................Contributing Editor
Alan Evans .......................Contributing Editor
Carl Contadini ...................Contributing Editor
Marilyn Heimburger ..........Production Assistant
**Desc.:** All staff-written and by-lined articles
    about model and prototype railroads of
    the nation, mostly how-to and feature
    articles on model railroad of 3/16 in.,= 1
    foot scale. Articles 2-4 pages long
    with many photos and drawings. Carry
    photo section also. Carry publicity when
    it refers to model railroading or to
    prototype railroads.
**Readers:** Persons of all age categories
    who have an interest in model
    railroading or an interest in prototype
    railroading & how it relates to models
    built to 3/16" to the foot; ratio of 1:64.

54018
### SN3 MODELER
7236 W. Madison
Forest Park, IL 60130
Telephone: (708) 366-1973
Year Established: 1984
Pub. Frequency: s-a.
Page Size: standard
Subscrip. Rate: $11/yr. US; $17/yr. foreign
Circulation: 2,000
Circulation Type: paid
**Owner(s):**
Heimburger House Publishing Co.
7236 W. Madison
Forest Park, IL 60130
Telephone: (708) 366-1973
**Management:**
Donald Heimburger ............................President
**Editorial:**
Donald Heimburger ...........................Editor
Gilbert Bennett ............................Artist
Susan O'brien ....................Editorial Assistant
Marilyn Heimburger ..........Production Assistant

**Desc.:** Model and prototype articles and photos on narrow gauge railroading, especially as it relates to S narrow gauge model railroading (3/16″ = 1 ft.).
**Readers:** Persons of all age categories who have interest in narrow gauge railroading, especially 3/16″ = 1 foot modeling

## SPORTS CARD PRICE GUIDE MONTHLY

65329

700 E. State St.
Iola, WI 54990
Telephone: (715) 445-2214
FAX: (715) 445-4087
Year Established: 1988
Pub. Frequency: m.
Page Size: standard
Subscrip. Rate: $2.95/copy; $18.95/yr.
Print Process: web offset
Circulation: 211,600
Circulation Type: paid
**Owner(s):**
Krause Publications, Inc.
700 E. State St.
Iola, WI 54990
Telephone: (715) 445-2214
**Management:**
Bob Lemke ...............................Publisher
**Editorial:**
Greg Ambrosius .........................Editor
**Desc.:** How to on buying, selling, trading and collecting sports cards, as well as card value information.
**Readers:** Active sports card collectors, 2nd dealers.
**Deadline:** story-2nd Tue. prior to pub. date; ads-2nd Tue. prior

## SPORTS CARDS MAGAZINE

58560

700 E. State St.
Iola, WI 54990
Telephone: (715) 445-2214
FAX: (715) 445-4087
Year Established: 1981
Pub. Frequency: m.
Page Size: standard
Subscrip. Rate: $2.95/copy; $18.95/yr.
Materials: 01,02,06,17,21,29,32,33
Freelance Pay: $150-$250/article
Print Process: web offset
Circulation: 182,500
Circulation Type: paid
**Owner(s):**
Krause Publications, Inc.
700 E. State St.
Iola, WI 54990
Telephone: (715) 445-2214
FAX: (715) 445-4087
Ownership %: 100
**Editorial:**
Greg Ambrosius .........................Editor
**Readers:** Beginning collector of sports memorabilia
**Deadline:** story-1st Tue. prior to pub. date; news-1st Tue. prior; photo-1st Tue. prior; ads-1st Tue. prior

## SPORTS CARD TRADER

67067

990 Grove St.
Evanston, IL 60201
Telephone: (708) 491-6440
FAX: (708) 491-0459
Year Established: 1990
Pub. Frequency: m.
Page Size: standard
Subscrip. Rate: $2.95 newsstand; $29.95/yr.
Circulation: 125,000
Circulation Type: paid

**Owner(s):**
Century Publishing Co.
990 Grove St.
Evanston, IL 60201
Telephone: (708) 491-6440
Ownership %: 100
**Management:**
Norman Jacobs ........................President
Norman Jacobs .........................Publisher
**Editorial:**
Douglas Kale ..............................Editor
Bob Kuenster .................Associate Editor

## SPORTS COLLECTORS DIGEST

58564

700 E. State St.
Iola, WI 54990
Telephone: (715) 445-2214
FAX: (715) 445-4087
Year Established: 1973
Pub. Frequency: w.
Page Size: tabloid
Subscrip. Rate: $3.75/copy; $49.95/yr.
Materials: 01,02,05,06,08,10,15,16,21,25, 28,29,32,33
Freelance Pay: $50-$95/pg.
Print Process: web
Circulation: 55,000
Circulation Type: paid
**Owner(s):**
Krause Publications, Inc.
700 E. State St.
Iola, WI 54990
Telephone: (715) 445-2214
**Management:**
Bob Lemke ...............................Publisher
**Editorial:**
Tom Mortenson ...........................Editor
**Desc.:** News, features and ads for the advanced collector, investor and dealer in sportscards and related memorabilia.
**Readers:** Advanced sports memorabilia collectors.
**Deadline:** story-Tue.; ads-Tue.

## STAMP COLLECTOR NEWSPAPER

26011

520 E. First Ave.
Albany, OR 97321
Telephone: (503) 928-5156
Year Established: 1931
Pub. Frequency: w.
Page Size: tabloid
Subscrip. Rate: $29.90/yr.
Materials: 01,02,05,06,10,16,20,25,27,28, 29,30,32,33
Freelance Pay: $30+/article
Print Process: web offset
Circulation: 18,000
Circulation Type: paid
**Owner(s):**
Van Dahl Publications
520 E. First Ave.
Albany, OR 97321
Telephone: (503) 928-3569
Ownership %: 100
**Management:**
James A. Magruder II ................Publisher
Kristi Lindgren .............Business Manager
**Editorial:**
Ken Palke ...................................Editor
Karen Murray .................Managing Editor
Mary Mansfield .........................Advertising
Anja Thompson ............Marketing Director
Linda Smith ...............Production Director
**Desc.:** Contains news and articles about stamp collecting for beginning and advanced collectors.
**Readers:** Stamp collectors and dealers.

## STAMP WHOLESALER, THE

26012

520 E. First Ave.
Albany, OR 97321
Telephone: (503) 928-4484
FAX: (503) 967-7262

Mailing Address:
P.O. Box 706
Albany, OR 97321
Year Established: 1936
Pub. Frequency: bi-w.
Page Size: tabloid
Subscrip. Rate: $25/yr.
Circulation: 5,000
Circulation Type: paid
**Owner(s):**
Van Dahl Publications
520 E. First Ave.
Albany, OR 97321
Telephone: (503) 928-4484
Ownership %: 100
**Management:**
James A. Magruder, II ..............Publisher
Mike Mathers ............Advertising Manager
**Editorial:**
Ken Palke ...................................Editor
**Desc.:** News and articles about stamp dealing.
**Readers:** World's largest stamp dealer newspaper.

## TEDDY BEAR & FRIENDS

66518

6405 Flank Ave.
Harrisburg, PA 17112
Telephone: (717) 657-9555
Year Established: 1983
Pub. Frequency: bi-m.
Page Size: standard
Subscrip. Rate: $17.95/yr. Canada; $22.95/yr.
Materials: 01,05,06,10,15,17,21,28,29
Freelance Pay: $65/published pg.
Circulation: 60,000
Circulation Type: paid
**Owner(s):**
Cowles Magazines, Inc.
6405 Flank Dr.
Harrisburg, PA 17112
Telephone: (717) 657-9555
Ownership %: 100
**Management:**
Steve Norton ...........................Publisher
**Editorial:**
Deborah Thompson .....................Editor
Pam Lefkowitz ..................Design Editor
**Desc.:** Historical bears, manufacturers, contemporary artist bears, events, values, question and answer.
**Readers:** Adult collectors of teddy bears and related toys, antique and modern.

## TOLE WORLD

25998

1041 Shary Circle
Concord, CA 94518
Telephone: (510) 671-9852
FAX: (510) 671-0692
Year Established: 1977
Pub. Frequency: bi-m.
Page Size: standard
Subscrip. Rate: $17/yr.; $30/2 yrs.
Freelance Pay: $150/project
Circulation: 110,000
Circulation Type: paid
**Owner(s):**
EGW Publishing Co.
1041 Shary Circle
Concord, CA 94518
Telephone: (510) 671-9852
Ownership %: 100
**Management:**
Wayne Lin ...............................President
Diana Sharp ............Circulation Manager
**Editorial:**
Judy Swager ..............................Editor
John Dixon ..............Advertising Director
Ginny Westland ...............Art Department
**Desc.:** Departments include: Our Readers' Page, Classified Ads, Your Letters, Book Review, Calendar, Jig Journals, Tricks of Trade, Tool Talk, Full-size pull-out plans.

**Readers:** Decorative painters.
**Deadline:** 2 mo. prior to pub. date

## TOPICAL TIME

26015

944 Ash St., Ste. 207
Johnstown, PA 15902
Telephone: (814) 539-6301
Mailing Address:
P.O. Box 630
Johnstown, PA 15907
Year Established: 1949
Pub. Frequency: bi-m.
Page Size: standard
Subscrip. Rate: $18/yr.
Materials: 02,06,10,28,32,33
Print Process: web offset
Circulation: 7,000
Circulation Type: paid
**Owner(s):**
American Topical Association
P.O. Box 630
Johnstown, PA 15907
Telephone: (814) 539-6301
Ownership %: 100
**Editorial:**
George Griffenhagen .....................Editor
**Desc.:** Contains background stories of all fields of human endeavor, as shown on postage stamps.
**Readers:** Collectors of stamps.

## TRAIN COLLECTORS QUARTERLY

69549

213 Fannie Ave.
Lancaster, PA 17602
Telephone: (717) 687-8623
Mailing Address:
PO Box 194
Willow Street, PA 17584-0194
Year Established: 1954
Pub. Frequency: q.
Page Size: standard
Subscrip. Rate: $12/yr.
Materials: 06,10,17,21
Print Process: web offset
Circulation: 26,700
Circulation Type: controlled
**Owner(s):**
Train Collectors Association
P.O. Box 194
Willow Street, PA 17584-0194
Telephone: (717) 687-8623
Ownership %: 100
**Editorial:**
Bruce D. Manson, Jr. ....................Editor

## TRAINS

24620

21027 Crossroads Cir.
Waukesha, WI 53187
Telephone: (414) 796-8776
Mailing Address:
P.O. Box 1612
Waukesha, WI 53187
Year Established: 1940
Pub. Frequency: m.
Page Size: standard
Subscrip. Rate: $3.50 newsstand; $39.95/yr.
Circulation: 111,381
Circulation Type: paid
**Owner(s):**
Kalmbach Publishing Co.
21027 Crossroads Cir.
Waukesha, WI 53186
Telephone: (414) 796-8776
FAX: (414) 796-1142
Ownership %: 100
**Management:**
Walter J. Mundschau ..................President
Russ Larson .............................Publisher
H. Michael Yuhas ..........Advertising Manager
**Editorial:**
Kevin Keefe ................................Editor
Mike Danneman .....................Art Director
Karin Frederickson ...........Production Director

---

**Materials Accepted/Included:** 01-Business news 02-By-line articles 03-Fashion news 04-Food news 05-Freelance copy 06-Letters to editor 07-Real estate news 08-Sports news 09-Travel news 10-Book rev. 11-Movie rev. 12-Music rev. 13-TV rev. 14-Theater rev. 15-Coming events 16-Obituaries 17-Question & answer 18-Social announcements 19-Artwork 20-Cartoons 21-Photos 22-TV listings 23-Audio rec. 24-Video rec. 25-Books 26-Films/film clips 27-Personnel news 28-Press releases 29-New product news/photos 30-Trade lit. 31-Contracts awarded 32-Display adv. 33-Classified adv.

6-65

**Desc.:** Reports the news, history and operations of railroading for the layman in an illustrated non-fiction magazine.
**Readers:** Professional and all others interested in railroading.

## U.S. BOAT & SHIP MODELER
71268

34249 Camino Capistrano
Capistrano Beach, CA 92624
Telephone: (714) 496-5411
FAX: (714) 496-5427
Mailing Address:
P.O. Box 2459
Capistrano Beach, CA 92624
Pub. Frequency: m.
Page Size: standard
Subscrip. Rate: $51/yr.
Materials: 32,33
Circulation: 60,000
Circulation Type: paid
**Owner(s):**
Gallant Models, Inc.
34249 Camino Capistrano
Capistrano Beach, CA 92624
Telephone: (714) 496-5411
FAX: (714) 496-5427
Ownership %: 100
**Management:**
Don Kremers .....................Advertising Manager
**Editorial:**
Mark Thiffault ........................................Editor

## WEEKEND WOODWORKING PROJECTS
65330

1716 Locust St.
Des Moines, IA 50336
Telephone: (515) 284-2160
FAX: (515) 284-2115
Year Established: 1988
Pub. Frequency: bi-m.
Page Size: standard
Subscrip. Rate: $4.95 newsstand;
$27.97/yr.
Freelance Pay: $100-125/page
Circulation: 200,000
Circulation Type: paid
**Owner(s):**
Meredith Corp.
1716 Locust St.
Des Moines, IA 50309
Ownership %: 100
**Management:**
William R. Reed ...........................Publisher
Allen Brush ..................Circulation Manager
**Editorial:**
Larry Clayton ................................Editor
Jim Harrold ......................Managing Editor
Chris Schraft ...............Advertising Director
**Desc.:** Short term woodworking projects with each issue.
**Readers:** Beginning and intermediate woodworkers.

## WESTERN & EASTERN TREASURES
26018

2955 80th Ave., S.E., Ste. 104
Ste. 104
Mercer Island, WA 98040
Telephone: (206) 230-9224
FAX: (206) 230-9248
Year Established: 1963
Pub. Frequency: m.
Page Size: standard
Subscrip. Rate: $5.50 newsstand;
$21.95/yr.
Freelance Pay: $.02/wd.
Circulation: 50,000
Circulation Type: paid

**Owner(s):**
People's Publishing Co., Inc.
2955 80th Ave. S.E.
Mercer Island, WA 98040
Telephone: (206) 230-9224
FAX: (206) 230-9248
Ownership %: 100
**Management:**
H.S. Burdette ..............................President
H.S. Burdette ..............................Publisher
Steve Anderson ...............Advertising Manager
**Editorial:**
Rosemary Anderson ...............Managing Editor
**Desc.:** Covers the fields of coin, glass, relic, rock, gold and silver and other forms of collecting. Gives product tests of metal detectors, camping and gold prospecting equipment. Offers instructions on how to build prospecting equipment, methods of gold prospecting, ghost towns to explore, where to find relic sites, and other off-road activities.
**Readers:** Treasure hunters and outdoors enthusiasts who use detectors and prospecting equipment to search for gold, goins, relics and collectibles.
**Deadline:** news-varies; ads-10th of each mo. prior to pub. date

## WINNING!
68903

15115 S. 76 E. Ave.
Bixby, OK 74008
Telephone: (918) 366-4441
FAX: (918) 366-4439
Year Established: 1976
Pub. Frequency: m.
Subscrip. Rate: $21/yr.
Materials: 02,05,06,10,11,12,19,20,21
Circulation: 225,000
Circulation Type: paid
**Owner(s):**
NatCom, Inc.
15115 S. 76 E. Ave.
Bixby, OK 74008
Telephone: (918) 366-4441
Ownership %: 100
**Editorial:**
Lawrence Taylor ........................Editor
**Desc.:** Guide to winning big money prizes in contests and sweepstakes, lotteries, bingo, slots and other games of chance.

## WOMAN'S DAY BEST IDEAS FOR CHRISTMAS
26019

1633 Broadway
New York, NY 10019
Telephone: (212) 767-6000
FAX: (212) 767-5912
Pub. Frequency: a.
Page Size: standard
Subscrip. Rate: $3.50 newsstand
Freelance Pay: variable
Circulation: 800,000
Circulation Type: paid
**Owner(s):**
Hachette Magazines, Inc.
1633 Broadway
New York, NY 10019
Telephone: (212) 767-6000
Ownership %: 100
**Management:**
Daniel Filipacchi .............Chairman of Board
David Pecker ..............................President
Susan Buckley .............................Publisher
**Editorial:**
Carolyn Gatto ........................Editor in Chief
**Desc.:** full of ideas for holiday gifts, festive foods and seasonal decorations that readers can make for family and friends in a short amount of time. Instructions and recipes included for all items shown.
**Readers:** Women

## WOODWORK
67236

42 Digital Dr., Ste. 5
Ste. 5
Novato, CA 94949
Telephone: (415) 382-0580
FAX: (415) 382-0587
Mailing Address:
P.O. Box 1529
Ross, CA 94957
Year Established: 1989
Pub. Frequency: bi-m.
Page Size: standard
Subscrip. Rate: $15/yr.
Freelance Pay: $150/printed page
Circulation: 70,000
Circulation Type: paid
**Owner(s):**
Ross Periodicals, Inc.
P.O. Box 1529
Ross, CA 94957
Telephone: (415) 382-0580
Ownership %: 100
**Management:**
Thomas Toldrian ........................Publisher
Stan Michelman ...............Advertising Manager
**Editorial:**
John McDonald ...............................Editor

## Group 640-Home & Garden

## AMERICAN HOMESTYLE
65384

110 Fifth Ave.
New York, NY 10011
Telephone: (212) 463-1636
FAX: (212) 463-1662
Year Established: 1986
Pub. Frequency: 8/yr.
Page Size: standard
Subscrip. Rate: $9.97/yr.
Circulation: 684,447
Circulation Type: paid
**Owner(s):**
New York Times, Inc.
110 Fifth Ave.
New York, NY 10011
Telephone: (212) 463-1636
Ownership %: 100
**Editorial:**
Catharine George ...........................Editor
Karen Saks ..................................Editor
Jesse W. Iverson ...............Associate Publisher
David Phapes ...............................Director
Karen A. Crawford ...............Marketing Director
Joseph Mamone ...............Production Director
Vivian Haberfeld ...............Research Director
**Desc.:** Edited for American homeowners and regularly features residential design in a variety of styles as an attainable goal. A commitment to retail sources-encourages the purchase process. It is the key element of the editorial philosophy.
**Readers:** Active in home decorating & design.

## AMERICAN HORTICULTURIST
26026

7931 E. Boulevard Dr.
Alexandria, VA 22308
Telephone: (703) 768-5700
FAX: (703) 768-7533
Year Established: 1922
Pub. Frequency: 6/yr.
Page Size: standard
Subscrip. Rate: $2.95 newsstand;
membership
Materials: 02,05,06,10,15,17,21,25,28,30
Freelance Pay: $100-$400/article
Print Process: web offset
Circulation: 25,000
Circulation Type: controlled & paid

**Owner(s):**
American Horticultural Society
7931 E. Boulevard Dr.
Alexandria, VA 22308
Telephone: (703) 768-5700
Ownership %: 100
**Editorial:**
Kathleen Fisher ............................Editor
Pat Jordan ............................Advertising
**Desc.:** Gardening views and commentary. Devoted to the dissemination of knowledge in the art and science of growing ornamental plants, fruits, vegetables and related subjects. Edited for the advanced amateur gardener with the intention of promoting and encouraging a better understanding of gardening and its impact on our lives and on the environment.
**Readers:** Advanced gardeners, both amateur & professional, nationwide.
**Deadline:** story-2 mo. prior to pub. date; news-2 mo.; photo-2 mo.; ads-2 mo.

## ARCHITECTURAL DIGEST
26029

6300 Wilshire Blvd., 11th Fl.
Los Angeles, CA 90048
Telephone: (213) 965-3700
FAX: (213) 937-1458
Year Established: 1920
Pub. Frequency: m.
Page Size: standard
Subscrip. Rate: $39.95/yr.
Circulation: 625,000
Circulation Type: paid
**Owner(s):**
Conde Nast Publ., Inc.
6300 Wilshire Blvd., 11th Fl.
Los Angeles, CA 90048
Telephone: (213) 965-3700
FAX: (213) 937-1458
Ownership %: 100
**Editorial:**
Paige Rense ........................Editor in Chief
Michael Wollaeger .................Senior Editor
**Desc.:** International magazine of fine residential interior design. Each issue showcases prestigious residences decorated by the leading international interior designers. Feature articles cover celebrity residences, architecture, historic houses, fine art and antiques and gardens in the grand manner.
**Readers:** Affluent house owners interested in the finest interior designs and furniture.

## BETTER HOMES & GARDENS
26030

1716 Locust St.
Des Moines, IA 50309-3023
Telephone: (515) 284-3000
FAX: (515) 284-3684
Year Established: 1924
Pub. Frequency: m.
Page Size: standard
Subscrip. Rate: $1.95/copy; $17/yr.
Materials: 04,09,19,20,21,28,29
Freelance Pay: varies
Circulation: 7,600,000
Circulation Type: paid
**Owner(s):**
Meredith Corp.
1716 Locust St.
Des Moines, IA 50309-3023
Telephone: (515) 284-3000
Ownership %: 100
**Management:**
Bill Kerr .................................President
Jerry Kaplan .............................Publisher
**Editorial:**
Jean LemMon ................................Editor
Lamont Olson ...................Managing Editor
Bradford W.S. Hong ...............Art Director
Jack D. Rehm .........Chairman of Board/CEO

Materials Accepted/Included: 01-Business news 02-By-line articles 03-Fashion news 04-Food news 05-Freelance copy 06-Letters to editor 07-Real estate news 08-Sports news 09-Travel news 10-Book rev. 11-Movie rev. 12-Music rev. 13-TV rev. 14-Theater rev. 15-Coming events 16-Obituaries 17-Question & answer 18-Social announcements 19-Artwork 20-Cartoons 21-Photos 22-TV listings 23-Audio rec. 24-Video rec. 25-Books 26-Films/film clips 27-Personnel news 28-Press releases 29-New product news/photos 30-Trade lit. 31-Contracts awarded 32-Display adv. 33-Classified adv.

6-66

Chris Little ..............Publishing Director
**Desc.:** To serve men and women who
have a serious interest in home and
family as the focal point of their lives;
and to provide this service in the form of
ideas, help, information and inspiration
to achieve a better home and family.
Inherent in this philosophy is the
editorial responsibility to move
these husbands and wives into action.
Articles cover building, remodeling, and
maintenance; gardening, cars in your
family, health, education, travel. 75
percent staff written, but do occasionally
buy freelance material.

26031
## BETTER HOMES & GARDENS BUILDING IDEAS
1716 Locust St.
Des Moines, IA 50309-3023
Telephone: (515) 284-2584
FAX: (515) 284-3697
Year Established: 1937
Pub. Frequency: q.
Page Size: 4 color photos/art
Subscrip. Rate: $3.95/issue
Freelance Pay: negotiable
Circulation: 450,000
Circulation Type: paid
**Owner(s):**
Meredith Corp.
1716 Locust St.
Des Moines, IA 50309-3023
Telephone: (515) 284-2584
Ownership %: 100
**Management:**
Jerry Ward ..............Publisher
**Editorial:**
William Yates ..............Editor in Chief
Pat Tomlinson ..............Advertising
Kathie Kull ..............New Products Editor
**Desc.:** Provides how-to and inspiration for
those planning to build a home.

26032
## BETTER HOMES & GARDENS CHRISTMAS IDEAS
1716 Locust St.
Des Moines, IA 50309
Telephone: (515) 284-3000
FAX: (515) 284-3697
Pub. Frequency: a.
Page Size: pg: 8 5/16 x 112; col: 2; photo:
yes; mat: no; cut
Subscrip. Rate: $3.50 newsstand
Circulation: 1,000,000
Circulation Type: paid
**Owner(s):**
Meredith Corp.
1716 Locust St.
Des Moines, IA 50309
Telephone: (515) 284-9011
Ownership %: 100
**Management:**
Steve Levinson ..............Publisher
Pat Tomlinson ..............Advertising Manager
**Editorial:**
Willam Yates ..............Editor in Chief
Linda Steuve ..............Editor
**Desc.:** Ideas on decorations for the home
settings, .
**Readers:** Handicrafting Homemakers

65990
## BETTER HOMES & GARDENS DECORATING IDEAS
17th & Locust St.
Des Moines, IA 50309-3023
Telephone: (515) 284-2999
FAX: (515) 284-3697
Year Established: 1941
Pub. Frequency: q.
Page Size: standard
Circulation: 500,000

**Owner(s):**
Meredith Corp.
17th & Locust St.
Des Moines, IA 50309-3023
Telephone: (515) 284-2999
Ownership %: 100
**Editorial:**
Heather Paper ..............Editor

26034
## BETTER HOMES & GARDENS GARDEN IDEAS & OUTDOOR LIVING
1716 Locust St.
Des Moines, IA 50309
Telephone: (515) 284-3000
FAX: (515) 284-3697
Year Established: 1940
Pub. Frequency: s-a.
Subscrip. Rate: $3.50 newsstand
Circulation: 550,000
Circulation Type: paid
**Owner(s):**
Meredith Corp.
1716 Locust St.
Des Moines, IA 50309
Telephone: (515) 284-3000
FAX: (515) 284-3697
Ownership %: 100
**Management:**
Steve Levinson ..............Publisher
Pat Tomlinson ..............Advertising Manager
**Editorial:**
William Yates ..............Editor in Chief
Greg Philby ..............Editor

26038
## BETTER HOMES & GARDENS KITCHEN & BATH IDEAS
1716 Locust St.
Des Moines, IA 50309
Telephone: (515) 284-3000
FAX: (515) 284-3697
Pub. Frequency: q.
Page Size: Standard
Subscrip. Rate: $3.99 newsstand
Circulation: 450000
Circulation Type: paid
**Owner(s):**
Meredith Corp.
1716 Locust St.
Des Moines, IA 50309
Telephone: (515) 284-3000
Ownership %: 100
**Management:**
Steve Levinson ..............Publisher
Pat Tomlinson ..............Advertising Manager
**Editorial:**
Willam Yates ..............Editor in Chief
Marsha Raisch ..............Editor
**Desc.:** Twenty-two Special Interest titles
for 1990. They offer something for
everyone - from building projects &
decorating, to crafts, cooking &
gardening.

26040
## BETTER HOMES & GARDENS REMODELING IDEAS
1716 Locust St.
Des Moines, IA 50309-3023
Telephone: (515) 284-2173
FAX: (515) 284-3697
Pub. Frequency: 4/yr.
Page Size: standard
Subscrip. Rate: $3.50/issue
Materials: 05,06,10,21,25,29
Circulation: 450,000
Circulation Type: paid
**Owner(s):**
Meredith Corp.
1716 Locust St.
Des Moines, IA 50336
Telephone: (515) 284-3000
Ownership %: 100

**Management:**
Stephen B. Levinson ..............Publisher
**Editorial:**
William J. Yates ..............Executive Editor
Robert G. Wilson ..............Editor
Patrick R. Tomlinson ..............Advertising
Don Nickell ..............Art Director
Jerry Ward ..............Publication Director
**Desc.:** Covers practical ideas for
remodeling and updating your home plus
advice on arranging financing
and working with contractors. Other
stories also detail low-budget fix-ups that
can be customized to suit any home's
decor.

59551
## BETTER HOMES & GARDENS WOOD
1716 Locust St.
Des Moines, IA 50336
Telephone: (515) 284-3000
FAX: (515) 284-2333
Year Established: 1984
Pub. Frequency: 9/yr.
Page Size: standard
Subscrip. Rate: $4.95/yr.; $25/yr. US;
$38/yr. foreign
Freelance Pay: negotiable
Circulation: 650,000
Circulation Type: paid
**Owner(s):**
Meredith Corp.
1716 Locust St.
Des Moines, IA 50336
Telephone: (515) 284-3000
Ownership %: 100
**Management:**
William Reed ..............Publisher
**Editorial:**
Larry Clayton ..............Editor
Kathy Garland ..............Administrative Assistant
**Desc.:** Covers woodworking projects for
homeowners.

66512
## BUILDER'S BEST HOME DESIGNS
One Thomas Circle, N.W., Ste. 600
Washington, DC 20005
Telephone: (202) 452-0800
FAX: (202) 785-1974
Year Established: 1991
Pub. Frequency: q.
Page Size: 4 color photos/art
Subscrip. Rate: $4.95/copy; $5.95/in
Canada
Circulation: 100,000
Circulation Type: paid
**Owner(s):**
Hanley-Wood, Inc.
One Thomas Circle, N.W., Ste.
Washington, DC 20005
Telephone: (202) 452-0800
Ownership %: 100
**Management:**
Michael J. Tucker ..............Publisher
**Editorial:**
Paul Kitzke ..............Editor

26067
## COLONIAL HOMES
1790 Broadway
New York, NY 10019
Telephone: (212) 830-2900
FAX: (212) 586-3455
Year Established: 1975
Pub. Frequency: 6/yr.
Page Size: standard
Subscrip. Rate: $3/copy
Circulation: 600,724
Circulation Type: paid
**Owner(s):**
Hearst Magazine Division, The
959 Eighth Ave.
New York, NY 10019
Telephone: (212) 262-5700
Ownership %: 100

**Management:**
Brian Doyle ..............Publisher
Jennifer Gallo ..............Advertising Manager
**Editorial:**
Diane Di Piero ..............Editor
Debra Muller ..............Managing Editor
Annette Stramesi ..............Editorial Director
Michael Liberatore ..............Art Director
Valerie Fony ..............Assistant Art Director
Debra Kanabis ..............Assistant Editor
Lisa Vahradian ..............Assistant Editor
Doretta Sperduto ..............Associate Editor
Jane Clancy ..............Associate Editor
Robert Mottley ..............Associate Editor
Claire Rooney ..............Associate Editor
Bobbie Dell'Aquilo ..............Copy Editor
Jason Kontos ..............Ed. in Chief
**Desc.:** Upscale shelter magazine for
readers with traditional design tastes.
**Readers:** Young, affluent, dual-income
homeowners.

67255
## COUNTRY AMERICA
1716 Locust St.
Des Moines, IA 50336
Telephone: (515) 284-3000
FAX: (515) 284-3035
Year Established: 1989
Pub. Frequency: 10/yr.
Page Size: standard
Subscrip. Rate: $16.97/yr.
Materials: 03,04,05,06,09,10,12,15,21,23,
24,25,32,33
Freelance Pay: $.25-$1 per word
Circulation: 1,000,000
Circulation Type: paid
**Owner(s):**
Meredith Corp.
1716 Locust St.
Des Moines, IA 50336
Telephone: (515) 284-3000
Ownership %: 100
**Management:**
Gail Healy ..............Publisher
Susan Harrington ..............Advertising Manager
**Editorial:**
Danita Allan ..............Editor
**Readers:** National distribution - 65%
female/35% male. For people who
enjoy the country life and country music
and entertainment.
**Deadline:** story-9th of mo. prior to pub.
date; news-3rd of mo. prior to pub. date;
ads-90 days prior to pub. date

59553
## COUNTRY HOME
1716 Locust St.
Des Moines, IA 50309-3023
Telephone: (515) 284-3000
FAX: (515) 284-3035
Year Established: 1979
Pub. Frequency: bi-m.
Page Size: standard
Subscrip. Rate: $3.95 newsstand
Circulation: 1,100,000
Circulation Type: paid
**Owner(s):**
Meredith Corp.
1716 Locust St.
Des Moines, IA 50309-3023
Telephone: (515) 284-3000
Ownership %: 100
**Management:**
Joseph Lagani ..............Publisher
**Editorial:**
Molly Culbertson ..............Editor
**Desc.:** We believe in lasting values, an
interest in history, respect for
craftsmanship, an appreciation
of traditions, and a deep commitment to
home. We are a life-style magazine for
and about people who share the same
beliefs.

**Materials Accepted/Included:** 01-Business news 02-By-line articles 03-Fashion news 04-Food news 05-Freelance copy 06-Letters to editor 07-Real estate news 08-Sports news 09-Travel news 10-Book rev. 11-Movie rev. 12-Music rev. 13-TV rev. 14-Theater rev. 15-Coming events 16-Obituaries 17-Question & answer 18-Social announcements 19-Artwork 20-Cartoons 21-Photos 22-TV listings 23-Audio rec. 24-Video rec. 25-Books 26-Films/film clips 27-Personnel news 28-Press releases 29-New product news/photos 30-Trade lit. 31-Contracts awarded 32-Display adv. 33-Classified adv.

6-67

**COUNTRY VICTORIAN ACCENTS**    67277
1700 Broadway
New York, NY 10019
Telephone: (212) 541-7100
FAX: (212) 245-1241
Year Established: 1989
Pub. Frequency: bi-m.
Page Size: standard
Subscrip. Rate: $12.97/yr.
Circulation: 225,000
Circulation Type: paid
**Owner(s):**
GCR Publishing Group, Inc.
1700 Broadway
New York, NY 10019
Telephone: (212) 541-7100
Ownership %: 100
**Management:**
Charles Goodman ................................Publisher
John Damboragean ..........Advertising Manager
**Editorial:**
Florine McCain ..........................................Editor

**CUSTOM HOME**    66514
One Thomas Circle, N.W., Ste. 600
Washington, DC 20005
Telephone: (202) 452-0800
FAX: (202) 785-1974
Year Established: 1991
Pub. Frequency: 6/yr.
Subscrip. Rate: $7.90/yr.
Circulation: 45,000
Circulation Type: paid
**Owner(s):**
Hanley Wood, Inc.
One Thomas Circle, N.W., Ste.
Washington, DC 20005
Telephone: (202) 452-0800
FAX: (202) 785-1974
Ownership %: 100
**Management:**
Michael J. Tucker ..............................Publisher
**Editorial:**
Paul Kitzke ..............................................Editor

**DALLAS/FT. WORTH HOME**    25843
   **BUYER'S GUIDE**
5501 LBJ Frwy., Ste. 300
Dallas, TX 75240
Telephone: (214) 239-2399
FAX: (214) 239-7850
Year Established: 1972
Pub. Frequency: bi-m.
Page Size: standard
Subscrip. Rate: free
Freelance Pay: $35/hr.
Circulation: 75,000
Circulation Type: free
**Owner(s):**
Living Partners, Ltd.
5501 LBJ Freeway, Ste. 300
Dallas, TX 75240
Telephone: (214) 239-2399
Ownership %: 100
**Management:**
Ray Baker ........................................Publisher
Sonia Lowery ....................Circulation Manager
Charlotte Llano ....................Office Manager
**Editorial:**
Nancy Meza ......................Managing Editor
Susan Taylor ........................Account Executive
Jim Augustine ..................Associate Publisher
Lynn Frank ............................Sales Assistant

**Desc.:** A comprehensive map guide covering all segments of the housing market with emphasis on new-home subdivisions. Articles include general features on the housing industry and home products and local features on new-home communities. Articles run 500-1,000 words. Departments include: New Home Section, New Communities Section, Necessary Numbers, Marketing Information.
**Readers:** Newcomers, corporate transfers, and local residents interested in a new home in Dallas/Ft. Worth area.

**EARLY AMERICAN LIFE**    26046
6405 Flank Dr.
Harrisburg, PA 17112
Telephone: (717) 657-9555
FAX: (717) 657-9552
Mailing Address:
   P.O. Box 8200
   Harrisburg, PA 17105
Year Established: 1970
Pub. Frequency: 7/yr.
Page Size: standard
Subscrip. Rate: $3.50 newsstand; $22/yr.
Freelance Pay: negotiable
Circulation: 150,000
Circulation Type: paid
**Owner(s):**
Cowles Media Co.
329 Portland Ave.
Minneapolis, MN 55415
Telephone: (612) 375-7000
Ownership %: 100
**Management:**
Bruce A. Barnet ................................President
Diane Myers ....................Advertising Manager
**Editorial:**
Mimi Handler ..................................Editor
Leah Stamos ..............................Art Director
**Desc.:** Contains material for persons interested in arts, crafts, furnishings, and architecture of the 17th, 18th, and 19th centuries, and in modern interpretations for their homes. Departments include: Travel (historic sites), Arts, Crafts, Antiques, American Social History, Architecture, Furnishings of the period.
**Readers:** People interested in early American designs.
**Deadline:** 4 wks. prior to pub. date

**ECONOMIC HOME OWNER**    69527
951 S. Oxford, #109
Los Angeles, CA 90006
Telephone: (213) 732-3477
Year Established: 1991
Pub. Frequency: q.
Subscrip. Rate: $26.99/yr.
Materials: 01,02,03,04,05,06,07,08,09,10,
   11,12,13,14,15,16,17,18,19,20,21,22,23,
   24,25,26,27,28,29,30,31,32,33
Freelance Pay: $.20-.50/wd.
Print Process: web
Circulation: 120,000
Circulation Type: controlled & paid
**Owner(s):**
Publishing & Business Consultants
951 S. Oxford, #109
Los Angeles, CA 90006
Telephone: (213) 732-3477
Ownership %: 100
**Editorial:**
Andeson Napoleon Atia ..........................Editor
**Desc.:** Provides helpful information on a variety of topics relating to home repair, with information on industry trends.
**Deadline:** story-2 wks. prior to pub. date; news-2 wks.; photo-2 wks.; ads-90 days

**ELLE DECOR**    67280
1633 Broadway, 44th Fl.
New York, NY 10019
Telephone: (800) 876-8775
FAX: (212) 789-4216
Year Established: 1989
Pub. Frequency: m.
Page Size: standard
Subscrip. Rate: $2.75 newsstand; $18/yr.
Circulation: 400,000
Circulation Type: paid
**Owner(s):**
Elle Publishing
1633 Broadway, 44th Fl.
New York, NY 10019
Telephone: (212) 767-5800
Ownership %: 100
**Management:**
John Miller ........................................Publisher
**Editorial:**
Marian McEvoy ................................Editor
**Desc.:** Provides an international design showcase of home products. Encourages readers to use their own creativity.

**EXTRA EQUITY FOR**    67283
   **HOMEBUYERS**
1720 Post Rd. E.
Westport, CT 06880
Telephone: (203) 255-0855
FAX: (203) 259-0724
Year Established: 1984
Pub. Frequency: 3/yr.
Page Size: standard
Subscrip. Rate: free
Circulation: 250,000
Circulation Type: controlled
**Owner(s):**
Homes & Land Publishing Corp.
1720 Post Rd. E.
Westport, CT 06880
Telephone: (203) 255-0855
Ownership %: 100
**Management:**
William O'Brien ................................President
William O'Brien ................................Publisher
James Boike ....................Advertising Manager
**Editorial:**
William O'Brien ..................................Editor
**Desc.:** Features promotional offers from national advertisers for people buying a single family home.

**FAMILY HANDYMAN, THE**    25975
7900 International Dr., Ste. 950
Minneapolis, MN 55425
Telephone: (612) 854-3000
FAX: (612) 854-8009
Year Established: 1951
Pub. Frequency: 10/yr.
Page Size: standard
Subscrip. Rate: $2.25 newsstand;
   $17.93/yr.
Freelance Pay: $100-$2000
Circulation: 1,000,000
Circulation Type: paid
**Owner(s):**
Reader's Digest Association, The
Pleasantville, NY 10570
Telephone: (914) 241-5249
Ownership %: 100
**Management:**
Thomas E. Kenney ............................President
Bob Amberg ....................Advertising Manager
Toby Roux ......................Circulation Manager
**Editorial:**
Art Rooze ................................Senior Editor
Gary Havens ..........................................Editor
Mark Thompson ....................Managing Editor
Gregg Weigand ........................Art Director
Bob Ungar ................................Art Director
Marcia Williston ........................Art Director

Bill Faber ................................Art Director
Don Prestly ..........................Associate Editor
Duane Johnson ....................Associate Editor
Ken Collier ..........................Associate Editor
Mike Smith ......................................Design
**Desc.:** Do-it-yourself homecraft projects with photos and sketches. Seasonal repairs, maintenance and improvements inside and out; how to use tools; yard and garden features; new products; how-to-tips. By-lines used. Average 1,000-1,500 words. Pay on acceptance.
**Readers:** Up-scale homeowners.

**FINE GARDENING**    65408
63 S. Main St.,
Newtown, CT 06470-5506
Telephone: (203) 426-8171
FAX: (203) 426-3434
Mailing Address:
   P.O. Box 5506
   Newtown, CT 06470-5506
Year Established: 1988
Pub. Frequency: bi-m.
Page Size: oversize
Subscrip. Rate: $5.50 newsstand; $28/yr.;
   $48/2 yrs.
Materials: 02,05,06,10,17,19,21,25,28,29,
   32,33
Freelance Pay: $150/pg.
Print Process: web offset
Circulation: 165,000
Circulation Type: paid
**Owner(s):**
Taunton Press, The
63 S. Main St.
Newtown, CT 06470-5506
Telephone: (203) 426-8171
FAX: (203) 426-3434
Ownership %: 100
**Management:**
Janice Roman ................................President
Anita Castelhano ..............Advertising Manager
Donna Pierpont .........Public Relations Manager
**Editorial:**
Nancy Beaubaire ....................Executive Editor
Elizabeth Eaton ........................Art Director
Rosalind Loeb Wanke ..................Assistant Art
   Director
Delilah Smittle ..........................Assistant Editor
Jeri Ann Geller ........................Assistant Editor
Amy Ziffer ............................Assistant Editor
Roy Swanson ....................Assistant Publisher
**Desc.:** Devoted exclusively to the home gardener. Primary focus is on landscaping and ornamental gardening, but also takes a selective interest in food gardening. Articles are written by experienced, active gardeners providing practical information ranging from the care of a single plant to the design of an entire landscape. Departments include: Letters, Tips, Basics, Q&A, Plants, Gleanings, Book Reviews, Last Word, and an Annual Index.
**Readers:** Readers range from novice home gardeners to professional horticulturists. Common to them all is a serious interest in gardening and a desire for breadth and depth of coverage. Nationwide readership.

**GARDENER, THE**    26051
5560 Merle Hay Rd.
Johnston, IA 50131-0241
Telephone: (515) 278-0295
FAX: (515) 278-6245
Mailing Address:
   P.O. Box 241
   Johnston, IA 50131-0241
Year Established: 1940
Pub. Frequency: bi-m.

**Materials Accepted/Included:** 01-Business news 02-By-line articles 03-Fashion news 04-Food news 05-Freelance copy 06-Letters to editor 07-Real estate news 08-Sports news 09-Travel news 10-Book rev. 11-Movie rev. 12-Music rev. 13-TV rev. 14-Theater rev. 15-Coming events 16-Obituaries 17-Question & answer 18-Social announcements 19-Artwork 20-Cartoons 21-Photos 22-TV listings 23-Audio rec. 24-Video rec. 25-Books 26-Films/film clips 27-Personnel news 28-Press releases 29-New product news/photos 30-Trade lit. 31-Contracts awarded 32-Display adv. 33-Classified adv.

Page Size: standard
Subscrip. Rate: $15/yr.
Materials: 01,02,04,19,20,29
Circulation: 9,000
Circulation Type: paid
**Owner(s):**
The Gardeners of America, Inc.
5560 Merle Hay Rd.
Johnston, IA 50131-0241
Telephone: (515) 278-0295
Ownership %: 100
**Management:**
O. Reeves Davis .................................President
Kimberley Press ................................Publisher
**Editorial:**
TGOA Staff ...........................................Editor
Executive Comm. TGOA ........Managing Editor
Carol Donovan ......................Associate Editor
**Desc.:** Edited for professional and amateur
gardeners in the U.S. Feature articles on
various aspects of gardening,
landscaping, planting, plants and
aspects of natural beautification.
**Readers:** Largest percentage are
members of Men's Garden Club of
America, Inc. Available to gardeners,
amateur & professional.

68723
## GARLINGHOUSE HOME PLAN GUIDE
34 Industrial Park Pl.
Middletown, CT 06457
Telephone: (203) 632-1064
FAX: (203) 632-0712
Mailing Address:
P.O. Box 1717
Middletown, CT 06457
Year Established: 1948
Pub. Frequency: q.
Subscrip. Rate: 12.64/yr.
Circulation: 115,720
Circulation Type: paid
**Owner(s):**
Garlinghouse Co., Inc.
34 Industrial Pk. Pl.
Middletown, CT 06457
Telephone: (203) 632-1064
Ownership %: 100
**Editorial:**
Whitney B. Garlinghouse .........................Editor
**Desc.:** Presents a collection of residential
home designs for the North American
market.

25858
## GOOD HOUSEKEEPING
959 Eighth Ave.
New York, NY 10019
*see Consumer Magazine, Women's
Magazines*

69275
## HIAWATHA HOMES
16700 Bollinger Dr.
Pacific Palisades, CA 90272
Telephone: (310) 454-4809
FAX: (310) 454-7527
Mailing Address:
P.O. Box 1148
Pacific Palisades, CA 90272-1148
Year Established: 1947
Pub. Frequency: a.
Page Size: standard
Subscrip. Rate: $4-7/issue
Circulation: 10,000
Circulation Type: paid
**Owner(s):**
Hiawatha Homes
P.O. Box 1148
Pacific Palisades, CA 90272-4809
Telephone: (310) 454-4809
Ownership %: 100
**Management:**
Richard Wilken .................................Publisher

68724
## HOME
1633 Broadway
New York, NY 10019
Telephone: (212) 767-6000
FAX: (212) 767-5600
Year Established: 1955
Pub. Frequency: m.
Subscrip. Rate: $18/yr.
Materials: 02,06,10,15,19,20,29,32,33
Freelance Pay: $1/wd.
Print Process: offset
Circulation: 1,000,000
Circulation Type: paid
**Owner(s):**
Hachette Filipacchi Magazines, Inc.
633 Broadway
New York, NY 10019
Telephone: (212) 767-6000
**Editorial:**
Gale C. Steves ....................................Editor
**Desc.:** Covers home design and
architecture, including creative, yet
practical, ideas aimed at the average
middle-income homeowner.

68746
## HOME PLANNER
3275 W. Ina Rd., Ste. 110
Tucson, AZ 85714
Telephone: (602) 297-8200
FAX: (602) 297-6219
Year Established: 1989
Pub. Frequency: 8/yr.
Subscrip. Rate: $4.95/copy; $21.95/yr.
Circulation: 100,000
Circulation Type: paid
**Owner(s):**
Home Planners, Inc.
3275 W. Ina Rd., Ste. 110
Tucson, AZ 85741
Telephone: (602) 297-8200
Ownership %: 100

68722
## HOME PLANS TO BUILD
34 Industrial Pk. Pl.
Middletown, CT 06457
Telephone: (203) 632-1064
Mailing Address:
P.O. Box 1717
Middletown, CT 06457
Year Established: 1985
Pub. Frequency: q.
Subscrip. Rate: 2.95 newsstand; $9.44/yr.
Materials: 30,32
Print Process: web offset
Circulation: 115,720
Circulation Type: paid
**Owner(s):**
Garlinghouse Co., Inc.
34 Industrial Pk. Pl.
Middletown, CT 06457
Telephone: (203) 632-1064
Ownership %: 100
**Editorial:**
Whitney B. Garlinghouse .........................Editor

26056
## HORTICULTURE, THE MAGAZINE OF AMERICAN GARDENING
98 N. Washington St.
Boston, MA 02114-1913
Telephone: (617) 742-5600
FAX: (617) 367-6364
Year Established: 1904
Pub. Frequency: 10/yr.
Page Size: standard
Subscrip. Rate: $24/yr.
Materials: 02,05,06,10,17,19,21,25,28,30,
32,33
Freelance Pay: varies
Print Process: web
Circulation: 330,000
Circulation Type: paid

**Owner(s):**
Horticulture Inc.
98 N. Washington St.
Boston, MA 02114-1913
Telephone: (617) 742-5600
FAX: (617) 367-6364
Ownership %: 100
**Bureau(s):**
Subscription Department, Horticulture
P.O. Box 53879
Boulder, CO 80321
Telephone: (800) 525-0643
**Management:**
Robert M. Cohn .................................President
Mary Dean ..........................................Controller
Robert M. Cohn ................................Publisher
Shirley A. Barry .................Circulation Manager
**Editorial:**
Thomas C. Cooper ................................Editor
Joel P. Toner .....................Associate Publisher
Linda Adams .....................Production Director
**Desc.:** By-line articles on all aspects of
gardening by experienced amateur and
professional horticulturists. Average
article runs about 1,500 words with
illustrations. Articles cover plants,
products, and environmental subjects.
Departments include: letters, questions
and answers, step-by-step, design,
books, native americans, and
hortjournal.
**Readers:** Amateur and professional
gardeners
**Deadline:** story-4 mos. prior to pub. date;
news-3 mos. prior; photo-varies; ads-1
mo. prior

26065
## HOUSE BEAUTIFUL
1700 Broadway
New York, NY 10019
Telephone: (212) 903-5000
FAX: (212) 765-8292
Year Established: 1896
Pub. Frequency: m.
Page Size: standard
Subscrip. Rate: $17.97/yr.
Freelance Pay: $500-$1000
Circulation: 1,000,000
Circulation Type: paid
**Owner(s):**
Hearst Corp.
959 Eighth Ave.
New York, NY 10019
Telephone: (212) 262-5700
**Management:**
Carole Ference ................................Publisher
**Editorial:**
Louis O. Gropp .....................................Editor
Jeff Burch ..........................Advertising Director
Elaine Greene .............................Feature Editor
Joseph Enterlin ..................Production Director
Elizabeth Hunter ...........................Travel Editor
**Desc.:** Emphasizes interior design,
architecture and home improvement.
Also covers food, entertainment, travel,
gardening and outdoor living.
**Readers:** Upper middle-class women
homeowners in their 30's & 40's.
**Deadline:** 2 mos. prior to pub. date

26066
## HOUSE BEAUTIFUL'S HOME BUILDING
1790 Broadway, 5th Fl.
New York, NY 10019
Telephone: (212) 841-8300
FAX: (212) 841-8392
Year Established: 1935
Pub. Frequency: s-a.
Page Size: standard
Subscrip. Rate: $2.95/issue
Circulation: 250,000
Circulation Type: paid

**Owner(s):**
Hearst Magazine Division, The
959 Eighth Ave.
New York, NY 10019
Telephone: (212) 262-5700
Ownership %: 100
**Management:**
Gilbert C. Maurer ...............................President
Sasha Lawer .....................................Publisher
Susan A. Costantino ..........Promotion Manager
**Editorial:**
Katherine Ball Ross ....................Editor in Chief
Karen Hoffman ......................Executive Editor
Jim Kemp .............................................Editor
Ron Renzullu .........................................Editor
Carolyn Feighner ......................Managing Editor
Brian Doyle .......................................Advertising
Susan Livoti ......................................Advertising
Edward Koon ...................................Art Director
Karen Hoffman ...............................Deputy Editor
**Desc.:** Building ideas, house plans &
product information.
**Readers:** Identifies families with serious
interest in building a custom home.

26069
## HOUSE BEAUTIFUL'S HOME REMODELING & DECORATING
1790 Broadway, 5th Fl.
New York, NY 10019
Telephone: (212) 841-8300
FAX: (212) 841-8392
Year Established: 1964
Pub. Frequency: 3/yr.
Page Size: standard
Subscrip. Rate: $3.50/issue
Circulation: 250,000
Circulation Type: paid
**Owner(s):**
Hearst Magazine Division, The
959 Eighth Ave.
New York, NY 10019
Telephone: (212) 262-5700
Ownership %: 100
**Management:**
Gilbert C. Maurer ...............................President
Sasha Lawer .....................................Publisher
Susan A. Costantino ..........Promotion Manager
**Editorial:**
Katherine Ball Ross ....................Editor in Chief
Karen Hoffman ......................Executive Editor
Jill Herbers ...........................................Editor
Jim Kemp .............................................Editor
Carolyn Feighner ......................Managing Editor
Brian Doyle .......................................Advertising
Susan Livoti ......................................Advertising
Edward Koons .................................Art Director
Karen Hoffman ...............................Deputy Editor
**Desc.:** Remodeling projects, decorating
ideas, and product information.
**Readers:** Targets families who are
remodeling or decorating their home
from small projects to whole house
renovation.

26070
## HOUSE BEAUTIFUL'S HOUSES & PLANS
1790 Broadway, 5th Fl.
New York, NY 10019
Telephone: (212) 841-8300
FAX: (212) 841-8392
Year Established: 1960
Pub. Frequency: 5/yr.
Page Size: standard
Subscrip. Rate: $2.95/issue
Circulation: 250,000
Circulation Type: paid
**Owner(s):**
Hearst Magazine Division, The
959 Eighth Ave.
New York, NY 10019
Telephone: (212) 262-5700
Ownership %: 100
**Management:**
Gilbert C. Maurer ...............................President

**Materials Accepted/Included:** 01-Business news 02-By-line articles 03-Fashion news 04-Food news 05-Freelance copy 06-Letters to editor 07-Real estate news 08-Sports news 09-Travel news 10-Book rev. 11-Movie rev. 12-Music rev. 13-TV rev. 14-Theater rev. 15-Coming events 16-Obituaries 17-Question & answer 18-Social announcements 19-Artwork 20-Cartoons 21-Photos 22-TV listings 23-Audio rec. 24-Video rec. 25-Books 26-Films/film clips 27-Personnel news 28-Press releases 29-New product news/photos 30-Trade lit. 31-Contracts awarded 32-Display adv. 33-Classified adv.

6-69

Sasha Lawer ........................Publisher
Susan A. Costantino ..........Promotion Manager
**Editorial:**
Rebecca Banks ..........................Editor in Chief
Karen Hoffman ........................Executive Editor
Jim Kemp ........................Editor
Carolyn Feighner ....................Managing Editor
Brian Doyle ........................Advertising
Susan Livoti ........................Advertising
Edward Koons ................Art Director
Karen Hoffman ........................Deputy Editor
**Desc.:** Architect designed houses, blueprints available for purchase.
**Readers:** Targets purchase-oriented families interested in custom home building.

26071

## HOUSE BEAUTIFUL'S KITCHENS/BATHS
1790 Broadway, 5th Floor
New York, NY 10019
Telephone: (212) 841-8325
Year Established: 1980
Pub. Frequency: 4/yr.
Page Size: standard
Subscrip. Rate: $2.95/copy
Circulation: 250,000
Circulation Type: paid
**Owner(s):**
Hearst Magazine Division, The
959 Eighth Ave.
New York, NY 10019
Telephone: (212) 262-5700
Ownership %: 100
**Editorial:**
Jim Kemp ........................Editor in Chief
Karen Hoffman ........................Editor
Laura Dye ........................Editor
Susan Livoti ........................Advertising
**Desc.:** Remodeling projects, decorating ideas for the kitchen and/or bath area of the home, also includes product information.
**Readers:** Targets families who are planning to remodel or decorate their kitchen and bathroom or build anew.

67269

## HOUSE PLANS & PRODUCTS
1350 E. Touhy Ave.
Des Plaines, IL 60018
Telephone: (708) 635-8800
FAX: (708) 635-9950
Year Established: 1988
Pub. Frequency: q.
Page Size: standard
Subscrip. Rate: $10/copy; $18/yr. US; $30/yr. foreign
Circulation: 194,000
Circulation Type: controlled & paid
**Owner(s):**
Reed Elsiver
1350 E. Touhy
Des Plaines, IL 60018
Telephone: (708) 635-8800
Ownership %: 100
**Management:**
Bob Krakoff ........................President
Peter Orsi ........................Publisher
**Editorial:**
Paul Gillen ........................Advertising Director
Roy L. Diez ........................Associate Editor
Roy L. Diez ........................Education Editor
**Desc.:** Offers new home deigns for sale and up-to-date building products.

26073

## HOUSTON LIFE MAGAZINE
5615 Kirby Dr., Ste. 600
Houston, TX 77005
Telephone: (713) 524-3000
Mailing Address:
P.O. Box 25386
Houston, TX 77265
Year Established: 1974
Pub. Frequency: m.

Page Size: 9.875 x 12
Subscrip. Rate: Available only in the Houston Post, 3rd Sun. of every month
Materials: 04,05,06,09,10,15,19,20,21
Freelance Pay: $50-$900/editorial feature
Circulation: 350,000
Circulation Type: paid
**Owner(s):**
Houston Metropolitan, Ltd.
P.O. Box 25386
Houston, TX 77265
Telephone: (713) 524-3000
Ownership %: 100
**Management:**
Mark Inabnit ........................Publisher
**Editorial:**
Maria Moss ........................Managing Editor
David Walker ........................Editorial Director
Jeff Stanton ........................Art Director
Jill Salomon ........................Editorial Assistant
**Desc.:** All editorial material must have a Houston eg. Since February 1994, focus has shifted to a more well-rounded view of Houston; home, garden, health, regional travel and city issues.
**Readers:** Median age 42, college educated

66516

## KITCHEN & BATH
One Thomas Circle, N.W., Ste. 600
Washington, DC 20005
Telephone: (202) 452-0800
FAX: (202) 785-1974
Year Established: 1989
Pub. Frequency: bi-m.
Subscrip. Rate: $3.95/copy; $4.95 in Canada
Circulation: 60,000
Circulation Type: controlled
**Owner(s):**
Hanley-Wood, Inc.
One Thomas Circle, N.W., Ste.
Washington, DC 20005
Telephone: (202) 452-0800
FAX: (202) 785-1974
Ownership %: 100
**Management:**
John M. Brannigan ........................Publisher
**Editorial:**
Paul Kitzke ........................Editor

67260

## LOG HOME LIVING
4451 Brookfield Corporate Dr., 101
Chantilly, VA 22021
Telephone: (703) 222-9411
FAX: (703) 222-3209
Mailing Address:
P.O. Box 220039
Chantilly, VA 22022
Year Established: 1982
Pub. Frequency: bi-m.
Page Size: standard
Subscrip. Rate: $21.95/yr.
Circulation: 200,000
Circulation Type: paid
**Owner(s):**
Home Buyer Publications, Inc.
4451 Brookfield Corp. 101
Chantilly, VA 22021
Telephone: (703) 222-9411
Ownership %: 100
**Management:**
John R. Kupferer ........................President
John R. Kupferer ........................Publisher
Patrick O'connell ........................Advertising Manager
**Editorial:**
Roland Sweet ........................Editor

69427

## LUXURY HOMES
1530 Touhy Ave.
Des Plaines, IL 60017-5080
Telephone: (708) 635-8800
FAX: (708) 635-6856

Pub. Frequency: 6/yr.
Subscrip. Rate: $18/yr. US; $30/yr. foreign
Circulation: 159,000
Circulation Type: paid
**Owner(s):**
Reed Publishing PLC
1350 E. Touhy Ave.
Des Plains, IL 60017-5080
Telephone: (708) 635-8800
Ownership %: 100
**Editorial:**
Roy L. Diez ........................Editor
**Readers:** Prospective buyers of custom homes.

67069

## MARTHA STEWART LIVING
20 W. 43rd St., 24th Fl.
New York, NY 10036
Telephone: (212) 522-2201
FAX: (212) 522-1499
Year Established: 1990
Pub. Frequency: m.
Page Size: standard
Subscrip. Rate: $3.50 newsstand
Circulation: 800,000
Circulation Type: paid
**Owner(s):**
Time Publishing Ventures, Inc.
11766 Wilshire Blvd.
Los Angeles, CA 90025
Telephone: (310) 478-8655
Ownership %: 100
**Management:**
Eric G. Thorkilsen ........................Publisher
**Editorial:**
Susan Wyland ........................Editor

26028

## METROPOLITAN HOME
1633 Broadway
New York, NY 10019
Telephone: (212) 767-6000
FAX: (212) 767-5636
Year Established: 1969
Pub. Frequency: bi-m.
Page Size: 4 color photos/art
Subscrip. Rate: $15.94/yr.; $27.94/2 yr.
Freelance Pay: by arrangement
Circulation: 750,000
Circulation Type: paid
**Owner(s):**
Hachette Magazines Inc.
1633 Broadway
New York, NY 10019
Telephone: (212) 767-6000
FAX: (212) 767-5636
Ownership %: 100
**Management:**
John Miller ........................Publisher
**Editorial:**
Donna Warner ........................Editor in Chief
**Desc.:** Edited for young, metropolitan oriented adults in the acquisitive stage of life. Showcases attainable, high - level ideas and products in a believable atmosphere of relevant service. Decorating, design, real estate, cooking, entertainment and collecting.
**Readers:** Primarily males and females, ages 25 - 44, upscale, live in major metropolitan areas.

59552

## MIDWEST LIVING
1912 Grand Ave.
Des Moines, IA 50309
Telephone: (515) 284-3000
FAX: (515) 284-3836
Year Established: 1987
Pub. Frequency: bi-m.
Page Size: standard
Subscrip. Rate: $17/yr. US; $23/yr. Canada
Circulation: 800,000
Circulation Type: paid

**Owner(s):**
Meredith Corp.
1716 Locust St.
Des Moines, IA 50336
Telephone: (515) 284-3000
Ownership %: 100
**Management:**
Tom E. Benson ........................Publisher
Matt Petersen ........................Advertising Manager
**Editorial:**
Dan Kaercher ........................Editor
**Desc.:** A regional service magazine that discusses the interests, values and lifestyles of Midwestern families. It provides a wealth of regional information on travel, events, food, dining, home and garden subjects. The magazine also features profiles of interesting Mid-Westerners and explores contemporary issues of particular relevance to people living in the nation's heartland.
**Readers:** Urban Midwestern Families

26075

## MINNESOTA HORTICULTURIST
1755 Prior Ave.
Falcon Heights, MN 55113
Telephone: (612) 645-7066
FAX: (612) 645-6709
Year Established: 1873
Pub. Frequency: 9/yr.
Page Size: standard
Subscrip. Rate: $2.50/copy; $25/yr.
Materials: 32,33
Print Process: offset
Circulation: 15,000
Circulation Type: paid
**Owner(s):**
Minnesota State Horticultural Society
1755 Prior Ave.
Falcon Heights, MN 55113
Telephone: (612) 645-7066
Ownership %: 100
**Bureau(s):**
Minnesota State Horticultural Society
161 Alderman Hall 1970 Folwell
Saint Paul, MN 55108
Telephone: (612) 645-7066
Contact: Dorothy Johnson, Executive Director
**Management:**
Michele Holzwarth ..........Advertising Manager
**Editorial:**
Lynn M. Steiner ........................Editor
Dorothy Johnson ........................Executive Director
**Desc.:** Designed for amateur northern gardeners. The bulk of the feature articles gives information on plants and their propagation and culture in a northern climate. Information is written for the experienced gardener or the gardener who wishes to become experienced. Other regular features include garden book reviews, a calendar of events, interviews of notable amateur gardeners. Most articles run 1,500 to 2,000 words. Publicity material on products is not used. Advertising rates available on request.
**Readers:** Amateur northern gardeners.
**Deadline:** story-3 mo. prior to pub. date; news-3 mo.; photo-3 mo.; ads-2 mo.

26076

## NATIONAL GARDENER, THE
4401 Magnolia Ave.
St. Louis, MO 63110
Telephone: (314) 776-7574
FAX: (314) 776-5108
Pub. Frequency: bi-m.
Page Size: standard
Subscrip. Rate: $6.50/yr.; $18/3 yr.
Circulation: 30,000
Circulation Type: paid

**Materials Accepted/Included:** 01-Business news 02-By-line articles 03-Fashion news 04-Food news 05-Freelance copy 06-Letters to editor 07-Real estate news 08-Sports news 09-Travel news 10-Book rev. 11-Movie rev. 12-Music rev. 13-TV rev. 14-Theater rev. 15-Coming events 16-Obituaries 17-Question & answer 18-Social announcements 19-Artwork 20-Cartoons 21-Photos 22-TV listings 23-Audio rec. 24-Video rec. 25-Books 26-Films/film clips 27-Personnel news 28-Press releases 29-New product news/photos 30-Trade lit. 31-Contracts awarded 32-Display adv. 33-Classified adv.

6-70

**Owner(s):**
National Council of State Garden Clubs, Inc.
4401 Magnolia Ave.
Saint Louis, MO 63110
Telephone: (314) 776-7574
Ownership %: 100
**Management:**
Eleanor Graem Yeates ........................President
Dorris Kracke ....................Advertising Manager
**Editorial:**
Susan Davidson ..........................................Editor
**Desc.:** Keeps the membership informed on organizational matters, civic development, beautification, pollution, conservation, education, garden therapy, world gardening, work with youth and aged, handicapped, underprivileged, land use, historic restoration and preservation, historic trails and scholarships to college and high school students.
**Readers:** Garden Club members, Plant Society members, conservation department, forest service, parks department, and universities.

66864

**NATIONAL GARDENING**
180 Flynn Ave.
Burlington, VT 05401
Telephone: (802) 863-1308
FAX: (802) 863-5962
Year Established: 1977
Pub. Frequency: bi-m.
Page Size: standard
Subscrip. Rate: $3 newsstand; $18/yr. US; $24/yr. foreign
Materials: 32,33
Circulation: 200,000
Circulation Type: paid
**Owner(s):**
National Gardening Association
180 Flynn Ave.
Burlington, VT 05401
Telephone: (802) 863-1308
Ownership %: 100
**Management:**
David E. Els ...........................................President
David E. Els ...........................................Publisher
Robert Bennett .................Advertising Manager
Betsy Pond ........................Circulation Manager
Alison Watt .......................Production Manager
**Editorial:**
Michael MacCaskey ..................Editor in Chief
Victoria Congdon ....................Managing Editor
**Desc.:** Provides complete, current and useful information about growing vegetables, fruit and flowers for the backyard gardener as well as advanced techniques for the more experienced gardener.

65421

**NORTHERN CALIFORNIA HOME & GARDEN**
P.O. Box 51823
Palo Alto, CA 94303-0724
Telephone: (415) 368-8800
FAX: (415) 368-6251
Year Established: 1987
Pub. Frequency: m.
Page Size: standard
Subscrip. Rate: $16/yr.
Circulation: 72,000
Circulation Type: controlled
**Owner(s):**
Westar Media, Inc.
656 Bair Island Rd., 2nd Fl.
Redwood City, CA 94063
Telephone: (415) 368-8800
Ownership %: 100
**Management:**
Sloane Citron ...........................................Publisher
**Editorial:**
Ann Bertelsen ..........................................Editor

Ellen Zaslow ..............................Art Director
Susannah Clark ........................Associate Editor
**Desc.:** Articles on California art, architecture, furniture, and interior design.
**Readers:** Aimed at design-conscious affluent homeowners in the northern California counties.

25901

**OLD-HOUSE JOURNAL, THE**
2 Main St.
Gloucester, MA 01930-5726
Telephone: (508) 283-3200
FAX: (508) 283-4629
Year Established: 1973
Pub. Frequency: 6/yr.
Page Size: standard
Subscrip. Rate: $4 newsstand; $24/yr.
Materials: 02,05,06,10,15,17,19,21,25,29, 30,32,33
Print Process: web offset
Circulation: 153,096
Circulation Type: paid
**Owner(s):**
Dovetale Publishers
2 Main St.
Gloucester, MA 01930-5726
Telephone: (508) 283-3200
Ownership %: 100
**Management:**
Patricia Poore ..........................................Publisher
**Editorial:**
Gordon Bock ..........................................Editor
Laura Marshall ........................Managing Editor
Lynn Elliott ..........................Assistant Editor
**Desc.:** Ideas, techniques, products, how-to articles all aimed at the restoration, maintenance and decoration of houses built prior to 1940. Articles run 2-4 pages. Emphasis on period decoration and historically appropriate restoration. By-lined articles sought that deal with vintage houses. Departments include: Products for the Old House, Book Reviews, Case Histories of Old-House Restoration.
**Readers:** Old-house owners, interior designers, architects, contractors.
**Deadline:** story-2 mo. prior to pub. date; news-2 mo. prior to pub. date; photo-2 mo. prior to pub. date; ads-75 days prior to pub. date

25522

**ORGANIC GARDENING**
33 E. Minor St.
Emmaus, PA 18049
Telephone: (215) 967-5171
FAX: (215) 967-8956
Year Established: 1942
Pub. Frequency: 9/yr.
Page Size: standard
Subscrip. Rate: $25/yr.
Circulation: 735,000
Circulation Type: paid
**Owner(s):**
Rodale Press
33 E. Minor St.
Emmaus, PA 18098
Telephone: (215) 967-5171
Ownership %: 100
**Editorial:**
Stevie O. Daniels ............................Exec. Editor
Michael McGrath ..........................................Editor
Scott M. Stephens ........................Art Director
Emilie Whitcomb ..............................Art Director
T. L. Gettings ..........................................Photo
Rob Cardillo ..........................................Photo

**Desc.:** Organic Gardening is America's leading gardening magazine, helping people build richer, more productive lives. The magazine covers fruit and vegetable growing, along with ornamentals, landscaping and lawn care. Organic Gardening also features processing and preparation of healthful food in the gardeners's kitchen; home and grounds improvements; home-working activities; and other aspects of an active lifestyle.
**Readers:** Gardeners.

68728

**ORIGINAL HOME PLANS**
34 Industrial Pl.
Middletown, CT 06457
Telephone: (203) 632-1064
FAX: (203) 632-0712
Mailing Address:
  P.O. Box 1717
  Middletown, CT 06457
Year Established: 1987
Pub. Frequency: q.
Subscrip. Rate: $12.64/yr.
Circulation: 115,720
Circulation Type: paid
**Owner(s):**
Garlinghouse Co., Inc.
34 Industrial Park Pl.
Middletown, CT 06457
Telephone: (203) 632-1064
Ownership %: 100
**Editorial:**
Whitney B. Garlinghouse .........................Editor

68729

**OWNER BUILT HOME PLANS**
34 Industrial Park Pl.
Middletown, CT 06457
Telephone: (203) 632-1064
FAX: (203) 632-0712
Mailing Address:
  P.O. Box 1717
  Middletown, CT 06457
Year Established: 1988
Pub. Frequency: q.
Subscrip. Rate: $12.64/yr.
Circulation: 115,720
Circulation Type: paid
**Owner(s):**
Garlinghouse Co., Inc.
34 Industrial Park Pl.
Middletown, CT 06457
Telephone: (203) 632-1064
Ownership %: 100
**Editorial:**
Whitney B. Garlinghouse .........................Editor

69455

**PHOENIX HOME & GARDEN**
P.O. Box 34308
Phoenix, AZ 85067
Telephone: (602) 234-0804
Year Established: 1980
Pub. Frequency: m.
Page Size: standard
Subscrip. Rate: $2.95 newsstand; $19/yr.
Circulation: 38,249
Circulation Type: paid
**Owner(s):**
H.G., Inc.
Box 34308
Phoenix, AZ 85067
Telephone: (602) 234-0804
Ownership %: 100
**Editorial:**
Mary Chesterfield ..........................................Editor

26082

**PLANTS & GARDENS: BROOKLYN BOTANIC GARDEN RECORD**
1000 Washington Ave.
Brooklyn, NY 11225-1099
Telephone: (718) 941-4044
FAX: (718) 857-2430

Year Established: 1945
Pub. Frequency: q.
Page Size: 4 color photos/art
Subscrip. Rate: $25/yr.
Circulation: 25,000
Circulation Type: controlled
**Owner(s):**
Brooklyn Botanic Garden
1000 Washington Ave.
Brooklyn, NY 11225
Telephone: (718) 941-4044
Ownership %: 100
**Editorial:**
Barbara Pesch ..........................Executive Editor
**Desc.:** By-line articles deal with horticulture and gardening. Each issue covers a specific phase of gardening, edited by a guest editor. A typical theme might be pruning, fragrance gardening, or bonsai. Also covers tools, methods, planting procedures, fertilizers, diseases, and plant foods.
**Readers:** Primarily owners of homes with gardens or persons generally interested in gardening.

66330

**REMODELED HOMES**
1350 E. Touhy
Des Plaines, IL 60018
Telephone: (708) 635-8800
FAX: (708) 635-9950
Mailing Address:
  P.O. Box 5080
  Des Plaines, IL 60018
Year Established: 1990
Pub. Frequency: q.
Page Size: standard
Subscrip. Rate: $3.95/copy
Circulation: 211,000
Circulation Type: controlled & paid
**Owner(s):**
Cahners Publishing Co.
1350 E. Touhy
Des Plaines, IL 60017-5080
Telephone: (708) 635-8800
Ownership %: 100
**Management:**
Arnold Consdorf ...........................................Publisher
**Editorial:**
Roy L. Diez ..........................................Editor
Laura Hengstler ........................Managing Editor
**Desc.:** Serves the two major influences that must come together to execute a successful addition/alteration remodeling project; the professional remodeler and the consumer. Offers residential remodeling ideas for the consumer.

26085

**SUNSET**
80 Willow Rd.
Menlo Park, CA 94025-3691
Telephone: (510) 321-3600
FAX: (510) 321-0551
Year Established: 1898
Pub. Frequency: m.
Page Size: standard
Subscrip. Rate: $21/yr.
Circulation: 1,750,000
Circulation Type: paid
**Owner(s):**
Sunset Publishing Corp.
80 Willow Rd.
Menlo Park, CA 94025-3691
Telephone: (510) 321-3600
Ownership %: 100
**Bureau(s):**
Sunset Magazine
11766 Wilshire Blvd.
Los Angeles, CA 90010
Telephone: (310) 268-7200

**Materials Accepted/Included:** 01-Business news 02-By-line articles 03-Fashion news 04-Food news 05-Freelance copy 06-Letters to editor 07-Real estate news 08-Sports news 09-Travel news 10-Book rev. 11-Movie rev. 12-Music rev. 13-TV rev. 14-Theater rev. 15-Coming events 16-Obituaries 17-Question & answer 18-Social announcements 19-Artwork 20-Cartoons 21-Photos 22-TV listings 23-Audio rec. 24-Video rec. 25-Books 26-Films/film clips 27-Personnel news 28-Press releases 29-New product news/photos 30-Trade lit. 31-Contracts awarded 32-Display adv. 33-Classified adv.

6-71

Sunset Magazine
500 Union St., Ste. 600
Seattle, WA 98101
Telephone: (206) 682-3993
Contact: Steve Lorton, Editor
**Management:**
Robin Wolauer .........................President
Stephen Seabolt ........................Publisher
Brianne Miller ..........Public Relations Manager
**Editorial:**
William Marken ..........................Editor
**Desc.:** Research & develop stories for four
　subject areas-travel, gardening, homes &
　food-which set the West apart from the
　rest of country.
**Readers:** Upscale western homeowners.

26088

**TEMAS, US EDITION**
300 W. 55th St., Ste. 14P
New York, NY 10019-5172
Telephone: (212) 582-4750
Year Established: 1950
Pub. Frequency: m.
Page Size: standard
Subscrip. Rate: $2 newsstand; $19/yr.
Circulation: 114,000
Circulation Type: paid
**Owner(s):**
Lolita De La Vega
300 W. 55th St., Ste. 14P
New York, NY 10019
Telephone: (212) 582-4750
Ownership %: 100
**Management:**
Lolita De La Vega ....................Publisher
**Editorial:**
Lolita De La Vega ....................Editor in Chief
Jose Luis Alvarez ....................Assistant Editor
**Desc.:** Edited for home families in general.
　Feature general topics include articles
　on fashions, home decorations, recipes,
　interviews with artists and celebrities,
　beauty and graphic current events of
　special interest for Spanish speaking
　people in the U.S.

65989

**TRADITIONAL HOME**
1716 Locust St.
Des Moines, IA 50309-3023
Telephone: (515) 284-3762
FAX: (515) 284-2083
Year Established: 1985
Pub. Frequency: bi-m.
Subscrip. Rate: $3.50 newsstand; $18/yr.
Materials: 06,25,29
Freelance Pay: varies
Circulation: 700,000
Circulation Type: paid
**Owner(s):**
Meredith Corp.
1716 Locust St.
Des Moines, IA 50336
Telephone: (515) 284-3762
Ownership %: 100
**Editorial:**
Karol DeWulf Nickell ....................Editor

66594

**UNIQUE HOMES**
801 Second Ave., No. 11
New York, NY 10017-4706
Telephone: (212) 599-3377
Year Established: 1972
Pub. Frequency: 8/yr.
Subscrip. Rate: $27.97/yr.
Materials: 33
Circulation: 70,746
Circulation Type: paid
**Owner(s):**
Unique Homes Magazine, Inc.
**Management:**
Richard Friese ..........................Publisher
**Editorial:**
Diane Berry ..........................Editor in Chief
Rick Goodwin ..........................Editor

26094

**WOMAN'S DAY GARDENING &
OUTDOOR LIVING IDEAS**
1633 Broadway
New York, NY 10019
Telephone: (212) 767-5924
FAX: (212) 767-5612
Year Established: 1988
Page Size: 4 color photos/art
Subscrip. Rate: $2.95/issue
Circulation: 450,000
Circulation Type: paid
**Owner(s):**
Hachette Filipacchi Magazines, Inc.
1633 Broadway
New York, NY 10019
Telephone: (212) 767-6000
Ownership %: 100
**Management:**
Susan S. Buckley ......................Vice President
Susan S. Buckley ......................Publisher
**Editorial:**
Carolyn Gatto ..........................Editor in Chief
Marion Lyons ..........................Editor
Shari Gurmain ..........................Associate Publisher

26092

**WOMAN'S DAY HOME
DECORATING IDEAS**
1633 Broadway
New York, NY 10019
Telephone: (212) 767-5924
FAX: (212) 767-5612
Year Established: 1962
Pub. Frequency: 4/yr.
Page Size: standard
Subscrip. Rate: $2.95/issue
Circulation: 600,000
Circulation Type: paid
**Owner(s):**
Hachette Filipacchi Magazines, Inc.
1633 Broadway
New York, NY 10019
Telephone: (212) 767-6000
Ownership %: 100
**Management:**
Susan S. Buckley ......................Vice President
Susan S. Buckley ......................Publisher
**Editorial:**
Carolyn Gatto ..........................Editor in Chief
Cynthia Edmends ......................Editor
Shari Gurmain ..........................Associate Publisher

56395

**WOMAN'S DAY SPECIALS & HOME
DESIGN**
1633 Broadway, 42nd Fl.
New York, NY 10019
Telephone: (212) 767-6815
Pub. Frequency: q.
Page Size: standard
Subscrip. Rate: $2.25/April issue;
　$2.50/other issues; $2.75/Canada
Freelance Pay: varies
Circulation: 800,000
Circulation Type: paid
**Owner(s):**
CBS Magazines, Div. of CBS, Inc.
1515 Broadway
New York, NY 10036
Telephone: (212) 719-6000
Ownership %: 100
**Management:**
Peter Diamandis ......................President
Gordon Burkhard ......................Publisher
**Editorial:**
Gale C. Steves ..........................Editor in Chief
Patricia Clemens ......................Editor
**Desc.:** Directed toward homeowners
　interested in decorating or renovating
　their homes. Focus is on photographs
　and articles showing new
　design concepts and the latest products
　available for their use.

**Readers:** Women. Profile determined by
　subject matter.

26023

**WORKBENCH**
700 W. 47th St., Ste. 310
Kansas City, MO 64112
Telephone: (816) 531-5730
FAX: (816) 531-3873
Year Established: 1957
Pub. Frequency: bi-m.
Page Size: standard
Subscrip. Rate: $2.95 newsstand;
　$12.95/yr.
Freelance Pay: varies
Circulation: 861427
Circulation Type: paid
**Owner(s):**
KC Publishing, Inc.
700 W. 47th St., Ste. 310
Kansas City, MO 64112
Telephone: (816) 531-5730
Ownership %: 100
**Bureau(s):**
New York Bureau
50 E. 42nd St.
New York, NY 10017
Telephone: (212) 697-7990
Contact: Pat Venegia, Manager

Sherborn Mass. Bureau
Telephone: (617) 655-4178
Contact: Richard Husselbee, Manager

Los Angeles Bureau
Telephone: (714) 859-4985
Contact: John Lawson, Manager

San Francisco Bureau
Telephone: (510) 932-7688
Contact: Ray Turpin, Manager

Chicago
230 N. Michigan Ave.
Chicago, IL 60601
Telephone: (312) 726-7012
Contact: Roger O'Sullivan, Manager
**Management:**
John C. Prebich ......................President
John C. Prebich ......................Publisher
Warren Lampe ..........Classified Adv. Manager
**Editorial:**
Lawrence F. Okrend ..................Senior Editor
A. Robert Gould ......................Editor
Ami Johnson ..........................Managing Editor
Kip Chen ..........................Assistant Editor
**Desc.:** Factual articles dealing with home
　workshop projects, home repair,
　improvement and maintenance from the
　do-it-yourself point of view. Virtually
　every article is illustrated with
　photographs, diagrams, sketches, etc.
　As much how-to-do-it detail as possible
　is provided in text and illustrations.
　Departments include: Shop Tips,
　Shopping with Bob Edwards (new
　products), Book Reviews, Energy
　Answers, Reader Service, Letters.
**Readers:** Home workshop & do-it-yourself
　home improvement enthusiasts and
　homeowners; median age 48.8; median
　income $31,134.
**Deadline:** 5 mos. prior to pub. date

## Group 642-Literary

69391

**AMERICAN VOICE, THE**
332 W. Broadway, Ste. 1215
Louisville, KY 40202
Telephone: (502) 562-0045
Year Established: 1985
Pub. Frequency: q.
Page Size: 14,17
Subscrip. Rate: $5 newsstand; $15/yr.
Circulation: 2,000
Circulation Type: paid

**Owner(s):**
Kentucky Foundation for Women, Inc.
332 W. Broadway, Ste. 1215
Louisville, KY 40202
Telephone: (502) 562-0045
Ownership %: 100
**Editorial:**
Frederick Smock ......................Editor
**Desc.:** Literary journal.

25617

**ANTAEUS**
100 W. Broad St.
Hopewell, NJ 08525
Telephone: (609) 466-4748
FAX: (609) 466-4706
Year Established: 1970
Pub. Frequency: s-a.
Page Size: standard
Subscrip. Rate: $15 newsstand; $30/4
　issues
Materials: 19,30
Freelance Pay: $10/printed page
Circulation: 5,000
Circulation Type: paid
**Owner(s):**
Ecco Press, Ltd.
100 W. Broad St.
Hopewell, NJ 08525
Telephone: (609) 466-4748
Ownership %: 100
**Management:**
Daniel Halpern ......................Publisher
Vincent Janoski ..................Production Manager
William Crager ....................Promotion Manager
**Editorial:**
Daniel Halpern ......................Executive Editor
Daniel Halpern ......................Editor
William Crager ......................Assistant Editor
Heather Winterer ....................Assistant Editor
**Desc.:** Features works by unknown or
　lesser known poets and writers along
　with those whose literary reputations are
　firmly established. Provides an
　international assemblage of fiction,
　essays and poetry, as well as interviews
　and rare and unusual literary documents.
　Each regular issue contains short
　stories, excerpts from novels, poems
　and non-fiction articles. Often there are
　special issues devoted to a particular
　subject: autobiography, writers on
　nature, literature as pleasure, journal
　writing, to name recent ones.
**Readers:** Writers, professors, people
　interested in serious literature.

25823

**ATLANTIC MONTHLY, THE**
745 Boylston St.
Boston, MA 02116
Telephone: (617) 536-9500
Year Established: 1857
Pub. Frequency: m.
Page Size: standard
Subscrip. Rate: $17.94/yr.
Circulation: 457,343
Circulation Type: paid
**Owner(s):**
Atlantic Monthly Co.
745 Boylston St.
Boston, MA 02116
Telephone: (617) 536-9500
Ownership %: 100
**Management:**
Mortiner B. Zuckerman ........Chairman of Board
Carol J. Ference ......................Manager
Susan Blank ....................Operations Manager
**Editorial:**
C. Michael Curtis ......................Senior Editor
Jack Beatty ..........................Senior Editor
William Whitworth ......................Editor
James Fallows ..........................Editor
Cullen Murphy ......................Managing Editor
Susannah Pask ......................Advertising
James Sheridan ......................Advertising

Judy Garlan ...................................Art Director
Fred Drasner ..........................Chief Operator
Joseph T. O'Connell ..........Production Director
**Desc.:** Magazine of public affairs and the
arts. Addresses contemporary issues
through commentary, criticism, humor,
fiction, and poetry.
**Readers:** Educated, sophisticated, active
professionals.

68958

**BABY SUE**
P.O. Box 1111
Decatur, GA 30031-1111
Telephone: (404) 875-8951
Year Established: 1985
Pub. Frequency: 2/yr.
Page Size: standard
Subscrip. Rate: $3/copy; $12/yr.
Materials: 06,12,19,20,23.25,28,32
Print Process: offset
Circulation: 5,000
Circulation Type: paid
**Owner(s):**
Baby Sue
P.O. Box 1111
Decatur, GA 30031-1111
Telephone: (404) 875-8951
Ownership %: 100
**Editorial:**
Don W. Seven ...................................Editor
**Desc.:** Contains humor and social satires.

68955

**BELLES LETTRES**
11151 Captain's Walk Ct.
North Potomac, MD 20878
Telephone: (301) 294-0278
FAX: (301) 294-0023
Year Established: 1985
Pub. Frequency: q.
Page Size: standard
Subscrip. Rate: $20/yr. individuals; $40/yr.
institutions
Materials: 05,10
Circulation: 5,000
Circulation Type: paid
**Owner(s):**
Belles Lettres
11151 Captain's Walk Ct.
North Potomac, MD 20878
Telephone: (301) 294-0278
Ownership %: 100
**Editorial:**
Janet Mullaney ...................................Editor
**Desc.:** Founded to preserve, promote, and
celebrate women's writing. Includes
interviews, rediscoveries, and
retrospectives.

25631

**BOSTON REVIEW**
33 Harrison Ave.
Boston, MA 02111
Telephone: (617) 350-5353
FAX: (617) 350-6633
Year Established: 1975
Pub. Frequency: bi-m.
Page Size: tabloid
Subscrip. Rate: $3 newsstand; $15/yr.
individual; $18/yr. institution
Freelance Pay: $100-$300
Circulation: 20,000
Circulation Type: controlled
**Owner(s):**
Boston Critic, Inc.
33 Harrison Ave.
Boston, MA 02111
Telephone: (617) 350-5353
Ownership %: 100
**Editorial:**
Kim Cooper ...................Managing Editor

**Desc.:** Publishes in-depth reviews and
comprehensive essays on the natural
and social sciences, literature, music,
painting, film, photography, dance and
theater. Also contains new fiction and
poetry, and excerpts from new books.
**Readers:** Well-educated, interested in
good writing.

58572

**CHAUCER REVIEW, THE**
820 N. University Dr., Ste. C
University Park, PA 16802
Telephone: (814) 865-1327
Year Established: 1966
Pub. Frequency: q.
Page Size: standard
Subscrip. Rate: $27.50/yr. individual US;
$35/yr. foreign; $40/yr. institution US;
$48/yr. foreign
Materials: 10
Circulation: 1,387
Circulation Type: paid
**Owner(s):**
Pennsylvania State University Press, The
USB-1c University Park
State College, PA 16802-1003
Telephone: (814) 865-1327
FAX: (814) 863-1408
Ownership %: 100
**Editorial:**
Robert W. Frank, Jr. ...........................Editor
**Desc.:** Publishes studies of the text,
sources and analogues, language, style,
structure, and themes of Chaucer's
poetry, as well as articles on medieval
literature, philosophy, theology, and
mythography relevant to a study of the
poet. Acts as a forum for the
presentation and discussion of the most
exciting new ideas about Chaucer and
the literature of the Middle Ages.
**Readers:** Scholars in the fields
represented.

68954

**CHICAGO REVIEW**
5801 S. Kenwood
Chicago, IL 60637
Telephone: (312) 702-0887
Year Established: 1946
Pub. Frequency: q.
Page Size: 6 X 9
Subscrip. Rate: $5 newsstand; $15/yr.
individual; $35/yr. institution; plus $5
foreign postage
Materials: 05,10,11,12,14,21,25,32
Freelance Pay: in copies
Print Process: offset
Circulation: 2,500
Circulation Type: paid
**Owner(s):**
Chicago Review, The University of Chicago
5801 S. Kenwood
Chicago, IL 60637
Telephone: (312) 702-0887
Ownership %: 100
**Editorial:**
David Nicholls ...................................Editor
**Desc.:** International journal of writing and
cultural exchange; includes poetry,
fiction, essays, reviews, and interviews.
**Readers:** Highly literate audience.

58575

**COMPARATIVE LITERATURE
STUDIES**
820 N. University Dr., Ste. C
University Park, PA 16802
Telephone: (814) 865-1327
Year Established: 1960
Pub. Frequency: q.
Page Size: standard
Subscrip. Rate: $27.50/yr. individual US;
$35/yr. foreign; $40/yr. institution US;
$48/yr. foreign
Materials: 10

Circulation: 1,000
Circulation Type: paid
**Owner(s):**
The Pennsylvania State University
USB 1C
University Park, PA 16802-1003
Telephone: (814) 865-1327
FAX: (814) 863-1408
Ownership %: 100
**Editorial:**
Robert R. Edwards ...........................Editor
Patrick Cheney ...............................Editor
Gerhard P. Strasser ...........................Editor
**Desc.:** Work of eminent critics, scholars,
theorists, and literary historians. Their
essays range across the rivh traditions
of Europe and North and South America
and examine the literary relations
between East Asia and the West. They
also explore movements, themes, forms,
the history of ideas, relations between
authors, and the foundations of criticism
and theory. Each issue includes reviews
of significant books by prominent
scholars.

69485

**CREAM CITY REVIEW**
413 Curtin Hall
Milwaukee, WI 53201
Telephone: (414) 229-4708
FAX: (414) 229-6329
Year Established: 1975
Pub. Frequency: s-a.
Subscrip. Rate: $10/yr.
Circulation: 2,500
Circulation Type: paid
**Owner(s):**
University of Wisconsin-Milwaukee
English Department
Curtin Hall, Box 413
Milwaukee, WI 53201
Telephone: (414) 229-4708
Ownership %: 100
**Editorial:**
Sandra Nelson, Ed. ...........................Editor

69492

**EARLY AMERICAN LITERATURE**
P.O. Box 2288
Chapel Hill, NC 27515-2288
Telephone: (919) 966-3561
FAX: (919) 966-3829
Year Established: 1966
Pub. Frequency: 3/yr.
Page Size: standard
Subscrip. Rate: $18/yr.
Circulation: 800
Circulation Type: paid
**Owner(s):**
University of North Carolina Press
P.O. Box 2288
Chapel Hill, NC 27515-2288
Telephone: (919) 966-3561
Ownership %: 100
**Editorial:**
Philip Gura ...................................Editor

54009

**EXPLICATOR, THE**
1319 18th St., N.W.
Washington, DC 20036-1802
Telephone: (202) 296-6267
FAX: (202) 296-5149
Year Established: 1941
Pub. Frequency: q.
Page Size: pocket
Subscrip. Rate: $29/yr. individuals; $52/yr.
institutions
Circulation: 1,952
Circulation Type: paid
**Owner(s):**
Heldref Publications
1319 18th St., N.W.
Washington, DC 20036-1802
Telephone: (202) 296-6267
Ownership %: 100

**Management:**
Walter E. Beach .............................Publisher
Raymond M. Rallo ...........Advertising Manager
Catherine Welker ...........Circulation Manager
**Editorial:**
Nancy Geltman ...................................Editor
Kerri P. Kilbane ...............Promotions Manager
**Desc.:** Offers insightful literary
interpretations. Focuses on "explication
de texte" in prose and poetry. Each
issue contains 25 to 30 essays.
**Readers:** Students & teachers of literature

25862

**HARPER'S MAGAZINE**
666 Broadway
New York, NY 10012
Telephone: (212) 614-6500
Year Established: 1850
Pub. Frequency: m.
Page Size: standard
Subscrip. Rate: $2.95/issue; $18/yr.
Freelance Pay: $2,500-$5,000
Circulation: 205,000
Circulation Type: paid
**Owner(s):**
Harper's Magazine Foundation
666 Broadway
New York, NY 10012
Telephone: (212) 614-6500
Ownership %: 100
**Management:**
John R. Macarthur ...........................Publisher
Jeanne Dubi ...........................Office Manager
**Editorial:**
Michael Pollan ...........................Exec. Editor
Lewis H. Lapham ...............................Editor
Lynn Carlson .............Vice President-Circulation
**Desc.:** Covers discussion of the arts,
letters, science, politics and economics.
Occasional short story, perhaps 2-3
times a year. No poetry.
**Readers:** They are affluent, well-educated
and active; both culturally and civically.

58576

**JOURNAL OF SPECULATIVE
PHILOSOPHY, THE**
Barbara Bldg., Ste. C
University Park, PA 16802
Telephone: (814) 865-1327
FAX: (814) 863-1408
Year Established: 1987
Pub. Frequency: q.
Page Size: 6 x 9
Subscrip. Rate: $27.50/yr. individual US;
$32.50/yr. foreign; $40/yr. institution US;
$45/yr. foreign
Materials: 10
Circulation: 330
Circulation Type: paid
**Owner(s):**
The Pennsylvania State University Press
USB 1C
University Park, PA 16802-1003
Telephone: (814) 865-1327
FAX: (814) 863-1408
Ownership %: 100
**Editorial:**
Henry W. Johnstone, Jr. .....................Editor
Carl R. Hausman ...............................Editor
**Desc.:** Systematic and interpretive essays
about basic philosophical questions.
Scholars examine the constructive
interaction between Continental and
American philosophy, as well as novel
developments in the ideas and theories
of past philosophers that have relevence
for contemporary thinkers. Also features
discussions of art, religion, and literature
that are not strictly or narrowly
philosophical. Book reviews and "News
from Abroad" are included in every
volume.
**Readers:** Scholars in the fields
represented.

**Materials Accepted/Included:** 01-Business news 02-By-line articles 03-Fashion news 04-Food news 05-Freelance copy 06-Letters to editor 07-Real estate news 08-Sports news 09-Travel news
10-Book rev. 11-Movie rev. 12-Music rev. 13-TV rev. 14-Theater rev. 15-Coming events 16-Obituaries 17-Question & answer 18-Social announcements 19-Artwork 20-Cartoons 21-Photos 22-TV listings
23-Audio rec. 24-Video rec. 25-Books 26-Films/film clips 27-Personnel news 28-Press releases 29-New product news/photos 30-Trade lit. 31-Contracts awarded 32-Display adv. 33-Classified adv.

6-73

## KENYON REVIEW, THE
64886

Kenyon College
Gambier, OH 43022
Telephone: (614) 427-3339
FAX: (614) 427-4240
Mailing Address:
  P.O. Box 8062
  Syracuse, NY 13217
Year Established: 1939
Pub. Frequency: 4/yr.
Page Size: standard
Subscrip. Rate: $7.00 newsstand; $22/yr.
  individuals; $24/yr. libraries
Materials: 02,10,25,28,20,32
Freelance Pay: $10-15/printed pg.
Print Process: web offset
Circulation: 5,500
Circulation Type: paid
Owner(s):
The Kenyon Review
Kenyon College
Gambier, OH 43022
Telephone: (614) 427-3339
FAX: (614) 427-5417
Ownership %: 100
Editorial:
Marilyn Hacker ...............................Editor
Cy Wainscott ...........................Managing Editor
Desc.: A challenging mix and meeting of
  the transgressive and the traditional in
  contemporary fiction, poetry and
  nonfiction prose. Multicultural,
  multigendered, contentious and lively.
Readers: Professionals and all sorts of
  followers of contemporary poetry and
  fiction.

## LITERARY REVIEW, THE
69505

285 Madison Ave.
Madison, NJ 07940
Telephone: (201) 593-8564
FAX: (201) 593-8510
Year Established: 1957
Pub. Frequency: q.
Page Size: 6X9
Subscrip. Rate: $5 newsstand; $18/yr. US;
  $21/yr. foreign
Materials: 34
Freelance Pay: 2 copies
Print Process: offset
Circulation: 2,150
Circulation Type: free & paid
Owner(s):
Fairleigh Dickinson University
Literary Review
285 Madison Ave.
Madison, NJ 07940
Telephone: (201) 593-8564
Ownership %: 100
Editorial:
Walter Cummins ...............................Editor
Desc.: Contemporary fiction, poetry, literary
  essays, often in English translation.
Readers: Libraries - university and large
  public, international subscriptions, book
  store sales.

## MAIRENA
69725

1656 C. Penasco
Paradise Hills
Rio Piedras, PR 00926-3127
Telephone: (809) 250-8197
Year Established: 1979
Pub. Frequency: s-a.
Page Size: standard
Subscrip. Rate: $6/yr. individuals; $15/yr.
  institutions
Circulation: 1,000
Circulation Type: paid

Owner(s):
Manuel de la Puebla
1656 C. Penasco
Paradise Hills
Rio Piedras, S.J., PR 00926-3127
Telephone: (809) 250-8197
Ownership %: 100
Management:
Manuel de la Puebla ............................Publisher
Desc.: Publishes articles on poetry,
  analysis, unpublished poems and
  commentary.

## MIDWEST POETRY REVIEW
68957

P.O. Box 4776
Rock Island, IL 61201
Telephone: (319) 391-1874
Year Established: 1980
Pub. Frequency: q.
Page Size: 8 1/2 x 10 1/2
Subscrip. Rate: $20/yr. US; $25/yr.
  Canada; $30/yr. elsewhere
Materials: 02,06,10
Freelance Pay: $10-$100
Print Process: offset
Circulation: 10000
Circulation Type: paid
Owner(s):
River City Publishers
P.O. Box 4776
Rock Island, IL 61201
Telephone: (319) 391-1874
Ownership %: 100
Editorial:
Tom Tilford, Ed. ...............................Editor
Desc.: Devoted only to poetry.

## NARRATIVE
69592

1070 Carmack Rd.
Columbus, OH 43210-1002
Telephone: (614) 292-6930
Year Established: 1993
Pub. Frequency: 3/yr.
Page Size: standard
Subscrip. Rate: $15/yr. individuals; $36
  institutions
Owner(s):
Ohio State University Press
1070 Carmack Rd.
Columbus, OH 43210-1002
Telephone: (614) 292-6930
Ownership %: 100
Editorial:
James Phelan ...............................Editor

## NEW YORKER, THE
25895

20 W. 43rd St.
New York, NY 10036
Telephone: (212) 840-3800
Year Established: 1925
Pub. Frequency: w.
Page Size: standard
Subscrip. Rate: $2.50 newsstand; $32/yr.
Materials: 32
Circulation: 808,545
Circulation Type: paid
Owner(s):
Advance Magazine Publishers, Inc.
950 Fingerboard Rd.
Staten Island, NY 10305
Telephone: (212) 840-3800
Ownership %: 100
Management:
Thomas A. Florio ...............................President
Larry Burstein ...............................Publisher
Editorial:
Tina Brown ...............................Editor
Matthew Roberts ...............................Marketing Director
Desc.: Articles, stories, verse, and artwork.
  Regular commentary on local, national,
  and international affairs.
Readers: 55% male, 45% female; 81%
  college educated, median HHI $61,515;
  median age 46.1.

## NEW YORK REVIEW OF BOOKS
25632

250 W. 57th St., Ste. 1321
New York, NY 10107
Telephone: (212) 757-8070
FAX: (212) 333-5374
Year Established: 1963
Pub. Frequency: 21/yr.
Page Size: tabloid
Subscrip. Rate: $2.95 newsstand; $45/yr.
Circulation: 120,000
Circulation Type: paid
Owner(s):
NYREV, Inc.
250 W. 57th St.
New York, NY 10107
Telephone: (212) 757-8070
Ownership %: 100
Management:
Rea S. Hederman ...............................Publisher
Mayda Sharrow ................Advertising Manager
Editorial:
Robert Silvers ...............................Editor
Barbara Epstein ...............................Editor
Catherine Tice ...................Associate Publisher
Desc.: A critical journal of books and
  ideas. Discusses such subjects as
  politics, science, education, economics,
  foreign affairs, and psychology, as well
  as the primary areas of literature and
  the arts.
Readers: Sophisticated audience of book
  readers on contemporary ideas at the
  highest level.

## PHILOSOPHY & RHETORIC
58574

820 N. Univ. Dr., Ste. C, Barbara Bldg.
University Park, PA 16802
Telephone: (814) 865-1327
Year Established: 1968
Pub. Frequency: q.
Page Size: standard
Subscrip. Rate: $27.50/yr. individuals US;
  $35/yr. foreign; $40/yr. institutions US;
  $48/yr. foreign
Materials: 10
Circulation: 783
Circulation Type: paid
Owner(s):
Pennsylvania State University Press, The
USB 1C
University Park, PA 16802-1003
Telephone: (814) 865-1327
FAX: (814) 863-1408
Ownership %: 100
Editorial:
Henry W. Johnstone, Jr. ...............................Editor
Stephen H. Browne ...............................Editor
Marie J. Secor ...............................Editor
Desc.: Publishes some of the most
  influential articles on the relations
  between philosophy and rhetoric. Topics
  include the connections between logic
  and rhetoric, the philosophical aspects
  of argumentation (including
  argumentation in philosopy itself),
  philosophical views on the nature of
  rhetoric among historical figures and
  during historical periods, philosophical
  analyses of the relation to rhetoric of
  other areas of human culture and
  thought, and psychological and
  sociological studies of rhetoric with a
  strong philosophical emphasis.
Readers: Scholars in the fields
  represented.

## POET LORE
54011

4508 Walsh St.
Bethesda, MD 20815-6006
Telephone: (202) 362-6445
Year Established: 1889
Pub. Frequency: q.

Page Size: standard
Subscrip. Rate: $24/yr. institutions; $15/yr.
  individuals
Materials: 10,32
Print Process: offset
Circulation: 650
Circulation Type: paid
Owner(s):
Writer's Center
4508 Walsh St.
Bethesda, MD 20815
Telephone: (301) 654-8664
FAX: (301) 654-8667
Ownership %: 100
Management:
Jane Fox ...............................Executive Director
Editorial:
S. Freeman ...............................Managing Editor
Desc.: Poet Lore presents the best work
  of both new and established writers.
  Interested in all schools of poetry.
Readers: 350 individuals, 300 libraries

## REVIEW OF CONTEMPORARY FICTION
69596

4241 Illinois State University
Normal, IL 61790-4241
Telephone: (309) 438-7555
FAX: (309) 437-7422
Year Established: 1981
Pub. Frequency: 3/yr.
Page Size: 6X9
Subscrip. Rate: $8 newsstand; $17/yr.
  individuals; $24/yr. institutions
Materials: 10,32
Print Process: offset
Circulation: 2,780
Circulation Type: paid
Owner(s):
Review of Contemporary Fiction, Inc.
4241 Illinois State University
Normal, IL 61790-4241
Telephone: (309) 438-7555
FAX: (309) 437-7422
Ownership %: 100
Editorial:
John O'Brien ...............................Editor
Desc.: Each issue profiles one or two
  significant but often neglected
  contemporary American authors.
  Includes fiction by the featured authors,
  interviews and critical discussions of the
  authors' work.

## SCRIBLERIAN, THE
58629

Temple University
English Dept.
Philadelphia, PA 19122
Telephone: (215) 204-4717
FAX: (215) 204-9620
Year Established: 1968
Pub. Frequency: s-a.
Page Size: pocket
Subscrip. Rate: $15/yr. individuals; $20/yr.
  libraries
Print Process: offset
Circulation: 1,300
Circulation Type: paid
Owner(s):
Arthur Weitzman
Northeastern University
Boston, MA 02115

Peter Tasch & Roy Wolper
Temple University
Dept. of English, Rm. 939
Philadelphia, PA 19122
Telephone: (215) 204-4717
Editorial:
Peter Tasch ...............................Editor
Deadline: ads-Sep., Apr.

Materials Accepted/Included: 01-Business news 02-By-line articles 03-Fashion news 04-Food news 05-Freelance copy 06-Letters to editor 07-Real estate news 08-Sports news 09-Travel news 10-Book rev. 11-Movie rev. 12-Music rev. 13-TV rev. 14-Theater rev. 15-Coming events 16-Obituaries 17-Question & answer 18-Social announcements 19-Artwork 20-Cartoons 21-Photos 22-TV listings 23-Audio rec. 24-Video rec. 25-Books 26-Films/film clips 27-Personnel news 28-Press releases 29-New product news/photos 30-Trade lit. 31-Contracts awarded 32-Display adv. 33-Classified adv.

## SPITBALL
68956
6224 Collegevue
Cincinnati, OH 45224-1922
Telephone: (513) 541-4296
Year Established: 1981
Pub. Frequency: q.
Page Size: pocket
Subscrip. Rate: $5 newsstand; $16/yr.
Materials: 02,10,19,20,21,32,33
Circulation: 10,000
Circulation Type: paid
**Owner(s):**
Spitball
6224 Collegevue
Cincinnati, OH 45224-1922
Telephone: (513) 541-4296
Ownership %: 100
**Editorial:**
Mike Shannon ..............................Editor
**Desc.:** Completely devoted to baseball
poetry and fiction.

## STUDIES IN AMERICAN FICTION
69602
Dept. of English
Northeastern University
Boston, MA 02115
Telephone: (617) 437-3687
Year Established: 1973
Pub. Frequency: s-a.
Page Size: standard
Subscrip. Rate: $7/yr. individuals; $12/yr.
  institutions
Circulation: 1,350
Circulation Type: controlled
**Owner(s):**
Northeastern University
Dept. of English
Boston, MA 02115
Telephone: (617) 437-3687
**Editorial:**
Mary Loeffelholz ..........................Editor

## SYMPOSIUM
54012
1319 18th St., N.W.
Washington, DC 20036-1802
Telephone: (202) 296-6267
FAX: (202) 296-5149
Year Established: 1946
Pub. Frequency: q.
Page Size: standard
Subscrip. Rate: $32/yr. individuals;
  $640/yr. institutions; add $10 outside of
  US
Circulation: 614
Circulation Type: paid
**Owner(s):**
Heldref Publications
1319 18th St., N.W.
Washington, DC 20036-1802
Telephone: (202) 296-6267
Ownership %: 100
**Management:**
Walter E. Beach ................................Publisher
Raymond M. Rollo ...........Advertising Manager
Catherine Welker ...............Circulation Manager
Kerri P. Kilbane ..................Promotion Manager
**Editorial:**
Jeanne Bebo ..............................Editor
**Desc.:** Includes research on authors,
  themes, periods, genres, works, and
  theory, frequently through comparative
  studies. Works are cited, and often
  discussed, in the original language.
**Readers:** Teachers, students and
  researchers.

## WEST HILLS BULLETIN
54004
5136 N.E. Glisan
Portland, OR 97213
Telephone: (503) 231-7628
Year Established: 1987
Pub. Frequency: m.

Page Size: tabloid
Subscrip. Rate: $5.95/yr.
Materials: 02,06,07,09,11,13,20,24,25
Freelance Pay: $.05/word
Print Process: web offset
Circulation: 7,000
Circulation Type: controlled & free
**Owner(s):**
Spectrum Publishing
5136 N.E. Glisan
Portland, OR 97213
Telephone: (503) 231-7628
Ownership %: 100
**Management:**
Lisa Lybrand ...........Customer Service Manager
**Editorial:**
Debbie West ..............................Editor
Bert Lybrand ..................Advertising Editor
Betty Sessions ..............................Miscellaneous
Luci Chiotti ..............................Miscellaneous
**Readers:** Upscale district of Portland.

## YELLOW SILK
69613
P.O. Box 6374
Albany, CA 94706
Telephone: (510) 644-4188
Year Established: 1981
Pub. Frequency: q.
Page Size: standard
Subscrip. Rate: $38/yr. institutions
Circulation: 16,000
Circulation Type: paid
**Owner(s):**
Verygraphics
P.O. Box 6374
Albany, CA 94706
Telephone: (510) 644-4188
**Editorial:**
Lily Pond ..............................Editor
Marnie Purple ..............................Editor

# Group 644-Mechanics & Science

## ASTRONOMY
26097
21027 Crossroads Circle
Waukesha, WI 53187-1612
Telephone: (414) 796-8776
FAX: (414) 796-1142
Mailing Address:
  P.O. Box 1612
  Waukeshau, WI 53187-1612
Year Established: 1973
Pub. Frequency: m.
Page Size: standard
Subscrip. Rate: $2.95 newsstand; $24/yr.
Freelance Pay: varies
Circulation: 169,059
Circulation Type: paid
**Owner(s):**
Kalmbach Publishing Co.
21027 Crossroads Circle
Waukesha, WI 53187-1612
Telephone: (414) 796-8776
Ownership %: 100
**Management:**
Russ Larson ..............................Publisher
Kim Bennett ..................Advertising Manager
**Editorial:**
Robert Burnham ..............................Editor
Rhoda Sherwood ..................Managing Editor
**Desc.:** Popular level consumer science
  magazine. Covers current research and
  developments in astronomy, celestial
  events almanac, astronomy news,
  constellation and mythology discussion,
  equipment, astronomical photography,
  and celestial observation.
**Readers:** Science-oriented people: novice,
  intermediate, and serious astronomy
  enthusiasts.

## AVIATION HERITAGE
66331
602 S. King St., Ste. 300
Leesburg, VA 22075
Telephone: (703) 771-9400
FAX: (703) 777-4627
Year Established: 1989
Pub. Frequency: bi- m.
Subscrip. Rate: $16.95/yr.
Freelance Pay: varies
Circulation: 90,000
Circulation Type: paid
**Owner(s):**
Cowles History Group
602 S. King St., Ste. 300
Leesburg, VA 22075
Telephone: (703) 771-9400
Ownership %: 100
**Management:**
Gregg Oehler ..............................Publisher
**Editorial:**
Arthur H. Sanfelici ..............................Editor

## DISCOVER
54062
500 S. Buena Vista
Burbank, CA 91521-6012
Telephone: (818) 973-4320
Year Established: 1980
Pub. Frequency: m.
Page Size: standard
Subscrip. Rate: $3.50 newsstand;
  $29.95/yr.
Materials: 32
Freelance Pay: negotiable
Circulation: 1,000,000
Circulation Type: paid
**Owner(s):**
Walt Disney Magazine Publishing Group
500 S. Buena Vista
Burbank, CA 91521-6012
Telephone: (818) 973-4320
Ownership %: 100
**Management:**
Lee Rosenbaum ..............................Publisher
**Editorial:**
Paul Hoffman ..................Editor in Chief
Bob Lee ..................Marketing Director
**Desc.:** A science newsmagazine which
  provides extensive coverage of science
  and technology in non-technical language. Contains articles on
  subjects such as astronomy, behavior,
  chemistry, computers, education,
  environment, mathematics, space and
  technology. Automation and robotics
  may occasionally be covered. Regularly
  features newsbriefs, essays, people in
  science, inventions, games and science-related arts reviews.
**Readers:** Upscale non-scientist audience.

## HOME MECHANIX
25993
2 Park Ave.
New York, NY 10016
Telephone: (212) 779-5000
FAX: (212) 725-3281
Year Established: 1928
Pub. Frequency: 10 issues/yr.
Page Size: standard
Subscrip. Rate: $9.97/yr.; $15.97/2 yrs.;
  $20.97/3 yrs.
Materials: 28,29,30,32,33
Circulation: 1,000,000
Circulation Type: paid
**Owner(s):**
Times Mirror Magazines, Inc.
2 Park Ave.
New York, NY 10016
Telephone: (212) 779-5000
Ownership %: 100
**Management:**
John Crawley ..............................Publisher
**Editorial:**
Michael K. Chotiner ..................Editor in Chief

**Desc.:** We cover all areas of interest to
  readers actively engaged in managing
  their houses and cars. Many of our
  articles show readers how to make
  improvements, repairs and maintenance
  tasks themselves. Others advise readers
  on how to get professional help. About
  40 percent of our material is done by
  outside contributors. Articles are
  presented with many photo, diagrams
  and charts.
**Readers:** Primarily male (42 years median)
  homeowner and car owner.

## INNOVATIONS & IDEAS
69105
951 S. Oxford, No. 109
Los Angeles, CA 90006
Telephone: (213) 732-3477
FAX: (213) 732-9123
Year Established: 1991
Pub. Frequency: q.
Subscrip. Rate: $29.99/yr.
Materials: 01,02,03,04,05,06,07,08,09,10,
  11,12,13,14,15,16,17,18,19,2,21,22,23,
  24,25,26,27,28,29,30,31,32,33
Freelance Pay: $.20-.50/wd.
Print Process: web
Circulation: 120000
Circulation Type: controlled & paid
**Owner(s):**
Publishing & Business Consultants
951 S. Oxford, No. 109
Los Angeles, CA 90006
Telephone: (213) 732-3477
FAX: (213) 732-9123
Ownership %: 100
**Editorial:**
Andeson Napoleon Atia ..............................Editor
**Desc.:** Covers breakthroughs in scientific
  research and high technology fields, with
  emphasis on human applications.
**Deadline:** story-2 wks. prior to pub. date;
  news-2 wks. prior to pub. date; photo-2
  wks. prior to pub. date; ads-90 days
  prior to pub. date

## MECANICA POPULAR
26099
6355 N.W. 36th St.
Virginia Gardens, FL 33166
Telephone: (305) 871-6400
FAX: (305) 871-6908
Year Established: 1947
Pub. Frequency: m.
Page Size: standard
Subscrip. Rate: $22.50/yr.
Circulation: 243,000
Circulation Type: paid
**Owner(s):**
Editorial America, S.A.
6355 N.W. 36th St.
Virginia Gardens, FL 33166
Telephone: (305) 871-6400
Ownership %: 100
**Management:**
Giorgio Cerboncini ...........Advertising Manager
**Editorial:**
Santiago J. Villazon ..............................Editor
**Deadline:** 90 days prior to pub. date

## NATURAL HISTORY
25891
79th St. & Central Pk., W.
New York, NY 10024
Telephone: (212) 769-5500
Year Established: 1900
Pub. Frequency: m.
Page Size: standard
Subscrip. Rate: $25/yr.
Freelance Pay: $600-$750
Circulation: 500,000
Circulation Type: paid

**Materials Accepted/Included:** 01-Business news 02-By-line articles 03-Fashion news 04-Food news 05-Freelance copy 06-Letters to editor 07-Real estate news 08-Sports news 09-Travel news 10-Book rev. 11-Movie rev. 12-Music rev. 13-TV rev. 14-Theater rev. 15-Coming events 16-Obituaries 17-Question & answer 18-Social announcements 19-Artwork 20-Cartoons 21-Photos 22-TV listings 23-Audio rec. 24-Video rec. 25-Books 26-Films/film clips 27-Personnel news 28-Press releases 29-New product news/photos 30-Trade lit. 31-Contracts awarded 32-Display adv. 33-Classified adv.

6-75

**Owner(s):**
American Museum of Natural History
79th & Central Pk., W.
New York, NY 10023
Telephone: (212) 769-5500
Ownership %: 100
**Management:**
L. Thomas Kelly .........................Publisher
John Moncure ...................Sales Manager
**Editorial:**
Alan Ternes ...................................Editor
Ellen Goldensohn ...........Managing Editor
Jenny Lawrence ...........Book Review Editor
Florence G. Edelstein ...............Copy Chief
Tom Page ...........................Design Director
Kay Zakariasen ...................................Photo
**Desc.:** By-line features and picture layouts
   cover various aspects of natural history
   and natural science. Articles deal with
   anthropology, geology, astronomy,
   zoology, botany, ecology, etc.
   Considerable text and pictorial space
   devoted to ethnological reports and
   other general natural history subjects.
   Articles run to maximum of 4,000 words.
   Reviews books on general theme of
   natural history. Does not use publicity
   releases.
**Readers:** People of all walks of life in the
   U.S.

69112
**OMNI**
324 W. Wendover Ave., Ste. 205
Greensboro, NC 27408
Telephone: (919) 275-9809
FAX: (919) 378-1862
Year Established: 1978
Pub. Frequency: m.
Page Size: standard
Subscrip. Rate: $24/yr.
Materials: 01,02,03,04,05,06,09,10,11,12,
   13,23,24,25,26,30,32,33
Freelance Pay: varies
Print Process: web
Circulation: 702,843
Circulation Type: paid
**Owner(s):**
General Media Publishing Group
1965 Broadway
New York, NY 10023-5965
Telephone: (212) 496-6100
Ownership %: 100
**Editorial:**
Keith Ferrell ..................................Editor
Peter Johnsmeyer ....................Advertising
Ellen Datlow ...........................Fiction Editor
**Desc.:** Covers science and technology for
   readers interested in their universe, past,
   present, and future. Publishes original
   science fiction stories.

26101
**POPULAR MECHANICS MAGAZINE**
224 W. 57th St.
New York, NY 10019
Telephone: (212) 649-3088
Year Established: 1902
Pub. Frequency: m.
Page Size: standard
Subscrip. Rate: $15.94/yr.
Circulation: 1,688,784
Circulation Type: paid
**Owner(s):**
Hearst Corp.
959 Eighth Ave.
New York, NY 10019
Telephone: (212) 649-2100
Ownership %: 100
**Management:**
Robert B. Dillingham ..................Publisher
**Editorial:**
Joe Oldham .........................Editor in Chief
Steve Willson ...............................Editor
Frank Vizard ...............................Editor
Joe Skorupa ...............................Editor

Deborah Frank .....................Managing Editor
Tony Swan .........................Automotive Editor
Bryan Canniff ...........................Graphics Editor
Abe Dane ...............................Science Editor
**Desc.:** By-line articles cover new and
   unusual developments in the fields of
   applied science, automobiles,
   technology, invention, discovery,
   industry, home maintenance, aviation,
   home workshop, electronics, computers
   and boating. Departments include:
   Automobiles, Science & Engineering,
   Aviation, Boating & Outdoors, Home &
   Yard, Shops & Crafts, Electronics, Radio
   & TV, Photography and
   Telecommunications.
**Readers:** Primarily men, interested in auto,
   home, and leisure activities.

26102
**POPULAR SCIENCE**
2 Park Ave.
New York, NY 10016
Telephone: (212) 779-5000
FAX: (212) 481-8062
Year Established: 1872
Pub. Frequency: m.
Page Size: standard
Subscrip. Rate: $13.94/yr.
Circulation: 2,000,000
Circulation Type: paid
**Owner(s):**
Times Mirror Magazines, Inc.
2 Park Ave.
New York, NY 10016
Telephone: (212) 779-5000
Ownership %: 100
**Bureau(s):**
Popular Science
875 N. Michigan Ave.
Chicago, IL 60611
Telephone: (312) 337-7717
Contact: Jim King, Manager

Popular Science
3550 Wilshire Blvd.
Los Angeles, CA 90010
Telephone: (310) 380-1936
Contact: Jacqueline Donnelly Kelly,
   Manager

Popular Science
755 W. Big Beaver Rd., #420
Troy, MI 48084
Telephone: (313) 362-9005
Contact: Edward A. Bartley, Manager

Joe Kelly & Assoc.
16990 Dallas Pkwy.
Dallas, TX 75248
Telephone: (214) 380-0416
Contact: Joe Kelly
**Management:**
James Kopper ...................Vice President
John Crawley ...........................Publisher
John Crawley ...............Advertising Manager
**Editorial:**
Fred Abatemarco ...................Editor in Chief
Fred Abatemarco .......................Editor
Wendy Black ...................Assistant Editor
Arthur Fisher ...................Science Editor
**Desc.:** Science and technology magazine
   covering new scientific and technical
   developments and new consumer
   products, plus do-it-yourself projects for
   the home owner.
**Readers:** Men of all ages interested in
   science, computers, technology,
   automobiles, and home improvement.

67240
**QUANTUM**
3140 N. Washington Blvd., 2nd Fl.
Arlington, VA 22201
Telephone: (703) 243-7100
FAX: (703) 243-7177
Year Established: 1990
Pub. Frequency: bi-m.

Page Size: standard
Subscrip. Rate: $15/yr. individuals; $20/yr.
   institutions; $34/yr. students
Freelance Pay: $100-$200
Circulation: 10,000
Circulation Type: paid
**Owner(s):**
National Science Teachers Association
3140 N. Washington Blvd.
Arlington, VA 22201
Telephone: (703) 243-7100
Ownership %: 100
**Management:**
Bill G. Aldridge ...........................Publisher
Paul Kuntzler ...............Advertising Manager
**Editorial:**
Timothy Weber ...................Managing Editor
Elisabeth Tobia ...........................Art Director
**Desc.:** The students magazine of math
   and science contains material translated
   from the Russian student magazine
   Kvant as well as original material. It is
   intended as supplementary enrichment
   for classroom use or for students to
   read on their own. In addition to feature
   articles and departmental pieces, many
   of which pose questions and problems,
   Quantum offers olympiad-style problems
   and brainteasers. Each issue contains
   an answer section.
**Readers:** Math and science students (high
   school, college); teachers.

53992
**ROCKS & MINERALS**
1319 18th St., N.W.
Washington, DC 20036-1802
Telephone: (202) 296-6267
FAX: (202) 296-5149
Year Established: 1926
Pub. Frequency: bi-m.
Page Size: standard
Subscrip. Rate: $37/yr. individuals; $62/yr.
   institutions; add $9/yr. for outside U.S.
Circulation: 3,295
Circulation Type: paid
**Owner(s):**
Heldref Publications
1319 18th St., NW
Washington, DC 20036-1802
Telephone: (202) 296-6267
Ownership %: 100
**Management:**
Walter E. Beach ...........................Publisher
Raymond M. Rallo ...........Advertising Manager
Catherine Welker ...........Circulation Manager
Kerri P. Kilbane ...................Promotion Manager
**Editorial:**
Marie Huizing ...............................Editor
Claire Wilson ...............................Editor
**Desc.:** Publishes articles of interest to all
   students of mineralogy, geology and
   paleontology. The magazine is designed
   to meet the needs of the amateur in the
   field.
**Readers:** Students of mineralogy, geology,
   and paleontology as well as amateurs
   in the field.

24896
**SCIENCE**
1333 H St., N.W.
Washington, DC 20005
Telephone: (202) 326-6500
FAX: (202) 681-0816
Year Established: 1880
Pub. Frequency: w.
Page Size: standard
Subscrip. Rate: $97/yr. individuals;
   $215/yr. institutions
Materials: 32,33
Circulation: 170,000
Circulation Type: paid

**Owner(s):**
American Assn. for the Advancement of
   Science
1333 H St., N.W.
Washington, DC 20005
Telephone: (202) 326-6400
Ownership %: 100
**Management:**
Richard S. Nicholson ...................Publisher
Susan A. Meredith ...........Advertising Manager
**Editorial:**
Daniel E. Koshland, Jr. ...................Editor
Monica M. Bradford ...............Managing Editor
Amy Henry ...............................Art Director
Colin Norman ...............Managing News Editor
Ellis Rubinstein ...................News Editor
**Desc.:** Publishes original research results,
   reviews, short features, and news of
   recent international developments and
   research in all fields of science.
**Readers:** Professional scientists and
   researchers.

24899
**SCIENCE NEWS**
1719 N St., N.W.
Washington, DC 20036
Telephone: (202) 785-2255
FAX: (202) 785-3751
Year Established: 1922
Pub. Frequency: w.
Page Size: standard
Subscrip. Rate: $44.50/yr.
Materials: 32
Circulation: 233,000
Circulation Type: paid
**Owner(s):**
Science Service, Inc.
1719 N St., N.W.
Washington, DC 20036
Telephone: (202) 785-2255
Ownership %: 100
**Management:**
Alfred Scott McLaren ...................President
Alfred Scott McLaren ...................Publisher
Donald Harless ...................Business Manager
**Editorial:**
Patrick Young ...................Editor in Chief
Blair Potter ...................Managing Editor
Greg Pearson ...................Assistant Editor
**Readers:** Scientists and science-oriented
   laymen.

24903
**SCIENTIFIC AMERICAN**
415 Madison Ave.
New York, NY 10017
Telephone: (212) 754-0550
FAX: (212) 754-1138
Year Established: 1845
Pub. Frequency: m.
Page Size: standard
Subscrip. Rate: $36/yr.
Materials: 32
Freelance Pay: none
Circulation: 637,000
Circulation Type: paid
**Owner(s):**
Scientific American, Inc.
415 Madison Ave.
New York, NY 10017
Telephone: (212) 754-0550
Ownership %: 100
**Management:**
John J. Hanley ...................Chairman of Board
John Moeling ...............................President
John Moeling ...............................Publisher
**Editorial:**
Jonathan B. Piel ...........................Editor
Kate Dobson ...................Advertising Director
Philip Morrison ...................Book Review Editor
Lorraine Terlecki ...................Circulation Director

---

**Materials Accepted/Included:** 01-Business news 02-By-line articles 03-Fashion news 04-Food news 05-Freelance copy 06-Letters to editor 07-Real estate news 08-Sports news 09-Travel news 10-Book rev. 11-Movie rev. 12-Music rev. 13-TV rev. 14-Theater rev. 15-Coming events 16-Obituaries 17-Question & answer 18-Social announcements 19-Artwork 20-Cartoons 21-Photos 22-TV listings 23-Audio rec. 24-Video rec. 25-Books 26-Films/film clips 27-Personnel news 28-Press releases 29-New product news/photos 30-Trade lit. 31-Contracts awarded 32-Display adv. 33-Classified adv.

**Desc.:** Articles report the new work of science, technological advances, history of science, etc. Departments include: science and the citizen, books, the amateur scientist, 50 and 100 years ago, computer recreations.
**Readers:** Engineers, scientists, professionals, executives in industry, government & universities.

## SKY & TELESCOPE
*26009*
49 Bay State Rd.
Cambridge, MA 02138
Telephone: (617) 864-7360
FAX: (617) 864-6117
Mailing Address:
   P.O. Box 9111
   Belmont, MA 02178
Year Established: 1941
Pub. Frequency: m.
Page Size: standard
Subscrip. Rate: $27/yr. US; $36.38/yr.
   Canada
Freelance Pay: $.10-$.25/word
Circulation: 100,000
Circulation Type: paid
**Owner(s):**
Sky Publishing Corp.
49 Bay State Rd.
Cambridge, MA 02138
Telephone: (617) 864-7360
Ownership %: 100
**Management:**
Richard T. Fienberg ...........................President
**Editorial:**
Leif J. Robinson .................................Editor
Dennis Di Cicco ......................Associate Editor
Roger W. Sinnott ....................Associate Editor
Alan M. MacRobert ................Associate Editor
Stephen James O'meara ........Associate Editor
Stuart J. Goldman ..............Book Review Editor
Douglas T. Dinsmoor ..........Marketing Director
**Desc.:** Contributed articles and semi-technical discussions on the various aspects of astronomy and space science. Departments include: Books and Beyond, Telescope Making, Backyard Astronomy, Observer's Page, Star Charts, News Notes, Celestial Calendar.
**Readers:** Amateur and professional astronomers.
**Deadline:** news-4 days before pub. date; ads-1st day of 3rd mo. prior to pub. date

## WEATHERWISE
*53993*
1319 18th St., N.W.
Washington, DC 20036-1802
Telephone: (202) 296-6267
FAX: (202) 296-5149
Year Established: 1948
Pub. Frequency: bi-m.
Page Size: standard
Subscrip. Rate: $32/yr. individual; $54/yr.
   institution; add $12/yr. foreign
Circulation: 9,817
Circulation Type: paid
**Owner(s):**
Heldref Publications
1319 18th St., N.W.
Washington, DC 20036-1802
Telephone: (202) 296-6267
Ownership %: 100
**Management:**
Walter E. Beach ...........................Publisher
Raymond M. Rallo ...........Advertising Manager
Catherine Welker ..............Circulation Manager
Kerri P. Kilbane .................Promotion Manager
**Editorial:**
Doublas Addison .................................Editor
Jeff Rosenfeld .................................Editor

**Desc.:** Captures the power, beauty, and excitement of the ever-changing elements of weather in vibrant color photographs and crisp, well-written articles.
**Readers:** Weather professionals, amateurs, nature lovers, photographers, print and broadcast journalists, teachers and students.

## WORLD & SCIENCE
*69108*
951 S. Oxford Ave., No. 109
Los Angeles, CA 90006
Telephone: (213) 732-3477
Year Established: 1991
Pub. Frequency: q.
Subscrip. Rate: $29.99/yr.
Materials: 01,02,03,04,05,06,07,08,09,10,
   11,12,13,14,15,16,17,18,19,20,21,22,23,
   24,25,26,27,28,29,30,31,32,33
Freelance Pay: $.20-.50/wd.
Print Process: web
Circulation: 120,000
Circulation Type: controlled & paid
**Owner(s):**
Publishing & Business Consultants
951 S. Oxford Ave., No. 109
Los Angeles, CA 90006
Telephone: (213) 732-3477
FAX: (213) 732-9123
Ownership %: 100
**Editorial:**
Andeson Napoleon Atia ..........................Editor
**Desc.:** Environmental Sciences in the area of biology, chemistry, physics, medicine, astrophysics and astronomy.
**Deadline:** story-2 wks. prior to pub. date; news-2 wks.; photo-2 wks.; ads-90 days

## Group 646-Men's Magazines

## ADAM
*69246*
8060 Melrose Ave.
Los Angeles, CA 90046
Telephone: (213) 653-8060
FAX: (213) 655-9452
Year Established: 1956
Pub. Frequency: m.
Subscrip. Rate: $4.95/copy
Materials: 02,20,23,24,25,29
Print Process: offset
Circulation: 150,000
Circulation Type: paid
**Owner(s):**
Knight Publishing Corp.
8060 Melrose Ave.
Los Angeles, CA 90046
Telephone: (213) 653-8060
Ownership %: 100
**Editorial:**
Jared Rutter .................................Editor

## DETAILS
*67278*
632 Broadway
New York, NY 10012
Telephone: (212) 420-0689
FAX: (212) 598-0284
Year Established: 1982
Pub. Frequency: m.
Page Size: standard
Subscrip. Rate: $2 newsstands; $12/yr.
Circulation: 465,205
Circulation Type: paid
**Owner(s):**
Conde Nast Publishing Co.
350 Madison Ave.
New York, NY 10017
Telephone: (212) 420-0689
Ownership %: 100
**Management:**
Michael Perlis ...........................Publisher
Gina Sanders ....................Advertising Manager
**Editorial:**
John Leland ........................Editor in Chief

**Desc.:** Covers mens' interests.

## DNR MONDAY
*65465*
7 W. 34th St., 3rd Fl.
New York, NY 10001
Telephone: (212) 630-4000
FAX: (212) 630-3602
Pub. Frequency: w.: Mon.
Page Size: oversize
Subscrip. Rate: $62/yr.
Circulation: 24,000
Circulation Type: paid
**Owner(s):**
Fairchild Publications, Inc.
7 W. 34th St., 3rd Fl.
New York, NY 10001
Telephone: (212) 630-4000
Ownership %: 100
**Management:**
David Hill .................................Publisher
**Editorial:**
Barry Van Lenten ..........................Editor
**Desc.:** Covers the men's fashion trade.

## ESQUIRE
*26111*
250 W. 55th St.
New York, NY 10019
Telephone: (212) 649-4020
Year Established: 1933
Pub. Frequency: m.
Page Size: standard
Subscrip. Rate: $15.94/yr.
Freelance Pay: $200-$1,500
Circulation: 702,611
Circulation Type: paid
**Owner(s):**
Hearst Corp.
959 Eighth Ave.
New York, NY 10019
Telephone: (212) 649-2000
**Management:**
Frank Bennack, Jr. ..............Chairman of Board
Ron Galotti ...........................Publisher
**Editorial:**
Edward Kosner ......................Editor in Chief
Rust Hills .........................Fiction Editor
**Desc.:** Interested in articles which will appeal to a large segment of the intelligent American public; colorful profiles of unusual personalities in the business, entertainment, and sports world; Short-shorts (1,200 words) both fiction and non-fiction; fiction of high literary caliber; picture stories which have universal appeal and which are of themselves outstanding photographic essays. Reviews new books, covers new articles for men.
**Readers:** Executive business men.

## ESQUIRE GENTLEMAN
*68825*
250 W. 55th St.
New York, NY 10019
Telephone: (212) 649-2000
Year Established: 1993
Pub. Frequency: s-a.
**Owner(s):**
Hearst Corp.
250 W. 55th St.
New York, NY 10019
Telephone: (212) 459-7500
Ownership %: 100
**Editorial:**
Terry McDonnell ...........................Editor
**Desc.:** Covers style and fashion for men.

## GENESIS
*26114*
1776 Broadway, 20th Fl.
New York, NY 10019
Telephone: (212) 265-3000
FAX: (212) 265-8087
Year Established: 1972
Pub. Frequency: 14/yr.

Page Size: standard
Subscrip. Rate: $5.99 newsstand; $41/yr.
Materials: 02,06,10,11,12,20,21,23,24,25,
   26,29,32
Freelance Pay: $500-$1,500
Circulation: 212,910
Circulation Type: paid
**Owner(s):**
Jakel Corp.
1776 Broadway, 20th Fl.
New York, NY 10019
Telephone: (212) 265-3500
Ownership %: 100
**Management:**
Michael Banka ...........................Publisher
**Desc.:** Newsmaking articles on politics, crime, exposes of national interest, humor, interviews with major celebrities in entertainment, service pictorials, new product material. Basketball, hockey, football and baseball ONLY in sports. Music, book and video reviews.
**Readers:** Sophisticated, intelligent 18-35 year-olds.

## GQ (GENTLEMEN'S QUARTERLY)
*22676*
350 Madison Ave.
New York, NY 10017
Telephone: (212) 880-8800
Year Established: 1957
Pub. Frequency: m.
Page Size: standard
Subscrip. Rate: $3 newsstand; $20/yr.
Circulation: 666,450
Circulation Type: paid
**Owner(s):**
Conde Nast Publications, Inc.
350 Madison Ave.
New York, NY 10017
Telephone: (212) 880-8800
Ownership %: 100
**Management:**
Michael Clinton ...........................Publisher
**Editorial:**
Arthur Cooper ......................Editor in Chief
Martin Beyser ...................Managing Editor
Michael Clinton ...............Advertising Director
Robert Priest ...........................Art Director
Nonnie Moore ......................Fashion Editor
Tanya Lenkow ...........................News Editor
**Desc.:** Magazine of personal style for American men. Features fashion, journalism, and contemporary fiction and humor. Edited for men who incorporate style into various aspects of his life, with solid service articles that encourage fitness, grooming and a healthy self-image.
**Readers:** Primarily men in all walks of life.

## HAWK
*69247*
801 Second Ave.
New York, NY 10017
Telephone: (212) 661-7878
Year Established: 1991
Pub. Frequency: 8/yr.
Page Size: standard
Subscrip. Rate: $21.95/yr.
Materials: 06,11,20,24,26,32
Freelance Pay: $.25/wd.
Print Process: web
Circulation: 250,000
Circulation Type: paid
**Owner(s):**
Killer Joe Productions
801 Second Ave.
New York, NY 10017
Telephone: (212) 661-7878
Ownership %: 100
**Editorial:**
Richard Dobbins ...........................Editor
**Desc.:** Covers fashion, fitness and music.
**Readers:** Men in their 20s and 30s.

**Materials Accepted/Included:** 01-Business news 02-By-line articles 03-Fashion news 04-Food news 05-Freelance copy 06-Letters to editor 07-Real estate news 08-Sports news 09-Travel news 10-Book rev. 11-Movie rev. 12-Music rev. 13-TV rev. 14-Theater rev. 15-Coming events 16-Obituaries 17-Question & answer 18-Social announcements 19-Artwork 20-Cartoons 21-Photos 22-TV listings 23-Audio rec. 24-Video rec. 25-Books 26-Films/film clips 27-Personnel news 28-Press releases 29-New product news/photos 30-Trade lit. 31-Contracts awarded 32-Display adv. 33-Classified adv.

6-77

**IN FASHION**
67267
29 W. 38th St., 15th Flr.
New York, NY 10018
Telephone: (212) 768-8450
FAX: (212) 768-8472
Year Established: 1985
Pub. Frequency: q.
Page Size: standard
Subscrip. Rate: $2.95 newsstand;
　$14.95/yr.
Circulation: 200,000
Circulation Type: controlled
**Owner(s):**
Opal Publishing
29 W. 38th St., 15th Flr.
New York, NY 10018
Telephone: (212) 768-8450
Ownership %: 100
**Management:**
Michael Belluomo ..............................Publisher
Gus Floris ..........................Associate Publisher
**Editorial:**
Carmen Tuttle ....................................Editor

**MEN'S HEALTH**
66597
33 E. Minor St.
Emmaus, PA 18049
Telephone: (215) 967-5171
Year Established: 1986
Pub. Frequency: 10/yr.
Subscrip. Rate: $19.97/yr.
Circulation: 1,100,000
Circulation Type: paid
**Owner(s):**
Rodale Press
33 E. Minor St.
Emmaus, PA 18049
Telephone: (215) 967-5171
**Editorial:**
Michael Lafavore ....................Executive Editor
Steve Sloan ..............................Design Editor

**MEN'S JOURNAL**
69248
1290 Ave. of the Americas
New York, NY 10104
Telephone: (212) 484-1616
Year Established: 1992
Pub. Frequency: 10/yr.
Circulation: 100,000
Circulation Type: paid
**Owner(s):**
Straight Arrow Publishers, Inc.
1290 Ave. of the Americas
New York, NY 10104
Telephone: (212) 484-1616
Ownership %: 100
**Editorial:**
John Rasmus ....................................Editor
**Desc.:** Features travel and adventure for
active men.

**OUI**
26118
28 W. 25th St.
New York, NY 10010
Telephone: (212) 647-0222
FAX: (212) 647-0236
Year Established: 1972
Pub. Frequency: m.
Page Size: standard
Subscrip. Rate: $4.95 newsstand US;
　$5.95 Canada
Freelance Pay: varies
Circulation: 395,000
Circulation Type: paid
**Owner(s):**
Laurant Publishing, Ltd.
28 W. 25th St.
New York, NY 10010
Telephone: (212) 647-0222
Ownership %: 100
**Management:**
Henry M. Mc Queeney ....................President
Henry M. McQueeney ......................Publisher

Gail Traub ..........................Advertising Manager
**Editorial:**
Mike Scott ....................................Editor
David Snow ..............................Managing Editor
**Desc.:** Covers travel, pop culture,
entertainment, sex, sports service, and
human behavior. Humor and satire are
especially welcome. All material should
be characterized by irreverences, wit
and humor.
**Readers:** Intelligent and sensuous urban
men, above average income.

## Group 648-Motorcycles

**AMERICAN IRON MAGAZINE**
70467
6 Prowitt St.
Norwalk, CT 06855
Telephone: (203) 855-0008
FAX: (203) 855-5962
Year Established: 1989
Pub. Frequency: m.
Page Size: standard
Subscrip. Rate: $3.50 newsstand; $25/yr.
Materials: 01,02,03,05,06,08,09,10,11,13,
　15,17,19,20,21,24,25,26,27,28,29,30,32
Circulation: 80,000
Circulation Type: paid
**Owner(s):**
TAM Communications, Inc.
6 Prowitt St.
Norwalk, CT 06855
Telephone: (203) 855-0008
FAX: (203) 852-9980
Ownership %: 100
**Management:**
Bod Petit ..........................Advertising Manager
**Desc.:** The best selling no-nonsense
Harley oriented magazine in the world.
No nudity or foul language. Plenty of
technical and how to articles, feature
motorcycles, history and product
reviews.

**CYCLE NEWS**
26390
2201 Cherry Ave.
Long Beach, CA 90806
Telephone: (310) 427-7433
FAX: (310) 427-6685
Mailing Address:
　P.O. Box 498
　Long Beach, CA 90801
Year Established: 1968
Pub. Frequency: w.
Page Size: tabloid
Subscrip. Rate: $35/yr.
Freelance Pay: on request
Circulation: 35,000
Circulation Type: paid
**Owner(s):**
Cycle News, Inc.
4190 First Ave.
Tucker, GA 30084
Telephone: (404) 934-7850
Ownership %: 100
**Management:**
Mike Klinger ..............................Publisher
Terry Pratt ..........................Advertising Manager
**Editorial:**
Paul Carruthers ....................................Editor
Kit Palmer ..............................Associate Editor
**Desc.:** Contains material interesting to
motorcycle competition enthusiasts;
touring, and other types of activities.
Departments include: Calendar
of Events, New Products, Race Results,
New Political Developments (helmet law,
land closure).
**Readers:** Motorcycle racing buffs and
motorcyclists.

**CYCLE WORLD**
24121
1499 Monrovia Ave.
Newport Beach, CA 92663
Telephone: (714) 720-5300
FAX: (714) 631-0651
Year Established: 1962
Pub. Frequency: m.
Page Size: standard
Subscrip. Rate: $19.94/yr.; $35.94/2 yrs.
Freelance Pay: $100/pg.
Circulation: 372,398
Circulation Type: paid
**Owner(s):**
Hachette Filipacchi Magazines, Inc.
1499 Monrovia Ave.
Neport Beach, CA 92663
Telephone: (714) 720-5300
Ownership %: 100
**Management:**
Larry Little ..............................Publisher
**Editorial:**
David Edward ..............................Editor in Chief
Jon Thompson ..............................Senior Editor
Matthew Miles ..............................Managing Editor
Paul Dean ..............................Editorial Director
Elaine Anderson ..............................Art Director
Rich Baker ..............................Assistant Art Director
Matthew Miles ..............................Associate Editor
Don Canet ..............................Associate Editor
Bob Starr ..............................Director
Jon F. Thompson ..............................Feature Editor
Robyn Figueroa ..............................Production Editor
**Desc.:** Staff production; road tests and
impressions of new motorcycles.
American and world racing coverage,
technical features, personality profiles,
new developments, new accessories,
apparel features. Freelance production:
We look for technical features; in-depth,
informative or humorous motorcycle
travel stories with professional quality
art, some racing, personality features,
etc.
**Readers:** Professional/technical
craftsmen; attended or graduated
college; the 18-34 age group, 97.4%
male; median age 30.2 years.

**DIRT BIKE MAGAZINE**
26394
25233 Amza
Valencia, CA 91355
Telephone: (805) 295-1910
Year Established: 1971
Pub. Frequency: m.
Page Size: standard
Subscrip. Rate: $14.98/yr.
Circulation: 131,930
Circulation Type: paid
**Owner(s):**
Hi-Torque Publishing, Inc.
25233 Amza
Valencia, CA 91355
Telephone: (805) 295-1910
Ownership %: 100
**Management:**
R.S. Hinz ..............................Publisher
Scott Wallenberg ..............................Advertising Manager
**Editorial:**
Ed Arnet ....................................Editor
Tim Tolleson ..............................Managing Editor
Joe Kosch ..............................Associate Editor

**Desc.:** Caters to the dirt bike motorcycle
riding and racing enthusiast. Coverage
includes events feature articles on
motocross, enduro, flat-track, speedway
and trials competitions; technical how-to
articles; tests of new motorcycles;
feature articles pertaining to off-road
riding; personality interviews. Dirt bike is
the largest and most widely read
magazine devoted totally to off-road
motorcycling. The editors should be
queried before submission. Stories and
photos which are accepted will be by-
lined.

**DIRT RIDER MAGAZINE**
69775
6420 Wilshire Blvd.
Los Angeles, CA 90048
Telephone: (213) 782-2000
Year Established: 1982
Pub. Frequency: m.
Subscrip. Rate: $2.95 newsstand;
　$19.94/yr.
Circulation: 159,900
Circulation Type: paid
**Owner(s):**
Peterson Publishing Co.
8490 Sunset Blvd.
Los Angeles, CA 90069
Telephone: (213) 854-2222
Ownership %: 100
**Editorial:**
Tom Webb ....................................Editor
Charlie Morey ..............................Executive Director

**EASYRIDERS**
26396
P.O. Box 3000
Agoura Hills, CA 91376
Telephone: (818) 889-8740
Year Established: 1971
Pub. Frequency: m.
Page Size: standard
Subscrip. Rate: $34.95/yr.
Freelance Pay: $.10/wd.
Circulation: 315,069
Circulation Type: paid
**Owner(s):**
Paisano Publications, Inc.
28210 Dorothy Dr.
Agoura Hills, CA 91301
Telephone: (818) 889-8740
Ownership %: 100
**Management:**
Joe Teresi ..............................Publisher
Lizette Hotinger ..............................Advertising Manager
**Editorial:**
Keith Ball ....................................Editor
Lou Kimzey ..............................Editorial Director
Lou Kimzey ..............................News Editor
**Readers:** Macho male.

**HARLEY WOMEN**
70427
P.O. Box 374
Streamwood, IL 60107
Telephone: (708) 888-2645
Pub. Frequency: bi-m.
Page Size: standard
Subscrip. Rate: $2.95/copy US;
　$3.50/copy Canada; $14/yr.; add $5 for
　foreign
Print Process: offset
**Owner(s):**
Asphalt Angels Publications, Inc.
P.O. Box 374
Streamwood, IL 60107
Telephone: (708) 888-2645
Ownership %: 100
**Management:**
Linda "Jo" Giovannoni ..............................Publisher
**Editorial:**
Linda "Jo" Giovannoni ....................................Editor
Bonnie Freese ..............................Advertising
Kathleen Richardson ..............................Copy Director

**Materials Accepted/Included:** 01-Business news 02-By-line articles 03-Fashion news 04-Food news 05-Freelance copy 06-Letters to editor 07-Real estate news 08-Sports news 09-Travel news 10-Book rev. 11-Movie rev. 12-Music rev. 13-TV rev. 14-Theater rev. 15-Coming events 16-Obituaries 17-Question & answer 18-Social announcements 19-Artwork 20-Cartoons 21-Photos 22-TV listings 23-Audio rec. 24-Video rec. 25-Books 26-Films/film clips 27-Personnel news 28-Press releases 29-New product news/photos 30-Trade lit. 31-Contracts awarded 32-Display adv. 33-Classified adv.

## INDIAN MOTORCYCLE ILLUSTRATED
68697
6 Prowitt St.
Norwalk, CT 06855
Telephone: (203) 855-0008
FAX: (203) 854-5962
Year Established: 1993
Pub. Frequency: q.
Page Size: standard
Subscrip. Rate: $4.95 newsstand;
$18.95/yr.
Materials: 02,05,06,10,19,20,21,25,29,30,32
Circulation: 50,000
Circulation Type: paid
**Owner(s):**
TAM Communications, Inc.
6 Prowitt St.
Norwalk, CT 06855
Telephone: (203) 855-0008
FAX: (203) 852-9980
Ownership %: 100
**Editorial:**
Mike Stankiewicz ............................Advertising
**Desc.:** Contains articles and news on the antique Indian motorcycle marque.

## MOTOCROSS ACTION MAGAZINE
26421
25233 Amza
Valencia, CA 91355
Telephone: (805) 295-1910
Year Established: 1973
Pub. Frequency: m.
Page Size: standard
Subscrip. Rate: $14.98/yr.
Freelance Pay: photo $10-$25 b&w, color $25-$50, ed $40/page
Circulation: 85,000
Circulation Type: paid
**Owner(s):**
Hi-Torque Publications, Inc.
25233 Amza
Valencia, CA 91355
Telephone: (805) 295-1910
Ownership %: 100
**Management:**
Roland S. Hinz ......................................Publisher
**Editorial:**
Jody Weisel ..................................................Editor
Dennis West ..................................Art Director
Mike Koger ..............................Associate Editor
**Desc.:** Appealing to the type of people who enjoy cross-country motorcycle racing, or motocross, as a sport. This includes the person interested in motor sports in general as well as the spectator and the participant. An open editorial policy considers any manuscript or layout that would be interesting and entertaining to the above group. Quality is stressed and everybody gets a by line. Race reports, technical articles and "how to's" are common. Publicity material is approached cautiously.
**Readers:** Survey indicated that 40% readership is young teenagers, male and female. Another 40% is 18 - 30 male. Both indicate a dirt motorcycle enthusiasts.

## MOTORCYCLE CONSUMER NEWS
26456
No. 3 Burroughs
Irvine, CA 92718
Telephone: (714) 855-8822
FAX: (714) 855-0654
Mailing Address:
P.O. Box 6050
Mission Viejo, CA 92690
Year Established: 1969
Pub. Frequency: m.
Page Size: standard
Subscrip. Rate: $19.97/yr.
Materials: 05,06,28,29,30

Freelance Pay: $150-$400
Print Process: web offset
Circulation: 52,000
Circulation Type: paid
**Owner(s):**
Aviation News Corp.
P.O. Box 57900
Los Angeles, CA 90057-0900
Telephone: (213) 385-2222
Ownership %: 100
**Management:**
Norman Ridker ....................................Publisher
Vera Geuther ..................Circulation Manager
**Editorial:**
Fred Rau ......................................Editor in Chief
**Desc.:** Dedicated to the touring motorcyclists. Covers long motorcycle trips, club and road-oriented events, humor relating to riding, safety tips, in-house cycle tests, and new product evaluations. Article length 1,500 words maximum; black & white photos are used.
**Readers:** Dedicated to experienced road rider motorcyclists. Readership age covers three generations of well-educated riders.

## MOTORCYCLE TOUR & TRAVEL
69436
6 Prowitt St.
Norwalk, CT 06855
Telephone: (203) 855-0008
FAX: (203) 852-9980
Year Established: 1991
Pub. Frequency: 8/yr.
Page Size: 4 color photos/art
Subscrip. Rate: $2.75 newsstand;
$17.97/yr.
Materials: 01,02,04,05,06,09,10,11,12,15,
17,18,19,20,21,23,24,25,28,29,30,32
Circulation: 75,000
Circulation Type: paid
**Owner(s):**
TAM Communications Inc.
6 Prowitt St.
Norwalk, CT 06855
Telephone: (203) 855-0008
Ownership %: 100
**Management:**
Buzz Canter ........................................Publisher
**Editorial:**
Buzz Canter ..............................Editor in Chief
Amy Hartnett ..............................................Editor
Mike Stankiewicz ..............Advertising Director
**Desc.:** Upscale travel magazine for motorcycling enthusiasts.

## MOTORCYCLIST
26424
6420 Wilshire Blvd.
Los Angeles, CA 90048-5515
Telephone: (213) 782-2230
FAX: (213) 782-2372
Year Established: 1912
Pub. Frequency: m.
Page Size: standard
Subscrip. Rate: $13.94/yr.
Materials: 03,05,08,09,10,15,17,19,20,21,29
Freelance Pay: $100-$250
Circulation: 260,000
Circulation Type: paid
**Owner(s):**
Petersen Publishing Co.
6420 Wilshire Blvd.
Los Angeles, CA 90048-5515
Telephone: (213) 782-2222
Ownership %: 100
**Management:**
Richard P. Lague ................................Publisher
Scott Goodwin ..................Advertising Manager
**Editorial:**
Art Friedman ................................Senior Editor
Mitch Boehm ..............................................Editor
Angela Barosso ..........................Managing Editor
Irma Hutton ................Administrative Assistant

Laura Morrison ........................................Art Editor
John Burns ..............................Associate Editor
Jason Black ..............................Associate Editor
Lydia Nieto ........................Coordinating Editor
Bob Griffith ......................................Copy Chief
Popi Buchanan ....................Editorial Assistant
**Desc.:** Devoted exclusively to street motorcycling. Aims at avid enthusiasts. Contains features, road tests of new models, travel articles, "how-to", technical articles, industry news, product releases, product evaluations and a sport section.
**Readers:** Cross-section ranging from the newcomer to members of the motorcycle industry (dealer, manufacturers).

## OLD BIKE JOURNAL
70466
6 Prowitt St.
Norwalk, CT 06855
Telephone: (203) 855-0008
FAX: (203) 854-5962
Pub. Frequency: m.
Page Size: standard
Subscrip. Rate: $2.95 newsstand;
$17.95/yr.
Materials: 02,05,06,08,10,15,17,19,20,21,
24,25,28,29,30,32,33
Circulation: 28,000
Circulation Type: paid
**Owner(s):**
TAM Communications, Inc.
6 Prowitt St.
Norwalk, CT 06855
Telephone: (203) 855-0008
FAX: (203) 852-9980
Ownership %: 100
**Management:**
Bob Martin ........................Advertising Manager
**Desc.:** Classic and vintage motorcycles. Editorial coverage of motorcycles, history and events. Very large classified ad section.

## RIDER
26451
3601 Calle Tecate
Camarillo, CA 93012
Telephone: (805) 389-0300
Year Established: 1974
Pub. Frequency: m.
Page Size: standard
Subscrip. Rate: $11.98/yr.
Freelance Pay: varies
Circulation: 120,000
Circulation Type: paid
**Owner(s):**
TL Enterprises, Inc.
3601 Calle Tecate
Camarillo, CA 93012
Telephone: (805) 389-0300
Ownership %: 100
**Management:**
Joseph McAdams ..............................President
Joseph E. McNeill ..............................Publisher
**Editorial:**
Mark Tuttle, Jr. ............................................Editor
Donya Carlson ........................Managing Editor
Joe Salluzzo ..........................................Advertising
Bob Price ......................................Technical Editor
**Desc.:** Specializes in motorcycle touring and commuting. Specific appeal is thus far to a relatively unserved segment of motorcyclists. Editorial content is hard-hitting and practical. Freelance features considered in every area covered by the magazine must be accompanied by high-quality photography, black, white and color slides.

**Readers:** Sport, touring and touring motorcyclists.

## Group 650-Music

## ACOUSTIC GUITAR
69639
P.O. Box 767
San Anselmo, CA 94797-0767
Telephone: (415) 485-6946
FAX: (415) 485-0831
Year Established: 1990
Pub. Frequency: bi-m.
Subscrip. Rate: $4.95 newsstand;
$23.95/yr. US; $31.45/yr. Canada;
$38.95/yr. elsewhere
Materials: 02,05,06,10,12,15,17,21,23,24,
25,32,33
Freelance Pay: $.12/wd.
Circulation: 45,000
Circulation Type: paid
**Owner(s):**
String Letter Press, Inc.
P.O. Box 767
San Anselmo, CA 94979-0767
Telephone: (415) 485-6946
FAX: (415) 485-0831
Ownership %: 100
**Editorial:**
Jeffrey Pepper Rodgers ............................Editor
**Desc.:** Covers a variety of musical styles. Includes transcriptions from recordings and solo pieces for guitar.
**Readers:** Musicians, specifically acoustic guitar players and enthusiasts.

## AMERICAN RECORD GUIDE
69610
4412 Braddock St.
Cincinnati, OH 45204-1006
Telephone: (513) 941-1116
Year Established: 1935
Pub. Frequency: bi-m.
Subscrip. Rate: $5.00 newsstand; $26/yr.
individuals; $36/yr. institutions
Materials: 12,23,25,32,33
Print Process: offset
Circulation: 12,500
Circulation Type: paid
**Owner(s):**
Record Guide Productions
4412 Braddock St.
Cincinnati, OH 45204
Telephone: (513) 941-1116
FAX: (513) 941-1112
**Editorial:**
Donald R. Vroon ......................................Editor
**Desc.:** Publishes feature articles and reviews music in concert and 600 classical recordings per issue.
**Deadline:** ads-6 wks. prior to pub. date

## BAM MAGAZINE
26130
3470 Buskirk Ave.
Pleasant Hill, CA 94523
Telephone: (510) 934-3700
FAX: (510) 934-2417
Mailing Address:
6767 Forest Lawn Dr.
Los Angeles, CA 90068
Year Established: 1976
Pub. Frequency: bi-w.
Page Size: tabloid
Subscrip. Rate: $25/yr.
Materials: 05,06,10,12,19,20,21,23,24,25,
26,27,28,29,30
Circulation: 130,000
Circulation Type: free
**Owner(s):**
Bam Publications, Inc.
3470 Buskirk Ave.
Pleasant Hill, CA 94523
Telephone: (510) 934-3700
Ownership %: 100

**Materials Accepted/Included:** 01-Business news 02-By-line articles 03-Fashion news 04-Food news 05-Freelance copy 06-Letters to editor 07-Real estate news 08-Sports news 09-Travel news 10-Book rev. 11-Movie rev. 12-Music rev. 13-TV rev. 14-Theater rev. 15-Coming events 16-Obituaries 17-Question & answer 18-Social announcements 19-Artwork 20-Cartoons 21-Photos 22-TV listings 23-Audio rec. 24-Video rec. 25-Books 26-Films/film clips 27-Personnel news 28-Press releases 29-New product news/photos 30-Trade lit. 31-Contracts awarded 32-Display adv. 33-Classified adv.

6-79

**Bureau(s):**
BAM Publications, Inc.
1800 Highland, #220
Los Angeles, CA 90028
Telephone: (310) 467-7878
Contact: Steve Stolder, Editor
**Management:**
Earl Adkins ..............................Publisher
Steve Gellman ..................Advertising Manager
**Editorial:**
Dennis Erokan ..............................Editor in Chief
Steve Stolder ..............................Editor
**Desc.:** Concerns itself with the music, film
& video news of Hollywood/Los Angeles
and San Francisco. We cover mainly the
personalities and events that are
important to music fans.
**Readers:** 18-39 (with an average age of
23.7) interested in popular music.

67291
**BASS PLAYER**
411 Borel Ave., Ste. 100
San Mateo, CA 94402-3516
Telephone: (415) 358-9500
FAX: (415) 358-8728
Year Established: 1990
Pub. Frequency: 8/yr.
Page Size: standard
Subscrip. Rate: $20/yr.
Materials: 01,02,05,06,15,16,17,19,21,23,
24,25,28,29,30,32,33
Freelance Pay: varies; $100 min.
Print Process: web
Circulation: 56,000
Circulation Type: paid
**Owner(s):**
Miller Freeman, Inc.
600 Harrison St.
San Francisco, CA 94107
Telephone: (415) 905-2200
FAX: (415) 905-2233
Ownership %: 100
**Management:**
Marshall Freeman ..............................President
Pat Cameron ..............................Publisher
Jim Roberts ..............................Associate Publisher
Ricc Sandoval ..................Advertising Manager
**Editorial:**
Jim Roberts ..............................Editor
**Desc.:** The only magazine for electric and
acoustic bass in all styles.
**Readers:** Amateur and professional bass
players.

26131
**BLUEGRASS UNLIMITED**
Rte. 5, Box 85
Warrenton, VA 22186-8418
Telephone: (703) 349-8181
FAX: (703) 341-0011
Mailing Address:
P.O. Box 111
Broad Run, VA 22014-0111
Year Established: 1966
Pub. Frequency: m.
Page Size: standard
Subscrip. Rate: $2.50/copy; $21/yr.; $40/2
yrs.; $58/3 yrs.
Materials: 01,02,05,06,09,10,12,15,16,17,
23,24,25,28,29,30,32,33
Freelance Pay: $.06-$.08/wd.
Print Process: web offset
Circulation: 23,500
Circulation Type: paid
**Owner(s):**
Bluegrass Unlimited, Inc.
P.O. Box 111
Broad Run, VA 22014-0111
Telephone: (703) 349-8181
Ownership %: 100
**Management:**
Pat Jeffries ..................Advertising Manager
**Editorial:**
Peter V. Kuykendall ..............................Editor
Sharon K. Watts ..............................Managing Editor

Richard K. Spottswood ........Contributing Editor
**Desc.:** Dedicated to the furtherance of
bluegrass music; bluegrass being a
branch of old-time traditional country
music. News of the artists' activities,
features include profiles on the artists,
articles on how to play instruments/build
and maintain them, etc., letters, songs,
bluegrass record reviews, personal
appearance calendar, monthly & regular
activities in bluegrass, classified ads.
Festival listing of summer events
featuring bluegrass and traditional string
music.
**Readers:** Listeners of bluegrass music
**Deadline:** story-1 mo.; news-1 mo.; photo-
1 mo.; ads-1 mo.

66725
**CD REVIEW**
86 Elm St.
Petersborough, NH 03458
Telephone: (603) 924-7271
FAX: (603) 924-7013
Year Established: 1984
Pub. Frequency: m.
Subscrip. Rate: $3.95 newsstand;
$19.97/yr.
Circulation: 86,000
Circulation Type: paid
**Owner(s):**
Connell Communication Inc.
86 Elm St.
Petersborough, NH 03458
Telephone: (603) 924-7271
FAX: (603) 924-7013
Ownership %: 100
**Management:**
Ellen A. Holmes ..............................Publisher
T. James Connell ..............................Publisher
**Editorial:**
Lou Waryncia ..............................Editor in Chief
Don O'Kane ..............................Senior Editor

69757
**COUNTRY MUSIC**
329 Riverside Ave.
Westport, CT 06880
Telephone: (203) 221-4950
Year Established: 1972
Pub. Frequency: bi-m.
Subscrip. Rate: $2.50 newsstand;
$15.98/yr.
Circulation: 700,000
Circulation Type: paid
**Owner(s):**
Silver Eagle Publishers
329 Riverside Ave.
Westport, CT 06880
Telephone: (203) 221-4950
Ownership %: 100
**Editorial:**
Helen Barnard ..............................Editor

26135
**COUNTRY SONG ROUNDUP**
63 Grand Ave.
River Edge, NJ 07661
Telephone: (201) 487-6124
Year Established: 1947
Pub. Frequency: m.
Page Size: standard
Subscrip. Rate: $2.95 newsstand; $25/yr.
Materials: 05,06,15,23,24,25,28
Freelance Pay: open
Circulation: 200,000
Circulation Type: paid
**Owner(s):**
Country Song Roundup, Inc.
210 Rt. 4 E., Ste. 401
Ste. 401
Paramus, NJ 07652
Telephone: (201) 843-4004
FAX: (201) 843-8636
**Editorial:**
Celeste Gomes ..............................Executive Editor

Jennifer Fusco Giacobbe ..........Assistant Editor
Brooks Johnson ..............Director of Licensing

26137
**CREEM**
28 W. 25th St.
New York, NY 10010
Telephone: (212) 647-0222
FAX: (212) 647-0236
Year Established: 1969
Pub. Frequency: 10/yr.
Page Size: standard
Subscrip. Rate: $17.50/yr.
Materials: 10,11,21,30,32,33
Circulation: 120,000
Circulation Type: paid
**Owner(s):**
John T. Edwards Publishing Ltd.
28 W. 25th St.
New York, NY 10010
Telephone: (212) 647-0222
Ownership %: 100
**Management:**
Arnold Levitt ..............................Publisher
**Editorial:**
Chris Nadler ..............................Editor
John Kordosh ..............................Editorial Director
Jeff Epstein ..............................Advertising
Pam Frankhauser ..............................Art Director
Pam Frankhauser ..............Photography Director
**Desc.:** Rock 'n' roll magazine which covers
pop culture from an iconoclastic and
irrevent point of view. Besides profiles of
rock stars, it featurs news and opinion
from the pop mileau, consumer
electronics and musical inst. columns as
well as film, book and record reviews.
**Readers:** Average age, 21.3, median 21,
18-24.

69010
**FACES ROCKS**
210 Rte. 4 E., Ste. 401
Paramus, NJ 07652
Telephone: (201) 843-8964
FAX: (201) 843-8636
Year Established: 1983
Pub. Frequency: bi-m.
Page Size: standard
Subscrip. Rate: $3.95 newsstand US &
Canada; $19/yr. US; $25/yr. foreign
Materials: 32
Print Process: offset
Circulation: 100,000
Circulation Type: paid
**Owner(s):**
Faces Magazines, Inc.
210 Rte. 4 E., Ste. 401
Paramus, NJ 08652
Telephone: (201) 843-8964
FAX: (201) 843-8636
Ownership %: 100
**Management:**
Scott Mitchell Figman ..............Publisher
**Editorial:**
Jennifer Rose ..............................Editor
Mitch Hershowitz ..............................Advertising
Victor Sierkowski ..............................Advertising
Ed Alves ..............................Art Assistant
John Gotto ..............................Art Director
**Desc.:** Covers various music, bands and
music groups.

69617
**FANFARE**
273 Woodland St.
Tenafly, NJ 07670
Mailing Address:
P.O. Box 720
Tenafly, NJ 07670
Year Established: 1977
Pub. Frequency: bi-m.
Page Size: standard
Subscrip. Rate: $34/yr.
Circulation: 13,200
Circulation Type: free & paid

**Owner(s):**
Fanfare, Inc.
273 Woodland St.
Tenafly, NJ 07670
Ownership %: 100
**Editorial:**
Joel Flegler ..............................Editor

69623
**GRAY AREAS**
P.O. Box 808
Broomall, PA 19008-0808
Telephone: (610) 353-8238
Year Established: 1992
Pub. Frequency: q.
Page Size: standard
Subscrip. Rate: $5.50 newsstand; $18/yr.
US; $34/yr. foreign
Materials: 06,10,11,12,13,19,20,21,23,24,
25,26,28,29,32
Freelance Pay: 5 free copies of issue work
appears in
Print Process: web
Circulation: 10,000
Circulation Type: paid
**Owner(s):**
Gray Areas, Inc.
P.O. Box 808
Broomall, PA 19008-0808
Telephone: (610) 353-8238
Ownership %: 100
**Editorial:**
Netta Gilboa ..............................Editor
**Desc.:** Examines gray areas of law and
morality including subject matter which is
illegal, immoral and/or controversial
such as drugs, porn, UFO's, computer
crimes, bootleg tapes, privacy issues,
etc.

69011
**GUITAR FOR THE PRACTICING
MUSICIAN**
10 Midland Ave.
Port Chester, NY 10573
Telephone: (914) 937-8601
FAX: (914) 937-0614
Year Established: 1983
Pub. Frequency: m.
Page Size: standard
Subscrip. Rate: $3.50 newsstand US;
$4.50 Canada; $27.95/yr.
Materials: 06,10,12,15,19,21,23,24,25,28,
29,32,33
Circulation: 1,000,000
Circulation Type: paid
**Owner(s):**
Cherry Lane Magazines, Inc.
10 Midland Ave.
Port Chester, NY 10573
Telephone: (914) 937-8601
FAX: (914) 937-0614
Ownership %: 100
**Management:**
Howard Cleff ..............................Publisher
**Editorial:**
John Stix ..............................Editor in Chief
Lorena Alexander ..............Executive Editor
Barbara Seerman ..............Director, Advertising
Sales
**Desc.:** Contains note-for-note
transcriptions to today's best selling
songs. Features interviews, music news,
instructional playing tips, artist profiles
and informative guitar techniques.
**Deadline:** story-15th of mo./4 mo. prior;
news-15th of mo./4 mo. prior; photo-1st
of mo./4 mo. prior; ads-15th of mo./4
mo. prior

26141
**GUITAR PLAYER**
411 Borel Ave.
San Mateo, CA 94402
Telephone: (415) 655-4100
FAX: (415) 358-9527
Year Established: 1967

**Materials Accepted/Included:** 01-Business news 02-By-line articles 03-Fashion news 04-Food news 05-Freelance copy 06-Letters to editor 07-Real estate news 08-Sports news 09-Travel news 10-Book rev. 11-Movie rev. 12-Music rev. 13-TV rev. 14-Theater rev. 15-Coming events 16-Obituaries 17-Question & answer 18-Social announcements 19-Artwork 20-Cartoons 21-Photos 22-TV listings 23-Audio rec. 24-Video rec. 25-Books 26-Films/film clips 27-Personnel news 28-Press releases 29-New product news/photos 30-Trade lit. 31-Contracts awarded 32-Display adv. 33-Classified adv.

Pub. Frequency: m.
Page Size: standard
Subscrip. Rate: $3.50 newsstand;
$29.95/yr.
Freelance Pay: $100-$300
Circulation: 150,000
Circulation Type: paid
**Owner(s):**
GPI Group, The, Miller Freeman, Inc.
600 Harrison St.
Cupertino, CA 94107
Telephone: (415) 905-2200
Ownership %: 100
**Management:**
Marshall W. Freeman ..................President
Pat Cameron ................................Publisher
**Editorial:**
Joe Gore ......................................Senior Editor
Dominic Milano ...........Editorial Director
Rich Leeds ..................................Art Director
Art Thompson ..........................Associate Editor
Tricia Pickens ...........................Associate Editor
Lonni Gause ..............................Production Editor
**Desc.:** Wide variety of articles pertaining to
guitars and guitarists: interviews, guitar
craftsmen profiles, how-to features-
anything amateur and pro guitarist would
find fascinating and/or helpful. In
interviews with name performers, be as
technical as possible regarding strings,
guitars, techniques, etc. We are not a
pop culture magazine but a magazine for
musicians. No reviews or timely pieces.
Photos preferred with stories.
Departments include: Books, LP,
Product Reviews, How-to Columns,
Editorials, History, Equipment Building.
All departments are staff- written.
**Readers:** 29 Years Old, 55%
Professional/Semi-Pro

**GUITAR WORLD** 54003
1115 Broadway
New York, NY 10010
Telephone: (212) 807-7100
FAX: (212) 627-4678
Year Established: 1980
Pub. Frequency: a.
Page Size: standard
Subscrip. Rate: $19.94/issue
Materials: 32,33
Freelance Pay: $200-$400/article
Circulation: 153,000
Circulation Type: paid
**Owner(s):**
Harris Publications, Inc.
1115 Broadway
New York, NY 10010
Telephone: (212) 807-7100
Ownership %: 100
**Management:**
Stanley Harris ..............................Publisher
**Editorial:**
Brad Tolinski ..............................Editor
Dennis Page ..............................Assistant Publisher
Greg DiBenedetto ...............Associate Publisher
**Desc.:** In the business of promoting the
guitar and the guitar player, through
sensitive interviews and appreciation of
guitarmanship. We are interested in the
love of the guitar and the relationship of
excellent players with their guitars.
**Readers:** Young and affluent, into hard
rock, heavy metal, new - funk, avant
garde.

**HIT PARADER** 24138
210 Rte. 4 E.
Paramus, NJ 07652
Telephone: (201) 843-5656
FAX: (201) 843-8775
Year Established: 1942
Pub. Frequency: m.

Page Size: standard
Subscrip. Rate: $3 newsstand; $29.50/yr.
Circulation: 100,000
Circulation Type: paid
**Owner(s):**
Charlton Publications, Inc.
40 Violet Ave.
Poughkeepsie, NY 12601
Telephone: (514) 454-7420
**Bureau(s):**
Hit Parader
441 Lexington Ave., Ste. 602
New York, NY 10017
Telephone: (212) 721-4454
Contact: Andy Secher, Editor
**Management:**
Mitch Herskowitz ...................Publisher
Victor Sierkowski .............Advertising Manager
**Editorial:**
Andy Secher ...........................Executive Editor
Andy Secher ...........................Editor
**Desc.:** Feature stories and photos on
Heavy Metal recording artists, analysis
of Heavy Metal music, record reviews,
song lyrics.
**Readers:** Heavy Metal music fans, median
age 16.5.

**JAZZTIMES** 69012
7961 Eastern Ave., Ste. 303
Silver Spring, MD 20910-4898
Telephone: (301) 588-4114
FAX: (301) 588-5531
Year Established: 1972
Pub. Frequency: 10/yr.
Page Size: standard
Subscrip. Rate: $21.95/yr. US; $35.95/yr.
Canada; $59.95/yr. elsewhere
Circulation: 65,000
Circulation Type: paid
**Owner(s):**
Jazz Times, Inc.
7961 Eastern Ave., Ste. 303
Silver Spring, MD 20910-4898
Telephone: (301) 588-4114
Ownership %: 100
**Editorial:**
Mike Joyce ................................Editor
**Desc.:** Covers swing and big band to
Brazilian, blues and contemporary jazz.

**KEYBOARD** 26133
411 Borel Ave.
San Mateo, CA 94402
Telephone: (415) 655-4100
FAX: (415) 358-9527
Year Established: 1975
Pub. Frequency: m.
Page Size: standard
Subscrip. Rate: $3.95 newsstand;
$29.95/yr.
Freelance Pay: $200-$350
Circulation: 70,000
Circulation Type: paid
**Owner(s):**
Miller Freeman, Inc.
600 Harrison Street
San Francisco, CA 94107
Telephone: (415) 905-2200
Ownership %: 100
**Management:**
Marshall W. Freeman ..................President
Pat Cameron ..............................Publisher
**Editorial:**
Tom Darter ..............................Managing Editor
Domininic Milano ...................Editorial Director
Vicki Hartung ..............................Advertising
Richard Leeds ...........................Art Director
Debra Greenberg ...................Editorial Assistant
Liz Ledgerwood ......................Graphics Editor

**Desc.:** Published for amateur and
professional keyboard players
(synthesizers, piano, electric piano,
computers, organ, electronic keyboards,
harpsichords) of all styles. Not for fans,
but for musicians. Covers history,
performers, equipment, MIDI, technique,
books, LPs, new products, how-to,
electronics, computers and music
software.
**Readers:** 31 years average age, 59%
professional/semi-pro playing styles.

**KICKS** 69608
P.O. Box 646
Cooper Station
New York, NY 10003
Telephone: (718) 789-4438
FAX: (718) 398-9215
Year Established: 1979
Pub. Frequency: a.
Page Size: standard
Subscrip. Rate: $5/newsstand
Materials: 02,04,06,10,11,12,16,19,20,21,
23,24,25,26,27,28
Print Process: web offset
Circulation: 5,000
Circulation Type: paid
**Owner(s):**
Miriam Linna & Billy Miller
P.O. Box 646, Cooper Station
New York, NY 10003
Telephone: (718) 789-4438
FAX: (718) 398-9215
Ownership %: 100
**Editorial:**
Billy Miller ...........................Editor
Miriam Linna ...........................Editor
**Desc.:** Covers rock & roll and popular
culture.

**MODERN DRUMMER** 26142
870 Pompton Ave.
Cedar Grove, NJ 07009
Telephone: (201) 239-4140
FAX: (201) 239-7139
Year Established: 1977
Pub. Frequency: m.
Page Size: standard
Subscrip. Rate: $3/yr.; $29.95/yr.
Materials: 01,02,06,10,12,17,20,21,23,24,
25,27,28,29,30,32,33
Freelance Pay: $50-$500
Print Process: offset
Circulation: 98,000
Circulation Type: paid
**Owner(s):**
Ronald L. Spagnardi
870 Pompton Ave.
Cedar Grove, NJ 07009
Telephone: (201) 239-4140
Ownership %: 50
**Management:**
Ronald L. Spagnardi ...................President
Ronald L. Spagnardi ...................Publisher
Bob Berenson ...................Advertising Manager
**Editorial:**
Ronald L. Spagnardi ...................Editor
Rick Van Horn ...................Managing Editor
Tracy Kearns ...................Administrative Assistant
Scott Bienstock ...................Art Director
Isabel Spagnardi ...................Associate Publisher
Adam Budofsky ...................Book Review Editor
William F. Miller ...................Fashion Editor
William F. Miller ...................Feature Editor
Scott Bienstock ...................Photo

**Desc.:** Exclusively directed towards the
varied specialized interest of drummers.
It is an up-to-date and reliable
information source concerning trends,
activities, materials, publications,
equipment, new ideas, educational
concepts, and the latest developments
of interest to student, semi-pro, and
professional drummers. Approximately
70 percent freelance written.
Departments include: feature interviews
with leading artists in the field; retail and
manufacturing level close-ups; complete
technical columns section covering all
phases of the instrument, industry
happenings, new products, books,
record reviews, and more.
**Readers:** Amateur, semi-pro and
professional.

**MUSIC CITY NEWS** 26144
United Artists Tower
50 Music Sq. W.
Nashville, TN 37203
Telephone: (615) 329-2200
FAX: (615) 327-2726
Mailing Address:
P.O. Box 22975
Nashville, TN 37202
Year Established: 1963
Pub. Frequency: m.
Page Size: standard
Subscrip. Rate: $2.50 newsstand, $18/yr.
special subcribers; $25.50/yr. others
Freelance Pay: $50-250/article
Circulation: 150,000
Circulation Type: paid
**Owner(s):**
Multimedia, Inc.
P.O. Box 1688
Greenville, SC 29602
Telephone: (803) 298-4203
Ownership %: 100
**Management:**
Bob Atkins ...........................Publisher
Bobbie Gorman ...................Advertising Manager
Mike Jones ...........................General Manager
**Editorial:**
Lydia Dixon Harden ...................Editor
Paige Easter ...................Art Director
**Desc.:** Edited for those involved with
country music, be it fan or professional.
Feature articles deal with country music
personalities and various aspects of the
country music industry. Monthly
departments include: LP Record
Reviews, Radio/TV/Film, Top Country
Sales Chart, Gospel, Fan Clubs, Star
Gazing, and New Faces.
**Readers:** Recent survey disclosed a
monthly readers families, and industry
professionals & executives. 500,000
readers, Median age 35, $25,000
income, 41% white collar, 65% married,
56% Female, 82% Homeowners, 57%
Urban, 78% Order by Mail, 34% Travel
over 2,000 miles on Vacation. Complete
kit available.

**MUSICIAN MAGAZINE** 26147
1515 Broadway, 11th Fl.
New York, NY 10036
Telephone: (212) 536-5208
FAX: (212) 536-6616
Year Established: 1976
Pub. Frequency: 12/yr.
Page Size: standard
Subscrip. Rate: $19.97/yr.
Materials: 01,02,06,10,12,21,23,24,25,28,
29,32,33
Circulation: 116,000
Circulation Type: paid

**Materials Accepted/Included:** 01-Business news 02-By-line articles 03-Fashion news 04-Food news 05-Freelance copy 06-Letters to editor 07-Real estate news 08-Sports news 09-Travel news
10-Book rev. 11-Movie rev. 12-Music rev. 13-TV rev. 14-Theater rev. 15-Coming events 16-Obituaries 17-Question & answer 18-Social announcements 19-Artwork 20-Cartoons 21-Photos 22-TV listings
23-Audio rec. 24-Video rec. 25-Books 26-Films/film clips 27-Personnel news 28-Press releases 29-New product news/photos 30-Trade lit. 31-Contracts awarded 32-Display adv. 33-Classified adv.

6-81

**Owner(s):**
Billboard Publications, Inc.
1515 Broadway
New York, NY 10036
Telephone: (212) 536-5208
Ownership %: 100
**Bureau(s):**
MUSICIAN MAGAZINE
5055 Wilshire Blvd.
Los Angeles, CA 90036
Telephone: (213) 525-2298
Contact: Mark Rowland, Editor
**Management:**
Paul Sacksman ........................Publisher
Andy Myers .................Advertising Manager
Stacey Zickerman ..............Circulation Manager
Devlin Sherlock ...............Promotion Manager
**Editorial:**
Mark Rowland ......................Executive Editor
Ted Greenwald ...........................Senior Editor
Bill Flanagan ...............................Editor
Keith Powers ...........................Managing Editor
Nathan Brackett ........................Administration
Miriam Campiz ...........................Art Director
Gary Krasner .....................Executive Publisher
**Desc.:** Contains insightful interviews with today's most acclaimed artists and tomorrow's brightest stars, in-depth record reviews and articles on the business side as well as on music.
**Readers:** 20 - 35 year-old musicians and music listeners.
**Deadline:** story-1st of mo.; news-1st of mo.; photo-1st of mo.; ads-1st of mo.

26148
**OPERA NEWS**
70 Lincoln Center Plz.
New York, NY 10023
Telephone: (212) 769-7080
Year Established: 1936
Pub. Frequency: m. (May-Nov.); bi-w. (Dec.-Apr.)
Page Size: standard
Subscrip. Rate: $2.95 newsstand; $30/yr.
Freelance Pay: negotiable
Print Process: web offset
Circulation: 120,000
Circulation Type: paid
**Owner(s):**
Metropolitan Opera Guild, Inc.
70 Lincoln Center Plz.
New York, NY 10023
Telephone: (212) 769-7000
FAX: (212) 769-7007
Ownership %: 100
**Management:**
Elaine Kones ....................Advertising Manager
**Editorial:**
Jane Poole ...............................Senior Editor
Patrick J. Smith ...............................Editor
Brian Kellow ...........................Managing Editor
Gregory Downer ...........................Art Director
John W. Freeman ........................Associate Editor
Marylis Sevilla - Gonzaga ........Associate Editor
Jeffrey Hildt ........................Associate Publisher
**Desc.:** World's largest circulation opera magazine. Features profiles of today's leading artists and rising young stars, articles on all aspects of opera, especially the weekly radio broadcasts from New York's Metropolitan Opera and to national opera telecasts. Also includes reviews of opera recordings, books and video releases.
**Readers:** Opera lovers the world around.

69643
**OPTION MAGAZINE**
2345 Westood Blvd., Ste. 2
Los Angeles, CA 90064
Telephone: (310) 449-1020
Year Established: 1985

Pub. Frequency: bi-m.
Subscrip. Rate: $3.50 newsstand; $15.95/yr.
Materials: 01,02,03,05,06,1012,19,21,23,24, 25,32,33,34
Print Process: web offset
Circulation: 27,000
Circulation Type: free & paid
**Owner(s):**
Sonic Options Network
1522-B Cloverfield Blvd.
Santa Monica, CA 90404
Telephone: (310) 449-0120
Ownership %: 100
**Management:**
Scott Becker ...............................Publisher
**Editorial:**
Mark Kemp ...............................Editor
**Desc.:** Covers non-mainstream music.

69014
**RELIX**
P.O. Box 94
Brooklyn, NY 11229
Telephone: (718) 258-0009
FAX: (718) 692-4345
Year Established: 1974
Pub. Frequency: bi-m.
Page Size: standard
Subscrip. Rate: $27/yr. US; $42/yr. foreign
Materials: 02,05,06,09,10,12,15,17,18,19, 20,21,23,24,25,28,29,30,31,32,33
Freelance Pay: varies
Print Process: web offset
Circulation: 50,000
Circulation Type: paid
**Owner(s):**
Relix Magazine, Inc.
P.O. Box 94
Brooklyn, NY 11229
Telephone: (718) 258-0009
FAX: (718) 692-4345
Ownership %: 100
**Editorial:**
Toni A. Brown ...............................Editor
**Desc.:** Specializes in music from San Francisco during the 1960's, with a focus on the Grateful Dead. Also covers current blues, folk, reggae and rock music.

26149
**ROLLING STONE**
1290 Ave. of the Americas, 2nd Fl.
New York, NY 10104
Telephone: (212) 484-1616
FAX: (212) 484-1713
Year Established: 1967
Pub. Frequency: bi-w.
Page Size: oversize
Subscrip. Rate: $3 newsstand; $25.95/yr.
Freelance Pay: negotiable
Circulation: 1,200,000
Circulation Type: paid
**Owner(s):**
Straight Arrow Publishers, Inc.
1290 Ave. of the Americas, 2nd
New York, NY 10104
Telephone: (212) 484-1616
Ownership %: 100
**Management:**
Jann S. Wenner ...............................Publisher
Howard Katz ....................Circulation Manager
**Editorial:**
Sid Holt ...............................Executive Editor
Jann S. Wenner ...............................Editor
Dana Fields ...............................Advertising
David Fricke ...............................Music Editor
Dana Fields ...............................Publicity Director
**Desc.:** General interest publication with a special interest in music and popular culture.
**Readers:** Ages 18-34.

26150
**SENSIBLE SOUND, THE**
403 Darwin Dr.
Buffalo, NY 14226
Telephone: (716) 681-3513
FAX: (716) 839-2264
Year Established: 1976
Pub. Frequency: q.
Page Size: pocket
Subscrip. Rate: $6 newsstand; $20/yr.
Materials: 02,05,06,10,12,19,20,21,23,24, 25,28,29,30,32,33
Freelance Pay: varies
Print Process: offset
Circulation: 11,500
Circulation Type: paid
**Owner(s):**
The Sensible Sound
403 Darwin Dr.
Buffalo, NY 14226
Telephone: (716) 681-3513
FAX: (716) 839-2264
Ownership %: 100
**Management:**
John A. Horan ...............................Publisher
Don Nowak ....................Circulation Manager
**Editorial:**
Karl Nehring ...............................Editor
Karl Nehring ...........................Publication Editor
**Desc.:** An audio equipment review publication. Covers the audio, audio equipment and recording industries. Departments include: Record Reviews, News Items, Technical Tips, Equipment Reviews.
**Readers:** Hi-Fi, audio hobbyists, manufacturer representatives and dealers.

26151
**SHEET MUSIC MAGAZINE**
223 Katonah Ave.
Katonah, NY 10536
Telephone: (914) 232-8108
Mailing Address:
    P.O. Box 58629
    Boulder, CO 80322
Year Established: 1976
Pub. Frequency: 6/yr.
Page Size: standard
Subscrip. Rate: $3/copy; $16.97/yr.
Materials: 12,14,15,28,29,32,33
Freelance Pay: $50/page
Print Process: web offset
Circulation: 192,388
Circulation Type: free & paid
**Owner(s):**
Shacor, Inc.
223 Katonah Ave.
Katonah, NY 10536
Telephone: (914) 232-8108
**Management:**
Edward J. Shanaphy ...........................President
Edward J. Shanaphy ...........................Publisher
**Editorial:**
Edward J. Shanaphy ...................Editor in Chief
**Desc.:** Musical self-help workshops with musical examples, occasional interviews with performers, articles about the various types of music or instruments; magazine oriented primarily to piano and organ players.
**Readers:** Home (amateurs) musician.
**Deadline:** story-6 wks. prior to pub. date; news-6 wks. prior; photo-6 wks. prior

26153
**SINGING NEWS, THE**
727-B Blowing Rock Rd.
Boone, NC 28607
Telephone: (704) 264-3700
FAX: (704) 264-4621
Mailing Address:
    P.O. Box 2810
    Boone, NC 28607
Year Established: 1969
Pub. Frequency: m.

Page Size: standard
Subscrip. Rate: $24/yr.
Materials: 06,12,15,17,21,23,27,28,29,30, 32,33
Print Process: web offset
Circulation: 128,000
Circulation Type: paid
**Owner(s):**
Jerry Kirksey
P.O. Box 2810
Boone, NC 28607
Telephone: (704) 264-3700
FAX: (704) 264-4621
Ownership %: 40

Maurice Templeton
P.O. Box 2810
Boone, NC 28607
Telephone: (704) 264-3700
FAX: (704) 465-4621
Ownership %: 60
**Management:**
Maurice Templeton ...........................Publisher
Jerry Kirksey ...........................Publisher
Rick Templeton ...............Advertising Manager
Jerry Kirksey ...............General Manager
**Editorial:**
Deana Surles ...........................Managing Editor
**Desc.:** Gospel music trade paper. News and features on the gospel music industry and its people, gospel record charts, gospel album reviews and Christian book reviews.
**Readers:** Gospel music industry, record companies, PS, talent agencies, recording studios, radio stations and stores. Southern gospel music fans.
**Deadline:** story-45 days prior to pub. date; news-45 days prior; photo-45 days prior

26152
**SING OUT! THE FOLK SONG MAGAZINE**
125 E. Third St.
Bethlehem, PA 18015
Telephone: (610) 865-5366
FAX: (610) 865-5129
Mailing Address:
    P.O. Box 5253
    Bethlehem, PA 18015
Year Established: 1950
Pub. Frequency: q.
Page Size: pocket
Subscrip. Rate: $4.50 newssstand; $18/yr.
Materials: 01,06,10,12,15,16,23,24,25,26, 27,28,29,30,31,32,33
Freelance Pay: $.07/wd.
Print Process: web offset
Circulation: 10,000
Circulation Type: free & paid
**Owner(s):**
The Sing Out Corporation
P.O. Box 5253
Bethlehem, PA 18015
Telephone: (215) 865-5366
Ownership %: 100
**Editorial:**
Mark D. Moss ...............................Editor
Diane Petro ...........................Managing Editor
Lynn Cohen Koehler ...........................Advertising
Kristen Morgan ...............................Art Director
**Desc.:** Contemporary and tradional folk music, dance, and storytelling.
**Readers:** Folk music and acoustic music enthusiasts.

67299
**2 HYPE**
210 Rte. 4 E., Ste. 401
Paramus, NJ 07652
Telephone: (201) 843-4004
Year Established: 1990
Pub. Frequency: bi-m.
Page Size: standard
Subscrip. Rate: $2.95/issue

**Materials Accepted/Included:** 01-Business news 02-By-line articles 03-Fashion news 04-Food news 05-Freelance copy 06-Letters to editor 07-Real estate news 08-Sports news 09-Travel news 10-Book rev. 11-Movie rev. 12-Music rev. 13-TV rev. 14-Theater rev. 15-Coming events 16-Obituaries 17-Question & answer 18-Social announcements 19-Artwork 20-Cartoons 21-Photos 22-TV listings 23-Audio rec. 24-Video rec. 25-Books 26-Films/film clips 27-Personnel news 28-Press releases 29-New product news/photos 30-Trade lit. 31-Contracts awarded 32-Display adv. 33-Classified adv.

**Owner(s):**
2Hype
210 Rte. 4 E., Ste. 401
Paramus, NJ 07652
Telephone: (201) 843-4004
Ownership %: 100
**Management:**
Scott Mitchell Figman ...........................Publisher

## Group 652-News

66732

### CITY JOURNAL, THE
52 Vanderbilt Ave.
New York, NY 10017
Telephone: (212) 599-7000
FAX: (212) 599-3494
Year Established: 1990
Pub. Frequency: q.
Page Size: standard
Subscrip. Rate: $6.95 newsstand; $24/yr.;
  $38/2 yr.
Freelance Pay: $.30/wd.
Circulation: 5,000
Circulation Type: paid
**Owner(s):**
Manhattan Institute, The
52 Vanderbilt Ave.
New York, NY 10017
Telephone: (212) 599-7000
Ownership %: 100
**Management:**
William Hammett ................................President
Maggie Gallagher ..............................Publisher
**Editorial:**
Myron Magnet .......................................Editor

64945

### CONTINENTAL NEWSTIME
341 W. Broadway, Ste. 265
San Diego, CA 92101
Telephone: (619) 492-8696
Year Established: 1987
Pub. Frequency: bi-w.
Page Size: standard
Subscrip. Rate: $52/6 mos.
Materials: 01,02,04,06,07,08,09,10,11,12,
  13,14,15,17,20,21,25,27,28,29,30,31,32,
  33
Print Process: offset
Circulation: 119,000
Circulation Type: free
**Owner(s):**
Continental Features/Continental News
  Service
341 W. Broadway, Ste. 265
San Diego, CA 92101
Telephone: (619) 492-8696
Ownership %: 100
**Management:**
Gary P. Salamone .............Advertising Manager
**Editorial:**
Gary P. Salamone ...............................Director
**Desc.:** A national magazine of news and
  commentary on national and
  international affairs.
**Deadline:** story-1st & 3rd Fri.; news-1st &
  3rd Fri.; photo-1st & 3rd Fri.; ads-1st &
  3rd Fri.

26167

### FOREIGN AFFAIRS
58 E. 68th St.
New York, NY 10021
Telephone: (212) 734-0400
Year Established: 1922
Pub. Frequency: 6/yr.
Page Size: pocket
Subscrip. Rate: $38/yr.
Circulation: 105,000
Circulation Type: paid
**Owner(s):**
Council On Foreign Relations, Inc.
58 E. 68th St.
New York, NY 10021
Telephone: (212) 734-0400
Ownership %: 100

**Management:**
David Kellogg ....................................Publisher
Chris Weyant ....................Advertising Manager
**Editorial:**
James F. Hoge, Jr. ...............................Editor
Fareed Zakeria .........................Managing Editor
Joseph O'Keefe ...................Book Review Editor
**Desc.:** Prestigious journal of international
  affairs.
**Readers:** Individuals interested in
  international affairs and businessmen.

66338

### HOUSTON PRESS
2000 W. Loop S., 19th Fl.
Houston, TX 77027
Telephone: (713) 624-1400
Year Established: 1989
Pub. Frequency: w.
Page Size: tabloid
Subscrip. Rate: $30/yr.; $50/2 yrs.
Freelance Pay: varies
Circulation: 85,000
Circulation Type: paid
**Owner(s):**
New Times Inc.
2000 W. Loop S., 19th Fl.
Houston, TX 77027
Telephone: (713) 624-1400
Ownership %: 100
**Management:**
Terry Coe .........................................Publisher
**Editorial:**
Jim Simmon ...........................................Editor

26173

### JET
820 S. Michigan Ave.
Chicago, IL 60605
Telephone: (312) 322-9300
FAX: (312) 322-9375
Year Established: 1951
Pub. Frequency: w.
Page Size: pocket
Subscrip. Rate: $36/yr.
Circulation: 975,000
Circulation Type: paid
**Owner(s):**
Johnson Publishing Co.
820 S. Michigan Ave.
Chicago, IL 60605
Telephone: (312) 322-9300
Ownership %: 100
**Bureau(s):**
Johnson Publishing Co. Washington
  Bureau
1750 Pennsylvania Ave., N.E.
Washington, DC 20006
Telephone: (202) 393-5860
Contact: Simeon Booker, Bureau Chief
**Management:**
John H. Johnson ...............................President
**Editorial:**
Robert E. Johnson ...............Executive Editor
Sylvia Flanagan ......................Senior Editor
John H. Johnson ....................................Editor
Malcolm West .......................Managing Editor
Pamela Cash ....................Book Review Editor
**Desc.:** Black news magazine covering
  features of general interest.
**Readers:** A cross section of the U.S.

67245

### MEMPHIS FLYER
460 Tennessee St.
Memphis, TN 38103
Telephone: (901) 521-9000
FAX: (901) 521-0129
Year Established: 1989
Pub. Frequency: w.
Page Size: tabloid
Subscrip. Rate: $50/yr.
Materials: 01,02,04,06,07,08,10,11,12,13,
  14,15,17,18,20,21,32,33
Print Process: web offset
Circulation: 130,000
Circulation Type: free

**Owner(s):**
Contemporary Media, Inc.
P.O. Box 687
Memphis, TN 38101
Telephone: (901) 521-9000
Ownership %: 100
**Management:**
Henry Turley, Jr. ...............................President
Kenneth Neill .....................................Publisher
Dennis Freeland ................Advertising Manager
Jeffrey Goldberg .......................Sales Manager
**Editorial:**
Tim Sampson .........................................Editor
**Desc.:** Contains only non-fiction articles on
  subjects directly related to Memphis &
  its immediate environments. Feature
  stories 1000-1500 words.
  Departments include: Letter to Editor,
  City Reporter, On Sports, Commentary,
  Steppin' Out, At the Movies, Memphis
  After Dark, On Music, On Theater and
  Backfire.
**Readers:** Average age 37.
**Deadline:** ads-Fri.

26183

### NEWSWEEK
1775 Broadway
New York, NY 10022
Telephone: (212) 350-4000
FAX: (212) 421-4993
Year Established: 1933
Pub. Frequency: w.
Page Size: standard
Subscrip. Rate: $41.08/yr.
Circulation: 3,240,131
Circulation Type: paid
**Owner(s):**
Washington Post Co., The
444 Madison Ave.
New York, NY 10022
Telephone: (212) 350-4000
Ownership %: 100
**Management:**
Richard M. Smith .............................President
Harold Shain ....................................Publisher
**Editorial:**
Richard M. Smith .....................Editor in Chief
Maynard Parker ......................................Editor
**Desc.:** Highly departmentalized news
  magazine covering every aspect of
  human endeavor including domestic and
  foreign affairs news, economics,
  entertainment, business, religion, books,
  education, people, etc. Special reports
  on important social, economic, and
  cultural trends are also featured
  periodically.
**Readers:** General readership among
  interested people.

26184

### SENTINEL, THE
150 N. Michigan, Ste. 2025
Chicago, IL 60604
Telephone: (312) 407-0060
FAX: (312) 407-0096
Year Established: 1911
Pub. Frequency: w.
Page Size: standard
Subscrip. Rate: $1 newsstand; $48.95/yr.
Freelance Pay: negotiable
Circulation: 46,000
Circulation Type: paid
**Owner(s):**
Sentinel Publishing Co.
150 N. Michigan, Ste. 3103
Chicago, IL 60604
Telephone: (312) 663-1101
Ownership %: 100
**Management:**
J. I. Fishbein ....................................Publisher
Janet Buzil ........................Advertising Manager
Lori Goldberg .......................Circulation Manager
Larry Pines .............................General Manager

**Editorial:**
J. I. Fishbein .........................................Editor
Ruth Marcus ............................Managing Editor
**Desc.:** Material deals with Jewish people
  and events with a Jewish nature on a
  local, national and international level.
**Readers:** Upper and middle class
  members.
**Deadline:** story-1 wk. prior to pub. date;
  ads-1 wk. prior

48949

### SPECTATOR MAGAZINE
1318 Dale St.
Raleigh, NC 27605
Telephone: (919) 828-7393
FAX: (919) 831-9217
Mailing Address:
  P.O. Box 12887
  Raleigh, NC 27605
Year Established: 1978
Pub. Frequency: w.
Page Size: tabloid
Subscrip. Rate: free; $24/yr.
Circulation: 60,000
Circulation Type: free & paid
**Owner(s):**
Spectator Publications, Inc.
1318 Dale St.
Raleigh, NC 27605
Telephone: (919) 828-7393
Ownership %: 100
**Management:**
R.B. Reeves ......................................Publisher
Candace Pirello .........................Sales Manager
**Editorial:**
R.B. Reeves .........................................Editor
**Desc.:** Represents an overview of The
  Triangle (Raleigh-Durham-Chapel Hill)
  lifestyle; features a calendar of events,
  restaurant guide, interviews, antique
  column, and a special pull-out section.
**Readers:** Upscale adults with high income
  and education levels.

26185

### TIME
Time & Life Bldg.
Rockefeller Ctr.
New York, NY 10020
Telephone: (212) 522-1212
Year Established: 1923
Pub. Frequency: w.
Page Size: standard
Subscrip. Rate: $1.19 newsstand;
  $61.88/yr.
Circulation: 4,103,772
Circulation Type: paid
**Owner(s):**
Time, Inc.
Time & Life Bldg.
New York, NY 10020
Telephone: (212) 522-1212
Ownership %: 100
**Management:**
Elizabeth Valk Long ...........................President
John Haire .........................................Publisher
Daniel Rubin ..........................General Manager
**Editorial:**
James R. Gaines ....................Managing Editor
Arthur Hochstein ..............................Art Director
Ken Godschall ...................Marketing Director
Michele Stephenson ................................Photo
**Desc.:** A complete coverage news
  magazine. Separate departments for
  each news category.
**Readers:** General readership in all
  communities.

26187

### U.S. NEWS & WORLD REPORT
2400 N St., N.W.
Washington, DC 20037
Telephone: (202) 955-2000
Year Established: 1933
Pub. Frequency: w.

---

**Materials Accepted/Included:** 01-Business news 02-By-line articles 03-Fashion news 04-Food news 05-Freelance copy 06-Letters to editor 07-Real estate news 08-Sports news 09-Travel news 10-Book rev. 11-Movie rev. 12-Music rev. 13-TV rev. 14-Theater rev. 15-Coming events 16-Obituaries 17-Question & answer 18-Social announcements 19-Artwork 20-Cartoons 21-Photos 22-TV listings 23-Audio rec. 24-Video rec. 25-Books 26-Films/film clips 27-Personnel news 28-Press releases 29-New product news/photos 30-Trade lit. 31-Contracts awarded 32-Display adv. 33-Classified adv.

Page Size: standard
Subscrip. Rate: $2.50 newsstand;
$34.50/yr.
Materials: 01,06
Print Process: web offset
Circulation: 2,150,000
Circulation Type: paid
**Owner(s):**
U.S. News & World Report, L.P.
1290 Ave. of the Americas
New York, NY 10104
Telephone: (212) 830-1500
Ownership %: 100
**Management:**
Fred Drasner ...........................President
Thomas R. Evans ...................Publisher
**Editorial:**
Merrill McLoughlin ......................Editor
Michael Ruby ..............................Editor
Rob Covey ..........................Art Director
Mark Godfrey ..............................Photo
**Desc.:** Reports and analyzes news of
government, business, industry, labor,
international relations, national defense,
tax and fiscal policies, economic
developments, politics, education,
science, medicine and world affairs.
**Readers:** Persons in business, industry
and government.

24846

**VITAL SPEECHES OF THE DAY**
P.O. Box 1247
Mt. Pleasant, SC 29465-1247
Telephone: (803) 881-8733
FAX: (803) 881-4007
Mailing Address:
P.O. Box 1247
Mt. Pleasant, SC 29465-1247
Year Established: 1934
Pub. Frequency: bi-m.
Page Size: standard
Subscrip. Rate: $37.50/yr.
Circulation: 14,000
Circulation Type: paid
**Owner(s):**
City News Publishing Company
P.O. Box 1247
Mt. Pleasant, SC 29465-1247
Telephone: (803) 881-8733
FAX: (803) 881-4007
Ownership %: 100
**Management:**
Genevieve T. Daly ...............President
Thomas F. Daly, III ...............Publisher
**Editorial:**
Thomas F. Daly, III ...........Executive Editor
**Desc.:** Carries speeches made by leaders
in economics, politics, education,
sociology, government, criminology,
finance, business, taxation, health, law,
labor and science on public questions.
**Readers:** Public, college and school
libraries, corporations

24852

**WILSON QUARTERLY, THE**
901 D St., S.W., Ste. 704
Washington, DC 20024
Telephone: (202) 287-3000
FAX: (202) 287-3772
Year Established: 1976
Pub. Frequency: q.
Page Size: standard
Subscrip. Rate: $24/yr.
Materials: 32
Circulation: 80,000
Circulation Type: paid
**Owner(s):**
Woodrow Wilson International for Scholars
Smithsonian Institution Bldg.
201 D St., S.W., Ste. 704
Washington, DC 20560
Telephone: (202) 357-2429
Ownership %: 100

**Management:**
Kathy Read ...........................Publisher
**Editorial:**
Steve Lagerfeld ..........................Editor
Jay Tolson ..................................Editor
Jeffery Paine ..............................Editor
James Carman ................Managing Editor
Robert Landers ................Associate Editor
**Desc.:** Explains and summarizes
development in serious research on
politics, the environment, the social
sciences, foreign affairs, history, arts, TV
and the press, economics, science, and
technology. Contains major essays and
reviews of both current books and
periodicals.
**Readers:** An educated, affluent general
audience; 96.4% college educated. $94,
700 average income; 84% business
executives, managers and professionals.

26188

**WORLD PRESS REVIEW**
200 Madison Ave., Ste. 2104
New York, NY 10016
Telephone: (212) 889-5155
FAX: (212) 889-5634
Year Established: 1961
Pub. Frequency: m.
Page Size: standard
Subscrip. Rate: $2.95 newsstand;
$24.95/yr.
Circulation: 53,000
Circulation Type: paid
**Owner(s):**
The Stanley Foundation
216 Sycamore St., Ste. 500
Muscatine, IA 52761
Telephone: (319) 264-1500
Ownership %: 100
**Management:**
Teri Schure ...........................Publisher
Tim O'Brien ...............Advertising Manager
Rita Polidori ...............Circulation Manager
**Editorial:**
Larry Martz ..................................Editor
Gail Robinson ................Managing Editor
**Desc.:** The only U.S. magazine devoted
entirely to selections from the press
outside the U.S. - reporting, comment
and cartoons from the great journals of
the world, translated and presented
each month in entertaining and
informative fashion. All text material
must first have been printed in the
foreign press. Departments include:
Viewpoints; Business; Economy and
Business Notes; Regional Reports -
Europe, Asia, Africa, Middle East; Living,
Cities, Books, Films, Art, Architecture,
Sports, Media, Looking at the U.S.,
Environment, Travel.
**Readers:** Thought and opinion leaders, all
535 members of Congress.
**Deadline:** news-4 wks. prior to pub. date;
ads-1 mo. prior

## Group 654-Occult

68811

**ASPECTS: ASTROLOGICAL
MAGAZINE**
P.O. Box 260556
Encino, CA 91426
Telephone: (818) 782-5573
Year Established: 1975
Pub. Frequency: q.
Subscrip. Rate: $7 newsstand; $25/yr.
Materials: 06,15,20,23,28,32
Circulation: 1,500
Circulation Type: controlled & paid

**Owner(s):**
Aquarius Workshops, Inc.
P.O. Box 260556
Encino, CA 91426
Telephone: (818) 782-5573
Ownership %: 100
**Editorial:**
Karen McCauley ..........................Editor
**Deadline:** story-Jan. I, Apr. 1, July 1, Oct.
1; ads-Feb. 1, May 1, Aug. 1, Nov. 1

25851

**FATE**
84 S. Wabasha
St. Paul, MN 55107
Telephone: (612) 291-1970
FAX: (612) 291-1908
Mailing Address:
P.O. Box 64383
St. Paul, MN 55164
Year Established: 1948
Pub. Frequency: m.
Page Size: standard
Subscrip. Rate: $2.95 newsstand;
$29.95/yr.
Materials: 02,05,06,10,15,19,20,21,32,33
Freelance Pay: $.10/word
Circulation: 120,000
Circulation Type: paid
**Owner(s):**
Llewellyn Worldwide, Ltd.
84 S. Wabasha
St. Paul, MN 55107
Telephone: (612) 291-1970
Ownership %: 100
**Management:**
Carl Llewellyn Weschcke ...................Publisher
**Editorial:**
Terry O'Neill ..................Editor in Chief
Les Stern ..................Managing Editor
Nancy M. ...............Advertising Representative
Trudelle
Amethust MacGregor ..................Advertising
Mark Chorvinsky ...................Consulting Editor
John Keel ...................Consulting Editor
Antonio Huneeus ..................Consulting Editor
Loyd Auerbach ...................Consulting Editor
Rosemary Guiley ..................Contributing Editor
Martin Caidin ...................Contributing Editor
**Desc.:** Publishes stories of strange or
mystical happenings. The
parapsychological fields we cover vary
widely: ESP, telepathy, ghosts and
hauntings, reincarnation, altered states
of consciousness, sorcery, divination,
possession, witchcraft, Fortean
phenomena, UFO's, monsters such as
the Loch Ness monster, abominable
snowmen, werewolves, vampires, types
of divination, biographies and
autobiographies of personalities in
psychic or occult fields, archaeological
topics. Departments include: I See By
The Papers, True Mystic Experiences,
My Proof Of Survival, Report From the
Readers, New Books.
**Readers:** Persons of all ages interested in
strange events, parapsychology,
Fortean phenomena, archaeology.

25983

**HOROSCOPE**
245 Park Ave.
New York, NY 10167
Telephone: (212) 354-6500
Year Established: 1935
Pub. Frequency: m.
Page Size: standard
Subscrip. Rate: $1.99 newsstand;
$19.97/yr.
Circulation: 240,000

**Owner(s):**
Bantam-Doubleday-Dell Publishing Group,
Inc.
666 Fifth Ave.
New York, NY 10103
Telephone: (212) 765-6500
Ownership %: 100
**Management:**
Fred Sabloff ...............Advertising Manager
Fred Sabloff ...................Sales Manager
**Editorial:**
Ronnie Grishman ..................Editor in Chief
Edward Kajkowski ..........................Editor
Jack Pettey ...................Associate Editor
**Desc.:** Astrology for beginners, advanced
and professionals.
**Readers:** Age group: teens to
octogenarians.

68817

**NEW AGE ASTROLOGY GUIDE
1995**
2640 Greenwich, Ste. 403
San Francisco, CA 94123
Telephone: (415) 921-1192
Year Established: 1972
Pub. Frequency: a.
Page Size: standard
Subscrip. Rate: $3.75 newsstand
Materials: 32
Print Process: web
Circulation: 20,000
Circulation Type: controlled
**Owner(s):**
Milo Kovar
2640 Greenwich, No. 403
San Francisco, CA 94123
Telephone: (415) 921-1192
Ownership %: 100
**Management:**
Milo Kovar ...........................Publisher
**Editorial:**
Milo Kovar ..................................Editor
**Desc.:** Explains the changes in planetary
patterns and the way they affect the
twelve zodical types during the ensuing
year.
**Readers:** Astrology buffs, psychoanalysts,
general public, astronomy researchers
on effects of planetary cycles on
mankind and its environment.
**Deadline:** story-Aug. 30; ads-Aug. 30

69089

**VISIONS**
4388 Amberwick Ln.
Moorpark, CA 93021
Telephone: (805) 523-1483
Year Established: 1975
Pub. Frequency: 6/yr.
Page Size: small
Subscrip. Rate: free
Materials: 02,04,06,10,11,12,13,14,15,19,
20,25,28,32
Circulation: 800
Circulation Type: paid
**Owner(s):**
Antonia Rodriguez
4388 Amberwick Ln.
Moorpark, CA 93021
Telephone: (805) 523-1483
Ownership %: 100
**Management:**
Antonia Rodriguez ...................Publisher
**Deadline:** story-1 wk. prior to pub. date;
news-1 wk. prior; photo-1 wk. prior; ads-
1 wk. prior

## Group 656-Parenting

26575

**AMERICAN BABY**
475 Park Ave., S.
New York, NY 10016
Telephone: (212) 689-3600
FAX: (212) 545-5400

Materials Accepted/Included: 01-Business news 02-By-line articles 03-Fashion news 04-Food news 05-Freelance copy 06-Letters to editor 07-Real estate news 08-Sports news 09-Travel news 10-Book rev. 11-Movie rev. 12-Music rev. 13-TV rev. 14-Theater rev. 15-Coming events 16-Obituaries 17-Question & answer 18-Social announcements 19-Artwork 20-Cartoons 21-Photos 22-TV listings 23-Audio rec. 24-Video rec. 25-Books 26-Films/film clips 27-Personnel news 28-Press releases 29-New product news/photos 30-Trade lit. 31-Contracts awarded 32-Display adv. 33-Classified adv.

Year Established: 1938
Pub. Frequency: m.
Page Size: standard
Subscrip. Rate: free
Freelance Pay: $300-$1,500/article
Circulation: 1,300,000
Circulation Type: controlled
**Owner(s):**
American Baby, A Sub. of Reed Publ.
(USA), Inc.
Cahners, 275 Washington St.
Newton, MA 02158
Telephone: (617) 964-3030
Ownership %: 100
**Management:**
Fern Greenberg .................Production Manager
**Editorial:**
Anne Winthrop .......................Managing Editor
Marjorie Crane Rosenstein .............Art Director
Robin Ruskin Linder .................Group Business
Director
Judith Nolte .................Group Editorial Director
Patricia Calderon .......Group Marketing Director
Sharon Summer .........Group Sales Director
Michael Arpino .................Production Supervisor
Judith Princz ...................Vice President/Group
Publisher
**Desc.:** Articles on various aspects of pre-
and postnatal care for mother and baby;
early learning features; nursery goods,
maternity and infant fashions. Articles
run from 1,500-2,000 words plus photos.
**Readers:** Expectant and new mothers.

## ATLANTA PARENT
69422
4330 Georgetown Sq., Ste. 506
Atlanta, GA 30338
Telephone: (404) 454-7599
FAX: (404) 454-7699
Year Established: 1983
Pub. Frequency: m.
Page Size: tabloid
Subscrip. Rate: $12/yr.
Materials: 02,05,17,29,32,33
Print Process: web offset
Circulation: 55,000
Circulation Type: controlled & paid
**Owner(s):**
Atlanta Parent, Inc.
4330 Georgetown Sq., Ste. 506
Atlanta, GA 30338
Telephone: (404) 454-7599
FAX: (404) 454-7699
Ownership %: 100
**Management:**
Liz White ..............................Publisher
**Desc.:** Covers family life, child care,
adolescence, motherhood, schools,
drugs, crafts and activities. Covers family
life, child care, adolescence,
motherhood, schools, drugs, crafts and
activities.
**Readers:** Families with children from birth
to 16-years old. 92% college educated;
60% make $50,000 or more per year;
74% own their own home; 94% are
women.
**Deadline:** story-3 mo. prior to pub. date;
news-3 mo. prior to pub. date; photo-3
mo. prior to pub. date; ads-10th of mo.
prior to pub. date

## BABY TALK
26577
25 W.43rd St.
New York, NY 10036
Telephone: (212) 840-2400
FAX: (212) 827-0019
Year Established: 1935
Pub. Frequency: m.
Page Size: standard
Subscrip. Rate: $12.95/yr.
Freelance Pay: $100-$300
Circulation: 1,300,000
Circulation Type: controlled

**Owner(s):**
Time Inc. Ventures
25 W. 43rd St.
New York, NY 10036
Telephone: (212) 840-4200
FAX: (212) 827-0019
Ownership %: 100
**Management:**
Carol Smith ............................President
Carol Smith ............................Publisher
**Editorial:**
Susan Strecker ...................Editor in Chief
Lori Fromm ............................Advertising
May Sugano Egner ....................Photo
Karen Palmieri ...................Production Director
**Desc.:** Pays on acceptance for short, true
experience articles on pregnancy and
caring for infant and young children.
Also buys articles on baby care
authored by physicians. Publicity
releases of new products sometimes
used in Shop Talk.
**Readers:** Expectant and new mothers.

## CHILD
65385
110 Fifth Ave.
New York, NY 10011
Telephone: (212) 463-1000
FAX: (212) 463-1553
Year Established: 1985
Pub. Frequency: 10/yr.
Page Size: standard
Subscrip. Rate: $15.94/yr.
Circulation: 650,000
Circulation Type: paid
**Owner(s):**
New York Times Co., The
110 Fifth Ave.
New York, NY 10011
Telephone: (212) 463-1000
Ownership %: 100
**Editorial:**
Freddi Greenberg ............................Editor
**Desc.:** In-depth yet personal articles for
self-assured parents raising children
today, a highly educated audience of
high achievers with a mindset for quality
information and advice. Helps parents
integrate kids into a high-pleasure, less
pressured life. Articles range from child
development and health, to education
and toys. features focus on travel,
beauty, food , fashion and home
furnishings. Also includes interactive
projects for parents and children to do
together.

## CONNECTICUT FAMILY
67276
141 Halstead, Ste. 3D
Mamaroneck, NY 10543
Telephone: (914) 381-7474
FAX: (914) 381-7672
Year Established: 1991
Pub. Frequency: m.
Page Size: standard
Subscrip. Rate: free
Circulation: 35,000
Circulation Type: free
**Owner(s):**
Family Publishing Group Inc.
141 Halstead Ave., Ste. 3D
Mamaroneck, NY 10543
Telephone: (914) 381-7474
Ownership %: 100
**Management:**
Felice Shapiro ......................Publisher
Cate Sanderson ...............Advertising Manager
**Editorial:**
Susan Ross Benamram ..........................Editor

## EMBARAZO
66728
685 Third Ave.
New York, NY 10017
Telephone: (212) 878-8700
FAX: (212) 878-4548
Year Established: 1990
Pub. Frequency: 2/yr.
Subscrip. Rate: free dist. in OBGYN's &
hospitals
Circulation: 250,000
Circulation Type: controlled & free
**Owner(s):**
Gruner & Jahr USA Publishing
685 Third Ave.
New York, NY 10017
Telephone: (212) 878-8700
Ownership %: 100
**Management:**
Dean Sanderson ............................Publisher
**Editorial:**
Johanna Bochholtz ...............Executive Editor
Jaceline Frank .......................Executive Editor
Anne George ....................Assistant Publisher
Ivette Cortes ............................Director

## EXCEPTIONAL PARENT
25848
290 Harvard St.
Brookline, MA 02146
Telephone: (617) 730-5800
FAX: (617) 730-8745
Year Established: 1971
Pub. Frequency: m.
Page Size: standard
Subscrip. Rate: $18/yr.
Freelance Pay: $25/pg.
Circulation: 50,000
Circulation Type: paid
**Owner(s):**
Joseph Valenzano
290 Harvard St.
Brookline, MA 02146
Telephone: (617) 730-5800
Ownership %: 100
**Management:**
Stanley D. Klein ...................Publisher
**Editorial:**
Stanley D. Klein ...........................Editor in Chief
**Desc.:** Articles for parents and
professionals concerned with children's
disabilities on practical, human, daily
questions as well as issues of long-
range planning, care and financing.
Technical information stripped of
professional jargon and practical advice
on day-to-day care. Departments
include: Family Forum, Parents Search,
Parents Respond, Book Reviews,
What's Happening.
**Readers:** Parents and professionals
concerned with the lives of children's
(infancy through adulthood) disabilities.

## EXPECTING
26587
685 Third Ave.
New York, NY 10017
Telephone: (212) 878-8700
Year Established: 1967
Pub. Frequency: q.
Page Size: 5 3/8 x 7 7/16
Subscrip. Rate: free
Circulation: 1,300,000
Circulation Type: controlled
**Owner(s):**
Gruner & Jahr USA Publishing
685 Third Ave.
New York, NY 10017
Telephone: (212) 878-8700
**Management:**
Linda Springett ...................Advertising Manager
**Editorial:**
Evelyn Podsiadlo ............................Editor
Bud Ward ...............Executive Publisher
**Readers:** Expectant mothers.

## FAMILIA DE HOY, LA
67259
529 Fifth Ave., 11th Fl.
New York, NY 10017
Telephone: (212) 916-3300
FAX: (212) 682-2952
Year Established: 1989
Pub. Frequency: bi-m.
Page Size: oversize
Subscrip. Rate: $11.95/yr.
Circulation: 52,000
Circulation Type: paid
**Owner(s):**
Covell Communications
529 Fifth Ave., 11th Fl.
New York, NY 10017
Telephone: (212) 916-3300
Ownership %: 100
**Management:**
Mara Covell ............................Publisher
Peter Winslow ....................Managing Director

## GRAND RAPIDS PARENT
69430
549 Ottawa Ave., N.W.
Grand Rapids, MI 49503-1444
Telephone: (616) 459-4545
FAX: (616) 459-4800
Year Established: 1989
Pub. Frequency: m.
Subscrip. Rate: $12/yr.
Circulation: 12,000
Circulation Type: free & paid
**Owner(s):**
Gemini Publications
549 Ottawa Ave., N.W.
Grand Rapids, MI 49503-1444
Telephone: (616) 459-4545
Ownership %: 100
**Management:**
Craig Rich .........................Advertising Manager
**Editorial:**
Carole Valade Smith ..............................Editor
**Desc.:** Covers finance, psychology, humor,
dining, education, food, new products,
events and recipes for parents.
**Deadline:** story-2 mo. prior to pub. date;
news-2 mo. prior; photo-2 mo. prior; ads-
6 wks. prior to pub. date

## HEALTHY KIDS
65375
475 Park Ave., S.
New York, NY 10016
Telephone: (212) 463-6582
FAX: (212) 545-5400
Year Established: 1989
Pub. Frequency: q.
Page Size: standard
Subscrip. Rate: free
Freelance Pay: $500 and over
Circulation: 1,500,000
Circulation Type: controlled
**Owner(s):**
Cahners Publishing Co.
475 Park Ave., S.
New York, NY 10016
Telephone: (212) 689-3600
Ownership %: 100
**Management:**
Joel J. Ehrlich ..............................Publisher
**Editorial:**
Phyllis Evans Steinberg ............................Editor
**Desc.:** Examines health issues of children
from infancy to three years of age.
**Readers:** Parents with young children.

## L.A. PARENT MAGAZINE
66718
443 E. Irving Dr.
Burbank, CA 91504
Telephone: (818) 846-0400
FAX: (818) 841-4380
Mailing Address:
P.O. Box 3204
Burbank, CA 91508
Year Established: 1981

**Materials Accepted/Included:** 01-Business news 02-By-line articles 03-Fashion news 04-Food news 05-Freelance copy 06-Letters to editor 07-Real estate news 08-Sports news 09-Travel news
10-Book rev. 11-Movie rev. 12-Music rev. 13-TV rev. 14-Theater rev. 15-Coming events 16-Obituaries 17-Question & answer 18-Social announcements 19-Artwork 20-Cartoons 21-Photos 22-TV listings
23-Audio rec. 24-Video rec. 25-Books 26-Films/film clips 27-Personnel news 28-Press releases 29-New product news/photos 30-Trade lit. 31-Contracts awarded 32-Display adv. 33-Classified adv.

6-85

Pub. Frequency: m.
Page Size: tabloid
Subscrip. Rate: $12/yr.; $18/2 yrs.
Freelance Pay: $.20/wd.
Circulation: 250,000
Circulation Type: controlled
**Owner(s):**
Wingate Enterprises, Inc.
443 E. Irving Dr.
Burbank, CA 91504
Telephone: (818) 846-0400
Ownership %: 100
**Management:**
Carey Bierman ...................................Publisher
**Editorial:**
Jack Bierman .........................................Editor
David Jamieson .......................Managing Editor
Harry Jigamian ....................Associate Publisher
Milli Militti ....................Special Projects Director
**Desc.:** Represents the most complete and
  only guide for parents in Los Angeles.
  Each issue contains reports and reviews
  on the places and pleasures of Southern
  California's largest community.

                                                    67261
**LONG ISLAND PARENTING NEWS**
2-12 W. Park Ave., Ste. 300
Long Beach, NY 11561
Telephone: (516) 889-5510
FAX: (516) 889-5513
Mailing Address:
  P.O. Box 214
  Island Park, NY 11558
Year Established: 1989
Pub. Frequency: m.
Page Size: tabloid
Subscrip. Rate: $20/yr.
Materials: 03,05,08,09,10,11,12,13,14,15,
  20,21,22,23,24,25,26,28,29,32,33
Freelance Pay: $25-$75
Print Process: web offset
Circulation: 50,000
Circulation Type: free
**Owner(s):**
Andrew Elias
P.O. Box 214
Island Park, NY 11558
Telephone: (516) 889-5510
Ownership %: 25

Pat Simms-Elias
Ownership %: 25

Arie Nadboy
Ownership %: 25

Annette Nadboy
Ownership %: 25
**Management:**
Arie Nadboy ......................................Publisher
Arie Nadboy ......................Advertising Manager
**Editorial:**
Pat Simms-Elias .....................................Editor
Andrew Elias .........................................Editor
**Readers:** Parents of pre-teens.

                                                    69536
**MOTHERING**
515 Don Gaspar
Santa Fe, NM 87501
Telephone: (505) 984-8116
FAX: (505) 986-8335
Mailing Address:
  P.O. Box 1690
  Santa Fe, NM 87504
Year Established: 1976
Pub. Frequency: q.
Page Size: standard
Subscrip. Rate: $4.95 newsstand;
  $18.95/yr.
Circulation: 70,000
Circulation Type: controlled & paid

**Owner(s):**
Peggy O'Mara
P.O. Box 1690
Santa Fe, NM 87504
Telephone: (505) 984-8116
Ownership %: 100
**Management:**
Peggy O'Mara ...................................Publisher
**Editorial:**
Peggy O'Mara .........................................Editor
**Desc.:** Articles and news covering all
  aspects of progressive childrearing,
  especially in the areas of health,
  learning, emotional and personal
  development.

                                                    67250
**NEW YORK FAMILY**
141 Halstead Ave., Ste. 3D
Mamaroneck, NY 10543
Telephone: (914) 381-7474
FAX: (914) 381-7672
Year Established: 1985
Pub. Frequency: m.
Page Size: standard
Subscrip. Rate: free
Circulation: 60,000
Circulation Type: controlled & free
**Owner(s):**
Family Publishing Inc.
141 Halstead, Ste. 3D
Mamaroneck, NY 10543
Telephone: (914) 381-7474
Ownership %: 100
**Management:**
Felice Shapiro ...................................Publisher
Cate Anderson ..................Advertising Manager
**Editorial:**
Susan Ross Benamuram .........................Editor

                                                    69743
**PARENTING**
301 Howard St., 18th Fl.
San Francisco, CA 94105-2252
Telephone: (415) 546-7575
FAX: (415) 546-0578
Year Established: 1987
Pub. Frequency: 10/yr.
Subscrip. Rate: $18/yr.
Circulation: 875,000
**Owner(s):**
Time Publishing Ventures, Inc.
301 Howard St., 18th Fl.
San Francisco, CA 94105-2252
Telephone: (415) 546-7575
Ownership %: 100
**Editorial:**
Steve Reddicliffe .........................Editor in Chief

                                                    26617
**PARENTS**
685 Third Ave.
New York, NY 10017
Telephone: (212) 878-8700
FAX: (212) 986-2656
Year Established: 1926
Pub. Frequency: m.
Page Size: standard
Subscrip. Rate: $2.50 newsstand;
  $12.97/yr.
Freelance Pay: $150-$2,000
Circulation: 1,825,000
Circulation Type: paid
**Owner(s):**
Gruner & Jahr USA Publishing
685 Third Ave.
New York, NY 10017
Telephone: (212) 878-8700
Ownership %: 100
**Management:**
Walter Ward .......................................Publisher
**Editorial:**
Ann Pleshette Murphy ...............Editor in Chief
Wendy Schuman .......................Executive Editor
Catherine Winters ..........................Senior Editor
Janet Gold .............................Managing Editor
Maxime Davidowitz ........................Art Director

Carol Straley ...............................Beauty Editor
Amy Genova ...............................Health Editor
**Desc.:** Covers all phases of infant and
  child care, prenatal to eighteen,
  including mental, physical, emotional,
  social development. This includes
  articles on child rearing, school and
  community problems, marriage and
  health pieces. Articles run about 2,
  000 words and most are written on a
  free-lance basis. Prefers friendly,
  colloquial style with quotes based on
  dependable research, specialists, etc.
  Does not want essays, lectures. Humor
  welcome, but not at the expense of
  children. Departments include: Home,
  Food, Fashion, Books.
**Readers:** Families with children, from
  infants to college age.

                                                    25907
**PARENTS' CHOICE**
1191 Chestnut St.
Newton, MA 02164
Telephone: (617) 965-5913
Mailing Address:
  P.O. Box 185
  Waban, MA 02168
Year Established: 1978
Pub. Frequency: q.
Page Size: tabloid
Subscrip. Rate: $18/yr.; $27/2 yrs.
Materials: 10,11,12,13,23,24,25,32,33
Freelance Pay: $150+
Print Process: web offset
Circulation: 175,000
Circulation Type: free & paid
**Owner(s):**
Parents' Choice Foundation
P.O. Box 185
Waban, MA 02168
Telephone: (617) 965-5913
Ownership %: 100
**Editorial:**
Diana H. Green ..........................Editor in Chief
Maggie Russell ...........................Managing Editor
**Desc.:** Articles designed to alert parents to
  trends and events in books, TV, records,
  films, toys, and computer software for
  children.
**Readers:** Concerned and involved parents
  & teachers.

                                                    68791
**PARENTS BABY**
685 Third Ave.
New York, NY 10017
Telephone: (212) 878-8700
Year Established: 1986
Pub. Frequency: a.
Circulation: 2,500,000
Circulation Type: paid
**Owner(s):**
Gruner & Jahr USA Publishing
685 Third Ave.
New York, NY 10017
Telephone: (212) 878-8700
Ownership %: 100
**Desc.:** Offers selected articles from
  Parents Magazine.

                                                    69435
**SAN FRANCISCO PENINSULA
  PARENT**
1131 Vancouver
Burlingame, CA 94010
Telephone: (415) 342-9203
FAX: (415) 342-9276
Year Established: 1984
Pub. Frequency: m.
Page Size: tabloid
Subscrip. Rate: $15/yr.
Circulation: 60,000
Circulation Type: controlled & paid

**Owner(s):**
Peninsula Parent Newspaper, Inc.
1131 Vancouver
Burlingame, CA 94010
Telephone: (415) 342-9203
Ownership %: 100
**Editorial:**
Lisa Rosenthal ..........................................Editor
**Desc.:** Resource guide for local events
  geared to parents.

                                                    66734
**SER PADRES**
685 Third Ave.
New York, NY 10017
Telephone: (212) 878-8700
FAX: (212) 286-0935
Year Established: 1990
Pub. Frequency: bi-m.
Page Size: standard
Subscrip. Rate: $1.50 newsstand; $6/yr.;
  free hospital dist.
Circulation: 400,000
Circulation Type: controlled & paid
**Owner(s):**
Gruner & Jahr USA Publishing
685 Third Ave.
New York, NY 10017
Telephone: (212) 878-8700
Ownership %: 100
**Management:**
Dean Sanderson ...................................Publisher
**Editorial:**
Jaceline Frank ...........................Executive Editor
Johanna Bochholtz ...................Executive Editor
Anne George .........................Assistant Publisher
Ivette Cortes ..............................................Director
**Desc.:** Covers day-to-day needs and
  concern of Hispanic parents.

                                                    68792
**TWINS**
6740 Antioch, Ste. 155
Merriam, KS 66204-1258
Telephone: (913) 722-1090
FAX: (913) 722-1767
Year Established: 1984
Pub. Frequency: bi-m.
Page Size: standard
Subscrip. Rate: $4.50 newsstand;
  $21.98/yr.
Materials: 02,06,10,17,19,20,21,23,24,25,
  26,28,29,32
Freelance Pay: varies
Print Process: web offset
Circulation: 50,954
Circulation Type: controlled & paid
**Owner(s):**
Twins Magazine, Inc.
6740 Antioch, Ste. 155
Merriam, KS 66204-1258
Telephone: (913) 722-1090
FAX: (913) 722-1767
Ownership %: 100
**Editorial:**
Barbara C. Unell .....................................Editor
Jean Cerne ...............................Managing Editor
Brenda Schifman ...............Advertising Director
Bob Hart ...............................Associate Editor
**Desc.:** Covers subjects from birth through
  the teenage years.
**Readers:** Parents of twins, triplets, or
  larger multiple births. Also -
  pediatricians, obstetricians, teachers,
  and childbirth educators.
**Deadline:** story-varies; news-varies; photo-
  varies; ads-2 mo. prior to pub. date

                                                    66727
**UNA NUEVA VIDA**
685 Third Ave.
New York, NY 10017
Telephone: (212) 878-8700
FAX: (212) 878-4548
Year Established: 1990
Pub. Frequency: a.
Subscrip. Rate: free in hospitals

**Materials Accepted/Included:** 01-Business news 02-By-line articles 03-Fashion news 04-Food news 05-Freelance copy 06-Letters to editor 07-Real estate news 08-Sports news 09-Travel news 10-Book rev. 11-Movie rev. 12-Music rev. 13-TV rev. 14-Theater rev. 15-Coming events 16-Obituaries 17-Question & answer 18-Social announcements 19-Artwork 20-Cartoons 21-Photos 22-TV listings 23-Audio rec. 24-Video rec. 25-Books 26-Films/film clips 27-Personnel news 28-Press releases 29-New product news/photos 30-Trade lit. 31-Contracts awarded 32-Display adv. 33-Classified adv.

Circulation: 450,000
Circulation Type: controlled & free
**Owner(s):**
Gruner and Jahr Publishing
685 Third Ave.
New York, NY 10017
Telephone: (212) 878-8700
Ownership %: 100
**Management:**
Dean Sanderson ..................................Publisher
**Editorial:**
Johanna Bochholtz ..................Executive Editor
Jaceline Frank ........................Executive Editor
Anne George ......................Assistant Publisher
Ivette Cortes ...................................Director
**Desc.:** Provides information on newborn
baby crae for Hispanic mothers.

67237

**WESTCHESTER FAMILY**
141 Halstead Ave., Ste. 3D
Mamaroneck, NY 10543
Telephone: (914) 381-7474
FAX: (914) 381-7672
Year Established: 1988
Pub. Frequency: m.
Page Size: standard
Subscrip. Rate: free
Circulation: 35,000
Circulation Type: controlled & free
**Owner(s):**
Family Publishing Group, Inc.
141 Halstead Ave., Ste. 3D
Mamaroneck, NY 10543
Telephone: (914) 381-7474
Ownership %: 100
**Management:**
Felice Shapiro ......................................Publisher
Cate Sanderson ................Advertising Manager
**Editorial:**
Susan Ross Benamram ..........................Editor

## Group 658-Pets

25719

**AMERICAN BRITTANY, THE**
103 E. Jackson
Marshfield, MO 65706
Telephone: (417) 468-6250
FAX: (417) 468-5860
Mailing Address:
P.O. Box 616
Marshfield, MO 65706
Year Established: 1934
Pub. Frequency: m.
Page Size: tabloid
Subscrip. Rate: $22/yr.
Materials: 06,08,15,16,21,32,33
Circulation: 3,900
Circulation Type: paid
**Owner(s):**
American Brittany Club, Inc.
P.O. Box 616
Marshfield, MO 65706
Telephone: (417) 468-6250
Ownership %: 100
**Editorial:**
Ron Smith ..................................Executive Editor
**Desc.:** Covers activities of local and
national brittany clubs. Feature articles
cover hunting, vet, hunting supplies,
bench shows and field trials, training,
pet ownership.
**Readers:** Owners of 1 or more dogs, and
hunters.
**Deadline:** story-1st of mo. prior to pub.
date; news-1st of mo. prior; photo-1st of
mo. prior; ads-1st of mo. prior

52636

**BIRD TALK**
3 Burroughs
Irvine, CA 92718
Telephone: (714) 855-8822
FAX: (714) 855-3045

Mailing Address:
P.O. Box 6050
Mission Viejo, CA 92690
Year Established: 1983
Pub. Frequency: m.
Page Size: standard
Subscrip. Rate: $2.95 newsstand;
$25.97/yr.; $40/2 yrs.
Materials: 32
Freelance Pay: varies
Circulation: 170,000
Circulation Type: paid
**Owner(s):**
Fancy Publications, Inc.
P.O. Box 57900
Los Angeles, CA 90057
Telephone: (213) 385-2222
Ownership %: 100
**Management:**
Norman Ridker ....................................Publisher
**Editorial:**
Julie Rach ...............................................Editor
Marian Engel ..........................Managing Editor
Kathleen Etchepare ..........................Art Editor
Mary Frederisy ..........................Assistant Editor
Vera Geuther ......................Circulation Director
Susan Stowe ......................Marketing Manager
Phil Samuelson ..............................News Editor
**Desc.:** Edited for the adult, pet bird owner
and provides medical information,
nutrition articles and tips on training and
breeding pet birds. Features include bird
training, human human interest
incidents, research developments,
caging tips, grooming how-tos, and
colorful photographs. Departments
include species profile in each issue with
four-color centerfold poster, bird show
calendar, breeder's directory, book and
new product reviews, and other articles
of interest to pet bird owners.
**Readers:** Both professional bird breeders
and especially general adult owners of
pet birds. Dedicated to pet owners
interested in staying aware of the latest
developments in the field of bird care
and ownership.

25725

**BLOODLINES**
100 E. Kilgore Rd.
Kalamazoo, MI 49001
Telephone: (616) 343-9020
FAX: (616) 343-7037
Year Established: 1905
Pub. Frequency: bi-m.
Page Size: standard
Subscrip. Rate: $2.50/copy; $12/yr. US;
$23 Canadian & foreign
Freelance Pay: varies, generally $100 per
submission
Circulation: 5,500
Circulation Type: paid
**Owner(s):**
United Kennel Club, Inc.
100 E. Kilgore Rd.
Kalamazoo, MI 49001
Telephone: (616) 343-9020
Ownership %: 100
**Management:**
Fred T. Miller ......................................President
Cindy Ftickley ..................Assistant Advertising
Manager
**Editorial:**
Kerry Knudsen ........................................Editor
Andy Johnson ....................Book Review Editor
Vicki Rand ..................................Feature Editor
Vicki Rand ........................New Products Editor
Lisa Watson ......................Production Assistant
Sondra McGee ......................Production Editor

**Desc.:** Features materials of interest to
dog owners and breeders. Includes
reports of shows, obedience trials,
working dog trials, weight
pulling retriever trials, and Schutzhund.
Reports from national and state breed
associations, plus articles on rearing,
training, showing, etc., profiles of
interesting people, veterinary and health
columns, book reviews, product reviews,
upcoming events, and U.K.C. rules and
policies regarding registration, events,
etc.
**Readers:** Dog Fanciers and owners and
breeders of various breeds of dogs.

25727

**BOXER REVIEW**
8760 Appian Way
Los Angeles, CA 90046
Telephone: (213) 654-3147
FAX: (213) 654-8318
Year Established: 1956
Pub. Frequency: 10/yr.
Page Size: standard
Subscrip. Rate: $30/yr.; $50/2 yr.; $45/yr.
foreign; $60/2 yr. foreign
Print Process: offset
Circulation: 2,000
Circulation Type: paid
**Owner(s):**
Drucker Publications
8760 Appian Way
Los Angeles, CA 90046
Telephone: (213) 654-3147
FAX: (213) 654-8318
Ownership %: 100
**Management:**
M. Drucker ..........................................Publisher
**Editorial:**
Kris Dahl ..................................................Editor
Kris Dahl ................................Managing Editor
**Desc.:** By-line articles deal with the
training of boxer, owning of dogs, etc.
Bulk of magazine devoted to reports of
shows, boxer club activities. Picture
coverage of dogs being shown, awards
received. Publicity material generally
handled as fillers.
**Readers:** Fanciers, breeders.

25832

**CAT FANCY MAGAZINE**
2401 Beverly Blvd.
Los Angeles, CA 90057
Telephone: (213) 385-2222
FAX: (213) 385-8565
Mailing Address:
P.O. Box 6050
Irvine, CA 92690
Year Established: 1965
Pub. Frequency: m.
Page Size: standard
Subscrip. Rate: $23.97/yr.
Circulation: 370,000
Circulation Type: paid
**Owner(s):**
Fancy Publications, Inc.
2401 Beverly Blvd.
Los Angeles, CA 90057
Telephone: (310) 385-2222
Ownership %: 100
**Bureau(s):**
Fancy Publications
3 Burroughs
Irvine, CA 92718
Telephone: (714) 855-8822
Contact: Barbara Kotowitz, Manager
**Management:**
Norman Ridker ....................................Publisher
Vera Geuther ......................Circulation Manager
**Editorial:**
Debra Phillips-Donaldson ..........................Editor
Bill Vernor ......................Production Director
Marc L. Fredman ....................................Sales
Mary Anne Murphy ....................................Sales

**Desc.:** A monthly magazine oriented
towards the general cat owning public.
Feature articles deal with health care,
grooming, showing and breeding.
Regular departments include latest show
schedules and reports and up-to-date
health care information written by some
of the leading veterinarians in the
country. Color photographs and articles
deal with the domestic as well as the
exotic cat. Departments include: Ask the
Vet, Litterbox, Poetry Page, Grooming
Your Cat.
**Readers:** Consumer audience, cat owner
show exhibitors, breeders, veterinarians.

25833

**CATS MAGAZINE**
2750-A S. Ridgewood Ave.
South Daytona, FL 32119
Telephone: (904) 788-2770
Mailing Address:
P.O. Box 290037
Port Orange, FL 32129
Year Established: 1945
Pub. Frequency: m.
Page Size: standard
Subscrip. Rate: $2.50 newsstand;
$21.97/yr.
Materials: 05,06,10,19,20,21,29,32,33
Freelance Pay: $50-$75/pg.
Print Process: web offset
Circulation: 148,000
Circulation Type: paid
**Owner(s):**
CATS Magazine, Inc.
P.O. Box 290037
Port Orange, FL 32129
Telephone: (904) 788-2770
Ownership %: 100
**Management:**
Ray Copeland ......................................President
Ray Copeland ....................................Publisher
Ruth Ann Copeland ..........Circulation Manager
Kelly Wells ..................New Products Manager
**Editorial:**
Tracey Copeland ....................................Editor
Roy Copeland ....................Production Director
**Desc.:** Contains articles on cat care and
health, history, literature, poems, light
fiction, cartoons, and photo stories.
Departments include: Letters to Editor,
Poetry Page, Book Reviews, Veterinarian
Column, Cat Show Calendar, Show
News, and New Products. Special
"Exhibitor Edition" is published for cat
breeders and exhibitors.
**Readers:** Pet cat owners, cat breeders
and veterinarians.

25730

**COLLIE REVIEW, THE**
3771 Longview Valley Rd.
Sherman Oaks, CA 91423
Telephone: (818) 990-7914
Year Established: 1946
Pub. Frequency: 10/yr.
Page Size: standard
Subscrip. Rate: $30/yr.; $50/2yr.; $45/yr.
foreign; $60/2 yr. foreign
Materials: 02,04,05,06,10,11,13,15
Circulation: 2,000
Circulation Type: paid
**Owner(s):**
The Collie Review
3771 Longview Valley Rd.
Sherman Oaks, CA 91423
Telephone: (818) 990-7914
Ownership %: 100
**Management:**
L.C. Rugg ................................................Owner
L.C. Rugg ............................................Publisher
**Editorial:**
L.C. Rugg ....................................Editor in Chief

**Materials Accepted/Included:** 01-Business news 02-By-line articles 03-Fashion news 04-Food news 05-Freelance copy 06-Letters to editor 07-Real estate news 08-Sports news 09-Travel news 10-Book rev. 11-Movie rev. 12-Music rev. 13-TV rev. 14-Theater rev. 15-Coming events 16-Obituaries 17-Question & answer 18-Social announcements 19-Artwork 20-Cartoons 21-Photos 22-TV listings 23-Audio rec. 24-Video rec. 25-Books 26-Films/film clips 27-Personnel news 28-Press releases 29-New product news/photos 30-Trade lit. 31-Contracts awarded 32-Display adv. 33-Classified adv.

6-87

**Desc.:** By-line articles deal with the training of collies, owning of dogs, etc. Bulk of magazine devoted to reports of shows, collie club activities. Picture coverage of dogs being shown, awards received. Publicity material generally handled as fillers. Educational & health articles requested. Personal interest stories included.
**Readers:** Fanciers, breeders.
**Deadline:** 1st of mo. for next mo. issue

25732

**DOG FANCY MAGAZINE**
2401 Beverly Blvd.
Los Angeles, CA 90057
Telephone: (213) 385-2222
Mailing Address:
P.O. Box 6050
Mission Viejo, CA 92690
Year Established: 1970
Pub. Frequency: m.
Page Size: standard
Subscrip. Rate: $15.97/yr.
Materials: 32,33
Circulation: 85,000
Circulation Type: paid
**Owner(s):**
Fancy Publications, Inc.
5509 Santa Monica Blvd.
Los Angeles, CA 90038
Telephone: (310) 466-1166
Ownership %: 100
**Management:**
Norman Ridker .............................Publisher
Penny Stewart ...................Circulation Manager
Marie Madera ....................Production Manager
**Editorial:**
Kim Thornton .................................Editor
Marty Gale ....................................Sales
Marc L. Fredman ..............................Sales
**Desc.:** A monthly magazine oriented towards the general dog-owning public. Feature articles deal with health care, grooming, showing and breeding. Regular departments include the latest show schedules and reports and up-to-date health care information written by some of the leading veterinarians in the country. There is a do-it-yourself department with new projects you can build for your dog as well as a section on dog denetics. Color photographs and articles deal with the domestic as well as the exotic dog. Departments include: Puppouri, Tell Me Why.
**Readers:** Consumer audience, dog owner show exhibitors, breeders, veterinarians.

25733

**DOG WORLD**
29 N. Wacker Dr.
Chicago, IL 60606
Telephone: (312) 726-2802
FAX: (312) 726-4103
Mailing Address:
P.O. Box 6500
Chicago, IL 60680
Year Established: 1916
Pub. Frequency: m.
Page Size: standard
Subscrip. Rate: $3.95/copy; $28/yr.
Materials: 01,02,04,0,06,10,15,19,20,21,25,
27,28,29,32,33
Print Process: web offset
Circulation: 55,000
Circulation Type: paid
**Owner(s):**
Maclean Hunter Publishing Co.
29 N. Wacker Dr.
Chicago, IL 60606
Telephone: (312) 726-2802
FAX: (312) 726-4103
Ownership %: 100

**Management:**
Gordon L. Coleman .........................Publisher
Gordon L. Coleman ..........Advertising Manager
Susan Stalioraitis ..................Business Manager
**Editorial:**
Donna Marcel ...............................Editor
**Desc.:** Highly specialized publication dealing with genetics, health, showing, training of purebred dogs. Writers must have necessary background and training to produce acceptable material. Carries news, reports, etc.
**Readers:** Dog breeders, exhibitors, kennel owners, dog owners, vets, handlers, judges, trainers.

54002

**FRESHWATER & MARINE AQUARIUM**
144 W. Sierra Madre Blvd.
Sierra Madre, CA 91024
Telephone: (818) 355-1476
FAX: (818) 355-6415
Mailing Address:
P.O. Box 487
Sierra Madre, CA 91025
Year Established: 1977
Pub. Frequency: m.
Page Size: standard
Subscrip. Rate: $2.95 newsstand US;
$3.50 newsstand Canada; $22/yr. US;
$27.50/yr. foreign
Materials: 32
Freelance Pay: $50-$350/article
Circulation: 60,000
Circulation Type: paid
**Owner(s):**
RC Publications Corp.
144 W. Sierra Madre Blvd.
Sierra Madre, CA 91024
Telephone: (818) 355-1476
Ownership %: 100
**Management:**
Don Dewey ................................Publisher
Barbara Richardson ..........Advertising Manager
**Editorial:**
Patricia Crews .........................Executive Editor
Susan Steele ...............................Art Director
Dick Kidd ..............................Technical Editor
**Desc.:** Geared to the beginning, intermediate and advanced aquarium hobbyist as well as the professional aquariologist.
**Readers:** Hobbyists and pet shop owners.

69045

**GOOD DOG! MAGAZINE**
511 Harbor View Cir.
Charleston, SC 29412-3205
Telephone: (803) 795-9555
FAX: (803) 795-2930
Mailing Address:
P.O. Box 31292
Charleston, SC 29417
Year Established: 1988
Pub. Frequency: bi-m.
Page Size: standard
Subscrip. Rate: $3 newsstand; $18/yr. US;
$25/yr. foreign
Circulation: 35,000
Circulation Type: paid
**Owner(s):**
Ross Becker
P.O Box 31292
Charleston, SC 29417
Telephone: (803) 795-9555
FAX: (803) 795-2930
Ownership %: 100
**Management:**
Ross Becker ...............................Publisher
Michael Goldberg .........New Products Manager
**Editorial:**
Judi Sklar ...................................Editor
Doug Furgeson .............................Advertising
Heather Siegel ........................Assistant Editor
Donna Schonker ...............................Sales

**Desc.:** Provides product test reports, plus articles on nutrition, health training, unusual dogs and fun with dogs.
**Readers:** Dog owners.

69046

**I LOVE CATS**
950 Third Ave., 16th Fl.
New York, NY 10022
Telephone: (212) 888-1855
FAX: (212) 838-8420
Year Established: 1988
Pub. Frequency: bi-m.
Page Size: standard
Subscrip. Rate: $3.50 newsstand; $21/yr.
Materials: 32
Circulation: 175,000
Circulation Type: paid
**Owner(s):**
Grass Roots Publishing Co., Inc.
950 Third Ave., 16th Fl.
New York, NY 10022
Telephone: (212) 888-1855
Ownership %: 100
**Management:**
Suzann Hochman .........................Publisher
Robert Miller ...................Advertising Manager
**Editorial:**
Lisa Sheets ...................................Editor
Renee Cajigal-Delgodo .......Marketing Manager
**Desc.:** Features information necessary for cat owners to help their cats live healthier and happier lives. Includes proper nutrition, veterinarian advice, dental care and stories about cat lovers and their adventures with cats.

59557

**INSECT CONTROL GUIDE**
37733 Euclid Ave.
Willoughby, OH 44094-5992
Telephone: (216) 942-2000
FAX: (216) 975-3447
Year Established: 1982
Pub. Frequency: a.
Page Size: standard
Subscrip. Rate: $39/yr. US; $47/yr. foreign
**Owner(s):**
Meister Publishing Co.
37733 Euclid Ave.
Willoughby, OH 44094-5992
Telephone: (216) 942-2000
Ownership %: 100
**Editorial:**
Stella K. Naegely ...........................Editor
Diane Sharp .........................Managing Editor
Charlotte Sine .....................Editorial Director
Alan C. Strohmaier ...........Advertising Director
Alan C. Strohmaier ............Associate Publisher
**Desc.:** Describes & explains the proper use of insecticides. Insecticides are listed by crops, recommended rates, pests controlled, tank mixes, applications & other data. Covers major & minor crops, as well as non-cropland. The information is indexed & cross-referenced by insecticide, pests & crops.

69047

**INTER ACTIONS**
321 Burnett Ave. S., 3rd Fl.
Renton, WA 98055
Telephone: (206) 226-7357
FAX: (206) 235-1076
Mailing Address:
P.O. Box 1080
Renton, WA 98057-9906
Year Established: 1983
Pub. Frequency: q.
Page Size: standard
Subscrip. Rate: $15/yr. individuals US;
$22/yr. foreign; or donations
Print Process: offset
Circulation: 5,000
Circulation Type: paid

**Owner(s):**
Delta Society
P.O. Box 1080
Renton, WA 98055
Telephone: (206) 226-7357
Ownership %: 100
**Editorial:**
Linda M. Hines ...........................Editor in Chief
**Desc.:** Covers interactions of people, animals and nature, animal-assisted, activity, therapy, and community people-pet programs.

25759

**POODLE REVIEW**
4401 Zephyr St.
Wheat Ridge, CO 80033
Telephone: (303) 420-2222
FAX: (303) 422-7000
Year Established: 1955
Pub. Frequency: bi-m.
Page Size: standard
Subscrip. Rate: $42/yr.; $57/yr. foreign
Materials: 05,06,10,15,16,17,18,19,20,21
Freelance Pay: complimentary issue in
which article appears
Print Process: offset
Circulation: 1,891
Circulation Type: paid
**Owner(s):**
Hoflin Publishing Ltd.
4401 Zephyr St.
Wheat Ridge, CO 80033
Telephone: (303) 420-2222
FAX: (303) 422-7000
Ownership %: 100
**Management:**
Don Hoflin ................................Publisher
Cindy Kerstiens ....................Business Manager
**Editorial:**
Don Hoflin ..............................Executive Editor
Laurie Neufeld .......................Assistant Editor
**Readers:** People who breed and show poodles.
**Deadline:** story-2 wks. prior to pub. date;
news-2 wks. prior; photo-2 wks. prior;
ads-8th of mo. prior

25761

**PURE-BRED DOGS/AKC GAZETTE**
51 Madison Ave.
New York, NY 10010
Telephone: (212) 696-8260
Year Established: 1889
Pub. Frequency: 12/yr.
Page Size: standard
Subscrip. Rate: $28/yr.
Materials: 02,06,10,15,21,32,33
Freelance Pay: $100+
Print Process: web
Circulation: 55,000
Circulation Type: paid
**Owner(s):**
American Kennel Club, Inc.
51 Madison Ave.
New York, NY 10010
Telephone: (212) 696-8200
Ownership %: 100
**Management:**
American Kennel Club .......................Publisher
**Editorial:**
Beth Adelman ..........................Executive Editor
Heather C. Hamilton ..........Advertising Director
**Desc.:** Devoted to all aspects of purebred dogs: health, care, study, breeding, exhibiting, etc. Annual photography & fiction contests.
**Readers:** Serious dog hobbyists.
**Deadline:** story-4 mos. prior to pub. date;
ads-2 mos prior

69053

**REPTILE & AMPHIBIAN MAGAZINE**
Box 3709, Rte. 61, R.D. 3
Pottsville, PA 17901-9219
Telephone: (717) 622-6050
FAX: (717) 622-5858

---

Materials Accepted/Included: 01-Business news 02-By-line articles 03-Fashion news 04-Food news 05-Freelance copy 06-Letters to editor 07-Real estate news 08-Sports news 09-Travel news 10-Book rev. 11-Movie rev. 12-Music rev. 13-TV rev. 14-Theater rev. 15-Coming events 16-Obituaries 17-Question & answer 18-Social announcements 19-Artwork 20-Cartoons 21-Photos 22-TV listings 23-Audio rec. 24-Video rec. 25-Books 26-Films/film clips 27-Personnel news 28-Press releases 29-New product news/photos 30-Trade lit. 31-Contracts awarded 32-Display adv. 33-Classified adv.

Year Established: 1989
Pub. Frequency: bi-m.
Page Size: pocket
Subscrip. Rate: $3.50 newsstand; $16/yr.
Materials: 02,06,10,15,17,21,23,24,25,32,33
Freelance Pay: $75-100
Print Process: sheetfed
Circulation: 14,000
Circulation Type: paid
**Owner(s):**
N.G. Publishing
Box 3709, Rte. 61, R.D. 3
Pottsville, PA 17901-9219
Telephone: (717) 622-6050
FAX: (717) 622-5858
Ownership %: 100
**Editorial:**
Norman Frank, DVM .................................Editor
Erica Ramus ...........................Associate Editor
**Readers:** Amateur reptile and amphibian hobbyists.
**Deadline:** ads-2 mo. prior to pub. date

---

**RESCUE** 67288
P.O. Box 116
Woodstock, NY 12498
Telephone: (914) 679-2355
Year Established: 1990
Pub. Frequency: q.
Page Size: standard
Subscrip. Rate: donations of $25 or more
Circulation: 30,000
Circulation Type: controlled
**Owner(s):**
National Dog Registry
P.O. Box 116
Woodstock, NY 12498
Telephone: (914) 679-2355
Ownership %: 100
**Management:**
Bette Rapoport ...........................Publisher
Greg Becker ...............Advertising Manager
**Editorial:**
Greg Becker ...............................Editor

---

**ROTTWEILER QUARTERLY** 69050
3355 Conant Ln.
Watsonville, CA 95076
Telephone: (408) 728-8461
FAX: (408) 728-4708
Mailing Address:
  P.O. Box 900
  Aromas, CA 95004
Year Established: 1987
Pub. Frequency: q.
Page Size: standard
Subscrip. Rate: $36/yr. US; $44/yr. foreign; $65/2 yrs. US; $85/2 yrs. foreign; $80/yr. airmail
Materials: 02,10,15,17,18,19,20,21,24,25, 28,29,30,32
Freelance Pay: $100 for published articles
Print Process: offset
Circulation: 3,850
Circulation Type: paid
**Owner(s):**
GRQ Publications
3355 Conant Ln.
Watsonville, CA 95076
Telephone: (408) 728-8461
FAX: (408) 728-4708
Ownership %: 50

Robin Stark
P.O. Box 900
Aromas, CA 95004
Ownership %: 50
**Management:**
Jill Kessler ...........................Circulation Manager
**Editorial:**
Robin Stark .................................Editor
**Desc.:** Covers training, breeding, working, health issues, statistics, show coverage, tip sharing and humor.

**Readers:** Rottweiler owners and fanciers.
**Deadline:** story-15th of every 3rd mo.; news-15th of every 3rd mo.; photo-15th of every 3rd mo.; ads-15th of every 3rd mo.

---

**TROPICAL FISH HOBBYIST** 26017
One TFH Plz.
Third & Union Aves.
Neptune City, NJ 07753
Telephone: (908) 988-8400
FAX: (908) 988-5466
Mailing Address:
  P.O. Box 427
  Neptune City, NJ 07753
Year Established: 1952
Pub. Frequency: m.
Page Size: standard
Subscrip. Rate: $30/yr.
Freelance Pay: $35-$200
Circulation: 60,000
Circulation Type: paid
**Owner(s):**
T.F.H. Publications, Inc.
One TFH Plz.
Third & Union Aves.
Neptune City, NJ 07753
Telephone: (908) 988-8400
Ownership %: 100
**Management:**
Dr. Herbert R. Axelrod ...................President
**Editorial:**
Dr. Herbert R. Axelrod ............Executive Editor
Dr. Warren E. Burgess .................Senior Editor
Ray Hunziker ...............................Editor
**Desc.:** Articles on tropical fish and aquariums are full color features and specializes in showing new tropicals in color. Breeding articles (how to breed and maintain new species) are carried.
**Readers:** Beginning and advanced acquarists.
**Deadline:** ads-2 mos. prior to pub. date

---

## Group 660-Photography

**AMERICAN PHOTO** 67295
1633 Broadway, 43rd Fl.
New York, NY 10009
Telephone: (212) 767-6000
FAX: (212) 767-5600
Year Established: 1978
Pub. Frequency: bi-m.
Page Size: broadsheet
Subscrip. Rate: $19.90/yr.
Circulation: 250,000
Circulation Type: paid
**Owner(s):**
Hachette Filipacchi Magazines, Inc.
1633 Broadway, 43rd Fl.
New York, NY 10009
Telephone: (212) 767-6000
**Management:**
David Pecker .................................President
Thomas Witschi ...............................Publisher
Steven Aaron ...................Advertising Manager
**Editorial:**
David Schomauer .........................Editor

---

**CAMERA & DARKROOM MAGAZINE** 67293
9171 Wilshire Blvd., Ste. 300
Beverly Hills, CA 90212
Telephone: (310) 858-7155
FAX: (310) 274-7985
Year Established: 1979
Pub. Frequency: m.
Page Size: standard
Subscrip. Rate: $3.99 newsstand; $24.95/yr.
Freelance Pay: $450-$750
Circulation: 43,000
Circulation Type: paid

---

**Owner(s):**
LFP Publishing, Inc.
9171 Wilshire Blvd., Ste. 300
Beverly Hills, CA 90210
Telephone: (310) 858-7100
Ownership %: 100
**Management:**
Jim Kohls .................................President
Donna Hahner ...........................Vice President
Larry Flynt ...............................Publisher
**Desc.:** Eclectic monthly photo magazine featuring fine-art portfolios, photographer's profiles, in-depth product reviews, technical how-to articles with emphasis on darkroom photography, industry news, monthly questions and answers, photo tips, critiques, book reviews and video reviews.
**Readers:** Beginner through advanced amateur photographers.

---

**CLUB MODELE** 71257
P.O. Box 15760
Stamford, CT 06901
Telephone: (203) 967-9952
FAX: (203) 975-1119
Year Established: 1994
Pub. Frequency: bi-m.
Subscrip. Rate: $24/yr.
Circulation: 100,000
Circulation Type: paid
**Owner(s):**
Aquino Productions, Inc.
P.O. Box 15760
Stamford, CT 06901
Telephone: (203) 967-9952
Ownership %: 100
**Management:**
Andres Aquino ...........................Publisher
**Editorial:**
Andres Aquino ...........................Editor

---

**PETERSEN'S PHOTOGRAPHIC** 24313
6420 Wilshire Blvd.
Los Angeles, CA 90048
Telephone: (213) 782-2000
FAX: (213) 782-2263
Year Established: 1972
Pub. Frequency: m.
Page Size: standard
Subscrip. Rate: $19.94/yr.
Freelance Pay: $60/pg.
Circulation: 209,000
Circulation Type: paid
**Owner(s):**
Petersen Publishing Co.
6420 Wilshire Blvd.
Los Angeles, CA 90048
Telephone: (213) 782-2000
Ownership %: 100
**Management:**
F.R. Waingrow ...........................President
Jaqueline Augustine ...........................Publisher
**Editorial:**
Karen Geller-Shinn .........................Exec. Editor
Mike Stensvold ...........................Senior Editor
David B. Brooks ...........................Senior Editor
Bill Hurter ...............................Editor
Franklin Cameron ...................Managing Editor
George Fukuda ...........................Art Director
Nigel P. Heaton ...........................Director
**Desc.:** Attention is on how-to articles, plus helpful ideas on lighting techniques, darkroom, cameras, lenses, films, etc. The entire photographic experience is explored and allows the reader to accumulate a reference library on photography. Departments include: One-To-One, Tools of the Trade, Pro Talk, Close-Up, Proof Sheet, Viewfinder, Monthly Photo Contest.
**Readers:** Advanced amateur photographers.

---

**PHOTO COMPETITION USA** 69060
4300 Chestnut St. #402
Philadelphia, PA 19104-2963
Telephone: (215) 569-8611
Year Established: 1992
Pub. Frequency: q.
Page Size: standard
Subscrip. Rate: $23.95/yr. US; $35/yr. foreign
Materials: 01,02,05,06,10,15,19,20,21,25, 28,32,33,34
Print Process: web
Circulation: 9,500
Circulation Type: free & paid
**Owner(s):**
Allan K. Marshall
3900 Ford Rd., #18-2
Philadelphia, PA 19131-1307
Telephone: (215) 878-1307
Ownership %: 100
**Editorial:**
Allan K. Marshall .................................Editor
**Desc.:** Publishes prize-winning photographs from amateurs all over the world, and general and technical articles on photography. Sponsors 5 competitions in each issue. Awards more than $4000 in prize money to amateurs. All color & glossy magazine.
**Deadline:** story-15 days prior; news-15 days prior; photo-15 days prior; ads-15 days prior

---

**PHOTOPRO** 67248
5211 S. Washington Ave.
Titusville, FL 32780
Telephone: (407) 268-5010
FAX: (407) 267-7216
Year Established: 1990
Pub. Frequency: bi-m.
Page Size: standard
Subscrip. Rate: $16.95/yr.
Circulation: 40,267
Circulation Type: paid
**Owner(s):**
Glenn Patch
5211 S. Washington Ave.
Titusville, FL 32780
Telephone: (407) 268-5010
Ownership %: 100
**Management:**
Christi Ashby ...........................Publisher
Eileen Tedder ...................Advertising Manager
**Editorial:**
Jerry O'neill ...............................Editor

---

**PICTURE PERFECT** 66335
P.O. Box 15760
Stamford, CT 06901
Telephone: (203) 967-9952
FAX: (203) 975-1119
Year Established: 1990
Pub. Frequency: bi-m.
Page Size: standard
Subscrip. Rate: $24/yr.
Freelance Pay: $.15/wd.
Circulation: 120,000
Circulation Type: paid
**Owner(s):**
Aquino Productions, Inc.
P.O. Box 15760
Stamford, CT 06901
Telephone: (203) 967-9952
Ownership %: 100
**Management:**
Andres Aquino ...........................Publisher
**Editorial:**
Andres Aquino ...........................Editor

---

Materials Accepted/Included: 01-Business news 02-By-line articles 03-Fashion news 04-Food news 05-Freelance copy 06-Letters to editor 07-Real estate news 08-Sports news 09-Travel news 10-Book rev. 11-Movie rev. 12-Music rev. 13-TV rev. 14-Theater rev. 15-Coming events 16-Obituaries 17-Question & answer 18-Social announcements 19-Artwork 20-Photos 21-Photos 22-TV listings 23-Audio rec. 24-Video rec. 25-Books 26-Films/film clips 27-Personnel news 28-Press releases 29-New product news/photos 30-Trade lit. 31-Contracts awarded 32-Display adv. 33-Classified adv.

6-89

**Desc.:** Covers all facets of photography: stock, travel, fashion, beauty, glamour, commercial, creative, and industrial. A showcase of photography in its many expressions. Ongoing photo contests. New photo products and industry trends. National and international travel pictorials. Model shoots and cover searches.

**Readers:** Photographers, art directors, modeling agencies, photo equipment manufacturers, dealers, and users.

26002
## POPULAR PHOTOGRAPHY
1633 Broadway
New York, NY 10019
Telephone: (212) 767-6000
FAX: (212) 767-5629
Year Established: 1937
Pub. Frequency: m.
Page Size: standard
Subscrip. Rate: 19.94/yr.
Freelance Pay: $125-B&W; $200 color
Circulation: 650,000
Circulation Type: paid
**Owner(s):**
Hachette Filipacchi Magazines, Inc.
1633 Broadway
New York, NY 10019
Telephone: (212) 719-6000
Ownership %: 100
**Management:**
Thomas Ph. Witschi .......................Publisher
**Editorial:**
Elinor Stecker ...................Senior Editor
Bob Schwalberg ...............................Editor
Barbara Lobron ...............................Editor
Renee Bruns .............................Managing Editor
Jason Schneider ...............Editorial Director
Annette Papps ...........................Advertising
Shinichiro Tora .............................Art Director
Peter Kolonia ...........................Associate Editor
Dana Rubin ...............Production Assistant
Larry White ...................Technical Director
**Desc.:** Edited for world's largest audience of amateur and professional photographers, on all levels from rank beginner to advanced worker. Articles on all phases of picture-taking and processing; factual how-to stories with clean, clear set-up pictures; intriguing off-beat picture features helpful to amateurs. Departments include: New Books, Travel, Photography, Letters, Tools & Techniques, Color Darkroom, Help, New Products, Just Out, Shoptalk, Time Exposure, Markets & Careers, Workshops.
**Readers:** Advanced hobbyists along with many professional photographers.

26005
## PSA JOURNAL
3000 United Founders Blvd., Ste. 103
Oklahoma City, OK 73112-3940
Telephone: (405) 843-1437
FAX: (405) 843-1438
Year Established: 1934
Pub. Frequency: m.
Page Size: standard
Subscrip. Rate: $35/yr. US; $40/yr. foreign
Freelance Pay: paid in copies
Circulation: 14,000
Circulation Type: paid
**Owner(s):**
Photographic Society of America, Inc.,
3000 United Founders. Blvd., S
Oklahoma City, OK 73112-3940
Telephone: (405) 843-1437
Ownership %: 100
**Management:**
James H. Turnbull ..........................President
Tammy Dresser ...............Advertising Manager
Mrs. Terry Stull ...............Operations Manager

**Editorial:**
Dennis J. Ramsey .............................Editor
**Desc.:** Aside from new products, publicity must have direct connection with society activities. Features include "how-to", new applications of photography, travel, amateur movie production, fine photography. Own correspondents write personality news on regional basis. Associate editors from coast to coast cover subject matter. Official organ of Photographic Society of America, with members in 81 countries. Departments include: new products, book reviews, camera clubs, recorded lectures, PSA services, salons and contests, cinema clinic, travel, and equipment classified.
**Readers:** Members of PSA, largely active advanced amateur photographers.

## Group 662-Regional, Metropolitan, Local

69726
## ACADIANA PROFILE MAGAZINE
100 Asma Blvd.
Lafayette, LA 70508
Telephone: (318) 235-7919
FAX: (318) 235-9925
Mailing Address:
  P.O. Box 52247
  Lafayette, LA 70505
Year Established: 1968
Pub. Frequency: q.
Page Size: standard
Subscrip. Rate: $2 newsstand; $9/yr.
Materials: 01,02,05,06,10,15,16,17,19,20,
  21,23,24,25,28,29,32,33
Freelance Pay: $25-$500/article
Print Process: offset
Circulation: 10,000
Circulation Type: controlled & paid
**Owner(s):**
Acadiana Profile Magazine
100 Asma Blvd.
Lafayette, LA 70508
Telephone: (318) 235-7919
Ownership %: 100
**Editorial:**
Trent Angers ...............................Editor
Tom Sommers ...........................Art Director
**Desc.:** General interest for the 22-county region of South Louisiana called Acadiana-otherwise known as Cajun country.

26241
## ADIRONDACK LIFE
Rte. 9N
Jay, NY 12941
Telephone: (518) 946-2191
FAX: (518) 946-7461
Mailing Address:
  P.O. Box 97
  Jay, NY 12941
Year Established: 1970
Pub. Frequency: bi-m.
Page Size: standard
Subscrip. Rate: $2.95 newsstand;
  $17.95/yr.
Materials: 32,33
Freelance Pay: $.25/wd.
Print Process: offset
Circulation: 50,000
Circulation Type: paid
**Owner(s):**
Adirondack Life, Inc.
P.O. Box 97
Jay, NY 12941
Telephone: (518) 946-2135
Ownership %: 100
**Management:**
Howard Fish ...........................Publisher
**Editorial:**
Tom Hughes ...............................Editor
Ann Eastman ...............Advertising Director

**Desc.:** Deals with all aspects of the Adirondack mountain region (northern N.Y. state), including history, nature, outdoor recreation, conservation, arts and crafts and public affairs. Feature articles emphasize outdoor recreation including skiing, backpacking, canoeing, fishing, natural history, human history, and issues relating to conservation of a wilderness area. Regular departments include a book review page.
**Readers:** Three quarters of readers are male, median age 45 and average income is $51,000, 35% post graduate degrees.

26244
## ALABAMA LIVING
340 Technacenter Dr.
Montgomery, AL 36117
Telephone: (205) 215-2732
FAX: (205) 215-2733
Mailing Address:
  P.O. Box 244014
  Montgomery, AL 36124
Year Established: 1948
Pub. Frequency: m.
Page Size: standard
Subscrip. Rate: $6/yr.
Materials: 01,02,04,25,32,33
Print Process: web offset
Circulation: 295,000
Circulation Type: paid
**Owner(s):**
Alabama Rural Electric Association
P.O. Box 244014
Montgomery, AL 36124
Telephone: (205) 215-2732
Ownership %: 100
**Management:**
Fred Clark ...........................Publisher
Lee Berry ...................Advertising Manager
**Editorial:**
Darryl Gates ...................Executive Editor
Kelly Windham ...............Editorial Assistant
**Desc.:** Stories, news and photos of interest to a rural and a growing suburban population.
**Readers:** Over 295,000 homes in rural and suburban Alabama.
**Deadline:** story-1 mo. prior to pub. date; news-1 mo. prior; photo-1 mo. prior; ads-1 mo. prior

26242
## ALASKA
808 E St., Ste. 200
Anchorage, AK 99501
Telephone: (907) 272-6070
FAX: (907) 272-2552
Year Established: 1935
Pub. Frequency: 10/yr.
Page Size: standard
Subscrip. Rate: $2.95 newsstand; $24/yr.
Materials: 32
Print Process: offset
Circulation: 242,000
Circulation Type: paid
**Owner(s):**
Yankee Publishing, Inc.
Main St.
Dublin, NH 03444
Telephone: (603) 563-8111
Ownership %: 100
**Management:**
Joe Meagher ...........................President
Dana Brockway ...........................Publisher
Jane Wilkens ...................Business Manager
**Editorial:**
Tobin Morrison ...............................Editor
**Desc.:** Heavily illustrated, true first-person stories of life on the Last Frontier, news of the North, travel, wildlife, history, hunting, fishing, boating, prospecting--subject area confined to Alaska and Northwestern Canada.

26243
## ALOHA: THE MAGAZINE OF HAWAII & THE PACIFIC
720 Kapiolani Blvd.
Honolulu, HI 96813
Telephone: (808) 593-1191
FAX: (808) 593-1327
Mailing Address:
  P.O. Box 3260
  Honolulu, HI 96813
Year Established: 1978
Pub. Frequency: bi-m.
Page Size: standard
Subscrip. Rate: $3.95/issue; $17.95/yr.
Materials: 03,06
Freelance Pay: $.10/wd.
**Owner(s):**
Davick Publications, Inc.
49 S. Hotel St., Ste. 309
Honolulu, HI 96813
Telephone: (808) 523-9871
Ownership %: 100
**Management:**
Rick Davis .............................Publisher
**Editorial:**
Cheryl Chee Tsutsumi .....................Editor
Sanford Mock ...........................Art Director
Rick Davis ...................Chief Executive Officer
Bruce Miller ...................Circulation Editor
Wendy Wakabayashi .........................Design
**Desc.:** Articles about Hawaii written for local people and visitors who love Hawaii. Use stories on art, business, interiors, entertainment, personalities, destinations, ethnic topics, sports, photo essays, history, hotels, food - all facets of Island life.
**Readers:** Affluent, college educated frequent traveler.

71254
## ARRIVE
111 Veterans Blvd., Ste. 1810
Metairie, LA 70005
Telephone: (504) 831-3731
FAX: (504) 837-2258
Pub. Frequency: m.
Page Size: standard
Subscrip. Rate: $3.95 newsstand; $16/yr.
Materials: 02,05,06,15,21,32,33
Print Process: offset
Circulation: 30,000
Circulation Type: controlled
**Owner(s):**
New Orleans Publishing Group
111 Veterans Blvd., Ste. 1810
Metairie, LA 70005
Telephone: (504) 831-3731
Ownership %: 100
**Management:**
William Metcalf ...........................President
Nancy Bourgois ...........................Publisher
Cassie Forman ...............Advertising Manager
Janel Durand ...................Circulation Manager
**Editorial:**
Errol Laborde ...............................Editor
Mary Beth Rumig ...................Managing Editor
Kathleen Joffrion ...........................Art Director

67298
## ATHENS MAGAZINE
One Press Pl.
Athens, GA 30601
Telephone: (706) 549-0123
FAX: (706) 543-5234
Mailing Address:
  P.O. Box 912
  Athens, GA 30603
Year Established: 1989
Pub. Frequency: bi-m.
Page Size: standard
Subscrip. Rate: $10/yr.
Circulation: 5,500
Circulation Type: paid

**Materials Accepted/Included:** 01-Business news 02-By-line articles 03-Fashion news 04-Food news 05-Freelance copy 06-Letters to editor 07-Real estate news 08-Sports news 09-Travel news 10-Book rev. 11-Movie rev. 12-Music rev. 13-TV rev. 14-Theater rev. 15-Coming events 16-Obituaries 17-Question & answer 18-Social announcements 19-Artwork 20-Cartoons 21-Photos 22-TV listings 23-Audio rec. 24-Video rec. 25-Books 26-Films/film clips 27-Personnel news 28-Press releases 29-New product news/photos 30-Trade lit. 31-Contracts awarded 32-Display adv. 33-Classified adv.

## Owner(s):
Athens Newspapers Inc.
One Press Pl.
Athens, GA 30601
Telephone: (706) 549-0123
Ownership %: 100
## Management:
William Morris ...................................President
A. Mark Smith ..................................Publisher
Kathy Russo .....................Advertising Manager
## Editorial:
Elaine Kalber .........................................Editor
**Desc.:** Articles about people and issues in Athens and Northeast Georgia; Includes short fiction essays, photographs, and visual art.

## ATLANTA MAGAZINE
26245
1360 Peachtree St.
2 Midtown Plz., Ste. 1800
Atlanta, GA 30309
Telephone: (404) 872-3100
FAX: (404) 876-2748
Year Established: 1961
Pub. Frequency: m.
Page Size: standard
Subscrip. Rate: $2.50/issue; $18/yr.; $31.80/2 yrs.
Materials: 02,03,05,06,18,32
Freelance Pay: varies
Print Process: offset
Circulation: 67,997
Circulation Type: paid
## Owner(s):
Emmis Broadcasting Corp.
950 N. Meridian St., Ste. 1200
Indianapolis, IN 46204
Ownership %: 100
## Management:
Chris Hoefer ....................................Publisher
Krsi Hoefer ......................Advertising Manager
## Editorial:
Lee Walburn ..............................Editor in Chief
Emma Edmunds .............................Senior Editor
Susan Percy ...............................Managing Editor
David Lauterborn ....................Chief Copy Editor
**Desc.:** Monthly metro publication. Covers metro Atlanta business, sports, politics, health and arts, lifestyles. 10 percent freelance, full by-line. Articles usually run from 1,000 to 2,000 words. Departments include: Politics, Business, Art, Education, Letters to Editor, Record Reviews, Fashion, Decor, and Gifts.
**Readers:** Upper income, highly educated professionals.

## ATLANTIC CITY MAGAZINE
26246
1000 W. Washington Ave.
Pleasantville, NJ 08232
Telephone: (609) 272-7900
FAX: (609) 272-7910
Mailing Address:
P.O. Box 2100
Pleasantville, NJ 08232
Year Established: 1977
Pub. Frequency: m.
Page Size: 4 color photos/art
Subscrip. Rate: $19.95/yr.
Materials: 05,17,32
Freelance Pay: varies
Print Process: offset
Circulation: 45,000
Circulation Type: paid
## Owner(s):
Abarta Metro Publsihing Co., Inc.
1000 W. Washington Ave.
Pleasantville, NJ 08232
Ownership %: 100
## Management:
John F. Bitzer, III ..............................Publisher
Barry Senoff ........................Associate Publisher
Jane Thompson .................Advertising Manager

## Editorial:
Deborah Ein ...........................Associate Editor
Susan Seabert ....................Production Director
**Desc.:** About Atlantic City, describing trends, development, entertainment and fine dining. Articles vary in length from 150 to 3,000 words, and must fit our editorial policy. Most are staff-assigned, but we will accept query letters and unsolicited manuscripts. Departments include: Art, Business, Real Estate, Entertainment, Casinos, History, Dining and Travel.

## BACK HOME IN KENTUCKY
26286
128 Holiday Ct., Ste. 116
Franklin, TN 37064
Telephone: (615) 794-4338
Mailing Address:
P.O. Box 681629
Franklin, TN 37068
Year Established: 1977
Pub. Frequency: bi-m.
Page Size: standard
Subscrip. Rate: $12/yr.; $19/2 yrs.; $25/3 yrs.
Freelance Pay: $15-$100
Circulation: 12,000
Circulation Type: controlled & paid
## Owner(s):
Greysmith Publishing, Inc.
P.O. Box 681629
Franklin, TN 37068
Telephone: (615) 794-4338
Ownership %: 100
## Management:
Bill Smith ..........................................President
Nanci P. Gregg ............................Vice President
Bill Smith ..........................................Publisher
## Editorial:
Nanci P. Gregg ..........................Managing Editor
Missy Estes ....................................Art Director
J. Holly McCall ...........................Associate Editor
Laura Clayton ...................................Food Editor
**Desc.:** Edited to inform and entertain those having root or interest in the Bluegrass State, its heritage, people, places and events. Contents include personalities, historical events, architecture, travel and recreation, coming events, arts and crafts, hobbies, gardening, recipes, gourmet cooking, restaurants, Kentucky books and authors. Deals with both historic and contemporary Kentucky.
**Readers:** Professionals, mature homeowners with income $40,000-$50,000.

## BALTIMORE
22263
16 S. Calvert St., Ste. 1000
Baltimore, MD 21202
Telephone: (410) 752-7375
FAX: (410) 625-0280
Year Established: 1977
Pub. Frequency: m.
Page Size: standard
Subscrip. Rate: $1.95/copy; $15/yr.
Materials: 01,05,06,15,23,24,25,28,32,33
Freelance Pay: $25-$2,000
Circulation: 51,615
Circulation Type: paid
## Owner(s):
Baltimore Magazine, Inc.
16 S. Calvert St.
Baltimore, MD 21202
Telephone: (301) 752-7375
FAX: (410) 220-2307
Ownership %: 100

## Bureau(s):
ESS Ventures, Inc.
6401 Golden Triangle Dr.
Greenbelt, MD 20770
Telephone: (301) 220-2300
Contact: John Roman, Assistant Chief Editor
## Management:
Jonathan Witty ..................................Publisher
Linda Sciuto ......................Advertising Manager
## Editorial:
Lois Perschetz ...........................Executive Editor
Ramsey Flynn ........................................Editor
Margaret Guroff ..........................Managing Editor
Claude Skelton .................................Art Director
Kathleen Renda ..........................Assistant Editor
Jim Duffy ...................................Associate Editor
Mariann Moery ..........................Circulation Editor
Paula Jaworski ...............................Miscellaneous
**Desc.:** Concerned primarily with lifestyle, cultural, and business interests of the city and metropolitan area. Insight, analysis, and consumer matters geared to Baltimore area residents. Editorial and Letter column sections. Regular columns on Politics, Health, Business, The Arts, Home & Garden, Fashion.
**Readers:** Well-educated, affluent Baltimore area residents.
**Deadline:** story-6 wks.

## BLUE RIDGE COUNTRY
65361
3424 Brambleton Ave., S.W.
Roanoke, VA 24018
Telephone: (703) 989-6138
FAX: (703) 989-7603
Mailing Address:
P.O. Box 21535
Roanoke, VA 24018
Year Established: 1988
Pub. Frequency: bi-m.
Page Size: standard
Subscrip. Rate: $2.95 newsstand; $14.95/yr.
Freelance Pay: $25-$250
Circulation: 75,000
Circulation Type: paid
## Owner(s):
Leisure Publishing Co.
P.O. Box 21535
Roanoke, VA 24018
Ownership %: 100
## Management:
Richard Wells ....................................Publisher
## Editorial:
Kurt Rheinheimer ...................................Editor
Jo Diedrich ..........................Advertising Director
**Desc.:** This publication celebrates the heritage of the mountains between western Maryland and northern Georgia. (The mountain regions of MD, VA, WV, NC, TN, KY, GA, SC).
**Readers:** Targets reisdents and vistors to this area of the U.S.

## BOSTON MAGAZINE
26250
300 Massachusetts Ave.
Boston, MA 02115
Telephone: (617) 262-9700
FAX: (617) 262-4925
Year Established: 1963
Pub. Frequency: m.
Page Size: standard
Subscrip. Rate: $2.50/issue; $15/yr.
Materials: 32
Freelance Pay: $500-$1,500/article
Circulation: 137,000
Circulation Type: paid
## Owner(s):
Metro Corp.
1500 Walnut St.
Philadelphia, PA 19102
Telephone: (215) 545-3500
Ownership %: 100

## Management:
D. Herbert Lipson ..............................President
Alan Klein .........................................Publisher
## Editorial:
Art Jahnke ...............................Managing Editor
Greg Klee .......................................Art Director
**Desc.:** City magazine covering cultural, investigative, humorous, and noteworthy items about and around Boston. Columns include the arts, country life, business academia, and first-person items and profiles.
**Readers:** Upscale Suburban/City people 25 and up. Median age 40.5

## BUFFALO SPREE
26253
4511 Harlem Rd.
Buffalo, NY 14226
Telephone: (716) 839-3405
FAX: (716) 839-4384
Mailing Address:
P.O. Box 38
Buffalo, NY 14226
Year Established: 1967
Pub. Frequency: q.
Page Size: 4 color photos/art
Subscrip. Rate: $2 newsstand; $8/yr.
Materials: 03,10,12,14,25,32
Freelance Pay: $75-$125/article
Circulation: 21,000
Circulation Type: controlled
## Owner(s):
Spree Publishing Co., Inc.
4511 Harlem Rd.
Buffalo, NY 14226
Telephone: (716) 839-3405
Ownership %: 100
## Management:
Johanna Van De Mark .......................Publisher
## Editorial:
Johanna Van De Mark .............................Editor
Alyssa Chase .............................Associate Editor
Ted Knight ...........................Book Review Editor
Janet Goldenberg .............................Poetry Editor
**Desc.:** Edited for the above-average income residents of the metropolitan Buffalo area. Special emphasis is placed on shopping, fashions, cultural events, the arts, theatre, dining out, gourmet cooking, leisure living and personality profiles. We strive to provide sophisticated and stimulating articles, poetry and short fiction. Our focus is not general interest, but literary and the humanities.
**Readers:** Educated, active, astute professionals and intellectuals. Readership is growing in areas outside Western New York.

## CENTERSTAGE
65344
196 Trumbull St.
Hartford, CT 06103-2207
Telephone: (203) 560-2699
FAX: (203) 541-6069
Year Established: 1993
Pub. Frequency: bi-m.
Page Size: standard
Materials: 15,32
Freelance Pay: $75-$500
Circulation: 70,000
Circulation Type: controlled
## Owner(s):
Parker Media, Inc.
196 Trumbull St.
Hartford, CT 06103
Telephone: (203) 560-2699
FAX: (203) 541-6069
Ownership %: 100
## Management:
Michael E. Parker ..............................Publisher
## Editorial:
Kenneth Ross .........................................Editor

**Materials Accepted/Included:** 01-Business news 02-By-line articles 03-Fashion news 04-Food news 05-Freelance copy 06-Letters to editor 07-Real estate news 08-Sports news 09-Travel news 10-Book rev. 11-Movie rev. 12-Music rev. 13-TV rev. 14-Theater rev. 15-Coming events 16-Obituaries 17-Question & answer 18-Social announcements 19-Artwork 20-Cartoons 21-Photos 22-TV listings 23-Audio rec. 24-Video rec. 25-Books 26-Films/film clips 27-Personnel news 28-Press releases 29-New product news/photos 30-Trade lit. 31-Contracts awarded 32-Display adv. 33-Classified adv.

6-91

**Desc.:** Feature stories & calendar related to performing arts organizations & art galleries in Connecticut.
**Readers:** Residents of the Hartford area as well as tourists.

26255

## CHARLOTTE MAGAZINE
220 King Owen Ct.
Charlotte, NC 28211
Telephone: (704) 366-5000
FAX: (704) 366-6148
Mailing Address:
  P.O. Box 11048
  Charlotte, NC 28220-1048
Year Established: 1968
Pub. Frequency: bi-m.
Page Size: standard
Subscrip. Rate: $2.95 newsstand; $12/yr.
Materials: 01,02,03,04,05,06,07,08,09,10,
  12,14,15,19,20,21,23,24,25,28,32
Freelance Pay: $.12/wd.
Circulation: 17,500
Circulation Type: paid
Owner(s):
New Charlotte Magazine, Inc.
6135 Park South Dr., Ste. 304
Charlotte, NC 28210
Ownership %: 100
Editorial:
Bob Dill ...........................................Editor
**Desc.:** Articles are regional in nature (North & South Carolina) concerning business, finance, personalities, events, and general information. Travel articles are run frequently, covering the United States and Europe. Use staff writers as well as free-lance and by-lines are always given. Departments run 750 to 1,300 words and features run 1,500 to 2,000 words. Color and black and white photos are used throughout the book. Departments include: Towntalk, Humor, Profile, Culture, Life Styles, Finance, Travel, Restaurant Guide (includes all major restaurants in city), Charlotte Guide (includes a list of antique shops, theatres, nightlife spots, galleries, etc.).
**Readers:** Upscale homeowners, women 25-50.

26256

## CHESAPEAKE BAY MAGAZINE
1819 Bay Ridge Ave.
Annapolis, MD 21403
Telephone: (410) 263-2662
FAX: (410) 267-6924
Year Established: 1971
Pub. Frequency: m.
Page Size: standard
Subscrip. Rate: $22.95/yr.
Freelance Pay: $50-$500/article
Circulation: 33,000
Circulation Type: paid
Owner(s):
Chesapeake Bay Communications, Inc.
1819 Bay Ridge Ave.
Annapolis, MD 21403
Telephone: (301) 263-2662
Ownership %: 100
Management:
Richard J. Royer .........................President
Richard J. Royer .........................Publisher
Jan Olekszyk ....................Circulation Manager
Editorial:
Jean Waller ...................................Editor
Ellen Honey .....................Associate Publisher
Bruce Harris .....................Marketing Director
**Desc.:** A regional monthly publication concentrating on boating, history, and ecology of the Chesapeake Bay and its tributaries. Strongly marine oriented.
**Readers:** College-educated, boat owners, living or vacation on Chesapeake Bay. Many are fishermen or are interested in water sports.

21758

## CHICAGO MAGAZINE
414 N. Orleans St.
Chicago, IL 60610
Telephone: (312) 222-8999
FAX: (312) 222-0287
Year Established: 1952
Pub. Frequency: m.
Page Size: standard
Subscrip. Rate: $19.90/yr.
Circulation: 177,103
Circulation Type: paid
Owner(s):
Chicago Publishing, Inc.
414 N. Orleans St.
Chicago, IL 60610
Telephone: (312) 222-8999
FAX: (312) 222-0287
Ownership %: 100
Management:
Richard F. Barry, III .....................President
Heidi Schultz .............................Publisher
Editorial:
Gale Kappe .........................Senior Editor
Gretchen Reynolds ...............Senior Editor
Christine Newman ................Senior Editor
Henry Hanson .....................Senior Editor
Jan Parr .............................Senior Editor
Ted Allen ...........................Senior Editor
Nancy Fowlds .....................Senior Editor
Richard Babcock ........................Editor
Shane Tritsch ...................Managing Editor
Sarah Walton .......................Art Director
Jeanne Rattenbury ...........Associate Editor
John Carroll ...................Associate Publisher
Meri Kessler ................Circulation Director
Constance Hall ......................Copy Editor
Penny Pollack .....................Dining Editor
Vicki Bales .....................Production Director
**Desc.:** Each issue contains feature articles and columns on dining, books, arts, politics, media, architecture.
  Departments include: Calendar of Chicago Events, Selective Guide to Dining.
**Readers:** Active, involved, Chicago area residents above average income and education.

26258

## CINCINNATI MAGAZINE
409 Broadway
Cincinnati, OH 45202
Telephone: (513) 421-4300
FAX: (513) 421-0105
Year Established: 1967
Pub. Frequency: m.
Page Size: standard
Subscrip. Rate: $1.95 newsstand; $16/yr.;
  $28/2 yrs.
Materials: 02,04,05,06,07,08,09,17,20,21,
  32,33
Freelance Pay: negotiable
Circulation: 32,000
Circulation Type: paid
Owner(s):
CM Media, Inc.
171 E. Livingston Ave.
Cincinnati, OH 45215
Telephone: (614) 464-4567
Ownership %: 100
Management:
Max S. Brown .............................President
Laura Pulfer .............................Publisher
Dianne Bohmer ................Associate Publsiher
Editorial:
Laura Pulfer .......................Editor in Chief
Lilia F. Brady ...................Managing Editor
Felix Winternitz .................Editorial Director
Thomas Hawley ......................Art Director

**Desc.:** A city magazine publishing regular columns, consumer how-to information and three or four lengthy features (about 3,000 words each) each month. The magazine accepts freelance submissions from writers, illustrators and photographers. The focus is on the quality of life, on surviving in the city of Cincinnati. We run in-depth features with a perspective, a point of view (a look at local news coverage, an analysis of why we don't get the movies we want, a profile of a segment of the community dissecting images and realities).
**Readers:** Affluent Cincinnati residents.

26260

## CLEVELAND MAGAZINE
1422 Euclid Ave., No. 730
Cleveland, OH 44115
Telephone: (216) 771-2833
FAX: (216) 781-6318
Year Established: 1972
Pub. Frequency: m.
Page Size: 4 color photos/art
Subscrip. Rate: $18/yr.
Materials: 01,02,03,04,05,06,07,08,09,10,
  11,12,13,14,15,18,19,20,21,23,24,25,27,
  28,29,32,33
Freelance Pay: based on assignment
Print Process: web
Circulation: 45,000
Circulation Type: free & paid
Owner(s):
City Magazines, Inc.
1422 Euclid Ave. #730
Cleveland, OH 44115
Telephone: (216) 771-2833
FAX: (216) 781-6318
Ownership %: 100
Management:
Lute Harmon ...........................Publisher
Paul Moskowitz ...............Advertising Manager
Editorial:
Tom Peric .........................Senior Editor
Liz Ludlow ...............................Editor
**Desc.:** Independent city magazine that publishes regional features, investigative reporting and area business news.
**Readers:** 130,000 young, affluent and influential adults.
**Deadline:** story-1st of the mo. prior to pub. date; news-1st of the mo. prior; photo-1st of the mo. prior; ads-1st of the mo. prior

25969

## COLLECTIONS
1020 Humbolt Pkwy.
Buffalo, NY 14211
Telephone: (716) 896-5200
Year Established: 1920
Pub. Frequency: bi-m.
Page Size: tabloid
Subscrip. Rate: $5/yr. US; $6/yr. Canada;
  $7/yr. foreign
Circulation: 10,000
Circulation Type: controlled
Owner(s):
Buffalo Society of Natural Sciences
1020 Humboldt Pkwy.
Buffalo, NY 14211
Telephone: (716) 896-5200
Ownership %: 100
Editorial:
Barbara Park Leggett ....................Editor
Joan Gilmartin-Manias ..............Art Director
**Desc.:** Devoted to activities and collections of the Buffalo Society of Natural Sciences, Buffalo Museum of Science and Tifft Nature Preserve.
**Readers:** Members of the Buffalo Society of Natural Sciences

66277

## COLUMBIA METROPOLITAN
3201 Devine St.
Columbia, SC 29205
Telephone: (803) 252-2327
FAX: (803) 765-9731
Mailing Address:
  P.O. Box 222
  Columbia, SC 29202
Year Established: 1990
Pub. Frequency: bi-m.
Page Size: standard
Subscrip. Rate: $13.97/yr.
Circulation: 10,000
Circulation Type: controlled & paid
Owner(s):
Columbia Metropolitan Magazine
3201 Devine St.
Columbia, SC 29205
Telephone: (803) 252-2327
Management:
Henry Clay ...............................Publisher
Editorial:
Emily Clay .................................Editor
**Desc.:** Covers people, places and events of interest in Columbia, S.C..

26263

## COLUMBUS MONTHLY
5255 Sinclair Rd.
Columbus, OH 43229
Telephone: (614) 888-4567
FAX: (614) 848-3838
Mailing Address:
  P.O. Box 29913
  Columbus, OH 43229
Year Established: 1975
Pub. Frequency: m.
Page Size: standard
Subscrip. Rate: $16/yr.
Materials: 01,03,05,08,15,32
Freelance Pay: varies
Print Process: offset
Circulation: 38,000
Circulation Type: paid
Owner(s):
CM Media, Inc.
5255 Sinclair Rd.
Columbus, OH 43229
Telephone: (614) 888-4567
Ownership %: 100
Management:
Max S. Brown ...........................President
Max S. Brown ...........................Publisher
Rheta Gallagher ...............Advertising Manager
Mary Fredrick ...................Circulation Manager
Editorial:
Lenore Brown ...............................Editor
**Desc.:** A metropolitan magazine aimed at the more sophisticated residents of Central Ohio. Editorial features include: Articles on the Arts, Media, Sports, Fashion, Business, Education and Politics, Restaurant Listings and Reviews, and a calendar of upcoming local events. Annual features include a comprehensive restaurant guide, an Arts Guide, and special sections on fitness, health care and homes. A portion of the material in each issue is free-lanced locally. Feature articles generally run 2,000 to 4,000 words; Department and Around Columbus articles are shorter. Releases and promotional material are welcome, but never used directly. Freelancers should submit a short query letter. All stories must have a Central Ohio slant.
**Readers:** Median age 40; average household income $53,123.

26264

## COMMONWEALTH, THE
595 Market St.
San Francisco, CA 94105
Telephone: (415) 597-6700
FAX: (415) 597-6729

---

Materials Accepted/Included: 01-Business news 02-By-line articles 03-Fashion news 04-Food news 05-Freelance copy 06-Letters to editor 07-Real estate news 08-Sports news 09-Travel news 10-Book rev. 11-Movie rev. 12-Music rev. 13-TV rev. 14-Theater rev. 15-Coming events 16-Obituaries 17-Question & answer 18-Social announcements 19-Artwork 20-Cartoons 21-Photos 22-TV listings 23-Audio rec. 24-Video rec. 25-Books 26-Films/film clips 27-Personnel news 28-Press releases 29-New product news/photos 30-Trade lit. 31-Contracts awarded 32-Display adv. 33-Classified adv.

Year Established: 1903
Pub. Frequency: w.
Page Size: standard
Subscrip. Rate: free membership, $17/yr.
institutions
Print Process: offset
Circulation: 21,000
Circulation Type: paid
**Owner(s):**
Commonwealth Club of California
595 Market St.
San Francisco, CA 94105
Telephone: (415) 597-6700
Ownership %: 100
**Management:**
Ambassador James D. ........Executive Director
Rosenthal
**Editorial:**
Gail Burns-Wax ...........................................Editor
James L. Coplan ....................Director Member
Services
**Desc.:** Contains editor-written reviews of
addresses and papers on public affairs
presented before the Commonwealth
Club. Also carries occasional
supplements containing reports on
public controversial issues, and
California Ballot proposition reports. (No
outside advertisements or reviews.)
**Readers:** Club members, libraries,
universities, and others interested in
public issues.

### CONCORD NORTH
66746

100 Main St.
Nashua, NH 03060
Telephone: (603) 883-3150
FAX: (603) 889-5557
Year Established: 1988
Pub. Frequency: m.
Page Size: standard
Subscrip. Rate: $2 newsstand; $24/yr.
Materials: 01,02,05,06,21
Freelance Pay: varies
Print Process: web offset
Circulation: 25,000
Circulation Type: controlled & paid
**Owner(s):**
Network Publications
Ownership %: 100
**Management:**
David Gregg ...........................................President
Patricia Gregg ......................................Publisher
**Editorial:**
Richard Broussard ...................................Editor
**Desc.:** Regional magazines for the state of
New Hampshire covering the people,
issues, and business of our state in an
in-depth and colorful form.
**Readers:** Primarily business owners,
CEO's, upper income families, and
young professionals.

### CONNECTICUT MAGAZINE
26266

789 Reservoir Ave.
Bridgeport, CT 06606
Telephone: (203) 374-3388
Year Established: 1971
Pub. Frequency: 12/yr.
Page Size: standard
Subscrip. Rate: $2.50 newsstand; $15/yr.
Materials: 02,05,06,17,32,33
Freelance Pay: $50-$1,200
Circulation: 87,000
Circulation Type: paid
**Owner(s):**
Communications International
789 Reservoir Ave.
Bridgeport, CT 06606
Telephone: (203) 374-3388
Ownership %: 100
**Management:**
Arthur Hill Diedrick ...........Chairman of Board
Michael Mims .....................................Publisher

L. Lee Healy .....................Circulation Manager
**Editorial:**
Charles A. Monagan ..............................Editor
Dale Salm ..............................Managing Editor
Joan Barrow .............................Art Director
Glen J. Johnson ...............Production Director
**Desc.:** Covers Connecticut issues and
lifestyle. Departments include: Calendar
of Events, Connecticut Interiors, Law &
Courts, Arts, Bargains, Restaurants,
Connecticut Home & Garden, Guides,
Profiles, Business, Real Estate and
more.
**Readers:** People interested in living well
and knowledgeably within their state of
residence.

### COUNTRY CONNECTIONS
70410

148 E. Third St.
Superior, NE 68908
Telephone: (402) 879-3293
Mailing Address:
P.O. Box 406
Superior, NE 68978
Year Established: 1986
Pub. Frequency: m.
Page Size: tabloid
Subscrip. Rate: $50/yr.
Print Process: offset
Circulation: 1,653
**Owner(s):**
Bill Blauvelt
**Management:**
Bill Blauvelt .........................................Publisher

### DAYTON MONTHLY MAGAZINE
26269

120 W. Third St., Ste. 200
Dayton, OH 45402
Telephone: (513) 222-1444
Year Established: 1964
Pub. Frequency: bi-m.
Page Size: 4 color photos/art
Subscrip. Rate: $9.95/yr.
Materials: 32
Circulation: 23,500
Circulation Type: controlled & paid
**Owner(s):**
Dayton Publishing Group, Inc.
120 W. Third St., Ste. 200
Dayton, OH 45402
Telephone: (513) 222-1011
Ownership %: 100
**Management:**
Jeff Ditmire ...........................................Publisher
Dinson Caldwell ...........Advertising Manager
Marc Stokoe ...........................Office Manager
**Editorial:**
Linda Lombard ...........................................Editor
Patrick Souhan .....................Managing Editor
Dan Meuller .............................Art Director
Peggie Barnes ...........................Food Editor
**Desc.:** 80% is written by free-lance writers.
Primarily interested in material about
Dayton as an attractive, inviting city in
which to live and work. We also publish
articles of interest to our readers which
are not necessarily about Dayton. Style
and emphasis may vary with subject, but
where possible, emphasis should be
placed on personality and information
told through revelation of character.
Space and layout make possible more
in-depth news stories than can be found
in the daily news, and we aim for the
interesting story behind the news story.
Again heavy emphasis on personality
profile.
**Readers:** Our primary audience is top-level
decision makers in business and
industry and their families, who are
between the ages of 35 and 55 income
(annual) of $42,500, college educated or
better.

### DELAWARE TODAY
26270

201 N. Walnut St., Ste. 1204
Wilmington, DE 19801
Telephone: (302) 656-1809
FAX: (302) 656-5843
Mailing Address:
P.O. Box 2087
Wilmington, DE 19899
Year Established: 1962
Pub. Frequency: m.
Page Size: standard
Subscrip. Rate: $18/yr.
Materials: 01,02,03,04,05,06,07,08,09,15,
21,25,27,28,29,30,32,33
Freelance Pay: $50-$400
Print Process: web offset
Circulation: 25,000
Circulation Type: paid
**Owner(s):**
Gazette Press, Inc.
16 School St.
Yonkers, NY 10701
Telephone: (914) 963-8300
Ownership %: 70

Robert Martinelli
111 Bellfield Ct.
Hockessin, DE 19707
Telephone: (302) 656-1809
Ownership %: 30
**Management:**
Angelo R. Martinelli ...........Chairman of Board
Robert F. Martinelli ...........................President
Robert Martinelli ...........................Publisher
Charles Tomlinson ...........Advertising Manager
**Editorial:**
Lisa Monty ...........................................Editor
Marsha Mah .....................Managing Editor
Cynthia Dwyer .................Associate Publisher
Ingrid Lynch .........................Design Director
**Desc.:** A monthly regional magazine
covering the entire state of Delaware
and reaching about 100,000 readers.
Features explore Delaware personalities,
trends, events. Service articles focus on
leisure activities, goods and services. No
fiction. Departments: Dining, film,
entertainment, investments, politics.
**Readers:** Average income $81,400
household; medium income $65,800
people; 35 to 55 years of age; 51-55%
college graduates or higher education.
**Deadline:** ads-6 wks. prior to pub. date

### DENVER HOUSING GUIDE, THE
26271

2323 S. Troy St., Ste. 103
Aurora, CO 80014
Telephone: (303) 695-8440
FAX: (303) 695-8449
Year Established: 1974
Pub. Frequency: bi-m.
Page Size: standard
Subscrip. Rate: $12/yr.
Freelance Pay: $.10/wd.
Print Process: web offset
Circulation: 70,000
Circulation Type: paid
**Owner(s):**
Baker Publications
2323 S. Troy St., Ste. 103
Aurora, CO 80014
Telephone: (303) 695-8440
Ownership %: 100
**Management:**
Dick B. Baker .......................................President
Dick B. Baker .......................................Publisher
Dick B. Baker .................Advertising Manager
Patt Dodd ...................Circulation Manager
Patt Dodd ........................Traffic Manager
**Editorial:**
Patt Dodd .........................Managing Editor
Patt Dodd .............................News Editor
Patt Dodd ...............................Photo
Peggy Jacobson ...............................Sales

**Desc.:** A housing guide-relocation
magazine for people interested in
housing in the Denver area. Regular
features include articles on housing
trends, updated financial facts, and
builder/ developer information. Also
included is a comprehensive map
system which locates all new home
developments, townhome and
condominium communities by location
and price range.
**Readers:** Home shoppers.

### DETROIT MONTHLY MAGAZINE
26301

1400 E. Woodbridge Ave.
Detroit, MI 48207
Telephone: (313) 446-0300
FAX: (313) 446-1687
Year Established: 1978
Pub. Frequency: m.
Page Size: standard
Subscrip. Rate: $2.50/copy; $19/yr.
Circulation: 93,950
Circulation Type: paid
**Owner(s):**
Crain Communications, Inc.
1400 E. Woodbridge Ave.
Detroit, MI 48207
Telephone: (313) 446-6000
Ownership %: 100
**Management:**
Keith E. Crain ...........................Vice Chairman
Jeanne Towar .....................................Publisher
**Editorial:**
Mary Kramer ...........................Executive Editor
Ric Bohy .............................Senior Editor
Carol Hopkins ...........................Senior Editor
John Barron ...........................................Editor
Megan Swoyer .....................Managing Editor
Judy Siner .............................Advertising
Margaret Kelly .........................Design Director
**Desc.:** Publish articles and information
about the greater Detroit metropolitan
area and of interest to metro Detroiters.
Freelance queries are welcome on any
such subjects. Unsolicited manuscripts
on nonfiction subjects up to 5,000 words
in length will be considered, but cannot
be returned without a self-addressed,
stamped envelope. Do not shy away
from controversial subjects, but reporting
and writing must be of professional
quality. Departments include: Politics,
Business/Labor, Arts & Letters,
Entertainment, Food, Shopping, Sports
and Human Drama.
**Readers:** Largely an educated, upscale
readership.

### DOWN EAST MAGAZINE
25845

Rt. 1, Roxmont
Rockport, ME 04856
Telephone: (207) 594-9544
FAX: (207) 594-7215
Mailing Address:
P.O. Box 679
Camden, ME 04843
Year Established: 1959
Pub. Frequency: m.
Page Size: standard
Subscrip. Rate: $2.95 newsstand;
$19.94/yr.
Materials: 02,04,05,06,07,10,11,14,15,19,
20,21,23,24,25,28,29,30,32,33
Print Process: web offset
Circulation: 67,000
Circulation Type: free & paid
**Owner(s):**
Down East Enterprises, Inc.
P.O. Box 679
Camden, ME 04843
Telephone: (207) 594-9544
Ownership %: 100

**Materials Accepted/Included:** 01-Business news 02-By-line articles 03-Fashion news 04-Food news 05-Freelance copy 06-Letters to editor 07-Real estate news 08-Sports news 09-Travel news 10-Book rev. 11-Movie rev. 12-Music rev. 13-TV rev. 14-Theater rev. 15-Coming events 16-Obituaries 17-Question & answer 18-Social announcements 19-Artwork 20-Cartoons 21-Photos 22-TV listings 23-Audio rec. 24-Video rec. 25-Books 26-Films/film clips 27-Personnel news 28-Press releases 29-New product news/photos 30-Trade lit. 31-Contracts awarded 32-Display adv. 33-Classified adv.

6-93

**Management:**
H. Allen Fernald ..............................President
H. Allen Fernald ..............................Publisher
Lynne Henry .......................Advertising Manager
Deb Dodge ........................Circulation Manager
**Editorial:**
D.W. Kuhnert ..............................Editor in Chief
**Desc.:** Illustrated articles about Maine and of interest to Maine. No fiction is used. Includes some Maine anecdotes and poems but no cartoons. Articles run about 2,500 to 3,000 words with either color or black and white illustrations. Departments include an editorial section North by East, Humor It Happened Down East, and news section Enterprise.
**Readers:** People interested in Maine, affluent, married.

26276

**EXCLUSIVELY YOURS**
161 W. Wisconsin Ave.
Milwaukee, WI 53203
Telephone: (414) 271-4270
FAX: (414) 271-0383
Year Established: 1947
Pub. Frequency: m.
Page Size: standard
Subscrip. Rate: $15.83/yr.
Freelance Pay: $.10/wd.
Circulation: 50,000
Circulation Type: controlled
**Owner(s):**
W.F. Patten
161 W. Wisconsin Ave.
Milwaukee, WI 53203
Telephone: (414) 271-4270
Ownership %: 100
**Management:**
W.F. Patten ..............................Publisher
Ed Liermann .....................Advertising Manager
**Editorial:**
W.F. Patten ..............................Senior Editor
Jack Pearson ..............................Editor
Lynne Piekraski ..............................Art Director
Lynne Piekarski ..............................Production Director
**Desc.:** General interest.
**Readers:** Affluent audience throughout Milwaukee and Wisconsin

26291

**GUEST INFORMANT**
21200 Erwin St.
Woodland Hills, CA 91367
Telephone: (818) 716-7484
FAX: (818) 716-7583
Year Established: 1937
Pub. Frequency: a.
Page Size: 4 color photos/art
Materials: 15,21,32
**Owner(s):**
Lin Communications
21200 Erwin St.
Woodland Hills, CA 91367
Telephone: (818) 716-7484
FAX: (818) 716-7583
Ownership %: 100
**Management:**
Edward Spitz ..............................Founder
Harold N. Spitz ...............Chairman of Board
Ronald E. Smith ..............................President
**Editorial:**
Andrea Zwerdling ..............................Editor
Linda Chase ..............................Managing Editor
Haines Wilkerson ..............................Art Director
Donald S. Palmer ..............................V.P., Controller
Geraldine Fitzgerald ..............................V.P., Marketing
Joe Kraynak ..............................V.P., Production
Michael Booker ............V.P., Sales & Marketing

**Desc.:** Distribution in the rooms of hotels in 30 different cities throughout the U.S. Each edition contains articles and editorials that introduce the traveler to the particular city. Special features focus on the history, personality and local color of the city as well. Pictorial articles guide the reader to dining and shopping establishments in the city and its surrounding area. Special sections give information about cultural and sports facilities that assist the traveler in planning his daily itinerary. Individual sections may have specific articles relating solely to that city or region.
**Readers:** Audience is composed of hotel guests.

25861

**GULFSHORE LIFE**
2900 S. Horseshoe Dr.
Ste. 400
Naples, FL 33942
Telephone: (813) 643-3933
FAX: (813) 643-5017
Year Established: 1969
Pub. Frequency: 10/yr.
Page Size: standard
Subscrip. Rate: $19.95/yr.
Freelance Pay: $.13-$.14/wd.
Circulation: 20,000
Circulation Type: paid
**Owner(s):**
Backe Group, Inc., The
327 E. 50th St.
New York, NY 10022
Telephone: (212) 355-6636
Ownership %: 100
**Management:**
John D. Backe ...................Chairman of Board
**Editorial:**
Lynne Groth ..............................Editor
Tim Cling ..............................Art Director
**Desc.:** Regional magazine reporting on the people and lifestyles of Southwest Florida. Departments and features include ecology, fashion, the arts, food, interior design, history, people, investment and business news. Primary coverage extends from Sarasota to Key West.
**Readers:** Upper income only; 45-65 years of age.

67234

**HARROWSMITH COUNTRY LIFE**
Ferry Rd.
Charlotte, VT 05445
Telephone: (802) 425-3961
FAX: (802) 425-3307
Year Established: 1986
Pub. Frequency: bi-m.
Page Size: standard
Subscrip. Rate: $2.95 newsstand; $18/yr.
Materials: 02,04,05,06,17,19,21,23,24,25, 28,29,32,33
Freelance Pay: $500-$2000/article
Circulation: 200,000
Circulation Type: paid
**Owner(s):**
Camden House Publishing
Ferry Rd.
Charlotte, VT 05445
Telephone: (802) 425-3961
Ownership %: 100
**Management:**
Fred Laflamme ..............................Publisher
Kathryn P. Hale ...............Advertising Manager
**Editorial:**
John Barstow ..............................Editor

25824

**HOME FINDER GUIDEBOOK**
1106 Clayton Ln., Ste. 528W
Austin, TX 78723
Telephone: (512) 451-5777
FAX: (512) 451-5779

Year Established: 1987
Pub. Frequency: bi-m.
Page Size: pocket
Subscrip. Rate: free
Materials: 07,32,33
Print Process: web offset
Circulation: 25,000
Circulation Type: free
**Owner(s):**
Southeast Publishing Ventures, Inc.
528 East Blvd.
Charlotte, NC 28203
Telephone: (704) 373-0051
Ownership %: 100
**Management:**
Jim Burris ..............................President
**Editorial:**
Angela Jones .......................Associate Publisher
**Desc.:** A comprehensive map guide covering all segments of the housing market with emphasis on new home subdivisions. articles include general features on the housing industry and local features on new home communities. articles run 200-500 words; departments include; financing section, industry news.
**Readers:** Newcomers, corporate transfers and local residents.

26282

**HONOLULU MAGAZINE**
36 Merchant St.
Honolulu, HI 96813
Telephone: (808) 524-7400
FAX: (808) 531-2306
Mailing Address:
P.O. Box 80
Honolulu, HI 96810
Year Established: 1888
Pub. Frequency: m.
Page Size: standard
Subscrip. Rate: $2.50/copy; $15/yr.
Materials: 01,02,03,04,05,06,09,10,15,19, 20,21,25,28,32
Freelance Pay: $15-$400/article
Print Process: offset
Circulation: 35,582
Circulation Type: paid
**Owner(s):**
Honolulu Publishing Co., Ltd.
36 Merchant St.
Honolulu, HI 96813
Telephone: (808) 524-7400
Ownership %: 100
**Management:**
David Pellegrin ..............................President
Patti O'Hara ..............................Vice President
Jim Myers ..............................Vice President
Nick Tinebra ..............................Vice President
Ed. Cassidy ..............................Publisher
**Editorial:**
John Heckathorn ..............................Editor
Janice Otaguro .......................Managing Editor
Teresa Black ..............................Art Director
Brett Uprichard ...................Associate Editor
Marilyn Kim ..............................Associate Editor
Pat Pitzer ..............................Associate Editor
**Desc.:** Written and edited for residents and frequent visitors to Hawaii, showcasing Hawaii's current issues and trends. Regular departments including dining reviews, politics, fashion, arts, history, calabah, and nakama'aina.
**Readers:** Well educated male/female, forties, married, average income of $88, 840 (household income). Homeowners, frequent travelers.
**Deadline:** story-2 mos. prior to pub. date; ads-7th of preceding mo.

26285

**HUDSON VALLEY MAGAZINE**
297 Main Mall
Poughkeepsie, NY 12601
Telephone: (914) 485-7844

Mailing Address:
P.O. Box 429
Poughkeepsie, NY 12601-3109
Year Established: 1972
Pub. Frequency: m.
Page Size: 4 color photos/art
Subscrip. Rate: $2.50 newsstand; $14.95/yr.
Freelance Pay: $100-$500/article
Circulation: 30,000
Circulation Type: paid
**Owner(s):**
Suburban Publishing, Inc.
16 School St.
Yonkers, NY 10701
Telephone: (914) 963-8300
Ownership %: 100
**Management:**
Thomas R. Martinelli ..............................Publisher
Bernard Rock ...................Advertising Manager
Laura Matarazi ..............................Business Manager
Coleen Mathers ...............Circulation Manager
**Editorial:**
Susan Agrest ..............................Managing Editor
**Desc.:** This is a regional monthly magazine. It covers 10 counties from north of NY city to the state capital in Albany. A general interest publication, our articles focus on topics of interest to our readers; restaurant listings and reviews, business, history, the arts, and the environment. We also feature personalities and subjects of our region.
**Readers:** Middle-to-upper class, affluent and well-educated and $87,758 average household income.

67266

**IOWA CITY MAGAZINE**
111 Wright St.
Iowa City, IA 52244
Telephone: (319) 351-0466
FAX: (319) 351-0466
Year Established: 1989
Pub. Frequency: 10/yr.
Page Size: broadsheet
Subscrip. Rate: $2.50/newsstand; $19.70/yr.
Materials: 04,05,06,10,11,12,13,14,15,19, 20,21,23,24,25,26,32
Print Process: web offset
Circulation: 15,000
Circulation Type: controlled
**Owner(s):**
Iowa City Magazine Publishing, Inc.
111 Wright St.
Iowa City, IA 52240
Telephone: (319) 351-0466
FAX: (319) 351-0466
Ownership %: 100
**Management:**
Christopher Green ..............................President
Christopher Green ..............................Publisher
Christopher Green ............Advertising Manager
**Editorial:**
Christopher Green ..............................Editor in Chief
**Desc.:** Combines local talent and ideas with a regional and national presentation, monthly 4-color.
**Readers:** Upper-income, educated.
**Deadline:** story-15th of each mo.; news-15th of each mo.; photo-15th of each mo.; ads-15th of each mo.

26287

**IOWAN MAGAZINE, THE**
108 Third St., Ste. 350
Des Moines, IA 50309
Telephone: (515) 282-8220
FAX: (515) 282-0125
Year Established: 1952
Pub. Frequency: q.
Page Size: 8 1/2 x 11 1/2
Subscrip. Rate: $4.50 newsstand; $18.50/yr.
Materials: 05,06,09,15,19,32

**Materials Accepted/Included:** 01-Business news 02-By-line articles 03-Fashion news 04-Food news 05-Freelance copy 06-Letters to editor 07-Real estate news 08-Sports news 09-Travel news 10-Book rev. 11-Movie rev. 12-Music rev. 13-TV rev. 14-Theater rev. 15-Coming events 16-Obituaries 17-Question & answer 18-Social announcements 19-Artwork 20-Cartoons 21-Photos 22-TV listings 23-Audio rec. 24-Video rec. 25-Books 26-Films/film clips 27-Personnel news 28-Press releases 29-New product news/photos 30-Trade lit. 31-Contracts awarded 32-Display adv. 33-Classified adv.

Freelance Pay: $200-$700/article
Print Process: web offset
Circulation: 27,000
Circulation Type: paid
**Owner(s):**
The Iowan, Inc.
P.O. Box 130
Shenandoah, IA 51601
Telephone: (712) 246-3586
Ownership %: 100
**Management:**
D.E. Archie ...........................Publisher
Sara De Cook Davis ........Advertising Manager
Betty VanNess ..................Business Manager
**Editorial:**
Karen Massetti Miller .............Managing Editor
Tim Stephany ......................Associate Publisher
**Desc.:** Interested exclusively in material on Iowa or about Iowans. Covers general non-fiction range of features; politics, state progress, homes and gardens, recipes, travel, history, personalities, industries, colleges, etc. Average article runs about 1,500 words with heavy use of pictures where possible. Uses transparencies on covers. Uses free lance writers intensively. Open to publicity material within its scope.
**Readers:** Mainly Iowans of above-average income.

## KANSAS CITY LIVE!
67251

201 E. Armour Blvd.
Kansas City, MO 64111
Telephone: (816) 968-5271
FAX: (816) 753-6802
Year Established: 1989
Pub. Frequency: q.
Page Size: standard
Subscrip. Rate: membership
Circulation: 97,000
Circulation Type: paid
**Owner(s):**
Blue Cross & Blue Shield of Kansas City
201 E. Armour Blvd.
Kansas City, MO 64111
Ownership %: 100
**Management:**
Warren Maus ........................Publisher
Clint Bradt .........................Advertising Manager
**Editorial:**
Warren Maus ........................Editor

## KEY MAGAZINE/THIS WEEK IN SAN FRANCISCO
23386

1508 Fillmore St., Ste. 211
San Francisco, CA 94115
Telephone: (415) 202-1900
FAX: (415) 931-0989
Year Established: 1900
Pub. Frequency: w.
Page Size: pocket
Subscrip. Rate: $65/yr.
Freelance Pay: negotiable
Circulation: 22,000
Circulation Type: controlled & paid
**Owner(s):**
Lou Levin Publishing Co.
1508 Fillmore St., Ste. 211
San Francisco, CA 94115
Telephone: (415) 202-1900
Ownership %: 100
**Management:**
Kate Devereau ......................Controller
Lou Levin ...........................Publisher
**Editorial:**
Brian Stott ..........................Editor
Choppy Oshiro ......................Art Director
Barbara Paul ........................Production Coordinator

**Desc.:** A weekly magazine designed to cover all phases of attractions in San Francisco. Departments include special events, theatre, music, art galleries & museums, night clubs, restaurants, smart shopping in San Francisco
**Readers:** Guests of hotels, motels and delegates at conventions.

## LOS ANGELES MAGAZINE
26293

1888 Century Park E.
Los Angeles, CA 90067
Telephone: (310) 557-7592
FAX: (310) 277-9087
Year Established: 1960
Pub. Frequency: m.
Page Size: standard
Subscrip. Rate: $2.50/issue; $19/yr.
Materials: 05,11,12,14,15,32
Freelance Pay: varies
Print Process: offset
Circulation: 156,000
Circulation Type: paid
**Owner(s):**
Capital Cities/ABC
77 W. 66th St.
New York, NY 10023
Ownership %: 100
**Management:**
Geoff Miller ........................Publisher
**Editorial:**
Rodger Claire .......................Executive Editor
Lew Harris ..........................Editor
Katie Marin .........................Advertising Director
Barbara Burden .....................Circulation Director
Katie Marin .........................Marketing Director
**Desc.:** Covers local and regional problems, pleasures, events, ideas and personalities. Average feature runs 1,500-2,500 words. Most publicity material revised. Pictorial features on Southern California life and leisure, preferred. Departments include: Music, Theatre, TV, Films, Books, Sports, Art, Coming Events, Calendar, Notes & Comment, Pictorial, etc.
**Readers:** Active, affluent Southern Californians.

## LOUISIANA LIFE
70419

111 Veterans Hwy., Ste. 1810
Metairie, LA 70005
Telephone: (504) 834-9698
FAX: (504) 837-2258
Year Established: 1981
Pub. Frequency: q.
Page Size: 4 color photos/art
Subscrip. Rate: $3.95 newsstand; $16/yr.
Materials: 02,05,06,15,21,32,33
Freelance Pay: $400-$500/article
Print Process: offset
Circulation: 30,000
Circulation Type: controlled
**Owner(s):**
William Metcalf
111 Veterans Blvd.
Ste. 1810
Metairie, LA 70005
Telephone: (504) 834-9698
FAX: (504) 837-2258
Ownership %: 100
**Management:**
William Metcalf .....................President
Errol Laborde ......................Publisher
Cassie Foreman ...................Advertising Manager
Janel Durand ......................Circulation Manager
**Editorial:**
Errol Laborde ......................Editor in Chief
Mary Beth Romig ..................Managing Editor
Kathleen Joffrion ..................Art Director
Shannon Gross .....................Listings Editor
**Desc.:** Four-color, high quality, glossy slick lifestyle magazine focused on life in Louisiana.

**Readers:** Middle-upper income professional, age 25-65.
**Deadline:** story-1st of mo., prior to pub. date; news-1st of mo.; photo-1st of mo.; ads-1st of mo.

## MADISON MAGAZINE
26294

625 Williamson St.
Madison, WI 53703
Telephone: (608) 255-9982
FAX: (608) 255-9351
Mailing Address:
   P.O. Box 1604
   Madison, WI 53701
Year Established: 1978
Pub. Frequency: m.
Page Size: standard
Subscrip. Rate: $18/yr.
Materials: 01,02,03,05,06,07,08,09,10,14, 15,17,18,19,21,23,24,25,26,27,28,29,30, 31,32,33
Freelance Pay: up to $1400/article
Print Process: offset
Circulation: 20,000,000
Circulation Type: controlled & paid
**Owner(s):**
Madison Magazine Inc.
625 Williamson St.
Madison, WI 53703
Telephone: (608) 255-9982
FAX: (608) 255-9351
Ownership %: 100
**Management:**
Gail B. Selk .........................Publisher
Gail B. Selk .........................Advertising Manager
**Editorial:**
Doug Moe ...........................Editor
Rachel Hart ........................Adv. Production Manager
Jan Lottig ..........................Adv. Sales Representative
Nora Whitney .......................Adv. Sales Representative
Nancy Lynch ........................Adv. Sales Representative
Penelope Johnson ..................Adv. Sales
Jill Johnson .........................Adv. Sales Representative
John Schultz .......................Art Director
**Desc.:** A city business, lifestyle magazine that focuses on political, cultural and social topics in and around the Madison and Dane County area. The publication reflects Madison's unique status as the state's capital, home to the university and a city with a healthy business climate.
**Readers:** Affluent, upscale audience.

## MARYLAND MAGAZINE
49866

100 S. Charles St., 13th Fl.
Baltimore, MD 21201
Telephone: (410) 539-3100
FAX: (410) 539-3188
Year Established: 1967
Pub. Frequency: bi-m.
Page Size: standard
Subscrip. Rate: $3.50 newsstand; $19.95/yr.
Materials: 32
Freelance Pay: varies
Circulation: 45,000
Circulation Type: paid
**Owner(s):**
Gerry Hartung & Scott Weber
100 S. Charles St., 13th Fl.
Baltimore, MD 21201
Telephone: (410) 539-3100
Ownership %: 100
**Management:**
Gerry Hartung .....................Publisher
**Editorial:**
Michele Burke ......................Editor
Trish Weber .........................Marketing Director

## MEMPHIS
26295

460 Tennessee St.
Memphis, TN 38103
Telephone: (901) 521-9000
FAX: (901) 521-0129
Mailing Address:
   P.O. Box 256
   Memphis, TN 38101
Year Established: 1976
Pub. Frequency: m.
Page Size: standard
Subscrip. Rate: $1.95 newsstand; $15/yr.
Materials: 01,02,03,04,06,08,09,15,19,21,32
Print Process: web offset
Circulation: 23,000
Circulation Type: controlled & paid
**Owner(s):**
MM Corp.
P.O. Box 256
Memphis, TN 38101
Telephone: (901) 521-9000
Ownership %: 100
**Management:**
Kenneth Neill .......................Publisher
Jeffrey Goldberg ...................Advertising Manager
Molly Zanone .......................Circulation Manager
**Editorial:**
Tim Sampson .......................Executive Editor
Murry Keith .........................Art Director
Marcus Villaca .....................Assistant Art Director
**Desc.:** Publishes only non-fiction articles on subjects directly related to Memphis and its immediate environs. In-depth investigative stories, consumer interest articles, and columns on a variety of subjects ranging from music and dining to sports and politics are welcome. Feature length stories should be 2,500-5,000 words long; columns, 1,000-2,500 words. All column and feature writers receive a by-line. 75 percent of editorial content is free-lance. Public event publicity welcomed for City Lights (events) section. Photo spreads welcome, but must be of professional qualify. Departments include: Backtalk (Letters to the Editor), City Lights (Events), Crosscurrents (Community affairs), City Dining (Restaurant reviews), Books (Book reviews), Back Porch (Humor).
**Readers:** 88.2% college graduates with an average age of 43.
**Deadline:** story-1 mo. prior to pub. date; news-1 mo. prior; photo-1 mo. prior; ads-1 mo. prior

## MID-ATLANTIC COUNTRY
52616

6401 Golden Triangle Dr., Ste. 120
Greenbelt, MD 20770
Telephone: (301) 220-2300
FAX: (301) 220-2304
Year Established: 1980
Pub. Frequency: m.
Page Size: standard
Subscrip. Rate: $2.50/newsstand; $18/yr.
Materials: 02,04,05,06,07,09,10,15,19,21, 28,32,33
Freelance Pay: $100-$800/article
Print Process: web offset
Circulation: 120,855
Circulation Type: paid
**Owner(s):**
ESS Ventures, Inc.
6401 Golden Triangle Dr.
Ste. 120
Greenbelt, MD 20770
Telephone: (301) 220-2300
Ownership %: 100
**Management:**
Susan Souders Obrecht ...........President
Laurin Ensslin ......................Publisher
Amy Freese .........................Production Manager

**Editorial:**
Sara Lowen .....................Senior Editor
Tim Sayles .................................Editor
Randy Clark .......................Art Director
Mariann Moery .........Circulation Director
**Desc.:** A regional travel and lifestyle
magazine devoted to Virginia, Maryland,
the District of Columbia, Pennsylvania,
New Jersey, North Carolina, and West
Virginia. Mid-Atlantic Country features
travel and leisure, home and garden,
food and entertaining, and property.
**Readers:** Active mid-Atlantic residents
(primarily metropolitan) who demand
quality leisure. Average age 51. Average
household income-$83,450. Female-
65.6%; male-34.4%. Home ownership-
91%. Average market value of home-
$215,000. Professional-70%

52580

**MIDWEST OUTDOORS**
111 Shore Dr.
Hinsdale, IL 60521
Telephone: (708) 887-7722
FAX: (708) 887-1958
Year Established: 1967
Pub. Frequency: m.
Page Size: tabloid
Subscrip. Rate: $11.95/yr.
Materials: 02,05,06,10,20,24,32,33
Freelance Pay: $15-$30/article
Circulation: 43,814
Circulation Type: paid
**Owner(s):**
Midwest Outdoors, Ltd.
111 Shore Dr.
Hinsdale, IL 60521
Telephone: (708) 887-7722
Ownership %: 100
**Management:**
Gene Laulunen ......................Publisher
Carolyn Kirtley ..........Circulation Manager
Carolyn Kirtley ..........Production Manager
**Editorial:**
Gene Laulunen ...........................Editor
Dan Ferris .................................Sales
**Desc.:** For the outdoorsmen who enjoy
fishing, hunting and camping in the
midwest. Those states include IL, IN, WI,
MI, MN, IA, MO, OH, KY, TN.
**Deadline:** story-35 days prior to pub. date;
news-35 days; photo-35 days; ads-35
days

26302

**MINNEAPOLIS ST. PAUL
  MAGAZINE**
220 S. Sixth St., Ste. 500
Pillsbury Ctr., South Twr.
Minneapolis, MN 55402-4507
Telephone: (612) 339-7571
FAX: (612) 339-5806
Year Established: 1971
Pub. Frequency: m.
Page Size: standard
Subscrip. Rate: $2.50/newsstand; $18/yr.
Materials: 02,03,04,05,06,08,09,15,19,20,
21,28,29
Freelance Pay: varies
Print Process: web offset
Circulation: 65,760
Circulation Type: paid
**Owner(s):**
M.S.P. Communications
220 S. 6th St., Ste. 500
Pillsbury Ctr., South Twr.
Minneapolis, MN 55402
Telephone: (612) 339-7571
FAX: (612) 339-5806
Ownership %: 100
**Management:**
Gary Johnson .............Vice President
Burton D. Cohen .......................Publisher
Pat Mathews ...........Advertising Manager

**Editorial:**
Brian Anderson ...........................Editor
Claude Peck ................Managing Editor
Jim Nelson .......................Art Director
Mary Authier ...........Production Director
**Desc.:** City magazine centering exclusively
on Twin Cities/Minnesota area. Features
can be from advocacy reporting,
investigative reporting, human interest,
humor. By-lines granted. Staff covers
most reviews (theater, movies, books,
short personality portraits). Over 2,000
words not generally desirable. Quality,
irresistible style, care with preparation,
research valued. Photo spreads used
occasionally.
**Readers:** Generally upper middle to upper
class, distribution to all in Twin Cities
and environs.

52631

**MINNESOTA MONTHLY**
15 S. Ninth St.
Minneapolis, MN 55402
Telephone: (612) 371-5800
FAX: (612) 371-5801
Year Established: 1968
Pub. Frequency: m.
Page Size: standard
Subscrip. Rate: $15/yr.
Freelance Pay: varies
Circulation: 82,064
Circulation Type: paid
**Owner(s):**
Minnesota Monthly Publications, Inc.
15 S. Ninth St.
Minneapolis, MN 55402
Telephone: (612) 371-5800
Ownership %: 100
**Management:**
William H. Kling ..........Chairman of Board
Steven Fox ...............................President
Steven Fox ...............................Publisher
Nancy Fazendin ...........Advertising Manager
**Editorial:**
Leonard Witt ..............................Editor
**Desc.:** Explores the vitality and variety of
life in the upper midwest. The region's
best writers, artists, and photographers
combine their talents to shed light on
the people, events, and issues that
matter most to people throughout the
region. Contains profiles of the region's
most compelling people-from business
executives to orchestra conductors;
discussions of the region's most vexing
issues-from medical ethics to farm
foreclosures; essays, fictions and poetry;
reports on books, food, personal
finance, records, musicians, artists,
health, fitness, and travel.
**Readers:** Reaches educated, upscale,
discriminating individuals. Though their
professions and interests are diverse,
they are intellectually curious, culturally
active, and community-conscious. They
have impressive standards, and pursue
the things they value.

65420

**MISSISSIPPI COAST**
P.O. Box 1209
Gulfport, MS 39502-1209
Telephone: (601) 868-1182
FAX: (601) 867-2986
Year Established: 1988
Pub. Frequency: bi-m.
Page Size: standard
Subscrip. Rate: $8/yr.
Circulation: 25,000
Circulation Type: paid
**Owner(s):**
Ship Island Holding Co.
Ownership %: 100
**Management:**
Jeff Bill ...................................Publisher

**Editorial:**
Karen Bryant ...............................Editor
**Desc.:** Examines contemporary people,
places and things, with columns on
business and art.
**Readers:** The active upscale audience
along the coast of Mississippi.

26299

**MISSOURI MAGAZINE**
P.O. Box 28830
St. Louis, MO 63123-4346
Telephone: (800) 451-0914
FAX: (618) 476-1616
Year Established: 1973
Pub. Frequency: q.
Page Size: standard
Subscrip. Rate: $16.95/yr.
Materials: 02,06,21,32
Circulation: 20,000
Circulation Type: paid
**Owner(s):**
ADmore, Inc.
P.O. Box 28830
St. Louis, MO 63123-4346
Telephone: (800) 451-0914
FAX: (618) 476-1616
Ownership %: 100
**Editorial:**
Tony Nolan Adrignola ...................Editor
**Desc.:** Use illustrated non-fiction features
and photo essays about almost any
aspect of life in Missouri: biography,
history, character sketches,
reminiscences, modern life styles, scenic
pieces with feel for the country
and cultural. Stress quality, originality of
approach and appeal to readers. No
poetry.
**Readers:** Missouri residents and others
interested; ages 35 and over,
professionals, newcomers and long-time
residents.

26300

**MONTANA MAGAZINE**
3020 Bozeman Ave.
Helena, MT 59601
Telephone: (406) 443-2842
FAX: (406) 443-5480
Mailing Address:
  P.O. Box 5630
  Helena, MT 59604
Year Established: 1970
Pub. Frequency: bi-m.
Page Size: standard
Subscrip. Rate: $3 newsstand; $18/yr.
Materials: 05,09,10,21,32,33
Freelance Pay: $.15/wd.
Print Process: web
Circulation: 56,000
Circulation Type: paid
**Owner(s):**
American & World Geographic Publishing
3020 Bozeman Ave.
Helena, MT 59601
Telephone: (406) 443-2842
Ownership %: 100
**Management:**
William Cordingley ....................President
Rick Graetz ...............................Publisher
**Editorial:**
Beverly R. Magley .......................Editor
Larry E. Sem ..........................Advertising
Barbara Fifer ...........Publication Manager
**Desc.:** A regional publication geared to the
quality-of-life features that interest
Montanans. That is, it features where-to,
how-to stories, recreation in season,
historical color, environmental and
natural resource issues, wildlife profiles,
scenic photography, in-state travel.
Departments include: Travel, Geology,
Economy, Agriculture, Weather,
Hunting and Fishing, Outdoor
Equipment.

**Readers:** Montana-oriented, travel-minded
readers.
**Deadline:** story-10 wks.; news-10 wks.;
photo-10 wks.

52620

**NEBRASKALAND MAGAZINE**
2200 N. 33rd St.
Lincoln, NE 68503
Telephone: (402) 471-0641
Mailing Address:
  P.O. Box 30370
  Lincoln, NE 68503
Year Established: 1926
Pub. Frequency: 10/yr. (Jan.-Feb., Aug.-
Sep. combined)
Page Size: standard
Subscrip. Rate: $2. newsstand; $14.27/yr.
Materials: 32
Circulation: 65,000
Circulation Type: paid
**Owner(s):**
State of Nebraska
Nebraska Game & Pks. Comm.
2200 N. 33rd St.
Lincoln, NE 68503
Telephone: (402) 471-0641
Ownership %: 100
**Management:**
Troy Kroeger .................Production Manager
**Editorial:**
Donald Cunningham .............Editor in Chief
Jon Farrar .........................Senior Editor
Ken Boric .........................Senior Editor
Paul Horton .........................Administrator
**Desc.:** As a state conservation and parks
agency, we deal with nearly all phases
of outdoor recreation, especially hunting,
fishing and camping. We also carry
historical and miscellaneous topics
of interest to Nebraskans and former
residents.
**Readers:** Most are Nebraskans, but in a
wide range of educational and income
levels. Most are outdoor oriented, from
avid hunters to casual bird watchers.

26306

**NEVADA**
1800 Highway 50 E., Ste. 200
Carson City, NV 89710
Telephone: (702) 687-5416
FAX: (702) 687-6159
Year Established: 1936
Pub. Frequency: bi-m.
Page Size: standard
Subscrip. Rate: $14.95/yr.
Materials: 02,05,06,09,10,15,21,25,28,32,33
Freelance Pay: $50-$400/article
Print Process: web offset
**Owner(s):**
State Of Nevada
Capitol Complex
Carson City, NV 89710
Telephone: (702) 687-5416
Ownership %: 100
**Management:**
Rich Moreno .............................Publisher
Patty Noll .................Advertising Manager
**Editorial:**
David E. Moore ...........................Editor
Paul Allee .........................Art Director
Debi Frame ...............Circulation Director
**Desc.:** The leading travel and leisure
magazine of Nevada seeks free-lance
photos and articles on Nevada history,
sports, events, recreation and
sightseeing areas. By-lines given and
articles should be 500-2,000 words, on
speculation only. Photos should be color
transparencies or black and white prints.
Departments include: Calendar, Show
Guide, Reading.
**Readers:** Mostly 35-70 of age, middle
class travelers, who are interested in
history and recreation.

**Materials Accepted/Included:** 01-Business news 02-By-line articles 03-Fashion news 04-Food news 05-Freelance copy 06-Letters to editor 07-Real estate news 08-Sports news 09-Travel news 10-Book rev. 11-Movie rev. 12-Music rev. 13-TV rev. 14-Theater rev. 15-Coming events 16-Obituaries 17-Question & answer 18-Social announcements 19-Artwork 20-Cartoons 21-Photos 22-TV listings 23-Audio rec. 24-Video rec. 25-Books 26-Films/film clips 27-Personnel news 28-Press releases 29-New product news/photos 30-Trade lit. 31-Contracts awarded 32-Display adv. 33-Classified adv.

## NEW HAMPSHIRE HIGHWAYS
25700

261 Sheep Davis Rd.
Concord, NH 03301
Telephone: (603) 224-1823
FAX: (603) 659-0650
Mailing Address:
P.O. Box 331
Concord, NH 03302-0331
Year Established: 1923
Pub. Frequency: m.
Page Size: standard
Subscrip. Rate: $25/yr.
Freelance Pay: varies
Circulation: 1,000
Circulation Type: controlled
**Owner(s):**
New Hampshire Highways
P.O. Box 331
Concord, NH 03302-0331
Telephone: (603) 224-1823
FAX: (603) 224-9399
Ownership %: 100
**Management:**
Kathleen A. LaBranche .........Executive Director
**Desc.:** An association publication of the
New Hampshire Good Roads
Association. Contains articles of interest
to general public, pertaining to good
roads, safety on the highways.
**Readers:** Road agents, highway
department personnels.

## NEW HAVEN LOCAL NEWS
69197

230 Grand Ave., Ste. 173
New Haven, CT 06513
Year Established: 1990
Pub. Frequency: m.
Page Size: standard
Subscrip. Rate: $30/yr.
Materials: 01,02,03,04,05,06,07,08,09,10,
11,12,13,14,15,17,18,19,20,21,22,25,26,
27,28,29,33
Freelance Pay: negotiable
Print Process: offset
Circulation: 10,000
Circulation Type: controlled
**Owner(s):**
Publishers Press
230 Grand Ave., No. 173
New Haven, CT 06513
Ownership %: 100
**Management:**
Willie Williams, Jr. ...............................Publisher
**Editorial:**
Willie Williams, Jr. .....................................Editor
**Deadline:** story-1st of mo.; news-1st of
mo.; photo-1st of mo.; ads-1st of mo.

## NEW JERSEY MONTHLY
65040

55 Park Pl.
Morristown, NJ 07960
Telephone: (201) 644-5570
FAX: (201) 538-2953
Mailing Address:
P.O. Box 920
Morristown, NJ 07960
Year Established: 1976
Pub. Frequency: m.
Page Size: tabloid
Subscrip. Rate: $2.95 newsstand; $12/yr.
Freelance Pay: $.50/wd.
Circulation: 88,000
Circulation Type: paid
**Owner(s):**
Micromedia Affiliates
7 Dumont Pl.
Morristown, NJ 07960
Telephone: (201) 644-5550
Ownership %: 100
**Management:**
Kate Tomlinson .....................................Publisher
**Editorial:**
Jennie DeMonte ........................................Editor
Michael Callahan ...................... Business Editor

**Desc.:** New Jersey's largest circulation
monthly magazine covering business,
entertainment, the arts as well as
fashion, home furnishing, health, travel,
fitness, etc.
**Readers:** Varied-almost all types.

## NEW MEXICO MAGAZINE
26553

495 Old Santa Fe Tr.
Lew Wallace Bldg.
Santa Fe, NM 87503
Telephone: (505) 827-7447
Year Established: 1923
Pub. Frequency: m.
Page Size: standard
Subscrip. Rate: $2.95/copy; $21.95/yr.
Materials: 05,25,32,33
Freelance Pay: $.30/wd.
Print Process: web offset
Circulation: 125,000
Circulation Type: paid
**Owner(s):**
State of New Mexico
495 Old Santa Fe Tr.
Santa Fe, NM 87503
Telephone: (505) 827-7447
Ownership %: 100
**Management:**
John McMahon ........................................Publisher
Patsy Martinez .................Advertising Manager
**Editorial:**
Emily Drabanski .........................Editor in Chief
Jon Bowman ...............................................Editor
John Vaughan ..................................Art Director
Fern Lyon ...........................Book Review Editor
**Desc.:** Features articles on the New
Mexico scene present and past. Only
New Mexico topics.
**Readers:** Tourists and cultural and
outdoors minded.
**Deadline:** story-6-12 mos. prior to pub.
date; news-6-12 mos. prior; photo-6-12
mos. prior; ads-1st of each mo. prior

## NEW ORLEANS MAGAZINE
26309

111 Veterans Blvd., Ste. 1810
Metairie, LA 70005
Telephone: (504) 831-3731
FAX: (504) 837-2258
Year Established: 1966
Pub. Frequency: m.
Page Size: standard
Subscrip. Rate: $3.95 newsstand; $16/yr.
Materials: 02,05,06,15,21,32,33
Freelance Pay: $100-$500/article
Circulation: 33,275
Circulation Type: paid
**Owner(s):**
New Orleans Publishing Group
111 Veterans Blvd.
Metairie, LA 70005
Telephone: (504) 246-2700
Ownership %: 100
**Management:**
William Metcalf .....................................President
Julio Melare ...........................................Publisher
Cassie Forman .................Advertising Manager
**Editorial:**
Errol Laborde ............................................Editor
Kathleen Joffrion ...........................Art Director
**Desc.:** Covers all aspects of New Orleans,
including politics, business,
entertainment, and restaurants. Most
editorial content is freelance.
Departments include: Business, and
Finance, Art, Real Estate, Fashion,
Women's News and Shopping,
Architecture, and Home Design,
Entertainment, Local Show Business
News, Calendar of Events, Local Color,
Characters, Restaurants and Music.
**Readers:** Mid to upper income, 35 and
over.

## NEW YORK MAGAZINE
26312

755 Second Ave.
New York, NY 10017
Telephone: (212) 880-0700
FAX: (212) 661-8518
Year Established: 1968
Pub. Frequency: w.
Page Size: standard
Subscrip. Rate: $39.98/yr.
Freelance Pay: $350-$4000/article
Circulation: 431,160
Circulation Type: paid
**Owner(s):**
K-III Magazine Corp.
755 Second Ave.
New York, NY 10017
Telephone: (212) 880-0700
Ownership %: 100
**Management:**
Edward Kosner ....................................President
Richard Kinsler .....................................Publisher
Kathy Viscardi ..................Advertising Manager
**Editorial:**
Edward Kosner ..........................................Editor
Peter Herbst ............................Managing Editor
**Desc.:** Covers current events,
contemporary life-styles and
personalities in the New York
metropolitan area.
**Readers:** Managers and other professional
people in the 25-49 year age group.

## NEW YORK OUTDOORS
71252

51 Atlantic Ave.
Floral Park, NY 11001
Telephone: (516) 352-9700
FAX: (516) 437-6941
Year Established: 1992
Pub. Frequency: 8/yr.
Subscrip. Rate: free newsstand
Circulation: 20,000
Circulation Type: free
**Owner(s):**
Allsport Publishing Co.
51 Atlantic Ave.
Floral Park, NY 11001
Telephone: (516) 352-9700
FAX: (516) 437-6941
Ownership %: 100
**Editorial:**
John T. Saousis ........................................Editor

## NORTH COAST JOURNAL
70461

83 Wilson Ln.
Arcata, CA 95521
Pub. Frequency: m.
**Owner(s):**
Miv Schaaf Associates

## NORTH SHORE
53999

874 Green Bay Rd.
Northfield, IL 60093
Telephone: (708) 441-7892
FAX: (708) 441-8505
Year Established: 1978
Pub. Frequency: m.
Page Size: standard
Subscrip. Rate: $1.95 newsstand; $12/yr.
Materials: 01,02,03,04,05,06,07,08,09,10,
11,12,15,18,19,20,21,27,28,29,32,33
Print Process: web offset
Circulation: 55,000
Circulation Type: paid
**Owner(s):**
Asher J. Birnbaum
874 Green Bay Rd.
Northfield, IL 60093
Telephone: (708) 441-7892
Ownership %: 60

S. William Pattis
4255 W. Touhy Ave.
Chicago, IL 60646
Telephone: (708) 679-5500
Ownership %: 40
**Management:**
Asher J. Birnbaum .................................Publisher
Asher J. Birnbaum .............Advertising Manager
Jon Michaels .................Circulation Manager
Randy Young .....................Production Manager
**Editorial:**
Irene Birnbaum ..................Associate Publisher
**Desc.:** For the sophisticated people who
enjoy the unique lifestyle of Chicago's
northern and northwestern suburbs. It
focuses attention on local events and
local people, utilizing good writing,
attractive graphics and a unique blend of
imagination and excitement.
**Readers:** Average household income
$184,200, 90.6% have attended college.
83% are professionals or business
managers/owners, 62% hold valid
passports.
**Deadline:** story-3 mos.; news-3 mos.;
photo-3 mos.; ads-25th of mo., 2 mos.
prior

## OHIO MAGAZINE
26314

62 E. Broad St.
Columbus, OH 43215-3522
Telephone: (614) 461-5083
FAX: (614) 461-5506
Year Established: 1978
Pub. Frequency: m.
Page Size: standard
Subscrip. Rate: $18/yr.
Materials: 06,32,33
Circulation: 85,705
Circulation Type: paid
**Owner(s):**
Ohio Magazine, Inc.
62 E. Broad St
Columbus, OH 43215
Telephone: (614) 461-5083
Ownership %: 100
**Bureau(s):**
Cleveland Office, Ohio Mag.
1701 E. 12Th St., Ste. 3-L W.
Cleveland, OH 44114
Telephone: (216) 861-3136

Akron-Canton-Youngstown Area Sales
Office
8035 Westfield Rd.
Medina, OH 44256
Telephone: (216) 887-5401
Contact: Lori Cantor

Toledo Area Sales Office
P.O. Box 4
Swanton, OH 43558
Telephone: (419) 825-1645
Contact: Nancy Allen
**Management:**
Karen Matusoff ..................Advertising Manager
Stacey Callahan ...................Circulation Manager
Roy Wolford ...........................General Manager
Dan Boyle .........................Production Manager
**Editorial:**
Cassie Ring ............................Managing Editor
**Desc.:** Features articles with a wide variety
of subjects. The common element is
that they have an angle oriented to
Ohioans. Departments include: Letters,
Country Journal, Ohioguide, Diners'
Digest, Ohio Journal, Last Word, Dining
In.
**Readers:** Upscale Ohioans interested in
travel, news, the state of their State and
who's in it.
**Deadline:** ads-25th of mo. 2 mos. prior to
pub. date

---

**Materials Accepted/Included:** 01-Business news 02-By-line articles 03-Fashion news 04-Food news 05-Freelance copy 06-Letters to editor 07-Real estate news 08-Sports news 09-Travel news
10-Book rev. 11-Movie rev. 12-Music rev. 13-TV rev. 14-Theater rev. 15-Coming events 16-Obituaries 17-Question & answer 18-Social announcements 19-Artwork 20-Cartoons 21-Photos 22-TV listings
23-Audio rec. 24-Video rec. 25-Books 26-Films/film clips 27-Personnel news 28-Press releases 29-New product news/photos 30-Trade lit. 31-Contracts awarded 32-Display adv. 33-Classified adv.

65116
## OMAHA MAGAZINE
7387 Pacific St.
Omaha, NE 68114
Telephone: (402) 391-4465
FAX: (402) 391-2848
Mailing Address:
P.O. Box 27405
Omaha, NE 68127
Year Established: 1983
Pub. Frequency: bi-m.
Page Size: standard
Subscrip. Rate: free/hotels; $2.50/copy
newsstand; $9.95/yr. mailed
Freelance Pay: $50-$100/200 wds.
Print Process: full heat set web
Circulation: 70,000
Circulation Type: paid
**Owner(s):**
Omaha Magazine, LLC
P.O. Box 27405
Omaha, NE 68127
Telephone: (402) 391-4465
Ownership %: 100
**Bureau(s):**
Vitality Magazine
P.O. Box 27405
Omaha, NE 68127
Telephone: (402) 391-8016
Contact: Todd Mills, Publisher
**Management:**
Todd Lemke .........................................President
Todd Lemke .........................................Publisher
Greg Bruns ........................Advertising Manager
Louise Casamento .............Circulation Manager
**Editorial:**
Mark Tatelman ......................................Editor
Sean Brennan ..............................Art Director
**Desc.:** A monthly consumer city magazine
about Omaha and its people. Monthly
features include Calendar of Events,
Heath, Restaurant Guide, Travel,
Motivation, Theatre and the Arts.
**Readers:** Three markets: (1) City-15,000;
(2) Hotels-20,000; (3) Relocation-5,000.

26317
## ORLANDO MAGAZINE
422 W. Fairbanks Ave., Ste. 300
Winter Park, FL 32789
Telephone: (407) 539-3939
FAX: (407) 539-0533
Year Established: 1946
Pub. Frequency: m.
Page Size: standard
Subscrip. Rate: $2.95 newsstand;
$14.95/yr.
Materials: 32
Freelance Pay: varies
Print Process: web offset
Circulation: 40,000
Circulation Type: controlled
**Owner(s):**
David F. Cook
Palm House Publishing, Inc.
422 W. Fairbanks Ave., Ste. 300
Winter Park, FL 32789
Telephone: (407) 539-3939
Ownership %: 100
**Management:**
David F. Cook .......................................Owner
Jeff Prutsman ...................................Publisher
**Editorial:**
Fred Abel ..............................................Editor
Jill Hamilton .....................Advertising Director
Bruce Borich .................................Art Director
**Desc.:** We are a metropolitan magazine
emphasizing editorial content useful to
people new to the area, and lifestyle
and business information for local
residents.
**Readers:** Local residents, potential new
residents.

25905
## PACIFIC NORTHWEST MAGAZINE
1115 N.W. Elford Rd.
Seattle, WA 98177
Telephone: (206) 364-2573
Year Established: 1966
Pub. Frequency: 10/yr.
Page Size: standard
Subscrip. Rate: $18.95/yr.
Materials: 04,09,10,11,12,14,23,24,25,32,
33,
Freelance Pay: negotiable
Circulation: 104,000
Circulation Type: paid
**Owner(s):**
Micro Media A.F., Inc.
7 Dumont Pl.
Morristown, NJ 07960
Ownership %: 100
**Management:**
Norman B. Tomlinson ....................President
Norman B. Tomlinson .........................Publisher
John Carnahan ................Advertising Manager
John Searight .......................General Manager
**Editorial:**
Ann Naumann .......................................Editor
Kate Roosevelt .....................Associate Editor
**Desc.:** In a straightforward graphic style
with emphasis on the appropriate use of
color photography and illustration;
reflects the unusual quality of life in the
region, provides a visually appealing
journal for the outstanding reporting of
issues that enhance, affect, or endanger
that quality of life, and offers to readers
hard and direct information on how to
use the unique recreational, cultural,
and economic resources to their best
personal advantage.
**Readers:** Average age 48, average income
$84,000

26318
## PALM BEACH LIFE
265 Royal Poinciana
Palm Beach, FL 33480
Telephone: (407) 655-5755
FAX: (407) 655-4594
Mailing Address:
P.O. Box 1176
Palm Beach, FL 33480
Year Established: 1906
Pub. Frequency: m.
Page Size: standard
Subscrip. Rate: $26/yr.
Freelance Pay: $150-$700/article
Circulation: 28,000
Circulation Type: controlled & paid
**Owner(s):**
Palm Beach News & Life
Telephone: (407) 655-5755
Ownership %: 100
**Management:**
Tom Giuffrida .....................................President
Joyce Harr ........................................Publisher
**Editorial:**
Michael Gaeta .......................Managing Editor
Leta Barnes .....................Assistant Publisher
Therese Christiano .............Circulation Director
Esa Jokela ..........................................Director
Amy Woodcox ....................................Director
**Desc.:** Catering to a sophisticated, high-
income readership and reflecting its
interests. Departments include: Art,
Society, Sports, Fashion, Travel,
Gourmet, Personality Profiles.
**Readers:** International society and Palm
Beach area.

26319
## PALM BEACH SOCIETY MAGAZINE
240 Worth Ave.
Palm Beach, FL 33480
Telephone: (407) 659-5555
FAX: (407) 655-6209

Mailing Address:
P.O. Box 591
Palm Beach, FL 33480
Year Established: 1953
Pub. Frequency: w.: Nov.-Apr.; m.: May-
Oct.
Page Size: oversize
Subscrip. Rate: $2 newsstand; $30/yr.
Materials: 01,02,03,05,09,15,18,21,28,29,32
Freelance Pay: negotiable
Print Process: offset
Circulation: 5,040
Circulation Type: paid
**Owner(s):**
James Jennings Sheeran
P.O. Box 591
Palm Beach, FL 33480
Telephone: (407) 659-5555
Ownership %: 80

Eric Friedheim
P.O. Box 591
Palm Beach, FL 33480
Telephone: (407) 659-5555
Ownership %: 20
**Bureau(s):**
James Sheehan
166 E. 61st St.
New York, NY 10022
Telephone: (212) 755-0505
**Management:**
James Jennings Sheeran ............Chairman of
Board
Eric Friedheim ...........................Vice Chairman
James Jennings Sheeran ...................Publisher
James Jennings .............Advertising Manager
Sheeran
**Editorial:**
Tamara Newell .................................Columnist
Judith Clemence ..............................Columnist
John Gander .....................................Columnist
Judy Schrafft ....................................Columnist
Tom Gates ........................................Columnist
**Desc.:** Contains photographs of the social,
charitable, cultural, and sports life of the
area, plus written columns covering both
public and private social and cultural
events. Departments include: Social
News, Gossip, New York Hotline,
London, International, West Coast.
**Readers:** Upscale and society.

26320
## PALM SPRINGS LIFE
303 N. Indian Canyon Dr.
Palm Springs, CA 92262
Telephone: (619) 325-2333
FAX: (619) 325-7008
Mailing Address:
P.O. Box 2724
Palm Springs, CA 92262
Year Established: 1948
Pub. Frequency: m.
Page Size: standard
Subscrip. Rate: $3.95 newsstand; $36/yr.
Materials: 03,04,32
Freelance Pay: $.20/wd.
Print Process: offset
Circulation: 24,000
Circulation Type: paid
**Owner(s):**
Desert Publications, Inc.
303 N. Indian Canyon Dr.
Palm Springs, CA 92262
Telephone: (619) 325-2333
Ownership %: 100
**Management:**
Milton W. Jones ................................President
Milton W. Jones ...............................Publisher
**Editorial:**
Stewart Weiner ....................................Editor
Bill Russon ....................................Art Director
Donna Coleman .................Associate Editor
Mary Anne Pinkston .............Associate Editor

**Desc.:** Carries news features of general
interest to the international society and
desert resort area, with emphasis on in-
depth personality profiles, plus
occasional travel pieces written primarily
by freelancers. Publicity material may be
used as a guide or tip to stories, but will
never be used by itself. Departments
include: Society, Fashion, Arts, Cuisine,
House & Garden.
**Readers:** Affluent Californians plus
national and international circulation.

26323
## PENNSYLVANIA MAGAZINE
P.O. Box 576
Camp Hill, PA 17001-0576
Telephone: (717) 761-6620
Year Established: 1981
Pub. Frequency: bi-m.
Page Size: standard
Subscrip. Rate: $2.95/copy; $18.97/yr.;
$33.92/2 yrs.
Freelance Pay: $.10-$.15/wd.
Circulation: 40,000
Circulation Type: paid
**Owner(s):**
Albert E. Holliday, General Partner
P.O. Box 576
Camp Hill, PA 17001
Telephone: (717) 761-6620
Ownership %: 100
**Management:**
Albert E. Holliday ..............................Publisher
Susan Getter ....................Advertising Manager
Joan M. Holliday .................Business Manager
**Editorial:**
Albert E. Holliday ......................Editor in Chief
Matt K. Holliday ....................Managing Editor
Patrick Reynolds ........................Miscellaneous
**Desc.:** Feature magazine about people
and developments in Pennsylvania.
Topics covered include: history, travel,
personalities, sports, entertainment,
major issues, lifestyles. Articles usually
run 250-2,500 words, always with
illustrations, b&w or color prints (do not
send original slides). Author by-lines and
art credits given. Publicity material used
when of editorial interest to readership.
Departments include: Books, Potpourri,
city/regional guide, genealogy and
calendar.
**Readers:** 35-60 years of age; median
family income $46,000

22387
## PHILADELPHIA MAGAZINE
1818 Market St.
Philadelphia, PA 19103
Telephone: (215) 564-7700
FAX: (215) 656-3502
Year Established: 1908
Pub. Frequency: m.
Page Size: standard
Subscrip. Rate: $2.95 newsstand; $7.95/yr.
Freelance Pay: $200-$1000/article
Circulation: 135,000
Circulation Type: paid
**Owner(s):**
Metrocorp
1818 Market St.
Philadelphia, PA 19103
Telephone: (215) 564-7700
Ownership %: 100
**Management:**
David H. Lipson ..................................President
David H. Lipson .................................Publisher
**Editorial:**
Loren Feldmen .........................Executive Editor
Lisa DePaulo ...........................Senior Editor
Carol Saline ................................Senior Editor
Eliot Kaplan ..........................................Editor
Laurenee Stains ........................Articles Editor
Ken Newbaker .....................Design Director

**Desc.:** Staff-written and contributed by-line features cover local business and political and entertainment scene as well as life style pieces. Articles run from 1,000 to 10,000 words.
**Readers:** Philadelphia area residents.

## PHOENIX MAGAZINE
5555 N. Seventh Ave., Ste. B-200
Phoenix, AZ 85013-1755
Telephone: (602) 207-3750
FAX: (602) 207-3777
Year Established: 1966
Pub. Frequency: m.
Page Size: standard
Subscrip. Rate: $1.95 newsstand; $14/yr.
Materials: 02,05,19,32,33
Freelance Pay: varies
Print Process: web
Circulation: 50,000
Circulation Type: paid
**Owner(s):**
Media America Corp.
5555 N. Seventh Ave., Ste. B-2
Phoenix, AZ 85013-1755
Telephone: (602) 207-3750
FAX: (602) 207-3777
Ownership %: 100
**Management:**
Jewell M. Lewis ...................Chairman of Board
Delbert R. Lewis ...............................President
**Editorial:**
Richard S. Vonier .........................................Editor
Beth Deveny ..........................Managing Editor
Ramona Kiyoshk .........................Copy Director
Laura Greenberg .........................Feature Editor
**Desc.:** City magazine covering primarily the metropolitan area of Phoenix and other matters of statewide interest.
**Readers:** Urban and suburban; social & civic leaders

## PITTSBURGH MAGAZINE
4802 Fifth Ave.
Pittsburgh, PA 15213
Telephone: (412) 622-1360
FAX: (412) 622-7066
Year Established: 1969
Pub. Frequency: m.
Page Size: standard
Subscrip. Rate: $2.50 newsstand; $15/yr.
Materials: 32
Freelance Pay: $50-$600/article
Print Process: web offset
Circulation: 65,000
Circulation Type: paid
**Owner(s):**
QED Communications, Inc.
4802 Fifth Ave.
Pittsburgh, PA 15213
Telephone: (412) 622-1300
Ownership %: 100
**Management:**
Donald Korb ...................................President
Meg Cheever ...................................Publisher
**Editorial:**
Christopher Fletcher ...............................Editor
Michelle Pilecki ......................Managing Editor
Renee Brown ...............Administrative Manager
Rhonda Goldblatts .............Advertising Director
**Desc.:** Reports on, analyzes, and evaluates public affairs, the arts, and people and places in the area including Pittsburgh, Western Pennsylvania, Northern West Virginia and Eastern Ohio. Regular columns and articles on politics, government, art, music, travel, history, humor. Departments include: Shopping, Dining, Personalities, Events, Movies, Sports, Lifestyles.
**Readers:** Educated, affluent, active adults.

## PLATEAU
Rte. 4, Box 720
Flagstaff, AZ 86001
Telephone: (602) 774-5211
FAX: (602) 779-1527
Year Established: 1928
Pub. Frequency: q.
Subscrip. Rate: $25/yr.
Circulation: 6,000
Circulation Type: paid
**Owner(s):**
Museum of Northern Arizona Press
Rte. 4, Box 270
Flagstaff, AZ 86001
Telephone: (602) 774-5211
Ownership %: 100

## SACRAMENTO MAGAZINE
4471 D St.
Sacramento, CA 95819
Telephone: (916) 452-6200
FAX: (916) 446-1238
Year Established: 1975
Pub. Frequency: 11/yr.
Page Size: standard
Subscrip. Rate: $18/yr.
Freelance Pay: varies
Circulation: 25,000
Circulation Type: paid
**Owner(s):**
Michael O'Brien
4471 D St.
Sacramento, CA 95819
Telephone: (916) 452-6200
Ownership %: 100
**Management:**
Michael O'Brien ...............................Publisher
**Editorial:**
Krista Hendricks-Minard ..........Managing Editor
Joe Chiodo .........................................Advertising
**Desc.:** Personalities, local or statewide issues, entertainment, gardening, decorating, publicity material; if it fits our needs and varies from several hundred words to 3,000.
**Readers:** Highly professional, high income.

## SALT LAKE CITY
1270 W. 2320 S., Ste. A
Salt Lake City, UT 84119
Telephone: (801) 975-1927
Year Established: 1989
Pub. Frequency: bi-m.
Page Size: standard
Subscrip. Rate: $3.25 newsstand; $15/yr.
Freelance Pay: varies
Circulation: 15,000
Circulation Type: paid
**Owner(s):**
JES Publishing Corp.
1270 W 2320 S., Ste. A
Salt Lake Cty, UT 84119
Telephone: (801) 975-1927
Ownership %: 100
**Management:**
Barbara Sivannisson ..........Associate Publisher
**Editorial:**
Ellen Fagg ...............................................Editor
**Desc.:** Lifestyle of Salt Lake City.
**Readers:** Households of $50,000-plus income

## SAN DIEGO MAGAZINE
4206 W. Point Loma Blvd.
San Diego, CA 92110
Telephone: (619) 225-8953
FAX: (619) 222-0773
Mailing Address:
  P.O. Box 85409
  San Diego, CA 92186
Year Established: 1948
Pub. Frequency: m.

Page Size: standard
Subscrip. Rate: $2.50/issue; $16/yr.
Freelance Pay: $200-$500/article
Circulation: 49,423
Circulation Type: paid
**Owner(s):**
Edwin & Gloria Self
4206 W. Point Loma Blvd.
San Diego, CA 92110
Telephone: (619) 225-8953
FAX: (619) 222-0773
Ownership %: 100
**Management:**
Edwin Self ...................................President
Gloria Self ...................................Publisher
Amy Van Buskirk .............Advertising Manager
**Editorial:**
Edwin Self ...........................Editor in Chief
Winke Self ...........................Managing Editor
Laurie Miller ...........................Art Director
Gloria Self ...........................Co-Publisher
Francis Bardacke ....................Theatrical Editor
**Desc.:** Directed to area's leadership audience (most college graduates). Departments include: theatre, books, restaurants, wine, night life, recreation, music, art, politics, health and diet, architecture, urban design.
**Readers:** Affluent on-the-go, educated audience.

## SANDLAPPER
334 Old Chapin Rd.
Lexington, SC 29072-1108
Telephone: (803) 359-9954
FAX: (803) 957-8226
Mailing Address:
  P.O. Box 1108
  Lexington, SC 29071
Year Established: 1968
Pub. Frequency: q.
Page Size: standard
Subscrip. Rate: $3.95 newsstand; $14.95/yr.
Materials: 02,06,15,28
Freelance Pay: negotiable
Print Process: web offset
Circulation: 6,300
Circulation Type: controlled & paid
**Owner(s):**
RPW Publishing Corp.
P.O. Box 1108
Lexington, SC 29071
Telephone: (803) 359-9954
Ownership %: 100
**Management:**
Robert P. Wilkins ...........................Publisher
Rose T. Wilkins .................Circulation Manager
**Editorial:**
Robert P. Wilkins ...............................Editor
Daniel Harmon .........................Managing Editor
**Desc.:** Covers entertainment, history, business, people, places and sports in the state of South Carolina.
**Readers:** Residents and tourists of South Carolina.

## SAN FRANCISCO FOCUS
2601 Mariposa St.
San Francisco, CA 94110-1400
Telephone: (415) 553-2800
FAX: (415) 553-2470
Year Established: 1953
Pub. Frequency: m.
Subscrip. Rate: $24/yr.
Materials: 01,03,05,06,07,08,09,10,11,12, 14,15,19,21,32,33
Freelance Pay: varies
Circulation: 180,000
Circulation Type: controlled & paid

**Owner(s):**
KQED, Inc.
2601 Mariposa St.
San Francisco, CA 94110
Telephone: (415) 553-2800
Ownership %: 100
**Editorial:**
Amy Rennert ...............................................Editor
**Desc.:** Features on travel, food and entertainment, fashion, entrepreneurship, health, and shopping in the city, with interviews, essays, and fiction of interest to a cosmopolitan audience.
**Deadline:** story-3 mos. prior to pub. date; news-3 mos. prior; photo-3 mos. prior; ads-2 mos. prior

## SAN GABRIEL VALLEY MAGAZINE
2908 W. Valley Blvd.
Alhambra, CA 91803
Telephone: (818) 284-7607
Year Established: 1976
Pub. Frequency: q.
Page Size: standard
Subscrip. Rate: $2.95 newsstand; $25/yr.
Materials: 32
Circulation: 300,000
Circulation Type: paid
**Owner(s):**
Miller Books, Inc.
2908 W. Valley Blvd.
Alhambra, CA 91803
Telephone: (818) 284-7607
Ownership %: 100
**Editorial:**
Joseph Miller ...............................................Editor

## SCANDINAVIAN REVIEW
725 Park Ave.
New York, NY 10021
Telephone: (212) 879-9779
FAX: (212) 249-3444
Year Established: 1913
Pub. Frequency: 3/yr.
Page Size: 6 x 9 1/4
Subscrip. Rate: $15/yr.
Freelance Pay: $100-$300/article
Circulation: 3,500
Circulation Type: paid
**Owner(s):**
American-Scandinavian Foundation
725 Park Ave.
New York, NY 10021
Telephone: (212) 879-9779
FAX: (212) 249-3444
Ownership %: 100
**Management:**
Lena Biorck Kaplan ...............................Publisher
**Desc.:** Articles cover travel, history, biography, education, literature, arts, science, industry, etc., of Scandinavia. General theme is the promotion of cultural relationships between the United States and Scandinavian countries. Departments include: Nordic Books in brief (capsule accounts of Scandinavian-theme books in English).

## SINGLES SOURCE
P.O. Box 1346
Salem, IL 62881
Telephone: (618) 548-2839
FAX: (618) 548-2583
Year Established: 1994
Pub. Frequency: m.
Subscrip. Rate: free/newsstand; $15/yr.
Materials: 01,02,03,04,05,06,09,10,11,12, 13,14,15,17,18,19,20,21,27,28,29,30,32, 33
Print Process: web offset

---

**Materials Accepted/Included:** 01-Business news 02-By-line articles 03-Fashion news 04-Food news 05-Freelance copy 06-Letters to editor 07-Real estate news 08-Sports news 09-Travel news 10-Book rev. 11-Movie rev. 12-Music rev. 13-TV rev. 14-Theater rev. 15-Coming events 16-Obituaries 17-Question & answer 18-Social announcements 19-Artwork 20-Cartoons 21-Photos 22-TV listings 23-Audio rec. 24-Video rec. 25-Books 26-Films/film clips 27-Personnel news 28-Press releases 29-New product news/photos 30-Trade lit. 31-Contracts awarded 32-Display adv. 33-Classified adv.

6-99

**Owner(s):**
Gretchen Rudd
3486 Robin Rd.
Salem, IL 62881
Telephone: (618) 548-2839
Ownership %: 100
**Management:**
Gretchen Rudd ..............................President
**Deadline:** story-20th of mo.; news-20th of mo.; photo-20th of mo.; ads-20th of mo.

26561

## SOUTHERN CALIFORNIA GUIDE
11385 Exposition Bl., #102
Los Angeles, CA 90064
Telephone: (310) 391-8255
Year Established: 1919
Pub. Frequency: m.
Page Size: digest
Subscrip. Rate: free
Materials: 01,03,09,28,29,32,33
Print Process: offset
Circulation: 34,000
Circulation Type: controlled
**Owner(s):**
Westworld Publishing Corp.
11835 Exposition Bl. #102
Los Angeles, CA 90064
Telephone: (310) 391-8255
Ownership %: 100
**Management:**
Valerie Summers ........................President
Valerie Summers ........................Publisher
Greg Rockmael ..............Circulation Manager
**Editorial:**
Sue Few .................Administrative Assistant
Keith Scott .................Motion Picture Editor
Valerie Summers .............New Product Editor
Valerie Summers ........................News Editor
Kevin Allen ..................................Photo
Valerie Summers ..................Technical Editor
**Desc.:** Brief items describe points of interest, events taking place in Southern California. Material slanted for business people, residents and visitors designed to promote stays in the area, restaurants, hotels, and resorts listed. Also restaurant reviews & world-wide travel features.
**Readers:** Traveling businessmen, conventioneers and tourists.

23251

## SOUTHERN EXPOSURE
P.O. Box 531
Durham, NC 27702
Telephone: (919) 419-8311
FAX: (919) 419-8315
Year Established: 1973
Pub. Frequency: q.
Page Size: standard
Subscrip. Rate: $5 newsstand; $24/yr.
Freelance Pay: $50-$200
Circulation: 5,000
Circulation Type: paid
**Owner(s):**
Institute For Southern Studies
P.O. Box 531
Durham, NC 27702
Telephone: (919) 419-8311
Ownership %: 100
**Management:**
Sharon Ugochukwu ..............Business Manager
**Editorial:**
Eric Bates ........................Managing Editor

**Desc.:** A quarterly review of politics and culture and of Southern affairs. It combines personalized interviews and detailed research to examine changes in the South & the region's popular traditions. We seek investigative journalism, political commentary, social essays, personal profiles and interviews with liberal or populist perspective. Native Southern writers preferred. Photos accepted. Length to 4,500 words. Articles on the meaning of southern music, who owns the south, the state of Black politics, profile of a farmer's cooperative, interview with William Fulbright, history of Appalachia's development.
**Readers:** Interdisciplinary academic and well-informed audience.

25940

## SOUTHERN LIVING
2100 Lakeshore Dr.
Birmingham, AL 35209
Telephone: (205) 877-6000
FAX: (205) 877-6700
Mailing Address:
  P.O. Box 523
  Birmingham, AL 35201
Year Established: 1966
Pub. Frequency: m.
Page Size: standard
Subscrip. Rate: $3.95 newsstand; $26/yr.
Circulation: 2,300,000
Circulation Type: paid
**Owner(s):**
Time, Inc.
Time Life Bldg.
New York, NY 10020
Telephone: (212) 522-2751
Ownership %: 100
**Management:**
Jim Nelson ..............................President
Scott Sheppard ........................Publisher
Betty Robb ..................General Manager
**Editorial:**
Michael Carlton ................Executive Editor
Eleanor Griffin ................Executive Editor
John Floyd ..................................Editor
Clay Nordan ........................Managing Editor
Greg Keyes ..............................Advertising
Tom Ford ..................................Art Director
Greg Keyes ..................Associate Publisher
Tom Ford ..................................Photo
**Desc.:** Magazine of today's south. Through a comprehensive editorial package highlighting foods, travel, homes and gardens. Addresses the bond between the South's traditional and cosmopolitan attitudes. Presented monthly to 10,000,000 readers. It is the definitive lifestyle guide for the ever-changing, ever-expanding South.
**Readers:** Home-owners in the upper income bracket; many are professional people.

26297

## SOUTH FLORIDA MAGAZINE
800 Douglas Rd., Ste. 500
Coral Gables, FL 33134
Telephone: (305) 445-4500
FAX: (305) 445-4600
Mailing Address:
  P.O. Box 019068
  Miami, FL 33101
Year Established: 1983
Pub. Frequency: m.
Page Size: standard
Subscrip. Rate: $3 newsstand; $24.95/yr.
Freelance Pay: $75-$1000/article
Circulation: 38,023
Circulation Type: paid

**Owner(s):**
Florida Media Affiliates, Inc.
Box 019068
Miami, FL 33101-9068
Telephone: (305) 445-4500
Ownership %: 100
**Management:**
Norman Tomlinson ..............................President
Shelly Iorfida ..................................Publisher
**Editorial:**
Glenn Albin ..................................Editor
Cynthia Magalin ........................Art Director
Eric Newill ........................Associate Editor
Barbara Shade ................Production Director
Suzanne Pallot ............Special Events Director
**Desc.:** Timely, topical provocative editorial content focusing on dynamic personalities, insiders, trends and topics.
**Readers:** Affluent cosmopolitan residents of South Florida area, including Miami, Fort Lauderdale, Palm Beach and Key West; 72% professionals and managers; median income $80,000, average value of home $200,000.

26338

## STATE, THE
128 S. Tryon St., Ste. 2200
Charlotte, NC 28202
Telephone: (704) 371-3265
Year Established: 1933
Pub. Frequency: m.
Page Size: 4 color photos/art
Subscrip. Rate: $2.50 newsstand; $19.75/yr.
Freelance Pay: varies
Circulation: 23,000
Circulation Type: paid
**Owner(s):**
Shaw Publishing, Inc.
128 S. Tryon St., Ste. 2200
Charlotte, NC 28202
Telephone: (704) 371-3265
Ownership %: 100
**Management:**
Sam Rogers ..................................Publisher
Dawn Johnson ..................Circulation Manager
**Editorial:**
Scott Smith ..................Managing Editor
**Desc.:** General articles about places, people, events, history, travel, general interest in North Carolina. Emphasizes travel in North Carolina and devotes features regularly to resorts, tourist attractions, dining and stopping places. All material printed must deal with North Carolina.
**Readers:** 85% inside North Carolina; 15% Carolinians. Older, conservative high income group.

24661

## TEXAS HIGHWAYS
1101 E. Anderson Ln.
Austin, TX 78752
Telephone: (512) 483-3675
FAX: (512) 483-3672
Mailing Address:
  P.O. Box 141009
  Austin, TX 78714
Year Established: 1974
Pub. Frequency: m.
Page Size: standard
Subscrip. Rate: $12.50/yr.; $20/yr. foreign
Materials: 02,04,05,06,09,15,19,21
Freelance Pay: $.40-.75/wd.
Print Process: web offset
Circulation: 430,000
Circulation Type: paid
**Owner(s):**
Texas Dept. of Transportation
P.O. Box 141009
Austin, TX 78714
Telephone: (512) 483-3675
Ownership %: 100

**Management:**
Herman Kelly ..................................Publisher
Jean Joanson ..................Circulation Manager
**Editorial:**
Jack Lowry ..................................Editor
Lori Moffatt ........................Assistant Editor
Nola McKey ........................Assistant Editor
Jill Bates ........................Associate Editor
Glenda Rogers ................Marketing Director
Michael A. Murphy ..........Photography Editor
Debbie Thompson ..................Products Editor
Ann Gallaway ..................Research Editor
**Desc.:** Interprets scenic, recreational, historical, cultural, and ethnic treasures of the state and preserves the best of Texas heritage. The official travel magazine of Texas, its purpose is to educate and to entertain, to encourage recreational travel to and within the state, and to tell the Texas story to readers around the world.
**Readers:** Over 1 million readership worldwide, magazine goes to all 50 states, 90 countries.

69750

## TEXAS MONTHLY
P.O. Box 1569
Austin, TX 78767
Telephone: (512) 320-6900
Year Established: 1973
Pub. Frequency: m.
Subscrip. Rate: $2.50 newsstand; $18/yr. in state; $21/yr. out of state
Circulation: 310,619
Circulation Type: paid
**Owner(s):**
Texas Monthly, Inc.
P.O. Box 1569
Austin, TX 78767
Telephone: (512) 320-6900
Ownership %: 100
**Editorial:**
Gregory Curtis ..................................Editor

26342

## VERMONT LIFE
6 Baldwin St.
Montpelier, VT 05602
Telephone: (802) 828-3241
FAX: (802) 828-3366
Year Established: 1946
Pub. Frequency: q.
Page Size: standard
Subscrip. Rate: $2.95 copy; $11.95/yr.
Freelance Pay: $.20/wd.
Circulation: 90,000
Circulation Type: paid
**Owner(s):**
State Of Vermont, Devel. Agency
Pavilion Bldg.
Montpelier, VT 05602
Telephone: (802) 828-3241
Ownership %: 100
**Editorial:**
Tom Slayton ..................................Editor
Linda Dean Paradee ................Managing Editor
Tom Slayton ........................Book Review Editor
Judith Powell ..................Editorial Assistant
**Desc.:** State publication designed to advertise the beauty, life, history and personalities of Vermont. Heavy emphasis on high quality black and white pictures and color transparencies as presentation is largely pictorial. All pictures and text must be factual and relate to Vermont. Gives by-lines.
**Readers:** General readership with interest in Vermont.

67241

## VERMONT MAGAZINE
14 School St.
Bristol, VT 05443
Telephone: (802) 453-3200
FAX: (802) 453-3940

**Materials Accepted/Included:** 01-Business news 02-By-line articles 03-Fashion news 04-Food news 05-Freelance copy 06-Letters to editor 07-Real estate news 08-Sports news 09-Travel news 10-Book rev. 11-Movie rev. 12-Music rev. 13-TV rev. 14-Theater rev. 15-Coming events 16-Obituaries 17-Question & answer 18-Social announcements 19-Artwork 20-Cartoons 21-Photos 22-TV listings 23-Audio rec. 24-Video rec. 25-Books 26-Films/film clips 27-Personnel news 28-Press releases 29-New product news/photos 30-Trade lit. 31-Contracts awarded 32-Display adv. 33-Classified adv.

Mailing Address:
  P.O. Box 288
  Bristol, VT 05443
Year Established: 1989
Pub. Frequency: bi-m.
Page Size: standard
Subscrip. Rate: $2.95 newsstand;
  $14.95/yr.
Circulation: 50,000
Circulation Type: paid
**Owner(s):**
David D. Sleeper
14 School St.
Bristol, VT 05443
Telephone: (802) 453-3200
Ownership %: 100
**Management:**
David D. Sleeper .........................President
David D. Sleeper .........................Publisher
Steave L'Heuzeux ...........Advertising Manager
**Editorial:**
John Rosenberg ..............................Editor

26347
## WASHINGTONIAN, THE
1828 L St., N.W., Ste. 200
Washington, DC 20036
Telephone: (202) 296-3600
Year Established: 1965
Pub. Frequency: m.
Page Size: standard
Subscrip. Rate: $2.75 newsstand;
  $21.95/yr.; $34.95 outside DC, MD, &
  VA
Materials: 02,03,04,06,09,11,15,21,32,33
Freelance Pay: $.50/wd.
Circulation: 157,055
Circulation Type: paid
**Owner(s):**
Washington Magazine, Inc.
1828 L St., N.W., Ste. 200
Washington, DC 20036
Telephone: (202) 296-3600
Ownership %: 100
**Management:**
Philip Merrill .............................Publisher
Edward Mansfield ............Advertising Manager
**Editorial:**
John A. Limpert ..............................Editor
Marilyn Dickey ....................Managing Editor
Mitchell Gerber ....................Managing Editor
Howard Means ..................Book Review Editor
Kathleen Hennessy ...........................Photo
**Desc.:** Uses wide variety of well-written,
  sophisticated feature material relating to
  life in Washington, D.C. 15 percent of
  editorial content done on assignment by
  free-lancers after consultation. By-lines
  used. Queries should reflect theme,
  outline, and treatment of proposed
  stories. 1,500-3,500 words preferred.
  Publicity material welcome for
  background only. Departments include:
  Politics, Profiles, Science, The Arts,
  Humor, History, Wining and Dining,
  Shopping.
**Readers:** Primarily well-educated, high-
  income.
**Deadline:** story-8 wks. prior to pub. date;
  news-8 wks. prior; photo-8 wks. prior;
  ads-1 mo. prior

26348
## WELCOME TO MIAMI & THE BEACHES
1751 N.E. 162 St.
Miami, FL 33162
Telephone: (305) 944-9444
Mailing Address:
  P.O. Box 630518
  Miami, FL 33163
Year Established: 1970
Pub. Frequency: w.
Page Size: pocket
Subscrip. Rate: $35/yr.
Circulation: 15,500

Circulation Type: paid
**Owner(s):**
Welcome Publishing
P.O. Box 630518
Miami, FL 33163
Telephone: (305) 944-9444
Ownership %: 100
**Management:**
Mona Levine ...............................Publisher
Alan Levine .................Advertising Manager
**Editorial:**
Lisa Masciovecchio ................Managing Editor
**Desc.:** Tourist publication. Welcomes
  visitors and conventioneers to the
  Miami/Miami Beach Area. Publication
  carries dining, shipping, sightseeing
  points of interest and other pertinent
  information about the South Florida
  area.
**Readers:** Tourists and conventioneers.

70482
## WILLIAMSBURG MAGAZINE
216 Ironbound Rd.
Williamsburg, VA 23188
Telephone: (804) 220-1736
FAX: (804) 220-1665
Pub. Frequency: m.
Page Size: standard
Subscrip. Rate: free
Materials: 32,33
Circulation: 77,000
Circulation Type: free
**Owner(s):**
Chesapeake Publishing Corp.
29088 Airpark Dr.
Easton, MD 21601
Ownership %: 100
**Management:**
William C. O'Donovan .....................Publisher
Michael Curry .................Advertising Manager
**Editorial:**
Nell Wickmann ..............................Editor
Hazel Richardson ...............Circulation Director
**Desc.:** Geared toward tourists sightseeing
  in Williamsburg and surrounding area.

25954
## YANKEE
Main St.
Dublin, NH 03444-0520
Telephone: (603) 563-8111
FAX: (603) 563-8252
Mailing Address:
  P.O. Box 520
  Dublin, OH 03444-0520
Year Established: 1935
Pub. Frequency: m.
Page Size: pocket
Subscrip. Rate: $22/yr.
Freelance Pay: $250-$800/article
Circulation: 700,000
Circulation Type: paid
**Owner(s):**
Yankee Publishing, Inc.
P.O. Box 520
Dublin, OH 03444-0520
Telephone: (603) 563-8111
Ownership %: 100
**Management:**
Joseph B. Meagher ......................President
James H. Fishman .......................Publisher
**Editorial:**
Mel Allen .............................Senior Editor
Judson D. Hale, Sr. .........................Editor
Timothy Clark ....................Managing Editor
Kevin Scully ...........................Advertising
Geoffrey Elan ..................Book Review Editor
J. Porter ...........................Design Editor
Edythe Clark .........................Fiction Editor
Ann Card .......................Photography Editor
Jean Burden ..........................Poetry Editor
James Dodson .......................Senior Writer
Mel Allen .............................Travel Editor

**Desc.:** Contains by-lined articles on the
  New England area. Carries general
  subjects and book reviews.
**Readers:** People in, and interested in New
  England.
**Deadline:** story-4 mos.

26351
## YANKEE MAGAZINE TRAVEL GUIDE TO NEW ENGLAND
33 Union St.
Boston, MA 02108
Telephone: (617) 723-4309
FAX: (617) 723-2435
Mailing Address:
  P.O. Box 520
  Dublin, NH 03444
Year Established: 1971
Pub. Frequency: a.
Page Size: standard
Subscrip. Rate: $4.95 newsstand
Materials: 09
Freelance Pay: negotiable
Circulation: 217,000
Circulation Type: paid
**Owner(s):**
Yankee Publishing, Inc.
Main St.
Dublin, NH 03444
Telephone: (603) 563-8111
Ownership %: 100
**Management:**
Joseph B. Meagher ......................President
**Editorial:**
Janice Brand ...............................Editor
Laura Yates Tyrrell .................Managing Editor
Lori Baird .............................Assistant Editor
**Desc.:** An insiders' guide to travel in New
  England; Offers articles, tips,
  suggestions, ideas for day trips,
  weekends, vacations, an extensive
  calendar of events, and suggestions for
  dining and lodging.
**Readers:** Northeast residents age 25-55;
  college-educated New England
  residents.

## Group 664-Religious

26190
## AMERICA
106 W. 56th St.
New York, NY 10019
Telephone: (212) 581-4640
FAX: (212) 399-3596
Year Established: 1909
Pub. Frequency: bi-w.
Page Size: standard
Subscrip. Rate: $33/yr.
Freelance Pay: varies
Print Process: offset
Circulation: 35,000
Circulation Type: paid
**Owner(s):**
America Press, Inc.
106 W. 56th St.
New York, NY 10019
Telephone: (212) 581-4640
Ownership %: 100
**Management:**
George W. Hunt ...........................President
George W. Hunt ...........................Publisher
Julia Sosa .................Advertising Manager
**Editorial:**
George W. Hunt ..............................Editor
Robert C. Collins ...................Managing Editor
Patrick H. Samway ...................Literary Editor
**Desc.:** Articles on politics, business ethics,
  education, books and theater, science
  and music, the United Nations, Latin
  America, Europe, Asia, Africa, the
  Middle East, religion, churches, and art.
**Readers:** Men and women including many
  engaged in education and other
  professions.

69290
## AMERICAN BAPTIST IN MISSION
P.O. Box 851
Valley Forge, PA 19482-0851
Telephone: (215) 768-2301
FAX: (610) 768-2320
Year Established: 1992
Pub. Frequency: bi-m.
Page Size: standard
Subscrip. Rate: free
Materials: 05,21,32
Freelance Pay: varies
Print Process: 4-color web
Wire service(s): RNS
Circulation: 45,000
Circulation Type: free
**Owner(s):**
American Baptist Churches U.S.A.
P.O. Box 851
Valley Forge, PA 19482-0851
Telephone: (610) 768-2077
Ownership %: 100
**Editorial:**
Dan Holland ................................Editor
Richard Schramm ...................Managing Editor
**Desc.:** Seeks to share the ministry of
  American Baptist individuals, churches
  and related organizations as they live
  out their faith in Jesus Christ in the U.S.
  and throughout the world.

26191
## AMERICAN BIBLE SOCIETY RECORD
1865 Broadway
New York, NY 10023
Telephone: (212) 408-1480
Mailing Address:
  P.O. Box 3575, Grand Cent. Sta.
  New York, NY 10164
Year Established: 1818
Pub. Frequency: m.
Page Size: pocket
Subscrip. Rate: free to all donors
Freelance Pay: negotiable
Print Process: web
Circulation: 250,000
Circulation Type: controlled
**Owner(s):**
American Bible Society
1865 Broadway
New York, NY 10023
Telephone: (212) 581-7400
Ownership %: 100
**Editorial:**
Clifford Macdonald ...................Managing Editor
**Desc.:** Articles and news stories
  concerning the work and mission of the
  American Bible Society-worldwide
  translation, publication and distribution of
  the scriptures. Both b & w and color
  photos are used. Articles should be no
  more than 2,000 words.
**Readers:** Donors to the American Bible
  Society.

69225
## ASPIRE
404 BNA Dr.
Bldg. 200, Ste. 600
Nashville, TN 37217
Telephone: (615) 872-8080
FAX: (615) 889-0437
Year Established: 1991
Pub. Frequency: bi-m.
Page Size: standard
Subscrip. Rate: $3.50 newsstand; $21/yr.
Materials: 32
Circulation: 100,000
Circulation Type: paid
**Owner(s):**
Royal Magazine Group, Inc.
404 BNA Dr., Bldg. 200, Ste. 6
Nashville, TN 37217
Telephone: (615) 872-8080
Ownership %: 100

**Materials Accepted/Included:** 01-Business news 02-By-line articles 03-Fashion news 04-Food news 05-Freelance copy 06-Letters to editor 07-Real estate news 08-Sports news 09-Travel news 10-Book rev. 11-Movie rev. 12-Music rev. 13-TV rev. 14-Theater rev. 15-Coming events 16-Obituaries 17-Question & answer 18-Social announcements 19-Artwork 20-Cartoons 21-Photos 22-TV listings 23-Audio rec. 24-Video rec. 25-Books 26-Films/film clips 27-Personnel news 28-Press releases 29-New product news/photos 30-Trade lit. 31-Contracts awarded 32-Display adv. 33-Classified adv.

6-101

**Management:**
Tim Gilmour ........................................Publisher
Larry Hornung ..................Advertising Manager
Tammie Kee ..................Circulation Manager
**Editorial:**
Mary Hopkins ..................Managing Editor
Frank Minirth ..............................Writer
Paul Meier ..................................Writer

26226
## B'NAI B'RITH INTERNATIONAL JEWISH MONTHLY, THE
1640 Rhode Island Ave., N.W.
Washington, DC 20036
Telephone: (202) 857-6645
Year Established: 1886
Pub. Frequency: 8/yr.
Page Size: standard
Subscrip. Rate: $1/issue; $12/yr.
Materials: 32
Freelance Pay: varies
Circulation: 45,000
Circulation Type: controlled
**Owner(s):**
B'nai B'rith
1640 Rhode Is. Ave. N.W.
Washington, DC 20036
Telephone: (202) 857-6600
**Management:**
Kent Schiner ................................President
Sidney Clearfield ........Executive Vice President
Ellen Zwecker ..................Advertising Manager
**Editorial:**
Jeff Rubin ..................................Editor
Kim Muller-Thym ..................Art Director
Stacy Weiner ..................Assistant Editor
Harvey Berk ..............Communications Director
Rachel Schwartz ..................Editorial Assistant
Dan Joseph ..................Editorial Assistant
**Desc.:** The editorial field is limited to material of general Jewish interest. Departments include: Arts, Letters to the Editor, Book Reviews, Analytical News Articles, and Features.
**Readers:** American Jewish families.

26194
## BAPTIST & REFLECTOR
P.O. Box 728
Brentwood, TN 37024
Telephone: (615) 371-2003
FAX: (615) 371-2080
Year Established: 1835
Pub. Frequency: Wed.
Page Size: standard
Subscrip. Rate: $7.50/yr.
Circulation: 67,300
Circulation Type: free & paid
**Owner(s):**
Executive Board, Tennessee Baptist Convention
P.O. Box 728
Brentwood, TN 37024
Telephone: (615) 371-2003
FAX: (615) 371-2080
Ownership %: 100
**Editorial:**
William Fletcher Allen ..............................Editor
Connie Davis ..................Assistant Editor
Lonnie Wilkey ..................Associate Editor
**Desc.:** News and comments of interest to Tennessee Baptists.
**Readers:** Members of Southern Baptist churches.

26193
## BAPTIST RECORD, THE
515 Mississippi St.
Jackson, MS 39201
Telephone: (601) 968-3800
FAX: (601) 968-3928
Mailing Address:
P.O. Box 530
Jackson, MS 39205
Year Established: 1877
Pub. Frequency: Thu.

Page Size: tabloid
Subscrip. Rate: $7.35/yr.
Materials: 06,10,15,16,21,27,28,32,33
Circulation: 108,000
Circulation Type: paid
**Owner(s):**
Mississippi Baptist Convention
P.O. Box 530
Jackson, MS 39205
Telephone: (601) 968-3800
Ownership %: 100
**Management:**
Mississippi Baptist Convention ............Publisher
Teresa Dickens ..................Advertising Manager
Renee Walley ..................Circulation Manager
**Editorial:**
Guy Henderson ..............................Editor
Betty Anne Bailey ........Administrative Assistant
Shannon Simpson ........Administrative Assistant
William H. Parkins, Jr. ..............Associate Editor
Florence Larrimore ..................Editorial Associate
**Desc.:** Our paper is the official journal of the Mississippi Baptist Convention. Its primary purpose is to help to implement the work of the churches of the Mississippi Baptist Convention through the dissemination of news and discussion of issues that affect Mississippi Baptists and Southern Baptists. However, a small portion of its circulation reaches all 50 states and more than 35 foreign countries so we seek to keep our material from being provincial, and do try to cover news and articles of a broad scope.
**Readers:** Principally members of Baptist churches.
**Deadline:** story-1 wk. prior to pub. date; news-1 wk. prior to pub. date; photo-1 wk. prior to pub. date; ads-2 wks. prior to pub. date

26195
## BAPTIST STANDARD
2343 Lone Star Dr.
Dallas, TX 75212
Telephone: (214) 630-4571
Mailing Address:
P.O. Box 660267
Dallas, TX 75266
Year Established: 1888
Pub. Frequency: Wed.
Page Size: standard
Subscrip. Rate: $9.95/yr.
Circulation: 276,988
Circulation Type: paid
**Owner(s):**
Baptist Standard Publishing Co.
P.O. Box 660267
Dallas, TX 75266
Telephone: (214) 630-4571
Ownership %: 100
**Management:**
Douglas A. Hylton ..............Advertising Manager
John Welch ..................Business Manager
**Editorial:**
Presnall H. Wood ..................Executive Editor
Toby Druin ..................Associate Editor
**Desc.:** Inspiration articles are used mostly with some historical ones on Baptist work and men spaced periodically. Articles are held to one page layouts. Occasionally very short features are used, and sometimes children's stories are used. By-lines are given on all articles and features. Photographs are sometimes used with articles.
**Readers:** Members of Baptist churches.

61666
## BIBLE REVIEW
3000 Connecticut Ave., N.W., Ste. 300
Washington, DC 20008
Telephone: (202) 387-8888
Year Established: 1985
Pub. Frequency: bi-m.

Page Size: standard
Subscrip. Rate: $24/yr.
Circulation: 55,000
Circulation Type: paid
**Owner(s):**
Biblical Archaeology Society
3000 Connecticut Ave Nw
Washington, DC 20008
Telephone: (202) 387-8888
Ownership %: 100
**Editorial:**
Adrian Mello ..................Editor in Chief
Hershel Shanks ..............................Editor
**Desc.:** Bible Review is a non-denominational magazine that brings biblical scholarship to the lay-person in literate, easily understood language by the world's most distinguished biblical scholars.

61665
## BIBLICAL ARCHAEOLOGY REVIEW
3000 Connecticut Ave., N.W., Ste. 300
Washington, DC 20008
Telephone: (202) 387-8888
Year Established: 1975
Pub. Frequency: bi-m.
Subscrip. Rate: $24/yr.
Circulation: 205,000
Circulation Type: paid
**Owner(s):**
Biblical Archaeology Society
3000 Connecticut Ave., N.W.
Washington, DC 20008
Telephone: (202) 387-8888
Ownership %: 100
**Editorial:**
Hershel Shanks ..............................Editor
**Desc.:** A publication devoted to the archaeology of the biblical world. Both Old & New Testament issues are covered by archaeologists and biblical scholars bringing new understanding to our biblical heritage.

26196
## CATECHIST
330 Progress Rd.
Dayton, OH 45449
Telephone: (513) 847-5900
FAX: (513) 847-5910
Year Established: 1967
Pub. Frequency: 7/yr.
Page Size: standard
Subscrip. Rate: $18.95/yr.
Freelance Pay: varies
Circulation: 46,000
Circulation Type: paid
**Owner(s):**
Peter Li, Inc.
330 Progress Rd.
Dayton, OH 45449
Telephone: (513) 847-5900
Ownership %: 100
**Management:**
James R. Sachs ..............................President
Peter Li ..................................Publisher
**Editorial:**
Carl Fischer ..................Editor in Chief
Patricia Fischer ..............................Editor
Ann Tomsic ..............................Advertising
Ellen Wright ..................Art Director
Rosemary E. Walker ..........Circulation Director
**Desc.:** Articles relating to philosophy, new techniques, experiences in catechetics and religious education. Departments include: Features, Audiovisual, Books, Early Childhood Education, Special Education.
**Readers:** Religious educators in Catholic schools & religion teachers in Parish programs, directors of religious education, and priests.

26197
## CATHOLIC DIGEST
475 Riverside Dr., Ste. 1268
New York, NY 10115
Telephone: (212) 870-2552
FAX: (212) 870-2540
Mailing Address:
P.O. Box 64090
St. Paul, MN 55164
Year Established: 1936
Pub. Frequency: m.
Page Size: standard
Subscrip. Rate: $1.95/issue; $16.97/yr.
Freelance Pay: $100/reprints; $200-$400/original
Circulation: 575,000
Circulation Type: paid
**Owner(s):**
St. Thomas University
2115 Summit Ave.
Saint Paul, MN 55105
Ownership %: 100
**Management:**
Philip Green ..................Chairman of Board
Philip Green ..................................Publisher
Thomas Rickert ..................Advertising Manager
Deborah Frey ..................Circulation Manager
**Editorial:**
Rich Reece ..............................Editor
Kathleen Stauffer ..................Managing Editor
Tami Cook ..................................Art Director
Rebecca Giusti ..................Assistant Editor
Susan Schaefer ..................Assistant Editor
Mary Byrne ..................Assistant Editor
Nick Cafarelli ..................Associate Editor
Howard Olson ..................Production Director
**Desc.:** A blend of information and inspiration for today's Catholic. Twenty-five articles, stories, and special features each month on Catholic lives, values, personal relationships, coping with problems, health, humor and human interest stories, and a daily inspirational guide.
**Readers:** Mature Catholics.

69227
## CATHOLIC WORLD, THE
997 Macarthur Blvd.
Mahwah, NJ 07430-2096
Telephone: (201) 825-7300
FAX: (201) 825-8345
Year Established: 1865
Pub. Frequency: bi-m.
Subscrip. Rate: $12/yr.
Circulation: 8,000
Circulation Type: paid
**Owner(s):**
Paulist Press
997 Mac Arthur Blvd.
Mahwah, NJ 07430-2096
Telephone: (201) 824-7300
FAX: (201) 825-8345
Ownership %: 100
**Editorial:**
Laurie Felknor ..............................Editor
**Desc.:** Thematic coverage of key religious questions from different perspectives.

71271
## CHARISMA CHRISTIAN LIFE MAGAZINE
600 Rinehart Rd.
Lake Mary, FL 32746
Telephone: (407) 333-0600
FAX: (407) 333-9753
Year Established: 1987
Pub. Frequency: bi-m.
Page Size: standard
Subscrip. Rate: $19.97/yr.
Materials: 32
Print Process: offset
Circulation: 200,000
Circulation Type: paid

**Materials Accepted/Included:** 01-Business news 02-By-line articles 03-Fashion news 04-Food news 05-Freelance copy 06-Letters to editor 07-Real estate news 08-Sports news 09-Travel news 10-Book rev. 11-Movie rev. 12-Music rev. 13-TV rev. 14-Theater rev. 15-Coming events 16-Obituaries 17-Question & answer 18-Social announcements 19-Artwork 20-Cartoons 21-Photos 22-TV listings 23-Audio rec. 24-Video rec. 25-Books 26-Films/film clips 27-Personnel news 28-Press releases 29-New product news/photos 30-Trade lit. 31-Contracts awarded 32-Display adv. 33-Classified adv.

**Owner(s):**
Strang Communications Co., Inc.
600 Rinehart Rd.
Lake Mary, FL 32746
Telephone: (407) 333-0600
Ownership %: 100
**Management:**
Steven Strang .......................Publisher
Bob Minotti ........................Advertising Manager
**Editorial:**
Steven Strang ...........................Editor
Larry Bergel .......................Marketing Manager

26200

## CHRISTIAN CENTURY, THE
407 S. Dearborn St., Rm. 1405
Chicago, IL 60605
Telephone: (312) 427-5380
FAX: (312) 427-1302
Year Established: 1884
Pub. Frequency: w.
Page Size: standard
Subscrip. Rate: $2 newsstand; $35/yr.
Materials: 02,05,06,10,11,12,13,14,15,16,
19,20,21,24,25,28,32,33
Freelance Pay: $50-$125/article
Print Process: web offset
Circulation: 32,000
Circulation Type: free & paid
**Owner(s):**
Christian Century Foundation, The
407 S. Dearborn St., Rm. 1405
Chicago, IL 60605
Telephone: (312) 427-5380
FAX: (312) 427-1302
Ownership %: 100
**Management:**
Rev. James M. Wall ...........................Publisher
Ann James ........................Advertising Manager
**Editorial:**
Martin E. Marty ......................Senior Editor
Dean Peerman .........................Senior Editor
Rev. James M. Wall ..................Editor
David Heim .......................Managing Editor
**Desc.:** Ecumenical weekly journal of news
and opinion whose readers include
leading clergy of all denominations and
influential lay people in all walks of life.
**Readers:** 95 percent of the readers are
professionals.

69103

## CHRISTIAN HISTORY MAGAZINE
465 Gundersen Dr.
Carol Stream, IL 60188
Telephone: (708) 260-6200
Year Established: 1982
Pub. Frequency: q.
Page Size: standard
Subscrip. Rate: $5 newsstand; $19.95/yr.
Circulation: 70,000
Circulation Type: paid
**Owner(s):**
Christianity Today, Inc.
465 Gundersen Dr.
Carol Stream, IL 60188
Telephone: (708) 260-6200
Ownership %: 100
**Editorial:**
Kevin Miller ...........................Edito..
Mark Galli ...........................Managing Editor
Mary Ann Jeffreys ....................Editorial Coord.
**Desc.:** Covers major persons, events,
issues in the history of the Christian
Church.

26205

## CHRISTIANITY TODAY
465 Gundersen Dr.
Carol Stream, IL 60188
Telephone: (708) 260-6200
FAX: (708) 260-0114
Year Established: 1956
Pub. Frequency: 15/yr.
Page Size: standard
Subscrip. Rate: $24/yr.
Materials: 02,05,06,10,25,28,32,33

Freelance Pay: $250-$300
Print Process: web offset
Circulation: 180,000
Circulation Type: paid
**Owner(s):**
Christianity Today, Inc.
465 Gundersen Dr.
Carol Stream, IL 60188
Telephone: (708) 260-6200
Ownership %: 100
**Management:**
Harold L. Myra ...........................President
Paul D. Robbins .........Executive Vice President
Harold Myra ...........................Publisher
**Editorial:**
David Neff ...........................Executive Editor
Roy Coffman ...........................Advertising
Tim Morgan ...........................News Editor
**Desc.:** Theologically oriented content
includes book reviews, news, editorials,
mostly commissioned articles.
**Readers:** Clergy and lay persons.

69101

## CHRISTIAN READER
465 Gundersen Dr.
Carol Stream, IL 60188-2498
Telephone: (708) 260-6200
FAX: (708) 260-0114
Year Established: 1963
Pub. Frequency: bi-m.
Page Size: standard
Subscrip. Rate: $14.95/yr.
Circulation: 220,000
Circulation Type: paid
**Owner(s):**
Christianity Today, Inc.
465 Gundersen Dr.
Carol Stream, IL 60188-2498
Telephone: (708) 260-6200
Ownership %: 100
**Management:**
Harold Myra ...........................Publisher
Linda Schambach ............Advertising Manager
**Editorial:**
Marshall Shelley ......................Executive Editor
Bonne Steffen ...........................Editor
Jennifer McGuire ......................Art Director

70432

## CHRISTIAN RESEARCH JOURNAL
P. O. Box 500
San Juan Capistrano, CA 92693-0500
Telephone: (714) 855-9926
Pub. Frequency: q.
Page Size: standard
Subscrip. Rate: $16/yr.
Materials: 05,06,10,17,23,24
**Owner(s):**
Christian Research Institute
P.O. Box 500
San Juan Capistrano, CA 92693-0500
Telephone: (714) 855-9926
Ownership %: 100
**Management:**
Hendrik H. Hanegraaff ..................President
**Editorial:**
Elliot Miller ...........................Editor in Chief
Melanie M. Cogdill ..................Managing Editor
Pamela Poll ...........................Art Director
Ron Rhodes ...........................Associate Editor
Paul Carden ...........................News Editor
**Desc.:** Dedicated to furthering the
proclamation and defense of the historic
gospel of Jesus Christ, and to facilitating
His people's growth in sound doctrine
and spiritual discernment. Thus it serves
both evangelistic and educational
purposes.

26206

## CHURCH HERALD, THE
4500 60th St., S.E.
Grand Rapids, MI 49512-9670
Telephone: (616) 698-7071
FAX: (616) 698-6606
Year Established: 1826

Pub. Frequency: m.
Page Size: standard
Subscrip. Rate: $15/yr. US; $18.25/yr.
Canada
Materials: 32
Freelance Pay: varies
Print Process: offset
Circulation: 108,000
Circulation Type: controlled
**Owner(s):**
The Church Herald, Inc.
4500 60th St., S.E.
Grand Rapids, MI 49512-9670
Telephone: (616) 698-7071
FAX: (616) 698-6606
Ownership %: 100
**Management:**
Jeffrey Japinga ...........................Publisher
Sandy Smith ...........................Business Manager
**Editorial:**
Jeffrey Japinga ...........................Editor
**Desc.:** We are interested in feature articles
on social, family, economic, and political
subjects, evaluated from the viewpoint
of the biblical Christian faith, between
700-2,200 words in length. We look
for articles that are intellectually
respectable, with reliability on facts
cited, good organization and progression
of thought taken into account.
Query first freelance material not
routinely reviewed.
**Readers:** Members of Reformed Church in
America.

26207

## CHURCHMAN'S HUMAN QUEST
1074 23rd Ave., N.
St. Petersburg, FL 33704-3228
Telephone: (813) 894-0097
Year Established: 1804
Pub. Frequency: bi-m.
Page Size: standard
Subscrip. Rate: $10/yr.; $3/yr. foreign
Circulation: 8,000
Circulation Type: paid
**Owner(s):**
Churchman Co.
1074 23rd Ave., N.
St. Petersburg, FL 33704
Telephone: (813) 894-0097
Ownership %: 100
**Management:**
James Oliver ...........................Advertising Manager
**Editorial:**
Edna Ruth Johnson ..................Executive Editor
John M. Swomley ..................Senior Editor
Edward Ericson ..........Administrative Assistant
Herbert Meridith Orrell ................Miscellaneous
William Winter ...........................Miscellaneous
**Desc.:** An independent journal of
humanistic, liberal religion in the liberal
tradition. A humanistic spiritual approach
to religion, ethics and education. Carries
articles on the free exchange of
humanistic religious and social ideas and
opinions. By-lined material and letters to
the editor accepted.
**Readers:** A quality readership/leaders in
education no religious affiliation-
humanistic religion, social action
oriented.

58631

## CIRCUIT RIDER
201 Eighth Ave., S.
Nashville, TN 37203
Telephone: (615) 749-6007
FAX: (615) 749-6079
Year Established: 1976
Pub. Frequency: 10/yr.
Page Size: standard
Subscrip. Rate: free to United Methodist
clergy
Materials: 06,20,21,28

Freelance Pay: $25-$150/article
Print Process: offset
Circulation: 37,000
Circulation Type: controlled
**Owner(s):**
United Methodist Publishing House
201 Eighth Ave., S.
Box 801
Nashville, TN 37202
Telephone: (615) 749-6000
**Editorial:**
J. Richard Peck ...........................Editor
Sheila McGee ...........................Associate Editor
**Readers:** United Methodist clergy.

26208

## COLUMBIA
One Columbus Plz.
New Haven, CT 06510-3326
Telephone: (203) 772-2130
FAX: (203) 777-0114
Mailing Address:
P.O. Drawer 1670
New Haven, CT 06507-0901
Year Established: 1920
Pub. Frequency: m.
Page Size: 4 color photos/art
Subscrip. Rate: $6/yr.
Freelance Pay: $200 & up
Circulation: 1,500,000
**Owner(s):**
Knights of Columbus
One Columbus Plz.
New Haven, CT 06510-3326
Telephone: (203) 772-2130
Ownership %: 100
**Bureau(s):**
Knights of Columbus
1275 Pennsylvania Ave, NW  #501
Washington, DC 20004
Telephone: (202) 628-2355
Contact: Russell Shaw, Publication Director
**Management:**
Virgil C. Dechant ...........................President
**Editorial:**
James Skorunski ...........................Senior Editor
Tim S. Hickey ...........................Managing Editor
Richard McMunn ..................Advertising Director
Richard Dowd ...........................Book Review Editor
Russell Shaw ...........................Columnist
Michael Gallagher ...........................Columnist
Bernard Casserly ...........................Columnist
**Desc.:** Contains factual articles directed to
the Catholic layman and family dealing
with current events, social problems,
education, rearing a family, literature,
science, arts, sports, and leisure. Also
contains photo stories, cartoons.
Departments include: Books, Vatican,
Family, Washington, Ottawa, Mail &
Knights in Action, Seniors, Media.
**Readers:** Knights of Columbus members &
families.

25838

## COMMONWEAL
15 Dutch St.
New York, NY 10038
Telephone: (212) 732-0800
Year Established: 1924
Pub. Frequency: bi-w.
Page Size: standard
Subscrip. Rate: $2/newsstand; $39/yr.
Materials: 02,06,10,20,32,33
Freelance Pay: $.03/wd.
Print Process: discs
Circulation: 18,000
Circulation Type: paid
**Owner(s):**
Commonweal Foundation
15 Dutch St.
New York, NY 10038
Telephone: (212) 732-0800
Ownership %: 100
**Management:**
Edward S. Skillin ...........................Publisher

**Materials Accepted/Included:** 01-Business news 02-By-line articles 03-Fashion news 04-Food news 05-Freelance copy 06-Letters to editor 07-Real estate news 08-Sports news 09-Travel news
10-Book rev. 11-Movie rev. 12-Music rev. 13-TV rev. 14-Theater rev. 15-Coming events 16-Obituaries 17-Question & answer 18-Social announcements 19-Artwork 20-Cartoons 21-Photos 22-TV listings
23-Audio rec. 24-Video rec. 25-Books 26-Films/film clips 27-Personnel news 28-Press releases 29-New product news/photos 30-Trade lit. 31-Contracts awarded 32-Display adv. 33-Classified adv.

6-103

Ruth Taylor ..................Advertising Manager
**Editorial:**
Margaret O'Brien Steinfels ..................Editor
**Desc.:** Published by Catholic lay people.
 Timely articles on political, social,
 religious and cultural subjects.
**Readers:** College graduate level.
**Deadline:** ads-5 wks. prior to pub. date

26209

**CONGRESS MONTHLY**
15 E. 84th St.
New York, NY 10028
Telephone: (212) 879-4500
Year Established: 1933
Pub. Frequency: bi-m.
Page Size: standard
Subscrip. Rate: $11/yr.
Freelance Pay: $75-$150/article
Circulation: 30,000
Circulation Type: controlled
**Owner(s):**
American Jewish Congress
15 E. 84th St.
New York, NY 10028
Telephone: (212) 879-4500
Ownership %: 100
**Editorial:**
Maier Deshell ..................Editor
**Desc.:** We publish topical articles, factual
 or opinion, on issues of interest to liberal
 Jewish readers-international relations,
 civil rights, civil liberties, Middle East,
 Israel, Jewish education, culture,
 communal affairs, politics, life abroad
 and personal essays. Particular fields of
 interest in literary and linguistic
 scholarship and literary criticism:
 Democratic American Institutions, Jewish
 interests, international relations, politics,
 Israel and Middle East. Particular
 approach-analytical, interpretative,
 descriptive (editorials, articles, book
 reviews).
**Readers:** Liberal American Jews-
 professionals, religious and lay leaders.

69102

**CORNERSTONE**
939 W. Wilson Ave.
Chicago, IL 60604
Telephone: (312) 989-2080
FAX: (312) 989-2076
Year Established: 1972
Pub. Frequency: 2-4/yr.
Page Size: standard
Subscrip. Rate: $2.00/issue; $15/12 issues
Materials: 32
Circulation: 45,000
Circulation Type: paid
**Owner(s):**
Cornerstone Communications, Inc.
939 W. Wilson Ave.
Chicago, IL 60640
Telephone: (312) 989-2080
Ownership %: 100
**Editorial:**
Dawn Mortimer ..................Editor in Chief
Jon Trott ..................Senior Editor
Eric Pement ..................Senior Editor
Mike Hertenstein ..................Senior Editor
**Desc.:** Avant garde evangelical publication
 dealing with social issues, scriptural
 truths, and cultural change.

26210

**DECISION**
1300 Harmon Pl.
Minneapolis, MN 55403
Telephone: (612) 338-0500
Mailing Address:
 P.O. Box 779
 Mineapolis, MN 55440-0779
Year Established: 1960
Pub. Frequency: m.: Sep.-July

Page Size: standard
Subscrip. Rate: $1/ copy; $7/yr.
Materials: 02,05,06
Freelance Pay: varies
Circulation: 1,800,000
Circulation Type: controlled & paid
**Owner(s):**
Billy Graham Evangelistic Association
1300 Harmon Pl.
P.O. Box 779
Minneapolis, MN 55403
Telephone: (612) 338-0500
Ownership %: 100
**Management:**
John R. Corts ..................President
**Editorial:**
Billy Graham ..................Editor in Chief
Roger C. Palms ..................Editor
Kersten Beckstrom ..................Managing Editor
**Desc.:** We use about 25 to 40% freelance
 material, best opportunity is in testimony
 areas and practical spiritual application
 (1,500 to 1,800 words). Also can use a
 few short narratives (400 to 1,000
 words) and short poems for "Quiet
 Heart" column.
**Readers:** General.

26211

**DISCIPLE, THE**
222 S. Downey Ave.
Indianapolis, IN 46219
Telephone: (317) 353-1491
FAX: (317) 359-7546
Mailing Address:
 P.O. Box 1986
 Indianapolis, IN 46206
Year Established: 1974
Pub. Frequency: m.
Page Size: standard
Subscrip. Rate: $14/yr.; $23/2 yrs.
Print Process: web
Circulation: 36,000
Circulation Type: free & paid
**Owner(s):**
Christian Board of Publication
P.O. Box 179
St. Louis, MO 63166
Telephone: (314) 231-8500
Ownership %: 100
**Management:**
James C. Suggs ..................Publisher
Fred A. Jones ..................Advertising Manager
Fred A. Jones ..................Circulation Manager
**Editorial:**
Robert L. Friedly ..................Editor
Patti R. Case ..................Associate Editor
**Desc.:** A Protestant, religious journal of the
 Christian Church (Disciples of Christ).
 Articles, 500-1,500 words on all aspects
 of the Christian life and work. News of
 general church world, as well as from
 the particular group served. Signed
 articles and occasional signed news
 reports, photos used.
**Readers:** Adults and especially older
 adults of the Christian Church who are
 laity in the church. Also Christian Church
 clergy plus regional and national church
 leaders and officers. Interested clergy
 from other denominations. Also some
 church members and clergy from
 Canada and several other foreign
 countries.

26213

**FAITH AT WORK**
150 S. Washington St., Ste. 204
Falls Church, VA 22046
Telephone: (703) 237-3426
FAX: (703) 237-0157
Pub. Frequency: q.
Page Size: standard
Subscrip. Rate: free
Materials: 32
Print Process: offset

Circulation: 20,000
Circulation Type: controlled
**Owner(s):**
Faith At Work, Inc.
150 S. Washington St., 204
Falls Church, VA 22046
Telephone: (703) 237-3426
**Editorial:**
Marjory Z. Bankson ..................Editor
Pat Minard ..................Assistant Editor
**Desc.:** Edited for an interdenominational
 group involved in personal and church
 renewal. Articles center on building
 relationships, discovering ministry,
 finding wholeness as persons and
 spiritual growth. Editorial content of each
 issue focuses on one particular aspect
 of church renewal, small group
 participation or personal growth. Articles
 welcomed which relate a Christian's
 journey towards new growth and
 wholeness. Departments include: Book
 Reviews, Bible Studies, Discussion
 Designs for Small Groups, listing of Area
 Conferences, Women's Events,
 Leadership Training.
**Readers:** Ecumenical audience of
 Christian Professionals with yearly
 income, $40,000-average age is 49
 years-many are ministers.

69406

**FIRST THINGS**
156 Fifth Ave., Ste. 400
New York, NY 10010
Telephone: (212) 627-2288
FAX: (212) 627-2184
Year Established: 1990
Pub. Frequency: 10/yr.
Page Size: standard
Subscrip. Rate: $3.75/issue; $29/yr.
Materials: 02,05,06,10
Freelance Pay: $125-$450/article & book
 reviews
Circulation: 25,000
Circulation Type: paid
**Owner(s):**
Institute on Religion & Public Life
156 Fifth Ave., Ste. 400
New York, NY 10010
Telephone: (212) 627-2288
Ownership %: 100
**Editorial:**
Richard John Neuhaus ..................Editor
**Desc.:** Examines issues arising at the
 crossroads of religion and public life
 today.

70373

**FOCUS ON THE FAMILY**
P.O. Box 35500
Colorado Springs, CO 80935-3550
Telephone: (800) 232-6459
Year Established: 1977
Pub. Frequency: m.
Page Size: standard
Subscrip. Rate: $.75/copy
Materials: 06,10,15
**Owner(s):**
Focus On the Family
P.O. Box 35500
Colorado Springs, CO 80935-3550
Ownership %: 100
**Management:**
James C. Dobson, Ph.D. ..................President
Rolf Zettersten ..................Executive Vice President
James C. Dobson, Ph.D. ..................Publisher
**Editorial:**
Sandra P. Aldrich ..................Senior Editor
Mike Yorkey ..................Editor
Timothy Jones ..................Art Editor
Kathleen Gray ..................Design

**Desc.:** A seventeen year old, non-profit
 organization dedicated to strengthening
 the home. Headed by psychologist Dr.
 James C. Dobson, the ministry produces
 several radio programs and magazines,
 as well as family-oriented books, films,
 videos and audiocassettes, all from a
 Christian perspective.
**Readers:** Christian families and individuals.

69221

**GESAR: PUBLICATION OF
NORTHERN BUDDHISM**
2425 Hillside Ave.
Berkeley, CA 94704
Telephone: (510) 548-5407
FAX: (510) 845-7540
Year Established: 1973
Pub. Frequency: q.
Subscrip. Rate: $12/yr.
Materials: 05,10,19,21
Print Process: offset
Circulation: 3,000
Circulation Type: paid
**Owner(s):**
Dharma Publishing
2425 Hillside Ave.
Berkeley, CA 94704
Telephone: (510) 548-5407
Ownership %: 100
**Editorial:**
Leslie Bradburn ..................Editor
Elizabeth Cook ..................Editor
**Desc.:** Covers activities of the Tibetan
 Nyingma Meditation Center, Dharma
 Publishing, Odiyan Monastery, Tibetan
 Aid Project, and Nyingma Institute.

26214

**HADASSAH MAGAZINE**
50 W. 58th St.
New York, NY 10019
Telephone: (212) 333-5946
FAX: (212) 333-5967
Year Established: 1921
Pub. Frequency: 10/yr.
Page Size: standard
Subscrip. Rate: $25/yr.
Freelance Pay: $.20/wd.
Circulation: 292,250
Circulation Type: controlled
**Owner(s):**
Hadassah
50 W. 58th St.
New York, NY 10019
Telephone: (212) 355-7900
Ownership %: 100
**Editorial:**
Alan M. Tigay ..................Executive Editor
Zelda Shluker ..................Senior Editor
Ruth Kinney ..................Advertising Coordinator
Barry J. Shrier ..................Advertising Director
Joan Michel ..................Associate Editor
Julie Gruenbaum ..................Editorial Assistant
**Desc.:** Feature articles and photo stories
 deal with social, economic and
 educational problems in the U.S. with
 the spiritual and economic development
 of Israel and with Jewish life in countries
 around the world. Departments include:
 Art, Theatre, Film, Book and Record
 Reviews, Travel Section.
**Readers:** American Jewish families.
**Deadline:** ads-18th of 2nd mo. prior to
 pub. date

26215

**JEWISH EXPONENT**
226 S. 16th St.
Philadelphia, PA 19102
Telephone: (215) 893-5700
FAX: (215) 893-0087
Year Established: 1887
Pub. Frequency: w.

**Materials Accepted/Included:** 01-Business news 02-By-line articles 03-Fashion news 04-Food news 05-Freelance copy 06-Letters to editor 07-Real estate news 08-Sports news 09-Travel news 10-Book rev. 11-Movie rev. 12-Music rev. 13-TV rev. 14-Theater rev. 15-Coming events 16-Obituaries 17-Question & answer 18-Social announcements 19-Artwork 20-Cartoons 21-Photos 22-TV listings 23-Audio rec. 24-Video rec. 25-Books 26-Films/film clips 27-Personnel news 28-Press releases 29-New product news/photos 30-Trade lit. 31-Contracts awarded 32-Display adv. 33-Classified adv.

Page Size: tabloid
Subscrip. Rate: $.85 newsstand; $31.95/yr.
Materials: 02,03,04,05,06,07,09,10,16,17,
18,19,20,21,25,32,33
Freelance Pay: $35-$100/article
Print Process: web offset
Circulation: 62,000
Circulation Type: paid
**Owner(s):**
Jewish Federation of Greater Philadelphia
226 S. 16th St.
Philadelphia, PA 19102
Telephone: (215) 893-5600
Ownership %: 100
**Management:**
Raymond L. Shapiro ...........................President
Richard Waloff .....................Business Manager
Rita Breskman ...........................Sales Manager
**Editorial:**
Sandra Sherman ...........................Senior Editor
Albert Erlick ...........................Managing Editor
Fredda Sacharow .....................Associate Editor
Michael Elkin .....................Entertainment Editor
Marshall Presbery .....................Graphics Editor
Lisa Hostein ...........................News Editor
Byron Fink ...........................Production Director
**Desc.:** Provides interpretation, education
and heritage preservation. Maintains a
vital link between the life of the Jewish
community here, throughout the world,
and in Israel. Also interprets the needs,
activities and services of those FJA
agencies which share in dollars from the
annual United Way campaign in the
Greater Philadelphia community.
Interested in material that impacts on
the Jewish community internationally,
nationally and locally. Inquiries to our
editors are welcome.
**Readers:** Jewish people in the Greater
Philadelphia area.
**Deadline:** story-8 days prior to pub. date;
news-5 days prior to pub. date; photo-8
days prior to pub. date; ads-5 days prior

26217
**LIGUORIAN**
One Liguori Dr.
Liguori, MO 63057-9999
Telephone: (314) 464-2500
FAX: (314) 464-8449
Year Established: 1913
Pub. Frequency: m.
Page Size: pocket
Subscrip. Rate: $1.75/newsstand; $15/yr.
Materials: 02,05,06,10,11,13
Freelance Pay: $.10-$.12/wd.
Circulation: 364,500
Circulation Type: paid
**Owner(s):**
Redemptorists, Liguori Publications
One Liguori Drive
Liguori, MO 63057
Telephone: (314) 464-2500
Ownership %: 100
**Management:**
Thomas Santa, CSSR ........................Publisher
Victor Karls, CSSR ............Circulation Manager
**Editorial:**
Allan Weinert ...........................Editor
Susan M. Schuster ...................Managing Editor
Myra Buechting ...........................Art & Design
Pam Hummelsheim ...........................Art Director
Cheryl Plass ...........................Associate Editor
Alicia Von Stamwitz .................Associate Editor
James J. Higgins, ............Book Review Editor
CSSR
Mary Bradley ...........................Editorial Assistant
John Meyer .................Vice President, Business
Operations
**Desc.:** Discusses current moral problems,
provides pastoral guidance, offers forum
for Catholic readers of all ages, book
reviews, children's page to aid families
in leading Christian lives.

**Readers:** Catholic families, singles, and
religious.

26218
**LIVING CHURCH, THE**
816 E. Juneau Ave.
P.O. Box 92936
Milwaukee, WI 53202
Telephone: (414) 276-5420
FAX: (414) 276-7483
Year Established: 1878
Pub. Frequency: w.
Page Size: standard
Subscrip. Rate: $1.50/newsstand;
$39.50/yr.
Materials: 05,06,10,12,32,33
Print Process: offset
Circulation: 9,000
Circulation Type: paid
**Owner(s):**
The Living Church Foundation, Inc.
Telephone: (414) 276-5420
FAX: (414) 276-7483
Ownership %: 100
**Management:**
Lila Thurber ...........................Advertising Manager
Betty Glatzel ...........................Business Manager
Barbara Pizzino .................Circulation Manager
**Editorial:**
David A. Kalvelage ...........................Editor
John E. Schuessler ...................Managing Editor
**Desc.:** News is of the Episcopal Church
primarily, with additional news about the
Anglican Communion throughout the
world. By-lined and news range from
minor practical matters, human interest,
to major issues. Few articles are staff-
written. This news is furnished by some
200 correspondents in the U.S.
and abroad. Unless of concern to
Church people, publicity material is
ignored. Articles run 800-1,200 words.
Photo spreads occasionally used as part
of articles. Departments include: Articles,
News, Letters to Editor, Columns,
Obituaries, Frontispiece, Occasional
Verse, Book Reviews.
**Readers:** Clergy and active laypeople in
Episcopal Church.
**Deadline:** story-1 mo. prior to pub. date;
news-1 mo.; photo-1 mo.; ads-1 mo.

26220
**LUTHERAN LAYMAN, THE**
2185 Hampton Ave.
St. Louis, MO 63139
Telephone: (314) 647-4900
Year Established: 1923
Pub. Frequency: 10/yr.
Page Size: tabloid
Subscrip. Rate: $5/yr.
Materials: 10,23,24,25,28
Circulation: 135,000
Circulation Type: controlled
**Owner(s):**
International Lutheran Laymen's League
2185 Hampton Ave.
St. Louis, MO 63139
Telephone: (314) 647-4900
Ownership %: 100
**Editorial:**
Gerald Perschbacher ...........................Editor
**Desc.:** News features, and information
material about the 127,000 member
International Lutheran Laymen's League,
its major projects including the world-
wide radio broadcast, The Lutheran
Hour, and information news about The
Lutheran Church-Missouri Synod
specifically, Lutheran churches generally
and other religious bodies. Departments
include: News, Features, Editorial,
Columnists, Pictures, Book Reviews,
Audio Tape and Video Tape Reviews.

**Readers:** Chiefly men and women who
occupy leading positions. All members
of the International Lutheran Laymen's
League. Also pastors and teachers.
**Deadline:** story-1st of mo. prior to pub.
date; news-1st of mo. prior; photo-1st of
mo. prior; ads-1st of mo. prior

26219
**LUTHERAN, THE**
8765 W. Higgins Rd.
Chicago, IL 60631
Telephone: (312) 380-2540
FAX: (312) 380-2751
Year Established: 1988
Pub. Frequency: m.
Page Size: standard
Subscrip. Rate: $1.50 newsstand; $10/yr.
Materials: 02,05,06,10,17,28,32,33
Freelance Pay: $100-$500/article
Circulation: 800,000
Circulation Type: paid
**Owner(s):**
Lutheran, The
8765 W. Higgins Rd.
Chicago, IL 60631
Telephone: (312) 380-2700
Ownership %: 100
**Management:**
Augsburg Fortress ...........................Publisher
Sigurd Hadland .................Advertising Manager
**Editorial:**
Edgar R. Trexler ...........................Editor
Roger R. Kahle ...................Managing Editor
Linda-Marie Delloff ...........Book Review Editor
David L. Miller ...........................Feature Editor
Sonia Groenewold ...........................News Editor
Jack Lund ...........................Photo
**Desc.:** Magazine of the Evangelical
Lutheran Church in America. Uses
features of interest to church
constituency; ideology, experience,
service in the church, Christian
personalities. Articles run up to 2,000
words. Will use photo stories if suitable.
Departments include: General Religious
News, Devotions, Answers to Questions,
Book Reviews.
**Readers:** Church membership, middle
class.

69223
**LUTHERAN WITNESS**
3358 S. Jefferson Ave.
St. Louis, MO 63122-7295
Telephone: (314) 965-9000
Year Established: 1882
Pub. Frequency: m.
Page Size: standard
Subscrip. Rate: $7.50/yr.
Materials: 17,20
Print Process: web offset
Circulation: 330,000
Circulation Type: paid
**Owner(s):**
The Lutheran Church-Missouri Synod
1333 S. Kirkwood Rd.
St. Louis, MO 63122-7295
Telephone: (314) 965-9000
Ownership %: 100
**Editorial:**
David Mahsman ...........................Editor
**Desc.:** Congregational magazine from the
Lutheran Church-Missouri Synod.

58632
**MATURE YEARS**
201 Eighth Ave., S.
Nashville, TN 37202
Telephone: (615) 749-6292
FAX: (615) 749-6512
Mailing Address:
P.O. Box 801
Nashville, TN 37202
Year Established: 1954
Pub. Frequency: q.

Page Size: standard
Subscrip. Rate: $3.50/newsstand; $12/yr.;
$20/2 yrs.
Materials: 02,06,20,28
Freelance Pay: $.05/wd.
Circulation: 75,000
Circulation Type: paid
**Owner(s):**
United Methodist Publishing House, The
201 Eighth Ave., S.
Nashville, TN 37202
Telephone: (615) 749-6000
Ownership %: 100
**Editorial:**
Mary Catherine Dean .................Editor in Chief
Marvin Cropsey ...........................Editor
Neil M. Alexander ...................Editorial Director
**Readers:** Senior citizens age 55 and plus.

26222
**MICHIGAN CHRISTIAN ADVOCATE**
316 Springbrook Ave.
Adrian, MI 49221
Telephone: (517) 265-2075
FAX: (517) 263-7422
Year Established: 1873
Pub. Frequency: bi-w.
Page Size: tabloid
Subscrip. Rate: $11/yr.
Materials: 32,33
Freelance Pay: varies
Print Process: web offset
Circulation: 13,000
Circulation Type: paid
**Owner(s):**
Michigan Christian Advocate Publishing Co.
316 Springbrook Ave.
Adrian, MI 49221
Telephone: (517) 265-2075
Ownership %: 100
**Management:**
M. Kay DeMoss ...........................Publisher
Diana Fields-Sell ...........Circulation Manager
**Editorial:**
M. Kay DeMoss ...........................Executive Editor
Kathy Goolian ...........................Advertising Editor
Bonnie Emerson ...........................Booklet Editor
Bonnie Emerson ...........Graphics Coordinator
Kathy Goolian ...........................Photo
**Desc.:** Articles should not be over 750
words in length. Illustrative photographs
are always welcome. Focuses on
materials with a religious or moral
lesson, or for the welfare of the people.
**Readers:** Members of the United
Methodist Church in Michigan, and 3,000
others elsewhere.

71270
**MINISTRIES TODAY**
600 Rinehart Rd.
Lake Mary, FL 32746
Telephone: (407) 333-0600
FAX: (407) 333-9753
Year Established: 1987
Pub. Frequency: bi-m.
Page Size: standard
Subscrip. Rate: $21.95/yr.
Materials: 32
Print Process: offset
Circulation: 30,000
Circulation Type: paid
**Owner(s):**
Strang Communications Co., Inc.
600 Rinehart Rd.
Lake Mary, FL 32746
Telephone: (407) 333-0600
Ownership %: 100
**Management:**
Steven Strang ...........................Publisher
Bob Minotti ...................Advertising Manager
**Editorial:**
Steven Strang ...........................Editor
Larry Bergel ...................Marketing Manager

**Materials Accepted/Included:** 01-Business news 02-By-line articles 03-Fashion news 04-Food news 05-Freelance copy 06-Letters to editor 07-Real estate news 08-Sports news 09-Travel news 10-Book rev. 11-Movie rev. 12-Music rev. 13-TV rev. 14-Theater rev. 15-Coming events 16-Obituaries 17-Question & answer 18-Social announcements 19-Artwork 20-Cartoons 21-Photos 22-TV listings 23-Audio rec. 24-Video rec. 25-Books 26-Films/film clips 27-Personnel news 28-Press releases 29-New product news/photos 30-Trade lit. 31-Contracts awarded 32-Display adv. 33-Classified adv.

6-105

**MOODY MAGAZINE** 26223
820 N. LaSalle Blvd.
Chicago, IL 60610
Telephone: (312) 329-2163
FAX: (312) 329-2149
Year Established: 1900
Pub. Frequency: 11/yr.
Page Size: standard
Subscrip. Rate: $2.95/copy; $23.95/yr.
Materials: 32
Freelance Pay: varies
Print Process: offset
Circulation: 150,000
Circulation Type: paid
**Owner(s):**
Moody Bible Institute
820 N. LaSalle Dr.
Chicago, IL 60610
Telephone: (312) 329-4420
Ownership %: 100
**Management:**
Dr. Joseph Stowell .........................President
Valerie Maze .....................Advertising Manager
Bruce Anderson ...................General Manager
Donna L. Hankins ............Operations Manager
**Editorial:**
Bruce Anderson ........................Executive Editor
Andrew Scheer ........................Managing Editor
Karen Beattie ....................Book Review Editor
Karen Sarian ........................Circulation Director
Janet McVay ...............................Miscellaneous
**Desc.:** This magazine seeks to encourage
and equip Christians through articles
that show the application of scriptural
principles to the human condition, as
well as reporting of relevant current
events and issues.
**Readers:** Evangelical Christian. Family
emphasis.

**NATIONAL CATHOLIC REPORTER** 26225
115 E. Armour Blvd.
Kansas City, MO 64111
Telephone: (816) 531-0538
FAX: (816) 531-7466
Mailing Address:
 P.O. Box 419281
 Kansas City, MO 64141
Year Established: 1964
Pub. Frequency: w.: Sep.-May
Page Size: tabloid
Subscrip. Rate: $32.95/yr.
Circulation: 47,000
Circulation Type: paid
**Owner(s):**
National Catholic Reporter Publishing Co.,
 Inc.
P.O. Box 419281
Kansas City, MO 64141
Telephone: (816) 531-0538
Ownership %: 100
**Bureau(s):**
Washington, D.C. Bureau
529 14th Street NW, Rm. 1292
Washington, DC 20045
Telephone: (202) 662-7191
Contact: Dorothy Vidulich
**Management:**
William L. McSweeney, Jr. ...................President
William L. McSweeney, Jr. ...................Publisher
Anna Fantasma ................Advertising Manager
**Editorial:**
Michael Farrell ..............................Senior Editor
Thomas C. Fox ...................................Editor
Gloria Murray .......................Marketing Director
**Desc.:** America's leading independent
Catholic weekly. Objective reporting of
Catholic social action and ecumenical
news and trends. Opinion magazine
section features well known national and
international writers and subjects.
**Readers:** Directed primarily to the Catholic
laity.

**NEW ERA, THE** 71281
50 E. North Temple
Salt Lake City, UT 84150
Telephone: (801) 240-1000
Pub. Frequency: m.
Page Size: standard
Subscrip. Rate: $.75/issue; $8/yr.
Print Process: offset
Circulation: 70,000
Circulation Type: controlled & paid
**Owner(s):**
The Church of Jesus Christ of Latter-Day
 Saints
50 E. North Temple
Salt Lake City, UT 84150
Ownership %: 100
**Management:**
Ronald L. Knighton ...............Managing Director
**Editorial:**
Rex D. Pinegar .................................Editor
Joe J. Christensen ............................Editor
Richard M. Romney ...................Managing Editor
Brian K. Kelly ........................Editorial Director
Bryan Lee Shaw ..........................Art Director
Linda Stahle Cooper ................Associate Editor
Janet Thomas ........................Associate Editor
Thomas L. Peterson ...........Circulation Director
Allan R. Loyborg .............Graphics Coordinator
Kent H. Sorensen ...............Marketing Manager

**NEW MAN MAGAZINE** 71273
600 Rinehart Rd.
Lake Mary, FL 32746
Telephone: (407) 333-0600
FAX: (407) 333-9753
Pub. Frequency: bi-m.
Page Size: standard
Subscrip. Rate: $15/yr.
Materials: 32
Print Process: offset
Circulation: 100,000
Circulation Type: paid
**Owner(s):**
Strang Communications Co., Inc.
600 Rinehart Rd.
Lake Mary, FL 32746
Telephone: (407) 333-0600
FAX: (407) 333-9753
Ownership %: 100
**Management:**
Steven Strang .........................Publisher
Bob Minotti ........................Advertising Manager
**Editorial:**
Steven Strang .................................Editor
Larry Bergel ........................Marketing Manager

**ORTHODOX OBSERVER** 26227
8 E. 79th St.
New York, NY 10021
Telephone: (212) 628-2590
Year Established: 1971
Pub. Frequency: m.
Page Size: tabloid
Subscrip. Rate: $5.50/yr.; $75/yr. foreign
Circulation: 130,000
Circulation Type: paid
**Owner(s):**
Greek Orthodox Archdiocese Press
8 E. 79th St.
New York, NY 10021
Telephone: (212) 628-2590
Ownership %: 100
**Management:**
P. J. Gazouleas .........................Publisher
**Editorial:**
Jim Golding .........................Editor in Chief

**Desc.:** Primarily coverage of Greek
Orthodox Christian news. Coverage of
orthodox news in general, i.e., Russian,
Syrian, Serbian, Ukrainian, Romanian,
ect. Major religious news, moral and
social issues that are current, Greek
American concerns e.g., Colleys Anemai.
Any ads that are appropriate in a
religious newspaper are accepted.
Departments include: Book Reviews,
Religious News, Letters, Youth
Supplement. On Social, Moral and
Religious Issues, Orthodox Education,
Culture and Heritage.
**Readers:** Greek Orthodox households.

**OUR SUNDAY VISITOR** 26228
200 Noll Plz.
Huntington, IN 46750
Telephone: (219) 356-8400
Year Established: 1912
Pub. Frequency: w.
Page Size: tabloid
Subscrip. Rate: 30/yr.
Freelance Pay: $100 minimum
Circulation: 120,000
Circulation Type: paid
**Owner(s):**
Our Sunday Visitor, Inc.
200 Noll Plaza
Huntington, IN 46750
Telephone: (219) 356-8400
Ownership %: 100
**Management:**
Robert P. Lockwood .........................President
Robert P. Lockwood .........................Publisher
Peter Schownir .................Advertising Manager
**Editorial:**
Joseph Isca .........................Marketing Director
**Desc.:** News magazine for the general
Catholic audience.
**Readers:** General Catholic audience.

**PENTECOSTAL EVANGEL** 26229
1445 Boonville Ave.
Springfield, MO 65802
Telephone: (417) 862-2781
FAX: (417) 862-0416
Year Established: 1913
Pub. Frequency: w.
Page Size: standard
Subscrip. Rate: $.50 newsstand; $15.95/yr.
Materials: 05
Freelance Pay: $.06/wd.
Circulation: 275,000
Circulation Type: paid
**Owner(s):**
Assemblies of God
1445 Boonville
Springfield, MO 65802
Telephone: (417) 862-2781
Ownership %: 100
**Management:**
Jodi Ohlin .........................Advertising Manager
Terry King .........................Circulation Manager
**Editorial:**
Richard Champion .........................Editor
John Maempa .........................Managing Editor
Randy Clute .........................Art Director
Christy Pryor .....................Book Review Editor
Barbara Long .....................Editorial Assistant
Cindy Replogle .............Graphics Coordinator
Gary Speer .........................News Editor
Cindy Replogle .........................Photo
John Maempa .........................Poetry Editor
Ann Floyd .........................Technical Editor

**Desc.:** This is a religious denominational
magazine. It is Protestant, Evangelical
and Evangelistic with a strong emphasis
on missionary work in the US. and
foreign lands. Sections include: Family,
World News, Church News, and
Missionary News. Articles are
Devotional, Bible Studies, Religious
Biographies, Personal Testimonials,
Sermons and Sermonettes, etc. We do
not sell advertising space.
**Readers:** Church members and clergymen.

**PENTECOSTAL MESSENGER, THE** 26230
4901 Pennsylvania
Joplin, MO 64804
Telephone: (417) 624-7050
FAX: (417) 624-7102
Mailing Address:
 P.O. Box 850
 Joplin, MO 64802
Year Established: 1926
Pub. Frequency: 11/yr.
Page Size: standard
Subscrip. Rate: $11/yr.; $18/2 yrs.; $26/3
 yrs.
Freelance Pay: $.15/wd.
Print Process: offset lithography
Circulation: 8,500
Circulation Type: paid
**Owner(s):**
Pentecostal Church Of God/Messenger
 Publ. House
P.O. Box 850
Joplin, MO 64802
Telephone: (417) 624-7050
Ownership %: 100
**Editorial:**
James D. Gee ...............................Editor in Chief
Don Allen ...............................Editor
Peggy Allen ...............................Managing Editor
**Desc.:** Edited primarily for the adult clergy
and lay members of The Pentecostal
Church of God, with special concern for
their spiritual growth. It carries news of
church happenings at home and abroad,
as well as news highlights generally
from the religious front. The features,
articles, editorials, and departments
discuss theological doctrines and treat
social and economic issues in the light
of Christian principles. It includes
material geared to the individual's
personal devotional life and to the
welfare of the Christian family.
**Readers:** Ministers, adult laymen, college-
age youths.

**PORTALS OF PRAYER** 69224
3558 S. Jefferson Ave.
St. Louis, MO 63118
Telephone: (314) 664-7000
Year Established: 1937
Pub. Frequency: q.
Subscrip. Rate: $4.90/yr.
Circulation: 900,000
Circulation Type: paid
**Owner(s):**
Concordia Publishing House
3558 S. Jefferson Ave.
St. Louis, MO 63118
Telephone: (314) 664-7000
Ownership %: 100
**Editorial:**
Arnold G. Kuntz ...............................Editor
**Desc.:** Daily devotions for adult Lutherans.

**PRESBYTERIAN SURVEY** 26231
100 Witherspoon St.
Louisville, KY 40202-1396
Telephone: (502) 569-5637
FAX: (502) 569-5018
Year Established: 1924
Pub. Frequency: m.

Page Size: standard
Subscrip. Rate: $11/yr.
Materials: 02,06,10,11,13,14,20,21,25,26,32, 33
Freelance Pay: $25-$200/article
Print Process: web offset
Circulation: 90,000
Circulation Type: paid
**Owner(s):**
Presbyterian Church (U.S.A.)
100 Witherspoon St.
Louisville, KY 40202
Telephone: (502) 569-5637
FAX: (502) 569-5018
Ownership %: 100
**Editorial:**
Catherine Cottingham ..............Managing Editor
Catherine Cottingham .......................Advertising
Linda Crittenden ...............................Art Director
Eva Stimson ...............................Associate Editor
**Desc.:** The magazine of the Presbyterian Church (U.S.A.), published primarily for members of the denomination. The magazines offers broad coverage and interpretation of the work of the Presbyterian Church and other religious news; articles that provide information and inspiration for both individuals and congregations, assistance with everyday Christian living, church activities; discussions of contemporary issues; book/film/TV reviews.
**Readers:** Presbyterian Church (U.S.A.) membership.
**Deadline:** story-3 mo. prior to pub. date; ads-2 mo. prior, display ads; 6 wks. prior, classifieds

26232
**REFORM JUDAISM**
838 Fifth Ave.
New York, NY 10021
Telephone: (212) 249-0100
Year Established: 1972
Pub. Frequency: q.
Page Size: standard
Subscrip. Rate: $12/yr.
Freelance Pay: $.10/wd.
Circulation: 295
Circulation Type: controlled
**Owner(s):**
Union of American Hebrew Congregations
838 Fifth Ave.
New York, NY 10021
Telephone: (212) 249-0100
Ownership %: 100
**Editorial:**
Erich Yoffie ..........................Executive Editor
Aron Hirt-Manheimer .........................Editor
Joy Weinberg ..........................Managing Editor
**Desc.:** Official publication of the Union of American Hebrew Congregations-the reform Jewish movement in North America.
**Readers:** Members of Reform Synagogues in U.S. and Canada.

58663
**SALT OF THE EARTH**
205 W. Monroe St.
Chicago, IL 60606
Telephone: (312) 236-7782
FAX: (312) 236-7230
Year Established: 1981
Pub. Frequency: bi-m.
Page Size: standard
Subscrip. Rate: $18/yr.
Print Process: sheet fed
Circulation: 9,000
Circulation Type: paid
**Owner(s):**
Claretian Publications
205 W. Monroe St.
Chicago, IL 60606
Telephone: (312) 236-7782

**Editorial:**
Rev. Mark J. Brummel, C.M.F. ................Editor
Mary Lynn Hendrickson ..........Managing Editor
Tom McGrath ..................Editorial Director
Catherine O'Connell-Cahill ......Associate Editor
**Desc.:** A magazine for Christians who have a concern for social justice. The name comes from the scripture passage wherein Jesus says, "You are the salt of the earth" (Matt. 5:13). Our readers are both would-be and part-time volunteers whose concerns encompass more than local parish activities. The objective is to continually raise people's awareness and offer concrete, hands-on suggestions for action.
**Readers:** Catholic laity

71295
**SINGLE PARENT FAMILY**
P.O. Box 3550
Colorado Springs, CO 80935-3550
Telephone: (800) 232-6459
Year Established: 1994
Pub. Frequency: m.
Page Size: tabloid
Subscrip. Rate: $12/yr.
**Owner(s):**
Focus On The Family
Colorado Springs, CO 80995-7451
Ownership %: 100
**Editorial:**
Lynda Hunter .........................................Editor
**Desc.:** 32 page full color magazine featuring financial advice, devotionals addressing spiritual needs of single families.
**Readers:** Single Christian parents.

53997
**SOUL MAGAZINE**
Mountain View Rd.
Washington, NJ 07882
Telephone: (908) 689-1700
FAX: (908) 689-6279
Mailing Address:
    P.O. Box 976
    Washington, NJ 07882
Year Established: 1950
Pub. Frequency: bi-m.
Page Size: standard
Subscrip. Rate: $3/yr.
Circulation: 100,000
Circulation Type: paid
**Owner(s):**
World Apostolate of Fatima (Blue Army)
Mountain View Rd.
Washington, NJ 07882
Telephone: (201) 689-1700
Ownership %: 100
**Management:**
Rev. Jerome J. Hastrich, D.D. ............Publisher
**Editorial:**
Rev. Jerome J. Hastrich, D.D. ................Editor
John Hauf ...............................Managing Editor
Sister Mary Celeste, ...........Contributing Editor
A.M.I.
**Desc.:** A Catholic family magazine with a strong Marian orientation. Promotes the message of Fatima and integrates it into the gospel message. Publishes timely features and news stories of interest to Catholics and news of the national and worldwide apostolate. Contains articles on the Message of Fatima, Catholic faith and spirituality, Marian devotion according to St. Louis de Montfort, the saints, Catholic family life and contemporary issues of concern to Catholics.
**Readers:** Roman Catholic predominant; most readership engaged in active promotion of message given by the Mother of Christ to three children at Fatima in 1917.

26233
**ST. ANTHONY MESSENGER**
1615 Republic St.
Cincinnati, OH 45210
Telephone: (513) 241-5615
FAX: (513) 241-0399
Year Established: 1893
Pub. Frequency: m.
Page Size: standard
Subscrip. Rate: $16/yr.
Materials: 02,05,06,10,11,13,17,20,21
Freelance Pay: $0.14/wd.
Print Process: web offset
Circulation: 318,250
Circulation Type: paid
**Owner(s):**
Franciscan Friars, Cincinnati
1615 Republic St.
Cincinnati, OH 45210
Telephone: (513) 241-5615
Ownership %: 100
**Management:**
John Bok ..................................President
Jeremy Harrington ..........................Publisher
Arthur Runnels .................Advertising Manager
**Editorial:**
Rev. Norman Perry ....................Editor in Chief
Rev. Norman Perry ..............................Editor
Barbara Beckwith ..................Managing Editor
Laura Barron-Stull ..........................Art Director
Catherine Walsh ........................Assistant Editor
Carol Ann Morrow ....................Assistant Editor
Mary Jo Dangel ......................Assistant Editor
John Bookser Feister ...............Assistant Editor
Rev. Jack Wintz ........................Associate Editor
**Desc.:** Carries fact articles on major events and movements in the Catholic Church; instruction in the application of the Christian faith to daily life; reportings on facts and opinions in the areas of family life, education, culture, psychology, and social problems. Personal human-interest narrative. Fiction stories are also carried, written with a Christian background.
**Readers:** Adult Roman Catholics.

69220
**SUFI REVIEW**
Colonial Green
256 Post Rd., E.
Westport, CT 06880
Telephone: (203) 221-7595
FAX: (203) 454-5873
Year Established: 1992
Pub. Frequency: q.
Page Size: tabloid
Subscrip. Rate: $12/yr.
Print Process: web offset
Circulation: 12,000
Circulation Type: controlled
**Owner(s):**
Pir Publications, Inc.
Colonial Green
256 Post Rd. E.
Westport, CT 06880
Telephone: (203) 221-7595
Ownership %: 100
**Editorial:**
Louis Rogers ..........................................Editor
**Desc.:** Discusses contemporary and classic Sufi mystical thought and teachings, and lists books available through the Sufi Book Club.

69104
**TODAY'S CHRISTIAN WOMAN**
465 Gundersen Dr.
Carol Stream, IL 60188-2498
*see Consumer Magazine, Women's Magazines*

67078
**TRICYCLE: THE BUDDHIST REVIEW**
163 W. 22nd St.
New York, NY 10011
Telephone: (212) 645-1143
FAX: (212) 645-1493
Year Established: 1991
Pub. Frequency: q.
Page Size: standard
Subscrip. Rate: $6 newsstand; $20/yr.
Materials: 32,33
Print Process: web
Circulation: 35,000
Circulation Type: paid
**Owner(s):**
Buddhist Ray, Inc.
163 W. 22nd St.
New York, NY 10011
Telephone: (212) 645-1143
Ownership %: 100
**Management:**
Lorraine Kissly ................................Publisher
Mark Copithorne ..............Advertising Manager
Elizabeth Lees ..................Business Manager
**Editorial:**
Helen Tworkov .......................Editor in Chief
Carol Tonkinson ....................Managing Editor
**Desc.:** A national magazine highlighting the people and issues at the intersection of western culture and Buddhist thought.
**Readers:** Upscale, intelligent, well educated, environmentally and socially conscious.

26236
**UNITED SYNAGOGUE REVIEW**
155 Fifth Ave.
New York, NY 10010
Telephone: (212) 533-7800
FAX: (212) 353-9439
Year Established: 1920
Pub. Frequency: s-a.
Page Size: tabloid
Subscrip. Rate: $3/yr.
Materials: 32,33
Circulation: 255,000
Circulation Type: free
**Owner(s):**
United Synagogue of Conservative Judaism
155 Fifth Ave.
New York, NY 10010
Telephone: (212) 533-7800
FAX: (212) 353-9439
Ownership %: 100
**Editorial:**
Lois Goldrich .........................................Editor
Ceil Skydell ......................................Advertising
Ceil Skydell ........................Associate Editor
**Desc.:** Major vehicle of communication for the conversative movement. Covers Judaism, synagogue life, moral issues, national and international events affecting the Jewish community. Carries feature articles, reports of newsworthy projects from the congregational and regional level, information on services, and activities of Central United Synagogue, and regular columns. House organ for Conservative Judaism in North America.
**Readers:** Rabbis, cantors, educators, executives and members of conservative congregations.

58662
**U.S. CATHOLIC**
205 W. Monroe St.
Chicago, IL 60606
Telephone: (312) 236-7782
FAX: (312) 236-7230
Year Established: 1963
Pub. Frequency: m.
Subscrip. Rate: $18/yr.
Circulation: 52,000

**Materials Accepted/Included:** 01-Business news 02-By-line articles 03-Fashion news 04-Food news 05-Freelance copy 06-Letters to editor 07-Real estate news 08-Sports news 09-Travel news
10-Book rev. 11-Movie rev. 12-Music rev. 13-TV rev. 14-Theater rev. 15-Coming events 16-Obituaries 17-Question & answer 18-Social announcements 19-Artwork 20-Cartoons 21-Photos 22-TV listings
23-Audio rec. 24-Video rec. 25-Books 26-Films/film clips 27-Personnel news 28-Press releases 29-New product news/photos 30-Trade lit. 31-Contracts awarded 32-Display adv. 33-Classified adv.

6-107

Circulation Type: paid
Owner(s):
Claretian Publications
205 W. Monroe St.
Chicago, IL 60606
Telephone: (312) 236-7782
Editorial:
Tom McGrath .............................Executive Editor
Rev. Mark J. Brummel, C.M.F. ................Editor
Patrice J. Tuohy .......................Managing Editor
Desc.: For intelligent Catholics who want to talk about the issues facing them in their daily lives. Encourages readers to take personal responsibility for their faith; to re-examine, and thereby strengthen, their religious beliefs; and to find new ways their faith can help them cope with the complex problems of modern living.
Readers: Catholic laity

26237

## WOMEN'S LEAGUE OUTLOOK
48 E. 74th St.
New York, NY 10021
Telephone: (212) 628-1600
FAX: (212) 772-3507
Year Established: 1930
Pub. Frequency: q.
Page Size: 4 color photos/art
Subscrip. Rate: $8/yr.; $10/yr. foreign
Freelance Pay: $50/article
Circulation: 135,000
Circulation Type: paid
Owner(s):
Women's League for Conservative Judaism
48 E. 74th St.
New York, NY 10021
Telephone: (212) 628-1600
Ownership %: 100
Management:
Audrey Citak ...............................President
Editorial:
Janis Popp ...................................Editor
Rhonda Kahn ......................Managing Editor
Desc.: Dedicated to the preservation of Judaism in the home and community; furthers Jewish education, stimulates religious observance and encourages participation in social action and community programs.
Readers: Sisterhood members of conservative Jewish congregations and members of their families.

69226

## YOUTHWORKER
1224 Greenfield Dr.
El Cajon, CA 92021
Telephone: (619) 440-2333
FAX: (619) 440-4939
Year Established: 1984
Pub. Frequency: q.
Page Size: standard
Subscrip. Rate: $25.95/yr.
Materials: 06,10,20,28,30,32
Circulation: 8000
Circulation Type: paid
Owner(s):
Youth Specialties
1224 Greenfield Dr.
El Cajon, CA 92021
Telephone: (619) 440-2333
Ownership %: 100
Editorial:
Wayne Rice ....................................Editor
Tim McLaughlin .....................Managing Editor
Mike Atkinson .............Director of Periodicals

Desc.: Addresses personal and professional issues of career youth workers in churches and parachurch organizations with in-depth articles.

## Group 666-Senior Citizens

68871

## A BETTER TOMORROW
5301 Wisconsin Ave., N.W., Ste. 620
Washington, DC 20015
Telephone: (202) 364-8000
FAX: (202) 364-8910
Year Established: 1992
Pub. Frequency: q.
Page Size: standard
Subscrip. Rate: $19.80/yr.
Circulation: 100,000
Circulation Type: paid
Owner(s):
Publishing Directions, Inc.
5301 Wisconsin Ave., N.W.
Ste. 620
Washington, DC 20015
Telephone: (202) 364-8000
Ownership %: 100
Editorial:
Dale Hanson Bourke ...............................Editor
Leslie Nunn ................................Advertising

68870

## AMERICAN SENIOR
951 S. Oxford, No. 109
Los Angeles, CA 00006
Telephone: (213) 732-3477
FAX: (213) 732-9123
Year Established: 1991
Pub. Frequency: q.
Subscrip. Rate: $29.99/yr.
Materials: 02,03,04,05,06,07,08,09,10,11, 13,14,15,16,17,18,19,20,21,22,23,24,25, 26,27,28,29,30,31,32,33
Freelance Pay: $.20-.50/word
Circulation: 120,000
Circulation Type: controlled & paid
Owner(s):
Publishing & Business Consultants
951 S. Oxford, No. 109
Los Angeles, CA 90006
Telephone: (213) 732-3477
FAX: (213) 732-9123
Ownership %: 100
Editorial:
Andeson Napoleon Atia ...........................Editor
Desc.: Covers medical breakthroughs, government programs and benefits affecting seniors and their lifestyles.
Deadline: story-2 wks. prior to pub. date; news-2 wks.; photo-2 wks.; ads-90 days prior to pub. date

25831

## CALIFORNIA SENIOR CITIZEN
4805 Alta Canyada Rd.
La Canada Flintridge, CA 91011
Telephone: (818) 790-0651
Year Established: 1961
Pub. Frequency: m.
Page Size: tabloid
Subscrip. Rate: $5/yr.
Materials: 06,09,20,21,28,32,33
Freelance Pay: $.75/in.
Print Process: web offset
Circulation: 69,000
Circulation Type: paid
Owner(s):
Osmon Publications, Inc.
4805 Alta Canyada Rd.
La Canada Flt, CA 91011
Telephone: (818) 790-0651
Ownership %: 100
Management:
Frank Osmon ..............................President
Carol Osmon .............................Publisher
Editorial:
Carol Osmon ...................................Editor

Desc.: Rarely use publicity generated by outsiders because most of our publication is staff written or submitted by established writers.
Readers: Senior citizens (mostly retired), in Los Angeles County, Northern Orange County and Inland Empire.
Deadline: story-15th of mo. prior to pub. date; news-15th of mo. prior; photo-15th of mo. prior; ads-15th of mo. prior

25079

## FLORIDA RETIREMENT LIFESTYLES MAGAZINE
P.O. Box 161848
Altamonte Springs, FL 32716
Telephone: (407) 774-8668
FAX: (407) 774-1095
Year Established: 1946
Pub. Frequency: 10/mo.
Page Size: standard
Subscrip. Rate: $18/yr.
Materials: 02,03,04,05,06,07,09,10,15,19, 21,29,32,33
Freelance Pay: negotiable
Print Process: web offset
Circulation: 45,000
Circulation Type: controlled & paid
Owner(s):
Gidder House Publishing, Inc.
Ownership %: 100
Management:
Dyeann Dummer ..............................President
R. H. Dummer .................................Publisher
R. H. Dummer ................Advertising Manager
Joyce Lee ........................Circulation Manager
Editorial:
Kay Fernandez ...................................Editor
Dyeann Dummer ......................Managing Editor
Bobbi Breadstill ..........................Art Director
R. H. Dummer ..................................Director
Desc.: Magazine is devoted to all news of interest to people looking into travel and retirement in Florida.
Readers: Pre-retirees and retirees wanting to learn about Florida senior housing & related subjects: travel, finances, activities, decorating and gardening, etc.
Deadline: story-2 mos. prior to pub. date; news-2 mos. prior; photo-2 mos. prior; ads-last Fri. prior to pub. date

68867

## GOOD LIFE
75 Fountain St.
Providence, RI 02902
Telephone: (401) 277-7022
FAX: (401) 277-7802
Year Established: 1992
Pub. Frequency: q.
Subscrip. Rate: $5/yr.
Circulation: 56,100
Circulation Type: paid
Owner(s):
Providence Journal Bulletin
75 Fountain St.
Providence, RI 02902
Telephone: (401) 277-7022
Ownership %: 100
Management:
Stephen Hamblett ..........................Publisher
Richard J. Murray .............Advertising Manager
Editorial:
Merrill Bailey ...................................Editor

65386

## IDAHO SENIOR NEWS
1111 S. Orchard, Ste. 114
Boise, ID 83705
Telephone: (208) 336-6707
FAX: (208) 336-6708
Mailing Address:
P.O. Box 6662
Boise, ID 83707
Year Established: 1979
Pub. Frequency: m.

Page Size: tabloid
Subscrip. Rate: free newsstand; $12/yr.
Freelance Pay: varies
Circulation: 54,000
Circulation Type: controlled
Owner(s):
Owen Krahn
1111 S. Orchard, Ste. 114
Boise, ID 83705
Telephone: (208) 336-6707
Ownership %: 100
Editorial:
Owen Krahn ...................................Editor
Desc.: Newspaper publishing and advertising. Statewide newspaper. Newspaper articles focus on health, finance, laws, insurance, state, local and national issues of interest to the 50 and over market.
Readers: For those 50 and over.

68868

## MATURE OUTLOOK
1912 Grand Ave.
Des Moines, IA 50309-3379
Telephone: (515) 284-2007
Year Established: 1983
Pub. Frequency: bi-m.
Page Size: standard
Subscrip. Rate: $9.95/yr. non-members; $6/yr. institutions
Materials: 02,04,05,06,32
Print Process: web offset
Circulation: 925,000
Circulation Type: free & paid
Owner(s):
Meredith Publishing Co.
1912 Grand Ave.
Des Moines, IA 50309-3379
Telephone: (800) 336-6330
Ownership %: 100
Editorial:
Marjorie Groves ...................................Editor
Desc.: Covers health and fitness, food and nutrition, travel, people and relationships, finance, and home decorating.
Deadline: story-6 mo. prior to pub. date; ads-2 mo. prior to pub. date

25695

## MODERN MATURITY
3200 E. Carson St.
Lakewood, CA 90712
Telephone: (310) 496-2277
FAX: (310) 496-4127
Year Established: 1958
Pub. Frequency: bi-m.
Page Size: standard
Subscrip. Rate: $8/yr.
Freelance Pay: $2,500
Circulation: 2,245,000
Circulation Type: controlled & paid
Owner(s):
American Association of Retired Persons
1909 K St. N.W.
Washington, DC 20049
Telephone: (202) 728-4700
Ownership %: 100
Management:
Leda Sanford ....................Advertising Manager
Patricia A. Mondello ..........Advertising Manager
Editorial:
Roy Hoopes ...............................Bureau Chief
Henry Fenwick ..............................Exec. Editor
Susan Taylor ..............................Senior Editor
David Black ..............................Senior Editor
Annette Winter ..........................Senior Editor
John Wood ...............................Senior Editor
Lorena F. Farrell ........................Senior Editor
Vanessa Orr ...............................Advertising
Tomiko Anderson .........................Advertising
Treesa W. Drury ..........................Advertising
James H. Richardson ......................Art Director
Karen C. Reyes ......................Articles Editor
Karen Sinrod ..........Assistant Program Director

Materials Accepted/Included: 01-Business news 02-By-line articles 03-Fashion news 04-Food news 05-Freelance copy 06-Letters to editor 07-Real estate news 08-Sports news 09-Travel news 10-Book rev. 11-Movie rev. 12-Music rev. 13-TV rev. 14-Theater rev. 15-Coming events 16-Obituaries 17-Question & answer 18-Social announcements 19-Artwork 20-Cartoons 21-Photos 22-TV listings 23-Audio rec. 24-Video rec. 25-Books 26-Films/film clips 27-Personnel news 28-Press releases 29-New product news/photos 30-Trade lit. 31-Contracts awarded 32-Display adv. 33-Classified adv.

David Fuller ..................Associate Art Director
Ian Ledgerwood ..........................Editor at Large
Daniel S. Brown ...............................Photographer
Michaelene Wadolny ....................Picture Editor
Brenda L. Allen ....................Production Assistant
Sharon L. Deeming ..........Production Assistant
Traci Wilson ..................Production Coordinator
Charles W. Allen ..................Publishing Director
**Desc.:** Covers everything of interest for
people over 50 years of age such as
travel, finance, hobbies, art, retirement
living, health, nostalgia, inspiration,
famous older Americans, and articles of
general entertainment. Departments
include: Laughing Matter, Spotlight,
Readers Write, What Should I Do,
Staying Well, Verse.
**Readers:** Men and women over 50.

25852
## NEW CHOICES FOR RETIREMENT LIVING
28 W. 23rd St.
New York, NY 10010
Telephone: (212) 366-8800
Year Established: 1961
Pub. Frequency: m.
Page Size: standard
Subscrip. Rate: $15.97/yr.
Circulation: 612,000
Circulation Type: paid
**Owner(s):**
Reader's Digest Association, Inc.
Pleasantville, NY 10570
Telephone: (800) 345-6563
Ownership %: 100
**Management:**
Richard M. Fontana, Jr. ......................Publisher
**Editorial:**
Al Braverman ......................................Art Director
Ellen Sweet ....................................Articles Editor
**Desc.:** Departments include: Health,
Money, Investments, Food, Nutrition,
Gardening, Fashion, Insurance, Taxes,
Law, Consumer Concerns, Home Repair
and Travel. No unsolicited material,
manuscripts or artwork acknowledged,
accepted or returned.

25703
## RETIREMENT LIFE
1533 New Hampshire Ave., N.W.
Washington, DC 20036-1279
Telephone: (202) 234-0832
FAX: (202) 797-9698
Year Established: 1921
Pub. Frequency: m.
Page Size: standard
Subscrip. Rate: $25/yr.
Materials: 32
Print Process: web offset
Circulation: 450,000
Circulation Type: paid
**Owner(s):**
National Association of Retired Federal
Employees
1533 New Hampshire Ave., N.W.
Washington, DC 20036-1279
Telephone: (202) 234-0832
FAX: (202) 797-9698
Ownership %: 100
**Bureau(s):**
National Headquarters
1533 New Hampshire Ave., N.W.
Washington, DC 20036-1279
Telephone: (202) 234-0832
FAX: (202) 797-9698
Contact: Kathleen E. Delaney, Editor
**Management:**
Charles W. Carter ..............................President
Al Golato ....................................Vice President
**Editorial:**
Kathleen E. Delaney ..............................Editor
Nola Agrular ..........................................Secretary
Benny L. Parker ..................................Treasurer

**Desc.:** Carries news of interest to and
about members and all other federal
retirees, and articles about association,
legislation, and retirement planning.
Advertising is also carried.
**Readers:** Retired and current federal civil
service employees.
**Deadline:** ads-1st of mo. prior to pub. date

68869
## RX REMEDY
120 Post Rd. W.
Westport, CT 06880
Telephone: (203) 221-4910
FAX: (203) 221-4913
Year Established: 1992
Pub. Frequency: bi-m.
Subscrip. Rate: $3 newsstand; $14.95/yr.
Circulation: 1,500,000
Circulation Type: paid
**Owner(s):**
Rx Remedy, Inc.
120 Post Rd. W.
Westport, CT 06880
Telephone: (203) 221-4910
Ownership %: 100
**Management:**
G. Douglas Johnston ..........................Publisher
**Editorial:**
Val Weaver ................................................Editor
Peter French ......................Advertising Director
Jill Webb ..........................Circulation Director
**Desc.:** Provides health information for the
over-55s.

49887
## SENIOR WORLD NEWSMAGAZINE
1000 Pioneer Way
El Cajon, CA 92020
Telephone: (619) 593-2900
Mailing Address:
P.O. Box 1565
El Cajon, CA 92022
Year Established: 1973
Pub. Frequency: m.
Page Size: tabloid
Subscrip. Rate: $30/yr.
Materials: 04,05,06,07,09,15,23,24,25,26,
32,33
Freelance Pay: $50-$100/article
Print Process: web offset
Circulation: 500,000
Circulation Type: free
**Owner(s):**
Kendell Communications, Inc.
1000 Pioneer Way
El Cajon, CA 92020
Telephone: (619) 593-2900
Ownership %: 100
**Management:**
Resa Trent ..............................General Manager
**Editorial:**
Laura Impastato ........................Executive Editor
Iris Neal ............................Entertainment Editor
Andrea Caughey ........................Financial Editor
Doug Brunk ......................................Health Editor
Carolyn Pantier ..............................Money Editor
Carolyn Pantier ..........................Life Style Editor
Jerry Goodrum ................................Travel Editor
**Desc.:** Targeted to active older adults, 55-
plus. It includes sections on travel,
finance, health, lifestyle, housing,
entertainment, sports, and news and
features of local, state and national
interest.
**Readers:** Senior citizens.

71267
## SUCCESSFUL RETIREMENT
950 Third Ave., 16th Fl.
New York, NY 10022
Telephone: (212) 888-1855
FAX: (212) 838-8420
Pub. Frequency: bi-m.
Page Size: standard
Subscrip. Rate: $3.50 newsstand; $21/yr.
Materials: 32

Circulation: 115,000
Circulation Type: paid
**Owner(s):**
Grass Roots Publishing Co., Inc.
950 Third Ave., 16th Fl.
New York, NY 10022
Telephone: (212) 888-1855
Ownership %: 100
**Management:**
Suzann Hochman ................................Publisher
Robert Miller ..................Advertising Manager
**Editorial:**
Marcio Vickers ............................................Editor
Renee Cajigal-Delgodo .......Marketing Manager

69363
## WORKING AGE NEWSLETTER
1601 E St., N.W.
Washington, DC 20049
Telephone: (202) 434-2277
FAX: (202) 434-6470
Year Established: 1984
Pub. Frequency: bi-m.
Subscrip. Rate: free
Circulation: 35,000
Circulation Type: controlled & free
**Owner(s):**
American Association of Retired Persons
Worker Equity Initiative
1601 E St., N.W.
Washington, DC 20049
Telephone: (202) 434-2277
Ownership %: 100
**Editorial:**
Ronald Allen ..............................................Editor
**Desc.:** Covers the latest employment facts
and demographic trends affecting
employees age 50 and over.
**Readers:** Personnel directors, policy
makers and specialists in aging.

69571
## 39 PLUS
66 Flint St.
Asheville, NC 28801
Telephone: (704) 251-5881
FAX: (704) 251-5881
Year Established: 1988
Pub. Frequency: m.
Page Size: tabloid
Subscrip. Rate: $.25/vending machines;
$12/yr.
Materials: 02,05,06,10,15,20,25,28,29,32,33
Print Process: web offset
Circulation: 60,000
Circulation Type: free & paid
**Owner(s):**
Westchester Publications
66 Flint St.
Asheville, NC 28801
Telephone: (704) 251-5881
FAX: (704) 251-5881
**Management:**
Josephine C. DeVaynes ......................President
Josephine C. DeVaynes ......................Publisher
David R. George ..................................Publisher
Josephine C. ..................Advertising Manager
DeVaynes
**Editorial:**
David R. George ..........................Editor in Chief

**Desc.:** Profiles mature adults and reports
on diverse subjects that pertain to their
interests. Includes crossword puzzles,
cartoons, restaurant reviews and
recipes.
**Deadline:** story-10th of mo. prior to pub.
date; ads-20th of mo. prior

## Group 668-Sewing & Needlework

68890
## AMERICAN QUILTER
P.O. Box 3290
Paducah, KY 42002-3290
Telephone: (502) 898-7903
FAX: (502) 898-8890
Year Established: 1985
Pub. Frequency: q.
Page Size: standard
Subscrip. Rate: $15/yr. US; $20/yr. foreign
Materials: 02,06,10,15,21,32,33
Print Process: web
Circulation: 70000
Circulation Type: controlled & paid
**Owner(s):**
American Quilter's Society
P.O. Box 3290
Paducah, KY 42002-3290
Telephone: (502) 898-7903
Ownership %: 100
**Editorial:**
Victoria Faoro ..........................................Editor
**Desc.:** Serves today's quilters with articles
on quilt designing techniques, study,
exhibition, issues events.
**Readers:** 70,000 members of AQS.

68891
## CREATIVE QUILTING
950 Third Ave., 16th Fl.
New York, NY 10022
Telephone: (212) 888-1855
FAX: (212) 838-8420
Year Established: 1986
Pub. Frequency: bi-m.
Page Size: standard
Subscrip. Rate: $3.50 newsstand; $21/yr.
Materials: 32
Circulation: 280,000
Circulation Type: paid
**Owner(s):**
Grass Roots Publishing Co., Inc.
950 Third Ave., 16th Fl.
New York, NY 10022
Telephone: (212) 888-1855
Ownership %: 100
**Management:**
Susan Hochman ................................Publisher
Robert Miller ..................Advertising Manager
**Editorial:**
Jan Burns ..................................................Editor
Renee Cajigal-Delgodo .......Marketing Manager
**Desc.:** Features step-by-step instructions
and diagrams for various levels of
quilters. Includes a buyer's guide and
articles on well-known quilters.

68892
## CROCHET FANTASY
243 Newton-Sparta Rd.
Newton, NJ 07860-2748
Telephone: (201) 383-8080
FAX: (201) 383-8133
Year Established: 1983
Pub. Frequency: 8/yr.
Page Size: 7 7/8 x 10 1/2
Subscrip. Rate: $3.50 US; $4.50 Can.;
$28/yr.
Materials: 02,06,10,32,33
Circulation: 198,000
Circulation Type: paid

**Materials Accepted/Included:** 01-Business news 02-By-line articles 03-Fashion news 04-Food news 05-Freelance copy 06-Letters to editor 07-Real estate news 08-Sports news 09-Travel news
10-Book rev. 11-Movie rev. 12-Music rev. 13-TV rev. 14-Theater rev. 15-Coming events 16-Obituaries 17-Question & answer 18-Social announcements 19-Artwork 20-Cartoons 21-Photos 22-TV listings
23-Audio rec. 24-Video rec. 25-Books 26-Films/film clips 27-Personnel news 28-Press releases 29-New product news/photos 30-Trade lit. 31-Contracts awarded 32-Display adv. 33-Classified adv.

6-109

**Owner(s):**
All American Crafts, Inc.
243 Newton-Sparta Rd.
Newton, NJ 07860-2748
Telephone: (201) 383-8080
FAX: (201) 383-8133
Ownership %: 100
**Editorial:**
Karen Manthey ......................Editor
Janice Utter ..........................Editor
**Desc.:** Features photographs, instructions,
and diagrams for traditional and
contemporary garments, accessories
and home decor.

69572

## CROSS-STITCHER
701 Lee St., Ste. 1000
Des Plaines, IL 60016-4570
Telephone: (708) 297-7400
FAX: (708) 297-8328
Year Established: 1983
Pub. Frequency: bi-m.
Page Size: standard
Subscrip. Rate: $3.50/issue; $14.97/yr.
Materials: 06,28,29,32,33
Print Process: web
Circulation: 77,452
Circulation Type: free & paid
**Owner(s):**
Clapper Communications Co.
701 Lee St., Ste. 1000
Des Plaines, IL 60016-4570
Telephone: (708) 297-7400
Ownership %: 100
**Editorial:**
B.J. McDonald ........................Editor
**Desc.:** This publication is edited for
counter cross-stitch enthusiasts. A
special feature in each issue is the
"Tired Eyes" section where the chart
and type are enlarged for easier
stitching. Other features include florals,
wildlife, inspirational, samplers and
educational articles.
**Deadline:** story-4 mos.; news-4 mos.;
photo-4 mos.; ads-5 wks.

69560

## CROSS STITCH & COUNTRY CRAFTS
1716 Locust St.
Des Moines, IA 50336
Telephone: (515) 284-3623
FAX: (515) 284-3863
Year Established: 1993
Pub. Frequency: bi-m.
Page Size: standard
Subscrip. Rate: $3.95 newsstand;
$19.97/yr.
Circulation: 1,000,000
Circulation Type: paid
**Owner(s):**
Meredith Corp., Special Interest
Publications
1716 Locust St.
Des Moines, IA 50336
Telephone: (515) 284-3000
Ownership %: 100
**Management:**
Jim Jarrell ..........................Publisher
**Editorial:**
Carol Field-Dahlstrom .............Editor
Peggy Daugherty .........Administrative Assistant

68894

## FASHION KNITTING
243 Newton-Sparta Rd.
Newton, NJ 07860-2748
Telephone: (201) 383-8080
FAX: (201) 383-8033
Year Established: 1981
Pub. Frequency: bi-m.
Page Size: standard
Subscrip. Rate: $3.95 newsstand;
$16.95/yr.
Materials: 32

Circulation: 30,000
Circulation Type: paid
**Owner(s):**
All American Crafts, Inc.
243 Newton-Sparta Rd.
Newton, NJ 08600-2748
Telephone: (201) 383-8080
Ownership %: 100
**Management:**
Jerry Cohen .......................Publisher
Barbara Smith ...............Advertising Manager
Marie Claire .....................Circulation Manager
MacDonald
**Editorial:**
Sally V. Klein .........................Editor
**Desc.:** Features contemporary knitted
garment designs, photographs,
instructions, diagrams and more.

56394

## HOLIDAY CRAFTS
1633 Broadway
New York, NY 10019
Telephone: (212) 767-6000
Pub. Frequency: a.
Page Size: standard
Freelance Pay: varies
Circulation: 950,000
Circulation Type: paid
**Owner(s):**
Hachette Magazines
1633 Broadway
New York, NY 10019
Telephone: (212) 767-6000
Ownership %: 100
**Management:**
Susan Buckley .....................Publisher
**Editorial:**
Carolyn Gatto ..................Editor in Chief
Rowan Gilman .......................Editor
**Desc.:** How-to magazine of crafts to make
ahead. Projects for skilled handicrafters
as well as novices. Complete directions
included in each issue.
**Readers:** Women. Profile of readership
depends on subject.

68893

## MCCALL'S CROCHET
New Plz.
P.O. Box 1790
Peoria, IL 61656
Telephone: (309) 682-6626
Year Established: 1980
Pub. Frequency: bi-m.
Page Size: standard
Subscrip. Rate: $3.95 newsstand;
$15.95/yr.
Materials: 32
Freelance Pay: varies
Circulation: 20,000
Circulation Type: paid
**Owner(s):**
Veronis Suhler Associates, Inc.
New Plz.
P.O. Box 1790
Peoria, IL 61656
Telephone: (309) 682-6626
Ownership %: 100
**Management:**
Kip DuBois ..................Advertising Manager
**Editorial:**
Ann Reed ............................Editor
Robin Hoffmann ................Circulation Director

25992

## MCCALL'S NEEDLEWORK
405 Riverhills Business Pk.
Birmingham, AL 35242
Telephone: (205) 995-8860
Year Established: 1930
Pub. Frequency: bi-m.
Page Size: standard
Subscrip. Rate: $3.95 newsstand;
$15.98/yr.
Materials: 01,02,03,05,06,09,10,15,19,21,
25,28,29,30,32,33

Freelance Pay: varies
Circulation: 300,000
Circulation Type: paid
**Owner(s):**
Symbol of Excellence
405 Riverhills Business Pk.
Birmingham, AL 35242
Ownership %: 100
**Bureau(s):**
McCall's Needlework
P.O. Box 1790
Chicago, IL 60690
**Management:**
Phyllis Hoffman ...................Publisher
Kip DuBois ..................Advertising Manager
**Editorial:**
Barbara Cockerham ............Executive Editor
Ashley C. Cobb ......................Editor
Yukie McLean .......................Art Director
**Desc.:** For the person who wants to create
beautiful things for herself and for her
home. Items are shown in a wide variety
of techniques, including knitting,
crocheting, needlepoint, quilting,
embroidery, smocking, cross stitch, and
needlework of all kinds.
**Readers:** Women who are actively
involved in a variety of techniques in
needlework and crafts.

69239

## MCCALL'S QUILTING
405 Riverhills Business Pk.
Birmingham, AL 35242
Telephone: (205) 995-8860
FAX: (205) 995-8428
Year Established: 1912
Pub. Frequency: 6/yr.
Page Size: standard
Subscrip. Rate: $3.95 newsstand US;
$4.75 newsstand Canada; $15.95/yr.
Materials: 02,03,04,05,06,10,15,21,23,24,
25,28,29,30,32,33
Circulation: 300,000
Circulation Type: controlled
**Owner(s):**
Symbol of Excellence
405 Riverhills Business Pk.
Birmingham, AL 35242
Ownership %: 100
**Management:**
Phyllis Hoffman ...................Publisher
Kip DuBois ..................Advertising Manager
**Editorial:**
Jan Grigsby ..........................Editor
Yukie McLean .......................Art Director
Robin Hoffmann ................Circulation Director
**Desc.:** Covers needlework, knitting, home
decorating, quilting and other crafts.

67064

## PATCHWORK QUILTS
152 Madison Ave.
Ste. 906
New York, NY 10016
Telephone: (212) 689-3933
Year Established: 1973
Pub. Frequency: 10/yr.
Page Size: standard
Subscrip. Rate: $3.95 newsstand;
$17.99/yr.
Circulation: 150,000
Circulation Type: paid
**Owner(s):**
Lopez Publications, Inc.
152 Madison Ave.
Ste. 906
New York, NY 10016
Telephone: (212) 689-3933
Ownership %: 100
**Management:**
Adrian Lopez .......................Publisher
**Desc.:** Photos and stories for the
experienced quilter.
**Readers:** 25-85 yr. old females.

71265

## QUICK & EASY CROCHET
950 Third Ave., 16th Fl.
New York, NY 10022
Telephone: (212) 888-1855
FAX: (212) 838-8420
Year Established: 1984
Pub. Frequency: bi-m.
Page Size: standard
Subscrip. Rate: $3.50 newsstand; $21/yr.
Materials: 32
Circulation: 325,000
Circulation Type: paid
**Owner(s):**
Grass Roots Publishing Co., Inc.
950 Third Ave., 16th Fl.
New York, NY 10022
Telephone: (212) 888-1855
Ownership %: 100
**Management:**
Suzann Hochman ...................Publisher
Robert Miller .....................Advertising Manager
**Editorial:**
Valier Kurita ..........................Editor
Renee Cajigal-Delgodo .......Marketing Manager
**Desc.:** Features step-by-step instructions
and diagrams for the beginner.

67063

## QUILT CRAFT
152 Madison Ave., Ste. 905
New York, NY 10016
Telephone: (212) 689-3933
FAX: (212) 725-2239
Year Established: 1991
Pub. Frequency: bi-m.
Page Size: standard
Subscrip. Rate: $3.95 newsstand;
$12.95/yr.
Circulation: 175,000
Circulation Type: paid
**Owner(s):**
Lopez Publications, Inc.
152 Madison Ave., Ste. 905
New York, NY 10016
Telephone: (212) 689-3933
Ownership %: 100
**Management:**
Adrian B. Lopez ...................Publisher
**Editorial:**
Wendie Blanchard ....................Editor
**Desc.:** Focuses on quilts for intermediate
and beginning quilters. Most designs are
original.

68895

## QUILTING INTERNATIONAL
243 Newton-Sparta Rd.
Newton, NJ 07860-2848
Telephone: (201) 383-8080
Year Established: 1987
Pub. Frequency: bi-m.
Subscrip. Rate: $23.70/yr.
Circulation: 121,000
Circulation Type: paid
**Owner(s):**
All American Crafts, Inc.
243 Newton-Sparta Rd.
Newton, NJ 07860-2848
Telephone: (201) 383-8080
Ownership %: 100
**Editorial:**
Marion Buccieri ......................Editor
**Desc.:** Features traditional and
contemporary quilting patterns,
techniques, interviews, show listings,
reviews, history and tips.

70355

## SEW NEWS
News Plz., P.O. Box 1790
Peoria, IL 61656
Telephone: (309) 682-6626
FAX: (309) 682-7394
Year Established: 1981
Pub. Frequency: m.

Materials Accepted/Included: 01-Business news 02-By-line articles 03-Fashion news 04-Food news 05-Freelance copy 06-Letters to editor 07-Real estate news 08-Sports news 09-Travel news 10-Book rev. 11-Movie rev. 12-Music rev. 13-TV rev. 14-Theater rev. 15-Coming events 16-Obituaries 17-Question & answer 18-Social announcements 19-Artwork 20-Cartoons 21-Photos 22-TV listings 23-Audio rec. 24-Video rec. 25-Books 26-Films/film clips 27-Personnel news 28-Press releases 29-New product news/photos 30-Trade lit. 31-Contracts awarded 32-Display adv. 33-Classified adv.

6-110

Page Size: 9 X 11 7/8
Subscrip. Rate: $3.95 newsstand;
$23.98/yr.
Materials: 03,05,10,17,25,28,29,32,33
Freelance Pay: $25-$1,000/article
Print Process: offset
Circulation: 260,000
Circulation Type: paid
**Owner(s):**
PJS Publications, Inc.
News Plz., P.O. Box 1790
Peoria, IL 61656
Telephone: (309) 682-6626
FAX: (309) 682-7394
Ownership %: 100
**Editorial:**
Linda Turner Griepentrog ..........................Editor
**Desc.:** Fashion magazine for people who
sew.
**Deadline:** story-4 mos.; news-4 mos.;
photo-4 mos.; ads-2 mos.

26008
**SHUTTLE, SPINDLE & DYEPOT**
1202 University Ave. W
Ste. 702
St. Paul, MN 55114
Telephone: (612) 646-0802
FAX: (612) 646-0806
Year Established: 1969
Pub. Frequency: q.
Page Size: Standard
Subscrip. Rate: $25/yr.; $48/2 yrs.; $29/yr.
foreign
Freelance Pay: up to $100
Circulation: 7,500
Circulation Type: paid
**Owner(s):**
Handweavers Guild of America, Inc.
1202 University Ave. W.
Ste. 702
St. Paul, MN 55114
Telephone: (612) 646-0802
Ownership %: 100
**Management:**
Ruth Gaskins ..................Advertising Manager
**Editorial:**
Sandra Bowles ..........................................Editor
**Desc.:** Features include how-to's,
historical, foreign, interviews, new
techniques in fiber arts and
handweaving fields; 1500 words max.
Color and b & w photos used. Articles
are by-lined. Stories on museum
collections and well-known people in
fiber arts field. Publicity matls.: calendar
of events for fiber shows, exhibition.
Departments include: Letters, Volunteer
services, Test & Report, Calendar,
Bookshelf, Suppliers News, and
Guildview, The Handweavers Guild of
America, is an international, non-profit
organization dedicated to serving
weavers, spinners and dyers.
**Readers:** Handweavers, Dyers, Spinners,
and related fiber artists.

66187
**THREADS**
63 S. Main St.
Newtown, CT 06470-5506
Telephone: (203) 426-8171
FAX: (203) 426-3434
Year Established: 1985
Pub. Frequency: bi-m.
Page Size: standard
Subscrip. Rate: $5.50 newsstand; $28/yr.;
$48/2 yrs.
Materials: 02,05,06,10,17,21,25,28,29,32,33
Freelance Pay: $150/pg.
Circulation: 150,000
Circulation Type: paid

**Owner(s):**
Taunton Press, The
63 S. Main St.
Newtown, CT 06470-5506
Telephone: (203) 426-8171
FAX: (203) 426-3434
Ownership %: 100
**Management:**
Betsy Levine ..........................Associate Publisher
Maureen Larkin .................Advertising Manager
Donna Pierpont ........Public Relations Manager
**Editorial:**
Amy Yanagi ...........................Executive Editor
Christine Timmons .......................Senior Editor
Vivian Dorman .......................Advertising Sales
Glee Barre ..................................Art Director
David Page Coffin ....................Associate Editor
Karen Morris ..........................Associate Editor
**Desc.:** Covers sewing and professional
garment making techniques, creative
hand or machine knitting ideas, and a
rich variety of today's most imaginative
needle work and textile arts. Full-color
photos and clearly detailed illustrations
show work-in-progress.
**Readers:** 98% are female and 86% have
attended college. Subscribers range
from serious amateurs to professionals.

69564
**TRADITIONAL QUILTER**
243 Newton Sparta Rd.
Newton, NJ 07860
Telephone: (201) 383-8080
FAX: (201) 383-8133
Year Established: 1989
Pub. Frequency: bi-m.
Page Size: standard
Subscrip. Rate: $3.95 newsstand;
$23.70/yr.
Materials: 03,05,06,30,32,33
Print Process: offset
Circulation: 65,000
Circulation Type: paid
**Owner(s):**
MSC Publishing, Inc.
243 Newton Sparta Rd.
Newton, NJ 07860
Telephone: (201) 383-8080
Ownership %: 100
**Editorial:**
Phyllis Barbieri ...........................................Editor
**Desc.:** Contains news on quilters and
exhibits, advanced quilting techniques
and quilt designs.

68824
**VOGUE PATTERNS**
161 Ave. of the Americas
New York, NY 10013
Telephone: (212) 620-2500
Year Established: 1915
Pub. Frequency: bi-m.
Subscrip. Rate: $12.95/yr.
Circulation: 225,000
Circulation Type: paid
**Owner(s):**
Butterick Co., Inc.
161 Ave. of the Americas
New York, NY 10013
Telephone: (212) 620-2500
Ownership %: 100
**Editorial:**
Meredith Gray ...........................................Editor

26638
**WORKBASKET, THE**
700 W. 47th St., Ste. 310
Kansas City, MO 64112
Telephone: (816) 531-5730
FAX: (816) 531-3873
Year Established: 1935
Pub. Frequency: bi-m.
Page Size: pocket
Subscrip. Rate: $2.95 newsstand;
$12.95/yr.
Materials: 32

Freelance Pay: varies
Print Process: offset
Circulation: 1,033,031
Circulation Type: paid
**Owner(s):**
KC Publishing, Inc.
700 W. 47th St., Ste. 310
Kansas City, MO 64112
Telephone: (816) 531-5730
Ownership %: 100
**Bureau(s):**
Modern Handcraft, Inc.
50 E. 42nd St.
New York, NY
Telephone: (212) 697-7990
Contact: Pat Venezia, Manager

Magazine Services, Inc.
500 N. Michigan Ave.
Chicago, IL 60611
Contact: Vicki Fuchs, Manager

Magazine Services, Inc.
9696 Culver Blvd.
Culver City, CA 90232
Telephone: (310) 842-8054
Contact: Joan Rubenstein, Manager
**Management:**
John C. Prebich ..............................President
**Editorial:**
Kay M. Olson ..........................................Editor
Beth Dawson ...............Advertising Research
Director
Jim Clark ....................................Art Director
Judy Dawson ................Financial Administrator
Cindy Lowe ...........................Production Director
Connie Moss ...........................VP Production
**Desc.:** Editorial stresses needlework and
home service features with directions for
crochet, knitting, tatting, quilting, crewel,
etc., plus special sections on cooking,
gardening, handicrafts, money making
ideas and general homemaker interests.
Article submissions are welcome.
**Readers:** Median age of readers 52.6,
median income $26,183; 80.7%
homeowners, 66.95% with no mortgage;
71.8% married. Needlecraft, cooking,
gardening, and homemaking enthusiasts.

## Group 670-Sports

3759
**ADVENTURE CYCLIST**
150 N. Pine St.
Missoula, MT 59802
Telephone: (406) 721-1776
Mailing Address:
P.O. Box 8308
Missoula, MT 59807
Year Established: 1985
Pub. Frequency: 9/yr.
Page Size: tabloid
Subscrip. Rate: $25/yr.
Materials: 32
Freelance Pay: negotiable
Print Process: offset
Circulation: 40,000
Circulation Type: paid
**Owner(s):**
Adventure Cycling Association
150 N. Pine St.
Missoula, MT 59802
Telephone: (406) 721-1776
Ownership %: 100
**Management:**
Julie Huck ...........................Circulation Manager
**Editorial:**
Daniel D'Ambrosio .......................................Editor
Kevin Condit ......................Marketing Manager

26355
**AMERICAN HANDGUNNER**
591 Camino de la Reina, Ste. 200
San Diego, CA 92108
Telephone: (619) 297-8520
Year Established: 1976

Pub. Frequency: bi-m.
Page Size: standard
Subscrip. Rate: $16.95/yr.
Circulation: 180,000
Circulation Type: paid
**Owner(s):**
Publishers Development Corp.
591 Camino de la Reina, Ste. 2
San Diego, CA 92108
Telephone: (619) 297-5350
Ownership %: 100
**Management:**
Tom von Rosen ..................................President
Thomas Hollander ......................Vice President
George E. von Rosen ........................Publisher
**Editorial:**
Cameron Hopkins ...................Editorial Director
John Hart ...........................................Art Director
**Desc.:** Editorial features of interest to all
who are interested in handguns,
shooters, collectors, hunters,
technicians. Departments include: Guns
& The Law, Leather Goods, Law
Enforcement, Combat Shooting, New
Products.
**Readers:** Firearms owner & shooting
sports competitors.

26356
**AMERICAN MOTORCYCLIST**
33 Collegeview Rd.
Westerville, OH 43081
Telephone: (614) 891-2425
FAX: (614) 891-5012
Year Established: 1947
Pub. Frequency: m.
Page Size: standard
Subscrip. Rate: $10/yr.
Materials: 05,06,15,24,25,27,28,29,32
Circulation: 176,169
Circulation Type: paid
**Owner(s):**
American Motorcyclist Association
33 College View Rd.
Westerville, OH 43081
Telephone: (614) 891-2425
FAX: (614) 891-5012
Ownership %: 100
**Editorial:**
Greg Harrison ...........................Executive Editor
Bill Wood ...........................Managing Editor
John Holliday ...........................Advertising
J.B. Norris ...................Advertising Sales-East
Beth J. Shaw ...............Advertising Sales-West
Roger Young ...........................Associate Editor
Ed Youngblood ...........................Columnist
Rob Rasor ...........................Columnist
**Desc.:** Covers all phases of the sport of
motorcycling, including national
championships, district and regional
championships and major events.
Departments include: Post Entry (Letters
to Ed.) AMA News, Gov't. Road, Top
Gear Sports and Classics.
**Readers:** Motorcycle riders, racers, and
entusiasts.

26357
**AMERICAN RIFLEMAN**
11250 Waples Mill Rd.
Fairfax, VA 22030-7400
Telephone: (703) 267-1300
Year Established: 1885
Pub. Frequency: m.
Page Size: standard
Subscrip. Rate: $25/yr. membership
Materials: 06,17,29,33
Freelance Pay: $250-$500/article
Circulation: 1,363,348
Circulation Type: paid
**Owner(s):**
National Rifle Association of America
11250 Waples Mill Rd.
Fairfax, VA 22030
Telephone: (703) 267-1000
Ownership %: 100

**Materials Accepted/Included:** 01-Business news 02-By-line articles 03-Fashion news 04-Food news 05-Freelance copy 06-Letters to editor 07-Real estate news 08-Sports news 09-Travel news 10-Book rev. 11-Movie rev. 12-Music rev. 13-TV rev. 14-Theater rev. 15-Coming events 16-Obituaries 17-Question & answer 18-Social announcements 19-Artwork 20-Cartoons 21-Photos 22-TV listings 23-Audio rec. 24-Video rec. 25-Books 26-Films/film clips 27-Personnel news 28-Press releases 29-New product news/photos 30-Trade lit. 31-Contracts awarded 32-Display adv. 33-Classified adv.

6-111

**Bureau(s):**
David Crosby & Associates
68 Silver Hill Rd.
Sudbury, MA 01776
Telephone: (617) 443-9910
Contact: David Crosby, Advertising
**Management:**
E.G. Bell, Jr. .............................Publisher
David Crosby ...............Advertising Manager
**Editorial:**
E.G. Bell, Jr. ................................Editor
Ronald Keysor .................Managing Editor
Diane Senesac .......................Advertising
Bill Fleegle ...............Production Director
Pete Dickey ..............Technical Editor
**Desc.:** Interested in all phases of sporting
firearms design, manufacturer,
modification, history, and in the use of
such arms for recreation and defense.
Contributed factual material deals
with hunting, target shooting, and other
activities in which firearms are used, as
well as on various technical and
historical aspects of firearms. Preferred
article length is from 2,000-2,500 words.
Uses short features running from 300-
750 words in length. Photos and photo
features used.
**Readers:** Members of the National Rifle
Association. Included are hunters,
gunsmiths, gun collectors, rifle, pistol &
shotgun tournament shooters, &
ordnance engineers.

26359
**AMERICAN TURF MONTHLY**
306 Broadway
Lynbrook, NY 11563
Telephone: (516) 599-2121
FAX: (516) 599-0451
Year Established: 1932
Pub. Frequency: m.
Page Size: standard
Subscrip. Rate: $29/yr.
Freelance Pay: $50-$125/article
Circulation: 15,000
Circulation Type: paid
**Owner(s):**
Star Sports Corp.
306 Broadway
Lynbrook, NY 11563
Telephone: (516) 599-2121
Ownership %: 100
**Management:**
Diane Karron .............................Publisher
**Editorial:**
I.C. Blair .................................Editor
**Desc.:** For those interested horse racing.
Also contains book reviews. Articles run
from 1500-2000 words.
**Readers:** Fans, and racing personnel.

26361
**APPALACHIA JOURNAL**
5 Joy St.
Boston, MA 02108
Telephone: (617) 523-0636
FAX: (617) 523-0722
Year Established: 1876
Pub. Frequency: s-a.
Page Size: standard
Subscrip. Rate: $10/yr.
Materials: 06,10,16,19,30
Print Process: offset
Circulation: 11,000
Circulation Type: paid
**Owner(s):**
Appalachian Mountain Club
5 Joy St.
Boston, MA 02108
Telephone: (617) 523-0636
Ownership %: 100
**Management:**
Carol Bast Tyler ........................Publisher
**Editorial:**
Sandy Stott ......................Editor in Chief

**Desc.:** The nation's oldest mountaineering
and conservation publication is
published semi-annually and edited for
those who enjoy the outdoors,
exploration and adventure. Reflects
the interest and knowledge of experts in
backcountry management, backpacking,
technical climbing, canoeing, trail
maintenance, mountain rescues, new
equipment and also includes book
reviews and photo essays. A respected
literary publication.
**Readers:** Literate, active outdoorsmen and
women with a strong interest in the
northeastern outdoors.
**Deadline:** story-Jul. 1, Dec. 1, prior to pub.
date; news-Jul. 1, Dec. 1, prior; photo-
Jul. 1, Dec. 1, prior

26366
**BACKPACKER**
33 E. Minor St.
Emmaus, PA 18098
Telephone: (215) 967-8296
FAX: (215) 967-8960
Year Established: 1973
Pub. Frequency: 9/yr.
Page Size: standard
Subscrip. Rate: $3.50/copy; $24/yr.
Materials: 05,06,08,10,32,33
Freelance Pay: $50-$1000/article
Circulation: 220,000
Circulation Type: paid
**Owner(s):**
Rodale Press, Inc.
33 E. Minor St.
Emmaus, PA 18098
Telephone: (215) 967-5171
Ownership %: 100
**Management:**
Peter Spiers .............................Publisher
**Editorial:**
John Viehman .............................Editor
**Readers:** Largely young and male, urban
professional, active campers, hikers,
canoeists, skiers, photographers,
bicyclists.

69780
**BASEBALL DIGEST**
990 Grove St.
Evanston, IL 60201-4370
Telephone: (708) 491-6440
Year Established: 1941
Pub. Frequency: m.
Subscrip. Rate: $22/yr.
Circulation: 350,000
Circulation Type: controlled & paid
**Owner(s):**
Century Publishing Co.
990 Grove St.
Evanston, IL 60201-4370
Telephone: (708) 491-6440
Ownership %: 100
**Editorial:**
John Kuenster .............................Editor

64871
**BASKETBALL WEEKLY**
8033 N. W. 36th St.
Miami, FL 33152
Telephone: (305) 594-0508
FAX: (305) 594-0518
Mailing Address:
P.O. Box 526600
Miami, FL 33152
Year Established: 1967
Pub. Frequency: 20/season
Page Size: tabloid
Subscrip. Rate: $2.95 newsstand;
$34.95/season
**Owner(s):**
Curtis Publications
P.O. Box 526600
Miami, FL 33152
Ownership %: 100

**Management:**
Tom Curtis .............................Publisher
**Editorial:**
Kevin Kaminski .............................Editor
**Desc.:** Covers professional, college and
high school basketball in depth. It is the
most informative publication in existence
and is read by more than 1,000
members of the media.

70479
**BECKETT TRIBUTE MAGAZINE**
15850 Dallas Pkwy.
Dallas, TX 75248
Telephone: (214) 991-6657
FAX: (214) 991-8930
Year Established: 1993
Pub. Frequency: bi-m.
Page Size: standard
Subscrip. Rate: $3.95 newsstand
Materials: 02,05,08,19,20,21,28,29,30,32
Freelance Pay: $200-300/article
Print Process: web offset
Circulation: 218,000
Circulation Type: paid
**Owner(s):**
Dr. James Beckett, III
15850 Dallas Pkwy.
Dallas, TX 75248
Telephone: (214) 991-6657
FAX: (214) 991-8930
**Management:**
Dr. James Beckett, III .................Publisher
**Editorial:**
Dr. James Beckett, III ....................Editor
Rudy Klanenik .........Assistant Managing Editor
Pepper Hastings ...............Editorial Director
**Desc.:** Each issue focuses on a single
sports personality.

66025
**BICYCLE GUIDE**
6420 Wilshire Blvd.
Los Angeles, CA 90048
Telephone: (800) 268-2504
Year Established: 1984
Pub. Frequency: m.
Page Size: standard
Subscrip. Rate: $19.94/yr.
Circulation: 165,000
Circulation Type: paid
**Owner(s):**
Peterson Publications
6420 Wilshire Blvd.
Los Angeles, CA 90048
Ownership %: 100
**Management:**
Christine Salem .................Circulation Manager
**Editorial:**
Tim Downs .............................Editor
Jeff Levy .............................Advertising
Marc Infield .............................Art Director

26370
**BICYCLING MAGAZINE**
33 E. Minor St.
Emmaus, PA 18098
Telephone: (215) 967-5171
Year Established: 1961
Pub. Frequency: 10/yr.
Page Size: standard
Subscrip. Rate: $17.97/yr.
Circulation: 380,000
Circulation Type: paid
**Owner(s):**
Rodale Press, Inc.
33 E. Minor St.
Emmaus, PA 18098
Telephone: (215) 967-5171
Ownership %: 100
**Management:**
James C. McCullagh .............Publisher
**Editorial:**
Ed Pavelka .............Executive Editor
Nelson Pena .............Senior Editor
John Kukoda .............Senior Editor
James C. McCullagh .............Editor

Don Cuerdon .............................Editor
Geoffrey Drake .............Managing Editor
John Pepper .............................Art Director
David S. McAfee .............Associate Publisher
Michael Shaw .............Photography Director
Joe Kita .............Senior Managing Editor
Fred Zahradnik .............Technical Editor
**Desc.:** Features articles about fitness,
training, nutrition, touring, racing
equipment, technology, industry
developments, and other topics of
interest to committed bicycle riders.
Editorially, we advocate for the sport
industry, and the cycling consumer.
**Readers:** Active Bicyclists and Bicycling
Enthusiasts

26373
**BLACK BELT MAGAZINE**
24715 Ave. Rockefeller
Santa Clarita, CA 91380-9018
Telephone: (805) 257-4066
FAX: (805) 257-3028
Mailing Address:
P.O. Box 918
Santa Clarita, CA 91380-9018
Year Established: 1961
Pub. Frequency: m.
Page Size: standard
Subscrip. Rate: $3.50/copy; $28/yr.
Materials: 02,05,06,08,15,16,17,18,19,20,
21,28,29,32
Freelance Pay: $75-$300/article
Circulation: 85,000
Circulation Type: paid
**Owner(s):**
Rainbow Publications, Inc.
24715 Ave. Rockefeller
Valencia, CA 91355
Telephone: (805) 257-4066
Ownership %: 100
**Management:**
M. James & G. Simon .................Publisher
Barbara Lessard ...............Advertising Manager
**Editorial:**
Jim Coleman .............................Editor
Deborah Brown .............................Art Director
Sandra E. Kessler .................Assistant Editor
Deborah Overman .............Copy Chief
Alice Negrete .............Miscellaneous
Doug Churchill .............................Photo
**Desc.:** Deals with all martial arts on a
worldwide scope. The editors think of
their magazine as the reader's digest of
the martial arts. Articles should be
typed, double-spaced with an
average length of approximately 7-10
pages. Black belt has something for
everyone who is interested in some
aspect of the martial arts, self-defense,
oriental culture extensions.
**Readers:** Male and female, semi
professional, sports-minded. Average
income $15,000 to $30,000.

66280
**BODY BOARDING**
950 Calle Amanecer St., Ste. C
San Clemente, CA 92674
Telephone: (714) 492-7873
FAX: (714) 498-6485
Mailing Address:
P.O. Box 3010
San Clemente, CA 92674
Year Established: 1985
Pub. Frequency: q.
Page Size: standard
Subscrip. Rate: $3.95 newsstand; $9.95/yr.
Freelance Pay: 32
Circulation: 4,000
Circulation Type: paid
**Owner(s):**
Western Empire Publishing
950 Calle Amanecer, Ste. C
San Clemente, CA 92672
Telephone: (714) 492-7873

**Management:**
Robert Mignogna .......................Publisher
**Editorial:**
N. Carroll ..........................................Editor
Steve Zeldin .................................Advertising
Larry Moor .........................................Photo
Denise Dorsey ..............Production Assistant

## BOWLING
26376

5301 S. 76th St.
Greendale, WI 53129
Telephone: (414) 421-6400
FAX: (414) 421-7977
Year Established: 1934
Pub. Frequency: bi-m.
Page Size: standard
Subscrip. Rate: $2.50/issue; $10/yr.
Materials: 01,02,05,06,08,21,32,33
Freelance Pay: varies
Print Process: web offset
Circulation: 131,350
Circulation Type: paid
**Owner(s):**
American Bowling Congress
5301 S. 76th St.
Greendale, WI 53129
Telephone: (414) 421-6400
Ownership %: 100
**Management:**
John Dill ...........................Advertising Manager
**Editorial:**
Bill Vint ...........................................Editor
**Desc.:** We use one selected feature
material relating to bowling. This would
include stories about adult male bowlers,
bowling proprietors, any activities at all
of an unusual nature having to do with
ABC sanctioned competition. New
developments in the game in any
respect are written up in popular
magazine style as against trade journal
treatment. We receive much publicity
material not applicable to the bowling
field and we do not use it. Length of
articles runs from 500 to 1,500 words.
**Readers:** ABC secretaries and presidents
120,000. Bowling centers 7,500.
**Deadline:** story-30-45 days prior to pub.
date; news-15-30 days; photo-30-45
days; ads-30 days

## BOWLING REVIEW, THE
26463

431 Chez Paree
Hazelwood, MO 63042
Telephone: (314) 831-4000
FAX: (314) 831-3610
Year Established: 1970
Pub. Frequency: bi-w.
Page Size: tabloid
Subscrip. Rate: $15/yr.
Freelance Pay: $.02/wd.
Circulation: 18,240
Circulation Type: paid
**Owner(s):**
Redbud Media Group, Inc.
427 Chez Paree
Hazelwood, MO 63042
Telephone: (314) 831-4000
Ownership %: 100
**Management:**
Bill Winders ...............................Publisher
H. Hansen .................Advertising Manager
**Editorial:**
V. L. Hansen ......................Executive Editor
V. L. Hansen ..................................Editor
V. L. Hansen .................Book Review Editor
**Desc.:** Covers bowling, sporting goods and
related subjects.

## CANOE & KAYAK MAGAZINE
26378

10526 N.E. 68th, Ste. 5
Kirkland, WA 98033
Telephone: (206) 827-6363
FAX: (206) 827-1893

Mailing Address:
P.O. Box 3146
Kirkland, WA 98083
Year Established: 1973
Pub. Frequency: bi-m.
Page Size: standard
Subscrip. Rate: $3.95/newsstand;
$17.97/yr.
Materials: 01,02,04,05,06,08,09,10,12,15,
19,20,21,25,27,28,29,30,32,33
Freelance Pay: $5/col. in.
Print Process: web offset
Circulation: 68,000
Circulation Type: paid
**Owner(s):**
Canoe America Associates
P.O. Box 3146
Kirkland, WA 98083
Telephone: (206) 827-6363
Ownership %: 100
**Management:**
Drew Deene ...............................Controller
Judy C. Harrison ...........................Publisher
Glen Bernard ...............Advertising Manager
Mary Lou Johnson ..........Circulation Manager
David F. Harrison ..............General Manager
**Editorial:**
Nancy Harrison ......................Senior Editor
Dennis Stuhaug ..................Managing Editor
Peter Becker ...........................Advertising
M. Katherine Therrien ................Art Director
**Desc.:** The magazine's editorial goal is to
inform and entertain the reader, with
lively articles related to the enjoyment of
all aspects of canoeing and kayaking,
including flatwater, wilderness tripping,
whitewater, racing, marathon, poling and
sailing, camping, fishing, photography,
etc. Articles vary to appeal to the
degree of proficiency of various readers,
raging from novice to expert.
Departments include: Conservation,
Safety, Camping, Canoe Sport, Fitness,
Destinations & Techniques.
**Readers:** High income (50 percent over
$35,000), college-educated.
**Deadline:** story-5 mo. prior to pub. date;
news-5 mo.; photo-5 mo.; ads-5 mo.

## CHICAGO SPORTS PROFILES
69423

4711 Golf Rd.
Ste. 900
Skokie, IL 60076
Telephone: (708) 673-0592
FAX: (708) 673-0633
Year Established: 1986
Pub. Frequency: bi-m.
Subscrip. Rate: $15/yr.
Circulation: 40,000
Circulation Type: paid
**Owner(s):**
Sports Profiles
4711 Golf St.
Ste. 900
Skokie, IL 60076
Telephone: (708) 673-0592
Ownership %: 100
**Management:**
Lisa Levine .................................Publisher
**Editorial:**
Paula Blaine .........................Editor in Chief
**Desc.:** Covers local professional and
college sports teams.

## CHRONICLE OF THE HORSE
26382

301 W. Washington St.
Middleburg, VA 22117
Telephone: (703) 687-6341
FAX: (703) 687-3937
Mailing Address:
P.O. Box 46
Middleburg, VA 22117
Year Established: 1937
Pub. Frequency: w.

Page Size: standard
Subscrip. Rate: $1.50/issue; $42/yr.
Freelance Pay: negotiable
Circulation: 23,400
Circulation Type: paid
**Owner(s):**
The Chronicle of the Horse, Inc.
P.O. Box 46
Middleburg, VA 22117
Telephone: (703) 687-6341
Ownership %: 100
**Management:**
Robert Banner, Jr. .......................Publisher
**Editorial:**
John Strassburger ...........................Editor
Nancy L. Comer ..................Managing Editor
Dale Hogoboom ..........................Treasurer
**Desc.:** Dedicated to those interested in
horse and horse sports. Emphasis on
breeding, hunting, showing,
steeplechase racing, combined
training dressage and driving.
**Readers:** Everyone who likes all phases of
horse sports.

## CIRCLE TRACK
66699

6420 Wilshire Blvd.
Los Angeles, CA 90048
Telephone: (213) 782-2000
FAX: (213) 782-2263
Year Established: 1982
Pub. Frequency: m.
Subscrip. Rate: $3.95; $23.95/yr.
Freelance Pay: $200/pg.
Circulation: 125,000
Circulation Type: paid
**Owner(s):**
Petersen Publishing Co.
6420 Wilshire Blvd.
Los Angeles, CA 90048
Telephone: (213) 782-2000
FAX: (213) 782-2263
Ownership %: 100
**Editorial:**
Bob Carpenter ....................Executive Editor
Gle Grissom ....................................Editor
Virginia Moore ........................Design Editor
**Desc.:** Combines an extensive array of
how-to and technical articles, features
action photos, event coverage and
inside information from home-built,
sportsman hobby-stock racing to the
exotic, state of the art, professional
world of Indy cars, and everything in
between.
**Readers:** Mostly male, age 30-40.

## CLIMBING
67275

1101 Village Rd.
Ste. LL1B
Carbondale, CO 81623
Telephone: (303) 963-9449
FAX: (303) 963-9442
Year Established: 1970
Pub. Frequency: 8/yr.
Page Size: Standard
Subscrip. Rate: $4.95 newsstand; $28/yr.
Circulation: 36075
Circulation Type: paid
**Owner(s):**
Michael & Julie Kennedy
502 Main
Carbondale, CO 81623
Telephone: (303) 963-9449
Ownership %: 100
**Management:**
Michael Kennedy ...........................President
Michael Kennedy ...........................Publisher
Julie Kennedy ...............Advertising Manager
Penn Newhard ........................Sales Manager

## COLORADO GOLF MAGAZINE
71264

559 Second Ave.
Castle Rock, CO 80104
Telephone: (303) 688-5853
Pub. Frequency: q.
Page Size: tabloid
Subscrip. Rate: $3.50 newsstand; $10/yr.
Circulation: 50,000
Circulation Type: paid
**Owner(s):**
Colorado Sports Publications
559 Second Ave.
Castle Rock, CO 80104
Ownership %: 100
**Management:**
Tim Pade ...................................Publisher
**Editorial:**
Tim Pade ......................................Editor

## CROSS COUNTRY SKIER
66713

1823 Freemont Ave. S.
Minneapolis, MN 55043
Telephone: (612) 337-0312
FAX: (612) 377-0312
Year Established: 1976
Pub. Frequency: 5/yr.
Subscrip. Rate: $12.97/yr.
Circulation: 75,000
Circulation Type: paid
**Owner(s):**
Collins Chase Inc.
1823 Freemont Ave. S.
Minneapolis, MN 55403
Telephone: (612) 337-0312
Ownership %: 100
**Management:**
Jim Chase ...................................Publisher
**Editorial:**
Jim Chase ......................................Editor
Peggy Ware ......................Assistant Editor
**Desc.:** Edited for the enthusiast cross
country skier who wants to learn more
about the sport.
**Readers:** Cross Country Skiers

## EXECUTIVE GOLFER
26386

2171 Campus Dr.
Ste. 330
Irvine, CA 92715-1499
Telephone: (714) 752-6474
FAX: (714) 752-0398
Year Established: 1972
Pub. Frequency: bi-m.
Page Size: standard
Subscrip. Rate: $9/yr.; $20/3 yrs.
Freelance Pay: varies
Circulation: 125,000
Circulation Type: controlled
**Owner(s):**
Pazdur Publishing Co.
2171 Campus Dr.
Irvine, CA 92715-1499
Telephone: (714) 752-6474
Ownership %: 100
**Management:**
Theda Pazdur .......................Vice President
Mark Pazdur .........................Vice President
Edward Pazdur ...........................Publisher
**Editorial:**
Edward Pazdur ................................Editor
Sho Kaneko .............................Art Director
Joyce Stevens ....................Associate Editor
**Desc.:** A golf oriented magazine that
contains articles of interest to a private
country club golfer, with special focus on
travel, golf communities and golf resorts.
**Readers:** America's richest golfers.
Average age is 52. Very affluent and
sophisticated, highly educated. Average
income $180,000 per year.

**Materials Accepted/Included:** 01-Business news 02-By-line articles 03-Fashion news 04-Food news 05-Freelance copy 06-Letters to editor 07-Real estate news 08-Sports news 09-Travel news
10-Book rev. 11-Movie rev. 12-Music rev. 13-TV rev. 14-Theater rev. 15-Coming events 16-Obituaries 17-Question & answer 18-Social announcements 19-Artwork 20-Cartoons 21-Photos 22-TV listings
23-Audio rec. 24-Video rec. 25-Books 26-Films/film clips 27-Personnel news 28-Press releases 29-New product news/photos 30-Trade lit. 31-Contracts awarded 32-Display adv. 33-Classified adv.

6-113

## FANTASY BASEBALL
67285

700 E. State St.
Iola, WI 54990
Telephone: (715) 445-2214
FAX: (715) 445-4087
Year Established: 1990
Pub. Frequency: q.
Page Size: standard
Subscrip. Rate: $9.95/yr.
Materials: 02,05,32,33
Print Process: web offset
Circulation: 110,400
Circulation Type: paid
**Owner(s):**
Krause Publications, Inc.
700 E. State St.
Iola, WI 54990
Telephone: (715) 445-2214
Ownership %: 100
**Management:**
Cliff Mishler ..............................President
Bob Lemke ..............................Publisher
Hugh McAloon .................Advertising Manager
**Editorial:**
Greg Ambrosius ..........................Editor
**Readers:** Participants in fantasy baseball, football, and basketball leagues. Mostly males; ages 25-45.

## FLEX
54010

21100 Erwin St.
Woodland Hills, CA 91367
Telephone: (818) 884-6800
FAX: (818) 704-5734
Year Established: 1983
Pub. Frequency: m.
Page Size: standard
Subscrip. Rate: $3.95 newsstand;
$29.97/yr.
Materials: 32
Freelance Pay: negotiable
Circulation: 145,000
Circulation Type: paid
**Owner(s):**
Weider Publications, Inc.
21100 Erwin St.
Woodland Hills, CA 91367
Telephone: (818) 884-6800
Ownership %: 100
**Management:**
Joseph Weider ..........................Publisher
Bob Washburn .................Advertising Manager
**Editorial:**
Kerry Kindela .....................Editor in Chief
Julian Schmidt ............................Editor
George De Pirro ................Managing Editor
Ruth Silverman .............Associate Publisher
Marty Withrow ................Creative Director
**Desc.:** Official publication of the International Federation of Body Builders. Covers major contests and gives in-depth behind-the-scenes view as well as training tips.
**Readers:** Men and women, 18-34 years old.

## FLORIDA SPORTSMAN
26400

5901 S.W. 74th St.
Miami, FL 33143
Telephone: (305) 661-4222
FAX: (305) 284-0277
Year Established: 1969
Pub. Frequency: m.
Page Size: standard
Subscrip. Rate: $16.95/yr.
Freelance Pay: $90-$400/article
Circulation: 106,500
Circulation Type: paid

**Owner(s):**
Wickstrom Publishers, Inc.
5901 S.W. 74th St.
Miami, FL 33143
Telephone: (305) 661-4222
FAX: (305) 284-0277
Ownership %: 100
**Management:**
Karl Wickstrom ..........................President
Karl Wickstrom ..........................Publisher
Bob L. Mitchell .................Advertising Manager
**Editorial:**
Biff Lampton ............................Editor
Don Mann .....................Associate Editor
Eric Paul .................New Product Editor
Ted Baker ..................................Photo
**Desc.:** Published for those with outdoor interests, concerning Florida, the Bahamas and tropical environments. Coverage includes: boating, fishing, diving, camping, hunting, ecology.
**Readers:** Affluent, mostly male, mostly boat-owners, in Florida and the surrounding Islands.

## FOOTBALL DIGEST
69130

990 Grove St.
Evanston, IL 60201-4370
Telephone: (708) 491-6440
Year Established: 1971
Pub. Frequency: 10/yr.
Page Size: standard
Subscrip. Rate: $22/yr. US; $20/yr. foreign
Circulation: 200,000
Circulation Type: paid
**Owner(s):**
Century Publishing Co.
990 Grove St.
Evanston, IL 60201-4370
Telephone: (708) 491-6440
Ownership %: 100
**Editorial:**
Vince Aversano ..........................Editor
**Desc.:** Provides statistics and features on pro and college football.

## FOOTBALL NEWS, THE
26401

P.O. Box 526600
Miami, FL 33152
Telephone: (305) 594-0508
Year Established: 1939
Pub. Frequency: 20/season: Mon.
Page Size: tabloid
Subscrip. Rate: $34.95/season
Freelance Pay: $50-$100/article; $10-$50/photo
**Owner(s):**
Curtis Publishing Co.
P.O. Box 526600
Miami, FL 33152
Telephone: (305) 594-0508
FAX: (305) 594-0518
Ownership %: 100
**Management:**
Thomas Curtis ..........................Publisher
Ken Keidel ................Advertising Manager
**Editorial:**
Andrew Cohen ............................Editor
**Desc.:** The "Bible" of the college and pro football worlds. It is well read by people in football and fans across the country who want more football information than they can find in their daily newspaper. It is to the football world what the Wall Street Journal is to the business world.
**Readers:** $40,000 plus salary. Average age is 40.

## FORE MAGAZINE
26402

3740 Cahuenga Blvd.
Studio City, CA 91604
Telephone: (818) 980-3630
FAX: (818) 980-1808

Mailing Address:
P.O. Box 8386
N. Hollywood, CA 91609
Year Established: 1968
Pub. Frequency: bi-m.
Page Size: standard
Subscrip. Rate: $1/yr. members only
Freelance Pay: negotiable
Print Process: web offset
Circulation: 130,000
Circulation Type: controlled & paid

**Owner(s):**
Southern California Golf Assoc.
3740 Cahuenga Blvd.
Studio City, CA 91604
Telephone: (818) 980-3630
Ownership %: 100
**Management:**
Robert D. Thomas ..........................Publisher
Robert D. Thomas ..........Advertising Manager
**Editorial:**
Robert D. Thomas .................Executive Editor
Mike Peck .................New Products Editor
**Desc.:** Published for and distributed to the members of the 800 golf and country clubs and affiliated golf clubs of the Southern California Golf Association. Covers professional and amateur tournaments, golf history, personality profiles on outstanding players and golf industry spokesmen, golf resort, new products, and special departments on golf rules and handicapping. Departments include: News in Brief, President's Message, Letters to the Editor, New Club Welcome, Resorts and Tours, Directory of Member Clubs, Organizational Chart, Desert Club Directory, New Products, Book Reviews.
**Readers:** Average family size of 2.6, with two golfing members was 67.7%. Average household income: $163,800, average home value: $332,239. More than 77% are college graduates. One third have more than one dwelling.
**Deadline:** story-1st of mo. prior to pub. mo.; news-1st of mo. prior; photo-1st of mo. prior; ads-20th of mo. 2 mos. prior to pub. date

## GAMECOCK
26403

Junction Hwy. 96 & 45 N.
Hartford, AR 72938
Telephone: (501) 639-2324
Mailing Address:
P.O. Box 158
Hartford, AR 72938
Year Established: 1937
Pub. Frequency: m.; Sep.-July
Page Size: pocket
Subscrip. Rate: $20/yr. US; $30/yr. foreign
Circulation: 16,000
Circulation Type: paid
**Owner(s):**
Marburger Publishing Co., Inc.
P.O. Box 158
Hartford, AR 72938
Telephone: (501) 639-2324
Ownership %: 100
**Management:**
J.C. Griffiths ..........................Publisher
Rose M. Griffiths ............Circulation Manager
**Desc.:** Essentially devoted to the raising of game fowl. Material is limited; uses only stories or articles that pertain to health and nutritional developments in general poultry industry. Reports on club activities, breeders association meetings, other news in the sport.
**Readers:** South and Southwest rural; East, Midwest Majority are small businessmen, working people, farmers.

## GOLF & TRAVEL
26518

7142 Fairway Bend Cir.
Sarasota, FL 34243
Telephone: (813) 355-8777
Year Established: 1968
Pub. Frequency: a.
Page Size: standard
Subscrip. Rate: free
Circulation: 75,650
Circulation Type: controlled
**Owner(s):**
Golf & Travel
7142 Fairway Bend Circle
Sarasota, FL 34243
Telephone: (813) 355-8777
Ownership %: 100
**Management:**
Al Forrest ..........................President
Al Forrest ..........................Publisher
Al Forrest ................Advertising Manager
**Editorial:**
Al Forrest ............................Editor
Carol Forrest .....................Assistant Editor
Al Forrest ................Book Review Editor
Al Forrest ..........................Columnist
**Desc.:** A local and regional golf and travel publication.
**Readers:** Consumer oriented.

## GOLF DIGEST
23188

5520 Park Ave.
Trumbull, CT 06611
Telephone: (203) 373-7000
FAX: (203) 373-7033
Year Established: 1950
Pub. Frequency: m.
Page Size: oversize
Subscrip. Rate: $23.94/yr.
Freelance Pay: negotiable
Circulation: 1,350,000
Circulation Type: paid
**Owner(s):**
New York Times Co., The
229 W. 43rd St.
New York, NY 10036
Telephone: (212) 556-1234
Ownership %: 100
**Bureau(s):**
Golf Digest
500 N. Michigan Ave.
Chicago, IL 60611
Telephone: (312) 467-4333
Contact: Robert Caldwell
**Management:**
Jay FitzGerald ..........................President
Carl Stitzer ................Executive Vice President
Hugh White ..........................Vice President
Joseph L. Mossa ..................Vice President
Alan M. Deyoe, Jr. ................Vice President
Marcia Strousse ..................Vice President
Jay FitzGerald ..........................Publisher
Bob Maxon ................Advertising Manager
Ross Fleckenstein ..............Public Relations Manager
Daryn Moffa ................Traffic Manager
**Editorial:**
Jerry Tarde ............................Exec. Editor
Dwayne Netland ................Senior Editor
Ross Goodner ................Senior Editor
Don Wade ................Senior Editor
Ron Whitten ............................Editor
Roger Schiffman ................Managing Editor
Cliff Schrock ............Assistant Managing Editor
Nick Seitz ................Editorial Director
Rick Bonti ..........................Advertising
Nick DiDio ..........................Art Director
Lois Hains .....................Assistant Editor
Lorin Anderson .....................Assistant Editor
Peter McCleery .................Associate Editor
Guy Yocom .................Associate Editor
Eileen Broderick ................Fashion Editor
Steve Szurlej ..........................Photographer

**Materials Accepted/Included:** 01-Business news 02-By-line articles 03-Fashion news 04-Food news 05-Freelance copy 06-Letters to editor 07-Real estate news 08-Sports news 09-Travel news 10-Book rev. 11-Movie rev. 12-Music rev. 13-TV rev. 14-Theater rev. 15-Coming events 16-Obituaries 17-Question & answer 18-Social announcements 19-Artwork 20-Cartoons 21-Photos 22-TV listings 23-Audio rec. 24-Video rec. 25-Books 26-Films/film clips 27-Personnel news 28-Press releases 29-New product news/photos 30-Trade lit. 31-Contracts awarded 32-Display adv. 33-Classified adv.

**Desc.:** Magazine for golfers divided into two general parts: instruction and features. Instruction is usually from professional teachers; an ordinary freelancer would not do them unless he worked with a pro. Personality stories are purchased from contributors. By-lined features on unusual golf-related events or persons are also used. Length of minor articles not more than 1,000 words; major not more than 3,000. Always looking for good photos of name golfers. Departments include: Letters, Golf Fashions, Humor, Cartoons, column material (short items).
**Readers:** Golfers at all levels of ability.

## GOLF FOR WOMEN
65430

P.O. Box 951989
Lake Mary, FL 32795-1989
Telephone: (407) 333-8821
FAX: (407) 333-8861
Year Established: 1988
Pub. Frequency: bi-m.
Page Size: standard
Subscrip. Rate: $3.50 newsstand; $14.97/yr.
Freelance Pay: $.40/wd.
Circulation: 300,000
Circulation Type: paid
**Owner(s):**
Meredith Corp.
1716 Locust St.
Des Moines, IA 50336
Telephone: (515) 284-3000
Ownership %: 100
**Management:**
David Cohen .................................Publisher
**Editorial:**
Patricia Baldwin .........................Editor in Chief
**Desc.:** Articles on instruction, equipment, and listings, results of golf tournaments, golf travel and fashion, features on women golfers, both professional and amateur.
**Readers:** Women golfers.

## GOLF INTERNATIONAL MAGAZINE
66680

559 Second Ave.
Castle Rock, CO 80104
Telephone: (303) 688-5853
Year Established: 1990
Pub. Frequency: q.
Page Size: standard
Subscrip. Rate: $3.50 newsstand; $19.95/yr.
Wire service(s): web
Circulation: 55,000
Circulation Type: paid
**Owner(s):**
Colorado Sports Publications
559 Second Ave.
Castle Rock, CO 80104
Telephone: (303) 688-5853
Ownership %: 100
**Management:**
Tim Pade ................................Publisher
**Editorial:**
Tim Pade ....................................Editor

## GOLF JOURNAL
26405

Liberty Corner Rd.
Far Hills, NJ 07931
Telephone: (201) 234-2300
  Far Hills, NJ 07931
Year Established: 1948
Pub. Frequency: 9/yr.
Page Size: standard
Subscrip. Rate: free
Materials: 05,06,08,10,11,12,15,16,20,21
Freelance Pay: varies
Circulation: 380,000
Circulation Type: paid

**Owner(s):**
United States Golf Association
Golf House, P.O. Box 708
Far Hills, NJ 07931
Telephone: (201) 234-2300
Ownership %: 100
**Editorial:**
David Earl .................................Editor
Rich Skyzinski ....................Managing Editor
Diane Chrenko-Becker ..............Art Director
Nancy Castiglione .....................Secretary
**Desc.:** Golf in general. Official publication of U.S. Golf Assn.
**Deadline:** story-1 mo. prior to pub. date; news-1 mo. prior; photo-1 mo. prior; ads-1 mo. prior

## GOLF MAGAZINE
26406

Two Park Ave.
New York, NY 10016
Telephone: (212) 779-5000
Year Established: 1959
Pub. Frequency: m.
Page Size: standard
Subscrip. Rate: $19.94/yr.
Freelance Pay: $100-$1500/article
Circulation: 1,250,000
Circulation Type: paid
**Owner(s):**
Times Mirror Magazines, Inc.
2 Park Ave.
New York, NY 10016
Telephone: (212) 779-5000
Ownership %: 100
**Management:**
Francis P. Pandolf .....................President
Peter Bonanni .........................Publisher
**Editorial:**
George Peper ......................Editor in Chief
John Andrisani .....................Senior Editor
David Barrett .......................Senior Editor
Mike Parkey ........................Senior Editor
Brian McCallen .....................Senior Editor
James A. Frank ..........................Editor
**Desc.:** Departments Include: Champs, Clinic, Hotline, Private Lessons, The Golf Course.
**Readers:** The recreational golfer.

## GOLF NEWS MAGAZINE
69735

P.O. Box 1040
Rancho Mirage, CA 92270
Telephone: (619) 324-8333
FAX: (619) 324-8011
Year Established: 1984
Pub. Frequency: 10/yr.
Page Size: oversize
Subscrip. Rate: $14/yr.; $22/2 yrs.; $34/3 yr.
Freelance Pay: negotiable
Print Process: web
Circulation: 28,000
Circulation Type: controlled
**Owner(s):**
Dan & Joan Poppers
P.O. Box 1040
Rancho Mirage, CA 92270
Telephone: (619) 324-8333
Ownership %: 100
**Management:**
Dan Poppers ...........................Publisher
Joan Poppers ..........................Publisher
**Desc.:** Covers news of golf events in Southern California.

## GOLF WORLD
69755

5520 Park Ave.
Trumbull, CT 06611
Telephone: (203) 373-7000
Mailing Address:
  P.O. Box 395
  Trumbull, CT 06611-0395
Year Established: 1947
Pub. Frequency: w.

Page Size: standard
Subscrip. Rate: $39.94/yr. US; $64/yr. Canada; $66/yr. foreign
Materials: 06,21,28,30,32,33
Circulation: 150,000
Circulation Type: paid
**Owner(s):**
New York Times Co. Magazine Group
5520 Park Ave.
Trumbull, CT 06611
Telephone: (203) 373-7000
Ownership %: 100
**Management:**
Jay Fitzgerald ..........................President
S.C. Croft ..........................Vice President
I.A. DiGeronimo ..................Vice President
Robert Maxon .........................Publisher
**Editorial:**
Nick Seitz .........................Editor in Chief
Terry Galvin ..............................Editor
Jim Herre ...........................Managing Editor
Bret Avery ...............Assistant Managing Editor
William G. Ridnour ............Advertising Director
Geoff Russell ......................Associate Editor
Rod Meiers ..............................Treasurer

## GORGE GUIDE
69424

500 Morton Rd.
Hood River, OR 97031
*see Consumer Magazine, Boating*

## GREYHOUND REVIEW, THE
25739

P.O. Box 543
Abilene, KS 67410
Telephone: (913) 263-4660
FAX: (913) 263-4689
Year Established: 1911
Pub. Frequency: m.
Page Size: standard
Subscrip. Rate: $3 newsstand; $30/yr. plus tax in FL & KS
Materials: 05,06,21,32,33
Freelance Pay: $50-$125/article
Circulation: 6,500
Circulation Type: paid
**Owner(s):**
National Greyhound Association
P.O. Box 543
Abilene, KS 67410
Telephone: (913) 263-4660
Ownership %: 100
**Editorial:**
Gary Guccione ......................Exec. Editor
Tim Horan ..........................Managing Editor
**Desc.:** Reports of recent news in greyhound racing industry, including racetrack features, articles about veterinary advancements in regard to greyhounds, breeding news, article about latest goings-on in greyhound racing and breeding; editorials, guest editorials, letters to the editor section; litters and breeding of greyhounds reported to the National Greyhound Association. Features on industry personalities, interviews with regional standouts and national stars.
**Readers:** Greyhound owners & breeders.

## GRIT & STEEL
26408

2148 Beach St.
Gaffney, SC 29340
Telephone: (803) 489-2324
FAX: (803) 489-2324
Mailing Address:
  P.O. Drawer 280
  Gaffney, SC 29342
Year Established: 1899
Pub. Frequency: m.
Page Size: standard
Subscrip. Rate: $16/yr. US; $20/yr. foreign
Circulation: 5,000
Circulation Type: paid

**Owner(s):**
DeCamp Publishing Co.
P.O. Drawer 280
Gaffney, SC 29342
Telephone: (803) 489-2324
**Management:**
Joe Mac Skinner ........................Manager
**Editorial:**
Joe Mac Skinner .........................Editor
**Desc.:** Articles on game fowl fighting, breeding, health. Reports on club activities and other news of the sports.
**Readers:** Game fowl enthusiasts.

## GUN REPORT, THE
25981

110 S. College Ave.
Aledo, IL 61231
Telephone: (309) 582-5311
FAX: (309) 582-5555
Mailing Address:
  P.O. Box 38
  Aledo, IL 61231
Year Established: 1955
Pub. Frequency: m.
Page Size: standard
Subscrip. Rate: $29.95/yr.
Materials: 02,06,16,17,21,32,33
Print Process: offset
Circulation: 6,000
Circulation Type: paid
**Owner(s):**
Gun Report
Aledo, IL
Ownership %: 100
**Management:**
Kenneth W. Liggett ......................President
Kenneth W. Liggett ......................Publisher
Kathy Jackson ...............Advertising Manager
Greg Liggett ...................Business Manager
Dory Liggett ...............Circulation Manager
**Editorial:**
Kenneth W. Liggett ...............Executive Editor
Eric Vaule ...........................Miscellaneous
Charles R. Suydam ..................Miscellaneous
Kandy Harrison ..............Publication Director
**Desc.:** Features and articles concerning history and facts about antique guns, cartridges, accessories and accoutrements. Columns include: Book Reviews, Gun Collectors' Club Meetings, Cartridge and Antique Arms Prices, Question and Answers, Cartridge Collector.
**Readers:** Gun enthusiasts and cartridge collectors.
**Deadline:** ads-1st of ea. mo.

## GUNS MAGAZINE
25982

591 Camino de la Reina, Ste. 200
San Diego, CA 92108
Telephone: (619) 297-5352
Year Established: 1955
Pub. Frequency: m.
Page Size: standard
Subscrip. Rate: $2.95/newsstand; $19.95/yr.
Freelance Pay: $100-$500/article
Circulation: 175,000
Circulation Type: paid
**Owner(s):**
Publishers Development Corp.
591 Camino de la Reina
San Diego, CA 92108
Telephone: (619) 297-8520
Ownership %: 100
**Management:**
Tom Von Rosen ........................President
George Von Rosen .....................Publisher
Denny Fallon ..............Advertising Manager
**Editorial:**
Jerry Lee .................................Editor
Bix Bigler ..............................Art Editor

**Materials Accepted/Included:** 01-Business news 02-By-line articles 03-Fashion news 04-Food news 05-Freelance copy 06-Letters to editor 07-Real estate news 08-Sports news 09-Travel news 10-Book rev. 11-Movie rev. 12-Music rev. 13-TV rev. 14-Theater rev. 15-Coming events 16-Obituaries 17-Question & answer 18-Social announcements 19-Artwork 20-Cartoons 21-Photos 22-TV listings 23-Audio rec. 24-Video rec. 25-Books 26-Films/film clips 27-Personnel news 28-Press releases 29-New product news/photos 30-Trade lit. 31-Contracts awarded 32-Display adv. 33-Classified adv.

6-115

**Desc.:** Articles are fact features on firearms use, design, hunting, sport and military shooting, collections and history. Authors must be responsible for the technical correctness of information presented, and for any security clearances required in the case of current military stories.
**Readers:** Collectors, hunters, target shooters and firearms enthusiasts.

26410
### GUN WORLD
34249 Camino Capistrano
Capistrano Beach, CA 92624
Telephone: (714) 493-2101
Mailing Address:
P.O. Box 2429
Capistrano Beach, CA 92624
Year Established: 1960
Pub. Frequency: 13/yr.
Page Size: standard
Subscrip. Rate: $20/yr.
Freelance Pay: varies
Circulation: 130,000
Circulation Type: paid
**Owner(s):**
Gallant/Charger Publications, Inc.
P.O. Box 2429
Capistrano Beach, CA 92624
Telephone: (714) 493-2101
Ownership %: 100
**Management:**
Jack Lewis .......................President
Jack Lewis .......................Publisher
Jack Mitchell ..................Advertising Manager
Mark Thiffault .........................General Manager
**Editorial:**
Jack Lewis ...............................Editor
Dean A. Grennell ....................Managing Editor
Rueselle Gilbert ......................Art Director
Roger Combs .................New Product Editor
**Desc.:** Covers all phases of small arms for recreation. Covering new product news, trade literature and general news. Staff articles, by-lined articles and photos are used. Departments include: New Products, Reloading Clinic, Law Enforcement, Antique Gun News, Shotgunning With Bob Stack, Varmint Hunting, Knife News.
**Readers:** Firearms enthusiasts.

68886
### HANDGUNNING
News Plz.
P.O. Box 1790
Peoria, IL 61656
Telephone: (309) 682-6626
FAX: (309) 682-7394
Year Established: 1987
Pub. Frequency: bi-m.
Page Size: standard
Subscrip. Rate: $3.95 newsstand;
$19.98/yr.
Materials: 08,29,32,33
Circulation: 80,000
Circulation Type: paid
**Owner(s):**
Veronis Suhler Associates, Inc.
350 Park Ave.
New York, NY 10022
Ownership %: 100
**Management:**
Chuck Boysen ..................Circulation Manager
**Editorial:**
John Crowley ...........................Editor
Art Setterlund ....................Advertising Director
**Desc.:** Premier journal of handgun enthusiasts.

26411
### HANDLOADER
6471 Airpark Dr.
Prescott, AZ 86301
Telephone: (602) 445-7810
FAX: (602) 778-5124

Year Established: 1964
Pub. Frequency: bi-m.
Page Size: standard
Subscrip. Rate: $29/yr.
Freelance Pay: $250-$400/article
Circulation: 36,000
Circulation Type: paid
**Owner(s):**
Wolfe Publishing Co., Inc.
6471 Airpark Dr.
Prescott, AZ 86301
Telephone: (602) 455-7810
Ownership %: 100
**Management:**
Mark Harris ..............................President
Mark Harris ..............................Publisher
Jana Kosco ........................Advertising Manager
Tammy Rossi ....................Circulation Manager
**Editorial:**
Dave Scovill ...............................Editor
**Desc.:** Semi-technical publication covering shooting, ballistics and the handloading of ammunition.

71269
### HEALTH CARE & GROOMING
12204 Covington Rd.
Fort Wayne, IN 46804
Telephone: (219) 625-4030
FAX: (219) 625-3480
Year Established: 1985
Pub. Frequency: a.: Apr.
Page Size: standard
Subscrip. Rate: $3.75
Materials: 32,33
Print Process: offset
Circulation: 29,000
Circulation Type: paid
**Owner(s):**
Midwest Hunter, Inc.
12204 Covington Rd.
Fort Wayn, IN 46804
Telephone: (219) 625-4030
Ownership %: 100
**Management:**
Laura Allen ..............................Publisher
Carol Craig ......................Advertising Manager
**Editorial:**
Laura Allen ...............................Editor
Lisa Allen ..............................Creative Director

68910
### HORSES INTERNATIONAL
21 Greenview
Carlsbad, CA 92009
Telephone: (619) 931-9958
FAX: (619) 931-0650
Year Established: 1962
Pub. Frequency: bi-m.
Subscrip. Rate: $7.50/newsstand;
$24.95/yr.
Materials: 02,05,06,08,10,21,30
Print Process: offset
Circulation: 10,000
Circulation Type: paid
**Owner(s):**
Horses International
21 Greenview
Carlsbad, CA 92009
Telephone: (619) 931-9958
Ownership %: 100
**Editorial:**
John Quirk ...............................Editor
**Desc.:** Covers international equestrian events.

68911
### HUNTER & SPORT HORSE
12204 Covington Rd.
Fort Wayne, IN 46804
Telephone: (219) 625-4030
FAX: (219) 625-3480
Year Established: 1989
Pub. Frequency: bi-m.

Page Size: standard
Subscrip. Rate: $3.75 newsstand;
$15.99/yr.
Materials: 32,33
Print Process: offset
Circulation: 29,000
Circulation Type: paid
**Owner(s):**
Midwest Hunter, Inc.
12204 Covington Rd.
Fort Wayne, IN 46804
Telephone: (219) 625-4030
Ownership %: 100
**Management:**
Laura Allen ..............................Publisher
Carol Craig ......................Advertising Manager
**Editorial:**
Laura Allen ...............................Editor
Lisa Allen ..............................Creative Director
**Desc.:** Covers dressage, combined training, hunter-jumper, and related equestrian sports.

69747
### INSIDE SPORTS
990 Grove St.
Evanston, IL 60201-4370
Telephone: (708) 491-6440
Year Established: 1979
Pub. Frequency: m.
Subscrip. Rate: $2.95 newsstand; $22/yr.
Circulation: 675,000
Circulation Type: paid
**Owner(s):**
Century Publishing Co.
990 Grove St.
Evanston, IL 60201
Telephone: (708) 491-6440
Ownership %: 100
**Management:**
Jerry Croft ..................Executive Vice President
Jerry Croft ..............................Publisher
Marty Michalek ..................Circulation Manager
**Editorial:**
Ken Leiker ...............................Editor

69499
### INSIDE TRIATHLON
1830 N. 55th St.
Boulder, CO 80301-2700
Telephone: (303) 440-0601
FAX: (303) 444-6788
Year Established: 1986
Pub. Frequency: 9/yr.
Subscrip. Rate: $19.95/yr.
**Owner(s):**
Inside Communications, Inc.
1830 N. 55th St.
Boulder, CO 80301-2700
Telephone: (303) 440-0601
Ownership %: 100
**Management:**
Felix Magawan ......................Publisher
**Editorial:**
Chris Newbound ...........................Editor
Randy Pelpon ....................Advertising Director

66716
### INSIGHTS
11250 Waples Mill Rd.
Fairfax, VA 22033
Telephone: (703) 267-1584
Year Established: 1981
Pub. Frequency: m.
Subscrip. Rate: $10/yr.
Materials: 02,05,21,28,32
Circulation: 48,000
Circulation Type: controlled
**Owner(s):**
National Rifle Association of America
11250 Waples Mill Rd.
Fairfax, VA 22033
Telephone: (703) 267-1584
Ownership %: 100
**Editorial:**
Brenda Balessandro ..................Executive Editor
John Robbins ...............................Editor

26416
### KARATE-KUNG FU ILLUSTRATED
24715 Ave. Rockefeller
Santa Clarita, CA 91380
Telephone: (805) 257-4066
FAX: (805) 257-3018
Mailing Address:
P.O. Box 918
Santa Clarita, CA 91380-0918
Year Established: 1971
Pub. Frequency: bi-m
Page Size: standard
Subscrip. Rate: $19.50/2 yrs.
Materials: 02,05,06,08,19,21,28,29,30,32
Freelance Pay: $75-$250/article
Print Process: web
Circulation: 55,000
Circulation Type: paid
**Owner(s):**
Rainbow Publications, Inc.
P.O. Box 918
Santa Clarita, CA 91380-0918
Telephone: (805) 257-4066
Ownership %: 100
**Management:**
Michael James ..............................Publisher
Barbara Lessard ..............Advertising Manager
**Editorial:**
Bob Young ...............................Editor
Debbie Brown ..............................Art Director
Geri Simon .........................Assistant Publisher
**Desc.:** Edited for those interested in karate and kung fu, for both beginning and advanced students. Features include profiles of well-known U.S players and instructors, national tournament coverage and departments.
**Readers:** Ages 15-60, male and female with self-defense interest and sport-minded.
**Deadline:** story-1st wk. of mo.; ads-2nd wk. of mo.

71262
### MARLIN MAGAZINE
330 W. Canton Ave.
Winter Park, FL 32789
Telephone: (407) 628-4802
FAX: (407) 628-7061
Mailing Address:
P.O. Box 2456
Winter Park, FL 32790
Pub. Frequency: 7/yr.
Page Size: standard
Subscrip. Rate: $3.95 newsstand;
$24.95/yr.
Materials: 05,32
Freelance Pay: $25-$500/article
Circulation: 32,252
Circulation Type: paid
**Owner(s):**
World Publications, Inc.
P.O. Box 2456
Winter Park, FL 32790
Telephone: (407) 628-4802
Ownership %: 100
**Management:**
Terry Snow ..............................Publisher
**Editorial:**
David Ritchie ...............................Editor
Glenn Hughes ....................Advertising Director
Trish Carter ........................Circulation Director
Jim Robinson ..................Circulation Systems Manager

69465
### METRO GOLF
2300 N St., N.W., Ste. 600
Washington, DC 20037
Telephone: (202) 663-9015
FAX: (202) 663-9016
Year Established: 1991
Pub. Frequency: 8/yr.
Page Size: standard
Subscrip. Rate: $3/newsstand; $14.95/yr.
Materials: 02,03,05,06,07,08,10,11,21,24,
25,28,29,32,33

Freelance Pay: varies
Circulation: 50,000
Circulation Type: controlled & paid
**Owner(s):**
Summerville Press, Inc.
2300 N St., N.W., Ste. 600
Washington, DC 20037
Telephone: (202) 663-9015
Ownership %: 100
**Editorial:**
John Holmes ...............................Editor
**Desc.:** Contains men's and women's
fashions, travel in the Mid-Atlantic
region, Southeast and elsewhere; a
holiday gift guide, equipment reviews,
regional tournament news; lessons and
instruction; and other golf-related
features.
**Deadline:** story-2 mo. prior to pub. date;
news-6 wks.; photo-2 mo.

69123
## METROSPORTS MAGAZINE
695 Washington St.
New York, NY 10014
Telephone: (212) 627-7040
FAX: (212) 242-3293
Year Established: 1974
Pub. Frequency: 11/yr.
Page Size: tabloid
Subscrip. Rate: $18/yr.
Materials: 32
Print Process: offset
Circulation: 185,000
Circulation Type: controlled
**Owner(s):**
Tate House Enterprises, Inc.
695 Washington St.
New York, NY 10014
Telephone: (212) 627-7040
Ownership %: 100
**Management:**
S. Dean ..............................Circulation Manager
**Editorial:**
Miles Tate ..............................Editor
Julie Tate ..............................Editor
Dominick Certelli ..............................Sales
**Desc.:** Covers all aspects of adult
recreational sports and fitness. Written
in 2 editions for the New York and
Boston areas.

26418
## MICHIGAN SNOWMOBILER
01615 Advance, E. Jordan Rd.
East Jordan, MI 49727
Telephone: (616) 536-2371
Mailing Address:
P.O. Box 417
East Jordan, MI 49727
Year Established: 1967
Pub. Frequency: bi-m.
Page Size: tabloid
Subscrip. Rate: $8/yr.; $14/2 yrs.; $20/3
yrs.
Freelance Pay: $.90/col. in.; $5/photo
accepted
Circulation: 28,900
Circulation Type: controlled
**Owner(s):**
Michigan Snowmobiler, Inc.
P.O. Box 417
East Jordan, MI 49727
Telephone: (616) 536-2371
Ownership %: 100
**Management:**
Wilma Sayles ..............................President
Lyle Shipe ..............................Advertising Manager
Nancy Shipe ..............................General Manager
**Editorial:**
Lyle Shipe ..............................Editor
Lyle Shipe ..............................Columnist
Patty Tisron ..............................New Products Editor
Karen Holcomb ..............................Writer

**Desc.:** A winter recreational snowmobile
vehicle newspaper. Feature articles deal
with snowmobiling, organized community
snowmobile events, and various aspects
of snowmobile production. Regular
monthly departments include:
Snowmobiling Editorials, The Snow
Scene, New Snowmobiling Products,
State Snowmobile Association News and
Snowmobile Racing. Previews of new
snowmobile units are featured annually.
One third or less of the editorial
contents is concerned with snowmobile
racing, two thirds with recreational
snowmobiling. Snowmobile Resorts-
places to stay, trails to ride on.
**Readers:** Great Lakes owners of
snowmobiles.

65400
## MID-SOUTH HUNTING & FISHING NEWS
2208 Central Ave.
Memphis, TN 38104
Telephone: (901) 722-9105
FAX: (901) 722-9107
Year Established: 1986
Pub. Frequency: bi-w.
Page Size: tabloid
Subscrip. Rate: $1.50 newsstand;
$17.95/yr.
Circulation: 15,000
Circulation Type: paid
**Owner(s):**
S.S. & J. Corporation, Inc.
2208 Central Ave.
Memphis, TN 38104
Telephone: (901) 722-9105
Ownership %: 100
**Management:**
Dorothy Boyett ..............................Circulation Manager
**Editorial:**
Peter Schutt ..............................Editor
Scott Liles ..............................Editor
Don Fancher ..............................Marketing Director
**Desc.:** Mid-South region (Arkansas,
Mississippi, Tennessee) outdoor news
about hunting and fishing. Covers new
laws, regulations, products for hunters
and fishermen as well as techniques
and equipments. Also contains regional
reports on weather conditions and game
herds, where to and how to enjoy sport
in this area.
**Readers:** 15,000 avid hunters and
fishermen. Affluent, 62 percent earn at
least $30,000 yearly, well-equipped
sportsmen who are active in the field.

25996
## MUZZLE BLASTS
P.O. Box 67
Friendship, IN 47021
Telephone: (812) 667-5131
FAX: (812) 667-5137
Year Established: 1939
Pub. Frequency: m.
Page Size: standard
Subscrip. Rate: $3.50 newsstand; $30/yr.
membership
Materials: 01,02,05,06,15,16,18,19,21,32,33
Freelance Pay: $50-$300/article
Print Process: offset
Circulation: 27,000
Circulation Type: controlled
**Owner(s):**
National Muzzle Loading Rifle Assn.
P.O. Box 67
Friendship, IN 47021
Telephone: (812) 667-5131
Ownership %: 100
**Management:**
David Arnold ..............................President
Denise Goodpaster ..............................Advertising Manager
**Editorial:**
Robert H. Wallace ..............................Executive Editor

Sharon Pollard ..............................Art Director
Marilyn Imel ..............................Computer Editor
Max Vickery ..............................Miscellaneous
James Crutchfield ..............................Miscellaneous
Lee Good ..............................Miscellaneous
Sharon Pollard ..............................Photo
James W. Carlson ..............................Research Editor
Jim O'meara ..............................Research Editor
Rick Hacker ..............................Research Editor
James C. Schneider ..............................Research Editor
John Bivins ..............................Technical Editor
**Desc.:** Covers news and activities of
owners and devotees of muzzle loading
rifles, pistols, and shotguns. Reports
regional and national meets, records,
results, etc. Uses some historical data
on powder and guns, developments, etc.
Lists contests, sales, describes various
collector's items and in general covers
the field of antique firearms. Has section
devoted to Charter Clubs affiliated with
the N.M.L.R.A. Departments include
Research (answering inquiries on
antique rifles, pistols, and shotguns);
Home Gunsmith (how to make and
repair firearms, home workshop tools,
etc.); Powder Horn Column (general
news, letters from members, etc.); Gun
Legislation Report; Hunting; Rendezvous
and Buckskinning.
**Readers:** All persons interested in
muzzleloading firearms.
**Deadline:** story-2-1/2 mos.; news-2-1/2
mos.; photo-2-1/2 mos.

56227
## NATIONAL MASTERS NEWS
6320 Van Nuys Blvd., Ste. 207
Van Nuys, CA 91401
Telephone: (818) 785-1895
FAX: (818) 782-1135
Mailing Address:
P.O. Box 2372
Van Nuys, CA 91404
Year Established: 1977
Pub. Frequency: m.
Page Size: tabloid
Subscrip. Rate: $2.50 newsstand; $24/yr.
Freelance Pay: $7.50/photo
Print Process: web
Circulation: 5,700
Circulation Type: paid
**Owner(s):**
National Masters News
P.O. Box 2372
Van Nuys, CA 91404
Telephone: (818) 785-1895
Ownership %: 100
**Editorial:**
Al Sheahen ..............................Editor
**Desc.:** Devoted exclusively to track and
field and long distance running for men
and women over age 35. Covers
competitions at local, national and
international levels.
**Readers:** People over age 35 who like to
participate in track and field and long
distance running.

69470
## NEW ENGLAND GOLF MAGAZINE
148 Old Westminster Rd.
Hubbardston, MA 01542
Telephone: (508) 928-5300
FAX: (508) 928-5311
Year Established: 1989
Pub. Frequency: bi-m.
Subscrip. Rate: $19.97/yr.
Circulation: 50,000
Circulation Type: paid
**Owner(s):**
New England Golf Magazine, Inc.
1853 N. Main St.
Leominster, MA 01453-1412
Telephone: (800) 627-7012
Ownership %: 100

**Management:**
Mark Mitchell ..............................Publisher
**Editorial:**
Joanne Mitchell ..............................Editor
**Desc.:** Focuses on local events,
tournaments, courses and players.

66295
## NEW ENGLAND WINDSURFING JOURNAL
P.O. Box 2120
Southbury, CT 06488
Telephone: (203) 264-9463
Year Established: 1983
Pub. Frequency: 11/yr.
Page Size: tabloid
Subscrip. Rate: $1.50 newsstand; $12/yr.
Materials: 08,09,32,33
Print Process: web offset
Circulation: 15,000
Circulation Type: paid
**Owner(s):**
New England Windsurfing Journal
P.O. Box 2120
Southbury, CT 06488
Telephone: (203) 264-9463
Ownership %: 100
**Management:**
Peter Bogucki ..............................Publisher
**Deadline:** ads-15th of mo.

69440
## NEW YORK RUNNING NEWS
9 E. 89th St.
New York, NY 10128
Telephone: (212) 860-4455
FAX: (212) 860-9754
Year Established: 1958
Pub. Frequency: bi-m.
Page Size: standard
Subscrip. Rate: membership
Circulation: 45,000
Circulation Type: controlled
**Owner(s):**
New York Road Runners Club
9 E. 89th St.
New York, NY 10128
Telephone: (212) 101-2800
Ownership %: 100
**Editorial:**
Raleigh Mayer ..............................Editor
**Desc.:** Regional sports magazine covering
running, racewalking, nutrition and
fitness.

71274
## NORTHWEST SAILBOARD
3702 W. Valley Highway N.
Ste. 106
Auburn, WA 98001
Telephone: (206) 351-6442
FAX: (206) 351-9274
Year Established: 1981
Pub. Frequency: bi-m.
Subscrip. Rate: 12.94/yr.
Circulation: 25000
Circulation Type: paid
**Owner(s):**
Extreme Publishing
3702 W. Valley Highway N.
Ste. 106
Auburn, WA 98001
Telephone: (206) 351-6442
Ownership %: 100
**Management:**
Scott Campbell ..............................Publisher
Golda Irvine ..............................Circulation Manager
**Editorial:**
Cary L. Ordway ..............................Editor
Cary Adams ..............................Advertising Director

69126
## OLYMPIAN
One Olympic Plz.
Colorado Springs, CO 80909
Telephone: (719) 636-2551
FAX: (719) 578-4677

**Materials Accepted/Included:** 01-Business news 02-By-line articles 03-Fashion news 04-Food news 05-Freelance copy 06-Letters to editor 07-Real estate news 08-Sports news 09-Travel news 10-Book rev. 11-Movie rev. 12-Music rev. 13-TV rev. 14-Theater rev. 15-Coming events 16-Obituaries 17-Question & answer 18-Social announcements 19-Artwork 20-Cartoons 21-Photos 22-TV listings 23-Audio rec. 24-Video rec. 25-Books 26-Films/film clips 27-Personnel news 28-Press releases 29-New product news/photos 30-Trade lit. 31-Contracts awarded 32-Display adv. 33-Classified adv.

6-117

Year Established: 1974
Pub. Frequency: bi-m.
Subscrip. Rate: $19.96/yr.
Circulation: 120,000
Circulation Type: controlled & paid
**Owner(s):**
United States Olympic Committee
One Olympic Plz.
Colorado Springs, CO 80909
Telephone: (719) 632-5551
Ownership %: 100
**Editorial:**
Frank Zang ...................................Editor

**ON-DIRT MAGAZINE**    69127
P.O. Box 6246
Woodland Hills, CA 91365
Telephone: (818) 340-5750
FAX: (818) 348-4648
Year Established: 1984
Pub. Frequency: m.
Page Size: standard
Subscrip. Rate: $3 newsstand; $35/yr.
Materials: 32
Circulation: 200,000
Circulation Type: paid
**Owner(s):**
Alta Publishing, Inc.
P.O. Box 6246
Woodland Hills, CA 91365
Telephone: (818) 340-5750
Ownership %: 100
**Management:**
Loni Peralta ...................Advertising Manager
**Editorial:**
Lori Peralta ...................................Editor

**OUTDOOR LIFE**    26435
2 Park Ave.
New York, NY 10016
Telephone: (212) 779-5000
Year Established: 1897
Pub. Frequency: m.
Page Size: standard
Subscrip. Rate: $11.97/yr.
Freelance Pay: $900-$1100 (National);
$350-$600 (Regional)
Circulation: 1,500,000
Circulation Type: paid
**Owner(s):**
Times Mirror, Inc.
2 Park Ave.
New York, NY 10016
Telephone: (212) 418-9600
Ownership %: 100
**Management:**
Bud Ward ...................................Publisher
**Editorial:**
Vin T. Sparano ...................................Editor
**Desc.:** Serves active outdoor sports
people. The magazine emphasizes
fishing, hunting, camping, boating,
conservation, and closely
related subjects. Reviews and reports of
various products such as clothing,
knives, boats, cars, and trucks,
books, camping equipment.
**Readers:** Hunters, fishermen, campers,
boaters. Outdoor sports enthusiasts.

**OUTSIDE MAGAZINE**    26437
400 Market St.
Santa Fe, NM 87501
Telephone: (505) 989-7100
Year Established: 1976
Pub. Frequency: m.
Page Size: standard
Subscrip. Rate: $18/yr.
Circulation: 450,000
Circulation Type: paid

**Owner(s):**
Mariah Publications Corp.
1165 N. Clark St.
Chicago, IL 60610
Telephone: (312) 951-0990
Ownership %: 100
**Management:**
Lawrence J. Burke ...............................President
**Editorial:**
Lawrence J. Burke ...............Editor in Chief
Mark Bryant ...................................Editor
Cathy Martin ...................Managing Editor
Susan Casey ...................................Art Director
Michele Givens ...........Consumer Affairs Editor
John Askwith ...................................Design Editor
Chris Czmyrid ...................Marketing Director
Susan Smith ...................Photography Director
**Desc.:** America's active lifestyle magazine
dedicated to inspiring people to enjoy
fuller, more rewarding lives through year-
round editorial coverage of participation
sports, travel, adventure, people, politics,
art and literature of the world outside.
**Readers:** Median age: 35; median yearly
income: $56,000; 73% male, 85%
college educated.

**PETERSEN'S HANDGUNS**    69142
6420 Wilshire Blvd.
Los Angeles, CA 90048
Telephone: (213) 782-2000
FAX: (213) 782-2263
Pub. Frequency: m.
Page Size: standard
Subscrip. Rate: $3.95 newsstand;
$23.94/yr.
Materials: 32
Circulation: 150,800
Circulation Type: paid
**Owner(s):**
Petersen Publsihing Co.
6420 Wilshire Blvd.
Los Angeles, CA 90048
Telephone: (213) 782-2000
Ownership %: 100
**Management:**
W. Jeff Young ...................................Publisher
**Editorial:**
J. Libourel ...................................Editor

**PRECISION SHOOTING MAGAZINE**    26442
37 Burnham St.
East Hartford, CT 06108
Telephone: (203) 249-6811
FAX: (203) 727-9690
Year Established: 1953
Pub. Frequency: m.
Page Size: standard
Subscrip. Rate: $25/yr.
Freelance Pay: negotiable
Circulation: 10,000
Circulation Type: paid
**Owner(s):**
Precision Shooting, Inc.
37 Burnham St.
East Hartford, CT 06108
Telephone: (203) 249-6811
Ownership %: 100
**Editorial:**
David Brennan ...................................Editor
**Desc.:** A target shooting oriented
magazine which also serves as the
House Organization for the International
Benchrest Shooters (IBS). Coverage of
the various shooting sports is welcome,
as are shooting reports and technical
features. News releases relative to the
shooting sports are accepted on a
space-available basis. Advertising is
accepted if it pertains to the shooting
sports. Pictures (no polaroids) are
welcome with all articles or news
releases.

**Readers:** Above average income and
education. Many are especially skilled in
the shooting sports. The professionals of
the shooting sports, ganser, etc.

**RACE & RALLY**    26447
Rte. 7 Box 614
Alexandria, MN 56308
Telephone: (612) 763-5411
Mailing Address:
P.O. Box 993
Alexandria, MN 56308
Year Established: 1968
Pub. Frequency: 3/yr.
Page Size: standard
Subscrip. Rate: $8/yr.; $12:50/2 yrs.;
$18/3 yrs.
Freelance Pay: varies
**Owner(s):**
Snowmobiler Publications, Inc.
Telephone: (612) 763-5411
Ownership %: 100
**Management:**
James E. Beilke ...................................Publisher
James E. Beilke ...................Advertising Manager
Kerry Infanger ...................Circulation Manager
**Editorial:**
James E. Beilke ...................Executive Editor
Al Skaar ...................................Photo
Vern Wieberdink ...................Technical Editor
**Desc.:** Devoted to snowmobile racing.
Covers the personalities, events, news
and related activities of high
performance snowmobiling. Use a heavy
amount of action pictures in both
color and black and white. Photo feature
stories can run as long as 28 pages.
Majority of photos used are black and
white-many of the color shots used go
full page and-or spreads. Articles are of
the informative type using illustrations
and photos. Vast majority of the photos,
features and illustrations are originated
in-house. Contributers should query first
about their ideas. Departments include:
Technical Questions, General Letters,
Ask the Factory Expert, Reader's Reply,
News & New Products.
**Readers:** Made up of people who both
race and feel they are basically outdoor
people.

**RACQUETBALL MAGAZINE**    69475
1685 W. Unintah St.
Colorado Springs, CO 80904-2921
Telephone: (719) 635-5396
FAX: (719) 635-0685
Year Established: 1990
Pub. Frequency: bi-m.
Page Size: standard
Subscrip. Rate: $15/yr.; $19.95/yr. benefit
membership
Materials: 05,06,08,11,13,15,17,19,20,21,
27,28,29,32,33
Print Process: web
Circulation: 35,000
Circulation Type: paid
**Owner(s):**
American Amateur Racquetball Association
1685 W. Uintah St.
Colorado Springs, CO 80904-2921
Telephone: (719) 635-5396
FAX: (719) 635-0685
Ownership %: 100
**Management:**
Luke St. Onge ...................................Publisher
Rebecca Maxedon ...........Production Manager
**Editorial:**
Linda L. Mojer ...................Editor in Chief

**Desc.:** This is the official publicatiion of the
American Amateur Racquetball
Association (AARA), the national
governing body for the sport. It is
geared toward a readership of informed,
active enthusiasts who seek
entertainment, instruction and coverage
of national events. Content includes:
player profiles, instructional articles by
top pros and teaching professionals,
men's and women's pro tour results;
amateur national event coverage,
national event calendar, national top-10
rankings, equipment reviews and product
updates.

**RECREATIONAL ICE SKATING**    69448
355 W. Dundee Rd.
Buffalo Grove, IL 60089-3500
Telephone: (708) 808-7528
FAX: (708) 808-8329
Year Established: 1976
Pub. Frequency: q.
Page Size: 8 1/8 x 10 3/4
Subscrip. Rate: $2.50 newsstand; $10/yr.
Materials: 02,04,06,08,11,15,28,32,33
Print Process: web offset
Circulation: 30,000
Circulation Type: paid
**Owner(s):**
Ice Skating Institute of America
355 W. Dundee Rd.
Buffalo Grove, IL 60089-3500
Telephone: (708) 808-7528
FAX: (708) 808-8329
Ownership %: 100
**Management:**
Craig Cichy ...................Advertising Manager
**Editorial:**
Justine T. Smith ...................Editor in Chief
Lara Dailey ...................Managing Editor
**Desc.:** The magazine for ice
skating/hockey enthusiasts. Features
celebrity/member profiles, event/travel
information, health/nutrition, competition
tips and more.
**Readers:** ISIA members both in the U.S.
and abroad.

**RECREATION RESOURCES**    52637
50 S. Ninth St.
Minneapolis, MN 55402
Telephone: (612) 333-0471
FAX: (612) 333-6526
Year Established: 1981
Pub. Frequency: 9/yr.
Page Size: tabloid
Subscrip. Rate: free qualified; $24/yr. non-
qualified
Materials: 25,28,29,30
Freelance Pay: varies
Circulation: 51,000
Circulation Type: controlled
**Owner(s):**
Lakewood Publications
50 S. Ninth St.
Minneapolis, MN 55402
Telephone: (612) 333-0471
Ownership %: 100
**Management:**
Jim Secord ...................................Publisher
**Editorial:**
Galynn Nordstrom ...................................Editor
**Desc.:** Provides for the informational
needs of readers in terms of products,
services and ideas for the efficient
operation of managed recreation and
leisure facilities.
**Readers:** Owners and operators of
managed recreation facilities, both public
and private.

**Materials Accepted/Included:** 01-Business news 02-By-line articles 03-Fashion news 04-Food news 05-Freelance copy 06-Letters to editor 07-Real estate news 08-Sports news 09-Travel news 10-Book rev. 11-Movie rev. 12-Music rev. 13-TV rev. 14-Theater rev. 15-Coming events 16-Obituaries 17-Question & answer 18-Social announcements 19-Artwork 20-Cartoons 21-Photos 22-TV listings 23-Audio rec. 24-Video rec. 25-Books 26-Films/film clips 27-Personnel news 28-Press releases 29-New product news/photos 30-Trade lit. 31-Contracts awarded 32-Display adv. 33-Classified adv.

## REFEREE

26450

2017 Lathrop Ave.
Racine, WI 53405
Telephone: (414) 632-8855
FAX: (414) 632-5460
Mailing Address:
P.O. Box 161
Franksville, WI 53126
Year Established: 1976
Pub. Frequency: m.
Page Size: standard
Subscrip. Rate: $47.40/yr.
Freelance Pay: $.04-$.10/wd.
Circulation: 35,000
Circulation Type: paid
**Owner(s):**
Referee Enterprises, Inc.
P.O. Box 161
Franksville, WI 53126
Telephone: (414) 632-8855
Ownership %: 100
**Management:**
Barry Mano .........................................President
Barry Mano .........................................Publisher
Tom Herre ..........................Advertising Manager
**Editorial:**
Barry Mano ..............................Executive Editor
Scott Ehret ..................................Senior Editor
Tom Hammill ...........................................Editor
Lisa Martin ......................................Art Director
Jerry Tapp ...................................Assistant Editor
Tom Hammill ...........................Book Review Editor
Tom Hammill .....................................News Editor
Tom Hammill ..............................................Photo
Tom Hammill ..........................Technical Editor
**Desc.:** Magazine by and for sports officials
who work primarily at the amateur level.
**Readers:** Umpires, sports officials,
coaches, and fans.

## RIFLE

26452

6471 Airpark Dr.
Prescott, AZ 86301
Telephone: (602) 445-7810
FAX: (602) 778-5124
Year Established: 1965
Pub. Frequency: bi-m
Page Size: standard
Subscrip. Rate: $19/yr.
Freelance Pay: $250-$400/article
Circulation: 26,000
Circulation Type: paid
**Owner(s):**
Wolfe Publishing Co., Inc.
6471 Airpark Dr.
Prescott, AZ 86301
Telephone: (602) 445-7810
Ownership %: 100
**Bureau(s):**
Wolfe Publishing Co.
6471 Airpark Dr.
Prescott, AZ 86301
Telephone: (602) 445-7810
**Management:**
Mark Harris ........................................President
Mark Harris ........................................Publisher
Jana Kosco .......................Advertising Manager
Tammy Rossi ....................Circulation Manager
**Editorial:**
Dave Scovill ...........................................Editor
**Readers:** Male, average age 48, Average
income $30,000, seriously involved in
shooting sports.

## ROCK & ICE

69495

603A S. Broadway
Boulder, CO 80303
Telephone: (303) 499-8410
Year Established: 1984
Pub. Frequency: bi-m.

Page Size: standard
Subscrip. Rate: $4.95 newsstand; $24/yr.
US; $36/yr. Canada & Mexico; $44/yr.
elsewhere
Materials: 02,05,06,08,09,10,19,20,21,24,
25,28,29,30,32,33
Freelance Pay: $200/pg.
Circulation: 36,000
Circulation Type: controlled & paid
**Owner(s):**
Eldorado Publishing
P.O. Box 3595
Boulder, CO 80307
Telephone: (303) 499-8410
Ownership %: 100
**Editorial:**
George Bracksieck .............................Editor
**Desc.:** Covers international climbing and
other related outdoor adventures.
**Deadline:** story-2.5 mo. prior to pub. date;
news-2 mo. prior; photo-2 mo. prior; ads-
1.5 mo. prior

## ROCKY MOUNTAIN SPORTS

69451

2025 Pearl St.
Boulder, CO 80302-5323
Telephone: (303) 440-5111
FAX: (303) 440-3313
Year Established: 1986
Pub. Frequency: m.
Page Size: tabloid
Subscrip. Rate: free/newsstand; $14.97/yr.
Materials: 05,06,08,09,10,15,21,23,24,25,
26,27,28,29,30,32,33
Print Process: web
Circulation: 45,000
Circulation Type: paid
**Owner(s):**
Rocky Mountain Sports
2025 Pearl St.
Boulder, CO 80302-5323
Telephone: (303) 440-5111
Ownership %: 100
**Editorial:**
Will Gadd .............................................Editor

## RODALE'S SCUBA DIVING

69143

6600 Abercom St., Ste. 208
Savannah, GA 31405
Telephone: (912) 351-0855
FAX: (912) 351-0890
Year Established: 1992
Pub. Frequency: 10/yr.
Page Size: standard
Subscrip. Rate: $2.95/yr.; $16.97/yr.
Materials: 02,05,06,08,09,15,17,21,28,29,
30,32
Print Process: web
Circulation: 200,000
Circulation Type: controlled & paid
**Owner(s):**
Rodale Press, Inc.
33 E. Minor St.
Emmanaus, PA 18098
Telephone: (610) 967-5171
FAX: (610) 967-7632
Ownership %: 100
**Management:**
John Griffin ........................................President
David McAfee ....................................Publisher
Brian Merritt .......................Circulation Manager
**Editorial:**
Steve Blount .............................Editor in Chief
David Taylor ...........................Managing Editor
**Readers:** Scuba enthusiasts and
professionals.

## RUGBY

69480

2350 Broadway, Ste. 220
New York, NY 10024
Telephone: (212) 787-1160
FAX: (212) 595-0934
Year Established: 1975
Pub. Frequency: 11/yr.

Page Size: tabloid
Subscrip. Rate: $3/copy; $29/yr. US;
$34/yr. Canada; $42/yr. elsewhere
Materials: 06,08,10,11,16,32,33
Print Process: web offset
Circulation: 10,300
Circulation Type: paid
**Owner(s):**
Rugby Press, Ltd.
2350 Broadway, Ste. 220
New York, NY 10024
Telephone: (212) 787-1160
FAX: (212) 595-0934
Ownership %: 100
**Editorial:**
Edward Hagerty ...................................Editor
**Desc.:** In-depth coverage of all U.S.
championships, news on the world rugby
scene, including Canada, Europe, South
Africa, Australia, New Zealand and the
South Pacific. Profiles clubs and
personalities, tournaments, and includes
regular coverage of topics from fitness
and nutrition to refereeing.

## RUNNER'S WORLD

26460

33 E. Minor St.
Emmaus, PA 18098
Telephone: (215) 967-5171
FAX: (610) 967-7725
Year Established: 1987
Pub. Frequency: m.
Page Size: standard
Subscrip. Rate: $24/yr.
Freelance Pay: $50-$1000/article
Circulation: 345,132
Circulation Type: paid
**Owner(s):**
Rodale Press, Inc.
33 E. Minor St.
Emmaus, PA 18098
Telephone: (215) 967-5171
Ownership %: 100
**Management:**
George Hirsch ....................................Publisher
**Editorial:**
Amby Burfoot .............................Exec. Editor
Megan Othersen .........................Senior Editor
Bob Wischnia ...............................Senior Editor
Mark Will Weber ..........................Senior Editor
Christina Negron .........................Senior Editor
Kenneth Kleppert ..............................Art Director
Mike Greehan ....................Associate Publisher
Charle Johnson ..................Photography Editor
Martin Post ...............................Statistical Editor
**Desc.:** Edited for people interested in
running as a lifestyle. Articles deal with
training advice, sports medicine,
nutrition, personalities, cross-training,
shoe evaluations, women's running and
major running events. Aims to enhance
a runner's enjoyment of the sport as
well as to improve performance.
**Readers:** Active runners and running
enthusiasts.

## RUNNING TIMES

26459

98 N. Washington St.
Boston, MA 02114
Telephone: (617) 367-2228
FAX: (617) 367-2350
Year Established: 1977
Pub. Frequency: 10/yr.
Page Size: standard
Subscrip. Rate: $19.95/yr.
Materials: 32,33
Freelance Pay: $15-$350; $25-$500
Circulation: 80,000
Circulation Type: paid

**Owner(s):**
Fitness Publishing, Inc.
98 N. Washington St.
Boston, MA 02114
Telephone: (617) 367-2228
FAX: (617) 367-2350
Ownership %: 100
**Management:**
Carol Lassiter ...................................Publisher
**Editorial:**
Scott Douglas ........................................Editor
**Desc.:** A monthly magazine for
recreational and competitive runners of
all ages.
**Readers:** Recreational and competive
runners of all ages.

## SHOOTING TIMES

26466

News Plz.
Peoria, IL 61656
Telephone: (309) 682-6626
FAX: (309) 682-7394
Mailing Address:
P.O. Box 1790
Peoria, IL 61656
Year Established: 1960
Pub. Frequency: m.
Page Size: standard
Subscrip. Rate: $2.95/issue; $21.98/yr.
Freelance Pay: negotiable
Circulation: 192,500
Circulation Type: paid
**Owner(s):**
PJS Publications, Inc.
News Plaza
Peoria, IL 61656
Telephone: (309) 682-6626
Ownership %: 100
**Management:**
Jerry Constantino ...............................President
Jerry Constantino ...............................Publisher
**Editorial:**
Jim Bequette ..........................................Editor
Ken Ramage ...................................Advertising
Randall Cook .................................Art Director
Joel J. Hutchcroft ......................Assistant Editor
**Desc.:** Articles covering every facet of
guns, shooting, hunting, reloading-both
shotshells and metallic, testing new
guns, components, outdoor, guns, gear,
outdoor equipment and clothing.
Departments include: Q & A from
Readers, Reloading, Handguns, Rifles,
Hunting, Firearms Law, Conservation,
Gunsmithing.
**Readers:** Gun enthusiasts, reloaders,
shooters, hunters, campers, back
packers, outdoor recreationalists.

## SKATING

26469

20 First St.
Colorado Springs, CO 80906
Telephone: (719) 635-5200
Year Established: 1923
Pub. Frequency: 10/yr.
Page Size: standard
Subscrip. Rate: $25/yr. U.S.; $35/yr.
Canada; $45/yr. foreign
Freelance Pay: $35-$100/article
Circulation: 36,000
Circulation Type: controlled
**Owner(s):**
United States Figure Skating Assn.
20 First St.
Colorado Spgs, CO 80906
Telephone: (719) 635-5200
Ownership %: 100
**Management:**
Claire W. Ferguson ...............................President
Luann Duda ....................Advertising Manager
**Editorial:**
Jay Miller ...............................................Editor
Mary Ann Purpura ...................Assistant Editor

**Materials Accepted/Included:** 01-Business news 02-By-line articles 03-Fashion news 04-Food news 05-Freelance copy 06-Letters to editor 07-Real estate news 08-Sports news 09-Travel news 10-Book rev. 11-Movie rev. 12-Music rev. 13-TV rev. 14-Theater rev. 15-Coming events 16-Obituaries 17-Question & answer 18-Social announcements 19-Artwork 20-Cartoons 21-Photos 22-TV listings 23-Audio rec. 24-Video rec. 25-Books 26-Films/film clips 27-Personnel news 28-Press releases 29-New product news/photos 30-Trade lit. 31-Contracts awarded 32-Display adv. 33-Classified adv.

6-119

**Desc.:** Articles deal with amateur figures skating, clubs and amateur skaters. Either staff-written or contributed by correspondents and free lancers. Run from 700-1,250 words. Departments include: full competition coverage and results, collectors pieces (figure skating), memorabilia, readers write, news from abroad, instructional articles, biographies of current competitors in U.S., Canada, and abroad, newsmakers in amateur figure skating.
**Readers:** Amateur and professional ice figure skaters and instructors. coaches, instructors, parents of skaters, spectators, researchers.

### SKEET SHOOTING REVIEW, THE
26470
5931 Roft Rd.
San Antonio, TX 78253
Telephone: (210) 688-3371
FAX: (210) 688-3014
Mailing Address:
 P.O. Box 680007
 San Antonio, TX 78268
Year Established: 1947
Pub. Frequency: m.
Page Size: standard
Subscrip. Rate: free to members; $15/yr.
Freelance Pay: negotiable
Circulation: 18,000
Circulation Type: controlled
**Owner(s):**
National Skeet Shooting Association
P.O. Box 680007
San Antonio, TX 78268
Telephone: (210) 688-3371
Ownership %: 100
**Management:**
Debby J. Smith .................Advertising Manager
**Editorial:**
Susie Fluckiger .........................Managing Editor
Richard Owen ...............................Columnist
Ed Scherer ....................................Field Editor
Nick Sisley ...................................Field Editor
Tom Roster .............................Technical Editor
**Desc.:** Official publication of the National Skeet Shooting Association. Dedicated to the promotion of skeet shooting in the United States and throughout the world. Features reports on skeet shoots, schedules of upcoming skeet tournaments, interviews with top competitors, and articles on subjects related specifically to skeet and clay target shooting game that originated in the United States in 1920.
**Readers:** Members of the National Skeet Shooting Association & non-member subscribers.

### SKIING
26473
2 Park Ave., 5th Fl.
New York, NY 10016
Telephone: (212) 779-5000
Year Established: 1948
Pub. Frequency: 7/yr.
Page Size: standard
Subscrip. Rate: $11.94
Materials: 32,33
Circulation: 450,000
Circulation Type: paid
**Owner(s):**
Times Mirror Magazines, Inc.
2 Park Ave.
New York, NY 10016
Telephone: (212) 779-5000
Ownership %: 100
**Management:**
Henry A. Kaiser .............................Publisher
**Editorial:**
Rick Kahl ................................Editor in Chief
William Grout .........................Executive Editor
James Flynn ....................Advertising Director

Andrew Clurman ...................Marketing Director
**Desc.:** Contains material for the active skier, beginner, as well as experienced skier who is interested in learning about the sport, its equipment, its technique; and reports on the world's great ski areas.

### SKI MAGAZINE
52579
2 Park Ave., 5th Fl.
New York, NY 10016
Telephone: (212) 779-5000
Year Established: 1936
Pub. Frequency: q.
Page Size: standard
Subscrip. Rate: $2.95 newsstand;
 $11.95/yr.
Materials: 05,32,33
Freelance Pay: $150-$500/article
Circulation: 441,172
Circulation Type: paid
**Owner(s):**
Times Mirror Magazines
2 Park Ave.
New York, NY 10016
Telephone: (212) 779-5000
Ownership %: 100
**Management:**
Edward Johnson .................Chairman of Board
Francis Pandolfi ..........................President
James Kopper .........Executive Vice President
**Editorial:**
Ed Pitoniak ....................................Editor
**Desc.:** Edited for new and veteran skiers, reports on What to Buy, Where to Go, and How to Ski Better.
**Readers:** Upscale readership, college-educated, high-income, variety of interests (particularly those athletic and involving the outdoors).

### SKIN DIVER
26474
6420 Wilshire Blvd.
Los Angeles, CA 90048
Telephone: (213) 782-2960
FAX: (213) 782-2121
Year Established: 1951
Pub. Frequency: m.
Page Size: standard
Subscrip. Rate: $21.94/yr.
Materials: 05,10,28,29
Freelance Pay: $50/printed pg.
Circulation: 218,473
Circulation Type: paid
**Owner(s):**
Petersen Publishing Co.
6420 Wilshire Blvd.
Los Angeles, CA 90048
Telephone: (213) 782-2960
FAX: (213) 782-2121
Ownership %: 100
**Management:**
Fred R. Waingrow .......................President
Paul Tzimoulis .........................Vice President
Bill Gleason .................................Publisher
**Editorial:**
Bonnie J. Cardone .................Executive Editor
Bill Gleason ....................................Editor
Jim R. Warner .........................Managing Editor
Suzanne Babcock ......................Art Director
Jim Walker ..............................Feature Editor
Paul J. Tzimoulis .........................Group Publisher
**Desc.:** Anything of interest to divers is considered for use such as personalities, diving equipment, new products, experience articles, etc. Departments include: Scuba IQ, New Gear, Diver's Directory, Technifacts, Medifacts, New Books, Fish of the Month, U/W Forum,. Shell Collector's Notebook, Shows 'n Events, Films 'n Symposiums.
**Readers:** World-wide including those who dive for sport and those who have an interest.

### SNOWBOARDER
67246
33046 Calle Avidor
San Juan Capistrano, CA 92675
Telephone: (714) 496-5922
FAX: (714) 496-7849
Mailing Address:
 P.O. Box 1028
 Dana Point, CA 92629
Year Established: 1988
Pub. Frequency: m.
Page Size: Standard
Subscrip. Rate: $3.50 newsstand;
 $12.95/yr.
Circulation: 90,000
Circulation Type: paid
**Owner(s):**
Surfer Publications, Inc.
P.O. Box 1028
Dana Point, CA 92629
Telephone: (714) 496-5922
Ownership %: 100
**Management:**
Donna Lewis-Gordon ...........................President
Brent Diamond .............................Publisher
Doug Palladini ...................Associate Publisher
Tim Reed ..........................Advertising Manager
**Editorial:**
Brent Diamond .................................Editor

### SNOW COUNTRY
65383
5520 Park Ave.
Trumbull, CT 06611
Telephone: (203) 373-7059
FAX: (203) 371-2127
Mailing Address:
 P.O. Box 395
 Trumbull, CT 06611-0395
Year Established: 1988
Pub. Frequency: 8/yr.
Page Size: standard
Subscrip. Rate: $13.97/yr.
Materials: 02,05,06,07,08,09,15,20,21
Circulation: 460,000
Circulation Type: controlled & paid
**Owner(s):**
New York Times
229 W. 43rd St.
New York, NY 10036
Ownership %: 100
**Management:**
Tom Brown .................................Publisher
Rip Warndorf ......................Advertising Manager
Julie Meier .........................Circulation Manager
**Editorial:**
John Fry ....................................Editor

### SNOWEST
26479
520 Park Ave.
Idaho Falls, ID 83402
Telephone: (208) 524-7000
FAX: (208) 522-5241
Year Established: 1974
Pub. Frequency: q.
Page Size: standard
Subscrip. Rate: $8/yr.
Materials: 06,08,15,28,29,32
Freelance Pay: $.10/wd.
Circulation: 161,000
Circulation Type: controlled & paid
**Owner(s):**
Harris Publishing Co, Inc.
520 Park Avenue
Idaho Falls, ID 83402
Telephone: (208) 524-7000
Ownership %: 100
**Management:**
Darryl W. Harris ...........................Publisher
Mel Erickson ......................Advertising Manager
**Editorial:**
Steve Janes ....................................Editor
Morgan Cloward ......................Assistant Editor
Janet Chase .........................Production Director
Gregg Manwaring .................................Sales

**Desc.:** Edited for Western snowmobilers with articles that feature trail riding in Idaho, Montana, Utah, Wyoming, Washington, Oregon, Colorado, Nevada, New Mexico, California, Arizona. Articles also cover how-to-do-its, snowmobile personalities, new machine previews, industry updates, some aspects of racing and other items related to snowmobiling. Photos (black and white) are a must. We appreciate both black and white and color photos and use stringer material, new products articles should accompany manuscript and business articles that relate.
**Readers:** Snowmobilers in all western states with snowmobiles.
**Deadline:** story-45 days prior to pub. date; news-45 days prior to pub. date; photo-45 days prior to pub. date; ads-30 days prior to pub. date

### SNOWMOBILE
26476
601 Lakeshore Pkwy., Ste. 600
Minnetonka, MN 55305-5215
Telephone: (612) 476-2200
FAX: (612) 476-8065
Year Established: 1980
Pub. Frequency: 4/yr. during winter
Page Size: standard
Subscrip. Rate: $11.80/season US;
 $18/season Canada
Freelance Pay: $50-$500/article
Circulation: 475,000
Circulation Type: controlled
**Owner(s):**
Ehlert Publishing Group, Inc.
601 Lakeshore Pkwy., Ste. 600
Minnetonka, MN 55305-5215
Telephone: (612) 476-2200
Ownership %: 100
**Management:**
John A. Ehlert ...............................President
Gary McEnelly ......................Vice President
John A. Ehlert .............................Publisher
Judy Willemsen ...................Circulation Manager
Susan Wilson ...................Production Manager
**Editorial:**
Dick Hendricks ....................................Editor
Paul James .........................Managing Editor
Dave Bortner ...............................Advertising
Mike Vaughan ...............................Advertising
Faith Williams .................................Director
Morris Woolery ...................Production Director
**Desc.:** The snowmobiler's magazine. Covers all aspects of recreational snowmobiling of interest to snowmobilers: Trails, People, Weather, News, Fashion, 4 x 4 Trucks, Travel & Tourism, Events, and Equipment.
**Readers:** Active snowmobiler-owning households.

### SOCCER AMERICA
69483
1235 Tenth St.
Burkley, CA 94710
Telephone: (510) 528-5000
FAX: (510) 528-5177
Mailing Address:
 P.O. Box 26704
 Oakland, CA 94623
Year Established: 1971
Pub. Frequency: 48/yr.
Subscrip. Rate: $46.94/yr.
Circulation: 35,000
Circulation Type: paid
**Owner(s):**
Berling Communications, Inc.
P.O. Box 23704
Oakland, CA 94623
Telephone: (510) 528-5000
Ownership %: 100

**Materials Accepted/Included:** 01-Business news 02-By-line articles 03-Fashion news 04-Food news 05-Freelance copy 06-Letters to editor 07-Real estate news 08-Sports news 09-Travel news 10-Book rev. 11-Movie rev. 12-Music rev. 13-TV rev. 14-Theater rev. 15-Coming events 16-Obituaries 17-Question & answer 18-Social announcements 19-Artwork 20-Cartoons 21-Photos 22-TV listings 23-Audio rec. 24-Video rec. 25-Books 26-Films/film clips 27-Personnel news 28-Press releases 29-New product news/photos 30-Trade lit. 31-Contracts awarded 32-Display adv. 33-Classified adv.

6-120

**Editorial:**
Lynn Berling Manuel .................................Editor
**Desc.:** Covers national and international soccer news, teams, the pros and college action for sophisticated soccer fans. Also features a monthly soccer events calendar, information and tips for adults working in youth soccer.

69486

## SOCCER DIGEST
990 Grove St.
Evanston, IL 60201-4370
Telephone: (708) 491-6440
Year Established: 1978
Pub. Frequency: bi-m.
Page Size: standard
Subscrip. Rate: $11.95/yr.
Materials: 08,10,11,24,25,28,32,33
Circulation: 65,000
Circulation Type: paid
**Owner(s):**
Century Publishing Co.
990 Grove St.
Evanston, IL 60201-4370
Telephone: (708) 491-6440
Ownership %: 100
**Desc.:** Presents statistics and features on soccer for serious soccer fans.

26483

## SOUTHERN OUTDOORS
5845 Carmichael Rd.
Montgomery, AL 36117
Telephone: (205) 277-3940
FAX: (205) 279-7148
Mailing Address:
　P.O. Box 179
　Montgomery, AL 36141
Year Established: 1952
Pub. Frequency: 9 issues/yr.
Page Size: standard
Subscrip. Rate: $2.50 newsstand;
　$14.97/yr.
Freelance Pay: $.15-$.20/wd.
Circulation: 250,000
Circulation Type: paid
**Owner(s):**
BASS Publications
5845 Carmichael Rd.
Montgomery, AL 36117
Telephone: (205) 277-3940
Ownership %: 100
**Management:**
Helen Sevier ................................Publisher
Mike Swain ...................Advertising Manager
**Editorial:**
Bob Cobb ..........................Executive Editor
Larry Teague ..................................Editor
Allison Hatfield ....................Assistant Editor
**Desc.:** Covers freshwater fishing, saltwater fishing, hunting, boating, camping, shooting, outdoor related travel.
**Readers:** The active sportsmen in 17 southern states.

26485

## SPORT
8490 Sunset Blvd.
Los Angeles, CA 90069
Telephone: (213) 854-2222
Year Established: 1946
Pub. Frequency: m.
Page Size: standard
Subscrip. Rate: $2.95/copy; $11.97/yr.
Circulation: 931,517
**Owner(s):**
Petersen Publishing Co.
8490 Sunset Blvd.
Los Angeles, CA 90069
Telephone: (213) 854-2222
**Management:**
Terry L. Shiver ...........................Publisher
Joseph Kensil ...................Advertising Manager
**Editorial:**
Don Evans .........................Executive Editor
Cameron Benty ..............................Editor

Joe Garza ..........................Managing Editor
Ira Gabriel ............................Picture Editor
**Readers:** Young, active, affluent, adult readership.

26486

## SPORT AVIATION
3000 Poberezny Rd.
Oshkosh, WI 54901
Telephone: (414) 426-4800
FAX: (414) 426-4828
Mailing Address:
　P.O. Box 3086
　Oshkosh, WI 54903
Year Established: 1953
Pub. Frequency: m.
Page Size: standard
Subscrip. Rate: $35/yr.
Circulation: 132,000
Circulation Type: paid
**Owner(s):**
Experimental Aircraft Association
3000 Pobeezny Rd.
Oshkosh, WI 54903
Telephone: (414) 426-4800
Ownership %: 100
**Management:**
Tom Poberezny ...........................Publisher
Golda Cox .................Advertising Manager
**Editorial:**
Jack Cox ...........................Editor in Chief
Golda Cox ........................Managing Editor
**Desc.:** Articles of technical, historical, and general nature accepted on free basis relating to amateur-built aircraft, antique aircraft, ex-military aircraft, racing aircraft and air racing, amateur-built rotary wing aircraft, aerobatic aircraft and aerobatic flying. Has Washington Report by EAA representative, David Scott and President's Report by EAA President, Paul Poberezny.
**Readers:** Sport aviation enthusiasts.

71260

## SPORT DIVER MAGAZINE
330 W. Canton Ave.
Winter Park, FL 32789
Telephone: (407) 628-4802
FAX: (407) 628-7061
Mailing Address:
　P.O. Box 2456
　Winter Park, FL 32789
Pub. Frequency: 5/yr.
Page Size: standard
Subscrip. Rate: $2.95 newsstand;
　$14.97/yr.
Materials: 05,32
Freelance Pay: $25-$500/article
Print Process: offset
Circulation: 84,885
Circulation Type: paid
**Owner(s):**
World Publications, Inc.
P.O. Box 2456
Winter Park, FL 32790
Telephone: (407) 628-4802
Ownership %: 100
**Management:**
Terry Snow ...............................Publisher
**Editorial:**
Pierce Hoover ..............................Editor
Glenn Hughes .................Advertising Director
Trish Carter .....................Circulation Director
Jim Robinson ...................Circulation Systems Manager

71261

## SPORT FISHING MAGAZINE
330 W. Canton Ave.
Winter Park, FL 32789
Telephone: (407) 628-4802
FAX: (407) 628-7061
Mailing Address:
　P.O. Box 2456
　Winter Park, FL 32790
Year Established: 1981

Pub. Frequency: 10/yr.
Page Size: standard
Subscrip. Rate: $2.95 newsstand;
　$18.97/yr.
Materials: 05,32
Freelance Pay: $25-$500/article
Circulation: 113,215
Circulation Type: paid
**Owner(s):**
World Publications, Inc.
P.O. Box 2456
Winter Park, FL 32790
Telephone: (407) 628-4802
Ownership %: 100
**Management:**
Terry Snow ...............................Publisher
**Editorial:**
Albia J. Dugger ..............................Editor
Sue Gilman ...................Advertising Director
Trish Carter .....................Circulation Director
Jim Robinson ...................Circulation Systems Manager

26487

## SPORTING NEWS, THE
1212 N. Lindbergh Blvd.
St. Louis, MO 63132
Telephone: (314) 997-7111
FAX: (314) 993-7726
Mailing Address:
　P.O. Box 56
　St. Louis, MO 63166
Year Established: 1886
Pub. Frequency: w.
Page Size: tabloid
Subscrip. Rate: $2.50 newsstand; $60/yr.
Freelance Pay: varies
Circulation: 535,000
Circulation Type: paid
**Owner(s):**
Times Mirror Co.
Times Mirror Sq.
Los Angeles, CA 90053
Telephone: (310) 237-3700
Ownership %: 100
**Management:**
Nicholas H. Niles ........................President
Francis X. Farrell ..........................Publisher
Robert Conklin ...............Circulation Manager
**Editorial:**
John Rawlings ..............................Editor
**Desc.:** Edited for followers of major spectator sports. Year round emphasis on baseball, pro and college football and pro and college basketball, and hockey.
**Readers:** Sports fans.

26488

## SPORTS AFIELD
250 W. 55th St.
New York, NY 10019
Telephone: (212) 649-4300
FAX: (212) 581-3923
Year Established: 1887
Pub. Frequency: m.
Page Size: standard
Subscrip. Rate: $13.97/yr.; 25.97/2 yrs.
Freelance Pay: $850-$1,500/article
Circulation: 500,000
Circulation Type: paid
**Owner(s):**
Hearst Magazine Division, The Hearst Corp.
959 Eighth Ave.
New York, NY 10019
Telephone: (212) 649-4302
Ownership %: 100
**Management:**
Terry McDonell ...........................Publisher
Drew de Carvaltho ............Promotion Manager
**Editorial:**
Terry McDonell ...................Editor in Chief
Fred Kesting .........................Exec. Editor
Francesca Rea ....................Managing Editor
Gary Gretter ............................Art Director

**Desc.:** Covers the non-competitive, non-commercial outdoor field: hunting, fishing, boating, camping, sporting dogs, etc. Interested in material in the following order: outdoor adventure, factual and instructive pieces, how-to, where-to-go, conservation articles, personal experience, humor. Articles should be between 1,500 and 2,000 words, accompanied by good photos. Various departments cover new products in their respective field.
**Readers:** All age groups and income brackets.

26493

## SPORTS ILLUSTRATED
1271 Ave of The Americas
New York, NY 10020
Telephone: (212) 522-1212
Year Established: 1954
Pub. Frequency: w.
Page Size: 7 x 10
Subscrip. Rate: $2.95 newsstand;
　$80.46/yr.
Circulation: 3,356,000
Circulation Type: paid
**Owner(s):**
Time Warner, Inc.
Time & Life Bldg.
1271 Ave. of the Americas
New York, NY 10020
Telephone: (212) 522-1212
Ownership %: 100
**Management:**
Mark Mulvoy ...........................Publisher
John Squires .................Circulation Manager
George P. Berger .............Promotion Manager
**Editorial:**
Kenneth Rudeen ..........................Exec. Editor
Mark Mulvoy ..............................Editor
Jerry Kirshenbaum ...........Assistant Managing Editor
Ray Cave .........................Editorial Director
Tracy T. Windrum ...........Production Director
**Desc.:** America's National Sports Weekly. Departments include: Baseball, Basketball, Boating, Boxing, Football, Golf, Hockey, Tennis, Track & Field, TV/Radio, Skiing, Swimming, Soccer, Sporting Look, Letters, Ecology, etc.
**Readers:** Sports enthusiasts.

67243

## SPORTS ILLUSTRATED FOR KIDS
Time & Life Bldg., Rockefeller Ctr.
New York, NY 10020-1393
Telephone: (212) 522-1212
FAX: (212) 522-0120
Year Established: 1989
Pub. Frequency: m.
Page Size: standard
Subscrip. Rate: $18.95/yr.
Circulation: 934,000
Circulation Type: paid
**Owner(s):**
Time Warner, Inc.
Time & Life Bldg.
Rockefeller Ctr.
New York, NY 10020
Telephone: (212) 522-1212
Ownership %: 100
**Management:**
Susan F. Sachs ...........................Publisher
Ed Willett ...................Advertising Manager
**Editorial:**
Craig Neff ..............................Editor

26497

## SURFER MAGAZINE
P.O. Box 1028
Dana Point, CA 92629
Year Established: 1960
Pub. Frequency: m.

**Materials Accepted/Included:** 01-Business news 02-By-line articles 03-Fashion news 04-Food news 05-Freelance copy 06-Letters to editor 07-Real estate news 08-Sports news 09-Travel news 10-Book rev. 11-Movie rev. 12-Music rev. 13-TV rev. 14-Theater rev. 15-Coming events 16-Obituaries 17-Question & answer 18-Social announcements 19-Artwork 20-Cartoons 21-Photos 22-TV listings 23-Audio rec. 24-Video rec. 25-Books 26-Films/film clips 27-Personnel news 28-Press releases 29-New product news/photos 30-Trade lit. 31-Contracts awarded 32-Display adv. 33-Classified adv.

6-121

Page Size: standard
Subscrip. Rate: $3.95 newsstand;
   $20.95/yr.
Materials: 06,08,19,21,32
Freelance Pay: $10-$350/article
Print Process: web offset
Circulation: 115,000
Circulation Type: paid
**Owner(s):**
Surfer Publications, Inc.
P.O. Box 1028
Dana Point, CA 92629
Telephone: (714) 496-5922
Ownership %: 100
**Management:**
Court Overin ...........................................Publisher
**Editorial:**
Steve Hawk ...................................................Editor
Jeff Divine .....................................................Photo
**Desc.:** For surfers worldwide, presents an
   expert point-of-view about swells, waves,
   coverage, equipment, events, history,
   travel and people.
**Readers:** Focuses on 16-24 year old male
   enthusiasts.

48841

**SURFING**
950 Calle Amanecer St., Ste. C
San Clemente, CA 92672
Telephone: (714) 492-7873
FAX: (714) 498-6485
Mailing Address:
   P.O. Box 3010
   San Clemente, CA 92674
Year Established: 1964
Pub. Frequency: m.
Page Size: standard
Subscrip. Rate: $3.95 newsstand;
   $19.95/yr.
Freelance Pay: varies
Circulation: 92,000
Circulation Type: paid
**Owner(s):**
Western Empire Publishing Co.
950 Calle Amanecer St., Ste. C
San Clemente, CA 92672
Telephone: (714) 492-7873
Ownership %: 100
**Management:**
Robert Mignogna .................................Publisher
**Editorial:**
N. Carroll ......................................................Editor
Steve Zeldin .........................................Advertising
Larry Moore ...................................................Photo
Denise Dorsey ..................Production Assistant
**Desc.:** Explores what it means to be a
   surfer: the attitude, the lifestyle, the
   classic competition of man versus
   nature, the symbol of a carefree and
   youthful culture.
**Readers:** Active, lifestyle oriented, upper
   income beach enthusiasts.

26498

**SWIMMING WORLD & JR.**
   **SWIMMER**
155 S. El Molino, Ste. 101
Pasadena, CA 91101
Telephone: (818) 304-7755
FAX: (818) 304-7759
Mailing Address:
   P.O. Box 91870
   Pasadena, CA 91109-1870
Year Established: 1960
Pub. Frequency: m.
Page Size: standard
Subscrip. Rate: $2.50/copy; $19/yr.
Materials: 05,06,08,10,20,21,24,32,33
Freelance Pay: $.12/wd.
Print Process: web
Circulation: 32,000
Circulation Type: paid

**Owner(s):**
Sports Publications, Inc.
155 S. El Molino
Pasadena, CA 91101
Telephone: (818) 304-7755
Ownership %: 100
**Management:**
Richard Deal ...........................................Publisher
Maria Blake .....................Advertising Manager
**Editorial:**
Phil Whitten ................................Editor in Chief
Robert Ingram ..............................................Editor
Russ Ewald ...............................Associate Editor
Brady Bingham ...............................News Editor
**Desc.:** Gives world-wide coverage from
   age group through open, high-prep,
   college, National and Olympic class.
   Features articles by leading coaches
   and authorities on body building,
   technique, nutrition and training, related
   to sports. Books and films related to
   these specialized fields are reviewed.
   Olympic and important international
   competitions are reported. As are news
   from countries which rank aquatics as a
   major sport. All-American selections,
   world and U.S. ranking are featured.
**Readers:** Athletes, coaches, parents
   involved in competitive aquatics.

26501

**TENNIS**
5520 Park Ave.
Trumbull, CT 06611
Telephone: (203) 373-7000
Mailing Address:
   P.O. Box 0395
   Trumbull, CT 06611
Year Established: 1965
Pub. Frequency: m.
Page Size: standard
Subscrip. Rate: $2.95 newsstand;
   $23.94/yr.
Materials: 03,06,08,09,15,17,18,28,29,30,
   31,32,33
Freelance Pay: varies
Circulation: 800,000
Circulation Type: paid
**Owner(s):**
New York Times Co., The
229 W. 43rd St.
New York, NY 10036
Telephone: (212) 556-1234
Ownership %: 100
**Management:**
Howard R. Gill, Jr. ....................Vice Chairman
Jay FitzGerald ........................................President
Mark Adorney ...............................Vice President
Joe Mossa .......................................Vice President
Marcia Strousse .............................Vice President
Diana O'Donnell .............................Vice President
Hugh White .....................................Vice President
Keith Levitt .....................................Vice President
Mark P. Adorney ......................................Publisher
Peter Griffin ......................Advertising Manager
Diana O'Donnell ...............Circulation Manager
Peter Francesconi ...............Managing Director
John Swain ..........................Promotion Manager
Stu Schneider ..........Public Relations Manager
**Editorial:**
Susan Festa Fiske .......................Senior Editor
Donna Doherty ...........................................Editor
Nick Seitz ..................................Editorial Director
Lori Wendin ...........................................Art Director
Mark Preston ..............................Associate Editor
Stuart Chirls ...............................Associate Editor
Denise Gumpper .....................Editorial Assistant
Debra Fratoni .........................Editorial Assistant
Tracy Leonard ........................Equipment Advisor
Nick Didio ..........................Graphics Coordinator
Liz Fernandez ..........................Marketing Director
Sandy Landsman ...........................Miscellaneous
Steve Szurlej ...........................................Photographer
Mary Elizabeth ...................Production Director
Zamboni
Jay Jennings ...............................Senior Writer

Brian Cleary ...............................Staff Writer
**Desc.:** For active tennis players of various
   levels and ages. Issues contain features
   on playing instruction, the mental aspect
   of the game, tips, equipment, fitness and
   travel to tennis camps and resorts. It
   covers the professional game with
   player profiles, tournament previews,
   professional circuit results and photo
   features.
**Readers:** Active, affluent fitness oriented
   tennis players of various levels and
   ages.

67244

**TEXAS BICYCLIST**
3804 El Campo
Ft. Worth, TX 76107
Telephone: (817) 731-2922
FAX: (817) 731-3353
Year Established: 1989
Pub. Frequency: 9/yr.
Page Size: tabloid
Subscrip. Rate: $15/yr.
Freelance Pay: varies
Print Process: web offset
Circulation: 40,000
Circulation Type: controlled
**Owner(s):**
Yellow Jersey Group
490 Second St., Ste. 304
San Francisco, CA 94107
Telephone: (415) 546-7291
Ownership %: 100
**Management:**
Stephan Roulac .....................................Publisher
Linda McDade ...................Advertising Manager
Bob Mack ...............................General Manager
**Editorial:**
Henry Kingman ............................................Editor
**Desc.:** A consumer magazine for bicycling
   enthusiasts.
**Deadline:** story-1st of mo. prior; news-1st
   of mo.; photo-1st of mo.; ads-1st of mo.

69133

**TEXAS FOOTBALL MAGAZINE**
904 N. Broadway
Lexington, KY 40505-8162
Telephone: (606) 226-4510
FAX: (606) 226-4575
Year Established: 1960
Pub. Frequency: a.
Subscrip. Rate: $6.95 newsstand
Circulation: 199562
Circulation Type: paid
**Owner(s):**
Host Communications
904 N. Broadway
Lexington, KY 40505-8162
Telephone: (606) 226-4510
FAX: (606) 226-4575
Ownership %: 100
**Editorial:**
Dave Campbell ..........................Editor in Chief
David Barron ............................Managing Editor
Craig Baroncelli .......................Managing Editor

69129

**THRASHER MAGAZINE**
1303 Underwood
San Francisco, CA 94124
Telephone: (415) 822-3083
FAX: (415) 822-8359
Mailing Address:
   P.O. Box 884570
   San Francisco, CA 94188-4570
Year Established: 1980
Pub. Frequency: m.
Subscrip. Rate: $18.50/yr.
Materials: 03,06,12,19,20,21,23,24,25,28,
   29,32,33
Circulation: 250,000
Circulation Type: paid

**Owner(s):**
High Speed Productions, Inc.
P.O. Box 884570
San Francisco, CA 94188-4570
Telephone: (415) 822-3083
FAX: (415) 822-8359
Ownership %: 100
**Editorial:**
Jake Phelps ...................................................Editor
**Desc.:** Covers skateboarding,
   snowboarding, music, video and
   aggressive youth-oriented lifestyle.
**Deadline:** story-1st of mo. prior to pub.
   date; news-1st of mo. prior; photo-1st of
   mo. prior; ads-Last day of mo. prior

26507

**TOUCHDOWN ILLUSTRATED**
2815 Mitchell Dr.
Ste. 202
Walnut Creek, CA 94598
Telephone: (510) 933-0230
FAX: (510) 933-0371
Pub. Frequency: 6/season
Subscrip. Rate: varies
Freelance Pay: $150-$750/article
Circulation: 3,000,000
Circulation Type: paid
**Owner(s):**
Delaware North Co.
700 Delaware Ave.
Buffalo, NY 14209
Telephone: (716) 881-6500
Ownership %: 100
**Management:**
Pamela Blawie ...........................Vice President
Robert Fulton ...................Operations Manager
**Editorial:**
Peggy Kearney .............................Senior Editor
Mike Goodwin .....................Advertising Director
Thom Hering ...........................Advertising Editor
**Readers:** People attending college regular
   season and Bowl Games.

26509

**TRACK & FIELD NEWS**
2570 El Camino
Ste. 606
Mountain View, CA 94040
Telephone: (415) 948-8188
FAX: (415) 948-9445
Year Established: 1948
Pub. Frequency: m.
Page Size: standard
Subscrip. Rate: $2.95 newsstand; $33/yr.
Materials: 06,08,20,21,32,33
Circulation: 30,000
Circulation Type: paid
**Owner(s):**
Track & Field News
2570 El Camino, Ste. 606
Mountain View, CA 94040
Telephone: (510) 948-8188
Ownership %: 100
**Management:**
Ed Fox ......................................................Publisher
Janet Vitu ...........................Advertising Manager
**Editorial:**
E. Garry Hill ................................................Editor
Jeff Hollobaugh .......................Managing Editor
Janet Vitu ........................Book Review Editor
Jon Hendershott ...........................................Photo
Shawn Price ...............................Staff Writer
**Desc.:** Worldwide coverage of track and
   field, from high school through the
   Olympics, including women's track,
   cross country, roadrunning, etc. All the
   major news of the sport, plus interviews,
   profiles, feature articles, action photos,
   statistical lists and rankings. Articles and
   meet reports obtained only from a cadre
   of voluntary correspondents around the
   world.
**Readers:** Coaches, athletes, officials and
   fans of track and field.

**Materials Accepted/Included:** 01-Business news 02-By-line articles 03-Fashion news 04-Food news 05-Freelance copy 06-Letters to editor 07-Real estate news 08-Sports news 09-Travel news 10-Book rev. 11-Movie rev. 12-Music rev. 13-TV rev. 14-Theater rev. 15-Coming events 16-Obituaries 17-Question & answer 18-Social announcements 19-Artwork 20-Cartoons 21-Photos 22-TV listings 23-Audio rec. 24-Video rec. 25-Books 26-Films/film clips 27-Personnel news 28-Press releases 29-New product news/photos 30-Trade lit. 31-Contracts awarded 32-Display adv. 33-Classified adv.

6-122

## TRAP & FIELD
26510

1200 Waterway Blvd.
Indianapolis, IN 46202-0567
Telephone: (317) 633-8800
FAX: (317) 264-2192
Year Established: 1890
Pub. Frequency: m.
Page Size: standard
Subscrip. Rate: $22/yr.
Materials: 16,32,33
Print Process: web
Circulation: 16,000
Circulation Type: paid
**Owner(s):**
Curtis Publishing Co.
1000 Waterway Blvd.
Indianapolis, IN 46202
Telephone: (317) 633-2043
Ownership %: 100
**Management:**
Bonnie Nash ..............................Publisher
**Editorial:**
Joan Davis ...........................Senior Editor
Sandy Tidwell .....................Senior Editor
Bonnie Nash ................................Editor
Sherry Galbreath .....................Advertising
**Desc.:** Official publications of Amateur
Trapshooting Association. Covers
trapshooting in the United States and
Canada, giving full reports (pictures,
stories, and scores) of registered
competitive clay target shooting. Feature
stories on champions in sports. All-
American team, techniques of shooting,
etc. Publishes the only official listing of
coming events registered with the ATA.
Departments include: Off the Firing Line
(news of gun club activities and
individuals), Completed Careers
(obituaries), Gun Club Scores (winners
of registered shoots), Legislative Review
(news on gun legislation), From Past
Pages (100, 75, 25 and 10 years ago in
the sport), Tips for Reloaders, Gun Test
Reports, 27-Yard Line (tips on shooting
technique), Lock, Stock and Barrel
(questions and answers), and New
Product Information.
**Readers:** High per capita income
sportsmen who choose their recreation.
**Deadline:** story-15th of 2nd mo. prior to
pub. date; news-15th of 2nd mo. prior;
ads-15th of 2nd mo. prior

## USA TODAY BASEBALL WEEKLY
69762

1000 Wilson Blvd.
Arlington, VA 22229-0020
Telephone: (703) 558-5630
FAX: (703) 558-4646
Year Established: 1991
Pub. Frequency: w.
Subscrip. Rate: $35/yr.
Materials: 02,06,10,15,17,20,21,22,23,24,
25,28,32,33
Print Process: offset
**Owner(s):**
USA Today
Arlington, VA
Ownership %: 100
**Management:**
Keith Cutler ..............................Publisher
Jim Schiekofer ...............Advertising Manager
Tom Kelly ...................Circulation Manager
Lynn Busby .......................Sales Manager
**Editorial:**
Lee Ivory ......................Executive Editor
Gary Kicinski .................Managing Editor
Paul White .....................Editor-in-Chief

## VELONEWS
26512

1830 N. 55th St.
Boulder, CO 80301
Telephone: (303) 440-0601
FAX: (303) 444-6788

Year Established: 1972
Pub. Frequency: 18/yr.
Page Size: tabloid
Subscrip. Rate: $33.97/yr.
Freelance Pay: $.05/word
Circulation: 48,000
Circulation Type: paid
**Owner(s):**
Inside Communications, Inc.
1830 N. 55th St.
Boulder, CO 80301
Telephone: (303) 440-0601
**Management:**
Felix Magowan ...........................Publisher
Nancy Grimes ...............Advertising Manager
Richard Rhinehart ...........Circulation Manager
**Editorial:**
John Wilcockson ...........................Editor
Tim Johnson .....................Managing Editor
W. David Walls ...........Publication Director
**Desc.:** Largest nationally circulated bicycle
racing journal in the country. Uses
photos, features and news stories on
racing, training, physiology, equipment,
personalities. Query recommended.
**Readers:** Enthusiasts of bicycle racing,
ages 8-80.

## VOLLEYBALL
66279

21700 Oxnard St., Ste. 1600
Woodland Hills, CA 91367
Telephone: (818) 593-3900
FAX: (818) 593-2274
Year Established: 1990
Pub. Frequency: m.
Subscrip. Rate: $17.95/yr.
Materials: 01,05,06,24,25,28,29,32
Freelance Pay: $100-$750/article
Circulation: 60,000
Circulation Type: paid
**Owner(s):**
AVCOM Publishing
21700 Oxnard St., Ste. 1600
Woodland Hills, CA 91367
Telephone: (818) 593-3900
Ownership %: 100
**Management:**
Carol Campbell ...........................Publisher
**Editorial:**
Rick Hazeltine ...........................Editor
**Desc.:** Contains instructions from coaches,
players and pros. Covers competition
including high school, Olympic and pro
beach tours and profiles top talent and
equipment.

## WAKEBOARDING MAGAZINE
71259

330 W. Canton Ave.
Winter Park, FL 32789
Telephone: (407) 628-4802
FAX: (407) 628-7061
Mailing Address:
P.O. Box 2456
Winter Park, FL 32789
Year Established: 1981
Pub. Frequency: q.
Page Size: standard
Subscrip. Rate: $2.95 newsstand; $9.97/yr.
Materials: 32
Circulation: 30,995
Circulation Type: paid
**Owner(s):**
World Publications, Inc.
P.O. Box 2456
Winter Park, FL 32790
Telephone: (407) 628-4802
Ownership %: 100
**Management:**
Terry Snow ..............................Publisher
**Editorial:**
Tom James ................................Editor
John McEver ...............Advertising Director
Trish Carter ...................Circulation Director
Jim Robinson ...........Circulation Systems

## WALKING MAGAZINE, THE
66022

9-11 Harcourt St.
Boston, MA 02116
Telephone: (617) 266-3322
FAX: (617) 266-7373
Year Established: 1986
Pub. Frequency: bi-m.
Page Size: standard
Subscrip. Rate: $2.95 newsstand;
$14.95/yr.
Circulation: 475,000
Circulation Type: paid
**Owner(s):**
Jan Bruce
Boston, MA 02116
Ownership %: 100
**Editorial:**
Seth Bauer ................................Editor
Linda Frahm .....................Managing Editor
**Desc.:** Contains information for
recreational and fitness walkers.
Focuses on health, fitness, nutrition,
travel, and equipments.

## WARREN MILLER'S SKI WORLD
49847

2540 Frontier Ave., Ste. 104
Boulder, CO 80301
Telephone: (303) 442-3430
FAX: (303) 442-3402
Year Established: 1983
Pub. Frequency: a.
Page Size: standard
Subscrip. Rate: free
Materials: 03,06,09,21
Print Process: web offset
Circulation: 200,000
Circulation Type: controlled
**Owner(s):**
Peter Speek
2540 Frontier Ave., Ste. 104
Boulder, CO 80301
Telephone: (303) 442-3430
Ownership %: 50

Kurt Miller
2540 Frontier Ave., Ste. 104
Boulder, CO 80301
Telephone: (303) 442-3430
Ownership %: 50
**Management:**
Peter Speek ..............................President
Bob Tunnell ..............................Publisher
**Editorial:**
Craig Altschul ...................Editor in Chief
Kurt Miller .............................Advertising
**Readers:** Annual program distributed at
Warren Miller's annual ski film.
**Deadline:** story-May 15; photo-May 15;
ads-July 15

## WATER SKIER, THE
26514

799 Overlook Dr.
Winter Haven, FL 33884
Telephone: (813) 324-4341
FAX: (813) 325-8259
Year Established: 1951
Pub. Frequency: 7/yr
Page Size: standard
Subscrip. Rate: $20/yr.
Freelance Pay: varies
Circulation: 30,000
Circulation Type: paid
**Owner(s):**
American Water Ski Association
799 Overlook Dr.
Winter Haven, FL 33884
Telephone: (813) 324-4341
Ownership %: 100
**Management:**
Don Cullimore ...........................Publisher
Leona Perry ...........Public Relations Manager

**Editorial:**
Don Cullimore ...........................Editor
Greg Nixon .....................Managing Editor
Duke Cullimore .................Executive Director
Dan Hargroves .................Marketing Director
**Desc.:** Encourages the safe enjoyment of
water skiing as a primary means of
family recreation. Also serves as
medium for information concerning water
ski competition and new products
related to the sport. The official
publication of the American Water Ski
Association.

## WATERSKI MAGAZINE
52558

330 W. Canton Ave.
Winter Park, FL 32789
Telephone: (407) 628-4802
FAX: (407) 628-7061
Mailing Address:
P.O. Box 2456
Winter Park, FL 32790
Year Established: 1979
Pub. Frequency: 10/yr.
Page Size: standard
Subscrip. Rate: $2.95 newsstand;
$18.95/yr.
Materials: 02,5,06,08,10,11,20,21,27,28,29,
32,33
Freelance Pay: $25-$500/article
Print Process: web offset
Circulation: 105,471
Circulation Type: free & paid
**Owner(s):**
World Publications, Inc.
P.O. Box 2456
Winter Park, FL 32790
Telephone: (407) 628-4802
FAX: (407) 628-7061
Ownership %: 100
**Management:**
Terry Snow ..............................Publisher
**Editorial:**
Rob Maye ................................Editor
John McEver ...............Advertising Director
Trish Carter ...................Circulation Director
Jim Robinson ...................Circulation Systems
Manager
**Desc.:** About the sport of water skiing.
**Deadline:** story-2 mo. prior to pub. date;
news-2 mo. prior; photo-2 mo. prior; ads-
2 mo. prior

## WB...FOR THE WOMAN WHO BOWLS
26519

5301 S. 76th St.
Greendale, WI 53129
Telephone: (414) 421-9000
FAX: (414) 421-3013
Year Established: 1936
Pub. Frequency: q.
Page Size: standard
Subscrip. Rate: free/membership
Freelance Pay: $25-$200/article
Circulation: 500,000
Circulation Type: controlled
**Owner(s):**
Women's International Bowling Congress
5301 S. 76th St.
Greendale, WI 53129
Telephone: (414) 421-9000
Ownership %: 100
**Bureau(s):**
Meredith Corp.
Telephone: (515) 284-3570
Contact: Paula Marshall, Advertising Editor
**Management:**
Joyce Deich ..............................President
Alicia Denzer .................Circulation Manager
**Editorial:**
Jeff Nowak ................................Editor
Paula Marshall .................Advertising Editor

**Materials Accepted/Included:** 01-Business news 02-By-line articles 03-Fashion news 04-Food news 05-Freelance copy 06-Letters to editor 07-Real estate news 08-Sports news 09-Travel news 10-Book rev. 11-Movie rev. 12-Music rev. 13-TV rev. 14-Theater rev. 15-Coming events 16-Obituaries 17-Question & answer 18-Social announcements 19-Artwork 20-Cartoons 21-Photos 22-TV listings 23-Audio rec. 24-Video rec. 25-Books 26-Films/film clips 27-Personnel news 28-Press releases 29-New product news/photos 30-Trade lit. 31-Contracts awarded 32-Display adv. 33-Classified adv.

6-123

**Desc.:** Official publication of Women's International Bowling Congress. Coverage is devoted to policies, procedures, achievements of women bowling in WIBC sanctioned competition. Answers queries, but rarely purchases unsolicited articles. Uses some publicity on bowling related products and events, gives bylines for major features and articles. Departments include: bowling instruction, rules, news articles on major events in bowling, wrapup of oddities or achievements by lower or medium average bowlers, letters, senior bowlers, bowling tips and junior bowlers.

**Readers:** WIBC leagues, bowling centers, sports writers, industry leaders and other sports.

26126

## WESTERN OUTDOORS
3197-E. Airport Loop
Costa Mesa, CA 92626
Telephone: (714) 546-4370
Mailing Address:
P.O. Box 2027
Newport Beach, CA 92659-1027
Year Established: 1960
Pub. Frequency: 9/yr.
Page Size: standard
Subscrip. Rate: $2.95 newsstand;
$3.50/Can.; $14.95/yr.
Materials: 02,05,06,10,19,20,21,25,28,29,
32,33
Freelance Pay: $400-500/feature
Print Process: web offset
Circulation: 130,000
Circulation Type: paid
**Owner(s):**
Western Outdoors Publications
3197-E. Airport Loop Dr.
Costa Mesa, CA 92626
Telephone: (714) 546-4370
Ownership %: 100
**Management:**
Robert Twilegar ...........................President
Robert Twilegar ...........................Publisher
Joe Higgins ....................Advertising Manager
**Editorial:**
Jack Brown .........................................Editor
Ron Eldridge ......................Managing Editor
Rich Holland ......................Associate Editor
Pat McDonell .....................Associate Editor
Bill Karr ...........................Associate Editor
Ron Eldridge ................................Columnist
John McKim ..................................Columnist
Jim Matthews .................................Columnist
Rich Holland ..................................Columnist
Mike Jones ....................................Columnist
**Desc.:** Edited for active sportsmen in the western states. The magazine stresses informative reports. Editorial coverage provides full details on Western fishing and hunting "how-to" techniques and where-to-go in the West for recreational activities with emphasis on new places for fishing, hunting, camping, and pleasure boating. Detailed maps and trip facts accompany each major feature. Regular columns cover fishing, guns and hunting, boating, bass fishing. All advertisements are coupon-keyed to Nielsen Reader Inquiry Service. Departments include: Fishing, Hunting, Boating, Camping, Sportsmen on Wheels, New Products Section, Test & Evaluation Section, Shopper Section.
**Readers:** The active sportsman.
**Deadline:** story-6 mo. prior to pub. date

26572

## WHEELERS RV RESORT & CAMPGROUND GUIDE
1310 Jarvis
Elk Grove Village, IL 60007
Telephone: (708) 981-0100
FAX: (708) 981-0106
Year Established: 1972
Pub. Frequency: a.
Page Size: standard
Subscrip. Rate: $12.95/yr.
Materials: 02,08,09,21,32
Freelance Pay: negotiable
Print Process: web offset
Circulation: 206,000
Circulation Type: controlled & paid
**Owner(s):**
Print Media Services, Ltd.
1310 Jarvis
Elk Grove Village, IL 60007
Telephone: (708) 981-0100
FAX: (708) 981-0106
Ownership %: 100
**Management:**
Gloria S. Telander .........................President
Gloria S. Telander .........................Publisher
**Editorial:**
Gerri Bussiere ..................................Editor
**Desc.:** Lists and quality rates, with complete information, phone numbers, and mail addresses, all significant private and public parks and campgrounds in the United States, Canada, and Mexico. The upfront 4/color feature section carries articles on camping, travel, border crossing, and general information on RVing and camping.
**Readers:** Campers and recreational vehicle tourists. Average age, 50-64; average income $45,000 with a college degree.
**Deadline:** story-Sep. 1; news-Sep. 1; photo-Sep. 1; ads-Nov. 1

69453

## WINDSURFING CALIFORNIA
3702 W. Valley Highway N.
Ste. 106
Auburn, WA 98001
Telephone: (206) 351-6442
FAX: (206) 351-9274
Year Established: 1990
Pub. Frequency: 7/yr.
Subscrip. Rate: $12.95/yr.
Circulation: 50000
Circulation Type: paid
**Owner(s):**
Extreme Publishing
3702 W. Valley Highway N.
Auburn, WA 98001
Telephone: (206) 351-6442
FAX: (206) 351-9274
Ownership %: 100
**Management:**
Scott Campbell ...........................Publisher
**Editorial:**
Cary L. Ordway ..............................Editor
Cary Adams ..................Advertising Director
Golda Irvin .....................Circulation Director

52559

## WINDSURFING MAGAZINE
330 W. Canton Ave.
Winter Park, FL 32789
Telephone: (407) 628-4802
FAX: (407) 628-7061
Mailing Address:
P.O. Box 2456
Winter Park, FL 32790
Year Established: 1981
Pub. Frequency: 9/yr.
Page Size: standard
Subscrip. Rate: $2.95 newsstand;
$18.97/yr.
Materials: 05,32

Freelance Pay: $25-$500/article
Circulation: 75,000
Circulation Type: paid
**Owner(s):**
World Publications, Inc.
P.O. Box 2456
Winter Park, FL 32790
Telephone: (407) 628-4802
Ownership %: 100
**Management:**
Terry Snow ...............................Publisher
**Editorial:**
Debbie L. Snow ...............................Editor
Sue Gilman ....................Advertising Director
Trish Carter .....................Circulation Director
Jim Robinson .................Circulation Systems Manager
**Desc.:** About the sport of boardsailing (a.k.a. windsurfing).

69462

## WINDY CITY SPORTS
1450 W. Randolph
Chicago, IL 60607
Telephone: (312) 421-1551
FAX: (312) 421-1454
Year Established: 1987
Pub. Frequency: 11/yr.
Page Size: tabloid
Subscrip. Rate: $15/yr.
Materials: 01,03,04,05,06,08,09,10,15,18,
19,20,21,25,28,29,30,32,33
Print Process: web
Circulation: 100,000
Circulation Type: controlled & free
**Owner(s):**
Chicago Sports Resources, Inc.
1450 W. Randolph
Chicago, IL 60607
Telephone: (312) 421-1551
Ownership %: 100
**Management:**
Mary Thorne ...............................Publisher
**Editorial:**
Shelley Berryhill .............................Editor
Doug Kaplan ..................................Sales
**Desc.:** Windy City Sports magazine is a monthly amateur sports magazine that reaches 100,000 readers in the Chicago area. The magazine covers topics including running, cycling, triatholons, in-line skating, health clubs, aerobics and various winter sports, including downhill and cross country skiing.

26517

## WINGED FOOT, THE
180 Central Pk. S.
New York, NY 10019
Telephone: (212) 247-5100
Year Established: 1892
Pub. Frequency: m.
Page Size: standard
Subscrip. Rate: $2.50/copy
Circulation: 8,000
Circulation Type: paid
**Owner(s):**
The Winged Foot
180 Central Park S.
New York, NY 10019
Ownership %: 100
**Management:**
Fred G. Jarvis ...............................Publisher
**Editorial:**
Fred G. Jarvis ................................Editor
Kevin Moccia ...................Managing Editor
**Desc.:** Athletic features of interest to New York Athletic Club members and articles pertaining to sports and activities of N.Y.A.C.
**Readers:** Members of N.Y.A.C.

26636

## WOMEN'S SPORTS & FITNESS MAGAZINE
2025 Pearl St.
Boulder, CO 80302
Telephone: (303) 440-5111
FAX: (303) 440-3313
Year Established: 1974
Pub. Frequency: 8/yr.
Page Size: standard
Subscrip. Rate: $19.97/yr.
Materials: 02,04,05,06,08,24,25,28,29
Freelance Pay: $100-$1500/article
Circulation: 155,000
Circulation Type: paid
**Owner(s):**
Sports & Fitness Publishing
2025 Pearl St.
Boulder, CO 80302
Telephone: (303) 440-5111
Ownership %: 100
**Bureau(s):**
Women's Sports & Fitness, Inc.
145 E. 57th St.
New York, NY 10022
Telephone: (212) 980-5580
Contact: Susan Sheerin
**Management:**
John T. Winsor ...........................President
Jane McConnell ...........................Publisher
Daemon Filson .................Advertising Manager
Sandra Llewelyn .................Production Manager
**Editorial:**
Jane McConnell ...................Editor in Chief
Allison Glock ......................Senior Editor
Mary Duffyonen .................................Editor
Lisa Goodman .............................Advertising
Michelle Theall ...........................Advertising
Janis Llewelyn ............................Art Director
Nancy Jordan ...............................Copy Chief
Laurie Jennings .............Photography Director
**Desc.:** Articles and stories should be submitted on a speculation basis, approximately 600-2,000 words for editor's consideration. It is preferable to send initial query. Interested in profiles, how-to fitness and sports, essays on sports and fitness, nutrition and health articles, as well as articles dealing with women's involvement in sports, fitness, health, as related to an active life style.
**Readers:** Women who lead an active lifestyle. Average age 35.

69759

## WORLD WRESTLING FEDERATION MAGAZINE
1241 E. Main St.
Stamford, CT 06902
Telephone: (203) 352-8600
FAX: (203) 352-8699
Mailing Address:
P.O. Box 3857
Stamford, CT 06902
Year Established: 1983
Pub. Frequency: m.
Subscrip. Rate: $20/yr., $35/2 yrs. in US;
$34.24/yr., $63.13/2 yrs. in Canada;
$32/yr., $59/2 yrs. foreign
Circulation: 364,306
Circulation Type: paid
**Owner(s):**
Titan Sports, Inc.
1241 E. Main St.
Stamford, CT 06902
Telephone: (203) 352-8600
Ownership %: 100
**Management:**
Thomas Emanuel ...........................Publisher
**Editorial:**
Vince Russo ..................................Editor

**Materials Accepted/Included:** 01-Business news 02-By-line articles 03-Fashion news 04-Food news 05-Freelance copy 06-Letters to editor 07-Real estate news 08-Sports news 09-Travel news 10-Book rev. 11-Movie rev. 12-Music rev. 13-TV rev. 14-Theater rev. 15-Coming events 16-Obituaries 17-Question & answer 18-Social announcements 19-Artwork 20-Cartoons 21-Photos 22-TV listings 23-Audio rec. 24-Video rec. 25-Books 26-Films/film clips 27-Personnel news 28-Press releases 29-New product news/photos 30-Trade lit. 31-Contracts awarded 32-Display adv. 33-Classified adv.

6-124

**Readers:** Fans of the World Wrestling Federation.

## Group 672-Travel

### AAA GOING PLACES MAGAZINE
26540

1515 N. Westshore Blvd.
Tampa, FL 33607
Telephone: (813) 289-5923
Mailing Address:
P.O. Box 31087
Tampa, FL 33631
Year Established: 1982
Pub. Frequency: bi-m.
Page Size: 4 color photos/art
Subscrip. Rate: free for AAA members
Freelance Pay: $15/printed pg.
Circulation: 865000
Circulation Type: free
**Owner(s):**
AAA Auto Club South
P.O. Box 31087
Tampa, FL 33631
Telephone: (813) 289-5000
Ownership %: 100
**Management:**
Robert R. Sharp ...................................Publisher
Sherry Gunia ......................Advertising Manager
**Editorial:**
Phyllis Zeno ...............................................Editor
Thom Shupp ..................................Art Director
**Desc.:** Policy is to inform AAA members in Florida, Georgia, and Tennessee of travel opportunities available by car, ship, motorcoach. Travel section uses features and photographs of interesting and different places including worldwide destinations and those within the US.
**Readers:** Members of AAA Auto Club South. It is primarily a motor club magazine with auto-related topics, club news, and travel stories both foreign and domestic.

### AAA MOTORIST OF NORTH EASTERN PA.
25117

1035 N. Washington Ave.
Scranton, PA 18509
Telephone: (717) 348-2511
FAX: (717) 384-2771
Pub. Frequency: bi-m.
Page Size: standard
Subscrip. Rate: membership
Materials: 32
Print Process: offset
Circulation: 90,000
Circulation Type: free
**Owner(s):**
AAA Motor Club of North Eastern PA.
Scranton, PA
Telephone: (717) 344-9661
Ownership %: 100
**Management:**
Larry Heckman ...........................Vice President
Craig H. Smith ..........Public Relations Manager
**Editorial:**
John D. Wilson .....................Managing Editor
**Desc.:** Anything pertaining to the ownership and operation of an automobile, highways and proposed highways, travel of all types including air and steamship.
**Readers:** Urban, rural county areas of North Eastern PA.

### AAA TODAY
25139

1025 N. Washington St.
Greenfield, OH 45123
Telephone: (614) 338-8222
Year Established: 1928
Pub. Frequency: bi-m.

---

Page Size: standard
Subscrip. Rate: membership
Materials: 09,21,32
Circulation: 1,000,000
**Owner(s):**
Automobile Club Publications
1025 N. Washington St.
Greenfield, OH 45123
Telephone: (614) 338-8222
Ownership %: 100
**Editorial:**
Pat Levak .................................................Editor
Ron Coffey .............................Managing Editor
Lisa Duac .............................Advertising Sales
**Desc.:** Material we use must relate to domestic and worldwide travel, covering not more than a page, including photos. Subjects include safety relating to autos, pedestrians, travel, as well as car care tips.
**Readers:** AAA members in Ohio, Alabama, Tennessee, West Virginia, Indiana, New York, Massachusetts, North Carolina, Vermont and Pennsylvania.
**Deadline:** story-5 mo. prior to pub. date; news-5 mo. prior; photo-5 mo. prior; ads-5 mo. prior

### AAA TODAY
25146

95 S. Hanover St.
Pottstown, PA 19464
Telephone: (215) 323-6300
FAX: (610) 323-6684
Mailing Address:
P.O. Box 559
Pottstown, PA 19464-0559
Year Established: 1908
Pub. Frequency: bi-m.
Page Size: standard
Subscrip. Rate: $2/yr. members; $1/copy non-members
Circulation: 37,000
Circulation Type: paid
**Owner(s):**
Greenfield Printing and Publishing Co.
Ownership %: 100
**Editorial:**
Franklin Mann, III .....................................Editor
**Desc.:** Endeavors to carry news items and stories of travel, Departments include: Travel and General Stories.
**Readers:** Diversified; business people, farmers.

### AAA TRAVELER
25134

1020 Hamilton St.
P.O. Box 1910
Allentown, PA 18105
Telephone: (215) 434-5141
FAX: (610) 778-3381
Year Established: 1909
Pub. Frequency: bi-m.
Page Size: tabloid
Subscrip. Rate: free/members
Circulation: 88,000
Circulation Type: controlled
**Owner(s):**
AAA Lehigh Valley
1020 Hamilton St.
P.O. Box 1910
Allentown, PA 18105
Telephone: (215) 434-5141
Ownership %: 100
**Management:**
Steven E. Wojnarowicz ......................President
**Editorial:**
Judith A. Barberich ...................Editor in Chief
**Desc.:** Contains articles on travel planning, reservation services, license and title services, auto insurance.
**Readers:** Members of AAA.

---

### AAA WORLD
25128

1000 AAA Dr.
Heathrow, FL 32746
Telephone: (407) 444-4300
FAX: (407) 444-4140
Year Established: 1947
Pub. Frequency: bi-m.
Page Size: standard
Subscrip. Rate: $4/yr. non-members; $2/yr. members
Materials: 32
Freelance Pay: negotiable
Circulation: 650,000
**Owner(s):**
American Automobile Association
1000 AAA Dr.
Heathrow, FL 32746
Telephone: (407) 444-4000
Ownership %: 100
**Management:**
Terry R. Farias ...................................Publisher
Dan Millott ......................Advertising Manager
**Editorial:**
William F. Dodd .....................Executive Editor
Janie Graziani ..........................................Editor
**Desc.:** News and features regarding motoring, travel, safety. Primary advertising media for agencies representing automobiles, auto service, auto financing, fuel and oil, tires, travel accommodations, resort area promotion, tourist attractions, foreign travel transportation, auto air conditioning.
**Readers:** Motorists, travellers.

### AAA WORLD
26548

118 Market St.
York, PA 15907
Telephone: (717) 848-8585
FAX: (717) 845-5444
Pub. Frequency: bi-m.
Page Size: pocket
Subscrip. Rate: $1/yr. members only
Circulation: 123,000
Circulation Type: controlled
**Owner(s):**
Triple A Traveler Auto Club of Southern PA
118 E. Market St.
York, PA 17401
Telephone: (714) 848-9723
Ownership %: 100
**Editorial:**
Donna Grove ............................................Editor
Bill Dixon ......................................Advertising
**Desc.:** Articles and items of interest to the general motoring public and members of the Mid-State Auto Club. All items of motoring interest, club services and activities, civic and safety matters.
**Readers:** AAA members.

### AAA WORLD MAGAZINE
26565

8030 Excelsior Dr.
Madison, WI 53717
Telephone: (608) 828-2487
FAX: (608) 828-2443
Mailing Address:
P.O. Box 33
Madison, WI 53701
Year Established: 1980
Pub. Frequency: bi-m.
Page Size: 4 color photos/art
Subscrip. Rate: $2/yr. AAA WI members; $4/yr. non-members
Freelance Pay: $.05-.10/wd.
Circulation: 263,535
Circulation Type: controlled
**Owner(s):**
AAA Wisconsin
P.O. Box 33
Madison, WI 53701
Telephone: (608) 828-2487
Ownership %: 100

---

**Management:**
Douglas Damerst ...................................Publisher
Matt Hamill .........................Advertising Manager
Louis Talluto ..................General Manager
Compton Boodhoo ..........Production Manager
**Editorial:**
Marianne Camas ........................Senior Editor
Ernest W. Stetenfeld ...........................Editor
Douglas Damerst ..................................Editor
Joseph Laubmeier ..................Associate Editor
Joseph D. Younger ....................Feature Editor
**Desc.:** Basically travel, also features on motoring, safety, legislation dealing with motoring, travel.
**Readers:** Members of the Wisconsin Div. of AAA.

### ACCENT MAGAZINE
61661

1720 Washington Blvd.
Ogden, UT 84404
Telephone: (801) 394-9446
FAX: (801) 627-1453
Mailing Address:
P.O. Box 10010
Ogden, UT 84409
Year Established: 1981
Pub. Frequency: m.
Page Size: standard
Materials: 02,09,28
Freelance Pay: $.15/wd.; photos/varies
Print Process: web
Circulation: 100,000
**Owner(s):**
Meridian International, Inc.
1720 Washington Blvd.
Ogden, UT 84404
Telephone: (801) 394-9446
Ownership %: 100
**Management:**
Carroll Shreeve ..........................Vice President
Carroll Shreeve ...................................Publisher
**Desc.:** Accent on travel, fun, fitness, sight-seeing, the ordinary and the unusual in foreign and domestic destinations, where you can spend money reasonable or lavishly.
**Readers:** Upper-Middle Income
**Deadline:** story-3 mos. prior to pub. date; news-6 mos. prior; photo-3 mos. prior

### ADVENTURE ROAD
25118

30400 Van Dyke Ave.
Warren, MI 48093
Telephone: (800) 334-3300
Year Established: 1964
Pub. Frequency: q.
Page Size: standard
Subscrip. Rate: free members; $1.50/issue
Materials: 32
Freelance Pay: $300-$500/article
Circulation: 1,500,000
Circulation Type: free & paid
**Owner(s):**
Amoco Enterprises, Inc.
200 E. Randolph
Chicago, IL 60601
Telephone: (312) 856-2583
Ownership %: 100
**Management:**
Bill Rowles ...............................................Publisher
Peggy Walsh ...........................Business Manager
Michael Cunningham ..........Managing Director
**Editorial:**
Michael Brudenell ................................Editor
Jeff Allen ...................................Art Director
Ann Phipps ..........................Art Supervisor
Rudy Marcinko ...............Business Coordinator
Christine Pett ...............Circulation Director
Greg Nelson ...............................Copy Director
Nadine Scodellatro ...............Department Editor
Carolyn Brooks ...............Production Coordinator

---

**Materials Accepted/Included:** 01-Business news 02-By-line articles 03-Fashion news 04-Food news 05-Freelance copy 06-Letters to editor 07-Real estate news 08-Sports news 09-Travel news 10-Book rev. 11-Movie rev. 12-Music rev. 13-TV rev. 14-Theater rev. 15-Coming events 16-Obituaries 17-Question & answer 18-Social announcements 19-Artwork 20-Cartoons 21-Photos 22-TV listings 23-Audio rec. 24-Video rec. 25-Books 26-Films/film clips 27-Personnel news 28-Press releases 29-New product news/photos 30-Trade lit. 31-Contracts awarded 32-Display adv. 33-Classified adv.

6-125

**Desc.:** A travel and recreation/leisure-oriented magazine that covers such subjects as: natural and man-made travel attractions; spectator and participant sports and sporting events; camping; trailering; cities, states and countries to visit; automotive subjects including auto maintenance; hotels; general travel tips. Publicity materials are used for article ideas. All photos/illustrations are in color. Departments include: Calendar of Events, Car Care Center, News Briefs, Camera Corner, Weekend Wanderer, Motor Club Mailbox.
**Readers:** 73% male; median age 48.6 years; median income $45,600; 80% own homes.

25119
### AIRFAIR INTERLINE VACATION GUIDE
6401 Congress Ave., Ste. 100
Boca Raton, FL 33487
Telephone: (407) 994-4509
FAX: (407) 997-7398
Year Established: 1971
Pub. Frequency: q.
Page Size: standard
Subscrip. Rate: $18/yr.
Materials: 32,33
Freelance Pay: negotiable
Circulation: 32,000
Circulation Type: paid
**Owner(s):**
Fair Weather Group, Inc.
6401 Congress Ave., Ste. 100
Boca Raton, FL 33487
Telephone: (407) 994-4509
Ownership %: 100
**Management:**
Robert A. Barrett ............................Publisher
Sandra J. Schocke ...........Circulation Manager
Dawn Silverberg .........................Sales Manager
**Editorial:**
Debra Fredel .............................Managing Editor
**Desc.:** Travel, airline industry news. Travel magazine for airline employees; source of reduced rate travel and discount information.
**Readers:** Airline employees.

69585
### AMTRAK EXPRESS
1301 Carolina St.
Greensboro, NC 27401
Telephone: (910) 378-6065
FAX: (910) 275-2864
Year Established: 1981
Pub. Frequency: bi-m.
Page Size: standard
Subscrip. Rate: $18/yr.
Materials: 05,06,15,25,32
Print Process: web offset
Circulation: 235,000
Circulation Type: controlled
**Owner(s):**
Pace Communications, Inc.
1301 Carolina St.
Greensboro, NC 27401
Telephone: (910) 378-6065
Ownership %: 100
**Editorial:**
Melinda L. Stovall ...............................Editor
Maryann Earley ...............................Advertising

**Desc.:** Amtrak Express is designed to speak to the mix of leisure and business travelers riding Amtrak. Capitalizing on the quality time afforded by rail travel, Amtrak Express presents thought-provoking articles on business, the arts, personal growth, technology, health and people, and travel articles that highlight the Amtrak rail experience. Amtrak Express brings America and its people to the reader as does Amtrak--in a friendly, engaging and personal way.
**Readers:** The riders of Amtrak trains nationwide.
**Deadline:** story-4 mos. prior to pub. date; news-4 mos. prior; photo-4 mos. prior; ads-2 mos. prior

26532
### ARIZONA HIGHWAYS MAGAZINE
2039 W. Lewis Ave.
Phoenix, AZ 85009
Telephone: (602) 258-6641
FAX: (602) 254-4505
Year Established: 1925
Pub. Frequency: m.
Page Size: oversize
Subscrip. Rate: $2.25 newsstand; $17/yr.; $29/2 yrs; $41/3 yrs.
Materials: 02,05,09,15,19,20,21,25
Freelance Pay: $.20-$.50/wd.
Print Process: web offset
Circulation: 385,500
Circulation Type: paid
**Owner(s):**
Arizona Department of Transportation
206 S. 17th Ave.
Phoenix, AZ 85007
Telephone: (602) 258-6641
Ownership %: 100
**Management:**
Hugh Harelson ...............................Publisher
Bethany Braley .......Customer Service Manager
Barbara Leonard .........................Sales Manager
**Editorial:**
Robert Early .............................................Editor
Richard G. Stahl ................Managing Editor
Christine Mitchell ...........................Art Director
Russ Wall ........................Associate Art Director
Becky Mong ..............................Associate Editor
Robert Steele ......................Business Director
Nina La France ................Circulation Marketing Director
Gary Bennett .........................Creative Director
Nina La France ....................Marketing Director
Larry Husband ....................Operations Director
Cindy Mackey .....................Production Director
**Desc.:** Official state publication featuring extended use of four color reproductions, history, flora and fauna. Covers tourism and travel articles of interest to Southwest.
**Readers:** Tourist-minded people of all 50 U.S. states and 110 foreign countries.

67297
### ASIA PACIFIC TRAVEL
1675 Rollins Rd., Ste. B3
Burlingame, CA 94010-2320
Telephone: (415) 697-4400
FAX: (415) 697-7937
Year Established: 1990
Pub. Frequency: q.
Page Size: standard
Subscrip. Rate: $12/yr. US; $30/yr. foreign
Materials: 01,05,06,09,10,19,210,21,25,32,33
Print Process: web offset
**Owner(s):**
Publishing Today
1675 Rollins Rd., Ste. B3
Burlingame, CA 94010
Telephone: (510) 697-4400
FAX: (510) 697-7937
Ownership %: 100

**Management:**
Dr. Kumai Pati ............................President
Dr. Kumai Pati ............................Publisher
Andy Krishen ....................Advertising Manager

61331
### ASU TRAVEL GUIDE
1525 E. Francisco Blvd.
San Rafael, CA 94901
Telephone: (415) 459-0300
FAX: (415) 459-0459
Year Established: 1970
Pub. Frequency: q.
Page Size: pocket
Subscrip. Rate: $16.50 newsstand; $32.95/yr.
Freelance Pay: $200/feature article 1,500-1,800 wds.
Circulation: 60,000
Circulation Type: paid
**Owner(s):**
Mr. Ronald Folkenflik, Publisher/ASU Travel Guide
1525 E. Francisco Blvd.
San Rafael, CA 94901
Telephone: (415) 459-0300
Ownership %: 100
**Editorial:**
Christopher Gil ...........................................Editor
Ron Heard ........................Marketing Director
**Desc.:** 16 feature destination pieces per year, or 4 per quarterly issue, each 1,500 to 1,800 words in length. Articles should be timely, newsworthy and reflective of trends in travel and destinations among a readership of diverse ages, all of whom have airline employer relationship.
**Readers:** Active Airline Employees, Retired Airline Employees, Spouses and Dependent Children of Airline Employees, Friends of Airline Employees; And Parents of Airline Employees; Ages 18-90.

71258
### COLUMBIA GORGE MAGAZINE
500 Morton Rd.
Hood River, OR 97031
Telephone: (503) 386-7440
FAX: (503) 386-7480
Mailing Address:
P.O. Box 918
Hood River, OR 97031
Year Established: 1990
Pub. Frequency: a.
Page Size: standard
Subscrip. Rate: $2.50 newsstand; $7.95/4 issues
Materials: 01,02,04,05,08,09,10,15,17,21, 28,29,32
Print Process: web offset
Circulation: 92,000
Circulation Type: free & paid
**Owner(s):**
Gorge Publishing, Inc.
500 Moron Rd.
Hood River, OR 97031
Telephone: (503) 386-7440
FAX: (503) 386-7480
Ownership %: 100
**Editorial:**
Carol York ...........................................Editor
**Desc.:** The official visitor and recreation guide for the Columbia River Gorge, covering the area from Troutdale to Arlington and Mt. Adams to Mt Hood.
**Readers:** Primarily West Coast residents plus national and international group tours. Families and senior citizens, day vistors to weeklong vacationers. Sightseers and active recreation participants, skiers and windsurfers.
**Deadline:** story-Apr. 18th; news-Apr. 18th; photo-Apr. 18th; ads-Apr. 18th

69744
### CONDE NAST'S TRAVELER
360 Madison Ave.
New York, NY 10017
Telephone: (212) 880-8800
FAX: (212) 880-2190
Year Established: 1954
Pub. Frequency: m.
Subscrip. Rate: $3.95 newsstand; $15/yr.
Circulation: 757,000
Circulation Type: paid
**Owner(s):**
Conde Nast Publications, Inc.
360 Madison Ave.
New York, NY 10017
Telephone: (212) 880-8800
Ownership %: 100
**Management:**
Richard Beckman ............................Publisher
**Editorial:**
Thomas J. Wallace ...............................Editor
Cara Ferragamo ...............................Advertising

65128
### COUNTRY INNS-BED & BREAKFAST
15 S. Orange Ave.
South Orange, NJ 07079
Telephone: (201) 762-7090
FAX: (201) 762-1491
Mailing Address:
P.O. Box 182
South Orange, NJ 07079
Pub. Frequency: bi-m.
Page Size: standard
Subscrip. Rate: $3.95 newsstand; $17.95/yr.
Circulation: 200,000
Circulation Type: paid
**Owner(s):**
Country Inns Publications, Inc.
P.O. Box 182
South Orange, NJ 07079
Telephone: (201) 762-7090
**Management:**
Charles Silver ............................Publisher
**Editorial:**
Gail Rudder Kent ........................Editor in Chief
Elise Margulis ...........................Classified Editor

67076
### CRUISES & TOURS
1502 Augusta
Ste. 415
Houston, TX 77057
Telephone: (713) 974-6903
FAX: (713) 974-0445
Year Established: 1992
Pub. Frequency: q.
Page Size: standard
Subscrip. Rate: $3.95 newsstand; $15.80/yr.
Circulation: 52,000
Circulation Type: paid
**Owner(s):**
Vacation Publications
1502 Augusta
Ste. 415
Houston, TX 77057
Telephone: (713) 974-6903
Ownership %: 100
**Management:**
Alan Fox ............................Publisher
**Editorial:**
Mary Lu Abbott ...............................Editor

66521
### CRUISE TRAVEL
990 Grove St.
Evanston, IL 60201-4370
Telephone: (708) 491-6440
Year Established: 1979
Pub. Frequency: bi-m.
Page Size: standard
Subscrip. Rate: $2.50/newsstand; $18/yr.
Materials: 01,02,04,05,06,09,10,21,24,25, 28,29,30,32,33

**Materials Accepted/Included:** 01-Business news 02-By-line articles 03-Fashion news 04-Food news 05-Freelance copy 06-Letters to editor 07-Real estate news 08-Sports news 09-Travel news 10-Book rev. 11-Movie rev. 12-Music rev. 13-TV rev. 14-Theater rev. 15-Coming events 16-Obituaries 17-Question & answer 18-Social announcements 19-Artwork 20-Cartoons 21-Photos 22-TV listings 23-Audio rec. 24-Video rec. 25-Books 26-Films/film clips 27-Personnel news 28-Press releases 29-New product news/photos 30-Trade lit. 31-Contracts awarded 32-Display adv. 33-Classified adv.

Freelance Pay: varies
Print Process: web offset
Circulation: 200,000
Circulation Type: paid
**Owner(s):**
World Publishing Co.
990 Grove St.
Evanston, IL 60201
Telephone: (708) 491-6440
Ownership %: 100
**Management:**
Norman Jacobs .............................Publisher
**Editorial:**
Robert Meyers ...........................Editor in Chief
Charles Doherty ......................Managing Editor
**Desc.:** A magazine aimed at those who
enjoy or dream of cruise vacations.
**Readers:** Cruise vacationers.
**Deadline:** story-5-7 mos. prior to pub.
date; news-3 mos. prior; photo-3 mos.
prior; ads-2 mos. prior

### DIVERSION
26538

1790 Broadway
6th Fl.
New York, NY 10019
Telephone: (212) 969-7500
FAX: (212) 969-7557
Year Established: 1973
Pub. Frequency: m.
Page Size: standard
Subscrip. Rate: $48/yr.
Circulation: 179,000
Circulation Type: controlled
**Owner(s):**
Hearst Professional Magazines, Inc.
60 E. 42nd St.
Ste. 2424
New York, NY 10165
Telephone: (212) 297-9600
Ownership %: 100
**Management:**
Edward B. Hughes ......................Vice President
Thomas E. Duffy ...........................Publisher
Leslie Dubin ........................Promotion Manager
**Editorial:**
Tom Passavant .............................Editor
Shari Hartford ........................Managing Editor
**Desc.:** Leisure and travel for physicians.
Departments include: Food & Wine,
Finance, Travel, Sports, and general
leisure activities.
**Readers:** Physicians and dentists.

### ENDLESS VACATION
69741

P.O. Box 80260
Indianapolis, IN 46280-0260
Telephone: (317) 871-9504
FAX: (317) 871-9507
Year Established: 1975
Pub. Frequency: bi-m.
Subscrip. Rate: $65/yr.
Circulation: 907,609
Circulation Type: paid
**Owner(s):**
Endless Vacation Publications
P.O. Box 80260
Indianapolis, IN 46280-0260
Telephone: (317) 871-9504
Ownership %: 100
**Editorial:**
Helen O'Guinn ...............................Editor

### ERIE MOTORIST, THE
25127

420 W. Sixth St.
Erie, PA 16507
Telephone: (814) 454-0123
FAX: (814) 455-5688
Year Established: 1904
Pub. Frequency: bi-m.
Page Size: standard
Subscrip. Rate: $.15-$1.50; with AAA
membership
Circulation: 35,000

Circulation Type: controlled
**Owner(s):**
Erie County Motor Club, The
420 W. Sixth St.
Erie, PA 16507
Telephone: (814) 454-0123
Ownership %: 100
**Management:**
James R. Brown .............................President
**Desc.:** Travel features, occasional new
product stories, local interest, local AAA.
All AAA oriented. Departments include:
No Fixed Breakdown, Editorial Page,
Letters to Editor, President's Message.
**Readers:** AAA members in Erie County. All
own cars, 50% buy new cars.

### FRIENDLY EXCHANGE
66036

c/o The Aegis Group
30400 Van Dyke Ave.
Warren, MI 48093
Telephone: (810) 558-7226
Mailing Address:
P.O. Box 2120
Warren, MI 48093
Year Established: 1981
Pub. Frequency: q.
Page Size: standard
Subscrip. Rate: free for qualified customers
Materials: 02,05,06,09,15,21,32
Freelance Pay: negotiable
Print Process: rotogravure
Circulation: 5,700,000
Circulation Type: controlled
**Owner(s):**
Farmers Insurance Group
4680 Wilshire Blvd.
Los Angeles, CA 90010
Telephone: (213) 932-3508
Ownership %: 100
**Editorial:**
Adele Malott ...............................Editor
**Desc.:** Magazine of domestic family travel
and leisure. Readers are frequent and
enthusiastic travels and are active
particpants in such recreational activities
as gardening, photography, entertaining,
the arts, camping and cooking.
**Readers:** Customers of Farmers Insurance
Group.

### GO
26541

720 E. Morehead St.
Charlotte, NC 28202
Telephone: (704) 377-3600
FAX: (704) 358-1585
Mailing Address:
P.O. Box 30008
Charlotte, NC 28230
Year Established: 1922
Page Size: tabloid
Subscrip. Rate: free to members only
Materials: 09,15,19,20,21,28,29,30,32
Freelance Pay: $.15/wd.
Print Process: web offset
Circulation: 375000
Circulation Type: controlled
**Owner(s):**
AAA Carolina Motor Club
720 E. Morehead St.
Charlotte, NC 28202
Telephone: (704) 377-3600
FAX: (704) 358-1585
Ownership %: 100
**Editorial:**
Tom Crosby ...............................Editor
Christine Wilkie ......................Managing Editor
**Desc.:** Reports on consumer safety issues,
travel (domestic and foreign), automotive
advice and driving/motoring issues.
**Readers:** Motorists and world travelers.
**Deadline:** story-1st of mo. prior to pub.
date; ads-1st of mo. prior to pub. date

### HARTFORD AUTOMOBILER
26543

815 Farmington Ave.
West Hartford, CT 06119
Telephone: (203) 236-3261
FAX: (203) 523-7688
Year Established: 1923
Pub. Frequency: m.
Page Size: pocket
Subscrip. Rate: free to members; $2/yr.
Circulation: 130,000
Circulation Type: free & paid
**Owner(s):**
Automobile Club of Hartford
815 Farmington Ave.
West Hartford, CT 06119
Telephone: (203) 236-3261
**Management:**
James H. Doraf ...........................Publisher
**Editorial:**
James L. Olbrys ...........................Editor
Jennifer Giorgio ...........................Editor
Linda Habermeir ....................Associate Publisher
**Desc.:** Primarily devoted to news of the
automobile club, as well as general
topics such as road safety, motoring,
and travel.
**Readers:** Members of the Automobile Club
of Hartford.

### HOME & AWAY, INDIANA
25129

3750 Guion Rd.
Indianapolis, IN 46222
Telephone: (317) 923-1500
Mailing Address:
P.O. Box 88505
Indianapolis, IN 46208
Year Established: 1913
Pub. Frequency: bi-m.
Page Size: standard
Subscrip. Rate: $6/yr.
Materials: 32
Freelance Pay: $100-$200/article
Circulation: 28,214
Circulation Type: controlled
**Owner(s):**
AAA Hoosier Motor Club
3750 Guion Rd.
P. O. Box 88505
Indianapolis, IN 46222
Telephone: (317) 923-1500
Ownership %: 100
**Management:**
Brian Nicol ...............................Publisher
Vern Cornish ......................Advertising Manager
**Editorial:**
Hugh F. Orr ...............................Editor
Stephanie Hinds ...........................Miscellaneous
**Desc.:** Publication devoted to car and
motoring news, insurance, traffic safety
and travel data.
**Readers:** Members of AAA Hoosier Motor
Club.

### HOME & AWAY, MINNESOTA
25137

7 Travelers Trail
Burnsville, MN 55337
Telephone: (612) 890-2500
FAX: (612) 891-8222
Year Established: 1980
Pub. Frequency: bi-m.
Page Size: standard
Subscrip. Rate: $6/yr.
Freelance Pay: $25-$350
Circulation: 212,000
Circulation Type: paid
**Owner(s):**
Minnesota State Automobile Association
7 Travelers Trail
Burnsville, MN 55337
Telephone: (612) 890-2500
Ownership %: 100
**Management:**
Duane Crandall ...........................Publisher
Ron Siegmund ......................Business Manager

**Editorial:**
Ron Siegmund ...............................Editor
**Desc.:** Official publication for AAA
members in Minnesota. Handles news
and features of interest to motorists,
developments in highways, highway
building, traffic engineering, education
and enforcement, travel news and
features/both foreign and domestic/by
automobile and all public carriers, tips
on car care and driving, Minnesota
people, places, events, outdoor
recreational activities, news of local
AAA auto clubs. Departments include:
Tips On Auto and Driving, Safety,
Outdoor Recreation News, Travel Notes.
Mostly staff-written; publicity releases
accepted.
**Readers:** AAA families in
Minnesota/mostly upper mobile and
foreign travel, leisure activities, a
membership.

### HOME & AWAY, NEBRASKA
26305

910 N. 96th St.
Omaha, NE 68114
Telephone: (402) 390-1000
FAX: (402) 390-0539
Mailing Address:
P.O. Box 3535
Omaha, NE 68103
Year Established: 1980
Pub. Frequency: bi-m.
Page Size: standard
Subscrip. Rate: $1/issue; $6/yr.
Materials: 05,06,09,15,21,32
Freelance Pay: $300-$1,200/article
Circulation: 1,980,000
Circulation Type: paid
**Owner(s):**
Home & Away, Inc.
910 N. 96th St.
Omaha, NE 68114
Telephone: (402) 390-1000
Ownership %: 100
**Management:**
Nels Pierson ......................Chairman of Board
Robert F. Stubblefield ......................President
Brian Nicol ...............................Publisher
Vern Cornish ...............................Publisher
Vern Cornish ......................Advertising Manager
Pat Meives ......................Production Manager
**Editorial:**
Brian Nicol ...............................Editor
Marge Peterson ......................Managing Editor
Jaquie Burgin ..............Administrative Assistant
Ann Taylor ...............................Advertising
Jill Faust ...........................Photography Editor
**Desc.:** Heavy emphasis on travel-domestic
and foreign, but foreign articles are
usually tie-in's to tours we operate so
inquiry important. Also use how-to's for
auto repair, features of consumer
interest for travelers and car owners.
Travel features should be critical, not all
gloss.
**Readers:** Members of 14 AAA Motor
Clubs
**Deadline:** story-3 mos. prior to pub. date;
news-3 mos. prior; photo-3 mos. prior;
ads-10 wks. prior

### HOME & AWAY, NORTH DAKOTA
26556

1801 38th St., S.W.
Fargo, ND 58103
Telephone: (701) 282-6222
FAX: (701) 282-8952
Mailing Address:
P.O. Box 10338
Fargo, ND 58106
Year Established: 1980
Pub. Frequency: q.
Page Size: standard
Subscrip. Rate: $2/yr.

**Materials Accepted/Included:** 01-Business news 02-By-line articles 03-Fashion news 04-Food news 05-Freelance copy 06-Letters to editor 07-Real estate news 08-Sports news 09-Travel news 10-Book rev. 11-Movie rev. 12-Music rev. 13-TV rev. 14-Theater rev. 15-Coming events 16-Obituaries 17-Question & answer 18-Social announcements 19-Artwork 20-Cartoons 21-Photos 22-TV listings 23-Audio rec. 24-Video rec. 25-Books 26-Films/film clips 27-Personnel news 28-Press releases 29-New product news/photos 30-Trade lit. 31-Contracts awarded 32-Display adv. 33-Classified adv.

6-127

Freelance Pay: negotiable
Circulation: 39,500
Circulation Type: paid
**Owner(s):**
AAA North Dakota
1801 38th St., S.W.
Fargo, ND 58103
Telephone: (701) 282-6222
Ownership %: 100
**Bureau(s):**
Home & Away
910 N. 96th St.
Omaha, NE 68114
Telephone: (402) 390-1000
Contact: Barc Wade, Robert Stubblefield
**Management:**
John B Wimbush .................Chairman of Board
Robert Stubblefield ............................Publisher
**Editorial:**
La Vonne Langord ...................Executive Editor
Barc Wade .............................................Editor
**Desc.:** Travel, car care, history, legislation
affecting the motorist; reminders to
members of services available;
automotive developments including new
car features, travel tips, restaurant
reviews, and consumer affairs.
**Readers:** AAA members, about 95 percent
of whom are middle class, fairly affluent.
**Deadline:** 75 days prior to pub. date

26525

**HOME & AWAY, OHIO**
90 E. Wilson Bridge Rd.
Worthington, OH 43085
Telephone: (614) 431-7919
Year Established: 1986
Pub. Frequency: bi-m.
Page Size: standard
Subscrip. Rate: free/members of OH. AAA
Club; $6/yr. non-members
Materials: 02,09,10,15,21,24,25,28,29,30,32
Freelance Pay: varies
Circulation: 407,330
Circulation Type: controlled
**Owner(s):**
Ohio Automobile Club
90 E. Wilson Bridge Rd.
Worthington, OH 43085
Telephone: (614) 431-7800
Ownership %: 100
**Editorial:**
William J. Purpura .................................Editor
**Desc.:** Uses news articles in the
automotive/travel, airline travel, travel
destinations, new products of interest to
members like labor saving devices,
general outdoors sports articles and
special events.
**Readers:** All members of the AAA, drivers,
most travel at least once a year, all own
cars.
**Deadline:** story-2 1/2 mo. prior to pub.
date; news-2 1/2; photo-2 1/2; ads-2
1/2

69428

**IDEAL TRAVELLER**
951 S. Oxford St., No. 109
Los Angeles, CA 90006
Telephone: (213) 732-3477
FAX: (213) 732-3477
Mailing Address:
P.O. Box 75392
Loa Angeles, CA 90075
Year Established: 1991
Pub. Frequency: q
Page Size: standard
Subscrip. Rate: $29.99/yr.
Materials: 01,02,03,04,05,06,07,08,09,10,
11,12,13,14,15,16,17,18,19,20,21,22,23,
24,25,26,27,28,29,30,31,32,33
Print Process: web
Circulation: 120,000
Circulation Type: controlled & paid

**Owner(s):**
Publishing & Business Consultants
951 S. Oxford., No. 109
Los Angeles, CA 90006
Telephone: (213) 732-3477
FAX: (213) 732-9123
Ownership %: 100
**Management:**
Andeson Napoleon Atia .....................Publisher
**Editorial:**
Andeson Napoleon Atia ...........................Editor
**Deadline:** story-2nd wk. prior to pub. date;
news-2nd wk. prior; photo-2nd wk. prior;
ads-90 days prior

65701

**INSIDE THE BLACK HILLS**
P.O. Box 9008
Rapid City, SD 57709
Telephone: (605) 341-7080
FAX: (605) 341-7180
Year Established: 1990
Pub. Frequency: q.
Page Size: standard
Subscrip. Rate: $2/issue; $8/yr.; $15/2
yrs.
Materials: 32
Circulation: 30,000
Circulation Type: paid
**Owner(s):**
Hagen Mktg. & Comm. Groups
P.O. Box 9008
Rapid City, SD 57709
Telephone: (605) 341-7080
Ownership %: 100
**Management:**
Janet Hagen ....................................Publisher
Ron Hagen ......................Advertising Manager
**Editorial:**
Ronald Hagen ...........................Editor in Chief
Sue Milne ...............................Managing Editor
**Desc.:** This is a regional publication for
residents and tourists covering business,
lifestyles, history, economy, tourism, etc.
**Readers:** Our readers are regional
residents and tourists. Of our residents
we have professionals, educators, and
seniors.

69176

**ISLANDS**
3886 State St.
Santa Barbara, CA 93105
Telephone: (805) 682-7177
FAX: (805) 569-0349
Year Established: 1981
Pub. Frequency: bi-m.
Page Size: standard
Subscrip. Rate: $3.95 newsstand;
$19.95/yr.
Materials: 32
Circulation: 177,000
Circulation Type: paid
**Owner(s):**
Islands Publishing Co.
3886 State St.
Santa Barbara, CA 93105
Telephone: (805) 682-7177
Ownership %: 100
**Management:**
William Kasch ....................................Publisher
Alan Rock ........................Advertising Manager
Barry Service ....................Circulation Manager
**Editorial:**
Joan Tapper ...........................................Editor
**Desc.:** Focuses on islands all over the
world; tropical and temperate,
undeveloped and urban, famous or
virtually undiscovered.

25133

**KEYSTONE AAA MOTORIST**
2040 Market St.
Philadelphia, PA 19103
Telephone: (215) 864-5455
Year Established: 1928
Pub. Frequency: bi-m.

Page Size: tabloid
Subscrip. Rate: $1/yr. members
Circulation: 336,000
Circulation Type: controlled
**Owner(s):**
AAA Mid-Atlantic, Inc.
2040 Market St.
Philadelphia, PA 19103
Telephone: (215) 864-5455
Ownership %: 100
**Management:**
Robert R. Rugel ..................................President
**Editorial:**
John C. Moyer ........................................Editor
**Desc.:** Material must be of automotive or
travel interest because paper is tailored
to a membership consisting of motorists
and travelers. Departments include:
Automotive, Travel, Government
Regulations, RVS, Camping Attractions,
Leisure Time Activities.
**Readers:** Circulation exclusively among
automobile club members.

52619

**LIFESTYLE MAGAZINE**
421 W. McArthur Blvd.
Oakland, CA 94609
Telephone: (510) 420-1091
FAX: (510) 420-1383
Year Established: 1976
Pub. Frequency: bi-m.
Page Size: 4 color photos/art
Subscrip. Rate: $1 newsstand; $7/yr.
Circulation: 50,000
Circulation Type: free
**Owner(s):**
Dave Sawle
421 W. McArthur Blvd.
Oakland, CA 94609
Telephone: (510) 420-1091
Ownership %: 50
**Management:**
Dave Sawle ......................................Publisher
Lindy Gray ........................Advertising Manager
**Editorial:**
Dave Sawle ...........................................Editor
Richard Elwas ................................Art Director
Bo Purtic ...............................Associate Editor
Suzanne Paiot .................Entertainment Editor
**Readers:** Singles/Business/New Age

26545

**MARYLAND MOTORIST, THE**
1401 Mt. Royal Ave.
Baltimore, MD 21217
Telephone: (301) 462-4000
Year Established: 1920
Pub. Frequency: bi-m.
Page Size: tabloid
Subscrip. Rate: $1/yr.
Circulation: 230,000
Circulation Type: controlled
**Owner(s):**
Automobile Club of Maryland
1401 Mt. Royal Ave.
Baltimore, MD 21217
Telephone: (301) 462-4000
Ownership %: 100
**Management:**
Garvin R. Kissinger ............................Publisher
Garvin R. Kissinger ..............................Manager
**Editorial:**
John C. Moyer ........................................Editor
**Desc.:** Useful information for auto owners,
counseling & legal aspects, as well as
promotion of AAA services, domestic &
world travel information.

69177

**MEXICO EVENTS &
DESTINATIONS**
5838 Edison Pl., Ste. 100
Carlsbad, CA 92008
Telephone: (619) 929-0707
FAX: (619) 929-0714

Mailing Address:
Box 188037
Carlsbad, CA 92009
Year Established: 1992
Pub. Frequency: q.
Page Size: 8 3/8 x 10 7/8
Subscrip. Rate: $2.95 newsstand; $11/yr.
Circulation: 121,500
Circulation Type: controlled & paid
**Owner(s):**
Travel Mexico Magazine Group
5838 Edison Pl., Ste. 100
Carlsbad, CA 92008
Telephone: (619) 929-0707
Ownership %: 100
**Management:**
Kirk Whisler .......................................Publisher
Jim Sullivan .......................Advertising Manager
Gabriela Flores .........................Sales Manager
**Editorial:**
Kathy Diaz .............................Editor-in-Chief
**Desc.:** Covers cultural, community and
entertainment events occuring
throughout the various regions of
Mexico.

26546

**MICHIGAN LIVING**
One Auto Club Dr.
Dearborn, MI 48126
Telephone: (313) 336-1506
FAX: (313) 336-1344
Year Established: 1918
Pub. Frequency: m.
Page Size: 4 color photos/art
Subscrip. Rate: $1/newsstand; $9/yr.
Materials: 01,02,05,06,09,10,14,15,19,20,
21,25,28,29,30,32,33
Freelance Pay: $45-$500/article
Print Process: offset
Circulation: 1,024,568
Circulation Type: paid
**Owner(s):**
Automobile Club of Michigan
One Auto Club Dr.
Dearborn, MI 48126
Telephone: (313) 336-1500
Ownership %: 100
**Management:**
Ron Garbinski ....................................Publisher
**Editorial:**
Leonard R. Barnes .....................Editor in Chief
Ron Garbinski ......................Executive Editor
Larry Keller .........................Managing Editor
William A. Semion ..................Associate Editor
Ron Garbinski ....................Book Review Editor
**Desc.:** Covers U.S., Canadian and world
travel, recreation in Michigan,
automotive news. Articles that contain
accurate current information on costs;
tips on trip planning; things to do
(camping, fishing, boating, etc.
throughout the United States and
Canada), especially articles on Michigan.
**Readers:** Travel-minded car owners. AAA
members in Michigan.
**Deadline:** story-25th of 2nd preceding mo.;
news-25th of 2nd preceding mo.; photo-
25th of 2nd preceding mo.; ads-25th of
2nd preceding mo.

21811

**MIDWEST MOTORIST, THE**
12901 N. Forty Dr.
St. Louis, MO 63141
Telephone: (314) 523-7350
FAX: (314) 523-7427
Year Established: 1971
Pub. Frequency: bi-m.
Page Size: standard
Subscrip. Rate: $3/yr.
Materials: 05,09,15,21,25,32
Freelance Pay: $50-$300/article
Print Process: web offset
Circulation: 390,000
Circulation Type: controlled

**Materials Accepted/Included:** 01-Business news 02-By-line articles 03-Fashion news 04-Food news 05-Freelance copy 06-Letters to editor 07-Real estate news 08-Sports news 09-Travel news 10-Book rev. 11-Movie rev. 12-Music rev. 13-TV rev. 14-Theater rev. 15-Coming events 16-Obituaries 17-Question & answer 18-Social announcements 19-Artwork 20-Cartoons 21-Photos 22-TV listings 23-Audio rec. 24-Video rec. 25-Books 26-Films/film clips 27-Personnel news 28-Press releases 29-New product news/photos 30-Trade lit. 31-Contracts awarded 32-Display adv. 33-Classified adv.

**Owner(s):**
Automobile Club of Missouri
12901 N. Forty Dr.
St. Louis, MO 63141
Telephone: (314) 523-7350
Ownership %: 100
**Management:**
Debbie Klein ......................Advertising Manager
**Editorial:**
Michael Right ..............................................Editor
Debbie Klein ...........................Managing Editor
Dennis Heintz ..........................Associate Editor
Martin Quigley ......................Contributing Editor
**Desc.:** Articles, features and photos of
interest to Midwesterners. Two theme
issues per year, including cruising and
European travel. Color artwork a big
plus.
**Readers:** A specialized, quality circulation,
to AAA members only.

69179

## MINNESOTA EXPLORER
100 Metro Sq.
121 Seventh Pl. E.
St. Paul, MN 55101-2112
Telephone: (800) 657-3700
Pub. Frequency: bi-m.
Subscrip. Rate: $6.99/yr.
Circulation: 800,000
Circulation Type: paid
**Owner(s):**
Minnesota Office of Tourism
100 Metro Sq.
121 Seventh Pl. E.
St. Paul, MN 55101-2112
Telephone: (800) 657-3700
Ownership %: 100

25138

## MOTOR CLUB NEWS
484 Central Ave.
Newark, NJ 07107
Telephone: (201) 733-4033
FAX: (201) 623-2469
Year Established: 1950
Pub. Frequency: bi-m.
Page Size: tabloid
Subscrip. Rate: $1/yr.
Freelance Pay: $150-$350/article
Circulation: 60,000
Circulation Type: paid
**Owner(s):**
Motor Club Of America
484 Central Ave.
Newark, NJ 07107
Telephone: (201) 733-4033
Ownership %: 100
**Management:**
Robert Fried .................................Publisher
**Editorial:**
Marlene Timm ...........................Editor in Chief
**Desc.:** Includes first hand travel articles,
automotive devices, and innovations in
transportation, safety, new products of
value to traveling and motoring public,
fashion, cookery, strong editorial page
angled to safety and consumer causes,
insurance, reports, community services,
and company benefits.
**Readers:** Members of Motor Club of
America and employees of MCA, which
is comprised of motor clubs,
an insurance company, travel agencies
and other service related companies.

26549

## MOTORLAND
150 Van Ness Ave.
San Francisco, CA 94102
Telephone: (415) 565-2451
Mailing Address:
P.O. Box 1860
San Francisco, CA 94101
Year Established: 1917
Pub. Frequency: bi-m.

Page Size: 4 color photos/art
Subscrip. Rate: $3/yr.
Freelance Pay: $.33/wd.
Circulation: 2,200,000
Circulation Type: paid
**Owner(s):**
California State Automobile Association
P.O. Box 1860
San Francisco, CA 94101
Telephone: (415) 565-2620
Ownership %: 100
**Management:**
Keith Radcliffe, Jr. ...........Advertising Manager
**Editorial:**
Lynn Ferrin ..................................................Editor
Albert R. Davidson ............................Art Director
John Goepel ..........................Associate Editor
Camille Cusumano ....................Associate Editor
Maria Streshinsky .........................Events Editor
Charles L. Beucher ............Production Director
**Desc.:** Features travel, attractions, events,
leisure activities, western history,
automobiles, transportation, safety, and
CSAA (AAA) news. Departments include:
Car Care, In The Driver's Seat, Car and
Consumer, On the Road, Travel Topics,
What's New, Events Calendar, Letters,
Commentary.
**Readers:** CSAA (AAA) Members in
California and Nevada

21814

## MOTOR NEWS
201 Kings Hwy., S.
Cherry Hill, NJ 08034
Telephone: (609) 428-9000
Year Established: 1927
Pub. Frequency: bi-m.
Page Size: tabloid
Subscrip. Rate: $1/copy; $6/yr.
Circulation: 132,000
Circulation Type: controlled
**Owner(s):**
Automobile Club Of Southern NJ.
201 Kings Hwy., S.
Cherry Hill, NJ 08034
Telephone: (609) 428-9000
Ownership %: 100
**Management:**
Joel L. Vittori ...............................Publisher
**Editorial:**
Richard Smith ......................................Editor
**Desc.:** Covers travel, traffic, highways,
resorts, history (US). Center spreads; 1
page of news/no charge; 1 page of
ads/charged. Departments include: New
Products, Motorist Book Review.
**Readers:** Principally airship and auto
travel.

69180

## NATIONAL GEOGRAPHIC TRAVELER
1145 17th St., N.W.
Washington, DC 20036
Telephone: (202) 857-7000
Year Established: 1984
Pub. Frequency: bi-m.
Page Size: standard
Subscrip. Rate: $17.95/yr.
Circulation: 700,000
Circulation Type: paid
**Owner(s):**
National Geographic Society
1145 17th St., N.W.
Washington, DC 20036
Telephone: (202) 857-7000
Ownership %: 100
**Editorial:**
Richard Busch ....................................Editor

**Desc.:** Offers articles on vacation places in
the US and Canada, plus popular spots
abroad. Includes columns on
photography, weekend destinations and
learning vacations, as well as a regional
calendar of events in the US, Canada,
Mexico and the Caribbean.

26550

## NATIONAL MOTORIST
188 The Embarcadero
San Francisco, CA 94105-1279
Telephone: (415) 777-4000
FAX: (415) 882-2141
Year Established: 1924
Pub. Frequency: q.
Page Size: standard
Subscrip. Rate: $.50 newsstand; $2/yr.
Materials: 01,02,09,10,15,21,25,28,32
Freelance Pay: $.10/wd. & up
Print Process: web offset
Circulation: 120,000
Circulation Type: paid
**Owner(s):**
National Automobile Club
188 The Embarcedro
San Francisco, CA 94105
Telephone: (415) 777-4000
FAX: (415) 882-2126
Ownership %: 100
**Editorial:**
Jane M. Offers ..........................................Editor
Jane M. Offers .....................................Advertising
**Desc.:** Motoring in the eleven Western
states. Plus domestic and international
travel and tour-cruising, special
packages for club members.
**Readers:** Members of National Automobile
Club, statewide in California only.
**Deadline:** story-6 mos.; news-4 mos.;
photo-6 mos.

26551

## NEGRO TRAVELER & CONVENTIONEER
11717 S. Vincennes Ave.
Chicago, IL 60643
Telephone: (312) 881-3712
Year Established: 1942
Pub. Frequency: bi-m.
Page Size: standard
Subscrip. Rate: $9.50/yr.
Freelance Pay: varies
Circulation: 73,000
Circulation Type: paid
**Owner(s):**
Travelers Research Publishing Co., Inc.
11717 S. Vincennes Ave.
Chicago, IL 60643
Telephone: (312) 881-3712

Travelers Research Publishing Co., Inc.
7831 E. Pima St.
Tucson, AZ 85715
Telephone: (602) 885-8360
**Bureau(s):**
Clarence Markham, III, V.P. Exec.
930 Butte St.
Claremont, CA 91711
Telephone: (714) 626-9900
Contact: Katie Markham, Travel Editor

Travelers Research Publishing Co., Inc.
11717 S. Vincennes Ave.
Chicago, IL 60643
Telephone: (312) 881-3712
Contact: C. M. Markham, Jr., Exec. Editor
**Management:**
Clarence M. Markham, Jr. ...Chairman of Board
Clarence M. Markham, III ............Vice President
Clarence M. Markham, Jr. ...................Publisher
Clarence M. Markham, III .........Advertising
Manager
Edwin Gorcyzca .................Editorial Production
Manager

**Editorial:**
Clarence M. Markham ............................Editor
Olga Markham .........................Managing Editor
Clarence Markham, III .............Assistant Editor
Paul Hughes .........................Consulting Editor
Julie Markham Westcost .............Design Editor
Aurelia Henton .............................Drama Editor
Clay Lee Guy .........................European Editor
Richard Byzinski .............Graphics Coordinator
Theresa Bell ................................News Editor
Freeman Bohannon ..................................Photo
**Desc.:** By-line articles and picture layouts
cover the various aspects of business or
vacation travel from the standpoint of
the Negro traveler. Deals with
accomodations, transporation, sightseeing, food, entertainment, new cars-
station wagons. Recommends places to
stay and eat, what to expect, what to
see, ways best to get there and best air
line and boat to take that will treat the
black man with respect and dignity when
traveling in a foreign country. Also
publishes human interest or news
stories concerning negroes. Uses some
fiction of short story type. Carries
suggestions for vacationers with stories
of vacation spots, fishing, sports, etc.
Departments include: Hotel Directory,
Negro convention listings, cities, dates
and place held, name of hotel
headquarters, and What's Going on
about the country; the latter being a
directory of entertainment spots,
performers featured there and type of
service, food and entertainment to be
expected. Also lists Negro radio
commentators, Negro business and
programs. Black colleges, Black travel
agencies, Black banks, mortgage
companies, Black conventions. Black
insurance co.'s, Black hospitals, Black
news papers, Black magazines, Black
advertising agencies-all found in the
once a year special directory "Economic
Impact of the Negro Traveler".
**Readers:** Primarily to Black travelers using
motels, hotels, restaurants, air lines,
buses, trains, ships and rent a cars and
those associated with some phase of
travel. Black travel agenccies.
Subscription-school teachers, lawyers,
doctors, upper middle class Blacks.

26554

## NEW YORK MOTORIST
1415 Kellum Pl.
Garden City, NY 11530
Telephone: (516) 746-7730
FAX: (516) 873-2355
Year Established: 1926
Pub. Frequency: m.
Page Size: tabloid
Subscrip. Rate: free to AAA members
Materials: 02,05,06,09,15,20,21,23,24,25,
28,30,32
Print Process: offset
Circulation: 700,000
Circulation Type: paid
**Owner(s):**
Automobile Club of New York, Inc.
1415 Kellum Pl.
Garden City, NY 11530
Telephone: (516) 746-7730
Ownership %: 100
**Management:**
Peter Crescenti .................Advertising Manager
Paul C. Petrillo .....................Business Manager
**Editorial:**
Sy Oshinsky ............................................Editor

---

**Materials Accepted/Included:** 01-Business news 02-By-line articles 03-Fashion news 04-Food news 05-Freelance copy 06-Letters to editor 07-Real estate news 08-Sports news 09-Travel news 10-Book rev. 11-Movie rev. 12-Music rev. 13-TV rev. 14-Theater rev. 15-Coming events 16-Obituaries 17-Question & answer 18-Social announcements 19-Artwork 20-Cartoons 21-Photos 22-TV listings 23-Audio rec. 24-Video rec. 25-Books 26-Films/film clips 27-Personnel news 28-Press releases 29-New product news/photos 30-Trade lit. 31-Contracts awarded 32-Display adv. 33-Classified adv.

6-129

**Desc.:** Official publication of the Automobile Club of New York. Informs its members about the latest developments in motoring comfort and efficiency, improvement in traffic and road conditions, and information concerning travel by air, road, rail and sea, resorts, vacation areas and hotels.
**Readers:** Members of Automobile Club of N.Y.

**NEW YORK TODAY**                    26555
80-34 Jamiaca Ave.
Woodhaven, NY 11421
Telephone: (718) 296-2655
Year Established: 1954
Pub. Frequency: w.
Page Size: tabloid
Subscrip. Rate: $18/yr.
Freelance Pay: negotiable
**Owner(s):**
Norman Cohen
80-34 Jamiaca Ave.
Woodhaven, NY 11421
Telephone: (718) 296-2655
Ownership %: 100
**Management:**
Andrew Cohen ..................................Publisher
**Editorial:**
Ray Wilson ...........................Managing Editor
Ray Wilson ..........................Book Review Editor
Ray Wilson ..........................Entertainment Editor
Ray Wilson ..........................New Product Editor
Ray Wilson ..........................Picture Editor
**Desc.:** Restaurant and traveling publication, and entertainment. Restaurants, theater, night life, movies and travel, "Tips on Tables" by Bob Dana, "Dana on Wine" by Bob Dana, "Travel with Hermes" by Ray Wilson.
**Readers:** Adult 20-45.

**NORTHEAST OUTDOORS**                22438
70 Edwin Ave.
Waterbury, CT 06708
Telephone: (203) 755-0158
FAX: (203) 755-3480
Mailing Address:
    P.O. Box 2180
    Waterbury, CT 06722
Year Established: 1968
Pub. Frequency: m.
Page Size: tabloid
Subscrip. Rate: $8/yr.
Materials: 02,05,06,09,19,20,21,28,32,33
Freelance Pay: $40 - $80
Print Process: web offset
Circulation: 140,000
Circulation Type: paid
**Owner(s):**
Northeast Outdoors, Inc.
70 Edwin Ave.
Waterbury, CT 06708
Telephone: (203) 755-0158
Ownership %: 100
**Management:**
David Zackin .................................President
David Zackin .................................Publisher
Linda Zackin ....................Advertising Manager
Silvia Purcaro ......................Office Manager
Henry Pacyna ...................Production Manager
**Editorial:**
Michael Griffin ................Managing Editor
John Florian ......................Editorial Director
Linda Herrmann ................Account Executive

**Desc.:** Stories on family camping and recreational vehicles, telling readers where to camp, what to see and do in the Northeast region of the U.S.; New England, N.Y., N.J. Related stories used on recreation vehicles, hiking, fishing, canoeing, winter sports, and any activity a camping family could participate in while on a trip. Departments include: New Products, Calendar of Events, Northeast Ski Report, Campground Report, Cartoons, New Recreational Vehicle Models.
**Readers:** Family campers and users of recreational vehicles.
**Deadline:** story-1st of mo. prior to pub. date; news-1st of mo. prior; photo-1st of mo. prior; ads-1st of mo. prior

**NORTHWEST TRAVEL**                  66675
1525 12th St.
Florence, OR 97439
Telephone: (503) 997-8401
FAX: (503) 997-1124
Mailing Address:
    P.O. Box 18000
    Florence, OR 97439-0130
Year Established: 1991
Pub. Frequency: bi-m.
Page Size: standard
Subscrip. Rate: $2.95 newsstand
Materials: 02,05,06,09,10,15,21,25,28,32,33
Freelance Pay: $75-$350/article
Circulation: 50,000
Circulation Type: paid
**Owner(s):**
Northwest Regional Magazines
P.O. Box 18000
Florence, OR 97439-0130
Telephone: (503) 997-8401
Ownership %: 100
**Management:**
Alicia Spooner ..............................Publisher
Robert Spooner .............................Publisher
**Editorial:**
Dave Peden ...................................Editor
Judy Fleagle ......................Managing Editor
Alicia Spooner ......................Design Editor
**Desc.:** A travel magazine about the Pacific Northwest which includes OR, WA, ID, B.C, and occasionally AK. Covers cities, towns, activities, special places and people, and history.
**Readers:** 40's and up, middle-class, well-educated and love to travel.
**Deadline:** story-3-1/2 mos.

**OHIO MOTORIST, THE**                25143
6000 S. Marginal Rd.
Cleveland, OH 44103
Telephone: (216) 361-6216
FAX: (216) 361-6109
Mailing Address:
    P.O. Box 6150
    Cleveland, OH 44101
Year Established: 1908
Pub. Frequency: m.
Page Size: tabloid
Subscrip. Rate: $1.50/yr.
Freelance Pay: $100-$300/article
Circulation: 395,000
Circulation Type: controlled
**Owner(s):**
AAA-Ohio Motorists Association
P.O. Box 6150
Cleveland, OH 44101
Telephone: (216) 361-6216
Ownership %: 100
**Management:**
F. Jerome Turk .............................Publisher
Thomas C. Michel ............Advertising Manager
**Editorial:**
F. Jerome Turk ...............................Editor

**Desc.:** Official publication of the Ohio Motorists Association. Reaches 575,000 members in Cleveland and 8 adjacent counties.
**Readers:** Automobile owners, frequent travelers, high income families.

**OREGON MOTORIST, THE**              25144
600 S.W. Market St.
Portland, OR 97201
Telephone: (503) 222-6729
FAX: (503) 222-6756
Pub. Frequency: bi-m.
Page Size: tabloid
Subscrip. Rate: $1/yr. members
Circulation: 373,000
Circulation Type: paid
**Owner(s):**
Automobile Club of Oregon
Telephone: (503) 222-6729
**Management:**
Roger Graybeal ..........................President
Douglas Peeples .............Advertising Manager
**Editorial:**
Ann O'Brien ...............................Editor
**Desc.:** We are interested in material pertaining to motoring/highways, safety, travel, etc. Articles not exceeding 1,000 words. By - lines acceptable. Little material outside staff - written stories are used, will consider free - lance, but don't usually accept. Publicity and editorial material used is as follows: safety, highways, mass transit, travel, recreation, hunting, fishing, skiing, arts and entertainment, legislation, automotive and related safety products and accessories.
**Readers:** AAA Club members only.

**OUT WEST**                          65391
408 Broad St., St. 11
Nevada City, CA 95959
Telephone: (916) 478-9080
FAX: (916) 478-9082
Year Established: 1988
Pub. Frequency: q.
Page Size: tabloid
Subscrip. Rate: $3.00 newsstand;
    $11.95/yr.; 21.95/2 yrs.
Materials: 02,05,06,09,10,20,21,24,25,28,
    32,33
Freelance Pay: $10-$100/article
Print Process: offset
Circulation: 10,000
Circulation Type: free & paid
**Owner(s):**
Out West Publishing
408 Broad St., Ste. 11
Nevada City, CA 95959
Telephone: (916) 478-9080
FAX: (916) 478-9082
Ownership %: 100
**Editorial:**
Chuck Woodbury ...........................Editor
Rodia Woodbury ..................Associate Editor
**Desc.:** Explores the back roads and small towns of the rural West, writing about the people and places he finds along the way.

**PUNCH IN INTERNATIONAL
(TRAVEL & ENTERTAINMENT)**            65372
400 E. 59th St., #9F
New York, NY 10022
Telephone: (212) 755-4363
FAX: (212) 755-4365
Year Established: 1986
Pub. Frequency: w.
Page Size: standard
Subscrip. Rate: members only
Materials: 04,09,10,11,12,13,14,22,23,24,
    25,26,28

Circulation: 4,000,000
Circulation Type: controlled & paid
**Owner(s):**
J. Walman
400 E. 59th St., #9F
New York, NY 10022
Telephone: (212) 755-4363
Ownership %: 100
**Editorial:**
J. Walman ...............................Editor
**Desc.:** Review on artistic format, travel, food, restaurants, wine and spirits, entertainment (movies, theatre, music, books, & financial news review), computer products and software review, hotels, resorts, airlines, cruise ships, railroads, and all travel services and products.
**Readers:** Upper income professions.

**QUE PASA**                          69722
P.O. Box 4435
Old San Juan Sta.
San Juan, PR 00905
Telephone: (809) 721-2676
FAX: (809) 725-4417
Year Established: 1948
Pub. Frequency: q.
Page Size: standard
Subscrip. Rate: free
Materials: 32
Print Process: web offset
Circulation: 150,000
Circulation Type: free
**Owner(s):**
Tourism Company of Puerto Rico
P.O. Box 4435
Old San Juan Sta.
San Juan, PR 00905
Ownership %: 100
**Editorial:**
Mary Ann Hopgood ...........................Editor
**Desc.:** Visitors guide to Puerto Rico.
**Deadline:** ads-45 days

**RECOMMEND**                         25147
5979 N.W. 151st St., Ste. 120
Miami Lakes, FL 33014
Telephone: (305) 828-0123
FAX: (305) 821-3829
Year Established: 1967
Pub. Frequency: m.
Page Size: standard
Subscrip. Rate: free
Freelance Pay: varies
Circulation: 55,000
Circulation Type: controlled
**Owner(s):**
Harold Herman
5979 N.W. 151st St.
Ste. 120
Miami Lakes, FL 33014
Telephone: (305) 653-0123
Ownership %: 100
**Bureau(s):**
PRI
37 W. 26th St. 10th Fl.
New York, NY 10010
Telephone: (212) 686-8042
Contact: Jeff Posner
**Management:**
Hal Herman ...............................President
Laurel Herman ...............................Publisher
Terry Murphy ..................Associate Publsiher
**Editorial:**
Laurel Herman ...............................Editor
Rick Shively ......................Managing Editor
Alys Bohn ......................Contributing Editor
Marcia Bayer ......................Miscellaneous

**Materials Accepted/Included:** 01-Business news 02-By-line articles 03-Fashion news 04-Food news 05-Freelance copy 06-Letters to editor 07-Real estate news 08-Sports news 09-Travel news 10-Book rev. 11-Movie rev. 12-Music rev. 13-TV rev. 14-Theater rev. 15-Coming events 16-Obituaries 17-Question & answer 18-Social announcements 19-Artwork 20-Cartoons 21-Photos 22-TV listings 23-Audio rec. 24-Video rec. 25-Books 26-Films/film clips 27-Personnel news 28-Press releases 29-New product news/photos 30-Trade lit. 31-Contracts awarded 32-Display adv. 33-Classified adv.

Desc.: Destination marketing information written for the travel agent industry. Editorial includes information on: The destination, new facilities, attractions, sporting events, tours, accommodations, dining, sightseeing, festivals, fishing tournaments, and general information needed by travel agents in order to sell travel. Publishes destination special supplements on a regular basis.
Readers: Travel agents throughout the U.S. & Canada.

65345

## RHODE ISLAND MONTHLY
18 Imperial Pl.
Providence, RI 02903-4628
Telephone: (401) 421-2552
FAX: (401) 831-5624
Year Established: 1988
Pub. Frequency: m.
Page Size: standard
Subscrip. Rate: $2.50 newsstand; $14.95/yr.
Circulation: 30,000
Circulation Type: paid
Owner(s):
Dan Kaplan
18 Imperial Pl.
Providence, RI 02903-4628
Telephone: (401) 421-2552
Ownership %: 100
Management:
Dan Kaplan ................................Publisher
Editorial:
Dan Kaplan ................................Editor
Konrad Schultz ..................Advertising Director
Desc.: People, places and anything pertaining to Rhode Island.
Readers: Residents as well as tourists.

69182

## SAN FRANCISCO BOOK
201 Third St., Ste. 900
San Francisco, CA 94103
Telephone: (415) 974-6900
FAX: (415) 227-2602
Year Established: 1984
Pub. Frequency: q.
Page Size: pocket
Subscrip. Rate: free
Materials: 32
Circulation: 600,000
Circulation Type: free
Owner(s):
San Francisco Convention & Visitors Bureau
201 Third St., Ste. 900
San Francisco, CA 94103
Telephone: (415) 974-6900
Ownership %: 100
Editorial:
Cynthia Hu ................................Editor
Desc.: Provides information on the San Francisco Bay area including sightseeing, restaurants, retail and events.

65417

## SEE MAGAZINES
3675 Clark Rd.
Sarasota, FL 34233
Telephone: (813) 922-3575
FAX: (813) 923-6309
Year Established: 1935
Pub. Frequency: varies
Page Size: pocket
Subscrip. Rate: free
Circulation: 55,000
Circulation Type: controlled
Owner(s):
Miles Media Group, Inc.
3675 Clark Rd.
Sarasota, FL 34233
Telephone: (813) 922-3575
FAX: (813) 923-6309
Ownership %: 100

Management:
Roger Miles ................................Owner
Editorial:
Pattie Lanier ................................Editor
Janet Fusco ................................Editor
Desc.: Contains information on tourist attractions, shopping, dining, recreation and real estate.
Readers: Visitors & new residents.

69699

## SEPTEMBER DAYS CLUB NEWS
339 Jefferson Rd.
Parsippany, NJ 07054
Telephone: (201) 428-9700
Pub. Frequency: q.
Page Size: standard
Subscrip. Rate: free to hotel guests; $10/yr. membership
Owner(s):
Days Inn of America
339 Jefferson Rd.
Parsippany, NJ 07054
Telephone: (201) 428-9700
Ownership %: 100
Editorial:
Phil Southard ................................Editor
Readers: Guests of Days Inn hotels 50 years and older.

56391

## SKY
600 Corporate Dr., Ste. 300
Ft. Lauderdale, FL 33334
Telephone: (305) 776-0066
FAX: (353) 493-8969
Year Established: 1972
Pub. Frequency: m.
Page Size: standard
Subscrip. Rate: $36/yr.
Freelance Pay: $300-$500/article
Print Process: web offset
Circulation: 500,000
Circulation Type: controlled
Owner(s):
Sky
Ft. Lauderdale, FL
Management:
Seymour Gerber ................................Publisher
John Masters ................Advertising Manager
Editorial:
Lidia de Leon ................................Editor
Barbara Whelehan ..............Associate Editor
Penny Rich ......................Production Editor
Desc.: A national magazine for passengers on Delta Airlines flights. Articles include human interest, travel, sports, personality interviews, arts, book reviews, special features and hi-tech and computer columns each month.
Readers: 73% professional, managerial and sales; 78% college educated, 79% with income $60,000 & up.

65605

## SOUTHERN LIVING TRAVEL GUIDES
2100 Lakeshore Dr.
Birmingham, AL 35209
Telephone: (205) 877-6000
FAX: (205) 877-6700
Year Established: 1989
Pub. Frequency: 5/yr.
Page Size: standard
Subscrip. Rate: $3.95 newsstand
Circulation: 200,000
Circulation Type: paid
Owner(s):
Time, Inc.
Time Life Bldg./Rockefeller Ct
New York, NY 10020
Telephone: (212) 522-2751
Ownership %: 100
Management:
Jim Nelson ................................President
Patti Hendrix ..................Business Manager
Betty Robb ......................General Manager

Editorial:
Karen Lingo ................................Editor
Victor Profis ..................Advertising Director
Jim DeVira ..................Associate Publisher
Desc.: Travel South-the tour guide for discovering the Nation's number one travel destination. Being the only magazine thats totally devoted to to travel in the South, our readers turn to Travel South for seasonal travel tips on where to stay and play, informative features on exciting destinations, maps and much more. And our unique reader response system provides our readers with easily attainable information about ads. This combination offers our advertisers an unusually high number of qualified leads.
Readers: Travelers living in the south or coming to the south.

69717

## ST. CROIX THIS WEEK
One Havensight Way
St. Thomas, VI 00802
Telephone: (809) 774-2500
FAX: (809) 776-1466
Mailing Address:
P.O. Box 11199
St. Thomas, VI 00807
Year Established: 1960
Pub. Frequency: m.
Materials: 32
Print Process: offset
Owner(s):
This Week Publishing, Inc.
P.O. Box 11199
St. Thomas, VI 00801
Telephone: (809) 774-2500
FAX: (809) 774-1466
Ownership %: 100

69183

## STRAND MAGAZINE
1359 21st Ave. N., No. 106
Myrtle Beach, SC 29577
Telephone: (803) 626-8911
FAX: (803) 626-6452
Year Established: 1986
Pub. Frequency: a.
Page Size: digest
Subscrip. Rate: free; $3/copy
Materials: 21,32
Print Process: web offset
Circulation: 1,100,000
Circulation Type: paid
Owner(s):
Strand Magazine
1359 21st Ave., N., No. 106
Myrtle Beach, SC 29577
Telephone: (615) 242-7747
Ownership %: 100
Management:
Delores Blount ................................Publisher
Susan Wagner ..................Circulation Manager
Editorial:
Delores Blount ......................Editor in Chief
Delores Blount ......................Managing Editor
Delores Blount ......................Advertising Editor
Kathy Smith ......................Business Editor
Kathy Smith ......................Fashion Editor
Kathy Smith ......................News Editor
Kathy Smith ......................Real Estate Editor
Deadline: ads-Mar. 30 (each yr.)

69716

## ST. THOMAS THIS WEEK
1 Havensight Way
St. Thomas, VI 00802
Telephone: (809) 774-2500
FAX: (809) 776-1466
Mailing Address:
P.O. Box 11199
St. Thomas, VI 00801
Year Established: 1960

Pub. Frequency: w.
Subscrip. Rate: free
Materials: 32
Owner(s):
This Week Publishing, Inc.
P.O. Box 11199
St. Thomas, VI 00801
Telephone: (804) 774-2500
FAX: (809) 776-1466
Ownership %: 100
Editorial:
Margot Bachman ................................Editor

64963

## SUN SCENE
2001 Killebrew Dr.
Ste. 105
Minneapolis, MN 55425
Telephone: (612) 854-0155
Year Established: 1973
Pub. Frequency: q.
Page Size: standard
Subscrip. Rate: $2/membership only
Freelance Pay: $75-$335/article
Circulation: 126,000
Circulation Type: controlled
Owner(s):
M.C. Club Services, Inc.
6007 N. Clark St.
Chicago, IL 60660
Telephone: (612) 690-7227
Ownership %: 100
Management:
Karel Laing ................................Publisher
Editorial:
Mary Lou Brooks ................................Editor
John Baskerville ..................Art Director
Sue Ritchie ......................Photo
Luann Eager ................Production Coordinator
Desc.: Carry 4 or 5 short feature stories per issue in the consumer, lifestyle, leisure, food and travel categories. Most stories are picked up from other magazines.
Readers: Travel club members.

67242

## SUN VALLEY MAGAZINE
500 S. Main St., Ste. 301
Ketchum, ID 83340
Telephone: (208) 726-1246
FAX: (208) 726-1268
Mailing Address:
P.O. Box 1469
Ketchum, ID 83340
Year Established: 1986
Pub. Frequency: s-a.
Page Size: standard
Subscrip. Rate: $3.50 newsstand; $7/yr.
Materials: 06,08,20,21,28,30,31,32,33
Freelance Pay: $50-$500/article
Print Process: web
Circulation: 15,000
Circulation Type: controlled
Owner(s):
Wood River Publishing, Inc.
P.O. Box 1469
Ketchum, ID 83340
Telephone: (208) 726-1246
Ownership %: 85

Peak Media, Inc.
P.O. Box 924
Hailey, ID 83333
Telephone: (208) 788-0057
Ownership %: 15
Management:
Michael Earls ................................President
Michael Earls ................................Publisher
Kelly Coles ..................Advertising Manager
Editorial:
Celeste Earls ................................Editor
Desc.: To provide the best medium representing the lifestyle of the Sun Valley area and its surroundings.

**Materials Accepted/Included:** 01-Business news 02-By-line articles 03-Fashion news 04-Food news 05-Freelance copy 06-Letters to editor 07-Real estate news 08-Sports news 09-Travel news 10-Book rev. 11-Movie rev. 12-Music rev. 13-TV rev. 14-Theater rev. 15-Coming events 16-Obituaries 17-Question & answer 18-Social announcements 19-Artwork 20-Cartoons 21-Photos 22-TV listings 23-Audio rec. 24-Video rec. 25-Books 26-Films/film clips 27-Personnel news 28-Press releases 29-New product news/photos 30-Trade lit. 31-Contracts awarded 32-Display adv. 33-Classified adv.

6-131

## TEL AVIV REVIEW, THE
65668

Brightleaf Sq., Ste. 18-B
805 W. Main St.
Durham, NC 27701
Telephone: (919) 684-2173
Mailing Address:
P.O. Box 90660
Durham, NC 27708
Pub. Frequency: a.: Aug.
Page Size: standard
Subscrip. Rate: membership
**Owner(s):**
Duke University Press
Brightleaf Sq., 18B
Durham, NC 27701
Telephone: (919) 687-3636
FAX: (919) 688-4574
Ownership %: 100
**Editorial:**
Janet Pursell .......................Journals Marketing
Schipporeit

## TOURING AMERICA
67073

P.O. Box 57900
Los Angeles, CA 90057-0900
Telephone: (714) 454-9755
FAX: (213) 385-8565
Year Established: 1991
Pub. Frequency: bi-m.
Page Size: standard
Subscrip. Rate: $3.95 newsstand; $15/yr.
Circulation: 116000
Circulation Type: paid
**Owner(s):**
Fancy Publications, Inc.
2401 Beverly Blvd.
Los Angeles, CA 90057
Telephone: (310) 385-2222
Ownership %: 100
**Management:**
Norman Ridker ..............................Publisher
**Editorial:**
Gene Booth ..........................................Editor
Richard Resnic ...............................Advertising

## TRAILS-A-WAY
26563

28167 N. Keith Dr.
Lake Forest, IL 60045-9952
Telephone: (708) 323-9076
FAX: (708) 362-8776
Year Established: 1970
Pub. Frequency: m.
Page Size: tabloid
Subscrip. Rate: $1/copy; $8/yr.
Freelance Pay: $.05/wd.; $15/photo
Circulation: 58,000
Circulation Type: paid
**Owner(s):**
Trails-A-Way
Lake Forest, IL
**Management:**
Frank Lockwood ..............................Publisher
Jean O'neill ......................Advertising Manager
**Desc.:** Dedicated to interests of
recreational vehicle owners in Michigan,
Ohio, Indiana, Illinois, Wisconsin.
**Readers:** Recreational vehicle owners.

## TRAVEL & LEISURE
26016

1120 Ave. of the Americas
New York, NY 10036
Telephone: (212) 382-5600
FAX: (212) 768-1568
Year Established: 1971
Pub. Frequency: m.
Page Size: standard
Subscrip. Rate: $32/yr.
Freelance Pay: $250-$4000/article
Circulation: 1,000,000
Circulation Type: paid

**Owner(s):**
American Express Publishing Corp.
1120 Ave. of the Americas
New York, NY 10036
Telephone: (212) 382-5600
Ownership %: 100
**Management:**
Richard Barthelmes ..........................Publisher
**Editorial:**
Nancy Novogrod ..........................Editor in Chief
Douglas Brenner ....................Executive Editor
Maria Shaw ..............................Managing Editor
**Desc.:** A sophisticated magazine covering
the field of travel and pleasurable leisure
time activities. All material assigned to
free-lance writers and photographers.
The magazine is planned by editors and
very little unsolicited material is used.
**Readers:** Active, sophisticated travelers.

## TRAVEL HOLIDAY
26566

28 W. 23rd St.
New York, NY 10010
Telephone: (212) 366-8700
FAX: (212) 366-8798
Year Established: 1977
Pub. Frequency: 10/yr.
Page Size: standard
Subscrip. Rate: $11.97/yr.
Circulation: 575,000
Circulation Type: paid
**Owner(s):**
Reader's Digest Association, Inc.
Pleasantville, NY 10570
Ownership %: 100
**Management:**
Ruth Halpert ....................Advertising Manager
**Editorial:**
Margaret Simmons ....................Editor in Chief
Elizabeth Hettich ....................Executive Editor
Teresa Fernandes ..........................Art Director
**Desc.:** Provides articles on where to go,
what to do and see for the best-value at
all times. Appropriate costs and prices
are covered. Major feature articles run
approximately 1600-1800 words. Shorter
pieces run from 800-1400 words.
Features both foreign and domestic
travel destinations as well as
special interest subjects (e.g., events,
museums. Administers Dining Circle
award, a guide to the best American
restaurants, published in the December
issue. Regular columns are: Food
(concerning food & wine, international
chefs), Photography (travel in focus),
Medical (health away from home), News
Items (e.g., travel advisor, travel digest,
travel fare), New & Notable (upcoming
events, new travel products).
**Readers:** Travel-conscious people, who
actively travel.

## TRAVELHOST
26567

10701 Stemmons Freeway
Dallas, TX 75220
Telephone: (214) 691-1163
FAX: (214) 869-1552
Year Established: 1968
Pub. Frequency: m.
Page Size: standard
Subscrip. Rate: free/hotel distrb.
Circulation: 1,180,000
Circulation Type: controlled & free
**Owner(s):**
Travelhost, Inc.
10701 Stemmons Freeway
Dallas, TX 75220
Telephone: (214) 691-1163
Ownership %: 100
**Management:**
James E. Buerger ..............................Publisher
Matt Carr ...........................General Manager

**Editorial:**
Jim South ..................................Chief Operator
**Desc.:** Serves as a local
entertainment/information guide for
hotel/motel guests in over 110 cities
nationwide. Emphasis placed on the
traveling market.
**Readers:** Over 2 million hotel/motel
guests per week.

## TRAVELORE REPORT
26569

1512 Spruce St., Ste. 100
Philadelphia, PA 19102
Telephone: (215) 735-3838
FAX: (215) 545-7976
Year Established: 1970
Pub. Frequency: m.
Page Size: standard
Subscrip. Rate: $28.50/yr. U.S. & Canada;
$48/yr. elsewhere
Freelance Pay: $10-$35/article
**Owner(s):**
TR Report
1512 Spruce St.
Philadelphia, PA 19102
Telephone: (215) 735-3838
Ownership %: 100
**Management:**
Ted Barkus ......................................Publisher
H. A. Jones ........................Circulation Manager
**Editorial:**
Ted Barkus ...............................Executive Editor
Rhoda S. Barkus .....................Associate Editor
Allen E. Barkus ....................Coordinating Editor
Harrieta Barkus ....................Coordinating Editor
Allen E. Barkus .......................Editorial Advisor
**Desc.:** Monthly newsletter reporting
concise, factual subjects on worldwide
travel. Editorial style geared to candid
appraisals, how to save money. Format
caters to affluent travelers, corporate
travel planners, travel agents. Uses
subjects when containing costs, how to
get there, what to do, what to avoid.
Contains warnings and alerts on
problems at destinations. Departments
include: Transportation, Lodgings,
Dining, Shopping, Book Reviews,
Photography.
**Readers:** Affluent travelers with time and
who travel often. Readers throughout
the world.

## TRAVEL SMART
26570

40 Beechdale Rd.
Dobbs Ferry, NY 10522
Telephone: (914) 693-8300
Year Established: 1976
Pub. Frequency: m.
Page Size: standard
Subscrip. Rate: $44/yr.; $37/yr.
introductory
Materials: 09
Freelance Pay: varies
Circulation: 12,000
Circulation Type: paid
**Owner(s):**
Communications House, Inc.
40 Beechdale Rd.
Dobbs Ferry, NY 10522
Telephone: (914) 693-8300
Ownership %: 100
**Management:**
H.J. Teison ........................................President
H.J. Teison ........................................Publisher
**Editorial:**
H.J. Teison ...........................................Editor
**Desc.:** Tells readers in detail how to travel
better for less. Desire short, informative
pieces that do just that.
**Readers:** Alert, sophisticated travelers,
who want to get maximum value for their
time and money.

## TRAVEL 50 & BEYOND
67289

1502 Augusta, Ste. 415
Houston, TX 77057
Telephone: (713) 974-6903
FAX: (713) 974-0445
Year Established: 1990
Pub. Frequency: q.
Page Size: standard
Subscrip. Rate: $3.95 newsstand;
$15.80/yr.
Circulation: 215,000
Circulation Type: paid
**Owner(s):**
Vacation Publications, Inc.
1502 Augusta, Ste. 415
Houston, TX 77057
Telephone: (713) 974-6903
Ownership %: 100
**Management:**
R. Alan Fox ......................................Publisher
Elizabeth Lewis .................Circulation Manager
**Editorial:**
Mary Lu Abbott .......................................Editor

## TRAVLTIPS
70429

163-07 Depot Rd.
Flushing, NY 11358-0188
Telephone: (718) 939-2400
Mailing Address:
P.O. Box 580188
Flushing, NY 11358
Year Established: 1966
Pub. Frequency: bi-m.
Page Size: standard
Subscrip. Rate: $30/yr. US; $35/yr.
Canada & Mexico
**Owner(s):**
Travltips, Inc.
163-07 Depot Rd.
Flushing, NY 11358-0188
Telephone: (718) 939-2400
Ownership %: 100
**Management:**
Travltips, Inc. ....................................Publisher
Pat McGowan ...................Circulation Manager
**Editorial:**
Edmund M. Kirk ....................................Editor
Bridgette Foley .....................Managing Editor
Catherine Gallagher .................Assistant Editor
Stephen K. Wellmeier ..........Contributing Editor
**Desc.:** Publication gives details and
combines features for traveling on
freighters, expeditions and unusual
cruises throughout the world.
**Readers:** For people who enjoy unusual
cruises throughout the world.

## USAIR MAGAZINE
21889

590 Madison Ave., 32nd Fl.
New York, NY 10022
Telephone: (212) 745-6414
Year Established: 1979
Pub. Frequency: m.
Page Size: standard
Subscrip. Rate: $50/yr.; $100/yr. foreign
Freelance Pay: $300-$600/dept.; $600-
$800/feature
Circulation: 450,000
Circulation Type: controlled
**Owner(s):**
NYT Custom Publishing
590 Madison Ave., 32nd Fl.
New York, NY 10022
Telephone: (212) 745-6414
**Management:**
Bonnie McElveen-Hunter .....................President
Gail Story ........................................Publisher
**Editorial:**
Terri Barnes ..........................................Editor
Gina L. Powell ..........Advertising Administrator
**Desc.:** General interest magazine for
passengers of USAir. Covers business,
technology, travel, sports, food, fashion,
and health articles.

**Readers:** Reaches affluent, upper management.

## VACATION GUIDES
`65126`

3675 Clark Rd.
Sarasota, FL 34233
Telephone: (813) 922-3575
FAX: (813) 923-6309
Year Established: 1954
Pub. Frequency: varies with location
Page Size: pocket
Subscrip. Rate: free
Freelance Pay: $25-$100/story
Circulation: 110,000
Circulation Type: free
**Owner(s):**
Miles Media Group, Inc.
3675 Clark Rd.
Sarasota, FL 34233
Telephone: (813) 922-3575
Ownership %: 100
**Management:**
Dennis Cobb .............................Publisher
**Editorial:**
Janet Fusco .................................Editor
Mary Johnson ....................Assistant Publisher
Paul Garris ....................Circulation Editor
**Desc.:** Aims to provide useful, timely information to visitors in 17 Florida markets. Details points of interest and area events. Also contains maps helping visitors get around the town.
**Readers:** Leisure and business travelers.

## VALLEY MOTORIST, THE
`25157`

100 Hazle St.
Wilkes Barre, PA 18702
Telephone: (717) 824-2444
FAX: (717) 824-9855
Year Established: 1927
Pub. Frequency: bi-m.
Page Size: tabloid
Subscrip. Rate: $1/issue
Materials: 09,21
Print Process: web offset
Circulation: 56,704
Circulation Type: controlled
**Owner(s):**
The Valley Automobile Club, Inc.
100 Hazle St.
Wilkes Barre, PA 18702
Telephone: (717) 824-2444
Ownership %: 100
**Editorial:**
Richard J. Myers .........................Editor
Charles J. Spitale ..................Managing Editor
**Desc.:** Features, photos, articles regarding domestic auto and worldwide travel. Devoted to informing its AAA members on matters of interest concerning products, highway conditions, locales and accommodations. Departments include International Travel, Legislation Information, Tips on Car Care, New Products.
**Readers:** Members of the Valley Automobile Club.
**Deadline:** story-1st mo. prior to pub. date

## WESTERN NEW YORK MOTORIST, THE
`25159`

100 International Dr.
Williamsville, NY 14221
Telephone: (716) 634-7900
Year Established: 1909
Pub. Frequency: m.
Page Size: tabloid
Subscrip. Rate: $1.20/yr. members
Circulation: 200,000
Circulation Type: paid

**Owner(s):**
Auto Club of Western New York
100 International Dr.
Williamsville, NY 14221
Telephone: (716) 634-7900
Ownership %: 100
**Editorial:**
Gerald J. Ryan .............................Editor
**Desc.:** Specialize in automotive and travel news. Cover automotive safety, legislation, highway and automotive products. Cover all subjects connected with automobile manufacturers and use.
**Readers:** Auto club members and their families.

## WESTWAYS
`25160`

2601 S. Figueroa St.
Los Angeles, CA 90007
Telephone: (310) 741-4760
FAX: (213) 741-3033
Mailing Address:
   P.O. Box 2890
   Los Angeles, CA 90051
Year Established: 1909
Pub. Frequency: m.
Page Size: standard
Subscrip. Rate: $11/yr.
Materials: 02,05,06,09,10,15,21,25
Freelance Pay: $.50/wd.
Circulation: 430,000
Circulation Type: paid
**Owner(s):**
Automobile Club of Southern California
2601 S. Figueroa St.
Los Angeles, CA 90007
Telephone: (310) 741-4760
Ownership %: 100
**Management:**
Tom McKernan .............................President
Marc Titel ....................................Publisher
Bob Bradley ....................Advertising Manager
**Editorial:**
Vivian Pupo ..............Administrative Assistant
Holly Caporale ......................Art Director
Monica Rowe ....................Editorial Assistant
**Desc.:** Covers travel, western history, modern civic and cultural developments, wildlife, typical and unusual activities and personalities. Articles run from 1,000-2, 500 words, with color photos as illustration. Picture features on an area, activity, wildlife require 40 to 60 photos with captions.
**Deadline:** story-6 mo. prior to pub. date; news-4 mo. prior; ads-3 mo. prior to pub. date

## Group 674-Women's Magazines

### ALLURE
`67070`

360 Madison Ave.
New York, NY 10017
Telephone: (212) 880-5550
FAX: (212) 370-1949
Year Established: 1991
Pub. Frequency: m.
Page Size: standard
Subscrip. Rate: $12/yr.
Circulation: 200,000
Circulation Type: paid
**Owner(s):**
Conde Nast Publications
360 Madison Ave.
New York, NY 10017
Telephone: (212) 880-5550
Ownership %: 100
**Management:**
Sandy Galinkin ...........................Publisher
**Editorial:**
Linda Wells .................................Editor

## AMERICAN WOMAN
`67072`

1700 Broadway, 34th Fl.
New York, NY 10019
Telephone: (212) 541-7100
FAX: (212) 245-1241
Year Established: 1990
Pub. Frequency: bi-m.
Page Size: standard
Subscrip. Rate: $2.50/copy; $14/yr.
Materials: 01,02,03,04,05,06,09,10,11,12, 13,26,28,29
Freelance Pay: $250-$500/article
Circulation: 167,000
Circulation Type: paid
**Owner(s):**
GCR Publishing Group, Inc.
1700 Broadway
New York, NY 10019
Telephone: (212) 541-7100
FAX: (212) 245-1241
Ownership %: 100
**Management:**
Charles Goodman ........................Publisher
Laura LaPatin ..............Advertising Manager
**Editorial:**
Lynn Varacalli .............................Editor
**Desc.:** A self-help, lifestyle magazine for women who want real answers to real problems in their relationships, jobs and personal life. The magazine is chock-full of inspiration and information.

## ATLANTA WEDDINGS
`71278`

7 Westchester Plz.
Elmsford, NY 10523
Telephone: (914) 347-2121
FAX: (914) 347-7330
Year Established: 1986
Pub. Frequency: s-a.
Page Size: standard
Subscrip. Rate: $3.95 newsstand
Materials: 32
Circulation: 25,000
Circulation Type: paid
**Owner(s):**
Opus Publishing Group, L.P.
7 Westchester Plz.
Elmsford, NY 10523
Telephone: (914) 347-2121
Ownership %: 100
**Management:**
Steven Portnoy .............................Publisher
**Editorial:**
Lisa Carse ............................Editor in Chief
Benjamin Bilbrough ..............Marketing Director
**Desc.:** Regional wedding magzine and resource directory for brides-to-be in the greater Atlanta area.

## BEAUTY HANDBOOK
`26578`

10100 Santa Monica Blvd., Ste. 450
Los Angeles, CA 90067
Telephone: (310) 286-0988
FAX: (310) 286-1293
Year Established: 1973
Pub. Frequency: q.
Page Size: 4 color photos/art
Subscrip. Rate: $.99 newstand only
Circulation: 1,350,000
**Owner(s):**
Beauty Handbook Corp.
10100 Santa Monica Blvd., 450
Los Angeles, CA 90067
Telephone: (310) 286-0988
Ownership %: 100
**Management:**
John McAuliffe .............................President
Kevin McGivney ....................Vice President
John McAuliffe .............................Publisher
Blair Howell ....................Production Manager
**Editorial:**
Andrea Sercu ........................Editor in Chief
Elizabeth M. Stallman ..................Advertising
Hawley Hilton McAuliffe ............ Feature Editor

**Desc.:** How-to beauty and health magazine sold at chain drugstores, mass merchandisers & supermarkets nationwide. Departments include: Articles and How-to, Health Updates and Your Body, Lifestyles, Careers, Travel Celebrities & Books With Health, Beauty and Self Help Advice.
**Readers:** Female, age 18-45.

## BLUSHING BRIDE
`66326`

114-02 Merrick Blvd.
Jamaica, NY 11434
Telephone: (718) 739-1296
FAX: (718) 526-5598
Year Established: 1989
Pub. Frequency: a.
Subscrip. Rate: $3 newsstand
Circulation: 20,000
Circulation Type: paid
**Owner(s):**
Baker - Brown Enterprise, Inc.
114 - 02 Merrick Blvd.
Jamaica, NY 11434
Telephone: (718) 739-1296
**Management:**
Angela Baker - Brown ....................Publisher

## BRIDAL GUIDE
`69749`

441 Lexington Ave.
New York, NY 10017
Telephone: (800) 472-7744
FAX: (212) 286-0772
Year Established: 1982
Pub. Frequency: bi-m.
Subscrip. Rate: $4.95 newsstand; $11.97/yr.
Materials: 02,09,10,11,17,19,21,25,26,28, 29,32,33
Freelance Pay: $500-$1000/article
Circulation: 225,000
Circulation Type: controlled & paid
**Owner(s):**
Globe Communications Corp.
441 Lexington Ave.
New York, NY 10017
Telephone: (800) 472-7744
Ownership %: 100
**Editorial:**
Judy Kuker ....................................Editor
**Desc.:** Articles about relationships, sexuality, health, nutrition, psychology, finance, and travel are accepted. All wedding-planning articles are produced in-house. We do not accept personal essays, poems, or fiction.
**Readers:** Engaged women, ages 18-35.

## BRIDE'S & YOUR NEW HOME
`26580`

140 E. 45th St.
New York, NY 10017
Telephone: (212) 880-8800
FAX: (212) 880-8331
Year Established: 1934
Pub. Frequency: bi-m.
Page Size: standard
Subscrip. Rate: $18/yr.; $34/2 yrs.
Freelance Pay: varies
Circulation: 458,769
Circulation Type: paid
**Owner(s):**
Conde Nast Publications, Inc.
350 Madison Ave.
Conde Nast Bldg.
New York, NY 10017
Telephone: (212) 880-8581
Ownership %: 100
**Management:**
Roger Antin ...............................Publisher
**Editorial:**
Barbara Tober ........................Editor in Chief

**Materials Accepted/Included:** 01-Business news 02-By-line articles 03-Fashion news 04-Food news 05-Freelance copy 06-Letters to editor 07-Real estate news 08-Sports news 09-Travel news 10-Book rev. 11-Movie rev. 12-Music rev. 13-TV rev. 14-Theater rev. 15-Coming events 16-Obituaries 17-Question & answer 18-Social announcements 19-Artwork 20-Cartoons 21-Photos 22-TV listings 23-Audio rec. 24-Video rec. 25-Books 26-Films/film clips 27-Personnel news 28-Press releases 29-New product news/photos 30-Trade lit. 31-Contracts awarded 32-Display adv. 33-Classified adv.

6-133

**Desc.:** A service magazine for the bride-to-be. It provides information and guidance in the expenditure of money in areas unfamiliar to her, for her wedding, honeymoon, decorating and furnishing her first home. Editorial coverage includes: bridal fashions, beauty, trousseau, honeymoon travel, wedding gifts, home furnishing, household appliances, equipment and entertaining. Regular features include wedding plans, etiquette, health and beauty questions and answers, marital and sexual adjustment, money matters, communication, where to buy information and reader service.
**Readers:** Prospective brides.

## BUZZ
65718
11835 W. Olympic Blvd., Ste. 450
Los Angeles, CA 90064
Telephone: (310) 467-4244
Year Established: 1990
Pub. Frequency: 10/yr.
Subscrip. Rate: $3/newsstand; $15/yr.
Materials: 02,05,06,19,21,32
Print Process: web offset
Circulation: 78,000
Circulation Type: controlled & paid
**Owner(s):**
Buzz, Inc.
11835 W. Olympic Blvd.,Ste.450
Los Angeles, CA 90064
Telephone: (310) 473-2721
Ownership %: 100
**Management:**
Eden Collinsworth .............................President
Susan Gates ...................................Publisher
**Editorial:**
Allan Mayer ........................................Editor

## COSMOPOLITAN
26583
224 W. 57th St.
New York, NY 10019
Telephone: (212) 649-3570
FAX: (212) 956-3268
Year Established: 1886
Pub. Frequency: m.
Page Size: 7 x 10 3/16
Subscrip. Rate: $24.97/yr.
Materials: 02,03,04,05,09,10,11,19,20,21,
23,25,28,29
Circulation: 2,741,784
Circulation Type: paid
**Owner(s):**
Hearst Corp.
959 Eighth Ave.
New York, NY 10019
Telephone: (212) 649-2000
Ownership %: 100
**Management:**
Tony Hoyt ...........................................Publisher
Pammy Brooks ..................Promotion Manager
**Editorial:**
Roberta Ashley ........................Executive Editor
Helen Gurley Brown ............................Editor
Guy Flatley .........................Managing Editor
Peg Farrell ...................................Advertising
Linda Cox .....................................Art Director
Andera Pomerantz Lynn ..........Beauty Director
Betty Kelly ...........................Books & Fiction
Pat Sadowsky ...............................Decorating
Sandy deNicolais ..................Fashion Director

**Desc.:** Uses personality stories running about 1,000 to 3,000 words. Interested in articles of broad, general appeal-expose, medical, career, health, personal problems, etc. Photo spreads used to cover personalities, travel, general interest stories, humor. Photographers, editors, and authors get by-lines. Fiction deals with adult romance, humor, exotic background material-sophisticated treatment.
**Readers:** Career women.

## COUNTRY HOME & GARDEN
66509
4151 Knob Dr.
Ste. 200
St. Paul, MN 55122
Telephone: (612) 452-0571
FAX: (612) 454-5791
Year Established: 1991
Pub. Frequency: bi-m.
Page Size: standard
Subscrip. Rate: $3.50 newsstand; $15/yr.
Materials: 03,04,05,06,07,09,10,11,12,13,
14,15,17,19,20,21,23,24,28,29,32,33,
Freelance Pay: $200-$300/1,000-1,500 wds.
Print Process: web offset
Circulation: 140,000
Circulation Type: paid
**Owner(s):**
Russ Moore & Associates, Inc.
4151 Knob Dr.
Ste. 200
St. Paul, MN 55122
Telephone: (612) 452-0571
FAX: (612) 454-5791
Ownership %: 100
**Management:**
Russ Moore ...................................Publisher
John Kramer .................Advertising Manager
Dick Cross ...................Production Manager
**Editorial:**
Carla Waldemar ..................Executive Editor
Karl Bowens ...............................Art Director
Judy Surano ........................Associate Editor
Lucina Spencer ........................Design Editor
**Desc.:** Covers travel, romance, and relationship editorials for women 20 to 50 years old.
**Readers:** Women 20-50 years of age.
**Deadline:** story-22nd of mo. prior to pub. date; news-22nd of mo. prior; photo-22nd of mo. prior; ads-10th of mo. prior

## DETROIT METROPOLITAN WOMAN
69198
17117 W. Nine Mile Rd., Ste. 1115
Southfield, MI  48075-4517
Telephone: (313) 443-6500
FAX: (313) 443-6501
Year Established: 1991
Pub. Frequency: m.
Page Size: standard
Subscrip. Rate: $15/yr.
Materials: 01,02,03,04,05,06,08,09,10,15,
18,19,23,24,25,27,28,29
Print Process: web offset
Circulation: 30,000
Circulation Type: paid
**Owner(s):**
Metropolitan Woman, Inc.
17117 W. Nine Mile Rd., #1115
Southfield, MI  48075-4517
Telephone: (313) 443-6500
Ownership %: 100
**Editorial:**
Patricia Banker Peart ...........................Editor
Alice Sieloff ...............................Advertising
**Desc.:** Lifestyle magazine aimed at women age 30-60. Regional
**Deadline:** story-2 mo. prior to pub. date; news-2 mo. prior

## ELEGANT BRIDE
65342
1301 Carolina St.
Greensboro, NC 27401
Telephone: (910) 378-6065
FAX: (910) 275-2864
Mailing Address:
P.O. Box 13607
Greensboro, NC 27415
Year Established: 1937
Pub. Frequency: bi-m.
Page Size: standard
Subscrip. Rate: $4.95 newsstand; $30/yr.
Circulation: 474,500
Circulation Type: paid
**Owner(s):**
Pace Communications, Inc.
1301 Carolina St.
Greensboro, NC 27401
Telephone: (910) 378-6065
Ownership %: 100
**Management:**
Bonnie McElveen-Hunter ...................Publisher
Cheryl Nichols ..................Advertising Manager
**Editorial:**
Jaclyn C. Barrett-Hirschant .....................Editor
**Desc.:** Features southern location photography of bridal gowns, wedding traditions of south and honeymoon travel.
**Readers:** Targets new brides in the southern region of the U.S. but also pertains to other areas of the U.S.

## ELLE
65412
1633 Broadway
New York, NY 10019
Telephone: (212) 767-5800
FAX: (212) 489-4216
Year Established: 1985
Pub. Frequency: m.
Page Size: standard
Subscrip. Rate: $26/yr.
Circulation: 875,000
Circulation Type: paid
**Owner(s):**
Hachette Filipacchi Publications, Inc.
1633 Broadway
New York, NY 10019
Telephone: (212) 767-5800
Ownership %: 100
**Bureau(s):**
Chicago Bureau
325 N. Michigan Ave.
Chicago, IL 60601
Telephone: (312) 280-0312
Contact: Corrine B. Kirby, Manager

Los Angeles Bureau
3807 Wilshire Blvd., #1204
Los Angeles, CA 90010
Telephone: (310) 739-5100
Contact: Anne Martino, Manager
**Management:**
Diane Wichard Silberstein ...................Publisher
Marilyn Carminio ..................Assistant Manager
John P. River .........................General Manager
Jean L. Fornasieri ................Managing Director
**Editorial:**
Amy Gross ..........................Editorial Director
Brenda G. Saget ............Advertising Director
Olivia Badrut-Giron ........................Art Director
John Kayser ..................Circulation Director
Gilles Bensimon ..................Creative Director
Cynthia R. Lewis ....................Fashion Editor
Lisa Loverro ........................Production Director
Regis Pagniez ....................Publishing Director
**Desc.:** International style magazine for the sophisticated, affluent, well traveled woman. Reports on global ideas and trends in fashion, personalities and lifestyles.

## ESSENCE
26586
1500 Broadway
New York, NY 10036
Telephone: (212) 642-0600
FAX: (212) 921-5173
Year Established: 1970
Pub. Frequency: m.
Page Size: standard
Subscrip. Rate: $2.25 newsstand;
$14.96/yr.
Freelance Pay: varies
Circulation: 950,000
Circulation Type: paid
**Owner(s):**
Essence Communications, Inc.
1500 Broadway
New York, NY 10036
Telephone: (212) 642-0600
Ownership %: 100
**Management:**
Clarence O. Smith .............................President
Edward Lewis .................................Publisher
James Forsythe ................Circulation Manager
Angela Perry ..........Public Relations Manager
**Editorial:**
Susan L. Taylor .........................Editor in Chief
Valerie Wilson Wesley ...................Exec. Editor
Stephanie Stokes Oliver .........................Editor
Barbara Britton ...............Advertising Director
Marlowe Goodson ...........................Art Director
Mikki Garth-Taylor ..........................Beauty Editor
Audrey Edwards ........................Editor at Large
Harriette Cole ...........................Fashion Editor
Pam Johnson ...........................Life Style Editor
Meleanie Howell ..................Sales Promotions
Williams                                    Manager
**Desc.:** Features on fashion, beauty, women service and how-to articles, recipes as well as editorial features concerning the role of black women in the world today. Departments Include: About People, Sign Time (Astrology), Mothering, Backtalk, In The Spirit, Total Well-Being, Travel Contemporary Living, Fashion, Beauty, Brothers, Essentials, Horoscope, Graffiti, Interiors, Windows and Legacy.
**Readers:** Black women ages 18-54.

## FAMILY CIRCLE
26588
110 Fifth Ave.
New York, NY 10011
Telephone: (212) 463-1000
FAX: (212) 463-1808
Year Established: 1932
Pub. Frequency: 17/yr.
Page Size: standard
Subscrip. Rate: $15.98/yr.
Circulation: 5,000,000
Circulation Type: paid
**Owner(s):**
The New York Times
229 W. 43rd St.
New York, NY 10036
Telephone: (212) 556-1234
Ownership %: 100
**Management:**
Wenda Harris-Millard .........................Publisher
Mike Golden .........................General Manager
**Editorial:**
Susan Ungaro .........................Editor in Chief
Barbara Winkler ........................Executive Editor
Cathy O'Haire ...........................Managing Editor
Jackie Leo .............................Editorial Director
Kathy Sagen ...................Book Review Editor
Doug Turshen ...................Creative Director
**Desc.:** Articles of interest to women. Features, Food, Home Furnishings, Equipment, Fashions and Needle Work, Beauty and Health, Your Children and You, Travel.
**Readers:** Homemakers, families.

---

**Materials Accepted/Included:** 01-Business news 02-By-line articles 03-Fashion news 04-Food news 05-Freelance copy 06-Letters to editor 07-Real estate news 08-Sports news 09-Travel news 10-Book rev. 11-Movie rev. 12-Music rev. 13-TV rev. 14-Theater rev. 15-Coming events 16-Obituaries 17-Question & answer 18-Social announcements 19-Artwork 20-Cartoons 21-Photos 22-TV listings 23-Audio rec. 24-Video rec. 25-Books 26-Films/film clips 27-Personnel news 28-Press releases 29-New product news/photos 30-Trade lit. 31-Contracts awarded 32-Display adv. 33-Classified adv.

## FAMILY CIRCLE GREAT IDEAS
25974

110 Fifth Ave.
New York, NY 10011
Year Established: 1975
Pub. Frequency: bi-m.
Page Size: standard
Subscrip. Rate: $2.95/Christmas,
$2.50/other
Freelance Pay: $500-$1250/article
Circulation: 600,000
Circulation Type: paid
**Owner(s):**
New York Times
488 Madison Ave.
New York, NY 10022
Telephone: (212) 463-1000
**Management:**
Marion Aaron ..............................Publisher
Marion Aaron ..................Advertising Manager
**Editorial:**
Karlys Brown ............................Managing Editor
**Desc.:** Features are: Best-Ever Barbecues,
Fashions & Crafts, Christmas Helps and
Holiday Baking. Departments include:
Food, Fashion, Craft, Health & Nutrition.

## FIRST FOR WOMEN
67286

270 Sylvan Ave.
Englewood Cliffs, NJ 07632
Telephone: (201) 569-6699
FAX: (201) 569-5303
Mailing Address:
P.O. Box 1649
Englewood Cliffs, NJ 07632
Year Established: 1989
Pub. Frequency: 17/yr.
Page Size: standard
Subscrip. Rate: $27/yr.
Circulation: 1,500,000
Circulation Type: paid
**Owner(s):**
Heinrich Bower North America, Inc.
270 Sylvan Ave.
Englewood Cliffs, NJ 07632
Telephone: (201) 569-6699
Ownership %: 100
**Management:**
Conrad Weiderholz ......................Publisher
Susan Orman ..................Advertising Manager
**Desc.:** Features fashion, food, health and
fitness, and things to do and make
around the house.

## GLAMOUR
26591

350 Madison Ave.
New York, NY 10017
Telephone: (212) 880-8800
FAX: (212) 880-6922
Year Established: 1939
Pub. Frequency: m.
Page Size: standard
Subscrip. Rate: $15/yr.
Circulation: 2,300,000
Circulation Type: paid
**Owner(s):**
Conde Nast Publications, Inc.
350 Madison Avenue
New York, NY 10017
Telephone: (212) 880-8800
Ownership %: 100
**Management:**
Steven Florio ..........................President
Charles Townsend ......................Publisher
**Editorial:**
Ruth Whitney ..........................Editor in Chief
Prescila Flood ........................Managing Editor
Debra Fine ..........................Advertising Director
Leslie Seymour ........................Beauty Editor
Charla Krupp ........................Entertainment Editor
Cindy Webber-Cleary ................Fashion Editor

**Desc.:** The fashion, beauty, and health
magazine for women who work. Devoted
to fashion, beauty, and health
complemented by informational
coverage on travel, careers,
entertainment, and home. By presenting
realistic fashion options that balance
style with affordability and availability.
Motivates readers to purchase the
merchandise featured within its pages.
**Readers:** Women between 18 and 39.

## HARPER'S BAZAAR
26594

1700 Broadway
New York, NY 10019-5970
Telephone: (212) 903-5000
FAX: (212) 581-4803
Year Established: 1867
Pub. Frequency: m.
Subscrip. Rate: $17.94/yr.
Circulation: 738,403
Circulation Type: paid
**Owner(s):**
Hearst Corp.
959 Eighth Ave.
New York, NY 10019
Telephone: (212) 935-5900
**Management:**
Carl Portale ..........................Publisher
**Editorial:**
Liz Tilberis ..........................Editor
Marguerite Kramer ................Managing Editor
Jeannette Chang ................Associate Publisher
**Desc.:** Articles cover fashions, pictures,
beauty, culture, and feature stories of
interest to women.
**Readers:** Fashion-conscious women.

## IMAGEN
69720

1700 Fernandez Juncos Ave., Stop 25
San Juan, PR 00909-2999
Telephone: (809) 728-3000
FAX: (809) 728-7325
Year Established: 1986
Pub. Frequency: m.
Subscrip. Rate: $2.75 newsstand; $24/yr.
Materials: 02,03,04,05,06,10,11,12,17,18,
19,21,29,32,33
Circulation: 200,000
Circulation Type: paid
**Owner(s):**
Casiano Communications, Inc.
1700 Fernandez Juncos Ave.
Stop 25
San Juan, PR 00909-2999
Telephone: (809) 728-3000
Ownership %: 100
**Editorial:**
Tere Paniagua ..........................Editor
**Desc.:** Focuses on fashion, beauty and
personalities.

## LADIES' HOME JOURNAL
26599

100 Park Ave.
New York, NY 10017
Telephone: (212) 351-3500
FAX: (212) 351-3650
Year Established: 1883
Pub. Frequency: m.
Page Size: standard
Subscrip. Rate: $19.95/yr.
Circulation: 5,000,000
Circulation Type: paid
**Owner(s):**
Meredith Corp.
750 3rd Ave.
New York, NY 10017
Telephone: (212) 351-3500
Ownership %: 100
**Management:**
Donna Galotti ..........................Publisher
**Editorial:**
Myrna Blyth ..........................Editor in Chief
Carolyn Noyes ........................Managing Editor

Jeffrey Saks ..........................Art Director
Lois Joy Johnson ........................Beauty Editor
Jane Farrell ..........................Fiction Editor
Jan Hazard ..........................Food Editor
**Desc.:** Women's magazine carrying service
and information articles, entertainment
profiles and interviews, and major
reporting on topics of
national/ international interest.
Unsolicited manuscripts occasionally
accepted. Departmental material staff -
written. Editorial offices located in New
York City.
**Readers:** Adult women-age 18 and older.

## LADY'S CIRCLE
26602

152 Madison Ave.
Ste. 906
New York, NY 10016
Telephone: (212) 689-3933
FAX: (212) 725-2239
Year Established: 1963
Pub. Frequency: bi-m.
Page Size: standard
Subscrip. Rate: $9.97/yr.
Freelance Pay: $75-$125
Circulation: 100,000
Circulation Type: paid
**Owner(s):**
Lopez Publications, Inc.
152 Madison Ave.
Ste. 906
New York, NY 10016
Telephone: (212) 689-3933
Ownership %: 100
**Management:**
Adrian Lopez ..........................President
Adrian Lopez ..........................Publisher
**Editorial:**
Mary Bemis ..........................Editor
**Desc.:** Articles on health, diet, child care,
hobbies, money making and sewing,
needlework, home management, doing
good for others,and people overcoming
handicaps. Length, 1,200-2,500 words.
**Readers:** Housewives and working
mothers.

## MADEMOISELLE
26604

350 Madison Ave.
New York, NY 10017
Telephone: (212) 880-8800
FAX: (212) 880-8165
Year Established: 1935
Pub. Frequency: m.
Page Size: standard
Subscrip. Rate: $2 newsstand; $15/yr.
Freelance Pay: $500-$1750/article
Circulation: 1,218,985
Circulation Type: paid
**Owner(s):**
Conde Nast Publications, Inc.
350 Madison Ave.
New York, NY 10017
Telephone: (212) 880-8800
Ownership %: 100
**Bureau(s):**
Conde Nast Publications/Mademoiselle
9100 Wilshire Blvd.
Beverly Hills , CA 90212
Telephone: (310) 205-7600
Contact: Jerry Bronow, Advertising
Manager

Detroit Office
3310 W. Beaver Rd.
Detroit, MI
Telephone: (313) 643-0540
Contact: Don Hager, Advertising Manager

Midwest Office
875 N. Michigan Ave.
Chicago, IL 60611
Telephone: (312) 943-2710
Contact: Shawn Cochrane, Advertising
Manager

Southeastern Office
1375 Peachtree St., N.E.
Atlanta, GA 30309
Telephone: (404) 892-3589
Contact: Diane Mann, Advertising Manager
**Management:**
Julie Lewit ..........................Publisher
Cathy Kruchko ................Advertising Manager
**Editorial:**
Elizabeth Crow ........................Editor in Chief
Amanda Lovell ........................Associate Editor
**Desc.:** Article and features run from 750
words to 2,500 words. Departments
include: General Features, Careers,
Health and Beauty, Health and Nutrition,
Fashion, Fiction. Editorial themes follow
the general outline listed. Works five full
months in advance. Query before
proceeding with specific articles.
**Readers:** Well-educated, successfully
employed, affluent, and interested in
what's coming in beauty, health, fashion,
and current affairs.

## MARYLAND BRIDE
71256

7 Westchester Plz.
Elmsford, NY 10523
Telephone: (914) 347-2121
FAX: (914) 347-7330
Year Established: 1986
Pub. Frequency: s-a.
Page Size: standard
Subscrip. Rate: $3.95 newsstand
Materials: 05,32
Freelance Pay: varies
Print Process: offset
Circulation: 50,000
Circulation Type: paid
**Owner(s):**
Opus Publishing Group
245 Park Ave.
New York, NY 10167
Ownership %: 100
**Management:**
Steve Portnoy ..........................Publisher
**Editorial:**
Lisa Carse ..........................Editor
Benjamine Bilbourgh ............Marketing Director
**Desc.:** Regional wedding magazine and
resource directory for brides-to-be.

## MCCALL'S
26605

110 Fifth Ave.
New York, NY 10011
Telephone: (212) 463-1000
FAX: (212) 463-1403
Year Established: 1876
Pub. Frequency: m.
Page Size: standard
Subscrip. Rate: $19.97/yr.
Freelance Pay: $50-$3500
Circulation: 4,600,000
Circulation Type: paid
**Owner(s):**
New York Times Magazine Group
110 5th Ave.
New York, NY 10011
Telephone: (212) 551-9500
Ownership %: 100
**Management:**
Charles M. Townsend ........................President
Barbara Litrell ..........................Publisher
**Editorial:**
Lynne Cosack ..........................Executive Editor
Kate White ..........................Editor
Leslie Smith ..........................Managing Editor
Marilu Lopez ..........................Creative Director
Lisel Eisenheimer ........................Deputy Editor

**Materials Accepted/Included:** 01-Business news 02-By-line articles 03-Fashion news 04-Food news 05-Freelance copy 06-Letters to editor 07-Real estate news 08-Sports news 09-Travel news
10-Book rev. 11-Movie rev. 12-Music rev. 13-TV rev. 14-Theater rev. 15-Coming events 16-Obituaries 17-Question & answer 18-Social announcements 19-Artwork 20-Cartoons 21-Photos 22-TV listings
23-Audio rec. 24-Video rec. 25-Books 26-Films/film clips 27-Personnel news 28-Press releases 29-New product news/photos 30-Trade lit. 31-Contracts awarded 32-Display adv. 33-Classified adv.

6-135

Ellen Kunes .........................Life Style Editor
**Desc.:** McCall's motivates readers to make positive changes in their lives and the world around them. It is the one women's service magazine that addresses the constant changes that affect American women and encourages readers to look beyond the obvious.
**Readers:** Women, nationally.

**MIRABELLA**                                    66709
200 Madison Ave.
New York, NY 10016
Telephone: (212) 447-4600
FAX: (212) 447-4762
Year Established: 1989
Pub. Frequency: m.
Page Size: standard
Subscrip. Rate: $2 newsstand; $24/yr.
Circulation: 575,000
Circulation Type: paid
**Owner(s):**
Murdock Mag., Div. of News America Publishing, Inc
1211 Ave. of the Americas
New York, NY 10036
Telephone: (212) 852-7000
Ownership %: 100
**Management:**
Grace Mirabella ........................Founder
Kathy Viscardi ........................Publisher
**Editorial:**
Gay Bryant ........................Editor in Chief
Grace Mirabella .................Publication Director
**Desc.:** Magazine about style and how it pertains to every aspect of a woman's life-the fashion she wears, the books she reads, the theater and film she enjoys, her travels, her home, her favorite restaurants, her health and sports activities. Business, politics, psychology, health, fiction, the performing arts-explores them all.
**Readers:** Aimed at the affluent woman, who is confident, secure and intelligent. The median age of the Mirabella subscriber is 41.

**MODERN BRIDE**                                26607
249 W. 17th St.
New York, NY 10011
Telephone: (212) 337-7000
FAX: (212) 337-7129
Year Established: 1949
Pub. Frequency: bi-m.
Page Size: standard
Subscrip. Rate: $22/yr.
Freelance Pay: varies
**Owner(s):**
Cahners Publishing Co., Div.-Reed Publishing USA
275 Washington St.
Newton, MA 02158
Telephone: (212) 503-3800
Ownership %: 100
**Bureau(s):**
Modern Bride
625 N. Michigan Ave., Ste 1500
Chicago, IL 60611
Telephone: (312) 915-4929
Contact: Carl Scichili, Sales Manager

Modern Bride
12233 W. Olympic Blvd. Ste 236
Los Angeles, CA 90064
Telephone: (800) 451-1457
Contact: Carl Scichili

Modern Bride
7200 Corp. Ctr. Dr., Ste. 610
Miami, FL 33126
Telephone: (305) 594-5680
Contact: Jerry Brennan, Sales Manager

**Management:**
Howard Friedberg ........................Publisher
Nancy Youngbeck ............Promotion Manager
**Editorial:**
Cele Goldsmith Lalli .................Editor in Chief
Mary Ann Cavlin ................Managing Editor
Debbra Gill ........................Art Director
Eleanor Simon ........................Booklet Editor
Martine Niddam ....................Fashion Editor
Carolyn Bartel ........................Home Editor
Michael Arpino ................Production Director
Suzanne Oppenheimer ..........Production Editor
Geri Bain ........................Travel Editor
**Desc.:** Service magazine for bride-to-be.
**Readers:** Brides-to-be

**MODERN ROMANCES**                            26609
233 Park Ave., S.
New York, NY 10003
Telephone: (212) 979-4800
FAX: (212) 979-7342
Year Established: 1924
Pub. Frequency: 11/yr.
Page Size: standard
Subscrip. Rate: $1.69 newsstand; $9.97/yr.
Freelance Pay: $.05/wd.
Circulation: 225,000
Circulation Type: paid
**Owner(s):**
Sterling Macfadden Partnership
233 Park Ave., S.
New York, NY 10003
Telephone: (212) 979-4000
Ownership %: 100
**Management:**
Peter Callahan ........................President
Barbara Hanna-Grufferman ................Publisher
John Fitzpatrick .................Advertising Manager
**Editorial:**
Ilene Fitzmaurice ........................Editor
Janet Tanke ...............New Production Editor
Constance Brukin ........................Photo
**Desc.:** Includes first-person confession stories. Occasionally, may print an article about marriage, sex, and birth control.

**MS**                                          26611
230 Park Ave.
7th Fl.
New York, NY 10169
Telephone: (212) 551-9595
FAX: (212) 551-9384
Year Established: 1972
Pub. Frequency: bi-m.
Page Size: standard
Subscrip. Rate: $45/yr. in US; $52/yr. in CN
Freelance Pay: negotiable
Circulation: 350,000
Circulation Type: paid
**Owner(s):**
Lang Communications, Inc.
230 Park Ave.
New York, NY 10169
Telephone: (212) 551-9500
Ownership %: 100
**Editorial:**
Marcia Ann Gillespie .................Editor in Chief
Barbara Findlen ................Managing Editor
**Desc.:** A general interest news magazine which charts the changes in women's lives and celebrates women's achievements. An advertising-free international feminist magazine.
**Readers:** Primarily women.

**NATIONAL BUSINESS WOMAN**                    26613
2012 Massachusetts Ave., N.W.
Washington, DC 20036
Telephone: (202) 293-1100
Year Established: 1919
Pub. Frequency: q.

Page Size: standard
Subscrip. Rate: $10/yr.
Materials: 01,02,06,32,33
Print Process: web
Circulation: 70,000
Circulation Type: controlled
**Owner(s):**
Natl. Fed. of Bus. & Prof. Womens Clubs, BPW/USA
2012 Massachusetts Ave., NW
Washington, DC 20036
Telephone: (202) 293-1100
Ownership %: 100
**Editorial:**
Marcia Eldrege ........................Editor
**Desc.:** Focuses on issues of concern to working women.
**Readers:** Association members-business and professional women.

**NETWORK MAGAZINE**                           70481
155 E. 4905 S.
Salt Lake City, UT 84107
Telephone: (801) 252-8091
FAX: (801) 262-5419
Mailing Address:
    P.O. Box 7187
    Salt Lake City, UT 84107
Year Established: 1978
Pub. Frequency: m.
Page Size: tabloid
Subscrip. Rate: $1 newsstand; $12/yr.
Circulation: 30,000
Circulation Type: controlled & paid
**Owner(s):**
Diversified Suburban Newspapers, Inc.
155 E. 4905 S.
Salt Lake City, UT 84107
Ownership %: 100
**Management:**
Peter Bernhard ........................Publisher
**Editorial:**
Lynne Tempest ........................Editor
**Desc.:** A magazine for today's woman.

**NEW JERSEY WEDDING**                         71283
7 Westcbester Plz.
Elmsford, NY 10523
Telephone: (914) 347-2121
FAX: (914) 347-7330
Year Established: 1986
Pub. Frequency: s-a.
Page Size: standard
Subscrip. Rate: $3.95 newsstand
Materials: 32
Circulation: 52,000
Circulation Type: paid
**Owner(s):**
Opus Publishing Group, L.P.
7 Westchester Plz.
Elmsford, NY 10523
Telephone: (914) 347-2121
Ownership %: 100
**Management:**
Steven Portnoy ........................Publisher
**Editorial:**
Lisa Carse ........................Editor in Chief
Benjamine Bilbrough ............Marketing Director
**Desc.:** Regional wedding magazine and resource directory for brides-to-be in Northern and Central New Jersey.

**NEW WOMAN**                                   26616
215 Lexington Ave.
New York, NY 10016
Telephone: (212) 251-1500
FAX: (212) 251-1590
Year Established: 1971
Pub. Frequency: m.
Page Size: standard
Subscrip. Rate: $16.97/yr.
Freelance Pay: negotiable
Circulation: 1,260,000
Circulation Type: paid

**Owner(s):**
K-III Magazines
200 Madison Ave.
New York, NY 10016
Telephone: (212) 447-4700
Ownership %: 100
**Editorial:**
Karen Walden ........................Editor in Chief
Susan Kane ........................Exec. Editor
Stephanie Von Hirschberg ..........Senior Editor
Kathy L. Green ................Managing Editor
Emma F. Segal ........................Feature Editor
**Desc.:** Edited for women seeking to improve the balance of their personal and professional lives. Self-improvement, self-esteem and self-discovery are prime editorial issues. Covers career, health, fitness, fashion, beauty, finance, and personal relationships.
**Readers:** Women ages 25-49

**NEW YORK WEDDING**                           71282
7 Westchester Plz.
Elmsford, NY 10523
Telephone: (914) 347-2121
FAX: (914) 347-7330
Year Established: 1986
Pub. Frequency: s-a.
Page Size: standard
Subscrip. Rate: $3.95 newsstand
Materials: 32
Circulation: 60,000
Circulation Type: paid
**Owner(s):**
Opus Publishing Group, L.P.
7 Westchester Plz.
Elmsford, NY 10523
Telephone: (914) 347-2121
Ownership %: 100
**Management:**
Steven Portnoy ........................Publisher
**Editorial:**
Lisa Carse ........................Editor in Chief
Benjamin Bilbrough ............Marketing Director
**Desc.:** Regional wedding magazine and resource directory for brides-to-be in the Greater Metropolitan New York area.

**PLAYGIRL**                                    26619
801 Second Ave.
Suite 1600
New York, NY 10017
Telephone: (212) 661-7878
FAX: (212) 697-6343
Year Established: 1973
Pub. Frequency: m. & 2 specials
Page Size: standard
Subscrip. Rate: $3.95 newsstand; $21.95/yr.
Materials: 02,05,06,10,11,12,13,20,21,23, 24,25,26,29,32,33
Freelance Pay: $25-$1500/article
Print Process: web offset
Circulation: 575,547
Circulation Type: paid
**Owner(s):**
Playgirl, Inc.
801 Second Ave.
New York, NY 10017
Ownership %: 100

**Editorial:**
Charmian Carl ........................Editor in Chief
Charlene Keel ................Managing Editor

**Desc.:** National women's magazine that uses pertinent, in-depth materials of interest to an aware, contemporary female audience. Articles must be well researched, approximately 2,000-3,000 words. Photography done by staff and freelancers. We use freelance illustrations. We accept both short and long (up to 4,000 words), fiction/stories may be sexually oriented but not salacious. Departments include: Articles, Fiction, Beauty, Fashion, Covers and Centerfolds.

**Readers:** Our readership is comprised of 86% women, who have had least one year of college. The Playgirl woman is an active, involved individual.

69207

## RADIANCE
P.O. Box 30246
Oakland, CA 94604
Telephone: (510) 482-0680
FAX: (510) 482-0680
Year Established: 1984
Pub. Frequency: q.
Page Size: standard
Subscrip. Rate: $5/newsstand US; $6/newsstand Canada; $20/yr. US; $26/yr. Canada; $34/yr. elsewhere
Materials: 01,02,03,04,05,06,09,10,11,12, 13,14,15,17,19,20,21,23,24,25,28,29,32, 33
Freelance Pay: $15-100
Print Process: offset
Circulation: 80,000
Circulation Type: paid
**Owner(s):**
Alice Ansfield
P.O. Box 30246
Oakland, CA 94604
Telephone: (510) 482-0680
Ownership %: 100
**Management:**
Alice Ansfield ......................Publisher
**Desc.:** Source of support, information and inspiration for women all sizes of large. Features dynamic large women from all walks of life, along with articles on health, media, fashion and politics.

25923

## REDBOOK
224 W. 57th St.
New York, NY 10019
Telephone: (212) 649-3331
FAX: (212) 581-7605
Year Established: 1903
Pub. Frequency: m.
Page Size: standard
Subscrip. Rate: $14.97/yr.
Circulation: 5,000,000
Circulation Type: paid
**Owner(s):**
The Hearst Corp.
959 Eighth Ave.
New York, NY 10019
Telephone: (212) 649-2000
Ownership %: 100
**Management:**
T.R. Sheppard, III ................Publisher
**Editorial:**
Ellen Levine ..............Editor in Chief
Sarah Scrymser ..........Managing Editor

**Desc.:** Articles deal with a wide variety of subjects of interest to women: relationships, marriage, parenting, child psychology, consumer interests, beauty, fashion, etc. Also publishes fiction. Departments include: Articles, Fiction, Beauty, Fashion, Food and Nutrition, Health, Home Furnishings. Regular columns include: Parents & Kids, Between Us, Young Mother's Story, Check Out. Contributing editors: Judith Viorst, Benjamin Spock, M.D., Helen Singer Kaplan, M.D., Ruth K. Westheimer, ED.D., Joel Rapp, Arlene Fisher.
**Readers:** Women in the 25- to 44-year age bracket.

69752

## SASSY
230 Park Ave., 7th Fl.
New York, NY 10169
Telephone: (212) 551-9500
FAX: (212) 764-7487
Year Established: 1988
Pub. Frequency: m.
Subscrip. Rate: $14.97/yr.
Circulation: 745,245
**Owner(s):**
Lang Communications, Inc.
230 Park Ave., 7th Fl.
New York, NY 10169
Telephone: (212) 551-9500
Ownership %: 100
**Management:**
Linda Cohen ......................Publisher
**Editorial:**
Jane Pratt ..................Editor in Chief

53994

## SHAPE
21100 Erwin St.
Woodland Hills, CA 91367
Telephone: (818) 595-0593
Year Established: 1981
Pub. Frequency: m.
Page Size: standard
Subscrip. Rate: $2.50 newsstand; $24.97/yr.
Materials: 04,06,09,25,29,32,33
Freelance Pay: negotiable
Circulation: 750,000
Circulation Type: paid
**Owner(s):**
Shape Magazine, Inc.
21100 Erwin St.
Woodland Hls, CA 91367
Telephone: (818) 595-0593
Ownership %: 100
**Management:**
Joseph Weider ....................Publisher
**Editorial:**
Barbara Harris ............Editor in Chief
Katherine Tomlinson ......Managing Editor
Peg Moline ..............Editorial Director
Peter Miller ............Advertising Director
Kathy Nenneker ..........Creative Director
**Desc.:** Active lifestyle magazine to take the no nonsense approach to all aspects of leading a healthy, productive life. Contributions from top professionals in their respective fields, is translated into laymen's terms for maximum information.
**Readers:** Primaily women of 18-34 years old who are interested in staying healthy and fit.
**Deadline:** story-5 mo. prior to pub. date; ads-3 mo. prior to pub. date

71280

## SOUTHERN CALIFORNIA WEDDING
7 Westchester Plz.
Elmsford, NY 10523
Telephone: (914) 347-2121
FAX: (914) 347-7330

Year Established: 1986
Pub. Frequency: s-a.
Page Size: standard
Subscrip. Rate: $3.95 newsstand
Materials: 32
Freelance Pay: varies
Print Process: offset
Circulation: 60,000
Circulation Type: paid
**Owner(s):**
Opus Publishing Group., L.P.
7 Westchester Plz.
Elmsford, NY 10523
Telephone: (914) 347-2121
Ownership %: 100
**Management:**
Steven Portnoy ....................Publisher
**Editorial:**
Lisa Carse ..............Editor in Chief
Benjamin Bilbrough ......Marketing Director
**Desc.:** Regional wedding magazine and resource directory for brides-to-be, in the Greater Santa Barbara to San Diego including Los Angeles area.

65024

## TODAY'S CHICAGO WOMAN
233 E. Ontario St., Ste. 1300
Chicago, IL 60611-3214
Telephone: (312) 951-7600
FAX: (312) 951-9083
Year Established: 1982
Pub. Frequency: m.
Page Size: tabloid
Subscrip. Rate: $12/yr.
Materials: 03
Freelance Pay: varies
Circulation: 160,000
Circulation Type: free
**Owner(s):**
Leigh Communications, Inc.
233 E. Ontario St., Ste. 1300
Chicago, IL 60611-3214
Telephone: (312) 951-7600
FAX: (312) 951-9083
Ownership %: 100
**Management:**
Pam Levy ..........Editorial Production Manager
Karen Iglar ................Sales Manager
**Editorial:**
Sherren Leigh ......................Editor
Suzanne Krill ..........Circulation Editor
**Desc.:** Contains personality profiles, career strategies, business trends, health, finance, fitness, fashion and activities for professional women.
**Deadline:** ads-18th of mo. prior to pub. date

69204

## TODAY'S LIFESTYLES
4151 Knob Dr.
St. Paul, MN 55122
Telephone: (612) 452-0571
FAX: (612) 454-5791
Year Established: 1992
Pub. Frequency: bi-m.
Freelance Pay: $250-$350/6,00-1,200 wds.
Circulation: 110000
Circulation Type: paid
**Owner(s):**
Prestige Publications, Inc.
4151 Knob Dr.
St. Paul, MN 55122
Telephone: (612) 452-0571
Ownership %: 100
**Editorial:**
Carla Waldemar ......................Editor

25945

## TRUE EXPERIENCE
233 Park Ave., S.
New York, NY 10003
Telephone: (212) 780-3500
FAX: (212) 979-7507
Year Established: 1925
Pub. Frequency: m.

Page Size: standard
Subscrip. Rate: $14.95/yr.
Freelance Pay: $.03/wd. min.
**Owner(s):**
Sterling MacFadden Partnership
233 Park Ave., S.
New York, NY 10003
Telephone: (212) 780-3500
Ownership %: 100
**Management:**
Michael Boylan ....................President
Barbara H. Marks ................Publisher
**Editorial:**
Sue Weiner ..............Editor in Chief
Peter Callahan ..........Editor in Chief
Jean Wallace ......................Editor
Jerome Leff ..................Art Director
Janis Keller ..............Associate Editor
Suzanne Mostacci ..........Miscellaneous
Janet Tanke ..........New Products Editor
Constance Brukin ....................Photo
**Desc.:** Features include child and baby care, pet care and pet photos, plant care, and self-help features. Departments include: Reader mail departments. First-person true stories about love and marriage and interpersonal relationships.
**Readers:** Young married and single middle-aged American women, primarily family oriented.

25947

## TRUE LOVE
233 Park Ave., S.
New York, NY 10003
Telephone: (212) 979-4800
FAX: (212) 979-7507
Year Established: 1924
Pub. Frequency: m.
Page Size: standard
Subscrip. Rate: $14.95/yr.
Freelance Pay: $.03/wd. min.
**Owner(s):**
Sterling MacFadden Partnership
233 Park Ave., S.
New York, NY 10003
Telephone: (212) 979-4800
Ownership %: 100
**Management:**
Michael Boylan ....................President
Barbara H. Marks ................Publisher
**Editorial:**
Sue Weiner ..............Editor in Chief
Peter Callahan ..........Editor in Chief
Cynthia DiMartino ..................Editor
Geraldine Thordsen ..........Art Director
Ella Schwartz ..............Associate Editor
Suzanne Mostacci ..........Miscellaneous
Constance Brukin ....................Photo
**Desc.:** Stories that deal with love and marriage problems of young and middle-aged American women.
**Readers:** Primarily young and middle-aged America women.

25948

## TRUE ROMANCE
233 Park Ave., S., 7th Fl.
New York, NY 10003
Telephone: (212) 979-4800
Year Established: 1923
Pub. Frequency: m.
Page Size: standard
Subscrip. Rate: $14.95/yr.
Materials: 03,04,06,09,10,13
Freelance Pay: $.03/wd. min.
**Owner(s):**
Sterling MacFadden Partnership
233 Park Ave., S., 6th Fl.
New York, NY 10003
Telephone: (212) 979-4800
**Management:**
Peter Callahan ....................President
John Fitzpatrick ....................Publisher
John Fitzpatrick ..........Advertising Manager

**Materials Accepted/Included:** 01-Business news 02-By-line articles 03-Fashion news 04-Food news 05-Freelance copy 06-Letters to editor 07-Real estate news 08-Sports news 09-Travel news 10-Book rev. 11-Movie rev. 12-Music rev. 13-TV rev. 14-Theater rev. 15-Coming events 16-Obituaries 17-Question & answer 18-Social announcements 19-Artwork 20-Cartoons 21-Photos 22-TV listings 23-Audio rec. 24-Video rec. 25-Books 26-Films/film clips 27-Personnel news 28-Press releases 29-New product news/photos 30-Trade lit. 31-Contracts awarded 32-Display adv. 33-Classified adv.

6-137

J. Robert Gallicano ............Circulation Manager
**Editorial:**
Patricia Byrdsong ............................................Editor
Frances M. Adrian ............................Art Director
Judith N. Newman ....................Associate Editor
Suzanne Mostacci ........................Miscellaneous
Suzanne Mostacci ................New Product Editor
Constance Brukin ......................................Photo
**Readers:** Young blue-collar women.

**VICTORIA**                                                69746
250 W. 55th St., 11th Fl.
New York, NY 10019
Telephone: (212) 649-3700
Year Established: 1987
Pub. Frequency: m.
Subscrip. Rate: $17.97/yr.; $33.97/2 yrs.
Circulation: 624,275
Circulation Type: paid
**Owner(s):**
Hearst Magazine Division, The
250 W. 55th St., 11th Fl.
New York, NY 10019
Telephone: (212) 649-3700
Ownership %: 100
**Editorial:**
Nancy Lindemeyer ....................Editor in Chief

**VOGUE**                                                   26632
350 Madison Ave.
New York, NY 10017
Telephone: (212) 880-8800
FAX: (212) 880-8169
Year Established: 1892
Pub. Frequency: m.
Page Size: standard
Subscrip. Rate: $24/yr.
Circulation: 1,227,003
Circulation Type: paid
**Owner(s):**
Conde Nast Publications, Inc.
350 Madison Ave.
New York, NY 10017
Telephone: (212) 880-8800
**Management:**
Ronald A. Galotti ..............................Publisher
Thomas Hartman ............Advertising Manager
**Editorial:**
Edward J. Menicheschi ............Executive Editor
Diane Oshin ........................Advertising Director
Norman Waterman ............Associate Publisher
**Desc.:** High-fashion publication for women.
  Places heavy emphasis on color and
  black and white photography. Feature
  articles include pieces by well-known
  writers. Departments include: People Are
  Talking About, Art, Sports, Collecting,
  Taxes, Restaurants, Sound

**W**                                                       26633
7 W. 34th St.
New York, NY 10001
Telephone: (212) 630-4199
FAX: (212) 630-4201
Year Established: 1972
Pub. Frequency: m.
Page Size: tabloid
Subscrip. Rate: $29.90/yr.
Circulation: 285,957
Circulation Type: paid
**Owner(s):**
Capital Cities-ABC, Inc.
7 W. 34th St.
New York, NY 10001
Telephone: (212) 630-4199
Ownership %: 100
**Bureau(s):**
Fairchild Publications
811 Wilshire Blvd
Los Angeles, CA 90017
Telephone: (510) 954-7738
Contact: Rita Tanos, Vanessa Lazo,
  Advertising Manager

Fairchild Publications
ABC Broadcast Ctr 900 Front St
San Francisco , CA 94111
Telephone: (310) 612-0688
Contact: Melissa Dunlap, Advertising
  Manager

Fairchild Publications
350 N. Orleans
Chicago, IL 60654
Telephone: (312) 644-6634
Contact: Leslie Weiss, Manager
**Management:**
Michael F. Cody ................................President
Olivia Thompson ........................Vice President
Martha Nype ....................Advertising Manager
**Editorial:**
Patrick McCarthy ........................Editor in Chief
Stephanie George ..........................Advertising
Mirta Soto ............................Circulation Director
**Desc.:** The magazine of fashion, social-
  lifestyle showing the finest, first.
**Readers:** Women 94%, average income
  $157,100 annually.

**WASHINGTON BRIDE**                                        71279
7 Westchester Plz.
Elmsford, NY 10523
Telephone: (914) 347-2121
FAX: (914) 347-7330
Year Established: 1986
Pub. Frequency: s-a.
Page Size: standard
Subscrip. Rate: $3.95 newsstand
Materials: 32
Freelance Pay: varies
Print Process: offset
Circulation: 50,000
Circulation Type: paid
**Owner(s):**
Opus Publishing Group., L.P.
7 Westchester Plz.
Elmsford, NY 10523
Telephone: (914) 347-2121
Ownership %: 100
**Management:**
Steven Portnoy ................................Publisher
**Editorial:**
Lise Carse ................................Editor in Chief
Benjamine Bilbrough ............Marketing Director
**Desc.:** Regional wedding magazine and
  resource directory for brides-to-be in the
  Greater Washington, DC and Northern
  Virginia area.

**WICHITA WOMEN MAGAZINE**                                  69205
250 N. Rock Rd. #100. 29
Wichita, KS 67206-2241
Telephone: (316) 684-3620
Year Established: 1986
Pub. Frequency: m.
Page Size: tabloid
Subscrip. Rate: $18/yr.
Materials: 01,02,03,04,05,08,09,10,11,14,
  15,19,20,21,28,29,32
Circulation: 5,000
Circulation Type: paid
**Owner(s):**
Watson Wordsmiths, Inc.
400 N. Woodlawn, Ste. 29
Wichita, KS 67208
Telephone: (316) 684-3620
Ownership %: 100
**Editorial:**
Kate Watson ........................................Editor
**Desc.:** To ease, enrich, and celebrate the
  lives of busy women.
**Deadline:** story-1st Mon. of mo. prior to
  pub. date; ads-15th of mo. prior to pub.
  date

**WOMAN'S DAY**                                             26091
1633 Broadway
New York, NY 10019
Telephone: (212) 767-6000
FAX: (212) 727-5610
Year Established: 1937
Pub. Frequency: 17/yr.
Page Size: standard
Subscrip. Rate: $.99 newsstand; $15.97/yr.
Circulation: 4,600,000
Circulation Type: paid
**Owner(s):**
Hachette Filipacchi Magazines, Inc.
1633 Broadway
New York, NY 10019
Telephone: (212) 767-6000
Ownership %: 100
**Bureaus(s):**
Woman's Day Midwest District
625 N. Michigan Ave Ste 400
Chicago, IL 60611
Telephone: (312) 280-0322
Contact: Jan Studin, Manager

Woman's Day Detroit Office
2300 W. Big Beaver Rd Ste 15
Troy, MI 48084
Telephone: (313) 643-8188
Contact: Susan Duvall, Manager

Los Angeles Office
3807 Wilshire Blvd, Ste 1200
Los Angeles, CA 90010
Telephone: (310) 739-5142
Contact: Mary Freeman, Manager

Woman's Day San Francisco Office
601 Montgomery St Ste 1215
San Francisco , CA 94111
Telephone: (415) 397-3441
Contact: Jon T. Werolin, Manager
**Management:**
Jane Chestnut ..........................Vice President
Susan Buckley ................................Publisher
John Fennell ....................Advertising Manager
Ronald Minutella ..................General Manager
Patrice Listfield ..................Promotion Manager
**Editorial:**
Jane Chestnut ........................Editor in Chief
Brad Pallas ................................Art Director
**Desc.:** Contains staff articles, by-lined
  articles, book excerpts. Covers child
  rearing, school problems, marriage,
  travel, family finance, healthand medical,
  food, creative crafts, fashion, decorating,
  kitchen planning and equipment,
  cosmetics and beauty, some fiction.
**Readers:** Women aged 18-45.

**WOMAN'S WORLD**                                           69737
270 Sylan Ave.
Englewood Cliffs, NJ 07632
Telephone: (201) 569-6699
FAX: (201) 569-3584
Year Established: 1981
Pub. Frequency: w.
Subscrip. Rate: $1.25 newsstand; $78/yr.
Circulation: 1,500,000
Circulation Type: paid
**Owner(s):**
Bauer Publishing Co.
270 Sylvan Ave.
Englewood Cliffs, NJ 07632
Telephone: (201) 569-6699
Ownership %: 100
**Editorial:**
Dena Vane ........................................Editor
Stephanie Saible ................................Editor

**WOMEN'S CIRCLE**                                          26635
P.O. Box 299
Lynnfield, MA 01940
Telephone: (219) 589-8741
FAX: (219) 589-8093
Year Established: 1957

Pub. Frequency: bi-m.
Page Size: 4 color photos/art
Subscrip. Rate: $9.95/yr.
Freelance Pay: varies
Circulation: 63,000
Circulation Type: paid
**Owner(s):**
House of White Birches, Inc.
306 E. Parr Rd.
Berne, IN 46711
Telephone: (219) 589-8741
Ownership %: 100
**Editorial:**
Marjorie Pearl ....................................Editor
**Desc.:** Tips and new ideas on arts and
  crafts, needlecrafts, homemaking,
  recipes, etc. Successful, home-based,
  female entrepreneurs.
**Readers:** Women of all ages.

**WOMEN'S STUDIES**                                         58630
**INTERNATIONAL FORUM**
660 White Plains Rd.
Tarrytown, NY 10591-5153
Telephone: (914) 524-9200
FAX: (914) 333-2444
Year Established: 1978
Pub. Frequency: bi-m.
Page Size: standard
Subscrip. Rate: $195 institutions
Circulation: 1,500
Circulation Type: paid
**Owner(s):**
Elsevier Science, Inc.
660 White Plains Rd.
Tarrytown, NY 10591-5153
Telephone: (914) 524-9200
Ownership %: 100
**Bureaus(s):**
Christine Zmroczek, Mng. Ed.
P.O. Box 181
Haywards Health
West Sussex, 00
**Management:**
Jay Feinman ....................Advertising Manager
Roger A. Dunn ....................General Manager
**Desc.:** Fosters the exchange of
  multidisciplinary feminist research. The
  journal seeks to critique and
  reconceptualize existing knowledge, and
  to examine and re-evaluate the manner
  in which knowledge is produced and
  distributed and the implications this has
  for women.

**WORKING MOTHER**                                          69748
230 Park Ave.
New York, NY 10169
Telephone: (212) 551-9399
FAX: (212) 551-9757
Year Established: 1978
Pub. Frequency: m.
Subscrip. Rate: $7.97/yr.
Circulation: 850,000
Circulation Type: controlled & paid
**Owner(s):**
Lang Communications, Inc.
230 Park Ave.
New York, NY 10169
Telephone: (212) 551-9399
Ownership %: 100
**Editorial:**
Judson Culbreth ................................Editor

**WORKING WOMAN**                                           26639
230 Park Ave.
New York, NY 10169
Telephone: (212) 551-9500
Year Established: 1976
Pub. Frequency: m.
Page Size: standard
Subscrip. Rate: $2.95 newsstand US;
  $3.50 newsstand Canada; $11.97/yr.
Materials: 02,05,29,32

**Materials Accepted/Included:** 01-Business news 02-By-line articles 03-Fashion news 04-Food news 05-Freelance copy 06-Letters to editor 07-Real estate news 08-Sports news 09-Travel news 10-Book rev. 11-Movie rev. 12-Music rev. 13-TV rev. 14-Theater rev. 15-Coming events 16-Obituaries 17-Question & answer 18-Social announcements 19-Artwork 20-Cartoons 21-Photos 22-TV listings 23-Audio rec. 24-Video rec. 25-Books 26-Films/film clips 27-Personnel news 28-Press releases 29-New product news/photos 30-Trade lit. 31-Contracts awarded 32-Display adv. 33-Classified adv.

Freelance Pay: $300-$750/article
Circulation: 900,000
Circulation Type: paid
**Owner(s):**
Lang Communications, Inc.
230 Park Ave.
New York, NY 10169
Telephone: (212) 551-9500
Ownership %: 100
**Management:**
Kristin A. Norrgard ..............................Publisher
**Editorial:**
Lyn Povich ....................................................Editor
Rosemary Ellis ..........................Managing Editor

**Desc.:** For women in management positions who need to be more informative concerning business as well as personal.
**Readers:** Professional/managerial women.

26669

**YM**
685 Third Ave.
New York, NY 10017
Telephone: (212) 878-8700
FAX: (212) 286-0935
Year Established: 1945
Pub. Frequency: 10/yr.

Page Size: standard
Subscrip. Rate: $2.50 newsstand;
 $13.97/yr.
Materials: 32
Freelance Pay: varies
Circulation: 1,300,000
Circulation Type: paid
**Owner(s):**
Gruner & Jahr USA Publishing Co., Inc.
685 Third Ave.
New York, NY 10017
Telephone: (212) 878-8700
Ownership %: 100
**Management:**
John Heins ..............................................President

Vicci Lansdon ......................................Publisher
**Editorial:**
Sally Lee ......................................................Editor
Lori Burgess ..........................Advertising Editor
**Desc.:** Aimed at girls from 12-19. Contains fiction, set in any locale or time period, concerning girls who manage to solve their problems through their own efforts. Young dating stories are also used. Non-fiction covers all matters of interest to girls in this age group. Good grooming, hobbies, food, self-improvement, etc., are all featured. We also use very short, simple how-to fillers.
**Readers:** Teenage girls, 12-19 years old.

**Materials Accepted/Included:** 01-Business news 02-By-line articles 03-Fashion news 04-Food news 05-Freelance copy 06-Letters to editor 07-Real estate news 08-Sports news 09-Travel news 10-Book rev. 11-Movie rev. 12-Music rev. 13-TV rev. 14-Theater rev. 15-Coming events 16-Obituaries 17-Question & answer 18-Social announcements 19-Artwork 20-Cartoons 21-Photos 22-TV listings 23-Audio rec. 24-Video rec. 25-Books 26-Films/film clips 27-Personnel news 28-Press releases 29-New product news/photos 30-Trade lit. 31-Contracts awarded 32-Display adv. 33-Classified adv.

6-139

# Section 7
# NEWSLETTERS

This section contains complete listings for newsletters. The newsletters are listed alphabetically within each subject group. Subject groups follow numerical order according to group number.

A subject listing is provided with a page reference to where each group heading may be found within the main listings.

Please refer to the Alphabetical Cross Index in Section 3 to locate related subject newsletters or related subject categories/listings in the magazine sections.

For materials accepted/included, refer to the coded list at the bottom of each page.

# SUBJECT GROUPS INCLUDED

## Group 302-Agriculture

**AGRARIAN ADVOCATE**                          69826
260 Russell Blvd, 3rd Fl.
Davis, CA 95616
Telephone: (916) 756-8518
FAX: (916) 756-7857
Mailing Address:
   P.O. Box 464
   Davis, CA 95617
Year Established: 1979
Pub. Frequency: q.
Page Size: tabloid
Subscrip. Rate: $15/yr.
Materials: 10,32
Print Process: offset
Circulation: 2,000
Circulation Type: controlled & paid
**Owner(s):**
California Action Network
P.O. Box 464
Davis, CA 95617
Telephone: (916) 756-8518
FAX: (916) 756-7857
Ownership %: 100
**Editorial:**
Erin Barnett ............................................Editor

**AGRICULTURAL CHEMICAL**                       70067
   **NEWSLETTER**
P.O. Box 9335
Fresno, CA 93791
Telephone: (209) 435-2163
FAX: (209) 435-8319
Year Established: 1979
Pub. Frequency: m.
Subscrip. Rate: $80/yr. US; $100/yr.
   foreign
Circulation: 375
Circulation Type: controlled & paid
**Owner(s):**
Thomson Publications
P.O. Box 9335
Fresno, CA 93791
Telephone: (209) 435-2163
FAX: (209) 435-8319
Ownership %: 100
**Editorial:**
W.T. Thomson ......................................Editor
**Desc.:** Presents new developments with
   agricultural chemicals. Features new
   registrations, use patterns, experimental
   permits on insecticides, herbicides,
   fungicides and miscellaneous pesticides
   used in the US.

**AGRICULTURAL CREDIT LETTER**                  69836
1530 N. Key Blvd., PH2
Arlington, VA 22209
Telephone: (703) 525-4512
FAX: (703) 525-4917
Year Established: 1981
Pub. Frequency: s-m.
Page Size: standard
Subscrip. Rate: $295/yr.
Materials: 223
**Owner(s):**
Webster Communications Corp.
1530 N. Key Blvd., PH2
Arlington, VA 22209
Telephone: (703) 525-4512
FAX: (703) 525-0000
Ownership %: 100
**Editorial:**
Fred J.C. Webster ..............................Editor

**AGRICULTURAL LAW DIGEST**                     69857
P.O. Box 5444
Madison, WI 53705
Telephone: (608) 277-8868
FAX: (608) 277-9660
Year Established: 1989
Pub. Frequency: s-m.

Page Size: standard
Subscrip. Rate: $100/yr.
**Owner(s):**
Agricultural Law Digest
P.O. Box 5444
Madison, WI 53705
Telephone: (608) 277-8868
FAX: (608) 277-9660
Ownership %: 100
**Editorial:**
Robert P. Achenbach ..........................Editor

**ALTERNATIVE AGRICULTURAL**                    69813
   **NEWS**
9200 Edmonston Rd.
Greenbelt, MD 20770-1551
Telephone: (301) 441-8777
FAX: (301) 220-0164
Year Established: 1983
Pub. Frequency: m.
Page Size: standard
Subscrip. Rate: $16/yr.
Circulation: 1,000
Circulation Type: controlled & paid
**Owner(s):**
Institute for Alternative Agriculture, Inc.
9200 Edmonston Rd.
Greenbelt, MD 20770-1551
Telephone: (301) 441-8777
FAX: (301) 220-0164
Ownership %: 100

**AMERICAN BEEKEEPING**                         69817
   **FEDERATION NEWSLETTER**
P.O. Box 1038
Jessup, GA 31545
Telephone: (912) 427-8447
FAX: (912) 427-8447
Year Established: 1944
Pub. Frequency: bi-m.
Page Size: standard
Subscrip. Rate: $25/yr. US; foreign $32/yr.
Materials: 10,32
Circulation: 2,000
Circulation Type: controlled & paid
**Owner(s):**
American Beekeeping Federation, Inc.
P.O. Box 1038
Jessup, GA 31545
Telephone: (912) 427-8447
FAX: (912) 427-8447
Ownership %: 100
**Editorial:**
Troy H. Fore ......................................Editor
**Desc.:** Keeps members current on
   activities of the organization and of
   happenings in the honey and
   beekeeping industry.

**AMERICAN POLYPAY SHEEP**                      69837
   **NEWS**
609 S. Central Ave., Ste. 9
Sidney, MT 59210
Telephone: (406) 482-7768
Pub. Frequency: m.
Page Size: standard
Subscrip. Rate: membership
Materials: 32
**Owner(s):**
American Polypay Sheep Association
609 S. Central Ave., Ste. 9
Sidney, MT 59210
Telephone: (406) 482-7768
Ownership %: 100
**Editorial:**
Sandy Petersen ..................................Editor
**Desc.:** Covers all areas of interest
   concerning polypay sheep--sales,
   production, health; inquiries and their
   breeders.

**AQUATIC FARMING NEWSLETTER**                  70252
P.O. Box 1004
Niland, CA 92257
Telephone: (619) 359-3474
Pub. Frequency: s-a.
Page Size: standard
Subscrip. Rate: free
Circulation: 4,500
Circulation Type: free
**Owner(s):**
California Aquaculture Association
P.O. Box 1004
Niland, CA 92257
Telephone: (619) 359-3474
Ownership %: 100
**Editorial:**
George Ray ........................................Editor
Fern Ray ............................................Editor
**Desc.:** Covers culture techniques, industry
   trends, and current concerns.

**ARID LANDS NEWSLETTER**                       69855
845 N. Park Ave.
Tucson, AZ 85719
Telephone: (602) 621-1955
FAX: (602) 621-3816
Year Established: 1975
Pub. Frequency: s-a.
Page Size: standard
Subscrip. Rate: free
Materials: 010
Circulation: 1,800
Circulation Type: controlled
**Owner(s):**
University of Arizona
845 N. Park Ave.
Tucson, AZ 85719
Telephone: (602) 621-1955
FAX: (602) 621-3816
Ownership %: 100
**Editorial:**
J.M. Bancroft ....................................Editor
**Desc.:** Contains articles by scientists,
   landowners, and conservationists about
   problems, potential, and sustainable
   uses of arid and semiarid lands
   worldwide.

**CALAVO NEWSLETTER**                           69873
P.O. Box 26081
Santa Ana, CA 92799-6081
Telephone: (714) 259-1166
FAX: (714) 259-1973
Year Established: 1959
Pub. Frequency: q.
Subscrip. Rate: free
Circulation: 2,500
Circulation Type: free
**Owner(s):**
Calavo Growers of California
P.O. Box 2608
Santa Ana, CA 92799-6081
Telephone: (714) 259-1166
FAX: (714) 259-1973
Ownership %: 100
**Desc.:** News and announcements
   pertaining to marketing and development
   in the avocado industry in California.

**FARM BUREAU NEWS**                            69827
600 Maryland Ave., S.W.
Washington, DC 20024
Telephone: (202) 484-3600
Year Established: 1921
Pub. Frequency: w.
Subscrip. Rate: $10/yr.
Circulation: 50,500
Circulation Type: paid

**Owner(s):**
American Farm Bureau Federation
600 Maryland Ave., S.W.
Washington, DC 20024
Telephone: (202) 484-3600
Ownership %: 100
**Editorial:**
Joan Waldoch ....................................Editor
**Desc.:** Newsletter updating legislative and
   regulatory developments affecting
   farmers and ranchers.

**FOOD & FIBER LETTER**                         69835
6708 Whittier Ave.
McClean, VA 22101
Telephone: (730) 734-8787
FAX: (703) 893-1065
Pub. Frequency: w.
Page Size: standard
Subscrip. Rate: $445/yr. US; $495/yr.
   foreign
Materials: 10,32
**Owner(s):**
Sparks Companies, Inc.
6708 Whittier Ave.
McClean, VA 22101
Telephone: (703) 734-8787
Ownership %: 100
**Editorial:**
James Webster ..................................Editor
**Desc.:** Covers agricultural policies.

**KENTUCKY FARM BUREAU NEWS**                   25387
9201 Bunsen Pkwy.
Louisville, KY 40220
Telephone: (502) 495-5112
FAX: (502) 495-5114
Mailing Address:
   P.O. Box 20700
   Louisville, KY 40250-0700
Year Established: 1937
Pub. Frequency: m.
Page Size: tabloid
Subscrip. Rate: $50/yr. non-members;
   $25/yr. members
Circulation: 345,737
Circulation Type: paid
**Owner(s):**
Kentucky Farm Bureau Federation
9201 Bunsen Pkwy.
Louisville, KY 40220
Telephone: (502) 495-5000
FAX: (502) 495-5114
Ownership %: 100
**Management:**
Lillie Shannon ..............Classified Adv. Manager
**Editorial:**
Gary Huddleston ................................Editor
**Desc.:** Newletter on issues affecting the
   farming and agricultural population of
   the state with editorial column on
   commodities and market analysis.
**Readers:** Members of the Kentucky Farm
   Bureau.

**NORTHEAST AGRICULTURE**                       69841
600 Maryland Ave., S.W.
Washington, DC 20024
Telephone: (202) 484-3600
Year Established: 1970
Pub. Frequency: m. except July/Aug.
Page Size: standard
Subscrip. Rate: $6.50/yr.
Materials: 32,10
Circulation: 80,000
Circulation Type: controlled & paid
**Owner(s):**
American Farm Bureau Federation
600 Maryland Ave., S.W.
Washington, DC 20024
Telephone: (202) 484-3600
Ownership %: 100
**Editorial:**
E. Rankin Lusby ................................Editor

---

**Materials Accepted/Included:** 01-Business news 02-By-line articles 03-Fashion news 04-Food news 05-Freelance copy 06-Letters to editor 07-Real estate news 08-Sports news 09-Travel news 10-Book rev. 11-Movie rev. 12-Music rev. 13-TV rev. 14-Theater rev. 15-Coming events 16-Obituaries 17-Question & answer 18-Social announcements 19-Artwork 20-Cartoons 21-Photos 22-TV listings 23-Audio rec. 24-Video rec. 25-Books 26-Films/film clips 27-Personnel news 28-Press releases 29-New product news/photos 30-Trade lit. 31-Contracts awarded 32-Display adv. 33-Classified adv.

**OLSEN'S AGRIBUSINESS REPORT** 69845
123 Picketts Ridge Rd.
W. Redding, CT 06896
Telephone: (203) 938-4188
FAX: (203) 938-4186
Year Established: 1979
Pub. Frequency: m.
Subscrip. Rate: $120/yr. US; $140/yr.
foreign
Materials: 32
**Owner(s):**
G.V. Olsen Associates
123 Picketts Ridge Rd.
W. Redding, CT 06896
Telephone: (203) 938-4188
FAX: (203) 938-4186
Ownership %: 100
**Editorial:**
Gus Olsen ..................................................Editor
**Desc.:** Information for executives in food
and agriculture, including biotechnology,
finance, marketing and production.

**OREGON FARM BUREAU NEWS** 25490
1701 Liberty St., S.E.
Salem, OR 97302-5158
Telephone: (503) 399-1701
Year Established: 1944
Pub. Frequency: s-m.
Page Size: standard
Subscrip. Rate: membership
Materials: 28,34
Print Process: offset
Circulation: 11,000
Circulation Type: controlled
**Owner(s):**
Oregon Farm Bureau Federation
1701 Liberty St., S.E.
Salem, OR 97302-5158
Telephone: (503) 399-1701
Ownership %: 100
**Management:**
Virginia M. Henley ................Business Manager
**Editorial:**
Rick Stevenson ..........................................Editor
**Desc.:** The official publication of the
Oregon Farm Bureau Federation.
**Readers:** Farm and ranch families in
Oregon.

**SMALL FARM NEWS** 69833
University of California
Davis, CA 95616
Telephone: (916) 757-8910
Year Established: 1981
Pub. Frequency: bi-m.
Page Size: standard
Subscrip. Rate: $10/yr.
Materials: 10
**Owner(s):**
Small Farm Center
University of California
Davis, CA 95616
Telephone: (916) 757-8910
Ownership %: 100
**Editorial:**
Claudia Myers ............................................Editor
**Readers:** Extension workers, researchers,
and operators of small farms and related
businesses.

**TRACTOR DIGEST** 69851
2001 The Alameda
San Jose, CA 95161
Telephone: (408) 296-1060
FAX: (408) 296-1300
Mailing Address:
P.O. Box 49006
San Jose, CA 95161
Year Established: 1982
Pub. Frequency: q.
Subscrip. Rate: $9.50/yr.

Circulation: 3,000
Circulation Type: paid
**Owner(s):**
Paramount Publishing
2001 The Alameda
San Jose, CA 95161
Telephone: (408) 296-1060
FAX: (408) 296-1300
Ownership %: 100
**Editorial:**
Daniel L. Doornbos ..............................Editor
**Desc.:** Covers agricultural equipment:
lubrication, maintenance and new
products.

### Group 304-Animals

**AAZPA COMMUNIQUE** 70041
Oglebay Park
Wheeling, WV 26003
Telephone: (304) 242-2160
FAX: (304) 242-2283
Year Established: 1959
Pub. Frequency: m.
Subscrip. Rate: membership
Materials: 10,11,33
Circulation: 6,300
Circulation Type: controlled & paid
**Owner(s):**
American Assn. of Zoological Parks and
Aquariums
Oglebay Park
Wheeling, WV 26003
Telephone: (304) 242-2160
FAX: (304) 242-2283
Ownership %: 100
**Editorial:**
Linda Boyd ..............................................Editor

**ACTION ALERT** 71094
175 W. 12th St., Ste. 16G
New York, NY 10011-8275
Telephone: (212) 989-8073
FAX: (212) 989-8073
Year Established: 1973
Pub. Frequency: 3/yr.
Subscrip. Rate: $15/yr.
Materials: 10
Circulation: 7,000
Circulation Type: controlled & paid
**Owner(s):**
Beauty Without Cruelty U.S.A.
175 12th St.
Ste. 16G
New York, NY 10011-8275
Telephone: (212) 989-8073
FAX: (212) 989-8073
Ownership %: 100
**Editorial:**
Ethel Thurston ..........................................Editor
**Desc.:** Consists of instructions to
individuals on how and where to write
letters protesting fur promotions: also
encourages the purchase of clothing
and cosmetics produced in ways that do
not involve suffering, confinement or
death of animals.

**ADVANCES IN SMALL ANIMAL** 70933
**MEDICINE & SURGERY**
Curtis Ctr.
Independence Sq., W.
Philadelphia, PA 19106-3399
Telephone: (215) 238-7800
FAX: (215) 238-6445
Year Established: 1988
Pub. Frequency: m.
Subscrip. Rate: $57/yr. individuals US;
$73/yr. individuals foreign; $75/yr.
institutions US; $90/yr. institutions
foreign

**Owner(s):**
W.B. Saunders Co.
Curtis Ctr.
Independence Sq., W.
Philadelphia, PA 19106-3399
Telephone: (215) 238-7800
FAX: (215) 238-6445
Ownership %: 100
**Editorial:**
Dr. Rhea V. Morgan ..............................Editor
**Desc.:** Provides insight into specific topics
and allows veterinarians and veterinary
technicians apply new tests and
treatments in their practices. Abstracts
material from recent publications and
presentations.

**ALTERNATIVE AQUACULTURE** 70239
**NETWORK NEWSLETTER**
P.O. Box 109
Breiningsville, PA 18031
Telephone: (215) 683-5854
FAX: (215) 683-9280
Year Established: 1981
Pub. Frequency: q.
Subscrip. Rate: $14/yr.
Materials: 10
Circulation: 500
Circulation Type: controlled & paid
**Owner(s):**
Alternative Aquaculture Association
P.O. Box 109
Breiningsville, PA 18031
Telephone: (215) 395-5854
FAX: (215) 683-9280
Ownership %: 100
**Editorial:**
Steven van Gorder ..................................Editor

**ANIMAL'S ADVOCATE** 71095
1363 Lincoln Ave., Ste. 7
San Rafael, CA 94901
Telephone: (415) 459-0885
FAX: (415) 459-3154
Year Established: 1982
Pub. Frequency: q.
Page Size: standard
Subscrip. Rate: $15/yr.
Circulation: 50,000
Circulation Type: controlled & paid
**Owner(s):**
Animal Legal Defense Fund (ALDF)
1363 Lincoln Ave., Ste. 7
San Rafael, CA 94901
Telephone: (415) 459-0885
FAX: (415) 459-3154
Ownership %: 100
**Editorial:**
Joyce Tischler ..........................................Editor
**Desc.:** Animal protection litigation reviews.

**BLACK SHEEP NEWSLETTER** 69327
25455 N.W. Dixie Mountain Rd.
Scappose, OR 97056
Telephone: (503) 621-3063
Year Established: 1974
Pub. Frequency: q.
Page Size: pocket
Subscrip. Rate: $12/yr. US; $16/yr. foreign
Materials: 05,06,10,17,19,28,32,33,34
Print Process: web
Circulation: 1,500
Circulation Type: paid
**Owner(s):**
Black Sheep Press
25455 N.W. Dixie Mountain Rd.
Scappose, OR 97056
Telephone: (503) 621-3063
Ownership %: 100
**Editorial:**
Peggy Lundquist ......................................Editor

**Readers:** Sheep and goat raisers, spinners
and textile artists interested in long wool
sheep, wool and other animal fibers.
Nationwide and international subscribers.
**Deadline:** story-2 wks.; news-2 wks.;
photo-2 wks.; ads-2 wks.

**BLUE GOOSE FLYER** 70180
10824 Fox Hunt Ln.
Potomac, MD 20854-0153
Telephone: (301) 983-1238
Year Established: 1975
Pub. Frequency: q.
Subscrip. Rate: $20/yr.
Materials: 10
Circulation: 1,000
Circulation Type: controlled & paid
**Owner(s):**
National Wildlife Refuge Association
10824 Fox Hunt Ln.
Potomac, MD 20854-1553
Telephone: (301) 983-1238
Ownership %: 100
**Editorial:**
Russel W. Clapper ..................................Editor
**Desc.:** Provides informational and
educational material on issues
concerning the National Wildlife Refuge
Association.

**CANINE LISTENER** 70177
10175 Wheeler Rd.
Central Point, OR 97502
Telephone: (503) 826-9220
FAX: (503) 826-6696
Year Established: 1977
Pub. Frequency: q.
Page Size: tabloid
Circulation: 28,000
Circulation Type: controlled & paid
**Owner(s):**
Dog for the Deaf, Inc.
10175 Wheeler Rd.
Central Point, OR 97502
Telephone: (503) 826-9220
FAX: (503) 826-6696
Ownership %: 100
**Editorial:**
Robin Wheeler ..........................................Editor

**CAT INDUSTRY NEWSLETTER** 69051
P.O. Box 31292
Charleston, SC 29417
Telephone: (803) 795-9555
FAX: (803) 795-2930
Year Established: 1992
Pub. Frequency: m.
Page Size: standard
Subscrip. Rate: $295/yr.
**Owner(s):**
Ross Becker
P.O. Box 31292
Charleston, SC 29417
Telephone: (803) 795-9555
Ownership %: 100
**Management:**
Ross Becker ..................................President
Ross Becker ..................................Publisher
**Desc.:** Covers new products, strategies,
industry data, new consumer
promotions, and cat food business.
**Readers:** Monthly newsletter for
executives in the pet products industry
and their advertisers and P.R. agencies.

**COMPASSIONATE SHOPPER** 71099
175 W. 12th St., Ste. 16G
New York, NY 10011-8275
Telephone: (212) 989-8073
FAX: (212) 989-8073
Year Established: 1973
Pub. Frequency: 3/yr.
Page Size: standard
Subscrip. Rate: $15/yr.

**Materials Accepted/Included:** 01-Business news 02-By-line articles 03-Fashion news 04-Food news 05-Freelance copy 06-Letters to editor 07-Real estate news 08-Sports news 09-Travel news 10-Book rev. 11-Movie rev. 12-Music rev. 13-TV rev. 14-Theater rev. 15-Coming events 16-Obituaries 17-Question & answer 18-Social announcements 19-Artwork 20-Cartoons 21-Photos 22-TV listings 23-Audio rec. 24-Video rec. 25-Books 26-Films/film clips 27-Personnel news 28-Press releases 29-New product news/photos 30-Trade lit. 31-Contracts awarded 32-Display adv. 33-Classified adv.

7-3

Circulation: 7,000
Circulation Type: controlled & paid
**Owner(s):**
Beauty Without Cruelty U.S.A.
175 W. 12th St.
Ste. 16G
New York, NY 10011-8275
Telephone: (212) 989-8073
Ownership %: 100
**Editorial:**
Ethel Thurston ...............................Editor

**DOG INDUSTRY NEWSLETTER**                 69052
P.O. Box 31292
Charleston, SC 29417
Telephone: (803) 795-9555
FAX: (803) 795-2930
Year Established: 1990
Pub. Frequency: m.
Page Size: standard
Subscrip. Rate: $295/yr.
**Owner(s):**
Ross Becker
P.O. Box 31292
Charleston, SC 29417
Telephone: (803) 795-9555
FAX: (803) 795-2930
Ownership %: 100
**Management:**
Ross Becker ...............................Publisher
**Desc.:** Provides marketing and competitive
  information to dog food manufacturers
  and other pet product makers, their
  advertising agencies and industry
  relations professionals. Covers new
  products due out in the next year,
  strategies, industry data, new consumer
  promotions, dog food business.
**Readers:** Monthly newsletter for
  executives in the pet products industry.

**FEDERAL VETERINARIAN**                      70941
1101 Vermont Ave., N.W., Ste. 710
Washington, DC 20005
Telephone: (202) 289-6334
Year Established: 1922
Pub. Frequency: m.
Page Size: standard
Subscrip. Rate: $30/yr. US; $50/yr. foreign
Materials: 10,32
Circulation: 2,000
Circulation Type: controlled & paid
**Owner(s):**
National Association of Federal
  Veterinarians
1101 Vermont Ave., N.W., Ste. 710
Washington, DC 20005
Telephone: (202) 289-6334
Ownership %: 100
**Editorial:**
Dr. Edward L. Menning ............................Editor
**Desc.:** Federal regulatory news, meat
  inspection, animal disease control,
  human disease from animals and federal
  personnel issues.

**FELINE HEALTH TOPICS**                      69186
Cornell University
College of Veterinary Medicine
Ithaca, NY 14853-6401
Telephone: (607) 253-3414
FAX: (607) 253-3419
Year Established: 1981
Pub. Frequency: q.
Page Size: standard
Subscrip. Rate: $25/yr.
Materials: 15,28
Print Process: offset lithography
Circulation: 25,803
Circulation Type: free & paid

**Owner(s):**
Cornell Feline Health Center
Cornell Univ.
Col. of Vet. Med.
Ithaca, NY 14853-6401
Telephone: (607) 253-3414
Ownership %: 100
**Editorial:**
June Tuttle ...............................Editor
**Readers:** Veterinary professionals.
**Deadline:** story-8 wks. prior to pub. date

**INTERNATIONAL BEAR NEWS**                   70048
333 Raspberry Rd.
Achorage, AK 99518-1599
Telephone: (907) 344-0541
FAX: (907) 344-7914
Year Established: 1968
Pub. Frequency: q.
Subscrip. Rate: $10/yr.
Circulation: 450
Circulation Type: paid
**Owner(s):**
International Assn. for Bear Research &
  Management
c/o Alaska Dept. of Fish & Gam
333 Raspberry Rd.
Anchorage, AK 99518-1599
Telephone: (907) 344-0541
FAX: (907) 344-7914
Ownership %: 100
**Editorial:**
T. DeLorenzo ...............................Editor
**Desc.:** Studies bear biology and
  management.

**INTERNATIONAL PET INDUSTRY**                70411
**NEWS**
P.O. Box 31292
Charleston, SC 29417
Telephone: (803) 795-9555
FAX: (803) 795-2930
Year Established: 1993
Pub. Frequency: m.
Subscrip. Rate: $295/yr.
**Owner(s):**
Ross Becker
P.O. Box 31292
Charleston, SC 29417
Telephone: (803) 795-9555
FAX: (803) 795-2930
Ownership %: 100
**Management:**
Ross Becker ...............................President
Ross Becker ...............................Publisher
**Desc.:** Covers marketing, new products
  and promotions for pet food and pet
  products around the world. Also keeps
  watch on developing markets for pet
  products, and provides trade leads.
**Readers:** Executives in the pet products
  industry.

**MATCH SHOW BULLETIN**                       70752
P.O. Box 214
Massapequa, NY 11758
Telephone: (516) 541-3442
FAX: (516) 541-3442
Year Established: 1969
Pub. Frequency: m.
Subscrip. Rate: $20/yr.
Circulation: 6,700
Circulation Type: controlled & paid
**Owner(s):**
Myrna Lieber
P.O. Box 214
Massapequa, NY 11758
Telephone: (516) 541-3442
FAX: (516) 541-3442
Ownership %: 100
**Editorial:**
Myrna Lieber ...............................Editor

**Desc.:** Lists locations and details of dog
  match shows, seminars, and training
  classes.

**NEW METHODS**                               69187
P.O. Box 22605
San Francisco, CA 94122-0605
Telephone: (415) 664-3469
Year Established: 1977
Pub. Frequency: irreg.
Page Size: standard
Subscrip. Rate: $29/copy
Materials: 10,32
Circulation: 6,000
Circulation Type: controlled
**Owner(s):**
New Methods Co.
P.O. Box 22605
San Francisco, CA 94122-0605
Telephone: (415) 664-3469
Ownership %: 100
**Editorial:**
Ronald S. Lippert ...............................Editor
**Desc.:** Information source that represents
  basic interest in the animal health
  profession.
**Deadline:** story-15th; news-15th; photo-
  15th; ads-15th

**NONGAME NEWS**                              70058
CN 400
Trenton, NJ 08625-0400
Telephone: (609) 292-9400
FAX: (908) 735-5689
Year Established: 1978
Pub. Frequency: q.
Subscrip. Rate: free
Circulation: 7,000
Circulation Type: free
**Owner(s):**
Department of Environmental Protection &
  Energy
Division of Fish, Game & Wildl
CN 400
Trenton, NJ 08625-0400
Telephone: (609) 292-9400
FAX: (908) 735-5689
Ownership %: 100
**Editorial:**
Michael Valent ...............................Editor
**Desc.:** Contains articles pertaining to the
  research, protection and management of
  native endangered, threatened and
  nongame wildlife in N.J. with
  occasional coverage of relevant national
  and international topics.

**PET PARTNERS**                              70754
321 Burnett Ave., S., 3rd Fl.
Renton, WA 98055
Telephone: (206) 226-7357
FAX: (206) 235-1076
Year Established: 1991
Pub. Frequency: 6/yr.
Subscrip. Rate: $6/yr. US; $9/yr. foreign
Circulation: 3,000
Circulation Type: controlled & paid
**Owner(s):**
Delta Society
321 Burnett Ave., S.
3rd Fl.
Renton, WA 98055
Telephone: (206) 226-7357
FAX: (206) 235-1076
Ownership %: 100
**Editorial:**
Maureen Fredrickson ...............................Editor
**Desc.:** Provides how-to information for
  health care professionals and volunteers
  involved in programs of animal assisted
  activities and therapy.

**RAT REPORT**                                70759
1010 1/2 Broadway
Chico, CA 95928
Year Established: 1992
Pub. Frequency: m.
Page Size: standard
Subscrip. Rate: $18/yr. US; $19.50/yr.
  Canada; $26/yr. foreign
**Owner(s):**
Pet-ables
1010 1/2 Broadway
Chico, CA 95928
Ownership %: 100
**Editorial:**
Debbie Ducommun ...............................Editor
**Desc.:** Covers all aspects of pet rates,
  including tips on getting started, care
  and feeding, health concerns, letters
  from pet owners, and features tricks or
  projects.

**UTAH CATTLEMAN, THE**                       25345
150 S. Sixth E., Ste. 10B
Salt Lake City, UT 84102
Telephone: (801) 355-5748
FAX: (801) 532-1669
Year Established: 1957
Pub. Frequency: m.
Page Size: standard
Subscrip. Rate: free members; $25/yr.
  non-members
Materials: 32,33
Freelance Pay: negotiable
Print Process: offset
Circulation: 4,000
Circulation Type: controlled
**Owner(s):**
Utah Cattlemen's Association
150 S. Sixth E., Ste. 10B
Salt Lake Cty, UT 84102
Telephone: (801) 355-5748
Ownership %: 100
**Editorial:**
Brent Tanner ...............................Editor
**Desc.:** Contains news of the beef cattle
  industry both state and national.
  Designed to inform both producers and
  feeders.
**Readers:** Rural residents.

**VET INDUSTRY NEWSLETTER**                   70412
P.O. Box 31292
Charleston, SC 29417
Telephone: (803) 795-9555
FAX: (803) 795-2930
Year Established: 1993
Pub. Frequency: m.
Subscrip. Rate: $295/yr.
**Owner(s):**
Ross Becker
P.O. Box 31292
Charleston, SC 29417
Telephone: (803) 795-9555
FAX: (803) 795-2930
Ownership %: 100
**Management:**
ross Becker ...............................Publisher
**Desc.:** Provides sensitive information about
  new products, strategies and promotions
  to the veterinary market. Also covers
  Animal Health Biotech news.
**Readers:** A monthly newsletter for
  executives at veterinary
  pharmaceuticals, pet product and pet
  food companies.

**VIRGINIA POULTRY FEDERATION**               5288
21 Terry Dr.
Harrisonburg, VA 22801
Telephone: (703) 433-2451
FAX: (703) 433-3256

---

Materials Accepted/Included: 01-Business news 02-By-line articles 03-Fashion news 04-Food news 05-Freelance copy 06-Letters to editor 07-Real estate news 08-Sports news 09-Travel news 10-Book rev. 11-Movie rev. 12-Music rev. 13-TV rev. 14-Theater rev. 15-Coming events 16-Obituaries 17-Question & answer 18-Social announcements 19-Artwork 20-Cartoons 21-Photos 22-TV listings 23-Audio rec. 24-Video rec. 25-Books 26-Films/film clips 27-Personnel news 28-Press releases 29-New product news/photos 30-Trade lit. 31-Contracts awarded 32-Display adv. 33-Classified adv.

Mailing Address:
P.O. Box 552
Harrisonburg, VA 22801
Pub. Frequency: q.
Page Size: standard
Subscrip. Rate: free
Print Process: offset
Circulation: 1,200
Circulation Type: controlled
**Owner(s):**
Virginia Poultry Federation
21 Terry Dr.
Harrisonburg, VA 22801
Telephone: (703) 433-2451
Ownership %: 100
**Editorial:**
Dick Moyers ........................................Editor
**Deadline:** news-1 mo.

## Group 306-Apparel

69482
**AMERICAN DIAMOND INDUSTRY ASSOCIATION NEWSLETTER**
71 W. 47th St.
New York, NY 10023
Telephone: (212) 575-0525
FAX: (212) 869-3721
Year Established: 1982
Pub. Frequency: unscheduled
Subscrip. Rate: free
Circulation: 16,000
Circulation Type: free
**Owner(s):**
American Diamond Industry Association Inc.
71 W. 47th St.
New York, NY 10023
Telephone: (212) 575-0525
Ownership %: 100
**Editorial:**
Lloyd Jaffe ........................................Editor
**Desc.:** Provides intelligence on the world's most important diamonds, future price indicators and key individuals in the industry.

2669
**BUREAU OF WHOLESALE SALES REPRESENTATIVES NEWS**
1801 Peachtree Rd., N.E., Ste. 200
Atlanta, GA 30309-1854
Telephone: (404) 351-7355
FAX: (404) 352-5298
Year Established: 1946
Pub. Frequency: m.
Subscrip. Rate: $10/yr.
Materials: 10,32
Circulation: 16,250
Circulation Type: paid
**Owner(s):**
Bureau of Wholesale Sales Representatives
1819 Peachtree Rd.
Atlanta, GA 30309-1854
Telephone: (404) 351-7355
FAX: (404) 352-5298
Ownership %: 100
**Editorial:**
Mike Blackman ........................................Editor

70125
**CAUS NEWS**
409 W. 44th St., 2nd Fl.
New York, NY 10036
Telephone: (212) 582-6884
Year Established: 1980
Pub. Frequency: m.
Subscrip. Rate: membership only
Materials: 10
Circulation: 6,000
Circulation Type: controlled & paid

**Owner(s):**
Color Association of the United States
409 W. 44th St., 2nd Fl.
New York, NY 10036
Telephone: (212) 582-6884
Ownership %: 100
**Editorial:**
Margaret Walch ........................................Editor
**Desc.:** News and articles on developments in the fashion and decorating industries, with announcements pertaining to the association's activities.

69489
**DIAMOND INSIGHT**
790 Madison Ave., Ste. 602
New York, NY 10021
Telephone: (212) 570-4180
FAX: (212) 772-1286
Year Established: 1988
Pub. Frequency: m.
Subscrip. Rate: $295/yr.
Materials: 10
Circulation: 200
Circulation Type: paid
**Owner(s):**
Tryon Mercantile, Inc.
790 Madison Ave.
New York, NY 10021
Telephone: (212) 570-4180
FAX: (212) 772-1286
Ownership %: 100
**Editorial:**
Guido Giovannini-Torelli ....................Editor
Leslie Tcheyan ....................Assistant Editor
Michael Kapok ........................................Research
**Desc.:** Provides intelligence on the world's most important diamonds, future price indicators and key individuals in the industry.
**Readers:** Diamond and Jewelry Manufacturers, Wholesalers, Dealers and Retailers, Auction Houses, Mining Concerns, and Financial Institutions.

68823
**FASHION INTERNATIONAL**
153 E. 87th St.
New York, NY 10128
Telephone: (212) 289-0420
Year Established: 1972
Pub. Frequency: m.
Subscrip. Rate: $100/yr.
**Owner(s):**
Fashion Calendar International
153 E. 87th St.
New York, NY 10128
Telephone: (212) 289-0420
Ownership %: 100
**Editorial:**
Deborah Brumfield ........................................Editor

22660
**I.F.I. FABRICARE NEWS**
12251 Tech Rd.
Silver Spring, MD 20904
Telephone: (301) 622-1900
FAX: (301) 236-9320
Year Established: 1972
Pub. Frequency: m.
Subscrip. Rate: $30/yr.
Circulation: 11,500
Circulation Type: paid
**Owner(s):**
International Fabricare Institute
12251 Tech Rd.
Silver Spring, MD 20904
Telephone: (301) 622-1900
FAX: (301) 236-9320
Ownership %: 100
**Editorial:**
Lynn Schweizer ........................................Editor
**Desc.:** Association newsletter for drycleaner/launderer membership. Most is staff written.
**Readers:** Drycleaning and laundry business owners and managers.

69501
**JEWELRY APPRAISER, THE**
P.O. Box 6558
Annapolis, MD 21401
Telephone: (301) 261-8270
FAX: (301) 261-8270
Year Established: 1980
Pub. Frequency: q.
Page Size: standard
Subscrip. Rate: $39/yr. US; $59/yr. foreign
Circulation: 1,200
Circulation Type: controlled & paid
**Owner(s):**
National Association of Jewelry Appraisers
P.O. Box 6558
Annapolis, MD 21401
Telephone: (301) 261-8270
**Editorial:**
James V. Jolliff ........................................Editor
**Desc.:** Discusses the value and evaluation techniques of jewels and gems.

70532
**JEWELRY NEWSLETTER INTERNATIONAL**
2600 S. Gessner Rd.
Houston, TX 77063
Telephone: (713) 783-0100
Year Established: 1973
Pub. Frequency: m.
Subscrip. Rate: $250/yr.
**Owner(s):**
Newsletters International, Inc.
2600 S. Gessner Rd.
Houston, TX 77063
Telephone: (713) 783-0100
Ownership %: 100
**Editorial:**
Len Fox ........................................Editor

70127
**RTW REVIEW**
8314 S. Tuckaway Shores
Franklin, WI 53132
Telephone: (414) 425-5503
FAX: (414) 425-2501
Year Established: 1986
Pub. Frequency: m.
Subscrip. Rate: $149/yr.
Materials: 10,32
Circulation: 5,000
Circulation Type: controlled & paid
**Owner(s):**
Danielle Consultants
8314 S. Tuckaway Shores
Franklin, WI 53132
Telephone: (414) 425-5503
FAX: (414) 425-2501
Ownership %: 100
**Editorial:**
Lauren Daniel-Falk ........................................Editor

## Group 308-Art

69896
**ALASKA STATE COUNCIL ON THE ARTS BULLETIN**
411 W. Fourth Ave.
Anchorage, AK 99501-2343
Telephone: (907) 279-1558
FAX: (907) 279-4330
Year Established: 1973
Pub. Frequency: m.
Subscrip. Rate: free
Circulation: 6,000
Circulation Type: controlled & paid
**Owner(s):**
Alaska State Council on the Arts
411 W. Fourth Ave.
Anchorage, AK 99501-2343
Telephone: (907) 279-1558
FAX: (907) 279-4330
Ownership %: 100

69898
**ART-WORLD**
55 Wheatley Rd.
Glen Head, NY 11545
Telephone: (516) 626-0914
Year Established: 1976
Pub. Frequency: a.
Subscrip. Rate: $20/yr.
Materials: 10,32
**Owner(s):**
Arts Review, Inc.
55 Wheatley Rd.
Glen Head, NY 11545
Telephone: (516) 626-0914
Ownership %: 100
**Editorial:**
Bruce Duff Hooton ........................................Editor

70990
**ART HAZARDS NEWS**
5 Beekman St.
New York, NY 10038
Telephone: (212) 227-6220
FAX: (212) 233-3846
Year Established: 1978
Pub. Frequency: 5/yr.
Subscrip. Rate: $21/yr.
Materials: 10
Circulation: 2,500
Circulation Type: paid
**Owner(s):**
Center for Safety in the Arts
5 Beekman St.
New York, NY 10038
Telephone: (212) 227-6220
FAX: (212) 233-3846
Ownership %: 100
**Editorial:**
Michael McCann ........................................Editor
**Desc.:** News on research and education pertaining to hazards in the arts (including visual and performing arts, museums, and educational facilities), covering such topics as precautions, legislation and regulations, lawsuits, and calendar of events.

69900
**ARTNEWSLETTER**
48 W. 38th St.
New York, NY 10018
Telephone: (212) 398-1690
Year Established: 1975
Pub. Frequency: bi-w.
Page Size: standard
Subscrip. Rate: $229/yr. US; $257/yr. foreign
**Owner(s):**
Artnews Associates
48 W. 38th St.
New York, NY 10018
Telephone: (212) 398-1690
Ownership %: 100
**Editorial:**
Bonnie Barrett Stretch ........................................Editor
**Desc.:** The international bi-weekly business report on the art market.

69905
**ART ON SCREEN**
980 Madison Ave.
New York, NY 10021
Telephone: (212) 988-4876
FAX: (212) 628-8963
Year Established: 1992
Pub. Frequency: 3/yr.
Subscrip. Rate: free
Circulation: 8,000
Circulation Type: controlled
**Owner(s):**
Program for Art on Film
980 Madison Ave.
New York, NY 10021
Telephone: (212) 988-4876
FAX: (212) 628-8963
Ownership %: 100

---

**Materials Accepted/Included:** 01-Business news 02-By-line articles 03-Fashion news 04-Food news 05-Freelance copy 06-Letters to editor 07-Real estate news 08-Sports news 09-Travel news 10-Book rev. 11-Movie rev. 12-Music rev. 13-TV rev. 14-Theater rev. 15-Coming events 16-Obituaries 17-Question & answer 18-Social announcements 19-Artwork 20-Cartoons 21-Photos 22-TV listings 23-Audio rec. 24-Video rec. 25-Books 26-Films/film clips 27-Personnel news 28-Press releases 29-New product news/photos 30-Trade lit. 31-Contracts awarded 32-Display adv. 33-Classified adv.

**Editorial:**
Susan Delson ..............................Editor
**Desc.:** Disseminates information on the presentation of the visual arts in film, video, television and interactive computer programs, including news of the program's activities and services, new releases on film and video, and events in the international art and media world.

**ARTSOURCE QUARTERLY**                    69902
13284 Rices Crossing
Renaissance, CA 95962-1355
Telephone: (916) 692-1355
FAX: (916) 692-1370
Mailing Address:
  P.O. Box 369
  Renaissance, CA 95962-1355
Pub. Frequency: q.
Subscrip. Rate: $19/yr.
**Owner(s):**
Artnetwork Press
P.O. Box 369
13284 Rices Crossing
Renaissance, CA 95962-1355
Telephone: (916) 692-1355
FAX: (916) 692-1370
Ownership %: 100
**Desc.:** Focuses on the latest marketing information, including interviews with artworld professionals, and strategies to make more sales.

**ARTSPACE**                               69909
727 E. Main St.
Columbus, OH 43205
Telephone: (614) 466-2613
Year Established: 1968
Pub. Frequency: q.
Page Size: standard
Subscrip. Rate: free
Materials: 10
Circulation: 8,000
Circulation Type: controlled & paid
**Owner(s):**
Ohio Arts Council
727 E. Main St.
Columbus, OH 43205
Telephone: (614) 466-2613
Ownership %: 100

**ARTWORLD EUROPE**                        69907
P.O. Box 1608
Largo, FL 34649
Telephone: (813) 581-7328
FAX: (813) 585-6398
Year Established: 1990
Pub. Frequency: bi-m.
Subscrip. Rate: $59/yr.
Materials: 10
Circulation: 1,000
Circulation Type: controlled & paid
**Owner(s):**
Humanities Exchange, Inc.
P.O. Box 1608
Largo, FL 34649
Telephone: (813) 581-7328
FAX: (813) 585-6398
Ownership %: 100
**Editorial:**
S.R. Howarth ..............................Editor
**Desc.:** Covers European art world including exhibitions, museum renovations, art fairs, galleries, restorations and interviews with art professionals. Covers European art world including exhibitions, museum renovations, art fairs, galleries, restorations and interviews with art professionals.

**CFA NEWS**                               69923
101 W. Flagler St.
Miami, FL 33130
Telephone: (305) 375-3000
FAX: (305) 375-1725
Year Established: 1982
Pub. Frequency: q.
Page Size: tabloid
Subscrip. Rate: membership
Circulation: 11,000
Circulation Type: controlled & paid
**Owner(s):**
Center for Fine Arts
101 W. Flagler St.
Miami, FL 33130
Telephone: (305) 375-3000
FAX: (305) 375-1725
Ownership %: 100
**Editorial:**
Brenda Williamson ..............................Editor
**Desc.:** Features fine art, design, photography, and sculpture at the center of current exhibitions.

**DETROIT FOCUS QUARTERLY**                69921
P.O. Box 32823
Detroit, MI 48232-0823
Telephone: (313) 882-1624
Year Established: 1982
Pub. Frequency: q.
Subscrip. Rate: $15/yr.
Materials: 32
Circulation: 3,000
Circulation Type: paid
**Owner(s):**
Detroit Focus Gallery
P.O. Box 32823
Detroit, MI 48232-0823
Telephone: (313) 882-1624
Ownership %: 100
**Editorial:**
Vince Carducci ..............................Editor

**ENTRY**                                  70788
P.O. Box 7648
Ann Arbor, MI 48107
Telephone: (313) 663-4686
Year Established: 1984
Pub. Frequency: 10/yr.
Page Size: standard
Subscrip. Rate: $22/yr.
Materials: 33
Circulation: 4,000
Circulation Type: controlled & paid
**Owner(s):**
Entry
P.O. Box 7648
Ann Arabor, MI 48107
Telephone: (313) 663-4686
Ownership %: 100
**Editorial:**
Jennifer Hill ..............................Editor

**ENVIRONMENT & ART LETTER**               69897
1800 N. Hermitage Ave.
Chicago, IL 60662-1101
Telephone: (312) 486-8970
FAX: (312) 486-7094
Year Established: 1988
Pub. Frequency: m.
Subscrip. Rate: $20/yr.
Materials: 10
Circulation: 2,450
Circulation Type: controlled & paid
**Owner(s):**
Liturgy Training Publications
1800 N. Hermitage Ave.
Chicago, IL 60662-1101
Telephone: (312) 486-8970
FAX: (312) 486-7094
Ownership %: 100
**Editorial:**
David Philippart ..............................Editor

**Desc.:** Provides a forum for the exchange of ideas on worship places.
**Readers:** For architects, artists, liturgy teams, pastors, and sacristans.

**FOR YOUR INFORMATION**                   69906
155 Ave. of the Americas
New York, NY 10013
Telephone: (212) 366-6900
FAX: (212) 366-1778
Year Established: 1985
Pub. Frequency: q.
Subscrip. Rate: contribution; $50/yr. libraries
Circulation: 25,000
Circulation Type: controlled & paid
**Owner(s):**
New York Foundation for the Arts
155 Ave. of the Americas
New York, NY 10013
Telephone: (212) 366-6900
FAX: (212) 366-1778
Ownership %: 100
**Editorial:**
Joseph Hannan ..............................Editor
**Desc.:** Practical information for those who create and work in the arts. Condensed information on issues, events and opportunities for artists and art workers. Includes funding deadlines and information on residencies.

**GETTY CONSERVATION INSTITUTE NEWSLETTER**    69911
4503 Glencoe Ave.
Marina del Rey, CA 90292-6537
Telephone: (213) 822-2299
FAX: (213) 821-9409
Year Established: 1986
Pub. Frequency: 3/yr.
Subscrip. Rate: free
Circulation: 13,500
Circulation Type: controlled & paid
**Owner(s):**
Getty Conservation Institute
4503 Glencoe Ave.
Marina Del Rey, CA 90292-6537
Telephone: (213) 822-2299
FAX: (213) 821-9409
Ownership %: 100
**Editorial:**
Jane Slate Siena ..............................Editor
**Desc.:** Covers the activities of the Institute's art and architecture conservation programs. Includes scientific research, conservation training, and information documentation.

**HEARD MUSEUM NEWSLETTER**                69919
22 E. Monte Vista Rd.
Phoenix, AZ 85004-1480
Telephone: (602) 252-8840
FAX: (602) 252-9757
Year Established: 1960
Pub. Frequency: q.
Subscrip. Rate: $30/yr. membership
Circulation: 4,000
Circulation Type: controlled & paid
**Owner(s):**
Heard Museum
22 E. Monte Vista Rd.
Phoenix, AZ 85004-1480
Telephone: (602) 252-8840
FAX: (602) 252-9757
Ownership %: 100
**Editorial:**
Mary Brennan ..............................Editor
**Desc.:** Covers art exhibits and educational programs. Covers art exhibits and educational programs.

**INSIDE BROOKS**                          69904
Overton Park
1934 Popular Ave.
Memphis, TN 38104
Telephone: (901) 722-3500
FAX: (901) 722-3522
Year Established: 1955
Pub. Frequency: m.
Subscrip. Rate: $12/yr.
**Owner(s):**
Memphis Brooks Museum of Art
Overton Park
1934 Popular Ave.
Memphis, TN 38104
Telephone: (901) 722-3500
FAX: (901) 722-3522
Ownership %: 100
**Editorial:**
Dorothy Lane McClure ..............................Editor
Mimi Snords ..............................Editor

**LETTER ARTS' BOOK CLUB NEWSLETTER**       69930
1833 Spring Garden St.
Greensboro, NC 27403
Telephone: (910) 272-7604
FAX: (910) 272-9015
Year Established: 1980
Pub. Frequency: q.
Subscrip. Rate: $7.50/yr.
Circulation: 5,000
Circulation Type: controlled & paid
**Owner(s):**
Letter Arts' Book Club
1833 Spring Garden St.
Greensboro, NC 27403
Telephone: (910) 272-7604
FAX: (910) 272-9015
Ownership %: 100
**Desc.:** How-to articles for calligraphers, marblers, book-binders and illuminators.

**LINKED RING LETTER**                     70780
163 Amsterdam Ave., No. 201
New York, NY 10023
Telephone: (212) 838-8640
FAX: (212) 873-7065
Year Established: 1990
Pub. Frequency: q.
Page Size: standard
Subscrip. Rate: $15/yr. US; $30/yr. foreign
Materials: 10,33
Circulation: 25,000
Circulation Type: controlled & paid
**Owner(s):**
Consultant Press, Ltd.
163 Amsterdam Ave., No. 201
New York, NY 10023
Telephone: (212) 838-8640
FAX: (212) 873-7065
Ownership %: 100
**Editorial:**
Robert S. Persky ..............................Editor
**Desc.:** For photographers who exhibit and sell fine art photography.

**MONTCLAIR ART MUSEUM BULLETIN-NEWSLETTER**    69908
13 S. Mountain
Montclair, NJ 07042-1747
Telephone: (201) 746-5555
FAX: (201) 746-9118
Year Established: 1929
Pub. Frequency: bi-m.
Circulation: 5,000
Circulation Type: controlled & paid
**Owner(s):**
Montclair Art Museum
13 S. Mountain
Montclair, NJ 07042-1747
Telephone: (201) 746-5555
FAX: (201) 746-9118
Ownership %: 100

**Materials Accepted/Included:** 01-Business news 02-By-line articles 03-Fashion news 04-Food news 05-Freelance copy 06-Letters to editor 07-Real estate news 08-Sports news 09-Travel news 10-Book rev. 11-Movie rev. 12-Music rev. 13-TV rev. 14-Theater rev. 15-Coming events 16-Obituaries 17-Question & answer 18-Social announcements 19-Artwork 20-Cartoons 21-Photos 22-TV listings 23-Audio rec. 24-Video rec. 25-Books 26-Films/film clips 27-Personnel news 28-Press releases 29-New product news/photos 30-Trade lit. 31-Contracts awarded 32-Display adv. 33-Classified adv.

**Editorial:**
Cathy Fazekas .....................................Editor

69914
**NAEA NEWS**
1916 Association Dr.
Reston, VA 22091
Telephone: (703) 860-8000
Year Established: 1958
Pub. Frequency: bi-m.
Subscrip. Rate: $50/yr. membership
Materials: 10,32
Circulation: 16,000
Circulation Type: controlled & paid
**Owner(s):**
Nation Art Education Association
1916 Association Dr.
Reston, VA 22091
Telephone: (703) 860-8000
Ownership %: 100
**Editorial:**
Thomas A. Hatfield .............................Editor
**Desc.:** List of current association events
and news affecting visual art education.

69932
**NEW HAMPSHIRE ARTS**
40 N. Main St.
Concord, NH 03301
Telephone: (603) 271-2789
FAX: (603) 271-3584
Year Established: 1987
Pub. Frequency: q.
Page Size: tabloid
Subscrip. Rate: free
Materials: 10
Circulation: 5,000
Circulation Type: free
**Owner(s):**
New Hampshire State Council on the Arts
40 N. Main St.
Concord, NH 03301
Telephone: (603) 271-2789
FAX: (603) 271-3584
Ownership %: 100
**Editorial:**
Rebecca Lawrence ...............................Editor
**Desc.:** Provides information of interest to
artists and art organizations in New
Hampshire.

69910
**NEW MUSEUM NEWSLETTER**
583 Broadway
New York, NY 10012
Telephone: (212) 219-1222
FAX: (212) 431-5328
Year Established: 1977
Pub. Frequency: q.
Subscrip. Rate: $35/yr.
Circulation: 15,000
Circulation Type: controlled & paid
**Owner(s):**
New Museum of Contemporary Art
583 Broadway
New York, NY 10012
Telephone: (212) 219-1222
FAX: (212) 431-5328
Ownership %: 100
**Editorial:**
Charlayne Haynes ...............................Editor

70833
**PHOTOFINISHING NEW LETTER**
10915 Bonita Beach Rd.
Bonita Springs, FL 33923
Telephone: (813) 992-4421
FAX: (813) 992-6328
Year Established: 1983
Pub. Frequency: bi-w.
Page Size: standard
Subscrip. Rate: $100/yr. US; $125/yr.
foreign
Materials: 10
Circulation: 500
Circulation Type: controlled & paid

**Owner(s):**
Photofinishing News, Inc.
10915 Beach Rd.
Bonita Beach, FL 33923
Telephone: (813) 992-4421
FAX: (813) 992-6328
Ownership %: 100
**Editorial:**
Don Franz .........................................Editor

70794
**PHOTOGRAPH COLLECTOR**
163 Amsterdam Ave., Ste. 201
New York, NY 10023
Telephone: (212) 838-8640
FAX: (212) 873-7065
Year Established: 1980
Pub. Frequency: m.
Subscrip. Rate: $125/yr.
Materials: 10,33
Circulation: 1,000
Circulation Type: controlled & paid
**Owner(s):**
Consultant Press, Ltd.
163 Amsterdam Ave., Ste. 201
New York, NY 10023
Telephone: (212) 838-8640
FAX: (212) 873-8640
Ownership %: 100
**Editorial:**
Robert S. Persky ...............................Editor
**Desc.:** For curators, dealers and collectors.
Covers all aspects of collecting and
selling collectible photographs. Provides
information and news on dealer and
collector activity, seminars, trade fairs,
auctions, court cases.

70834
**PHOTOGRAPHY**
6 N. Water St.
Greenwich, CT 06830
Telephone: (203) 531-7755
FAX: (203) 622-6688
Year Established: 1990
Pub. Frequency: q.
Subscrip. Rate: $250/yr.
Materials: 10,33
Circulation: 4,800
Circulation Type: controlled
**Owner(s):**
Devin-Adair Publishers, Inc.
6 N. Water St.
Greenwich, CT 06830
Telephone: (203) 531-7755
FAX: (203) 622-6688
Ownership %: 100
**Editorial:**
W. Dows ...........................................Editor
**Desc.:** Covers new books on photography,
reviews of exhibitions, photographers,
photo reproduction, illustrations, auction
results, gallery openings, and
international exhibits.

70781
**PHOTO REVIEW NEWSLETTER**
301 Hill Ave.
Langhorne, PA 19047
Year Established: 1976
Pub. Frequency: 8/yr.
Subscrip. Rate: $25/yr.
Materials: 10
Circulation: 1,200
Circulation Type: controlled & paid
**Owner(s):**
Photo Review
1303 Hill Ave.
Langhorne, PA 19047
Ownership %: 100
**Editorial:**
Stephen Perloff ...............................Editor
**Desc.:** Photography exhibition listings for
New York, Philadelphia, Baltimore,
Washington, Pittsburgh; news and
exhibition opportunities.

69912
**PORTLAND ART MUSEUM
NEWSLETTER**
1219 S.W. Park Ave
Portland, OR 97205
Telephone: (503) 226-2811
FAX: (503) 226-2842
Year Established: 1949
Pub. Frequency: m.
Subscrip. Rate: membership
Circulation: 20,000
Circulation Type: controlled
**Owner(s):**
Portland Art Musuem
1219 S.W. Park Ave.
Portland, OR 97205
Telephone: (503) 226-2811
FAX: (503) 226-2842
Ownership %: 100
**Editorial:**
Diane Kantor ...................................Editor

69936
**PRINT COLLECTOR'S
NEWSLETTER**
119 E. 79th St.
New York, NY 10021
Telephone: (212) 988-5959
FAX: (212) 988-6107
Year Established: 1970
Pub. Frequency: bi-m.
Subscrip. Rate: $60/yr.
Materials: 10,32
Circulation: 5,000
Circulation Type: paid
**Owner(s):**
Print Collector's Newsletter Inc.
119 E. 79th St.
New York, NY 10021
Telephone: (212) 988-5959
FAX: (212) 988-6107
Ownership %: 100
**Editorial:**
Jacqueline Brody ...............................Editor

69941
**SEATTLE ARTS**
312 First Ave., N.
Seattle, WA 98109
Telephone: (206) 684-7172
Year Established: 1972
Pub. Frequency: m.
Page Size: tabloid
Subscrip. Rate: free
Circulation: 12,000
Circulation Type: free
**Owner(s):**
City of Seattle Arts Commission
312 First Ave., N.
Seattle, WA 98109
Telephone: (206) 684-7171
FAX: (206) 684-7172
Ownership %: 100
**Editorial:**
Doug Lauen .......................................Editor

69918
**SOTHEBY'S NEWSLETTER**
1334 York Ave.
New York, NY 10021
Telephone: (212) 606-7000
Year Established: 1973
Pub. Frequency: 7/yr.
Subscrip. Rate: $25/yr. US & Canada;
$35/yr. elsewhere
Circulation: 55,000
Circulation Type: controlled & paid
**Owner(s):**
Sotheby's, Inc.
1334 York Ave.
New York, NY 10021
Telephone: (212) 606-7000
Ownership %: 100
**Editorial:**
Lynn Stowell Pearson ...........................Editor

69920
**STREET ARTISTS' NEWSLETTER**
P.O. Box 867
Cambridge, MA 02238
Telephone: (617) 522-3407
FAX: (617) 522-3407
Mailing Address:
P.O. Box 570
Cambridge, MA 02238
Year Established: 1979
Pub. Frequency: s-a.
Subscrip. Rate: $25/yr. membership
Materials: 10,32
Circulation: 1,000
Circulation Type: controlled & paid
**Owner(s):**
Folk Arts Network, Inc.
P.O. Box 867
Cambridge, MA 02238
Telephone: (617) 522-3407
FAX: (617) 522-3407
Ownership %: 100
**Editorial:**
Stephen Baird ...................................Editor
**Desc.:** Covers locations, legal issues,
profiles and reviews, festival and event
listings.

69944
**TENNESSEE ARTS REPORT**
320 Sixth Ave., N.
Nashville, TN 37219
Telephone: (615) 741-1701
FAX: (615) 741-8559
Year Established: 1974
Pub. Frequency: q.
Page Size: tabloid
Subscrip. Rate: free
Materials: 10,11,14
Circulation: 4,000
Circulation Type: free
**Owner(s):**
Tennessee Arts Commission
320 Sixth Ave., N.
Nashville, TN 37219
Telephone: (615) 741-1701
FAX: (615) 741-8559
Ownership %: 100
**Editorial:**
Kyle Stirling ...................................Editor

69924
**UNIVERSITY OF KENTUCKY ART
MUSEUM NEWSLETTER**
Rose & Euclid Sts.
Lexington, KY 40506-0241
Telephone: (606) 257-5716
FAX: (606) 258-1994
Year Established: 1986
Pub. Frequency: s-a.
Page Size: tabloid
Circulation: 3,000
Circulation Type: controlled & paid
**Owner(s):**
University of Kentucky Art Museum
Rose & Euclid Sts.
Lexington, KY 40506-0241
Telephone: (606) 257-5716
FAX: (606) 258-1994
Ownership %: 100
**Editorial:**
Harriet Fowler ...................................Editor
**Desc.:** Information on acquisitions,
exhibitions and programs of the
museum. Information on acquisitions,
exhibitions and programs of the
museum.

## Group 310-Business

70130
**ACCOUNTING & AUDITING
UPDATE SERVICE**
One Penn Plz.
New York, NY 10119
Telephone: (212) 971-5000
FAX: (212) 971-5240

---

**Materials Accepted/Included:** 01-Business news 02-By-line articles 03-Fashion news 04-Food news 05-Freelance copy 06-Letters to editor 07-Real estate news 08-Sports news 09-Travel news 10-Book rev. 11-Movie rev. 12-Music rev. 13-TV rev. 14-Theater rev. 15-Coming events 16-Obituaries 17-Question & answer 18-Social announcements 19-Artwork 20-Cartoons 21-Photos 22-TV listings 23-Audio rec. 24-Video rec. 25-Books 26-Films/film clips 27-Personnel news 28-Press releases 29-New product news/photos 30-Trade lit. 31-Contracts awarded 32-Display adv. 33-Classified adv.

7-7

Mailing Address:
The Park Sq. Bldg.
31 St. James St.
Boston, MA 02116-4112
Year Established: 1984
Pub. Frequency: bi-w.
Page Size: standard
Subscrip. Rate: 256.50/yr. US; $331/yr.
foreign
Owner(s):
Warren Gorham Lamont
One Penn Plz.
New York, NY 10119
Telephone: (212) 971-5000
FAX: (212) 971-5240
Ownership %: 100
Editorial:
Allan B. Afterman ...................................Editor
Desc.: Analyzes and interprets all FASB
and AICPA pronouncements as they are
issued.

70104
**ACCOUNTING FOR LAW FIRMS**
111 Eighth Ave.
New York, NY 10110
Telephone: (212) 741-8300
FAX: (212) 463-5522
Year Established: 1988
Pub. Frequency: m.
Subscrip. Rate: $175/yr.
Owner(s):
New York Law Publishing Co.
111 Eighth Ave.
New York, NY 10011
Telephone: (212) 741-8300
FAX: (212) 463-5522
Ownership %: 100
Editorial:
Mark Hopkins ........................................Editor
Desc.: Provides analysis of new and
pending statutes, regulations and cases,
as well as practical strategies for
increasing firms' profitability to law
firm partners, chief financial officers,
administrators, accountants and financial
planners.

70935
**AEF NEWSLETTER**
1215 Terminal Tower
Cleveland, OH 44113-2253
Telephone: (216) 781-1212
Year Established: 1977
Pub. Frequency: bi-m.
Subscrip. Rate: $24/yr.
Circulation: 12,000
Circulation Type: controlled & paid
Owner(s):
American Economic Foundation
1215 Terminal Tower
Cleveland, OH 44113-2253
Telephone: (216) 781-1212
Ownership %: 100
Editorial:
Homer W. Giles ....................................Editor

70066
**AFFLUENT MARKETS ALERT**
488 E. 18th St.
Brooklyn, NY 11226-6702
Telephone: (718) 469-9330
FAX: (718) 469-7124
Year Established: 1989
Pub. Frequency: m.
Subscrip. Rate: $235/yr.
Owner(s):
EPM Communications
488 E. 18th St.
Brooklyn, NY 11226-6702
Telephone: (718) 469-9330
FAX: (718) 469-7124
Ownership %: 100
Editorial:
Michael Schav .....................................Editor

Desc.: Covers the affluent consumer; taps
into the lifestyles and media styles of all
segments of the wealthy marketplace.

70851
**ALABAMA AFL-CIO**
297 W. Valley Ave.
Birmingham, AL 35209
Telephone: (205) 942-5260
FAX: (205) 945-8207
Year Established: 1957
Pub. Frequency: w.
Page Size: standard
Subscrip. Rate: membership
Circulation: 1,000
Circulation Type: controlled
Owner(s):
AFL-CIO
297 W. Valley Ave.
Birmingham, AL 35209
Telephone: (205) 942-5260
FAX: (205) 945-8207
Ownership %: 100
Editorial:
James E. Albright ........................Editor
Desc.: State and local labor news.

67660
**AMERICAN MARKETPLACE**
951 Pershing Dr.
Silver Spring, MD 20910-4464
Telephone: (301) 587-6300
FAX: (301) 587-1081
Year Established: 1980
Pub. Frequency: bi-w.
Page Size: standard
Subscrip. Rate: $338/yr.
Materials: 01,07,09,25,28
Owner(s):
Business Publishers, Inc.
951 Pershing Dr.
Silver Spring, MD 20910
Telephone: (301) 587-6300
Ownership %: 100
Management:
Lawrence Fishbein ................................Publisher
Editorial:
Dave Speights ...........................................Editor

70602
**AT WORK**
155 Montgomery St.
San Francisco, CA 94104-4109
Telephone: (415) 288-0260
Year Established: 1992
Pub. Frequency: bi-m.
Page Size: standard
Subscrip. Rate: $75/yr.
Owner(s):
Berrett-Koehler Publishers, Inc.
155 Montgomery St.
San Francisco, CA 94104-4109
Telephone: (415) 288-0260
Ownership %: 100
Editorial:
Alis Valencia .............................................Editor
Desc.: Focuses on innovative practices
that are being implemented in
organizations around the world.

70069
**BARNARD'S RETAIL MARKETING
REPORT**
25 Sutton Pl., S.
New York, NY 10022
Telephone: (212) 752-9810
Year Established: 1984
Pub. Frequency: m.
Subscrip. Rate: $125/yr.
Materials: 10
Owner(s):
Barnard Enterprises, Inc.
25 Sutton Pl., S.
New York, NY 10022
Telephone: (212) 752-9810
Ownership %: 100

Editorial:
Kurt Barnard .............................................Editor
Desc.: Covers and forecasts retailing
trends with an emphasis on marketing.

70982
**BARTER UPDATE**
P.O. Box 416
Denver, CO 80201-0416
Year Established: 1983
Pub. Frequency: a.
Subscrip. Rate: $4/yr.
Materials: 32
Circulation: 1,000
Circulation Type: controlled & paid
Owner(s):
Prosperity & Profits Unlimited
P.O. Box 416
Denver, CO 80201-0416
Ownership %: 100
Editorial:
A. Doyle ...................................................Editor

61269
**BBI'S NEWSLETTER OF
TECHNOLOGY ASSESSMENT
AND REIMBURSEMENT**
1524 Brookhollow Dr.
Santa Ana, CA 92705
Telephone: (714) 755-5757
FAX: (714) 755-5704
Year Established: 1992
Pub. Frequency: m.
Page Size: standard
Subscrip. Rate: $425/yr.
Materials: 01,28,29,30
Freelance Pay: negotiable
Owner(s):
Biomedical Business International, Inc.
Ownership %: 100
Management:
Peggy Pargoff ...................................Publisher
Editorial:
Mike Gibb .............................Executive Editor
Dona Watson ....................................Editor
Anna Lee .............................Associate Editor
Cheryl Scaglioni ..................Circulation Editor
Desc.: Cost outcome and payment data
critical to medical product markets.
Readers: Executives of medical devices
and diagnostics manufacturing firms

70960
**BLUE CHIP ECONOMIC
INDICATORS**
1101 King St., Ste. 444
Alexandria, VA 22314
Telephone: (703) 683-4100
FAX: (703) 739-6517
Year Established: 1975
Pub. Frequency: m.
Subscrip. Rate: $498/yr. US; $510/yr.
foreign
Owner(s):
Capitol Publications Inc.
1101 King St., Ste. 444
Alexandria, VA 22314
Telephone: (703) 383-4100
FAX: (703) 739-6517
Ownership %: 100
Editorial:
Robert J. Eggert ...................................Editor
Desc.: Current economic forecasts for top
management, corporate planners,
market research directors, economists,
bankers, brokers, and investors.

70132
**BOOKKEEPER'S TAX LETTER**
49 Van Syckel Ln.
Wyckoff, NJ 07481
Telephone: (201) 891-6430
FAX: (201) 891-1131
Year Established: 1991
Pub. Frequency: m.
Subscrip. Rate: $119.40/yr.

Owner(s):
ProPub, Inc.
49 Van Syckel Ln.
Wyckoff, NJ 07481
Telephone: (201) 891-6430
FAX: (201) 891-1131
Ownership %: 100

70109
**BOWMAN'S ACCOUNTING
REPORT**
905 E. Paces Ferry Rd., Ste. 2425
Atlanta, GA 30326
Telephone: (404) 264-9977
FAX: (404) 264-9968
Year Established: 1987
Pub. Frequency: m.
Subscrip. Rate: $195/yr. US; $250/yr.
foreign
Materials: 10
Owner(s):
Hudson Sawyer Professional Svcs. Mktg.,
Inc.
905 E. Paces Ferry Rd.
Atlanta, GA 30326
Telephone: (404) 264-9977
FAX: (404) 264-9968
Ownership %: 100
Editorial:
Arthur W. Bowman ...................................Editor
Desc.: News, analysis and commentary of
events, trends, strategies, and politics in
the accounting profession.

70952
**BRAZIL WATCH**
1924 47th St., N.W.
Washington, DC 20007
Telephone: (202) 625-2702
FAX: (202) 333-8740
Year Established: 1984
Pub. Frequency: fortn.
Subscrip. Rate: $645/yr.; $345/yr.
universities
Owner(s):
Orbis Publications, Ltd.
1924 47th St., N.W.
Washington, DC 20007
Telephone: (202) 625-2702
FAX: (202) 333-8740
Ownership %: 100
Editorial:
Richard W. Foster ...................................Editor
Desc.: Reports of political, economic and
business events in Brazil.

2536
**BRIEFING NEWSLETTER**
1331 Pennsylvania Ave., N.W., Ste. 1500N
Washington, DC 20004
Telephone: (202) 637-3000
FAX: (202) 637-3182
Pub. Frequency: w.
Page Size: standard
Subscrip. Rate: $250/yr. non-members
Circulation: 26,500
Circulation Type: paid
Owner(s):
National Association of Manufacturers
1331 Pennyslvania Ave., N.W.,
Washington, DC 20004
Telephone: (202) 637-3000
Ownership %: 100
Management:
Bevolin Ashley ..................Circulation Manager
Editorial:
Doug Kurkul ...................................Editor
Darlene Megahan ..................Vice President of
Publishing

70103
**BRONG'S BUSINESS SUCCESS
NEWS**
RR 1, Box 1130
Mamatash Rd.
Ellensburg, WA 98926-9733
Telephone: (509) 962-8238

Year Established: 1990
Pub. Frequency: bi-m.
Materials: 10,32
**Owner(s):**
GMB Partnership
RR 1, Box 1130
Mamatash Rd.
Ellensberg, WA 98926-9733
Telephone: (509) 962-8238
Ownership %: 100
**Editorial:**
Gerald Brong .................................................Editor

## BUSINESS EUROPE
70054

111 W. 57th St.
New York, NY 10019
Telephone: (800) 938-4685
FAX: (212) 586-1182
Year Established: 1960
Pub. Frequency: w.
Subscrip. Rate: $1150/yr.
**Owner(s):**
Economist Intelligence Unit
111 W. 57th St.
New York, NY 10019
Telephone: (212) 554-0600
FAX: (212) 586-1182
Ownership %: 100
**Desc.:** Management advisory report for
executives responsible for European
operations, with latest issues, trends,
policies, and corporate strategies in 16
countries, EEC developments and
forecasts for each country and industrial
sector. Covers finance, marketing,
taxation, personnel, organization, politics
and actual corporate experience.

## BUSINESS LATIN AMERICA
70958

111 W. 57th St.
New York, NY 10019
Telephone: (212) 554-0600
FAX: (212) 586-1182
Year Established: 1966
Pub. Frequency: w.
Page Size: standard
Subscrip. Rate: $945/yr.
**Owner(s):**
Economist Intelligence Unit
111 W. 57th St.
New York, NY 10019
Telephone: (212) 554-0600
FAX: (212) 554-0600
Ownership %: 100
**Editorial:**
Anna Szterenfeld .........................................Editor
**Desc.:** Interprets and evaluates changing
political, economic and business-related
trends, government policy changes,
regulatory developments, regional
integration moves and actions taken by
government and leading agencies to
cope with the region's debt.

## BUSINESS OWNER
70122

383 S. Broadway
Hicksville, NY 11801
Telephone: (516) 681-2111
FAX: (516) 681-2197
Year Established: 1977
Pub. Frequency: bi-m.
Subscrip. Rate: $88/yr.
**Owner(s):**
Thomar Publications, Inc.
383 S. Broadway
Hicksville, NY 11801
Telephone: (516) 681-2111
FAX: (516) 681-2197
Ownership %: 100
**Editorial:**
Thomas J. Martin .........................................Editor

## BUSINESS STRATEGIES BULLETIN
70107

4025 W. Peterson Ave.
Chicago, IL 60646
Telephone: (312) 583-8500
FAX: (708) 940-0113
Year Established: 1983
Pub. Frequency: m.
Subscrip. Rate: $125/yr.
**Owner(s):**
Commerce Clearing House, Inc.
4025 W. Peterson Ave.
Chicago, IL 60646
Telephone: (312) 583-8500
FAX: (708) 940-0113
Ownership %: 100
**Editorial:**
Sidney Kess .................................................Editor

## BUYOUTS NEWSLETTER
70111

40 W. 57th St., 8th Fl.
New York, NY 10019
Telephone: (212) 765-5311
FAX: (212) 765-6123
Year Established: 1985
Pub. Frequency: bi-m.
Subscrip. Rate: $495/yr.
Materials: 10
**Owner(s):**
SDC Publishing
40 W. 57th St., 8th Fl.
New York, NY 10019
Telephone: (212) 765-5311
FAX: (212) 765-6123
Ownership %: 100
**Editorial:**
Ted Weissberg .............................................Editor
**Desc.:** Contains interviews with and
articles about successful buyouts,
restructurings and leveraged
acquisitions.

## CALIFORNIA INSURANCE REPORT
70526

4635 Nicols Rd.,
Ste. 100
Eagan, MN 55122
Telephone: (612) 452-8267
FAX: (612) 452-8694
Year Established: 1986
Pub. Frequency: m.
Subscrip. Rate: $217/yr.
**Owner(s):**
Data Research, Inc.
4635 Nicols Rd., Ste. 100
Eagan, MN 55122
Telephone: (612) 452-8267
Ownership %: 100
**Editorial:**
Warren Cody .................................................Editor

## CARIBBEAN TREND WATCH
70047

P.O. Box 1052
Port Washington, NY 10050
Telephone: (516) 741-8877
Year Established: 1986
Pub. Frequency: m.
Subscrip. Rate: $100/yr.
**Owner(s):**
Hank Boerner
P.O. Box 1052
Port Washington, NY 10050
Telephone: (516) 741-8877
Ownership %: 100
**Management:**
Hank Boerner .......................................Publisher
**Editorial:**
Hank Boerner .............................................Editor
**Desc.:** Newsletter and briefing service for
executives and business owners with an
interest in USA-Caribbean Basin
Commerce.

## CARLSON REPORT FOR SHOPPING MANAGEMENT
70644

9595 Whitley Dr., Ste.100
Indianapolis, IN 46240
Telephone: (317) 844-9024
FAX: (317) 848-6953
Year Established: 1982
Pub. Frequency: m.
Subscrip. Rate: $112/yr.
**Owner(s):**
Report Communications
595 Whitley Dr.
Ste. 100
Indianapolis, IN 46240
Telephone: (317) 844-9024
FAX: (317) 848-6953
Ownership %: 100
**Editorial:**
William R. Wilburn .......................................Editor
**Desc.:** Industry newsletter for shopping
center management professionals at the
mall and corporate level.

## CHANNELS
24519

The Dudley House
14 Front St.
Exeter, NH 03833
Telephone: (603) 778-0514
FAX: (603) 778-1741
Mailing Address:
   P.O. Box 600
   Exeter, NH 03833
Year Established: 1923
Pub. Frequency: m.
Subscrip. Rate: $40/yr.
Materials: 01,02,06,10,15,25,28,32
Freelance Pay: free
**Owner(s):**
PR Publishing Co., Inc.
P.O. Box 600
Exeter, NH 03833
Telephone: (603) 778-0514
FAX: (603) 778-1741
Ownership %: 100
**Editorial:**
Janet Barber .................................................Editor
**Desc.:** Issues, trends, and tactics relevant
to the communication and management
concerns of nonprofit, government and
business in dealing with public relations.
Covers programs and campaigns,
especially on the community level, and
reviews journals, reports, and books of
interest to communicators. Departments
include: Communications Forum & Ideas
That Communicate.
**Readers:** Nonprofit agency executives,
public relations professionals, fund
raisers and others.

## CHIEF EXECUTIVE OPINION
70113

845 Third Ave.
New York, NY 10022
Telephone: (212) 759-0900
FAX: (212) 980-7014
Year Established: 1989
Pub. Frequency: irreg.
Subscrip. Rate: $5/yr. members; $15/yr.
   non-members
Circulation: 8,700
Circulation Type: controlled & paid
**Owner(s):**
Conference Board, Inc.
845 Third Ave.
New York, NY 10022
Telephone: (212) 759-0900
FAX: (212) 980-7014
Ownership %: 100
**Editorial:**
Fabian Linden .............................................Editor
**Desc.:** Analysis of US CEO's views on
major policy issues and business trends.

## CHRONICLE OF LATIN AMERICAN ECONOMIC AFFAIRS
70961

801 Yale, N.E.
Albuquerque, NM 87131-1016
Year Established: 1986
Pub. Frequency: w.
Subscrip. Rate: $125/yr. individuals;
   $225/yr. institutions
**Owner(s):**
Chronicle of Latin American Economic
   Affairs
801 Yale, N.E.
Albuquerque, NM 87131-1016
Telephone: (505) 277-6839
FAX: (505) 277-5989
Ownership %: 100
**Editorial:**
Carlos M. Navarro .......................................Editor
**Desc.:** Monitors economic and political
climates of Latin America. Covers news
and trends concerning investment, trade,
capital flow, foreign debt and general
economic performance.

## CONSULTANTS NEWS
70625

Templeton Rd.
Fitzwilliam, NH 03447
Telephone: (603) 585-2200
FAX: (603) 585-9555
Year Established: 1970
Pub. Frequency: m.
Subscrip. Rate: $144/yr.
**Owner(s):**
Kennedy Publications
Templeton Rd.
Fitzwilliam, NH 03447
Telephone: (603) 585-2200
FAX: (603) 585-9555
Ownership %: 100
**Editorial:**
James H. Kennedy .......................................Editor
**Desc.:** Covers trends and developments in
management consulting.

## CONTINENTAL FRANCHISE REVIEW
70126

P.O. Box 3283
Englewood, CO 80155
Telephone: (303) 649-1044
FAX: (303) 649-1059
Year Established: 1968
Pub. Frequency: bi-w.
Subscrip. Rate: $155/yr. US; $175/yr.
   foreign
Materials: 10
**Owner(s):**
Sparks Publishing Co., Inc.
P.O. Box 3285
Englewood, CO 80155
Telephone: (303) 649-1044
FAX: (303) 649-1059
Ownership %: 100
**Editorial:**
Ron Vlieger .................................................Editor

## COORDINATOR
68768

1755 Lynnfield Rd., Ste. 222
Memphis, TN 38119-7235
Telephone: (901) 680-0470
FAX: (901) 680-0505
Year Established: 1953
Pub. Frequency: m.
Page Size: tabloid
Subscrip. Rate: $12/yr. non-members
Materials: 32,33
Circulation: 8,500
Circulation Type: controlled & paid

---

**Materials Accepted/Included:** 01-Business news 02-By-line articles 03-Fashion news 04-Food news 05-Freelance copy 06-Letters to editor 07-Real estate news 08-Sports news 09-Travel news 10-Book rev. 11-Movie rev. 12-Music rev. 13-TV rev. 14-Theater rev. 15-Coming events 16-Obituaries 17-Question & answer 18-Social announcements 19-Artwork 20-Cartoons 21-Photos 22-TV listings 23-Audio rec. 24-Video rec. 25-Books 26-Films/film clips 27-Personnel news 28-Press releases 29-New product news/photos 30-Trade lit. 31-Contracts awarded 32-Display adv. 33-Classified adv.

**Owner(s):**
American Society of Women Accountants
1755 Lynnfield Rd., Ste. 222
Memphis, TN 38119-7235
Telephone: (901) 680-0470
FAX: (901) 680-0505
Ownership %: 100
**Editorial:**
Allison Conte .................................Editor

70632
## COPIER REVIEW
20 Railroad Ave.
Hackensack, NJ 07601-3309
Telephone: (201) 488-0404
FAX: (201) 488-0461
Pub. Frequency: m.
Subscrip. Rate: $365/yr.
Circulation: 2,600
Circulation Type: controlled & paid
**Owner(s):**
Buyers Laboratory, Inc.
20 Railroad Ave.
Hackensack, NJ 07601-3309
Telephone: (201) 488-0404
FAX: (201) 488-0461
Ownership %: 100
**Desc.:** Provides news and analysis of copy
machines, new products, new
technologies, market trends and options
for copiers.

70761
## CORPORATE JOBS OUTLOOK
Drawer 100
Boerne, TX 78006-0100
Telephone: (512) 755-8810
FAX: (512) 755-2410
Year Established: 1986
Pub. Frequency: bi-m.
Subscrip. Rate: $159.99/yr.
Circulation: 1,000
Circulation Type: controlled & paid
**Owner(s):**
Corporate Jobs Outlook
Drawer 100
Boerne, TX 78006-0100
Telephone: (512) 755-8810
FAX: (512) 755-2410
Ownership %: 100
**Editorial:**
Jack W. Pluckett ..............................Editor
**Desc.:** Objective reports on growing, hiring
employees. Includes ratings for salaries,
benefits, and advancement
opportunities. Covers training, corporate
growth, financial stability, marketing,
products and services, and mid-term
outlook for America's top employers.

70072
## CREATIVE EXHIBITING
## TECHNIQUES
745 Marquette Bank Bldg.
Rochester, MN 55904
Telephone: (507) 289-6556
FAX: (507) 289-5253
Year Established: 1992
Pub. Frequency: m.
Subscrip. Rate: $89/yr. new subscribers;
$98/yr. renewal
Circulation: 1,000
Circulation Type: controlled & paid
**Owner(s):**
Exhibitor Publications, Inc.
745 Marquette Bank Bldg.
Rochester, MN 55904
Telephone: (507) 289-6556
FAX: (507) 289-5253
Ownership %: 100
**Editorial:**
Lee Knight ..................................Editor
**Desc.:** Newsletter of tips, tactics and how-
tos for effective trade show marketing.

70656
## CUSTOMER COMMUNICATOR
215 Park Ave. S., Ste. 1301
New York, NY 10003
Telephone: (212) 228-0246
FAX: (212) 228-0376
Pub. Frequency: m.
Subscrip. Rate: $129/yr.
**Owner(s):**
Alexander Research & Communications,
Inc.
215 Park Ave. S., Ste. 1301
New York, NY 10003
Telephone: (212) 228-0246
FAX: (212) 228-0376
Ownership %: 100
**Editorial:**
Leslie Hansen Harps ........................Editor
**Desc.:** For customer contact personnel,
covers customer relations skills.

70627
## CUSTOMER SERVICE
## NEWSLETTER
215 Park Ave., S.
Ste. 1301
New York, NY 10003
Telephone: (212) 228-0246
FAX: (212) 228-0376
Year Established: 1973
Pub. Frequency: m.
Subscrip. Rate: $117/yr.
**Owner(s):**
Alexander Research & Communications,
Inc.
215 Park Ave. S.
Ste. 1301
New York, NY 10003
Telephone: (212) 228-0246
FAX: (212) 228-0376
Ownership %: 100
**Editorial:**
Leslie Hanson Harps ........................Editor
**Desc.:** Addresses overall customer service
problems: performance standards,
boosting productivity, evaluating reps,
and running an effective customer
service department.

70136
## DIRECT RESPONSE SPECIALIST
P.O. Box 1075
Tarpon Springs, FL 34688-1075
Telephone: (813) 786-1411
Year Established: 1982
Pub. Frequency: m.
Subscrip. Rate: $77/yr.
Materials: 10,32
**Owner(s):**
Stilson & Stilson
P.O. Box 7430
Tarpon Springs, FL 34688-1075
Telephone: (813) 786-1411
Ownership %: 100
**Editorial:**
Galen Stilson .................................Editor
**Desc.:** Newsletter for effective response
and profit techniques.

70805
## DISCOUNT & WHOLESALE
## PRINTING NEWSLETTER
P.O. Box 416
Denver, CO 80201-0416
Telephone: (303) 575-5676
Year Established: 1990
Pub. Frequency: bi-a.
Subscrip. Rate: $4.50/yr.
Circulation: 3,000
Circulation Type: controlled & paid
**Owner(s):**
Prosperity & Profits Unlimited
P.O. Box 416
Denver, CO 80201-0416
Telephone: (303) 575-5676
Ownership %: 100

**Editorial:**
A. Doyle .....................................Editor
**Desc.:** Lists sources for discount and
wholesale printing

70112
## DISTRIBUTION CENTER
## MANAGEMENT
215 Park Ave., S., Ste. 1301
New York, NY 10003
Telephone: (212) 228-0246
FAX: (212) 228-0376
Year Established: 1966
Pub. Frequency: m.
Subscrip. Rate: $119/yr.
**Owner(s):**
Alexander Research & Communications,
Inc.
215 Park Ave., S., Ste. 1301
New York, NY 10003
Telephone: (212) 228-0246
FAX: (212) 228-0376
Ownership %: 100
**Editorial:**
Laurence Alexander ........................Editor
**Desc.:** Provides practical strategies and
industry news to help distribution center
and warehouse professionals improve
distribution center efficiency.

70115
## DISTRIBUTION MANAGEMENT
## DIGEST
P.O. Box 7457
Wilton, CT 06897
Year Established: 1987
Pub. Frequency: q.
Materials: 32
**Owner(s):**
Business Marketing & Publishing Inc.
P.O. Box 7457
Wilton, CT 06897
Ownership %: 100
**Editorial:**
George B. Young ...................Advertising Editor

70962
## EARLY WARNING FORECAST
275 Washington St.
Newton, MA 02158-1630
Telephone: (617) 630-2105
FAX: (617) 630-2100
Mailing Address:
P.O. Box 59-Newton Branch
Boston, MA 02258
Year Established: 1975
Pub. Frequency: m.
Subscrip. Rate: $259/yr.
Circulation: 1,000
Circulation Type: controlled & paid
**Owner(s):**
Cahners Publishing Co.
275 Washington St.
Newton, MA 02158-1630
Telephone: (617) 630-2105
FAX: (617) 630-2100
Ownership %: 100
**Editorial:**
Bill Wood ...................................Editor

70687
## EMPLOYEE BENEFITS REPORT
One Penn Plz.
New York, NY 10119
Telephone: (212) 971-5000
FAX: (212) 971-5024
Year Established: 1974
Pub. Frequency: m.
Subscrip. Rate: $120.98/yr. US; $167/yr.
foreign
**Owner(s):**
Warren Gorham Lamont
One Penn Plz.
New York, NY 10119
Telephone: (212) 971-5000
FAX: (212) 971-5024
Ownership %: 100

**Editorial:**
John D. Reynolds .............................Editor
**Desc.:** Provides information on the latest
ideas and developments in the field of
employee benefits. Offers advice and
up-to-date coverage on IRS actions,
employment law, benefits planning,
social security developments and related
topics.

70657
## EMPLOYEE COMMUNICATION
379 W. Broadway
New York, NY 10012
Telephone: (212) 966-8966
Year Established: 1982
Pub. Frequency: m.
Subscrip. Rate: $95/yr.
**Owner(s):**
Management Resources, Inc.
379 W. Broadway
New York, NY 10012
Telephone: (212) 966-8966
Ownership %: 100
**Editorial:**
John Carpenter ..............................Editor
**Desc.:** Making communication between
companies and their employees more
productive and profitable.

70691
## EMPLOYEE HIRING LAW
## BULLETIN
23 Drydock Ave.
Boston, MA 02210-2387
Telephone: (800) 229-2084
FAX: (617) 345-9646
Pub. Frequency: m.
Subscrip. Rate: $66/yr.
**Owner(s):**
Quinlan Publishing Co., Inc.
23 Drydock Ave.
Boston, MA 02210-2387
Telephone: (800) 229-2084
FAX: (617) 345-9646
Ownership %: 100
**Desc.:** Covers laws and decisions affecting
the hiring process, including issues such
as policy implementation, employee
fraud, misrepresentation, replacement
policy, and related concerns.

70501
## EMPLOYER'S HEALTH BENEFITS
## BULLETIN
1725 K St., N.W., Ste. 200
Washington, DC 20006
Telephone: (202) 827-4000
FAX: (301) 543-2921
Year Established: 1987
Pub. Frequency: m.
Subscrip. Rate: $227/yr.
**Owner(s):**
Thompson Publishing Group
1725 K St., N.W., Ste. 200
Washington, DC 20006
Telephone: (202) 872-4000
FAX: (301) 543-2921
Ownership %: 100
**Editorial:**
John Ortman ..................................Editor

70651
## ENTREPRENEURIAL
## MANAGEMENT
180 Varick St.
Penthouse
New York, NY 10014
Telephone: (212) 633-0060
FAX: (212) 633-0063
Year Established: 1979
Pub. Frequency: m.
Subscrip. Rate: $96/yr.

**Owner(s):**
Center For Entrepreneurial Managment,
Inc.
180 Varick St.
Penthouse
New York, NY 10014
Telephone: (212) 633-0060
FAX: (212) 633-0063
Ownership %: 100
**Editorial:**
Joseph R. Mancuso ....................Editor
**Desc.:** For the entrepreneurial manager
and the professionals who advise him.

70628
## EXECUTIVE REPORT ON CUSTOMER SATISFACTION
215 Park Ave., S., Ste. 1301
New York, NY 10003
Telephone: (212) 228-0246
FAX: (212) 228-0376
Pub. Frequency: m.
Subscrip. Rate: $199/yr.
**Owner(s):**
Alexander Research & Communications,
Inc.
215 Park Ave., S., Ste. 1301
New York, NY 10003
Telephone: (212) 228-0246
FAX: (212) 228-0376
Ownership %: 100
**Editorial:**
Leslie Hansen Harps ....................Editor
**Desc.:** Covers how successful companies
of all sizes are using innovative
strategies to retain their best customers
and attract new ones. Plus trends,
statistics, timely news and information.

65726
## FAIR EMPLOYMENT REPORT
951 Pershing Dr.
Silver Spring, MD 20910
Telephone: (301) 587-6300
FAX: (301) 585-9075
Year Established: 1963
Pub. Frequency: bi-w.
Page Size: standard
Subscrip. Rate: $254.54/yr.
Materials: 10
**Owner(s):**
Business Publishers, Inc.
951 Pershing Dr.
Silver Spring, MD 20910
Telephone: (301) 587-6300
FAX: (301) 585-9075
Ownership %: 100
**Editorial:**
Steve Lash ....................Editor
**Desc.:** Studies developments in federal
programs aimed at eliminating
employment discrimination.

70530
## FEDERAL & STATE INSURANCE WEEK
P.O. Box 6654
McLean, VA 22106
Telephone: (703) 532-2235
Year Established: 1987
Pub. Frequency: w.
Subscrip. Rate: $347/yr.
**Owner(s):**
J.R. Publishing
Box 6654
McLean, VA 22106
Telephone: (703) 532-2235
Ownership %: 100
**Editorial:**
John V. Reistrup ....................Editor

70114
## GOVERNMENT ACCOUNTING & AUDITING UPDATE
One Penn Plz.
New York, NY 10119
Telephone: (212) 971-5000
FAX: (212) 971-5240
Year Established: 1990
Pub. Frequency: m.
Subscrip. Rate: $161.25/yr. US;
$217.70/yr. foreign
**Owner(s):**
Warren Gorham Lamont
One Penn Plz.
New York, NY 10119
Telephone: (212) 971-5000
FAX: (212) 971-5240
Ownership %: 100
**Desc.:** Informs readers on changes in
government accounting and financial
reporting and how they affect their
businesses.

70706
## HR REPORTER
1350 Connecticut Ave., N.W.
Ste. 1000
Washington, DC 20036
Telephone: (202) 862-0990
FAX: (202) 862-0999
Year Established: 1984
Pub. Frequency: m.
Subscrip. Rate: $325/yr. US; $347/yr.
foreign
Materials: 10
**Owner(s):**
Buraff Publications, Inc.
1350 Connecticut Ave., N.W.
Ste. 1000
Washington, DC 20036
Telephone: (202) 862-0990
FAX: (202) 862-0999
**Editorial:**
Tessa Jolls ....................Editor
**Desc.:** Reports on issues in human
relations, corporate policies and
programs, and new concepts, theories,
and trends.

70710
## HUMAN RESOURCE MANAGEMENT NEWS
350 W. Hubbard St., No. 440
Chicago, IL 60610-4011
Telephone: (312) 464-0300
Year Established: 1951
Pub. Frequency: w.
Subscrip. Rate: $240/yr.
**Owner(s):**
Remy Publishing Co.
350 W. Hubbard St., No. 440
Chicago, IL 60060-4011
Telephone: (312) 464-0300
Ownership %: 100
**Editorial:**
John Hickey ....................Editor
**Readers:** Weekly newsletter for the human
resource management field.

70374
## IL AFL-CIO LABORLETTER
828 S. Second St., Ste. 200
Springfield, IL 62704
Telephone: (217) 544-4014
FAX: (217) 544-0225
Year Established: 1926
Pub. Frequency: m.
Page Size: standard
Subscrip. Rate: $10/yr.
Print Process: offset
**Owner(s):**
IL CIO-AFL
828 S. Second St., Ste. 200
Springfield, IL 62704
Telephone: (217) 544-4014
FAX: (217) 544-0225
Ownership %: 100

**Editorial:**
Loren Billings ....................Editor

70049
## INDIA BUSINESS & INVESTMENT REPORT
75 Maiden Ln.
New York, NY 10038
Telephone: (212) 806-8840
FAX: (212) 269-0420
Year Established: 1990
Pub. Frequency: m.
Subscrip. Rate: $385/yr. US; $410/yr.
foreign
**Owner(s):**
PSI, Inc.
75 Maiden Ln.
New York, NY 10038
Telephone: (212) 806-8840
FAX: (212) 269-0420
Ownership %: 100
**Editorial:**
John Pitt ....................Editor
**Desc.:** Covers international trade and
investment in India, including
automotive, textiles, electronics,
chemicals and pharmaceuticals,
telecommunications, regulation and
political risk issues.

64947
## INDUSTRIES IN TRANSITION
25 Van Zant St.
Norwalk, CT 06855
Telephone: (203) 853-4266
FAX: (203) 853-0348
Year Established: 1977
Pub. Frequency: m.
Page Size: standard
Subscrip. Rate: $305/yr.
**Owner(s):**
Business Communications Co., Inc.
25 Van Zant St.
Norwalk, CT 06855
Telephone: (203) 853-4266
Ownership %: 100
**Management:**
Louis Naturman ....................Manager
**Editorial:**
Robert Butler ....................Editor
**Desc.:** Industry trends specifically
addressing markets where primary and
radical changes are taking place,
analyzing the causes and the effects
that are revelent to industry decision
makers.
**Readers:** Corporate executives, industry
watchers, and industry decision makers.

70520
## INSURANCE & RISK MANAGEMENT
1350 Connecticut Ave., N.W.
Ste. 1000
Washington, DC 20036
Telephone: (202) 862-0990
FAX: (202) 862-0999
Year Established: 1987
Pub. Frequency: bi-w.
Subscrip. Rate: $348/yr. US; $370/yr.
foreign
**Owner(s):**
Buraff Publications
1350 Connecticut Ave., N.W.
Ste. 1000
Washington, DC 20036
Telephone: (202) 862-0990
FAX: (202) 862-0999
Ownership %: 100
**Editorial:**
Louis LaBrecque ....................Editor
**Desc.:** Covers risk management and loss
prevention and control, including news
briefs, tax tips, state developments, and
coverage of specific insurance and risk
management topics.

70511
## INSURANCE ACCOUNTANT
One State St. Plz.
New York, NY 10004-1549
Telephone: (800) 733-4371
FAX: (212) 943-2224
Pub. Frequency: w.
Subscrip. Rate: $465/yr. US; $495/yr.
foreign
**Owner(s):**
American Banker-Bond Buyer
One State St. Plz.
New York, NY 10004-1549
Telephone: (800) 733-4371
FAX: (212) 943-2224
Ownership %: 100
**Desc.:** Concentrates on the regulatory,
legislative, and accounting policy
developments affecting the insurance
industry accounting practices. Covers all
relevant major developments within the
National Association of Insurance
Commissioners, the AICPA, the FASB,
the IRS, and the SEC, as well as
relevant court cases impacting insurance
accounting.

70535
## INSURANCE REGULATOR
One State Street Plz
New York, NY 10004-1549
Telephone: (800) 733-4371
FAX: (212) 943-2224
Pub. Frequency: w.
Subscrip. Rate: $465/yr. US; $495/yr.
foreign
**Owner(s):**
American Banker-Bond Buyer
Newsletter Division
One State Street Plaza
New York, NY 10004
Telephone: (800) 733-4371
**Desc.:** Covers statae regulation and gives
a national overview of developing trends
in the industry. Includes ledger of state
commissions' and "Behind the Scenes"
column by those involved in policy
affecting insurance.

70601
## INTERNATIONAL CONTRACT ADVISOR
Six Bigelow St.
Cambridge, MA 02139
Telephone: (617) 354-0140
FAX: (617) 354-8595
Year Established: 1988
Pub. Frequency: m.
Subscrip. Rate: $250/yr.
**Owner(s):**
Kluwer Law & Taxation Publishers
Six Bigelow St.
Cambridge, MA 02139
Telephone: (617) 354-0140
FAX: (617) 354-8595
Ownership %: 100
**Editorial:**
M.F. Klingenberg ....................Editor
J.E. Pattison ....................Editor
**Desc.:** Provides concise and practical
information regarding international
business, including analysis of
international contract clauses, reports on
arbitration and litigation developments
affecting global business, negotiation
strategies.

70921
## INTERNATIONAL ECONOMIC SCOREBOARD
845 Third Ave.
New York, NY 10022
Telephone: (212) 759-0900
FAX: (212) 980-7014
Year Established: 1979
Pub. Frequency: a.
Subscrip. Rate: free

---

**Materials Accepted/Included:** 01-Business news 02-By-line articles 03-Fashion news 04-Food news 05-Freelance copy 06-Letters to editor 07-Real estate news 08-Sports news 09-Travel news 10-Book rev. 11-Movie rev. 12-Music rev. 13-TV rev. 14-Theater rev. 15-Coming events 16-Obituaries 17-Question & answer 18-Social announcements 19-Artwork 20-Cartoons 21-Photos 22-TV listings 23-Audio rec. 24-Video rec. 25-Books 26-Films/film clips 27-Personnel news 28-Press releases 29-New product news/photos 30-Trade lit. 31-Contracts awarded 32-Display adv. 33-Classified adv.

**Owner(s):**
Conference Board, Inc.
845 Third Ave.
New York, NY 10022
Telephone: (212) 759-0900
FAX: (212) 980-7014
Ownership %: 100
**Desc.:** Indexes of economic performance
of major industrial countries presented in
chart and tabular form with commentary.

58609
**JACK O'DWYER'S NEWSLETTER**
271 Madison Ave.
New York, NY 10016
Telephone: (212) 679-2471
FAX: (212) 683-2750
Year Established: 1968
Pub. Frequency: w.
Page Size: standard
Subscrip. Rate: $175/yr.
**Owner(s):**
J.R. O'Dwyer Co., Inc.
271 Madison Ave.
New York, NY 10016
Telephone: (212) 679-2497
Ownership %: 100
**Editorial:**
Jack O'Dwyer ...................................Editor

70927
**JOHN NAISBITT'S TREND LETTER**
1101 30th St., N.W., Ste. 130
Washington, DC 20007
Telephone: (202) 337-5960
Year Established: 1982
Pub. Frequency: fortn.
Subscrip. Rate: $195/yr.
Circulation: 8,000
Circulation Type: paid
**Owner(s):**
Global Network, Inc.
1101 30th St., N.W., Ste. 130
Washington, DC 20007
Telephone: (202) 337-5960
Ownership %: 100
**Editorial:**
Jerry Kline ......................................Editor

70137
**JONESREPORT FOR SHOPPING
CENTER MARKETING**
9595 Whitley Dr., Ste. 100
Indianapolis, IN 46240
Telephone: (317) 844-9024
FAX: (317) 848-6953
Year Established: 1978
Pub. Frequency: m.
Subscrip. Rate: $112/yr.
Materials: 32
Circulation: 2,100
Circulation Type: paid
**Owner(s):**
Report Communications
9595 Whitley Dr., Ste. 100
Indianapolis, IN 46240
Telephone: (317) 844-9024
FAX: (317) 848-6953
Ownership %: 100
**Editorial:**
William R. Wilburn ...........................Editor
**Desc.:** Industry newsletter about shopping
center marketing and promotions for
marketing directors of malls at the
corporate level.

70116
**JOURNEY**
800 Main St.
Antioch, IL 60002
Telephone: (708) 395-7990
FAX: (708) 395-8093
Year Established: 1991
Pub. Frequency: q.
Subscrip. Rate: $39.95/yr.
Materials: 10,32

**Owner(s):**
David W. Bucker, Inc.
800 Main St.
Antioch, IL 60002
Telephone: (708) 395-7990
FAX: (708) 395-8093
Ownership %: 100
**Editorial:**
James W. Bieal ..............................Editor
Mike Stickler ...................Advertising Editor
**Desc.:** Provides business managers with
proven methods of improving their
operating performance.

70938
**LAGNIAPPE QUARTERLY
MONITOR**
159 W. 53rd St., 28th Fl.
New York, NY 10019
Telephone: (212) 765-5520
FAX: (212) 765-2929
Pub. Frequency: q.
Subscrip. Rate: $625/yr.
**Owner(s):**
Latin American Information Services, Inc.
159 W. 53rd St., 28th Fl.
New York, NY 10019
Telephone: (212) 765-5520
FAX: (212) 765-2929
Ownership %: 100
**Editorial:**
Rosemary H. Werrett ......................Editor
**Desc.:** Statistics of financial indicators,
short-term forecasts and production
trends of Latin America's nine key
markets.

71277
**LAND LETTER**
1800 N. Kent St., Ste. 1120
Arlington, VA 22209
Telephone: (703) 522-8008
FAX: (703) 525-4610
Year Established: 1982
Pub. Frequency: 34/yr.
Page Size: standard
Subscrip. Rate: $100/yr. introductory;
$165/yr. regular
Circulation: 600
Circulation Type: paid
**Owner(s):**
Conservation Fund
1800 N. Kent St., Ste.1120
Arlington, VA 22209
Telephone: (703) 522-8008
FAX: (703) 525-4610
Ownership %: 100
**Editorial:**
Jason Rhilander ....................Managing Editor
**Desc.:** The newsletter for natural resource
professionals.

70075
**LEADER**
10 Paragon Dr.
Montvale, NJ 07645-1760
Telephone: (201) 573-6154
FAX: (201) 573-8601
Pub. Frequency: m.
Circulation: 12,000
**Owner(s):**
Institute of Management Accountants
10 Paragon Dr.
Montvale, NJ 07645-1760
Telephone: (201) 573-6154
FAX: (201) 573-8601
Ownership %: 100
**Editorial:**
Kathryn Hogan ...........................Editor
**Desc.:** Focuses on improving
communication between members and
the national office.

70043
**MAGNET MARKETING**
40 Oval Rd.
Quincy, MA 02170
Telephone: (617) 328-0069
FAX: (617) 471-1504
Year Established: 1976
Pub. Frequency: q.
Subscrip. Rate: free
Circulation: 3,500
Circulation Type: controlled
**Owner(s):**
Graham Communications
40 Oval Rd.
Quincy, MA 02170
Telephone: (617) 328-0069
FAX: (617) 471-1504
Ownership %: 100
**Editorial:**
John Graham ..................................Editor
**Desc.:** Features results-oriented articles
and information on advertising,
marketing, public relations, design,
creative sales and fundraising for
businesses.

70635
**MANAGEMENT MATTERS**
P.O. Box 15640
Plantation, FL 33318-5640
Telephone: (305) 473-9560
FAX: (305) 473-0544
Pub. Frequency: m.
Subscrip. Rate: $249/yr. US; $269/yr.
Canada; $309/yr. elsewhere
**Owner(s):**
Marton Allan/InfoTeam, Inc.
P.O. Box 15640
Plantation, FL 33318-5640
Telephone: (305) 473-9560
FAX: (305) 473-0544
Ownership %: 100
**Editorial:**
David R. Allen ...............................Editor
**Desc.:** Covers all facts, topics, and issues
of effective management.

70143
**MANAGING THE HUMAN CLIMATE**
155 N. Harbor Dr., No. 2201
Chicago, IL 60601
Telephone: (312) 819-3590
FAX: (312) 819-3592
Year Established: 1970
Pub. Frequency: bi-m.
Subscrip. Rate: $30/yr.
Materials: 32
Circulation: 2,500
Circulation Type: paid
**Owner(s):**
Philip Lesly Co.
155 N. Harbor Dr., No. 2201
Chicago, IL 60601
Telephone: (312) 819-3590
FAX: (312) 819-3592
Ownership %: 100
**Editorial:**
Philip Lesly ...................................Editor
**Desc.:** Editorial newsletter on mass
attitudes and dynamics of the human
climate affecting all organizations.

70045
**MANUFACTURING AUTOMATION**
321 Carrera Dr.
Mill Valley, CA 94941-3995
Telephone: (415) 389-8671
FAX: (415) 345-7018
Pub. Frequency: m.
Subscrip. Rate: $325/yr. US; $345/yr.
foreign

**Owner(s):**
Vital Information Publications
321 Carrera Dr.
Mill Valley, CA 94941-3995
Telephone: (415) 389-8671
FAX: (415) 345-7018
Ownership %: 100
**Editorial:**
Peter Adrian ..................................Editor
**Desc.:** Provides information on worldwide
markets in key areas of manufacturing
and industrial automation.

71220
**MARKETSCAN EUROPE**
17 Arlington St.
Boston, MA 02116
Telephone: (617) 424-9291
Year Established: 1989
Pub. Frequency: 10/yr.
Subscrip. Rate: $299/yr.
Circulation: 1,000
Circulation Type: paid
**Owner(s):**
Marketscan Europe
17 Arlington St.
Boston, MA 02116
Telephone: (617) 424-9291
Ownership %: 100
**Editorial:**
Robert Sprung ...............................Editor

70932
**MARPLE'S BUSINESS
NEWSLETTER**
117 W. Mercer St., Ste. 200
Seattle, WA 98119
Telephone: (206) 281-9609
FAX: (206) 285-8035
Year Established: 1949
Pub. Frequency: fortn.
Subscrip. Rate: $72/yr.
Circulation: 4,100
Circulation Type: paid
**Owner(s):**
Newsletter Publishing Corp.
117 W. Mercer St., Ste. 200
Seattle, WA 98119-3960
Telephone: (206) 281-9609
FAX: (206) 285-8035
Ownership %: 100
**Editorial:**
Michael J. Parks ............................Editor
**Desc.:** Covers business trends affecting
the Pacific Northwest, with company
profiles, news of recent acquisitions,
demographic issues, and evaluation of
international business conditions.

65110
**MEDIA INDUSTRY NEWSLETTER**
1201 Seven Locks Rd., Ste. 300
Potomac, MD 20854
Telephone: (301) 424-3338
FAX: (301) 309-3847
Year Established: 1948
Pub. Frequency: w.
Page Size: standard
Subscrip. Rate: $395/yr.
Materials: 01,10,15,28,29,30,31
Circulation: 2,143
Circulation Type: paid
**Owner(s):**
Phillips Business Information, Inc.
1201 Seven Locks Rd., Ste. 300
Potomac, MD 20854
Telephone: (301) 424-4297
FAX: (301) 309-3847
Ownership %: 100
**Bureau(s):**
NY-Editorial Bureau
305 Madison Ave., Ste. 4417
New York, NY 10165
Telephone: (212) 983-5170
FAX: (212) 983-5144
Contact: Steve Cohn, Editor

---

Materials Accepted/Included: 01-Business news 02-By-line articles 03-Fashion news 04-Food news 05-Freelance copy 06-Letters to editor 07-Real estate news 08-Sports news 09-Travel news
10-Book rev. 11-Movie rev. 12-Music rev. 13-TV rev. 14-Theater rev. 15-Coming events 16-Obituaries 17-Question & answer 18-Social announcements 19-Artwork 20-Cartoons 21-Photos 22-TV listings
23-Audio rec. 24-Video rec. 25-Books 26-Films/film clips 27-Personnel news 28-Press releases 29-New product news/photos 30-Trade lit. 31-Contracts awarded 32-Display adv. 33-Classified adv.

**Management:**
Thomas L. Phillips ...............Chairman of Board
Thomas C. Thompson ......................President
Thomas Phillips ...............................Publisher
Ellen H. Stuhlmann ..........................Publisher
**Editorial:**
Kismet Toksu Gould ..........Associate Publisher
Maggie Jackman .....................Marketing Editor
Lisa S. Kelley .......................Marketing Manager
Anne Holland .......................Marketing Manager
John Masterton ..................Media Group Editor
Richard Gorrio .....................Research Reporter
**Desc.:** Exclusive, inside look at media
 industry with a smart snippy style.
 Includes coverage of circulation and
 advertising trends in the media industry,
 especially magazine and newspaper
 publications, plus a monthly stock watch.
**Readers:** Publishers and other top
 executives in the Media Industry.

70936
**MONEY WATCH BULLETIN**
24 Cantebury Rd.
Rockville Center, NY 11570
Telephone: (516) 766-5850
Year Established: 1984
Pub. Frequency: m.
Subscrip. Rate: $95/yr.
Materials: 10
**Owner(s):**
International Wealth Success, Inc.
24 Cantebury Rd.
Rockville Center, NY 11570
Telephone: (516) 766-5850
Ownership %: 100
**Editorial:**
Tyler G. Hicks ....................................Editor
**Desc.:** Information on 100 lenders for real
 estate, business and other income-
 producing activities every month.

70124
**MULTINATIONAL PR REPORT**
P.O. Box 9588
Washington, DC 20016
Telephone: (202) 244-2580
FAX: (202) 244-2581
Year Established: 1984
Pub. Frequency: m.
Subscrip. Rate: $75/yr.
Materials: 10
**Owner(s):**
Pigafetta Press
P.O. Box 9588
Washington, DC 20016
Telephone: (202) 244-2580
FAX: (202) 244-2581
Ownership %: 100
**Editorial:**
John M. Reed ....................................Editor

70939
**NICARAGUA MONITOR**
1247 E St., N.E.
Washington, DC 20003-2221
Telephone: (202) 544-9355
Year Established: 1986
Pub. Frequency: m.
Subscrip. Rate: $15/yr.
Materials: 10,32
Circulation: 5,000
Circulation Type: controlled & paid
**Owner(s):**
Nicaragua Network
1247 E St., N.E.
Washington, DC 20003-2221
Telephone: (202) 544-9355
Ownership %: 100
**Editorial:**
Chuck Kaufman ....................................Editor
**Desc.:** News and analysis of the effects of
 US policy on the people of Nicaragua.
 Seeks to establish ties of peace and
 friendship between the people of the US
 and Nicaragua. Text mainly in English,
 occasionally in Spanish.

64913
**NONPROFIT INSIGHTS**
313 South Ave.
Fanwood, NJ 07023
Telephone: (908) 889-6336
FAX: (908) 889-6339
Mailing Address:
 P.O. Box 340
 Fanwood, NJ 07023
Year Established: 1980
Pub. Frequency: bi-w.
Page Size: standard
Subscrip. Rate: $239/yr.
**Owner(s):**
Whitaker Newsletters, Inc.
313 South Ave.
Fanwood, NJ 07023
Telephone: (908) 889-6336
FAX: (908) 889-6339
Ownership %: 100
**Management:**
Joel Whitaker .........................................President
Sandra Smith ....................Operations Manager
**Editorial:**
Fred Rossi .............................................Editor
**Desc.:** Summarizes new developments
 affecting the non-profit community
 including colleges and universities such
 as Federal and state legislation, IRS
 rulings and court rulings.
**Readers:** Non-profit professionals.

70081
**NONPROFIT REPORT**
One Penn Plz.
New York, NY 10119
Telephone: (212) 971-5000
FAX: (212) 971-5240
Year Established: 1991
Pub. Frequency: m.
Subscrip. Rate: $113.98/yr. US;
 $157.90/yr. foreign
**Owner(s):**
Warren Gorham Lamont
One Penn Plz.
New York, NY 10119
Telephone: (212) 971-5000
Ownership %: 100
**Editorial:**
Murray Dropkin ....................................Editor
**Desc.:** Offers certified public accountants
 working with nonprofit organizations
 insight into key financial and tax
 legislation.

70639
**OFFICE PROFESSIONAL**
210 Commerce Blvd.
Round Rock, TX 78664-2189
Telephone: (512) 255-6006
FAX: (512) 255-7532
Year Established: 1981
Pub. Frequency: m.
Subscrip. Rate: $39/yr.
**Owner(s):**
Professional Training Associates, Inc.
210 Commerce Blvd.
Round Rock, TX 78664-2189
Telephone: (512) 255-6006
FAX: (512) 255-7532
Ownership %: 100
**Editorial:**
Marilyn C. Johnson ..................................Editor

70128
**PARTYLINE**
35 Sutton Pl.
New York, NY 10022
Telephone: (212) 755-3487
FAX: (212) 755-3488
Year Established: 1960
Pub. Frequency: w.
Subscrip. Rate: $150/yr.

**Owner(s):**
PartyLine Publishing
35 Sutton Pl.
New York, NY 10022
Telephone: (212) 755-3487
FAX: (212) 755-3488
Ownership %: 100
**Editorial:**
Betty Yarmon ....................................Editor
**Desc.:** For public relations professionals.

70661
**PERSONNEL PRACTICE IDEAS**
One Penn Plz.
New York, NY 10119
Telephone: (212) 971-5000
FAX: (212) 971-5240
Pub. Frequency: m.
Subscrip. Rate: $123.98/yr. US; $170.90
 overseas
**Owner(s):**
Warren Gorham Lamont
One Penn Plz.
New York, NY 10019
Telephone: (212) 971-5000
FAX: (212) 971-5240
Ownership %: 100
**Desc.:** Addresses current employment law
 problems confronting human resources
 managers. Provides how-to information
 on complying with regulations, preparing
 employee handbooks, and interviewing
 job applicants in order to avoid costly
 errors.

70669
**PRACTICAL SUPERVISION**
210 Commerce Blvd.
Round Rock, TX 78664-2189
Telephone: (512) 255-6006
FAX: (512) 255-7532
Year Established: 1984
Pub. Frequency: m.
Subscrip. Rate: $48/yr.
**Owner(s):**
Professional Training Associates, Inc.
210 Commerce Blvd.
Round Rock, TX 78664-2189
Telephone: (512) 255-6006
FAX: (512) 255-7532
Ownership %: 100
**Editorial:**
Mark Gozonsky ....................................Editor

70630
**PRODUCTIVITY**
101 Merritt, 5th Fl.
Norwalk, CT 06851
Telephone: (203) 846-6883
Year Established: 1980
Pub. Frequency: 10/yr.
Subscrip. Rate: $110/yr.
Circulation: 4,000
Circulation Type: controlled & paid
**Owner(s):**
Productivity, Inc.
101 Merritt, 5th Fl.
Norwalk, CT 06851
Telephone: (203) 846-6883
Ownership %: 100
**Editorial:**
Norman Bodek ....................................Editor
**Desc.:** Improving productivity and quality
 by learning what is working at other
 companies.

70053
**PROMOTING STORE TRAFFIC**
224 Seventh Ave.
Garden City, NY 11530-5771
Telephone: (800) 229-6700
FAX: (516) 294-8141
Year Established: 1990
Pub. Frequency: m.
Subscrip. Rate: $60/yr.
Circulation: 500
Circulation Type: controlled & paid

**Owner(s):**
Hoke Communications, Inc.
224 Seventh Ave.
Garden City, NY 11530-5771
Telephone: (800) 229-6700
FAX: (516) 294-8141
Ownership %: 100
**Desc.:** Designed to help retailers use their
 existing customer base to the best
 advantage and to build this base
 through the use of the latest affordable
 marketing techniques.

24520
**PR REPORTER**
The Dudley House
14 Front St.
Exeter, NH 03833
Telephone: (603) 778-0514
FAX: (603) 778-1741
Mailing Address:
 P.O. Box 600
 Exeter, NH 03833
Year Established: 1958
Pub. Frequency: w.
Subscrip. Rate: $185/yr.
Materials: 01,02,06,10,15,25,28,30
**Owner(s):**
PR Publishing Co., Inc.
P.O. Box 600
Exeter, NH 03833
Telephone: (603) 778-0514
Ownership %: 100
**Management:**
Otto Lerbinger ....................................Publisher
Laurie Eldridge ....................................Manager
**Editorial:**
Patrick Jackson ....................................Editor
June Barber ..............................Associate Editor
**Desc.:** Interested in new PR techniques,
 application of old techniques to new PR
 problems, PR speeches, case histories,
 general organization and PR
 counselor news with public relations
 overtones. Departments include: Editorial
 Box, General News, PR Briefs
 & Comments, Tips & Tactics, Crisis &
 Issues Management, Trends & Issues
 Affecting PR.
**Readers:** Public relations and public affairs
 professionals.

70776
**PRYOR REPORT**
P.O. Box 1766
Clemson, SC 29633
Telephone: (800) 237-7967
FAX: (803) 654-7275
Year Established: 1984
Pub. Frequency: m.
Subscrip. Rate: $69/yr.
Materials: 10
Circulation: 27,000
Circulation Type: controlled & paid
**Owner(s):**
Image, Inc.
P.O. Box 1766
Clemson, SC 29633
Telephone: (800) 237-7967
FAX: (803) 654-7275
Ownership %: 100
**Editorial:**
Paul G. Friedman ....................................Editor

70676
**RECRUITING TRENDS**
350 W. Hubbard St., Ste. 440
Chicago, IL 60610-4011
Telephone: (312) 464-0300
Year Established: 1962
Pub. Frequency: m.
Subscrip. Rate: $140/yr.

**Materials Accepted/Included:** 01-Business news 02-By-line articles 03-Fashion news 04-Food news 05-Freelance copy 06-Letters to editor 07-Real estate news 08-Sports news 09-Travel news 10-Book rev. 11-Movie rev. 12-Music rev. 13-TV rev. 14-Theater rev. 15-Coming events 16-Obituaries 17-Question & answer 18-Social announcements 19-Artwork 20-Cartoons 21-Photos 22-TV listings 23-Audio rec. 24-Video rec. 25-Books 26-Films/film clips 27-Personnel news 28-Press releases 29-New product news/photos 30-Trade lit. 31-Contracts awarded 32-Display adv. 33-Classified adv.

7-13

**Owner(s):**
Remy Publishing Co.
350 W. Hubbard St., Ste. 440
Chicago, IL 60610-4011
Telephone: (312) 464-0300
Ownership %: 100
**Editorial:**
Elizabeth Hintch ...............................Editor
**Readers:** Recruiting executives.

70966

**REGIONAL ECONOMIES & MARKETS**
845 Third Ave.
New York, NY 10022
Telephone: (212) 759-0900
FAX: (212) 980-7014
Year Established: 1986
Pub. Frequency: q.
Subscrip. Rate: free members; $295/yr. non-members
Circulation: 9,000
Circulation Type: paid
**Owner(s):**
Conference Board, Inc.
845 Third Ave.
New York, NY 10022
Telephone: (212) 759-0900
FAX: (212) 980-7014
Ownership %: 100
**Desc.:** Examines trends and prospects in the nine major US regions.

70079

**RESEARCH ALERT**
488 E. 18th St.
Brooklyn, NY 11226-6702
Telephone: (718) 469-9330
FAX: (718) 469-7124
Year Established: 1981
Pub. Frequency: bi-w.
Subscrip. Rate: $345/yr. US; $405/yr. foreign
**Owner(s):**
EPM Communications
488 E. 18th St.
Brooklyn, NY 11226-6702
Telephone: (718) 469-9330
FAX: (718) 469-7124
Ownership %: 100
**Editorial:**
Ira Mayer ...................................Editor
**Desc.:** Bi-weekly report of consumer marketing studies.

70085

**RETAILING TODAY**
P.O. Box 249
Lafayette, CA 94549
Telephone: (510) 254-4434
FAX: (510) 284-5612
Year Established: 1966
Pub. Frequency: m.
Subscrip. Rate: $48/yr. US; $60/yr. foreign
Circulation: 1,200
Circulation Type: controlled & paid
**Owner(s):**
Robert Kahn & Associates
P.O. Box 249
Lafayette, CA 94549
Telephone: (510) 254-4434
FAX: (510) 284-5612
Ownership %: 100
**Editorial:**
Robert Kahn ...............................Editor
**Desc.:** For CEO'S in retailing. Commentary on current trends, with emphasis on ethical business practices.

70096

**SALES AUTOMATION SUCCESS**
2815 N.W. Pine Cone Dr., Ste. 100
Issaquah, WA 98027-8698
Telephone: (206) 392-3514
FAX: (206) 391-7982
Year Established: 1985

Pub. Frequency: 10/yr.
Subscrip. Rate: $97/yr.
Materials: 10
**Owner(s):**
Denali Group, Inc.
2815 N.W. Pine Cone Dr., Ste.
Issaquah, WA 98027-8698
Telephone: (206) 392-3514
FAX: (206) 391-7982
Ownership %: 100
**Editorial:**
Steven P. Pokin ...........................Editor
**Desc.:** Discusses how to use computer technology in direct sales to close more orders.

70985

**SALES REP'S ADVISOR**
215 Park Ave., S., Ste. 1301
New York, NY 10003
Telephone: (212) 228-0246
FAX: (212) 228-0376
Year Established: 1981
Pub. Frequency: s-m.
Subscrip. Rate: $117/yr.
Materials: 10
**Owner(s):**
Alexander Research & Communications, Inc.
215 Park Ave., S., Ste. 1301
New York, NY 10003
Telephone: (212) 228-0246
FAX: (212) 228-0376
Ownership %: 100
**Editorial:**
Laurence A. Alexander .....................Editor
**Desc.:** For independent manufacturer's representatives. Provides case studies, how-to-do-it reports, and industry news to help sales reps run their businesses more efficiently. Typical articles focus on management strategies, legal issues, working with principals, tax information, staffing and more.

70093

**SEC ACCOUNTING & REPORTING UPDATE SERVICE**
One Penn Plz.
New York, NY 10119
Telephone: (212) 971-5000
FAX: (212) 971-5240
Year Established: 1984
Pub. Frequency: 48/yr.
Subscrip. Rate: $326.50/yr. US; $427/yr. foreign
**Owner(s):**
Warren Gorham Lamont
One Penn Plz.
New York, NY 10119
Telephone: (212) 971-5000
FAX: (212) 971-5240
Ownership %: 100
**Editorial:**
Charles Maurer ...........................Editor
Allan B. Afterman ........................Editor
**Desc.:** Reports on SEC pronouncements within three weeks, including detailed analysis and practical examples.

70098

**SEC ACCOUNTING REPORT**
One Penn Plz.
New York, NY 10119
Telephone: (212) 971-5000
FAX: (212) 971-5240
Year Established: 1974
Pub. Frequency: m.
Subscrip. Rate: $214.75/yr. US; $284/yr. foreign
**Owner(s):**
Warren Gorham Lamont
One Penn Plz.
New York, NY 10119
Telephone: (212) 971-5000
FAX: (212) 971-5240
Ownership %: 100

**Editorial:**
Paul J. Wendell ...........................Editor
**Desc.:** Covers SEC, FASB, and related financial reporting matters. Offers up-to-date information on new SEC developments and federal regulations.

70988

**SELF-EMPLOYMENT UPDATE**
P.O. Box 416
Denver, CO 80201-0416
Telephone: (303) 575-5676
Year Established: 1983
Pub. Frequency: a.
Circulation: 1,500
Circulation Type: controlled & paid
**Owner(s):**
Prosperity & Profits Unlimited
P.O. Box 416
Denver, CO 80201-0416
Telephone: (303) 575-5676
Ownership %: 100
**Editorial:**
A. Doyle ...................................Editor

70637

**SERVICE EDGE**
50 S. Ninth St.
Minneapolis, MN 55402
Telephone: (612) 333-0471
FAX: (612) 333-6526
Year Established: 1988
Pub. Frequency: m.
Page Size: standard
Subscrip. Rate: $98/yr. US; $108/yr. Canada; $118/yr. elsewhere
**Owner(s):**
Lakewood Publishing
50 S. Ninth St.
Minneapolis, MN 55402
Telephone: (612) 333-0471
FAX: (612) 333-6526
Ownership %: 100
**Management:**
Stella Dean ............Customer Service Manager
**Editorial:**
Brian McDermott .........................Editor
**Desc.:** Provides practical ideas and information about implementing a service strategy that can result in better customer service and improved profits.

70118

**SHOPPING CENTER NEWSLETTER**
121 Chanlon Rd.
New Providence, NJ 07974
Telephone: (800) 521-8110
FAX: (908) 665-6688
Mailing Address:
    Order Dept.
    P.O. Box 31
    New Providence, NJ 07974
Year Established: 1959
Pub. Frequency: m.
Subscrip. Rate: $49.15/yr.
**Owner(s):**
R.R. Bowker
121 Chanlon Rd.
New Providence, NJ 07974
Telephone: (800) 521-8110
FAX: (908) 665-6688
Ownership %: 100
**Editorial:**
Teresa Levinson .........................Editor

70100

**SIEDLECKI ON BUSINESS**
2996 Grandview Ave.
Ste. 305
Atlanta, GA 30305
Telephone: (404) 816-4040
Year Established: 1990
Pub. Frequency: 10/yr.
Subscrip. Rate: $29/yr.
Materials: 10
Circulation: 1,000

Circulation Type: controlled & paid
**Owner(s):**
Seidlecki Marketing & Management
2996 Grandview Ave.
Ste. 305
Atlanta, GA 30305
Telephone: (404) 816-4040
Ownership %: 100
**Editorial:**
R. Seidlecki ...............................Editor
**Desc.:** Covers ideas, tips, and techniques for more successful marketing and business development.

70732

**TELECOMMUTING REVIEW; THE GORDON REPORT**
10 Donner Ct.
Monmouth Junction, NJ 08852
Telephone: (908) 329-2266
Year Established: 1984
Pub. Frequency: m.
Subscrip. Rate: $157/yr. US; $177/yr. foreign
Materials: 10
**Owner(s):**
Gill Gordon Associates
10 Donner Ct.
Monmouth Junction, NJ 08852
Telephone: (908) 329-2266
Ownership %: 100
**Editorial:**
Gil Gordon ...............................Editor
**Desc.:** Features case studies, legal, supervisory and technical issues; telecommuting (work-at-home) programs sponsored by employers.

70151

**TELEMARKETING UPDATE**
P.O. Box 416
Denver, CO 80201-0416
Telephone: (303) 575-5676
Year Established: 1985
Pub. Frequency: m.
Subscrip. Rate: $200/yr.
Circulation: 5,000
Circulation Type: controlled & paid
**Owner(s):**
Prosperity & Profits Unlimited
P.O. Box 416
Denver, CO 80201-0416
Telephone: (303) 575-5676
Ownership %: 100
**Editorial:**
A. Doyle ...................................Editor
**Desc.:** Provides ideas on telemarketing, scripts and how to.

70120

**THRIFT ACCOUNTANT**
One State St. Plz.
New York, NY 10040-1549
Telephone: (800) 733-4371
FAX: (212) 943-2224
Pub. Frequency: w.
Subscrip. Rate: $465/yr. new subscribers; $675/yr. renewal
**Owner(s):**
Thomson Financial Services Co.
One State St. Plz.
New York, NY 10004-1549
Telephone: (800) 733-4371
FAX: (212) 943-2224
Ownership %: 100
**Editorial:**
Dave Postal ...............................Editor
**Desc.:** Analyses and interpretations and regulatory changes, new examination standards, market value disclosure notations and other developments affecting accounting for thrift institutions.

## TODAY'S HOSPITAL GIFT SHOP BUSINESS
71215

P.O. Box 8204
Asheville, NC 28814
Telephone: (704) 258-1322
FAX: (704) 253-3726
Year Established: 1978
Pub. Frequency: q.
Circulation: 8,000
Circulation Type: controlled
**Owner(s):**
Mason & Associates
P.O. Box 8204
Asheville, NC 28814
Telephone: (704) 258-1322
FAX: (704) 253-3726
Ownership %: 100
**Editorial:**
Marilyn Mason ...........................................Editor
**Readers:** For persons involved with hospital gift shops.

## TOTAL QUALITY NEWSLETTER
70638

50 S. Ninth St.
Minneapolis, MN 55402
Telephone: (612) 333-0471
FAX: (612) 333-6526
Year Established: 1990
Pub. Frequency: m.
Subscrip. Rate: $128/yr. US; $138/yr. Canada; $148/yr. elsewhere
**Owner(s):**
Lakewood Publications
50 S. Ninth St.
Minneapolis, MN 55402
Telephone: (612) 333-0471
FAX: (612) 333-6526
Ownership %: 100

## TRAINING & DEVELOPMENT ALERT
71035

801 Riverside Ave.
Roseville, CA 95678
Telephone: (916) 781-2900
FAX: (916) 781-2901
Mailing Address:
   P.O. Box 1438
   Roseville, CA 95678
Year Established: 1979
Pub. Frequency: bi-m.
Subscrip. Rate: $95/yr.
Materials: 10
Circulation: 1,000
Circulation Type: controlled & paid
**Owner(s):**
Advanced Personnel Systems
801 Riverside Ave.
Roseville, CA 95678
Telephone: (916) 781-2900
FAX: (916) 781-2901
Ownership %: 100
**Editorial:**
Richard B. Frantzreb ...........................Editor
**Desc.:** Consists of 180-200 abstracts (200-300 words) of articles on training and development from over 225 professional journals, as well as new books.

## TYNDALL REPORT, THE
65334

135 Rivington St.
New York, NY 10002
Telephone: (212) 674-8913
FAX: (212) 979-7304
Year Established: 1988
Pub. Frequency: bi-m.
Page Size: standard
Subscrip. Rate: $60/yr.; $260/yr. newsletter & fax
Circulation: 500
Circulation Type: paid

**Owner(s):**
ADT Research
135 Rivington St.
New York, NY 10002
Telephone: (212) 674-8913
Ownership %: 100
**Management:**
Andrew Tyndall ....................Publisher
**Editorial:**
Bruno Pajaczkowski .................Editor
**Desc.:** Analyzes top news stories, along with features, tracking data, and commentary. Information is gathered from monitoring of the three television network nightly newscasts (ABC,CBS, NBC). Summary of each week's news available each Saturday on the Tyndall Weekly Faxsheet.
**Readers:** The news media, public relations and press officers, newsmakers, news analysists.

## TYPELINE
70642

20 Railroad Ave.
Hackensack, NJ 07601
Telephone: (201) 488-0404
FAX: (201) 488-0461
Year Established: 1980
Pub. Frequency: m.
Subscrip. Rate: $345/yr.
**Owner(s):**
Buyers Laboratory, Inc.
20 Railroad Ave.
Hackensack, NJ 07601
Telephone: (201) 488-0404
FAX: (201) 488-0461
Ownership %: 100
**Editorial:**
Kathleen Dwyer ...........................Editor
**Desc.:** Provides news and analysis of dot-matrix, ink-jet, laser and LED- array printers; word processors and typewriters. Reports on new products, new technology, market trends and options for each product category.

## UPDATE: THE EXECUTIVE'S PURCHASING ADVISOR
70654

20 Railroad Ave.
Hackensack, NJ 07601
Telephone: (201) 488-0404
FAX: (201) 488-0461
Pub. Frequency: m.
Subscrip. Rate: $95/yr.
Circulation: 2,200
Circulation Type: controlled & paid
**Owner(s):**
Buyers Laboratory, Inc.
20 Railroad Ave.
Hackensack, NJ 07601
Telephone: (201) 488-0404
FAX: (201) 488-0461
Ownership %: 100
**Editorial:**
Daria Hoffman ...........................Editor
**Desc.:** offers advice on purchasing and using office equipment, supplies and office services.

## VOICE OF 1319
70854

69 Public Sq., Rm. 1217
Wilkes Barre, PA 18701
Telephone: (717) 823-2078
FAX: (717) 824-9025
Pub. Frequency: m.
Page Size: standard
Subscrip. Rate: free
Circulation: 800
Circulation Type: free

**Owner(s):**
Local 1319
69 Public Sq., Rm. 1217
Pittsburgh, PA 18701
Telephone: (717) 823-2078
Ownership %: 100
**Management:**
David Blauer ......................President
Henry Stanski .............Business Manager

## WASHINGTON TARIFF & TRADE LETTER
70607

P.O. Box 467
Washington, DC 20044
Telephone: (301) 570-4544
FAX: (301) 570-4545
Year Established: 1981
Pub. Frequency: w.
Subscrip. Rate: $447/yr. US; $477/yr. foreign
**Owner(s):**
Gilston Communications Group
P.O. Box 467
Washington, DC 20044
Telephone: (301) 570-4544
FAX: (301) 570-4545
Ownership %: 100
**Editorial:**
Samuel M. Gilston ......................Editor

## WENDELL'S REPORT FOR CONTROLLERS
70119

One Penn Plz.
New York, NY 10119
Telephone: (800) 950-1217
Year Established: 1979
Pub. Frequency: m.
Subscrip. Rate: $126.50/yr. US; $183.90/yr. foreign
**Owner(s):**
Warren Gorham Lamont
One Penn Plz.
New York, NY 10119
Telephone: (800) 950-1217
Ownership %: 100
**Desc.:** Focuses exclusively on all areas of crucial interest to chief financial officers, from taxes and legal developments to operations and compensation, giving quick access to the latest ideas and methods.

## WHAT'S AHEAD IN HUMAN RESOURCES
70681

350 W. Hubbard St., No. 440
Chicago, IL 60610-4011
Telephone: (312) 464-0300
Year Established: 1973
Pub. Frequency: s-m.
Subscrip. Rate: $145/yr.
Materials: 10
**Owner(s):**
Remy Publishing Co.
350 W. Hubbard St., No. 440
Chicago, IL 60610-4011
Telephone: (312) 464-0300
Ownership %: 100
**Editorial:**
John Hickey ...........................Editor

## WHO'S MAILING WHAT
70102

401 N. Broad St.
Philadelphia, PA 19108
Telephone: (215) 238-5300
FAX: (215) 238-5270
Year Established: 1984
Pub. Frequency: m.
Subscrip. Rate: $195/yr.
Circulation: 40,000
Circulation Type: controlled & paid

**Owner(s):**
North American Publishing Co.
401 N. Broad St.
Philadelphia, PA 19108
Telephone: (215) 238-5300
FAX: (215) 238-5270
Ownership %: 100
**Editorial:**
Denison Hatch ...........................Editor

## WORK-FAMILY ROUNDTABLE
70684

845 Third Ave.
New York, NY 10022
Telephone: (212) 759-0900
FAX: (212) 980-7014
Year Established: 1991
Pub. Frequency: q.
Subscrip. Rate: $150/yr. non-members
**Owner(s):**
Conference Board, Inc.
845 Third Ave.
New York, NY 10022
Telephone: (212) 759-0900
FAX: (212) 980-7014
Ownership %: 100
**Desc.:** Provides information on how businesses are implementing work-family programs.

## WORLD ARBITRATION & MEDIATION REPORT
70610

One Bridge St.
Irvington-On-Hudson, NY 10533
Telephone: (914) 591-4288
FAX: (914) 591-2688
Year Established: 1990
Pub. Frequency: m.
Subscrip. Rate: $455/yr.
**Owner(s):**
Transnational Juris Publications, Inc.
One Bridge St.
Irvington-On-Hudson, NY 10533
Telephone: (914) 591-4288
FAX: (914) 591-2688
Ownership %: 100
**Editorial:**
S. Gale Dick ...........................Editor
**Desc.:** Covers arbitration and other alternatives to litigation in international commercial disputes.

## YOUTH MARKETS ALERT
70105

488 E. 18th St.
Brooklyn, NY 11226-6702
Telephone: (718) 469-9330
FAX: (718) 469-7124
Year Established: 1989
Pub. Frequency: m.
Subscrip. Rate: $235/yr.
**Owner(s):**
EPM Communications
488 E. 18th St.
New York, NY 11226-6702
Telephone: (718) 469-9330
FAX: (718) 469-7124
Ownership %: 100
**Editorial:**
Mary Porter ...........................Editor
**Desc.:** Covers all the latest research on youth markets.

## Group 312-Buildings & Furnishings

## BOCA BULLETIN
70052

4051 W. Flossmor Rd.
Country Club Hills, IL 60478-5795
Telephone: (708) 799-2300
Year Established: 1950
Pub. Frequency: bi-m.
Subscrip. Rate: membership
Circulation: 12,000
Circulation Type: controlled & paid

---

Materials Accepted/Included: 01-Business news 02-By-line articles 03-Fashion news 04-Food news 05-Freelance copy 06-Letters to editor 07-Real estate news 08-Sports news 09-Travel news 10-Book rev. 11-Movie rev. 12-Music rev. 13-TV rev. 14-Theater rev. 15-Coming events 16-Obituaries 17-Question & answer 18-Social announcements 19-Artwork 20-Cartoons 21-Photos 22-TV listings 23-Audio rec. 24-Video rec. 25-Books 26-Films/film clips 27-Personnel news 28-Press releases 29-New product news/photos 30-Trade lit. 31-Contracts awarded 32-Display adv. 33-Classified adv.

**Owner(s):**
Building Officials & Code Administrators
Interntl.
4051 W. Flossmor Rd.
Country Club Hills, IL 60478-5795
Telephone: (708) 799-2300
Ownership %: 100

69894

## BOSTON SOCIETY OF ARCHITECTS CHAPTERLETTER
152 Broad St.
Boston, MA 02109-4301
Telephone: (617) 951-1433
FAX: (617) 951-0845
Year Established: 1914
Pub. Frequency: m.
Subscrip. Rate: $45/yr.
Materials: 32
Circulation: 5,000
Circulation Type: controlled & paid
**Owner(s):**
Boston Society of Architects
152 Broad St.
Boston, MA 02109-4301
Telephone: (617) 951-1433
FAX: (617) 951-0845
Ownership %: 100
**Editorial:**
Richard Fitzgerald .............................Editor

70065

## BUILDING & CONSTRUCTION MARKET FORECAST
275 Washington St.
Newton, MA 02158-1630
Telephone: (617) 630-2124
FAX: (617) 630-2100
Year Established: 1983
Pub. Frequency: m.
Subscrip. Rate: $197/yr. US; $219/yr.
  foreign
Circulation: 80,000
Circulation Type: controlled & paid
**Owner(s):**
Cahners Publishing Co.
Div. of Reed Elsevier Inc.
275 Washington St.
Newton, MA 02158-1630
Telephone: (617) 630-2124
FAX: (617) 630-2100
Ownership %: 100
**Editorial:**
Kermit Baker ....................................Editor
Daryl Delano ....................................Editor

69889

## COMPETITIONS
P.O. Box 20445
Louisville, KY 40250
Telephone: (502) 451-3623
Year Established: 1991
Pub. Frequency: q.
Subscrip. Rate: $28/yr.
Circulation: 1,200
Circulation Type: controlled & paid
**Owner(s):**
Competitions
P.O. Box 20445
Louisville, KY 40250
Telephone: (502) 451-3623
Ownership %: 100
**Editorial:**
G. Stanley Collyer ..........................Editor
**Desc.:** Provides information on
  competitions for participants.
**Readers:** Artists, planners, and architects.

70059

## CONSTRUCTION CONTRACTOR
1120 20th St., N.W., Ste. 500 S.
Washington, DC 20036
Telephone: (202) 377-7000
FAX: (202) 659-2233
Pub. Frequency: bi-w.
Subscrip. Rate: $580/yr.

**Owner(s):**
Federal Publications, Inc.
1120 20th St., N.W., Ste. 500
Washington, DC 20036
Telephone: (202) 377-7000
FAX: (202) 659-2233
Ownership %: 100
**Editorial:**
Richard L. Shea ..............................Editor
**Desc.:** Contains news and analysis of
  construction contract developments and
  cases.

70078

## CONSTRUCTION LAW ADVISER
155 Pfingsten Rd.
Deerfield, IL 60015
Telephone: (800) 323-1336
FAX: (708) 948-9340
Year Established: 1983
Pub. Frequency: m.
Subscrip. Rate: $275/yr.
**Owner(s):**
Callaghan & Co.
155 Pfingsten Rd.
Deerfield, IL 60015
Telephone: (800) 323-1336
FAX: (708) 948-9340
Ownership %: 100
**Editorial:**
C. Allen Foster ...............................Editor
John A. Ramsey ..............................Editor
**Desc.:** Monthly practical advice for lawyers
  and construction professionals.

70084

## CONSTRUCTION LITIGATION REPORTER
P.O. Box 35300
Colorado Springs, CO 80935-3530
Telephone: (719) 475-7230
Year Established: 1979
Pub. Frequency: m.
Subscrip. Rate: $310/yr.
**Owner(s):**
Shepard's McGraw-Hill, Inc.
P.O. Box 35300
Colorado Springs, CO 80935-3530
Telephone: (719) 475-7230
Ownership %: 100
**Editorial:**
Mark Schneier .................................Editor
**Desc.:** Legal developments and summaries
  of cases affecting construction law.

70094

## ENERGY DESIGN UPDATE
37 Broadway
Arlington, MA 02174
Telephone: (617) 648-8700
FAX: (617) 648-8707
Year Established: 1982
Pub. Frequency: m.
Subscrip. Rate: $297/yr. US; $347/yr.
  foreign
**Owner(s):**
Cutter Information Corp.
37 Broadway
Arlington, MA 02174
Telephone: (617) 648-8700
FAX: (617) 648-8707
Ownership %: 100
**Editorial:**
J.D. Ned Nisson ..............................Editor
**Desc.:** Covers new products, research and
  techniques for building energy-efficient,
  high-quality and healthful houses.
  Includes discussion of mechanical
  systems, major appliances and an
  objective look at products' promotional
  claims.

70097

## ENVIRONMENTAL BUILDING NEWS
RR 1, Box 161
Brattleboro, VT 05301-0161
Telephone: (802) 257-7300
FAX: (802) 257-7304
Year Established: 1992
Pub. Frequency: 6/yr.
Subscrip. Rate: $60/yr. individuals; $95/yr.
  institutions
Materials: 10
Circulation: 1,400
Circulation Type: controlled & paid
**Owner(s):**
Alex Wilson
RR 1, Box 161
Brattleboro, VT 05301-0161
Telephone: (802) 257-7300
FAX: (802) 257-7304
Ownership %: 100
**Management:**
Alex Wilson ...............................Publisher
**Editorial:**
Alex Wilson ...................................Editor
**Desc.:** A newsletter on environmentally
  sustainable design and construction.
  Environmental news, product reviews,
  issues and concerns for professional
  architects, builders and policy-makers.

69895

## GUIDELINES LETTER
P.O. Box 456
Orinda, CA 94563
Telephone: (415) 254-9393
FAX: (510) 254-9397
Year Established: 1972
Pub. Frequency: m.
Page Size: standard
Subscrip. Rate: $56/yr.
Materials: 10
Circulation: 3,000
Circulation Type: controlled
**Owner(s):**
Guidelines
P.O. Box 456
Orinda, CA 94563
Telephone: (415) 254-9393
FAX: (415) 254-9397
Ownership %: 100
**Editorial:**
Fred Stitt ........................................Editor
**Desc.:** Focuses on the needs of small
  office practice for the design
  professions.

70346

## HEALTHY HOME & WORKPLACE
248 Lafayette St.
New York, NY 10012
Telephone: (212) 226-5152
Year Established: 1991
Pub. Frequency: q.
Subscrip. Rate: $12/yr.
Circulation: 1,000
Circulation Type: controlled & paid
**Owner(s):**
Healthy Home & Workplace
248 Lafayette St.
New York, NY 10012
Telephone: (212) 226-5152
Ownership %: 100
**Editorial:**
Mimi Weisbord ...............................Editor
**Desc.:** Provides a guide to non-toxic living.
  Cautions about products and common
  workplace situations detrimental to
  health.

70842

## HOUSING MARKET REPORT
8204 Fenton St.
Silver Spring, MD 20910-2889
Telephone: (301) 588-6380
FAX: (301) 588-6385
Year Established: 1976

Pub. Frequency: s-m.
Subscrip. Rate: $289/yr.
**Owner(s):**
Community Development Services, Inc.
8204 Fenton St.
Silver Spring, MD 20910-2889
Telephone: (301) 588-6380
FAX: (301) 588-6385
Ownership %: 100
**Editorial:**
Joe Poduska ...................................Editor
**Desc.:** Focuses on national and regional
  markets. Includes monthly forecasts of
  starts, interest rates, and other key
  indicators.

69899

## INDOOR AIR QUALITY UPDATE
37 Broadway
Arlington, MA 02174
Telephone: (617) 648-8700
FAX: (617) 648-8707
Year Established: 1988
Pub. Frequency: m.
Subscrip. Rate: $287/yr. US; $357/yr.
  foreign
**Owner(s):**
Cutter Information Corp.
37 Broadway
Arlington, MA 02174
Telephone: (617) 648-8700
FAX: (617) 648-8707
Ownership %: 100
**Editorial:**
Carlton Vogt ...................................Editor
**Desc.:** Covers current research, case
  studies, trends, and news in the field of
  indoor air quality (IAQ). Includes
  resource reviews, information exchange,
  industry events, and feature articles.

70870

## ISLAND PROPERTIES REPORT
P.O. Box 1596
Bonita Springs, FL 33959
Telephone: (813) 495-1604
FAX: (813) 495-1738
Year Established: 1983
Pub. Frequency: m.
Subscrip. Rate: $44/yr.
Materials: 10
Circulation: 10,210
Circulation Type: controlled & paid
**Owner(s):**
Island Properties Report
P.O. Box 1596
Bonita Springs, FL 33959
Telephone: (813) 495-1604
FAX: (813) 495-1738
Ownership %: 100
**Editorial:**
Joan Kelly-Plate ............................Editor
**Desc.:** Reports on Caribbean Island
  economy, politics, taxes and purchase
  regulations. Also lists properties for sale.

70858

## MANAGING HOUSING LETTER
8204 Fenton St.
Silver Spring, MD 20910-2889
Telephone: (301) 588-6380
FAX: (301) 588-6385
Year Established: 1978
Pub. Frequency: m.
Subscrip. Rate: $127/yr.
**Owner(s):**
CD Publications
8204 Fenton St.
Silver Spring, MD 20910-2889
Telephone: (301) 588-6380
Ownership %: 100
**Editorial:**
James Kelder ..................................Editor
**Desc.:** News and advice for owners and
  managers of public, private and
  subsidized rental housing.

---

**Materials Accepted/Included:** 01-Business news 02-By-line articles 03-Fashion news 04-Food news 05-Freelance copy 06-Letters to editor 07-Real estate news 08-Sports news 09-Travel news 10-Book rev. 11-Movie rev. 12-Music rev. 13-TV rev. 14-Theater rev. 15-Coming events 16-Obituaries 17-Question & answer 18-Social announcements 19-Artwork 20-Cartoons 21-Photos 22-TV listings 23-Audio rec. 24-Video rec. 25-Books 26-Films/film clips 27-Personnel news 28-Press releases 29-New product news/photos 30-Trade lit. 31-Contracts awarded 32-Display adv. 33-Classified adv.

**MATRIX** 70099
P.O. Box 3731
Washington, DC 20007
Telephone: (202) 333-8190
FAX: (202) 337-3809
Year Established: 1992
Pub. Frequency: 24/yr.
Subscrip. Rate: $95/yr.
Materials: 10
Circulation: 500
Circulation Type: controlled & paid
**Owner(s):**
Robert N. Pyle & Associates
P.O. Box 3731
Washington, DC 20007
Telephone: (202) 333-8190
FAX: (202) 337-3809
Ownership %: 100
**Editorial:**
Nicholas A. Pyle ..........................................Editor
**Desc.:** Industry news report for the
integrated building system control and
automation professional. Provides timely
reports of new products, legislative
and regulatory issues, industry
standards, activities and
announcements, with analysis of trends
affecting the intelligent building and
home automation field.

**MR. LANDLORD** 70872
P.O. Box 1366
Norfolk, VA 23501
Telephone: (804) 495-5809
FAX: (804) 467-1427
Year Established: 1985
Pub. Frequency: m.
Subscrip. Rate: $59/yr.
Materials: 32
Circulation: 15,000
Circulation Type: controlled & paid
**Owner(s):**
Home Rental Publishing
P.O. Box 1366
Norfolk, VA 23501
Telephone: (804) 495-5809
FAX: (804) 467-1427
Ownership %: 100
**Editorial:**
Jeffrey E. Taylor .........................................Editor
**Desc.:** Survival newsletter for landlords
and landladies. Aims to help landlords to
attain and maintain maximum cashflow,
control and gain cooperation from
tenants, and to serve as a forum for
rental owners to share ideas and
concerns.

**PRESERVATION PERSPECTIVE** 69901
170 Township Line Rd.
Belle Mead, NJ 08502
Year Established: 1981
Pub. Frequency: m.
Subscrip. Rate: $20/yr. individuals; $35/yr.
institutions; $10/yr. students
Materials: 10,32
Circulation: 3,000
Circulation Type: controlled
**Owner(s):**
Preservation New Jersey, Inc.
170 Township Line Rd.
Belle Mead, NJ 08502
Telephone: (908) 359-4557
FAX: (908) 874-6044
Ownership %: 100
**Desc.:** Covers architecture and historic
preservation in New Jersey.

**RANDOM LENGTHS** 68850
450 Country Club Rd.
Eugene, OR 97401
Telephone: (503) 686-9925
FAX: (503) 874-7979

Mailing Address:
P.O. Box 867
Eugene, OR 97440-0867
Year Established: 1944
Pub. Frequency: w.
Subscrip. Rate: $193.50/yr.
Materials: 01,28
Circulation: 13,000
Circulation Type: paid
**Owner(s):**
Random Lengths Publications, Inc.
P.O. Box 867
Eugene, OR 97440-0867
Telephone: (503) 686-9925
Ownership %: 100
**Management:**
Jon P. Anderson ................................Publisher
**Editorial:**
Burrle Elmore ...........................................Editor

**RANDOM LENGTHS EXPORT** 70271
450 Country Club Rd.
Eugene, OR 97440-0867
Telephone: (503) 686-9925
FAX: (800) 874-7979
Mailing Address:
P.O. Box 867
Eugene, OR 97440
Year Established: 1968
Pub. Frequency: fortn.
Subscrip. Rate: $98.50/yr. US; $125/yr.
foreign
Circulation: 1,450
Circulation Type: controlled & paid
**Owner(s):**
Random Lengths Publications, Inc.
P.O. Box 867
Eugene, OR 97440-0867
Telephone: (503) 686-9925
FAX: (800) 874-7979
Ownership %: 100
**Editorial:**
Jessie Taylor ...........................................Editor
**Desc.:** Prices and market summaries
covering North American lumber and
panel items sold in international
markets.

**REAL ESTATE INSIDER** 65758
1541 Morris Ave.
Bronx, NY 10457-8702
Telephone: (718) 583-8060
FAX: (718) 583-8258
Year Established: 1968
Pub. Frequency: bi-w.
Page Size: standard
Subscrip. Rate: $225/yr.
Materials: 10
Circulation: 1,000
Circulation Type: controlled & paid
**Owner(s):**
Walker Communications, Inc.
1541 Morris Ave.
Bronx, NY 10457-8702
Telephone: (718) 583-8060
Ownership %: 100
**Editorial:**
Suzie Mitchell ...........................................Editor
**Desc.:** Business newsletter for owners,
managers and real estate firms of
residential and commercial real estate.
**Readers:** Real estate brokers.

**REAL ESTATE NEWSLETTER** 70881
121 Chanlon Rd.
New Providence, NJ 07974
Telephone: (800) 521-8110
FAX: (908) 665-6688
Pub. Frequency: m.
Subscrip. Rate: $51.55/yr.

**Owner(s):**
Reed Reference Publishing Co.
121 Chanlon Rd.
New Providence, NJ 07974
Telephone: (800) 521-8110
FAX: (908) 665-6688
Ownership %: 100
**Editorial:**
Barbara Boeding ......................................Editor
**Desc.:** Real estate news and trends for
realtors, developers, title companies and
finanacial personnel.

**SOCIETY OF ARCHITECTURAL** 69903
**HISTORIANS NEWSLETTER**
1232 Pine St.
Philadelphia, PA 19107-5944
Year Established: 1957
Pub. Frequency: 6/yr.
Subscrip. Rate: membership
Materials: 32
Circulation: 4,000
Circulation Type: controlled & paid
**Owner(s):**
Society of Architectural Historians
1232 Pine St.
Philadelphia, PA 19107-5944
Ownership %: 100
**Editorial:**
Marjorie Pearson ......................................Editor

**WOOD DESIGN FOCUS** 70251
4033 S.W. Canyon Rd.
Portland, OR 97221
Telephone: (503) 228-0819
FAX: (503) 228-3624
Year Established: 1989
Pub. Frequency: q.
Subscrip. Rate: $25/yr.
Materials: 10,32
**Owner(s):**
Wood Information Center
4033 S.W. Canyon Rd.
Portland, OR 97221
Telephone: (503) 228-0819
FAX: (503) 228-3624
Ownership %: 100
**Editorial:**
Robert Leichti ...........................................Editor
**Desc.:** Covers the design and application
of solid timber and structural wood
engineered products.

**YOUR HOME** 70861
1820 W. 48th St.
Cleveland, OH 44102
Telephone: (216) 281-4663
FAX: (216) 651-0914
Year Established: 1987
Pub. Frequency: m.
Subscrip. Rate: $15/yr.
Materials: 10
Circulation: 4,500
Circulation Type: controlled & paid
**Owner(s):**
Housing Resource Center
1820 W. 48th St.
Cleveland, OH 44102
Telephone: (216) 281-4663
FAX: (216) 651-0914
Ownership %: 100
**Desc.:** Features home improvement
information.

## Group 314-Children & Youth

**ALATEEN TALK** 70070
1372 Broadway, 7th Fl.
New York, NY 10018-6106
Telephone: (212) 302-7240
FAX: (212) 869-7240

Mailing Address:
P.O. Box 862, Midtown Sta.
New York, NY 10018-0862
Year Established: 1965
Pub. Frequency: q.
Subscrip. Rate: $2.50/yr.
Circulation: 9,000
Circulation Type: controlled & paid
**Owner(s):**
AFG, Inc.
1372 Broadway, 7th Fl.
New York, NY 10018-6106
Telephone: (212) 302-7240
FAX: (212) 869-3757
Ownership %: 100
**Desc.:** Alateen members, young people
whose lives have been affected by
someone else's drinking, share their
experiences through articles of interest
to teenagers and professionals working
with adolescents.

**AMERICAN NEWSPAPER CARRIER** 24156
P.O. Box 2225
Kernersville, NC 27285
Telephone: (919) 788-4336
Year Established: 1927
Pub. Frequency: m.
Subscrip. Rate: varies
Circulation: 35,000
Circulation Type: controlled
**Owner(s):**
W.H. Lowry
P.O. Box 2225
Kernersville, NC 27285
Telephone: (919) 725-3400
Ownership %: 100
**Management:**
W.H. Lowry .........................................Publisher
**Editorial:**
W.H. Lowry .............................................Editor
**Desc.:** Contains light fiction and upbeat,
inspirational articles about newspaper
carriers which would be of interest to
teenagers and adults.
**Readers:** Newspaper carriers.

**CHILD PROTECTION REPORT** 70086
951 Pershing Dr.
Silver Spring, MD 20910-4432
Telephone: (301) 587-6300
FAX: (301) 585-9075
Year Established: 1975
Pub. Frequency: bi-w.
Subscrip. Rate: $189.54/yr.
Materials: 10
**Owner(s):**
Business Publishers, Inc.
951 Pershing Dr.
Silver Spring, MD 20910-4432
Telephone: (301) 587-6300
FAX: (301) 585-9075
Ownership %: 100
**Editorial:**
Linda Roeder .............................................Editor
**Desc.:** Advice and funding information for
managers of child-assistance programs.

**CHILDWORLD** 70091
P.O. Box 85066
Richmond, VA 23286-8912
Telephone: (800) 776-6767
FAX: (804) 756-2718
Year Established: 1976
Pub. Frequency: q.
Subscrip. Rate: free
Circulation: 300,000
Circulation Type: controlled & paid

**Materials Accepted/Included:** 01-Business news 02-By-line articles 03-Fashion news 04-Food news 05-Freelance copy 06-Letters to editor 07-Real estate news 08-Sports news 09-Travel news 10-Book rev. 11-Movie rev. 12-Music rev. 13-TV rev. 14-Theater rev. 15-Coming events 16-Obituaries 17-Question & answer 18-Social announcements 19-Artwork 20-Cartoons 21-Photos 22-TV listings 23-Audio rec. 24-Video rec. 25-Books 26-Cartoons/film clips 27-Personnel news 28-Press releases 29-New product news/photos 30-Trade lit. 31-Contracts awarded 32-Display adv. 33-Classified adv.

7-17

**Owner(s):**
Christian Children's Fund, Inc.
P.O. Box 85066
Richmond, VA 23286-8912
Telephone: (800) 776-6767
FAX: (804) 756-2718
Ownership %: 100
**Editorial:**
Cheri Whitlock Dahl ....................................Editor

70073
## KIDS RHYME NEWSLETTER
P.O. Box 416
Denver, CO 80201-0416
Telephone: (303) 575-5676
Year Established: 1991
Pub. Frequency: a.
Subscrip. Rate: $6/yr.
Circulation: 10,000
Circulation Type: controlled & paid
**Owner(s):**
Prosperity & Profits Unlimited
P.O. Box 416
Denver, CO 80201-0416
Telephone: (303) 575-5676
Ownership %: 100
**Editorial:**
A.E. Doyle ....................................................Editor

70088
## PARENT & PRESCHOOLER NEWSLETTER
P.O. Box 1851
Garden City, NY 11530
Telephone: (516) 742-9557
FAX: (516) 742-5007
Year Established: 1986
Pub. Frequency: m.
Subscrip. Rate: $27/yr. US; $37/yr.
   bilingual edition
Materials: 10
Circulation: 3,000
Circulation Type: controlled & paid
**Owner(s):**
Preschool Publications, Inc.
P.O. Box 1851
Garden City, NY 11530
Telephone: (516) 742-9557
FAX: (516) 742-5007
Ownership %: 100
**Editorial:**
Betty Farber ...................................................Editor
**Desc.:** Each issue presents a child
   development theme, along with
   activities, recipes, and books for children
   and parents.

70089
## SPECTRUM NEWSLETTER
60 Academy Rd.
Albany, NY 11203-3198
Telephone: (518) 426-2600
Year Established: 1979
Pub. Frequency: q.
Subscrip. Rate: free
Circulation: 25,000
Circulation Type: controlled & paid
**Owner(s):**
Parsons Child and Family Center
60 Academy Rd.
Albany, NY 11203-3198
Telephone: (518) 426-2600
Ownership %: 100
**Editorial:**
B.A. Unser ....................................................Editor

70076
## STORY RHYME NEWSLETTER FOR SCHOOLS
P.O. Box 416
Denver, CO 80201-0416
Telephone: (303) 575-5676
Year Established: 1992
Pub. Frequency: 10/yr.
Subscrip. Rate: $2/yr. US; $3/yr. Canada;
   4/yr. elsewhere

**Owner(s):**
Properity & Profits Unlimited
P.O. Box 416
Denver, CO 80201-0416
Telephone: (303) 575-5676
Ownership %: 100

70080
## STORY TIME STORIES THAT RYHME NEWSLETTER
P.O. Box 416
Denver, CO 80201-0416
Telephone: (303) 575-5676
Year Established: 1990
Pub. Frequency: q.
Subscrip. Rate: $20/yr.
**Owner(s):**
Prosperity & Profits Unlimited
P.O. Box 416
Denver, CO 80201-0416
Telephone: (303) 575-5676
Ownership %: 100
**Editorial:**
A. Doyle ........................................................Editor

70090
## TOTLINE NEWSLETTER
P.O. Box 2250
Everett, WA 98203
Telephone: (206) 353-3100
FAX: (206) 355-7007
Year Established: 1979
Pub. Frequency: bi-m.
Subscrip. Rate: $24/yr.
Materials: 10
Circulation: 9,000
Circulation Type: controlled & paid
**Owner(s):**
Warren Publishing House, Inc.
P.O. Box 2250
Everett, WA 98203
Telephone: (206) 353-3100
FAX: (206) 355-7007
Ownership %: 100
**Editorial:**
Susan Hodges ...............................................Editor
**Desc.:** Provides parents and teachers with
   activities and songs for children three to
   five years old.

70082
## TZIVOS HASHEM CHILDREN'S NEWSLETTER
332 Kingston Ave.
Brooklyn, NY 11213
Telephone: (718) 467-6630
FAX: (718) 467-8527
Year Established: 1981
Pub. Frequency: 5/yr.
Subscrip. Rate: $3/yr. non-members
Materials: 10
Circulation: 130,000
Circulation Type: controlled & paid
**Owner(s):**
Tzivos ha-Shem
332 Kingston Ave.
Brooklyn, NY 11213
Telephone: (718) 467-6630
FAX: (718) 467-8527
Ownership %: 100
**Editorial:**
David S. Pape ...............................................Editor

**Desc.:** Contains stories, contests and
   activities that teach about Jewish
   holidays and good behavior. Children
   submit pictures of themselves and write
   about their interests and family.

# Group 316-Communications & Media

70167
## ADVANCED WIRELESS COMMUNICATIONS
1101 King St., Ste. 444
Alexandria, VA 22313-2055
Telephone: (800) 327-7205
FAX: (703) 739-6490
Mailing Address:
   P.O. Box 1455
   Alexandria, VA 22313-2055
Year Established: 1990
Pub. Frequency: 24/yr.
Subscrip. Rate: $446/yr. US; $470/yr.
   foreign
**Owner(s):**
Capitol Publications, Inc.
1101 King St., Ste. 444
Alexandria, VA 20852-3030
Telephone: (800) 327-7205
FAX: (703) 739-6490
Ownership %: 100
**Editorial:**
Ed Warner .....................................................Editor
**Desc.:** Covers the business of personal
   communications, digital radio, miniature
   paging, in-flight phones, local loop
   alternatives, low-orbit satellites, security
   and alarm technology, specialized
   mobile radio, spectrum allocation,
   telepoint, vehicle location, wireless
   payphones, wireless PBXs and LANs,
   and other next-generation wireless
   technologies.

70134
## BOARD REPORT FOR GRAPHIC ARTISTS
P.O. Box 300789
Denver, CO 80203
Telephone: (303) 839-9058
Year Established: 1978
Pub. Frequency: m.
Subscrip. Rate: $96/yr.
Materials: 10,32
**Owner(s):**
Board Report Publishing Co., Inc.
P.O. Box 300789
Denver, CO 80203
Telephone: (303) 839-9058
Ownership %: 100
**Editorial:**
Drew Allen Miller .........................................Editor

70095
## BOOK MARKETING UPDATE
P.O. Box 205
Fairfield, IA 52556-0205
Telephone: (512) 472-6130
FAX: (515) 472-3186
Year Established: 1986
Pub. Frequency: m.
Subscrip. Rate: $60/yr. US; $98/yr. foreign
Materials: 10,32
Circulation: 2,000
Circulation Type: controlled & paid
**Owner(s):**
Open Horizons Publishing
P.O. Box 205
Fairfield, IA 52556-0205
Telephone: (512) 472-6130
FAX: (515) 472-3186
Ownership %: 100
**Editorial:**
John Kremer ..................................................Editor

**Desc.:** Features ideas, tips, case histories,
   and articles on book marketing, publicity,
   and promotions for large and small book
   publishers and authors.

70071
## BOOK PROMOTION HOTLINE
51 1/2 W. Adams
Fairfield, IA 52556-1102
Telephone: (800) 669-0773
FAX: (515) 472-3186
Mailing Address:
   P.O. Box 1102
   Fairfield, IA 52556-1102
Year Established: 1989
Pub. Frequency: w.
Subscrip. Rate: $150/yr.
**Owner(s):**
Ad-Lib Publications
P.O. Box 1102
Fairfield, IA 52556-1102
Telephone: (800) 669-0773
FAX: (515) 472-3186
Ownership %: 100
**Editorial:**
Marie Kiefer .................................................Editor
**Desc.:** Lists 75 to 100 key media and book
   marketing contacts.

70155
## CALIFORNIA CABLETTER
P.O. Box 7600
Santa Cruz, CA 95061-7600
Telephone: (408) 426-5981
FAX: (408) 426-5981
Year Established: 1992
Pub. Frequency: m.
Subscrip. Rate: $48/yr.
Materials: 10
Circulation: 120
Circulation Type: controlled & paid
**Owner(s):**
Thomas Karwin & Associates
P.O. Box 7600
Santa Cruz, CA 95061-7600
Telephone: (408) 426-5981
FAX: (408) 426-5981
Ownership %: 100
**Editorial:**
Thomas J. Karwin .........................................Editor
**Desc.:** News articles and commentary on
   legal cases, legislation, and commercial
   issues that affect cable television.

54068
## CAPELLS CIRCULATION REPORT
313 South Ave.
Fanwood, NJ 07023
Telephone: (908) 889-6336
FAX: (212) 949-7294
Mailing Address:
   P.O. Box 192
   Fanwood, NJ 07023-0192
Year Established: 1982
Pub. Frequency: 20/yr.
Subscrip. Rate: $344/yr.US; $384/yr.
   foreign
Materials: 10
Circulation: 1,000
Circulation Type: paid
**Owner(s):**
Whitaker Newsletters, Inc.
313 South Ave.
Fanwood, NJ 07023
Telephone: (908) 889-6336
FAX: (908) 889-6339
Ownership %: 100
**Editorial:**
Dan Capell ....................................................Editor
**Desc.:** Provides current information on
   what's happening in circulation trends,
   strategies, tactics and analysis.
**Readers:** Circulation directors, publishers,
   advertising agencies.

Materials Accepted/Included: 01-Business news 02-By-line articles 03-Fashion news 04-Food news 05-Freelance copy 06-Letters to editor 07-Real estate news 08-Sports news 09-Travel news 10-Book rev. 11-Movie rev. 12-Music rev. 13-TV rev. 14-Theater rev. 15-Coming events 16-Obituaries 17-Question & answer 18-Social announcements 19-Artwork 20-Cartoons 21-Photos 22-TV listings 23-Audio rec. 24-Video rec. 25-Books 26-Films/film clips 27-Personnel news 28-Press releases 29-New product news/photos 30-Trade lit. 31-Contracts awarded 32-Display adv. 33-Classified adv.

## CENSORSHIP NEWS
70580
275 Seventh Ave., 20th Fl.
New York, NY 10001
Telephone: (212) 807-6222
FAX: (212) 807-6245
Year Established: 1975
Pub. Frequency: q.
Subscrip. Rate: $30/yr.
Materials: 10
Circulation: 5,000
Circulation Type: controlled & paid
**Owner(s):**
National Coalition Against Censorship
275 Seventh Ave.
New York, NY 10001
Telephone: (212) 807-6222
FAX: (212) 807-6245
Ownership %: 100
**Editorial:**
Leanne Katz ...............................Editor
**Desc.:** Covers current school book
censorship controversies, threats to the
free flow of information, obscenity laws,
and creationism and school textbooks.

## CHIPS OFF THE WRITER'S BLOCK
70584
P.O. Box 83371
Los Angeles, CA 90083
Year Established: 1986
Pub. Frequency: bi-m.
Subscrip. Rate: $15/yr.
Materials: 10,32
Circulation: 500
Circulation Type: controlled & paid
**Owner(s):**
Chips Off the Writer's Block
P.O. Box 83371
Los Angeles, CA 90083
Ownership %: 100
**Editorial:**
Wanda Windham ...............................Editor
**Desc.:** How-to articles and inspiration for
writers with market and contest
information.

## CITY COUNTY COMMUNICATIONS
69555
P.O. Box 16645
Tampa, FL 33687
Telephone: (813) 622-8484
FAX: (813) 664-0051
Mailing Address:
P.O. Box 16645
Tampa, FL 33687-6645
Year Established: 1987
Pub. Frequency: q.
Page Size: standard
Subscrip. Rate: $19/yr.
Materials: 10,32
Print Process: offset
Circulation: 4,000
Circulation Type: controlled & paid
**Owner(s):**
Innovation Groups, Inc.
P.O. Box 16645
Tampa, FL 33687
Telephone: (813) 622-8484
FAX: (813) 664-0054
Ownership %: 100
**Editorial:**
Mary Floyd ...............................Editor
**Desc.:** Studies videos, cable, TV, radio,
communication programs, training
programs on video and multi-media
computer presentations and means of
communications beteen local
government, employees and the public.
**Readers:** Cable administrators,
telecommunication specialists,
purchasing managers, city/county
administrators, city/county department
heads, all local government
professionals, and public information
officers.

## CLASSIFIED ADVERTISING REPORT
70350
213 Danbury Rd.
Wilton, CT 06897
Telephone: (203) 834-0033
FAX: (203) 834-1771
Mailing Address:
P.O. Box 7430
Wilton, CT 06897
Year Established: 1987
Pub. Frequency: m.
Subscrip. Rate: $396/yr. US; $420/yr.
foreign
**Owner(s):**
SIMBA-Communications Trends
213 Danbury Rd.
Wilton, CT 06897
Telephone: (203) 834-0033
FAX: (203) 834-1771
Ownership %: 100
**Editorial:**
Efrem Sigel ...............................Editor
**Desc.:** Newsletter for classified publishers
and advertisers.

## COMMON CARRIER WEEK
70168
2115 Ward Ct., N.W.
Washington, DC 20037
Telephone: (202) 872-9200
FAX: (202) 293-3435
Year Established: 1984
Pub. Frequency: w.
Subscrip. Rate: $651/yr. US; $693/yr.
foreign
**Owner(s):**
Warren Publishing, Inc.
2115 Ward Ct., N.W.
Washington, DC 20037
Telephone: (202) 872-9200
FAX: (202) 293-3435
Ownership %: 100
**Editorial:**
Brock Meeks ...............................Editor

## COMMUNICATION BRIEFINGS
70156
700 Black House Pike, Ste. 110
Blackwood, NJ 08012-1455
Telephone: (609) 232-6380
FAX: (609) 232-8245
Year Established: 1981
Pub. Frequency: m.
Subscrip. Rate: $69/yr. US; $79/yr.
Canada; $99/yr. elsewhere
Materials: 10
Circulation: 45,000
Circulation Type: controlled & paid
**Owner(s):**
Encoders, Inc.
1700 Black Horse Pike, Ste. 11
Blackwood, NJ 08012-1455
Telephone: (609) 232-6380
FAX: (609) 232-8245
Ownership %: 100
**Editorial:**
Frank Grazian ...............................Editor
**Desc.:** Articles, excerpts, news items, and
departments on ideas and techniques to
help improve writing, speaking, listening,
organizing, problem-solving, and
decision-making skills at the managerial
and administrative levels.

## COMMUNICATIONS DAILY
49834
2115 Ward Ct., N.W.
Washington, DC 20037
Telephone: (202) 872-9200
FAX: (202) 293-3435
Year Established: 1981
Pub. Frequency: 5/wk.
Page Size: standard
Subscrip. Rate: $2300/yr. US; $2520/yr.
foreign

**Owner(s):**
Warren Publishing, Inc.
2115 Ward Ct., N.W.
Washington, DC 20037
Telephone: (202) 872-9200
FAX: (202) 293-3435
Ownership %: 100
**Bureau(s):**
Warren Publishing, Inc.
475 Fifth Ave., Ste. 1202
New York, NY 10017
Telephone: (212) 686-5410
Contact: David Lachenbruch, Editorial
Director
**Management:**
Roy W. Easley, III ...............................Controller
Albert Warren ...............................Publisher
Gene Edwards ...............................Advertising Manager
Betty Alvine ...............................Circulation Manager
**Editorial:**
Dawson B. Nail ...............................Executive Editor
Martin Brockstein ...............................Senior Editor
Paul Warren ...............................Senior Editor
Daniel Warren ...............................Senior Editor
Art Brodsky ...............................Senior Editor
Michael Feazel ...............................Senior Editor
Albert Warren ...............................Editor
David Lachenbruch ...............................Editorial Director
Gary Madderom ...............................Marketing Director
**Desc.:** Covers all aspects of electronic
communications, including telephone
and data communications, cable TV,
broadcasting, satellites, electronic
publishing, and emerging technologies.
**Readers:** Executives in foregoing fields.

## COPY EDITOR
69566
P.O. Box 604, Ansonia Sta.
New York, NY 10023-0604
Telephone: (212) 757-2645
Year Established: 1990
Pub. Frequency: bi-m.
Page Size: standard
Subscrip. Rate: $69/yr.
Materials: 01,02,05,06,10,17,29,30
Print Process: offset
Circulation: 1,400
Circulation Type: controlled & paid
**Owner(s):**
Copy Editor
P.O. Box 604, Ansonia Sta.
New York, NY 10023-0604
Telephone: (212) 757-2645
Ownership %: 100
**Editorial:**
Mary Beth Protomastro ...............................Editor
**Desc.:** Copy Editor keeps professional
copy editions up-to-date with usage,
neologisms, reference books,
technology, and more.
**Readers:** Professional copy editors.

## EDITOR'S WORKSHOP NEWSLETTER
70568
212 W. Superior St., Ste. 200
Chicago, IL 60610-3533
Telephone: (312) 335-0037
Year Established: 1984
Pub. Frequency: w.
Subscrip. Rate: $119/yr.
Materials: 10
Circulation: 6,000
Circulation Type: controlled & paid
**Owner(s):**
Lawrence Ragan Communications, Inc.
212 W. Superior St., Ste. 200
Chicago, IL 60610-3533
Telephone: (312) 335-0037
Ownership %: 100
**Editorial:**
Charles Shields ...............................Editor

## EDITORIAL EYE
70101
66 Canal Ctr. Plz., Ste. 200
Alexandria, VA 22314-5570
Telephone: (703) 683-0683
FAX: (703) 683-4915
Year Established: 1978
Pub. Frequency: 12/yr.
Subscrip. Rate: $87/yr.
Materials: 10
Circulation: 2,500
Circulation Type: controlled & paid
**Owner(s):**
Editorial Experts, Inc.
66 Canal Ctr. Plz., Ste. 200
Alexandria, VA 22314-5570
Telephone: (703) 683-0683
FAX: (703) 683-4915
Ownership %: 100
**Editorial:**
Linda Jorgensen ...............................Editor
**Desc.:** Covers editing, proofreading,
publications management and language
usage. Includes reviews of publishing
software.

## EDITORS ONLY
70540
P.O. Box 17108
Fountain Hills, AZ 85269
Telephone: (602) 837-6492
FAX: (602) 837-6872
Year Established: 1982
Pub. Frequency: m.
Page Size: standard
Subscrip. Rate: $89/yr. US; $95/yr.
Canada; $105/yr. elsewhere
Materials: 10
Circulation: 450
Circulation Type: paid
**Owner(s):**
Editors Only Publications
P.O. Box 17108
Fountain Hills, AZ 85269
Telephone: (602) 837-6492
FAX: (602) 837-6872
Ownership %: 100
**Editorial:**
William Dunkerley ...............................Editor

## ELECTRIC PAGES
70106
405 Fourth St.
Brooklyn, NY 11215
Telephone: (718) 499-1884
FAX: (718) 499-1970
Year Established: 1991
Pub. Frequency: m.
Subscrip. Rate: $245/yr.
Materials: 10
**Owner(s):**
Graphic Research Laboratory, Inc.
405 Fourth St.
Brooklyn, NY 11215
Telephone: (718) 499-1884
FAX: (718) 499-1970
Ownership %: 100
**Editorial:**
Jack Powers ...............................Editor
**Desc.:** Devoted to new publishing and
media technologies including fax
publishing, CD-ROM, electronic
photography and other tools for
commercial, corporate and government
publications.

## EURO-EAST TELECOMMUNICATIONS
70144
3 Wing Dr., Ste. 240
Cedar Knolls, NJ 07927-1000
Telephone: (201) 285-1500
FAX: (201) 285-1519
Year Established: 1991
Pub. Frequency: m.
Subscrip. Rate: $347/yr. US; $367/yr.
foreign

---

**Owner(s):**
Probe Research, Inc.
3 Wing Dr., Ste. 240
Cedar Knolls, NJ 07927-1000
Telephone: (201) 285-1500
FAX: (201) 285-1519
Ownership %: 100
**Editorial:**
Gerhard Kafka .....................................Editor
Peter Bernstein ................................Editor

71224
**EUROPEAN MEDIA BUSINESS & FINANCE**
1201 Seven Locks Rd.
Potomac, MD 20854
Telephone: (301) 424-3338
FAX: (301) 309-3847
Year Established: 1993
Pub. Frequency: bi-w.
Subscrip. Rate: $795/yr.
**Owner(s):**
Phillips Business Information, Inc.
1201 Seven Locks Rd.
Potomac, MD 20854
Telephone: (301) 424-3338
FAX: (301) 309-3847
Ownership %: 100

70169
**EUROPEAN TELECOMMUNICATIONS**
3 Wing Dr., Ste. 240
Cedar Knolls, NJ 07927-1000
Telephone: (201) 285-1500
FAX: (201) 285-1519
Year Established: 1983
Pub. Frequency: s-m.
Subscrip. Rate: $497/yr. US; $527/yr.
foreign
**Owner(s):**
Probe Research, Inc.
3 Wing Dr., Ste. 240
Cedar Knolls, NJ 07927-1000
Telephone: (201) 285-1500
FAX: (201) 285-1519
Ownership %: 100
**Editorial:**
Paul Broadhead ...............................Editor
**Desc.:** Covers European
telecommunications developments,
regulations and issues.

70629
**EXECUTIVE SPEECHWRITER NEWSLETTER**
Emerson Falls
St. Johnsbury, VT 05819
Telephone: (802) 748-4472
FAX: (802) 748-1939
Year Established: 1986
Pub. Frequency: bi-m.
Subscrip. Rate: $79/yr.
**Owner(s):**
Words, Inc.
Emerson Falls
St. Johnsbury, VT 05819
Telephone: (802) 748-4472
FAX: (802) 748-1939
Ownership %: 100
**Desc.:** Contains anecdotal information and
material for speechwriters.

70146
**FACSIMILE & VOICE SERVICES**
3 Wing Dr., Ste. 240
Cedar Knolls, NJ 07927-1000
Telephone: (201) 285-1500
FAX: (201) 285-1519
Year Established: 1991
Pub. Frequency: m.
Subscrip. Rate: $347/yr. US; $367/yr.
foreign

**Owner(s):**
Probe Research, Inc.
3 Wing Dr., Ste. 240
Cedar Knolls, NJ 07927-1000
Telephone: (201) 285-1500
FAX: (201) 285-1519
Ownership %: 100
**Editorial:**
David Toll ..........................................Editor

70157
**FCC REPORT**
1101 King St., Ste. 444
Alexandria, VA 22313-2055
Telephone: (800) 327-7205
FAX: (703) 739-6490
Mailing Address:
P.O. Box 1455
Alexandria, VA 22313-2055
Year Established: 1981
Pub. Frequency: 24/yr.
Subscrip. Rate: $579/yr. US; $627/yr.
foreign
**Owner(s):**
Capitol Publications, Inc.
1101 King St., Ste. 444
Alexandria, VA 22313-2055
Telephone: (800) 327-7205
FAX: (703) 739-6490
Ownership %: 100
**Editorial:**
Anne F. LaLena .............................Editor

70171
**FIBER OPTICS BUSINESS**
214 Harvard Ave.
Boston, MA 02134
Telephone: (617) 232-3111
FAX: (617) 734-8562
Year Established: 1986
Pub. Frequency: bi-w.
Subscrip. Rate: $480/yr. US; $525/yr.
foreign
**Owner(s):**
Information Gatekeepers, Inc.
214 Harvard Ave.
Boston, MA 02134
Telephone: (617) 232-3111
FAX: (617) 734-8562
Ownership %: 100
**Editorial:**
Paul Polishuk ................................Editor
**Desc.:** Covers business developments in
fiber optics, procurements, contract
awards, price trends, markets, business
developments, and conferences.

70141
**FIBER OPTICS NEWS**
7811 Montrose Rd.
Potomac, MD 20854
Telephone: (301) 340-2100
FAX: (301) 424-4297
Year Established: 1981
Pub. Frequency: q.
Subscrip. Rate: $697/yr.
**Owner(s):**
Phillips Publishing, Inc.
7811 Montrose Ave.
Potomac, MD 20854
Telephone: (301) 340-2100
FAX: (301) 424-4297
Ownership %: 100
**Editorial:**
Charlie Hartley .................................Editor

71199
**FMEDIA!**
P.O. Box 24
Adolph, MN 55701
Telephone: (218) 879-7676
Year Established: 1987
Pub. Frequency: m.
Subscrip. Rate: $30/6 mo.
Circulation: 300
Circulation Type: controlled & paid

**Owner(s):**
FM Atlas Publishing
P.O. Box 24
Adolph, MN 55701
Telephone: (218) 879-7676
Ownership %: 100
**Editorial:**
Bruce F. Elving .............................Editor
**Desc.:** Contains fact and opinion about FM
radio and related technologies.

70551
**FREELANCE WRITER'S NEWSLETTER**
P.O. Box 3491
Knoxville, TN 37927
Telephone: (615) 637-9243
Pub. Frequency: irr.
Page Size: standard
Subscrip. Rate: $100/yr.
**Owner(s):**
Fine Arts Press
P.O. Box 3491
Knoxville, TN 37927
Telephone: (615) 637-9243
Ownership %: 100
**Desc.:** Contains the latest news, ideas,
advice and inside information for writers,
editors and publishers.

70172
**GLOBAL TELCOM REPORT**
7811 Montrose Rd.
Potomac, MD 20854
Telephone: (301) 340-2100
FAX: (301) 309-3847
Year Established: 1991
Pub. Frequency: fortn.
Subscrip. Rate: $897/yr.
**Owner(s):**
Phillips Publishing, Inc.
7811 Montrose Rd.
Potomac, MD 20854
Telephone: (301) 340-2100
FAX: (301) 309-3847
Ownership %: 100
**Editorial:**
Ray Py ..............................................Editor

70170
**GPS REPORT**
7811 Montrose Rd.
Potomac, MD 20854
Telephone: (301) 340-2100
FAX: (301) 309-3847
Year Established: 1991
Pub. Frequency: fortn.
Subscrip. Rate: $497/yr.
**Owner(s):**
Phillips Publishing, Inc.
7811 Montrose Rd.
Potomac, MD 20854
Telephone: (301) 340-2100
FAX: (301) 309-3847
Ownership %: 100
**Editorial:**
Kevin Dennehy ...............................Editor

71110
**GREAT AMERICAN VIDEO BUSINESS NEWSLETTER**
1900 S. Eads St.
Arlington, VA 22202
Telephone: (703) 892-1993
Year Established: 1990
Pub. Frequency: m.
Subscrip. Rate: $60/yr.
**Owner(s):**
V. Parrish Publishing
1900 S. Eads St.
Arlington, VA 22202
Telephone: (703) 892-1993
Ownership %: 100
**Desc.:** Provides issue analysis, feature
stories, market evaluations, business
and product news, and strategies for the
video business person.

70166
**HDTV REPORT**
7811 Montrose Rd.
Potomac, MD 20854
Telephone: (301) 340-2100
FAX: (301) 424-4297
Year Established: 1991
Pub. Frequency: fortn.
Subscrip. Rate: $447/yr.
**Owner(s):**
Phillips Publishing, Inc.
7811 Montrose Ave.
Potomac, MD 20854
Telephone: (301) 340-2100
FAX: (301) 424-4297
Ownership %: 100
**Editorial:**
Chris McConnell ...............................Editor
**Desc.:** Provides current information on
developments in the U.S., Europe and
Japan in all areas of the race toward all-
digital television, including displays,
transmission, production and
broadcasting, and computers.

71116
**IMAGING NEWS**
1101 King St., Ste. 444
Alexandria, VA 22313-2055
Telephone: (800) 327-7505
FAX: (703) 739-6490
Mailing Address:
P.O. Box 1455
Alexandria, VA 22313
Pub. Frequency: 24/yr.
Subscrip. Rate: $380/yr. US; $404/yr.
foreign
**Owner(s):**
Capitol Publications, Inc.
1101 King St., Ste. 444
Alexandria, VA 22313-2055
Telephone: (800) 327-7505
FAX: (703) 739-6490
Ownership %: 100
**Desc.:** Covers video conferencing, high-
resolution imaging and broadband
services.

70074
**INDEPENDENT BOOKSELLING TODAY**
212 Sloan Rd.
Nashville, TN 37209
Telephone: (615) 298-2303
FAX: (615) 298-9864
Year Established: 1993
Pub. Frequency: m.
Subscrip. Rate: $65/yr.
Circulation: 400
Circulation Type: controlled
**Owner(s):**
Paz & Associates
212 Sloan Rd.
Nashville, TN 37209
Telephone: (615) 298-2303
FAX: (615) 298-9864
Ownership %: 100
**Editorial:**
Donna Paz .......................................Editor
**Desc.:** Covers business management
issues for owners and managers of
independent bookstores. Helps them
fine tune their business operations and
meet the challenges of the changing
market. Features include a manager's
checklist, marketing and display ideas,
and sidelines tips.

71089
**INFORMATION & INTERACTIVE SERVICES REPORT**
1333 H St., N.W., Ste. 1100-W.
Washington, DC 20005
Telephone: (202) 842-0520
FAX: (202) 842-3047
Year Established: 1980

---

Materials Accepted/Included: 01-Business news 02-By-line articles 03-Fashion news 04-Food news 05-Freelance copy 06-Letters to editor 07-Real estate news 08-Sports news 09-Travel news 10-Book rev. 11-Movie rev. 12-Music rev. 13-TV rev. 14-Theater rev. 15-Coming events 16-Obituaries 17-Question & answer 18-Social announcements 19-Artwork 20-Cartoons 21-Photos 22-TV listings 23-Audio rec. 24-Video rec. 25-Books 26-Films/film clips 27-Personnel news 28-Press releases 29-New product news/photos 30-Trade lit. 31-Contracts awarded 32-Display adv. 33-Classified adv.

Pub. Frequency: bi-w.
Subscrip. Rate: $495/yr.
Materials: 10
**Owner(s):**
Telecommunications Reports
1333 H St., N.W., Ste. 1100-W.
Washington, DC 20005
Telephone: (202) 842-0520
FAX: (202) 842-3047
Ownership %: 100
**Editorial:**
Kevin McGilly .....................................Editor
**Desc.:** Monitors policy, technology, and
market developments in wireless
telecommunications. Covers new
services, corporate activity, and licensing
& spectrum allocation in personal
communication services, cellular, land
mobile radio, messaging, RF devices,
mobile satellites, and more.

70179
## INFORMATION NETWORKS
101 King St., Ste. 444
Alexandria, VA 22313-2055
Telephone: (800) 327-7205
FAX: (703) 739-6490
Mailing Address:
    P.O. Box 1455
    Alexandria, VA 22313-2055
Year Established: 1987
Pub. Frequency: m.
Subscrip. Rate: $397/yr. US; $421/yr.
    foreign
**Owner(s):**
Capitol Publications, Inc.
101 King St., Ste. 444
Alexandria, VA 22313-2055
Telephone: (800) 327-7205
FAX: (703) 739-6490
Ownership %: 100
**Editorial:**
Ed Warner ........................................Editor
**Desc.:** Newsletter reporting interactive
video and data networks business.
Includes reports about current
technologies, product and services,
corporate alliances, investment and
financial climate and regulation.
Identifies market opportunities and
analyzes public policy.

70173
## ISDN REPORT
3 Wing Dr., Ste. 240
Cedar Knolls, NJ 07927-1000
Telephone: (201) 285-1500
FAX: (201) 285-1519
Year Established: 1986
Pub. Frequency: s-m.
Subscrip. Rate: $497/yr. US; $527/yr.
    foreign
**Owner(s):**
Probe Research, Inc.
3 Wing Dr., Ste. 240
Cedar Knolls, NJ 07927-1000
Telephone: (201) 285-1500
FAX: (201) 285-1519
Ownership %: 100
**Editorial:**
Jeff Berger ......................................Editor

70148
## JAPANESE
## TELECOMMUNICATIONS
Three Wing Dr.
Ste. 240
Cedar Knolls, NJ 07927-1000
Telephone: (201) 285-1500
FAX: (201) 285-1519
Year Established: 1990
Pub. Frequency: m.
Subscrip. Rate: $347/yr. US; $367/yr.
    foreign

**Owner(s):**
Probe Research, Inc.
Three Wing Dr.
Ste. 240
Cedar Knolls, NJ 07927-1000
Telephone: (201) 285-1500
FAX: (201) 285-1519
Ownership %: 100
**Editorial:**
Michael Galbraith ..........................Editor

71173
## JON SULLIVAN'S RADIO
## PROMOTION BULLETIN
P.O. Box 841002
Houston, TX 77284
Telephone: (713) 684-6914
FAX: (713) 855-3475
Year Established: 1989
Pub. Frequency: m.
Subscrip. Rate: $133/yr.
Circulation: 450
Circulation Type: controlled & paid
**Owner(s):**
Sullivan Co.
P.O. Box 841002
Houston, TX 77284
Telephone: (713) 684-6914
FAX: (713) 855-3475
Ownership %: 100
**Editorial:**
Jon Sullivan ....................................Editor
**Desc.:** Contains sales promotion ideas for
commercial radio sales managers,
marketing directors and promotion
executives.

70174
## LAND MOBILE RADIO NEWS
7811 Montrose Rd.
Potomac, MD 20854
Telephone: (301) 340-2100
FAX: (301) 424-4297
Year Established: 1983
Pub. Frequency: w.
Subscrip. Rate: $597/yr.
**Owner(s):**
Phillips Publishing, Inc.
7811 Montrose Rd.
Potomac, MD 20854
Telephone: (301) 340-2100
FAX: (301) 424-4297
Ownership %: 100
**Editorial:**
Jane Bryant ....................................Editor

70077
## LAUGHING BEAR NEWSLETTER
P.O. Box 36159
Denver, CO 80236
Telephone: (303) 989-5614
Year Established: 1976
Pub. Frequency: m.
Subscrip. Rate: $10/yr. US; $12/yr.
    Canada; $20/yr. elsewhere
Materials: 10,32
Circulation: 150
Circulation Type: controlled & paid
**Owner(s):**
Laughing Bear Press
P.O. Box 36159
Denver, CO 80236
Telephone: (303) 989-5614
Ownership %: 100
**Editorial:**
Tom Person ....................................Editor
**Desc.:** Contains practical information for
independent publishers.

70176
## LOCAL COMPETITION REPORT
1101 King St., Ste. 444
Alexandria, VA 22313-2055
Telephone: (800) 327-7205
FAX: (703) 739-6490

Mailing Address:
    P.O. Box 1455
    Alexandria, VA 22313-2055
Pub. Frequency: 24/yr.
Subscrip. Rate: $387/yr. US; $411/yr.
    foreign
**Owner(s):**
Capitol Publications, Inc.
1101 King St., Ste. 444
Alexandria, VA 22313-2055
Telephone: (800) 327-7205
FAX: (703) 739-6490
Ownership %: 100
**Desc.:** Reports regulation, technology, and
competitive strategies in the local
telephone exchange market. Features
interviews with top decision makers.
Covers CAPS, teleco strategies, cable
TV participation, and new technologies.

71235
## LOCAL TELECOM COMPETITION
## NEWS
1201 Seven Locks Rd.
Potomac, MD 20854
Telephone: (301) 424-3380
FAX: (301) 309-3847
Year Established: 1993
Pub. Frequency: bi-w.
Subscrip. Rate: $597/yr. US; $630/yr.
    foreign
**Owner(s):**
Phillips Business Information, Inc.
1201 Seven Locks Rd.
Potomac, MD 20854
Telephone: (301) 424-3338
FAX: (301) 309-3847
Ownership %: 100

71030
## MEDIA LETTER
P.O. Box 218
Newton Centre, MA 02159-9746
Telephone: (617) 965-7691
FAX: (617) 969-7901
Pub. Frequency: 4/yr.
Subscrip. Rate: $195/yr. US; $225/yr.
    foreign
**Owner(s):**
Hurwitz Consulting Group
P.O. Box 218
Newton Centre, MA 02159-9746
Telephone: (617) 965-7691
FAX: (617) 969-7901
Ownership %: 100
**Editorial:**
Dena Brody ....................................Editor
**Desc.:** Provides analysis and information
about the trends, tools, and products
relating to interactive media technology.

70123
## MICROCELL NEWS
3 Wing Dr., Ste. 240
Cedar Knolls, NJ 07927-1000
Telephone: (201) 285-1500
FAX: (201) 285-1519
Year Established: 1989
Pub. Frequency: s-m.
Subscrip. Rate: $497/yr.US; $527/yr.
    foreign
**Owner(s):**
Probe Research, Inc.
3 Wing Dr., Ste. 240
Cedar Knolls, NJ 07927-1000
Telephone: (201) 285-1500
FAX: (201) 285-1519
Ownership %: 100
**Editorial:**
John Benson ....................................Editor
Gary Kim ........................................Editor

70181
## MICROCELL REPORT
150 W. 22nd St., Ste. 1000
New York, NY 10011-2421
Telephone: (212) 366-9788
FAX: (212) 366-9798
Year Established: 1990
Pub. Frequency: m.
Subscrip. Rate: $397/yr.
**Owner(s):**
Microcell Strategies, Inc.
150 W. 22nd St., Ste. 1000
New York, NY 10011-2421
Telephone: (212) 366-9788
FAX: (212) 366-9798
Ownership %: 100
**Editorial:**
Roger P. Newell ..............................Editor
**Desc.:** Covers business, technical and
regulatory aspects of personal
communications services and personal
communication networks, including
telepoints and wireless PBXs, and
wireless LANs.

70185
## MOBILE PHONE NEWS
7811 Montrose Rd.
Potomac, MD 20854
Telephone: (301) 340-2100
FAX: (301) 309-3847
Year Established: 1983
Pub. Frequency: fortn.
Subscrip. Rate: $597/yr.
**Owner(s):**
Phillips Publishing, Inc.
7811 Montrose Rd.
Potomac, MD 20854
Telephone: (301) 340-2100
FAX: (301) 309-3847
Ownership %: 100
**Editorial:**
Andrea Bona ..................................Editor

70187
## MOBILE SATELLITE NEWS
7811 Montrose Rd.
Potomac, MD 20854
Telephone: (301) 340-2100
FAX: (301) 309-3847
Year Established: 1989
Pub. Frequency: m.
Subscrip. Rate: $597/yr.
**Owner(s):**
Phillips Publishing, Inc.
7811 Montrose Rd.
Potoma, MD 20854
Telephone: (300) 000-0000
FAX: (301) 309-3847
Ownership %: 100
**Editorial:**
Jane Bryant ....................................Editor

70062
## MORGAN REPORT ON
## DIRECTORY PUBLISHING
2200 Sansom St.
Phiadelphia, PA 19103
Telephone: (215) 557-8200
FAX: (215) 557-8414
Year Established: 1986
Pub. Frequency: m.
Subscrip. Rate: $115/yr. US; $140/yr.
    foreign
Circulation: 1,000
Circulation Type: controlled & paid
**Owner(s):**
Morgan-Rand Publishing Co.
2200 Sansom St.
Philadelphia, PA 19103
Telephone: (215) 557-8200
FAX: (215) 557-8414
Ownership %: 100
**Editorial:**
Kathy Wolden ..................................Editor

**Materials Accepted/Included:** 01-Business news 02-By-line articles 03-Fashion news 04-Food news 05-Freelance copy 06-Letters to editor 07-Real estate news 08-Sports news 09-Travel news
10-Book rev. 11-Movie rev. 12-Music rev. 13-TV rev. 14-Theater rev. 15-Coming events 16-Obituaries 17-Question & answer 18-Social announcements 19-Artwork 20-Cartoons 21-Photos 22-TV listings
23-Audio rec. 24-Video rec. 25-Books 26-Films/film clips 27-Personnel news 28-Press releases 29-New product news/photos 30-Trade lit. 31-Contracts awarded 32-Display adv. 33-Classified adv.

7-21

**Desc.:** News on contemporary legislative and business issues affecting the informational publishing industry.

**NATIONAL SCANNING REPORT** 71162
P.O. Box 360
Wagontown, PA 19376
Telephone: (800) 423-1331
Year Established: 1990
Pub. Frequency: 6/yr.
Subscrip. Rate: $17.50/yr.
Materials: 10,32
Circulation: 10,000
Circulation Type: controlled & paid
**Owner(s):**
L.J. Miller, Inc.
P.O. Box 360
Wagontown, PA 19376
Telephone: (800) 423-1331
Ownership %: 100
**Editorial:**
Laura Quarantiello .......................................Editor
**Desc.:** Non-technical magazine for those who enjoy monitoring police, fire, emergency medical and other communications on their scanners. Includes tips on hearing more, system profiles, frequency information, new products and a reader information exchange.

**NEWSLETTER** 70161
11300 Rockville Pike, Ste. 1100
Rockville, MD 20852-3030
Telephone: (301) 816-8950
FAX: (301) 816-8945
Year Established: 1979
Pub. Frequency: bi-w.
Subscrip. Rate: $279/yr.
**Owner(s):**
United Communications Group
11300 Rockville Pike, Ste. 110
Rockville, MD 20852-3030
Telephone: (301) 816-8950
FAX: (301) 816-8945
Ownership %: 100
**Editorial:**
Lori Walsh .......................................Editor
**Desc.:** Directed to professionals who oversee voice communications; it gives advice for trimming expenses, boosting productivity, and the pros and cons of new systems.

**NEWSLETTER ON NEWSLETTERS** 70557
44 W. Market St.
Rhinebeck, NY 12572
Telephone: (914) 876-2081
FAX: (914) 876-2561
Mailing Address:
  P.O. Box 311
  Rhinebeck, NY 12572
Year Established: 1964
Pub. Frequency: m.
Page Size: standard
Subscrip. Rate: $120/yr. US; $140/yr. foreign
Materials: 10
**Owner(s):**
Newsletter Clearinghouse
44 W. Market St.
Rhinebeck, NY 12572
Telephone: (914) 876-2081
FAX: (914) 876-2561
Ownership %: 100
**Editorial:**
Howard Penn Hudson .......................Editor
**Desc.:** Reporting on the newsletter world: editing, graphics, management, promotion, newsletter reviews, and surveys.

**ONCE UPON A TIME** 70110
553 Winston Ct.
St. Paul, MN 55118
Pub. Frequency: q.
Subscrip. Rate: $15/yr.
Circulation: 1,000
Circulation Type: controlled & paid
**Owner(s):**
Audrey Baird
553 Winston Ct.
St. Paul, MN 55118
Ownership %: 100
**Readers:** For children's writers and illustrators.

**PCS NEWS** 70191
7811 Montrose Rd.
Potomac, MD 20854
Telephone: (301) 340-2100
FAX: (301) 309-3847
Year Established: 1990
Pub. Frequency: fortn.
Subscrip. Rate: $597/yr.
**Owner(s):**
Phillips Publishing, Inc.
7811 Montrose Rd.
Potomac, MD 20854
Telephone: (301) 340-2100
FAX: (301) 309-3847
Ownership %: 100
**Editorial:**
Andrea Bona ................................Editor

**PMA NEWSLETTER** 70083
2401 Pacific Coast Hwy.
Ste. 102
Hermosa Beach, CA 90254
Telephone: (310) 372-2732
FAX: (310) 374-3342
Year Established: 1982
Pub. Frequency: m.
Subscrip. Rate: $40/yr. membership
Materials: 10,32
Circulation: 6,000
Circulation Type: controlled & paid
**Owner(s):**
Publishers Marketing Association
4201 Pacific Coast Hwy.
Ste. 102
Hermosa Beach, CA 90254
Telephone: (310) 372-2732
FAX: (310) 374-3342
Ownership %: 100
**Editorial:**
Jan Nathan ................................Editor
**Desc.:** Provides news of industry trends, publisher profiles and cooperative marketing ideas and information for small to medium-sized independent publishers.

**POSTAL WATCH** 70832
9800 Metcalf
Overland Park, KS 66212-2213
Telephone: (913) 341-1300
FAX: (913) 967-1898
Year Established: 1990
Pub. Frequency: bi-w.
Subscrip. Rate: $183/yr.
**Owner(s):**
Intertec Publishing Co.
9800 Metcalf
Overland Park, KS 66212-2215
Telephone: (913) 341-1300
FAX: (913) 967-1898
Ownership %: 100
**Editorial:**
Lori Billington ................................Editor
**Desc.:** Covers changes in postal regulations and outlines options available to reduce mailing costs and to speed delivery.

**POST GUTENBERG** 70811
Grand St., W.
Palatine Bridge, NY 13428
Telephone: (518) 673-3237
FAX: (518) 673-2699
Mailing Address:
  P.O. Box 121
  Palatine Bridge, NY 13428
Year Established: 1986
Pub. Frequency: fortn.
Subscrip. Rate: Free
Materials: 32
**Owner(s):**
Lee Publications, Inc.
P.O. Box 121
Palatine Bridge, NY 13428
Telephone: (518) 673-3237
Ownership %: 100
**Editorial:**
Sally-Jean Taylor ...............................Editor
**Desc.:** Contains articles & announcements of interest to graphic artists located in the northeastern United States.

**PRC NEWS** 71126
2554 Lincoln Blvd., Ste. 1015
Marina Del Rey, CA 90291
Telephone: (310) 821-6675
FAX: (310) 641-9769
Year Established: 1988
Pub. Frequency: w.
Subscrip. Rate: $397/yr.
**Owner(s):**
Corbell Publishing
2554 Lincoln Blvd., Ste. 1015
Marina Del Rey, CA 90291
Telephone: (310) 821-6675
FAX: (310) 641-9769
Ownership %: 100
**Editorial:**
Deborah Rolfe ................................Editor
**Desc.:** Covers weekly news, mergers and acquisitions, people on the move, calender of events, statistics, new releases, and sell-through products.

**PUBLIC BROADCASTING REPORT** 49830
2115 Ward Ct., N.W.
Washington, DC 20037
Telephone: (202) 872-9200
FAX: (202) 293-3435
Year Established: 1978
Pub. Frequency: bi-w.
Page Size: standard
Subscrip. Rate: $390/yr. US; $411/yr. foreign
Materials: 01,06,15,16,23,24,25,27,28,29, 30,31,32,33
**Owner(s):**
Warren Publishing, Inc.
2115 Ward Ct.
Washington, DC 20037
Telephone: (202) 872-9200
FAX: (202) 293-3435
Ownership %: 100
**Management:**
Albert Warren ...............................Publisher
**Editorial:**
Dawson B. Nail .......................Executive Editor
Albert Warren ...........................Senior Editor
Paul Warren ...........................Senior Editor
Dan Warren ...........................Senior Editor
Jeff Kole ................................Editor
Betty Alvine ..................Marketing Director
**Desc.:** Analytical news and information on public broadcasting, including funding and technical and regulatory news.
**Readers:** Executives in public television, public radio and related fields.
**Deadline:** photo-Wed. prior to pub. date

**PUBLISHING MARKETS** 68745
275 Washington St.
Newton, MA 02158-1630
Telephone: (617) 630-2105
FAX: (617) 630-2100
Year Established: 1986
Pub. Frequency: bi-m.
Page Size: standard
Subscrip. Rate: $129/yr.
Materials: 01
**Owner(s):**
Cahners Publishing Co.
275 Washington St.
Newton, MA 02158-1630
Telephone: (617) 630-2105
Ownership %: 100
**Editorial:**
Jennifer Aaronson ..........................Editor

**PUBLISHING POYNTERS** 70057
P.O. Box 4232-462
Santa Barbara, CA 93140-4232
Telephone: (805) 968-7277
FAX: (805) 968-1379
Year Established: 1986
Pub. Frequency: q.
Subscrip. Rate: $9.95/8 issues
Materials: 10
Circulation: 13,000
Circulation Type: controlled & paid
**Owner(s):**
Para Publishing
P.O. Box 4232-462
Santa Barbara, CA 93140-4232
Telephone: (805) 968-7277
FAX: (805) 968-1379
Ownership %: 100
**Editorial:**
Dan Poynter ................................Editor

**PUBLISHING TRENDS & TRENDSETTERS** 70117
150 Fifth Ave.
New York, NY 10011
Telephone: (212) 741-0231
FAX: (212) 633-2938
Year Established: 1978
Pub. Frequency: 10/yr.
Subscrip. Rate: $197/yr.
Materials: 10
Circulation: 320
Circulation Type: controlled & paid
**Owner(s):**
Oxbridge Communications, Inc.
150 Fifth Ave.
New York, NY 10011
Telephone: (212) 741-0231
FAX: (212) 633-2938
Ownership %: 100
**Editorial:**
Jim Mann ................................Editor
**Desc.:** Contains interviews with magazine publishing executives, analysis of publishing industry trends.

**REPORT ON AT&T** 71096
1101 King St. Ste. 444
P.O. Box 1455
Alexandria, VA 22313-2055
Telephone: (800) 327-7205
FAX: (703) 739-6490
Year Established: 1983
Pub. Frequency: w.
Subscrip. Rate: $697/yr. US; $747/yr. foreign
**Owner(s):**
Capitol Publications, Inc.
1101 King St., Ste. 444
P.O. Box 145
Alexandria, VA 22313-2055
Telephone: (800) 327-7205
FAX: (703) 739-6490
Ownership %: 100

**Editorial:**
Mark Kellner ...................................Editor
**Desc.:** Independent business intelligence
on all of AT&T's activities. Briefings on
new products and services, computers,
and networking equiptment, prices, and
marketing. Full coverage of long
distance activities, joint ventures,
regulatory action, and personal
decisions.

## RUNDOWN
71037
P.O. Box 335
Ardmore, PA 19003
Telephone: (215) 664-3322
FAX: (215) 667-5148
Year Established: 1981
Pub. Frequency: w.
Subscrip. Rate: $325/yr.
Circulation: 400
Circulation Type: controlled & paid
**Owner(s):**
Standish Publishing Co.
P.O. Box 335
Ardmore, PA 19003
Telephone: (215) 664-3322
FAX: (215) 667-5148
Ownership %: 100
**Editorial:**
Kim Standish ...................................Editor
**Desc.:** Reports on trends in local television
news and information programming and
on televsion news management issues.

## SATELLITE NEWS
70145
7811 Montrose Rd.
Potomac, MD 20854
Telephone: (301) 340-2100
Year Established: 1978
Pub. Frequency: w.
Subscrip. Rate: $797/yr.
**Owner(s):**
Phillips Publishing, Inc.
7811 Montrose Rd.
Potomac, MD 20854
Telephone: (301) 340-2100
Ownership %: 100
**Editorial:**
Dave Bross ...................................Editor

## SHARING IDEAS
70152
18825 Hicrest Ave.
Glendora, CA 91740
Telephone: (818) 335-8069
FAX: (818) 335-6127
Mailing Address:
P.O. Box 1120
Glendora, CA 91740
Year Established: 1978
Pub. Frequency: bi-m.
Subscrip. Rate: $95/yr. for 2 years
Materials: 10,32
Circulation: 3,000
Circulation Type: controlled & paid
**Owner(s):**
Royal Publishing Inc.
18825 Hicrest Ave.
P.O. Box 1120
Glendora, CA 91740
Telephone: (818) 335-8069
FAX: (818) 335-6127
Ownership %: 100
**Editorial:**
Dorothy M. Walters ...................................Editor
**Desc.:** Provides news, tips, and articles on
speaking.

## SIPAPU
70608
23311 County Rd. 88
Winters, CA 95694-9008
Telephone: (916) 662-3364
Year Established: 1970
Pub. Frequency: s-a.
Subscrip. Rate: $8/yr.

**Owner(s):**
Noel Peattie
23311 County Rd. 88
Winters, CA 95694-9008
Telephone: (916) 662-3364
Ownership %: 100
**Management:**
Noel Peattie ...................................Publisher
**Editorial:**
Noel Peattie ...................................Editor
**Desc.:** Newsletter for librarians, collectors,
and others interested in the alternative
press, which includes small and
"underground" presses, Third World,
dissent, feminist, peace, and other types
of publishing.

## SPECTRUM REPORT
70149
7811 Montrose Ave.
Potomac, MD 20854
Telephone: (301) 340-2100
FAX: (301) 309-3847
Year Established: 1991
Pub. Frequency: fortn.
Subscrip. Rate: $697/yr.
**Owner(s):**
Phillips Publishing, Inc.
7811 Montrose Ave.
Potomac, MD 20854
Telephone: (301) 340-2100
FAX: (301) 309-3847
Ownership %: 100
**Editorial:**
Angela M. Duff ...................................Editor

## SPEECHWRITER'S NEWSLETTER
70591
212 W. Superior St., Ste. 200
Chicago, IL 60610-3533
Telephone: (312) 335-0037
Year Established: 1980
Pub. Frequency: w.
Subscrip. Rate: $287/yr.
Materials: 10
Circulation: 1,500
Circulation Type: controlled & paid
**Owner(s):**
Lawrence Ragan Communications, Inc.
212 W. Superior St., Ste. 200
Chicago, IL 60610
Telephone: (312) 335-0037
Ownership %: 100
**Editorial:**
John Cowan ...................................Editor

## STATE TELEPHONE REGULATION REPORT
70196
1101 King St., Ste. 444
Alexandria, VA 22313-2055
Telephone: (800) 327-7205
FAX: (703) 739-6490
Mailing Address:
P.O. Box 1455
Alexandria, VA 22313-2055
Year Established: 1983
Pub. Frequency: bi-w.
Subscrip. Rate: $487/yr. US; $511/yr.
foreign
**Owner(s):**
Capitol Publications, Inc.
1101 King St., Ste. 444
Alexandria, VA 22313-2055
Telephone: (800) 327-7205
FAX: (703) 739-6490
Ownership %: 100
**Editorial:**
Herb Kirchhoff ...................................Editor

## TELCO BUSINESS REPORT
70175
1101 King St., Ste. 444
Alexandria, VA 22313-2055
Telephone: (800) 327-7205
FAX: (703) 739-6490

Mailing Address:
P.O. Box 1455
Alexandria, VA 22313-2055
Year Established: 1985
Pub. Frequency: w.
Subscrip. Rate: $617/yr. US; $667/yr.
foreign
**Owner(s):**
Capitol Publications, Inc.
1101 King St., Ste. 1455
Alexandria, VA 22313-2055
Telephone: (800) 327-7205
FAX: (703) 739-6490
Ownership %: 100
**Editorial:**
Kristine Loosley ...................................Editor

## TELCO COMPETITION REPORT
71198
1333 H St., N.W., 11th Fl.-W.
Washington, DC 20005
Telephone: (202) 842-3006
FAX: (202) 842-3047
Pub. Frequency: bi-w.
Subscrip. Rate: $495/yr.
**Owner(s):**
Telecommunications Reports
1333 H St., N.W., 11th Fl.-W.
Washington, DC 20005
Telephone: (202) 842-3006
FAX: (202) 842-3047
Ownership %: 100
**Editorial:**
Kevin McGilly ...................................Editor
Victoria Mason ...................................Editor
**Desc.:** Provides news on events resulting
from F.C.C. decisions.

## TELECOM DATA NETWORKS
70153
1101 King St., Ste. 444
Alexandria, VA 22313-2055
Telephone: (703) 739-6490
FAX: (703) 739-6490
Mailing Address:
P. O. Box 1455
Alexandria, VA 22313-2055
Pub. Frequency: 24/yr.
Subscrip. Rate: $446/yr. US; $470/yr.
foreign
**Owner(s):**
Capitol Publications, Inc.
1101 King St., Ste. 444
P.O. Box 1455
Alexandria, VA 22313-2055
Telephone: (703) 739-6490
FAX: (703) 739-6490
Ownership %: 100
**Editorial:**
Ed Warner ...................................Editor
**Desc.:** Covers the services, technologies,
markets, and trends that drive the
development of data services worldwide.

## TELECOM DATA REPORT
71193
1333 H St., N.W., 2nd Fl.-W.
Washington, DC 20005
Telephone: (202) 842-3022
FAX: (202) 842-1875
Pub. Frequency: bi-w.
Subscrip. Rate: $498/yr.
**Owner(s):**
Telecommunications Report
1333 H St., N.W., 2nd Fl.-W.
Washington, DC 20005
Telephone: (202) 842-3022
FAX: (202) 842-1875
Ownership %: 100
**Editorial:**
Rod Kukro ...................................Editor
**Desc.:** Reports on telecommunications
services, products, and technology
developments.

## TELEPHONE NEWS
70202
7811 Montrose Rd.
Potomac, MD 20854
Telephone: (301) 340-2100
FAX: (301) 309-3847
Year Established: 1980
Pub. Frequency: w.
Subscrip. Rate: $597/yr.
**Owner(s):**
Phillips Publishing, Inc.
7811 Montrose Rd.
Potomac, MD 20854
Telephone: (301) 340-2100
FAX: (301) 309-3847
Ownership %: 100
**Editorial:**
Ian McCaleb ...................................Editor

## TELEVISION & RADIO NEWSLETTER
71213
201 Elden St., Ste. 167
Herndon, VA 22070
Year Established: 1988
Pub. Frequency: m.
Subscrip. Rate: $125/yr.
**Owner(s):**
Restivo Communications
201 Elden St., Ste. 167
Herndon, VA 22070
Ownership %: 100
**Editorial:**
P.J. Restivo ...................................Editor

## TRAVELWRITER MARKETLETTER
70595
Waldorf-Astoria
301 Park Ave., Ste. 1850
New York, NY 10022
Telephone: (212) 759-6744
FAX: (212) 758-9209
Year Established: 1979
Pub. Frequency: m.
Subscrip. Rate: $60/yr.
Materials: 10
Circulation: 1,000
Circulation Type: controlled & paid
**Owner(s):**
Robert Scott Milne
Waldorf-Astoria
301 Park Ave., Ste. 1850
New York, NY 10022
Telephone: (212) 759-6744
FAX: (212) 758-9209
Ownership %: 100
**Editorial:**
Robert Scott Milne ...................................Editor
**Desc.:** Marketing informations for travel
writers and photographers. Includes
information on free trips
for professionals.

## TYPOGRAPHY DESIGN & USE
70087
P.O. Box 19107
Arlington, TX 76019
Telephone: (817) 273-2658
Year Established: 1992
Pub. Frequency: q.
Subscrip. Rate: $12/yr.
Materials: 10
Circulation: 5,430
Circulation Type: controlled & paid
**Owner(s):**
Doron-Byrd Publishing
P.O. Box 19107
Arlington, TX 76019
Telephone: (817) 273-2658
Ownership %: 100
**Editorial:**
Tom Doron ...................................Editor
**Desc.:** Covers typography design, use,
supplies, guidelines, and trends.

**Materials Accepted/Included:** 01-Business news 02-By-line articles 03-Fashion news 04-Food news 05-Freelance copy 06-Letters to editor 07-Real estate news 08-Sports news 09-Travel news 10-Book rev. 11-Movie rev. 12-Music rev. 13-TV rev. 14-Theater rev. 15-Coming events 16-Obituaries 17-Question & answer 18-Social announcements 19-Artwork 20-Cartoons 21-Photos 22-TV listings 23-Audio rec. 24-Video rec. 25-Records 26-Films/film clips 27-Personnel news 28-Press releases 29-New product news/photos 30-Trade lit. 31-Contracts awarded 32-Display adv. 33-Classified adv.

7-23

## US TELECOMMUNICATIONS
70178

3 Wing Dr., Ste. 240
Cedar Knolls, NJ 07927-1000
Telephone: (201) 285-1500
FAX: (201) 285-1519
Year Established: 1980
Pub. Frequency: s-m.
Subscrip. Rate: $497/yr. US; $527/yr.
    foreign
**Owner(s):**
Probe Research, Inc.
3 Wing Dr., Ste. 240
Cedar Knolls, NJ 07927-1000
Telephone: (201) 285-1500
FAX: (201) 285-1519
Ownership %: 100
**Editorial:**
Peter Bernstein ...................................Editor
**Desc.:** Reports on telecommunications
    issues.

## VIDEO SERVICES NEWS
71240

1201 Seven Locks Rd.
Potomac, MD 20854
Telephone: (301) 424-3338
FAX: (301) 309-3847
Year Established: 1993
Pub. Frequency: bi-w.
Subscrip. Rate: $597/yr. US; $630/yr.
    foreign
**Owner(s):**
Phillips Business Information, Inc.
1201 Seven Locks Rd.
Potomac, MD 20854
Telephone: (301) 424-3338
FAX: (301) 309-3847
Ownership %: 100

## VIDEO TECHNOLOGY NEWS
71121

7811 Montrose St.
Potomac, MD 20854
Telephone: (301) 340-2100
FAX: (301) 309-3847
Pub. Frequency: fortn.
Subscrip. Rate: $595/yr.
**Owner(s):**
Phillips Publishing, Inc.
7811 Montrose Rd.
Potomac, MD 20854
Telephone: (301) 340-2100
FAX: (301) 309-3847
Ownership %: 100
**Editorial:**
Charlotte Wolter ...........................Editor

## VOICENEWS
71097

P.O. Box 1891
Rockville, MD 20849
Telephone: (001) 424-0114
FAX: (301) 424-8971
Year Established: 1981
Pub. Frequency: 12/yr.
Subscrip. Rate: $297/yr. US; $327/yr.
    foreign
**Owner(s):**
Stoneridge Technical Services
P.O. Box 1891
Rockville, MD 20849
Telephone: (301) 424-0114
FAX: (301) 424-8971
Ownership %: 100
**Editorial:**
William W. Creitz ..........................Editor
**Desc.:** Covers voice processing
    technology, products and companies.
    Offers information on voice mail,
    voice response, speech recognition, and
    speech synthesis.

## VOICE PROCESSING NEWSLETTER
67227

3 Wing Dr., Ste. 240
Cedar Knolls, NJ 07927-1000
Telephone: (201) 285-1500
FAX: (201) 285-1519
Year Established: 1982
Pub. Frequency: s-m.
Page Size: standard
Subscrip. Rate: $497/yr. US; $527/yr.
    foreign
**Owner(s):**
Probe Research, Inc.
3 Wing Dr., Ste. 240
Cedar Knolls, NJ 07927-1000
Telephone: (201) 285-1500
FAX: (201) 285-1500
Ownership %: 100
**Management:**
Victor Schree .........................President
Victor Schree .........................Publisher
**Desc.:** The publication of record of the
    voice (messaging, response, synthesis,
    recognition) industries.

## VOICE TECHNOLOGY NEWS
70160

7811 Montrose Rd.
Potomac, MD 20854
Telephone: (301) 340-2100
FAX: (301) 309-3847
Year Established: 1989
Pub. Frequency: fortn.
Subscrip. Rate: $497/yr.
**Owner(s):**
Phillips Publishing, Inc.
7811 Montrose Rd.
Potomac, MD 20854
Telephone: (301) 340-2100
FAX: (301) 309-3847
Ownership %: 100
**Editorial:**
Ian McCaleb ...................................Editor

## WALL STREET NETWORK NEWS
71210

P.O. Box 2248
Binghamton, NY 13902-2248
Telephone: (607) 770-9242
FAX: (607) 770-9435
Year Established: 1992
Pub. Frequency: fortn.
Subscrip. Rate: $495/yr. US; $395/yr.
    Europe; $645/yr. elsewhere
**Owner(s):**
Waters Information Services
P.O. Box 2248
Binghamton, NY 13902
Telephone: (607) 770-9242
FAX: (607) 770-9435
Ownership %: 100
**Desc.:** Covers the business concerns of
    Wall Street professionals responsible for
    data and voice communications in
    metropolitan and wide-area networks.

## WHO'S PRINTING WHAT
70820

150 Fifth Ave., Ste. 302
New York, NY 10011
Telephone: (212) 741-0231
FAX: (212) 633-2938
Year Established: 1991
Pub. Frequency: m.
Subscrip. Rate: $195/yr.
**Owner(s):**
Oxbridge Communications, Inc.
150 Fifth Ave., Ste.302
New York, NY 10011
Telephone: (212) 741-0231
Ownership %: 100
**Editorial:**
Jennifer Howland ..........................Editor
**Desc.:** Follows developments & trends in
    the printing industry

## WIC NEWS
70163

500 N. Michigan Ave., Ste. 14000
Chicago, IL 60611
Telephone: (312) 661-1700
FAX: (312) 661-0769
Year Established: 1984
Pub. Frequency: bi-m.
Subscrip. Rate: $75/yr.
Materials: 10
Circulation: 20,000
Circulation Type: controlled & paid
**Owner(s):**
P.M. Haeger & Associates
500 N. Michigan Ave., Ste. 140
Chicago, IL 60611
Telephone: (312) 661-1700
FAX: (312) 661-0769
Ownership %: 100
**Editorial:**
C. Kane ...........................................Editor
**Desc.:** Supports professional development
    opportunities and issues that concern
    working women in the cable industry.

## WORLD SCANNER REPORT
71177

P.O. Box 262478-C
San Diego, CA 92196-2478
Year Established: 1991
Pub. Frequency: m.
Subscrip. Rate: $25/yr.
Materials: 10,32
**Owner(s):**
Commtronics Engineering
P.O. Box 262478-C
San Diego, CA 92196-2478
Ownership %: 100
**Desc.:** Features do-it-yourself mods, soup-
    ups, hints and kinks for serious scanner
    needs.

## WRITER'S CONNECTION
70121

1601 Saratoga Sunnyvale Rd., Ste. 180
Cupertino, CA 95014
Telephone: (408) 554-2090
FAX: (408) 554-2099
Year Established: 1983
Pub. Frequency: m.
Subscrip. Rate: $45/yr. US; $55/yr.
    Canada
Materials: 10,32
Circulation: 3,000
Circulation Type: controlled & paid
**Owner(s):**
Writer's Connection
1601 Saratoga Sunnyvale Rd., Ste. 180
Cupertino, CA 95014
Telephone: (408) 554-2090
FAX: (408) 554-2099
Ownership %: 100
**Editorial:**
Jan Stiles .......................................Editor

## WRITER'S NOOK NEWS
70577

38114 Third St., Ste.181
Willoughby, OH 44094
Telephone: (216) 953-9292
FAX: (216) 354-6403
Year Established: 1985
Pub. Frequency: q.
Subscrip. Rate: $18/yr.
Materials: 10,32
Circulation: 1,000
Circulation Type: controlled & paid
**Owner(s):**
Writer's Nook Press
38114 Third St., Ste. 181
Willoughby, OH 44094
Telephone: (216) 953-9292
FAX: (216) 354-6403
Ownership %: 100
**Editorial:**
Eugene Ortiz ...................................Editor

**Desc.:** Contains news and tips for working
    and aspiring writers.

## WRITING RIGHT
70044

P.O. Box 35132
Elmwood Park, IL 60635
Telephone: (708) 453-5023
Year Established: 1992
Pub. Frequency: m.
Subscrip. Rate: $30/yr.
Materials: 10
**Owner(s):**
Elmwood Park Publishing Co.
P.O. Box 35132
Elmwood Park, IL 60635
Telephone: (708) 453-5023
Ownership %: 100
**Editorial:**
John C. Biardo ...............................Editor
**Desc.:** Newsletter with the sole focus on
    helping writers and publishers with their
    careers. Features writing tips, research,
    promotion and publicity, book reviews,
    writer's convention, book exhibit news
    and sources for writers.

## YELLOW PAGES & DIRECTORY REPORT
70046

213 Danbury Rd.
Wilton, CT 06897
Telephone: (203) 834-0033
FAX: (203) 834-1771
Mailing Address:
    P.O. Box 7430
    Danbury, CT 06897
Year Established: 1985
Pub. Frequency: s-m.
Subscrip. Rate: $480/yr. US; $516/yr.
    foreign
Materials: 32
**Owner(s):**
SIMBA-Communications Trends
213 Danbury Rd.
Wilton, CT 06897
Telephone: (203) 834-0033
FAX: (203) 834-1771
Ownership %: 100
**Editorial:**
Efrem Sigel ....................................Editor
**Desc.:** Newsletter for the yellow page and
    directory publishing industry.

## Group 318-Computers

## A-E-C AUTOMATION NEWSLETTER
61301

5920 Roswell Rd., B107336
Atlanta, GA 30328-4922
Telephone: (404) 565-3282
FAX: (404) 565-3286
Year Established: 1977
Pub. Frequency: m.
Page Size: standard
Subscrip. Rate: $189/yr.
Materials: 01,10,28,29,30
Print Process: offset
Circulation: 3,300
Circulation Type: paid
**Owner(s):**
Technology Publications, Inc.
5920 Roswell Rd., B-107336
Atlanta, GA 30328-4922
Telephone: (404) 565-3282
FAX: (404) 565-3286
Ownership %: 100
**Editorial:**
Carleton R. Howk ..........................Editor

**Desc.:** Analyzes and describes useful applications of systems and software for geographic information systems (GIS), and for the design-build industry; computer aided engineering (CAE); computer aided design/drafting (CAD) personal computers (PC) workstations (WS) and multimedia (MM).
**Readers:** Serves mapping, design, engineering, fabrication and construction management, automation systems, development and marketing managements.

71059
## AIN REPORT
7811 Montrose Rd.
Potomac, MD 20854
Telephone: (301) 340-2100
FAX: (301) 309-3847
Year Established: 1991
Pub. Frequency: fortn.
Subscrip. Rate: $497/yr.
**Owner(s):**
Phillips Publishing, Inc.
7811 Montrose Rd.
Potomac, MD 20854
Telephone: (301) 340-2100
FAX: (301) 309-3847
Ownership %: 100
**Editorial:**
John Roper ...................................Editor

71038
## AI TRENDS
8232 E. Buckskin Trail
Scottsdale, AZ 85255-2132
Telephone: (602) 585-8587
FAX: (602) 585-3066
Year Established: 1984
Pub. Frequency: m.
Subscrip. Rate: $295/yr.
**Materials:** 10
**Owner(s):**
Relayer Group
8232 E. Buckskin Trail
Scottsdale, AZ 85255-2132
Telephone: (602) 585-8587
FAX: (602) 585-3066
Ownership %: 100
**Editorial:**
Harvey P. Newquist III .............................Editor
**Desc.:** Analysis of the business of intelligent systems.

71025
## ANDERSON REPORT
1901 E. Fourth St., Ste. 310
Santa Ana, CA 92705
Telephone: (714) 542-0700
FAX: (714) 542-0783
Year Established: 1978
Pub. Frequency: m.
Subscrip. Rate: $345/yr. US; $395/yr. foreign
**Materials:** 10
**Owner(s):**
Altus, Inc.
1901 E. Fourth St.. Ste. 310
Santa Ana, CA 92705
Telephone: (714) 542-0700
FAX: (714) 542-0783
Ownership %: 100
**Editorial:**
Marcia Brooks ...........................................Editor
**Desc.:** Covers engineering productivity tools and computer graphics. Includes current news, industry happenings, information on new products (both hardware and software), and insights into new technology.

71087
## BITS & BYTES REVIEW
623 N. Iowa Ave.
Whitefish, MT 59937
Telephone: (406) 862-7280
FAX: (406) 862-1124

Year Established: 1987
Pub. Frequency: q.
Subscrip. Rate: $55/yr.
**Materials:** 10
Circulation: 2,000
Circulation Type: controlled & paid
**Owner(s):**
Bits & Bytes Computer Resources
623 N. Iowa Ave.
Whitefish, MT 59937
Telephone: (406) 862-7280
FAX: (406) 862-1124
Ownership %: 100
**Editorial:**
John J. Hughes ...............................Editor
**Desc.:** Provides moderately technical, detailed product reviews and reports on a broad spectrum of computing-related activites.

71061
## BROADBAND NETWORKING NEWS
7811 Montrose Rd.
Potomac, MD 20854
Telephone: (301) 340-2100
FAX: (301) 309-3847
Year Established: 1991
Pub. Frequency: bi-w.
Subscrip. Rate: $497/yr.
**Owner(s):**
Phillips Publishing, Inc.
7811 Montrose Rd.
Potomac, MD 20854-3300
Telephone: (301) 340-2100
FAX: (301) 309-3847
Ownership %: 100
**Editorial:**
Patty Brown ...........................................Editor
**Desc.:** Covers developments, trends and applications of high band width data transmission and communications.

71054
## CAD-CAM UPDATE
P.O. Box 3273
Boynton Beach, FL 33424-3273
Telephone: (407) 738-2276
Year Established: 1989
Pub. Frequency: m.
**Materials:** 10
**Owner(s):**
Worldwide Videotex
P.O. Box 3273
Boynton Beach, FL 33424-3273
Telephone: (407) 738-2276
Ownership %: 100
**Editorial:**
Mark Wright ...........................................Editor
**Desc.:** Provides timely news and information about CAD-CAM industry, including CAD, CAM, CADD, CASE products, services, companies, marketing strategies, and research and development.

71067
## CAPITAL PC MONITOR
51 Monroe St.
Rockille, MD 20850
Telephone: (301) 762-9372
Year Established: 1982
Pub. Frequency: m.
Subscrip. Rate: $35/yr.
**Materials:** 10,33
Circulation: 5,000
Circulation Type: paid
**Owner(s):**
Capital PC User Group, Inc.
51 Monroe St.
Rockville, MD 20850
Telephone: (301) 762-9372
Ownership %: 100
**Editorial:**
Alan Blandamer ...........................................Editor

**Desc.:** News, anouncements, advertisements, and special features for users of IBM personal computers and compatibles.

71055
## CD COMPUTING NEWS
P.O. Box 3273
Boynton Beach, FL 33424-3273
Telephone: (407) 738-2276
Year Established: 1987
Pub. Frequency: m.
Subscrip. Rate: $150/yr. US; $165/yr. foreign
**Owner(s):**
Worldwide Videotex
P.O. Box 3273
Boynton Beach, FL 33424-3273
Telephone: (407) 738-2276
Ownership %: 100
**Desc.:** Covers CD-ROM technology, products, and news, with emphasis on marketing strategies.

71053
## CHEMICAL DESIGN AUTOMATION NEWS
16 New England Executive Pk.
Burlington, MA 01803-5297
Telephone: (617) 229-9800
FAX: (617) 229-9899
Year Established: 1986
Pub. Frequency: m.
Subscrip. Rate: $300/yr. US; $345/yr. foreign; $55/yr. institutions; $175/yr. non-profit
**Materials:** 10,32
**Owner(s):**
Molecular Simulations, Inc.
16 New England Executive Pk.
Burlington, MA 01803-5297
Telephone: (617) 229-9800
FAX: (617) 229-9899
Ownership %: 100
**Editorial:**
Barbara F. Graham ...................................Editor
**Desc.:** Covers computer-assisted molecular materials design.

71043
## COMPUTER BOOK REVIEW
735 Ekekela Pl.
Honolulu, HI 96817
Year Established: 1983
Pub. Frequency: 6/yr.
Subscrip. Rate: $30/yr.
**Materials:** 10,32
**Owner(s):**
Computer Book Review
735 Ekekela Pl.
Honolulu, HI 96817
Ownership %: 100
**Editorial:**
Carlene Char ...........................................Editor
**Desc.:** For computer professionals, users, librarians, managers, and information specialists. Offers critical reviews of computer-related books.

71044
## COMPUTER COUNSEL
641 W. Lake St., Ste. 403
Chicago, IL 60661
Telephone: (312) 207-6900
FAX: (312) 207-1045
Year Established: 1988
Pub. Frequency: m.
Subscrip. Rate: $130/yr.
**Materials:** 32
Circulation: 1,200
Circulation Type: controlled & paid

**Owner(s):**
Computer Counsel, Inc.
641 W. Lake St., Ste. 403
Chicago, IL 60661
Telephone: (312) 207-6900
FAX: (312) 207-1045
Ownership %: 100
**Editorial:**
Richard L. Robbins ...................................Editor
**Desc.:** Helps lawyers, managing partners of law firms, and MIS directors decide what software and hardware to buy to automate their offices, and how to improve productivity.

71072
## COMPUTER ECONOMICS REPORT
5841 Edison Pl.
Carlsbad, CA 92008
Telephone: (619) 438-8100
FAX: (619) 431-1126
Year Established: 1979
Pub. Frequency: m.
Subscrip. Rate: $595/yr.
**Owner(s):**
Computer Economics, Inc.
5841 Edison Pl.
Carlsbad, CA 92008
Telephone: (619) 438-8100
FAX: (619) 431-1126
Ownership %: 100
**Editorial:**
Eva Young ...........................................Editor
**Desc.:** Provides financial advisement for data processing users. Offers information on lease provisions, used and new equipment systems and management techniques. May occasionally contain office automation applications. Features include a new product analysis and marketplace news. Provides financial advice for data processing users. Offers information on lease provisions, used and new equipment systems and management techniques.

70541
## COMPUTER INDUSTRY LITIGATION REPORTER
646 West Chester Pike
P.O. Box 1000
Westtown, PA 19395
*see Newsletters, Legal*

71077
## COMPUTER PUBLICITY NEWS
101 Howard St., 2nd Fl.
San Francisco, CA 94105-1616
Telephone: (415) 904-7000
FAX: (415) 904-7025
Year Established: 1981
Pub. Frequency: m.
Subscrip. Rate: $230/yr.
Circulation: 250
Circulation Type: paid
**Owner(s):**
Hi-Tech Communications
101 Howard St., 2nd Fl.
San Francisco, CA 94105-1616
Telephone: (415) 904-7000
FAX: (415) 904-7025
Ownership %: 100
**Editorial:**
Tony Reveaux ...........................................Editor
**Desc.:** Informative articles cover all aspects of publicity and advertising within the computer and computer-related industries.

71088
## COMPUTER PUBLISHING & ADVERTISING REPORT
213 Danbury Rd.
Wilton, CT 06897
Telephone: (203) 834-0033
FAX: (203) 834-1771

---

**Materials Accepted/Included:** 01-Business news 02-By-line articles 03-Fashion news 04-Food news 05-Freelance copy 06-Letters to editor 07-Real estate news 08-Sports news 09-Travel news 10-Book rev. 11-Movie rev. 12-Music rev. 13-TV rev. 14-Theater rev. 15-Coming events 16-Obituaries 17-Question & answer 18-Social announcements 19-Artwork 20-Cartoons 21-Photos 22-TV listings 23-Audio rec. 24-Video rec. 25-Books 26-Films/film clips 27-Personnel news 28-Press releases 29-New product news/photos 30-Trade lit. 31-Contracts awarded 32-Display adv. 33-Classified adv.

7-25

Mailing Address:
  P.O. Box 7430
  Wilton, CT 06897
Year Established: 1983
Pub. Frequency: 24/yr.
Subscrip. Rate: $432/yr. US; $468/yr.
  foreign
Materials: 10
**Owner(s):**
SIMBA-Communications Trends
213 Danbury Rd.
Wilton, CT 06897
Telephone: (203) 384-0033
FAX: (203) 834-1771
Ownership %: 100
**Editorial:**
Efrem Sigel ..................................Editor
**Desc.:** Provides coverage of computer
  publishing and distibution, international
  industry news, advertising campaigns for
  computer conpanies, new products
  and publication.

71074
**DATA CHANNELS**
7811 Montrose Rd.
Potomac, MD 20854
Telephone: (301) 340-2100
FAX: (301) 309-3847
Year Established: 1975
Pub. Frequency: fortn.
Subscrip. Rate: $597/yr.
**Owner(s):**
Phillips Publishing, Inc.
7811 Montrose Rd.
Potomac, MD 20854
Telephone: (301) 340-2100
FAX: (301) 309-3847
Ownership %: 100
**Editorial:**
Lana Sansur ..................................Editor
Joanne M. Connelly ...........Associate Editor
**Desc.:** For data communications industry
  executives. Features articles on packet
  networks, electronic mail, micro-to-
  mainframe communications, local area
  networks and other pertinent topics in
  data communications.

71075
**DATA STORAGE REPORT**
53 Park Belmont Pl.
San Jose, CA 95136-2505
Telephone: (408) 629-8249
Year Established: 1985
Pub. Frequency: m.
Subscrip. Rate: $385/yr. US; $424/yr.
  foreign
Materials: 10
**Owner(s):**
Jonas Press Publishing Co.
53 Park Belmont Pl.
San Jose, CA 95136-2506
Telephone: (408) 629-8249
Ownership %: 100
**Editorial:**
Jonas McCloud ..................................Editor
**Desc.:** Covers all aspects of the mass
  storage industry; technology, legislation,
  finance and marketing.

71085
**DENTAL COMPUTER
NEWSLETTER**
1000 North Ave.
Waukegan, IL 60085
Telephone: (708) 223-5077
Year Established: 1978
Pub. Frequency: q.
Subscrip. Rate: $20/yr.
Materials: 10,33
**Owner(s):**
Andent, Inc.
1000 North Ave.
Waukegan, IL 60085
Telephone: (708) 223-5077
Ownership %: 100

**Editorial:**
E. J. Neiburger ..................................Editor
**Desc.:** For dentists and other medical
  practitioners interested in office
  compters. Offers notes on hardware,
  software, peripherals and integration
  with office personnel.

71076
**DP BUDGET**
5841 Edison Pl.
Carlsbad, CA 92008-6519
Telephone: (619) 438-8100
FAX: (619) 431-1126
Year Established: 1982
Pub. Frequency: m.
Subscrip. Rate: $495/yr.
**Owner(s):**
Computer Economics, Inc.
5841 Edison Pl.
Carlsbad, CA 92008-6519
Telephone: (619) 438-8100
FAX: (619) 431-1126
Ownership %: 100
**Editorial:**
John Graf ..................................Editor
**Desc.:** Provides financial advice and
  analysis to DP executives in charge of
  data processing budgets. Reports on
  and evaluates the financial management
  of DP operations, DP equipment
  acquisition methods and more.

71068
**EDI NEWS**
7811 Montrose Rd.
Potomac, MD 20854
Telephone: (301) 340-2100
FAX: (301) 309-3847
Year Established: 1987
Pub. Frequency: fortn.
Subscrip. Rate: $397/yr.
**Owner(s):**
Phillips Publishing, Inc.
7811 Montrose Rd.
Potomac, MD 20854
Telephone: (301) 340-2100
FAX: (301) 309-3847
Ownership %: 100
**Editorial:**
John Zyskowski ..................................Editor
**Desc.:** Provides timely updates on EDI
  industry trends, events, new products
  and services, and advances in paperless
  trading technology.

71081
**ELECTRONIC COMMERCE
BULLETIN**
34 Beacon St.
Boston, MA 02108
Telephone: (617) 859-5676
FAX: (617) 536-8310
Year Established: 1992
Pub. Frequency: m.
Subscrip. Rate: $169/yr.
**Owner(s):**
Little, Brown & Co.
34 Beacon St.
Boston, MA 02108
Telephone: (617) 859-5676
FAX: (617) 536-8310
Ownership %: 100
**Editorial:**
Benjamin Wright ..................................Editor
**Desc.:** Includes electronic mail, electronic
  funds transfer, fax and electronic data
  interchange, electronic signatures,
  computerized tax records and computer
  system controls.

71070
**ELECTRONIC IMAGING REPORT**
7811 Montrose Rd.
Potomac, MD 20854
Telephone: (301) 340-2100
FAX: (301) 309-3847

Year Established: 1991
Pub. Frequency: fortn.
Subscrip. Rate: $397/yr.
**Owner(s):**
Phillips Publishing, Inc.
7811 Montrose Rd.
Potomac, MD 20854
Telephone: (301) 340-2100
FAX: (301) 309-3847
Ownership %: 100
**Editorial:**
John Zyskowski ..................................Editor
**Desc.:** Discusses strategies and
  applications of imaging technology of
  interest to executives and
  corporate planners.

71091
**ELECTRONIC MESSAGING NEWS**
7811 Montrose Rd.
Potomac, MD 20854
Telephone: (301) 340-2100
FAX: (301) 309-3847
Year Established: 1989
Pub. Frequency: fortn.
Page Size: standard
Subscrip. Rate: $497/yr.
**Owner(s):**
Phillips Publishing, Inc.
7811 Montrose Rd.
Potomac, MD 20854
Telephone: (301) 340-2100
FAX: (301) 309-3847
Ownership %: 100
**Editorial:**
Lana Sansur ..................................Editor
**Desc.:** Case studies and applications of
  recent developments in messaging
  technologies for corporate
  communications.

71050
**ENTERPRISE INTEGRATION
STRATEGIES**
37 Broadway
Arlington, MA 02174
Telephone: (617) 648-8700
FAX: (617) 648-8707
Year Established: 1984
Pub. Frequency: m.
Subscrip. Rate: $377/yr. US; $437/yr.
  foreign
**Owner(s):**
Cutter Information Corp.
37 Broadway
Arlington, MA 02174
Telephone: (617) 694-8870
FAX: (617) 648-8707
Ownership %: 100
**Editorial:**
Lee Hales ..................................Editor
**Desc.:** Covers new technologies, methods,
  and practices for information
  management, specifically in firms that
  manufacture goods. Includes trends,
  product reviews, and hands-on
  integration advice.

64966
**FEDERAL COMPUTER MARKET
REPORT**
3918 Prosperity Ave., Ste. 310
Fairfax, VA 22031
Telephone: (703) 573-8400
FAX: (703) 573-8594
Year Established: 1976
Pub. Frequency: s-m.
Page Size: standard
Subscrip. Rate: $495/yr. US; $519/yr.
  foreign
Materials: 01,02,05,06,10,15,21,23,24,25,
  26,27,28,29,30,31
Freelance Pay: negotiable
Print Process: offset
Circulation: 975
Circulation Type: paid

**Owner(s):**
Computer Age & EDP News Services
3918 Prosperity Ave., Ste. 310
Fairfax, VA 22031
Telephone: (703) 573-8400
FAX: (703) 573-8594
Ownership %: 100
**Management:**
S.L. Millin ..................................Publisher
Mike Cotter ...........Managing Director
**Editorial:**
Terry Miller ..................................Editor
Thomas G. Shack III ...........Marketing Director
**Desc.:** Analyzes government procurement
  regulations, technical evaluation criteria,
  minority subcontracting, RFP instructions
  and other issues of interest to vendors
  and government buyers. Each issue also
  lists Delegations of Procurement
  Authority (DPA's) approved by the GSA
  months before they appear in
  Commerce Business Daily.
**Readers:** CEOs, VPs, marketing directors,
  researchers, vendors and corporate
  libraries for computer and
  communications companies and their
  counterparts in academia and
  government; large end users of
  hardware and software.

71058
**IMAGING UPDATE**
P.O. Box 3273
Boynton Beach, FL 33424-3273
Telephone: (407) 738-2276
Year Established: 1989
Pub. Frequency: m.
Subscrip. Rate: $150/yr.
Materials: 10
**Owner(s):**
Worldwide Videotex
P.O. Box 3273
Boynton Beach, FL 33424-3273
Telephone: (407) 738-2276
Ownership %: 100
**Editorial:**
Mark Wright ..................................Editor
**Desc.:** Provides news and information on
  the digitized image and computer
  graphics industry, covering new
  hardware and software products, as well
  as research and development. Special
  emphasis is on the marketing strategies
  of manufacturers and vendors, along
  with articles on publishing and
  information storage and retrieval.

71051
**INCREMENTAL MOTION CONTROL
SYSTEMS & DEVICES
NEWSLETTER**
P.O. Box 2772, Sta. A
Champaign, IL 61825
Telephone: (217) 356-1523
FAX: (217) 356-2356
Year Established: 1972
Pub. Frequency: s-a.
Subscrip. Rate: $10/yr.; free to qualified
  personnel & institutions
Materials: 10,32
Circulation: 4,000
Circulation Type: controlled & paid
**Owner(s):**
Incremental Motion Control Systems
  Society
P.O. Box 2772, Sta. A
Champaign, IL 61825
Telephone: (217) 356-1523
FAX: (217) 356-2356
Ownership %: 100
**Editorial:**
B.C. Kuo ..................................Editor
**Desc.:** Provides an up-to-date review of
  existing technology and hardware.

**Materials Accepted/Included:** 01-Business news 02-By-line articles 03-Fashion news 04-Food news 05-Freelance copy 06-Letters to editor 07-Real estate news 08-Sports news 09-Travel news 10-Book rev. 11-Movie rev. 12-Music rev. 13-TV rev. 14-Theater rev. 15-Coming events 16-Obituaries 17-Question & answer 18-Social announcements 19-Artwork 20-Cartoons 21-Photos 22-TV listings 23-Audio rec. 24-Video rec. 25-Books 26-Films/film clips 27-Personnel news 28-Press releases 29-New product news/photos 30-Trade lit. 31-Contracts awarded 32-Display adv. 33-Classified adv.

## INTELLIGENT SOFTWARE STRATEGIES
71049
37 Broadway
Arlington, MA 02174
Telephone: (617) 648-8700
FAX: (617) 648-8707
Year Established: 1985
Pub. Frequency: m.
Subscrip. Rate: $395/yr. US; $455/yr.
    foreign
**Owner(s):**
Cutter Information Corp.
37 Broadway
Arlington, MA 02174
Telephone: (617) 648-8700
FAX: (617) 648-8707
Ownership %: 100
**Editorial:**
Paul Harmon ...................................Editor
**Desc.:** Discusses technology and market
    trends related to advanced, "intelligent"
    software technologies, i.e., artificial
    intelligence.

## ISR: INTELLIGENT SYSTEMS REPORT
71039
2555 Cumberland Pkwy., Ste. 299
Atlanta, GA 30339
Telephone: (404) 434-2187
FAX: (404) 432-6969
Year Established: 1983
Pub. Frequency: m.
Subscrip. Rate: $299/yr. US; $349/yr.
    foreign
Materials: 10,32
Circulation: 10,000
Circulation Type: controlled & paid
**Owner(s):**
AI Week, Inc.
2555 Cumberland Pkwy., Ste. 29
Atlanta, GA 30339
Telephone: (404) 434-2187
FAX: (404) 432-6969
Ownership %: 100
**Desc.:** Covers issues and events in the
    advanced computing field, such as
    expert systems, neural networks, fuzzy
    logic, and CASE (computer-aided
    software engineering).

## LAN PRODUCT NEWS
71062
P.O. Box 3273
Boynton Beach, FL 33424-3273
Telephone: (407) 738-2276
Year Established: 1989
Pub. Frequency: m.
Subscrip. Rate: $150/yr.
Materials: 10
**Owner(s):**
Worldwide Videotex
P.O. Box 3273
Boynton Beach, FL 33424-3273
Telephone: (407) 738-2276
Ownership %: 100
**Editorial:**
Mark Wright ...................................Editor
**Desc.:** Provides news and information on
    the computer local area network
    industry. Covers new hardware and
    software products, as well as research
    and development. With special emphasis
    on the marketing strategies of LAN
    manufacturers and vendors, user
    applications, and development of
    industry standards.

## MACINTOSH UPDATE
71066
P.O. Box 1209
Amherst, NH 03031
Telephone: (603) 672-6544
Year Established: 1984

Pub. Frequency: bi-m.
Subscrip. Rate: $98/yr.
Materials: 10
**Owner(s):**
Macintosh Update
P.O. Box 1209
Amherst, NH 03031
Telephone: (603) 672-6544
Ownership %: 100
**Desc.:** For computer related businesses.
    Provides information about business
    systems products. Articles cover
    business systems, systems software and
    hardware news. Provides how-to
    information and reviews for Macintosh
    users.

## MOBILE DATA REPORT
71092
1101 King St., Ste. 444
Alexandria, VA 22313
Telephone: (800) 327-7025
FAX: (703) 739-6490
Mailing Address:
    P.O. Box 1455
    Alexandria, VA 22313
Pub. Frequency: 24/yr.
Subscrip. Rate: $495/yr. US; $519/yr.
    foreign
**Owner(s):**
Capitol Publications, Inc.
1101 King St., Ste. 444
Alexandria, VA 22313
Telephone: (800) 327-7025
FAX: (703) 739-6490
Ownership %: 100
**Editorial:**
Alan Reiter ...................................Editor
**Desc.:** Concentrates on wireless
    computing and messaging. Includes
    news and analysis about the latest
    technologies, applications and
    competitive strategies in mobile data
    communications; covers E-mail, cellular
    data, alphanumeric paging, public mobile
    data networks, and portable computer
    connectivity.

## NETWORK MANAGEMENT SYSTEMS & STRATEGIES
71065
8130 Boone Blvd., Ste. 210
Vienna, VA 22182
Telephone: (703) 760-0660
FAX: (703) 760-9365
Year Established: 1989
Pub. Frequency: fortn.
Subscrip. Rate: $445/yr. US; $493/yr.
    foreign
**Owner(s):**
DataTrends Publications, Inc.
8130 Boone Blvd., Ste. 210
Vienna, VA 22182
Telephone: (703) 760-0660
FAX: (703) 760-9365
Ownership %: 100
**Editorial:**
Patricia Everett ...................................Editor
**Desc.:** Examines the latest products,
    strategies, and techniques for managing
    corporate information networks.

## OBJECT-ORIENTED STRATEGIES
71071
37 Broadway
Arlington, MA 02174
Telephone: (617) 648-8700
FAX: (617) 648-8707
Year Established: 1991
Pub. Frequency: m.
Subscrip. Rate: $495/yr. US; $565/yr.
    foreign

**Owner(s):**
Cutter Information Corp.
37 Broadway
Arlington, MA 02174
Telephone: (617) 648-8700
FAX: (617) 648-8707
Ownership %: 100
**Editorial:**
Paul Harmon ...................................Editor
Paul Heidt ...................................Editor
**Desc.:** Covers new technologies, new
    products, market developments and
    industry trends in the capabilities and
    uses of object-oriented software
    technologies. Includes discussion of
    techniques, and methodologies.
**Readers:** For managers and devlopers of
    object-oriented systems.

## ONLINE NEWSLETTER
71073
P.O. Box 31098
Phoenix, AZ 85046
Telephone: (800) 228-9982
Year Established: 1980
Pub. Frequency: 10/yr.
Subscrip. Rate: $43.75/yr. to individuals;
    $62.50/yr. institutions; $25/yr. students
Materials: 10
**Owner(s):**
Information Intelligence Inc.
P.O. Box 31098
Phoenix, AZ 85046
Telephone: (800) 228-9982
Ownership %: 100
**Editorial:**
Richard S. Huleatt ...................................Editor
**Desc.:** Covers all aspects of online use;
    features events, mergers, acquisitions,
    new products and relevant news.

## OPEN
71078
8130 Boone Blvd., Ste. 210
Vienna, VA 22182
Telephone: (703) 760-0660
FAX: (703) 760-9365
Year Established: 1988
Pub. Frequency: m.
Subscrip. Rate: $525/yr. US; $573/yr.
    foreign
Materials: 10
**Owner(s):**
Data Trends Publications, Inc.
8130 Boone Blvd., Ste. 210
Vienna, VA 22182
Telephone: (703) 760-0660
FAX: (703) 760-9365
Ownership %: 100
**Editorial:**
Patricia Everett ...................................Editor
**Desc.:** International newsletter of
    multivendor networking technologies,
    trends and products. Provides news on
    computer hardware and software
    products that work toward multivendor
    networking.

## OPEN SYTEMS COMMUNICATIONS
71069
7811 Montrose Rd.
Potomac, MD 20854
Telephone: (301) 340-2100
FAX: (301) 424-4297
Year Established: 1982
Pub. Frequency: bi-w.
Subscrip. Rate: $497/yr.
**Owner(s):**
Phillips Publishing, Inc.
7811 Montrose Rd.
Potomac, MD 30854
Telephone: (301) 340-2100
FAX: (301) 424-4297
Ownership %: 100

## OPTICAL MEMORY NEWS
61630
7811 Montrose Rd.
Potomac, MD 20854
Telephone: (301) 340-2100
FAX: (301) 309-3847
Year Established: 1982
Pub. Frequency: fortn.
Page Size: standard
Subscrip. Rate: $397/yr.
Circulation: 1,000
Circulation Type: paid
**Owner(s):**
Phillips Publishing, Inc.
7811 Montrose Rd.
Potomac, MD 20854
Telephone: (301) 340-2100
Ownership %: 100
**Editorial:**
Patty Brown ...................................Editor
**Desc.:** Covers the optical storage
    marketplace from the vendor
    perspective, including industry trends,
    new products, and corporate alliances
    and partnerships.

## PLC INSIDER'S NEWSLETTER
71063
P.O. Box 5268
Carefree, AZ 85377
Telephone: (602) 488-1462
Year Established: 1981
Pub. Frequency: m.
Subscrip. Rate: $140/yr.
Materials: 10
**Owner(s):**
Carefree Communications, Inc.
P.O. Box 5268
Carefree, AZ 85377
Telephone: (602) 488-1462
Ownership %: 100
**Desc.:** For marketing and other executives
    who make and sell programmable logic
    controllers, peripherals, and industrial
    computers.

## RAISED DOT COMPUTING NEWSLETTER
70055
408 S. Baldwin
Madison, WI 53703
Telephone: (608) 257-9595
FAX: (608) 255-1800
Year Established: 1984
Pub. Frequency: bi-m.
Subscrip. Rate: $18/yr. large print; $20/yr.
    cassette; $24/yr., diskette
Materials: 10
**Owner(s):**
Raised Dot Computing, Inc.
408 S. Baldwin
Madison, WI 53703
Telephone: (608) 257-9595
FAX: (608) 255-1800
Ownership %: 100
**Desc.:** Brief articles about the use of small
    computers for the blind; topics include
    low-cost braille devices, voice synthesis,
    paperless braille, use of computers by
    transcribers, and braille translation.

## REPORT ON IBM
71064
8130 Boone Blvd., Ste. 210
Vienna, VA 22182
Telephone: (703) 760-0660
FAX: (703) 760-9365
Mailing Address:
    P.O. Box 657
    Merrifield, VA 22116
Year Established: 1984
Pub. Frequency: w.
Subscrip. Rate: $745/yr. US; $795/yr.
    foreign

**Materials Accepted/Included:** 01-Business news 02-By-line articles 03-Fashion news 04-Food news 05-Freelance copy 06-Letters to editor 07-Real estate news 08-Sports news 09-Travel news 10-Book rev. 11-Movie rev. 12-Music rev. 13-TV rev. 14-Theater rev. 15-Coming events 16-Obituaries 17-Question & answer 18-Social announcements 19-Artwork 20-Cartoons 21-Photos 22-TV listings 23-Audio rec. 24-Video rec. 25-Books 26-Films/film clips 27-Personnel news 28-Press releases 29-New product news/photos 30-Trade lit. 31-Contracts awarded 32-Display adv. 33-Classified adv.

7-27

**Owner(s):**
DataTrends Publications, Inc.
8130 Boone Blvd., Ste. 210
Vienna, VA 22182
Telephone: (703) 760-0660
FAX: (703) 760-9365
Ownership %: 100
**Desc.:** Independent newsletter reporting and providing analysis on the activities and plans of the IBM Corporation.

71031
**RISC MANAGEMENT**
P.O. Box 1300
Freedom, CA 95019
Telephone: (408) 626-4361
FAX: (408) 626-4362
Year Established: 1988
Pub. Frequency: m. (except July
Subscrip. Rate: $575/yr. US; $625/yr. foreign
**Owner(s):**
Elk Horn Publishing Co.
P.O. Box 1300
Freedom, CA 95019
Telephone: (408) 626-4361
FAX: (408) 626-4362
Ownership %: 100
**Editorial:**
Andrew Allison ...........................................Editor
**Desc.:** Features strategic implication of impact of open systems and reduced instruction set computer technology on the computer industry.

71052
**SCAN NEWSLETTER**
11 Middle Neck Rd.
Great Neck, NY 11021
Telephone: (516) 487-6370
FAX: (516) 487-6449
Year Established: 1977
Pub. Frequency: m.
Subscrip. Rate: $175/yr. US; $195/yr. foreign
Materials: 10
**Owner(s):**
Scanning, Coding & Automation Newsletter Ltd.
11 Middle Neck Rd.
Great Neck, NY 11021
Telephone: (516) 487-6370
FAX: (516) 487-6449
Ownership %: 100
**Editorial:**
George Goldberg ....................................Editor
**Desc.:** Contains information for all industries involved with bar code scanning and other automatic identification technologies and applications.

71186
**SELECTED BOOK REVIEWS**
206 Davison Ave.
Lynbrook, NY 11563
Pub. Frequency: q.
Page Size: standard
Subscrip. Rate: $2.50/copy; $10/yr.
Materials: 10,32
Circulation: 973
Circulation Type: paid
**Owner(s):**
Vector Graphiques
206 Davison Ave.
Lynbrook, NY 11563
Ownership %: 100
**Editorial:**
John R. Cartmell, Jr. .............................Editor
**Desc.:** An independent newsletter that gives experts' opinions on the latest computer books.
**Readers:** For Computer Clubs, Libraries, Computer Professionals, Publishers, Bulletin Board Sys Ops, and Book Wholesalers.

71048
**SIXTH GENERATION SYSTEMS**
P.O. Box 155
Vicksburg, MI 49007
Telephone: (616) 649-3772
FAX: (616) 649-3592
Year Established: 1987
Pub. Frequency: m.
Subscrip. Rate: $79/yr.
Materials: 10
Circulation: 500
Circulation Type: controlled & paid
**Owner(s):**
Gallifrey Publishing
P.O. Box 155
Vicksburg, MI 49007
Telephone: (616) 649-3772
FAX: (616) 649-3592
Ownership %: 100
**Editorial:**
Derek F. Stubbs .........................................Editor
**Desc.:** Presents findings and news in the field of neural networks, whether natural, theoretical or artificial.

71033
**SMALLTALK REPORT**
588 Broadway, Ste. 604
New York, NY 10012
Telephone: (212) 274-0640
FAX: (212) 274-0646
Year Established: 1991
Pub. Frequency: 9/yr.
Subscrip. Rate: $69/yr. US; $94/yr. foreign
Materials: 10,33
Circulation: 4,000
Circulation Type: paid
**Owner(s):**
Sigs Publications, Inc.
588 Broadway, Ste. 604
New York, NY 10012
Telephone: (212) 274-0640
FAX: (212) 274-0646
Ownership %: 100
**Editorial:**
John Pugh ......................................................Editor
Paul White .....................................................Editor
**Desc.:** Covers programming techniques, language issues, analysis and design , methodologies, project management, training and education, application case studies and experience reports.

71079
**SOFTWARE ECONOMICS LETTER**
5841 Edison Pl.
Carlsbad, CA 92008-6519
Telephone: (619) 438-8100
FAX: (619) 431-1126
Year Established: 1992
Pub. Frequency: m.
Subscrip. Rate: $395/yr.
**Owner(s):**
Computer Economics, Inc.
5841 Edison Pl.
Carlsbad, CA 92008-6519
Telephone: (619) 438-8100
FAX: (619) 431-1126
Ownership %: 100
**Desc.:** Maximizing your return on corporate software. Provides the corporate and IS communities with a concise analysis of software issues and enables them to stay informed of the latest trends in software and software licensing.

64967
**SOFTWARE INDUSTRY REPORT**
3918 Prosperity Ave., Ste. 310
Fairfax, VA 22031-3300
Telephone: (703) 573-5400
FAX: (703) 573-8594
Year Established: 1968
Pub. Frequency: s-m.

Page Size: standard
Subscrip. Rate: $495/yr. US; $519/yr. foreign
Materials: 01,02,06,10,15,21,23,24,25,26, 27,28,29,30,31
Freelance Pay: negotiable
Print Process: offset
Circulation: 1,100
Circulation Type: paid
**Owner(s):**
Computer Age
3918 Prosperity Ave., Ste. 310
Fairfax, VA 22031
Telephone: (703) 573-8400
FAX: (703) 573-8594
Ownership %: 100
**Editorial:**
Mike Cotter ...................................................Editor
Terry Miller ...................................................Editor
S.L. Millin ..................................................Director
Chuck Bailey ..................Technical Editor
**Desc.:** Tracks worldwide industry and government software activities and opportunities with an emphasis on innovative strategies for MIS executives, market research and new developments in systems technology. Topics covered include CASE, Ada, AI, Cals, ISDN, open systems, MAP/TOP, object-oriented design, EDI, expert systems and neural networks.
**Readers:** CEOs, VPs, marketing directors, researchers, vendors and corporate libraries for computer and communications companies and their counterparts in academia and government; large end users of hardware and software.
**Deadline:** story-Thu.; news-Thu.

71080
**SOFTWARE MANAGEMENT NEWS**
141 St. Marks Pl., Ste. 5F
Staten Island, NY 10301
Telephone: (718) 816-5522
FAX: (718) 816-9038
Mailing Address:
4546 El Camino Real, B10, Ste. 237
Los Altos, CA 94022
Year Established: 1983
Pub. Frequency: bi-m.
Subscrip. Rate: $60/yr. US; $95/yr. foreign
Materials: 10,32
Circulation: 3,500
Circulation Type: controlled & paid
**Owner(s):**
Software Maintenance News, Inc.
141 St. Marks Pl., Ste. 5F
Staten Island, NY 10301
Telephone: (718) 816-5522
FAX: (718) 816-9038
Ownership %: 100
**Editorial:**
Nicholas Zvegintzov .................................Editor
**Desc.:** Reports on the people who manage installed software systems and the technology they use to control, enhance, adapt, test, document, or correct software and to support nontechnical users.

71034
**TECHNICAL COMPUTING**
9714 S. Rice Ave.
Houston, TX 77096-4138
Telephone: (713) 723-6658
FAX: (713) 728-2150
Year Established: 1988
Pub. Frequency: m.
Subscrip. Rate: $175/yr.
Materials: 10

**Owner(s):**
Stics, Inc.
9714 S. Rice Ave.
Houston, TX 77096-4138
Telephone: (713) 723-6658
FAX: (713) 728-2150
Ownership %: 100
**Editorial:**
John Chappelear .......................................Editor

71056
**TERRY SHANNON ON DEC**
8130 Boone Blvd., Ste. 210
Vienna, VA 22182-2640
Telephone: (703) 760-0660
FAX: (703) 760-9365
Year Established: 1980
Pub. Frequency: m.
Subscrip. Rate: $595/yr. US; $643/yr. foreign
**Owner(s):**
DataTrends Publications, Inc.
8130 Boone Blvd., Ste. 210
Vienna, VA 22182-2640
Telephone: (703) 760-0660
FAX: (703) 760-9365
Ownership %: 100
**Editorial:**
Terry Shannon .............................................Editor
**Desc.:** Analyzes issues and activity in the Digital Equipment Corporation computing environment. Evaluates DEC products, positioning and strategies.

70491
**VDT NEWS**
552 Grand Central Sta.
New York, NY 10163
Telephone: (212) 517-2802
Mailing Address:
P.O. Box 1799
New York, NY 10163
Year Established: 1984
Pub. Frequency: bi-m.
Subscrip. Rate: $87/yr.; $97/yr.
**Owner(s):**
Microwave News
P.O. Box 1799
New York, NY 10163
Ownership %: 100
**Editorial:**
Louis Slesin ................................................Editor

71057
**VIRTUAL REALITY WORLD**
11 Ferry Ln., W.
Westport, CT 06880-5808
Telephone: (203) 226-6967
FAX: (203) 454-8540
Year Established: 1993
Pub. Frequency: bi-m.
Page Size: standard
Subscrip. Rate: $33/yr. individuals; $59/yr. institutions
**Owner(s):**
Meckler Publishing Corp.
11 Ferry Ln., W.
Westport, CT 06880-5808
Telephone: (203) 226-6967
FAX: (203) 454-8540
Ownership %: 100
**Management:**
Alan M. Meckler ................................President

71241
**WIRELESS DATA NEWS**
1201 Seven Locks Rd.
Potomac, MD 20854
Telephone: (301) 424-3338
FAX: (301) 309-3847
Year Established: 1993
Pub. Frequency: bi-w.
Subscrip. Rate: $397/yr. US; $430/yr. foreign

---

Materials Accepted/Included: 01-Business news 02-By-line articles 03-Fashion news 04-Food news 05-Freelance copy 06-Letters to editor 07-Real estate news 08-Sports news 09-Travel news 10-Book rev. 11-Movie rev. 12-Music rev. 13-TV rev. 14-Theater rev. 15-Coming events 16-Obituaries 17-Question & answer 18-Social announcements 19-Artwork 20-Cartoons 21-Photos 22-TV listings 23-Audio rec. 24-Video rec. 25-Books 26-Films/film clips 27-Personnel news 28-Press releases 29-New product news/photos 30-Trade lit. 31-Contracts awarded 32-Display adv. 33-Classified adv.

Owner(s):
Phillips Business Information, Inc.
1201 Seven Locks Rd.
Potomac, MD 20854
Telephone: (301) 424-3338
FAX: (301) 309-3847
Ownership %: 100

## Group 320-Engineering & Industrial Materials

### ACM MONTHLY
70279
7670 Opportunity Rd., Ste. 250
San Diego, CA 92111-0002
Telephone: (619) 560-1085
FAX: (619) 560-0234
Year Established: 1971
Pub. Frequency: m.
Owner(s):
Composite Market Reports, Inc.
7670 Opportunity Rd., Ste. 250
San Diego, CA 92111-2222
Telephone: (619) 560-1085
FAX: (619) 560-0234
Ownership %: 100
**Desc.:** Non-aerospace application of advanced composites.

### ADHESIVES & SEALANTS NEWSLETTER
70266
P.O. Box 1123
Mishawaka, IN 46546-1123
Telephone: (219) 255-6794
Year Established: 1977
Pub. Frequency: m.
Subscrip. Rate: $165/yr. US; $185/yr. foreign
Materials: 10
Owner(s):
Adhesive Information Services
P.O. Box 1123
Mishawaka, IN 46546-1123
Telephone: (219) 255-6794
Ownership %: 100
Editorial:
W.F. Harrington ...................................Editor
**Desc.:** News digest of adhesive and sealant information.

### ADVANCED COMPOSITES MONTHLY
70289
7670 Opportunity Rd., Ste. 250
San Diego, CA 92111-2222
Telephone: (619) 560-1085
FAX: (619) 560-0234
Year Established: 1972
Pub. Frequency: m.
Subscrip. Rate: $2535/yr.
Owner(s):
Composite Market Reports, Inc.
7670 Opportunity Rd., Ste. 250
San Diego, CA 92111-2222
Telephone: (619) 560-1085
FAX: (619) 560-0234
Ownership %: 100
Editorial:
Steve Loud ...........................................Editor
**Desc.:** Prepared for engineering, program, and manufacturing management at primes and their subcontractors where aerospace components made of high-performance composite materials are designed, fabricated or assembled.

### ADVANCED MATERIALS
61720
P.O. Box 6249
Hilton Head, SC 29938
Telephone: (803) 842-4940
FAX: (803) 842-4940
Year Established: 1979

Pub. Frequency: s-m.
Subscrip. Rate: $187/yr. US; $210/yr. foreign
Materials: 10
Owner(s):
Advanced Publications, Inc.
P.O. Box 6249
Hilton Head, SC 29938
Telephone: (803) 842-4940
FAX: (803) 842-4940
Ownership %: 100
Editorial:
Philip West ...........................................Editor
**Desc.:** Newsletter covering high-performance composites, alloys, ceramics, plastics, adhesives, and elastomers. Emphasis on technical developments and new applications and processes.
**Readers:** Those in engineering, R & D, marketing in industrial fields, universities and consultants.

### ALKALINE PAPER ADVOCATE
70789
7105 Geneve Dr.
Austin, TX 78723
Telephone: (512) 929-3992
FAX: (512) 929-3992
Year Established: 1988
Pub. Frequency: bi-m.
Page Size: standard
Subscrip. Rate: $35/yr.; $45/yr. institutions
Materials: 32
Circulation: 227
Circulation Type: controlled & paid
Owner(s):
Abbey Publications, Inc.
7105 Geneve Dr.
Austin, TX 78723
Telephone: (512) 929-3992
Ownership %: 100
Editorial:
Ellen McCrady ......................................Editor
**Desc.:** For those interested (papermakers, librarians, and paper industry suppliers) in trends in conversion to alkaline papermaking, world wide. Includes current news and events.

### BOARD CONVERTING NEWS
69367
43 Main St.
Avon by Sea, NJ 07717
Telephone: (908) 502-0500
FAX: (908) 502-9606
Year Established: 1984
Pub. Frequency: w.
Page Size: standard
Subscrip. Rate: $120/yr.
Materials: 01,02,06,16,32,33
Circulation: 9,575
Circulation Type: paid
Owner(s):
NV Business Publishers Corp.
43 Main St.
Avon by Sea, NJ 07717
Telephone: (908) 502-0500
Ownership %: 100
Editorial:
Jim Curley ...........................................Editor
**Desc.:** Covers product and current news.
**Deadline:** story-1 wk. prior to pub. date; news-1 wk.; photo-1 wk.; ads-1 wk.

### BOARD CONVERTING NEWS INTERNATIONAL
70768
43 Main St.
Avon By Sea, NJ 07717
Telephone: (908) 502-0500
FAX: (908) 502-9606
Pub. Frequency: fortn.
Subscrip. Rate: $110/yr.
Circulation: 3,075
Circulation Type: controlled & paid

Owner(s):
NV Business Publishers Corp.
43 Main St.
Avon By The Sea, NJ 07717
Telephone: (908) 502-0500
Ownership %: 100
Editorial:
Michael Brunton ...................................Editor
**Desc.:** Covers product news and general news.

### CENTER FOR THE HISTORY OF ELECTRICAL ENGINEERING NEWSLETTER
70331
39 Union St.
New Brunswick, NJ 08903
Telephone: (908) 932-1066
FAX: (908) 932-1193
Year Established: 1982
Pub. Frequency: 3/yr.
Subscrip. Rate: free
Circulation: 5,000
Circulation Type: controlled & paid
Owner(s):
Center for the History of Electrical Engineering
39 Union St.
New Brunswick, NJ 08903
Telephone: (908) 932-1066
FAX: (908) 932-1193
Ownership %: 100
Editorial:
William Aspray ....................................Editor

### COAL OUTLOOK
70705
1616 N. Ft. Myer Dr., Ste. 1000
Arlington, VA 22209-3107
Telephone: (703) 528-1244
FAX: (703) 528-1253
Year Established: 1975
Pub. Frequency: w.
Subscrip. Rate: $695/yr. US; $725/yr. foreign
Owner(s):
Pasha Publications
1616 N. Ft. Myer Dr., Ste. 100
Arlington, VA 22209-3107
Telephone: (703) 528-1244
FAX: (703) 528-1253
Ownership %: 100
Editorial:
Barry Cassell .......................................Editor
**Desc.:** Reports on coal market trends.

### COMPOSITES & ADHESIVES NEWSLETTER
70782
P.O. Box 36006
Los Angeles, CA 90036
Telephone: (213) 938-6923
Year Established: 1984
Pub. Frequency: bi-m.
Subscrip. Rate: $150/yr. US; $170/yr. foreign
Materials: 10,32
Circulation: 150
Circulation Type: controlled & paid
Owner(s):
TC Press
P.O. Box 36006
Los Angeles, CA 90036
Telephone: (213) 938-6923
Ownership %: 100
Editorial:
George Epstein ....................................Editor
**Desc.:** Covers composite and adhesive materials. Includes information on new applications, alerts or problems to avoid, technology developments, plus industry news about companies, schools, and professional societies.

### CURELETTER
70779
P.O. Box 504
Brick, NJ 08723-0504
Telephone: (908) 840-1224
FAX: (908) 840-1211
Year Established: 1984
Pub. Frequency: m.
Subscrip. Rate: $225/yr. US; $247/yr. foreign
Materials: 10,32
Owner(s):
Captan Associates, Inc.
P.O. Box 504
Brick, NJ 08723-0504
Telephone: (908) 840-1244
Ownership %: 100
Editorial:
C. Bluestein .........................................Editor

### DESIGN & DRAFTING NEWS
70260
P.O. Box 799
Rockville, MD 20848-0799
Telephone: (301) 460-6875
FAX: (301) 460-8591
Pub. Frequency: bi-m.
Subscrip. Rate: membership
Materials: 10,32
Circulation: 2,500
Circulation Type: controlled & paid
Owner(s):
American Design Drafting Assn.
P.O. Box 799
Rockville, MD 20848-0799
Telephone: (301) 460-6875
FAX: (301) 460-8591
Ownership %: 100
Editorial:
R. Howard ...........................................Editor

### DIAMOND & STRUCTURAL CARBON NEWS (DASC NEWS)
70400
25 Van Zant St.
Norwalk, CT 06855
Telephone: (203) 853-4266
FAX: (203) 853-0348
Pub. Frequency: m.
Page Size: standard
Subscrip. Rate: $295/yr.
Owner(s):
Business Communications Co., Inc.
25 Van Zant St.
Norwalk, CT 06855
Telephone: (203) 853-4266
FAX: (203) 853-0348
Ownership %: 100
Management:
Robert Butler ....................................Manager
**Desc.:** New developments and applications of carbon, graphite and natural diamonds in: 1) structural materials, with the emergence of graphite fibers and new applications in extreme environmental conditions, and 2) industrial diamonds which have revolutionized such operations as grinding, cutting, drilling and finishing, and in diamond and diamond-like films on a variety of substrates, which have opened up opportunities for a wide variety of applications. Up-dates on crucial information on trends in materials, technology, systems, concepts; who is making, buying testing and using what; international developments; industry analysis, including business & economic trends.
**Readers:** Professionals in structural engineering, manufacturing and those who incorporate operations using diamonds in grinding, cutting, drilling and finishing.

**Materials Accepted/Included:** 01-Business news 02-By-line articles 03-Fashion news 04-Food news 05-Freelance copy 06-Letters to editor 07-Real estate news 08-Sports news 09-Travel news 10-Book rev. 11-Movie rev. 12-Music rev. 13-TV rev. 14-Theater rev. 15-Coming events 16-Obituaries 17-Question & answer 18-Social announcements 19-Artwork 20-Cartoons 21-Photos 22-TV listings 23-Audio rec. 24-Video rec. 25-Books 26-Films/film clips 27-Personnel news 28-Press releases 29-New product news/photos 30-Trade lit. 31-Contracts awarded 32-Display adv. 33-Classified adv.

7-29

## E & MJ MINING ACTIVITY DIGEST
70707
29 N. Wacker Dr.
Chicago, IL 60606
Telephone: (312) 726-2802
FAX: (312) 726-2574
Year Established: 1974
Pub. Frequency: m.
Subscrip. Rate: $110/yr.
Circulation: 162
Circulation Type: controlled & paid
**Owner(s):**
Maclean Hunter Publishing Co.
29 N. Wacker Dr.
Chicago, IL 60606
Telephone: (312) 726-2802
FAX: (312) 726-2574
Ownership %: 100
**Editorial:**
Charles Richardson .................................Editor
**Desc.:** Summarizes mining company
activities and markets for metals
thoughtout the world.

## EERC NEWS
70273
1301 S. 46th St.
Richmond, CA 94804
Telephone: (510) 231-9554
FAX: (510) 231-9471
Year Established: 1977
Pub. Frequency: q.
Subscrip. Rate: free
Circulation: 5,000
Circulation Type: controlled & paid
**Owner(s):**
University of California, Berkeley
Earthquake & Engineering Resea
1301 S. 46th St.
Richmond, CA 94804
Telephone: (510) 231-9554
FAX: (510) 231-9471
Ownership %: 100
**Editorial:**
Ruth C. Wrentmore ..................................Editor
**Desc.:** Publishes news and new
developments in the field of earthquake
engineering.

## ELECTRONIC BUSINESS FORECAST
71128
275 Washington St.
Newton, MA 02158-1630
Telephone: (617) 630-2124
FAX: (617) 630-2100
Year Established: 1982
Pub. Frequency: s-m.
Subscrip. Rate: $337/yr.; $387/yr. foreign
Circulation: 500
Circulation Type: controlled & paid
**Owner(s):**
Cahners Publishing Co.
275 Washington St.
Newton, MA 02158-2124
Telephone: (617) 630-2124
FAX: (617) 630-2100
Ownership %: 100
**Editorial:**
Maddy Franchi ..................................Editor

## ELECTRONIC MATERIALS TECHNOLOGY NEWS
66131
25 Van Zant St.
Norwalk, CT 06855
Telephone: (203) 853-4266
FAX: (203) 853-0348
Year Established: 1986
Pub. Frequency: m.
Page Size: standard
Subscrip. Rate: $305/yr.
Materials: 01,19,20,21,26

**Owner(s):**
Business Communications Co., Inc.
25 Van Zant St.
Norwalk, CT 06855
Telephone: (203) 853-4266
Ownership %: 100
**Management:**
Louis Naturman ..................................Owner
**Editorial:**
Robert Butler ..................Circulation Editor
**Desc.:** Provides timely anaysis of new
products, patent and industry trends in
the major new market for the chemicals
and materials industries. Late
breaking news in the rapidly evolving
electronic materials industry.
**Readers:** Maunfacturers, materials
suppliers and end users for new
materials and specialty chemicals in
electronic components and systems.

## EQUIPMENT & MATERIALS UPDATE
71185
P.O. Box 15640
Plantation, FL 33318-5640
Telephone: (304) 473-9560
FAX: (304) 473-0544
Pub. Frequency: m.
Subscrip. Rate: $269/yr. US; $289/yr.
Canada; $319/yr. foreign
**Owner(s):**
Merton Allen Associates
P.O. Box 15640
Plantation, FL 33318-5640
Telephone: (305) 473-9560
FAX: (305) 473-0544
Ownership %: 100
**Editorial:**
Walter Treff ..................................Editor

## EUROPEAN PACKAGING NEWSLETTER & WORLD REPORT
70763
669 S. Washington St.
Alexandria, VA 22314-4109
Telephone: (703) 519-3907
FAX: (703) 519-7732
Year Established: 1961
Pub. Frequency: m.
Subscrip. Rate: $240/yr. US; $255/yr.
foreign
**Owner(s):**
IPN Inc.
669 S. Washington St.
Alexandria, VA 22314
Telephone: (703) 519-3907
Ownership %: 100
**Editorial:**
PierreJ. Louis ..................................Editor
**Desc.:** Serves the packaging industry as a
clearinghouse for information on
techniques, new machinery, and
processes from Europe and Asia.

## FIBERWORKS QUARTERLY
70902
P.O. Box 49770
Austin, TX 78765-9770
Telephone: (512) 343-6112
Year Established: 1985
Pub. Frequency: q.
Subscrip. Rate: $14/yr.
Materials: 10,33
**Owner(s):**
Fiberworks Publications
P.O. Box 49l770
Austin, TX 78765-9770
Telephone: (512) 343-6112
Ownership %: 100
**Editorial:**
Bobbi A. McRae ..................................Editor

## FLAME RETARDANCY NEWS
66587
25 Van Zant St.
Norwalk, CT 06855
Telephone: (203) 853-4266
FAX: (203) 853-0348
Year Established: 1991
Pub. Frequency: m.
Page Size: standard
Subscrip. Rate: $325/yr.
**Owner(s):**
Business Communications Co., Inc.
25 Van Zant St.
Norwalk, CT 06855
Telephone: (203) 853-4266
Ownership %: 100
**Management:**
Louis Naturman ..................................Owner
Robert Butler ..................................Manager
**Desc.:** Describes and details advances in
flame retardancy of polymeric materials
applications industry developments and
markets. News and analysis of
worldwide R&D, product descriptions
and comparisons, corporate activities
and attitudes.
**Readers:** Commercial development-
corporate management-technical
management/research and market
research people in industries making,
buying or using new flame retardant
materials.

## GLOBAL ELECTRONICS
71134
222B View St.
Moutain View, CA 94041
Telephone: (415) 969-1545
FAX: (415) 968-1126
Year Established: 1980
Pub. Frequency: m.
Subscrip. Rate: $12/yr.
Materials: 10
Circulation: 350
Circulation Type: controlled & paid
**Owner(s):**
Pacific Studies Center
222B View St.
Moutain View, CA 94041
Telephone: (415) 969-1545
FAX: (415) 968-1126
Ownership %: 100
**Editorial:**
Lenny Siegel ..................................Editor
**Desc.:** Covers current trends in the
computer and semiconductor industries,
emphasizing the impact on the
workforce and environment.

## GMP LETTER
70518
117 N. 19th St., Ste. 200
Arlington, VA 22209
Telephone: (703) 247-3434
FAX: (703) 247-3421
Year Established: 1980
Pub. Frequency: m.
Subscrip. Rate: $337/yr.
Materials: 10
**Owner(s):**
Washington Business Information, Inc.
1117 N. 19th St., Ste. 200
Arlington, VA 22209
Telephone: (703) 247-3434
Ownership %: 100
**Editorial:**
Samuel Gilston ..................................Editor
**Desc.:** Covers Good Manufacturing
Practice according to FDA rules dictating
controls on producttion and quality
control.

## GRAFIBER NEWS
70352
7670 Opportunity Rd., Ste. 250
San Diego, CA 92111-2222
Telephone: (619) 560-1085
FAX: (619) 560-0234
Year Established: 1971
Pub. Frequency: m.
Subscrip. Rate: $2535/yr.
**Owner(s):**
Composite Market Reports, Inc.
7670 Opportunity Rd., Ste. 250
San Diego, CA 92111-2222
Telephone: (619) 560-1085
FAX: (619) 560-0234
Ownership %: 100
**Editorial:**
Steve Loud ..................................Editor
**Desc.:** For marketing, manufacturing, and
technical management personnel at US
and overseas suppliers of advanced
composite fibers, resins, fabrics and
related materials, plus process
equipment manufacturers.

## INFRASTRUCTURE
70275
951 Pershing Dr.
Silver Spring, MD 20901-4464
Telephone: (301) 587-6300
FAX: (301) 585-9075
Year Established: 1992
Pub. Frequency: bi-w.
Subscrip. Rate: $390/yr.
**Owner(s):**
Business Publishers, Inc.
951 Pershing Dr.
Silver Spring, MD 20901-4464
Telephone: (301) 587-6300
FAX: (301) 585-9075
Ownership %: 100

## INSIDE TEXTILES
70898
P.O. Box 1309
Point Pleasant Beach, NJ 08742
Telephone: (201) 295-8258
Year Established: 1980
Pub. Frequency: m.
Subscrip. Rate: $167/yr. US; $197/yr.
foreign
Materials: 10
**Owner(s):**
Point Publishing Co., Inc.
P.O. Box 1309
Point Pleasant Beach, NJ 08742
Telephone: (201) 295-8258
Ownership %: 100
**Editorial:**
Noreen C. Heimboldt ..................................Editor

## JETS REPORT
70264
1420 King St., Ste. 405
Alexandria, VA 22314-2794
Telephone: (703) 548-5387
FAX: (703) 836-4875
Year Established: 1980
Pub. Frequency: s-a.
Subscrip. Rate: free qualified personnel
Circulation: 35,000
Circulation Type: controlled & paid
**Owner(s):**
Junior Engineering Technical Society
1420 King St., Ste. 405
Alexandria, VA 22314-2794
Telephone: (703) 548-5387
FAX: (703) 836-4875
Ownership %: 100
**Editorial:**
Cathy McGowan ..................................Editor
**Desc.:** Promoting interest in engineering,
technology, mathmatics and science in
high school.

## KEYSTONE NEWS BULLETIN
70697

29 N. Wacker Dr.
Chicago, IL 60606
Telephone: (312) 726-2802
FAX: (312) 726-4103
Pub. Frequency: m.
Subscrip. Rate: $120/yr.
Circulation: 600
Circulation Type: controlled & paid
**Owner(s):**
Maclean Hunter Publishing Co.
29 N. Wacker Dr.
Chicago, IL 60606
Telephone: (312) 726-2802
FAX: (312) 726-4103
Ownership %: 100
**Editorial:**
M.J. Martin ...............................Editor
**Desc.:** Summarizes American news that
affects coal mining and marketing.
Emphasizes government actions, coal
company acquisitions and production,
and consumption statistics.

## MAGNESIUM MONTHLY REVIEW
70671

106 Spring Forest Rd.
Greenville, SC 29615-2241
Telephone: (803) 244-5718
Year Established: 1971
Pub. Frequency: m.
Subscrip. Rate: $45/yr.
Materials: 10
Circulation: 416
Circulation Type: controlled & paid
**Owner(s):**
Magnesium Monthly Review
106 Spring Forest Rd.
Greenville, SC 29615-2241
Telephone: (803) 224-5718
Ownership %: 100
**Editorial:**
David C. Brown ...........................Editor
**Desc.:** Updates on and predictions for this
structural metal industry, covering
production, markets, techniques, and
foreign developments.

## MEMBRANE & SEPARATION TECHNOLOGY NEWS
64948

25 Van Zant St.
Norwalk, CT 06855
Telephone: (203) 853-4266
FAX: (203) 853-0348
Year Established: 1982
Pub. Frequency: m.
Page Size: standard
Subscrip. Rate: $395/yr.
**Owner(s):**
Business Communications Co., Inc.
25 Van Zant St.
Norwalk, CT 06855
Telephone: (203) 853-4266
Ownership %: 100
**Management:**
Louis Naturman ...........................Owner
Robert Butler .............................Manager
**Desc.:** Explores and analyzes the latest
developments in the science, technology
and business of microfiltration, reverse
osmosis, ultrafiltration, gas separation,
electrodialysis, specialty chromatography
and an array of other membrane and
separation opportunities.
**Readers:** Pharmaceutical, biotechnology
and electronics professionals and those
interested in commercial applications in
light of membrane technology's cost-
effective, energy efficient properties.

## METALS WEEK
24029

1221 Avenue of the Americas
New York, NY 10020
Telephone: (212) 512-2224
FAX: (212) 512-2504
Year Established: 1930
Pub. Frequency: w.
Page Size: standard
Subscrip. Rate: $770/yr.
**Owner(s):**
S & P Information Services
1221 Ave. of the Americas
New York, NY 10020
Telephone: (212) 512-2823
Ownership %: 100
**Editorial:**
Andy Blamey .....................Senior Editor
Karen McBeth ...........................Editor
Mary Ann Wright ..............Managing Editor
John Burger ....................Assistant Editor
Marjorie Coeyman .............Assistant Editor
Jackie Roche ..................Assistant Editor
Nancy Stair ....................Assistant Editor
Ovid Abrams ...................Associate Editor
Melanie Lovatt .................Associate Editor
Mary Ann Whalen ..........Conference Manager
Jackie Roche ................Editorial Assistant
Rieko Suda ...................Hong Kong Editor
Sandra Pucciarelli .........................Sales
Wakako Ishibashi .................Tokyo Editor
**Desc.:** Reports news affecting the world
nonferrous metals industries, with
special emphasis on prices and
marketing information, government-
related action, and international
developments affecting metals trading,
supply and demand. Many of Metals
Week's daily and weekly prices are
exclusive and used by both industry and
government as the basis for contracts.

## M TECHNOLOGY NEWSLETTER
70690

105 College Rd., E.
Princeton, NJ 08540
Telephone: (609) 452-7700
FAX: (609) 987-8523
Year Established: 1960
Pub. Frequency: m.
Page Size: standard
Subscrip. Rate: $70/yr. individuals ;
    $135/yr. institutions
Materials: 10
Circulation: 3,000
Circulation Type: controlled & paid
**Owner(s):**
American Powder Metallurgy Institute
105 College Rd. E.
Princeton, NJ 08540
Telephone: (609) 452-7700
FAX: (609) 987-8523
Ownership %: 100
**Editorial:**
Peter K. Johnson .........................Editor
**Desc.:** Covers international developments
in metal powder industry and
technology; R & D reports, company and
industry news, meetings, and new
products.

## NONWOVENS PATENT NEWS
70937

3112 E. Hampton Ave.
Mesa, AZ 85204
Telephone: (602) 924-0813
FAX: (602) 924-6966
Year Established: 1990
Pub. Frequency: m.
Subscrip. Rate: $857/yr.
**Owner(s):**
D.K. Smith
3112 E. Hampton Ave.
Mesa, AZ 85204
Telephone: (602) 924-0813
FAX: (602) 924-6966
Ownership %: 100

**Management:**
D.K. Smith ...........................Publisher
**Editorial:**
D.K. Smith ...............................Editor
**Desc.:** Contains articles, patent abstracts,
and diagrams of U.S., European and
Japanese patents that affect the
nonwoven textile industry. Includes
polymlers, films, tissues, proccsses,
equipment, converted products, and
related items.

## PAPER STOCK REPORT
69037

13727 Holland Rd.
Cleveland, OH 44142-3920
Telephone: (216) 362-7979
FAX: (216) 362-4623
Year Established: 1990
Pub. Frequency: bi-w.
Page Size: standard
Subscrip. Rate: $99/yr. US; $125/yr.
    Canada & Mexico; $235/yr. elsewhere
Materials: 01,02,05,06,27,28,29,30,31,32,33
Print Process: offset lithography
Circulation: 2,000
Circulation Type: paid
**Owner(s):**
McEntee Media Corp.
13727 Holland Rd.
Cleveland, OH 44142-3920
Telephone: (216) 362-7979
FAX: (216) 362-4623
Ownership %: 100
**Editorial:**
Ken McEntee .............................Editor
Richard Downing ...................Advertising
**Desc.:** Features news and trends
impacting markets for recovered scrap
paper.

## PERSPECTIVES IN ENGINEERING
70334

150 W. State St.
Trenton, NJ 08608
Telephone: (609) 393-0099
FAX: (609) 396-5361
Year Established: 1939
Pub. Frequency: q.
Subscrip. Rate: membership only
Circulation: 3,000
Circulation Type: controlled & paid
**Owner(s):**
New Jersey Society of Professional
    Engineers
150 W. State St.
Trenton, NJ 08608
Telephone: (609) 393-0099
FAX: (609) 396-5361
Ownership %: 100
**Editorial:**
John Patterson ...........................Editor
**Desc.:** Newsletter of the society.

## PLASTICS FOCUS
61719

358 N. Pleasant St.
Amherst, MA 01002
Telephone: (413) 549-5020
FAX: (413) 549-9955
Mailing Address:
    P.O. Box 814
    Amherst, MA 01004
Year Established: 1968
Pub. Frequency: bi-w.
Page Size: standard
Subscrip. Rate: $250/yr.
Materials: 01,28,27,29
Print Process: offset
**Owner(s):**
Plastics Connection, Inc.
P.O. Box 814
Amherst, MA 01004
Telephone: (413) 549-5020
FAX: (413) 549-9955
Ownership %: 100

**Editorial:**
Michael L. Berins .......................Editor
**Desc.:** Interpretive news report covering
developments in plastic materials,
equipment, processes, and applications.
**Readers:** Users, buyers, and sellers of
plastics
**Deadline:** news-Tue. prior to pub. date

## PRINCETON UNIVERSITY SCHOOL OF ENGINEERING & APPLIED SCIENCES
70335

School of Engineering & Applied Sciences
Princeton, NJ 08544
Telephone: (609) 258-3617
Pub. Frequency: 3/yr.
Circulation: 12,000
Circulation Type: controlled & paid
**Owner(s):**
Princeton University
School of Engineering & Applied Sciences
Princeton, NJ 08544
Telephone: (609) 258-3617
Ownership %: 100
**Editorial:**
Ann Haver-Allen .........................Editor

## PROFESSIONAL REPORT
70304

1834 Mayfair Rd., Ste. 111
Milwaukee, WI 53226-1406
Telephone: (414) 257-0910
FAX: (414) 257-4092
Year Established: 1957
Pub. Frequency: 6/yr.
Subscrip. Rate: membership
Circulation: 2,500
Circulation Type: controlled & paid
**Owner(s):**
Fluid Power Society
1834 Mayfair Rd., Ste. 111
Milwaukee, WI 53226-1406
Telephone: (414) 257-0910
FAX: (414) 257-4092
Ownership %: 100
**Editorial:**
Jim Morgan ..............................Editor

## REFRACTORY NEWS
70270

500 Wood St., Ste. 326
Pittsburgh, PA 15222
Telephone: (412) 281-6781
FAX: (412) 281-6881
Year Established: 1098
Pub. Frequency: m.
Page Size: standard
Subscrip. Rate: $24/yr. non-members
Circulation: 800
Circulation Type: controlled & paid
**Owner(s):**
Refractories Institute
500 Wood St., Ste. 326
Pittsburgh, PA 15222
Telephone: (412) 281-6781
FAX: (412) 281-6881
Ownership %: 100
**Editorial:**
C.G. Marvin .............................Editor
**Desc.:** News of refractories industry,
covering suppliers of raw materials,
manufacturers and consumers.

## SEMICONDUCTOR INDUSTRY & BUSINESS SURVEY NEWSLETTER
71138

400 Oyster Point Blvd., Ste. 220
San Francisco, CA 94080
Telephone: (415) 871-4377
FAX: (415) 871-0513
Year Established: 1979
Pub. Frequency: 18/yr.
Subscrip. Rate: $495/yr. US; $595/yr.
    foreign
Materials: 10

**Materials Accepted/Included:** 01-Business news 02-By-line articles 03-Fashion news 04-Food news 05-Freelance copy 06-Letters to editor 07-Real estate news 08-Sports news 09-Travel news
10-Book rev. 11-Movie rev. 12-Music rev. 13-TV rev. 14-Theater rev. 15-Coming events 16-Obituaries 17-Question & answer 18-Social announcements 19-Artwork 20-Cartoons 21-Photos 22-TV listings
23-Audio rec. 24-Video rec. 25-Books 26-Films/film clips 27-Personnel news 28-Press releases 29-New product news/photos 30-Trade lit. 31-Contracts awarded 32-Display adv. 33-Classified adv.

7-31

Circulation: 2,000
Circulation Type: controlled & paid
**Owner(s):**
HTE Research, Inc.
400 Oyster Point Blvd., Ste. 2
San Francisco, CA 94080
Telephone: (415) 871-4377
FAX: (415) 871-0513
Ownership %: 100
**Editorial:**
Steve Z. Szirom ...........................Editor
**Desc.:** Presents business analyses,
company profiles, growth market trends,
and a survey of the semiconductor
industry's developments.

**SKILLINGS' MINING REVIEW**  24105
130 W. Superior St., Ste. 728
Duluth, MN 55802-2083
Telephone: (218) 722-2310
FAX: (218) 722-0134
Year Established: 1912
Pub. Frequency: w.
Page Size: standard
Subscrip. Rate: $30/yr.
Materials: 15,16,21,27,28,29,30,32,33
Circulation: 4,000
Circulation Type: controlled & paid
**Owner(s):**
Skillings' Mining Review
130 W. Superior St., Ste. 728
Duluth, MN 55802-2083
Telephone: (218) 722-2310
FAX: (218) 722-0134
Ownership %: 100
**Management:**
David N. Skillings ...............................Publisher
**Editorial:**
David N. Skillings ...................Executive Editor
David N. Skillings ...................Managing Editor
**Desc.:** News publication covering metal
mining and associated industries.
Features include reviews of various
mines, mining areas, mining methods
plus occasional features on shipping and
use of metals. Departments include:
News (and Rumor) From the Bush,
Personal Mention, 70-60-50 Years Ago,
Iron & Steel, Finance, Coming Events,
Mining & Industrial Share Markets,
Metal/Ore Prices, Marine, Trade Notes.
**Readers:** Management level in mining.

**SP NEWS**  70785
10 Lombard St., Ste. 250
San Francisco, CA 94111
Telephone: (415) 433-1000
FAX: (415) 391-7890
Pub. Frequency: bi-m.
Subscrip. Rate: $59/yr.
Circulation: 25,000
Circulation Type: controlled & paid
**Owner(s):**
Conservative Paper Co.
10 Lombard St., Ste. 250
SanFrancisco, CA 94111
Telephone: (415) 433-1000
Ownership %: 100
**Editorial:**
David Assmann ...........................Editor
**Desc.:** Discusses enviornmentally sound
paper issues, including recycled paper
and chlorine-free paper issues.

**TREND IN ENGINEERING**  68837
University of Washington
College of Engineering
Seattle, WA 98195
Telephone: (206) 543-2520
FAX: (206) 685-0666
Year Established: 1948
Pub. Frequency: s-a.

Page Size: tabloid
Subscrip. Rate: free qualified personnel
Materials: 10
Circulation: 25,000
Circulation Type: controlled
**Owner(s):**
University of Washington, College of
Engineering
Dean's Office of Engineering
Seattle, WA 98195
Telephone: (206) 543-2520
FAX: (206) 685-0666
Ownership %: 100

**VXIBUS**  70333
8380 Hercules Dr., Ste. P3
La Mesa, CA 91942
Telephone: (619) 697-8790
FAX: (619) 697-5955
Year Established: 1989
Pub. Frequency: 10/yr.
Subscrip. Rate: $195/yr.
Circulation: 300
Circulation Type: controlled & paid
**Owner(s):**
Bode Enterprises
8380 Hercules Dr.
La Mesa, CA 91942
Telephone: (619) 697-8790
FAX: (619) 697-5955
Ownership %: 100
**Editorial:**
Fred R. Bode .............................Editor
**Desc.:** Covers technical and marketing
developments relating to VXI modular
instrumentation standards.

**WASTE RECOVERY REPORT**  70256
211 S. 45th St.
Philadelphia, PA 19104
Telephone: (215) 349-6500
FAX: (215) 349-6502
Year Established: 1096
Pub. Frequency: m.
Subscrip. Rate: $50/yr. US; $75/yr. foreign
Materials: 10
Circulation: 450
Circulation Type: controlled & paid
**Owner(s):**
ICON Information Concepts
211 S. 45th St.
Philadelphia, PA 19104
Telephone: (215) 349-6500
FAX: (215) 349-6502
Ownership %: 100
**Editorial:**
Alan Krigman .............................Editor
**Desc.:** Recycling and reprocessing of
resources.

## Group 322-Entertainment

**BANJO NEWSLETTER**  70714
P.O. Box 364
Greensboro, MD 21639
Telephone: (410) 482-6278
FAX: (410) 482-7252
Year Established: 1973
Pub. Frequency: m.
Subscrip. Rate: $22/yr. US; $28/yr. foreign
Materials: 10,32
Circulation: 6,900
Circulation Type: controlled & paid
**Owner(s):**
Banjo Newsletter, Inc.
P.O. Box 364
Greensboro, MD 21639
Telephone: (410) 482-6278
FAX: (410) 482-7252
Ownership %: 100
**Editorial:**
Hub Nitchie .............................Editor

**Desc.:** Contains information on the 5-string
banjo, a musical instrument used in folk
and classical music. Includes tablature
for the instrument.

**BULLET**  70165
42 Music Sq., W., Ste. 146
Nashville, TN 37203
Year Established: 1982
Pub. Frequency: q.
Subscrip. Rate: $8/yr.
Materials: 10,32
Circulation: 10,000
Circulation Type: controlled & paid
**Owner(s):**
Andy Griffith Show Rerun Watchers Club
42 Music Sq. W.
Ste. 146
Nashville, TN 37203
Ownership %: 100
**Editorial:**
Jim Clark .............................Editor

**CALENDAR FOR NEW MUSIC**  70715
P.O. Box 850
Philmont, NY 12565-0850
FAX: (518) 672-4775
Year Established: 1979
Pub. Frequency: 9/yr.
Subscrip. Rate: $20/2 yrs.; $8/yr. student;
$16/yr. foreign
Materials: 32
Circulation: 6,500
Circulation Type: controlled & paid
**Owner(s):**
SoundArt Foundation, Inc.
P.O. Box 850
Philmont, NY 12565-0850
FAX: (518) 672-4775
Ownership %: 100

**CHURCH MUSIC REPORT**  70730
P.O. Box 1179
Grapevine, TX 76099-1179
Telephone: (817) 488-0141
FAX: (817) 481-4191
Year Established: 1984
Pub. Frequency: m.
Subscrip. Rate: $39.95/yr.
Circulation: 6,600
Circulation Type: controlled & paid
**Owner(s):**
CMR Communications
P.O. Box 1179
Grapevine, TX 76099-1179
Telephone: (817) 488-0141
FAX: (817) 481-4191
Ownership %: 100
**Editorial:**
William H. Rayborn .............................Editor

**CONCERTINA & SQUEEZEBOX**  70716
P.O. Box 6706
Ithaca, NY 14851
Year Established: 1983
Pub. Frequency: q.
Subscrip. Rate: $15/yr.
Materials: 10,32
Circulation: 750
Circulation Type: controlled & paid
**Owner(s):**
J.M. Cowan
P.O. Box 6706
Ithaca, NY 14851
Ownership %: 100
**Editorial:**
J.M. Cowan .............................Editor
**Desc.:** Covers concertinas, accordions,
bandoliers, and other reed instruments.

**CURRENT BLACKJACK NEWS**  71217
7910 Ivanhoe Ave.
No. 34
La Jolla, CA 92037-4511
Telephone: (619) 456-4080
FAX: (619) 456-8076
Year Established: 1979
Pub. Frequency: m. (plus irreg. special
issues)
Subscrip. Rate: $99/yr.; $145/yr. with
special issues; $199/yr. with fax service
Circulation: 350
Circulation Type: paid
**Owner(s):**
Pi Yee Press
7910 Ivanhoe Ave.
No.34
LA Jolla, CA 92037-4511
Telephone: (619) 456-4080
FAX: (619) 456-8076
Ownership %: 100
**Editorial:**
Stanford Wong .............................Editor
**Desc.:** Contains news and updates on the
rules and playing conditions for the
casino game of blackjack in legal
casinos, as well as reports on other
casino games that can be beaten.

**DISC COLLECTOR**  70733
P.O. Box 315
Cheswold, DE 19936
Telephone: (302) 674-3149
Year Established: 1950
Pub. Frequency: m.
Subscrip. Rate: $5/yr. US; $10/yr. foreign
**Owner(s):**
Disc Collector Publications
P.O. Box 315
Cheswold, DE 19936
Telephone: (302) 674-3149
Ownership %: 100
**Editorial:**
Lou Deneumoustier .............................Editor

**DRAMATISTS GUILD NEWSLETTER**  69513
234 W. 44th St.
New York, NY 10036
Telephone: (212) 398-9366
Year Established: 1977
Pub. Frequency: m.
Page Size: tabloid
Subscrip. Rate: membership
Materials: 33
Circulation: 7,500
Circulation Type: paid
**Owner(s):**
Dramatists Guild, Inc.
234 W. 44th St.
New York, NY 10036
Telephone: (212) 398-9366
Ownership %: 100
**Editorial:**
Scott Segal .............................Editor
**Readers:** The professional association of
playwrights, composers & lyricists.

**ENTERTAINMENT INDUSTRY OUTLOOK**  71208
249 W. 17th St.
New York, NY 10011
Telephone: (212) 463-6834
FAX: (212) 463-6500
Mailing Address:
P.O. Box 59
New Town Branch
Boston, MA 02258-9908
Pub. Frequency: m.
Subscrip. Rate: $149/yr.

**Materials Accepted/Included:** 01-Business news 02-By-line articles 03-Fashion news 04-Food news 05-Freelance copy 06-Letters to editor 07-Real estate news 08-Sports news 09-Travel news 10-Book rev. 11-Movie rev. 12-Music rev. 13-TV rev. 14-Theater rev. 15-Coming events 16-Obituaries 17-Question & answer 18-Social announcements 19-Artwork 20-Cartoons 21-Photos 22-TV listings 23-Audio rec. 24-Video rec. 25-Books 26-Films/film clips 27-Personnel news 28-Press releases 29-New product news/photos 30-Trade lit. 31-Contracts awarded 32-Display adv. 33-Classified adv.

**Owner(s):**
Cahners Publishing Co.
249 W. 17th St.
New York, NY 10011
Telephone: (212) 463-6834
FAX: (212) 463-6500
Ownership %: 100
**Desc.:** Provides economic analysis and forecasts relevant to decision makers in the entertainment industry.

70717

## EXPERIMENTAL MUSICAL INSTRUMENTS
P.O. Box 784
Nicasio, CA 94946
Telephone: (415) 662-2182
Year Established: 1985
Pub. Frequency: q.
Subscrip. Rate: $24/yr. US; $34/yr. foreign
Materials: 10,32
Circulation: 650
Circulation Type: controlled & paid
**Owner(s):**
Experimental Musical Instruments
P.O. Box 784
Nicasio, CA 94946
Telephone: (415) 662-2182
Ownership %: 100
**Editorial:**
Bart Hopkin .................................Editor
**Desc.:** Devoted to new and unusual acoustic and electro-acoustic musical instruments and sound sculpture.

70718

## GIRL GROUPS GAZETTE
P.O. Box 69A04
Dept. UL
W. Hollywood, CA 90069
Telephone: (213) 650-5112
Year Established: 1987
Pub. Frequency: q.
Subscrip. Rate: $20/yr.
Materials: 10,32
Circulation: 10,000
Circulation Type: controlled & paid
**Owner(s):**
Fan Club Publishing
P.O. Box 69A04
Dept. UL
W. Hollywood, CA 90069
Telephone: (213) 650-5112
Ownership %: 100
**Editorial:**
Louis Wendruck .................................Editor
**Desc.:** Covers news and developments relating to female rock'n roll groups of the 1960's, 70's, and 80's.

70737

## GOOD DAY SUNSHINE
397 Edgwood Ave.
New Haven, CT 06511-4013
Telephone: (203) 865-8131
FAX: (203) 562-5260
Year Established: 1980
Pub. Frequency: bi-m.
Subscrip. Rate: $10/yr. US; $20/yr. foreign
Circulation: 4,800
Circulation Type: controlled & paid
**Owner(s):**
Liverpool Productions
397 Edgwood Ave.
New Haven, CT 06511-4013
Telephone: (203) 865-8131
FAX: (203) 562-5260
Ownership %: 100
**Editorial:**
Charles F. Rosenay .................................Editor
**Desc.:** For Beatles fans, collectors and appreciators of music from the 60's, including news, reviews, convention reports, and photos.

70711

## INTERNATIONAL DOCUMENTARY
1551 S. Robertson Blvd., Ste. 201
Los Angeles, CA 90035
Telephone: (310) 284-8422
FAX: (310) 785-9334
Year Established: 1982
Pub. Frequency: m.
Subscrip. Rate: $25/yr. individuals; $30/yr. institutions; $35/yr. foreign
Materials: 10,32
Circulation: 2,000
Circulation Type: controlled & paid
**Owner(s):**
International Documentary Foundation
1551 S. Roberson Blvd.
Ste. 201
Los Angeles, CA 90035
Telephone: (310) 284-8422
FAX: (310) 785-9334
Ownership %: 100
**Editorial:**
Diana Rico .................................Editor
**Desc.:** Devoted to non-fiction film and video. Provides valuable information for documentary filmmakers and their audience.

70720

## KURT WEILL NEWSLETTER
7 E. 20th St.
New York, NY 10003-1106
Telephone: (212) 505-5240
FAX: (212) 353-9663
Year Established: 1983
Pub. Frequency: 2/yr.
Subscrip. Rate: free
Materials: 10
Circulation: 6,000
Circulation Type: controlled & paid
**Owner(s):**
Kurt Weill Foundation for Music
7 E. 20th St.
New York, NY 10003-1106
Telephone: (212) 505-5240
FAX: (212) 353-9663
Ownership %: 100
**Editorial:**
David Farneth .................................Editor

71205

## LAS VEGAS ADVISOR
5280 S. Valley View Blvd., Ste. B
Las Vegas, NV 89118
Telephone: (702) 597-1884
FAX: (702) 597-5208
Year Established: 1983
Pub. Frequency: m.
Subscrip. Rate: $45/yr. US; $50/yr. foreign
Materials: 10
Circulation: 6,500
Circulation Type: paid
**Owner(s):**
Huntington Press
5280 S. Valley View Blvd.
Ste. B
Las Vegas, NV 89118
Telephone: (702) 597-1884
FAX: (702) 597-5208
Ownership %: 100
**Editorial:**
Deke Castleman .................................Editor
**Desc.:** For Las Vegas visitors. Covers dining, gambling, entertainment and accomodations, with an emphasis on bargain and value.

71158

## LEISURE INDUSTRY REPORT
P.O. Box 43563
Washington, DC 20010
Telephone: (202) 232-7107
Year Established: 1981
Pub. Frequency: 10/yr.
Subscrip. Rate: $65/yr.
Materials: 10,32

**Owner(s):**
Leisure Industry-Recreation News
P.O. Box 43563
Washington, DC 20010
Telephone: (202) 232-7107
Ownership %: 100
**Editorial:**
Marj Jensen .................................Editor
**Desc.:** Compiles news reports from a wide range of sources into summary reviews of trends and developments on leisure and discretionary spending.

71242

## MUSIC FOR THE LOVE OF IT
67 Parkside Dr.
Berkeley, CA 94705
Telephone: (510) 654-9134
FAX: (510) 654-4656
Year Established: 1988
Pub. Frequency: bi-m.
Subscrip. Rate: $20/yr.
Materials: 33
**Owner(s):**
Music for the Love of It
67 Parkside Dr.
Berkeley, CA 94705
Telephone: (510) 654-9134
FAX: (510) 654-4656
Ownership %: 100
**Editorial:**
Ted Rust .................................Editor

70721

## NEW YORK OPERA NEWSLETTER
P.O. Box 278
Maplewood, NJ 07040
Telephone: (201) 378-9549
FAX: (201) 278-2372
Year Established: 1987
Pub. Frequency: m.
Subscrip. Rate: $48/yr.
Circulation: 2,200
Circulation Type: controlled & paid
**Owner(s):**
New York Opera Newsletter, Inc.
P.O. Box 278
Maplewood, NJ 07040
Telephone: (201) 378-9549
FAX: (201) 278-2372
Ownership %: 100
**Editorial:**
David D. Wood .................................Editor
**Desc.:** Provides specific information for classical vocal artists at all levels, with interviews, articles, and coverage of auditions, competitions, and training programs.

70712

## PAST TIMES: THE NOSTALGIA ENTERTAINMENT NEWSLETTER
7308 Filmore Dr.
Buena Park, CA 90620
Telephone: (714) 956-2246
Year Established: 1990
Pub. Frequency: q.
Subscrip. Rate: $12/yr.
Materials: 10,11,32
Circulation: 5,000
Circulation Type: controlled & paid
**Owner(s):**
Moonstone Press
7308 Filmore Dr.
Buena Park, CA 90620
Telephone: (714) 956-2246
Ownership %: 100
**Editorial:**
Jordan R. Young .................................Editor
**Desc.:** Celebrates the entertainment of the 1920's through the 1940's, covering movies, music, radio programs, pop culture, actors, musicians, and personalities.

71160

## RECREATION INDUSTRY REPORT
P.O. Box 43563
Washington, DC 20010
Telephone: (202) 232-7107
Year Established: 1973
Pub. Frequency: 10/yr.
Subscrip. Rate: $65/yr.
Materials: 10, 32
Circulation: 600
Circulation Type: controlled & paid
**Owner(s):**
Leisure Industry-Recreation News
P.O. Box 43563
Washington, DC 20010
Telephone: (202) 232-7107
Ownership %: 100
**Editorial:**
Marj Jensen .................................Editor
**Desc.:** Presents coverage of recreation issues, directed primarily to those involved in public recreation.

70731

## REMEMBER THAT SONG
5623 N. 64th Ave.
Glendale, AZ 85301
Telephone: (602) 931-2835
Year Established: 1981
Pub. Frequency: m.
Subscrip. Rate: $19/yr.
Materials: 10
Circulation: 425
Circulation Type: controlled & paid
**Owner(s):**
Lois A. Cordrey
5623 N. 64th Ave.
Glendale, AZ 85301
Telephone: (602) 931-2835
Ownership %: 100
**Editorial:**
Lois A. Cordrey .................................Editor
**Desc.:** Covers the historical aspects and implications of collecting American popular music, and the evolution of song, from pre-Civil War to the present day.

70742

## SACRED MUSIC NEWS & REVIEW
P.O. Box 1179
Grapevine, TX 76099-1179
Telephone: (817) 488-0141
FAX: (817) 488-4191
Year Established: 1992
Pub. Frequency: m.
Subscrip. Rate: $39.95/yr.
**Owner(s):**
CMR Communications
P.O. Box 1179
Grapevine, TX 76099-1179
Telephone: (817) 488-0141
FAX: (817) 488-4191
**Editorial:**
Timothy Sharp .................................Editor
**Desc.:** Discusses issues in music ministry, news and information pertaining to choral music, notices of publications and recorded music, and employment listings.

70722

## SCHIRMER-NEWS
225 Park Ave. S., 18th Fl.
New York, NY 10003
Telephone: (212) 254-2100
FAX: (212) 254-2013
Year Established: 1987
Pub. Frequency: 1-4/yr.
Subscrip. Rate: free
**Owner(s):**
G. Schirmer Inc.
225 Park Ave., S., 18th Fl.
New York, NY 10003
Telephone: (212) 254-2100
FAX: (212) 254-2013
Ownership %: 100

**Materials Accepted/Included:** 01-Business news 02-By-line articles 03-Fashion news 04-Food news 05-Freelance copy 06-Letters to editor 07-Real estate news 08-Sports news 09-Travel news 10-Book rev. 11-Movie rev. 12-Music rev. 13-TV rev. 14-Theater rev. 15-Coming events 16-Obituaries 17-Question & answer 18-Social announcements 19-Artwork 20-Cartoons 21-Photos 22-TV listings 23-Audio rec. 24-Video rec. 25-Books 26-Films/film clips 27-Personnel news 28-Press releases 29-New product news/photos 30-Trade lit. 31-Contracts awarded 32-Display adv. 33-Classified adv.

7-33

**Editorial:**
E. Matthew ...............................Editor
**Desc.:** Contains articles, calendars, and announcements of interest to performers, conductors, and the classical music business.

70723
## STACKHOUSE-ROOSTER BLUES NEWSLETTER
232 Sunflower Ave.
Clarkside, MS 38614
Telephone: (601) 627-2209
FAX: (601) 627-9861
Year Established: 1989
Pub. Frequency: a.
Subscrip. Rate: free
Circulation: 10,000
Circulation Type: controlled & paid
**Owner(s):**
Stackhouse-Rooster Blues Records
232 Sunflower Ave.
Clarkside, MS 38614
Telephone: (601) 627-2209
FAX: (601) 627-9861
Ownership %: 100
**Editorial:**
Jim O'Neal ...............................Editor
**Desc.:** Gives news, descriptions, and commentary about the blues in the Mississippi Delta.

70713
## TEN THOUSAND WORDS!
901 E. Grove St., Ste. A4
Bloomington, IL 61701
Telephone: (309) 829-3931
FAX: (309) 829-9677
Year Established: 1976
Pub. Frequency: 10/yr.
Subscrip. Rate: $75/yr.
Materials: 10
Circulation: 3,000
Circulation Type: controlled & paid
**Owner(s):**
Behavioral Images, Inc.
901 E. Grove St., Ste. A4
Bloomington, IL 61701
Telephone: (309) 829-3931
FAX: (309) 829-9677
Ownership %: 100
**Editorial:**
Steve Johnson ...............................Editor
**Desc.:** Strategies, research, terminology, bibliographies, and case studies about appraisal of all AV media for any purpose.

65333
## TRAVERSO
R.D. 3, Box 56
Hudson, NY 12534
Telephone: (518) 828-9779
FAX: (518) 822-1416
Year Established: 1989
Pub. Frequency: q.
Page Size: standard
Subscrip. Rate: $12/yr.; $15/yr. foreign
**Owner(s):**
Folkers & Powell
R.D. 3, Box 56
Hudson, NY 12534
Telephone: (518) 828-9779
Ownership %: 100
**Editorial:**
Ardal Powell ...............................Editor
**Desc.:** Carries news, information and ideas for all interested in the Baroque flute and its music. It lists articles, new books, and general information for Baroque flutists.
**Readers:** Flute players and Baroque flute players

70724
## TUROK'S CHOICE
250 W. 15th St.
New York, NY 10113-0202
Telephone: (212) 691-9229
Year Established: 1990
Pub. Frequency: 11/yr.
Subscrip. Rate: $13.95/yr.
Circulation: 1,000
Circulation Type: controlled & paid
**Owner(s):**
P. Turok
250 W. 15th St.
New York, NY 10113-0202
Telephone: (212) 691-9229
Ownership %: 100
**Editorial:**
P. Turok ...............................Editor
**Desc.:** Examines new classical recordings (on cassette or CD) with information about the artist, format, and commentary.

71129
## VIDEO MOVIES
P.O. Box 2725
Bremerton, WA 98310
Telephone: (206) 377-2231
FAX: (206) 373-6805
Year Established: 1992
Pub. Frequency: m.
Subscrip. Rate: $42/yr. US; $47/yr. Canada; $64/yr. foreign
**Owner(s):**
Video Librarian
P.O. Box 2725
Bremerton, WA 98310
Telephone: (206) 377-2231
FAX: (206) 373-6805
Ownership %: 100
**Editorial:**
Randy Pitman ...............................Editor
**Desc.:** Critical reviews of forthcoming video movie releases for libraries and collectors, with information on stars, original production date for theaters or TV, price, distributor, and potential audience.

# Group 324-Environment & Energy

23192
## AIR/WATER POLLUTION REPORT
951 Pershing Dr.
Silver Spring, MD 20910
Telephone: (301) 587-6300
FAX: (301) 587-1081
Year Established: 1963
Pub. Frequency: w.
Page Size: standard
Subscrip. Rate: $595/yr.
**Owner(s):**
Business Publishers, Inc.
951 Pershing Dr.
Silver Spring, MD 20910
Telephone: (301) 587-6300
Ownership %: 100
**Management:**
Lawrence Fishbein ...............................President
Lawrence Fishbein ...............................Publisher
**Editorial:**
David Goeller ...............................Editor
**Desc.:** This 10 page newsletter provides weekly reports on the entire enviromental field: Legislation (federal & state), Markets, Technology. Special reports are frequent.
**Readers:** The newsletter is aimed specifically at top environmental managers in both industry and government.

69839
## AIR TOXIC REPORTS
951 Pershing Dr.
Silver Spring, MD 20910-4464
Telephone: (301) 587-6300
FAX: (301) 585-9075
Year Established: 1988
Pub. Frequency: m.
Subscrip. Rate: $279.48/yr.
**Owner(s):**
Business Publishers, Inc.
951 Pershing Dr.
Silver Spring, MD 20910-4464
Telephone: (301) 587-6300
Ownership %: 100
**Editorial:**
Charles Knebl ...............................Editor
**Desc.:** Briefing on politics and business technology of toxic air pollutants, with affective emphasis on the 1990 Clean air Act.

70912
## ALTERNATIVE ENERGY
205 S. Beverly Dr.
Ste. 208
Beverly Hills, CA 90212-3873
Telephone: (310) 273-3486
Year Established: 1979
Pub. Frequency: m.
Subscrip. Rate: $90/yr. US; $104/yr. foreign
**Owner(s):**
Alternative Energy
205 S. Beverly Dr.
Ste. 208
Beverly Hills, CA 90212-3873
Telephone: (310) 273-3486
Ownership %: 100
**Editorial:**
Irwin Stambler ...............................Editor

69874
## AMERICAN SHORE & BEACH PRESERVATION ASSOCIATION NEWSLETTER
412 O'Brien Hall
University of California at Berkeley
Berkeley, CA 94720
Telephone: (510) 000-0007
FAX: (510) 642-9143
Mailing Address:
  3000 Citrus Circle
  Ste. 230
  Walnut Creek, CA 94598
Year Established: 1954
Pub. Frequency: q.
Subscrip. Rate: $40/yr. US; $52/yr. foreign; $20/yr. student US; $32/yr. student foreign
Circulation: 1,200
Circulation Type: controlled & paid
**Owner(s):**
American Shore & Beach Preservation Association
412 O'Brien Hall
University of California at Berkeley
Berkeley, CA 94720
Telephone: (510) 642-6777
FAX: (510) 642-9143
Ownership %: 100
**Editorial:**
Gerald J. Giefer ...............................Editor

70438
## ATMOSPHERIC POLLUTION & ABATEMENT NEWS
25 Van Zant St.
Norwalk, CT 06855
Telephone: (203) 853-4266
FAX: (203) 853-0348
Pub. Frequency: m.
Subscrip. Rate: $295/yr.

**Owner(s):**
Business Communications Co., Inc.
25 Van Zant St.
Norwalk, CT 06855
Telephone: (203) 853-4266
Ownership %: 100
**Management:**
Louis Naturman ...............................Owner
Robert Butler ...............................Manager
**Desc.:** Reports on: recent data concerning atmospheric testing; new advances in equipment and technology; news from important federal and corporate sources.

71191
## BIOREDMEDIATION REPORT
627 National Press Bldg.
Washington, DC 20045
Telephone: (202) 638-4260
Year Established: 1991
Pub. Frequency: m.
Subscrip. Rate: $395/yr.
**Owner(s):**
King Communications Group
627 National Press Bldg.
Washington, DC 20045
Telephone: (202) 638-4260
Ownership %: 100
**Editorial:**
Mick Rood ...............................Editor

68718
## BUSINESS & THE ENVIRONMENT
37 Broadway
Arlington, MA 02174-5539
Telephone: (617) 641-5123
FAX: (617) 648-8708
Year Established: 1990
Pub. Frequency: s-m.
Page Size: standard
Subscrip. Rate: $397/yr.
Materials: 01,15,25,27,28,29,30
**Owner(s):**
Cutter Information Corp.
37 Broadway
Arlington, MA 02174-5539
Telephone: (617) 647-8700
FAX: (617) 648-8708
Ownership %: 100
**Editorial:**
Kathleen M. Victory ...............................Editor
**Desc.:** Covers corporate initiatives to protect the environment. Includes product development, process redesign, packaging, business strategy, responses to changing regulatory environment.
**Readers:** Corporate executives, policymakers worldwide.

69886
## CHEMICAL WASTE LITIGATION REPORT
1519 Connecticut Ave. N.W., Ste. 200
Washington, DC 20036
Telephone: (202) 462-5755
FAX: (202) 328-2430
Year Established: 1980
Pub. Frequency: m.
Page Size: LL
Subscrip. Rate: $1500/yr.
**Owner(s):**
Computer Law Reporter, Inc.
1519 Connecticut Ave., N.W., S
Washington, DC 20036
Telephone: (202) 462-5755
FAX: (202) 328-2430
Ownership %: 100
**Editorial:**
John Clewett ...............................Editor

69848
## CITIZEN ALERT NEWSLETTER
3680 Grant Dr.
Reno, NV 89513
Telephone: (702) 827-4200
FAX: (702) 827-4299
Year Established: 1976

**Materials Accepted/Included:** 01-Business news 02-By-line articles 03-Fashion news 04-Food news 05-Freelance copy 06-Letters to editor 07-Real estate news 08-Sports news 09-Travel news 10-Book rev. 11-Movie rev. 12-Music rev. 13-TV rev. 14-Theater rev. 15-Coming events 16-Obituaries 17-Question & answer 18-Social announcements 19-Artwork 20-Cartoons 21-Photos 22-TV listings 23-Audio rec. 24-Video rec. 25-Books 26-Films/film clips 27-Personnel news 28-Press releases 29-New product news/photos 30-Trade lit. 31-Contracts awarded 32-Display adv. 33-Classified adv.

Pub. Frequency: q.
Subscrip. Rate: $15/yr.
Materials: 10
Circulation: 12,500
**Owner(s):**
Citizen Alert
3680 Grant Dr.
Reno, NV 89513
Telephone: (702) 827-4200
FAX: (702) 827-4299
Ownership %: 100
**Editorial:**
Fielding M. McGeehee, III .......................Editor

71132

## CLEAN AIR REPORT
P.O. Box 7167
Benjamin Franklin Sta.
Washington, DC 20044
Telephone: (202) 892-8500
FAX: (202) 685-2606
Pub. Frequency: bi-w.
Subscrip. Rate: $460/yr. US; $510/yr.
   foreign
**Owner(s):**
Inside Washington Publishers
P.O. Box 7167
Benjamin Franklin Sta.
Washington, DC 20044
Telephone: (202) 892-8500
FAX: (202) 685-2606
Ownership %: 100

71141

## CLEAN WATER REPORT
951 Pershing Dr.
Silver Spring, MD 20910-4464
Telephone: (301) 587-6300
FAX: (301) 587-1081
Year Established: 1964
Pub. Frequency: bi-w.
Subscrip. Rate: $242.50/yr.
**Owner(s):**
Business Publishers, Inc.
951 Pershing Dr.
Silver Spring, MD 20910-4464
Telephone: (301) 587-6300
FAX: (301) 587-1081
Ownership %: 100
**Editorial:**
Elaine Eiserer ...............................Editor
**Desc.:** Provides current information from
   the offices of the EPA for wastewater
   treatment plant operators, equiptment
   manufactures, consulting engineers, or
   government regulators.

70917

## COAL & SYNFUELS TECHNOLOGY
1616 N. Fort Myer Dr.
Ste. 1000
Arlington, VA 22209-3107
Telephone: (212) 528-1244
FAX: (703) 528-1253
Year Established: 1979
Pub. Frequency: w.
Subscrip. Rate: $790/yr. US; $820/yr.
   foreign
**Owner(s):**
Pasha Publications Inc.
1616 N. Fort Myer Dr.
Ste. 1000
Arlington, VA 22209-3107
Telephone: (703) 528-1244
FAX: (703) 528-1253
Ownership %: 100
**Editorial:**
Mary Anne Gozewski ....................Editor
**Desc.:** Reports on coal technology project
   financing, environmental issues, oil
   shale, coal liquefaction and gasification
   and synfuels projects.

70200

## COASTAL ZONE MANAGEMENT
201 National Press Bldg.
Washington, DC 20045
Telephone: (202) 347-6643

Year Established: 1969
Pub. Frequency: 3/m.(every 10 days)
Subscrip. Rate: $355/yr. US; $375/yr.
   foreign
Materials: 10
**Owner(s):**
Nautilus Press, Inc.
1201 National Press Bldg.
Washington, DC 20045
Telephone: (202) 347-6643
Ownership %: 100
**Editorial:**
John R. Botzum ...........................Editor
**Desc.:** Specializes in reporting on federal-
   state relationships in the U.S. Coastal
   Zone and Exclusive Economic Zone,
   including information on oil, gas, and
   mineral activities on the outer
   continental shelf; also covers technical
   side of coastal management community
   development, and certain aspects of
   tourism.

71169

## DEFENSE CLEANUP
1616 N. Ft. Meyer Dr., Ste. 1000
Arrlington, VA 22209-3107
Telephone: (703) 528-1244
FAX: (703) 528-1253
Year Established: 1990
Pub. Frequency: w.
Subscrip. Rate: $450/yr. US; $480/yr.
   foreign
**Owner(s):**
Pasha Publications Inc.
1616 N. Ft. Myer Dr., Ste. 100
Arlington, VA 22209-3107
Telephone: (703) 528-1244
FAX: (703) 528-1253
Ownership %: 100
**Editorial:**
Bowman Cox ...............................Editor
**Desc.:** Covers environmental cleanup
   issues, including new waste
   management laws, technology,
   businesses, evolving regulations and
   standards, and political factors
   influencing the cleanup industry.

70772

## E & P ENVIRONMENT
1616 N. Ft. Myer Dr., Ste. 1000
Arlington, VA 22209
Telephone: (703) 528-1244
FAX: (703) 528-1253
Year Established: 1990
Pub. Frequency: bi-w.
Subscrip. Rate: $377/yr.; $392/yr. foreign
**Owner(s):**
Pasha Publications inc.
1616 N. Ft. Myer Dr., Ste. 100
Arlington, VA 22209-3107
Telephone: (703) 528-1244
FAX: (703) 528-1253
Ownership %: 100
**Editorial:**
Jerry Grisham ...............................Editor
**Desc.:** Covers environmental issues
   affecting the oil and gas industries,
   including news of federal and state
   actions, enforcement and regulation, as
   well as trends in risk management and
   liability.

69861

## ECO-PROFITEER
350 Center Dr., Ste. 1000
Dunwoody, GA 30338-4134
Telephone: (404) 668-0432
FAX: (404) 668-0692
Year Established: 1991
Pub. Frequency: m.
Subscrip. Rate: $96/yr.
Circulation: 3,000

**Owner(s):**
Soundview Publications
350 Center Dr., Ste. 1000
Dunwoody, GA 30338-4134
Telephone: (404) 668-0432
FAX: (404) 668-0692
Ownership %: 100
**Editorial:**
Franklin Sanders ...........................Editor

69875

## ECOLOGY USA
951 Pershing Dr.
Silver Spring, MD 20910-4464
Telephone: (301) 587-6300
FAX: (301) 587-1081
Year Established: 1976
Pub. Frequency: bi-w.
Subscrip. Rate: $104.50/yr.
**Owner(s):**
Business Publishers, Inc.
951 Pershing Dr.
Silver Spring, MD 20910-4464
Telephone: (301) 587-6300
FAX: (301) 587-1081
Ownership %: 100
**Editorial:**
Elaine Eiserer ...............................Editor
**Desc.:** Comprehensive coverage of the
   ecosystem as a whole with its complex
   interrelationships.

69878

## ECONEWS
879 Ninth St.
Arcata, CA 95521
Telephone: (707) 822-6918
FAX: (707) 822-0827
Year Established: 1971
Pub. Frequency: m.
Subscrip. Rate: $20/yr.
Materials: 10,32
Circulation: 8,500
Circulation Type: controlled & paid
**Owner(s):**
Northcoast Environmental Center, Inc.
879 Ninth St.
Arcata, CA 95521
Telephone: (707) 822-6918
FAX: (707) 822-0827
Ownership %: 100
**Editorial:**
Sidney Dominitz ...........................Editor
Andrew Alm ...............................Editor
**Desc.:** Presents articles on environmental
   issues including old-growth forests,
   public landsl, pollution and energy.

69879

## EDF LETTER
257 Park Ave., S.
New York, NY 10010
Telephone: (212) 505-2100
FAX: (212) 505-2375
Year Established: 1970
Pub. Frequency: bi-m.
Subscrip. Rate: $20/yr.
Circulation: 200,000
Circulation Type: paid
**Owner(s):**
Environmental Defense Fund
257 Park Ave., S.
New York, NY 10010
Telephone: (212) 505-2100
FAX: (212) 505-2375
Ownership %: 100
**Editorial:**
Norma H. Watson ...........................Editor
**Desc.:** Covers issues relating to the
   environment and public health.

70332

## ELECTRIC POWER ALERT
P.O. 7167
Benjamin Franklin Sta.
Washington, DC 20044
Telephone: (703) 892-8500
FAX: (703) 685-2606

Year Established: 1991
Pub. Frequency: bi-w.
Subscrip. Rate: $445/yr. US; $495/yr.
   foreign
**Owner(s):**
Inside Washington Publishers
P.O. Box 7167
Benjamin Franklin Sta.
Washington, DC 20044
Telephone: (703) 892-8500
FAX: (703) 685-2606
Ownership %: 100
**Editorial:**
Rick Weber ...............................Editor

70405

## ENERGY
25 Van Zant St.
Norwalk, CT 06855
Telephone: (203) 853-4266
FAX: (203) 853-0348
Pub. Frequency: 5/yr.
Subscrip. Rate: $185/yr.
**Owner(s):**
Business Communications Co., Inc.
25 Van Zant St.
Norwalk, CT 06855
Telephone: (203) 853-4266
FAX: (203) 853-0348
Ownership %: 100
**Management:**
Louis Naturman ...........................Owner
Robert Butler ...........................Manager
**Desc.:** Serves the hybrid functions of a
   journal of record and interdisciplinary
   magazine that reports analyzes major
   energy developments as they occur.
**Readers:** Governmental officials, industry
   associations, energy engineers and
   interest groups, energy companies,
   foreign energy ministries.

70904

## ENERGY & ENVIRONMENT ALERT
4169 Westport Rd.
P.O. Box 7732
Louisville, KY 40257-0732
Telephone: (502) 896-8731
Year Established: 1978
Pub. Frequency: q.
Subscrip. Rate: $20/yr. individuals; $25/yr.
   institutions
Materials: 10
Circulation: 1,000
Circulation Type: controlled & paid
**Owner(s):**
National Council for Environmental
   Balance
4169 Westport Rd.
P.O. Box 7732
Louisville, KY 40257-0732
Telephone: (502) 896-8731
Ownership %: 100
**Editorial:**
Irwin W. Tucker ...........................Editor

65020

## ENERGY & HOUSING REPORT
9124 Bradford Rd.
Silver Spring, MD 20901-4918
Telephone: (301) 565-2532
FAX: (301) 587-1081
Year Established: 1981
Pub. Frequency: m.
Subscrip. Rate: $132/yr. (foreign $142/yr.)
**Owner(s):**
ALFA Publishing
9124 Bradford Rd.
Silver Spring, MD 20901-4918
Telephone: (301) 565-2532
Ownership %: 100
**Management:**
Leonard A. Eiser ...........................Publisher
**Editorial:**
Allan F. Frank ...........................Editor
Kevin Adler ...........................Marketing Director

**Materials Accepted/Included:** 01-Business news 02-By-line articles 03-Fashion news 04-Food news 05-Freelance copy 06-Letters to editor 07-Real estate news 08-Sports news 09-Travel news 10-Book rev. 11-Movie rev. 12-Music rev. 13-TV rev. 14-Theater rev. 15-Coming events 16-Obituaries 17-Question & answer 18-Social announcements 19-Artwork 20-Cartoons 21-Photos 22-TV listings 23-Audio rec. 24-Video rec. 25-Books 26-Films/film clips 27-Personnel news 28-Press releases 29-New product news/photos 30-Trade lit. 31-Contracts awarded 32-Display adv. 33-Classified adv.

7-35

**Desc.:** Covers new technologies and
marketing techniques; local, state and
federal energy conservation programs;
current news on corporate activities;
updates on recent laboratory research
findings; and pre-implementation details
on consensus standards.

64952

## ENERGY CONSERVATION NEWS
25 Van Zant St.
Norwalk, CT 06855
Telephone: (203) 853-4266
FAX: (203) 853-0348
Year Established: 1978
Pub. Frequency: m.
Page Size: standard
Subscrip. Rate: $275/yr.
**Owner(s):**
Business Communications Co., Inc.
25 Van Zant St.
Norwalk, CT 06855
Telephone: (203) 853-4266
Ownership %: 100
**Management:**
Louis Naturman ...........................................Owner
Robert Butler ...........................................Manager
**Desc.:** Focuses on the technology and
economics of energy conservation at
industrial, commercial and institutional
facilities, reporting on the complex and
dynamic issues that can mean the
difference between profits and losses.
**Readers:** Facilities managers, energy
engineers, utility companies, equipment
manufacturers and the business
community.

69881

## ENERGY, ECONOMICS & CLIMATE CHANGE
137 Broadway
Arlington, MA 02174
Telephone: (617) 648-8700
FAX: (617) 648-8707
Year Established: 1991
Pub. Frequency: m.
Subscrip. Rate: $547/yr. US; $647/yr.
foreign
**Owner(s):**
Cutter Information Corp.
137 Broadway
Arlington, MA 02174
Telephone: (617) 648-6700
FAX: (617) 648-8707
Ownership %: 100
**Editorial:**
Bradford J. Hurley ...........................................Editor
Nicholas A. Sundt ...........................................Editor
**Desc.:** Reviews economic models used to
develop energy policies for national and
international regions.

70907

## ENERGY REPORT
1616 N. Fort Myer Dr., Ste. 1000
Arlington, VA 22209-3107
Telephone: (703) 528-1244
FAX: (703) 528-1253
Year Established: 1973
Pub. Frequency: w.
Subscrip. Rate: $675/yr. US; $749/yr.
foreign
Materials: 10
**Owner(s):**
Pasha Publications Inc.
1616 N. Ft. Myer Dr., Ste. 100
Arlington, VA 22209-3107
Telephone: (703) 528-1244
FAX: (703) 528-1253
Ownership %: 100
**Editorial:**
Beth McConnell ...........................................Editor
**Desc.:** Reports on law and policy for the
oil, gas, coal, nuclear, solar and
alternative energy industries as well as
major energy consumers.

64950

## ENHANCED ENERGY RECOVERY NEWS
25 Van Zant St.
Norwalk, CT 06855
Telephone: (203) 853-4266
FAX: (203) 853-0348
Year Established: 1980
Pub. Frequency: m.
Page Size: standard
Subscrip. Rate: $305/yr.
**Owner(s):**
Business Communications Co., Inc.
25 Van Zant St.
Norwalk, CT 06855
Telephone: (203) 853-4266
Ownership %: 100
**Management:**
Robert Butler ...........................................Manager
**Desc.:** Informs its readership as to who is
involved, what technologies are used,
where the fields are, which events are
likely to shape the trends in the industry
of energy recovery.
**Readers:** Energy producing and operating
companies, chemical formulators,
government officials, materials scientists,
new venture and market analysts,
equipment manufacturers, systems
designers academicians and
administrators.

69893

## ENVIRONMENTAL BRIEFING
20 S. Wacker Dr., Ste. 2900
Chicago, IL 60606
Telephone: (312) 207-1000
FAX: (312) 207-6400
Pub. Frequency: q.
Subscrip. Rate: free
Circulation: 1,200
Circulation Type: controlled & free
**Owner(s):**
Sachnoff & Weaver, Ltd.
20 S. Wacker Dr., Ste. 2900
Chicago, IL 60606
Telephone: (312) 207-1000
FAX: (312) 207-6400
Ownership %: 100
**Editorial:**
J.J. Brown ...........................................Editor

69888

## ENVIRONMENTAL CONTROL NEWS FOR SOUTHERN INDUSTRY
P.O. Box 241813
Memphis, TN 38124-1813
Telephone: (901) 685-2077
FAX: (901) 684-1852
Year Established: 1971
Pub. Frequency: m.
Subscrip. Rate: $29.95/yr.
Materials: 32
Circulation: 300
Circulation Type: controlled & paid
**Owner(s):**
E.F.W. Commercial Ventures, Inc.
P.O. Box 241813
Memphis, TN 38124-1813
Telephone: (901) 685-2077
FAX: (901) 684-1852
Ownership %: 100
**Editorial:**
Edward F. Williams III ...........................................Editor

69850

## ENVIRONMENTAL ENGINEERING NEWSLETTER
Perdue University
School of Civil Engineering
West Lafayette, IN 47907
Telephone: (317) 494-2194
FAX: (317) 496-1107
Year Established: 1944
Pub. Frequency: m.
Subscrip. Rate: free

Circulation: 3,000
Circulation Type: free
**Owner(s):**
Perdue University
School of Civil Engineering
West Lafayette, IN 47907
Telephone: (317) 494-2194
FAX: (317) 496-1107
**Editorial:**
John M. Bell ...........................................Editor
**Desc.:** Presents new facts on
environmental issues.

66099

## ENVIRONMENTAL MANAGER
22 W. 21st St.
New York, NY 10010-6990
Telephone: (212) 645-7880
FAX: (212) 645-1160
Year Established: 1989
Pub. Frequency: m.
Subscrip. Rate: $162/yr.
**Owner(s):**
Executive Enterprises Publications Co., Inc.
22 W. 21st St.
New York, NY 10010
Telephone: (212) 645-7880
Ownership %: 100
**Editorial:**
Sarah Magee ...........................................Editor
**Desc.:** Provides regulatory & legislative
news, environmental case studies,
reports on key court decisions; also
provides recycling updates and in depth
coverage of important health and safety
issues, cleanup and waste control.
**Readers:** Environmental managers.

69856

## ENVIRONMENTAL OUTLOOK
University of Washington
Institute for Environmental Studies
Seattle, WA 98195
Telephone: (206) 543-1812
Pub. Frequency: 10/yr. (except July &
Aug.)
Subscrip. Rate: varies
Circulation: 2,100
**Owner(s):**
University of Washington
Institute for Environmental St
Engineering Annex
Seattle, WA 98195
Telephone: (206) 543-1812
Ownership %: 100
**Desc.:** Provides a calendar of
environmental courses, conferences,
meetings and hearings, as well as
information about faculty activities.
Includes short notes on environmental
curricula at the University and on
regional environmental topics.

69860

## ENVIRONMENTAL POLICY ALERT
P.O. Box 7167
Benjamin Franklin Sta.
Washington, DC 20044
Telephone: (703) 892-8500
FAX: (703) 685-2606
Pub. Frequency: bi-w.
Subscrip. Rate: $485/yr.; $535/yr. foreign
**Owner(s):**
Inside Washington Publishers
P.O. Box 7167
Benjamin Franklin Sta.
Washington, DC 20044
Telephone: (703) 892-8500
FAX: (703) 685-2606
Ownership %: 100

71204

## ENVIRONMENTAL REMEDIATION TECHNOLOGY
951 Pershing Dr.
Silver Spring, MD 20910-4464
Telephone: (301) 587-6300
FAX: (301) 589-5103
Year Established: 1993
Pub. Frequency: bi-w.
Subscrip. Rate: $390/yr.
**Owner(s):**
Business Publishers, Inc.
951 Pershing Dr.
Silver Spring, MD 20910-4464
Telephone: (301) 587-6300
FAX: (301) 589-5103
Ownership %: 100
**Desc.:** Provides the latest news and
analysis of technological developments
in the field of environmental remediation
technology.

71086

## ENVIRONMENTAL SOFTWARE REPORT
P.O. Box 335
Garrisonville, VA 22463
Telephone: (703) 659-1954
Year Established: 1988
Pub. Frequency: 8/yr.
Subscrip. Rate: $95/yr.
Materials: 33
**Owner(s):**
Donley Technology
P.O. Box 335
Gariisonville, VA 22463
Telephone: (703) 659-1954
Ownership %: 100
**Editorial:**
Veronica Deschambault ...........................................Editor
**Desc.:** Covers the latest developments in
the environmental software industry.
Examines commercial and government
software packages, database and on-
line systems for the environmental
professionals.

69883

## ENVIRONMENT WATCH: EAST EUROPE, RUSSIA & EURASIA
37 Broadway
Arlington, MA 02174-5539
Telephone: (800) 888-8939
FAX: (617) 648-8707
Year Established: 1992
Pub. Frequency: m.
Subscrip. Rate: $577/yr. US; $637/yr.
foreign
**Owner(s):**
Cutter Information Corp.
37 Broadway
Arlington, MA 02174-5539
Telephone: (800) 888-8939
FAX: (617) 648-8707
Ownership %: 100
**Editorial:**
Phillip Clendenning ...........................................Editor
**Desc.:** Covers business and regulatory
trends and their implications for
companies doing business in the former
Soviet bloc. Features global funding
sources, resource alert and decision of
developments in these regions.

69887

## ENVIRONMENT WATCH: LATIN AMERICA
37 Broadway
Arlington, MA 02174-5539
Telephone: (800) 888-8939
FAX: (617) 648-8707
Year Established: 1991
Pub. Frequency: m.
Subscrip. Rate: $537/yr. US; $597/yr.
foreign

**Owner(s):**
Cutter Information Corp.
37 Broadway
Arlington, MA 02174-5539
Telephone: (800) 888-8939
FAX: (671) 648-8707
Ownership %: 100
**Editorial:**
James Lahive .......................Editor
**Desc.:** Covers the business implications of policy developments in the environmental area; includes corporate initiatives, regulatory trends and research in Brazil, the Southern Cone, the Andean Nations and Central America.

## ENVIRONMENT WATCH: WEST EUROPE
69892
37 Broadway
Arlington, MA 02174-5539
Telephone: (800) 888-8939
FAX: (617) 648-8707
Year Established: 1992
Pub. Frequency: m.
Subscrip. Rate: $555/yr US; $657/yr. foreign
**Owner(s):**
Cutter Information Corp.
37 Broadway
Arlington, MA 02179
Telephone: (800) 888-8939
FAX: (617) 648-8707
Ownership %: 100
**Editorial:**
Tony Carritt .......................Editor
**Desc.:** Covers policy developments, regulatory trends and research.

## EXPLORATION DAILY
70791
P.O. Box 2162
Denver, CO 80201-2162
Telephone: (303) 740-7100
FAX: (303) 694-1754
Pub. Frequency: d.
Subscrip. Rate: $50/yr. fax deliv. available
**Owner(s):**
Petroleum Information Corp.
P.O. Box 2162
Denver, CO 80201-2162
Telephone: (303) 740-7100
FAX: (303) 694-1754
Ownership %: 100
**Desc.:** Covers important worldwide petroleum exploration news, including wildcats, new discoveries, and land plays.

## FEDERAL PARKS & RECREATION
70203
1010 Vermont Ave., N.W., Ste. 708
Washington, DC 20005
Telephone: (202) 638-7529
FAX: (202) 393-2075
Year Established: 1983
Pub. Frequency: fortn.
Subscrip. Rate: $167/yr.
**Owner(s):**
Resources Publishing Co.
1010 Vermont Ave., N.W., Ste. 708
Washington, DC 20005
Telephone: (202) 638-7529
FAX: (202) 393-2075
Ownership %: 100
**Editorial:**
James B. Coffin .......................Editor

## FUSION POWER REPORT
64900
951 Pershing Dr.
Silver Spring, MD 20910-4464
Telephone: (301) 587-6300
FAX: (301) 587-1081
Year Established: 1980
Pub. Frequency: m.

Page Size: standard
Subscrip. Rate: $666/yr.
Materials: 01
**Owner(s):**
Business Publishers, Inc.
951 Pershing Dr.
Silver Spring, MD 20910-4464
Telephone: (301) 587-6300
Ownership %: 100
**Editorial:**
Thecla Fabian .......................Editor
**Desc.:** Covers worldwide new technology and government support of fusion power research.

## GAS BUYERS GUIDE
70793
1616 N. Ft. Myer Dr., Ste. 1000
Arlington, VA 22209-3107
Telephone: (703) 528-1244
FAX: (703) 528-1253
Year Established: 1974
Pub. Frequency: w.
Subscrip. Rate: $457/yr. US; $487/yr. foreign
**Owner(s):**
Petroleum Information Corp.
1616 N. Ft. Myer Dr., Ste. 100
Arlington, VA 22209-3107
Telephone: (703) 528-1244
FAX: (703) 528-1253
Ownership %: 100
**Editorial:**
Daniel Macey .......................Editor
**Desc.:** Covers legal, technological and legislative matters affecting the gas industry.

## GAS DAILY
70797
1616 N. Ft. Myer Dr., Ste. 1000
Arlington, VA 22209-3107
Telephone: (703) 528-1244
FAX: (703) 528-1253
Year Established: 1974
Pub. Frequency: d.
Subscrip. Rate: $947/yr. US; $1035/yr. foreign
Circulation: 1,400
Circulation Type: controlled & paid
**Owner(s):**
Pasha Publications, Inc.
1616 N. Ft. Myer Dr., Ste. 100
Arlington, VA 22209
Telephone: (703) 528-1244
Ownership %: 100
**Editorial:**
Daniel Macey .......................Editor

## GAS STORAGE REPORT
70800
1616 N. Ft. Myer Dr., Ste. 1000
Arlington, VA 22209-3107
Telephone: (703) 528-1244
FAX: (703) 528-1253
Year Established: 1991
Pub. Frequency: m.
Subscrip. Rate: $397/yr. US; $412/yr. foreign
**Owner(s):**
Pasha Publications, Inc.
1616 N. Ft. Myer Dr., Ste. 100
Arlington, VA 22209-3107
Telephone: (703) 528-1244
FAX: (703) 528-1253
Ownership %: 100
**Editorial:**
Daniel Macey .......................Editor
**Desc.:** Monitors natural gas storage inventories, withdrawals and injections, open-access storage programs, federal and state regulatory actions, new business ventures, technological innovations and business trends.

## GLOBAL ENVIRONMENTAL CHANGE REPORT
69877
37 Broadway
Arlington, MA 02174
Telephone: (617) 648-8700
FAX: (617) 648-8707
Year Established: 1990
Pub. Frequency: s-m.
Subscrip. Rate: $447/yr. US; $547/yr. foreign
**Owner(s):**
Cutter Information Corp.
37 Broadway
Arlington, MA 02174
Telephone: (617) 648-8700
FAX: (617) 648-8707
Ownership %: 100
**Editorial:**
Bradford J. Hurley .......................Editor
**Desc.:** Covers developments around the world relating to climate change including global warming, acid rain, deforestation, biodiversity and sustainable development. Reports on scientific governmental and industrial developments.

## GOLOB'S OIL POLLUTION BULLETIN
71114
P.O. Box 535
Harvard Sq. Sta.
Cambridge, MA 02238
Telephone: (617) 491-5100
Year Established: 1989
Pub. Frequency: fortn.
Subscrip. Rate: $335/yr. US; $375/yr. foreign
Materials: 32
**Owner(s):**
World Information Systems
P.O. Box 535
Harvard Sq. Sta.
Cambridge, MA 02238
Telephone: (617) 491-5100
Ownership %: 100
**Editorial:**
Richard S. Golob .......................Editor
**Desc.:** Provides news analysis on oil pollution prevention, control, and cleanup. Covers oil spills worldwide, regulations, legislation and rulings, court decisions, new equiptment and products, contract opportunities and awards, and conference notices.

## GREENHOUSE EFFECT REPORT
64899
951 Pershing Dr.
Silver Spring, MD 20910-4464
Telephone: (301) 587-6300
FAX: (301) 585-9075
Year Established: 1975
Pub. Frequency: bi-w.
Subscrip. Rate: $423.54/yr.
**Owner(s):**
Business Publishers, Inc.
951 Pershing Dr.
Silver Spring, MD 20910-4464
Telephone: (301) 587-6300
Ownership %: 100
**Editorial:**
Hiram Reisner .......................Editor
**Desc.:** Studies large-scale activities designed to ease global environment problems, such as greenhouse effects, deforestation, CFCs.

## GREEN MARKET ALERT
69885
345 Wood Creek Rd.
Bethlehem, CT 06751-1014
Telephone: (203) 266-7209
FAX: (203) 266-5049
Year Established: 1990

Pub. Frequency: m.
Subscrip. Rate: $295/yr.
**Owner(s):**
Bridge Group
345 Wood Creek Rd.
Bethlehem, CT 06751-1014
Telephone: (203) 266-7209
FAX: (203) 266-5049
Ownership %: 100
**Editorial:**
Molly Barnes .......................Editor
**Desc.:** Analyzing the business impacts of green consumerism.

## GREEN MARKETING REPORT
71153
951 Pershing Dr.
Silver Spring, MD 20910-4464
Telephone: (301) 587-6300
FAX: (301) 585-9075
Year Established: 1990
Pub. Frequency: fortn.
Subscrip. Rate: $354.96/yr.
**Owner(s):**
Business Publlishers, Inc.
951 Pershing Dr.
Silver Spring, MD 20910-4464
Telephone: (301) 587-6300
FAX: (301) 585-9075
Ownership %: 100
**Editorial:**
Hiram Reisner .......................Editor
**Desc.:** Innovative ways manufacturers and advertisers are telling consumers about their environmentally friendly products; developments in federal disclosure regulations.

## GROUND WATER MONITOR
64898
951 Pershing Dr.
Silver Spring, MD 20910-4464
Telephone: (301) 587-6300
FAX: (301) 585-9075
Year Established: 1985
Pub. Frequency: fortn.
Subscrip. Rate: $474.54/yr.
**Owner(s):**
Business Publishers, Inc.
951 Pershing Dr.
Silver Spring, MD 20910-4464
Telephone: (301) 587-6300
Ownership %: 100
**Management:**
Leonard A. Eiser .......................Publisher
**Editorial:**
Charles Anderson .......................Editor
Kevin Adler .......................Marketing Director
**Desc.:** News from Congress, EPA and states on cleanup of ground water contamination across the US.

## GROUNDWATER NEWSLETTER
25244
1099 18th St., Ste. 1800
Denver, CO 80202
Telephone: (303) 294-1200
FAX: (303) 391-8799
Year Established: 1972
Pub. Frequency: s-m.
Page Size: standard
Subscrip. Rate: $327/yr. US; $357/yr. foreign
Materials: 10
**Owner(s):**
Water Information Center, Inc.
1099 18th St., Ste. 2150
Denver, CO 80202
Telephone: (303) 391-8799
Ownership %: 100
**Management:**
David W. Miller .......................President
Fred L. Troise .......................Publisher
Michelle Hankins .......................Manager
**Editorial:**
Judith Schoeck .......................Editor
Fred L. Troise .......................Managing Editor

**Materials Accepted/Included:** 01-Business news 02-By-line articles 03-Fashion news 04-Food news 05-Freelance copy 06-Letters to editor 07-Real estate news 08-Sports news 09-Travel news 10-Book rev. 11-Movie rev. 12-Music rev. 13-TV rev. 14-Theater rev. 15-Coming events 16-Obituaries 17-Question & answer 18-Social announcements 19-Artwork 20-Cartoons 21-Photos 22-TV listings 23-Audio rec. 24-Video rec. 25-Books 26-Films/film clips 27-Personnel news 28-Press releases 29-New product news/photos 30-Trade lit. 31-Contracts awarded 32-Display adv. 33-Classified adv.

7-37

Janet L. Sterling .....................Assistant Editor
**Desc.:** Provides news on groundwater exploration, development, management, recharge, pollution, and waste disposal.
**Readers:** Technical personnel in water field.

70806
## GULF OF MEXICO NEWSLETTER
P.O. Box 19909
Houston, TX 77224-1909
Telephone: (713) 781-2713
FAX: (713) 781-9594
Year Established: 1986
Pub. Frequency: w.
Subscrip. Rate: $77/yr.
Circulation: 2,175
Circulation Type: controlled & paid
**Owner(s):**
Offshore Data Services, Inc.
P.O. Box 19909
Houston, TX 77224
Telephone: (713) 781-2713
FAX: (713) 781-9594
Ownership %: 100
**Editorial:**
Richard Maddox .............................Editor

71194
## HAZARDOUS EMERGENCY RESPONSE
225 N. New Rd.
Waco, TX 76710
Telephone: (817) 776-9000
FAX: (817) 776-9018
Pub. Frequency: m.
Subscrip. Rate: $299/yr. US; $335/yr. Canada; $349/yr. Mexico; $383/yr. elsewhere
**Owner(s):**
Stevens Publishing
225 N. New Rd.
Waco, TX 76710
Telephone: (817) 776-9000
FAX: (817) 776-9018
Ownership %: 100
**Editorial:**
Adam Glen ....................................Editor
**Desc.:** Discusses the legislation, enforcement, and technology of emergency reponse to spills of hazardous materials.

71100
## HAZARDOUS MATERIALS INTELLIGENCE REPORT
P.O. Box 535
Harvard Sq. Sta.
Cambridge, MA 02238
Telephone: (617) 491-5100
FAX: (617) 492-3312
Year Established: 1980
Pub. Frequency: w.
Subscrip. Rate: $375/yr. US; $445/yr. foreign
**Owner(s):**
World Information Systems
P.O. Box 535
Harvard Sq. Sta.
Cambridge, MA 02238
Telephone: (617) 491-5100
FAX: (617) 492-3312
Ownership %: 100
**Editorial:**
George Stubbs .............................Editor
**Desc.:** Provides news analysis on environmental business, hazardous materials, waste management, and pollution prevention and control. Covers regulations, legislation and court decisions, new technology, contract opportunites and awards, and conference notices.

70343
## HAZARDOUS MATERIALS NEWSLETTER
P.O. Box 204
Barre, VT 05641
Telephone: (802) 479-2307
FAX: (802) 479-2307
Year Established: 1980
Pub. Frequency: bi-m.
Subscrip. Rate: $47/yr. US; $50/yr. foreign
Materials: 10,32
Circulation: 705
Circulation Type: controlled & paid
**Owner(s):**
Hazardous Materials Publishing
P.O. Box 204
Barre, VT 05641
Telephone: (802) 479-2307
FAX: (802) 479-2307
Ownership %: 100
**Editorial:**
John R. Cashman .....................Editor
**Desc.:** Addresses leak, fire, spill control for incident commanders and experienced responders, including incident causes, prevention, and remedial action.

64891
## HAZARDOUS WASTE NEWS
951 Pershing Dr.
Silver Spring, MD 20910-4464
Telephone: (301) 587-6300
FAX: (301) 587-1081
Year Established: 1979
Pub. Frequency: w.
Subscrip. Rate: $514.50/yr.
**Owner(s):**
Business Publishers, Inc.
951 Pershing Dr.
Silver Spring, MD 20910-4464
Telephone: (301) 587-6300
**Management:**
Leonard A. Eiser ....................Publisher
**Editorial:**
Robert W. Thompson ....................Editor
Kevin Adler .....................Marketing Director
**Desc.:** Covers federal and state regulations on hazardous waste, cleanup funding, new technology, business news. Includes a special liability feature.

70344
## HAZARDOUS WASTE REPORT
200 Orchard Ridge Dr.
Gaithersburg, MD 20878
Telephone: (301) 417-7500
FAX: (301) 417-7550
Year Established: 1979
Pub. Frequency: fortn.
Subscrip. Rate: $499/yr. US; $599/yr. foreign
**Owner(s):**
Aspen Publishers, Inc.
200 Orchard Ridge Dr.
Gaithersburg, MD 20878
Telephone: (301) 417-7500
FAX: (301) 417-7550
Ownership %: 100

70183
## HI SIERRAN
3820 Ray St.
San Diego, CA 92104-3623
Telephone: (619) 233-7143
FAX: (619) 299-1742
Year Established: 1950
Pub. Frequency: m.
Subscrip. Rate: $12/yr.
Materials: 10,32
Circulation: 15,000
Circulation Type: controlled & paid

**Owner(s):**
Sierra Club
3820 Ray St.
San Diego, CA 92104-3623
Telephone: (619) 233-7143
FAX: (619) 299-1742
Ownership %: 100
**Editorial:**
P.R. Dahlberg ..............................Editor

71111
## HYDROWIRE
410 Archibald St.
Kansas City, MO 64111-3046
Telephone: (816) 931-1311
FAX: (816) 931-2015
Year Established: 1980
Pub. Frequency: bi-w.
Subscrip. Rate: $295/yr. US; $375/yr. foreign
**Owner(s):**
HCI Publications
410 Archibald St.
Kansas City, MO 64111-3046
Telephone: (816) 931-1311
FAX: (816) 931-2015
Ownership %: 100
**Editorial:**
John Braden ..............................Editor
**Desc.:** Covers the hydroelectric market including business, finance and regulatory news in both the US and Canada.

70916
## IMPROVED RECOVERY WEEK
1616 N. Ft. Myer Dr., Ste. 1000
Arlington, VA 22209-3107
Telephone: (703) 528-1244
FAX: (703) 528-1253
Year Established: 1980
Pub. Frequency: w.
Subscrip. Rate: $495/yr. US; $660/yr. foreign
**Owner(s):**
Pasha Publications Inc.
1616 N. Ft. Myer Dr., Ste. 100
Arlington, VA 22209-3107
Telephone: (703) 528-1244
FAX: (703) 528-1253
Ownership %: 100
**Editorial:**
F. Jay Schempf .............................Editor
**Desc.:** Updates economic analysis of improved oil and gas recovery projects such as horizontal drilling, teriary oil recover, profile modification and more.

54035
## INDEPENDENT POWER REPORT
1221 Aveue of the Americas
New York, NY 10020
Telephone: (212) 512-6410
Year Established: 1985
Pub. Frequency: bi-w.
Page Size: standard
Subscrip. Rate: $815/yr. US & Canada; $840/yr. elsewhere
Freelance Pay: $15-$17/col. in.
**Owner(s):**
McGraw-Hill, Inc.
1221 Avenue of the Americas
New York, NY 10020
Telephone: (212) 512-2904
Ownership %: 100
**Bureau(s):**
Washington, DC
1120 Vermont Ave., N.W.
Ste. 1200
Washington, DC 20005
Telephone: (202) 463-1655
Contact: Brian Jordan, Bureau Chief
**Management:**
John E. Slater ..............................Publisher
**Editorial:**
Brian Jordan ..............................Bureau Chief
Richard Schwartz .....................Chief Editor

Ray Pospisil ..........................Associate Editor
Paul Carlsen ..........................Associate Editor
Rob Ingraham ..........................Associate Editor
Kathy Carolin Larsen ...............Associate Editor
Ron Dionne ..........................Associate Editor
**Desc.:** National and state news on the congeneration and independent power market.
**Readers:** Cogeneration and small power developers, consultants, equipment manufacturers, utility management, lawyers, federal and state regulators, bankers, and equipment suppliers.

71146
## INDOOR AIR BULLETIN
2548 Empire Grade
Santa Cruz, CA 95060
FAX: (408) 426-6522
Year Established: 1991
Pub. Frequency: m.
Subscrip. Rate: $195/yr. US; $235/yr. foreign
Materials: 10
**Owner(s):**
Indoor Information Service, Inc.
2548 Empire Grade
Santa Cruz, CA 95060
FAX: (408) 426-6522
Ownership %: 100
**Editorial:**
Hal Levin ..............................Editor

48845
## INSIDE N.R.C.
1200 G. St. N.W., Ste. 1100
Washington, DC 20005
Telephone: (202) 383-2167
FAX: (202) 383-2125
Year Established: 1979
Pub. Frequency: bi-w.
Page Size: standard
Subscrip. Rate: $1,415/yr. US/Canada; $1,510/yr. elsewhere
**Owner(s):**
McGraw-Hill, Inc.
1221 Avenue of Americas
New York, NY 10020
Telephone: (212) 997-3194
Ownership %: 100
**Management:**
John E. Slater ..............................Publisher
**Editorial:**
Michael Knapik ..........................Editor in Chief
**Desc.:** Industry newsletter reporting on nuclear industry and government agencies.
**Readers:** Nuclear/uranium corporations, government agencies, utilities.

70808
## INTERNATIONAL BUTANE-PROPANE NEWSLETTER
338 E. Foothill Blvd.
Arcadia, CA 91006
Telephone: (818) 357-2168
FAX: (818) 303-2854
Mailing Address:
P.O. Box 419
Arcadia, CA 91006
Year Established: 1977
Pub. Frequency: s-m.
Subscrip. Rate: $215/yr.
**Owner(s):**
Butane-Propane News, Inc.
338 E. Foothill Blvd.
Arcadia, CA 91006
Telephone: (818) 303-2168
FAX: (818) 303-2854
Ownership %: 100
**Editorial:**
Ann Rey ..............................Editor

**Materials Accepted/Included:** 01-Business news 02-By-line articles 03-Fashion news 04-Food news 05-Freelance copy 06-Letters to editor 07-Real estate news 08-Sports news 09-Travel news 10-Book rev. 11-Movie rev. 12-Music rev. 13-TV rev. 14-Theater rev. 15-Coming events 16-Obituaries 17-Question & answer 18-Social announcements 19-Artwork 20-Cartoons 21-Photos 22-TV listings 23-Audio rec. 24-Video rec. 25-Books 26-Films/film clips 27-Personnel news 28-Press releases 29-New product news/photos 30-Trade lit. 31-Contracts awarded 32-Display adv. 33-Classified adv.

## INTERNATIONAL TRENDS IN OIL & GAS
70809

P.O. Box 2612
Denver, CO 80201-2612
Telephone: (303) 740-7100
FAX: (303) 694-1754
Pub. Frequency: m.
Subscrip. Rate: $300/yr. US; $360/yr.
  foreign
**Owner(s):**
Petroleum Information Corp.
P.O. Box 2612
Denver, CO 80201-2612
Telephone: (303) 740-7100
FAX: (303) 694-1754
Ownership %: 100
**Desc.:** Covers worldwide statistics of
  petroleum: rigs, seismic crews,
  production, exports.

## JOBS FROM RECYCLABLES POSSIBILITY NEWSLETTER
70753

P.O. Box 416
Denver, CO 80201-0416
Telephone: (303) 575-5676
Year Established: 1991
Pub. Frequency: a.
Subscrip. Rate: $4.50/yr.
Circulation: 2,000
Circulation Type: controlled & paid
**Owner(s):**
Prosperity and Profits Unlimited
P.O. Box 416
Denver, CO 80201-0416
Telephone: (303) 575-5676
Ownership %: 100
**Editorial:**
A. C. Doyle ..................................Editor

## LAND RIG NEWSLETTER
70813

P.O. Box 6645
Lubbock, TX 79493-6645
Telephone: (806) 741-1531
FAX: (806) 741-1553
Year Established: 1978
Pub. Frequency: m.
Subscrip. Rate: $250/yr. includes q.
  summary
**Owner(s):**
JM Communications
P.O. Box 6645
Lubbock, TX 79493-6645
Telephone: (806) 741-1531
FAX: (806) 741-1553
Ownership %: 100
**Editorial:**
Richard Mason ...........................Editor
**Desc.:** Provides market intelligence for the
  onshore drilling industry and includes
  business news on emerging onshore
  drilling markets, financial reports on
  acquisitions, rig sales, and company
  performance.

## LEAD DETECTION & ABATEMENT REPORT
71184

4520 East-West Hwy., Ste. 610
Bethesda, MD 20814
Telephone: (301) 913-0115
FAX: (301) 913-0119
Year Established: 1992
Pub. Frequency: m.
Subscrip. Rate: $325/yr.
**Owner(s):**
IAQ Publications, Inc.
4520 East-West Hwy., Ste. 610
Bethesda, MD 20814
Telephone: (301) 913-0115
FAX: (301) 913-0119
Ownership %: 100

## MAINE ENVIRONMENT
70186

271 State St.
Augusta, ME 04330
Telephone: (207) 622-3101
Year Established: 1974
Pub. Frequency: 7/yr.
Subscrip. Rate: $28/yr.
Materials: 10
Circulation: 8,000
Circulation Type: controlled & paid
**Owner(s):**
Natural Resources Council of Maine
271 State St.
Augusta, ME 04330
Telephone: (207) 622-3101
Ownership %: 100
**Editorial:**
Judy Berk ..................................Editor

## MEDICAL WASTE NEWS
71118

951 Pershing Dr.
Silver Spring, MD 20910-4432
Telephone: (301) 587-6300
FAX: (301) 585-9075
Year Established: 1989
Pub. Frequency: fortn.
Subscrip. Rate: $345.54/yr.
**Owner(s):**
Business Publishers, Inc.
951 Pershing Dr.
Silver Spring, MD 20910-4432
Telephone: (301) 587-6300
FAX: (301) 585-9075
Ownership %: 100
**Desc.:** Studies regulation and litigation in
  reducing problems of medical waste,
  including hazardous and radioactive
  wastes.

## NATURAL GAS
58687

22 W. 21st St.
New York, NY 10010-6990
Telephone: (212) 645-7880
FAX: (212) 645-1160
Year Established: 1985
Pub. Frequency: m.
Page Size: standard
Subscrip. Rate: $295/yr.
**Owner(s):**
Executive Enterprises Publications Co., Inc.
22 W. 21st St.
New York, NY 10010
Telephone: (212) 645-7880
Ownership %: 100
**Editorial:**
Robert Willett ...........................Editor
Isabelle Cohen ..............Managing Editor
**Desc.:** Covers the financial and regulatory
  concerns of the natural gas industry,
  including contract pricing, purchasing,
  mergers and acquisitions.
**Readers:** Industry executives, advisors and
  regulators.

## NATURAL GAS INTELLIGENCE
70756

22648 Glenn Dr.
Sterling, VA 20164-4495
Telephone: (212) 645-7880
FAX: (212) 645-1160
Year Established: 1981
Pub. Frequency: w.
Subscrip. Rate: $675/yr.; $754/yr. foreign
**Owner(s):**
Intelligence Press Inc.
22648 Glenn Dr.
Sterling, VA 20164-4495
Telephone: (703) 318-8848
FAX: (703) 318-0597
Ownership %: 100
**Editorial:**
Ellen Beswick ...........................Editor

## NEW FUELS REPORT
70919

P.O. Box 7167
Benjamin Franklin Sta.
Washington, DC 20044
Telephone: (703) 892-8500
FAX: (703) 685-2606
Pub. Frequency: w.
Subscrip. Rate: $610/yr. US; $660/yr.
  foreign
**Owner(s):**
Inside Washington Publishers
P.O. Box 7167
Benjamin Franklin Sta.
Washington, DC 20044
Telephone: (703) 892-8500
FAX: (703) 685-2606
Ownership %: 100

## NOISE REGULATION REPORT
64897

951 Pershing Dr.
Silver Spring, MD 20910-4464
Telephone: (301) 587-6300
FAX: (301) 585-9075
Year Established: 1971
Pub. Frequency: bi-w.
Page Size: standard
Subscrip. Rate: $384.54/yr.
**Owner(s):**
Business Publishers, Inc.
951 Pershing Dr.
Silver Spring, MD 20910-4464
Telephone: (301) 587-6300
Ownership %: 100
**Management:**
Leonard A. Eiser ..................Publisher
**Editorial:**
Brian K. Morris ...........................Editor
**Desc.:** Regulation and technology in noise
  control, especially for industrial
  machinery and airport noises.

## NUCLEAR PLANT MAINTENANCE NEWSLETTER
69070

799 Roosevelt Rd.
Bldg. 6, Ste. 208
Glen Ellyn, IL 60137-5925
Telephone: (708) 858-6161
FAX: (708) 858-8787
Year Established: 1981
Pub. Frequency: m.
Page Size: standard
Subscrip. Rate: $220/yr. US; $252/yr.
  foreign
Materials: 28,29,30,31
Circulation: 70
Circulation Type: paid
**Owner(s):**
EQES, Inc.
Bldg. 6, Ste. 208
799 Roosevelt Rd.
Glen Ellyn, IL 60137-5925
Telephone: (708) 858-6161
Ownership %: 100
**Editorial:**
Newal K. Agnihotri ...........................Editor
**Desc.:** Contains information about the
  latest nuclear power industry
  maintenance products and practices.
**Readers:** Managers, supervisors, and
  engineers in nuclear energy related
  industries, including utilities and power
  plants.

## NUCLEAR WASTE NEWS
64892

951 Pershing Dr.
Silver Spring, MD 20910-4464
Telephone: (301) 587-6300
FAX: (301) 585-9075
Year Established: 1980
Pub. Frequency: w.
Page Size: standard
Subscrip. Rate: $650/yr.
Freelance Pay: $.20/wd.

**Owner(s):**
Business Publishers, Inc.
951 Pershing Dr.
Silver Spring, MD 20910-4464
Telephone: (301) 587-6300
Ownership %: 100
**Management:**
Lawrence Fishbein ..............................Publisher
**Editorial:**
Thecla Fabian .............................................Editor
**Desc.:** News about management of
  radioactive waste from energy
  production, weapons production, and
  medical science.
**Readers:** Professionals in radioactive
  waste management

## OFFSHORE INTERNATIONAL NEWSLETTER
70760

P.O. Box 19909
Houston, TX 77224-1909
Telephone: (713) 781-2713
FAX: (713) 781-2713
Year Established: 1973
Pub. Frequency: w.
Page Size: standard
Subscrip. Rate: $475/yr. US; $510/yr.
  foreign
Circulation: 695
Circulation Type: controlled & paid
**Owner(s):**
Offshore Data Services, Inc.
P.O. Box 19909
Houston, TX 77224-1909
Telephone: (713) 781-2713
FAX: (713) 781-9594
Ownership %: 100
**Editorial:**
Susanne S. Pagano .................................Editor
**Desc.:** Follows offshore oil developments
  and related concerns worldwide.

## OFFSHORE RIG NEWSLETTER, THE
61641

3200 Wilcrest, Ste. 170
Houston, TX 77042
Telephone: (713) 781-2713
FAX: (713) 781-9594
Mailing Address:
  P.O. Box 19909
  Houston, TX 77224
Year Established: 1973
Pub. Frequency: m.
Page Size: standard
Subscrip. Rate: $190/yr. US; $205/yr.
  foreign
Circulation: 1,650
Circulation Type: paid
**Owner(s):**
Shore Data Services, Inc.
P.O. Box 19909
Houston, TX 77224
Telephone: (713) 781-2713
FAX: (713) 781-9594
Ownership %: 100
**Editorial:**
Tom Marsh .............................................Editor
**Desc.:** Covers the offshore rig market
  worldwide-utilization, trends, labor
  problems, accidents, new orders,
  developing markets, designs, financing,
  etc.
**Readers:** Oil company personnel,
  contractor personnel, supplies & service
  companies.

## OIL IN THE ROCKIES
70764

P.O. Box 2612
Denver, CO 80201-2612
Telephone: (303) 740-7100
FAX: (303) 694-1754
Pub. Frequency: m.
Subscrip. Rate: $33.50/yr.

---

**Materials Accepted/Included:** 01-Business news 02-By-line articles 03-Fashion news 04-Food news 05-Freelance copy 06-Letters to editor 07-Real estate news 08-Sports news 09-Travel news 10-Book rev. 11-Movie rev. 12-Music rev. 13-TV rev. 14-Theater rev. 15-Coming events 16-Obituaries 17-Question & answer 18-Social announcements 19-Artwork 20-Cartoons 21-Photos 22-TV listings 23-Audio rec. 24-Video rec. 25-Books 26-Films/film clips 27-Personnel news 28-Press releases 29-New product news/photos 30-Trade lit. 31-Contracts awarded 32-Display adv. 33-Classified adv.

7-39

**Owner(s):**
Petroleum Information Corp.
P.O. Box 2612
Denver, CO 80201-2612
Telephone: (303) 740-7100
FAX: (303) 694-1754
Ownership %: 100
**Desc.:** Regional activity summary featuring
exploration highlights, land and leasing
information, pipline and refining activity,
completion and production statistics, and
more.

70773

**OIL SPILL INTELLIGENCE REPORT**
37 Broadway
Arlington, VA 22209-3107
Telephone: (617) 648-8700
FAX: (617) 648-8707
Year Established: 1978
Pub. Frequency: w.
Subscrip. Rate: $537/yr.; $637/yr. foreign
Materials: 33
**Owner(s):**
Cutter Information Corp.
37 Broadway
Arlington, VA 02174
Telephone: (617) 648-8700
FAX: (617) 648-8707
Ownership %: 100
**Editorial:**
Faith Yando ..................................Editor
**Desc.:** News and developments around
the world relating to oil spills and related
events. Covers advances in technology
for preventing, controlling, and cleaning
up oil spills, also covers regulations,
ligislation, treaties and litigators.

70205

**PEAK & PRAIRIE**
777 Grant St., Ste. 606
Denver, CO 80203
Telephone: (303) 861-8819
Pub. Frequency: bi-m.
Subscrip. Rate: $5/yr. to non-members
Materials: 10,11
Circulation: 12,000
Circulation Type: controlled & paid
**Owner(s):**
Sierra Club
777 Grant St., Ste. 606
Denver, CO 80203
Telephone: (303) 861-8819
Ownership %: 100
**Editorial:**
Jeff Holland ..................................Editor
Gail Spencer ..................................Editor
**Desc.:** Covers environmental issues,
legislative news, Chapter activities, and
events.

69561

**PLASTICS RECYCLING UPDATE**
P.O. Box 10540
Portland, OR 97210-0540
Telephone: (503) 227-1319
FAX: (503) 227-6135
Year Established: 1988
Pub. Frequency: m.
Page Size: standard
Subscrip. Rate: $49/yr.
Materials: 01,06,15,28,30,31,32
Circulation: 2,000
Circulation Type: paid
**Owner(s):**
Resource Recycling, Inc.
P.O. Box 10540
Portland, OR 97210-0540
Telephone: (503) 227-1319
FAX: (503) 227-6135
Ownership %: 100
**Editorial:**
Jerry Powell ..................................Editor

**Desc.:** Provides information on all aspects
of the plastics recycling process,
including markets, current and proposed
legislation, research, collection
techniques, recycled plastic products,
and economic issues and trends.

70207

**PUBLIC LAND NEWS**
1010 Vermont Ave., N.W., Ste. 708
Washington, DC 20005
Telephone: (202) 638-7529
FAX: (202) 393-2075
Year Established: 1976
Pub. Frequency: fortn.
Subscrip. Rate: $187/yr.
**Owner(s):**
Resources Publishing Co.
1010 Vermont Ave., N.W., Ste. 708
Washington, DC 20005
Telephone: (202) 638-7529
FAX: (202) 393-2075
Ownership %: 100
**Editorial:**
James B. Coffin ..................................Editor

70923

**PURPA LINES**
410 Archibald St.
Kansas City, MO 64111-3046
Telephone: (816) 931-1311
FAX: (816) 931-2015
Year Established: 1985
Pub. Frequency: bi-w.
Subscrip. Rate: $295/yr. US; $375/yr.
foreign
**Owner(s):**
HCI Publications
410 Archibald St.
Kansas City, MO 64111-3046
Telephone: (816) 931-1311
FAX: (816) 931-2015
Ownership %: 100
**Editorial:**
John Braden ..................................Editor
**Desc.:** Covers the cogeneration and
independent power industry; including
relevant business, finance, project and
tax news.

70775

**RECYCLING MARKETS**
143 Main St.
Avon By The Sea, NJ 07717
Telephone: (908) 502-0500
FAX: (908) 502-0500
Year Established: 1963
Pub. Frequency: w.
Subscrip. Rate: $90/yr.
Materials: 10,32
**Owner(s):**
NV Business Publishers Corp.
43 Main St.
Avon By The Sea, NJ 07717
Telephone: (908) 502-0500
Ownership %: 100
**Editorial:**
Ted Vilardi ..................................Editor

71101

**RECYCLING UPDATE**
P.O. Box 416
Denver, CO 80201-0416
Telephone: (303) 575-5676
Year Established: 1983
Pub. Frequency: s-a.
Subscrip. Rate: $6/yr.
Materials: 32
Circulation: 2,000
Circulation Type: controlled & paid
**Owner(s):**
Prosperity & Profits Unlimited
P.O. Box 416
Denver, CO 80201-0416
Telephone: (303) 575-5676
Ownership %: 100
**Editorial:**
A. Doyle ..................................Editor

**Desc.:** Lists new products, publications
and conventions.

70926

**SAVING ENERGY**
5411 117th Ave., S.E.
Bellevue, WA 98006
Telephone: (206) 643-4248
Year Established: 1977
Pub. Frequency: m.
Subscrip. Rate: $75/yr. US; $100/yr.
foreign
**Owner(s):**
Saving Energy
5411 117th Ave., S.E.
Bellevue, WA 98006
Telephone: (206) 643-4248
Ownership %: 100
**Editorial:**
Larry Liebman ..................................Editor
**Desc.:** Describes what business, industry,
and instittions can and are doing to save
energy.

70947

**SEICHE**
1518 Cleveland Ave., N.
St. Paul, MN 55108
Telephone: (612) 625-9790
FAX: (612) 625-1263
Year Established: 1976
Pub. Frequency: q.
Subscrip. Rate: free
Circulation: 3,500
Circulation Type: controlled & paid
**Owner(s):**
University of Minnesota
1518 Cleveland Ave., N.
St. Paul, MN 55108
Telephone: (612) 625-9790
FAX: (612) 625-1263
Ownership %: 100
**Editorial:**
Alice Tibbetts ..................................Editor
**Desc.:** Covers issues related to the Great
Lakes: fisheries, policy, research and
education.

70210

**SIERRA ATLANTIC**
353 Hamilton St.
Albany, NY 12210
Telephone: (518) 426-9144
Year Established: 1974
Pub. Frequency: q.
Subscrip. Rate: $5/yr. membership
Materials: 10,32
Circulation: 45,000
Circulation Type: controlled & paid
**Owner(s):**
Sierra Club
353 Hamilton St.
Albany, NY 12210
Telephone: (518) 426-9144
Ownership %: 100
**Editorial:**
Ann Botshon ..................................Editor
**Desc.:** Chapter newsletter on
environmental issues of interest to club
members in New York State.

64893

**SLUDGE NEWSLETTER**
951 Pershing Dr.
Silver Spring, MD 20910-4464
Telephone: (301) 587-6300
FAX: (301) 587-1081
Year Established: 1978
Pub. Frequency: bi-w.
Subscrip. Rate: $287.04/yr.
**Owner(s):**
Business Publishers, Inc.
951 Pershing Dr.
Silver Spring, MD 20910-4464
Telephone: (301) 587-6300
**Management:**
Leonard A. Eiser ..................................Publisher

**Editorial:**
Chuck Anderson ..................................Editor
Kevin Adler ..................................Marketing Director
**Desc.:** Monitors sludge management
developments in Washington and around
the country.

71201

**SOLAR ENERGY TODAY**
2303 Cedros Cir.
Santa Fe, NM 87505
Telephone: (505) 473-1067
Pub. Frequency: a.
Subscrip. Rate: $7/yr.
**Owner(s):**
PV Network News
2303 Cedros Cir.
Santa Fe, NM 87505
Telephone: (505) 473-1067
Ownership %: 100
**Editorial:**
Paul Wilkins ..................................Editor

71117

**SOLAR LETTER**
9124 Bradford Rd.
Silver Spring, MD 20901-4918
Telephone: (301) 565-2532
Year Established: 1991
Pub. Frequency: bi-w.
Subscrip. Rate: $360/yr. US; $384/yr.
foreign
**Owner(s):**
ALFA Publishing
9124 Bradford Rd.
Silver Spring, MD 20901-4918
Telephone: (301) 565-2532
Ownership %: 100
**Desc.:** Covers new developments and
regulations in the field.

64894

**SOLID WASTE REPORT**
951 Pershing Dr.
Silver Spring, MD 20910-4464
Telephone: (301) 587-6300
FAX: (301) 585-9075
Year Established: 1970
Pub. Frequency: w.
Page Size: standard
Subscrip. Rate: $500/yr.
Materials: 31
**Owner(s):**
Business Publishers, Inc.
951 Pershing Dr.
Silver Spring, MD 20910-4464
Telephone: (301) 587-6300
FAX: (301) 585-9075
Ownership %: 100
**Management:**
Lawrence Fishbein ..................................Publisher
Mary Anvari ..................................Promotion Manager
**Editorial:**
Ruhan Memishi ..................................Editor
**Desc.:** Covers municipal, commercial,
agricultural and non-hazardous industrial
refuse; generation, collection,
transportation, processing, resource
recovery, recycling and ultimate
disposal.
**Readers:** For waste managers, collectors,
transporters, site operators, equipment
vendors, regulators, and consultants.

70190

**SPECIAL PLACES**
572 Essex St.
Beverly, MA 01915-1530
Telephone: (508) 921-1944
FAX: (508) 921-1948
Pub. Frequency: 4/yr.
Subscrip. Rate: membership
Circulation: 15,000
Circulation Type: controlled & paid

**Materials Accepted/Included:** 01-Business news 02-By-line articles 03-Fashion news 04-Food news 05-Freelance copy 06-Letters to editor 07-Real estate news 08-Sports news 09-Travel news 10-Book rev. 11-Movie rev. 12-Music rev. 13-TV rev. 14-Theater rev. 15-Coming events 16-Obituaries 17-Question & answer 18-Social announcements 19-Artwork 20-Cartoons 21-Photos 22-TV listings 23-Audio rec. 24-Video rec. 25-Books 26-Films/film clips 27-Personnel news 28-Press releases 29-New product news/photos 30-Trade lit. 31-Contracts awarded 32-Display adv. 33-Classified adv.

**Owner(s):**
Trustees of Reservations
572 Essex St.
Beverly, MA 01915-1530
Telephone: (508) 921-1944
FAX: (508) 921-1948
Ownership %: 100
**Editorial:**
Marah Ren ...................................Editor
**Desc.:** Directed to members and contributors to the Massachusetts land conservation organization. Covers specific management practices, new land acquisitions, and events on the organization's 73 properties.

64895
## STATE ENVIRONMENT REPORT
951 Pershing Dr.
Silver Spring, MD 20910-4464
Telephone: (301) 587-6300
FAX: (301) 585-9075
Year Established: 1981
Pub. Frequency: w.
Subscrip. Rate: $431.50/yr.
**Owner(s):**
Business Publishers, Inc.
951 Pershing Dr.
Silver Spring, MD 20910-4464
Telephone: (301) 587-6300
**Management:**
Leonard A. Eiser .........................Publisher
Mary Anvari .........................Promotion Manager
**Editorial:**
Phil Zahodiakin ...........................Editor
**Desc.:** Provides news on state-level activities to reduce pollution and clean contaminated land and water.

69882
## SUPERFUND WEEK
1616 N. Ft. Myer Dr., Ste. 1000
Arlington, VA 22209-3107
Telephone: (703) 528-1244
FAX: (703) 528-1253
Year Established: 1987
Pub. Frequency: w.
Subscrip. Rate: $445/yr. US; $475/yr. foreign
**Owner(s):**
Pasha Publications, Inc.
1616 N. Ft. Myer Dr., Ste. 100
Arlington, VA 22209-3107
Telephone: (703) 528-1244
FAX: (703) 528-1253
Ownership %: 100
**Editorial:**
Jeff Stanfield .............................Editor
**Desc.:** Reports on Superfund litigation cases, innovative cleanup methods and costs, cleanup standards and noncompliance penalties.

64896
## TOXIC MATERIALS NEWS
951 Pershing Dr.
Silver Spring, MD 20910-4464
Telephone: (301) 587-6300
FAX: (301) 585-9075
Year Established: 1974
Pub. Frequency: w.
Subscrip. Rate: $540/yr.
**Owner(s):**
Business Publishers, Inc.
951 Pershing Dr.
Silver Spring, MD 20910-4464
Telephone: (301) 587-6300
**Editorial:**
Charles Knebl ...........................Editor
**Desc.:** Provides current information on the myriad laws, regulations and court cases that affect toxic chemicals.

70778
## U.S. OIL WEEK
1101 King St., Ste. 444
Alexandria, VA 22314
Telephone: (703) 683-4100
FAX: (703) 739-6517
Year Established: 1967
Pub. Frequency: w.
Subscrip. Rate: $259/yr.; $309/yr. foreign
**Owner(s):**
Capitol Publications, Inc.
1101 King St., Ste. 444
Alexandria, VA 22314
Telephone: (703) 683-4100
FAX: (703) 739-6517
Ownership %: 100
**Editorial:**
Jack Peckham ...........................Editor
**Desc.:** Focuses on ways to thrive in a changing marketplace. Covers industry news; current and pending government regulations; underground tank, insurance and environment issues.

70945
## UTILITY REPORTER-FUELS ENERGY & POWER
P.O. Box 15640
Plantation, FL 33318-5640
Telephone: (305) 473-9560
FAX: (305) 473-0544
Pub. Frequency: m.
Subscrip. Rate: $249/yr. US; $269/yr. Canada; $309/yr. elsewhere
**Owner(s):**
InfoTeam Inc.
P.O. Box 15640
Plantation, FL 33318-5640
Telephone: (305) 473-9560
FAX: (305) 473-0544
Ownership %: 100
**Desc.:** Covers the energy arena: fuels, energy power, utilities, exploration and production, research and development, transmission, equipment, systems, exotic and alternative energy, conservation, cogeneration and regulation.

57284
## UTILITY SPOTLIGHT
P.O. Box 819
McLean, VA 22101
Telephone: (703) 847-6344
FAX: (703) 847-0544
Year Established: 1947
Pub. Frequency: w.
Page Size: standard
Subscrip. Rate: $547/yr.
Freelance Pay: $7/col. in.
**Owner(s):**
Shumway Communication, Inc.
P.O. Box 819
Mc Lean, VA 22101
Telephone: (703) 847-6344
FAX: (703) 847-0544
Ownership %: 100
**Management:**
DeVan Shumway ...........................Publisher
**Editorial:**
Gene Smith ...........................Editor
**Desc.:** Provides late-breaking news in the electric, gas, water, telephone and nuclear utility industries, written in brief, terse copy style for busy executives. Covers technological, legal, political, financial and management developments.
**Readers:** Executives and managers of utility industry.

70192
## VOICE OF WALDEN
P.O. Box 275
Concord, MA 01742
Telephone: (508) 369-9393
Year Established: 1981

Pub. Frequency: q.
Subscrip. Rate: $15/yr.
Materials: 10
**Owner(s):**
Walden Forever Wild, Inc.
P.O. Box 275
Concord, MA 01742
Telephone: (508) 369-9393
Ownership %: 100
**Editorial:**
Edmund A. Schofield ...........................Editor
**Desc.:** Provides support for changing the status of Walden from a recreational park to a nature-preserve sanctuary.

71190
## WASTE MANAGEMENT NEWS
225 N. New Rd.
Waco, TX 76710
Telephone: (817) 776-9000
FAX: (817) 776-9018
Pub. Frequency: bi-m.
Subscrip. Rate: $322/yr. US; $360/yr. Canada; $374/yr. Mexico; $408/yr. elsewhere
**Owner(s):**
Stevens Publishing
225 N. New Rd.
Waco, TX 76710
Telephone: (817) 776-9000
FAX: (817) 776-9018
Ownership %: 100
**Editorial:**
Adam Glenn ...........................Editor
**Desc.:** Covers news and regulatory developments in the field of waste management.

64949
## WASTE TREATMENT TECHNOLOGY NEWS
25 Van Zant St.
Norwalk, CT 06855
Telephone: (203) 853-4266
FAX: (203) 853-0348
Year Established: 1985
Pub. Frequency: m.
Page Size: standard
Subscrip. Rate: $350/yr.
**Owner(s):**
Business Communications Co, Inc.
25 Van Zant St.
Norwalk, CT 06855
Telephone: (203) 853-4266
Ownership %: 100
**Management:**
Louis Naturman ...........................Owner
Robert Butler ...........................Manager
**Desc.:** Profiles existing and developing industrial waste treatment techniques and businesses, concentrating on new technologies developed for and applied to industrial waste management.
**Readers:** Professionals interested in government news, patenting, funding, legislation, market introduction, new products, R&D efforts and international events.

70943
## WATER POLICY REPORT
P.O. Box 7176
Benjamin Franklin Sta.
Washington, DC 20044
Telephone: (703) 892-8500
FAX: (703) 685-2606
Pub. Frequency: bi-w.
Subscrip. Rate: $455/yr. US; $505/yr. foreign
**Owner(s):**
Inside Washington Publishers
P.O. Box 7176
Benjamin Franklin Sta.
Washington, DC 20044
Telephone: (703) 892-8500
FAX: (703) 685-2606
Ownership %: 100

70439
## WATER TECHNOLOGY NEWS
25 Van Zant St.
Norwalk, CT 06855
Telephone: (203) 853-4266
FAX: (203) 853-0348
Year Established: 1993
Pub. Frequency: m.
Subscrip. Rate: $295/yr.
**Owner(s):**
Business Communications Co., Inc.
25 Van Zant St.
Norwalk, CT 06855
Telephone: (203) 853-4266
FAX: (203) 853-0348
Ownership %: 100
**Management:**
Louis Naturman ...........................Owner
Robert Butler ...........................Manager
**Desc.:** Informs readers of: worldwide research and development projects in water; technology insights, product descriptions, analyses, comparisons, technology; important corporate activity, attitudes, development; supply and demand analyses for new chemicals, products, and systems.
**Readers:** For technical planners, analysts, users, vendors and investment analysts

70770
## WEEKLY PROPANE NEWSLETTER
338 E. Foothill Blvd.
Arcadia, CA 91066
Telephone: (818) 357-2168
FAX: (818) 303-2854
Mailing Address:
  P.O. Box 419
  Arcadia, CA 91066
Year Established: 1971
Pub. Frequency: w.
Subscrip. Rate: $150/yr.
**Owner(s):**
Butane-Propane Newsletter
338 E. Foothill Blvd.
P.O. Box 419
Arcadia, CA 91066
Telephone: (818) 357-2168
FAX: (818) 303-2854
Ownership %: 100
**Editorial:**
Hal McWilliams ...........................Editor

70197
## WILDERNESS RECORD
2655 Portage Bay E., Ste. 5
Davis, CA 95616
Telephone: (916) 758-0380
Year Established: 1976
Pub. Frequency: m.
Subscrip. Rate: $25/yr.
Materials: 10
Circulation: 3,000
Circulation Type: controlled & paid
**Owner(s):**
California Wilderness Coalition
2655 Portage Bay E., Ste. 5
Davis, CA 95616
Telephone: (916) 758-0380
Ownership %: 100
**Editorial:**
Lucy Rosenau ...........................Editor
**Desc.:** Covers California's existing and potential wilderness areas.

70194
## WILD RANCH REVIEW
P.O. Box 91
Gulnare, CO 81042
Year Established: 1991
Pub. Frequency: q.
Subscrip. Rate: $15/yr.
**Owner(s):**
Tim Haugh
P.O. Box 91
Gulnare, CO 81042
Ownership %: 100

**Materials Accepted/Included:** 01-Business news 02-By-line articles 03-Fashion news 04-Food news 05-Freelance copy 06-Letters to editor 07-Real estate news 08-Sports news 09-Travel news 10-Book rev. 11-Movie rev. 12-Music rev. 13-TV rev. 14-Theater rev. 15-Coming events 16-Obituaries 17-Question & answer 18-Social announcements 19-Artwork 20-Cartoons 21-Photos 22-TV listings 23-Audio rec. 24-Video rec. 25-Books 26-Films/film clips 27-Personnel news 28-Press releases 29-New product news/photos 30-Trade lit. 31-Contracts awarded 32-Display adv. 33-Classified adv.

7-41

**Management:**
Tim Haugh ..............................Publisher
**Editorial:**
Tim Haugh ..................................Editor
**Desc.:** Offers in-depth profiles of grass-roots environmental groups.

71135

**WIND ENERGY NEWS**
P.O. Box 4008
St. Johnsbury, VT 05819-4008
Telephone: (802) 748-5148
FAX: (802) 748-3286
Year Established: 1987
Pub. Frequency: m.
Subscrip. Rate: $96/yr.
Materials: 10,33
Circulation: 2,000
Circulation Type: paid
**Owner(s):**
WindBooks, Inc.
P.O. Box 4008
St. Johnsbury, VT 05818-4008
Telephone: (802) 748-5148
FAX: (802) 748-3286
Ownership %: 100
**Editorial:**
Farrell Smith Seiler ......................Editor
**Desc.:** Focuses on business, marketing and international policies of the windmill industry.

## Group 326-Ethnic Interest

70965

**A. MAGAZINE: THE ASIAN AMERICAN QUARTERLY**
296 Elizabeth St., No. 2F
New York, NY 10012
Telephone: (212) 505-1416
Year Established: 1991
Pub. Frequency: q.
Subscrip. Rate: $10/yr.
**Owner(s):**
Metro East Publications, Inc.
296 Elizabeth St., No. 2F
New York, NY 10012
Telephone: (212) 505-1416
Ownership %: 100
**Editorial:**
Jeff Yang ....................................Editor
**Desc.:** Covers political, social and cultural issues of interest to young Asian Americans.

70979

**ASC NEWSLETTER**
African Studies Ctr.
100 International Ctr.
East Lansing, MI 48824-1035
Telephone: (517) 353-1700
FAX: (517) 535-7254
Pub. Frequency: s-a.
Subscrip. Rate: free
Circulation: 1,000
Circulation Type: controlled
**Owner(s):**
Michigan State University
100 International Ctr.
East Lansing, MI 48824-1035
Telephone: (517) 353-1700
FAX: (517) 535-7254
Ownership %: 100
**Desc.:** Contains African-related articles on African visitors, African accomplishments by MSU scholars, literature, film, and general announcements.

71003

**BELGIAN LACE**
62073 Fruitdale Ln.
La Grande, OR 97850-5312
Telephone: (503) 963-6697
Year Established: 1976
Pub. Frequency: q.
Subscrip. Rate: $12/yr. US; $14/yr. foreign
Materials: 10

Circulation: 350
Circulation Type: controlled & paid
**Owner(s):**
Belgian Researchers
62073 Fruitdale Ln.
La Grande, OR 97850-5312
Telephone: (503) 963-6697
Ownership %: 100
**Editorial:**
Leen J. Enghels ..........................Editor
**Desc.:** Covers the history of the Belgian generation in the US.

70971

**NEWS OF NORWAY**
2720 34th St., N.W.
Washington, DC 20008
Telephone: (202) 333-6000
FAX: (202) 337-0870
Year Established: 1941
Pub. Frequency: m.
Subscrip. Rate: free
Materials: 10
Circulation: 16,000
Circulation Type: controlled & paid
**Owner(s):**
Royal Norwegian Embassy
2720 34th St., N.W.
Washington, DC 20008
Telephone: (202) 333-6000
FAX: (202) 337-0870
Ownership %: 100
**Desc.:** Covers Norwegian interests.

71006

**OFARI'S BI-MONTHLY**
5517 Secrest Dr.
Los Angeles, CA 90043
Telephone: (213) 298-0266
Year Established: 1984
Pub. Frequency: bi-m.
Page Size: standard
Subscrip. Rate: $10/yr. individuals; $18/yr. institutions
Circulation: 50
Circulation Type: controlled
**Owner(s):**
Middle Passage Press
5517 Secrest Dr.
Los Angeles, CA 90043
Telephone: (213) 298-0266
Ownership %: 100
**Editorial:**
Earl Ofari Hutchinson ....................Editor
**Desc.:** Black domestic news issues including annual reports, media analysis, and political criticism.

70973

**POLISH STUDIES NEWSLETTER**
3433 Gregg Rd.
Brookeville, MD 20833
Telephone: (301) 774-4560
Year Established: 1979
Pub. Frequency: m.
Subscrip. Rate: $17/yr.
Materials: 10,32
Circulation: 350
Circulation Type: controlled & paid
**Owner(s):**
Polish Studies Newsletter
3433 Gregg Rd.
Brookeville, MD 20833
Telephone: (301) 774-4560
Ownership %: 100
**Editorial:**
Albin S. Wozniak ........................Editor
**Desc.:** Covers Polish interests.

70976

**SANGBAD BICHITRA**
101 Iden Ave.
Pelham Manor, NY 10803
Telephone: (914) 738-5727
FAX: (914) 738-4775
Year Established: 1971

Pub. Frequency: bi-w.
Subscrip. Rate: $15/yr.
Materials: 10,32
Circulation: 1,000
Circulation Type: controlled & paid
**Owner(s):**
Cultural Association of Bengal
101 Iden Ave.
Pelham Manor, NY 10803
Telephone: (914) 738-5727
FAX: (914) 738-4775
Ownership %: 100
**Editorial:**
Mira Das ..................................Editor
**Desc.:** News and literary articles concerning India and Bangladesh.

## Group 328-Finance

69946

**ACQUISITION MART**
9605 Scranton Rd., Ste. 840
San Diego, CA 92121-1774
Telephone: (619) 457-7577
FAX: (619) 453-1091
Year Established: 1982
Pub. Frequency: m.
Subscrip. Rate: $195/yr.
**Owner(s):**
Business Publications, Inc.
9605 Scranton Rd.
San Diego, CA 92121-1774
Telephone: (619) 457-7577
FAX: (619) 453-1091
Ownership %: 100
**Editorial:**
Lynn Mason ..............................Editor

69947

**ADRIAN DAY'S INVESTMENT ANALYSIS**
P.O. Box 6644
Annapolis, MD 21401
Telephone: (410) 224-8885
FAX: (410) 224-8229
Year Established: 1987
Pub. Frequency: m.
Subscrip. Rate: $87/yr.
Materials: 10
Circulation: 41,000
Circulation Type: controlled & paid
**Owner(s):**
Investment Consultants International
P.O. Box 6644
Annapolis, MD 21401
Telephone: (410) 224-8885
FAX: (410) 224-8229
Ownership %: 100
**Editorial:**
Adrian Day ................................Editor
**Desc.:** Covers analysis, forecasts, recommendations, techniques on all major markets. Covers analysis, forecasts, recommendations, techniques on all major markets.

69948

**AFRICA INVESTMENT MONITOR**
P.O. Box 25683
Washington, DC 20007
Telephone: (202) 338-4440
FAX: (202) 338-4440
Year Established: 1991
Pub. Frequency: bi-m.
Subscrip. Rate: $345/yr.
Materials: 32
Circulation: 4,000
Circulation Type: controlled & paid
**Owner(s):**
Media International, Inc.
P.O. Box 25683
Washington, DC 20007
Telephone: (202) 338-4440
FAX: (202) 338-4440
Ownership %: 100

**Editorial:**
Richard Synget ..........................Editor

70010

**AGBIOTECH STOCK LETTER**
P.O. Box 40460
Berkeley, CA 94704
Telephone: (510) 843-1842
FAX: (510) 843-0901
Year Established: 1989
Pub. Frequency: 12/yr.
Subscrip. Rate: $165/yr.
**Owner(s):**
Piedmont Venture Group
P.O. Box 40460
Berkeley, CA 94704
Telephone: (510) 843-1842
FAX: (510) 843-0901
Ownership %: 100
**Editorial:**
Jim McCamant ..........................Editor
**Desc.:** Covers non-medical biotechnology stocks, with specific buy and sell recommendations for investors.

69949

**AL HANSON'S ECONOMIC NEWSLETTER**
P.O. Box 9
Ottertail, MN 56571
Telephone: (218) 367-2404
Year Established: 1972
Pub. Frequency: m.
Subscrip. Rate: $120/yr.
Circulation: 100,000
Circulation Type: controlled & paid
**Owner(s):**
Al Hanson
P.O. Box 9
Ottertail, MN 56571
Telephone: (218) 367-2404
Ownership %: 100
**Management:**
Al Hanson ..............................Publisher

69925

**AMERICAN BANKER'S WASHINGTON WATCH**
One State St. Plz.
New York, NY 10004-1549
Telephone: (800) 733-4371
FAX: (212) 943-2224
Mailing Address:
   P.O. Box 28315
   Washington, DC 20038-8315
Pub. Frequency: w.
Page Size: standard
Subscrip. Rate: $695/yr. US; $725/yr. foreign
Materials: 32
**Owner(s):**
American Banker-Bond Buyer
One State St. Plz.
New York, NY 10004-1549
Telephone: (800) 733-4371
FAX: (212) 943-2224
Ownership %: 100
**Editorial:**
Miles Maguire ............................Editor
**Desc.:** Analysis of the developing regulatory and legislative initiative affecting insured financial institutions. Covers events at the FDIC, the Federal Reserve Board, and the Office of the Comptroller of the Currency.

69950

**ASSET SALES REPORT**
One State St. Plz.
New York, NY 10004-1549
Telephone: (800) 733-4371
FAX: (212) 943-2224
Pub. Frequency: w.
Page Size: standard
Subscrip. Rate: $775/yr. US; $1125/yr. foreign
Materials: 32

**Materials Accepted/Included:** 01-Business news 02-By-line articles 03-Fashion news 04-Food news 05-Freelance copy 06-Letters to editor 07-Real estate news 08-Sports news 09-Travel news 10-Book rev. 11-Movie rev. 12-Music rev. 13-TV rev. 14-Theater rev. 15-Coming events 16-Obituaries 17-Question & answer 18-Social announcements 19-Artwork 20-Cartoons 21-Photos 22-TV listings 23-Audio rec. 24-Video rec. 25-Books 26-Films/film clips 27-Personnel news 28-Press releases 29-New product news/photos 30-Trade lit. 31-Contracts awarded 32-Display adv. 33-Classified adv.

7-42

**Owner(s):**
American Banker-Bond Buyer
One State St. Plz.
New York, NY 10004-1549
Telephone: (800) 733-4371
FAX: (212) 943-2224
Ownership %: 100
**Editorial:**
Brian Sullivan ............................Editor
Thomas Curtin .................Advertising Editor
**Desc.:** Covers the field of loan sales and
asset securitization, including reports on
industry developments and trends, the
volume of commercial loans sold by ten
of North America's largest banks,
closing prices, and yield on activity
traded asset-backed securities, and
interviews with market leaders.

70024
## ASTUTE INVESTOR
Rt. 3
P.O. Box 310-D
Kingston, TN 37763
Telephone: (615) 376-2732
Year Established: 1982
Pub. Frequency: m.
Subscrip. Rate: $125/yr.
Materials: 10
Circulation: 1,000
Circulation Type: controlled & paid
**Owner(s):**
Charles E. Cardwell
Rt. 3
P.O. Box 310-D
Kingston, TN 37763
Telephone: (615) 376-2732
Ownership %: 100
**Management:**
Charles E. Cardwell .....................Publisher
**Readers:** Benjamin-Graham stock screens
service for value-oriented investors.
Reviews investment strategies.

70026
## ATLANTIC CITY ACTION
33 S. Presbyterian Ave.
Atlantic City, NJ 08404
Telephone: (609) 347-1225
FAX: (609) 345-4168
Mailing Address:
   P.O. Box 5059
   Atlantic City, NJ 08404
Year Established: 1978
Pub. Frequency: m.
Page Size: standard
Subscrip. Rate: $125/yr.
Materials: 10
Circulation: 2,000
Circulation Type: controlled & paid
**Owner(s):**
Glasco Associates, Inc.
33 S. Presbyterian Ave.
Atlantic City, NJ 08404
Telephone: (609) 347-1225
FAX: (609) 345-4168
Ownership %: 100
**Editorial:**
Al Glasgow ...............................Editor

69929
## BANK BAILOUT LITIGATION
   NEWS
350 Connecticut Ave., N.W.
Ste. 1000
Washington, DC 20036
Telephone: (202) 862-0990
FAX: (202) 862-0999
Year Established: 1989
Pub. Frequency: w.
Subscrip. Rate: $595/yr. US; $617/yr.
   foreign

**Owner(s):**
Buraff Publications
1350 Connecticut Ave., N.W.
Ste. 1000
Washington, DC 20036
Telephone: (202) 862-0990
FAX: (202) 862-0999
Ownership %: 100
**Editorial:**
David B. Kirby .............................Editor
**Desc.:** Reports and analyzes litigation
stemming from the failure of banks and
thrifts, including evolving case law and
litigation strategies under the Financial
Institutions Reform, Recovery, and
Enforcement Act and other statutes.

69938
## BANKER'S LETTER OF THE LAW
One Penn Plz.
New York, NY 10119
Telephone: (212) 971-5000
FAX: (212) 971-5240
Year Established: 1967
Pub. Frequency: m.
Subscrip. Rate: $188.75/yr.; $251.50/yr.
   overseas
**Owner(s):**
Warren Gorham Lamont
One Penn Plz.
New York, NY 10119
Telephone: (212) 971-5000
FAX: (212) 971-5240
Ownership %: 100
**Desc.:** Alerts bank attorneys to the latest
rulings involving federal and state
banking issues. Cites specific cases and
translates "legalese" into everyday
language.

69967
## BANKERS RESEARCH
P.O. Box 431
Westport, CT 06881-0431
Telephone: (203) 227-1237
Pub. Frequency: m.
Subscrip. Rate: $286/yr.; $316/yr. foreign
**Owner(s):**
Bankers Research, Inc.
P.O. Box 431
Westport, CT 06881
Telephone: (203) 227-1237
Ownership %: 100
**Editorial:**
Theodore Volckhausen ....................Editor

69957
## BANK FAILURE LITIGATION NEWS
P.O. Box 248
Chalfont, PA 18914
Telephone: (215) 822-9158
Year Established: 1988
Pub. Frequency: m.
Subscrip. Rate: $597/yr.
Materials: 10
**Owner(s):**
Litigation Reporting Service
P.O. Box 248
Chalfont, PA 18914
Telephone: (215) 822-9158
Ownership %: 100
**Editorial:**
William Keough ...........................Editor

61626
## BANKING LAW BRIEFS
125 E. 74th St.
New York, NY 10021
Telephone: (212) 472-0917
Mailing Address:
   P.O. Box 426 Lenox Sta.
   New York, NY 10021
Year Established: 1983
Pub. Frequency: s-m.
Page Size: standard
Subscrip. Rate: $67/yr.

**Owner(s):**
Elsah Associates
125 E. 74th St.
New York, NY 10021
Telephone: (212) 472-0917
Ownership %: 100
**Management:**
Donald Faerber .........................Manager
**Editorial:**
Donald Faerber ..........................Editor
**Desc.:** Important developments in
Commercial Banking Law.
**Readers:** Bankers & lawyers in
commercial banking

69972
## BANKING WEEK
One State St. Plz.
New York, NY 10004-1549
Telephone: (800) 733-4371
FAX: (212) 943-2224
Year Established: 1986
Pub. Frequency: w.
Subscrip. Rate: $110/yr.
Materials: 32
**Owner(s):**
Thomson Financial Services Co.
One State St. Plz.
New York, NY 10004-1549
Telephone: (800) 733-4371
FAX: (212) 943-2224
Ownership %: 100
**Editorial:**
Tom Ferris ...............................Editor
**Desc.:** Information for financial services
executives.

69961
## BANK LETTER
488 Madison Ave.
New York, NY 10022-5782
Telephone: (212) 303-3233
FAX: (212) 303-3353
Year Established: 1977
Pub. Frequency: w.
Page Size: standard
Subscrip. Rate: $1275/yr. US; $1300/yr.
   Canada; $1340/yr. elsewhere
Materials: 32
**Owner(s):**
Institutional Investor, Inc.
488 Madison Ave.
New York, NY 10022-5782
Telephone: (212) 303-3233
FAX: (212) 303-3333
Ownership %: 100
**Editorial:**
Tom Lamont ..............................Editor
**Desc.:** Examines the news events, key
issues and trends at both money center
and middle market banks. Emphasis on
regulatory affairs, new products,
corporate borrowings, marketing, trusts,
strategy shifts and senior personnel
moves.

71214
## BANK SECURITIES REPORT
1201 Seven Locks Rd.
Potomac, MD 20854
Telephone: (301) 424-3338
FAX: (301) 309-3847
Year Established: 1993
Pub. Frequency: bi-w.
Subscrip. Rate: $595/yr. US; $630/yr.
   foreign
**Owner(s):**
Phillips Business Information, Inc.
1201 Seven Locks Rd.
Potomac, MD 20854
Telephone: (301) 424-3338
FAX: (301) 309-3847

58700
## BANKS IN INSURANCE REPORT
22 W. 21st St.
New York, NY 10010-6904
Telephone: (212) 645-7880
FAX: (212) 645-1160
Year Established: 1985
Pub. Frequency: m.
Page Size: standard
Subscrip. Rate: $345/yr.
Materials: 01,02,28,29,30
**Owner(s):**
Executive Enterprises Publications Co., Inc.
22 W. 21st St.
New York, NY 10010-6904
Telephone: (212) 645-7880
FAX: (212) 645-1160
Ownership %: 100
**Editorial:**
Edward J. Stone ..........................Editor
Isabelle Cohen ..................Managing Editor
**Desc.:** Provides very specific information
on bank's expansion into insurance. It
covers new developments; legal,
legislative, and regulatory news; and
business and selling strategies.
**Readers:** Bankers selling insurance,
insurers concerned with bank-insurance
business.

56290
## BANK TELLER'S REPORT
One Penn Plz.
New York, NY 10119
Telephone: (212) 971-5000
FAX: (212) 971-5240
Year Established: 1969
Pub. Frequency: m.
Page Size: standard
Subscrip. Rate: $108.98/yr. US;
   $141.40/yr. foreign
Materials: 01,06,10,15
**Owner(s):**
Warren Gorham Lamont
One Penn Plz.
New York, NY 10119
Telephone: (212) 971-5000
Ownership %: 100
**Editorial:**
Joan German-Grapes ......................Editor
**Desc.:** Training tool providing bank tellers
with practical pointers on all phases of
banking: cross selling, security,
operations, money- handling techniques,
and customer relations.
**Readers:** Tellers on a nationwide basis
employed by banks, savings institutions,
and credit unions.

69951
## BARCLAY MANAGED FUTURES
   REPORT
508 N. Second St., Ste. 201
Fairfield, IA 52556
Telephone: (515) 472-3456
FAX: (515) 472-7320
Year Established: 1990
Pub. Frequency: q.
Subscrip. Rate: $150/yr.
Materials: 32
Circulation: 6,000
Circulation Type: controlled & paid
**Owner(s):**
Barclay Trading Group, Ltd.
508 N. Second St., Ste. 201
Fairfield, IA 52556
Telephone: (515) 472-3456
FAX: (515) 472-7320
Ownership %: 100
**Editorial:**
Sol Waksman ............................Editor
**Desc.:** Overview of performance of money
managers specializing in futures
markets. Includes interviews with money
managers on current issues facing
investors.

---

**Materials Accepted/Included:** 01-Business news 02-By-line articles 03-Fashion news 04-Food news 05-Freelance copy 06-Letters to editor 07-Real estate news 08-Sports news 09-Travel news 10-Book rev. 11-Movie rev. 12-Music rev. 13-TV rev. 14-Theater rev. 15-Coming events 16-Obituaries 17-Question & answer 18-Social announcements 19-Artwork 20-Cartoons 21-Photos 22-TV listings 23-Audio rec. 24-Video rec. 25-Books 26-Films/film clips 27-Personnel news 28-Press releases 29-New product news/photos 30-Trade lit. 31-Contracts awarded 32-Display adv. 33-Classified adv.

7-43

### BENDER'S FEDERAL TAX WEEK
70182
11 Penn Plz.
New York, NY 10001
Telephone: (212) 967-7707
FAX: (212) 967-1069
Year Established: 1951
Pub. Frequency: w.
Subscrip. Rate: $250/yr.
**Owner(s):**
Matthew Bender & Co., Inc.
11 Penn Plz.
New York, NY 10001
Telephone: (212) 967-7707
FAX: (212) 967-1069
Ownership %: 100

### BOND COUNSEL
69978
One State St. Plz.
New York, NY 10004-1549
Telephone: (800) 733-4371
FAX: (212) 943-2224
Year Established: 1989
Pub. Frequency: 48/yr.
Subscrip. Rate: $465/yr. new subscribers;
 $645/yr. renewal
**Owner(s):**
Thomson Financial Services Co.
One State St. Plz.
New York, NY 10004-1549
Telephone: (800) 733-4371
FAX: (212) 943-2224
Ownership %: 100
**Editorial:**
Ed McFadden .............................................Editor

### BOWNE REVIEW FOR CFOS & INVESTMENT BANKERS
69984
124 Harvard St.
Brookline, MA 02146
Telephone: (617) 734-1979
FAX: (617) 734-1989
Year Established: 1989
Pub. Frequency: m.
Subscrip. Rate: free
**Owner(s):**
Brumberg Publications, Inc.
124 Harvard St.
Brookline, MA 02146
Telephone: (617) 734-1979
FAX: (617) 734-1989
Ownership %: 100
**Editorial:**
Susan Koffman ..........................................Editor

### BOWSER REPORT
69969
P.O. Box 6278
Newport News, VA 23606
Telephone: (804) 877-5979
Year Established: 1976
Pub. Frequency: m.
Page Size: standard
Subscrip. Rate: $48/yr.
Circulation: 10,000
Circulation Type: controlled & paid
**Owner(s):**
R. Max Bowser
P.O. Box 6278
Newport News, VA 23606
Telephone: (804) 877-5979
Ownership %: 100
**Editorial:**
R. Max Bowser .........................................Editor
**Desc.:** Up-to-date information on stocks
 selling for $3 a share or less.

### BUSINESS & ACQUISITION NEWSLETTER
69988
2600 S. Gessner Rd.
Houston, TX 77063
Telephone: (713) 783-0100
Year Established: 1966

Pub. Frequency: m.
Subscrip. Rate: $300/yr.
Materials: 10
**Owner(s):**
Newsletters International, Inc.
2600 S. Gessner Rd.
Houston, TX 77063
Telephone: (713) 783-0100
Ownership %: 100
**Editorial:**
Len Fox ......................................................Editor

### CALIFORNIA PUBLIC FINANCE
70195
One State St. Plz.
New York, NY 10004-1549
Telephone: (800) 733-4371
FAX: (212) 943-2224
Pub. Frequency: w.
Subscrip. Rate: $420/yr. new subscriber;
 $545/yr. renewal
**Owner(s):**
American Banker-Bond Buyer
One State St. Plz.
New York, NY 10004-1549
Telephone: (800) 733-4371
FAX: (212) 943-2224
Ownership %: 100
**Desc.:** Latest developments affecting
 municipal bonds in the state that issues
 more municipal bonds than any other
 state. Reports on new issues by the
 state's 457 cities and 58 counties that
 follows legislative developments
 affecting public finance in Sacramento
 and Washington.

### CARD NEWS
69994
7811 Montrose Rd.
Potomac, MD 20854
Telephone: (301) 340-2100
FAX: (302) 309-3847
Pub. Frequency: fortn.
Subscrip. Rate: $445/yr.
**Owner(s):**
Phillips Publishing, Inc.
7811 Montrose Rd.
Potomac, MD 20854
Telephone: (301) 340-2100
FAX: (301) 309-3847
Ownership %: 100
**Desc.:** Provides information on
 developments affecting credit card
 issuers and manufacturers of equipment
 for credit card transactions and
 management.

### CATALYST
69973
P.O. Box 1308
Montpelier, VT 05601-1308
Telephone: (802) 223-7943
Year Established: 1984
Pub. Frequency: q.
Subscrip. Rate: $25/yr.
Materials: 10
Circulation: 1,000
Circulation Type: controlled & paid
**Owner(s):**
Catalyst Press
P.O. Box 1308
Montpelier, VT 05601-1308
Telephone: (802) 223-7943
Ownership %: 100
**Editorial:**
Susan Meeker-Lowry ...............................Editor
**Desc.:** Profiles of and articles on social
 investing: small businesses, revolving
 loan funds, co-ops, land trusts, and
 other organizations to support positive
 economic change for disadvantaged
 populations and to save and regenerate
 existing farm and forestland. Focuses on
 small-scale, grass roots enterprises
 seeking some form of capital: loans,
 partnerships, equity, and grants.

### CLARK'S BANK DEPOSITS & PAYMENTS MONTHLY
70001
One Penn Plz.
New York, NY 10199
Telephone: (212) 971-5000
FAX: (212) 971-5240
Year Established: 1992
Pub. Frequency: m.
Subscrip. Rate: $152.25/yr. US; $206/yr.
 foreign
**Owner(s):**
Warren Gorham Lamont
One Penn Plz.
New York, NY 10119
Telephone: (212) 971-5000
FAX: (212) 971-5240
Ownership %: 100
**Editorial:**
Barkley Clark .............................................Editor
Barbara Brewer Clark ...............................Editor
**Desc.:** Reports on legal developments
 affecting bank deposits, collections, and
 credit cards.

### CLARK'S SECURED TRANSACTIONS MONTHLY
70009
One Penn Plz.
New York, NY 10119
Telephone: (212) 971-5000
FAX: (212) 971-5240
Year Established: 1984
Pub. Frequency: m.
Subscrip. Rate: $141.50/yr. US; $193/yr.
 foreign
**Owner(s):**
Warren Gorham Lamont
One Penn Plz.
New York, NY 10119
Telephone: (212) 971-5000
FAX: (212) 971-5240
Ownership %: 100
**Editorial:**
Barkley Clark .............................................Editor
Barbara Brewer Clark ...............................Editor
**Desc.:** Provides how-to guidance on
 drafting air-tight lending agreements.

### CLEAN YIELD
69977
P.O. Box 1880
Greensboro Bend, VT 05842
Telephone: (802) 533-7178
FAX: (802) 533-2907
Year Established: 1985
Pub. Frequency: m.
Subscrip. Rate: $95/yr. individuals;
 $125/yr. businesses
Materials: 10
Circulation: 1,200
Circulation Type: controlled & paid
**Owner(s):**
Clean Yield Publications
P.O. Box 1880
Greensboro Bend, VT 05842
Telephone: (802) 533-7178
FAX: (802) 533-2907
Ownership %: 100
**Editorial:**
Rian Fried ..................................................Editor
**Desc.:** Stock market newsletter for
 investors concerned with the social
 responsibilities of publicly held
 companies.

### COMMUNITY BANK PRESIDENT
70028
P.O. Box 1384
Storm Lake, IA 50588
Telephone: (712) 732-7340
Year Established: 1980
Pub. Frequency: bi-m.
Subscrip. Rate: $279/yr.
Circulation: 1,750
Circulation Type: paid

**Owner(s):**
Siefer Consultants, Inc.
P.O. Box 1384
Storm Lake, IA 50588
Telephone: (712) 732-7340
Ownership %: 100
**Editorial:**
Joe Sheller ................................................Editor
**Desc.:** Profit making ideas for community
 banks.

### CONSERVATIVE SPECULATOR
69952
3 Myrtle Bank Rd.
Hilton Head, SC 29926
Telephone: (803) 681-3399
Mailing Address:
 P.O. Drawer 22509
 Hilton Head Island, SC 29925
Year Established: 1988
Pub. Frequency: m.
Subscrip. Rate: $198/yr.
Materials: 10
Circulation: 13,000
Circulation Type: controlled & paid
**Owner(s):**
Guidera Publishing Corp.
3 Myrtle Bank Rd.
Hilton Head Island, SC 29926
Telephone: (803) 681-3399
Ownership %: 100
**Desc.:** Helps readers make more with the
 ten percent they put into special
 situations than they make with the ninety
 percent put into everything else.
 Includes 3-4 special situations, inflation-
 interest rate forecasts and Dow 30
 timing.

### CONSUMER FINANCE NEWSLETTER
70189
82 Brookline Ave.
Boston, MA 02215
Telephone: (617) 262-4040
FAX: (617) 247-0136
Year Established: 1975
Pub. Frequency: m.
Subscrip. Rate: $24.50/yr.
Circulation: 1,000
Circulation Type: controlled & paid
**Owner(s):**
Financial Publishing Co.
82 Brookline Ave.
Boston, MA 02215
Telephone: (617) 262-4040
FAX: (617) 247-0136
Ownership %: 100
**Editorial:**
James C. Senay .......................................Editor

### CONSUMER LENDING REPORT
70030
One Penn Plz.
New York, NY 10119
Telephone: (800) 950-1201
FAX: (212) 971-5240
Year Established: 1973
Pub. Frequency: m.
Subscrip. Rate: $180/yr.
**Owner(s):**
Warren Gorham Lamont
One Penn Plz.
New York, NY 10119
Telephone: (800) 950-1201
FAX: (212) 971-5240
Ownership %: 100
**Desc.:** Highlights news business ideas and
 time-saving tips to improve efficiency
 and profitability of consumer loan
 portfolios.

**Materials Accepted/Included:** 01-Business news 02-By-line articles 03-Fashion news 04-Food news 05-Freelance copy 06-Letters to editor 07-Real estate news 08-Sports news 09-Travel news 10-Book rev. 11-Movie rev. 12-Music rev. 13-TV rev. 14-Theater rev. 15-Coming events 16-Obituaries 17-Question & answer 18-Social announcements 19-Artwork 20-Cartoons 21-Photos 22-TV listings 23-Audio rec. 24-Video rec. 25-Books 26-Films/film clips 27-Personnel news 28-Press releases 29-New product news/photos 30-Trade lit. 31-Contracts awarded 32-Display adv. 33-Classified adv.

7-44

## CORPORATE E.F.T. REPORT
69955

7811 Montrose Rd.
Potomac, MD 20854
Telephone: (301) 340-2100
FAX: (301) 424-4297
Year Established: 1983
Pub. Frequency: fortn.
Subscrip. Rate: $595/yr.
**Owner(s):**
Phillips Publishing, Inc.
7811 Montrose Rd.
Potomac, MD 20854
Telephone: (301) 340-2100
FAX: (301) 424-4297
Ownership %: 100
**Editorial:**
Claire Taylor ................................Editor

## CORPORATE FINANCE LETTER
69922

900 19th St. N.W., Ste. 400
Washington, DC 20006
Telephone: (202) 857-3100
FAX: (202) 296-8716
Pub. Frequency: m.
Subscrip. Rate: $395/yr.
**Owner(s):**
Savings & Community Bankers of America
900 19th St. N.W., Ste. 400
Washington, DC 20006
Telephone: (202) 857-3100
FAX: (202) 296-8716
Ownership %: 100
**Desc.:** Focuses on the structuring and
management of commercial loans.
**Readers:** Chief financial officers and
managers.

## CORPORATE VENTURING QUARTERLY
69954

40 W. 57th St.
New York, NY 10019
Year Established: 1987
Pub. Frequency: q.
Subscrip. Rate: $395/yr.
**Owner(s):**
SDC Publishing
40 W. 57th St.
New York, NY 10019
Ownership %: 100
**Editorial:**
Matt Yost ..................................Editor

## CREDIT UNION ACCOUNTANT
69959

One State St. Plz.
New York, NY 10004-1549
Telephone: (800) 733-4371
FAX: (212) 943-2224
Mailing Address:
    P.O. Box 28315
    Washington, DC 20038-8315
Pub. Frequency: w.
Subscrip. Rate: $420/yr. new subscriber;
    $510/yr. renewal
**Owner(s):**
American Banker-Bond Buyer
One State St. Plz.
New York, NY 10004-1549
Telephone: (800) 733-4371
FAX: (212) 943-2224
Ownership %: 100
**Desc.:** Focuses on accounting policy
changes for credit unions emanating
from government agencies. Includes a
ledger summarizing the most critical
developments in legal and regulatory
issues affecting how the books of credit
unions are kept as well as the latest
actions being considered by the FASB,
the AICPA, and the National Credit
Union Administration.

## CREDIT UNION DIRECTORS NEWSLETTER
69940

5710 Mineral Point Rd.
Madison, WI 53701
Telephone: (608) 231-4000
FAX: (608) 231-4370
Mailing Address:
    P.O. Box 431
    Madison, WI 53701
Year Established: 1946
Pub. Frequency: m.
Subscrip. Rate: $58/yr.
Circulation: 6,358
Circulation Type: controlled & paid
**Owner(s):**
Credit Union National Association, Inc.
5710 Mineral Point Rd.
Madison, WI 53701
Telephone: (608) 231-4000
Ownership %: 100
**Editorial:**
Steve Rodgers ................................Editor

## CREDIT UNION MANAGER NEWSLETTER
69993

5710 Mineral Point Rd.
Madison, WI 53701
Telephone: (608) 231-4000
FAX: (608) 231-4370
Mailing Address:
    P.O. Box 431
    Madison, WI 53701
Year Established: 1946
Pub. Frequency: fortn.
Subscrip. Rate: $120/yr.
Circulation: 2,400
Circulation Type: controlled & paid
**Owner(s):**
Credit Union National Association, Inc.
5710 Mineral Point Rd.
P.O. Box 431
Madison, WI 53701
Telephone: (608) 231-4000
FAX: (608) 231-4858
Ownership %: 100
**Editorial:**
Steve Rodgers ................................Editor
**Desc.:** Credit Union information.

## DINES LETTER
69958

P.O. Box 22
Belvedere, CA 94920
Telephone: (800) 845-8259
Year Established: 1960
Pub. Frequency: bi-m.
Subscrip. Rate: $195/yr.
Materials: 10
**Owner(s):**
James Dines & Co., Inc.
P.O. Box 22
Belvedere, CA 94920
Telephone: (800) 845-8259
Ownership %: 100
**Editorial:**
James Dines ................................Editor
**Desc.:** Contains buy and sell advice based
on mass psychology, technical analysis
and fundamental considerations for
stocks, options and the economy.

## DONOGHUE'S MONEYLETTER
69981

P.O. Box 9104
Ashland, MA 01721-9104
Telephone: (508) 881-2800
FAX: (508) 881-0982
Year Established: 1980
Pub. Frequency: fortn.
Subscrip. Rate: $109/yr.
Circulation: 30,000
Circulation Type: controlled & paid

**Owner(s):**
IBC-Donoghue, Inc.
P.O. Box 9104
Ashland, MA 01721-9104
Telephone: (508) 881-2800
FAX: (508) 881-0982
Ownership %: 100
**Editorial:**
Ann Needle ................................Editor

## EASTERN EUROPE FINANCE
70042

P.O. Box 7188
Fairfax Station, VA 22039
Telephone: (703) 425-1322
FAX: (703) 425-7911
Year Established: 1990
Pub. Frequency: fortn.
Subscrip. Rate: $437/yr.
Materials: 10
**Owner(s):**
D.P. Publications Co.
P.O. Box 7188
Fairfax Station, VA 22039
Telephone: (703) 425-1322
FAX: (703) 425-7911
Ownership %: 100
**Editorial:**
Michael Morrison ................................Editor
**Desc.:** Intelligence on new trends and
innovations in East-West trade, project
and opportunity finance.

## EFT REPORT
71083

7811 Montrose Rd.
Potomac, MD 20854
Telephone: (301) 340-2100
Year Established: 1978
Pub. Frequency: fortn.
Subscrip. Rate: $445/yr.
**Owner(s):**
Phillips Publishing, Inc.
7811 Montrose Rd.
Potomac, MD 20854
Telephone: (301) 340-2100
Ownership %: 100
**Editorial:**
Claire Taylor ................................Editor
**Desc.:** For administrators and bankers
interested in the electronic funds transfer
market. Contains reports on automated
teller machine systems, personal
identification systems, home banking,
home security, and regional and national
networks.

## ELECTRONIC CLAIMS PROCESSING REPORT
71225

1201 Seven Locks Rd.
Potomac, MD 20854
Telephone: (301) 309-3847
FAX: (301) 309-3847
Year Established: 1993
Pub. Frequency: bi-w.
Subscrip. Rate: $395/yr. US; $430/yr.
    foreign
**Owner(s):**
Phillips Business Information, Inc.
1201 Seven Locks Rd.
Potomac, MD 20854
Telephone: (301) 424-3338
FAX: (301) 309-3847
Ownership %: 100

## FEE INCOME REPORT
69870

P.O. Box 1384
Storm Lake, IA 50588
Telephone: (712) 732-7340
FAX: (712) 732-7906
Year Established: 1986
Pub. Frequency: bi-m.
Subscrip. Rate: $297/yr.
Circulation: 2,300

**Owner(s):**
Siefer Consultants, Inc.
P.O. Box 1384
Storm Lake, IA 50588
Telephone: (712) 732-7340
FAX: (712) 732-7906
Ownership %: 100
**Editorial:**
Steve Herron ................................Editor
**Desc.:** How-to tips for banks on increasing
non-interest income.

## FINANCIAL SERVICES REPORT
69963

7811 Montrose Rd.
Potomac, MD 20854
Telephone: (301) 340-2100
FAX: (301) 424-4297
Pub. Frequency: fortn.
Subscrip. Rate: $795/yr.
**Owner(s):**
Phillips Publishing, Inc.
7811 Montrose Rd.
Potomac, MD 20854
Telephone: (301) 340-2100
FAX: (301) 424-4297
Ownership %: 100
**Editorial:**
Eric Williams ................................Editor
**Desc.:** Covers the latest legal, regulatory
and business developments in the
banking and financial services industries.

## FINANCIAL WOMAN TODAY
66104

7910 Woodmont Ave., Ste. 1430
Bethesda, MD 20814-3015
Telephone: (301) 657-8288
FAX: (301) 913-0001
Year Established: 1985
Pub. Frequency: 8/yr.
Page Size: standard
Subscrip. Rate: $24/yr.
Materials: 01,10,19,20,21,25,28,30,32
Circulation: 14,000
Circulation Type: controlled & paid
**Owner(s):**
Financial Women International, Inc.
7910 Woodmont Ave., Ste. 1430
Bethesda, MD 20814-3015
Telephone: (301) 657-8288
FAX: (301) 913-0001
Ownership %: 100
**Management:**
Barbara Ralston ................................President
**Editorial:**
Sylvia Straub ................................Editor
**Desc.:** Reaches executives in banks,
savings and loans, credit unions,
diversified financials, insurance, and all
other types of financial services
companies. The newsletter contains
short news items and features on the
industry, career and management
issues, contributions made by women in
the industry, and, less frequently,
association activities. Industry, their
effects on individuals and companies,
and how institutions are facing the
challenges induced by change. Special
attention is given to workforce issues
such as employee diversity, productivity,
child care, training, and education.
**Readers:** Commercial banks, savings &
loans credit unions, and other financial
service institutions.

## FRASER OPINION LETTER
69962

309 S. Willard St.
Burlington, VT 05402
Telephone: (802) 658-0322
FAX: (802) 658-0260
Mailing Address:
    P.O. Box 494
    Burlington, VT 05402
Year Established: 1949

**Materials Accepted/Included:** 01-Business news 02-By-line articles 03-Fashion news 04-Food news 05-Freelance copy 06-Letters to editor 07-Real estate news 08-Sports news 09-Travel news 10-Book rev. 11-Movie rev. 12-Music rev. 13-TV rev. 14-Theater rev. 15-Coming events 16-Obituaries 17-Question & answer 18-Social announcements 19-Artwork 20-Cartoons 21-Photos 22-TV listings 23-Audio rec. 24-Video rec. 25-Books 26-Films/film clips 27-Personnel news 28-Press releases 29-New product news/photos 30-Trade lit. 31-Contracts awarded 32-Display adv. 33-Classified adv.

7-45

Pub. Frequency: fortn.
Subscrip. Rate: $70/yr.
Materials: 10
**Owner(s):**
Fraser Management Associates, Inc.
309 S. Willard St.
P.O. Box 494
Burlington, VT 05402
Telephone: (802) 658-0322
FAX: (802) 658-0260
Ownership %: 100
**Editorial:**
James L. Fraser .........................Editor
**Desc.:** Contrary comments in a survey of
current economic events and trends in
business, finance and public thinking.

**FUNDLINE**
P.O. Box 663
Woodland Hills, CA 91365
Telephone: (818) 346-5637
Year Established: 1968
Pub. Frequency: 12/yr.
Subscrip. Rate: $127/yr.
Circulation: 2,000
Circulation Type: controlled & paid
**Owner(s):**
David H. Menashe & Co.
P.O. Box 663
Woodland Hills, CA 91365
Telephone: (818) 346-5637
Ownership %: 100
**Editorial:**
David H. Menashe .........................Editor
**Desc.:** Graphs and indexes depicting long-
term indicators, trading oscillators,
selling signals, boundaries and
composites for U.S. and international
gold funds.

70964
**FXC REPORT**
162-19 Cooper Ave.
Glendale, NY 11385
Telephone: (718) 417-1330
FAX: (718) 417-5950
Year Established: 1972
Pub. Frequency: s-m.
Subscrip. Rate: $290/yr.
Circulation: 2,000
Circulation Type: paid
**Owner(s):**
F X C Report
62-19 Cooper Ave.
Glendale, NY 11385
Telephone: (718) 417-1330
FAX: (718) 417-5950
Ownership %: 100
**Editorial:**
Francis Xavier Curzio .....................Editor
**Desc.:** Provides conservative and
speculative recommendations, allocated
to six categories: asset play, growth, hi-
tech, income, special and turnaround
situtations.

69966
**GEORGIA CONTRARIAN**
P.O. Box 464731
Lawrenceville, NJ 08648-4731
Year Established: 1993
Pub. Frequency: m.
Subscrip. Rate: $60/yr.
**Owner(s):**
P&A Communications, Inc.
P.O. Box 464731
Lawrenceville, NJ 08648-4731
Ownership %: 100
**Editorial:**
Patrick C. Carroll .........................Editor

69971
**GLOBAL ASSET BACKED
   MONITOR**
One State St.Plz
New York, NY 10004-1549
Telephone: (800) 733-4371
FAX: (212) 943-2224
Pub. Frequency: w.
Subscrip. Rate: $675/yr. new; $850/yr.
renewal
**Owner(s):**
American Banker-Bond Buyer
Newsletter Division
One State St. Plz.
New York, NY 10004-1549
Telephone: (800) 733-4371
FAX: (212) 943-2224
Ownership %: 100
**Desc.:** Covers regulatory changes and
shifting market conditions affecting asset
securitization around the world; provides
country-by-country picture of the shifts in
the rules banks and others must
consider in the asset-backed sescurities
marketplace.

69871
**GUARANTOR**
One State St. Plz.
New York, NY 10004-1549
Telephone: (800) 733-4371
FAX: (212) 943-2224
Pub. Frequency: w.
Subscrip. Rate: $995/yr.; $1025/yr. foreign
**Owner(s):**
American Banker-Bond Buyer
One State St. Plz.
New York, NY 10040-1549
Telephone: (800) 733-4371
FAX: (212) 943-2224
Ownership %: 100

69960
**HIGH YIELD REPORT**
One State St. Plz.
New York, NY 10004-1549
Telephone: (800) 733-4371
FAX: (212) 943-2224
Pub. Frequency: w.
Subscrip. Rate: $465/yr. US; $495/yr.
foreign
Materials: 32
**Owner(s):**
American Banker-Bond Buyer
One State St. Plz.
New York, NY 10004-1549
Telephone: (800) 733-4371
FAX: (212) 943-2224
Ownership %: 100
**Editorial:**
Dave Feldheim .........................Editor
**Desc.:** Reports on high-yield bond market,
workouts, bankruptcies and distressed
securities. Includes pricing information
for both primary and secondary markets,
and analysis of high yield sector.

69982
**INCOME STOCKS**
4016 S. Michigan St.
South Bend, IN 46614-2544
Telephone: (219) 291-3823
Year Established: 1972
Pub. Frequency: a.
Subscrip. Rate: $45/yr.
Circulation: 3,000
Circulation Type: paid
**Owner(s):**
Elton Stephens Investments
4016 S. Michigan St.
South Bend, IN 46614-2544
Telephone: (219) 291-3823
Ownership %: 100
**Editorial:**
Elton Stephens .........................Editor

69968
**INSIDERS' CHRONICLE**
One State St. Plz.
New York, NY 10004-1549
Telephone: (800) 733-4371
FAX: (212) 943-2224
Year Established: 1976
Pub. Frequency: w.
Subscrip. Rate: $445/yr.
Materials: 32
**Owner(s):**
American Banker-Bond Buyer
One State St. Plz.
New York, NY 10004-1549
Telephone: (800) 733-4371
FAX: (212) 943-2224
Ownership %: 100
**Editorial:**
William Mehlman .........................Editor
Thomas Curtin .................Advertising Editor
**Desc.:** Reports on buy-sell stock
transactions of corporate officers,
directors and beneficial owners,
providing a guage of corporate
confidence levels and expectations.

69931
**INTERNATIONAL BANK
   ACCOUNTANT**
One State St. Plaza
New York, NY 10004-1549
Telephone: (800) 733-4371
FAX: (212) 943-2224
Pub. Frequency: w.
Subscrip. Rate: $465/yr.; $645/yr. renewal
**Owner(s):**
American Banker-Bond Buyer
One State St. Plaza
New York, NY 10004-1549
Telephone: (800) 733-4371
FAX: (212) 943-2224
Ownership %: 100
**Desc.:** Accounting issues of interest to
banks in the US, Canada and Europe.
Contains a US ledger that summarizes
events in the UK, France, Germany and
Canada, as well as others on a periodic
basis.

69939
**INTERNATIONAL BANKING
   REGULATOR**
One State St. Plaza
New York, NY 10004-1549
Telephone: (800) 733-4371
FAX: (212) 943-2224
Pub. Frequency: w.
Subscrip. Rate: $850/yr.; foreign $880/yr.
**Owner(s):**
American Banker-Bond Buyer
One State St. Plaza
New York, NY 10004-1549
Telephone: (800) 733-4371
FAX: (212) 943-2224
Ownership %: 100
**Desc.:** Provides analysis detailing the
imperative regulatory and legislative
decisions being made in key international
financial centers, and insights on
debates in the US on banking and
securities deregulation.

69985
**INTERNATIONAL SECURITIES
   REGULATION REPORT**
1350 Connecticut Ave. N.W., Ste. 1000
Washington, DC 20036
Telephone: (202) 862-0990
FAX: (202) 862-0999
Year Established: 1987
Pub. Frequency: bi-w.
Subscrip. Rate: $745/yr.; $767/yr. foreign

**Owner(s):**
Buraff Publications
1350 Connecticut Ave. N.W., St
Washington, DC 20036
Telephone: (202) 862-0990
FAX: (202) 862-0999
Ownership %: 100
**Editorial:**
Paul Kelash .........................Editor
**Desc.:** Provides information on regulation
of international securities trading, new
trading links among markets, and
cooperation among governments in
enforcing securities law.

69975
**INVESTMENT MANAGEMENT
   WEEKLY**
One Liberty Sq.
12th Fl.
Boston, MA 02109
Telephone: (617) 426-5450
Pub. Frequency: w.
Subscrip. Rate: $995/yr.
Materials: 32
**Owner(s):**
Investment Management Weekly
One Liberty Sq.
12th Fl.
Boston, MA 02109
Telephone: (617) 426-5450
Ownership %: 100
**Editorial:**
Richard Chimburg .........................Editor

70035
**INVESTMENT QUALITY TRENDS**
7440 Girard Ave.
Ste. 4
La Jolla, CA 92037
Telephone: (619) 459-3818
FAX: (619) 459-3819
Year Established: 1966
Pub. Frequency: bi-m.
Subscrip. Rate: $275/yr.
**Owner(s):**
Value Trend Analysis
7440 Girard Ave.
Ste. 4
La Jolla, CA 92037
Telephone: (619) 459-3818
FAX: (619) 459-3819
Ownership %: 100
**Editorial:**
Geraldine Weiss .........................Editor

69976
**IRA-INDIVIDUAL RETIREMENT
   ACCOUNT STOCKS**
4016 S. Michigan St.
South Bend, IN 46614-2544
Telephone: (219) 291-3823
Year Established: 1972
Pub. Frequency: a.
Subscrip. Rate: $45/yr.
Circulation: 3,000
Circulation Type: paid
**Owner(s):**
Elton Stephens Investments
4016 S. Michigan St.
South Bend, IN 46614-2544
Telephone: (219) 291-3823
Ownership %: 100
**Editorial:**
Elton Stephens .........................Editor
**Desc.:** Lists IRA stocks, arranged by
category.

69979
**JAKE BERNSTEIN'S LETTER OF
   LONG TERM TRENDS**
2 Northbrook Pl.
Northbrook, IL 60062
Telephone: (708) 291-1870
FAX: (708) 291-9435
Pub. Frequency: m.
Subscrip. Rate: $400/yr.

**Materials Accepted/Included:** 01-Business news 02-By-line articles 03-Fashion news 04-Food news 05-Freelance copy 06-Letters to editor 07-Real estate news 08-Sports news 09-Travel news
10-Book rev. 11-Movie rev. 12-Music rev. 13-TV rev. 14-Theater rev. 15-Coming events 16-Obituaries 17-Question & answer 18-Social announcements 19-Artwork 20-Cartoons 21-Photos 22-TV listings
23-Audio rec. 24-Video rec. 25-Books 26-Films/film clips 27-Personnel news 28-Press releases 29-New product news/photos 30-Trade lit. 31-Contracts awarded 32-Display adv. 33-Classified adv.

7-46

**Owner(s):**
M.B.H. Commodity Advisors, Inc.
60 Revere Dr.
Ste. 888
Northbrook, IL 60062
Telephone: (708) 291-1870
FAX: (708) 291-9435
Ownership %: 100
**Editorial:**
Jake Bernstein ............................................Editor

## LETTERS OF CREDIT REPORT
*58701*
122 W. 21st St.
New York, NY 10010-6990
Telephone: (212) 645-7880
FAX: (212) 645-1160
Year Established: 1986
Pub. Frequency: bi-m.
Page Size: standard
Subscrip. Rate: $245/yr.
Materials: 02,06,32
Circulation: 300
Circulation Type: paid
**Owner(s):**
Executive Enterprises Publications Co., Inc.
22 W. 21st St.
New York, NY 10010
Telephone: (212) 645-7880
Ownership %: 100
**Editorial:**
Gerald McLaughlin ......................Editor in Chief
Thomas Whitehill .......................................Editor
Deborah Wenger ....................Managing Editor
**Desc.:** A bi-monthly newsletter covering
the latest legal and financial
developments affecting letters of credit,
bank acceptances, and bank
guarantees, both domestically and
internationally.
**Readers:** Bankers, lawyers and financial
executives.

## LOAN OFFICERS LEGAL ALERT
*58703*
22 W. 21st St.
New York, NY 10010-6990
Telephone: (212) 645-7880
Year Established: 1984
Pub. Frequency: m.
Page Size: standard
Subscrip. Rate: $195/yr.; $359/2 yrs.;
$486/3 yrs.
**Owner(s):**
Executive Enterprises Publications Co., Inc.
22 W. 21st St.
New York, NY 10010
Telephone: (212) 645-7880
Ownership %: 100
**Editorial:**
Lewis Koflowitz .........................................Editor
Isabelle Cohen ........................Managing Editor
**Desc.:** Covers the practical legal issues
underlying commercial lenders policies
and procedures.
**Readers:** Commercial bank lending
officers.

## LOW PRICED STOCKS
*69986*
4016 S. Michigan St.
South Bend, IN 46614-2544
Telephone: (219) 291-3823
Year Established: 1972
Pub. Frequency: a.
Subscrip. Rate: $45/yr.
Circulation: 3,000
Circulation Type: paid
**Owner(s):**
Elton Stephens Investments
4016 S. Michigan St.
South Bend, IN 46614-2544
Telephone: (219) 291-3823
Ownership %: 100
**Editorial:**
Elton Stephens ..........................................Editor

## MARGO'S MARKET MONITOR
*69989*
P.O. Box 642
Lexington, MA 02173
Telephone: (617) 861-0302
FAX: (617) 861-1489
Year Established: 1980
Pub. Frequency: m.
Subscrip. Rate: $125/yr.
Materials: 10
**Owner(s):**
Margo's Market Monitor
P.O. Box 642
Lexington, MA 02173
Telephone: (617) 861-0302
FAX: (617) 861-1489
Ownership %: 100
**Editorial:**
Margo Parrish .............................................Editor

## MARKET CYCLE INVESTING
*70038*
995 Oak Pk. Dr.
Morgan Hill, CA 95037-4747
Telephone: (408) 778-2925
Year Established: 1974
Pub. Frequency: 17/yr.
Subscrip. Rate: $98.50/yr.
**Owner(s):**
Andrews Publications
995 Oak Pk. Dr.
Morgan Hill, CA 95037-4747
Telephone: (408) 778-2925
Ownership %: 100
**Editorial:**
R. Earl Andrews .........................................Editor
**Desc.:** Growth stocks for long-term
investors.

## MONEYLETTER
*69992*
835 Franklin Ct.
Atlanta, GA 30348
Telephone: (404) 426-1920
FAX: (404) 423-7349
Mailing Address:
P.O. Box 105627
Atlanta, GA 30348
Year Established: 1979
Pub. Frequency: m.
Subscrip. Rate: $95/yr.
Circulation: 3,600
Circulation Type: paid
**Owner(s):**
Hume Group, Inc.
835 Franklin Ct.
Atlanta, GA 30348
Telephone: (404) 426-1920
FAX: (404) 423-7349
Ownership %: 100
**Editorial:**
Ron Davis ....................................................Editor
**Desc.:** Offers current financial advice to
Hume clients and recommends specific
investment and tax-planning strategies.

## MONEY MANAGEMENT LETTER
*69991*
488 Madison Ave.
New York, NY 10022
Telephone: (212) 303-3233
FAX: (212) 303-3353
Year Established: 1980
Pub. Frequency: bi-w.
Subscrip. Rate: $1275/yr. US;
$1287.50/yr. Canada; $1307/yr.
elsewhere
Materials: 32
**Owner(s):**
Institutional Investor, Inc.
488 Madison Ave.
New York, NY 10022
Telephone: (212) 303-3233
FAX: (212) 303-3353
Ownership %: 100
**Editorial:**
Tom Lamont .................................................Editor

**Desc.:** Covers the business of U.S.
pension fund investment managers.
Reports on which funds are hiring
new money managers and why, what
new strategies and products are being
used, personnel changes that shift
market power, and trends in master trust
and custodial services.

## MORTGAGE MARKETPLACE
*70000*
One State St. Plz.
New York, NY 10004-1549
Telephone: (800) 733-4371
FAX: (212) 943-2224
Year Established: 1970
Pub. Frequency: w.
Subscrip. Rate: $465/yr. new subscriber;
$495/yr. foreign; $675/yr. renewal;
$705/yr. foreign
**Owner(s):**
American Banker-Bond Buyer
One State St. Plz.
New York, NY 10004-1549
Telephone: (800) 733-4371
FAX: (212) 943-2224
Ownership %: 100
**Editorial:**
James Byrne ...............................................Editor
**Desc.:** Covers political developments,
regulatory changes, and accounting
issues affecting the market for
mortgages, and mortgage-backed
securities traded by banks and other
financial institutions in the US.

## MUTUAL FUND SPECIALIST
*70032*
P.O. Box 1025
Eau Claire, WI 54702
Telephone: (800) 547-1025
FAX: (715) 834-7425
Year Established: 1978
Pub. Frequency: m.
Subscrip. Rate: $95/yr.
**Owner(s):**
Royal R. Lemier & Co.
P.O. Box 1025
Eau Claire, WI 54702
Telephone: (800) 547-1025
FAX: (715) 834-7425
Ownership %: 100
**Editorial:**
Royal R. Lemier .........................................Editor
**Desc.:** Provides analysis of equity markets
and mutual fund trends. Focus on family
of funds concept to mutual funds
investing.

## NATIONAL REVIEW OF CORPORATE ACQUISITIONS
*69928*
49 Main St.
Tiburon, CA 94920
Telephone: (415) 435-2175
FAX: (415) 435-6310
Year Established: 1974
Pub. Frequency: w.
Subscrip. Rate: $295/yr.
Circulation: 2,200
**Owner(s):**
Tweed Publishing Co.
49 Main St.
Tiburon, CA 94920
Telephone: (415) 435-2175
FAX: (415) 435-6310
Ownership %: 100
**Editorial:**
Sonja J. Mahoney ......................................Editor

## NOLOAD FUND
*70023*
Russ Bldg., Ste. 662
235 Montgomery St.
San Francisco, CA 94104
Telephone: (415) 986-7979
FAX: (415) 986-1595

Year Established: 1976
Pub. Frequency: m.
Subscrip. Rate: $114/yr.
**Owner(s):**
Dal Investment Co.
235 Montgomery St.
Russ Bldg., Ste. 662
San Francisco, CA 94104
Telephone: (415) 986-7979
FAX: (415) 986-1595
Ownership %: 100
**Editorial:**
Burton Berry ...............................................Editor
**Desc.:** Investment system and
performance data covering all no-load
and low-load funds.

## NYSE WEEKLY STOCK BUYS
*70013*
4016 S. Michigan St.
South Bend, IN 46624-0476
Telephone: (219) 291-3823
Year Established: 1991
Pub. Frequency: w.
Subscrip. Rate: $45/yr.
**Owner(s):**
Elton Stephens Investments
4016 S. Michigan St.
South Bend, IN 46624-0476
Telephone: (219) 291-3823
Ownership %: 100
**Editorial:**
Elton Stephens ..........................................Editor

## PETER DAG INVESTMENT LETTER
*69933*
65 Lakefront Dr.
Akron, OH 44319
Telephone: (216) 644-2782
Year Established: 1977
Pub. Frequency: 29/yr.
Subscrip. Rate: $250/yr.
Materials: 10
Circulation: 2,000
**Owner(s):**
Peter Dag & Associates
65 Lakefront Dr.
Akron, OH 44319
Telephone: (216) 644-2782
Ownership %: 100
**Editorial:**
George Dagnino .........................................Editor

## PRACTICAL CASH MANAGEMENT
*69943*
P.O. Box 431
Westport, CT 06881-0431
Telephone: (203) 227-1237
Pub. Frequency: m.
Subscrip. Rate: $292/yr.; $322/yr. foreign
**Owner(s):**
Bankers Research, Inc.
P.O. Box 431
Westport, CT 06881-0431
Telephone: (203) 227-1237
Ownership %: 100
**Editorial:**
Theodore Volckhausen ...........................Editor

## PRICE PERCEPTIONS
*69996*
211 N. Robinson Ave., Ste. 3000
Oklahoma City, OK 73102-7101
Telephone: (405) 235-5687
FAX: (405) 232-4354
Year Established: 1970
Pub. Frequency: s-m.
Subscrip. Rate: $360/yr.
Circulation: 1,000
Circulation Type: controlled & paid
**Owner(s):**
Commodity Information Systems
211 N. Robinson Ave., Ste. 300
Oklahoma City, OK 73102-7101
Telephone: (405) 235-5687
FAX: (405) 232-4354
Ownership %: 100

**Materials Accepted/Included:** 01-Business news 02-By-line articles 03-Fashion news 04-Food news 05-Freelance copy 06-Letters to editor 07-Real estate news 08-Sports news 09-Travel news 10-Book rev. 11-Movie rev. 12-Music rev. 13-TV rev. 14-Theater rev. 15-Coming events 16-Obituaries 17-Question & answer 18-Social announcements 19-Artwork 20-Cartoons 21-Photos 22-TV listings 23-Audio rec. 24-Video rec. 25-Books 26-Films/film clips 27-Personnel news 28-Press releases 29-New product news/photos 30-Trade lit. 31-Contracts awarded 32-Display adv. 33-Classified adv.

7-47

**Editorial:**
William K. Gary .......................... Editor
**Desc.:** Commodity market research and analysis.

69937
**PRIVATE PLACEMENT REPORTER**
One State Plz.
New York, NY 10004-1549
Telephone: (800) 733-4371
FAX: (212) 943-2224
Pub. Frequency: w.
Subscrip. Rate: $645/yr.
Materials: 32
**Owner(s):**
American Banker-Bond Buyer
One State St. Plz.
New York, NY 10004-1549
Telephone: (800) 733-4371
FAX: (212) 943-2224
Ownership %: 100
**Editorial:**
Gracian Mack .......................... Editor
Thomas Curtin .................. Advertising Editor
**Desc.:** Covers buying, selling and trading unregistered securities. Includes deal structure and pricing, covenant packages and spreads; surveilliance and the "new" private placement market in post-144A environment; stories affecting the marketplace.

70027
**PROFESSIONAL TAPE READER**
P.O. Box 2407
Hollywood, FL 33022
Telephone: (800) 868-7857
Year Established: 1972
Pub. Frequency: m.
Subscrip. Rate: $350/yr.
Circulation: 12,000
Circulation Type: paid
**Owner(s):**
Radcap, Inc.
P.O. Box 2407
Hollywood, FL 33022
Telephone: (800) 868-7857
Ownership %: 100
**Editorial:**
Stan Weinstein .......................... Editor
**Desc.:** Stock market advisory service with charts, advice, information, and forecasts for long and short-term trends, analysis of promising and vulnerable stocks, and fund performance data.

69970
**PRUDENT SPECULATOR**
P.O. Box 1767
Santa Monica, CA 90406-1767
Telephone: (310) 315-9888
FAX: (310) 315-9883
Year Established: 1977
Pub. Frequency: m.
Subscrip. Rate: $175/yr.
Materials: 10
Circulation: 2,500
Circulation Type: controlled & paid
**Owner(s):**
Al Frank Asset Management, Inc.
P.O. Box 1767
Santa Monica, CA 90406-1767
Telephone: (310) 315-9888
FAX: (310) 315-9883
Ownership %: 100
**Editorial:**
Al Frank .......................... Editor
**Desc.:** Stock advisory letter showing investors what to consider in buying and selling stocks, managing a portfolio and adjusting to significant market-wide changes.

69998
**PUBLIC FINANCE WATCH**
One State St. Plaza
New York, NY 10004-1549
Telephone: (800) 733-4371
FAX: (212) 943-2224
Pub. Frequency: w.
Subscrip. Rate: $645/yr.
**Owner(s):**
American Banker-Bond Buyer
One State St. Plaza
New York, NY 10004-1549
Telephone: (800) 733-4371
FAX: (212) 943-2224
Ownership %: 100
**Desc.:** State and local insurance of public finance instruments and the market for those securities.

69942
**REGULATORY COMPLIANCE WATCH**
One State St. Plz.
New York, NY 10004-1549
Telephone: (800) 733-4371
FAX: (212) 943-2224
Pub. Frequency: w.
Subscrip. Rate: $465/yr. US; $495/yr. foreign
**Owner(s):**
American Banker-Bond Buyer
Newsletter Div.
One State St. Plz.
New York, NY 10004-1549
Telephone: (800) 733-4371
FAX: (212) 943-2224
Ownership %: 100
**Editorial:**
Anthony Kimberly .......................... Editor
**Desc.:** Covers the legal, regulatory and legislative developments in Washington, affecting the nation's banks, S&L's and credit unions. Contains analysis and interpretations of all the critical regulatory changes in progress.

69974
**RUSS REPORTS**
506 Old Mill Rd.
Mauldin, SC 29662-1717
Telephone: (803) 281-1561
Year Established: 1981
Pub. Frequency: m.
Subscrip. Rate: $90/yr.
Circulation: 3,750
Circulation Type: controlled & paid
**Owner(s):**
Russ Reports
506 Old Mill Rd.
Mauldin, SC 29662-1717
Telephone: (803) 281-1561
Ownership %: 100
**Editorial:**
Russ Klein .......................... Editor
**Desc.:** Provides investment advice, with buy and sell recommendations for selected stocks.

70934
**SAFE MONEY REPORT**
2200 N. Florida Mango Rd.
W. Palm Beach, FL 33409
Telephone: (407) 684-9039
FAX: (407) 684-9039
Year Established: 1971
Pub. Frequency: m.
Subscrip. Rate: $145/yr.
Circulation: 6,000
Circulation Type: controlled & paid
**Owner(s):**
Martin D. Weiss Publishing
2200 N. Florida Mango Rd.
W. Palm Beach, FL 33409
Telephone: (407) 684-9039
FAX: (407) 684-9039
Ownership %: 100

**Desc.:** A forum for investors that deals with high returns, maximum liquidity, and speculative strategies along with bank, insurance, and brokerage safety.

70002
**SECURITIES ARBITRATION COMMENTOR**
6 1/2 Highland Pl.
Maplewood, NJ 07040
Telephone: (201) 761-5880
FAX: (201) 761-1504
Year Established: 1988
Pub. Frequency: m.
Subscrip. Rate: $295/yr.
**Owner(s):**
Richard Ryder
**Editorial:**
Richard Ryder .......................... Editor

69980
**SILVER BARON'S MONEY FEVER**
5025 S. Eastern Ave.
Ste. 24
Las Vegas, NV 89119
Telephone: (702) 597-9980
FAX: (702) 597-9510
Year Established: 1984
Pub. Frequency: 18/yr.
Subscrip. Rate: $150/yr.
Materials: 32
Circulation: 1,900
Circulation Type: controlled
**Owner(s):**
SB Stocks USA
5025 S. Eastern Ave.
Ste. 24
Las Vegas, NV 89119
Telephone: (702) 597-9980
FAX: (702) 597-9510
Ownership %: 100
**Editorial:**
Elliot R. Pearson .......................... Editor
**Desc.:** Picks winners with as little risk as possible under the circumstances.

69983
**SLANKER REPORT**
Rte. 9
P.O. Box 610
Texarkana, TX 75501
Telephone: (903) 832-3809
FAX: (903) 832-3918
Year Established: 1992
Pub. Frequency: m.
Subscrip. Rate: $95/yr.
**Owner(s):**
Saturn Five, Inc.
Rte. 9
P.O. Box 610
Texarkana, TX 75501
Telephone: (903) 832-3809
FAX: (903) 832-3918
Ownership %: 100
**Editorial:**
Ted E. Slanker, Jr. .......................... Editor

69987
**SOLID VALUE**
4410 S.W. Pt. Robinson Rd.
Vashon Island, WA 98070-7399
Telephone: (206) 463-9399
FAX: (206) 463-9255
Year Established: 1986
Pub. Frequency: s-m.
Subscrip. Rate: $276/yr.
Materials: 10,32
**Owner(s):**
Happy Man Corporation
4410 S.W. Pt. Robinson Rd.
Vashon Island, WA 98070-7399
Telephone: (206) 463-9399
FAX: (206) 463-9255
Ownership %: 100
**Editorial:**
Irving Scott Wolfe .......................... Editor

**Desc.:** Lists the market's most under-priced stocks; includes commentaries and updates on recommendations and market analysis.

69945
**TAX INSIGHT**
900 19th St. N.W., Ste. 400
Washington, DC 20006
Telephone: (202) 857-3100
FAX: (202) 857-5581
Pub. Frequency: m.
Subscrip. Rate: $295/yr. to non-members; $195/yr. to members
**Owner(s):**
Savings & Community Bankers of America
900 19th St. N.W., Ste. 400
Washington, DC 20006
Telephone: (202) 857-3100
FAX: (202) 857-5581
Ownership %: 100
**Editorial:**
Beth Neese .......................... Editor
**Desc.:** rovides clear explanations of federal tax legislation, regulations and rulings important to financial institutions.

69956
**THRIFT REGULATOR**
One State St. Plz.
New York, NY 10040-1549
Telephone: (800) 733-4371
FAX: (212) 943-2224
Year Established: 1982
Pub. Frequency: w.
Subscrip. Rate: $565/yr. US; $595/yr. foreign
**Owner(s):**
American Banker-Bond Buyer
One State St. Plz.
New York, NY 10004-1549
Telephone: (800) 733-4371
FAX: (212) 943-2224
Ownership %: 100
**Editorial:**
Bob Duke .......................... Editor
**Desc.:** News on regulatory, congressional and judicial developments affecting saving and loan industry.

69990
**TRADING CYCLES**
995 Oak Park Dr.
Morgan Hill, CA 95037
Telephone: (408) 778-2925
Year Established: 1974
Pub. Frequency: 17/yr.
Subscrip. Rate: $97.99/yr.
**Owner(s):**
Andrews Publications
995 Oak Park Dr.
Morgan Hill, CA 95037
Telephone: (408) 778-2925
Ownership %: 100
**Editorial:**
R. Earl Andrews .......................... Editor
**Desc.:** Market timing service for stocks, bonds, precious metals; currencies, options, computer generated decisions.

71239
**TREASURY MANAGER'S REPORT**
1201 Seven Locks Rd.
Potomac, MD 20854
Telephone: (301) 424-3338
FAX: (301) 309-3847
Year Established: 1993
Pub. Frequency: bi-w.
Subscrip. Rate: $495/yr. US; $530/yr. foreign
**Owner(s):**
Phillips Business Information, Inc.
1201 Seven Locks Rd.
Potomac, MD 20854
Telephone: (301) 424-3338
FAX: (301) 309-3847
Ownership %: 100

**Materials Accepted/Included:** 01-Business news 02-By-line articles 03-Fashion news 04-Food news 05-Freelance copy 06-Letters to editor 07-Real estate news 08-Sports news 09-Travel news 10-Book rev. 11-Movie rev. 12-Music rev. 13-TV rev. 14-Theater rev. 15-Coming events 16-Obituaries 17-Question & answer 18-Social announcements 19-Artwork 20-Cartoons 21-Photos 22-TV listings 23-Audio rec. 24-Video rec. 25-Books 26-Films/film clips 27-Personnel news 28-Press releases 29-New product news/photos 30-Trade lit. 31-Contracts awarded 32-Display adv. 33-Classified adv.

## VALUE FORECASTER
69995
P.O. Box 50
Pilot Hill, CA 95664
Year Established: 1988
Pub. Frequency: m.
Subscrip. Rate: $195/yr.
Materials: 10
Circulation: 500
Circulation Type: controlled & paid
**Owner(s):**
Value Forecaster
P.O. Box 50
Pilot Hill, CA 95664
Ownership %: 100
**Editorial:**
Robert Freitas, Jr. ...............................Editor
**Desc.:** Investment research service using
 nonlinear econometrics to forecast
 investments.

## ZWEIG FORECAST
69999
P.O. Box 2900
Wantagh, NY 11793
Telephone: (516) 785-1300
Year Established: 1971
Pub. Frequency: every 3 wks.
Subscrip. Rate: $265/yr.
Circulation: 13,000
Circulation Type: controlled & paid
**Owner(s):**
Zweig Securities Advisory Service
P.O. Box 2900
Wantagh, NY 11793
Telephone: (516) 785-1300
Ownership %: 100
**Editorial:**
Martin E. Zweig ...............................Editor

## ZWEIG PERFORMANCE RATINGS REPORT
70004
P.O. Box 2900
Wantagh, NY 11793
Telephone: (516) 785-1300
Pub. Frequency: s-m.
Subscrip. Rate: $205/yr.
Circulation: 6,000
Circulation Type: controlled & paid
**Owner(s):**
Zweig Securities Advisory Service
P.O. Box 2900
Wantagh, NY 11793
Telephone: (516) 785-1300
Ownership %: 100
**Editorial:**
Timothy Clark ...............................Editor
**Desc.:** Ratings of more than 3,000 stocks
 with model portfolio and 3 individual
 stock picks each issue

## 401(K) REPORTER
70006
P.O. Box 979
Brainerd, MN 56401
Telephone: (218) 829-4781
FAX: (218) 829-2106
Year Established: 1985
Pub. Frequency: m.
Subscrip. Rate: $75/yr.
**Owner(s):**
Universal Pensions, Inc.
P.O. Box 979
Brainerd, MN 56401
Telephone: (218) 829-4781
FAX: (218) 829-2106
Ownership %: 100
**Editorial:**
Pamela O'Rourke ...............................Editor

**Desc.:** Details information and recent
 developments concerning "401 K"
 plans.

## Group 330-Food

### ALCOHOLIC BEVERAGE EXECUTIVES' NEWSLETTER
61306
1120 S. 96th St.
Omaha, NE 68124-1122
Telephone: (402) 397-5514
FAX: (402) 397-3843
Mailing Address:
 P.O. Box 3188
 Omaha, NE 68103-0188
Year Established: 1940
Pub. Frequency: w.
Page Size: standard
Subscrip. Rate: $225/yr.
Materials: 32
Circulation: 3,000
Circulation Type: paid
**Owner(s):**
Alcoholic Beverage Committee
Ownership %: 100
**Editorial:**
Patricia Kennedy ...............................Editor
**Desc.:** Covers beer, wine & spirits.
**Readers:** Executives of beer, wine &
 spirits industries.

### ALCOHOL ISSUES INSIGHTS
70011
51 Virginia Ave.
W. Nyack, NY 10994
Telephone: (914) 358-7751
Year Established: 1983
Pub. Frequency: m.
Subscrip. Rate: $187/yr.
**Owner(s):**
Beer Marketer's Insights, Inc.
51 Virginia Ave.
W. Nyack, NY 10994
Telephone: (914) 358-7751
Ownership %: 100
**Editorial:**
Benj Steinman ...............................Editor
**Desc.:** Covers alcohol policy issues,
 including excise tax, drunk driving laws,
 advertising and availability restrictions,
 and alcohol and health.

### BAKERY NEWSLETTER
71228
Division of Reed Elsevier Inc.
455 N. Cityfront Plaza Dr., 24th Fl.
Chicago, IL 60611-5503
Telephone: (312) 222-2000
FAX: (312) 222-2026
Pub. Frequency: w.
Subscrip. Rate: $245/yr. US; $295/yr.
 foreign
**Owner(s):**
Delta Communications, Inc.
Division of Reed Elsevier Inc.
455 N. Cityfront Plaza Dr., 24th Fl.
Chicago, IL 60611-5503
Telephone: (312) 222-2000
FAX: (312) 222-2026
Ownership %: 100
**Desc.:** Keeps readers on top of market
 and product trends, commodity reports,
 advertising and marketing strategies,
 mergers and acquisitions, competitive
 moves, and government regulations.

### BEER MARKETER'S INSIGHTS
70015
51 Virginia Ave.
W. Nyack, NY 10994
Telephone: (914) 358-7751
Year Established: 1970
Pub. Frequency: 23/yr.
Subscrip. Rate: $289/yr.
Materials: 10

**Owner(s):**
Beer Marketer's Insights, Inc.
51 Virginia Ave.
W. Nyack, NY 10994
Telephone: (914) 358-7751
Ownership %: 100
**Editorial:**
Jerry Steinman ...............................Editor
**Desc.:** Analyzes shipments, sales in beer
 industry (domestic and import), plus
 social, political, legal trends which affect
 sales.

### BEVERAGE ALCOHOL MARKET REPORT
61580
160 E. 48th St.
New York, NY 10017
Telephone: (212) 371-5237
Year Established: 1982
Pub. Frequency: 6/yr.
Page Size: standard
Subscrip. Rate: $175/yr.; $195/yr. foreign
Materials: 01,04,10,15,16,23,24,25,27,28,
 29,30,32
Freelance Pay: none
Print Process: offset
Circulation: 3,000
Circulation Type: paid
**Owner(s):**
Peregine Communications
160 E. 48th St.
New York, NY 10017
Telephone: (212) 371-5237
Ownership %: 100
**Management:**
Perry Luntz ...............................Manager
**Editorial:**
Perry Luntz ...............................Editor
Carol Luntz ...............................Circulation Editor
**Desc.:** For executives in the international
 beer, wine and spirits industry. Including
 producers, wholesalers and retailers.
**Readers:** Middle and top management
 executives.
**Deadline:** story-Mon.; news-Mon.; photo-
 Mon.; ads-Mon.

### BEVERAGE DIGEST
69374
P.O. Box 238
Old Greenwich, CT 06870
Telephone: (203) 358-8198
FAX: (203) 327-9761
Year Established: 1982
Pub. Frequency: 22/yr.
Page Size: standard
Subscrip. Rate: $400/yr. US; $450/yr.
 foreign
Materials: 10
**Owner(s):**
Tomac & Company, Inc.
P.O. Box 238
Old Greenwich, CT 06870
Telephone: (203) 358-8198
Ownership %: 100
**Editorial:**
Jesse Myers ...............................Editor
Michael Hayes ...............................Editor
**Desc.:** Covers the soft drink industry plus
 related markets. Primary focus is
 marketing and statistics.

### BREAD PUDDING UPDATE
70499
c/o Posperity & Profits Unlimited
P.O. Box 416
Denver, CO 80201-0416
Telephone: (303) 575-5676
Year Established: 1989
Pub. Frequency: a.
Subscrip. Rate: $5/yr. US; $7/yr. Canada;
 $9/yr. foreign
Circulation: 1500
Circulation Type: controlled & paid

**Owner(s):**
Continnuus
P.O. Box 416
Denver, CO 80201-0416
Telephone: (303) 575-5676
Ownership %: 100
**Editorial:**
A.C. Doyle ...............................Editor

### CALIFORNIA BEVERAGE HOTLINE
69997
3284 Barham Blvd.
Los Angeles, CA 90068-1008
Telephone: (213) 876-7590
FAX: (213) 876-4090
Year Established: 1983
Pub. Frequency: m.
Subscrip. Rate: $120/yr.
Materials: 10,32
**Owner(s):**
GE Publications
3284 Barham Blvd.
Los Angeles, CA 90068-1008
Telephone: (213) 876-7590
FAX: (213) 876-4090
Ownership %: 100
**Editorial:**
Harold Metz ...............................Editor

### CALIFORNIA WINELETTER
70003
P.O. Box 70
Mill Valley, CA 94942
Telephone: (415) 388-2578
Year Established: 1948
Pub. Frequency: m.
Subscrip. Rate: $65/yr.
Materials: 10,32
Circulation: 1,200
Circulation Type: paid
**Owner(s):**
California Wineletter
P.O. Box 70
Mill Valley, CA 94942
Telephone: (415) 388-2578
Ownership %: 100
**Management:**
Phyllis van Kriedt ...............................Publisher
**Desc.:** Newsletter for the wine trade.

### CAMERON'S FOODSERVICE MARKETING REPORTER
70291
5325 Sheridan Dr.
Williamsville, NY 14231-1160
Telephone: (716) 833-4369
FAX: (716) 834-4159
Mailing Address:
 P.O. Box 1160
 Williamsville, NY 14231-1160
Year Established: 1982
Pub. Frequency: s-m.
Subscrip. Rate: $197/yr.
Circulation: 10,000
Circulation Type: controlled & paid
**Owner(s):**
Cameron's Foodservice Marketing
 Reporter
5325 Sheridan Dr.
Williamsville, NY 14231-1160
Telephone: (716) 833-4369
FAX: (716) 834-4159
Ownership %: 100
**Editorial:**
Nina Cameron ...............................Editor
**Desc.:** Food service promotions and
 advertising newsletter for hotels,
 restaurants, military and country clubs.

### DAIRY-DELI-BAKE DIGEST
70267
313 Price Pl.
Ste. 202
Madison, WI 53705-0528
Telephone: (608) 238-7908
FAX: (608) 238-6330

**Materials Accepted/Included:** 01-Business news 02-By-line articles 03-Fashion news 04-Food news 05-Freelance copy 06-Letters to editor 07-Real estate news 08-Sports news 09-Travel news 10-Book rev. 11-Movie rev. 12-Music rev. 13-TV rev. 14-Theater rev. 15-Coming events 16-Obituaries 17-Question & answer 18-Social announcements 19-Artwork 20-Cartoons 21-Photos 22-TV listings 23-Audio rec. 24-Video rec. 25-Books 26-Films/film clips 27-Personnel news 28-Press releases 29-New product news/photos 30-Trade lit. 31-Contracts awarded 32-Display adv. 33-Classified adv.

7-49

Pub. Frequency: m.
Subscrip. Rate: membership
Materials: 10
Circulation: 10,000
Circulation Type: controlled & paid
**Owner(s):**
International Dairy-Deli-Bakery Association
313 Price Pl.
Ste. 202
Madison, WI 53705-0528
Telephone: (608) 238-7908
FAX: (608) 238-6330
Ownership %: 100
**Editorial:**
Carol Christison .............................Editor
**Desc.:** Covers management trends, new
products and ideas, resources,
legislation for dairy, deli and
bakery professionals.

68672
### DAIRY FOODS MAGAZINE
455 N. Cityfront Plz. Dr., 24th Fl.
Chicago, IL 60611-5503
Telephone: (312) 222-2000
FAX: (312) 222-2026
Year Established: 1959
Pub. Frequency: w.
Subscrip. Rate: $282/yr.; $289/yr. foreign
Materials: 01,04,06,16,21,27,28,29,30,31
Circulation: 24,000
Circulation Type: controlled
**Owner(s):**
Cahners Publishing Company, Inc.
455 N. Cityfront Plz. Dr.
Chicago, IL 60611-5503
Telephone: (312) 222-2000
FAX: (312) 222-2026
Ownership %: 100
**Editorial:**
Jeff Reiter .........................Senior Editor

70318
### FMI ISSUES BULLETIN
800 Connecticut Ave., N.W.
Washington, DC 20006
Telephone: (202) 452-8444
Year Established: 1977
Pub. Frequency: m.
Subscrip. Rate: $35/yr. to non-members
Circulation: 4,000
Circulation Type: controlled & paid
**Owner(s):**
Food Marketing Institute
800 Connecticut Ave., N.W.
Washington, DC 20006
Telephone: (202) 452-8444
Ownership %: 100
**Editorial:**
Judy Smith ................................Editor
**Desc.:** Covers issues and ideas important
to the food distribution industry. Includes
industry trends, interviews with business
and government leaders, and
information on programs and services
provided by the institute.

70293
### FOOD & DRINK DAILY
627 National Press Bldg.
Washingtonf, DC 20045
Telephone: (202) 638-4260
FAX: (202) 662-9744
Year Established: 1985
Pub. Frequency: d.
Subscrip. Rate: $825/yr.
Materials: 10
Circulation: 168
Circulation Type: controlled & paid
**Owner(s):**
King Publishing Group, Inc.
627 National Press Bldg.
Washington, DC 20045
Telephone: (202) 638-4260
FAX: (202) 662-9744
Ownership %: 100

**Editorial:**
Linda Gasparello ..........................Editor
**Desc.:** Covers all aspects of the food and
beverage industry, its international
markets, and its regulators. Reports on
government agencies.

70744
### FOOD & NUTRITION NEWS
444N. Michigan Ave.
Chicago, IL 60611
Telephone: (312) 467-5520
FAX: (312) 467-9729
Year Established: 1930
Pub. Frequency: 5/yr.
Page Size: standard
Subscrip. Rate: free
Materials: 10
Circulation: 55000
Circulation Type: free
**Owner(s):**
National Live Stock and Meat Board
444 N. Michigan Ave.
Chicago, IL 60611
Telephone: (312) 467-5520
FAX: (312) 467-9729
Ownership %: 100
**Editorial:**
E. Urenos .................................Editor

71230
### FOOD HISTORY NEWS
HC 60
P.O. Box 354A
Islesboro, ME 04848
Telephone: (207) 734-8140
FAX: (207) 734-8883
Year Established: 1989
Pub. Frequency: q.
Subscrip. Rate: $12/yr.
Materials: 10
Circulation: 525
Circulation Type: paid
**Owner(s):**
Food History News
HC 60
P.O. Box 354A
Islesboro, ME 04848
Telephone: (207) 734-8140
FAX: (207) 734-8883
Ownership %: 100
**Editorial:**
Sandra L. Oliver ..........................Editor
**Desc.:** News and announcements of
upcoming events in food history studies,
history of specific dishes and or foods,
practical information on reconstructing
historic foods, and food history
methodology.

70269
### FOOD INDUSTRY FUTURES: A STRATEGY SERVICE
P.O. Box 430
Fayetteville, NY 13066
Year Established: 1972
Pub. Frequency: s-m.
Subscrip. Rate: $150/yr.
Materials: 10
**Owner(s):**
Cuthill Research Services, Inc.
P.O. Box 430
Fayetteville, NY 13066
Ownership %: 100
**Editorial:**
Ian D. Cuthill ............................Editor

70272
### FOOD INDUSTRY NEWSLETTER
P.O. Box 2730
Bethesda, MD 20827
Telephone: (301) 469-8507
FAX: (301) 469-7271
Year Established: 1972
Pub. Frequency: 22/yr.
Subscrip. Rate: $245/yr.
Materials: 10

**Owner(s):**
Newsletters, Inc.
P.O. Box 2730
Bethesda, MD 20827
Telephone: (301) 469-8507
FAX: (301) 469-7271
Ownership %: 100
**Editorial:**
Max Busetti ..............................Editor

70441
### FOOD INGREDIENT NEWS
25 Van Zant St.
Norwalk, CT 06855
Telephone: (203) 853-4266
FAX: (203) 853-0348
Year Established: 1994
Pub. Frequency: m.
Subscrip. Rate: $295/yr.
**Owner(s):**
Business Communications Co., Inc.
25 Van Zant St.
Norwalk, CT 06855
Telephone: (203) 853-4266
FAX: (203) 853-0348
Ownership %: 100
**Management:**
Robert Butler .........................Manager
**Editorial:**
Dorothy Kroll ............................Editor
**Desc.:** Covers product development,
technology, patents, research and other
news relating to the food industry.
**Readers:** Ingredient Companies and
Ingredient Scientists; new venture and
market analysts; advanced
manufacturers of processed food; R&D
Managers, planners, marketers of food
products; food and packaging engineers
and chemists.

70296
### FOOD INVESTMENT REPORT
Two Corporate Dr.
Trumbull, CT 06611
Telephone: (203) 261-8587
FAX: (203) 261-9724
Mailing Address:
P.O. Box 374
Trumbull, CT 06611
Year Established: 1993
Pub. Frequency: 15/yr.
Subscrip. Rate: $79/yr.
**Owner(s):**
Food & Nutrition Press, Inc.
Two Corporate Dr.
Trumbull, CT 06611
Telephone: (203) 261-8587
FAX: (203) 261-9724
Ownership %: 100
**Editorial:**
Gerald C. Melson .........................Editor
**Desc.:** Provides market analysis as well as
the fundamentals and technical
approach (charting). Deals with the food
and related industries and all of the
ramifications for the investor.

70300
### FOOD MARKETING BRIEFS
P.O. Box 2730
Bethesda, MD 20827
Telephone: (301) 469-8507
FAX: (301) 469-7271
Year Established: 1987
Pub. Frequency: m.
Subscrip. Rate: $89/yr.
**Owner(s):**
Newsletters, Inc.
P.O. Box 2730
Bethesda, MD 20827
Telephone: (301) 469-8507
FAX: (301) 469-7271
Ownership %: 100
**Editorial:**
Ray Marsili ..............................Editor

**Desc.:** Marketing report for food
companies and retailers.

70302
### FOOD, NUTRITION & HEALTH NEWSLETTER
Two Corporate Dr.
Trumbull, CT 06611
Telephone: (203) 261-8587
FAX: (203) 261-9724
Year Established: 1977
Pub. Frequency: m.
Subscrip. Rate: $74/yr.
Materials: 10
**Owner(s):**
Food & Nutrition Press, Inc.
Two Corporate Dr.
Trumbull, CT 06611
Telephone: (203) 261-8587
FAX: (203) 261-9724
Ownership %: 100
**Editorial:**
Paul A. Lachance .........................Editor
Michele C. Fisher .........................Editor
**Desc.:** Covers food, nutrition and health
research, education, and policy issues.

70277
### FOOD PACKAGING & LABELING NEWSLETTER
Two Corporate Dr.
Trumbull, CT 06611
Telephone: (203) 261-8587
FAX: (203) 261-9724
Mailing Address:
P.O. Box 374
Trumbull, CT 06611
Year Established: 1977
Pub. Frequency: m.
Subscrip. Rate: $74/yr.
Materials: 10
**Owner(s):**
Food & Nutrition Press, Inc.
Two Corporate Dr.
Trumbull, CT 06611
Telephone: (203) 261-8587
FAX: (203) 261-9724
Ownership %: 100
**Editorial:**
Stanley Sacharow .........................Editor
**Desc.:** Informs readers of the latest trends,
emerging markets and legislation in food
packaging and labeling.

71219
### FOOD PLANT STRATEGIES
122 S. Church St.
West Chester, PA 19382-3223
Telephone: (215) 436-4220
FAX: (215) 436-6277
Year Established: 1993
Pub. Frequency: m.
Subscrip. Rate: $295/yr. US; $345/yr.
foreign
**Owner(s):**
Packaging Strategies, Inc.
122 S. Church St.
West Chester, PA 19382-3223
Telephone: (215) 436-4220
FAX: (215) 436-6277
Ownership %: 100
**Management:**
William H. LeMaire .....................Publisher
**Editorial:**
Mike Pehanich ...........................Editor
**Desc.:** Covers innovations and trends in
the design and construction of new food
factories, factory expansions and
renovations. Also examines location
strategies and new manufacturing
technologies.

70305
### FOODTALK
P.O. Box 42-6543
San Fransisco, CA 94142
Telephone: (415) 386-3067

Materials Accepted/Included: 01-Business news 02-By-line articles 03-Fashion news 04-Food news 05-Freelance copy 06-Letters to editor 07-Real estate news 08-Sports news 09-Travel news 10-Book rev. 11-Movie rev. 12-Music rev. 13-TV rev. 14-Theater rev. 15-Coming events 16-Obituaries 17-Question & answer 18-Social announcements 19-Artwork 20-Cartoons 21-Photos 22-TV listings 23-Audio rec. 24-Video rec. 25-Books 26-Films/film clips 27-Personnel news 28-Press releases 29-New product news/photos 30-Trade lit. 31-Contracts awarded 32-Display adv. 33-Classified adv.

Year Established: 1978
Pub. Frequency: q.
Subscrip. Rate: $18/yr.
Materials: 10
Circulation: 10,000
Circulation Type: controlled & paid
**Owner(s):**
Foodtalk
Telephone: (415) 386-3067
Ownership %: 100
**Editorial:**
Elaine Douglas Cahn .................................Editor
**Desc.:** Focuses on the cultural uses of food in ritual, history, folklore and ceremony.

## KANE'S BEVERAGE WEEK
64902

313 South Ave.
Fanwood, NJ 07023-0340
Telephone: (908) 889-6336
FAX: (908) 889-6339
Mailing Address:
 P.O. Box 340
 Fanwood, NJ 07023
Year Established: 1938
Pub. Frequency: w.
Page Size: standard
Subscrip. Rate: $347/yr.
Materials: 01,02,16,23,24,25,27,28,29,30
**Owner(s):**
Whitaker Newsletters, Inc.
313 South Ave.
Fanwood, NJ 07023
Telephone: (908) 889-6336
FAX: (908) 889-6339
Ownership %: 100
**Management:**
Joel Whitaker .........................................President
Sandra Smith ....................Circulation Manager
**Editorial:**
Joel Whitaker ................................Senior Editor
**Desc.:** Contains news pertaining to the beverage industry, with particular emphasis on beer, wine, and spirits. Includes new products, federal and state regulations, market trends and advertising research.
**Readers:** Senior executives of suppliers and wholesalers.

## KITCHEN TIMES
70500

185 Marlborough
Boston, MA 02116
Telephone: (617) 437-9983
Year Established: 1975
Pub. Frequency: m.
Subscrip. Rate: $66/yr.
Materials: 10
Circulation: 350
Circulation Type: controlled & paid
**Owner(s):**
Howard Wilson & Co., Inc.
185 Marlborough
Boston, MA 02116
Telephone: (617) 437-9983
Ownership %: 100
**Editorial:**
Howard Wilson .......................................Editor
**Desc.:** Information on restaurants, cooks, packaged goods, and wines. Emphasis is on "simple" recipes, not haute cuisine.

## LEISURE BEVERAGE INSIDER NEWSLETTER
65284

313 South Ave.
Fanwood, NJ 07023
Telephone: (908) 889-6336
FAX: (908) 889-6339
Mailing Address:
 P.O. Box 340
 Fanwood, NJ 07023
Year Established: 1968
Pub. Frequency: bi-w.

Page Size: standard
Subscrip. Rate: $269/yr.; $310/yr. foreign
Materials: 01,04,06,15,27,28,29,30,31
Print Process: photocopy
Circulation: 409
Circulation Type: paid
**Owner(s):**
Whitaker Newsletters, Inc.
313 South Ave.
P.O. Box 340
Fanwood, NJ 07023
Telephone: (908) 889-6336
FAX: (908) 889-6339
Ownership %: 100
**Management:**
Joel Whitaker .......................................Publisher
Sandra Smith ....................Circulation Manager
**Editorial:**
Patrick Curren ........................................Editor
**Desc.:** Covers the news of the beverage industry with particular emphasis on soft drinks, mixers, and bottled water. Includes new products, federal and state regulations, marketing trends and advertising research.
**Readers:** Soft drink bottlers, distributors, manufacturers, marketers, and allied industries.
**Deadline:** story-Wed. prior to pub. date; news-Wed. prior to pub. date

## LOSS PREVENTION NEWSLETTER FOR SUPERMARKET EXECUTIVES
70322

800 Connecticut Ave., N.W.
Washington, DC 20006
Telephone: (202) 452-8444
Pub. Frequency: m.
Subscrip. Rate: $50/yr. non-members; $25/yr. members
**Owner(s):**
Food Marketing Institute
800 Connecticut Ave., N.W.
Washington, DC 20006
Telephone: (202) 452-8444
Ownership %: 100

## MICROWAVES & FOOD NEWSLETTER
70280

Two Corporate Dr.
Trumbull, CT 06611
Telephone: (203) 261-8587
FAX: (203) 261-9724
Mailing Address:
 P.O. Box 374
 Trumbull, CT 06611
Year Established: 1991
Pub. Frequency: m.
Subscrip. Rate: $55/yr.
**Owner(s):**
Food & Nutrition Press, Inc.
Two Corporate Dr.
Trumbull, CT 06611
Telephone: (203) 261-8587
FAX: (203) 261-9274
Ownership %: 100
**Editorial:**
Dr. Robert V. Decareau ...........................Editor
**Desc.:** Discusses new food products, production, packaging, quality assurance, microbiology, shelf-life, and microwave equipment.

## NATIONAL PACKING NEWS
69032

P.O. Box 1349
Murphys, CA 95247
Telephone: (209) 728-1455
FAX: (209) 728-3277
Year Established: 1937
Pub. Frequency: m.
Page Size: standard
Subscrip. Rate: $25/yr.
Materials: 01,04,27,28,29,30,31,32,33
Print Process: offset

Circulation: 2,100
Circulation Type: controlled & paid
**Owner(s):**
National Packing News
P.O. Box 1349
Murphys, CA 95247
Telephone: (209) 728-1455
FAX: (209) 728-3277
Ownership %: 100
**Editorial:**
Jack W. Soward ......................................Editor
**Desc.:** Contains news about the food processing industry, including new products, plants, R&D, marketing, staff and line management personnel.

## ORGANIC FOOD BUSINESS NEWS
70283

P.O. Box 208
Williston, ND 58802-0208
Telephone: (701) 774-8757
FAX: (701) 774-0419
Year Established: 1989
Pub. Frequency: m.
Subscrip. Rate: $72/yr.
Materials: 10, 32
Circulation: 450
Circulation Type: controlled & paid
**Owner(s):**
Hotline Printing & Publishing
P.O. Box 208
Williston, ND 58802-0208
Telephone: (701) 774-8757
FAX: (701) 774-0419
Ownership %: 100
**Editorial:**
Dennis Blank ..........................................Editor

## SIMPLE COOKING
70284

P.O. Box 88
Steuben, ME 04680-0088
Year Established: 1980
Pub. Frequency: q.
Subscrip. Rate: $16/yr.
Materials: 10
Circulation: 2,000
Circulation Type: controlled & paid
**Owner(s):**
Simple Cooking
P.O. Box 88
Steuben, ME 04680-0088
Ownership %: 100
**Desc.:** Contains news and essays about gastronomy.

## SPROUTLETTER
70750

P.O. Box 62
Ashland, OR 97520
Telephone: (503) 488-2326
Year Established: 1980
Pub. Frequency: q.
Subscrip. Rate: $12/yr.
Circulation: 3,000
Circulation Type: controlled & paid
**Owner(s):**
Sprouting Publications
P.O. Box 62
Ashland, OR 97520
Telephone: (503) 488-2326
Ownership %: 100
**Editorial:**
Michael Linden ......................................Editor
**Desc.:** Explores nutrition, holistic health, vegetarianism, sprouting, live foods, blue-green algae, acidophillus, enzymes, indoor food gardening; includes recipes and product listings.

## SUPERMARKET STRATEGIC ALERT
70320

140 E. 81st St.
Ste. 5E
New York, NY 10028
Telephone: (212) 734-0753
FAX: (212) 988-9394
Year Established: 1990
Pub. Frequency: m.
Subscrip. Rate: $795/yr.
Circulation: 100
Circulation Type: controlled & paid
**Owner(s):**
Pollack Associates
140 E. 81st St.
Ste. 5E
New York, NY 10028
Telephone: (212) 734-0753
FAX: (212) 988-9394
Ownership %: 100
**Editorial:**
Mary Pollack .........................................Editor
**Desc.:** Provides an overview of the supermarket industry from articles in 70 daily to monthly general business and trade publications.

## TEA TALK
70287

419 N. Larchmont
Los Angeles, CA 90004-3000
Telephone: (310) 659-9650
Mailing Address:
 P.O. Box 225
 Los Angeles, CA 90004-3000
Year Established: 1989
Pub. Frequency: q.
Subscrip. Rate: $17.95/yr.
Materials: 10
Circulation: 2,000
Circulation Type: controlled & paid
**Owner(s):**
R&R Publications
419 Larchmont St.
Los Angeles, CA 90004-3000
Telephone: (310) 659-9650
Ownership %: 100
**Editorial:**
Diana Rosen ..........................................Editor
**Desc.:** For tea fanciers, teapot collectors, and hosts of afternoon teas. Profiles restaurants, tearooms and hotels, new products, and tea industry personnel.

## UPPERCRUST
68854

361 Virginia St.
Crystal Lake, IL 60014
Telephone: (815) 459-1000
Year Established: 1987
Pub. Frequency: bi-m.
Page Size: tabloid
Subscrip. Rate: $12/yr.
Materials: 04,10,28
Print Process: offset
Circulation: 5,700
Circulation Type: controlled & paid
**Owner(s):**
Upper Crust Publications
361 Virginia St.
Crystal Lake, IL 60014
Telephone: (815) 459-1000
Ownership %: 100
**Editorial:**
Sharon Myers .......................................Editor
**Desc.:** Appeals to both novice and experienced chef alike with recipes featuring fresh ingredients rather than artificial or prepared mixes.
**Readers:** Restaurant chefs, homemakers, food services, food professionals, others with culinary interests.

**Materials Accepted/Included:** 01-Business news 02-By-line articles 03-Fashion news 04-Food news 05-Freelance copy 06-Letters to editor 07-Real estate news 08-Sports news 09-Travel news 10-Book rev. 11-Movie rev. 12-Music rev. 13-TV rev. 14-Theater rev. 15-Coming events 16-Obituaries 17-Question & answer 18-Social announcements 19-Artwork 20-Cartoons 21-Photos 22-TV listings 23-Audio rec. 24-Video rec. 25-Books 26-Films/film clips 27-Personnel news 28-Press releases 29-New product news/photos 30-Trade lit. 31-Contracts awarded 32-Display adv. 33-Classified adv.

7-51

**1932 BUICK REGISTRY** [71209]
3000 Warren Rd.
Indiana, PA 15701
Telephone: (412) 463-3372
Year Established: 1974
Pub. Frequency: s-a.
Subscrip. Rate: free
**Owner(s):**
1932 Buick Registry
3000 Warren Rd.
Indiana, PA 15701
Telephone: (412) 463-3372
Ownership %: 100
**Desc.:** For owners of 1925-1935 Buicks.
Provides lists of parts for sale, literature,
and restoration tips.

## Group 332-Gay & Lesbian

**ADVENT** [71016]
566 Vallejo St., Ste. 25
San Francisco, CA 94133
Telephone: (415) 956-2069
Year Established: 1979
Pub. Frequency: q.
Subscrip. Rate: $30/yr.
Materials: 33
Circulation: 800
Circulation Type: paid
**Owner(s):**
Advent
566 Vallejo St., Ste. 25
San Francisco, CA 94133
Telephone: (415) 956-2069
Ownership %: 100
**Editorial:**
James Lokken ............................................Editor
**Desc.:** Promotes gay and lesbian
understanding in Lutheran churches.

**BWMT-ATLANTA NEWSLETTER** [70963]
P.O. Box 1334
Atlanta, GA 30301-1334
Telephone: (404) 892-2968
Year Established: 1981
Pub. Frequency: m.
Subscrip. Rate: $18/yr.
Materials: 10
Circulation: 200
Circulation Type: controlled & paid
**Owner(s):**
Black & White Men Together-Atlanta
P.O. Box 1334
Atlanta, GA 30301-1334
Telephone: (404) 892-2968
Ownership %: 100
**Editorial:**
John Nicholson ..........................................Editor
**Desc.:** Contains articles, announcements,
calendar of events, and discussion
topics.

**GAY AIRLINE CLUB NEWSLETTER** [71026]
P.O. Box 69A04
Dept. UL
Hollywood, CA 90069
Telephone: (213) 650-5112
Year Established: 1993
Pub. Frequency: q.
Subscrip. Rate: $20/yr.
Materials: 10,33
Circulation: 10,000
Circulation Type: paid
**Owner(s):**
Fan Club Publishing
P.O. Box 69A04
W. Hollywood, CA 90069
Telephone: (213) 650-5112
Ownership %: 100
**Editorial:**
Louis Wendruck ........................................Editor

**Desc.:** Provides a forum for gay airline or
travel industry workers who travel or
collect airline memorabilia.

**GLB AMES NEWSLETTER** [71022]
P.O. Box 176
Ames, IA 50010-1761
Telephone: (515) 382-3223
Year Established: 1980
Pub. Frequency: m.
Subscrip. Rate: $7/yr.
Materials: 10,33
Circulation: 125
Circulation Type: paid
**Owner(s):**
G L A, Inc.
P.O. Box 1761
Ames, IA 50010-1761
Telephone: (515) 382-3223
Ownership %: 100
**Editorial:**
Allan Beatty ..............................................Editor

**LIP NEWSLETTER** [70983]
P.O. Box 761
Utica, NY 13503
Year Established: 1982
Pub. Frequency: q.
Subscrip. Rate: $10/yr.
Materials: 10
Circulation: 200
Circulation Type: controlled & paid
**Owner(s):**
Women's Collective
P.O. Box 761
Utica, NY 13503
Ownership %: 100

**LOVING BROTHERHOOD** [70989]
**NEWSLETTER**
P.O. Box 556
Sussex, NJ 07461
Telephone: (201) 875-4710
Year Established: 1977
Pub. Frequency: m.
Subscrip. Rate: $15/yr.
Materials: 10, 32
Circulation: 500
Circulation Type: controlled & paid
**Owner(s):**
Lightning Press
P.O. Box 556
Sussex, NJ 07461
Telephone: (201) 875-4710
Ownership %: 100
**Editorial:**
Robertbruce Walker ...................................Editor
**Desc.:** Directed to gay men; keeps
members posted on the growing process
and expanding impact of love worldwide.
Includes information about members,
letters from readers, news of workshops,
and editorials.

**RICHMOND LESBIAN FEMINIST** [70993]
**FLYER**
P.O. Box 7216
Richmond, VA 23221-0216
Telephone: (804) 379-6422
Year Established: 1973
Pub. Frequency: m.
Subscrip. Rate: $10/yr.
Materials: 10, 32
Circulation: 700
Circulation Type: controlled & paid

**Owner(s):**
Richmond Lesbian Feminists
P.O. Box 7216
Richmond, VA 23221-0216
Telephone: (804) 379-6422
Ownership %: 100

## Group 334-General Interest

**BARGAIN HUNTERS &** [70498]
**BUDGETEERS OPPORTUNITY**
**NEWSLETTER**
c/o Prosperity & Profits Unlimited
P.O. Box 416
Denver, CO 80201-0416
Telephone: (303) 575-5676
Year Established: 1990
Pub. Frequency: bi-a.
Subscrip. Rate: $5/yr.
Circulation: 2000
Circulation Type: controlled & paid
**Owner(s):**
Continnuus
P.O. Box 416
Denver, CO 80201-0416
Telephone: (303) 575-5676
Ownership %: 100
**Editorial:**
A.C. Doyle ................................................Editor
**Desc.:** Tips on saving money.

**CLOTHING FOR LESS** [70949]
**NEWSLETTER**
c/o Prosperity & Profits Unlimited
P.O. Box 416
Denver, CO 80201-0416
Telephone: (303) 575-5676
Year Established: 1990
Pub. Frequency: bi-a.
Subscrip. Rate: $5/yr.
Circulation: 3,999
Circulation Type: controlled & paid
**Owner(s):**
Continnuus
c/o Prosperity & Profits Unlimited
P.O. Box 416
Denver, CO 80201-0416
Telephone: (303) 575-5676
Ownership %: 100
**Editorial:**
A.C. Doyle ................................................Editor
**Desc.:** Contains ideas on getting clothing
for less.

**CONSUMER FORUM** [70968]
436 W. Wisconsin Ave.
Milwaukee, WI 53203-2105
Year Established: 1980
Pub. Frequency: s-m.
Subscrip. Rate: $15/yr.
Circulation: 3,999
Circulation Type: controlled & paid
**Owner(s):**
Concerned Consumers League
436 W. Wisconsin Ave.
Milwaukee, WI 53203-2105
Ownership %: 100
**Editorial:**
Cheryl Gurlik ............................................Editor
**Desc.:** Contaiians consumer news and
self-help information.

**COUPON TREASURE HUNT** [70954]
**NEWSLETTER**
c/o Prosperity & Profits Unlimited
P.O. Box 416
Denver, CO 80201-0416
Telephone: (303) 575-5676
Year Established: 1990
Pub. Frequency: bi-a.
Subscrip. Rate: $3/yr.
Circulation: 1,500
Circulation Type: controlled & paid

**Owner(s):**
Continnuus
c/o Prosperity & Profits
P.O. Box 416
Denver, CO 80201-0416
Telephone: (303) 575-5676
Ownership %: 100
**Editorial:**
A.C. Doyle ................................................Editor
**Desc.:** Information on finding and
redeeming coupons.

**FREE TIME** [70951]
20 Waterside Plz., Ste. 6F
New York, NY 10010
Telephone: (212) 545-8900
FAX: (212) 213-3469
Year Established: 1987
Pub. Frequency: m.
Subscrip. Rate: $11.90/yr. individuals;
$36/yr. institutions
**Owner(s):**
Concerned Consumers League
436 W. Wisconsin Ave.
Milwaukee, WI 53203-2105
Ownership %: 100
**Editorial:**
Natella Vaidman .......................................Editor
**Desc.:** Calendar of free and low budget
cultural events in Manhattan.

**GOLD COAST NEWS** [70956]
P.O. Box 2115
Miami Beach, FL 33140-0115
Telephone: (305) 674-9746
FAX: (305) 674-1939
Year Established: 1983
Pub. Frequency: m.
Subscrip. Rate: $20/yr.
Materials: 10
Circulation: 100,000
Circulation Type: controlled & paid
**Owner(s):**
Charles Hesser & Co.
P.O. Box 2115
Miami Beach, FL 33140-0115
Telephone: (305) 674-9746
FAX: (305) 674-1939
Ownership %: 100
**Editorial:**
Charles Hesser .........................................Editor
**Desc.:** Covers events in Southeast Florida.

**GREEN LINE** [70957]
P.O. Box 144
Asheville, NC 28802
Telephone: (704) 251-1333
FAX: (704) 251-1311
Year Established: 1987
Pub. Frequency: m.
Subscrip. Rate: free
Materials: 10,32
Circulation: 23,000
Circulation Type: controlled & paid
**Owner(s):**
Green Lined Media, Inc.
P.O. Box 144
Asheville, NC 28802
Telephone: (704) 251-1333
FAX: (704) 251-1311
Ownership %: 100
**Editorial:**
Peter Gregutt ...........................................Editor
**Desc.:** Covers trends and events in
western North Carolina. Focuses on
environmental issues, citizen action, arts,
outdoors and media.

**HAWAIIAN EXPRESS MAGAZINE** [70953]
10 Kamehameha Hwy.
Wahiawa, HI 96876
Telephone: (808) 622-2679
FAX: (808) 621-3329
Year Established: 1989

---

**Materials Accepted/Included:** 01-Business news 02-By-line articles 03-Fashion news 04-Food news 05-Freelance copy 06-Letters to editor 07-Real estate news 08-Sports news 09-Travel news 10-Book rev. 11-Movie rev. 12-Music rev. 13-TV rev. 14-Theater rev. 15-Coming events 16-Obituaries 17-Question & answer 18-Social announcements 19-Artwork 20-Cartoons 21-Photos 22-TV listings 23-Audio rec. 24-Video rec. 25-Books 26-Films/film clips 27-Personnel news 28-Press releases 29-New product news/photos 30-Trade lit. 31-Contracts awarded 32-Display adv. 33-Classified adv.

Pub. Frequency: bi-m.
Subscrip. Rate: free
Materials: 10,32
Circulation: 10,000
Circulation Type: controlled & paid
**Owner(s):**
Al Plant
10 Kamehameha Hwy.
Wahiawa, HI 96876
Telephone: (808) 622-2679
FAX: (808) 621-3329
Ownership %: 100
**Editorial:**
Al Plant ..................................Editor
**Desc.:** Community-focused articles on business, arts, and sports.

70612
## HUMOR DEFENSE
7953 Stonehurst Ct.
Pleasanton, CA 94588
Telephone: (510) 462-5710
FAX: (510) 786-1826
Mailing Address:
   P.O. Box 10944
   Pleasanton, CA 94588
Year Established: 1981
Pub. Frequency: q.
Subscrip. Rate: free
Materials: 10
Circulation: 600
Circulation Type: free
**Owner(s):**
Humor Defense Publishing
P.O. Box 10944
Pleasanton, CA 94588
Telephone: (510) 462-5710
Ownership %: 100
**Editorial:**
Virginia Tooper ..........................Editor
**Desc.:** Explores the positive and negative uses of humor with a light apporach.

70771
## INTERNATIONAL EMPLOYMENT HOTLINE
P.O. Box 3030
Oakton, VA 22124
Telephone: (703) 620-1972
Year Established: 1980
Pub. Frequency: m.
Subscrip. Rate: $36/yr.
Materials: 33
Circulation: 5,000
Circulation Type: controlled & paid
**Owner(s):**
Cantrell Corporation
P.O Box 3030
Oakton, VA 22124
Telephone: (703) 620-1972
Ownership %: 100
**Editorial:**
Will Cantrell ..........................Editor
**Desc.:** Reports on developments in the international job market, covering a wide range of overseas job openings for US citizens.

71108
## INTUITIVE EXPLORATIONS
P.O. Box 561
Quincy, IL 62306-0561
Telephone: (217) 222-9082
Year Established: 1987
Pub. Frequency: m.
Subscrip. Rate: $15/yr.
Materials: 10
Circulation: 1,000
Circulation Type: controlled & paid
**Owner(s):**
Intuitive Explorations
P.O. Box 561
Quincy, IL 62306-0561
Telephone: (217) 222-9082
Ownership %: 100
**Editorial:**
Gloria Reiser ..........................Editor

**Desc.:** Covers all areas of metaphysics, magic, mysticism, manifesting human potential. Acts as a free-flow exchange among those individuals who take metaphysics seriously.

70751
## JOB SEEKER
P.O. Box 16
Rt. 2
Warrens, WI 54666
Telephone: (608) 378-4290
Year Established: 1988
Pub. Frequency: fortn.
Subscrip. Rate: $60/yr.; $84/yr. instn.
**Owner(s):**
Job Seeker
P.O. Box 16
Rt. 2
Warrens, WI 54666
Telephone: (608) 378-4290
Ownership %: 100

70757
## JOBS IN RECESSIONARY TIMES POSSIBILITY NEWSLETTER
P.O. Box 416
Denver, CO 80201-0416
Telephone: (303) 575-5676
Year Established: 1990
Pub. Frequency: a.
Subscrip. Rate: $7/yr.
Circulation: 1500
Circulation Type: controlled & paid
**Owner(s):**
Continnuus
P.O. Box 416
Denver, CO 80201-0416
Telephone: (303) 575-5676
Ownership %: 100
**Editorial:**
A. C. Doyle ..........................Editor

70774
## ORGANIZE YOUR LUCK!
901 E. Groove St.
Carrage House, Ste. A4
Bloomington, IL 61701
Telephone: (309) 829-3931
FAX: (309) 829-9677
Year Established: 1976
Pub. Frequency: 10/yr.
Subscrip. Rate: $75/yr.
Materials: 10,33
Circulation: 3000
Circulation Type: controlled & paid
**Owner(s):**
Behavioral Images, Inc.
901 E. Groove St.
Carrage House, Ste. A4
Bloomington, IL 61701
Telephone: (309) 829-3931
FAX: (309) 829-9677
Ownership %: 100
**Editorial:**
Stephen C. Johnson ..........................Editor
**Desc.:** Assists people in finding, getting, and keeping their jobs through self-marketing methods.

71212
## PERSONAL DISCOVERY REPORT
P.O. Box 10883
Portland, OR 97210-0882
Telephone: (503) 223-9117
Year Established: 1990
Pub. Frequency: m.
Subscrip. Rate: $49/yr.
**Owner(s):**
Personal Advantage
P.O. Box 10883
Portland, OR 97210-0882
Telephone: (503) 223-9117
Ownership %: 100
**Editorial:**
Maggie Conolly-Jensen ..........................Editor

**Desc.:** Promotes positive ideas and approaches for better living and personal health.

71093
## SINGLE SOURCE NEWSLETTER
P.O. Box 416
Denver, CO 80201-0416
Telephone: (303) 575-5676
Year Established: 1987
Pub. Frequency: a.
Subscrip. Rate: $5/yr.
Circulation: 1,500
Circulation Type: controlled & paid
**Owner(s):**
Bibliotheca Press
P.O. Box 416
Denver, CO 80201-0416
Telephone: (303) 575-5676
Ownership %: 100

71122
## SUBCONSCIOUSLY SPEAKING
4110 Edgeland
Dept. 800
Royal Oak, MI 48073
Telephone: (313) 549-5594
Year Established: 1985
Pub. Frequency: bi-m.
Subscrip. Rate: $12/yr. in US; $15/yr. CN; $18/yr. foreign
Materials: 32,10
Circulation: 3500
Circulation Type: controlled & paid
**Owner(s):**
Harriman Publishing Co.
4110 Edgeland
Dept. 800
Royal Oak, MI 48073
Telephone: (313) 549-5594
Ownership %: 100
**Editorial:**
Anne H. Spencer ..........................Editor
**Desc.:** To elevate the consciousness of all who read through current information regarding hynosis, imagery, and healing of body, mind and spirit.

71171
## TO US
5405 Alton Pkwy.
Ste. A344
Irvine, CA 92714
Telephone: (714) 733-9150
Year Established: 1991
Pub. Frequency: bi-m.
Subscrip. Rate: $12/yr.
Materials: 10
Circulation: 2000
Circulation Type: controlled & paid
**Owner(s):**
Innovisions Unlimited
5405 Alton Pkwy.
Ste. A344
Irvine, CA 92714
Telephone: (714) 733-9150
Ownership %: 100
**Editorial:**
Faith A. Boyle ..........................Editor
**Desc.:** An upbeat, comprehensive resource that couples can use to educate themselves about the realitites and rewards of lifelong committment. Features ideas, insights, humor and proven techniques from relationship experts and other couples.

70950
## WEEKLY NEWS UPDATE ON NICARAGUA & THE AMERICAS
339 Lafayette St.
New York, NY 10012
Telephone: (212) 674-9499
Pub. Frequency: w.
Subscrip. Rate: $25/yr.

**Owner(s):**
Nicaragua Solidarity Network
339 Lafayette St.
New York, NY 10012
Telephone: (212) 674-9499
Ownership %: 100
**Desc.:** Up-to-date news from a variety of sources covering Central and South America and the Caribbean.

70758
## WORKAMPER NEWS
201 Hiram Rd.
Heber Springs, AR 72543
Telephone: (501) 362-2637
FAX: (501) 362-2637
Year Established: 1987
Pub. Frequency: bi-m.
Subscrip. Rate: $23/yr.
Materials: 10,32
Circulation: 6000
Circulation Type: controlled & paid
**Owner(s):**
Workamper News
201 Hiram Rd.
Heber Springs, AR 72543
Telephone: (501) 366-2267
Ownership %: 100
**Editorial:**
Greg Robus ..........................Editor
**Desc.:** Provides information on seasonal and year-round employment opportunities in parks and resort areas.

## Group 336-Hobbies & Clubs

70505
## ALPCA NEWSLETTER
P.O. Box 77
Horner, WV 26372
Mailing Address:
   P.O. Box 77
   Gary Brent Kincade
   Horner, WV 26372
Year Established: 1954
Pub. Frequency: bi-m.
Subscrip. Rate: $22/yr. US; $25/yr. foreign
Materials: 32
Circulation: 2,320
Circulation Type: controlled & paid
**Owner(s):**
Automobile License Plate Collectors Association
P.O. Box 77
Horner, WV 26372
Ownership %: 100
**Editorial:**
Paul M. Maginnity ..........................Editor

70492
## ANTIQUE COMB COLLECTOR
3748 Sunray Dr.
Holiday, FL 34691-3239
Telephone: (813) 942-7354
Year Established: 1986
Pub. Frequency: bi-m.
Subscrip. Rate: $25/yr. includes membership; $27/yr. foreign
Materials: 33
Circulation: 100
Circulation Type: controlled & paid
**Owner(s):**
Belva Green
3748 Sunray Dr.
Holiday, FL 34691-3239
Telephone: (813) 942-7354
Ownership %: 100
**Editorial:**
Belva Green ..........................Editor
**Desc.:** Research on the current cost, history, dating, manufacturing, materials, design and styles and care of head jewelry.

## BALLROOM REVIEW
70249

60 Gramercy Park N.
New York, NY 10010
Telephone: (212) 673-3442
FAX: (212) 673-3442
Year Established: 1991
Pub. Frequency: every 5-6 wks.
Subscrip. Rate: $25/yr.
Materials: 10,11,14
Circulation: 3,000
Circulation Type: controlled & paid
**Owner(s):**
TBR Communications, Ltd.
60 Gramercy Park N.
New York, NY 10010
Telephone: (212) 673-3442
FAX: (212) 673-3442
Ownership %: 100
**Editorial:**
Nicholas M. Ullo .................................Editor
**Desc.:** Features selective listings of
ballroom dance events and news items.
Carries feature articles on the history of
dance and dance music (ballroom and
modern) and on people who have
contributed to the field of dance.

## BILL NELSON NEWSLETTER
70487

P.O. Box 41630
Tucson, AZ 85717-1630
Telephone: (602) 629-0868
FAX: (602) 629-0387
Year Established: 1985
Pub. Frequency: m.
Subscrip. Rate: $20/yr.; $30/yr. foreign
Circulation: 87,000
Circulation Type: controlled & paid
**Owner(s):**
Nelson Newsletter Publishing Corp.
P.O. Box 41630
Tuscon, AZ 85717-1630
Telephone: (602) 629-0868
FAX: (602) 629-0387
Ownership %: 100
**Editorial:**
Bill Nelson ....................................Editor
**Desc.:** Features news, ads, and tips for pin
collectors.

## CAT COLLECTORS
70509

33161 Wendy Dr.
Sterling Hts., MI 48310
Telephone: (313) 264-0285
Year Established: 1982
Pub. Frequency: bi-m.
Subscrip. Rate: $18/yr. US; $22/yr. CN;
$25/yr. elsewhere
Materials: 10,32
Circulation: 1,000
Circulation Type: controlled & paid
**Owner(s):**
Cat Collectors
33161 Wendy Dr.
Sterling Hts., MI 48310
Ownership %: 100
**Editorial:**
Marilyn Dipboye ...........................Editor
**Desc.:** News, articles, and illustrations on
antique and new cat collectibles, artists
and craftspersons. Includes book
reviews, museum holdings, and
catalog shopping advice.

## CERTIFIED COIN DEALER NEWSLETTER
70513

P.O. Box 11099
Torrance, CA 90510-1099
Telephone: (310) 515-7369
FAX: (310) 515-7534
Year Established: 1986
Pub. Frequency: w.
Subscrip. Rate: $99/yr.

**Owner(s):**
Coin Dealer Newsletter
P.O. Box 11099
Torrance, CA 90510-1099
Telephone: (310) 515-7369
FAX: (310) 515-7534
Ownership %: 100
**Editorial:**
Dennis r. Baker ............................Editor

## CHRYSLER 300 CLUB NEWS
70490

4900 Jonesville Rd.
Jonesville, MI 49250
Telephone: (517) 849-2783
Year Established: 1970
Pub. Frequency: q.
Subscrip. Rate: $20/yr.
Materials: 32
Circulation: 900
Circulation Type: controlled & paid
**Owner(s):**
Chrysler 300 Club International, Inc.
4900 Jonesville Rd.
Jonesville, MI 49250
Telephone: (517) 849-2783
Ownership %: 100
**Editorial:**
Eleanor Riehl ..............................Editor
**Desc.:** Provides technical statistics on
automobiles represented by the Club,
restoration information, and member
stories.

## CRAFTS NEWS
71125

1001 Connecticut Ave.
Ste. 1138
Washington, DC 20036
Telephone: (202) 728-9603
FAX: (202) 457-0549
Year Established: 1986
Pub. Frequency: q.
Subscrip. Rate: $25/yr.
Materials: 33
Circulation: 5,000
Circulation Type: controlled & paid
**Owner(s):**
Crafts Center
1001 Connecticut Ave.
Ste. 1138
Washington, DC 20036
Telephone: (202) 728-9603
FAX: (202) 457-0549
Ownership %: 100
**Editorial:**
Sheila Mooney ...........................Editor
**Desc.:** International crafts effort, artisan
profiles, sources of technical assistance,
equipment, materials.

## CREATIVE OUTLETS
71130

P.O. Box 5024
Durango, CO 81301
Year Established: 1984
Pub. Frequency: q.
Subscrip. Rate: $5/copy
**Owner(s):**
Country Press
P.O. Box 5024
Durango, CO 81301
Ownership %: 100
**Editorial:**
J.L. Walker ................................Editor
**Desc.:** Dedicated to home based business
with an emphasis on the arts and crafts
industry. Features listings of shops and
shows buying or consigning handicrafts.

## CURRENCY DEALER NEWSLETTER
70516

P.O. Box 11099
Torrence, CA 90510-1099
Telephone: (310) 515-7369
FAX: (310) 515-7534

Year Established: 1979
Pub. Frequency: m.
Subscrip. Rate: $44/yr.
**Owner(s):**
Coin Dealer Newsletter
P.O. Box 11099
Torrence, CA 90510-1099
Telephone: (310) 515-7369
FAX: (310) 515-7534
Ownership %: 100
**Editorial:**
Dennis R. Baker ..........................Editor
**Desc.:** Wholesale price guide to old U.S.
paper money.

## ELVIS NOW FAN CLUB
70129

P.O. Box 6581
San Jose, CA 95150
Telephone: (408) 923-0978
Year Established: 1973
Pub. Frequency: q.
Subscrip. Rate: $11/yr. US; $15/yr. foreign
Materials: 10,32
Circulation: 356
Circulation Type: paid
**Owner(s):**
Sue McCasland
P.O. Box 6581
San Jose, CA 95150
Telephone: (408) 923-0978
Ownership %: 100
**Editorial:**
Sue McCasland ..........................Editor

## FARM ANTIQUES NEWS
71232

812 N. Third St.
Tarkio, MO 64491
Telephone: (816) 736-4528
Year Established: 1991
Pub. Frequency: bi-m.
Subscrip. Rate: $14/yr.
Materials: 10,32
Circulation: 2,500
Circulation Type: paid
**Owner(s):**
Farm Antiques News
812 N. Third St.
Tarkio, MO 64491
Telephone: (816) 736-4528
Ownership %: 100
**Editorial:**
Gary VanHoozer ..........................Editor
**Desc.:** Covers anything old from the farm:
collecting and pricing.

## FRIENDSHIP EXPRESS
70495

P.O. Box 167492
Irving, TX 75062
Year Established: 1988
Pub. Frequency: bi-m.
Subscrip. Rate: $15/yr.
Materials: 32
Circulation: 5,000
Circulation Type: controlled & paid
**Owner(s):**
Penpals at Large
P.O. Box 167492
Irving, TX 75062
Ownership %: 100
**Editorial:**
Karie Rochelle Koutz ....................Editor
**Desc.:** Contains hundreds of listings of US
and international pen pals. Promotes
peace through world friendship.

## GUARDIAN ENGEL
70131

3024 Fourth Ave.
Carney
Baltimore, MD 21234
Telephone: (410) 665-0744
Year Established: 1971
Pub. Frequency: m.
Subscrip. Rate: $10/yr.
Circulation: 95

Circulation Type: paid
**Owner(s):**
Engel's Angels in Humperdinck Heaven
Fan Club
3024 Fourth Ave.
Baltimore, MD 21234
Telephone: (410) 665-0744
Ownership %: 100
**Editorial:**
Jean R. Marshalek ......................Editor
**Desc.:** Established for the fans of
Englebert Humperdink regarding his
concerts, records, and club activities.

## HEISEY NEWS
70503

169 W. Church St.
Newark, OH 43055
Telephone: (614) 345-2932
FAX: (614) 345-9638
Year Established: 1972
Pub. Frequency: m.
Subscrip. Rate: $18.50/yr. membership
Materials: 33
Circulation: 2,650
Circulation Type: controlled & paid
**Owner(s):**
Heisely Collectors of America
169 W. Church St.
Newark, OH 43055
Telephone: (614) 345-2932
FAX: (614) 345-9638
Ownership %: 100
**Editorial:**
Karen D. Kneisley .......................Editor
**Desc.:** Promotes education and study of
Heisey glassware, made in Newark,
Ohio from 1896 to 1957.

## JACKPOTUNITIES
70493

P.O. Box 393
Centuck Station
Yonkers, NY 10710
Telephone: (914) 723-6427
Year Established: 1978
Pub. Frequency: bi-m.
Page Size: tabloid
Subscrip. Rate: $8.99/yr.
Materials: 32
Circulation: 100,000
Circulation Type: controlled & paid
**Owner(s):**
Jackpotunities, Inc.
P.O. Box 393
Centuck Station
Yonkers, NY 10710
Telephone: (914) 723-6427
Ownership %: 100
**Editorial:**
Shirley Liss ...............................Editor
**Desc.:** Sweepstakes guide.

## KOVELS ON ANTIQUES & COLLECTIBLES
70506

30799 Pinetree Rd.
Pepper Pike, OH 44124
Telephone: (800) 829-9158
Year Established: 1974
Pub. Frequency: m.
Subscrip. Rate: $36/yr.
**Owner(s):**
Antiques, Inc.
30799 Pinetree Rd., Ste.127
Pepper Pike, OH 44127
Telephone: (800) 829-9158
Ownership %: 100
**Editorial:**
Ralph Kovel ..............................Editor
Terry Kovel ..............................Editor
**Desc.:** The newsletter for dealers,
collectors and investors.

**Materials Accepted/Included:** 01-Business news 02-By-line articles 03-Fashion news 04-Food news 05-Freelance copy 06-Letters to editor 07-Real estate news 08-Sports news 09-Travel news 10-Book rev. 11-Movie rev. 12-Music rev. 13-TV rev. 14-Theater rev. 15-Coming events 16-Obituaries 17-Question & answer 18-Social announcements 19-Artwork 20-Cartoons 21-Photos 22-TV listings 23-Audio rec. 24-Video rec. 25-Books 26-Films/film clips 27-Personnel news 28-Press releases 29-New product news/photos 30-Trade lit. 31-Contracts awarded 32-Display adv. 33-Classified adv.

**LACE COLLECTOR** 70508
P.O. Box 222
Plainwell, MI 49080
Telephone: (616) 685-9792
Year Established: 1991
Pub. Frequency: q.
Subscrip. Rate: $20/yr.
Materials: 33
**Owner(s):**
Lace Merchant
P.O. Box 222
Plainwell, MI 49080
Telephone: (616) 685-9792
Ownership %: 100
**Management:**
Elizabeth M. Kurella ............................Publisher
**Editorial:**
Elizabeth M. Kurella ...............................Editor
**Desc.:** Features a photographic and
textual exploration of a particular type of
lace, comparisons that distinguish it from
other lace work, reference works helpful
to the study of lace, a guide to
museums with collections of antique
laces, market information including
pieces for sale, and prices realized at
auction.

**MARBLE MART NEWSLETTER** 70494
P.O. Box 206
Northboro, MA 01532
Telephone: (508) 393-2923
Pub. Frequency: q.
Subscrip. Rate: $10/yr.
Materials: 32
Circulation: 800
Circulation Type: controlled & paid
**Owner(s):**
Marble Collectors Unlimited
P.O. Box 206
Northboro, MA 01532
Telephone: (508) 393-2923
Ownership %: 100
**Editorial:**
Beverly Brule ........................................Editor

**MINERAL NEWS** 70496
P.O. Box 2043
Coeur d'Alene, ID 83816-2043
Telephone: (208) 667-0453
Year Established: 1985
Pub. Frequency: m.
Subscrip. Rate: $15/yr. US; $19/yr. foreign
Materials: 10,32
Circulation: 900
Circulation Type: controlled & paid
**Owner(s):**
L.R. Ream Publishing
P.O. Box 2043
Coeur d'Alene, ID 83816-2043
Telephone: (208) 667-0453
Ownership %: 100
**Editorial:**
Lanny R. Ream .....................................Editor
**Desc.:** Details localities, new minerals,
mineral shows and symposiums.

**MONKEES, BOYCE & HART**
**PHOTO FAN CLUB** 70133
P.O. Box 411
Watertown, SD 57201-0411
Telephone: (603) 886-3017
Year Established: 1969
Pub. Frequency: bi-m.
Subscrip. Rate: $8.50/yr. US; $11/yr.
foreign
Materials: 10,32
Circulation: 15,000
Circulation Type: paid

**Owner(s):**
Jodi Hammrich
P.O. Box 411
Watertown, SD 57201-0411
Telephone: (603) 886-3017
**Editorial:**
Jodi Hammrich ......................................Editor
Shari S. Cain .......................................Editor

**MYSTIC LIGHT OF THE ALADDIN**
**KNIGHTS** 70486
R.1
Simpson, IL 62985

Year Established: 1973
Pub. Frequency: bi-m.
Subscrip. Rate: $20/yr.
Circulation: 1,400
Circulation Type: controlled & paid
**Owner(s):**
J.W. Courter
R.1
Simpson, IL 62985
Telephone: (618) 949-3884
Ownership %: 100
**Management:**
J.W. Courter .......................................Publisher
**Editorial:**
J.W. Courter ........................................Editor
**Desc.:** Covers antique oil and electric
lighting.

**POSTCARD EXAMINER** 70525
P.O. Box 4177
Carson City, NV 89702
Telephone: (702) 882-5312
Year Established: 1984
Pub. Frequency: 5/yr.
Subscrip. Rate: $5.50/yr.; $7.50/yr. foreign
**Owner(s):**
Postcard Examiner
P.O. Box 4177
Carson City, NV 89702
Telephone: (702) 882-5312
Ownership %: 100
**Editorial:**
Ann Rusnak .........................................Editor
**Desc.:** Discusses new and unusual findings
in the field of modern postcard
collecting and illustrates new postcard
designs.

**REBA MCENTIRE INTERNATIONAL**
**FAN CLUB NEWSLETTER** 70135
P.O. Box 121996
Nashville, TN 37212-1996
Telephone: (615) 259-4009
Year Established: 1979
Pub. Frequency: bi-m.
Subscrip. Rate: $12/yr.
Circulation: 34
Circulation Type: paid
**Owner(s):**
Reba McEntire International Fan Club
P.O. Box 121996
Nashville, TN 37212-1996
Telephone: (615) 259-4009
Ownership %: 100
**Editorial:**
Cindy Owen ........................................Editor

**SMURF COLLECTORS CLUB**
**INTERNATIONAL NEWSLETTER** 70502
24U Cabot Rd. W.
Massapequa, NY 11758
Telephone: (516) 799-3221
Year Established: 1986
Pub. Frequency: q.
Subscrip. Rate: $15/yr.
Materials: 10,32
Circulation: 800
Circulation Type: controlled & paid

**Owner(s):**
Smurf Collectors Club
24U Cabot Rd. W.
552 Massapequa, NY 11758
Ownership %: 100
**Editorial:**
Suzanne Lipschitz ................................Editor

**TOBACCO ANTIQUES AND**
**COLLECTIBLES MARKET** 71187
P.O. Box 11652
Houston, TX 77293
Year Established: 1994
Pub. Frequency: bi-m.
Subscrip. Rate: $6.95/yr. US; $19.95/yr.
Canada & Mexico; $30/yr. elsewhere
**Owner(s):**
Tobacco Antiques and Collectibles Market
P.O. Box 11653
Houston, TX 77293
Ownership %: 100
**Management:**
Chuck Thompson ...............................Publisher
**Editorial:**
Chuck Thompson .................................Editor

**WATERCRAFT PHILATELY** 70528
P.O. Box 23092
Washington, DC 20026
Telephone: (703) 671-6484
Year Established: 1954
Pub. Frequency: bi-m.
Subscrip. Rate: $6.50/yr.
Materials: 33
Circulation: 350
Circulation Type: controlled & paid
**Owner(s):**
Robert L. Tessier
P.O. Box 23092
Washington, DC 20026
Telephone: (703) 671-6484
Ownership %: 100
**Editorial:**
Robert L. Tessier .................................Editor

## Group 338-Law Enforcement
## & Military

**ARREST LAW BULLETIN** 70211
23 Drydock Ave., Second Fl.
Boston, MA 02210-2387
Telephone: (800) 229-2084
FAX: (617) 345-9646
Year Established: 1976
Pub. Frequency: m.
Subscrip. Rate: $60/yr.
**Owner(s):**
Quinlan Publishing Co., Inc.
23 Drydock Ave., Second Fl.
Boston, MA 02210-2387
Telephone: (800) 229-2084
FAX: (617) 345-9646
Ownership %: 100
**Editorial:**
E. Michael Quinlan ...............................Editor
**Desc.:** Summaries of current cases
discussing arrest procedures.

**CAMPUS CRIME** 71106
951 Pershing Dr.
Silver Spring, MD 20910-4464
Telephone: (301) 587-6300
FAX: (301) 585-9075
Year Established: 1991
Pub. Frequency: m.
Subscrip. Rate: $231.48/yr.
**Owner(s):**
Business Publishers, Inc.
951 Pershing Dr.
Silver Spring, MD 20910-4464
Telephone: (301) 587-6300
FAX: (301) 585-9075
Ownership %: 100

**Editorial:**
Anthony R. Cooke ................................Editor
**Desc.:** Advice for university security
officers and university officals on
reducing incidents of crime on campus.
Tracks federal crime reporting
legislation.

**CAMPUS SECURITY REPORT** 71109
402 Main St.
Port Washington, NY 11050
Telephone: (516) 883-1440
FAX: (516) 883-1683
Pub. Frequency: m.
Subscrip. Rate: $199/yr.; $224/yr. foreign
**Owner(s):**
Rusting Publications
P.O. Box 190
Port Washington, NY 11050
Telephone: (516) 883-1440
FAX: (516) 883-1683
Ownership %: 100
**Editorial:**
Robert R. Rusting ................................Editor

**CJN DRUG LETTER** 70243
443 Park Ave., S.
New York, NY 10016
Telephone: (212) 685-5450
FAX: (212) 679-4701
Year Established: 1992
Pub. Frequency: m.
Subscrip. Rate: $149/yr.
**Owner(s):**
Pace Publications
443 Park Ave., S.
New York, NY 10016
Telephone: (212) 685-5450
FAX: (212) 679-4701
Ownership %: 100
**Desc.:** Reports on legislative, legal,
administrative and technical
developments affecting drug testing
and treatment in the criminal justice
system.

**COMMISH** 71028
23 Drydock Ave.
2nd Fl.
Boston, MA 02210-2387
Telephone: (800) 229-2084
FAX: (617) 345-9646
Pub. Frequency: m.
Subscrip. Rate: $68/yr.
**Owner(s):**
Quinlan Publishing Co.
23 Drydock Ave.
2nd Fl.
Boston, MA 02210-2387
Telephone: (800) 229-2084
Ownership %: 100
**Editorial:**
Leo D. Stapelton .................................Editor
**Desc.:** For fire chiefs, firefighters, and
other members of the firefighting
community.

**COMMUNITY CRIME PREVENTION**
**DIGEST** 70213
3918 Prosperity Ave., Ste. 318
Fairfax, VA 22031-3334
Telephone: (703) 573-1600
FAX: (703) 573-1604
Year Established: 1973
Pub. Frequency: m.
Subscrip. Rate: $75/yr.
**Owner(s):**
Washington Crime News Services
3918 Prosperity Ave., Ste. 318
Fairfax, VA 22031-3334
Telephone: (703) 573-1600
FAX: (703) 573-1604
Ownership %: 100

**Materials Accepted/Included:** 01-Business news 02-By-line articles 03-Fashion news 04-Food news 05-Freelance copy 06-Letters to editor 07-Real estate news 08-Sports news 09-Travel news 10-Book rev. 11-Movie rev. 12-Music rev. 13-TV rev. 14-Theater rev. 15-Coming events 16-Obituaries 17-Question & answer 18-Social announcements 19-Artwork 20-Cartoons 21-Photos 22-TV listings 23-Audio rec. 24-Video rec. 25-Books 26-Films/film clips 27-Personnel news 28-Press releases 29-New product news/photos 30-Trade lit. 31-Contracts awarded 32-Display adv. 33-Classified adv.

7-55

**Editorial:**
Susan Kernus .........................Editor
**Desc.:** Focuses on federal and state budgets, and programs for the community crime prevention professional.

71112

**CORPORATE CRIME REPORTER**
P.O. Box 18384
Washington, DC 20036
Telephone: (202) 429-6928
Year Established: 1987
Pub. Frequency: 48/yr.
Subscrip. Rate: $795/yr.
**Owner(s):**
American Communications & Publishing Co.
P.O. Box 18384
Washington, DC 20036
Telephone: (202) 429-6928
Ownership %: 100
**Editorial:**
Russell Mokhibert .........................Editor

70217

**CORRECTIONS COMPENDIUM**
3900 Industrial Ave., N., Second Fl.
Lincoln, NE 68501-1826
Telephone: (402) 464-0602
FAX: (402) 464-5931
Mailing Address:
   P.O. Box 81826
   Lincoln, NE 68501-1826
Year Established: 1976
Pub. Frequency: m.
Subscrip. Rate: $48/yr.
Circulation: 2,000
Circulation Type: controlled & paid
**Owner(s):**
CEGA Publishing Services
3900 Industrial Ave., N., Seco
Lincoln, NE 68501-1826
Telephone: (402) 464-0602
FAX: (402) 464-5931
Ownership %: 100
**Editorial:**
Su Perk Davis .........................Editor
**Readers:** The national journal for corrections professionals.

70219

**CORRECTIONS DIGEST**
3918 Prosperity Ave., Ste. 318
Fairfax, VA 22031-3334
Telephone: (703) 573-1600
Year Established: 1969
Pub. Frequency: bi-w.
Subscrip. Rate: $249.50/yr.
Materials: 10
**Owner(s):**
Washington Crime News Services
3918 Prosperity Ave., Ste. 318
Fairfax, VA 22031-3334
Telephone: (703) 573-1600
Ownership %: 100
**Editorial:**
Betty B. Bosarge .........................Editor
**Readers:** A complete information exchange for the rehabilitation and correction professional.

70221

**CRIME CONTROL DIGEST**
3918 Prosperity Ave., Ste. 318
Fairfax, VA 22031-3334
Telephone: (703) 573-1600
Year Established: 1967
Pub. Frequency: w.
Subscrip. Rate: $295/yr.
Materials: 10
**Owner(s):**
Washington Crime News Services
3918 Prosperity Ave., Ste. 318
Fairfax, VA 22031-3334
Telephone: (703) 573-1600
Ownership %: 100

**Editorial:**
Betty B. Bosarge .........................Editor

70224

**CRIME VICTIMS DIGEST**
3918 Prosperity Ave., Ste. 318
Fairfax, VA 22031-3334
Telephone: (703) 573-1600
Year Established: 1983
Pub. Frequency: m.
Subscrip. Rate: $75/yr.
**Owner(s):**
Washington Crime News Services
3918 Prosperity Ave., Ste. 318
Fairfax, VA 22031-3334
Telephone: (703) 573-1600
Ownership %: 100
**Editorial:**
Susan Kernus .........................Editor

70227

**CRIMINAL JUSTICE DIGEST**
3918 Prosperity Ave., Ste. 318
Fairfax, VA 22031-3334
Telephone: (703) 573-1600
Year Established: 1982
Pub. Frequency: m.
Subscrip. Rate: $140/yr.
Materials: 10
**Owner(s):**
Washington Crime News Services
3918 Prosperity Ave., Ste. 318
Fairfax, VA 22031-3334
Telephone: (703) 573-1600
Ownership %: 100
**Editorial:**
Betty B. Bosarge .........................Editor

70230

**CRIMINAL JUSTICE NEWSLETTER**
443 Park Ave., S.
New York, NY 10016
Telephone: (212) 685-5450
FAX: (212) 679-4701
Year Established: 1970
Pub. Frequency: s-m.
Subscrip. Rate: $198/yr.
Materials: 10
**Owner(s):**
Pace Publications
443 Park Ave., S.
New York, NY 10016
Telephone: (212) 685-5450
FAX: (212) 679-4701
Ownership %: 100
**Editorial:**
Craig Fischer .........................Editor
**Desc.:** Systemwide perspective on the criminal justice system, covering law enforcement, courts, and corrections.

71234

**C4I NEWS**
1201 Seven Locks Rd.
Potomac, MD 20854
Telephone: (301) 424-3338
FAX: (301) 309-3847
Year Established: 1993
Pub. Frequency: bi-w.
Subscrip. Rate: $495/yr. US; $530/yr. foreign
**Owner(s):**
Phillips Business Information, Inc.
1201 Seven Locks Rd.
Potomac, MD 20854
Telephone: (301) 424-3338
FAX: (301) 309-3847
Ownership %: 100

70696

**DEFENSE & AEROSPACE ELECTRONICS**
1616 N. Ft. Myer Dr.
Ste. 1000
Arlington, VA 22209-3107
Telephone: (703) 528-1244
FAX: (703) 528-1253
Year Established: 1985

Pub. Frequency: w.
Subscrip. Rate: $497/yr. US; $527/yr. foreign
**Owner(s):**
Pasha Publications Inc.
1616 N. Ft. Myer Dr.
Ste. 1000
Arlington, VA 22209-3107
Telephone: (703) 528-1244
Ownership %: 100
**Editorial:**
Len Famiglietti .........................Editor
**Desc.:** Business opportunities and technological innovations of interest to government contractors,

70704

**DEFENSE & ECONOMY WORLD REPORT**
P.O. Box 5997
Washington, DC 20016
Telephone: (202) 244-7050
FAX: (202) 244-5410
Year Established: 1972
Pub. Frequency: s-m.
Subscrip. Rate: $350/yr.
Materials: 10
**Owner(s):**
Government Business Worldwide Reports
P.O. Box 5997
Washington, DC 20016
Telephone: (202) 244-7050
Ownership %: 100
**Editorial:**
J.H. Wagner .........................Editor
**Desc.:** Presents information on international and military-economic affairs, with emphasis on defense plans and requirements, force changes, procurement, arms transfer, defense budget, and industry.

71200

**DEFENSE CONVERSION**
1616 N. Fort Meyer Dr.
Ste. 1000
Arlington, VA 22209-3107
Telephone: (703) 528-1244
FAX: (703) 528-1253
Year Established: 1992
Pub. Frequency: bi-w.
Subscrip. Rate: $387/yr. US; $418/yr. foreign
**Owner(s):**
Pasha Publications Inc.
1616 N. Fort Myer Dr.
Ste. 1000
Arlington, VA 22209-3107
Telephone: (703) 528-1244
FAX: (703) 528-1253
Ownership %: 100
**Editorial:**
Pat Cooper .........................Editor
**Desc.:** Covers developments relating to defense conversion in industry, at the local, state and federal levels, including Department of Energy, Department of Defense, and Department of Commerce activities, as well as news of relevant international matters.

70708

**DI MONITOR**
1616 N. Ft. Myer Dr.
Ste. 1000
Arlington, VA 22209-3107
Telephone: (703) 528-1244
FAX: (703) 528-1253
Year Established: 1986
Pub. Frequency: fortn.
Subscrip. Rate: $747/yr. US; $762/ yr. foreign

**Owner(s):**
Pasha Publications, Inc.
1616 N. Ft. Myer Dr.
Ste. 1000
Arlington, VA 22209-3107
Telephone: (703) 528-1244
FAX: (703) 528-1253
Ownership %: 100
**Editorial:**
Jeff W. Schomisch .........................Editor
**Desc.:** Follows technical, political, and policy aspects of the SDI program.

70244

**DRUG DETECTION REPORT**
443 Park Ave., S.
New York, NY 10016
Telephone: (212) 685-5450
FAX: (212) 679-4701
Year Established: 1991
Pub. Frequency: 24/yr.
Subscrip. Rate: $295/yr.
**Owner(s):**
Pace Publications
443 Park Ave., S.
New York, NY 10016
Telephone: (212) 685-5450
FAX: (212) 679-4701
Ownership %: 100
**Editorial:**
Dave McIntyre .........................Editor

70232

**DRUG ENFORCEMENT REPORT**
443 Park Ave., S.
New York, NY 10016
Telephone: (212) 685-5450
FAX: (212) 679-4701
Year Established: 1984
Pub. Frequency: s-m.
Subscrip. Rate: $197/yr.
**Owner(s):**
Pace Publications
443 Park Ave., S.
New York, NY 10016
Telephone: (212) 685-5450
FAX: (212) 679-4701
Ownership %: 100
**Editorial:**
Molly R. Parrish .........................Editor
**Desc.:** Reports on federal developments in drug enforcement policy.

71115

**HOSPITAL SECURITY & SAFETY MANAGEMENT**
402 Main St.
Port Washington, NY 11050
Telephone: (516) 883-1440
FAX: (516) 883-1683
Mailing Address:
   P.O. Box 190
   Port Washington, NY 11050
Year Established: 1980
Pub. Frequency: m.
Subscrip. Rate: $169/yr.; $194/yr. foreign
Circulation: 1,200
Circulation Type: controlled & paid
**Owner(s):**
Rusting Publications
402 Main St.
P.O. Box 190
Port Washington, NY 11050
Telephone: (516) 883-1440
FAX: (516) 883-1683
Ownership %: 100
**Editorial:**
Robert R. Rusting .........................Editor

70672

**INSIDE DEFENSE ELECTRONICS**
P.O. Box 7167
Benjamin Franklin Sta.
Washington, DC 20044
Telephone: (703) 892-8500
FAX: (703) 685-2606

**Materials Accepted/Included:** 01-Business news 02-By-line articles 03-Fashion news 04-Food news 05-Freelance copy 06-Letters to editor 07-Real estate news 08-Sports news 09-Travel news 10-Book rev. 11-Movie rev. 12-Music rev. 13-TV rev. 14-Theater rev. 15-Coming events 16-Obituaries 17-Question & answer 18-Social announcements 19-Artwork 20-Cartoons 21-Photos 22-TV listings 23-Audio rec. 24-Video rec. 25-Books 26-Films/film clips 27-Personnel news 28-Press releases 29-New product news/photos 30-Trade lit. 31-Contracts awarded 32-Display adv. 33-Classified adv.

Pub. Frequency: w.
Subscrip. Rate: $565/yr. US; $615/yr.
foreign
**Owner(s):**
Inside Washington Publishers
P.O. Box 7167
Benjamin Franklin Sta.
Washington, DC 20044
Telephone: (703) 892-8500
FAX: (703) 685-2606
Ownership %: 100

## INSIDE THE AIR FORCE
70692

P.O. Box 7167
Benjamin Franklin Sta.
Washington, DC 20044
Telephone: (703) 892-8500
FAX: (703) 685-2606
Pub. Frequency: w.
Subscrip. Rate: $495/yr. US; $545/yr.
foreign
**Owner(s):**
Inside Washington Publishers
P.O. Box 7167
Benjamin Franklin Sta.
Washington, DC 20044
Telephone: (703) 892-8500
FAX: (703) 685-2606
Ownership %: 100

## INSIDE THE ARMY
70699

P.O. Box 7167
Benjamin Franklin Sta.
Washington, DC 20044
Telephone: (703) 829-8500
FAX: (703) 685-2606
Pub. Frequency: w.
Subscrip. Rate: $495/yr. US; $545/yr.
foreign
**Owner(s):**
Inside Washington Publishers
P.O. Box 7167
Benjamin Franklin Sta.
Washington, DC 20044
Telephone: (703) 829-8500
FAX: (703) 685-2606
Ownership %: 100

## INSIDE THE NAVY
70701

P.O. Box 7167
Benjamin Franklin Sta.
Washington, DC 20044
Telephone: (703) 892-8500
FAX: (703) 685-2606
Pub. Frequency: w.
Subscrip. Rate: $510/yr. US; $560/yr.
foreign
**Owner(s):**
Inside Washington Publishers
P.O. Box 7167
Benjamin Franklin Sta.
Washington, DC 20044
Telephone: (703) 892-8500
FAX: (703) 685-2606
Ownership %: 100

## INSIDE THE PENTAGON
70703

P.O. Box 7167
Benjamin Franklin Sta.
Washington, DC 20044
Telephone: (703) 892-8500
FAX: (703) 685-2606
Pub. Frequency: w.
Subscrip. Rate: $695/yr. US; $745/yr.
foreign
**Owner(s):**
Inside Washington Publishers
P.O. Box 7167
Benjamin Franklin Sta.
Washington, DC 20044
Telephone: (703) 892-8500
FAX: (703) 685-2606
Ownership %: 100

## JUVENILE JUSTICE DIGEST
70245

3918 Prosperity Ave., Ste. 318
Fairfax, VA 22031-3334
Telephone: (703) 573-1600
Year Established: 1973
Pub. Frequency: s-m.
Subscrip. Rate: $175/yr.
Materials: 10
**Owner(s):**
Washington Crime News Letter
3918 Prosperity Ave., Ste. 318
Fairfax, VA 22031-3334
Telephone: (703) 573-1600
Ownership %: 100
**Editorial:**
Susan M. Kernus ........................Editor
**Desc.:** Focuses on delinquency issues.

## LAW ENFORCEMENT LEGAL REPORTER
69660

P.O. Box 1356
Torrance, CA 90505
Telephone: (213) 379-3214
FAX: (310) 379-3835
Year Established: 1977
Pub. Frequency: m.
Page Size: 8 1/2*11
Subscrip. Rate: $29.50/yr.
Print Process: offset
Circulation: 2,750
Circulation Type: paid
**Owner(s):**
Law Enforcement Legal Reporter
P.O. Box 1356
Torrance, CA 90505
Telephone: (213) 379-3214
FAX: (310) 379-3835
Ownership %: 100
**Editorial:**
Elliot Alhadeff ..........................Editor

## LAW ENFORCEMENT PERSONNEL NOTES
71174

P.O. Box 662
Latham, NY 12110
Telephone: (800) 281-8582
FAX: (518) 456-8582
Pub. Frequency: m.
Subscrip. Rate: $60/yr.
**Owner(s):**
Nyper Publications
P.O. Box 662
Latham, NY 12110
Telephone: (800) 281-8582
FAX: (518) 456-8582
Ownership %: 100
**Editorial:**
Harvey Randall ..........................Editor
**Desc.:** Discusses legal developments
concerning police and corrections
personnel.

## MILITARY ROBOTICS NEWSLETTER
71175

119 Rock Creek Church Rd., N.W.
Washington, DC 20011-6005
Telephone: (202) 723-5031
FAX: (202) 726-2979
Year Established: 1987
Pub. Frequency: s-m.
Subscrip. Rate: $325/yr. US; $350/yr.
foreign
Circulation: 250
Circulation Type: paid
**Owner(s):**
L & B Limited
119 Rock Creek Church Rd., N.W
Washington, DC 20011-6005
Telephone: (202) 723-5031
FAX: (202) 726-2979
Ownership %: 100
**Editorial:**
Joseph A. Lovece ......................Editor

**Desc.:** Covers military and government use
of robotics.

## NARCOTICS CONTROL DIGEST
70234

3918 Prosperity Ave., Ste. 318
Fairfax, VA 22031-3334
Telephone: (703) 573-1600
Year Established: 1971
Pub. Frequency: bi-w.
Subscrip. Rate: $249.50/yr.
Materials: 10
**Owner(s):**
Washington Crime News Services
3918 Prosperity Ave., Ste. 318
Fairfax, VA 22031-3337
Telephone: (703) 573-1600
Ownership %: 100
**Editorial:**
Betty B. Bosarge ......................Editor

## NARCOTICS DEMAND REDUCTION DIGEST
70237

3918 Prosperity Ave., Ste. 318
Fairfax, VA 22031
Telephone: (703) 573-1600
FAX: (703) 573-1604
Year Established: 1989
Pub. Frequency: m.
Subscrip. Rate: $150/yr.
Materials: 10,32
Circulation: 1,000
Circulation Type: controlled & paid
**Owner(s):**
Washington Crime News Services
3918 Prosperity Ave., Ste. 318
Fairfax, VA 22031
Telephone: (703) 573-1600
FAX: (703) 573-1604
Ownership %: 100
**Editorial:**
Robert H. Feldkamp ..................Editor
**Desc.:** Provides education about
substance abuse.

## NARCOTICS LAW BULLETIN
70246

23 Drydock Ave.
Boston, MA 02210-2387
Telephone: (617) 542-0048
FAX: (617) 345-9646
Year Established: 1974
Pub. Frequency: m.
Subscrip. Rate: $59/yr.
**Owner(s):**
Quinlan Publishing Co., Inc.
23 Drydock Ave.
Boston, MA 02210-2387
Telephone: (617) 542-0048
FAX: (617) 345-9646
Ownership %: 100
**Editorial:**
Ed. M. Quinlan ..........................Editor

## NATIONAL BULLETIN ON POLICE MISCONDUCT
70247

23 Drydock Ave.
Boston, MA 02210-2387
Telephone: (800) 229-2084
FAX: (617) 345-9646
Pub. Frequency: m.
Subscrip. Rate: $60/yr.
**Owner(s):**
Quinlan Publishing Co., Inc.
23 Drydock Ave.
Boston, MA 02210-2387
Telephone: (800) 229-2084
FAX: (617) 345-9646
Ownership %: 100
**Desc.:** Covers legal aspects of police
misconduct and challenges to law
enforcement personnel on such issues
as wrongful death, civil rights, immunity,
confessions, false arrest, brutality, use
of force, and entrapment.

## ORGANIZED CRIME DIGEST
70238

3918 Prosperity Ave., Ste. 318
Fairfax, VA 22031-3334
Telephone: (703) 573-1600
Year Established: 1980
Pub. Frequency: bi-m.
Subscrip. Rate: $249.50/yr.
**Owner(s):**
Washington Crime News Services
3918 Prosperity Ave., Ste. 318
Fairfax, VA 22031-3334
Telephone: (703) 573-1600
Ownership %: 100
**Editorial:**
Betty B. Bosarge ......................Editor

## PARKING SECURITY REPORT
71104

402 Main St.
Port Washington, NY 11050
Telephone: (516) 883-1440
FAX: (516) 883-1683
Mailing Address:
P.O. Box 190
Port Washington, NY 11050
Pub. Frequency: m.
Subscrip. Rate: $169/yr.; $194 foreign
**Owner(s):**
Rusting Publications
402 Main St.
P.O. Box 190
Port Washington, NY
Telephone: (516) 883-1440
FAX: (516) 883-1683
Ownership %: 100
**Editorial:**
Robert R. Rusting ......................Editor

## SCHOOL SECURITY REPORT
71119

402 Main St.
Port Washington, NY 11050
Telephone: (516) 883-1440
FAX: (516) 883-1683
Mailing Address:
P.O. Box 190
Port Washington, NY 11050
Pub. Frequency: m.
Subscrip. Rate: $169/yr.
**Owner(s):**
Rusting Publications
402 Main St.
P.O. Box 490
Port Washington, NY 11050
Telephone: (516) 883-1440
FAX: (516) 883-1683
Ownership %: 100
**Editorial:**
Robert R. Rusting ......................Editor

## SEARCH & SEIZURE BULLETIN
70248

23 Drydock Ave.
Boston, MA 22031-2387
Telephone: (617) 542-0048
FAX: (617) 345-9646
Year Established: 1964
Pub. Frequency: m.
Subscrip. Rate: $62/yr.
**Owner(s):**
Quinlan Publishing Co., Inc.
23 Drydock Ave.
Boston, MA 22031-2387
Telephone: (617) 542-0048
FAX: (617) 345-9646
Ownership %: 100
**Editorial:**
Ed M. Quinlan ..........................Editor
**Desc.:** Summarizes current cases involving
search and seizure. For non-lawyer law
enforcement personnel.

**Materials Accepted/Included:** 01-Business news 02-By-line articles 03-Fashion news 04-Food news 05-Freelance copy 06-Letters to editor 07-Real estate news 08-Sports news 09-Travel news 10-Book rev. 11-Movie rev. 12-Music rev. 13-TV rev. 14-Theater rev. 15-Coming events 16-Obituaries 17-Question & answer 18-Social announcements 19-Artwork 20-Cartoons 21-Photos 22-TV listings 23-Audio rec. 24-Video rec. 25-Books 26-Films/film clips 27-Personnel news 28-Press releases 29-New product news/photos 30-Trade lit. 31-Contracts awarded 32-Display adv. 33-Classified adv.

7-57

## SECURITY TECHNOLOGY NEWS
71238

1201 Seven Locks Rd.
Potomac, MD 20854
Telephone: (301) 424-3338
FAX: (301) 309-3847
Year Established: 1993
Pub. Frequency: bi-w.
Subscrip. Rate: $495/yr. US; $530/yr.
   foreign
**Owner(s):**
Phillips Business Information, Inc.
1201 Seven Locks Rd.
Potomac, MD 20854
Telephone: (301) 424-3338
FAX: (301) 309-3847
Ownership %: 100

## SURVEILLANT
71036

Lockbox Mail Unit 18757
Washington, DC 20036-8757
Telephone: (202) 785-4334
FAX: (202) 331-7456
Year Established: 1990
Pub. Frequency: bi-m.
Subscrip. Rate: $58/yr. US; $65/yr. CN;
   $75/yr. foreign
Materials: 10,32
Circulation: 8,000
Circulation Type: controlled & paid
**Owner(s):**
Surveillant - NIBC Press
Lockbox Mail Unit 18757
Washington, DC 20036
Telephone: (202) 785-4334
FAX: (202) 331-7456
Ownership %: 100
**Desc.:** Covers the newest non-fiction
   espionage and intelligence publications
   worldwide, on a wide variety of current
   and historical topics in all media,
   for librarians, academics, politicians,
   researchers, government and corporate
   security professionals, and diplomats.

## TRAINING AIDS DIGEST
70241

3918 Prosperity Ave., Ste. 318
Fairfax, VA 22031-3334
Telephone: (703) 573-1600
Year Established: 1976
Pub. Frequency: m.
Subscrip. Rate: $150/yr.
**Owner(s):**
Washington Crime News Services
3918 Prosperity Ave., Ste. 318
Fairfax, VA 22031-3334
Telephone: (703) 573-1600
Ownership %: 100
**Editorial:**
Betty B. Bosarge ............................Editor

## Group 340-Legal

## ARIZONA ENVIRONMENTAL LAW LETTER
70552

162 Fourth Ave. N.
Nashville, TN 37219-8867
Telephone: (615) 242-7395
FAX: (615) 256-6601
Year Established: 1990
Pub. Frequency: m.
Subscrip. Rate: $137/yr.
**Owner(s):**
Lee/Smith Publishers & Printers
162 Fourth Ave. N.
Nashville, TN 37219-8867
Telephone: (615) 242-7395
Ownership %: 100
**Editorial:**
Steve Owens ............................Editor
**Desc.:** Reports the latest Arizona
   environmental law developments that
   affect Arizona companies.

## ARKANSAS LEGISLATIVE REPORT
71120

P.O. Box 1304
Little Rock, AR 72203
Telephone: (501) 663-5081
FAX: (501) 375-3163
Year Established: 1983
Pub. Frequency: d.
Subscrip. Rate: $525/yr.
**Owner(s):**
Legislative Reports, Inc.
P.O. Box 1304
Little Rock, AR 72203
Telephone: (501) 663-5081
FAX: (501) 375-3163
Ownership %: 100
**Editorial:**
Ken Parker ............................Editor

## ASBESTOS MONITOR
71036... 70559

P.O. Box 19976
Houston, TX 77224
Telephone: (713) 531-7229
FAX: (713) 531-7229
Year Established: 1989
Pub. Frequency: m.
Subscrip. Rate: $247/yr.
**Owner(s):**
Monitor Communications
P.O. Box 19976
Houston, TX 77224-9965
Telephone: (713) 531-7229
Ownership %: 100
**Editorial:**
Susan Hale Abbot ............................Editor

## ASBESTOS PRODUCT LIABILITY LITIGATION M D L REPORTER
70539

P.O. Box 315
Springfield, PA 19064
Telephone: (215) 328-4388
FAX: (215) 328-0566
Year Established: 1991
Pub. Frequency: s-m.
Subscrip. Rate: $650/yr.
**Owner(s):**
McGuire Publications
P.O. Box 315
Springfield, PA 19064
Telephone: (215) 328-4388
FAX: (215) 328-0566
Ownership %: 100
**Editorial:**
Authur McGuire ............................Editor

## ATTORNEYS MARKETING REPORT
70565

3520 Cadillac Ave.
Ste. E
Costa Mesa, CA 92626
Telephone: (714) 755-5450
FAX: (714) 549-8835
Year Established: 1981
Pub. Frequency: m.
Subscrip. Rate: $197 US; $227 CN; $252
   elsewhere
Circulation: 400
Circulation Type: controlled & paid
**Owner(s):**
James Publishing Group
3520 Cadillac Ave.
Ste. E
Costa Mesa, CA 92626
Telephone: (714) 755-5450
Ownership %: 100
**Editorial:**
Linda M. Standke ............................Editor
**Desc.:** To help law firm marketers design,
   implement and evaluate effective
   programs to attract new clients, enhance
   the firm's image, improve client
   relations, and build a sound practice.

## BANKING ATTORNEY
70576

One State St. Plaza
New York, NY 10004-1549
Telephone: (800) 733-4371
FAX: (212) 943-2224
Pub. Frequency: w.
Subscrip. Rate: $465/yr. US; $495/yr.
   foreign
Materials: 32
**Owner(s):**
Thomson Financial Services Compan;y
One State St. Plaza
New York, NY 10004-1549
Telephone: (800) 733-4371
Ownership %: 100
**Editorial:**
Dave Postal ............................Editor
**Desc.:** Provides analyses of legal issues,
   legal ruling, and litigation affecting all
   depository institutions. Reports on recent
   court decisions in bank-related cases,
   comments on the impact of those
   decisions, and provides a summary of
   upcoming court cases that will influence
   banking.

## BANKRUPTCY COUNSELLOR
70544

P.O. Box 19070
Alexandria, VA 22320
Telephone: (703) 684-9156
FAX: (703) 739-0489
Year Established: 1988
Pub. Frequency: 24/yr.
Subscrip. Rate: $345/yr.
**Owner(s):**
Counsellor Publications, Inc.
P.O. Box 19070
Alexandria, VA 22320
Telephone: (703) 684-9156
FAX: (703) 739-0489
Ownership %: 100
**Editorial:**
Gregory Lee ............................Editor

## BREAST IMPLANT LITIGATION REPORTER
70583

1646 West Chester Pike
Westtown, PA 19395
Telephone: (215) 399-6600
FAX: (215) 399-6610
Mailing Address:
   P.O. Box 1000
   Westtown, PA 19395
Year Established: 1992
Pub. Frequency: m.
Subscrip. Rate: $600/yr.
**Owner(s):**
Andrews Publications
1646 West Chester Pike
Westtown, PA 19395
Telephone: (215) 399-6600
Ownership %: 100
**Desc.:** Provides current information on
   developments in breast implant suits
   nationally.

## BURAFF'S LITIGATION REPORT
71139

1350 Connecticut Ave., N.W.
Washington, DC 20036
Telephone: (202) 862-0990
FAX: (202) 822-8092
Year Established: 1992
Pub. Frequency: w.
Subscrip. Rate: $295/yr.; $317/yr. foreign
**Owner(s):**
Millin Publications, Inc.
1350 Connecticut Ave., N.W.
Washington, DC 20036
Telephone: (202) 862-0990
FAX: (202) 822-8092
Ownership %: 100

**Desc.:** Text and anaylsis of RTC, FDIC,
   OTS, and legislative and regulatory
   activity affecting the liability of counsel
   to open institutions. Text and anaylsis of
   RTC, FDIC, OTS, and related actions
   against bank lawyers. Includes listings
   of all RTC and FCIC suits filed against
   attorneys as well as legislative and
   regulatory activity affecting the liability of
   counsel to open institutions.

## CALIFORNIA CRIMINAL LAW REPORTER
71167

5580 La Jolla Blvd.
Ste. 116
La Jolla, CA 92037
Telephone: (619) 236-0679
Year Established: 1983
Pub. Frequency: bi-w.
Subscrip. Rate: $327.50/yr.
**Owner(s):**
La Jolla Publications, Inc.
5580 La Jolla Blvd.
Ste. 116
La Jolla, CA 92037
Telephone: (619) 236-0679
Ownership %: 100
**Editorial:**
Patrick M. Ford ............................Editor

## CALIFORNIA EMPLOYMENT LAW LETTER
70590

162 Fourth Ave. N.
Nashville, TN 37219
Telephone: (615) 242-7395
FAX: (615) 256-6601
Year Established: 1990
Pub. Frequency: m.
Subscrip. Rate: $95/yr.
**Owner(s):**
Lee/Smith Publishers & Printers
162 Fourth Ave. N.
Nashville, TN 37219-8867
Telephone: (615) 242-7395
Ownership %: 100
**Editorial:**
S. Pepe ............................Editor
C. Hagen ............................Editor
**Desc.:** Reports the latest California
   employment law developments that
   affect California employers.

## CALIFORNIA ENVIRONMENTAL LAW REPORTER
69884

11 Penn Plaza
New York, NY 10001
*see Newsletters, Environment & Energy*

## CALIFORNIA FAMILY LAW FIRST ALERT
71137

P.O. Box 5917
Sausalito, CA 94966
Telephone: (415) 332-9000
Year Established: 1982
Pub. Frequency: 48/yr.
Subscrip. Rate: $250/yr.
**Owner(s):**
California Family Law Report
P.O. Box 5917
Sausalito, CA 94966
Telephone: (415) 332-9000
Ownership %: 100
**Editorial:**
Stephen Adams ............................Editor

## CALIFORNIA FAMILY LAW REPORT
71140

P.O. Box 5917
Sausalito, CA 94966
Telephone: (415) 332-9000
Year Established: 1977
Pub. Frequency: m.
Subscrip. Rate: $280/yr.

---

**Materials Accepted/Included:** 01-Business news 02-By-line articles 03-Fashion news 04-Food news 05-Freelance copy 06-Letters to editor 07-Real estate news 08-Sports news 09-Travel news 10-Book rev. 11-Movie rev. 12-Music rev. 13-TV rev. 14-Theater rev. 15-Coming events 16-Obituaries 17-Question & answer 18-Social announcements 19-Artwork 20-Cartoons 21-Photos 22-TV listings 23-Audio rec. 24-Video rec. 25-Books 26-Films/film clips 27-Personnel news 28-Press releases 29-New product news/photos 30-Trade lit. 31-Contracts awarded 32-Display adv. 33-Classified adv.

**Owner(s):**
California Family Law Report
P.O. Box 5917
Sausalito, CA 94966
Telephone: (415) 332-9000
Ownership %: 100
**Editorial:**
Stephen Adams ..........................Editor

70549
## CALIFORNIA TORT REPORTER
P.O. Box 35300
Colorado Spring, CO 80935-3530
Telephone: (719) 475-7230
FAX: (800) 525-0053
Year Established: 1980
Pub. Frequency: 10/yr.
Subscrip. Rate: $290/yr.
**Owner(s):**
Shepard's - McGraw-Hill, Inc.
P.O. Box 35300
Colorado Spring, CO 80935-3530
Telephone: (719) 475-7230
FAX: (800) 525-0053

70597
## CALIFORNIA WATER LAW & POLICY REPORTER
555 Middle Creek Pkwy.
Colorado Springs, CO 80935
Telephone: (719) 488-3000
FAX: (800) 525-0053
Year Established: 1990
Pub. Frequency: m.
Subscrip. Rate: $270/yr.
**Owner(s):**
Shepard's/McGraw-Hill, Inc.
555 Middle Creek Pkwy.
Colorado Springs, CO
Telephone: (719) 488-3000
Ownership %: 100
**Editorial:**
Rafael Bernardino ......................Editor

69219
## CEMETERY BUSINESS & LEGAL GUIDE
555 Skokie Blvd., Ste. 500
Northbrook, IL 60062-2845
Telephone: (708) 480-1020
FAX: (708) 509-1022
Year Established: 1973
Pub. Frequency: 10/yr.
Subscrip. Rate: $95/yr.
Circulation: 500
Circulation Type: paid
**Owner(s):**
CB Legal Publishing Corp.
555 Skokie Blvd.
Ste. 500
Northbrook, IL 60025
Telephone: (708) 480-1020
Ownership %: 100
**Editorial:**
Harvey Lapin ..........................Editor

71123
## CHAPTER 11 UPDATE
1646 West Chester Pike
P.O. Box 1000
Westtown, PA 19395
Telephone: (215) 399-6600
FAX: (215) 399-6610
Year Established: 1991
Pub. Frequency: s-m.
Subscrip. Rate: $450/yr.
**Owner(s):**
Andrews Publications
1646 West Chester Pike
P.O. Box 1000
Westtown, PA 19395
Telephone: (215) 399-6600
FAX: (215) 399-6610
Ownership %: 100
**Editorial:**
Mary Jeffers ..........................Editor
Kathy Knaub ..........................Editor

71124
## COMMERCIAL LAW ADVISER
11630 Chillicothe Rd.
Chesterland, OH 44026
Telephone: (216) 729-7996
FAX: (216) 729-0645
Year Established: 1988
Pub. Frequency: m.
Subscrip. Rate: $225/yr.
**Owner(s):**
Business Laws, Inc.
11630 Chillicothe Rd.
Chesterland, OH 44026
Telephone: (216) 729-7996
FAX: (216) 729-0645
Ownership %: 100
**Editorial:**
William A. Hancock ....................Editor
**Desc.:** Reports on developments pertaining to commercial law.

71045
## COMPUTER LAW & TAX REPORT
954 Lexington Ave.
Ste. 163
New York, NY 10021-5013
*see Newsletters, Computers*

71046
## COMPUTER LAW MONITOR
92 Fairway Dr.
Asheville, NC 28805
*see Newsletters, Computers*

71047
## COMPUTER LAW REPORTER
519 Connecticut Ave., N.W.
Ste. 200
Washington, DC 20036
*see Newsletters, Computers*

70555
## CONSUMER BANKRUPTCY NEWS
747 Dresher Rd.
Horsham, PA 19044
Telephone: (215) 784-0860
FAX: (215) 784-0870
Year Established: 1991
Pub. Frequency: w.
Subscrip. Rate: $245/yr.
**Owner(s):**
L R P Publications
747 Dresher Rd.
Horsham, PA 19044
Telephone: (215) 784-0860
FAX: (215) 784-0870
**Editorial:**
David Light ..........................Editor

70543
## CONSUMER CREDIT & TRUTH IN LENDING COMPLIANCE REPORT
One Penn Plaza
New York, NY 10119
Telephone: (212) 971-5000
FAX: (212) 971-5240
Mailing Address:
The Park Square Building
31 St. James Ave.
Boston, MA 02116-4112
Year Established: 1969
Pub. Frequency: m.
Subscrip. Rate: $176.75/yr. US;
$235.90/yr. foreign
**Owner(s):**
Warren Gorham Lamont
One Penn Plaza
New York, NY 10119
Telephone: (212) 971-5000
FAX: (212) 971-5240
Ownership %: 100
**Editorial:**
Earl Phillips ..........................Editor
**Desc.:** Focuses on the latest regulatory rulings and findings involving consumer lending and credt activitiy.

70562
## CONSUMER PRODUCT LITIGATION REPORTER
1646 West Chester Pike
Westtown, PA 19395
Telephone: (215) 399-6600
FAX: (215) 399-6600
Mailing Address:
P.O. Box 1000
Westtown, PA 19395
Year Established: 1990
Pub. Frequency: m.
Subscrip. Rate: $500/yr.
Materials: 32
**Owner(s):**
Andrews Publications
P.O. Box 1000
Westtown, PA 19395
Telephone: (215) 399-6600
FAX: (215) 399-6610
Ownership %: 100
**Editorial:**
Kathy Knaub ..........................Editor
**Desc.:** Covers product liability issues such as strict liability, adequacy of warning, and merchantability. Also covers state and federal legislation.

71131
## CORPORATE COUNSEL'S MONITOR
11630 Chillicothe Rd.
Chesterland, OH 44026
Telephone: (216) 729-7996
FAX: (216) 729-0645
Year Established: 1986
Pub. Frequency: m.
Subscrip. Rate: $275/yr.
**Owner(s):**
Business Laws, Inc.
11630 Chillicothe Rd.
Chesterland, OH 44026
Telephone: (216) 729-7996
FAX: (216) 729-0645
Ownership %: 100
**Editorial:**
William A. Hancock ....................Editor
**Desc.:** Developments in the US federal laws that are pertinent information to corporate attorneys.

71127
## CORPORATE COUNSELLOR
Marketing Dept.
111 Eighth Ave.
New York, NY 10011
Telephone: (212) 741-8300
FAX: (212) 741-8300
Year Established: 1986
Pub. Frequency: m.
Subscrip. Rate: $220/yr.
**Owner(s):**
New York Law Publishing Co.
Marketing Dept.
111 Eighth Ave.
New York, NY 10011
Telephone: (212) 741-8300
Ownership %: 100
**Desc.:** Provides reports on legal and regulatory issues faced in an in-house practice, as well as administrative, recruitment and financial issues involved in running an in-house firm.

71143
## CORPORATE CRIMINAL & CONSTITUTIONAL LAW REPORTER
233 Broadway
Ste. 944
New York, NY 10279
Telephone: (212) 964-6173
Year Established: 1989
Pub. Frequency: 15/yr.
Subscrip. Rate: $295/yr.
Materials: 10

**Owner(s):**
Lexline Publishing Co.
233 Broadway
Ste. 944
New York, NY 10279
Telephone: (212) 964-6173
Ownership %: 100
**Editorial:**
Norman A. Olch ........................Editor

71133
## CORPORATE OFFICERS & DIRECTORS LIABILITY LITIGATION REPORTER
1646 West Chester Pike
P.O. Box 1000
Westtown, PA 19395
Telephone: (215) 399-6600
FAX: (215) 399-6610
Year Established: 1985
Pub. Frequency: s-m.
Subscrip. Rate: $800/yr.
**Owner(s):**
Andrews Publications
1646 West Chester Pike
P.O. Box 1000
Westtown, PA 19395
Telephone: (215) 399-6600
FAX: (215) 399-6610
Ownership %: 100
**Editorial:**
Frank Reynolds ........................Editor

71206
## COUNTERFEIT PRODUCTS INTELLIGENCE REPORT
9124 Bradford Rd.
Silver Spring, MD 20901-4918
Telephone: (301) 565-2532
FAX: (301) 565-3298
Year Established: 1994
Pub. Frequency: m.
Subscrip. Rate: $372/yr. US; $384/yr. foreign
**Owner(s):**
A L F A Publishing
9124 Bradford Rd.
Silver Spring, MD 20901-4918
Telephone: (301) 565-2532
FAX: (301) 565-3298
Ownership %: 100
**Editorial:**
Steven Rizer ..........................Editor
**Desc.:** Covers product piracy, copyright and trademark infringement, and currency fraud, focusing on detection, prevention, interdiction, and prosecution of illegal copying of software, records, compact discs, audio and video tapes, and books; counterfeiting of metal fasteners, automotive parts, plumbing parts, collectables; misrepresented clothing brands and unauthorized use of a company brand name or trademark.

71144
## COURT'S CHARGE REPORTER
Echelon II, Ste. 100
9430 Research Blvd.
Auston, TX 78759
Telephone: (512) 346-9686
FAX: (512) 346-9373
Year Established: 1973
Pub. Frequency: a.
Subscrip. Rate: $175/yr.
**Owner(s):**
Butterworth Legal Publishers
Echelon II, Ste. 100
9430 Research Blvd.
Austin, TX 78759
Telephone: (512) 346-9686
FAX: (512) 346-9373
Ownership %: 100
**Editorial:**
Will G. Barber ........................Editor

**Materials Accepted/Included:** 01-Business news 02-By-line articles 03-Fashion news 04-Food news 05-Freelance copy 06-Letters to editor 07-Real estate news 08-Sports news 09-Travel news 10-Book rev. 11-Movie rev. 12-Music rev. 13-TV rev. 14-Theater rev. 15-Coming events 16-Obituaries 17-Question & answer 18-Social announcements 19-Artwork 20-Cartoons 21-Photos 22-TV listings 23-Audio rec. 24-Video rec. 25-Books 26-Films/film clips 27-Personnel news 28-Press releases 29-New product news/photos 30-Trade lit. 31-Contracts awarded 32-Display adv. 33-Classified adv.

7-59

**Desc.:** Contains condensed transcripts of actual charges from Texas civil jury cases.

**COURT CASE DIGEST** 71145
10 Signal Rd.
Stamford, CT 06902
Telephone: (203) 975-7070
FAX: (203) 975-7002
Year Established: 1981
Pub. Frequency: m.
Subscrip. Rate: $440/yr.
Circulation: 185
Circulation Type: controlled & paid
**Owner(s):**
Maritime Advisory Services Inc.
10 Signal Rd.
Stamford, CT 06902
Telephone: (203) 975-7070
FAX: (203) 975-7002
Ownership %: 100
**Desc.:** Reviews all major American and Canadian court decisions.

**COURT MANAGEMENT & ADMINISTRATIVE REPORT** 71142
88 Post Rd., W.
Westport, CT 06881-5007
Telephone: (203) 226-3571
FAX: (203) 685-0285
Mailing Address:
P.O. Box 5007
Westport, CT 06881-5007
Year Established: 1990
Pub. Frequency: 11/yr.
Subscrip. Rate: $145/yr.
**Owner(s):**
GP Subscription Publications
88 Post Rd., W.
Westport, CT 06881-5007
Telephone: (203) 226-3571
FAX: (203) 685-0284
Ownership %: 100
**Editorial:**
Clifford Kirsch ...............................Editor
**Desc.:** Newsletter for professionals in justice systems management.

**CRIMINAL PRACTICE LAW REVIEW** 71170
P.O. Box 7587
Charlottesville, VA 22906-7587
Telephone: (804) 972-7600
FAX: (804) 972-7666
Year Established: 1988
Pub. Frequency: q.
Subscrip. Rate: $80/yr.
**Owner(s):**
Michie Co.
P.O. Box 7587
Charlottesville, VA 22906-7587
Telephone: (804) 972-7600
FAX: (804) 972-7666
Ownership %: 100

**DRUNK DRIVING-LIQUOR LIABILITY REPORTER** 70574
11 Penn Plaza
New York, NY 10001-2006
Telephone: (212) 967-7707
FAX: (212) 967-1069
Year Established: 1987
Pub. Frequency: m.
Subscrip. Rate: $225/yr.
**Owner(s):**
Matthew/Bender & Co., Inc.
11 Penn Plaza
New York, NY 10001-2006
Telephone: (212) 967-7707
FAX: (212) 967-1069
Ownership %: 100
**Editorial:**
Laurie Wood ...............................Editor

**EMPLOYMENT LAW UPDATE** 70548
P.O. Box 15250
Evansville, IN 47716-0250
Telephone: (812) 476-4520
Year Established: 1986
Pub. Frequency: m.
Subscrip. Rate: $97.50/yr.
**Owner(s):**
Rutkowski & Associates Inc.
P.O. Box 15250
Evansville, IN 47716-0250
Telephone: (812) 476-4520
Ownership %: 100
**Editorial:**
Arthur D. Rutkowski ...............................Editor
Barbara Lang Rutkowski ...............................Editor
**Desc.:** Provides timely news for human resources executives on relevant issues, including critical legislation and legal decisions, current trends, helpful policies and checklists, and authoritative legal analysis.

**EMPLOYMENT LITIGATION REPORTER** 70553
1646 West Chester Pike
P.O. Box 1000
Westtown, PA 19395
Telephone: (215) 399-6600
FAX: (215) 399-6610
Year Established: 1986
Pub. Frequency: s-m.
Subscrip. Rate: $800/yr.
**Owner(s):**
Andrews Publications
1646 West Chester Pike
P.O. Box 1000
Westtown, PA 19395
Telephone: (215) 399-6600
FAX: (215) 399-6610
Ownership %: 100
**Editorial:**
Linda Coady ...............................Editor

**ENTERTAINMENT LAW REPORTER** 70556
2210 Wilshire Blvd.
Ste. 311
Santa Monica, CA 90403
Telephone: (310) 829-9335
Year Established: 1979
Pub. Frequency: m.
Subscrip. Rate: $175/yr.
Materials: 10,32
Circulation: 825
Circulation Type: controlled & paid
**Owner(s):**
Entertainment Law Reporter Publishing Co.
2210 Wilshire Blvd.
Ste. 311
Santa Monica, CA 90403
Telephone: (310) 829-9335
Ownership %: 100
**Editorial:**
Lionel S. Sobel ...............................Editor

**EUROPEAN COMMUNITY LAW & BUSINESS REPORTER** 70592
P.O. Box 8219
Boston, MA 02114
Telephone: (617) 742-7959
Year Established: 1990
Pub. Frequency: 5/yr.
Subscrip. Rate: $150/yr.
**Owner(s):**
Legal Medical Studies, Inc.
P.O. Box 8219
Boston, MA 02114
Telephone: (617) 742-0000
Ownership %: 100
**Editorial:**
Patricia Kindregant ...............................Editor

**EUROSCOPE** 70594
46679 Winchester Dr.
Sterling, VA 22170
Telephone: (703) 430-5417
Year Established: 1991
Pub. Frequency: w.
Subscrip. Rate: $300/yr.
**Owner(s):**
Euroscope, Inc.
46679 Winchester Dr.
Sterling, VA 22170
Telephone: (703) 430-5417
Ownership %: 100
**Editorial:**
John Baird ...............................Editor
**Desc.:** Reports legislative developments in the European Community nations.

**FEDERAL COURT APPOINTMENTS REPORT** 71149
1511 K St., N.W.
Washington, DC 20005
Telephone: (202) 783-1887
FAX: (202) 393-5106
Year Established: 1992
Pub. Frequency: 6/yr.
Subscrip. Rate: $125/yr.
**Owner(s):**
Want Publishing Co.
1511 K St., N.W.
Washington, DC 20005
Telephone: (202) 783-1887
FAX: (202) 393-5106
Ownership %: 100
**Editorial:**
Robert Want ...............................Editor

**FEDERAL DRUG ENFORCEMENT LAW BULLETIN** 71164
P.O. Box 134
Pitman, NJ 08071
Telephone: (800) 234-8358
FAX: (609) 582-3940
Year Established: 1991
Pub. Frequency: 10/yr.
Subscrip. Rate: $195/yr.
**Owner(s):**
Paks Publishing Group
P.O. Box 134
Pitman, NJ 08071
Telephone: (800) 234-8358
FAX: (609) 582-3940
Ownership %: 100
**Editorial:**
Matthew Christopher ...............................Editor

**FEDERAL LITIGATOR** 70582
P.O. Box 35300
Colorado Springs, CO 80935-3530
Telephone: (719) 488-3000
Year Established: 1985
Pub. Frequency: 10/yr.
Subscrip. Rate: $290/yr.
**Owner(s):**
Shepards/McGraw-Hill, Inc.
P.O. Box 35300
Colorado Springs, CO 80935-3530
Telephone: (719) 488-3000
Ownership %: 100
**Editorial:**
Jeffery Brand ...............................Editor
Neil Levy ...............................Editor

**FEDERAL RULES OF EVIDENCE NEWS** 70588
Acqueduct Bldg.
Rochester, NY 14694
Telephone: (800) 527-0430
Year Established: 1976
Pub. Frequency: m.
Subscrip. Rate: $180/yr.

**Owner(s):**
Lawyers Cooperative Publishing
Acqueduct Bldg.
Rochester, NY 14694
Telephone: (800) 527-0430
Ownership %: 100
**Editorial:**
John R. Schmertz, Jr. ...............................Editor

**FIREHOUSE LAWYER MONTHLY NEWSLETTER** 71032
23 Drydock Ave.
Boston, MA 02210-2387
Telephone: (800) 229-2084
FAX: (617) 345-9646
Pub. Frequency: m.
Subscrip. Rate: $57/yr.
**Owner(s):**
Quinlan Publishing Co., Inc.
23 Drydock Ave.
Boston, MA 02210-2387
Telephone: (800) 229-2084
Ownership %: 100
**Desc.:** Covers recent court decisions and legal issues affecting firefighting personnel.

**FLORIDA EMPLOYMENT LAW LETTER** 70547
162 Fourth Ave., N.
Nashville, TN 37219-8867
Telephone: (615) 242-7395
FAX: (615) 256-6601
Year Established: 1989
Pub. Frequency: m.
Subscrip. Rate: $93/yr.
**Owner(s):**
Lee Smith Publishers & Printers
162 Fourth Ave., N.
Nashville, TN 37219-8867
Telephone: (615) 242-7395
FAX: (615) 256-6601
Ownership %: 100
**Editorial:**
T. Harper ...............................Editor
**Desc.:** Review of Florida employment law developments.

**FLORIDA ENVIRONMENTAL & COMPLIANCE UPDATE** 70550
162 Fourth Ave., N.
Nashville, TN 37219-8867
Telephone: (615) 242-7395
FAX: (615) 256-6601
Year Established: 1990
Pub. Frequency: m.
Subscrip. Rate: $147/yr.
**Owner(s):**
Lee Smith Publishers & Printers
162 Fourth Ave., N.
Nashville, TN 37219-8867
Telephone: (615) 242-7395
FAX: (615) 256-6601
Ownership %: 100
**Editorial:**
S. Ansbacher ...............................Editor
**Desc.:** Reports the latest Florida environmental law developments that affect Florida companies.

**FOURTH CIRCUIT REVIEW** 71151
400 Oyster Point Blvd., Ste. 500
San Francisco, CA 94080
Telephone: (415) 588-1155
FAX: (415) 244-6619
Year Established: 1990
Pub. Frequency: bi-w.
Subscrip. Rate: $215/yr.

**Materials Accepted/Included:** 01-Business news 02-By-line articles 03-Fashion news 04-Food news 05-Freelance copy 06-Letters to editor 07-Real estate news 08-Sports news 09-Travel news 10-Book rev. 11-Movie rev. 12-Music rev. 13-TV rev. 14-Theater rev. 15-Coming events 16-Obituaries 17-Question & answer 18-Social announcements 19-Artwork 20-Cartoons 21-Photos 22-TV listings 23-Audio rec. 24-Video rec. 25-Books 26-Films/film clips 27-Personnel news 28-Press releases 29-New product news/photos 30-Trade lit. 31-Contracts awarded 32-Display adv. 33-Classified adv.

**Owner(s):**
Barclays Law Publishers
400 Oyster Point Blvd, Ste. 50
San Francisco, CA 94080
Telephone: (415) 588-1155
FAX: (415) 244-6619
Ownership %: 100
**Editorial:**
Frank Gomez ......................................Editor

70554

## GEORGIA EMPLOYMENT LAW LETTER
162 Fourth Ave., N.
Nashville, TN 37219-8867
Telephone: (800) 274-6774
FAX: (615) 256-6601
Year Established: 1988
Pub. Frequency: m.
Subscrip. Rate: $94/yr.
**Owner(s):**
Lee Smith Publishers & Printers
162 Fourth Ave., N.
Nashville, TN 37219-8867
Telephone: (800) 274-6774
FAX: (615) 256-6601
Ownership %: 100
**Editorial:**
D. Hagaman ....................................Editor
**Desc.:** Survey of Georgia law developments.

70558

## GEORGIA ENVIRONMENTAL LAW LETTER
162 Fourth Ave., N.
Nashville, TN 37219-8867
Telephone: (615) 242-7395
FAX: (615) 256-6601
Year Established: 1989
Pub. Frequency: m.
Subscrip. Rate: $147/yr.
**Owner(s):**
Lee Smith Publishers & Printers
162 Fourth Ave., N.
Nashville, TN 37219-8867
Telephone: (615) 242-7395
FAX: (615) 256-6601
**Editorial:**
A. Jean Tolman ..............................Editor
**Desc.:** Reports the latest Georgia environmental law developments that affect Georgia companies.

70521

## HEALTH LABOR RELATIONS REPORTS
P.O. Box 20241
Cincinnati, OH 45220
Telephone: (513) 221-3715
Year Established: 1976
Pub. Frequency: 24/yr.
Subscrip. Rate: $149/yr.
**Owner(s):**
Interwood Publications
P.O. Box 20241
Cincinnati, OH 45220
Telephone: (513) 221-3715
Ownership %: 100
**Editorial:**
Frank J. Bardack ..........................Editor
**Desc.:** Covers court and National Labor Review Board decisions, including wrongful discharge, employment-at-will, contract settlements, arbitration awards, and discrimination.

70560

## HEALTH LAW WEEK
1201 Peachtree St., N.E.
Ste. 1150
Atlanta, GA 30361
Telephone: (404) 881-1141
FAX: (404) 881-0074
Year Established: 1992
Pub. Frequency: w.
Subscrip. Rate: $647/yr.

**Owner(s):**
Strattford Communications, Inc.
1201 Peachtree St., N.E.
Ste. 1150
Atlanta, GA 30361
Telephone: (404) 881-1141
FAX: (404) 881-0074
Ownership %: 100
**Editorial:**
Nancy Johnson ..........................Editor

70564

## HEALTH LAWYER
750 N. Lake Shore Dr.
Chicago, IL 60611
Telephone: (312) 988-6067
Pub. Frequency: 3-4/yr. membership only
Circulation: 3,220
Circulation Type: controlled & paid
**Owner(s):**
B.A. Press
750 N. Lake Shore Dr.
Chicago, IL 60611
Telephone: (312) 988-6067
Ownership %: 100
**Editorial:**
Lawrence Manson ........................Editor
**Desc.:** Legal trends in health law.

70522

## HOSPITAL LAW NEWSLETTER
200 Orchard Ridge Dr.
Gaithersburg, MD 20878
Telephone: (301) 417-7500
FAX: (301) 417-7550
Year Established: 1984
Pub. Frequency: m.
Subscrip. Rate: $255/yr. US; $306/yr. foreign
**Owner(s):**
Aspen Publishers, Inc.
200 Orchard Ridge Dr.
Gaithersburg, MD 20878
Telephone: (301) 417-7500
FAX: (301) 417-7550
Ownership %: 100

70534

## HUMAN RESOURCE MANAGER'S LEGAL REPORTER
39 Academy St.
Madison, CT 06443-1513
Telephone: (203) 245-7448
FAX: (203) 245-2559
Year Established: 1978
Pub. Frequency: m.
Subscrip. Rate: $95/yr.
Circulation: 2,700
Circulation Type: controlled & paid
**Owner(s):**
Business & Legal Reports, Inc.
39 Academy St.
Madison, CT 06443-1513
Telephone: (203) 245-7448
FAX: (203) 245-2559
Ownership %: 100
**Editorial:**
Maureen Gallagher ......................Editor
**Desc.:** Reports and advises on the practical aspects of EEO and human resource compliance.

71166

## IDAHO BANKRUPTCY COURT REPORT
P.O. Box 2756
Boise, ID 83701
Telephone: (208) 336-4715
Year Established: 1980
Pub. Frequency: m.
Subscrip. Rate: $120/yr.
**Owner(s):**
Goller Publishing Corp.
P.O. Box 2756
Boise, ID 83701
Telephone: (208) 336-4715
Ownership %: 100

**Editorial:**
Jane Crosby ..............................Editor

70570

## IDAHO LEGISLATIVE REPORT
P.O. Box 2756
Boise, ID 83701
Telephone: (208) 336-4715
Pub. Frequency: d. during legislative session
**Owner(s):**
Goller Publishing Corp.
P.O. Box 2756
Boise, ID 83701
Telephone: (208) 336-4715
Ownership %: 100
**Editorial:**
Jane Crosby ..............................Editor

70572

## ILLINOIS ENVIRONMENTAL LAW LETTER
162 Fourth Ave., N.
Nashville, TN 37219-8867
Telephone: (615) 242-7385
FAX: (615) 256-6601
Year Established: 1992
Pub. Frequency: m.
Subscrip. Rate: $137/yr.
**Owner(s):**
Lee Smith Publishers & Printers
162 Fourth Ave., N.
Nashville, TN 37219-8867
Telephone: (615) 242-7385
FAX: (615) 256-6601
Ownership %: 100
**Editorial:**
S. Stein ......................................Editor
P. Fleischauer ............................Editor
**Desc.:** Reports the latest developments in Illinois environmental laws.

70575

## INSURANCE SETTLEMENTS INSIDER
3520 Cadillac Ave.
Ste. E
Costa Mesa, CA 92626
Telephone: (714) 755-5450
FAX: (714) 549-8835
Year Established: 1988
Pub. Frequency: m.
Subscrip. Rate: $19.97/yr.
**Owner(s):**
James Publishing Group, Inc.
3520 Cadillac Ave.
Ste. E
Costa Mesa, CA 92626
Telephone: (714) 755-5450
FAX: (714) 549-8835
Ownership %: 100
**Editorial:**
Wendi Webb ..............................Editor

70598

## INTERNATIONAL LAWYERS' NEWSLETTER
Six Bigelow St.
Cambridge, MA 02139
Telephone: (617) 354-0140
FAX: (617) 354-8595
Year Established: 1979
Pub. Frequency: bi-m.
Subscrip. Rate: $95/yr.
**Owner(s):**
Kluwer Law & Taxation Publishers
Six Bigelow St.
Cambridge, MA 02139
Telephone: (617) 354-0140
FAX: (617) 354-8595
Ownership %: 100
**Editorial:**
Carol A. Emory ..........................Editor
Arthur G. Kroos ........................Editor

**Desc.:** Contains timely legal news and information from around the globe, including coverage of recent political, legal and social developments, important statutes and rulings with an impact on international transactions, and other matters of interest to members of the international legal profession.

71152

## INVESTMENT LIMITED PARNERSHIPS LAW REPORT
375 Hudson St.
New York, NY 10014
Telephone: (800) 232-1336
FAX: (212) 924-0460
Year Established: 1981
Pub. Frequency: 10/yr.
Subscrip. Rate: $185/yr.
**Owner(s):**
Clark-Boardman-Callaghan Co., Inc.
375 Hudson St.
New York, NY 10014
Telephone: (800) 323-1336
FAX: (212) 924-0460
Ownership %: 100
**Editorial:**
Robert J. Haft & Peter M. Fass ..........Editors

70578

## KANSAS-IOWA ENVIRONMENTAL LAW LETTER
162 Fourth Ave., N.
Nashville, TN 37219
Telephone: (615) 242-7385
FAX: (615) 256-6601
Year Established: 1990
Pub. Frequency: m.
Subscrip. Rate: $137/yr.
**Owner(s):**
Lee Smith Publishers & Printers
162 Fourth Ave., N.
Nashville, TN 37219
Telephone: (615) 242-7385
FAX: (615) 256-6601
Ownership %: 100
**Editorial:**
George M. von Stamwitz ..............Editor
**Desc.:** Reports the latest developments in Kansas and Iowa environmental laws.

71147

## LANDLORD TENANT LAW BULLETIN
23 Drydock Ave.
Boston, MA 02110
Telephone: (800) 229-2084
FAX: (617) 345-9646
Year Established: 1979
Pub. Frequency: m.
Subscrip. Rate: $60/yr.
**Owner(s):**
Quinlan Publishing Co., Inc.
23 Drydock Ave.
Boston, MA 02110
Telephone: (800) 229-2084
FAX: (617) 345-9646
Ownership %: 100
**Editorial:**
E. Michael Quinlan ......................Editor
**Desc.:** Contains court decisions on tenancy law.

70589

## LAW & STRATEGY
111 Eighth Ave.
New York, NY 10011
Telephone: (212) 463-5709
FAX: (212) 463-5523
Year Established: 1989
Pub. Frequency: m.
Subscrip. Rate: $295/yr.

Group 340-Legal

NEWSLETTERS

**Owner(s):**
Leader Publications, Inc.
111 Eighth Ave.
New York, NY 10011
Telephone: (212) 463-5709
FAX: (212) 463-5523
Ownership %: 100
**Editorial:**
John Sarna ..............................Editor

70545

## LAW FIRM BENEFITS
111 Eighth Ave.
New York, NY 10011
Telephone: (212) 463-5733
FAX: (212) 463-5573
Year Established: 1992
Pub. Frequency: m.
**Owner(s):**
Leader Publications, Inc.
111 Eighth Ave.
New York, NY 10011
Telephone: (212) 463-5733
Ownership %: 100
**Editorial:**
Patricia L. Johnson ..................Editor

67062

## LEGAL INFORMATION ALERT
401 W. Fullerton Pkwy.
Chicago, IL 60614
Telephone: (312) 525-7594
FAX: (312) 525-7015
Year Established: 1981
Pub. Frequency: 10/yr.
Page Size: standard
Subscrip. Rate: $149/yr.
**Owner(s):**
Alert Publications, Inc.
401 W. Fullerton Pkwy.
Chicago, IL 60614
Telephone: (312) 525-7594
Ownership %: 100
**Management:**
Donna Tuke Heroy ...............Publisher
**Editorial:**
Donna Tuke Heroy ..................Editor
**Desc.:** A newsletter for law librarians with
news and reviews of new books and
databases.
**Readers:** Law librarians.

71156

## LENDER LIABILITY LAW REPORT
One Penn Plz.
New York, NY 10019
Telephone: (212) 971-5000
FAX: (212) 971-5340
Year Established: 1987
Pub. Frequency: m.
Subscrip. Rate: $173/yr.
**Owner(s):**
Warren Gorham Lamont
One Penn Plz.
New York, NY 10019
Telephone: (212) 971-5000
FAX: (212) 971-5240
Ownership %: 100
**Editorial:**
Helen Davis Chaitman ............Editor
**Desc.:** Analyzes recent court decisions
and new legislation. Provides
suggestions for developing
protective mechanisms for lenders and
the means of defending borrowers' suits.

71157

## LENDER LIABILITY NEWS
1350 Connecticut Ave., N.W.
Ste. 1000
Washington, DC 20036
Telephone: (202) 862-0990
FAX: (202) 822-8092
Year Established: 1988
Pub. Frequency: bi-w.
Subscrip. Rate: $545/yr.; $567/yr. foreign

**Owner(s):**
Burraff Publications
1350 Connectitcut Ave., N.W.
Ste. 1000
Washington, DC 20036
Telephone: (202) 862-0990
FAX: (202) 822-8092
Ownership %: 100
**Editorial:**
Rose Lally ..............................Editor
**Desc.:** Liability issues facing lenders in all
areas; fraud, breach of fidicuary duty,
environmental cleanup. Covers litigation,
legislation and regulation, and new
industry practice (how lenders are
reducing their exposure in negotiating,
administrating, and enforcing loan
agreements).

70542

## MARKETING FOR LAWYERS NEWSLETTER
111 Eighth Ave.
New York, NY 10011
Telephone: (212) 741-8300
Year Established: 1987
Pub. Frequency: m.
Subscrip. Rate: $175/yr.
**Owner(s):**
New York Law Publishing Co.
111 Eighth Ave.
New York, NY 10011
Telephone: (212) 741-8300
Ownership %: 100
**Desc.:** Helps attorneys to expand their
practices by covering marketing
techniques and strategies such as
cross-marketing, using newsletters and
seminars, opening branch offices, and
servicing existing clients.

70567

## MICHIGAN ENVIROMENTAL LAW LETTER
162 Fourth Ave. N.
Nashville, TN 37219-8867
Telephone: (615) 242-7395
FAX: (615) 256-6601
Year Established: 1990
Pub. Frequency: m.
Subscrip. Rate: $137/yr.
**Owner(s):**
M. Lee Smith Publishers & Printers
162 Fourth Ave. N.
Nashville, TN 37219-8867
Telephone: (615) 242-7395
FAX: (615) 256-6601
Ownership %: 100
**Editorial:**
J. Polito ..................................Editor
R. Hykan ................................Editor
**Desc.:** Reports the latest Michigan
environmental law developments that
affect Michigan companies.

70571

## MISSOURI EMPLOYMENT LAW LETTER
162 Fourth Ave. N.
Nashville, TN 37219-8867
Telephone: (615) 252-7395
FAX: (615) 256-6601
Year Established: 1991
Pub. Frequency: m.
Subscrip. Rate: $95/yr.
**Owner(s):**
M. Lee Smith Publishers & Printers
162 Fourth Ave. N.
Nashville, TN 37219-8867
Telephone: (615) 252-7395
FAX: (615) 256-6601
Ownership %: 100
**Editorial:**
Robert A. Kaiser ....................Editor
Vance D. Miller ......................Editor

**Desc.:** Reports the latest Missouri
employment law developments that
affect Missouri employers.

70573

## NEW JERSEY ENVIRONMENTAL LAW LETTER
162 Fourth Ave. N.
Nashville, TN 37219-8867
Telephone: (615) 242-7385
FAX: (615) 256-7385
Year Established: 1992
Pub. Frequency: m.
Subscrip. Rate: $137/yr.
**Owner(s):**
M. Lee Smith Publlishers & Printers
162 Fourth Ave. N.
Nashville, TN 37219-8867
Telephone: (615) 242-7385
FAX: (615) 256-6601
Ownership %: 100
**Editorial:**
Gail H. Allyn ..........................Editor

70579

## NORTH CAROLINA EMPLOYMENT LAW LETTER
162 Fourth Ave. N.
Nashville, TN 37219-8867
Telephone: (615) 242-7395
FAX: (615) 256-6601
Year Established: 1991
Pub. Frequency: m.
Subscrip. Rate: $97/yr.
**Owner(s):**
M. Lee Smith Publishers & Printers
162 Fourth Ave. N.
Nashville, TN 37219-8867
Telephone: (615) 242-7395
FAX: (615) 256-6601
Ownership %: 100
**Editorial:**
D. Irvin ..................................Editor
R. Rainey ..............................Editor
**Desc.:** Reports the latest North Carolina
employment law developments that
affect Noth Carolina employers.

70586

## OHIO ENVIRONMENTAL LAW LETTER
162 Fourth Ave. N.
Nashville, TN 37219-8867
Telephone: (615) 242-7395
FAX: (615) 256-6601
Year Established: 1990
Pub. Frequency: m.
Subscrip. Rate: $137/yr.
**Owner(s):**
M. Lee Smith Publishers & Printers
162 Fourth Ave. N.
Nashville, TN 37219-8867
Telephone: (615) 242-7395
FAX: (615) 242-7395
Ownership %: 100
**Editorial:**
Martin S. Seltzer ....................Editor
**Desc.:** Reports the latest Ohio
environmental law developments that
affect Ohio companies.

69270

## ORTHODOX HERALD
P.O. Box 9
Hunlock Creek, PA 18621-0009
Telephone: (717) 256-7232
Year Established: 1952
Pub. Frequency: m.
Page Size: tabloid
Subscrip. Rate: $5/yr.
Print Process: offset
Circulation: 5,000
Circulation Type: controlled & paid

**Owner(s):**
Orthodox Herald, Inc.
P.O. Box 9
Hunlock Creek, PA 18621
Telephone: (717) 256-7232
Ownership %: 100
**Editorial:**
Rev. W. Basil Stroyen ............Editor
**Desc.:** News about the Orthodox Christian
faith and church, and the traditions and
culture of people whose ancestors came
from the former Austro-Hungarian
empire and Russia.

70593

## PENNSYLVANIA EMPLOYMENT LAW LETTER
162 Fourth Ave. N.
Nashville, TN 37219-8867
Telephone: (615) 256-6601
FAX: (615) 256-6601
Year Established: 1990
Pub. Frequency: m.
Subscrip. Rate: $95/yr.
**Owner(s):**
M. Lee Smith Publlishers & Printers
162 Fourth Ave. N.
Nashville, TN 37219-8867
Telephone: (615) 242-7395
FAX: (615) 256-7395
Ownership %: 100
**Editorial:**
John E. Krampf ......................Editor
Harry Reagan ........................Editor
**Desc.:** Reports the latest Pennsylvania
employment law developments that
affect Pennsylvania employers.

66503

## PERFECT LAWYER, THE
P.O. Box 35300
Colorado Springs, CO 80935-3530
Telephone: (719) 488-3000
Mailing Address:
P.O. Box 1108
Lexington, SC 29071
Year Established: 1990
Pub. Frequency: m.
Page Size: standard
Subscrip. Rate: $110/yr.
Freelance Pay: $50/pg.
Print Process: offset
Circulation: 4,000
Circulation Type: controlled
**Owner(s):**
Shepard's McGraw-Hill, Inc.
Box 35300
Colorado Springs, CO 80935-3530
Telephone: (719) 488-3000
Ownership %: 100
**Editorial:**
Robert P. Wilkins ....................Editor
Dan Harmon ..................Design Editor
**Desc.:** Legal newsletter for lawyers & staff
who use Word Perfect.

71168

## PROBATION & PAROLE LAW REPORTS
P.O. Box 88
Warrensburg, MD 64093
Telephone: (816) 429-1102
Year Established: 1979
Pub. Frequency: m.
Subscrip. Rate: $98/yr.
**Owner(s):**
Knehans-Miller Publications
P.O. Box 88
Warrensburg, MD 64093
Telephone: (816) 429-1102
Ownership %: 100
**Editorial:**
Dane C. Miller ........................Editor

**Desc.:** Summaries and verbatim excerpts of all Federal and State Appellate Court decisions relating to probation and parole. Indexed by subject and jurisdiction.

70561

## REAL ESTATE-ENVIRONMENTAL LIABILITY NEWS
1350 Connecticut Ave.
Ste. 1000
Washington, DC 20036
Telephone: (800) 333-1291
FAX: (202) 862-0999
Year Established: 1989
Pub. Frequency: bi-w.
Subscrip. Rate: $497/yr. US; $519/yr. foreign
**Owner(s):**
Buraff Publications
1350 Connecticut Ave.
Ste. 1000
Washington, DC 20036
Telephone: (800) 333-1291
FAX: (202) 862-0999
Ownership %: 100
**Editorial:**
Susan Winchurch .....................Editor
**Desc.:** Reports and analyzes litigation involving environmental liability in business transactions, innovative solutions to liability problems, changing federal and state requirements, and industry practices.

71165

## RISK MANAGER LAW BULLETIN
23 Drydock Ave.
Boston, MA 02110
Telephone: (617) 542-0048
FAX: (617) 345-9646
Year Established: 1986
Pub. Frequency: m.
Subscrip. Rate: $60/yr.
**Owner(s):**
Quinlan Publishing Co., Inc.
23 Drydock Ave.
Boston, MA 02110
Telephone: (617) 542-0048
FAX: (617) 345-9646
Ownership %: 100
**Desc.:** Discusses isssues and concerns relating to insurance coverage of interest to company directors, financial officers, insurance executives and insurance purchasers.

71155

## SECOND CIRCUIT REVIEW
400 Oyster Point Blvd., Ste. 500
San Francisco, CA 94080
Telephone: (415) 588-1155
FAX: (415) 244-6619
Year Established: 1988
Pub. Frequency: bi-w.
Subscrip. Rate: $215/yr
**Owner(s):**
Barclays Law Publishers
400 Oyster Point Blvd., Ste. 500
San Francisco, CA 94080
Telephone: (415) 588-1155
FAX: (415) 244-6619
Ownership %: 100
**Editorial:**
Frank Gomez .....................Editor

71159

## SEVENTH CIRCUIT REVIEW
400 Oyster Point Blvd., Ste. 500
San Francisco, CA 94080
Telephone: (415) 588-1155
FAX: (415) 244-6619
Year Established: 1988
Pub. Frequency: bi-w.
Subscrip. Rate: $215/yr.

**Owner(s):**
Barclays Law Publishers
400 Oyster Point Blvd., Ste. 500
San Francisco, CA 94080
Telephone: (415) 588-1155
FAX: (415) 244-6619
Ownership %: 100
**Editorial:**
Frank Gomez .....................Editor

71163

## SIXTH CIRCUIT REVIEW
400 Oyster Point Blvd., Ste. 500
San Francisco, CA 94080
Telephone: (415) 588-1155
FAX: (415) 244-6619
Year Established: 1987
Pub. Frequency: bi-w.
Subscrip. Rate: $215/yr.
**Owner(s):**
Barclays Law Publishers
400 Oyster Point Blvd., Ste. 500
San Francisco, CA 94080
Telephone: (415) 588-1155
FAX: (415) 244-6619
Ownership %: 100
**Editorial:**
Frank Gomez .....................Editor

70566

## SPORTS MEDICINE STANDARDS & MALPRACTICE REPORTER
4571 Stephen Circle, NW
Canton, OH 44718
Telephone: (800) 336-0083
FAX: (216) 499-6609
Pub. Frequency: q.
Subscrip. Rate: $39.95/yr.
**Owner(s):**
Professional Reports Corporation
4571 Stephen Circle NW
Canton, OH 44718-3629
Telephone: (800) 669-0083
FAX: (216) 499-6609
Ownership %: 100
**Desc.:** Covers legal issues of interest to sports medicine professionals, including current trends in liability, professional standards, drug screening, legal aspects of athletic programs, and more.

70569

## SPORTS, PARKS & RECREATION LAW REPORTER
4571 Stepen Circle, NW
Canton, OH 44718-3629
Telephone: (800) 336-0083
FAX: (216) 499-6609
Pub. Frequency: q.
Subscrip. Rate: $39.95/yr.
**Owner(s):**
Professional Reports Corporation
4571 Stephen Circle, NW
Canton, OH 44718-3629
Telephone: (800) 336-0083
FAX: (216) 499-6609
Ownership %: 100
**Desc.:** Covers legal issues of interest to sports, parks and recreation professionals, including liability, releases and waivers, drug testing, professional standerds, and more.

70581

## TENNESSEE REAL ESTATE LAW LETTER
162 Fourth Ave. N.
Nashville, TN 37219-8867
Telephone: (615) 242-7395
FAX: (615) 256-6601
Year Established: 1983
Pub. Frequency: m.
Subscrip. Rate: $92/yr.

**Owner(s):**
M. Lee Smith Publishers & Printers
162 Fourth Ave. N.
Nashville, TN 37219-8867
Telephone: (615) 242-7395
FAX: (615) 256-6601
Ownership %: 100
**Editorial:**
C. Dewees Berry .....................Editor
**Desc.:** Surveys Tennessee and federal real estate law developments.

70585

## TEXAS ENVIRONMENTAL LAW LETTER
162 Fourth St. N.
Nashville, TN 37219-8867
Telephone: (615) 242-7395
FAX: (615) 256-6601
Year Established: 1991
Pub. Frequency: m.
Subscrip. Rate: $147/yr.
**Owner(s):**
M. Lee Smith Publishers & Printers
162 Fourth St. N.
Nashville, TN 37219-8867
Telephone: (615) 242-7395
FAX: (615) 256-6601
Ownership %: 100
**Editorial:**
Neil R. Mitchell .....................Editor
Rebecca A. Leigh .....................Editor
**Desc.:** Reports the latest Texas environmental law developments that affect Texas companies.

70587

## VIRGINIA EMPLOYMENT LAW LETTER
162 Fourth Ave. N.
Nashville, TN 37219-8867
Telephone: (615) 242-7395
FAX: (615) 256-6601
Year Established: 1989
Pub. Frequency: m.
Subscrip. Rate: $95/yr.
**Owner(s):**
M. Lee Smith Publishers & Printers
162 Fourth Ave. N.
Nashville, TN 37219-8867
Telephone: (615) 242-7395
FAX: (615) 256-6601
Ownership %: 100
**Editorial:**
James V. Meath .....................Editor
**Desc.:** Surveys of employment law developments in Virginia.

# Group 342-Libraries

70615

## ABBEY NEWSLETTER
7105 Geneva Dr.
Austin, TX 78723-1510
Telephone: (512) 929-3992
FAX: (512) 929-3995
Year Established: 1975
Pub. Frequency: 8/yr.
Subscrip. Rate: $40/yr. individuals; $49/yr. institutions
Materials: 10
Circulation: 1,300
Circulation Type: controlled & paid
**Owner(s):**
Abbey Publications, Inc.
7105 Geneva Dr.
Austin, TX 78723-1510
Telephone: (512) 929-3992
FAX: (512) 929-3995
Ownership %: 100
**Editorial:**
Ellen R. McCrady .....................Editor
**Desc.:** Covers bookbinding and conservation of book and paper materials, world wide. Includes current news and events.

70619

## ASSISTANT EDITOR
857 Twin Harbor Dr.
Ste.1300
Arnold, MD 21012-1027
Telephone: (410) 647-6708
FAX: (410) 647-0415
Year Established: 1991
Pub. Frequency: q.
Subscrip. Rate: $75/yr. US; $78/yr. CN; $90/yr. foreign
**Owner(s):**
Chris Olsen & Associates
857 Twin Harbor Dr.
Ste. 1300
Arnold, MD 21012-1027
Telephone: (410) 647-6708
FAX: (410) 647-0415
Ownership %: 100

70016

## BOOKWATCH
166 Miramar Ave.
San Francisco, CA 94112
Telephone: (415) 587-7009
Year Established: 1981
Pub. Frequency: m.
Subscrip. Rate: $12/yr.
Materials: 10,32
Circulation: 50,000
Circulation Type: controlled & paid
**Owner(s):**
Midwest Book Review
166 Miramar Ave.
San Francisco, CA 94112
Telephone: (415) 587-7009
Ownership %: 100
**Editorial:**
James A. Cox .....................Editor
Diane C. Donovan .....................Editor
**Desc.:** Capsule reviews of quality publications from large and small presses throughout the United States, targeted toward acquisitions librarians and subscribers.

69811

## FAIS NOTES
1429 Walnut St.
Philadelphia, PA 19102
Telephone: (215) 563-2406
FAX: (215) 563-2848
Pub. Frequency: m.
Subscrip. Rate: membership only
**Owner(s):**
Nat'l. Fed. of Abstracting & Information Services
1429 Walnut St.
Philadelphia, PA 19102
Telephone: (215) 563-2406
FAX: (215) 563-2848
Ownership %: 100
**Desc.:** Provides news of current developments affecting the information industry.

70618

## FOCUS: LIBRARY SERVICE TO OLDER ADULTS, PEOPLE WITH DISABILITIES
216 N. Frederick Ave.
Daytona Beach, FL 32114
Year Established: 1983
Pub. Frequency: m.
Subscrip. Rate: $12/yr.
Materials: 10
Circulation: 150
Circulation Type: controlled & paid
**Owner(s):**
Michael G. Gunde
216 N. Frederick Ave.
Daytona Beach, FL 32114
Ownership %: 100
**Management:**
Michael G. Gunde .....................Publisher
**Editorial:**
Michael G. Gunde .....................Editor

**Materials Accepted/Included:** 01-Business news 02-By-line articles 03-Fashion news 04-Food news 05-Freelance copy 06-Letters to editor 07-Real estate news 08-Sports news 09-Travel news 10-Book rev. 11-Movie rev. 12-Music rev. 13-TV rev. 14-Theater rev. 15-Coming events 16-Obituaries 17-Question & answer 18-Social announcements 19-Artwork 20-Cartoons 21-Photos 22-TV listings 23-Audio rec. 24-Video rec. 25-Books 26-Films/film clips 27-Personnel news 28-Press releases 29-New product news/photos 30-Trade lit. 31-Contracts awarded 32-Display adv. 33-Classified adv.

7-63

**Desc.:** Newsletter of library resources and sevices pertaining to elderly persons and persons with disabilities.

70596

## INFORMATION BROKER
Burwell Enterprises
Houston, TX 77068
Telephone: (713) 537-9051
FAX: (713) 537-8332
Year Established: 1978
Pub. Frequency: 6/yr.
Subscrip. Rate: $35/yr.
**Owner(s):**
Burwell Enterprises
Houston, TX 77068
Telephone: (713) 537-9051
FAX: (713) 537-8332
Ownership %: 100
**Editorial:**
Helen P. Burwell .................................Editor
**Desc.:** Newsletter for, by, and about the companies which offer information for a fee.

70631

## INFORMATION MANAGEMENT BULLETIN
4811 Jonestown Rd.
Ste. 230
Harrisburg, PA 17109-1751
Telephone: (717) 541-9150
FAX: (717) 541-9159
Year Established: 1988
Pub. Frequency: s-a.
Subscrip. Rate: $40/yr. individuals; $60/yr. institutions
Circulation: 5,000
Circulation Type: controlled & paid
**Owner(s):**
Idea Group Publishing
4811 Jonestown Rd.
Ste. 230
Harrisburg, PA 17109-1751
Telephone: (717) 541-9150
FAX: (717) 541-9159
Ownership %: 100
**Editorial:**
Medhi Khosrowpour ...............................Editor
**Desc.:** Digest of information advancements in the information resources management field. Enumerates current and future issues and trends in the field of information technology.

70624

## INFORMATION SOLUTIONS
300 Pearl St., Ste. 200
Buffalo, NY 14202
Telephone: (716) 852-2220
Year Established: 1984
Pub. Frequency: bi-m.
Subscrip. Rate: $65/yr.
**Owner(s):**
Information Plus, Inc.
300 Pearl St., Ste. 200
Buffalo, NY 14202
Telephone: (716) 852-2220
Ownership %: 100
**Editorial:**
D.C. Sawyer .........................................Editor
**Desc.:** Newsletter of ideas and techniques about how to profit from information.

70633

## INFORMATION TECHNOLOGY NEWSLETTER
4811 Jonestown Rd.
Ste. 230
Harrisburg, PA 17109-1751
Telephone: (717) 541-9150
FAX: (717) 541-5195
Year Established: 1990
Pub. Frequency: a.
Subscrip. Rate: $20/yr. individuals; $35/yr. institutions

**Owner(s):**
Idea Group Publishing
4811 Jonestown Rd.
Ste. 230
Harrisburg, PA 17109-1751
Telephone: (717) 541-9150
FAX: (717) 541-9159
Ownership %: 100
**Editorial:**
Karen Cullings .....................................Editor
**Desc.:** Designed to help librarians strategically plan aspects of implementing information technology resources.

70603

## LAC NEWSLETTER
State University of New York at Buffalo
Lockwood Library Bldg.
Buffalo, NY 14260-2200
FAX: (716) 645-5955
Mailing Address:
    285 Sharp Rd.
    Baton Rouge, LA 70815
Year Established: 1981
Pub. Frequency: q.
Subscrip. Rate: $10/yr. individuals; $16/yr. institutions
Materials: 10
Circulation: 705
Circulation Type: controlled & paid
**Owner(s):**
Online Audiovisual Cataloger, Inc.
State University of New York a
Lockwood Library Bldg.
Buffalo, NY 14260-2200
FAX: (914) 645-5955
Ownership %: 100
**Editorial:**
Susan M. Neumeister ...............................Editor
**Desc.:** For cataloguers of audiovisual media in an online enivironment.

71082

## LIBRARY HI TECH NEWS
P.O. Box 1808
Ann Arbor, MI 48106
Telephone: (313) 434-5530
FAX: (313) 434-6409
Year Established: 1984
Pub. Frequency: 10/yr.
Subscrip. Rate: $70/yr. individuals; $95/yr. institutions
Circulation: 5,000
Circulation Type: paid
**Owner(s):**
Pierian Press
P.O. Box 1808
Ann Arbor, MI 48106
Telephone: (313) 434-5530
FAX: (313) 434-6409
Ownership %: 100
**Editorial:**
C. Edward Wall ...................................Editor
**Desc.:** News about all aspects of technology related to library operations for professionals in the information management-science field.

70600

## LIBRARY ISSUES
321 S. Main St.
P.O. Box 8330
Ann Arbor, MI 48107
Telephone: (313) 662-3925
FAX: (313) 662-4450
Pub. Frequency: bi-m.
Subscrip. Rate: $35/yr.
**Owner(s):**
Mountainside Publishing, Inc.
321 S. Main St.
P.O Box 8330
Ann Arbor, MI 48107
Telephone: (313) 662-3925
FAX: (313) 662-4450
Ownership %: 100

**Editorial:**
Richard M. Dougherty .............................Editor
**Desc.:** In layman's terms, explains academic library problems as they relate to faculty, administrators, and the parent institution.

70621

## LIBRARY PR NEWS
Rd. One, P.O. Box 219
New Albany, PA 18833
Telephone: (717) 746-1842
FAX: (717) 746-1114
Year Established: 1978
Pub. Frequency: bi-m.
Subscrip. Rate: $29.95/yr. US; $31.95/yr. Canada; $40.95/yr. elsewhere
Materials: 10
Circulation: 5,000
Circulation Type: controlled & paid
**Owner(s):**
L E I, Inc.
Rd. One, P.O. Box 219
New Albany, PA 18833
Telephone: (717) 746-1842
FAX: (717) 746-1114
Ownership %: 100
**Editorial:**
Phillip J. Bradbury ...............................Editor
**Desc.:** For public, school, and academic libraries. Devoted to library public relations, programming, promotion exhibits, and graphic arts.

61255

## MICROGRAPHICS NEWSLETTER
2140 Boston Post Rd.
Larchmont, NY 10538
Telephone: (914) 834-3044
FAX: (914) 834-3993
Mailing Address:
    P.O. Box 950
    Larchmont, NY 10538
Year Established: 1969
Pub. Frequency: m.
Page Size: standard
Subscrip. Rate: $168/yr. US; $186/yr. foreign
Materials: 01,10,27,28,29,30
Freelance Pay: varies
Print Process: offset
**Owner(s):**
Microfilm Publishing, Inc.
P.O. Box 950
Larchmont, NY 10538
Telephone: (914) 834-3044
Ownership %: 100
**Management:**
Mitchell M. Badler ..........................Publisher
**Editorial:**
Mitchell M. Badler ...............................Editor
Dorothy Miceli ...................Associate Publisher
**Desc.:** Summary news, company profiles, and classified advertising pertaining to the industry, for executives who market or use services and equipment.
**Readers:** Users of microfilm, micrographics, optical disk systems, vendors, and dealers in the industry.
**Deadline:** story-end of each mo.; news-end of each mo.; photo-end of each mo.; ads-end of each mo.

70434

## MSRRT NEWSLETTER
4645 Columbus Ave. S.
Minneapolis, MN 55407
Year Established: 1988
Pub. Frequency: 10/yr.
Page Size: standard
Subscrip. Rate: $15/yr.
Materials: 10,12,15,19,20,23,24,25,30
**Owner(s):**
Minnesota Library Association
4645 Columbus Ave., S.
Minneapolis, MN 55407
Ownership %: 100

**Management:**
Christopher Dodge ............................Publisher
**Editorial:**
Christopher Dodge .................................Editor
Jan DeSirey .....................................Copy Editor
**Desc.:** Alternative news and criticism, focusing on independent media productions, small presses and magazines. Subjects covered include ethnicity, human and civil rights, labor, environment, gays and lesbians, women, peace, counter-culture and the arts.
**Readers:** Librarians, cultural workers, writers, teachers, social workers.
**Deadline:** story-20th of mo.

70606

## ONE-PERSON LIBRARY
Murray Hill Sta.
P.O. Box 948
New York, NY 10156-0614
Telephone: (212) 683-6285
Year Established: 1984
Pub. Frequency: m.
Subscrip. Rate: $75/yr. US; $80/yr. Canada; $85/yr. foreign
Materials: 10
Circulation: 2,000
Circulation Type: controlled & paid
**Owner(s):**
PL Resources, Ltd.
Murray Hill Station
P.O. Box 948
New York, NY 10156-0614
Telephone: (212) 683-6285
Ownership %: 100
**Editorial:**
Andrew Berner ...................................Editor

71084

## ONLINE LIBRARIES & MICROCOMPUTERS
P.O. Box 31098
Phoenix, AZ 85046
Telephone: (800) 228-9982
Year Established: 1983
Pub. Frequency: 10/yr.
Subscrip. Rate: $43.75/yr. individuals; $62.50/yr. institutions; $25/yr. students
Materials: 10
**Owner(s):**
Information Intelligence, Inc.
P.O. Box 31098
Phoenix, AZ 85046
Telephone: (800) 228-9982
Ownership %: 100
**Editorial:**
George S. Machovec ..............................Editor
**Desc.:** Aimed at library and information center developments and applications throughout North America. Features articles covering new online library and automation applications using a wide variety of microcomputers and software.

70623

## READMORE REPORTER
22 Cortlandt St.
New York, NY 10007
Telephone: (212) 349-5540
FAX: (212) 233-0746
Year Established: 1982
Pub. Frequency: q.
Subscrip. Rate: free
Materials: 33
Circulation: 2,100
Circulation Type: controlled & free
**Owner(s):**
Readmore Publications, Inc.
22 Cortlandt St.
New York, NY 10007
Telephone: (212) 349-5540
FAX: (212) 233-0746
Ownership %: 100
**Management:**
Lisa Bogutz ......................Advertising Manager

**Materials Accepted/Included:** 01-Business news 02-By-line articles 03-Fashion news 04-Food news 05-Freelance copy 06-Letters to editor 07-Real estate news 08-Sports news 09-Travel news 10-Book rev. 11-Movie rev. 12-Music rev. 13-TV rev. 14-Theater rev. 15-Coming events 16-Obituaries 17-Question & answer 18-Social announcements 19-Artwork 20-Cartoons 21-Photos 22-TV listings 23-Audio rec. 24-Video rec. 25-Books 26-Films/film clips 27-Personnel news 28-Press releases 29-New product news/photos 30-Trade lit. 31-Contracts awarded 32-Display adv. 33-Classified adv.

**Editorial:**
Lisa Bogutz ........................................Editor
**Desc.:** Covers developments in international periodical publishing for libraries, publishers, and CD-Rom manufacturers.

## SCHOOL LIBRARIAN'S WORKSHOP
70599

61 Greenbriar Dr.
Berkeley Heights, NJ 07922
Telephone: (201) 635-1833
FAX: (201) 635-2614
Year Established: 1980
Pub. Frequency: m.; except July & Aug.
Subscrip. Rate: $42/yr.
Circulation: 7,800
Circulation Type: controlled & paid
**Owner(s):**
Library Resources, Inc.
61 Greenbriar Dr.
Berkeley Heights, NJ 07922
Telephone: (201) 635-1833
FAX: (201) 635-2614
Ownership %: 100
**Editorial:**
Ruth Toor ........................................Editor
Hilda K. Weisburg ..............................Editor
**Desc.:** For school librarians grades K-12. Contains teaching units, professional development concerns, bulletin boards, reference questions, pencil games, and annual survey.

## TECHNOLOGY CONNECTION
71229

480 E. Wilson Bridge Rd.
Ste. L
Worthington, OH 43085
Year Established: 1994
Pub. Frequency: m. (except July & Aug.)
Subscrip. Rate: $22/yr.
**Owner(s):**
Linworth Publishing, Inc.
480 E. Wilson Bridge Rd.
Ste. L
Worthington, OH 43085
Ownership %: 100

## VIDEO LIBRARIAN
70604

P.O. Box 2725
Bremerton, WA 98310
Telephone: (206) 377-2231
FAX: (206) 373-6805
Year Established: 1986
Pub. Frequency: m.
Subscrip. Rate: $47/yr. US; $52/yr. CN; $69/yr. elsewhere
Materials: 10
Circulation: 764
Circulation Type: controlled & paid
**Owner(s):**
Video Librarian
P.O. Box 2725
Bremerton, WA 98310
Telephone: (206) 377-2231
Ownership %: 100
**Editorial:**
Randy Pitman ........................................Editor
**Desc.:** Articles, news, and reviews on the subject of video in public and school libraries.

## YARDSTICK
70650

56 Top Gallant Rd.
Stamford, CT 06902
Telephone: (203) 000-0006
FAX: (203) 967-6191
Year Established: 1979
Pub. Frequency: q.
Subscrip. Rate: $2000/yr.
Circulation: 130
Circulation Type: controlled & paid

**Owner(s):**
Gartner Group
56 Top Gallant Rd.
Stamford, CT 06902
Telephone: (203) 964-0096
FAX: (203) 967-6191
Ownership %: 100
**Editorial:**
Randall F. Brophy ..............................Editor
**Desc.:** Market reference data on the information processing industry worldwide, for planning professionals, consultants, market researchers and investors.

## Group 344-Literature

### AFRICAN AMERICAN LITERARY REVIEW
71172

5381 La Paseo, Ste. 105
Fort Worth, TX 76112
Telephone: (817) 429-6150
FAX: (817) 336-7527
Year Established: 1993
Pub. Frequency: q.
Subscrip. Rate: $12/yr. individuals; $15/yr. institutions
Materials: 10
Circulation: 800
Circulation Type: controlled & paid
**Owner(s):**
John Posey
5381 La Paseo, Ste. 105
Fort Worth, TX 76112
Telephone: (817) 429-6150
FAX: (817) 336-7527
Ownership %: 100
**Management:**
John Posey ..............................Publisher
**Editorial:**
Monica Marchi ........................................Editor

### CAROUSEL
69484

4508 Walsh St.
Bethesda, MD 20815
Telephone: (301) 654-8664
Year Established: 1977
Pub. Frequency: bi-m.
Subscrip. Rate: $30/yr.
**Owner(s):**
Writer's Center
4508 Walsh St.
Bethesda, MD 20815
Telephone: (301) 654-8664
Ownership %: 100
**Editorial:**
A. Lefcowitz ........................................Editor

### FAULKNER NEWSLETTER & YOKNAPATAWPHA REVIEW
70634

739 Clematis Dr.
Nashville, TN 37205
Telephone: (601) 234-0909
Year Established: 1981
Pub. Frequency: q.
Subscrip. Rate: $12.50/yr.; $15; yr. foreign
Materials: 10,33
Circulation: 500
Circulation Type: controlled & paid
**Owner(s):**
Yoknapatawpha Press
739 Clematis Dr.
Nashville, TN 37205
Telephone: (601) 234-0909
Ownership %: 100
**Management:**
William Boozer ..............................President
**Desc.:** Devoted to the life and works of William Faulkner.

### IT GOES ON THE SHELF
71192

713 Paul St.
Newport News, VA 23605
Telephone: (804) 380-6595
Year Established: 1979
Pub. Frequency: irreg.
Subscrip. Rate: free
Materials: 10,32
Circulation: 350
Circulation Type: controlled & paid
**Owner(s):**
Purple Mouth Press
713 Paul St.
Newport News, VA 23605
Telephone: (804) 380-6595
Ownership %: 100
**Editorial:**
Ned Brooks ........................................Editor
**Desc.:** Reviews books and related materials of interest to science fiction and fantasy readers and collectors.

### MINNESOTA LITERATURE
70605

1 Nord Circle
St. Paul, MN 55127
Telephone: (612) 483-3904
Year Established: 1973
Pub. Frequency: m. (Sep.-June)
Subscrip. Rate: $10+/yr.
Materials: 32
Circulation: 750
Circulation Type: controlled & paid
**Owner(s):**
Minnesota Literature
1 Nord Circle
St. Paul, MN 55127
Telephone: (612) 483-3904
Ownership %: 100
**Editorial:**
Mary Bround Smith ..............................Editor
**Desc.:** Announcements, opportunities, and publication news affecting writers and supporters of literature in the state. Also includes opinion essays.

### NEW LOVECRAFT COLLECTOR
71196

P.O. Box 1304
West Warwick, RI 02893
Telephone: (401) 828-7161
FAX: (401) 738-6125
Year Established: 1993
Pub. Frequency: q.
Subscrip. Rate: $5/yr. US; $7/yr. foreign
**Owner(s):**
Necronomicon Press
P.O. Box 1304
West Warwick, RI 02893
Telephone: (401) 828-7161
FAX: (401) 738-6125
Ownership %: 100
**Desc.:** Covers past, present, and forthcoming publications and adaptations of works by H.P. Lovecraft, including appearances in anthologies, translations, movies and non-book oddities. Also discusses noteworthy editions, advice to collectors, and a sampling of current prices.

### POETRY PROJECT NEWSLETTER
70611

St. Mark's Church in-the-Bowery
131 E. Tenth St.
New York, NY 10003
Telephone: (212) 674-0910
Year Established: 1967
Pub. Frequency: 4/yr.
Subscrip. Rate: $20/yr.
Materials: 10,32
Circulation: 3,500
Circulation Type: controlled & paid

**Owner(s):**
Poetry Project Ltd.
St. Mark's Church in-the-Bower
131 E. Tenth St.
New York, NY 10003
Telephone: (212) 674-0910
Ownership %: 100
**Desc.:** Contains poetry, articles, transcripts of symposia presentations, and annotated calendars of readings and events at the Poetry Project.

### RISING STAR
71176

47 Byledge Rd.
Manchester, NH 03104
Telephone: (603) 623-9796
Year Established: 1983
Pub. Frequency: bi-m.
Subscrip. Rate: $7.50/yr.
Materials: 10, 32
Circulation: 120
Circulation Type: controlled & paid
**Owner(s):**
Star-Sword Publications
47 Byledge Rd.
Manchester, NH 03104
Telephone: (603) 623-9796
Ownership %: 100
**Editorial:**
Scott E. Green ........................................Editor
**Desc.:** Publishes market information for writers and artists in the sci-fi, fantasy and horror genres.

### SCIENCE FICTION & FANTASY WORKSHOP
71179

1193 S. 1900 E.
Salt Lake City, UT 84108
Telephone: (801) 582-2090
Year Established: 1980
Pub. Frequency: m.
Subscrip. Rate: $10/yr.
Circulation: 450
Circulation Type: controlled & paid
**Owner(s):**
Science Fiction & Fantasy Workshop
1193 S. 1900 E.
Salt Lake City, UT 84108
Telephone: (801) 582-2090
Ownership %: 100
**Editorial:**
Kathleen D. Woodbury ........................Editor
**Desc.:** Covers writing and marketing of science fiction, fantasy and horror stories of all lengths.

### TALKING RAVEN
69607

P.O. Box 45758
Seattle, WA 98145
Telephone: (206) 781-5691
Year Established: 1991
Pub. Frequency: q.
Subscrip. Rate: $11/yr.
Circulation: 5,000
**Owner(s):**
ParaTheatrical Research
P.O. Box 45758
Seattle, WA 98145
Telephone: (206) 781-5691
Ownership %: 100
**Desc.:** Publishes poetry, fiction, essays, brief interviews, and artwork with an emphasis on rebelliousness. Each issue is devoted to a single theme.

### WOMAN OF MYSTERY
70646

P.O. Box 1616
Canal St. Sta.
New York, NY 10013
Telephone: (212) 732-5154
Year Established: 1986
Pub. Frequency: m.
Subscrip. Rate: $30/yr.

**Materials Accepted/Included:** 01-Business news 02-By-line articles 03-Fashion news 04-Food news 05-Freelance copy 06-Letters to editor 07-Real estate news 08-Sports news 09-Travel news 10-Book rev. 11-Movie rev. 12-Music rev. 13-TV rev. 14-Theater rev. 15-Coming events 16-Obituaries 17-Question & answer 18-Social announcements 19-Artwork 20-Cartoons 21-Photos 22-TV listings 23-Audio rec. 24-Video rec. 25-Books 26-Films/film clips 27-Personnel news 28-Press releases 29-New product news/photos 30-Trade lit. 31-Contracts awarded 32-Display adv. 33-Classified adv.

7-65

Circulation: 600
Circulation Type: controlled & paid
**Owner(s):**
Wom'n
P.O. box 1616
Canal St. Sta.
New York, NY 10013
Telephone: (212) 732-5154
Ownership %: 100
**Editorial:**
Amy Lubelski ............................Editor
**Desc.:** Devoted to annotating the mystery novels of Agatha Christie.

## Group 346-Medicine & Health

**ADHD REPORT** 70804
72 Spring St.
New York, NY 10012
Telephone: (212) 431-9800
FAX: (212) 966-6708
Year Established: 1993
Pub. Frequency: bi-m.
Subscrip. Rate: $65/yr.; $70/yr. foreign individuals; $80/yr. foreign institutions
Materials: 10,33
**Owner(s):**
Guilford Publications, Inc.
72 Spring St.
New York, NY 10012
Telephone: (212) 431-9800
FAX: (212) 966-6708
Ownership %: 100
**Editorial:**
Russell A. Barkley ....................Editor
**Desc.:** Offers relevant information from research, workshops, and clinical work on ADHD, as well as from recent scientific publications and conferences from around the world.

**ADULT DAY CARE LETTER** 70314
Brinley Professional Plaza
3100 Hwy. 138
Wall Township, NJ 07719-1442
Telephone: (908) 681-0490
FAX: (908) 681-0490
Mailing Address:
  P.O. Box 1442
  Wall Township, NJ 07719-1442
Year Established: 1985
Pub. Frequency: m.
Subscrip. Rate: $127/yr.
**Owner(s):**
Health Resources Publishing
Brinley Professional Plaza
3100 Hwy. 138
Wall Township, NJ 07719-1442
Telephone: (908) 681-1133
FAX: (908) 681-0490
Ownership %: 100
**Editorial:**
Robert K. Jenkins ....................Editor
**Desc.:** Provides administrators and directors with current news on the services involved in running an adult day care center including social services health care, mental health, nutrition, recreation and rehabilitation activities.

**AFTERLOSS** 70649
P.O. Box 599
Summerland, CA 93067-0599
Telephone: (805) 969-6666
FAX: (805) 565-3369
Year Established: 1989
Pub. Frequency: m.
Subscrip. Rate: $48/yr.
Circulation: 2,000
Circulation Type: controlled & paid

**Owner(s):**
Harbor House Publishers, Inc.
P.O. Box 599
Summerland, CA 93067-0599
Telephone: (805) 969-6666
FAX: (805) 565-3365
Ownership %: 100
**Editorial:**
Margie Kennedy-Reeves ..........Editor
**Desc.:** Deals with the management of and education about grief following the death of a loved one. Functions to help the survivors deal with the death of a spouse, child, other relations, and friends.

**AIDS REPORT** 70981
2 Corporate Dr.
Trumbull, CT 06611
Telephone: (203) 261-8587
FAX: (203) 261-9724
Mailing Address:
  P.O. Box 374
  Trumbull, CT 06611
Year Established: 1987
Pub. Frequency: m.
Page Size: 10
Subscrip. Rate: $27/yr.
**Owner(s):**
Food & Nutrition Press, Inc.
2 Corporate Dr.
Trumbull, CT 06611
Telephone: (203) 261-8587
**Editorial:**
Gerald C. Melson ....................Editor
**Desc.:** Dedicated to the distribution of information on AIDS. Provides current developments in the medical, social, economic, regulatory, and political aspects of AIDS.

**AIDS TREATMENT NEWS** 70986
San Francisco, CA 94141
Telephone: (415) 255-0588
FAX: (415) 255-4659
Mailing Address:
  P.O. Box 411256
  San Francisco, CA 94141
Year Established: 1986
Pub. Frequency: s-m.
Subscrip. Rate: $230/yr.; $100/yr. institutions
Materials: 10
Circulation: 6,000
Circulation Type: controlled & paid
**Owner(s):**
ATN Publications
P.O. Box 411256
San Francisco, CA 94141
Telephone: (415) 255-0588
Ownership %: 100
**Editorial:**
John S. James ..........................Editor
**Desc.:** Chronicles current developments in experimental and alternative treatments and deals with public policy issues.

**ALCOHOL & DRUG ABUSE PULSE BEATS NEWSLETTER** 70729
P.O. Box 24244
Louisville, KY 40224
Telephone: (502) 491-5857
FAX: (502) 491-5905
Year Established: 1984
Pub. Frequency: m.
Subscrip. Rate: $57/yr.
**Owner(s):**
Insurance Field Co.
P.O. Box 24244
Louisville, KY 50200-4917
Telephone: (502) 491-5857
FAX: (502) 491-5905
Ownership %: 100

**Editorial:**
George Smith ............................Editor
**Desc.:** Provides current information in all areas of alcohol and drug abuse.

**ALCOHOL & DRUG ABUSE WEEKLY** 70728
P.O. Box 3357
Providence, RI 02906-0757
Telephone: (800) 333-7771
FAX: (401) 861-6370
Year Established: 1986
Pub. Frequency: w.
Subscrip. Rate: $297/yr. individuals; $317/yr. Canada; $437/yr. elsewhere
**Owner(s):**
Manisses Communications Group, Inc.
P.O. Box 3357
Providence, RI 02906-0757
Telephone: (800) 333-7771
FAX: (401) 861-6370
Ownership %: 100
**Editorial:**
Robert Curley ..........................Editor
**Desc.:** Covers public policy and economic issues for those in the public, private and non-profit sectors.

**ALTERNATIVES** 70695
P.O. Box 829
Ingram, TX 78025
Telephone: (512) 367-4492
Year Established: 1989
Pub. Frequency: bi-m.
**Owner(s):**
Mountain Home Publishing
P.O. Box 829
Ingram, TX 78025
Telephone: (512) 367-4492
Ownership %: 100

**ALZHEIMER'S ASSOCIATION NEWSLETTER** 70319
919 N. Michigan Ave.
Ste. 1000
Chicago, IL 60611-1676
Telephone: (312) 335-8700
FAX: (312) 335-1110
Year Established: 1981
Pub. Frequency: q.
Subscrip. Rate: free
Materials: 10
Circulation: 650,000
Circulation Type: controlled & free
**Owner(s):**
Alzheimer's Association, Inc.
919 N. Michigan Ave.
Ste. 1000
Chicago, IL 60611-1676
Telephone: (312) 335-8700
FAX: (312) 335-1110
Ownership %: 100
**Editorial:**
Mary Anne Pecora ....................Editor

**ANRED ALERT** 70836
P.O. Box 5102
Eugene, OR 97405
Telephone: (503) 344-1144
Year Established: 1979
Pub. Frequency: 10/yr.
Subscrip. Rate: $10/yr.
Materials: 10
Circulation: 15,000
Circulation Type: controlled & paid
**Owner(s):**
Anorexia Nervosa & Related Eating Disorders, Inc.
P.O. Box 5102
Eugene, OR 97405
Telephone: (503) 344-1144
Ownership %: 100

**Editorial:**
Dr. J. Bradley Rubel ................Editor
**Desc.:** Causes, consequences, symptoms, and treatment of anorexia nervosa and bulimia nervosa.

**ARTHUR ANDERSON WASHINGTON HEALTHCARE NEWSLETTER** 70515
1666 K St., NW
Washington, DC 20006
Telephone: (202) 862-6732
FAX: (202) 862-7098
Pub. Frequency: 11/yr.
Subscrip. Rate: free
**Owner(s):**
Arthur Andersen & Co.
1666 K St.
Washington, DC 20006
Telephone: (202) 862-6732
FAX: (202) 862-7098
Ownership %: 100
**Editorial:**
Don Yesukaitis ........................Editor

**ASPEN'S NURSE EXECUTIVE NETWORK** 70666
200 Orchard Ridge Dr.
Gaithersburg, MD 20878
Telephone: (301) 417-7500
FAX: (301) 417-7550
Year Established: 1985
Pub. Frequency: m.
Subscrip. Rate: $145/yr. US; $174/yr. foreign
**Owner(s):**
Aspen Publishers, Inc.
200 Orchard Ridge Dr.
Gaithersburg, MD 20878
Telephone: (301) 417-7500
FAX: (301) 417-7550
Ownership %: 100

**ASTHMA & ALLERGY ADVOCATE** 70978
611 E. Wells St.
Milwaukee, WI 53202
Telephone: (414) 272-6071
FAX: (414) 276-2349
Year Established: 1985
Pub. Frequency: q.
Subscrip. Rate: $70/yr.
Materials: 10
Circulation: 75,000
Circulation Type: controlled & paid
**Owner(s):**
American Academy of Allergy & Immunology
611 E. Wells St.
Milwaukee, WI 53202
Telephone: (414) 272-6071
Ownership %: 100
**Editorial:**
S.E. Kaluzny ............................Editor
**Desc.:** Patient newsletter with information in the field

**ASTHMA UPDATE** 71010
123 Monticello Ave.
Annapolis, MD 21401
Telephone: (410) 267-8329
FAX: (410) 267-0309
Year Established: 1985
Pub. Frequency: q.
Subscrip. Rate: $10/yr.
**Owner(s):**
David Jamison
123 Monticello Ave.
Annapolis, MD 21401
Telephone: (410) 267-8329
FAX: (410) 267-0309
Ownership %: 100
**Editorial:**
David Jamison ..........................Editor

**Desc.:** Contains annotated abstracts from current medical journals.
**Readers:** Newsletter for people with asthma.

## ATIN: AIDS TARGETED INFORMATION NEWSLETTER
428 E. Preston St.
Baltimore, MD 21202
Telephone: (410) 528-4000
FAX: (410) 528-4312
Year Established: 1987
Pub. Frequency: m.
Page Size: standard
Subscrip. Rate: $295/yr. individual;
  $350/yr. institution
Circulation: 8,500
Circulation Type: paid
**Owner(s):**
Williams & Wilkins Co.
428 E. Preston St.
Baltimore, MD 21202
Telephone: (410) 528-4000
Ownership %: 100
**Management:**
Don Pfarr ............................Advertising Manager
Alma Wills .....................................Manager
**Editorial:**
Russell E. McDonald, Ph.D. ......................Editor
Nancy Collins ........................Marketing Director
**Desc.:** Compendium of the latest articles on medical knowledge and research about AIDS from over 300 journals.

## BIOLOGICAL THERAPIES IN PSYCHIATRY NEWSLETTER
11830 Westline Industrial Dr.
St. Louis, MO 63146
Telephone: (800) 325-4177
Year Established: 1977
Pub. Frequency: m.
Page Size: standard
Subscrip. Rate: $52/yr. individuals; $70/yr. institutions
Circulation: 6,000
Circulation Type: paid
**Owner(s):**
Mosby-Year Book, Inc.
11830 Westline Industrial Dr.
St. Louis, MO 63146
Telephone: (800) 325-4177
Ownership %: 100
**Editorial:**
Dr. Alan J. Gelenberg ..............................Editor
**Desc.:** Provides updates on the clinical use of psychotropic drugs to practicing psychiatrists, psychiatric house staff, residents and students.

## BIOMEDICAL SAFETY & STANDARDS NEWSLETTER
1351 Titan Way
Brea, CA 92621-3787
Telephone: (714) 738-6400
Year Established: 1971
Pub. Frequency: s-m.; m. Jan. & Aug.
Page Size: standard
Subscrip. Rate: $210/yr. US; $248/yr. foreign
Materials: 10
**Owner(s):**
Quest Publishing Co.
1351 Titan Way
Brea, CA 92621-3787
Telephone: (714) 738-6400
Ownership %: 100
**Management:**
Allan F. Pacela .............................Publisher
**Editorial:**
Gregory Nighshowner ..............Managing Editor

**Desc.:** Covers the safety of medical products, medical devices and facilities. Covers hazardous products, recalls, standards, regulations, and government activities that affect safety. Reviews law suits, publications, and meetings on topic of medical device safety.
**Readers:** Primarily read by biomedical and clinical engineers and technicians located in hospitals throughout the U.S. and 38 other countries. Also read by hospital administrators, clinical personnel, medical device industry personnel, and investment analysts.

## BRIEFINGS ON PRACTICE MANAGEMENT
P.O. Box 1168
Marblehead, MA 00005
Telephone: (617) 639-1872
FAX: (617) 639-2982
Pub. Frequency: m.
**Owner(s):**
Opus Communications
P.O. Box 1168
Marblehead, MA 01945
Telephone: (617) 639-1872
FAX: (617) 639-2982
Ownership %: 100
**Desc.:** Provides information on effective medical practice management, including compliance and regulations, reimbursement, money management, and related issues such as managed care.

## CARETAKER GAZETTE
221 Wychwood Rd.
Westfield, NJ 07090-1933
Telephone: (908) 654-6600
Year Established: 1983
Pub. Frequency: bi-m.
Subscrip. Rate: $18/yr.
Circulation: 2,000
Circulation Type: controlled & paid
**Owner(s):**
Dunn, Inc.
221 Wychwood Rd.
Westfield, NJ 07090-1933
Telephone: (908) 654-6600
Ownership %: 100
**Management:**
Gary C. Dunn ...........................Publisher
**Editorial:**
Thea K. Dunn ...............................Editor
**Desc.:** Provides information on caretaker positions available in U.S. and abroad, includes reader correspondence and profiles successful caretakers. Provides free ads for landowners seeking to hire caretakers.

## CHRONIC PAIN LETTER
P.O. Box 1303 Old Chelsea Sta.
New York, NY 10011
Telephone: (212) 614-9266
Year Established: 1984
Pub. Frequency: bi-m.
Subscrip. Rate: $20/yr. individuals; $35/yr. institutions & professionals
**Owner(s):**
Robert J. Fabian Memorial Foundation
P.O. Box 1303 Old Chelsea Sta.
New York, NY 10011
Telephone: (718) 797-0015
Ownership %: 100
**Editorial:**
Alice Delury ...............................Editor
**Desc.:** Contains current information on the management of chronic pain for the sufferer and the professional.

## CIVIL ABOLITIONIST
P.O. Box 26
Swain, NY 14884
Telephone: (607) 545-6213
Year Established: 1986
Pub. Frequency: q.
Subscrip. Rate: $5/yr.
**Owner(s):**
Civil Abolitionist
P.O. Box 26
Swain, NY 14884
Telephone: (607) 545-6213
Ownership %: 100
**Editorial:**
Bina Robinson ...............................Editor
**Desc.:** Aims to promote better human health care (as opposed to sickness care), by abolishing the practice of vivisection, i.e. animal experimentation.

## CLINICAL CANCER LETTER
P.O. Box 15189
Washington, DC 20003
Telephone: (202) 543-7665
FAX: (202) 543-6879
Year Established: 1978
Pub. Frequency: m.
Subscrip. Rate: $65/yr. US; $77/yr. foreign
**Owner(s):**
Cancer Letter Inc.
P.O. Box 15189
Washington, DC 20003
Telephone: (202) 543-7665
Ownership %: 100
**Editorial:**
Kirsten B. Goldberg ...............................Editor
**Desc.:** Covers new clinical developments, clinical trials, and research on cancer.

## CLINICAL IMMUNOLOGY NEWSLETTER
655 Ave. of the Americas
New York, NY 10010
Telephone: (212) 989-5800
FAX: (212) 633-3990
Year Established: 1980
Pub. Frequency: m.
Subscrip. Rate: $168/yr. US; $217/yr. foreign
**Owner(s):**
Elsevier Science Publishing Co., Inc.
655 Ave. of the Americas
New York, NY 10010
Telephone: (212) 989-5800
Ownership %: 100
**Editorial:**
Alan L. Landay ...............................Editor
Henry Homburger ...............................Editor
**Desc.:** For clinical immunologists, pathologists, microbiologists & infectious disease physicians

## CLINICAL INVESTIGATOR NEWS
33 Bleeker St.
Millburn, NJ 07041
Telephone: (201) 379-7749
FAX: (201) 379-1158
Mailing Address:
  P.O. Box 218
  Maplewood, NJ 07040-0218
Year Established: 1993
Pub. Frequency: m.
Page Size: standard
Subscrip. Rate: $628/yr. US; $658/yr. foreign
Materials: 01,15,27,28,29,30,31,
Print Process: offset

**Owner(s):**
CTB International Publishing, Inc.
P.O. Box 218
Maplewood, NJ 07040-0218
Telephone: (201) 379-7749
FAX: (201) 379-1158
Ownership %: 100
**Management:**
Oykue Brogna ..............................President
William Robinson ...............Circulation Manager
**Editorial:**
Christopher Brogna .....................Editor in Chief
Mark Via ...............................Editor
**Desc.:** Covers new drug study opportunities, which companies are targeting, what compounds, when they plan to begin trials, and where they stand in their research.
**Readers:** Presidents, researchers and executives in upper management.

## CLINICAL LAB LETTER
1351 Titan Way
Brea, CA 92621
Telephone: (714) 738-6400
Year Established: 1980
Pub. Frequency: s-m.
Page Size: standard
Subscrip. Rate: $204/yr. US, Mexico & Canada; $242/yr. airmail
**Owner(s):**
Quest Publishing Co.
1351 Titan Way
Brea, CA 92621
Telephone: (714) 738-6400
Ownership %: 100
**Management:**
Allan F. Pacela .............................Publisher
**Editorial:**
Gregory F. Nighshowner .........Managing Editor
**Desc.:** Written exclusively for clinical lab personnel; this newsletter presents timely, factual reports on the technology, regulations, and important issues affecting the clinical lab. Included are accurate, verified reports of potential safety hazards and product recalls involving lab equipment or diagnostic products. We welcome new product and new technology news releases in the health care field.
**Readers:** Clinical personnel, technologists, technicians, lab supervisors, hospital administrators, manufacturers, research labs and government agencies.

## CLINICAL TRIALS MONITOR
33 Bleeker St.
Millburn, NJ 07041
Telephone: (201) 379-7749
FAX: (201) 379-1158
Mailing Address:
  P.O. Box 218
  Maplewood, NJ 07040-0218
Year Established: 1992
Pub. Frequency: m.
Page Size: standard
Subscrip. Rate: $1102/yr. U.S. & Canada; $1164/yr. foreign
Materials: 01,15,27,28,29,30,31
Print Process: offset
**Owner(s):**
CTB International Publishing, Inc.
P.O. Box 218
Maplewood, NJ 07040-0218
Telephone: (201) 379-7749
FAX: (201) 379-1158
Ownership %: 100
**Management:**
Oykue Brogna ..............................President
William Robinson ...............Circulation Manager
**Editorial:**
Christopher Brogna ................Editor in Chief
Christina Petrolas ...............................Editor

**Materials Accepted/Included:** 01-Business news 02-By-line articles 03-Fashion news 04-Food news 05-Freelance copy 06-Letters to editor 07-Real estate news 08-Sports news 09-Travel news 10-Book rev. 11-Movie rev. 12-Music rev. 13-TV rev. 14-Theater rev. 15-Coming events 16-Obituaries 17-Question & answer 18-Social announcements 19-Artwork 20-Cartoons 21-Photos 22-TV listings 23-Audio rec. 24-Video rec. 25-Books 26-Films/film clips 27-Personnel news 28-Press releases 29-New product news/photos 30-Trade lit. 31-Contracts awarded 32-Display adv. 33-Classified adv.

7-67

Mark Via ..............................................Editor
Susan Krakowiecki ............................Editor
**Desc.:** Tracks clinical trials of drugs, in
vivo imaging agents and extra corpeal
therapies from beginning to end.
Sections include: Trials Planned, Trials
Underway, Contractors Sought,
Cancellations/Suspensions; results
presented at meetings and published
results.
**Readers:** Presidents, researchers and
executives in upper management.

70694
## COLON & RECTAL SURGERY
## OUTLOOK
11970 Borman Dr.
Ste. 222
St. Louis, MO 63146
Telephone: (800) 423-6865
FAX: (314) 878-9937
Year Established: 1988
Pub. Frequency: 10/yr.
Subscrip. Rate: $145/yr. individuals;
$194.50/yr. foreign individuals; $224/yr.
institutions; $281.50/yr. foreign
institutions
**Owner(s):**
Quality Medical Publishing, Inc.
11970 Borman Dr.
Ste. 222
St. Louis, MO 63146
Telephone: (800) 423-6865
FAX: (314) 878-9937
Ownership %: 100
**Editorial:**
Dr. Theodore R. Schrock ......................Editor

58706
## CRITICAL CARE NURSING
## QUARTERLY
200 Orchard Ridge Dr.
Gaithersburg, MD 20878
Telephone: (301) 698-7100
Year Established: 1978
Pub. Frequency: q.
Page Size: standard
Subscrip. Rate: $63/yr. US; $76/yr. foreign
Materials: 06,10,15,32
Print Process: DTP
Circulation: 4,429
Circulation Type: paid
**Owner(s):**
Aspen Publishers, Inc.
200 Orchard Ridge Dr.
Gaithersburg, MD 20878
Telephone: (301) 417-7500
Ownership %: 100
**Editorial:**
Lenda Hill ..............................Managing Editor
Jane Garwood ....................Acquisitions Editor
Jack Bruggeman ...............Associate Publisher
**Desc.:** Peer reviewed journal providing
current practice-oriented information for
the continuing education and improved
clinical care professionals, including
nurses, physicians and allied health care
professionals.
**Readers:** Critical care nurses and
physicians, ICU department, graduate
programs in critical care nursing.

70675
## DENTAL OFFICE
225 N. New Rd.
Waco, TX 76710
Telephone: (817) 776-9000
FAX: (817) 776-9018
Year Established: 1981
Pub. Frequency: m.
Subscrip. Rate: $79/yr.
Materials: 32
Circulation: 7,000
Circulation Type: controlled & paid

**Owner(s):**
Stevens Publishing Corporation
225 N. New Rd.
Waco, TX 76710
Telephone: (817) 776-9000
Ownership %: 100
**Editorial:**
Kathy Witherspoon ......................................Editor

70682
## DENTIST'S PATIENT
## NEWSLETTER
P.O. Box 11177
Lancaster, PA 17605
Telephone: (717) 393-1010
Year Established: 1983
Pub. Frequency: q.
Subscrip. Rate: $398/qtr. 500 copies
**Owner(s):**
Doctor's Press
P.O. Box 11177
Lancaster, PA 17605-1177
Telephone: (717) 393-1010
Ownership %: 100
**Editorial:**
Lee Dmitzak ..............................................Editor
**Desc.:** Provides dental health information
for dentists to use to market their
practice.

70678
## DEVICES & DIAGNOSTICS LETTER
1117 N. 19th St.
Ste. 200
Arlington, VA 22209
Telephone: (703) 247-3434
FAX: (703) 247-3421
Year Established: 1974
Pub. Frequency: w.
Subscrip. Rate: $627/yr.
**Owner(s):**
Washington Business Information, Inc.
1117 N. 19th St., Ste. 200
c/o Karen Harrington
Arlington, VA 22209
Telephone: (703) 247-3434
FAX: (703) 247-3421
Ownership %: 100
**Editorial:**
Steve Mardon ...............................................Editor
**Desc.:** For business leaders concerned
with government regulation of medical
devices and in vitro diagnostics. Covers
compliance and inspection programs,
defect reporting, labeling, and testing
rules.

69293
## DIAGNOSTICS INTELLIGENCE
1980 Springfield Ave.
Maplewood, NJ 07040
Telephone: (201) 379-7749
FAX: (201) 379-1158
Mailing Address:
P.O. Box 218
Maplewood, NJ 07040-0218
Year Established: 1989
Pub. Frequency: m.
Page Size: standard
Subscrip. Rate: $389/yr. US; $409/yr.
foreign
Materials: 01,15,27,28,29,30,31
Freelance Pay: negotiable
Print Process: offset
**Owner(s):**
CTB International Publishing, Inc.
P.O. Box 218
Maplewood, NJ 07040-0218
Telephone: (201) 379-7749
FAX: (201) 379-1158
Ownership %: 100
**Management:**
Oykue Brogna .........................................President
William Robinson ...............Circulation Manager
**Editorial:**
Christopher Brogna ....................Editor in Chief
David Richards ..........................................Editor

Christina Petroulas ..............................Editor
**Desc.:** Covers the latest research, new
markets, new products, regulatory
affairs, patents, litigations, business
opportunities, finance and more on the
in-vitro diagnostics field.
**Readers:** Presidents, researchers, and
executives in upper-management.

70755
## DICKINSON'S FDA INSPECTION
P.O. Box 367
La Cruces, NM 88004
Telephone: (505) 527-8634
FAX: (505) 527-8858
Year Established: 1992
Pub. Frequency: s-m.
Subscrip. Rate: $395/yr.; $455/yr. foreign
**Owner(s):**
Ferdic Inc.
P.O. Box 367
Las Cruces, NM 88004
Telephone: (505) 527-8634
FAX: (505) 527-8858
Ownership %: 100
**Editorial:**
James G. Dickinson ...................................Editor

22753
## DLANY NEWSLETTER
42-01 215 Pl.
Flushing, NY 11361
Telephone: (718) 229-1001
FAX: (718) 224-9661
Year Established: 1929
Pub. Frequency: m.
Page Size: standard
Subscrip. Rate: $12/yr.
Circulation: 1,500
Circulation Type: paid
**Owner(s):**
Dental Lab Assn. of the State of New
York, Inc.
42-01 215 Pl.
Flushing, NY 11361
Telephone: (718) 229-1001
Ownership %: 100
**Bureau(s):**
Dental Lab. Assn.-State-NY, Inc.
42 - 01 215 Pl.
Flushing, NY 11361
Telephone: (712) 229-1001
**Management:**
Paul Barton ...........................................President
Mark J. Polevoy ...................................Publisher
Mark J. Polevoy ....................Executive Director
**Editorial:**
Teresa M. Sager .........................................Editor
Teresa M. Sager .................New Products Editor
**Desc.:** Trade association newsletter of
interest to owners & operators of
commercial dental laboratories and
dentists with G. P. including prosthetics.
**Readers:** Dental laboratories, dentists,
distributors to dentists & labs.

70739
## DOCTOR'S OFFICE
1861 Colonial Village Ln.
Lancaster, PA 17605-0488
Telephone: (800) 331-5196
Mailing Address:
P.O. Box 10488
Lancaster, PA 17605
Year Established: 1982
Pub. Frequency: m.
Subscrip. Rate: $98/yr.
**Owner(s):**
Wentworth Publishing
1861 Colonia Village Ln.
Lancaster, PA 17605-0488
Ownership %: 100
**Editorial:**
Ann Mead Ash .........................................Editor

**Desc.:** Provides information to clarify
insurance regulations, collection
techniques, marketing ideas and other
practice management techniques.

70740
## DR. ALEXANDER GRANT'S
## HEALTH GAZETTE
P.O. Box 1786
Indianapolis, IN 46206
Telephone: (317) 253-8582
Year Established: 1978
Pub. Frequency: 10/yr.
Subscrip. Rate: $21.95/yr.
Circulation: 40,000
Circulation Type: controlled & paid
**Owner(s):**
Alexander Grant & Associates, Inc.
P.O. Box 1786
Indianapolis, IN 46206
Telephone: (317) 253-8582
Ownership %: 100
**Desc.:** Monthly digest of medical facts and
news.

70636
## DRUG ABUSE & ALCOHOLISM
## NEWSLETTER
2355 Northside Dr.
San Diego, CA 92108-2705
Telephone: (619) 563-1770
Year Established: 1971
Pub. Frequency: 6/yr.
Page Size: tabloid
Subscrip. Rate: Free
Circulation: 32500
Circulation Type: free
**Owner(s):**
Vista Hill Foundation
2355 Northside Dr.
San Diego, CA 92180-2705
Telephone: (619) 563-1770
Ownership %: 100

70762
## DRUG GMP REPORT
c/o Karen Harrington
1117 N. 19th St.
Arlington, VA 22209
Telephone: (703) 247-3434
FAX: (703) 247-3421
Year Established: 1992
Pub. Frequency: m.
Subscrip. Rate: $39/yr.
**Owner(s):**
Washington Business Information, Inc.
1117 N. 19th St.
Arlington, VA 22209
Telephone: (703) 247-3434
FAX: (703) 247-3421
Ownership %: 100
**Editorial:**
Dennis Melamed ........................................Editor
**Desc.:** Reports on good manufacturing
practices as they relate to the
pharmaceutical industry.

70766
## DRUG NEWSLETTER
111 W. Port Plaza
Ste. 423
St. Louis, MO 63146-3098
Telephone: (800) 223-0554
FAX: (314) 878-5563
Pub. Frequency: m.
Subscrip. Rate: $54/yr.
**Owner(s):**
Facts and Comparisons
111 W. Port Plaza
Ste. 423
St. Louis, MO 63146-3098
Telephone: (800) 223-0554
FAX: (314) 878-5563
Ownership %: 100

---

**Materials Accepted/Included:** 01-Business news 02-By-line articles 03-Fashion news 04-Food news 05-Freelance copy 06-Letters to editor 07-Real estate news 08-Sports news 09-Travel news 10-Book rev. 11-Movie rev. 12-Music rev. 13-TV rev. 14-Theater rev. 15-Coming events 16-Obituaries 17-Question & answer 18-Social announcements 19-Artwork 20-Cartoons 21-Photos 22-TV listings 23-Audio rec. 24-Video rec. 25-Books 26-Films/film clips 27-Personnel news 28-Press releases 29-New product news/photos 30-Trade lit. 31-Contracts awarded 32-Display adv. 33-Classified adv.

**Desc.:** Summarizes new findings and recent developments in drug therapy. Information on investigational drugs, OTC's, actions, reactions and interactions, and more.

67654

## DRUGS IN THE WORKPLACE
817 Broadway, Third Fl.
New York, NY 10003
Telephone: (212) 673-4700
FAX: (212) 475-1790
Year Established: 1986
Pub. Frequency: m.
Page Size: standard
Subscrip. Rate: $245/yr.
**Owner(s):**
Business Research Publications, Inc.
817 Broadway, Third Fl.
New York, NY 10003
Telephone: (212) 673-4700
Ownership %: 100
**Management:**
John Roche ........................................Publisher
**Editorial:**
Alison Knopf ...........................................Editor
**Desc.:** Practical report on the lawful prevention, detection, and treatment of alcohol and drug abuse.

68876

## EMERGING PHARMACEUTICALS
33 Bleeker St.
Millburn, NJ 07041
Telephone: (201) 379-7749
FAX: (201) 379-1158
Mailing Address:
   P.O. Box 218
   Maplewood, NJ 07040-0218
Year Established: 1992
Pub. Frequency: m.
Page Size: standard
Subscrip. Rate: $457/yr. US & Canada;
   $477/yr. foreign
Materials: 01,15,27,28,29,30,31
Print Process: offset
**Owner(s):**
CTB International Publishing, Inc.
P.O. Box 218
Maplewood, NJ 07040-0218
Telephone: (201) 379-7749
FAX: (201) 379-1158
Ownership %: 100
**Management:**
Oykue Brogna ...................................President
William Robinson ...............Circulation Manager
**Editorial:**
Christopher Brogna ....................Editor in Chief
John Gever ............................................Editor
**Desc.:** A monthly newsletter covering preclinical drug development.
**Readers:** Presidents, researchers and executives in upper management.

70683

## ENVIRONMENTAL HEALTH LETTER
951 Pershing Dr.
Silver Spring, MD 20910-4464
Telephone: (301) 587-6300
FAX: (301) 585-9075
Year Established: 1961
Pub. Frequency: fortn.
Subscrip. Rate: $267.54/yr.
**Owner(s):**
Business Publishers, Inc.
951 Pershing Dr.
Silver Spring, MD 20910-4464
Telephone: (301) 587-6300
FAX: (301) 585-9075
Ownership %: 100
**Editorial:**
Kathleen Hart ........................................Editor

70769

## EUROPE DRUG & DEVICE REPORT
c/o Karen Harrington
1117 N. 19th St.
Arlington, VA 22209
Telephone: (703) 247-3434
FAX: (703) 247-3421
Year Established: 1991
Pub. Frequency: bi-m.
Subscrip. Rate: $767.yr.
**Owner(s):**
Washington Business Information, Inc.
1117 N. 19th St.
Arlington, VA 22209
Telephone: (703) 247-3434
FAX: (703) 247-3421
Ownership %: 100
**Editorial:**
Sara Lewis .............................................Editor
**Desc.:** Reports on European, rules and standards for the pharmaceutical and device and dianostic products industries.

71015

## FAMILY FOCUS
30 E. 33rd St.
New York, NY 10016
Telephone: (212) 889-2210
Pub. Frequency: q.
Subscrip. Rate: Free
Circulation: 100000
Circulation Type: controlled & free
**Owner(s):**
National Kidney Foundation
Family Focus
30 E. 33rd St.
New York, NY 10016
Telephone: (212) 889-2210
Ownership %: 100
**Desc.:** Information for dialysis and transplant patients and their families.

70685

## FANLIGHT NEWS
47 Halifax St.
Boston, MA 02130
Telephone: (617) 524-0980
FAX: (617) 524-8838
Year Established: 1992
Pub. Frequency: a.
Subscrip. Rate: free
**Owner(s):**
Fanlight Productions
47 Halifax St.
Boston, MA 02130
Telephone: (617) 524-0980
FAX: (617) 524-8838
Ownership %: 100
**Editorial:**
Ben Achtenberg ......................................Editor
**Desc.:** Describes new media resources and general information of interest to health care and social service professionals, educators, librarians and administrators.

70741

## FELIX LETTER
P.O. Box 7094
Berkeley, CA 94707
Telephone: (510) 526-6268
Year Established: 1981
Pub. Frequency: 6/yr.
Subscrip. Rate: $11/yr.
Materials: 10
Circulation: 2000
Circulation Type: controlled
**Owner(s):**
Clara Felix
P.O. Box 7094
Berkeley, CA 94707
Telephone: (510) 526-6268
Ownership %: 100
**Management:**
Clara Felix ........................................Publisher
**Editorial:**
Clara Felix ............................................Editor

**Desc.:** Critical review and commentary on nutrition research. Promotes nutrition as an alternative to or adjunctive to medical approaches to illness.

70310

## FOCUS ON GERIATRIC CARE AND REHABILITATION
200 Orchard Ridge Dr.
Gaithersburg, MD 20878
Telephone: (301) 417-7500
FAX: (301) 417-7550
Year Established: 1987
Pub. Frequency: 10/yr.
Subscrip. Rate: $67/yr. US; $80/yr. foreign
**Owner(s):**
Aspen Publishers, Inc.
200 Orchard Ridge Dr.
Gaithersburg, MD 20878
Telephone: (301) 417-7500
FAX: (301) 417-7550
Ownership %: 100

71020

## FOR THOSE WHO GIVE & GRIEVE
30 E. 33rd St.
New York, NY 10016
Telephone: (212) 889-2210
FAX: (212) 689-9261
Year Established: 1991
Pub. Frequency: q.
Subscrip. Rate: Free
Circulation: 20,000
Circulation Type: controlled & free
**Owner(s):**
National Kidney Foundation
30 E. 33rd St.
New York, NY 10016
Telephone: (212) 889-2210
Ownership %: 100
**Editorial:**
Maggie Coolican .....................................Editor
**Desc.:** Discusses grief amoug families of kidney donors, advances in kidney transplant techniques and support organizations to assist families.

70323

## GERIATRIC CARE
P.O. 3577
Reno, NV 89505
Telephone: (702) 333-6651
Year Established: 1968
Pub. Frequency: m.
Subscrip. Rate: $75/yr. for 25 copies
Materials: 10
Circulation: 50,000
Circulation Type: controlled & paid
**Owner(s):**
Eymann Publications
P.O. Box 3577
Reno, NV 89505
Telephone: (702) 333-6651
Ownership %: 100
**Editorial:**
Ken Eymann ...........................................Editor

70655

## HABILITATIVE MENTAL HEALTHCARE NEWSLETTER
P.O. Box 57
Bear Creek, NC 27207-0057
Telephone: (919) 581-3700
FAX: (919) 581-3766
Year Established: 1982
Pub. Frequency: bi-m.
Page Size: tabloid
Subscrip. Rate: $44/yr. US; $60/yr. foreign; $57/yr. US institutions; $79/yr. foreign institutions
Materials: 32
Circulation: 5,000
Circulation Type: controlled & paid

**Owner(s):**
Psych-Media, Inc.
P.O. Box 57
Bear Creek, NC 27207-0057
Telephone: (919) 581-3700
FAX: (919) 581-3766
Ownership %: 100
**Editorial:**
Dr. Robert Sovner ...................................Editor
Anne DesNoyers Hurely ...........................Editor
**Desc.:** Provides clinicians and habilitative caregivers with information regarding the diagnosis and treatment of neuropsychiatric disorders and therapeutic interventions which can improve the quality of psychosocial fuctioning of persons with developmental disabilities.

70645

## HAZELDEN NEWS & PROFESSIONAL UPDATE
1400 Park Ave. S.
Minneapolis, MN 55404
Telephone: (612) 349-4290
FAX: (612) 339-5195
Year Established: 1990
Pub. Frequency: 3/yr.
Subscrip. Rate: free
**Owner(s):**
Hazelden Foundation
1400 Park Ave. S.
Minneapolis, MN 55404
Telephone: (612) 349-4290
Ownership %: 100
**Editorial:**
Mary Duda ............................................Editor
**Desc.:** Covers a broad range of issues for professionals in the chemical health field and for those in search of recovery from chemical dependecy and other related addictive behaviors.

70339

## HEALTH & HEALING
7811 Montrose Rd.
Potomac, MD 20854
Telephone: (800) 777-5005
FAX: (301) 424-7034
Year Established: 1991
Pub. Frequency: m.
Subscrip. Rate: $39.95/yr.
**Owner(s):**
Phillips Publishing, Inc.
7811 Montrose Rd.
Potomac, MD 20854
Telephone: (800) 777-5005
FAX: (301) 424-7034
Ownership %: 100
**Editorial:**
Dr. Julian Whitaker ...............................Editor

70688

## HEALTHCARE COMMUNITY RELATIONS & MARKETING LETTER
3100 Hwy. 138
Wall Township, NJ 07719-1442
Telephone: (908) 681-1133
FAX: (908) 681-0490
Year Established: 1987
Pub. Frequency: m.
Subscrip. Rate: $197/yr.
**Owner(s):**
Health Resources Publishing
3100 Hwy. 138
Wall Township, NJ 07719-1442
Telephone: (908) 681-1133
FAX: (908) 681-0490
Ownership %: 100
**Editorial:**
Robert K. Jenkins ...................................Editor
**Desc.:** Provides current news and innovations for the public and community relations and marketing professionals.

**Materials Accepted/Included:** 01-Business news 02-By-line articles 03-Fashion news 04-Food news 05-Freelance copy 06-Letters to editor 07-Real estate news 08-Sports news 09-Travel news 10-Book rev. 11-Movie rev. 12-Music rev. 13-TV rev. 14-Theater rev. 15-Coming events 16-Obituaries 17-Question & answer 18-Social announcements 19-Artwork 20-Cartoons 21-Photos 22-TV listings 23-Audio rec. 24-Video rec. 25-Books 26-Films/film clips 27-Personnel news 28-Press releases 29-New product news/photos 30-Trade lit. 31-Contracts awarded 32-Display adv. 33-Classified adv.

7-69

## HEALTH CARE COMPETITION WEEK

70519

1101 King St.
Ste. 444
Alexandria, VA 22314
Telephone: (703) 683-4100
FAX: (703) 739-6517
Year Established: 1983
Pub. Frequency: bi-w.
Subscrip. Rate: $417/yr. US; $441/yr.
   foreign
**Owner(s):**
Capitol Publications, Inc.
1101 King St.
Ste. 444
Alexandria, VA 22314
Telephone: (703) 683-4100
FAX: (703) 739-6517
Ownership %: 100
**Desc.:** Critical coverage of the health care
   services business, marketing and
   management strategies.

## HEALTHCARE FUND RAISING NEWSLETTER

70504

Brinley Professional Plz.
3100 Hwy. 138
Wall Township, NJ 07719-1442
Telephone: (908) 681-1133
FAX: (908) 681-0490
Mailing Address:
   P.O. Box 1442
   Wall Township, NJ 07719
Year Established: 1979
Pub. Frequency: 6/yr.
Subscrip. Rate: $77/yr.
Circulation: 400
Circulation Type: controlled & paid
**Owner(s):**
Health Resources Publishing
Brinley Professional Plz.
3100 Hwy. 138
Wall Township, NJ 07719-1442
Telephone: (908) 681-1133
FAX: (908) 681-0490
Ownership %: 100
**Editorial:**
Robert K. Jenkins ........................................Editor
**Desc.:** Exchange of information among
   hospitals, summarizing ways they are
   raising funds to meet competitive
   pressures and demands for services.

## HEALTHCARE HUMAN RESOURCES

70510

P.O. Box 40959
Santa Barbara, CA 93140
Telephone: (805) 564-2177
Year Established: 1992
Pub. Frequency: m.
Subscrip. Rate: $128/yr.
Materials: 10
**Owner(s):**
COR Research, Inc.
P.O. Box 40959
Santa Barbara, CA 93140
Ownership %: 100
**Editorial:**
Paul Engstrom ...........................................Editor
**Desc.:** Case studies and analysis of trends
   in the strategic management of human
   resources in hospitals and other
   healthcare organizations.

## HEALTHCARE PACKAGING

71216

122 S. Church St.
West Chester, PA 19382-3223
Telephone: (215) 436-4220
FAX: (215) 436-6277
Year Established: 1992
Pub. Frequency: m.
Subscrip. Rate: $295/yr. US; $345/yr.
   foreign

**Owner(s):**
Packaging Strategies, Inc.
122 S. Church St.
West Chester, PA 19382-3223
Telephone: (215) 436-4220
FAX: (215) 436-6277
Ownership %: 100
**Management:**
William H. LeMaire ..............................Publisher
**Editorial:**
Jim Wagner ...............................................Editor
**Desc.:** Provides news and analysis of
   technological and business issues
   related to the development of product
   packaging for the pharmaceutical,
   medical device and diagnostics
   industries.

## HEALTHCARE PR & MARKETING NEWS

71227

1201 Seven Locks Rd.
Potomac, MD 20854
Telephone: (301) 424-3338
FAX: (301) 309-3847
Year Established: 1992
Pub. Frequency: bi-w.
Subscrip. Rate: $397/yr. US; $430/yr.
   foreign
**Owner(s):**
Phillps Business Information, Inc.
1201 Seven Locks Rd.
Potomac, MD 20854
Telephone: (301) 424-3338
FAX: (301) 309-3847
Ownership %: 100

## HEALTHCARE TECHNOLOGY & BUSINESS OPPORTUNITIES

70693

1524 Brookhollow Rd.
Santa Ana, CA 92705-5426
Telephone: (714) 755-5757
FAX: (714) 755-5724
Year Established: 1980
Pub. Frequency: m.
Subscrip. Rate: $325/yr.
**Owner(s):**
Biomedical Business International
1524 Brookhollow Rd.
Santa Ana, CA 92705-5426
Telephone: (714) 755-5757
FAX: (714) 755-5724
Ownership %: 100
**Desc.:** Includes listing of technologies
   available for license and transfer,
   business opportunities, U.S., Japanese
   and European patent activity, and
   resources. Includes listing of
   technologies available for license and
   transfer, business opportunities, U.S.,
   Japanese and European patent activity,
   and resources.

## HEALTH EDUCATION REPORTS

70341

4401-A Connecticut Ave., N.W., Ste. 212
Washington, DC 20008
Telephone: (202) 362-3444
FAX: (202) 362-3493
Pub. Frequency: 24/yr.
Subscrip. Rate: $198/yr.
**Owner(s):**
Feistritzer Publications
4401-A Connecticut Ave., N.W.,
Washington, DC 20008
Telephone: (202) 362-3444
FAX: (202) 362-3493
Ownership %: 100
**Desc.:** Covers health promotion and
   disease prevention. Reports on policy
   and legislation, reviews literature and
   meetings.

## HEALTH POLICY WEEK

70345

11300 Rockville Pike., Ste. 1100
Rockville, MD 20852-3030
Telephone: (301) 816-8950
FAX: (301) 816-8945
Year Established: 1971
Pub. Frequency: w.
Subscrip. Rate: $395/yr.
**Owner(s):**
United Communications Group
11300 Rockville Pike, Ste. 110
Rockville, MD 20852-3030
Telephone: (301) 816-8950
FAX: (301) 816-8945
Ownership %: 100
**Editorial:**
Burt Schorr ...............................................Editor
**Desc.:** Offers an inside look at federal and
   state government actions affecting the
   financing and delivery of health care
   services.

## HEALTH PROFESSIONS REPORT

22039

313 South Ave.
Fanwood, NJ 07023
Telephone: (908) 889-6336
FAX: (908) 889-6339
Mailing Address:
   P.O. Box 340
   Fanwood, NJ 07023
Year Established: 1971
Pub. Frequency: bi-w.
Page Size: standard
Subscrip. Rate: $260/yr.
Materials: 01,06,15,27,28,29,30,31
Print Process: photocopy
**Owner(s):**
Whitaker Newsletters, Inc.
313 South Ave.
Fanwood, NJ 07023
Telephone: (908) 889-6336
FAX: (908) 889-6339
Ownership %: 100
**Management:**
Joel Whitaker ......................................President
Sandra Smith ..................Operations Manager
**Editorial:**
Anne Bittner ..............................................Editor
Joel Whitaker .......................Marketing Director
**Desc.:** Reports on the education and
   training of doctors, nurses and allied
   health professionals. Includes pending
   legislation, information on public and
   private funding sources, cost-cutting
   measures, new medical breakthroughs,
   curriculum ideas, and admissions
   policies.
**Readers:** Deans, admissions officers,
   financial aid officers.
**Deadline:** story-Wed. prior to pub. date;
   news-Wed. prior

## HOSPITAL MANAGEMENT REVIEW

70529

P.O. Box 40959
Santa Barbara, CA 93140
Telephone: (805) 564-2177
Year Established: 1982
Pub. Frequency: m. (except July)
Subscrip. Rate: $87/yr.
Materials: 10
**Owner(s):**
OR Research Inc.
P.O. Box 40959
Santa Barbara, CA 93140
Telephone: (805) 564-2177
Ownership %: 100
**Editorial:**
Dean H. Anderson ....................................Editor
**Desc.:** Information summaries of articles
   selected from more than 140 healthcare
   management periodicals.

## HOSPITAL MATERIALS MANAGEMENT

70531

5350 S. Roslyn St., Ste. 400
Englewood, CO 80111-2145
Telephone: (303) 290-8500
FAX: (303) 290-9025
Year Established: 1976
Pub. Frequency: m.
Subscrip. Rate: $187/yr.; $205/yr. foreign
Materials: 33
**Owner(s):**
Business World, Inc.
5350 S. Roslyn St.
Ste. 400
Englewood, CO 80111-2145
Telephone: (303) 290-8500
FAX: (303) 290-9025
Ownership %: 100
**Editorial:**
Donald E.L. Johnson ................................Editor
**Desc.:** Contains news about hospital group
   purchasing organizations; articles on
   materials management issues.

## HOSPITAL STRATEGY REPORT

70523

200 Orchard Ridge Dr.
Gaithersburg, MD 20878
Telephone: (301) 417-7500
FAX: (301) 417-7550
Year Established: 1985
Pub. Frequency: m.
Subscrip. Rate: $181/yr. US; $217/yr.
   foreign
**Owner(s):**
Aspen Publishers, Inc.
200 Orchard Ridge Dr.
Gaithersburg, MD 20878
Telephone: (301) 417-7500
FAX: (301) 417-7550
Ownership %: 100

## INDUSTRIAL HEALTH & HAZARDS UPDATE

71001

P.O. Box 15640
Plantation, FL 33318-5640
Telephone: (305) 473-9560
FAX: (305) 473-0544
Year Established: 1984
Pub. Frequency: m.
Subscrip. Rate: $249/yr. US; $269/yr.
   Canada; $309/yr. elsewhere
**Owner(s):**
Merton Allen Associates
P.O. Box 15640
Plantation, FL 33318-5640
Telephone: (305) 473-9560
FAX: (305) 473-0544
Ownership %: 100
**Editorial:**
Merton Allen .............................................Editor
David R. Allen ...........................................Editor
**Desc.:** Covers occupational health, safety,
   hazards, and related subjects. Designed
   for busy executives in the health,
   medical, environmental, legal,
   management, and technological fields of
   industry, government, commerce, and
   academia.

## INTERNATIONAL DRUG THERAPY NEWSLETTER

70660

1130 E. Cold Spring Ln.
Baltimore, MD 21239
Telephone: (410) 433-9220
FAX: (410) 532-5419
Year Established: 1966
Pub. Frequency: m. (Sep.-June)
Subscrip. Rate: $45/yr.
Materials: 10
Circulation: 7,000
Circulation Type: controlled & paid

**Materials Accepted/Included:** 01-Business news 02-By-line articles 03-Fashion news 04-Food news 05-Freelance copy 06-Letters to editor 07-Real estate news 08-Sports news 09-Travel news 10-Book rev. 11-Movie rev. 12-Music rev. 13-TV rev. 14-Theater rev. 15-Coming events 16-Obituaries 17-Question & answer 18-Social announcements 19-Artwork 20-Cartoons 21-Photos 22-TV listings 23-Audio rec. 24-Video rec. 25-Books 26-Films/film clips 27-Personnel news 28-Press releases 29-New product news/photos 30-Trade lit. 31-Contracts awarded 32-Display adv. 33-Classified adv.

7-70

**Owner(s):**
Ayd Medical Communications
1130 E. Cold Spring Ln.
Baltimore, MD 21239
Telephone: (410) 433-9220
FAX: (410) 532-5419
Ownership %: 100
**Editorial:**
Frank J. Ayd, Jr., M.D. ..............Editor
**Desc.:** Psychoactive drug therapy.

70668
## INTERVENTIONAL CARDIOLOGY NEWSLETTER
655 Avenue of the Americas
New York, NY 10010
Telephone: (212) 633-3950
FAX: (212) 633-3990
Year Established: 1993
Pub. Frequency: 6/yr.
Subscrip. Rate: $89/yr. US; $113/yr. foreign
**Owner(s):**
Elsevier Science Publishing Co., Inc.
655 Ave. of the Americas
New York, NY 10010
Telephone: (212) 633-3950
Ownership %: 100

70700
## JAPAN MEDICAL REVIEW
41 Sutter St., Ste. 1112
San Francisco, CA 94104
Telephone: (415) 772-5555
FAX: (415) 772-5659
Year Established: 1986
Pub. Frequency: m.
Subscrip. Rate: $450/yr.
**Owner(s):**
Japanese Publications, Inc.
41 Sutter St.
Ste. 1112
San Francisco, CA 94104
Telephone: (415) 772-5555
FAX: (415) 772-5679
Ownership %: 100
**Editorial:**
S. Nakamura ......................Editor
**Desc.:** Contains latest Ministry of Health regulations, policies, research and development licenses, manufacturer and distributor profiles, research and development breakthroughs, company profiles and competitive activity.

67653
## JOB SAFETY CONSULTANT
817 Broadway
New York, NY 10003
Telephone: (212) 673-4700
FAX: (212) 475-1790
Year Established: 1973
Pub. Frequency: m.
Page Size: standard
Subscrip. Rate: $169/yr.
**Owner(s):**
Business Research Publications, Inc.
817 Broadway
New York, NY 10003
Telephone: (212) 673-4700
Ownership %: 100
**Management:**
John Roche .......................Publisher
**Editorial:**
Marcia Waggol .......................Editor
**Desc.:** Tells what one needs to know to comply with OSHA and other government safety regulations and how to reduce worker injuries and production losses, medical bills, and worker's compensation costs.

70643
## LEGISLATIVE NETWORK FOR NURSES
951 Pershing Dr.
Silver Springs, MD 20910-4464
Telephone: (301) 587-6300
FAX: (301) 585-9075
Year Established: 1984
Pub. Frequency: fortn.
Subscrip. Rate: $275/yr.
**Owner(s):**
Business Publishers, Inc.
951 Pershing Dr.
Silver Springs, MD 20910-4464
Telephone: (301) 587-6300
FAX: (301) 585-9075
Ownership %: 100
**Editorial:**
B. K. Morris .......................Editor
**Desc.:** Regulations and how they impact the nursing profession - salaries, training, recruiting, and unionizing.

70726
## MANAGED CARE OUTLOOK
1101 King St.
Alexandria, VA 22314
Telephone: (703) 683-4100
FAX: (703) 739-6517
Year Established: 1986
Pub. Frequency: bi-w.
Subscrip. Rate: $399/yr.
**Owner(s):**
Capitol Publications, Inc.
1101 King St., Ste. 444
Alexandria, VA 22314
Telephone: (703) 683-4100
FAX: (703) 739-6517
Ownership %: 100
**Desc.:** Includes reports on new business, industry trends, regional happenings, legal and policy news, conference coverage, case studies.

70745
## MAYO CLINIC HEALTH LETTER
200 First St., S.W.
Rochester, MN 55905
Telephone: (507) 284-4730
FAX: (507) 284-5410
Year Established: 1983
Pub. Frequency: m.
Subscrip. Rate: $24/yr.
Circulation: 375,000
Circulation Type: controlled & paid
**Owner(s):**
Mayo Foundation
200 First St., S.W.
Rochester, MN 55905
Telephone: (507) 284-4730
FAX: (507) 284-5410
Ownership %: 100
**Editorial:**
David E. Swanson .......................Editor
**Desc.:** Presents timely facts and findings on a broad variety of health issues.

70725
## MDR WATCH
1117 N. 19th St., Ste. 200
Arlington, VA 22209
Telephone: (703) 247-3434
FAX: (703) 247-3427
Year Established: 1986
Pub. Frequency: m.
Subscrip. Rate: $597/yr.
**Owner(s):**
Business Information, Inc.
1117 N. 19th St., Ste. 200
c/o Karen Harrington
Arlington, VA 22209
Telephone: (703) 247-3434
FAX: (703) 247-3427
Ownership %: 100
**Editorial:**
Sean Oberle .......................Editor

**Desc.:** Monitors compliance with the FDA's MDR regulation with charts by manufacturer, product, and company. Includes current year-to-date figures.

70746
## MEDICAL-MORAL NEWSLETTER
1130 E. Cold Spring Ln.
Baltimore, MD 21239
Telephone: (410) 433-9220
FAX: (410) 532-5419
Year Established: 1964
Pub. Frequency: 10/yr.
Subscrip. Rate: $25/yr.
Materials: 10
**Owner(s):**
Ayd Medical Communications
1130 E. Cold Spring Ln.
Baltimore, MD 21239
Telephone: (410) 433-9220
FAX: (410) 532-5419
Ownership %: 100
**Editorial:**
Dr. Frank J. Ayd, Jr. .......................Editor
**Desc.:** Discusses medical ethics.

70538
## MEDICAL LIABILITY MONITOR
P.O. Box 9011
Winnetka, IL 60093-9011
Telephone: (708) 996-3000
FAX: (706) 998-1930
Year Established: 1975
Pub. Frequency: m.
Subscrip. Rate: $150/yr.
Materials: 10
Circulation: 1,750
Circulation Type: controlled & paid
**Owner(s):**
Malpractice Lifeline
P.O. Box 9011
Winnetka, IL 60093-9011
Telephone: (708) 996-3000
Ownership %: 100
**Editorial:**
Carol Brierly Golin .......................Editor
**Desc.:** News updates on legal and policy issues that affect premiums for malpractice insurance

70626
## MEDICAL OFFICE MANAGER
P.O. Box 1168
Marblehead, MA 01945
Telephone: (617) 639-1872
FAX: (617) 639-2982
Year Established: 1988
Pub. Frequency: m.
Subscrip. Rate: $132/yr.
Materials: 10
Circulation: 3,300
Circulation Type: controlled & paid
**Owner(s):**
Opus III Communications
P.O. Box 1168
Marblehead, MA 01945
Telephone: (617) 639-1872
FAX: (617) 639-2982
Ownership %: 100
**Editorial:**
Susan Crawford .......................Editor
**Desc.:** Covers issues and regulations affecting the management of medical practice offices.
**Readers:** For physician office administrators.

70765
## MEDICAL SCIENCES BULLETIN
2761 Trenton Rd.
Levittown, PA 19056
FAX: (215) 949-2594
Year Established: 1977
Pub. Frequency: m.
Subscrip. Rate: $27/yr. US individuals; $40/yr. foreign; $34/yr. institutions
Circulation: 1,800
Circulation Type: controlled & paid

**Owner(s):**
Pharmaceutical Information Associates, Ltd.
2761 Trenton Rd.
Levittown, PA 19056
FAX: (215) 949-2594
Ownership %: 100
**Editorial:**
Robert Hand, Ed. .......................Editor
**Desc.:** Provides an account of new advances in phamacology and therapeutics.

70727
## MEDICAL STAFF BRIEFING
P.O. Box 1168
Marblehead, MA 01945
Telephone: (617) 639-1872
FAX: (617) 639-2982
Year Established: 1991
Pub. Frequency: m.
Subscrip. Rate: $175/yr.
Circulation: 7,000
Circulation Type: controlled & paid
**Owner(s):**
OPUS Communications
P.O. Box 1168
Marblehead, MA 01945
Telephone: (617) 639-1872
FAX: (617) 639-2982
Ownership %: 100
**Management:**
Cathy A. Ross .......................Publisher
**Desc.:** Covers issues affecting medical staff administration, staff relations, and physician-patient relations.

70839
## MEDICAL TOYS & BOOKS
P.O. Box 571555
Tarzana, CA 91357
Telephone: (818) 705-3660
Year Established: 1989
Pub. Frequency: q.
Subscrip. Rate: $14/yr.; $18/yr. foreign
Materials: 10
**Owner(s):**
Pediatric Projects Inc.
P.O. Box 571555
Tarzana, CA 91357
Telephone: (818) 705-3660
Ownership %: 100
**Editorial:**
Pat Azarnoff .......................Editor

70336
## MEDICAL UPDATE
1100 Waterway Blvd.
Indianapolis, IN 46202
Telephone: (317) 637-0126
Mailing Address:
  P.O. Box 567
  Indianapolis, IN 46202
Year Established: 1976
Pub. Frequency: m.
Subscrip. Rate: $12/yr.
Circulation: 21,000
Circulation Type: controlled & paid
**Owner(s):**
Benjamin Franklin Literary & Medical Society, Inc.
1100 Waterway Blvd.
Indianapolis, IN 46202
Telephone: (317) 637-0126
Ownership %: 100

70524
## MEDICARE REVIEW
9441 Lyndon B. Johnson Fwy.
Ste. 510
Dallas, TX 75243-4541
Telephone: (214) 644-0159
FAX: (214) 644-1538
Pub. Frequency: m.
Subscrip. Rate: $125/yr.
Circulation: 3,226
Circulation Type: controlled & paid

**Materials Accepted/Included:** 01-Business news 02-By-line articles 03-Fashion news 04-Food news 05-Freelance copy 06-Letters to editor 07-Real estate news 08-Sports news 09-Travel news 10-Book rev. 11-Movie rev. 12-Music rev. 13-TV rev. 14-Theater rev. 15-Coming events 16-Obituaries 17-Question & answer 18-Social announcements 19-Artwork 20-Cartoons 21-Photos 22-TV listings 23-Audio rec. 24-Video rec. 25-Books 26-Films/film clips 27-Personnel news 28-Press releases 29-New product news/photos 30-Trade lit. 31-Contracts awarded 32-Display adv. 33-Classified adv.

7-71

**Owner(s):**
Shannon Publications, Inc.
9441 Lyndon B. Johnson Fwy.
Ste. 510
Dallas, TX 75243-4541
Telephone: (214) 644-0159
FAX: (214) 644-1538
Ownership %: 100
**Editorial:**
Brian Buchan ............................Editor
**Desc.:** In-depth coverage of billing-coding
policies, coverage issues,
reimbursements, legislation, ect.

71154

**MENTAL HEALTH LAW NEWS**
3 E. Interwood Pl.
P.O. Box 20241
Cincinnati, OH 45220
Telephone: (513) 221-3715
Year Established: 1986
Pub. Frequency: m.
Subscrip. Rate: $79/yr.
**Owner(s):**
Interwood Publications
Three E. Interwood Pl.
P.O. Box 20241
Cincinnati, OH 45220
Telephone: (513) 221-3715
Ownership %: 100
**Editorial:**
Frank J. Bardack ......................Editor
**Desc.:** Provides case law summaries on
mental health malpractice, commitment,
appropriate treatment, consent, and
patient danger to community.

71161

**MENTAL HEALTH LAW
REPORTER**
951 Pershing Dr.
Silver Spring, MD 20910-4464
Telephone: (301) 587-6300
FAX: (301) 585-9075
Year Established: 1983
Pub. Frequency: m.
Subscrip. Rate: $192.48/yr.
**Owner(s):**
Business Publishers, Inc.
951 Pershing Dr.
Silver Spring, MD 20910-4464
Telephone: (301) 587-6300
FAX: (301) 585-9075
Ownership %: 100
**Editorial:**
Bonita Becker ..........................Editor
**Desc.:** Covers the avoidance of mental
health lawsuits for mental health
professionals and advice on winning
suits that are brought.

70864

**MENTAL HEALTH REPORT**
951 Pershing Dr.
Silver Spring, MD 20910-4464
Telephone: (301) 587-6300
FAX: (301) 585-9075
Year Established: 1976
Pub. Frequency: fortn.
Subscrip. Rate: $280.54/yr.
**Owner(s):**
Business Publishers, Inc.
951 Pershing Dr.
Silver Spring, MD 20910-4464
Telephone: (301) 587-6300
FAX: (301) 585-9075
Ownership %: 100
**Editorial:**
Lisa Rabasca ............................Editor
**Desc.:** Provides funding and operational
tips for managers of mental health
programs in public and private sectors.

70841

**MENTAL HEALTH WEEKLY**
P.O. Box 3357
Providence, RI 02906
Telephone: (800) 333-7771
FAX: (401) 861-6370
Pub. Frequency: w.
Subscrip. Rate: $295/yr. individuals US;
$315/yr. CN; $335/yr. elsewhere;
$390/yr. institutions US; $410/yr. CN;
$430/yr. elsewhere
**Owner(s):**
Manisses Communications Group, Inc.
P.O. Box 3357
Providence, RI 02906
Telephone: (800) 333-7771
FAX: (401) 861-6370
Ownership %: 100
**Editorial:**
Keith Rosen ............................Editor
**Desc.:** Contains reports on state and
federal legislative and administrative
developments. Covers news of the
mental and health field, and public and
private policy issues.

70641

**NATIONAL HEADACHE
FOUNDATION NEWSLETTER**
5252 N. Western Ave.
Chicago, IL 60625
Telephone: (312) 878-7715
FAX: (312) 878-2782
Year Established: 1970
Pub. Frequency: q.
Page Size: tabloid
Subscrip. Rate: $15/yr.
Circulation: 45,000
Circulation Type: controlled & paid
**Owner(s):**
National Headache Foundation
5252 N. Western Ave.
Chicago, IL 60625
Telephone: (312) 878-7715
FAX: (312) 878-2782
Ownership %: 100
**Desc.:** Research and information on
headache causes and treatments.

70665

**NEWS BRIEF**
9041 Colgate St.
Indianapolis, IN 46268-1210
Telephone: (317) 872-9913
Year Established: 1982
Pub. Frequency: q.
Subscrip. Rate: $25/yr.
Materials: 10,33
Circulation: 500
Circulation Type: controlled & paid
**Owner(s):**
Parent Care, Inc.
9041 Colgate St.
Indianapolis, IN 46268-1210
Telephone: (317) 872-9913
Ownership %: 100
**Editorial:**
Sarah Killion ............................Editor

70337

**NEWSLETTER FOR PEOPLE WITH
LACTOSE INTOLERANCE &
MILK ALLERGY**
P.O. Box 3074
Iowa City, IA 52244
Telephone: (319) 351-1353
Year Established: 1987
Pub. Frequency: q.
Subscrip. Rate: $15/yr.
Materials: 10
Circulation: 1,000
Circulation Type: controlled & paid

**Owner(s):**
Commercial Writing Service
P.O. Box 3074
Iowa City, IA 52244
Telephone: (319) 351-1353
Ownership %: 100
**Editorial:**
Jane Zukin ............................Editor
**Desc.:** Provides information, support, and
recipes for those with lactose
intolerance or milk protein allergy.

71183

**NURSING QUALITY CONNECTION**
200 N. LaSalle St.
Chicago, IL 60601-1080
Telephone: (312) 726-9733
FAX: (312) 726-6075
Year Established: 1992
Pub. Frequency: bi-m.
Subscrip. Rate: $49.95/yr.
**Owner(s):**
Mosby-Yearbook, Inc./Times Mirror Co.
200 N. LaSalle St.
Chicago, IL 60601-1080
Telephone: (312) 726-9733
FAX: (312) 726-6075
Ownership %: 100

70648

**NURSING RECRUITMENT &
RETENTION**
951 Pershing Dr.
Silver Springs, MD 20910-4464
Telephone: (301) 587-6300
FAX: (301) 585-9075
Year Established: 1988
Pub. Frequency: m.
Subscrip. Rate: $321.48/yr.
**Owner(s):**
Business Publishers, Inc.
951 Pershing Dr.
Silver Springs, MD 20910-4464
Telephone: (301) 587-6300
FAX: (301) 585-9075
Ownership %: 100
**Editorial:**
B. K. Morris ............................Editor
**Desc.:** Teaches health care managers how
to recruit and retain qualified nurses for
their staff.

71181

**NURSING STAFF DEVELOPMENT
INSIDER**
200 N. LaSalle St.
Chicago, IL 60601-1080
Telephone: (312) 726-9733
FAX: (312) 726-6075
Year Established: 1992
Pub. Frequency: bi-m.
Subscrip. Rate: $49.95/yr.
**Owner(s):**
Mosby - Year Book, Inc.
Times Mirror Company
200 N. LaSalle St.
Chicago, IL 60601-1080
Telephone: (312) 726-9733
FAX: (312) 726-6075
Ownership %: 100
**Editorial:**
Donna Richards Sheridan ............Editor
**Desc.:** Features original articles and
commentary on issues pertinent to
nursing staff development.

70749

**NUTRITION & THE M.D.**
P.O. Box 10172
Van Nuys, CA 91410
Telephone: (800) 365-2468
FAX: (818) 997-1316
Year Established: 1974
Pub. Frequency: m.
Subscrip. Rate: $48/yr.
Circulation: 10,000
Circulation Type: controlled & paid

**Owner(s):**
P.M. Inc.
P.O. Box
Van Nuys, CA 91410
Telephone: (800) 365-2468
FAX: (818) 997-1316
Ownership %: 100
**Editorial:**
Dr. Russell Merritt, M.D. ............Editor
**Desc.:** Continuing education service for
physicians and nutritionists.

69022

**NUTRITION NEWS**
4108 Watkins Dr.
Riverside, CA 92507-4752
Telephone: (909) 784-7500
Year Established: 1976
Pub. Frequency: m.
Subscrip. Rate: $18/yr. US; $22/yr. CN &
MX; $29/yr. elsewhere
Print Process: offset
Circulation: 90,000
Circulation Type: paid
**Owner(s):**
Nutrition News
4108 Watkins Dr.
Riverside, CA 92507-4752
Telephone: (909) 784-7500
Ownership %: 100
**Editorial:**
Siri Kahlsa ............................Editor
**Desc.:** Reviews health and nutrition related
topics, primarily on dietary, herbal, and
vitamin supplements, for a general
audience.

70987

**OCCUPATIONAL HEALTH &
SAFETY LETTER**
951 Pershing Dr.
Silver Spring, MD 20910-4464
Telephone: (301) 587-6300
FAX: (301) 585-9075
Year Established: 1971
Pub. Frequency: fortn.
Subscrip. Rate: $254.54/yr.
**Owner(s):**
Business Publishers, Inc.
951 Pershing Dr.
Silver Spring, MD 20910-4464
Telephone: (301) 587-6300
FAX: (301) 585-9075
Ownership %: 100
**Editorial:**
Bryan Morris ............................Editor
**Desc.:** News for workplace managers on
maintaining staff safety; includes
Americans with Disablilites Act
regulations.

70647

**OPTOMETRIST'S PATIENT
NEWSLETTER**
P.O. Box 11177
Lancaster, PA 17605
Telephone: (717) 393-1010
Year Established: 1988
Pub. Frequency: q.
Subscrip. Rate: $398/per issue for 500
copies
**Owner(s):**
Doctor's Press
P.O. Box 11177
Lancaster, PA 17605
Telephone: (717) 393-1010
Ownership %: 100
**Editorial:**
Lee Dmitzak ............................Editor

70670

**PEDIATRIC ALERT**
P.O. Box 338
Newton Highlands, MA 02161
Year Established: 1976

---

**Materials Accepted/Included:** 01-Business news 02-By-line articles 03-Fashion news 04-Food news 05-Freelance copy 06-Letters to editor 07-Real estate news 08-Sports news 09-Travel news 10-Book rev. 11-Movie rev. 12-Music rev. 13-TV rev. 14-Theater rev. 15-Coming events 16-Obituaries 17-Question & answer 18-Social announcements 19-Artwork 20-Cartoons 21-Photos 22-TV listings 23-Audio rec. 24-Video rec. 25-Books 26-Films/film clips 27-Personnel news 28-Press releases 29-New product news/photos 30-Trade lit. 31-Contracts awarded 32-Display adv. 33-Classified adv.

Pub. Frequency: bi-w.
Subscrip. Rate: $59/yr. individuals; $75/yr. institutions; $39/yr. students
**Owner(s):**
Medical Alert, Inc.
P.O. Box 338
Newton Highlands, MA 02161
Ownership %: 100
**Editorial:**
Dr. Allen A. Mitchell .................................Editor

71014

## PEDIATRIC EMERGENCY & CRITICAL CARE
P.O. Box 23
Jersey City, NJ 07303-0023
Telephone: (201) 434-5073
FAX: (201) 434-7230
Year Established: 1988
Pub. Frequency: m.
Subscrip. Rate: $55/yr. individuals; $85/yr. institutions; $35/yr. residents & nurses
Circulation: 1,100
Circulation Type: controlled & paid
**Owner(s):**
Riverpress, Inc.
P.O. Box 23
Jersey City, NJ 07303-0023
Telephone: (201) 434-5072
FAX: (201) 434-7230
Ownership %: 100
**Editorial:**
Douglas W.E. Wagner .................................Editor
**Desc.:** Clinical update for those who care for infants and children. Digest of clinically useful literature and papers; each abstract has an expert's comment focusing on the clinical point.

70673

## PEDIATRIC REPORT'S CHILD HEALTH NEWSLETTER
71 Hope St.
P.O. Box 155
Providence, RI 02906-2062
Telephone: (401) 434-7390
FAX: (401) 434-7390
Year Established: 1984
Pub. Frequency: m.; 11/yr.
Subscrip. Rate: $35/yr.
**Owner(s):**
I G M Enterprises, Inc.
71 Hope St.
P.O. Box 155
Providence, RI 02906-2062
Telephone: (401) 434-7390
FAX: (401) 435-3634
Ownership %: 100
**Editorial:**
Dr. Linda Tartell .........................................Editor

71018

## PEDIATRIC THERAPEUTICS & TOXICOLOGY
P.O. Box 23
Jersey City, NJ 07303-0023
Telephone: (201) 434-5073
FAX: (201) 434-7230
Year Established: 1987
Pub. Frequency: m.
Subscrip. Rate: $45/yr. individuals; $80/yr. institutions; $28/yr. residents & nurses
**Owner(s):**
Riverpress, Inc.
P.O. Box 23
Jersey City, NJ 07303-0023
Telephone: (201) 434-5073
FAX: (201) 434-7230
Ownership %: 100
**Editorial:**
Douglas W.E. Wagner .................................Editor
**Desc.:** Practical pediatrics for the pediatric practitioner. Digest of clinically useful articles, each abstract has an expert's comment focusing on the clinical point.

70652

## PHARMCHEM NEWSLETTER
1505A O'Brien Dr.
Menlo Park, CA 94025
Year Established: 1972
Pub. Frequency: 4/yr.
Subscrip. Rate: free
Materials: 10
Circulation: 900
Circulation Type: free
**Owner(s):**
PharmChem Laboratories, Inc.
1505A O'Brien Dr.
Menlo Park, CA 94025
Telephone: (415) 328-6200
Ownership %: 100
**Editorial:**
Matt Moore .................................................Editor

70748

## PHYSICIAN'S PATIENT NEWSLETTER
P.O. Box 11177
Lancaster, PA 17605-1177
Telephone: (717) 393-1010
Year Established: 1983
Pub. Frequency: q.
Subscrip. Rate: $398/qtr. for 500 copies
**Owner(s):**
Doctor's Press
P.O. Box 11177
Lancaster, PA 17605-1177
Telephone: (717) 393-1010
Ownership %: 100
**Editorial:**
Lee Dmitzak .................................................Editor
**Desc.:** For family practice physicians and general practitioners to use to market their practice by providing health information.

70686

## PLASTIC SURGERY OUTLOOK
11970 Borman Dr.
Ste. 222
St. Louis, MO 63146
Telephone: (800) 423-6865
FAX: (314) 878-9937
Year Established: 1987
Pub. Frequency: 10/yr.
Subscrip. Rate: $185/yr. individuals; $238.50/yr. foreign individuals; $244/yr. institutions; $303.50 foreign institutions
**Owner(s):**
Quality Medical Publishing, Inc.
11970 Borman Dr.
Ste. 222
St. Louis, MO 63146
Telephone: (800) 423-6865
FAX: (314) 878-9937
Ownership %: 100

70659

## PODIATRIST'S PATIENT NEWSLETTER
P.O. Box 11177
Lancaster, PA 17605-1177
Telephone: (717) 393-1010
Year Established: 1983
Pub. Frequency: q.
Subscrip. Rate: $398/per issue for 500 copies
**Owner(s):**
Doctor's Press
P.O. Box 11177
Lancaster, PA 17605-1177
Telephone: (717) 393-1010
Ownership %: 100
**Editorial:**
Lee Dmitzak .................................................Editor

70653

## POST ANESTHESIA & AMBULATORY SURGERY NURSING UPDATE
Curtis Center
Independence Square W.
Philadelphia, PA 19106-3399
Telephone: (215) 238-7800
FAX: (215) 238-6445
Year Established: 1993
Pub. Frequency: bi-m.
Subscrip. Rate: $49/yr US; $100/yr. foreign; $85/yr. US instn.; $100/yr. foreign instn.; $39/yr. residents; $60/yr. foreign residents
**Owner(s):**
W.B./Saunders Co.
Curtis Center
Independence Square W.
Philadelphia, PA 19106-3399
Telephone: (215) 238-7800
FAX: (215) 238-6445
Ownership %: 100
**Editorial:**
Nancy Burden .............................................Editor
**Desc.:** Informs post-anesthesia nurses, nurse aneshetists, and nurses in ambulatory surgery about developments in their field. Also summarizes current literature.

70338

## PRESIDENT'S COUNCIL OF PHYSICAL FITNESS & SPORTS NEWSLETTER
450 Fifth St., N.W., Ste. 7103
Washington, DC 20001
Telephone: (202) 272-3430
Year Established: 1965
Pub. Frequency: 6/yr.
Subscrip. Rate: free
Circulation: 10,000
Circulation Type: controlled & free
**Owner(s):**
U.S. Department of Health & Human Services
450 Fifth St.,N.W., Ste. 7103
Washington, DC 20001
Telephone: (319) 351-1353
Ownership %: 100
**Editorial:**
Phil Wiephorn .............................................Editor

70485

## PRODUCT SAFETY LETTER
1117 N. 19th St.
Ste. 200
Arlington, VA 22209
Telephone: (703) 247-3434
FAX: (703) 247-3421
Year Established: 1972
Pub. Frequency: w.
Subscrip. Rate: $767/yr.
Materials: 10
**Owner(s):**
Washington Business Information, Inc.
1117 N. 19th St.
Ste. 200
Arlington, VA 22209
Telephone: (703) 247-3434
FAX: (703) 247-3421
Ownership %: 100
**Editorial:**
Dave Kramer .............................................Editor
**Desc.:** Contains information for executives concerned with government regulation of consumer products.

70815

## PSYCHOTHERAPY LETTER
P.O. Box 3357
Providence, RI 02906-0757
Telephone: (800) 333-7771
FAX: (401) 861-6370
Year Established: 1989

Pub. Frequency: m.
Subscrip. Rate: $67/yr. individuals; $77/yr. Canada; $87/yr. elsewhere; $97/yr. institutions; $107/yr. Canada; $117/yr. elsewhere
**Owner(s):**
Manisses Communications Group, Inc.
P.O. Box 3357
Providence, RI 02906-0757
Telephone: (800) 333-7771
FAX: (401) 861-6370
Ownership %: 100

70507

## QRC ADVISOR
200 Orchard Ridge Dr.
Gaithersburg, MD 20878
Telephone: (301) 417-7500
Year Established: 1984
Pub. Frequency: m.
Subscrip. Rate: $192/yr.; $230/yr. foreign
**Owner(s):**
Aspen Publishers Inc.
500 Orchard Ridge Dr.
Gaithersburg, MD 20878
Telephone: (301) 417-7500
FAX: (301) 417-7550
Ownership %: 100

70880

## REPORT ON DISABLITY PROGRAMS
951 Pershing Dr.
Silver Spring, MD 20910-4464
Telephone: (301) 587-6300
FAX: (301) 585-9075
Year Established: 1978
Pub. Frequency: fortn.
Subscrip. Rate: $248.04
**Owner(s):**
Business Publishers, Inc.
951 Pershing Dr.
Silver Spring, MD 20910-4464
Telephone: (301) 857-6300
FAX: (301) 585-9075
Ownership %: 100
**Editorial:**
Lisa Rabasca .............................................Editor
**Desc.:** Covers funding advice, new programs for managers of disabled programs; especially for occupational development of disabled.

70658

## REPORT ON MEDICAL GUIDELINES & OUTCOMES RESEARCH
1101 King St.
Ste. 444
Alexandria, VA 22314
Telephone: (703) 683-4100
FAX: (703) 739-6517
Pub. Frequency: m.
Subscrip. Rate: $495/yr.; $519/yr. foreign
**Owner(s):**
Capitol Publications, Inc.
1101 King St.
Ste. 444
Alexandria, VA 22314
Telephone: (703) 683-4100
FAX: (703) 739-6517
Ownership %: 100
**Editorial:**
Mary Darby .................................................Editor

71182

## RESPIRATORY CARE MANAGER
P.O. Box 1168
Marblehead, MA 01945
Telephone: (617) 639-1872
FAX: (617) 639-2982
Year Established: 1992
Pub. Frequency: m.
Subscrip. Rate: $117/yr.

Materials Accepted/Included: 01-Business news 02-By-line articles 03-Fashion news 04-Food news 05-Freelance copy 06-Letters to editor 07-Real estate news 08-Sports news 09-Travel news 10-Book rev. 11-Movie rev. 12-Music rev. 13-TV rev. 14-Theater rev. 15-Coming events 16-Obituaries 17-Question & answer 18-Social announcements 19-Artwork 20-Cartoons 21-Photos 22-TV listings 23-Audio rec. 24-Video rec. 25-Books 26-Films/film clips 27-Personnel news 28-Press releases 29-New product news/photos 30-Trade lit. 31-Contracts awarded 32-Display adv. 33-Classified adv.

7-73

**Owner(s):**
Opus Communications
P.O. Box 1168
Marblehead, MA 01945
Telephone: (617) 639-1872
FAX: (617) 639-2982
Ownership %: 100

71013

## SAFETY & SECURITY FOR SUPERVISORS
817 Broadway
New York, NY 10003
Telephone: (212) 673-4700
FAX: (212) 475-1790
Year Established: 1973
Pub. Frequency: m.
Subscrip. Rate: price varies
**Owner(s):**
Business Research Publications, Inc.
817 Broadway
New York, NY 10003
Telephone: (212) 673-4700
FAX: (212) 475-1790
Ownership %: 100
**Editorial:**
Marcia Wagghol ..............................Editor
**Desc.:** Includes safety checklists, case decisions covering the legal problems of safety and security, questions and answers that probe all aspects of industrial safety and security, and safety and security ideas that work.

70821

## SEX OVER FORTY
P.O. Box 1600
Chapel Hill, NC 27515
Year Established: 1982
Pub. Frequency: m.
Subscrip. Rate: $36/yr.
Materials: 10
Circulation: 40,000
Circulation Type: controlled & paid
**Owner(s):**
D K T International, Inc.
P.O. Box 1600
Chapel Hill, NC 27515
Ownership %: 100
**Editorial:**
Dr. Douglas Whitehead ..............................Editor
Dr. Shirley Zussman ..............................Editor

70662

## SMART'S HEALTH CARE REFORM REPORT
One Waters Park Dr.
Ste. 104
San Mateo, CA 94403
Telephone: (415) 341-2432
FAX: (415) 341-3304
Year Established: 1993
Pub. Frequency: w.
Subscrip. Rate: $395/yr.
**Owner(s):**
Smart's Publishing Group
One Waters Park Dr.
Ste. 104
San Mateo, CA 94403
Telephone: (415) 341-2432
FAX: (415) 341-3304
Ownership %: 100
**Editorial:**
Fred Pilot ..............................Editor
**Desc.:** Covers government and market trends in health care reform for business, risk management, benefit and health care industry leaders.

70640

## SPECIAL DELIVERY
P.O. Box 3675
Ann Arbor, MI 48106-3675
Telephone: (313) 662-6857
Year Established: 1977

Pub. Frequency: q.
Subscrip. Rate: $15/yr.
Materials: 10,33
Circulation: 2,000
Circulation Type: controlled & paid
**Owner(s):**
Informed Homebirth
P.O. Box 3675
Ann Arbor, MI 48106-3675
Telephone: (313) 662-6857
Ownership %: 100
**Editorial:**
Rahima Baldwin ..............................Editor
**Desc.:** Discusses midwifery alternatives in birth, parenting, and early childhood education.

71090

## SPORTS MEDICINE DIGEST
P.O. Box 10172
Van Nuys, CA 91410
Telephone: (800) 365-2468
FAX: (818) 997-1316
Year Established: 1979
Pub. Frequency: m.
Subscrip. Rate: $49/yr.
Materials: 10
Circulation: 2,500
Circulation Type: paid
**Owner(s):**
P. M. Inc.
P.O. Box 10172
Van Nuys, CA 91410
Telephone: (800) 365-2468
FAX: (818) 997-1316
Ownership %: 100
**Editorial:**
Dr. James C. Puffer ..............................Editor

70512

## STRATEGIES FOR HEALTHCARE EXCELLENCE
P.O. Box 40959
Santa Barbara, CA 93140-0959
Telephone: (805) 564-2177
Year Established: 1988
Pub. Frequency: m.
Subscrip. Rate: $197/yr.
Materials: 10
**Owner(s):**
OR Research Inc.
P.O. Box 40959
Santa Barbara, CA 93140-0959
Telephone: (805) 564-2177
Ownership %: 100
**Editorial:**
Susan J. Anthony ..............................Editor
**Desc.:** Case studies and commentary on quality, efficiency, and productivity in healthcare delivery.

70005

## STURZA'S MEDICAL INVESTMENT LETTER
424 W. End Ave., Ste. 7J
New York, NY 10024
*see Newsletters, Finance*

70689

## SUN & SKIN NEWS
245 Fifth Ave.
Ste. 2402
New York, NY 10016
Telephone: (212) 725-5176
Pub. Frequency: q.
Subscrip. Rate: $25/yr.; donation
**Owner(s):**
Skin Cancer Foundation
245 Fifth Ave.
Ste. 2402
New York, NY 10016
Telephone: (212) 725-5176
Ownership %: 100
**Desc.:** Covers a range of topics related to skin health: prevention and treatment of sun-induced skin cancer and other damage.

70825

## TERRAP TIMES
932 Evelyn St.
Menlo Park, CA 94025
Telephone: (415) 321-0300
Year Established: 1970
Pub. Frequency: m.
Subscrip. Rate: $18/yr.; $20/yr. foreign
Materials: 10,33
Circulation: 2,500
Circulation Type: controlled & paid
**Owner(s):**
T S C Management Corporation
932 Evelyn St.
Menlo Park, CA 94025
Telephone: (415) 321-0300
Ownership %: 100
**Editorial:**
Kathy Anderson ..............................Editor
**Desc.:** Features a support column and helpful hints for people with phobias.

71024

## TRANSPLANT CHRONICLES
30 E. 33rd St.
New York, NY 10016
Telephone: (212) 889-2210
Pub. Frequency: q.
Subscrip. Rate: Free
Circulation: 25,000
Circulation Type: controlled & free
**Owner(s):**
National Kidney Foundation
30 E. 33rd St.
New York, NY 10016
Telephone: (212) 889-2210
Ownership %: 100
**Desc.:** News and information for transplant patients and their families.

70999

## TREATMENT ISSUES
129 W. 20th St.
New York, NY 10011
Year Established: 1987
Pub. Frequency: m.
Subscrip. Rate: $30/yr. US; $40/yr. foreign
Circulation: 18,000
Circulation Type: controlled & paid
**Owner(s):**
GMHC Inc.
129 W. 20th St.
New York, NY 10011
Ownership %: 100
**Editorial:**
David Gold ..............................Editor
**Desc.:** Addresses the various medical aspects of AIDS such as experimental treatments, descriptions of opportunistic infections often seen in AIDS, drug licensing issues, & medical articles of general interest to people who are HIV-infected.

70698

## VASCULAR SURGERY OUTLOOK
11970 Borman Dr.
Ste. 222
St. Louis, MO 63146
Telephone: (800) 423-6865
FAX: (314) 878-9937
Year Established: 1988
Pub. Frequency: 10/yr.
Subscrip. Rate: $165/yr. individuals; $194.50/yr. foreign individuals; $224/yr. institutions; $281.50/yr. foreign institutions
**Owner(s):**
Quality Medical Publishing, Inc.
11970 Borman Dr.
Ste. 222
St. Louis, MO 63146
Telephone: (800) 423-6865
FAX: (314) 878-9937
Ownership %: 100
**Editorial:**
Dr. Jerry Goldstone ..............................Editor

70767

## WASHINGTON DRUG LETTER
1117 N. 19th St.
Arlington, VA 22209
Telephone: (703) 247-3434
FAX: (703) 247-3421
Year Established: 1969
Pub. Frequency: w.
Subscrip. Rate: $667/yr.
Materials: 10
**Owner(s):**
Washington Business Information, Inc.
1117 N. 19th St.
Arlington, VA 22209
Telephone: (703) 247-3434
FAX: (703) 247-3421
Ownership %: 100
**Editorial:**
John Briley ..............................Editor

70340

## WELLNESS NEWSLETTER
3451 Central Ave.
St. Petersburg, FL 33713-8522
Year Established: 1980
Pub. Frequency: bi-m.
Subscrip. Rate: $30/yr.
Materials: 10
**Owner(s):**
Carolyn Chambers Clark, Publ.
3451 Central Ave.
St. Petersburg, FL 33713-8522
Ownership %: 100
**Management:**
Carolyn Chambers Clark ..............................Publisher
**Editorial:**
Carolyn Chambers Clark ..............................Editor
**Desc.:** Each issue focuses on a different aspect of health: self-care, nutrition, fitness, stress, management, environment, or "positive" relationships.

71008

## WORLD GASTROENTEROLOGY NEWS
20 N. Third St.
Philadelphia, PA 19106
Telephone: (215) 574-2285
FAX: (215) 574-2270
Year Established: 1993
Pub. Frequency: 3/yr.
Materials: 32
Circulation: 60,000
Circulation Type: controlled & paid
**Owner(s):**
Current Science
120 N. Third St.
Philadelphia, PA 19106
Telephone: (215) 574-2285
Ownership %: 100
**Management:**
Fred Wood ..............................Advertising Manager
**Editorial:**
Meinhard Classen ..............................Editor
**Desc.:** Covers topics of interest to practicing gastroenterologists worldwide.

70743

## YOUR HEALTH
P.O. Box 18433
Asheville, NC 28814-0433
Telephone: (704) 258-3243
Year Established: 1979
Pub. Frequency: bi-m.
Page Size: tabloid
Subscrip. Rate: $30/yr. members
Materials: 10,32
Circulation: 1,000
Circulation Type: controlled & paid
**Owner(s):**
Int'l Academy of Nutrition & Preventive Medicine
P.O. Box 18433
Asheville, NC 28814-0433
Telephone: (704) 258-3243
Ownership %: 100

**Materials Accepted/Included:** 01-Business news 02-By-line articles 03-Fashion news 04-Food news 05-Freelance copy 06-Letters to editor 07-Real estate news 08-Sports news 09-Travel news 10-Book rev. 11-Movie rev. 12-Music rev. 13-TV rev. 14-Theater rev. 15-Coming events 16-Obituaries 17-Question & answer 18-Social announcements 19-Artwork 20-Cartoons 21-Photos 22-TV listings 23-Audio rec. 24-Video rec. 25-Books 26-Films/film clips 27-Personnel news 28-Press releases 29-New product news/photos 30-Trade lit. 31-Contracts awarded 32-Display adv. 33-Classified adv.

**Editorial:**
Dr. Joel Yager .................................Editor
**Desc.:** Written for lay people to inform readers of developments in nutrition and preventive medicine.

## Group 348-Plants

70292
### AMERICAN HERB ASSOCIATION NEWSLETTER
P.O. Box 1673
Nevada City, CA 95959-1673
Year Established: 1981
Pub. Frequency: q.
Subscrip. Rate: $20/yr. US; $28/yr. foreign
Materials: 10,11,32
Circulation: 800
Circulation Type: controlled & paid
**Owner(s):**
American Herb Association
P.O. Box 1673
Nevada City, CA 95959
Ownership %: 100
**Editorial:**
Kathi Keville .................................Editor

70274
### BETWEEN THE VINES
P.O. Box 520
W. Carrolton, OH 45449-0520
Telephone: (513) 434-7069
Year Established: 1989
Pub. Frequency: s-a.
Subscrip. Rate: $15/yr.
Circulation: 375
Circulation Type: controlled & paid
**Owner(s):**
American Ivy Society
P.O. Box 520
W. Carrolton, OH 45449-0520
Telephone: (513) 434-7069
Ownership %: 100
**Desc.:** Contains short pieces with news, research, and growing tips.

70276
### BEV DOBSON'S ROSE LETTER
215 Harriman Rd.
Irvington, NY 10533
Telephone: (914) 591-6736
Pub. Frequency: 6/yr.
Subscrip. Rate: $12/yr.
Materials: 10
Circulation: 1,000
Circulation Type: controlled & paid
**Owner(s):**
Beverly R. Dobson
215 Harriman Rd.
Irvington, NY 10533
Telephone: (914) 591-6736
Ownership %: 100
**Management:**
Beverly R. Dobson .................................Publisher
**Desc.:** Contains articles on any rose-related topics, announcements of rose events, reports on rose conventions and symposiums, and book reviews.

71113
### COMPOSTING NEWS
13727 Holland Rd.
Cleveland, OH 44142
Telephone: (216) 362-7979
FAX: (216) 362-4623
Year Established: 1992
Pub. Frequency: m.
Subscrip. Rate: $120/yr. US; $140/yr. CN & MX; $200/yr. foreign
Circulation: 5,000
Circulation Type: controlled & paid

**Owner(s):**
McEntee Media Corp.
13727 Holland Rd.
Cleveland, OH 44142
Telephone: (216) 362-7979
FAX: (216) 362-4623
Ownership %: 100
**Desc.:** Features news, trends, and legislation in private, public and home composting.

70295
### FLORA-LINE
7336 Berry Hill
Palos Verdes, CA 90274-4404
Year Established: 1981
Pub. Frequency: q.
Subscrip. Rate: $16.95/yr.
Materials: 10,32
Circulation: 2,000
Circulation Type: controlled & paid
**Owner(s):**
Berry Hill Press
7336 Berry Hill
Palos Verdes, CA 90274-4404
Telephone: (310) 377-7040
Ownership %: 100
**Editorial:**
Dody Lyness .................................Editor
**Desc.:** For both professional and amateur dried herbal-floral and fragrance designers.

70278
### GREEN MARKETS
4600 East-West Hwy.
Ste. 200
Bethesda, MD 20814
Telephone: (301) 654-6262
FAX: (301) 654-6297
Year Established: 1977
Pub. Frequency: w.
Subscrip. Rate: $860/yr. US; $1095/yr. foreign
**Owner(s):**
Pike & Fischer, Inc.
4600 East-West Hwy.
Ste. 200
Bethesda, MD 20814
Telephone: (301) 654-6262
FAX: (301) 654-6297
Ownership %: 100
**Editorial:**
Steve Seay .................................Editor

70299
### GREEN MARKETS DEALER REPORT
4600 East-West Hwy., Ste. 200
Bethesda, MD 20814
Telephone: (301) 654-6262
FAX: (301) 654-6297
Pub. Frequency: w.
Subscrip. Rate: $410/yr.
**Owner(s):**
Pike & Fischer, Inc.
4600 East-West Hwy.
Bethesda, MD 20814
Telephone: (301) 654-6262
FAX: (301) 654-6297
Ownership %: 100
**Editorial:**
Steve Seay .................................Editor

70282
### HORTIDEAS
460 Black Lick Rd.
Gravel Switch, KY 40328
Telephone: (606) 332-7606
FAX: (606) 332-7606
Year Established: 1984
Pub. Frequency: m.
Subscrip. Rate: $15/yr.

**Owner(s):**
Gregory & Patricia Williams
460 Black Lick Rd.
Gravel Switch, KY 40328
Telephone: (606) 332-7606
FAX: (606) 332-7606
Ownership %: 100
**Management:**
Gregory Williams .................................Publisher
Patricia Williams .................................Publisher
**Editorial:**
Gregory Williams .................................Editor
Patricia Williams .................................Editor
**Desc.:** Contains reports on the latest research, methods, tools, plants and books of interest to food and ornamental gardeners, from hundreds of worldwide sources.

70285
### ORNAMENTALS NORTHWEST NEWSLETTER
Cooperative Extension Service
Dept. of Horticulture
Corvallis, OR 97331
Telephone: (503) 737-5452
FAX: (503) 737-3479
Year Established: 1992
Pub. Frequency: bi-m.
Subscrip. Rate: $10/yr.; $15/yr. foreign
Circulation: 5,000
Circulation Type: controlled & paid
**Owner(s):**
Oregon State University
Cooperative Extension Service
Dept. of Horticulture
Corvallis, OR 97331
Telephone: (503) 737-5452
FAX: (503) 737-3479
Ownership %: 100
**Editorial:**
James L. Green .................................Editor

70288
### PLANTS & GARDENS NEWS
1000 Washington Ave.
Brooklyn, NY 11225
Telephone: (718) 941-4044
FAX: (718) 857-2430
Year Established: 1986
Pub. Frequency: 4/yr.
Page Size: tabloid
Materials: 10
Circulation: 25,000
Circulation Type: controlled & paid
**Owner(s):**
Brooklyn Botanic Garden
1000 Washington Ave.
Brooklyn, NY 11225
Telephone: (718) 941-4044
FAX: (718) 857-2430
Ownership %: 100
**Editorial:**
Betsy Kissam .................................Editor

70250
### WOODLAND REPORT
374 Maple Ave., E., Ste. 204
Vienna, VA 22180
Telephone: (703) 255-2700
Year Established: 1984
Pub. Frequency: 8/yr.
Subscrip. Rate: $15/yr.
Circulation: 3,000
Circulation Type: controlled & paid
**Owner(s):**
National Woodland Owners Association
374 Maple Ave., E., Ste. 204
Vienna, VA 22180
Telephone: (703) 255-2700
Ownership %: 100
**Editorial:**
Keith A. Argow .................................Editor

**Desc.:** Contains practical forestry information for woodland owners.

## Group 350-Politics & Government

70810
### ACCESS RESOURCE BRIEF
1511 K St., N.W., Ste. 643
Washington, DC 20005
Telephone: (202) 785-6630
FAX: (202) 223-2737
Pub. Frequency: 6-8/yr.
Subscrip. Rate: $275/yr. individuals; $45/yr. foreign
Circulation: 2,500
Circulation Type: controlled & paid
**Owner(s):**
A Security Information Service
1511 K St., N.W., Ste. 643
Washington, DC 20005
Telephone: (202) 785-6630
FAX: (202) 223-2737
Ownership %: 100
**Editorial:**
Bruce Seymore, II .................................Editor
**Desc.:** Provides an overview of timely issues relating to international affairs, peace and security; lists sources of information from diverse viewpoints and suggested readings representing the political spectrum.

70847
### ARIZONA CAPITOL TIMES
14 N. 18th Ave.
Phoenix, AZ 85007
Telephone: (602) 258-7026
Year Established: 1945
Pub. Frequency: w.
Subscrip. Rate: $32/yr.
**Owner(s):**
Arizona News Service
14 N. 18th Ave.
Phoenix, AZ 85007
Telephone: (602) 258-7026
Ownership %: 100
**Editorial:**
Ned Creighton .................................Editor
**Desc.:** Covers Arizona political, legislative and state agency news.

70822
### BLACK CONGRESSIONAL MONITOR
P.O. Box 75035
Washington, DC 20013
Telephone: (202) 488-8879
Year Established: 1987
Pub. Frequency: m.
Subscrip. Rate: $41.95/yr.
**Owner(s):**
Len Mor Publications
P.O. Box 75035
Washington, DC 20013
Telephone: (202) 488-8879
Ownership %: 100
**Editorial:**
Lenora Moragne, Ed. .................................Editor
**Desc.:** Coverage of bills and resolutions introduced, hearings held, congressional comments made, available grant awards, contract and subcontract opportunities, public notices, proposed and final regulations, and public policy documents.

70848
### CALIFORNIA PLANNING & DEVELOPMENT REPORT
1275 Sunny Crest Ave.
Ventura, CA 93003-1212
Telephone: (805) 642-7838
Year Established: 1986
Pub. Frequency: m.
Subscrip. Rate: $179/yr.

**Materials Accepted/Included:** 01-Business news 02-By-line articles 03-Fashion news 04-Food news 05-Freelance copy 06-Letters to editor 07-Real estate news 08-Sports news 09-Travel news 10-Book rev. 11-Movie rev. 12-Music rev. 13-TV rev. 14-Theater rev. 15-Coming events 16-Obituaries 17-Question & answer 18-Social announcements 19-Artwork 20-Cartoons 21-Photos 22-TV listings 23-Audio rec. 24-Video rec. 25-Books 26-Films/film clips 27-Personnel news 28-Press releases 29-New product news/photos 30-Trade lit. 31-Contracts awarded 32-Display adv. 33-Classified adv.

7-75

**Owner(s):**
Torf Fulton Associates
1275 Sunny Crest Ave.
Ventura, CA 93003-1212
Telephone: (805) 642-7838
Ownership %: 100
**Editorial:**
William Fulton .............................Editor
**Desc.:** Covers local government, real estate and urban planning issues.

**CALIFORNIA POLITICAL WEEK**                    70827
P.O. Box 1468
Beverly Hills, CA 90213
Telephone: (310) 659-0205
FAX: (310) 657-4340
Year Established: 1979
Pub. Frequency: w.
Subscrip. Rate: $90/yr.
Materials: 33
Circulation: 3,000
Circulation Type: controlled & paid
**Owner(s):**
California Political Week, Inc.
P.O. Box 1468
Beverly Hills, CA 90213
Telephone: (310) 659-0205
FAX: (310) 657-4340
Ownership %: 100
**Editorial:**
Dick Rosengarten ........................Editor
**Desc.:** California and western U.S. state and local government and political developments and trends.

**CAROLINA REPORT**                               70801
P.O. Box 12074
Rock Hill, SC 29731
Telephone: (803) 323-2200
Year Established: 1986
Pub. Frequency: m.
Subscrip. Rate: $48/yr.
**Owner(s):**
Broach, Mijeski & Associates
P.O. Box 12074
Rock Hill, SC 29731
Telephone: (803) 323-2200
Ownership %: 100
**Editorial:**
Glen Broach ...............................Editor

**CLINTON MONTHLY**                               70616
P.O. Box 5656
Buena Park, CA 90622-5656
Telephone: (714) 220-9415
Year Established: 1993
Pub. Frequency: m.
Subscrip. Rate: $33.95/yr.
Materials: 32
**Owner(s):**
Politically Unique Publications
P.O. Box 5656
Buena Park, CA 90622
Telephone: (714) 220-9415
Ownership %: 100
**Editorial:**
Mark S. Kennedy ........................Editor
**Desc.:** Acts as a forum for public praise and public outrage, providing conservative views and evaluations of how the Clinton administration is handling foreign, domestic, military, congressional, and economic policy.

**COMMUNITY DEVELOPMENT**                         70835
**DIGEST**
8204 Fenton St.
Silver Spring, MD 20910
Telephone: (301) 588-6380
FAX: (301) 588-6385
Year Established: 1965

Pub. Frequency: m.
Subscrip. Rate: $359/yr.
Materials: 10
**Owner(s):**
CD Publications
8204 Fenton St.
Silver Spring, MD 20910
Telephone: (301) 588-6380
FAX: (301) 588-6385
Ownership %: 100
**Editorial:**
Byron Fielding ...........................Editor
**Desc.:** Covers U.S. community development programs.

**COMMUNITY HEALTH FUNDING**                      70849
**REPORT**
8204 Fenton St.
Silver Spring, MD 20910-2889
Telephone: (301) 588-6380
FAX: (301) 588-6385
Year Established: 1990
Pub. Frequency: s-m.
Subscrip. Rate: $229/yr.
**Owner(s):**
CD Publications
8204 Fenton St.
Silver Spring, MD 20910-2889
Telephone: (301) 588-6380
FAX: (301) 588-6385
Ownership %: 100
**Editorial:**
Mary Lehman ...........................Editor
**Desc.:** Reviews of public and private health grant opportunities, including reports on eligibility requirements, funding levels and deadlines.

**CONGRESSIONAL INSIGHT**                         70783
1414 22nd St., N.W.
Washington, DC 20037
Telephone: (800) 432-2250
FAX: (202) 728-1863
Year Established: 1976
Pub. Frequency: w.
Subscrip. Rate: $319/yr.
**Owner(s):**
Congressional Quarterly Inc.
1414 22nd St., N.W.
Washington, DC 20037
Telephone: (800) 432-2250
FAX: (202) 728-1863
Ownership %: 100
**Editorial:**
Brian Nutting ...........................Editor
**Desc.:** Coverage devoted exclusively to the U.S. Congress including its priorities, power struggles, and personalities.

**DOWNTOWN IDEA EXCHANGE**                        70837
215 Park Ave., S.
Ste. 1301
New York, NY 10003
Telephone: (212) 228-9246
FAX: (212) 228-0376
Year Established: 1954
Pub. Frequency: s-m.
Subscrip. Rate: $127/yr.
Materials: 10
**Owner(s):**
Alexander Research & Communications, Inc.
215 Park Ave., S.
Ste. 1301
New York, NY 10003
Telephone: (212) 228-0246
FAX: (212) 228-0376
Ownership %: 100
**Editorial:**
Laurence A. Alexander ...............Editor
**Desc.:** Newsletter of downtown revitilization for downtown leaders and officials in local and state government.

**ECONOMIC OPPORTUNITY**                          70859
**REPORT**
951 Pershing Dr.
Silver Spring, MD 20910-4464
Telephone: (301) 587-6300
FAX: (301) 585-9075
Year Established: 1966
Pub. Frequency: w.
Subscrip. Rate: $307/ yr.
**Owner(s):**
Business Publishers, Inc.
951 Pershing Dr.
Silver Spring, MD 20910-4464
Telephone: (301) 587-6300
FAX: (301) 585-9075
Ownership %: 100
**Editorial:**
Jay Fletcher ............................Editor
**Desc.:** Provides inside news from Washington on money, trends, innovations, and research results for antipoverty administrators.

**FACT FINDER**                                   70784
P.O. Box A
Scottsdale, AZ 85252
Telephone: (602) 947-4466
Year Established: 1942
Pub. Frequency: fortn.
Subscrip. Rate: $30/yr.
Circulation: 12000
Circulation Type: controlled & paid
**Owner(s):**
Harry T. Everingham
P.O. Box A
Scottsdale, AZ 85252
Telephone: (602) 947-4466
Ownership %: 100
**Editorial:**
Harry T. Everingham ..................Editor

**FEDERAL ASSISTANCE MONITOR**                    70818
8204 Fenton St.
Silver Spring, MD 20910-2889
Telephone: (301) 588-6380
FAX: (301) 588-6385
Year Established: 1986
Pub. Frequency: s-m.
Subscrip. Rate: $239/yr.
**Owner(s):**
CD Publications, Inc.
8204 Fenton St.
Silver Spring, MD 10910-2889
Telephone: (301) 588-6380
FAX: (301) 588-6385
Ownership %: 100
**Editorial:**
David Kittross ...........................Editor
**Desc.:** Covers federal regulations, funding availability, legislative developments affecting funding of social and exonomic programs.

**FEDERAL GRANTS & CONTRACTS**                    70850
**WEEKLY**
1101 King St., Ste. 444
Alexandria, VA 22314
Telephone: (703) 683-4100
FAX: (703) 739-6517
Year Established: 1977
Pub. Frequency: w.
Subscrip. Rate: $349/yr. US; $339/yr. foreign
**Owner(s):**
Capitol Publications, Inc.
1101 King St., Ste. 444
Alexandria, VA 22314
Telephone: (703) 683-4100
FAX: (703) 739-6571
Ownership %: 100
**Editorial:**
Leslie Ratzlaff ..........................Editor

**Desc.:** Provides funding news, analysis, profiles of key agencies, updates on new legislation and regulations, budget development.

**FLORIDA INSIGHT**                               70812
P.O. Box 2099
Gainesville, FL 32602
Year Established: 1989
Pub. Frequency: fortn.
Subscrip. Rate: $95/yr.
Circulation: 200
Circulation Type: controlled & paid
**Owner(s):**
Florida Communications Network, Inc.
P.O. Box 2099
Gainesville, FL 32602
Ownership %: 100
**Editorial:**
Jon Mills ...............................Editor
**Desc.:** Reports on all facets of government and politics in Florida, including the state legislature.

**GOVERNMENT & POLITICS ALERT**                   71021
701 Jackson St.
Topeka, KS 66603
Telephone: (913) 232-7720
FAX: (913) 232-1615
Year Established: 1989
Pub. Frequency: 6/yr.
Subscrip. Rate: $87.50/yr.
**Owner(s):**
Government Research Service
701 Jackson St.
Topeka, KS 66603
Telephone: (913) 232-7720
FAX: (913) 232-1615
Ownership %: 100
**Editorial:**
Lynn Hellebust ........................Editor
**Desc.:** Provides news and information about new publications, videos and databases dealing with Congress, state legislatures and lobbying in particular, as well as American government and politics in general.

**GOVERNMENT MICROCOMPUTER**                      70824
**LETTER**
P.O. Box 16645
Tampa, FL 33687
Telephone: (813) 622-8484
FAX: (813) 664-0051
Year Established: 1983
Pub. Frequency: bi-m.
Subscrip. Rate: $19/yr.
Circulation: 2,700
Circulation Type: controlled & paid
**Owner(s):**
Innovations Groups, Inc.
P.O. Box 16645
Tampa, FL 33687
Telephone: (813) 622-8484
FAX: (813) 664-0051
Ownership %: 100
**Editorial:**
Liz Weisberg .........................Editor
**Desc.:** For local goverments using computer systems.

**GOVERNMENT PRODUCTIVITY**                       70823
**NEWS**
P.O. Box 27435
Austin, TX 78755-0435
Telephone: (512) 343-1884
Year Established: 1987
Pub. Frequency: 10/yr.
Subscrip. Rate: $57/yr. US; $65/yr. foreign
Materials: 10

**Materials Accepted/Included:** 01-Business news 02-By-line articles 03-Fashion news 04-Food news 05-Freelance copy 06-Letters to editor 07-Real estate news 08-Sports news 09-Travel news 10-Book rev. 11-Movie rev. 12-Music rev. 13-TV rev. 14-Theater rev. 15-Coming events 16-Obituaries 17-Question & answer 18-Social announcements 19-Artwork 20-Cartoons 21-Photos 22-TV listings 23-Audio rec. 24-Video rec. 25-Books 26-Films/film clips 27-Personnel news 28-Press releases 29-New product news/photos 30-Trade lit. 31-Contracts awarded 32-Display adv. 33-Classified adv.

**Owner(s):**
James Jarrett, Publ.
P.O. Box 27435
Austin, TX 78755-0435
Telephone: (512) 343-1884
Ownership %: 100

70840
## HOUSING & DEVELOPMENT REPORTER-CURRENT DEVELOPMENTS
One Penn Plz.
New York, NY 10119
Telephone: (212) 971-5000
FAX: (212) 971-5240
Year Established: 1973
Pub. Frequency: bi-w.
Subscrip. Rate: $602.95/yr.
Materials: 10
**Owner(s):**
Warren Gorham Lamont
One Penn Plz.
New York, NY 10119
Telephone: (212) 971-5000
FAX: (212) 971-5240
Ownership %: 100
**Editorial:**
Warren Gorham Lamont ...........................Editor
**Desc.:** Reports on legislative
developments, administrative actions,
and judicial opinions affecting housing
and urban affairs and community
development. Provides comprehensive
coverage.

70838
## HOUSING AFFAIRS LETTER
8204 Fenton St.
Silver Spring, MD 20910-2889
Telephone: (301) 588-6380
FAX: (301) 588-6385
Year Established: 1961
Pub. Frequency: w.
Subscrip. Rate: $339/yr.
**Owner(s):**
CD Publications
8204 Fenton St.
Silver Spring, MD 20910-2889
Telephone: (301) 588-6380
FAX: (301) 588-6385
Ownership %: 100
**Editorial:**
Byron Fielding ...........................Editor
**Desc.:** Covers the housing market, its
legislation and regulations

70972
## INNOVATIVE PRODUCTS
P.O. Box 16645
Tampa, FL 33687
Telephone: (813) 622-8484
FAX: (813) 664-0051
Year Established: 1988
Pub. Frequency: q.
Subscrip. Rate: $19
Materials: 10,32
Circulation: 2,900
Circulation Type: controlled & paid
**Owner(s):**
Innovation Groups, Inc.
P.O. Box 16645
Tampa, FL 33687
Telephone: (813) 622-8484
FAX: (813) 664-0051
Ownership %: 100
**Desc.:** Discusses new and existing
products of interest to local
governments.

70830
## INSIDE MICHIGAN POLITICS
2029 S. Waverly Rd.
Lansing, MI 48917-4263
Telephone: (517) 394-2441
FAX: (517) 487-3830
Year Established: 1987

Pub. Frequency: bi-w.
Subscrip. Rate: $200/yr.
Circulation: 1,025
Circulation Type: controlled & paid
**Owner(s):**
Inside Michigan Politics
2029 S. Waverly Rd.
Lansing, MI 48917-4263
Telephone: (517) 394-2441
FAX: (517) 487-3830
Ownership %: 100
**Editorial:**
William S. Ballenger ...........................Editor
**Desc.:** Covers Michigan government,
politics, and business.

70828
## INSIDE THE WHITE HOUSE
P.O. Box 7167, Benjamin Franklin Sta.
Washington, DC 20044
Telephone: (703) 892-8500
FAX: (703) 685-2606
Year Established: 1983
Pub. Frequency: w.
Subscrip. Rate: $565/yr. US; $615/yr.
foreign
**Owner(s):**
Inside Washington Publishers
P.O. Box 7167, Benjamin Frankl
Washington, DC 20044
Telephone: (703) 892-8500
FAX: (703) 685-2606
Ownership %: 100
**Editorial:**
Peter Busowski ...........................Editor
**Desc.:** Reports on national administration,
economic, trade and regulatory policies.

70831
## JAG
10 E. Charles
Oelwein, IA 50662
Telephone: (319) 283-3491
FAX: (319) 283-3926
Year Established: 1962
Pub. Frequency: 9-10/yr.
Subscrip. Rate: free
Materials: 10
Circulation: 1000
Circulation Type: free
**Owner(s):**
Jag, Inc.
10 E. Charles
Oelwein, IA 50662
Telephone: (319) 283-3491
FAX: (319) 283-3926
Ownership %: 100
**Editorial:**
Dr. R.S. Jaggard ...........................Editor
**Desc.:** Covers politics as it relates to
medicine.

70843
## MARYLAND REPORT
P.O. Box 65360
Baltimore, MD 21209
Telephone: (410) 358-0658
FAX: (410) 764-1967
Year Established: 1989
Pub. Frequency: bi-w.
Subscrip. Rate: $200/yr.
**Owner(s):**
Bancroft Information Group, Inc.
P.O. Box 65360
Baltimore, MD 21209
Telephone: (410) 358-0658
FAX: (410) 764-1967
Ownership %: 100
**Editorial:**
Bruce L. Bortz ...........................Editor
**Desc.:** News analysis of Maryland
government, politics, and business.

70796
## MICHIGAN: AROUND & ABOUT
304 1-2 S. State St.
Ann Arbor, MI 48104
Telephone: (313) 668-6097

Year Established: 1985
Pub. Frequency: m.
Subscrip. Rate: $10/yr.
Circulation: 1,200
Circulation Type: controlled & paid
**Owner(s):**
George Wahr Publishing Co.
304 1-2 S. State St.
Ann Arbor, MI 48104
Telephone: (313) 668-6097
Ownership %: 100
**Editorial:**
Elizabeth Davenport ...........................Editor
**Desc.:** Contains commentary and analysis
on domestic and international events
and issues.

70816
## MIDDLE EAST MONITOR
P.O. Box 236
Ridgewood, NJ 07451
Telephone: (908) 545-1058
Year Established: 1971
Pub. Frequency: m.
Subscrip. Rate: $98/yr.
**Owner(s):**
Middle East Monitor
P.O. Box 236
Ridgewood, NJ 07451-0236
Telephone: (908) 545-1058
Ownership %: 100
**Editorial:**
Amir N. Ghazaii ...........................Editor

70829
## MUNICIPAL IMMUNITY LAW BULLETIN
23 Drydock Ave.
Boston, MA 02210-2387
Telephone: (800) 229-2084
FAX: (617) 345-9646
Pub. Frequency: m.
Subscrip. Rate: $60/yr.
**Owner(s):**
Quinlan Publishing co.
123 Drydock
Boston, MA 02210
Telephone: (800) 229-2084
FAX: (617) 345-9646
Ownership %: 100
**Desc.:** Covers issues relating to immunity
in lawsuits brought against
municipalities, including official
misconduct, injuries on city property,
street maintenance, civil rights violations,
wrongful prosecution or arrest, and
similar issues.

70807
## NATIONAL MINORITY POLITICS
5757 Westheimer
Ste. 3-296
Houston, TX 77057
Telephone: (713) 444-4265
FAX: (713) 580-0011
Year Established: 1988
Pub. Frequency: m.
Subscrip. Rate: $89/yr.
Materials: 10
Circulation: 400
Circulation Type: controlled & paid
**Owner(s):**
Lionshare, Inc.
5757 Westheimer
Ste. 3-296
Houston, TX 77057
Telephone: (713) 444-4265
FAX: (713) 580-0011
Ownership %: 100
**Editorial:**
Gwenevere Daye Richardson ...................Editor
**Desc.:** Provides the latest information on
issues, trends, and election involving
minority groups.

70819
## NEAR EAST REPORT
440 First St., N.W.
Ste. 607
Washington, DC 20001
Telephone: (202) 638-1225
FAX: (202) 638-1225
Year Established: 1957
Pub. Frequency: w.
Subscrip. Rate: $30/yr.
**Owner(s):**
Near East Research, Inc.
440 First St., N.W.
Ste 607
Washington, DC 20001
Telephone: (202) 638-1225
FAX: (202) 347-4916
Ownership %: 100
**Editorial:**
Raphael Danziger ...........................Editor

70814
## NONVIOLENT ANARCHIST NEWSLETTER
P.O. Box 1385
Austin, TX 78767
Year Established: 1983
Pub. Frequency: a.
Subscrip. Rate: $3/yr.
Materials: 10,33
Circulation: 500
Circulation Type: controlled & paid
**Owner(s):**
Slough Press
P.O. Box 1385
Austin, TX 78767
Ownership %: 100
**Editorial:**
Chuck Taylor ...........................Editor

70980
## O S H A WEEK
225 N. New Rd.
Waco, TX 76710-6931
Telephone: (817) 776-9000
Pub. Frequency: w.
Subscrip. Rate: $468/yr.
**Owner(s):**
Stevens Publishing Corporation
225 N. New Rd.
Waco, TX 76710-6931
Telephone: (817) 776-9000
Ownership %: 100
**Editorial:**
Jerome Ashton ...........................Editor

70786
## PACS & LOBBIES
2000 National Press Bldg.
Washington, DC 20045
Telephone: (301) 251-9009
FAX: (301) 251-9058
Year Established: 1980
Pub. Frequency: s-m.
Subscrip. Rate: $287/yr.
**Owner(s):**
Amward Publications, Inc.
2000 National Press Bldg.
Washington, DC 20045
Telephone: (301) 251-9009
FAX: (301) 251-9058
Ownership %: 100
**Desc.:** Covers campaign finance and
lobbying developments.

70871
## PLANNING COMMISSIONERS JOURNAL
Burlington, VT 05406
Telephone: (802) 458-9423
FAX: (802) 862-1882
Mailing Address:
P.O. Box 4295
Burlington, VT 05406
Year Established: 1991
Pub. Frequency: 4/yr.
Subscrip. Rate: $15/yr

**Materials Accepted/Included:** 01-Business news 02-By-line articles 03-Fashion news 04-Food news 05-Freelance copy 06-Letters to editor 07-Real estate news 08-Sports news 09-Travel news
10-Book rev. 11-Movie rev. 12-Music rev. 13-TV rev. 14-Theater rev. 15-Coming events 16-Obituaries 17-Question & answer 18-Social announcements 19-Artwork 20-Cartoons 21-Photos 22-TV listings
23-Audio rec. 24-Video rec. 25-Books 26-Films/film clips 27-Personnel news 28-Press releases 29-New product news/photos 30-Trade lit. 31-Contracts awarded 32-Display adv. 33-Classified adv.

7-77

Circulation: 3,000
Circulation Type: controlled & paid
**Owner(s):**
Champlain Planning Press
P.O. Box 4295
Burlington, VT 05406
Telephone: (802) 864-9083
Ownership %: 100
**Editorial:**
Wayne M. Senville .........................Editor
**Desc.:** Aimed at local planning
    commissioners US & others interested in
    local planning - covers transportation,
    land use, zoning, housing & urban
    design

70787
**POLITICAL WOMAN**
276 Chatterton Pkwy.
White Plains, NY 10606
Telephone: (914) 285-9761
Year Established: 1992
Pub. Frequency: 11/yr.
Subscrip. Rate: $45/yr.
**Owner(s):**
Political Woman, Inc.
276 Chatterton Pkwy.
White Plains, NY 10606
Telephone: (605) 285-9761
Ownership %: 100
**Editorial:**
Antonia Stolper ..........................Editor

70613
**PROGRESSIVE REVIEW**
1739 Connecticut Ave., N.W.
Washington, DC 20009
Telephone: (202) 232-5544
FAX: (202) 234-6222
Year Established: 1966
Pub. Frequency: 9/yr.
Subscrip. Rate: $15/yr. US; $26/yr. foreign
Materials: 10
Circulation: 1,500
Circulation Type: controlled & paid
**Owner(s):**
Progressive Review
1739 Connecticut Ave., N.W.
Washington, DC 20009
Telephone: (202) 232-5544
Ownership %: 100
**Editorial:**
Sam Smith ..............................Editor
**Desc.:** Newsletter of progressive politics.

70803
**RESIST NEWSLETTER**
One Summer St.
Sommerville, MA 02143
Telephone: (617) 623-5110
Year Established: 1967
Pub. Frequency: m.
Subscrip. Rate: $15/yr.
Circulation: 5,000
Circulation Type: controlled & paid
**Owner(s):**
Resist Newsletter
One Summer St.
Sommerville, MA 02143
Telephone: (617) 623-5110
Ownership %: 100
**Editorial:**
Tatiana Schreiber .........................Editor
**Desc.:** Covers AIDS, reproductive rights,
    homelessness, ecology movements,
    Middle East and Third World organizing
    efforts. Articles on topics of interest to
    all those concerned with peace and
    social justice.

70790
**SCIENCE & GOVERNMENT
REPORT**
P.O. Box 6226A
Northwest Sta.
Washington, DC 20015
Telephone: (800) 522-1970

Year Established: 1971
Pub. Frequency: s-m.
Subscrip. Rate: $395/yr.
Circulation: 1,500
Circulation Type: controlled & paid
**Owner(s):**
Science & Government Reports, Inc.
P.O. Box 6226A
Northwest Sta.
Washington, DC 20015
Telephone: (800) 522-1970
Ownership %: 100

70846
**TENNESSEE JOURNAL**
162 Fourth Ave., N.
Nashville, TN 37219-8867
Telephone: (615) 242-7395
FAX: (615) 256-6601
Year Established: 1974
Pub. Frequency: w.
Subscrip. Rate: $187/yr.
Circulation: 1,400
Circulation Type: controlled & paid
**Owner(s):**
M. Lee Smith Publishers & Printers
162 Fourth Ave., N.
Nashville, TN 37219-8867
Telephone: (615) 242-7395
FAX: (615) 256-6601
Ownership %: 100
**Editorial:**
Bradford N. Forrister .......................Editor
**Desc.:** Insider's newsletter on Tennessee
    government and politics.

70792
**TEXAS GOVERNMENT
NEWSLETTER**
P.O. Box 13274
Austin, TX 78711
Telephone: (512) 323-5051
Year Established: 1973
Pub. Frequency: 40/yr.
Subscrip. Rate: $26/yr.
Circulation: 1,400
Circulation Type: controlled & paid
**Owner(s):**
Texas Government Newsletter
P.O. Box 13274
Austin, TX 78711
Telephone: (512) 323-5051
Ownership %: 100
**Editorial:**
Thomas L. Whatley .......................Editor
**Desc.:** Contains information about Texas
    state government and politics; includes
    reviews of news and in-depth analysis of
    single topics.

70795
**TEXAS WEEKLY**
P.O. Box 5306
Austin, TX 78763
Telephone: (512) 322-9332
FAX: (512) 453-0027
Year Established: 1984
Pub. Frequency: w.
Subscrip. Rate: $150/yr.
**Owner(s):**
Texas Weekly
P.O. Box 5306
Autin, TX 78763
Telephone: (512) 322-9332
FAX: (512) 453-0027
Ownership %: 100
**Editorial:**
Sam Kinch, Jr. ..........................Editor
**Desc.:** Nonpartisan reports on Texas
    government and politics.

70868
**URBAN OUTLOOK**
215 Park Ave., S.
Ste. 1301
New York, NY 10003
Telephone: (212) 228-0246
FAX: (212) 228-0376
Year Established: 1977
Pub. Frequency: s-m.
Subscrip. Rate: $157/yr.
**Owner(s):**
Alexander Research & Communications,
    Inc.
215 Park Ave., S.
Ste. 1301
New York, NY 10003
Telephone: (212) 228-0246
Ownership %: 100
**Editorial:**
Laurence A. Alexander .....................Editor
**Desc.:** For professionals concerned with
    meeting unique challenges of urban
    areas. Focuses on planning & land use,
    energy, envrionment health,
    infrastaructure, economics, grants,
    crime, housing, education

71189
**WASHINGTON PACIFIC REPORT**
1615 New Hampshire Ave., N.W.
Ste. 400
Washington, DC 20009-2520
Telephone: (202) 387-8100
FAX: (202) 332-9162
Year Established: 1982
Pub. Frequency: bi-m.
Subscrip. Rate: $159/yr.
**Owner(s):**
Washington Pacific Publications
1615 New Hampshire Ave., N.W.
Ste. 400
Washington, DC 20009-2520
Telephone: (202) 387-8100
FAX: (202) 332-9162
Ownership %: 100
**Editorial:**
Fred Radewagon ...........................Editor
**Desc.:** Covers current events in the Pacific
    islands and offers analysis on political
    topics, especially U.S. government
    actions that effect these nations.

70817
**WASHINGTON REPORT**
P.O. Box 10309
St. Petersburg, FL 33733-0309
Telephone: (813) 866-1598
FAX: (813) 866-1598
Year Established: 1979
Pub. Frequency: m.
Subscrip. Rate: $25/yr.
Circulation: 17,000
Circulation Type: controlled & paid
**Owner(s):**
Editors Release Service
P.O. Box 10309
St. Petersburg, FL 33733-0309
Telephone: (812) 866-1598
FAX: (812) 866-1598
Ownership %: 100
**Editorial:**
William A. Leavell .........................Editor
**Desc.:** Alternative reports of the
    Washington political scene not generally
    covered by the media.

70799
**WOLFE'S VERSION**
P.O. Box 99
Blue Springs, MO 64015
Telephone: (314) 635-3154
Year Established: 1975
Pub. Frequency: m.
Subscrip. Rate: $24/yr.

**Owner(s):**
Wolf's Version
P.O. Box 99
Blue Springs, MO 64015
Telephone: (314) 635-3154
Ownership %: 100
**Editorial:**
James F. Wolfe ..........................Editor
**Desc.:** Discusses economics and how they
    affect Missouri and national politics.

## Group 352-Religion

71007
**ACTS & FACTS**
P.O. Box 2667
El Cajon, CA 92021
FAX: (619) 448-3469
Year Established: 1972
Pub. Frequency: m.
Subscrip. Rate: free
Materials: 32
Circulation: 120,000
Circulation Type: controlled & free
**Owner(s):**
Institute for Creation Research
P.O. Box 2667
El Cajon, CA 92021
FAX: (619) 448-3469
Ownership %: 100
**Desc.:** Newsletter on the creation and
    evolution questions, including scientific
    articles.

70984
**AMUDIM**
401 Grinter Hall
University of Florida
Gainesville, FL 32611
Telephone: (904) 392-9247
FAX: (904) 392-5378
Year Established: 1986
Pub. Frequency: a.
Subscrip. Rate: free
Circulation: 6,500
Circulation Type: controlled
**Owner(s):**
University of Florida
Gainesville, FL 32611
Telephone: (904) 392-9247
FAX: (904) 392-5378
Ownership %: 100
**Editorial:**
Warren Bargad ...........................Editor
**Desc.:** Provides information on events and
    lectures sponsored by the center, gifts,
    Judaica library, graduates, courses, and
    special programs in Jewish studies.

70889
**BIBLE-SCIENCE NEWS**
P.O. Box 32547
Minneapolis, MN 55432-0457
Telephone: (612) 755-8606
FAX: (612) 755-8606
Year Established: 1963
Pub. Frequency: 9/yr.
Subscrip. Rate: $25/yr.
Materials: 10
Circulation: 15,000
Circulation Type: controlled & paid
**Owner(s):**
Bible-Science Association, Inc.
P.O. Box 32457
Minneapolis, MN 55432-0457
Telephone: (612) 755-8606
FAX: (612) 755-8606
Ownership %: 100
**Editorial:**
Paul A. Bartz ............................Editor
**Desc.:** Non-technical publication of Bible
    and science issues for a Christian
    audience.

**Materials Accepted/Included:** 01-Business news 02-By-line articles  03-Fashion news  04-Food news  05-Freelance copy  06-Letters to editor  07-Real estate news  08-Sports news  09-Travel news 10-Book rev. 11-Movie rev. 12-Music rev. 13-TV rev. 14-Theater rev. 15-Coming events 16-Obituaries 17-Question & answer 18-Social announcements 19-Artwork 20-Cartoons 21-Photos 22-TV listings 23-Audio rec. 24-Video rec. 25-Books 26-Films/film clips 27-Personnel news 28-Press releases 29-New product news/photos 30-Trade lit. 31-Contracts awarded 32-Display adv. 33-Classified adv.

7-78

**BIBLICAL ERRANCY** 70895
3158 Sherwood Park Dr.
Springfield, OH 45505
Telephone: (513) 323-6146
Year Established: 1983
Pub. Frequency: m.
Subscrip. Rate: $12/yr. US; $14/yr.
   Canada
Circulation: 330
Circulation Type: controlled & paid
**Owner(s):**
Dennis McKinsey
3158 Sherwood Park Dr.
Springfield, OH 45505
Telephone: (513) 323-6146
Ownership %: 100
**Management:**
Dennis McKinsey ...............................Publisher
**Editorial:**
Dennis McKinsey ...................................Editor
**Desc.:** Exposes and critiques fallacies and
   contradictions in the Bible. Includes
   letters from readers and critics. Exposes
   and critiques fallacies and contradictions
   in the Bible. Includes letters from
   readers and critics.

**BRINGING RELIGION HOME** 70991
205 W. Monroe St.
Chicago, IL 60606
Telephone: (312) 236-7782
FAX: (312) 236-7230
Year Established: 1976
Pub. Frequency: m.
Subscrip. Rate: $12/yr.
Circulation: 69,862
Circulation Type: controlled & paid
**Owner(s):**
Claretian Publications
205 W. Monroe St.
Chicago, IL 60606
Telephone: (312) 236-7782
FAX: (312) 236-7230
Ownership %: 100
**Editorial:**
Rev. Mark J. Brummel ...............................Editor

**CALL TO PEACEMAKING** 71009
P.O. Box 500
Akron, PA 17501
Telephone: (717) 859-1958
Year Established: 1983
Pub. Frequency: q.
Subscrip. Rate: free
Materials: 10
Circulation: 650
Circulation Type: controlled & free
**Owner(s):**
New Call to Peacemaking
P.O. Box 500
Akron, PA 17501
Telephone: (717) 859-1958
Ownership %: 100
**Editorial:**
John K. Stoner ...................................Editor
**Desc.:** Discusses nonviolence, alternatives
   to war, and related issues for a church
   audience.

**CARING COMMUNITY** 70994
115 E. Armour Blvd.
P.O. Box 419281
Kansas City, MO 64141
Telephone: (800) 444-8910
FAX: (816) 931-5082
Year Established: 1985
Pub. Frequency: m.
Circulation: 30,000
Circulation Type: controlled & paid

**Owner(s):**
National Catholic Reporter Publishing Co.,
   Inc.
115 E. Armour Blvd.
P.O. Box 419281
Kansas City, MO 64141
Telephone: (800) 444-8910
FAX: (816) 931-5082
Ownership %: 100
**Editorial:**
Carolyn Hoff ...................................Editor
Rich Heffren ...................................Editor
**Desc.:** Newsletter of support and
   inspiration for homebound and
   hospitalized Catholics.

**CRUX OF THE NEWS** 70899
3 Enterprise Dr.
Albany, NY 12204
Telephone: (518) 465-4591
FAX: (518) 465-4333
Year Established: 1966
Pub. Frequency: w.
Subscrip. Rate: $59.50/yr.
Materials: 10,32
Circulation: 3,400
Circulation Type: controlled & paid
**Owner(s):**
Gabriel Publishing Co., Inc.
3 Enterprise Dr.
Albany, NY 12204
Telephone: (518) 465-4591
FAX: (518) 465-4333
Ownership %: 100
**Editorial:**
Richard A. Dowd ...................................Editor

**DENSAL** 71019
352 Mead Mountain Rd.
Woodstock, NY 12498
Telephone: (914) 679-7541
FAX: (914) 679-4625
Year Established: 1979
Pub. Frequency: q.
Subscrip. Rate: $14/yr.
Materials: 10, 32
Circulation: 2000
Circulation Type: controlled & paid
**Owner(s):**
Karma Triyana Dharmachakra (K.T.D.)
352 Mead Mountain Rd.
Woodstock, NY 12498
Telephone: (914) 679-7541
FAX: (914) 679-4625
Ownership %: 100
**Editorial:**
Naomi Schmidt ...................................Editor
**Desc.:** Teaching the news of the Karma
   Kagyu Lineage of Tibetan Buddhism.

**DIOCESAN DIALOGUE** 70995
16160 S. Seton Dr.
Holland, IL 60473
Telephone: (708) 331-5485
Year Established: 1986
Pub. Frequency: s-a.
Subscrip. Rate: $5/yr.
Circulation: 550
Circulation Type: controlled & paid
**Owner(s):**
American Catholic Press
16160 S. Seton Dr.
Holland, IL 60473
Telephone: (708) 331-5485
Ownership %: 100
**Editorial:**
Raquel Ryan ...................................Editor
**Desc.:** Includes news about the work of
   offices of communication in various
   Roman Catholic dioceses in the US,
   especially those that produce religious
   services on television

**DOVETAIL** 71202
3014 A Folsom St.
Boulder, CO 80304
Year Established: 1993
Pub. Frequency: bi-m.
Subscrip. Rate: $24.99/yr.
**Owner(s):**
Dovetail Publishing
3014 A Folsom St.
Boulder, CO 80304
Ownership %: 100
**Desc.:** Aimed at interfaith Jewish-Christian
   families.

**FOCUS ON MISSIONS** 71027
P.O. Box 136
Middletown, DE 19409-0136
Telephone: (302) 378-1525
Year Established: 1970
Pub. Frequency: 3/yr.
Subscrip. Rate: free
Materials: 10
Circulation: 24000
Circulation Type: controlled & free
**Owner(s):**
Fellowship of Mission
P.O. Box 136
Middletown, DE 19409
Telephone: (302) 378-1525
Ownership %: 100
**Editorial:**
Henry J. Heijermans ...............................Editor
**Desc.:** Covers news on missions
   worldwide.

**GENERATION** 70997
205 W. Monroe St.
Chicago, IL 60606
Telephone: (312) 236-7782
FAX: (312) 236-7230
Year Established: 1980
Pub. Frequency: m.
Subscrip. Rate: $12/yr.
Circulation: 25,366
Circulation Type: controlled & paid
**Owner(s):**
Claretian Publications
205 W. Monroe St.
Chicago, IL 60606
Telephone: (312) 236-7782
FAX: (312) 236-7230
Ownership %: 100
**Editorial:**
Rev. Mark J. Brummel ...............................Editor
**Desc.:** Each newsletter examines one
   topic of special interest to older
   Catholics.

**JEWISH CHRONICLE LEADER** 71197
131 Lincoln St.
Worchester, MA 01605
Telephone: (508) 752-2512
FAX: (508) 752-9057
Year Established: 1926
Pub. Frequency: fortn.
Page Size: tabloid
Subscrip. Rate: $11/yr.
Materials: 10,32
Circulation: 3500
Circulation Type: paid
**Owner(s):**
Mar-Len Publications
131 Lincoln St.
Worcester, MA 01605
Telephone: (508) 251-2000
FAX: (508) 752-9057
Ownership %: 100
**Editorial:**
Sondra Shapiro ...................................Editor

**JEWS FOR JESUS NEWSLETTER** 71005
60 Haight St.
San Francisco, CA 94102
Telephone: (415) 864-2600
FAX: (415) 552-8325
Year Established: 1973
Pub. Frequency: m.
Subscrip. Rate: free
Circulation: 23,000
Circulation Type: controlled
**Owner(s):**
Jews for Jesus
60 Haight St.
San Francisco, CA 94102
Telephone: (415) 864-2600
FAX: (415) 552-8325
Ownership %: 100
**Editorial:**
Ceil Rosen ...................................Editor

**NATIONAL & INTERNATIONAL
RELIGION REPORT** 71244
P.O. Box 21433
Roanoke, VA 24018
Telephone: (703) 989-1330
Year Established: 1987
Pub. Frequency: fortn.
Subscrip. Rate: $49/yr.
**Owner(s):**
Media Management
P.O. Box 21433
Roanoke, VA 24018
Telephone: (703) 989-1330
Ownership %: 100

**NEW TREND** 70996
P.O. Box 356
Kingsville, MD 21087
Telephone: (410) 435-4046
Year Established: 1977
Pub. Frequency: m.
Subscrip. Rate: $7.50/yr.
Materials: 10
Circulation: 5,000
Circulation Type: controlled & paid
**Owner(s):**
American Society for Education & Religion,
   Inc.
P.O. Box 356
Kingsville, MD 21087
Telephone: (410) 435-4046
Ownership %: 100
**Editorial:**
K. Siddique ...................................Editor
**Desc.:** Islamic perspective on change and
   conflict in the world.

**OPTIONS** 71017
P.O. Box 311
Wayne, NJ 07474-0311
Telephone: (201) 694-2327
Year Established: 1974
Pub. Frequency: m.
Subscrip. Rate: $18/yr.
Materials: 10
**Owner(s):**
Options Publishing Co.
P.O. Box 311
Wayne, NJ 07474-0311
Telephone: (201) 694-2327
Ownership %: 100
**Editorial:**
Betty J. Singer ...................................Editor
**Desc.:** American Jewish resources:
   cultural, educational, religious, and more.

**PARISH COMMUNICATION** 71004
Rte. 1
P.O. Box 142
New Hampton, NH 03256-9713
Telephone: (603) 744-6316
FAX: (603) 744-6318
Year Established: 1981

**Materials Accepted/Included:** 01-Business news 02-By-line articles 03-Fashion news 04-Food news 05-Freelance copy 06-Letters to editor 07-Real estate news 08-Sports news 09-Travel news
10-Book rev. 11-Movie rev. 12-Music rev. 13-TV rev. 14-Theater rev. 15-Coming events 16-Obituaries 17-Question & answer 18-Social announcements 19-Artwork 20-Cartoons 21-Photos 22-TV listings
23-Audio rec. 24-Video rec. 25-Books 26-Films/film clips 27-Personnel news 28-Press releases 29-New product news/photos 30-Trade lit. 31-Contracts awarded 32-Display adv. 33-Classified adv.

7-79

Pub. Frequency: q.
Subscrip. Rate: $23/yr. US; $28/yr. foreign
Materials: 10
Circulation: 1,100
Circulation Type: controlled & paid
**Owner(s):**
Fred B. Estabrook Company, Inc.
Rte. 1
P.O. Box 142
New Hampton, NH 03256-9713
Telephone: (603) 744-6316
FAX: (603) 744-6318
Ownership %: 100
**Editorial:**
Veronica Dicomo ..........................Editor
**Desc.:** Seasonal graphics, quotes from
　saints and modern leaders, weekly
　essays, puzzles, calendars, and
　sketches to be used in parish bulletins
　and newsletters.

71040

**REACH**
2850 Kalamazoo Ave., S.E.
Grand Radids, MI 49560
Telephone: (616) 246-0767
FAX: (616) 246-0834
Pub. Frequency: bi-m.
Subscrip. Rate: $22.50/yr.
Circulation: 14,500
Circulation Type: controlled & paid
**Owner(s):**
Christian Reformed Home Missions
2850 Kalamazoo Ave., S.E.
Grand Rapids, MI 49560
Telephone: (616) 146-0767
FAX: (616) 579-0834
Ownership %: 100
**Desc.:** Deals with church growth issues for
　pastors and church leaders in the
　Christian Reformed Church of North
　America.

70998

**RELIGIOUS LIFE**
P.O. Box 41007
Chicago, IL 60641
Telephone: (312) 267-2044
Year Established: 1976
Pub. Frequency: 10/yr.
Subscrip. Rate: $10/yr.
Materials: 10,32
Circulation: 3,800
Circulation Type: controlled & paid
**Owner(s):**
Institute on Religious Life
P.O. Box 41007
Chicago, IL 60641
Telephone: (312) 267-2044
Ownership %: 100
**Editorial:**
Fr. L. Dudley Day ..........................Editor
**Desc.:** Serves the Catholic religious
　communities by fostering a more
　effective understanding of the Church's
　teaching on religious life.

71023

**SNOW LION NEWSLETTER &**
　**CATALOG**
P.O. Box 6483
Ithaca, NY 14851
Telephone: (607) 273-8506
FAX: (607) 273-8508
Year Established: 1986
Pub. Frequency: q.
Subscrip. Rate: $1/yr.
Materials: 10, 32
Circulation: 18000
Circulation Type: controlled & paid
**Owner(s):**
Snow Lion Publications
P.O. Box 6483
Ithaca, NY 14851
Telephone: (607) 273-8506
FAX: (607) 273-8508
Ownership %: 100

71002

**US PARISH**
205 W. Monroe St.
Chicago, IL 60606
Telephone: (312) 236-7782
FAX: (312) 236-7230
Year Established: 1983
Pub. Frequency: m.
Subscrip. Rate: $24.95/yr.
Circulation: 1,938
Circulation Type: controlled & paid
**Owner(s):**
Claretian Publications
205 W. Monroe St.
Chicago, IL 60606
Telephone: (312) 236-7782
FAX: (312) 236-7230
Ownership %: 100
**Editorial:**
Rev. Mark J. Brummel ..........................Editor

70901

**WORLD MISSIONARY PRESS**
　**NEWS**
P.O. Box 120
New Paris, IN 46553-0120
Telephone: (219) 831-2111
FAX: (219) 831-2161
Year Established: 1961
Pub. Frequency: 5/yr.
Subscrip. Rate: free
Circulation: 12,000
Circulation Type: controlled & free
**Owner(s):**
World Missionary Press, Inc.
P.O. Box 120
New Paris, IN 46553-0120
Telephone: (219) 831-2111
FAX: (219) 831-2161
Ownership %: 100
**Editorial:**
Deborah Crist ..........................Editor

71042

**YOUTHWORKER UPDATE**
1224 Greenfield Dr.
El Cajon, CA 92021
Telephone: (619) 440-2333
FAX: (619) 440-1939
Mailing Address:
　P.O. Box 17017
　North Hollywood, CA 91615-9937
Year Established: 1986
Pub. Frequency: m.
Subscrip. Rate: $23.95/yr.
**Owner(s):**
Youth Specialties
1224 Greenfield Dr.
El Cajon, CA 92021
Telephone: (619) 440-2333
FAX: (619) 440-4939
Ownership %: 100
**Editorial:**
Wayne Rice ..........................Editor
**Desc.:** Provides informaton on the latest
　youth culture trends, research,
　resources, and news.

## Group 354-Schools & Education

71243

**ACADEMIC LEADER**
2718 Dryden Dr.
Madison, WI 53704
Telephone: (608) 246-3580
FAX: (608) 249-0355
Year Established: 1985
Pub. Frequency: m.
Subscrip. Rate: $73/yr.
Materials: 10

**Owner(s):**
Magna Publications
2718 Dryden Dr.
Madison, WI 53700
Telephone: (608) 246-3580
FAX: (608) 249-0355
Ownership %: 100
**Editorial:**
Doris Green ..........................Editor

70229

**ADMINISTRATORS NEWSLETTER**
P.O. Box 2079
Yucca Valley, CA 92286-2079
Telephone: (619) 365-9718
FAX: (619) 228-1567
Pub. Frequency: m.
Circulation: 26,711
Circulation Type: controlled & paid
**Owner(s):**
CMA Microcomputers
P.O. Box 2079
Yucca Valley, CA 92286-2079
Telephone: (619) 365-9718
FAX: (619) 228-1567
Ownership %: 100
**Editorial:**
Ray Burr ..........................Editor

70199

**AP SPECIAL**
1904 Association Dr.
Reston, VA 22091
Telephone: (703) 860-0200
FAX: (703) 476-5432
Year Established: 1985
Pub. Frequency: q.
Circulation: 10,000
Circulation Type: controlled & paid
**Owner(s):**
National Association of Secondary School
　Principal
1904 Association Dr.
Reston, VA 22091
Telephone: (703) 860-0200
FAX: (703) 476-5432
Ownership %: 100
**Editorial:**
Jackie Rough ..........................Editor
**Desc.:** Addresses issues of interest to
　secondary school assistant principals.

58582

**AV GUIDE: LEARNING MEDIA**
　**NEWSLETTER, THE**
380 Northwest Hwy.
Des Plaines, IL 60016-2282
Telephone: (708) 298-6622
FAX: (708) 390-0408
Pub. Frequency: m.
Page Size: standard
Subscrip. Rate: $15/yr.
Materials: 23,24,26,28,29,30
Print Process: offset
Circulation: 1,000
Circulation Type: paid
**Owner(s):**
Educational Screen, Inc.
380 Northwest Hwy.
Des Plaines, IL 60016
Telephone: (708) 298-6622
Ownership %: 100
**Management:**
H.S. Gillette ..........................Publisher
**Editorial:**
Natalie Ferguson ..........................Editor
**Deadline:** story-15th of mo.; news-15th of
　mo.; photo-15th of mo.; ads-15th of mo.

71211

**BLUMENFELD EDUCATION**
　**LETTER**
P.O. Box 54161
Boise, ID 83711
Telephone: (208) 343-3790
Year Established: 1986

Pub. Frequency: m.
Subscrip. Rate: $36/yr.
**Owner(s):**
Paradigm Co.
P.O. Box 45161
Boise, ID 83711
Telephone: (208) 343-3790
Ownership %: 100
**Editorial:**
Samuel L. Blumenfeld ..........................Editor

70198

**CAREER PLANNING & ADULT**
　**DEVELOPMENT NETWORK**
　**NEWSLETTER**
4965 Sierra Rd.
San Jose, CA 95132
Telephone: (408) 559-4946
FAX: (408) 559-8211
Year Established: 1979
Pub. Frequency: m.
Subscrip. Rate: $50/yr. non-members;
　$70/yr. foreign
Materials: 10,11
Circulation: 1,000
Circulation Type: controlled & paid
**Owner(s):**
Career Planning and Adult Development
　Network
4965 Sierra Rd.
San Jose, CA 95132
Telephone: (408) 559-4946
FAX: (408) 559-8211
Ownership %: 100
**Editorial:**
Richard L. Knowdell ..........................Editor
**Desc.:** Listing of workshops, conferences,
　films, books and counseling techniques
　for career counselors.

70257

**CENTER FOR LAW & EDUCATION**
955 Massachusetts Ave.
Cambridge, MA 02139
Telephone: (617) 876-6611
FAX: (617) 876-0202
Year Established: 1979
Pub. Frequency: q.
Subscrip. Rate: free
Materials: 10
Circulation: 5,500
Circulation Type: controlled & free
**Owner(s):**
Center for Law & Education, Inc.
955 Massachusetts Ave.
Cambridge, MA 02139
Telephone: (617) 876-6611
FAX: (617) 876-0203
Ownership %: 100
**Editorial:**
Sharon Schumack ..........................Editor
**Desc.:** Covers education advocacy, key
　legal developments, noteworthy
　advocacy efforts, and useful resources
　for persons who represent low-income
　parents and students.

70218

**COLLEGE BOUND**
P.O. Box 6536
Evanston, IL 60204
Telephone: (312) 262-5810
FAX: (312) 262-5806
Year Established: 1986
Pub. Frequency: 10/yr.
Subscrip. Rate: $59/yr. US; $69/yr. foreign
Materials: 10
Circulation: 2,500
Circulation Type: controlled & paid
**Owner(s):**
College Bound Publications, Inc.
P.O. Box 6536
Evanston, IL 60204
Telephone: (312) 262-5810
FAX: (312) 262-5806
Ownership %: 100

**Materials Accepted/Included:** 01-Business news 02-By-line articles 03-Fashion news 04-Food news 05-Freelance copy 06-Letters to editor 07-Real estate news 08-Sports news 09-Travel news 10-Book rev. 11-Movie rev. 12-Music rev. 13-TV rev. 14-Theater rev. 15-Coming events 16-Obituaries 17-Question & answer 18-Social announcements 19-Artwork 20-Cartoons 21-Photos 22-TV listings 23-Audio rec. 24-Video rec. 25-Books 26-Films/film clips 27-Personnel news 28-Press releases 29-New product news/photos 30-Trade lit. 31-Contracts awarded 32-Display adv. 33-Classified adv.

**Editorial:**
R. Craig Sautter ................................Editor
**Desc.:** Covers college admissions, financial aid, issues and trends.

70206

## COLLEGE BY MAIL
P.O. Box 416
Denver, CO 80201-0416
Telephone: (303) 575-5676
Year Established: 1991
Pub. Frequency: a.
Subscrip. Rate: $6.95/yr.
Circulation: 10,000
Circulation Type: controlled & paid
**Owner(s):**
Prosperity & Profits Unlimited
P.O. Box 416
Denver, CO 80201-0416
Telephone: (303) 575-5676
Ownership %: 100
**Editorial:**
A. Doyle ........................................Editor

70329

## COLLOQUY
312 Sutter St., Ste. 200
San Francisco, CA 94108
Telephone: (415) 982-3263
FAX: (415) 982-5028
Year Established: 1980
Pub. Frequency: q.
Subscrip. Rate: free; $2/yr. out of state
Circulation: 3,000
Circulation Type: controlled & paid
**Owner(s):**
World Affairs Council
312 Sutter St., Ste. 200
San Francisco, CA 94108
Telephone: (415) 982-3263
FAX: (415) 982-5028
Ownership %: 100
**Editorial:**
Diana M. Wolf ................................Editor
**Desc.:** Examines international studies of teaching, teaching methods and curriculum, the humanities, history, and social studies.

70235

## COMMUNICATOR
1615 Duke St.
Alexandria, VA 22314-3483
Telephone: (703) 684-3345
FAX: (703) 548-6021
Pub. Frequency: m.
Subscrip. Rate: $20/yr.
Circulation: 29,000
Circulation Type: controlled & paid
**Owner(s):**
National Assn. of Elementary School
Principals
1615 Duke St.
Alexandria, VA 22314-3483
Telephone: (703) 684-3345
FAX: (703) 548-6021
Ownership %: 100
**Editorial:**
Betsy Berlin ....................................Editor
**Desc.:** For elementary and middle school educators. Covers educational, legislative and other issues.

70138

## COMMUNIQUE
55 Brown Rd.
Ithaca, NY 14850-1266
Telephone: (607) 254-7111
FAX: (607) 254-7167
Year Established: 1978
Pub. Frequency: 4/yr.
Subscrip. Rate: free
Circulation: 17,000
Circulation Type: controlled

**Owner(s):**
Cornell University
55 Brown Rd.
Ithaca, NY 14850-1266
Telephone: (607) 254-7111
FAX: (607) 254-7167
Ownership %: 100
**Editorial:**
Jeannette Knapp ................................Editor
**Desc.:** Published as a leadership report to alumni and friends of Cornell University.

70139

## CONCORDIA ALUMNI NEWS
901 S. Eighth St.
Moorhead, MN 56562
Telephone: (218) 299-4000
FAX: (218) 299-3646
Year Established: 1961
Pub. Frequency: 3/yr.
Circulation: 34,000
Circulation Type: controlled
**Owner(s):**
Concordia College
901 S. Eighth St.
Moorhead, MN 56562
Telephone: (218) 299-4000
FAX: (218) 299-3646
Ownership %: 100
**Editorial:**
Maureen Zimmerman ............................Editor
**Desc.:** Covers news and features for alumni and friends of the college.

70309

## COTTONWOOD MONTHLY
P.O. Box 802
Henderson, KS 42420
Year Established: 1987
Pub. Frequency: m
Subscrip. Rate: $21.95
Circulation: 300
Circulation Type: controlled & paid
**Owner(s):**
Class Act
P.O. Box 802
Henderson, KS 42420
Ownership %: 100
**Editorial:**
Cheryl Thurston ................................Editor

69493

## CUE NEWSLETTER
1210 Marina Village Pkwy., #100
Alameda, CA 94501-1045
Telephone: (408) 496-2935
Year Established: 1978
Pub. Frequency: bi-m
Subscrip. Rate: $25/yr. membership
Circulation: 9,500
Circulation Type: paid
**Owner(s):**
Computer Using Educators, Inc.
4655 Old Ironsides Dr., No.200
Santa Clara, CA 95054-1808
Telephone: (408) 496-2935
Ownership %: 100
**Desc.:** Articles and news discussing the application of computer systems to learning and education.
**Readers:** California educators at all levels.

70142

## DANA REVIEW
Dana College
Blair, NE 68008
Telephone: (402) 426-7235
FAX: (402) 426-7386
Year Established: 1944
Pub. Frequency: 4/yr.
Subscrip. Rate: free
Circulation: 11,000
Circulation Type: controlled & free

**Owner(s):**
Dana College
Blair, NE 68008
Telephone: (402) 426-7235
FAX: (402) 426-7236
Ownership %: 100
**Editorial:**
Ann George ....................................Editor

70253

## DEPARTMENT CHAIR
176 Ballville Rd.
Bolton, MA 01740-0249
Telephone: (508) 779-6190
FAX: (508) 779-6296
Mailing Address:
    P.O. Box 249
    Bolton, MA 01740-0249
Year Established: 1990
Pub. Frequency: q.
Subscrip. Rate: $69/yr.
Materials: 10,32
Circulation: 2,100
Circulation Type: controlled & paid
**Owner(s):**
Anker Publishing Co., Inc.
176 Ballville Rd.
Bolton, MA 01740-0249
Telephone: (508) 779-6190
FAX: (508) 779-6296
Ownership %: 100
**Editorial:**
James D. Anker ................................Editor
**Desc.:** Contains original articles, news, and resources for department chairs, division heads, and deans for any discipline at four-year or two-year schools.

70262

## EDUCATION DAILY
1101 King St., Ste. 444
Alexandria, VA 22314
Telephone: (703) 683-4100
FAX: (703) 739-6517
Mailing Address:
    P.O. Box 1455
    Alexandria, VA 22314
Year Established: 1968
Pub. Frequency: 5/w.
Subscrip. Rate: $564/yr.; $814/yr. foreign
**Owner(s):**
Capitol Publications, Inc.
1101 King St., Ste. 444
Alexandria, VA 22314
Telephone: (703) 683-4100
FAX: (703) 739-6517
Ownership %: 100
**Editorial:**
Joe McGavin ....................................Editor
**Desc.:** Current reports on national, state and local events pertinent to top-level education officials everywhere. Includes news from the Education Department, Congress, the White House and the courts. Reports on the latest education research, education of handicapped children, and higher education.

70204

## EDUCATION GRANTS ALERT
1101 King St., Ste. 444
Alexandria, VA 22314
Telephone: (703) 683-4100
FAX: (703) 739-6517
Year Established: 1991
Pub. Frequency: w.
Subscrip. Rate: $299/yr.US; $349/yr. foreign
**Owner(s):**
Capitol Publications, Inc.
1101 King St.
Alexandria, VA 22314
Telephone: (703) 683-4100
FAX: (703) 739-6517
Ownership %: 100
**Editorial:**
Leslie Ratzlaff ................................Editor

**Desc.:** Covers federal and private funding opportunities and funding trends in education, especially designed for those seeking grants for elementary and secondary education programs.

70208

## EDUCATION MONITOR
1101 King St.
Alexandria, VA 22314
Telephone: (703) 683-4100
FAX: (703) 739-6517
Mailing Address:
    P.O. Box 1453
    Alexandria, VA 22314
Year Established: 1988
Pub. Frequency: s-m. during school yr.; m. Jun. & Jul.
Subscrip. Rate: $158/yr. US; $180/yr. foreign
**Owner(s):**
Capitol Publications, Inc.
1101 King St., Ste. 444
Alexandria, VA 22314
Telephone: (703) 683-4100
FAX: (703) 739-6517
Ownership %: 100
**Editorial:**
Maggie Rosen ..................................Editor
**Desc.:** For administrators, principals, and curriculum specialists. Includes a digest of current information on education research, curriculum development, and leadership.

70348

## EDUCATION PERSONNEL NEWS
P.O. Box 662
Latham, NY 12110
Telephone: (518) 786-1654
FAX: (518) 456-8582
Pub. Frequency: m.
Subscrip. Rate: $70/yr.
**Owner(s):**
Nyper Publications
P.O. Box 662
Latham, NY 12110
Telephone: (518) 786-1654
FAX: (518) 456-8582
Ownership %: 100
**Editorial:**
Harvey Randall ................................Editor

65729

## EDUCATION TECHNOLOGY NEWS
951 Pershing Dr
Silver Spring, MD 20910-4464
Telephone: (301) 587-6300
FAX: (301) 585-9075
Year Established: 1984
Pub. Frequency: fortn.
Subscrip. Rate: $267.54/yr.
**Owner(s):**
Business Publishers
951 Pershing Dr
Silver Spring, MD 20910
Telephone: (301) 587-6300
**Editorial:**
David Ritchie ..................................Editor
**Desc.:** For teachers and those interested in the educational uses of computers in the classroom. Feature articles on applications, educational software and pertinent programs.

70215

## EDUCATION USA
1101 King St., Ste. 444
Alexandria, VA 22314
Telephone: (703) 683-4100
FAX: (703) 739-6517
Year Established: 1958
Pub. Frequency: fortn.
Subscrip. Rate: $123/yr. US; $149/yr. foreign
Materials: 10

---

**Materials Accepted/Included:** 01-Business news 02-By-line articles 03-Fashion news 04-Food news 05-Freelance copy 06-Letters to editor 07-Real estate news 08-Sports news 09-Travel news 10-Book rev. 11-Movie rev. 12-Music rev. 13-TV rev. 14-Theater rev. 15-Coming events 16-Obituaries 17-Question & answer 18-Social announcements 19-Artwork 20-Cartoons 21-Photos 22-TV listings 23-Audio rec. 24-Video rec. 25-Books 26-Films/film clips 27-Personnel news 28-Press releases 29-New product news/photos 30-Trade lit. 31-Contracts awarded 32-Display adv. 33-Classified adv.

**Owner(s):**
Capitol Publications, Inc.
1101 King St., Ste. 444
Alexandria, VA 22314
Telephone: (703) 683-4100
FAX: (703) 739-6517
Ownership %: 100
**Editorial:**
Joe McGavin .............................Editor

70735
**FOLKSONG IN THE CLASSROOM**
P.O. Box 264
Holyoke, MA 10141
Year Established: 1980
Pub. Frequency: 3/yr.
Subscrip. Rate: $7/yr. individuals; $8/yr.
   foreign; $12/yr. institutions
Circulation: 1,500
Circulation Type: controlled & paid
**Owner(s):**
Folksong in the Classroom
P.O. Box 264
Holyoke, MA 01041
Ownership %: 100
**Desc.:** Contains sheet music and lyrics,
   historical analysis, correspondence from
   readers.

70306
**FORUM**
1118 22nd St., N.W.
Washington, DC 20037-1214
Telephone: (800) 321-6223
FAX: (202) 429-9766
Year Established: 1978
Pub. Frequency: bi-m.
Subscrip. Rate: free
Materials: 10
Circulation: 30,000
Circulation Type: free
**Owner(s):**
National Clearinghouse for Bilingual
   Education
1118 22nd St., N.W.
Washington, DC 20037-1214
Telephone: (800) 321-6223
FAX: (202) 429-9766
Ownership %: 100
**Editorial:**
Omar Shabka ...........................Editor
**Desc.:** Contains research articles and
   news of instructional materials for
   bilingual educators.

70294
**GIFTED EDUCATION PRESS
   QUARTERLY**
10201 Yuma Ct.
Manassas, VA 22110
Telephone: (703) 369-5017
Mailing Address:
   P.O. Box 1586
   Manassas, VA 22110
Year Established: 1987
Pub. Frequency: q.
Subscrip. Rate: $12/yr.
Materials: 10
Circulation: 1,000
Circulation Type: controlled & paid
**Owner(s):**
Gifted Education Press
10201 Yuma Ct.
Manassas, VA 22110
Telephone: (703) 369-5017
Ownership %: 100
**Editorial:**
Maurice D. Fisher .......................Editor
**Desc.:** Covers current problems and issues
   concerned with educating the gifted, and
   using the humanities and sciences with
   the gifted.

70259
**GRANTS FOR SCHOOL DISTRICTS
   MONTHLY HOTLINE**
23 Drydock Ave.
Boston, MA 02210-2387
Telephone: (800) 229-2084
FAX: (617) 345-9646
Pub. Frequency: m.
Subscrip. Rate: $83/yr.
**Owner(s):**
Quinlan Publishing Co., Inc.
23 Drydock Ave.
Boston, MA 02210-2387
Telephone: (800) 229-2084
FAX: (617) 345-9646
Ownership %: 100
**Desc.:** Information on available grants,
   schools programs and business
   partnerships throughout the country, of
   interest to school administrators, grants,
   writers, district officials and
   superintendents.

70220
**HARVARD EDUCATION LETTER**
Six Appian Way
Gutman Library, No. 301
Cambridge, MA 02138-3752
Telephone: (617) 496-9984
Year Established: 1985
Pub. Frequency: bi-m.
Subscrip. Rate: $26/yr.
Circulation: 14,000
Circulation Type: controlled & paid
**Owner(s):**
Harvard University, Graduate School of
   Education
Six Appian Way
Gutman Library No. 301
Cambridge, MA 02138-3752
Telephone: (617) 496-9984
Ownership %: 100
**Editorial:**
Adria Steinberg ...........................Editor
**Desc.:** Applies the latest educational
   research to practical concerns in
   education today; for parents and
   educators.

70147
**HOPKINS NEWS-LETTER**
P.O. Box 1230
Baltimore, MD 21218
Telephone: (410) 516-7647
Year Established: 1897
Pub. Frequency: w.
Page Size: tabloid
Subscrip. Rate: $35/yr.
Materials: 10,11,14,32
Circulation: 6,500
Circulation Type: controlled & paid
**Owner(s):**
Johns Hopkins University Press
P.O. Box 1230
Baltimore, MD 21218
Telephone: (410) 516-7647
Ownership %: 100

70150
**INTERFRATERNITY BULLETIN**
3901 W. 86th St.
Ste. 380
Indianapolis, IN 46268
Telephone: (317) 872-3304
Year Established: 1950
Pub. Frequency: m.
Subscrip. Rate: $8/yr.
Materials: 10
Circulation: 3,000
Circulation Type: controlled & paid
**Owner(s):**
National Fraternity Foundation
3901 W. 86th St.
Ste. 380
Indianapolis, IN 46268
Telephone: (317) 872-3304
Ownership %: 100

**Editorial:**
Kris Brandt Riske .......................Editor
**Desc.:** Digest of articles on national
   Greek-letter fraternities and sororities,
   professional fraternities, campus and
   student trends; calendar of related
   events.

70268
**ISTE UPDATE**
1787 Agate St.
Eugene, OR 97403-1923
Telephone: (503) 346-4414
FAX: (503) 346-5890
Year Established: 1988
Pub. Frequency: 7/yr.
Subscrip. Rate: free; $12/yr. non-members
**Owner(s):**
International Society for Technology in
   Education
1787 Agate St.
Eugene, OR 97403-1923
Telephone: (503) 346-4414
FAX: (503) 346-5890
Ownership %: 100
**Editorial:**
Anita Best .............................Editor
**Desc.:** Articles on current issues by
   leaders in the field of technology in
   education.

70159
**JAMESTOWN COLLEGE ALUMNI &
   FRIENDS**
6082 Jamestown College
Jamestown, ND 58401
Telephone: (701) 252-3467
FAX: (701) 453-2318
Pub. Frequency: q.
Page Size: tabloid
Subscrip. Rate: free
Circulation: 11,000
Circulation Type: controlled
**Owner(s):**
Jamestown College
6082 Jamestown College
Jamestown, ND 58401
Telephone: (701) 252-3467
FAX: (701) 453-2318
Ownership %: 100
**Editorial:**
Lori Sims .............................Editor
**Desc.:** Covers college events, alumni and
   student news.

68799
**KEY REPORTER**
1811 Q St., N.W.
Washington, DC 20009
Telephone: (202) 265-3808
Year Established: 1936
Pub. Frequency: q.
Page Size: standard
Subscrip. Rate: $3/yr. nonmembers
Materials: 10
Print Process: web
Circulation: 400,100
Circulation Type: controlled & paid
**Owner(s):**
Phi Beta Kappa Society
1811 Q St. N.W.
Washington, DC 20009
Telephone: (202) 265-3808
Ownership %: 100
**Editorial:**
Priscilla S. Taylor .......................Editor
**Desc.:** Contains news of the society's
   activities, feature articles and scholarly
   book recommendations.

70327
**LEARNING EDGE**
1289 Jewett
Ann Arbor, MI 48104
Telephone: (313) 769-4515
Year Established: 1984

Pub. Frequency: 6/yr.
Subscrip. Rate: $15/yr. US; $20/yr. foreign
Materials: 10
Circulation: 2,000
Circulation Type: controlled & paid
**Owner(s):**
Clonlara Publications
1289 Jewett
Ann Arbor, MI 48104
Telephone: (313) 769-4515
Ownership %: 100
**Editorial:**
Jo Hindsdale .............................Editor
**Desc.:** Features information for families
   enrolled in a home-based education
   program, including articles of general
   interest to home educators. Covers
   teaching, learning methods and
   materials.

70222
**LEX COLLEGII**
P.O. Box 150541
Nashville, TN 37215
Telephone: (615) 383-3332
Year Established: 1978
Pub. Frequency: q.
Subscrip. Rate: $36/yr.
**Owner(s):**
College Legal Information, Inc.
P.O. Box 150541
Nashville, TN 37215
Telephone: (615) 383-3332
Ownership %: 100
**Editorial:**
Kent M. Weeks .......................Editor
**Desc.:** Legal newsletter for independent
   higher education.

70212
**MARKETING HIGHER EDUCATION
   NEWSLETTER**
280 Easy St.
No. 114
Mountain View, CA 94043-3736
Telephone: (415) 962-1105
Year Established: 1987
Pub. Frequency: m.
Subscrip. Rate: $94.95/yr.
Materials: 10
Circulation: 700
Circulation Type: controlled
**Owner(s):**
Topor & Associates
280 Easy St.
No. 114
Mountain View, CA 94043-3736
Telephone: (415) 962-1105
Ownership %: 100

70162
**MCC NEWS**
1415 Anderson
Manhattan, KS 66502
Telephone: (913) 539-3571
Year Established: 1930
Pub. Frequency: q.
Page Size: tabloid
Subscrip. Rate: free
Circulation: 15,000
Circulation Type: controlled & free
**Owner(s):**
Manhattan Christian College
1415 Anderson
Manhattan, KS 66502
Telephone: (913) 539-3571
Ownership %: 100
**Management:**
Tara Griffin ...........................Development Mgr.
**Desc.:** Informational newsletter for
   constituents of the Manhattan Christian
   College.

**Materials Accepted/Included:** 01-Business news 02-By-line articles 03-Fashion news 04-Food news 05-Freelance copy 06-Letters to editor 07-Real estate news 08-Sports news 09-Travel news 10-Book rev. 11-Movie rev. 12-Music rev. 13-TV rev. 14-Theater rev. 15-Coming events 16-Obituaries 17-Question & answer 18-Social announcements 19-Artwork 20-Cartoons 21-Photos 22-TV listings 23-Audio rec. 24-Video rec. 25-Books 26-Films/film clips 27-Personnel news 28-Press releases 29-New product news/photos 30-Trade lit. 31-Contracts awarded 32-Display adv. 33-Classified adv.

## MLA NEWSLETTER
70209

10 Astor Pl.
New York, NY 10003
Telephone: (212) 475-9100
FAX: (212) 477-9863
Year Established: 1969
Pub. Frequency: 4/yr.
Subscrip. Rate: $6/yr.
Materials: 32
Circulation: 32,000
Circulation Type: controlled & paid
**Owner(s):**
Modern Language Association of America
10 Astor Pl.
New York, NY 10003
Telephone: (212) 475-9100
FAX: (212) 477-9863
Ownership %: 100
**Editorial:**
Phyllis P. Franklin ..........................Editor
**Desc.:** Information about the activities of
the Modern Language Association,
deadlines for fellowships and grants,
and news of the language and literature
profession.

## MONTESSORI OBSERVER
70226

912 Thayer Ave.
Silver Spring, MD 20910
Telephone: (301) 589-1127
Year Established: 1980
Pub. Frequency: 4/yr.
Subscrip. Rate: $20/yr. individuals; $25/yr.
institutions
Materials: 10,32
Circulation: 2,000
Circulation Type: paid
**Owner(s):**
International Montessori Society
912 Thayer Ave.
Silver Spring, MD 20910
Telephone: (301) 589-1127
Ownership %: 100
**Editorial:**
Lee Havis ..........................Editor
**Desc.:** Provides news and information
about the development of Montessori
education and attempts to promote an
awareness of its principles.

## NASSP TIPS FOR PRINCIPALS
70216

1904 Association Dr.
Reston, VA 22091
Telephone: (703) 860-0200
FAX: (703) 476-5432
Pub. Frequency: m.
Circulation: 42,000
Circulation Type: controlled & paid
**Owner(s):**
Nat'l. Assn. of Secondary School Principals
1904 Association Dr.
Reston, VA 22091
Telephone: (703) 860-0200
FAX: (703) 476-5432
Ownership %: 100
**Editorial:**
Patricia George ..........................Editor
**Desc.:** Tips for administrators on a variety
of topics.

## OPTIONS IN LEARNING
70321

P.O. Box 59
Chatham, NY 12060-0059
Telephone: (518) 392-6900
Year Established: 1990
Pub. Frequency: q.
Subscrip. Rate: $20/yr.
Materials: 10
Circulation: 2,000
Circulation Type: paid

**Owner(s):**
Alliance for Parental Involvement in
Education
P.O. Box 59
Chatham, NY 12060-0059
Telephone: (518) 392-6900
Ownership %: 100
**Editorial:**
Katharine Houk ..........................Editor
Seth Rockmuller ..........................Editor
**Desc.:** Offers parents information about
educational options (public, private, and
homeschooling), resources and
encouragement.

## PARENTS' CHOICE
70231

927 S. Walter Reed Dr., Ste. 1
Arlington, VA 22204
Telephone: (703) 486-8311
Year Established: 1959
Pub. Frequency: q.
Page Size: tabloid
Subscrip. Rate: $20/yr.
Circulation: 10,000
Circulation Type: controlled & paid
**Owner(s):**
Citizens for Educational Freedom
927 Walter Reed Dr., Ste. 1
Arlington, VA 22204
Telephone: (703) 486-8311
Ownership %: 100
**Editorial:**
Martin Duggan ..........................Editor
Mae Duggan ..........................Editor

## PENNSYLVANIA ADVOCATE
70853

53 S. Tenth St.
Pittsburgh, PA 15203
Telephone: (412) 431-5900
FAX: (412) 431-6882
Pub. Frequency: q.
Page Size: standard
Subscrip. Rate: $5/yr. members
Freelance Pay: varies
Circulation: 43,000
Circulation Type: paid
**Owner(s):**
Pennsylvania Federation of Teachers
53 S. Tenth St.
Pittsburgh, PA 15203
Telephone: (412) 431-5900
Ownership %: 100
**Editorial:**
John Tarka ..........................Editor

## PHI KAPPA PHI NEWSLETTER
70140

P.O. Box 16000
Louisiana State University
Baton Rouge, LA 70893
Telephone: (504) 388-3202
Year Established: 1969
Pub. Frequency: bi-m.
Subscrip. Rate: membership
Materials: 10
Circulation: 120,000
Circulation Type: controlled & paid
**Owner(s):**
Honor Society of Phi Kappa Phi
Louisiana State University
P.O. Box 70893
Baton Rouge, LA 70893
Ownership %: 100
**Editorial:**
John E. Braithwaite, Jr. ..........................Editor
**Desc.:** Articles on outstanding Phi Kappa
Phi members and national and regional
organization activities.

## PRACTITIONER
70223

1904 Association Dr.
Reston, VA 22091-1537
Telephone: (703) 860-0200
FAX: (703) 476-5432
Year Established: 1976

Pub. Frequency: q.
Subscrip. Rate: $4/yr.
Circulation: 42,000
Circulation Type: controlled & paid
**Owner(s):**
National Assn. of Secondary School
Principals
1904 Association Dr.
Reston, VA 22091-1537
Telephone: (703) 860-0200
FAX: (703) 476-5432
Ownership %: 100
**Editorial:**
Patricia George ..........................Editor
**Desc.:** Addresses administrative issues in
secondary school education.

## READER
70193

5795 Widewaters Pkwy.
Syracuse, NY 13214
Telephone: (315) 445-8000
FAX: (315) 445-8006
Year Established: 1979
Pub. Frequency: 4/yr.
Subscrip. Rate: $25/lifetime subscription
Materials: 10
Circulation: 50,000
Circulation Type: controlled & paid
**Owner(s):**
Literacy Volunteers of America, Inc.
5795 Widewaters Pkwy.
Syracuse, NY 13214
Telephone: (315) 445-8000
FAX: (315) 445-8006
Ownership %: 100
**Editorial:**
Beverly Miller ..........................Editor
**Desc.:** Addresses the problem of adult
illiteracy and describes US efforts to
promote literacy.

## REGIONAL SPOTLIGHT
70214

592 Tenth St., N.W.
Atlanta, GA 30318-5790
Telephone: (404) 875-9211
Year Established: 1974
Pub. Frequency: irreg.
Subscrip. Rate: $.50/per no.
Circulation: 8,500
Circulation Type: controlled & paid
**Owner(s):**
Southern Regional Education Board
592 Tenth St., N.W.
Atlanta, GA 30318-5790
Telephone: (404) 875-9211
Ownership %: 100
**Editorial:**
Margaret Sullivan ..........................Editor

## REPORT ON CORPORATE EDUCATIONAL SUPPORT
70281

951 Pershing Dr.
Silver Spring, MD 20910-4464
Telephone: (301) 587-6300
FAX: (301) 585-9075
Year Established: 1992
Pub. Frequency: bi-w.
Subscrip. Rate: $274.54/yr.
**Owner(s):**
Business Publishers, Inc.
951 Pershing Dr.
Silver Spring, MD 20910-4464
Telephone: (301) 587-6300
FAX: (301) 585-9075
Ownership %: 100
**Editorial:**
Rosemary Lally ..........................Editor
**Desc.:** Issues in improving America's
workforce capability, including corporate
support for public education.

## REPORT ON EDUCATION OF THE DISADVANTAGED
70298

951 Pershing Dr.
Silver Spring, MD 20910-4464
Telephone: (301) 587-6300
FAX: (301) 585-9075
Year Established: 1968
Pub. Frequency: fortn.
Subscrip. Rate: $241.54/yr.
**Owner(s):**
Business Publishers, Inc.
951 Pershing Dr.
Silver Spring, MD 20910-4464
Telephone: (301) 587-6300
FAX: (301) 585-9075
Ownership %: 100
**Editorial:**
Rosemary Lally ..........................Editor
**Desc.:** Advice and funding info for
managers of programs to assist
disadvantaged youth, with an emphasis
on Head Start and other programs.

## REPORT ON EDUCATION RESEARCH
70236

1101 King St., Ste. 444
Alexandria, VA 22314
Telephone: (703) 683-4100
FAX: (703) 739-6517
Year Established: 1969
Pub. Frequency: bi-w.
Subscrip. Rate: $240/yr.; $266/yr. foreign
**Owner(s):**
Capitol Publications, Inc.
1101 King St., Ste. 444
Alexandria, VA 22314
Telephone: (703) 683-4100
FAX: (703) 739-6517
Ownership %: 100
**Editorial:**
Annette Licitra ..........................Editor
**Desc.:** Provides current research initiatives,
results and funding from the Education
Department, its labs and centers, and
education policy group.

## REPORT ON LITERACY PROGRAM
70242

951 Pershing Dr.
Silver Spring, MD 20910-4464
Telephone: (301) 587-6300
FAX: (301) 585-9075
Year Established: 1989
Pub. Frequency: fortn.
Subscrip. Rate: $228.54/yr.
**Owner(s):**
Business Publishers, Inc.
951 Pershing Dr.
Silver Spring, MD 20910-4464
Telephone: (301) 587-6300
FAX: (301) 585-9075
Ownership %: 100
**Editorial:**
Dave Speights ..........................Editor
**Desc.:** Provides news and information on
ways and efforts to improve literacy in
the United States, both in the workplace
and at home.

## REPORT ON PRESCHOOL PROGRAMS
70254

951 Pershing Dr.
Silver Spring, MD 20910-4464
Telephone: (301) 587-6300
FAX: (301) 585-9075
Year Established: 1969
Pub. Frequency: bi-w.
Subscrip. Rate: $254.54/yr.

**Materials Accepted/Included:** 01-Business news 02-By-line articles 03-Fashion news 04-Food news 05-Freelance copy 06-Letters to editor 07-Real estate news 08-Sports news 09-Travel news 10-Book rev. 11-Movie rev. 12-Music rev. 13-TV rev. 14-Theater rev. 15-Coming events 16-Obituaries 17-Question & answer 18-Social announcements 19-Artwork 20-Cartoons 21-Photos 22-TV listings 23-Audio rec. 24-Video rec. 25-Books 26-Films/film clips 27-Personnel news 28-Press releases 29-New product news/photos 30-Trade lit. 31-Contracts awarded 32-Display adv. 33-Classified adv.

7-83

**Owner(s):**
Business Publishers, Inc.
951 Pershing Dr.
Silver Spring, MD 20910-4464
Telephone: (301) 587-6300
FAX: (301) 585-9075
Ownership %: 100
**Editorial:**
Charles Devaries ........................Editor
**Desc.:** Ideal for administrators of preschool programs, includes reports of new studies of the most effective teaching methods.

70092
## REPORT ON SCHOOL-AGED CHILD CARE
951 Pershing Dr.
Silver Spring, MD 20910-4464
Telephone: (301) 587-6300
FAX: (301) 585-9075
Year Established: 1988
Pub. Frequency: m.
Subscrip. Rate: $159.48/yr.
**Owner(s):**
Business Publishers, Inc.
951 Pershing Dr.
Silver Spring, MD 20910-4464
Telephone: (301) 587-6300
FAX: (301) 585-9075
Ownership %: 100
**Editorial:**
Charles Devaries ........................Editor
**Desc.:** Provides education tips and covers sources of funding for program administrators in preschool and elementary school programs.

70286
## SCHOOL LAW BULLETIN
23 Drydock Ave., 2nd Fl.
Boston, MA 02210-2387
Telephone: (617) 542-0048
FAX: (617) 345-9646
Year Established: 1974
Pub. Frequency: m.
Subscrip. Rate: $60/yr.
**Owner(s):**
Quinlan Publishing Co., Inc.
23 Drydock Ave., 2nd Fl.
Boston, MA 00210-2387
Telephone: (617) 542-0048
FAX: (617) 345-9646
Ownership %: 100
**Editorial:**
M. Quinlan ........................Editor
**Desc.:** Summarizes current cases concerning labor relations, tort liability, special education and other issues facing schools and school district.

70228
## SCHOOL LAW NEWS
1101 King St., Ste. 444
Alexandria, VA 22314
Telephone: (703) 683-4100
FAX: (703) 739-6517
Year Established: 1973
Pub. Frequency: bi-w.
Subscrip. Rate: $225/yr. US; $281/yr. foreign
**Owner(s):**
Capitol Publications, Inc.
1101 King St., Ste. 444
Alexandria, VA 22314
Telephone: (703) 683-4100
FAX: (703) 739-6517
Ownership %: 100
**Editorial:**
Douglas Onley ........................Editor

**Desc.:** Keeps school administrators and legal advisors informed of legal decisions, pending court cases and issues that affect schools. Covers the federal juiciary, the US Supreme Court, state courts, and legal developments in federal agencies and Congress.

70290
## SCHOOL MARKETING NEWSLETTER
P.O. Box 10
Haddam, CT 06438
Telephone: (203) 345-8183
FAX: (203) 345-3985
Year Established: 1981
Pub. Frequency: m.
Subscrip. Rate: $119/yr.
Circulation: 500
Circulation Type: paid
**Owner(s):**
School Market Research Institute
P.O. Box 10
Haddam, CT 06438
Telephone: (203) 345-8183
FAX: (203) 345-3985
Ownership %: 100
**Editorial:**
Lynn O. Vosburgh ........................Editor

70201
## SEMINARS, WORKSHOPS & CLASSES
P.O. Box 416
Denver, CO 80201-0416
Telephone: (303) 575-5676
Year Established: 1985
Pub. Frequency: biennial
Subscrip. Rate: $4/yr.
Circulation: 1,500
Circulation Type: controlled & paid
**Owner(s):**
Prosperity & Profits Unlimited
P.O. Box 416
Denver, CO 80201-0416
Telephone: (303) 575-5676
Ownership %: 100
**Desc.:** Provides information on educational opportunities.

70301
## SPECIAL EDUCATION REPORT
1101 King St., Ste. 444
Alexandria, VA 22314
Telephone: (703) 683-4100
FAX: (703) 739-6517
Year Established: 1975
Pub. Frequency: bi-w.
Subscrip. Rate: $257/yr. US; $283/yr. foreign
**Owner(s):**
Capitol Publications, Inc.
1101 King St., Ste. 444
Alexandria, VA 22314
Telephone: (703) 683-4100
FAX: (703) 739-6517
Ownership %: 100
**Desc.:** Covers federal and state legislation on the Education for All Handicapped Children Act and other relevant laws. Looks at innovations and research in the field.

70315
## SPECIAL EDUCATION UPDATE
4635 Nichols Rd., Ste. 100
Eagan, MN 55122
Telephone: (612) 452-8267
FAX: (612) 452-8694
Year Established: 1983
Pub. Frequency: m.
Subscrip. Rate: $107/yr.

**Owner(s):**
Data Research, Inc.
4635 Nichols Rd., Ste. 100
Eagan, MN 55122
Telephone: (612) 452-8267
FAX: (612) 452-8695
Ownership %: 100
**Editorial:**
Warren Cody ........................Editor

70308
## SPECIAL EDUCATOR
747 Dresher Rd.
Horsham, PA 19044
Telephone: (215) 628-3113
FAX: (215) 784-0870
Year Established: 1982
Pub. Frequency: 18/yr.
Subscrip. Rate: $150/yr.
**Owner(s):**
LRP Publications
747 Dresher Rd.
horsham, PA 19044
Telephone: (215) 628-3113
FAX: (215) 784-0870
Ownership %: 100
**Editorial:**
Melinda Maloney ........................Editor

70225
## STUDENT AID NEWS
1101 King St.
Ste. 444
Alexandria, VA 22314
Telephone: (703) 683-4100
FAX: (703) 739-6517
Year Established: 1974
Pub. Frequency: bi-w.
Subscrip. Rate: $252/yr. US; $278/yr. foreign
**Owner(s):**
Capitol Publications, Inc.
1101 King St.
Ste. 444
Alexandria, VA 22314
Telephone: (703) 683-4100
FAX: (703) 739-6517
Ownership %: 100
**Desc.:** Covers federal student aid programs and the student aid community. Provides news on federal policies affecting financial aid to post-secondary students, including Pell Grants, Stafford Student Loans and Perkins Loans, College Work-Study, Supplemental Education Opportunity Grants and State Student Incentive Grants.

70326
## TEACHER UPDATE
P.O. Box 233
Barryville, NY 12719
Telephone: (914) 557-8713
FAX: (914) 557-6770
Year Established: 1977
Pub. Frequency: q.
Subscrip. Rate: $25/yr.
Materials: 10
Circulation: 7,500
Circulation Type: controlled & paid
**Owner(s):**
NAR Publications
P.O. Box 233
Barryville, NY 12719
Telephone: (914) 557-8713
FAX: (914) 557-6770
Ownership %: 100

NAR Publications
P.O. Box 233
Barryville, NY 12719
Telephone: (914) 557-8713
FAX: (914) 557-6770
Ownership %: 100
**Editorial:**
Nicholas A. Roes ........................Editor

**Desc.:** Contains suggestions for art projects, unit ideas, math and science games, and other projects of interest to teachers of younger children.

70184
## TEACHING FOR CHANGE
118 22nd St., N.W.
Washington, DC 20037
Telephone: (202) 429-0137
FAX: (202) 429-9766
Year Established: 1987
Pub. Frequency: q.
Subscrip. Rate: $15/yr. individuals; $25/yr. institutions
Materials: 10, 32
Circulation: 1,000
Circulation Type: controlled & paid
**Owner(s):**
Network of Educators on the Americas
1118 22nd St., N.W.
Washington, DC 20037
Telephone: (202) 429-0137
FAX: (202) 429-9766
Ownership %: 100
**Editorial:**
Katie Rawson ........................Editor
**Desc.:** Serves as a forum for educators to share strategies, ideas and concerns. Includes news, classroom handouts and activities.

70855
## UNIONGRAM
3315 W. Broad St.
Richmond, VA 23230
Telephone: (804) 355-7444
Year Established: 1994
Pub. Frequency: q.
Page Size: standard
Subscrip. Rate: free
Circulation: 112,000
Circulation Type: controlled
**Owner(s):**
AFL-CIO State of Virginia
3515 W. Broad St.
Richmond, VA 23230
Telephone: (804) 355-7444
Ownership %: 100
**Management:**
Daniel G. LeBlanc ........................President
**Editorial:**
James R. Leamar ..........Secretary & Treasurer

70233
## UPDATING SCHOOL BOARD POLICIES
1680 Duke St.
Alexandria, VA 22314
Telephone: (703) 838-6722
FAX: (703) 683-7590
Year Established: 1970
Pub. Frequency: m.
Subscrip. Rate: $250/yr.
Circulation: 20,000
Circulation Type: controlled & paid
**Owner(s):**
National School Boards Association
1680 Duke St.
Alexandria, VA 22314
Telephone: (703) 838-6722
FAX: (703) 683-7590
Ownership %: 100
**Editorial:**
Karen Powe ........................Editor
**Desc.:** Includes articles, trends, tips and legal analyses on subjects relating to school policies and issues of concern to school boards and superintendents.

70164
## VISIONS
Columbus Drive & Jackson Blvd.
Chicago, IL 60604
Telephone: (312) 263-0141
Year Established: 1982
Pub. Frequency: s-a.

Circulation: 12,000
Circulation Type: controlled & paid
**Owner(s):**
School of the Art Institute of Chicago
Columbus Dr. & Jackson Blvd.
Chicago, IL 60604
Telephone: (312) 263-0141
Ownership %: 100
**Editorial:**
Howard Brimson ........................................Editor

70188
## WHAT'S HAPPENING IN WASHINGTON
2000 L. St., N.W.
Ste. 600
Washington, DC 20036
Telephone: (202) 331-1380
Mailing Address:
700 N. Rush St.
Chicago, IL 60611-2571
Year Established: 1992
Pub. Frequency: bi-m.
Subscrip. Rate: $4/yr.
Circulation: 34,000
Circulation Type: controlled & paid
**Owner(s):**
National Parent-Teacher Association
2000 L. St., N.W.
Ste. 600
Washington, DC 20036
Telephone: (202) 331-1380
Ownership %: 100
**Editorial:**
Susan Kushner ........................................Editor
**Desc.:** Informs PTA members and concerned citizens about federal legislation that has an impact on the education, health and welfare of children.

70240
## WISCONSIN CENTER FOR EDUCATION RESEARCH HIGHLIGHTS
1025 W. Johnson St.
Madison, WI 53706
Telephone: (608) 263-8814
FAX: (608) 263-6448
Year Established: 1970
Pub. Frequency: q.
Subscrip. Rate: free
Circulation: 7,000
Circulation Type: free
**Owner(s):**
Wisconsin Center for Education Research
1025 W. Johnson St.
Madison, WI 53706
Telephone: (608) 263-8814
FAX: (608) 263-6448
Ownership %: 100
**Editorial:**
Paul Baker ........................................Editor
**Desc.:** Examines university research on teaching methods and curriculum, organization and administration, higher education, special education and rehabilitation.

## Group 356-Science

69953
## AMS NEWSLETTER
45 Beacon St.
Boston, MA 02108-3693
Telephone: (617) 227-2425
FAX: (617) 742-8718
Year Established: 1980
Pub. Frequency: m.
Subscrip. Rate: $80/yr.; $100/yr. foreign
Circulation: 610
Circulation Type: paid

**Owner(s):**
American Meteorological Society
45 Beacon St.
Boston, MA 02108-3693
Telephone: (617) 227-2425
FAX: (617) 742-8718
Ownership %: 100
**Editorial:**
Roland D. Paine ........................................Editor
**Desc.:** Contains news briefs, dates, notes on people, information on grants, and contracts for meteorologists, oceanographers, and hydrologists.

64946
## APPLIED GENETICS NEWS
25 Van Zant St.
Norwalk, CT 06855
Telephone: (203) 853-4266
FAX: (203) 853-0348
Year Established: 1980
Pub. Frequency: m.
Page Size: standard
Subscrip. Rate: $350/yr.
**Owner(s):**
Louis Naturman
25 Van Zant St.
Norwalk, CT 06855
Telephone: (203) 853-4266
Ownership %: 100
**Management:**
Robert Butler ........................................Manager
**Desc.:** Unique technical-economic perspective on biotechnology projects under way and future projects in academia and industry. Analysis and highlights of basic research, genetic production, technology, patents, joint ventures, mergers, company activities, clinical licenses, industry structure, key personnel, finance, funding, regulation and legal developments in the U.S., Europe, and Japan.
**Readers:** Industry watchers, corporate executives and scientists worldwide who need to keep their finger on the pulse of the biotechnology industry with news, trends, forecasts and analyses.

23745
## ASM NEWS
1325 Massachusetts Ave., N.W.
Washington, DC 20005-4171
Telephone: (202) 737-3600
Year Established: 1935
Pub. Frequency: m.
Page Size: standard
Subscrip. Rate: $25/yr.
Materials: 02,06,10,16,29,32,33
Print Process: web offset
Circulation: 40,600
Circulation Type: paid
**Owner(s):**
American Society for Microbiology
1325 Massachusetts Ave., N.W.
Washington, DC 20005-4171
Telephone: (202) 737-3600
Ownership %: 100
**Editorial:**
Michael I. Goldberg ........................Editor in Chief
Linda M. Illig ........................................Director
Pamela M. Winters ................Production Editor
**Desc.:** Provides information on a broad range of scientific and policy issues to microbiologists; letters, opinion pieces, meetings calendar; reports of legislative activity; and classified employment listings.
**Readers:** Members of ASM, industry and university scientists, and legislators.

64951
## BATTERY & EV TECHNOLOGY NEWS
25 Van Zant St.
Norwalk, CT 06855
*see Newsletters, Environment & Energy*

70031
## BAYLOR GENOME CENTER NEWS
One Baylor Plaza
Houston, TX 77030
Telephone: (713) 798-5669
FAX: (713) 798-5386
Year Established: 1991
Pub. Frequency: q.
**Owner(s):**
Baylor College of Medicine
One Baylor Plaza
Houston, TX 77030
Telephone: (713) 798-5669
FAX: (713) 798-5386
Ownership %: 100
**Desc.:** Covers recent advances related to the center's areas of genome research, details of data and materials that are available to other researchers, lists of recent publications and reports on other center activities.

71105
## BIOTECHNOLOGY INFORMATION PACKAGE
P.O. Box 1304
Ft. Lee, NJ 07024-9967
Telephone: (201) 568-4744
Pub. Frequency: m.
Subscrip. Rate: $897/yr. US; $872/yr. foreign
**Owner(s):**
Technical Insights, Inc.
P.O. Box 1304
Fort Lee, NJ 07024-9967
Telephone: (201) 568-4744
Ownership %: 100

71103
## BIOTECHNOLOGY IN JAPAN NEWSSERVICE
467 Hamilton Ave.. Ste. 2
Palo Alto, CA 94301
Telephone: (415) 322-8441
FAX: (415) 322-8454
Year Established: 1982
Pub. Frequency: m.
Subscrip. Rate: $525/yr.
**Owner(s):**
Japan Pacific Associates
467 Hamilton Ave., Ste. 2
Palo Alto, CA 94301
Telephone: (415) 322-8441
FAX: (415) 322-8454
Ownership %: 100
**Editorial:**
Yoriko Kishimoto ........................................Editor
**Desc.:** Focuses on current biotechnology research and developments in Japan.

61273
## BIOTECHNOLOGY NEWS
33 Bleeker St.
Millburn, NJ 07041
Telephone: (201) 379-7749
FAX: (201) 379-1158
Mailing Address:
P.O. Box 218
Maplewood, NJ 07040
Year Established: 1981
Pub. Frequency: 30/yr.
Page Size: standard
Subscrip. Rate: $498/yr. US & Can.; $534/yr. foreign
Materials: 01,10
Print Process: offset
**Owner(s):**
CTB International Publishing, Inc.
P.O. Box 218
Maplewood, NJ 07040
Telephone: (201) 763-6855
Ownership %: 100
**Management:**
Oykve Brogna ........................................President
William Robinson ..............Circulation Manager
**Editorial:**
Christopher Brogna ........................................Editor

David Richards ........................Associate Editor
**Desc.:** Written for executives in the biotechnology industry. Covers company news, regulatory changes, financial trends, technical developments, market analyses and patents.
**Readers:** Presidents, researchers and executives in upper management.

71107
## BIOVENTURE VIEW
300 W. 23rd Ave.
San Mateo, CA 94403
Telephone: (415) 574-7128
FAX: (415) 574-8319
Year Established: 1986
Pub. Frequency: m.
Subscrip. Rate: $499/yr. US; $699/yr. foreign
**Owner(s):**
BioVenture Publishing
300 W. 23rd Ave.
San Mateo, CA 94403
Telephone: (415) 574-7128
FAX: (415) 574-8319
Ownership %: 100

71188
## BIOWORLD WEEK
P.O. Box 740056
Atlanta, GA 30374
Telephone: (404) 262-7436
FAX: (404) 814-0759
Pub. Frequency: w.
Subscrip. Rate: $160/yr.
**Owner(s):**
American Health Consultants Group
P.O. Box 740056
Atlanta, GA
Telephone: (404) 262-7436
FAX: (404) 814-0759
Ownership %: 100

70033
## BIRDSCOPE
159 Sapsucker Woods Rd.
Ithaca, NY 14850
Telephone: (607) 254-2473
FAX: (607) 254-2415
Year Established: 1987
Pub. Frequency: 3/yr.
Subscrip. Rate: membership
Circulation: 14,000
Circulation Type: controlled & paid
**Owner(s):**
Cornell University
159 Sapsucker Woods Rd.
Ithaca, NY 14850
Telephone: (607) 254-2473
FAX: (607) 254-2415
Ownership %: 100
**Editorial:**
Tim Gallagher ........................................Editor
**Desc.:** Explains research programs of the laboratory in lay terms.

70036
## CARNIVOROUS PLANT NEWSLETTER
California State University
Fullerton, CA 92634
Telephone: (714) 773-2766
FAX: (714) 773-3426
Year Established: 1971
Pub. Frequency: q.
Subscrip. Rate: $15/yr. US; $20/yr. foreign
Materials: 10,32
Circulation: 950
Circulation Type: controlled & paid
**Owner(s):**
International Carnivorous Plant Society
California State Univeristy
Fullerton, CA 92634
Telephone: (714) 773-2766
FAX: (714) 773-3426
Ownership %: 100

**Materials Accepted/Included:** 01-Business news 02-By-line articles 03-Fashion news 04-Food news 05-Freelance copy 06-Letters to editor 07-Real estate news 08-Sports news 09-Travel news 10-Book rev. 11-Movie rev. 12-Music rev. 13-TV rev. 14-Theater rev. 15-Coming events 16-Obituaries 17-Question & answer 18-Social announcements 19-Artwork 20-Cartoons 21-Photos 22-TV listings 23-Audio rec. 24-Video rec. 25-Books 26-Films/film clips 27-Personnel news 28-Press releases 29-New product news/photos 30-Trade lit. 31-Contracts awarded 32-Display adv. 33-Classified adv.

7-85

**Editorial:**
Leo C. Song, Jr. ........................Editor
**Desc.:** Covers anything pertaining to carnivorous plants, natural history, and culture. Covers anything pertaining to carnivorous plants, natural history, and culture.

70063

**CHEMICAL MONITOR**
P.O. Box 314
Lindenhurst, NY 11757-0314
Telephone: (516) 669-7817
Year Established: 1985
Pub. Frequency: m.
Subscrip. Rate: $95/yr. US; $110/yr. foreign
**Owner(s):**
Desktop Publishing
P.O. Box 314
Lindenhurst, NY 11757-0314
Telephone: (516) 669-8147
Ownership %: 100
**Editorial:**
Angelo Tulumello ........................Editor
**Desc.:** Covers developments that influence changes in the field of chemical instrumentation.

70454

**COMPOSITES NEWS: INFRASTRUCTURE**
991 Lomas Santa Fe Dr., C469
Solona Beach, CA 92075-7010
*see Newsletters, Engineering & Industrial Materials*

70736

**CONSORTIUM**
57 Bedford St., Ste. 210
Lexington, MA 02173-4428
Year Established: 1984
Pub. Frequency: q.
Subscrip. Rate: $32/yr. US; $37/yr. foreign
**Owner(s):**
Consortium for Mathematics & Its Applications
57 Bedford St., Ste. 210
Lexington, MA 02173-4428
Ownership %: 100
**Editorial:**
Margaret B. Cozzens ........................Editor

70777

**ELECTRONIC PHOTOGRAPHY NEWS**
10915 Bonita Beach Rd.
Bonita Springs, FL 33923
Telephone: (813) 992-4421
FAX: (813) 992-6328
Year Established: 1986
Pub. Frequency: m.
Subscrip. Rate: $90/yr.; $112/yr. foreign
Materials: 10
**Owner(s):**
Photofinishing News, Inc.
10915 Bonita Beach Rd.
Bonita Springs, FL 33923
Telephone: (813) 992-4421
FAX: (813) 992-6328
Ownership %: 100
**Editorial:**
Don Franz ........................Editor
John Larish ........................Editor

23843

**ESA NEWSLETTER**
9301 Annapolis Rd.
Lanham, MD 20706-3115
Telephone: (301) 731-4535
FAX: (301) 731-4538
Year Established: 1978
Pub. Frequency: m.
Page Size: standard
Subscrip. Rate: $18/yr. individuals; $35/yr. institutions
Materials: 32
Circulation: 9,000

Circulation Type: paid
**Owner(s):**
Entomological Society of America
9301 Annapolis Rd.
Lanham, MD 20706-3115
Telephone: (301) 731-4535
FAX: (301) 731-4538
Ownership %: 100
**Editorial:**
Victoria Morehead ........................Editor
Rob Headrick ........................Editor
**Desc.:** Contains feature articles, meeting announcements, listing of employment opportunities, notices of grants and awards, member profiles, and branch and section news.
**Readers:** Primarily professional entomologists and libraries throughout the world.

71231

**FUTURE TECHNOLOGY INTELLIGENCE REPORT**
P.O. Box 423652
San Francisco, CA 94142-3652
Telephone: (415) 359-3757
Year Established: 1990
Pub. Frequency: m.
Subscrip. Rate: $150/yr.
Materials: 10
**Owner(s):**
F T I R Inc.
P.O. Box 423652
San Francisco, CA 94142-3652
Telephone: (415) 359-3757
Ownership %: 100
**Editorial:**
Anthony C. Sutton ........................Editor
**Desc.:** Predicts future techology emphasizing little known and unpublicized developments from world network of contacts. Includes such topics as: cold fusion, weather engineering and energy medicine.

70039

**GULL**
2530 San Pablo Ave.
Ste. G
Berkeley, CA 94702
Telephone: (510) 843-2222
Year Established: 1917
Pub. Frequency: 11/yr.
Subscrip. Rate: $10/yr.
Materials: 10
Circulation: 6,000
Circulation Type: controlled & paid
**Owner(s):**
Golden Gate Audobon Society
2530 San Pablo Ave.
Ste. G
Berkeley, CA 94702
Telephone: (510) 843-2222
Ownership %: 100
**Editorial:**
Don Sanford ........................Editor

70029

**HUMAN GENOME NEWS**
Oak Ridge National Laboratory
P.O. Box 2008
Oak Ridge, TN 37831-6050
Telephone: (615) 576-6669
FAX: (615) 574-9888
Pub. Frequency: bi-m.
Circulation: 13,000
Circulation Type: controlled
**Owner(s):**
Human Genome Management Information System
Oak Ridge National Library
P.O. Box 2008
Oak Ridge, TN 37831-6050
Telephone: (615) 576-6669
FAX: (615) 574-9888
Ownership %: 100

**Editorial:**
Betty K. Mansfield ........................Editor
**Desc.:** Facilitates communication among genome researchers and informs persons interested in genome research.

69292

**IMAGING TECHNOLOGY REPORT**
2140 Boston Post Rd.
Larchmont, NY 10538
Telephone: (914) 834-3044
FAX: (914) 834-3993
Mailing Address:
  P.O. Box 950
  Larchmont, NY 10538
Year Established: 1987
Pub. Frequency: m.
Page Size: standard
Subscrip. Rate: $168/yr. US; $186/yr. foreign
Materials: 01
Freelance Pay: varies
Print Process: offset
**Owner(s):**
Microfilm Publishing, Inc.
P.O. Box 950
Larchmont, NY 10538
Telephone: (914) 834-3044
FAX: (914) 834-3993
Ownership %: 100
**Management:**
Mitchell M. Badler ........................Publisher
**Editorial:**
Mitchell M. Badler ........................Editor
Dorothy Miceti ........................Associate Publisher
**Desc.:** Covers business imaging. Reports on technology, applications, vendors, markets, problems, research, innovations, products and trends in electronic imaging.

70857

**INNOVATOR'S DIGEST**
P.O. Box 15640
Plantation, FL 33318-5640
Telephone: (305) 473-9560
FAX: (305) 473-0544
Year Established: 1979
Pub. Frequency: bi-w.
Subscrip. Rate: $269/yr. US; $309/yr. CN; $389/yr. foreign
**Owner(s):**
Merton Allen Associates
InfoTeam, Inc.
P.O. 15640
Plantation, FL 33318-5640
Telephone: (305) 473-9560
FAX: (305) 473-0544
Ownership %: 100
**Desc.:** Covers worldwide innovative activites, accomplishments, and happenings in science, engineering, technology, manufacture, finance, management, marketing, and regulation.

71195

**LASER BULLETIN**
Seven Placid Harbor
Dana Point, CA 92629-3245
Telephone: (714) 496-6577
FAX: (714) 496-8963
Year Established: 1994
Pub. Frequency: m.
Subscrip. Rate: $150/yr.
**Owner(s):**
Opto-Laser Info
Seven Placid Harbor
Dana Point, CA 92629-3245
Telephone: (714) 496-6577
FAX: (714) 496-8963
Ownership %: 100
**Editorial:**
Randy Schroeter ........................Editor

**Desc.:** Covers advances in laser design and application, business news, market trends and new patents related to laser components, systems and laser-based processes.

71237

**MARINE TECHNOLOGY NEWS**
1201 Seven Locks Rd.
Potomac, MD 20854
Telephone: (301) 424-3338
FAX: (301) 309-3847
Year Established: 1993
Pub. Frequency: bi-w.
Subscrip. Rate: $495/yr. US; $530/yr. foreign
**Owner(s):**
Phillips Business Information, Inc.
1201 Seven Locks Rd.
Potomac, MD 20854
Telephone: (301) 424-3338
FAX: (301) 309-3847
Ownership %: 100

23682

**OCEAN SCIENCE NEWS**
1201 National Press Bldg.
Washington, DC 20045
Telephone: (202) 347-6643
Year Established: 1959
Pub. Frequency: 3/m.
Page Size: standard
Subscrip. Rate: $365/yr.; $385/yr. foreign
Freelance Pay: varies
**Owner(s):**
Nautilus Press, Inc.
1201 National press Bldg.
Washington, DC 20045
Telephone: (202) 347-3043
Ownership %: 100
**Management:**
John Botzum ........................President
Edward W. Scripps, II ........................Publisher
**Editorial:**
John R. Botzum, Jr. ........................Editor
**Desc.:** Reports on U.S. and international developments in ocean and atmosphere science, technology, research, and engineering, and offers detailed coverage of Capitol Hill.
**Readers:** Industry, academia, government (1/3 each).

70037

**ORNITHOLOGICAL NEWSLETTER**
Business Office
P.O. Box 1897
Lawrence, KS 66044
Telephone: (913) 843-1221
FAX: (913) 843-1274
Year Established: 1976
Pub. Frequency: bi-m.
Subscrip. Rate: membership
Materials: 10
Circulation: 4,600
Circulation Type: controlled & paid
**Owner(s):**
Ornithological Societies of North America
Business Office
P.O. Box 1897
Lawrence, KS 66044
Telephone: (913) 843-1221
FAX: (913) 843-1274
Ownership %: 100
**Editorial:**
Kevin McGowan ........................Editor

70021

**PROTEIN INFORMATION RESOURCE NEWSLETTER**
3900 Reservoir Rd., N.W.
Washington, DC 20007
Telephone: (202) 687-2121
FAX: (202) 687-1662
Year Established: 1985
Pub. Frequency: irreg.
Subscrip. Rate: free to qualified personnel

---

**Materials Accepted/Included:** 01-Business news 02-By-line articles 03-Fashion news 04-Food news 05-Freelance copy 06-Letters to editor 07-Real estate news 08-Sports news 09-Travel news 10-Book rev. 11-Movie rev. 12-Music rev. 13-TV rev. 14-Theater rev. 15-Coming events 16-Obituaries 17-Question & answer 18-Social announcements 19-Artwork 20-Cartoons 21-Photos 22-TV listings 23-Audio rec. 24-Video rec. 25-Books 26-Films/film clips 27-Personnel news 28-Press releases 29-New product news/photos 30-Trade lit. 31-Contracts awarded 32-Display adv. 33-Classified adv.

Circulation: 1,000
Circulation Type: controlled
**Owner(s):**
National Biomedical Research Foundation
3900 Reservoir Rd., N.W.
Washington, DC 20007
Telephone: (202) 687-2121
FAX: (202) 687-1662
Ownership %: 100
**Editorial:**
Kathryn E. Sidman .............................Editor

**REFLECTOR NEWSLETTER**

69926

5027 W. Stanford
Dallas, TX 75209-3319
Telephone: (214) 754-1461
FAX: (214) 754-1330
Year Established: 1956
Pub. Frequency: q.
Subscrip. Rate: $4/yr. non-members
Materials: 10,32
Circulation: 12,000
Circulation Type: controlled & paid
**Owner(s):**
Astronomical League
5027 W. Stanford
Dallas, TX 75209-3319
Telephone: (214) 754-1461
FAX: (214) 754-1330
Ownership %: 100
**Editorial:**
Ed Flaspoehler .............................Editor
**Desc.:** Covers amateur astronomy news.

**RLBL NEWSLETTER**

70034

Dept. of Chemistry
University of Pennslyvania
Philadelphia, PA 19104-6323
Telephone: (215) 898-3605
FAX: (215) 898-0590
Year Established: 1977
Pub. Frequency: 2/yr.
Circulation: 2,000
Circulation Type: controlled & paid
**Owner(s):**
Regional Laser & Biotechnology
Laboratories
Dept. of Chemistry
University of Pennslyvania
Philadelphia, PA 19104-6323
Telephone: (215) 898-3605
FAX: (215) 898-0590
Ownership %: 100
**Editorial:**
Charles M. Phillips .............................Editor
**Desc.:** Covers ultrafast laser spectroscopy.

**SCIENCE BOOKS & FILMS**

71029

1333 H St., N.W.
Washington, DC 20005
Telephone: (202) 326-6454
Year Established: 1965
Pub. Frequency: 9/yr.
Subscrip. Rate: $40/yr.
Materials: 10,32
Circulation: 4,500
Circulation Type: controlled & paid
**Owner(s):**
American Assoc. for the Advancement of
Science
1333 H St., N.W.
Washington, DC 20005
Telephone: (202) 326-6454
Ownership %: 100
**Editorial:**
Maria Sosa .............................Editor
**Desc.:** Reviews of print, film, and software
materials in all sciences for all age
levels, for librarians and educators.

**SPACE BUSINESS NEWS**

69814

7811 Montrose Rd.
Potomac, MD 20854
Telephone: (800) 777-5006
FAX: (301) 309-3847
Year Established: 1984
Pub. Frequency: fortn.
Subscrip. Rate: $497/yr.; $515/yr. out of
country
**Owner(s):**
Phillips Business Information
7811 Montrose Rd.
Potomac, MD 20854
Telephone: (800) 777-5006
Ownership %: 100
**Editorial:**
Joe Anselmo .............................Editor

**SPACE PRESS**

69822

645 West End Ave.
New York, NY 10025
Telephone: (212) 724-5919
Year Established: 1981
Pub. Frequency: m.
Subscrip. Rate: $50/yr.
Materials: 10,32
Circulation: 1,000
Circulation Type: paid
**Owner(s):**
Vernuccio Publications
645 West End Ave.
New York, NY 10025
Telephone: (212) 724-5919
Ownership %: 100
**Editorial:**
Frank V. Vernuccio, Jr. .............................Editor
**Desc.:** Complete coverage of all US and
international space news.

**SPECTRA: CIW NEWSLETTER**

69916

1530 P St., N.W.
Washington, DC 20005
Telephone: (202) 387-6411
FAX: (202) 387-8092
Year Established: 1971
Pub. Frequency: 3/yr.
Subscrip. Rate: free
Circulation: 3,000
Circulation Type: free
**Owner(s):**
Carnegie Institution of Washington
1530 P St., N.W.
Washington, DC 20005
Telephone: (202) 387-6411
Ownership %: 100
**Editorial:**
R. Bowers .............................Editor
**Desc.:** Features current activities of the
Institution's astronomers, biologists, and
earth scientists.

**TECHNOLOGY ALERT**

70887

P.O. Box 15640
Plantation, FL 33318-5640
Telephone: (305) 473-9560
FAX: (305) 473-0544
Year Established: 1987
Pub. Frequency: 6/yr.
Subscrip. Rate: $109/yr. US; $129/yr.
Canada; $159/yr. elsewhere
**Owner(s):**
Merton Allen Associates
P.O. Box 15640
Plantation, FL 33318-5640
Telephone: (305) 473-9560
FAX: (305) 473-0544
Ownership %: 100
**Editorial:**
Merton Allen .............................Editor

**Desc.:** Presents on-line descriptions of
available technical papers and reports
abstracted from publishers' subscription
newsletters. Contains summary and
listings of available database searches
on a variety of specific technological,
management, marketing and finance
subjects.

**TECHNOTRENDS NEWSLETTER**

70893

P.O. Box 26413
Milwaukee, WI 53226-0413
Telephone: (414) 774-7790
FAX: (414) 774-8330
Year Established: 1985
Pub. Frequency: m.
Subscrip. Rate: $49.95/yr.
**Owner(s):**
Burrus Research Associates, Inc.
P.O. Box 26413
Milwaukee, WI 53226-0413
Telephone: (414) 774-7790
FAX: (414) 774-8330
Ownership %: 100
**Editorial:**
Patti A. Thomsen .............................Editor

**TRIPOD**

69935

L.W. Chase Hall
P.O. Box 830728
Lincoln, NE 68583-0728
Telephone: (402) 472-6704
FAX: (402) 472-6614
Year Established: 1988
Pub. Frequency: 2/yr.
Subscrip. Rate: $307/yr.
**Owner(s):**
University of Nebraska, Lincoln
L.W. Chase Hall
P.O. Box 830728
Lincoln, NE 68583-0728
Telephone: (402) 472-6704
FAX: (402) 472-6614
Ownership %: 100
**Editorial:**
Deborah Wood .............................Editor
**Desc.:** Covers the operation of weather
stations in an automated environment,
measurement and calibration of sensors,
programming techniques for dataloggers,
data retrieval, storage quality control
and disssemination mechanism.

**TURBOMACHINERY
MAINTENANCE NEWSLETTER**

70614

P.O. Box 5550
Norwalk, CT 06856-5550
Telephone: (203) 853-6015
FAX: (203) 852-8175
Year Established: 1959
Pub. Frequency: m.
Subscrip. Rate: $49/yr. membership
Materials: 10,32
Circulation: 10,631
Circulation Type: controlled & paid
**Owner(s):**
Turbomachinery Maintenance Institute, Inc.
P.O. Box 5550
Norwalk, CT 06856-5550
Telephone: (203) 853-6015
FAX: (203) 852-8175
Ownership %: 100
**Editorial:**
Rena Hines .............................Editor

**UNIVERSE IN A CLASSROOM**

69927

390 Ashton Ave.
San Francisco, CA 94112
Telephone: (415) 337-1100
FAX: (415) 337-5205
Year Established: 1984
Pub. Frequency: 3/yr.
Subscrip. Rate: free

Circulation: 15,000
Circulation Type: controlled & free
**Owner(s):**
Astronomical Society of the Pacific
390 Ashton Ave.
San Francisco, CA
Telephone: (415) 337-1100
FAX: (415) 337-5205
Ownership %: 100
**Editorial:**
Andrew Fraknoi .............................Editor
**Desc.:** For teachers of astronomy for
grades 3-12, with information, activities
and resource lists.

**WILDFLOWER, NEWSLETTER OF
THE NWRC**

70022

2600 FM 973 N.
Austin, TX 78725
Telephone: (512) 929-3600
Year Established: 1983
Pub. Frequency: bi-m.
Subscrip. Rate: $25/yr.
Circulation: 18,000
Circulation Type: controlled & paid
**Owner(s):**
National Wildflower Research Center
2600 FM 973 N.
Austin, TX 78725
Telephone: (512) 929-3600
Ownership %: 100
**Editorial:**
Tela Goodwin Mange .............................Editor
**Desc.:** Promotes reestablishment of
wildflowers and native plants to repair
the environment in North America.

## Group 358-Senior Citizens

**AGING NETWORK NEWS**

70303

P.O. Box 1223
McLean, VA 22101
Telephone: (703) 734-3266
FAX: (703) 847-0573
Year Established: 1984
Pub. Frequency: m.
Subscrip. Rate: $55/yr.
Materials: 10,32
Circulation: 1,000
Circulation Type: controlled & paid
**Owner(s):**
Hansan Group, Inc.
P.O. Box 1223
McLean, VA 22101
Telephone: (703) 734-3266
FAX: (703) 847-0573
Ownership %: 100
**Editorial:**
John Hansan .............................Editor

**AGING NEWS ALERT**

70307

8204 Fenton St.
Silver Spring, MD 20910
Telephone: (301) 588-6380
FAX: (301) 588-6385
Year Established: 1984
Pub. Frequency: m.
Subscrip. Rate: $194/yr.
**Owner(s):**
CD Publications
8204 Fenton St.
Silver Spring, MD 20910
Telephone: (301) 588-6380
FAX: (301) 588-6385
Ownership %: 100
**Editorial:**
Steve Albright .............................Editor
**Desc.:** For all professionals working with
the elderly. Covers news and
developments in the geriatric field.

**Materials Accepted/Included:** 01-Business news 02-By-line articles 03-Fashion news 04-Food news 05-Freelance copy 06-Letters to editor 07-Real estate news 08-Sports news 09-Travel news 10-Book rev. 11-Movie rev. 12-Music rev. 13-TV rev. 14-Theater rev. 15-Coming events 16-Obituaries 17-Question & answer 18-Social announcements 19-Artwork 20-Cartoons 21-Photos 22-TV listings 23-Audio rec. 24-Video rec. 25-Books 26-Films/film clips 27-Personnel news 28-Press releases 29-New product news/photos 30-Trade lit. 31-Contracts awarded 32-Display adv. 33-Classified adv.

7-87

**AGING RESEARCH & TRAINING NEWS**
70342
951 Pershing Dr.
Silver Spring, MD 20910-4464
Telephone: (301) 587-6300
FAX: (301) 585-9075
Year Established: 1978
Pub. Frequency: bi-w.
Subscrip. Rate: $182.38/yr.
**Owner(s):**
Business Publishers, Inc.
951 Pershing Dr.
Silver Spring, MD 20910-4464
Telephone: (301) 587-6300
FAX: (301) 585-9075
Ownership %: 100
**Editorial:**
Audrey Osborne .............................Editor
**Desc.:** Provides information on current
grants and contracts for aging research
and training.

**BOISE SENIOR CENTER NEWSLETTER**
65389
690 Robbins Rd.
Boise, ID 83702
Telephone: (208) 345-9921
Pub. Frequency: m.
Page Size: standard
Subscrip. Rate: free
Circulation: 5,400
Circulation Type: free
**Owner(s):**
Boise Senior Ctr.
690 Robbins Rd.
Boise, ID 83702
Telephone: (208) 345-9921
Ownership %: 100
**Editorial:**
Tamie Hopkins .............................Editor
**Desc.:** Educational, health, social security
information.
**Readers:** Senior citizens.

**GERONTOLOGY NEWS**
70311
1275 K St., N.W., Ste. 350
Washington, DC 20005-4006
Telephone: (202) 842-1275
Year Established: 1978
Pub. Frequency: m.
Subscrip. Rate: $50/yr.
Circulation: 7,200
Circulation Type: controlled & paid
**Owner(s):**
Gerontological Society of America
1275 K St., N.W., Ste. 350
Washington, DC 20005-4006
Telephone: (202) 842-1275
Ownership %: 100
**Editorial:**
Linda Krogh Harootyan .............................Editor
**Desc.:** Reports on policy issues,
fellowships and grants in the field of
aging.

**GOLDEN AGE**
70312
2330 S. Main St., Ste. 2
Salt Lake City, UT 84115-2777
Telephone: (801) 486-5051
FAX: (801) 486-5065
Pub. Frequency: m.
Subscrip. Rate: $10/yr.
Materials: 32
Circulation: 28,000
Circulation Type: controlled & paid
**Owner(s):**
Senior Media Network
2330 S. Main St., Ste. 2
Salt Lake City, UT 84115-2777
Telephone: (801) 486-5051
FAX: (801) 486-5065
Ownership %: 100

**Editorial:**
Miriam Murphy .............................Editor

**OLDERS AMERICANS REPORT**
70874
951 Pershing Dr.
Silver Spring, MD 20910-4464
Telephone: (301) 587-6300
FAX: (301) 585-9075
Year Established: 1976
Pub. Frequency: w.
Subscrip. Rate: $294.50/yr.
**Owner(s):**
Business Publishers, Inc.
951 Pershing Dr.
Silver Spring, MD 20910-4464
Telephone: (301) 587-6300
FAX: (301) 585-9075
Ownership %: 100
**Editorial:**
Nancy Aldrich .............................Editor
**Desc.:** News for directors of senior citizens
programs; includes funding, nutritions
and social security news.

**RESOURCES IN AGING**
70328
21946 Pine Trace
Boca Raton, FL 33428
Telephone: (407) 482-6271
Year Established: 1987
Pub. Frequency: bi-m.
Subscrip. Rate: 25/yr.
Materials: 10,32
**Owner(s):**
Demko Publishing
21946 Pine Trace
Boca Raton, FL 33428
Telephone: (407) 482-6271
Ownership %: 100
**Editorial:**
David J. Demko .............................Editor

**SENIOR CARE PROFESSIONAL**
70316
8204 Fenton St.
Silver Spring, MD 20910-2889
Telephone: (301) 588-6380
FAX: (301) 588-6385
Year Established: 1987
Pub. Frequency: m.
Subscrip. Rate: $197/yr.
**Owner(s):**
Community Development Services, Inc.
8204 Fenton St.
Silver Spring, MD 20910-2889
Telephone: (301) 588-6380
FAX: (301) 588-6385
Ownership %: 100
**Editorial:**
James Kelder .............................Editor
**Desc.:** Practical advice for senior care
professionals on how to work more
effectively with families of the aged.

## Group 360-Social Sciences

**AFGHANISTAN FORUM**
70488
201 E. 71st St.
Apt. 2K
New York, NY 10021
Telephone: (212) 861-4272
Year Established: 1972
Pub. Frequency: bi-m.
Subscrip. Rate: $25/yr.; $35/yr. US
institutions; $45/yr. foreign institutions
Materials: 10
Circulation: 250
Circulation Type: controlled & paid
**Owner(s):**
Afghanistan Forum, Inc.
201 E. 71st St.
Apt. 2K
New York, NY 10021
Telephone: (212) 861-4272
Ownership %: 100

**Editorial:**
Mary Ann Siegfried .............................Editor
**Desc.:** Contains a chronology of events,
including items from the Kabul
government, articles from national and
international publications, notices of
conferences, exhibitions and lectures,
information on organizations and
projects concerned with Afghanistan.

**AMERICAN FOLKLORE SOCIETY NEWSLETTER**
70255
1703 New Hampshire Ave., N.W.
Washington, DC 20009
Telephone: (202) 232-8800
Pub. Frequency: 6/yr.
Subscrip. Rate: $16/yr.
Circulation: 2,000
Circulation Type: controlled & paid
**Owner(s):**
American Anthropological Association
1703 New Hampshire Ave., N.W.
Washington, DC 20009
Telephone: (202) 232-8800
Ownership %: 100
**Editorial:**
Shalom Staub .............................Editor
**Desc.:** Covers folklore, material culture,
music, art and local history.

**ANTHROPOLOGY NEWSLETTER**
69862
1703 New Hampshire Ave., N.W.
Washington, DC 20009
Telephone: (202) 232-8800
Year Established: 1947
Pub. Frequency: m.: Sep.-May
Subscrip. Rate: $45/yr.
**Owner(s):**
American Anthropological Assn.
1703 New Hampshire Ave.
Washington, DC 20009
Telephone: (202) 232-8800
Ownership %: 100
**Editorial:**
David Givens .............................Editor
**Desc.:** News of interest to anthropologists;
association affairs, departments and
people, jobs, grants and support, brief
research reports and announcements.

**ARCHAEOLOGICAL CONSERVANCY NEWSLETTER**
69866
415 Orchard Dr.
Santa Fe, NM 87501
Telephone: (505) 982-3278
Year Established: 1980
Pub. Frequency: q.
Subscrip. Rate: $25/yr.
Circulation: 13,000
**Owner(s):**
Archaeological Conservancy
415 Orchard Dr.
Santa Fe, NM 87501
Telephone: (505) 982-3278
Ownership %: 100
**Editorial:**
Mark Michel .............................Editor
**Desc.:** Reports on the Archaeological
Conservancy's preservation projects and
on research conducted on
archaeological preserves.

**ASIA FOUNDATION NEWS**
70497
P.O. Box 1932231
San Francisco, CA 94119-3223
Telephone: (415) 982-4640
FAX: (415) 392-8863
Year Established: 1987
Pub. Frequency: q.
Subscrip. Rate: free
Circulation: 4,000
Circulation Type: controlled & free

**Owner(s):**
Asia Foundation
P.O. Box 1932231
San Francisco, CA 94119-3223
Telephone: (415) 982-4640
FAX: (415) 392-8863
Ownership %: 100
**Editorial:**
Jim Mullins .............................Editor

**ASOR NEWSLETTER**
69865
P.O. Box 15399
Atlanta, GA 30333-0399
Telephone: (404) 727-2320
FAX: (404) 727-2348
Year Established: 1992
Pub. Frequency: q.
Subscrip. Rate: $20/yr.
Circulation: 1,500
**Owner(s):**
Scholars Press
P.O. Box 15399
Atlanta, GA 30333-0399
Telephone: (404) 727-2320
FAX: (404) 727-2348
Ownership %: 100
**Editorial:**
Victor Matthews .............................Editor
**Desc.:** Newsletter of the American School
of Oriental Research.

**COME-ALL-YE**
70265
12 Meetinghouse Rd.
Hatboro, PA 19040-0494
Telephone: (215) 675-6762
FAX: (215) 674-2826
Mailing Address:
P.O. Box 494
Hatboro, PA 19040-0494
Year Established: 1977
Pub. Frequency: q.
Subscrip. Rate: $6/yr.
Materials: 10,32
Circulation: 2,000
Circulation Type: controlled & paid
**Owner(s):**
Legacy Books
12 Meetinghouse Rd.
Hatboro, PA 19040-0494
Telephone: (215) 675-6762
FAX: (215) 674-2826
Ownership %: 100
**Editorial:**
Richard Burns .............................Editor
**Desc.:** Covers folklore and folklife, social
history and community culture.

**COUNCIL COLUMNS**
70860
1828 L St., N.W.
Ste. 300
Washington, DC 20036
Telephone: (202) 466-6512
FAX: (202) 785-3926
Year Established: 1980
Pub. Frequency: s-m.
Subscrip. Rate: $60/yr.
Circulation: 8,000
Circulation Type: controlled & paid
**Owner(s):**
Council on Foundations, Inc.
1828 L St., N.W.
Ste. 300
Washington, DC 20036
Telephone: (202) 466-6512
FAX: (202) 785-3926
Ownership %: 100
**Editorial:**
Robin Hettleman .............................Editor

**FOLKLIFE CENTER NEWS**
70258
Library of Congress
Washington, DC 20540
Telephone: (202) 707-6590
Year Established: 1978

**Materials Accepted/Included:** 01-Business news 02-By-line articles 03-Fashion news 04-Food news 05-Freelance copy 06-Letters to editor 07-Real estate news 08-Sports news 09-Travel news 10-Book rev. 11-Movie rev. 12-Music rev. 13-TV rev. 14-Theater rev. 15-Coming events 16-Obituaries 17-Question & answer 18-Social announcements 19-Artwork 20-Cartoons 21-Photos 22-TV listings 23-Audio rec. 24-Video rec. 25-Books 26-Films/film clips 27-Personnel news 28-Press releases 29-New product news/photos 30-Trade lit. 31-Contracts awarded 32-Display adv. 33-Classified adv.

Pub. Frequency: q.
Page Size: tabloid
Subscrip. Rate: free
Circulation: 10,000
Circulation Type: controlled & free
**Owner(s):**
U.S. Library of Congress
Washington, DC 20540
Telephone: (202) 707-6590
Ownership %: 100
**Editorial:**
James Hardin ............................................Editor
**Desc.:** Reports on the activities and
programs of the center, along with
articles about the traditional
and expressive culture of the United
States.

70261
## FOOTNOTES FROM THE ARID ZONE
P.O. Box 5268
Carefree, AZ 85377
Telephone: (602) 488-1462
Year Established: 1990
Pub. Frequency: m.
Subscrip. Rate: $10/yr.
Materials: 10
**Owner(s):**
Carefree Communications, Inc.
P.O. Box 5268
Carefree, AZ 85377
Telephone: (602) 488-1462
Ownership %: 100
**Editorial:**
Jack Grenard ............................................Editor
**Desc.:** Takes a light, humorous look at
Arizona, its people and wildlife, pre-
history, history and future.

71178
## FORMER PRESIDENTS QUARTERLY
P.O. Box 6443
Fullerton, CA 92634
Telephone: (714) 738-4386
Year Established: 1993
Pub. Frequency: q.
Subscrip. Rate: $12/yr.
Materials: 10
**Owner(s):**
RHL Enterprises
P.O. Box 6443
Fullerton, CA 92634
Telephone: (714) 738-4386
Ownership %: 100
**Editorial:**
Robert H. Lewandowski ............................Editor
**Desc.:** Report on the activities of retired
U.S. presidents, including notable
speeches, overseas travel, articles and
books they have written or agreed to
write.

70527
## FREETHOUGHT HISTORY
Box 5224
Kansas City, KS 66119
Telephone: (913) 588-1996
Year Established: 1992
Pub. Frequency: q.
Subscrip. Rate: $10/yr.
Materials: 10,33
Circulation: 200
Circulation Type: controlled & paid
**Owner(s):**
People's Culture
Box 5224
Kansas City, KS 66119
Telephone: (913) 588-1996
Ownership %: 100
**Editorial:**
Fred Whitehead ............................................Editor

70533
## GEORGIA HUMANITIES
Emory University
1556 Clifton Rd., N.E.
Atlanta, GA 30322
Telephone: (404) 727-7500
FAX: (404) 727-0206
Year Established: 1981
Pub. Frequency: q.
Subscrip. Rate: free
Circulation: 5,000
Circulation Type: controlled
**Owner(s):**
Georgia Humanities Council
Emory University
1556 Clifton Rd., N.E.
Atlanta, GA 30322
Telephone: (404) 727-7500
FAX: (404) 727-0206
Ownership %: 100
**Editorial:**
Patricia Suhrcke ............................................Editor
**Desc.:** Provides a forum to foster
understanding and appreciation of the
humanities among the citizens of
Georgia.

69863
## HISTORY OF ANTHROPOLOGY NEWSLETTER
University of Chicago
1126 E. 59th St.
Chicago, IL 60637
Telephone: (312) 232-7022
Year Established: 1974
Pub. Frequency: a.
Subscrip. Rate: $5/yr. individuals; $6/yr.
institutions
**Owner(s):**
University of Chicago
1126 E. 59th St.
Chicago, IL 60637
Telephone: (312) 702-7702
Ownership %: 100
**Editorial:**
George W. Stocking ............................Editor

70263
## MAINE FOLKLORE CENTER NEWSLETTER
South Stevens Hall
University of Maine
Orono, ME 04469
Telephone: (207) 581-1891
Year Established: 1920
Pub. Frequency: s-a.
**Owner(s):**
Maine Folklore Center
South Stevens Hall
University of Maine
Orono, ME 04469
Telephone: (207) 581-1891
Ownership %: 100

71233
## MEMORIES PLUS
201 First St., N.W.
Ste. 114
Albany, OR 97321
Telephone: (503) 928-4798
Year Established: 1992
Pub. Frequency: m.
Subscrip. Rate: $5/yr.
Circulation: 750
Circulation Type: paid
**Owner(s):**
Memories Plus
201 First St., N.W.
Ste. 114
Albany, OR 97321
Telephone: (503) 928-4798
Ownership %: 100
**Editorial:**
Margaret Ingram ............................................Editor

70867
## PHILANTHROPIC TRENDS DIGEST
545 Madison Ave.
New York, NY 10022
Telephone: (212) 759-5660
FAX: (212) 759-1893
Year Established: 1983
Pub. Frequency: s-m.
Subscrip. Rate: $48/yr.
Materials: 10
Circulation: 2,000
Circulation Type: controlled & paid
**Owner(s):**
Douglas M. Lawson Associates, Inc.
545 Madison Ave.
New York, NY 10022
Telephone: (212) 759-5660
FAX: (212) 759-1893
Ownership %: 100
**Editorial:**
Joyce Rosen ............................................Editor
**Desc.:** News of issues, events, legislation
and trends in philanthropy of interest to
non-profit organizations.

70489
## PRESIDENTS' JOURNAL
79 Drakes Ridge
Bennington, IN 47011
Telephone: (812) 427-3914
Year Established: 1985
Pub. Frequency: q.
Subscrip. Rate: $12/yr.
Materials: 10
**Owner(s):**
Cottontail Publications
79 Drakes Ridge
Bennington, IN 47011
Telephone: (812) 427-3914
Ownership %: 100
**Editorial:**
Ellyn Kern, Ed. ............................................Editor
**Desc.:** Covers homes, history, and
collectibles related to presidential lore.

69868
## SOCIETY FOR AMERICAN ARCHAEOLOGY BULLETIN
900 Second St., N.W.
No. 12
Washington, DC 20002
Telephone: (202) 223-9774
Year Established: 1983
Pub. Frequency: 5/yr.
Subscrip. Rate: $15/yr.
**Owner(s):**
Society for American Archaeology
900 Second St., N.W.
No. 12
Washington, DC 20002
Telephone: (202) 223-9774
Ownership %: 100

69891
## SOCIETY FOR HISTORICAL ARCHAEOLOGY NEWSLETTER
P.O. Box 30446
Tucson, AZ 85751
Year Established: 1968
Pub. Frequency: q.
Subscrip. Rate: $50/yr. individuals; $65/yr.
institutions
Circulation: 1,900
Circulation Type: controlled & paid
**Owner(s):**
Society for Historical Archaeology
P.O. Box 30446
Tucson, AZ 85751
Ownership %: 100
**Editorial:**
Norman F. Barka ............................................Editor
**Desc.:** Contains forums on archaeological
conservation, urban archaeology,
information on society activities, and
current research.

69867
## SOPA NEWSLETTER
Southern Methodist University
Dallas, TX 75275
Year Established: 1977
Pub. Frequency: m.
Subscrip. Rate: membership
Circulation: 800
Circulation Type: controlled & paid
**Owner(s):**
Society of Professional Archeologists
Southern Methodist University
Dallas, TX 75275
Ownership %: 100
**Editorial:**
Sue Linder-Linsley ............................................Editor
**Desc.:** Covers cultural resource
management issues, ethical problems,
contract archaeology and society news.

69964
## SOUTH DAKOTA ARCHAEOLOGICAL SOCIETY NEWSLETTER
P.O. Box 1257
Rapid City, SD 57709-1257
Telephone: (605) 394-1936
FAX: (605) 394-1941
Year Established: 1970
Pub. Frequency: q.
Subscrip. Rate: $12/yr.
Materials: 10,11
**Owner(s):**
South Dakota Archeological Society
Newsletter
P.O. Box 1257
Rapid City, IA 57709-1257
Telephone: (605) 394-1936
FAX: (605) 394-1941
Ownership %: 100
**Editorial:**
Michael R. Fosha ............................................Editor

69869
## W.A.S. NEWSLETTER
120 Lakewood Dr.
Hollister, MO 65672
Year Established: 1971
Pub. Frequency: 4/yr.
Subscrip. Rate: $12/yr. US members;
$16/yr. overseas
**Owner(s):**
World Archaeological Society
120 Lakewood Dr.
Hollister, MO 65672
Ownership %: 100
**Editorial:**
Ron Miller ............................................Director

70622
## WHAT IS TO BE READ
1736 Columbia Rd., NW
Ste. 202
Washington, DC 20009
Telephone: (202) 387-1753
Year Established: 1984
Pub. Frequency: bi-m.
Subscrip. Rate: $25/yr.
Circulation: 2,500
Circulation Type: controlled & paid
**Owner(s):**
Cooperative Economics News Service
1736 Columbia Rd., NW
Ste. 202
Washington, DC 20009
Telephone: (202) 387-1753
Ownership %: 100
**Editorial:**
Henry Leland ............................................Editor

**Materials Accepted/Included:** 01-Business news 02-By-line articles 03-Fashion news 04-Food news 05-Freelance copy 06-Letters to editor 07-Real estate news 08-Sports news 09-Travel news
10-Book rev. 11-Movie rev. 12-Music rev. 13-TV rev. 14-Theater rev. 15-Coming events 16-Obituaries 17-Question & answer 18-Social announcements 19-Artwork 20-Cartoons 21-Photos 22-TV listings
23-Audio rec. 24-Video rec. 25-Books 26-Films/film clips 27-Personnel news 28-Press releases 29-New product news/photos 30-Trade lit. 31-Contracts awarded 32-Display adv. 33-Classified adv.

7-89

**Desc.:** Read primarily by academic social scientists. Publishes book reviews of current academic, scholarly, and college textbooks in economics, sociology, labor studies, women's studies, urban affairs, and educational software.

## Group 362-Sports

70068

### AMERICAN WHITE WATER
P.O. Box 85
Phoenicia, NY 12464
Telephone: (914) 688-5569
Year Established: 1967
Pub. Frequency: bi-m.
Subscrip. Rate: 20/yr.
Materials: 10
Circulation: 5,000
Circulation Type: controlled & paid
**Owner(s):**
American Whitewater Affiliation
P.O. Box 85
Phoenicia, NY 12464
Telephone: (914) 688-5569
Ownership %: 100
**Editorial:**
Chris Koll ..............................Editor
**Desc.:** Covers canoeing and kayaking and river conservation.

70900

### APBA JOURNAL
P.O. Box 5405
San Francisco, CA 94083-5405
Telephone: (415) 772-0907
FAX: (415) 757-1122
Year Established: 1967
Pub. Frequency: m.
Subscrip. Rate: $24/yr.
Circulation: 2,650
Circulation Type: controlled & paid
**Owner(s):**
APBA Journal
P.O. Box 5405
San Francisco, CA 94083-5405
Telephone: (415) 772-0907
FAX: (415) 757-1122
Ownership %: 100
**Management:**
Ed Naftaly ...........................Publisher
**Editorial:**
Ed Naftaly ...............................Editor

70878

### AUTORACER'S MONTHLY
P.O. Box 21447
Reno, NV 89515
Telephone: (415) 424-1334
FAX: (415) 858-0727
Year Established: 1990
Pub. Frequency: m.
Subscrip. Rate: $50/yr.
Materials: 10
Circulation: 600
Circulation Type: controlled & paid
**Owner(s):**
LP Inc.
P.O. Box 21447
Reno, NV 89515
Telephone: (415) 424-1334
FAX: (415) 858-0727
Ownership %: 100
**Editorial:**
Jim Crockett ...............................Editor
**Desc.:** Covers everything from driving techniques and sponsor search hints to tax-planning and safety tips. For the serious amateur and semi-pro racecar driver.

70906

### BASEBALL INSIGHT
P.O. Box 23205
Portland, OR 97223
Telephone: (503) 244-8975
Year Established: 1982

Pub. Frequency: 27/yr. (w. Apr.-Oct.)
Subscrip. Rate: $139/yr.
Materials: 10
Circulation: 600
Circulation Type: controlled & paid
**Owner(s):**
Parrish Publications
P.O. Box 23205
Portland, OR 97223
Telephone: (415) 757-1122
Ownership %: 100
**Editorial:**
Phil Erwin ...............................Editor
**Desc.:** Inside stats for serious fans.

70886

### BAY SPORTS REVIEW
P.O. Box 4520
Berkeley, CA 94704
Telephone: (510) 845-2062
FAX: (510) 444-6698
Year Established: 1991
Pub. Frequency: bi-m.
Subscrip. Rate: $20/yr.
Materials: 10, 33
Circulation: 10,000
Circulation Type: controlled & paid
**Owner(s):**
Bay Sports Review
P.O. Box 4520
Berkeley, CA 94704
Telephone: (510) 845-2062
FAX: (510) 444-6698
Ownership %: 100
**Editorial:**
Paul Matson ...............................Editor
**Desc.:** Contains fans' responses to and opinions on sports questions and topics. Lists wagering odds on NFL, Super Bowl, NL, AL, World Series, NBA, Stanley Cup, and more.

70884

### BETWEEN THE LINES
227 Park Ave.
New York, NY 10172
Telephone: (212) 773-1634
Pub. Frequency: q.
Subscrip. Rate: free
**Owner(s):**
Ernst & Young
Media & Entertainment Group
227 Park Ave.
New York, NY 10172
Telephone: (212) 773-1634
Ownership %: 100
**Editorial:**
Michael Breit ...............................Editor
**Desc.:** Financial newsletter for the sports world.

70875

### BOWHUNTING NEWS
1-B Airport Dr.
Hopedale, MA 01747
Telephone: (508) 478-4754
FAX: (508) 478-3541
Year Established: 1989
Pub. Frequency: m.
Subscrip. Rate: $15/yr.
Materials: 10,33
Circulation: 15,000
Circulation Type: paid
**Owner(s):**
Eastern Publishing & Distributing, Inc.
1-B
Hopedale, MA 01747
Telephone: (508) 478-4754
FAX: (508) 478-3541
Ownership %: 100
**Editorial:**
Roy Goodwind ...............................Editor

**Desc.:** Official newsletter of six statewide bowhunting organizations. Contains stories by bowhunters relating actual hunting experiences, and industry news, hunting programs and updates on pending legislation.

70892

### CASINO CHRONICLE
1412 Chanticleer
Cherry Hill, NJ 08003
Telephone: (609) 751-8620
FAX: (609) 751-8620
Year Established: 1983
Pub. Frequency: w.
Subscrip. Rate: $155/yr.; $165/yr. Canada; $205/yr. elsewhere
Circulation: 1,500
Circulation Type: controlled & paid
**Owner(s):**
Casino Chronicle, Inc.
1412 Chanticleer
Cherry Hill, NJ 08003
Telephone: (609) 751-8620
FAX: (609) 751-8620
Ownership %: 100
**Editorial:**
Ben A. Borowsky ...............................Editor
**Desc.:** Focuses on gaming industry in U.S.

70897

### COMPUTER CHESS REPORTS
21 Walt Whitman Rd.
Huntington Station, NY 11746
Telephone: (516) 424-3300
Year Established: 1983
Pub. Frequency: s-a.
Subscrip. Rate: $10.99/yr.; $15.99/yr. Canada; $22.99/yr. elsewhere
**Owner(s):**
Computer Chess Digest, Inc.
21 Walt Whitman Rd.
Huntington Station, NY 11746
Telephone: (516) 424-3300
Ownership %: 100
**Desc.:** Detailed comparison of chess computer boards and programs for consumer and retailer info and clearinghouse.

70017

### CYCLING USA
11 Olympic Plz.
Colorado Springs, CO 80909
Telephone: (719) 578-4628
FAX: (719) 578-4628
Year Established: 1980
Pub. Frequency: m.
Subscrip. Rate: $15/yr.
Materials: 10,32
Circulation: 35,000
Circulation Type: controlled & paid
**Owner(s):**
U.S. Cycling Federation
11 Olympic Plz.
Colorado Springs, CO 80909
Telephone: (719) 578-4628
FAX: (719) 578-4628
Ownership %: 100
**Editorial:**
Steve Penny ...............................Editor
**Desc.:** Offers federation-related news reports and releases, feature articles on all aspects of bicycle racing, profiles of coaches and cyclists, and information on events and programs of interest to federation members.

70051

### FEELING SPORTS MAGAZINE
4601 Excelsior Ave., S.
St. Louis Park, MN 55416
Telephone: (612) 920-9363
Year Established: 1975
Pub. Frequency: bi-m.
Subscrip. Rate: free

**Owner(s):**
Braille Sports Foundation
4601 Excelsior Ave., S.
St. Louis Park, MN 55416
Telephone: (612) 920-9363
Ownership %: 100
**Editorial:**
John Ross ...............................Editor
**Desc.:** Information about tournaments and other activities sponsored by organizations promoting sports and mobility for visually impaired persons.

70856

### GAME MANAGER
P.O. Box 1330
West Point, CA 95255-1330
Telephone: (209) 293-7087
Year Established: 1987
Pub. Frequency: m.
Subscrip. Rate: $45/yr.
Materials: 33
**Owner(s):**
Multiple Use Managers, Inc.
P.O. Box 1330
West Point, CA 95255-1330
Telephone: (209) 293-7087
Ownership %: 100
**Editorial:**
Wayne Long ...............................Editor
**Desc.:** Designed for land owners and game managers.

70862

### INSIDERS SKI LETTER
115 Lilly Pond Ln.
Katonah, NY 10536
Telephone: (914) 232-5094
Year Established: 1989
Pub. Frequency: 10/yr.
Subscrip. Rate: $33/yr.
**Owner(s):**
Skiletter, Inc.
115 Lilly Pond Ln.
Katonah, NY 10536
Telephone: (914) 232-5094
Ownership %: 100
**Editorial:**
I. William Berry ...............................Editor
**Desc.:** Covers skiing for serious skiers.

70060

### LOG & SAN DIEGO LOG
1025 Rosecrans St.
San Diego, CA 92106
Telephone: (619) 226-1608
FAX: (619) 226-0573
Year Established: 1971
Pub. Frequency: fortn.
Subscrip. Rate: $24.95/yr.
Materials: 10,32
Circulation: 60,000
Circulation Type: controlled & paid
**Owner(s):**
Log Newspapers
1025 Rosecrans St.
San Diego, CA 92106
Telephone: (619) 226-1608
FAX: (619) 226-0573
Ownership %: 100
**Editorial:**
Kevin Featherly III ...............................Editor
**Desc.:** Covers boating in Southern California and Western Arizona.

70019

### MASS CYCLIST
P.O. Box 1015
Kendall Square Branch
Cambridge, MA 02142-0008
Telephone: (617) 491-7423
Year Established: 1979
Pub. Frequency: bi-m.
Subscrip. Rate: $25/yr. includes membership
Materials: 10

**Materials Accepted/Included:** 01-Business news 02-By-line articles 03-Fashion news 04-Food news 05-Freelance copy 06-Letters to editor 07-Real estate news 08-Sports news 09-Travel news 10-Book rev. 11-Movie rev. 12-Music rev. 13-TV rev. 14-Theater rev. 15-Coming events 16-Obituaries 17-Question & answer 18-Social announcements 19-Artwork 20-Cartoons 21-Photos 22-TV listings 23-Audio rec. 24-Video rec. 25-Books 26-Films/film clips 27-Personnel news 28-Press releases 29-New product news/photos 30-Trade lit. 31-Contracts awarded 32-Display adv. 33-Classified adv.

7-90

**Owner(s):**
Bicycle Coalition of Massachusetts
P.O. Box 1015
Kendall Square Branch
Cambridge, MA 02142-0008
Telephone: (617) 491-7423
Ownership %: 100
**Desc.:** Newsletter of the Coalition, a
bicycle advocacy group working to
promote the safe and practical use of
the bicycle for both transportation and
recreation.

70050

## MOTORSPORTS MARKETING NEWS
1448 Hollywood Ave.
Langhorne, PA 19047
Telephone: (215) 752-2392
FAX: (215) 752-1518
Year Established: 1985
Pub. Frequency: m.
Subscrip. Rate: $80/yr.
Materials: 10,32
**Owner(s):**
Ernie Saxton Communications
1448 Hollywood Ave.
Langhorne, PA 19047
Telephone: (215) 752-2392
FAX: (215) 752-1518
Ownership %: 100
**Editorial:**
Marilyn Saxton .............................Editor

70911

## NASCAR NEWS
1801 Volusia Ave.
Daytona Beach, FL 32114-1243
Telephone: (904) 253-0611
FAX: (904) 252-8804
Year Established: 1949
Pub. Frequency: fortn.
Page Size: 10,33
Subscrip. Rate: $35/yr. non-members
Circulation: 40,000
Circulation Type: controlled & paid
**Owner(s):**
National Assn. for Stock Car Auto Racing,
Inc.
1801 Volusia Ave.
Daytona Beach, FL 32114-1243
Telephone: (904) 253-0611
FAX: (904) 252-8804
Ownership %: 100
**Editorial:**
Paul C. Schaefer .........................Editor

70064

## NAUTIQUE NEWS
6100 S. Orange Ave.
Orlando, FL 32809
Telephone: (407) 855-4141
FAX: (407) 851-7844
Year Established: 1961
Pub. Frequency: 3/yr.
Subscrip. Rate: free
Materials: 32
Circulation: 80,000
Circulation Type: controlled & paid
**Owner(s):**
Correct Craft, Inc.
6100 S. Orange Ave.
Orlando, FL 32809
Telephone: (407) 855-4141
FAX: (407) 851-7844
Ownership %: 100
**Editorial:**
Teresa "Terry" Dunagin ...........................Editor
**Desc.:** News for boating and water sports
enthusiasts, with special emphasis on
Correct Craft boats.

71207

## PHYS ED JOURNAL OF SPORTS MEDICINE
250 Mercer St.
New York, NY 10012
Telephone: (212) 777-7462
FAX: (212) 777-7556
Mailing Address:
P.O. Box 408
New York, NY 10012
Year Established: 1992
Pub. Frequency: m.
Subscrip. Rate: $157/yr.
**Owner(s):**
Phys Ed Fitness Ltd.
250 Mercer St.
P.O. Box 408
New York, NY 10012
Telephone: (212) 777-7462
FAX: (212) 777-7556
Ownership %: 100
**Editorial:**
Ken Hom .............................Editor
**Desc.:** Helps physicians keep up with
developments in sports medicine, recent
research studies, and related issues,
including practice management and
health care reform.

70879

## SKI INDUSTRY LETTER
115 Lilly Pond Lane
Katonah, NY 10536
Telephone: (914) 232-5094
Year Established: 1979
Pub. Frequency: m.
Subscrip. Rate: $197/yr.
Materials: 10
**Owner(s):**
Skiletter, Inc.
115 Lilly Pond Lane
Katonah, NY 10536
Telephone: (914) 232-5094
Ownership %: 100
**Editorial:**
I. William Berry .............................Editor
**Desc.:** Covers the ski trade.

70869

## SURF REPORT
P.O. Box 1028
Dana Point, CA 92629
Telephone: (714) 496-5922
FAX: (714) 496-7849
Year Established: 1980
Pub. Frequency: m.
Subscrip. Rate: $35/yr. US; $42/yr. foreign
**Owner(s):**
Surf Report
P.O. Box 1028
Dana Point, CA 92629
Telephone: (714) 496-5922
FAX: (714) 496-7849
Ownership %: 100
**Editorial:**
Donna Oakley .............................Editor

65692

## TEAM MARKETING REPORT
660 W. Grand Ave. #100E
Chicago, IL 60610-3906
Telephone: (312) 829-7060
FAX: (312) 733-4071
Year Established: 1988
Pub. Frequency: m.
Page Size: standard
Subscrip. Rate: $159/yr.
Materials: 08,10
Circulation: 5,000
Circulation Type: paid
**Owner(s):**
Team Marketing Report
660 W. Grand Ave. #100E
Chicago, IL 60610-3906
Telephone: (312) 829-7060
FAX: (312) 733-4071
Ownership %: 100

**Management:**
Alan Friedman .............................Publisher
**Editorial:**
Alan Friedman .............................Editor
**Desc.:** Covers innovative and successful
sports marketing and promotion
activities of sports teams sports
sponsors and sports marketing
agencies.
**Readers:** Sports marketing and sports
business executives for sports teams,
corporate sponsors and sports
marketing agencies.

70865

## WRESTLING OBSERVER LETTER
P.O. Box 1228
Campbell, CA 95001
Telephone: (408) 379-8067
FAX: (408) 379-6562
Year Established: 1982
Pub. Frequency: w
Subscrip. Rate: $72/yr.
Circulation: 5,600
Circulation Type: controlled & paid
**Owner(s):**
Wrestling Observer Newsletter
P.O. Box 1228
Campbell, CA 95009
Telephone: (408) 379-8067
FAX: (408) 379-6562
Ownership %: 100
**Editorial:**
Dave Meltzeer .............................Editor
**Desc.:** Examines the business aspects of
pro-wrestling.

## Group 364-Travel & Transportation

69818

## ACCIDENT PREVENTION
2200 Wilson Blvd.
Ste. 500
Arlington, VA 22201-3306
Telephone: (703) 522-8300
FAX: (703) 525-6047
Year Established: 1948
Pub. Frequency: m.
Subscrip. Rate: $70/yr. US; $75/yr. foreign
**Owner(s):**
Flight Safety Foundation, Inc.
2200 Wilson Blvd.
Ste. 500
Arlington, VA 22201-3306
Telephone: (703) 522-8300
Ownership %: 100

71221

## AIRCRAFT VALUE NEWSLETTER
1201 Seven Locks Rd.
Potomac, MD 20854
Telephone: (301) 424-3338
FAX: (301) 309-3847
Year Established: 1992
Pub. Frequency: bi-w.
Subscrip. Rate: $595/yr.; $630/yr. foreign
**Owner(s):**
Phillips Business Information, Inc.
1201 Seven Locks Rd.
Potomac, MD 20854
Telephone: (301) 424-3338
FAX: (301) 309-3847
Ownership %: 100

71223

## AIRLINE MARKETING NEWS
1201 Seven Locks Rd.
Potomac, MD 20854
Telephone: (301) 424-3338
FAX: (301) 309-3847
Year Established: 1993
Pub. Frequency: bi-w.
Subscrip. Rate: $495/yr.; $530/yr. foreign

**Owner(s):**
Phillips Business Information, Inc.
1201 Seven Locks Rd.
Potomac, MD 20854
Telephone: (301) 424-3338
FAX: (301) 309-3847
Ownership %: 100

71236

## ASIAN AVIATION NEWS
1201 Seven Locks Rd.
Potomac, MD 20854
Telephone: (301) 424-3338
FAX: (301) 309-3847
Year Established: 1993
Pub. Frequency: bi-w.
Subscrip. Rate: $495/yr.; $530/yr. foreign
**Owner(s):**
Phillips Business Information, Inc.
1201 Seven Locks Rd.
Potomac, MD 20854
Telephone: (301) 424-3338
FAX: (301) 309-3847
Ownership %: 100

48944

## AUTOMOTIVE WEEK
P.O. Box 3495
Wayne, NJ 07474-3495
Telephone: (201) 694-7792
FAX: (201) 694-2817
Year Established: 1975
Pub. Frequency: w.
Page Size: standard
Subscrip. Rate: $120/yr.; $185/2 yrs.;
$245/3 yrs.
Materials: 32
**Owner(s):**
Automotive Week Publishing Co.
P.O. Box 3495
Wayne, NJ 07474-3495
Telephone: (201) 694-7792
FAX: (201) 694-2817
Ownership %: 100
**Editorial:**
Chuck Laverty .............................Editor
Barbara Lanni ...............Associate Publisher
**Desc.:** Merchandising, marketing and
business news and trends in the auto
parts, accessories, chemicals
and service aftermarket are treated in
news style. Aim is to help readers profit
from experiences of others in retailing
and distribution operations. Stress on
promotions -- their launching, and
comparison with results during periods
without such promotions. Covers
mergers, acquisitions, bankruptcies,
litigation.
**Readers:** Retailers, distributors &
manufacturers of auto parts, accessories
and service. Presidents, owners,
executive V.P./marketing, merchandise
managers and buyers.

70873

## AUTO PARTS REPORT
P.O. Box 5950
Bethesda, MD 20824-5950
Telephone: (301) 229-2077
FAX: (301) 229-3995
Year Established: 1986
Pub. Frequency: s-m.
Subscrip. Rate: $425/yr.
**Owner(s):**
International Trade Services
P.O. Box 5950
Bethesda, MD 20824-5950
Telephone: (301) 229-2077
FAX: (301) 229-3995
Ownership %: 100
**Editorial:**
Ronald J. DeMarines .............................Editor
**Desc.:** Reports on news and trends
involving the OE and aftermarket auto
parts industry worldwide.

**Materials Accepted/Included:** 01-Business news 02-By-line articles 03-Fashion news 04-Food news 05-Freelance copy 06-Letters to editor 07-Real estate news 08-Sports news 09-Travel news 10-Book rev. 11-Movie rev. 12-Music rev. 13-TV rev. 14-Theater rev. 15-Coming events 16-Obituaries 17-Question & answer 18-Social announcements 19-Artwork 20-Cartoons 21-Photos 22-TV listings 23-Audio rec. 24-Video rec. 25-Books 26-Films/film clips 27-Personnel news 28-Press releases 29-New product news/photos 30-Trade lit. 31-Contracts awarded 32-Display adv. 33-Classified adv.

7-91

## AVIATION EDUCATION NEWS BULLETIN

69831

1900 Arch St.
Philadelphia, PA 19103-1498
Telephone: (215) 564-3484
Pub. Frequency: bi-m.
**Owner(s):**
Aviation Distributors & Manufacturers Assn.
1900 Arach St.
Philadelphia, PA 19103-1498
Telephone: (215) 564-3484
Ownership %: 100

## BUSINESS FLYER

69530

P.O. Box 276
Newton Center, MA 02159-0002
Telephone: (800) 359-3774
Year Established: 1986
Pub. Frequency: m.
Subscrip. Rate: $24.95/yr.
Print Process: offset
Circulation: 80,000
Circulation Type: controlled & paid
**Owner(s):**
Holcon
P.O. Box 276
Newton Center, MA 02159
Telephone: (800) 359-3774
Ownership %: 100
**Editorial:**
Jane Costello .................................Editor
**Desc.:** Designed to enable business and
leisure travelers to make the most of
their travel.

## CABIN CREW SAFETY

69824

2200 Wilson Blvd.
Ste. 500
Arlington, VA 22201-3306
Telephone: (703) 522-8300
FAX: (703) 525-6047
Year Established: 1956
Pub. Frequency: bi-m.
Subscrip. Rate: $55/yr. US; $60/yr. foreign
**Owner(s):**
Flight Safety Foundation, Inc.
2200 Wilson Blvd.
Ste. 500
Arlington, VA 22201-3306
Telephone: (703) 522-8300
Ownership %: 100
**Desc.:** Focuses attention on the cabin
crew, especially in airline operations, but
the special requirements of corporate
operations are also presented.

## DISCERNING TRAVELER

70944

504 W. Mermaid Ln.
Philadelphia, PA 19118
Telephone: (215) 247-5578
Year Established: 1987
Pub. Frequency: bi-m.
Subscrip. Rate: $50/yr.
Materials: 10
**Owner(s):**
Lida Limited
504 W. Mermaid Ln.
Philadelphia, PA 19118
Telephone: (215) 247-5578
Ownership %: 100
**Editorial:**
David L. Glickstein ...........................Editor
**Desc.:** East coast of the US & Canada

## EDUCATED TRAVELER

70948

Chantilly, VA 22022
Telephone: (703) 471-1063
FAX: (703) 471-4439
Mailing Address:
P.O. Box 220822
Chantilly, VA 22022
Year Established: 1990

Pub. Frequency: bi-m.
Subscrip. Rate: $45/yr. incl. free directory
of tours
Materials: 10,32
Circulation: 1,500
Circulation Type: controlled & paid
**Owner(s):**
Educated Traveler
P.O. Box 220822
Philadelphia, PA 19118
Telephone: (703) 471-1063
Ownership %: 100
**Editorial:**
Ann H. Waigand .............................Editor
**Desc.:** International speciality travel incl.
tourism, educational travel, special
interest tours, ecotourism, museums,
intercultural & activity holidays

## ELECTRIC VEHICLE PROGRESS

70876

215 Park Ave., S.
Ste. 1301
New York, NY 10003
Telephone: (212) 228-0246
FAX: (212) 228-0376
Year Established: 1979
Pub. Frequency: s-m.
Subscrip. Rate: $367/yr.
**Owner(s):**
Alexander Research & Communications,
Inc.
215 Park Ave., S.
Ste. 1301
New York, NY 10003
Telephone: (212) 228-0246
FAX: (212) 228-0376
Ownership %: 100
**Editorial:**
Laurence A. Alexander ......................Editor
**Desc.:** Newsletter of electric vehicle
commercialization. World wide coverage
coverage focuses on news and data on
both the technical and business aspect
of the electrical vehicle industry.

## ENTREE

70918

1470 E. Valey Rd., Ste. W
Santa Barbara, CA 93108
Telephone: (805) 969-5848
FAX: (805) 966-7095
Year Established: 1982
Pub. Frequency: m.
Subscrip. Rate: $59/yr.
Materials: 10
Circulation: 6,000
Circulation Type: controlled & paid
**Owner(s):**
Entree Travel
1470 E. Valley Rd., Ste. W
Santa Barbara, CA 93108
Telephone: (805) 969-5848
FAX: (805) 966-7095
Ownership %: 100
**Editorial:**
William Tomick ...............................Editor
**Desc.:** Hotel and restaurant critiques; an
insider's look at travel and eating; book
spas, cruises, shopping reviews.

## HAZMAT TRANSPORT

66007

951 Pershing Dr.
Silver Spring, MD 20910
Telephone: (301) 587-6300
Year Established: 1980
Pub. Frequency: fortn.
Page Size: standard
Subscrip. Rate: $345.54/yr.
**Owner(s):**
Business Publishers, Inc.
951 Pershing Dr.
Silver Spring, MD 20910
Telephone: (301) 587-6300
Ownership %: 100

**Editorial:**
Roger Gilroy .................................Editor
Marjorie Weiner ..................Marketing Director

## HELICOPTER SAFETY

69825

2200 Wilson Blvd., Ste. 500
Arlington, VA 22201-3306
Telephone: (703) 522-8300
FAX: (703) 525-6047
Year Established: 1967
Pub. Frequency: bi-m.
Subscrip. Rate: $70/yr. US; $75/yr. foreign
**Owner(s):**
Flight Safety Foundation, Inc.
2200 Wilson Blvd., Ste. 500
Arlington, VA 22201-3306
Telephone: (703) 522-8300
Ownership %: 100
**Desc.:** Highlights the broad spectrum of
real-world helicopter operations.

## HIGHWAY & VEHICLE - SAFETY REPORT

70908

178 Thimble Islands Rd.
Branford, CT 06405
Telephone: (203) 488-9808
FAX: (203) 488-3129
Mailing Address:
P.O. Box 3367
Branford, CT 06405
Year Established: 1974
Pub. Frequency: 26/yr.
Subscrip. Rate: $327/yr. US; $352/yr.
foreign
Materials: 10
**Owner(s):**
Stamler Publishing Co.
178 Thimble Islands Rd.
Branford, CT 06405
Telephone: (203) 488-9808
FAX: (203) 488-3129
Ownership %: 100
**Editorial:**
S. Paul Stamler ..............................Editor
**Desc.:** Covers new developments in
transportation and vehicle safety.

## HISTORIC TRAVELER

71218

19400 Vintage St.
Northridge, CA 91324
Telephone: (818) 349-2161
Year Established: 1988
Pub. Frequency: 10/yr.
Subscrip. Rate: $24/yr.
**Owner(s):**
Allan Mann Communications
19400 Vintage St.
Northridge, CA 91324
Telephone: (818) 349-2161
Ownership %: 100
**Editorial:**
Allan Mann ...................................Editor
**Desc.:** Publishes features and news about
travel to historic towns, districts and
homes for enthusiasts of historic
architecture.

## HOTEL-MOTEL SECURITY & SAFETY MANAGEMENT

68927

402 Main St.
Port Washington, NY 11050
Telephone: (516) 883-1440
FAX: (516) 883-1683
Year Established: 1982
Pub. Frequency: m.
Subscrip. Rate: $169/yr. US; $194/yr.
foreign
Circulation: 750
Circulation Type: paid

**Owner(s):**
Rusting Publications
402 Main St.
Port Washington, NY 11050
Telephone: (516) 883-1440
Ownership %: 100
**Editorial:**
Robert R. Rusting ...........................Editor

## HOTEL UPDATE NEWSLETTER

70514

2125 Butterfield Rd.
Troy, MI 48084
Telephone: (313) 637-8432
FAX: (313) 637-2035
Year Established: 1990
Pub. Frequency: m.
Subscrip. Rate: $24/yr.
**Owner(s):**
Entertainment Publications, Inc.
2125 Butterfield Rd.
Troy, MI 48084
Telephone: (313) 637-8432
FAX: (313) 637-2035
Ownership %: 100
**Editorial:**
Robert McHenry .............................Editor
**Desc.:** Provides information of attractive
industry offerings for lodging, dining,
leisure activities, and travel.

## HUMAN FACTORS & AVIATION MEDICINE

69812

2200 Wilson Blvd.
Ste. 500
Arlington, VA 22201-3306
Telephone: (703) 522-8300
FAX: (703) 525-6047
Year Established: 1957
Pub. Frequency: bi-m.
Subscrip. Rate: $70/yr. US; $75/yr. foreign
**Owner(s):**
Flight Safety Foundation, Inc.
2200 Wilson Blvd.
Ste. 500
Arlington, VA 22201-3306
Telephone: (703) 522-8300
FAX: (703) 525-6047
Ownership %: 100
**Desc.:** Allows specialists, researchers, and
physicians to present information critical
to the training, performance, and health
of aviation professionals.

## I B QUARTERLY INDEX

70915

1325 G St., N.W.
Ste. 1005
Washington, DC 20005
Telephone: (202) 347-2275
FAX: (202) 347-2278
Pub. Frequency: 4/yr.
Subscrip. Rate: $225/yr. US; $307/yr.
foreign
**Owner(s):**
Congressional Information Bureau, Inc.
1325 G. St., N.W.
Ste. 1005
Washington, DC 20005
Telephone: (202) 347-2275
Ownership %: 100
**Editorial:**
Robert P. Cazalas ...........................Editor

## INTERNATIONAL RAILWAY TRAVELER

70920

The Belknap Bldg.
1810 Sils Ave., Ste. 306B
Louisville, KY 40205
Telephone: (502) 454-0277
FAX: (502) 454-1542
Year Established: 1983

Pub. Frequency: bi-m.
Subscrip. Rate: $39.95 US; $41.45
    Canada; $45.95 elsewhere
Materials: 10,32
Circulation: 5,000
Circulation Type: controlled & paid
**Owner(s):**
Hardy Publishing Co., Inc.
The Belknap Bldg.
1810 Sils Ave., Ste. 306B
Louisville, KY 40205
Telephone: (502) 454-0277
FAX: (502) 454-1542
Ownership %: 100
**Editorial:**
Owen Hardy .............................Editor
**Desc.:** For all who love to travel by trains,
    whether by Amtrak or the East African
    Railway.

70883

## ISLAND ESCAPES
3886 State St.
Santa Barbara, CA 93105
Telephone: (805) 682-7177
FAX: (805) 569-0349
Pub. Frequency: m.
Subscrip. Rate: $39/yr.
Circulation: 4,000
Circulation Type: controlled & paid
**Owner(s):**
Islands Publishing Company
3886 State St.
Santa Barbara, CA 93105
Telephone: (805) 682-7177
FAX: (805) 569-0349
Ownership %: 100
**Editorial:**
Joan Tapper .............................Editor
**Desc.:** Provides ratings and evaluations of
    where to go, how to get there, where to
    stay, where and what to eat and what to
    do.

70909

## LAKE LOG CHIPS
221 Water St.
Boyne City, MI 49712
Telephone: (616) 582-2814
FAX: (616) 582-3392
Year Established: 1972
Pub. Frequency: bi-w.
Subscrip. Rate: $25/yr.
Materials: 10
Circulation: 1,200
Circulation Type: controlled & paid
**Owner(s):**
Harbor House Publishers, Inc.
221 Water St.
Boyne City, MI 49712
Telephone: (616) 582-2814
Ownership %: 100
**Editorial:**
David Knight .............................Editor

70924

## LAS VEGAS INSIDER
P.O. Box 29274
Las Vegas, NV 89126
Telephone: (602) 636-1649
Year Established: 1973
Pub. Frequency: m.
Subscrip. Rate: $42/yr.
Materials: 32
Circulation: 5,100
Circulation Type: controlled & paid
**Owner(s):**
Lucky Publishing Co.
P.O. Box 29274
Las Vegas, NV 89126
Telephone: (602) 636-1649
Ownership %: 100
**Editorial:**
Donald Currier .............................Editor

**Desc.:** Contains the latest gaming,
    tournament and travel information.
    Includes tourist tips, freebies,
    and discounts.

70922

## MARITIME RESEARCH CHARTER NEWSLETTER
Parlin, NJ 00009
Telephone: (908) 727-8040
FAX: (908) 727-0243
Mailing Address:
    P.O. Box 805
    Parlin, NJ 08859
Year Established: 1953
Pub. Frequency: w.
Subscrip. Rate: $240/yr. US; $250/yr.
    foreign
Materials: 32
Circulation: 5,000
Circulation Type: controlled & paid
**Owner(s):**
Maritime Research, Inc.
P.O. Box 805
Parlin, NJ 08859
Telephone: (908) 727-8040
**Editorial:**
Jay Lillianthal .............................Editor
**Desc.:** Listing of all charter fixtures
    reported worldwide in the tramp charter
    market

65416

## MATURE TRAVELER NEWSLETTER, THE
P.O. Box 50820
Reno, NV 89513-0820
Telephone: (702) 786-7419
Year Established: 1984
Pub. Frequency: m.
Page Size: 9 1/2 x 11
Subscrip. Rate: $29.95/yr.
Materials: 02,05,06,09,15,21,28,32,33
Freelance Pay: $25-$100/article
Print Process: offset
Circulation: 2,500
Circulation Type: paid
**Owner(s):**
GEM Publishing Group, Inc.
250 E. Riverview Cir.
Reno, NV 89509
Telephone: (702) 786-7419
Ownership %: 100
**Management:**
Adele R. Malott .............................Manager
**Editorial:**
Gene E. Malott .............................Editor
**Desc.:** A monthly newsletter that gives 49-
    plus the information they need to be
    travel insiders. Aims to alert mature
    travelers to the very best bargains
    available, wherever they travel, to trips
    especially planned for them, to special
    places they will enjoy, and to ways they
    can make travel easier and more fun.
**Readers:** Active seniors over 49 years old,
    with the time and resources to make
    several major trips each year.

70877

## NUTZ & BOLTZ NEWSLETTER
P.O. Box 123
Butler, MD 21023
Telephone: (410) 584-7574
Year Established: 1989
Pub. Frequency: m.
Subscrip. Rate: $25/yr.
**Owner(s):**
Nutz & Boltz
P.O. Box 123
Butler, MD 21023
Telephone: (410) 584-7574
Ownership %: 100
**Editorial:**
David R. Solomon .............................Editor
**Desc.:** Covers all things automotive.

69828

## ORGANIZATION OF BLACK AIRLINE PILOTS NEWSLETTER
P.O. Box 5793
Englewood, NJ 07631
Telephone: (201) 568-8145
Pub. Frequency: q.
**Owner(s):**
Organization of Black Airline Pilots
P.O. Box 5793
Englewood, NJ 07631
Telephone: (201) 568-8145
Ownership %: 100

24648

## RESTAURATEUR
7926 Jones Brance Dr., Ste. 530
Mclean, VA 22102-3303
Telephone: (703) 356-1315
FAX: (703) 893-4926
Year Established: 1947
Pub. Frequency: m.
Page Size: tabloid
Subscrip. Rate: $20/yr.
Circulation: 4,000
Circulation Type: controlled
**Owner(s):**
Restaurant Association of Metro
    Washington, Inc.
7926 Jones Branch Dr., Ste.530
Mclean, VA 22102-3303
Telephone: (703) 356-1315
Ownership %: 100
**Editorial:**
J. Thomas Rouland ...........Executive Editor
Carol Morgan .............................Editor
**Desc.:** Articles pertaining to the food-
    service industry, new products,
    restaurants, and personnel. Uses
    publicity releases as fillers; interested in
    materials pertaining to the Metro
    Washington, DC, area. Publicity pictures
    used in addition to pictures taken by
    staff. Most articles run 100-250 words.
    Departments include: Business News,
    Viewpoint (written by the president of
    the association), Calendar, Buyer's
    Guide, Tips Lists, Short Summaries.
**Readers:** Owners and managers of
    restaurants and other food-service
    establishments and suppliers in Metro
    Washington, DC, area.

70931

## ROAD WORK SAFETY REPORT
Burke, VA 22009
Telephone: (703) 239-2122
FAX: (703) 239-9055
Mailing Address:
    P.O. Box 10735
    Burke, VA 20099
Year Established: 1991
Pub. Frequency: bi-m.
Subscrip. Rate: $59/yr.
**Owner(s):**
TranSafety Inc.
P.O. Box 10735
Burke, VA 22009
Telephone: (703) 239-2122
Ownership %: 100
**Editorial:**
Roy Anderson .............................Editor

69823

## RTCA DIGEST
1140 Connecticut Ave., N.W.
Ste. 1020
Washington, DC 20036-4001
Telephone: (202) 833-9339
FAX: (202) 833-9434
Year Established: 1965
Pub. Frequency: q.
Circulation: 3,600
Circulation Type: controlled & paid

**Owner(s):**
Radio Technical Commission for
    Aeronautics
1140 Connecticut Ave., N.W.
Ste. 1020
Washington, DC 20036-4001
Telephone: (202) 833-9339
FAX: (202) 833-9339
Ownership %: 100

70894

## SHOESTRING TRAVELER
8 S. J St.
Lake Worth, FL 33460
Telephone: (407) 582-8320
Mailing Address:
    P.O. Box 1349
    Lake Worth, FL 33460
Year Established: 1990
Pub. Frequency: bi-m.
Subscrip. Rate: $42/yr.
Materials: 10,32
Circulation: 9,300
Circulation Type: controlled & paid
**Owner(s):**
International Features, Inc.
8 S. J St.
Lake Worth, FL 33460
Telephone: (407) 582-8320
Ownership %: 100
**Editorial:**
Byron Lutz .............................Editor
**Desc.:** Budget travel tips for the
    international traveler with an emphasis
    on air courier travel.

70903

## SPEEDNEWS
1801 Ave. of the Stars
Ste. 210
Los Angeles, CA 90067
Telephone: (213) 203-9603
FAX: (213) 203-9352
Year Established: 1979
Pub. Frequency: w.
Subscrip. Rate: $497/yr.
Circulation: 3,000
Circulation Type: controlled & paid
**Owner(s):**
Ann More
1801 Ave. of the Stars
Ste. 210
Los Angeles, CA 90067-5904
Telephone: (213) 203-9603
Ownership %: 100
**Editorial:**
Ann More .............................Editor
**Desc.:** Keeps executives up-to-date on the
    week's aviation news, including new
    aircraft orders, leases, new product
    orders, and innovations.

70905

## STATION BREAK
300 Seventh St., S.W.
Ste. 110
Washington, DC 20024-2520
FAX: (202) 863-0265
Pub. Frequency: m.
Subscrip. Rate: free
**Owner(s):**
Lee Ann Landers
300 Seventh St., S.W.
Ste. 110
Washington, DC 20024-2520
Ownership %: 100
**Editorial:**
Lee Ann Landers .............................Editor
**Desc.:** General-audience publication about
    NASA's Space Station Freedom
    Program.

70882

## TRAFFIC LAW REPORTS
Warrenburg, MO 64093
Telephone: (816) 429-1102

**Materials Accepted/Included:** 01-Business news 02-By-line articles 03-Fashion news 04-Food news 05-Freelance copy 06-Letters to editor 07-Real estate news 08-Sports news 09-Travel news
10-Book rev. 11-Movie rev. 12-Music rev. 13-TV rev. 14-Theater rev. 15-Coming events 16-Obituaries 17-Question & answer 18-Social announcements 19-Artwork 20-Cartoons 21-Photos 22-TV listings
23-Audio rec. 24-Video rec. 25-Books 26-Films/film clips 27-Personnel news 28-Press releases 29-New product news/photos 30-Trade lit. 31-Contracts awarded 32-Display adv. 33-Classified adv.

7-93

Mailing Address:
 P.O. Box 88
 Warrenburg, MO 64093
Year Established: 1987
Pub. Frequency: m.
Subscrip. Rate: $98/yr.
Owner(s):
Knehans-Miller
P.O. Box 88
Warrenburg, MO 64093
Telephone: (816) 429-1102
Ownership %: 100
Editorial:
Dane C. Miller ............................Editor
Desc.: Summaries of all Federal and State
 Appellate Court decisions relating to
 traffic. Indexed by subject and
 jurisdiction.

**TRANSITPULSE**        70914
P.O. Box 249
Fields Corner Station
Boston, MA 02122
Telephone: (617) 825-2318
FAX: (617) 482-7417
Year Established: 1983
Pub. Frequency: bi-m.
Page Size: tabloid
Subscrip. Rate: $75/yr. US; $90/yr. foreign
Materials: 10
Circulation: 850
Circulation Type: paid
Owner(s):
Trans21
P.O. Box 249
Fields Corner Station
Boston, MA 02122
Telephone: (617) 825-2318
FAX: (617) 482-7417
Ownership %: 100
Editorial:
Lawrence J. Fabian ....................Editor
Desc.: Covers worldwide developments in
 automated passenger transport systems
 for urban, suburban and airport travel.

**TRAVEL & TOURISM EXECUTIVE**   70896
 **REPORT**
P.O. Box 43563
Washington, DC 20010
Telephone: (202) 232-7107
Year Established: 1979
Pub. Frequency: m.
Subscrip. Rate: $65/yr. non-members
Materials: 32
Circulation: 4,000
Circulation Type: controlled & paid
Owner(s):
Leisure Industry - Recreation News
P.O. Box 43563
Washington, DC 20010
Telephone: (202) 232-7107
Ownership %: 100
Editorial:
Marj Jensen ..............................Editor
Desc.: Focuses on the marketing and
 promotion of travel destination products.
 Presents information and data on trends
 and demographics.

**TRAVELING HEALTHY &**     70929
 **COMFORTABLE**
108-48 70th Rd.
Forest Hills, NY 11375
Telephone: (718) 268-7290
Year Established: 1988
Pub. Frequency: bi-m.
Subscrip. Rate: $32/yr.
Owner(s):
Mercury Marketing
108-48 70th Rd.
Forest Hills, NY 11375
Telephone: (718) 268-7290
Ownership %: 100

Editorial:
Karl Neumann ............................Editor
Desc.: Alerts travelers about health and
 medical issues.

**TRAVEL MANAGEMENT DAILY**   66780
1775 Broadway, 19th Fl.
New York, NY 10019
Telephone: (212) 237-3000
FAX: (212) 237-3007
Year Established: 1970
Pub. Frequency: 5/wk.
Page Size: standard
Subscrip. Rate: $675/yr.
Owner(s):
Official Airline Guides, Inc.
1775 Broadway, 19th Fl.
New York, NY 10019
Telephone: (212) 237-3000
Ownership %: 100
Editorial:
Steve Ballinger ..........................Editor

**UNITED STATES PILOTS**     69829
 **ASSOCIATION NEWSLETTER**
483 S. Kirkwood Rd., Ste. 10
St. Louis, MO 63122
Telephone: (314) 849-8772
Pub. Frequency: q.
Owner(s):
United States Pilots Association
483 S. Kirkwood Rd., Ste. 10
St. Louis, MO 63122
Telephone: (314) 849-8772
Ownership %: 100

**URBAN TRANSPORT NEWS**    67652
951 Pershing Dr.
Silver Spring, MD 20910
Telephone: (301) 587-6300
FAX: (301) 587-1081
Year Established: 1973
Pub. Frequency: bi-w.
Page Size: standard
Subscrip. Rate: $312/yr.
Owner(s):
Business Publishers, Inc.
951 Pershing Dr.
Silver Spring, MD 20910
Telephone: (301) 587-6300
Ownership %: 100
Management:
Eric Easton ..........................Publisher
Editorial:
Tom Ramstack ..........................Editor

**U.S. RAIL NEWS**        67658
951 Pershing Dr.
Silver Spring, MD 20910
Telephone: (301) 587-6300
FAX: (301) 587-1081
Year Established: 1978
Pub. Frequency: bi-w.
Page Size: standard
Subscrip. Rate: $390/yr.
Owner(s):
Business Publications, Inc.
951 Pershing Dr.
Silver Spring, MD 20910
Telephone: (301) 587-6300
Ownership %: 100
Management:
Lawrence Fishbein ..................Publisher
Editorial:
Steve Lash ..............................Editor
Desc.: Provides objective views of laws
 and new technologies affecting rail
 transport business, both passenger and
 goods transport.

**WASHINGTON INTERNATIONAL**   70913
1090 Vermont Ave., N.W.
Ste. 700
Washington, DC 20005
Telephone: (202) 223-3180
FAX: (301) 946-0779
Year Established: 1986
Pub. Frequency: bi-m.
Subscrip. Rate: $12/yr.
Materials: 10,32
Circulation: 25,000
Circulation Type: controlled & paid
Owner(s):
Washington International
1090 Vermont Ave., N.W.
Ste. 700
Washington, DC 20005
Telephone: (202) 223-3180
FAX: (301) 946-0779
Ownership %: 100
Editorial:
Patricia Keegan ..........................Editor
Desc.: Contains diplomatic news and travel
 articles directed toward the international,
 travel, and cultural community of
 Washington, DC. Includes
 interviews with personalities, and
 features international hotel spotlights
 and a calendar of cultural events.

**WOMEN WITH WHEELS**     70891
1718A Northfield Sq.
Northfield, IL 60093
Telephone: (708) 501-3519
Year Established: 1989
Pub. Frequency: q.
Subscrip. Rate: $15/yr.; $20/yr. institutions
Materials: 10,32
Owner(s):
Susan Frissell
1718A Northfield Sq.
Northfield, IL 60093
Telephone: (708) 501-3519
Ownership %: 100
Management:
Susan Frissell ........................Publisher
Editorial:
Susan Frissell ..........................Editor
Desc.: Provides information on cars and
 their maintenance. Features articles on
 subjects such as: safety, leasing vs.
 buying, talking with auto salespeople,
 and choosing a mechanic.

## Group 366-Women

**AACS NEWS**         70008
5201 Leesburg Pike, No. 205
Falls Church, VA 22041
Telephone: (703) 845-1333
FAX: (703) 845-1336
Pub. Frequency: m.
Materials: 32
Owner(s):
Association of Accredited Cosmetology
 Schools
5201 Leesburg Pike, No. 205
Falls Church, VA 22041
Telephone: (703) 845-1333
FAX: (703) 845-1336
Ownership %: 100
Editorial:
Katie Atkinson ..........................Editor

**COSMETIC WORLD**      68689
530 Fifth Ave., Ste. 430
New York, NY 10036-5101
Telephone: (212) 840-8800
FAX: (212) 840-7246
Year Established: 1967

Pub. Frequency: w.
Subscrip. Rate: $175/yr. US; $250/yr.
 foreign
Materials: 10,32
Circulation: 4,073
Circulation Type: paid
Owner(s):
Cosmetic World, Inc.
530 Fifth Ave., Ste. 430
New York, NY 10036-5101
Telephone: (212) 840-8800
Ownership %: 100
Editorial:
John G. Ledes ..........................Editor
Desc.: Covers marketing, sales, retailing
 and technical management of the
 cosmetic, fragrance and toiletry industry.

**MENOPAUSE NEWS**      70325
2074 Union St.
San Francisco, CA 94123
Telephone: (415) 567-2368
Year Established: 1991
Pub. Frequency: bi-m.
Subscrip. Rate: $24/yr. individuals; $30/yr.
 institutions
Materials: 10
Owner(s):
Menopause News
2074 Union St.
San Francisco, CA 94123
Telephone: (415) 567-2368
Ownership %: 100
Editorial:
Judith Stiles Askew ....................Editor
Desc.: Contains the latest medical and
 psychological information, as well as
 first-person accounts.

**VISIBLE**          70313
P.O. Box 1494
Mendocino, CA 95460
*see Newsletters, Senior Citizens*

**WELCOME HOME**       70910
8310A Old Courthouse Rd.
Vienna, VA 22182
Telephone: (703) 827-5903
Year Established: 1984
Pub. Frequency: m.
Subscrip. Rate: $15/yr. US; $25/yr. foreign
Materials: 10
Circulation: 15,000
Circulation Type: controlled & paid
Owner(s):
Mothers-at-Home
8310A Old Courthouse Rd.
Vienna, VA 22182
Telephone: (703) 827-5903
Ownership %: 100
Editorial:
Pam Goresh ..............................Editor

**WOMEN'S HISTORY NETWORK**   71102
 **NEWS**
7738 Bell Rd.
Windsor, CA 95492
Telephone: (707) 838-6000
FAX: (707) 838-0478
Year Established: 1983
Pub. Frequency: q.
Subscrip. Rate: $25/yr.
Circulation: 800
Circulation Type: controlled & paid
Owner(s):
National Women's History Project
7738 Bell Rd.
Windsor, CA 95492
Telephone: (707) 838-6000
FAX: (707) 838-0478
Ownership %: 100
Editorial:

# Section 8
# INDEX OF INTERNAL PUBLICATIONS BY TITLE

This section contains an alphabetical listing of internal publication titles. It shows at a glance titles already appropriated. Each entry gives the publication title and the sponsoring company, so the complete listing in section 11 can be found.

'ROUND THE CENTER CHILDREN'S HOSPITAL MEDICAL CENTER Cincinnati, OH
'TWEEN CUES QUALITY STORES, INC. N. Muskegon, MI

## A

A A A MICHIGAN LIVING AUTO CLUB OF MICHIGAN Dearborn, MI
A A A WORLD - WISCONSIN EDITION AMERICAN AUTOMOBILE ASSOCIATION (WISCONSIN) Madison, WI
A A O M S FORUM AMERICAN ASSOCIATION OF ORAL & MAXILLOFACIAL SURGEONS Rosemont, IL
A B F BY-LINES ABF FREIGHT SYSTEM, INC. Fort Smith, AR
A B Y C NEWS AMERICAN BOAT & YACHT COUNCIL INC. Edgewater, MD
A C F TODAY ACF INDUSTRIES, INC. Earth City, MO
A C L CURRENTS AMERICAN COMMERCIAL LINES, INC. Jeffersonvlle, IN
A C P DIRECTORY ASSOCIATED CHURCH PRESS Grand Rapids, MI
A C W A NEWS ASSOCIATION OF CALIFORNIA WATER AGENCIES Sacramento, CA
A G C NEWS SERVICE ASSOCIATED GENERAL CONTRACTORS OF HOUSTON Houston, TX
A H C A NOTES AMERICAN HEALTH CARE ASSOCIATION Washington, DC
A H P VISTA AMERICAN HOME PRODUCTS New York, NY
A I D C REPORT ARKANSAS INDUSTRIAL DEVELOPMENT COMMISSION Little Rock, AR
A L NEWS U.S. DEPARTMENT OF ENERGY Albuquerque, NM
A LITTLE LIGHT READING SEATTLE CITY LIGHT Seattle, WA
A M KTVE-TV Monroe, LA
A N I C O AMERICAN NATIONAL INSURANCE CO. Galveston, TX

A P A MEMBER BULLETIN ARKANSAS PRESS ASSOCIATION Little Rock, AR
A P C O BULLETIN ASSOCIATED PUBLIC-SAFETY COMMUNICATIONS OFFICE Daytona Beach, FL
A R T B A NEWSLETTER AMERICAN ROAD & TRANSPORTATION BUILDERS ASSOCIATION Washington, DC
A S I D REPORT AMERICAN SOCIETY OF INTERIOR DESIGNERS Washington, DC
A S T C ANNUAL DIRECTORY OF MEMBERS ASSOCIATION OF SCIENCE-TECHNOLOGY CENTERS Washington, DC
A S T C ANNUAL REPORT ASSOCIATION OF SCIENCE-TECHNOLOGY CENTERS Washington, DC
A S T C NEWSLETTER ASSOCIATION OF SCIENCE-TECHNOLOGY CENTERS Washington, DC
A U L NEWS AMERICAN UNITED LIFE INSURANCE COMPANY Indianapolis, IN
A. G. FOCUS AMERICAN GENERAL FINANCE Evansville, IN
A-C D NEWS ITT AEROSPACE, COMMUNICATIONS DIVISION Fort Wayne, IN
AAA HIGHROADS ARIZONA AUTOMOBILE ASSOCIATION Phoenix, AZ
ABBOTT WORLD ABBOTT LABORATORIES North Chicago, IL
ACADEMIC BULLETIN PINEY WOODS COUNTRY LIFE SCHOOL Piney Woods, MS
ACCELERATOR, THE AUBURN-CORD-DUESENBERG MUSEUM Auburn, IN
ACCENT WEST AMARILLO CHAMBER OF COMMERCE Amarillo, TX
ACCOUNT IOWA CREDIT UNION LEAGUE Des Moines, IA
ACHIEVER MIDLAND MUTUAL LIFE INSURANCE CO. Columbus, OH
ACHIEVER, THE UNITED UNIONS OF JOB CORPS Washington, DC
ACIPCO NEWS BULLETIN AMERICAN CAST IRON PIPE COMPANY Birmingham, AL
ACROSS COPPERWELD COPPERWELD CORP. Pittsburgh, PA
ACTION DURHAM CHAMBER OF COMMERCE Durham, NC

ACTION TEXAS MEDICAL ASSOCIATION Austin, TX
ACTION LINE EMPLOYERS GROUP Los Angeles, CA
ACTION NEWSBANK-VIDEO NEWS MAGAZINE BARNETT BANKS, INC. Jacksonville, FL
ADJUDICATOR INDUSTRIAL COMMISSION Columbus, OH
ADVANCE NEWS FAMILY CIRCLE, INC. New York, NY
ADVANCED MATERIALS & PROCESSES ASM INTERNATIONAL Metals Park, OH
ADVANCES CARDIAC PACEMAKERS INC. New Brighton, MN
ADVANCES METHODIST HOSPITAL Minneapolis, MN
ADVANTAGE BEST FOODS, DIVISION OF CPC INTERNATIONAL, INC. Englewood Cliffs, NJ
ADVANTAGE PYRAMID LIFE INSURANCE CO. Shawnee Mission, KS
ADVANTAGE, THE WHIRLPOOL CORPORATION Evansville, IN
ADVOCATE AMERICAN LUNG ASSOCIATION OF TEXAS Austin, TX
ADVOCATE, THE BALTIMORE ASSOCIATION FOR RETARDED CITIZENS, INC. Baltimore, MD
ADVOCATE, THE URBAN APPALACHIAN COUNCIL Cincinnati, OH
AEROQUIP AEROQUIP CORP. Maumee, OH
AETNASPHERE AETNA LIFE & CASUALTY Hartford, CT
AGENCY NEWS EQUITABLE LIFE ASSURANCE SOCIETY New York, NY
AGENT EXCHANGE ERIE INSURANCE GROUP Erie, PA
AGENT NEWS NORTHWESTERN NATIONAL INSURANCE GROUP Brookfield, WI
AGENTS NEWS INDIANA FARMERS INSURANCE GROUP Indianapolis, IN
AGVENTURE WISCONSIN FARM BUREAU FEDERATION Madison, WI
AGWAY COOPERATOR AGWAY INC. De Witt, NY
AIR LINE PILOT AIR LINE PILOTS ASSOCIATION Herndon, VA
ALA OF GEORGIA ANNUAL REPORT AMERICAN LUNG ASSOCIATION OF GEORGIA Smyrna, GA
ALABAMA FORESTS ALABAMA FORESTRY ASSN. Montgomery, AL
ALABAMA SCHOOL JOURNAL ALABAMA EDUCATION ASSN. Montgomery, AL

**ALABAMA'S HEALTH** ALABAMA DEPT. OF PUBLIC HEALTH Montgomery, AL

**ALBERTO** ALBERTO-CULVER CO. Melrose Park, IL

**ALCOA NEWS** ALUMINUM COMPANY OF AMERICA Pittsburgh, PA

**ALEUTIAN CURRENT** ALEUT CORP. Anchorage, AK

**ALL A-BOARD** U.S. RAILROAD RETIREMENT BOARD Chicago, IL

**ALL AMERICAN** AMERICAN FAMILY INSURANCE GROUP Madison, WI

**ALLSTATE NOW** ALLSTATE INSURANCE COMPANY Northbrook, IL

**ALMOND FACTS** BLUE DIAMOND GROWERS Sacramento, CA

**ALONG THE TRACK** LONG ISLAND RAILROAD Jamaica, NY

**ALUMNEWS** BRISTOL-MYERS CO. New York, NY

**ALUMNEWS** CREIGHTON UNIVERSITY Omaha, NE

**ALUMNI ACTION** BURLINGTON COUNTY COLLEGE Pemberton, NJ

**AMBASSADOR, THE** UNITED TELEPHONE CO. OF FLORIDA Altamonte Springs, FL

**AMERICAN CHRISTMAS TREE JOURNAL** NATIONAL CHRISTMAS TREE ASSOCIATION Milwaukee, WI

**AMERICAN EAGLE** AMERICAN MUTUAL LIFE INSURANCE CO. Des Moines, IA

**AMERICAN GAS** AMERICAN GAS ASSOCIATION Arlington, VA

**AMERICAN JOURNAL OF OCCUPATIONAL THERAPY** AMERICAN OCCUPATIONAL THERAPY ASSOCIATION Rockville, MD

**AMERICAN PHILOSOPHICAL SOCIETY YEAR BOOK** AMERICAN PHILOSOPHICAL SOCIETY Philadelphia, PA

**AMERICAN PODIATRIC WRITERS ASSOCIATION NEWSLETTER** AMERICAN PODIATRIC WRITERS ASSOCIATION New York, NY

**AMERICAN TIMES** AMERICAN FAMILY INSURANCE GROUP Madison, WI

**AMERICAN WANDERER, THE** AMERICAN VOLKSSPORT ASSOCIATION Universal City, TX

**AMERICAN WAY** AMERICAN AIRLINES INC. DFW Airport, TX

**AMERON NEWS** AMERON, INC. Pasadena, CA

**AMONG OURSELVES** CAPITAL BLUE CROSS Harrisburg, PA

**AMONG OURSELVES** LOS ANGELES TIMES Los Angeles, CA

**AMONG OURSELVES** NATIONAL GRANGE MUTUAL INSURANCE CO. Keene, NH

**AMPERSAND** ALEXANDER & BALDWIN, INC. Honolulu, HI

**AMTRAK TIMES** AMTRAK Washington, DC

**ANALOG BRIEFINGS** ANALOG DEVICES, INC. Norwood, MA

**ANALOG DIALOGUE** ANALOG DEVICES, INC. Norwood, MA

**ANDERSEN INSIGHTS** ANDERSEN CORP. Bayport, MN

**ANHEUSER-BUSCH EAGLE** ANHEUSER-BUSCH COMPANIES, INC. Saint Louis, MO

**ANNALS OF EMERGENCY MEDICINE** AMERICAN COLLEGE OF EMERGENCY PHYSICIANS Irving, TX

**ANNUAL EMPLOYEE REPORT** UNITED TELEPHONE CO. OF INDIANA, INC. Warsaw, IN

**ANNUAL REPORT** BANK SOUTH Atlanta, GA

**ANNUAL REPORT** DALLAS LIGHTHOUSE FOR THE BLIND, INC. Dallas, TX

**ANNUAL REPORT** EASTER SEAL SOCIETY OF WISCONSIN, INC. Madison, WI

**ANNUAL REPORT** FAIRCHILD CORPORATION Chantilly, VA

**ANNUAL REPORT** MEMORIAL SLOAN-KETTERING CANCER CENTER New York, NY

**ANNUAL REPORT** MID-AMERICA DAIRYMEN INC. Springfield, MO

**ANNUAL REPORT** MIDWEST RESEARCH INSTITUTE Kansas City, MO

**ANNUAL REPORT** NAVAJO TRIBAL UTILITY AUTHORITY Fort Defiance, AZ

**ANNUAL REPORT** RESEARCH TRIANGLE INSTITUTE Durham, NC

**ANNUAL REPORT** ST. LOUIS POLICE DEPARTMENT St. Louis, MO

**ANNUAL REPORT** UNION CENTRAL LIFE Cincinnati, OH

**ANNUAL REPORT** US SMALL BUSINESS ADMINISTRATION Washington, DC

**ANNUAL REPORT TO EMPLOYEES** HOOVER CO. North Canton, OH

**ANTHONY MERCHANT** C.R. ANTHONY CO. Oklahoma City, OK

**ANTONIAN** PROVENANT HEALTH CENTERS Denver, CO

**ANVIL** BOSTWICK-BRAUN CO. Toledo, OH

**AOG QUARTERLY** AIR FORCE INSTITUTE OF TECHNOLOGY Dayton, OH

**APACHE CORP., ANNUAL REPORT** APACHE CORPORATION Houston, TX

**APL NEWS** APPLIED PHYSICS LABORATORY Laurel, MD

**APOGEE HIGHLITES** APOGEE ENTERPRISES, INC. Minneapolis, MN

**APPLAUSE** ORLEANS PARRISH SCHOOL BOARD New Orleans, LA

**ARA NEWS** ARA SERVICES INC. Philadelphia, PA

**ARBOR NEWS** GLEANER LIFE INSURANCE SOCIETY Adrian, MI

**ARC TODAY** ARC, NATIONAL HEADQUARTERS Arlington, TX

**ARCATAGRAPH** ARCATA GRAPHICS CORP. Depew, NY

**AREA CHAIRMAN MAILING** CHESAPEAKE BAY GIRL SCOUT COUNCIL Newark, DE

**ARGUS** AMERICAN ACADEMY OF OPHTHALMOLOGY San Francisco, CA

**ARMSTRONG TODAY** ARMSTRONG WORLD INDUSTRIES Lancaster, PA

**AROUND THE CIRCUIT** PUBLIC SERVICE CO. OF NEW HAMPSHIRE Manchester, NH

**AROUND THE CLOCK** READING HOSPITAL & MEDICAL CENTER, THE West Reading, PA

**AROUND THE SYSTEM** CONSOLIDATED EDISON CO. OF NEW YORK New York, NY

**AROUND ZALES** ZALE CORP. Irving, TX

**ARROWS** APACHE CORPORATION Houston, TX

**ARTHRITIS & RHEUMATISM** AMERICAN COLLEGE OF RHEUMATOLOGY Atlanta, GA

**ASI INTERACTION** ALADDIN SYNERGETICS INC. Nashville, TN

**ASSOCIATE** MARION LABORATORIES, INC. Kansas City, MO

**ASSOCIATES MAGAZINE, THE** ASSOCIATES CORPORATION OF NORTH AMERICA Dallas, TX

**ASSOCIATES' VIEW, THE** GOLUB CORP./PRICE CHOPPER SUPERMARKETS Schenectady, NY

**ASSOCIATION OF BIRTH DEFECT CHILDREN** ASSOCIATION OF BIRTH DEFECT CHILDREN, INC. Orlando, FL

**ASSOCIATIONS** FEDERAL EXPRESS CORP. Memphis, TN

**AT THE MARKET** NEW YORK STOCK EXCHANGE New York, NY

**ATC NEWS BULLETIN** APPLIED TECHNOLOGY COUNCIL Redwood City, CA

**ATLANTIC LOG, THE** ATLANTIC MUTUAL COS. New York, NY

**ATLANTIC MESSENGER** ATLANTIC MUTUAL COS. New York, NY

**ATLAS AMPLIFIER** ATLAS VAN-LINES, INC. Evansville, IN

**ATLAS BULLETIN** ATLAS SUPPLY CO. Atlanta, GA

**ATTITUDE** AMERICA'S FAVORITE CHICKEN Atlanta, GA

**ATTLEGRAM** TEXAS INSTRUMENTS INC. Attleboro, MA

**AUTOMOTIVE ENGINEER & AEROSPACE ENGINEER** SOCIETY OF AUTOMOTIVE ENGINEERS INC. Warrendale, PA

**AUTOMOTIVE EXECUTIVE** NATIONAL AUTO DEALERS ASSN. McLean, VA

**AUTUMN IN THE CITY** CITY OF DETROIT Detroit, MI

**AVA CHECKPOINT** AMERICAN VOLKSSPORT ASSOCIATION Universal City, TX

**AVENUES** HERSHEY FOODS CORP. Hershey, PA

**AVIS NEWS** AVIS, INC. Garden City, NY

**AVONDALE SUN** AVONDALE MILLS, INC. Sylacauga, AL

**AWARE** AMERICA WEST AIRLINES Phoenix, AZ

**AWARE** VIRGINIA DEPARTMENT OF MENTAL HEALTH, RETARDATION-SUBSTANCE ABUSE SERVICES Richmond, VA

**AWARE VIEW** AMERICA WEST AIRLINES Phoenix, AZ

**AXIA ACTION** AXIA, INC. Hinsdale, IL

# B

**B & L E EMPLOYEE NEWSLETTER** BESSEMER & LAKE ERIE RAILROAD Monroeville, PA

**B B & T CHRONICLE** BB & T Wilson, NC

**B C NEWS** BOISE CASCADE CORP. Boise, ID

**B C U N BRIEFING** BUSINESS COUNCIL FOR THE UNITED NATIONS New York, NY

**B F G TODAY** B.F. GOODRICH Fairlawn, OH

**B F I BLUELINE** BROWNING FERRIS INDUSTRIES Houston, TX

**B M A BULLETIN** BUSINESS MEN'S ASSURANCE CO. Kansas City, MO

**B M A SKYLINES** BUSINESS MEN'S ASSURANCE CO. Kansas City, MO

**B N A'S REVIEW OF WHAT'S NEW** BUREAU OF NATIONAL AFFAIRS, INC. Washington, DC

**B N W NEWS** NAVAL NUCLEAR FUEL DIVISION Lynchburg, VA

**BADGER BEACON** BADGER MUTUAL INSURANCE COMPANY Milwaukee, WI

**BALL LINE** BALL CORP. Muncie, IN

**BANK BRIEFS** NATIONAL CITY BANK, INDIANA Indianapolis, IN

**BANK NOTES** FIRST INTERSTATE BANK OF DENVER Denver, CO

**BANK ONE** BANK OF NEW YORK, THE New York, NY

**BANKER, THE** FIRST INTERSTATE BANCORP. Los Angeles, CA

**BANKER, THE** FIRST NATIONAL BANK OF CINCINNATI CORP. Cincinnati, OH

**BANKERS NOTES** BANKERS SECURITY LIFE INSURANCE SOCIETY Arlington, VA

**BANKERS' HOURS** TEXAS COMMERCE BANCSHARES, INC. Houston, TX

**BANKING NEWS** VIRGINIA BANKERS ASSOCIATION Richmond, VA

**BANKNOTES** PACIFIC FIRST BANK Seattle, WA

**BANKNOTES, JOINT VENTURE** FIRST COMMERCIAL BANK, N.A. Little Rock, AR

**BAPTIST BEAT** BAPTIST HEALTH SYSTEM, THE Knoxville, TN

**BARKER** P.H. GLATFELTER CO. Spring Grove, PA

**BARNES MAGAZINE** BARNES HOSPITAL St. Louis, MO

**BARNETT ACTION** BARNETT BANKS, INC. Jacksonville, FL

**BARROW** ST. JOSEPH'S HOSPITAL & MEDICAL CTR. Phoenix, AZ

**BASF INFORMATION** BASF CORPORATION CHEMICALS DIVISION Parsippany, NJ

**BAUSCH & LOMB WORLD** BAUSCH & LOMB, INC. Rochester, NY

**BAY STATER** BAY STATE GAS CO. Westborough, MA

**BAY WINDOW** CHESAPEAKE BAY GIRL SCOUT COUNCIL Newark, DE

**BAYLOR MEDICINE** BAYLOR COLLEGE OF MEDICINE Houston, TX

**BAYLOR PROGRESS** BAYLOR UNIVERSITY MEDICAL CENTER Dallas, TX

**BAYTOWN BRIEFS** EXXON CO., U.S.A. Houston, TX

**BEAUMONITOR** WILLIAM BEAUMONT HOSPITAL Royal Oak, MI

**BEDSIDE BANNER** ROCKINGHAM MEMORIAL HOSPITAL Harrisonburg, VA

**BEECHCRAFTER** BEECH AIRCRAFT CORP. Wichita, KS

**BELL HELICOPTER NEWS** BELL HELICOPTER TEXTRON, INC. Fort Worth, TX

**BELLRINGER** STATE FARM MUTUAL AUTO INSURANCE CO. St. Paul, MN

**BENCHMARKS** INDIANA JUDICIAL CENTER Indianapolis, IN

**BENEFICIAL BENEFACTOR** BENEFICIAL LIFE INS. CO. Salt Lake City, UT

**BENEFICIAL NEWS BRIEFS** BENEFICIAL MANAGEMENT CORP. Peapack, NJ

**BERKSHIRE LIFE AFIELD** BERKSHIRE LIFE INSURANCE COMPANY Pittsfield, MA

**BERKSHIRE LIFE NEWSLETTER** BERKSHIRE LIFE INSURANCE COMPANY Pittsfield, MA

**BERRY LEADER, THE** BERRY CO., THE Dayton, OH

**BEST TIMES** BEST PRODUCTS CO., INC. Richmond, VA

**BETTER FIBERS; POINTERS FOR PROFITS** ANDRITZ-SPROUT-BAUER, INC. Muncy, PA

**BETTER HEALTH MAGAZINE** BETTER HEALTH PRESS New Haven, CT

# INTERNAL PUBLICATIONS BY TITLE

**BETWEEN AWARE** AMERICA WEST AIRLINES Phoenix, AZ
**BIB AMERICA** MICHELIN NORTH AMERICA, INC. Greenville, SC
**BIC PICTURE** BIC CORP. Milford, CT
**BIENNIAL REPORT** OREGON DEPARTMENT OF INSURANCE & FINANCE Salem, OR
**BIG G** GROVE WORLDWIDE, INC. Shady Grove, PA
**BISCUIT VISION** RJR NABISCO, NABISCO FOODS GROUP Parsippany, NJ
**BLADE:** GILLETTE COMPANY, THE Boston, MA
**BLOWER OUTLET** DRESSER INDUSTRIES, INC. Connersville, IN
**BLUE ALUMNI** BLUE CROSS & BLUE SHIELD Columbia, SC
**BLUE BLAZE** LONE STAR GAS CO. Dallas, TX
**BLUE CHIP NEWS** CONNECTICUT MUTUAL LIFE INSURANCE Hartford, CT
**BLUE FLAME NEWS:** ATLANTA GAS LIGHT CO. Atlanta, GA
**BLUE PRINT** BLUE CROSS & BLUE SHIELD Columbia, SC
**BLUE STREAK RELEASE** W. H. BRADY CO. Milwaukee, WI
**BLUES WEEK** BLUE CROSS & BLUE SHIELD Columbia, SC
**BOARD OF TRADE NEWS** GREATER WASHINGTON BOARD OF TRADE, THE Washington, DC
**BODINE MOTORGRAM** BODINE ELECTRIC CO. Chicago, IL
**BOEING MANAGEMENT INFORMATION** BOEING CO. Seattle, WA
**BOEING NEWS** BOEING CO. Seattle, WA
**BOILERMAKER** NOOTER CORP. Saint Louis, MO
**BOISE CASCADE INSIGHT** BOISE CASCADE CORP. Boise, ID
**BOND TELLER, THE** U.S. SAVINGS BONDS DIVISION Washington, DC
**BORAX PIONEER** U.S. BORAX INC. Valencia, CA
**BOSTON GAS NEWS** BOSTON GAS COMPANY Boston, MA
**BOTTOMLINE, THE** INTERNATIONAL ASSOCIATION OF HOSPITALITY ACCOUNTANTS Austin, TX
**BOWLING PROPRIETOR, THE** BOWLING PROPRIETORS' ASSOCIATION OF AMERICA Arlington, TX
**BOYS TOWN QUARTERLY** FATHER FLANAGAN'S BOY'S HOME Boys Town, NE
**BRAILLE BOOK REVIEW** LIBRARY OF CONGRESS Washington, DC
**BRANCH CLEARINGS** FIRST SECURITY CORP. Salt Lake City, UT
**BRANCH NEWSLETTERS** CNA INSURANCE Chicago, IL
**BRANCHING OUT** FLEET BANK N.A. Nashua, NH
**BREADWINNER** ARNOLD BAKERS, INC. Greenwich, CT
**BREATHTAKING NEWS** AMERICAN LUNG ASSOCIATION OF GEORGIA Smyrna, GA
**BRICKBATS & BOUQUETS** EMPLOYERS CASUALTY Dallas, TX
**BRIDGESTONE/FIRESTONE NETWORK** BRIDGESTONE/FIRESTONE, INC. Nashville, TN
**BRIEF UPDATE** CHILDREN'S HOSPITAL OF THE KING'S DAUGHTERS Norfolk, VA
**BRIEFINGS** GILBERT/COMMONWEALTH, INC. Reading, PA
**BRIEFLY STATED** STATE DEPARTMENT OF EDUCATION Jackson, MS
**BRIEFS** AMERICAN ASSOCIATION OF COLLEGES FOR TEACHER EDUCATION Washington, DC
**BRISTOL MYERS NEW YORK** BRISTOL-MYERS CO. New York, NY
**BRISTOL-MYERS WORLD** BRISTOL-MYERS CO. New York, NY
**BROADCASTER** CITY PUBLIC SERVICE San Antonio, TX
**BROKER & AGENT NEWS** PENNSYLVANIA MANUFACTURERS' ASSOCIATION INSURANCE CO. Philadelphia, PA
**BROWN FORUM** BROWN-FORMAN, CORP. Louisville, KY
**BRULIN NEWS, THE** BRULIN & CO., INC. Indianapolis, IN
**BRUNSWICK OPERATIONS UPDATE** GEORGIA-PACIFIC BRUNSWICK OPERATIONS Brunswick, GA
**BRUNSWICK WEEK** GEORGIA-PACIFIC CORP., BRUNSWICK OPERATIONS Brunswick, GA
**BUCKET** KFC CORP. Louisville, KY

**BUCKEYE FARM NEWS** OHIO FARM BUREAU FEDERATION Columbus, OH
**BUCKEYE MONITOR** BUCKEYE PIPE LINE COMPANY Allentown, PA
**BUGLE** EBSCO INDUSTRIES, INC. Birmingham, AL
**BUILDER NEWS** HOME BUILDERS ASSOCIATION OF GREATER ST. LOUIS St. Louis, MO
**BULLETIN** AMERICAN ACADEMY OF ORTHOPAEDIC SURGEONS Rosemont, IL
**BULLETIN** AMERICAN SOCIETY OF MAGAZINE PHOTOGRAPHERS Princeton Junction, NJ
**BULLETIN** CINCINNATI GAS & ELECTRIC CO. Cincinnati, OH
**BULLETIN** NATIONAL ASSOCIATION OF WATCH & CLOCK COLLECTORS Columbia, PA
**BULLETIN** OHIO NATIONAL LIFE INSURANCE CO. Cincinnati, OH
**BULLETIN** PACIFIC POWER & LIGHT CO. Portland, OR
**BULLETIN** STATE LIFE INSURANCE CO. Indianapolis, IN
**BULLETIN** USF & A. INSURANCE Baltimore, MD
**BULLETIN** VIRGINIA DEPARTMENT OF TRANSPORTATION Richmond, VA
**BULLETIN ADJUNCT** TEACHERS ASSOCIATION OF BALTIMORE COUNTY MD., INC. Baltimore, MD
**BULLETIN WEEKLY, THE** FIRST BAPTIST CHURCH MODESTO Modesto, CA
**BULLETIN, THE** BAPTIST HOSPITAL INC. Nashville, TN
**BULLETIN, THE** MITRE CORP. Bedford, MA
**BULLETIN, THE** SAINT ANTHONY MEDICAL CENTER Rockford, IL
**BUREAU BRIEFING** GREATER MADISON CONVENTION & VISITORS BUREAU Madison, WI
**BURLINGTON LOOK, THE** BURLINGTON INDUSTRIES Greensboro, NC
**BURNS & MIXES** HARBISON-WALKER REFRACTORIES CO. Pittsburgh, PA
**BUS RIDE** FRIENDSHIP PUBLICATIONS Spokane, WA
**BUSINESS ACTION** GREATER SAN DIEGO CHAMBER OF COMMERCE San Diego, CA
**BUSINESS REPORT** KANSAS CITY KANSAS CHAMBER OF COMMERCE Kansas City, KS
**BY THE WAY** UNITED WAY OF KING COUNTY Seattle, WA
**BYLINE** ROCKFORD REGISTER STAR Rockford, IL

## C

**C A M MAGAZINE** CONSTRUCTION ASSOCIATION OF MICHIGAN (CAM) Detroit, MI
**C B A LEGAL DIRECTORY** CINCINNATI BAR ASSOCIATION Cincinnati, OH
**C B I A NEWS** CONNECTICUT BUSINESS & INDUSTRY ASSOCIATION Hartford, CT
**C E A ADVISOR** CONNECTICUT EDUCATION ASSOCIATION Hartford, CT
**C H H NOW** CARTER HAWLEY HALE STORES, INC. Los Angeles, CA
**C I B A U.S.** CIBA-GEIGY CORP. Ardsley, NY
**C I G WORLD** COLORADO INTERSTATE GAS CO. Colorado Springs, CO
**C I P S NEWS** CENTRAL ILLINOIS PUBLIC SERVICE CO. Springfield, IL
**C L E A NEWSLETTER** SEATTLE CITY LIGHT Seattle, WA
**C M I** CHATHAM MANUFACTURING CO. Elkin, NC
**C M I NEWS** CMI CORP. Oklahoma City, OK
**C M L NEWSLETTER** COLORADO MUNICIPAL LEAGUE Denver, CO
**C P C U JOURNAL** SOCIETY OF CHARTERED PROPERTY & CASUALTY UNDERWRITERS Malvern, PA
**C P C U NEWS** SOCIETY OF CHARTERED PROPERTY & CASUALTY UNDERWRITERS Malvern, PA
**C P NEWS** UNITED CEREBRAL PALSY ASSOCIATION OF NASSAU COUNTY, INC. Roosevelt, NY
**C S B A NEWS** CALIFORNIA SCHOOL BOARDS ASSOCIATION W Sacramento, CA
**C S X TODAY** CSX CORP. Jacksonville, FL
**C T A ACTION** CALIFORNIA TEACHERS ASSOCIATION Burlingame, CA
**C U NEWS** COMMERCIAL UNION INS. CO. Boston, MA
**C. BREWER TODAY** C. BREWER & CO. LTD. Honolulu, HI
**C-TEC COMMUNICATOR** C-TEC CORP. Wilkes Barre, PA

**CABLE VIEWS** ROCKFORD/PARK CABLEVISION, INC. Rockford, IL
**CABOT WORLD** CABOT CORP. Boston, MA
**CAL-TAX NEWS** CALIFORNIA TAXPAYERS ASSOCIATION Sacramento, CA
**CALENDAR OF EVENTS** CITY OF DETROIT Detroit, MI
**CALIFORNIA PACIFIC QUARTERLY** CALIFORNIA PACIFIC MEDICAL CENTER San Francisco, CA
**CALIFORNIA REAL ESTATE MAGAZINE** CALIFORNIA ASSOCIATION OF REALTORS Los Angeles, CA
**CALIFORNIA SCHOOLS** CALIFORNIA SCHOOL BOARDS ASSOCIATION W Sacramento, CA
**CALMATTERS** CALMAT CO. Los Angeles, CA
**CALUNDERWRITER** CALIFORNIA ASSOCIATION OF LIFE UNDERWRITERS, INC. Oakland, CA
**CAPIA CAPSULES** CAROLINA ASSOCIATION OF PROFESSIONAL INSURANCE AGENTS Raleigh, NC
**CAPITAL CADENCE** SALVATION ARMY, THE Washington, DC
**CAPITOL REVIEW** EMPLOYERS GROUP Los Angeles, CA
**CAPSULE** GROSSMONT HOSPITAL La Mesa, CA
**CAPSULE** KOHLER CO. Kohler, WI
**CAPSULE** SAINT ANTHONY MEDICAL CENTER Rockford, IL
**CAPSULE** SOUTHWEST GENERAL HOSPITAL Cleveland, OH
**CAPSULE REPORT** MASTER BUILDERS' ASSOCIATION OF WESTERN PA/AGC Pittsburgh, PA
**CAPSULES** LOUISIANA STATE MEDICAL SOCIETY Metairie, LA
**CAPTIONS** CAP GEMINI AMERICA New York, NY
**CARAVAN** RJR TOBACCO CO. Winston-Salem, NC
**CARILLON MAGAZINE** UNION CENTRAL LIFE Cincinnati, OH
**CARING** MEMORIAL HEALTHCARE SYSTEM Houston, TX
**CARNEGIE MELLON MAGAZINE** CARNEGIE MELLON UNIVERSITY Pittsburgh, PA
**CAROLINA AGENT** CAROLINA ASSOCIATION OF PROFESSIONAL INSURANCE AGENTS Raleigh, NC
**CAROLINA COUNTRY** NORTH CAROLINA ASSOCIATION OF ELECTRIC COOPERATIVES Raleigh, NC
**CARPENTER NEWS** CARPENTER TECHNOLOGY CORPORATION Reading, PA
**CARRIER LINES** PENNSYLVANIA ELECTRIC CO. Johnstown, PA
**CARRIER WORLD** CARRIER CORP. Syracuse, NY
**CASCADE FLAME** CASCADE NATURAL GAS CORP. Seattle, WA
**CASE CLIPS** INDIANA JUDICIAL CENTER Indianapolis, IN
**CASE CURRENTS** COUNCIL FOR ADVANCEMENT & SUPPORT OF EDUCATION Washington, DC
**CASTING ABOUT** EMI CO. Erie, PA
**CASUAL OBSERVER** LINCOLN TELECOMMUNICATIONS CO. Lincoln, NE
**CAT FOLKS** CATERPILLAR INDUSTRIAL, INC. Peoria, IL
**CATERPILLAR WORLD:** CATERPILLAR INDUSTRIAL, INC. Peoria, IL
**CATHOLIC JOURNALIST, THE** CATHOLIC PRESS ASSOCIATION Rockville Center, NY
**CATHOLIC PRESS DIRECTORY** CATHOLIC PRESS ASSOCIATION Rockville Center, NY
**CBPC ANNUAL REPORT** CORN BELT POWER COOPERATIVE Humboldt, IA
**CDC NEWS** COLUMBIA GAS DISTRIBUTION CO. Columbus, OH
**CENTER BULLETIN** MEMORIAL SLOAN-KETTERING CANCER CENTER New York, NY
**CENTER CIRCLE** PEACHTREE CENTER Atlanta, GA
**CENTER LIFELINES** UNIVERSITY OF WISCONSIN MADISON CENTER Madison, WI
**CENTER NEWS** MEMORIAL SLOAN-KETTERING CANCER CENTER New York, NY
**CENTER REVIEW** SHELL OIL CO. Houston, TX
**CENTER STAT** ST. MARY'S HEALTH CENTER St. Louis, MO
**CENTERLINE, THE** KINDER CARE LEARNING CENTERS, INC. Montgomery, AL
**CENTERSPREAD** MITRE CORP. Bedford, MA
**CENTRA HEALTH MAGAZINE** LYNCHBURG GENERAL-MARSHALL LODGE HOSPITALS Lynchburg, VA

**CENTURY NOTES** CENTURY COMPANIES OF AMERICA Waverly, IA

**CERGRAM** CERTIFIED GROCERS OF CALIFORNIA, LTD. Los Angeles, CA

**CERITAS** SISTERS OF PROVIDENCE HEALTH SYSTEM Seattle, WA

**CESSNA** CESSNA AIRCRAFT CO. Wichita, KS

**CHAIN LINK, THE** FIRST NATIONAL SUPERMARKETS, INC. Windsor Locks, CT

**CHAIN REACTION** LONGS DRUG STORES, INC. Walnut Creek, CA

**CHALLENGE** LONG BEACH MEMORIAL MEDICAL CENTER Long Beach, CA

**CHALLENGER** NATIONWIDE INSURANCE Columbus, OH

**CHAMBER BUSINESS** GREATER RENO-SPARKS CHAMBER OF COMMERCE Reno, NV

**CHAMBER MONTHLY** AMARILLO CHAMBER OF COMMERCE Amarillo, TX

**CHAMBER NEWSLETTER** ERIE AREA CHAMBER OF COMMERCE Erie, PA

**CHAMBER OF COMMERCE NEWSLETTER** SAN FRANCISCO CHAMBER OF COMMERCE San Francisco, CA

**CHAMBER VISION** GREATER CINCINNATI CHAMBER OF COMMERCE Cincinnati, OH

**CHAMBERLETTER** FORT WORTH CHAMBER OF COMMERCE Fort Worth, TX

**CHANCE TIPS** A.B. CHANCE CO. Centralia, MO

**CHANGES** UNION PACIFIC RAILROAD Omaha, NE

**CHASE BUSINESS** CHASE MANHATTAN CORP. New York, NY

**CHECKUP** NORTH MISSISSIPPI MEDICAL CENTER Tupelo, MS

**CHEMICAL TOPICS** CHEMICAL BANKING CORP. New York, NY

**CHESAPEAKE** CHESAPEAKE CORP. Richmond, VA

**CHILD HEALTH TALK** ALFRED I DUPONT INSTITUTE Wilmington, DE

**CHILDREN'S HOSPITAL TIMES** CHILDREN'S HOSPITAL OF PHILADELPHIA, THE Philadelphia, PA

**CHILDREN'S VIEW** CHILDREN'S HOSPITAL OF PHILADELPHIA, THE Philadelphia, PA

**CHOCOLATE SHAKE** WORLD'S FINEST CHOCOLATE, INC. Chicago, IL

**CHOP TALK** CHILDREN'S HOSPITAL OF PHILADELPHIA, THE Philadelphia, PA

**CHRONICLE NEWSPAPER** EAST VIRGINIA MEDICAL SCHOOL OF THE MEDICAL COLLEGE HAMPTON Norfolk, VA

**CHRONICLE, THE** KELLY SERVICES, INC. Troy, MI

**CHRONICLE, THE** UNION BANKERS INSURANCE CO. Dallas, TX

**CHRYSLER TIMES** CHRYSLER CORP. Detroit, MI

**CILCO SCENE** CENTRAL ILLINOIS LIGHT CO. Peoria, IL

**CINCINNATI HORIZONS** UNIVERSITY OF CINCINNATI Cincinnati, OH

**CIRAS NEWS** IOWA STATE UNIVERSITY Ames, IA

**CIRCLE** BAPTIST SUNDAY SCHOOL BOARD Nashville, TN

**CIRCUIT** DELCO ELECTRONICS CORPORATION Kokomo, IN

**CIRCUIT** LORAL DEFENSE SYSTEMS-AKRON Akron, OH

**CIRCULATOR** HONEYWELL, INC. Minneapolis, MN

**CITIBANK WORLD** CITIBANK New York, NY

**CITINEWS** NEW ORLEANS, CITY OF New Orleans, LA

**CITINGS** CIT GROUP Livingston, NJ

**CITIZEN WEEKLY, THE** GEORGIA POWER CO. Atlanta, GA

**CITY BEAT** CITY OF DAYTON Dayton, OH

**CITY OF RICHMOND ANNUAL REPORT** CITY OF RICHMOND VIRGINIA Richmond, VA

**CITY RECORD** CITY OF BOSTON Boston, MA

**CITY SCENES** CITY OF CINCINNATI Cincinnati, OH

**CITY WIDE NEWSLETTER** CITY OF RICHARDSON TEXAS Richardson, TX

**CITYWORKS** CITY OF JACKSON MISSISSIPPI Jackson, MS

**CIVITAN MAGAZINE** CIVITAN INTERNATIONAL Birmingham, AL

**CLAIROL HIGHLIGHTS:** CLAIROL INC. New York, NY

**CLEVELANDER, THE** GREATER CLEVELAND GROWTH ASSOCIATION Cleveland, OH

**CLIENTELL** UTAH DEPARTMENT OF HUMAN SERVICES Salt Lake City, UT

**CLIPBOARD** AURORA PUBLIC SCHOOLS Aurora, CO

**CLOCK DIAL** DR. PEPPER CO. Dallas, TX

**CO & S NEWS** CHASE MANHATTAN CORP. New York, NY

**COACHMEN CAPERS** COACHMAN INDUSTRIES, INC. Elkhart, IN

**COACHMEN WORLD** COACHMAN INDUSTRIES, INC. Elkhart, IN

**COASTAL WORLD** COASTAL CORP., THE Houston, TX

**COASTLINES** CENTRAL LINCOLN PEOPLE'S UTILITY DISTRICT Newport, OR

**COATS & CLARK HIGHLIGHTS** COATS & CLARK, INC. Greenville, SC

**CODE ONE** LOCKHEED FORT WORTH CO. Fort Worth, TX

**COFFEE COMMUNICATOR** OTTER TAIL POWER CO. Fergus Falls, MN

**COLLEGE CONNECTION, THE** BURLINGTON COUNTY COLLEGE Pemberton, NJ

**COLLEGIATE SPORTS REPORT** INTERNATIONAL UNIVERSITY FOUNDATION Independence, MO

**COLLINS COUNTRY** SIZZLER INTERNATIONAL, INC. Los Angeles, CA

**COLONIAL WILLIAMSBURG NEWS** COLONIAL WILLIAMSBURG FOUNDATION Williamsburg, VA

**COLORADO MUNICIPALITIES** COLORADO MUNICIPAL LEAGUE Denver, CO

**COLORADO REALTOR NEWS** COLORADO ASSN. OF REALTORS Englewood, CO

**COLSO-QUIPS** COLSO-QUIPS Paris, IL

**COLUMBIA TODAY** COLUMBIA GAS SYSTEM Wilmington, DE

**COLUMNS** NORTH WESTERN NATIONAL LIFE Minneapolis, MN

**COMMENT:** PRINCIPAL FINANCIAL GROUP, THE Des Moines, IA

**COMMERCE** GREATER BATON ROUGE CHAMBER OF COMMERCE Baton Rouge, LA

**COMMERCE FOLIO** OKLAHOMA DEPARTMENT OF COMMERCE Oklahoma City, OK

**COMMERCIAL LENDING NEWSLETTER** ROBERT MORRIS ASSOCIATES Philadelphia, PA

**COMMERCIAL MERCHANDISER MAGAZINE** MAYTAG CO. Newton, IA

**COMMITMENT** CYSTIC FIBROSIS FOUNDATION Bethesda, MD

**COMMON GROUND** UNITED WAY OF SUMMIT COUNTY Akron, OH

**COMMON THREAD, THE** SARA LEE KNIT PRODUCTS Winston Salem, NC

**COMMONER** BRYAN MEMORIAL HOSPITAL Lincoln, NE

**COMMONWEALTH COMMENTS** COMMONWEALTH LIFE INSURANCE CO. Louisville, KY

**COMMUNICATION WORLD** INTERNATIONAL ASSOCIATION OF BUSINESS COMMUNICATORS San Francisco, CA

**COMMUNICATIONS INDUSTRIES REPORT** INTERNATIONAL COMMUNICATIONS INDUSTRIES ASSN., THE Fairfax, VA

**COMMUNICATOR** AVISTAR INTERNATIONAL TRANSPORTATION CORP. Melrose Park, IL

**COMMUNICATOR** CERTIFIED GROCERS OF CALIFORNIA, LTD. Los Angeles, CA

**COMMUNICATOR** COPELAND CORP. Sidney, OH

**COMMUNICATOR** COPPERWELD STEEL CO. Warren, OH

**COMMUNICATOR** FIRST NATIONAL BANK OF MARYLAND Baltimore, MD

**COMMUNICATOR** INCO ALLOYS INTERNATIONAL, INC. Huntington, WV

**COMMUNICATOR** OHIO CASUALTY INSURANCE GROUP, THE Hamilton, OH

**COMMUNICATOR** STATE CHEMICAL MANUFACTURING CO. Cleveland, OH

**COMMUNICATOR** SWEDISH AMERICAN HEALTH SYSTEM Rockford, IL

**COMMUNICATOR** TANDYCRAFTS, INC. Fort Worth, TX

**COMMUNICATOR** WISCONSIN ASSOCIATION OF HOMES FOR THE AGING Madison, WI

**COMMUNICATOR PLUS** SWEDISH AMERICAN HEALTH SYSTEM Rockford, IL

**COMMUNIQUE** FIRST COMMERCE CORP. New Orleans, LA

**COMMUNIQUE** ROCKWELL INTERNATIONAL, COMMAND & CONTROL SYSTEMS DIVISION Richardson, TX

**COMMUNIQUE** SOUTHERN STATES COOPERATIVE Richmond, VA

**COMMUNIQUES** ROSES STORES, INC. Henderson, NC

**COMPANION HEALTHWORLD** BLUE CROSS & BLUE SHIELD Columbia, SC

**COMPANY PUBLICATION, THE** HACKENSACK WATER CO. Harrington Park, NJ

**COMPAQ COMPASS** COMPAQ COMPUTER CORP. Houston, TX

**COMPASS** MARINE OFFICE OF AMERICA CORP. New York, NY

**COMPASS, THE** CENTRAL NEW YORK GIRL SCOUT COUNCIL INC. Syracuse, NY

**COMPASS, THE** COMPASS, The Brooklyn, NY

**COMPASS, THE** MOBIL OIL CORP. Fairfax, VA

**COMPASSION CORPS** PEOPLE FOR THE ETHICAL TREATMENT OF ANIMALS (PETA) Washington, DC

**CONCESSIONAIRE, THE** NATIONAL ASSOCIATION OF CONCESSIONAIRES Chicago, IL

**CONFIDENT LIVING** GOOD NEWS BROADCASTING ASSOCIATION, INC. Lincoln, NE

**CONNECTICUT TRAVELER** CONNECTICUT MOTOR CLUB Hamden, CT

**CONNECTION** ALLEN-BRADLEY CO. Milwaukee, WI

**CONNECTION** CHUBB LIFEAMERICA Concord, NH

**CONNECTION, THE** MICHIGAN CAPITAL HEALTHCARE Lansing, MI

**CONNECTIONS** ARIZONA PUBLIC SERVICE CO. Phoenix, AZ

**CONNECTIONS** CALIFORNIA PACIFIC MEDICAL CENTER San Francisco, CA

**CONNECTIONS** DALLAS AREA RAPID TRANSIT Dallas, TX

**CONNECTIONS** HOSPICE OF THE FLORIDA SUNCOAST Largo, FL

**CONNECTIONS** HUMANE SOCIETY FOR TACOMA & PIERCE COUNTIES, THE Tacoma, WA

**CONNECTIONS** NATIONAL WESTMINSTER BANCORP Jersey City, NJ

**CONNECTIONS** PACIFIC BELL San Francisco, CA

**CONNECTIONS** QUANTUM CHEMICAL CORP., USI DIV. Cincinnati, OH

**CONNECTIONS** SOUTHERN CALIFORNIA WATER CO. San Dimas, CA

**CONNECTIONS** VETCO, INC. Houston, TX

**CONNECTIONS** WISCONSIN POWER & LIGHT CO. Madison, WI

**CONNECTOR** MINNESOTA STATE COUNCIL ON DISABILITY St. Paul, MN

**CONSECO COMMENTS** CONSECO, INC. Carmel, IN

**CONSTRUCTION BUYERS GUIDE** CONSTRUCTION ASSOCIATION OF MICHIGAN (CAM) Detroit, MI

**CONSTRUCTION MARKETING RESEARCH** CONSTRUCTION ASSOCIATION OF MICHIGAN (CAM) Detroit, MI

**CONSTRUCTION UPDATE** SAINT ANTHONY MEDICAL CENTER Rockford, IL

**CONSULTANT** ABBOTT NORTHWESTERN HOSPITAL INC. Minneapolis, MN

**CONSUMER LINES** HAWAIIAN ELECTRIC CO., INC. Honolulu, HI

**CONSUMER NEWS** KENTUCKY UTILITIES CO. Lexington, KY

**CONTACT** ALLSTATE INSURANCE COMPANY Northbrook, IL

**CONTACT** CONTINENTAL WESTERN INDUSTRIES Des Moines, IA

**CONTACT** MINNESOTA POWER Duluth, MN

**CONTACT** SHELTER INSURANCE COMPANY Columbia, MO

**CONTACT** ST. JOSEPH LIGHT & POWER CO. St. Joseph, MO

**CONTACT** TOWERS PERRIN New York, NY

**CONTACT MAGAZINE** AMERICAN INTERNATIONAL GROUP, INC. New York, NY

**CONTACT VIDEO** AMP INC., VALLEY FORGE Harrisburg, PA

**CONTINENTAL BULLETIN** CONTINENTAL CORP. New York, NY

**CONTINENTAL CURRENCY** CONTINENTAL BANK Chicago, IL

**CONTINUING EDUCATION BULLETIN** CHURCH DIVINITY SCHOOL OF THE PACIFIC Berkeley, CA
**CONVEYOR** MISSISSIPPI CHEMICAL CORP. Yazoo City, MS
**CONVEYOR, THE** STERLING DRUG, INC. Myerstown, PA
**COOP CONNECTION** COUNTRYMARK COOP Indianapolis, IN
**COOPER NEWS** COOPER INDUSTRIES, INC. Houston, TX
**COOPERATIVE FARMER** SOUTHERN STATES COOPERATIVE Richmond, VA
**COOPERATIVE PARTNERS** CENEX/LAND O'LAKES Inver Grove, MN
**COORS COURIER** COORS COURIER Golden, CO
**COPY** HOUSTON CHRONICLE Houston, TX
**CORE DRILLER** GEORGE E. FAILING CO. Enid, OK
**CORN ANNUAL** CORN REFINERS ASSOCIATION, INC. Washington, DC
**CORNING WORLD** CORNING INCORPORATED Corning, NY
**CORNSTALK** HUBINGER CO., THE Keokuk, IA
**CORPORATE BULLETIN** KOHLER CO. Kohler, WI
**CORPORATE OFFICE COURIER:** PRUDENTIAL INSURANCE CO. OF AMERICA Newark, NJ
**CORPORATE REPORT** KELLY-SPRINGFIELD TIRE CO. Cumberland, MD
**CORRESPONDENT** AID ASSOCIATION FOR LUTHERANS (AAL) Appleton, WI
**COUNTDOWN** CIVITAN INTERNATIONAL Birmingham, AL
**COUNTRY LIVING MAGAZINE** OHIO RURAL ELECTRIC COOPS INC. Columbus, OH
**COUNTY LINES, THE** SHELBY COUNTY GOVERNMENT Memphis, TN
**COURIER** FIRST-CITIZENS BANK & TRUST CO. Raleigh, NC
**COVERAGE** GENERAL ACCIDENT INSURANCE Philadelphia, PA
**COVERALL** TRI STATE INDUSTRIAL LAUNDRIES, INC. Utica, NY
**CRAFTSMAN, THE** WEST BEND CO. West Bend, WI
**CREDIT UNION DIGEST** CALIFORNIA CREDIT UNION LEAGUE Pomona, CA
**CREDIT UNION EXECUTIVE** CREDIT UNION NATIONAL ASSOCIATION INC. Madison, WI
**CREDIT UNION MAGAZINE** CREDIT UNION NATIONAL ASSOCIATION INC. Madison, WI
**CREDIT WORLD** INTERNATIONAL CREDIT ASSOCIATION St. Louis, MO
**CREDITLINE** NATIONS CREDIT Allentown, PA
**CRIER, THE** INDIANA FARMERS INSURANCE GROUP Indianapolis, IN
**CRITTENSCRIBE** CRITTENTON HOSPITAL Rochester, MI
**CROSSINGS** CHURCH DIVINITY SCHOOL OF THE PACIFIC Berkeley, CA
**CROSSROADS-INTERNAL NEWSLETTER** INDIANA DEPT. OF TRANSPORTATION Indianapolis, IN
**CUBIC CIRCUIT** CUBIC CORP. San Diego, CA
**CURRENCY** BOATMEN'S BANK Saint Louis, MO
**CURRENCY** DESERT SCHOOLS FEDERAL CREDIT UNION Phoenix, AZ
**CURRENT MATTERS** DAIRYLAND POWER COOPERATIVE La Crosse, WI
**CURRENT NEWS** EASTERN IOWA LIGHT POWER COOPERATIVE Wilton, IA
**CURRENTLY** SANTEE COOPER Moncks Corner, SC
**CURRENTLY** WISCONSIN ELECTRIC POWER CO. Milwaukee, WI
**CURRENTS** MUTUAL OF OMAHA COMPANIES Omaha, NE
**CURRENTS** NEW ENGLAND MUTUAL LIFE INSURANCE CO. Boston, MA
**CURRENTS** PEOPLES SECURITY LIFE INSURANCE CO. Durham, NC
**CURTIS ADE** CURTIS 1000, INC. Atlanta, GA
**CURTIS COURIER** CURTIS 1000, INC. Atlanta, GA
**CURTIS LINE, THE** CURTIS CIRCULATION CO. Camden, NJ
**CUTTING EDGE** GLEASON WORKS Rochester, NY
**CUTTING EDGE** ZALE CORP. Irving, TX
**CYANAMID NEWS** AMERICAN CYANAMID CO. Wayne, NJ

## D

**D & B REPORTS** DUN & BRADSTREET CORP., THE New York, NY
**D N R DIGEST** WISCONSIN DEPARTMENT OF NATURAL RESOURCES Madison, WI
**D O E THIS MONTH** U.S. DEPARTMENT OF ENERGY Washington, DC
**D P & L ENERGY UPDATE** DAYTON POWER & LIGHT CO. Dayton, OH
**D-M-E FAMILY:** D-M-E CO. Madison Heights, MI
**DAILY COMMUNICATIONS** GENERAL MOTORS CORP. Marion, IN
**DAILY, THE** MERCK & CO., INC. Whitehouse Station, NJ
**DAIRY EXPRESS** WISCONSIN DAIRIES COOPERATIVE Baraboo, WI
**DAIRY MEN'S DIGEST, SOUTHERN REGION** ASSOCIATED MILK PRODUCERS, INC. San Antonio, TX
**DAIRYLEADER** DAIRYLEA COOPERATIVE INC. E. Syracuse, NY
**DAIRYMEN'S DIGEST, MORNING GLORY FARMS REGION** ASSOCIATED MILK PRODUCERS, INC. San Antonio, TX
**DAIRYMEN'S DIGEST, N. CENTRAL REGION** ASSOCIATED MILK PRODUCERS, INC. San Antonio, TX
**DAIRYNEWS** DAIRYLEA COOPERATIVE INC. E. Syracuse, NY
**DALLASITE** TEXAS INSTRUMENTS, INC. Dallas, TX
**DATA** INTEGON Winston Salem, NC
**DATELINE** ARMSTRONG WORLD INDUSTRIES Lancaster, PA
**DATELINE** EAST OHIO GAS CO. Cleveland, OH
**DATELINE** NATIONS BANK CORP. Charlotte, NC
**DATELINE** ST. LOUIS COMMUNITY COLLEGE AT FOREST PARK Saint Louis, MO
**DATELINE INTERNATIONAL** AMERICAN EXPRESS CO. New York, NY
**DAVOL WORLD CLASS BULLETIN** DAVOL INC. Cranston, RI
**DAYTON UPDATE** CITY OF DAYTON Dayton, OH
**DDC BULLETIN** TEXAS SAFETY ASSOCIATION Austin, TX
**DEALER NEWS** KENTUCKY UTILITIES CO. Lexington, KY
**DEALER WORLD** FORD MOTOR COMPANY Dearborn, MI
**DEALERS' CHOICE** TEXAS AUTOMOBILE DEALERS ASSOCIATION Austin, TX
**DECISIONS** PRINTING INDUSTRIES OF AMERICA, INC. Alexandria, VA
**DELTA DIGEST** DELTA AIR LINES Atlanta, GA
**DELTA DISPATCH** DELTA AIR LINES Atlanta, GA
**DENTSPLY DIMENSIONS** DENTSPLY INTERNATIONAL INC. York, PA
**DEPAUL NEWS** DEPAUL HEALTH CTR. Hazelwood, MO
**DETAILS** DATAPOINT CORP. San Antonio, TX
**DEVELOPING KANSAS** KANSAS DEPARTMENT OF COMMERCE Topeka, KS
**DI CYAN BULLETIN** ERWIN DI CYAN Brooklyn, NY
**DIALOG** MERIDIAN BANK Reading, PA
**DIALOGUE** DAVOL INC. Cranston, RI
**DIALOGUE** MISSISSIPPI POWER CO. Gulfport, MS
**DIALOGUE** PRUDENTIAL INSURANCE CO. OF AMERICA Newark, NJ
**DIALOGUE** S.C. JOHNSON & SON INC. Racine, WI
**DIALOGUE** SENTARA HEALTH SYSTEM Norfolk, VA
**DIGEST, THE** IOWA DEPARTMENT OF ECONOMIC DEVELOPMENT Des Moines, IA
**DIGESTER, THE** UNION CAMP CORPORATION Savannah, GA
**DIMENSIONS** CUNA MUTUAL INSURANCE GROUP Madison, WI
**DIRECT LINE** VETCO, INC. Houston, TX
**DIRECTION** AC ROCHESTER DIVISION, GENERAL MOTORS CORPORATION Flint, MI
**DIRECTION 79** ELF ATOCHEM NORTH AMERICA, INC. Philadelphia, PA
**DIRECTIONS** GTE DIRECTORIES CORP. DFW Airport, TX
**DIRECTIONS** PENNSYLVANIA MANUFACTURERS' ASSOCIATION INSURANCE CO. Philadelphia, PA
**DIRECTIONS** RAND MCNALLY & CO. Skokie, IL

**DIRECTORY OF COMPANY MEMBERS** NORTHWEST ELECTRIC LIGHT & POWER ASSOCIATION Portland, OR
**DISCOVER HEALTH** CLARKSON HOSPITAL Omaha, NE
**DISPATCHER** NEBRASKA PUBLIC POWER DISTRICT Columbus, NE
**DISTRIBUTOR NEWS** VICKERS, INC. Troy, MI
**DISTRICT, THE** SALT LAKE CITY SCHOOL DISTRICT Salt Lake City, UT
**DITTLER HOT LINE** DITTLER BROTHERS, INC. Atlanta, GA
**DIVERSEY ADVANTAGE, THE** DIVERSEY CORP. Livonia, MI
**DIXIE NEWS** DIXIE YARNS, INC. Chattanooga, TN
**DOCKSIDE NEWS** MISSISSIPPI CHEMICAL CORP. Yazoo City, MS
**DOCKSIDE NEWSLETTER** MARYLAND PORT ADMINISTRATION Baltimore, MD
**DOCTOR'S DIGEST** BATON ROUGE GENERAL MEDICAL CTR. Baton Rouge, LA
**DOIN' IT** AMSCO AMERICAN STERILIZER CO. Erie, PA
**DOINGS AT THE DEPOT** HOME DEPOT, INC., THE Atlanta, GA
**DONREY MEDIAGRAM** DONREY MEDIA GROUP Ft. Smith, AR
**DONTECH CONNECTIONS** DONTECH Chicago, IL
**DOW CORNING WORLD** DOW CORNING CORP. Midland, MI
**DRESSER QUALTIY CONNECTION** DRESSER INDUSTRIES, INC. Dallas, TX
**DRIVE LINE** FORD MOTOR COMPANY, SHARONVILLE PLANT Cincinnati, OH
**DRIVING FORCE** DUNLOP TIRE CORP. Buffalo, NY
**DSM COPOLYMER NEWS** DSM COPOLYMER Baton Rouge, LA
**DUCAS** IRISH AMERICAN CULTURAL INSTITUTE St. Paul, MN
**DUCOMMUN NEWSREEL:** DUCOMMUN, INC. Carson, CA
**DUFFEL BAG** ST. LOUIS AREA COUNCIL, B.S.A. St. Louis, MO
**DUKE POWER JOURNAL** DUKE POWER CO. Charlotte, NC
**DUPONT MAGAZINE** E I DUPONT DE NEMOURS Wilmington, DE
**DUQUESNE LIGHT NEWS** DUQUESNE LIGHT CO. Pittsburgh, PA
**DUQUESNE UNIVERSITY RECORD** DUQUESNE UNIVERSITY Pittsburgh, PA
**DURACLEAN JOURNAL** DURACLEAN INTERNATIONAL Deerfield, IL
**DYNAMO** NATIONAL TRAVELERS LIFE CO. Des Moines, IA

## E

**E A B PEOPLE** EUROPEAN AMERICAN BANK Uniondale, NY
**E B S CONVEYOR** EDISON BROS. STORES St. Louis, MO
**E L C O NEWSLETTER** ELCO INDUSTRIES, INC. Rockford, IL
**E L C O TIMES** ELCO INDUSTRIES, INC. Rockford, IL
**E M KAYAN** MORRISON KNUDSEN CORP. Boise, ID
**E U A SPECTRUM** EUA SERVICE CORP. W. Bridgewater, MA
**E-BEE** ENSIGN-BICKFORD INDUSTRIES, INC. Simsbury, CT
**EA ITEMS** ELECTRONIC ASSOCIATES, INC. W. Long Branch, NJ
**EAGLE** BANK OF BOSTON CORP. Boston, MA
**EAGLE** BANK ONE OF ARIZONA Phoenix, AZ
**EAGLE, THE** ELECTRONICS INFORMATION & MISSILES GROUP Orlando, FL
**EASTMAN NEWS** EASTMAN CHEMICAL COMPANY Kingsport, TN
**EATON TODAY** EATON CORP. Cleveland, OH
**EBASCO NEWS** EBASCO SERVICES INC. New York, NY
**ECHO** ELDEC CORP. Lynnwood, WA
**ECHOES** LYONS FALLS PULP & PAPER Lyons Falls, NY
**ECOLAB NEWS** ECOLAB INC. St. Paul, MN
**ECONOMIC BULLETIN** GREATER SAN DIEGO CHAMBER OF COMMERCE San Diego, CA
**ECONOMIC DEVELOPMENTS** SOUTH CAROLINA DEPARTMENT OF COMMERCE Columbia, SC

**EDISON LIFE** BOSTON EDISON CO. Boston, MA
**EDISON TODAY** DETROIT EDISON CO. Detroit, MI
**EDITORIAL EYE, THE** EEI Alexandria, VA
**EDUCATION FIRST** OREGON DEPARTMENT OF EDUCATION Salem, OR
**EDWARDIAN, THE** ST. EDWARD'S UNIVERSITY Austin, TX
**EIA MARKET DATA BOOK** ELECTRONIC INDUSTRIES ASSOCIATION Washington, DC
**EIRE-IRELAND, JOURNAL OF IRISH STUDIES** IRISH AMERICAN CULTURAL INSTITUTE St. Paul, MN
**ELECTRIC LEAGUER** ELECTRIC POWER BOARD CHATTANOOGA Chattanooga, TN
**ELECTRIC TIMES** WEST TEXAS UTILITIES CO. Abilene, TX
**ELECTRON OPTICS BULLETIN** PHILIPS ELECTRONICS INSTRUMENTS Mahwah, NJ
**EMANCIPATOR** LINCOLN NATIONAL LIFE INSURANCE COMPANY Fort Wayne, IN
**EMBLEM** AUTO-OWNERS INSURANCE Lansing, MI
**EMBROIDERY DIRECTORY** SCHIFFLI LACE & EMBROIDERY MANUFACTURERS ASSN. North Bergen, NJ
**EMBROIDERY NEWS** SCHIFFLI LACE & EMBROIDERY MANUFACTURERS ASSN. North Bergen, NJ
**EMPIRE DISPATCH** EMPIRE DISTRICT ELECTRIC CO. Joplin, MO
**EMPIRE NEWS** EMPIRE BRUSHES INC. Greenville, NC
**EMPLOYEE GAZETTE** JACOBS ENGINEERING Baton Rouge, LA
**EMPLOYEE HILINES** SACRAMENTO MUNICIPAL UTILITY DISTRICT Sacramento, CA
**EMPLOYEE NEWS** NORTHWESTERN NATIONAL INSURANCE GROUP Brookfield, WI
**EMPLOYEE NEWS DAILY** CHRYSLER CORP. Detroit, MI
**EMPLOYEES ARE THE FIRST TO KNOW** AMERICA WEST AIRLINES Phoenix, AZ
**EMPLOYS' NEWS** KENTUCKY UTILITIES CO. Lexington, KY
**ENCOR RESPONDANCE** EASTERN NEBRASKA COMMUNITY OFFICE OF RETARDATION Omaha, NE
**ENCORE** CORESTATES FIRST PENNSYLVANIA BANK Philadelphia, PA
**ENERGIZER** KN ENERGY, INC. Hastings, NE
**ENERGY EXCHANGE** MAXUS ENERGY CORP. Dallas, TX
**ENEWS** EL PASO ELECTRIC CO. El Paso, TX
**ENGINES IN ACTION** KOHLER CO. Kohler, WI
**ENTERPRISE** EQUITABLE LIFE ASSURANCE SOCIETY New York, NY
**ENTERTAINMENT GUIDE** AMARILLO CHAMBER OF COMMERCE Amarillo, TX
**ENTHUSIAST** HARLEY-DAVIDSON MOTOR CO. INC. Milwaukee, WI
**ENVIRONMENT NEWS DIGEST** FOODSERVICE & PACKAGING INSTITUTE, INC. Arlington, VA
**ENVIRONMENTAL PROTECTION NEWS** STEVENS PUBLISHING CORP. Waco, TX
**EPISTLES** GLEANER LIFE INSURANCE SOCIETY Adrian, MI
**EQUIOWA** EQUITABLE LIFE INS. CO. OF IOWA Des Moines, IA
**EQUITABLE NEWS** EQUITABLE RESOURCES Pittsburgh, PA
**ERECTOR** NOOTER CORP. Saint Louis, MO
**ERIE FAMILY** ERIE INSURANCE GROUP Erie, PA
**ESCO LADLE** ESCO CORP. Portland, OR
**ETHYL INTERCOM** ETHYL CORP. Richmond, VA
**EVERYBODY'S MONEY** CREDIT UNION NATIONAL ASSOCIATION INC. Madison, WI
**EXCEL** MINNESOTA MUTUAL LIFE INSURANCE CO. St. Paul, MN
**EXCEL** WOODMEN ACCIDENT & LIFE CO. Lincoln, NE
**EXCHANGE POST, THE** ARMY & AIR FORCE EXCHANGE SERVICE Dallas, TX
**EXECUTIVE REPORT** AMERICA WEST AIRLINES Phoenix, AZ
**EXECUTIVE REPORT TO THE ELECTRONIC INDUSTRIES** ELECTRONIC INDUSTRIES ASSOCIATION Washington, DC
**EXPRESS** BANCOKLAHOMA CORP. Tulsa, OK
**EXPRESS** MINNESOTA DEPARTMENT OF TRANSPORTATION St. Paul, MN
**EXTENSION TODAY** TEXAS A & M UNIVERSITY SYSTEM College Station, TX

**EXTRA** MINNESOTA MUTUAL LIFE INSURANCE CO. St. Paul, MN

# F

**F H W A NEWS** FEDERAL HIGHWAY ADMINISTRATION Washington, DC
**F M S UPDATE** FINANCIAL MANAGERS SOCIETY, INC. Chicago, IL
**F Y I** AMERICAN TELEPHONE & TELEGRAPH CO. Basking Ridge, NJ
**F Y I** GTE WISCONSIN Bloomington, WI
**F Y I** MIDWEST RESEARCH INSTITUTE Kansas City, MO
**F Y I** NIAGARA FRONTIER TRANSPORTATION AUTHORITY Buffalo, NY
**F Y I** MAGAZINE HARRIS CORP. Melbourne, FL
**FACE TO FACE** HOOVER CO. North Canton, OH
**FACE-TO-FACE** PENNSYLVANIA ELECTRIC CO. Johnstown, PA
**FACTORY MUTUAL RECORD** FACTORY MUTUAL ENGINEERING AND RESEARCH Norwood, MA
**FACTS ABOUT DETROIT** CITY OF DETROIT Detroit, MI
**FALK TALK** FALK CORP. Milwaukee, WI
**FAMILY ALBUM** AMERICAN FAMILY INSURANCE GROUP Madison, WI
**FAMILY TIES** WHITTIER HOSPITAL MEDICAL CENTER Whittier, CA
**FARM BUREAU PRESS** ARKANSAS FARM BUREAU FEDERATION Little Rock, AR
**FARM FAMILY SPIRIT** FARM FAMILY INSURANCE COMPANIES Glenmont, NY
**FARM LIFE** EASTERN MILK PRODUCERS CO-OP ASSN. INC. Syracuse, NY
**FARWEST MAGAZINE** OREGON ASSOCIATION OF NURSERYMEN Milwaukie, OR
**FEATURES** STRIDE RITE CORP. Cambridge, MA
**FED** FEDERAL RESERVE BANK OF NEW YORK New York, NY
**FEDERAL CREDIT UNION** NATIONAL ASSOCIATION OF FEDERAL CREDIT UNIONS Arlington, VA
**FEDERAL RESERVE NOTES** FEDERAL RESERVE BANK OF CLEVELAND Cleveland, OH
**FEDERAL-MOGUL WORLD** FEDERAL-MOGUL CORP. Southfield, MI
**FEL-PROGRAM** FELT PRO INC. Skokie, IL
**FHP ENCORE** FHP INTERNATIONAL CORP. Fountain Valley, CA
**FIBERLUX PROFILE** FIBERLUX, INC. Purchase, NY
**FIELD** MONROE SYSTEMS FOR BUSINESS Morris Plains, NJ
**FIELD EXTRACT** MERCK & CO. INC. West Point, PA
**FIELD FOCUS** AMERICAN GENERAL LIFE/ACCIDENT INSURANCE CO. Nashville, TN
**FIELDCREST CANNON** FIELDCREST CANNON, INC. Eden, NC
**FILENE'S FORUM** FILENE'S Boston, MA
**FINANCIAL DIRECTIONS** BANK OF HAWAII Honolulu, HI
**FIRE NEWS** NATIONAL FIRE PROTECTION ASSOCIATION Quincy, MA
**FIRST & FOREMOST** FIRST FEDERAL S & L ASSOCIATION OF ROCHESTER Rochester, NY
**FIRST CHICAGOAN** FIRST CHICAGO CORPORATION Chicago, IL
**FIRST FIDELITY JOURNAL** FIRST FIDELITY BANCORPORATION Newark, NJ
**FIRST FOCUS** FIRST AMERICAN CORP. Nashville, TN
**FIRST NEVADAN** FIRST INTERSTATE BANK OF NEVADA, N.A. Reno, NV
**FIRST VIRGINIAN** FIRST VIRGINIA BANK Falls Church, VA
**FIRST WORD, THE** SOUTHEAST MICHIGAN, N.A. Royal Oak, MI
**FIRSTFOCUS** FIRST SECURITY CORP. Salt Lake City, UT
**FIRSTTEAM** FIRST SECURITY CORP. Salt Lake City, UT
**FLAGSHIP NEWS** AMERICAN AIRLINES INC. DFW Airport, TX
**FLASH** OMAHA PUBLIC POWER DIST. Omaha, NE
**FLASH** UTICA NATIONAL INSURANCE GROUP New Hartford, NY
**FLASHES** AMERICAN STORES CO. Salt Lake City, UT
**FLASHES** JEWEL FOOD STORES Melrose Park, IL
**FLEMING ASSOCIATE, THE** FLEMING COS. INC. Oklahoma City, OK

**FLORIDA RURAL ELECTRIC NEWS** FLORIDA RURAL ELECTRIC CO-OP ASSOCIATION Tallahassee, FL
**FLORIST** FLORISTS TRANSWORLD DELIVERY ASSOCIATION Southfield, MI
**FLOW** BDP BRANDS, CARRIER CORP. Indianapolis, IN
**FOCAL POINT** RICH'S, INC. Atlanta, GA
**FOCAL POINT** SUPERMARKETS, INC. Albuquerque, NH
**FOCUS** ALLIED GROUP Des Moines, IA
**FOCUS** AURORA PUBLIC SCHOOLS Aurora, CO
**FOCUS** BEST FOODS, DIVISION OF CPC INTERNATIONAL, INC. Englewood Cliffs, NJ
**FOCUS** COX ENTERPRISES, INC. Atlanta, GA
**FOCUS** FIRST COMMERCE CORP. New Orleans, LA
**FOCUS** GREAT LAKES DIVISION-NATIONAL STEEL Ecorse, MI
**FOCUS** MEDICAL CENTER OF DELAWARE, THE Wilmington, DE
**FOCUS** NATIONAL LIFE OF VERMONT Montpelier, VT
**FOCUS** NORFOLK SOUTHERN CORP. Norfolk, VA
**FOCUS** OKLAHOMA CITY UNIVERSITY Oklahoma City, OK
**FOCUS MAGAZINE (FOR MANAGERS)** CAROLINA POWER & LIGHT CO. Raleigh, NC
**FOCUS NEWSLETTER** SPIEGEL, INC. Downer Grove, IL
**FOCUS ON COMMISSIONS** INTER-STATE ASSURANCE CO. Des Moines, IA
**FOCUS ON OHIO DENTISTRY** OHIO DENTAL ASSOCIATION Columbus, OH
**FOCUS ON SAKS FIFTH AVENUE** SAKS FIFTH AVENUE New York, NY
**FOCUS ON ST. LOUIS** ANHEUSER-BUSCH COMPANIES, INC. Saint Louis, MO
**FOCUS ON THE BEST** FIRST NATIONWIDE BANK San Francisco, CA
**FOCUS ON US** U.S. BANCORP Portland, OR
**FOLEY'S INTERVIEW** FOLEY'S Houston, TX
**FOLK ARTS NOTES** SOUTHERN ARTS FEDERATION, INC. Atlanta, GA
**FOODLINE** COCA-COLA FOODS Houston, TX
**FOODLINE CLUB NEWSLETTER** COCA-COLA FOODS Houston, TX
**FOOTNOTE** MINNESOTA SOCIETY OF CERTIFIED PUBLIC ACCOUNTANTS Minneapolis, MN
**FOR MEMBERS ONLY** JEWISH COMMUNITY CENTER Dallas, TX
**FORD TIMES** FORD MOTOR COMPANY Dearborn, MI
**FORD WORLD** FORD MOTOR COMPANY Dearborn, MI
**FOREFRONT** MERCY HOSPITAL Iowa City, IA
**FORESIGHT** FARMLAND INSURANCE COMPANIES Des Moines, IA
**FOREST LOG** OREGON DEPT. OF FORESTRY Salem, OR
**FOREST PRESCRIPTION** WASHINGTON DEPARTMENT OF NATURAL RESOURCES Olympia, WA
**FORESTS & PEOPLE** LOUISIANA FORESTRY ASSOCIATION Alexandria, LA
**FORM & FUNCTION** USG CORP. Chicago, IL
**FORUM** EMPLOYERS GROUP Los Angeles, CA
**FORUM** GRAND VALLEY STATE UNIVERSITY Allendale, MI
**FORUM** PRINTING INDUSTRIES OF AMERICA, INC. Alexandria, VA
**FORUM** UARCO, INC. Barrington, IL
**FORUM MAGAZINE** METROPOLITAN LIFE INSURANCE CO. New York, NY
**FORWARD** MONTGOMERY WARD & CO. Chicago, IL
**FRAME MAKER** ANDERSEN CORP. Bayport, MN
**FRANKLIN FIELD** FRANKLIN, THE Springfield, IL
**FREELANCE EDITOR-WRITER** WARNER ENTERPRISES Rochester, NY
**FREIGHTLINER NEWS REPORT** FREIGHTLINER CORP. Portland, OR
**FRIDAY FACTS** NATIONAL INDEMNITY CO. Omaha, NE
**FRIDAY MORNING** GLEANER LIFE INSURANCE SOCIETY Adrian, MI
**FRONT LINE** IES UTILITIES Cedar Rapids, IA
**FRONT LINE** MERCK & CO. INC. West Point, PA
**FRONT LINE** U-HAUL INTERNATIONAL, INC. Phoenix, AZ
**FRONT LINES** AGENCY FOR INTERNATIONAL DEVELOPMENT Washington, DC
**FRONT LINES** SEARS ROEBUCK & CO. Hoffman Estates, IL
**FRONTLINE** COOK COMPOSITES Kansas City, MO
**FRONTLINE** MILLER BREWING CO. Milwaukee, WI

**FUEL FOR THOUGHT** CONNECTICUT NATURAL GAS CORP. Hartford, CT
**FULLCOVERAGE** MOTORISTS INSURANCE COMPANIES Columbus, OH
**FULLER WORLD** H.B. FULLER CO. St. Paul, MN
**FURNAS TODAY** FURNAS ELECTRIC CO. Batavia, IL
**FYI INTERNATIONAL** EQUIFAX, INC. Atlanta, GA

## G

**G E NEWS** GE Fort Wayne, IN
**G P M MESSENGER** GOVERNMENT PERSONNEL MUTUAL LIFE INSURANCE CO San Antonio, TX
**G T E MONTHLY** GTE CORP. Stamford, CT
**G T E WEEKLY** GTE CORP. Stamford, CT
**G. S. NEWS** CENTRAL NEW YORK GIRL SCOUT COUNCIL INC. Syracuse, NY
**GARLIC VINE, THE** GILROY FOODS, INC. Gilroy, CA
**GAS LINES** ALABAMA GAS CORP. Birmingham, AL
**GAS LINES** BOSTON GAS COMPANY Boston, MA
**GASETTE** OKLAHOMA NATURAL GAS CO. Tulsa, OK
**GATEWAY NEWS:** GATEWAY YOUTH & FAMILY SERVICES Williamsville, NY
**GAZETTE** AMERICAN OLEAN TILE CO. Lansdale, PA
**GAZETTE** GENERAL ACCIDENT INSURANCE Philadelphia, PA
**GEISINGER MAGAZINE** GEISINGER SYSTEM Danville, PA
**GENCORP BUSINESS REVIEW** GENCORP Fairlawn, OH
**GENIUS AT WORK** KANO LABS INC. Nashville, TN
**GEORGIA ANCHORAGE** GEORGIA PORTS AUTHORITY Savannah, GA
**GEORGIA'S CITIES** GEORGIA MUNICIPAL ASSOCIATION Atlanta, GA
**GILBARCO GAZETTE** GILBARCO INC. Greensboro, NC
**GIRL SCOUTING** GIRL SCOUT COUNCIL OF GREATER MINNEAPOLIS Minneapolis, MN
**GO-DEVIL** SHELL OIL CO. Houston, TX
**GOLDEN CARES** SAINT ANTHONY MEDICAL CENTER Rockford, IL
**GOLDEN CUSTOMER NEWSLETTER** TRUSTMARK NATIONAL BANK Brookhaven, MS
**GOOD LIVING** BOULEVARD PUBLICATIONS INC. Columbus, OH
**GOOD NEWS BEARER** CHILDREN'S HOSPITAL OF ORANGE COUNTY Orange, CA
**GOODWILL FORUM** GOODWILL INDUSTRIES INTERNATIONAL, INC. Bethesda, MD
**GOODWILL NEWS-NEWSLETTER** GOODWILL INDUSTRIES OF HOUSTON Houston, TX
**GOULDS PROFESSIONAL DEALERS ASSOCIATION** GOULDS PUMPS INC. Seneca Falls, NY
**GOVERNMENT REPORT** ARC, NATIONAL HEADQUARTERS Arlington, TX
**GRACE INSIDER UPDATE** W.R. GRACE & CO. Boca Raton, FL
**GRAND STAND** GRAND UNION CO. Wayne, NJ
**GRAPEVINE** FOREST LAWN MEMORIAL PARK Glendale, CA
**GRAPEVINE** ROWAN COMPANIES, INC. Houston, TX
**GRAPEVINE** SOUTHWESTERN PUBLIC SERVICE CO. Amarillo, TX
**GRAPHICOPY** MEREDITH GRAPHICS, INC. Cleveland, OH
**GRAYBAR OUTLOOK** GRAYBAR ELECTRIC CO. INC. St. Louis, MO
**GREAT NEWS** MEAD CORPORATION Dayton, OH
**GREENBRIER MAGAZINE** GREENBRIER HOTEL White Sulphur Springs, WV
**GROUP UPDATE / MEMBERS PLUS / OUT OF THE BLUE** BLUE CROSS & BLUE SHIELD OF WEST VIRGINIA, INC. Charleston, WV
**GROWING TOGETHER** CHILDREN'S MEDICAL CENTER Dayton, OH
**GRUMMAN WORLD** GRUMMAN CORP. Bethpage, NY
**GRUNAU GRAM** GRUCON CORP. Milwaukee, WI
**GUARANTEE MUTUAL FIELD NEWS** GUARANTEE MUTUAL LIFE CO. Omaha, NE
**GUARANTOR** CHICAGO TITLE & TRUST CO. Chicago, IL
**GUARDIAN GRAPHICS** GUARDIAN CORPORATION Rocky Mount, NC
**GUILD AT A GLANCE** ST. JOSEPH MEDICAL CENTER Burbank, CA

**GULF COAST PLUMBING, HEATING, COOLING NEWS** PLUMBING MECHANICAL CONTRACTORS COUNCIL HARRIS COUNTY Houston, TX
**GULF RESEARCH REPORTS** GULF COAST RESEARCH LABORATORY Ocean Springs, MS
**GUNDERSON NEWS** GUNDERSON, INC. Portland, OR
**GUTHRIE THEATER PROGRAM MAGAZINE** GUTHRIE THEATRE Minneapolis, MN

## H

**H B A NEWSLETTER** HOME BUILDERS ASSOCIATION OF GREATER ST. LOUIS St. Louis, MO
**H M O MAGAZINE** GROUP HEALTH ASSOCIATION OF AMERICA, INC. Washington, DC
**H R MAGAZINE** SOCIETY FOR HUMAN RESOURCE MANAGEMENT Alexandria, VA
**H S C THIS WEEK** STATE UNIVERSITY OF N.Y. HEALTH SCIENCE CTR. AT SYRACUSE Syracuse, NY
**H S C TODAY** STATE UNIVERSITY OF N.Y. HEALTH SCIENCE CTR. AT SYRACUSE Syracuse, NY
**H T B TODAY** HTB, INC. Oklahoma City, OK
**HAGGAR HIGHLIGHTS** HAGGAR CO. Dallas, TX
**HALLIBURTON PRIDE** HALLIBURTON ENERGY SERVICES Houston, TX
**HAND IN HAND** MICHIGAN MUTUAL INSURANCE CO. Detroit, MI
**HANDSIGNALS, THE** OPPENHEIMER MANAGEMENT CORP. New York, NY
**HANFORD REACH** WESTINGHOUSE HANFORD COMPANY Richland, WA
**HAPPENINGS** PHILIP MORRIS, USA New York, NY
**HAPPENINGS** UNITED INSURANCE CO. OF AMERICA Chicago, IL
**HARD HAT** FLUOR DANIEL INC. Irvine, CA
**HARRISON COMMUNICATOR** HARRISON RADIATOR DIV. Lockport, NY
**HASBRO HERALD** HASBRO, INC. Pawtucket, RI
**HASBRO NEWS** HASBRO, INC. Pawtucket, RI
**HAZMAT NEWS** STEVENS PUBLISHING CORP. Waco, TX
**HEADLINE** INDIANAPOLIS LIFE INSURANCE CO. Indianapolis, IN
**HEADLINER** ATLANTA JOURNAL-CONSTITUTION Atlanta, GA
**HEADLINER** SECURITY MUTUAL LIFE INSURANCE CO. OF NEW YORK Binghamton, NY
**HEADLINES** GE AIRCRAFT ENGINES Cincinnati, OH
**HEALTH & BENEFIT BRIEFS** NALCO CHEMICAL CO. Naperville, IL
**HEALTH AT WORK** ALLIANT HEALTH SYSTEM Louisville, KY
**HEALTH CONNECTIONS** BROWN GROUP, INC. St. Louis, MO
**HEALTH MAGAZINE** GROSSMONT HOSPITAL La Mesa, CA
**HEALTH MATTERS** BLUE CROSS & BLUE SHIELD Columbia, SC
**HEALTH NEWS** MEDICAL COLLEGE OF WISCONSIN Milwaukee, WI
**HEALTH PICX** NEBRASKA METHODIST HOSPITAL Omaha, NE
**HEALTH REVIEW:** ST. VINCENT HOSPITAL Green Bay, WI
**HEALTH SCIENCES REPORT** UNIVERSITY OF UTAH MEDICAL CENTER Salt Lake City, UT
**HEALTH WATCH** VALLEY PRESBYTERIAN HOSPITAL Van Nuys, CA
**HEALTH-O-GRAM** P.H. GLATFELTER CO. Spring Grove, PA
**HEALTHCARING** MISSISSIPPI BAPTIST MEDICAL CENTER Jackson, MS
**HEALTHPARTNERS TODAY** GROUP HEALTH, INC. Minneapolis, MN
**HEALTHPLEX MAGAZINE** CHILDREN'S HOSPITAL Omaha, NE
**HEALTHPOINT (COMMUNITY NEWSLETTER)** MILLS-PENINSULA HOSPITALS Burlingame, CA
**HEALTHREACH** ARLINGTON HOSPITAL Arlington, VA
**HEALTHTALK** ST. ELIZABETH MEDICAL CENTER Granite City, IL
**HEART TO HEART** AMERICAN HEART ASSOCIATION St. Louis, MO
**HEART-TO-HEART** BLOOD SYSTEMS Scottsdale, AZ

**HEARTBEAT** SETON MEDICAL CENTER Austin, TX
**HEAT ENGINEERING** FOSTER WHEELER CORP. Clinton, NJ
**HEDMAN FLASH** HEDMAN CO. Chicago, IL
**HEINZLINE** HEINZ U.S.A. Pittsburgh, PA
**HELPING BUILD MISSISSIPPI** MISSISSIPPI POWER & LIGHT CO. Jackson, MS
**HERALD OF HOPE** AMERICAN CANCER SOCIETY Edina, MN
**HERE & NOW** HOLMES & NARVER, INC. Orange, CA
**HEWLETT-PACKARD JOURNAL** HEWLETT-PACKARD CO. Palo Alto, CA
**HI-LIGHTS** CORAL GABLES FEDERAL SAVINGS & LOAN ASSOCIATION Miami, FL
**HI-LITES** OTTER TAIL POWER CO. Fergus Falls, MN
**HI-TECH ALERT FOR THE PRO. COMMUNICATOR** COMMUNICATION RESEARCH ASSOCIATES, INC. Silver Spring, MD
**HIGH SPOTS** OHIO CREDIT UNION LEAGUE Columbus, OH
**HIGHEST PROFIT PROGRAM** HIGHEST PROFIT CORP. Pewaukee, WI
**HIGHLANDER** REGIS UNIVERSITY Denver, CO
**HIGHWAY BUILDER** ASSOCIATED PENNSYLVANIA CONSTRUCTORS Harrisburg, PA
**HILLENBRAND INDUSTRIES VISION** HILLENBRAND INDUSTRIES, INC. Batesville, IN
**HILLSDALE MAGAZINE** HILLSDALE COLLEGE Hillsdale, MI
**HILLTOP VIEWS** ST. EDWARD'S UNIVERSITY Austin, TX
**HISPANIC PHYSICIAN** CALIFORNIA HISPANIC AMERICAN MEDICAL ASSOCIATION Pasadena, CA
**HOA HANA** HAWAIIAN ELECTRIC CO., INC. Honolulu, HI
**HOLSTEIN NEWS** HOLSTEIN ASSOCIATION OF AMERICA Brattleboro, VT
**HOME & AWAY-IOWA** AAA IOWA Bettendorf, IA
**HOME OFFICE NEWS** SUPERVALU, INC. Eden Prairie, MN
**HOME OFFICE NEWS** WESTERN/SOUTHERN LIFE INSURANCE CO. Cincinnati, OH
**HOME TOPICS** HOME BENEFICIAL LIFE INSURANCE CO. Richmond, VA
**HONEYWELL PRIDE** HONEYWELL, INC. Phoenix, AZ
**HOOSIER BANKER** INDIANA BANKERS ASSOCIATION, INC. Indianapolis, IN
**HOOSIER FARMER** INDIANA FARM BUREAU, INC. Indianapolis, IN
**HOOVER NEWS** HOOVER CO. North Canton, OH
**HORIZON** RESEARCH MEDICAL CENTER Kansas City, MO
**HORIZON-MED STAFF** RESEARCH MEDICAL CENTER Kansas City, MO
**HORIZONS** ALLIED-SIGNAL AEROSPACE CO. Torrance, CA
**HORIZONS** APPLETON MILLS Appleton, WI
**HORIZONS** FLUOR DANIEL INC. Irvine, CA
**HORIZONS** GRAND VALLEY STATE UNIVERSITY Allendale, MI
**HORIZONS** HIA (HOBBY INDUSTRY ASSOCIATION OF AMERICA) Elmwood Park, NJ
**HORIZONS** LIMA MEMORIAL HOSPITAL Lima, OH
**HORIZONS** WILKES-BARRE GENERAL HOSPITAL Wilkes Barre, PA
**HORIZONS:** SAINT JOHN HOSPITAL Detroit, MI
**HOSPICE TODAY** HOSPICE OF THE FLORIDA SUNCOAST Largo, FL
**HOT LINE** NORTH CAROLINA MUTUAL LIFE INSURANCE CO. Durham, NC
**HOT SHEET** SAN DIEGO MUNICIPAL EMPLOYEES ASSOCIATION San Diego, CA
**HOTLINE** FOODLAND INTERNATIONAL CORP. Hazelwood, PA
**HOTLINE** FUTURE BUSINESS LEADERS OF AMERICA-PHI BETA LAMBDA Reston, VA
**HOTLINE** SIZZLER INTERNATIONAL, INC. Los Angeles, CA
**HOUGHTON LINE** E.F. HOUGHTON & CO. Valley Forge, PA
**HOUGHTONEWS** E.F. HOUGHTON & CO. Valley Forge, PA
**HOUSTON BUILDER** GREATER HOUSTON BUILDERS ASSOCIATION Houston, TX
**HQ REVIEW** DUNLOP TIRE CORP. Buffalo, NY
**HUGHES CHRISTIANSEN HORIZON** HUGHES CHRISTIANSEN CO. The Woodlands, TX

**HUGHES RIGWAY** HUGHES CHRISTIANSEN CO. The Woodlands, TX
**HUGHESNEWS** HUGHES AIRCRAFT CO. Los Angeles, CA
**HUMAN SIDE, THE** GEORGIA DEPARTMENT OF HUMAN RESOURCES Atlanta, GA
**HUMAN TOUCH** UTAH DEPARTMENT OF HUMAN SERVICES Salt Lake City, UT
**HUNTINGTON HIGHLIGHTS** HUNTINGTON BANCSHARES, INC. Columbus, OH
**HUPDATE** HOSPITAL OF THE UNIVERSITY OF PENNSYLVANIA Philadelphia, PA
**HYPOTENUSE** RESEARCH TRIANGLE INSTITUTE Durham, NC

# I

**I A H A INFOLINE** INTERNATIONAL ASSOCIATION OF HOSPITALITY ACCOUNTANTS Austin, TX
**I B MAGAZINE (INDEPENDENT BUSINESS)** NATIONAL FEDERATION OF INDEPENDENT BUSINESS Washington, DC
**I G A GROCERGRAM** IGA, INC. Chicago, IL
**I I A TODAY** INSTITUTE OF INTERNAL AUDITORS Altamonte Springs, FL
**I P L C O NEWS** IPALCO ENTERPRISES, INC. Indianapolis, IN
**I T T HARTFORD AGENT** ITT HARTFORD INSURANCE GROUP Hartford, CT
**I T T HARTFORD WORLD** ITT HARTFORD INSURANCE GROUP Hartford, CT
**IDEAS FOR BETTER LIVING** BOULEVARD PUBLICATIONS INC. Columbus, OH
**ILLINOIS ENGINEER** ILLINOIS SOCIETY OF PROFESSIONAL ENGINEERS Springfield, IL
**ILLINOIS REPORTER** ILLINOIS LEAGUE OF SAVINGS INSTITUTIONS Springfield, IL
**ILLINOIS RURAL ELECTRIC NEWS** ASSOCIATION OF ILLINOIS ELECTRIC COOPERATIVES Springfield, IL
**ILLUMINATOR** APPALACHIAN POWER CO. Roanoke, VA
**IMAGE** APPLIED TECHNOLOGY San Jose, CA
**IMAGE** KONICA BUSINESS MACHINES U.S.A., INC. Windsor, CT
**IMAGE** MARION LABORATORIES, INC. Kansas City, MO
**IMAGE, THE** WHIRLPOOL CORPORATION Evansville, IN
**IMAGES OF SOUTHWEST TEXAS METHODIST HOSPITAL** SOUTHWEST TEXAS METHODIST HOSPITAL San Antonio, TX
**IMANET** INDIANA MANUFACTURERS ASSOCIATION, INC. Indianapolis, IN
**IMPACT** UNIVERSITY OF NEBRASKA MEDICAL CENTER Omaha, NE
**IMPACT ON WESTERN NEW YORK** UNITED WAY OF BUFFALO & ERIE COUNTY Buffalo, NY
**IMPRESSIONS** GARDNER DENVER MACHINERY INC. Quincy, IL
**IMPRIMIS** HILLSDALE COLLEGE Hillsdale, MI
**IMPRINT** INDIANA MICHIGAN POWER CO. Fort Wayne, IN
**IMPULSE** ELECTRIC COUNCIL OF NEW ENGLAND Bedford, MA
**IN ACTION MANAGEMENT MEMO** EMPLOYERS GROUP Los Angeles, CA
**IN BRIEF** SISTERS OF PROVIDENCE HEALTH SYSTEM Seattle, WA
**IN DEPTH** ILLINOIS CREDIT UNION LEAGUE Naperville, IL
**IN FOCUS** LIBERTY NATIONAL BANK & TRUST CO. Louisville, KY
**IN FOCUS** SAN DIEGO GAS & ELECTRIC CO. San Diego, CA
**IN FOCUS** SANWA BANK CALIFORNIA Los Angeles, CA
**IN GENERAL** AMERICAN GENERAL LIFE/ACCIDENT INSURANCE CO. Nashville, TN
**IN GENERAL** NEW BRITAIN GENERAL HOSPITAL New Britain, CT
**IN GENERAL NEWSLETTER** BATON ROUGE GENERAL MEDICAL CTR. Baton Rouge, LA
**IN PERSPECTIVE** WILLIAMS CO., THE Tulsa, OK
**IN SEARCH EXPLORATION** LONE STAR GAS CO. Dallas, TX
**IN SYNC** ERIE INSURANCE GROUP Erie, PA
**IN THE LARGE** ZALE CORP. Irving, TX
**IN TOUCH** ETHICON INC. Somerville, NJ

**IN TOUCH WITH SAFETY** UNION CAMP CORPORATION Savannah, GA
**IN TRANSIT** ATLANTIC ENVELOPE CO. Atlanta, GA
**IN-GRAIN** GRAIN ELEVATOR AND PROCESSING SOCIETY Minneapolis, MN
**INDIAN HILLS ECHOES** GUARANTEE MUTUAL LIFE CO. Omaha, NE
**INDIANA CAPITOL MONITOR** HILLENBRAND INDUSTRIES, INC. Batesville, IN
**INDIANAPOLIS LIFE TIMES** INDIANAPOLIS LIFE INSURANCE CO. Indianapolis, IN
**INDUSTRIAL** INDUSTRIAL COMMISSION Columbus, OH
**INDUSTRY OUTLOOK** BLUE CROSS & BLUE SHIELD Columbia, SC
**INFO** UNION PACIFIC RAILROAD Omaha, NE
**INFOAAU** AMATEUR ATHLETIC UNION OF THE U.S. Indianapolis, IN
**INFOBITS** SETON MEDICAL CENTER Austin, TX
**INFORM** MOORE BUSINESS FORMS, INC. Lake Forest, IL
**INFORMATION EDGE** SOUTHERN BELL TELEPHONE CO. Atlanta, GA
**INFORMATION MEMO** ALBANY INTERNATIONAL CORP. Albany, NY
**INGALLS NEWS** INGALLS SHIPBUILDING DIVISION, LITTON INDUSTRIES Pascagoula, MS
**INGENUITY** UNIVERSITY OF MISSOURI Columbia, MO
**INGERSOLLETTER** INGERSOLL INTERNATIONAL, INC. Rockford, IL
**INNOVATOR** CONTINENTAL GRAIN CO., WAYNE FEED DIVISION Chicago, IL
**INS-SPIRE** CHURCH MUTUAL INSURANCE CO. Merrill, WI
**INSIDE** HORMEL FOODS CORP. Austin, MN
**INSIDE** SOUTHERN COMPANY SERVICES, INC. Atlanta, GA
**INSIDE & OUT** COMPAQ COMPUTER CORP. Houston, TX
**INSIDE A G C S** AG COMMUNICATIONS CORP. Genda, IL
**INSIDE AT F P L** FLORIDA POWER & LIGHT CO. Miami, FL
**INSIDE B N** BURLINGTON NORTHERN RAILROAD Fort Worth, TX
**INSIDE BANK SOUTH** BANK SOUTH Atlanta, GA
**INSIDE C N A** CNA INSURANCE Chicago, IL
**INSIDE C N A** CONTINENTAL ASSURANCE CO. Chicago, IL
**INSIDE CENTRAL** GTE TELEPHONE OPERATIONS Wentzville, MO
**INSIDE CURTIS** CURTIS 1000, INC. Atlanta, GA
**INSIDE D N R** WASHINGTON DEPARTMENT OF NATURAL RESOURCES Olympia, WA
**INSIDE ETHICON** ETHICON INC. Somerville, NJ
**INSIDE G V S U** GRAND VALLEY STATE UNIVERSITY Allendale, MI
**INSIDE I P M A** IN-PLANT MANAGEMENT ASSOCIATION Liberty, MO
**INSIDE I S O** INSURANCE SERVICES OFFICE INC. New York, NY
**INSIDE INFORMATION** BAYLOR COLLEGE OF MEDICINE Houston, TX
**INSIDE INFORMATION** UNISYS Great Neck, NY
**INSIDE J P** JEFFERSON PILOT LIFE INSURANCE CO. Greensboro, NC
**INSIDE LUTHERAN** LUTHERAN MEDICAL CENTER Cleveland, OH
**INSIDE M S** NATIONAL MULTIPLE SCLEROSIS SOCIETY New York, NY
**INSIDE M S BULLETIN** NATIONAL MULTIPLE SCLEROSIS SOCIETY New York, NY
**INSIDE NORTH** GENERAL TELEPHONE CO. OF PA. Westfield, IN
**INSIDE OG & E** OKLAHOMA GAS & ELECTRIC CO. Oklahoma City, OK
**INSIDE OUT** KOSS CORP. Milwaukee, WI
**INSIDE P M A** PENNSYLVANIA MANUFACTURERS' ASSOCIATION INSURANCE CO. Philadelphia, PA
**INSIDE S A S INTERNATIONAL** SCANDINAVIAN AIRLINES SYSTEM INC. Lindhurst, NY
**INSIDE SHAWNEE MISSION PUBLIC SCHOOLS** SHAWNEE MISSION PUBLIC SCHOOLS Shawnee Mission, KS
**INSIDE SPIRITS** VIRGINIA DEPARTMENT OF ALCOHOLIC BEVERAGE CONTROL Richmond, VA

**INSIDE STORY** WASHINGTON GAS Washington, DC
**INSIDE THE BLADE** TOLEDO BLADE CO. Toledo, OH
**INSIDE TRACK** NATIONAL CITY CORP. Cleveland, OH
**INSIDE TRACK** SUBARU OF AMERICA, INC. Cherry Hill, NJ
**INSIDER** MEREDITH CORP. Des Moines, IA
**INSIDER** MIAMI VALLEY HOSPITAL Dayton, OH
**INSIDER** QUANTUM CHEMICAL CORP., USI DIV. Cincinnati, OH
**INSIDER** WILMINGTON SAVINGS FUND SOCIETY Wilmington, DE
**INSIGHT** BB & T Wilson, NC
**INSIGHT** BLUE CROSS & BLUE SHIELD ASSOCIATION Chicago, IL
**INSIGHT** BRANCH BANKING AND TRUST CO. Wilson, NC
**INSIGHT** CHUBB LIFEAMERICA Concord, NH
**INSIGHT** GIRL SCOUT COUNCIL OF GREATER ST. LOUIS Saint Louis, MO
**INSIGHT** OHIO BELL TELEPHONE CO. Cleveland, OH
**INSIGHT** OWENS-ILLINOIS INC. Toledo, OH
**INSIGHT** STATE COMPENSATION INSURANCE FUND San Francisco, CA
**INSIGHTS** CMP INDUSTRIES, INC. Albany, NY
**INSIGHTS** COLUMBIA GAS TRANSMISSION CORP. Charleston, WV
**INSIGHTS** COLUMBIA GULF TRANSMISSION Houston, TX
**INSIGHTS** ILLINOIS FARM BUREAU Bloomington, IL
**INSIGHTS FOR AGENTS** HARLEYSVILLE INSURANCE COMPANIES Harleysville, PA
**INSIGHTS FOR EMPLOYEES** HARLEYSVILLE INSURANCE COMPANIES Harleysville, PA
**INSITE MAGAZINE** NATIONAL ASSOCIATION OF CONCESSIONAIRES Chicago, IL
**INSTANT ITEMS** APPLIED TECHNOLOGY San Jose, CA
**INTAKE MAGAZINE** LOS ANGELES DEPARTMENT OF WATER & POWER Los Angeles, CA
**INTERCHANGE** DEKALB GENETICS CORP. De Kalb, IL
**INTERCHANGE** TRANSPORTATION COMMUNICATIONS INTERNATIONAL UNION Rockville, MD
**INTERCOM** BALL CORP. Muncie, IN
**INTERCOM** DALLAS MORNING NEWS Dallas, TX
**INTERCOM** HCA PRESBYTERIAN HOSPITAL Oklahoma City, OK
**INTERCOM** JOHN H HARLAND CO. Atlanta, GA
**INTERCOM** JOURNAL COMMUNICATIONS Milwaukee, WI
**INTERCOM** ST. FRANCIS HOSPITAL CENTER Beech Grove, IN
**INTERCOMM** INDUSTRIAL COMMISSION Columbus, OH
**INTERFACE** SMITHS INDUSTRIES AEROSPACE & DEFENSE SYSTEMS, INC. Grand Rapids, MI
**INTERMET NEWS** INTERMET FOUNDRY Lynchburg, VA
**INTERNAL AUDITOR** INSTITUTE OF INTERNAL AUDITORS Altamonte Springs, FL
**INTERNAL NEWSLETTER** SARA LEE KNIT PRODUCTS Winston Salem, NC
**INTERNATIONAL FLYING FARMER** INTERNATIONAL FLYING FARMERS Wichita, KS
**INTERNATIONAL NEWS** NATIONAL SEMICONDUCTOR CORP. Santa Clara, CA
**INTERNATIONAL UNIVERSITY POETRY QUARTERLY, THE** INTERNATIONAL UNIVERSITY FOUNDATION Independence, MO
**INTERNIST: HEALTH POLICY IN PRACTICE** AMERICAN SOCIETY OF INTERNAL MEDICINE Washington, DC
**INTERSTATE NEWS** INTERSTATE POWER CO. Dubuque, IA
**INTERVIEW** PHOENIX BAPTIST HOSPITAL & MEDICAL CENTER Phoenix, AZ
**INTERVIEWS** ALLIANT HEALTH SYSTEM Louisville, KY
**INVESTMENT BLUE BOOK** SECURITIES INVESTIGATIONS, INC. Woodstock, NY
**IOWA COUNTY, THE** IOWA STATE ASSOCIATION OF COUNTIES Des Moines, IA
**IOWA INTERLINK** LEAGUE OF IOWA MUNICIPALITIES Des Moines, IA
**IOWA MUNICIPALITIES:** LEAGUE OF IOWA MUNICIPALITIES Des Moines, IA
**IOWA REC NEWS** IOWA ASSOCIATION OF ELECTRIC COOPERATIVES Des Moines, IA
**IT STARTS IN THE CLASSROOM** NATIONAL SCHOOL PUBLIC RELATIONS ASSOCIATION Arlington, VA

# INTERNAL PUBLICATIONS BY TITLE

**IT STARTS ON THE FRONT LINE** NATIONAL SCHOOL PUBLIC RELATIONS ASSOCIATION Arlington, VA

**ITALIC HARDWRITING NEWSLETTER** CONTINUING EDUCATION PRESS Portland, OR

**ITEM** ITEK OPTICAL SYSTEMS, DIV. OF LITTON INDUSTRIES Lexington, MA

## J

**J C PENNEY TODAY** JC PENNEY COMPANY Plano, TX

**J D JOURNAL** DEERE & CO. Moline, IL

**J L G INK, THE** JLG INDUSTRIES, INC. McConnellsburg, PA

**J P HOME SERVICE TODAY** JEFFERSON PILOT LIFE INSURANCE CO. Greensboro, NC

**J P LIFE MAGAZINE** JEFFERSON PILOT LIFE INSURANCE CO. Greensboro, NC

**J P NEWS** JEFFERSON PILOT LIFE INSURANCE CO. Greensboro, NC

**JAMES JOURNAL, THE** T.L. JAMES & CO., INC. Ruston, LA

**JANTZEN YARNS** JANTZEN INC. Portland, OR

**JAYCEES MAGAZINE** UNITED STATES JUNIOR CHAMBER OF COMMERCE, THE Tulsa, OK

**JAZZ SOUTH** SOUTHERN ARTS FEDERATION, INC. Atlanta, GA

**JOB INFORMATION SERVICE** RADIO-TELEVISION NEWS DIRECTORS ASSOCIATION Washington, DC

**JONATHAN** JONATHAN CLUB Los Angeles, CA

**JOURNAL OF COLLEGE SCIENCE TEACHING** NATIONAL SCIENCE TEACHERS ASSOCIATION Washington, DC

**JOURNAL OF ORAL & MAXILLOFACIAL SURGERY** AMERICAN ASSOCIATION OF ORAL & MAXILLOFACIAL SURGEONS Rosemont, IL

**JOURNAL OF RURAL HEALTH** NATIONAL RURAL HEALTH ASSOCIATION Kansas City, MO

**JOURNAL OF TEACHER EDUCATION** AMERICAN ASSOCIATION OF COLLEGES FOR TEACHER EDUCATION Washington, DC

**JOURNAL OF THE AMERICAN SOCIETY OF C L U & C H F C** AMERICAN SOCIETY OF CLU & CHFC Bryn Mawr, PA

**JOURNAL OF THE L A STATE MEDICAL SOCIETY** LOUISIANA STATE MEDICAL SOCIETY Metairie, LA

**JOURNAL-AMERICAN HELICOPTER SOCIETY** AMERICAN HELICOPTER SOCIETY, INC. Alexandria, VA

**JOURNAL, THE** METHODIST HOSPITAL, THE Houston, TX

**JOURNAL, THE** STONE & WEBSTER ENGINEERING CORP. Boston, MA

**JOURNEY** COCA-COLA COMPANY, THE Atlanta, GA

**JUST KIDS** CHILDREN'S HOSPITAL Omaha, NE

## K

**K G F FOCUS** KRAFT-GENERAL FOODS Northfield, IL

**K M NEWS** KERR-MCGEE CORPORATION Oklahoma City, OK

**K MERCHANTS** KMART CORPORATION Troy, MI

**K P L GAS SERVICE** KPL GAS SERVICE Topeka, KS

**K U B REPORTER:** KNOXVILLE UTILITIES BOARD Knoxville, TN

**KA LEO REFLECTIONS** ST. FRANCIS HOSPITAL Honolulu, HI

**KA MANU** REHABILITATION HOSPITAL OF THE PACIFIC Honolulu, HI

**KADYDID CHRONICLE** NESTLE-BEICH, INC. Wilmington, DE

**KALEIDOSCOPE** BLUE CROSS & BLUE SHIELD Columbia, SC

**KANSAS MAGAZINE** KANSAS DEPARTMENT OF COMMERCE Topeka, KS

**KANSAS OIL MARKETER** KANSAS OIL MARKETERS ASSOCIATION Topeka, KS

**KEEPING IN TOUCH** BERGEN BRUNSWICK CORP. Orange, CA

**KEEPING TABS** ESSELTE PENDAFLEX CORP. Garden City, NY

**KEITH SCHOOL NEWS** KEITH SCHOOL Rockford, IL

**KELLOGG NEWS** KELLOGG COMPANY Littleton, CO

**KENTUCKY JOURNAL OF COMMERCE & INDUSTRY** ASSOCIATED INDUSTRIES OF KENTUCKY Louisville, KY

**KENTUCKY TEACHER** KENTUCKY DEPARTMENT OF EDUCATION Frankfort, KY

**KEYNOTE** MONROE SYSTEMS FOR BUSINESS Morris Plains, NJ

**KEYNOTER** CNA INSURANCE Chicago, IL

**KEYTIPS** ILCO UNICAN CORP. Rocky Mount, NC

**KIDS HEALTH** CHILDREN'S HOSPITAL OF ORANGE COUNTY Orange, CA

**KIDSTUFF** CHILDREN'S HOSPITAL OF THE KING'S DAUGHTERS Norfolk, VA

**KIE-WAYS** PETER KIEWIT SONS, INC. Omaha, NE

**KINDRED SPIRIT** DALLAS THEOLOGICAL SEMINARY Dallas, TX

**KINNEY WORLD** KINNEY SHOE CORPORATION New York, NY

**KINSHIP** GLENMARY SISTERS Owensboro, KY

**KIRBY QUARTERLY** KIRBY CO. Cleveland, OH

**KOA DIRECTORY, ROAD ATLAS AND CAMPING GUIDE** KAMPGROUNDS OF AMERICA, INC. Billings, MT

**KOHLER SHOPPER** KOHLER CO. Kohler, WI

## L

**L & F TOPICS** L & F PRODUCTS Montvale, NJ

**L A C M A PHYSICIAN** LOS ANGELES COUNTY MEDICAL ASSOCIATION Los Angeles, CA

**L A OIL & GAS FACTS** LOUISIANA MID-CONTINENT OIL & GAS Baton Rouge, LA

**L B L CURRENTS, THE** LAWRENCE BERKELEY LABORATORY Berkeley, CA

**L B L RESEARCH REVIEW** LAWRENCE BERKELEY LABORATORY Berkeley, CA

**L I F E NEWSLETTER** ROBERT F. KENNEDY MEDICAL CENTER Hawthorne, CA

**L T T MAGAZINE** LINCOLN TELECOMMUNICATIONS CO. Lincoln, NE

**L T V TIMES** LTV STEEL-MINING CO. Hoyt Lakes, MN

**LAB NEWS** OAK RIDGE NATIONAL LABORATORY Oak Ridge, TN

**LACLEDE NEWS:** LACLEDE GAS COMPANY St. Louis, MO

**LAMINATOR, THE** RALPH WILSON PLASTICS CO. Temple, TX

**LAMPPOST** ORANGE & ROCKLAND UTILITIES, INC. Pearl River, NY

**LANDIS LINE** TELEDYNE, INC. Waynesboro, PA

**LAWRENCE TECHNOLOGICAL UNIVERSITY MAGAZINE** LAWRENCE TECHNOLOGICAL UNIVERSITY Southfield, MI

**LAWYERS TITLE NEWS** LAWYERS TITLE INSURANCE CORP. Richmond, VA

**LEADER DIGEST** LEADER FEDERAL SAVINGS & LOAN ASSOCIATION Memphis, TN

**LEADER, THE** CENTURY 21, REAL ESTATE CORP. Irvine, CA

**LEADER, THE** PRICE WATERHOUSE & CO. New York, NY

**LEADER'S LETTER** TENNESSEE ELECTRIC COOP ASSOCIATION Nashville, TN

**LEADERS' DIGEST** HONEYWELL, INC. Phoenix, AZ

**LEADING EDGE** RUSSELL HARRINGTON CUTLERY CO. Southbridge, MA

**LEADING TO EXCELLENCE** NORTHWESTERN NATIONAL INSURANCE GROUP Brookfield, WI

**LEAGUE UPDATE** CONNECTICUT CREDIT UNION LEAGUE Wallingford, CT

**LEAGUE UPDATE EXTRA** CONNECTICUT CREDIT UNION LEAGUE Wallingford, CT

**LEASE LINE** HICKORY FARMS OF OHIO INC. Maumee, OH

**LEDERLE HORIZONS** LEDERLE LABORATORIES DIV. Wayne, NJ

**LEGISLATIVE BULLETIN** ENVIRONMENTAL LOBBY OF MASSACHUSETTS Boston, MA

**LENNOX NEWS** LENNOX INDUSTRIES INC. Richardson, TX

**LENS** OLAN MILLS OF TENNESSEE Chattanooga, TN

**LET'S TALK** UNITED ILLUMINATING CO. New Haven, CT

**LETTER OF RECOGNITION** RECOGNITION INTERNATIONAL INC. Irving, TX

**LEWIS NEWS** NASA LEWIS RESEARCH CENTER Cleveland, OH

**LIFE HEALTH** CAROLINAS MEDICAL CENTER Charlotte, NC

**LIFE LINES** MONUMENTAL LIFE INS. CO. Baltimore, MD

**LIFELINE** PAN-AMERICAN LIFE INSURANCE CO. New Orleans, LA

**LIFELINES** ALLIANCE LIFE Minneapolis, MN

**LIFETIME** KANSAS CITY LIFE INSURANCE CO. Kansas City, MO

**LIGHT** BRAILLE INSTITUTE OF AMERICA, INC. Los Angeles, CA

**LIMELITE** U.S. AIR FORCE Loring AFB, ME

**LINE MARKER** WILLIAMS CO., THE Tulsa, OK

**LINES OF ARGUMENT** REDDY CORP. INTERNATIONAL Albuquerque, NM

**LINK** LITTON GUIDANCE & CONTROL SYSTEMS Woodland Hills, CA

**LITELINES:** COLUMBUS SOUTHERN POWER CO. Columbus, OH

**LOCOMOTIVE ENGINEERS NEWSLETTER** INTERNATIONAL BROTHERHOOD OF LOCOMOTIVE ENGINEERS Cleveland, OH

**LOG** COLUMBUS LIFE INSURANCE CO. Columbus, OH

**LONG ISLAND NEWS** UNISYS Great Neck, NY

**LOOKING AHEAD** NATIONAL EDUCATION PROGRAM Oklahoma City, OK

**LOOKING AHEAD** USG CORP. Chicago, IL

**LOOKING GLASS** NEWELL CO. Freeport, IL

**LOOKING IN** ANAHEIM MEMORIAL HOSPITAL Anaheim, CA

**LORDFACTS** LORD CORP. Erie, PA

**LOUISIANA BANKER** LOUISIANA BANKERS ASSOCIATION Baton Rouge, LA

**LOUISIANA PHARMACIST** LOUISIANA PHARMACISTS ASSOCIATION Baton Rouge, LA

**LUBRIZOL REPORTS** LUBRIZOL CORP. THE Wickliffe, OH

**LUKENS LIFE** LUKENS INC. Coatesville, PA

**LUMBER CO-OPERATOR** NORTHEASTERN RETAIL LUMBERMENS ASSOCIATION Rochester, NY

**LUTHERAN BROTHERHOOD BOND** LUTHERAN BROTHERHOOD Minneapolis, MN

## M

**M & T OBSERVER:** M & T BANK Buffalo, NY

**M A S C JOURNAL** MASSACHUSETTS ASSOCIATION OF SCHOOL COMMITTEES Boston, MA

**M A S C BULLETIN** MASSACHUSETTS ASSOCIATION OF SCHOOL COMMITTEES Boston, MA

**M C W ALUMNI NEWS** MEDICAL COLLEGE OF WISCONSIN Milwaukee, WI

**M D N A NEWS** MACHINERY DEALERS NATIONAL ASSOCIATION Silver Spring, MD

**M E S C MESSENGER** MICHIGAN EMPLOYMENT SECURITY COMMISSION Detroit, MI

**M G NEWS** MEDIA GENERAL Richmond, VA

**M H I REPORT** MANUFACTURED HOUSING INSTITUTE Arlington, VA

**M M D EXCHANGE** MARION MERRELL DOW INC. Cincinnati, OH

**M N C NOW** MNC FINANCIAL, INC. Baltimore, MD

**M S T A ACTION LINE** MARYLAND STATE TEACHERS ASSOCIATION Baltimore, MD

**M S U MANUAL OF PERSONNEL POLICIES AND PROGRAMS** MICHIGAN STATE UNIVERSITY East Lansing, MI

**MACK BULLDOG** MACK TRUCKS INC. Allentown, PA

**MACKTIVITIES** MACK TRUCKS INC. Allentown, PA

**MADISON AREA TRAVEL PLANNER & VISITORS GUIDE** GREATER MADISON CONVENTION & VISITORS BUREAU Madison, WI

**MAINE POTATO NEWS** MAINE POTATO BOARD Presque Isle, ME

**MALL STREET JOURNAL** PEACHTREE CENTER Atlanta, GA

**MANAGE MAGAZINE** NATIONAL MANAGEMENT ASSOCIATION Dayton, OH

**MANAGEMENT FOCUS** FIRST-CITIZENS BANK & TRUST CO. Raleigh, NC

**MANAGEMENT NEWS** SCHERING-PLOUGH CORP. Madison, NJ

**MANAGEMENT NEWSLETTER** SENTRY INSURANCE Stevens Point, WI

**MANAGEMENT PORTFOLIO** PRINTING INDUSTRIES OF AMERICA, INC. Alexandria, VA

**MANAGEMENT QUARTERLY** PUBLIC SERVICE ELECTRIC & GAS CO. Newark, NJ

**MANAGEMENT UPDATE** INDIANA CREDIT UNION LEAGUE, INC. Indianapolis, IN

**MANAGER'S JOURNAL** SAMARITAN HEALTH SERVICE Phoenix, AZ

**MANAGERS CALENDAR** RAYMOND CORP. Greene, NY

**MANAGERS MONTHLY** MUTUAL OF OMAHA COMPANIES Omaha, NE

**MANUFACTURED HOUSING QUARTERLY** MANUFACTURED HOUSING INSTITUTE Arlington, VA

**MANUFACTURING REPORT** MANUFACTURED HOUSING INSTITUTE Arlington, VA

**MARINE BRIEFS** GULF COAST RESEARCH LABORATORY Ocean Springs, MS

**MARKET ADMINISTRATOR'S BULLETIN** MILK MARKET ADMINISTRATOR Berkley, MI

**MARKET MONITOR** INTERNATIONAL COMMUNICATIONS INDUSTRIES ASSN., THE Fairfax, VA

**MARKET-EAR, THE** LAWYERS TITLE INSURANCE CORP. Richmond, VA

**MARKETEER** AMERICAN STORES CO. Salt Lake City, UT

**MARKETING MINUTE** UNION CENTRAL LIFE Cincinnati, OH

**MARKETING UPDATE** PHILLIPS PETROLEUM CO. Bartlesville, OK

**MARKETING UPDATE** SECURITY MUTUAL LIFE INSURANCE CO. OF NEW YORK Binghamton, NY

**MARLEY LEADER** MARLEY CO., THE Shawnee Mission, KS

**MARQUETTE** MARQUETTE UNIVERSITY Milwaukee, WI

**MARYKNOLL** CATHOLIC FOREIGN MISSION SOCIETY Maryknoll, NY

**MARYLAND AVENEWS** BROWN GROUP, INC. St. Louis, MO

**MASSMUTUAL NEWS** MASSACHUSETTS MUTUAL LIFE INSURANCE CO. Springfield, MA

**MASTER BUILDER** MASTER BUILDERS' ASSOCIATION OF WESTERN PA/AGC Pittsburgh, PA

**MASTER LOCK NEWS TODAY** MASTER LOCK CO. Milwaukee, WI

**MAYO TODAY** ST. MARYS HOSPITAL Rochester, MN

**MAYTAG MONTHLY BULLETIN** MAYTAG CO. Newton, IA

**MC CORMICK PEOPLE NEWSPAPER** MCCORMICK & CO., INC. Sparks Glenco, MD

**MC GRAW-HILL WORLD** MCGRAW-HILL INC. New York, NY

**MC KESSON TODAY** MCKESSON CORPORATION San Francisco, CA

**MEASURE** HEWLETT-PACKARD CO. Palo Alto, CA

**MED STAFF NEWS** CHILDREN'S HOSPITAL OF ORANGE COUNTY Orange, CA

**MED-A-NEWS** BLUE CROSS & BLUE SHIELD Columbia, SC

**MEDIA GENERAL ANNUAL REPORT** MEDIA GENERAL Richmond, VA

**MEDIA GUIDE** WOMEN'S INTERNATIONAL BOWLING CONGRESS Greendale, WI

**MEDIA REPORT TO WOMEN** COMMUNICATION RESEARCH ASSOCIATES, INC. Silver Spring, MD

**MEDICAL BULLETIN OF ST JOHN HOSPITAL:** SAINT JOHN HOSPITAL Detroit, MI

**MEDICAL REPORT** MOUNT SINAI MEDICAL CENTER Miami Beach, FL

**MEDICAL STAFF NEWS** BRYAN MEMORIAL HOSPITAL Lincoln, NE

**MEDICAL STAFF OUTLOOK** CALIFORNIA PACIFIC MEDICAL CENTER San Francisco, CA

**MEDICAL STAFF UPDATE** SAINT ANTHONY MEDICAL CENTER Rockford, IL

**MEDICARE BRIEFLY** BLUE CROSS & BLUE SHIELD Columbia, SC

**MEDICARE MATTERS** BLUE CROSS & BLUE SHIELD Columbia, SC

**MEDICARE MESSENGER** BLUE CROSS & BLUE SHIELD Columbia, SC

**MEDICINE & SCIENCE IN SPORTS & EXERCISE** AMERICAN COLLEGE OF SPORTS MEDICINE Indianapolis, IN

**MEDSTAFF NEWS** SETON MEDICAL CENTER Austin, TX

**MEMBERS LISTING IN SPOTLIGHT MAGAZINE** WLIW CHANNEL 21 Plainview, NY

**MEMBERSHIP DIRECTORY** GREATER WASHINGTON BOARD OF TRADE, THE Washington, DC

**MEMBERSHIP DIRECTORY** GREATER WINSTON-SALEM CHAMBER OF COMMERCE Winston Salem, NC

**MEMBERSHIP DIRECTORY** METROPOLITAN MILWAUKEE ASSOCIATION OF COMMERCE Milwaukee, WI

**MEMBERSHIP DIRECTORY-BUYERS GUIDE** AMERICAN ROAD & TRANSPORTATION BUILDERS ASSOCIATION Washington, DC

**MEMO** AUTO-OWNERS INSURANCE Lansing, MI

**MEMO** ROCKFORD MEMORIAL HOSPITAL Rockford, IL

**MEMORIAL MERCURY** LONG BEACH MEMORIAL MEDICAL CENTER Long Beach, CA

**MENTOR LIFT-LINES** CATERPILLAR INDUSTRIAL, INC. Mentor, OH

**MERCHANDISER** AMOCO CORPORATION Chicago, IL

**MERCHANDISER MAGAZINE** MAYTAG CO. Newton, IA

**MERCK WORLD** MERCK & CO., INC. Whitehouse Station, NJ

**MERCURY** LAACO, INC. Los Angeles, CA

**MERCY LIFE** MERCY MEDICAL CENTER Baltimore, MD

**MERCY PHYSICIAN, THE** MERCY MEDICAL CENTER Baltimore, MD

**MERCY TODAY** MERCY MEDICAL CENTER Baltimore, MD

**MESSENGER** MERCHANTS INSURANCE GROUP Buffalo, NY

**MESSENGER** SALEM HOSPITAL Salem, OR

**MESSENGER, THE** SHAWNEE MISSION PUBLIC SCHOOLS Shawnee Mission, KS

**MESSENGER, THE** ST. PATRICK HOSPITAL Missoula, MT

**METER** OKLAHOMA GAS & ELECTRIC CO. Oklahoma City, OK

**METHODIST HOSPITAL HAPPENINGS** METHODIST HOSPITAL, THE Houston, TX

**METRO'S PLUS BUSINESS** METRO CREATIVE GRAPHICS, INC. New York, NY

**METROPOLITAN BEAUMONT** BEAUMONT CHAMBER OF COMMERCE Beaumont, TX

**MIAMI SYSTEMS FAMILY NEWS & PEOPLE REPORT** MIAMI SYSTEMS-SHELBY DIVISION Shelby, OH

**MICHAEL REESE NEWS** MICHAEL REESE HOSPITAL & MEDICAL CENTER Chicago, IL

**MICHELIN RADIAL TIMES** MICHELIN NORTH AMERICA, INC. Greenville, SC

**MICHIGAN MILK MESSENGER** MICHIGAN MILK PRODUCERS ASSOCIATION Novi, MI

**MICHIGRAM, THE** STATE FARM MUTUAL AUTO INSURANCE CO. Marshall, MI

**MICROSCOPE** WAKE MEDICAL CENTER Raleigh, NC

**MID-AM PROCESSOR (FOR EMPLOYEES)** MID-AMERICA DAIRYMEN INC. Springfield, MO

**MID-AM REPORTER** MID-AMERICA DAIRYMEN INC. Springfield, MO

**MIDLANTIC TODAY** MIDLANTIC CORPORATION Edison, NJ

**MIDSOUTHWEST RESTAURANT MAGAZINE** OKLAHOMA RESTAURANT ASSOCIATION Oklahoma City, OK

**MIDWEEK** QUAKER OATS CO. Chicago, IL

**MIDWEST FOCUS** MIDWEST RESEARCH INSTITUTE Kansas City, MO

**MIDWEST REGION NEWSLINE** GTE TELEPHONE OPERATIONS Wentzville, MO

**MIGHTY TO MINI NEWS** AMERICAN HONDA MOTOR CO., INC. Torrance, CA

**MILKY WAY** CUMBERLAND FARMS, INC. Canton, MA

**MILLER HIGH-LITES** MILLER BREWING CO. Milwaukee, WI

**MILLWHEEL** LAKE ERIE GIRL SCOUT COUNCIL Cleveland, OH

**MILLWIDE MONITOR** GEORGIA-PACIFIC CORP., BRUNSWICK OPERATIONS Brunswick, GA

**MILTON BRADLEY NEWS** MILTON BRADLEY CO. East Longmeadow, MA

**MILWAUKEE COMMERCE HOTLINE** METROPOLITAN MILWAUKEE ASSOCIATION OF COMMERCE Milwaukee, WI

**MINER DETAILS:** BUCYRUS-ERIE CO. South Milwaukee, WI

**MINIVIEWS** ROBERT F. KENNEDY MEDICAL CENTER Hawthorne, CA

**MINUTE** KELLY-SPRINGFIELD TIRE CO. Cumberland, MD

**MISSISSIPPI MESSAGES** STATE DEPARTMENT OF EDUCATION Jackson, MS

**MISSISSIPPI REVIEW OF OUTDOOR** EDUCATION & RESEARCH CTR. OF MISSISSIPPI Jackson, MS

**MISSOURI FARM BUREAU NEWS** MISSOURI FARM BUREAU FEDERATION Jefferson, MO

**MITRE MATTERS** MITRE CORP. Bedford, MA

**MIXING BOWL, THE** MIRRO CORP. Manitowoc, WI

**MOBIL WORLD** MOBIL OIL CORP. Fairfax, VA

**MOMENTOM** SACHS PROPERTIES, INC. Chesterfield, MO

**MONARCH FIELD NEWS** MONARCH CAPITAL CORP. Springfield, MA

**MONARCH NEWS** MONARCH CAPITAL CORP. Springfield, MA

**MONDAKONIA** MDU RESOURCES GROUP, INC. Bismarck, ND

**MONDAY MORNING** FIRST INTERSTATE BANCORP. Los Angeles, CA

**MONDAY MORNING MEMO** ROCK VALLEY COLLEGE Rockford, IL

**MONITOR** COMMUNITY MEDICAL CENTER Scranton, PA

**MONONGAHELA NEWS** MONONGAHELA POWER CO. Fairmont, WV

**MONROE LA-Z-NEWS** LA-Z-BOY CHAIR CO. Monroe, MI

**MONTANA JOURNALISM REVIEW** UNIVERSITY OF MONTANA SCHOOL OF JOURNALISM Missoula, MT

**MONTHLY COMMUNICATIONS** TOLEDO EDISON CO. Toledo, OH

**MONTHLY EMPLOYEE NEWSLETTER** NAVAJO TRIBAL UTILITY AUTHORITY Fort Defiance, AZ

**MORBARK REPORT** MORBARK INDUSTRIES INC. Winn, MI

**MORGAN NEWS, THE** MORGAN GUARANTY TRUST CO. OF N.Y. New York, NJ

**MORGAN TODAY** MORGAN GUARANTY TRUST CO. OF N.Y. New York, NJ

**MORSE CODE** MORSE SHOE, INC. Canton, MA

**MOSBY TIMES** MOSBY-YEAR BOOK, INC. St. Louis, MO

**MOTORS NEWS** GE Fort Wayne, IN

**MOUNTAIN STATE** MOUNTAIN STATE BLUE CROSS & BLUE SHIELD Parkersburg, WV

**MP & L NEWS** MISSISSIPPI POWER & LIGHT CO. Jackson, MS

**MRINSIDE** MIDWEST RESEARCH INSTITUTE Kansas City, MO

**MULTILINER** FEDERATED INSURANCE COS. Owatonna, MN

**MURPHY NEWS** MURPHY OIL CORPORATION El Dorado, AR

**MUSEUM OF SCIENCE NEWSLETTER** MUSEUM OF SCIENCE Boston, MA

**MUSTANG NEWS CONNECTION** MUSTANG FUEL CORP. Oklahoma City, OK

**MUTUAL MAGAZINE, THE** MUTUAL BENEFICIAL ASSN. OF RAILROAD TRANSPORTATION EMPLOYEES Philadelphia, PA

# N

**N A W C C MART** NATIONAL ASSOCIATION OF WATCH & CLOCK COLLECTORS Columbia, PA

**N B C NOTES** NATIONAL BANK OF COMMERCE Memphis, TN

**N B D CONNECTIONS** NBD BANK Indianapolis, IN

**N B D NEWS** NATIONAL BANK OF DETROIT Detroit, MI

**N B D: INDIANAPOLIS REGION REPORT** NBD BANK Indianapolis, IN

**N C B A COOPERATIVE BUSINESS JOURNAL** NATIONAL COOPERATIVE BUSINESS ASSOCIATION Washington, DC

**N E A TODAY** NATIONAL EDUCATION ASSOCIATION Washington, DC

**N E S NEWS** NASHVILLE ELECTRIC SERVICE Nashville, TN

**N F G TODAY** RJR NABISCO, NABISCO FOODS GROUP Parsippany, NJ

**N M NEWS** NIAGARA MOHAWK POWER CORP. Syracuse, NY

**N S F R E JOURNAL** NATIONAL SOCIETY OF FUND RAISING EXECUTIVES Alexandria, VA

**N W D A EXECUTIVE NEWSLETTER** NATIONAL WHOLESALE DRUGGISTS' ASSOCIATION Reston, VA

**N Y L I C REVIEW** NEW YORK LIFE INSURANCE CO. New York, NY

**N-W: INTERNAL COMMUNICATIONS** NEWSWEEK New York, NY

**NACDS FEDERAL REPORT** NATIONAL ASSOCIATION OF CHAIN DRUG STORES Alexandria, VA

**NALCO NEWS** NALCO CHEMICAL CO. Naperville, IL

**NALLEVENTS** NALLEYS FINE FOODS Tacoma, WA

**NASH REPORTER** NASH ENGINEERING CO. Trumbull, CT

**NATIONAL ASSOCIATION OF HOME & WORKSHOP WRITERS** NATIONAL ASSOCIATION OF HOME & WORKSHOP WRITERS NEWSLETTER Palomar Mountain, CA

**NATIONAL ASSOCIATION OF RAILROAD PASSENGERS NEWS** NATIONAL ASSOCIATION OF RAILROAD PASSENGERS Washington, DC

**NATIONAL GLEANER FORUM** GLEANER LIFE INSURANCE SOCIETY Adrian, MI

**NATIONAL NEWS** AMERICAN LEGION AUXILIARY Indianapolis, IN

**NATIONAL'S COMPASS** NATIONAL STARCH & CHEMICAL CO. Bridgewater, NJ

**NATIONS BANK TIMES** NATIONS BANK CORP. Charlotte, NC

**NATIONWIDE DIVIDEND** NATIONWIDE INSURANCE Columbus, OH

**NEBRASKA DEVELOPMENT NEWSLETTER** NEBRASKA DEPT. OF ECONOMIC DEVELOPMENT Lincoln, NE

**NEBRASKA DIRECTORY OF MANUFACTURERS** NEBRASKA DEPT. OF ECONOMIC DEVELOPMENT Lincoln, NE

**NEEDLE, THE** RAYMOND CORP. Greene, NY

**NEESPAPER** NEW ENGLAND ELECTRIC SYSTEM Westborough, MA

**NEIGHBORS MAGAZINE** ALABAMA FARMERS FEDERATION Montgomery, AL

**NELPA NEWS** NORTHWEST ELECTRIC LIGHT & POWER ASSOCIATION Portland, OR

**NESTLE U S A 2000** NESTLE USA, INC. Glendale, CA

**NETWORK** ALLEN-BRADLEY CO. Milwaukee, WI

**NETWORK** NATIONAL SCHOOL PUBLIC RELATIONS ASSOCIATION Arlington, VA

**NETWORK** NORWEST FINANCIAL, INC. Des Moines, IA

**NETWORK** SEATTLE CITY LIGHT Seattle, WA

**NETWORK** SENTARA HEALTH SYSTEM Norfolk, VA

**NETWORK** UTAH POWER, A DIVISION OF PACIFICORP, OREGON Salt Lake City, UT

**NETWORK NEWS** EASTER SEAL SOCIETY OF WISCONSIN, INC. Madison, WI

**NEVADA EVENTS** NEVADA COMMISSION ON TOURISM Carson City, NV

**NEW DETROIT NOW** NEW DETROIT, INC. Detroit, MI

**NEW DIRECTIONS** FLEET FINANCIAL GROUP, INC. Providence, RI

**NEW ENGLAND PRINTER & PUBLISHER** NEW ENGLAND PRINTER & PUBLISHER INC. Salem, NH

**NEW FARM, THE** NEW FARM MAGAZINE Emmaus, PA

**NEW HORIZONS** COMMERCIAL UNION INS. CO. Boston, MA

**NEW HORIZONS** EASTERN NEBRASKA OFFICE ON AGING Omaha, NE

**NEW HORIZONS** FLORIDA HORIZONS FEDERAL CREDIT UNION Homestead, FL

**NEW JERSEY LAWYER** N.J. STATE BAR ASSN. New Brunswick, NJ

**NEW ORLEANS REVIEW** LOYOLA UNIVERSITY New Orleans, LA

**NEW YORK LIFE NEWS** NEW YORK LIFE INSURANCE CO. New York, NY

**NEW YORK STATE DENTAL JOURNAL** DENTAL SOCIETY OF THE STATE OF NEW YORK Albany, NY

**NEWS** BARNES GROUP, INC. Bristol, CT

**NEWS** CONSOLIDATED PAPERS, INC. Wisconsin Rapids, WI

**NEWS** HORMEL FOODS CORP. Austin, MN

**NEWS** LIBRARY OF CONGRESS Washington, DC

**NEWS & REVIEW** MINING & SPECIALTY EQUIP. DIV. OF INDRESCO, INC., MARION OPERATIONS Marion, OH

**NEWS & VIEWS** ACACIA GROUP, THE Washington, DC

**NEWS & VIEWS** CPI CORP. St. Louis, MO

**NEWS & VIEWS** MARQUETTE UNIVERSITY Milwaukee, WI

**NEWS & VIEWS** SOUTHERN CONNECTICUT GAS CO. Bridgeport, CT

**NEWS BEEPS** SHERWOOD MEDICAL CO. St. Louis, MO

**NEWS BULLETIN** NATIONAL ASSOCIATION OF PHARMACEUTICAL MANUFACTURERS New York, NY

**NEWS CIRCUIT** ANALOG DEVICES, INC. Norwood, MA

**NEWS FOR DAIRY COOPS** NATIONAL MILK PRODUCERS FEDERATION Arlington, VA

**NEWS FROM ARKANSAS, THE NATURAL STATE** ARKANSAS DEPARTMENT OF PARKS & TOURISM Little Rock, AR

**NEWS LETTER** PIGGLY WIGGLY CORP. Memphis, TN

**NEWS LETTER** WESTVACO CORP. Covington, VA

**NEWS LINE** GREATER WINSTON-SALEM CHAMBER OF COMMERCE Winston Salem, NC

**NEWS LINES** COLUMBIA GAS TRANSMISSION CORP. Charleston, WV

**NEWS PIX** NEW YORK DAILY New York, NY

**NEWS PRINT** JOURNAL COMMUNICATIONS Milwaukee, WI

**NEWS WHEEL** GOVERNMENT EMPLOYEES INSURANCE CO. Washington, DC

**NEWSACCOUNT** COLORADO SOCIETY OF CERTIFIED PUBLIC ACCOUNTANTS Denver, CO

**NEWSBREAK** UTAH POWER, A DIVISION OF PACIFICORP, OREGON Salt Lake City, UT

**NEWSBRIEFS** DENTAL SOCIETY OF THE STATE OF NEW YORK Albany, NY

**NEWSBULLETIN** LOS ALMOS NATIONAL LABORATORY Los Alamos, NM

**NEWSCASTER** CORAL GABLES FEDERAL SAVINGS & LOAN ASSOCIATION Miami, FL

**NEWSCLIPS** RESEARCH MEDICAL CENTER Kansas City, MO

**NEWSCLIPS** TRINITY LUTHERAN HOSPITAL Kansas City, MO

**NEWSLETTER** AMERICAN DIABETES ASSOCIATION Santa Ana, CA

**NEWSLETTER** SPACE COAST DISABILITY RIGHTS ASSOCIATION Coco Beach, FL

**NEWSLETTER** THOMPSON INTERNATIONAL, INC. Henderson, KY

**NEWSLETTER** UNIVERSITY CIRCLE INC. Cleveland, OH

**NEWSLINE** ATLANTIC CITY ELECTRIC CO. Pleasantville, NJ

**NEWSLINE** FIRST INTERSTATE BANK OF DENVER Denver, CO

**NEWSLINE** GRACO INC. Minneapolis, MN

**NEWSLINE** GTE SOUTH Durham, NC

**NEWSLINE** SHAWNEE MISSION PUBLIC SCHOOLS Shawnee Mission, KS

**NEWSLINE** TAMPA ELECTRIC CO. Tampa, FL

**NEWSLINES** PHOENIX HOME LIFE INSURANCE CO. Hartford, CT

**NEWSLINES ON THE LINE** LINN COUNTY RURAL ELECTRIC COOPERATIVE ASSOCIATION Marion, IA

**NEWSLOG** ASSOCIATED CHURCH PRESS Grand Rapids, MI

**NEWSMAKERS** LOMAS FINANCIAL CORP. Dallas, TX

**NEWSORAMA** KINGSBROOK JEWISH MEDICAL CENTER Brooklyn, NY

**NEXUS** INDIANA CREDIT UNION LEAGUE, INC. Indianapolis, IN

**NIAGARA MOHAWK UPDATE** NIAGARA MOHAWK POWER CORP. Syracuse, NY

**NIPSCOFOLKS** NORTHERN INDIANA PUBLIC SERVICE CO. Hammond, IN

**NITTY GRITTY:** GARDEN CITY HOSPITAL Garden City, MI

**NOLAND NEWS** NOLAND CO. Newport News, VA

**NOON NEWS** HARNISCHFEGER INDUSTRIES, INC. Milwaukee, WI

**NORFOLK SOUTHERN WORLD** NORFOLK SOUTHERN CORP. Norfolk, VA

**NORTH CENTRAL MANAGER** STATE FARM MUTUAL AUTO INSURANCE CO. St. Paul, MN

**NORTH NEWS** GTE NORTH Johnstown, NY

**NORTHBOUND** TREES FOR TOMMORROW INC., NATURAL RESOURCES EDUCATION Eagle River, WI

**NORTHERN NEWS** NORTHERN TRUST CO. Chicago, IL

**NORTHROP-GRUMMAN NEWS** NORTHROP-GRUMMAN CORP. Hawthorne, CA

**NORTHWEST BANKER** FIRST INTERSTATE BANK OF NORTHWEST REGION Portland, OR

**NORTHWEST DISCOVERY** NORTHWEST PIPELINE CORP. Salt Lake Cty, UT

**NORTHWEST ELECTRIC UTILITY DIRECTORY** NORTHWEST PUBLIC POWER ASSOCIATION Vancouver, WA

**NORTHWEST PASSAGES** NORTHWEST AIRLINES, INC. Eagan, MN

**NORTHWEST PUBLIC POWER BULLETIN** NORTHWEST PUBLIC POWER ASSOCIATION Vancouver, WA

**NORWEST WORLD** NORWEST CORPORATION Minneapolis, MN

**NOTES** NATIONS BANK CORP. Charlotte, NC

**NURSE CHRONICLE** CHILDREN'S HOSPITAL OF ORANGE COUNTY Orange, CA

## O

**O M C CURRENTS** OUTBOARD MARINE CORP. Waukegan, IL

**O N L I ECHOES** OHIO NATIONAL LIFE INSURANCE CO. Cincinnati, OH

**O T WEEK** AMERICAN OCCUPATIONAL THERAPY ASSOCIATION Rockville, MD

**O T C TODAY** OTC DIVISION OF SPX Owatonna, MN

**O-K NEWS** CINCINNATI GAS & ELECTRIC CO. Cincinnati, OH

**OAN DIGGER** OREGON ASSOCIATION OF NURSERYMEN Milwaukie, OR

**OAN DIRECTORY & BUYER'S GUIDE** OREGON ASSOCIATION OF NURSERYMEN Milwaukie, OR

**OASIS: SOCIAL SECURITY ADMINISTRATION** Baltimore, MD

**OCCUPATIONAL HEALTH & SAFETY NEWS** STEVENS PUBLISHING CORP. Waco, TX

**OHA HARD LINES** OHIO HARDWARE ASSOCIATION Columbus, OH

**OHA MEMBERSHIP DIRECTORY** OHIO HARDWARE ASSOCIATION Columbus, OH

**OHIO CHAMBER NETWORK & SMALL BUSINESS NEWS** OHIO CHAMBER OF COMMERCE Columbus, OH

**OHIO EDISONIAN** OHIO EDISON CO. Akron, OH

**OHIO GOVERNMENT DIRECTORY** OHIO TRUCKING ASSOCIATION Columbus, OH

**OHIO LEGISLATIVE REPORT** OHIO CHAMBER OF COMMERCE Columbus, OH

**OHIO MONITOR** OHIO BUREAU OF WORKER'S COMPENSATION Columbus, OH

**OHIO PHARMACIST** OHIO PHARMACISTS ASSOCIATION Dublin, OH

**OHIO POWER REVIEW** OHIO POWER CO. Canton, OH

**OHIO REALTOR** OHIO ASSOCIATION OF REALTORS Columbus, OH

**OHIO STATE MEDICAL JOURNAL** OHIO STATE MEDICAL ASSOCIATION Columbus, OH

**OHSU VIEWS** OREGON HEALTH SCIENCES UNIVERSITY Portland, OR

**OIL & IRON** COOPER OIL, TOOL DIV. Houston, TX

**OIL PROGRESS** CALTEX PETROLEUM CORP. Dallas, TX

**OKLAHOMA BANKER** OKLAHOMA BANKERS ASSOCIATION Oklahoma City, OK

**OKLAHOMA BAR JOURNAL** OKLAHOMA BAR ASSOCIATION Oklahoma City, OK

**OKLAHOMA LIVING** OKLAHOMA ASSOCIATION OF ELECTRIC COOPERATIVES Oklahoma City, OK

**OLDS LINE** OLDSMOBILE/DIV. GENERAL MOTORS Lansing, MI

**OMAHA PROFILE** GREATER OMAHA CHAMBER OF COMMERCE Omaha, NE

**OMARK 80** BLOUNT, INC. Montgomery, AL

**ON CALL** MERCY HOSPITAL, INC. Charlotte, NC

**ON CENTER** ST. LUKE'S-ROOSEVELT HOSPITAL CENTER New York, NY

**ON CUE** QUALITY STORES, INC. N. Muskegon, MI

**ON LINE WITH BENTON** BENTON CITY ELECTRIC COOPERATIVE ASSOCIATION Vinton, IA

**ON LOCATION** SIGNET BANKING CORP. Richmond, VA

**ON MAGAZINE** ARKANSAS POWER & LIGHT CO. Little Rock, AR
**ON STREAM** JACOBS ENGINEERING Baton Rouge, LA
**ON STREAM** QUESTAR CORPORATION Salt Lake City, UT
**ON THE MOVE** NATIONAL CITY CORP. Cleveland, OH
**ON THE MOVE** SAFECO INSURANCE CO. Seattle, WA
**ON THE SCENE** ST. PAUL PIONEER PRESS DISPATCH Saint Paul, MN
**ON-LINE** JERSEY CENTRAL POWER & LIGHT CO. Morristown, NJ
**ON-LINE** KOHLER CO. Kohler, WI
**ON-LINE** NORWEST FINANCIAL, INC. Des Moines, IA
**ON-SITE** NALCO CHEMICAL CO. Naperville, IL
**ONAN NEWS** ONAN CORP. Minneapolis, MN
**ONE NALCO CENTER** NALCO CHEMICAL CO. Naperville, IL
**OPEN LINE** AMERICAN OLEAN TILE CO. Lansdale, PA
**OPEN LINE** COMMONWEALTH LIFE INSURANCE CO. Louisville, KY
**OPERATIONS NEWS** RAX RESTAURANTS INC. Dublin, OH
**OPTIMIST MAGAZINE** OPTIMIST INTERNATIONAL St. Louis, MO
**ORBITER** AEROSPACE CORP. Los Angeles, CA
**ORCHID ISLE AUTO CENTER NEWSLETTER** ORCHID ISLE AUTO CTR. Hilo, HI
**OREGON STATER** OREGON STATE UNIVERSITY Corvallis, OR
**OREGON-IZER** BLOUNT, INC. Montgomery, AL
**ORYX OUTLOOK** ORYX ENERGY CO. Dallas, TX
**OSHA WEEK** STEVENS PUBLISHING CORP. Waco, TX
**OTIS BULLETIN** OTIS ELEVATOR CO. Farmington, CT
**OTIS MAGAZINE** OTIS ELEVATOR CO. Farmington, CT
**OUR ANIMALS** SAN FRANCISCO SPCA San Francisco, CA
**OUR HOUSE** UNITED METHODIST PUBLISHING HOUSE, THE Nashville, TN
**OUR NEWS - CITY EMPLOYEES NEWSLETTER** CITY OF RICHMOND VIRGINIA Richmond, VA
**OUR PEOPLE** IOWA-ILLINOIS GAS & ELECTRIC CO. Davenport, IA
**OUR WORLD** MAGIC CHEF COMPANY Cleveland, TN
**OUTLET** PUGET SOUND POWER & LIGHT CO. Bellevue, WA
**OUTLOOK** BANKERS SECURITY LIFE INSURANCE SOCIETY Arlington, VA
**OUTLOOK** COPPERWELD-SHELBY DIV. Shelby, OH
**OUTLOOK** FARMLAND INSURANCE COMPANIES Des Moines, IA
**OUTLOOK** KONICA BUSINESS MACHINES U.S.A., INC. Windsor, CT
**OUTLOOK** METHODIST HOSPITALS OF DALLAS Dallas, TX
**OUTLOOK** PITNEY BOWES, INC. Stamford, CT
**OUTLOOK** UTAH STATE UNIVERSITY Logan, UT
**OVER THE WIRES** CENTRAL LINCOLN PEOPLE'S UTILITY DISTRICT Newport, OR
**OZONE NEWSLETTER** OZONE INDUSTRIES INC. Jamaica, NY

## P

**P B L BUSINESS LEADER** FUTURE BUSINESS LEADERS OF AMERICA-PHI BETA LAMBDA Reston, VA
**P E T A'S ANIMAL TIMES** PEOPLE FOR THE ETHICAL TREATMENT OF ANIMALS (PETA) Washington, DC
**P G & E WEEK** PACIFIC GAS & ELECTRIC CO. San Francisco, CA
**P G W NEWSLINE** PHILADELPHIA GAS WORKS Philadelphia, PA
**P M A BULLETIN** PHARMACEUTICAL MANUFACTURERS ASSOCIATION Washington, DC
**P M A NEWSLETTER** PHARMACEUTICAL MANUFACTURERS ASSOCIATION Washington, DC
**P M E A NEWS** PENNSYLVANIA MUSIC EDUCATORS ASSOCIATION West Chester, PA
**P N C BANK NEWS** PNC BANK Pittsburgh, PA
**P N G TODAY** PEOPLES NATURAL GAS CO. Pittsburgh, PA
**P S CO TIMES** PUBLIC SERVICE CO. OF COLORADO Denver, CO

**P S E & G NEWS** PUBLIC SERVICE ELECTRIC & GAS CO. Newark, NJ
**P T A TODAY** NATIONAL PTA Chicago, IL
**P U L** SAN DIEGO MUNICIPAL EMPLOYEES ASSOCIATION San Diego, CA
**P W C BAYGRAM** NAVY PUBLIC WORKS CENTER SAN FRANCISCO BAY Oakland, CA
**PACE MAGAZINE** PACE UNIVERSITY New York, NY
**PACE 55** AMERICAN STORES CO. Salt Lake City, UT
**PACEMAKER** AKRON CITY HOSPITAL Akron, OH
**PACEMAKER** TARRANT COUNTY HOSPITAL DISTRICT Fort Worth, TX
**PACEMAKER** UNIVERSITY OF IOWA HOSPITALS & CLINICS Iowa City, IA
**PACESETTER** SOUTHERN STATES COOPERATIVE Richmond, VA
**PACESETTERS** MUTUAL OF OMAHA COMPANIES Omaha, NE
**PAGE 317 E. CAPITOL** LAMAR LIFE INSURANCE CO. Jackson, MS
**PAGER** ST. JOHN MEDICAL CENTER Tulsa, OK
**PANAKO** FIRST HAWAIIAN, INC. Honolulu, HI
**PANORAMA** DALLAS LIGHTHOUSE FOR THE BLIND, INC. Dallas, TX
**PAPER & PEOPLE** GEORGIA-PACIFIC CORP. Port Edwards, WI
**PAPER NEWS** GEORGIA-PACIFIC CORP. Port Edwards, WI
**PARA-SCOPE** PARAGON ELECTRIC COMPANY, INC. Two Rivers, WI
**PARK NOTES** CHICAGO PARK DISTRICT Chicago, IL
**PARKS TODAY** PARKS COLLEGE OF ST. LOUIS UNIVERSITY Cahokia, IL
**PARTS BUSINESS** BILL COMMUNICATIONS, INC. New York, NY
**PARTS PUPS** GENUINE PARTS CO., INC. Atlanta, GA
**PATHWAYS** UNITED TELEPHONE CO. OF OHIO Mansfield, OH
**PAYDAY** NATIONAL STEEL CORP. Mishawaka, IN
**PEDIATRIC FORUM** CHILDREN'S MEDICAL CENTER Dayton, OH
**PEDIATRIC PROGRESS** CHILDREN'S HOSPITAL OF THE KING'S DAUGHTERS Norfolk, VA
**PEN CATALOG** ARTHUR BROWN & BROS., INC. New York, NY
**PEN OF I N C O** INCO UNITED STATES, INC. New York, NY
**PEN POINTS** SHEAFFER, INC. Fort Madison, IA
**PENETRANT PROGRESS** SHERWIN, INC. South Gate, CA
**PENN POWER NEWS** PENNSYLVANIA POWER CO. New Castle, PA
**PENNSYLVANIA LAWYER, THE** PENNSYLVANIA BAR ASSOCIATION Harrisburg, PA
**PENNSYLVANIA MEDICINE** PENNSYLVANIA MEDICAL SOCIETY Harrisburg, PA
**PENNTRUX** PENNSYLVANIA MOTOR TRUCK ASSOCIATION Camp Hill, PA
**PEOPLE** KOHLER CO. Kohler, WI
**PEOPLE 'N PRIDE** GENERAL MOTORS CORP.-U.A.W. Flint, MI
**PEOPLE'S NEWSLETTER** PEOPLE'S BANK Bridgeport, CT
**PEP TALK** UNION CENTRAL LIFE Cincinnati, OH
**PEP-PROGRAM EMPLOYEE PARTICIPATION** SANTEE COOPER Moncks Corner, SC
**PEPCO COMMUNICATOR, THE** POTOMAC ELECTRIC POWER CO. Washington, DC
**PEPP TALK** PEPPERIDGE FARM, INC. Norwalk, CT
**PEPSI SPIRIT** PEPSI-COLA CO. Somers, NY
**PERCEPRION** MDU RESOURCES GROUP, INC. Bismarck, ND
**PERINI PAGES** PERINI CORP. Framingham, MA
**PERINI SECOND CENTURY** PERINI CORP. Framingham, MA
**PERSONAL TOUCH** MARSHALL & ILSLEY BANK Milwaukee, WI
**PERSPECTIVE** MSI INSURANCE Arden Hills, MN
**PERSPECTIVE** MUTUAL TRUST LIFE INSURANCE CO. Oak Brook, IL
**PERSPECTIVE** PEPPERIDGE FARM, INC. Norwalk, CT
**PERSPECTIVE** PRUDENTIAL INSURANCE CO. OF AMERICA Newark, NJ
**PERSPECTIVE** STA-RITE INDUSTRIES Delavan, WI

**PERSPECTIVES** IN-PLANT MANAGEMENT ASSOCIATION Liberty, MO
**PERSPECTIVES** OREGON PUBLIC EMPLOYEES RETIREMENT SYSTEM Portland, OR
**PERSPECTIVES** PECO ENERGY COMPANY Philadelphia, PA
**PERSPECTIVES** PENNZOIL CO. Houston, TX
**PFIZER SCENE** PFIZER, INC. New York, NY
**PHILADELPHIA BAR REPORTER, THE** PHILADELPHIA BAR ASSOCIATION Philadelphia, PA
**PHILADELPHIA LAWYER, THE** PHILADELPHIA BAR ASSOCIATION Philadelphia, PA
**PHILLIPS U S A EXPRESS, THE** PHILLIPS CONSUMER ELECTRONICS CORP. Greeneville, TN
**PHILNEWS** PHILLIPS PETROLEUM CO. Bartlesville, OK
**PHOS PHOLKS** CARGILL FERTILIZER, INC. Riverview, FL
**PHOTOMARKET** PHOTOSOURCE INTERNATIONAL Osceola, WI
**PHYSICAL THERAPY** AMERICAN PHYSICAL THERAPY ASSOCIATION, INC. Alexandria, VA
**PHYSICIAN DIRECTORY** BLUE CROSS & BLUE SHIELD OF WEST VIRGINIA, INC. Charleston, WV
**PHYSICIAN RESOURCE** GOOD SAMARITAN HOSPITAL AND HEALTH CENTER Dayton, OH
**PHYSICIAN'S NEWS** LIMA MEMORIAL HOSPITAL Lima, OH
**PIFELINES** PRINTING INDUSTRIES OF AMERICA, INC. Alexandria, VA
**PILLSBURY TODAY** PILLSBURY CO., THE Minneapolis, MN
**PILOT** SOUTHERN CONNECTICUT GAS CO. Bridgeport, CT
**PINE TORCH, THE** PINEY WOODS COUNTRY LIFE SCHOOL Piney Woods, MS
**PINE-AIRE** STATE FARM MUTUAL AUTO INSURANCE CO. St. Paul, MN
**PINELLAS PEN** PINELLAS COUNTY GOVERNMENT Clearwater, FL
**PIONEER** GIRL SCOUT COUNCIL OF GREATER MINNEAPOLIS Minneapolis, MN
**PIONEERING** PIONEER MUTUAL LIFE INSURANCE CO. Fargo, ND
**PIPE LINES** PANHANDLE EASTERN CORP. Houston, TX
**PIPE PROGRESS** AMERICAN CAST IRON PIPE COMPANY Birmingham, AL
**PIPELINE** DENVER WATER BOARD Denver, CO
**PIPELINE** NORTH WESTERN NATIONAL LIFE Minneapolis, MN
**PIPELINER** EL PASO NATURAL GAS CO. El Paso, TX
**PIPER MARKET DIGEST** PIPER JAFFRAY Minneapolis, MN
**PIREPS** STATE OF NEBRASKA Lincoln, NE
**PITCH PIPE, THE** SWEET ADELINES INTERNATIONAL Tulsa, OK
**PITMAN RECORD** CBS, INC. New York, NY
**PITTSBURGH FACTORY NEWS** HEINZ U.S.A. Pittsburgh, PA
**PIZZA HUT TODAY** PIZZA HUT, INC. Wichita, KS
**PLAINTALK** WISCO INDUSTRIES INC. Oregon, WI
**PLANNING AND ACTION** FEDERATION FOR COMMUNITY PLANNING Cleveland, OH
**PLUMBLINE** KOHLER CO. Kohler, WI
**PO'OKELA** ALEXANDER & BALDWIN, INC. Honolulu, HI
**POINT** SENTRY INSURANCE Stevens Point, WI
**POINT OF VIEW** ETHICON INC. Somerville, NJ
**POINTER, THE** GREEN POINT SAVINGS BANK Flushing, NY
**POINTERS MAGAZINE** OHIO CASUALTY INSURANCE GROUP, THE Hamilton, OH
**POLICE JOURNAL** ST. LOUIS POLICE DEPARTMENT St. Louis, MO
**PORT OF BALTIMORE MAGAZINE** MARYLAND PORT ADMINISTRATION Baltimore, MD
**PORT OF HOUSTON MAGAZINE** PORT OF HOUSTON MAGAZINE Houston, TX
**PORT PROGRESS** PORT OF OAKLAND Oakland, CA
**PORT PROGRESS** PORT OF PORTLAND Portland, OR
**PORTABLE SANITATION QUARTERLY** SATELLITE INDUSTRIES INC. Minneapolis, MN
**POSTAL LIFE** U.S. POSTAL SERVICE, COMMUNICATIONS DEPT. Washington, DC
**POWER NOTES** NASHVILLE ELECTRIC SERVICE Nashville, TN

**POWER SOURCE, THE** NC ASSOCIATION OF ELECTRICAL CONTRACTORS Raleigh, NC
**POWERGRAMS** ALABAMA POWER CO. Birmingham, AL
**POWERLINES** MISSISSIPPI POWER CO. Gulfport, MS
**POWERLINES** UNITED ILLUMINATING CO. New Haven, CT
**PRACTICAL PROSECUTOR** NATIONAL COLLEGE OF DISTRICT ATTORNEYS Houston, TX
**PRAIRIE LINES** SEARS ROEBUCK & CO. Hoffman Estates, IL
**PREMIER BANKING NEWSLETTER** NATIONAL BANK OF COMMERCE Memphis, TN
**PREMIER CONNECTION** PREMIER BANK Baton Rouge, LA
**PRESIDENT'S REPORT** BARTON COUNTY COMMUNITY COLLEGE Great Bend, KS
**PRESTIGE BOOK** ROBERT F. KENNEDY MEDICAL CENTER Hawthorne, CA
**PRETRIAL REPORTER** PRETRIAL SERVICES RESOURCE CENTER Washington, DC
**PREVIEW** SANDY CORPORATION Troy, MI
**PREVIEW** WDCN CHANNEL 8 Nashville, TN
**PRIDE** CALIFORNIA STATE EMPLOYEES ASSOCIATION Sacramento, CA
**PRIME INTEREST** FIRST TENNESSEE NATIONAL CORP. Memphis, TN
**PRINCIPAL** MILLER BREWING CO. Milwaukee, WI
**PRINT OUT** NASHVILLE STATE TECHNICAL INSTITUTE Nashville, TN
**PRINTER, THE** R.R. DONNELLEY & SONS CO. Chicago, IL
**PRO HEALTH MAGAZINE** MIAMI VALLEY HOSPITAL Dayton, OH
**PRO PUBLICATION** SANDY CORPORATION Troy, MI
**PRO-FILE** UNION INSURANCE GROUP Bloomington, IL
**PROBER** ROSEMOUNT INC. Eden Prairie, MN
**PROBINGS** SHANNON & WILSON INC. Seattle, WA
**PROCEEDINGS** SOUTHERN ASSOCIATION OF COLLEGES & SCHOOLS Decatur, GA
**PROCESSION** BLAIR, CORP. Warren, PA
**PRODUCTION AND INVENTORY MANAGEMENT** AMERICAN PRODUCTION & INVENTORY CONTROL SOCIETY (APICS) Falls Church, VA
**PROFESSIONAL COMMUNICATIOR, THE** WOMEN IN COMMUNICATIONS INC. Arlington, VA
**PROFILE** FARM BUREAU INS. Manhattan, KS
**PROFILE** LOS ANGELES JR. CHAMBER OF COMMERCE Los Angeles, CA
**PROFILE** UNION PLANTERS Memphis, TN
**PROFILE NEWSMAGAZINE PEOPLE-BRUNSWICK** BRUNSWICK CORP. Lake Forest, IL
**PROFILES** GOOD SAMARITAN HOSPITAL AND HEALTH CENTER Dayton, OH
**PROFITLINE** MISSISSIPPI CHEMICAL CORP. Yazoo City, MS
**PROGRESS** MUSEUM OF SCIENCE & INDUSTRY Chicago, IL
**PROGRESS NOTES** PROVENANT HEALTH CENTERS Denver, CO
**PROGRESS REPORT** HANDGUN CONTROL, INC. Washington, DC
**PROMOTIONAL PUBLICATIONS** STONE & WEBSTER ENGINEERING CORP. Boston, MA
**PROTECTION** TRAVELERS INSURANCE CO. Hartford, CT
**PROTECTIVE COVER** PROTECTIVE LIFE INS. CO. Birmingham, AL
**PROTECTIVE LIFE LINES** PROTECTIVE LIFE INS. CO. Birmingham, AL
**PROVIDENT PERSPECTIVE** PROVIDENT MUTUAL LIFE INSURANCE CO. OF PHILADELPHIA Philadelphia, PA
**PROVIDER** AMERICAN HEALTH CARE ASSOCIATION Washington, DC
**PRUDENTIAL'S REAL ESTATE DIMENSIONS** PRUDENTIAL INSURANCE CO. OF AMERICA Newark, NJ
**PSI** PINELLAS COUNTY GOVERNMENT Clearwater, FL
**PT-MAGAZINE OF PHYSICAL THERAPY** AMERICAN PHYSICAL THERAPY ASSOCIATION, INC. Alexandria, VA
**PUBLIC EMPLOYEE, THE** AFSCME Washington, DC
**PUBLIC EMPLOYEE, THE** HAWAII GOVERNMENT EMPLOYEES ASSN., AFSCME LOCAL 15 Honolulu, HI
**PUBLIC RELATIONS REVIEW:** COMMUNICATION RESEARCH ASSOCIATES, INC. Silver Spring, MD

**PUBLIX NEWS** PUBLIX SUPER MARKETS, INC. Lakeland, FL
**PULSE** CIGNA CORP. Philadelphia, PA
**PULSE** COOPER HOSPITAL/UNIVERSITY MEDICAL CENTER Camden, NJ
**PULSE** ROCKFORD MEMORIAL HOSPITAL Rockford, IL
**PULSE** ZURICH-AMERICAN INSURANCE GROUP Schaumburg, IL
**PULSE:** COMMUNITY HOSPITAL OF THE MONTEREY PENINSULA Monterey, CA
**PULSEBEAT** SALEM HOSPITAL Salem, OR
**PUMPLINE** VIKING PUMP, INC./A UNIT OF IDEX CORP. Cedar Falls, IA
**PUMPLINES EXTRA** GOULDS PUMPS INC. Seneca Falls, NY
**PUNCH LINES** DAYTON PROGRESS CORP. Dayton, OH

## Q

**Q-MUNICATOR** FRED MEYER INC. Portland, OR
**Q-MUNICATOR** ROADWAY SERVICES, INC. Akron, OH
**QUAKER INSIDER** QUAKER OATS CO. Chicago, IL
**QUAKER QUARTERLY** QUAKER OATS CO. Chicago, IL
**QUALITY SPOTLIGHT** MEDRAD INC. Pittsburgh, PA
**QUANTUM UPDATE** QUANTUM CHEMICAL CORP., USI DIV. Cincinnati, OH
**QUARTERLY FINANCIAL REPORTER** SANTEE COOPER Moncks Corner, SC
**QUARTERLY INTEREST** BANK SOUTH Atlanta, GA
**QUARTERLY REPORT** BANK SOUTH Atlanta, GA
**QUARTERLY REPORT TO STOCKHOLDERS** FAIRCHILD CORPORATION Chantilly, VA
**QUEEN'S VISION, THE** QUEEN'S MEDICAL CENTER Honolulu, HI
**QUEST** SHELL OIL CO. Houston, TX
**QUICK MIXES** HARBISON-WALKER REFRACTORIES CO. Pittsburgh, PA
**QUOTE** PIPER JAFFRAY Minneapolis, MN

## R

**R C S B PREVIEW** ROCHESTER COMMUNITY SAVINGS BANK Rochester, NY
**R G & E NEWS** ROCHESTER GAS & ELECTRIC CORP. Rochester, NY
**R P TODAY** RALSTON PURINA CO. St. Louis, MO
**R S R LEAD PRESS** RSR CORPORATION Dallas, TX
**R T ITEMS** RESEARCH TRIANGLE INSTITUTE Durham, NC
**R T N D A COMMUNICATOR** RADIO-TELEVISION NEWS DIRECTORS ASSOCIATION Washington, DC
**RADIO SHACK INTERCOM** RADIO SHACK DIVISION, TANDY CORP. Fort Worth, TX
**RAGAN REPORT** LAWRENCE RAGAN COMMUNICATIONS, INC. Chicago, IL
**RALPH'S NEWS:** RALPH'S GROCERY CO. Los Angeles, CA
**RANGER RESOURCES** RANGER INSURANCE CO. Houston, TX
**RAYTHEON NEWS** RAYTHEON CO. Lexington, MA
**REACTOR** ZIMPRO ENVIRONMENTAL, INC. Rothschild, WI
**REAL ESTATE CENTER LAW LETTER** REAL ESTATE CENTER College Station, TX
**REAL ESTATE CENTER TRENDS** REAL ESTATE CENTER College Station, TX
**REAL ESTATE INVESTMENT JOURNAL** CENTURY 21, REAL ESTATE CORP. Irvine, CA
**REAL ESTATEMENTS** BARCLAYS AMERICAN/MORTGAGE Charlotte, NC
**RECORD** JIII SALES PROMOTION ASSOCIATES, INC. Coshocton, OH
**RECORD GUIDE** WOMEN'S INTERNATIONAL BOWLING CONGRESS Greendale, WI
**RECORD, THE** UNION NATIONAL LIFE INSURANCE CO. Baton Rouge, LA
**RECORDER, THE** DRESSER INDUSTRIES, INC. Dallas, TX
**REEL PEOPLE NEWS** WIRE ROPE COROPRATION OF AMERICA, INC. St. Joseph, MO
**REFLECTION, THE** HALLIBURTON-GEOPHYSICAL SERVICES, INC. Houston, TX
**REFLECTOR** NAVAL AIR WARFARE CENTER Warminster, PA

**REFLECTOR:** PITTSBURGH BLIND ASSOCIATION Pittsburgh, PA
**REGION 10 NEWS** KTVE-TV Monroe, LA
**REGIONAL BANKER, THE** CHASE MANHATTAN BANK, N.A., THE Rochester, NY
**REGIS UNIVERSITY MAGAZINE** REGIS UNIVERSITY Denver, CO
**REHAB JOURNAL** REHABILITATION HOSPITAL OF THE PACIFIC Honolulu, HI
**REINSURANCE REPORTER** LINCOLN NATIONAL CORP. Fort Wayne, IN
**REPORT** CINCINNATI BAR ASSOCIATION Cincinnati, OH
**REPORT** TEXAS SOCIETY OF ARCHITECTS Austin, TX
**REPORT CARD-ANNUAL REPORT TO THE COMMUNITY** SALT LAKE CITY SCHOOL DISTRICT Salt Lake City, UT
**REPORT TO THE COMMUNITY** AMERICAN HEART ASSOCIATION St. Louis, MO
**REPORTER MAGAZINE** AMERICAN HOECHST CORP. Somerville, NJ
**REPORTER MAGAZINE** HOECHST CELANESE CORP. Somerville, NJ
**REPORTER, THE** RAYMOND CORP. Greene, NY
**RESEARCH REVIEW** UNIVERSITY OF ROCHESTER Rochester, NY
**RESERVE 7** FEDERAL RESERVE BANK OF CHICAGO Chicago, IL
**RESIN REVIEW** ROHM & HAAS CO. Philadelphia, PA
**RESOURCE** ALLIED GROUP Des Moines, IA
**RESOURCE** WISCONSIN NATURAL GAS CO. Racine, WI
**RESOURCE, THE** WESTERN RESOURCES, INC. Topeka, KS
**RESPONSE MAGAZINE** SIMON WIESENTHAL CENTER Los Angeles, CA
**RETAIL UPDATE** SUPERVALU, INC. Eden Prairie, MN
**RETIREE'S NEWSLETTER** STATE COMPENSATION INSURANCE FUND San Francisco, CA
**REVCO SCRIPTS** REVCO, D.S. INC. Twinsburg, OH
**REVENEWS** GEORGIA REVENUE DEPT. Atlanta, GA
**REVENUE QUARTERLY** GEORGIA REVENUE DEPT. Atlanta, GA
**REVIEW** GENERAL MILLS, INC. Minneapolis, MN
**REVIEW** NORTH CAROLINA MUTUAL LIFE INSURANCE CO. Durham, NC
**REVIEW, THE** OAKITE PRODUCTS, INC. Berkeley Hts, NJ
**REVISTA MARYKNOLL** CATHOLIC FOREIGN MISSION SOCIETY Maryknoll, NY
**REYNOLDS REVIEW** REYNOLDS METALS CO. Richmond, VA
**RHODE ISLAND BUILDER REPORT, THE** RHODE ISLAND BUILDERS ASSOCIATION East Providence, RI
**RICHARDSON EMPLOYEE NEWSLETTER** CITY OF RICHARDSON TEXAS Richardson, TX
**RIO** PASEO DEL RIO ASSOCIATION San Antonio, TX
**RIPPLES & CURRENTS** JORDAN SCHOOL DISTRICT Sandy, UT
**RIVERSIDE MONTHLY** RIVERSIDE METHODIST HOSPITALS Columbus, OH
**ROCKHURST MAGAZINE** ROCKHURST COLLEGE Kansas City, MO
**ROCKHURST REPORT** ROCKHURST COLLEGE Kansas City, MO
**ROCKWELL NEWS** ROCKWELL INTERNATIONAL, COMMAND & CONTROL SYSTEMS DIVISION Richardson, TX
**ROCKY MOUNTAIN MOTORIST** ROCKY MOUNTAIN AAA CLUB Denver, CO
**ROHM & HAAS REPORTER** ROHM & HAAS CO. Philadelphia, PA
**ROPE TALK MAGAZINE** WIRE ROPE COROPRATION OF AMERICA, INC. St. Joseph, MO
**ROSEBURG NEWS & VIEWS** ROSEBURG FOREST PRODUCTS CO. Roseburg, OR
**ROSEBURG WOODSMAN** ROSEBURG FOREST PRODUCTS CO. Roseburg, OR
**ROSICRUCIAN DIGEST** ROSICRUCIAN ORDER AMORC San Jose, CA
**ROTO-ROOTER EXCHANGE** ROTO-ROOTER CORP. West Des Moines, IA
**ROTOR BREEZE** BELL HELICOPTER TEXTRON, INC. Fort Worth, TX
**ROUNDTABLE** JIII SALES PROMOTION ASSOCIATES, INC. Coshocton, OH
**ROUNDUP** ACME BOOT COMPANY INC. Clarksville, TN

**RUBBERMAID REVIEW** RUBBERMAID, INC. Wooster, OH

**RULES REGULATIONS FOR RECREATIONAL BOATS** AMERICAN BOAT & YACHT COUNCIL INC. Edgewater, MD

**RURAL CLINICIAN QUARTERLY** NATIONAL RURAL HEALTH ASSOCIATION Kansas City, MO

**RURAL HEALTH CARE** NATIONAL RURAL HEALTH ASSOCIATION Kansas City, MO

**RURAL KENTUCKIAN** KENTUCKY ASSOCIATION OF ELECTRIC COOPERATIVES Louisville, KY

**RURAL LIVING** VA., MD., & DE. ASSOCIATION OF ELECTRIC CO-OP. Glen Allen, VA

**RYDER DEALER** RYDER SYSTEM, INC. Miami, FL

**RYDER PEOPLE** RYDER SYSTEM, INC. Miami, FL

# S

**S A IN THE NEWS** SCIENTIFIC-ATLANTA, INC. Norcross, GA

**S B NEWS** SMITHKLINE BEECHAM Philadelphia, PA

**S C E & G NEWS** SOUTH CAROLINA ELECTRIC & GAS CO. Columbia, SC

**S C J THIS WEEK** S.C. JOHNSON & SON INC. Racine, WI

**S F NEWSLETTER** SOUTHERN FOREST PRODUCTS ASSOCIATION New Orleans, LA

**S I G E C O NEWS** SOUTHERN INDIANA GAS & ELECTRIC CO. Evansville, IN

**S J JOURNAL:** ST. JOSEPH MEDICAL CENTER Fort Wayne, IN

**S M U MAGAZINE** SOUTHERN METHODIST UNIVERSITY Dallas, TX

**S N E NEWS** SOUTHERN NEW ENGLAND TELEPHONE CO. New Haven, CT

**S N E TIMES** SOUTHERN NEW ENGLAND TELEPHONE CO. New Haven, CT

**S S B NEWS LETTER** SYRACUSE SAVINGS BANK Syracuse, NY

**S W E** SOCIETY OF WOMEN ENGINEERS New York, NY

**SAE UPDATE** SOCIETY OF AUTOMOTIVE ENGINEERS INC. Warrendale, PA

**SAFE CYCLING** MOTORCYCLE SAFETY FOUNDATION Irvine, CA

**SAFECO AGENT** SAFECO INSURANCE CO. Seattle, WA

**SAFETY & HEALTH** NATIONAL SAFETY COUNCIL Itasca, IL

**SAFETY BRIEFS** NEW JERSEY STATE SAFETY COUNCIL Cranford, NJ

**SAFETY NEWS, THE** MICHIGAN MUTUAL INSURANCE CO. Detroit, MI

**SAFETY TALK** TEXAS SAFETY ASSOCIATION Austin, TX

**SAFETY TIMES** UTAH POWER, A DIVISION OF PACIFICORP, OREGON Salt Lake City, UT

**SAGINAW DIVISIONAL NEWSLETTER** SAGINAW DIVISION-GENERAL MOTORS CORP. Saginaw, MI

**SAINT JOHN'S NEWS** ST. JOHN'S HOSPITAL & HEALTH CENTER Santa Monica, CA

**SALADMASTER SALUT!** SALADMASTER, INC. Arlington, TX

**SALES & MARKETING NEWSLETTER** BEST FOODS, DIVISION OF CPC INTERNATIONAL, INC. Englewood Cliffs, NJ

**SALES BOOSTER** JII SALES PROMOTION ASSOCIATES, INC. Coshocton, OH

**SALES PROSPECTOR** SALES PROSPECTOR Waltham, MA

**SAMARITAN TODAY, THE** SAMARITAN HEALTH SERVICE Phoenix, AZ

**SAMPLE CASE** UNITED COMMERCIAL TRAVELERS OF AMERICA Columbus, OH

**SAN DIEGO PHYSICIAN** SAN DIEGO COUNTY MEDICAL SOCIETY San Diego, CA

**SAN LUIS OBISPO BUSINESS** SAN LUIS OBISPO CHAMBER OF COMMERCE San Luis Obispo, CA

**SAN LUIS OBISPO VISITOR GUIDE** SAN LUIS OBISPO CHAMBER OF COMMERCE San Luis Obispo, CA

**SANTA MARIA RECORD** CBS, INC. New York, NY

**SANTEE COOPER ANNUAL REPORT** SANTEE COOPER Moncks Corner, SC

**SAVANNAH MILL WEEKLY** UNION CAMP CORPORATION Savannah, GA

**SBRC NEWS:** SANTA BARBARA RESEARCH CENTER Santa Barbara, CA

**SCANNER** ITT GILFILLAN Van Nuys, CA

**SCENE:** PACIFIC LUTHERAN UNIVERSITY Tacoma, WA

**SCHERING-PLOUGH GRASSROOTS NETWORK VOICE** SCHERING-PLOUGH CORP. Madison, NJ

**SCHERING-PLOUGH WORLD** SCHERING-PLOUGH CORP. Madison, NJ

**SCHWINN CYCLING & FITNESS, INC. DEALER NEWS LETTER** SCHWINN CYCLING & FITNESS, INC. Boulder, CO

**SCIENCE SCOPE** NATIONAL SCIENCE TEACHERS ASSOCIATION Washington, DC

**SCIENCE SCREEN REPORT** ALLEGRO PRODUCTIONS, INC. Boca Raton, FL

**SCOOP, THE** BRESLER'S ICE CREAM & YOGURT, INC. Des Plaines, IL

**SCOPE** LONG BEACH MEMORIAL MEDICAL CENTER Long Beach, CA

**SCOPE** VALSPAR CORP. Minneapolis, MN

**SCOPE** WAKE MEDICAL CENTER Raleigh, NC

**SCOPE: COMP NEWS** SAIF CORP. Salem, OR

**SCRAPS** HANDY & HARMAN CO. Rye, NY

**SCRIBE** MULTNOMAH COUNTY MEDICAL SOCIETY Portland, OR

**SEAFIRST NEWS** SEAFIRST CORP. Seattle, WA

**SELLING 66** PHILLIPS PETROLEUM CO. Bartlesville, OK

**SEMAPHORE** BLACK HAWK COUNCIL OF GIRL SCOUTS Madison, WI

**SENDOUT** BROOKLYN UNION GAS CO. Brooklyn, NY

**SENDOUT** WISCONSIN NATURAL GAS CO. Racine, WI

**SENIOR HEALTH NEWS** TENNESSEE HOSPITAL ASSOCIATION Nashville, TN

**SENIOR NEWSLETTER** RICH'S, INC. Atlanta, GA

**SENTRY NEWS** SENTRY INSURANCE Stevens Point, WI

**SERVICE LIFE** FORD MOTOR COMPANY Dearborn, MI

**SETON GOOD HEALTH MAGAZINE** SETON MEDICAL CENTER Austin, TX

**SEU NEWS** ST. EDWARD'S UNIVERSITY Austin, TX

**SEVEN-UP LEADER** DR. PEPPER CO. Dallas, TX

**SEVENTY SIX** UNOCAL CORP. Los Angeles, CA

**SHAKLEE NEWS** SHAKLEE CORP. San Francisco, CA

**SHAREHOLDER UPDATE** MISSISSIPPI CHEMICAL CORP. Yazoo City, MS

**SHARING** UNITED WAY OF METROPOLITAN TARRANT COUNTY Fort Worth, TX

**SHAVINGS** WOODMAN OF THE WORLD LIFE INSURANCE SOCIETY Omaha, NE

**SHAWMUT NEWS** SHAWMUT BANK, CONNECTICUT Hartford, CT

**SHEAFFER NEWSLETTER** SHEAFFER, INC. Fort Madison, IA

**SHELL ALUMNI NEWS** SHELL OIL CO. Houston, TX

**SHELL MARKETER** SHELL OIL CO. Houston, TX

**SHELL NEWS** SHELL OIL CO. Houston, TX

**SHELL PROGRESS** SHELL OIL CO. Houston, TX

**SHENANDOAH** SHENANDOAH LIFE INSURANCE CO. Roanoke, VA

**SHERWOOD REPORTER** SHERWOOD MEDICAL CO. St. Louis, MO

**SHIELD** SPARTAN STORES, INC. Grand Rapids, MI

**SHIELD, THE** SHELTER INSURANCE COMPANY Columbia, MO

**SHIFTING TIMES** BORG-WARNER AUTOMOTIVE, TRANSMISSION SYSTEMS Muncie, IN

**SHOP TALK** WASHINGTON POST Washington, DC

**SHORT CIRCUITS** DAIRYLAND POWER COOPERATIVE La Crosse, WI

**SHRINKSTOPPERS** ZALE CORP. Irving, TX

**SIERRA SCENE** SIERRA PACIFIC POWER CO. Reno, NV

**SIGLETTER** AL SIGL CENTER FOR REHABILITATION AGENCIES, INC. Rochester, NY

**SIGNAL** TEXAS SAFETY ASSOCIATION Austin, TX

**SIGNAL, THE** SIGNET BANKING CORP. Richmond, VA

**SIGNALS** CIGNA CORP. Philadelphia, PA

**SIKORSKY LIFELINE** SIKORSKY AIRCRAFT Bridgeport, CT

**SIKORSKY NEWS** SIKORSKY AIRCRAFT Bridgeport, CT

**SIMA "WAVELENGTHS"** SIMA-SURF INDUSTRY MANUFACTURERS ASSOCATION Dana Point, CA

**SINGLE SERVICE NEWS** FOODSERVICE & PACKAGING INSTITUTE, INC. Arlington, VA

**SKYLINER:** TRANS WORLD AIRLINES INC. Hazelwood, MO

**SLICES** SUNKIST GROWERS, INC. Van Nuys, CA

**SMALL BUSINESS NEWS** OHIO CHAMBER OF COMMERCE Columbus, OH

**SMITH & NEPHEW RICHARDS REPORTER** SMITH & NEPHEW RICHARDS INC. Memphis, TN

**SNAP-ON DEALER NEWS:** SNAP-ON TOOLS CORP. Kenosha, WI

**SNAP-ON INDUSTRIAL NEWS:** SNAP-ON TOOLS CORP. Kenosha, WI

**SOCI CORPORATE NOTES:** SOCIETY CORP. Cleveland, OH

**SOCIAL SCIENCE MONITOR** COMMUNICATION RESEARCH ASSOCIATES, INC. Silver Spring, MD

**SOCIETY** TRANSACTION-PUBLISHERS New Brunswick, NJ

**SOCIETY NOW** SOCIETY CORPORATION Cleveland, OH

**SOFT DRINK LINES** NATIONAL SOFT DRINK ASSOCIATION Washington, DC

**SOLDIERS** UNITED STATES ARMY Fort Belvoir, VA

**SONAT TIELINES** SONAT, INC. Birmingham, AL

**SONOCO WORLD** SONOCO PRODUCTS CO. Hartsville, SC

**SOROPTIMIST OF THE AMERICAS** SOROPTIMIST INTERNATIONAL OF THE AMERICAS, INC. Philadelphia, PA

**SOUNDBOARD** KIMBALL INTERNATIONAL, INC. Jasper, IN

**SOURCE** MICHIGAN STATE UNIVERSITY East Lansing, MI

**SOURCE, THE** ASHLAND OIL, INC. Russell, KY

**SOURCEBOOK** REDDY CORP. INTERNATIONAL Albuquerque, NM

**SOUTH CAROLINA PORT NEWS** SOUTH CAROLINA STATE PORTS AUTHORITY Charleston, SC

**SOUTHEAST TEXAS BUSINESS MONTHLY** BEAUMONT CHAMBER OF COMMERCE Beaumont, TX

**SOUTHERN AIR** AMERICAN LUNG ASSOCIATION OF ALABAMA Birmingham, AL

**SOUTHERN BELL VIEWS** SOUTHERN BELL TELEPHONE CO. Atlanta, GA

**SOUTHERN HIGHLIGHTS** SOUTHERN COMPANY SERVICES, INC. Atlanta, GA

**SOUTHERN PACIFIC BULLETIN** SOUTHERN PACIFIC TRANSPORTATION CO. San Francisco, CA

**SOUTHERN UNION COMPANY FORUM** SOUTHERN UNION CO. Austin, TX

**SOUTHSIDE HEALTH** SOUTHSIDE HOSPITAL Bay Shore, NY

**SOUTHSIDE PHYSICIAN** SOUTHSIDE HOSPITAL Bay Shore, NY

**SOUTHWEST ECONOMY** FEDERAL RESERVE BANK OF DALLAS Dallas, TX

**SOUTHWEST TODAY** SOUTHWEST GENERAL HOSPITAL Cleveland, OH

**SOUTHWESTERN** SOUTHWESTERN ELECTRIC POWER CO. Shreveport, LA

**SOUTHWESTERNER** SOUTHWESTERN PUBLIC SERVICE CO. Amarillo, TX

**SPAN** STANDARD OIL CO. Chicago, IL

**SPARK, THE** ARCO Los Angeles, CA

**SPARTAN NEWS** SPARTAN STORES, INC. Grand Rapids, MI

**SPECTRA** JERSEY CENTRAL POWER & LIGHT CO. Morristown, NJ

**SPECTRUM** AMERICAN GREETINGS CORP. Cleveland, OH

**SPECTRUM** BANK OF HAWAII Honolulu, HI

**SPECTRUM** COMERICA, INC. Detroit, MI

**SPECTRUM** GATES CORPORATION, THE Denver, CO

**SPECTRUM** HORACE MANN COS., THE Springfield, IL

**SPECTRUM** ST. FRANCIS HOSPITAL CENTER Beech Grove, IN

**SPINNIT, THE** DYERSBURG FABRICS INC. Dyersburg, TN

**SPIRIT** MERCY MEDICAL CENTER Baltimore, MD

**SPIRIT** PACIFIC FIRST BANK Seattle, WA

**SPIRIT** UNITED WAY OF THE GREATER DAYTON AREA Dayton, OH

**SPIRIT MAGAZINE** ATLANTA GAS LIGHT CO. Atlanta, GA

**SPIRIT, THE** UNITED TELEPHONE CO. OF OHIO Mansfield, OH

**SPORTS MEDICINE BULLETIN** AMERICAN COLLEGE OF SPORTS MEDICINE Indianapolis, IN

**SPORTS SUPPLEMENT** UNITED STATES SPORTS ACADEMY Daphne, AL
**SPOTLIGHT** ELECTRIC POWER BOARD CHATTANOOGA Chattanooga, TN
**SPOTLIGHT** GREAT SOUTHERN LIFE INSURANCE CO. Dallas, TX
**SPOTLIGHT** T.U. ELECTRIC Dallas, TX
**SPOTLIGHT ON SPIRIT** ST. JOSEPH MEDICAL CENTER Burbank, CA
**SPOTLIGHT, THE** NATIONAL INSURANCE CRIME BUREAU Palos Hills, IL
**SPOTLIGHT:** CAROLINA POWER & LIGHT CO. Raleigh, NC
**SPOTLIGHT:** SCRIPTURE PRESS PUBLICATIONS, INC. Wheaton, IL
**SPOTLITE** FBG SERVICE CORP. Omaha, NE
**SPRINGS BULLETIN THE** SPRINGS INDUSTRIES, INC. Fort Mill, SC
**SPRINT MID-ATLANTIC TELECOM TODAY** SPRINT MID-ATLANTIC TELECOM Wake Forest, NC
**SQUARE TALK** RALSTON PURINA CO. St. Louis, MO
**ST JOSEPH'S NEWS:** ST. JOSEPH'S HOSPITAL Parkersburg, WV
**ST. AGNES NEWS** ST. AGNES HOSPITAL Baltimore, MD
**ST. FRANCIS CAPSULE** ST. FRANCIS HOSPITAL, INC. Wilmington, DE
**ST. PAUL NEWS** ST. PAUL COMPANIES, INC., THE Saint Paul, MN
**ST. THOMAS MAGAZINE** UNIVERSITY OF ST. THOMAS Houston, TX
**STABILIZER** LINCOLN ELECTRIC CO., THE Cleveland, OH
**STABILIZER** SCHWEIZER AIRCRAFT CORP. Elmira, NY
**STAINLESS SPIRIT** STAINLESS FOUNDRY & ENGINEERING INC. Milwaukee, WI
**STANDARDS** SECURITY MUTUAL LIFE INSURANCE CO. OF NEW YORK Binghamton, NY
**STANDARDS & RECOMMENDED PRACTICES FOR SMALL CRAFT** AMERICAN BOAT & YACHT COUNCIL INC. Edgewater, MD
**STAR** LOCKHEED ADVANCED DEVELOPMENT CO. Palmdale, CA
**STAR BULLETIN** AMERICAN NATIONAL INSURANCE CO. Galveston, TX
**STAR NEWS** STAR MARKET CO. Cambridge, MA
**STAR-TELEGRAM CHASER** FORT WORTH STAR-TELEGRAM Fort Worth, TX
**STAT SHEET, THE** MERCY HOSPITAL, INC. Charlotte, NC
**STATE STREET NOW** STATE STREET BOSTON CORP. Boston, MA
**STATEMENT** STATE CHEMICAL MANUFACTURING CO. Cleveland, OH
**STATESMAN** SOUTHERN STATES COOPERATIVE Richmond, VA
**STETHOSCOPE** COOPER HOSPITAL/UNIVERSITY MEDICAL CENTER Camden, NJ
**STONE & WEBSTER INCORPORATE NEWSLETTER** STONE & WEBSTER ENGINEERING CORP. Boston, MA
**STORE CHAT** STRAWBRIDGE & CLOTHIER Philadelphia, PA
**STRAIGHT-TALK** WESTIN HOTEL Seattle, WA
**STRIDE RITER** STRIDE RITE CORP. Cambridge, MA
**SUCCESS EXTRA** MSI INSURANCE Arden Hills, MN
**SUGAR EXCHANGE** IMPERIAL HOLLY CORP. Sugar Land, TX
**SUGAR SCOOP** VALHI, INC. Dallas, TX
**SUGARBEET** VALHI, INC. Dallas, TX
**SUMMER IN THE CITY** CITY OF DETROIT Detroit, MI
**SUN MAGAZINE** SUN COMPANY INC. Philadelphia, PA
**SUNFLOWER, THE** NATIONAL SUNFLOWER ASSOCIATION Bismarck, ND
**SUNKIST MAGAZINE** SUNKIST GROWERS, INC. Van Nuys, CA
**SUNSCRIBE** CITY OF ST. PETERSBURG St. Petersburg, FL
**SUPERINTENDENTS BULLETIN** ORLEANS PARRISH SCHOOL BOARD New Orleans, LA
**SUPERVALU PEOPLE** SUPERVALU, INC. Eden Prairie, MN
**SURFACE MINER** BUCYRUS-ERIE CO. South Milwaukee, WI
**SYMBOLS** INTEGON Winston Salem, NC
**SYNCHRONIZER** T.U. ELECTRIC Dallas, TX

**SYNERGY** OHIO STATE MEDICAL ASSOCIATION Columbus, OH
**SYNERGY** WISCONSIN ELECTRIC POWER CO. Milwaukee, WI

# T

**T A B C O BULLETIN** TEACHERS ASSOCIATION OF BALTIMORE COUNTY MD., INC. Baltimore, MD
**T E A NEWS** TENNESSEE EDUCATION ASSOCIATION Nashville, TN
**T I P R O REPORTER** TEXAS INDEPENDENT PRODUCERS & ROYALTY OWNERS ASSOCIATIOIN Austin, TX
**T I TOPICS** THOMAS INDUSTRIES Louisville, KY
**T I U NEWSLETTER** INTERNATIONAL UNIVERSITY FOUNDATION Independence, MO
**T P A MESSENGER** TEXAS PRESS ASSOCIATION Austin, TX
**TABLET, THE** MELROSE-WAKEFIELD HOSPITAL Melrose, MA
**TAKE 10** RAYMOND CORP. Greene, NY
**TALKING BOOK TOPICS** LIBRARY OF CONGRESS Washington, DC
**TALKING POINTS** ARMSTRONG WORLD INDUSTRIES Lancaster, PA
**TAPS & JETS** METROPOLITAN UTILITIES DISTRICT Omaha, NE
**TEAM** E-SYSTEMS, INC. Dallas, TX
**TEAM TALK** ANHEUSER-BUSCH COMPANIES, INC. Saint Louis, MO
**TEAM TIDBITS** AMERICAN LUNG ASSOCIATION OF GEORGIA Smyrna, GA
**TEAMWORK** FIRSTIER BANK Omaha, NE
**TEAMWORKS** MIDWEST RESOURCES INC. Des Moines, IA
**TEAMWORKS** NORTHWESTERN MEMORIAL HOSPITAL Chicago, IL
**TECHNOLOGY** ENGINEERING SOCIETY OF DETROIT St. Clair Shores, MI
**TELCO TODAY** INDIANA TELCO FEDERAL CREDIT UNION Indianapolis, IN
**TELENEWS** WISCONSIN ELECTRIC POWER CO. Milwaukee, WI
**TELEPHONE TIMES** SOUTHWESTERN BELL TELEPHONE CO. Dallas, TX
**TELLING IT LIKE IT IS** TRANSPORTATION COMMUNICATIONS INTERNATIONAL UNION Rockville, MD
**TELOPS NEWS** GTE TELEPHONE OPERATIONS Muskegon, MI
**TELSTAR** BOSTON MUTUAL LIFE INS. CO. Canton, MA
**TEMPO** KANSAS CITY LIFE INSURANCE CO. Kansas City, MO
**TEMPO** NORTH AMERICAN OPERATIONS-DRESSER INDUSTRY Canton, MA
**TENNESSEE HOSPITALS** TENNESSEE HOSPITAL ASSOCIATION Nashville, TN
**TENNESSEE MAGAZINE, THE** TENNESSEE ELECTRIC COOP ASSOCIATION Nashville, TN
**TENNESSEE TEACHER** TENNESSEE EDUCATION ASSOCIATION Nashville, TN
**TERRA TODAY** TERRA CHEMICALS INT'L., INC. Sioux City, IA
**TERRASOL** MITCHELL ENERGY & DEVELOPMENT CORP. The Woodlands, TX
**TERRE HAUTE RECORD** CBS, INC. New York, NY
**TESCO ROUNDUP** T.U. ELECTRIC Dallas, TX
**TEXACO MARKETER, THE** TEXACO, INC. White Plains, NY
**TEXACO TODAY** TEXACO, INC. White Plains, NY
**TEXAS AGGIE** ASSOCIATION OF FORMER STUDENTS TEXAS A&M UNIVERSITY College Station, TX
**TEXAS ALCALDE** EX-STUDENTS ASSOCIATION Austin, TX
**TEXAS ARCHITECT** TEXAS SOCIETY OF ARCHITECTS Austin, TX
**TEXAS BAR JOURNAL** STATE BAR OF TEXAS Austin, TX
**TEXAS CO-OP POWER** TEXAS ELECTRIC COOPS INC. Austin, TX
**TEXAS COACH** TEXAS HIGH SCHOOL COACHES ASSOCIATION INC. Austin, TX

**TEXAS EASTMAN NEWS** TEXAS EASTMAN DIV., EASTMAN CHEMICAL CO. Longview, TX
**TEXAS MEDICINE** TEXAS MEDICAL ASSOCIATION Austin, TX
**TEXAS NURSING** TEXAS NURSES ASSOCIATION Austin, TX
**TEXAS P T A COMMUNICATOR** TEXAS CONGRESS OF PARENTS & TEACHERS Austin, TX
**TEXAS PROFESSIONAL ENGINEER** TEXAS SOCIETY OF PROFESSIONAL ENGINEERS Austin, TX
**TEXAS PUBLIC EMPLOYEE** TEXAS PUBLIC EMPLOYEES ASSOCIATION Austin, TX
**TEXAS REALTOR** TEXAS ASSOCIATION OF REALTORS Austin, TX
**TEXAS WESLEYAN TODAY** TEXAS WESLEYAN UNIVERSITY Fort Worth, TX
**TEXAS WIRE** BANK ONE Dallas, TX
**THE BIG IDEA** UNITED PARCEL SERVICE Atlanta, GA
**THE BULLETIN** PRESBYTERIAN-UNIV. OF PENNSYLVANIA MEDICAL CTR. Philadelphia, PA
**THE CITIZEN** COLORADO ASSOCIATION OF PUBLIC EMPLOYEES Denver, CO
**THE DIAMOND EXCHANGE** L.G. BALFOUR CO. Attleboro, MA
**THE GOOD WORK** SISTERS OF PROVIDENCE HEALTH SYSTEM Seattle, WA
**THE IMAGE** BIG BROTHERS OF GREATER LOS ANGELES, INC. Los Angeles, CA
**THE KEY:** KYOCERA INTERNATIONAL, INC. San Diego, CA
**THE LEGAL BULLETIN** EMPLOYERS GROUP Los Angeles, CA
**THE OPEN LINE** PENN TRAFFIC CO. Syracuse, NY
**THE ROUNDUP** NEWHALL LAND & FARMING CO. Valencia, CA
**THE TRADEWINDS** MOTOROLA, INC. Schaumburg, IL
**THERMOSPHERE** THERMO ELECTRON CORP. Boston, MA
**THINK** INTERNATIONAL BUSINESS MACHINES CORP. Armonk, NY
**THIOKOL MAGAZINE** THIOKOL CORP. Ogden, UT
**THIS WEEK** CHASE MANHATTAN BANK, N.A., THE Rochester, NY
**THIS WEEK** DELMARVA POWER & LIGHT CO. Wilmington, DE
**THIS WEEK** PIER 1 IMPORTS, INC. Ft. Worth, TX
**THIS WEEK** SIERRA PACIFIC POWER CO. Reno, NV
**THIS WEEK** STA-RITE INDUSTRIES Delavan, WI
**THREAD TIPS** TELEDYNE, INC. Waynesboro, PA
**TIDINGS:** GOODWILL INDUSTRIES OF SOUTHERN CALIFORNIA Los Angeles, CA
**TIE LINES** MICHIGAN BELL TELEPHONE CO. Detroit, MI
**TIERRA GRANDE MAGAZINE** REAL ESTATE CENTER College Station, TX
**TIMBER TIMES** ALASKA FOREST ASSN. INC. Ketchikan, AK
**TIME OUT** MARION MERRELL DOW INC. Cincinnati, OH
**TIMES COMPANY REPORT** NEW YORK TIMES New York, NY
**TIMES TALK** NEW YORK TIMES New York, NY
**TIMES TALK** TIMES PUBLISHING CO. St. Petersburg, FL
**TIMES, THE** DUQUESNE UNIVERSITY Pittsburgh, PA
**TIRE TRACKS** COOPER TIRE & RUBBER COMPANY Findlay, OH
**TITELINES** LAWYERS TITLE INSURANCE CORP. Richmond, VA
**TOASTMASTERS NEWSLETTER** NALCO CHEMICAL CO. Naperville, IL
**TOBACCOTALK** BROWN & WILLIAMSON TOBACCO CORP. Louisville, KY
**TODAY** KELLY-SPRINGFIELD TIRE CO. Cumberland, MD
**TODAY** METHODIST HOSPITAL Brooklyn, NY
**TODAY** MICHIGAN TRUCKING ASSOCIATION Lansing, MI
**TODAY - MENTAL HEALTH IN YOUR COMMUNITY** MENTAL HEALTH ASSOCIATION OF ERIE COUNTY INC. Buffalo, NY
**TODAY AT B M A** BUSINESS MEN'S ASSURANCE CO. Kansas City, MO
**TODAY'S C P A** TEXAS SOCIETY CERTIFIED PUBLIC ACCOUNTANTS Dallas, TX
**TODAY'S HEADLINES** DANIEL FREEMAN MEMORIAL HOSPITAL Inglewood, CA
**TOGETHER** UNITED WAY OF ORANGE COUNTY Irvine, CA

**TOMORROW'S BUSINESS LEADER** FUTURE BUSINESS LEADERS OF AMERICA-PHI BETA LAMBDA Reston, VA

**TOPFLIGHT TODAY** TOPFLIGHT CORP. York, PA

**TOPICS** TEACHERS INSURNACE & ANNUITY ASSOCIATION New York, NY

**TOPICS IN VETERINARY MEDICINE** SMITHKLINE BEECHAM ANIMAL HEALTH Exton, PA

**TORCH, THE** LIBERTY NATIONAL LIFE INSURANCE CO. Birmingham, AL

**TOW LINE** MORAN TOWING & TRANSPORTATION CO., INC. Greenwich, CT

**TOWER TALK** MERCY MEDICAL CENTER Baltimore, MD

**TOWER, THE** ST. EDWARD'S UNIVERSITY Austin, TX

**TOYOTA TODAY** TOYOTA MOTOR SALES USA, INC. Torrance, CA

**TRACT, THE** LAWYERS TITLE INSURANCE CORP. Richmond, VA

**TRADER** AMERICA WEST AIRLINES Phoenix, AZ

**TRAIL GUIDE** QUIVIRA COUNCIL, INC. Wichita, KS

**TRANSMISSION LINES** ANR PIPELINE CO. Detroit, MI

**TRANSMISSIONS** HOUSTON LIGHTING & POWER CO. Houston, TX

**TRANSMITTER** WEOKIE CREDIT UNION Oklahoma City, OK

**TRANSPORTATION BUILDER** AMERICAN ROAD & TRANSPORTATION BUILDERS ASSOCIATION Washington, DC

**TRAVELERS TRIBUNE** TRAVELERS INSURANCE CO. Hartford, CT

**TREATMENT ISSUES** GMHC, INC. New York, NY

**TREND** WISCONSIN BELL, INC. Milwaukee, WI

**TRENDS** AVCO FINANCIAL SERVICES Irvine, CA

**TRENDS** BURGER KING CORP. Miami, FL

**TRENDS** MEDICAL COLLEGE OF WISCONSIN Milwaukee, WI

**TRI-STATE EXPRESS** FLEMING COS. INC. Oklahoma City, OK

**TRIANGLE NEWS** TRIANGLE DISTRIBUTING CO. Santa Fe Springs, CA

**TRIANGLE, THE** AMERICAN DIABETES ASSOC. LOUISIANA AFFILIATE, INC Baton Rouge, LA

**TRINITY LUTHERAN TODAY** TRINITY LUTHERAN HOSPITAL Kansas City, MO

**TRINITY TIMES** TRINITY UNIVERSAL INSURANCE CO. Dallas, TX

**TRINOVA** AEROQUIP CORP. Maumee, OH

**TRISKELION, THE** STONE & WEBSTER ENGINEERING CORP. Boston, MA

**TROY-BILT OWNER NEWS** GARDEN WAY MFG. CO. INC. Troy, NY

**TRUCKBUILDERS PROGRESS** FREIGHTLINER CORP. Portland, OR

**TRUMPETER, THE** ACME MARKETS INC. Malvern, PA

**TURNING WHEELS** STUDEBAKER DRIVERS CLUB, INC. Oswego, IL

**TURNSTILE** PIGGLY WIGGLY CORP. Memphis, TN

**TWIN DISC** TWIN DISC INC. Racine, WI

**TYSON UPDATE** TYSON FOODS Springdale, AR

## U

**U A NEWS** UNITED AMERICAN INSURANCE CO. Dallas, TX

**U G I HORIZONS** UGI CORP. Valley Forge, PA

**U M COMMUNITY** UNITED METHODIST COMMUNICATIONS Nashville, TN

**U N M C NEWS** UNIVERSITY OF NEBRASKA MEDICAL CENTER Omaha, NE

**U P REPORTER** UNION PACIFIC RESOURCES CO. Ft. Worth, TX

**U P RESOURCES** UNION PACIFIC RESOURCES CO. Ft. Worth, TX

**U R R EMPLOYEE NEWSLETTER** UNION RAILROAD CO. Monroeville, PA

**U S D A EMPLOYEE NEWSLETTER** U.S. DEPARTMENT OF AGRICULTURE Washington, DC

**U S I A WORLD** U.S. INFORMATION AGENCY Washington, DC

**U-HAUL INTERNATIONAL NEWS** U-HAUL INTERNATIONAL, INC. Phoenix, AZ

**UNDERMOUND** EG & G MOUND APPLIED TECHNOLOGIES Miamisburg, OH

**UNICANEWS** ILCO UNICAN CORP. Rocky Mount, NC

**UNION ELECTRIC NEWS** UNION ELECTRIC CO. St. Louis, MO

**UNITED WAY ANNUAL REPORT** UNITED WAY OF BUFFALO & ERIE COUNTY Buffalo, NY

**UNITED WAY LEADER** UNITED WAY SERVICES Cleveland, OH

**UNITED WAY NEWSLETTER** UNITED WAY OF THE NATIONAL CAPITAL AREA Washington, DC

**UNITY** UNION BANK San Francisco, CA

**UNIVERSE** JET PROPULSION LABORATORY, CIT Pasadena, CA

**UNIVERSITY OF DAYTON CAMPUS REPORT, THE** UNIVERSITY OF DAYTON Dayton, OH

**UNIVERSITY OF DAYTON QUARTERLY** UNIVERSITY OF DAYTON Dayton, OH

**UNIVERSITY OF ROCHESTER CURRENTS** UNIVERSITY OF ROCHESTER Rochester, NY

**UNIWORLD** UNISTRUT CORPORATION Ann Arbor, MI

**UNUM TODAY** UNUM CORP. Portland, ME

**UP FRONT** BURGER KING CORP. Miami, FL

**UP FRONT** THERMO KING Minneapolis, MN

**UP FRONT WISCONSIN** GEORGIA-PACIFIC CORP. Port Edwards, WI

**UPBEAT** DEPAUL HEALTH CTR. Hazelwood, MO

**UPDATE** CAROLINA POWER & LIGHT CO. Raleigh, NC

**UPDATE** CHILDREN'S HOSPITAL OF THE KING'S DAUGHTERS Norfolk, VA

**UPDATE** ILLINOIS TOOL WORKS Glenview, IL

**UPDATE** JLG INDUSTRIES, INC. McConnellsburg, PA

**UPDATE** LEHIGH VALLEY BANK Bethlehem, PA

**UPDATE** LIBRARY OF CONGRESS Washington, DC

**UPDATE** MILES, INC. Pittsburgh, PA

**UPDATE** OHIO DEPARTMENT OF YOUTH SERVICES Columbus, OH

**UPDATE** PACIFIC HEALTH RESOURCES Los Angeles, CA

**UPDATE** PHILADELPHIA NATIONAL BANK Philadelphia, PA

**UPDATE** REGIS UNIVERSITY Denver, CO

**UPDATE** UTAH POWER, A DIVISION OF PACIFICORP, OREGON Salt Lake City, UT

**UPDATE, THE** GENERAL ATOMICS TECHNOLOGIES, INC. San Diego, CA

**URBAN APPALACHIAN VOICE** URBAN APPALACHIAN COUNCIL Cincinnati, OH

**US AIR NEWS** U.S. AIR GROUP, INC. Arlington, VA

**US MILEPOSTS** CP RAIL SYSTEM Minneapolis, MN

**US PIPER** UNITED STATES PIPE & FOUNDRY CO. Birmingham, AL

**US!** SHAKLEE CORP. San Francisco, CA

**UTILIBITS** TACOMA PUBLIC UTILITIES Tacoma, WA

## V

**V F W AUXILIARY** LADIES AUXILIARY TO VFW OF THE US Kansas City, MO

**VALENTINE NEWS** VALENTINE, THE MUSEUM OF THE LIFE & HISTORY OF RICHMOND Richmond, VA

**VALLEY REPORTS** VALLEY HOSPITAL Ridgewood, NJ

**VALUATION & THE LAW** AMERICAN APPRAISAL ASSOCIATES Milwaukee, WI

**VALUATION VIEWPOINT** AMERICAN APPRAISAL ASSOCIATES Milwaukee, WI

**VALVOLINE WORLD** VALVOLINE, INC. Lexington, KY

**VANGUARD** MUTUAL TRUST LIFE INSURANCE CO. Oak Brook, IL

**VANGUARD, THE** ALPHA BETA CO. La Habra, CA

**VANTAGE POINT** GREEN POINT SAVINGS BANK Flushing, NY

**VARIAN ASSOCIATES MAGAZINE** VARIAN ASSOCIATES, INC. Palo Alto, CA

**VECTORS** HUGHES AIRCRAFT CO. Los Angeles, CA

**VENTURE** SHELL OIL CO. Houston, TX

**VEPCO CURRENTS** VIRGINIA POWER CO. Richmond, VA

**VERITAS** UNIVERSITY OF MIAMI Coral Gables, FL

**VERNON MIRROR** VERNON CO. Newton, IA

**VERTIFLITE MAGAZINE** AMERICAN HELICOPTER SOCIETY, INC. Alexandria, VA

**VIA I T T** ITT CORP. New York, NY

**VIA INTERNATIONAL PORT OF NEW YORK-NEW JERSEY** PORT AUTHORITY OF NEW YORK & NEW JERSEY New York, NY

**VIACOMMENTS** VIACOM INTERNATIONAL INC. New York, NY

**VICKERS IN PRINT** VICKERS, INC. Troy, MI

**VIDEO MERCHANDISER** MAYTAG CO. Newton, IA

**VIDEO MONITOR** COMMUNICATION RESEARCH ASSOCIATES, INC. Silver Spring, MD

**VIEW** BELK STORES SERVICES INC. Charlotte, NC

**VIEWPOINT** KTVE-TV Monroe, LA

**VIEWPOINT** MARSH & MCLENNAN COMPANIES INC. New York, NY

**VIEWPOINT** OGILVY & MATHER Chicago, IL

**VIEWPOINT** SAN DIEGO MUNICIPAL EMPLOYEES ASSOCIATION San Diego, CA

**VIEWPOINT** SECURA INSURANCE Appleton, WI

**VIEWPOINT MAGAZINE** CNA INSURANCE Chicago, IL

**VILTER BOOSTER** VILTER MANUFACTURING CORP. Milwaukee, WI

**VIRGINIA P H C IMAGE** VIRGINIA ASSOCIATION OF PLUMBING HEATING COOLING CONTRACTORS Richmond, VA

**VIRGINIAN** VIRGINIA CREDIT UNION LEAGUE Lynchburg, VA

**VISION** MARTIN MARIETTA ELECTRONICS Orlando, FL

**VISION** SPRINT MID-ATLANTIC TELECOM Wake Forest, NC

**VISION** ST. JOSEPH'S HOSPITAL & MEDICAL CTR. Phoenix, AZ

**VISIONS** MALLINCKRODT MEDICAL, INC. St. Louis, MO

**VISIONS** 21ST CENTURY GENETICS COOPERATIVE Shawano, WI

**VISITOR** FIRST BAPTIST CHURCH MODESTO Modesto, CA

**VITAL LINES** ROBERT F. KENNEDY MEDICAL CENTER Hawthorne, CA

**VITAL SIGNS** SOUTHWEST TEXAS METHODIST HOSPITAL San Antonio, TX

**VITAL SIGNS** ST. VINCENT CHARITY HOSPITAL & HEALTH CTR. Cleveland, OH

**VOGT VIEWS** HENRY VOGT MACHINE CO. Louisville, KY

**VOICE** AKRON GENERAL MEDICAL CENTER Akron, OH

**VOICE** SAINT JOHN HOSPITAL Detroit, MI

**VOICE** ST. MARY'S HEALTH CENTER St. Louis, MO

**VOICE, THE** ORE-IDA FOODS, INC. Boise, ID

**VOLUNTEER-LINE** SALVATION ARMY, THE Washington, DC

## W

**W & R WORLD** WADDELL & REED INC. Overland Park, KS

**W F S JOURNAL** WILLIAMS CO., THE Tulsa, OK

**W I C I MEMBERSHIP & RESOURCE DIRECTORY** WOMEN IN COMMUNICATIONS Arlington, VA

**W N G MAINLINE** WILLIAMS CO., THE Tulsa, OK

**W P L PIPELINE** WILLIAMS CO., THE Tulsa, OK

**WACHOVIA NEWS** WACHOVIA BANK OF GEORGIA Atlanta, GA

**WALGREEN WORLD** WALGREEN CO. Deerfield, IL

**WARD'S BULLETIN** WARD'S NATURAL SCIENCE ESTABLISHMENT, INC. Rochester, NY

**WASHINGTON CAPITOL MONITOR** HILLENBRAND INDUSTRIES, INC. Batesville, IN

**WASHINGTON LEARNING** SUPERINTENDENT OF PUBLIC INSTRUCTION Olympia, WA

**WASHINGTON MOTORIST** AAA WASHINGTON Bellevue, WA

**WATER LINES** INDIANAPOLIS WATER CO. Indianapolis, IN

**WATER QUALITY MONITOR** ASSOCIATION OF CALIFORNIA WATER AGENCIES Sacramento, CA

**WATER SKIER, THE** AMERICAN WATER SKI ASSOCIATION Winter Haven, FL

**WATERWEEK** AMERICAN WATER WORKS ASSOCIATION Denver, CO

**WATKINS WORLD** WATKINS PRODUCTS INC. Winona, MN

**WATT'S HAPPENING, THE** COMMONWEALTH EDISON Chicago, IL

**WATT'S NEW** WEST PENN POWER CO. Greensburg, PA

**WATTS N' WATER NEWS** KANSAS CITY BOARD OF PUBLIC UTILITIES Kansas City, KS

**WATTS WATT** CORN BELT POWER COOPERATIVE Humboldt, IA

**WAVELENGHT** PACIFIC MUTUAL LIFE INS. CO. Newport Beach, CA

**WAYN-E-GRAM** CONTINENTAL GRAIN CO., WAYNE FEED DIVISION Chicago, IL

**WBC BULLETIN** WASHINGTON BUILDING CONGRESS, INC. Washington, DC

**WE NEWS** GIANT FOOD, INC. Landover, MD

**WE THE PEOPLE** MERRILL LYNCH & CO., INC. New York, NY

**WEB, THE** ADAMS BUSINESS FORMS, INC. Topeka, KS

**WEDNESDAY UPDATE** PROTECTIVE LIFE INS. CO. Birmingham, AL

**WEEKLY** NATIONAL LIFE OF VERMONT Montpelier, VT

**WEEKLY** WASHINGTON WATER POWER CO., THE Spokane, WA

**WEEKLY EXPOSURE** OLAN MILLS OF TENNESSEE Chattanooga, TN

**WEEKLY NEWS SUMMARY** GENERAL MOTORS CORP. Marion, IN

**WEEKLY UPDATE** CENTRAL MAINE POWER CO. Augusta, ME

**WEEKLY, THE** ST. JOSEPH MEDICAL CENTER Fort Wayne, IN

**WELCH'S NEWS** WELCH'S Concord, MA

**WELL LOG** NATIONAL GROUND WATER ASSOCIATION Dublin, OH

**WELL SAID** CONTINENTAL BANK Chicago, IL

**WELLCOME NEWS** BURROUGHS WELLCOME CO. Durham, NC

**WELLNESS** SETON MEDICAL CENTER Austin, TX

**WELLNESS NEWS** WASHINGTON DEPARTMENT OF NATURAL RESOURCES Olympia, WA

**WEST PENN NEWS** WEST PENN POWER CO. Greensburg, PA

**WESTERN WATER** WATER EDUCATION FOUNDATION Sacramento, CA

**WESTERNER** WESTERN STATE EQUIPMENT CO. Boise, ID

**WESTIMES** CIBA-GEIGY CORP. Ardsley, NY

**WESTINGHOUSE NEWS** WESTINGHOUSE ELECTRIC CORP. Pittsburgh, PA

**WESTWORDS:** CUNA MUTUAL INSURANCE GROUP Pomona, CA

**WHAT'S COOKIN'** COOK'S PEST CONTROL, INC. Decatur, AL

**WHAT'S GOING ON** AMERICAN UNITED LIFE INSURANCE COMPANY Indianapolis, IN

**WHAT'S HAPPENING** SCHRAMM INC. West Chester, PA

**WHEEL** NEW ENGLAND MUTUAL LIFE INSURANCE CO. Boston, MA

**WHETSTONE** NORTH CAROLINA MUTUAL LIFE INSURANCE CO. Durham, NC

**WHIRLPOOL WORLD** WHIRLPOOL CORPORATION Benton Harbor, MI

**WHITING NEWS** WHITING CORPORATION Harvey, IL

**WICK-LIFE** LUBRIZOL CORP. THE Wickliffe, OH

**WIN-WOMEN'S INFORMATION NETWORK** GROSSMONT HOSPITAL La Mesa, CA

**WINDJAMMER** GAST MFG. CORP. Benton Harbor, MI

**WINDOWS TO YOUR SCHOOL** JORDAN SCHOOL DISTRICT Sandy, UT

**WIRE, THE** BANK ONE, INDIANAPOLIS, NA Indianapolis, IN

**WISCONSIN IDEAS** UNIVERSITY OF WISCONSIN SYSTEM Madison, WI

**WISCONSIN NATURAL RESOURCES MAGAZINE** WISCONSIN DEPARTMENT OF NATURAL RESOURCES Madison, WI

**WISCONSIN REC NEWS** WISCONSIN ELECTRIC COOPERATIVE ASSOCIATION Madison, WI

**WITNESS** LAWYERS CO-OP PUBLISHING CO. Rochester, NY

**WITTS-WITHIN THE I T T SYSTEM** ITT CORP. New York, NY

**WOLVERINE NEWS** WOLVERINE WORLD WIDE Rockford, MI

**WOMAN BOWLER** WOMEN'S INTERNATIONAL BOWLING CONGRESS Greendale, WI

**WOMEN'S HEALTH FOCUS QUARTERLY** ROCKINGHAM MEMORIAL HOSPITAL Harrisonburg, VA

**WOODLOTHIAN** WOODWARD & LATHROP, INC. Washington, DC

**WORKSTYLE NEWSLETTER** KELLY SERVICES, INC. Troy, MI

**WORLD BANK NEWS** WORLD BANK Washington, DC

**WORLD BOOK OF MEMBERS & SERVICES** INTERNATIONAL ASSOCIATION OF BUSINESS COMMUNICATORS San Francisco, CA

**WORLD BOOKER, THE** WORLD BOOK, INC. Omaha, NE

**WORLD PARISH** CATHOLIC FOREIGN MISSION SOCIETY Maryknoll, NY

**WORLDWIDE UPDATE** FEDERAL EXPRESS CORP. Memphis, TN

**WRITINGS ON THE WALL** NATIONAL GYPSUM CO. Charlotte, NC

## X

**XEROX WORLD** XEROX Stanford, CT

## Y

**YARDLINES** NEWPORT NEWS SHIPBUILDING & DRY DOCK CO. Newport News, VA

**YIELDS** FARM CREDIT SERVICES Spokane, WA

**YOU** COLONIAL PENN GROUP INC. Philadelphia, PA

**YOU** UTICA NATIONAL INSURANCE GROUP New Hartford, NY

**YOUNG AMBASSADOR** GOOD NEWS BROADCASTING ASSOCIATION, INC. Lincoln, NE

**YOUNG NEWS & VIEWS** YOUNG RADIATOR CO. Racine, WI

**YOUNKERS REPORTER** YOUNKERS, INC. Des Moines, IA

**YOUR HEALTH & FITNESS** GENERAL HEARING CORP. Northbrook, IL

**YOUR HEALTH CARE BENEFITS & HOW TO USE THEM** BLUE CROSS & BLUE SHIELD OF WEST VIRGINIA, INC. Charleston, WV

**YOUR WAY** UNITED WAY OF GREATER GREENSBORO Greensboro, NC

## Z

**ZIP-A-GRAM** ZIPPO MANUFACTURING CO. Bradford, PA

**141 EXPRESS** STATE LIFE INSURANCE CO. Indianapolis, IN

**3-C** FEDERAL RESERVE BANK OF PHILADELPHIA Philadelphia, PA

**32 E EVENTS** SERVICE EMPLOYEES INTERNATIONAL UNION, LOCAL 32E Bronx, NY

This section contains an alphabetical listing of internal publication sponsors arranged by industry affiliation.

## ADVERTISING, ART, PUBLIC RELATIONS

ASM INTERNATIONAL
BILL COMMUNICATIONS, INC.
BUCYRUS-ERIE CO.
BURLINGTON INDUSTRIES
BUSINESS COUNCIL FOR THE UNITED NATIONS
COMMUNICATION RESEARCH ASSOCIATES, INC.
DATAPOINT CORP.
GEORGIA-PACIFIC BRUNSWICK OPERATIONS
JII SALES PROMOTION ASSOCIATES, INC.
KAMPGROUNDS OF AMERICA, INC.
KENTUCKY DEPARTMENT OF EDUCATION
METRO CREATIVE GRAPHICS, INC.
NATIONAL SCHOOL PUBLIC RELATIONS ASSOCIATION
PHILIP MORRIS, USA
PIPER JAFFRAY
SANDY CORPORATION
SOCIETY CORP.
TRANSACTION-PUBLISHERS
U.S. SAVINGS BONDS DIVISION
VERNON CO.
WATKINS PRODUCTS INC.
WESTINGHOUSE HANFORD COMPANY

## AGRICULTURE, SERVICES

AGWAY INC.
ALABAMA FARMERS FEDERATION
C. BREWER & CO. LTD.
CARGILL FERTILIZER, INC.
CENEX/LAND O'LAKES
COUNTRYMARK COOP
DEERE & CO.
FARM CREDIT SERVICES
ILLINOIS FARM BUREAU
INDIANA FARM BUREAU, INC.
MISSISSIPPI CHEMICAL CORP.
NATIONAL SUNFLOWER ASSOCIATION
NEW FARM MAGAZINE
NEWHALL LAND & FARMING CO.
SOUTHERN STATES COOPERATIVE
TERRA CHEMICALS INT'L., INC.
UNION PLANTERS
URBAN APPALACHIAN COUNCIL
WILLIAMS CO., THE
21ST CENTURY GENETICS COOPERATIVE

## AIRCRAFT, AEROSPACE, DEFENSE

AEROQUIP CORP.
AEROSPACE CORP.
ALLIED-SIGNAL AEROSPACE CO.
BEECH AIRCRAFT CORP.
BELL HELICOPTER TEXTRON, INC.
BOEING CO.
DUCOMMUN, INC.
ELECTRONICS INFORMATION & MISSILES GROUP
GE AIRCRAFT ENGINES
GENCORP
GRUMMAN CORP.
HONEYWELL, INC.
HUGHES AIRCRAFT CO.
ITT AEROSPACE, COMMUNICATIONS DIVISION
LITTON GUIDANCE & CONTROL SYSTEMS
LOCKHEED FORT WORTH CO.
LORAL DEFENSE SYSTEMS-AKRON
MARTIN MARIETTA ELECTRONICS
NASA LEWIS RESEARCH CENTER
NAVAL AIR WARFARE CENTER
NAVAL NUCLEAR FUEL DIVISION
NORTHROP-GRUMMAN CORP.
ROCKWELL INTERNATIONAL, COMMAND & CONTROL SYSTEMS DIVISION
SCHWEIZER AIRCRAFT CORP.
SIKORSKY AIRCRAFT
SMITHS INDUSTRIES AEROSPACE & DEFENSE SYSTEMS, INC.
STATE OF NEBRASKA
THIOKOL CORP.

## AIRLINES

AMERICA WEST AIRLINES
AMERICAN AIRLINES INC.
DELTA AIR LINES
NORTHWEST AIRLINES, INC.
SCANDINAVIAN AIRLINES SYSTEM INC.
TRANS WORLD AIRLINES INC.
U.S. AIR GROUP, INC.

## ALUMINUM

ALUMINUM COMPANY OF AMERICA
MIRRO CORP.

## ARCHITECTS, ENGINEERS, BUSINESS SERVICE

APPLIED TECHNOLOGY COUNCIL
EBASCO SERVICES INC.
FACTORY MUTUAL ENGINEERING AND RESEARCH
FOSTER WHEELER CORP.
GILBERT/COMMONWEALTH, INC.
GRUCON CORP.
HOLMES & NARVER, INC.
HTB, INC.
JACOBS ENGINEERING
MASTER BUILDERS' ASSOCIATION OF WESTERN PA/AGC
OGILVY & MATHER
PORT OF HOUSTON MAGAZINE
REDDY CORP. INTERNATIONAL
REVCO, D.S. INC.
STAINLESS FOUNDRY & ENGINEERING INC.
TEXAS SOCIETY OF ARCHITECTS
TEXAS SOCIETY OF PROFESSIONAL ENGINEERS

## ASSOCIATIONS: CITY, STATE, FEDERAL

AFSCME
AGENCY FOR INTERNATIONAL DEVELOPMENT
ALBANY INTERNATIONAL CORP.
ALBERTO-CULVER CO.
ALEUT CORP.
AMARILLO CHAMBER OF COMMERCE
AMERICAN ASSOCIATION OF COLLEGES FOR
  TEACHER EDUCATION
ARKANSAS DEPARTMENT OF PARKS & TOURISM
ARKANSAS INDUSTRIAL DEVELOPMENT COMMISSION
ARMY & AIR FORCE EXCHANGE SERVICE
ASSOCIATED PUBLIC-SAFETY COMMUNICATIONS
  OFFICE
BEAUMONT CHAMBER OF COMMERCE
BIG BROTHERS OF GREATER LOS ANGELES, INC.
BUREAU OF NATIONAL AFFAIRS, INC.
CALIFORNIA CREDIT UNION LEAGUE
CALIFORNIA HISPANIC AMERICAN MEDICAL
  ASSOCIATION
CALIFORNIA SCHOOL BOARDS ASSOCIATION
CALIFORNIA STATE EMPLOYEES ASSOCIATION
CALIFORNIA TAXPAYERS ASSOCIATION
CHICAGO PARK DISTRICT
CITY OF BOSTON
CITY OF CINCINNATI
CITY OF DAYTON
CITY OF DETROIT
CITY OF JACKSON MISSISSIPPI
CITY OF RICHARDSON TEXAS
CITY OF RICHMOND VIRGINIA
CITY OF ST. PETERSBURG
COLONIAL WILLIAMSBURG FOUNDATION
COLORADO MUNICIPAL LEAGUE
CONNECTICUT BUSINESS & INDUSTRY ASSOCIATION
COUNCIL FOR ADVANCEMENT & SUPPORT OF
  EDUCATION
EASTERN NEBRASKA OFFICE ON AGING
ELECTRIC COUNCIL OF NEW ENGLAND
ENVIRONMENTAL LOBBY OF MASSACHUSETTS
ERIE AREA CHAMBER OF COMMERCE
FEDERAL HIGHWAY ADMINISTRATION
FEDERATION FOR COMMUNITY PLANNING
FORT WORTH CHAMBER OF COMMERCE
GEORGIA MUNICIPAL ASSOCIATION
GEORGIA REVENUE DEPT.
GOVERNMENT EMPLOYEES INSURANCE CO.
GREATER BATON ROUGE CHAMBER OF COMMERCE
GREATER CINCINNATI CHAMBER OF COMMERCE
GREATER CLEVELAND GROWTH ASSOCIATION
GREATER MADISON CONVENTION & VISITORS
  BUREAU
GREATER SAN DIEGO CHAMBER OF COMMERCE
GREATER WASHINGTON BOARD OF TRADE, THE
HANDGUN CONTROL, INC.
INDIANA DEPT. OF TRANSPORTATION
INDIANA JUDICIAL CENTER
INDUSTRIAL COMMISSION
IOWA DEPARTMENT OF ECONOMIC DEVELOPMENT
IOWA STATE ASSOCIATION OF COUNTIES
KANSAS CITY KANSAS CHAMBER OF COMMERCE
LEAGUE OF IOWA MUNICIPALITIES
METROPOLITAN MILWAUKEE ASSOCIATION OF
  COMMERCE
MICHIGAN EMPLOYMENT SECURITY COMMISSION
MINNESOTA DEPARTMENT OF TRANSPORTATION
MINNESOTA STATE COUNCIL ON DISABILITY
MISSOURI FARM BUREAU FEDERATION
NATIONAL FIRE PROTECTION ASSOCIATION
NEBRASKA DEPT. OF ECONOMIC DEVELOPMENT
NEVADA COMMISSION ON TOURISM
NEW DETROIT, INC.
NEW JERSEY STATE SAFETY COUNCIL
NEW ORLEANS, CITY OF
OHIO BUREAU OF WORKER'S COMPENSATION
OHIO CHAMBER OF COMMERCE
OHIO DEPARTMENT OF YOUTH SERVICES
OHIO STATE MEDICAL ASSOCIATION
OKLAHOMA ASSOCIATION OF ELECTRIC
  COOPERATIVES
OKLAHOMA DEPARTMENT OF COMMERCE
OREGON DEPARTMENT OF EDUCATION

OREGON DEPT. OF FORESTRY
PASEO DEL RIO ASSOCIATION
PINELLAS COUNTY GOVERNMENT
SAN DIEGO MUNICIPAL EMPLOYEES ASSOCIATION
SAN LUIS OBISPO CHAMBER OF COMMERCE
SHELBY COUNTY GOVERNMENT
SOCIAL SECURITY ADMINISTRATION
SOUTH CAROLINA DEPARTMENT OF COMMERCE
ST. LOUIS POLICE DEPARTMENT
STATE DEPARTMENT OF EDUCATION
SUPERINTENDENT OF PUBLIC INSTRUCTION
TEXAS HIGH SCHOOL COACHES ASSOCIATION INC.
TEXAS SAFETY ASSOCIATION
U.S. AIR FORCE
U.S. DEPARTMENT OF AGRICULTURE
U.S. DEPARTMENT OF ENERGY
U.S. DEPARTMENT OF ENERGY
U.S. INFORMATION AGENCY
U.S. POSTAL SERVICE, COMMUNICATIONS DEPT.
UNITED STATES ARMY
UNITED WAY OF KING COUNTY
UNITED WAY OF METROPOLITAN TARRANT COUNTY
UNITED WAY OF ORANGE COUNTY
UNITED WAY OF SUMMIT COUNTY
UNITED WAY OF THE NATIONAL CAPITAL AREA
UNITED WAY SERVICES
VIRGINIA DEPARTMENT OF ALCOHOLIC BEVERAGE
  CONTROL
VIRGINIA DEPARTMENT OF TRANSPORTATION
WASHINGTON DEPARTMENT OF NATURAL
  RESOURCES
WISCONSIN ASSOCIATION OF HOMES FOR THE
  AGING
WISCONSIN DEPARTMENT OF NATURAL RESOURCES
WOLVERINE WORLD WIDE
WOODWARD & LATHROP, INC.

## ASSOCIATIONS: HEALTH GROUPS

ALABAMA DEPT. OF PUBLIC HEALTH
AMERICAN ACADEMY OF ORTHOPAEDIC SURGEONS
AMERICAN CANCER SOCIETY
AMERICAN COLLEGE OF RHEUMATOLOGY
AMERICAN DIABETES ASSOC. LOUISIANA AFFILIATE,
  INC
AMERICAN DIABETES ASSOCIATION
AMERICAN HEALTH CARE ASSOCIATION
AMERICAN HEART ASSOCIATION
AMERICAN LUNG ASSOCIATION OF ALABAMA
AMERICAN LUNG ASSOCIATION OF GEORGIA
AMERICAN LUNG ASSOCIATION OF TEXAS
AMERICAN PODIATRIC WRITERS ASSOCIATION
AMERICAN SOCIETY OF INTERNAL MEDICINE
AMERICAN VOLKSSPORT ASSOCIATION
ARC, NATIONAL HEADQUARTERS
ASSOCIATION OF BIRTH DEFECT CHILDREN, INC.
BALTIMORE ASSOCIATION FOR RETARDED CITIZENS,
  INC.
BAUSCH & LOMB, INC.
BLOOD SYSTEMS
CAPITAL BLUE CROSS
CATHOLIC PRESS ASSOCIATION
CYSTIC FIBROSIS FOUNDATION
DALLAS LIGHTHOUSE FOR THE BLIND, INC.
DEKALB GENETICS CORP.
DURACLEAN INTERNATIONAL
EASTER SEAL SOCIETY OF WISCONSIN, INC.
EASTERN NEBRASKA COMMUNITY OFFICE OF
  RETARDATION
ELCO INDUSTRIES, INC.
FHP INTERNATIONAL CORP.
GATEWAY YOUTH & FAMILY SERVICES
GMHC, INC.
GROUP HEALTH ASSOCIATION OF AMERICA, INC.
GROUP HEALTH, INC.
HUMANE SOCIETY FOR TACOMA & PIERCE
  COUNTIES, THE
LOUISIANA STATE MEDICAL SOCIETY
MALLINCKRODT MEDICAL, INC.
MCKESSON CORPORATION
MENTAL HEALTH ASSOCIATION OF ERIE COUNTY INC.
MULTNOMAH COUNTY MEDICAL SOCIETY
NATIONAL MULTIPLE SCLEROSIS SOCIETY
NATIONAL RURAL HEALTH ASSOCIATION

NATIONAL SAFETY COUNCIL
PITTSBURGH BLIND ASSOCIATION
SMITH & NEPHEW RICHARDS INC.
UNITED CEREBRAL PALSY ASSOCIATION OF NASSAU
  COUNTY, INC.
UNITED WAY OF GREATER GREENSBORO
UNITED WAY OF THE GREATER DAYTON AREA
UTAH DEPARTMENT OF HUMAN SERVICES
VIRGINIA DEPARTMENT OF MENTAL HEALTH,
  RETARDATION-SUBSTANCE ABUS SERVICES

## ASSOCIATIONS: TRADE, FRATERNAL

AAA IOWA
AAA WASHINGTON
AIR LINE PILOTS ASSOCIATION
ALADDIN SYNERGETICS INC.
ALLIED GROUP
AMERICAN ASSOCIATION OF ORAL & MAXILLOFACIAL
  SURGEONS
AMERICAN AUTOMOBILE ASSOCIATION (WISCONSIN)
AMERICAN BOAT & YACHT COUNCIL INC.
AMERICAN HELICOPTER SOCIETY, INC.
AMERICAN LEGION AUXILIARY
AMERICAN PHYSICAL THERAPY ASSOCIATION, INC.
AMERICAN SOCIETY OF INTERIOR DESIGNERS
AMERICAN WATER SKI ASSOCIATION
AMERON, INC.
ARKANSAS FARM BUREAU FEDERATION
ARKANSAS PRESS ASSOCIATION
ASSOCIATED INDUSTRIES OF KENTUCKY
ASSOCIATED PENNSYLVANIA CONSTRUCTORS
ASSOCIATION OF FORMER STUDENTS TEXAS A&M
  UNIVERSITY
AUTO CLUB OF MICHIGAN
BLACK HAWK COUNCIL OF GIRL SCOUTS
BOWLING PROPRIETORS' ASSOCIATION OF AMERICA
BRAILLE INSTITUTE OF AMERICA, INC.
CALIFORNIA TEACHERS ASSOCIATION
CATHOLIC FOREIGN MISSION SOCIETY
CENTRAL NEW YORK GIRL SCOUT COUNCIL INC.
CHESAPEAKE BAY GIRL SCOUT COUNCIL
CINCINNATI BAR ASSOCIATION
CIVITAN INTERNATIONAL
COLORADO ASSN. OF REALTORS
COLORADO ASSOCIATION OF PUBLIC EMPLOYEES
COLORADO SOCIETY OF CERTIFIED PUBLIC
  ACCOUNTANTS
CONNECTICUT EDUCATION ASSOCIATION
COOK COMPOSITES
COOK'S PEST CONTROL, INC.
COOPER INDUSTRIES, INC.
CORN REFINERS ASSOCIATION, INC.
CP RAIL SYSTEM
CREDIT UNION NATIONAL ASSOCIATION INC.
DRESSER INDUSTRIES, INC.
DRESSER INDUSTRIES, INC.
DURHAM CHAMBER OF COMMERCE
EASTERN MILK PRODUCERS CO-OP ASSN. INC.
ELECTRONIC INDUSTRIES ASSOCIATION
EMPLOYERS GROUP
ENGINEERING SOCIETY OF DETROIT
FATHER FLANAGAN'S BOY'S HOME
FIRST BAPTIST CHURCH MODESTO
FIRST HAWAIIAN, INC.
FLORIDA RURAL ELECTRIC CO-OP ASSOCIATION
FLORISTS TRANSWORLD DELIVERY ASSOCIATION
FUTURE BUSINESS LEADERS OF AMERICA-PHI BETA
  LAMBDA
GENERAL HEARING CORP.
GIRL SCOUT COUNCIL OF GREATER MINNEAPOLIS
GIRL SCOUT COUNCIL OF GREATER ST. LOUIS
GLENMARY SISTERS
GOODWILL INDUSTRIES INTERNATIONAL, INC.
GOODWILL INDUSTRIES OF HOUSTON
GOODWILL INDUSTRIES OF SOUTHERN CALIFORNIA
GRACO INC.
GREATER HOUSTON BUILDERS ASSOCIATION
GREATER OMAHA CHAMBER OF COMMERCE
GREATER RENO-SPARKS CHAMBER OF COMMERCE
GREATER WINSTON-SALEM CHAMBER OF
  COMMERCE
GUARDIAN CORPORATION
GUTHRIE THEATRE

HAGGAR CO.
HANDY & HARMAN CO.
HARBISON-WALKER REFRACTORIES CO.
HARRIS CORP.
HAWAII GOVERNMENT EMPLOYEES ASSN., AFSCME LOCAL 15
HIA (HOBBY INDUSTRY ASSOCIATION OF AMERICA)
HOME BUILDERS ASSOCIATION OF GREATER ST. LOUIS
HONEYWELL, INC.
ILLINOIS CREDIT UNION LEAGUE
ILLINOIS SOCIETY OF PROFESSIONAL ENGINEERS
IN-PLANT MANAGEMENT ASSOCIATION
INDIANA CREDIT UNION LEAGUE, INC.
INDIANA MANUFACTURERS ASSOCIATION, INC.
INTERNATIONAL ASSOCIATION OF BUSINESS COMMUNICATORS
INTERNATIONAL BROTHERHOOD OF LOCOMOTIVE ENGINEERS
INTERNATIONAL COMMUNICATIONS INDUSTRIES ASSN., THE
INTERNATIONAL CREDIT ASSOCIATION
INTERNATIONAL FLYING FARMERS
IOWA ASSOCIATION OF ELECTRIC COOPERATIVES
IRISH AMERICAN CULTURAL INSTITUTE
JEWISH COMMUNITY CENTER
JONATHAN CLUB
L.G. BALFOUR CO.
LAACO, INC.
LADIES AUXILIARY TO VFW OF THE US
LAKE ERIE GIRL SCOUT COUNCIL
LAWRENCE RAGAN COMMUNICATIONS, INC.
LORD CORP.
LOS ANGELES JR. CHAMBER OF COMMERCE
LOUISIANA BANKERS ASSOCIATION
LOUISIANA FORESTRY ASSOCIATION
LOUISIANA PHARMACISTS ASSOCIATION
MACHINERY DEALERS NATIONAL ASSOCIATION
MANUFACTURED HOUSING INSTITUTE
MARINE OFFICE OF AMERICA CORP.
MARION MERRELL DOW INC.
MARSH & MCLENNAN COMPANIES INC.
MARYLAND STATE TEACHERS ASSOCIATION
METHODIST HOSPITAL
METHODIST HOSPITAL, THE
MICHIGAN MILK PRODUCERS ASSOCIATION
MICHIGAN TRUCKING ASSOCIATION
MID-AMERICA DAIRYMEN INC.
MINNESOTA SOCIETY OF CERTIFIED PUBLIC ACCOUNTANTS
N.J. STATE BAR ASSN.
NATIONAL ASSOCIATION OF FEDERAL CREDIT UNIONS
NATIONAL ASSOCIATION OF HOME & WORKSHOP WRITERS NEWSLETTER
NATIONAL ASSOCIATION OF RAILROAD PASSENGERS
NATIONAL ASSOCIATION OF WATCH & CLOCK COLLECTORS
NATIONAL AUTO DEALERS ASSN.
NATIONAL CHRISTMAS TREE ASSOCIATION
NATIONAL COLLEGE OF DISTRICT ATTORNEYS
NATIONAL COOPERATIVE BUSINESS ASSOCIATION
NATIONAL EDUCATION ASSOCIATION
NATIONAL EDUCATION PROGRAM
NATIONAL FEDERATION OF INDEPENDENT BUSINESS
NATIONAL MANAGEMENT ASSOCIATION
NATIONAL SCIENCE TEACHERS ASSOCIATION
NATIONAL SOCIETY OF FUND RAISING EXECUTIVES
NATIONAL SOFT DRINK ASSOCIATION
NOLAND CO.
NORTHWEST ELECTRIC LIGHT & POWER ASSOCIATION
NORTHWEST PUBLIC POWER ASSOCIATION
OHIO CREDIT UNION LEAGUE
OHIO FARM BUREAU FEDERATION
OHIO HARDWARE ASSOCIATION
OHIO PHARMACISTS ASSOCIATION
OHIO TRUCKING ASSOCIATION
OKLAHOMA BAR ASSOCIATION
OKLAHOMA RESTAURANT ASSOCIATION
ONAN CORP.
OPTIMIST INTERNATIONAL
OREGON ASSOCIATION OF NURSERYMEN
OREGON PUBLIC EMPLOYEES RETIREMENT SYSTEM
PENNSYLVANIA BAR ASSOCIATION

PENNSYLVANIA MUSIC EDUCATORS ASSOCIATION
PEOPLE FOR THE ETHICAL TREATMENT OF ANIMALS (PETA)
PHILADELPHIA BAR ASSOCIATION
PRETRIAL SERVICES RESOURCE CENTER
QUIVIRA COUNCIL, INC.
RADIO-TELEVISION NEWS DIRECTORS ASSOCIATION
RHODE ISLAND BUILDERS ASSOCIATION
ROCKY MOUNTAIN AAA CLUB
ROSICRUCIAN ORDER AMORC
SALVATION ARMY, THE
SAN FRANCISCO SPCA
SCRIPTURE PRESS PUBLICATIONS, INC.
SERVICE EMPLOYEES INTERNATIONAL UNION, LOCAL 32E
SIMON WIESENTHAL CENTER
SISTERS OF PROVIDENCE HEALTH SYSTEM
SOCIETY FOR HUMAN RESOURCE MANAGEMENT
SOCIETY OF AUTOMOTIVE ENGINEERS INC.
SOCIETY OF WOMEN ENGINEERS
SOROPTIMIST INTERNATIONAL OF THE AMERICAS, INC.
SOUTHERN ARTS FEDERATION, INC.
ST. LOUIS AREA COUNCIL, B.S.A.
STATE BAR OF TEXAS
STUDEBAKER DRIVERS CLUB, INC.
T.L. JAMES & CO., INC.
TEACHERS ASSOCIATION OF BALTIMORE COUNTY MD., INC.
TENNESSEE EDUCATION ASSOCIATION
TENNESSEE ELECTRIC COOP ASSOCIATION
TEXAS ASSOCIATION OF REALTORS
TEXAS CONGRESS OF PARENTS & TEACHERS
TEXAS ELECTRIC COOPS INC.
TEXAS INDEPENDENT PRODUCERS & ROYALTY OWNERS ASSOCIATIOIN
TEXAS MEDICAL ASSOCIATION
TEXAS NURSES ASSOCIATION
TEXAS PRESS ASSOCIATION
TEXAS PUBLIC EMPLOYEES ASSOCIATION
TOPFLIGHT CORP.
TOWERS PERRIN
TRANSPORTATION COMMUNICATIONS INTERNATIONAL UNION
TRIANGLE DISTRIBUTING CO.
UNITED COMMERCIAL TRAVELERS OF AMERICA
UNITED METHODIST COMMUNICATIONS
UNITED STATES JUNIOR CHAMBER OF COMMERCE, THE
UNITED STATES SPORTS ACADEMY
UNITED WAY OF BUFFALO & ERIE COUNTY
VIRGINIA ASSOCIATION OF PLUMBING HEATING COOLING CONTRACTORS
WASHINGTON BUILDING CONGRESS, INC.
WISCONSIN FARM BUREAU FEDERATION
WOMAN'S MISSIONARY UNION SBC
WOMEN IN COMMUNICATIONS INC.
WOMEN'S INTERNATIONAL BOWLING CONGRESS
ZALE CORP.
ZIMPRO ENVIRONMENTAL, INC.
ZIPPO MANUFACTURING CO.

## AUTO SUPPLIERS

ATLAS SUPPLY CO.
AVIS, INC.
BORG-WARNER AUTOMOTIVE, TRANSMISSION SYSTEMS
CHRYSLER CORP.
FELT PRO INC.
FORD MOTOR COMPANY, SHARONVILLE PLANT
GENUINE PARTS CO., INC.
MOTOROLA, INC.
OTC DIVISION OF SPX
SUBARU OF AMERICA, INC.
TOYOTA MOTOR SALES USA, INC.

## AUTOS, TRUCKS

AC ROCHESTER DIVISION, GENERAL MOTORS CORPORATION
AMERICAN HONDA MOTOR CO., INC.
ARIZONA AUTOMOBILE ASSOCIATION
COACHMAN INDUSTRIES, INC.

CONNECTICUT MOTOR CLUB
FEDERAL-MOGUL CORP.
FORD MOTOR COMPANY
GENERAL MOTORS CORP.
GENERAL MOTORS CORP.-U.A.W.
MACK TRUCKS INC.
OLDSMOBILE/DIV. GENERAL MOTORS
ORCHID ISLE AUTO CTR.
TEXAS AUTOMOBILE DEALERS ASSOCIATION
U-HAUL INTERNATIONAL, INC.

## BAKERY PRODUCTS

ARNOLD BAKERS, INC.
PEPPERIDGE FARM, INC.

## BANKS, SAVINGS & LOANS

ASSOCIATES CORPORATION OF NORTH AMERICA
BANCOKLAHOMA CORP.
BANK OF BOSTON CORP.
BANK OF HAWAII
BANK OF NEW YORK, THE
BANK ONE
BANK ONE OF ARIZONA
BANK ONE, INDIANAPOLIS, NA
BANK SOUTH
BARNES GROUP, INC.
BARNETT BANKS, INC.
BB & T
BOATMEN'S BANK
BRANCH BANKING AND TRUST CO.
CHASE MANHATTAN BANK, N.A., THE
CHASE MANHATTAN CORP.
CHEMICAL BANKING CORP.
CITIBANK
COMERICA, INC.
CONTINENTAL BANK
CORAL GABLES FEDERAL SAVINGS & LOAN ASSOCIATION
CORESTATES FIRST PENNSYLVANIA BANK
EUROPEAN AMERICAN BANK
FEDERAL RESERVE BANK OF CHICAGO
FEDERAL RESERVE BANK OF CLEVELAND
FEDERAL RESERVE BANK OF DALLAS
FEDERAL RESERVE BANK OF NEW YORK
FEDERAL RESERVE BANK OF PHILADELPHIA
FIRST AMERICAN CORP.
FIRST CHICAGO CORPORATION
FIRST COMMERCE CORP.
FIRST COMMERCIAL BANK, N.A.
FIRST FEDERAL S & L ASSOCIATION OF ROCHESTER
FIRST FIDELITY BANCORPORATION
FIRST INTERSTATE BANCORP.
FIRST INTERSTATE BANK OF DENVER
FIRST INTERSTATE BANK OF NEVADA, N.A.
FIRST INTERSTATE BANK OF NORTHWEST REGION
FIRST NATIONAL BANK OF CINCINNATI CORP.
FIRST NATIONAL BANK OF MARYLAND
FIRST NATIONWIDE BANK
FIRST TENNESSEE NATIONAL CORP.
FIRST VIRGINIA BANK
FIRST-CITIZENS BANK & TRUST CO.
FIRSTIER BANK
FLEET BANK N.A.
GREEN POINT SAVINGS BANK
HUNTINGTON BANCSHARES, INC.
ILLINOIS LEAGUE OF SAVINGS INSTITUTIONS
INDIANA BANKERS ASSOCIATION, INC.
IOWA CREDIT UNION LEAGUE
LEADER FEDERAL SAVINGS & LOAN ASSOCIATION
LEHIGH VALLEY BANK
LIBERTY NATIONAL BANK & TRUST CO.
LOMAS FINANCIAL CORP.
M & T BANK
MARSHALL & ILSLEY BANK
MERIDIAN BANK
MIDLANTIC CORPORATION
MNC FINANCIAL, INC.
MORGAN GUARANTY TRUST CO. OF N.Y.
NATIONAL BANK OF COMMERCE
NATIONAL BANK OF DETROIT
NATIONAL CITY BANK, INDIANA
NATIONAL CITY CORP.

NATIONS BANK CORP.
NBD BANK
NORTHERN TRUST CO.
OKLAHOMA BANKERS ASSOCIATION
PACIFIC FIRST BANK
PEOPLE'S BANK
PHILADELPHIA NATIONAL BANK
PNC BANK
PREMIER BANK
ROBERT MORRIS ASSOCIATES
ROCHESTER COMMUNITY SAVINGS BANK
ROCKFORD MEMORIAL HOSPITAL
SANWA BANK CALIFORNIA
SEAFIRST CORP.
SHAWMUT BANK, CONNECTICUT
SIGNET BANKING CORP.
SYRACUSE SAVINGS BANK
TEXAS COMMERCE BANCSHARES, INC.
TRUSTMARK NATIONAL BANK
U.S. BANCORP
UNION BANK
VIRGINIA BANKERS ASSOCIATION
WACHOVIA BANK OF GEORGIA
WEOKIE CREDIT UNION
WORLD BANK

## BREWERS, DISTILLERS

ANHEUSER-BUSCH COMPANIES, INC.
BROWN-FORMAN, CORP.
COORS COURIER
MILLER BREWING CO.

## BRONZE, BRASS, COPPER

COPPERWELD CORP.

## BUS, TRANSIT

DALLAS AREA RAPID TRANSIT
NIAGARA FRONTIER TRANSPORTATION AUTHORITY
PENN TRAFFIC CO.

## CANDY

NESTLE USA, INC.
WORLD'S FINEST CHOCOLATE, INC.

## CEMENT, CERAMICS, CLAY

AMERICAN OLEAN TILE CO.
CALMAT CO.
KYOCERA INTERNATIONAL, INC.
NEWELL CO.

## CHEMICALS, PLASTICS

AMERICAN HOECHST CORP.
BASF CORPORATION CHEMICALS DIVISION
BRULIN & CO., INC.
BRUNSWICK CORP.
D-M-E CO.
DIVERSEY CORP.
DOW CORNING CORP.
E I DUPONT DE NEMOURS
E.F. HOUGHTON & CO.
EASTMAN CHEMICAL COMPANY
ECOLAB INC.
EG & G MOUND APPLIED TECHNOLOGIES
ELF ATOCHEM NORTH AMERICA, INC.
ETHYL CORP.
FALK CORP.
H.B. FULLER CO.
HOECHST CELANESE CORP.
KERR-MCGEE CORPORATION
MARION LABORATORIES, INC.
MILES, INC.
NALCO CHEMICAL CO.
NATIONAL GYPSUM CO.
NATIONAL STARCH & CHEMICAL CO.
QUANTUM CHEMICAL CORP., USI DIV.

RALPH WILSON PLASTICS CO.
S.C. JOHNSON & SON INC.
SHERWIN, INC.
STATE CHEMICAL MANUFACTURING CO.
TEXAS EASTMAN DIV., EASTMAN CHEMICAL CO.
U.S. BORAX INC.
W.R. GRACE & CO.

## COLLEGES, INSTITUTIONS, SCIENCE RESEARCH

AIR FORCE INSTITUTE OF TECHNOLOGY
ALABAMA EDUCATION ASSN.
AMERICAN COLLEGE OF EMERGENCY PHYSICIANS
AMERICAN COLLEGE OF SPORTS MEDICINE
AMERICAN PHILOSOPHICAL SOCIETY
APPLIED PHYSICS LABORATORY
ASSOCIATION OF SCIENCE-TECHNOLOGY CENTERS
AURORA PUBLIC SCHOOLS
BARTON COUNTY COMMUNITY COLLEGE
BAYLOR COLLEGE OF MEDICINE
BURLINGTON COUNTY COLLEGE
CARNEGIE MELLON UNIVERSITY
CHURCH DIVINITY SCHOOL OF THE PACIFIC
CONTINUING EDUCATION PRESS
CORNING INCORPORATED
CREIGHTON UNIVERSITY
DALLAS THEOLOGICAL SEMINARY
DUQUESNE UNIVERSITY
EAST VIRGINIA MEDICAL SCHOOL OF THE MEDICAL
   COLLEGE HAMPTON
EDUCATION & RESEARCH CTR. OF MISSISSIPPI
EX-STUDENTS ASSOCIATION
GEORGIA DEPARTMENT OF HUMAN RESOURCES
GRAND VALLEY STATE UNIVERSITY
GULF COAST RESEARCH LABORATORY
HILLSDALE COLLEGE
INTERNATIONAL UNIVERSITY FOUNDATION
IOWA STATE UNIVERSITY
JET PROPULSION LABORATORY, CIT
JORDAN SCHOOL DISTRICT
KEITH SCHOOL
KINDER CARE LEARNING CENTERS, INC.
LAWRENCE BERKELEY LABORATORY
LAWRENCE TECHNOLOGICAL UNIVERSITY
LOS ALMOS NATIONAL LABORATORY
LOYOLA UNIVERSITY
LUTHERAN MEDICAL CENTER
MASSACHUSETTS ASSOCIATION OF SCHOOL
   COMMITTEES
MEDICAL COLLEGE OF WISCONSIN
MICHIGAN STATE UNIVERSITY
MIDWEST RESEARCH INSTITUTE
MOTORCYCLE SAFETY FOUNDATION
MUSEUM OF SCIENCE
MUSEUM OF SCIENCE & INDUSTRY
NASHVILLE STATE TECHNICAL INSTITUTE
NATIONAL PTA
OAK RIDGE NATIONAL LABORATORY
OKLAHOMA CITY UNIVERSITY
OREGON STATE UNIVERSITY
ORLEANS PARRISH SCHOOL BOARD
OZONE INDUSTRIES INC.
PACE UNIVERSITY
PACIFIC LUTHERAN UNIVERSITY
PARKS COLLEGE OF ST. LOUIS UNIVERSITY
PINEY WOODS COUNTRY LIFE SCHOOL
PRESBYTERIAN-UNIV. OF PENNSYLVANIA MEDICAL
   CTR.
REGIS UNIVERSITY
RESEARCH MEDICAL CENTER
RESEARCH TRIANGLE INSTITUTE
ROCK VALLEY COLLEGE
ROCKHURST COLLEGE
SHANNON & WILSON INC.
SHAWNEE MISSION PUBLIC SCHOOLS
SOUTHERN ASSOCIATION OF COLLEGES & SCHOOLS
SOUTHERN METHODIST UNIVERSITY
ST. EDWARD'S UNIVERSITY
ST. LOUIS COMMUNITY COLLEGE AT FOREST PARK
STATE UNIVERSITY OF N.Y. HEALTH SCIENCE CTR. AT
   SYRACUSE
TEXAS A & M UNIVERSITY SYSTEM
TEXAS WESLEYAN UNIVERSITY

UNIVERSITY CIRCLE INC.
UNIVERSITY OF CINCINNATI
UNIVERSITY OF DAYTON
UNIVERSITY OF IOWA HOSPITALS & CLINICS
UNIVERSITY OF MIAMI
UNIVERSITY OF MISSOURI
UNIVERSITY OF MONTANA SCHOOL OF JOURNALISM
UNIVERSITY OF NEBRASKA MEDICAL CENTER
UNIVERSITY OF ROCHESTER
UNIVERSITY OF ST. THOMAS
UNIVERSITY OF UTAH MEDICAL CENTER
UNIVERSITY OF WISCONSIN MADISON CENTER
UNIVERSITY OF WISCONSIN SYSTEM
UTAH STATE UNIVERSITY
VALENTINE, THE MUSEUM OF THE LIFE & HISTORY
   OF RICHMOND
WARD'S NATURAL SCIENCE ESTABLISHMENT, INC.

## CONTAINERS, PACKAGES

AUBURN-CORD-DUESENBERG MUSEUM
BALL CORP.
WESTVACO CORP.

## COOLING, HEATING

CARRIER CORP.
COPELAND CORP.
HARRISON RADIATOR DIV.
MARLEY CO., THE
PLUMBING MECHANICAL CONTRACTORS COUNCIL
   HARRIS COUNTY
THERMO KING CORP.
VILTER MANUFACTURING CORP.
YOUNG RADIATOR CO.

## DAIRY PRODUCTS

ASSOCIATED MILK PRODUCERS, INC.
BRESLER'S ICE CREAM & YOGURT, INC.
CUMBERLAND FARMS, INC.
DAIRYLEA COOPERATIVE INC.
HOLSTEIN ASSOCIATION OF AMERICA
MILK MARKET ADMINISTRATOR
NATIONAL MILK PRODUCERS FEDERATION
WISCONSIN DAIRIES COOPERATIVE

## DENTAL, MEDICAL

CMP INUSTRIES, INC.
DENTAL SOCIETY OF THE STATE OF NEW YORK
DENTSPLY INTERNATIONAL INC.
ETHICON INC.
OHIO DENTAL ASSOCIATION

## DRUGS, COSMETICS, PHARMACEUTICALS

ABBOTT LABORATORIES
AMERICAN CYANAMID CO.
AMERICAN HOME PRODUCTS
BERGEN BRUNSWICK CORP.
BRISTOL-MYERS CO.
BURROUGHS WELLCOME CO.
CARDIAC PACEMAKERS INC.
CIBA-GEIGY CORP.
CLAIROL INC.
DAVOL INC.
GILLETTE COMPANY, THE
LEDERLE LABORATORIES DIV.
LONGS DRUG STORES, INC.
MERCK & CO. INC.
MERCK & CO., INC.
NATIONAL ASSOCIATION OF PHARMACEUTICAL
   MANUFACTURERS
NATIONAL WHOLESALE DRUGGISTS' ASSOCIATION
PFIZER, INC.
PHARMACEUTICAL MANUFACTURERS ASSOCIATION
SCHERING-PLOUGH CORP.
SHERWOOD MEDICAL CO.
SMITHKLINE BEECHAM

SMITHKLINE BEECHAM ANIMAL HEALTH
STERLING DRUG, INC.

## ELECTRICAL, ELECTRONIC, MANUFACTURING

A.B. CHANCE CO.
ALLEN-BRADLEY CO.
AMP INC., VALLEY FORGE
ANALOG DEVICES, INC.
APPLIED TECHNOLOGY
CORN BELT POWER COOPERATIVE
CUBIC CORP.
DELCO ELECTRONICS CORPORATION
E-SYSTEMS, INC.
EATON CORP.
ELDEC CORP.
ELECTRONIC ASSOCIATES, INC.
ENSIGN-BICKFORD INDUSTRIES, INC.
FURNAS ELECTRIC CO.
GE
GEORGIA POWER CO.
GTE CORP.
HEWLETT-PACKARD CO.
HOOVER CO.
ILCO UNICAN CORP.
INTERNATIONAL BUSINESS MACHINES CORP.
ITT CORP.
ITT GILFILLAN
JLG INDUSTRIES, INC.
KENTUCKY ASSOCIATION OF ELECTRIC
    COOPERATIVES
KOSS CORP.
LENNOX INDUSTRIES INC.
LINCOLN ELECTRIC CO., THE
LOCKHEED ADVANCED DEVELOPMENT CO.
MEDRAD INC.
MITRE CORP.
NATIONAL SEMICONDUCTOR CORP.
NC ASSOCIATION OF ELECTRICAL CONTRACTORS
OHIO RURAL ELECTRIC COOPS INC.
OTIS ELEVATOR CO.
PARAGON ELECTRIC COMPANY, INC.
PHILIPS ELECTRONICS INSTRUMENTS
PHILLIPS CONSUMER ELECTRONICS CORP.
RADIO SHACK DIVISION, TANDY CORP.
RAYTHEON CO.
SCIENTIFIC-ATLANTA, INC.
TANDYCRAFTS, INC.
TELEDYNE, INC.
TEXAS INSTRUMENTS, INC.
THERMO ELECTRON CORP.
THOMAS INDUSTRIES
UNISYS
UNITED ILLUMINATING CO.
VARIAN ASSOCIATES, INC.
WESTINGHOUSE ELECTRIC CORP.

## FINANCE, SERVICES

AMERICAN APPRAISAL ASSOCIATES
AMERICAN EXPRESS CO.
AMERICAN GENERAL FINANCE
ARA SERVICES INC.
AVCO FINANCIAL SERVICES
BENEFICIAL MANAGEMENT CORP.
CAP GEMIMI AMERICA
CIT GROUP
CONNECTICUT CREDIT UNION LEAGUE
DESERT SCHOOLS FEDERAL CREDIT UNION
EQUITABLE LIFE ASSURANCE SOCIETY
ERWIN DI CYAN
FIRST SECURITY CORP.
FLEET FINANCIAL GROUP, INC.
FLORIDA HORIZONS FEDERAL CREDIT UNION
HIGHEST PROFIT CORP.
INDIANA TELCO FEDERAL CREDIT UNION
INSTITUTE OF INTERNAL AUDITORS
INTERNATIONAL ASSOCIATION OF HOSPITALITY
    ACCOUNTANTS
KANSAS DEPARTMENT OF COMMERCE
MERRILL LYNCH & CO., INC.
MONARCH CAPITAL CORP.

MONROE SYSTEMS FOR BUSINESS
NATIONAL WESTMINSTER BANCORP
NATIONS CREDIT
NEW YORK STOCK EXCHANGE
NORWEST CORPORATION
NORWEST FINANCIAL, INC.
OPPENHEIMER MANAGEMENT CORP.
PRICE WATERHOUSE & CO.
PRINCIPAL FINANCIAL GROUP, THE
SAN FRANCISCO CHAMBER OF COMMERCE
SECURITIES INVESTIGATIONS, INC.
SOUTHEAST MICHIGAN, N.A.
STATE STREET BOSTON CORP.
TEXAS SOCIETY CERTIFIED PUBLIC ACCOUNTANTS
US SMALL BUSINESS ADMINISTRATION
VIRGINIA CREDIT UNION LEAGUE
WADDELL & REED INC.
WILMINGTON SAVINGS FUND SOCIETY

## FOOD, GENERAL

ALPHA BETA CO.
AMERICA'S FAVORITE CHICKEN
BEST FOODS, DIVISION OF CPC INTERNATIONAL, INC.
BLUE DIAMOND GROWERS
BURGER KING CORP.
COCA-COLA FOODS
FIRST NATIONAL SUPERMARKETS, INC.
FLEMING COS. INC.
GENERAL MILLS, INC.
GIANT FOOD, INC.
GILROY FOODS, INC.
GRAIN ELEVATOR AND PROCESSING SOCIETY
GRAND UNION CO.
HEINZ U.S.A.
HERSHEY FOODS CORP.
HICKORY FARMS OF OHIO INC.
HUBINGER CO., THE
IGA, INC.
JEWEL FOOD STORES
KANO LABS INC.
KELLOGG COMPANY
KFC CORP.
KRAFT-GENERAL FOODS
MAINE POTATO BOARD
MCCORMICK & CO., INC.
NALLEYS FINE FOODS
NATIONAL ASSOCIATION OF CONCESSIONAIRES
NESTLE-BEICH, INC.
ORE-IDA FOODS, INC.
PILLSBURY CO., THE
PIZZA HUT, INC.
PUBLIX SUPER MARKETS, INC.
QUAKER OATS CO.
RALPH'S GROCERY CO.
RALSTON PURINA CO.
RAX RESTAURANTS INC.
RJR NABISCO, NABISCO FOODS GROUP
SHAKLEE CORP.
SIZZLER INTERNATIONAL, INC.
STAR MARKET CO.
SUNKIST GROWERS, INC.
TYSON FOODS
WELCH'S

## GLASS

ANDERSEN CORP.
APOGEE ENTERPRISES, INC.
FOODSERVICE & PACKAGING INSTITUTE, INC.
OWENS-ILLINOIS INC.

## HARDWARE, PLUMBING

KOHLER CO.
MAYTAG CO.
STA-RITE INDUSTRIES

## HOME APPLIANCES, FURNISHINGS

BOSTWICK-BRAUN CO.
KIRBY CO.

LA-Z-BOY CHAIR CO.
MAGIC CHEF COMPANY
WEST BEND CO.
WHIRLPOOL CORPORATION
WHIRLPOOL CORPORATION

## HOSPITALS

ABBOTT NORTHWESTERN HOSPITAL INC.
AKRON CITY HOSPITAL
AKRON GENERAL MEDICAL CENTER
AL SIGL CENTER FOR REHABILITATION AGENCIES,
    INC.
ALFRED I DUPONT INSTITUTE
ALLIANT HEALTH SYSTEM
AMERICAN OCCUPATIONAL THERAPY ASSOCIATION
ANAHEIM MEMORIAL HOSPITAL
ARLINGTON HOSPITAL
BAPTIST HEALTH SYSTEM, THE
BAPTIST HOSPITAL INC.
BARNES HOSPITAL
BATON ROUGE GENERAL MEDICAL CTR.
BAYLOR UNIVERSITY MEDICAL CENTER
BETTER HEALTH PRESS
BRYAN MEMORIAL HOSPITAL
CALIFORNIA PACIFIC MEDICAL CENTER
CAROLINAS MEDICAL CENTER
CHILDREN'S HOSPITAL
CHILDREN'S HOSPITAL MEDICAL CENTER
CHILDREN'S HOSPITAL OAKLAND
CHILDREN'S HOSPITAL OF ORANGE COUNTY
CHILDREN'S HOSPITAL OF PHILADELPHIA, THE
CHILDREN'S HOSPITAL OF THE KING'S DAUGHTERS
CHILDREN'S MEDICAL CENTER
CLARKSON HOSPITAL
COMMUNITY HOSPITAL OF THE MONTEREY
    PENINSULA
COMMUNITY MEDICAL CENTER
COOPER HOSPITAL/UNIVERSITY MEDICAL CENTER
CRITTENTON HOSPITAL
DANIEL FREEMAN MEMORIAL HOSPITAL
DEPAUL HEALTH CTR.
GARDEN CITY HOSPITAL
GEISINGER SYSTEM
GOOD SAMARITAN HOSPITAL AND HEALTH CENTER
GROSSMONT HOSPITAL
HCA PRESBYTERIAN HOSPITAL
HOSPICE OF THE FLORIDA SUNCOAST
HOSPITAL OF THE UNIVERSITY OF PENNSYLVANIA
KINGSBROOK JEWISH MEDICAL CENTER
LIMA MEMORIAL HOSPITAL
LONG BEACH MEMORIAL MEDICAL CENTER
LOS ANGELES COUNTY MEDICAL ASSOCIATION
LYNCHBURG GENERAL-MARSHALL LODGE
    HOSPITALS
MEDICAL CENTER OF DELAWARE, THE
MELROSE-WAKEFIELD HOSPITAL
MEMORIAL HEALTHCARE SYSTEM
MEMORIAL SLOAN-KETTERING CANCER CENTER
MERCY HOSPITAL
MERCY HOSPITAL, INC.
MERCY MEDICAL CENTER
METHODIST HOSPITAL
METHODIST HOSPITALS OF DALLAS
MIAMI VALLEY HOSPITAL
MICHAEL REESE HOSPITAL & MEDICAL CENTER
MICHIGAN CAPITAL HEALTHCARE
MILLS-PENINSULA HOSPITALS
MISSISSIPPI BAPTIST MEDICAL CENTER
MOUNT SINAI MEDICAL CENTER
NEBRASKA METHODIST HOSPITAL
NEW BRITAIN GENERAL HOSPITAL
NORTH MISSISSIPPI MEDICAL CENTER
NORTHWESTERN MEMORIAL HOSPITAL
PACIFIC HEALTH RESOURCES
PENNSYLVANIA MEDICAL SOCIETY
PHOENIX BAPTIST HOSPITAL & MEDICAL CENTER
PROVENANT HEALTH CENTERS
QUEEN'S MEDICAL CENTER
READING HOSPITAL & MEDICAL CENTER, THE
REHABILITATION HOSPITAL OF THE PACIFIC
RIVERSIDE METHODIST HOSPITALS
ROBERT F. KENNEDY MEDICAL CENTER
ROCKINGHAM MEMORIAL HOSPITAL

SAINT ANTHONY MEDICAL CENTER
SAINT JOHN HOSPITAL
SALEM HOSPITAL
SAMARITAN HEALTH SERVICE
SCANNERS
SENTARA HEALTH SYSTEM
SETON MEDICAL CENTER
SOUTHSIDE HOSPITAL
SOUTHWEST GENERAL HOSPITAL
SOUTHWEST TEXAS METHODIST HOSPITAL
SPACE COAST DISABILITY RIGHTS ASSOCIATION
ST. AGNES HOSPITAL
ST. ELIZABETH MEDICAL CENTER
ST. FRANCIS HOSPITAL
ST. FRANCIS HOSPITAL CENTER
ST. FRANCIS HOSPITAL, INC.
ST. JOHN MEDICAL CENTER
ST. JOHN'S HOSPITAL & HEALTH CENTER
ST. JOSEPH MEDICAL CENTER
ST. JOSEPH MEDICAL CENTER
ST. JOSEPH'S HOSPITAL
ST. JOSEPH'S HOSPITAL & MEDICAL CTR.
ST. LUKE'S-ROOSEVELT HOSPITAL CENTER
ST. MARY'S HEALTH CENTER
ST. MARYS HOSPITAL
ST. PATRICK HOSPITAL
ST. VINCENT CHARITY HOSPITAL & HEALTH CTR.
ST. VINCENT HOSPITAL
SWEDISH AMERICAN HEALTH SYSTEM
TARRANT COUNTY HOSPITAL DISTRICT
TENNESSEE HOSPITAL ASSOCIATION
TRINITY LUTHERAN HOSPITAL
VALLEY HOSPITAL
VALLEY PRESBYTERIAN HOSPITAL
WAKE MEDICAL CENTER
WHITTIER HOSPITAL MEDICAL CENTER
WILKES-BARRE GENERAL HOSPITAL
WILLIAM BEAUMONT HOSPITAL

### HOTELS, MOTELS

GREENBRIER HOTEL
WESTIN HOTEL

### INDUSTRY: HEAVY CONSTRUCTION, MACHINERY

ACF INDUSTRIES, INC.
AMERICAN CAST IRON PIPE COMPANY
AMERICAN ROAD & TRANSPORTATION BUILDERS
   ASSOCIATION
ANDRITZ-SPROUT-BAUER, INC.
AXIA, INC.
BLOUNT, INC.
CATERPILLAR INDUSTRIAL, INC.
CATERPILLAR INDUSTRIAL, INC.
CMI CORP.
CONSTRUCTION ASSOCIATION OF MICHIGAN (CAM)
FLUOR DANIEL INC.
GARDNER DENVER MACHINERY INC.
GEORGE E. FAILING CO.
GILBARCO INC.
GROVE WORLDWIDE, INC.
HARNISCHFEGER INDUSTRIES, INC.
HENRY VOGT MACHINE CO.
HUGHES CHRISTIANSEN CO.
LTV STEEL-MINING CO.
LUKENS INC.
MINING & SPECIALTY EQUIP. DIV. OF INDRESCO, INC.,
   MARION OPERATINS
MORRISON KNUDSEN CORP.
NEWPORT NEWS SHIPBUILDING & DRY DOCK CO.
PERINI CORP.
PETER KIEWIT SONS, INC.
RAYMOND CORP.
SCHRAMM INC.
STONE & WEBSTER ENGINEERING CORP.
THOMPSON INTERNATIONAL, INC.
UNISTRUT CORPORATION
UNITED UNIONS OF JOB CORPS
VICKERS, INC.
WESTERN STATE EQUIPMENT CO.
WHITING CORPORATION

### INDUSTRY: LIGHT TOOLS, EQUIPMENT

ARMSTRONG WORLD INDUSTRIES
BIC CORP.
DAYTON PROGRESS CORP.
EMPIRE BRUSHES INC.
GARDEN WAY MFG. CO. INC.
GAST MFG. CORP.
GLEASON WORKS
GOULDS PUMPS INC.
ILLINOIS TOOL WORKS
ITEK OPTICAL SYSTEMS, DIV. OF LITTON INDUSTRIES
MASTER LOCK CO.
NASH ENGINEERING CO.
NORTH AMERICAN OPERATIONS-DRESSER INDUSTRY
RECOGNITION INTERNATIONAL INC.
ROTO-ROOTER CORP.
RUSSELL HARRINGTON CUTLERY CO.
SNAP-ON TOOLS CORP.
TWIN DISC INC.
VIKING PUMP, INC./A UNIT OF IDEX CORP.
W. H. BRADY CO.
WIRE ROPE CORORATION OF AMERICA, INC.

### INDUSTRY: MATERIAL HANDLING

AG COMMUNICATIONS CORP.
AMERICAN PRODUCTION & INVENTORY CONTROL
   SOCIETY (APICS)
ASNT (AMERICAN SOCIETY FOR NONDESTRUCTIVE
   TESTING)
COOPER OIL, TOOL DIV.
OAKITE PRODUCTS, INC.
RSR CORPORATION
SIMA-SURF INDUSTRY MANUFACTURERS
   ASSOCATION
WISCO INDUSTRIES INC.

### INSURANCE

ACACIA GROUP, THE
AETNA LIFE & CASUALTY
AID ASSOCIATION FOR LUTHERANS (AAL)
ALLIANCE LIFE
ALLSTATE INSURANCE COMPANY
AMERICAN FAMILY INSURANCE GROUP
AMERICAN GENERAL LIFE/ACCIDENT INSURANCE CO.
AMERICAN INTERNATIONAL GROUP, INC.
AMERICAN MUTUAL LIFE INSURANCE CO.
AMERICAN NATIONAL INSURANCE CO.
AMERICAN SOCIETY OF CLU & CHFC
AMERICAN UNITED LIFE INSURANCE COMPANY
ATLANTIC MUTUAL COS.
AUTO-OWNERS INSURANCE
BADGER MUTUAL INSURANCE COMPANY
BANKERS SECURITY LIFE INSURANCE SOCIETY
BENEFICIAL LIFE INS. CO.
BERKSHIRE LIFE INSURANCE COMPANY
BLUE CROSS & BLUE SHIELD
BLUE CROSS & BLUE SHIELD ASSOCIATION
BLUE CROSS & BLUE SHIELD OF WEST VIRGINIA, INC.
BOSTON MUTUAL LIFE INS. CO.
BUSINESS MEN'S ASSURANCE CO.
CALIFORNIA ASSOCIATION OF LIFE UNDERWRITERS,
   INC.
CAROLINA ASSOCIATION OF PROFESSIONAL
   INSURANCE AGENTS
CENTURY COMPANIES OF AMERICA
CHUBB LIFEAMERICA
CHURCH MUTUAL INSURANCE CO.
CIGNA CORP.
CNA INSURANCE
COLONIAL PENN GROUP INC.
COLUMBUS LIFE INSURANCE CO.
COMMERCIAL UNION INS. CO.
COMMONWEALTH LIFE INSURANCE CO.
CONNECTICUT MUTUAL LIFE INSURANCE
CONSECO, INC.
CONTINENTAL ASSURANCE CO.
CONTINENTAL CORP.
CONTINENTAL WESTERN INDUSTRIES
CUNA MUTUAL INSURANCE GROUP

CUNA MUTUAL INSURANCE GROUP
EMPLOYERS CASUALTY
EQUIFAX, INC.
EQUITABLE LIFE INS. CO. OF IOWA
ERIE INSURANCE GROUP
FARM BUREAU INS.
FARM FAMILY INSURANCE COMPANIES
FARMLAND INSURANCE COMPANIES
FEDERATED INSURANCE COS.
FRANKLIN, THE
GENERAL ACCIDENT INSURANCE
GLEANER LIFE INSURANCE SOCIETY
GOVERNMENT PERSONNEL MUTUAL LIFE INSURANCE
   CO
GREAT SOUTHERN LIFE INSURANCE CO.
GUARANTEE MUTUAL LIFE CO.
HARLEYSVILLE INSURANCE COMPANIES
HILLENBRAND INDUSTRIES, INC.
HOME BENEFICIAL LIFE INSURANCE CO.
HORACE MANN COS., THE
INDIANA FARMERS INSURANCE GROUP
INDIANAPOLIS LIFE INSURANCE CO.
INSURANCE SERVICES OFFICE INC.
INTEGON
INTER-STATE ASSURANCE CO.
ITT HARTFORD INSURANCE GROUP
JEFFERSON PILOT LIFE INSURANCE CO.
KANSAS CITY LIFE INSURANCE CO.
LAMAR LIFE INSURANCE CO.
LAWYERS TITLE INSURANCE CORP.
LIBERTY NATIONAL LIFE INSURANCE CO.
LINCOLN NATIONAL CORP.
LINCOLN NATIONAL LIFE INSURANCE COMPANY
LUTHERAN BROTHERHOOD
MASSACHUSETTS MUTUAL LIFE INSURANCE CO.
METROPOLITAN LIFE INSURANCE CO.
MICHIGAN MUTUAL INSURANCE CO.
MIDLAND MUTUAL LIFE INSURANCE CO.
MINNESOTA MUTUAL LIFE INSURANCE CO.
MONUMENTAL LIFE INS. CO.
MOTORISTS INSURANCE COMPANIES
MOUNTAIN STATE BLUE CROSS & BLUE SHIELD
MSI INSURANCE
MUTUAL OF OMAHA COMPANIES
MUTUAL TRUST LIFE INSURANCE CO.
NATIONAL GRANGE MUTUAL INSURANCE CO.
NATIONAL INDEMNITY CO.
NATIONAL INSURANCE CRIME BUREAU
NATIONAL LIFE OF VERMONT
NATIONAL TRAVELERS LIFE CO.
NATIONWIDE INSURANCE
NEW ENGLAND MUTUAL LIFE INSURANCE CO.
NEW YORK LIFE INSURANCE CO.
NORTH CAROLINA MUTUAL LIFE INSURANCE CO.
NORTH WESTERN NATIONAL LIFE
NORTHWESTERN NATIONAL INSURANCE GROUP
OHIO CASUALTY INSURANCE GROUP, THE
OHIO NATIONAL LIFE INSURANCE CO.
OREGON DEPARTMENT OF INSURANCE & FINANCE
PACIFIC MUTUAL LIFE INS. CO.
PAN-AMERICAN LIFE INSURANCE CO.
PENNSYLVANIA MANUFACTURERS' ASSOCIATION
   INSURANCE CO.
PEOPLES SECURITY LIFE INSURANCE CO.
PHOENIX HOME LIFE INSURANCE CO.
PIONEER MUTUAL LIFE INSURANCE CO.
PROTECTIVE LIFE INS. CO.
PROVIDENT MUTUAL LIFE INSURANCE CO. OF
   PHILADELPHIA
PRUDENTIAL INSURANCE CO. OF AMERICA
PYRAMID LIFE INSURANCE CO.
RANGER INSURANCE CO.
SAFECO INSURANCE CO.
SAIF CORP.
SECURA INSURANCE
SECURITY MUTUAL LIFE INSURANCE CO. OF NEW
   YORK
SENTRY INSURANCE
SHELTER INSURANCE COMPANY
SHENANDOAH LIFE INSURANCE CO.
SOCIETY OF CHARTERED PROPERTY & CASUALTY
   UNDERWRITERS
ST. PAUL COMPANIES, INC., THE
STATE COMPENSATION INSURANCE FUND
STATE FARM MUTUAL AUTO INSURANCE CO.

STATE FARM MUTUAL AUTO INSURANCE CO.
STATE LIFE INSURANCE CO.
TEACHERS INSURANCE & ANNUITY ASSOCIATION
TRAVELERS INSURANCE CO.
TRINITY UNIVERSAL INSURANCE CO.
UNION BANKERS INSURANCE CO.
UNION CENTRAL LIFE
UNION INSURANCE GROUP
UNION NATIONAL LIFE INSURANCE CO.
UNITED AMERICAN INSURANCE CO.
UNITED INSURANCE CO. OF AMERICA
UNUM CORP.
USF & A. INSURANCE
UTICA NATIONAL INSURANCE GROUP
WESTERN/SOUTHERN LIFE INSURANCE CO.
WOODMEN ACCIDENT & LIFE CO.
ZURICH-AMERICAN INSURANCE GROUP

## LUMBER, FORESTRY, BUILDING MATERIALS

ALABAMA FORESTRY ASSN.
ALASKA FOREST ASSN. INC.
CHESAPEAKE CORP.
KIMBALL INTERNATIONAL, INC.
MORBARK INDUSTRIES INC.
NORTHEASTERN RETAIL LUMBERMENS ASSOCIATION
ROSEBURG FOREST PRODUCTS CO.
SOUTHERN FOREST PRODUCTS ASSOCIATION
TREES FOR TOMMORROW INC., NATURAL
   RESOURCES EDUCATION
USG CORP.
WOODMAN OF THE WORLD LIFE INSURANCE
   SOCIETY

## MEAT PRODUCTS

HORMEL FOODS CORP.

## MUSIC

SWEET ADELINES INTERNATIONAL

## NEWSPAPERS

ATLANTA JOURNAL-CONSTITUTION
DALLAS MORNING NEWS
DONREY MEDIA GROUP
FORT WORTH STAR-TELEGRAM
HOUSTON CHRONICLE
JOURNAL COMMUNICATIONS
LOS ANGELES TIMES
NEW YORK DAILY
NEW YORK TIMES
ST. PAUL PIONEER PRESS DISPATCH
TIMES PUBLISHING CO.
TOLEDO BLADE CO.
WASHINGTON POST

## NICKEL

INCO ALLOYS INTERNATIONAL, INC.
INCO UNITED STATES, INC.

## OFFICE EQUIPMENT, SERVICES, SUPPLIES

ADAMS BUSINESS FORMS, INC.
AMSCO AMERICAN STERILIZER CO.
COMPAQ COMPUTER CORP.
CURTIS 1000, INC.
ESSELTE PENDAFLEX CORP.
FBG SERVICE CORP.
HEDMAN CO.
KELLY SERVICES, INC.
KONICA BUSINESS MACHINES U.S.A., INC.
PITNEY BOWES, INC.
SHEAFFER, INC.
TEXAS INSTRUMENTS INC.
XEROX

## OPTICAL

AMERICAN ACADEMY OF OPHTHALMOLOGY

## PAINT

VALSPAR CORP.

## PAPER PRODUCTS

AMERICAN GREETINGS CORP.
APPLETON MILLS
ATLANTIC ENVELOPE CO.
BOISE CASCADE CORP.
CONSOLIDATED PAPERS, INC.
GEORGIA-PACIFIC CORP.
GEORGIA-PACIFIC CORP., BRUNSWICK OPERATIONS
LYONS FALLS PULP & PAPER
MEAD CORPORATION
MIAMI SYSTEMS-SHELBY DIVISION
MOORE BUSINESS FORMS, INC.
P.H. GLATFELTER CO.
SONOCO PRODUCTS CO.
UARCO, INC.
UNION CAMP CORPORATION

## PETROLEUM, GAS

AMERICAN GAS ASSOCIATION
AMOCO CORPORATION
ANR PIPELINE CO.
APACHE CORPORATION
ARCO
ASHLAND OIL, INC.
CALTEX PETROLEUM CORP.
COMPASS, THE
EQUITABLE RESOURCES
HALLIBURTON ENERGY SERVICES
HALLIBURTON-GEOPHYSICAL SERVICES, INC.
KANSAS OIL MARKETERS ASSOCIATION
KN ENERGY, INC.
LOUISIANA MID-CONTINENT OIL & GAS
LUBRIZOL CORP. THE
MAXUS ENERGY CORP.
MURPHY OIL CORPORATION
MUSTANG FUEL CORP.
ORYX ENERGY CO.
PANHANDLE EASTERN CORP.
PENNZOIL CO.
PHILADELPHIA GAS WORKS
PHILLIPS PETROLEUM CO.
QUESTAR CORPORATION
ROWAN COMPANIES, INC.
SAN DIEGO GAS & ELECTRIC CO.
SHELL OIL CO.
SONAT, INC.
STANDARD OIL CO.
SUN COMPANY INC.
TEXACO, INC.
UNION PACIFIC RESOURCES CO.
UNOCAL CORP.
VALVOLINE, INC.

## PHOTOGRAPHY

AMERICAN SOCIETY OF MAGAZINE PHOTOGRAPHERS
CPI CORP.
OLAN MILLS OF TENNESSEE
PHOTOSOURCE INTERNATIONAL
VETCO, INC.

## PRINTERS, SERVICES

ARCATA GRAPHICS CORP.
COLSO-QUIPS
DITTLER BROTHERS, INC.
JOHN H HARLAND CO.
MEREDITH GRAPHICS, INC.
PRINTING INDUSTRIES OF AMERICA, INC.

## PUBLISHERS, BOOKS, MAGAZINES

ARTHUR BROWN & BROS., INC.
ASSOCIATED CHURCH PRESS
BAPTIST SUNDAY SCHOOL BOARD
BERRY CO., THE
BOULEVARD PUBLICATIONS INC.
CURTIS CIRCULATION CO.
DUN & BRADSTREET CORP., THE
EBSCO INDUSTRIES, INC.
EEI
FAMILY CIRCLE, INC.
FRIENDSHIP PUBLICATIONS
GTE DIRECTORIES CORP.
LAWYERS CO-OP PUBLISHING CO.
LIBRARY OF CONGRESS
MCGRAW-HILL INC.
MOSBY-YEAR BOOK, INC.
NEW ENGLAND PRINTER & PUBLISHER INC.
NEWSWEEK
R.R. DONNELLEY & SONS CO.
RAND MCNALLY & CO.
ROCKFORD REGISTER STAR
SALES PROSPECTOR
STEVENS PUBLISHING CORP.
UNITED METHODIST PUBLISHING HOUSE, THE
WARNER ENTERPRISES
WORLD BOOK, INC.

## RADIO, TV, MOVIES

ALLEGRO PRODUCTIONS, INC.
COX ENTERPRISES, INC.
GOOD NEWS BROADCASTING ASSOCIATION, INC.
KTVE-TV
MEREDITH CORP.
ROCKFORD/PARK CABLEVISION, INC.
SATELLITE INDUSTRIES INC.
VIACOM INTERNATIONAL INC.
WDCN CHANNEL 8
WLIW CHANNEL 21

## RAILROADS

AMTRAK
BESSEMER & LAKE ERIE RAILROAD
BROWN GROUP, INC.
BROWNING FERRIS INDUSTRIES
BURLINGTON NORTHERN RAILROAD
CSX CORP.
GUNDERSON, INC.
LONG ISLAND RAILROAD
MUTUAL BENEFICIAL ASSN. OF RAILROAD
   TRANSPORTATION EMPLOYEES
NORFOLK SOUTHERN CORP.
U.S. RAILROAD RETIREMENT BOARD
UNION PACIFIC RAILROAD
UNION RAILROAD CO.

## REAL ESTATE

BARCLAYS AMERICAN/MORTGAGE
CALIFORNIA ASSOCIATION OF REALTORS
CENTURY 21, REAL ESTATE CORP.
CERTIFIED GROCERS OF CALIFORNIA, LTD.
FOREST LAWN MEMORIAL PARK
MITCHELL ENERGY & DEVELOPMENT CORP.
OHIO ASSOCIATION OF REALTORS
PEACHTREE CENTER
REAL ESTATE CENTER
SACHS PROPERTIES, INC.

## RETAIL STORES

ACME MARKETS INC.
AMERICAN STORES CO.
BELK STORES SERVICES INC.
BEST PRODUCTS CO., INC.
BLAIR, CORP.
C.R. ANTHONY CO.
CARTER HAWLEY HALE STORES, INC.
EDISON BROS. STORES

FILENE'S
FINANCIAL MANAGERS SOCIETY, INC.
FOLEY'S
FOODLAND INTERNATIONAL CORP.
FRED MEYER INC.
GOLUB CORP./PRICE CHOPPER SUPERMARKETS
HOME DEPOT, INC., THE
JC PENNEY COMPANY
KMART CORPORATION
L & F PRODUCTS
MONTGOMERY WARD & CO.
NATIONAL ASSOCIATION OF CHAIN DRUG STORES
PIER 1 IMPORTS, INC.
PIGGLY WIGGLY CORP.
QUALITY STORES, INC.
RICH'S, INC.
ROSES STORES, INC.
SAKS FIFTH AVENUE
SALADMASTER, INC.
SEARS ROEBUCK & CO.
SPARTAN STORES, INC.
SPIEGEL, INC.
STRAWBRIDGE & CLOTHIER
SUPERMARKETS, INC.
SUPERVALU, INC.
WALGREEN CO.
YOUNKERS, INC.

### RUBBER, TIRES

B.F. GOODRICH
BRIDGESTONE/FIRESTONE, INC.
COOPER TIRE & RUBBER COMPANY
DUNLOP TIRE CORP.
GATES CORPORATION, THE
KELLY-SPRINGFIELD TIRE CO.
MICHELIN NORTH AMERICA, INC.
RUBBERMAID, INC.

### SHIPPING

AMERICAN COMMERCIAL LINES, INC.
FEDERAL EXPRESS CORP.
GEORGIA PORTS AUTHORITY
INGALLS SHIPBUILDING DIVISION, LITTON INDUSTRIES
MARYLAND PORT ADMINISTRATION
MEDIA GENERAL
MORAN TOWING & TRANSPORTATION CO., INC.
PORT AUTHORITY OF NEW YORK & NEW JERSEY
PORT OF OAKLAND
PORT OF PORTLAND
SOUTH CAROLINA STATE PORTS AUTHORITY

### SHOES

ACME BOOT COMPANY INC.
KINNEY SHOE CORPORATION
MORSE SHOE, INC.
STRIDE RITE CORP.

### SOFT DRINKS

COCA-COLA COMPANY, THE
DR. PEPPER CO.
PEPSI-COLA CO.

### SPORTS, EQUIPMENT

AMATEUR ATHLETIC UNION OF THE U.S.
OUTBOARD MARINE CORP.
SANTA BARBARA RESEARCH CENTER
SCHWINN CYCLING & FITNESS, INC.

### STEEL, IRON

CABOT CORP.
CARPENTER TECHNOLOGY CORPORATION
COPPERWELD STEEL CO.
COPPERWELD-SHELBY DIV.
EMI CO.
ESCO CORP.

GREAT LAKES DIVISION-NATIONAL STEEL
INTERMET FOUNDRY
NATIONAL STEEL CORP.
NOOTER CORP.
REYNOLDS METALS CO.
UNITED STATES PIPE & FOUNDRY CO.

### SUGAR

ALEXANDER & BALDWIN, INC.
IMPERIAL HOLLY CORP.
VALHI, INC.

### TEXTILES, APPAREL, MILLS, MACHINERY

CHATHAM MANUFACTURING CO.
COATS & CLARK, INC.
DIXIE YARNS, INC.
DYERSBURG FABRICS INC.
FIBERLUX, INC.
FIELDCREST CANNON, INC.
INGERSOLL INTERNATIONAL, INC.
JANTZEN INC.
SARA LEE KNIT PRODUCTS
SCHIFFLI LACE & EMBROIDERY MANUFACTURERS ASSN.
SPRINGS INDUSTRIES, INC.

### TOBACCO

BROWN & WILLIAMSON TOBACCO CORP.
RJR TOBACCO CO.

### TOYS, CRAFTS

HASBRO, INC.
MILTON BRADLEY CO.

### TRUCKING

ABF FREIGHT SYSTEM, INC.
ATLAS VAN-LINES, INC.
AVISTAR INTERNATIONAL TRANSPORTATION CORP.
BDP BRANDS, CARRIER CORP.
FREIGHTLINER CORP.
PENNSYLVANIA MOTOR TRUCK ASSOCIATION
ROADWAY SERVICES, INC.
UNITED PARCEL SERVICE

### UTILITY: ELECTRIC

ALABAMA POWER CO.
APPALACHIAN POWER CO.
ARIZONA PUBLIC SERVICE CO.
ARKANSAS POWER & LIGHT CO.
ASSOCIATION OF ILLINOIS ELECTRIC COOPERATIVES
ATLANTIC CITY ELECTRIC CO.
BENTON CITY ELECTRIC COOPERATIVE ASSOCIATION
BODINE ELECTRIC CO.
BOSTON EDISON CO.
CAROLINA POWER & LIGHT CO.
CENTRAL ILLINOIS LIGHT CO.
CENTRAL ILLINOIS PUBLIC SERVICE CO.
CENTRAL LINCOLN PEOPLE'S UTILITY DISTRICT
COASTAL CORP., THE
COLUMBUS SOUTHERN POWER CO.
COMMONWEALTH EDISON
CONSOLIDATED EDISON CO. OF NEW YORK
DAIRYLAND POWER COOPERATIVE
DAYTON POWER & LIGHT CO.
DELMARVA POWER & LIGHT CO.
DUKE POWER CO.
DUQUESNE LIGHT CO.
EASTERN IOWA LIGHT POWER COOPERATIVE
EL PASO ELECTRIC CO.
ELECTRIC POWER BOARD CHATTANOOGA
EMPIRE DISTRICT ELECTRIC CO.
EUA SERVICE CORP.
FLORIDA POWER & LIGHT CO.

GRAYBAR ELECTRIC CO. INC.
HAWAIIAN ELECTRIC CO., INC.
HOUSTON LIGHTING & POWER CO.
IES UTILITIES
INDIANA MICHIGAN POWER CO.
INTERSTATE POWER CO.
IOWA-ILLINOIS GAS & ELECTRIC CO.
JERSEY CENTRAL POWER & LIGHT CO.
KENTUCKY UTILITIES CO.
LINN COUNTY RURAL ELECTRIC COOPERATIVE ASSOCIATION
MDU RESOURCES GROUP, INC.
MIDWEST RESOURCES INC.
MINNESOTA POWER
MISSISSIPPI POWER & LIGHT CO.
MISSISSIPPI POWER CO.
MONONGAHELA POWER CO.
NASHVILLE ELECTRIC SERVICE
NEBRASKA PUBLIC POWER DISTRICT
NEW ENGLAND ELECTRIC SYSTEM
NIAGARA MOHAWK POWER CORP.
NORTH CAROLINA ASSOCIATION OF ELECTRIC COOPERATIVES
OHIO EDISON CO.
OHIO POWER CO.
OKLAHOMA GAS & ELECTRIC CO.
OMAHA PUBLIC POWER DIST.
ORANGE & ROCKLAND UTILITIES, INC.
OTTER TAIL POWER CO.
PACIFIC GAS & ELECTRIC CO.
PACIFIC POWER & LIGHT CO.
PECO ENERGY COMPANY
PENNSYLVANIA ELECTRIC CO.
PENNSYLVANIA POWER CO.
POTOMAC ELECTRIC POWER CO.
PUBLIC SERVICE CO. OF COLORADO
PUBLIC SERVICE CO. OF NEW HAMPSHIRE
PUGET SOUND POWER & LIGHT CO.
SACRAMENTO MUNICIPAL UTILITY DISTRICT
SANTEE COOPER
SEATTLE CITY LIGHT
SOUTH CAROLINA ELECTRIC & GAS CO.
SOUTHERN COMPANY SERVICES, INC.
SOUTHERN INDIANA GAS & ELECTRIC CO.
SOUTHWESTERN ELECTRIC POWER CO.
SOUTHWESTERN PUBLIC SERVICE CO.
ST. JOSEPH LIGHT & POWER CO.
T.U. ELECTRIC
TAMPA ELECTRIC CO.
TOLEDO EDISON CO.
UNION ELECTRIC CO.
VA., MD., & DE. ASSOCIATION OF ELECTRIC CO-OP.
VIRGINIA POWER CO.
WEST PENN POWER CO.
WESTERN RESOURCES, INC.
WISCONSIN ELECTRIC COOPERATIVE ASSOCIATION
WISCONSIN ELECTRIC POWER CO.
WISCONSIN POWER & LIGHT CO.

### UTILITY: GAS

ALABAMA GAS CORP.
ATLANTA GAS LIGHT CO.
BAY STATE GAS CO.
BOSTON GAS COMPANY
BROOKLYN UNION GAS CO.
CASCADE NATURAL GAS CORP.
CINCINNATI GAS & ELECTRIC CO.
COLORADO INTERSTATE GAS CO.
COLUMBIA GAS DISTRIBUTION CO.
COLUMBIA GAS SYSTEM
COLUMBIA GAS TRANSMISSION CORP.
COLUMBIA GULF TRANSMISSION
CONNECTICUT NATURAL GAS CORP.
EAST OHIO GAS CO.
EL PASO NATURAL GAS CO.
EXXON CO., U.S.A.
KPL GAS SERVICE
LACLEDE GAS COMPANY
LONE STAR GAS CO.
NORTHERN INDIANA PUBLIC SERVICE CO.
NORTHWEST PIPELINE CORP.
OKLAHOMA NATURAL GAS CO.
PEOPLES NATURAL GAS CO.

PUBLIC SERVICE ELECTRIC & GAS CO.
SOUTHERN CONNECTICUT GAS CO.
SOUTHERN UNION CO.
UGI CORP.
WASHINGTON GAS
WISCONSIN NATURAL GAS CO.

## UTILITY: RELATED

ASSOCIATED GENERAL CONTRACTORS OF HOUSTON
BUCKEYE PIPE LINE COMPANY
CITY PUBLIC SERVICE
GENERAL ATOMICS TECHNOLOGIES, INC.
IPALCO ENTERPRISES, INC.
KNOXVILLE UTILITIES BOARD
METROPOLITAN UTILITIES DISTRICT
NAVAJO TRIBAL UTILITY AUTHORITY
NAVY PUBLIC WORKS CENTER SAN FRANCISCO BAY
ROCHESTER GAS & ELECTRIC CORP.
SIERRA PACIFIC POWER CO.

UTAH POWER, A DIVISION OF PACIFICORP, OREGON
WASHINGTON WATER POWER CO., THE
WEST TEXAS UTILITIES CO.

## UTILITY: TELEPHONE

AMERICAN TELEPHONE & TELEGRAPH CO.
C-TEC CORP.
GENERAL TELEPHONE CO. OF PA.
GTE NORTH
GTE SOUTH
GTE TELEPHONE OPERATIONS
GTE TELEPHONE OPERATIONS
GTE WISCONSIN
LINCOLN TELECOMMUNICATIONS CO.
MICHIGAN BELL TELEPHONE CO.
NEW ENGLAND TELEPHONE CO.
OHIO BELL TELEPHONE CO.
PACIFIC BELL
SOUTHERN BELL TELEPHONE CO.

SOUTHERN NEW ENGLAND TELEPHONE CO.
SOUTHWESTERN BELL TELEPHONE CO.
SPRINT MID-ATLANTIC TELECOM
UNITED TELEPHONE CO. OF FLORIDA
UNITED TELEPHONE CO. OF INDIANA, INC.
UNITED TELEPHONE CO. OF OHIO

## UTILITY: WATER

AMERICAN WATER WORKS ASSOCIATION
ASSOCIATION OF CALIFORNIA WATER AGENCIES
DENVER WATER BOARD
HACKENSACK WATER CO.
INDIANAPOLIS WATER CO.
KANSAS CITY BOARD OF PUBLIC UTILITIES
LOS ANGELES DEPARTMENT OF WATER & POWER
NATIONAL GROUND WATER ASSOCIATION
SOUTHERN CALIFORNIA WATER CO.
TACOMA PUBLIC UTILITIES
WATER EDUCATION FOUNDATION

# INDEX OF INTERNAL PUBLICATIONS BY SUBJECT

This section contains an alphabetical listing of internal publication sponsors and their title(s), arranged by editorial subject.

## BABY CARE

**BANK ONE OF ARIZONA:** EAGLE
**BLUE CROSS & BLUE SHIELD OF WEST VIRGINIA, INC.:** GROUP UPDATE / MEMBERS PLUS / OUT OF THE BLUE
**CUMBERLAND FARMS, INC.:** MILKY WAY
**GUARANTEE MUTUAL LIFE CO.:** GUARANTEE MUTUAL FIELD NEWS
**MERCY HOSPITAL:** FOREFRONT
**MOUNT SINAI MEDICAL CENTER:** MEDICAL REPORT
**NASA LEWIS RESEARCH CENTER:** LEWIS NEWS
**NAVY PUBLIC WORKS CENTER SAN FRANCISCO BAY:** P W C BAYGRAM
**SOUTHERN CALIFORNIA WATER CO.:** CONNECTIONS
**SOUTHWEST TEXAS METHODIST HOSPITAL:** IMAGES OF SOUTHWEST TEXAS METHODIST HOSPITAL
**ST. VINCENT HOSPITAL:** HEALTH REVIEW
**UNITED WAY OF SUMMIT COUNTY:** COMMON GROUND

## BEAUTY HINTS

**BANK ONE OF ARIZONA:** EAGLE
**FAMILY CIRCLE, INC.:** ADVANCE NEWS
**GTE TELEPHONE OPERATIONS:** TELOPS NEWS
**GUARANTEE MUTUAL LIFE CO.:** GUARANTEE MUTUAL FIELD NEWS
**NASA LEWIS RESEARCH CENTER:** LEWIS NEWS
**NAVY PUBLIC WORKS CENTER SAN FRANCISCO BAY:** P W C BAYGRAM
**OHIO EDISON CO.:** OHIO EDISONIAN
**OLAN MILLS OF TENNESSEE:** LENS
**ROSEBURG FOREST PRODUCTS CO.:** ROSEBURG NEWS & VIEWS
**SHELL OIL CO.:** SHELL NEWS
**SOUTHERN CALIFORNIA WATER CO.:** CONNECTIONS

## BOOK REVIEWS

**AAA WASHINGTON:** WASHINGTON MOTORIST

**ALABAMA EDUCATION ASSN.:** ALABAMA SCHOOL JOURNAL
**AMERICAN COLLEGE OF RHEUMATOLOGY:** ARTHRITIS & RHEUMATISM
**AMERICAN COLLEGE OF SPORTS MEDICINE:** SPORTS MEDICINE BULLETIN
**BANK OF HAWAII:** SPECTRUM
**BOEING CO.:** BOEING NEWS
**BUCYRUS-ERIE CO.:** SURFACE MINER
**BURLINGTON COUNTY COLLEGE:** COLLEGE CONNECTION, THE
**CALIFORNIA ASSOCIATION OF REALTORS:** CALIFORNIA REAL ESTATE MAGAZINE
**CALIFORNIA PACIFIC MEDICAL CENTER:** CALIFORNIA PACIFIC QUARTERLY
**CALIFORNIA TEACHERS ASSOCIATION:** C T A ACTION
**CATHOLIC PRESS ASSOCIATION:** CATHOLIC JOURNALIST, THE
**CITY OF ST. PETERSBURG:** SUNSCRIBE
**CIVITAN INTERNATIONAL:** COUNTDOWN
**COLORADO MUNICIPAL LEAGUE:** COLORADO MUNICIPALITIES
**CORNING INCORPORATED:** CORNING WORLD
**DRESSER INDUSTRIES, INC.:** RECORDER, THE
**ERIE INSURANCE GROUP:** ERIE FAMILY
**ERWIN DI CYAN:** DI CYAN BULLETIN
**GARDEN CITY HOSPITAL:** NITTY GRITTY
**HOME BENEFICIAL LIFE INSURANCE CO.:** HOME TOPICS
**LAWRENCE RAGAN COMMUNICATIONS, INC.:** RAGAN REPORT
**LIBRARY OF CONGRESS:** BRAILLE BOOK REVIEW
**LIBRARY OF CONGRESS:** TALKING BOOK TOPICS
**LOUISIANA PHARMACISTS ASSOCIATION:** LOUISIANA PHARMACIST
**LOYOLA UNIVERSITY:** NEW ORLEANS REVIEW
**NAVY PUBLIC WORKS CENTER SAN FRANCISCO BAY:** P W C BAYGRAM
**NEW ENGLAND MUTUAL LIFE INSURANCE CO.:** CURRENTS
**OHIO NATIONAL LIFE INSURANCE CO.:** O N L I ECHOES
**OZONE INDUSTRIES INC.:** OZONE NEWSLETTER

**PENNSYLVANIA MUSIC EDUCATORS ASSOCIATION:** P M E A NEWS
**PHARMACEUTICAL MANUFACTURERS ASSOCIATION:** P M A BULLETIN
**SATELLITE INDUSTRIES INC.:** PORTABLE SANITATION QUARTERLY
**SCANDINAVIAN AIRLINES SYSTEM INC.:** INSIDE S A S INTERNATIONAL
**SCRIPTURE PRESS PUBLICATIONS, INC.:** SPOTLIGHT
**SHAWNEE MISSION PUBLIC SCHOOLS:** INSIDE SHAWNEE MISSION PUBLIC SCHOOLS
**SOUTHERN CALIFORNIA WATER CO.:** CONNECTIONS
**STA-RITE INDUSTRIES:** PERSPECTIVE
**TEXAS SOCIETY OF ARCHITECTS:** TEXAS ARCHITECT
**TEXAS SOCIETY OF PROFESSIONAL ENGINEERS:** TEXAS PROFESSIONAL ENGINEER
**UNISYS:** INSIDE INFORMATION
**UNITED WAY OF SUMMIT COUNTY:** COMMON GROUND
**UNIVERSITY OF ST. THOMAS:** ST. THOMAS MAGAZINE
**WESTERN/SOUTHERN LIFE INSURANCE CO.:** HOME OFFICE NEWS

## BUSINESS

**AGENCY FOR INTERNATIONAL DEVELOPMENT:** FRONT LINES
**AMARILLO CHAMBER OF COMMERCE:** ACCENT WEST
**AMERICAN APPRAISAL ASSOCIATES:** VALUATION VIEWPOINT
**AMERICAN INTERNATIONAL GROUP, INC.:** CONTACT MAGAZINE
**ANALOG DEVICES, INC.:** ANALOG DIALOGUE
**ANALOG DEVICES, INC.:** NEWS CIRCUIT
**ARKANSAS INDUSTRIAL DEVELOPMENT COMMISSION:** A I D C REPORT
**ASSOCIATED INDUSTRIES OF KENTUCKY:** KENTUCKY JOURNAL OF COMMERCE & INDUSTRY
**ASSOCIATED PENNSYLVANIA CONSTRUCTORS:** HIGHWAY BUILDER

BANK ONE: TEXAS WIRE
BANK ONE, INDIANAPOLIS, NA: WIRE, THE
BEAUMONT CHAMBER OF COMMERCE: METROPOLITAN BEAUMONT
BEST FOODS, DIVISION OF CPC INTERNATIONAL, INC.: FOCUS
BEST FOODS, DIVISION OF CPC INTERNATIONAL, INC.: SALES & MARKETING NEWSLETTER
BODINE ELECTRIC CO.: BODINE MOTORGRAM
C-TEC CORP.: C-TEC COMMUNICATOR
CALIFORNIA ASSOCIATION OF LIFE UNDERWRITERS, INC. : CALUNDERWRITER
CALIFORNIA CREDIT UNION LEAGUE: CREDIT UNION DIGEST
CALTEX PETROLEUM CORP.: OIL PROGRESS
CAROLINA ASSOCIATION OF PROFESSIONAL INSURANCE AGENTS: CAROLINA AGENT
CHESAPEAKE BAY GIRL SCOUT COUNCIL: BAY WINDOW
CHUBB LIFEAMERICA: INSIGHT
CNA INSURANCE: BRANCH NEWSLETTERS
CNA INSURANCE: KEYNOTER
COMMONWEALTH LIFE INSURANCE CO.: COMMONWEALTH COMMENTS
CONTINENTAL CORP.: CONTINENTAL BULLETIN
COPPERWELD STEEL CO.: COMMUNICATOR
CP RAIL SYSTEM: US MILEPOSTS
CREDIT UNION NATIONAL ASSOCIATION INC.: CREDIT UNION EXECUTIVE
CREDIT UNION NATIONAL ASSOCIATION INC.: CREDIT UNION MAGAZINE
CREDIT UNION NATIONAL ASSOCIATION INC.: EVERYBODY'S MONEY
DAVOL INC.: DAVOL WORLD CLASS BULLETIN
DESERT SCHOOLS FEDERAL CREDIT UNION: CURRENCY
DR. PEPPER CO.: CLOCK DIAL
EASTERN IOWA LIGHT POWER COOPERATIVE: CURRENT NEWS
EMPLOYERS GROUP: ACTION LINE
EMPLOYERS GROUP: CAPITOL REVIEW
EMPLOYERS GROUP: FORUM
EMPLOYERS GROUP: IN ACTION MANAGEMENT MEMO
ERIE AREA CHAMBER OF COMMERCE: CHAMBER NEWSLETTER
FAIRCHILD CORPORATION: QUARTERLY REPORT TO STOCKHOLDERS
FARMLAND INSURANCE COMPANIES: FORESIGHT
FEDERAL RESERVE BANK OF CHICAGO: RESERVE 7
FIRST INTERSTATE BANK OF NORTHWEST REGION: NORTHWEST BANKER
FIRST NATIONWIDE BANK: FOCUS ON THE BEST
FLEMING COS. INC.: FLEMING ASSOCIATE, THE
FLORIDA HORIZONS FEDERAL CREDIT UNION: NEW HORIZONS
FLORISTS TRANSWORLD DELIVERY ASSOCIATION: FLORIST
FUTURE BUSINESS LEADERS OF AMERICA-PHI BETA LAMBDA: TOMORROW'S BUSINESS LEADER
GOULDS PUMPS INC.: GOULDS PROFESSIONAL DEALERS ASSOCIATION
GOVERNMENT PERSONNEL MUTUAL LIFE INSURANCE CO: G P M MESSENGER
GREATER RENO-SPARKS CHAMBER OF COMMERCE: CHAMBER BUSINESS
GREATER SAN DIEGO CHAMBER OF COMMERCE: BUSINESS ACTION
GREATER SAN DIEGO CHAMBER OF COMMERCE: ECONOMIC BULLETIN
GREATER WASHINGTON BOARD OF TRADE, THE: BOARD OF TRADE NEWS
GREATER WASHINGTON BOARD OF TRADE, THE: MEMBERSHIP DIRECTORY
HARRISON RADIATOR DIV.: HARRISON COMMUNICATOR
HASBRO, INC.: HASBRO HERALD
HAWAIIAN ELECTRIC CO., INC.: CONSUMER LINES
HILLENBRAND INDUSTRIES, INC.: WASHINGTON CAPITOL MONITOR
HOOVER CO.: ANNUAL REPORT TO EMPLOYEES
HOOVER CO.: FACE TO FACE
INSTITUTE OF INTERNAL AUDITORS: I I A TODAY
INSTITUTE OF INTERNAL AUDITORS: INTERNAL AUDITOR

INTERMET FOUNDRY: INTERMET NEWS
INTERNATIONAL ASSOCIATION OF HOSPITALITY ACCOUNTANTS: BOTTOMLINE, THE
INTERNATIONAL COMMUNICATIONS INDUSTRIES ASSN., THE: COMMUNICATIONS INDUSTRIES REPORT
INTERNATIONAL CREDIT ASSOCIATION: CREDIT WORLD
IOWA CREDIT UNION LEAGUE: ACCOUNT
IOWA STATE UNIVERSITY: CIRAS NEWS
ITT HARTFORD INSURANCE GROUP: I T T HARTFORD AGENT
KANSAS DEPARTMENT OF COMMERCE: KANSAS MAGAZINE
KANSAS OIL MARKETERS ASSOCIATION: KANSAS OIL MARKETER
LAWYERS TITLE INSURANCE CORP.: TRACT, THE
LOCKHEED FORT WORTH CO.: CODE ONE
LONE STAR GAS CO.: IN SEARCH EXPLORATION
LORAL DEFENSE SYSTEMS-AKRON: CIRCUIT
LUBRIZOL CORP. THE: WICK-LIFE
MARYLAND PORT ADMINISTRATION: PORT OF BALTIMORE MAGAZINE
MASTER LOCK CO.: MASTER LOCK NEWS TODAY
MCKESSON CORPORATION: MC KESSON TODAY
MEDICAL COLLEGE OF WISCONSIN: HEALTH NEWS
METROPOLITAN MILWAUKEE ASSOCIATION OF COMMERCE: MEMBERSHIP DIRECTORY
MINNESOTA SOCIETY OF CERTIFIED PUBLIC ACCOUNTANTS: FOOTNOTE
MISSISSIPPI POWER & LIGHT CO.: HELPING BUILD MISSISSIPPI
MUTUAL OF OMAHA COMPANIES: MANAGERS MONTHLY
NATIONAL CITY CORP.: ON THE MOVE
NATIONAL FEDERATION OF INDEPENDENT BUSINESS: I B MAGAZINE (INDEPENDENT BUSINESS)
NATIONAL MANAGEMENT ASSOCIATION: MANAGE MAGAZINE
NATIONAL SEMICONDUCTOR CORP.: INTERNATIONAL NEWS
NAVAL NUCLEAR FUEL DIVISION: B N W NEWS
NEBRASKA DEPT. OF ECONOMIC DEVELOPMENT: NEBRASKA DIRECTORY OF MANUFACTURERS
NEW YORK STOCK EXCHANGE: AT THE MARKET
NORTHEASTERN RETAIL LUMBERMENS ASSOCIATION: LUMBER CO-OPERATOR
NORTHERN INDIANA PUBLIC SERVICE CO.: NIPSCOFOLKS
OHIO ASSOCIATION OF REALTORS: OHIO REALTOR
OHIO CREDIT UNION LEAGUE: HIGH SPOTS
OHIO HARDWARE ASSOCIATION: OHA HARD LINES
OKLAHOMA BAR ASSOCIATION: OKLAHOMA BAR JOURNAL
OKLAHOMA NATURAL GAS CO.: GASETTE
PACIFIC MUTUAL LIFE INS. CO.: WAVELENGHT
PEOPLE'S BANK: PEOPLE'S NEWSLETTER
PORT OF HOUSTON MAGAZINE: PORT OF HOUSTON MAGAZINE
PRINCIPAL FINANCIAL GROUP, THE: COMMENT:
PRUDENTIAL INSURANCE CO. OF AMERICA: PRUDENTIAL'S REAL ESTATE DIMENSIONS
QUALITY STORES, INC.: ON CUE
REYNOLDS METALS CO.: REYNOLDS REVIEW
ROBERT MORRIS ASSOCIATES: COMMERCIAL LENDING NEWSLETTER
RSR CORPORATION: R S R LEAD PRESS
SAN LUIS OBISPO CHAMBER OF COMMERCE: SAN LUIS OBISPO BUSINESS
SANTEE COOPER: QUARTERLY FINANCIAL REPORTER
SANWA BANK CALIFORNIA: IN FOCUS
SARA LEE KNIT PRODUCTS: COMMON THREAD, THE
SATELLITE INDUSTRIES INC.: PORTABLE SANITATION QUARTERLY
SCHWEIZER AIRCRAFT CORP.: STABILIZER
SCHWINN CYCLING & FITNESS, INC.: SCHWINN CYCLING & FITNESS, INC. DEALER NEWS LETTER
SENTRY INSURANCE: MANAGEMENT NEWSLETTER
SISTERS OF PROVIDENCE HEALTH SYSTEM: THE GOOD WORK
SOUTH CAROLINA ELECTRIC & GAS CO.: S C E & G NEWS
SPIEGEL, INC.: FOCUS NEWSLETTER

ST. JOSEPH LIGHT & POWER CO.: CONTACT
STONE & WEBSTER ENGINEERING CORP.: STONE & WEBSTER INCORPORATE NEWSLETTER
TEXAS SOCIETY CERTIFIED PUBLIC ACCOUNTANTS: TODAY'S C P A
TRANSPORTATION COMMUNICATIONS INTERNATIONAL UNION : INTERCHANGE
TRAVELERS INSURANCE CO.: PROTECTION
TRAVELERS INSURANCE CO.: TRAVELERS TRIBUNE
U.S. SAVINGS BONDS DIVISION: BOND TELLER, THE
VIRGINIA BANKERS ASSOCIATION: BANKING NEWS
VIRGINIA CREDIT UNION LEAGUE: VIRGINIAN
WEOKIE CREDIT UNION: TRANSMITTER
WISCONSIN POWER & LIGHT CO.: CONNECTIONS
WOMEN IN COMMUNICATIONS INC.: W I C I MEMBERSHIP & RESOURCE DIRECTORY
WOODMEN ACCIDENT & LIFE CO.: EXCEL
XEROX: XEROX WORLD

## CHILDREN-TEENS

BLACK HAWK COUNCIL OF GIRL SCOUTS: SEMAPHORE
FATHER FLANAGAN'S BOY'S HOME: BOYS TOWN QUARTERLY

## CIVIC

BUSINESS COUNCIL FOR THE UNITED NATIONS: B C U N BRIEFING
CITY OF RICHARDSON TEXAS: RICHARDSON EMPLOYEE NEWSLETTER
COLORADO ASSOCIATION OF PUBLIC EMPLOYEES: THE CITIZEN
GREATER WINSTON-SALEM CHAMBER OF COMMERCE: MEMBERSHIP DIRECTORY
JEWISH COMMUNITY CENTER: FOR MEMBERS ONLY
LEAGUE OF IOWA MUNICIPALITIES: IOWA MUNICIPALITIES:
MANUFACTURED HOUSING INSTITUTE: M H I REPORT
ORLEANS PARRISH SCHOOL BOARD: APPLAUSE
PACIFIC MUTUAL LIFE INS. CO.: WAVELENGHT
PINELLAS COUNTY GOVERNMENT: PINELLAS PEN

## ECOLOGY

ALABAMA FORESTRY ASSN.: ALABAMA FORESTS
ALASKA FOREST ASSN. INC.: TIMBER TIMES
ALLIED GROUP: FOCUS
ALPHA BETA CO.: VANGUARD, THE
ALUMINUM COMPANY OF AMERICA: ALCOA NEWS
AMERICAN HONDA MOTOR CO., INC.: MIGHTY TO MINI NEWS
BANK ONE OF ARIZONA: EAGLE
BAUSCH & LOMB, INC.: BAUSCH & LOMB WORLD
BAY STATE GAS CO.: BAY STATER
BENTON CITY ELECTRIC COOPERATIVE ASSOCIATION: ON LINE WITH BENTON
BLUE CROSS & BLUE SHIELD OF WEST VIRGINIA, INC.: GROUP UPDATE / MEMBERS PLUS / OUT OF THE BLUE
BRISTOL-MYERS CO.: BRISTOL MYERS NEW YORK
BROOKLYN UNION GAS CO.: SENDOUT
BUCYRUS-ERIE CO.: SURFACE MINER
CALIFORNIA ASSOCIATION OF REALTORS: CALIFORNIA REAL ESTATE MAGAZINE
CASCADE NATURAL GAS CORP.: CASCADE FLAME
CATERPILLAR INDUSTRIAL, INC.: MENTOR LIFT-LINES
CITY OF BOSTON: CITY RECORD
CITY OF ST. PETERSBURG: SUNSCRIBE
CIVITAN INTERNATIONAL: COUNTDOWN
COLUMBUS SOUTHERN POWER CO.: LITELINES:
COOK COMPOSITES: FRONTLINE
COOK'S PEST CONTROL, INC.: WHAT'S COOKIN'
COORS COURIER: COORS COURIER
CORNING INCORPORATED: CORNING WORLD
COUNTRYMARK COOP: COOP CONNECTION
DATAPOINT CORP.: DETAILS
DRESSER INDUSTRIES, INC.: RECORDER, THE
DUN & BRADSTREET CORP., THE: D & B REPORTS
DUQUESNE LIGHT CO.: DUQUESNE LIGHT NEWS

**E.F. HOUGHTON & CO.:** HOUGHTON LINE
**E.F. HOUGHTON & CO.:** HOUGHTONEWS
**E-SYSTEMS, INC.:** TEAM
**EBASCO SERVICES INC.:** EBASCO NEWS
**ELCO INDUSTRIES, INC.:** E L C O NEWSLETTER
**ELECTRIC COUNCIL OF NEW ENGLAND:** IMPULSE
**ELF ATOCHEM NORTH AMERICA, INC.:** DIRECTION 79
**ENVIRONMENTAL LOBBY OF MASSACHUSETTS:** LEGISLATIVE BULLETIN
**FLEMING COS. INC.:** FLEMING ASSOCIATE, THE
**FLORIDA RURAL ELECTRIC CO-OP ASSOCIATION:** FLORIDA RURAL ELECTRIC NEWS
**FREIGHTLINER CORP.:** TRUCKBUILDERS PROGRESS
**GARDEN CITY HOSPITAL:** NITTY GRITTY
**GARDEN WAY MFG. CO. INC.:** TROY-BILT OWNER NEWS
**GEORGIA MUNICIPAL ASSOCIATION:** GEORGIA'S CITIES
**GIANT FOOD, INC.:** WE NEWS
**GILBARCO INC.:** GILBARCO GAZETTE
**GRAND UNION CO.:** GRAND STAND
**GREAT LAKES DIVISION-NATIONAL STEEL:** FOCUS
**GRUCON CORP.:** GRUNAU GRAM
**GRUMMAN CORP.:** GRUMMAN WORLD
**GUARANTEE MUTUAL LIFE CO.:** GUARANTEE MUTUAL FIELD NEWS
**GUARANTEE MUTUAL LIFE CO.:** INDIAN HILLS ECHOES
**HAWAIIAN ELECTRIC CO., INC.:** HOA HANA
**INTERSTATE POWER CO.:** INTERSTATE NEWS
**IPALCO ENTERPRISES, INC.:** I P L C O NEWS
**JET PROPULSION LABORATORY, CIT:** UNIVERSE
**KAMPGROUNDS OF AMERICA, INC.:** KOA DIRECTORY, ROAD ATLAS AND CAMPING GUIDE
**KANO LABS INC.:** GENIUS AT WORK
**LAKE ERIE GIRL SCOUT COUNCIL:** MILLWHEEL
**LEADER FEDERAL SAVINGS & LOAN ASSOCIATION:** LEADER DIGEST
**LOS ANGELES DEPARTMENT OF WATER & POWER:** INTAKE MAGAZINE
**LTV STEEL-MINING CO.:** L T V TIMES
**MEREDITH GRAPHICS, INC.:** GRAPHICOPY
**MIDLAND MUTUAL LIFE INSURANCE CO.:** ACHIEVER
**MONONGAHELA POWER CO.:** MONONGAHELA NEWS
**MUSEUM OF SCIENCE:** MUSEUM OF SCIENCE NEWSLETTER
**NASA LEWIS RESEARCH CENTER:** LEWIS NEWS
**NAVY PUBLIC WORKS CENTER SAN FRANCISCO BAY:** P W C BAYGRAM
**NESTLE-BEICH, INC.:** KADYDID CHRONICLE
**NEW YORK LIFE INSURANCE CO.:** NEW YORK LIFE NEWS
**OAK RIDGE NATIONAL LABORATORY:** LAB NEWS
**OPPENHEIMER MANAGEMENT CORP.:** HANDSIGNALS, THE
**ORANGE & ROCKLAND UTILITIES, INC.:** LAMPPOST
**ORE-IDA FOODS, INC.:** VOICE, THE
**OTTER TAIL POWER CO.:** HI-LITES
**OZONE INDUSTRIES INC.:** OZONE NEWSLETTER
**PACIFIC BELL:** CONNECTIONS
**PAN-AMERICAN LIFE INSURANCE CO.:** LIFELINE
**PHILLIPS PETROLEUM CO.:** PHILNEWS
**PITNEY BOWES, INC.:** OUTLOOK
**PLUMBING MECHANICAL CONTRACTORS COUNCIL HARRIS COUNTY:** GULF COAST PLUMBING, HEATING, COOLING NEWS
**PUBLIC SERVICE CO. OF NEW HAMPSHIRE:** AROUND THE CIRCUIT
**QUAKER OATS CO.:** MIDWEEK
**QUAKER OATS CO.:** QUAKER INSIDER
**RADIO SHACK DIVISION, TANDY CORP.:** RADIO SHACK INTERCOM
**RALPH'S GROCERY CO.:** RALPH'S NEWS:
**RESEARCH MEDICAL CENTER:** HORIZON
**ROCKY MOUNTAIN AAA CLUB:** ROCKY MOUNTAIN MOTORIST
**ROSICRUCIAN ORDER AMORC:** ROSICRUCIAN DIGEST
**SANTA BARBARA RESEARCH CENTER:** SBRC NEWS
**SATELLITE INDUSTRIES INC.:** PORTABLE SANITATION QUARTERLY
**SCANDINAVIAN AIRLINES SYSTEM INC.:** INSIDE S A S INTERNATIONAL
**SCHRAMM INC.:** WHAT'S HAPPENING

**SHAWNEE MISSION PUBLIC SCHOOLS:** INSIDE SHAWNEE MISSION PUBLIC SCHOOLS
**SHELL OIL CO.:** SHELL NEWS
**SHELL OIL CO.:** VENTURE
**SIZZLER INTERNATIONAL, INC.:** COLLINS COUNTRY
**SIZZLER INTERNATIONAL, INC.:** HOTLINE
**SONAT, INC.:** SONAT TIELINES
**SOUTHERN CALIFORNIA WATER CO.:** CONNECTIONS
**SOUTHERN NEW ENGLAND TELEPHONE CO.:** S N E TIMES
**STAR MARKET CO.:** STAR NEWS
**STERLING DRUG, INC.:** CONVEYOR, THE
**T.U. ELECTRIC:** SYNCHRONIZER
**TENNESSEE EDUCATION ASSOCIATION:** TENNESSEE TEACHER
**TEXAS SOCIETY OF ARCHITECTS:** TEXAS ARCHITECT
**TREES FOR TOMMORROW INC., NATURAL RESOURCES EDUCATION:** NORTHBOUND
**UNITED STATES ARMY:** SOLDIERS
**UNITED WAY OF SUMMIT COUNTY:** COMMON GROUND
**VALHI, INC.:** SUGAR SCOOP
**VALHI, INC.:** SUGARBEET
**VETCO, INC.:** DIRECT LINE
**WEST BEND CO.:** CRAFTSMAN, THE
**WESTERN/SOUTHERN LIFE INSURANCE CO.:** HOME OFFICE NEWS
**WESTINGHOUSE HANFORD COMPANY:** HANFORD REACH
**WORLD'S FINEST CHOCOLATE, INC.:** CHOCOLATE SHAKE
**ZIMPRO ENVIRONMENTAL, INC.:** REACTOR
**ZIPPO MANUFACTURING CO.:** ZIP-A-GRAM

## EDUCATIONAL

**ALABAMA GAS CORP.:** GAS LINES
**AMERICAN WATER SKI ASSOCIATION:** WATER SKIER, THE
**CALIFORNIA SCHOOL BOARDS ASSOCIATION:** C S B A NEWS
**CALIFORNIA SCHOOL BOARDS ASSOCIATION:** CALIFORNIA SCHOOLS
**CALIFORNIA TEACHERS ASSOCIATION:** C T A ACTION
**COLORADO SOCIETY OF CERTIFIED PUBLIC ACCOUNTANTS :** NEWSACCOUNT
**DOW CORNING CORP.:** DOW CORNING WORLD
**EASTERN NEBRASKA OFFICE ON AGING:** NEW HORIZONS
**FUTURE BUSINESS LEADERS OF AMERICA-PHI BETA LAMBDA:** HOTLINE
**GROSSMONT HOSPITAL:** WIN-WOMEN'S INFORMATION NETWORK
**GROUP HEALTH, INC.:** HEALTHPARTNERS TODAY
**INDUSTRIAL COMMISSION:** INDUSTRIAL
**INTERNATIONAL UNIVERSITY FOUNDATION:** T I U NEWSLETTER
**MIAMI VALLEY HOSPITAL:** PRO HEALTH MAGAZINE
**NATIONAL EDUCATION ASSOCIATION:** N E A TODAY
**NATIONAL EDUCATION PROGRAM:** LOOKING AHEAD
**NATIONAL PTA:** P T A TODAY
**NATIONAL SCHOOL PUBLIC RELATIONS ASSOCIATION:** IT STARTS ON THE FRONT LINE
**NATIONAL SCHOOL PUBLIC RELATIONS ASSOCIATION:** NETWORK
**OHIO PHARMACISTS ASSOCIATION:** OHIO PHARMACIST
**OREGON DEPARTMENT OF EDUCATION:** EDUCATION FIRST
**PACE UNIVERSITY:** PACE MAGAZINE
**PINEY WOODS COUNTRY LIFE SCHOOL:** ACADEMIC BULLETIN
**PINEY WOODS COUNTRY LIFE SCHOOL:** PINE TORCH, THE
**RAX RESTAURANTS INC.:** OPERATIONS NEWS
**RJR NABISCO, NABISCO FOODS GROUP:** N F G TODAY
**SALT LAKE CITY SCHOOL DISTRICT:** REPORT CARD-ANNUAL REPORT TO THE COMMUNITY
**SAN FRANCISCO SPCA:** OUR ANIMALS
**SHAWNEE MISSION PUBLIC SCHOOLS:** INSIDE SHAWNEE MISSION PUBLIC SCHOOLS

**SHAWNEE MISSION PUBLIC SCHOOLS:** NEWSLINE
**SOUTHERN ASSOCIATION OF COLLEGES & SCHOOLS:** PROCEEDINGS
**SOUTHERN METHODIST UNIVERSITY:** S M U MAGAZINE
**STATE DEPARTMENT OF EDUCATION:** MISSISSIPPI MESSAGES
**SUPERINTENDENT OF PUBLIC INSTRUCTION:** WASHINGTON LEARNING
**TENNESSEE EDUCATION ASSOCIATION:** T E A NEWS
**TEXAS CONGRESS OF PARENTS & TEACHERS:** TEXAS P T A COMMUNICATOR
**TEXAS HIGH SCHOOL COACHES ASSOCIATION INC.:** TEXAS COACH
**UNIVERSITY CIRCLE INC.:** NEWSLETTER
**UNIVERSITY OF DAYTON:** UNIVERSITY OF DAYTON CAMPUS REPORT, THE
**WASHINGTON WATER POWER CO., THE:** WEEKLY

## ENTERTAINMENT

**ALABAMA GAS CORP.:** GAS LINES
**DUN & BRADSTREET CORP., THE:** D & B REPORTS
**GUTHRIE THEATRE:** GUTHRIE THEATER PROGRAM MAGAZINE
**INTERNATIONAL UNIVERSITY FOUNDATION:** INTERNATIONAL UNIVERSITY POETRY QUARTERLY, THE
**MENTAL HEALTH ASSOCIATION OF ERIE COUNTY INC.:** TODAY - MENTAL HEALTH IN YOUR COMMUNITY
**ROBERT F. KENNEDY MEDICAL CENTER:** PRESTIGE BOOK
**SHAWNEE MISSION PUBLIC SCHOOLS:** INSIDE SHAWNEE MISSION PUBLIC SCHOOLS
**ST. LUKE'S-ROOSEVELT HOSPITAL CENTER:** ON CENTER
**WISCONSIN DEPARTMENT OF NATURAL RESOURCES:** WISCONSIN NATURAL RESOURCES MAGAZINE

## FARM

**AGWAY INC.:** AGWAY COOPERATOR
**ARKANSAS FARM BUREAU FEDERATION:** FARM BUREAU PRESS
**CENEX/LAND O'LAKES:** COOPERATIVE PARTNERS
**DAIRYLEA COOPERATIVE INC.:** DAIRYNEWS
**HIGHEST PROFIT CORP.:** HIGHEST PROFIT PROGRAM
**MAINE POTATO BOARD:** MAINE POTATO NEWS
**MICHIGAN MILK PRODUCERS ASSOCIATION:** MICHIGAN MILK MESSENGER
**MILK MARKET ADMINISTRATOR:** MARKET ADMINISTRATOR'S BULLETIN
**MISSOURI FARM BUREAU FEDERATION:** MISSOURI FARM BUREAU NEWS
**NEW FARM MAGAZINE:** NEW FARM, THE
**OHIO FARM BUREAU FEDERATION:** BUCKEYE FARM NEWS
**SHAWNEE MISSION PUBLIC SCHOOLS:** INSIDE SHAWNEE MISSION PUBLIC SCHOOLS
**SOUTHERN STATES COOPERATIVE:** COOPERATIVE FARMER
**STA-RITE INDUSTRIES:** PERSPECTIVE
**STA-RITE INDUSTRIES:** THIS WEEK
**TEXAS ELECTRIC COOPS INC.:** TEXAS CO-OP POWER
**WISCONSIN FARM BUREAU FEDERATION:** AGVENTURE

## FASHIONS MEN'S

**AMERICAN STORES CO.:** PACE 55
**COLUMBUS LIFE INSURANCE CO.:** LOG
**ENSIGN-BICKFORD INDUSTRIES, INC.:** E-BEE
**FREIGHTLINER CORP.:** TRUCKBUILDERS PROGRESS
**GENERAL MILLS, INC.:** REVIEW
**GUARANTEE MUTUAL LIFE CO.:** GUARANTEE MUTUAL FIELD NEWS
**HAGGAR CO.:** HAGGAR HIGHLIGHTS
**KINNEY SHOE CORPORATION:** KINNEY WORLD
**MEREDITH GRAPHICS, INC.:** GRAPHICOPY
**MIDLAND MUTUAL LIFE INSURANCE CO.:** ACHIEVER
**MORSE SHOE, INC.:** MORSE CODE

NASA LEWIS RESEARCH CENTER: LEWIS NEWS
OHIO EDISON CO.: OHIO EDISONIAN
RICH'S, INC.: FOCAL POINT
SAKS FIFTH AVENUE: FOCUS ON SAKS FIFTH AVENUE
SHELTER INSURANCE COMPANY: CONTACT
SOUTHERN CALIFORNIA WATER CO.: CONNECTIONS
STRAWBRIDGE & CLOTHIER: STORE CHAT
WESTERN/SOUTHERN LIFE INSURANCE CO.: HOME OFFICE NEWS

## FASHIONS WOMEN'S

AMERICAN STORES CO.: PACE 55
ENSIGN-BICKFORD INDUSTRIES, INC.: E-BEE
FAMILY CIRCLE, INC.: ADVANCE NEWS
FLORIDA RURAL ELECTRIC CO-OP ASSOCIATION: FLORIDA RURAL ELECTRIC NEWS
GENERAL MILLS, INC.: REVIEW
GTE TELEPHONE OPERATIONS: TELOPS NEWS
GUARANTEE MUTUAL LIFE CO.: GUARANTEE MUTUAL FIELD NEWS
KINNEY SHOE CORPORATION: KINNEY WORLD
MIDLAND MUTUAL LIFE INSURANCE CO.: ACHIEVER
MORSE SHOE, INC.: MORSE CODE
NASA LEWIS RESEARCH CENTER: LEWIS NEWS
OHIO EDISON CO.: OHIO EDISONIAN
OHIO NATIONAL LIFE INSURANCE CO.: O N L I ECHOES
OKLAHOMA ASSOCIATION OF ELECTRIC COOPERATIVES: OKLAHOMA LIVING
RICH'S, INC.: FOCAL POINT
SAKS FIFTH AVENUE: FOCUS ON SAKS FIFTH AVENUE
SHELTER INSURANCE COMPANY: CONTACT
SOUTHERN CALIFORNIA WATER CO.: CONNECTIONS
STRAWBRIDGE & CLOTHIER: STORE CHAT
TENNESSEE ELECTRIC COOP ASSOCIATION: TENNESSEE MAGAZINE, THE
WESTERN/SOUTHERN LIFE INSURANCE CO.: HOME OFFICE NEWS

## FOOD

ADAMS BUSINESS FORMS, INC.: WEB, THE
ALPHA BETA CO.: VANGUARD, THE
AMERICAN HEART ASSOCIATION: HEART TO HEART
AMERICAN STORES CO.: FLASHES
AMERICAN STORES CO.: PACE 55
ASSOCIATED MILK PRODUCERS, INC.: DAIRYMEN'S DIGEST, N. CENTRAL REGION
BENTON CITY ELECTRIC COOPERATIVE ASSOCIATION: ON LINE WITH BENTON
BLUE CROSS & BLUE SHIELD OF WEST VIRGINIA, INC.: GROUP UPDATE / MEMBERS PLUS / OUT OF THE BLUE
BROOKLYN UNION GAS CO.: SENDOUT
CASCADE NATURAL GAS CORP.: CASCADE FLAME
CENTRAL LINCOLN PEOPLE'S UTILITY DISTRICT: COASTLINES
CITY OF ST. PETERSBURG: SUNSCRIBE
COOK'S PEST CONTROL, INC.: WHAT'S COOKIN'
COOPER OIL, TOOL DIV.: OIL & IRON
CORN REFINERS ASSOCIATION, INC.: CORN ANNUAL
CORNING INCORPORATED: CORNING WORLD
CUMBERLAND FARMS, INC.: MILKY WAY
DUQUESNE LIGHT CO.: DUQUESNE LIGHT NEWS
EASTERN MILK PRODUCERS CO-OP ASSN. INC.: FARM LIFE
ELF ATOCHEM NORTH AMERICA, INC.: DIRECTION 79
ENSIGN-BICKFORD INDUSTRIES, INC.: E-BEE
EQUITABLE RESOURCES: EQUITABLE NEWS
ERWIN DI CYAN: DI CYAN BULLETIN
FAMILY CIRCLE, INC.: ADVANCE NEWS
FLEMING COS. INC.: FLEMING ASSOCIATE, THE
FLORIDA RURAL ELECTRIC CO-OP ASSOCIATION: FLORIDA RURAL ELECTRIC NEWS
FOODLAND INTERNATIONAL CORP.: HOTLINE
GARDEN CITY HOSPITAL: NITTY GRITTY:
GARDEN WAY MFG. CO. INC.: TROY-BILT OWNER NEWS
GENERAL MILLS, INC.: REVIEW
GIANT FOOD, INC.: WE NEWS
GILROY FOODS, INC.: GARLIC VINE, THE

GOLUB CORP./PRICE CHOPPER SUPERMARKETS: ASSOCIATES' VIEW, THE
GRAND UNION CO.: GRAND STAND
GREEN POINT SAVINGS BANK: POINTER, THE
GTE TELEPHONE OPERATIONS: TELOPS NEWS
GUARANTEE MUTUAL LIFE CO.: GUARANTEE MUTUAL FIELD NEWS
GUARANTEE MUTUAL LIFE CO.: INDIAN HILLS ECHOES
H.B. FULLER CO.: FULLER WORLD
HICKORY FARMS OF OHIO INC.: LEASE LINE
IGA, INC.: I G A GROCERGRAM
IPALCO ENTERPRISES, INC.: I P L C O NEWS
KAMPGROUNDS OF AMERICA, INC.: KOA DIRECTORY, ROAD ATLAS AND CAMPING GUIDE
KOSS CORP.: INSIDE OUT
KRAFT-GENERAL FOODS: K G F FOCUS
LEADER FEDERAL SAVINGS & LOAN ASSOCIATION: LEADER DIGEST
LINN COUNTY RURAL ELECTRIC COOPERATIVE ASSOCIATION: NEWSLINES ON THE LINE
MIRRO CORP.: MIXING BOWL, THE
MONONGAHELA POWER CO.: MONONGAHELA NEWS
NASA LEWIS RESEARCH CENTER: LEWIS NEWS
NATIONAL ASSOCIATION OF CONCESSIONAIRES: CONCESSIONAIRE, THE
NATIONAL ASSOCIATION OF CONCESSIONAIRES: INSITE MAGAZINE
NAVY PUBLIC WORKS CENTER SAN FRANCISCO BAY: P W C BAYGRAM
OHIO EDISON CO.: OHIO EDISONIAN
OHIO NATIONAL LIFE INSURANCE CO.: O N L I ECHOES
OHIO RURAL ELECTRIC COOPS INC.: COUNTRY LIVING MAGAZINE
OKLAHOMA ASSOCIATION OF ELECTRIC COOPERATIVES: OKLAHOMA LIVING
ORCHID ISLE AUTO CTR.: ORCHID ISLE AUTO CENTER NEWSLETTER
ORE-IDA FOODS, INC.: VOICE, THE
OZONE INDUSTRIES INC.: OZONE NEWSLETTER
PACIFIC BELL: CONNECTIONS
PIZZA HUT, INC.: PIZZA HUT TODAY
PRICE WATERHOUSE & CO.: LEADER, THE
RALPH'S GROCERY CO.: RALPH'S NEWS
RJR NABISCO, NABISCO FOODS GROUP: N F G TODAY
ROSEBURG FOREST PRODUCTS CO.: ROSEBURG NEWS & VIEWS
SCANDINAVIAN AIRLINES SYSTEM INC.: INSIDE S A S INTERNATIONAL
SHELL OIL CO.: SHELL NEWS
SIZZLER INTERNATIONAL, INC.: HOTLINE
SOUTHERN CALIFORNIA WATER CO.: CONNECTIONS
ST. JOSEPH'S HOSPITAL: ST JOSEPH'S NEWS
STA-RITE INDUSTRIES: PERSPECTIVE
STAR MARKET CO.: STAR NEWS
T.U. ELECTRIC: SYNCHRONIZER
TENNESSEE ELECTRIC COOP ASSOCIATION: TENNESSEE MAGAZINE, THE
U.S. DEPARTMENT OF AGRICULTURE: U S D A EMPLOYEE NEWSLETTER
UNION RAILROAD CO.: U R R EMPLOYEE NEWSLETTER
UNITED WAY OF SUMMIT COUNTY: COMMON GROUND
VALHI, INC.: SUGAR SCOOP
VALHI, INC.: SUGARBEET
WELCH'S: WELCH'S NEWS
WEST BEND CO.: CRAFTSMAN, THE
WISCONSIN DAIRIES COOPERATIVE: DAIRY EXPRESS
WORLD'S FINEST CHOCOLATE, INC.: CHOCOLATE SHAKE

## GARDEN

ADAMS BUSINESS FORMS, INC.: WEB, THE
BANK ONE OF ARIZONA: EAGLE
BDP BRANDS, CARRIER CORP.: FLOW
BROOKLYN UNION GAS CO.: SENDOUT
BUCYRUS-ERIE CO.: MINER DETAILS:
BURLINGTON COUNTY COLLEGE: COLLEGE CONNECTION, THE

BUSINESS MEN'S ASSURANCE CO.: B M A SKYLINES
CITY OF ST. PETERSBURG: SUNSCRIBE
COLUMBUS SOUTHERN POWER CO.: LITELINES
COOPER OIL, TOOL DIV.: OIL & IRON
CORNING INCORPORATED: CORNING WORLD
COUNTRYMARK COOP: COOP CONNECTION
DONREY MEDIA GROUP: DONREY MEDIAGRAM
ELF ATOCHEM NORTH AMERICA, INC.: DIRECTION 79
ENSIGN-BICKFORD INDUSTRIES, INC.: E-BEE
EUA SERVICE CORP.: E U A SPECTRUM
FAMILY CIRCLE, INC.: ADVANCE NEWS
FEDERATED INSURANCE COS.: MULTILINER
FLORIDA RURAL ELECTRIC CO-OP ASSOCIATION: FLORIDA RURAL ELECTRIC NEWS
GARDEN CITY HOSPITAL: NITTY GRITTY:
GARDEN WAY MFG. CO. INC.: TROY-BILT OWNER NEWS
GUARANTEE MUTUAL LIFE CO.: GUARANTEE MUTUAL FIELD NEWS
GUARANTEE MUTUAL LIFE CO.: INDIAN HILLS ECHOES
H.B. FULLER CO.: FULLER WORLD
IPALCO ENTERPRISES, INC.: I P L C O NEWS
LEADER FEDERAL SAVINGS & LOAN ASSOCIATION: LEADER DIGEST
MEREDITH GRAPHICS, INC.: GRAPHICOPY
NASA LEWIS RESEARCH CENTER: LEWIS NEWS
NAVY PUBLIC WORKS CENTER SAN FRANCISCO BAY: P W C BAYGRAM
OHIO EDISON CO.: OHIO EDISONIAN
OHIO NATIONAL LIFE INSURANCE CO.: O N L I ECHOES
OHIO RURAL ELECTRIC COOPS INC.: COUNTRY LIVING MAGAZINE
OKLAHOMA ASSOCIATION OF ELECTRIC COOPERATIVES: OKLAHOMA LIVING
OLAN MILLS OF TENNESSEE: LENS
OPPENHEIMER MANAGEMENT CORP.: HANDSIGNALS, THE
OREGON ASSOCIATION OF NURSERYMEN: OAN DIGGER
OREGON ASSOCIATION OF NURSERYMEN: OAN DIRECTORY & BUYER'S GUIDE
OZONE INDUSTRIES INC.: OZONE NEWSLETTER
PAN-AMERICAN LIFE INSURANCE CO.: LIFELINE
PRICE WATERHOUSE & CO.: LEADER, THE
PUBLIC SERVICE CO. OF NEW HAMPSHIRE: AROUND THE CIRCUIT
ROSEBURG FOREST PRODUCTS CO.: ROSEBURG NEWS & VIEWS
RUBBERMAID, INC.: RUBBERMAID REVIEW
SAKS FIFTH AVENUE: FOCUS ON SAKS FIFTH AVENUE
SCANDINAVIAN AIRLINES SYSTEM INC.: INSIDE S A S INTERNATIONAL
SHELL OIL CO.: SHELL NEWS
T.U. ELECTRIC: SYNCHRONIZER
UNION RAILROAD CO.: U R R EMPLOYEE NEWSLETTER
UNITED WAY OF SUMMIT COUNTY: COMMON GROUND
WESTERN/SOUTHERN LIFE INSURANCE CO.: HOME OFFICE NEWS

## GENERAL INTEREST

ALABAMA POWER CO.: POWERGRAMS
ALBANY INTERNATIONAL CORP.: INFORMATION MEMO
ALEXANDER & BALDWIN, INC.: PO'OKELA
AMERICAN GENERAL LIFE/ACCIDENT INSURANCE CO.: FIELD FOCUS
AMERICAN MUTUAL LIFE INSURANCE CO.: AMERICAN EAGLE
APOGEE ENTERPRISES, INC.: APOGEE HIGHLITES
BAYLOR COLLEGE OF MEDICINE: BAYLOR MEDICINE
BROWNING FERRIS INDUSTRIES: B F I BLUELINE
BURLINGTON COUNTY COLLEGE: ALUMNI ACTION
BURROUGHS WELLCOME CO.: WELLCOME NEWS
CARNEGIE MELLON UNIVERSITY: CARNEGIE MELLON MAGAZINE
CARPENTER TECHNOLOGY CORPORATION: CARPENTER NEWS

**CITY OF RICHARDSON TEXAS:** CITY WIDE NEWSLETTER
**CMP INUSTRIES, INC.:** INSIGHTS
**DELTA AIR LINES:** DELTA DIGEST
**EL PASO ELECTRIC CO.:** ENEWS
**FEDERAL RESERVE BANK OF CLEVELAND:** FEDERAL RESERVE NOTES
**FIRST INTERSTATE BANCORP.:** BANKER, THE
**FLEMING COS. INC.:** FLEMING ASSOCIATE, THE
**GENERAL ACCIDENT INSURANCE:** GAZETTE
**GEORGIA-PACIFIC CORP.:** PAPER & PEOPLE
**GLEANER LIFE INSURANCE SOCIETY:** EPISTLES
**HAWAII GOVERNMENT EMPLOYEES ASSN., AFSCME LOCAL 15:** PUBLIC EMPLOYEE, THE
**HUNTINGTON BANCSHARES, INC.:** HUNTINGTON HIGHLIGHTS
**ITT HARTFORD INSURANCE GROUP:** I T T HARTFORD AGENT
**ITT HARTFORD INSURANCE GROUP:** I T T HARTFORD WORLD
**JEFFERSON PILOT LIFE INSURANCE CO.:** J P LIFE MAGAZINE
**KENTUCKY DEPARTMENT OF EDUCATION:** KENTUCKY TEACHER
**KIRBY CO.:** KIRBY QUARTERLY
**KOHLER CO.:** CAPSULE
**KOHLER CO.:** PEOPLE
**KOSS CORP.:** INSIDE OUT
**LOS ANGELES JR. CHAMBER OF COMMERCE:** PROFILE
**MARTIN MARIETTA ELECTRONICS:** VISION
**MENTAL HEALTH ASSOCIATION OF ERIE COUNTY INC.:** TODAY - MENTAL HEALTH IN YOUR COMMUNITY
**MOBIL OIL CORP.:** COMPASS, THE
**NATIONAL ASSOCIATION OF RAILROAD PASSENGERS:** NATIONAL ASSOCIATION OF RAILROAD PASSENGERS NEWS
**NATIONAL CHRISTMAS TREE ASSOCIATION:** AMERICAN CHRISTMAS TREE JOURNAL
**OREGON ASSOCIATION OF NURSERYMEN:** FARWEST MAGAZINE
**PACIFIC HEALTH RESOURCES:** UPDATE
**PENNSYLVANIA BAR ASSOCIATION:** PENNSYLVANIA LAWYER, THE
**PORT OF OAKLAND:** PORT PROGRESS
**ROBERT F. KENNEDY MEDICAL CENTER:** MINIVIEWS
**SAFECO INSURANCE CO.:** ON THE MOVE
**SAN LUIS OBISPO CHAMBER OF COMMERCE:** SAN LUIS OBISPO VISITOR GUIDE
**SANWA BANK CALIFORNIA:** IN FOCUS
**SISTERS OF PROVIDENCE HEALTH SYSTEM:** IN BRIEF
**SOCIETY FOR HUMAN RESOURCE MANAGEMENT:** H R MAGAZINE
**SOCIETY OF CHARTERED PROPERTY & CASUALTY UNDERWRITERS:** C P C U JOURNAL
**SOCIETY OF CHARTERED PROPERTY & CASUALTY UNDERWRITERS:** C P C U NEWS
**STA-RITE INDUSTRIES:** PERSPECTIVE
**STONE & WEBSTER ENGINEERING CORP.:** TRISKELION, THE
**TEXAS MEDICAL ASSOCIATION:** ACTION
**U.S. DEPARTMENT OF ENERGY:** A L NEWS
**UNITED WAY OF ORANGE COUNTY:** TOGETHER
**VA., MD., & DE. ASSOCIATION OF ELECTRIC CO-OP.:** RURAL LIVING
**WASHINGTON GAS:** INSIDE STORY
**WDCN CHANNEL 8:** PREVIEW

## HOBBIES

**ADAMS BUSINESS FORMS, INC.:** WEB, THE
**AKRON CITY HOSPITAL:** PACEMAKER
**ALLIED GROUP:** FOCUS
**ALUMINUM COMPANY OF AMERICA:** ALCOA NEWS
**AMERICAN STORES CO.:** FLASHES
**APPLIED PHYSICS LABORATORY:** APL NEWS
**APPLIED TECHNOLOGY:** IMAGE
**ARCATA GRAPHICS CORP.:** ARCATAGRAPH
**ASSOCIATED MILK PRODUCERS, INC.:** DAIRYMEN'S DIGEST, N. CENTRAL REGION
**ATLANTA JOURNAL-CONSTITUTION:** HEADLINER

**AUBURN-CORD-DUESENBERG MUSEUM:** ACCELERATOR, THE
**BALL CORP.:** BALL LINE
**BANK ONE OF ARIZONA:** EAGLE
**BARCLAYS AMERICAN/MORTGAGE:** REAL ESTATEMENTS
**BAUSCH & LOMB, INC.:** BAUSCH & LOMB WORLD
**BDP BRANDS, CARRIER CORP.:** FLOW
**BESSEMER & LAKE ERIE RAILROAD:** B & L E EMPLOYEE NEWSLETTER
**BLOUNT, INC.:** OMARK 80
**BLOUNT, INC.:** OREGON-IZER
**BOEING CO.:** BOEING NEWS
**BROOKLYN UNION GAS CO.:** SENDOUT
**BURLINGTON COUNTY COLLEGE:** COLLEGE CONNECTION, THE
**BUSINESS MEN'S ASSURANCE CO.:** B M A SKYLINES
**CABOT CORP.:** CABOT WORLD
**CENTRAL LINCOLN PEOPLE'S UTILITY DISTRICT:** COASTLINES
**CITY OF ST. PETERSBURG:** SUNSCRIBE
**CIVITAN INTERNATIONAL:** COUNTDOWN
**COLONIAL PENN GROUP INC.:** YOU
**COLUMBUS LIFE INSURANCE CO.:** LOG
**COLUMBUS SOUTHERN POWER CO.:** LITELINES
**CONNECTICUT NATURAL GAS CORP.:** FUEL FOR THOUGHT
**COOK COMPOSITES:** FRONTLINE
**COOK'S PEST CONTROL, INC.:** WHAT'S COOKIN'
**COOPER OIL, TOOL DIV.:** OIL & IRON
**CORNING INCORPORATED:** CORNING WORLD
**COUNTRYMARK COOP:** COOP CONNECTION
**CUNA MUTUAL INSURANCE GROUP:** DIMENSIONS
**CUNA MUTUAL INSURANCE GROUP:** WESTWORDS
**DALLAS MORNING NEWS:** INTERCOM
**DELTA AIR LINES:** DELTA DIGEST
**DRESSER INDUSTRIES, INC.:** RECORDER, THE
**DUQUESNE LIGHT CO.:** DUQUESNE LIGHT NEWS
**E.F. HOUGHTON & CO.:** HOUGHTON LINE
**E.F. HOUGHTON & CO.:** HOUGHTONEWS
**ELF ATOCHEM NORTH AMERICA, INC.:** DIRECTION 79
**EMPLOYERS CASUALTY:** BRICKBATS & BOUQUETS
**EQUITABLE RESOURCES:** EQUITABLE NEWS
**ERIE INSURANCE GROUP:** ERIE FAMILY
**EUA SERVICE CORP.:** E U A SPECTRUM
**FEDERAL RESERVE BANK OF NEW YORK:** FED
**FEDERATED INSURANCE COS.:** MULTILINER
**FIRST AMERICAN CORP.:** FIRST FOCUS
**FIRST VIRGINIA BANK:** FIRST VIRGINIAN
**FLORIDA RURAL ELECTRIC CO-OP ASSOCIATION:** FLORIDA RURAL ELECTRIC NEWS
**GARDEN CITY HOSPITAL:** NITTY GRITTY
**GARDEN WAY MFG. CO. INC.:** TROY-BILT OWNER NEWS
**GEORGE E. FAILING CO.:** CORE DRILLER
**GIANT FOOD, INC.:** WE NEWS
**GILBARCO INC.:** GILBARCO GAZETTE
**GLEASON WORKS:** CUTTING EDGE
**GOLUB CORP./PRICE CHOPPER SUPERMARKETS:** ASSOCIATES' VIEW, THE
**GRAND UNION CO.:** GRAND STAND
**GREAT LAKES DIVISION-NATIONAL STEEL:** FOCUS
**GREEN POINT SAVINGS BANK:** POINTER, THE
**GRUMMAN CORP.:** GRUMMAN WORLD
**GTE TELEPHONE OPERATIONS:** TELOPS NEWS
**GUARANTEE MUTUAL LIFE CO.:** INDIAN HILLS ECHOES
**HARRIS CORP.:** F Y I MAGAZINE
**HAWAIIAN ELECTRIC CO., INC.:** HOA HANA
**HIA (HOBBY INDUSTRY ASSOCIATION OF AMERICA):** HORIZONS
**HOUSTON CHRONICLE:** COPY
**HOUSTON LIGHTING & POWER CO.:** TRANSMISSIONS
**INTERSTATE POWER CO.:** INTERSTATE NEWS
**IPALCO ENTERPRISES, INC.:** I P L C O NEWS
**KANO LABS INC.:** GENIUS AT WORK
**KANSAS DEPARTMENT OF COMMERCE:** KANSAS MAGAZINE
**KIMBALL INTERNATIONAL, INC.:** SOUNDBOARD
**LAKE ERIE GIRL SCOUT COUNCIL:** MILLWHEEL
**LEADER FEDERAL SAVINGS & LOAN ASSOCIATION:** LEADER DIGEST
**LONGS DRUG STORES, INC.:** CHAIN REACTION
**LORD CORP.:** LORDFACTS

**LOS ANGELES DEPARTMENT OF WATER & POWER:** INTAKE MAGAZINE
**LUTHERAN MEDICAL CENTER:** INSIDE LUTHERAN
**LYNCHBURG GENERAL-MARSHALL LODGE HOSPITALS:** CENTRA HEALTH MAGAZINE
**MAGIC CHEF COMPANY:** OUR WORLD
**MARSHALL & ILSLEY BANK:** PERSONAL TOUCH
**MERCHANTS INSURANCE GROUP:** MESSENGER
**MEREDITH GRAPHICS, INC.:** GRAPHICOPY
**MERIDIAN BANK:** DIALOG
**METHODIST HOSPITAL:** ADVANCES
**MICHELIN NORTH AMERICA, INC.:** BIB AMERICA
**MIDLAND MUTUAL LIFE INSURANCE CO.:** ACHIEVER
**MORSE SHOE, INC.:** MORSE CODE
**MUTUAL BENEFICIAL ASSN. OF RAILROAD TRANSPORTATION EMPLOYEES:** MUTUAL MAGAZINE, THE
**NATIONAL INDEMNITY CO.:** FRIDAY FACTS
**NAVY PUBLIC WORKS CENTER SAN FRANCISCO BAY:** P W C BAYGRAM
**OHIO EDISON CO.:** OHIO EDISONIAN
**OHIO NATIONAL LIFE INSURANCE CO.:** O N L I ECHOES
**OHIO RURAL ELECTRIC COOPS INC.:** COUNTRY LIVING MAGAZINE
**OKLAHOMA ASSOCIATION OF ELECTRIC COOPERATIVES:** OKLAHOMA LIVING
**OLAN MILLS OF TENNESSEE:** LENS
**OPPENHEIMER MANAGEMENT CORP.:** HANDSIGNALS, THE
**ORANGE & ROCKLAND UTILITIES, INC.:** LAMPPOST
**ORE-IDA FOODS, INC.:** VOICE, THE
**OZONE INDUSTRIES INC.:** OZONE NEWSLETTER
**PAN-AMERICAN LIFE INSURANCE CO.:** LIFELINE
**PHILADELPHIA BAR ASSOCIATION:** PHILADELPHIA LAWYER, THE
**PHILLIPS PETROLEUM CO.:** PHILNEWS
**PUBLIC SERVICE CO. OF NEW HAMPSHIRE:** AROUND THE CIRCUIT
**RALPH'S GROCERY CO.:** RALPH'S NEWS
**RANGER INSURANCE CO.:** RANGER RESOURCES
**RESEARCH MEDICAL CENTER:** HORIZON
**ROSEBURG FOREST PRODUCTS CO.:** ROSEBURG NEWS & VIEWS
**RUBBERMAID, INC.:** RUBBERMAID REVIEW
**SAFECO INSURANCE CO.:** ON THE MOVE
**SAKS FIFTH AVENUE:** FOCUS ON SAKS FIFTH AVENUE
**SCANDINAVIAN AIRLINES SYSTEM INC.:** INSIDE S A S INTERNATIONAL
**SCHRAMM INC.:** WHAT'S HAPPENING
**SCRIPTURE PRESS PUBLICATIONS, INC.:** SPOTLIGHT
**SHELL OIL CO.:** SHELL ALUMNI NEWS
**SHERWOOD MEDICAL CO.:** SHERWOOD REPORTER
**SIZZLER INTERNATIONAL, INC.:** COLLINS COUNTRY
**SMITH & NEPHEW RICHARDS INC.:** SMITH & NEPHEW RICHARDS REPORTER
**SONAT, INC.:** SONAT TIELINES
**SOUTHEAST MICHIGAN, N.A.:** FIRST WORD, THE
**SOUTHERN COMPANY SERVICES, INC.:** INSIDE
**ST. JOSEPH'S HOSPITAL:** ST JOSEPH'S NEWS
**STAINLESS FOUNDRY & ENGINEERING INC.:** STAINLESS SPIRIT
**STERLING DRUG, INC.:** CONVEYOR, THE
**STUDEBAKER DRIVERS CLUB, INC.:** TURNING WHEELS
**T.U. ELECTRIC:** SYNCHRONIZER
**TENNESSEE ELECTRIC COOP ASSOCIATION:** TENNESSEE MAGAZINE, THE
**U.S. BORAX INC.:** BORAX PIONEER
**UGI CORP.:** U G I HORIZONS
**UNION RAILROAD CO.:** U R R EMPLOYEE NEWSLETTER
**UNISYS:** INSIDE INFORMATION
**UNITED STATES ARMY:** SOLDIERS
**UNITED WAY OF SUMMIT COUNTY:** COMMON GROUND
**VIRGINIA POWER CO.:** VEPCO CURRENTS
**WALGREEN CO.:** WALGREEN WORLD
**WEST BEND CO.:** CRAFTSMAN, THE
**WEST PENN POWER CO.:** WATT'S NEW
**WESTERN/SOUTHERN LIFE INSURANCE CO.:** HOME OFFICE NEWS
**WOLVERINE WORLD WIDE:** WOLVERINE NEWS
**YOUNG RADIATOR CO.:** YOUNG NEWS & VIEWS

ZIPPO MANUFACTURING CO.: ZIP-A-GRAM

## HOME APPLIANCES

ASSOCIATED MILK PRODUCERS, INC.: DAIRYMEN'S
DIGEST, N. CENTRAL REGION
BANK ONE OF ARIZONA: EAGLE
BDP BRANDS, CARRIER CORP.: FLOW
BENTON CITY ELECTRIC COOPERATIVE
ASSOCIATION: ON LINE WITH BENTON
BOSTWICK-BRAUN CO.: ANVIL
BROOKLYN UNION GAS CO.: SENDOUT
CASCADE NATURAL GAS CORP.: CASCADE FLAME
CENTRAL LINCOLN PEOPLE'S UTILITY DISTRICT:
COASTLINES
COLUMBUS SOUTHERN POWER CO.: LITELINES
CONNECTICUT NATURAL GAS CORP.: FUEL FOR
THOUGHT
DONREY MEDIA GROUP: DONREY MEDIAGRAM
DUQUESNE LIGHT CO.: DUQUESNE LIGHT NEWS
ELF ATOCHEM NORTH AMERICA, INC.: DIRECTION 79
EQUITABLE RESOURCES: EQUITABLE NEWS
EUA SERVICE CORP.: E U A SPECTRUM
FLORIDA RURAL ELECTRIC CO-OP ASSOCIATION:
FLORIDA RURAL ELECTRIC NEWS
GREATER HOUSTON BUILDERS ASSOCIATION:
HOUSTON BUILDER
GUARANTEE MUTUAL LIFE CO.: INDIAN HILLS
ECHOES
HAWAIIAN ELECTRIC CO., INC.: HOA HANA
IPALCO ENTERPRISES, INC.: I P L C O NEWS
LINN COUNTY RURAL ELECTRIC COOPERATIVE
ASSOCIATION: NEWSLINES ON THE LINE
MEREDITH GRAPHICS, INC.: GRAPHICOPY
MIRRO CORP.: MIXING BOWL, THE
MONONGAHELA POWER CO.: MONONGAHELA NEWS
NAVY PUBLIC WORKS CENTER SAN FRANCISCO
BAY: P W C BAYGRAM
OHIO EDISON CO.: OHIO EDISONIAN
OHIO RURAL ELECTRIC COOPS INC.: COUNTRY
LIVING MAGAZINE
OKLAHOMA ASSOCIATION OF ELECTRIC
COOPERATIVES: OKLAHOMA LIVING
PLUMBING MECHANICAL CONTRACTORS COUNCIL
HARRIS COUNTY: GULF COAST PLUMBING,
HEATING, COOLING NEWS
RICH'S, INC.: FOCAL POINT
T.U. ELECTRIC: SYNCHRONIZER
TENNESSEE ELECTRIC COOP ASSOCIATION:
TENNESSEE MAGAZINE, THE
UNITED WAY OF SUMMIT COUNTY: COMMON
GROUND
WEST BEND CO.: CRAFTSMAN, THE

## HOME FURNISHINGS

AMERICAN HOME PRODUCTS: A H P VISTA
CALIFORNIA ASSOCIATION OF REALTORS:
CALIFORNIA REAL ESTATE MAGAZINE
CENTRAL LINCOLN PEOPLE'S UTILITY DISTRICT:
COASTLINES
DONREY MEDIA GROUP: DONREY MEDIAGRAM
ELF ATOCHEM NORTH AMERICA, INC.: DIRECTION 79
ENSIGN-BICKFORD INDUSTRIES, INC.: E-BEE
EUA SERVICE CORP.: E U A SPECTRUM
FAMILY CIRCLE, INC.: ADVANCE NEWS
FLORIDA RURAL ELECTRIC CO-OP ASSOCIATION:
FLORIDA RURAL ELECTRIC NEWS
GREATER HOUSTON BUILDERS ASSOCIATION:
HOUSTON BUILDER
GUARANTEE MUTUAL LIFE CO.: INDIAN HILLS
ECHOES
INTERSTATE POWER CO.: INTERSTATE NEWS
JEFFERSON PILOT LIFE INSURANCE CO.: J P HOME
SERVICE TODAY
OHIO EDISON CO.: OHIO EDISONIAN
OHIO NATIONAL LIFE INSURANCE CO.: O N L I
ECHOES
OKLAHOMA ASSOCIATION OF ELECTRIC
COOPERATIVES: OKLAHOMA LIVING
OLAN MILLS OF TENNESSEE: LENS
PLUMBING MECHANICAL CONTRACTORS COUNCIL
HARRIS COUNTY: GULF COAST PLUMBING,
HEATING, COOLING NEWS

RICH'S, INC.: FOCAL POINT
TENNESSEE ELECTRIC COOP ASSOCIATION:
TENNESSEE MAGAZINE, THE
VALSPAR CORP.: SCOPE
WEST BEND CO.: CRAFTSMAN, THE

## HOME WORKSHOP

ALLIED GROUP: FOCUS
ALPHA BETA CO.: VANGUARD, THE
BDP BRANDS, CARRIER CORP.: FLOW
BENTON CITY ELECTRIC COOPERATIVE
ASSOCIATION: ON LINE WITH BENTON
BUCYRUS-ERIE CO.: MINER DETAILS
BURLINGTON COUNTY COLLEGE: COLLEGE
CONNECTION, THE
BUSINESS MEN'S ASSURANCE CO.: B M A SKYLINES
CENTRAL LINCOLN PEOPLE'S UTILITY DISTRICT:
COASTLINES
CITY OF ST. PETERSBURG: SUNSCRIBE
COLUMBUS SOUTHERN POWER CO.: LITELINES
COOPER OIL, TOOL DIV.: OIL & IRON
DONREY MEDIA GROUP: DONREY MEDIAGRAM
ELF ATOCHEM NORTH AMERICA, INC.: DIRECTION 79
ENSIGN-BICKFORD INDUSTRIES, INC.: E-BEE
EUA SERVICE CORP.: E U A SPECTRUM
FAMILY CIRCLE, INC.: ADVANCE NEWS
FEDERATED INSURANCE COS.: MULTILINER
FLORIDA RURAL ELECTRIC CO-OP ASSOCIATION:
FLORIDA RURAL ELECTRIC NEWS
GARDEN WAY MFG. CO. INC.: TROY-BILT OWNER
NEWS
GUARANTEE MUTUAL LIFE CO.: INDIAN HILLS
ECHOES
H.B. FULLER CO.: FULLER WORLD
INTERSTATE POWER CO.: INTERSTATE NEWS
KANO LABS INC.: GENIUS AT WORK
LEADER FEDERAL SAVINGS & LOAN ASSOCIATION:
LEADER DIGEST
MEREDITH GRAPHICS, INC.: GRAPHICOPY
MUTUAL BENEFICIAL ASSN. OF RAILROAD
TRANSPORTATION EMPLOYEES: MUTUAL
MAGAZINE, THE
OHIO NATIONAL LIFE INSURANCE CO.: O N L I
ECHOES
OHIO RURAL ELECTRIC COOPS INC.: COUNTRY
LIVING MAGAZINE
OKLAHOMA ASSOCIATION OF ELECTRIC
COOPERATIVES: OKLAHOMA LIVING
OZONE INDUSTRIES INC.: OZONE NEWSLETTER
PLUMBING MECHANICAL CONTRACTORS COUNCIL
HARRIS COUNTY: GULF COAST PLUMBING,
HEATING, COOLING NEWS
PUBLIC SERVICE CO. OF NEW HAMPSHIRE: AROUND
THE CIRCUIT
SALT LAKE CITY SCHOOL DISTRICT: DISTRICT, THE
SECURITY MUTUAL LIFE INSURANCE CO. OF NEW
YORK: HEADLINER
T.U. ELECTRIC: SYNCHRONIZER
TENNESSEE ELECTRIC COOP ASSOCIATION:
TENNESSEE MAGAZINE, THE
U.S. BORAX INC.: BORAX PIONEER
UNION RAILROAD CO.: U R R EMPLOYEE
NEWSLETTER
WESTERN/SOUTHERN LIFE INSURANCE CO.: HOME
OFFICE NEWS

## HOW-TO-STORIES

AAA WASHINGTON: WASHINGTON MOTORIST
ADAMS BUSINESS FORMS, INC.: WEB, THE
ALLIED GROUP: FOCUS
AMERICAN ASSOCIATION OF COLLEGES FOR
TEACHER EDUCATION: BRIEFS
AMERICAN NATIONAL INSURANCE CO.: A N I C O
AMERICAN STORES CO.: FLASHES
AMP INC., VALLEY FORGE: CONTACT VIDEO
BANCOKLAHOMA CORP.: EXPRESS
BANK ONE OF ARIZONA: EAGLE
BARCLAYS AMERICAN/MORTGAGE: REAL
ESTATEMENTS
BENEFICIAL LIFE INS. CO.: BENEFICIAL
BENEFACTOR

RICH'S, INC.: FOCAL POINT

BESSEMER & LAKE ERIE RAILROAD: B & L E
EMPLOYEE NEWSLETTER
BLOUNT, INC.: OREGON-IZER
BUCYRUS-ERIE CO.: SURFACE MINER
CALIFORNIA ASSOCIATION OF REALTORS:
CALIFORNIA REAL ESTATE MAGAZINE
CATHOLIC PRESS ASSOCIATION: CATHOLIC
JOURNALIST, THE
CITY OF ST. PETERSBURG: SUNSCRIBE
CIVITAN INTERNATIONAL: COUNTDOWN
COLONIAL PENN GROUP INC.: YOU
COLUMBUS LIFE INSURANCE CO.: LOG
COOK COMPOSITES: FRONTLINE
COOK'S PEST CONTROL, INC.: WHAT'S COOKIN'
COOPER HOSPITAL/UNIVERSITY MEDICAL CENTER:
STETHOSCOPE
CORNING INCORPORATED: CORNING WORLD
CPI CORP.: NEWS & VIEWS
CUMBERLAND FARMS, INC.: MILKY WAY
DALLAS MORNING NEWS: INTERCOM
DATAPOINT CORP.: DETAILS
DEERE & CO.: J D JOURNAL
E.F. HOUGHTON & CO.: HOUGHTONEWS
E-SYSTEMS, INC.: TEAM
ELF ATOCHEM NORTH AMERICA, INC.: DIRECTION 79
ENSIGN-BICKFORD INDUSTRIES, INC.: E-BEE
EUA SERVICE CORP.: E U A SPECTRUM
FIRST AMERICAN CORP.: FIRST FOCUS
FIRST NATIONAL BANK OF MARYLAND:
COMMUNICATOR
FIRST VIRGINIA BANK: FIRST VIRGINIAN
GARDEN WAY MFG. CO. INC.: TROY-BILT OWNER
NEWS
GEORGE E. FAILING CO.: CORE DRILLER
GOLUB CORP./PRICE CHOPPER SUPERMARKETS:
ASSOCIATES' VIEW, THE
GOVERNMENT PERSONNEL MUTUAL LIFE
INSURANCE CO: G P M MESSENGER
GRAND UNION CO.: GRAND STAND
GRUMMAN CORP.: GRUMMAN WORLD
H.B. FULLER CO.: FULLER WORLD
HARLEY-DAVIDSON MOTOR CO. INC.: ENTHUSIAST
HICKORY FARMS OF OHIO INC.: LEASE LINE
HOUSTON CHRONICLE: COPY
HOUSTON LIGHTING & POWER CO.: TRANSMISSIONS
IGA, INC.: I G A GROCERGRAM
INTERSTATE POWER CO.: INTERSTATE NEWS
IOWA DEPARTMENT OF ECONOMIC DEVELOPMENT:
DIGEST, THE
IPALCO ENTERPRISES, INC.: I P L C O NEWS
KAMPGROUNDS OF AMERICA, INC.: KOA
DIRECTORY, ROAD ATLAS AND CAMPING GUIDE
KANO LABS INC.: GENIUS AT WORK
KIMBALL INTERNATIONAL, INC.: SOUNDBOARD
LAWRENCE RAGAN COMMUNICATIONS, INC.: RAGAN
REPORT
MEREDITH GRAPHICS, INC.: GRAPHICOPY
MERIDIAN BANK: DIALOG
MICHIGAN STATE UNIVERSITY: SOURCE
MID-AMERICA DAIRYMEN INC.: MID-AM REPORTER
MIDLAND MUTUAL LIFE INSURANCE CO.: ACHIEVER
MORSE SHOE, INC.: MORSE CODE
NATIONAL ASSOCIATION OF FEDERAL CREDIT
UNIONS: FEDERAL CREDIT UNION
NATIONAL FEDERATION OF INDEPENDENT
BUSINESS: I B MAGAZINE (INDEPENDENT
BUSINESS)
NATIONAL INDEMNITY CO.: FRIDAY FACTS
NEW ENGLAND MUTUAL LIFE INSURANCE CO.:
CURRENTS
NEW YORK LIFE INSURANCE CO.: NEW YORK LIFE
NEWS
OAK RIDGE NATIONAL LABORATORY: LAB NEWS
OHIO NATIONAL LIFE INSURANCE CO.: BULLETIN
OHIO RURAL ELECTRIC COOPS INC.: COUNTRY
LIVING MAGAZINE
OHIO TRUCKING ASSOCIATION: OHIO GOVERNMENT
DIRECTORY
OKLAHOMA ASSOCIATION OF ELECTRIC
COOPERATIVES: OKLAHOMA LIVING
OKLAHOMA DEPARTMENT OF COMMERCE:
COMMERCE FOLIO
OZONE INDUSTRIES INC.: OZONE NEWSLETTER
PAN-AMERICAN LIFE INSURANCE CO.: LIFELINE
QUAKER OATS CO.: MIDWEEK

QUAKER OATS CO.: QUAKER INSIDER
QUAKER OATS CO.: QUAKER QUARTERLY
QUIVIRA COUNCIL, INC.: TRAIL GUIDE
RADIO-TELEVISION NEWS DIRECTORS ASSOCIATION: R T N D A COMMUNICATOR
RANGER INSURANCE CO.: RANGER RESOURCES
RESEARCH MEDICAL CENTER: HORIZON
ROSICRUCIAN ORDER AMORC: ROSICRUCIAN DIGEST
SAIF CORP.: SCOPE: COMP NEWS
SAKS FIFTH AVENUE: FOCUS ON SAKS FIFTH AVENUE
SANDY CORPORATION: PRO PUBLICATION
SATELLITE INDUSTRIES INC.: PORTABLE SANITATION QUARTERLY
SCANDINAVIAN AIRLINES SYSTEM INC.: INSIDE S A S INTERNATIONAL
SCHRAMM INC.: WHAT'S HAPPENING
SCRIPTURE PRESS PUBLICATIONS, INC.: SPOTLIGHT:
SHELL OIL CO.: VENTURE
SIZZLER INTERNATIONAL, INC.: COLLINS COUNTRY
SIZZLER INTERNATIONAL, INC.: HOTLINE
SONAT, INC.: SONAT TIELINES
SOUTHERN COMPANY SERVICES, INC.: INSIDE
SOUTHERN NEW ENGLAND TELEPHONE CO.: S N E TIMES
ST. JOSEPH'S HOSPITAL: ST JOSEPH'S NEWS:
ST. VINCENT HOSPITAL: HEALTH REVIEW
STATE BAR OF TEXAS: TEXAS BAR JOURNAL
T.U. ELECTRIC: SYNCHRONIZER
TENNESSEE EDUCATION ASSOCIATION: TENNESSEE TEACHER
TENNESSEE ELECTRIC COOP ASSOCIATION: TENNESSEE MAGAZINE, THE
US SMALL BUSINESS ADMINISTRATION: ANNUAL REPORT
VALSPAR CORP.: SCOPE
VERNON CO.: VERNON MIRROR
WALGREEN CO.: WALGREEN WORLD
WASHINGTON POST: SHOP TALK
WESTERN/SOUTHERN LIFE INSURANCE CO.: HOME OFFICE NEWS
WESTVACO CORP.: NEWS LETTER
WISCONSIN DAIRIES COOPERATIVE: DAIRY EXPRESS
ZIPPO MANUFACTURING CO.: ZIP-A-GRAM
21ST CENTURY GENETICS COOPERATIVE: VISIONS

## MAGAZINE SUPPLEMENT

BAPTIST SUNDAY SCHOOL BOARD: CIRCLE
FRANKLIN, THE: FRANKLIN FIELD
NESTLE USA, INC.: NESTLE U S A 2000
OHIO CASUALTY INSURANCE GROUP, THE: POINTERS MAGAZINE
OREGON DEPT. OF FORESTRY: FOREST LOG
SALES PROSPECTOR: SALES PROSPECTOR

## MERCHANDISING PUBLICATION

A.B. CHANCE CO.: CHANCE TIPS
AMERICAN OLEAN TILE CO.: GAZETTE
AMERICAN ROAD & TRANSPORTATION BUILDERS ASSOCIATION: TRANSPORTATION BUILDER
ATLANTIC ENVELOPE CO.: IN TRANSIT
AUTO-OWNERS INSURANCE: EMBLEM
BERRY CO., THE: BERRY LEADER, THE
CURTIS CIRCULATION CO.: CURTIS LINE, THE
FURNAS ELECTRIC CO.: FURNAS TODAY
METRO CREATIVE GRAPHICS, INC.: METRO'S PLUS BUSINESS
OUTBOARD MARINE CORP.: O M C CURRENTS
RAX RESTAURANTS INC.: OPERATIONS NEWS
RYDER SYSTEM, INC.: RYDER DEALER
RYDER SYSTEM, INC.: RYDER PEOPLE
SONOCO PRODUCTS CO.: SONOCO WORLD
STATE LIFE INSURANCE CO.: BULLETIN
STONE & WEBSTER ENGINEERING CORP.: JOURNAL, THE
TANDYCRAFTS, INC.: COMMUNICATOR
YOUNKERS, INC.: YOUNKERS REPORTER

## MISCELLANEOUS

AID ASSOCIATION FOR LUTHERANS (AAL): CORRESPONDENT
AMERICAN COLLEGE OF SPORTS MEDICINE: SPORTS MEDICINE BULLETIN
AMERICAN LUNG ASSOCIATION OF GEORGIA: BREATHTAKING NEWS
AMERICAN PRODUCTION & INVENTORY CONTROL SOCIETY (APICS): PRODUCTION AND INVENTORY MANAGEMENT
AMERICAN ROAD & TRANSPORTATION BUILDERS ASSOCIATION: A R T B A NEWSLETTER
AMERICAN SOCIETY OF INTERIOR DESIGNERS: A S I D REPORT
AMTRAK: AMTRAK TIMES
ANHEUSER-BUSCH COMPANIES, INC.: FOCUS ON ST. LOUIS
ASSOCIATES CORPORATION OF NORTH AMERICA: ASSOCIATES MAGAZINE, THE
BIG BROTHERS OF GREATER LOS ANGELES, INC.: THE IMAGE
BOULEVARD PUBLICATIONS INC.: GOOD LIVING
BOULEVARD PUBLICATIONS INC.: IDEAS FOR BETTER LIVING
BRISTOL-MYERS CO.: ALUMNEWS
CARPENTER TECHNOLOGY CORPORATION: CARPENTER NEWS
CHESAPEAKE BAY GIRL SCOUT COUNCIL: AREA CHAIRMAN MAILING
CHESAPEAKE BAY GIRL SCOUT COUNCIL: BAY WINDOW
CHILDREN'S HOSPITAL OF PHILADELPHIA, THE: CHILDREN'S VIEW
COLORADO ASSN. OF REALTORS: COLORADO REALTOR NEWS
CONNECTICUT NATURAL GAS CORP.: FUEL FOR THOUGHT
CORN BELT POWER COOPERATIVE: WATTS WATT
DALLAS MORNING NEWS: INTERCOM
ECOLAB INC.: ECOLAB NEWS
EEI: EDITORIAL EYE, THE
GENERAL ACCIDENT INSURANCE: COVERAGE
GEORGIA PORTS AUTHORITY: GEORGIA ANCHORAGE
GIRL SCOUT COUNCIL OF GREATER MINNEAPOLIS: GIRL SCOUTING
GIRL SCOUT COUNCIL OF GREATER MINNEAPOLIS: PIONEER
HEINZ U.S.A.: HEINZLINE
HTB, INC.: H T B TODAY
IN-PLANT MANAGEMENT ASSOCIATION: PERSPECTIVES
INDIANAPOLIS WATER CO.: WATER LINES
INTER-STATE ASSURANCE CO.: FOCUS ON COMMISSIONS
INTERNATIONAL FLYING FARMERS: INTERNATIONAL FLYING FARMER
KELLY SERVICES, INC.: WORKSTYLE NEWSLETTER
KYOCERA INTERNATIONAL, INC.: THE KEY
LEHIGH VALLEY BANK: UPDATE
LUTHERAN BROTHERHOOD: LUTHERAN BROTHERHOOD BOND
MERCK & CO. INC.: FRONT LINE
MINNESOTA MUTUAL LIFE INSURANCE CO.: EXCEL
MORBARK INDUSTRIES INC.: MORBARK REPORT
NASHVILLE STATE TECHNICAL INSTITUTE: PRINT OUT
NATIONAL RURAL HEALTH ASSOCIATION: JOURNAL OF RURAL HEALTH
NATIONAL RURAL HEALTH ASSOCIATION: RURAL CLINICIAN QUARTERLY
NATIONAL RURAL HEALTH ASSOCIATION: RURAL HEALTH CARE
NEW ENGLAND PRINTER & PUBLISHER INC.: NEW ENGLAND PRINTER & PUBLISHER
NEW YORK TIMES: TIMES COMPANY REPORT
OHIO STATE MEDICAL ASSOCIATION: OHIO STATE MEDICAL JOURNAL
OKLAHOMA BANKERS ASSOCIATION: OKLAHOMA BANKER

OREGON DEPARTMENT OF INSURANCE & FINANCE: BIENNIAL REPORT
OREGON HEALTH SCIENCES UNIVERSITY: OHSU VIEWS
PHILADELPHIA BAR ASSOCIATION: PHILADELPHIA BAR REPORTER, THE
PHOTOSOURCE INTERNATIONAL: PHOTOMARKET
SHANNON & WILSON INC.: PROBINGS
SOCIETY OF AUTOMOTIVE ENGINEERS INC.: SAE UPDATE
SOCIETY OF WOMEN ENGINEERS: S W E
SOUTH CAROLINA STATE PORTS AUTHORITY: SOUTH CAROLINA PORT NEWS
SOUTHWESTERN PUBLIC SERVICE CO.: SOUTHWESTERNER
STAR MARKET CO.: STAR NEWS
STONE & WEBSTER ENGINEERING CORP.: PROMOTIONAL PUBLICATIONS
STRAWBRIDGE & CLOTHIER: STORE CHAT
SUBARU OF AMERICA, INC.: INSIDE TRACK
TEXAS ELECTRIC COOPS INC.: TEXAS CO-OP POWER
TYSON FOODS: TYSON UPDATE
U.S. AIR FORCE: LIMELITE
UNIVERSITY OF WISCONSIN SYSTEM: WISCONSIN IDEAS
W.R. GRACE & CO.: GRACE INSIDER UPDATE
WATER EDUCATION FOUNDATION: WESTERN WATER
WESTERN STATE EQUIPMENT CO.: WESTERNER
WISCO INDUSTRIES INC.: PLAINTALK
WISCONSIN NATURAL GAS CO.: RESOURCE
WLIW CHANNEL 21: MEMBERS LISTING IN SPOTLIGHT MAGAZINE

## MUSIC

APACHE CORPORATION: APACHE CORP., ANNUAL REPORT
ROCHESTER GAS & ELECTRIC CORP.: R G & E NEWS
SWEET ADELINES INTERNATIONAL: PITCH PIPE, THE

## NEW PRODUCTS

ALABAMA FARMERS FEDERATION: NEIGHBORS MAGAZINE
ALPHA BETA CO.: VANGUARD, THE
AMERICAN ASSOCIATION OF COLLEGES FOR TEACHER EDUCATION: BRIEFS
AMERICAN HOME PRODUCTS: A H P VISTA
AMERICAN HONDA MOTOR CO., INC.: MIGHTY TO MINI NEWS
AMERICAN STORES CO.: FLASHES
AMP INC., VALLEY FORGE: CONTACT VIDEO
ATLANTIC MUTUAL COS.: ATLANTIC MESSENGER
AXIA, INC.: AXIA ACTION
BALL CORP.: BALL LINE
BANK ONE OF ARIZONA: EAGLE
BANKERS SECURITY LIFE INSURANCE SOCIETY: BANKERS NOTES
BENTON CITY ELECTRIC COOPERATIVE ASSOCIATION: ON LINE WITH BENTON
BESSEMER & LAKE ERIE RAILROAD: B & L E EMPLOYEE NEWSLETTER
BOEING CO.: BOEING NEWS
BORG-WARNER AUTOMOTIVE, TRANSMISSION SYSTEMS: SHIFTING TIMES
BOSTWICK-BRAUN CO.: ANVIL
BROOKLYN UNION GAS CO.: SENDOUT
BUCYRUS-ERIE CO.: SURFACE MINER
BURLINGTON COUNTY COLLEGE: COLLEGE CONNECTION, THE
CABOT CORP.: CABOT WORLD
CALIFORNIA ASSOCIATION OF REALTORS: CALIFORNIA REAL ESTATE MAGAZINE
CASCADE NATURAL GAS CORP.: CASCADE FLAME
CATERPILLAR INDUSTRIAL, INC.: MENTOR LIFT-LINES
CATHOLIC PRESS ASSOCIATION: CATHOLIC JOURNALIST, THE
CENTRAL LINCOLN PEOPLE'S UTILITY DISTRICT: COASTLINES
CHASE MANHATTAN CORP.: CHASE BUSINESS
CITY OF ST. PETERSBURG: SUNSCRIBE

CIVITAN INTERNATIONAL: CIVITAN MAGAZINE
CLAIROL INC.: CLAIROL HIGHLIGHTS
CNA INSURANCE: BRANCH NEWSLETTERS
CNA INSURANCE: KEYNOTER
COLONIAL PENN GROUP INC.: YOU
CONNECTICUT BUSINESS & INDUSTRY ASSOCIATION: C B I A NEWS
CONNECTICUT NATURAL GAS CORP.: FUEL FOR THOUGHT
COOK COMPOSITES: FRONTLINE
COOPER INDUSTRIES, INC.: COOPER NEWS
COPPERWELD CORP.: ACROSS COPPERWELD
CORNING INCORPORATED: CORNING WORLD
CPI CORP.: NEWS & VIEWS
CUMBERLAND FARMS, INC.: MILKY WAY
CUNA MUTUAL INSURANCE GROUP: DIMENSIONS
DALLAS LIGHTHOUSE FOR THE BLIND, INC.: PANORAMA
DAVOL INC.: DIALOGUE
DSM COPOLYMER: DSM COPOLYMER NEWS
E.F. HOUGHTON & CO.: HOUGHTONEWS
E-SYSTEMS, INC.: TEAM
EAST OHIO GAS CO.: DATELINE
ELCO INDUSTRIES, INC.: E L C O NEWSLETTER
ERWIN DI CYAN: DI CYAN BULLETIN
EX-STUDENTS ASSOCIATION: TEXAS ALCALDE
FAMILY CIRCLE, INC.: ADVANCE NEWS
FIRST NATIONAL BANK OF MARYLAND: COMMUNICATOR
GARDEN WAY MFG. CO. INC.: TROY-BILT OWNER NEWS
GENERAL TELEPHONE CO. OF PA.: INSIDE NORTH
GEORGE E. FAILING CO.: CORE DRILLER
GILBARCO INC.: GILBARCO GAZETTE
GILROY FOODS, INC.: GARLIC VINE, THE
GLEASON WORKS: CUTTING EDGE
GRAND UNION CO.: GRAND STAND
GREATER HOUSTON BUILDERS ASSOCIATION: HOUSTON BUILDER
GRUCON CORP.: GRUNAU GRAM
GTE CORP.: G T E WEEKLY
GTE SOUTH: NEWSLINE
HARRIS CORP.: F Y I MAGAZINE
HEINZ U.S.A.: HEINZLINE
HOME BUILDERS ASSOCIATION OF GREATER ST. LOUIS: BUILDER NEWS
HORACE MANN COS., THE: SPECTRUM
HUGHES AIRCRAFT CO.: HUGHESNEWS
ILCO UNICAN CORP.: KEYTIPS
INDIANA FARMERS INSURANCE GROUP: CRIER, THE
INTERNATIONAL BUSINESS MACHINES CORP.: THINK
INTERNATIONAL COMMUNICATIONS INDUSTRIES ASSN., THE: COMMUNICATIONS INDUSTRIES REPORT
INTERSTATE POWER CO.: INTERSTATE NEWS
ITT CORP.: WITTS-WITHIN THE I T T SYSTEM
JLG INDUSTRIES, INC.: UPDATE
KANO LABS INC.: GENIUS AT WORK
KANSAS DEPARTMENT OF COMMERCE: DEVELOPING KANSAS
KELLOGG COMPANY: KELLOGG NEWS
KELLY-SPRINGFIELD TIRE CO.: TODAY
KIMBALL INTERNATIONAL, INC.: SOUNDBOARD
KOHLER CO.: ENGINES IN ACTION
KOHLER CO.: ON-LINE
KOHLER CO.: PLUMBLINE
LAWRENCE RAGAN COMMUNICATIONS, INC.: RAGAN REPORT
LEADER FEDERAL SAVINGS & LOAN ASSOCIATION: LEADER DIGEST
LEHIGH VALLEY BANK: UPDATE
LENNOX INDUSTRIES INC.: LENNOX NEWS
LINN COUNTY RURAL ELECTRIC COOPERATIVE ASSOCIATION: NEWSLINES ON THE LINE
LOUISIANA PHARMACISTS ASSOCIATION: LOUISIANA PHARMACIST
LYNCHBURG GENERAL-MARSHALL LODGE HOSPITALS: CENTRA HEALTH MAGAZINE
MARION LABORATORIES, INC.: ASSOCIATE
MARION LABORATORIES, INC.: IMAGE
MARLEY CO., THE: MARLEY LEADER
MEREDITH GRAPHICS, INC.: GRAPHICOPY
METHODIST HOSPITAL: ADVANCES
MISSOURI FARM BUREAU FEDERATION: MISSOURI FARM BUREAU NEWS

MONONGAHELA POWER CO.: MONONGAHELA NEWS
MOORE BUSINESS FORMS, INC.: INFORM
MORSE SHOE, INC.: MORSE CODE
NASH ENGINEERING CO.: NASH REPORTER
NATIONAL INDEMNITY CO.: FRIDAY FACTS
NATIONAL STARCH & CHEMICAL CO.: NATIONAL'S COMPASS
NATIONS BANK CORP.: DATELINE
NESTLE-BEICH, INC.: KADYDID CHRONICLE
NEW ENGLAND MUTUAL LIFE INSURANCE CO.: CURRENTS
OHIO RURAL ELECTRIC COOPS INC.: COUNTRY LIVING MAGAZINE
OKLAHOMA DEPARTMENT OF COMMERCE: COMMERCE FOLIO
OPPENHEIMER MANAGEMENT CORP.: HANDSIGNALS, THE
ORE-IDA FOODS, INC.: VOICE, THE
OTTER TAIL POWER CO.: HI-LITES
PACIFIC BELL: CONNECTIONS
PAN-AMERICAN LIFE INSURANCE CO.: LIFELINE
PENN TRAFFIC CO.: THE OPEN LINE
PHILADELPHIA BAR ASSOCIATION: PHILADELPHIA LAWYER, THE
PLUMBING MECHANICAL CONTRACTORS COUNCIL HARRIS COUNTY: GULF COAST PLUMBING, HEATING, COOLING NEWS
PUBLIC SERVICE CO. OF NEW HAMPSHIRE: AROUND THE CIRCUIT
QUAKER OATS CO.: MIDWEEK
QUAKER OATS CO.: QUAKER INSIDER
QUAKER OATS CO.: QUAKER QUARTERLY
RALSTON PURINA CO.: SQUARE TALK
RANGER INSURANCE CO.: RANGER RESOURCES
READING HOSPITAL & MEDICAL CENTER, THE: AROUND THE CLOCK
RICH'S, INC.: FOCAL POINT
RUBBERMAID, INC.: RUBBERMAID REVIEW
SAFECO INSURANCE CO.: SAFECO AGENT
SANTA BARBARA RESEARCH CENTER: SBRC NEWS:
SATELLITE INDUSTRIES INC.: PORTABLE SANITATION QUARTERLY
SCANDINAVIAN AIRLINES SYSTEM INC.: INSIDE S A S INTERNATIONAL
SCHRAMM INC.: WHAT'S HAPPENING
SCRIPTURE PRESS PUBLICATIONS, INC.: SPOTLIGHT
SECURITY MUTUAL LIFE INSURANCE CO. OF NEW YORK: MARKETING UPDATE
SHELL OIL CO.: SHELL PROGRESS
SIZZLER INTERNATIONAL, INC.: HOTLINE
SMITH & NEPHEW RICHARDS INC.: SMITH & NEPHEW RICHARDS REPORTER
SMITHKLINE BEECHAM: S B NEWS
SOUTHEAST MICHIGAN, N.A.: FIRST WORD, THE
ST. FRANCIS HOSPITAL: KA LEO REFLECTIONS
ST. VINCENT HOSPITAL: HEALTH REVIEW
STAR MARKET CO.: STAR NEWS
STATE BAR OF TEXAS: TEXAS BAR JOURNAL
STATE FARM MUTUAL AUTO INSURANCE CO.: PINE-AIRE
STERLING DRUG, INC.: CONVEYOR, THE
T.U. ELECTRIC: SYNCHRONIZER
TENNESSEE EDUCATION ASSOCIATION: TENNESSEE TEACHER
TEXAS SOCIETY OF PROFESSIONAL ENGINEERS: TEXAS PROFESSIONAL ENGINEER
UNISYS: INSIDE INFORMATION
UNITED STATES ARMY: SOLDIERS
USF & A. INSURANCE: BULLETIN
USG CORP.: FORM & FUNCTION
VALSPAR CORP.: SCOPE
VERNON CO.: VERNON MIRROR
VETCO, INC.: DIRECT LINE
VICKERS, INC.: VICKERS IN PRINT
VIKING PUMP, INC./A UNIT OF IDEX CORP.: PUMPLINE
WEST BEND CO.: CRAFTSMAN, THE
WESTVACO CORP.: NEWS LETTER
WILLIAMS CO., THE: LINE MARKER
YOUNG RADIATOR CO.: YOUNG NEWS & VIEWS
ZIPPO MANUFACTURING CO.: ZIP-A-GRAM
21ST CENTURY GENETICS COOPERATIVE: VISIONS

## NEWS COMMENTARY

BOSTON EDISON CO.: EDISON LIFE
GEORGIA POWER CO.: CITIZEN WEEKLY, THE
OHIO DEPARTMENT OF YOUTH SERVICES: UPDATE
REAL ESTATE CENTER: REAL ESTATE CENTER TRENDS

## NEWS

ACME BOOT COMPANY INC.: ROUNDUP
AEROSPACE CORP.: ORBITER
AETNA LIFE & CASUALTY: AETNASPHERE
AIR FORCE INSTITUTE OF TECHNOLOGY: AOG QUARTERLY
AIR LINE PILOTS ASSOCIATION: AIR LINE PILOT
AKRON GENERAL MEDICAL CENTER: VOICE
ALABAMA GAS CORP.: GAS LINES
ALEXANDER & BALDWIN, INC.: AMPERSAND
ALLEN-BRADLEY CO.: CONNECTION
ALLEN-BRADLEY CO.: NETWORK
ALLIANCE LIFE: LIFELINES
ALLIED-SIGNAL AEROSPACE CO.: HORIZONS
AMATEUR ATHLETIC UNION OF THE U.S.: INFOAAU
AMERICA'S FAVORITE CHICKEN: ATTITUDE
AMERICAN ACADEMY OF ORTHOPAEDIC SURGEONS: BULLETIN
AMERICAN ASSOCIATION OF ORAL & MAXILLOFACIAL SURGEONS: A A O M S FORUM
AMERICAN BOAT & YACHT COUNCIL INC.: A B Y C NEWS
AMERICAN FAMILY INSURANCE GROUP: ALL AMERICAN
AMERICAN FAMILY INSURANCE GROUP: AMERICAN TIMES
AMERICAN FAMILY INSURANCE GROUP: FAMILY ALBUM
AMERICAN GAS ASSOCIATION: AMERICAN GAS
AMERICAN GENERAL FINANCE: A. G. FOCUS
AMERICAN GENERAL LIFE/ACCIDENT INSURANCE CO.: IN GENERAL
AMERICAN GREETINGS CORP.: SPECTRUM
AMERICAN HELICOPTER SOCIETY, INC.: VERTIFLITE MAGAZINE
AMERICAN OLEAN TILE CO.: OPEN LINE
AMERICAN PODIATRIC WRITERS ASSOCIATION: AMERICAN PODIATRIC WRITERS ASSOCIATION NEWSLETTER
AMERICAN WATER WORKS ASSOCIATION: WATERWEEK
AMSCO AMERICAN STERILIZER CO.: DOIN' IT
ANALOG DEVICES, INC.: ANALOG BRIEFINGS
ANR PIPELINE CO.: TRANSMISSION LINES
APPLETON MILLS: HORIZONS
ARA SERVICES INC.: ARA NEWS
ARIZONA PUBLIC SERVICE CO.: CONNECTIONS
ARKANSAS DEPARTMENT OF PARKS & TOURISM: NEWS FROM ARKANSAS, THE NATURAL STATE
ARKANSAS POWER & LIGHT CO.: ON MAGAZINE
ARKANSAS PRESS ASSOCIATION: A P A MEMBER BULLETIN
ARMY & AIR FORCE EXCHANGE SERVICE: EXCHANGE POST, THE
ARNOLD BAKERS, INC.: BREADWINNER
ASHLAND OIL, INC.: SOURCE, THE
ASSOCIATED GENERAL CONTRACTORS OF HOUSTON: A G C NEWS SERVICE
ASSOCIATED INDUSTRIES OF KENTUCKY: KENTUCKY JOURNAL OF COMMERCE & INDUSTRY
ASSOCIATES CORPORATION OF NORTH AMERICA: ASSOCIATES MAGAZINE, THE
ASSOCIATION OF ILLINOIS ELECTRIC COOPERATIVES: ILLINOIS RURAL ELECTRIC NEWS
ATLANTA GAS LIGHT CO.: BLUE FLAME NEWS
ATLANTIC CITY ELECTRIC CO.: NEWSLINE
AUTO-OWNERS INSURANCE: MEMO
AVCO FINANCIAL SERVICES: TRENDS
AVISTAR INTERNATIONAL TRANSPORTATION CORP.: COMMUNICATOR
AXIA, INC.: AXIA ACTION
BADGER MUTUAL INSURANCE COMPANY: BADGER BEACON
BANK OF BOSTON CORP.: EAGLE
BANK SOUTH: INSIDE BANK SOUTH

HILLENBRAND INDUSTRIES, INC.: INDIANA CAPITOL MONITOR
HILLSDALE COLLEGE: HILLSDALE MAGAZINE
HOECHST CELANESE CORP.: REPORTER MAGAZINE
HOME BUILDERS ASSOCIATION OF GREATER ST. LOUIS: BUILDER NEWS
HOME BUILDERS ASSOCIATION OF GREATER ST. LOUIS: H B A NEWSLETTER
HONEYWELL, INC.: CIRCULATOR
HONEYWELL, INC.: HONEYWELL PRIDE
HOOVER CO.: HOOVER NEWS
HORMEL FOODS CORP.: INSIDE
HORMEL FOODS CORP.: NEWS
HOSPITAL OF THE UNIVERSITY OF PENNSYLVANIA: HUPDATE
HUBINGER CO., THE: CORNSTALK
HUMANE SOCIETY FOR TACOMA & PIERCE COUNTIES, THE : CONNECTIONS
IES UTILITIES: FRONT LINE
ILLINOIS CREDIT UNION LEAGUE: IN DEPTH
ILLINOIS LEAGUE OF SAVINGS INSTITUTIONS: ILLINOIS REPORTER
IN-PLANT MANAGEMENT ASSOCIATION: INSIDE I P M A
INDIANA CREDIT UNION LEAGUE, INC.: NEXUS
INDIANA FARMERS INSURANCE GROUP: CRIER, THE
INDIANA MANUFACTURERS ASSOCIATION, INC.: IMANET
INDUSTRIAL COMMISSION: ADJUDICATOR
INGALLS SHIPBUILDING DIVISION, LITTON INDUSTRIES : INGALLS NEWS
INSURANCE SERVICES OFFICE INC.: INSIDE I S O
INTEGON: SYMBOLS
INTERMET FOUNDRY: INTERMET NEWS
INTERNATIONAL ASSOCIATION OF BUSINESS COMMUNICATORS: COMMUNICATION WORLD
INTERNATIONAL BROTHERHOOD OF LOCOMOTIVE ENGINEERS : LOCOMOTIVE ENGINEERS NEWSLETTER
INTERNATIONAL COMMUNICATIONS INDUSTRIES ASSN., THE: COMMUNICATIONS INDUSTRIES REPORT
IOWA ASSOCIATION OF ELECTRIC COOPERATIVES: IOWA REC NEWS
ITEK OPTICAL SYSTEMS, DIV. OF LITTON INDUSTRIES: ITEM
ITT GILFILLAN: SCANNER
ITT HARTFORD INSURANCE GROUP: I T T HARTFORD AGENT
JEFFERSON PILOT LIFE INSURANCE CO.: INSIDE J P
JERSEY CENTRAL POWER & LIGHT CO.: ON-LINE
JERSEY CENTRAL POWER & LIGHT CO.: SPECTRA
JLG INDUSTRIES, INC.: J L G INK, THE
JOHN H HARLAND CO.: INTERCOM
JONATHAN CLUB: JONATHAN
JORDAN SCHOOL DISTRICT: RIPPLES & CURRENTS
JORDAN SCHOOL DISTRICT: WINDOWS TO YOUR SCHOOL
KELLY SERVICES, INC.: CHRONICLE, THE
KELLY-SPRINGFIELD TIRE CO.: MINUTE
KENTUCKY ASSOCIATION OF ELECTRIC COOPERATIVES: RURAL KENTUCKIAN
KENTUCKY DEPARTMENT OF EDUCATION: KENTUCKY TEACHER
KINDER CARE LEARNING CENTERS, INC.: CENTERLINE, THE
KN ENERGY, INC.: ENERGIZER
KOHLER CO.: KOHLER SHOPPER
KONICA BUSINESS MACHINES U.S.A., INC.: OUTLOOK
KTVE-TV: REGION 10 NEWS
KYOCERA INTERNATIONAL, INC.: THE KEY
L & F PRODUCTS: L & F TOPICS
L.G. BALFOUR CO.: THE DIAMOND EXCHANGE
LA-Z-BOY CHAIR CO.: MONROE LA-Z-NEWS
LAMAR LIFE INSURANCE CO.: PAGE 317 E. CAPITOL
LAWRENCE TECHNOLOGICAL UNIVERSITY: LAWRENCE TECHNOLOGICAL UNIVERSITY MAGAZINE
LAWYERS TITLE INSURANCE CORP.: LAWYERS TITLE NEWS
LAWYERS TITLE INSURANCE CORP.: MARKET-EAR, THE
LAWYERS TITLE INSURANCE CORP.: TITLELINES
LAWYERS TITLE INSURANCE CORP.: TRACT, THE
LEHIGH VALLEY BANK: UPDATE

LIBERTY NATIONAL BANK & TRUST CO.: IN FOCUS
LIMA MEMORIAL HOSPITAL: HORIZONS
LINCOLN ELECTRIC CO., THE: STABILIZER
LOCKHEED ADVANCED DEVELOPMENT CO.: STAR
LONE STAR GAS CO.: BLUE BLAZE
LONG ISLAND RAILROAD: ALONG THE TRACK
LORAL DEFENSE SYSTEMS-AKRON: CIRCUIT
LOS ANGELES DEPARTMENT OF WATER & POWER: INTAKE MAGAZINE
LUBRIZOL CORP. THE: LUBRIZOL REPORTS
LUKENS INC.: LUKENS LIFE
MARION MERRELL DOW INC.: M M D EXCHANGE
MARION MERRELL DOW INC.: TIME OUT
MARQUETTE UNIVERSITY: MARQUETTE
MARQUETTE UNIVERSITY: NEWS & VIEWS
MASTER LOCK CO.: MASTER LOCK NEWS TODAY
MAXUS ENERGY CORP.: ENERGY EXCHANGE
MCGRAW-HILL INC.: MC GRAW-HILL WORLD
MEAD CORPORATION: GREAT NEWS
MEDIA GENERAL: M G NEWS
MEDIA GENERAL: MEDIA GENERAL ANNUAL REPORT
MEDICAL CENTER OF DELAWARE, THE: FOCUS
MELROSE-WAKEFIELD HOSPITAL: TABLET, THE
MEMORIAL SLOAN-KETTERING CANCER CENTER: CENTER BULLETIN
MERCK & CO., INC.: MERCK WORLD
MERCY HOSPITAL, INC.: STAT SHEET, THE
MERCY MEDICAL CENTER: MERCY LIFE
MERCY MEDICAL CENTER: MERCY PHYSICIAN, THE
METHODIST HOSPITAL, THE: JOURNAL, THE
METHODIST HOSPITALS OF DALLAS: OUTLOOK
METROPOLITAN LIFE INSURANCE CO.: FORUM MAGAZINE
METROPOLITAN MILWAUKEE ASSOCIATION OF COMMERCE: MILWAUKEE COMMERCE HOTLINE
METROPOLITAN UTILITIES DISTRICT: TAPS & JETS
MIAMI SYSTEMS-SHELBY DIVISION: MIAMI SYSTEMS FAMILY NEWS & PEOPLE REPORT
MICHIGAN CAPITAL HEALTHCARE: CONNECTION, THE
MID-AMERICA DAIRYMEN INC.: MID-AM PROCESSOR (FOR EMPLOYEES)
MID-AMERICA DAIRYMEN INC.: MID-AM REPORTER
MIDWEST RESEARCH INSTITUTE: F Y I
MILES, INC.: UPDATE
MILLER BREWING CO.: FRONTLINE
MILLER BREWING CO.: MILLER HIGH-LITES
MILTON BRADLEY CO.: MILTON BRADLEY NEWS
MINING & SPECIALTY EQUIP. DIV. OF INDRESCO, INC., MARION OPERATIONS: NEWS & REVIEW
MINNESOTA DEPARTMENT OF TRANSPORTATION: EXPRESS
MISSISSIPPI POWER & LIGHT CO.: MP & L NEWS
MISSISSIPPI POWER CO.: DIALOGUE
MISSISSIPPI POWER CO.: POWERLINES
MISSOURI FARM BUREAU FEDERATION: MISSOURI FARM BUREAU NEWS
MITCHELL ENERGY & DEVELOPMENT CORP.: TERRASOL
MITRE CORP.: MITRE MATTERS
MONARCH CAPITAL CORP.: MONARCH FIELD NEWS
MONARCH CAPITAL CORP.: MONARCH NEWS
MONROE SYSTEMS FOR BUSINESS: KEYNOTE
MONUMENTAL LIFE INS. CO.: LIFE LINES
MORGAN GUARANTY TRUST CO. OF N.Y.: MORGAN NEWS, THE
MOTORISTS INSURANCE COMPANIES: FULLCOVERAGE
MOUNTAIN STATE BLUE CROSS & BLUE SHIELD: MOUNTAIN STATE
MSI INSURANCE: PERSPECTIVE
MSI INSURANCE: SUCCESS EXTRA
MUSTANG FUEL CORP.: MUSTANG NEWS CONNECTION
MUTUAL OF OMAHA COMPANIES: CURRENTS
MUTUAL OF OMAHA COMPANIES: PACESETTERS
MUTUAL TRUST LIFE INSURANCE CO.: PERSPECTIVE
MUTUAL TRUST LIFE INSURANCE CO.: VANGUARD
N.J. STATE BAR ASSN.: NEW JERSEY LAWYER
NALCO CHEMICAL CO.: NALCO NEWS
NALLEYS FINE FOODS: NALLEVENTS
NASHVILLE ELECTRIC SERVICE: N E S NEWS
NATIONAL AUTO DEALERS ASSN.: AUTOMOTIVE EXECUTIVE
NATIONAL BANK OF DETROIT: N B D NEWS

NATIONAL CITY BANK, INDIANA: BANK BRIEFS
NATIONAL FEDERATION OF INDEPENDENT BUSINESS: I B MAGAZINE (INDEPENDENT BUSINESS)
NATIONAL FIRE PROTECTION ASSOCIATION: FIRE NEWS
NATIONAL GROUND WATER ASSOCIATION: WELL LOG
NATIONAL INSURANCE CRIME BUREAU: SPOTLIGHT, THE
NATIONAL STARCH & CHEMICAL CO.: NATIONAL'S COMPASS
NATIONAL STEEL CORP.: PAYDAY
NATIONS BANK CORP.: NATIONS BANK TIMES
NAVAL AIR WARFARE CENTER: REFLECTOR
NBD BANK: N B D CONNECTIONS
NEBRASKA METHODIST HOSPITAL: HEALTH PICX
NEW ORLEANS, CITY OF: CITINEWS
NEW YORK DAILY: NEWS PIX
NEWPORT NEWS SHIPBUILDING & DRY DOCK CO.: YARDLINES
NIAGARA MOHAWK POWER CORP.: N M NEWS
NOLAND CO.: NOLAND NEWS
NORFOLK SOUTHERN CORP.: NORFOLK SOUTHERN WORLD
NORTH CAROLINA MUTUAL LIFE INSURANCE CO.: HOT LINE
NORTH MISSISSIPPI MEDICAL CENTER: CHECKUP
NORTH WESTERN NATIONAL LIFE: PIPELINE
NORTHROP-GRUMMAN CORP.: NORTHROP-GRUMMAN NEWS
NORTHWEST ELECTRIC LIGHT & POWER ASSOCIATION: NELPA NEWS
NORTHWESTERN NATIONAL INSURANCE GROUP: AGENT NEWS
NORTHWESTERN NATIONAL INSURANCE GROUP: EMPLOYEE NEWS
NORTHWESTERN NATIONAL INSURANCE GROUP: LEADING TO EXCELLENCE
NORWEST FINANCIAL, INC.: NETWORK
OAKITE PRODUCTS, INC.: REVIEW, THE
OHIO BUREAU OF WORKER'S COMPENSATION: OHIO MONITOR
OHIO PHARMACISTS ASSOCIATION: OHIO PHARMACIST
OKLAHOMA CITY UNIVERSITY: FOCUS
OKLAHOMA GAS & ELECTRIC CO.: INSIDE OG & E
OKLAHOMA GAS & ELECTRIC CO.: METER
OKLAHOMA RESTAURANT ASSOCIATION: MIDSOUTHWEST RESTAURANT MAGAZINE
OMAHA PUBLIC POWER DIST.: FLASH
ONAN CORP.: ONAN NEWS
OPTIMIST INTERNATIONAL: OPTIMIST MAGAZINE
OTIS ELEVATOR CO.: OTIS BULLETIN
OTIS ELEVATOR CO.: OTIS MAGAZINE
OTTER TAIL POWER CO.: HI-LITES
OWENS-ILLINOIS INC.: INSIGHT
P.H. GLATFELTER CO.: BARKER
PACIFIC FIRST BANK: SPIRIT
PACIFIC POWER & LIGHT CO.: BULLETIN
PARKS COLLEGE OF ST. LOUIS UNIVERSITY: PARKS TODAY
PEACHTREE CENTER: CENTER CIRCLE
PEACHTREE CENTER: MALL STREET JOURNAL
PENNSYLVANIA ELECTRIC CO.: CARRIER LINES
PEOPLE'S BANK: PEOPLE'S NEWSLETTER
PEOPLES NATURAL GAS CO.: P N G TODAY
PEOPLES SECURITY LIFE INSURANCE CO.: CURRENTS
PETER KIEWIT SONS, INC.: KIE-WAYS
PHARMACEUTICAL MANUFACTURERS ASSOCIATION: P M A NEWSLETTER
PHILADELPHIA BAR ASSOCIATION: PHILADELPHIA LAWYER, THE
PHILADELPHIA GAS WORKS: P G W NEWSLINE
PHILIP MORRIS, USA: HAPPENINGS
PHILLIPS CONSUMER ELECTRONICS CORP.: PHILLIPS U S A EXPRESS, THE
PIER 1 IMPORTS, INC.: THIS WEEK
PIGGLY WIGGLY CORP.: TURNSTILE
PIONEER MUTUAL LIFE INSURANCE CO.: PIONEERING
PIPER JAFFRAY: PIPER MARKET DIGEST
PIPER JAFFRAY: QUOTE
PNC BANK: P N C BANK NEWS

**PORT AUTHORITY OF NEW YORK & NEW JERSEY:** VIA INTERNATIONAL PORT OF NEW YORK-NEW JERSEY
**PROTECTIVE LIFE INS. CO.:** PROTECTIVE COVER
**PROTECTIVE LIFE INS. CO.:** PROTECTIVE LIFE LINES
**PROTECTIVE LIFE INS. CO.:** WEDNESDAY UPDATE
**PROVIDENT MUTUAL LIFE INSURANCE CO. OF PHILADELPHIA:** PROVIDENT PERSPECTIVE
**PRUDENTIAL INSURANCE CO. OF AMERICA:** CORPORATE OFFICE COURIER
**PRUDENTIAL INSURANCE CO. OF AMERICA:** DIALOGUE
**PUBLIC SERVICE CO. OF COLORADO:** P S CO TIMES
**PUBLIC SERVICE ELECTRIC & GAS CO.:** MANAGEMENT QUARTERLY
**PUBLIC SERVICE ELECTRIC & GAS CO.:** P S E & G NEWS
**PUBLIX SUPER MARKETS, INC.:** PUBLIX NEWS
**PUGET SOUND POWER & LIGHT CO.:** OUTLET
**PYRAMID LIFE INSURANCE CO.:** ADVANTAGE
**QUALITY STORES, INC.:** ON CUE
**QUESTAR CORPORATION:** ON STREAM
**R.R. DONNELLEY & SONS CO.:** PRINTER, THE
**RADIO SHACK DIVISION, TANDY CORP.:** RADIO SHACK INTERCOM
**RAND MCNALLY & CO.:** DIRECTIONS
**REAL ESTATE CENTER:** REAL ESTATE CENTER LAW LETTER
**REDDY CORP. INTERNATIONAL:** LINES OF ARGUMENT
**REGIS UNIVERSITY:** HIGHLANDER
**REGIS UNIVERSITY:** REGIS UNIVERSITY MAGAZINE
**REGIS UNIVERSITY:** UPDATE
**RESEARCH TRIANGLE INSTITUTE:** HYPOTENUSE
**RIVERSIDE METHODIST HOSPITALS:** RIVERSIDE MONTHLY
**ROBERT F. KENNEDY MEDICAL CENTER:** L I F E NEWSLETTER
**ROCHESTER COMMUNITY SAVINGS BANK:** R C S B PREVIEW
**ROCKHURST COLLEGE:** ROCKHURST REPORT
**ROCKWELL INTERNATIONAL, COMMAND & CONTROL SYSTEMS DIVISION:** COMMUNIQUE
**ROCKWELL INTERNATIONAL, COMMAND & CONTROL SYSTEMS DIVISION:** ROCKWELL NEWS
**RSR CORPORATION:** R S R LEAD PRESS
**SAFECO INSURANCE CO.:** SAFECO AGENT
**SAIF CORP.:** SCOPE: COMP NEWS
**SAINT ANTHONY MEDICAL CENTER:** CAPSULE
**SALADMASTER, INC.:** SALADMASTER SALUT!
**SALEM HOSPITAL:** MESSENGER
**SALEM HOSPITAL:** PULSEBEAT
**SALES PROSPECTOR:** SALES PROSPECTOR
**SAMARITAN HEALTH SERVICE:** SAMARITAN TODAY, THE
**SAN DIEGO GAS & ELECTRIC CO.:** IN FOCUS
**SAN FRANCISCO CHAMBER OF COMMERCE:** CHAMBER OF COMMERCE NEWSLETTER
**SANTEE COOPER:** SANTEE COOPER ANNUAL REPORT
**SARA LEE KNIT PRODUCTS:** INTERNAL NEWSLETTER
**SCHERING-PLOUGH CORP.:** SCHERING-PLOUGH WORLD
**SCHIFFLI LACE & EMBROIDERY MANUFACTURERS ASSN.:** EMBROIDERY NEWS
**SEAFIRST CORP.:** SEAFIRST NEWS
**SEARS ROEBUCK & CO.:** FRONT LINES
**SEARS ROEBUCK & CO.:** PRAIRIE LINES
**SECURA INSURANCE:** VIEWPOINT
**SENTARA HEALTH SYSTEM:** DIALOGUE
**SENTRY INSURANCE:** POINT
**SENTRY INSURANCE:** SENTRY NEWS
**SETON MEDICAL CENTER:** INFOBITS
**SHAWMUT BANK, CONNECTICUT:** SHAWMUT NEWS
**SHEAFFER, INC.:** SHEAFFER NEWSLETTER
**SHELBY COUNTY GOVERNMENT:** COUNTY LINES, THE
**SIERRA PACIFIC POWER CO.:** SIERRA SCENE
**SIERRA PACIFIC POWER CO.:** THIS WEEK
**SIGNET BANKING CORP.:** ON LOCATION
**SIGNET BANKING CORP.:** SIGNAL, THE
**SIKORSKY AIRCRAFT:** SIKORSKY LIFELINE
**SIKORSKY AIRCRAFT:** SIKORSKY NEWS
**SIMON WIESENTHAL CENTER:** RESPONSE MAGAZINE

**SMITHS INDUSTRIES AEROSPACE & DEFENSE SYSTEMS, INC.:** INTERFACE
**SOUTH CAROLINA ELECTRIC & GAS CO.:** S C E & G NEWS
**SOUTHERN BELL TELEPHONE CO.:** SOUTHERN BELL VIEWS
**SOUTHERN CONNECTICUT GAS CO.:** NEWS & VIEWS
**SOUTHERN FOREST PRODUCTS ASSOCIATION:** S F NEWSLETTER
**SOUTHERN INDIANA GAS & ELECTRIC CO.:** S I G E C O NEWS
**SOUTHERN NEW ENGLAND TELEPHONE CO.:** S N E NEWS
**SOUTHERN UNION CO.:** SOUTHERN UNION COMPANY FORUM
**SOUTHWEST GENERAL HOSPITAL:** CAPSULE
**SOUTHWEST GENERAL HOSPITAL:** SOUTHWEST TODAY
**SPRINT MID-ATLANTIC TELECOM:** SPRINT MID-ATLANTIC TELECOM TODAY
**SPRINT MID-ATLANTIC TELECOM:** VISION
**ST. AGNES HOSPITAL:** ST. AGNES NEWS
**ST. EDWARD'S UNIVERSITY:** EDWARDIAN, THE
**ST. EDWARD'S UNIVERSITY:** SEU NEWS
**ST. JOSEPH'S HOSPITAL & MEDICAL CTR.:** VISION
**ST. MARY'S HEALTH CENTER:** CENTER STAT
**ST. PAUL COMPANIES, INC., THE:** ST. PAUL NEWS
**ST. PAUL PIONEER PRESS DISPATCH:** ON THE SCENE
**ST. VINCENT CHARITY HOSPITAL & HEALTH CTR.:** VITAL SIGNS
**STATE COMPENSATION INSURANCE FUND:** INSIGHT
**STATE FARM MUTUAL AUTO INSURANCE CO.:** BELLRINGER
**STATE FARM MUTUAL AUTO INSURANCE CO.:** NORTH CENTRAL MANAGER
**STATE FARM MUTUAL AUTO INSURANCE CO.:** PINE-AIRE
**STATE UNIVERSITY OF N.Y. HEALTH SCIENCE CTR. AT SYRACUSE:** H S C THIS WEEK
**STRIDE RITE CORP.:** FEATURES
**STRIDE RITE CORP.:** STRIDE RITER
**SUNKIST GROWERS, INC.:** SLICES
**SUNKIST GROWERS, INC.:** SUNKIST MAGAZINE
**SUPERMARKETS, INC.:** FOCAL POINT
**SYRACUSE SAVINGS BANK:** S S B NEWS LETTER
**T.U. ELECTRIC:** SPOTLIGHT
**TEACHERS ASSOCIATION OF BALTIMORE COUNTY MD., INC.:** T A B C O BULLETIN
**TENNESSEE ELECTRIC COOP ASSOCIATION:** LEADER'S LETTER
**TEXAS COMMERCE BANCSHARES, INC.:** BANKERS' HOURS
**TEXAS EASTMAN DIV., EASTMAN CHEMICAL CO.:** TEXAS EASTMAN NEWS
**TEXAS MEDICAL ASSOCIATION:** TEXAS MEDICINE
**TEXAS PUBLIC EMPLOYEES ASSOCIATION:** TEXAS PUBLIC EMPLOYEE
**TEXAS SOCIETY OF ARCHITECTS:** REPORT
**THERMO ELECTRON CORP.:** THERMOSPHERE
**THOMAS INDUSTRIES:** T I TOPICS
**THOMPSON INTERNATIONAL, INC.:** NEWSLETTER
**TOLEDO BLADE CO.:** INSIDE THE BLADE
**TOLEDO EDISON CO.:** MONTHLY COMMUNICATIONS
**TRANSPORTATION COMMUNICATIONS INTERNATIONAL UNION :** TELLING IT LIKE IT IS
**U.S. AIR GROUP, INC.:** US AIR NEWS
**U.S. BANCORP:** FOCUS ON US
**U.S. INFORMATION AGENCY:** U S I A WORLD
**U.S. RAILROAD RETIREMENT BOARD:** ALL A-BOARD
**U-HAUL INTERNATIONAL, INC.:** U-HAUL INTERNATIONAL NEWS
**UNION BANK:** UNITY
**UNION ELECTRIC CO.:** UNION ELECTRIC NEWS
**UNION INSURANCE GROUP:** PRO-FILE
**UNION PACIFIC RESOURCES CO.:** U P REPORTER
**UNION PACIFIC RESOURCES CO.:** U P RESOURCES
**UNISTRUT CORPORATION:** UNIWORLD
**UNITED AMERICAN INSURANCE CO.:** U A NEWS
**UNITED ILLUMINATING:** POWERLINES
**UNITED INSURANCE CO. OF AMERICA:** HAPPENINGS
**UNITED METHODIST PUBLISHING HOUSE, THE:** OUR HOUSE
**UNITED PARCEL SERVICE:** THE BIG IDEA

**UNITED STATES JUNIOR CHAMBER OF COMMERCE, THE:** JAYCEES MAGAZINE
**UNITED TELEPHONE CO. OF FLORIDA:** AMBASSADOR, THE
**UNITED TELEPHONE CO. OF INDIANA, INC.:** ANNUAL EMPLOYEE REPORT
**UNITED TELEPHONE CO. OF OHIO:** PATHWAYS
**UNITED WAY OF METROPOLITAN TARRANT COUNTY:** SHARING
**UNIVERSITY OF DAYTON:** UNIVERSITY OF DAYTON CAMPUS REPORT, THE
**UNIVERSITY OF DAYTON:** UNIVERSITY OF DAYTON QUARTERLY
**UNIVERSITY OF MIAMI:** VERITAS
**UNIVERSITY OF NEBRASKA MEDICAL CENTER:** IMPACT
**UNIVERSITY OF ROCHESTER:** UNIVERSITY OF ROCHESTER CURRENTS
**UNUM CORP.:** UNUM TODAY
**URBAN APPALACHIAN COUNCIL:** ADVOCATE, THE
**USF & A. INSURANCE:** BULLETIN
**UTAH POWER, A DIVISION OF PACIFICORP, OREGON:** NETWORK
**UTICA NATIONAL INSURANCE GROUP:** YOU
**VALENTINE, THE MUSEUM OF THE LIFE & HISTORY OF RICHMOND:** VALENTINE NEWS
**VILTER MANUFACTURING CORP.:** VILTER BOOSTER
**VIRGINIA ASSOCIATION OF PLUMBING HEATING COOLING CONTRACTORS:** VIRGINIA P H C IMAGE
**WACHOVIA BANK OF GEORGIA:** WACHOVIA NEWS
**WAKE MEDICAL CENTER:** SCOPE
**WASHINGTON GAS:** INSIDE STORY
**WHITTIER HOSPITAL MEDICAL CENTER:** FAMILY TIES
**WILMINGTON SAVINGS FUND SOCIETY:** INSIDER
**WISCONSIN ASSOCIATION OF HOMES FOR THE AGING:** COMMUNICATOR
**WISCONSIN DEPARTMENT OF NATURAL RESOURCES:** D N R DIGEST
**WISCONSIN ELECTRIC POWER CO.:** TELENEWS
**WISCONSIN NATURAL GAS CO.:** SENDOUT
**WOODMAN OF THE WORLD LIFE INSURANCE SOCIETY:** SHAVINGS
**WOODMEN ACCIDENT & LIFE CO.:** EXCEL
**WORLD BOOK, INC.:** WORLD BOOKER, THE
**ZURICH-AMERICAN INSURANCE GROUP:** PULSE

## OUTDOOR SPORTS

**AAA WASHINGTON:** WASHINGTON MOTORIST
**AKRON CITY HOSPITAL:** PACEMAKER
**ALPHA BETA CO.:** VANGUARD, THE
**AMERICAN COLLEGE OF SPORTS MEDICINE:** SPORTS MEDICINE BULLETIN
**AMERICAN HOME PRODUCTS:** A H P VISTA
**AMERICAN HONDA MOTOR CO., INC.:** MIGHTY TO MINI NEWS
**APPLIED PHYSICS LABORATORY:** APL NEWS
**APPLIED TECHNOLOGY:** IMAGE
**ARCATA GRAPHICS CORP.:** ARCATAGRAPH
**ATLANTA JOURNAL-CONSTITUTION:** HEADLINER
**BARCLAYS AMERICAN/MORTGAGE:** REAL ESTATEMENTS
**BDP BRANDS, CARRIER CORP.:** FLOW
**BESSEMER & LAKE ERIE RAILROAD:** B & L E EMPLOYEE NEWSLETTER
**BLUE CROSS & BLUE SHIELD OF WEST VIRGINIA, INC.:** GROUP UPDATE / MEMBERS PLUS / OUT OF THE BLUE
**BOEING CO.:** BOEING NEWS
**BROOKLYN UNION GAS CO.:** SENDOUT
**CASCADE NATURAL GAS CORP.:** CASCADE FLAME
**CITY OF BOSTON:** CITY RECORD
**CIVITAN INTERNATIONAL:** COUNTDOWN
**COLONIAL PENN GROUP INC.:** YOU
**CONNECTICUT NATURAL GAS CORP.:** FUEL FOR THOUGHT
**COOK COMPOSITES:** FRONTLINE
**COOK'S PEST CONTROL, INC.:** WHAT'S COOKIN'
**COOPER OIL, TOOL DIV.:** OIL & IRON
**COORS COURIER:** COORS COURIER
**CUBIC CORP.:** CUBIC CIRCUIT
**CUNA MUTUAL INSURANCE GROUP:** WESTWORDS:
**DRESSER INDUSTRIES, INC.:** RECORDER, THE

**DUQUESNE LIGHT CO.:** DUQUESNE LIGHT NEWS
**DYERSBURG FABRICS INC.:** SPINNIT, THE
**E.F. HOUGHTON & CO.:** HOUGHTON LINE
**EMI CO.:** CASTING ABOUT
**EMPLOYERS CASUALTY:** BRICKBATS & BOUQUETS
**ENSIGN-BICKFORD INDUSTRIES, INC.:** E-BEE
**EUA SERVICE CORP.:** E U A SPECTRUM
**EUROPEAN AMERICAN BANK:** E A B PEOPLE
**GEORGE E. FAILING CO.:** CORE DRILLER
**GILBARCO INC.:** GILBARCO GAZETTE
**GREEN POINT SAVINGS BANK:** POINTER, THE
**GRUMMAN CORP.:** GRUMMAN WORLD
**HARRIS CORP.:** F Y I MAGAZINE
**HOUSTON LIGHTING & POWER CO.:** TRANSMISSIONS
**HUGHES AIRCRAFT CO.:** HUGHESNEWS
**INTERSTATE POWER CO.:** INTERSTATE NEWS
**KAMPGROUNDS OF AMERICA, INC.:** KOA
   DIRECTORY, ROAD ATLAS AND CAMPING GUIDE
**KANSAS DEPARTMENT OF COMMERCE:** KANSAS
   MAGAZINE
**LAKE ERIE GIRL SCOUT COUNCIL:** MILLWHEEL
**LEADER FEDERAL SAVINGS & LOAN ASSOCIATION:**
   LEADER DIGEST
**LONGS DRUG STORES, INC.:** CHAIN REACTION
**LORD CORP.:** LORDFACTS
**LTV STEEL-MINING CO.:** L T V TIMES
**MARSHALL & ILSLEY BANK:** PERSONAL TOUCH
**MERIDIAN BANK:** DIALOG
**MICHELIN NORTH AMERICA, INC.:** BIB AMERICA
**MIRRO CORP.:** MIXING BOWL, THE
**MUTUAL BENEFICIAL ASSN. OF RAILROAD
   TRANSPORTATION EMPLOYEES:** MUTUAL
   MAGAZINE, THE
**NASH ENGINEERING CO.:** NASH REPORTER
**NORTHERN TRUST CO.:** NORTHERN NEWS
**OPPENHEIMER MANAGEMENT CORP.:** HANDSIGNALS,
   THE
**PACIFIC BELL:** CONNECTIONS
**PHILADELPHIA BAR ASSOCIATION:** PHILADELPHIA
   LAWYER, THE
**PUBLIC SERVICE CO. OF NEW HAMPSHIRE:** AROUND
   THE CIRCUIT
**RANGER INSURANCE CO.:** RANGER RESOURCES
**ROSEBURG FOREST PRODUCTS CO.:** ROSEBURG
   NEWS & VIEWS
**RUBBERMAID, INC.:** RUBBERMAID REVIEW
**SANTA BARBARA RESEARCH CENTER:** SBRC NEWS:
**SCANDINAVIAN AIRLINES SYSTEM INC.:** INSIDE S A
   S INTERNATIONAL
**SCHRAMM INC.:** WHAT'S HAPPENING
**SHELL OIL CO.:** SHELL ALUMNI NEWS
**SMITH & NEPHEW RICHARDS INC.:** SMITH & NEPHEW
   RICHARDS REPORTER
**SONAT, INC.:** SONAT TIELINES
**SOUTHEAST MICHIGAN, N.A.:** FIRST WORD, THE
**SOUTHERN COMPANY SERVICES, INC.:** INSIDE
**STAINLESS FOUNDRY & ENGINEERING INC.:**
   STAINLESS SPIRIT
**TENNESSEE ELECTRIC COOP ASSOCIATION:**
   TENNESSEE MAGAZINE, THE
**U.S. BORAX INC.:** BORAX PIONEER
**UNITED STATES ARMY:** SOLDIERS
**VERNON CO.:** VERNON MIRROR
**VETCO, INC.:** DIRECT LINE
**WALGREEN CO.:** WALGREEN WORLD
**WILLIAMS CO., THE:** LINE MARKER
**WISCONSIN DEPARTMENT OF NATURAL
   RESOURCES:** WISCONSIN NATURAL RESOURCES
   MAGAZINE
**YOUNG RADIATOR CO.:** YOUNG NEWS & VIEWS
**ZIPPO MANUFACTURING CO.:** ZIP-A-GRAM

## PUBLIC AFFAIRS

**AMERICAN OCCUPATIONAL THERAPY
   ASSOCIATION:** O T WEEK
**ARLINGTON HOSPITAL:** HEALTHREACH
**CITY OF DAYTON:** DAYTON UPDATE
**CITY OF JACKSON MISSISSIPPI:** CITYWORKS
**CITY OF RICHMOND VIRGINIA:** CITY OF RICHMOND
   ANNUAL REPORT
**CITY OF RICHMOND VIRGINIA:** OUR NEWS - CITY
   EMPLOYEES NEWSLETTER

**COMMUNICATION RESEARCH ASSOCIATES, INC.:**
   PUBLIC RELATIONS REVIEW:
**DOW CORNING CORP.:** DOW CORNING WORLD
**FOODSERVICE & PACKAGING INSTITUTE, INC.:**
   ENVIRONMENT NEWS DIGEST
**GREATER CINCINNATI CHAMBER OF COMMERCE:**
   CHAMBER VISION
**GREATER CLEVELAND GROWTH ASSOCIATION:**
   CLEVELANDER, THE
**HEINZ U.S.A.:** HEINZLINE
**HILLSDALE COLLEGE:** IMPRIMIS
**IOWA STATE ASSOCIATION OF COUNTIES:** IOWA
   COUNTY, THE
**KANSAS CITY KANSAS CHAMBER OF COMMERCE:**
   BUSINESS REPORT
**KANSAS DEPARTMENT OF COMMERCE:** KANSAS
   MAGAZINE
**KTVE-TV:** A M
**KTVE-TV:** VIEWPOINT
**MERCK & CO., INC.:** MERCK WORLD
**NATIONS BANK CORP.:** NOTES
**ROCKFORD MEMORIAL HOSPITAL:** MEMO
**ST. LOUIS POLICE DEPARTMENT:** POLICE JOURNAL
**TEXAS AUTOMOBILE DEALERS ASSOCIATION:**
   DEALERS' CHOICE
**TEXAS INDEPENDENT PRODUCERS & ROYALTY
   OWNERS ASSOCIATIOIN:** T I P R O REPORTER
**UNION BANKERS INSURANCE CO.:** CHRONICLE, THE
**USG CORP.:** LOOKING AHEAD

## PUBLIC SERVICE MATERIAL

**AAA IOWA:** HOME & AWAY-IOWA
**AAA WASHINGTON:** WASHINGTON MOTORIST
**ABBOTT LABORATORIES:** ABBOTT WORLD
**ACACIA GROUP, THE:** NEWS & VIEWS
**ACF INDUSTRIES, INC.:** A C F TODAY
**AKRON CITY HOSPITAL:** PACEMAKER
**AL SIGL CENTER FOR REHABILITATION AGENCIES,
   INC.:** SIGLETTER
**ALABAMA EDUCATION ASSN.:** ALABAMA SCHOOL
   JOURNAL
**ALADDIN SYNERGETICS INC.:** ASI INTERACTION
**ALLIED GROUP:** FOCUS
**AMERICAN ASSOCIATION OF COLLEGES FOR
   TEACHER EDUCATION:** BRIEFS
**AMERICAN CAST IRON PIPE COMPANY:** ACIPCO
   NEWS BULLETIN
**AMERICAN COLLEGE OF SPORTS MEDICINE:**
   SPORTS MEDICINE BULLETIN
**AMERICAN HOME PRODUCTS:** A H P VISTA
**AMERICAN HONDA MOTOR CO., INC.:** MIGHTY TO
   MINI NEWS
**AMERICAN STORES CO.:** FLASHES
**APPALACHIAN POWER CO.:** ILLUMINATOR
**APPLIED PHYSICS LABORATORY:** APL NEWS
**APPLIED TECHNOLOGY:** IMAGE
**ARCATA GRAPHICS CORP.:** ARCATAGRAPH
**ASSOCIATED MILK PRODUCERS, INC.:** DAIRYMEN'S
   DIGEST, N. CENTRAL REGION
**ASSOCIATION OF CALIFORNIA WATER AGENCIES:** A
   C W A NEWS
**ATLANTA JOURNAL-CONSTITUTION:** HEADLINER
**BALL CORP.:** BALL LINE
**BANKERS SECURITY LIFE INSURANCE SOCIETY:**
   BANKERS NOTES
**BARCLAYS AMERICAN/MORTGAGE:** REAL
   ESTATEMENTS
**BAY STATE GAS CO.:** BAY STATER
**BDP BRANDS, CARRIER CORP.:** FLOW
**BENTON CITY ELECTRIC COOPERATIVE
   ASSOCIATION:** ON LINE WITH BENTON
**BLOOD SYSTEMS:** HEART-TO-HEART
**BLOUNT, INC.:** OMARK 80
**BLUE CROSS & BLUE SHIELD OF WEST VIRGINIA,
   INC.:** GROUP UPDATE / MEMBERS PLUS / OUT OF
   THE BLUE
**BOEING CO.:** BOEING NEWS
**BOSTWICK-BRAUN CO.:** ANVIL
**BRISTOL-MYERS CO.:** BRISTOL MYERS NEW YORK
**BROOKLYN UNION GAS CO.:** SENDOUT
**BRUNSWICK CORP.:** PROFILE NEWSMAGAZINE
   PEOPLE-BRUNSWICK
**BUCYRUS-ERIE CO.:** MINER DETAILS

**BUCYRUS-ERIE CO.:** SURFACE MINER
**BURLINGTON COUNTY COLLEGE:** COLLEGE
   CONNECTION, THE
**BUSINESS MEN'S ASSURANCE CO.:** B M A SKYLINES
**CABOT CORP.:** CABOT WORLD
**CALIFORNIA ASSOCIATION OF REALTORS:**
   CALIFORNIA REAL ESTATE MAGAZINE
**CALIFORNIA PACIFIC MEDICAL CENTER:**
   CALIFORNIA PACIFIC QUARTERLY
**CALIFORNIA TEACHERS ASSOCIATION:** C T A
   ACTION
**CARPENTER TECHNOLOGY CORPORATION:**
   CARPENTER NEWS
**CASCADE NATURAL GAS CORP.:** CASCADE FLAME
**CATERPILLAR INDUSTRIAL, INC.:** MENTOR LIFT-
   LINES
**CENTRAL LINCOLN PEOPLE'S UTILITY DISTRICT:**
   COASTLINES
**CHASE MANHATTAN CORP.:** CHASE BUSINESS
**CIGNA CORP.:** SIGNALS
**CITY OF BOSTON:** CITY RECORD
**CITY OF CINCINNATI:** CITY SCENES
**CITY PUBLIC SERVICE:** BROADCASTER
**CIVITAN INTERNATIONAL:** CIVITAN MAGAZINE
**CIVITAN INTERNATIONAL:** COUNTDOWN
**COLONIAL PENN GROUP INC.:** YOU
**COLUMBIA GAS SYSTEM:** COLUMBIA TODAY
**COLUMBUS LIFE INSURANCE CO.:** LOG
**COLUMBUS SOUTHERN POWER CO.:** LITELINES
**COMMUNICATION RESEARCH ASSOCIATES, INC.:**
   PUBLIC RELATIONS REVIEW:
**CONNECTICUT MUTUAL LIFE INSURANCE:** BLUE
   CHIP NEWS
**CONNECTICUT NATURAL GAS CORP.:** FUEL FOR
   THOUGHT
**COOK COMPOSITES:** FRONTLINE
**COOK'S PEST CONTROL, INC.:** WHAT'S COOKIN'
**COOPER HOSPITAL/UNIVERSITY MEDICAL CENTER:**
   STETHOSCOPE
**COOPER OIL, TOOL DIV.:** OIL & IRON
**COORS COURIER:** COORS COURIER
**COPPERWELD CORP.:** ACROSS COPPERWELD
**COUNCIL FOR ADVANCEMENT & SUPPORT OF
   EDUCATION:** CASE CURRENTS
**COUNTRYMARK COOP:** COOP CONNECTION
**CPI CORP.:** NEWS & VIEWS
**CUBIC CORP.:** CUBIC CIRCUIT
**DALLAS LIGHTHOUSE FOR THE BLIND, INC.:**
   PANORAMA
**DATAPOINT CORP.:** DETAILS
**DELTA AIR LINES:** DELTA DIGEST
**DENTSPLY INTERNATIONAL INC.:** DENTSPLY
   DIMENSIONS
**DONREY MEDIA GROUP:** DONREY MEDIAGRAM
**DRESSER INDUSTRIES, INC.:** RECORDER, THE
**DSM COPOLYMER:** DSM COPOLYMER NEWS
**DUCOMMUN, INC.:** DUCOMMUN NEWSREEL
**DUKE POWER CO.:** DUKE POWER JOURNAL
**DUN & BRADSTREET CORP., THE:** D & B REPORTS
**DUNLOP TIRE CORP.:** HQ REVIEW
**DUQUESNE LIGHT CO.:** DUQUESNE LIGHT NEWS
**DURHAM CHAMBER OF COMMERCE:** ACTION
**DYERSBURG FABRICS INC.:** SPINNIT, THE
**E.F. HOUGHTON & CO.:** HOUGHTON LINE
**E.F. HOUGHTON & CO.:** HOUGHTONEWS
**E-SYSTEMS, INC.:** TEAM
**EASTERN NEBRASKA COMMUNITY OFFICE OF
   RETARDATION :** ENCOR RESPONDANCE
**EBASCO SERVICES INC.:** EBASCO NEWS
**ELCO INDUSTRIES, INC.:** E L C O NEWSLETTER
**ELECTRIC COUNCIL OF NEW ENGLAND:** IMPULSE
**EMI CO.:** CASTING ABOUT
**EMPLOYERS CASUALTY:** BRICKBATS & BOUQUETS
**EQUITABLE RESOURCES:** EQUITABLE NEWS
**ERIE INSURANCE GROUP:** ERIE FAMILY
**ERWIN DI CYAN:** DI CYAN BULLETIN
**EUA SERVICE CORP.:** E U A SPECTRUM
**FACTORY MUTUAL ENGINEERING AND RESEARCH:**
   FACTORY MUTUAL RECORD
**FEDERAL RESERVE BANK OF NEW YORK:** FED
**FEDERATED INSURANCE COS.:** MULTILINER
**FIRST NATIONAL BANK OF MARYLAND:**
   COMMUNICATOR
**FIRST VIRGINIA BANK:** FIRST VIRGINIAN
**FIRSTIER BANK:** TEAMWORK

FLEMING COS. INC.: FLEMING ASSOCIATE, THE
GARDEN CITY HOSPITAL: NITTY GRITTY
GARDEN WAY MFG. CO. INC.: TROY-BILT OWNER NEWS
GAST MFG. CORP.: WINDJAMMER
GENERAL TELEPHONE CO. OF PA.: INSIDE NORTH
GENUINE PARTS CO., INC.: PARTS PUPS
GEORGE E. FAILING CO.: CORE DRILLER
GEORGIA MUNICIPAL ASSOCIATION: GEORGIA'S CITIES
GEORGIA REVENUE DEPT.: REVENEWS
GIANT FOOD, INC.: WE NEWS
GILBARCO INC.: GILBARCO GAZETTE
GILROY FOODS, INC.: GARLIC VINE, THE
GLEANER LIFE INSURANCE SOCIETY: NATIONAL GLEANER FORUM
GLEASON WORKS: CUTTING EDGE
GMHC, INC.: TREATMENT ISSUES
GOLUB CORP./PRICE CHOPPER SUPERMARKETS: ASSOCIATES' VIEW, THE
GOODWILL INDUSTRIES INTERNATIONAL, INC.: GOODWILL FORUM
GOODWILL INDUSTRIES OF SOUTHERN CALIFORNIA: TIDINGS
GRAND UNION CO.: GRAND STAND
GREATER BATON ROUGE CHAMBER OF COMMERCE: COMMERCE
GREATER OMAHA CHAMBER OF COMMERCE: OMAHA PROFILE
GREATER WINSTON-SALEM CHAMBER OF COMMERCE: NEWS LINE
GROVE WORLDWIDE, INC.: BIG G
GRUCON CORP.: GRUNAU GRAM
GRUMMAN CORP.: GRUMMAN WORLD
GTE SOUTH: NEWSLINE
GTE TELEPHONE OPERATIONS: TELOPS NEWS
GUARDIAN CORPORATION: GUARDIAN GRAPHICS
H.B. FULLER CO.: FULLER WORLD
HARRIS CORP.: F Y I MAGAZINE
HOLMES & NARVER, INC.: HERE & NOW
HOME BENEFICIAL LIFE INSURANCE CO.: HOME TOPICS
HORACE MANN COS., THE: SPECTRUM
HOUSTON CHRONICLE: COPY
IGA, INC.: I G A GROCERGRAM
ILCO UNICAN CORP.: UNICANEWS
IMPERIAL HOLLY CORP.: SUGAR EXCHANGE
INTERNATIONAL ASSOCIATION OF BUSINESS COMMUNICATORS: WORLD BOOK OF MEMBERS & SERVICES
INTERSTATE POWER CO.: INTERSTATE NEWS
IPALCO ENTERPRISES, INC.: I P L C O NEWS
ITT CORP.: WITTS-WITHIN THE I T T SYSTEM
JERSEY CENTRAL POWER & LIGHT CO.: ON-LINE
JET PROPULSION LABORATORY, CIT: UNIVERSE
JOURNAL COMMUNICATIONS: INTERCOM
KANSAS DEPARTMENT OF COMMERCE: DEVELOPING KANSAS
KELLOGG COMPANY: KELLOGG NEWS
KFC CORP.: BUCKET
KIMBALL INTERNATIONAL, INC.: SOUNDBOARD
L & F PRODUCTS: L & F TOPICS
LACLEDE GAS COMPANY: LACLEDE NEWS
LAKE ERIE GIRL SCOUT COUNCIL: MILLWHEEL
LAWRENCE RAGAN COMMUNICATIONS, INC.: RAGAN REPORT
LEADER FEDERAL SAVINGS & LOAN ASSOCIATION: LEADER DIGEST
LEDERLE LABORATORIES DIV.: LEDERLE HORIZONS
LIBERTY NATIONAL LIFE INSURANCE CO.: TORCH, THE
LINN COUNTY RURAL ELECTRIC COOPERATIVE ASSOCIATION: NEWSLINES ON THE LINE
LITTON GUIDANCE & CONTROL SYSTEMS: LINK
LOMAS FINANCIAL CORP.: NEWSMAKERS
LONGS DRUG STORES, INC.: CHAIN REACTION
LOUISIANA BANKERS ASSOCIATION: LOUISIANA BANKER
LOUISIANA PHARMACISTS ASSOCIATION: LOUISIANA PHARMACIST
LTV STEEL-MINING CO.: L T V TIMES
LUTHERAN MEDICAL CENTER: INSIDE LUTHERAN
LYNCHBURG GENERAL-MARSHALL LODGE HOSPITALS: CENTRA HEALTH MAGAZINE
MARSHALL & ILSLEY BANK: PERSONAL TOUCH

MEMORIAL SLOAN-KETTERING CANCER CENTER: ANNUAL REPORT
MEMORIAL SLOAN-KETTERING CANCER CENTER: CENTER NEWS
MERCHANTS INSURANCE GROUP: MESSENGER
MERCY HOSPITAL: FOREFRONT
MERCY MEDICAL CENTER: TOWER TALK
MERIDIAN BANK: DIALOG
METHODIST HOSPITAL: ADVANCES
MIAMI VALLEY HOSPITAL: INSIDER
MICHELIN NORTH AMERICA, INC.: BIB AMERICA
MICHIGAN BELL TELEPHONE CO.: TIE LINES
MICHIGAN EMPLOYMENT SECURITY COMMISSION: M E S C MESSENGER
MIDLAND MUTUAL LIFE INSURANCE CO.: ACHIEVER
MINNESOTA MUTUAL LIFE INSURANCE CO.: EXCEL
MIRRO CORP.: MIXING BOWL, THE
MNC FINANCIAL, INC.: M N C NOW
MONONGAHELA POWER CO.: MONONGAHELA NEWS
MONROE SYSTEMS FOR BUSINESS: FIELD
MORSE SHOE, INC.: MORSE CODE
MOSBY-YEAR BOOK, INC.: MOSBY TIMES
MURPHY OIL CORPORATION: MURPHY NEWS
MUSEUM OF SCIENCE: MUSEUM OF SCIENCE NEWSLETTER
MUTUAL BENEFICIAL ASSN. OF RAILROAD TRANSPORTATION EMPLOYEES: MUTUAL MAGAZINE, THE
NASH ENGINEERING CO.: NASH REPORTER
NATIONAL ASSOCIATION OF RAILROAD PASSENGERS: NATIONAL ASSOCIATION OF RAILROAD PASSENGERS NEWS
NATIONAL GRANGE MUTUAL INSURANCE CO.: AMONG OURSELVES
NATIONAL INDEMNITY CO.: FRIDAY FACTS
NEBRASKA DEPT. OF ECONOMIC DEVELOPMENT: NEBRASKA DEVELOPMENT NEWSLETTER
NEBRASKA PUBLIC POWER DISTRICT: DISPATCHER
NESTLE-BEICH, INC.: KADYDID CHRONICLE
NEW DETROIT, INC.: NEW DETROIT NOW
NEW ENGLAND MUTUAL LIFE INSURANCE CO.: CURRENTS
NEW YORK LIFE INSURANCE CO.: NEW YORK LIFE NEWS
NEWELL CO.: LOOKING GLASS
NIAGARA FRONTIER TRANSPORTATION AUTHORITY: F Y I
NORTHERN TRUST CO.: NORTHERN NEWS
OAK RIDGE NATIONAL LABORATORY: LAB NEWS
OHIO CHAMBER OF COMMERCE: OHIO CHAMBER NETWORK & SMALL BUSINESS NEWS
OHIO NATIONAL LIFE INSURANCE CO.: BULLETIN
OHIO NATIONAL LIFE INSURANCE CO.: O N L I ECHOES
OHIO RURAL ELECTRIC COOPS INC.: COUNTRY LIVING MAGAZINE
OLAN MILLS OF TENNESSEE: LENS
OPPENHEIMER MANAGEMENT CORP.: HANDSIGNALS, THE
ORANGE & ROCKLAND UTILITIES, INC.: LAMPPOST
ORCHID ISLE AUTO CTR.: ORCHID ISLE AUTO CENTER NEWSLETTER
ORE-IDA FOODS, INC.: VOICE, THE
OREGON PUBLIC EMPLOYEES RETIREMENT SYSTEM: PERSPECTIVES
PACIFIC BELL: CONNECTIONS
PARAGON ELECTRIC COMPANY, INC.: PARA-SCOPE
PENN TRAFFIC CO.: THE OPEN LINE
PENNSYLVANIA POWER CO.: PENN POWER NEWS
PHILADELPHIA BAR ASSOCIATION: PHILADELPHIA LAWYER, THE
PLUMBING MECHANICAL CONTRACTORS COUNCIL HARRIS COUNTY: GULF COAST PLUMBING, HEATING, COOLING NEWS
PRESBYTERIAN-UNIV. OF PENNSYLVANIA MEDICAL CTR.: THE BULLETIN
PRICE WATERHOUSE & CO.: LEADER, THE
QUAKER OATS CO.: MIDWEEK
QUAKER OATS CO.: QUAKER INSIDER
QUAKER OATS CO.: QUAKER QUARTERLY
QUEEN'S MEDICAL CENTER: QUEEN'S VISION, THE
QUIVIRA COUNCIL, INC.: TRAIL GUIDE
RADIO SHACK DIVISION, TANDY CORP.: RADIO SHACK INTERCOM
RALPH'S GROCERY CO.: RALPH'S NEWS

RALSTON PURINA CO.: R P TODAY
RALSTON PURINA CO.: SQUARE TALK
RANGER INSURANCE CO.: RANGER RESOURCES
RESEARCH MEDICAL CENTER: HORIZON
RICH'S, INC.: FOCAL POINT
RJR NABISCO, NABISCO FOODS GROUP: N F G TODAY
ROCK VALLEY COLLEGE: MONDAY MORNING MEMO
ROSES STORES, INC.: COMMUNIQUES
ROTO-ROOTER CORP.: ROTO-ROOTER EXCHANGE
ROWAN COMPANIES, INC.: GRAPEVINE
RUBBERMAID, INC.: RUBBERMAID REVIEW
SACRAMENTO MUNICIPAL UTILITY DISTRICT: EMPLOYEE HILINES
SAINT JOHN HOSPITAL: HORIZONS:
SAINT JOHN HOSPITAL: MEDICAL BULLETIN OF ST JOHN HOSPITAL
SAINT JOHN HOSPITAL: VOICE
SAKS FIFTH AVENUE: FOCUS ON SAKS FIFTH AVENUE
SANTA BARBARA RESEARCH CENTER: SBRC NEWS
SATELLITE INDUSTRIES INC.: PORTABLE SANITATION QUARTERLY
SCANNERS: SCANNERS
SCHRAMM INC.: WHAT'S HAPPENING
SHELTER INSURANCE COMPANY: CONTACT
SHERWOOD MEDICAL CO.: SHERWOOD REPORTER
SIERRA PACIFIC POWER CO.: SIERRA SCENE
SOCIAL SECURITY ADMINISTRATION: OASIS
SOCIETY CORP.: SOCI CORPORATE NOTES
SONAT, INC.: SONAT TIELINES
SOUTHEAST MICHIGAN, N.A.: FIRST WORD, THE
SOUTHERN ARTS FEDERATION, INC.: JAZZ SOUTH
SOUTHERN COMPANY SERVICES, INC.: INSIDE
SOUTHWESTERN BELL TELEPHONE CO.: TELEPHONE TIMES
ST. FRANCIS HOSPITAL CENTER: INTERCOM
ST. FRANCIS HOSPITAL: KA LEO REFLECTIONS
ST. JOSEPH MEDICAL CENTER: WEEKLY, THE
ST. JOSEPH'S HOSPITAL: ST JOSEPH'S NEWS
ST. LOUIS POLICE DEPARTMENT: ANNUAL REPORT
ST. VINCENT HOSPITAL: HEALTH REVIEW
STAR MARKET CO.: STAR NEWS
STERLING DRUG, INC.: CONVEYOR, THE
TEACHERS INSURNACE & ANNUITY ASSOCIATION: TOPICS
TENNESSEE EDUCATION ASSOCIATION: TENNESSEE TEACHER
TEXAS A & M UNIVERSITY SYSTEM: EXTENSION TODAY
TEXAS SOCIETY OF PROFESSIONAL ENGINEERS: TEXAS PROFESSIONAL ENGINEER
THIOKOL CORP.: THIOKOL MAGAZINE
TRANS WORLD AIRLINES INC.: SKYLINER
TRINITY UNIVERSAL INSURANCE CO.: TRINITY TIMES
U.S. BORAX INC.: BORAX PIONEER
U.S. DEPARTMENT OF AGRICULTURE: U S D A EMPLOYEE NEWSLETTER
U.S. POSTAL SERVICE, COMMUNICATIONS DEPT.: POSTAL LIFE
UARCO, INC.: FORUM
UGI CORP.: U G I HORIZONS
UNION NATIONAL LIFE INSURANCE CO.: RECORD, THE
UNION PACIFIC RAILROAD: CHANGES
UNION PACIFIC RAILROAD: INFO
UNITED STATES ARMY: SOLDIERS
UNITED WAY OF GREATER GREENSBORO: YOUR WAY
UNITED WAY OF KING COUNTY: BY THE WAY
UNITED WAY OF THE NATIONAL CAPITAL AREA: UNITED WAY NEWSLETTER
UNIVERSITY OF ST. THOMAS: ST. THOMAS MAGAZINE
US SMALL BUSINESS ADMINISTRATION: ANNUAL REPORT
VALHI, INC.: SUGAR SCOOP
VALHI, INC.: SUGARBEET
VALSPAR CORP.: SCOPE
VERNON CO.: VERNON MIRROR
VETCO, INC.: DIRECT LINE
VICKERS, INC.: VICKERS IN PRINT
VIRGINIA DEPARTMENT OF TRANSPORTATION: BULLETIN
VIRGINIA POWER CO.: VEPCO CURRENTS

WALGREEN CO.: WALGREEN WORLD
WEST BEND CO.: CRAFTSMAN, THE
WEST PENN POWER CO.: WATT'S NEW
WESTINGHOUSE HANFORD COMPANY: HANFORD REACH
WESTVACO CORP.: NEWS LETTER
WILLIAMS CO., THE: LINE MARKER
WOLVERINE WORLD WIDE: WOLVERINE NEWS
WOODWARD & LATHROP, INC.: WOODLOTHIAN
YOUNG RADIATOR CO.: YOUNG NEWS & VIEWS
ZIPPO MANUFACTURING CO.: ZIP-A-GRAM

## QUIZ

OHIO PHARMACISTS ASSOCIATION: OHIO PHARMACIST

## RELIGIOUS

CATHOLIC FOREIGN MISSION SOCIETY: MARYKNOLL
CATHOLIC FOREIGN MISSION SOCIETY: REVISTA MARYKNOLL
CATHOLIC FOREIGN MISSION SOCIETY: WORLD PARISH
FIRST BAPTIST CHURCH MODESTO: BULLETIN WEEKLY, THE
GLENMARY SISTERS: KINSHIP
GOOD NEWS BROADCASTING ASSOCIATION, INC.: CONFIDENT LIVING
SALVATION ARMY, THE: CAPITAL CADENCE
SISTERS OF PROVIDENCE HEALTH SYSTEM: CERITAS
SISTERS OF PROVIDENCE HEALTH SYSTEM: THE GOOD WORK

## SAFETY

AMERICAN AUTOMOBILE ASSOCIATION (WISCONSIN): A A A WORLD - WISCONSIN EDITION
ASSOCIATED PUBLIC-SAFETY COMMUNICATIONS OFFICE: A P C O BULLETIN
CORN BELT POWER COOPERATIVE: WATTS WATT
FIELDCREST CANNON, INC.: FIELDCREST CANNON
MICHIGAN MUTUAL INSURANCE CO.: SAFETY NEWS, THE
MOTORCYCLE SAFETY FOUNDATION: SAFE CYCLING
NATIONAL SAFETY COUNCIL: SAFETY & HEALTH
NEW JERSEY STATE SAFETY COUNCIL: SAFETY BRIEFS
RAX RESTAURANTS INC.: OPERATIONS NEWS
ROCKINGHAM MEMORIAL HOSPITAL: BEDSIDE BANNER
RSR CORPORATION: R S R LEAD PRESS
TEXAS SAFETY ASSOCIATION: SAFETY TALK
TEXAS SAFETY ASSOCIATION: SIGNAL

## SCENIC PHOTOS

AAA WASHINGTON: WASHINGTON MOTORIST
AMERICAN STORES CO.: FLASHES
BALL CORP.: BALL LINE
BANKERS SECURITY LIFE INSURANCE SOCIETY: BANKERS NOTES
BOEING CO.: BOEING NEWS
BUCYRUS-ERIE CO.: SURFACE MINER
CITY OF BOSTON: CITY RECORD
CIVITAN INTERNATIONAL: COUNTDOWN
COLUMBUS LIFE INSURANCE CO.: LOG
COLUMBUS SOUTHERN POWER CO.: LITELINES
COOK'S PEST CONTROL, INC.: WHAT'S COOKIN'
COPPERWELD CORP.: ACROSS COPPERWELD
CUNA MUTUAL INSURANCE GROUP: DIMENSIONS
DALLAS THEOLOGICAL SEMINARY: KINDRED SPIRIT
DELTA AIR LINES: DELTA DIGEST
DRESSER INDUSTRIES, INC.: RECORDER, THE
E.F. HOUGHTON & CO.: HOUGHTON LINE
ENVIRONMENTAL LOBBY OF MASSACHUSETTS: LEGISLATIVE BULLETIN
FLEMING COS. INC.: FLEMING ASSOCIATE, THE
GEORGE E. FAILING CO.: CORE DRILLER
GOODWILL INDUSTRIES OF SOUTHERN CALIFORNIA: TIDINGS:

HARLEY-DAVIDSON MOTOR CO. INC.: ENTHUSIAST
HOME BENEFICIAL LIFE INSURANCE CO.: HOME TOPICS
ILCO UNICAN CORP.: UNICANEWS
KAMPGROUNDS OF AMERICA, INC.: KOA DIRECTORY, ROAD ATLAS AND CAMPING GUIDE
KANSAS DEPARTMENT OF COMMERCE: KANSAS MAGAZINE
LEDERLE LABORATORIES DIV.: LEDERLE HORIZONS
LOS ANGELES DEPARTMENT OF WATER & POWER: INTAKE MAGAZINE
MERIDIAN BANK: DIALOG
METHODIST HOSPITAL: ADVANCES
MICHELIN NORTH AMERICA, INC.: BIB AMERICA
MIDLAND MUTUAL LIFE INSURANCE CO.: ACHIEVER
MONONGAHELA POWER CO.: MONONGAHELA NEWS
MUTUAL BENEFICIAL ASSN. OF RAILROAD TRANSPORTATION EMPLOYEES: MUTUAL MAGAZINE, THE
NESTLE-BEICH, INC.: KADYDID CHRONICLE
OHIO NATIONAL LIFE INSURANCE CO.: BULLETIN
OPPENHEIMER MANAGEMENT CORP.: HANDSIGNALS, THE
OTTER TAIL POWER CO.: HI-LITES
PACIFIC BELL: CONNECTIONS
PAN-AMERICAN LIFE INSURANCE CO.: LIFELINE
PENN TRAFFIC CO.: THE OPEN LINE
PHILADELPHIA BAR ASSOCIATION: PHILADELPHIA LAWYER, THE
PUBLIC SERVICE CO. OF NEW HAMPSHIRE: AROUND THE CIRCUIT
QUIVIRA COUNCIL, INC.: TRAIL GUIDE
RESEARCH MEDICAL CENTER: HORIZON
ROADWAY SERVICES, INC.: Q-MUNICATOR
ROCKY MOUNTAIN AAA CLUB: ROCKY MOUNTAIN MOTORIST
SANTA BARBARA RESEARCH CENTER: SBRC NEWS
SCHRAMM INC.: WHAT'S HAPPENING
SHELL OIL CO.: VENTURE
SOCIAL SECURITY ADMINISTRATION: OASIS:
SOUTHWESTERN BELL TELEPHONE CO.: TELEPHONE TIMES
TEXAS SOCIETY OF PROFESSIONAL ENGINEERS: TEXAS PROFESSIONAL ENGINEER
TRINITY UNIVERSAL INSURANCE CO.: TRINITY TIMES
U.S. BORAX INC.: BORAX PIONEER
UNITED STATES ARMY: SOLDIERS
VETCO, INC.: DIRECT LINE
WEST PENN POWER CO.: WATT'S NEW
WILLIAMS CO., THE: LINE MARKER
YOUNG RADIATOR CO.: YOUNG NEWS & VIEWS

## SCIENCE

AKRON CITY HOSPITAL: PACEMAKER
ALABAMA DEPT. OF PUBLIC HEALTH: ALABAMA'S HEALTH
ALFRED I DUPONT INSTITUTE: CHILD HEALTH TALK
ALLEGRO PRODUCTIONS, INC.: SCIENCE SCREEN REPORT
ALUMINUM COMPANY OF AMERICA: ALCOA NEWS
AMERICAN COLLEGE OF EMERGENCY PHYSICIANS: ANNALS OF EMERGENCY MEDICINE
AMERICAN COLLEGE OF RHEUMATOLOGY: ARTHRITIS & RHEUMATISM
AMERICAN COLLEGE OF SPORTS MEDICINE: MEDICINE & SCIENCE IN SPORTS & EXERCISE
AMERICAN COLLEGE OF SPORTS MEDICINE: SPORTS MEDICINE BULLETIN
AMP INC., VALLEY FORGE: CONTACT VIDEO
APPLIED PHYSICS LABORATORY: APL NEWS
ASSOCIATED MILK PRODUCERS, INC.: DAIRYMEN'S DIGEST, N. CENTRAL REGION
BALL CORP.: BALL LINE
BLOUNT, INC.: OREGON-IZER
BOEING CO.: BOEING NEWS
BUCYRUS-ERIE CO.: MINER DETAILS:
BUCYRUS-ERIE CO.: SURFACE MINER
BURLINGTON COUNTY COLLEGE: COLLEGE CONNECTION, THE
CABOT CORP.: CABOT WORLD
CALIFORNIA PACIFIC MEDICAL CENTER: CALIFORNIA PACIFIC QUARTERLY
CASCADE NATURAL GAS CORP.: CASCADE FLAME

CENTRAL LINCOLN PEOPLE'S UTILITY DISTRICT: COASTLINES
CIVITAN INTERNATIONAL: CIVITAN MAGAZINE
COASTAL CORP., THE: COASTAL WORLD
COOK COMPOSITES: FRONTLINE
COOK'S PEST CONTROL, INC.: WHAT'S COOKIN'
COOPER OIL, TOOL DIV.: OIL & IRON
CPI CORP.: NEWS & VIEWS
DELTA AIR LINES: DELTA DIGEST
DENTAL SOCIETY OF THE STATE OF NEW YORK: NEW YORK STATE DENTAL JOURNAL
DRESSER INDUSTRIES, INC.: RECORDER, THE
DSM COPOLYMER: DSM COPOLYMER NEWS
E.F. HOUGHTON & CO.: HOUGHTON LINE
E.F. HOUGHTON & CO.: HOUGHTONEWS
E-SYSTEMS, INC.: TEAM
EBASCO SERVICES INC.: EBASCO NEWS
ELECTRIC COUNCIL OF NEW ENGLAND: IMPULSE
ENGINEERING SOCIETY OF DETROIT: TECHNOLOGY
ENVIRONMENTAL LOBBY OF MASSACHUSETTS: LEGISLATIVE BULLETIN
ERWIN DI CYAN: DI CYAN BULLETIN
FACTORY MUTUAL ENGINEERING AND RESEARCH: FACTORY MUTUAL RECORD
GARDEN CITY HOSPITAL: NITTY GRITTY
GE AIRCRAFT ENGINES: HEADLINES
GREAT LAKES DIVISION-NATIONAL STEEL: FOCUS
GULF COAST RESEARCH LABORATORY: GULF RESEARCH REPORTS
GULF COAST RESEARCH LABORATORY: MARINE BRIEFS
HUGHES AIRCRAFT CO.: HUGHESNEWS
IPALCO ENTERPRISES, INC.: I P L C O NEWS
ITT CORP.: WITTS-WITHIN THE I T T SYSTEM
JET PROPULSION LABORATORY, CIT: UNIVERSE
KANO LABS INC.: GENIUS AT WORK
LAWRENCE BERKELEY LABORATORY: L B L RESEARCH REVIEW
LAWRENCE TECHNOLOGICAL UNIVERSITY: LAWRENCE TECHNOLOGICAL UNIVERSITY MAGAZINE
LEDERLE LABORATORIES DIV.: LEDERLE HORIZONS
LOS ALMOS NATIONAL LABORATORY: NEWSBULLETIN
LOS ANGELES DEPARTMENT OF WATER & POWER: INTAKE MAGAZINE
LOUISIANA PHARMACISTS ASSOCIATION: LOUISIANA PHARMACIST
LUTHERAN MEDICAL CENTER: INSIDE LUTHERAN
MERCHANTS INSURANCE GROUP: MESSENGER
METHODIST HOSPITAL: ADVANCES
MICHELIN NORTH AMERICA, INC.: BIB AMERICA
MICHIGAN BELL TELEPHONE CO.: TIE LINES
MOBIL OIL CORP.: COMPASS, THE
MOUNT SINAI MEDICAL CENTER: MEDICAL REPORT
MUSEUM OF SCIENCE & INDUSTRY: PROGRESS
MUSEUM OF SCIENCE: MUSEUM OF SCIENCE NEWSLETTER
MUTUAL BENEFICIAL ASSN. OF RAILROAD TRANSPORTATION EMPLOYEES: MUTUAL MAGAZINE, THE
NASH ENGINEERING CO.: NASH REPORTER
NATIONAL SCIENCE TEACHERS ASSOCIATION: JOURNAL OF COLLEGE SCIENCE TEACHING
NATIONAL SCIENCE TEACHERS ASSOCIATION: SCIENCE SCOPE
NATIONAL SUNFLOWER ASSOCIATION: SUNFLOWER, THE
OAK RIDGE NATIONAL LABORATORY: LAB NEWS
OHIO TRUCKING ASSOCIATION: OHIO GOVERNMENT DIRECTORY
PACIFIC BELL: CONNECTIONS
PHILIPS ELECTRONICS INSTRUMENTS: ELECTRON OPTICS BULLETIN
PLUMBING MECHANICAL CONTRACTORS COUNCIL HARRIS COUNTY: GULF COAST PLUMBING, HEATING, COOLING NEWS
PRESBYTERIAN-UNIV. OF PENNSYLVANIA MEDICAL CTR.: THE BULLETIN
RADIO SHACK DIVISION, TANDY CORP.: RADIO SHACK INTERCOM
RANGER INSURANCE CO.: RANGER RESOURCES
RESEARCH MEDICAL CENTER: HORIZON
ROSICRUCIAN ORDER AMORC: ROSICRUCIAN DIGEST

**ROWAN COMPANIES, INC.:** GRAPEVINE
**SANTA BARBARA RESEARCH CENTER:** SBRC NEWS
**SHELL OIL CO.:** QUEST
**SHELL OIL CO.:** SHELL NEWS
**SHELL OIL CO.:** VENTURE
**SHERWOOD MEDICAL CO.:** SHERWOOD REPORTER
**SMITH & NEPHEW RICHARDS INC.:** SMITH & NEPHEW RICHARDS REPORTER
**ST. FRANCIS HOSPITAL CENTER:** INTERCOM
**ST. JOHN MEDICAL CENTER:** PAGER
**ST. VINCENT HOSPITAL:** HEALTH REVIEW
**STATE CHEMICAL MANUFACTURING CO.:** STATEMENT
**STERLING DRUG, INC.:** CONVEYOR, THE
**SUN COMPANY INC.:** SUN MAGAZINE
**TACOMA PUBLIC UTILITIES:** UTILIBITS
**TEXAS SOCIETY OF PROFESSIONAL ENGINEERS:** TEXAS PROFESSIONAL ENGINEER
**TRANSACTION-PUBLISHERS:** SOCIETY
**UNION RAILROAD CO.:** U R R EMPLOYEE NEWSLETTER
**UNISYS:** INSIDE INFORMATION
**UNIVERSITY OF ST. THOMAS:** ST. THOMAS MAGAZINE
**VALHI, INC.:** SUGAR SCOOP
**VALHI, INC.:** SUGARBEET
**VALSPAR CORP.:** SCOPE
**VARIAN ASSOCIATES, INC.:** VARIAN ASSOCIATES MAGAZINE
**WEST BEND CO.:** CRAFTSMAN, THE
**WESTINGHOUSE HANFORD COMPANY:** HANFORD REACH
**WILLIAMS CO., THE:** LINE MARKER

## SEWING & PATTERNS

**FAMILY CIRCLE, INC.:** ADVANCE NEWS
**FOODLAND INTERNATIONAL CORP.:** HOTLINE
**GTE TELEPHONE OPERATIONS:** TELOPS NEWS
**RICH'S, INC.:** FOCAL POINT

## SPORTS

**AMERICAN COLLEGE OF SPORTS MEDICINE:** MEDICINE & SCIENCE IN SPORTS & EXERCISE
**AMERICAN VOLKSSPORT ASSOCIATION:** AMERICAN WANDERER, THE
**AMERICAN WATER SKI ASSOCIATION:** WATER SKIER, THE
**INTERNATIONAL UNIVERSITY FOUNDATION:** COLLEGIATE SPORTS REPORT
**LAACO, INC.:** MERCURY
**WOMEN'S INTERNATIONAL BOWLING CONGRESS:** RECORD GUIDE
**WOMEN'S INTERNATIONAL BOWLING CONGRESS:** WOMAN BOWLER

## TALK

**MINNESOTA STATE COUNCIL ON DISABILITY:** CONNECTOR

## TEXTILES, APPAREL, MILLS, MACHINERY

**TRI STATE INDUSTRIAL LAUNDRIES, INC.:** COVERALL

## TRAVEL

**AAA WASHINGTON:** WASHINGTON MOTORIST
**ADAMS BUSINESS FORMS, INC.:** WEB, THE
**ALABAMA EDUCATION ASSN.:** ALABAMA SCHOOL JOURNAL
**ALPHA BETA CO.:** VANGUARD, THE
**AMERICAN AUTOMOBILE ASSOCIATION (WISCONSIN):** A A A WORLD - WISCONSIN EDITION
**AMERICAN HOME PRODUCTS:** A H P  VISTA
**APPLIED PHYSICS LABORATORY:** APL NEWS
**ARIZONA AUTOMOBILE ASSOCIATION:** AAA HIGHROADS
**AUTO CLUB OF MICHIGAN:** A A A MICHIGAN LIVING
**BDP BRANDS, CARRIER CORP.:** FLOW
**BESSEMER & LAKE ERIE RAILROAD:** B & L E EMPLOYEE NEWSLETTER
**BLOUNT, INC.:** OREGON-IZER
**BOEING CO.:** BOEING NEWS
**BUCYRUS-ERIE CO.:** MINER DETAILS:
**BURLINGTON COUNTY COLLEGE:** COLLEGE CONNECTION, THE
**CERTIFIED GROCERS OF CALIFORNIA, LTD.:** CERGRAM
**CIVITAN INTERNATIONAL:** CIVITAN MAGAZINE
**CIVITAN INTERNATIONAL:** COUNTDOWN
**COACHMAN INDUSTRIES, INC.:** COACHMEN CAPERS
**COLONIAL PENN GROUP INC.:** YOU
**COLUMBIA GAS SYSTEM:** COLUMBIA TODAY
**CONNECTICUT MOTOR CLUB:** CONNECTICUT TRAVELER
**CONNECTICUT NATURAL GAS CORP.:** FUEL FOR THOUGHT
**COPPERWELD CORP.:** ACROSS COPPERWELD
**COUNTRYMARK COOP:** COOP CONNECTION
**CUBIC CORP.:** CUBIC CIRCUIT
**DELTA AIR LINES:** DELTA DIGEST
**DONREY MEDIA GROUP:** DONREY MEDIAGRAM
**DUN & BRADSTREET CORP., THE:** D & B REPORTS
**E.F. HOUGHTON & CO.:** HOUGHTON LINE
**EMPLOYERS CASUALTY:** BRICKBATS & BOUQUETS
**FEDERAL EXPRESS CORP.:** WORLDWIDE UPDATE
**FEDERATED INSURANCE COS.:** MULTILINER
**FIRST NATIONAL BANK OF MARYLAND:** COMMUNICATOR
**FLEMING COS. INC.:** FLEMING ASSOCIATE, THE
**FORD MOTOR COMPANY:** FORD TIMES
**GEORGE E. FAILING CO.:** CORE DRILLER
**GREATER MADISON CONVENTION & VISITORS BUREAU:** MADISON AREA TRAVEL PLANNER & VISITORS GUIDE
**HARLEY-DAVIDSON MOTOR CO. INC.:** ENTHUSIAST
**HOUSTON CHRONICLE:** COPY
**JOURNAL COMMUNICATIONS:** INTERCOM

**KAMPGROUNDS OF AMERICA, INC.:** KOA DIRECTORY, ROAD ATLAS AND CAMPING GUIDE
**KANSAS DEPARTMENT OF COMMERCE:** KANSAS MAGAZINE
**LOMAS FINANCIAL CORP.:** NEWSMAKERS
**LORD CORP.:** LORDFACTS
**MARSHALL & ILSLEY BANK:** PERSONAL TOUCH
**MERCHANTS INSURANCE GROUP:** MESSENGER
**MICHELIN NORTH AMERICA, INC.:** BIB AMERICA
**MIDLAND MUTUAL LIFE INSURANCE CO.:** ACHIEVER
**MONONGAHELA POWER CO.:** MONONGAHELA NEWS
**MOSBY-YEAR BOOK, INC.:** MOSBY TIMES
**MUTUAL BENEFICIAL ASSN. OF RAILROAD TRANSPORTATION EMPLOYEES:** MUTUAL MAGAZINE, THE
**NESTLE-BEICH, INC.:** KADYDID CHRONICLE
**OPPENHEIMER MANAGEMENT CORP.:** HANDSIGNALS, THE
**PAN-AMERICAN LIFE INSURANCE CO.:** LIFELINE
**PASEO DEL RIO ASSOCIATION:** RIO
**PHILADELPHIA BAR ASSOCIATION:** PHILADELPHIA LAWYER, THE
**PHILLIPS PETROLEUM CO.:** PHILNEWS
**PRICE WATERHOUSE & CO.:** LEADER, THE
**RADIO SHACK DIVISION, TANDY CORP.:** RADIO SHACK INTERCOM
**RANGER INSURANCE CO.:** RANGER RESOURCES
**RESEARCH MEDICAL CENTER:** HORIZON
**ROCKY MOUNTAIN AAA CLUB:** ROCKY MOUNTAIN MOTORIST
**SCHRAMM INC.:** WHAT'S HAPPENING
**SHELL OIL CO.:** SHELL ALUMNI NEWS
**SHELL OIL CO.:** SHELL NEWS
**SOUTHERN COMPANY SERVICES, INC.:** INSIDE
**TENNESSEE EDUCATION ASSOCIATION:** TENNESSEE TEACHER
**TEXAS WESLEYAN UNIVERSITY:** TEXAS WESLEYAN TODAY
**TRANS WORLD AIRLINES INC.:** SKYLINER:
**UNITED COMMERCIAL TRAVELERS OF AMERICA:** SAMPLE CASE
**UNITED STATES ARMY:** SOLDIERS
**VERNON CO.:** VERNON MIRROR
**VETCO, INC.:** DIRECT LINE
**WALGREEN CO.:** WALGREEN WORLD
**WEST PENN POWER CO.:** WATT'S NEW
**WILLIAMS CO., THE:** LINE MARKER
**YOUNG RADIATOR CO.:** YOUNG NEWS & VIEWS

## WOMEN

**COMMUNICATION RESEARCH ASSOCIATES, INC.:** MEDIA REPORT TO WOMEN
**LADIES AUXILIARY TO VFW OF THE US:** V F W AUXILIARY
**ROCKINGHAM MEMORIAL HOSPITAL:** WOMEN'S HEALTH FOCUS QUARTERLY
**SOROPTIMIST INTERNATIONAL OF THE AMERICAS, INC.:** SOROPTIMIST OF THE AMERICAS
**WOMEN IN COMMUNICATIONS INC.:** PROFESSIONAL COMMUNICATIOR, THE

This section contains complete listings for internal publications in the United States. They are listed alphabetically by sponsor, with each entry containing the name and address of the sponsor, industry affiliation, internal publication title, editor, year established, frequency, page size, printing method, and editorial description.

For materials accepted/included, refer to the code explanations at the bottom of each page.

---

**AAA IOWA**  3072
2900 AAA Ct.
Bettendorf, IA 52722
Telephone: (319) 332-7400
FAX: (319) 332-7991
Mailing Address:
 P.O. Box 4290
 Davenport, IA 52808
Industry Affiliation: Associations: Trade, Fraternal
**Publication(s):**
*Home & Away-Iowa*
Day Published: bi-m.
Lead Time: 2 mos.
Mtls Deadline: 2 mos. prior to pub. date
Contact: Sheree K. Freese, Ed.-Home & Away
 2900 AAA Ct.
 Bettendorf, IA 52722
Spec. Requirements: 16-24 pg.; regional edition insert; 8 x 10 7/8
Personnel: Sherry K. Freese, Editor

**AAA WASHINGTON**  5294
1745-114th Ave. S.E.
Bellevue, WA 98004-6930
Telephone: (206) 462-2222
FAX: (206) 646-2193
Mailing Address:
 P.O. Box 34995
 Seattle, WA 98124-1995
Industry Affiliation: Associations: Trade, Fraternal

**Publication(s):**
*Washington Motorist*
Day Published: 11/yr.
Mtls Deadline: 1st of mo. prior to pub. date
Contact: Washington Motorist
Spec. Requirements: 12-16 pg.; offset newspaper; 114 x 174
Personnel: Janet E. Ray, Editor
 Bruce D. Olson, Advertising Manager

**ABBOTT LABORATORIES**  2724
One Abbott Park Rd.
North Chicago, IL 60064
Telephone: (708) 937-6100
Industry Affiliation: Drugs, Cosmetics, Pharmaceuticals
**Publication(s):**
*Abbott World*
Day Published: q.
Lead Time: 4 mo.
Spec. Requirements: 4-10 pg; offset tabloid; 11 x 17
Personnel: Don Brokman, Editor

**ABBOTT NORTHWESTERN HOSPITAL INC.**  3535
800 E. 28th St.
Minneapolis, MN 55407
Telephone: (612) 863-4000
Industry Affiliation: Hospitals
**Publication(s):**
*Consultant*
Day Published: q.
Spec. Requirements: 8 pg; offset; 11 x 14
Personnel: Charles F. Williams, Editor

**A.B. CHANCE CO.**  3672
210 N. Allen
Centralia, MO 65240
Telephone: (314) 682-5521

Mailing Address:
 210 N. Allen
 Centralia, MO 65240
Industry Affiliation: Electrical, Electronic, Manufacturing
**Publication(s):**
*Chance Tips*
Day Published: q.
Spec. Requirements: 12-16 pgs.; offset magazine; 8 1/2 x 11
Personnel: R.S. Erdel, Editor

**ABF FREIGHT SYSTEM, INC.**  2034
301 S. 11th St.
Fort Smith, AR 72901-3798
Telephone: (501) 785-6347
FAX: (501) 785-8783
Mailing Address:
 P.O. Box 48
 Fort Smith, AR 72902-0048
Industry Affiliation: Trucking
**Publication(s):**
*A B F by-Lines*
Day Published: m.
Mtls Deadline: 1st of mo. prior to pub. date
Contact: Training
Spec. Requirements: 12-page; offset; 8 1/2 x 11
Personnel: Jan Cutsinger, Editor

**ACACIA GROUP, THE**  2502
51 Louisiana Ave., N.W.
Washington, DC 20001
Telephone: (202) 628-4506
Industry Affiliation: Insurance

**Publication(s):**
*News & Views*
Day Published: q.
Lead Time: 3 wks. prior to pub. date
Mtls Deadline: 2 mos. prior to pub. date
Spec. Requirements: 4 Page; Offset; 11 x 17
Personnel: Christine M. Feheley, Editor

**ACF INDUSTRIES, INC.**  3928
3301 Rider Trail, S.
Earth City, MO 63045
Industry Affiliation: Industry: Heavy Construction, Machinery
**Publication(s):**
*A C F today*
Day Published: q.
Contact: ACF Industries Horizons
 620 N 2nd St
 St. Charles, MO 63301
Spec. Requirements: 4 pg, 8 1/2 x 11
Personnel: Donald J. Reilly, Editor

**ACME BOOT COMPANY INC.**  4847
1002 Stafford St.
Clarksville, TN 37040
Telephone: (615) 552-2000
Mailing Address:
 P.O. Box 749
 Clarksville, TN 37041
Industry Affiliation: Shoes

---

**Materials Accepted/Included:** 01-Business news 02-By-line articles 03-Fashion news 04-Food news 05-Freelance copy 06-Letters to editor 07-Real estate news 08-Sports news 09-Travel news 10-Book rev. 11-Movie rev. 12-Music rev. 13-TV rev. 14-Theater rev. 15-Coming events 16-Obituaries 17-Question & answer 18-Social announcements 19-Artwork 20-Cartoons 21-Photos 22-TV listings 23-Audio rec. 24-Video rec. 25-Books 26-Films/film clips 27-Personnel news 28-Press releases 29-New product news/photos 30-Trade lit. 31-Contracts awarded 32-Display adv. 33-Classified adv.

11-1

**Publication(s):**
*Roundup*
Day Published: bi-m.
Lead Time: 15 days prior to pub. date
Mtls Deadline: 15th mo. prior to pub. date
Spec. Requirements: 10 pg.; offset
   magazine; 9 x 12
Personnel: Pam McCaslin, Editor

4624

**ACME MARKETS INC.**
75 Valley Stream Pkwy.
P.O. Box 3010
Malvern, PA 19355
Telephone: (215) 889-4000
Industry Affiliation: Retail Stores
**Publication(s):**
*Trumpeter, The*
Day Published: m.
Lead Time: 2 mos. prior to pub. date
Contact: American Stores Company
Spec. Requirements: 16 pg.; offset
   magazine
Personnel: Rosemary Delzingaro, Editor

68386

**AC ROCHESTER DIVISION,
GENERAL MOTORS
CORPORATION**
4800 S. Saginaw St.
Flint, MI 48501-1360
Telephone: (313) 257-7720
FAX: (313) 257-7728
Industry Affiliation: Autos, Trucks
**Publication(s):**
*Direction*
Day Published: q.
Mtls Deadline: By AC Rochester Request
   Only
Personnel: Daniel L. Dolan

3139

**ADAMS BUSINESS FORMS, INC.**
200 Jackson
Topeka, KS 66603
Telephone: (913) 233-4101
FAX: (913) 233-4291
Mailing Address:
   P.O. Box 91
   Topeka, KS 66601
Industry Affiliation: Office Equipment,
   Services, Supplies
**Publication(s):**
*Web, The*
Day Published: q.
Spec. Requirements: 12-page; offset
   tabloid; 8 x 10
Personnel: Sandy Becker, Editor

3415

**AEROQUIP CORP.**
3000 Strayer
Maumee, OH 43537
Telephone: (419) 891-7600
Mailing Address:
   P.O. Box 631
   Maumee, OH 43537
Industry Affiliation: Aircraft, Aerospace,
   Defense
**Publication(s):**
*Trinova*
Day Published: d.
Personnel: Chuck Kingdom, Editor

*Aeroquip*
Day Published: bi-m.
Personnel: Kathy Goulette, Editor

2054

**AEROSPACE CORP.**
P.O. Box 92957, M1/450
Los Angeles, CA 90009
Telephone: (310) 336-5444
Industry Affiliation: Aircraft, Aerospace,
   Defense

**Publication(s):**
*Orbiter*
Day Published: bi-w.
Lead Time: 2 wks.
Mtls Deadline: 2 wks. prior to pub. date
Spec. Requirements: 6 page; offset
   newspaper; 11 x 17
Personnel: Mabel Oshiro, Editor

2401

**AETNA LIFE & CASUALTY**
151 Farmington Ave.
Hartford, CT 06156
Telephone: (203) 273-0123
FAX: (203) 273-0079
Industry Affiliation: Insurance
**Publication(s):**
*Aetnasphere*
Day Published: bi-m.
Lead Time: 2 wks. prior to pub. date
Mtls Deadline: 2 wks. prior to pub. date
Spec. Requirements: 8-pages; offset; 11 x
   15
Personnel: Carol Atlas, Editor

71253

**AFSCME**
1625 L St.
Washington, DC 20036
Telephone: (202) 429-1144
Industry Affiliation: Associations: City,
   State, Federal
**Publication(s):**
*Public Employee, The*
Day Published: 8/yr.
Materials: 02,03,04,06,10,11,19,20
Contact: Marshall O. Donley, Jr.
   Telephone: (202) 429-1144
   1625 L. St.
   Washington, DC 20036

2818

**AG COMMUNICATIONS CORP.**
333 E. First St.
Genda, IL 60135-1087
Telephone: (708) 681-7100
FAX: (601) 581-4967
Industry Affiliation: Industry: Material
   Handling
**Publication(s):**
*Inside A G C S*
Day Published: bi-m.
Spec. Requirements: 6-8 pg; offset
   newspaper; 11 x 14 1/2
Personnel: Jim Kasseblum, Editor

5289

**AGENCY FOR INTERNATIONAL
DEVELOPMENT**
320 21st St., N.W., Rm. 4889 NS
Washington, DC 20523
Telephone: (202) 647-4330
FAX: (202) 647-3945
Industry Affiliation: Associations: City,
   State, Federal
**Publication(s):**
*Front Lines*
Day Published: 11/yr.
Lead Time: 3 wks. prior to pub. date
Mtls Deadline: 10 working days prior to
   pub. date
Contact: Publications Division
Spec. Requirements: 16-pages; offset; 11
   1/2 x 17
Personnel: Nancy Long, Editor

3930

**AGWAY INC.**
333 Butternut Dr.
De Witt, NY 13214
Telephone: (315) 449-7061
Mailing Address:
   P.O. Box 4933
   Syracuse, NY 13221
Industry Affiliation: Agriculture, Services

**Publication(s):**
*Agway Cooperator*
Day Published: 7/yr.
Materials: 32
Spec. Requirements: 32 pgs.; offset
   magazine; 8 1/8 x 10 15/16
Personnel: Susan Zarris, Editor

5356

**AID ASSOCIATION FOR
LUTHERANS (AAL)**
4321 N. Ballard Rd.
Appleton, WI 54919
Telephone: (414) 734-5721
FAX: (414) 730-3757
Industry Affiliation: Insurance
**Publication(s):**
*Correspondent*
Day Published: bi-m.
Lead Time: 90 days prior to pub. date
Spec. Requirements: 4 pg.; Offset
   Magazine; 84 x 11
Personnel: Cindy Zirbel, Editor
          Linda Peterson

4285

**AIR FORCE INSTITUTE OF
TECHNOLOGY**
Bldg. 125, Area B
Dayton, OH 45433
Telephone: (513) 255-2135
Industry Affiliation: Colleges, Institutions,
   Science Research
**Publication(s):**
*Aog Quarterly*
Day Published: q.: Jan., Apr., July, Dec.
        Telephone: (513) 255-9623
Personnel: Tom Stivers, Editor

2503

**AIR LINE PILOTS ASSOCIATION**
535 Herndon Pkwy.
Herndon, VA 22070
Telephone: (703) 689-4174
Industry Affiliation: Associations: Trade,
   Fraternal
**Publication(s):**
*Air Line Pilot*
Day Published: 10/yr.
Lead Time: 2 mos.
Mtls Deadline: 1st of mo. prior to pub. date
Spec. Requirements: 48-64 pages; 8 1/4 x
   11
Personnel: Esperison Martinez, Editor

4286

**AKRON CITY HOSPITAL**
525 E. Market St.
Akron, OH 44304
Telephone: (216) 375-3000
Industry Affiliation: Hospitals
**Publication(s):**
*Pacemaker*
Day Published: bi-m.
Spec. Requirements: 8 page; offset; 84 x
   11

4287

**AKRON GENERAL MEDICAL
CENTER**
400 Wabash Ave.
Akron, OH 44307
Telephone: (216) 384-6376
FAX: (216) 996-2384
Industry Affiliation: Hospitals

**Publication(s):**
*Voice*
Day Published: q.
Mtls Deadline: 1 mo.
Spec. Requirements: 8-page; offset; 11 x
   15
Personnel: Sue Hobson, Editor

1977

**ALABAMA DEPT. OF PUBLIC
HEALTH**
Normandale Shopping Ctr., Patton Ave.
Montgomery, AL 36130
Telephone: (205) 613-5300
FAX: (205) 240-3097
Mailing Address:
   434 Monroe St.
   Montgomery, AL 36130-3017
Industry Affiliation: Associations: Health
   Groups
**Publication(s):**
*Alabama's Health*
Day Published: m.
Lead Time: 10th prior to pub. date
Materials: 02,06,17,21,28
Mtls Deadline: 21 days prior to pub. date
Spec. Requirements: offset magazine 8
   1/2 x 11
Personnel: Arrol Sheehan, Editor

1978

**ALABAMA EDUCATION ASSN.**
422 Dexter Ave.
Montgomery, AL 36104
Telephone: (205) 834-9790
Mailing Address:
   P.O. Box 4177
   Montgomery, AL 36103-4177
Industry Affiliation: Colleges, Institutions,
   Science Research
**Publication(s):**
*Alabama School Journal*
Day Published: w.
Lead Time: 2 wks. prior to pub. date
Mtls Deadline: 2 wks. prior to pub. date
Spec. Requirements: 16 page; offset
   tabloid; 10 X 12 1/2
Personnel: Dr. Paul R. Hubbert, Editor

1979

**ALABAMA FARMERS
FEDERATION**
P.O. Box 11000
Montgomery, AL 36191-0001
Telephone: (205) 288-3900
FAX: (205) 284-3957
Industry Affiliation: Agriculture, Services
**Publication(s):**
*Neighbors Magazine*
Day Published: m.
Lead Time: 1 mo.
Materials: 01,04,32,33
Mtls Deadline: 1st of mo. prior
Personnel: Mark Morrison, Editor

1980

**ALABAMA FORESTRY ASSN.**
555 Alabama St.
Montgomery, AL 36104
Telephone: (205) 265-8733
Industry Affiliation: Lumber, Forestry,
   Building Materials
**Publication(s):**
*Alabama Forests*
Day Published: bi-m.
Lead Time: 30 days
Spec. Requirements: 28-34 pg.; offset
   magazine; 82 x 11
Personnel: Rei Boyce, Editor

2006

**ALABAMA GAS CORP.**
2101 Sixth Ave., N.
Birmingham, AL 35203
Telephone: (205) 326-8196
FAX: (205) 326-2704
Industry Affiliation: Utility: Gas

**Materials Accepted/Included:** 01-Business news 02-By-line articles 03-Fashion news 04-Food news 05-Freelance copy 06-Letters to editor 07-Real estate news 08-Sports news 09-Travel news 10-Book rev. 11-Movie rev. 12-Music rev. 13-TV rev. 14-Theater rev. 15-Coming events 16-Obituaries 17-Question & answer 18-Social announcements 19-Artwork 20-Cartoons 21-Photos 22-TV listings 23-Audio rec. 24-Video rec. 25-Books 26-Films/film clips 27-Personnel news 28-Press releases 29-New product news/photos 30-Trade lit. 31-Contracts awarded 32-Display adv. 33-Classified adv.

**Publication(s):**
*Gas Lines*
Day Published: bi-m.
Lead Time: 4 wks.
Mtls Deadline: 2nd wk. of odd mos.
Spec. Requirements: 20-30-page; offset
   magazine; 8 x 11
Personnel: Beverly Stone, Editor

**ALABAMA POWER CO.**    2007
P.O. Box 2641
Birmingham, AL 35291
Telephone: (205) 250-2403
Industry Affiliation: Utility:  Electric
**Publication(s):**
*Powergrams*
Day Published: m.
Spec. Requirements: 36 page; offset; 8
   1/2 x 11
Personnel: Julia Thomas, Editor

**ALADDIN SYNERGETICS INC.**    4848
P.O. Box 100888
Nashville, TN 37224
Telephone: (615) 748-3000
Industry Affiliation: Associations:  Trade,
   Fraternal
**Publication(s):**
*Asi Interaction*
Day Published: bi-m.
Spec. Requirements: 6 pg.; letterpress; 8
   1/2 x 11
Personnel: Bill Griggs, Editor

**ALASKA FOREST ASSN. INC.**    2009
111 Stedman St., Ste. 200
Ketchikan, AK 99901
Telephone: (907) 225-6114
FAX: (907) 225-5920
Industry Affiliation: Lumber, Forestry,
   Building Materials
**Publication(s):**
*Timber Times*
Day Published: m.
Lead Time: 1 mo.
Materials: 01,02,17,27,28
Mtls Deadline: 25th of mo. prior to pub.
   date
Spec. Requirements: 6 page; offset; 8 1/2
   x 11
Personnel: Troy Reinhart, Editor

**ALBANY INTERNATIONAL CORP.**    3931
One Sage Rd.
Albany, NY 12204
Telephone: (518) 447-6400
Mailing Address:
   P.O. Box 1109
   Albany, NY 12201
Industry Affiliation: Associations:  City,
   State, Federal
**Publication(s):**
*Information Memo*
Day Published: bi-m.
Lead Time: 2 mos.
Spec. Requirements: 12 pg; offset; 2 color;
   8 1/2 11
Personnel: Charles Buchanan, Editor
        Susan Tenerowicz, Assistant
        Editor

**ALBERTO-CULVER CO.**    2728
2525 Armitage
Melrose Park, IL 60160
Telephone: (708) 450-3000
Industry Affiliation: Associations:  City,
   State, Federal

**Publication(s):**
*Alberto*
Day Published: q.
Spec. Requirements: 20 page; offset
   magazine; 8 1/2 x 11
Personnel: Nancy Shields, Editor

**ALEUT CORP.**    68585
4000 Old Seward Hwy., 300
Anchorage, AK 99503
Telephone: (907) 561-4300
Industry Affiliation: Associations:  City,
   State, Federal
**Publication(s):**
*Aleutian Current*
Day Published: bi-m.
Personnel: Lori Waisanen, Editor
        Sharon Guenther, Lay-out

**ALEXANDER & BALDWIN, INC.**    2693
822 Bishop St.
Honolulu, HI 96813
Telephone: (808) 525-8439
FAX: (808) 525-6677
Mailing Address:
   P.O. Box 3440
   Honolulu, HI 96801-3440
Industry Affiliation: Sugar
**Publication(s):**
*Ampersand*
Day Published: q.
Materials: 01,02,04,05,06,07,17,19,20,21
Spec. Requirements: 4 pg.; offset; 8 1/2 x
   11
Personnel: Melissa Chang, Editor
        Donne Dawson, Editor in Chief

*Po'okela*
Day Published: m.
Materials: 01,02,04,05,06,07,17,20,21
Mtls Deadline: 2nd wk. of mo.
Personnel: Donne Dawson, Editor in Chief
        Melissa Chang, Editor

**ALFRED I DUPONT INSTITUTE**    2501
1600 Rockland Rd.
Wilmington, DE 19899
Telephone: (302) 651-6090
Mailing Address:
   P.O. Box 269
   Wilmington, DE 19899
Industry Affiliation: Hospitals
**Publication(s):**
*Child Health Talk*
Day Published: m.
Lead Time: 4 wks. prior to pub. date
Mtls Deadline: 4 wks. prior to pub. date
Spec. Requirements: 8 Page; 8 1/2 X 11
Personnel: Karen Bengston, Editor

**ALLEGRO PRODUCTIONS, INC.**    3932
1000 Clint Moore Rd.
Boca Raton, FL 33487-2806
Telephone: (407) 994-9111
FAX: (407) 241-0707
Industry Affiliation: Radio, TV, Movies
**Publication(s):**
*Science Screen Report*
Day Published: 8/yr.
Materials: 21,26
Personnel: Jerome G. Forman, President

**ALLEN-BRADLEY CO.**    5357
1201 S. Second St.
Milwaukee, WI 53204
Telephone: (414) 382-2000
Mailing Address:
   P.O. Box 2086
   Milwaukee, WI 53201
Industry Affiliation: Electrical, Electronic,
   Manufacturing

**Publication(s):**
*Network*
Day Published: q.
Spec. Requirements: 8 pgs.; offset; 11 x
   17, tabloid
Personnel: Shawna Todd, Managing Editor

*Connection*
Day Published: q.
Lead Time: 3 mos.
Contact: Headquarters
Spec. Requirements: 4-6 pgs., 11 x 7;
   tabloid
Personnel: Ted Hutton, Editor

**ALLIANCE LIFE**    3599
1750 Hennepin Ave.
Minneapolis, MN 55403
Telephone: (612) 347-6500
FAX: (612) 347-6515
Industry Affiliation: Insurance
**Publication(s):**
*Lifelines*
Day Published: m.
Lead Time: 2nd wk. of mo.
Mtls Deadline: 2nd wk. of mo.
Contact: Mktg.
Spec. Requirements: 6-8-page; offset
   magazine; 84 x 11
Personnel: Charles Clayton, Editor

**ALLIANT HEALTH SYSTEM**    3187
234 E. Gray, Ste. 154
Louisville, KY 40202
Telephone: (502) 629-2000
FAX: (502) 629-2688
Mailing Address:
   P.O. Box 35070
   Louisville, KY 40232-5070
Industry Affiliation: Hospitals
**Publication(s):**
*Interviews*
Day Published: q.
Lead Time: 2 wks.
Contact: Public Relations
Personnel: Daniel G. Shaw, Editor

*Health At Work*
Day Published: q.
Lead Time: 3 wks.
Personnel: Nancy McElwain

**ALLIED-SIGNAL AEROSPACE CO.**    3836
2525 W. 190th St.
Torrance, CA 90504
Telephone: (310) 323-9500
FAX: (310) 512-2490
Industry Affiliation: Aircraft, Aerospace,
   Defense
**Publication(s):**
*Horizons*
Day Published: m.
Lead Time: 1 wk. prior to pub. date
Mtls Deadline: 1 wk. prior to pub. date
Spec. Requirements: circ. 56,000; tabloid

**ALLIED GROUP**    3073
701 Fifth Ave.
Des Moines, IA 50309
Telephone: (515) 280-4270
Mailing Address:
   P.O. Box 974
   Des Moines, IA 50304
Industry Affiliation: Associations: Trade,
   Fraternal
**Publication(s):**
*Focus*
Day Published: m.
Lead Time: 1 mo.
Spec. Requirements: 6-12 pgs; offset
   newspaper; 11 x 17
Personnel: Jeff Abbas, Editor

*Resource*
Day Published: m.
Lead Time: 1 mo.
Personnel: Jeff Abbas, Editor

**ALLSTATE INSURANCE COMPANY**    2944
Allstate Plaza N., F4
Northbrook, IL 60062
Telephone: (708) 402-5631
Industry Affiliation: Insurance
**Publication(s):**
*Contact*
Day Published: bi-m.
Spec. Requirements: 24 pg.; offset
   magazine; 84 x 11
Personnel: Catherine Driscoll, Editor

*Allstate Now*
Day Published: irreg.
Personnel: Marilyn Abbey, Editor

**ALPHA BETA CO.**    2058
777 S. Harbor Blvd.
La Habra, CA 90631
Telephone: (714) 738-2000
Industry Affiliation: Food, General
**Publication(s):**
*Vanguard, The*
Day Published: q.
Spec. Requirements: tabloid; 11 x 14
Personnel: Ron Kim Cammock, Editor

**AL SIGL CENTER FOR**    3933
   **REHABILITATION AGENCIES,**
   **INC.**
1000 Elmwood Ave
Rochester, NY 14620
Telephone: (716) 442-4100
Industry Affiliation: Hospitals
**Publication(s):**
*Sigletter*
Day Published: 3/yr.
Spec. Requirements: 4-8 pg.; offset; 8 1/2
   x 11
Personnel: B. J. Yudelson, Editor

**ALUMINUM COMPANY OF**    4629
   **AMERICA**
1501 Alcoa Bldg.
Pittsburgh, PA 15219
Telephone: (412) 553-3655
FAX: (412) 553-3129
Industry Affiliation: Aluminum
**Publication(s):**
*Alcoa News*
Day Published: bi-m.
Lead Time: 5 mos. prior the pub. date
Spec. Requirements: 24-pg.; offset
   lithography; 8 3/8 x 10 5/8
Personnel: Karita L. Malhotra, Editor

**AMARILLO CHAMBER OF**    4909
   **COMMERCE**
1000 S. Polk
Amarillo, TX 79101
Telephone: (806) 373-7800
FAX: (806) 373-3909
Mailing Address:
   P.O. Box 9480
   Amarillo, TX 79105
Industry Affiliation: Associations: City,
   State, Federal
**Publication(s):**
*Chamber Monthly*
Day Published: m.
Personnel: Cathy Dixon, Editor

*Entertainment Guide*
Day Published: q.
Personnel: Mindy Bradley, Editor

---

**Materials Accepted/Included:** 01-Business news 02-By-line articles 03-Fashion news 04-Food news 05-Freelance copy 06-Letters to editor 07-Real estate news 08-Sports news 09-Travel news 10-Book rev. 11-Movie rev. 12-Music rev. 13-TV rev. 14-Theater rev. 15-Coming events 16-Obituaries 17-Question & answer 18-Social announcements 19-Artwork 20-Cartoons 21-Photos 22-TV listings 23-Audio rec. 24-Video rec. 25-Books 26-Films/film clips 27-Personnel news 28-Press releases 29-New product news/photos 30-Trade lit. 31-Contracts awarded 32-Display adv. 33-Classified adv.

11-3

*Accent West*
Day Published: m.
Personnel: Don Cantrell, Editor

## AMATEUR ATHLETIC UNION OF THE U.S.    2977
AAU House 3400 W. 86th St.
Indianapolis, IN 46268
Telephone: (317) 872-2900
Mailing Address:
    P.O. Box 68207
    Indianapolis, IN 46268
Industry Affiliation: Sports, Equipment
Publication(s):
*Infoaau*
Day Published: bi-m.
Lead Time: 30 days prior to pub. date
Mtls Deadline: 30 days prior to pub. date
Contact: Sports
Spec. Requirements: 16 pg., trim size is 8 3/8″ x 10 13/16″
Personnel: David Morton, Editor

## AMERICA'S FAVORITE CHICKEN    3230
6 Concourse Pkwy., Ste. 1700
Atlanta, GA 30328
Telephone: (404) 391-9500
Industry Affiliation: Food, General
Publication(s):
*Attitude*
Day Published: q.
Contact: Dave Eisnaugle
        Telephone: (404) 391-9500
        6 Concourse Pkwy., Ste. 1700
        Atlanta, GA 30328
Spec. Requirements: 20-24-page; offset; 8 1/2 x 11
Personnel: Webb Williams, Editor

## AMERICAN ACADEMY OF OPHTHALMOLOGY    2060
655 Beach St.
San Francisco, CA 94109
Telephone: (415) 561-8500
FAX: (415) 561-8567
Mailing Address:
    P.O. Box 7424
    San Francisco, CA 94120
Industry Affiliation: Optical
Publication(s):
*Argus*
Day Published: m.
Lead Time: 6 wks. prior to pub. date
Materials: 32
Mtls Deadline: 5th of mo. prior to pub. date
Contact: Communications
Spec. Requirements: 16-32 pg; tabloid; web press; 4 color; 10 x 14 1/2
Personnel: Pamela Beach, Editor
        Robin Brandes, Marketing Director

## AMERICAN ACADEMY OF ORTHOPAEDIC SURGEONS    2732
6300 N. River Rd.
Rosemont, IL 60018
Telephone: (708) 823-7186
Industry Affiliation: Associations: Health Groups

Publication(s):
*Bulletin*
Day Published: q.
Lead Time: 3 mos.
Contact: Comm. Div.
Spec. Requirements: 36-44 pg.; offset; 8 1/2 x 11
Personnel: Alvin Nagelberg, Editor
        Mark W. Wieting

## AMERICAN AIRLINES INC.    4910
P.O. Box 619616
DFW Airport, TX 75261
Telephone: (817) 963-1234
Industry Affiliation: Airlines
Publication(s):
*Flagship News*
Day Published: bi-w.
Lead Time: 14 days prior to pub. date
Materials: 09
Spec. Requirements: 8-12 pg.; tabloid; 8-1/2 x 11
Personnel: Don Bedwell, Editor

*American Way*
Day Published: bi-w.
Lead Time: 4 mos. prior to pub. date
Personnel: Doug Crichton, Editor

## AMERICAN APPRAISAL ASSOCIATES    5359
100 E. Wisconsin Ave.
Ste. 2100
Milwaukee, WI 53202
Telephone: (414) 271-7240
Industry Affiliation: Finance, Services
Publication(s):
*Valuation Viewpoint*
Day Published: q.
Spec. Requirements: 8 pgs.; offset bulletin; 81/2 x 11
Personnel: Lorrie LiBrizzie, Editor

*Valuation & The Law*
Day Published: q.
Spec. Requirements: 8 pgs.: 8 1/2 x 11
Personnel: Lorrie LiBrizzie, Editor

## AMERICAN ASSOCIATION OF COLLEGES FOR TEACHER EDUCATION    2505
One Dupont Cir., Ste. 610
Washington, DC 20036-1186
Telephone: (202) 293-2450
FAX: (202) 457-8095
Industry Affiliation: Associations: City, State, Federal
Publication(s):
*Briefs*
Day Published: bi-m.
Materials: 15,28,32
Mtls Deadline: 1st of mo. prior to pub. date
Spec. Requirements: 4 & 8 Page; Offset; 8 1/2 x 11
Personnel: Elizabeth Foxwell, Editor

*Journal Of Teacher Education*
Day Published: 5/yr.
Lead Time: 4 mos./articles
Spec. Requirements: camera-ready adv.; 80 pg.; offset; 8 3/8 x 11
Personnel: Sharon Givens
        Ed Ducharme, Director

## AMERICAN ASSOCIATION OF ORAL & MAXILLOFACIAL SURGEONS    2733
9700 W. Bryn Mawr Ave.
Rosemont, IL 60018-5701
Telephone: (708) 678-6200
FAX: (708) 678-6286
Industry Affiliation: Associations: Trade, Fraternal

Publication(s):
*A A O M S Forum*
Day Published: q.
Lead Time: 1 mo. prior to pub. date
Spec. Requirements: 16 pg.; 8 1/2 x 11
Personnel: Dr. Daniel Laskin, Editor

*Journal Of Oral & Maxillofacial Surgery*
Day Published: m.
Lead Time: 2 mos.
Mtls Deadline: 2 mos. prior to pub. date
Personnel: Dr. Daniel M. Laskin, Editor

## AMERICAN AUTOMOBILE ASSOCIATION (WISCONSIN)    5473
P.O. Box 33
Madison, WI 53701-0033
Telephone: (608) 236-1300
FAX: (608) 828-2443
Industry Affiliation: Associations: Trade, Fraternal
Publication(s):
*A A A World - Wisconsin Edition*
Day Published: bi-m.
Lead Time: 10 wks.
Mtls Deadline: 10 wks. prior to pub. date
Spec. Requirements: 8 x 10 3/4 high-web offset, coated stock
Personnel: Ernest Stetenfeld, Editor

## AMERICAN BOAT & YACHT COUNCIL INC.    3935
3069 Solomon's Island Rd.
Edgewater, MD 21037
Telephone: (410) 956-1050
FAX: (410) 956-2737
Industry Affiliation: Associations: Trade, Fraternal
Publication(s):
*A B Y C News*
Day Published: q.
Lead Time: 60 days prior to pub. date
Materials: 10,30
Mtls Deadline: 1 mo. prior to pub. date
Spec. Requirements: 8 pg.; offset; 8-1/2 x 11
Personnel: Susan Canfield, Editor

*Rules Regulations For Recreational Boats*
Day Published: intermittently
Personnel: Lysle B. Gray, Executive Director

*Standards & Recommended Practices For Small Craft*
Day Published: 3/yr.
Personnel: Jennifer Ruppert, Publication Director

## AMERICAN CANCER SOCIETY    3536
3316 W. 66th St.
Edina, MN 55435
Telephone: (612) 925-2772
Industry Affiliation: Associations: Health Groups
Publication(s):
*Herald Of Hope*
Day Published: bi-m.
Mtls Deadline: 1 mo. prior the pub. date
Spec. Requirements: 4-pg; offset; 11 x 17 to 8 1/2 x 11
Personnel: Brian L. Nelson, Editor

## AMERICAN CAST IRON PIPE COMPANY    1981
2930 N. 16th St.
Birmingham, AL 35207
Telephone: (205) 325-7701
Mailing Address:
    P.O. Box 2727
    Birmingham, AL 35207
Industry Affiliation: Industry: Heavy Construction, Machinery

Publication(s):
*Pipe Progress*
Day Published: s-a.
Spec. Requirements: 16-page; offset; 84 x 11
Personnel: Cynthia Lovoy, Editor

*Acipco News Bulletin*
Day Published: m.
Spec. Requirements: 24-page
Personnel: Myra Hunter, Editor

## AMERICAN COLLEGE OF EMERGENCY PHYSICIANS    3416
1125 Executive Cir.
Irving, TX 75038
Telephone: (214) 550-0911
Mailing Address:
    P.O. Box 619911
    Dallas, TX 75261
Industry Affiliation: Colleges, Institutions, Science Research
Publication(s):
*Annals Of Emergency Medicine*
Day Published: m.
Lead Time: 15th of 2nd mo. prior to mo. of pub.
Mtls Deadline: 20th of 2nd mo. prior to date of issue
Spec. Requirements: 104 pgs.; offset; 8 1/8 x 11
Personnel: Joseph Waeckerle, Editor in Chief
        Michael Callahan, Editor

## AMERICAN COLLEGE OF RHEUMATOLOGY    2627
60 Executive Park S., Ste. 150
Atlanta, GA 30329
Telephone: (404) 633-3777
Industry Affiliation: Associations: Health Groups
Publication(s):
*Arthritis & Rheumatism*
Day Published: m.
Lead Time: 1st of mth.
Spec. Requirements: 104-112-page; offset; 8 1/2 x 11
Personnel: J.B. Lippincott Co., Publisher
        Peter H. Schur, M.D., Editor in Chief
        Jane Diamond, Managing Editor

## AMERICAN COLLEGE OF SPORTS MEDICINE    5360
P.O. Box 1440
Indianapolis, IN 46206
Telephone: (317) 637-9200
Industry Affiliation: Colleges, Institutions, Science Research
Publication(s):
*Medicine & Science In Sports & Exercise*
Day Published: m.
Spec. Requirements: 96 pg.; offset; 8 1/2 x 11
Personnel: Deanna Gamillo, Managing Editor

*Sports Medicine Bulletin*
Day Published: q.
Lead Time: 6 wks. prior to pub. date
Mtls Deadline: 6 wks. prior to pub. date
Spec. Requirements: 12 pgs.
Personnel: Carol L. Christison, Editor

## AMERICAN COMMERCIAL LINES, INC.    2979
1701 E. Market St.
Jeffersonvlle, IN 47130
Telephone: (812) 288-0100
Mailing Address:
    P.O. Box 610
    Jeffersonvlle, IN 47131
Industry Affiliation: Shipping

Materials Accepted/Included: 01-Business news 02-By-line articles 03-Fashion news 04-Food news 05-Freelance copy 06-Letters to editor 07-Real estate news 08-Sports news 09-Travel news 10-Book rev. 11-Movie rev. 12-Music rev. 13-TV rev. 14-Theater rev. 15-Coming events 16-Obituaries 17-Question & answer 18-Social announcements 19-Artwork 20-Cartoons 21-Photos 22-TV listings 23-Audio rec. 24-Video rec. 25-Books 26-Films/film clips 27-Personnel news 28-Press releases 29-New product news/photos 30-Trade lit. 31-Contracts awarded 32-Display adv. 33-Classified adv.

**Publication(s):**
*A C L currents*
Day Published: q.
Lead Time: 2 mos.
Mtls Deadline: 10th of mo. prior to pub.
    date
Spec. Requirements: 12 pgs. offset; 8 1/2
    x 11
Personnel: Chris Kirk, Editor

68576

**AMERICAN CYANAMID CO.**
1 Cyanamid Plz.
Wayne, NJ 07470
Telephone: (201) 831-2224
Industry Affiliation: Drugs, Cosmetics,
    Pharmaceuticals
**Publication(s):**
*Cyanamid News*
Day Published: q.
Spec. Requirements: 8 pg.; offset tabloid;
    11 x 15
Personnel: Ron Keel, Editor

68375

**AMERICAN DIABETES**
    **ASSOCIATION**
1570 Brookhollow Dr., Ste. 120
Santa Ana, CA 92705
Telephone: (714) 662-7940
FAX: (714) 662-0247
Industry Affiliation: Associations: Health
    Groups
**Publication(s):**
*Newsletter*
Day Published: q.

68374

**AMERICAN DIABETES ASSOC.**
    **LOUISIANA AFFILIATE, INC**
9420 Lindale, Ste. B
Baton Rouge, LA 70815
Telephone: (504) 927-7732
FAX: (504) 927-7736
Industry Affiliation: Associations: Health
    Groups
**Publication(s):**
*Triangle, The*
Day Published: q.
Mtls Deadline: 10th of Jan., Apr., July, Oct.
Personnel: Roberta M. Madden

3938

**AMERICAN EXPRESS CO.**
American Express Tower, 200 Vessey St.
New York, NY 10285-4895
Telephone: (212) 640-2000
Industry Affiliation: Finance, Services
**Publication(s):**
*Dateline International*
Day Published: m.
Spec. Requirements: 6-8 pg.; offset
    magazine 2/c; 84 x 11
Personnel: Fran Aller Goldstein, Editor

5361

**AMERICAN FAMILY INSURANCE**
    **GROUP**
6000 American Pkwy.
Madison, WI 53783
Telephone: (608) 249-2111
FAX: (608) 249-0100
Industry Affiliation: Insurance
**Publication(s):**
*All American*
Day Published: m.
Lead Time: 6 wks.
Mtls Deadline: 15th of mo.
Contact: Pub. Rels.
Spec. Requirements: 12-16 pg.; offset
    news-magazine; 8 1/2 x 11
Personnel: Drew Lawrence, Editor

*Family Album*
Day Published: q.
Lead Time: 6 wks.
Mtls Deadline: 15th of mo.
Contact: Corp. Comms.
    P.O. Box 7430
    Madison, WI 53707
Spec. Requirements: 20 pg. offset news
    mag. to employees 8 1/2 x 11
Personnel: Mary Vertacic, Editor
    Shirley A. Baumann, Associate
        Editor

*American Times*
Day Published: m.
Lead Time: 3 wks.
Mtls Deadline: 15th of prior mo.
Contact: Corporate Communications
Spec. Requirements: tabloid for employees
Personnel: Julie S. Minix
    Mark Inciong
    Mary Bigus
    Glenn C. Harrison, Editor

5218

**AMERICAN GAS ASSOCIATION**
1515 Wilson Blvd.
Arlington, VA 22209
Telephone: (703) 841-8400
FAX: (703) 841-8687
Industry Affiliation: Petroleum, Gas
**Publication(s):**
*American Gas*
Day Published: 10/yr.
Lead Time: 1st of mo.
Spec. Requirements: 40-page; offset
    magazine; 84 x 112
Personnel: Lois Whetzel, Editor

2992

**AMERICAN GENERAL FINANCE**
601 N.W. Second St.
Evansville, IN 47708
Telephone: (812) 424-8031
Industry Affiliation: Finance, Services
**Publication(s):**
*A. G. Focus*
Day Published: q.
Lead Time: 2 mos. prior to pub. date
Mtls Deadline: 2 mos. prior to issue date
Contact: Public Relations
Spec. Requirements: 8-16 pg.; offset; 84 x
    11
Personnel: Barry Roberts, Editor

2590

**AMERICAN GENERAL**
    **LIFE/ACCIDENT INSURANCE**
    **CO.**
American General Center
Mail Code 0365
Nashville, TN 37250
Telephone: (615) 749-1264
FAX: (615) 749-1264
Industry Affiliation: Insurance
**Publication(s):**
*In General*
Day Published: bi-w.
Lead Time: 4 wks.
Mtls Deadline: 8th of mo.
Contact: Home Office
Spec. Requirements: 4-6 pages 11 x 14
Personnel: Mitch Petroff, Editor

*Field Focus*
Day Published: m.
Materials: 01,03,04,08,09,10,11,12,13,14,
    15,17,29
Contact: Sales Promotion
Spec. Requirements: 16-20 pages; offset;
    8 1/2 x 11
Personnel: Karen Shanks, Editor in Chief
    Ian Campbell, Editor

4289

**AMERICAN GREETINGS CORP.**
10500 American Rd.
Cleveland, OH 44144
Telephone: (216) 252-7300
FAX: (216) 252-6979
Industry Affiliation: Paper Products
**Publication(s):**
*Spectrum*
Day Published: bi-m.
Lead Time: 3 wks. prior to pub. date
Mtls Deadline: 3 wks. prior to pub. date
Personnel: Barbara Rook, Publication
    Director
    Patricia Dowd, Editor

2507

**AMERICAN HEALTH CARE**
    **ASSOCIATION**
1201 L St., N.W.
Washington, DC 20005
Telephone: (202) 842-4444
FAX: (202) 842-3860
Industry Affiliation: Associations: Health
    Groups
**Publication(s):**
*Provider*
Day Published: m.
Lead Time: 3 mos. prior to pub. date
Mtls Deadline: 3 mos. prior the pub. date
Contact: Editorial Department
Spec. Requirements: 52 pg.; web; 8 1/2 x
    11
Personnel: Marla F. Gold, Editor

*A H C A notes*
Day Published: m.
Lead Time: 2 wks. prior to pub. date
Mtls Deadline: 2 wks. prior to pub. date
Contact: Editorial Services
Personnel: Marla F. Gold

3754

**AMERICAN HEART ASSOCIATION**
4643 Lindell Blvd.
St. Louis, MO 63108
Telephone: (314) 367-3383
Industry Affiliation: Associations: Health
    Groups
**Publication(s):**
*Heart To Heart*
Day Published: 3/yr.
Personnel: Mike McLaughlin, Editor

*Report To The Community*
Day Published: a.
Personnel: Mike McLaughlin, Editor

2508

**AMERICAN HELICOPTER**
    **SOCIETY, INC.**
217 N. Washington St.
Alexandria, VA 22314
Telephone: (703) 684-6777
FAX: (703) 739-9279
Industry Affiliation: Associations: Trade,
    Fraternal
**Publication(s):**
*Vertiflite Magazine*
Day Published: bi-m.
Lead Time: 2 mos. prior to pub. date
Mtls Deadline: 6 wks. prior to 1st day of
    issue mo.
Spec. Requirements: 80 pgs.; coated
    stock; 8 1/2 x 11
Personnel: L. Kim Smith, Editor

*Journal-American Helicopter Society*
Day Published: q.
Lead Time: 3 mos. prior to pub. date
Personnel: Walter W. Bacak, Jr.
    Christopher R. Colligan, Editor
    David A. Peters
    Jing G. Yen

68613

**AMERICAN HOECHST CORP.**
Rte. 202-206
Somerville, NJ 08876
Telephone: (908) 231-2735
Industry Affiliation: Chemicals, Plastics
**Publication(s):**
*Reporter Magazine*
Day Published: q.
Personnel: Mary Nowicki, Editor

3940

**AMERICAN HOME PRODUCTS**
685 Third Ave.
New York, NY 10017
Telephone: (212) 878-5000
Industry Affiliation: Drugs, Cosmetics,
    Pharmaceuticals
**Publication(s):**
*A H P vista*
Day Published: q.
Lead Time: 1 mo. prior to pub. date
Contact: Industrial Relations Dept.
Spec. Requirements: 16 pg.; offset; 8 1/2
    x 11
Personnel: Craig Porter, Editor

2061

**AMERICAN HONDA MOTOR CO.,**
    **INC.**
1919 Torrance Blvd.
Torrance, CA 90501
Telephone: (310) 783-3171
FAX: (310) 783-3622
Industry Affiliation: Autos, Trucks
**Publication(s):**
*Mighty To Mini News*
Day Published: m.
Spec. Requirements: 12 pg.; offset; 8 1/2
    x 11
Personnel: Robert H. Murphy, Editor

3941

**AMERICAN INTERNATIONAL**
    **GROUP, INC.**
70 Pine St.
New York, NY 10270
Telephone: (212) 770-6037
Industry Affiliation: Insurance
**Publication(s):**
*Contact Magazine*
Day Published: bi-m.
Lead Time: 12 wks.
Spec. Requirements: 24-pg.; offset
    magazine; 8 1/2 x 11
Personnel: Shawn Armstrong, Editor

2981

**AMERICAN LEGION AUXILIARY**
777 N. Meridian St., Third Flr.
Indianapolis, IN 46204
Telephone: (317) 635-6291
FAX: (317) 636-5590
Industry Affiliation: Associations: Trade,
    Fraternal

---

**Materials Accepted/Included:** 01-Business news 02-By-line articles 03-Fashion news 04-Food news 05-Freelance copy 06-Letters to editor 07-Real estate news 08-Sports news 09-Travel news
10-Book rev. 11-Movie rev. 12-Music rev. 13-TV rev. 14-Theater rev. 15-Coming events 16-Obituaries 17-Question & answer 18-Social announcements 19-Artwork 20-Cartoons 21-Photos 22-TV listings
23-Audio rec. 24-Video rec. 25-Books 26-Films/film clips 27-Personnel news 28-Press releases 29-New product news/photos 30-Trade lit. 31-Contracts awarded 32-Display adv. 33-Classified adv.

11-5

**Publication(s):**
*National News*
Day Published: bi-m.
Lead Time: 2 mos. prior to pub. date
Mtls Deadline: 45 days prior to issue mo.
Contact: National News
Spec. Requirements: 32 pg.; web press 8
   1/8 x 10 7/8 trim size
Personnel: Lauralyn T. Mohr, Editor

2008
**AMERICAN LUNG ASSOCIATION
OF ALABAMA**
900 S. 18th St.
Birmingham, AL 35205
Telephone: (205) 933-8821
FAX: (205) 930-1717
Mailing Address:
   P.O. Box 55209
   Birmingham, AL 35255
Industry Affiliation: Associations: Health
   Groups
**Publication(s):**
*Southern Air*
Day Published: q.
Lead Time: 3 wks. prior to pub. date
Spec. Requirements: 8-16 pg.; offset; 8
   1/2 x 11
Personnel: Laura L. Vann, Editor
         Karen Greene, Art Director
         Pamela Thomas,
            Communications Assistant

2660
**AMERICAN LUNG ASSOCIATION
OF GEORGIA**
2452 Spring Rd.
Smyrna, GA 30080
Telephone: (404) 434-5864
Industry Affiliation: Associations: Health
   Groups
**Publication(s):**
*Breathtaking News*
Day Published: q.
Lead Time: 30 days prior to pub. date
Mtls Deadline: 30 days prior to pub. date
Spec. Requirements: 6-12 pg.; offset; 84 x
   11
Personnel: Eloise Thomas, Editor

*Ala Of Georgia Annual Report*
Day Published: a.
Lead Time: 60 days prior to pub. date
Contact: Comm. Dept.
Personnel: Eloise Thomas, Editor

*Team Tidbits*
Day Published: m.
Mtls Deadline: 1st of mo. prior to pub. date
Contact: Comm. Dept.
Personnel: Eloise Thomas, Editor

4914
**AMERICAN LUNG ASSOCIATION
OF TEXAS**
3520 Executive Center Dr., Ste. G-100
Austin, TX 78731
Telephone: (512) 343-0502
Mailing Address:
   P.O. Box 26460
   Austin, TX 78755
Industry Affiliation: Associations: Health
   Groups
**Publication(s):**
*Advocate*
Day Published: q.
Lead Time: 2 mos.
Spec. Requirements: 4 pg. 11 x 17
Personnel: Lisa Kerth, Editor

3075
**AMERICAN MUTUAL LIFE
INSURANCE CO.**
418 Sixth Ave.
Des Moines, IA 50309-2499
Telephone: (515) 280-1331
FAX: (515) 280-3908
Industry Affiliation: Insurance

**Publication(s):**
*American Eagle*
Day Published: m.
Lead Time: 1 mo. prior to pub. date
Mtls Deadline: 1st of mo. prior to pub. mo.
Spec. Requirements: 20 pg.; offset
   magazine; 8 1/2 x 11
Personnel: Linda Knodle, Editor

4915
**AMERICAN NATIONAL
INSURANCE CO.**
One Moody Plz.
Galveston, TX 77550
Telephone: (409) 763-4661
Industry Affiliation: Insurance
**Publication(s):**
*Star Bulletin*
Day Published: q.
Spec. Requirements: 50-80 pgs.; offset; 84
   x 11
Personnel: Judith A. Baxter, Editor

*A N I C O*
Day Published: m.
Spec. Requirements: 36-44-page
Personnel: Judith A. Baxter, Editor

3260
**AMERICAN OCCUPATIONAL
THERAPY ASSOCIATION**
1383 Piccard Dr.
Rockville, MD 20850-4375
Telephone: (301) 948-9626
FAX: (301) 948-5512
Mailing Address:
   P.O. Box 1725
   Rockville, MD 20850
Industry Affiliation: Hospitals
**Publication(s):**
*O T week*
Day Published: w.
Lead Time: 6 wks. prior to pub. date
Mtls Deadline: 6 wks. prior to pub. date
Contact: Public Affairs
         164 Rollins Ave.
         Ste. 301
         Rockville, MD 20852-4043
Spec. Requirements: 56-116 pg.; 8-1/2 x
   11; offset
Personnel: Bruce Tapper, Editor

*American Journal Of Occupational Therapy*
Day Published: m.
Lead Time: 8 wks. prior to pub. date
Mtls Deadline: 6 wks. prior to pub. date
Contact: Communications
         1383 Picard Dr.
         P.O. Box 1725
         Rockville, MD 20850-4375
Spec. Requirements: 8-1/8 x 11; offset;
   perfect bound
Personnel: Elaine Viseltear, Editor
         Jennifer Jones, Managing Editor

4632
**AMERICAN OLEAN TILE CO.**
1000 Cannon Ave.
Lansdale, PA 19446
Telephone: (215) 393-2705
FAX: (215) 393-2784
Industry Affiliation: Cement, Ceramics, Clay
**Publication(s):**
*Open Line*
Day Published: q.
Mtls Deadline: 15th of preceding mo.
Contact: Ceramic Tile Div.
         4100 First Int'l. Bldg.
         Dallas, TX 75270
Spec. Requirements: offset tabloid; 8 1/2 x
   11
Personnel: Susan Van Voorhees, Editor

*Gazette*
Day Published: q.
Mtls Deadline: 15th of mo. prior to pub.
Contact: Ceramic Tile Div.
Spec. Requirements: offset tabloid; 8 1/2 x
   11
Personnel: Susan Van Voorhees
         Sara Robins

68611
**AMERICAN PHILOSOPHICAL
SOCIETY**
104 S. Fifth St.
Philadelphia, PA 19106
Telephone: (215) 440-3427
FAX: (215) 440-3450
Industry Affiliation: Colleges, Institutions,
   Science Research
**Publication(s):**
*American Philosophical Society Year Book*
Day Published: a.
Personnel: Carole LeFaivre

2510
**AMERICAN PHYSICAL THERAPY
ASSOCIATION, INC.**
1111 N. Fairfax St.
Alexandria, VA 22314
Telephone: (703) 684-2782
FAX: (703) 706-3169
Industry Affiliation: Associations: Trade,
   Fraternal
**Publication(s):**
*Physical Therapy*
Day Published: m.
Lead Time: 2 mos.
Materials: 32,33
Mtls Deadline: call for media kit
Spec. Requirements: Articles-Personal
   Experience-Interest-P.T. Clinic
Personnel: Julie Hilenberg, Editor
         Karin Quantrille, Managing
            Editor

*Pt-Magazine Of Physical Therapy*
Day Published: m.
Materials: 01,06,28,29,30,32
Mtls Deadline: call for media kit
Personnel: Jan P. Reynolds, Editor
         Ellen N. Woods, Editor
         Karin Quantrille, Managing
            Editor

69583
**AMERICAN PODIATRIC WRITERS
ASSOCIATION**
P.O. Box 50
Island Station
New York, NY 10044
Telephone: (212) 355-5216
FAX: (212) 486-7706
Industry Affiliation: Associations: Health
   Groups
**Publication(s):**
*American Podiatric Writers Association
   Newsletter*
Day Published: bi-m.
Personnel: Barry Block, Editor

5291
**AMERICAN PRODUCTION &
INVENTORY CONTROL SOCIETY
(APICS)**
500 W. Annandale Rd.
Falls Church, VA 22046
Telephone: (703) 237-8344
Industry Affiliation: Industry: Material
   Handling

**Publication(s):**
*Production And Inventory Management*
Day Published: q.
Lead Time: 6 mos. prior to pub. date
Mtls Deadline: 6 mos. prior to pub. date
Spec. Requirements: cir. 70,000
Personnel: David Strickland, Editor

2568
**AMERICAN ROAD &
TRANSPORTATION BUILDERS
ASSOCIATION**
501 School St., S.W.
Washington, DC 20024
Telephone: (202) 488-2722
Industry Affiliation: Industry: Heavy
   Construction, Machinery
**Publication(s):**
*Transportation Builder*
Day Published: bi-w.
Lead Time: 2 mos. prior to pub. date
Mtls Deadline: 2 mos. prior the pub. date
Spec. Requirements: 32-page; offset
   magazine; 8 1/2 x 11

*A R T B A newsletter*
Day Published: irreg.
Lead Time: 1 mo. prior to pub. date
Personnel: John Yago

*Membership Directory-Buyers Guide*
Day Published: a.
Lead Time: 3 mos. prior to pub. date
Mtls Deadline: 1 mo. prior to pub. date
Contact: Communication
Personnel: William Toohey, Jr.

4633
**AMERICAN SOCIETY OF CLU &
CHFC**
270 Bryn Mawr Ave.
Bryn Mawr, PA 19010
Telephone: (215) 526-2500
FAX: (215) 527-4010
Industry Affiliation: Insurance
**Publication(s):**
*Journal Of The American Society Of C L U
   & C H F C*
Day Published: bi-m.
Lead Time: 8 wks. prior to pub. date
Mtls Deadline: 2 mos. prior to issue date
Contact: publications dept.
Spec. Requirements: 72-pg.; offset
   magazine; 8 1/2 x 11
Personnel: Kenneth Black, Jr., Editor
         Deanne Sherman, Managing
            Editor
         John R. Driskill, Publisher

3943
**AMERICAN SOCIETY OF INTERIOR
DESIGNERS**
608 Massachusetts Ave., N.E.
Washington, DC 20002
Telephone: (202) 546-3480
FAX: (202) 546-3240
Industry Affiliation: Associations: Trade,
   Fraternal
**Publication(s):**
*A S I D report*
Day Published: bi-m.
Lead Time: 2 mos. prior to pub. date
Mtls Deadline: 2 mos. prior to pub. date
Contact: Communications Dept.
Spec. Requirements: 24 pg.; 8 1/2 x 11
Personnel: Joseph Pryweller, Editor

2063
**AMERICAN SOCIETY OF
INTERNAL MEDICINE**
2011 Pennsylvania Ave., N.W., Ste. 800
Washington, DC 20006-1808
Telephone: (202) 835-2746
Industry Affiliation: Associations: Health
   Groups

**Publication(s):**
*Internist: Health Policy In Practice*
Day Published: 10/yr.
Lead Time: 1st of mo.
Mtls Deadline: 45 days prior to pub. date
Spec. Requirements: 40-48 pages; offset;
8 1/2 X 10 7/8
Personnel: C. Burns Roehrig, M.D., Medical
Editor
Diana L. Madden, Managing
Editor

69380

## AMERICAN SOCIETY OF MAGAZINE PHOTOGRAPHERS
14 Washington Rd., Ste. 502
Princeton Junction, NJ 08550-1033
Telephone: (212) 889-9144
Industry Affiliation: Photography
**Publication(s):**
*Bulletin*
Day Published: m.
Materials: 01,02,10,21,28,32,33
Personnel: Peter Skinner, Editor in Chief
Cilla Skinner, Production
Manager

2836

## AMERICAN STORES CO.
P.O. Box 27447
Salt Lake City, UT 84127-0447
Industry Affiliation: Retail Stores
**Publication(s):**
*Flashes*
Day Published: w.
Spec. Requirements: 16-20-page; offset
magazine; 7 x 84
Personnel: Virginia Novinger, Editor

*Marketeer*
Day Published: w.
Spec. Requirements: 6-page
Personnel: A.C. Haberichter, Editor

*Pace 55*
Day Published: m.
Spec. Requirements: 8-page
Personnel: Angela Gram, Editor

3944

## AMERICAN TELEPHONE & TELEGRAPH CO.
295 N. Maple Ave.
Basking Ridge, NJ 07920
Telephone: (908) 221-2000
Industry Affiliation: Utility: Telephone
**Publication(s):**
*F Y I*
Day Published: w.
Contact: Gus Merkel
Spec. Requirements: 4-page
Personnel: John A. Krug, Editor

2982

## AMERICAN UNITED LIFE INSURANCE COMPANY
One American Sq.
Indianapolis, IN 46204
Telephone: (317) 263-1877
FAX: (317) 263-1979
Mailing Address:
P.O. Box 368
Indianapolis, IN 46206-0368
Industry Affiliation: Insurance
**Publication(s):**
*A U L News*
Day Published: bi-m.
Lead Time: 2 wks. prior to pub. date
Materials: 01,30
Contact: Corporate Communications
Spec. Requirements: 12-16 pg.; 8-1/2 x 11
Personnel: Amber D. Gray, Editor
Stephanie B. Vare, Editor

*What's Going On*
Day Published: w.
Lead Time: 2 days prior to pub. date
Materials: 15,28,30
Mtls Deadline: Mon., 12:00pm
Contact: Corporate Communications
Spec. Requirements: 2 sided/typeset in-
house/8-1/2 x 14 bi-fold
Personnel: S. Eric Freeman
Deborah A. King, Editor

68438

## AMERICAN VOLKSSPORT ASSOCIATION
1001 Pat Booker Rd., Ste. 101
Universal City, TX 78148-4147
Telephone: (210) 659-2112
FAX: (210) 659-1212
Industry Affiliation: Associations: Health
Groups
**Publication(s):**
*American Wanderer, The*
Day Published: bi-m.
Lead Time: 60 days prior to pub. date
Materials: 02,04,05,06,08,09,15,19,20,21,
24,25,28,29,32
Mtls Deadline: 1st of mo. prior to issue mo.
Personnel: Sandra Ward, Editor

*Ava Checkpoint*
Day Published: m.
Lead Time: 15 days prior to pub. date
Mtls Deadline: 15th of mo. prior to pub.
date
Personnel: Sandra Ward, Editor

2576

## AMERICAN WATER SKI ASSOCIATION
799 Overlook Drive
Winter Haven, FL 33884
Telephone: (813) 324-4341
FAX: (813) 325-8259
Industry Affiliation: Associations: Trade,
Fraternal
**Publication(s):**
*Water Skier, The*
Day Published: 7/yr.
Lead Time: 8 wks.
Materials: 08,28,29,30,32,33
Spec. Requirements: 80-page; offset
magazine; 64 x 92
Personnel: Greg Nixon, Editor
Don Cullimore, Editor in Chief
Heidi Ingram, Production
Manager
Dan Hargroves, Marketing
Director

69441

## AMERICAN WATER WORKS ASSOCIATION
6666 W. Quincy Ave.
Denver, CO 80235
Telephone: (303) 794-7711
Industry Affiliation: Utility: Water
**Publication(s):**
*Waterweek*
Day Published: bi-w.
Spec. Requirements: news and analysis of
the drinking water industry
Personnel: Mark Scharfenaker, Editor

66460

## AMERICA WEST AIRLINES
4000 E. Sky Harbor Blvd.
Phoenix, AZ 85034
Telephone: (602) 693-5729
FAX: (602) 693-5546
Industry Affiliation: Airlines
**Publication(s):**
*Aware*
Day Published: m.
Lead Time:
Mtls Deadline: 1 mo. prior to pub. date
Contact: Corporate Communications
Personnel: Janet Conrad, Editor

*Employees Are The First To Know*
Day Published: irreg.
Contact: Corporate Communications

*Trader*
Day Published: m.
Lead Time: 2 wks. prior to pub. date
Materials: 32,33
Mtls Deadline: last Fri. of mo. prior to pub.
date
Contact: Corporate Communications
Spec. Requirements: classified & display
adv.
Personnel: Janet Conrad, Editor

*Executive Report*
Day Published: irreg.
Contact: Corporate Communications

*Between Aware*
Contact: Corporate Communications

*Aware View*
Contact: Corporate Communications

68518

## AMERON, INC.
245 Los Robles Ave.
Pasadena, CA 91101-2894
Telephone: (818) 683-4000
FAX: (818) 683-4060
Mailing Address:
P.O. Box 7007
Pasadena, CA 91109
Industry Affiliation: Associations: Trade,
Fraternal
**Publication(s):**
*Ameron News*
Day Published: q.
Materials: 21,27,28,29,31
Contact: Communications & Public Affairs
Personnel: Dan Strachner, Editor
Christina Lucio, Editor
Jeanne Daleo, Production
Manager

52331

## AMOCO CORPORATION
P.O. Box 87703
Chicago, IL 60680
Telephone: (312) 856-6111
Industry Affiliation: Petroleum, Gas
**Publication(s):**
*Merchandiser*
Day Published: q.
Personnel: Neil Geary, Editor

4634

## AMP INC., VALLEY FORGE
P.O. Box 3608
Harrisburg, PA 17105
Telephone: (215) 647-6060
Industry Affiliation: Electrical, Electronic,
Manufacturing
**Publication(s):**
*Contact Video*
Day Published: q.
Lead Time: 6 wks.
Spec. Requirements: 20-28 pqs.; offset; 8
1/2 x 11
Personnel: Robert Costello, Audiovis. Spvr.

4789

## AMSCO AMERICAN STERILIZER CO.
2424 W. 23rd St.
Erie, PA 16506
Telephone: (814) 452-3100
Industry Affiliation: Office Equipment,
Services, Supplies

**Publication(s):**
*Doin' It*
Day Published: m.
Lead Time: 60 days
Spec. Requirements: 16-pgs.; offset; 8 1/2
x 11
Personnel: Kevin Marsh, Editor

5338

## AMTRAK
60 Massachusetts Ave. N.E.
Washington, DC 20002
Telephone: (202) 906-3000
Industry Affiliation: Railroads
**Publication(s):**
*Amtrak Times*
Day Published: m.
Lead Time: 3 wks.
Mtls Deadline: 15th of mo. prior to pub.
date
Spec. Requirements: 12-pgs.; offset; 11 x
17
Personnel: Janice W. Irwin, Managing
Editor

2066

## ANAHEIM MEMORIAL HOSPITAL
1111 W. LaPalma Ave
Anaheim, CA 92801
Telephone: (714) 774-1450
Industry Affiliation: Hospitals
**Publication(s):**
*Looking In*
Day Published: q.
Mtls Deadline: Aug. lst prior to pub. date
Spec. Requirements: 24 pg.; offset; 8 1/2
x 11
Personnel: Dorothy Coleman, Editor

3313

## ANALOG DEVICES, INC.
One Technology Way
Norwood, MA 02062
Telephone: (617) 461-3392
Mailing Address:
P.O. Box 9106
Norwood, MA 02062
Industry Affiliation: Electrical, Electronic,
Manufacturing
**Publication(s):**
*News Circuit*
Day Published: bi-m.
Lead Time: 2 wks. prior to pub. date
Mtls Deadline: 2 wks.
Contact: Communications
24 Wilson Way
Westwood, MA 02090
Spec. Requirements: 12-20 pg.; offset; 8 x
11
Personnel: Susan Loffredo, Editor

*Analog Dialogue*
Day Published: q.
Lead Time: 10 wks.
Mtls Deadline: 10 wks.
Contact: Technical Communications
Spec. Requirements: 24-36 pp., 8 1/2 x
11, 4 color process
Personnel: Daniel H. Sheingold

*Analog Briefings*
Day Published: q.
Lead Time: 8 wks.
Mtls Deadline: 10 wks.
Contact: Technical Publicity Dept.
Spec. Requirements: up to 10 pages; 2
color only
Personnel: Mark Logan
Pamela Whittaker

3541

## ANDERSEN CORP.
100 Fourth Ave., N.
Bayport, MN 55003
Telephone: (612) 439-5150
Industry Affiliation: Glass

Materials Accepted/Included: 01-Business news 02-By-line articles 03-Fashion news 04-Food news 05-Freelance copy 06-Letters to editor 07-Real estate news 08-Sports news 09-Travel news
10-Book rev. 11-Movie rev. 12-Music rev. 13-TV rev. 14-Theater rev. 15-Coming events 16-Obituaries 17-Question & answer 18-Social announcements 19-Artwork 20-Cartoons 21-Photos 22-TV listings
23-Audio rec. 24-Video rec. 25-Books 26-Films/film clips 27-Personnel news 28-Press releases 29-New product news/photos 30-Trade lit. 31-Contracts awarded 32-Display adv. 33-Classified adv.

11-7

**Publication(s):**
*Frame Maker*
Day Published: bi-w.
Lead Time: 2 wks.
Spec. Requirements: 4-pg.; letterpress
　bulletin; 7 x 9
Personnel: John Palmer, Editor

*Andersen Insights*
Day Published: bi-m.
Lead Time: 4 wks.
Personnel: Steve Sherod

4792
**ANDRITZ-SPROUT-BAUER, INC.**
Sherman St.
Muncy, PA 17756
Telephone: (717) 546-8211
FAX: (717) 546-1306
Industry Affiliation: Industry: Heavy
　Construction, Machinery
**Publication(s):**
*Better Fibers; Pointers For Profits*
Day Published: q.
Spec. Requirements: 4-8 pgs.; offset; 8
　1/2 x 11
Personnel: Gary Staggs, Editor

3663
**ANHEUSER-BUSCH COMPANIES,**
　**INC.**
One Busch Pl.
Saint Louis, MO 63118
Telephone: (314) 577-4012
FAX: (314) 577-4013
Industry Affiliation: Brewers, Distillers
**Publication(s):**
*Focus On St. Louis*
Day Published: m.
Contact: Corporate Communications
　　　　721 Pestalozzi St
　　　　Saint Louis, MO 63118
Spec. Requirements: 12-pg.; offset; 8 1/2
　x 11
Personnel: Dave Lange, Editor

*Anheuser-Busch Eagle*
Day Published: bi-m.
Contact: Corporate Communications
Spec. Requirements: 12 pg.
Personnel: Bill Mueller, Editor

*Team Talk*
Day Published: bi-m.
Spec. Requirements: 24 pg.
Personnel: Carol Warner, Editor

3526
**ANR PIPELINE CO.**
500 Renaissance Ctr.
Detroit, MI 48243
Telephone: (313) 496-5079
Industry Affiliation: Petroleum, Gas
**Publication(s):**
*Transmission Lines*
Day Published: bi-m.
Lead Time: 4 mos.
Spec. Requirements: 28-pg.; offset; 11 x 8
　1/2
Personnel: Martha Roemer Kurtz, Editor

68409
**APACHE CORPORATION**
2000 Post Oak Blvd.
Houston, TX 77056-4400
Telephone: (713) 296-6000
Industry Affiliation: Petroleum, Gas
**Publication(s):**
*Arrows*
Day Published: bi-m.
Mtls Deadline: varies
Personnel: Melissa Reynolds, Editor

*Apache Corp., Annual Report*
Day Published: a.
Personnel: Jeanne Buchanan

3543
**APOGEE ENTERPRISES, INC.**
7900 Xerxes Ave. S., Ste. 1800
Minneapolis, MN 55431
Telephone: (612) 835-1874
Industry Affiliation: Glass
**Publication(s):**
*Apogee Highlites*
Day Published: q.
Lead Time: 1 mo.
Mtls Deadline: 5 wks. prior to pub. date
Spec. Requirements: 12-16 pgs.; offset; 8
　1/2 x 11
Personnel: Marcia Parle, Editor

5220
**APPALACHIAN POWER CO.**
40 Franklin Rd., S.W.
Roanoke, VA 24011
Telephone: (703) 985-2300
Mailing Address:
　P.O. Box 2021
　Roanoke, VA 24022
Industry Affiliation: Utility: Electric
**Publication(s):**
*Illuminator*
Day Published: m.
Lead Time: 3 wks. prior to pub. date
Mtls Deadline: 3 wks. prior to pub. date
Spec. Requirements: 14-page; offset
　newspaper; 114 x 16
Personnel: Betty Lou Carter, Editor

5363
**APPLETON MILLS**
2100 N. Ballard Rd.
Appleton, WI 54911
Telephone: (414) 734-9876
Mailing Address:
　P.O. Box 1899
　Appleton, WI 54913
Industry Affiliation: Paper Products
**Publication(s):**
*Horizons*
Day Published: q.
Spec. Requirements: 6-pg.; offset; 8 1/2 x
　11

3281
**APPLIED PHYSICS LABORATORY**
Johns Hopkins Rd.
Laurel, MD 20707
Telephone: (301) 953-5225
Industry Affiliation: Colleges, Institutions,
　Science Research
**Publication(s):**
*Apl News*
Day Published: m.
Lead Time: 1 wk.
Mtls Deadline: 15th of mo.
Spec. Requirements: 8 pg.; offset; 8 1/2 x
　11
Personnel: John Wilhelm, Editor
　　　　Helen Worth, Managing Editor

2068
**APPLIED TECHNOLOGY**
4747 Hellyer Ave.
San Jose, CA 95138
Telephone: (408) 365-4747
Industry Affiliation: Electrical, Electronic,
　Manufacturing
**Publication(s):**
*Image*
Day Published: bi-m.
Spec. Requirements: 8-12 pgs.; offset
　magazine; 8 1/2 x 11
Personnel: Judy Horst, Editor
　　　　Joan Powell, Managing Editor

*Instant Items*
Day Published: w.
Lead Time: 1 day prior to pub. date
Mtls Deadline: Mon. prior to pub. date
Contact: ATD

68393
**APPLIED TECHNOLOGY COUNCIL**
555 Twin Dolphin Dr., Ste. 550
Redwood City, CA 94065
Telephone: (510) 595-1542
FAX: (415) 593-2320
Industry Affiliation: Architects, Engineers,
　Business Service
**Publication(s):**
*Atc News Bulletin*
Day Published: 2-4/yr.
Personnel: Patty Christofferson

4635
**ARA SERVICES INC.**
1101 Market St.
Philadelphia, PA 19107
Telephone: (215) 238-3320
Industry Affiliation: Finance, Services
**Publication(s):**
*Ara News*
Day Published: 8/yr.
Lead Time: 6 wks.
Spec. Requirements: 8 pg.; offset
　newspaper; 11 x 14
Personnel: John Gribbin, Editor

3946
**ARCATA GRAPHICS CORP.**
TC Industrial Pk.
Depew, NY 14043
Telephone: (716) 686-2500
Mailing Address:
　P.O. Box 90
　Depew, NY 14043
Industry Affiliation: Printers, Services
**Publication(s):**
*Arcatagraph*
Day Published: q.
Lead Time: 20 days
Mtls Deadline: 15th of mo. prior to pub.
　date
Contact: Arcata Graphics-Buffalo
Spec. Requirements: 8-12 pg.; magazine; 8
　1/2 x 11
Personnel: Denise Hauser, Editor

5031
**ARC, NATIONAL HEADQUARTERS**
500 E. Border St., 3rd Fl.
Arlington, TX 76010
Telephone: (817) 261-6003
FAX: (817) 277-3491
Mailing Address:
　P.O. Box 1047
　Arlington, TX 76004
Industry Affiliation: Associations: Health
　Groups
**Publication(s):**
*Arc Today*
Day Published: bi-m.
Lead Time: 90 days prior to pub. date
Mtls Deadline: 60 days prior to pub. date
Spec. Requirements: Typewritten copy;
　black-and-white photos
Personnel: Dick Collier, Editor

*Government Report*
Day Published: s-m.

2071
**ARCO**
515 S. Flower
Los Angeles, CA 90071
Telephone: (213) 486-3511
Mailing Address:
　Box 2679-TA
　Los Angeles, CA 90051
Industry Affiliation: Petroleum, Gas

**Publication(s):**
*Spark, The*
Day Published: m.
Lead Time: 6 wks. prior to pub. date
Mtls Deadline: 6 wks. prior to pub. date,
　2nd Fri. of mo.
Contact: Corp. Human Res.
Spec. Requirements: 20 pg.; offset; 8 1/2
　x 11
Personnel: Wally Conger, Editor

2010
**ARIZONA AUTOMOBILE**
　**ASSOCIATION**
3144 N. 7th Ave.
Phoenix, AZ 85013
Telephone: (602) 274-1116
FAX: (602) 277-1194
Mailing Address:
　P.O. Box 33119
　Phoenix, AZ 85067
Industry Affiliation: Autos, Trucks
**Publication(s):**
*Aaa Highroads*
Day Published: bi-m.
Lead Time: 12 wks.
Materials: 05,09,21
Mtls Deadline: 12 wks.
Spec. Requirements: 40-pg.; offset
　magazine; 8 1/2 x 11; four color
Personnel: Pamela Heck, Editor

2012
**ARIZONA PUBLIC SERVICE CO.**
400 N. 5th St., Ste. 8528
Phoenix, AZ 85004
Telephone: (602) 250-2251
Mailing Address:
　P.O. Box 53999, Station 8528
　Phoenix, AZ 85072
Industry Affiliation: Utility: Electric
**Publication(s):**
*Connections*
Day Published: m.
Personnel: Lynne Adams, Editor

2045
**ARKANSAS DEPARTMENT OF**
　**PARKS & TOURISM**
One Capitol Mall
Little Rock, AR 72201
Telephone: (501) 682-7777
FAX: (501) 682-1364
Industry Affiliation: Associations: City,
　State, Federal
**Publication(s):**
*News From Arkansas, The Natural State*
Day Published: q.
Lead Time: 2 mos. prior to pub. date
Materials: 01,09,15,21,28,29,30
Mtls Deadline: Mar. 1, May 15, Sep. 1,
　Dec. 1
Personnel: Tyler Hardeman, Editor

2046
**ARKANSAS FARM BUREAU**
　**FEDERATION**
10720 Kanis
Little Rock, AR 72211
Telephone: (501) 224-4400
Mailing Address:
　P.O. Box 31
　Little Rock, AR 72203
Industry Affiliation: Associations: Trade,
　Fraternal

Materials Accepted/Included: 01-Business news 02-By-line articles 03-Fashion news 04-Food news 05-Freelance copy 06-Letters to editor 07-Real estate news 08-Sports news 09-Travel news 10-Book rev. 11-Movie rev. 12-Music rev. 13-TV rev. 14-Theater rev. 15-Coming events 16-Obituaries 17-Question & answer 18-Social announcements 19-Artwork 20-Cartoons 21-Photos 22-TV listings 23-Audio rec. 24-Video rec. 25-Books 26-Films/film clips 27-Personnel news 28-Press releases 29-New product news/photos 30-Trade lit. 31-Contracts awarded 32-Display adv. 33-Classified adv.

**Publication(s):**
*Farm Bureau Press*
Day Published: m.
Lead Time: 1 mo. prior to pub. date
Mtls Deadline: 1 mo. prior to pub. date
Contact: Editor
Spec. Requirements: 20 pg.; offset; 9 3/8 x 12 1/2
Personnel: A. Audie Ayer, Editor

69697

## ARKANSAS INDUSTRIAL DEVELOPMENT COMMISSION
One Capitol Mall, 4C - 300
Little Rock, AR 72201
Telephone: (501) 682-5154
FAX: (501) 682-7341
Industry Affiliation: Associations: City, State, Federal
**Publication(s):**
*A I D C Report*
Day Published: bi-m.
Lead Time: 1 mo. prior the pub. date
Materials: 28,29
Mtls Deadline: 1 mo. prior the pub. date
Contact: Communications Section
Spec. Requirements: black & white only
Personnel: H.K. Stewart, Editor

2050

## ARKANSAS POWER & LIGHT CO.
P.O. Box 551
Little Rock, AR 72203
Telephone: (501) 377-4000
Industry Affiliation: Utility: Electric
**Publication(s):**
*On Magazine*
Day Published: m.
Lead Time: 10 days prior to pub. date
Mtls Deadline: 5th & 20th of mo.
Spec. Requirements: 8 pg.; offset; 11 x 15 tabloid
Personnel: Kelle Barfield, Editor

69570

## ARKANSAS PRESS ASSOCIATION
1701 Broadway
Little Rock, AR 72206-1249
Telephone: (501) 374-1500
FAX: (501) 374-7509
Industry Affiliation: Associations: Trade, Fraternal
**Publication(s):**
*A P A Member Bulletin*
Day Published: w.
Personnel: Dennis Schick, Editor

5281

## ARLINGTON HOSPITAL
1701 N. George Mason Dr.
Arlington, VA 22205
Telephone: (703) 558-5000
FAX: (703) 276-9854
Industry Affiliation: Hospitals
**Publication(s):**
*Healthreach*
Day Published: q.
Lead Time: 2 mos. prior to pub. date
Mtls Deadline: 1st of mo. prior to pub. date
Contact: Public Affairs Office
Spec. Requirements: 2 pages

68615

## ARMSTRONG WORLD INDUSTRIES
P.O. Box 3001
Lancaster, PA 17604
Telephone: (717) 396-4398
FAX: (717) 396-4598
Industry Affiliation: Industry: Light Tools, Equipment
**Publication(s):**
*Armstrong Today*
Day Published: q.
Lead Time: 1 mo.
Mtls Deadline: 1 mo. prior to pub. date
Personnel: Joseph DiSanto, Editor in Chief

*Dateline*
Day Published: q.
Lead Time: 1 mo.
Mtls Deadline: 1 mo. prior to pub. date
Personnel: Joseph DiSanto, Editor in Chief

*Talking Points*
Day Published: q.
Lead Time: 1 mo.
Mtls Deadline: 1 mo. prior to pub. date
Personnel: Joseph DiSanto, Editor in Chief

4919

## ARMY & AIR FORCE EXCHANGE SERVICE
3911 S. Walton Walker Blvd.
Dallas, TX 75266
Telephone: (214) 312-2763
Mailing Address:
　P.O. Box 660202 (PA-I)
　Dallas, TX 75266
Industry Affiliation: Associations: City, State, Federal
**Publication(s):**
*Exchange Post, The*
Day Published: bi-m.
Lead Time: 2 mos. prior to pub. date
Mtls Deadline: 10th of mo. prior to pub. date
Contact: Pub. Affrs. Div.
Spec. Requirements: 28 pg.; offset newspaper; 11 1/2 x 17 1/2
Personnel: Nancy Pantusa, Editor
　　　　　Fred Bluhm, Editor

68548

## ARNOLD BAKERS, INC.
12 Hamilton Ave.
Greenwich, CT 06830
Telephone: (203) 531-2000
FAX: (203) 531-2345
Industry Affiliation: Bakery Products
**Publication(s):**
*Breadwinner*
Day Published: q.
Lead Time: 5 days prior to pub. date
Mtls Deadline: 5 days prior to pub. date
Personnel: Ann Scott, Editor

68580

## ARTHUR BROWN & BROS., INC.
Two W. 46th St.
New York, NY 10036
Telephone: (212) 575-5555
FAX: (212) 575-5825
Industry Affiliation: Publishers, Books, Magazines
**Publication(s):**
*Pen Catalog*
Day Published: a.
Contact: Advertiser
Personnel: Norman Adler

3169

## ASHLAND OIL, INC.
1000 Ashland Dr.
Russell, KY 41169
Telephone: (606) 329-3333
Mailing Address:
　P.O. Box 391
　Ashland, KY 41114
Industry Affiliation: Petroleum, Gas
**Publication(s):**
*Source, The*
Day Published: m.
Lead Time: 3 mos.
Mtls Deadline: 3 mos. prior to pub. date
Spec. Requirements: 20 or more pgs.; offset; 8 1/2 x 11
Personnel: Lesli S. Christian, Editor

4291

## ASM INTERNATIONAL
Rte. 87
Metals Park, OH 44073
Telephone: (216) 338-5151
FAX: (216) 338-4634
Industry Affiliation: Advertising, Art, Public Relations

**Publication(s):**
*Advanced Materials & Processes*
Day Published: m.
Lead Time: 30 days prior to pub. date
Materials: 01,02,05,06,10,15,16,25,27,28, 29,30,32,33
Spec. Requirements: 100+ pgs.; web-offset; 8 1/4 x 10 7/8; mag.
Personnel: Patricia E. Brooks, Publisher
　　　　　Margaret Hunt, Editor in Chief
　　　　　Donald Baxter, Managing Editor
　　　　　Faye Balser, Production Manager
　　　　　Barbara Brody, Art Director

70462

## ASSOCIATED CHURCH PRESS
502 Edgeworthe S.E.
Grand Rapids, MI 49546-9263
Telephone: (616) 676-1190
FAX: (616) 676-3759
Mailing Address:
　P.O. Box 162
　Ada, MI 49301-0162
Industry Affiliation: Publishers, Books, Magazines
**Publication(s):**
*A C P Directory*
Day Published: a.

*Newslog*
Day Published: 5/yr.
Spec. Requirements: offset; standard size

4920

## ASSOCIATED GENERAL CONTRACTORS OF HOUSTON
2404 Crawford St.
Houston, TX 77004
Telephone: (713) 659-4845
Mailing Address:
　P.O. Box 662
　Houston, TX 77001
Industry Affiliation: Utility: Related
**Publication(s):**
*A G C News Service*
Day Published: w.
Spec. Requirements: 8-pg.; letterpress newspaper; 11 x 16
Personnel: Coleen Ludwig, Editor

3170

## ASSOCIATED INDUSTRIES OF KENTUCKY
2303 Greene Way
Louisville, KY 40220-4009
Telephone: (502) 491-4737
FAX: (502) 491-5322
Industry Affiliation: Associations: Trade, Fraternal
**Publication(s):**
*Kentucky Journal Of Commerce & Industry*
Day Published: bi-w.
Lead Time: 14 days prior to pub. date
Materials: 01,02,06,07,29,30,31,32
Mtls Deadline: 2 wks. prior to pub. date
Spec. Requirements: 8-pg; offset
Personnel: Larry A. Maggard, Editor

4921

## ASSOCIATED MILK PRODUCERS, INC.
6609 Blanco Rd.
San Antonio, TX 78216
Telephone: (210) 340-9100
FAX: (210) 340-9112

Mailing Address:
　P.O. Box 790287
　San Antonio, TX 78279-0287
Industry Affiliation: Dairy Products
**Publication(s):**
*Dairymen's Digest, N. Central Region*
Day Published: m.
Lead Time: 20 days
Mtls Deadline: 10th of mo. prior to pub. date
Contact: AMPI, North Central Region
　　　　　PO Box 455
　　　　　New Ulm, MN 56073
Spec. Requirements: 32 pg.; offset magazine; 8 1/2 x 11
Personnel: Sheryl Doering Meshke, Editor

*Dairy Men's Digest, Southern Region*
Day Published: m.
Lead Time: 20 days
Mtls Deadline: 10th of each month
Personnel: Raymond Crouch, Editor in Chief
　　　　　Ken McKenzie

*Dairymen's Digest, Morning Glory Farms Region*
Day Published: q.
Personnel: Pam Tadych, Managing Editor
　　　　　Raymond Crouch

4637

## ASSOCIATED PENNSYLVANIA CONSTRUCTORS
800 N. Third St.
Harrisburg, PA 17102-2099
Telephone: (717) 238-2513
FAX: (717) 238-5060
Industry Affiliation: Associations: Trade, Fraternal
**Publication(s):**
*Highway Builder*
Day Published: q.: Jan., Apr., July, Oct.
Lead Time: 1 mo. prior to pub. date
Mtls Deadline: 1 mo. prior to pub. date
Spec. Requirements: 44 pg.; offset; 82 x 112
Personnel: Robert E. Hetherington, Editor

2577

## ASSOCIATED PUBLIC-SAFETY COMMUNICATIONS OFFICE
2040 S. Ridgewood Ave., Ste. 100
Daytona Beach, FL 32119-8437
Telephone: (904) 322-2500
FAX: (904) 322-2501
Industry Affiliation: Associations: City, State, Federal
**Publication(s):**
*A P C O Bulletin*
Day Published: m.
Lead Time: 2 mos.
Mtls Deadline: 2 mos.
Spec. Requirements: 64 pg.; offset; 8 1/2 x 11; 64-88 pg.
Personnel: Allan W. Chase, Editor

4922

## ASSOCIATES CORPORATION OF NORTH AMERICA
250 Carpenter Frwy.
Dallas, TX 75222
Telephone: (214) 541-4500
Mailing Address:
　P.O. Box 660237
　Dallas, TX 75266
Industry Affiliation: Banks, Savings & Loans

---

Materials Accepted/Included: 01-Business news 02-By-line articles 03-Fashion news 04-Food news 05-Freelance copy 06-Letters to editor 07-Real estate news 08-Sports news 09-Travel news 10-Book rev. 11-Movie rev. 12-Music rev. 13-TV rev. 14-Theater rev. 15-Coming events 16-Obituaries 17-Question & answer 18-Social announcements 19-Artwork 20-Cartoons 21-Photos 22-TV listings 23-Audio rec. 24-Video rec. 25-Books 26-Films/film clips 27-Personnel news 28-Press releases 29-New product news/photos 30-Trade lit. 31-Contracts awarded 32-Display adv. 33-Classified adv.

11-9

**Publication(s):**
*Associates Magazine, The*
Day Published: s-a.
Spec. Requirements: 20-24 pg.; offset; 8 1/2 x 11
Personnel: Becky Briening, Editor

70435

**ASSOCIATION OF BIRTH DEFECT CHILDREN, INC.**
5400 Diplomat Cir., Ste. 270
Orlando, FL 32810
Industry Affiliation: Associations: Health Groups
**Publication(s):**
*Association Of Birth Defect Children*
Day Published: q.
Contact: Association of Birth Defect Children, Inc.
    5400 Diplomat Cir., Ste. 270
    Orlando, FL 32810
Personnel: William G. McBride, Founder

2069

**ASSOCIATION OF CALIFORNIA WATER AGENCIES**
910 K St., 250
Sacramento, CA 95814-3577
Telephone: (916) 441-4545
FAX: (916) 441-7893
Industry Affiliation: Utility: Water
**Publication(s):**
*A C W A News*
Day Published: bi-w.
Lead Time: 2 wks.
Materials: 01,10,28,29
Mtls Deadline: 2 wks. prior to pub. date
Contact: Communications Department
Spec. Requirements: 16 pg.; offset; 8 1/2 x 11
Personnel: Cindy Bundock, Editor

*Water Quality Monitor*
Day Published: bi-m.
Lead Time: 2 wks.
Mtls Deadline: 2 wks. prior to pub. date
Personnel: Cindy Bundock, Editor

5126

**ASSOCIATION OF FORMER STUDENTS TEXAS A&M UNIVERSITY**
Clayton Williams, Jr., Alumni Center, TAMU
College Station, TX 77840
Telephone: (409) 845-7514
FAX: (409) 845-9263
Mailing Address:
    P.O. Box 7368
    College Station, TX 77844
Industry Affiliation: Associations: Trade, Fraternal
**Publication(s):**
*Texas Aggie*
Day Published: 8/yr.
Lead Time: 1 1/2 mos.
Materials: 25,28,32
Mtls Deadline: 1 1/2 mos.
Spec. Requirements: 72 page; offset magazine; 8 1/2 x 11
Personnel: Jerry C. Cooper, Editor

2740

**ASSOCIATION OF ILLINOIS ELECTRIC COOPERATIVES**
6460 S. Sixth Frontage Rd.
Springfield, IL 62707
Telephone: (217) 529-5561
Mailing Address:
    P.O. Box 3787
    Springfield, IL 62708
Industry Affiliation: Utility: Electric

**Publication(s):**
*Illinois Rural Electric News*
Day Published: m.
Lead Time: 60 days prior to pub. date
Mtls Deadline: 1st of mo. prior to pub. date
Spec. Requirements: 32 pg.; offset; 8 1/2 x 11
Personnel: Larry Elledge, Editor
       Jack Halstead, Associate Editor

68363

**ASSOCIATION OF SCIENCE-TECHNOLOGY CENTERS**
1025 Vermont Ave., N.W., Ste. 500
Washington, DC 20005
Telephone: (202) 783-7200
FAX: (202) 783-7207
Industry Affiliation: Colleges, Institutions, Science Research
**Publication(s):**
*A S T C Newsletter*
Day Published: bi-m.
Lead Time: 7 wks. prior to pub. date
Materials: 02,06,10,15,21,25,27,28
Contact: Publications
Spec. Requirements: job announcement must be for professional positios
Personnel: Chris Raymond, Editor in Chief

*A S T C Annual Directory Of Members*
Day Published: a.
Lead Time: 3 mos. prior to end of yr.
Materials: 32
Mtls Deadline: late Nov.
Contact: Publications
Spec. Requirements: camera-ready art
Personnel: Chris Raymond, Editor in Chief
       Todd Happer, Managing Editor

*A S T C Annual Report*
Day Published: a.
Personnel: Chris Raymond, Editor in Chief

2629

**ATLANTA GAS LIGHT CO.**
303 Peachtree St., Rm. 4036
Atlanta, GA 30308-3251
Telephone: (404) 584-3830
Mailing Address:
    P.O. Box 4569
    Atlanta, GA 30302-4569
Industry Affiliation: Utility: Gas
**Publication(s):**
*Blue Flame News:*
Day Published: bi-m.
Lead Time: 2 mos. prior to pub. date
Materials: 01,15,17,30
Mtls Deadline: 1st working day wk. prior to pub. date
Spec. Requirements: 8 1/2 x 14
Personnel: Lydia Parker, Editor
       Cass M. Lievsay

*Spirit Magazine*
Day Published: q.
Mtls Deadline: 1st day of mo. 2 mos. prior to pub. date
Personnel: Lydia Parker, Editor

2630

**ATLANTA JOURNAL-CONSTITUTION**
72 Marietta St., N.W.
Atlanta, GA 30303
Telephone: (404) 526-5151
Mailing Address:
    P.O. Box 4689
    Atlanta, GA 30302
Industry Affiliation: Newspapers

**Publication(s):**
*Headliner*
Day Published: bi-m.
Lead Time: 2 wks.
Mtls Deadline: 15th of mo.
Spec. Requirements: 12-plus page; tabloid 14 1/2 x 11 1/2
Personnel: Randy Jay, Editor

3841

**ATLANTIC CITY ELECTRIC CO.**
6801 Black Horse Pike
Pleasantville, NJ 08232
Telephone: (609) 645-3500
Mailing Address:
    P.O. Box 1264
    Pleasantville, NJ 08232
Industry Affiliation: Utility: Electric
**Publication(s):**
*Newsline*
Day Published: m.
Lead Time: 3 wks. prior to pub. date
Mtls Deadline: 2nd Mon. of mo. prior to pub. date
Spec. Requirements: 8-page; tabloid; 11 x 17
Personnel: Elizabeth Kennedy, Editor

2631

**ATLANTIC ENVELOPE CO.**
1700 Northside Dr., N.W.
Atlanta, GA 30318
Telephone: (404) 351-5011
Mailing Address:
    P.O. Box 1267
    Atlanta, GA 30374-1267
Industry Affiliation: Paper Products
**Publication(s):**
*In Transit*
Day Published: bi-m.
Lead Time: 1 mo.
Mtls Deadline: 15th of 2nd mo. prior to pub. date
Contact: Aeco Products Division
       P.O. Box 1267
       Atlanta, GA 30301
Spec. Requirements: 8-page; offset magazine; 54 x 84
Personnel: Jerry Gallagher, Editor

3947

**ATLANTIC MUTUAL COS.**
45 Wall St.
New York, NY 10005
Telephone: (201) 408-6148
Industry Affiliation: Insurance
**Publication(s):**
*Atlantic Messenger*
Day Published: q.
Lead Time: 2 mos.
Spec. Requirements: 16 pg.; offset; 8 1/2 x 12
Personnel: Judy Samuelson, Editor

*Atlantic Log, The*
Day Published: bi-m.
Spec. Requirements: 12-16 pgs. tabloid size
Personnel: Judy Samuelson, Managing Editor

3842

**ATLAS SUPPLY CO.**
2625 Cumberland Pkwy., Ste. 300
Atlanta, GA 30339
Telephone: (404) 431-3880
FAX: (404) 431-3893
Industry Affiliation: Auto Suppliers

**Publication(s):**
*Atlas Bulletin*
Day Published: bi-m.
Spec. Requirements: 28 pg.; offset magazine; 8 1/2 x 11
Personnel: Joan T. Monahan, Editor

68527

**ATLAS VAN-LINES, INC.**
1212 St. George Rd.
Evansville, IN 47711
Telephone: (812) 424-2222
FAX: (812) 421-7142
Industry Affiliation: Trucking
**Publication(s):**
*Atlas Amplifier*
Day Published: s-a.
Personnel: James Huth

65156

**AUBURN-CORD-DUESENBERG MUSEUM**
1600 S. Wayne St.
Auburn, IN 46706
Telephone: (219) 925-1444
FAX: (219) 925-6266
Mailing Address:
    P.O. Box 271
    Auburn, IN 46706
Industry Affiliation: Institutions
**Publication(s):**
*Accelerator, The*
Day Published: q.
Lead Time: 2 mos.
Mtls Deadline: 1 mo. prior to new quarter
Contact: Archives-Publicity
Personnel: Gregg Buttermore, Editor

2354

**AURORA PUBLIC SCHOOLS**
1085 Peoria St.
Aurora, CO 80011
Telephone: (303) 344-8060
Industry Affiliation: Colleges, Institutions, Science Research
**Publication(s):**
*Clipboard*
Day Published: m.
Lead Time: 1 wk.
Personnel: Debbie Lynch, Editor

*Focus*
Day Published: 4-6/yr.
Personnel: Debbie Lynch, Editor

3421

**AUTO-OWNERS INSURANCE**
6101 Anacapri Blvd.
Lansing, MI 48917
Telephone: (517) 323-1200
FAX: (517) 323-8796
Mailing Address:
    P.O. Box 30660
    Lansing, MI 48909
Industry Affiliation: Insurance
**Publication(s):**
*Memo*
Day Published: bi-m.
Lead Time: 6 wks. prior to pub. date
Materials: 03,04,05,09,10,15,16,17,29,30
Mtls Deadline: 6 wks. prior to pub. date
Contact: Marketing
Spec. Requirements: 32-40 pg.; 84 x 11
Personnel: Bill Pamerleau, Editor

**Materials Accepted/Included:** 01-Business news 02-By-line articles 03-Fashion news 04-Food news 05-Freelance copy 06-Letters to editor 07-Real estate news 08-Sports news 09-Travel news 10-Book rev. 11-Movie rev. 12-Music rev. 13-TV rev. 14-Theater rev. 15-Coming events 16-Obituaries 17-Question & answer 18-Social announcements 19-Artwork 20-Cartoons 21-Photos 22-TV listings 23-Audio rec. 24-Video rec. 25-Books 26-Films/film clips 27-Personnel news 28-Press releases 29-New product news/photos 30-Trade lit. 31-Contracts awarded 32-Display adv. 33-Classified adv.

*Emblem*
Day Published: bi-m.
Lead Time: 6 wks.
Materials: 30
Mtls Deadline: 6 wks. prior to pub. date
Contact: Marketing
Spec. Requirements: 32-52-page
Personnel: Bill Pamerleau, Editor

**AUTO CLUB OF MICHIGAN**                    3420
One Auto Club Dr.
Dearborn, MI 48126
Telephone: (313) 336-1211
FAX: (313) 336-1344
Industry Affiliation: Associations: Trade,
   Fraternal
**Publication(s):**
*A A A Michigan Living*
Day Published: m.
Lead Time: 2 mo. prior to pub. date
Materials: 04,05,09,10
Mtls Deadline: 2 mo. prior to pub. date
Spec. Requirements: 4-8 pg.; offset; 8 1/2
   x 11
Personnel: Len Barnes, Editor

**AVCO FINANCIAL SERVICES**          2073
3349 Michelson Dr.
Irvine, CA 92715-1606
Telephone: (714) 553-1200
FAX: (714) 553-7722
Mailing Address:
   P.O. Box 19701
   Irvine, CA 92713-9702
Industry Affiliation: Finance, Services
**Publication(s):**
*Trends*
Day Published: bi-m.
Lead Time: 1 mo. prior to pub. date
Mtls Deadline: 1 mo. prior to pub. date
Contact: Corporate Communications
Spec. Requirements: newsletter; 2 color; 8
   1/2 x 11
Personnel: Donn Silver

**AVIS, INC.**                                  3948
900 Old Country Rd.
Garden City, NY 11530
Telephone: (516) 222-3000
FAX: (516) 222-4381
Industry Affiliation: Auto Suppliers
**Publication(s):**
*Avis News*
Day Published: 8/yr.
Spec. Requirements: 12 pg.; offset; 8 1/2
   x 11
Personnel: Janet Wood, Editor

**AVISTAR INTERNATIONAL**           2832
   **TRANSPORTATION CORP.**
10400 W. North Ave.
Melrose Park, IL 60160
Telephone: (708) 865-4366
FAX: (708) 865-3887
Industry Affiliation: Trucking
**Publication(s):**
*Communicator*
Day Published: w.
Lead Time: 1 day prior to pub. date
Mtls Deadline: Wed., 8:00 am prior to pub.
   date
Contact: Engine Div.
   10400 W. North Ave.
   Melrose Park, IL 60160
Spec. Requirements: 4 pg.; 8 1/2 x 11
Personnel: Beverly Love, Editor
   Dave Baron

**AVONDALE MILLS, INC.**              1982
900 Avondale Ave.
Sylacauga, AL 35150
Telephone: (205) 249-1200
Industry Affiliation: Trucking

**Publication(s):**
*Avondale Sun*
Day Published: m.
Lead Time: 10 days
Personnel: Kelley Wasserman, Editor

**AXIA, INC.**                                  68533
2001 Spring Rd., Ste. 300
Hinsdale, IL 60521
Telephone: (708) 571-3350
FAX: (708) 571-3360
Industry Affiliation: Industry: Heavy
   Construction, Machinery
**Publication(s):**
*Axia Action*
Day Published: a.
Personnel: Diane LaFauce, Editor

**BADGER MUTUAL INSURANCE**       5365
   **COMPANY**
1635 W. National Ave.
Milwaukee, WI 53204
Telephone: (414) 383-1234
Industry Affiliation: Insurance
**Publication(s):**
*Badger Beacon*
Day Published: 2-3/yr.
Spec. Requirements: 24 pgs.; offset; 7 x
   96
Personnel: Meribeth Waldrop, Editor
   Judy Courtis

**BALL CORP.**                                2985
345 S. High St.
Muncie, IN 47305
Telephone: (317) 747-6100
FAX: (317) 747-6203
Mailing Address:
   P.O. Box 2407
   Muncie, IN 47307
Industry Affiliation: Containers, Packages
**Publication(s):**
*Ball Line*
Day Published: q.
Spec. Requirements: 20-32 pg.; offset; 8
   1/2 x 11
Personnel: Scott McCarty, Editor

*Intercom*
Day Published: m.
Personnel: Scott McCarty, Editor

**BALTIMORE ASSOCIATION FOR**      3262
   **RETARDED CITIZENS, INC.**
4800 York Rd.
Baltimore, MD 21212
Telephone: (410) 323-5600
FAX: (410) 323-6326
Industry Affiliation: Associations:  Health
   Groups
**Publication(s):**
*Advocate, The*
Day Published: bi-m.
Lead Time: 3 wks.
Mtls Deadline: 1 mo. prior to pub. date
Spec. Requirements: 4-6 pg.; 8 x 10
Personnel: Lisa Singer, Editor
   Mary Page Sater, Art Director

**BANCOKLAHOMA CORP.**              4522
Bank of Oklahoma Tower
Tulsa, OK 74182
Telephone: (918) 588-6000
Mailing Address:
   P.O. Box 2300
   Tulsa, OK 74192
Industry Affiliation: Banks, Savings &
   Loans

**Publication(s):**
*Express*
Day Published: w.
Lead Time: 1 wk.
Contact: Bank of Oklahoma NA
Spec. Requirements: 16-page; offset; 8
   1/2 x 11
Personnel: Becky J. Frank, Editor

**BANKERS SECURITY LIFE**          2513
   **INSURANCE SOCIETY**
4601 Fairfax Dr.
Arlington, VA 22203
Telephone: (703) 875-3500
Industry Affiliation: Insurance
**Publication(s):**
*Bankers Notes*
Day Published: q.
Lead Time: 30 days prior to pub. date
Mtls Deadline: 30 days prior to pub.
Spec. Requirements: 8-12 pg.; offset; 84 x
   11
Personnel: Maria Yannopoulos, Senior
   Editor

*Outlook*
Day Published: a.
Lead Time: 90 days days prior to pub. date
Mtls Deadline: 90 days prior to pub. date
Personnel: Maria Yannopoulos, Senior
   Editor

**BANK OF BOSTON CORP.**           2415
100 Federal St.
Boston, MA 02110
Telephone: (617) 434-5593
FAX: (617) 434-4555
Industry Affiliation: Banks, Savings &
   Loans
**Publication(s):**
*Eagle*
Day Published: m.
Lead Time: 1 mo. prior to pub. date
Mtls Deadline: 1 mo. prior to pub.
Personnel: Janine Fondon, Editor

**BANK OF HAWAII**                      2695
111 S. King St.
Honolulu, HI 96813
Telephone: (808) 537-8111
Mailing Address:
   P.O. Box 2900
   Honolulu, HI 96846
Industry Affiliation: Banks, Savings &
   Loans
**Publication(s):**
*Spectrum*
Day Published: bi-m.
Lead Time: 2 mos.
Mtls Deadline: vary
Contact: Corp. Comms.-Mktg.
Personnel: Sam Vigil Jr., Editor

*Financial Directions*
Day Published: q.
Lead Time: 2 mos.
Contact: Corp. Comms.-Mktg.
Personnel: Sharlene Bliss, Editor

**BANK OF NEW YORK, THE**          3951
One Wall St., 13th Fl.
New York, NY 10286
Telephone: (212) 635-7736
FAX: (212) 635-7470
Industry Affiliation: Banks, Savings &
   Loans

**Publication(s):**
*Bank One*
Day Published: q.
Lead Time: 1 mo. prior to pub. date
Materials: 01,15,16,18,19,21
Contact: Comm. Dept. Personnel
   90 Washington St.
   New York, NY 10006
Spec. Requirements: 12 pg.; 11 x 15-1/2
Personnel: Nora E. Walsh, Assistant Editor

**BANK ONE**                               5051
1600 Pacific Ave., 16th Fl.
Dallas, TX 75201
Telephone: (214) 290-2000
Mailing Address:
   P.O. Box 655415
   Dallas, TX 75265-5415
Industry Affiliation: Banks, Savings &
   Loans
**Publication(s):**
*Texas Wire*
Day Published: m.
Lead Time: 5 wks. prior to pub. date
Mtls Deadline: 5 wks. prior to pub. date
Spec. Requirements: 8 pg.; offset; 9 2/3 x
   13 1/4
Personnel: Cindy Speaker, Editor
   Linda A. Barton, Editor

**BANK ONE, INDIANAPOLIS, NA**     2980
111 Monument Cir.
Indianapolis, IN 46277
Telephone: (317) 321-3000
FAX: (317) 321-8840
Industry Affiliation: Banks, Savings &
   Loans
**Publication(s):**
*Wire, The*
Day Published: 45 days
Lead Time: 1 mo.
Mtls Deadline: 1 mo. prior to pub. date
Contact: Bank One, Indianapolis, NA
Spec. Requirements: 4 pg; offset; 8 1/2 x
   11
Personnel: Keith Gran, Editor

**BANK ONE OF ARIZONA**            2032
241 N. Central
Phoenix, AZ 85004
Telephone: (602) 221-2900
Mailing Address:
   P.O. Box 71
   Phoenix, AZ 85001
Industry Affiliation: Banks, Savings &
   Loans
**Publication(s):**
*Eagle*
Day Published: q.
Lead Time: 1 mo. prior to pub. date
Mtls Deadline: 1 mo. prior to pub. date
Contact: Mktg.
Spec. Requirements: 8 page; offset
   newspaper; 11 1/2 x 16 1/2

**BANK SOUTH**                             66452
55 Marietta St.
Atlanta, GA 30303
Telephone: (404) 529-4150
FAX: (404) 529-4655
Industry Affiliation: Banks, Savings &
   Loans
**Publication(s):**
*Inside Bank South*
Day Published: bi-m.
Mtls Deadline: Mon. prior to pub.; pub.
   date-15th & 30th
Personnel: Lori Brannen, Editor

*Quarterly Interest*
Day Published: q.
Lead Time: 1 mo.
Mtls Deadline: 1 mo. prior to pub. date
Spec. Requirements: tabloid
Personnel: Lori Brannen, Editor

Materials Accepted/Included: 01-Business news 02-By-line articles 03-Fashion news 04-Food news 05-Freelance copy 06-Letters to editor 07-Real estate news 08-Sports news 09-Travel news
10-Book rev. 11-Movie rev. 12-Music rev. 13-TV rev. 14-Theater rev. 15-Coming events 16-Obituaries 17-Question & answer 18-Social announcements 19-Artwork 20-Cartoons 21-Photos 22-TV listings
23-Audio rec. 24-Video rec. 25-Books 26-Films/film clips 27-Personnel news 28-Press releases 29-New product news/photos 30-Trade lit. 31-Contracts awarded 32-Display adv. 33-Classified adv.

11-11

*Quarterly Report*
Day Published: 3/yr.
Personnel: Lori Brannen, Editor

*Annual Report*
Day Published: a.
Personnel: Lori Brannen, Editor

**BAPTIST HEALTH SYSTEM, THE** 4857
Blount Bldg., Ste. 501
137 Blount Ave.
Knoxville, TN 37920
Telephone: (615) 632-5677
FAX: (615) 632-5113
Mailing Address:
    P.O. Box 1788
    Knoxville, TN 37901
Industry Affiliation: Hospitals
**Publication(s):**
*Baptist Beat*
Day Published: m.
Lead Time: 6 wks. prior to pub. date
Mtls Deadline: 8 wks. prior to pub. date
Contact: Mktng. & Comm. Dept.
Spec. Requirements: 8-12 pgs.; offset; 11
    x 17
Personnel: Kim Nicley
          Donna Creech
          Roger Ricker, Editor

**BAPTIST HOSPITAL INC.** 4849
2000 Church St.
Nashville, TN 37236
Telephone: (615) 329-5300
Industry Affiliation: Hospitals
**Publication(s):**
*Bulletin, The*
Day Published: Fri.
Mtls Deadline: Wed., 12:00 pm prior to Fri.
    pub. date
Spec. Requirements: 2 pg; offset; 8 1/2 x
    11

**BAPTIST SUNDAY SCHOOL** 4850
    **BOARD**
127 Ninth Ave., N.
Nashville, TN 37234
Industry Affiliation: Publishers, Books,
    Magazines
**Publication(s):**
*Circle*
Day Published: m.
Lead Time: 2 mos.
Contact: Comms. Dept.
Personnel: Terri Lackey, Editor

**BARCLAYS** 2946
    **AMERICAN/MORTGAGE**
5032 Parkway Plz. Blvd., Bldg. 81
Charlotte, NC 28217
Telephone: (704) 357-7065
FAX: (704) 329-6818
Industry Affiliation: Real Estate
**Publication(s):**
*Real Estatements*
Day Published: bi-m.
Lead Time: 30 days
Spec. Requirements: 8-pg.; offset; 11 x 14
Personnel: Julie Thordarson McGuire,
          Editor
          Laura Mercer, Editorial
          Assistant

**BARNES GROUP, INC.** 2407
Executive Office
123 Main St.
Bristol, CT 06010
Telephone: (203) 583-7070
Industry Affiliation: Banks, Savings &
    Loans

**Publication(s):**
*News*
Day Published: m.
Lead Time: 2 wks. prior to pub. date
Mtls Deadline: 25th of mo. prior to pub.
    date
Spec. Requirements: 8-page; offset; 8 x 11
Personnel: Barbara Puffer, Editor

**BARNES HOSPITAL** 65906
Barnes Hospital Plz.
St. Louis, MO 63110
Telephone: (314) 362-4350
Industry Affiliation: Hospitals
**Publication(s):**
*Barnes Magazine*
Day Published: q.
Personnel: Scott Ragan, Editor

**BARNETT BANKS, INC.** 2579
50 N. Laura St.
Jacksonville, FL 32202
Telephone: (904) 791-7668
FAX: (904) 791-5382
Industry Affiliation: Banks, Savings &
    Loans
**Publication(s):**
*Barnett Action*
Day Published: m.
Contact: Internal Communications
Spec. Requirements: 40-page; offset
    magazine; 84 x 11
Personnel: Sherry McGlamory, Editor

*Action Newsbank-Video News Magazine*
Day Published: q.
Contact: Media Communications
Personnel: Dale Stephenson, Editor

**BARTON COUNTY COMMUNITY** 3140
    **COLLEGE**
Rte. 3
Great Bend, KS 67530
Telephone: (316) 792-2701
Industry Affiliation: Colleges, Institutions,
    Science Research
**Publication(s):**
*President's Report*
Day Published: q.
Lead Time: 2 mos. prior to pub. date
Personnel: Dick Wade, Editor

**BASF CORPORATION CHEMICALS** 3846
    **DIVISION**
Eight Campus Dr.
Parsippany, NJ 07054
Telephone: (201) 397-2800
FAX: (201) 397-4525
Industry Affiliation: Chemicals, Plastics
**Publication(s):**
*Basf Information*
Day Published: m.
Lead Time: 6 wks.
Spec. Requirements: 6-pg.; newspaper;
    11" x 15"
Personnel: Marsha S. Westfall, Editor

**BATON ROUGE GENERAL** 3204
    **MEDICAL CTR.**
3600 Florida Blvd.
Baton Rouge, LA 70806
Telephone: (504) 387-7773
Mailing Address:
    P.O. Box 2511
    Baton Rouge, LA 70821
Industry Affiliation: Hospitals
**Publication(s):**
*In General Newsletter*
Day Published: m.
Lead Time: 1 mo.
Mtls Deadline: 1 mo. prior to pub. mo.
Contact: Publications
Spec. Requirements: 4 pg.
Personnel: Bob Gohannessen, Editor

*Doctor's Digest*
Day Published: bi-m.
Lead Time: 1 mo.
Mtls Deadline: 1 mo. prior to pub. date
Personnel: Jaynie Barham

**BAUSCH & LOMB, INC.** 3953
One Lincoln First Sq.
Rochester, NY 14604
Telephone: (716) 338-6000
Mailing Address:
    P.O. Box 54
    Rochester, NY 14604
**Publication(s):**
*Bausch & Lomb World*
Day Published: m.
Lead Time: 3 wks.
Mtls Deadline: 3 wks. prior to pub. date
Spec. Requirements: 8 pg.; 8 1/2 x 14
Personnel: Cynthia M. Serve', Editor

**BAYLOR COLLEGE OF MEDICINE** 4927
One Baylor Plaza
Houston, TX 77030
Telephone: (713) 798-4726
FAX: (713) 798-3348
Industry Affiliation: Colleges, Institutions,
    Science Research
**Publication(s):**
*Baylor Medicine*
Day Published: 11/yr.
Lead Time: 2 mos.
Spec. Requirements: 4-8 pgs.; offset; 17 x
    11
Personnel: B.J. Almond, Editor

*Inside Information*
Day Published: 11/yr.
Lead Time: 2 mos. prior to pub. date
Spec. Requirements: issues & info. of
    interest to colleges
Personnel: B. J. Almond, Editor
          Dana Morrison

**BAYLOR UNIVERSITY MEDICAL** 68600
    **CENTER**
3500 Gaston Ave.
Dallas, TX 75246
Telephone: (214) 820-2116
Industry Affiliation: Hospitals
**Publication(s):**
*Baylor Progress*
Day Published: m.
Lead Time: 6 wks. prior to pub. date
Mtls Deadline: 6 wks. prior to pub. date
Personnel: Robin Stricklin, Editor

**BAY STATE GAS CO.** 3317
300 Friberg Pkwy.
Westborough, MA 01581-5039
Telephone: (508) 836-7000
Industry Affiliation: Utility: Gas
**Publication(s):**
*Bay Stater*
Day Published: m.
Lead Time: 1 mo.
Materials: 01
Mtls Deadline: 1st of mo. prior to pub. date
Contact: Public Affairs
Spec. Requirements: 14 pg.; offset; 8 1/2
    x 11
Personnel: Heather Fitzgerald, Editor

**BB & T** 68435
223 W. Lash St.
Wilson, NC 27893
Telephone: (919) 399-4647
FAX: (919) 399-4369
Industry Affiliation: Banks, Savings &
    Loans

**Publication(s):**
*Insight*
Day Published: q.
Personnel: Mike Kohler, Editor

*B B & T Chronicle*
Day Published: m.
Mtls Deadline: 1 Wed. of mo.
Personnel: Mike Kohler, Editor

**BDP BRANDS, CARRIER CORP.** 3955
P.O. Box 70
Indianapolis, IN 46206
Telephone: (317) 243-0851
Industry Affiliation: Trucking
**Publication(s):**
*Flow*
Day Published: q.
Lead Time: 60 days prior to pub. date
Mtls Deadline: 60 days prior to pub. date
Personnel: Carl Wochele, Editor

**BEAUMONT CHAMBER OF** 4928
    **COMMERCE**
450 Bowie
Beaumont, TX 77701
Telephone: (409) 838-6581
FAX: (409) 833-6718
Mailing Address:
    P.O. Box 3150
    Beaumont, TX 77704
Industry Affiliation: Associations: City,
    State, Federal
**Publication(s):**
*Metropolitan Beaumont*
Day Published: bi-m.
Lead Time: 45 days prior to pub. date
Mtls Deadline: 45 days prior to pub. date
Spec. Requirements: 48-64 pages; offset;
    8 1/2 x 11
Personnel: Harry Wood, Editor
          Jamie Jacobson, Public
          Relations Manager

*Southeast Texas Business Monthly*
Day Published: m.
Lead Time: 30 days
Mtls Deadline: 30 days prior to pub. date
Personnel: Harry Wood, Editor

**BEECH AIRCRAFT CORP.** 3141
9709 East Central
Wichita, KS 67205-2599
Telephone: (316) 676-7111
Mailing Address:
    P.O. Box 85
    Wichita, KS 67201
Industry Affiliation: Aircraft, Aerospace,
    Defense
**Publication(s):**
*Beechcrafter*
Day Published: m.
Lead Time: 2 wks.
Mtls Deadline: 10 days prior to pub. date
Spec. Requirements: 8-page; letterpress
    tabloid
Personnel: Mike Potts, Editor

**BELK STORES SERVICES INC.** 4217
2801 W. Tyvola Rd.
Charlotte, NC 28217
Telephone: (704) 357-1000
Industry Affiliation: Retail Stores

**Materials Accepted/Included:** 01-Business news 02-By-line articles 03-Fashion news 04-Food news 05-Freelance copy 06-Letters to editor 07-Real estate news 08-Sports news 09-Travel news 10-Book rev. 11-Movie rev. 12-Music rev. 13-TV rev. 14-Theater rev. 15-Coming events 16-Obituaries 17-Question & answer 18-Social announcements 19-Artwork 20-Cartoons 21-Photos 22-TV listings 23-Audio rec. 24-Video rec. 25-Books 26-Films/film clips 27-Personnel news 28-Press releases 29-New product news/photos 30-Trade lit. 31-Contracts awarded 32-Display adv. 33-Classified adv.

**Publication(s):**
*View*
Day Published: m.
Spec. Requirements: 8 pages; offset; 10 x 14
Personnel: Sidney S. Dixon, Editor

68602

**BELL HELICOPTER TEXTRON, INC.**
P.O. Box 482, MS 010105
Fort Worth, TX 76101
Telephone: (817) 280-8417
FAX: (817) 280-8221
Industry Affiliation: Aircraft, Aerospace, Defense
**Publication(s):**
*Bell Helicopter News*
Day Published: bi-w.
Contact: Public Affairs
Personnel: Gale Baird, Editor

*Rotor Breeze*
Day Published: bi-m.
Spec. Requirements: newsletter
Personnel: Susan Green, Editor

5198

**BENEFICIAL LIFE INS. CO.**
36 S. State St.
Salt Lake City, UT 84136
Telephone: (801) 531-7979
Mailing Address:
P.O. Box 2654
Salt Lake City, UT 84136
Industry Affiliation: Insurance
**Publication(s):**
*Beneficial Benefactor*
Day Published: bi-m.
Lead Time: 30 days prior to pub. date
Mtls Deadline: 30 days prior to pub. date
Spec. Requirements: 8-page; offset magazine; 84 x 11
Personnel: Steven Fisher, Editor

3848

**BENEFICIAL MANAGEMENT CORP.**
200 Beneficial Ctr.
Peapack, NJ 07977
Telephone: (908) 781-3882
Industry Affiliation: Finance, Services
**Publication(s):**
*Beneficial News Briefs*
Day Published: bi-m.
Lead Time: 4 mos. prior to pub. date
Mtls Deadline: 4 mos. prior to pub. date
Spec. Requirements: 16 pg.; offset; 84 x 11
Personnel: William H. Meagher, III, Editor

3079

**BENTON CITY ELECTRIC COOPERATIVE ASSOCIATION**
1006 W. Fourth St.
Vinton, IA 52349
Telephone: (319) 472-2367
FAX: (319) 472-5006
Mailing Address:
P.O. Box 488
Vinton, IA 52349
Industry Affiliation: Utility: Electric
**Publication(s):**
*On Line With Benton*
Day Published: q.: Feb., May, Aug., Nov.
Mtls Deadline: 2 wks. prior to pub. date
Spec. Requirements: 10-12 pgs.; offset; 8 1/2 x 11
Personnel: Maribell Hesson, Editor

5146

**BERGEN BRUNSWICK CORP.**
4000 Metropolitian Dr.
Orange, CA 92668
Telephone: (714) 385-4000
FAX: (714) 385-1442
Industry Affiliation: Drugs, Cosmetics, Pharmaceuticals

**Publication(s):**
*Keeping In Touch*
Day Published: bi-m.
Spec. Requirements: 4-8 pg.; letterpress; 11 x 15
Personnel: Susan Delay, Editor

68395

**BERKSHIRE LIFE INSURANCE COMPANY**
700 South St.
Pittsfield, MA 01201
Telephone: (413) 499-4321
FAX: (413) 499-4831
Industry Affiliation: Insurance
**Publication(s):**
*Berkshire Life Newsletter*
Day Published: bi-w.
Mtls Deadline: Thu. of w. prior to pub. date
Personnel: Susan B. LeBourdais, Manager

*Berkshire Life Afield*
Day Published: m.
Mtls Deadline: 30th of mo.
Personnel: Susan B. LeBourdais, Manager

4298

**BERRY CO., THE**
3170 Kettering Blvd.
Dayton, OH 45439
Telephone: (513) 296-2121
Mailing Address:
P.O. Box 6000
Dayton, OH 45401
Industry Affiliation: Publishers, Books, Magazines
**Publication(s):**
*Berry Leader, The*
Day Published: m.
Lead Time: 2 mos. prior to pub. date
Mtls Deadline: 10th of mo. prior to pub. date
Contact: Planning & Communications
Spec. Requirements: 6 pg.; offset; 11-1/2 x 17
Personnel: Chris Socki, Editor
Jane Pierce

4639

**BESSEMER & LAKE ERIE RAILROAD**
135 Jamison Ln.
Monroeville, PA 15146
Telephone: (412) 829-6696
FAX: (412) 829-6624
Mailing Address:
P.O. Box 68
Monroeville, PA 15146
Industry Affiliation: Railroads
**Publication(s):**
*B & L E Employee Newsletter*
Day Published: m.
Lead Time: 3 wks.
Spec. Requirements: 1 page both sides typed; 8 1/2 x 11
Personnel: Alice C. Saylor, Editor

3855

**BEST FOODS, DIVISION OF CPC INTERNATIONAL, INC.**
International Plz.
Englewood Cliffs, NJ 07632
Telephone: (201) 894-2435
Industry Affiliation: Food, General
**Publication(s):**
*Focus*
Day Published: 3/yr.
Lead Time: 4 wks. prior to pub. date
Mtls Deadline: 4 wks. prior to pub. date
Contact: Best Foods
Spec. Requirements: 8-12 pg.; offset; 9 x 12
Personnel: Dana Lee Wood, Editor

*Sales & Marketing Newsletter*
Day Published: 3/yr.
Lead Time: 4 wks. prior to pub. date
Mtls Deadline: 4 wks. prior to pub. date
Contact: Best Foods
Spec. Requirements: 6-8 pg.; offset; 8-1/2 x 11
Personnel: Dana Lee Wood, Editor

*Advantage*
Day Published: 3/yr.
Lead Time: 4 wks. prior to pub. date
Mtls Deadline: 4 wks. prior to pub. date
Contact: Best Foods
Personnel: Tom DiPizza, Editor

5223

**BEST PRODUCTS CO., INC.**
1400 Best Plz.
Richmond, VA 23227
Telephone: (804) 261-2000
Mailing Address:
P.O. Box 26303
Richmond, VA 23227
Industry Affiliation: Retail Stores
**Publication(s):**
*Best Times*
Day Published: m.
Lead Time: 3 wks. prior to pub. date
Mtls Deadline: 3 wks. prior to pub. date
Spec. Requirements: 11 x 15
Personnel: Ross Richardson, Editor

2433

**BETTER HEALTH PRESS**
1384 Chapel St.
New Haven, CT 06511
Telephone: (203) 789-3972
Industry Affiliation: Hospitals
**Publication(s):**
*Better Health Magazine*
Day Published: bi-m.
Lead Time: 3-5 mos. prior to pub. date
Mtls Deadline: 3-5 mos. prior to pub. date
Spec. Requirements: 48 pg.; web; 8-1/2 x 11
Personnel: James F. Malerba, Editor

66556

**B.F. GOODRICH**
3925 Embassy Pkwy.
Fairlawn, OH 44333
Telephone: (216) 374-2000
Industry Affiliation: Rubber, Tires
**Publication(s):**
*B F G Today*
Day Published: m.
Lead Time: 1 mo.
Mtls Deadline: 1st of mo. prior to pub. date
Personnel: Denise Bowler, Editor

68552

**BIC CORP.**
500 Bic Dr.
Milford, CT 06460
Telephone: (203) 783-2000
FAX: (203) 783-2081
Industry Affiliation: Industry: Light Tools, Equipment
**Publication(s):**
*Bic Picture*
Day Published: bi-m.
Personnel: April Chaplin, Editor

2082

**BIG BROTHERS OF GREATER LOS ANGELES, INC.**
1486 Colorado Blvd.
Los Angeles, CA 90041
Telephone: (213) 258-3333
Mailing Address:
1486 Colorado Blvd.
Los Angeles, CA 90041
Industry Affiliation: Associations: City, State, Federal

**Publication(s):**
*The Image*
Day Published: s-a.
Spec. Requirements: 3 pgs; offset; 8 1/2 x 11
Personnel: Nancy Dufford, Editor

3957

**BILL COMMUNICATIONS, INC.**
355 Park Ave. S. #3 Fl.
New York, NY 10010-1706
Telephone: (212) 592-6200
Industry Affiliation: Advertising, Art, Public Relations
**Publication(s):**
*Parts Business*
Day Published: m.
Spec. Requirements: 60-pg; offset; 10 x 14 1/2
Personnel: Rusty Pierson, Editor

5367

**BLACK HAWK COUNCIL OF GIRL SCOUTS**
2710 Ski Ln.
Madison, WI 53713
Telephone: (608) 276-8500
Industry Affiliation: Associations: Trade, Fraternal
**Publication(s):**
*Semaphore*
Day Published: q.
Lead Time: 1 mo. prior to pub. date
Mtls Deadline: 1 mo. prior to pub. date
Spec. Requirements: 8 pg.; 8-1/2 x 11
Personnel: Scott Williams, Editor

4734

**BLAIR, CORP.**
220 Hickory St.
Warren, PA 16366-0001
Telephone: (814) 723-3600
Industry Affiliation: Retail Stores
**Publication(s):**
*Procession*
Day Published: m.
Lead Time: 2 wks.
Materials: 01,02,04,08,15,18,21,27,29,32,33
Mtls Deadline: 2 wks. prior to pub. date
Contact: Employee and Public Relations
Spec. Requirements: 10-16 page; offset tabloid; 8 1/2 x 11
Personnel: Deborah J. Ward, Editor

2031

**BLOOD SYSTEMS**
P.O. Box 1867
Scottsdale, AZ 85252-1867
Industry Affiliation: Associations: Health Groups
**Publication(s):**
*Heart-To-Heart*
Day Published: m.
Materials: 19,20
Mtls Deadline: 15th of mo. prior to pub. date
Spec. Requirements: 4 pg.; offset; 8-1/2 x 11
Personnel: Carol Brugman, Editor

4596

**BLOUNT, INC.**
4520 Executive Park Dr.
Montgomery, AL 36116
Telephone: (205) 244-4000
FAX: (205) 244-4000
Industry Affiliation: Industry: Heavy Construction, Machinery
**Publication(s):**
*Omark 80*
Day Published: bi-m.
Spec. Requirements: 28-pgs.; offset magazine; 84 x 11
Personnel: John Bernard, Editor

**Materials Accepted/Included:** 01-Business news 02-By-line articles 03-Fashion news 04-Food news 05-Freelance copy 06-Letters to editor 07-Real estate news 08-Sports news 09-Travel news 10-Book rev. 11-Movie rev. 12-Music rev. 13-TV rev. 14-Theater rev. 15-Coming events 16-Obituaries 17-Question & answer 18-Social announcements 19-Artwork 20-Cartoons 21-Photos 22-TV listings 23-Audio rec. 24-Video rec. 25-Books 26-Films/film clips 27-Personnel news 28-Press releases 29-New product news/photos 30-Trade lit. 31-Contracts awarded 32-Display adv. 33-Classified adv.

11-13

*Oregon-Izer*
Day Published: bi-m.
Contact: Oregon Saw Chain Division
　　　9701 SE McLoughlin Blvd
　　　Milwaukie, OR 97222
Spec. Requirements: 16-24 pgs.
Personnel: Rhys Campbell, Editor

## BLUE CROSS & BLUE SHIELD
　　　　　　　　　　　　　　　　68595
I-20 E. Alpine Rd.
Columbia, SC 29219
Telephone: (803) 788-3860
Industry Affiliation: Insurance
**Publication(s):**
*Blues Week*
Day Published: bi-w.
Personnel: Jackie Hazzard, Editor

*Kaleidoscope*
Day Published: m.
Personnel: Jackie Hazzard, Editor

*Industry Outlook*
Day Published: m.
Personnel: Jackie Hazzard, Editor

*Blue Alumni*
Day Published: bi-m.
Personnel: Jackie Hazzard, Editor

*Health Matters*
Day Published: bi-m.
Personnel: Jackie Hazzard, Editor

*Medicare Briefly*
Day Published: q.

*Medicare Messenger*
Day Published: q.

*Medicare Matters*
Day Published: q.

*Companion Healthworld*
Day Published: q.

*Med-A-News*
Day Published: q.

*Blue Print*
Day Published: w.

## BLUE CROSS & BLUE SHIELD
## ASSOCIATION
　　　　　　　　　　　　　　　　2753
676 N. St. Clair St.
Chicago, IL 60611
Telephone: (312) 440-6000
Industry Affiliation: Insurance
**Publication(s):**
*Insight*
Day Published: bi-m.
Contact: Pub. Rels Dept.
Spec. Requirements: 5-6 pgs.; standard
Personnel: Ann Rukavina, Editor

## BLUE CROSS & BLUE SHIELD OF
## WEST VIRGINIA, INC.
　　　　　　　　　　　　　　　　5341
200 Kanawha Blvd., E.
Charleston, WV 25301
Telephone: (800) 852-5471
Industry Affiliation: Insurance
**Publication(s):**
*Group Update / Members Plus / Out Of
The Blue*
Day Published: q.
Lead Time: 1 mo. prior to pub. date
Mtls Deadline: 2 wks. prior to pub. date
Contact: Pub. Rels./Mktg.
Spec. Requirements: 4 pg.; offset; 11 x 17
Personnel: Susan Moore

*Physician Directory*
Day Published: q.
Lead Time: 2 mos. prior to pub. date
Mtls Deadline: 1 mo. prior to pub. date
Contact: Provider Rels.
Spec. Requirements: 32 pg.; 4 x 8-1/2
　　　booklet; offset
Personnel: Katherine Rollison, Editor

---

*Your Health Care Benefits & How To Use
Them*
Lead Time: 3 wks. prior to pub. date
Contact: Mktg.

## BLUE DIAMOND GROWERS
　　　　　　　　　　　　　　　　2088
P.O. Box 1768
Sacramento, CA 95812
Telephone: (916) 442-0771
Industry Affiliation: Food, General
**Publication(s):**
*Almond Facts*
Day Published: bi-m.
Spec. Requirements: 40-48 page; offset;
　　　84 x 11
Personnel: Susan Brauner, Editor

## BOATMEN'S BANK
　　　　　　　　　　　　　　　　3682
One Boatmen's Plz.
Saint Louis, MO 63101
Telephone: (314) 466-6000
Industry Affiliation: Banks, Savings &
　　　Loans
**Publication(s):**
*Currency*
Day Published: m.
Lead Time: 1 mo.

## BODINE ELECTRIC CO.
　　　　　　　　　　　　　　　　2754
2500 W. Bradley Pl.
Chicago, IL 60618
Telephone: (312) 478-3515
Industry Affiliation: Utility: Electric
**Publication(s):**
*Bodine Motorgram*
Day Published: bi-m.
Lead Time: 2 mos.
Mtls Deadline: 2 mos. prior to pub. date
Contact: BECO Adv.
Spec. Requirements: 4-pgs.; offset; 84 x
　　　11
Personnel: C.B. Bodine, Editor

## BOEING CO.
　　　　　　　　　　　　　　　　5295
P.O. Box 3707
Seattle, WA 98124
Telephone: (206) 655-1131
FAX: (206) 237-3491
Industry Affiliation: Aircraft, Aerospace,
　　　Defense
**Publication(s):**
*Boeing News*
Day Published: w.
Spec. Requirements: 8-12 pgs; offset; 114
　　　x 146
Personnel: Barbara R. Minor, Editor

*Boeing Management Information*
Day Published: 50/yr.
Spec. Requirements: pages vary
Personnel: Elmer C. Vogel, Editor

## BOISE CASCADE CORP.
　　　　　　　　　　　　　　　　2712
One Jefferson Sq.
Boise, ID 83702
Telephone: (208) 384-6161
FAX: (208) 384-7224
Mailing Address:
　　　P.O. Box 50
　　　Boise, ID 83728
Industry Affiliation: Paper Products
**Publication(s):**
*B C News*
Day Published: bi-m.
Lead Time: 3 mos.
Mtls Deadline: 1st of the mo.
Spec. Requirements: 8-page sheet-fed
　　　tabloid
Personnel: Sue Rourke, Editor
　　　　　Ann Nauis, Communications
　　　　　Associate
　　　　　Jana McAdams, Art Director

---

*Boise Cascade Insight*
Day Published: 3/yr.
Spec. Requirements: circ. 31,000
Personnel: Karla Haun, Editor

## BORG-WARNER AUTOMOTIVE,
## TRANSMISSION SYSTEMS
　　　　　　　　　　　　　　　　3046
P.O. Box 2688
Muncie, IN 47307
Telephone: (317) 286-6100
Industry Affiliation: Auto Suppliers
**Publication(s):**
*Shifting Times*
Day Published: q.
Lead Time: 1 mo. prior to pub. date
Mtls Deadline: 1 mo. prior to pub. date
Spec. Requirements: 4 pgs.; offset
　　　newsletter; 11 x 17
Personnel: Peggy Myers, Editor

## BOSTON EDISON CO.
　　　　　　　　　　　　　　　　3322
800 Boylston St.
P.O. Box P-203
Boston, MA 02199
Telephone: (617) 424-2251
Industry Affiliation: Utility: Electric
**Publication(s):**
*Edison Life*
Day Published: bi-m.
Lead Time: 6 wks. prior to pub. date
Mtls Deadline: 6 wks. prior to pub. date
Contact: Employee Communication Dept.
Spec. Requirements: 20 pg. offset
　　　magazine; 8-1/2 x 11
Personnel: Editorial Brd & Staff Writers ,
　　　Editor

## BOSTON GAS COMPANY
　　　　　　　　　　　　　　　　3323
One Beacon St.
Boston, MA 02108
Telephone: (617) 742-8400
Industry Affiliation: Utility: Gas
**Publication(s):**
*Gas Lines*
Day Published: m.
Lead Time: 1 mo.
Mtls Deadline: 1 mo. prior to pub. date
Spec. Requirements: 4-page; offset; 11 x
　　　16
Personnel: Richard D. Hull, Editor

*Boston Gas News*
Day Published: s-a.
Personnel: Richard D. Hull, Editor

## BOSTON MUTUAL LIFE INS. CO.
　　　　　　　　　　　　　　　　3324
120 Royall St.
Canton, MA 02021
Telephone: (617) 828-7000
Industry Affiliation: Insurance
**Publication(s):**
*Telstar*
Day Published: m.
Lead Time: 1 mo.
Mtls Deadline: 1 mo. prior to pub. date
Contact: Communications
Spec. Requirements: 4-page; offset tabloid;
　　　84 x 11
Personnel: James E. Chisholm, Editor

## BOSTWICK-BRAUN CO.
　　　　　　　　　　　　　　　　4302
1946 N. 13th St.
Toledo, OH 43624
Telephone: (419) 259-3600
Mailing Address:
　　　P.O. Box 912
　　　Toledo, OH 43697
Industry Affiliation: Home Appliances,
　　　Furnishings

---

**Publication(s):**
*Anvil*
Day Published: q.
Lead Time: 1 mo. prior to pub. date
Mtls Deadline: 15th of Feb., May, Aug.,
　　　Nov.
Spec. Requirements: 8 pg.; offset; 8-1/2 x
　　　11
Personnel: Jennifer Truss, Editor

## BOULEVARD PUBLICATIONS INC.
　　　　　　　　　　　　　　　　4472
3380 Tremont Rd.
Columbus, OH 43221
Telephone: (614) 451-6548
Mailing Address:
　　　P.O. Box 12098
　　　Columbus, OH 43212
Industry Affiliation: Publishers, Books,
　　　Magazines
**Publication(s):**
*Ideas For Better Living*
Day Published: m.
Lead Time: 5 mos.
Materials: 03,04,09,10,19,20,21,25,28,29,
　　　32,33
Mtls Deadline: 5 mos. prior to pub. date
Contact: Savings & Loan Publications
Spec. Requirements: 16-page; offset
　　　magazine; 7 3/8 x 10 1/2
Personnel: Steve Bulkley, Editor
　　　　　Robert F. West, Publisher

*Good Living*
Day Published: m.
Lead Time: 5 mos.
Materials: 03,04,09,10,19,20,21,25,28,29,
　　　32,33
Mtls Deadline: 5 mos. prior to pub. date
Contact: Public Relations Publications
Spec. Requirements: 16-page
Personnel: Steve Bulkley, Editor
　　　　　Robert F. West, Publisher

## BOWLING PROPRIETORS'
## ASSOCIATION OF AMERICA
　　　　　　　　　　　　　　　　4932
615 Six Flags Dr.
Arlington, TX 76011
Telephone: (817) 649-5105
FAX: (817) 633-2940
Mailing Address:
　　　P.O. Box 5802
　　　Arlington, TX 76005
Industry Affiliation: Associations: Trade,
　　　Fraternal
**Publication(s):**
*Bowling Proprietor, The*
Day Published: m.
Lead Time: 5th of mo. prior to pub. date
Materials: 01,02,04,,06,07,08,09,10,25,27,
　　　28,29,30,32,33
Mtls Deadline: adv.-26th of mo. 2 mos.
　　　prior to pub. date
Spec. Requirements: 64 pg.; offset; 8-1/4
　　　x 10-3/4
Personnel: Daniel Burgess, Editor

## BRAILLE INSTITUTE OF AMERICA,
## INC.
　　　　　　　　　　　　　　　　2084
741 N. Vermont Ave.
Los Angeles, CA 90029
Telephone: (213) 663-1111
Industry Affiliation: Associations: Trade,
　　　Fraternal

---

**Materials Accepted/Included:** 01-Business news 02-By-line articles 03-Fashion news 04-Food news 05-Freelance copy 06-Letters to editor 07-Real estate news 08-Sports news 09-Travel news 10-Book rev. 11-Movie rev. 12-Music rev. 13-TV rev. 14-Theater rev. 15-Coming events 16-Obituaries 17-Question & answer 18-Social announcements 19-Artwork 20-Cartoons 21-Photos 22-TV listings 23-Audio rec. 24-Video rec. 25-Books 26-Films/film clips 27-Personnel news 28-Press releases 29-New product news/photos 30-Trade lit. 31-Contracts awarded 32-Display adv. 33-Classified adv.

**Publication(s):**
*Light*
Day Published: a.
Spec. Requirements: 32 pg.; offset magazine; 82 x 11
Personnel: Paul J. Porrelli, Editor

**BRANCH BANKING AND TRUST CO.**                    4220
P.O. Box 1847
Wilson, NC 27894
Telephone: (919) 399-4111
Industry Affiliation: Banks, Savings & Loans
**Publication(s):**
*Insight*
Day Published: q.
Lead Time: 1 mo.
Contact: Marketing & Banking Services
Spec. Requirements: 16-page; offset; 8 1/2 x 11
Personnel: Mike Kohler, Editor
Gail S. Tharrington, Administrative Assistant

**BRESLER'S ICE CREAM & YOGURT, INC.**              2757
999 E. Touhy Ave., Ste. 333
Des Plaines, IL 60018
Telephone: (708) 298-1100
FAX: (708) 298-0697
Industry Affiliation: Dairy Products
**Publication(s):**
*Scoop, The*
Day Published: q.
Lead Time: 90 days
Spec. Requirements: 4 pg; offset; 8 1/2 x 17
Personnel: Michael Rappaport, Editor

**BRIDGESTONE/FIRESTONE, INC.**                     4341
50 Century Blvd.
Nashville, TN 37214
Telephone: (615) 872-5000
FAX: (615) 872-1599
Industry Affiliation: Rubber, Tires
**Publication(s):**
*Bridgestone/firestone Network*
Day Published: m.

**BRISTOL-MYERS CO.**                               3960
345 Park Ave.
New York, NY 10154
Telephone: (212) 546-4372
Industry Affiliation: Drugs, Cosmetics, Pharmaceuticals
**Publication(s):**
*Bristol Myers New York*
Day Published: q.
Spec. Requirements: 8-pg.; offset tabloid; 10 x 13
Personnel: Arlene Elzweig, Editor

*Bristol-Myers World*
Day Published: q.
Spec. Requirements: tabloid
Personnel: M. Friedman, Editor

*Alumnews*
Day Published: q.
Personnel: Madelien Drefack
Mary Evans

**BROOKLYN UNION GAS CO.**                          3962
195 Montague St
Brooklyn, NY 11201
Telephone: (718) 403-2000
Industry Affiliation: Utility: Gas

**Publication(s):**
*Sendout*
Day Published: bi-w.
Spec. Requirements: 8 pg.; offset tabloid; 9 x 11
Personnel: Denis Szabaga, Editor

**BROWN & WILLIAMSON TOBACCO CORP.**                3172
1600 W. Hill St.
Louisville, KY 40210
Telephone: (502) 568-7000
Mailing Address:
P.O. Box 35090
Louisville, KY 40232
Industry Affiliation: Tobacco
**Publication(s):**
*Tobaccotalk*
Day Published: q.
Lead Time: 4 wks.
Spec. Requirements: 16-24 pg.; 2-color; 8 1/2 x 11
Personnel: Charles Springer, Editor

**BROWN-FORMAN, CORP.**                             68620
850 Dixie Hwy.
Louisville, KY 40210
Telephone: (502) 585-1100
FAX: (502) 774-7876
Industry Affiliation: Brewers, Distillers
**Publication(s):**
*Brown Forum*
Day Published: q.
Personnel: Jean Ashburn, Editor

**BROWN GROUP, INC.**                               3747
8300 Maryland Ave.
St. Louis, MO 63105-3662
Telephone: (314) 854-4093
FAX: (314) 854-4091
Mailing Address:
P.O. Box 29
St. Louis, MO 63166-0029
Industry Affiliation: Shoes
**Publication(s):**
*Maryland Avenews*
Day Published: bi-m.
Lead Time: 6-8 wks.
Personnel: Mary L. Sylvia, Public Relations Manager

*Health Connections*
Day Published: m.
Personnel: Mary L. Sylvia, Public Relations Manager

**BROWNING FERRIS INDUSTRIES**                      4934
14701 St. Mary's
Houston, TX 77079
Telephone: (713) 870-8100
Mailing Address:
P.O. Box 3151
Houston, TX 77253
Industry Affiliation: Railroads
**Publication(s):**
*B F I Blueline*
Day Published: m.
Lead Time: 30 days
Spec. Requirements: 16 pg.; offset; 12 x 18
Personnel: Peter Block, Editor

**BRULIN & CO., INC.**                              2987
2920 Dr. Andrew J. Brown Ave.
Indianapolis, IN 46205
Telephone: (317) 923-3211
FAX: (317) 925-4596
Mailing Address:
P.O. Box 270
Indianapolis, IN 46206
Industry Affiliation: Chemicals, Plastics

**Publication(s):**
*Brulin News, The*
Day Published: bi-m.
Materials: 01,17,27,29,31
Mtls Deadline: last Fri. of mo. prior to bi-m. pub. date
Contact: Marketing Division
Spec. Requirements: 8 pgs; 8 1/2 x 11 folded
Personnel: Janet Cleary Salisbury, Editor

**BRUNSWICK CORP.**                                 2758
One N. Field Ct.
Lake Forest, IL 60045-4811
Telephone: (708) 375-4457
FAX: (708) 375-4455
Industry Affiliation: Chemicals, Plastics
**Publication(s):**
*Profile Newsmagazine People-Brunswick*
Day Published: q.
Lead Time: 90 days
Spec. Requirements: 20 pg.; 8 1/2 x 11; 2-4 color pgs.
Personnel: Arthur K. Serbo, Editor

**BRYAN MEMORIAL HOSPITAL**                         3767
1600 S. 48th St.
Lincoln, NE 68506
Telephone: (402) 489-0200
Industry Affiliation: Hospitals
**Publication(s):**
*Commoner*
Day Published: bi-m.
Lead Time: 2 mos. prior to pub. date
Mtls Deadline: 15th of mo. prior to pub. date
Spec. Requirements: 12-page; offset; 8 1/2 x 11
Personnel: Paul Hadley, Editor

*Medical Staff News*
Day Published: bi-m.
Lead Time: 8 wks. prior to pub. date
Mtls Deadline: mid of mo. prior to pub. date
Personnel: Paul Hadley, Editor

**BUCKEYE PIPE LINE COMPANY**                       4643
3900 Hamilton Blvd.
Allentown, PA 18103
Telephone: (610) 820-8300
FAX: (610) 820-3823
Mailing Address:
P.O. Box 368
Emmaus, PA 18049
Industry Affiliation: Utility: Related
**Publication(s):**
*Buckeye Monitor*
Day Published: q.
Lead Time: 6 wks.
Materials: 19,20
Spec. Requirements: 30-32 pages; offset; 8 5/16 x 10 3/4
Personnel: Robin L. Clark, Editor
Carl A. Ostach, Editor

**BUCYRUS-ERIE CO.**                                5372
P.O. Box 56
South Milwaukee, WI 53172
Telephone: (414) 768-4747
Industry Affiliation: Advertising, Art, Public Relations
**Publication(s):**
*Miner Details:*
Day Published: 3/yr.
Spec. Requirements: 8-10 pg.; newsletter
Personnel: Petti Barfield, Editor

*Surface Miner*
Day Published: bi-m.
Spec. Requirements: 20-30 pgs.
Personnel: Lois Schroeder, Editor

**BUREAU OF NATIONAL AFFAIRS, INC.**                68581
1231 25th St., N.W.
Washington, DC 20037
Telephone: (202) 452-4200
Industry Affiliation: Associations: City, State, Federal
**Publication(s):**
*B N A's Review Of What's New*
Day Published: q.
Mtls Deadline: varies
Contact: Sales & Marketing
Spec. Requirements: 4-4 pages; offset; 8 1/2 x 11
Personnel: Sarita Cabrera, Editor

**BURGER KING CORP.**                               2580
17777 Old Cutlee Rd.
Miami, FL 33157
Telephone: (305) 378-7011
FAX: (305) 378-7262
Mailing Address:
P.O. Box 520783
Miami, FL 33152
Industry Affiliation: Food, General
**Publication(s):**
*Up Front*
Day Published: q.
Materials: no materials accepted
Personnel: Chuck Uckert, Editor

*Trends*
Day Published: q.
Materials: no materials accepted
Spec. Requirements: 12 pg.-4 Col. 8 1/2 x 11
Personnel: Chuck Uckert, Editor

**BURLINGTON COUNTY COLLEGE**                       3849
Pemberton-Browns Mills Rd.
Pemberton, NJ 08068
Telephone: (609) 894-9311
Industry Affiliation: Colleges, Institutions, Science Research
**Publication(s):**
*College Connection, The*
Day Published: every 3 wks.
Lead Time: 1 wk. prior to pub. date
Mtls Deadline: 1 wk. prior to pub. date
Spec. Requirements: 4-10 pg.; offset; 8 1/2 x 11
Personnel: Linda Dickman, Editor

*Alumni Action*
Day Published: 3-4/yr.
Lead Time: 2 mos. prior to pub. date
Mtls Deadline: 2 mos. prior to pub. date
Personnel: Linda Dickman, Editor

**BURLINGTON INDUSTRIES**                           4222
3330 W. Friendly Ave.
Greensboro, NC 27410
Telephone: (919) 379-2512
Mailing Address:
P.O. Box 21207
Greensboro, NC 27420
Industry Affiliation: Advertising, Art, Public Relations

**Materials Accepted/Included:** 01-Business news 02-By-line articles 03-Fashion news 04-Food news 05-Freelance copy 06-Letters to editor 07-Real estate news 08-Sports news 09-Travel news 10-Book rev. 11-Movie rev. 12-Music rev. 13-TV rev. 14-Theater rev. 15-Coming events 16-Obituaries 17-Question & answer 18-Social announcements 19-Artwork 20-Cartoons 21-Photos 22-TV listings 23-Audio rec. 24-Video rec. 25-Books 26-Films/film clips 27-Personnel news 28-Press releases 29-New product news/photos 30-Trade lit. 31-Contracts awarded 32-Display adv. 33-Classified adv.

11-15

**Publication(s):**
*Burlington Look, The*
Day Published: bi-m.
Materials: 03,20
Mtls Deadline: varies
Spec. Requirements: 8-12 pg.; web offset;
11 1/2 x 17
Personnel: Melissa M. Staples, Editor
Bryant Haskins, Exec. Editor

68584
**BURLINGTON NORTHERN
RAILROAD**
2900 Continental Plz.
Fort Worth, TX 76102
Telephone: (817) 333-3042
FAX: (817) 333-7997
Industry Affiliation: Railroads
**Publication(s):**
*Inside B N*
Day Published: m.
Lead Time: 1 mo.
Materials: 06
Mtls Deadline: 1 mo. prior to pub. date
Personnel: Robin Russell McCasland,
Editor

4223
**BURROUGHS WELLCOME CO.**
3030 Cornwallis Rd.
Durham, NC 27709
Telephone: (919) 248-3000
Industry Affiliation: Drugs, Cosmetics,
Pharmaceuticals
**Publication(s):**
*Wellcome News*
Day Published: bi-m.
Lead Time: 6 wks.
Spec. Requirements: 12 pg.; offset; 134 x
11
Personnel: Nancy Herndon, Editor

4165
**BUSINESS COUNCIL FOR THE
UNITED NATIONS**
60 E. 42nd St., Rm. 2925
New York, NY 10165
Telephone: (212) 661-1772
Industry Affiliation: Advertising, Art, Public
Relations
**Publication(s):**
*B C U N Briefing*
Day Published: q.
Spec. Requirements: 8 pgs; offset; 84 x 10
Personnel: Janice Caswell, Editor

3670
**BUSINESS MEN'S ASSURANCE
CO.**
31st & Southwest Trafficway
Kansas City, MO 64108
Telephone: (816) 753-8000
FAX: (816) 751-5563
Mailing Address:
P.O. Box 419458
Kansas City, MO 64141
Industry Affiliation: Insurance
**Publication(s):**
*B M A Skylines*
Day Published: m.
Lead Time: 2 wks.
Spec. Requirements: 8 pg; tabloid; 10 x 13
1/2
Personnel: Ann Clifford, Editor

*Today At B M A*
Day Published: Mon.-Fri.
Lead Time: 1 day
Mtls Deadline: 9:00 am, day of publication
Spec. Requirements: 8 1/2 x 11
Personnel: Dana Ruppert, Editor

*B M A Bulletin*
Day Published: m.
Mtls Deadline: 1st wk. prior to end of mo.
pub. date
Spec. Requirements: 16-24 pgs; 8 1/2 x
11
Personnel: Marty Moseman, Editor

4790
**C-TEC CORP.**
46 Public Sq.
Wilkes Barre, PA 18701
Telephone: (717) 825-1100
Mailing Address:
Box 3000
Wilkes Barre, PA 18703
Industry Affiliation: Utility: Telephone
**Publication(s):**
*C-Tec Communicator*
Day Published: bi-m.
Lead Time: Jan. 15th, Mar. 15th, May 15th
Mtls Deadline: last day of Feb., Apr., June.,
Aug., Oct., Dec.
Contact: Pub. Rels. Dept.
Spec. Requirements: 20-24 pg. offset 8
1/2 x 11
Personnel: Carrie Thorpe, Editor
D. OToole

3327
**CABOT CORP.**
75 State St.
Boston, MA 02109
Telephone: (617) 345-0100
Industry Affiliation: Steel, Iron
**Publication(s):**
*Cabot World*
Day Published: q.
Spec. Requirements: 4-6 pgs.; offset; 8
1/2 x 11
Personnel: Susan Urbanetti, Editor

2089
**CALIFORNIA ASSOCIATION OF
LIFE UNDERWRITERS, INC.**
70 Washington St., Ste. #325
Oakland, CA 94607
Telephone: (510) 834-2258
FAX: (510) 834-1453
Industry Affiliation: Insurance
**Publication(s):**
*Calunderwriter*
Day Published: m.
Lead Time: 1-2 mos. prior to pub. date
Materials: 01,02,06,28,30,32
Mtls Deadline: 1-2 mos. prior to pub. date
Spec. Requirements: 12-24 pgs. offset;
image area 7 x 10
Personnel: Dan Crouch, Director

2296
**CALIFORNIA ASSOCIATION OF
REALTORS**
525 S. Virgil Ave.
Los Angeles, CA 90020
Telephone: (310) 739-8200
Industry Affiliation: Real Estate
**Publication(s):**
*California Real Estate Magazine*
Day Published: 10/yr.
Lead Time: 6-8 wk.
Spec. Requirements: 56, 64, or 72 pg.;
web offset; 7 x 10
Personnel: Anne Framroze, Editor

2334
**CALIFORNIA CREDIT UNION
LEAGUE**
2350 S. Garey Ave.
Pomona, CA 91766-5898
Telephone: (909) 628-6044
FAX: (909) 590-7121
Industry Affiliation: Associations: City,
State, Federal

**Publication(s):**
*Credit Union Digest*
Day Published: m.
Lead Time: 1 wk. prior to pub. date
Materials: 02,28
Mtls Deadline: Mon. by 12:00 pm
Contact: Communications
Spec. Requirements: 16 pg.; offset
newsletter; 8 1/2 x 11
Personnel: Carol Payne, Editor in Chief
Dan Niegrugge, Managing
Editor
Kecia Doyle

68381
**CALIFORNIA HISPANIC
AMERICAN MEDICAL
ASSOCIATION**
1020 S. Arroyo Pkwy., Ste. 200
Pasadena, CA 91105
Telephone: (818) 799-5456
FAX: (818) 799-6136
Industry Affiliation: Associations: City,
State, Federal
**Publication(s):**
*Hispanic Physician*
Day Published: s-a.
Personnel: Aliza Lifshitz, MD, President

2225
**CALIFORNIA PACIFIC MEDICAL
CENTER**
Clay & Buchanan Sts.
San Francisco, CA 94120
Telephone: (415) 923-3260
FAX: (415) 923-6595
Mailing Address:
P.O. Box 7999
San Francisco, CA 94120
Industry Affiliation: Hospitals
**Publication(s):**
*California Pacific Quarterly*
Day Published: q.
Lead Time: 3 wks. prior to pub. date
Mtls Deadline: 3 wks. prior to pub. date
Personnel: Terry Hastings, Editor

*Medical Staff Outlook*
Day Published: m.
Personnel: Terry Hastings, Editor

*Connections*
Day Published: bi-w.
Lead Time: 2 wks. prior to pub. date
Mtls Deadline: 2 wks. prior to pub. date
Personnel: Terry Hastings, Editor

2343
**CALIFORNIA SCHOOL BOARDS
ASSOCIATION**
3100 Beacon Blvd.
W Sacramento, CA 95691
Telephone: (916) 371-4691
FAX: (916) 371-3407
Mailing Address:
P.O. Box 1660
W Sacramento, CA 95691
Industry Affiliation: Associations: City,
State, Federal
**Publication(s):**
*California Schools*
Day Published: q.
Materials: 02,05,06,15,17,19,21,28,29,32
Spec. Requirements: 48 pg.; offset; 9 x 11;
4C
Personnel: Kevin Swartzendruber, Editor
Brian Lewis, Editor in Chief
Joe Carrasco, Art Director

*C S B A News*
Day Published: m.
Materials: 21,28
Personnel: Kevin Swartzendruber, Editor
Joe Carrasco, Art Director
Brian Lewis, Editor in Chief

2345
**CALIFORNIA STATE EMPLOYEES
ASSOCIATION**
1108 O St
Sacramento, CA 95814
Telephone: (916) 326-4249
Industry Affiliation: Associations: City,
State, Federal
**Publication(s):**
*Pride*
Day Published: bi-m.
Lead Time: 2 wks. prior to pub. date
Materials: 19,20,25,32
Mtls Deadline: 2 wks. prior to pub. date
Spec. Requirements: 30 pgs.; offset
newspaper; 174 x 11
Personnel: Robert Striegel, Editor
George Clark

2347
**CALIFORNIA TAXPAYERS
ASSOCIATION**
921 11TH St., Ste. 800
Sacramento, CA 95814
Telephone: (916) 441-0490
FAX: (916) 441-1619
Industry Affiliation: Associations: City,
State, Federal
**Publication(s):**
*Cal-Tax News*
Day Published: s-m.
Lead Time: 1 mo. prior to pub. date
Mtls Deadline: 1 mo. prior to pub. date
Spec. Requirements: 12 pg.; offset; 8 1/2
x 11
Personnel: Ron Roach, Editor

2348
**CALIFORNIA TEACHERS
ASSOCIATION**
1705 Murchison Dr.
Burlingame, CA 94011
Telephone: (415) 697-1400
FAX: (415) 697-0786
Mailing Address:
P.O. Box 921
Burlingame, CA 94011-0921
Industry Affiliation: Associations: Trade,
Fraternal
**Publication(s):**
*C T A Action*
Day Published: 9/yr.
Lead Time: 2 mos. prior to pub. date
Mtls Deadline: 1 mo. prior to pub. date
Contact: Advertising Dept.
1905 E. 17th St., Ste. 309
Santa Ana, CA 92701
Spec. Requirements: 24-28 pgs; Web; 10 x
15 1/2
Personnel: Trudy S. Willis, Editor

2111
**CALMAT CO.**
3200 San Fernando Rd.
Los Angeles, CA 90065
Telephone: (213) 258-2777
FAX: (213) 258-1583
Mailing Address:
P.O. Box 2950
Los Angeles, CA 90051
Industry Affiliation: Cement, Ceramics, Clay

**Materials Accepted/Included:** 01-Business news 02-By-line articles 03-Fashion news 04-Food news 05-Freelance copy 06-Letters to editor 07-Real estate news 08-Sports news 09-Travel news 10-Book rev. 11-Movie rev. 12-Music rev. 13-TV rev. 14-Theater rev. 15-Coming events 16-Obituaries 17-Question & answer 18-Social announcements 19-Artwork 20-Cartoons 21-Photos 22-TV listings 23-Audio rec. 24-Video rec. 25-Books 26-Films/film clips 27-Personnel news 28-Press releases 29-New product news/photos 30-Trade lit. 31-Contracts awarded 32-Display adv. 33-Classified adv.

**Publication(s):**
*Calmatters*
Day Published: q.
Spec. Requirements: 16 pgs.; offset; 84 x 11
Personnel: Kathy Cameron, Editor

3966
**CALTEX PETROLEUM CORP.**
P.O. Box 61500
Dallas, TX 75261
Telephone: (214) 830-1000
Industry Affiliation: Petroleum, Gas
**Publication(s):**
*Oil Progress*
Day Published: q.
Spec. Requirements: 24 pg.; offset magazine; 9 x 12
Personnel: Richard A. Coccola, Editor

5381
**CAP GEMIMI AMERICA**
1114 Ave. of Americas, 29th Fl.
New York, NY 10036
Telephone: (212) 944-6464
Industry Affiliation: Finance, Services
**Publication(s):**
*Captions*
Day Published: q.
Lead Time: 6 wks. prior to pub. date
Spec. Requirements: 16 pg.; offset; 8 x 11
Personnel: Larry Schlegel, Editor
Virginia Vann

4645
**CAPITAL BLUE CROSS**
2500 Elmerton Ave.
Harrisburg, PA 17110
Telephone: (717) 541-7000
Industry Affiliation: Associations: Health Groups
**Publication(s):**
*Among Ourselves*
Day Published: m.
Lead Time: 6-8 wks.
Mtls Deadline: 4 wks. prior to pub. date
Contact: Public Affrs.
Spec. Requirements: 16-20 pgs.; offset; 8 1/2 x 11
Personnel: Laurie Vogelsang, Editor

3547
**CARDIAC PACEMAKERS INC.**
4100 Hamline Ave., N.
New Brighton, MN 55112
Telephone: (612) 638-4000
Industry Affiliation: Drugs, Cosmetics, Pharmaceuticals
**Publication(s):**
*Advances*
Day Published: q.
Lead Time: 3 mo.
Mtls Deadline: 2 mo. prior to pub.
Spec. Requirements: 16 pg.; offset; 8 1/2 x 11
Personnel: Carol Lindahl, Editor
Donna Hadland

2588
**CARGILL FERTILIZER, INC.**
8813 Hwy. 41, S.
Riverview, FL 33569
Telephone: (813) 677-9111
FAX: (813) 671-6146
Industry Affiliation: Agriculture, Services
**Publication(s):**
*Phos Pholks*
Day Published: bi-m.
Lead Time: 2 mos. prior to pub. date
Mtls Deadline: 2 mos. prior to pub. date
Contact: Human Resources Dept.
Spec. Requirements: 10-12 pgs.; offset; 8 1/2 x 11
Personnel: Diane Markley, Editor

4647
**CARNEGIE MELLON UNIVERSITY**
5000 Forbes Ave.
Pittsburgh, PA 15213
Telephone: (412) 268-2000

Mailing Address:
Bramer House
Pittsburgh, PA 15213
Industry Affiliation: Colleges, Institutions, Science Research
**Publication(s):**
*Carnegie Mellon Magazine*
Day Published: q.
Lead Time: 2 mo.
Spec. Requirements: 52 pg.; offset; 9 x 11 1/2
Personnel: Ann Curran, Editor

4274
**CAROLINA ASSOCIATION OF PROFESSIONAL INSURANCE AGENTS**
3109 Charles B. Root Wynd.
Raleigh, NC 27612
Telephone: (919) 782-5807
FAX: (919) 781-6189
Industry Affiliation: Insurance
**Publication(s):**
*Carolina Agent*
Day Published: q.
Lead Time: 2 mos.
Materials: 01,32
Mtls Deadline: 1st of mo. prior to pub. date
Spec. Requirements: 4-44 pgs.; 8 1/2 x 11
Personnel: Sally Sherman, Editor

*Capia Capsules*
Day Published: s-m.
Lead Time: 1-2 wks.
Materials: 01,28
Mtls Deadline: 1 wk. prior to pub.
Spec. Requirements: ads-3 1/2 x 3 1/2, 7 x 4 3/4, 7 x 9 3/4
Personnel: Evelyn Bickley
Jenny Brading
Sally Sherman, Editor

4224
**CAROLINA POWER & LIGHT CO.**
411 Fayetteville St.
Raleigh, NC 27601
Telephone: (919) 836-6111
Mailing Address:
P.O. Box 1551
Raleigh, NC 27602
Industry Affiliation: Utility: Electric
**Publication(s):**
*Spotlight:*
Day Published: m.
Lead Time: 6 wk.
Mtls Deadline: 90 days before pub.
Spec. Requirements: 20 pg.; tabloid
Personnel: Susan Crutchfield, Editor

*Update*
Day Published: bi-m.
Lead Time: 6 wk.
Mtls Deadline: 90 days
Spec. Requirements: videotape magazine, original done on 1 inch tape
Personnel: Barbara Nicely, Producer

*Focus Magazine (for Managers)*
Day Published: q.
Lead Time: 6 wk.
Mtls Deadline: 90 days
Spec. Requirements: 20 pg.; 8 1/2 x 11; B & W (Color Cover)
Personnel: Susan Crutchfield, Editor

4227
**CAROLINAS MEDICAL CENTER**
1000 Blythe Blvd.
Charlotte, NC 28203
Telephone: (704) 355-2000
FAX: (704) 355-4084
Mailing Address:
P.O. Box 32861
Charlotte, NC 28232
Industry Affiliation: Hospitals

**Publication(s):**
*Life Health*
Day Published: q.
Lead Time: 2 wks. prior to pub. date
Personnel: Scott White, Editor

4648
**CARPENTER TECHNOLOGY CORPORATION**
101 W. Bern St.
Reading, PA 19601
Telephone: (215) 208-2639
FAX: (215) 208-3242
Industry Affiliation: Steel, Iron
**Publication(s):**
*Carpenter News*
Day Published: bi-m.
Lead Time: 1 mo.
Materials: 01,15,20,21
Mtls Deadline: 1 mo. before pub. date
Contact: Cathy Souders
Telephone: (215) 208-2000
Carpenter Technology
101 W. Bern St.
Reading, PA 19601
Spec. Requirements: 8 pg.; newsletter; 11 x 17 tabloid
Personnel: Cathy Souders, Editor
Keith Daubert, Art Director

3967
**CARRIER CORP.**
P.O. Box 4808
Syracuse, NY 13221
Telephone: (315) 432-6000
Industry Affiliation: Cooling, Heating
**Publication(s):**
*Carrier World*
Day Published: q.
Spec. Requirements: 16 pg.; offset magazine; 84 x 11
Personnel: Bob Strickland, Editor

2092
**CARTER HAWLEY HALE STORES, INC.**
3880 N. Mission Rd.
Los Angeles, CA 90031
Telephone: (213) 227-2000
FAX: (213) 227-3361
Industry Affiliation: Retail Stores
**Publication(s):**
*C H H Now*
Day Published: m.
Mtls Deadline: 10th; mo. prior to pub. date
Spec. Requirements: 4-6 pgs; offset; 2 color; photos
Personnel: John Sherman, Editor

5296
**CASCADE NATURAL GAS CORP.**
222 Fairview Ave.
Seattle, WA 99109
Telephone: (206) 624-3900
FAX: (206) 624-7215
Mailing Address:
P.O. Box 24464
Seattle, WA 98124
Industry Affiliation: Utility: Gas
**Publication(s):**
*Cascade Flame*
Day Published: bi-m.
Lead Time: 30 days prior to pub. date
Mtls Deadline: 1st of mo. prior to pub. date
Spec. Requirements: 16-24 pgs.; offset magazine; 84 x 11
Personnel: Frank Mansell, Editor

2764
**CATERPILLAR INDUSTRIAL, INC.**
100 N.E. Adams St.
Peoria, IL 61629
Telephone: (309) 675-1000
FAX: (309) 675-5815
Industry Affiliation: Industry: Heavy Construction, Machinery

**Publication(s):**
*Caterpillar World:*
Day Published: q.
Spec. Requirements: 32-page; offset magazine; 84 x 11
Personnel: Joyce Luster, Editor

*Cat Folks*
Day Published: bi-w.
Spec. Requirements: 8-12-page
Personnel: Gary Ortman, Editor

4445
**CATERPILLAR INDUSTRIAL, INC.**
5960 Heisley Rd.
Mentor, OH 44060
Telephone: (216) 357-2200
Industry Affiliation: Industry: Heavy Construction, Machinery
**Publication(s):**
*Mentor Lift-Lines*
Day Published: bi-w.
Spec. Requirements: 4-6 pg.; offset newspaper; 14 x 15
Personnel: Steve Vitale, Editor

3968
**CATHOLIC FOREIGN MISSION SOCIETY**
55 Rider Rd.
Maryknoll, NY 10545
Telephone: (914) 941-7590
FAX: (914) 945-0670
Industry Affiliation: Associations: Trade, Fraternal
**Publication(s):**
*Maryknoll*
Day Published: m.
Lead Time: 6 mos. prior to pub. date
Materials: 02,05,06,21
Mtls Deadline: 4-6 mos. prior to pub. date
Spec. Requirements: 64 pg.; offset magazine; 5 3/8 x 8 1/2
Personnel: Stephen T. De Mott, M.M., Publisher
Frank Maurovich, Managing Editor
Joseph R. Veneroso, M.M., Editor
Norman Kluepfel, Production Manager
Alicia Grant, Art Director
Robert J. Carleton, M.M., Fulfillment Director

*World Parish*
Day Published: bi-m.
Materials: 21
Spec. Requirements: 4 pgs.; 8 1/2 x 11
Personnel: Stephen De Mott, M.M., Publisher
Daniel Jensen, M.M., Associate Editor
Moises Sandoval, Editor

*Revista Maryknoll*
Day Published: m.
Materials: 02,05,06,21
Spec. Requirements: 32-page, offset mag.
　5 3/8 x 8 1/2
Personnel: Moises Sandoval, Editor
　　　　　Stephen T. De Mott, M.M.,
　　　　　　Publisher
　　　　　Linda Unger, Associate Editor
　　　　　Joseph Veneroso, M.M.,
　　　　　　Associate Editor
　　　　　Daniel Jensen, M.M., Associate
　　　　　　Editor
　　　　　Norman Kluepfel, Production
　　　　　　Manager
　　　　　Alicia Grant, Art Director
　　　　　Robert J. Carleton, M.M.,
　　　　　　Fulfillment Director

4178
**CATHOLIC PRESS ASSOCIATION**
119 N. Park Ave.
Rockville Center, NY 11570
Telephone: (516) 766-3400
FAX: (516) 766-3416
Industry Affiliation: Associations: Health
　Groups
**Publication(s):**
*Catholic Journalist, The*
Day Published: m.
Lead Time: 1 mo.
Materials: 01,02,05,06,10,15,16,20,21,28,
　30,32,33
Mtls Deadline: 15th of mo. prior to pub.
　date
Spec. Requirements: 8 pg.; offset; 11 x 16
Personnel: Jo Ann Dickerson, Editor
　　　　　Judy Dickerson
　　　　　Rev. Owen F. Campion
　　　　　James A. Doyle
　　　　　Rev. Albert Nevins
　　　　　Thomas Orr

*Catholic Press Directory*
Day Published: a.
Lead Time: Jan. 31
Materials: 32,33
Mtls Deadline: Dec. 20; year prior to pub.
　date
Spec. Requirements: offset; 1 pg. 4 3/4 x
　7 3/4
Personnel: Jo-Ann Wilson, Editor

2697
**C. BREWER & CO. LTD.**
827 Fort St.
Honolulu, HI 96813
Telephone: (808) 536-4461
Mailing Address:
　P.O. Box 1826
　Honolulu, HI 96805
Industry Affiliation: Agriculture, Services
**Publication(s):**
*C. Brewer Today*
Day Published: bi-m.
Spec. Requirements: 4 pg.; offset tabloid;
　11 1/4 x 14
Personnel: Brenda J. Hicks, Editor
　　　　　James G. Higgins

4198
**CBS, INC.**
51 W 52nd St
New York, NY 10019
Industry Affiliation: Agriculture, Services
**Publication(s):**
*Pitman Record*
Day Published: q.
Spec. Requirements: 4-8-page; offset; 8
　1/2 x 11
Personnel: Margery Harrison, Editor

*Terre Haute Record*

*Santa Maria Record*

3549
**CENEX/LAND O'LAKES**
5500 Cenex Dr.
Inver Grove, MN 55077
Telephone: (612) 451-5151
Mailing Address:
　P.O. Box 64089
　St. Paul, MN 55164
Industry Affiliation: Agriculture, Services
**Publication(s):**
*Cooperative Partners*
Day Published: 8/yr.
Lead Time: 2 mos. prior to pub. date
Mtls Deadline: 2 mos. prior to pub. date
Contact: Marketing Communications
Spec. Requirements: 24 pg.; magazine; 8
　1/2 x 11
Personnel: Linda Tank, Editor

2765
**CENTRAL ILLINOIS LIGHT CO.**
300 Liberty St.
Peoria, IL 61602
Telephone: (309) 672-5252
FAX: (309) 677-5282
Industry Affiliation: Utility: Electric
**Publication(s):**
*Cilco Scene*
Day Published: bi-m.
Lead Time: 3 wk.
Mtls Deadline: 3 wk. prior to pub. date
Spec. Requirements: 4-8 pg. offset
　newspaper; 114 x 164, 2-color
Personnel: Chris Muir, Editor

2948
**CENTRAL ILLINOIS PUBLIC
　SERVICE CO.**
607 E. Adams
Springfield, IL 62739
Telephone: (217) 523-3600
FAX: (217) 525-5825
Industry Affiliation: Utility: Electric
**Publication(s):**
*C I P S News*
Day Published: m.
Lead Time: 30 days
Contact: Pub. Rels.
Spec. Requirements: 32 pg.; offset
　magazine

4579
**CENTRAL LINCOLN PEOPLE'S
　UTILITY DISTRICT**
2129 N. Coast Hwy.
Newport, OR 97365
Telephone: (503) 265-3211
FAX: (503) 263-5208
Mailing Address:
　P.O. Box 1126
　Newport, OR 97365
Industry Affiliation: Utility: Electric
**Publication(s):**
*Coastlines*
Day Published: m.
Spec. Requirements: 4 pg.; offset bulletin;
　6 x 9
Personnel: Gary Cockrum, Editor

*Over The Wires*
Day Published: m.
Spec. Requirements: 8 pg.; 8 1/2 x 11
Personnel: Gary Cockrum, Editor

66451
**CENTRAL MAINE POWER CO.**
Edison Dr.
Augusta, ME 04330
Telephone: (207) 623-3521
Industry Affiliation: Utility: Electric

**Publication(s):**
*Weekly Update*
Day Published: w.: Thu.
Personnel: Sara Hammond

3969
**CENTRAL NEW YORK GIRL
　SCOUT COUNCIL INC.**
6724 Thompson Road N.
Syracuse, NY 13217
Telephone: (315) 437-6531
FAX: (315) 437-0559
Mailing Address:
　P.O. Box 6505
　Syracuse, NY 13217
Industry Affiliation: Associations:  Trade,
　Fraternal
**Publication(s):**
*Compass, The*
Day Published: bi-m.
Lead Time: 10th of prior mo.
Mtls Deadline: 10th of prior mo.
Spec. Requirements: 4-pg.; offset; 8 1/2 x
　11
Personnel: Ann M. Kochan, Editor

*G. S. News*
Day Published: 3/yr.
Lead Time: 1 mo.
Mtls Deadline: Aug. 1, Jan. 1, May 1
Personnel: Jean B. Howe
　　　　　Linda Tyminski

3107
**CENTURY COMPANIES OF
　AMERICA**
2000 Heritage Way
Waverly, IA 50677
Telephone: (319) 352-4090
FAX: (319) 352-2702
Industry Affiliation: Insurance
**Publication(s):**
*Century Notes*
Day Published: m.
Lead Time: 30 days
Mtls Deadline: 1 mo. prior to pub. date
Spec. Requirements: 20-28 pg.; offset
　magazine; 8 1/2 x 11
Personnel: Rick Feldkamp, Editor
　　　　　Marcia Janssen, Reporter

2098
**CENTURY 21, REAL ESTATE
　CORP.**
2601 S.E. Main St., Century Ctr.
Irvine, CA 92714
Telephone: (714) 553-2100
FAX: (714) 553-2199
Industry Affiliation: Real Estate
**Publication(s):**
*Real Estate Investment Journal*
Day Published: bi-m.
Lead Time: 30 days
Mtls Deadline: 1 mo. prior to pub. date
Spec. Requirements: 4 pg.; 8 1/2 x 11
Personnel: Monte Helme, Editor

*Leader, The*
Day Published: bi-m.
Mtls Deadline: 1 mo. prior to pub. date
Personnel: Monte Helme, Editor

2297
**CERTIFIED GROCERS OF
　CALIFORNIA, LTD.**
2601 S. Eastern Ave.
Los Angeles, CA 90040
Telephone: (213) 726-2601
Industry Affiliation: Food, General
**Publication(s):**
*Cergram*
Day Published: m.
Lead Time: 1 mo.
Materials: 04,27,28,30
Mtls Deadline: 1 mo. prior to pub.
Spec. Requirements: 4 pg.; offset; 8 x 11
Personnel: Shelley Machock, Editor

*Communicator*
Day Published: m.
Lead Time: 1 mo.
Materials: 01,04
Personnel: Shelley Machock, Editor

3144
**CESSNA AIRCRAFT CO.**
P.O. Box 7704
Wichita, KS 67277
Telephone: (316) 941-6488
Industry Affiliation: Aircraft
**Publication(s):**
*Cessna*
Day Published: bi-m.
Personnel: Sharon Prophet, Editor

4186
**CHASE MANHATTAN BANK, N.A.,
　THE**
One Lincoln First Sq.
Rochester, NY 14643
Telephone: (716) 258-5000
FAX: (716) 258-7462
Industry Affiliation: Banks, Savings &
　Loans
**Publication(s):**
*Regional Banker, The*
Day Published: bi-m.
Lead Time: 6 wks. prior to pub. date
Mtls Deadline: 1st & 3rd Mon. of mo.
Contact: Corporate
Spec. Requirements: 12 pg. prepared on
　dsktp publisher
Personnel: Norine E. Jones
　　　　　Amy Metal

*This Week*
Day Published: w.
Lead Time: 1 wk. prior to pub. date

3971
**CHASE MANHATTAN CORP.**
One Chase Manhattan Plz.
New York, NY 10081
Telephone: (212) 552-1849
Industry Affiliation: Banks, Savings &
　Loans
**Publication(s):**
*Chase Business*
Day Published: w.
Mtls Deadline: Thu.
Spec. Requirements: 6 pg.; 16 x 10 1/2
Personnel: Rachel Goldman, Editor

*Co & S News*
Day Published: m.
Contact: Pub. Affrs.
Personnel: Sheila Eby

4228
**CHATHAM MANUFACTURING CO.**
P.O. Box 620
Elkin, NC 28621
Telephone: (919) 835-2211
FAX: (919) 526-6063
Industry Affiliation: Textiles, Apparel, Mills,
　Machinery
**Publication(s):**
*C M I*
Day Published: q.
Spec. Requirements: 8-pgs.; offset
　newspaper; 92 x 122
Personnel: Mack Parsons, Editor

3972
**CHEMICAL BANKING CORP.**
270 Park Ave.
New York, NY 10017
Telephone: (212) 270-7455
FAX: (212) 270-2866
Industry Affiliation: Banks, Savings &
　Loans

Materials Accepted/Included: 01-Business news 02-By-line articles  03-Fashion news  04-Food news  05-Freelance copy  06-Letters to editor  07-Real estate news  08-Sports news 09-Travel news 10-Book rev. 11-Movie rev. 12-Music rev. 13-TV rev. 14-Theater rev. 15-Coming events 16-Obituaries 17-Question & answer 18-Social announcements 19-Artwork 20-Cartoons 21-Photos 22-TV listings 23-Audio rec. 24-Video rec. 25-Books 26-Films/film clips 27-Personnel news 28-Press releases 29-New product news/photos 30-Trade lit. 31-Contracts awarded 32-Display adv. 33-Classified adv.

**Publication(s):**
*Chemical Topics*
Day Published: m.
Spec. Requirements: 16-pg.; offset
 newspaper; 11 x 14 1/2
Personnel: Donna Lewis, Editor

2484
**CHESAPEAKE BAY GIRL SCOUT
 COUNCIL**
501 S. College Ave.
Newark, DE 19713
Telephone: (302) 456-7150
FAX: (302) 456-7188
Industry Affiliation: Associations: Trade,
 Fraternal
**Publication(s):**
*Bay Window*
Day Published: q.
Lead Time: 3 wks. prior to pub. date
Materials: 06,15,21,27,29
Contact: Communications
Spec. Requirements: 6-8 pgs.; offset; 8
 1/4 x 11
Personnel: Renee Patton, Editor

*Area Chairman Mailing*
Day Published: m.
Materials: 15,17,18,19,20,21,28,29
Mtls Deadline: 15th of mo.
Spec. Requirements: 8 1/2 x 11
Personnel: Bette Stauffer, Editor in Chief
 Sandy Mauser, Editor

52339
**CHESAPEAKE CORP.**
1021 E. Cary St., James Center II
Richmond, VA 23219
Telephone: (804) 697-1110
Mailing Address:
 P.O. Box 2350
 Richmond, VA 23219
Industry Affiliation: Lumber, Forestry,
 Building Materials
**Publication(s):**
*Chesapeake*
Day Published: m.
Lead Time: 15 days
Mtls Deadline: 15th of mo. prior to pub.
 date
Personnel: Madge Bush, Editor

2963
**CHICAGO PARK DISTRICT**
425 E. McFetridge Dr
Chicago, IL 60605
Telephone: (312) 294-2490
Industry Affiliation: Associations: City,
 State, Federal
**Publication(s):**
*Park Notes*
Day Published: m.

52600
**CHICAGO TITLE & TRUST CO.**
171 N. Clark St.
Chicago, IL 60601
Telephone: (312) 223-2959
Industry Affiliation: Associations: City,
 State, Federal
**Publication(s):**
*Guarantor*
Day Published: q.
Mtls Deadline: 2 mos. prior to pub. date
Personnel: Stephen W. Flanagan, Editor

3768
**CHILDREN'S HOSPITAL**
8301 Dodge St.
Omaha, NE 68114
Telephone: (402) 390-4810
Industry Affiliation: Hospitals

**Publication(s):**
*Healthplex Magazine*
Day Published: q.
Lead Time: 3 mo. prior to pub. date
Mtls Deadline: 3 mo. prior to pub. date
Spec. Requirements: 40 pg.; offset; 9 x 11
 1/2
Personnel: Gini Goldsmith, Editor

*Just Kids*
Day Published: q.
Lead Time: 3 mo. prior to pub. date
Mtls Deadline: 3 mo. prior to pub. date
Personnel: Mary Fernau, Editor

4306
**CHILDREN'S HOSPITAL MEDICAL
 CENTER**
3333 Burnett Ave.
Cincinnati, OH 45229-3039
Telephone: (513) 559-4200
Industry Affiliation: Hospitals
**Publication(s):**
*'round The Center*
Day Published: bi-w.
Lead Time: 2 wks. prior to pub. date
Mtls Deadline: 2 wks. prior to pub. date
Spec. Requirements: 4-pg.; offset; 8 1/2 x
 14
Personnel: Charlie Whaton, Editor

2298
**CHILDREN'S HOSPITAL OF
 ORANGE COUNTY**
455 S. Main St.
Orange, CA 92668
Telephone: (714) 997-3000
Mailing Address:
 P.O. Box 5700
 Orange, CA 92613
Industry Affiliation: Hospitals
**Publication(s):**
*Kids Health*
Day Published: q.
Contact: Public Relations
Spec. Requirements: 8 pg.; offset; 8 1/2 x
 11
Personnel: Debbie Shaw, Editor
 Jena Jensen, Marketing
 Director

*Med Staff News*
Day Published: m.
Lead Time: 6 wk.
Mtls Deadline: 6 wk.
Personnel: Mishele Kishmoian, Editor

*Good News Bearer*
Day Published: s-m.
Materials: 04,15,19,20,28
Contact: Public Relations
Personnel: Andrea Pronk, Editor

*Nurse Chronicle*
Day Published: m.
Materials: 19,20
Contact: Public Relations
Personnel: Judy Howard, Editor in Chief
 Andrea Pronk, Editor

4649
**CHILDREN'S HOSPITAL OF
 PHILADELPHIA, THE**
34th St. & Civic Str Blvd.
Philadelphia, PA 19104
Telephone: (215) 590-4100
Industry Affiliation: Hospitals
**Publication(s):**
*Children's View*
Day Published: q.
Mtls Deadline: 2 mos.
Personnel: Karen Yoon, Editor

*Children's Hospital Times*
Day Published: bi-m.
Mtls Deadline: 1 mo.
Personnel: Susan Soiferman, Editor

*Chop Talk*
Day Published: bi-w.
Mtls Deadline: 4 days
Personnel: Tamara Calkins

5225
**CHILDREN'S HOSPITAL OF THE
 KING'S DAUGHTERS**
601 Children's Ln.
Norfolk, VA 23507
Telephone: (804) 628-7043
FAX: (804) 628-7350
Industry Affiliation: Hospitals
**Publication(s):**
*Kidstuff*
Day Published: q.
Spec. Requirements: 16 pg.; 8 1/2 x 11
Personnel: Loretta Coureas, Editor
 Denise M. Dowd

*Update*
Day Published: bi-m.
Personnel: Patty Jo Nachman
 Denise M. Dowd
 Loretta Coureas

*Pediatric Progress*
Day Published: q.
Personnel: Beth M. Duke
 Denise M. Dowd
 Loretta Coureas

*Brief Update*
Day Published: w.

4307
**CHILDREN'S MEDICAL CENTER**
One Children's Plz.
Dayton, OH 45404-1815
Telephone: (513) 226-8300
FAX: (513) 226-8454
Industry Affiliation: Hospitals
**Publication(s):**
*Growing Together*
Day Published: q.
Lead Time: 60 days
Materials: 10,11,13,25,28
Mtls Deadline: 2 mos. prior to pub. date
Contact: Marketing and Comms
Spec. Requirements: 16-pg. offset
Personnel: Susan A. Brockman, Editor

*Pediatric Forum*
Day Published: q.
Lead Time: s-a.
Materials: 10,25
Mtls Deadline: 2 mo. prior to pub. date
Contact: Marketing and Comms.
Personnel: Susan A. Brockman, Editor

68542
**CHRYSLER CORP.**
1200 Chrysler Dr.
Detroit, MI 48288
Telephone: (313) 956-2894
FAX: (313) 956-2595
Industry Affiliation: Auto Suppliers
**Publication(s):**
*Chrysler Times*
Day Published: w.
Personnel: Allan Nahajewski

*Employee News Daily*
Day Published: d.
Personnel: Judith Griffie

3853
**CHUBB LIFEAMERICA**
1 Granite Pl.
Concord, NH 03301
Telephone: (603) 226-5000
Industry Affiliation: Insurance

**Publication(s):**
*Connection*
Day Published: q.
Lead Time: 1 mo.
Contact: Public Relations
Spec. Requirements: loose sheets
Personnel: Michael Holmes, Editor

*Insight*
Day Published: q.
Lead Time: 1 mo.
Contact: Marketing Communications
Spec. Requirements: 16-pg.
Personnel: Byron Champlin, Editor

2101
**CHURCH DIVINITY SCHOOL OF
 THE PACIFIC**
2451 Ridge Rd.
Berkeley, CA 94709
Telephone: (510) 848-3282
Industry Affiliation: Colleges, Institutions,
 Science Research
**Publication(s):**
*Crossings*
Day Published: q.
Lead Time: 3 mo.
Spec. Requirements: 8 pg.; offset; 8 1/2 x
 11
Personnel: Dolly Patterson, Editor

*Continuing Education Bulletin*
Day Published: s-a.
Spec. Requirements: Produced in-house
 educational programs
Personnel: Alda Marsh Morgan, Editor

5374
**CHURCH MUTUAL INSURANCE
 CO.**
3000 Schuster Ln.
Merrill, WI 54452
Industry Affiliation: Insurance
**Publication(s):**
*Ins-Spire*
Day Published: q.
Spec. Requirements: 6 pg.; offset bulletin;
 66 x 104
Personnel: Patrick Moreland, Editor

3973
**CIBA-GEIGY CORP.**
444 Saw Mill River Rd.
Ardsley, NY 10502
Telephone: (914) 479-5000
FAX: (914) 479-4218
Industry Affiliation: Drugs, Cosmetics,
 Pharmaceuticals
**Publication(s):**
*C I B A u.s.*
Day Published: q.
Mtls Deadline: 2 mos. prior to pub. date
Contact: Corporate
Spec. Requirements: 12 pg.; offset; 8 1/2
 x 11
Personnel: Linda Spear, Editor

*Westimes*
Day Published: m.
Lead Time: 1 mo.
Mtls Deadline: 1 mo. prior to pub. date
Personnel: Linda Spear, Editor

4705
**CIGNA CORP.**
1601 Chestnut St.
TLP-6
Philadelphia, PA 19192
Telephone: (215) 761-1000
Industry Affiliation: Insurance

---

Materials Accepted/Included: 01-Business news 02-By-line articles 03-Fashion news 04-Food news 05-Freelance copy 06-Letters to editor 07-Real estate news 08-Sports news 09-Travel news 10-Book rev. 11-Movie rev. 12-Music rev. 13-TV rev. 14-Theater rev. 15-Coming events 16-Obituaries 17-Question & answer 18-Social announcements 19-Artwork 20-Cartoons 21-Photos 22-TV listings 23-Audio rec. 24-Video rec. 25-Books 26-Films/film clips 27-Personnel news 28-Press releases 29-New product news/photos 30-Trade lit. 31-Contracts awarded 32-Display adv. 33-Classified adv.

**Publication(s):**
*Signals*
Day Published: q.
Lead Time: 2 mos. prior to pub. date
Contact: Barry Nelson
       1650 Market St.
       OLP-53
       Philadelphia, PA 19192
Spec. Requirements: 16-20 pg.; offset; 10 x 13
Personnel: Barry Nelson, Managing Editor

*Pulse*
Day Published: s-m.
Lead Time: 2 wks. prior to pub. date
Mtls Deadline: 2 wks. prior to pub. date
Contact: Gene Morris
       1601 Chestnut St.
       TLP-6
       Philadelphia, PA 19192
Spec. Requirements: 4 pg.; 10 x 13; offset
Personnel: Gene Morris, Editor

**CINCINNATI BAR ASSOCIATION**   4309
35 E. Seventh St., Ste. 800
Cincinnati, OH 45202-2492
Telephone: (513) 381-8213
Industry Affiliation: Associations: Trade, Fraternal
**Publication(s):**
*Report*
Day Published: m.
Lead Time: 2 mos. prior to pub. date
Mtls Deadline: 1st of mo. prior to pub.
Spec. Requirements: 8 1/2 x 11 magazine
Personnel: Leah Silverman Gales, Editor
       Nancy V. Nolan
       Suzanne Pettett
       Melanie A. Grace, Art Director

*C B A Legal Directory*
Day Published: a.
Lead Time: 6 mos. prior to pub. date
Mtls Deadline: 6 mos. prior to May pub.
Personnel: Nancy V. Nolan

**CINCINNATI GAS & ELECTRIC CO.**   4490
P.O. Box 960
Cincinnati, OH 45201
Telephone: (513) 287-2637
Industry Affiliation: Utility: Gas
**Publication(s):**
*O-K News*
Day Published: bi-w.
Spec. Requirements: 8 pg.; offset newspaper; 11 x 16
Personnel: Marshall Hacker, Editor

*Bulletin*
Day Published: d.
Personnel: Marshall Hacker, Editor

**CIT GROUP**   3974
650 Cit Dr.
Livingston, NJ 07039
Telephone: (201) 740-5136
FAX: (201) 740-5132
Industry Affiliation: Finance, Services
**Publication(s):**
*Citings*
Day Published: q.
Spec. Requirements: 20 pg; offset; 84 x 11
Personnel: Elenor Spalmacin, Editor

**CITIBANK**   4013
850 Third Ave., 13th Fl.
New York, NY 10043
Telephone: (212) 559-8403
FAX: (212) 793-5945
Industry Affiliation: Banks, Savings & Loans

**Publication(s):**
*Citibank World*
Day Published: 6-8/yr.
Spec. Requirements: 24-pg; offset magazine; 82 x 112
Personnel: Andrew Daniels, Editor

**CITY OF BOSTON**   3329
One City Hall Plz., New City Hall
Boston, MA 02201
Telephone: (617) 635-4000
Industry Affiliation: Associations: City, State, Federal
**Publication(s):**
*City Record*
Day Published: bi-m.
Contact: Office of Communications
Spec. Requirements: 8-page; offset; 10 3/4 x 15
Personnel: William D. Stanton, Editor

**CITY OF CINCINNATI**   4310
City Hall, Rm. 152
Cincinnati, OH 45202
Telephone: (513) 352-3241
FAX: (513) 352-6284
Industry Affiliation: Associations: City, State, Federal
**Publication(s):**
*City Scenes*
Day Published: q.
Lead Time: 6 wks. prior to pub. date
Mtls Deadline: 3rd wk. of qtr. prior to pub. date
Contact: Personnel
Spec. Requirements: 11 x 17.5; accordion-fold; 8 panels
Personnel: Michelle Jones, Editor

**CITY OF DAYTON**   4311
101 W. Third St.
Dayton, OH 45402
Telephone: (513) 443-3750
FAX: (513) 443-4282
Mailing Address:
       P.O. Box 22
       Dayton, OH 45402
Industry Affiliation: Associations: City, State, Federal
**Publication(s):**
*City Beat*
Day Published: bi-m.
Lead Time: 4 wks. prior to pub. date
Mtls Deadline: 4 wks. prior to pub. date
Contact: Division of Marketing
Spec. Requirements: 8-16 pgs.; offset; 17 x 11
Personnel: Lorraine Russell, Editor

*Dayton Update*
Day Published: q.
Lead Time: 4 wks. prior to pub. date
Mtls Deadline: 4 wks. prior to pub. date
Contact: Division of Marketing
Spec. Requirements: 8-12 pg. tabloid
Personnel: Thomas J. Biedenharn
       Lorraine Russell

**CITY OF DETROIT**   3439
608 City Council Bldg.
Detroit, MI 48226
Telephone: (313) 224-3755
FAX: (313) 224-1647
Industry Affiliation: Associations: City, State, Federal
**Publication(s):**
*Facts About Detroit*
Day Published: irreg.
Lead Time: 60 days

*Calendar Of Events*
Day Published: irreg.
Lead Time: 60 days

*Summer In The City*
Day Published: irreg.
Lead Time: 60 days

*Autumn In The City*
Day Published: irreg.
Lead Time: 60 days

**CITY OF JACKSON MISSISSIPPI**   3640
P.O. Box 17
Jackson, MS 39205
Telephone: (601) 960-1084
Industry Affiliation: Associations: City, State, Federal
**Publication(s):**
*Cityworks*
Day Published: m.
Lead Time: 1 mo.
Mtls Deadline: 30 days
Spec. Requirements: 6-pg.; offset; 8 1/2 x 11
Personnel: Robert Lesley, Editor

**CITY OF RICHARDSON TEXAS**   4943
411 W. Arapaho Rd.
Richardson, TX 75080
Telephone: (214) 235-8331
Mailing Address:
       P.O. Box 830309
       Richardson, TX 75083
Industry Affiliation: Associations: City, State, Federal
**Publication(s):**
*City Wide Newsletter*
Day Published: m.
Lead Time: 4 wks. prior to pub. date
Mtls Deadline: 1st of mo. prior to pub. date
Contact: Public Information
Spec. Requirements: 20 pg.; offset; 11 x 17
Personnel: Amy McGuire, Editor

*Richardson Employee Newsletter*
Day Published: m.
Lead Time: 2 wks. prior to pub. date
Mtls Deadline: 1st of mo. prior to pub. date
Contact: Public Information
Spec. Requirements: 4-pg.
Personnel: Rick McGarry, Editor

**CITY OF RICHMOND VIRGINIA**   5227
900 E. Broad St.
Richmond, VA 23219
Telephone: (804) 780-7985
FAX: (804) 780-6931
Industry Affiliation: Associations: City, State, Federal
**Publication(s):**
*Our News - City Employees Newsletter*
Day Published: q.
Lead Time: 3 wks. of 1st mo.
Materials: 02,19,20
Mtls Deadline: 5 wks. prior to pub.
Contact: City Manager's Public Info. Office
Spec. Requirements: 4-pg.; offset; 8 1/2 x 11
Personnel: Anne Amoury, Editor

*City Of Richmond Annual Report*
Day Published: a.
Lead Time: 6 mos.
Mtls Deadline: July 30 for Nov. 30 pub. date
Contact: City Manager's Public Info. Office
Personnel: Anne Amoury

**CITY OF ST. PETERSBURG**   2581
175 5th St., N.
St. Petersburg, FL 33701
Telephone: (813) 893-7465
FAX: (813) 892-5372
Mailing Address:
       P.O. Box 2842
       St Petersburg, FL 33731
Industry Affiliation: Associations: City, State, Federal

**Publication(s):**
*Sunscribe*
Day Published: m.
Lead Time: 15 days
Materials: 01,30
Mtls Deadline: 15th of ea. mo.
Spec. Requirements: 6 pg., 8 1/2 x 11
Personnel: Joan Ann Riedmiller, Editor

**CITY PUBLIC SERVICE**   4944
P.O. Box 1771
San Antonio, TX 78296
Telephone: (210) 978-2545
FAX: (210) 978-3058
Industry Affiliation: Utility: Related
**Publication(s):**
*Broadcaster*
Day Published: bi-m.
Spec. Requirements: 20-pg. offset; 8 1/2 x 11
Personnel: Steve School, Editor

**CIVITAN INTERNATIONAL**   1988
P.O. Box 130744
Birmingham, AL 35213-0744
Telephone: (205) 591-8910
FAX: (205) 592-6307
Industry Affiliation: Associations: Trade, Fraternal
**Publication(s):**
*Civitan Magazine*
Day Published: 8/yr.
Lead Time: 3-6 mos.
Spec. Requirements: 32-pg.; offset; 8 1/2 x 11
Personnel: Dorothy M. Wellborn, Editor
       Civitan International, Publisher
       Connie Manier, Art Director

*Countdown*
Day Published: q.
Spec. Requirements: 16 page
Personnel: Dorothy Wellborn, Editor
       Connie Manier, Art Director

**CLAIROL INC.**   3976
345 Park Ave.
New York, NY 10154
Telephone: (212) 546-5000
Industry Affiliation: Drugs, Cosmetics, Pharmaceuticals
**Publication(s):**
*Clairol Highlights:*
Day Published: m.
Spec. Requirements: 4-pg.; offset; 9 x 12
Personnel: Connie Kain, Editor

**CLARKSON HOSPITAL**   3765
44th & Dewey Ave.
Omaha, NE 68105
Telephone: (402) 552-2000
Industry Affiliation: Hospitals
**Publication(s):**
*Discover Health*
Day Published: 3/yr.
Lead Time: 10 wks. prior to pub. date
Mtls Deadline: 10 wks. prior to pub. date
Spec. Requirements: 20 pg., 4-color
Personnel: Susan Meyers, Editor

**CMI CORP.**   4526
P.O. Box 1985
Oklahoma City, OK 73101
Telephone: (405) 787-6020
FAX: (405) 491-2417
Industry Affiliation: Industry: Heavy Construction, Machinery

**Materials Accepted/Included:** 01-Business news 02-By-line articles 03-Fashion news 04-Food news 05-Freelance copy 06-Letters to editor 07-Real estate news 08-Sports news 09-Travel news 10-Book rev. 11-Movie rev. 12-Music rev. 13-TV rev. 14-Theater rev. 15-Coming events 16-Obituaries 17-Question & answer 18-Social announcements 19-Artwork 20-Cartoons 21-Photos 22-TV listings 23-Audio rec. 24-Video rec. 25-Books 26-Films/film clips 27-Personnel news 28-Press releases 29-New product news/photos 30-Trade lit. 31-Contracts awarded 32-Display adv. 33-Classified adv.

**Publication(s):**
*C M I News*
Day Published: q.
Lead Time: 90 Days
Materials: 01,02,05,21,24,25,28
Mtls Deadline: Contact Editor
Spec. Requirements: 48-page; offset; 8 1/2 x 11
Personnel: Jim Rodriguez, Editor

4155
**CMP INUSTRIES, INC.**
413 N. Pearl St.
Albany, NY 12207
Telephone: (518) 434-3147
FAX: (518) 434-1288
Mailing Address:
  P.O. Box 350
  Albany, NY 12201-0350
Industry Affiliation: Dental, Medical
**Publication(s):**
*Insights*
Day Published: q.
Lead Time: 3-4 mos. prior to pub. date
Materials: 01,02,06,20,30
Mtls Deadline: 1-2 mos. prior to pub. date
  P.O. Box 407
  North Chatham, NY 12132
Spec. Requirements: 4-pg. 11 x 17
Personnel: Dean Quackenbush, Editor
  Joseph Strack
  Richard Adamson, Marketing Director

2770
**CNA INSURANCE**
CNA Plaza
Chicago, IL 60685
Telephone: (312) 822-7402
Mailing Address:
  P.O. Box 90210
  Beverly Hills, CA 90210
Industry Affiliation: Insurance
**Publication(s):**
*Inside C N A*
Day Published: bi-m.
Lead Time: 1 mo. prior to pub. date
Materials: 01
Spec. Requirements: 8 pg.; offset; tabloid
Personnel: Robert Ghelardi, Editor
  Ellen Grindy, Editor in Chief
  Ellen Grindy, Publisher

*Viewpoint Magazine*
Day Published: q.
Spec. Requirements: 32 pg.; 8 x 10
Personnel: Sandra Carcione, Editor
  Ellen Grindy, Marketing Director

*Keynoter*
Day Published: q.
Spec. Requirements: 12-16 pg.; 8 1/2 x 11; magazine
Personnel: Kay Athey, Editor

*Branch Newsletters*
Day Published: bi-m.
Spec. Requirements: 8 1/2 x 11; 2 pg.; newsletter
Personnel: Joan Johnston, Editor
  Helen Raece, Marketing Director
  Joan Cocciatore, Publisher

2990
**COACHMAN INDUSTRIES, INC.**
601 E. Beardsley
Elkhart, IN 46514
Telephone: (219) 825-8514
FAX: (219) 825-7868
Mailing Address:
  P.O. Box 30, 423 N. Main St.
  Middlebury, IN 46540
Industry Affiliation: Autos, Trucks

**Publication(s):**
*Coachmen Capers*
Day Published: q.
Lead Time: 45 days
Materials: 09,15
Spec. Requirements: 80-92 pg.; offset; 8 1/2 x 11
Personnel: Lon Huffman, Editor
  Rosalie Corson, Managing Editor

*Coachmen World*
Day Published: m.
Materials: 27
Personnel: Lon Huffman, Editor

4946
**COASTAL CORP., THE**
9 Greenway Plz., Ste. 704A
Houston, TX 77046
Telephone: (713) 877-3041
FAX: (713) 877-3299
Industry Affiliation: Utility: Electric
**Publication(s):**
*Coastal World*
Day Published: q.
Lead Time: 1 mo. prior to pub. date
Mtls Deadline: 1 mo. prior to pub. date
Spec. Requirements: 8-12 pg.; offset; 10 x 12-1/2
Personnel: Allyson K. Edwards, Editor

2638
**COATS & CLARK, INC.**
30 Patewood Dr.
Greenville, SC 29615
Telephone: (803) 234-0331
Mailing Address:
  P.O. Box 757
  Toccoa, GA 30577
Industry Affiliation: Textiles, Apparel, Mills, Machinery
**Publication(s):**
*Coats & Clark Highlights*
Day Published: q.
Contact: Finishing Div.
Spec. Requirements: 12-16 pgs.; offset; 11 x 15
Personnel: William W. Chism, Editor

4947
**COCA-COLA COMPANY, THE**
One Coca-Cola Plaza
Atlanta, GA 30313
Telephone: (404) 676-2121
Mailing Address:
  P.O. Drawer 1734
  Atlanta, GA 30301
Industry Affiliation: Soft Drinks
**Publication(s):**
*Journey*
Day Published: q.
Personnel: Robert Byrd, Managing Editor

68424
**COCA-COLA FOODS**
P.O. Box 2079
Houston, TX 77252
Telephone: (713) 888-5423
FAX: (713) 888-5054
Industry Affiliation: Food, General
**Publication(s):**
*Foodline*
Day Published: bi-m.
Mtls Deadline: 5th of ea. mo. prior to pub. date
Personnel: Laura Watts

*Foodline Club Newsletter*
Day Published: bi-w.
Mtls Deadline: Thu.
Personnel: Laura Watts

4651
**COLONIAL PENN GROUP INC.**
1818 Market St.
Philadelphia, PA 19181
Telephone: (215) 988-8000
FAX: (215) 988-7703
Industry Affiliation: Insurance

**Publication(s):**
*You*
Day Published: m.
Contact: Corp. Affrs.
Spec. Requirements: 2-pg.; offset; 11 x 17
Personnel: William McBratney, Editor

68437
**COLONIAL WILLIAMSBURG FOUNDATION**
P.O. Box 1776
Williamsburg, VA 23187
Telephone: (804) 220-7120
FAX: (804) 220-7702
Industry Affiliation: Associations: City, State, Federal
**Publication(s):**
*Colonial Williamsburg News*
Day Published: w.
Mtls Deadline: Mon. 5 pm
Personnel: Patrick R. Saylor, Editor

2357
**COLORADO ASSN. OF REALTORS**
300 Inverness Way S.
Englewood, CO 80112-5819
Telephone: (303) 770-6550
Industry Affiliation: Associations: Trade, Fraternal
**Publication(s):**
*Colorado Realtor News*
Day Published: 10/yr.
Lead Time: 15th of mo. prior to pub. date
Materials: 01,28,29,32
Mtls Deadline: 15th of mo. prior to pub. date
Spec. Requirements: 12-16 pg. (varies); tabloid
Personnel: John Van Blaricum, Editor in Chief

2356
**COLORADO ASSOCIATION OF PUBLIC EMPLOYEES**
1390 Logan St., Rm. 402
Denver, CO 80203
Telephone: (303) 832-1001
FAX: (303) 832-1004
Industry Affiliation: Associations: Trade, Fraternal
**Publication(s):**
*The Citizen*
Day Published: m.
Lead Time: 2 wks. prior to pub. date
Mtls Deadline: 2 wks. prior to pub. date
Spec. Requirements: 12-page; offset; 11 1/4 x 17
Personnel: Phil Christie, Editor

2395
**COLORADO INTERSTATE GAS CO.**
2 N. Nevada
Colorado Springs, CO 80903
Telephone: (719) 520-4451
FAX: (719) 520-4318
Industry Affiliation: Utility: Gas
**Publication(s):**
*C I G World*
Day Published: bi-m.
Lead Time: 2 mos.
Mtls Deadline: 2 mos.
Spec. Requirements: 16 pg.; offset; 10 3/4 x 8 1/4
Personnel: Wayne Tiller, Editor

2396
**COLORADO MUNICIPAL LEAGUE**
1660 Lincoln, Ste. 2100
Denver, CO 80264
Telephone: (303) 831-6411
Industry Affiliation: Associations: City, State, Federal

**Publication(s):**
*Colorado Municipalities*
Day Published: bi-m.
Lead Time: 2 mos.
Materials: 02,06,32
Mtls Deadline: 15th of Feb., Apr., Jun., Aug., Oct., Dec.
Spec. Requirements: 32-36 pg.; offset; 8 1/2 x 11
Personnel: Kay Mariea, Editor

*C M L Newsletter*
Day Published: bi-w.
Lead Time: 2 wks.
Mtls Deadline: Fri. before pub. date
Spec. Requirements: 8 pg.; offset; 8 1/2 x 11
Personnel: Kay Mariea, Editor

2398
**COLORADO SOCIETY OF CERTIFIED PUBLIC ACCOUNTANTS**
7979 E. Tufts Ave., Ste. 500
Denver, CO 80237
Telephone: (303) 773-2877
Industry Affiliation: Associations: Trade, Fraternal
**Publication(s):**
*Newsaccount*
Day Published: 8/yr.
Lead Time: 5 wks. prior to pub. date
Mtls Deadline: 5 wks. prior to pub. date
Spec. Requirements: 20 pg.; offset; 8-1/2 x 11
Personnel: Liz Julin, Editor

66424
**COLSO-QUIPS**
901 N. Main St.
Paris, IL 61944-0490
Telephone: (217) 465-7535
Mailing Address:
  P.O. Box 490
  Paris, IL 61944-0490
Industry Affiliation: Printers, Services
**Publication(s):**
*Colso-Quips*
Day Published: q.
Lead Time: 2 mos. prior to pub. date
Mtls Deadline: 2 mos. prior to start of calendar quarter
Personnel: John E. Jedd, Editor

4317
**COLUMBIA GAS DISTRIBUTION CO.**
200 Civic Center Dr.
Columbus, OH 43215
Telephone: (614) 460-6000
FAX: (614) 460-4672
Mailing Address:
  P.O. Box 117
  Columbus, OH 43216
Industry Affiliation: Utility: Gas
**Publication(s):**
*Cdc News*
Day Published: m.
Lead Time: 4 wks. prior to pub. date
Mtls Deadline: 4 wks. prior to pub. date
Personnel: Paul Collins, Editor

2485
**COLUMBIA GAS SYSTEM**
20 Montchanin Rd.
Wilmington, DE 19807
Telephone: (302) 429-5000
Mailing Address:
  P.O. Box 4020
  Wilmington, DE 19807
Industry Affiliation: Utility: Gas

---

Materials Accepted/Included: 01-Business news 02-By-line articles 03-Fashion news 04-Food news 05-Freelance copy 06-Letters to editor 07-Real estate news 08-Sports news 09-Travel news 10-Book rev. 11-Movie rev. 12-Music rev. 13-TV rev. 14-Theater rev. 15-Coming events 16-Obituaries 17-Question & answer 18-Social announcements 19-Artwork 20-Cartoons 21-Photos 22-TV listings 23-Audio rec. 24-Video rec. 25-Books 26-Films/film clips 27-Personnel news 28-Press releases 29-New product news/photos 30-Trade lit. 31-Contracts awarded 32-Display adv. 33-Classified adv.

**Publication(s):**
*Columbia Today*
Day Published: bi-m.
Contact: Tom Hauck, Ed.
    Telephone: (614) 481-4376
    P.O. Box 2318
    Columbus, OH 43276-2318
Spec. Requirements: 20 pg.; offset; 8 x 11
Personnel: Tom Hauck, Editor

**COLUMBIA GAS TRANSMISSION**  68394
  **CORP.**
P.O. Box 1273
Charleston, WV 25325
Industry Affiliation: Utility: Gas
**Publication(s):**
*Insights*
Day Published: bi-w.
Mtls Deadline: 2 wks. prior to pub. date
Personnel: Karl Brack, Editor

*News Lines*
Day Published: s-w.
Mtls Deadline: ongoing
Personnel: E. Kelly Merritt, Editor

**COLUMBIA GULF TRANSMISSION**  68396
P.O. Box 683
Houston, TX 77001
Telephone: (713) 267-4181
FAX: (713) 267-4110
Industry Affiliation: Utility: Gas
**Publication(s):**
*Insights*
Day Published: m.
Personnel: K. Smith Leonard,
    Communications
    Representative

**COLUMBUS LIFE INSURANCE CO.**  4319
303 E. Broad St.
Columbus, OH 43215
Telephone: (614) 221-5875
Industry Affiliation: Insurance
**Publication(s):**
*Log*
Day Published: m.
Spec. Requirements: 12-pg.; offset
  magazine; 8 1/2 x 11
Personnel: Kathleen O'Neill, Editor

**COLUMBUS SOUTHERN POWER**  4318
  **CO.**
215 N. Front St
Columbus, OH 43215
Telephone: (614) 836-2570
FAX: (614) 464-7144
Industry Affiliation: Utility: Electric
**Publication(s):**
*Litelines:*
Day Published: m.
Lead Time: 2 mos. prior to pub. date
Mtls Deadline: 2 mos. prior to pub. date
Spec. Requirements: 16 page-mag. is
  quarterly 8 page-tabloid 8 time/yr
Personnel: Greg Grant, Editor

**COMERICA, INC.**  3444
211 W. Fort St.
Detroit, MI 48275
Telephone: (313) 222-7350
Industry Affiliation: Banks, Savings &
  Loans

**Publication(s):**
*Spectrum*
Day Published: m.
Lead Time: 1 mo.
Spec. Requirements: 6 pg.; magapaper
  (tabloid)
Personnel: Elaine McRee, Editor

**COMMERCIAL UNION INS. CO.**  3330
One Beacon St.
Boston, MA 02108
Telephone: (617) 725-6000
Industry Affiliation: Insurance
**Publication(s):**
*C U News*
Day Published: bi-m.
Lead Time: 3 wks.
Spec. Requirements: 16 pg.; 9 x 12 glossy
Personnel: John Lempesis, Editor
    Breda Shernan Monchick,
      Production Manager
    Louis Mucci, Art Director

*New Horizons*
Day Published: q.
Personnel: John Lempesis, Editor
    Breda Shernan Monchick,
      Production Manager
    Louis Mucci, Art Director

**COMMONWEALTH EDISON**  2775
One First National Plz.
Chicago, IL 60690
Telephone: (312) 394-4321
Industry Affiliation: Utility: Electric
**Publication(s):**
*Watt's Happening, The*
Day Published: q.
Spec. Requirements: 12-16 pg.; offset
  magazine; 8 1/2 x 11
Personnel: Kelly Martin, Editor

**COMMONWEALTH LIFE**  3175
  **INSURANCE CO.**
680 Fourth Ave.
Louisville, KY 40202-4306
Telephone: (502) 560-3669
FAX: (502) 560-2148
Mailing Address:
    P.O. Box 32800
    Louisville, KY 40232
Industry Affiliation: Insurance
**Publication(s):**
*Commonwealth Comments*
Day Published: m.
Lead Time: 3 wks.
Materials: 01,15,27,28,29,30
Spec. Requirements: 20-40 page; offset; 8
  1/2 x 11
Personnel: Stacy Crabtree, Editor
    Casey Arterburn,
      Communications Associate

*Open Line*
Day Published: m.
Materials: 01,15,27,28,29
Mtls Deadline: 25th of mo.
Contact: Human Resources
    Telephone: (502) 560-3669
Personnel: Betsey Shirey, Editor in Chief

**COMMUNICATION RESEARCH**  3275
  **ASSOCIATES, INC.**
10606 Mantz Rd.
Silver Spring, MD 20903
Telephone: (301) 445-3230
Industry Affiliation: Advertising, Art, Public
  Relations
**Publication(s):**
*Public Relations Review:*
Day Published: q.
Lead Time: 3 mos.
Spec. Requirements: 64-pg.; offset; 6 x 9
Personnel: Ray E. Hiebert, Editor

*Social Science Monitor*
Day Published: m.
Spec. Requirements: 8-pg. newsletter
Personnel: Ray E. Hiebert

*Video Monitor*
Day Published: m.
Lead Time: 1 mo.
Spec. Requirements: 8-pg. newsletter
Personnel: Ray E. Hiebert
    Sheila Gibbons

*Hi-Tech Alert For The Pro. Communicator*
Day Published: m.
Spec. Requirements: 8-Pg. Newsletter
Personnel: Michael R. Naver

*Media Report To Women*
Day Published: bi-m.
Lead Time: 1 mo.
Spec. Requirements: 12 Page Newsletter
Personnel: Sheila Gibbons

**COMMUNITY HOSPITAL OF THE**  2106
  **MONTEREY PENINSULA**
P.O. Box HH
Monterey, CA 93942
Telephone: (408) 625-4505
Industry Affiliation: Hospitals
**Publication(s):**
*Pulse:*
Day Published: q.
Lead Time: 2 mos.
Spec. Requirements: 32 pgs; offset; 8 x 11
Personnel: Laurie Slothower, Editor

**COMMUNITY MEDICAL CENTER**  4653
1822 Mulberry St.
Scranton, PA 18510
Telephone: (717) 969-8000
FAX: (717) 969-8007
Industry Affiliation: Hospitals
**Publication(s):**
*Monitor*
Day Published: bi-m.
Lead Time: 1 mo.
Spec. Requirements: 4-8 pgs; offset; 8 1/2
  x 11
Personnel: Mary Louise Ruane, Editor

**COMPAQ COMPUTER CORP.**  66557
20555 S. H. 249
Houston, TX 77070
Industry Affiliation: Office Equipment,
  Services, Supplies
**Publication(s):**
*Inside & Out*
Day Published: bi-m.
Lead Time: 3 wks.
Mtls Deadline: 3rd Mon. of prior mo.
Personnel: Kira Giffin

*Compaq Compass*
Day Published: q.
Lead Time: 3 wks.
Mtls Deadline: 1st mo. of quarter

**CONNECTICUT BUSINESS &**  2467
  **INDUSTRY ASSOCIATION**
370 Asylum St.
Hartford, CT 06103
Telephone: (203) 244-1900
FAX: (203) 278-2582
Industry Affiliation: Associations: City,
  State, Federal
**Publication(s):**
*C B I A news*
Day Published: 8/yr.
Lead Time: 8 wks.
Materials: 32
Mtls Deadline: 8 wks. prior to pub. date
Spec. Requirements: 16-32 pg.; offset; 22
  x 17
Personnel: Diane Friend Edwards, Editor

**CONNECTICUT CREDIT UNION**  2474
  **LEAGUE**
P.O. Box 5001
Wallingford, CT 06492
Telephone: (203) 265-5657
FAX: (203) 284-8194
Industry Affiliation: Finance, Services
**Publication(s):**
*League Update Extra*
Day Published: q.
Materials: 01,07,17,19,20,21,28,29,30
Mtls Deadline: Jan., Apr., Jul., Oct.
Contact: Publications
Spec. Requirements: 8-12 pg.; offset; 8
  1/2 x 11
Personnel: Diane Tye, Editor

*League Update*
Day Published: w.
Materials: 01,07,17,19,20,21,28,29,30
Contact: Publications
Spec. Requirements: 2 pg.; newsletter; 8
  1/2 x 11
Personnel: Diane Tye, Editor

**CONNECTICUT EDUCATION**  2476
  **ASSOCIATION**
Capital Pl., Ste. 500, 21 Oak St.
Hartford, CT 06106-8001
Telephone: (203) 525-5641
Industry Affiliation: Associations: Trade,
  Fraternal
**Publication(s):**
*C E A advisor*
Day Published: 9/yr.
Lead Time: 1 mo. prior to pub. date
Mtls Deadline: 1 mo. prior to pub. date
Spec. Requirements: 16-page; offset; 11
  3/4 x 17 1/2
Personnel: Michael G. Lydick, Editor

**CONNECTICUT MOTOR CLUB**  2478
2276 Whitney Ave.
Hamden, CT 06518
Telephone: (203) 288-7441
Industry Affiliation: Autos, Trucks

**Publication(s):**
*Connecticut Traveler*
Day Published: m.
Lead Time: 3 mos.
Mtls Deadline: 2 mos. prior to pub. date
Spec. Requirements: 32 pages; offset 10 x 14; trim 10 1/2 x 14 1/2
Personnel: Annette Cormany, Editor

2479
**CONNECTICUT MUTUAL LIFE INSURANCE**
140 Garden St
Hartford, CT 06154
Telephone: (203) 727-6500
Industry Affiliation: Insurance
**Publication(s):**
*Blue Chip News*
Day Published: bi-w.
Lead Time: 2 wks. prior to pub. date
Mtls Deadline: 8 days prior to pub. date
Contact: Communications Div.
Spec. Requirements: 6-8 page; desktop publishing; 11 x 13
Personnel: David Conrad, Associate Editor

2480
**CONNECTICUT NATURAL GAS CORP.**
100 Columbus Blvd.
Hartford, CT 06103
Telephone: (203) 727-3000
FAX: (203) 727-3271
Mailing Address:
    P.O. Box 1500
    Hartford, CT 06144
Industry Affiliation: Utility:  Gas
**Publication(s):**
*Fuel For Thought*
Day Published: bi-m.
Lead Time: 6 wks. prior to pub. date
Mtls Deadline: 6 wks. prior to pub. date
Spec. Requirements: 4-pg.; offset tabloid; 12 x 7 1/2
Personnel: Martha McGann, Editor

4998
**CONSECO, INC.**
11815 N. Pennsylvania St.
Carmel, IN 46032
Telephone: (800) 824-2726
FAX: (317) 573-6818
Industry Affiliation: Insurance
**Publication(s):**
*Conseco Comments*
Day Published: m.
Lead Time: 1 mo. prior to pub. date
Materials: 01
Mtls Deadline: 15th of mo. prior to pub. date
Spec. Requirements: 16-20-page
Personnel: Lisa Hullinger, Editor

3979
**CONSOLIDATED EDISON CO. OF NEW YORK**
4 Irving Pl., Rm. 1627
New York, NY 10003
Telephone: (212) 460-4109
Industry Affiliation: Utility:  Electric
**Publication(s):**
*Around The System*
Day Published: 10/yr.
Lead Time: 3 mo.
Spec. Requirements: 32-pg.; offset; 8 1/2 x 11
Personnel: Allen Pinto, Editor

5376
**CONSOLIDATED PAPERS, INC.**
231 First Ave., N.
Wisconsin Rapids, WI 54495
Telephone: (715) 422-3111
Industry Affiliation: Paper Products

**Publication(s):**
*News*
Day Published: bi-m.
Lead Time: 2 mo. minimum
Spec. Requirements: 16-pg.; offset magazine; 9 x 12
Personnel: Robert Walker, Editor

3431
**CONSTRUCTION ASSOCIATION OF MICHIGAN (CAM)**
1351 E. Jefferson Ave.
Detroit, MI 48207
Telephone: (313) 567-5500
FAX: (313) 567-1372
Industry Affiliation: Industry:  Heavy Construction, Machinery
**Publication(s):**
*C A M magazine*
Day Published: m.
Lead Time: 1 mo.
Mtls Deadline: 5th of mo. prior to pub. date
Spec. Requirements: 15-pg.; offset; 8 1/2 x 11
Personnel: Marla Janess, Editor

*Construction Marketing Research*
Day Published: w.
Mtls Deadline: 2 wks. prior to pub. date
Personnel: Rachel Lichtman, Editor

*Construction Buyers Guide*
Day Published: a.
Lead Time: Dec. 1st
Personnel: Kathryn Winkeljohn

68528
**CONTINENTAL ASSURANCE CO.**
CNA Plz.
333 S. Wabash
Chicago, IL 60604
Telephone: (312) 822-5000
FAX: (312) 822-2481
Industry Affiliation: Insurance
**Publication(s):**
*Inside C N A*
Day Published: bi-m.
Personnel: Paul Brucker

66450
**CONTINENTAL BANK**
231 S. LaSalle St.
Chicago, IL 60697
Telephone: (312) 974-5210
Industry Affiliation: Banks, Savings & Loans
**Publication(s):**
*Continental Currency*
Day Published: bi-m.
Lead Time: 2-4 wks. prior to pub. date
Mtls Deadline: 2 wks. prior to pub. date
Contact: Corporate Relations
Personnel: Deborah Storms, Editor

*Well Said*
Day Published: q.
Contact: Corporate Relations
            Telephone: (312) 974-5210
            231 S. LaSalle St.
            Chicago, IL 60697
Personnel: Dr. Richard Hughes, Managing Editor
            Deborah Storms, Editor
            Continental Bank, Publisher

3981
**CONTINENTAL CORP.**
180 Maiden Ln.
New York, NY 10038
Telephone: (212) 440-7727
Industry Affiliation: Insurance

**Publication(s):**
*Continental Bulletin*
Day Published: q.
Lead Time: 2 mos. prior to pub. date
Spec. Requirements: 16-24 pg.; offset magazine; 8-1/2 x 11
Personnel: Jodi H. Dorman, Editor

68444
**CONTINENTAL GRAIN CO., WAYNE FEED DIVISION**
10 S. Riverside Plaza
Chicago, IL 60606
Telephone: (312) 466-6520
FAX: (312) 466-6614
Industry Affiliation: Agriculture
**Publication(s):**
*Innovator*
Day Published: q.
Personnel: Barbara Becker, Editor

*Wayn-E-Gram*
Day Published: q.
Personnel: Barbara Becker, Editor

3083
**CONTINENTAL WESTERN INDUSTRIES**
11021 Douglas Ave.
Des Moines, IA 50322
Telephone: (515) 278-3000
FAX: (515) 278-3451
Mailing Address:
    P.O. Box 1594
    Des Moines, IA 50322
Industry Affiliation: Insurance
**Publication(s):**
*Contact*
Day Published: bi-m.
Spec. Requirements: 4 pg.; 8-1/2 x 11
Personnel: Bonnie Barnes, Editor

68414
**CONTINUING EDUCATION PRESS**
1633 SW Park
Portland, OR 97202
Telephone: (503) 725-4846
FAX: (503) 725-4840
Industry Affiliation: Colleges, Institutions, Science Research
**Publication(s):**
*Italic Hardwriting Newsletter*
Day Published: s-a.
Materials: 25
Personnel: Tena Spears, Marketing Director
            Tony Midson, Publisher

1989
**COOK'S PEST CONTROL, INC.**
1627 Wolverine Dr., S.E.
Decatur, AL 35601
Telephone: (404) 288-8233
Industry Affiliation: Associations:  Trade, Fraternal
**Publication(s):**
*What's Cookin'*
Day Published: m.
Lead Time: 1 mo. prior to pub. date
Mtls Deadline: 1st of mo. prior to pub. date
Spec. Requirements: 16-20 pg.; offset; 8-1/2 x 11
Personnel: Lyn S. Cook, Editor

3676
**COOK COMPOSITES**
P.O. Box 419389
Kansas City, MO 64141
Telephone: (816) 391-6000
Industry Affiliation: Associations:  Trade, Fraternal

**Publication(s):**
*Frontline*
Day Published: q.
Lead Time: 1 mo.
Spec. Requirements: 6-8 pg. offset; 8 1/2 x 11

3854
**COOPER HOSPITAL/UNIVERSITY MEDICAL CENTER**
One Cooper Plz.
Camden, NJ 08103
Telephone: (609) 342-2000
FAX: (609) 342-3299
Industry Affiliation: Hospitals
**Publication(s):**
*Pulse*
Day Published: m.
Spec. Requirements: 4-6 pg.; offset; 8 1/2 x 11
Personnel: Rhonda Wexler, Editor

*Stethoscope*
Day Published: m.
Lead Time: 2 wks. prior to pub. date
Mtls Deadline: 2 wks. prior to pub. date
Spec. Requirements: 4 pg.
Personnel: Robinia Phoenix, Editor

4952
**COOPER INDUSTRIES, INC.**
First City Tower
1001 Fannin, 40th Fl.
Houston, TX 77002
Telephone: (713) 739-5400
FAX: (713) 739-5555
Mailing Address:
    P.O. Box 4446
    Houston, TX 77210
Industry Affiliation: Associations:  Trade, Fraternal
**Publication(s):**
*Cooper News*
Day Published: q.
Contact: Cooper Energy Services
            N. Sandusky St.
            Mount Vernon, OH 43050
Spec. Requirements: 16-24 pg.; offset; 8 1/2 x 11
Personnel: Pat Meinecke, Editor

4937
**COOPER OIL, TOOL DIV.**
P.O. Box 1212
Houston, TX 77251-1212
Telephone: (713) 499-8511
Industry Affiliation: Industry:  Material Handling
**Publication(s):**
*Oil & Iron*
Day Published: q.
Spec. Requirements: 20-pg.; 8 1/2 x 11
Personnel: Don Kingsley, Editor

4321
**COOPER TIRE & RUBBER COMPANY**
Lima & Western Aves.
Findlay, OH 45840
Telephone: (419) 423-1321
FAX: (419) 427-4719
Mailing Address:
    P.O. Box 550
    Findlay, OH 45839
Industry Affiliation: Rubber, Tires
**Publication(s):**
*Tire Tracks*
Day Published: m.
Spec. Requirements: 8-page; offset; 8 1/2 x 11
Personnel: Debbie Scherf, Editor

2358
**COORS COURIER**
311 10th St.
Golden, CO 80401
Telephone: (303) 277-2555
FAX: (303) 277-6246

Materials Accepted/Included: 01-Business news 02-By-line articles 03-Fashion news 04-Food news 05-Freelance copy 06-Letters to editor 07-Real estate news 08-Sports news 09-Travel news 10-Book rev. 11-Movie rev. 12-Music rev. 13-TV rev. 14-Theater rev. 15-Coming events 16-Obituaries 17-Question & answer 18-Social announcements 19-Artwork 20-Cartoons 21-Photos 22-TV listings 23-Audio rec. 24-Video rec. 25-Books 26-Films/film clips 27-Personnel news 28-Press releases 29-New product news/photos 30-Trade lit. 31-Contracts awarded 32-Display adv. 33-Classified adv.

11-23

Mailing Address:
Corporate Communications Dept.
Mail #NH470
Golden, CO 80401
Industry Affiliation: Brewers, Distillers
**Publication(s):**
*Coors Courier*
Day Published: w.
Lead Time: 1 wk.
Materials: 01,06,08,15,17,21,27,28,29,33
Mtls Deadline: 5 days prior to pub. date
Contact: Corporate Communications Dept.
Spec. Requirements: 16-20 pgs.
Personnel: Angie Fry, Editor
        Libby Farrar, Managing Editor

4322

**COPELAND CORP.**
1675 W. Campbell Rd.
Sidney, OH 45365-0669
Telephone: (513) 498-3685
Industry Affiliation: Cooling, Heating
**Publication(s):**
*Communicator*
Day Published: q.
Lead Time: 1 mo. prior to pub. date
Mtls Deadline: 1st wk. of mo. prior to pub. date
Spec. Requirements: 8 pg.; offset; 11 x 17

4519

**COPPERWELD-SHELBY DIV.**
132 W. Main St.
Shelby, OH 44875
Telephone: (419) 342-1420
FAX: (419) 342-1473
Industry Affiliation: Steel, Iron
**Publication(s):**
*Outlook*
Day Published: w.
Lead Time: 2 days prior to pub. date
Materials: 01,02,08,16,17,18
Spec. Requirements: 6-8 pgs.; offset; 11 x 16
Personnel: Bob Bland, Editor

2777

**COPPERWELD CORP.**
Four Gateway Ctr., Ste. 2200
Pittsburgh, PA 15222
Telephone: (412) 263-3200
Industry Affiliation: Bronze, Brass, Copper
**Publication(s):**
*Across Copperweld*
Day Published: q.
        7401 S. Linder Ave.
        Chicago, IL 60638
Spec. Requirements: 8 pg.; offset; 8 1/2 x 11

4323

**COPPERWELD STEEL CO.**
4000 Mahoning Ave.
Warren, OH 44483
Telephone: (216) 841-6011
Industry Affiliation: Steel, Iron
**Publication(s):**
*Communicator*
Day Published: q.
Lead Time: 1 mo. prior to pub. date
Mtls Deadline: 1 mo. prior to pub. date
Personnel: Terri Gilbert, Editor

2582

**CORAL GABLES FEDERAL
SAVINGS & LOAN ASSOCIATION**
2511 Ponce De Leon Blvd.
Miami, FL 33134
Telephone: (305) 447-4710
Mailing Address:
P.O. Box 141488
Miami, FL 33114
Industry Affiliation: Banks, Savings & Loans

**Publication(s):**
*Newscaster*
Day Published: s-a.
Lead Time: 1 mo.
Mtls Deadline: 1 mo. prior to pub. date
Contact: Marketing
Spec. Requirements: 24-48 page; offset; 8 1/2 x 11 typeset
Personnel: Virginia B. Jones, Editor

*Hi-Lights*
Day Published: bi-w.
Lead Time: 2 days
Mtls Deadline: 3 days prior to pub. date
Contact: Marketing
Personnel: Virginia B. Jones, Editor

4679

**CORESTATES FIRST
PENNSYLVANIA BANK**
16th & Market Sts.
Philadelphia, PA 19101
Telephone: (215) 786-5000
FAX: (215) 786-8333
Industry Affiliation: Banks, Savings & Loans
**Publication(s):**
*Encore*
Day Published: m.
Lead Time: 1 mo prior to pub. date
Mtls Deadline: 1 mo. prior to pub. date
Spec. Requirements: 2 color
Personnel: Patti Kiernan, Editor

3084

**CORN BELT POWER
COOPERATIVE**
1300 13th St., N.
Humboldt, IA 50548
Telephone: (515) 332-2571
Mailing Address:
P.O. Box 508
Humboldt, IA 50548
Industry Affiliation: Electrical, Electronic, Manufacturing
**Publication(s):**
*Watts Watt*
Day Published: m.
Lead Time: 1st of mo.
Mtls Deadline: Beginning of mo.
Spec. Requirements: 8 pg.; offset; 8 1/2 x 11
Personnel: Kathy Taylor, Editor

*Cbpc annual Report*
Day Published: a.
Lead Time: 3 mo.
Mtls Deadline: Jan. 1
Spec. Requirements: rural electric industry.
Personnel: Kathy Taylor, Editor

3982

**CORNING INCORPORATED**
One Riverfront Plaza
Corning, NY 14831
Telephone: (607) 974-9000
Industry Affiliation: Colleges, Institutions, Science Research
**Publication(s):**
*Corning World*
Day Published: bi-m.
Lead Time: 2 mo.
Spec. Requirements: 12-16 pg.; offset tabloid; 10 x 13
Personnel: Carole R. Hedden, Editor
        Martn J. Rome

2517

**CORN REFINERS ASSOCIATION, INC.**
1701 Pennsylvania Ave. NW #950
Washington, DC 20006
Telephone: (202) 331-1634
FAX: (202) 331-2054
Industry Affiliation: Associations: Trade, Fraternal

**Publication(s):**
*Corn Annual*
Day Published: a.
Lead Time: 2 mos. prior to pub. date
Spec. Requirements: 32 pgs.; letterpress magazine; 84 x 11
Personnel: Edith M. Munro, Editor

2518

**COUNCIL FOR ADVANCEMENT &
SUPPORT OF EDUCATION**
11 Dupont Cir., Ste. 400
Washington, DC 20036
Telephone: (202) 328-5900
Industry Affiliation: Associations: City, State, Federal
**Publication(s):**
*Case Currents*
Day Published: 10/yr.
Lead Time: 4 mos. prior to pub. date
Mtls Deadline: 4 months. prior to pub. date
Spec. Requirements: 64 pg.; web; 8 1/4 x 11
Personnel: Karla Taylor, Editor

4367

**COUNTRYMARK COOP**
950 N. Meridian St.
Indianapolis, IN 46204
Telephone: (317) 685-3000
Industry Affiliation: Agriculture, Services
**Publication(s):**
*Coop Connection*
Day Published: bi-m.
Spec. Requirements: 4-12 pg.; offset newsletter; 8 1/2 x 11
Personnel: Ray Volpe, Editor

2640

**COX ENTERPRISES, INC.**
1400 Lake Hearn Dr., N.E.
Atlanta, GA 30319
Telephone: (404) 843-5125
Mailing Address:
P.O. Box 105357
Atlanta, GA 30348
Industry Affiliation: Radio, TV, Movies
**Publication(s):**
*Focus*
Day Published: bi-mo.
Lead Time: 2 mo.
Mtls Deadline: 15th-mo. before pub. date Apr. 15-May/Jun. issue
Spec. Requirements: 12 pg.; offset; 11 x 16 1/2
Personnel: Anthony Surratt, Editor

5132

**CPI CORP.**
1706 Washington St.
St. Louis, MO 63103
Telephone: (314) 621-9286
Industry Affiliation: Photography
**Publication(s):**
*News & Views*
Day Published: m.
Spec. Requirements: 12-page; offset; 112 x 14
Personnel: Nancy Murphy Boyle, Editor

3619

**CP RAIL SYSTEM**
105 S. 5th St.
P.O. Box 530
Minneapolis, MN 55440
Telephone: (612) 347-8209
FAX: (612) 337-8800
Industry Affiliation: Associations: Trade, Fraternal

**Publication(s):**
*Us Mileposts*
Day Published: m.
Spec. Requirements: 12-24 pg.; offset tabloid; 8 1/2 x 11
Personnel: Tim Hedin, Editor

68599

**C.R. ANTHONY CO.**
P.O. Box 25725
Oklahoma City, OK 73125
Telephone: (405) 235-3711
Mailing Address:
PO Box 25725
Oklahoma City, OK 73125-0725
Industry Affiliation: Retail Stores
**Publication(s):**
*Anthony Merchant*
Day Published: m.
Materials: 03
Mtls Deadline: end of mo.
Personnel: Karis Barnett, Editor

5465

**CREDIT UNION NATIONAL
ASSOCIATION INC.**
5710 Mineral Point Rd.
Madison, WI 53705
Telephone: (608) 231-4000
Mailing Address:
P.O. Box 431
Madison, WI 53701
Industry Affiliation: Associations: Trade, Fraternal
**Publication(s):**
*Everybody's Money*
Day Published: q.
Contact: Communications Div
Spec. Requirements: 24 pg.; offset; 8 x 5
Personnel: Susan Tiffany, Editor
        Philip Heckman, Associate Editor
        Mark Condon, Publisher
        Linda Des Lauriens, Art Director

*Credit Union Magazine*
Day Published: m.
Personnel: Mark Condon, Publisher
        Eugene Johnson, Editor
        Roger Napiwocki, Art Director

*Credit Union Executive*
Day Published: bi-m.
Materials: 32
Personnel: Mark Condon, Publisher
        Leigh Gregg, Editor
        Roger Napiwocki, Art Director

3772

**CREIGHTON UNIVERSITY**
California St. at 24th
Omaha, NE 68178
Telephone: (402) 280-2810
Industry Affiliation: Colleges, Institutions, Science Research
**Publication(s):**
*Alumnews*
Day Published: q.
Lead Time: 60 days prior to pub. date
Mtls Deadline: 60 days prior to pub. date
Spec. Requirements: 12 pg.; offset newspaper; 11 x 16
Personnel: Pamela Adams Vaughn, Editor

3442

**CRITTENTON HOSPITAL**
1101 W. University Dr.
Rochester, MI 48307
Telephone: (313) 652-5000
Industry Affiliation: Hospitals

**Materials Accepted/Included:** 01-Business news 02-By-line articles 03-Fashion news 04-Food news 05-Freelance copy 06-Letters to editor 07-Real estate news 08-Sports news 09-Travel news 10-Book rev. 11-Movie rev. 12-Music rev. 13-TV rev. 14-Theater rev. 15-Coming events 16-Obituaries 17-Question & answer 18-Social announcements 19-Artwork 20-Cartoons 21-Photos 22-TV listings 23-Audio rec. 24-Video rec. 25-Books 26-Films/film clips 27-Personnel news 28-Press releases 29-New product news/photos 30-Trade lit. 31-Contracts awarded 32-Display adv. 33-Classified adv.

**Publication(s):**
*Crittenscribe*
Day Published: bi-w.
Spec. Requirements: 3-4 page; offset; 8 1/2 x 17
Personnel: Peggy Hayes, Editor

3176

**CSX CORP.**
500 Water St.
Jacksonville, FL 32202
Telephone: (904) 359-1504
Industry Affiliation: Railroads
**Publication(s):**
*C S X today*
Day Published: m.
Lead Time: 2 wks.
Mtls Deadline: 15th of ea. mo. prior to pub.
Spec. Requirements: offset tabloid newspaper; 9 1/2 x 15 1/2
Personnel: Gary Sease, Editor

2117

**CUBIC CORP.**
9333 Balboa Ave.
San Diego, CA 92123
Telephone: (619) 277-6780
FAX: (619) 277-9329
Mailing Address:
    P.O. Box 85587
    San Diego, CA 92186-5587
Industry Affiliation: Electrical, Electronic, Manufacturing
**Publication(s):**
*Cubic Circuit*
Day Published: m.
Lead Time: 15 days
Mtls Deadline: 15th of mo. prior to pub. date
Spec. Requirements: 4-page; offset; 15 x 22
Personnel: Deb Jordon, Editor
                Cubic Corp., Publisher

3332

**CUMBERLAND FARMS, INC.**
777 Dedham St
Canton, MA 02021
Telephone: (617) 828-4900
Industry Affiliation: Dairy Products
**Publication(s):**
*Milky Way*
Day Published: m.
Lead Time: 2 wk.
Spec. Requirements: letterpress; 6-8 pg. offset, 11 x 14
Personnel: Donna Michael, Editor

2118

**CUNA MUTUAL INSURANCE GROUP**
2350 S. Garey
Pomona, CA 91766
Telephone: (714) 627-2644
Industry Affiliation: Insurance
**Publication(s):**
*Westwords:*
Day Published: bi-m.
Spec. Requirements: 4 pg.; letterpress; 8 1/2 x 11
Personnel: Nancy Grigas, Editor

5378

**CUNA MUTUAL INSURANCE GROUP**
5910 Mineral Point Rd.
Madison, WI 53705
Telephone: (608) 238-5851
FAX: (608) 238-2449
Mailing Address:
    P.O. Box 391
    Madison, WI 53701
Industry Affiliation: Insurance

**Publication(s):**
*Dimensions*
Day Published: bi-m.
Lead Time: 60 days prior to pub. date
Mtls Deadline: 60 days prior to pub. date
Spec. Requirements: 32 pg.; offset; 8 1/2 x 11; 4-color
Personnel: Carla Mills, Editor

4657

**CURTIS CIRCULATION CO.**
2500 McClellan Ave.
Camden, NJ 08109
Telephone: (609) 488-5700
FAX: (609) 488-2219
Mailing Address:
    P.O. Box 9102
    Camden, NJ 08101
Industry Affiliation: Publishers, Books, Magazines
**Publication(s):**
*Curtis Line, The*
Day Published: bi-m.
Lead Time: 10 wks prior to pub. date
Mtls Deadline: 2 mos. prior to issue date
Spec. Requirements: 8 pgs.; offset; 8 1/2 x 11
Personnel: Lisa M. Fahoury, Editor
                Jaime G. Conte

2642

**CURTIS 1000, INC.**
2100 River Edge Pkwy., 1100
Atlanta, GA 30328
Telephone: (404) 951-1000
FAX: (404) 955-0707
Industry Affiliation: Office Equipment, Services, Supplies
**Publication(s):**
*Curtis Ade*
Day Published: m.
Spec. Requirements: 16-20 page; offset; 54 x 8
Personnel: Wynell Lauver, Editor

*Inside Curtis*
Day Published: bi-m.
Spec. Requirements: 16-28 page
Personnel: Wynell Hauver, Editor

*Curtis Courier*
Day Published: q.
Spec. Requirements: 16-page
Personnel: Wynell Hauver, Editor

2643

**CYSTIC FIBROSIS FOUNDATION**
6931 Arlington Rd.
Bethesda, MD 20814
Telephone: (301) 951-4422
Industry Affiliation: Associations: Health Groups
**Publication(s):**
*Commitment*
Day Published: s-a.
Lead Time: 6 wks.
Mtls Deadline: 6 wks. prior to pub. date
Contact: Comm. Dept.
Spec. Requirements: 8 1/2 x 11
Personnel: Mary Beth Kilduff Ross

3446

**D-M-E CO.**
29111 Stephenson Hwy.
Madison Heights, MI 48071
Telephone: (313) 398-6000
Industry Affiliation: Chemicals, Plastics

**Publication(s):**
*D-M-E Family:*
Day Published: q.
Spec. Requirements: 8-12 pgs.; offset; 11 x 16
Personnel: Sharon Simon

5380

**DAIRYLAND POWER COOPERATIVE**
3200 East Ave., S.
La Crosse, WI 54602
Telephone: (608) 787-1323
FAX: (608) 787-1420
Industry Affiliation: Utility: Electric
**Publication(s):**
*Current Matters*
Day Published: bi-m.
Lead Time: 3 mos. prior to pub. date
Mtls Deadline: 3 mos. prior to pub. date
Spec. Requirements: 12-24 pg.; offset 8-1/2 x 11
Personnel: Don Walsh, Editor in Chief
                Debbie Mirasola, Editor

*Short Circuits*
Day Published: d.
Personnel: Debbie Mirasola, Editor

52343

**DAIRYLEA COOPERATIVE INC.**
5001 Brittonfield Pkwy.
E. Syracuse, NY 13057
Mailing Address:
    P.O. Box 4844
    Syracuse, NY 13202
Industry Affiliation: Dairy Products
**Publication(s):**
*Dairynews*
Day Published: q.
Lead Time: 1 mo.
Materials: 01,02,05,19,21,28,30,32,33
Mtls Deadline: 1 mo.
Personnel: Kris Green, Editor
                Pam Brunet, Advertising Manager
                Mark Kenville, Editor in Chief
                Monica Novelle Coleman, Production Manager

*Dairyleader*
Day Published: 8/yr.
Lead Time: 4 wk.
Materials: 05,28
Mtls Deadline: 4 wk.
Personnel: Mark Kenville, Editor in Chief
                Kris Green, Editor
                Monica Novelle Coleman, Production Manager

5160

**DALLAS AREA RAPID TRANSIT**
1401 Pacific Ave.
Dallas, TX 75266
Telephone: (214) 749-3278
FAX: (214) 749-3668
Mailing Address:
    P.O. Box 660163
    Dallas, TX 75266
Industry Affiliation: Bus, Transit

**Publication(s):**
*Connections*
Day Published: m.
Lead Time: 4 wks. prior to pub.
Materials: 04,15,20,23,24,27
Mtls Deadline: 4 wks. prior to pub.
Spec. Requirements: 1 pg.; offset magazine; 8 1/2 x 11
Personnel: Elaine Srnka, Editor
                Roz Theesfeld, Production Manager

5128

**DALLAS LIGHTHOUSE FOR THE BLIND, INC.**
4245 Office Pkwy.
Dallas, TX 75204-3680
Telephone: (214) 821-2375
Industry Affiliation: Associations: Health Groups
**Publication(s):**
*Panorama*
Day Published: q.
Lead Time: 1 mo. prior to pub. date
Mtls Deadline: 1st of Jun., Aug., Nov., Mar.
Contact: Public Relations
Spec. Requirements: 8 pg.; offset; 11 x 17
Personnel: Maria Leahey, Editor

*Annual Report*
Day Published: a.
Lead Time: 1 mo. prior to pub. date
Mtls Deadline: Dec. 15th prior to pub. date
Contact: Public Relations
Spec. Requirements: 12 pgs.; offset; 8-1/2 x 11
Personnel: Maria Leahey, Editor

5156

**DALLAS MORNING NEWS**
400 S. Record
Dallas, TX 75202
Telephone: (214) 977-7775
FAX: (214) 977-7046
Mailing Address:
    Communications Ctr.
    P.O. Box 655237
    Dallas, TX 75265
Industry Affiliation: Newspapers
**Publication(s):**
*Intercom*
Day Published: m.
Lead Time: 2 wks. prior to pub. date
Mtls Deadline: 15th of mo. 2 mos. prior to pub. date
Spec. Requirements: 20-24 pg.; offset
Personnel: Michelle Medley, Editor

4958

**DALLAS THEOLOGICAL SEMINARY**
3909 Swiss Ave.
Dallas, TX 75204
Telephone: (214) 824-3094
FAX: (214) 841-3535
Industry Affiliation: Colleges, Institutions, Science Research
**Publication(s):**
*Kindred Spirit*
Day Published: 3/yr.
Lead Time: 4 mos. prior to pub. date
Mtls Deadline: 4 mos. prior to pub. date
Spec. Requirements: 16 pg.; offset; 8-1/4 x 11-1/4
Personnel: Michael Edwards, Editor
                Philip E. Raw, Managing Editor

2147

**DANIEL FREEMAN MEMORIAL HOSPITAL**
333 N. Prairie Ave.
Inglewood, CA 90301
Telephone: (310) 674-7050
Mailing Address:
    P.O. Box 100
    Inglewood, CA 90306
Industry Affiliation: Hospitals

---

Materials Accepted/Included: 01-Business news 02-By-line articles 03-Fashion news 04-Food news 05-Freelance copy 06-Letters to editor 07-Real estate news 08-Sports news 09-Travel news 10-Book rev. 11-Movie rev. 12-Music rev. 13-TV rev. 14-Theater rev. 15-Coming events 16-Obituaries 17-Question & answer 18-Social announcements 19-Artwork 20-Cartoons 21-Photos 22-TV listings 23-Audio rec. 24-Video rec. 25-Books 26-Films/film clips 27-Personnel news 28-Press releases 29-New product news/photos 30-Trade lit. 31-Contracts awarded 32-Display adv. 33-Classified adv.

**Publication(s):**
*Today's Headlines*
Day Published: d.
Lead Time: 24 hrs. prior to pub. date
Mtls Deadline: 24 hrs. prior to pub. date
Spec. Requirements: 2 pg.; offset; 8 1/2 x 11
Personnel: Nary Ellen Brown, Editor
Christie A. Ciraulo

**DATAPOINT CORP.** 4959
8400 Datapoint Dr.
San Antonio, TX 78229-8500
Telephone: (210) 593-7000
FAX: (210) 593-7946
Industry Affiliation: Advertising, Art, Public Relations
**Publication(s):**
*Details*
Day Published: q.
Lead Time: 30 days
Materials: 01,04,08,15,17,20,21,27,28,29
Spec. Requirements: 8 pg.; offset; 8 1/2 x 11
Personnel: Maggie Thorschmidt, Editor

**DAVOL INC.** 4819
P.O. Box 8500
Cranston, RI 02920
Telephone: (401) 463-7000
Industry Affiliation: Drugs, Cosmetics, Pharmaceuticals
**Publication(s):**
*Dialogue*
Day Published: bi-m.
Materials: 19,21
Spec. Requirements: 4 pgs.; 11 x 17
Personnel: Lisa Baumler, Information Director

*Davol World Class Bulletin*
Day Published: bi-m.
Materials: 19,20
Spec. Requirements: 2 pgs. 8.5 x 11

**DAYTON POWER & LIGHT CO.** 4326
1065 Woodman Dr.
Dayton, OH 45432
Telephone: (513) 224-6000
Mailing Address:
P.O. Box 1247
Dayton, OH 45401
Industry Affiliation: Utility: Electric
**Publication(s):**
*D P & L energy Update*
Day Published: m.
Lead Time: 1 mo. prior to pub. date
Mtls Deadline: 1 mo. prior to pub. date
Spec. Requirements: 4-Page; Offset Newspaper; 8 1/2 x 11
Personnel: Michele Gutt, Editor

**DAYTON PROGRESS CORP.** 4327
500 Progress Rd.
Dayton, OH 45449
Telephone: (513) 859-5111
FAX: (513) 859-5353
Industry Affiliation: Industry: Light Tools, Equipment
**Publication(s):**
*Punch Lines*
Day Published: q.
Lead Time: 60 days prior to pub. date
Mtls Deadline: 60 days prior to pub. date
Spec. Requirements: 12 pg.; offset; 8-1/2 x 11
Personnel: Rosemary Domansky, Editor

**DEERE & CO.** 2780
John Deere Rd.
Moline, IL 61265
Telephone: (309) 765-4974
Industry Affiliation: Agriculture, Services

**Publication(s):**
*J D Journal*
Day Published: 3/yr.
Lead Time: 3-4 mo. prior to pub. date
Materials: 02
Spec. Requirements: 28 pg.; offset; 9 x 11

**DEKALB GENETICS CORP.** 2781
3100 Sycamore Rd.
De Kalb, IL 60115
Telephone: (815) 758-3461
Industry Affiliation: Associations: Health Groups
**Publication(s):**
*Interchange*
Day Published: bi-m.
Lead Time: 30-60 days
Mtls Deadline: May 1, Aug. 1, Oct. 1, Feb. 1
Spec. Requirements: 8 pg.; offset magtabloid; 8 1/2 x 11
Personnel: Rod Everhart, Editor

**DELCO ELECTRONICS CORPORATION** 68621
One Corporate Center
Kokomo, IN 46904-9005
Telephone: (317) 451-0906
Industry Affiliation: Electrical, Electronic, Manufacturing
**Publication(s):**
*Circuit*
Day Published: m.
Spec. Requirements: 4 pg.; tabloid
Personnel: Marie Becker, Editor

**DELMARVA POWER & LIGHT CO.** 2489
800 King St
Wilmington, DE 19801
Telephone: (302) 429-3491
Mailing Address:
P.O. Box 231
Wilmington, DE 19899
Industry Affiliation: Utility: Electric
**Publication(s):**
*This Week*
Day Published: w.
Lead Time: 2 wks. prior to pub. date
Mtls Deadline: 2 wks. prior to pub. date
Spec. Requirements: 2 pg.; desktop-published newsletter; 8 1/2 x 11
Personnel: Drew Vallorano, Managing Editor
Adrienne Kent, Contributing Editor

**DELTA AIR LINES** 2646
Hartsfield Atlanta Intl. Airport
Dept. 954
Atlanta, GA 30320
Telephone: (404) 765-2341
FAX: (404) 715-2100
Industry Affiliation: Airlines
**Publication(s):**
*Delta Digest*
Day Published: m.
Lead Time: 30 days prior to pub. date
Mtls Deadline: 30 days prior to pub. date
Contact: Personnel Dept.
Spec. Requirements: 36-44 pg.; offset magazine: 8-1/2 x 11
Personnel: Nancy Snyder, Editor
James H. Lundy, Editor

*Delta Dispatch*
Day Published: s-m.
Lead Time: 7 days prior to pub. date
Mtls Deadline: 7 days prior to pub. date
Contact: Personnel
Personnel: Nancy Snyder, Editor

**DENTAL SOCIETY OF THE STATE OF NEW YORK** 3986
7 Elk St.
Albany, NY 12207
Telephone: (518) 465-0044
FAX: (518) 427-0461
Industry Affiliation: Dental, Medical
**Publication(s):**
*New York State Dental Journal*
Day Published: 10/yr.
Lead Time: 2 mos. prior to pub. date
Mtls Deadline: 2 mos. prior to pub. date
Spec. Requirements: 60 pg.; offset; 8 1/2 x 11
Personnel: Bernard P. Tillis, Editor
Roberta R. Armstrong, Communications Director

*Newsbriefs*
Day Published: q.
Lead Time: 2 mos. prior to pub. date
Personnel: Roberta R. Armstrong, Editor

**DENTSPLY INTERNATIONAL INC.** 4659
570 W. College Ave.
York, PA 17404-0872
Telephone: (717) 845-7511
FAX: (717) 848-3739
Mailing Address:
P.O. Box 872
York, PA 17405-0872
Industry Affiliation: Dental, Medical
**Publication(s):**
*Dentsply Dimensions*
Day Published: q.
Lead Time: 30 days prior to pub. date
Mtls Deadline: 30 days prior to pub. date
Spec. Requirements: 8-16 pg.; 8-1/2 x 11
Personnel: George Rhodes, Editor

**DENVER WATER BOARD** 2394
1600 W. 12th Ave.
Denver, CO 80254
Telephone: (303) 628-6000
FAX: (303) 628-6349
Industry Affiliation: Utility: Water
**Publication(s):**
*Pipeline*
Day Published: m.
Spec. Requirements: 4-8 pg.; offset tabloid; 8 1/2 x 11
Personnel: Amy Hudson, Editor

**DEPAUL HEALTH CTR.** 3678
12303 DePaul Dr.
Hazelwood, MO 63044
Telephone: (314) 344-6277
FAX: (314) 344-7512
Industry Affiliation: Hospitals
**Publication(s):**
*Depaul News*
Day Published: bi-w.
Lead Time: 2 wks. prior to pub. date
Mtls Deadline: 3 days prior to pub. date
Contact: St. Vincent Psychiatric Div.
Spec. Requirements: 8-1/2 x 11
Personnel: Lori D. Leemann, Editor
Diana J. Kiernan

*Upbeat*
Day Published: m.
Lead Time: 3 wks. prior to pub. date
Mtls Deadline: 2 wks. prior to pub. date
Contact: St. Anne (Skilled Nursing) Div.

**DESERT SCHOOLS FEDERAL CREDIT UNION** 2014
6633 N. Black Canyon
Phoenix, AZ 85015
Telephone: (602) 433-7000
FAX: (602) 433-4200
Mailing Address:
P.O. Box 11350
Phoenix, AZ 85061
Industry Affiliation: Finance, Services
**Publication(s):**
*Currency*
Day Published: q.
Lead Time: 30 days prior to pub. date
Mtls Deadline: 10th of mo. prior to pub. date
Contact: Mktg. Dept.
Spec. Requirements: 4 pg.; 8 1/2 x 11
Personnel: Lee Goodman Brice, Editor

**DETROIT EDISON CO.** 3520
2000 Second Ave.
Detroit, MI 48226
Telephone: (313) 237-9434
Industry Affiliation: Utility: Electric
**Publication(s):**
*Edison Today*
Day Published: bi-w.
Lead Time: 4 wks. prior to pub. date
Personnel: Guy D. Cerullo, Editor

**DITTLER BROTHERS, INC.** 68593
1375 Seaboard Industrial Blvd.
Atlanta, GA 30318
Telephone: (404) 355-3423
Industry Affiliation: Printers, Services
**Publication(s):**
*Dittler Hot Line*
Day Published: q.
Personnel: Beth Greene

**DIVERSEY CORP.** 2782
12025 Tech Center Dr.
Livonia, MI 48150
Telephone: (800) 521-8140
Industry Affiliation: Chemicals, Plastics
**Publication(s):**
*Diversey Advantage, The*
Day Published: m.
Lead Time: 30 days prior to pub. date
Mtls Deadline: 30 days prior to pub. date
Contact: Thomas Steiner, Mktg.
Spec. Requirements: 8-12 pg.; Heidelberg 18 x 24

**DIXIE YARNS, INC.** 68589
P.O. Box 751
Chattanooga, TN 37401
Telephone: (615) 698-2501
FAX: (615) 493-7353
Industry Affiliation: Textiles, Apparel, Mills, Machinery
**Publication(s):**
*Dixie News*
Day Published: q.
Mtls Deadline: 10th of mo. prior to pub. date
Personnel: Sandy Harrison, Editor

**DONREY MEDIA GROUP** 2035
P.O. Box 17017
Ft. Smith, AR 72917
Telephone: (501) 785-9404
Industry Affiliation: Newspapers

**Materials Accepted/Included:** 01-Business news 02-By-line articles 03-Fashion news 04-Food news 05-Freelance copy 06-Letters to editor 07-Real estate news 08-Sports news 09-Travel news 10-Book rev. 11-Movie rev. 12-Music rev. 13-TV rev. 14-Theater rev. 15-Coming events 16-Obituaries 17-Question & answer 18-Social announcements 19-Artwork 20-Cartoons 21-Photos 22-TV listings 23-Audio rec. 24-Video rec. 25-Books 26-Films/film clips 27-Personnel news 28-Press releases 29-New product news/photos 30-Trade lit. 31-Contracts awarded 32-Display adv. 33-Classified adv.

11-26

**Publication(s):**
*Donrey Mediagram*
Day Published: bi-m.
Lead Time: 30 days prior to pub. date
Spec. Requirements: 24-32 pg.; offset; 10 x 13-1/2
Personnel: Terry V. Johnson, Editor

66430

**DONTECH**
205 N. Michigan
Chicago, IL 60601
Telephone: (312) 861-3500
FAX: (312) 856-8612
Industry Affiliation: Newspapers
**Publication(s):**
*Dontech Connections*
Day Published: m.
Lead Time: 1 mo. prior to pub. date
Mtls Deadline: 1st of mo. prior to pub. date
Personnel: Anne Goreoki, Communications Director

3448

**DOW CORNING CORP.**
2200 W. Salzburg Rd.
Midland, MI 48686-0994
Telephone: (517) 496-8689
FAX: (517) 496-6487
Industry Affiliation: Chemicals, Plastics
**Publication(s):**
*Dow Corning World*
Day Published: q.
Spec. Requirements: 20-24 pg; offset; 8 1/2 x 11
Personnel: Mary Lou Benecke, Editor

4966

**DRESSER INDUSTRIES, INC.**
2001 Ross Ave.
Dallas, TX 75201
Telephone: (214) 740-6000
Mailing Address:
　P.O. Box 718
　Dallas, TX 75221
Industry Affiliation: Associations: Trade, Fraternal
**Publication(s):**
*Recorder, The*
Day Published: bi-m.
Contact: Corporate Headquarters
Spec. Requirements: 16-20 page; offset; 8 1/2 x 11
Personnel: Jim Basham, Editor

*Dresser Qualtiy Connection*
Day Published: m.
Lead Time: 2 wks. prior to pub. date
Mtls Deadline: 2 wks. prior to pub. date
Personnel: Kathy Bolen, Editor

68623

**DRESSER INDUSTRIES, INC.**
900 W. Mount St.
Connersville, IN 47331
Telephone: (317) 827-9200
Industry Affiliation: Associations: Trade, Fraternal
**Publication(s):**
*Blower Outlet*
Day Published: 3/yr.
Personnel: Connie Chandler

4964

**DR. PEPPER CO.**
8144 Walnut Hill Ln.
Dallas, TX 75231
Telephone: (214) 360-7000
Mailing Address:
　P.O. Box 655086
　Dallas, TX 75265
Industry Affiliation: Soft Drinks

**Publication(s):**
*Clock Dial*
Day Published: q.
Lead Time: 3 wks. prior to pub. date
Mtls Deadline: 30th of mo. prior to pub. date
Spec. Requirements: 28-23 pg.; offset magazine; 8 1/2 x 11
Personnel: Jill Haerle, Editor

*Seven-Up Leader*
Day Published: q.
Lead Time: 3 wks. prior to pub. date
Mtls Deadline: 3 wks. prior to pub. date
Spec. Requirements: 28-32 pg.; offset magazine; 8 1/2 x 11
Personnel: Bridget Barry, Editor

3209

**DSM COPOLYMER**
5955 Scenic Hwy.
Baton Rouge, LA 70805
Telephone: (504) 355-5655
Mailing Address:
　P.O. Box 2591
　Baton Rouge, LA 70821
Industry Affiliation: Soft Drinks
**Publication(s):**
*Dsm Copolymer News*
Day Published: q.
Lead Time: 2 wk.
Mtls Deadline: 1st Tue. of Feb., Apr., Jun., Aug., Oct., Dec.
Spec. Requirements: 10-12 pg.; offset magazine; 8 1/2 x 11
Personnel: Sally Genovese, Editor

2127

**DUCOMMUN, INC.**
23301 S. Wilmington Ave.
Carson, CA 90745-6209
Telephone: (310) 513-7200
FAX: (310) 518-0176
Industry Affiliation: Aircraft, Aerospace, Defense
**Publication(s):**
*Ducommun Newsreel:*
Day Published: m.
Spec. Requirements: 16-page; offset magazine; 84 x 11
Personnel: Ron Palmer, Editor

4231

**DUKE POWER CO.**
P.O. Box 1009
Charlotte, NC 28201-1009
Telephone: (704) 382-8343
Industry Affiliation: Utility: Electric
**Publication(s):**
*Duke Power Journal*
Day Published: m.
Lead Time: 6 wk.
Materials: 01
Spec. Requirements: 12 pgs.; 9 1/2 x 15 1/2
Personnel: Jeremy Dreier, Editor

3993

**DUN & BRADSTREET CORP., THE**
299 Park Ave.
New York, NY 10171
Telephone: (212) 593-8695
Industry Affiliation: Publishers, Books, Magazines
**Publication(s):**
*D & B Reports*
Day Published: bi-m.
Mtls Deadline: 2 mos. prior to pub. date
Spec. Requirements: 28-32 pg.; photo composition; 8-1/2 x 11
Personnel: Patricia W. Hamilton, Editor

3995

**DUNLOP TIRE CORP.**
P.O. Box 1109
Buffalo, NY 14240
Telephone: (716) 639-5200
Industry Affiliation: Rubber, Tires

**Publication(s):**
*Hq Review*
Day Published: m.
Lead Time: 30 days prior to pub. date
Personnel: Colleen Low-Larkin, Editor

*Driving Force*
Day Published: m.
Personnel: Tom Dziekan, Editor

4663

**DUQUESNE LIGHT CO.**
301 Grant St.
Pittsburgh, PA 15279
Telephone: (412) 393-6000
FAX: (412) 393-6449
Industry Affiliation: Utility: Electric
**Publication(s):**
*Duquesne Light News*
Day Published: m.
Lead Time: 2 mos.
Mtls Deadline: 2 mos. prior
Spec. Requirements: 20 pgs; offset magazine; 8 1/2 x 11
Personnel: Jerry Lewis, Managing Editor

4664

**DUQUESNE UNIVERSITY**
406 Administration Bldg.
Duquesne University
Pittsburgh, PA 15282
Telephone: (412) 434-6050
FAX: (412) 434-5779
Industry Affiliation: Colleges, Institutions, Science Research
**Publication(s):**
*Duquesne University Record*
Day Published: q.
Lead Time: 2 mos. prior to pub. date
Materials: 28
Mtls Deadline: 2 mos. prior to pub. date
Contact: Public Relations
Spec. Requirements: 24-32 pg. 8-1/2 x 11
Personnel: Ann D'Amico Rago, Editor
　　　　　John Wdowiak

*Times, The*
Day Published: w.
Lead Time: 1 wk. prior to pub. date
Materials: 27,28
Mtls Deadline: 1 wk. prior to pub date.
Contact: Public Relations
Spec. Requirements: query before submitting materials
Personnel: Ann Rago, Executive Editor

2786

**DURACLEAN INTERNATIONAL**
2151 Waukegan Rd.
Deerfield, IL 60015
Telephone: (708) 945-2000
Industry Affiliation: Associations: Health Groups
**Publication(s):**
*Duraclean Journal*
Day Published: q.
Spec. Requirements: 8-12 pgs.; offset; 8 1/2 x 11
Personnel: Kay Henrichsen, Editor

4232

**DURHAM CHAMBER OF COMMERCE**
300 W. Morgan St.
Durham, NC 27701
Telephone: (919) 682-2133
FAX: (919) 688-8351
Mailing Address:
　P.O. Box 3829
　Durham, NC 27702
Industry Affiliation: Associations: Trade, Fraternal

**Publication(s):**
*Action*
Day Published: m.
Lead Time: 20 days prior to pub. date
Materials: 01,07,32
Mtls Deadline: 20 days prior to pub. date
Contact: Membership/Communications-DCC
Spec. Requirements: 12 pg.; offset; 11 x 14
Personnel: Bll K. Baucom Jr., Managing Editor
　　　　　Robert H. Book, Publisher
　　　　　Linda S. Roggli, Art Director

4856

**DYERSBURG FABRICS INC.**
East Phillips St.
Dyersburg, TN 38024
Telephone: (901) 285-2323
FAX: (901) 286-3474
Mailing Address:
　P.O. Box 767
　Dyersburg, TN 38024
Industry Affiliation: Textiles, Apparel, Mills, Machinery
**Publication(s):**
*Spinnit, The*
Day Published: m.
Spec. Requirements: 8-16 pgs.; offset; 86 x 116
Personnel: Lewis Norman, Editor

4972

**E-SYSTEMS, INC.**
6250 LBJ Fwy.
Dallas, TX 75240
Telephone: (214) 661-1000
Industry Affiliation: Electrical, Electronic, Manufacturing
**Publication(s):**
*Team*
Day Published: bi-m.
Lead Time: 45 days prior to pub. date
Mtls Deadline: 45 days prior to pub. date
Spec. Requirements: 16 pg.; offset; 8-3/8 x 10-7/8
Personnel: Joe Curtis, Editor

3089

**EASTERN IOWA LIGHT POWER COOPERATIVE**
E. Fifth & Sycamore
Wilton, IA 52778
Telephone: (319) 732-2211
Mailing Address:
　P.O. Box 869
　Wilton, IA 52778
Industry Affiliation: Utility: Electric
**Publication(s):**
*Current News*
Day Published: m.
Lead Time: 2 wks. prior to pub. date
Spec. Requirements: 12 pg; offset newspaper; 11 x 16
Personnel: Jim Williams, Editor
　　　　　Ed Bomberger, Managing Editor
　　　　　Mel Nicholas, Publisher

3996

**EASTERN MILK PRODUCERS CO-OP ASSN. INC.**
2401 Burnet Ave.
Syracuse, NY 13206
Telephone: (315) 463-0781
FAX: (315) 437-1225
Industry Affiliation: Associations: Trade, Fraternal

---

**Materials Accepted/Included:** 01-Business news 02-By-line articles 03-Fashion news 04-Food news 05-Freelance copy 06-Letters to editor 07-Real estate news 08-Sports news 09-Travel news 10-Book rev. 11-Movie rev. 12-Music rev. 13-TV rev. 14-Theater rev. 15-Coming events 16-Obituaries 17-Question & answer 18-Social announcements 19-Artwork 20-Cartoons 21-Photos 22-TV listings 23-Audio rec. 24-Video rec. 25-Books 26-Films/film clips 27-Personnel news 28-Press releases 29-New product news/photos 30-Trade lit. 31-Contracts awarded 32-Display adv. 33-Classified adv.

11-27

**Publication(s):**
*Farm Life*
Day Published: m.
Lead Time: 1-2 mos. prior to pub. date
Mtls Deadline: 1-2 mos. prior to pub. date
Contact: Co-op. Rels.
Spec. Requirements: 24-pgs.; offset; 8 1/2 x 11
Personnel: Patricia Stokes, Editor

**EASTERN NEBRASKA** [3775]
**COMMUNITY OFFICE OF RETARDATION**
885 S. 72nd St.
Omaha, NE 68114
Telephone: (402) 444-6669
FAX: (402) 444-6504
Industry Affiliation: Associations: Health Groups
**Publication(s):**
*Encor Respondance*
Day Published: q.
Lead Time: 1 mo. prior to pub. date
Mtls Deadline: 1 mo. prior to pub. date
Contact: Public Education & Information
Spec. Requirements: 4-pgs.; offset; 8 1/2 x 11
Personnel: Billie Dawson, Editor

**EASTERN NEBRASKA OFFICE ON** [3776]
**AGING**
885 S. 72nd St.
Omaha, NE 68114
Telephone: (402) 444-6654
Industry Affiliation: Associations: City, State, Federal
**Publication(s):**
*New Horizons*
Day Published: m.
Lead Time: 15th of mo. prior to pub. date
Materials: 09,10,15,18,19,21,25,28,29,32,33
Mtls Deadline: 15th of mo. prior to pub. date
Contact: Jeff Reinhardt, Ed.
          Telephone: (402) 444-6654
Spec. Requirements: 20-24 pg.; offset; 11 x 15-1/2
Personnel: Rovert V. Whitmore, Publisher

**EASTER SEAL SOCIETY OF** [68412]
**WISCONSIN, INC.**
101 Nob Hill Rd., Ste. 301
Madison, WI 53713
Telephone: (608) 277-8288
FAX: (608) 277-8333
Industry Affiliation: Associations: Health Groups
**Publication(s):**
*Network News*
Day Published: s-a.
Materials: 01,06,17,32
Personnel: Andrew Sagan, Editor

*Annual Report*
Day Published: a.
Personnel: Andrew Sagan, Editor

**EASTMAN CHEMICAL COMPANY** [4893]
P.O. Box 1973
Kingsport, TN 37662-5284
Telephone: (615) 229-2196
FAX: (615) 224-0667
Industry Affiliation: Chemicals, Plastics

**Publication(s):**
*Eastman News*
Day Published: bi-w.
Lead Time: 1 wk.
Materials: 01,08,15,16,19,21,27,28,29,33
Mtls Deadline: 1 wk.
Contact: Corp. Emp. Communications
Spec. Requirements: 8-page; offset newspaper; 11 1/2 x 17
Personnel: Gary W. Quillen, Editor

**EAST OHIO GAS CO.** [4333]
1717 E. Ninth, Rm. 704
Cleveland, OH 44114
Telephone: (216) 736-6225
Industry Affiliation: Utility: Gas
**Publication(s):**
*Dateline*
Day Published: 3/yr.
Lead Time: 2 mos. prior to pub. date
Mtls Deadline: 2 mos. prior to pub. date
Spec. Requirements: 4-6 pg.; offset; 11 x 174
Personnel: Bernard Holmes, Editor

**EAST VIRGINIA MEDICAL SCHOOL** [5234]
**OF THE MEDICAL COLLEGE HAMPTON**
358 Mowbray Arch, Ste. 411
Norfolk, VA 23507
Telephone: (804) 446-6050
FAX: (804) 640-0311
Mailing Address:
  P.O. Box 1980
  Norfolk, VA 23501
Industry Affiliation: Colleges, Institutions, Science Research
**Publication(s):**
*Chronicle Newspaper*
Day Published: m.
Lead Time: 2 mos. prior to pub. date
Mtls Deadline: 2 mos. prior to pub. date
Contact: Community Mental Health Center
Spec. Requirements: 8 pgs.
Personnel: Sheila Edelheit, Editor

**EATON CORP.** [68603]
1111 Superior Ave., Eaton Ctr.
Cleveland, OH 44114
Telephone: (216) 523-4738
FAX: (216) 479-7080
Industry Affiliation: Electrical, Electronic, Manufacturing
**Publication(s):**
*Eaton Today*
Day Published: m.
Lead Time: 1 mo. prior to pub. date
Contact: World Headquarters
Spec. Requirements: 4-6 pg.; offset newsletter; 11 x 15-1/2
Personnel: Tim Weidner, Editor

**EBASCO SERVICES INC.** [3999]
2 World Trade Ctr.
New York, NY 10048
Telephone: (212) 839-1000
Industry Affiliation: Architects, Engineers, Business Service
**Publication(s):**
*Ebasco News*
Day Published: bi-m.
Spec. Requirements: 4-6 pgs.; tabloid; offset magazine; 11 x 16
Personnel: Michael Ketcham, Reporter

**EBSCO INDUSTRIES, INC.** [68568]
5724 Hwy. 280 E.
Birmingham, AL 35242
Telephone: (205) 991-6600
FAX: (205) 991-1479

Mailing Address:
  P.O. Box 1943
  Birmingham, AL 35201
Industry Affiliation: Publishers, Books, Magazines
**Publication(s):**
*Bugle*
Day Published: 5/yr.
Personnel: Karen Ingram, Editor

**ECOLAB INC.** [3554]
Ecolab Ctr.
St. Paul, MN 55102
Telephone: (612) 293-2419
FAX: (612) 225-3034
Industry Affiliation: Chemicals, Plastics
**Publication(s):**
*Ecolab News*
Day Published: bi-m.
Lead Time: 2 mos. prior to pub. date
Materials: 01,17,21,29
Contact: Communications
Spec. Requirements: 4-12 pg.; offset; 11 x 17
Personnel: Keralyn Groff, Editor
          Helen Carciofini, Managing Editor

**EDISON BROS. STORES** [68605]
501 N. Broadway
St. Louis, MO 63102
Telephone: (314) 331-6000
Industry Affiliation: Retail Stores
**Publication(s):**
*E B S Conveyor*
Day Published: bi-m.
Personnel: John Twombly, Editor

**EDUCATION & RESEARCH CTR.** [3656]
**OF MISSISSIPPI**
3825 Ridgewood Rd.
Jackson, MS 39211
Telephone: (601) 982-6334
FAX: (601) 982-6129
Industry Affiliation: Colleges, Institutions, Science Research
**Publication(s):**
*Mississippi Review Of Outdoor*
Day Published: a.
Lead Time: Jan. prior to pub. date
Spec. Requirements: 16 pg.; offset; 8 x 11
Personnel: Phil Pepper, M. D., Editor

**EEI** [5235]
66 Canal Ctr. Plz., Ste. 200
Alexandria, VA 22314-5507
Telephone: (703) 683-0683
FAX: (703) 683-4915
Industry Affiliation: Publishers, Books, Magazines
**Publication(s):**
*Editorial Eye, The*
Day Published: m.
Lead Time: 2 mos. prior to pub. date
Materials: 05,06,10,19,25
Mtls Deadline: 2 mos. prior to pub. date
Contact: Linda Jorgensen, Ed.
Spec. Requirements: 12 pg.; offset; 8-1/2 x 11
Personnel: Linda Jorgensen, Editor
          Daniel Horowitz, Publisher
          Andrea Sutcliffe, Editor in Chief
          Candee Wilson, Production Manager

**E.F. HOUGHTON & CO.** [4704]
P.O. Box 930
Valley Forge, PA 19482-0930
Telephone: (215) 666-4000
FAX: (215) 666-1376
Industry Affiliation: Chemicals, Plastics

**Publication(s):**
*Houghton Line*
Day Published: q.
Spec. Requirements: 52 pg.; offset; 4 x 7
Personnel: Richard Geiselman, Editor

*Houghtonews*
Day Published: q.
Spec. Requirements: 12 pg.
Personnel: Richard Geiselman, Editor

**EG & G MOUND APPLIED** [4393]
**TECHNOLOGIES**
P.O. Box 3000
Miamisburg, OH 45343-3000
Telephone: (513) 865-4450
FAX: (513) 865-3972
Industry Affiliation: Chemicals, Plastics
**Publication(s):**
*Undermound*
Day Published: s-m.
Lead Time: 2 wks. prior to pub. date
Materials: 01
Mtls Deadline: 15th of mo. prior to pub. date
Spec. Requirements: 4 pg.; 8-1/2 x 11
Personnel: Jennifer Beavers, Editor

**E I DUPONT DE NEMOURS** [68557]
Nemours 9442
Wilmington, DE 19898
Telephone: (800) 228-2558
Industry Affiliation: Chemicals, Plastics
**Publication(s):**
*Dupont Magazine*
Day Published: bi-m.
Personnel: James L. Moore, Editor

**ELCO INDUSTRIES, INC.** [2788]
1111 Samuelson Rd.
Rockford, IL 61109
Telephone: (815) 397-5151
FAX: (815) 398-4569
Industry Affiliation: Associations: Health Groups
**Publication(s):**
*E L C O newsletter*
Day Published: s-w.
Spec. Requirements: 1-pg.
Personnel: Mel Gorman, Editor

*E L C O times*
Day Published: s-a.
Spec. Requirements: 16-pgs.
Personnel: Mel Gorman, Editor

**ELDEC CORP.** [68569]
16700 13th Ave., W.
Lynnwood, WA 98037
Telephone: (206) 743-1313
FAX: (206) 743-8234
Mailing Address:
  P.O. Box 100
  Lynwood, WA 98037
Industry Affiliation: Electrical, Electronic, Manufacturing
**Publication(s):**
*Echo*
Day Published: m.
Personnel: Steve Clarke

**ELECTRIC COUNCIL OF NEW** [3337]
**ENGLAND**
54 Middlesex Tpke.
Bedford, MA 01730
Telephone: (617) 271-9002
Industry Affiliation: Associations: City, State, Federal

---

Materials Accepted/Included: 01-Business news 02-By-line articles 03-Fashion news 04-Food news 05-Freelance copy 06-Letters to editor 07-Real estate news 08-Sports news 09-Travel news 10-Book rev. 11-Movie rev. 12-Music rev. 13-TV rev. 14-Theater rev. 15-Coming events 16-Obituaries 17-Question & answer 18-Social announcements 19-Artwork 20-Cartoons 21-Photos 22-TV listings 23-Audio rec. 24-Video rec. 25-Books 26-Films/film clips 27-Personnel news 28-Press releases 29-New product news/photos 30-Trade lit. 31-Contracts awarded 32-Display adv. 33-Classified adv.

**Publication(s):**
*Impulse*
Day Published: m.
Spec. Requirements: 6-pgs.; offset; 84 x 11
Personnel: Frank A. Swierz, Editor

**ELECTRIC POWER BOARD CHATTANOOGA** [4859]
P.O. Box 182255
Chattanooga, TN 37422-7255
Telephone: (615) 629-3227
FAX: (615) 629-3577
Industry Affiliation: Utility: Electric
**Publication(s):**
*Spotlight*
Day Published: q.
Spec. Requirements: 20 pg; offset; 8 1/2 x 11
Personnel: Hal Morris, Editor

*Electric Leaguer*
Day Published: q.
Mtls Deadline: flexible
Personnel: Hal Morris, Editor

**ELECTRONIC ASSOCIATES, INC.** [3860]
185 Monmouth Pkwy.
W. Long Branch, NJ 07764
Telephone: (908) 229-1100
FAX: (908) 229-4341
Industry Affiliation: Electrical, Electronic, Manufacturing
**Publication(s):**
*Ea Items*
Day Published: q.
Spec. Requirements: 2 pg; offset; 11 x 17
Personnel: Barbara Everson, Editor

**ELECTRONIC INDUSTRIES ASSOCIATION** [2521]
2001 Pennsylvania Ave., N.W.
Washington, DC 20006
Telephone: (202) 457-4900
FAX: (202) 457-4985
Industry Affiliation: Associations: Trade, Fraternal
**Publication(s):**
*Executive Report To The Electronic Industries*
Day Published: irreg.
Spec. Requirements: 6-8 pg.; offset newsletter; 84 x 11
Personnel: Mark V. Rosenker, Editor

*Eia Market Data Book*
Day Published: a.
Personnel: Mark V. Rosenker, Editor

**ELECTRONICS INFORMATION & MISSILES GROUP** [68590]
P.O. Box 55837
Orlando, FL 32855-5837
Telephone: (407) 356-2211
FAX: (407) 356-2080
Industry Affiliation: Aircraft, Aerospace, Defense
**Publication(s):**
*Eagle, The*
Day Published: m.
Lead Time: 2 wks. prior to pub. date
Mtls Deadline: last Fri. of mo. prior to pub. date
Contact: Public Affairs
Personnel: Al Kamhi, Director of Public Affairs

**ELF ATOCHEM NORTH AMERICA, INC.** [4108]
2000 Market St.
Philadelphia, PA 19103-3222
Telephone: (215) 419-7000
FAX: (215) 419-7591
Industry Affiliation: Chemicals, Plastics

**Publication(s):**
*Direction 79*
Day Published: q.
Spec. Requirements: 12-16 pg; offset bulletin; 8 1/2 x 11
Personnel: Michael J. Poteran, Editor

**EL PASO ELECTRIC CO.** [4969]
303 N. Oregon
El Paso, TX 79901
Telephone: (915) 543-5916
FAX: (915) 521-4766
Mailing Address:
   P.O. Box 982
   El Paso, TX 79960
Industry Affiliation: Utility: Electric
**Publication(s):**
*Enews*
Day Published: m.
Lead Time: 1 mo. prior to pub. date
Materials: 01,12
Mtls Deadline: 1 mo. prior to pub. date
Personnel: John Hupfer, Editor

**EL PASO NATURAL GAS CO.** [5130]
304 Texas
El Paso, TX 79978
Telephone: (915) 541-2600
Mailing Address:
   P.O. Box 1492
   El Paso, TX 79978
Industry Affiliation: Utility: Gas
**Publication(s):**
*Pipeliner*
Day Published: m.
Spec. Requirements: 8 x 11 1/2; offset
Personnel: Beth Ford, Editor

**EMI CO.** [4670]
603 W. 12th St.
Erie, PA 16501
Telephone: (814) 452-6431
FAX: (814) 452-3439
Industry Affiliation: Steel, Iron
**Publication(s):**
*Casting About*
Day Published: bi-m.
Lead Time: 1 mo. prior to pub. date
Mtls Deadline: 15th of mo. prior to pub. date
Spec. Requirements: 4 pg.; offset; 8-1/2 x 11
Personnel: Judith W. Cuthbert, Editor

**EMPIRE BRUSHES INC.** [4000]
U.S. Hwy. 13, N.
Greenville, NC 27834
Telephone: (719) 758-4111
Mailing Address:
   P.O. Box 1606
   Greenville, NC 27835
Industry Affiliation: Industry: Light Tools, Equipment
**Publication(s):**
*Empire News*
Day Published: q.
Personnel: Beverly Vanderly, Editor

**EMPIRE DISTRICT ELECTRIC CO.** [68628]
602 Joplin St.
Joplin, MO 64801
Telephone: (417) 623-4700
FAX: (417) 625-5169
Mailing Address:
   P.O. Box 127
   Joplin, MO 64801
Industry Affiliation: Utility: Electric

**Publication(s):**
*Empire Dispatch*
Day Published: bi-w.
Lead Time: 2 wks. prior to pub. date
Mtls Deadline: 2 wks. prior to pub. date
Personnel: Marsha Wallace, Editor

**EMPLOYERS CASUALTY** [4970]
1301 Young St.
Dallas, TX 75202
Telephone: (214) 760-6282
Mailing Address:
   P.O. Box 2759
   Dallas, TX 75221
Industry Affiliation: Insurance
**Publication(s):**
*Brickbats & Bouquets*
Day Published: q.
Lead Time: 4 wks. prior to pub. date
Mtls Deadline: 1st of mo. prior to pub. date
Spec. Requirements: 16-20 pgs.; offset magazine; 8 1/2 x 11
Personnel: Curtis Broyles, Editor

**EMPLOYERS GROUP** [2200]
1150 S. Olive St., 23rd Fl.
Los Angeles, CA 90015
Telephone: (213) 748-0421
Mailing Address:
   P.O. Box 15013
   Los Angeles, CA 90015
Industry Affiliation: Associations: Trade, Fraternal
**Publication(s):**
*In Action Management Memo*
Day Published: m.
Lead Time: 1 mo. prior to pub. date
Mtls Deadline: 2 mos. prior to middle of pub. mo.
Spec. Requirements: 4 pg.; offset magazine; 8 1/2 x 11
Personnel: Karen Kukurin, Editor

*Action Line*
Day Published: irreg.
Lead Time: 1 mo. prior to pub. date
Mtls Deadline: 1 mo. prior to pub. date
Spec. Requirements: 4 pg.
Personnel: Karen Kukurin, Editor

*Capitol Review*
Day Published: bi-m.
Lead Time: 2 mos. prior to pub. date
Mtls Deadline: middle of mo. prior to pub. date
Spec. Requirements: 4 pg. newsletter
Personnel: Karen Kukurin, Editor

*Forum*
Day Published: irreg.
Lead Time: 1 mo. prior to pub. date
Mtls Deadline: middle of mo. prior to pub. date
Personnel: Karen Kukurin, Editor

*The Legal Bulletin*
Day Published: bi-m.
Lead Time: 1 mo. prior to pub. date
Mtls Deadline: 1 mo. prior to pub. date
Personnel: Karen Kukurin, Editor

**ENGINEERING SOCIETY OF DETROIT** [3450]
274 21 Harper Ave.
St. Clair Shores, MI 48081
Telephone: (313) 832-5400
FAX: (313) 774-3530
Industry Affiliation: Associations: Trade, Fraternal

**Publication(s):**
*Technology*
Day Published: 10/yr.
Materials: 02,05,28,32
Mtls Deadline: 20th of 2nd mo. prior to pub. date
Contact: Editorial
Spec. Requirements: 40 pg; offset magazine; 8-1/2 x 11
Personnel: Karen Shellie, Publisher
   Andrea Mogielnicki, Art Director
   Kevin Campbell, Marketing Director

**ENSIGN-BICKFORD INDUSTRIES, INC.** [2422]
10 Mill Pond Ln.
Simsbury, CT 06070
Telephone: (203) 843-2000
Mailing Address:
   P.O. Box 7
   Simsbury, CT 06070
Industry Affiliation: Electrical, Electronic, Manufacturing
**Publication(s):**
*E-Bee*
Day Published: bi-m.
Spec. Requirements: 4-8 pg; 8 1/2 x 11
Personnel: Linda Angelastro, Editor

**ENVIRONMENTAL LOBBY OF MASSACHUSETTS** [3363]
3 Joy St.
Boston, MA 02108
Telephone: (617) 742-2553
Industry Affiliation: Associations: City, State, Federal
**Publication(s):**
*Legislative Bulletin*
Day Published: q.
Spec. Requirements: 6-pgs.; offset newsletter; 84 x 11
Personnel: James R. Gomes, Editor

**EQUIFAX, INC.** [2650]
1600 Peachtree St., N.W.
Atlanta, GA 30309
Telephone: (404) 885-8000
Mailing Address:
   P.O. Box 4081
   Atlanta, GA 30302
Industry Affiliation: Insurance
**Publication(s):**
*Fyi International*
Day Published: m.
Lead Time: 2 mos. prior to pub. date
Spec. Requirements: 16 pg. offset; 9 x 12
Personnel: Halle Holland, Editor

**EQUITABLE LIFE ASSURANCE SOCIETY** [4002]
787 Seventh Ave.
New York, NY 10019
Telephone: (212) 554-1838
Industry Affiliation: Finance, Services
**Publication(s):**
*Enterprise*
Day Published: 9/yr.
Lead Time: 4 wks. prior to pub. date
Mtls Deadline: 4 wks. prior to pub. date
Contact: Corp. Comms.
Spec. Requirements: 8 pg.; offset; 8-1/2 x 11; 2 color
Personnel: James Lacey, Editor
   Carl Barbati
   Thomas R. Stanton

**Materials Accepted/Included:** 01-Business news 02-By-line articles 03-Fashion news 04-Food news 05-Freelance copy 06-Letters to editor 07-Real estate news 08-Sports news 09-Travel news 10-Book rev. 11-Movie rev. 12-Music rev. 13-TV rev. 14-Theater rev. 15-Coming events 16-Obituaries 17-Question & answer 18-Social announcements 19-Artwork 20-Cartoons 21-Photos 22-TV listings 23-Audio rec. 24-Video rec. 25-Books 26-Films/film clips 27-Personnel news 28-Press releases 29-New product news/photos 30-Trade lit. 31-Contracts awarded 32-Display adv. 33-Classified adv.

11-29

*Agency News*
Day Published: bi-w.
Lead Time: 1 mo. prior to pub. date
Contact: Agency Oper.
Spec. Requirements: 4 pg.
Personnel: Tom Donlon, Editor

3090
## EQUITABLE LIFE INS. CO. OF IOWA
604 Locust St.
Des Moines, IA 50309
Telephone: (515) 245-6911
FAX: (515) 245-6794
Mailing Address:
  P.O. Box 1635
  Des Moines, IA 50306
Industry Affiliation: Insurance
**Publication(s):**
*Equiowa*
Day Published: bi-m.
Lead Time: 2 mos. prior to pub. date
Spec. Requirements: 28 pgs.; offset magazine; 84 x 11
Personnel: Sheryl McAtee, Editor

4667
## EQUITABLE RESOURCES
420 Blvd. of Allies
Pittsburgh, PA 15219
Telephone: (412) 261-3000
Industry Affiliation: Petroleum, Gas
**Publication(s):**
*Equitable News*
Day Published: q.
Lead Time: 6 wks. prior to pub. date
Contact: Corp. Comms. Div.
Spec. Requirements: 16-pgs.; offset; 11 x 8 1/2
Personnel: Sydney Reid, Editor

4668
## ERIE AREA CHAMBER OF COMMERCE
1006 State St.
Erie, PA 16501
Telephone: (814) 454-7191
FAX: (814) 459-0241
Industry Affiliation: Associations:  City, State, Federal
**Publication(s):**
*Chamber Newsletter*
Day Published: m.
Lead Time: 1 mo.
Mtls Deadline: 1 mo. prior to pub. date
Spec. Requirements: 8-10 pg; offset; 8 1/2 x 11
Personnel: Ray Horton, Editor

4669
## ERIE INSURANCE GROUP
144 E. Sixth St.
Erie, PA 16530
Telephone: (814) 452-6831
Industry Affiliation: Insurance
**Publication(s):**
*Erie Family*
Day Published: m.
Lead Time: 1 mo. prior to pub. date
Mtls Deadline: 1st mo. prior to pub. date
Spec. Requirements: 12-pgs.; offset; 8 1/2 x 11
Personnel: Lisa Miller, Editor

*In Sync*
Day Published: q.
Lead Time: 6 mos. prior to pub. date
Spec. Requirements: 20 pgs.; standard
Personnel: Pamela Gilchrist, Editor

*Agent Exchange*
Day Published: bi-m.
Lead Time: 2 mos. prior to pub. date
Spec. Requirements: 24 pgs.; standard
Personnel: Pamela Gilchrist, Editor

3988
## ERWIN DI CYAN
1486 E. 33rd St.
Brooklyn, NY 11234-3435
Telephone: (718) 252-8844
Industry Affiliation: Finance, Services
**Publication(s):**
*Di Cyan Bulletin*
Day Published: m.
Spec. Requirements: 4 pg; letterpress; 8 1/2 x 11
Personnel: Dr. Erwin Di Cyan, Editor

4582
## ESCO CORP.
2141 N.W. 25th Ave.
Portland, OR 97210
Telephone: (503) 228-2141
Industry Affiliation: Steel, Iron
**Publication(s):**
*Esco Ladle*
Day Published: q.
Spec. Requirements: 32-pgs.; offset magazine; 84 x 11
Personnel: John Howard, Editor

2128
## ESSELTE PENDAFLEX CORP.
71 Clinton Rd.
Garden City, NY 11530
Telephone: (516) 741-3200
Industry Affiliation: Office Equipment, Services, Supplies
**Publication(s):**
*Keeping Tabs*
Day Published: q.
Lead Time: 1 mo.
Mtls Deadline: Feb. 15; May 15; Aug. 15; Nov. 15.
Spec. Requirements: 8 pgs. standard size
Personnel: Bob Perkins, Editor

3861
## ETHICON INC.
P.O. Box 151
Div. Johnson & Johnson Corp.
Somerville, NJ 08876-0151
Telephone: (908) 218-2683
FAX: (908) 218-3150
Industry Affiliation: Dental, Medical
**Publication(s):**
*Inside Ethicon*
Day Published: q.
Lead Time: 1 mo. prior to pub. date
Mtls Deadline: 2 mos. prior to pub. date
Spec. Requirements: 8-12 pgs.; offset newspaper; 11 x 17
Personnel: Liz Slavin, Editor

*Point Of View*
Day Published: 3/yr.
Spec. Requirements: 24 pgs.
Personnel: Janice Hamel, Editor

*In Touch*
Day Published: w.
Lead Time: 3 wks.
Mtls Deadline: Fri. am
Spec. Requirements: 8 1/2 x 11
Personnel: Ralph Maratta, Editor

5238
## ETHYL CORP.
330 S. Fourth St.
Richmond, VA 23217
Telephone: (804) 788-5000
Mailing Address:
  P.O. Box 2189
  Richmond, VA 23217
Industry Affiliation: Chemicals, Plastics

**Publication(s):**
*Ethyl Intercom*
Day Published: bi-m.
Lead Time: 1 mo. prior to pub. date
Mtls Deadline: 1 mo. prior to pub. date
Personnel: Susan Sadler, Editor

4820
## EUA SERVICE CORP.
750 W. Center St.
W. Bridgewater, MA 02379
Telephone: (508) 559-1000
FAX: (508) 559-8932
Industry Affiliation: Utility:  Electric
**Publication(s):**
*E U A Spectrum*
Day Published: m.
Spec. Requirements: 12-16 pg.; offset bulletin; 8 1/2 x 11
Personnel: Hauk Sennott, Editor

4003
## EUROPEAN AMERICAN BANK
EAB Plz.
Uniondale, NY 11555
Telephone: (212) 557-3700
Industry Affiliation: Banks, Savings & Loans
**Publication(s):**
*E A B  people*
Day Published: m.
Contact: Mktg. Dept.
Spec. Requirements: 8-pgs.; offset; 9 x 12
Personnel: Linda M. Strongin, Editor

4974
## EX-STUDENTS ASSOCIATION
2110 San Jacinto
Austin, TX 78705
Telephone: (512) 471-8086
FAX: (512) 471-8088
Mailing Address:
  P.O. Box 7278
  Austin, TX 78713-7278
Industry Affiliation: Colleges, Institutions, Science Research
**Publication(s):**
*Texas Alcalde*
Day Published: bi-m.
Lead Time: 2 mos.
Materials: 01,02,05,06,08,10,16,17,19,32
Mtls Deadline: 6 wks. prior to pub. date
Spec. Requirements: 56-64 pg; offset; 8 1/2 x 11
Personnel: Ernestine Wheelock, Editor
          Tracy Shuford, Assistant Editor
          Homer Williams
          Teo Furtado
          Valerie Davis
          Mary Barminski, Art Director

68601
## EXXON CO., U.S.A.
P.O. Box 2180
Houston, TX 77252
Telephone: (713) 425-3332
Industry Affiliation: Utility:  Gas
**Publication(s):**
*Baytown Briefs*
Day Published: bi-m.
Personnel: G.R. Pfennig

3338
## FACTORY MUTUAL ENGINEERING AND RESEARCH
1151 Boston-Providence Turnpike
Norwood, MA 02062
Telephone: (617) 762-4300
Mailing Address:
  P.O. Box 9102
  Norwood, MA 02062
Industry Affiliation: Architects, Engineers, Business Service

**Publication(s):**
*Factory Mutual Record*
Day Published: q.
Spec. Requirements: 20 pgs.; web offset printed; 84 x 11
Personnel: Ellen Casaccio, Managing Editor

3273
## FAIRCHILD CORPORATION
300 W. Service Rd.
Chantilly, VA 22021
Telephone: (703) 478-5800
FAX: (703) 478-5915
Mailing Address:
  P.O. Box 10803
  Chantilly, VA 22021
Industry Affiliation: Architects, Engineers, Business Service
**Publication(s):**
*Quarterly Report To Stockholders*
Day Published: q.
Lead Time: 3 wks.
Personnel: John D. Jackson, Editor

*Annual Report*
Day Published: a.
Lead Time: 3 wks.
Personnel: John D. Jackson, Editor

68535
## FALK CORP.
3001 W. Canal St.
Milwaukee, WI 53208
Telephone: (414) 342-3131
FAX: (414) 937-4359
Mailing Address:
  P.O. Box 492
  Milwaukee, WI 53201
Industry Affiliation: Chemicals, Plastics
**Publication(s):**
*Falk Talk*
Day Published: m.
Personnel: William O'Keefe, Editor

4007
## FAMILY CIRCLE, INC.
110 Fifth Ave.
New York, NY 10011
Telephone: (212) 463-1000
Industry Affiliation: Publishers, Books, Magazines
**Publication(s):**
*Advance News*
Day Published: m.
Spec. Requirements: 8-12 pg; offset newspaper; 11 1/8 x 14 1/4

3145
## FARM BUREAU INS.
2627 KFB Plz.
Manhattan, KS 66502
Telephone: (913) 587-6000
Industry Affiliation: Insurance
**Publication(s):**
*Profile*
Day Published: bi-m.
Lead Time: 60 days prior to pub. date
Mtls Deadline: 60 days prior to pub. date
Spec. Requirements: 20-24 pgs.; offset; 8 1/2 x 11
Personnel: Ed Keck, Editor

5300
## FARM CREDIT SERVICES
601 W. First Ave.
Spokane, WA 99204
Telephone: (509) 838-9210
FAX: (509) 838-9410
Mailing Address:
  P.O. Box TAF-C5
  Spokane, WA 99220
Industry Affiliation: Agriculture, Services

**Materials Accepted/Included:** 01-Business news 02-By-line articles 03-Fashion news 04-Food news 05-Freelance copy 06-Letters to editor 07-Real estate news 08-Sports news 09-Travel news 10-Book rev. 11-Movie rev. 12-Music rev. 13-TV rev. 14-Theater rev. 15-Coming events 16-Obituaries 17-Question & answer 18-Social announcements 19-Artwork 20-Cartoons 21-Photos 22-TV listings 23-Audio rec. 24-Video rec. 25-Books 26-Films/film clips 27-Personnel news 28-Press releases 29-New product news/photos 30-Trade lit. 31-Contracts awarded 32-Display adv. 33-Classified adv.

**Publication(s):**
*Yields*
Day Published: q.
Lead Time: 3 mos. prior to pub. date
Mtls Deadline: 3 mos. prior to pub. date

68559

### FARM FAMILY INSURANCE COMPANIES
Rte. 9W
Glenmont, NY 12077
Telephone: (518) 436-9751
FAX: (518) 436-5471
Mailing Address:
  P.O. Box 656
  Albany, NY 12201
Industry Affiliation: Insurance
**Publication(s):**
*Farm Family Spirit*
Day Published: m.
Lead Time: 4 mos.
Materials: 20,27,28,29,30,32
Mtls Deadline: 4 mos. prior to pub. date
Contact: Marketing Services
Personnel: Monica Gray, Editor

3091

### FARMLAND INSURANCE COMPANIES
1963 Bell Ave.
Des Moines, IA 50315
Telephone: (515) 245-8800
Industry Affiliation: Insurance
**Publication(s):**
*Outlook*
Day Published: bi-m.
Lead Time: 30 days
Mtls Deadline: 15th of mo. prior to pub. date
Contact: Communications
Spec. Requirements: 8-12 pg; offset; 11 x 17
Personnel: Mary Wolfe, Editor

*Foresight*
Day Published: bi-m.
Lead Time: 30 days
Mtls Deadline: 1st of mo. prior to pub. date
Contact: Communications Dept.
Spec. Requirements: 12 pg; 8 1/2 x 11

69414

### FATHER FLANAGAN'S BOY'S HOME
Father Flanagan's Boy's Home
Boys Town, NE 68010
Telephone: (402) 498-1301
FAX: (402) 498-1348
Industry Affiliation: Associations: Trade, Fraternal
**Publication(s):**
*Boys Town Quarterly*
Day Published: q.
Contact: Boy's Town Public Relations
Spec. Requirements: tabloid
Personnel: John Melingagio, Editor

3778

### FBG SERVICE CORP.
27th & Harney St.
Omaha, NE 68131
Telephone: (402) 346-4422
Industry Affiliation: Office Equipment, Services, Supplies
**Publication(s):**
*Spotlite*
Day Published: m.
Lead Time: 3 wks. prior to pub. date
Mtls Deadline: 3 wks. prior to pub. date
Spec. Requirements: 2 pgs.; offset; 11 x 17
Personnel: Mike Lucy, Editor

3452

### FEDERAL-MOGUL CORP.
26555 Northwestern Hwy.
Southfield, MI 48034
Telephone: (810) 354-7700

Mailing Address:
  P.O. Box 1966
  Detroit, MI 48235
Industry Affiliation: Autos, Trucks
**Publication(s):**
*Federal-Mogul World*
Day Published: q.
Spec. Requirements: 20-pg; offset; 8 1/2 x 11
Personnel: Lonnie Ross, Editor

4860

### FEDERAL EXPRESS CORP.
2005 Corporate
Memphis, TN 38132
Industry Affiliation: Shipping
**Publication(s):**
*Worldwide Update*
Day Published: m.
Spec. Requirements: 8-pgs.; offset; 11 x 17
Personnel: Mary Harvey Gurley, Editor

*Associations*
Day Published: q.
  P.O. Box 727
  Memphis, TN 38194
Personnel: Mary Murphy, Editor

2522

### FEDERAL HIGHWAY ADMINISTRATION
400 Seventh St., S.W.
Washington, DC 20590
Telephone: (202) 366-0660
Industry Affiliation: Associations: City, State, Federal
**Publication(s):**
*F H W A  news*
Day Published: q.
Spec. Requirements: 4-pgs.; offset; 8 1/2 x 11
Personnel: Z. English, Editor

68598

### FEDERAL RESERVE BANK OF CHICAGO
230 S. LaSalle St.
Chicago, IL 60604
Telephone: (312) 322-5111
Industry Affiliation: Banks, Savings & Loans
**Publication(s):**
*Reserve 7*
Day Published: q.
Personnel: Margaret Malochleb, Editor

4338

### FEDERAL RESERVE BANK OF CLEVELAND
E. Sixth St. & Superior Ave.
Cleveland, OH 44114
Telephone: (216) 579-2000
Mailing Address:
  P.O. Box 6387
  Cleveland, OH 44101
Industry Affiliation: Banks, Savings & Loans
**Publication(s):**
*Federal Reserve Notes*
Day Published: bi-m.
Lead Time: 1-2 mos. prior to pub. date
Mtls Deadline: 2 mos. prior to pub. date
Contact: Personnel Department
Spec. Requirements: garamond typeface 4 column 11 x 17 finished size
Personnel: Jeff Bendix, Editor

4976

### FEDERAL RESERVE BANK OF DALLAS
400 S. Akard
Dallas, TX 75202
Telephone: (214) 922-6000
Mailing Address:
  Station K
  Dallas, TX 75222
Industry Affiliation: Banks, Savings & Loans

**Publication(s):**
*Southwest Economy*
Day Published: bi-m.
Spec. Requirements: 4 pg; offset tabloid; 8 1/2 x 11
Personnel: Rhonda Harris, Editor

4009

### FEDERAL RESERVE BANK OF NEW YORK
33 Liberty St.
New York, NY 10045
Telephone: (212) 720-5000
FAX: (212) 720-4947
Industry Affiliation: Banks, Savings & Loans
**Publication(s):**
*Fed*
Day Published: m.
Spec. Requirements: 16 pg; offset magazine; 84 x 11
Personnel: Brook Jacey, Editor

4673

### FEDERAL RESERVE BANK OF PHILADELPHIA
10 Independence Mall
Philadelphia, PA 19106
Telephone: (215) 574-6089
Mailing Address:
  P.O. Box 66
  Philadelphia, PA 19105
Industry Affiliation: Banks, Savings & Loans
**Publication(s):**
*3-C*
Day Published: m.
Lead Time: 60 days
Spec. Requirements: 30-32 pg; offset; 8 1/2 x 11
Personnel: Carol J. Shanks, Editor

3560

### FEDERATED INSURANCE COS.
121 E. Park Sq.
Owatonna, MN 55060
Telephone: (507) 455-5200
Mailing Address:
  P.O. Box 328
  Owatonna, MN 55060
Industry Affiliation: Insurance
**Publication(s):**
*Multiliner*
Day Published: 8/yr.
Spec. Requirements: 24-pgs.; offset magazine; 84 x 11
Personnel: Tim Lueck, Editor

4339

### FEDERATION FOR COMMUNITY PLANNING
614 Superior Ave., N.W., Rm. 300
Cleveland, OH 44113
Telephone: (216) 781-2944
Industry Affiliation: Associations: City, State, Federal
**Publication(s):**
*Planning And Action*
Day Published: bi-m.
Lead Time: 30 days prior to pub. date
Mtls Deadline: 30 days prior to pub. date
Contact: Public Information Comm. Educ.
Spec. Requirements: 4 pg; offset newspaper; 8 1/2 x 11
Personnel: Frederic E. Markowitz, Editor
  Jan Blank

2798

### FELT PRO INC.
7450 N. McCormick Blvd.
Skokie, IL 60076
Telephone: (708) 674-7700
FAX: (708) 674-7721
Mailing Address:
  P.O. Box C1103
  Skokie, IL 60076
Industry Affiliation: Auto Suppliers

**Publication(s):**
*Fel-Program*
Day Published: bi-m.
Spec. Requirements: 16 pg; offset magazine; 8 1/2 x 11
Personnel: Marian Bloomfield, Editor

2134

### FHP INTERNATIONAL CORP.
9900 Talbert Ave.
Fountain Valley, CA 92708
Telephone: (714) 963-7233
FAX: (714) 378-5655
Industry Affiliation: Associations: Health Groups
**Publication(s):**
*Fhp Encore*
Day Published: q.
Lead Time: 100 days prior to pub. date
Mtls Deadline: Mar. 15, Jun. 15, Sep. 15, Dec. 15
Spec. Requirements: 16 pgs.; offset; 8 1/2 x 11
Personnel: Ria Marie Carlson, Editor

4011

### FIBERLUX, INC.
3010 Westchester Ave.
Purchase, NY 10577-2524
Telephone: (914) 253-6400
FAX: (914) 253-6565
Industry Affiliation: Textiles, Apparel, Mills, Machinery
**Publication(s):**
*Fiberlux Profile*
Day Published: m.
Lead Time: 3 wks. prior to pub. date
Spec. Requirements: 8 1/2 x 11; offset
Personnel: J. Amendola, Editor

4234

### FIELDCREST CANNON, INC.
326 E. Stadium Dr.
Eden, NC 27288
Telephone: (919) 627-3000
Industry Affiliation: Textiles, Apparel, Mills, Machinery
**Publication(s):**
*Fieldcrest Cannon*
Day Published: 11/yr.
Lead Time: 1 mo. prior to pub. date
Spec. Requirements: textile-related 12-pgs; offset tabloid; 12 x 15
Personnel: Karen S. Cobb, Editor

3340

### FILENE'S
426 Washington St.
Boston, MA 02108
Telephone: (617) 357-2499
FAX: (617) 357-2434
Industry Affiliation: Retail Stores
**Publication(s):**
*Filene's Forum*
Day Published: bi-m.
Materials: 01,03,06,15,19,20,21,27,28,29
Contact: Human Resources
Spec. Requirements: 8-16 pg; offset; 74 x 10
Personnel: Chris Berger, Editor in Chief

2800

### FINANCIAL MANAGERS SOCIETY, INC.
8 S. Michigan Ave.
Chicago, IL 60603
Telephone: (312) 578-1300
Industry Affiliation: Retail Stores

---

Materials Accepted/Included: 01-Business news 02-By-line articles 03-Fashion news 04-Food news 05-Freelance copy 06-Letters to editor 07-Real estate news 08-Sports news 09-Travel news 10-Book rev. 11-Movie rev. 12-Music rev. 13-TV rev. 14-Theater rev. 15-Coming events 16-Obituaries 17-Question & answer 18-Social announcements 19-Artwork 20-Cartoons 21-Photos 22-TV listings 23-Audio rec. 24-Video rec. 25-Books 26-Films/film clips 27-Personnel news 28-Press releases 29-New product news/photos 30-Trade lit. 31-Contracts awarded 32-Display adv. 33-Classified adv.

**Publication(s):**
*F M S update*
Day Published: s-m.
Lead Time: 2 wks.
Mtls Deadline: 1st & 15th of mo. prior to pub. date
Spec. Requirements: short/2-3 paragraphs
Personnel: Bea McLean, Editor
    Karla L. Heuer

**FIRST-CITIZENS BANK & TRUST CO.**  4236
3128 Smoketree Ct.
Raleigh, NC 27604
Telephone: (919) 755-7458
FAX: (919) 755-2844
Mailing Address:
    P.O. Box 27131
    Raleigh, NC 27611-7131
Industry Affiliation: Banks, Savings & Loans
**Publication(s):**
*Courier*
Day Published: 10/yr.
Lead Time: 60 days prior to pub. date
Materials: 01,19,20,21
Mtls Deadline: 15th of mo. prior to pub. date
Spec. Requirements: 16-20 pgs.; offset; 8 1/2 x 11
Personnel: Terry Haggerty, Editor

*Management Focus*
Day Published: q.
Materials: 01,10,19,20,21
Mtls Deadline: mid-Feb., May, Aug., Nov.
Spec. Requirements: 6 pgs., offset, 8 1/2 x 11
Personnel: Tom Haggerty, Managing Editor
    Noel McLaughlin, Editor

**FIRST AMERICAN CORP.**  4863
First American Ctr.
Nashville, TN 37237
Telephone: (615) 248-2000
Industry Affiliation: Banks, Savings & Loans
**Publication(s):**
*First Focus*
Day Published: m.
Lead Time: 30 days
Spec. Requirements: 24 pg; offset; 84 x 11
Personnel: Jamie Webb, Editor

**FIRST BAPTIST CHURCH MODESTO**  2139
808 Needham St.
Modesto, CA 95354
Telephone: (209) 521-0181
Mailing Address:
    P.O. Box 4309
    Modesto, CA 95352
Industry Affiliation: Associations: Trade, Fraternal
**Publication(s):**
*Visitor*
Day Published: w.
Lead Time: 5 days
Spec. Requirements: 14 pg; offset; 7 x 8 1/2
Personnel: Jane Baten, Editor

*Bulletin Weekly, The*
Day Published: w.
Lead Time: 1 mo.
Personnel: Jane Baten, Editor

**FIRST CHICAGO CORPORATION**  66419
One First National Plz.
Chicago, IL 60670
Telephone: (312) 732-6209
FAX: (312) 732-5976
Industry Affiliation: Banks, Savings & Loans

**Publication(s):**
*First Chicagoan*
Day Published: m.
Lead Time: 3-4 wks.
Materials: 01,06,15,21,28
Mtls Deadline: 3-4 wks. prior to pub. date
Contact: Corporate Affairs
Personnel: Donna Gist Coleman, Editor

**FIRST COMMERCE CORP.**  3213
925 Common St., 5th Fl.
New Orleans, LA 70112
Telephone: (504) 582-7493
FAX: (504) 582-7385
Mailing Address:
    P.O. Box 60279
    New Orleans, LA 70160
Industry Affiliation: Banks, Savings & Loans
**Publication(s):**
*Communique*
Day Published: m.
Lead Time: 1 mo.
Materials: 01,02,15,21,28,29
Mtls Deadline: 15th of each mo.
Contact: Corporate Training
Spec. Requirements: 4-8 pg; 8 1/2 x 11
Personnel: Yolanda Pollard, Editor

*Focus*
Day Published: m.
Materials: 01,02,15,21,28,29
Mtls Deadline: 15th of each mo.
Contact: Corporate Training
Spec. Requirements: 4-8 pgs.; 8 1/2 x 11
Personnel: Yolanda Pollard, Editor

**FIRST COMMERCIAL BANK, N.A.**  2037
Capitol & Broadway
Little Rock, AR 72201
Telephone: (501) 371-7000
FAX: (501) 371-7457
Mailing Address:
    P.O. Box 1471
    Little Rock, AR 72203
Industry Affiliation: Banks, Savings & Loans
**Publication(s):**
*Banknotes, Joint Venture*
Day Published: q.
Personnel: Arlene Lovelace, Editor

**FIRST FEDERAL S & L ASSOCIATION OF ROCHESTER**  4012
One First Federal Plaza
Rochester, NY 14614
Telephone: (716) 238-2225
FAX: (716) 238-2483
Industry Affiliation: Banks, Savings & Loans
**Publication(s):**
*First & Foremost*
Day Published: bi-m.
Lead Time: 3 wks.
Mtls Deadline: 3 wks. prior to pub. date
Contact: Marketing
Spec. Requirements: 8-16 -page; 8 1/2 x 11
Personnel: Robert E. Nolan, Editor

**FIRST FIDELITY BANCORPORATION**  3864
550 Broad St.
Newark, NJ 07102
Telephone: (201) 565-3200
FAX: (201) 565-2876
Industry Affiliation: Banks, Savings & Loans

**Publication(s):**
*First Fidelity Journal*
Day Published: 10/yr.
Personnel: Henry T. Wallhauser, Editor

**FIRST HAWAIIAN, INC.**  2699
165 S. King St.
Honolulu, HI 96813
Telephone: (808) 525-7000
FAX: (808) 525-7619
Mailing Address:
    P.O. Box 3200
    Honolulu, HI 96847
Industry Affiliation: Associations: Trade, Fraternal
**Publication(s):**
*Panako*
Day Published: bi-m.
Lead Time: 1 mo. prior to pub. date
Spec. Requirements: 16-20 pgs.;offset magazine; 8 1/2 x 11
Personnel: Barbara Yamato, Editor

**FIRSTIER BANK**  3799
1700 Farnam St.
Omaha, NE 68102
Telephone: (402) 348-6000
FAX: (402) 348-7805
Industry Affiliation: Banks, Savings & Loans
**Publication(s):**
*Teamwork*
Day Published: bi-m.
Lead Time: 1 mo. prior to pub. date
Mtls Deadline: 1 mo. prior to pub. date
Spec. Requirements: 6-10 pg.; offset newspaper; 8 1/2 x 11
Personnel: Don Peterson, Editor

**FIRST INTERSTATE BANCORP.**  2286
633 W. 5th St.
Los Angeles, CA 90071
Telephone: (213) 614-3656
FAX: (213) 614-5137
Mailing Address:
    P. O. Box 54068
    Los Angeles, CA 90054
Industry Affiliation: Banks, Savings & Loans
**Publication(s):**
*Banker, The*
Day Published: m.
Mtls Deadline: 15th of mo. prior to pub. date
Contact: First Interstate Bank of California
Spec. Requirements: 32 page; 8 1/2 x 11
Personnel: Anne Reeves, Editor

*Monday Morning*
Day Published: w.
Mtls Deadline: Thu.
Contact: First Interstate Bank of California
Personnel: Tom Unger, Editor

**FIRST INTERSTATE BANK OF DENVER**  2363
633 17th St.
Denver, CO 80270
Telephone: (303) 293-2211
Industry Affiliation: Banks, Savings & Loans
**Publication(s):**
*Newsline*
Day Published: w.
Lead Time: Thu. prior to pub. date
Mtls Deadline: Thu. prior to pub. date
Personnel: Larry Pierce, Editor

*Bank Notes*
Day Published: w.
Personnel: Larry Pierce, Editor

**FIRST INTERSTATE BANK OF NEVADA, N.A.**  3818
1 E. First St.
Reno, NV 89501
Telephone: (702) 784-3000
FAX: (702) 784-3360
Mailing Address:
    P.O. Box 11007
    Reno, NV 89520
Industry Affiliation: Banks, Savings & Loans
**Publication(s):**
*First Nevadan*
Day Published: bi-m.
Lead Time: 1 mo. prior to pub. date
Mtls Deadline: 15th of alternate mos. prior to pub. date
Spec. Requirements: 20-pg.; offset magazine; 8 1/2 x 11
Personnel: Caryn Swobe, Editor

**FIRST INTERSTATE BANK OF NORTHWEST REGION**  5309
1300 S.W. Fifth Ave.
Portland, OR 97208
Telephone: (503) 225-2203
FAX: (503) 220-4999
Mailing Address:
    P.O. Box 3131
    Portland, OR 97208-3131
Industry Affiliation: Banks, Savings & Loans
**Publication(s):**
*Northwest Banker*
Day Published: m.
Contact: Marketing
Spec. Requirements: 4-6 page; offset; 11 x 17
Personnel: Evelyn Jung, Editor

**FIRST NATIONAL BANK OF CINCINNATI CORP.**  4342
425 Walnut St.
Cincinnati, OH 45202
Telephone: (513) 632-4902
Industry Affiliation: Banks, Savings & Loans
**Publication(s):**
*Banker, The*
Day Published: q.
Lead Time: 3 wks. prior to pub. date
Mtls Deadline: 20th of mo. prior to pub. date
Spec. Requirements: 8-pgs.; offset; 8 1/2 x 11
Personnel: Kathy M. Marshall, Editor

**FIRST NATIONAL BANK OF MARYLAND**  3274
25 S. Charles St.
Baltimore, MD 21201
Telephone: (410) 244-4000
Mailing Address:
    P.O. Box 1596
    Baltimore, MD 21201
Industry Affiliation: Banks, Savings & Loans

Materials Accepted/Included: 01-Business news 02-By-line articles 03-Fashion news 04-Food news 05-Freelance copy 06-Letters to editor 07-Real estate news 08-Sports news 09-Travel news 10-Book rev. 11-Movie rev. 12-Music rev. 13-TV rev. 14-Theater rev. 15-Coming events 16-Obituaries 17-Question & answer 18-Social announcements 19-Artwork 20-Cartoons 21-Photos 22-TV listings 23-Audio rec. 24-Video rec. 25-Books 26-Films/film clips 27-Personnel news 28-Press releases 29-New product news/photos 30-Trade lit. 31-Contracts awarded 32-Display adv. 33-Classified adv.

**Publication(s):**
*Communicator*
Day Published: 5-6/yr.
Lead Time: 3 wks.
Mtls Deadline: 3 wks.
Spec. Requirements: 24-28 page; offset; 8 1/2 X 11
Personnel: Therese Cashen, Editor

2426
**FIRST NATIONAL SUPERMARKETS, INC.**
500 North St.
Windsor Locks, CT 06096
Telephone: (203) 627-0241
Industry Affiliation: Food, General
**Publication(s):**
*Chain Link, The*
Day Published: q.
Lead Time: 1 mo.
Mtls Deadline: 1st of mo. prior to pub. date
Personnel: Ernest Monschein, Editor

2102
**FIRST NATIONWIDE BANK**
135 Main St.
San Francisco, CA 94105
Telephone: (415) 904-1100
FAX: (415) 904-1157
Industry Affiliation: Banks, Savings & Loans
**Publication(s):**
*Focus On The Best*
Day Published: q.
Lead Time: 3 wks.
Mtls Deadline: 3 wks.
Spec. Requirements: 16 page; offset; 8 1/2 x 11
Personnel: Janis Tarter, Editor

68571
**FIRST SECURITY CORP.**
29 E. First S.
Salt Lake City, UT 84101
Telephone: (801) 246-5534
FAX: (801) 246-2680
Mailing Address:
　P.O. Box 30006
　Salt Lake City, UT 84130
Industry Affiliation: Finance, Services
**Publication(s):**
*Firstfocus*
Day Published: bi-m.
Lead Time: 2 mos.
Materials: 01,02,16,17,21,27,28,29
Personnel: Patricia Kay, Editor

*Firstteam*
Day Published: bi-m.
Lead Time: 2 mos.
Mtls Deadline: 2 mos. prior to pub. date
Personnel: Patricia Kay, Editor

*Branch Clearings*
Day Published: bi-m.
Lead Time: 1 mo. prior to pub. date
Mtls Deadline: 1 mo. prior to pub. date
Contact: Communications
Spec. Requirements: 24-page; offset; 8 1/2 x 11
Personnel: Patricia Pace, Editor

4864
**FIRST TENNESSEE NATIONAL CORP.**
165 Madison Ave.
Memphis, TN 38103
Telephone: (901) 523-4444
Mailing Address:
　P.O. Box 84
　Memphis, TN 38101
Industry Affiliation: Banks, Savings & Loans

**Publication(s):**
*Prime Interest*
Day Published: bi-m.
Lead Time: 2 wks.
Mtls Deadline: every other Fri.
Contact: Corp. Communications
Personnel: Kathie Alexander, Editor

5240
**FIRST VIRGINIA BANK**
6400 Arlington Blvd
Falls Church, VA 22042
Telephone: (703) 241-4404
Industry Affiliation: Banks, Savings & Loans
**Publication(s):**
*First Virginian*
Day Published: bi-m.
Lead Time: 6 wks. prior to pub. date
Mtls Deadline: 6 wks. prior to pub. date
Spec. Requirements: 4-pgs.; ; 11 x 15
Personnel: Douglas M. Church, Jr., Editor

3828
**FLEET BANK N.A.**
1 Indian Head Plz., Rm. 58
Nashua, NH 03060
Telephone: (603) 594-5000
FAX: (603) 594-5670
Industry Affiliation: Banks, Savings & Loans
**Publication(s):**
*Branching Out*
Day Published: irreg.
Mtls Deadline: 13th of mo. prior to pub. date
Contact: Human Resources
Spec. Requirements: 12 page; offset newsletter; 8 1/2 x 11
Personnel: Louise A. Lindenberger, Editor

4823
**FLEET FINANCIAL GROUP, INC.**
50 Kennedy Plz.
Providence, RI 02903
Telephone: (401) 278-6242
Industry Affiliation: Finance, Services
**Publication(s):**
*New Directions*
Day Published: m.
Lead Time: 7-8 wks.
Mtls Deadline: 3rd wk. of mo.
Spec. Requirements: 8 pgs.; offset; 12 1/2 x 18
Personnel: Therese Myers, Editor

4534
**FLEMING COS. INC.**
6301 Waterford Blvd.
Oklahoma City, OK 73118
Telephone: (405) 840-7200
FAX: (405) 841-8158
Mailing Address:
　P.O. Box 26647
　Oklahoma City, OK 73126
Industry Affiliation: Food, General
**Publication(s):**
*Fleming Associate, The*
Day Published: q.
Lead Time: 1 mo.
Mtls Deadline: 1 mo.
Spec. Requirements: 28 page; offset; 8 1/2 x 11
Personnel: Susan Wallace, Editor

*Tri-State Express*
Day Published: m.
Lead Time: 1 mo.
Mtls Deadline: 1 mo.
Personnel: Susan Wallace, Editor

2593
**FLORIDA HORIZONS FEDERAL CREDIT UNION**
12171 Moody Dr.
Homestead, FL 33032
Telephone: (305) 258-1000
FAX: (305) 258-6505
Industry Affiliation: Finance, Services

**Publication(s):**
*New Horizons*
Day Published: q.
Lead Time: 6 wks.
Materials: 01,02,06,19,20,21,30
Mtls Deadline: 1st wk. of Mar., June, Sep., Dec.
Contact: Marketing Dept.
Personnel: Bill Moody, Editor

68388
**FLORIDA POWER & LIGHT CO.**
9250 W. Flagler St.
Miami, FL 33174
Telephone: (305) 552-2369
FAX: (305) 552-2144
Industry Affiliation: Utility: Electric
**Publication(s):**
*Inside At F P L*
Day Published: m.
Lead Time: 30 days
Mtls Deadline: 30 days prior to pub. date
Personnel: Tom Veenstra, Editor

2624
**FLORIDA RURAL ELECTRIC CO-OP ASSOCIATION**
P.O. Box 590
Tallahassee, FL 32302
Telephone: (904) 877-6166
FAX: (904) 656-5485
Industry Affiliation: Associations: Trade, Fraternal
**Publication(s):**
*Florida Rural Electric News*
Day Published: m.
Spec. Requirements: 16-page; offset; 8 1/2 x 11
Personnel: Laura Harrod, Editor

69334
**FLORISTS TRANSWORLD DELIVERY ASSOCIATION**
29200 N.W. Hwy.
Southfield, MI 48034
Telephone: (810) 355-9300
FAX: (810) 948-6415
Mailing Address:
　P.O. Box 2227
　Southfield, MI 49037
Industry Affiliation: Associations: Trade, Fraternal
**Publication(s):**
*Florist*
Day Published: m.
Lead Time: 3 mos.
Mtls Deadline: 3 mos. prior to pub. date
Spec. Requirements: 90 page; offset; 8 3/8 x 10 7/8
Personnel: William P. Golden, Editor

66558
**FLUOR DANIEL INC.**
3333 Michelson Dr.
Irvine, CA 92730
Telephone: (714) 975-2000
FAX: (714) 975-6549
Industry Affiliation: Industry: Heavy Construction, Machinery
**Publication(s):**
*Horizons*
Day Published: 10/yr.
Lead Time: 1 mo.
Mtls Deadline: 1 mo.
Personnel: Debbie Durell, Editor

*Hard Hat*
Day Published: bi-m.
Lead Time: 6 wks.
Mtls Deadline: 2 wks.
Personnel: Debbie Durell, Editor

69315
**FOLEY'S**
1110 Main St.
Houston, TX 77002
Telephone: (713) 651-6555
FAX: (713) 651-2599

Mailing Address:
　P.O. Box 1971
　Houston, TX 77251
Industry Affiliation: Retail Stores
**Publication(s):**
*Foley's Interview*
Day Published: bi-m.
Lead Time: 1-2 mos.
Mtls Deadline: 1-2 mos.
Contact: Jamie Hartwell

4682
**FOODLAND INTERNATIONAL CORP.**
8920 Pershall Rd.
Hazelwood, PA 63042
Telephone: (314) 524-5000
FAX: (314) 595-1749
Industry Affiliation: Retail Stores
**Publication(s):**
*Hotline*
Day Published: m.
Spec. Requirements: 4 pg; offset tabloid; 10 1/2 x 17
Personnel: Vesper McDonald, Editor

2556
**FOODSERVICE & PACKAGING INSTITUTE, INC.**
1901 N. Moore St., Ste. 1111
Arlington, VA 22209
Telephone: (703) 527-7505
FAX: (703) 527-7512
Industry Affiliation: Food, General
**Publication(s):**
*Environment News Digest*
Day Published: q.
Lead Time: 1 mo.
Mtls Deadline: 1 mo.
Spec. Requirements: 24-page; offset magazine; 4 x 8 1/2
Personnel: Charles W. Felix, Editor

*Single Service News*
Day Published: m.
Lead Time: 1 mo.
Mtls Deadline: 1 mo.
Personnel: Nancy Sherman, Editor
　Joe Spina

3454
**FORD MOTOR COMPANY**
The American Rd., Rm. 918
Dearborn, MI 48121
Telephone: (313) 322-1262
FAX: (313) 845-0179
Industry Affiliation: Autos, Trucks
**Publication(s):**
*Ford Times*
Day Published: m.
Lead Time: 6 mos.
Mtls Deadline: 6 mos. prior to pub. date
Contact: Ford North American Automotive
Spec. Requirements: 52 pg.; web offset; 7x10
Personnel: Jan Bronghton, Editor

*Dealer World*
Day Published: 9/yr.
Lead Time: 2 1/2 mos.
Mtls Deadline: 2 1/2 mos. prior to publication
Spec. Requirements: articles and photographs; assignment only.
Personnel: Hal Watts, Editor

*Ford World*
Day Published: 10/yr.
Materials: 32
Spec. Requirements: circ.: 250,000; tabloid
Personnel: Edward Miller, Editor

Materials Accepted/Included: 01-Business news 02-By-line articles 03-Fashion news 04-Food news 05-Freelance copy 06-Letters to editor 07-Real estate news 08-Sports news 09-Travel news 10-Book rev. 11-Movie rev. 12-Music rev. 13-TV rev. 14-Theater rev. 15-Coming events 16-Obituaries 17-Question & answer 18-Social announcements 19-Artwork 20-Cartoons 21-Photos 22-TV listings 23-Audio rec. 24-Video rec. 25-Books 26-Films/film clips 27-Personnel news 28-Press releases 29-New product news/photos 30-Trade lit. 31-Contracts awarded 32-Display adv. 33-Classified adv.

11-33

*Service Life*
Day Published: q.
Contact: Ford Parts & Service Div.
Personnel: Bob Girling, Editor

**FORD MOTOR COMPANY, SHARONVILLE PLANT**    68632
3000 Sharon Rd.
Cincinnati, OH 45241
Telephone: (513) 782-7317
FAX: (513) 782-7399
Industry Affiliation: Auto Suppliers
**Publication(s):**
*Drive Line*
Day Published: m.
Mtls Deadline: 1st Fri.
Personnel: Terry Bernard, Associate Editor

**FOREST LAWN MEMORIAL PARK**    68423
1712 S. Glendale Ave.
Glendale, CA 91205
Telephone: (818) 241-4151
FAX: (213) 344-9035
Industry Affiliation: Real Estate
**Publication(s):**
*Grapevine*
Day Published: m.
Materials: 24,25,29
Personnel: J. Carol Winn, Editor
         Dick Fisher, Editor in Chief
         John Mlyner, Managing Editor

**FORT WORTH CHAMBER OF COMMERCE**    4985
777 Taylor St., Ste. 900
Fort Worth, TX 76102
Telephone: (817) 336-2491
FAX: (817) 879-4034
Industry Affiliation: Associations: City, State, Federal
**Publication(s):**
*Chamberletter*
Day Published: m.
Lead Time: 2 mos.
Mtls Deadline: 2 mos. prior to pub. date
Spec. Requirements: 60-page; offset magazine; 8 1/2 x 11
Personnel: Denise Wentworth, Editor

**FORT WORTH STAR-TELEGRAM**    4938
400 Seventh St.
Fort Worth, TX 76102
Telephone: (817) 390-7400
FAX: (817) 390-7553
Mailing Address:
   P.O. Box 1870
   Fort Worth, TX 76101
Industry Affiliation: Newspapers
**Publication(s):**
*Star-Telegram Chaser*
Day Published: s-w.
Lead Time: 30 days prior to pub. date
Personnel: Karla Uecher, Editor

**FOSTER WHEELER CORP.**    3865
Perryville Corporate Pk.
Clinton, NJ 08809
Telephone: (908) 730-4000
FAX: (908) 730-5315
Industry Affiliation: Architects, Engineers, Business Service

**Publication(s):**
*Heat Engineering*
Day Published: q.
Lead Time: 2 mos.
Mtls Deadline: 2 mos.
Spec. Requirements: 20-page; offset; 8 1/2 x 11
Personnel: Harry Levy, Editor

**FRANKLIN, THE**    2804
Franklin Sq.
Springfield, IL 62713
Telephone: (217) 528-2011
Industry Affiliation: Insurance
**Publication(s):**
*Franklin Field*
Day Published: m.
Materials: 01,23,24,27,28,29,30,31
Spec. Requirements: 24 pg.; offset magazine; 8 1/2 x 11
Personnel: Jeff Tarr, Editor

**FRED MEYER INC.**    4591
3800 S.E. 22nd Ave.
Portland, OR 97202
Telephone: (503) 232-8844
FAX: (503) 797-5609
Mailing Address:
   P.O. Box 42121
   Portland, OR 97242
Industry Affiliation: Retail Stores
**Publication(s):**
*Q-Municator*
Day Published: bi-m.
Lead Time: 1 mo.
Materials: 01,03,04,19,20
Mtls Deadline: 1 mo. prior to pub. date
Spec. Requirements: 20 page; offset tabloid; 84 x 11
Personnel: Paul Casey, Editor

**FREIGHTLINER CORP.**    68570
4747 N. Channel Ave.
Portland, OR 97217
Telephone: (503) 735-8820
FAX: (503) 735-8921
Industry Affiliation: Trucking
**Publication(s):**
*Truckbuilders Progress*
Day Published: q.
Lead Time: 1 mo.
Mtls Deadline: 1 mo. prior to pub. date
Contact: Public Affairs
Spec. Requirements: 12-20 page; offset; 8 1/2 x 11
Personnel: Brooks Sanders, Editor

*Freightliner News Report*
Day Published: w.: Tue.
Mtls Deadline: Thu. prior to pub. date
Personnel: Brooks Sanders, Editor

**FRIENDSHIP PUBLICATIONS**    68369
P.O. Box 1472
Spokane, WA 99210
Telephone: (509) 328-9181
FAX: (509) 325-0405
Industry Affiliation: Publishers, Books, Magazines
**Publication(s):**
*Bus Ride*
Day Published: 9/yr.
Personnel: William A. Luke, Editor

**FURNAS ELECTRIC CO.**    2807
1000 McKee St.
Batavia, IL 60510
Telephone: (708) 879-6000
Industry Affiliation: Electrical, Electronic, Manufacturing

**Publication(s):**
*Furnas Today*
Day Published: m.
Lead Time: 2 mos.
Spec. Requirements: 8-page; offset magazine; 84 x 11
Personnel: Steve Wilcox, Editor

**FUTURE BUSINESS LEADERS OF AMERICA-PHI BETA LAMBDA**    5241
1912 Association Dr.
Reston, VA 22091
Telephone: (703) 998-2534
FAX: (703) 379-4561
Industry Affiliation: Associations: Trade, Fraternal
**Publication(s):**
*Hotline*
Day Published: q.
Lead Time: 6 wks. prior to pub. date
Mtls Deadline: 6 wks. prior to pub. date
Spec. Requirements: offset; 8 pg.; 8 1/2 x 11
Personnel: Angela Angerosa, Editor

*Tomorrow's Business Leader*
Day Published: q.
Lead Time: 10 wks.
Mtls Deadline: 10 wks. prior to pub. date
Spec. Requirements: 32 pgs.; 8 1/4 x 10 7/8; web press
Personnel: Angela Angerosa, Editor

*P B L Business Leader*
Day Published: 3/yr.
Lead Time: 10 wks.
Mtls Deadline: 10 wks. prior to pub. date
Personnel: Angela M. Angerosa, Editor

**GARDEN CITY HOSPITAL**    3456
6245 N. Inkster Rd.
Garden City, MI 48135
Telephone: (313) 458-4277
Industry Affiliation: Hospitals
**Publication(s):**
*Nitty Gritty:*
Day Published: b-m.
Lead Time: 60 days prior to pub. date
Mtls Deadline: as submitted
Spec. Requirements: 12-16-page; offset; 8 x 11
Personnel: Mitchell Nimmoor, Editor

**GARDEN WAY MFG. CO. INC.**    4020
102nd St. & Ninth Ave.
Troy, NY 12180
Telephone: (518) 235-6010
Industry Affiliation: Industry: Light Tools, Equipment
**Publication(s):**
*Troy-Bilt Owner News*
Day Published: q.
Spec. Requirements: 20-32 pg.; offset; tabloid
Personnel: Julie Needham, Editor

**GARDNER DENVER MACHINERY INC.**    2809
1800 Gardner Expwy.
Quincy, IL 62301
Telephone: (217) 222-5400
FAX: (217) 223-5897
Industry Affiliation: Industry: Heavy Construction, Machinery

**Publication(s):**
*Impressions*
Day Published: q.
Lead Time: 30 days prior to pub. date
Mtls Deadline: 30 days prior to pub. date
Contact: Cooper Machinery Group
Spec. Requirements: 4-12 pg.; offset magazine; 84 x 11
Personnel: Connie Frese, Editor

**GAST MFG. CORP.**    3457
2300 M139, P.O. Box 97
Benton Harbor, MI 49022
Telephone: (616) 926-6171
FAX: (616) 927-0808
Industry Affiliation: Industry: Light Tools, Equipment
**Publication(s):**
*Windjammer*
Day Published: m.
Lead Time: 1 mo. prior to pub. date
Materials: 01,02,15,18,19,20,21
Mtls Deadline: 1 mo. prior to pub. date
Contact: Marian Edinger, Ed.
Spec. Requirements: 8-page; offset; 8 1/2 x 11
Personnel: Glenn W. Eckert, Editor

**GATES CORPORATION, THE**    66425
900 S. Broadway
Denver, CO 80209
Telephone: (303) 744-5113
FAX: (303) 744-4000
Mailing Address:
   P.O. Box 5887
   Denver, CO 80217
Industry Affiliation: Rubber, Tires
**Publication(s):**
*Spectrum*
Day Published: m.
Mtls Deadline: 1st of mo. prior to pub. date
Contact: Worldwide Gates Corp., The
Personnel: Glenn R. Troester

**GATEWAY YOUTH & FAMILY SERVICES**    4021
6350 Main St.
Williamsville, NY 14221
Telephone: (716) 633-7266
Industry Affiliation: Associations: Health Groups
**Publication(s):**
*Gateway News:*
Day Published: q.
Lead Time: 1 mo.
Mtls Deadline: 1 mo. prior to pub. date
Spec. Requirements: 8-pg.; offset; 8 1/2 x 11
Personnel: Vernon Bigler, Editor

**GE**    68442
1635 Broadway
Fort Wayne, IN 46802
Telephone: (219) 439-3249
FAX: (219) 439-2740
Industry Affiliation: Electrical, Electronic, Manufacturing
**Publication(s):**
*G E News*
Day Published: w.
Mtls Deadline: Wed.
Personnel: Karen Horn, Editor

**Materials Accepted/Included:** 01-Business news 02-By-line articles 03-Fashion news 04-Food news 05-Freelance copy 06-Letters to editor 07-Real estate news 08-Sports news 09-Travel news 10-Book rev. 11-Movie rev. 12-Music rev. 13-TV rev. 14-Theater rev. 15-Coming events 16-Obituaries 17-Question & answer 18-Social announcements 19-Artwork 20-Cartoons 21-Photos 22-TV listings 23-Audio rec. 24-Video rec. 25-Books 26-Films/film clips 27-Personnel news 28-Press releases 29-New product news/photos 30-Trade lit. 31-Contracts awarded 32-Display adv. 33-Classified adv.

11-34

*Motors News*
Day Published: m.
Mtls Deadline: 15th of each mo.
Personnel: Karen Horn, Editor

**GE AIRCRAFT ENGINES**
1 Neumann Way, M-D N4
Cincinnati, OH 45215
Telephone: (513) 243-5635
FAX: (513) 243-9968
Industry Affiliation: Aircraft, Aerospace, Defense
**Publication(s):**
*Headlines*
Day Published: w.
Lead Time: 2 wks. prior to pub. date
Mtls Deadline: 2 wks. prior to pub. date
Personnel: Angela Genty, Editor

**GEISINGER SYSTEM**
100 N. Academy Ave.
Danville, PA 17822
Telephone: (717) 271-8860
FAX: (717) 271-6929
Industry Affiliation: Hospitals
**Publication(s):**
*Geisinger Magazine*
Day Published: q.
Spec. Requirements: 8 1/2 x 11; magazine
Personnel: Marcia Elliott, Editor

**GENCORP**
175 Ghent Rd.
Fairlawn, OH 44333
Telephone: (216) 869-4200
Industry Affiliation: Aircraft, Aerospace, Defense
**Publication(s):**
*Gencorp Business Review*
Day Published: bi-m.
Lead Time: 6 wks. prior to pub. date
Mtls Deadline: 4-6 wks. prior to pub. date
Spec. Requirements: 12 pgs.; web; 8 1/2 X 11
Personnel: George R. Carson, Jr., Editor

**GENERAL ACCIDENT INSURANCE**
436 Walnut St.
Philadelphia, PA 19106-3786
Telephone: (215) 625-2208
Industry Affiliation: Insurance
**Publication(s):**
*Coverage*
Day Published: 9/yr.
Lead Time: 1-1/2 mos. prior to pub. date
Materials: 01,02,05,06,09,21,25,27,28,30
Mtls Deadline: 6 wks. prior to pub. date
Contact: Communications
Spec. Requirements: 16 pg.; sheet-feed offset; 8 1/2 x 11
Personnel: Christine Norris, Editor
          Christy McCabe, Assistant Editor

*Gazette*
Day Published: bi-m.
Lead Time: 2 wks.
Materials: 01,02,05,25,28
Mtls Deadline: 2 wks. prior to pub. date
Contact: Communications
Personnel: Christine A. Norris, Editor
          Christy McCabe, Assistant Editor
          Jeanne Sabatino, Art Director

**GENERAL ATOMICS TECHNOLOGIES, INC.**
10955 John Jay Hopkins Dr.
San Diego, CA 92121
Telephone: (619) 455-2100
Mailing Address:
    P.O. Box 85608
    San Diego, CA 92186-9784
Industry Affiliation: Utility: Related

**Publication(s):**
*Update, The*
Day Published: bi-m.
Lead Time: 3 wks.
Mtls Deadline: 10th of mo.
Contact: Pub. Rels.
Spec. Requirements: 8-12-page; offset; 8 1/2 x 11
Personnel: Douglas M. Fouguet, Editor

**GENERAL HEARING CORP.**
60 Revere Dr.
Northbrook, IL 60062
Telephone: (708) 564-4070
Industry Affiliation: Associations: Trade, Fraternal
**Publication(s):**
*Your Health & Fitness*
Day Published: bi-m.
Personnel: Phyllis Hyman, Editor

**GENERAL MILLS, INC.**
One General Mills Blvd.
Minneapolis, MN 55440
Telephone: (612) 540-2311
Mailing Address:
    P.O. Box 1113
    Minneapolis, MN 55440
Industry Affiliation: Food, General
**Publication(s):**
*Review*
Day Published: q.
Lead Time: 8 wks. prior to pub. date
Contact: Kris Wenker, Ed.
Spec. Requirements: 12-20 pg.; 8 1/2 x 11
Personnel: Kris Wenker, Editor

**GENERAL MOTORS CORP.**
2400 W. Second St.
Marion, IN 46952
Telephone: (317) 668-2106
FAX: (317) 668-2010
Industry Affiliation: Autos, Trucks
**Publication(s):**
*Daily Communications*
Day Published: d.
Materials: 16,27,34
Personnel: Marilyn Stewart, Editor

*Weekly News Summary*
Day Published: w.
Materials: 01,02,28,29,30
Contact: Communications Dept.
Personnel: Jon Jonson, Editor
          Marilyn Stewart, Editor

**GENERAL MOTORS CORP.-U.A.W.**
G-3248 Van Slyke
Flint, MI 48552
Telephone: (313) 236-7622
FAX: (313) 236-3802
Industry Affiliation: Autos, Trucks
**Publication(s):**
*People 'n Pride*
Day Published: m.
Spec. Requirements: circ. 5,000
Personnel: Dennis S. Wisnewski, Editor

**GENERAL TELEPHONE CO. OF PA.**
19845 N. U.S. 31
Westfield, IN 46074
Telephone: (317) 896-6658
FAX: (317) 896-6290
Industry Affiliation: Utility: Telephone

**Publication(s):**
*Inside North*
Day Published: m.
Lead Time: 1st Tue. of mo. prior to pub. date
Spec. Requirements: 4 pg.; offset; 8 1/2 x 11
Personnel: Jim Hinkle, Editor

**GENUINE PARTS CO., INC.**
2999 Circle 75 Pkwy., N.W.
Atlanta, GA 30339
Telephone: (404) 953-1700
FAX: (404) 956-2211
Industry Affiliation: Auto Suppliers
**Publication(s):**
*Parts Pups*
Day Published: m.
Lead Time: 6-8 wks. prior to pub. date
Mtls Deadline: 8 wks. prior to pub. date
Spec. Requirements: 8 pg.; offset; 8 1/4 x 10 7/8
Personnel: Don Kite, Editor

**GEORGE E. FAILING CO.**
2215 S. Van Buren
Enid, OK 73703
Telephone: (405) 234-4141
FAX: (405) 233-6807
Mailing Address:
    P.O. Box 872
    Enid, OK 73702
Industry Affiliation: Industry: Heavy Construction, Machinery
**Publication(s):**
*Core Driller*
Day Published: q.
Spec. Requirements: 6-pg.; offset magazine; 7 1/2 x 9
Personnel: Kyle Barry, Editor

**GEORGIA-PACIFIC BRUNSWICK OPERATIONS**
P.O. Box 1438
Brunswick, GA 31521
Telephone: (912) 265-5780
FAX: (912) 765-8060
Industry Affiliation: Paper Products

**Publication(s):**
*Brunswick Operations Update*
Day Published: m.
Materials: 01,02,05,06,28,30
Mtls Deadline: 10th of mo. prior to pub. date
Spec. Requirements: 4-page; offset tabloid
Personnel: Curtis Carter, Editor

**GEORGIA-PACIFIC CORP.**
100 Wisconsin River Dr.
Port Edwards, WI 54469
Telephone: (715) 887-5061
FAX: (715) 887-5675
Industry Affiliation: Paper Products
**Publication(s):**
*Paper & People*
Day Published: bi-m.
Lead Time: 3 mos.
Materials: 05,20
Contact: Ellen Zettel, Ed.
Personnel: Ellen L. Zettel, Editor

*Up Front Wisconsin*
Day Published: irreg.
Contact: Ellen Zettel, Ed.
Personnel: Ellen Zettel, Editor

*Paper News*
Day Published: q.
Lead Time: 3 mos.
Mtls Deadline: 2 mos. prior to pub. date
Spec. Requirements: 8-12 pgs.; offset magazine; 8 1/2 x ll
Personnel: Ellen Zettel, Editor

**GEORGIA-PACIFIC CORP., BRUNSWICK OPERATIONS**
Ninth St.
Brunswick, GA 31521
Telephone: (912) 265-5780
FAX: (912) 265-8060
Mailing Address:
    P.O. Box 1438
    Brunswick, GA 32521
Industry Affiliation: Paper Products
**Publication(s):**
*Brunswick Week*
Day Published: w.
Mtls Deadline: Tue. prior to pub. date
Personnel: Curtis Carter

*Millwide Monitor*
Day Published: bi-m.
Mtls Deadline: 15th of mo. prior to pub. date
Personnel: Curtis Carter, Editor

**GEORGIA DEPARTMENT OF HUMAN RESOURCES**
47 Trinity Ave., S.W.
Atlanta, GA 30334
Telephone: (404) 656-5680
Industry Affiliation: Colleges, Institutions, Science Research
**Publication(s):**
*Human Side, The*
Day Published: bi-m.
Lead Time: 6 wks.
Mtls Deadline: 4 wks. prior to pub. date
Spec. Requirements: 2-page; offset
Personnel: Fran Buchanan, Editor

**GEORGIA MUNICIPAL ASSOCIATION**
201 Pryor St., S.W.
Atlanta, GA 30303
Telephone: (404) 688-0472
FAX: (404) 577-6663
Industry Affiliation: Associations: City, State, Federal
**Publication(s):**
*Georgia's Cities*
Day Published: m.
Lead Time: 6 wks.
Materials: 02,05,06,15,24,25,26,28,32,33
Mtls Deadline: 1st of mo. prior to pub. date
Contact: Publications Editor
Spec. Requirements: scannable copy-no faxes
Personnel: Charles C. Craig, Editor
          James V. Burgess, Jr., Publisher
          Preston Steckel, Marketing Director

**GEORGIA PORTS AUTHORITY**
P.O. Box 2406
Savannah, GA 31402
Telephone: (912) 964-3811
FAX: (912) 964-3921
Industry Affiliation: Shipping

Materials Accepted/Included: 01-Business news 02-By-line articles 03-Fashion news 04-Food news 05-Freelance copy 06-Letters to editor 07-Real estate news 08-Sports news 09-Travel news 10-Book rev. 11-Movie rev. 12-Music rev. 13-TV rev. 14-Theater rev. 15-Coming events 16-Obituaries 17-Question & answer 18-Social announcements 19-Artwork 20-Cartoons 21-Photos 22-TV listings 23-Audio rec. 24-Video rec. 25-Books 26-Films/film clips 27-Personnel news 28-Press releases 29-New product news/photos 30-Trade lit. 31-Contracts awarded 32-Display adv. 33-Classified adv.

11-35

**Publication(s):**
*Georgia Anchorage*
Day Published: q.
Lead Time: 26th of odd mos.
Mtls Deadline: 26th of odd mos. prior to pub. date
Contact: Amy Rhodes, Ed.
Spec. Requirements: 44 page; offset magazine; 8 1/2 x 11
Personnel: Amy Rhodes, Editor

2691
**GEORGIA POWER CO.**
333 Piedmont Ave., 22nd Fl.
Atlanta, GA 30308
Telephone: (404) 526-6526
FAX: (404) 526-2995
Industry Affiliation: Electrical, Electronic, Manufacturing
**Publication(s):**
*Citizen Weekly, The*
Day Published: w.
Lead Time: 1 wk.
Materials: 01,02,06,15,16,17,19,21
Mtls Deadline: 10 days prior to pub. date
Contact: Corporate Communication
Personnel: Barry Inman, Editor
          Vicki Gardocki, Art Director

2692
**GEORGIA REVENUE DEPT.**
Trinity-Washington Bldg.
270 Washington St., Ste. 434
Atlanta, GA 30334
Telephone: (404) 656-0568
FAX: (404) 651-9490
Industry Affiliation: Associations: City, State, Federal
**Publication(s):**
*Revenews*
Day Published: m.
Materials: 27,28
Spec. Requirements: 8-12-page; offset tabloid; 84 x 11
Personnel: John Brady, Editor

*Revenue Quarterly*
Day Published: q.: Jan., Apr., July, Oct.
Materials: 01,28
Personnel: Beryl Sellers, Editor

2524
**GIANT FOOD, INC.**
6300 Sheriff Rd.
Landover, MD 20785
Telephone: (301) 341-4100
FAX: (301) 618-4967
Mailing Address:
   P.O. Box 1804 - Dept. 599
   Washington, DC 20013
Industry Affiliation: Food, General
**Publication(s):**
*We News*
Day Published: bi-m.
Spec. Requirements: 12 page; 11 x 17
Personnel: Paula Fink, Editor

4240
**GILBARCO INC.**
7300 W. Friendly Ave.
Greensboro, NC 27410
Telephone: (919) 292-3011
Mailing Address:
   P.O. Box 22087
   Greensboro, NC 27410
Industry Affiliation: Industry: Heavy Construction, Machinery

**Publication(s):**
*Gilbarco Gazette*
Day Published: m.
Lead Time: 2 wks.
Mtls Deadline: 2 wks.
Spec. Requirements: 4-12-page; offset; 8 1/2 x 11
Personnel: Beth Cross, Editor

3463
**GILBERT/COMMONWEALTH, INC.**
P.O. Box 1498
Reading, PA 19603
Telephone: (610) 775-2600
FAX: (610) 775-2670
Industry Affiliation: Architects, Engineers, Business Service
**Publication(s):**
*Briefings*
Day Published: m.
Lead Time: 1 mo.
Materials: 1 mo. prior to pub. date
Spec. Requirements: 4-8 page; offset; 11 x 17
Personnel: C. Elizabeth Sterner, Editor

3347
**GILLETTE COMPANY, THE**
Prudential Tower Bldg.
Boston, MA 02199
Telephone: (617) 421-7000
Industry Affiliation: Drugs, Cosmetics, Pharmaceuticals
**Publication(s):**
*Blade:*
Day Published: 10/yr.
Lead Time: 2-6 wk. prior to pub. daate
Mtls Deadline: varied with publ. flow cycle
Contact: North American Shaving Div.
         1 Gillette Park
         Boston, MA 02127
Spec. Requirements: 8-12-page; offset; 8 1/2 x 11
Personnel: Susan Warzel, Editor

2155
**GILROY FOODS, INC.**
1280 Pacheco Pass Hwy., Ste. 1350
Gilroy, CA 95020
Telephone: (408) 842-8261
Mailing Address:
   P.O. Box 1088
   Gilroy, CA 95021
Industry Affiliation: Food, General
**Publication(s):**
*Garlic Vine, The*
Day Published: q.
Spec. Requirements: 4-page; offset bulletin; 84 x 11
Personnel: Elena Crandell, Editor

3570
**GIRL SCOUT COUNCIL OF GREATER MINNEAPOLIS**
5601 Brooklyn Blvd.
Minneapolis, MN 55429
Telephone: (612) 535-4602
FAX: (612) 535-7524
Industry Affiliation: Associations: Trade, Fraternal
**Publication(s):**
*Pioneer*
Day Published: bi-m.
Lead Time: 3 wks.
Mtls Deadline: q.
Contact: Pub. Rels. Dept.
Spec. Requirements: 12-page; offset; 8 1/2 x 11
Personnel: Kate Brehe, Editor

Girl Scouting
Day Published: q.
Lead Time: 3 wks.
Contact: Pub. Rels. Dept.
Personnel: Joan Kryshak

3687
**GIRL SCOUT COUNCIL OF GREATER ST. LOUIS**
911 Washington St.
Saint Louis, MO 63101
Telephone: (314) 241-1270
FAX: (314) 241-3155
Industry Affiliation: Associations: Trade, Fraternal
**Publication(s):**
*Insight*
Day Published: 3/yr.
Lead Time: 6 wks.
Mtls Deadline: 6 wks. prior to pub. date
Contact: Pub. Rels. Dept.
Spec. Requirements: 4-8-page; letterpress; 11 1/2 x 16
Personnel: Dorothy Hutchinson-Gross, Editor

3464
**GLEANER LIFE INSURANCE SOCIETY**
5200 West U.S. 223
Adrian, MI 49221
Telephone: (517) 263-2244
Mailing Address:
   P.O. Box 1894
   Adrian, MI 49221
Industry Affiliation: Insurance
**Publication(s):**
*National Gleaner Forum*
Day Published: q.
Spec. Requirements: 20-page; offset; 54 x 8
Personnel: Mary Ward Eaton, Editor

*Arbor News*
Day Published: m.
Lead Time: 60 days
Mtls Deadline: 1st of mo. prior to pub. date
Contact: Communications
Spec. Requirements: 6-8 pages; 8 1/2 x 11; offset
Personnel: Gregory Warfield, Editor

*Friday Morning*
Day Published: bi-w.
Lead Time: 3 days
Mtls Deadline: 3 days prior to pub. date
Contact: Communications
Spec. Requirements: 1-4 pages; 8 1/2 x 11
Personnel: Gregory Warfield, Editor

*Epistles*
Day Published: w.
Lead Time: 2 wks.
Mtls Deadline: Fri. prior to pub. date
Contact: Communications
Spec. Requirements: 1-4 pages; 8 X 11
Personnel: Gregory L. Warfield, Editor

4032
**GLEASON WORKS**
1000 University Ave.
Rochester, NY 14607
Telephone: (716) 473-1000
Industry Affiliation: Industry: Light Tools, Equipment
**Publication(s):**
*Cutting Edge*
Day Published: bi-m.
Spec. Requirements: 1-4 pg.; offset; 8 1/2 x 11
Personnel: Ginny Lalka, Editor

4349
**GLENMARY SISTERS**
405 W. Parrish Ave.
Owensboro, KY 42302
Telephone: (502) 686-8401
FAX: (502) 686-8759

Mailing Address:
   P.O. Box 2264
   Owensboro, KY 42302
Industry Affiliation: Associations: Trade, Fraternal
**Publication(s):**
*Kinship*
Day Published: q.
Spec. Requirements: 12-page; offset; 8 1/4 x 10 7/8
Personnel: Sr. Christine Beckett, Editor
          Linda Lehmann, Managing Editor

69457
**GMHC, INC.**
129 W. 20th St.
New York, NY 10011
Telephone: (212) 337-3593
FAX: (212) 337-3656
Industry Affiliation: Associations: Health Groups
**Publication(s):**
*Treatment Issues*
Day Published: m.
Contact: Dept. of Medical Information
Spec. Requirements: newsletter on medical aspects of AIDS & ARC
Personnel: David Gold, Editor

4033
**GOLUB CORP./PRICE CHOPPER SUPERMARKETS**
501 Duanesburg Rd.
Schenectady, NY 12306
Telephone: (518) 356-9413
Mailing Address:
   P.O. Box 1074
   Schenectady, NY 12301
Industry Affiliation: Retail Stores
**Publication(s):**
*Associates' View, The*
Day Published: 6 wks.
Lead Time: 5 wks.
Contact: Human Res.
Spec. Requirements: 16-36 pgs; offset; 8 1/2 x 11
Personnel: Lotte Meers, Editor
          Kelly Van Aller, Associate Editor

3780
**GOOD NEWS BROADCASTING ASSOCIATION, INC.**
301 S. 12th St.
Lincoln, NE 68508
Telephone: (402) 474-4567
Mailing Address:
   P.O. Box 82808
   Lincoln, NE 68501
Industry Affiliation: Radio, TV, Movies
**Publication(s):**
*Young Ambassador*
Day Published: m.: except July-Aug.

*Confident Living*
Day Published: m.: except Aug.
Lead Time: 9 mo.
Mtls Deadline: 9 mos. prior to pub. date
Contact: Adult Dept.
Spec. Requirements: material must relate to the Bible.
Personnel: Warren W. Wiersbe, Editor

4475
**GOOD SAMARITAN HOSPITAL AND HEALTH CENTER**
2222 Philadelphia Dr.
Dayton, OH 45406
Telephone: (513) 278-2612
FAX: (513) 276-8244
Industry Affiliation: Hospitals

---

**Publication(s):**
*Profiles*
Day Published: w.
Lead Time: 1 wk.
Mtls Deadline: 1 wk. prior to pub. date
Contact: Director of Communications
Spec. Requirements: 2-page; offset; 8 1/2 x 11
Personnel: Sharon Keeter

*Physician Resource*
Day Published: bi-m.
Lead Time: 2 mos.
Mtls Deadline: 2 mos. prior to pub. date
Contact: Director of Communications
Spec. Requirements: Short Articles

3008
**GOODWILL INDUSTRIES INTERNATIONAL, INC.**
9200 Wisconsin Ave.
Bethesda, MD 20814
Telephone: (301) 530-6500
FAX: (301) 530-1516
Industry Affiliation: Associations: Trade, Fraternal
**Publication(s):**
*Goodwill Forum*
Day Published: 10/yr.
Lead Time: 8 wks. prior to pub. date
Mtls Deadline: 1st of mo. prior to pub. mo.
Contact: 182 Autonomous Units-US/Can.
1635 W. Michigan St.
Indianapolis, IN 46222
Spec. Requirements: 40 pg.; 8 1/2 x 11
Personnel: Eric Ries, Editor
Hossain Hastaie, Art Director

68425
**GOODWILL INDUSTRIES OF HOUSTON**
5200 Jensen Dr.
Houston, TX 77026
Telephone: (713) 692-6221
FAX: (713) 692-0923
Industry Affiliation: Associations: Trade, Fraternal
**Publication(s):**
*Goodwill News-Newsletter*
Day Published: a.: Jan.
Mtls Deadline: Dec. 1, prior to pub. date
Personnel: Sherri Lowe

2158
**GOODWILL INDUSTRIES OF SOUTHERN CALIFORNIA**
342 San Fernando Rd.
Los Angeles, CA 90031
Telephone: (310) 223-1211
Industry Affiliation: Associations: Trade, Fraternal
**Publication(s):**
*Tidings*
Day Published: q.
Lead Time: 3-4 wks.
Materials: 01,15,19,21
Mtls Deadline: 1st of mo. prior to pub. date
Contact: Community Relations
Spec. Requirements: 6-8-page; offset; 8 1/2 x 11
Personnel: Rholan Wong, Editor
Michele Johnsen, Writer

4034
**GOULDS PUMPS INC.**
240 Fall St.
Seneca Falls, NY 13148
Telephone: (315) 568-2811
FAX: (315) 568-2418
Mailing Address:
P.O. Box 330
Seneca Falls, NY 13148
Industry Affiliation: Industry: Light Tools, Equipment

**Publication(s):**
*Goulds Professional Dealers Association*
Day Published: q.
Contact: Water Systems Div.
Bayard St. Ext.
Seneca Falls, NY 13148
Spec. Requirements: 20-36 pgs.
Personnel: James Flanders, Editor

*Pumplines Extra*
Day Published: m.
Lead Time: 1 mo.
Personnel: Gerald Abbott, Editor

2525
**GOVERNMENT EMPLOYEES INSURANCE CO.**
5260 Western Ave., N.W.
Washington, DC 20015
Telephone: (301) 986-2757
FAX: (301) 718-5234
Mailing Address:
One Geico Plz.
Washington, DC 20076-0001
Industry Affiliation: Associations: City, State, Federal
**Publication(s):**
*News Wheel*
Day Published: 11/yr.
Lead Time: 2 mos. prior to pub. date
Mtls Deadline: 2 mos. prior to pub. date
Contact: Comm. Dept. Pub.
Spec. Requirements: 8-page
Personnel: Jody Goulden, Editor

4997
**GOVERNMENT PERSONNEL MUTUAL LIFE INSURANCE CO**
GPM Life Bldg.
P.O. Box 790270
San Antonio, TX 78284-4199
Telephone: (210) 341-6161
FAX: (210) 341-3034
Industry Affiliation: Insurance
**Publication(s):**
*G P M Messenger*
Day Published: m.
Contact: Marketing Div.
Spec. Requirements: 12-20 pg; desktop; 8 1/2 x 11
Personnel: Anne LaFave, Editor

3569
**GRACO INC.**
4050 Olson Memorial Hwy.
Minneapolis, MN 55422
Telephone: (612) 623-6000
FAX: (612) 623-6777
Mailing Address:
P.O. Box 1441
Minneapolis, MN 55440
Industry Affiliation: Associations: Trade, Fraternal
**Publication(s):**
*Newsline*
Day Published: m.
Lead Time: 2 wks. prior to pub. date
Mtls Deadline: 2 wks. prior to pub. date
Spec. Requirements: 12-20 pgs.; offset; 8 1/2 x 11
Personnel: Von Sille, Editor

68379
**GRAIN ELEVATOR AND PROCESSING SOCIETY**
301 Fourth Ave., S., Ste. 365
Minneapolis, MN 55415-0026
Telephone: (612) 339-4625
FAX: (612) 339-4644
Mailing Address:
P.O. Box 15026
Minneapolis, MN 55415
Industry Affiliation: Food, General

**Publication(s):**
*In-Grain*
Day Published: m.
Lead Time: 1 mo. prior to pub. date
Mtls Deadline: 1 mo. prior to pub. date
Contact: Kathryn Hendricks, Ed.
Spec. Requirements: 12 pgs.; offset; 8 1/2 x 11
Personnel: Kathryn Hendricks, Editor

3868
**GRAND UNION CO.**
201 Willowbrook Blvd.
Wayne, NJ 07470
Telephone: (201) 890-6100
Industry Affiliation: Food, General
**Publication(s):**
*Grand Stand*
Day Published: q.
Lead Time: 5-6 wks. prior to pub. date
Mtls Deadline: 6 wks. prior to pub. date
Spec. Requirements: 40 pgs.; offset; 8 1/2 x 11
Personnel: D.C. Vaillancourt, Editor

3465
**GRAND VALLEY STATE UNIVERSITY**
1 Campus Dr., 24-26 JHZ
Allendale, MI 49401-9403
Telephone: (616) 895-2221
FAX: (616) 895-3503
Industry Affiliation: Colleges, Institutions, Science Research
**Publication(s):**
*Forum*
Day Published: w.: Mon.
Lead Time: 5 days prior to pub. date
Mtls Deadline: Wed. prior to pub. date
Contact: Public Relations Office
Spec. Requirements: 4-Page; Offset; 8 1/2 x 11
Personnel: Sue Squire, Editor
Clarice Geels, Editor in Chief
Bob Bauer, Art Director

*Horizons*
Day Published: q.: Oct., Jan., Apr., July
Lead Time: 3 mos. prior to pub. date
Mtls Deadline: 3 mos. prior to pub date
Contact: Foundation Office
Spec. Requirements: 8 Pg.; Offset; 17 1/2 x 11 1/4
Personnel: Clarice Geels, Editor in Chief
Bob Bauer, Art Director

*Inside G V S U*
Day Published: 3/yr.: Dec., May, Aug.
Lead Time: 2 mos. prior to pub. date
Mtls Deadline: 2 mos. prior to pub. date
Contact: Public Relations Office
Spec. Requirements: 4 Pg.; Offset; 8 1/2 x 11
Personnel: Clarice Geels, Editor in Chief
Nancee Miller, Managing Editor

4036
**GRAYBAR ELECTRIC CO. INC.**
34 N. Merrimac Ave.
St. Louis, MO 63105
Telephone: (314) 727-3900
FAX: (314) 727-0788
Mailing Address:
P.O Box 7231
St. Louis, MO 63177
Industry Affiliation: Utility: Electric
**Publication(s):**
*Graybar Outlook*
Day Published: m.
Spec. Requirements: 12 pg.; offset; 9 x 12
Personnel: Daniel E. Hayes, Editor

3203
**GREATER BATON ROUGE CHAMBER OF COMMERCE**
564 Laurel St.
Baton Rouge, LA 70801
Telephone: (504) 381-7125
FAX: (504) 336-4306

Mailing Address:
P.O. Box 3217
Baton Rouge, LA 70821
Industry Affiliation: Associations: City, State, Federal
**Publication(s):**
*Commerce*
Day Published: m.
Lead Time: 3 wks.
Mtls Deadline: 10th of mo.
Contact: Communications
Spec. Requirements: 16-24 page; 8 1/2 x 11
Personnel: Jace Dobrowolski, Editor

4353
**GREATER CINCINNATI CHAMBER OF COMMERCE**
441 Vine St., Ste. 300
Cincinnati, OH 45202
Telephone: (513) 579-3195
Industry Affiliation: Associations: City, State, Federal
**Publication(s):**
*Chamber Vision*
Day Published: m.
Lead Time: 3 wks. prior to pub. date
Mtls Deadline: 3 wks. prior to pub. date
Spec. Requirements: 4-page; offset newsletter; 84 x 11
Personnel: Keith Stichtenoth, Editor

4476
**GREATER CLEVELAND GROWTH ASSOCIATION**
200 Towers City Ctr.
Cleveland, OH 44113
Telephone: (216) 621-3300
Industry Affiliation: Associations: City, State, Federal
**Publication(s):**
*Clevelander, The*
Day Published: m.
Lead Time: 1 mo. prior to pub. date
Mtls Deadline: 1st of mo. prior to pub. date
Spec. Requirements: 8 pg.; offset; 8 1/2 x 11
Personnel: Melissa Beight, Editor

5000
**GREATER HOUSTON BUILDERS ASSOCIATION**
6120 Tarnef, Ste. 100
Houston, TX 77074
Telephone: (713) 776-1445
FAX: (713) 776-1624
Mailing Address:
P.O. Box 741189
Houston, TX 77274
Industry Affiliation: Associations: Trade, Fraternal
**Publication(s):**
*Houston Builder*
Day Published: m.
Lead Time: 10 days
Materials: 01,32,33
Mtls Deadline: 10 days prior to pub. date
Contact: Communications Dept.
Spec. Requirements: 12-page; offset; 11 x 17
Personnel: Kristen Baker, Editor
Susan Anderson, Publisher

5394
**GREATER MADISON CONVENTION & VISITORS BUREAU**
615 E. Washington Ave.
Madison, WI 53703
Telephone: (608) 255-2537
FAX: (608) 258-4950
Industry Affiliation: Associations: City, State, Federal

**Materials Accepted/Included:** 01-Business news 02-By-line articles 03-Fashion news 04-Food news 05-Freelance copy 06-Letters to editor 07-Real estate news 08-Sports news 09-Travel news 10-Book rev. 11-Movie rev. 12-Music rev. 13-TV rev. 14-Theater rev. 15-Coming events 16-Obituaries 17-Question & answer 18-Social announcements 19-Artwork 20-Cartoons 21-Photos 22-TV listings 23-Audio rec. 24-Video rec. 25-Books 26-Films/film clips 27-Personnel news 28-Press releases 29-New product news/photos 30-Trade lit. 31-Contracts awarded 32-Display adv. 33-Classified adv.

11-37

**Publication(s):**
*Bureau Briefing*
Day Published: bi-m.
Lead Time: 2 wks. prior to pub. date
Mtls Deadline: 2 wks. prior to pub. date
Contact: Communications Dept.
Spec. Requirements: legal size tabloid
Personnel: Sandy Sobek Leslie, Editor

*Madison Area Travel Planner & Visitors Guide*
Day Published: a.
Lead Time: Dec. 15 prior to pub. date
Mtls Deadline: Dec. 15 prior to pub. date
Contact: Communications Dept.
Personnel: Sandy Sobek Leslie, Editor

3781
**GREATER OMAHA CHAMBER OF COMMERCE**
1301 Harney St.
Omaha, NE 68102
Telephone: (402) 346-5000
Industry Affiliation: Associations: Trade, Fraternal
**Publication(s):**
*Omaha Profile*
Day Published: 21/yr.
Lead Time: 2 wks. prior to pub. date
Mtls Deadline: 2 wks. prior to pub. date
Contact: Vicki Krecek, V.P. Communications
Spec. Requirements: 8-page; offset; 8 1/2 x 11
Personnel: Liz Cajka, Editor

3819
**GREATER RENO-SPARKS CHAMBER OF COMMERCE**
405 Marsh Ave.
Reno, NV 89509
Telephone: (702) 786-3030
Mailing Address:
   P.O. Box 3499
   Reno, NV 89505
Industry Affiliation: Associations: Trade, Fraternal
**Publication(s):**
*Chamber Business*
Day Published: m.
Lead Time: 6 wks. prior to pub. date
Mtls Deadline: 6 wks. prior to pub date
Contact: Public Affairs
Spec. Requirements: 8 page; offset; tabloid
Personnel: Patti Pietsch, Editor

2236
**GREATER SAN DIEGO CHAMBER OF COMMERCE**
402 W. Broadway, Ste. 1000
San Diego, CA 92101
Telephone: (619) 544-1312
FAX: (619) 234-0571
Industry Affiliation: Associations: City, State, Federal
**Publication(s):**
*Business Action*
Day Published: m.
Lead Time: 15-20 days prior to pub. date
Mtls Deadline: 15th of mo. prior to pub. date
Spec. Requirements: 16 page; 8 1/2 x 11
Personnel: Debbie Brown, Editor
   Anthony LeSasne, Assistant Editor

*Economic Bulletin*
Day Published: m.
Lead Time: 30 days
Mtls Deadline: 30 days prior to pub. date
Personnel: Kelly Cunningham, Editor

2534
**GREATER WASHINGTON BOARD OF TRADE, THE**
1129 20th St., N.W., Ste. 260
Washington, DC 20036
Telephone: (202) 857-5900
FAX: (202) 223-2648
Industry Affiliation: Associations: City, State, Federal
**Publication(s):**
*Board Of Trade News*
Day Published: bi-m.
Lead Time: 1 mo.
Materials: 01,02,07,09,15,21,27,28,29,31,32
Mtls Deadline: 1 mo. prior to pub. date
Contact: Community Development Group
Spec. Requirements: 20-page; offset; tabloid
Personnel: Sandra W. Rubenstein, Editor
   Suzanne L. Trump, Advertising Representative

*Membership Directory*
Day Published: a.: Nov.-Dec.
Lead Time: 3 mos.
Materials: 32
Mtls Deadline: 2 wks. to 3 mos. prior to pub. date
Contact: Administration
Spec. Requirements: 128 pg.; offset, 4-color cover
Personnel: Sandra W. Rubenstein, Editor
   Suzanne L. Trump, Advertising Representative

4241
**GREATER WINSTON-SALEM CHAMBER OF COMMERCE**
601 W. Fourth St.
Winston Salem, NC 27101
Telephone: (919) 725-2361
FAX: (919) 773-1404
Mailing Address:
   P.O. Box 1408
   Winston Salem, NC 27102-1408
Industry Affiliation: Associations: Trade, Fraternal
**Publication(s):**
*News Line*
Day Published: m.
Lead Time: 3 wks. prior to pub. date
Mtls Deadline: 1st of ea. mo. prior to pub. date
Contact: Communications
Spec. Requirements: 8-1/2 x 11, 8 pages photos
Personnel: Rosalind Chostner, Editor

*Membership Directory*
Day Published: a.
Lead Time: 6 mos. prior to pub. date
Mtls Deadline: June 15 prior to pub. date
Contact: Communications
Personnel: Rosalind Chostner, Editor
   Carole Crosslin

3467
**GREAT LAKES DIVISION-NATIONAL STEEL**
One Quality Dr.
Ecorse, MI 48229
Telephone: (313) 297-2100
FAX: (313) 297-2312
Industry Affiliation: Steel, Iron

**Publication(s):**
*Focus*
Day Published: 10/yr.
Lead Time: 3 wks.
Mtls Deadline: 15th of mo.
Spec. Requirements: 8-page; offset tabloid; 11 x 14
Personnel: John Jakcsy, Editor

4999
**GREAT SOUTHERN LIFE INSURANCE CO.**
500 N. Akard
Dallas, TX 75201
Telephone: (800) 231-0801
FAX: (214) 954-8148
Mailing Address:
   P.O. Box 2699
   Dallas, TX 75221
Industry Affiliation: Insurance
**Publication(s):**
*Spotlight*
Day Published: m.
Lead Time: 2 wks. prior to pub. date
Mtls Deadline: 10th of mo. prior to pub. date
Personnel: Lynn Phillips, Editor

5347
**GREENBRIER HOTEL**
Rte. 60
White Sulphur Springs, WV 24986
Telephone: (304) 536-1110
FAX: (304) 536-7834
Industry Affiliation: Hotels, Motels
**Publication(s):**
*Greenbrier Magazine*
Day Published: s-a.
Lead Time: 1 mo.
Mtls Deadline: 1 mo. prior to pub. date
Contact: Sharon Rowe, Ed.
Spec. Requirements: 12-16 page; offset bulletin; 9 x 12
Personnel: Sharon Rowe, Editor

4037
**GREEN POINT SAVINGS BANK**
41-60 Main St.
Flushing, NY 11355
Telephone: (718) 670-7500
Industry Affiliation: Banks, Savings & Loans
**Publication(s):**
*Pointer, The*
Day Published: m.
Lead Time: 2 wks.
Mtls Deadline: 15th of mo.
Spec. Requirements: 14-pg.; offset magazine; 8 1/2 x 11
Personnel: Collen Kolesnik, Editor in Chief

*Vantage Point*
Day Published: q.
Personnel: Paul Rizzo, Editor

2160
**GROSSMONT HOSPITAL**
5555 Grossmont Center Dr.
La Mesa, CA 91942
Telephone: (619) 465-0711
FAX: (619) 668-4201
Mailing Address:
   P.O. Box 158
   La Mesa, CA 91944
Industry Affiliation: Hospitals
**Publication(s):**
*Capsule*
Day Published: m.
Lead Time: 1 mo. prior to pub. date
Mtls Deadline: 1 mo. prior to pub. date
Contact: Publications
Spec. Requirements: 4-8 pg.; offset; 8 1/2 x 11
Personnel: Janie Blessinger, Editor

*Win-Women's Information Network*
Day Published: 1/3 yrs.
Lead Time: 8 wks. prior to pub. date
Contact: Publications
Personnel: Janie Blessinger

*Health Magazine*
Day Published: q.
Lead Time: 1 mo. prior to pub. date
Mtls Deadline: 1 mo. prior to pub. date
Contact: Publications
Personnel: Janie Blessinger

2527
**GROUP HEALTH ASSOCIATION OF AMERICA, INC.**
1129 20th St., N.W., Ste. 600
Washington, DC 20036
Telephone: (202) 778-3200
Industry Affiliation: Associations: Health Groups
**Publication(s):**
*H M O Magazine*
Day Published: bi-m.
Lead Time: 7 wks.
Materials: 01,05,06,10,
Mtls Deadline: 3rd Mon. of the mo. prior to pub. date
Spec. Requirements: 40 page; 4 color; 8 1/2 x 11
Personnel: Susan Pisano, Editor
   Lisa Lopez, Managing Editor
   Debbie Wells, Production Manager

3572
**GROUP HEALTH, INC.**
2829 University Ave., S.E.
Minneapolis, MN 55414
Telephone: (612) 883-6000
FAX: (612) 883-5260
Mailing Address:
   8100 34th Ave., S.
   Bloomington, MN 55425-1309
Industry Affiliation: Associations: Health Groups
**Publication(s):**
*Healthpartners Today*
Day Published: 8/yr.
Lead Time: 3 mos. prior to pub. date
Mtls Deadline: 3·mos. prior to pub. date
Spec. Requirements: 8-pg.; offset; 8 1/2 x 11
Personnel: Marcia Kelly, Editor

4694
**GROVE WORLDWIDE, INC.**
1565 Buchanan Trail, E.
Shady Grove, PA 17256
Telephone: (717) 597-8121
FAX: (717) 597-4062
Mailing Address:
   P.O. Box 21
   Shady Grove, PA 17256
Industry Affiliation: Industry: Heavy Construction, Machinery
**Publication(s):**
*Big G*
Day Published: m.
Spec. Requirements: 10-12 pgs.; offset; 8 1/2 x 11
Personnel: Robert C. Kannel, Editor

5395
**GRUCON CORP.**
P.O. Box 479
Milwaukee, WI 53201
Telephone: (414) 223-6900
FAX: (414) 223-6950
Industry Affiliation: Architects, Engineers, Business Service

Materials Accepted/Included: 01-Business news 02-By-line articles 03-Fashion news 04-Food news 05-Freelance copy 06-Letters to editor 07-Real estate news 08-Sports news 09-Travel news 10-Movie rev. 11-Movie rev. 12-Music rev. 13-TV rev. 14-Theater rev. 15-Coming events 16-Obituaries 17-Question & answer 18-Social announcements 19-Artwork 20-Cartoons 21-Photos 22-TV listings 23-Audio rec. 24-Video rec. 25-Books 26-Films/film clips 27-Personnel news 28-Press releases 29-New product news/photos 30-Trade lit. 31-Contracts awarded 32-Display adv. 33-Classified adv.

11-38

**Publication(s):**
*Grunau Gram*
Day Published: q.
Lead Time: 1 mo.
Spec. Requirements: 4-6-pg.; offset
   bulletin; 84 x 11
Personnel: Loris Reichard, Editor

**GRUMMAN CORP.** 4038
1111 Stewart
Bethpage, NY 11714
Telephone: (516) 575-0574
Industry Affiliation: Aircraft, Aerospace,
   Defense
**Publication(s):**
*Grumman World*
Day Published: 22/yr.
Lead Time: 1 wk. prior to pub. date
Spec. Requirements: 8-12 pg.; offset
   tabloid; 11 x 17
Personnel: Kathleen M. Housley, Editor

**GTE CORP.** 48948
One Stamford Forum
Stamford, CT 06904
Telephone: (203) 965-2000
FAX: (203) 965-2277
Industry Affiliation: Electrical, Electronic,
   Manufacturing
**Publication(s):**
*G T E Weekly*
Day Published: w.
Spec. Requirements: 4-8 pgs.; offset,
   tabloid
Personnel: Charlie Ernst, Editor

*G T E Monthly*
Day Published: m.
Personnel: Charlie Ernst, Editor

**GTE DIRECTORIES CORP.** 2813
W. Airfield Dr.
DFW Airport, TX 75261-9810
Telephone: (214) 453-7629
FAX: (214) 453-7231
Mailing Address:
   P.O. Box 619810
   DFW Airport, TX 75261
Industry Affiliation: Publishers, Books,
   Magazines
**Publication(s):**
*Directions*
Day Published: m.
Lead Time: 8 wks. prior to pub. date
Materials: 01,02,05,21
Mtls Deadline: 8 wks. prior to pub. date
Contact: Jacqueline Fowler, Ed.
Spec. Requirements: 12 page; offset; 114
   x 16
Personnel: Jacqueline Fowler, Editor

**GTE NORTH** 4029
850 Harrison St. Ext.
Johnstown, NY 12095
Telephone: (518) 773-1117
FAX: (518) 773-6654
Industry Affiliation: Utility: Telephone
**Publication(s):**
*North News*
Day Published: m.
Lead Time: 1 mo.
Mtls Deadline: 1 mo. prior to pub. date
Contact: Debbie Mazzone, Ed.
Spec. Requirements: 4-8-page; offset; 11 x
   16
Personnel: Debbie Mazzone, Editor

**GTE SOUTH** 4271
300 W. Morgan St.
Durham, NC 27701
Telephone: (919) 687-9421
FAX: (919) 471-2538

Mailing Address:
   P.O. Box 611
   Durham, NC 27702
Industry Affiliation: Utility: Telephone
**Publication(s):**
*Newsline*
Day Published: q.
Lead Time: 3 wks. prior to pub. date
Mtls Deadline: 3 wks. prior to pub.date
Spec. Requirements: 8-12-page; offset
   tabloid; 16 x 11 1/2
Personnel: Cindy Gardiner, Editor

**GTE TELEPHONE OPERATIONS** 3095
1000 GTE Dr.
Wentzville, MO 63385
Telephone: (314) 639-7432
FAX: (314) 639-3287
Industry Affiliation: Utility: Telephone
**Publication(s):**
*Inside Central*
Day Published: m.
Personnel: Darrell Hollinger, Editor

*Midwest Region Newsline*
Day Published: bi-m.
Lead Time: 1 mo.
Mtls Deadline: 1 mo.
Personnel: Darell Hollinger, Editor

**GTE TELEPHONE OPERATIONS** 3461
455 Ellis Rd.
Muskegon, MI 49443
Telephone: (616) 798-5366
FAX: (616) 798-2258
Industry Affiliation: Utility: Telephone
**Publication(s):**
*Telops News*
Day Published: m.
Spec. Requirements: 6-page; offset
   newspaper; 114 x 16
Personnel: Charley Wilson, Editor

**GTE WISCONSIN** 5392
1312 E. Empire St.
Bloomington, WI 61701
Telephone: (309) 663-3858
FAX: (309) 663-3051
Industry Affiliation: Utility: Telephone
**Publication(s):**
*F Y I*
Day Published: w.
Spec. Requirements: 6-8 pgs.; offset
   newspaper; 11 1/2 x 16
Personnel: Kate Arthur, Editor

**GUARANTEE MUTUAL LIFE CO.** 3782
8801 Indian Hills Dr.
Omaha, NE 68114
Telephone: (402) 391-2121
Industry Affiliation: Insurance
**Publication(s):**
*Guarantee Mutual Field News*
Day Published: m.
Lead Time: 2 wks. prior to pub. date
Mtls Deadline: 2 wks. prior to pub. date
Spec. Requirements: 16-20 pgs.; offset
   magazine; 8 1/2 x 11
Personnel: Ruth Brase, Editor

*Indian Hills Echoes*
Day Published: q.
Lead Time: 2 wks. prior to pub. date
Mtls Deadline: 2 wks. prior to pub. date
Spec. Requirements: 8 pg.
Personnel: Jen Swotek, Editor

**GUARDIAN CORPORATION** 4242
3801 Sunset Ave., W.
Rocky Mount, NC 27804
Telephone: (919) 443-4101

Mailing Address:
   P.O. Box 7397
   Rocky Mount, NC 27804
Industry Affiliation: Associations: Trade,
   Fraternal
**Publication(s):**
*Guardian Graphics*
Day Published: q.
Lead Time: 1st mo. of qtr. prior to pub.
   date
Mtls Deadline: 1st mo. of qtr. prior to pub.
   date
Contact: Corporate Relations
Spec. Requirements: 20 pg.; offset; 9 x 13;
   1 color ink
Personnel: Genie Dunn-Andracchio, Editor

**GULF COAST RESEARCH** 3642
   **LABORATORY**
703 E. Beach Dr.
Ocean Springs, MS 39566-7000
Telephone: (601) 872-4273
FAX: (601) 872-4204
Mailing Address:
   P.O. Box 7000
   Ocean Springs, MS 39566-7000
Industry Affiliation: Colleges, Institutions,
   Science Research
**Publication(s):**
*Marine Briefs*
Day Published: m.
Lead Time: 15th of prior mo.
Mtls Deadline: 15th of mo. prior to pub.
   date
Contact: Pub. Info./Pub. Section
Spec. Requirements: 4-8 pages; 8 1/2 x
   11
Personnel: Susan Griggs, Editor
   Dr. Thomas D. McIlwain,
   Laboratory Director

*Gulf Research Reports*
Day Published: a.: Dec.
Mtls Deadline: Apr. 1 prior to pub. date
Spec. Requirements: approx. 100 pg.; 8
   1/2 x 11
Personnel: Dr. Thomas D. McIlwain, Editor

**GUNDERSON, INC.** 69732
4350 N.W. Front Ave.
Portland, OR 97210
Telephone: (503) 228-9281
FAX: (503) 242-0683
Industry Affiliation: Railroads
**Publication(s):**
*Gunderson News*
Day Published: q.
Contact: Bruce Harmon, Ed.

**GUTHRIE THEATRE** 3573
Vineland Pl.
Minneapolis, MN 55403
Telephone: (612) 347-1103
Industry Affiliation: Associations: Trade,
   Fraternal
**Publication(s):**
*Guthrie Theater Program Magazine*
Day Published: irreg.
Lead Time: 10 wks. prior to pub. date
Mtls Deadline: 10 wks. prior to pub. date
Contact: Public Relations Director
Spec. Requirements: 36-page; offset; 8
   1/2 x 11
Personnel: Amy Forton, Managing Editor
   Jim Lewis, Editor

**HACKENSACK WATER CO.** 3870
200 Old Hook Rd.
Harrington Park, NJ 07640
Telephone: (201) 767-9300
FAX: (201) 767-2892
Industry Affiliation: Utility: Water

**Publication(s):**
*Company Publication, The*
Day Published: irreg.
Spec. Requirements: 8 page; offset; 11 x
   17
Personnel: Carol Horne, Editor

**HAGGAR CO.** 5003
6113 Lemmon Ave.
Dallas, TX 75209
Telephone: (214) 352-8481
Industry Affiliation: Associations: Trade,
   Fraternal
**Publication(s):**
*Haggar Highlights*
Day Published: q.
Spec. Requirements: 16 pg.; offset
   magazine; 76 x 106
Personnel: Peter Mitchell, Editor

**HALLIBURTON-GEOPHYSICAL** 4991
   **SERVICES, INC.**
6909 Southwest Fwy.
Houston, TX 77074
Telephone: (713) 774-7561
FAX: (713) 778-3487
Industry Affiliation: Petroleum, Gas
**Publication(s):**
*Reflection, The*
Day Published: bi-m.
Spec. Requirements: 20-24 pg.; offset
   magazine; 8-1/2 x 11
Personnel: Gary White, Editor

**HALLIBURTON ENERGY** 4538
   **SERVICES**
5950 N. Course Dr.
Houston, TX 77072
Telephone: (713) 561-1579
FAX: (713) 495-9866
Industry Affiliation: Petroleum, Gas
**Publication(s):**
*Halliburton Pride*
Day Published: q.
Materials: 05,21
Mtls Deadline: 1st wk. of each qtr.
Contact: Employee Communications
Spec. Requirements: 36-page; offset;
   standard
Personnel: Mark McFarlane, Editor

**HANDGUN CONTROL, INC.** 68365
1225 Eye St., N.W., Ste. 1100
Washington, DC 20005
Telephone: (202) 898-0792
FAX: (202) 371-9615
Industry Affiliation: Associations: City,
   State, Federal
**Publication(s):**
*Progress Report*
Day Published: s-a.
Personnel: Susan Whitmore, Editor

**HANDY & HARMAN CO.** 4041
555 Theodore Fremd Ave.
Rye, NY 10580
Telephone: (212) 661-2400
Industry Affiliation: Associations: Trade,
   Fraternal

**Materials Accepted/Included:** 01-Business news 02-By-line articles 03-Fashion news 04-Food news 05-Freelance copy 06-Letters to editor 07-Real estate news 08-Sports news 09-Travel news 10-Book rev. 11-Movie rev. 12-Music rev. 13-TV rev. 14-Theater rev. 15-Coming events 16-Obituaries 17-Question & answer 18-Social announcements 19-Artwork 20-Cartoons 21-Photos 22-TV listings 23-Audio rec. 24-Video rec. 25-Books 26-Films/film clips 27-Personnel news 28-Press releases 29-New product news/photos 30-Trade lit. 31-Contracts awarded 32-Display adv. 33-Classified adv.

11-39

**Publication(s):**
*Scraps*
Day Published: q.
Lead Time: 3 mos. prior to pub. date
Mtls Deadline: 3 mos. prior to pub. date
Contact: Advertising Div.
Spec. Requirements: 16-20 pg.; offset; 8
　1/2 x 11
Personnel: Sheila Sheehey, Editor

68554

**HARBISON-WALKER**
**REFRACTORIES CO.**
1 Gateway Ctr.
Pittsburgh, PA 15222
Telephone: (412) 562-6200
FAX: (412) 562-6331
Industry Affiliation: Associations: Trade,
　Fraternal
**Publication(s):**
*Burns & Mixes*
Day Published: q.
Lead Time: 1st of mo. prior to pub. date
Mtls Deadline: 1 mo. prior to pub. date
Spec. Requirements: 20 pgs.; 8 1/2 x 11
Personnel: Phil Rydeski, Editor

*Quick Mixes*
Day Published: m.
Lead Time: 3 wks. prior to pub. date
Mtls Deadline: 3 wks. prior to pub. date
Spec. Requirements: 2 pg.; offset; 8 1/2 x
　11
Personnel: Phil Rydeski, Editor

5398

**HARLEY-DAVIDSON MOTOR CO.**
**INC.**
P.O. Box 653
Milwaukee, WI 53201
Telephone: (414) 342-4680
FAX: (414) 935-4800
Industry Affiliation: Associations: Trade,
　Fraternal
**Publication(s):**
*Enthusiast*
Day Published: q.
Spec. Requirements: 20 pg.; offset
　magazine; 8 1/2 x 11
Personnel: Steve Piehl, Editor

4699

**HARLEYSVILLE INSURANCE**
**COMPANIES**
355 Maple Ave.
Harleysville, PA 19438
Telephone: (215) 256-5000
FAX: (215) 256-5340
Industry Affiliation: Insurance
**Publication(s):**
*Insights For Employees*
Day Published: bi-m.
Lead Time: 60 days prior to pub. date
Materials: 01,05,19,20,21
Mtls Deadline: 60-90 days prior to pub.
　date
Contact: Harleysville Communications
Spec. Requirements: 20 pg.; offset; 8-1/2
　x 11
Personnel: Beth Gavis, Editor
　　　　Randy Buckwalter, Editor
　　　　Donald E. Diehl

*Insights For Agents*
Day Published: q.
Lead Time: 90 days
Materials: 01,05,19,20,21
Mtls Deadline: 90 days prior to pub. date
Contact: Harleysville Communications
Spec. Requirements: 24 page; offset; 8-
　1/2 x 11
Personnel: Linda K. Manero
　　　　Donald E. Diehl
　　　　Randy Buckwalter
　　　　Frederick W. Baker

5399

**HARNISCHFEGER INDUSTRIES,**
**INC.**
395 Bishops Way
Milwaukee, WI 53201
Telephone: (414) 797-6625
FAX: (414) 797-6747
Mailing Address:
　P.O. Box 554
　Milwaukee, WI 53201
Industry Affiliation: Industry: Heavy
　Construction, Machinery
**Publication(s):**
*Noon News*
Day Published: w.
Lead Time: 1 wk. prior to pub. date
Mtls Deadline: Tue. prior to pub. date
Spec. Requirements: 2 pg.; offset; 8-1/2 x
　11
Personnel: Mark Dietz, Editor

4043

**HARRIS CORP.**
1025 W. Nasa Blvd.
Melbourne, FL 32919
Telephone: (407) 727-9100
FAX: (407) 727-9646
Industry Affiliation: Associations: Trade,
　Fraternal
**Publication(s):**
*F Y I Magazine*
Day Published: s-a.
Lead Time: 2 mos. prior to pub. date
Contact: Corp. Hqtrs.
Spec. Requirements: 24 pg.; offset; 8 1/2
　x 11
Personnel: Tom Hausman, Editor

4044

**HARRISON RADIATOR DIV.**
200 Upper Mountain Rd.
Lockport, NY 14094
Telephone: (716) 439-2011
FAX: (716) 439-2474
Industry Affiliation: Cooling, Heating
**Publication(s):**
*Harrison Communicator*
Day Published: q.
Spec. Requirements: 16 pg.; offset
　magazine; 84 x 11
Personnel: Deborah Perkins, Editor

4822

**HASBRO, INC.**
1027 Newport Ave.
Pawtucket, RI 02862-1059
Telephone: (401) 431-8697
FAX: (401) 727-5099
Mailing Address:
　P.O. Box 200
　Pawtucket, RI 02862-1059
Industry Affiliation: Toys, Crafts
**Publication(s):**
*Hasbro Herald*
Day Published: q.
Lead Time: 2 mos. prior to pub. date
Mtls Deadline: 2 mos. prior to pub. date
Contact: Employee Relations
Spec. Requirements: offset; 11 x 14
Personnel: Kathy Miltimore, Editor

*Hasbro News*
Day Published: m.
Lead Time: 2 mos. prior to pub. date
Mtls Deadline: 2 mos. prior to pub. date
Spec. Requirements: offset; 11 x 14
Personnel: Kathy Beeler

2700

**HAWAIIAN ELECTRIC CO., INC.**
900 Richards St.
Honolulu, HI 96813
Telephone: (808) 543-7736
FAX: (808) 543-7790
Mailing Address:
　P.O. Box 2750
　Honolulu, HI 96840-0001
Industry Affiliation: Utility: Electric
**Publication(s):**
*Hoa Hana*
Day Published: q.
Lead Time: 2 mos.
Mtls Deadline: 1 mo. prior to pub. date
Spec. Requirements: 8-page; offset; 8 1/2
　x 11
Personnel: Debbie Malilay, Editor

*Consumer Lines*
Day Published: m.
Lead Time: 30 days
Mtls Deadline: 30 days prior to pub. date
Personnel: Marc Beauchamp, Editor

2710

**HAWAII GOVERNMENT**
**EMPLOYEES ASSN., AFSCME**
**LOCAL 15**
888 Mililani St., Ste. 601
Honolulu, HI 96813
Telephone: (808) 536-2351
Mailing Address:
　P.O. Box 2930
　Honolulu, HI 96802
Industry Affiliation: Associations: Trade,
　Fraternal
**Publication(s):**
*Public Employee, The*
Day Published: m.
Lead Time: 2 wks.
Mtls Deadline: 2 wks. prior to pub. date
Contact: Communications Dept.
Spec. Requirements: 6-8-page; offset
　tabloid; 102 x 15
Personnel: Ben V. Cruz, Jr., Editor
　　　　Betsey Y. Shinkawa, Editor
　　　　Randall T. Kusaka, Editor

3565

**H.B. FULLER CO.**
Energy Pk. Dr.
St. Paul, MN 55108
Telephone: (612) 645-3401
FAX: (612) 645-6936
Industry Affiliation: Chemicals, Plastics
**Publication(s):**
*Fuller World*
Day Published: bi-m.
Spec. Requirements: 16 pg.; 8-1/2 x 11
Personnel: Kathy Mueller, Editor

4551

**HCA PRESBYTERIAN HOSPITAL**
N.E. 13th at Lincoln Blvd.
Oklahoma City, OK 73104
Telephone: (405) 271-5100
FAX: (405) 524-2812
Industry Affiliation: Hospitals

**Publication(s):**
*Intercom*
Day Published: bi-w.
Lead Time: 1 wk. prior to pub. date
Spec. Requirements: 6 pg.; 8-1/2 x 11
Personnel: Lil Kennic, Editor

2824

**HEDMAN CO.**
1158 W. Armitage Ave.
Chicago, IL 60614
Telephone: (312) 871-6500
FAX: (312) 248-0603
Industry Affiliation: Office Equipment,
　Services, Supplies
**Publication(s):**
*Hedman Flash*
Day Published: bi-m.
Spec. Requirements: 8 pg; offset bulletin;
　54 x 84
Personnel: R.J. Abramson, Editor

4701

**HEINZ U.S.A.**
1062 Progress St.
Pittsburgh, PA 15230
Telephone: (412) 237-5743
FAX: (412) 237-4230
Mailing Address:
　P.O. Box 57
　Pittsburgh, PA 15230
Industry Affiliation: Food, General
**Publication(s):**
*Heinzline*
Day Published: q.
Lead Time: 3 mos. prior to pub. date
Mtls Deadline: 1st of Feb., May, Aug., Nov.
Contact: Communications Dept.
Spec. Requirements: 12-20 pg.; offset
　newsletter; 8 1/2 x 11
Personnel: Cheryl Stewart - Miller, Editor

*Pittsburgh Factory News*
Day Published: s-a.
Lead Time: 3 mos. prior to pub. date
Mtls Deadline: 3 mos. prior to pub. date
Contact: Communications Dept.
Spec. Requirements: 8-16 pg.; offset
　newsletter; 8 1/2 X 11
Personnel: Cheryl Stewart-Miller, Editor

3195

**HENRY VOGT MACHINE CO.**
P.O. Box 1918
Louisville, KY 40201
Telephone: (502) 634-1500
Industry Affiliation: Industry: Heavy
　Construction, Machinery
**Publication(s):**
*Vogt Views*
Day Published: q.
Lead Time: 30 days prior to pub. date
Mtls Deadline: 30 days prior to pub. date
Contact: Corp. Communications
Spec. Requirements: 12 pg.; 8 1/2 x 11; 4-
　color
Personnel: Don Durs, Editor
　　　　Ben Ruiz

4702

**HERSHEY FOODS CORP.**
100 Crystal A Dr.
Hershey, PA 17033
Telephone: (717) 534-6799
Mailing Address:
　P.O. Box 810
　Hershey, PA 17033
Industry Affiliation: Food, General

**Publication(s):**
*Avenues*
Day Published: bi-m.
Lead Time: 60 days
Mtls Deadline: 60 days
Spec. Requirements: 16 pg; 8 1/2 x 11
Personnel: Mike Kinney, Assistant Editor

2163

### HEWLETT-PACKARD CO.
3000 Hanover St.
Palo Alto, CA 94304
Telephone: (415) 859-1501
FAX: (415) 857-7299
Industry Affiliation: Electrical, Electronic, Manufacturing
**Publication(s):**
*Measure*
Day Published: bi-m.
Lead Time: 2 mos. prior to pub. date
Spec. Requirements: 24 pg.; offset; 8-1/2 x 11
Personnel: Jay Coleman, Editor

*Hewlett-Packard Journal*
Day Published: bi-m.
Spec. Requirements: circ.: 200,000; free
Personnel: Richard P. Dolan, Editor

3871

### HIA (HOBBY INDUSTRY ASSOCIATION OF AMERICA)
319 E. 54th St.
Elmwood Park, NJ 07407
Telephone: (201) 794-1133
FAX: (201) 797-0657
Mailing Address:
P.O. Box 348
Elmwood Park, NJ 07407
Industry Affiliation: Associations: Trade, Fraternal
**Publication(s):**
*Horizons*
Day Published: q.
Lead Time: 2 mos. prior to pub. date
Materials: 01,06,15,27,28
Mtls Deadline: 2 mo. prior to pub. date
Spec. Requirements: 4-12 page; offset newspaper; 11 x 14
Personnel: Susan Brandt, Editor

4355

### HICKORY FARMS OF OHIO INC.
1505 Holland Rd.
Maumee, OH 43537
Telephone: (419) 893-7611
FAX: (419) 893-0164
Industry Affiliation: Food, General
**Publication(s):**
*Lease Line*
Day Published: q.
Spec. Requirements: 4-8 pg.; offset; 8 1/2 x 11
Personnel: Anita Gardner, Editor

52328

### HIGHEST PROFIT CORP.
N. 35, 21100 W. Capitol Dr.
Pewaukee, WI 53072
Telephone: (414) 783-5157
Industry Affiliation: Finance, Services
**Publication(s):**
*Highest Profit Program*
Day Published: 3/yr.
Lead Time: 2 mos.
Mtls Deadline: 2 mos.
Personnel: Carol Trabbold, Editor

66416

### HILLENBRAND INDUSTRIES, INC.
700 State Rte. 46 E.
Batesville, IN 47006-8835
Telephone: (812) 934-8197
FAX: (812) 934-1963
Industry Affiliation: Insurance

**Publication(s):**
*Hillenbrand Industries Vision*
Day Published: m.
Lead Time: 2 mos.
Mtls Deadline: photo-15th of mo.; copy-20th of mo.
Contact: Senior Management
Personnel: Mark E. Craft, Editor

*Washington Capitol Monitor*
Day Published: w.
Lead Time: Thu.
Mtls Deadline: Thu. prior to pub. date
Contact: Senior Management
Personnel: Mark E. Craft, Editor

*Indiana Capitol Monitor*
Day Published: w.
Lead Time: Thu.
Mtls Deadline: Thu. prior to pub. date
Contact: Senior Management
Personnel: Mark E. Craft, Editor

3471

### HILLSDALE COLLEGE
33 E. College St.
Hillsdale, MI 49242
Telephone: (517) 437-7341
FAX: (517) 437-0106
Industry Affiliation: Colleges, Institutions, Science Research
**Publication(s):**
*Hillsdale Magazine*
Day Published: q.
Contact: Public Affairs
Spec. Requirements: 32 pg.; offset magazine; 84 x 11
Personnel: William Koshelnyk, Editor
J.S. McNamara, Executive Editor

*Imprimis*
Day Published: m.
Lead Time: 2 mos. prior to pub. date
Contact: Constructive Alternatives Ctr.
Spec. Requirements: 6-8 pg.; offset journal; 84 x 11
Personnel: Ronald Trowbridge, M. D., Executive Editor
Peter C. McCarty

68429

### HOECHST CELANESE CORP.
Rte. 202-206
Somerville, NJ 08876
Telephone: (908) 231-2735
FAX: (908) 231-4405
Mailing Address:
P.O. Box 2500
Somerville, NJ 08876
Industry Affiliation: Chemicals, Plastics
**Publication(s):**
*Reporter Magazine*
Day Published: q.
Lead Time: 3 mos. prior to pub. date
Spec. Requirements: 20-32 pg.; 8 1/2 x 11
Personnel: M. L. Nowicki, Editor

2167

### HOLMES & NARVER, INC.
999 Town & Country Rd.
Orange, CA 92668
Telephone: (714) 567-2400
FAX: (714) 567-2632
Industry Affiliation: Architects, Engineers, Business Service

**Publication(s):**
*Here & Now*
Day Published: m.
Lead Time: 2 wks.
Mtls Deadline: 24th of each mo.
Spec. Requirements: 10-page; offset magazine; 8 1/2 x 11
Personnel: Amy Racin, Editor

68436

### HOLSTEIN ASSOCIATION OF AMERICA
One Holstein Pl.
Brattleboro, VT 05302-0802
Telephone: (802) 254-4551
FAX: (802) 254-8251
Industry Affiliation: Dairy Products
**Publication(s):**
*Holstein News*
Day Published: bi-m.
Lead Time: 3 wks.
Personnel: Jim Yanizyn, Editor

5247

### HOME BENEFICIAL LIFE INSURANCE CO.
3901 W. Broad St.
Richmond, VA 23230
Telephone: (804) 358-8431
FAX: (804) 254-9601
Mailing Address:
P.O. Box 27572
Richmond, VA 23261
Industry Affiliation: Insurance
**Publication(s):**
*Home Topics*
Day Published: m.
Lead Time: 3 wks.
Materials: 3 wks. prior to pub. date
Spec. Requirements: 16 pg.; offset magazine; 8 1/4 x 11
Personnel: R. Leon Smith, Jr., Editor

3688

### HOME BUILDERS ASSOCIATION OF GREATER ST. LOUIS
10104 Old Olive St. Rd.
St. Louis, MO 63141
Telephone: (314) 994-7700
Industry Affiliation: Associations: Trade, Fraternal
**Publication(s):**
*Builder News*
Day Published: m.
Lead Time: 3 wks.
Materials: 01,02,07,15,16,18,19,20,21,27, 28,29,30,32,33
Mtls Deadline: 15th of mo. prior to pub. date
Spec. Requirements: 36-44 page; offset; 8 1/2 x 11
Personnel: Nancy McKee, Editor
John L. Gutmann, Publisher
Felicia Watkins, Advertising

*H B A Newsletter*
Day Published: bi-w.
Materials: 07,15,18,19,28
Mtls Deadline: morning of pub. date
Personnel: Nancy McKee, Editor

66459

### HOME DEPOT, INC., THE
2727 Paces Ferry Rd., N.W.
Atlanta, GA 30339
Telephone: (404) 431-5161
Industry Affiliation: Retail Stores

**Publication(s):**
*Doings At The Depot*
Day Published: bi-m.
Lead Time: 2 mos. prior to pub. date
Mtls Deadline: 2 mos. prior to pub. date
Personnel: Valerie Bertrand

2027

### HONEYWELL, INC.
21111 N. 19th Ave.
Phoenix, AZ 85027
Telephone: (602) 436-2311
FAX: (602) 436-2252
Industry Affiliation: Aircraft, Aerospace, Defense
**Publication(s):**
*Honeywell Pride*
Day Published: bi-m.
Lead Time: 1 mo. prior to pub. date
Mtls Deadline: 1 mo. prior to pub. date
Contact: Headquarters
Spec. Requirements: 8 pg.; offset; 11 x 17
Personnel: M. Honicker, Editor

*Leaders' Digest*
Day Published: bi-w.
Lead Time: 2 wks. prior to pub. date
Mtls Deadline: Wed. prior to pub. date
Contact: Headquarters
Personnel: M. Honicker, Editor

3575

### HONEYWELL, INC.
Honeywell Plz.
Minneapolis, MN 55408
Telephone: (612) 951-0065
Industry Affiliation: Associations: Trade, Fraternal
**Publication(s):**
*Circulator*
Day Published: w.
Spec. Requirements: 4-8 pg.; offset newspaper; 12 x 15
Personnel: Sarah Stonehouse, Editor

4358

### HOOVER CO.
101 E. Maple St.
North Canton, OH 44720
Telephone: (216) 497-5825
FAX: (216) 966-5439
Industry Affiliation: Electrical, Electronic, Manufacturing
**Publication(s):**
*Hoover News*
Day Published: m.
Lead Time: 1 mo. prior to pub. date
Mtls Deadline: 10 days prior to pub. date
Contact: Public Relations
Spec. Requirements: 8-16 pg.; 8 1/2 x 11
Personnel: Jacquelyn Love, Editor

*Face To Face*
Day Published: 3-4/yr.
Lead Time: 2 mos. prior to pub. date
Mtls Deadline: 3-4 wks. prior to pub. date
Contact: Public Relations
Spec. Requirements: 10-20 pg.; 8 1/2 x 11
Personnel: Jacquelyn B. Love, Editor

*Annual Report To Employees*
Day Published: a.

2846

### HORACE MANN COS., THE
One Horace Mann Plz.
Box L069
Springfield, IL 62715
FAX: (217) 788-5161
Industry Affiliation: Insurance

Materials Accepted/Included: 01-Business news 02-By-line articles 03-Fashion news 04-Food news 05-Freelance copy 06-Letters to editor 07-Real estate news 08-Sports news 09-Travel news 10-Book rev. 11-Movie rev. 12-Music rev. 13-TV rev. 14-Theater rev. 15-Coming events 16-Obituaries 17-Question & answer 18-Social announcements 19-Artwork 20-Cartoons 21-Photos 22-TV listings 23-Audio rec. 24-Video rec. 25-Books 26-Films/film clips 27-Personnel news 28-Press releases 29-New product news/photos 30-Trade lit. 31-Contracts awarded 32-Display adv. 33-Classified adv.

11-41

**Publication(s):**
*Spectrum*
Day Published: m.: mag.; w.: newsletter
Lead Time: 1 wk. prior to pub. date
Mtls Deadline: 1 wk. prior to pub. date
Contact: Assoc. Relt and Comm
Spec. Requirements: 28 pg.; offset; 9 x 11 1/2

3576
**HORMEL FOODS CORP.**
510 N. E. 16th Ave.
Austin, MN 55912
Telephone: (507) 473-5448
FAX: (507) 437-5489
Mailing Address:
 1 Hormel Pl.
 Austin, MN 55912-3680
Industry Affiliation: Meat Products
**Publication(s):**
*News*
Day Published: m.
Lead Time: 2 mos. prior to pub. date
Materials: 01,04,16,21,27,28,29
Mtls Deadline: 2 mos. prior to pub. date
Spec. Requirements: 20 pg.; offset; 8 x 104; 4 color
Personnel: Len Schulke, Editor
 Meri Everhart

*Inside*
Day Published: bi-m.
Lead Time: 1 mo. prior to pub. date
Materials: 01,04,15,27,28,29
Mtls Deadline: 1 mo. prior to pub. date
Spec. Requirements: b/w; 11 x 17
Personnel: Len Schulke, Editor

69421
**HOSPICE OF THE FLORIDA SUNCOAST**
300 E. Bay Dr.
Largo, FL 34640
Telephone: (813) 586-4432
Industry Affiliation: Hospitals
**Publication(s):**
*Hospice Today*
Day Published: q.
Personnel: Kimberly Walter, Editor

*Connections*
Day Published: 3/yr.
Materials: 28,30
Contact: Development and Community Relations
Spec. Requirements: must be related to terminal illness or bereavement

4703
**HOSPITAL OF THE UNIVERSITY OF PENNSYLVANIA**
34th & Spruce Sts.
Philadelphia, PA 19104-2265
Telephone: (215) 662-4000
FAX: (215) 349-8312
Industry Affiliation: Hospitals
**Publication(s):**
*Hupdate*
Day Published: 11/yr.
Lead Time: 1 mo. prior to pub. date
Materials: 01,02,05,06,15,16,19,20,21,27
Spec. Requirements: 16 pg.; 11 x 17
Personnel: Jacquelin Sufak, Editor
 Michelle Maloney, Art Director

5134
**HOUSTON CHRONICLE**
801 Texas Ave.
Houston, TX 77002
Telephone: (713) 220-7171
Mailing Address:
 P.O. Box 4260
 Houston, TX 77210
Industry Affiliation: Newspapers

**Publication(s):**
*Copy*
Day Published: m.
Spec. Requirements: 16-pg.; offset magazine; 8 1/2 x 11
Personnel: Angie Gage, Editor

5136
**HOUSTON LIGHTING & POWER CO.**
611 Walker
Houston, TX 77002
Telephone: (713) 228-9211
FAX: (713) 220-5016
Mailing Address:
 P.O. Box 1700
 Houston, TX 77251
Industry Affiliation: Utility: Electric
**Publication(s):**
*Transmissions*
Day Published: bi-m.
Lead Time: 10 days prior to pub. date
Mtls Deadline: 10 days prior to pub. date
Contact: Public Affairs
Spec. Requirements: 4 pg.; offset newspaper; 12 1/2 x 16-1/2
Personnel: Tal Gribbens, Editor

4540
**HTB, INC.**
900 N. Stiles
Oklahoma City, OK 73104
Telephone: (405) 239-4700
FAX: (405) 239-4750
Mailing Address:
 P.O. Box 1845
 Oklahoma City, OK 73101
Industry Affiliation: Architects, Engineers, Business Service
**Publication(s):**
*H T B Today*
Day Published: m.
Lead Time: 6 wks.
Mtls Deadline: 6 wks. prior to pub. date
Contact: Marketing & Communications
Spec. Requirements: 4-6 pg.; offset; 8 1/2 x 11
Personnel: Peggy Dailey, Editor
 Rex M. Ball, Editor

3097
**HUBINGER CO., THE**
One Progress St.
Keokuk, IA 52632
Telephone: (319) 524-5757
Industry Affiliation: Food, General
**Publication(s):**
*Cornstalk*
Day Published: bi-m.
Lead Time: 3 wks.
Mtls Deadline: 2 wks. prior to pub. date
Spec. Requirements: 8 pg.; offset magazine; 8 1/2 x 11
Personnel: Rita Noe, Editor

2170
**HUGHES AIRCRAFT CO.**
7200 Hughes Terr.
Los Angeles, CA 90045
Telephone: (310) 568-7200
Mailing Address:
 P.O. Box 45066
 Los Angeles, CA 90045
Industry Affiliation: Aircraft, Aerospace, Defense
**Publication(s):**
*Hughesnews*
Day Published: bi-w.
Spec. Requirements: 8-page; offset; 11 x 16 1/2
Personnel: Barbara Hugh, Editor

*Vectors*
Day Published: q.
Lead Time: 3 mos.
Spec. Requirements: 24-page
Personnel: Gary T. Panton, Art Director

5007
**HUGHES CHRISTIANSEN CO.**
9110 Grogan's Mill Rd.
The Woodlands, TX 77380-1130
Telephone: (713) 363-6000
FAX: (713) 363-6080
Industry Affiliation: Industry: Heavy Construction, Machinery
**Publication(s):**
*Hughes Christiansen Horizon*
Day Published: q.
Spec. Requirements: 12 pg.; offset tabloid; 11 x 15
Personnel: Jim Redden, Editor

*Hughes Rigway*
Day Published: irreg.
Spec. Requirements: 32 pg.
Personnel: Howard Batt, Editor

5326
**HUMANE SOCIETY FOR TACOMA & PIERCE COUNTIES, THE**
2608 Center St.
Tacoma, WA 98409
Telephone: (206) 572-8708
Industry Affiliation: Associations: Health Groups
**Publication(s):**
*Connections*
Day Published: q.
Lead Time: 3-4 wks. prior to pub. date
Spec. Requirements: 8-12 pg.; 8-1/2 x 11
Personnel: Lynne Hoffman, Editor

4359
**HUNTINGTON BANCSHARES, INC.**
41 S. High St.
Columbus, OH 43287
Telephone: (614) 463-4531
Industry Affiliation: Banks, Savings & Loans
**Publication(s):**
*Huntington Highlights*
Day Published: m.
Lead Time: 2 wks. prior to pub. date
Mtls Deadline: 2 wks. prior to pub. date
Contact: Corporate Communications
Spec. Requirements: 4-page; offset; 11 x 14
Personnel: Paula G. Jurcenko, Editor

3129
**IES UTILITIES**
200 First St., S.E.
Cedar Rapids, IA 52401
Telephone: (319) 398-4411
FAX: (319) 398-4146
Mailing Address:
 P.O. Box 351
 Cedar Rapids, IA 52406
Industry Affiliation: Utility: Electric
**Publication(s):**
*Front Line*
Day Published: bi-m.
Lead Time: 30 days prior to pub. date
Mtls Deadline: 1st of mo. prior to pub. date
Contact: Corp. Affairs
Spec. Requirements: 4 pg.; offset; 10 x 13
Personnel: Tom Peterson, Editor

2829
**IGA, INC.**
8725 W. Higgins Rd.
Chicago, IL 60631
Telephone: (312) 693-4520
FAX: (312) 693-1271
Industry Affiliation: Food, General

**Publication(s):**
*I G A Grocergram*
Day Published: m. & 2 spec. issues
Lead Time: 1 mo. prior to pub. date
Spec. Requirements: 50 pg.; offset; 8 1/4 x 11 1/4
Personnel: Bill Hayes, Editor

4244
**ILCO UNICAN CORP.**
400 Jeffreys Rd.
Rocky Mount, NC 27804
Mailing Address:
 P.O. Box 2627
 Rocky Mount, NC 27802
Industry Affiliation: Electrical, Electronic, Manufacturing
**Publication(s):**
*Unicanews*
Day Published: bi-m.
Lead Time: 2 mos.
Materials: 01,02,03,06,08,15,18,19,20,21
Mtls Deadline: 2 mos. prior to pub. date
Contact: Advertising
Spec. Requirements: 4-6 page
Personnel: Donna Lancaster, Editor
 Joyce Bailey, Production Manager

*Keytips*
Day Published: q.
Lead Time: 2-3 mos.
Materials: 01,06,17,19,20
Mtls Deadline: 2-3 mos. prior to pub. date
Spec. Requirements: 8 pg; offset; 8 1/2x11
Personnel: Lynn Best, Publisher
 Steve Spiwar, Editor
 Karen Blount, Production Manager

2969
**ILLINOIS CREDIT UNION LEAGUE**
1807 W. Diehl
Naperville, IL 60566
Telephone: (708) 983-3400
FAX: (708) 983-4261
Industry Affiliation: Associations: Trade, Fraternal
**Publication(s):**
*In Depth*
Day Published: m.
Lead Time: 5 wks. prior to pub. date
Mtls Deadline: 5 wks. prior to pub. date
Spec. Requirements: 8 pg.; offset; 8-1/2 x 11
Personnel: Lynn Cust, Editor

2827
**ILLINOIS FARM BUREAU**
1701 Towanda Ave.
Bloomington, IL 61701
Telephone: (309) 557-2236
FAX: (309) 557-2559
Mailing Address:
 P.O. Box 2901
 Bloomington, IL 61702
Industry Affiliation: Agriculture, Services
**Publication(s):**
*Insights*
Day Published: q.
Spec. Requirements: 24 pg.; offset tabloid; 84 x 11
Personnel: Steve Sims, Editor

2973
**ILLINOIS LEAGUE OF SAVINGS INSTITUTIONS**
133 S. Fourth St., Ste. 206
Springfield, IL 62701-1203
Telephone: (217) 522-5575
FAX: (217) 789-9115
Industry Affiliation: Banks, Savings & Loans

**Publication(s):**
*Illinois Reporter*
Day Published: bi-m.
Lead Time: 1 mo. prior to pub. date
Mtls Deadline: 5th of mo. prior to pub. date
Spec. Requirements: 36 pg.; 8 1/2 x 11;
   ads 7 x 9; offset
Personnel: Norma Altman, Editor

**ILLINOIS SOCIETY OF** 2974
**PROFESSIONAL ENGINEERS**
1304 S. Lowell
Springfield, IL 62704
Telephone: (217) 544-7424
FAX: (217) 544-3349
Industry Affiliation: Associations: Trade,
   Fraternal
**Publication(s):**
*Illinois Engineer*
Day Published: bi-m.
Lead Time: 4 wks.
Mtls Deadline: 15th of mo., 1 mo. prior to
   pub. date
Spec. Requirements: 16-20 pg.; offset
   magazine; 84 x 11
Personnel: Chuck Stockus, Editor

**ILLINOIS TOOL WORKS** 2975
3600 W. Lake
Glenview, IL 60025
Telephone: (708) 724-7500
FAX: (708) 657-4321
Industry Affiliation: Industry: Light Tools,
   Equipment
**Publication(s):**
*Update*
Day Published: bi-m.
Mtls Deadline: varies
Spec. Requirements: 4-12 pgs; offset; 8
   1/2 x 11
Personnel: Nancy Christopherson, Editor

**IMPERIAL HOLLY CORP.** 5010
8016 Hwy. 908
Sugar Land, TX 77478
Telephone: (713) 491-9181
Mailing Address:
   P.O. Box 9
   Sugar Land, TX 77478
Industry Affiliation: Sugar
**Publication(s):**
*Sugar Exchange*
Day Published: bi-m.
Lead Time: 2 mos. prior to pub. date
Mtls Deadline: 2 mos. prior to pub. date
Spec. Requirements: 16-20 pg.; offset
   bulletn; 10 x 14
Personnel: William M. Krocak, Editor

**IN-PLANT MANAGEMENT** 2831
**ASSOCIATION**
1205 W. College St.
Liberty, MO 64068-3733
Telephone: (816) 781-1111
FAX: (816) 781-2790
Industry Affiliation: Associations: Trade,
   Fraternal
**Publication(s):**
*Perspectives*
Day Published: m.
Lead Time: 30 days
Materials: 01,02,06,10,15,17,28,29,32,33
Mtls Deadline: 30 days prior to pub. date
Contact: Communications
Spec. Requirements: 20 pg.; offset; 8 1/2
   x 11; recycled paper
Personnel: Barbara Schaaf Petty, Editor

*Inside I P M A*
Day Published: m.
Lead Time: 30 days
Mtls Deadline: 30 days
Contact: Membership Services
Personnel: Jayne Nixon, Editor

**INCO ALLOYS INTERNATIONAL,** 5348
**INC.**
Guyan River Rd.
Huntington, WV 25720
Telephone: (304) 526-5100
Mailing Address:
   P.O. Box 1958
   Huntington, WV 25720
Industry Affiliation: Nickel
**Publication(s):**
*Communicator*
Day Published: q.
Spec. Requirements: 4 pg.; offset; 11 x 16
Personnel: Jean Neal, Editor

**INCO UNITED STATES, INC.** 4052
One New York Plz.
New York, NY 10004
Telephone: (212) 612-5500
Industry Affiliation: Nickel
**Publication(s):**
*Pen Of I N C O*
Day Published: q.
Personnel: Visual Communications Dept.,
   Editor

**INDIANA BANKERS ASSOCIATION,** 3049
**INC.**
One N. Capitol, Ste. 315
Indianapolis, IN 46204
Telephone: (317) 236-0750
FAX: (317) 236-0754
Industry Affiliation: Banks, Savings &
   Loans
**Publication(s):**
*Hoosier Banker*
Day Published: m.
Lead Time: 1 mo.
Mtls Deadline: 2 mos. prior to pub. date
Spec. Requirements: 48-72-pgs; offset; 8
   1/2 x 11
Personnel: Laura Wilson, Editor

**INDIANA CREDIT UNION LEAGUE,** 3055
**INC.**
8440 Allison Ponte Blvd., Ste. 400
Indianapolis, IN 46250
Telephone: (317) 594-5300
FAX: (317) 594-5301
Mailing Address:
   P.O. Box 50425
   Indianapolis, IN 46250
Industry Affiliation: Associations: Trade,
   Fraternal
**Publication(s):**
*Nexus*
Day Published: q.-15th of Mar., June, Sep.,
   Dec.
Lead Time: 45 days
Mtls Deadline: 45 days
Contact: Pub. Rels. Dept.
Spec. Requirements: 2 pg; offset; 8 1/2 x
   11
Personnel: Wendy Roepke, Editor

*Management Update*
Day Published: bi-w.
Lead Time: 1 wk.
Mtls Deadline: 1 wk.
Contact: Pub. Rels. Dept.
Personnel: Wendy Roepke, Public
   Relations Manager

**INDIANA DEPT. OF** 3015
**TRANSPORTATION**
100 N. Senate, Rm. N-755
Indianapolis, IN 46204
Telephone: (317) 232-5115
FAX: (317) 232-0238
Industry Affiliation: Associations: City,
   State, Federal
**Publication(s):**
*Crossroads-Internal Newsletter*
Day Published: q.
Mtls Deadline: 1 mo. prior to pub. date
Contact: Pub. Affrs.

**INDIANA FARM BUREAU, INC.** 3014
225 S. East St.
Indianapolis, IN 46202
Telephone: (317) 692-7819
FAX: (317) 692-7854
Industry Affiliation: Agriculture, Services
**Publication(s):**
*Hoosier Farmer*
Day Published: bi-m.
Mtls Deadline: 1st wk. of Jan., Mar., May,
   Jul., Oct., Nov.
Contact: The Hoosier Farmer
Spec. Requirements: 24 page
Personnel: Shirley Richardson, Editor

**INDIANA FARMERS INSURANCE** 3057
**GROUP**
10 W. 106th St.
Indianapolis, IN 46290
Telephone: (317) 846-4211
Mailing Address:
   P.O. Box 527
   Indianapolis, IN 46206
Industry Affiliation: Insurance
**Publication(s):**
*Crier, The*
Day Published: bi-m.
Lead Time: 1 mo.
Spec. Requirements: 4-6 pgs; 8 1/2" x 11"
Personnel: Susan M. Andrews, Editor

*Agents News*
Day Published: bi-m.
Lead Time: 30 days
Mtls Deadline: 1st of mo. prior to pub. date
Personnel: Susan M. Andrews, Managing
   Editor

**INDIANA JUDICIAL CENTER** 3062
115 W. Washington St., Ste. 1075
Indianapolis, IN 46204-3417
Telephone: (317) 232-1313
Industry Affiliation: Associations: City,
   State, Federal
**Publication(s):**
*Benchmarks*
Day Published: q.
Spec. Requirements: 4 pg.; offset; 8 1/2 x
   11
Personnel: George R. Glass, Editor

*Case Clips*
Day Published: 40/yr.
Personnel: George Glass, Editor

**INDIANA MANUFACTURERS** 3063
**ASSOCIATION, INC.**
One American Sq., Ste. 2400
Indianapolis, IN 46282
Telephone: (317) 632-2474
FAX: (317) 264-3281

Mailing Address:
   P.O. Box 82012
   Indianapolis, IN 46282
Industry Affiliation: Associations: Trade,
   Fraternal
**Publication(s):**
*Imanet*
Day Published: m.
Lead Time: 2 wks. prior to pub. date
Materials: 01,20
Mtls Deadline: 15th of mo. prior to pub.
   date
Spec. Requirements: 16 pg.; 8 1/2 x 11;
   offset
Personnel: Bob O'Bannon, Editor

**INDIANA MICHIGAN POWER CO.** 3013
110 E. Wayne St.
Fort Wayne, IN 46802
Telephone: (219) 425-2111
FAX: (219) 425-2157
Mailing Address:
   P.O. Box 60
   Fort Wayne, IN 46801
Industry Affiliation: Utility: Electric
**Publication(s):**
*Imprint*
Day Published: m.
Lead Time: 1 mo. prior to pub. date
Mtls Deadline: 1st of mo. prior to pub. date
Contact: Public Affairs
Spec. Requirements: 28 pg.; offset
   magazine; 8 1/2 x 11
Personnel: Vince LaBarbera, Editor

**INDIANAPOLIS LIFE INSURANCE** 3069
**CO.**
2960 N. Meridian St.
Indianapolis, IN 46208
Telephone: (317) 927-6500
Mailing Address:
   P.O. Box 1230
   Indianapolis, IN 46206
Industry Affiliation: Insurance
**Publication(s):**
*Indianapolis Life Times*
Day Published: bi-m.: Jan., Mar., May, July,
   Sep., Nov.
Lead Time: 1 mo. prior to pub. date
Mtls Deadline: 3rd wk. of Dec., Feb., Apr.,
   June, Aug., Oct.
Contact: Communications Dept.
Personnel: Nancy Adams, Editor

*Headline*
Day Published: m.
Contact: Human Resources Dept.

**INDIANAPOLIS WATER CO.** 3071
1220 Waterway Blvd.
Indianapolis, IN 46202
Telephone: (317) 639-1501
FAX: (317) 263-6414
Mailing Address:
   P.O. Box 1220
   Indianapolis, IN 46206
Industry Affiliation: Utility: Water
**Publication(s):**
*Water Lines*
Day Published: q.
Lead Time: 1 mo. prior to pub. date
Mtls Deadline: 1st of mo. prior to pub. date
Spec. Requirements: 8 pg.; offset
   magazine; 64 x 84
Personnel: Jeb Conran, Editor
   Pat Chastain

**INDIANA TELCO FEDERAL** 3066
**CREDIT UNION**
P.O. Box 50738
Indianapolis, IN 46250
Telephone: (317) 845-8383
Industry Affiliation: Finance, Services

Materials Accepted/Included: 01-Business news 02-By-line articles 03-Fashion news 04-Food news 05-Freelance copy 06-Letters to editor 07-Real estate news 08-Sports news 09-Travel news
10-Book rev. 11-Movie rev. 12-Music rev. 13-TV rev. 14-Theater rev. 15-Coming events 16-Obituaries 17-Question & answer 18-Social announcements 19-Artwork 20-Cartoons 21-Photos 22-TV listings
23-Audio rec. 24-Video rec. 25-Books 26-Films/film clips 27-Personnel news 28-Press releases 29-New product news/photos 30-Trade lit. 31-Contracts awarded 32-Display adv. 33-Classified adv.
11-43

**Publication(s):**
*Telco Today*
Day Published: m.
Lead Time: 1 mo. prior to pub. date
Spec. Requirements: 4 pg.; tabloid; 12 x 9
Personnel: Gary Gosch, Editor

4360

## INDUSTRIAL COMMISSION
30 W. Spring St.
Columbus, OH 43266-0589
Telephone: (614) 466-8650
Industry Affiliation: Associations: City, State, Federal
**Publication(s):**
*Intercomm*
Day Published: bi-m.
Lead Time: 2 mos. prior to pub. date
Mtls Deadline: 2 mos. prior to pub date.
Contact: Safety & Hygiene
Spec. Requirements: 24-32 page; offset; 8 1/2 x 11
Personnel: Robert Macon, Editor

*Adjudicator*
Day Published: m.
Lead Time: 3 wks. prior to pub. date
Mtls Deadline: 3 wks. prior to pub. date
Personnel: Lou Forrest, Editor

*Industrial*
Day Published: w.
Lead Time: 1 wk. prior to pub. date
Mtls Deadline: 1 wk. prior to pub. date
Personnel: Lou Forrest, Editor

3645

## INGALLS SHIPBUILDING DIVISION, LITTON INDUSTRIES
1000 Access Rd.
Pascagoula, MS 39568-0149
Telephone: (601) 935-3971
FAX: (601) 935-5766
Mailing Address:
P.O. Box 149
Pascagoula, MS 39568
Industry Affiliation: Shipping
**Publication(s):**
*Ingalls News*
Day Published: w.
Lead Time: Mon. prior to pub. date
Mtls Deadline: Mon. prior to pub. date
Contact: Ingalls Shipbuilding
Spec. Requirements: 4 pg.; offset; 8 1/2 x 11
Personnel: Mark Sullivan, Editor
Cherie Cole

2830

## INGERSOLL INTERNATIONAL, INC.
707 Fulton Ave.
Rockford, IL 61103
Telephone: (815) 987-6000
Industry Affiliation: Textiles, Apparel, Mills, Machinery
**Publication(s):**
*Ingersolletter*
Day Published: bi-m.
Spec. Requirements: 8 pg.; offset tabloid; 8 1/2 x 11
Personnel: Jill Carmichael, Editor

2594

## INSTITUTE OF INTERNAL AUDITORS
249 Maitland Ave.
Altamonte Springs, FL 32701-4201
Telephone: (407) 830-7600
FAX: (407) 831-5171
Industry Affiliation: Finance, Services

**Publication(s):**
*Internal Auditor*
Day Published: bi-m.
Mtls Deadline: editorial-90 days prior to pub. date
Spec. Requirements: 96-page; 6 x 9
Personnel: Anne Graham, Editor
Mary Ellen Kammert, Production Editor
Doug Nelson, Art Director
Gretchen Gorfine, Editorial Assistant
Jo An Shultz, Advertising Coordinator

*I I A Today*
Day Published: bi-m.
Lead Time: 60 days
Materials: 01
Mtls Deadline: 30 days prior to pub. date
Contact: Professional Services
Personnel: Lisa Krist, Editor

4050

## INSURANCE SERVICES OFFICE INC.
7 World Trade Ctr.
New York, NY 10048
Telephone: (212) 898-6000
FAX: (212) 898-6616
Industry Affiliation: Insurance
**Publication(s):**
*Inside I S O*
Day Published: m.
Lead Time: 6 wks. prior to pub. date
Mtls Deadline: 2 wks. prior to pub. date
Contact: Communications Div.
Spec. Requirements: 16 pg.; offset; 8-1/2 x 11
Personnel: Leslie Fellows, Editor

4245

## INTEGON
500 W. Fifth St.
Winston Salem, NC 27152
Telephone: (919) 770-2000
FAX: (919) 770-2122
Mailing Address:
P.O. Box 3199
Winston Salem, NC 27152
Industry Affiliation: Insurance
**Publication(s):**
*Symbols*
Day Published: m.
Lead Time: 15th of mo. prior to pub. date
Mtls Deadline: 15th of mo. prior to pub. date

*Data*
Day Published: bi-w.
Lead Time: 1 wk.
Mtls Deadline: 1 wk. prior to pub. date

3099

## INTER-STATE ASSURANCE CO.
1206 Mulberry
Des Moines, IA 50309
Telephone: (515) 283-2501
FAX: (515) 283-0278
Industry Affiliation: Insurance
**Publication(s):**
*Focus On Commissions*
Day Published: 6 wks.
Lead Time: 1 mo. prior to pub. date
Spec. Requirements: 4 pg.; offset; 8 1/2 x 11
Personnel: Randy Timm, Editor

5251

## INTERMET FOUNDRY
620 Court St.
Lynchburg, VA 24504
Telephone: (804) 528-8317
FAX: (804) 528-8301
Industry Affiliation: Steel, Iron

**Publication(s):**
*Intermet News*
Day Published: q.
Lead Time: 60 days prior to pub. date
Mtls Deadline: 60 days prior to pub. date
Spec. Requirements: 28-32 pg.; offset magazine; 8-1/2 x 11
Personnel: Janis J. Toennisson, Editor

2174

## INTERNATIONAL ASSOCIATION OF BUSINESS COMMUNICATORS
One Hallidie Plz., Ste. 600
San Francisco, CA 94102
Telephone: (415) 433-3400
FAX: (415) 382-8762
Industry Affiliation: Associations: Trade, Fraternal
**Publication(s):**
*Communication World*
Day Published: m.
Lead Time: 60 days
Materials: 01,02,06,10
Mtls Deadline: 30-45 days prior to pub. date
Contact: Kyie Heger
Spec. Requirements: 48 pg; web
Personnel: Gloria Gordon, Editor
Kyie Heger, Managing Editor

*World Book Of Members & Services*
Day Published: a.
Lead Time: 60 days
Mtls Deadline: Sep. 30
Contact: Communication
Personnel: Kyie Heger, Managing Editor
Gloria Gordon, Editor

68380

## INTERNATIONAL ASSOCIATION OF HOSPITALITY ACCOUNTANTS
9171 Capital of Texas Hwy., Ste. H-350
Austin, TX 78759
Telephone: (512) 346-5680
FAX: (512) 346-5760
Mailing Address:
P.O. Box 203008
Austin, TX 78720-3008
Industry Affiliation: Finance, Services
**Publication(s):**
*Bottomline, The*
Day Published: bi-m.
Lead Time: 6 wks.
Materials: 32,33
Mtls Deadline: 6 wks. prior to pub. date
Contact: Communications
Personnel: Frank Wolfe, Editor in Chief

*I A H A Infoline*
Day Published: bi-m.
Lead Time: 4-6 wks.
Materials: 33
Mtls Deadline: 4 wks. prior to pub. date
Contact: Communications
Personnel: Frank Wolfe, Editor in Chief

69425

## INTERNATIONAL BROTHERHOOD OF LOCOMOTIVE ENGINEERS
1370 Ontario St., Mezz.
Cleveland, OH 44113-1702
Telephone: (216) 241-2630
FAX: (216) 861-0932
Industry Affiliation: Associations: Trade, Fraternal

**Publication(s):**
*Locomotive Engineers Newsletter*
Day Published: q.
Personnel: S.W. FitzGerald, Editor

4047

## INTERNATIONAL BUSINESS MACHINES CORP.
Old Orchard Rd.
Armonk, NY 10504
Telephone: (914) 765-1900
FAX: (914) 765-7690
Industry Affiliation: Electrical, Electronic, Manufacturing
**Publication(s):**
*Think*
Day Published: m.
Lead Time: 2 wks. prior to pub. date
Contact: General Products Div.
5600 Cottle Rd.
San Jose, CA 95193
Spec. Requirements: 24 pg.; offset; 8 1/2 x 11
Personnel: Doug Miller, Editor

5255

## INTERNATIONAL COMMUNICATIONS INDUSTRIES ASSN., THE
3150 Spring St.
Fairfax, VA 22031
Telephone: (703) 273-7200
Industry Affiliation: Associations: Trade, Fraternal
**Publication(s):**
*Communications Industries Report*
Day Published: m.
Lead Time: 1 mo. prior to pub. date
Mtls Deadline: 1st of mo. prior to pub. date
Spec. Requirements: 16 - Page; Offset; 8 1/2 x 11
Personnel: Jane Gould, Editor

*Market Monitor*
Day Published: M.
Lead Time: 1 mo.
Mtls Deadline: 1 mo. prior to pub. date
Personnel: Guy Philbin

3690

## INTERNATIONAL CREDIT ASSOCIATION
243 N. Lindbergh Blvd.
St. Louis, MO 63141
Telephone: (314) 991-3030
FAX: (314) 991-3029
Mailing Address:
P.O. Box 419057
St. Louis, MO 63141-1757
Industry Affiliation: Associations: Trade, Fraternal
**Publication(s):**
*Credit World*
Day Published: bi-m.
Lead Time: 45 days
Materials: 01,02,06,10,17,19,20,21,25,27, 28,29,30,32,33
Mtls Deadline: 45 days prior to pub. date
Spec. Requirements: offset magazine; 81 x 107
Personnel: Janet Lipkind, Editor

3150

## INTERNATIONAL FLYING FARMERS
2120 Airport Rd.
Wichita, KS 67209
Telephone: (316) 943-4234
FAX: (316) 943-4235
Mailing Address:
P.O. Box 9124
Wichita, KS 67277
Industry Affiliation: Associations: Trade, Fraternal

Materials Accepted/Included: 01-Business news 02-By-line articles 03-Fashion news 04-Food news 05-Freelance copy 06-Letters to editor 07-Real estate news 08-Sports news 09-Travel news 10-Book rev. 11-Movie rev. 12-Music rev. 13-TV rev. 14-Theater rev. 15-Coming events 16-Obituaries 17-Question & answer 18-Social announcements 19-Artwork 20-Cartoons 21-Photos 22-TV listings 23-Audio rec. 24-Video rec. 25-Books 26-Films/film clips 27-Personnel news 28-Press releases 29-New product news/photos 30-Trade lit. 31-Contracts awarded 32-Display adv. 33-Classified adv.

11-44

**Publication(s):**
*International Flying Farmer*
Day Published: 9/yr.
Lead Time: 30 days prior to pub. date
Mtls Deadline: 30 days prior to pub. date
Spec. Requirements: film or camera-ready art
Personnel: Angie Blakely, Editor
    Kyle Ann Stream, Executive Director

3692

## INTERNATIONAL UNIVERSITY FOUNDATION
1301 S. Noland Rd.
Independence, MO 64055
Telephone: (816) 461-3633
Industry Affiliation: Colleges, Institutions, Science Research
**Publication(s):**
*T I U Newsletter*
Day Published: q.
Lead Time: 6 wks.
Materials: 01,15,19,21,27,28
Mtls Deadline: 6 wks.
Spec. Requirements: 1-6 pg; 8 1/2 x 11
Personnel: Dr. John Wayne Johnston, Editor

*Collegiate Sports Report*
Day Published: q.
Lead Time: 30 days
Materials: 08,15,19,21,27
Spec. Requirements: 1-10 pg; 8 1/2 X 11
Personnel: Dr. John Wayne Johnston, Editor

*International University Poetry Quarterly, The*
Day Published: q.
Lead Time: 4-6 wks.
Materials: 15,19,21
Spec. Requirements: short selections greatly preferred
Personnel: Dr. John Wayne Johnston, Editor

3100

## INTERSTATE POWER CO.
1000 Main St.
Dubuque, IA 52004
Telephone: (319) 582-5421
FAX: (319) 557-2247
Mailing Address:
    P.O. Box 769
    Dubuque, IA 52004
Industry Affiliation: Utility: Electric
**Publication(s):**
*Interstate News*
Day Published: m.
Lead Time: 20th of mo. prior to pub.
Spec. Requirements: 4-6 pg.; offset tabloid; 11 x 14
Personnel: Jim Esmoil, Editor

3132

## IOWA-ILLINOIS GAS & ELECTRIC CO.
206 E. Second St.
Davenport, IA 52801
Telephone: (319) 326-7350
FAX: (319) 326-7016
Industry Affiliation: Utility: Electric
**Publication(s):**
*Our People*
Day Published: bi-m.
Spec. Requirements: 12-24 pg.; offset magazine; 8 1/2 x 11
Personnel: Ron Oelke, Editor

3101

## IOWA ASSOCIATION OF ELECTRIC COOPERATIVES
8525 Douglas, Ste. 48
Des Moines, IA 50322-2992
Telephone: (515) 276-5350
FAX: (515) 276-7946
Industry Affiliation: Associations: Trade, Fraternal

**Publication(s):**
*Iowa Rec News*
Day Published: m.
Lead Time: 8 wks. prior to pub. date
Materials: 02,04,05,29,32,33
Mtls Deadline: 8 wks. prior to pub. date
Contact: Judy Garlock
Spec. Requirements: 24 pg.; offset magazine; 84 x 11
Personnel: Jody Garlock, Editor

68520

## IOWA CREDIT UNION LEAGUE
3737 Westown Pkwy.
Des Moines, IA 50265
Telephone: (515) 226-9999
FAX: (515) 226-7970
Mailing Address:
    P.O. Box 10409
    Des Moines, IA 50306
Industry Affiliation: Banks, Savings & Loans
**Publication(s):**
*Account*
Day Published: q.
Spec. Requirements: 12-16 pg.; offset; 94 x 76
Personnel: Katie Swalla, Editor

3103

## IOWA DEPARTMENT OF ECONOMIC DEVELOPMENT
200 E. Grand Ave.
Des Moines, IA 50309
Telephone: (515) 242-4700
FAX: (515) 242-4859
Industry Affiliation: Associations: City, State, Federal
**Publication(s):**
*Digest, The*
Day Published: bi-m.
Lead Time: 1-1/2 mos. prior to pub. date
Materials: 01
Mtls Deadline: 1 mo. prior to pub. date
Spec. Requirements: 12 pg.; offset; 8-1/2 x 11
Personnel: Anita Walker, Editor
    Robert Boyd

3137

## IOWA STATE ASSOCIATION OF COUNTIES
701 E. Court Ave.
Des Moines, IA 50309
Telephone: (515) 244-7181
FAX: (515) 244-6397
Industry Affiliation: Associations: City, State, Federal
**Publication(s):**
*Iowa County, The*
Day Published: m.
Lead Time: 2 wks.
Mtls Deadline: 15th of mo. prior to pub. date
Spec. Requirements: 20 pg; offset; 8 1/2 x 11
Personnel: Sandra K. Longfellow, Layout Director
    Tricia Fazzini, Managing Editor

3138

## IOWA STATE UNIVERSITY
2501 N. Loop Dr., Ste. 500
Research Pk.
Ames, IA 50010
Telephone: (515) 294-3420
FAX: (515) 294-4925
Industry Affiliation: Colleges, Institutions, Science Research

**Publication(s):**
*Ciras News*
Day Published: q.
Lead Time: 2 mos.
Mtls Deadline: 2nd mo. of quarter
Contact: University Extension
    110 Curtiss Hall
Spec. Requirements: 8 pg; offset; 8 1/2 x 11
Personnel: William R. Berkland, Editor

3070

## IPALCO ENTERPRISES, INC.
25 Monument Cir.
Indianapolis, IN 46204
Telephone: (317) 261-8261
FAX: (317) 261-8912
Mailing Address:
    P.O. Box 1595B
    Indianapolis, IN 46204
Industry Affiliation: Utility: Related
**Publication(s):**
*I P L C O News*
Day Published: m.
Spec. Requirements: 8-12 pg.; offset tabloid; 11 x 17
Personnel: Susan Poole, Editor

68376

## IRISH AMERICAN CULTURAL INSTITUTE
2115 Summit Ave., Mail 5026
St. Paul, MN 55105
Telephone: (612) 962-6040
FAX: (612) 962-6043
Industry Affiliation: Associations: Trade, Fraternal
**Publication(s):**
*Eire-Ireland, Journal Of Irish Studies*
Day Published: q.
Spec. Requirements: fully annotated, scholarly article
Personnel: Thomas Redshaw, Editor

*Ducas*
Day Published: q.
Personnel: James Rogers, Editor

3356

## ITEK OPTICAL SYSTEMS, DIV. OF LITTON INDUSTRIES
10 Maguire Rd.
Lexington, MA 02173
Telephone: (617) 276-2000
FAX: (617) 276-2000
Industry Affiliation: Industry: Light Tools, Equipment
**Publication(s):**
*Item*
Day Published: m.
Lead Time: 6 wks.
Spec. Requirements: 8 pg.; offset; 11 x 14
Personnel: Diana Tempel, Editor

3019

## ITT AEROSPACE, COMMUNICATIONS DIVISION
1919 W. Cook Rd.
Fort Wayne, IN 46818
Telephone: (219) 487-6000
Mailing Address:
    P.O. Box 3700
    Fort Wayne, IN 46801
Industry Affiliation: Aircraft, Aerospace, Defense
**Publication(s):**
*A-C D News*
Day Published: m.
Spec. Requirements: 4-6 pg; offset tabloid; 8 1/2 x 11
Personnel: Joan Lynn, Editor

4055

## ITT CORP.
320 Park Ave.
New York, NY 10022
Telephone: (212) 258-1000
Industry Affiliation: Electrical, Electronic, Manufacturing

**Publication(s):**
*Witts-Within The I T T System*
Day Published: m.
Spec. Requirements: 4-8 pg.; 11 x 15
Personnel: Marion F. Kurtz, Editor

*Via I T T*
Day Published: 10/yr.
Contact: Communications Operations Grou
Spec. Requirements: 4-6 pg.
Personnel: Katherine G. Thomas, Editor

2175

## ITT GILFILLAN
7821 Orion Ave.
Van Nuys, CA 91409
Telephone: (818) 988-2600
FAX: (818) 901-2435
Mailing Address:
    P.O. Box 7713
    Van Nuys, CA 91409
Industry Affiliation: Electrical, Electronic, Manufacturing
**Publication(s):**
*Scanner*
Day Published: m.
Lead Time: 1 mo.
Mtls Deadline: 1 mo.
Contact: ITT Gilfillan
Spec. Requirements: 6 pg; offset; 8 1/2 X 11
Personnel: Jhana Petersen, Editor

2432

## ITT HARTFORD INSURANCE GROUP
Hartford Plz.
Hartford, CT 06115
Telephone: (203) 547-4959
FAX: (203) 547-3799
Industry Affiliation: Insurance
**Publication(s):**
*I T T Hartford Agent*
Day Published: bi-m.
Lead Time: 4 mos.
Materials: 01,02,05,06,19,21
Mtls Deadline: 1 mo. prior to pub. date
Spec. Requirements: 20-page; offset magazine; 8 1/2 x 11
Personnel: Robert Proctor, Editor
    Randy Richards, Art Director

*I T T Hartford World*
Day Published: bi-m.
Lead Time: 6 wks.
Materials: 01,02,05,06,19,21
Mtls Deadline: 15th of odd-numbered months
Spec. Requirements: 16-page
Personnel: John Lord, Editor
    Barry Kramer, Art Director

3241

## JACOBS ENGINEERING
P.O. Box 98033
Baton Rouge, LA 98033
Telephone: (504) 769-2700
FAX: (504) 768-5046
Industry Affiliation: Architects, Engineers, Business Service
**Publication(s):**
*Employee Gazette*
Day Published: q.
Mtls Deadline: 1st of Sep., Dec., Mar., June
Contact: Construction Div.
Spec. Requirements: 4 pg.; offset; 8-1/2 x 11
Personnel: Kim Ruiz, Editor

---

Materials Accepted/Included: 01-Business news 02-By-line articles 03-Fashion news 04-Food news 05-Freelance copy 06-Letters to editor 07-Real estate news 08-Sports news 09-Travel news 10-Book rev. 11-Movie rev. 12-Music rev. 13-TV rev. 14-Theater rev. 15-Coming events 16-Obituaries 17-Question & answer 18-Social announcements 19-Artwork 20-Cartoons 21-Photos 22-TV listings 23-Audio rec. 24-Video rec. 25-Books 26-Films/film clips 27-Personnel news 28-Press releases 29-New product news/photos 30-Trade lit. 31-Contracts awarded 32-Display adv. 33-Classified adv.

*On Stream*
Day Published: q.
Mtls Deadline: Nov. 1, Feb. 1, May 1, Aug. 1
Contact: Construction Div.
Spec. Requirements: 4-page

**JANTZEN INC.**      4590
411 N. E. 19th.
Portland, OR 97232
Telephone: (503) 238-5000
FAX: (503) 238-5087
Mailing Address:
  P.O. Box 3001
  Portland, OR 97208
Industry Affiliation: Textiles, Apparel, Mills, Machinery
**Publication(s):**
*Jantzen Yarns*
Day Published: q.
Lead Time: 1-2 mos.
Mtls Deadline: 1-2 mos. prior to pub. date
Personnel: Stacy Davis, Editor

**JC PENNEY COMPANY**      4107
6501 Legacy Dr.
Plano, TX 75024-3698
Telephone: (214) 431-1000
Mailing Address:
  P.O. Box 10001
  Dallas, TX 75301-2205
Industry Affiliation: Retail Stores
**Publication(s):**
*J C Penney Today*
Day Published: 5/yr.
Lead Time: 12 wks. prior to pub. date
Spec. Requirements: 12 pg.; offset magazine 9-1/2 x 12-1/4
Personnel: Tim Lyons, Editor

**JEFFERSON PILOT LIFE INSURANCE CO.**      4246
100 N. Green St.
Greensboro, NC 27401
Telephone: (919) 691-3000
FAX: (919) 691-3938
Mailing Address:
  P.O. Box 21008
  Greensboro, NC 27420
Industry Affiliation: Insurance
**Publication(s):**
*J P News*
Day Published: w.
Spec. Requirements: 4 pg.; offset; 9 x 124
Personnel: Nancy Elkins, Editor

*Inside J P*
Day Published: m.
Personnel: Nancy Elkins, Editor

*J P Life Magazine*
Day Published: m.

*J P Home Service Today*
Day Published: m.
Personnel: Nancy Elkins, Editor

**JERSEY CENTRAL POWER & LIGHT CO.**      3874
300 Madison Ave.
Morristown, NJ 07960
Telephone: (800) 452-9155
FAX: (201) 455-8976
Industry Affiliation: Utility: Electric
**Publication(s):**
*On-Line*
Day Published: w.
Lead Time: 2-3 wks. prior to pub. date
Mtls Deadline: 15th of mo. prior to pub. date
Spec. Requirements: 8 pg.; newsletter; 8 1/2 x 11
Personnel: Lucille Andeloro, Editor

*Spectra*
Day Published: bi-m.
Lead Time: 2 mos. prior to pub. date
Mtls Deadline: 2 mos. prior to pub. date
Spec. Requirements: Utility Industry News (E.E. New Products, Services
Personnel: Mary Irons, Editor

**JET PROPULSION LABORATORY, CIT**      2341
4800 Oak Grove Dr., MS/186-120
Pasadena, CA 91109
Industry Affiliation: Colleges, Institutions, Science Research
**Publication(s):**
*Universe*
Day Published: s-m.
Contact: Public Affairs Division
Spec. Requirements: 4 pg.; offset tabloid; 17 x 22
Personnel: Mark Whalen, Editor

**JEWEL FOOD STORES**      68633
1955 W. North Ave.
Melrose Park, IL 60160
Telephone: (708) 531-6942
FAX: (708) 288-2151
Industry Affiliation: Food, General
**Publication(s):**
*Flashes*
Day Published: bi-w.
Materials: 01,02,04,15,16,17,21,27,29
Contact: Communications & Training
Spec. Requirements: 24-28 pg.; 6 1/2" x 8 1/2"
Personnel: Mary Anne Vydra, Editor

**JEWISH COMMUNITY CENTER**      5012
7900 Northaven Rd.
Dallas, TX 75230
Telephone: (214) 739-2737
FAX: (214) 768-4709
Industry Affiliation: Associations: Trade, Fraternal
**Publication(s):**
*For Members Only*
Day Published: bi-m.
Lead Time: 40 days prior to pub. date
Mtls Deadline: 30 days prior to pub. date
Contact: Publicity And Promotions
Spec. Requirements: 24 pg.; offset; 8-1/2 x 7
Personnel: Elaine Schrager, Editor

**JII SALES PROMOTION ASSOCIATES, INC.**      4431
545 Walnut St.
Coshocton, OH 43812
Telephone: (614) 622-4422
FAX: (614) 622-5868
Industry Affiliation: Advertising, Art, Public Relations
**Publication(s):**
*Sales Booster*
Day Published: m.
Lead Time: 30 days prior to pub. date
Mtls Deadline: 30 days prior to pub. date
Spec. Requirements: 24 pgs.; offset magazine; 8 1/2 x 11
Personnel: James R. Yarrington, Marketing Manager
    William Siedrist

*Record*
Day Published: m.
Lead Time: 30 days
Personnel: James R. Yarrington, Marketing Manager
    Roger Foster, Assistant Editor

*Roundtable*
Day Published: m.
Lead Time: 1 mo.
Mtls Deadline: 1 mo.
Spec. Requirements: b & w only
Personnel: James R. Yarrington, Marketing Manager

**JLG INDUSTRIES, INC.**      4708
JLG Dr.
McConnellsburg, PA 17233
Telephone: (717) 485-5161
FAX: (717) 485-6466
Industry Affiliation: Electrical, Electronic, Manufacturing
**Publication(s):**
*J L G Ink, The*
Day Published: q.
Lead Time: 2 wks. prior to pub. date
Mtls Deadline: 2 wks. prior to pub. date
Spec. Requirements: 6-8 pg.; offset; 8 1/2 x 11
Personnel: Jeanne M. Wakefield, Editor

*Update*
Day Published: bi-w.
Lead Time: 1 wk. prior to pub. date
Personnel: Terri Smith
    Lynn Foster
    Deborah R. Fagley, Editor

**JOHN H HARLAND CO.**      2665
P.O. Box 105250
Atlanta, GA 30348
Telephone: (404) 981-9460
FAX: (404) 593-5347
Industry Affiliation: Printers, Services
**Publication(s):**
*Intercom*
Day Published: q.
Lead Time: 2 mos. prior to pub. date
Materials: 01,02
Mtls Deadline: 15th of last mo. prior to pub. date
Contact: Marketing
Spec. Requirements: 6 pg., 8-1/2 x 11
Personnel: Gina Niederhauser, Editor
    Lamar Ussery, Art Director

**JONATHAN CLUB**      2177
545 S. Figueroa St.
Los Angeles, CA 90071
Telephone: (310) 624-0881
Industry Affiliation: Associations: Trade, Fraternal
**Publication(s):**
*Jonathan*
Day Published: m.
Lead Time: 10th of mo. prior to pub. date
Mtls Deadline: 10th of mo. prior to pub. date
Contact: Johnathan Beach Facility
    850 Palisades Beach Rd.
    Santa Monica, CA 90403
Spec. Requirements: 32 pg.; offset; 9 x 12 1 suplication
Personnel: Sally R. Guthrie, Editor

**JORDAN SCHOOL DISTRICT**      5204
9361 S. 300, E.
Sandy, UT 84070
Telephone: (801) 565-8290
Industry Affiliation: Colleges, Institutions, Science Research
**Publication(s):**
*Windows To Your School*
Day Published: m.
Spec. Requirements: 4 pg.; offset; 8 1/2 x 11
Personnel: Patty Dahl, Editor

*Ripples & Currents*
Day Published: w.
Mtls Deadline: Tue. (Sep.-June)
Personnel: Patty Dahl

**JOURNAL COMMUNICATIONS**      5404
P.O. Box 661
Milwaukee, WI 53201-0661
Telephone: (414) 224-2000
Industry Affiliation: Newspapers
**Publication(s):**
*Intercom*
Day Published: m.
Spec. Requirements: offset mag. 10 x 14
Personnel: Dawn Finnegan, Editor

*News Print*
Day Published: m.
Spec. Requirements: 10-14 pg. 10 x 14 offset mag.
Personnel: Dawn Finnegan, Editor

**KAMPGROUNDS OF AMERICA, INC.**      3760
550 N. 31st St.
Billings, MT 59101
Telephone: (406) 248-7444
Industry Affiliation: Advertising, Art, Public Relations
**Publication(s):**
*Koa Directory, Road Atlas And Camping Guide*
Day Published: a.
Materials: 32
Mtls Deadline: mid-Oct.
Contact: Kent Zimmerman
Spec. Requirements: 144-pg.; offset; 8 x 10 3/4
Personnel: Kent Zimmerman, Editor

**KANO LABS INC.**      4871
1000 S. Thompson Ln.
Nashville, TN 37211
Telephone: (615) 833-4101
FAX: (615) 833-5790
Mailing Address:
  P.O. Box 110098
  Nashville, TN 37222
Industry Affiliation: Food, General
**Publication(s):**
*Genius At Work*
Day Published: q.
Spec. Requirements: 4 pg.; offset bulletin; 84 x 11
Personnel: Peter J. Zimmerman, Editor

**KANSAS CITY BOARD OF PUBLIC UTILITIES**      3151
700 Minnesota Ave.
Kansas City, KS 66101
Telephone: (913) 573-9190
FAX: (913) 573-9990
Industry Affiliation: Utility: Water
**Publication(s):**
*Watts N' Water News*
Day Published: bi-m.
Personnel: Carol Irish, Editor

**KANSAS CITY KANSAS CHAMBER OF COMMERCE**      3152
727 Minnesota Ave.
Kansas City, KS 66101
Telephone: (913) 371-3070
FAX: (913) 371-3732
Mailing Address:
  P.O. Box 171337
  Kansas City, KS 66117
Industry Affiliation: Associations: City, State, Federal

Materials Accepted/Included: 01-Business news 02-By-line articles 03-Fashion news 04-Food news 05-Freelance copy 06-Letters to editor 07-Real estate news 08-Sports news 09-Travel news 10-Book rev. 11-Movie rev. 12-Music rev. 13-TV rev. 14-Theater rev. 15-Coming events 16-Obituaries 17-Question & answer 18-Social announcements 19-Artwork 20-Cartoons 21-Photos 22-TV listings 23-Audio rec. 24-Video rec. 25-Books 26-Films/film clips 27-Personnel news 28-Press releases 29-New product news/photos 30-Trade lit. 31-Contracts awarded 32-Display adv. 33-Classified adv.

**Publication(s):**
*Business Report*
Day Published: bi-m.
Lead Time: 3 wks. prior to pub. date
Mtls Deadline: 20th of mo. prior to pub. date
Spec. Requirements: done in-house on laserjet computer printer
Personnel: Marsha Luce, Editor

**KANSAS CITY LIFE INSURANCE CO.**                           66449
3520 Broadway
Kansas City, MO 64111
Telephone: (816) 753-7000
Mailing Address:
    P.O. Box 419139-6139
    Kansas City, MO 64141
Industry Affiliation: Insurance
**Publication(s):**
*Lifetime*
Day Published: m.
Lead Time: 1 wk. prior to pub. date
Mtls Deadline: 20th of mo. prior to pub. date
Personnel: Eileen Jenkins, Editor

*Tempo*
Day Published: bi-w.
Lead Time: 3 days prior to pub. date
Mtls Deadline: 2nd & 4th Thu. prior to pub. date
Personnel: Nancy Vilmer

**KANSAS DEPARTMENT OF COMMERCE**                            3153
700 S.W. Harrison, Ste. 1300
Topeka, KS 66603
Telephone: (913) 296-3481
FAX: (913) 296-6988
Industry Affiliation: Finance, Services
**Publication(s):**
*Kansas Magazine*
Day Published: q.
Lead Time: 6 mos.-1 yr. prior to pub. date
Mtls Deadline: 1 yr. prior to pub. date
Contact: Travel and Tourism
Spec. Requirements: 38 pg.; offset mag.; 8 1/2 x 11
Personnel: Andrea Glenn, Editor
          Galen Senogles
          Mary Lou McPhail, Production Manager

*Developing Kansas*
Day Published: q.
Lead Time: 3 mos.
Mtls Deadline: 1 mo.
Contact: Industrial Development
Spec. Requirements: 12 - Page
Personnel: Andrea Glen, Editor

**KANSAS OIL MARKETERS ASSOCIATION**                         3154
201 N.W. Hwy. 24, Ste. 320
Topeka, KS 66608-0479
Telephone: (913) 233-9655
Mailing Address:
    P.O. Box 8479
    Topeka, KS 66608-0479
Industry Affiliation: Petroleum, Gas

**Publication(s):**
*Kansas Oil Marketer*
Day Published: bi-m.
Materials: 01,02,04,15,20,32,33
Mtls Deadline: 1st of Feb., Apr., Jun., Aug., Oct., Dec.
Spec. Requirements: 32-36 page; offset; 8 1/2 x 11
Personnel: Dennis Anderson, Editor

**KEITH SCHOOL**                                             2838
One Jacoby Pl.
Rockford, IL 61107
Telephone: (815) 399-8823
FAX: (815) 399-2470
Industry Affiliation: Colleges, Institutions, Science Research
**Publication(s):**
*Keith School News*
Day Published: m.
Lead Time: 15th prior to pub. date
Spec. Requirements: 4 pg.; 8-1/2 x 11
Personnel: Sharon Dittel, Editor

**KELLOGG COMPANY**                                          3472
26 W. Dry Creek Cir.
Littleton, CO 80120
Telephone: (303) 794-1818
Industry Affiliation: Food, General
**Publication(s):**
*Kellogg News*
Day Published: q.
Materials: 01,06,17,30,31
Spec. Requirements: 4-6 pg.; offset; 17 x 22
Personnel: J. M. Becica, Editor

**KELLY-SPRINGFIELD TIRE CO.**                               3282
Willowbrook Rd.
Cumberland, MD 21502-2599
Telephone: (301) 777-6000
Industry Affiliation: Rubber, Tires
**Publication(s):**
*Minute*
Day Published: q.
Lead Time: 1 mo.
Mtls Deadline: 1 mo. prior to pub. date
Contact: Public Affairs
Spec. Requirements: 16 pg; offset magazine; 8 1/2 x 11
Personnel: G.N. Hess, Editor

*Today*
Day Published: bi-m.
Lead Time: 1 mo.
Spec. Requirements: 6-8 pgs
Personnel: Barbara Cadwallader, Assistant Editor
          G.N. Hess, Editor

*Corporate Report*
Day Published: d.
Spec. Requirements: Electronics
Personnel: Barbara Cadwallader, Editor

**KELLY SERVICES, INC.**                                     3516
999 W. Big Beaver Rd.
Troy, MI 48084
Telephone: (313) 362-4444
FAX: (313) 244-4154
Mailing Address:
    P.O. Box 1179
    Detroit, MI 48266
Industry Affiliation: Office Equipment, Services, Supplies
**Publication(s):**
*Workstyle Newsletter*
Day Published: m.
Lead Time: 3 mos. prior to pub. date
Spec. Requirements: 16 pg.; offset; 8-1/2 x 11
Personnel: Jeanne Nicol, Editor

*Chronicle, The*
Day Published: q.
Personnel: Jeanne Nicol, Editor

**KENTUCKY ASSOCIATION OF ELECTRIC COOPERATIVES**            3182
4515 Bishop Ln.
Louisville, KY 40218
Telephone: (502) 451-2430
FAX: (502) 459-1611
Mailing Address:
    P.O. Box 32170
    Louisville, KY 40232
Industry Affiliation: Electrical, Electronic, Manufacturing
**Publication(s):**
*Rural Kentuckian*
Day Published: m.
Lead Time: 60 days prior to pub. date
Contact: Exec. Rels.
          4515 Bishop Ln.
          Louisville, KY 40218
Spec. Requirements: 32-40 pg.; offset; 8-1/2 x 11
Personnel: Gary W. Luhr, Editor

**KENTUCKY DEPARTMENT OF EDUCATION**                         3196
Capital Plz. Tower
Frankfort, KY 40601
Telephone: (502) 564-3421
FAX: (502) 564-7749
Mailing Address:
    500 Mero St., Rm. 1935
    Frankfort, KY 40601
Industry Affiliation: Advertising, Art, Public Relations
**Publication(s):**
*Kentucky Teacher*
Day Published: 9/yr.
Lead Time: 1 mo. prior to pub. date
Mtls Deadline: 1 mo. prior to pub. date
Contact: Publications
Spec. Requirements: 12-16 pg.; tabloid
Personnel: Fran Salyers, Editor
          Mike Gray, Art Director

**KENTUCKY UTILITIES CO.**                                   3201
One Quality St.
Lexington, KY 40507
Telephone: (606) 255-1461
FAX: (606) 288-1169
Industry Affiliation: Utility: Electric
**Publication(s):**
*Employes' News*
Day Published: m.
Spec. Requirements: 12 pg.; offset newspaper; 8-1/2 x 11
Personnel: Martin Baker, Editor

*Consumer News*
Day Published: m.
Spec. Requirements: 6 pg.
Personnel: Jeff Rhodes, Editor

*Dealer News*
Day Published: bi-m.
Spec. Requirements: 4-6 pg.
Personnel: Joey Barr, Editor

**KERR-MCGEE CORPORATION**                                   66417
123 Robert S. Kerr
Oklahoma City, OK 73102
Telephone: (405) 270-1313
FAX: (405) 270-3940
Mailing Address:
    P.O. Box 25861
    Oklahoma City, OK 73125
Industry Affiliation: Chemicals, Plastics

**Publication(s):**
*K M News*
Day Published: q.
Lead Time: 15th of mo. prior to pub. date
Mtls Deadline: 15th of mo. prior to pub. date
Contact: Corp. Comm.

**KFC CORP.**                                                3184
1441 Gardiner Ln.
Louisville, KY 40213
Telephone: (502) 456-8300
Mailing Address:
    P.O. Box 32070
    Louisville, KY 40232
Industry Affiliation: Food, General
**Publication(s):**
*Bucket*
Day Published: q.
Personnel: Jean D. Litterst, Public Affairs Director

**KIMBALL INTERNATIONAL, INC.**                              3022
1600 Royal St.
Jasper, IN 47549
Telephone: (812) 482-1600
Industry Affiliation: Lumber, Forestry, Building Materials
**Publication(s):**
*Soundboard*
Day Published: m.
Lead Time: 3 wks. prior to pub. date
Materials: 01,19,20
Spec. Requirements: 8 pg; offset tabloid; 8 1/2 x 11
Personnel: Greg Eckerle, Editor

**KINDER CARE LEARNING CENTERS, INC.**                       1994
2400 Presidents Dr.
Montgomery, AL 36116
Telephone: (205) 277-5090
FAX: (205) 277-7865
Mailing Address:
    P.O. Box 2151
    Montgomery, AL 36102-2151
Industry Affiliation: Colleges, Institutions, Science Research
**Publication(s):**
*Centerline, The*
Day Published: m.
Lead Time: 15th of mo. prior to pub. date
Spec. Requirements: 4 pg.; letterpress; 8-1/2 x 11
Personnel: Sherry Garner, Editor
          Peggy Paugh
          Sallye Skipper

**KINGSBROOK JEWISH MEDICAL CENTER**                         4059
585 Schenectady Ave.
Brooklyn, NY 11203
Telephone: (718) 604-5000
Industry Affiliation: Hospitals
**Publication(s):**
*Newsorama*
Day Published: w.
Lead Time: 5 days prior to pub. date
Mtls Deadline: Wed. prior to pub. date
Contact: Public Relations
Personnel: Robert Blalock

**KINNEY SHOE CORPORATION**                                  4185
233 Broadway
New York, NY 10279
Telephone: (212) 720-3700
Industry Affiliation: Shoes

**Materials Accepted/Included:** 01-Business news 02-By-line articles 03-Fashion news 04-Food news 05-Freelance copy 06-Letters to editor 07-Real estate news 08-Sports news 09-Travel news 10-Book rev. 11-Movie rev. 12-Music rev. 13-TV rev. 14-Theater rev. 15-Coming events 16-Obituaries 17-Question & answer 18-Social announcements 19-Artwork 20-Cartoons 21-Photos 22-TV listings 23-Audio rec. 24-Video rec. 25-Books 26-Films/film clips 27-Personnel news 28-Press releases 29-New product news/photos 30-Trade in. 31-Contracts awarded 32-Display adv. 33-Classified adv.

11-47

**Publication(s):**
*Kinney World*
Day Published: 10/yr.
Lead Time: 2 mos. prior to pub. date
Spec. Requirements: 8-16 pg.; offset; 11 x 14
Personnel: Linda DeJacomo, Editor
         Todd Dawson, Assistant Editor
         Vicki Lynn Crafton, Editorial Assistant

**KIRBY CO.**     4364
1920 W. 114th St
Cleveland, OH 44102
Telephone: (216) 228-2400
Industry Affiliation: Home Appliances, Furnishings
**Publication(s):**
*Kirby Quarterly*
Day Published: q.
Lead Time: 8 wks. prior to pub. date
Mtls Deadline: 4 wks. prior to pub. date.
Spec. Requirements: 24-60 page; offset magazine; standard
Personnel: Julie Klein, Editor

**KMART CORPORATION**     66418
3100 W. Big Beaver
Troy, MI 48084
Telephone: (313) 643-1000
Industry Affiliation: Retail Stores
**Publication(s):**
*K Merchants*
Day Published: bi-m.
Lead Time: 1 mo. prior to pub. date
Mtls Deadline: 1 mo. prior to pub date
Spec. Requirements: 8 pg.; tabloid
Personnel: Maria Seyrig, Editor

**KN ENERGY, INC.**     3785
300 N. St. Joseph
Hastings, NE 68901
Telephone: (402) 462-2141
FAX: (402) 461-4382
Mailing Address:
   P.O. Box 608
   Hastings, NE 68902
Industry Affiliation: Petroleum, Gas
**Publication(s):**
*Energizer*
Day Published: m.
Lead Time: 6 wks. prior to pub. date
Mtls Deadline: 6 wks. prior to pub. date
Spec. Requirements: 12-40 pg.; offset newsp. 12 x 18; mag. 8-1/2 x 11
Personnel: Bill Gasper, Editor

**KNOXVILLE UTILITIES BOARD**     4872
626 Gay St., S.W.
Knoxville, TN 37902
Telephone: (615) 524-2911
FAX: (615) 558-2168
Mailing Address:
   4515 Middle Brook Pk.
   Knoxville, TN 37921
Industry Affiliation: Utility: Related
**Publication(s):**
*K U B Reporter:*
Day Published: q.
Lead Time: 30 days
Mtls Deadline: 1st wk. of mo.
Spec. Requirements: 20-pg.; offset; 84 x 11
Personnel: Lynnda Tenpenny, Editor

**KOHLER CO.**     5467
444 Highland Dr.
Kohler, WI 53044
Telephone: (414) 457-4441
Industry Affiliation: Hardware, Plumbing

**Publication(s):**
*People*
Day Published: q.
Lead Time: 2 mos.
Mtls Deadline: 60 days
Contact: Public Affairs Dept.
Personnel: Ann Pirrung

*Capsule*
Day Published: w.
Lead Time: 1 wk.
Mtls Deadline: 1 wk.
Contact: Public Affairs Dept.
Personnel: Jennifer Reibel, Editor

*Plumbline*
Day Published: q.
Mtls Deadline: 6 wks.
Contact: Public Affairs Dept.
Spec. Requirements: for plumbing contractors & distributors
Personnel: Nancy Deptolla, Editor

*Corporate Bulletin*
Day Published: q.
Contact: Public Affairs Dept.
Spec. Requirements: for supervisory personnel
Personnel: Jennifer Reibel, Editor

*Engines In Action*
Day Published: q.
Contact: Public Affairs Dept.
Spec. Requirements: for engine distributors
Personnel: Jeff Gabin, Editor

*Kohler Shopper*
Day Published: bi-w.
Contact: Public Affairs Dept.
Spec. Requirements: for Wisconsin employees

*On-Line*
Day Published: q.
Contact: Public Affairs Dept.
Spec. Requirements: for generator distributors
Personnel: Jeff Gabin, Editor

**KONICA BUSINESS MACHINES U.S.A., INC.**     2451
500 Day Hill Rd.
Windsor, CT 06095
Telephone: (203) 683-2222
FAX: (203) 285-7617
Industry Affiliation: Office Equipment, Services, Supplies
**Publication(s):**
*Outlook*
Day Published: bi-m.
Lead Time: 1 mo. prior to pub. date
Mtls Deadline: 10th of mo. prior to pub. date
Contact: Direct Sales
Spec. Requirements: 8-20 pgs.
Personnel: Suzanne Schumann, Editor
         Debbie Kerfoot, Art Director

*Image*
Day Published: q.
Lead Time: 6 wks. prior to pub. date
Mtls Deadline: 15th of mo. prior to pub. date
Contact: Wholesale
Spec. Requirements: 8-20 pgs.
Personnel: Suzanne Schumann, Editor
         Debbie Kerfoot, Art Director

**KOSS CORP.**     5407
4129 N. Port Washington Ave.
Milwaukee, WI 53212
Telephone: (414) 964-5000
FAX: (414) 964-8615
Industry Affiliation: Electrical, Electronic, Manufacturing

**Publication(s):**
*Inside Out*
Day Published: m.
Lead Time: 2 mos. prior to pub. date
Materials: 01,27,28,29
Mtls Deadline: 1 mo. prior to pub. date
Contact: Marketing
Spec. Requirements: 4 pg.; offset; 11 x 17
Personnel: Cameryne Roberts, Editor

**KPL GAS SERVICE**     3683
818 Kansas Ave.
Topeka, KS 66612
Telephone: (816) 221-4765
Mailing Address:
   P.O. Box 889
   Topeka, KS 66601
Industry Affiliation: Utility: Gas
**Publication(s):**
*K P L Gas Service*
Day Published: m.
Lead Time: 1 mo.
Mtls Deadline: 1st day of mo. prior to pub. date
Personnel: Sue Henke

**KRAFT-GENERAL FOODS**     2842
3 Lakes Dr.
Northfield, IL 60093
Telephone: (708) 646-2000
FAX: (708) 644-3070
Industry Affiliation: Food, General
**Publication(s):**
*K G F Focus*
Day Published: q.
Spec. Requirements: 24 pg.; offset magazine; 9 x 12
Personnel: Sally Maier, Editor
         Polly Youngberg

**KTVE-TV**     5115
2909 Kilpatrick Blvd.
Monroe, LA 71201
Telephone: (318) 323-1300
FAX: (318) 322-9718
Mailing Address:
   P.O. Box 4339
   Monroe, LA 71211
Industry Affiliation: Radio, TV, Movies
**Publication(s):**
*Viewpoint*
Day Published: w.
Lead Time: 2 wks. prior to pub. date
Mtls Deadline: 7 working days prior to pub. date
Contact: Jerry Mayer
Spec. Requirements: 6-8 pg.; letterpress; 8 1/2 x 11
Personnel: Renae Willis
         Leighton Spann

*A M*
Day Published: d.
Lead Time: 2 wks. prior to pub. date
Mtls Deadline: 7 working days prior to pub. date
Contact: GeGe Roulame
Spec. Requirements: 6-8 pg.; letterpress; 8 1/2 x 11
Personnel: John Young

*Region 10 News*
Day Published: d.
Lead Time: 2-5 days prior to pub. date
Mtls Deadline: 2-4 days prior to pub. date
Contact: Nan Goss
Personnel: Jerry Mayer
         Kynn Bilbo

**KYOCERA INTERNATIONAL, INC.**     2181
8611 Balboa Ave
San Diego, CA 92123
Telephone: (619) 279-8310
Industry Affiliation: Cement, Ceramics, Clay

**Publication(s):**
*The Key:*
Day Published: 10/yr.
Lead Time: 1 mo.
Mtls Deadline: 1 mo.
Spec. Requirements: 8-pg.; offset; 11 1/2 x 15
Personnel: Jay Scovie, Editor

**L & F PRODUCTS**     3878
225 Summit Ave.
Montvale, NJ 07645
Telephone: (201) 573-5700
Industry Affiliation: Retail Stores
**Publication(s):**
*L & F Topics*
Day Published: bi-m.
Lead Time: 2 mos. prior to pub. date
Mtls Deadline: 2 mos. prior to pub. date
Spec. Requirements: 16-pg.; offset magazine; 9 x 12
Personnel: Patricia Jones, Editor

**LA-Z-BOY CHAIR CO.**     3476
1284 N. Telegraph Rd.
Monroe, MI 48161
Telephone: (313) 242-1444
Industry Affiliation: Home Appliances, Furnishings
**Publication(s):**
*Monroe La-Z-News*
Day Published: q.
Lead Time: 2 mos.
Spec. Requirements: 16-24 pgs.; offset; 8 1/2 x 11
Personnel: Bonnie Tomkinson, Editor

**LAACO, INC.**     2182
431 W. Seventh St.
Los Angeles, CA 90014
Telephone: (310) 625-2211
Industry Affiliation: Associations: Trade, Fraternal
**Publication(s):**
*Mercury*
Day Published: m.
Lead Time: 1 mo. prior to pub. date
Mtls Deadline: 1 mo. prior to pub. date
Contact: Public Relations Dept.
Spec. Requirements: 44 pg.; offset; 8 1/2 x 11
Personnel: Marcelle Greene, Editor
         Christina Warren, Editor

**LACLEDE GAS COMPANY**     3695
720 Olive St
St. Louis, MO 63101
Telephone: (314) 621-6920
Industry Affiliation: Utility: Gas
**Publication(s):**
*Laclede News:*
Day Published: m.
Spec. Requirements: 16-pg.; offset magazine; 84 x 11
Personnel: Richard Hargraves

**LADIES AUXILIARY TO VFW OF THE US**     3751
406 W. 34th St.
Kansas City, MO 64111
Telephone: (816) 561-7663
Industry Affiliation: Associations: Trade, Fraternal

Materials Accepted/Included: 01-Business news 02-By-line articles 03-Fashion news 04-Food news 05-Freelance copy 06-Letters to editor 07-Real estate news 08-Sports news 09-Travel news 10-Book rev. 11-Movie rev. 12-Music rev. 13-TV rev. 14-Theater rev. 15-Coming events 16-Obituaries 17-Question & answer 18-Social announcements 19-Artwork 20-Cartoons 21-Photos 22-TV listings 23-Audio rec. 24-Video rec. 25-Books 26-Films/film clips 27-Personnel news 28-Press releases 29-New product news/photos 30-Trade lit. 31-Contracts awarded 32-Display adv. 33-Classified adv.

**Publication(s):**
*V F W Auxiliary*
Day Published: 8/yr.
Lead Time: 3 mos. prior to pub. date
Mtls Deadline: 2 mos. prior to pub. date
Spec. Requirements: 40 pg.; offset; 8 x 10-3/4
Personnel: Marilyn Ebersole, Editor in Chief
Rosemary Mazer, Chairman of Board

**LAKE ERIE GIRL SCOUT COUNCIL**            4366
19201 Villaview Rd.
Cleveland, OH 44119-3074
Telephone: (216) 481-1313
FAX: (216) 692-4060
Industry Affiliation: Associations: Trade, Fraternal
**Publication(s):**
*Millwheel*
Day Published: q.
Lead Time: 4-6 wks. prior to pub. date
Contact: Communications
Spec. Requirements: 10 pg.; offset; 11 1/2 x 17; 2 color
Personnel: Suzanne Collart, Editor

**LAMAR LIFE INSURANCE CO.**            3644
317 E. Capitol St.
Jackson, MS 39201
Telephone: (601) 949-3100
Mailing Address:
P.O. Box 880
Jackson, MS 39205
Industry Affiliation: Insurance
**Publication(s):**
*Page 317 E. Capitol*
Day Published: m.
Lead Time: 1 wk.
Spec. Requirements: 10 pgs.; offset magazine
Personnel: Bob Ahlschewede, Editor

**LAWRENCE BERKELEY LABORATORY**            2081
One Cyclotron Rd.
Berkeley, CA 94720
Telephone: (510) 486-4000
Industry Affiliation: Colleges, Institutions, Science Research
**Publication(s):**
*L B L Research Review*
Day Published: q.
Contact: Public Information
Spec. Requirements: 32-40 pg; offset; 8 1/4 x 10 3/4
Personnel: Pamela Patterson, Editor

*L B L Currents, The*
Day Published: w.: Fri.
Personnel: Mary Bodvarsson, Editor

**LAWRENCE RAGAN COMMUNICATIONS, INC.**            2883
212 W. Superior St., Ste. 200
Chicago, IL 60610-3533
Telephone: (312) 335-0037
Industry Affiliation: Associations: Trade, Fraternal

**Publication(s):**
*Ragan Report*
Day Published: w.
Lead Time: 2-4 wks. prior to pub. date
Mtls Deadline: Tue. eve prior to pub. date
Spec. Requirements: 8 pg.; offset newsletter; 8-1/2 x 11
Personnel: Janine Ragan, Editor
Steve Crescenzo, Editor

**LAWRENCE TECHNOLOGICAL**            3475
**UNIVERSITY**
21000 W. Ten Mile Rd.
Southfield, MI 48075-1058
Telephone: (810) 356-0200
Industry Affiliation: Colleges, Institutions, Science Research
**Publication(s):**
*Lawrence Technological University Magazine*
Day Published: 3/yr.
Lead Time: 12 wks. prior to pub. date
Materials: 02,05,06,16,19,21,27,28
Mtls Deadline: open
Spec. Requirements: 36 pg.; offset; 8-1/2 x 11
Personnel: Bruce J. Annett, Editor

**LAWYERS CO-OP PUBLISHING**            4061
**CO.**
50 Broad St., E.
Rochester, NY 14604
Telephone: (716) 546-5530
Industry Affiliation: Publishers, Books, Magazines
**Publication(s):**
*Witness*
Day Published: q.
Personnel: Dave Read, Editor

**LAWYERS TITLE INSURANCE**            5249
**CORP.**
6630 W. Broad St.
Richmond, VA 23230
Telephone: (804) 281-6841
FAX: (804) 282-5453
Mailing Address:
P.O. Box 27567
Richmond, VA 23261
Industry Affiliation: Insurance
**Publication(s):**
*Lawyers Title News*
Day Published: q.
Lead Time: 2 mos. prior to pub. date
Mtls Deadline: 2 mos. prior to pub. date
Spec. Requirements: 24 pg.; offset; 8 1/2 x 11
Personnel: Eleanor Anders, Editor

*Tract, The*
Day Published: bi-m.
Lead Time: 2 mos. prior to pub. date
Mtls Deadline: 2 mos. prior to pub. date
Personnel: Ginny Purcell, Editor

*Market-Ear, The*
Day Published: bi-m.
Lead Time: 6 wks. prior to pub. date
Mtls Deadline: 2 mos. prior to pub. date
Personnel: Vonda Stokely, Editor

*Titlelines*
Day Published: q.
Lead Time: 6 wks. prior to pub. date
Mtls Deadline: 2 mos. prior to pub. date
Personnel: Vonda Stokely, Editor

**LEADER FEDERAL SAVINGS &**            4874
**LOAN ASSOCIATION**
158 Madison Ave.
Memphis, TN 38103
Telephone: (901) 578-2345

Mailing Address:
P.O. Box 3410
Memphis, TN 38173
Industry Affiliation: Banks, Savings & Loans
**Publication(s):**
*Leader Digest*
Day Published: bi-m.
Lead Time: 3 wks. prior to pub. date
Mtls Deadline: 3 wks. prior to pub. date
Spec. Requirements: 8-12 pg.; offset; 8-1/2 x 11
Personnel: Ed Pruitt, Editor

**LEAGUE OF IOWA**            3105
**MUNICIPALITIES**
100 Court Ave., Ste. 209
Des Moines, IA 50309
Telephone: (515) 244-7282
FAX: (515) 244-0740
Industry Affiliation: Associations: City, State, Federal
**Publication(s):**
*Iowa Municipalities:*
Day Published: bi-m.
Lead Time: 10th of mo. prior
Mtls Deadline: 10th of mo. prior
Spec. Requirements: 28-32 pgs.; offset magazine; 8 1/2 x 11
Personnel: Joy M. Newcom, Editor

*Iowa Interlink*
Day Published: bi-m.
Lead Time: 10th mo.
Mtls Deadline: 10th mo. prior to pub. date
Spec. Requirements: 8 Pg.; offset newsletter; 8 1/2 x 11f Two - Color
Personnel: Joy M. Newcom
Joy M. Newcom

**LEDERLE LABORATORIES DIV.**            4062
One Cyanamid Plz.
Wayne, NJ 07470
Telephone: (201) 831-3250
FAX: (201) 831-2813
Industry Affiliation: Drugs, Cosmetics, Pharmaceuticals
**Publication(s):**
*Lederle Horizons*
Day Published: bi-m.
Lead Time: 8 wks. prior to pub. date
Spec. Requirements: 8 pg. tabloid, offset, 2 color/4-color lead photo
Personnel: Carol Dornbush, Editor

**LEHIGH VALLEY BANK**            4774
65 E. Elizabeth Ave.
Bethlehem, PA 18018
Telephone: (215) 861-1700
Industry Affiliation: Banks, Savings & Loans
**Publication(s):**
*Update*
Day Published: bi-w.
Mtls Deadline: 20th of mo. prior to pub.
Spec. Requirements: 2-4 pgs.; multilith; 8 1/2 x 11
Personnel: Mike Jupina, Editor

**LENNOX INDUSTRIES INC.**            5014
2100 Lake Park Blvd.
Richardson, TX 75080
Telephone: (214) 497-5000
Industry Affiliation: Electrical, Electronic, Manufacturing

**Publication(s):**
*Lennox News*
Day Published: q.
Contact: Public Relations
Spec. Requirements: 8 pg.; tabloid
Personnel: Rhonda Hewitt, Editor
Corwin Hall

**L.G. BALFOUR CO.**            68586
25 County St.
Attleboro, MA 02703
Telephone: (508) 222-3600
Industry Affiliation: Associations: Trade, Fraternal
**Publication(s):**
*The Diamond Exchange*
Day Published: m.
Personnel: Jeff Cambridge

**LIBERTY NATIONAL BANK &**            3197
**TRUST CO.**
416 W. Jefferson St.
Louisville, KY 40202
Telephone: (502) 566-2000
FAX: (502) 566-1800
Mailing Address:
P.O. Box 32500
Louisville, KY 40232-2500
Industry Affiliation: Banks, Savings & Loans
**Publication(s):**
*In Focus*
Day Published: m.: 3rd Mon.
Lead Time: 1 mo. prior to pub. date
Mtls Deadline: 15th of mo. prior to pub. date
Contact: Marketing
Spec. Requirements: offset
Personnel: Nancy L. Norris, Editor in Chief
Maria I. Gerwing, Marketing Director

**LIBERTY NATIONAL LIFE**            1995
**INSURANCE CO.**
2001 Third Ave., S.
Birmingham, AL 35233
Telephone: (205) 325-2722
Mailing Address:
P.O. Box 2612
Birmingham, AL 35202
Industry Affiliation: Insurance
**Publication(s):**
*Torch, The*
Day Published: m.
Contact: Corporate Communications Dept.
Spec. Requirements: 8-20 pg.; offset; tabloid
Personnel: Brant Beene, Editor

**LIBRARY OF CONGRESS**            2531
1291 Taylor St., N.W.
Washington, DC 20542
Telephone: (202) 707-5100
FAX: (202) 707-0712
Industry Affiliation: Publishers, Books, Magazines
**Publication(s):**
*Talking Book Topics*
Day Published: bi-m.
Lead Time: 2 mos. prior to pub. date
Mtls Deadline: 4 mos. prior to pub. date
Contact: National Library Service
Spec. Requirements: 100-110 pgs.; offset; 8 1/2 x 11
Personnel: George Thuronyi, Editor

*Braille Book Review*
Day Published: bi-m.
Lead Time: 2 mos. prior to pub. date
Mtls Deadline: 4 mos. prior to pub. date
Contact: National Library Service
Spec. Requirements: 50-75 pgs.; offset: 8 1/2 x 11
Personnel: Ruth Nieland, Editor

**Materials Accepted/Included:** 01-Business news 02-By-line articles 03-Fashion news 04-Food news 05-Freelance copy 06-Letters to editor 07-Real estate news 08-Sports news 09-Travel news 10-Book rev. 11-Movie rev. 12-Music rev. 13-TV rev. 14-Theater rev. 15-Coming events 16-Obituaries 17-Question & answer 18-Social announcements 19-Artwork 20-Cartoons 21-Photos 22-TV listings 23-Audio rec. 24-Video rec. 25-Books 26-Films/film clips 27-Personnel news 28-Press releases 29-New product news/photos 30-Trade lit. 31-Contracts awarded 32-Display adv. 33-Classified adv.

11-49

*News*
Day Published: q.
Lead Time: 2 mos. prior to pub. date
Mtls Deadline: 4 mos. prior to pub. date
Contact: National Library Service
Spec. Requirements: 4-16 pgs.; offset; 8
1/2 x 11
Personnel: Vicki Fitzpatrick, Editor

*Update*
Day Published: q.
Lead Time: 2 mos. prior to pub. date
Spec. Requirements: 4-12 pgs.; offset; 8
1/2 x 11
Personnel: Freddie Peaco, Editor

**LIMA MEMORIAL HOSPITAL** ⁴³⁷²
1001 Bellefontaine Ave.
Lima, OH 45804
Telephone: (419) 228-3335
FAX: (419) 226-5128
Industry Affiliation: Hospitals
**Publication(s):**
*Horizons*
Day Published: 10/yr.
Lead Time: 4 wks. prior to pub. date
Mtls Deadline: 1st of mo. prior to pub. date
Spec. Requirements: 12 pg.; offset; 8 1/2
x 11
Personnel: Chris McClure, Editor

*Physician's News*
Day Published: bi-m.
Personnel: Chris McClure, Editor

**LINCOLN ELECTRIC CO., THE** ⁴⁴⁷⁸
22801 St. Clair Ave.
Cleveland, OH 44117
Telephone: (216) 481-8100
Industry Affiliation: Electrical, Electronic,
Manufacturing
**Publication(s):**
*Stabilizer*
Day Published: q.
Lead Time: 30 days prior to pub. date
Mtls Deadline: 30 days prior to pub. date
Spec. Requirements: 16 pg.; offset; 8-1/2
x 11
Personnel: Randy Glassburn, Editor

**LINCOLN NATIONAL CORP.** ³⁰²⁴
200 E. Berry St.
Fort Wayne, IN 46802
Telephone: (219) 455-7512
FAX: (219) 455-2733
Mailing Address:
P.O. Box 7822
Fort Wayne, IN 46801-7822
Industry Affiliation: Insurance
**Publication(s):**
*Reinsurance Reporter*
Day Published: q.
Lead Time: 4 mos. prior to pub. date
Mtls Deadline: 1st of Dec., Mar., June,
Aug.
Contact: Reinsurance Marketing
Spec. Requirements: 20 pg.; offset; 8-1/2
x 11
Personnel: Barbara Wachtman, Editor

**LINCOLN NATIONAL LIFE** ⁶⁸⁶²⁹
**INSURANCE COMPANY**
1300 S. Clinton St.
Fort Wayne, IN 46802
Telephone: (219) 455-2000
FAX: (219) 455-2733
Mailing Address:
P.O. Box 1110
Fort Wayne, IN 46802
Industry Affiliation: Insurance

**Publication(s):**
*Emancipator*
Day Published: m.
Personnel: Cindy Purvis

**LINCOLN TELECOMMUNICATIONS** ³⁷⁸⁸
**CO.**
1440 M
Lincoln, NE 68508
Telephone: (402) 476-4321
FAX: (402) 476-4711
Mailing Address:
P.O. Box 81309
Lincoln, NE 68501
Industry Affiliation: Utility: Telephone
**Publication(s):**
*L T T Magazine*
Day Published: bi-m.
Lead Time: 3 mos. prior to pub. date
Mtls Deadline: 3 mos. prior to pub. date
Spec. Requirements: 16 pgs.; offset mag.;
84 x 11
Personnel: Bob Hoppe, Editor

*Casual Observer*
Day Published: bi-w.
Lead Time: 2 wks. prior to pub. date
Personnel: Kerry Shepherd, Editor

**LINN COUNTY RURAL ELECTRIC** ³¹⁰⁶
**COOPERATIVE ASSOCIATION**
999 35th St.
Marion, IA 52302
Telephone: (319) 377-1587
FAX: (319) 377-5875
Mailing Address:
P.O. Box 69
Marion, IA 52302-0069
Industry Affiliation: Utility: Electric
**Publication(s):**
*Newslines On The Line*
Day Published: m.
Lead Time: 1 mo. prior to pub. date
Mtls Deadline: 1st wk. prior to pub. mo.
Spec. Requirements: 8 pg.; offset; 8-1/2 x
11
Personnel: Phyllis Ann Barber, Editor

**LITTON GUIDANCE & CONTROL** ²¹⁸⁷
**SYSTEMS**
5500 Canoga Ave.
Woodland Hills, CA 91367
Telephone: (818) 712-7225
FAX: (818) 715-2488
Industry Affiliation: Aircraft, Aerospace,
Defense
**Publication(s):**
*Link*
Day Published: m.
Lead Time: 1st of mo. 1 mo. prior to pub.
date
Spec. Requirements: 4-8 pgs.; offset
newspaper; 114 x 164
Personnel: Ron Palmer, Editor

**LOCKHEED ADVANCED** ²³⁰⁵
**DEVELOPMENT CO.**
1011 Lockheed Way, Unit 10
Palmdale, CA 93599-3740
Telephone: (805) 572-4155
FAX: (805) 572-4163
Industry Affiliation: Electrical, Electronic,
Manufacturing

**Publication(s):**
*Star*
Day Published: m.
Lead Time: 8 days prior to pub. date
Mtls Deadline: 8 days prior to pub. date
Contact: Lockheed Advanced Developmt
Co
Spec. Requirements: 8 pg.; offset
newspaper; 11 x 15
Personnel: Jerry Hall, Editor
Patti Thomas
Al Dubiel

**LOCKHEED FORT WORTH CO.** ⁶⁹⁷³³
Mail Zone 1793
P.O. Box 748
Fort Worth, TX 76101
Telephone: (817) 777-5542
FAX: (817) 777-5557
Industry Affiliation: Aircraft, Aerospace,
Defense
**Publication(s):**
*Code One*
Day Published: q.
Personnel: Eric Hehs, Editor

**LOMAS FINANCIAL CORP.** ⁵¹³⁹
1600 Viceroy Dr., 8th Fl.
Dallas, TX 75235
Telephone: (214) 879-4000
Industry Affiliation: Banks, Savings &
Loans
**Publication(s):**
*Newsmakers*
Day Published: m.
Spec. Requirements: 8-12 pg.; offset; 8-
1/2 x 11
Personnel: Barbie Deborah, Editor

**LONE STAR GAS CO.** ⁶⁸⁵⁹¹
301 S. Harwood St., Ste. 130 S
Dallas, TX 75201
Telephone: (214) 670-2968
FAX: (214) 747-1187
Industry Affiliation: Utility: Gas
**Publication(s):**
*Blue Blaze*
Day Published: q.
Personnel: Lisa Geyer, Editor

*In Search Exploration*
Day Published: q.
Personnel: Lisa Geyer, Editor

**LONG BEACH MEMORIAL** ²¹⁹⁸
**MEDICAL CENTER**
2801 Atlantic Ave.
Long Beach, CA 90806
Telephone: (310) 933-2000
Mailing Address:
P.O. Box 1428
Long Beach, CA 90801-1428
Industry Affiliation: Hospitals
**Publication(s):**
*Memorial Mercury*
Day Published: q.
Spec. Requirements: 36-52 pg.; offset; 9 x
12
Personnel: Lori Brandt, Editor

*Challenge*
Day Published: m.
Personnel: Jennifer Merrell

*Scope*
Day Published: m.
Lead Time: 6 wks. prior to pub. date
Mtls Deadline: 6 wks. prior to 1st of mo.

**LONG ISLAND RAILROAD** ⁶⁸⁶¹²
Jamaica Sta.
Jamaica, NY 11435
Telephone: (718) 990-8228
FAX: (718) 990-7633
Industry Affiliation: Railroads

**Publication(s):**
*Along The Track*
Day Published: bi-m.
Personnel: Don Malone

**LONGS DRUG STORES, INC.** ²¹⁸⁹
P.O. Box 5222
Walnut Creek, CA 94596
Telephone: (510) 937-1170
FAX: (510) 210-6997
Industry Affiliation: Drugs, Cosmetics,
Pharmaceuticals
**Publication(s):**
*Chain Reaction*
Day Published: 3/yr.
Spec. Requirements: 24 pg.; offset; 8 1/2
x 11
Personnel: Dianne Clement, Editor

**LORAL DEFENSE SYSTEMS-** ²⁰¹⁷
**AKRON**
1210 Massillon Rd.
Akron, OH 44315-0001
Telephone: (216) 796-8458
FAX: (216) 796-3274
Industry Affiliation: Aircraft, Aerospace,
Defense
**Publication(s):**
*Circuit*
Day Published: m.
Lead Time: 2 wks. prior to pub. date
Materials: 28,30,31
Mtls Deadline: 20th of mo. prior to pub.
date
Contact: Akron Div.
Litchfield Pk., AZ 85340
Spec. Requirements: 4 pg.; offset; 8 1/2 x
11
Personnel: Cary J. Dell, Editor

**LORD CORP.** ⁴⁷¹⁷
2000 W. Grandview Blvd.
Erie, PA 16514
Telephone: (814) 868-0924
Industry Affiliation: Associations: Trade,
Fraternal
**Publication(s):**
*Lordfacts*
Day Published: q.
Lead Time: 2 mos. prior to pub. date
Spec. Requirements: 8 pg.; offset; 11 x 14
Personnel: Carl P. Mann, Editor

**LOS ALMOS NATIONAL** ³⁹²¹
**LABORATORY**
MS-F318
Los Alamos, NM 87545
Telephone: (505) 667-6103
FAX: (505) 665-5552
Mailing Address:
MS-C318
Los Alamos, NM 87545
Industry Affiliation: Colleges, Institutions,
Science Research
**Publication(s):**
*Newsbulletin*
Day Published: 48/yr.
Lead Time: 2 wks. prior to pub. date
Mtls Deadline: 2 wks. prior to pub. date
Spec. Requirements: 8-12 pg.; tabloid;
newsprint
Personnel: Kathy Haq, Editor
Judy Goldie, Managing Editor

**LOS ANGELES COUNTY MEDICAL** ²¹⁹⁰
**ASSOCIATION**
P.O. Box 3465
Los Angeles, CA 90051
Telephone: (213) 483-1581
Industry Affiliation: Hospitals

**Publication(s):**
*L A C M A Physician*
Day Published: 20/yr.
Lead Time: 6 wks. prior to pub. date
Mtls Deadline: 6 wks. prior to pub. date
Spec. Requirements: 48 pg.; offset; 8 1/4 x 11
Personnel: Janice Nagano, Editor

2191
**LOS ANGELES DEPARTMENT OF WATER & POWER**
111 N. Hope St., Rm. 1514
Los Angeles, CA 90012
Telephone: (213) 367-1370
FAX: (213) 367-1434
Mailing Address:
   P.O. Box 111
   Los Angeles, CA 90051
Industry Affiliation: Utility: Water
**Publication(s):**
*Intake Magazine*
Day Published: bi-m.
Lead Time: 1 mo. prior to pub. date
Contact: Public Affairs
Spec. Requirements: 24 pg.; offset; 8 1/2x11
Personnel: Karen Denne, Editor

2192
**LOS ANGELES JR. CHAMBER OF COMMERCE**
404 S. Bixel St.
Los Angeles, CA 90017
Telephone: (213) 482-1311
FAX: (213) 482-0865
Industry Affiliation: Associations: Trade, Fraternal
**Publication(s):**
*Profile*
Day Published: bi-m.
Lead Time: 2 wks. prior to pub. date
Mtls Deadline: 2 wks. prior to pub. date
Spec. Requirements: 4 pg.; offset bulletin; 9 x 11 3/4
Personnel: Marva R. Murphy, Editor

2193
**LOS ANGELES TIMES**
Times Mirror Sq.
Los Angeles, CA 90053
Telephone: (213) 237-5000
Industry Affiliation: Newspapers
**Publication(s):**
*Among Ourselves*
Day Published: m.
Spec. Requirements: 10 pg.
Personnel: Ed Gilbert, Editor

3219
**LOUISIANA BANKERS ASSOCIATION**
666 North St.
Baton Rouge, LA 70802
Telephone: (504) 387-3282
FAX: (504) 343-3159
Mailing Address:
   P.O. Box 2871
   Baton Rouge, LA 70821
Industry Affiliation: Associations: Trade, Fraternal

**Publication(s):**
*Louisiana Banker*
Day Published: s-m.
Lead Time: 2nd to last Fri. of mo. prior to pub. date
Materials: 01
Mtls Deadline: 15th & 30th of each mo. prior to pub. date
Spec. Requirements: 6 pg.; offset; 8 1/2 x 11
Personnel: Heidi Picard, Editor

3243
**LOUISIANA FORESTRY ASSOCIATION**
2316 S. MacArthur Dr.
Alexandria, LA 71301
Telephone: (318) 443-2558
Mailing Address:
   P.O. Drawer 5067
   Alexandria, LA 71307
Industry Affiliation: Associations: Trade, Fraternal
**Publication(s):**
*Forests & People*
Day Published: q.
Lead Time: 3 mos. prior to pub. date
Personnel: Georgiann Gullett, Editor

3224
**LOUISIANA MID-CONTINENT OIL & GAS**
801 North Blvd. Ste 201
Baton Rouge, LA 70802
Telephone: (504) 387-3205
Industry Affiliation: Petroleum, Gas
**Publication(s):**
*L A Oil & Gas Facts*
Day Published: a.
Lead Time: 2 wks.
Mtls Deadline: 2 wks. prior to pub. date

3250
**LOUISIANA PHARMACISTS ASSOCIATION**
P.O. Box 14446
Baton Rouge, LA 70898-4446
Telephone: (504) 767-7115
Industry Affiliation: Associations: Trade, Fraternal
**Publication(s):**
*Louisiana Pharmacist*
Day Published: bi-m.
Spec. Requirements: 24-32 pg.; offset magazine; 8-1/2 x 11
Personnel: Mona Davis, Editor
   Jody Miller, Managing Editor

3249
**LOUISIANA STATE MEDICAL SOCIETY**
3501 N. Causeway Blvd., Ste. 800
Metairie, LA 70002
Telephone: (504) 832-9815
Industry Affiliation: Associations: Health Groups
**Publication(s):**
*Capsules*
Day Published: m.
Lead Time: 2 mos. prior to pub. date
Mtls Deadline: 25th of mo. prior to pub. date
Spec. Requirements: 4-8 pgs.; offset; 8 1/2 x 11
Personnel: Gene Bailey, Editor

*Journal Of The L A State Medical Society*
Day Published: m.
Lead Time: 2 mos. prior to pub. date
Mtls Deadline: 2 mos. prior to pub. daye
Personnel: Gene Bailey

3220
**LOYOLA UNIVERSITY**
6363 St. Charles
New Orleans, LA 70118
Telephone: (504) 865-2295

Mailing Address:
   P.O. Box 195
   New Orleans, LA 70118
Industry Affiliation: Colleges, Institutions, Science Research
**Publication(s):**
*New Orleans Review*
Day Published: 3/yr.
Spec. Requirements: 96 pg; offset; 8 1/2 x 11
Personnel: John Mosier, Editor

3555
**LTV STEEL-MINING CO.**
P.O. Box 847
Hoyt Lakes, MN 55750
Telephone: (218) 225-4215
Industry Affiliation: Industry: Heavy Construction, Machinery
**Publication(s):**
*L T V Times*
Day Published: q.
Spec. Requirements: 6-8 pg.; offset; 11 x 17
Personnel: Charles Mattson, Editor

4373
**LUBRIZOL CORP. THE**
29400 Lakeland Blvd.
Wickliffe, OH 44092
Telephone: (216) 943-4200
FAX: (216) 942-1377
Industry Affiliation: Petroleum, Gas
**Publication(s):**
*Lubrizol Reports*
Day Published: q.
Spec. Requirements: 20-24-page; offset magazine; 8 1/2 x 11
Personnel: Gail S. Rhodes, Editor

*Wick-Life*
Day Published: q.

4718
**LUKENS INC.**
50 S. First Ave.
Coatesville, PA 19320
Telephone: (215) 383-2504
FAX: (215) 383-2440
Mailing Address:
   ARC Bldg. B500, Modena Rd.
   Coatesville, PA 19320-0911
Industry Affiliation: Industry: Heavy Construction, Machinery
**Publication(s):**
*Lukens Life*
Day Published: m.
Lead Time: 3 wks. prior to pub. date
Mtls Deadline: 15th of Mar., May, July, Sep., Nov.
Spec. Requirements: 4 pg.; offset; 11 x 17
Personnel: Debbie Wexler, Editor

3585
**LUTHERAN BROTHERHOOD**
625 Fourth Ave., S.
Minneapolis, MN 55415
Telephone: (612) 340-8589
FAX: (612) 340-8447
Industry Affiliation: Insurance

**Publication(s):**
*Lutheran Brotherhood Bond*
Day Published: q.
Lead Time: 2 mos. prior to pub. date
Materials: 02,05
Mtls Deadline: 3-6 mos. prior to pub. date
Contact: Fraternal & Corp. Pub. Div. Comm.
Spec. Requirements: 24 pg.; 4 color; 8 1/2 x 11
Personnel: Gaelyn Beal, Editor

4375
**LUTHERAN MEDICAL CENTER**
2609 Franklin Blvd.
Cleveland, OH 44113
Telephone: (216) 696-4300
FAX: (216) 363-2282
Industry Affiliation: Colleges, Institutions, Science Research
**Publication(s):**
*Inside Lutheran*
Day Published: m.
Spec. Requirements: 4 pg.; offset; 8 1/2 x 11
Personnel: Jennifer Foye, Editor

5274
**LYNCHBURG GENERAL-MARSHALL LODGE HOSPITALS**
Tate Springs Rd.
Lynchburg, VA 24504
Telephone: (804) 947-3000
FAX: (804) 947-3298
Industry Affiliation: Hospitals
**Publication(s):**
*Centra Health Magazine*
Day Published: q.
Lead Time: 2 mos. prior to pub. date
Mtls Deadline: 2 mos. prior to pub. date
Contact: Fund Development and Community
Spec. Requirements: 8 pg.; offset; 11 x 16
Personnel: Susan Brandt, Editor

66448
**LYONS FALLS PULP & PAPER**
P.O. Box 338
Lyons Falls, NY 13368
Telephone: (315) 348-8411
FAX: (315) 348-8629
Industry Affiliation: Paper Products
**Publication(s):**
*Echoes*
Day Published: q.
Personnel: Mike Virga, Editor

4070
**M & T BANK**
One M & T Plz.
Buffalo, NY 14203
Telephone: (716) 842-5385
FAX: (716) 842-5601
Industry Affiliation: Banks, Savings & Loans
**Publication(s):**
*M & T Observer:*
Day Published: m.
Lead Time: 1 mo.
Mtls Deadline: 10th of mo. prior to pub. date
Spec. Requirements: 8-10-page; offset; 9 1/4 x 12 1/4
Personnel: Jessica Stein Diamond, Editor

3283
**MACHINERY DEALERS NATIONAL ASSOCIATION**
1110 Spring St.
Silver Spring, MD 20910
Telephone: (301) 585-9494
FAX: (301) 588-7830
Industry Affiliation: Associations: Trade, Fraternal

**Materials Accepted/Included:** 01-Business news 02-By-line articles 03-Fashion news 04-Food news 05-Freelance copy 06-Letters to editor 07-Real estate news 08-Sports news 09-Travel news 10-Book rev. 11-Movie rev. 12-Music rev. 13-TV rev. 14-Theater rev. 15-Coming events 16-Obituaries 17-Question & answer 18-Social announcements 19-Artwork 20-Cartoons 21-Photos 22-TV listings 23-Audio rec. 24-Video rec. 25-Books 26-Films/film clips 27-Personnel news 28-Press releases 29-New product news/photos 30-Trade lit. 31-Contracts awarded 32-Display adv. 33-Classified adv.

11-51

**Publication(s):**
*M D N A News*
Day Published: m.
Lead Time: 15th of mo. prior to pub. mo.
Mtls Deadline: 15th of mo. prior to pub. mo.
Spec. Requirements: 8-16 pg.; offset; tabloid 11-1/2 x 15-1/4
Personnel: Lois F. Brand, Editor

### MACK TRUCKS INC.
4794

2100 Mack Blvd.
Allentown, PA 18103-5000
Telephone: (610) 439-3121
FAX: (610) 439-3364
Mailing Address:
   P.O. Box M
   Allentown, PA 18105-5000
Industry Affiliation: Autos, Trucks
**Publication(s):**
*Mack Bulldog*
Day Published: q.
Mtls Deadline: 1st mo. each qtr. prior to pub. date
Spec. Requirements: 32 pg.; offset; 8 1/2 x 11
Personnel: John Mies, Editor
       Robin Crawford, Director

*Macktivities*
Day Published: m.
Personnel: Debbie Morgan

### MAGIC CHEF COMPANY
4876

740 King Edward St.
Cleveland, TN 37320
Telephone: (615) 472-3371
FAX: (615) 478-4680
Mailing Address:
   P.O. Box 2790
   Cleveland, TN 37320-2790
Industry Affiliation: Home Appliances, Furnishings
**Publication(s):**
*Our World*
Day Published: m.
Lead Time: 1 wk. prior to pub. date
Materials: 01,02,04,15,19,20,21,27,28,29
Mtls Deadline: 28th of mo. prior to pub. date
Spec. Requirements: offset tabloid; 11 x 18
Personnel: Pamela Simmons, Editor

### MAINE POTATO BOARD
3256

Agricultural Ctr.
744 Main St., Rm. 1
Presque Isle, ME 04769
Telephone: (207) 769-5061
FAX: (207) 764-4148
Industry Affiliation: Food, General
**Publication(s):**
*Maine Potato News*
Day Published: m.
Lead Time: 3rd wk. of mo. prior to pub. date
Mtls Deadline: 1 mo. prior to pub. date
Spec. Requirements: 16-32 pg.; offset tabloid; 5 col. x 13 col.
Personnel: David R. Lavway, Editor

### MALLINCKRODT MEDICAL, INC.
68390

675 McDonnell Blvd.
St. Louis, MO 63134
Telephone: (314) 895-2000
FAX: (314) 895-2242
Mailing Address:
   P.O. Box 5840
   St. Louis, MO 63134
Industry Affiliation: Associations: Health Groups

**Publication(s):**
*Visions*
Day Published: q.
Lead Time: 1 mo. prior to pub. date
Mtls Deadline: 15th of mo. prior to pub. mo.
Spec. Requirements: 32 pg.; 8 1/2 x 11
Personnel: Pamela A. McGrath, Editor

### MANUFACTURED HOUSING INSTITUTE
5252

1745 Jeff Davis Hwy., Ste. 511
Arlington, VA 22202
Telephone: (703) 413-6620
FAX: (703) 413-6621
Industry Affiliation: Associations: Trade, Fraternal
**Publication(s):**
*M H I Report*
Day Published: bi-w.
Spec. Requirements: 2 pg.; 8 1/2 x 11
Personnel: Patrick U. Di Chiro
       Susan M. Fiske

*Manufacturing Report*
Day Published: m.

*Manufactured Housing Quarterly*
Day Published: q.
Lead Time: 3 mos. prior to pub. date

### MARINE OFFICE OF AMERICA CORP.
4211

1 Continental Dr.
New York, NY 10038
Telephone: (609) 395-2000
Industry Affiliation: Associations: Trade, Fraternal
**Publication(s):**
*Compass*
Day Published: s-a.
Lead Time: 6-7 mos. prior to pub. date
Spec. Requirements: 32 pg.; offset magazine; 8 1/2 x 11
Personnel: Gillian Sterling, Editor

### MARION LABORATORIES, INC.
3698

Marion Park Dr.
Kansas City, MO 64137
Telephone: (816) 966-5000
Mailing Address:
   9300 Ward Pkwy.
   Kansas City, MO 64114
Industry Affiliation: Chemicals, Plastics
**Publication(s):**
*Associate*
Day Published: bi-m.
Spec. Requirements: 4 pg.; offset; 10 x 14

*Image*
Day Published: bi-m.
Spec. Requirements: 4 pg.

### MARION MERRELL DOW INC.
4387

10123 Alliance Rd.
Cincinnati, OH 45242
Telephone: (513) 948-6066
FAX: (513) 948-6087
Industry Affiliation: Associations: Trade, Fraternal
**Publication(s):**
*M M D Exchange*
Day Published: q.
Lead Time: 30 days prior to pub. date
Mtls Deadline: 30 days prior to pub. date
Spec. Requirements: 12 pg. magazine style; offset newspaper; 11 x 15
Personnel: Linda Salvay, Editor
       Becky Carr, Editor

*Time Out*
Day Published: bi-w.
Personnel: Toni T. Sweeney

### MARLEY CO., THE
3155

1900 Shawnee Mission Pkwy.
Shawnee Mission, KS 66205
Telephone: (913) 362-5440
FAX: (913) 432-1451
Industry Affiliation: Cooling, Heating
**Publication(s):**
*Marley Leader*
Day Published: q.
Lead Time: 1 mo. prior to pub. date
Mtls Deadline: 1 mo. prior to pub. date
Contact: Corp. Communs.
Spec. Requirements: 8 pg.; offset; 9-1/4 x 12-1/8
Personnel: Abby Sims, Editor

### MARQUETTE UNIVERSITY
5411

1212 W. Wisconsin Ave.
Milwaukee, WI 53233
Telephone: (414) 288-6712
FAX: (609) 288-6519
Industry Affiliation: Colleges, Institutions
**Publication(s):**
*News & Views*
Day Published: bi-w.
Lead Time: 3 wks. prior to pub. date
Spec. Requirements: offset; tabloid newspaper
Personnel: Cathy Jakick, Editor

*Marquette*
Day Published: q.
Lead Time: 2 mos. prior to pub. date
Personnel: Paul M. McInerny, Editor

### MARSH & MCLENNAN COMPANIES INC.
4073

1166 Ave. of the Americas
New York, NY 10036
Telephone: (212) 345-5000
Industry Affiliation: Associations: Trade, Fraternal
**Publication(s):**
*Viewpoint*
Day Published: q.
Lead Time: 8 wks. prior to pub. date
Personnel: Dong Kingman, Jr., Editor

### MARSHALL & ILSLEY BANK
5412

770 N. Water St.
Milwaukee, WI 53202
Telephone: (414) 765-7700
Industry Affiliation: Banks, Savings & Loans
**Publication(s):**
*Personal Touch*
Day Published: bi-m
Spec. Requirements: 16-24 pgs.; offset; 8 1/2 x 11
Personnel: James Letkiewicz, Editor

### MARTIN MARIETTA ELECTRONICS
2595

5600 Sand Lake Rd.
Orlando, FL 32855
Telephone: (407) 356-2211
Mailing Address:
   P.O. Box 555837, MP-455
   Orlando, FL 32855
Industry Affiliation: Aircraft, Aerospace, Defense

**Publication(s):**
*Vision*
Day Published: m.
Lead Time: 2 wks. prior to pub. date
Mtls Deadline: 2 wks. prior to pub. date
Contact: Public Affairs
Spec. Requirements: 8 pg.; offset; tabloid newspaper
Personnel: Chip Glisson, Editor

### MARYLAND PORT ADMINISTRATION
3307

The World Trade Center
Baltimore, MD 21202
Telephone: (410) 385-4480
FAX: (410) 333-1126
Industry Affiliation: Shipping
**Publication(s):**
*Port Of Baltimore Magazine*
Day Published: m.
Lead Time: 2 mos. prior to pub. date
Materials: 01,02,21,27,28,30,32
Mtls Deadline: 2 mos. prior to pub. date
Contact: Public Affairs
Spec. Requirements: 32 pg.; offset; 8 1/2 x 11
Personnel: Jim Gring, Editor
       Sara Moriarity, Publisher

*Dockside Newsletter*
Day Published: m.
Lead Time: 2 mos. prior to pub. date
Mtls Deadline: 1 mo. prior to pub. date
Contact: Public Affairs
Personnel: Jim Gring
       Rebecca Barber, Editor

### MARYLAND STATE TEACHERS ASSOCIATION
3308

344 N. Charles St.
Baltimore, MD 21201
Telephone: (410) 727-7676
Industry Affiliation: Associations: Trade, Fraternal
**Publication(s):**
*M S T A Action Line*
Day Published: 10/yr.
Lead Time: 2 wks.
Mtls Deadline: 2 wks. prior to pub. date
Contact: Communications
Spec. Requirements: offset tabloid newspaper; no advertising
Personnel: Roger Kuhn, Editor

### MASSACHUSETTS ASSOCIATION OF SCHOOL COMMITTEES
68434

179 South St.
Boston, MA 02111
Telephone: (617) 542-3225
FAX: (617) 542-6313
Industry Affiliation: Colleges, Institutions, Science Research
**Publication(s):**
*M A S C journal*
Day Published: q.
Lead Time: 6 wks. prior to pub. date
Mtls Deadline: 6 wks. prior to pub. date
Personnel: Jenifer Handy

*M A S C Bulletin*
Day Published: bi-m.
Mtls Deadline: 3 wks. prior to pub. date
Personnel: Jenifer Handy

### MASSACHUSETTS MUTUAL LIFE INSURANCE CO.
66446

1295 State St.
Springfield, MA 01111
Telephone: (413) 788-8411
Industry Affiliation: Insurance

**Materials Accepted/Included:** 01-Business news 02-By-line articles 03-Fashion news 04-Food news 05-Freelance copy 06-Letters to editor 07-Real estate news 08-Sports news 09-Travel news 10-Book rev. 11-Movie rev. 12-Music rev. 13-TV rev. 14-Theater rev. 15-Coming events 16-Obituaries 17-Question & answer 18-Social announcements 19-Artwork 20-Cartoons 21-Photos 22-TV listings 23-Audio rec. 24-Video rec. 25-Books 26-Films/film clips 27-Personnel news 28-Press releases 29-New product news/photos 30-Trade lit. 31-Contracts awarded 32-Display adv. 33-Classified adv.

11-52

**Publication(s):**
*Massmutual News*
Day Published: w.
Lead Time: 1 wk. prior to pub. date
Mtls Deadline: 1 wk. prior to pub. date
Contact: Corp. Comms.
Personnel: Anne Ligenza, Editor

**MASTER BUILDERS'**          68368
**ASSOCIATION OF WESTERN**
**PA/AGC**
2270 Noblestown Rd.
Pittsburgh, PA 15205
Telephone: (412) 922-3912
FAX: (412) 922-3729
Industry Affiliation: Architects, Engineers,
   Business Service
**Publication(s):**
*Master Builder*
Day Published: q.
Materials: 01,06,07,30,31
Mtls Deadline: 1st of Dec., Mar., Jun., Sep.
Contact: Public Relations
Personnel: Ann Billak

*Capsule Report*
Day Published: bi-m.
Materials: 01,07,28,30
Mtls Deadline: 7th & 21st of mo. prior to
   pub. date
Personnel: Ann Billak

**MASTER LOCK CO.**          5413
2600 N. 32nd St.
Milwaukee, WI 53210
Telephone: (414) 444-2800
FAX: (414) 449-3193
Industry Affiliation: Industry: Light Tools,
   Equipment
**Publication(s):**
*Master Lock News Today*
Day Published: q.
Spec. Requirements: 28 pgs.; 8 1/2 x 11
Personnel: Richard P. Simons, Editor
   Karl K. Loehrer

**MAXUS ENERGY CORP.**          4330
717 N. Harwood St.
Maxus Energy Twr.
Dallas, TX 75201-6594
Telephone: (214) 956-3284
FAX: (214) 979-1977
Industry Affiliation: Petroleum, Gas
**Publication(s):**
*Energy Exchange*
Day Published: irreg.
Contact: Public Relations Group, Human
   Resources Dept.
Spec. Requirements: 4 pgs. 8 1/2 x 11
Personnel: Tom Sullivan, Editor in Chief
   Maxus Energy Group, Publisher

**MAYTAG CO.**          3110
One Dependability Sq.
Newton, IA 50208
Telephone: (515) 792-7000
Industry Affiliation: Hardware, Plumbing
**Publication(s):**
*Commercial Merchandiser Magazine*
Day Published: bi-m.
Contact: Public Relations Dept.
Spec. Requirements: 8-page
Personnel: Donna Christensen, Advertising
   Manager
   Linda Eggerss

*Merchandiser Magazine*
Day Published: q.
Contact: Public Relations Dept.
Spec. Requirements: 20 pg.
Personnel: Donna Christensen
   Ronald Krajnovich
   Barbara Schei Heki

*Video Merchandiser*
Day Published: q.
Contact: Public Relations Dept.
Personnel: Kurt Funke

*Maytag Monthly Bulletin*
Day Published: m.
Spec. Requirements: 8 1/2 x 11

**MCCORMICK & CO., INC.**          3286
18 Loveton Cir.
Sparks Glenco, MD 21152
Telephone: (410) 771-7803
FAX: (410) 527-8289
Industry Affiliation: Food, General
**Publication(s):**
*Mc Cormick People Newspaper*
Day Published: q.
Lead Time: 2 mos. prior to pub. date

**MCGRAW-HILL INC.**          4076
1221 Ave. of the Americas
29th Fl., Rm. 2917
New York, NY 10020
Telephone: (212) 512-2435
FAX: (212) 512-3050
Industry Affiliation: Publishers, Books,
   Magazines
**Publication(s):**
*Mc Graw-Hill World*
Day Published: bi-w.
Lead Time: 2 wks.
Mtls Deadline: 2 wks. prior to pub. date
Spec. Requirements: 4-8 pg.; offset
   newspaper; 11 x 17
Personnel: Daniel H. Aug., Editor

**MCKESSON CORPORATION**          66447
One Post St., Ste. 3275
San Francisco, CA 94104
Telephone: (415) 983-8416
FAX: (415) 983-7654
Industry Affiliation: Associations: Health
   Groups
**Publication(s):**
*Mc Kesson Today*
Day Published: q.
Materials: 01,02,17,19,20,21,27,29
Contact: Corporate Communications
Spec. Requirements: articles by
   assignment only
Personnel: Joan Kampe, Editor in Chief
   Marvin Krasnansky, Publisher
   Grant Opperman, Editor
   Clara Degen, Production
      Manager
   Mark Coleman, Art Director

**MDU RESOURCES GROUP, INC.**          4279
400 N. Fourth St.
Bismarck, ND 58501-4092
Telephone: (701) 222-7900
Industry Affiliation: Utility: Electric
**Publication(s):**
*Mondakonia*
Day Published: m.
Lead Time: 1 mo. prior to pub. date
Mtls Deadline: 10th of prior mo. to pub.
   date.
Spec. Requirements: 12-24 pg.; offset; 10
   1/2 x 14 1/2
Personnel: Steve Van Dyke, Editor

*Perceprion*
Day Published: q.: Jan., Apr., July, Oct.
Lead Time: 1 mo. prior to pub. date
Mtls Deadline: 1 mo. prior to pub. date.
Spec. Requirements: color; B & W; 150
   line screen
Personnel: Tim Rasmussen, Editor

**MEAD CORPORATION**          4383
Courthouse Plz., N.E.
Dayton, OH 45463
Telephone: (513) 495-6323
Industry Affiliation: Paper Products
**Publication(s):**
*Great News*
Day Published: m.
Spec. Requirements: 4-6 pg.; offset; 8 1/2
   x 11
Personnel: Thomas P. Schwartz, Editor

**MEDIA GENERAL**          65907
333 E. Grace St.
Richmond, VA 23219
Telephone: (804) 649-6000
Mailing Address:
   P.O. Box C-32333
   Richmond, VA 23293
Industry Affiliation: Shipping
**Publication(s):**
*Media General Annual Report*
Day Published: a.
Contact: Robert Pendergast, V.P. of Corp.
   Communications
   Telephone: (804) 649-6103
Personnel: Bill Millsaps, Editor

*M G News*
Day Published: bi-m.
Contact: Robert Pendergast, V.P. Corp.
   Communications
   Telephone: (804) 649-6103
Personnel: Susan Poveromo, Editor

**MEDICAL CENTER OF**          2498
**DELAWARE, THE**
501 W. 14th St.
Wilmington, DE 19801
Telephone: (302) 428-2122
Mailing Address:
   P.O. Box 1668
   Wilmington, DE 19801
Industry Affiliation: Hospitals
**Publication(s):**
*Focus*
Day Published: bi-m.
Lead Time: 10 days prior to pub. date
Mtls Deadline: 10 days prior to pub. date
Personnel: Michele Schiavoni, Editor

**MEDICAL COLLEGE OF**          5415
**WISCONSIN**
8701 Watertown Plank Rd.
Milwaukee, WI 53226-4801
Telephone: (414) 266-4740
FAX: (414) 266-4739 .
Mailing Address:
   P.O. Box 26509
   Milwaukee, WI 53226-4801
Industry Affiliation: Colleges, Institutions,
   Science Research
**Publication(s):**
*Health News*
Day Published: 3/yr.
Lead Time: 3 mos. prior to pub. date
Mtls Deadline: 3 mos. prior to pub. date
Contact: Off. of Pub. Affrs.
Spec. Requirements: 12-16 pgs.; offset; 8
   1/2 x 11
Personnel: Diane Herman, Editor

*Trends*
Day Published: 3/yr.
Lead Time: 3 mos. prior to pub. date
Mtls Deadline: 3 mos. prior to pub. date
Contact: Off. of Pub. Affrs.
Spec. Requirements: articles about MCW
   faculty
Personnel: Carrie A. Wiss, Editor

*M C W Alumni News*
Day Published: 3/yr.
Lead Time: 3 mos. prior to pub. date
Mtls Deadline: 3 mos. prior to pub. date
Contact: Office Public Affairs
Spec. Requirements: 16-20 pgs.; offset; 8
   1/2 x 11
Personnel: Andrea Schneider, Editor

**MEDRAD INC.**          4724
271 Kappa Dr.
Pittsburgh, PA 15238
Telephone: (412) 967-9700
FAX: (412) 963-0859
Industry Affiliation: Electrical, Electronic,
   Manufacturing
**Publication(s):**
*Quality Spotlight*
Day Published: s-a.
Lead Time: 2 mos. prior to pub. date
Mtls Deadline: 2 mos. prior to pub. date

**MELROSE-WAKEFIELD HOSPITAL**          3365
585 Lebanon St.
Melrose, MA 02176
Telephone: (617) 979-3507
Industry Affiliation: Hospitals
**Publication(s):**
*Tablet, The*
Day Published: m.
Spec. Requirements: 4-8 pg. offset
   newspaper; 11 x 14
Personnel: Kelly Carrasio, Editor

**MEMORIAL HEALTHCARE**          5022
**SYSTEM**
7737 Southwest Fwy., Ste. 240
Houston, TX 77074
Telephone: (713) 776-5313
Industry Affiliation: Hospitals
**Publication(s):**
*Caring*
Day Published: 3/yr.
Lead Time: 3 mos. prior to pub. date
Mtls Deadline: 3 mos. prior to pub. date.
Spec. Requirements: 8-12 pg.; offset; 8
   1/2 x 11
Personnel: Karen Kephart, Editor

**MEMORIAL SLOAN-KETTERING**          4077
**CANCER CENTER**
1275 York Ave.
New York, NY 10021
Telephone: (212) 639-3573
Industry Affiliation: Hospitals
**Publication(s):**
*Center News*
Day Published: bi-m.
Spec. Requirements: 8-pg; offset
   newspaper; 11 x 14
Personnel: Debby Rosenberg Bush, Editor

*Center Bulletin*
Day Published: w.
Personnel: Debby Rosenberg Bush, Editor

Materials Accepted/Included: 01-Business news 02-By-line articles 03-Fashion news 04-Food news 05-Freelance copy 06-Letters to editor 07-Real estate news 08-Sports news 09-Travel news
10-Book rev. 11-Movie rev. 12-Music rev. 13-TV rev. 14-Theater rev. 15-Coming events 16-Obituaries 17-Question & answer 18-Social announcements 19-Artwork 20-Cartoons 21-Photos 22-TV listings
23-Audio rec. 24-Video rec. 25-Books 26-Films/film clips 27-Personnel news 28-Press releases 29-New product/photos 30-Trade lit. 31-Contracts awarded 32-Display adv. 33-Classified adv.

11-53

*Annual Report*
Day Published: a.
Personnel: Debby Rosenberg Bush, Editor

**MENTAL HEALTH ASSOCIATION** 4078
**OF ERIE COUNTY INC.**
999 Delaware Ave.
Buffalo, NY 14209
Telephone: (716) 886-1242
FAX: (716) 881-6428
Industry Affiliation: Associations: Health
   Groups
**Publication(s):**
*Today - Mental Health In Your Community*
Day Published: m.
Materials: 02,06,15,20,21,28,30
Mtls Deadline: 10th of mo.
Spec. Requirements: 12 pg.; offset; 15 x
   10 image size
Personnel: Patricia Van Remmen, Editor

**MERCHANTS INSURANCE GROUP** 4079
250 Main St.
Buffalo, NY 14202
Telephone: (716) 849-3333
Industry Affiliation: Associations: Health
   Groups
**Publication(s):**
*Messenger*
Day Published: m.
Spec. Requirements: 4-6 pgs.; offset; 8
   1/2 x 11
Personnel: Robert Baker, Editor

**MERCK & CO., INC.** 3881
One Merck Dr.
Whitehouse Station, NJ 08889-0100
Telephone: (908) 423-1000
Mailing Address:
   P.O. Box 100
   Whithouse Station, NJ 08889-0100
Industry Affiliation: Drugs, Cosmetics,
   Pharmaceuticals
**Publication(s):**
*Merck World*
Day Published: m.
Lead Time: 2 mos. prior to pub. date
Spec. Requirements: 12 pg.; offset
   magapaper; 11 x 14
Personnel: Maria Martino, Editor in Chief
   Kim Bradley, Editor

*Daily, The*
Day Published: d.
Spec. Requirements: 2 pg.; 8 1/2 x 11;
   duplicated 2-color
Personnel: Maria Martino, Editor in Chief
   Sharyn Bearse, Editor

**MERCK & CO. INC.** 4727
Sumnytown Pike
West Point, PA 19486
Telephone: (215) 652-5000
FAX: (215) 652-4283
Mailing Address:
   Mail Code 37 C 1
   West Point, PA 19486
Industry Affiliation: Drugs, Cosmetics,
   Pharmaceuticals
**Publication(s):**
*Field Extract*
Day Published: bi-w.
Spec. Requirements: 4 pg.
Personnel: Madeleine Kaye, Editor

*Front Line*
Day Published: q.
Spec. Requirements: 32 pg.
Personnel: Madeleine Kaye, Editor

**MERCY HOSPITAL** 3112
500 E. Market St.
Iowa City, IA 52245
Telephone: (319) 339-0300
FAX: (319) 339-3788
Industry Affiliation: Hospitals
**Publication(s):**
*Forefront*
Day Published: q.
Lead Time: 6 wks. prior to pub. date
Spec. Requirements: 4 pg.; offset; 8 1/2 x
   11
Personnel: Denice Connell, Editor

**MERCY HOSPITAL, INC.** 4251
2001 Vail Ave.
Charlotte, NC 28207
Telephone: (704) 379-5000
FAX: (704) 379-6045
Industry Affiliation: Hospitals
**Publication(s):**
*Stat Sheet, The*
Day Published: w.
Lead Time: 2 wks. prior to pub. date
Mtls Deadline: 2 wks. prior to pub. date
Spec. Requirements: 6 pg; offset; 8 1/2 x
   11
Personnel: Angie Scarlett, Editor

*On Call*
Day Published: m.
Lead Time: 30 days prior to pub. date
Mtls Deadline: 30 days prior to pub. date
Spec. Requirements: 2 pgs.
Personnel: Barbara B. Lockman, Editor

**MERCY MEDICAL CENTER** 3288
301 St. Paul Pl.
Baltimore, MD 21202
Telephone: (410) 332-9239
FAX: (410) 685-7469
Industry Affiliation: Hospitals
**Publication(s):**
*Tower Talk*
Day Published: m.
Contact: Public Relations
Spec. Requirements: 8-Page; Offset
   Magazine; 8 1/2 X 11
Personnel: Peg Benzinger, Editor

*Mercy Physician, The*
Day Published: bi-m.
Contact: Public Relations
Spec. Requirements: 6 pg; 8-1/2 x 11
Personnel: Peg Benzinger, Editor

*Mercy Life*
Day Published: m.
Mtls Deadline: 1st of mo.
Contact: Public Relations
Spec. Requirements: 8 pg; magazine; 8-
   1/2 x 12
Personnel: Peg Benzinger, Editor

*Mercy Today*
Day Published: w.
Spec. Requirements: 2 pg; 8-1/2 x 11
Personnel: Peg Benzinger, Editor

*Spirit*
Day Published: q.
Personnel: Tom Hooper, Editor

**MEREDITH CORP.** 3114
1716 Locust St.
Des Moines, IA 50309-3023
Telephone: (515) 284-2059
FAX: (515) 284-3153
Industry Affiliation: Radio, TV, Movies

**Publication(s):**
*Insider*
Day Published: 10/yr.
Lead Time: 2 mos. prior to pub. date
Materials: 01,10,20
Mtls Deadline: 2 mos. prior to pub. date
Spec. Requirements: 16 pg.; offset
   magazine; 11 x 14
Personnel: Kathi Woods, Editor

**MEREDITH GRAPHICS, INC.** 4386
1231 E. 286th St.
Cleveland, OH 44132
Telephone: (216) 261-6333
FAX: (216) 261-3961
Industry Affiliation: Printers, Services
**Publication(s):**
*Graphicopy*
Day Published: q.
Spec. Requirements: 4 pg.; offset
   newsletter; 8 1/2 x 11
Personnel: K.L. Meredith, Editor

**MERIDIAN BANK** 4631
35 N. Sixth St.
Reading, PA 19601
Telephone: (215) 655-2499
Mailing Address:
   P.O. Box 1102
   Reading, PA 19603
Industry Affiliation: Banks, Savings &
   Loans
**Publication(s):**
*Dialog*
Day Published: bi-m.
Lead Time: 1 mo. prior to pub. date
Mtls Deadline: end of Feb., May, Aug.,
   Nov.
Contact: Corporate Communications Div.
   431 Penn St.
   Reading, PA 19601
Spec. Requirements: 16 pg; offset; 8 1/2 x
   11
Personnel: Carlene Rozzi, Editor

**MERRILL LYNCH & CO., INC.** 66561
World Financial Ctr., S. Tower
New York, NY 10080
Telephone: (212) 449-1000
FAX: (212) 236-8005
Industry Affiliation: Finance, Services
**Publication(s):**
*We The People*
Day Published: 10/yr.
Lead Time: 4-6 wks. prior to pub. date
Personnel: Brian Thomas, Editor

**METHODIST HOSPITAL** 3589
6500 Excelsior Blvd.
Minneapolis, MN 55426
Telephone: (612) 932-6058
FAX: (612) 932-5936
Mailing Address:
   P.O. Box 650
   Minneapolis, MN 55440
Industry Affiliation: Associations: Trade,
   Fraternal

**Publication(s):**
*Advances*
Day Published: q.
Lead Time: 2 mos. prior to pub. mo.
Mtls Deadline: 1 mo. prior to pub. date
Spec. Requirements: 12 or 16 pg.; offset;
   11 x 17
Personnel: Eileen Smith, Editor
   Jim Bayer, Staff Writer
   Donna Morton
   Chris Reynolds

**METHODIST HOSPITAL** 4081
506 Sixth St.
Brooklyn, NY 11215
Telephone: (718) 780-3000
FAX: (718) 780-3372
Industry Affiliation: Hospitals
**Publication(s):**
*Today*
Day Published: q.
Spec. Requirements: 6 pg.; offset; 8 1/2 x
   11
Personnel: Lyn Hill, Editor

**METHODIST HOSPITALS OF** 5025
**DALLAS**
1441 N. Beckley
Dallas, TX 75203
Telephone: (214) 944-2393
Mailing Address:
   P.O. Box 655999
   Dallas, TX 75625
Industry Affiliation: Hospitals
**Publication(s):**
*Outlook*
Day Published: m.
Lead Time: 4 wks. prior to pub. date
Mtls Deadline: 4 wks. prior to pub. date
Spec. Requirements: 12 pg.; offset; 8 1/2
   x 11
Personnel: Laurie Ponder, Editor

**METHODIST HOSPITAL, THE** 5024
6565 Fannin, MS-131
Houston, TX 77030
Telephone: (713) 790-2795
Industry Affiliation: Associations: Trade,
   Fraternal
**Publication(s):**
*Journal, The*
Day Published: q.
Lead Time: 4 mos. prior to pub. date
Mtls Deadline: 3 mos. prior to pub. date
Contact: Public Affairs
Spec. Requirements: 32 pg.; offset; 8-1/2
   x 11
Personnel: Kathleen Much, Editor
   Nancy Brown

*Methodist Hospital Happenings*
Day Published: m.
Lead Time: 6 wks. prior to pub. date
Mtls Deadline: 1st of mo. prior to pub. date
Contact: Public Affairs
Personnel: Kathleen Much, Editor
   Nancy Brown

**METRO CREATIVE GRAPHICS,** 4082
**INC.**
33 W. 34th St.
New York, NY 10001
Telephone: (212) 947-5100
FAX: (212) 967-4602
Industry Affiliation: Advertising, Art, Public
   Relations

**Materials Accepted/Included:** 01-Business news 02-By-line articles 03-Fashion news 04-Food news 05-Freelance copy 06-Letters to editor 07-Real estate news 08-Sports news 09-Travel news 10-Book rev. 11-Movie rev. 12-Music rev. 13-TV rev. 14-Theater rev. 15-Coming events 16-Obituaries 17-Question & answer 18-Social announcements 19-Artwork 20-Cartoons 21-Photos 22-TV listings 23-Audio rec. 24-Video rec. 25-Books 26-Films/film clips 27-Personnel news 28-Press releases 29-New product news/photos 30-Trade lit. 31-Contracts awarded 32-Display adv. 33-Classified adv.

**Publication(s):**
*Metro's Plus Business*
Day Published: m.
Lead Time: 4 mos.
Mtls Deadline: 4 mos. prior to pub. date
Spec. Requirements: 12 pg.; offset
   magazine; 8.5 x 11
Personnel: Maria Manliclic, Editor
   Joan Seittelman
   Nancee B. Kukich

68560
**METROPOLITAN LIFE INSURANCE CO.**
1 Madison Ave.
New York, NY 10010
Telephone: (212) 578-7466
FAX: (212) 679-5621
Industry Affiliation: Insurance
**Publication(s):**
*Forum Magazine*
Day Published: bi-m.
Personnel: Mike Dynan, Editor
   Lisa Tishler, Editor

5417
**METROPOLITAN MILWAUKEE ASSOCIATION OF COMMERCE**
756 N. Milwaukee St.
Milwaukee, WI 53202-3767
Telephone: (414) 287-4100
Industry Affiliation: Associations: City,
   State, Federal
**Publication(s):**
*Milwaukee Commerce Hotline*
Day Published: 3/mo.
Lead Time: 4 wks. prior to pub. date
Mtls Deadline: 4 wks. prior to pub. date
Contact: Communications
Spec. Requirements: 8 pg.; offset; 8-1/2 x
   11
Personnel: Ann Dee Allen, Editor

*Membership Directory*
Day Published: a.
Materials: 32
Spec. Requirements: members only

3790
**METROPOLITAN UTILITIES DISTRICT**
1723 Harney St.
Omaha, NE 68102
Telephone: (402) 449-8157
FAX: (702) 554-7929
Industry Affiliation: Utility: Related
**Publication(s):**
*Taps & Jets*
Day Published: q.
Lead Time: 1 mo. prior to pub. date
Mtls Deadline: 1 mo. prior to pub. date
Contact: Public Relations
Spec. Requirements: 4 pg.; offset; 22 x 17
Personnel: Mari Matulka, Editor

68631
**MIAMI SYSTEMS-SHELBY DIVISION**
40 High School Ave.
Shelby, OH 44875
Telephone: (419) 342-3515
FAX: (419) 347-8330
Industry Affiliation: Paper Products
**Publication(s):**
*Miami Systems Family News & People
Report*
Day Published: bi-m.
Spec. Requirements: 20-30 pgs; offset; 8-
   1/2 x 11
Personnel: Margaret Myers, Editor

4389
**MIAMI VALLEY HOSPITAL**
1 Wyoming St.
Dayton, OH 45409
Telephone: (513) 223-6192
Industry Affiliation: Hospitals

**Publication(s):**
*Insider*
Day Published: bi-w.
Lead Time: 2 wks. prior to pub. date
Mtls Deadline: 1 mo. prior to pub. date
Spec. Requirements: 12 pg.; offset; 11 1/2
   x 17
Personnel: Teri Holmes, Editor

*Pro Health Magazine*
Day Published: q.
Lead Time: 3 mos. prior to pub. date
Personnel: Ian Kaufman, Editor

2885
**MICHAEL REESE HOSPITAL & MEDICAL CENTER**
Lake Shore Dr. & 31st St.
Chicago, IL 60616
Telephone: (312) 791-2000
Industry Affiliation: Hospitals
**Publication(s):**
*Michael Reese News*
Day Published: bi-m.
Lead Time: 4 wks. prior to pub. date
Mtls Deadline: 4 wks. prior to pub. date
Spec. Requirements: 12 pg.; offset; 11 x
   17

4084
**MICHELIN NORTH AMERICA, INC.**
One Parkway, S.
Greenville, SC 29615
Telephone: (803) 458-5000
Mailing Address:
   P.O. Box 19001
   Greenville, SC 29602
Industry Affiliation: Rubber, Tires
**Publication(s):**
*Bib America*
Day Published: q.
Contact: Commercial
Spec. Requirements: 8 pg. offset; 8 1/2 x
   17
Personnel: Jim Billig, Editor
   Paige Lockridge

*Michelin Radial Times*
Day Published: q.
Personnel: Bill Pattrtson, Editor
   Kevin Clemens

3479
**MICHIGAN BELL TELEPHONE CO.**
1365 Cass, Ste. 1812
Detroit, MI 48226
Telephone: (313) 223-7250
FAX: (313) 496-9337
Industry Affiliation: Utility: Telephone
**Publication(s):**
*Tie Lines*
Day Published: s-m.
Spec. Requirements: 8 pg.; offset; 11 1/2
   x 14 1/2
Personnel: Tom Andrew, Editor

3474
**MICHIGAN CAPITAL HEALTHCARE**
2727 S. Pennsylvania Ave.
Lansing, MI 48910-3490
Telephone: (517) 374-2693
FAX: (517) 487-2100
Industry Affiliation: Hospitals

**Publication(s):**
*Connection, The*
Day Published: w.
Lead Time: 1 wk. prior to pub. date
Materials: 01,02,06,17,20,21,27,28,29,33
Mtls Deadline: 1 wk. prior to pub. date
Spec. Requirements: 4-6 pg.; tabloid
Personnel: Greg Melvin, Editor
   Chris Henning, Managing Editor
   Mark Holoweiko, Director

3517
**MICHIGAN EMPLOYMENT SECURITY COMMISSION**
7310 Woodward, Rm. 612
Detroit, MI 48202
Telephone: (313) 876-5488
Industry Affiliation: Associations: City,
   State, Federal
**Publication(s):**
*M E S C Messenger*
Day Published: m.
Lead Time: 6-8 wks. prior to pub. date
Mtls Deadline: 6-8 wks. prior to pub. date
Contact: Pub. Inform. Svcs. Div.
Spec. Requirements: 12 pg.; offset; 8 1/2
   x 11
Personnel: Frank Lee, Editor
   Ann Costa, Editor

3481
**MICHIGAN MILK PRODUCERS ASSOCIATION**
P.O. Box 8002
Novi, MI 48376
Telephone: (810) 474-6672
FAX: (810) 474-0924
Industry Affiliation: Associations: Trade,
   Fraternal
**Publication(s):**
*Michigan Milk Messenger*
Day Published: m.
Lead Time: 30 days prior to pub. date
Mtls Deadline: 5th of mo. prior to pub. date
Spec. Requirements: 28-36 pg.; 8 1/2 x 11
Personnel: Laura Child, Editor

3482
**MICHIGAN MUTUAL INSURANCE CO.**
28 W. Adams Ave.
Detroit, MI 48226
Telephone: (313) 965-8600
Industry Affiliation: Insurance
**Publication(s):**
*Hand In Hand*
Day Published: bi-m.
Mtls Deadline: 1 wk.-1 mo. prior to
   typesetting
Contact: Adv.
Spec. Requirements: 16-24 pg.; offset
   magazine; 84 x 11
Personnel: Judith J. Willis, Editor
   Donald A. Wozniak

*Safety News, The*
Day Published: q.
Mtls Deadline: 1 wk.-1 mo. prior to
   typesetting
Contact: Adv.
Spec. Requirements: 4 pg.
Personnel: Judith Willis, Editor

3483
**MICHIGAN STATE UNIVERSITY**
Dept. of Communication, Michigan State
   Univ.
East Lansing, MI 48824
Telephone: (517) 355-1855
FAX: (517) 336-1192
Industry Affiliation: Colleges, Institutions,
   Science Research

**Publication(s):**
*Source*
Day Published: m.
Contact: Personnel & Employee Relations
   40 Nisbet Bldg.
   East Lansing, MI 48824
Spec. Requirements: 8 pg.; offset; 8-1/2 x
   11

*M S U Manual Of Personnel Policies And
Programs*
Spec. Requirements: 8 pg.

3524
**MICHIGAN TRUCKING ASSOCIATION**
5800 Executive Dr.
Lansing, MI 48911
Telephone: (517) 393-2053
FAX: (517) 393-1120
Industry Affiliation: Associations: Trade,
   Fraternal
**Publication(s):**
*Today*
Day Published: m.
Lead Time: 2 wks. prior to pub. date
Mtls Deadline: 1st of mo. prior to pub. date
Spec. Requirements: 16 pg.; offset; 8 1/2
   x 11
Personnel: Nancy Aurand, Editor

3704
**MID-AMERICA DAIRYMEN INC.**
3253 E. Chestnut Expy.
Springfield, MO 65802
Telephone: (417) 865-7100
Industry Affiliation: Associations: Trade,
   Fraternal
**Publication(s):**
*Mid-Am Reporter*
Day Published: m.
Lead Time: 1 mo. prior to pub. date
Mtls Deadline: 1 mo. prior to pub. date
Contact: Corp. Hdqtrs.
Spec. Requirements: 24 pg.; offset; tabloid
Personnel: Lydia Decarlis, Communications
   Director

*Mid-Am Processor (for Employees)*
Day Published: m.
Lead Time: 1 mo. prior to pub. date
Mtls Deadline: 1 mo. prior to pub. date
Spec. Requirements: tabloid
Personnel: Lydia DeCarlis,
   Communications Director

*Annual Report*
Day Published: a.
Lead Time: 2 mos. prior to pub. date
Mtls Deadline: 2 mos. prior to pub. date
Personnel: Forrest Bradley
   Lydia Decarlis
   Dan Reuwee, Communications
   Director

4391
**MIDLAND MUTUAL LIFE INSURANCE CO.**
250 E. Broad St.
Columbus, OH 43215
Telephone: (614) 228-2001
Industry Affiliation: Insurance
**Publication(s):**
*Achiever*
Day Published: m.
Lead Time: 2-3 wks. prior to pub. date
Mtls Deadline: 3 wks. prior to pub. date
Spec. Requirements: 4-6 pg.; offset; 10 x
   14
Personnel: Mary Pollman, Editor

3882
**MIDLANTIC CORPORATION**
Metropark Plz.
Edison, NJ 08818
Telephone: (908) 321-8294
FAX: (908) 321-2636

---

**Materials Accepted/Included:** 01-Business news 02-By-line articles 03-Fashion news 04-Food news 05-Freelance copy 06-Letters to editor 07-Real estate news 08-Sports news 09-Travel news 10-Book rev. 11-Movie rev. 12-Music rev. 13-TV rev. 14-Theater rev. 15-Coming events 16-Obituaries 17-Question & answer 18-Social announcements 19-Artwork 20-Cartoons 21-Photos 22-TV listings 23-Audio rec. 24-Video rec. 25-Books 26-Films/film clips 27-Personnel news 28-Press releases 29-New product news/photos 30-Trade lit. 31-Contracts awarded 32-Display adv. 33-Classified adv.

11-55

Mailing Address:
P.O. Box 600
Edison, NJ 08818
Industry Affiliation: Banks, Savings &
Loans
**Publication(s):**
*Midlantic Today*
Day Published: m.
Materials: 01
Contact: Corporate Communications
Spec. Requirements: 8 pg; magapaper; 11
x 14
Personnel: Barbara Maddox, Editor

**MIDWEST RESEARCH INSTITUTE**   3705
425 Volker Blvd.
Kansas City, MO 64110
Telephone: (816) 753-7600
Industry Affiliation: Colleges, Institutions,
Science Research
**Publication(s):**
*Mrinside*
Day Published: m.
Personnel: Mary Walker, Editor

*F Y I*
Day Published: w.
Personnel: Mary Lou Lillis, Editor

*Annual Report*
Day Published: a.

*Midwest Focus*
Day Published: 3-4/yr.
Personnel: Mary Lou Lillis, Editor

**MIDWEST RESOURCES INC.**   3134
P.O. Box 657
Des Moines, IA 50303
Telephone: (515) 281-2222
FAX: (515) 242-4250
Industry Affiliation: Utility: Electric
**Publication(s):**
*Teamworks*
Day Published: m.
Lead Time: 3 wks. prior to pub. date
Mtls Deadline: 3 wks. prior to pub. date
Contact: Pub. Rels. Dept.
Spec. Requirements: 6-8 pg.; offset; 8 1/2
x 11
Personnel: Kelly Sankey, Editor

**MILES, INC.**   3030
One Mellon Ctr.
500 Grant St.
Pittsburgh, PA 15219-2507
Telephone: (412) 394-5504
FAX: (412) 394-5586
Industry Affiliation: Chemicals, Plastics
**Publication(s):**
*Update*
Day Published: q.
Lead Time: 1 1/2 mos. prior to pub. date
Spec. Requirements: 12 pg.; offset tabloid
newspaper; 11 x 15
Personnel: Gregory Coffey, Editor
Elizabeth S. Lott, Ph.D.

**MILK MARKET ADMINISTRATOR**   3484
2684 W. 11th Mile Rd.
Berkley, MI 48072
Telephone: (313) 548-1603
Industry Affiliation: Dairy Products

**Publication(s):**
*Market Administrator's Bulletin*
Day Published: m.
Lead Time: 1 mo. prior to pub. date
Spec. Requirements: 8 pg.; offset bulletin;
8 1/2 x 11
Personnel: Terri Gerhardt, Editor

**MILLER BREWING CO.**   5419
3939 W. Highland Blvd.
Milwaukee, WI 53208
Telephone: (414) 931-2000
Industry Affiliation: Brewers, Distillers
**Publication(s):**
*Miller High-Lites*
Day Published: m.
Lead Time: 5 wks. prior to pub. date
Mtls Deadline: 1st of mo. prior to pub. date
Contact: Communications
Personnel: Eileen Hammer, Managing
Editor
Robert Peacock, Editor

*Frontline*
Day Published: bi-m.
Lead Time: 6 wks. prior to pub. date
Mtls Deadline: 10th of mo. prior to pub.
date
Contact: Communications
Spec. Requirements: 24 pg.; offset
magazine; 12 x 9 1/4
Personnel: Janet M. Gottfredsen
Karen J. Birk
Linda Bryson
Mahin Motamedi
Jeff Waalkes, Editor

*Principal*
Day Published: q.
Lead Time: 2 mos. prior to pub. date
Mtls Deadline: 2 mos. prior to pub. date
Personnel: Jeff Waalkes, Editor

**MILLS-PENINSULA HOSPITALS**   2219
1783 El Camino Real
Burlingame, CA 94010
Telephone: (415) 696-5400
FAX: (415) 696-5374
Industry Affiliation: Hospitals
**Publication(s):**
*Healthpoint (community Newsletter)*
Day Published: q.
Lead Time: 2 mos. prior to pub. date
Mtls Deadline: 2 mos. prior to pub. date
Spec. Requirements: 12 pg.; offset; 11 x
17
Personnel: Margie O'Claire, Editor

**MILTON BRADLEY CO.**   3366
443 Shaker Rd.
East Longmeadow, MA 01028
Telephone: (413) 525-6411
FAX: (413) 525-4365
Industry Affiliation: Toys, Crafts
**Publication(s):**
*Milton Bradley News*
Day Published: m.
Materials: 21,27,29
Mtls Deadline: 15th of mo. prior to pub.
date
Contact: Sharon Mello Reis

**MINING & SPECIALTY EQUIP. DIV.**   4379
**OF INDRESCO, INC., MARION**
**OPERATIONS**
617 W. Center St.
Marion, OH 43302
Telephone: (614) 383-5211
FAX: (614) 382-2052
Mailing Address:
P.O. Box 505
Marion, OH 43301-0505
Industry Affiliation: Industry: Heavy
Construction, Machinery

**Publication(s):**
*News & Review*
Day Published: q.
Lead Time: 1 mo. prior to pub. date
Contact: Marion Operations
Spec. Requirements: 8 pg.; offset; 9 x 12
Personnel: Tom Lusch, Editor

**MINNESOTA DEPARTMENT OF**   3634
**TRANSPORTATION**
395 John Ireland Blvd., Rm. 404
St. Paul, MN 55155
Telephone: (612) 296-1411
Industry Affiliation: Associations: City,
State, Federal
**Publication(s):**
*Express*
Day Published: 10/yr.
Lead Time: 2 mos. prior to pub. date
Mtls Deadline: 1st of mo. prior to pub. date
Contact: Commun. & Media Svcs.
Spec. Requirements: 4 pg.; offset; 11 x 17
Personnel: Michael Stirens, Editor

**MINNESOTA MUTUAL LIFE**   3636
**INSURANCE CO.**
400 N. Robert St.
St. Paul, MN 55101
Telephone: (612) 298-3500
Industry Affiliation: Insurance
**Publication(s):**
*Excel*
Day Published: m.
Lead Time: 1 mo. prior to pub. date
Spec. Requirements: 36 pg.
Personnel: Peter Stathopoulos, Editor

*Extra*
Day Published: m.
Lead Time: 1 mo. prior to pub. date

**MINNESOTA POWER**   66562
30 W. Superior St.
Duluth, MN 55802
Telephone: (218) 722-2641
FAX: (218) 723-3983
Industry Affiliation: Utility: Electric
**Publication(s):**
*Contact*
Day Published: m.
Lead Time: 1 mo. prior to pub. date
Materials: 01,02,06,10,17,19,20,21,27,29
Mtls Deadline: 2nd wk. of mo. prior to pub.
date

**MINNESOTA SOCIETY OF**   3638
**CERTIFIED PUBLIC**
**ACCOUNTANTS**
7900 Xerxes Ave., S., Ste. 1230
Minneapolis, MN 55431
Telephone: (612) 831-2707
FAX: (612) 831-7875
Industry Affiliation: Associations: Trade,
Fraternal
**Publication(s):**
*Footnote*
Day Published: m.
Lead Time: 1st of mo. prior to pub. mo.
Materials: 02,28,32,33
Mtls Deadline: 1st of mo. prior to pub. mo.
Contact: Communications
Spec. Requirements: 24 pg.; offset; 8-1/2
x 11
Personnel: Lissa Reitz, Editor

**MINNESOTA STATE COUNCIL ON**   3594
**DISABILITY**
121 E. Seventh St., Ste. 107
St. Paul, MN 55101
Telephone: (612) 296-6785
Industry Affiliation: Associations: City,
State, Federal

**Publication(s):**
*Connector*
Day Published: q.
Lead Time: 2 wks. prior to pub. date
Mtls Deadline: 15th of mo. prior to pub.
date
Spec. Requirements: 8 pg.; offset; 8 1/2 x
11
Personnel: Tom Brick, Editor

**MIRRO CORP.**   5424
1512 Washington St.
Manitowoc, WI 54220
Telephone: (414) 684-4421
FAX: (414) 684-1929
Mailing Address:
P.O. Box 1330
Manitowoc, WI 54221-1330
Industry Affiliation: Aluminum
**Publication(s):**
*Mixing Bowl, The*
Day Published: bi-m.
Lead Time: 2 wks. prior to pub. date
Spec. Requirements: 16 pg.; offset
magazine; 8 1/2 X 11
Personnel: Cindee Vogel, Editor

**MISSISSIPPI BAPTIST MEDICAL**   3648
**CENTER**
1225 N. State St.
Jackson, MS 39202
Telephone: (601) 968-5135
FAX: (601) 968-4137
Industry Affiliation: Hospitals
**Publication(s):**
*Healthcaring*
Day Published: q.
Spec. Requirements: 12 pg.; offset; 8 1/2
x 11
Personnel: Jean B. May, Editor
Laura Jones, Associate Editor

**MISSISSIPPI CHEMICAL CORP.**   3652
P.O. Box 388
Yazoo City, MS 39194
Telephone: (601) 746-4131
FAX: (601) 746-9158
Industry Affiliation: Agriculture, Services
**Publication(s):**
*Conveyor*
Day Published: bi-m.
Lead Time: 2 wks. prior to pub. date
Materials: 01,15,16,18,21,27
Contact: Communications
Spec. Requirements: 16 pgs.; 8 1/2 x 11
Personnel: Wendy Weathersby, Editor

*Profitline*
Day Published: m.
Lead Time: 1 wk. prior to pub. date
Materials: 01,02
Contact: Marketing & Sales
Spec. Requirements: 4 pgs.; 8 1/2 x 11
Personnel: Wendy Weathersby, Editor
Tommy Thompson, Marketing
Director

*Shareholder Update*
Day Published: q.
Lead Time: 1 wk. prior to pub. date
Materials: 01
Contact: Stock
Spec. Requirements: 4 pgs.; 8 1/2 x 11
Personnel: Wendy Weathersby, Editor
Rosalyn Glascoe, Marketing
Director

**Materials Accepted/Included:** 01-Business news 02-By-line articles 03-Fashion news 04-Food news 05-Freelance copy 06-Letters to editor 07-Real estate news 08-Sports news 09-Travel news 10-Book rev. 11-Movie rev. 12-Music rev. 13-TV rev. 14-Theater rev. 15-Coming events 16-Obituaries 17-Question & answer 18-Social announcements 19-Artwork 20-Cartoons 21-Photos 22-TV listings 23-Audio rec. 24-Video rec. 25-Books 26-Films/film clips 27-Personnel news 28-Press releases 29-New product news/photos 30-Trade lit. 31-Contracts awarded 32-Display adv. 33-Classified adv.

*Dockside News*
Day Published: bi-m.
Materials: 01,15,16,18,19,21
Contact: Corporate Communications
Spec. Requirements: 4 pgs.; 8 1/2 x 11
Personnel: Wendy Weathersby, Editor

**MISSISSIPPI POWER & LIGHT CO.** 3654
308 E. Pearl St.
Jackson, MS 39201
Telephone: (601) 969-2330
FAX: (609) 969-4878
Mailing Address:
P.O. Box 1640
Jackson, MS 39215
Industry Affiliation: Utility: Electric
**Publication(s):**
*Mp & L News*
Day Published: m.
Lead Time: 3 wks. prior to pub. date
Mtls Deadline: 10th of mo. prior to pub. date
Contact: Publications
Spec. Requirements: 24 pg.; offset magazine; 84 x 11
Personnel: Beth Moore, Editor

*Helping Build Mississippi*
Day Published: s-a.
Lead Time: 3 mos. prior to pub. date
Mtls Deadline: Feb 1st & July 1st
Contact: Publications
Spec. Requirements: 36 pg.; 4-color magazine
Personnel: Checky Herrington

**MISSISSIPPI POWER CO.** 3655
2992 W. Beach Blvd.
Gulfport, MS 39501
Telephone: (601) 864-1211
FAX: (601) 865-5771
Mailing Address:
P.O. Box 4079
Gulfport, MS 39502
Industry Affiliation: Utility: Electric
**Publication(s):**
*Powerlines*
Day Published: bi-m.
Lead Time: 45 days prior to pub. date
Spec. Requirements: 28 pg.; offset; 8 1/2 x 11
Personnel: Teresa Taylor, Editor

*Dialogue*
Day Published: w.
Lead Time: 1 wk. prior to pub. date
Mtls Deadline: Mon. prior to pub. date
Spec. Requirements: 4 pg.; 8 1/2 x 11
Personnel: Sharon Ward, Editor
Teresa Taylor
Tim Foley

**MISSOURI FARM BUREAU FEDERATION** 3756
P.O. Box 658
Jefferson, MO 65102
Telephone: (314) 893-1400
Industry Affiliation: Associations: City, State, Federal
**Publication(s):**
*Missouri Farm Bureau News*
Day Published: 9/yr.
Lead Time: 1 mo. prior to pub. date
Mtls Deadline: 1 mo. prior to pub. date
Spec. Requirements: 12-24 pg.; 10 1/4 x 11 1/4
Personnel: Chris Fennewald, Editor

**MITCHELL ENERGY & DEVELOPMENT CORP.** 5028
2001 Timberloch Pl.
The Woodlands, TX 77380
Telephone: (713) 377-5661
FAX: (713) 377-5802

Mailing Address:
P.O. Box 4000
The Woodlands, TX 77387
Industry Affiliation: Real Estate
**Publication(s):**
*Terrasol*
Day Published: bi-m.
Lead Time: 1 mo. prior to pub. date
Mtls Deadline: 1 mo. prior to pub. date
Contact: Public Affairs
Spec. Requirements: 12 pg.; offset; 8-1/2 x 11; B & W
Personnel: Patrick Cassidy, Editor

**MITRE CORP.** 3367
Burlington Rd.
Bedford, MA 01730
Telephone: (617) 271-2000
FAX: (617) 271-2185
Industry Affiliation: Electrical, Electronic, Manufacturing
**Publication(s):**
*Mitre Matters*
Day Published: bi-m.
Lead Time: 1 mo. prior to pub. date
Mtls Deadline: 3 wks. prior to pub. date
Spec. Requirements: 4-6 pg.; offset; 11 1/2 x 17
Personnel: Maryanne Connors, Editor
Pamela Mehos

*Bulletin, The*
Day Published: w.
Lead Time: 1 wk. prior to pub. date
Mtls Deadline: 1 wk. prior to pub. date
Personnel: Pamela Mehos
Fran Jonuskis, Editor

*Centerspread*
Day Published: w.
Lead Time: 1 wk. prior to pub. date
Mtls Deadline: 1 wk. prior to pub. date
Personnel: Jeff Livesay, Editor

**MNC FINANCIAL, INC.** 3306
100 S. Charles St.
Baltimore, MD 21201
Telephone: (410) 605-5000
Industry Affiliation: Banks, Savings & Loans
**Publication(s):**
*M N C Now*
Day Published: m.
Contact: Corporate Communications
Spec. Requirements: 8 pg.; offset; 8 x 12
Personnel: Jim Choplick, Editor

**MOBIL OIL CORP.** 4086
3225 Gallows Rd.
Fairfax, VA 22037
Telephone: (703) 846-3000
Industry Affiliation: Petroleum, Gas

**Publication(s):**
*Compass, The*
Day Published: q.
Lead Time: 4 mos.
Contact: Marine & Aviation Sales
Spec. Requirements: 40-pgs.; offset magazine; 9 x 12
Personnel: James Randall, Editor

*Mobil World*
Day Published: 9-10/yr.
Contact: Pub. Rels.
Spec. Requirements: 12-page; 11 x 15 1/2; circ.: 75,000
Personnel: Carole Edwards, Editor

**MONARCH CAPITAL CORP.** 3368
One Monarch Pl.
Springfield, MA 01144
Telephone: (413) 781-3000
FAX: (708) 480-5378
Industry Affiliation: Finance, Services

**Publication(s):**
*Monarch News*
Day Published: bi-w.
Lead Time: 2 wks. prior to pub. date
Spec. Requirements: 8 pg.; offset newsletter; 17 x 22
Personnel: Virginia Page, Editor
Susan Fentin

*Monarch Field News*
Day Published: bi-m.
Lead Time: 1 mo. prior to pub. date
Personnel: Virginia Page, Editor

**MONONGAHELA POWER CO.** 5351
1310 Fairmont Ave.
Fairmont, WV 26554
Telephone: (304) 366-3000
FAX: (304) 367-3377
Mailing Address:
P.O. Box 1392
Fairmont, WV 26555-1392
Industry Affiliation: Utility: Electric
**Publication(s):**
*Monongahela News*
Day Published: m.
Materials: 01,02,04,08,09,15,16,18,21,27, 29,30
Spec. Requirements: 36-52 pg.; offset newspaper; 9 x 12
Personnel: Angenette Rice-Figueroa, Editor

**MONROE SYSTEMS FOR BUSINESS** 3883
American Rd.
Morris Plains, NJ 07950
Telephone: (201) 993-2510
Industry Affiliation: Finance, Services
**Publication(s):**
*Keynote*
Day Published: bi-m.
Spec. Requirements: 6-8 pg.; offset newspaper; 11 x 15
Personnel: Norma V. Backster, Editor

*Field*
Day Published: m.
Spec. Requirements: 6-12 pg.
Personnel: Norma V. Backster, Editor

**MONTGOMERY WARD & CO.** 2853
One Montgomery Ward Plz. 8-3
Chicago, IL 60671
Telephone: (312) 467-6649
Industry Affiliation: Retail Stores
**Publication(s):**
*Forward*
Day Published: q.
Contact: Public Relations
Spec. Requirements: 12 pg.; offset magazine; 8 1/2 x 11 3/4
Personnel: Faith Mazzuca, Editor

**MONUMENTAL LIFE INS. CO.** 3289
2 E. Chase St.
Baltimore, MD 21202
Telephone: (410) 685-2900
FAX: (410) 347-8666
Industry Affiliation: Insurance
**Publication(s):**
*Life Lines*
Day Published: m.
Lead Time: 45 days prior to pub. date
Mtls Deadline: 30-45 days prior to pub. date
Spec. Requirements: 16-pg.; offset tabloid; 11 x 17 folded
Personnel: Chris Boerner, Editor

**MOORE BUSINESS FORMS, INC.** 2855
275 North Field Dr.
Lake Forest, IL 60045
Telephone: (708) 615-6000
FAX: (708) 803-6717
Industry Affiliation: Paper Products

**Publication(s):**
*Inform*
Day Published: q.
Spec. Requirements: 8-12 pg.; offset magazine; 8 1/2 x 11
Personnel: Donna Eckert, Editor

**MORAN TOWING & TRANSPORTATION CO., INC.** 4088
2 Greenwich Plz., 3rd Fl.
Greenwich, CT 06830
Telephone: (203) 625-7809
FAX: (203) 625-7857
Industry Affiliation: Shipping
**Publication(s):**
*Tow Line*
Day Published: a.
Mtls Deadline: Dec. 31; Mar. 30; June 30; Sep. 30
Spec. Requirements: 20 pg.; photo offset; 8 1/2 x 11
Personnel: Tony Watt, Editor

**MORBARK INDUSTRIES INC.** 3486
P.O. Box 1000
Winn, MI 48896
Telephone: (517) 866-2381
FAX: (517) 866-2280
Industry Affiliation: Lumber, Forestry, Building Materials
**Publication(s):**
*Morbark Report*
Day Published: q.
Lead Time: 30 days prior to pub. date
Spec. Requirements: 4 pg.; offset; 7 x 10
Personnel: Dan Brandon, Editor

**MORGAN GUARANTY TRUST CO. OF N.Y.** 4089
60 Wall St.
New York, NY 10005
Telephone: (212) 483-2323
FAX: (212) 698-5193
Industry Affiliation: Banks, Savings & Loans
**Publication(s):**
*Morgan News, The*
Day Published: m.
Mtls Deadline: 1 mo. prior to pub. date
Spec. Requirements: 28-32 pg.; offset; 9 3/8 x 9 3/8
Personnel: Elizabeth Roth, Editor

*Morgan Today*
Day Published: d.

**MORRISON KNUDSEN CORP.** 68415
720 Park Blvd.
Boise, ID 83729
Telephone: (208) 386-6630
FAX: (208) 386-5065
Mailing Address:
P.O. Box 73
Boise, ID 83729
Industry Affiliation: Industry: Heavy Construction, Machinery
**Publication(s):**
*E M Kayan*
Day Published: bi-m.
Personnel: Rodney L. Hunt

**MORSE SHOE, INC.** 3369
555 Turnpike St.
Canton, MA 02021
Telephone: (617) 828-9300
Industry Affiliation: Shoes

Materials Accepted/Included: 01-Business news 02-By-line articles 03-Fashion news 04-Food news 05-Freelance copy 06-Letters to editor 07-Real estate news 08-Sports news 09-Travel news 10-Book rev. 11-Movie rev. 12-Music rev. 13-TV rev. 14-Theater rev. 15-Coming events 16-Obituaries 17-Question & answer 18-Social announcements 19-Artwork 20-Cartoons 21-Photos 22-TV listings 23-Audio rec. 24-Video rec. 25-Books 26-Films/film clips 27-Personnel news 28-Press releases 29-New product news/photos 30-Trade lit. 31-Contracts awarded 32-Display adv. 33-Classified adv.

11-57

**Publication(s):**
*Morse Code*
Day Published: 9/yr.
Spec. Requirements: 4 pg.; offset; 8 1/2 x 11
Personnel: Virginia Driscoll, Editor

3708
**MOSBY-YEAR BOOK, INC.**
11830 Westline Industrial Dr.
St. Louis, MO 63146
Telephone: (314) 872-8370
FAX: (314) 432-1380
Industry Affiliation: Publishers, Books, Magazines
**Publication(s):**
*Mosby Times*
Day Published: q.
Lead Time: 4 mos. prior to pub. date
Spec. Requirements: 16-24 pg.; offset; 8 1/2 x 11
Personnel: Gretchen Jaspering, Editor

3290
**MOTORCYCLE SAFETY FOUNDATION**
2 Jenner St., Ste. 150
Irvine, CA 92718-3812
Telephone: (714) 727-3227
FAX: (714) 727-4217
Industry Affiliation: Colleges, Institutions, Science Research
**Publication(s):**
*Safe Cycling*
Day Published: q.
Lead Time: 1 mo. prior to pub. date
Materials: 06,23,24,25,27,28,29
Mtls Deadline: 2 mos. prior to issue date
Contact: Communications
Spec. Requirements: 16 pg.; offset; 8 1/2 x 11
Personnel: Nate Rauba, Editor
       Peter Fassnacht, Publisher
       Julie Filatoff, Editor in Chief

4396
**MOTORISTS INSURANCE COMPANIES**
471 E. Broad St.
Columbus, OH 43215
Telephone: (614) 225-8211
FAX: (614) 225-8407
Industry Affiliation: Insurance
**Publication(s):**
*Fullcoverage*
Day Published: m.
Lead Time: 3 wks. prior to pub. date
Mtls Deadline: 3rd of mo. prior to pub. date
Spec. Requirements: 16 pg.; offset; 8 1/2 x 10 7/8
Personnel: Sherry Habry, Editor

2857
**MOTOROLA, INC.**
1303 E. Algonquin Rd.
Schaumburg, IL 60173
Telephone: (708) 576-5000
Industry Affiliation: Auto Suppliers
**Publication(s):**
*The Tradewinds*
Day Published: m.
Spec. Requirements: 2 pg.; offset; 8 1/2 x 11
Personnel: Yvor Stoakley, Editor

68549
**MOUNTAIN STATE BLUE CROSS & BLUE SHIELD**
700 Market St.
Parkersburg, WV 26102
Telephone: (304) 424-7700
FAX: (304) 424-7730
Industry Affiliation: Insurance

**Publication(s):**
*Mountain State*
Day Published: m.
Personnel: Carl Calleson

2597
**MOUNT SINAI MEDICAL CENTER**
4300 Alton Rd.
Miami Beach, FL 33140
Telephone: (305) 674-2121
FAX: (305) 674-2663
Industry Affiliation: Hospitals
**Publication(s):**
*Medical Report*
Day Published: q.
Lead Time: 3 wks. prior to pub. date
Mtls Deadline: 3 wks. prior to pub. date
Personnel: Margie Kenin, Editor
       Lori Brookins, Editor

3596
**MSI INSURANCE**
2 Pine Tree Dr.
Arden Hills, MN 55112-3793
Telephone: (612) 631-7271
Mailing Address:
   P.O. Box 64035
   St Paul, MN 55164-0035
Industry Affiliation: Insurance
**Publication(s):**
*Success Extra*
Day Published: m.
Lead Time: 1 mo. prior to pub. date
Mtls Deadline: 1 mo. prior to pub. date
Contact: Lori Worner, Ed.
Spec. Requirements: 16-24 pg.; offset; 8 1/2 x 11
Personnel: Lori Worner, Editor
       Michelle Johnson, Art Director

*Perspective*
Day Published: m.
Spec. Requirements: 12 pg.
Personnel: Pat Ryan Greene, Editor
       Michelle Johnson, Art Director

4592
**MULTNOMAH COUNTY MEDICAL SOCIETY**
4540 S.W. Kelly St.
Portland, OR 97201
Telephone: (503) 222-3326
FAX: (503) 222-3164
Industry Affiliation: Associations: Health Groups
**Publication(s):**
*Scribe*
Day Published: s-m.
Lead Time: 1 mo. prior to pub. date
Mtls Deadline: 2 mos. prior to pub. date
Spec. Requirements: 12 pg.; 11 x 13
Personnel: Mindt, Editor

2040
**MURPHY OIL CORPORATION**
200 Peach
El Dorado, AR 71730
Telephone: (501) 862-6411
FAX: (501) 862-9057
Mailing Address:
   P.O. Box 7000
   El Dorado, AR 71731-7000
Industry Affiliation: Petroleum, Gas

**Publication(s):**
*Murphy News*
Day Published: 8/yr.
Lead Time: 1 mo.
Mtls Deadline: 2nd wk. of ea. mo.
Contact: General Service Division, Publication Section
Spec. Requirements: 16 pg.; offset; 8 1/2 x 11
Personnel: Lisa Coleman, Editor
       Kenna Williams, Art Director

3370
**MUSEUM OF SCIENCE**
Science Park
Boston, MA 02114-1099
Telephone: (617) 723-2500
FAX: (617) 589-0363
Industry Affiliation: Colleges, Institutions, Science Research
**Publication(s):**
*Museum Of Science Newsletter*
Day Published: 5/yr.
Lead Time: 2 wks. prior to pub. date
Spec. Requirements: 6 pg.; offset; 6 x 11
Personnel: Ben Brooks, Editor
       Jack Curtis, Editor in Chief
       Pauline Gobeil, Art Director

52329
**MUSEUM OF SCIENCE & INDUSTRY**
57th St. & Lake Shore Dr.
Chicago, IL 60637
Telephone: (312) 684-1414
FAX: (312) 684-2907
Industry Affiliation: Colleges, Institutions, Science Research
**Publication(s):**
*Progress*
Day Published: q.
Lead Time: 4 mos. prior
Mtls Deadline: 4 mos. prior to pub. date
Personnel: Scott Harms Rose, Editor

4543
**MUSTANG FUEL CORP.**
2000 Classen Ctr., Ste. 800 E.
Oklahoma City, OK 73106
Telephone: (405) 557-9400
FAX: (405) 557-9550
Industry Affiliation: Petroleum, Gas
**Publication(s):**
*Mustang News Connection*
Day Published: s-a.
Lead Time: 6 wks. prior to pub. date
Mtls Deadline: 6 wks. prior to pub. date
Spec. Requirements: 8-10 pg.; letterpress; 9 x 12
Personnel: Marion Story, Editor

4731
**MUTUAL BENEFICIAL ASSN. OF RAILROAD TRANSPORTATION EMPLOYEES**
1617 JFK Blvd., Ste. 366
Philadelphia, PA 19103
Telephone: (215) 596-3578
FAX: (215) 596-3580
Industry Affiliation: Railroads
**Publication(s):**
*Mutual Magazine, The*
Day Published: m.
Lead Time: 10th of mo. prior to pub. date
Mtls Deadline: 10th of mo. prior to pub. date
Spec. Requirements: 48 pg.; offset magazine; 8 1/2 x 5 1/2
Personnel: Stephen M. Santarlasci, Editor

3791
**MUTUAL OF OMAHA COMPANIES**
Mutual of Omaha Plz.
3301 Dodge St.
Omaha, NE 68175
Telephone: (402) 342-7600
FAX: (402) 978-5302
Industry Affiliation: Insurance

**Publication(s):**
*Pacesetters*
Day Published: m.
Lead Time: 8 wks. prior to pub. date
Mtls Deadline: 6 wks. prior to pub. date
Contact: Advertising/Communication
Spec. Requirements: 28 pg.; offset; 84 x 11
Personnel: Steve Pacholski, Editor

*Managers Monthly*
Day Published: m.
Lead Time: 8 wks. prior to pub. date
Mtls Deadline: 6 wks. prior to pub. date
Contact: Advertising/Communication
Spec. Requirements: 12 pg.
Personnel: Steve Pacholski, Editor

*Currents*
Day Published: m.
Lead Time: 3 wks.
Mtls Deadline: 3 wks. prior to pub. date
Contact: Advertising/Communication
Personnel: Georgene Lahm, Editor

2859
**MUTUAL TRUST LIFE INSURANCE CO.**
1200 Jorie Blvd.
Oak Brook, IL 60521
Telephone: (708) 990-1000
Industry Affiliation: Insurance
**Publication(s):**
*Vanguard*
Day Published: s-m.
Spec. Requirements: 16 pg.; offset; 10 3/4 x 14 magapaper
Personnel: Jennie Stevens, Editor

*Perspective*
Day Published: m.
Lead Time: 3 wks.
Personnel: Ray Rolff
       Barbara Boland
       Gail Hoecker, Editor

2861
**NALCO CHEMICAL CO.**
One Nalco Ctr.
Naperville, IL 60563
Telephone: (708) 305-1697
FAX: (708) 305-2900
Industry Affiliation: Chemicals, Plastics
**Publication(s):**
*Nalco News*
Day Published: 4-5/yr.
Lead Time: 1 mo.
Mtls Deadline: end of ea. mo.
Spec. Requirements: 8-12 pg.; offset; 12 x 16 1/2
Personnel: Lisa C. Beyer, Editor

*One Nalco Center*
Day Published: q.
Lead Time: 1 mo.
Contact: Corporate Communications
Personnel: Andy Rauwerda, Editor

*Health & Benefit Briefs*
Day Published: irreg.
Lead Time: 2 mos.
Personnel: Lisa C. Beyer, Editor

*Toastmasters Newsletter*
Day Published: q.
Lead Time: 2 mos.
Personnel: Ellen Delordo, President

*On-Site*
Day Published: m.
Personnel: Irene Sosa, Editor

5302
**NALLEYS FINE FOODS**
3303 S. 35th St.
Tacoma, WA 98409
Telephone: (206) 383-1621
FAX: (206) 272-2730

---

**Materials Accepted/Included:** 01-Business news 02-By-line articles 03-Fashion news 04-Food news 05-Freelance copy 06-Letters to editor 07-Real estate news 08-Sports news 09-Travel news 10-Book rev. 11-Movie rev. 12-Music rev. 13-TV rev. 14-Theater rev. 15-Coming events 16-Obituaries 17-Question & answer 18-Social announcements 19-Artwork 20-Cartoons 21-Photos 22-TV listings 23-Audio rec. 24-Video rec. 25-Books 26-Films/film clips 27-Personnel news 28-Press releases 29-New product news/photos 30-Trade lit. 31-Contracts awarded 32-Display adv. 33-Classified adv.

Mailing Address:
  P.O. Box 11046
  Tacoma, WA 98411
Industry Affiliation: Food, General
**Publication(s):**
*Nallevents*
Day Published: m.
Lead Time: 1 mo. prior to pub. date
Mtls Deadline: 2 wks. prior to pub. date
Contact: Corporate
Spec. Requirements: 8 pg.; offset tabloid;
  10 x 16
Personnel: Paul Benson, Editor

**NASA LEWIS RESEARCH CENTER** 4398
21000 Brookpark Rd.
Cleveland, OH 44135
Telephone: (216) 433-4000
FAX: (216) 433-8143
Industry Affiliation: Aircraft, Aerospace,
  Defense
**Publication(s):**
*Lewis News*
Day Published: 28/yr.
Spec. Requirements: 4-8 pgs.; 112 x 172
Personnel: Doreen Zudell, Editor

**NASH ENGINEERING CO.** 2437
9 Trefoil Dr.
Trumbull, CT 06611-1330
Telephone: (203) 852-3900
FAX: (203) 459-3880
Industry Affiliation: Industry: Light Tools,
  Equipment
**Publication(s):**
*Nash Reporter*
Day Published: 3-4/yr.
Lead Time: 1 mo. prior to pub. date
Mtls Deadline: 1 mo. prior to pub. date
Spec. Requirements: 8-12 pgs.; 8 1/2 X 11
Personnel: Theresa M. Tucci, Editor

**NASHVILLE ELECTRIC SERVICE** 4880
1214 Church St.
Nashville, TN 37203
Industry Affiliation: Utility: Electric
**Publication(s):**
*N E S News*
Day Published: m.
Lead Time: 2 mos.
Mtls Deadline: 2 mos. prior to pub. date
Spec. Requirements: 16 pg.; offset; 9 x 12
Personnel: Tim Hill, Editor

*Power Notes*
Day Published: m.
Lead Time: 2 mos.
Personnel: Tim Hill, Editor

**NASHVILLE STATE TECHNICAL** 4882
  **INSTITUTE**
120 White Bridge Rd.
Nashville, TN 37209
Telephone: (615) 353-3222
Mailing Address:
  P.O. Box 90285
  Nashville, TN 37209
Industry Affiliation: Colleges, Institutions,
  Science Research

**Publication(s):**
*Print Out*
Day Published: q.
Lead Time: 2 mos. prior to pub. date
Mtls Deadline: adv.-11 wks. prior to pub.
  date
Contact: Pub. Rels. Div.
Spec. Requirements: 24 pgs.; offset; 8 X
  10 1/2
Personnel: Martha Henegar, Editor

**NATIONAL ASSOCIATION OF** 69373
  **CHAIN DRUG STORES**
413 N. Lee St.
Alexandria, VA 22314
Telephone: (703) 549-3001
FAX: (703) 836-4869
Mailing Address:
  P.O. Box 1417-D49
  Alexandria, VA 22313
Industry Affiliation: Retail Stores
**Publication(s):**
*Nacds Federal Report*
Day Published: m.
Personnel: David Lambert, Editor

**NATIONAL ASSOCIATION OF** 2862
  **CONCESSIONAIRES**
35 E. Wacker Dr., Ste. 1545
Chicago, IL 60601
Telephone: (312) 236-3858
FAX: (312) 236-7809
Industry Affiliation: Food, General
**Publication(s):**
*Concessionaire, The*
Day Published: bi-m.
Lead Time: 1 mo.
Materials: 27,28,29
Mtls Deadline: 10th of mo. prior to pub.
  date
Spec. Requirements: 12-20 pg.; letterpress
  tabloid; 8 1/2 x 11
Personnel: Susan Cross, Editor

*Insite Magazine*
Day Published: a.
Lead Time: 6 mos.
Mtls Deadline: fall - for Jan. pub.
Personnel: Susan Cross, Editor

**NATIONAL ASSOCIATION OF** 2535
  **FEDERAL CREDIT UNIONS**
3138 N. 10th St.
Arlington, VA 22201
Telephone: (703) 522-4770
FAX: (703) 524-1082
Mailing Address:
  P.O. Box 3769
  Washington, DC 20007
Industry Affiliation: Associations: Trade,
  Fraternal
**Publication(s):**
*Federal Credit Union*
Day Published: bi-m.
Lead Time: 3 mos. prior to pub. date
Mtls Deadline: 3 mos. prior to pub. date
Contact: Communications
Spec. Requirements: 48 pg.; offset; 8 1/2
  x 11
Personnel: Patrick M. Keefe, Editor

**NATIONAL ASSOCIATION OF** 69598
  **HOME & WORKSHOP WRITERS**
  **NEWSLETTER**
P.O. Box 10
Palomar Mountain, CA 92060-0010
Industry Affiliation: Associations: Trade,
  Fraternal

**Publication(s):**
*National Association Of Home & Workshop
Writers*
Day Published: q.
Personnel: Richard Day, Managing Editor

**NATIONAL ASSOCIATION OF** 69378
  **PHARMACEUTICAL**
  **MANUFACTURERS**
747 Third Ave.
New York, NY 10017
Telephone: (212) 838-3720
FAX: (212) 753-6832
Industry Affiliation: Drugs, Cosmetics,
  Pharmaceuticals
**Publication(s):**
*News Bulletin*
Day Published: m.
Materials: 23,30
Personnel: Robert S. Milanese, Editor

**NATIONAL ASSOCIATION OF** 69418
  **RAILROAD PASSENGERS**
900 Second St., N.E., Ste. 308
Washington, DC 20002-3557
Telephone: (202) 408-8632
FAX: (202) 408-8287
Industry Affiliation: Associations: Trade,
  Fraternal
**Publication(s):**
*National Association Of Railroad
Passengers News*
Day Published: 11/yr.
Spec. Requirements: news and advocacy
  articles on railroad issues
Personnel: Ross Capon, Editor

**NATIONAL ASSOCIATION OF** 69521
  **WATCH & CLOCK COLLECTORS**
1514 Poplar St.
Columbia, PA 17512
Telephone: (717) 684-8261
FAX: (717) 684-0878
Industry Affiliation: Associations: Trade,
  Fraternal
**Publication(s):**
*Bulletin*
Day Published: bi-m.
Personnel: Kathy I. Everett, Editor
  NAWCC, Inc., Publisher

*N A W C C Mart*
Day Published: bi-m.
Materials: 32,33
Personnel: Kathy I. Everett, Editor

**NATIONAL AUTO DEALERS ASSN.** 5275
8400 Westpark Dr.
McLean, VA 22102
Telephone: (703) 821-7000
Industry Affiliation: Associations: Trade,
  Fraternal
**Publication(s):**
*Automotive Executive*
Day Published: m.
Lead Time: 2 mos. prior to pub. date
Mtls Deadline: 2 mos. prior to pub. date
Spec. Requirements: 32-124 pgs.; offset; 8
  1/4 x 11 1/4
Personnel: Joe Phillips, Editor

**NATIONAL BANK OF COMMERCE** 4883
One Commerce Sq.
Memphis, TN 38150-3101
Telephone: (901) 523-3101
FAX: (901) 523-3266
Mailing Address:
  P.O. Box 357
  Memphis, TN 38150
Industry Affiliation: Banks, Savings &
  Loans

**Publication(s):**
*N B C Notes*
Day Published: m.
Lead Time: 5th of mo. prior to pub. date
Contact: Personnel Div.
Spec. Requirements: 4 pg.; offset; tabloid
Personnel: Nancy Prince, Editor

*Premier Banking Newsletter*
Day Published: q.
Lead Time: 1st wk. of last mo. of ea.
  quarter
Materials: 01,02,09,20
Contact: Marketing Div.
Personnel: Janice Warner, Editor

**NATIONAL BANK OF DETROIT** 3489
611 Woodward Ave.
Detroit, MI 48226
Telephone: (313) 225-1000
FAX: (313) 225-2012
Industry Affiliation: Banks, Savings &
  Loans
**Publication(s):**
*N B D News*
Day Published: bi-w.
Lead Time: 2 wks. prior to pub. date
Mtls Deadline: 2 wks. prior to pub. date
Contact: Personnel Div.
Spec. Requirements: 4 pg.; offset; 11 x 15
Personnel: Sylvia O'Neill, General Manager
  Patricia Zarzecki, Editor

**NATIONAL CHRISTMAS TREE** 5426
  **ASSOCIATION**
611 E. Wells St.
Milwaukee, WI 53202
Telephone: (414) 276-6410
FAX: (414) 276-3349
Industry Affiliation: Associations: Trade,
  Fraternal
**Publication(s):**
*American Christmas Tree Journal*
Day Published: q.
Lead Time: 6 wks.
Materials: 01,02,05,06,25,29,32
Mtls Deadline: 6 wks. prior to pub. date
Spec. Requirements: 60-72 pg.; offset; 8-
  1/2 x 11
Personnel: Dennis Tompkins, Editor
  Joan Geiger, Managing Editor
  David Bowmann, Publisher

**NATIONAL CITY BANK, INDIANA** 3029
101 W. Washington
Indianapolis, IN 46255
Telephone: (317) 267-7000
Industry Affiliation: Banks, Savings &
  Loans
**Publication(s):**
*Bank Briefs*
Day Published: m.
Lead Time: 1 mo. prior to pub. date
Mtls Deadline: Mon., 5:00 pm prior to pub.
  date
Contact: Adv. Dept.
Spec. Requirements: 4 pg.; offset; 8 1/2 x
  11
Personnel: Beth Muir, Editor

**NATIONAL CITY CORP.** 4399
1900 E. Ninth St.
Cleveland, OH 44114
Telephone: (216) 575-2000
Mailing Address:
  P.O. Box 5756
  Cleveland, OH 44101
Industry Affiliation: Banks, Savings &
  Loans

**Materials Accepted/Included:** 01-Business news 02-By-line articles 03-Fashion news 04-Food news 05-Freelance copy 06-Letters to editor 07-Real estate news 08-Sports news 09-Travel news
10-Book rev. 11-Movie rev. 12-Music rev. 13-TV rev. 14-Theater rev. 15-Coming events 16-Obituaries 17-Question & answer 18-Social announcements 19-Artwork 20-Cartoons 21-Photos 22-TV listings
23-Audio rec. 24-Video rec. 25-Books 26-Films/film clips 27-Personnel news 28-Press releases 29-New product news/photos 30-Trade lit. 31-Contracts awarded 32-Display adv. 33-Classified adv.

11-59

**Publication(s):**
*On The Move*
Day Published: m.
Lead Time: 3 wks.
Mtls Deadline: 1st of mo. prior to pub. date
Contact: National City Bank
Spec. Requirements: 8 pg.; web tabloid
  newspaper 11 x 17
Personnel: Margie Flynn, Editor
      Barb Brown, Editor

*Inside Track*
Day Published: bi-w.
Lead Time: 1 wk.
Personnel: Marianne Wascak, Editor

**NATIONAL COLLEGE OF**   5035
**DISTRICT ATTORNEYS**
University Of Houston-Law Center
Houston, TX 77204
Telephone: (713) 743-1840
Industry Affiliation: Associations: Trade,
  Fraternal
**Publication(s):**
*Practical Prosecutor*
Day Published: a.
Lead Time: 3 mos.
Personnel: Candace Mosley
      Robin S. Breaux, Marketing
      Manager

**NATIONAL COOPERATIVE**   68370
**BUSINESS ASSOCIATION**
1401 New York Ave., N.W., Ste. 1100
Washington, DC 20005
Telephone: (202) 638-6222
FAX: (202) 638-1374
Industry Affiliation: Associations: Trade,
  Fraternal
**Publication(s):**
*N C B A Cooperative Business Journal*
Day Published: 10/yr.
Lead Time: 3 wks. prior to pub. date
Mtls Deadline: 15th of mo. prior to pub.
  date
Personnel: Leta M. Mach

**NATIONAL EDUCATION**   2539
**ASSOCIATION**
1201 16th St., N.W.
Washington, DC 20036
Telephone: (202) 823-7207
Industry Affiliation: Associations: Trade,
  Fraternal
**Publication(s):**
*N E A Today*
Day Published: 8/yr.
Spec. Requirements: 96 pg.; letterpress
  and offset; 82 x 112
Personnel: Bill Fischer, Editor
      Sam Pizzagati, Publisher

**NATIONAL EDUCATION PROGRAM**   70463
2501 E. Memorial Rd.
Oklahoma City, OK 73111
Telephone: (405) 425-5035
FAX: (405) 425-5108
Mailing Address:
  P.O. Box 11000
  Oklahoma City, OK 73136-1100
Industry Affiliation: Associations: Trade,
  Fraternal
**Publication(s):**
*Looking Ahead*
Day Published: q.
Spec. Requirements: offset; $10/yr.

**NATIONAL FEDERATION OF**   2203
**INDEPENDENT BUSINESS**
600 Maryland Ave., S.W., Ste. 700
Washington, DC 20024
Telephone: (202) 554-9000
Industry Affiliation: Associations: Trade,
  Fraternal

**Publication(s):**
*I B Magazine (independent Business)*
Day Published: bi-m.
Lead Time: 6 wks.
Materials: 01,02,05,06,15,28,32
Mtls Deadline: 6-8 wks. prior to pub. date
Contact: Group IV Communications
    Telephone: (805) 496-6156
    875 S. Westlake Blvd., Ste. 211
    Westlake Village, CA 91361
Spec. Requirements: 64 pgs.; web.; 8 x 10
  3/4
Personnel: Don Phillipson, Editor

**NATIONAL FIRE PROTECTION**   3371
**ASSOCIATION**
1 Batterymarch Pk.
Quincy, MA 02269
Telephone: (617) 770-3000
Mailing Address:
  P.O. Box 9101
  Quincy, MA 02269
Industry Affiliation: Associations: City,
  State, Federal
**Publication(s):**
*Fire News*
Day Published: bi-m.
Lead Time: 6 wks. prior to pub. date
Materials: 01,02,06,15,27,28
Mtls Deadline: 6 wks. prior to pub. date
Spec. Requirements: 8 pg.; offset; 13 1/4
  x 10 1/2
Personnel: Michael Hazell, Managing
      Editor

**NATIONAL GRANGE MUTUAL**   3830
**INSURANCE CO.**
55 West St.
Keene, NH 03431
Telephone: (603) 352-4000
FAX: (603) 358-1173
Industry Affiliation: Insurance
**Publication(s):**
*Among Ourselves*
Day Published: m.
Spec. Requirements: 8-12-page; offset
  tabloid; 84 x 11
Personnel: Ron Woods, Editor

**NATIONAL GROUND WATER**   69443
**ASSOCIATION**
6375 Riverside Dr.
Dublin, OH 40317
Telephone: (614) 761-1711
FAX: (614) 761-3446
Industry Affiliation: Utility: Water
**Publication(s):**
*Well Log*
Day Published: m.
Spec. Requirements: water industry news

**NATIONAL GYPSUM CO.**   5036
2001 Rexford Rd.
Charlotte, NC 28211
Telephone: (704) 365-7300
FAX: (704) 365-7289
Industry Affiliation: Chemicals, Plastics
**Publication(s):**
*Writings On The Wall*
Day Published: q.
Spec. Requirements: 8-12 pgs.; newsletter
Personnel: Jonathan Scott, Editor

**NATIONAL INDEMNITY CO.**   3792
3024 Harney St
Omaha, NE 68131
Telephone: (402) 346-7400
FAX: (402) 536-3030
Industry Affiliation: Insurance

**Publication(s):**
*Friday Facts*
Day Published: w.
Spec. Requirements: 8 pg.; offset; 8 1/2 x
  11
Personnel: Cheryl Schmid, Editor

**NATIONAL INSURANCE CRIME**   2435
**BUREAU**
10330 S. Roberts Rd.
Palos Hills, IL 60465
Telephone: (708) 430-2430
FAX: (708) 430-2446
Industry Affiliation: Insurance
**Publication(s):**
*Spotlight, The*
Day Published: q.
Spec. Requirements: 16 pg.; offset; 11 x
  14
Personnel: Marcy Clay, Editor

**NATIONAL LIFE OF VERMONT**   68397
National Life Dr.
Montpelier, VT 05604
Telephone: (802) 229-3882
FAX: (802) 229-9281
Industry Affiliation: Insurance
**Publication(s):**
*Weekly*
Day Published: w.
Mtls Deadline: Tue. of ea. wk. prior to pub.
  date
Personnel: Jane Robb

*Focus*
Day Published: m.
Mtls Deadline: 1st of ea. mo. prior to pub.
  date
Personnel: Brian Vachon

**NATIONAL MANAGEMENT**   4401
**ASSOCIATION**
2210 Arbor Blvd.
Dayton, OH 45439
Telephone: (513) 294-0421
FAX: (513) 294-2374
Industry Affiliation: Associations: Trade,
  Fraternal
**Publication(s):**
*Manage Magazine*
Day Published: q.
Lead Time: 90 days prior to pub. date
Spec. Requirements: 32 pg.; 8 1/2 x 11;
  84 x 11
Personnel: Douglas Shaw, Editor
      K. Stephen Bailey, President

**NATIONAL MILK PRODUCERS**   2541
**FEDERATION**
1840 Wilson Blvd.
Arlington, VA 22201
Telephone: (703) 243-6111
Industry Affiliation: Dairy Products
**Publication(s):**
*News For Dairy Coops*
Day Published: w.
Lead Time: 2 wks. prior to pub. date
Mtls Deadline: 2 wks. prior to pub. date
Spec. Requirements: 4 pg.; offset; 8-1/2 x
  11
Personnel: Karl Hoyle, Editor

**NATIONAL MULTIPLE SCLEROSIS**   69586
**SOCIETY**
733 Third Ave.
New York, NY 10017-3288
Telephone: (212) 986-3240
FAX: (212) 986-7981
Industry Affiliation: Associations: Health
  Groups

**Publication(s):**
*Inside M S*
Day Published: q.
Materials: 02,05,06,10,17,19,20,21,24,25,
  28,29,32
Mtls Deadline: 1st Aug., Nov., Feb., May
Contact: Publications
Spec. Requirements: 32 pg. consumer
  magazine
Personnel: Martha King, Editor

*Inside M S Bulletin*
Day Published: q.
Materials: 02,17,19,20,21
Mtls Deadline: 1st Feb., May, Aug., Nov.
Contact: Publications
Personnel: Martha King, Editor

**NATIONAL PTA**   2867
330 N. Wabash Ave.
Ste. 2100
Chicago, IL 60611-3690
Telephone: (312) 670-6782
FAX: (312) 670-6783
Industry Affiliation: Colleges, Institutions,
  Science Research
**Publication(s):**
*P T A Today*
Day Published: 7/yr.
Lead Time: 3 mos. prior to pub. date
Mtls Deadline: 3 mos. prior to pub. date
Spec. Requirements: 40-48 pg.; offset; 8-
  1/2 x 11
Personnel: Pamela Schrom Reynolds,
      Editor
      Joan Kuersten

**NATIONAL RURAL HEALTH**   65222
**ASSOCIATION**
One W. Armour Blvd., Ste. 301
Kansas City, MO 64111
Telephone: (816) 756-3140
FAX: (816) 756-3144
Mailing Address:
  National Rural Health Association
  1320 19th St., NW, Ste. 350
  Washington, DC 20036-1610
Industry Affiliation: Associations: Health
  Groups
**Publication(s):**
*Rural Health Care*
Day Published: bi-m.
Lead Time: 1 mo. prior to pub. date
Materials: 01,02,05,06,15,17,21,27,28,29,
  30,31,33
Mtls Deadline: 1 mo. prior to pub. date
Contact: Communications
Personnel: Robert Quick
      Mary Boyd
      Jenifer Bockelman, Editor

*Journal Of Rural Health*
Day Published: q.
Lead Time: 3 mos. prior to pub. date
Materials: 06,10,25,32,33
Mtls Deadline: 3 mos. prior to pub. date
Contact: Communications
Personnel: Michael K. Miller, Ph.D.
      Robert Quick, Managing
      Publisher
      Thomas Ricketts, Ph.D., Editor

Materials Accepted/Included: 01-Business news 02-By-line articles 03-Fashion news 04-Food news 05-Freelance copy 06-Letters to editor 07-Real estate news 08-Sports news 09-Travel news 10-Book rev. 11-Movie rev. 12-Music rev. 13-TV rev. 14-Theater rev. 15-Coming events 16-Obituaries 17-Question & answer 18-Social announcements 19-Artwork 20-Cartoons 21-Photos 22-TV listings 23-Audio rec. 24-Video rec. 25-Books 26-Films/film clips 27-Personnel news 28-Press releases 29-New product news/photos 30-Trade lit. 31-Contracts awarded 32-Display adv. 33-Classified adv.

*Rural Clinician Quarterly*
Day Published: q.
Lead Time: 1 mo. prior to pub. date
Materials: 02,05,21,27,28,29,30,31
Mtls Deadline: 1 mo. prior to pub. date
Contact: Communications
Personnel: Mary Boyd
          Jenifer Bockelman, Editor

### NATIONAL SAFETY COUNCIL
2868
1121 Spring Lake Dr. #558
Itasca, IL 60143-3200
Telephone: (708) 775-2288
FAX: (708) 775-2285
Industry Affiliation: Associations: Health
  Groups
**Publication(s):**
*Safety & Health*
Day Published: m.
Lead Time: 2 mos. prior
Mtls Deadline: 2 mos. prior
Contact: Publications
Spec. Requirements: 100-300 pg.; offset; 8
  1/8 x 10 7/8 trim size
Personnel: Austin Weber, Editor
          James W. Lahey
          Edward D. Dionn
          James W. Lahey
          Peter D. Minetos

### NATIONAL SCHOOL PUBLIC RELATIONS ASSOCIATION
5256
1501 Lee Hwy., 201
Arlington, VA 22209
Telephone: (703) 528-5840
Industry Affiliation: Advertising, Art, Public
  Relations
**Publication(s):**
*Network*
Day Published: m.
Lead Time: 1 wk. prior to pub. date
Mtls Deadline: 1 wk. prior to pub. date
Spec. Requirements: 8 pgs.; offset; 8 1/2
  x 11; educ. coverage only
Personnel: Judi Cowan, Editor
          Rich Bagin, Editor in Chief

*It Starts In The Classroom*
Day Published: m.: Sep.-May
Lead Time: 6 wks. prior to pub. date
Mtls Deadline: 6 wks. prior to pub. date
Spec. Requirements: 8-pg./1 color, offset;
  8 1/2 x 11
Personnel: Virginia M. Ross, Editor

*It Starts On The Front Line*
Day Published: m.
Spec. Requirements: 6 pgs.; 11 x 25 1/2
Personnel: Rich Bagin, Editor in Chief

### NATIONAL SCIENCE TEACHERS ASSOCIATION
52337
1742 Connecticut Ave., N.W.
Washington, DC 20009
Telephone: (202) 328-5800
Mailing Address:
  3140 N.Washington Blvd.
  Arlington, VA 22201
Industry Affiliation: Associations: Trade,
  Fraternal
**Publication(s):**
*Science Scope*
Day Published: 8/yr.
Lead Time: 4 mos. prior to pub. date
Personnel: Marily DeWall

*Journal Of College Science Teaching*
Day Published: bi-m.
Lead Time: 12 mos.
Personnel: Michael Byrnes, Managing
          Editor
          Lester G. Paldy, Field Editor

### NATIONAL SEMICONDUCTOR CORP.
2133
2900 Semiconductor Dr.
Santa Clara, CA 95052
Telephone: (408) 721-5000
FAX: (408) 721-4089
Mailing Address:
  P.O. Box 58090 MS 16-410
  Santa Clara, CA 95052
Industry Affiliation: Electrical, Electronic,
  Manufacturing
**Publication(s):**
*International News*
Day Published: m.
Lead Time: 60-90 days prior to pub. date
Mtls Deadline: 60-90 days prior to pub.
  date
Spec. Requirements: 16-24 pg.; offset; 8
  1/2 x 11; B&W photos
Personnel: Mike Brozda, Editor

### NATIONAL SOCIETY OF FUND RAISING EXECUTIVES
69417
1101 King St., Ste. 700
Alexandria, VA 22314
Telephone: (703) 684-0410
FAX: (703) 684-0540
Industry Affiliation: Associations: Trade,
  Fraternal
**Publication(s):**
*N S F R E Journal*
Day Published: q.
Personnel: Gael Clarke, Editor

### NATIONAL SOFT DRINK ASSOCIATION
2546
1101 16th St., N.W.
Washington, DC 20036
Telephone: (202) 463-6732
FAX: (202) 463-8178
Industry Affiliation: Associations: Trade,
  Fraternal
**Publication(s):**
*Soft Drink Lines*
Day Published: bi-m.
Contact: Public Affairs
Spec. Requirements: 4-6 pg.; offset
  newsletter; 84 x 11
Personnel: Leslie Schreiber, Editor
          Sherry Aguirre, Senior
            Managing Editor
          Venus Adkins, Production
            Assistant

### NATIONAL STARCH & CHEMICAL CO.
3887
10 Finderne Ave.
Bridgewater, NJ 08807
Telephone: (908) 685-5000
FAX: (908) 685-5300
Mailing Address:
  P.O. Box 6500
  Bridgewater, NJ 08807
Industry Affiliation: Chemicals, Plastics

*National's Compass*
**Publication(s):**
Day Published: bi-m.
Lead Time: 1 mo. prior to pub. date
Mtls Deadline: 1 mo. prior to pub. date
Spec. Requirements: 20 pg.; offset; 8 1/2
  x 11
Personnel: Damian Proulx, Editor

### NATIONAL STEEL CORP.
2869
4100 Edison Lakes Pkwy.
Mishawaka, IN 46545-3422
Telephone: (219) 273-0000
FAX: (219) 273-7579
Industry Affiliation: Steel, Iron
**Publication(s):**
*Payday*
Day Published: bi-m.

### NATIONAL SUNFLOWER ASSOCIATION
4282
4023 State St.
Bismarck, ND 58501
Telephone: (701) 221-5100
FAX: (701) 221-5101
Industry Affiliation: Agriculture, Services
**Publication(s):**
*Sunflower, The*
Day Published: bi-m.
Lead Time: 1 mo. prior to pub. date
Mtls Deadline: 1 mo. prior to pub. date
Contact: Editorial
Spec. Requirements: 24-48 pg.; 8-1/2 x 11
Personnel: Larry Kleingartner, Editor
          Don Lilleboe, Consulting Editor
          Ruth Isaak, Business Manager

### NATIONAL TRAVELERS LIFE CO.
3115
820 Keo Way
Des Moines, IA 50309
Telephone: (515) 283-0101
FAX: (515) 283-3070
Industry Affiliation: Insurance
**Publication(s):**
*Dynamo*
Day Published: m.
Spec. Requirements: 16 pgs; offset; 84 x
  11
Personnel: Michelle Miller, Editor

### NATIONAL WESTMINSTER BANCORP
66426
10 Exchange Pl.
Jersey City, NJ 07302
Telephone: (201) 547-7516
Industry Affiliation: Finance, Services
**Publication(s):**
*Connections*
Day Published: bi-m.
Lead Time: 2 wks. prior to pub. date
Materials: 10,15,19,20,21,25,28,30
Mtls Deadline: 1st of mo. prior to pub. date
Contact: Entire Bancorp
Personnel: Marya McMorrow, Desktop
            Publishing
          Robin Hulkower, Editor

### NATIONAL WHOLESALE DRUGGISTS' ASSOCIATION
69377
P.O. Box 2219
Reston, VA 22090
Telephone: (703) 787-0000
FAX: (703) 787-6930
Industry Affiliation: Drugs, Cosmetics,
  Pharmaceuticals

**Publication(s):**
*N W D A Executive Newsletter*
Day Published: m.
Contact: Barbara Jennings, Ed.
Personnel: Lauren Asplen, Editor

### NATIONS BANK CORP.
4980
901 Main St.
Charlotte, NC 28255
Telephone: (704) 386-5000
Industry Affiliation: Banks, Savings &
  Loans
**Publication(s):**
*Nations Bank Times*
Day Published: bi-w.
Lead Time: 2 wks. prior to pub. date
Mtls Deadline: 2 wks. prior to pub. date
Contact: Public Affairs
Spec. Requirements: 8-12 pgs. tabloid,
  newsprint
Personnel: Karen Hill, Editor

*Dateline*
Day Published: q.
Lead Time: 6 wks. prior to pub. date
Mtls Deadline: 6 wks. prior to pub. date
Contact: Corporate Communications
Spec. Requirements: 1-6 pg. 8 1/2 x 11
  newsletter

*Notes*
Day Published: w.
Lead Time: 3 days prior to pub. date
Mtls Deadline: Wed., 12:00 pm prior to
  pub. date
Contact: Public Affairs

### NATIONS CREDIT
4676
1105 Hamilton St.
Allentown, PA 18101
Telephone: (610) 437-8000
FAX: (610) 437-8377
Industry Affiliation: Finance, Services
**Publication(s):**
*Creditline*
Day Published: m.
Personnel: Anne L. Morris, Editor

### NATIONWIDE INSURANCE
68606
One Nationwide Plz.
Columbus, OH 43215
Telephone: (614) 249-6353
FAX: (614) 249-6794
Industry Affiliation: Insurance
**Publication(s):**
*Nationwide Dividend*
Day Published: bi-w.
Personnel: Cynthia Pryor, Editor

*Challenger*
Day Published: m.
Personnel: Terry Leach, Editor

### NAVAJO TRIBAL UTILITY AUTHORITY
68401
P.O. Box 170
Fort Defiance, AZ 86504
Telephone: (602) 729-5721
FAX: (602) 729-2135
Industry Affiliation: Utility: Related
**Publication(s):**
*Annual Report*
Day Published: a.
Mtls Deadline: Mar. 1
Personnel: Dora Cheschilly

---

**Materials Accepted/Included:** 01-Business news 02-By-line articles 03-Fashion news 04-Food news 05-Freelance copy 06-Letters to editor 07-Real estate news 08-Sports news 09-Travel news 10-Book rev. 11-Movie rev. 12-Music rev. 13-TV rev. 14-Theater rev. 15-Coming events 16-Obituaries 17-Question & answer 18-Social announcements 19-Artwork 20-Cartoons 21-Photos 22-TV listings 23-Audio rec. 24-Video rec. 25-Books 26-Films/film clips 27-Personnel news 28-Press releases 29-New product news/photos 30-Trade lit. 31-Contracts awarded 32-Display adv. 33-Classified adv.

*Monthly Employee Newsletter*
Day Published: m.
Mtls Deadline: 25th of ea. mo.
Personnel: Dora Cheschilly

**NAVAL AIR WARFARE CENTER** [4733]
Code 041
Warminster, PA 18974
Telephone: (215) 441-3067
FAX: (215) 441-1955
Industry Affiliation: Aircraft, Aerospace, Defense
**Publication(s):**
*Reflector*
Day Published: m.
Lead Time: 30 days prior to pub. date
Mtls Deadline: 1st of mo. prior to pub. date
Contact: Pub. Affrs. Office
Spec. Requirements: 8-12 pg.; offset; 114 x 16
Personnel: Heather H. Myllenbeck, Editor

**NAVAL NUCLEAR FUEL DIVISION** [5257]
Rte. 726  Mount Athos Rd.
Lynchburg, VA 24504
Telephone: (804) 522-6000
FAX: (804) 522-5922
Mailing Address:
  P.O. Box 785
  Lynchburg, VA 24505
Industry Affiliation: Aircraft, Aerospace, Defense
**Publication(s):**
*B N W News*
Day Published: q.
Lead Time: 2 mos. prior to pub. date
Mtls Deadline: 2 mos. prior to pub. date
Spec. Requirements: 4-6 pg.; offset; 11 x 17
Personnel: Nathaniel Marshall, Editor
        James Conner, General Manager

**NAVY PUBLIC WORKS CENTER** [2205]
  **SAN FRANCISCO BAY**
P.O. Box 24003
Oakland, CA 94623
Telephone: (510) 869-1400
FAX: (510) 466-3486
Industry Affiliation: Utility: Related
**Publication(s):**
*P W C Baygram*
Day Published: bi-w.
Contact: Jerry Boling, Ed.
        P.O. Box 24003
        Oakland, CA 94623
Spec. Requirements: 12 pg.; offset; 8 1/2 x 11 1/2
Personnel: Jerry Boling, Editor

**NBD BANK** [68543]
1 Indiana Sq., Ste. 540
Indianapolis, IN 46266
Telephone: (317) 266-6000
FAX: (317) 266-6305
Industry Affiliation: Banks, Savings & Loans
**Publication(s):**
*N B D: Indianapolis Region Report*
Day Published: m.
Lead Time: 2 wks. prior to pub. date
Mtls Deadline: 15th of mo. prior to pub. date
Personnel: Roberta Gardner, Editor

*N B D Connections*
Day Published: m.
Lead Time: 30 days prior the pub. date
Materials: 19,20
Personnel: Roberta Gardner, Editor

**NC ASSOCIATION OF** [68367]
  **ELECTRICAL CONTRACTORS**
920 E-12 Paverstone Dr.
Raleigh, NC 27615
Telephone: (919) 847-6067
FAX: (919) 847-6091
Industry Affiliation: Electrical, Electronic, Manufacturing
**Publication(s):**
*Power Source, The*
Day Published: q.
Lead Time: 1 mo.
Materials: 01,02,06,17,29,30,32
Mtls Deadline: end of Feb., May., Aug., Nov.
Spec. Requirements: 24-pg., camera-ready advertising
Personnel: Perri Morgan, Editor in Chief

**NEBRASKA DEPT. OF ECONOMIC** [3793]
  **DEVELOPMENT**
301 Centennial Mall S.
Lincoln, NE 68508
Telephone: (800) 426-6505
FAX: (402) 471-3778
Mailing Address:
  P.O. Box 94666
  Lincoln, NE 68509
Industry Affiliation: Associations: City, State, Federal
**Publication(s):**
*Nebraska Development Newsletter*
Day Published: 11/yr.
Lead Time: 4 wks. prior to pub. date
Mtls Deadline: 10th of mo. prior to pub. mo.
Spec. Requirements: 10-20 pg.
Personnel: Don Wright, Editor
        Susan Sitzmann, Assistant Editor

*Nebraska Directory Of Manufacturers*
Day Published: bi-a.
Lead Time: 6 mos. prior to pub. date
Mtls Deadline: 6 mos. prior to pub. date
Spec. Requirements: $50/yr. subscription
Personnel: Don Wright, Editor

**NEBRASKA METHODIST** [3811]
  **HOSPITAL**
8303 Dodge St.
Omaha, NE 68114
Telephone: (402) 390-4000
FAX: (402) 390-4819
Industry Affiliation: Hospitals
**Publication(s):**
*Health Picx*
Day Published: 3/yr.
Lead Time: 3 mos. prior to pub. date
Mtls Deadline: 3 mos. prior to pub. date
Spec. Requirements: 20 pg., 9 x 7 1/2
Personnel: Ginny Goldsmith, Editor

**NEBRASKA PUBLIC POWER** [3815]
  **DISTRICT**
1414 15th St.
Columbus, NE 68601
Telephone: (402) 564-8561
Mailing Address:
  P. O. Box 499
  Columbus, NE 68602-0499
Industry Affiliation: Utility: Electric

**Publication(s):**
*Dispatcher*
Day Published: m.
Lead Time: 1st of mo.prior to pub. mo.
Mtls Deadline: 1st of mo. prior to pub. mo.
Contact: External Affairs
Spec. Requirements: 20 pg.; offset magazine; 84 x 11
Personnel: Sharon Saltero, Editor

**NESTLE-BEICH, INC.** [2947]
300 Delaware Ave., 706
Wilmington, DE 19801
Telephone: (309) 828-1311
Mailing Address:
  P.O. Box 2914
  Bloomington, IL 61702
Industry Affiliation: Food, General
**Publication(s):**
*Kadydid Chronicle*
Day Published: irreg.
Spec. Requirements: 16 pg.; offset magazine; 54 x 84
Personnel: David D. Elder, Editor

**NESTLE USA, INC.** [2091]
800 N. Brand Blvd.
Glendale, CA 91203
Telephone: (818) 549-6000
Industry Affiliation: Candy
**Publication(s):**
*Nestle U S A 2000*
Day Published: q.
Spec. Requirements: 36 pg.; offset magazine; 8 1/2 x 11
Personnel: Julie Thomas-Lowe, Editor

**NEVADA COMMISSION ON** [3816]
  **TOURISM**
5151 S. Carson St.
Carson City, NV 89710
Telephone: (702) 687-4322
Mailing Address:
  Capitol Complex
  Carson City, NV 89710
Industry Affiliation: Associations: City, State, Federal
**Publication(s):**
*Nevada Events*
Day Published: bi-m.
Lead Time: 3 mos. prior to pub. date
Personnel: Jim Joelson

**NEW BRITAIN GENERAL** [2438]
  **HOSPITAL**
100 Grand St.
New Britain, CT 06050
Telephone: (203) 224-5695
FAX: (203) 224-5740
Industry Affiliation: Hospitals
**Publication(s):**
*In General*
Day Published: m.
Lead Time: 2 mos. prior to pub. date
Mtls Deadline: 2 mos. prior to pub. date
Spec. Requirements: 8-12 pg.; offset; 8 1/2 x 11
Personnel: Terri Dixey, Editor

**NEW DETROIT, INC.** [3490]
2900 Penobscot Bldg.
645 Griswold, Ste.2900
Detroit, MI 48226-4234
Telephone: (313) 496-2000
Industry Affiliation: Associations: City, State, Federal

**Publication(s):**
*New Detroit Now*
Day Published: irreg.
Lead Time: 2 mos. prior to pub. date
Materials: 06
Mtls Deadline: 2 mos. prior to pub. date
Contact: Communications
Spec. Requirements: 16 pg.; two color; 8 1/2 x 11
Personnel: John Huls, Editor

**NEWELL CO.** [4292]
Newell Ctr.
29 E. Stephenson St.
Freeport, IL 61032
Telephone: (614) 687-2111
Industry Affiliation: Cement, Ceramics, Clay
**Publication(s):**
*Looking Glass*
Day Published: q.
Lead Time: 4 wks. prior to pub. date
Mtls Deadline: 1 mo. prior to pub. date
Spec. Requirements: 8 pg.; offset magazine; 9 3/4 x 13 3/4
Personnel: Brenda Hammond, Editor

**NEW ENGLAND ELECTRIC** [3410]
  **SYSTEM**
25 Research Dr.
Westborough, MA 01581
Telephone: (508) 366-9011
FAX: (508) 389-3198
Industry Affiliation: Utility: Electric
**Publication(s):**
*Neespaper*
Day Published: m.
Spec. Requirements: 12 pg.; offset; 9 1/2 x 13
Personnel: Maureen Wright

**NEW ENGLAND MUTUAL LIFE** [3374]
  **INSURANCE CO.**
501 Boylston St.
Boston, MA 02116
Telephone: (617) 578-2000
FAX: (617) 578-5507
Industry Affiliation: Insurance
**Publication(s):**
*Currents*
Day Published: bi-w.
Contact: Ed. Svcs.
Personnel: Pat Crowley, Editor

*Wheel*
Day Published: bi-w.
Spec. Requirements: 4-6 pgs.
Personnel: Linda Hilliard, Editor

**NEW ENGLAND PRINTER &** [3832]
  **PUBLISHER INC.**
P.O. Box 170
Salem, NH 03079
Telephone: (603) 898-2822
Industry Affiliation: Publishers, Books, Magazines

**Materials Accepted/Included:** 01-Business news 02-By-line articles 03-Fashion news 04-Food news 05-Freelance copy 06-Letters to editor 07-Real estate news 08-Sports news 09-Travel news 10-Book rev. 11-Movie rev. 12-Music rev. 13-TV rev. 14-Theater rev. 15-Coming events 16-Obituaries 17-Question & answer 18-Social announcements 19-Artwork 20-Cartoons 21-Photos 22-TV listings 23-Audio rec. 24-Video rec. 25-Books 26-Films/film clips 27-Personnel news 28-Press releases 29-New product news/photos 30-Trade lit. 31-Contracts awarded 32-Display adv. 33-Classified adv.

11-62

**Publication(s):**
*New England Printer & Publisher*
Day Published: m.: 1st of mo.
Lead Time: 30 days prior to pub. date
Mtls Deadline: 30 days prior to pub. date
Spec. Requirements: 64 pg.; offset; 8 1/2 x 11
Personnel: Jean Hanson, Editor

3375
**NEW ENGLAND TELEPHONE CO.**
125 High St., Rm. 1258
Boston, MA 02110
Telephone: (617) 743-9800
FAX: (617) 743-9080
Industry Affiliation: Utility: Telephone

2208
**NEWHALL LAND & FARMING CO.**
23823 W. Valencia Blvd.
Valencia, CA 91355
Telephone: (805) 255-4000
Industry Affiliation: Agriculture, Services
**Publication(s):**
*The Roundup*
Day Published: q.
Lead Time: 2 wks. prior to pub. date
Mtls Deadline: 2 wks. prior to pub. date
Spec. Requirements: 6 pg.; offset; 11 x 17
Personnel: Linda Pointer, Editor

3919
**NEW JERSEY STATE SAFETY COUNCIL**
6 Commerce Dr.
Cranford, NJ 07016
Telephone: (908) 272-7712
FAX: (908) 376-6622
Industry Affiliation: Associations: City, State, Federal
**Publication(s):**
*Safety Briefs*
Day Published: irreg. (4-6/yr.)
Spec. Requirements: 8 pg.; offset; 8 1/2 x 11
Personnel: Carol Ann Dylan, Editor

3208
**NEW ORLEANS, CITY OF**
1300 Perdido St.
City Hall Rm. 1WO2
New Orleans, LA 70112
Telephone: (504) 565-6580
FAX: (504) 565-6588
Industry Affiliation: Associations: City, State, Federal
**Publication(s):**
*Citinews*
Day Published: bi-m.
Lead Time: 4 wks. prior to pub. date
Mtls Deadline: 2nd wk. of every other mo.
Contact: Pub. Inform. Office
Personnel: Jinx Broussard, Editor

5258
**NEWPORT NEWS SHIPBUILDING & DRY DOCK CO.**
4101 Washington Ave.
Newport News, VA 23607
Telephone: (804) 380-2000
Industry Affiliation: Industry: Heavy Construction, Machinery

**Publication(s):**
*Yardlines*
Day Published: m.
Spec. Requirements: 8 pg.; offset tabloid
Personnel: Pam Curley, Editor
    Jerri Dicksseski, Editor

4190
**NEWSWEEK**
444 Madison Ave
New York, NY 10022
Telephone: (212) 350-4000
FAX: (212) 421-4993
Industry Affiliation: Publishers, Books, Magazines
**Publication(s):**
*N-W: Internal Communications*
Day Published: w.
Lead Time: 2 wks. prior to pub. date
Mtls Deadline: 2 wks. prior to pub. date
Contact: N-W Internal Communcations
Spec. Requirements: 4-pg. offset bulletin; 8 1/2 x 11
Personnel: Cliff Chase, Editor

4192
**NEW YORK DAILY**
220 E. 42nd St.
New York, NY 10017
Telephone: (212) 210-2100
FAX: (212) 661-2597
Industry Affiliation: Newspapers
**Publication(s):**
*News Pix*
Day Published: bi-m.
Lead Time: 4 wks. prior to pub. date
Mtls Deadline: 30 days prior to pub. date
Spec. Requirements: 16 pg.; offset; 10 1/2 x 7 1/2
Personnel: Vickie McCormick, Editor

4191
**NEW YORK LIFE INSURANCE CO.**
51 Madison Ave.
New York, NY 10010
Telephone: (212) 576-7000
FAX: (212) 576-6928
Industry Affiliation: Insurance
**Publication(s):**
*N Y L I C Review*
Day Published: 9/yr.
Spec. Requirements: 32 pg.; offset; 8 1/2 x 11
Personnel: Douglas Davin, Editor

*New York Life News*
Day Published: 10/yr.
Spec. Requirements: 6-8 pgs.
Personnel: Angela M. Vega, Managing Editor

4098
**NEW YORK STOCK EXCHANGE**
11 Wall St.
New York, NY 10005
Telephone: (212) 656-3000
FAX: (212) 269-4030
Industry Affiliation: Finance, Services
**Publication(s):**
*At The Market*
Day Published: q.
Lead Time: 1 mo. prior to pub. date
Mtls Deadline: 10th of mo., 1 mo. prior to pub. date
Contact: Communications Div.
Spec. Requirements: 8 pg.; offset; 11 x 15
Personnel: Richard Bryan, Editor

4206
**NEW YORK TIMES**
229 W. 43rd St.
New York, NY 10036
Telephone: (212) 556-7078
Industry Affiliation: Newspapers

**Publication(s):**
*Times Company Report*
Day Published: 3/yr.
Spec. Requirements: 8 pg.; offset magazine; 10 x 14
Personnel: Nancy Pelkus, Editor

*Times Talk*
Day Published: irreg. (8-9/yr.)
Spec. Requirements: 16-24 pgs.
Personnel: Susan Sloan, Editor

4212
**NIAGARA FRONTIER TRANSPORTATION AUTHORITY**
181 Ellicott St.
Buffalo, NY 14203
Telephone: (716) 855-7300
FAX: (716) 855-6677
Mailing Address:
  P.O. Box 5008
  Buffalo, NY 14205
Industry Affiliation: Bus, Transit
**Publication(s):**
*F Y I*
Day Published: q.
Lead Time: 1 mo. prior to pub. date
Mtls Deadline: 1 mo. prior to pub. date
Contact: NFTA - Public Relations
Spec. Requirements: 12 pg.; offset; 8 1/2 x 11
Personnel: Robert Rakozzi, General Manager
    Darrel Rasuli, Manager of Communications

4214
**NIAGARA MOHAWK POWER CORP.**
300 Erie Blvd., W.
Syracuse, NY 13202
Telephone: (315) 428-6923
FAX: (315) 428-5524
Industry Affiliation: Utility: Electric
**Publication(s):**
*N M News*
Day Published: m.
Lead Time: 1 wk. prior to pub. date
Materials: 01,02,15,16,17,18,20,21
Mtls Deadline: 15th of mo. prior to pub. date
Contact: Corporate Public Relations
Spec. Requirements: 8-pg.; tabloid newspaper; 15 x 11
Personnel: Joe Della Posta, Editor
    Monica Dooley, Art Director

*Niagara Mohawk Update*
Day Published: w.
Lead Time: 2 days
Personnel: Emilye Alfino, Editor

3915
**N.J. STATE BAR ASSN.**
One Constitution Sq.
New Brunswick, NJ 08901
Telephone: (908) 249-5000
FAX: (908) 249-2815
Industry Affiliation: Associations: Trade, Fraternal
**Publication(s):**
*New Jersey Lawyer*
Day Published: 8/yr.
Lead Time: 3 mos. prior to pub. date
Mtls Deadline: 3 mos. prior to pub. date
Spec. Requirements: 48-64-pgs.; offset; 8 1/2 x 11
Personnel: Sharon Komitas, Editor
    Linda Kozloff

5259
**NOLAND CO.**
2700 Warwick Blvd
Newport News, VA 23607
Telephone: (804) 928-9000
FAX: (804) 244-9817
Industry Affiliation: Associations: Trade, Fraternal

**Publication(s):**
*Noland News*
Day Published: m.
Lead Time: 3 wks. prior to pub. date
Mtls Deadline: 15th of mo.
Contact: Corporate Communications
Spec. Requirements: 4 pgs.; offset; 11 x 14
Personnel: Kathy W. Bryant, Editor

3711
**NOOTER CORP.**
1400 S. Third St.
Saint Louis, MO 63104
Telephone: (314) 621-6000
FAX: (314) 421-7704
Mailing Address:
  P.O. Box 451
  Saint Louis, MO 63166
Industry Affiliation: Steel, Iron
**Publication(s):**
*Boilermaker*
Day Published: q.
Lead Time: 1 1/2 mos. prior to pub. date
Contact: Missouri Boiler & Tank Co.
    2300 Papin St.
    Saint Louis, MO 63103
Spec. Requirements: 16-24 pg.; magazine; 8 1/2 x 11
Personnel: William H. Schawacker, II, Editor
    Connie Treber, Associate Editor

*Erector*
Day Published: bi-m.
Personnel: William H. Schawacker, II

2557
**NORFOLK SOUTHERN CORP.**
3 Commercial Pl.
Norfolk, VA 23510
Telephone: (804) 629-2707
FAX: (804) 629-2822
Industry Affiliation: Railroads
**Publication(s):**
*Focus*
Day Published: q.
Lead Time: 1 mo. prior to pub. date
Mtls Deadline: 1 mo. prior to pub. date
Spec. Requirements: 24 pg.; 8 x 11
Personnel: Susan M. Terpay, Editor
    Rebecca Burcher

*Norfolk Southern World*
Day Published: m.
Lead Time: 1 wk. prior to pub. date
Mtls Deadline: 1 wk. prior to pub. date
Contact: Public Relations Dept.
Spec. Requirements: circ. 47,000 controlled; bk. rev.; illus.
Personnel: Rebecca Burcher
    Susan M. Terpay, Editor

3361
**NORTH AMERICAN OPERATIONS-DRESSER INDUSTRY**
275 Turnpike St.
Canton, MA 02021
Telephone: (508) 586-4600
FAX: (617) 828-8971
Industry Affiliation: Industry: Light Tools, Equipment
**Publication(s):**
*Tempo*
Day Published: q.
Lead Time: 60 days prior to pub. date
Mtls Deadline: 60 days prior to pub. date
Spec. Requirements: 4 pg.; offset; 84 x 11
Personnel: Mary Kay Quails, Editor

4252
**NORTH CAROLINA ASSOCIATION OF ELECTRIC COOPERATIVES**
P.O. Box 27306
Raleigh, NC 27611
Telephone: (919) 872-0800
FAX: (919) 872-3970
Industry Affiliation: Utility: Electric

---

Materials Accepted/Included: 01-Business news 02-By-line articles 03-Fashion news 04-Food news 05-Freelance copy 06-Letters to editor 07-Real estate news 08-Sports news 09-Travel news 10-Book rev. 11-Movie rev. 12-Music rev. 13-TV rev. 14-Theater rev. 15-Coming events 16-Obituaries 17-Question & answer 18-Social announcements 19-Artwork 20-Cartoons 21-Photos 22-TV listings 23-Audio rec. 24-Video rec. 25-Books 26-Films/film clips 27-Personnel news 28-Press releases 29-New product news/photos 30-Trade lit. 31-Contracts awarded 32-Display adv. 33-Classified adv.

**Publication(s):**
*Carolina Country*
Day Published: m.
Lead Time: 4 wks. prior to pub. date
Materials: 01,05,17,32
Mtls Deadline: 5 wks. prior to mo. of pub.
Personnel: Michael E.C. Gery, Editor

4253
## NORTH CAROLINA MUTUAL LIFE INSURANCE CO.
Mutual Plz.
Durham, NC 27701
Telephone: (919) 682-9201
FAX: (919) 683-1694
Industry Affiliation: Insurance
**Publication(s):**
*Whetstone*
Day Published: q.
Lead Time: 60 days prior to pub. date
Mtls Deadline: Mar. 1, July 1, Nov. 1
Spec. Requirements: 24 pg.
Personnel: Charles Blackman, Chairman
Editorial Board

*Review*
Day Published: s-m.
Lead Time: 4 wks. prior to pub. date
Mtls Deadline: 1st & 15th of ea. mo. prior
to pub. date
Spec. Requirements: 16 pg.; offset
Personnel: J.E. Wiggins, Editor
Debbie Gates, Assistant Editor

*Hot Line*
Day Published: bi-w.
Lead Time: 1 mo. prior to pub. date
Mtls Deadline: 1st & 15th of ea. mo. prior
to pub. date
Personnel: Joyce Holloway, Editor

4068
## NORTHEASTERN RETAIL LUMBERMENS ASSOCIATION
339 East Ave.
Rochester, NY 14604-2672
Telephone: (716) 325-1626
FAX: (716) 325-6179
Industry Affiliation: Lumber, Forestry,
Building Materials
**Publication(s):**
*Lumber Co-Operator*
Day Published: m.
Lead Time: 6 wks. prior to pub. date
Materials: 32,33
Mtls Deadline: 6 wks. prior to pub. date
Contact: Editorial Div.
Spec. Requirements: 48-180 pg.; offset; 8-
1/2 x 11
Personnel: Ellen Rye, Editor
John J. Brill, Publisher
Gabriele Lodder, Publications
Director

3032
## NORTHERN INDIANA PUBLIC SERVICE CO.
5265 Hohman Ave.
Hammond, IN 46320
Telephone: (219) 647-6210
FAX: (219) 647-6216
Industry Affiliation: Utility: Gas
**Publication(s):**
*Nipscofolks*
Day Published: bi-m.
Materials: 01,05,16,19,21,27
Contact: Corporate Communications
Spec. Requirements: 20-24 pg.; offset 8
1/2 x 11

2874
## NORTHERN TRUST CO.
50 S La Salle St
Chicago, IL 60675
Telephone: (312) 630-6000

Mailing Address:
50 S. LaSalle St.
Chicago, IL 60675
Industry Affiliation: Banks, Savings &
Loans
**Publication(s):**
*Northern News*
Day Published: w.
Contact: Pub. Rels.
Spec. Requirements: 2-4 pg. standard size
Personnel: Judy Mohan, Editor

3649
## NORTH MISSISSIPPI MEDICAL CENTER
830 S. Gloster St.
Tupelo, MS 38801
Telephone: (601) 841-3000
FAX: (601) 841-3822
Industry Affiliation: Hospitals
**Publication(s):**
*Checkup*
Day Published: fortn.
Lead Time: 2 wks.
Mtls Deadline: 2 wks. prior to pub. date
Contact: North Mississippi Medical Center
830 S. Gloster St.
Tupelo, MS 38801
Spec. Requirements: 4 pgs.
Personnel: Ed Darling, Editor

2212
## NORTHROP-GRUMMAN CORP.
One Northrop Ave.
Hawthorne, CA 90250
Telephone: (310) 332-1000
FAX: (310) 332-3396
Industry Affiliation: Aircraft, Aerospace,
Defense
**Publication(s):**
*Northrop-Grumman News*
Day Published: bi-w.
Lead Time: 2 mos. prior to pub. date
Mtls Deadline: 10 days prior to pub. date
Contact: All Divisions
Spec. Requirements: 11 x 16; tabloid; 8
pgs.
Personnel: Robert Judge, Editor in Chief

3601
## NORTHWEST AIRLINES, INC.
2700 Lone Oak Pkwy.
Eagan, MN 55121
Telephone: (612) 727-4505
Mailing Address:
5101 Northwest Dr.
Dept. A-1310
Saint Paul, MN 55111-3034
Industry Affiliation: Airlines
**Publication(s):**
*Northwest Passages*
Day Published: s-m.
Materials: 32,33
Spec. Requirements: 16 pg.: offset
newspaper; 114 x 14
Personnel: John Heenehan, Editor
Chris Clauser, Publisher
Mark Abels, Editor in Chief
Jeff Smith, Managing Editor

4593
## NORTHWEST ELECTRIC LIGHT & POWER ASSOCIATION
827 NE Oregon St., Ste. 200
Portland, OR 97232-2108
Telephone: (503) 231-1994
Industry Affiliation: Associations: Trade,
Fraternal
**Publication(s):**
*Nelpa News*
Day Published: 7/yr.
Lead Time: 30 days
Spec. Requirements: 8-16 pgs.; offset: 8
1/2 X 11
Personnel: Julie Icenogle, Editor

*Directory Of Company Members*
Day Published: a.
Lead Time: Jan. 1, prior to pub. date
Mtls Deadline: Nov. prior to pub. date
Personnel: Julie Icenogle

2958
## NORTHWESTERN MEMORIAL HOSPITAL
Superior St. & Fairbanks Ct.
Chicago, IL 60611
Telephone: (312) 908-2000
FAX: (312) 908-2937
Mailing Address:
215 E. Chicago Ave.
Chicago, IL 60611
Industry Affiliation: Hospitals
**Publication(s):**
*Teamworks*
Day Published: bi-m.
Lead Time: 3 mos.
Mtls Deadline: 8 wks. prior to pub.
Contact: Pub. Rels. Dept.
Personnel: Barb Storms, Editor

5429
## NORTHWESTERN NATIONAL INSURANCE GROUP
18650 W. Corporate Dr.
Brookfield, WI 53045-6344
Telephone: (414) 792-3165
FAX: (414) 792-3444
Mailing Address:
P.O. Box 2070
Milwaukee, WI 53201-2070
Industry Affiliation: Insurance
**Publication(s):**
*Employee News*
Day Published: m.
Contact: Communications
Spec. Requirements: 2 pg.; offset; 8 1/2 x
11
Personnel: Daniel J. Zautis, Editor
Catherine E. Bretl
Elizabeth P. Rafferty

*Agent News*
Day Published: q.
Spec. Requirements: 4 pg.; offset; 17 x 11
Personnel: Elizabeth P. Rafferty
Amy L. Bley
Kristine Sobczak, Editor

*Leading To Excellence*
Day Published: q.
Spec. Requirements: 4 pg., photocopied, 8
1/2 x 11
Personnel: Kristine Sobczak, Editor

3603
## NORTH WESTERN NATIONAL LIFE
20 Washington Ave., S.
Minneapolis, MN 55401
Telephone: (612) 372-5432
Industry Affiliation: Insurance
**Publication(s):**
*Columns*
Day Published: bi-w.
Mtls Deadline: Wed. prior
Contact: Corp. Comms.
Spec. Requirements: 8 pg.; offset; 8 1/2 X
11
Personnel: Tom Schnetz, Editor

*Pipeline*
Day Published: w.
Mtls Deadline: Wed. prior to pub. date
Contact: Corp. Communications
Spec. Requirements: 4 pg.; offset; 8 1/2 x
11
Personnel: P. Racquel Wright, Editor

5207
## NORTHWEST PIPELINE CORP.
295 Chipeta Way
Salt Lake Cty, UT 84108
Telephone: (801) 583-8800

Mailing Address:
P.O. Box 58900
Salt Lake Cty, UT 84158
Industry Affiliation: Utility: Gas
**Publication(s):**
*Northwest Discovery*
Day Published: q.
Spec. Requirements: 24 pg.; offset; 8 1/2
x 11
Personnel: John Nicksich, Editor

5304
## NORTHWEST PUBLIC POWER ASSOCIATION
9817 N.E. 54th St.
Vancouver, WA 98662
Telephone: (206) 254-0109
FAX: (206) 254-5731
Mailing Address:
P.O. Box 4576
Vancouver, WA 98662
Industry Affiliation: Associations: Trade,
Fraternal
**Publication(s):**
*Northwest Public Power Bulletin*
Day Published: m.
Lead Time: 30 days prior to pub. date
Materials: 01,02,05,15,16,21,27,28,29,30,
32,33
Mtls Deadline: last day of mo. prior to pub.
date
Spec. Requirements: 32 page; offset; 8
1/2 x 11
Personnel: Jack Vogel, Editor
Don Noel, Editor in Chief

*Northwest Electric Utility Directory*
Day Published: a.
Lead Time: 45 days prior to pub. date
Mtls Deadline: Feb. 28th prior to pub. date
Spec. Requirements: 128-pg.
Personnel: Don Noel, Editor

68420
## NORWEST CORPORATION
Norwest Ctr.-Sixth & Marquette
Minneapolis, MN 55479-1006
Telephone: (612) 667-9650
FAX: (612) 667-9555
Industry Affiliation: Finance, Services
**Publication(s):**
*Norwest World*
Day Published: m.
Lead Time: 3 wks. prior to pub. date
Personnel: Janet Grant

3087
## NORWEST FINANCIAL, INC.
206 Eighth St.
Des Moines, IA 50309
Telephone: (515) 243-2131
Industry Affiliation: Finance, Services
**Publication(s):**
*Network*
Day Published: m.
Lead Time: 1 mo.
Spec. Requirements: 20 pgs.; offset; 8 1/2
x 11
Personnel: Klare Black Logan, Editor

*On-Line*
Day Published: q.
Lead Time: 6 wks.
Spec. Requirements: 6 pgs.
Personnel: Klare Black Logan

3890
## OAKITE PRODUCTS, INC.
50 Valley Rd.
Berkeley Hts., NJ 07922
Telephone: (908) 464-6900
Industry Affiliation: Industry: Material
Handling

**Materials Accepted/Included:** 01-Business news 02-By-line articles 03-Fashion news 04-Food news 05-Freelance copy 06-Letters to editor 07-Real estate news 08-Sports news 09-Travel news 10-Book rev. 11-Movie rev. 12-Music rev. 13-TV rev. 14-Theater rev. 15-Coming events 16-Obituaries 17-Question & answer 18-Social announcements 19-Artwork 20-Cartoons 21-Photos 22-TV listings 23-Audio rec. 24-Video rec. 25-Books 26-Films/film clips 27-Personnel news 28-Press releases 29-New product news/photos 30-Trade lit. 31-Contracts awarded 32-Display adv. 33-Classified adv.

**Publication(s):**
*Review, The*
Day Published: q.
Lead Time: 3-6 mos.
Mtls Deadline: 3 mos. prior to pub. date
Spec. Requirements: 8-page
Personnel: Judy King, Editor

4884
## OAK RIDGE NATIONAL LABORATORY
P.O. Box 2008
Oak Ridge, TN 37831
Telephone: (615) 574-4160
Industry Affiliation: Colleges, Institutions, Science Research
**Publication(s):**
*Lab News*
Day Published: m.
Lead Time: 1 mo.
Spec. Requirements: 8-12 pg; offset; 8 1/2 x 11
Personnel: Bill Cabage, Editor

68421
## OGILVY & MATHER
676 St. Clair
Chicago, IL 60611
Telephone: (312) 988-2522
FAX: (312) 988-4329
Industry Affiliation: Architects, Engineers, Business Service
**Publication(s):**
*Viewpoint*
Day Published: s-a.
Personnel: Peg Bala, Production Manager

4408
## OHIO ASSOCIATION OF REALTORS
200 E. Town St.
Columbus, OH 43215
Telephone: (614) 228-6675
FAX: (614) 228-2601
Industry Affiliation: Real Estate
**Publication(s):**
*Ohio Realtor*
Day Published: m.
Lead Time: 30 days
Mtls Deadline: 1st Mon. of mo. prior to pub. date
Contact: Communications
Spec. Requirements: 16 pg.; 2-color; 11 3/8 x 15 1/2 tabloid
Personnel: Nikki Gasbarro, Editor

4479
## OHIO BELL TELEPHONE CO.
45 Erieview Plz., Rm. 862
Cleveland, OH 44114
Telephone: (216) 822-9700
FAX: (216) 822-5522
Industry Affiliation: Utility: Telephone
**Publication(s):**
*Insight*
Day Published: bi-w.
Spec. Requirements: 8 pg.; 8 1/2 x 11
Personnel: Irma Baker, Editor

71294
## OHIO BUREAU OF WORKER'S COMPENSATION
30 Spring St.
Columbus, OH 43266-0589
Telephone: (614) 752-8504
Industry Affiliation: Associations: City, State, Federal

**Publication(s):**
*Ohio Monitor*
Day Published: bi-m.
Lead Time: 2 mos. prior to pub. date
Mtls Deadline: 2 mos. prior to pub. date
Personnel: Robert L. McCullough, Editor

66455
## OHIO CASUALTY INSURANCE GROUP, THE
136 N. Third St.
Hamilton, OH 45025
Telephone: (513) 867-3000
Industry Affiliation: Insurance
**Publication(s):**
*Communicator*
Day Published: m.
Lead Time: 3 wks. prior to pub. date
Contact: Employee & Retiree Dept.
Personnel: Marcia Larison

*Pointers Magazine*
Day Published: q.

4494
## OHIO CHAMBER OF COMMERCE
35 E. Gay St., 2nd Fl.
Columbus, OH 43215-3181
Telephone: (614) 228-4201
FAX: (614) 228-6403
Industry Affiliation: Associations: City, State, Federal
**Publication(s):**
*Ohio Chamber Network & Small Business News*
Day Published: q.
Materials: 01
Spec. Requirements: 6-8 pg; offset; 11 x 17; 2 color ink
Personnel: Linda E. Deitch, Editor

*Small Business News*
Day Published: approx. 6-8/yr.
Mtls Deadline: ongoing
Spec. Requirements: 2-4 pg; 8 1/2 x 11; offset; 2 color ink
Personnel: Linda E. Deitch, Editor

*Ohio Legislative Report*
Day Published: m.
Lead Time: ongoing
Personnel: Linda E. Deitch, Editor

4496
## OHIO CREDIT UNION LEAGUE
1201 Dublin Rd.
Columbus, OH 43215
Telephone: (614) 486-2917
FAX: (614) 486-6044
Industry Affiliation: Associations: Trade, Fraternal
**Publication(s):**
*High Spots*
Day Published: a.
Lead Time: 1 mo. prior to pub. date
Mtls Deadline: 1 mo. prior to pub. date
Spec. Requirements: 4 pg.; offset tabloid; 11 x 17
Personnel: Catharine West, Editor

4498
## OHIO DENTAL ASSOCIATION
1370 Dublin Rd.
Columbus, OH 43215
Telephone: (614) 486-2700
FAX: (614) 486-0381
Industry Affiliation: Dental, Medical

**Publication(s):**
*Focus On Ohio Dentistry*
Day Published: m.
Lead Time: 4 wks. prior to pub. date
Personnel: Dr. Donald Bowers, Editor

4410
## OHIO DEPARTMENT OF YOUTH SERVICES
51 N. High St.
Columbus, OH 43215
Telephone: (614) 466-4314
FAX: (614) 752-9078
Industry Affiliation: Associations: City, State, Federal
**Publication(s):**
*Update*
Day Published: q.
Lead Time: 2 wks. prior to pub. date
Materials: 02,05,06,15,28,30
Mtls Deadline: 1st of mo. prior to pub. date
Contact: Public Information
Spec. Requirements: Material must relate to juvenile corrections field

4501
## OHIO EDISON CO.
76 S. Main St.
Akron, OH 44308
Telephone: (216) 384-5428
Industry Affiliation: Utility: Electric
**Publication(s):**
*Ohio Edisonian*
Day Published: bi-m.
Materials: 01
Spec. Requirements: 24 pg.; offset magazine; 8 1/2 x 11
Personnel: Gretchan Sekulich, Editor

4502
## OHIO FARM BUREAU FEDERATION
280 N. High St.
Columbus, OH 43215
Telephone: (614) 249-2479
FAX: (614) 249-2200
Mailing Address:
   P.O. Box 479
   Columbus, OH 43216-0479
Industry Affiliation: Associations: Trade, Fraternal
**Publication(s):**
*Buckeye Farm News*
Day Published: 11/yr.
Lead Time: 60 days prior to pub. date
Mtls Deadline: 60 days prior to pub. date
Spec. Requirements: 32 pg; offset magazine; 8 3/8 x 10 7/8
Personnel: Curt Dunham, Editor

4506
## OHIO HARDWARE ASSOCIATION
P.O. Box 1828
Columbus, OH 43216
Telephone: (614) 486-5278
Industry Affiliation: Associations: Trade, Fraternal
**Publication(s):**
*Oha Hard Lines*
Day Published: m.
Lead Time: 30 days days prior to pub. date
Mtls Deadline: 1st of mo. prior to pub. date
Spec. Requirements: 12 pg; offset; 8 1/2 x 11
Personnel: Andria Holmquist, Editor

*Oha Membership Directory*
Day Published: a.
Mtls Deadline: May 1st prior to pub. date
Spec. Requirements: 104 pgs.
Personnel: Andria Holmquist, Editor

4513
## OHIO NATIONAL LIFE INSURANCE CO.
P.O. Box 237
Cincinnati, OH 45201
Telephone: (513) 861-3600
FAX: (513) 559-6212
Industry Affiliation: Insurance
**Publication(s):**
*Bulletin*
Day Published: m.
Spec. Requirements: 12-16 pg.; offset; 84 x 11
Personnel: Karen Taravella, Editor

*O N L I Echoes*
Day Published: m.
Spec. Requirements: 4-6 pg.
Personnel: Debbie Hernan, Editor

4518
## OHIO PHARMACISTS ASSOCIATION
6037 Frantz Rd., Ste. 106
Dublin, OH 43017
Telephone: (614) 798-0037
FAX: (614) 798-0978
Industry Affiliation: Associations: Trade, Fraternal
**Publication(s):**
*Ohio Pharmacist*
Day Published: m.
Lead Time: 4 wks. prior to pub. date
Mtls Deadline: 4 wks. prior to issue mo.
Spec. Requirements: 28-32 pg.; offset lithography; 8 1/2 x 11
Personnel: Amy Bennett, R. Ph., Editor

4514
## OHIO POWER CO.
301 Cleveland Ave., S.W.
Canton, OH 44702
Telephone: (216) 456-8173
FAX: (216) 438-7340
Mailing Address:
   P.O. Box 24400
   Canton, OH 44712
Industry Affiliation: Utility: Electric
**Publication(s):**
*Ohio Power Review*
Day Published: m.
Spec. Requirements: 24-28 pg.; offset; 11 x 16
Personnel: David Hagelin, Editor

4515
## OHIO RURAL ELECTRIC COOPS INC.
6677 Busch Blvd.
Columbus, OH 43229
Telephone: (614) 846-5757
FAX: (618) 846-7108
Mailing Address:
   P.O. Box 26036
   Columbus, OH 43226-0036
Industry Affiliation: Electrical, Electronic, Manufacturing

**Materials Accepted/Included:** 01-Business news 02-By-line articles 03-Fashion news 04-Food news 05-Freelance copy 06-Letters to editor 07-Real estate news 08-Sports news 09-Travel news 10-Book rev. 11-Movie rev. 12-Music rev. 13-TV rev. 14-Theater rev. 15-Coming events 16-Obituaries 17-Question & answer 18-Social announcements 19-Artwork 20-Cartoons 21-Photos 22-TV listings 23-Audio rec. 24-Video rec. 25-Books 26-Films/film clips 27-Personnel news 28-Press releases 29-New product news/photos 30-Trade lit. 31-Contracts awarded 32-Display adv. 33-Classified adv.

11-65

**Publication(s):**
*Country Living Magazine*
Day Published: m.
Lead Time: 45 days prior to pub. date
Materials: 02,05,06,15,23,24,25,26,32
Mtls Deadline: 6 wks. prior to pub. date
Contact: Ed. Dept.
Spec. Requirements: 24-32 pgs.; offset magazine, 8.3 x 11
Personnel: Jeff Brehm, Editor

### OHIO STATE MEDICAL ASSOCIATION
4517
1500 Lake Shore Dr.
Columbus, OH 43204
Telephone: (614) 486-2401
Industry Affiliation: Associations: City, State, Federal
**Publication(s):**
*Ohio State Medical Journal*
Day Published: m.
Lead Time: 1st of mo. prior to pub. date
Mtls Deadline: 1st of mo. prior to pub. mo.
Spec. Requirements: 28-32 pg.; offset; 11 x 17
Personnel: Karen S. Edwards, Editor

*Synergy*
Day Published: m.
Mtls Deadline: 1st of mo. prior to mo. of pub.

### OHIO TRUCKING ASSOCIATION
4520
50 W. Broad St., Ste. 1111
Columbus, OH 43215
Telephone: (614) 221-5375
FAX: (614) 221-3717
Industry Affiliation: Associations: Trade, Fraternal
**Publication(s):**
*Ohio Government Directory*
Day Published: bi-a.
Lead Time: Feb.-Mar. prior to pub. date
Mtls Deadline: Feb.-Mar. even yrs.
Spec. Requirements: 96 pg.; offset; 84 x 11
Personnel: David F. Bartosic, Editor
　　　　　Tom King, Publisher

### OKLAHOMA ASSOCIATION OF ELECTRIC COOPERATIVES
4544
P.O. Box 54309
Oklahoma City, OK 73154-1309
Telephone: (405) 478-1455
FAX: (405) 478-0246
Industry Affiliation: Associations: City, State, Federal
**Publication(s):**
*Oklahoma Living*
Day Published: m.
Lead Time: 15th of mo. prior to pub. date
Spec. Requirements: 16-32 pgs.; offset; 9 3/4 x 13 3/4
Personnel: Mary Logan Kouts, Editor
　　　　　Fred Albert, Editor

### OKLAHOMA BANKERS ASSOCIATION
4545
PO Box 18246
Oklahoma City, OK 73154
Telephone: (405) 424-5252
FAX: (405) 424-4518
Mailing Address:
　P.O. Box 18246
　Oklahoma City, OK 73154
Industry Affiliation: Banks, Savings & Loans

**Publication(s):**
*Oklahoma Banker*
Day Published: bi-m.
Lead Time: 1 mo.
Mtls Deadline: 10 days prior to pub. date
Spec. Requirements: offset: 11 1/2 x 14 1/2
Personnel: Darrell McClendon, Editor
　　　　　Beth Payne, Ad Director

### OKLAHOMA BAR ASSOCIATION
4546
1901 N. Lincoln Blvd.
Oklahoma City, OK 73105
Telephone: (405) 524-2365
FAX: (405) 524-1115
Mailing Address:
　P.O. Box 53036
　Oklahoma City, OK 73152
Industry Affiliation: Associations: Trade, Fraternal
**Publication(s):**
*Oklahoma Bar Journal*
Day Published: w.; except Aug.
Lead Time: Tue., 12:00 pm prior to pub. date
Mtls Deadline: Tue., 12:00 pm prior to pub. date
Spec. Requirements: 48 pg.; offset; 8 x 10 1/2
Personnel: Martha M. Snow, Editor
　　　　　Stuart B. Strasner

### OKLAHOMA CITY UNIVERSITY
4547
2501 N. Blackwelder
Oklahoma City, OK 73106
Telephone: (405) 521-5348
FAX: (405) 523-4798
Industry Affiliation: Colleges, Institutions, Science Research
**Publication(s):**
*Focus*
Day Published: 5/yr.
Lead Time: 2 mos. prior to pub. date
Spec. Requirements: 16 or 48 pg.; offset; 8 1/2 x 11
Personnel: Lisa Pitsiri, Editor

### OKLAHOMA DEPARTMENT OF COMMERCE
4528
6601 N. Broadway
Oklahoma City, OK 73116
Telephone: (405) 843-9770
FAX: (405) 841-5199
Mailing Address:
　P.O. Box 26980
　Oklahoma City, OK 73126
Industry Affiliation: Associations: City, State, Federal
**Publication(s):**
*Commerce Folio*
Day Published: bi-m.
Lead Time: 1 mo. prior to pub. date
Contact: Communications & Media
Spec. Requirements: 8-pg; tabloid; 114 x 17
Personnel: Norma Vincent, Editor

### OKLAHOMA GAS & ELECTRIC CO.
4548
101 N. Robinson
Oklahoma City, OK 73101
Telephone: (405) 272-3280
Mailing Address:
　P.O. Box 321, MC 1200
　Oklahoma City, OK 73101
Industry Affiliation: Utility: Electric
**Publication(s):**
*Meter*
Day Published: m.
Contact: Electric Utility
Spec. Requirements: 24 pg; offset magazine; 8 1/2 x 11
Personnel: Ken Biddle, Editor

*Inside Og & E*
Day Published: m.
Lead Time: 2 wks.

### OKLAHOMA NATURAL GAS CO.
4571
P.O. Box 871
Tulsa, OK 74102
Telephone: (918) 588-7570
FAX: (918) 508-7372
Industry Affiliation: Utility: Gas
**Publication(s):**
*Gasette*
Day Published: 10-11/yr.
Lead Time: 45 days prior to pub. date
Mtls Deadline: 1st of mo. prior to pub. date
Spec. Requirements: 24-32 pg.; offset; 84 x 11
Personnel: Sue Hunsicker, Editor

### OKLAHOMA RESTAURANT ASSOCIATION
4573
3800 N. Portland
Oklahoma City, OK 73112
Telephone: (405) 942-8181
Industry Affiliation: Associations: Trade, Fraternal
**Publication(s):**
*Midsouthwest Restaurant Magazine*
Day Published: bi-m.
Lead Time: 30 days prior to pub. date
Materials: 04,32,33
Spec. Requirements: 16 pg.; offset; 84 x 11
Personnel: Cheryl Walker, Editor
　　　　　Robert T. Clift, Publisher

### OLAN MILLS OF TENNESSEE
4885
1101 Carter St.
Chattanooga, TN 37402
Telephone: (615) 622-5141
Industry Affiliation: Photography
**Publication(s):**
*Weekly Exposure*
Day Published: w.
Spec. Requirements: 14 pg.; mimeo bulletin; 54 x 84
Personnel: Billie Messner, Editor

*Lens*
Day Published: q.
Spec. Requirements: 8-12 pgs.
Personnel: Josie Sibold, Editor

### OLDSMOBILE/DIV. GENERAL MOTORS
66444
920 Townsend
Lansing, MI 48921
Telephone: (517) 377-5660
FAX: (517) 377-2706
Industry Affiliation: Autos, Trucks
**Publication(s):**
*Olds Line*
Day Published: bi-w.
Lead Time: 1 wk. prior to pub. date
Contact: Oldsmobile Employees
Spec. Requirements: 6 pg.; 8 1/2 x 11
Personnel: Ann Cornell, Editor

### OMAHA PUBLIC POWER DIST.
3800
444 S. 16th St.
Omaha, NE 68102
Telephone: (402) 636-2000
Industry Affiliation: Utility: Electric

**Publication(s):**
*Flash*
Day Published: m.
Lead Time: 30 days prior to pub. date
Mtls Deadline: 5th of mo. prior to pub. date
Contact: Pub. Rels. Div.
Spec. Requirements: 16-20 pgs. offset magazine; 8 1/2 x 11
Personnel: Paula Lukowski, Editor

### ONAN CORP.
3605
1400 73rd Ave., N.E.
Minneapolis, MN 55432
Telephone: (612) 574-5000
FAX: (612) 574-8087
Industry Affiliation: Associations: Trade, Fraternal
**Publication(s):**
*Onan News*
Day Published: q.
Mtls Deadline: 3 wks. prior to ea. calendar qrtr.
Contact: Corp. Comm.
Spec. Requirements: 8 pg.; offset; 8 1/2 x 11
Personnel: Allen Guidry III, Editor

### OPPENHEIMER MANAGEMENT CORP.
2366
2 World Trade Ctr., 34th Fl.
New York, NY 10048
Telephone: (800) 255-2755
FAX: (212) 323-0557
Industry Affiliation: Finance, Services
**Publication(s):**
*Handsignals, The*
Day Published: q.
Spec. Requirements: 26 pg.; offset; 8 1/2 x 11
Personnel: Ellen Batt, Editor

### OPTIMIST INTERNATIONAL
3712
4494 Lindell Blvd.
St. Louis, MO 63108
Telephone: (314) 371-6000
FAX: (314) 371-6006
Industry Affiliation: Associations: Trade, Fraternal
**Publication(s):**
*Optimist Magazine*
Day Published: 9/yr.
Lead Time: 8 wks. prior to pub. date
Mtls Deadline: 6 wks. prior to pub. date
Spec. Requirements: 32 pg.; offset; 8 1/2 x 11
Personnel: Gary Bradley, Editor

### ORANGE & ROCKLAND UTILITIES, INC.
4103
One Blue Hill Plz.
Pearl River, NY 10965
Telephone: (914) 577-2546
FAX: (914) 577-6913
Industry Affiliation: Utility: Electric
**Publication(s):**
*Lamppost*
Day Published: m.
Lead Time: 1 mo. prior to pub. date
Materials: 01
Spec. Requirements: 16-20 pg.; offset; 11 x 14 1/2
Personnel: Jonathan L. Yoder, Editor

### ORCHID ISLE AUTO CTR.
2704
P.O. Box 4397
Hilo, HI 96720
Telephone: (808) 935-1191
FAX: (808) 935-5960
Industry Affiliation: Autos, Trucks

**Publication(s):**
*Orchid Isle Auto Center Newsletter*
Day Published: m.
Lead Time: 6 wks. prior to pub. date
Mtls Deadline: 6 wks. prior to pub. date
Spec. Requirements: 2 pg; offset; 8 1/2 x
    14; 19 & 20 on C.D. Rom
Personnel: Katherine S. Hanley, Editor

2718
**ORE-IDA FOODS, INC.**
220 W. Parkcenter Blvd.
Boise, ID 83706
Telephone: (208) 383-6570
Mailing Address:
    P.O. Box 10
    Boise, ID 83707
Industry Affiliation: Food, General
**Publication(s):**
*Voice, The*
Day Published: q.
Lead Time: 2 mos. prior to pub. date
Mtls Deadline: 1st of mo. prior to pub. date
Spec. Requirements: 16 pg; letterpress; 84
    x 11
Personnel: Grant C. Jones, Editor

4597
**OREGON ASSOCIATION OF
    NURSERYMEN**
2780 S.E. Harrison, Ste. 102
Milwaukie, OR 97222
Telephone: (503) 653-8733
FAX: (503) 653-1528
Industry Affiliation: Associations: Trade,
    Fraternal
**Publication(s):**
*Oan Digger*
Day Published: m.
Lead Time: 30 days prior to pub. date
Materials: 02,05,10,15,21,25,27,28,29,30,
    32,33
Mtls Deadline: 1st of mo. prior to pub. date
Contact: Publications
Spec. Requirements: 56 pg.; offset; 8 1/2
    x 11; 3 col. fmt.
Personnel: Don Grey, Editor
        Lucinda Wagenblast, Art
        Director

*Oan Directory & Buyer's Guide*
Day Published: a.
Lead Time: June 1st prior to pub. date
Mtls Deadline: May 1st prior to pub. date
Contact: Publications
Spec. Requirements: 556 pgs.; web press;
    8 1/2 x 11; col. adv. avail.
Personnel: Don Grey, Editor
        Lucinda Wagenblast, Art
        Director

*Farwest Magazine*
Day Published: a.
Materials: 02,05,10,15,19,21,25,27,28,29,
    30,32,33
Mtls Deadline: June 15
Contact: Publications
Spec. Requirements: 200 pgs.; web offset;
    8 1/2 x 11; 3 col.
Personnel: Don Grey, Editor
        Lucinda Wagenblast, Art
        Director

4617
**OREGON DEPARTMENT OF
    EDUCATION**
700 Pringle Pkwy. S.E.
Salem, OR 97310
Telephone: (503) 378-3569
Industry Affiliation: Associations: City,
    State, Federal

**Publication(s):**
*Education First*
Day Published: bi-m.
Lead Time: 1 mo. prior to pub. date
Mtls Deadline: 1 mo. prior to pub. date
Personnel: Larry Austin, Editor

4615
**OREGON DEPARTMENT OF
    INSURANCE & FINANCE**
21 Labor & Industries Bldg.
Salem, OR 97310
Telephone: (503) 378-4100
FAX: (503) 378-6444
Mailing Address:
    Oregon Dept. of Consumer & Business
    Services
    21 Labor & Industries Bldg.
    Salem, OR 97310
Industry Affiliation: Insurance
**Publication(s):**
*Biennial Report*
Day Published: bi-a.

4622
**OREGON DEPT. OF FORESTRY**
2600 State St.
Salem, OR 97310
Telephone: (503) 945-7422
FAX: (503) 945-7212
Industry Affiliation: Associations: City,
    State, Federal
**Publication(s):**
*Forest Log*
Day Published: bi-m.
Spec. Requirements: 8 pg.; offset; 8 1/2 x
    11
Personnel: Brian Ballou, Editor

4618
**OREGON HEALTH SCIENCES
    UNIVERSITY**
3181 S.W. Sam Jackson Pk. Rd.
Portland, OR 97201
Telephone: (503) 494-8231
FAX: (503) 494-8246
Industry Affiliation: Associations: City,
    State, Federal
**Publication(s):**
*Ohsu Views*
Day Published: q.
Lead Time: 2 mos. prior to pub. date
Spec. Requirements: 32 pgs.; 8 1/2 x 11
Personnel: Marlys Levin, Editor
        Dick Baltus
        Shannon Stroud

4620
**OREGON PUBLIC EMPLOYEES
    RETIREMENT SYSTEM**
P.O. Box 73
Portland, OR 97207
Telephone: (503) 229-5824
FAX: (503) 222-5504
Industry Affiliation: Associations: Trade,
    Fraternal
**Publication(s):**
*Perspectives*
Day Published: q.
Materials: 17,21,27,28
Spec. Requirements: 4-8 pg.; offset; 8 1/2
    x 11
Personnel: David Amick, Editor

4623
**OREGON STATE UNIVERSITY**
Admin. Services Bldg.
Corvallis, OR 97331
Telephone: (503) 737-0780
Industry Affiliation: Colleges, Institutions,
    Science Research

**Publication(s):**
*Oregon Stater*
Day Published: bi-m.
Contact: Dept. of Information
Spec. Requirements: 24-32 pg; offset
    tabloid newspaper; 114 x 144
Personnel: George P. Edmonston, Jr.,
        Editor

3244
**ORLEANS PARRISH SCHOOL
    BOARD**
4100 Touro St.
New Orleans, LA 70122
Telephone: (504) 942-3529
Industry Affiliation: Colleges, Institutions,
    Science Research
**Publication(s):**
*Applause*
Day Published: m.
Lead Time: 3 wks.
Mtls Deadline: 15th of ea. mo.
Contact: Information & Community Svcs.
        Dept.
Spec. Requirements: 4 pg.; offset; 17 x 22
Personnel: Al Kennedy, Editor

*Superintendents Bulletin*
Day Published: w.
Lead Time: 1 wk.
Mtls Deadline: Wed., 12:00 pm

5093
**ORYX ENERGY CO.**
13155 Noel Rd.
Dallas, TX 75240-5067
Telephone: (214) 715-4000
Mailing Address:
    P.O. Box 2880
    Dallas, TX 75221-2880
Industry Affiliation: Petroleum, Gas
**Publication(s):**
*Oryx Outlook*
Day Published: s-m.
Spec. Requirements: 8-12 pg; offset; 8 1/2
    x 11
Personnel: Christine Caffey, Editor

3607
**OTC DIVISION OF SPX**
655 Eisenhower Dr.
Owatonna, MN 55060
Telephone: (507) 455-7000
FAX: (507) 455-7186
Industry Affiliation: Auto Suppliers
**Publication(s):**
*O T C Today*
Day Published: bi-m.
Lead Time: 1 wk. prior to pub. date
Mtls Deadline: 1 wk. prior to pub. date
Spec. Requirements: 4-6 pg.; offset; 8 1/2
    x 11
Personnel: Diane Lageson, Editor

2441
**OTIS ELEVATOR CO.**
One Farm Springs
Farmington, CT 06032
Telephone: (203) 676-6000
Industry Affiliation: Electrical, Electronic,
    Manufacturing
**Publication(s):**
*Otis Bulletin*
Day Published: 5/yr.
Lead Time: 30 days prior to pub. date
Contact: Otis North American Operations
Spec. Requirements: 12-16 pg.; offset; 9
    1/2 x 12
Personnel: Michael Jordan-Reilly, Editor

*Otis Magazine*
Day Published: q.
Lead Time: 60 days prior to pub. date
Mtls Deadline: 60 days prior to pub. date
Personnel: John Kwelak, Editor

3606
**OTTER TAIL POWER CO.**
215 S. Cascade
Fergus Falls, MN 56537
Telephone: (218) 739-8200
FAX: (218) 739-8218
Mailing Address:
    P.O. Box 496
    Fergus Falls, MN 56538
Industry Affiliation: Utility: Electric
**Publication(s):**
*Hi-Lites*
Day Published: m.
Spec. Requirements: 20-28 pg.; offset; 8
    1/2 x 11
Personnel: Tom Hintgen, Editor
        Theresa Drexler, Assistant
        Editor

*Coffee Communicator*
Day Published: d.
Spec. Requirements: 1 pg.; 8 1/2 x 11
Personnel: Tom Hintgen, Editor

2837
**OUTBOARD MARINE CORP.**
100 Seahorse Dr.
Waukegan, IL 60085
Telephone: (708) 689-5422
FAX: (708) 689-5789
Industry Affiliation: Sports, Equipment
**Publication(s):**
*O M C Currents*
Day Published: q.
Lead Time: 1 1/2 mos. prior to pub. date
Spec. Requirements: 14-16 pgs. offset; 8
    1/2 X 11
Personnel: Chuck Merritt, Editor

4413
**OWENS-ILLINOIS INC.**
One SeaGate
Toledo, OH 43666
Telephone: (419) 247-5000
Industry Affiliation: Glass
**Publication(s):**
*Insight*
Day Published: q.
Contact: Corp. Staff
Spec. Requirements: 4 pg.; offset
    newspaper; 114 x 16
Personnel: John Hoff, Editor

4104
**OZONE INDUSTRIES INC.**
101-32 101st St.
Jamaica, NY 11416
Telephone: (718) 845-5200
FAX: (718) 641-6221
Industry Affiliation: Colleges, Institutions,
    Science Research
**Publication(s):**
*Ozone Newsletter*
Day Published: s-a.
Materials: 01,04,27,28,29,31
Contact: Personnel
Spec. Requirements: 12 pg.; 8 1/2 x 11
Personnel: Marie Fertitta, Editor

4105
**PACE UNIVERSITY**
Pace Plz.
New York, NY 10038
Telephone: (212) 346-1712
Industry Affiliation: Colleges, Institutions,
    Science Research

---

**Materials Accepted/Included:** 01-Business news 02-By-line articles 03-Fashion news 04-Food news 05-Freelance copy 06-Letters to editor 07-Real estate news 08-Sports news 09-Travel news 10-Book rev. 11-Movie rev. 12-Music rev. 13-TV rev. 14-Theater rev. 15-Coming events 16-Obituaries 17-Question & answer 18-Social announcements 19-Artwork 20-Cartoons 21-Photos 22-TV listings 23-Audio rec. 24-Video rec. 25-Books 26-Films/film clips 27-Personnel news 28-Press releases 29-New product news/photos 30-Trade lit. 31-Contracts awarded 32-Display adv. 33-Classified adv.

11-67

**Publication(s):**
*Pace Magazine*
Day Published: q.
Lead Time: 1 mo. prior to pub. date
Mtls Deadline: 1 mo. prior to pub. date
Contact: University Communications
Spec. Requirements: 4-16 pg.; typeset; 8-1/2 x 11; offset
Personnel: Jim Kayton, Editor

### PACIFIC BELL [2218]
140 New Montgomery St., Rm. 611
San Francisco, CA 94105
Telephone: (415) 542-9000
Industry Affiliation: Utility: Telephone
**Publication(s):**
*Connections*
Day Published: w.
Lead Time: 2 wks. prior to pub. date
Mtls Deadline: 2 wks. prior to pub. date
Spec. Requirements: 8 pg.; offset; 11 x 17
Personnel: Eleanor Vincent, Editor

### PACIFIC FIRST BANK [5306]
1420 Fifth Ave., Ste. 1300
Seattle, WA 98101
Telephone: (202) 224-3368
Mailing Address:
P.O. Box 91029
Seattle, WA 98111
Industry Affiliation: Banks, Savings & Loans
**Publication(s):**
*Spirit*
Day Published: 11/yr.
Lead Time: 2 wks. prior to pub. date
Mtls Deadline: 2 wks. prior to pub. date
Contact: Employee Communications
Spec. Requirements: 4 pg.; offset tabloid
Personnel: Robb Zerr, Editor

*Banknotes*
Day Published: q.
Lead Time: 20 days prior to pub. date
Mtls Deadline: 20 days prior to pub. date
Contact: Employee Communications
Personnel: Robb Zerr, Editor

### PACIFIC GAS & ELECTRIC CO. [66443]
77 Beale St., Rm. 2925B
San Francisco, CA 94177
Telephone: (415) 973-1868
FAX: (415) 973-9446
Industry Affiliation: Utility: Electric
**Publication(s):**
*P G & E Week*
Day Published: w.

### PACIFIC HEALTH RESOURCES [2307]
1423 S. Grand
Los Angeles, CA 90015
Telephone: (213) 748-2411
Industry Affiliation: Hospitals
**Publication(s):**
*Update*
Day Published: bi-w.
Lead Time: 2 wks. prior to pub. date
Mtls Deadline: 2 wks. prior to pub. date
Contact: Public Relations
Spec. Requirements: 20 pg.; offset; magazine
Personnel: Kathy Fisher, Editor

### PACIFIC LUTHERAN UNIVERSITY [5307]
121st & S. Park
Tacoma, WA 98447
Telephone: (206) 535-7430
FAX: (206) 535-8331
Industry Affiliation: Colleges, Institutions, Science Research

**Publication(s):**
*Scene:*
Day Published: Oct., Dec., Mar., June
Lead Time: 15th of mo. prior
Spec. Requirements: 20-28-page; offset; 17 1/2 x 11 1/2
Personnel: James L. Peterson, Editor

### PACIFIC MUTUAL LIFE INS. CO. [2336]
700 Newport Center Dr.
Newport Beach, CA 92660
Telephone: (714) 640-3768
Mailing Address:
700 Newport Center Dr.
Newport Beach, CA 92660
Industry Affiliation: Insurance
**Publication(s):**
*Wavelenght*
Day Published: m.
Lead Time: 3 wks.s
Mtls Deadline: 4 wks.
Spec. Requirements: 12 pge.; offset; 8 1/2 X 11
Personnel: Barbara Assadi, Editor

### PACIFIC POWER & LIGHT CO. [4598]
920 S.W. Sixth Ave.
Public Service Bldg.
Portland, OR 97204
Telephone: (503) 256-6800
Industry Affiliation: Utility: Electric
**Publication(s):**
*Bulletin*
Day Published: m.
Lead Time: 1 mo. prior to pub. date
Mtls Deadline: 20th of ea. mo. prior to pub. date
Spec. Requirements: 16 pgs.; offset; 8 1/2 x 11
Personnel: Jan Mitchell, Editor

### PAN-AMERICAN LIFE INSURANCE CO. [3229]
P.O. Box 60219
New Orleans, LA 70160
Telephone: (504) 566-1300
Industry Affiliation: Insurance
**Publication(s):**
*Lifeline*
Day Published: m.
Contact: Corporate Communications
Spec. Requirements: 4 pg.; offset; 8 1/2 x 11
Personnel: Eileen Lumar-Johnson, Editor

### PANHANDLE EASTERN CORP. [66442]
5400 Westheimer Ct.
Houston, TX 77056
Telephone: (713) 627-5400
FAX: (713) 627-4091
Mailing Address:
P.O. Box 1642
Houston, TX 77251
Industry Affiliation: Petroleum, Gas
**Publication(s):**
*Pipe Lines*
Day Published: bi-m.
Lead Time: 6 wks. prior to pub. date
Contact: Corp. Comms.
Personnel: Tom Overton, Editor

### PARAGON ELECTRIC COMPANY, INC. [5431]
606 Parkway Blvd.
Two Rivers, WI 54241
Telephone: (414) 793-1161
FAX: (414) 793-3736
Industry Affiliation: Electrical, Electronic, Manufacturing

**Publication(s):**
*Para-Scope*
Day Published: s-a.
Materials: 17,19,21,27,28,29,31
Spec. Requirements: 4-8 pg.; offset magazine; 84 x 11
Personnel: Sandra Murray, Editor

### PARKS COLLEGE OF ST. LOUIS UNIVERSITY [2879]
500 Falling Springs Rd.
Cahokia, IL 62206
Telephone: (618) 337-7500
FAX: (618) 332-6802
Industry Affiliation: Colleges, Institutions, Science Research
**Publication(s):**
*Parks Today*
Day Published: 4/yr.
Lead Time: 3 mos. prior to pub. date
Mtls Deadline: 1st of Feb., Apr., Jul., Nov.
Spec. Requirements: 12-16 pg.; offset; 11 x 17
Personnel: Nita S. Browning, Editor

### PASEO DEL RIO ASSOCIATION [5041]
213 Broadway, Ste. 5
San Antonio, TX 78205-1923
Telephone: (210) 227-4262
Industry Affiliation: Associations: City, State, Federal
**Publication(s):**
*Rio*
Day Published: m.
Materials: 09,23,24,25,32
Mtls Deadline: 15th of mo. prior to pub. date
Spec. Requirements: coated cover magazine
Personnel: Richard Marini, Editor

### PEACHTREE CENTER [2670]
225 Peachtree St., N.E., Ste. 300
Atlanta, GA 30303
Telephone: (404) 614-5000
FAX: (404) 614-5346
Industry Affiliation: Real Estate
**Publication(s):**
*Center Circle*
Day Published: bi-m.
Lead Time: 1 mo. prior to pub. date
Mtls Deadline: 2 wks. prior to pub. date
Spec. Requirements: 12-16 pg.; offset; 7 x 7
Personnel: Wendy Giddes, Editor

*Mall Street Journal*
Day Published: m.
Lead Time: 2 wks. prior prior to pub. date
Personnel: Wendy Giddes, Editor

### PECO ENERGY COMPANY [4742]
2301 Market St., S13-1
Philadelphia, PA 19103
Telephone: (215) 841-4130
FAX: (215) 841-5323
Mailing Address:
P.O. Box 8699
Philadelphia, PA 19101
Industry Affiliation: Utility: Electric
**Publication(s):**
*Perspectives*
Day Published: bi-w.
Personnel: Lisa E.R. Balestra, Editor

### PENNSYLVANIA BAR ASSOCIATION [4737]
100 South St.
Harrisburg, PA 17108
Telephone: (717) 238-6715
FAX: (717) 238-7182
Industry Affiliation: Associations: Trade, Fraternal

**Publication(s):**
*Pennsylvania Lawyer, The*
Day Published: bi-m.
Lead Time: 1 mo. prior to pub. date
Mtls Deadline: 1 mo. prior to pub. date
Spec. Requirements: 32-44 pgs.; offset; 8 1/2 x 11
Personnel: Donald C. Sarvey, Editor

### PENNSYLVANIA ELECTRIC CO. [4796]
1001 Broad St.
Johnstown, PA 15906
Telephone: (814) 533-8846
FAX: (814) 533-8875
Industry Affiliation: Utility: Electric
**Publication(s):**
*Carrier Lines*
Day Published: m.
Lead Time: 8 wks. prior to pub. date
Spec. Requirements: 16 or 20 pg.; offset; 8 1/2 x 11
Personnel: Larry R. O'Reilly, Editor

*Face-To-Face*
Day Published: m.
Lead Time: 1 mo. prior to pub. date
Mtls Deadline: 1st of mo. prior to pub. date
Personnel: Larry R. O'Reilly, Editor

### PENNSYLVANIA MANUFACTURERS' ASSOCIATION INSURANCE CO. [4805]
925 Chestnut St.
Philadelphia, PA 19107
Telephone: (215) 629-5000
FAX: (215) 629-5144
Industry Affiliation: Insurance
**Publication(s):**
*Inside P M A*
Day Published: q.
Contact: Human Resources Dept.
Spec. Requirements: 12-16 pgs.; offset; 8 1/2 x 11
Personnel: Kathleen Travaline, Editor

*Broker & Agent News*
Day Published: q.
Personnel: Kathleen Travaline, Editor

*Directions*
Day Published: q.
Personnel: Kathleen Travaline, Editor

### PENNSYLVANIA MEDICAL SOCIETY [4804]
777 E. Park Dr.
Harrisburg, PA 17105
Telephone: (717) 558-7750
FAX: (717) 558-7840
Mailing Address:
P.O. Box 8820
Harrisburg, PA 17105
Industry Affiliation: Hospitals
**Publication(s):**
*Pennsylvania Medicine*
Day Published: m.
Mtls Deadline: 1st of mo. prior to pub. mo.
Spec. Requirements: 58 pg.; offset; 8 x 11
Personnel: Elaine Herrmann, Editor

### PENNSYLVANIA MOTOR TRUCK ASSOCIATION [4806]
910 Linda Ln.
Camp Hill, PA 17011-6401
Telephone: (717) 761-7122
FAX: (717) 761-8434
Industry Affiliation: Trucking

**Materials Accepted/Included:** 01-Business news 02-By-line articles 03-Fashion news 04-Food news 05-Freelance copy 06-Letters to editor 07-Real estate news 08-Sports news 09-Travel news 10-Book rev. 11-Movie rev. 12-Music rev. 13-TV rev. 14-Theater rev. 15-Coming events 16-Obituaries 17-Question & answer 18-Social announcements 19-Artwork 20-Cartoons 21-Photos 22-TV listings 23-Audio rec. 24-Video rec. 25-Books 26-Films/film clips 27-Personnel news 28-Press releases 29-New product news/photos 30-Trade lit. 31-Contracts awarded 32-Display adv. 33-Classified adv.

**Publication(s):**
*Penntrux*
Day Published: m.
Lead Time: 6 wks. prior to pub. date
Mtls Deadline: 6 wks. prior to pub. date
Personnel: Charles A. Schulz, Editor

4807

## PENNSYLVANIA MUSIC EDUCATORS ASSOCIATION
823 Old Westtown Rd.
West Chester, PA 19382-5276
Telephone: (610) 436-9281
FAX: (610) 430-2169
Industry Affiliation: Associations: Trade, Fraternal
**Publication(s):**
*P M E A News*
Day Published: q.
Lead Time: 6 wks. prior to pub. date
Materials: 06,10,25,28,29,32,33
Mtls Deadline: 6 wks. prior to pub. date
Spec. Requirements: 64-80 pg.; offset; 8-1/2 x 11
Personnel: Dr. Richard C. Merrell, Editor

4808

## PENNSYLVANIA POWER CO.
One E. Washington St.
New Castle, PA 16103-0891
Telephone: (412) 652-5531
FAX: (412) 656-5318
Industry Affiliation: Utility: Electric
**Publication(s):**
*Penn Power News*
Day Published: bi-m.
Lead Time: 1 mo. prior to pub. date
Materials: 01,02,15,16,17,18,21,31
Mtls Deadline: 10th of mo. prior to pub. date
Spec. Requirements: 16-20 pg.; offset magazine; 8-1/2 x 11
Personnel: Ellen Ramicone, Editor

4803

## PENN TRAFFIC CO.
P.O. Box 4965
Syracuse, NY 13221
Telephone: (315) 453-7284
FAX: (315) 453-0474
Industry Affiliation: Bus, Transit
**Publication(s):**
*The Open Line*
Day Published: q.
Contact: Emp. Rels. Dept.
Spec. Requirements: 20-pgs.; offset; 8 1/2 x 11
Personnel: Vi Schlereth, Editor

5042

## PENNZOIL CO.
700 Milam St.
Houston, TX 77002
Telephone: (713) 546-4000
FAX: (713) 546-6051
Mailing Address:
P.O. Box 2967
Houston, TX 77252
Industry Affiliation: Petroleum, Gas
**Publication(s):**
*Perspectives*
Day Published: bi-m.
Lead Time: 3-6 mos. prior to pub. date
Mtls Deadline: 3 mos. prior to pub. date
Spec. Requirements: 24-28 pg.; offset; 8 1/2 x 11
Personnel: Carol Mancini-Price, Editor

2442

## PEOPLE'S BANK
850 Main St.
Bridgeport, CT 06604
Telephone: (203) 338-7433
Industry Affiliation: Banks, Savings & Loans

**Publication(s):**
*People's Newsletter*
Day Published: 8/yr.
Lead Time: 15 days prior to pub. date
Mtls Deadline: 15 days prior to pub. date
Spec. Requirements: 20-pg.; offset; 8 1/2 x 11
Personnel: Jane Sharpe, Editor

68403

## PEOPLE FOR THE ETHICAL TREATMENT OF ANIMALS (PETA)
P.O. Box 42516
Washington, DC 20015
Telephone: (301) 770-7388
FAX: (301) 770-8969
Industry Affiliation: Associations: Trade, Fraternal
**Publication(s):**
*P E T A's Animal Times*
Day Published: bi-m.
Personnel: Kathryn Fisher

*Compassion Corps*
Day Published: q.
Personnel: Kathryn Fisher

4739

## PEOPLES NATURAL GAS CO.
CNG Tower
625 Liberty Ave.
Pittsburgh, PA 15222
Telephone: (412) 471-5100
FAX: (412) 497-6600
Industry Affiliation: Utility: Gas
**Publication(s):**
*P N G Today*
Day Published: 11/yr.
Lead Time: 3 mos. prior to pub. date
Spec. Requirements: 8 pg., offset, 11 x 7

2548

## PEOPLES SECURITY LIFE INSURANCE CO.
300 Morgan St.
Durham, NC 27702
Telephone: (919) 682-5431
FAX: (919) 687-8575
Mailing Address:
P.O. Box 61
Durham, NC 27702
Industry Affiliation: Insurance
**Publication(s):**
*Currents*
Day Published: m.
Lead Time: 6 wks. prior to pub. date
Mtls Deadline: 15th of the mo. prior to pub. date
Spec. Requirements: 16-20 pgs.; offset magazine; 84 x 11
Personnel: David C. Nowakowski, Editor

68428

## PEPPERIDGE FARM, INC.
595 Westport Ave.
Norwalk, CT 06851
Telephone: (203) 846-7000
FAX: (203) 846-7369
Industry Affiliation: Bakery Products
**Publication(s):**
*Perspective*
Day Published: 2-3/yr.
Personnel: Leslie Weaver, Editor in Chief

*Pepp Talk*
Day Published: 2-4/yr.
Personnel: Leslie Weaver

4109

## PEPSI-COLA CO.
Rte. 100
Somers, NY 10589
Telephone: (914) 767-6000
FAX: (914) 767-6553
Industry Affiliation: Soft Drinks

**Publication(s):**
*Pepsi Spirit*
Day Published: q.
Lead Time: 1 mo. prior to pub. date
Personnel: Ann Ward, Editor

3380

## PERINI CORP.
73 Mt. Wayte Ave.
Framingham, MA 01701
Telephone: (508) 628-2000
FAX: (508) 628-2960
Industry Affiliation: Industry: Heavy Construction, Machinery
**Publication(s):**
*Perini Pages*
Day Published: s-a.
Lead Time: 4 wks. prior to pub. date
Spec. Requirements: 6 pg.; tabloid; offset newsletter
Personnel: Kathleen Fyfe, Editor

*Perini Second Century*
Day Published: s-a.
Spec. Requirements: 12 pg.; magazine style
Personnel: Kathleen Fyfe, Managing Editor

3786

## PETER KIEWIT SONS, INC.
1000 Kiewit Plz.
Omaha, NE 68131
Telephone: (402) 342-2052
Industry Affiliation: Industry: Heavy Construction, Machinery
**Publication(s):**
*Kie-Ways*
Day Published: bi-m.
Lead Time: 1-1 1/2 mos. prior to pub. date
Mtls Deadline: 1-1 1/2 mos. prior to pub. date
Spec. Requirements: 32-48 pgs.; offset magazine; 8 1/2 x 11
Personnel: John Maher, Editor

4110

## PFIZER, INC.
235 E. 42nd St.
New York, NY 10017
Telephone: (212) 573-2255
Industry Affiliation: Drugs, Cosmetics, Pharmaceuticals
**Publication(s):**
*Pfizer Scene*
Day Published: 7/yr.
Materials: 01
Spec. Requirements: 16 pg.; offset magazine; 8 1/2 x 11
Personnel: Tom McDonough, Editor

69379

## PHARMACEUTICAL MANUFACTURERS ASSOCIATION
1100 15th St., N.W.
Washington, DC 20005
Telephone: (202) 835-3400
FAX: (202) 835-3414
Industry Affiliation: Drugs, Cosmetics, Pharmaceuticals
**Publication(s):**
*P M A Newsletter*
Day Published: w.
Personnel: Duffy Miller, Editor

*P M A Bulletin*
Day Published: 10/yr.
Spec. Requirements: offset; 84 x 11
Personnel: Claudia Baskin, Editor

4693

## P.H. GLATFELTER CO.
228 S. Main St.
Spring Grove, PA 17362
Telephone: (717) 225-4711
Industry Affiliation: Paper Products

**Publication(s):**
*Barker*
Day Published: q.
Lead Time: 2 mos.
Mtls Deadline: 1st wk.: Feb., May, Aug., Nov.
Spec. Requirements: 24-pgs.; offset magazine; 8 1/4 x 11
Personnel: Patricia Sweeney, Editor

*Health-O-Gram*
Day Published: irreg.
Lead Time: 6 wks.
Mtls Deadline: 6 wks.
Spec. Requirements: 1 pg. format; reproduced in-house
Personnel: J. Cauffiel-Zinn

4740

## PHILADELPHIA BAR ASSOCIATION
1101 Market St., 11th Fl.
Philadelphia, PA 19107
Telephone: (215) 238-6300
Industry Affiliation: Associations: Trade, Fraternal
**Publication(s):**
*Philadelphia Bar Reporter, The*
Day Published: 21/yr.
Lead Time: 2 wks. prior to pub. date
Mtls Deadline: 2 wks. prior to pub. date
Contact: Comms. Dept.
Spec. Requirements: 8-16 pg.; offset; 11 1/2 x 15
Personnel: Nancy L. Hebble, Managing Editor

*Philadelphia Lawyer, The*
Day Published: q.
Lead Time: 2 mos. prior to pub. date
Mtls Deadline: 2 mos. prior to pub. date
Contact: Comms. Dept.
Spec. Requirements: 72-96 pg.; 8 1/2 x 11; color cover
Personnel: Nancy L. Hebble, Managing Editor

4743

## PHILADELPHIA GAS WORKS
800 W. Montgomery Ave.
Philadelphia, PA 19122
Telephone: (215) 684-6564
Industry Affiliation: Petroleum, Gas
**Publication(s):**
*P G W Newsline*
Day Published: m.
Lead Time: 2 mos. prior to pub. date
Mtls Deadline: 15th of mo. prior to pub. date
Spec. Requirements: 16 pgs.; offset magazine 8 1/2 x 11; circ.: 4500
Personnel: Peter A. Hussie, Editor

4798

## PHILADELPHIA NATIONAL BANK
P.O. Box 7558
Philadelphia, PA 19101
Telephone: (215) 973-3100
Industry Affiliation: Banks, Savings & Loans
**Publication(s):**
*Update*
Day Published: s-m.
Spec. Requirements: 16 pg.; offset; 8 x 10
Personnel: Carol Verona, Managing Editor

68575

## PHILIP MORRIS, USA
120 Park Ave.
New York, NY 10017
Telephone: (212) 880-5000
Industry Affiliation: Advertising, Art, Public Relations

Materials Accepted/Included: 01-Business news 02-By-line articles 03-Fashion news 04-Food news 05-Freelance copy 06-Letters to editor 07-Real estate news 08-Sports news 09-Travel news 10-Book rev. 11-Movie rev. 12-Music rev. 13-TV rev. 14-Theater rev. 15-Coming events 16-Obituaries 17-Question & answer 18-Social announcements 19-Artwork 20-Cartoons 21-Photos 22-TV listings 23-Audio rec. 24-Video rec. 25-Books 26-Films/film clips 27-Personnel news 28-Press releases 29-New product news/photos 30-Trade lit. 31-Contracts awarded 32-Display adv. 33-Classified adv.

11-69

**Publication(s):**
*Happenings*
Day Published: 10/yr.
Materials: 01,02,06,15,16,17,18,19,20,21,
28,29,30
Contact: Diane Sansverie, Editor
Telephone: (212) 880-5000
120 Park Ave.
New York, NY 10017
Personnel: Diane Sanoverie, Editor

3893

**PHILIPS ELECTRONICS
INSTRUMENTS**
85 McKee Dr.
Mahwah, NJ 07430
Telephone: (201) 529-3800
Industry Affiliation: Electrical, Electronic,
Manufacturing
**Publication(s):**
*Electron Optics Bulletin*
Day Published: q.
Telephone: (201) 529-6168
Spec. Requirements: 40 pg.; offset
magazine; 8-1/2 x 11
Personnel: Karen Knizik, Editor

4877

**PHILLIPS CONSUMER
ELECTRONICS CORP.**
P.O. Box 1210
Greeneville, TN 37744
Telephone: (615) 636-5100
Industry Affiliation: Electrical, Electronic,
Manufacturing
**Publication(s):**
*Phillips U S A express, The*
Day Published: bi-m.
Personnel: Paula Berstein, Editor

4550

**PHILLIPS PETROLEUM CO.**
Fourth & Keeler Sts.
Bartlesville, OK 74004
Telephone: (918) 661-6600
Industry Affiliation: Petroleum, Gas
**Publication(s):**
*Selling 66*
Day Published: q.
Contact: Mktg. Dept.
Spec. Requirements: 36-80 pgs.; 84 x 11
Personnel: Vic McLeran, Editor

*Marketing Update*
Personnel: Vic McLeran, Editor

*Philnews*
Day Published: m.
Spec. Requirements: 32 pg.
Personnel: William E. Miller, Editor

2021

**PHOENIX BAPTIST HOSPITAL &
MEDICAL CENTER**
6025 N. 20th Ave.
Phoenix, AZ 85015
Telephone: (602) 249-0212
Industry Affiliation: Hospitals
**Publication(s):**
*Interview*
Day Published: a.
Spec. Requirements: 8-pg.; b & w; offset
11 x 14
Personnel: Joel Hobbs, Editor
Carol Donaldson

66441

**PHOENIX HOME LIFE INSURANCE
CO.**
One American Row
Communicators 12 Fl.
Hartford, CT 06115
Telephone: (203) 275-5000
FAX: (203) 275-5755
Industry Affiliation: Insurance

**Publication(s):**
*Newslines*
Day Published: m.
Lead Time: 4 wks.
Materials: 01
Contact: Carla Carpenter, Editor, Public
Affairs Dept.
Personnel: Carla Carpenter, Editor

56348

**PHOTOSOURCE INTERNATIONAL**
Pine Lake Farm
Osceola, WI 54020
Telephone: (715) 248-3800
FAX: (715) 248-7394
Industry Affiliation: Photography
**Publication(s):**
*Photomarket*
Day Published: bi-m.
Lead Time: 10 days prior to pub. date
Mtls Deadline: 2nd & 4th Wed. of mo. prior
to pub. date
Personnel: Angela Larson
Lori Johnson
Lynette Layer

5045

**PIER 1 IMPORTS, INC.**
301 Commerce St., Ste. 600
Ft. Worth, TX 76102
Telephone: (817) 878-8155
Industry Affiliation: Retail Stores
**Publication(s):**
*This Week*
Day Published: w.
Lead Time: 1 wk. prior to pub. date
Mtls Deadline: Wed. prior to pub. date
Contact: Human Resources
Spec. Requirements: company-interest only
Personnel: Lisa Mosier, Editor

2601

**PIGGLY WIGGLY CORP.**
1991 Corporate Ave.
Memphis, TN 38132
Telephone: (901) 395-8215
Industry Affiliation: Retail Stores
**Publication(s):**
*Turnstile*
Day Published: bi-m.
Lead Time: 15 days
Materials: 01,28,30
Mtls Deadline: 15 days prior to pub.
Contact: Marketing Communications
Spec. Requirements: 8-10 pgs.; special
editions 20-48 pgs.; offset
Personnel: Melinda Ingram, Editor

*News Letter*
Day Published: w.
Lead Time: 15 days
Contact: Trade Relations Div.
Personnel: Ed Matthews

3571

**PILLSBURY CO., THE**
3783 Pillsbury Ctr.
Minneapolis, MN 55402
Telephone: (612) 330-4768
Industry Affiliation: Food, General
**Publication(s):**
*Pillsbury Today*
Day Published: q.
Personnel: Karen Gustavson, Editor

2602

**PINELLAS COUNTY GOVERNMENT**
400 S. Ft. Harrison Ave.
Clearwater, FL 34616
Telephone: (813) 462-4807
FAX: (813) 462-3949
Industry Affiliation: Associations: City,
State, Federal

**Publication(s):**
*Pinellas Pen*
Day Published: m.
Lead Time: 4-6 wks. prior to pub. date
Mtls Deadline: 8 wks. prior to pub. date
Spec. Requirements: 6-10 pgs. offset; 8
1/2 x 11
Personnel: Al Collins, Editor

*Psi*
Day Published: bi-m.
Lead Time: 6 wks. prior to pub. date
Mtls Deadline: 6 wks. prior to pub. date
Contact: Public Service & Information
Personnel: Al Collins, Editor

3650

**PINEY WOODS COUNTRY LIFE
SCHOOL**
Hwy. 49 S.
Piney Woods, MS 39148
Telephone: (601) 845-2214
Industry Affiliation: Colleges, Institutions,
Science Research
**Publication(s):**
*Pine Torch, The*
Day Published: q.
Lead Time: 4-6 wks. prior to pub. date
Mtls Deadline: 1 mo. prior to pub. date
Contact: Special Projects
Personnel: Beverly Young, Editor
Wilda Harrison

*Academic Bulletin*
Day Published: bi-m.
Lead Time: 2 wks. prior to pub. date
Mtls Deadline: 2 wks. prior to pub. date
Contact: Special Projects
Personnel: Maxine O. Beady

4280

**PIONEER MUTUAL LIFE
INSURANCE CO.**
203 N. Tenth St.
Fargo, ND 58102
Telephone: (701) 293-3300
Mailing Address:
P.O. Box 2546
Fargo, ND 58108
Industry Affiliation: Insurance
**Publication(s):**
*Pioneering*
Day Published: m.
Lead Time: 2 wks. prior to pub. date
Mtls Deadline: 1st wk. of mo. prior to pub.
date
Contact: Advertising & Sales Promotion
Spec. Requirements: 8-16 pgs.; offset
magazine; 8.5 x 11
Personnel: James M. Sorensen, Editor

3610

**PIPER JAFFRAY**
222 S. Ninth St.
Minneapolis, MN 55402
Telephone: (612) 342-5800
Industry Affiliation: Advertising, Art, Public
Relations
**Publication(s):**
*Quote*
Day Published: bi-m.
Lead Time: 1 mo.
Mtls Deadline: 2 mos. prior to pub. date
Contact: Julie Swanson, Editor
Telephone: (612) 342-6591
Spec. Requirements: 16-pg.; offset; 8 1/2
x 11

*Piper Market Digest*
Day Published: q.
Lead Time: 1 mo.
Mtls Deadline: 6 wks. prior to pub.
Personnel: Wally May

2446

**PITNEY BOWES, INC.**
World Headquarters
Stamford, CT 06926
Telephone: (203) 356-5000
FAX: (203) 351-6303
Industry Affiliation: Office Equipment,
Services, Supplies
**Publication(s):**
*Outlook*
Day Published: 3/yr.
Lead Time: 2 mos. prior to pub. date
Mtls Deadline: 2 mos. prior to pub. date
Contact: Corporate Communications
Spec. Requirements: 8-pg.; 8 1/2 x 12
Personnel: Rick Petreycik, Senior Editor

4744

**PITTSBURGH BLIND
ASSOCIATION**
300 S. Craig St.
Pittsburgh, PA 15213
Telephone: (412) 682-5600
Industry Affiliation: Associations: Health
Groups
**Publication(s):**
*Reflector:*
Day Published: q.
Lead Time: 2 mos.
Mtls Deadline: January 28, April 30, July
31, Oct 31
Spec. Requirements: 4 pg. letterpress; 8
1/2 x 11; appropriate subject
Personnel: Jane S. Clark, Editor

3156

**PIZZA HUT, INC.**
9111 E. Douglas
Wichita, KS 67201
Telephone: (316) 681-9000
Mailing Address:
P.O. Box 428
Wichita, KS 67201
Industry Affiliation: Food, General
**Publication(s):**
*Pizza Hut Today*
Day Published: bi-m.
Mtls Deadline: 1 mo. prior to pub. date
Spec. Requirements: 16 pg.; offset; 8-1/2
x 11
Personnel: Theresa Marshall, Editor

5049

**PLUMBING MECHANICAL
CONTRACTORS COUNCIL
HARRIS COUNTY**
812 Wakefield
Houston, TX 77018
Telephone: (713) 691-6200
Mailing Address:
P.O. Box 430434
Houston, TX 77243
Industry Affiliation: Cooling, Heating
**Publication(s):**
*Gulf Coast Plumbing, Heating, Cooling
News*
Day Published: m.
Spec. Requirements: 12-16 pgs.; offset
tabloid; 102 x 14
Personnel: Joseph R. Zimmerman, Editor

4745

**PNC BANK**
One PNC Plz.
Fifth Ave. at Wood
Pittsburgh, PA 15265
Telephone: (412) 762-2000
Industry Affiliation: Banks, Savings &
Loans

**Materials Accepted/Included:** 01-Business news 02-By-line articles 03-Fashion news 04-Food news 05-Freelance copy 06-Letters to editor 07-Real estate news 08-Sports news 09-Travel news
10-Book rev. 11-Movie rev. 12-Music rev. 13-TV rev. 14-Theater rev. 15-Coming events 16-Obituaries 17-Question & answer 18-Social announcements 19-Artwork 20-Cartoons 21-Photos 22-TV listings
23-Audio rec. 24-Video rec. 25-Books 26-Films/film clips 27-Personnel news 28-Press releases 29-New product news/photos 30-Trade lit. 31-Contracts awarded 32-Display adv. 33-Classified adv.

**Publication(s):**
*P N C Bank News*
Day Published: m.
Contact: Jeff Worden, Editor
Spec. Requirements: 2 8-pgs; ; 8 1/2 x 11
Personnel: William H. Lloyd, Editor

4112
**PORT AUTHORITY OF NEW YORK & NEW JERSEY**
One World Trade Ctr., Ste. 34-E
New York, NY 10048
Telephone: (212) 435-6605
FAX: (212) 435-6032
Industry Affiliation: Shipping
**Publication(s):**
*Via International Port Of New York-New Jersey*
Day Published: m.
Lead Time: 10 wks. prior to pub. date
Mtls Deadline: 8 wks. prior to mo. of pub.
Contact: Port Communications
Spec. Requirements: 32 pgs.
Personnel: Shirley Fraenkel, Editor
    Arnold Davis, Publisher
    Gerard Ekedal
    Dorothy Rosciszewski

5050
**PORT OF HOUSTON MAGAZINE**
111 E. Loop, N.
Houston, TX 77029
Telephone: (713) 670-2594
FAX: (713) 670-2564
Mailing Address:
  P.O. Box 2562
  Houston, TX 77252-2562
Industry Affiliation: Architects, Engineers, Business Service
**Publication(s):**
*Port Of Houston Magazine*
Day Published: m.
Lead Time: 60 days prior to pub. date
Mtls Deadline: 6 wks. prior to pub. date
Spec. Requirements: 28 pgs.; offset; 7 1/2 x 10
Personnel: Ann Bordelon, Editor
    Marcella Cabrera, Art Director
    Marcella Cabrera, Production Manager
    H. Thomas Kornegay, Executive Director
    Ria Griffin, Communications Director

2222
**PORT OF OAKLAND**
530 Water St.
Oakland, CA 94607
Telephone: (510) 272-1100
FAX: (510) 839-1766
Mailing Address:
  P.O. Box 2064
  Oakland, CA 94604
Industry Affiliation: Shipping
**Publication(s):**
*Port Progress*
Day Published: q.
Lead Time: 6 wks. prior to pub. date
Mtls Deadline: 6 wks. prior to pub. date
Spec. Requirements: 8 pgs.; offset tabloid; 8 1/2 x 11
Personnel: Robert Middleton, Editor

4602
**PORT OF PORTLAND**
PO Box 3529
Portland, OR 97208
Telephone: (510) 272-1100
FAX: (510) 839-1766
Mailing Address:
  P.O. Box 3529
  Portland, OR 97208
Industry Affiliation: Shipping

**Publication(s):**
*Port Progress*
Day Published: q.
Spec. Requirements: 8 pg.; offset; 11 x 14
Personnel: Bob Middleton, Editor

68391
**POTOMAC ELECTRIC POWER CO.**
1900 Pennsylvania Ave., N.W.
Washington, DC 20068
Telephone: (202) 872-2337
Industry Affiliation: Utility:  Electric
**Publication(s):**
*Pepco Communicator, The*
Day Published: m.
Personnel: Jean Crider

3247
**PREMIER BANK**
451 Florida
Baton Rouge, LA 70801
Telephone: (504) 389-4241
Industry Affiliation: Banks, Savings & Loans
**Publication(s):**
*Premier Connection*
Day Published: m.
Spec. Requirements: 8-10 pg.; offset; 8-1/2 x 11
Personnel: Chris Ross, Editor

4748
**PRESBYTERIAN-UNIV. OF PENNSYLVANIA MEDICAL CTR.**
39th St. above Market
Philadelphia, PA 19104
Telephone: (215) 662-8000
Mailing Address:
  39th St. above Market
  Philadelphia, PA 19104
Industry Affiliation: Colleges, Institutions, Science Research
**Publication(s):**
*The Bulletin*
Day Published: bi-w.
Spec. Requirements: 2 pgs. offset; 11 x 14
Personnel: Diana Lewis, Editor

68402
**PRETRIAL SERVICES RESOURCE CENTER**
1325 G Street, N.W. Ste., 1020
Washington, DC 20005
Telephone: (202) 638-3080
FAX: (202) 347-0493
Industry Affiliation: Associations:  Trade, Fraternal
**Publication(s):**
*Pretrial Reporter*
Day Published: bi-m.
Lead Time: 5th of mo. 1 mo. prior to pub. mo.
Mtls Deadline: 15th of Feb., Apr., June, Aug., Oct., Dec.
Personnel: Jolanta Juszkiewicz
    D. Alan Henry, Publisher

4114
**PRICE WATERHOUSE & CO.**
1251 Ave. of the Americas
New York, NY 10020
Telephone: (212) 819-5000
Industry Affiliation: Finance, Services

**Publication(s):**
*Leader, The*
Day Published: 10/yr.
Lead Time: 1-1/2 mos. prior to pub. date
Mtls Deadline: 1-1/2 mos. prior to pub. date
Spec. Requirements: 24-32 pg.
Personnel: Deborah Rothchild, Editor

3078
**PRINCIPAL FINANCIAL GROUP, THE**
711 High St.
Des Moines, IA 50392
Telephone: (515) 247-5111
FAX: (515) 247-5930
Industry Affiliation: Finance, Services
**Publication(s):**
*Comment:*
Day Published: m.
Lead Time: 1 mo.
Mtls Deadline: end of mo.
Contact: Corp. Rels.
Spec. Requirements: 20-24 pgs.; offset magazine; 8 X 11
Personnel: Kristin Crouse, Editor

69389
**PRINTING INDUSTRIES OF AMERICA, INC.**
100 Daingerfield Rd.
Alexandria, VA 22314-2888
Telephone: (703) 519-8100
FAX: (703) 548-3227
Industry Affiliation: Printers, Services
**Publication(s):**
*Management Portfolio*
Day Published: m.
Materials: 02,05
Mtls Deadline: 60 days prior to pub. date
Contact: Marketing & Publications
Personnel: Cliff Weiss, Editor

*Decisions*
Day Published: q.
Materials: 01,02,05,28,29,30
Mtls Deadline: 60 days prior to pub. date
Contact: Marketing & Publications

*Forum*
Day Published: q.
Materials: 01,02,05
Mtls Deadline: 60 days prior to pub. date

*Pifelines*
Day Published: q.
Materials: 01,02,05
Mtls Deadline: 60 days prior to pub. date

1999
**PROTECTIVE LIFE INS. CO.**
P.O. Box 2606
Birmingham, AL 35202
Telephone: (205) 868-3118
Industry Affiliation: Insurance
**Publication(s):**
*Protective Life Lines*
Day Published: m.
Lead Time: 2 wks.
Mtls Deadline: 5th of mo.
Contact: Jane French, Editor
    Telephone: (205) 868-3118
Spec. Requirements: 20-24 pg.; offset; 8 1/2 x 11
Personnel: Jane French, Editor

*Wednesday Update*
Day Published: w.
Contact: Jane French, Editor
    Telephone: (205) 868-3118

*Protective Cover*
Day Published: m.
Contact: Jane French, Editor
    Telephone: (205) 868-3118

2383
**PROVENANT HEALTH CENTERS**
4231 W. 16th Ave.
Denver, CO 80204
Telephone: (303) 629-3511
FAX: (303) 595-6142
Industry Affiliation: Hospitals
**Publication(s):**
*Antonian*
Day Published: bi-m.
Spec. Requirements: 8 pg.; offset magazine; 8 1/2 x 11
Personnel: Leslie Hackett, Editor

*Progress Notes*
Day Published: m.
Spec. Requirements: 8 pg.
Personnel: Leslie Hackett, Editor

4749
**PROVIDENT MUTUAL LIFE INSURANCE CO. OF PHILADELPHIA**
1600 Market St.
Philadelphia, PA 19103
Telephone: (215) 636-5000
FAX: (215) 636-5039
Industry Affiliation: Insurance
**Publication(s):**
*Provident Perspective*
Day Published: bi-w.
Lead Time: 3 wks. prior to pub. date
Mtls Deadline: 3 wks. prior to pub. date
Contact: Internal Communications
Spec. Requirements: 8-pgs.; offset; 11 x 17
Personnel: Bob Evanoski, Editor

3895
**PRUDENTIAL INSURANCE CO. OF AMERICA**
Prudential Plz.
Newark, NJ 07102
Telephone: (201) 802-6147
Industry Affiliation: Insurance
**Publication(s):**
*Corporate Office Courier:*
Day Published: 23/yr.
Spec. Requirements: 6 pg.; offset tabloid; 11 1/2 x 17 1/4

*Prudential's Real Estate Dimensions*
Day Published: 3/yr.
Spec. Requirements: 40-44 pg.
Personnel: Leah Berton, Editor

*Dialogue*
Day Published: q.
Spec. Requirements: 20-56 pg.
Personnel: Alice Shiller, Editor

*Perspective*
Day Published: m.
Contact: Prupac
    PO Box 419
    Holmdel, NJ 07733
Spec. Requirements: 8 pg.

2379
**PUBLIC SERVICE CO. OF COLORADO**
550 15th St., Rm. 620
Denver, CO 80202
Telephone: (303) 571-7511
Mailing Address:
  P.O. Box 840
  Denver, CO 80201
Industry Affiliation: Utility:  Electric

---

**Materials Accepted/Included:** 01-Business news 02-By-line articles 03-Fashion news 04-Food news 05-Freelance copy 06-Letters to editor 07-Real estate news 08-Sports news 09-Travel news 10-Book rev. 11-Movie rev. 12-Music rev. 13-TV rev. 14-Theater rev. 15-Coming events 16-Obituaries 17-Question & answer 18-Social announcements 19-Artwork 20-Cartoons 21-Photos 22-TV listings 23-Audio rec. 24-Video rec. 25-Books 26-Films/film clips 27-Personnel news 28-Press releases 29-New product news/photos 30-Trade lit. 31-Contracts awarded 32-Display adv. 33-Classified adv.

11-71

**Publication(s):**
*P S Co Times*
Day Published: fortn.
Lead Time: 2 wks. prior to pub. date
Mtls Deadline: 2 wks. prior to pub. date
Contact: Kevin Graham, Ed.
 Telephone: (303) 571-7511
 P.O. Box 840
 Denver, CO 80201
Personnel: Kevin Graham, Editor

**PUBLIC SERVICE CO. OF NEW HAMPSHIRE** [3833]
1000 Elm St.
Manchester, NH 03101
Telephone: (603) 669-4000
Mailing Address:
 P.O. Box 330
 Manchester, NH 03101-0330
Industry Affiliation: Utility: Electric
**Publication(s):**
*Around The Circuit*
Day Published: m.
Spec. Requirements: 12-pg.; offset; 11 x 14
Personnel: David Johnson, Editor

**PUBLIC SERVICE ELECTRIC & GAS CO.** [3896]
80 Park Plz.
Newark, NJ 07102
Telephone: (201) 621-7500
Mailing Address:
 P.O. Box 570
 Newark, NJ 07102
Industry Affiliation: Utility: Gas
**Publication(s):**
*P S E & G News*
Day Published: fortn.
Contact: Pete Laning
 Telephone: (800) 672-1073
 P.O. Box 570
 Newark, NJ 07102
Spec. Requirements: 24-40 pgs.; offset; 84 x 11
Personnel: Eugene Murphy, Editor

*Management Quarterly*
Day Published: q.
Contact: Joe Murphy, Editor
 Telephone: (800) 672-1073
 P.O. Box 570
 Newark, NJ 07102

**PUBLIX SUPER MARKETS, INC.** [2604]
P.O. Box 407
Lakeland, FL 33802
Telephone: (813) 688-1188
Industry Affiliation: Food, General
**Publication(s):**
*Publix News*
Day Published: m.
Mtls Deadline: 1st of mo.
Contact: Stacy Smith, Editor
 Telephone: (813) 688-1188
 P.O. Box 407
 Lakeland, FL 33802
Personnel: Stacy Smith, Editor
 Susan Krause

**PUGET SOUND POWER & LIGHT CO.** [5313]
One Bellevue Ctr. Bldg.
411 108th Ave., N.E., 9th Fl.
Bellevue, WA 98004
Telephone: (206) 454-6363
Mailing Address:
 P.O. Box 97034 OBC-09s
 Bellevue, WA 98009
Industry Affiliation: Utility: Electric

**Publication(s):**
*Outlet*
Day Published: w.
Lead Time: 10 days prior to pub. date
Mtls Deadline: 10 days prior to pub. date
Spec. Requirements: 4 pg., offset tabloid
Personnel: Allison Turner

**PYRAMID LIFE INSURANCE CO.** [3157]
6201 Johnson Dr.
Shawnee Mission, KS 66202
Telephone: (913) 722-1110
FAX: (913) 722-4015
Mailing Address:
 P.O. Box 772
 Shawnee Mission, KS 66201
Industry Affiliation: Insurance
**Publication(s):**
*Advantage*
Day Published: q.
Lead Time: 1 mo.
Contact: Melinda Dabney, Ed.
 Telephone: (913) 722-1110
 P.O. Box 772
 Shawnee Mission, KS 66201
Spec. Requirements: 20-pg.; offset; 8 1/2 x 11
Personnel: Melinda Dabney, Editor
 Jennifer Segale, Art Director
 Larry Mogolov, Marketing Director

**QUAKER OATS CO.** [2882]
321 N. Clark, Quaker Tower
Chicago, IL 60610
Telephone: (312) 222-7111
Industry Affiliation: Food, General
**Publication(s):**
*Quaker Insider*
Day Published: bi-m.
Spec. Requirements: 12 pg.; photoletter and coldtype; 84 x 11
Personnel: L. Theisen, Editor

*Quaker Quarterly*
Day Published: q.
Spec. Requirements: 12 pg.
Personnel: L. Theisen, Editor

*Midweek*
Day Published: w.
Personnel: Carol A. Haag, Editor

**QUALITY STORES, INC.** [3497]
1460 Whitehall Road
N. Muskegon, MI 49445
Telephone: (616) 744-2491
Industry Affiliation: Retail Stores
**Publication(s):**
*On Cue*
Day Published: q.
Spec. Requirements: 4 pg.; offset
Personnel: Kristin Mullinnex, Editor

*'tween Cues*
Day Published: q.
Lead Time: 12 days
Personnel: Kristin Mullinex, Editor

**QUANTUM CHEMICAL CORP., USI DIV.** [4092]
11500 Northlake Dr.
Cincinnati, OH 45249-1694
Telephone: (212) 949-5000
Industry Affiliation: Chemicals, Plastics
**Publication(s):**
*Quantum Update*
Day Published: bi-m.
Lead Time: 1 mo.
Spec. Requirements: 6 pg.; offset; 8 1/2 x 11
Personnel: Don Congram, Editor

*Insider*
Day Published: bi-m.
Contact: USI
Spec. Requirements: 8 pg.; offset magazine; 8 1/2 x 11

*Connections*
Day Published: bi-m.

**QUEEN'S MEDICAL CENTER** [2706]
P.O. Box 861
Honolulu, HI 96808
Telephone: (808) 538-9011
Mailing Address:
 P.O. Box 861
 Honolulu, HI 96808
Industry Affiliation: Hospitals
**Publication(s):**
*Queen's Vision, The*
Day Published: q.
Spec. Requirements: 4 pg.; magapaper; 11 x 17
Personnel: Henry Yamamoto, Editor

**QUESTAR CORPORATION** [5206]
180 E. First, S.
Salt Lake City, UT 84111
Telephone: (801) 534-5521
Mailing Address:
 P.O. Box 11150
 Salt Lake City, UT 84147
Industry Affiliation: Petroleum, Gas
**Publication(s):**
*On Stream*
Day Published: 3/yr.
Lead Time: 6 wks. prior to pub. date
Mtls Deadline: 1st of mo. prior to pub. date
Contact: Questar Corp.
Spec. Requirements: 8 1/2 x 11
Personnel: Dave Hampshire, Editor

**QUIVIRA COUNCIL, INC.** [3143]
1555 E. Second St.
Wichita, KS 67214
Telephone: (316) 264-3386
FAX: (316) 264-6054
Industry Affiliation: Associations: Trade, Fraternal
**Publication(s):**
*Trail Guide*
Day Published: m.
Lead Time: 15 days prior to pub. date
Mtls Deadline: 10th of mo. prior to pub. date
Spec. Requirements: 4-6 pg.; offset; 11 x 17
Personnel: Chuck Lang, Editor

**RADIO-TELEVISION NEWS DIRECTORS ASSOCIATION** [2554]
1000 Connecticut Ave., N. W.
Ste. 615
Washington, DC 20036
Telephone: (202) 659-6510
FAX: (202) 223-4007
Industry Affiliation: Associations: Trade, Fraternal
**Publication(s):**
*R T N D A Communicator*
Day Published: m.
Lead Time: 3 1/2 wks. prior to pub. date
Mtls Deadline: 5th of mo. prior to pub. date
Spec. Requirements: 52 pg.; offset; 8-1/2 x 11
Personnel: Joe Tiernan, Editor

*Job Information Service*
Day Published: m.
Lead Time: 2 wks. prior to 1st of mo.
Personnel: Michele Fitzgerald, Editor

**RADIO SHACK DIVISION, TANDY CORP.** [5052]
300 One Tandy Ctr.
Fort Worth, TX 76102
Telephone: (817) 390-3257
FAX: (817) 390-2103
Industry Affiliation: Electrical, Electronic, Manufacturing
**Publication(s):**
*Radio Shack Intercom*
Day Published: m.
Lead Time: 30 days prior to pub. date
Materials: 27,29
Mtls Deadline: 1st of mo. prior to cover date
Contact: Radio Shack
Spec. Requirements: 68 pg; web offset; 8 1/2 x 11; 56 pg.
Personnel: Bill Kneer, Editor

**RALPH'S GROCERY CO.** [2227]
1100 W. Artesia Blvd.
Los Angeles, CA 90220
Telephone: (310) 884-9000
Mailing Address:
 P.O. Box 54143
 Los Angeles, CA 90054
Industry Affiliation: Food, General
**Publication(s):**
*Ralph's News:*
Day Published: m.
Lead Time: 3 wks. prior to pub. date
Mtls Deadline: 3 wks. prior to pub. date
Spec. Requirements: 8-16 pg.; offset; 8 1/2 x 11
Personnel: Terry O'Neil, Editor

**RALPH WILSON PLASTICS CO.** [5122]
600 General Bruce Dr.
Temple, TX 76501
Telephone: (817) 778-2711
Mailing Address:
 P.O. Box 6110
 Temple, TX 76503
Industry Affiliation: Chemicals, Plastics
**Publication(s):**
*Laminator, The*
Day Published: w.
Lead Time: 2 wks. prior to pub. date
Mtls Deadline: 2 wks. prior to pub. date
Spec. Requirements: 8 pg.; offset; 8 1/2 x 11
Personnel: Gail Benavidez

**RALSTON PURINA CO.** [3718]
Checkerboard Sq.
St. Louis, MO 63164
Telephone: (314) 982-1000
Industry Affiliation: Food, General
**Publication(s):**
*R P Today*
Day Published: bi-m.
Spec. Requirements: 32 pgs.
Personnel: Brian Westich, Editor

*Square Talk*
Day Published: m.
Spec. Requirements: 2-pg.
Personnel: Brian Westich, Editor

**RAND MCNALLY & CO.** [2884]
8255 N. Central Park Ave.
Skokie, IL 60076
Telephone: (708) 329-2296
Industry Affiliation: Publishers, Books, Magazines

**Publication(s):**
*Directions*
Day Published: bi-m.
Contact: Joyce Hodel
Personnel: Joyce Hodel, Editor

**RANGER INSURANCE CO.** 5053
10777 Westheimer Rd.
Houston, TX 77042
Telephone: (713) 954-8100
FAX: (713) 954-8803
Mailing Address:
P.O. Box 2807
Houston, TX 77252
Industry Affiliation: Insurance
**Publication(s):**
*Ranger Resources*
Day Published: bi-m.
Spec. Requirements: 20 pg.; offset
magazine; 6 x 9
Personnel: Joscelyn Darby, Editor

**RAX RESTAURANTS INC.** 4420
4150 Tuller Rd.
Dublin, OH 43017
Telephone: (614) 766-2500
FAX: (614) 766-4706
Industry Affiliation: Food, General
**Publication(s):**
*Operations News*
Day Published: w.
Personnel: Karen Longtine, Editor

**RAYMOND CORP.** 4117
S. Canal St
Greene, NY 13778
Telephone: (607) 656-2390
FAX: (607) 656-9005
Mailing Address:
P.O. Box 130
Greene, NY 13778
Industry Affiliation: Industry: Heavy
Construction, Machinery
**Publication(s):**
*Reporter, The*
Day Published: bi-m.
Lead Time: 3 wks. prior to pub. date
Mtls Deadline: 2 wks. prior to pub. date
Spec. Requirements: 16-20 pg.; offset; 8-
1/2 x 11
Personnel: Valerie Mahar, Editor

*Managers Calendar*
Day Published: m.
Lead Time: 3 wks. prior to pub. date
Mtls Deadline: 2 wks. prior to pub. date
Spec. Requirements: 8-1/2 x 11
Personnel: Valerie Mahar, Editor

*Take 10*
Day Published: w.
Lead Time: 1 wk. prior to pub. date
Mtls Deadline: 2 wks. prior to pub. date
Spec. Requirements: 8-1/2 x 11
Personnel: Valerie Mahar, Editor

*Needle, The*
Day Published: m.
Lead Time: 3 wks. prior to pub. date
Contact: Marketing/Sales
Personnel: Brenda Wrigley, Marketing
Director

**RAYTHEON CO.** 3386
141 Spring
Lexington, MA 02173
Telephone: (617) 862-6600
Industry Affiliation: Electrical, Electronic,
Manufacturing

**Publication(s):**
*Raytheon News*
Day Published: m.
Spec. Requirements: 4 pg.; letterpress
newspaper; 11 x 15
Personnel: Ralph Williams, Editor

**READING HOSPITAL & MEDICAL** 4750
**CENTER, THE**
Sixth Ave. & Spruce St.
West Reading, PA 19611
Telephone: (610) 378-6000
FAX: (610) 208-5192
Mailing Address:
P.O. Box 16052
Reading, PA 19612-6052
Industry Affiliation: Hospitals
**Publication(s):**
*Around The Clock*
Day Published: q.
Lead Time: 2 mos. prior to pub. date
Mtls Deadline: 2 mos. prior to pub. date
Contact: Communication Services
Spec. Requirements: 12-16 pg.; offset; 8-
1/2 x 11
Personnel: Wendie Waschitsch, Editor

**REAL ESTATE CENTER** 5179
Texas A & M University
College Station, TX 77843-2115
Telephone: (409) 845-0369
FAX: (409) 845-0460
Industry Affiliation: Real Estate
**Publication(s):**
*Tierra Grande Magazine*
Day Published: q.
Lead Time: 2 mos. prior to pub. date
Materials: 07
Mtls Deadline: 1st of Jan., Apr., Jul., Oct.
Contact: Communications Div.
Spec. Requirements: 24 pg.; 8-1/2 x 11
Personnel: David S. Jones, Editor in Chief
James W. Christian, Publisher
Shirley Bovey, Editor
Kammy Senter, Production
Manager
Robert Beals, Art Director
David Jones, Marketing Director

*Real Estate Center Trends*
Day Published: m.
Lead Time: 2 wks. prior to pub. date
Materials: 07
Contact: Communications
Personnel: James W. Christian, Publisher
Ted Jones, Editor in Chief
Oran Jones, Production
Manager
Robert Beals, Art Director
David Jones, Marketing Director

*Real Estate Center Law Letter*
Day Published: q.
Lead Time: 2 mos. prior to pub. date
Materials: 07
Contact: Communications
Personnel: Shirley E. Bovey

**RECOGNITION INTERNATIONAL** 5055
**INC.**
2701 E. Grauwyler
Irving, TX 75061
Telephone: (214) 579-6000
Industry Affiliation: Industry: Light Tools,
Equipment

**Publication(s):**
*Letter Of Recognition*
Day Published: m.
Spec. Requirements: 20-24 pg.; offset; 84
x 11
Personnel: Beth Black, Editor

**REDDY CORP. INTERNATIONAL** 2448
5801 Osuna Rd., N.E.
Albuquerque, NM 87109
Telephone: (505) 884-7500
FAX: (505) 883-1753
Mailing Address:
P.O. Box 3209
Albuquerque, NM 87190
Industry Affiliation: Architects, Engineers,
Business Service
**Publication(s):**
*Lines Of Argument*
Day Published: bi-m.
Lead Time: 2 mos. prior to pub. date
Mtls Deadline: 2 mos. prior to pub. date
Contact: Energy Communication Services
Personnel: Noel Fletcher, Managing Editor

*Sourcebook*
Day Published: m.
Lead Time: 3 mo. prior to pub. date
Mtls Deadline: 3 mo. prior to pub. date
Contact: Issues Management services
Personnel: Noel Fletcher, Editor

**REGIS UNIVERSITY** 2380
3333 Regis Blvd.
Denver, CO 80221
Telephone: (303) 458-3544
FAX: (303) 458-4387
Industry Affiliation: Colleges, Institutions,
Science Research
**Publication(s):**
*Highlander*
Day Published: 20/yr.
Lead Time: 2 wks. prior to pub. date
Mtls Deadline: 2 wks. prior to pub. date
Personnel: Craig Scott

*Regis University Magazine*
Day Published: q.
Lead Time: 2 mos. prior to pub. date
Mtls Deadline: 2 mos. prior to pub. date
Contact: Public Affairs
Personnel: Jefferson Sheppard, Publication
Director
Paul Brocker
Lisa C. Rogers

*Update*
Day Published: bi-w.
Lead Time: 2 wks. prior to pub. date
Mtls Deadline: 2 wks. prior to pub. date
Contact: Public Affairs
Personnel: Becky Zachmeier, Publication
Assistant

**REHABILITATION HOSPITAL OF** 2707
**THE PACIFIC**
226 N. Kuakini St.
Honolulu, HI 96817
Telephone: (808) 531-3511
Industry Affiliation: Hospitals
**Publication(s):**
*Ka Manu*
Day Published: q.
Lead Time: 4-6 wks. prior to pub. date
Mtls Deadline: 3 wks. prior to pub. date
Contact: Marketing & Public Affairs
Spec. Requirements: 6 pg.; offset; 8-1/2 x
11
Personnel: Jay Conley, Editor

*Rehab Journal*
Day Published: s-a.
Lead Time: 4-6 wks. prior to pub. date
Mtls Deadline: 6 wks. prior to pub. date
Contact: Public Relations
Spec. Requirements: 4 pg.; offset; 8-1/2 x
11
Personnel: Mike Levin

**RESEARCH MEDICAL CENTER** 3720
2316 E. Meyer Blvd.
Kansas City, MO 64132
Telephone: (816) 276-4000
FAX: (816) 276-9222
Mailing Address:
2304 E. Meyer Blvd., A-21
Kansas City, MO 64132
Industry Affiliation: Colleges, Institutions,
Science Research
**Publication(s):**
*Horizon*
Day Published: bi-m.
Lead Time: 8 wks.
Mtls Deadline: 4 wks.
Spec. Requirements: 4-8; 8 1/2 x 11
Personnel: Robin Harrison, Editor

*Horizon-Med Staff*
Day Published: m.
Lead Time: 1 mo.
Mtls Deadline: 1 mo.
Personnel: Robin Harrison, Editor

*Newsclips*
Day Published: w.
Lead Time: 7 days
Spec. Requirements: 2-pg.; newsletter

**RESEARCH TRIANGLE INSTITUTE** 4258
3040 Cornwallis Rd.
Durham, NC 27705
Telephone: (919) 541-6000
Mailing Address:
P.O. Box 12194
Durham, NC 27709
Industry Affiliation: Colleges, Institutions,
Science Research
**Publication(s):**
*Hypotenuse*
Day Published: q.
Spec. Requirements: 20-28 pg.; offset; 8-
1/2 x 11
Personnel: Mike Chitwood, Editor

*R T Items*
Day Published: m.
Personnel: Mike Chitwood
Bill Newton

*Annual Report*
Day Published: a.: Jan.
Personnel: Bill Newton, Editor

**REVCO, D.S. INC.** 4423
1925 Enterprise Pkwy.
Twinsburg, OH 44087
Telephone: (216) 425-9811
Industry Affiliation: Architects, Engineers,
Business Service
**Publication(s):**
*Revco Scripts*
Day Published: bi-m.
Lead Time: 2 mo.
Spec. Requirements: 4 pg.; tabloid; offset;
11 x 17
Personnel: Mark Weinberg, Editor

**REYNOLDS METALS CO.** 5262
6601 W. Broad St.
Richmond, VA 23230
Telephone: (804) 281-2000
Mailing Address:
P.O. Box 27003
Richmond, VA 23261
Industry Affiliation: Steel, Iron

Materials Accepted/Included: 01-Business news 02-By-line articles 03-Fashion news 04-Food news 05-Freelance copy 06-Letters to editor 07-Real estate news 08-Sports news 09-Travel news 10-Book rev. 11-Movie rev. 12-Music rev. 13-TV rev. 14-Theater rev. 15-Coming events 16-Obituaries 17-Question & answer 18-Social announcements 19-Artwork 20-Cartoons 21-Photos 22-TV listings 23-Audio rec. 24-Video rec. 25-Books 26-Films/film clips 27-Personnel news 28-Press releases 29-New product news/photos 30-Trade lit. 31-Contracts awarded 32-Display adv. 33-Classified adv.

11-73

**Publication(s):**
*Reynolds Review*
Day Published: q.
Lead Time: 3 mo.
Materials: 01,02,15,17,21
Mtls Deadline: Jan., Apr., July, Oct.
Spec. Requirements: 8 pg.; tabloid
　newsletter; 11 x 17
Personnel: Anne Waring, Editor

4824

## RHODE ISLAND BUILDERS ASSOCIATION
450 Veterans Memorial Pkwy.
East Providence, RI 02914
Telephone: (401) 438-7400
FAX: (401) 438-7446
Industry Affiliation: Associations: Trade,
　Fraternal
**Publication(s):**
*Rhode Island Builder Report, The*
Day Published: m.
Lead Time: 1 mo. prior to pub. date
Mtls Deadline: 12th day of mo. prior to
　issue date
Spec. Requirements: 12-32 pgs; offset 8
　1/2 x 11; some desktop publ.
Personnel: Paul F. Eno, Editor

2671

## RICH'S, INC.
Perimenta Ctr. Pkwy.
Atlanta, GA 30346
Telephone: (404) 913-4000
FAX: (404) 913-4549
Industry Affiliation: Retail Stores
**Publication(s):**
*Focal Point*
Day Published: 10/yr.
Contact: Human Resources
　7 W. Seventh St.
　Cincinnati, OH 45202
Spec. Requirements: 16 pgs.; offset
　magazine; 84 x 11
Personnel: Michelle Hauser, Editor

*Senior Newsletter*
Day Published: 3-4/yr.
Contact: Rich's Inc.
　7 W. Seventh St.
　Cincinnati, OH 45202
Personnel: Diane Green, Editor

4426

## RIVERSIDE METHODIST HOSPITALS
3535 Olentangy River Rd.
Columbus, OH 43214
Telephone: (619) 566-5000
Industry Affiliation: Hospitals
**Publication(s):**
*Riverside Monthly*
Day Published: m.
Lead Time: 6-8 wks. prior to pub. date
Spec. Requirements: 12 pg. magazine, 8
　1/2 X 11; 2-color
Personnel: Greg Reynolds, Editor

3886

## RJR NABISCO, NABISCO FOODS GROUP
7 Campus Dr.
Parsippany, NJ 07054-0311
Telephone: (201) 503-7155
Industry Affiliation: Food, General
**Publication(s):**
*N F G Today*
Day Published: bi-m.
Lead Time: 5 mo.
Mtls Deadline: 3 mo.
Contact: Public Relations
Spec. Requirements: 48 pg.; offset
　magazine; 8 1/2 x 11; four-color
Personnel: Victor DePalo, Editor

*Biscuit Vision*
Day Published: bi-m.
Contact: Public Relations
Spec. Requirements: 24-28 pg.; offset
　magazine; 8 1/2 x 11
Personnel: Bill Brown, Editor

4259

## RJR TOBACCO CO.
401 N. Main St.
Winston-Salem, NC 27102
Telephone: (919) 741-5000
Mailing Address:
　P.O. Box 2959
　Winston-Salem, NC 27102
Industry Affiliation: Tobacco
**Publication(s):**
*Caravan*
Day Published: bi-m.
Spec. Requirements: 8 pg.; tabloid
Personnel: Jan Fulton, Editor

4427

## ROADWAY SERVICES, INC.
1077 Gorge Blvd.
P.O. Box 88
Akron, OH 44309
Telephone: (216) 258-2547
FAX: (216) 258-6258
Industry Affiliation: Trucking
**Publication(s):**
*Q-Municator*
Day Published: m.
Materials: 01,02,05,06,07,17,18,19,20,21,
　27,29
Contact: Corporate Communications
Spec. Requirements: B-16 pg.; offset
　magazine; 84 x 11
Personnel: Mara Benjamin, Editor
　　Mark Axel, Production Manager
　　Lewis Demis, Art Director

2162

## ROBERT F. KENNEDY MEDICAL CENTER
4500 W. 116th St.
Hawthorne, CA 90250
Telephone: (310) 973-1711
FAX: (310) 219-3715
Industry Affiliation: Hospitals
**Publication(s):**
*L I F E newsletter*
Day Published: bi-a.
Spec. Requirements: 16 pgs.; offset; 9 1/2
　x 12 1/2

*Prestige book*
Day Published: a.: Nov.
Materials: 32
Mtls Deadline: Oct. 15 prior to pub. date
Contact: Public Relations
Personnel: Monique Murphy Mijares, Editor

*Miniviews*
Day Published: q.
Materials: 04,11,19,20
Mtls Deadline: 1st of Mar., June, Sep.,
　Dec.
Contact: Public Relations
Personnel: Monique Murphy Mijares

*Vital Lines*
Day Published: q.
Mtls Deadline: Ist of Mar., June, Sep., Dec.
Personnel: Monique Murphy Mijares

4730

## ROBERT MORRIS ASSOCIATES
One Liberty Pl.
1650 Market St.
Philadelphia, PA 19103-7398
Telephone: (215) 851-9100
FAX: (215) 851-9206
Industry Affiliation: Banks, Savings &
　Loans

**Publication(s):**
*Commercial Lending Newsletter*
Day Published: m.
Lead Time: 2 mos. prior to pub. date
Materials: 01,07,28
Spec. Requirements: 4 pg.; offset; 8 1/2 x
　11
Personnel: Luis W. Morales, Editor in Chief
　　Daniel E. Weekerly, Managing
　　Editor
　　Elizabeth Bond, Editor

4123

## ROCHESTER COMMUNITY SAVINGS BANK
235 E. Main St.
Rochester, NY 14604
Telephone: (716) 423-7364
FAX: (716) 423-7365
Industry Affiliation: Banks, Savings &
　Loans
**Publication(s):**
*R C S B Preview*
Day Published: q.
Lead Time: 8 wks. prior to pub. date
Materials: 01,05,17,21
Mtls Deadline: 8 wks. prior to pub. date
Contact: Corp. Comms.
Spec. Requirements: 4-8 pgs; 8 1/2 x 11
Personnel: Jean VanEtten, Editor
　　Jane Argenta, Production
　　Manager

4122

## ROCHESTER GAS & ELECTRIC CORP.
89 East Ave.
Rochester, NY 14649-0001
Telephone: (716) 724-8413
FAX: (716) 724-8799
Mailing Address:
　Corporate Communications
　Rochester, NY 14649-0001
Industry Affiliation: Utility: Related
**Publication(s):**
*R G & E News*
Day Published: m.
Lead Time: 6 wks. prior to pub. date
Materials: 17,19,21,28,29,30
Mtls Deadline: 1st of mo. prior to pub. date
Contact: Corporate Communications
Spec. Requirements: 8-12 pg.; offset; 17 x
　22
Personnel: Richard D. Meier, Editor

2888

## ROCKFORD/PARK CABLEVISION, INC.
227 N. Wyman
Rockford, IL 61101
Telephone: (815) 987-4510
FAX: (815) 962-9643
Industry Affiliation: Radio, TV, Movies
**Publication(s):**
*Cable Views*
Day Published: s-a.: Feb.& Sep.
Lead Time: 4 wks. prior to pub. date
Mtls Deadline: 4 wks. prior to pub. date
Personnel: K. C. McWilliams, Editor

2959

## ROCKFORD MEMORIAL HOSPITAL
2400 N. Rockton Ave.
Rockford, IL 61103
Telephone: (815) 968-6861
Industry Affiliation: Hospitals

**Publication(s):**
*Pulse*
Day Published: q.
Lead Time: 3 mo.
Spec. Requirements: 16-pg.; offset; 11 x
　16
Personnel: Paul Arco, Editor

*Memo*
Day Published: bi-m.
Lead Time: 1 wk.
Contact: Pub. Rels.
Spec. Requirements: 12 pg.; 8 1/2 x 11
Personnel: Heidi Tennant, Editor

68430

## ROCKFORD REGISTER STAR
99 E. State St.
Rockford, IL 61104
Telephone: (815) 987-1322
FAX: (815) 961-5833
Industry Affiliation: Publishers, Books,
　Magazines
**Publication(s):**
*Byline*
Day Published: m.
Mtls Deadline: 1st of mo. prior to pub. date
Personnel: Marion F. Wilke

3721

## ROCKHURST COLLEGE
1100 Rockhurst Rd.
Kansas City, MO 64110
Telephone: (816) 926-4000
Industry Affiliation: Colleges, Institutions,
　Science Research
**Publication(s):**
*Rockhurst Report*
Day Published: bi-m.
Lead Time: 2 wks. prior to pub. date
Contact: Development/Public Information
Spec. Requirements: 4 pg.; offset; 11 x 17
Personnel: Bob Jacobi, Editor

*Rockhurst Magazine*
Day Published: q.
Lead Time: 4 wks. prior to pub. date
Contact: Public Information
Spec. Requirements: 8-1/2 x 11
Personnel: Kate Pope
　　Rosita E. McCoy, Editor

5265

## ROCKINGHAM MEMORIAL HOSPITAL
235 Cantrell Ave.
Harrisonburg, VA 22801
Telephone: (703) 433-4100
Industry Affiliation: Hospitals
**Publication(s):**
*Bedside Banner*
Day Published: m.
Lead Time: 1 mo. prior to pub. date
Mtls Deadline: 1 mo. prior to pub. date
Spec. Requirements: 8-12 pg.; letterpress;
　8-1/2 x 11
Personnel: Debra Thompson, Editor
　　John Green

*Women's Health Focus Quarterly*
Day Published: q.
Lead Time: 1 mo. prior to pub. date
Mtls Deadline: 1 mo. prior to pub. date
Personnel: Debra Thompson, Managing
　　Editor

2891

## ROCK VALLEY COLLEGE
3301 N. Mulford Rd.
Rockford, IL 61114
Telephone: (815) 654-4250
Industry Affiliation: Colleges, Institutions,
　Science Research

---

**Materials Accepted/Included:** 01-Business news 02-By-line articles 03-Fashion news 04-Food news 05-Freelance copy 06-Letters to editor 07-Real estate news 08-Sports news 09-Travel news 10-Book rev. 11-Movie rev. 12-Music rev. 13-TV rev. 14-Theater rev. 15-Coming events 16-Obituaries 17-Question & answer 18-Social announcements 19-Artwork 20-Cartoons 21-Photos 22-TV listings 23-Audio rec. 24-Video rec. 25-Books 26-Films/film clips 27-Personnel news 28-Press releases 29-New product news/photos 30-Trade lit. 31-Contracts awarded 32-Display adv. 33-Classified adv.

**Publication(s):**
*Monday Morning Memo*
Day Published: w.
Contact: College Rels./Pub.
Spec. Requirements: 1-2 pg.; offset; 8 1/2 x 11
Personnel: Mrs. Sterling, Editor

69706

**ROCKWELL INTERNATIONAL, COMMAND & CONTROL SYSTEMS DIVISION**
3200 E. Renner Rd.
Richardson, TX 75082-2402
Telephone: (214) 705-0000
Industry Affiliation: Aircraft, Aerospace, Defense
**Publication(s):**
*Rockwell News*
Day Published: m.
Spec. Requirements: 4-6 pg.; tabloid
Personnel: Jo Bishop, Editor

*Communique*
Day Published: w.
Spec. Requirements: 4 pg.; newsletter; 8 1/2 x 11
Personnel: Jo Bishop, Editor

2382

**ROCKY MOUNTAIN AAA CLUB**
4100 E. Arkansas Ave.
Denver, CO 80222
Telephone: (303) 753-8800
Industry Affiliation: Associations: Trade, Fraternal
**Publication(s):**
*Rocky Mountain Motorist*
Day Published: m.
Lead Time: 6 wk.
Spec. Requirements: 36 pg.; offset magazine; 8 1/8 x 10 5/8
Personnel: Barbara Bauerle, Editor

4753

**ROHM & HAAS CO.**
Independence Mall W.
Philadelphia, PA 19105
Telephone: (215) 592-3000
Industry Affiliation: Associations: Trade, Fraternal
**Publication(s):**
*Rohm & Haas Reporter*
Day Published: q.
Spec. Requirements: 32 pg.; offset; 8 1/2 x 11
Personnel: Dr. Henry Gambino, Editor

*Resin Review*
Day Published: q.
Spec. Requirements: 24-32 pg.
Personnel: Tom Hansen, Editor

4606

**ROSEBURG FOREST PRODUCTS CO.**
Highway 99, S.
Roseburg, OR 97470
Telephone: (503) 679-3311
FAX: (503) 679-9683
Mailing Address:
  P.O. Box 1088
  Roseburg, OR 97470
Industry Affiliation: Lumber, Forestry, Building Materials
**Publication(s):**
*Roseburg News & Views*
Day Published: m.
Lead Time: 2 mo. prior to pub. date
Mtls Deadline: 15th of mo. prior to pub. date
Spec. Requirements: 12-16 pgs.
Personnel: Frank Teracio, Editor

*Roseburg Woodsman*
Lead Time: 6 mo. prior to pub. date
Spec. Requirements: 12-18 pgs.

3613

**ROSEMOUNT INC.**
12001 Technology Dr.
Eden Prairie, MN 55344
Telephone: (612) 941-5560
Industry Affiliation: Lumber, Forestry, Building Materials
**Publication(s):**
*Prober*
Day Published: bi-m.
Spec. Requirements: 16-24 pg.; offset; 8 1/2 x 11
Personnel: Deanna Juergens, Editor

4260

**ROSES STORES, INC.**
218-220 Garnett St.
Henderson, NC 27536
Telephone: (919) 430-2600
Mailing Address:
  P.O. Drawer 947
  Henderson, NC 27536
Industry Affiliation: Retail Stores
**Publication(s):**
*Communiques*
Day Published: m.
Spec. Requirements: 32-36 pg.; offset magazine; 8 1/2 x 11
Personnel: Bob Gorham, Editor

2231

**ROSICRUCIAN ORDER AMORC**
Rosicrucian Park
San Jose, CA 95191
Telephone: (408) 947-3600
FAX: (408) 947-3677
Industry Affiliation: Associations: Trade, Fraternal
**Publication(s):**
*Rosicrucian Digest*
Day Published: q.
Lead Time: 1 mo. prior to pub. date
Mtls Deadline: 1 mo. prior to pub. date
Spec. Requirements: 40-pgs.; offset; 7 1/2 x 10 1/4
Personnel: Robin M. Thompson, Editor
  Kristy Knutson, President

3120

**ROTO-ROOTER CORP.**
300 Ashworth Rd.
West Des Moines, IA 50265
Telephone: (515) 223-1345
Industry Affiliation: Industry: Light Tools, Equipment
**Publication(s):**
*Roto-Rooter Exchange*
Day Published: m.
Lead Time: 2 mos. prior to pub. date
Mtls Deadline: 2 mos. prior to pub. date
Spec. Requirements: 4 pg.; letterpress tabloid; 84 x 11
Personnel: M. Schettler, Editor

5062

**ROWAN COMPANIES, INC.**
5450 Transco Tower
2800 Post Oak Blvd.
Houston, TX 77056-6196
Telephone: (713) 621-7800
FAX: (713) 960-7560
Industry Affiliation: Petroleum, Gas

**Publication(s):**
*Grapevine*
Day Published: q.
Spec. Requirements: 28-32 pg.; offset; 8 1/2 x 11
Personnel: Charles Wharton, Editor

2783

**R.R. DONNELLEY & SONS CO.**
R.R. Donnelley Bldg.
77 W. Wacker Dr.
Chicago, IL 60610-1696
Telephone: (312) 326-8000
Industry Affiliation: Publishers, Books, Magazines
**Publication(s):**
*Printer, The*
Day Published: q.
Lead Time: 3 mo.
Spec. Requirements: 32 pg.; sheetfed offset magazine; 8 1/2 x 11
Personnel: Diane M. Dunne, Editor

5063

**RSR CORPORATION**
1111 W. Mockingbird Ln., Ste. 1000
Dallas, TX 75247
Telephone: (214) 631-6070
Industry Affiliation: Industry: Material Handling
**Publication(s):**
*R S R Lead Press*
Day Published: s-a.
Lead Time: 30 days prior to pub. date
Mtls Deadline: June & Nov.1st, prior to pub. date
Spec. Requirements: 8 pg.; offset; 8 1/2 x 11
Personnel: Kate Jeffries, Editor

4428

**RUBBERMAID, INC.**
1147 Akron Rd.
Wooster, OH 44691
Telephone: (216) 264-6464
Industry Affiliation: Rubber, Tires
**Publication(s):**
*Rubbermaid Review*
Day Published: bi-m.
Contact: Home Prod. Div.
Spec. Requirements: 8 pg.; offset newspaper; 9 1/2 x 12 1/2
Personnel: Marjorie Kamen, Editor

3389

**RUSSELL HARRINGTON CUTLERY CO.**
44 River St.
Southbridge, MA 01550
Telephone: (508) 765-0201
Industry Affiliation: Industry: Light Tools, Equipment
**Publication(s):**
*Leading Edge*
Day Published: q.
Spec. Requirements: 6 pg.; 8 1/2 x 11
Personnel: Alice Forrester, Editor

4951

**RYDER SYSTEM, INC.**
3600 N.W. 82nd Ave.
Miami, FL 33166
Telephone: (305) 593-3726
Mailing Address:
  P.O. Box 020816
  Miami, FL 33102-0816
Industry Affiliation: Industry: Light Tools, Equipment
**Publication(s):**
*Ryder People*
Day Published: q.
Lead Time: 2 mo.
Personnel: Beth Lawrence, Managing Editor

*Ryder Dealer*
Day Published: 11/yr.
Lead Time: 2 mo.
Spec. Requirements: 6 pg.; tabloid; 2-color

3722

**SACHS PROPERTIES, INC.**
400 Chesterfield Ctr., #600
Chesterfield, MO 63017
Telephone: (314) 537-1000
FAX: (314) 537-0718
Mailing Address:
  P.O. Box 7104
  Saint Louis, MO 63177
Industry Affiliation: Real Estate
**Publication(s):**
*Momentom*
Day Published: s-a.
Lead Time: 6 wks. prior to pub. date
Mtls Deadline: 6 wks. prior to pub. date
Personnel: Marie Casey, Editor

2232

**SACRAMENTO MUNICIPAL UTILITY DISTRICT**
6201 S St.
Sacramento, CA 95817
Telephone: (916) 452-3211
Mailing Address:
  P.O. Box 15830
  Sacramento, CA 95852
Industry Affiliation: Utility: Electric
**Publication(s):**
*Employee Hilines*
Day Published: m.
Contact: Media Services Dept.
Spec. Requirements: 8 pg.
Personnel: Cindy Arvin, Editor

5317

**SAFECO INSURANCE CO.**
SAFECO Plz. T-8
Seattle, WA 98185
Telephone: (206) 545-5000
FAX: (206) 545-5776
Industry Affiliation: Insurance
**Publication(s):**
*Safeco Agent*
Day Published: bi-m.
Spec. Requirements: 3 pg.; offset; 8 1/2 x 11
Personnel: Dan Pedersen, Editor

*On The Move*
Day Published: m.
Lead Time: 1 mo. prior to pub. date
Mtls Deadline: 1 mo. prior to pub. date
Spec. Requirements: 4 pg., offset newsletter

66423

**SAGINAW DIVISION-GENERAL MOTORS CORP.**
3900 Holland Ave.
Saginaw, MI 48601
Telephone: (517) 757-4004
FAX: (517) 757-4022
Industry Affiliation: Autos, Trucks
**Publication(s):**
*Saginaw Divisional Newsletter*
Day Published: Mon.-Fri.
Personnel: Gene Bishop, Editor

4609

**SAIF CORP.**
400 High St., S.E.
Salem, OR 97312
Telephone: (503) 373-8011
FAX: (503) 373-8181
Industry Affiliation: Insurance

**Materials Accepted/Included:** 01-Business news 02-By-line articles 03-Fashion news 04-Food news 05-Freelance copy 06-Letters to editor 07-Real estate news 08-Sports news 09-Travel news 10-Book rev. 11-Movie rev. 12-Music rev. 13-TV rev. 14-Theater rev. 15-Coming events 16-Obituaries 17-Question & answer 18-Social announcements 19-Artwork 20-Cartoons 21-Photos 22-TV listings 23-Audio rec. 24-Video rec. 25-Books 26-Films/film clips 27-Personnel news 28-Press releases 29-New product news/photos 30-Trade lit. 31-Contracts awarded 32-Display adv. 33-Classified adv.

11-75

**Publication(s):**
*Scope: Comp News*
Day Published: bi-m.
Spec. Requirements: 6-pgs.; offset; 8 1/2 x 11
Personnel: Tom Powslee, Editor

2892

**SAINT ANTHONY MEDICAL CENTER**
5666 E. State St.
Rockford, IL 61108
Telephone: (815) 226-2000
FAX: (815) 395-5449
Industry Affiliation: Hospitals
**Publication(s):**
*Golden Cares*
Day Published: q.

*Capsule*
Day Published: m.
Mtls Deadline: 10th of mo.
Personnel: Gerrie Gustafson, Director
          Elizabeth Ennenga, Editor

*Medical Staff Update*
Day Published: m.

*Bulletin, The*
Day Published: s-w.

*Construction Update*
Day Published: 2-3/yr.

3500

**SAINT JOHN HOSPITAL**
22101 Moross Rd
Detroit, MI 48236
Telephone: (313) 343-7479
Industry Affiliation: Hospitals
**Publication(s):**
*Horizons:*
Day Published: q.
Lead Time: 30 Days
Spec. Requirements: 24-pgs; offset; 8 1/2 x 11
Personnel: Molly Hunter, Editor

*Voice*
Day Published: bi-m.
Mtls Deadline: 30 days
Spec. Requirements: 4-pg.
Personnel: Molly Hunter, Editor

*Medical Bulletin Of St John Hospital:*
Day Published: a.
Lead Time: 60 days
Mtls Deadline: 60 days
Spec. Requirements: 24-pg.
Personnel: Molly Hunter, Editor

4128

**SAKS FIFTH AVENUE**
12 E. 49th St.
New York, NY 10017
Telephone: (212) 940-5468
FAX: (212) 940-5455
Industry Affiliation: Retail Stores
**Publication(s):**
*Focus On Saks Fifth Avenue*
Day Published: q.
Spec. Requirements: 8-20 pg; offset; 11 x 14
Personnel: Suzanne McAndrews, Editor

5066

**SALADMASTER, INC.**
912 113th St.
Arlington, TX 76011
Telephone: (817) 633-3555
FAX: (817) 633-5544
Industry Affiliation: Retail Stores

**Publication(s):**
*Saladmaster Salut!*
Day Published: m.
Lead Time: 2-3 wks. prior to pub. date
Mtls Deadline: 2 wks. prior to pub. date
Spec. Requirements: 20-60 pgs.; offset; 8 1/2 x 11
Personnel: Lisa Peterson, Editor

4607

**SALEM HOSPITAL**
665 Winter St., S.E.
Salem, OR 97301
Telephone: (503) 370-5200
FAX: (503) 370-5372
Mailing Address:
   P.O. Box 14001
   Salem, OR 97309
Industry Affiliation: Hospitals
**Publication(s):**
*Messenger*
Day Published: q.
Lead Time: 60 days
Contact: Comms. Rels.
Spec. Requirements: 16 pg; offset; 8 1/2 x 11
Personnel: Tina Richards, Editor

*Pulsebeat*
Day Published: q.
Lead Time: 60 days
Personnel: Sherry Partridge, Editor

3383

**SALES PROSPECTOR**
751 Main St.
Waltham, MA 02254
Telephone: (617) 899-1271
Mailing Address:
   P.O. Box 9079
   Waltham, MA 02254
Industry Affiliation: Publishers, Books, Magazines
**Publication(s):**
*Sales Prospector*
Day Published: bi-m.
Spec. Requirements: 7-10 pg.; offset; 8 1/2 x 12 3/4
Personnel: Sherry Levin, Editor

5209

**SALT LAKE CITY SCHOOL DISTRICT**
440 E. First, S.
Salt Lake City, UT 84111
Telephone: (801) 578-8599
FAX: (801) 578-8248
Industry Affiliation: Publishers, Books, Magazines
**Publication(s):**
*District, The*
Lead Time: 2 days
Mtls Deadline: every other Mon., 5 pm
Contact: Public Information Office
Spec. Requirements: 1-6 pages; typed; 8 1/2 x 11
Personnel: Sherri Clark

*Report Card-Annual Report To The Community*
Day Published: a.
Personnel: Sherri Clark, Editor

2555

**SALVATION ARMY, THE**
503 E. St. N.W.
Washington, DC 20001
Telephone: (202) 783-9085
FAX: (202) 347-4070
Mailing Address:
   P.O. Box 2166
   Washington, DC 20013
Industry Affiliation: Associations: Trade, Fraternal

**Publication(s):**
*Capital Cadence*
Day Published: q.
Lead Time: 1 mo.
Mtls Deadline: 1 mo.
Spec. Requirements: 4-8 pgs.; offset; 8 1/2 x 11
Personnel: Glenn D. Fite, Jr., Editor

*Volunteer-Line*
Day Published: m.
Lead Time: 1 mo. prior to pub. date.
Spec. Requirements: 4-8 pgs.
Personnel: Joe Demato, Editor

2025

**SAMARITAN HEALTH SERVICE**
1441 N. 12th St.
Phoenix, AZ 85004
Telephone: (602) 495-4000
FAX: (602) 495-4559
Mailing Address:
   P.O. Box 25489
   Phoenix, AZ 85002
Industry Affiliation: Hospitals
**Publication(s):**
*Samaritan Today, The*
Day Published: m.
Lead Time: 30 days prior to pub. date
Contact: Corp. Pub. Rels.
Spec. Requirements: 8-pgs.; offset; 14 1/2 x 11
Personnel: Renee Moe, Editor

*Manager's Journal*
Day Published: bi-m.
Lead Time: 30 days
Mtls Deadline: 30 days prior to pub. date
Personnel: Chad Madden

2238

**SAN DIEGO COUNTY MEDICAL SOCIETY**
3702 Ruffin Rd.
San Diego, CA 92123
Mailing Address:
   P.O. Box 23581
   San Diego, CA 92193
Industry Affiliation: Hospitals
**Publication(s):**
*San Diego Physician*
Day Published: m.
Lead Time: 1st of mo. prior to pub. date
Mtls Deadline: 1st of mo. prior to pub. date
Spec. Requirements: 48-pgs.; 84 x 11
Personnel: Helen Westcott, Editor

2239

**SAN DIEGO GAS & ELECTRIC CO.**
101 Ash St.
San Diego, CA 92101
Telephone: (619) 696-2000
FAX: (619) 696-2792
Mailing Address:
   P.O. Box 1831
   San Diego, CA 92112
Industry Affiliation: Petroleum, Gas
**Publication(s):**
*In Focus*
Day Published: m.
Contact: Public Relations
Spec. Requirements: 4 pg.
Personnel: Tom Murnane, Editor

2313

**SAN DIEGO MUNICIPAL EMPLOYEES ASSOCIATION**
4185 Home Ave.
San Diego, CA 92105
Telephone: (619) 264-6632
FAX: (619) 264-0405
Industry Affiliation: Associations: City, State, Federal

**Publication(s):**
*Viewpoint*
Day Published: q.
Lead Time: 1 mo. prior to pub. date
Mtls Deadline: 1 mo. prior to pub. date
Spec. Requirements: 8 pg; offset; 8 1/2 x 11
Personnel: Kelly Cruz, Editor

*P U L*
Day Published: bi-w.
Lead Time: 2 wks. prior to pub. date
Mtls Deadline: 2 wks. prior to pub. date
Spec. Requirements: 2 pg; 8 1/2 x 14
Personnel: Judie Italiano, Editor

*Hot Sheet*
Day Published: irreg.
Spec. Requirements: 2 pg; 8 1/2 x 11
Personnel: Kathy Rollins, Editor

3502

**SANDY CORPORATION**
1500 W. Big Beaver
Troy, MI 48084
Telephone: (313) 649-0800
Industry Affiliation: Advertising, Art, Public Relations
**Publication(s):**
*Pro Publication*
Day Published: m.
Lead Time: 2 mos.
Spec. Requirements: 35 pg; 8 1/2 x 11
Personnel: Leslie Schneider, Editor

*Preview*
Day Published: m.
Lead Time: 2 mos.
Personnel: Jennifer Wohletz, Editor

2240

**SAN FRANCISCO CHAMBER OF COMMERCE**
465 California St., 9th Fl.
San Francisco, CA 94104
Telephone: (415) 392-4511
Industry Affiliation: Finance, Services
**Publication(s):**
*Chamber Of Commerce Newsletter*
Day Published: m.
Lead Time: 2 mos. prior to pub. date
Mtls Deadline: 6 wks. prior to pub. date
Spec. Requirements: 2-8 pgs.
Personnel: Carol Piasente, Editor

2241

**SAN FRANCISCO SPCA**
2500 16th St.
San Francisco, CA 94103
Industry Affiliation: Associations: Trade, Fraternal
**Publication(s):**
*Our Animals*
Day Published: q.
Lead Time: 2 mos. prior to pub. date
Materials: 32
Spec. Requirements: 32 pg; offset; 8 3/8 x 10 7/8
Personnel: Paul Glassner, Editor

2314

**SAN LUIS OBISPO CHAMBER OF COMMERCE**
1039 Chorro St.
San Luis Obispo, CA 93401
Telephone: (805) 781-2777
FAX: (805) 543-1255
Industry Affiliation: Associations: City, State, Federal
**Publication(s):**
*San Luis Obispo Business*
Day Published: m.
Lead Time: 6-8 wks. prior to pub. date
Mtls Deadline: 1st of mo. prior to pub. date
Spec. Requirements: 4-pgs.; offset; 11 x 17
Personnel: Rebecca Burner, Editor

**Materials Accepted/Included:** 01-Business news 02-By-line articles 03-Fashion news 04-Food news 05-Freelance copy 06-Letters to editor 07-Real estate news 08-Sports news 09-Travel news 10-Book rev. 11-Movie rev. 12-Music rev. 13-TV rev. 14-Theater rev. 15-Coming events 16-Obituaries 17-Question & answer 18-Social announcements 19-Artwork 20-Cartoons 21-Photos 22-TV listings 23-Audio rec. 24-Video rec. 25-Books 26-Films/film clips 27-Personnel news 28-Press releases 29-New product news/photos 30-Trade lit. 31-Contracts awarded 32-Display adv. 33-Classified adv.

*San Luis Obispo Visitor Guide*
Day Published: a.
Lead Time: 3 mos. prior to pub. date
Mtls Deadline: 3 mos. prior to pub. date
Personnel: Rebecca Burner, Editor

2242

## SANTA BARBARA RESEARCH CENTER
75 Coromar Dr.
Santa Barbara, CA 93117
Telephone: (805) 968-3511
Industry Affiliation: Sports, Equipment
**Publication(s):**
*Sbrc News:*
Day Published: m.
Lead Time: 1 mo. prior to pub. date
Mtls Deadline: 1 mo. prior to pub. date
Spec. Requirements: 2-page; ; 8 1/2 x 11
Personnel: Thomas R. Ball, Editor

4842

## SANTEE COOPER
One Riverwood Dr.
Moncks Corner, SC 29461
Telephone: (803) 761-8000
FAX: (803) 761-7060
Industry Affiliation: Utility:  Electric
**Publication(s):**
*Quarterly Financial Reporter*
Day Published: q.
Spec. Requirements: 8-32 pgs; offset; 8 1/2 x 11
Personnel: Beth Oliver, Editor

*Currently*
Day Published: w.
Lead Time: 1-2 days prior to pub. date
Mtls Deadline: Wed. prior to pub. date
Personnel: Beth Oliver, Editor

*Santee Cooper Annual Report*
Day Published: a.
Lead Time: 3 wks. prior to pub. date
Personnel: Beth Oliver, Editor

*Pep-Program Employee Participation*
Day Published: q.
Personnel: Cile Spivey, Editor

2188

## SANWA BANK CALIFORNIA
601 S. Figueroa St.
Los Angeles, CA 90017
Telephone: (213) 896-7000
Mailing Address:
   P.O. Box 54445
   Los Angeles, CA 90054
Industry Affiliation: Banks, Savings & Loans
**Publication(s):**
*In Focus*
Day Published: m.
Lead Time: 3 mos.
Mtls Deadline: 1 mo. prior to pub. date
Contact: Corp. Comm.
Spec. Requirements: 8 pg; offset; 11 x 17

4243

## SARA LEE KNIT PRODUCTS
450 Hanes Mill Rd.
Winston Salem, NC 27105
Telephone: (919) 744-4400
FAX: (919) 519-4966
Mailing Address:
   P.O. Box 3019
   Winston Salem, NC 27102
Industry Affiliation: Textiles, Apparel, Mills, Machinery
**Publication(s):**
*Common Thread, The*
Day Published: q.
Lead Time: 6 wks. prior to pub. date
Mtls Deadline: 1st of Feb., Jun., Aug., Oct., & Dec.
Spec. Requirements: 28 pg; offset 8 1/2 x 11 1/2
Personnel: Paige Simpson, Editor

*Internal Newsletter*
Day Published: m.
Lead Time: 2 wks. prior to pub. date
Mtls Deadline: 2 wks. prior to pub. date
Personnel: Paige Simpson, Editor

3617

## SATELLITE INDUSTRIES INC.
2530 Xenium Lane, N.
Minneapolis, MN 55441
Telephone: (612) 553-1900
FAX: (612) 553-1905
Industry Affiliation: Radio, TV, Movies
**Publication(s):**
*Portable Sanitation Quarterly*
Day Published: q.
Lead Time: 6 wks. prior to pub. date
Spec. Requirements: 4-pgs.; 8 1/2 x 11
Personnel: John L. Taylor, Editor

4131

## SCANDINAVIAN AIRLINES SYSTEM INC.
9 Toledo Ave.
Lindhurst, NY 07071
Telephone: (201) 896-3691
Industry Affiliation: Airlines
**Publication(s):**
*Inside S A S International*
Day Published: bi-w.
Contact: North American Division/SAS
   138-02 Queens Blvd.
   Jamaica, NY 11435
Spec. Requirements: 22-30 pgs.; 72 x 102
Personnel: Michael Notrica, Editor in Chief

3898

## SCHERING-PLOUGH CORP.
One Giralda Farms
Madison, NJ 07940
Telephone: (201) 822-7000
FAX: (201) 822-7447
Industry Affiliation: Drugs, Cosmetics, Pharmaceuticals
**Publication(s):**
*Schering-Plough World*
Day Published: bi-m.
Lead Time: 2 mos.
Mtls Deadline: 1 mo.
Spec. Requirements: 8 pg; offset; 11-1/2 x 15
Personnel: Claudia Robinson, Editor

*Management News*
Day Published: q.
Lead Time: 1 mo.
Mtls Deadline: 1 mo.
Spec. Requirements: 8 pg; offset; 8 1/2 x 11
Personnel: Claudia Robinson, Editor

*Schering-Plough Grassroots Network Voice*
Day Published: q.
Lead Time: 1 mo.
Mtls Deadline: 1 mo.
Spec. Requirements: 12 pg; offset, 8 1/2 x 11
Personnel: Claudia Robinson, Editor

3917

## SCHIFFLI LACE & EMBROIDERY MANUFACTURERS ASSN.
8555 Tonnelle Ave.
North Bergen, NJ 07047-4738
Telephone: (201) 868-7200
FAX: (201) 869-9833
Industry Affiliation: Textiles, Apparel, Mills, Machinery
**Publication(s):**
*Embroidery Directory*
Day Published: a.: Nov.
Lead Time: 4 mos. prior to pub. date
Materials: 03
Mtls Deadline: Aug. 31st
Spec. Requirements: 180-pg.; offset; 8 1/2 x 11
Personnel: I. Leonard Seiler, Editor
   Sciffli Association, Publisher

*Embroidery News*
Day Published: bi-m.
Lead Time: 4 wks.
Materials: 01,02,03,06,09,1011,14,15,17,20, 30,33
Mtls Deadline: 2 wks. prior to pub. date
Spec. Requirements: 12 pgs.
Personnel: I. Leonard Seiler, Editor

4755

## SCHRAMM INC.
800 E. Virginia Ave.
West Chester, PA 19380
Telephone: (215) 696-2500
FAX: (215) 696-6950
Industry Affiliation: Industry:  Heavy Construction, Machinery
**Publication(s):**
*What's Happening*
Day Published: w.
Lead Time: 1 mo. prior to pub. date
Mtls Deadline: 1st & 15th of mo. prior to pub. date
Spec. Requirements: 6-pgs.; offset newsletter; 84 x 11
Personnel: Horman Greet, Editor
   A.H Williams, Editor

4132

## SCHWEIZER AIRCRAFT CORP.
P.O. Box 147
Elmira, NY 14902
Telephone: (607) 739-3821
FAX: (607) 796-2488
Industry Affiliation: Aircraft, Aerospace, Defense
**Publication(s):**
*Stabilizer*
Day Published: q.
Spec. Requirements: 4 pg; photocopied; 9 x 12
Personnel: Thomas Walton, Editor

2897

## SCHWINN CYCLING & FITNESS, INC.
1690 38th St.
Boulder, CO 80301-2602
Telephone: (303) 939-0100
FAX: (303) 939-0260
Industry Affiliation: Sports, Equipment

**Publication(s):**
*Schwinn Cycling & Fitness, Inc. Dealer News Letter*
Day Published: m.
Lead Time: 16 wks. prior to pub. date
Personnel: Tracy Hickey

2674

## SCIENTIFIC-ATLANTA, INC.
One Technology Pkwy.
Norcross, GA 30092-2967
Telephone: (404) 903-4000
Industry Affiliation: Electrical, Electronic, Manufacturing
**Publication(s):**
*S A  in The News*
Day Published: w.
Personnel: Bob Myers, Director of Communications

5403

## S.C. JOHNSON & SON INC.
1525 Howe St.
Racine, WI 53403
Telephone: (414) 631-2000
Industry Affiliation: Chemicals, Plastics
**Publication(s):**
*Dialogue*
Day Published: m.
Contact: Corp. Comms. Worldwide
Spec. Requirements: 12 pgs.
Personnel: Susan E. Bukacek, Editor

*S C J This Week*
Day Published: w.
Contact: Corp. Comms. Worldwide
Personnel: Susan Bukacek, Editor
   Dave Buchanan, Editor

2899

## SCRIPTURE PRESS PUBLICATIONS, INC.
1825 College Ave
Wheaton, IL 60187
Telephone: (708) 668-6000
Industry Affiliation: Associations:  Trade, Fraternal
**Publication(s):**
*Spotlight:*
Day Published: w.
Spec. Requirements: 2-pg.; mimeo bulletin; 84 x 11
Personnel: Stephanie Parsons, Editor

5319

## SEAFIRST CORP.
701 Fifth Ave.
Seattle, WA 98104
Telephone: (206) 358-3432
FAX: (206) 358-3697
Mailing Address:
   P.O. Box 3586
   Seattle, WA 98124
Industry Affiliation: Banks, Savings & Loans
**Publication(s):**
*Seafirst News*
Day Published: s-m.
Lead Time: 2 wks. prior to pub. date
Mtls Deadline: 2 wks. prior to pub. date
Spec. Requirements: 8 pgs.
Personnel: Jerri Etchason, Editor

68532

## SEARS ROEBUCK & CO.
3333 Beverly Rd.,
Hoffman Estates, IL 60179
Telephone: (708) 286-2500
FAX: (708) 286-5918
Industry Affiliation: Retail Stores
**Publication(s):**
*Front Lines*
Day Published: bi-m.
Personnel: Melissa Breyette, Editor
   Peggy Palter, Assistant Editor

---

Materials Accepted/Included: 01-Business news 02-By-line articles 03-Fashion news 04-Food news 05-Freelance copy 06-Letters to editor 07-Real estate news 08-Sports news 09-Travel news 10-Book rev. 11-Movie rev. 12-Music rev. 13-TV rev. 14-Theater rev. 15-Coming events 16-Obituaries 17-Question & answer 18-Social announcements 19-Artwork 20-Cartoons 21-Photos 22-TV listings 23-Audio rec. 24-Video rec. 25-Books 26-Films/film clips 27-Personnel news 28-Press releases 29-New product news/photos 30-Trade lit. 31-Contracts awarded 32-Display adv. 33-Classified adv.

*Prairie Lines*
Day Published: s-m.
Personnel: Melissa Breyette, Editor
Peggy Palter, Assistant Editor

**SEATTLE CITY LIGHT** 5321
1015 Third Ave., Rm. 809
Seattle, WA 98104
Telephone: (206) 684-3112
FAX: (206) 233-2509
Industry Affiliation: Utility: Electric
**Publication(s):**
*Network*
Day Published: bi-w.
Lead Time: 2 mos.
Contact: Community Relations Division
Spec. Requirements: 8 pg; offset; 11 x 17
Personnel: Kathy Sugiyama, Editor

*C L E A Newsletter*
Day Published: m.
Personnel: Ruby Haywood, Editor

*A Little Light Reading*
Day Published: bi-m.
Personnel: Gina Santo Domingo, Editor

**SECURA INSURANCE** 5400
2401 S. Memorial Dr.
Appleton, WI 54915
Telephone: (414) 739-3161
FAX: (414) 739-4496
Mailing Address:
P.O. Box 819
Appleton, WI 54912
Industry Affiliation: Insurance
**Publication(s):**
*Viewpoint*
Day Published: q.
Lead Time: 60 days prior to pub.
Mtls Deadline: 60 days prior to pub.
Contact: Sales Division
Spec. Requirements: 4-6 pgs.; offset; 84 x 11
Personnel: Sandy Whight, Editor

**SECURITIES INVESTIGATIONS, INC.** 56347
P.O. Box 888
Woodstock, NY 12498-0888
Telephone: (914) 679-2300
FAX: (914) 679-2301
Industry Affiliation: Finance, Services
**Publication(s):**
*Investment Blue Book*
Day Published: s-a.
Lead Time: 3 mos. prior to pub. date
Materials: 32
Personnel: Stuart A. Ober, Editor in Chief

**SECURITY MUTUAL LIFE INSURANCE CO. OF NEW YORK** 4137
100 Court St.
Binghamton, NY 13901
Telephone: (607) 723-3551
FAX: (607) 723-0619
Mailing Address:
P.O. Box 1625
Binghamton, NY 13902
Industry Affiliation: Insurance
**Publication(s):**
*Marketing Update*
Day Published: bi-m.
Lead Time: 1st Mon. of mo.
Materials: 01,15,30
Mtls Deadline: 1st Mon. of mo.
Contact: Communications
Spec. Requirements: b & w photos
Personnel: Colleen Kenny-Kuk, Editor
Robert L. Dalke, Editor in Chief
Cindi Eaton, Production Manager

*Headliner*
Day Published: bi-m.
Lead Time: 3 wks.
Materials: 10,11,12,19,20
Mtls Deadline: 3 wks. prior to pub. date
Contact: Communications
Spec. Requirements: 2 pg.
Personnel: Colleen Lewis, Editor
Colleen Kenny-Kuk, Managing Editor

*Standards*
Day Published: q.
Lead Time: 3 wks.
Mtls Deadline: 3 wks. prior to pub. date
Personnel: Terri M. Barden, Editor

**SENTARA HEALTH SYSTEM** 5254
6015 Poplar Hall Dr.
Norfolk, VA 23502
Telephone: (804) 455-7170
Mailing Address:
600 Gresham Dr.
Norfolk, VA 23507
Industry Affiliation: Hospitals
**Publication(s):**
*Network*
Day Published: m.
Lead Time: 2 mos. prior to pub. date
Mtls Deadline: 1 1/2 mos. prior to pub. date
Contact: Sentara Health System
Spec. Requirements: b & w photos

*Dialogue*
Day Published: bi-m.
Lead Time: 1 mo. prior to pub. date
Mtls Deadline: 1 mo. prior to pub. date

**SENTRY INSURANCE** 5438
1800 N. Point Dr.
Stevens Point, WI 54481
Telephone: (715) 346-6781
FAX: (715) 346-7516
Industry Affiliation: Insurance
**Publication(s):**
*Sentry News*
Day Published: q.
Lead Time: 2 mos.
Spec. Requirements: 16-24 pgs.; offset newspaper
Personnel: Nick Schultz, Editor

*Management Newsletter*
Day Published: bi-m.
Lead Time: 1-6 wks.
Personnel: Nick Schultz, Editor

*Point*
Day Published: m.
Lead Time: 1 wk.
Mtls Deadline: 15th of prior mo.
Personnel: Nick Schultz, Editor

**SERVICE EMPLOYEES INTERNATIONAL UNION, LOCAL 32E** 69797
4234 Bronx Blvd.
Bronx, NY 10466-2611
Telephone: (718) 324-6556
FAX: (718) 994-4910
Industry Affiliation: Associations: Trade, Fraternal
**Publication(s):**
*32 E Events*
Day Published: q.
Personnel: Diana D. DeGroat, Editor

**SETON MEDICAL CENTER** 5072
1201 W. 38th St.
Austin, TX 78705
Telephone: (512) 323-1000
FAX: (512) 323-1972
Industry Affiliation: Hospitals

**Publication(s):**
*Seton Good Health Magazine*
Day Published: q.
Spec. Requirements: 30-40 pg; offset; 6 x 10-3/4
Personnel: Travis Froehlich, Executive Editor
Gayle Granberry, Copy Editor
Diana Smith, Copy Editor

*Heartbeat*
Day Published: q.
Personnel: Susan Bell, Editor

*Medstaff News*
Day Published: m.
Lead Time: 2 wks. prior to pub. date
Mtls Deadline: 15th of mo. prior to pub. date

*Infobits*
Day Published: m.
Mtls Deadline: varies
Personnel: Diana Smith, Editor

*Wellness*
Day Published: q.

**SHAKLEE CORP.** 2245
444 Market St., Ste. T-321
San Francisco, CA 94111
Telephone: (415) 954-2007
FAX: (415) 986-0808
Industry Affiliation: Food, General
**Publication(s):**
*Shaklee News*
Day Published: 8/yr.
Lead Time: 8-10 wks. prior to pub. date
Mtls Deadline: 8 wks. prior to pub. date
Spec. Requirements: Photographs of successful Shaklee sales leaders
Personnel: Jim Jardine, Editor
Rhonda Andronico

*Us!*
Day Published: q.
Lead Time: 2-3 mos. prior to pub. date
Mtls Deadline: 2-3 mos. prior to pub. date
Personnel: Jim Jardine, Editor

**SHANNON & WILSON INC.** 5322
400 N. 34th St., Ste. 100
Seattle, WA 98103
Telephone: (206) 632-8020
FAX: (206) 633-6777
Industry Affiliation: Colleges, Institutions, Science Research
**Publication(s):**
*Probings*
Day Published: q.
Spec. Requirements: 4 pgs
Personnel: Richard Gates, P.E., Editor
Mary Lou Reslock, Assistant Editor

**SHAWMUT BANK, CONNECTICUT** 2469
777 Main St.
13th Fl.
Hartford, CT 06115
Telephone: (203) 986-4529
d, 06115
Industry Affiliation: Banks, Savings & Loans

**Publication(s):**
*Shawmut News*
Day Published: bi-w.
Lead Time: 10 days
Materials: 02,05,21,27,28,33
Mtls Deadline: Wed. prior to pub. date
Contact: Shawmut Bank, Connecticut
Spec. Requirements: 4 page; offset; 11 x 17
Personnel: Carl C. Mueller, Editor
Melody Guy-Boston, Assistant Editor
Hal Tovin, Marketing Director

**SHAWNEE MISSION PUBLIC SCHOOLS** 3158
7235 Antioch
Shawnee Mission, KS 66204
Telephone: (913) 831-1900
FAX: (913) 831-1450
Industry Affiliation: Colleges, Institutions, Science Research
**Publication(s):**
*Newsline*
Day Published: s-m.
Contact: Communications
Spec. Requirements: 16-page; offset; 8 1/2 x 11
Personnel: Mary Charles, Editor

*Inside Shawnee Mission Public Schools*
Day Published: 3/yr.
Spec. Requirements: 12 page; offset; 11 x 17
Personnel: Mary Charles, Editor

*Messenger, The*
Day Published: w.
Mtls Deadline: Fri., 12:00 pm
Contact: Communications
Spec. Requirements: 8 1/2 x 11
Personnel: Mary Charles, Editor

**SHEAFFER, INC.** 68544
301 Ave. H
Fort Madison, IA 52627
Telephone: (319) 372-3300
FAX: (319) 372-7539
Industry Affiliation: Office Equipment, Services, Supplies
**Publication(s):**
*Pen Points*
Day Published: s-a.
Personnel: Cheryl Knox, Editor
Darla Boeding, Editor

*Sheaffer Newsletter*
Day Published: m.
Mtls Deadline: 1st wk. of mo.
Spec. Requirements: 2 pg.
Personnel: Cheryl Knox, Editor

**SHELBY COUNTY GOVERNMENT** 4891
160 N. Main St. Mall, Ste. 850
Memphis, TN 38103
Telephone: (901) 576-4588
FAX: (901) 576-4759
Industry Affiliation: Associations: City, State, Federal

Materials Accepted/Included: 01-Business news 02-By-line articles 03-Fashion news 04-Food news 05-Freelance copy 06-Letters to editor 07-Real estate news 08-Sports news 09-Travel news 10-Book rev. 11-Movie rev. 12-Music rev. 13-TV rev. 14-Theater rev. 15-Coming events 16-Obituaries 17-Question & answer 18-Social announcements 19-Artwork 20-Cartoons 21-Photos 22-TV listings 23-Audio rec. 24-Video rec. 25-Books 26-Films/film clips 27-Personnel news 28-Press releases 29-New product news/photos 30-Trade lit. 31-Contracts awarded 32-Display adv. 33-Classified adv.

**Publication(s):**
*County Lines, The*
Day Published: bi-m.
Lead Time: 3 mos.
Materials: 01,09,15,17,27,28,30
Mtls Deadline: 10th of Feb., Apr., June,
  Aug., Oct., Dec.
Contact: Public Affairs
Spec. Requirements: 4 pgs.; offset; 11 x
  16 1/2
Personnel: Ruth Ann Hale, Editor

### SHELL OIL CO.    5074
900 Louisiana St.
Houston, TX 77002
Telephone: (713) 241-6161
FAX: (713) 241-6781
Industry Affiliation: Petroleum, Gas
**Publication(s):**
*Shell News*
Day Published: bi-m.
Spec. Requirements: 36 pg; offset
  magazine; 9 x 11
Personnel: Bill Scrimpshire, Editor

*Shell Progress*
Day Published: 3/yr.
Spec. Requirements: 32 pg.
Personnel: Dillon Scott, Editor

*Center Review*
Day Published: q.
Contact: Shell Information Ctr.
  P.O. Box 20329
  Houston, TX 77225
Spec. Requirements: 6-8 pg.
Personnel: Kathleen Abel, Editor

*Go-Devil*
Day Published: bi-m.
Contact: Shell Pipe Line Corp.
  P.O. Box 2648
  Houston, TX 77252
Spec. Requirements: 8 pg.; circ. 3000; free
Personnel: Mark Woodruff, Editor

*Venture*
Day Published: bi-m.
Contact: E & P Organization, Subsidiaries
  P.O. Box 576
  Houston, TX 77001
Spec. Requirements: 12 pgs.
Personnel: Jane Taylor, Editor

*Quest*
Day Published: a.
Contact: Shell Development Co.
Spec. Requirements: 32-36 pg.; insert in
  Shell News
Personnel: Teresa Hurst, Editor

*Shell Alumni News*
Day Published: q.
Spec. Requirements: 4-6 pg.; tabloid
Personnel: K. R. Bruce, Editor

*Shell Marketer*
Day Published: q.
Personnel: Dillon Scott, Editor

### SHELTER INSURANCE COMPANY    3703
1817 W. Broadway
Columbia, MO 65218
Telephone: (314) 445-8441
FAX: (314) 445-3199
Industry Affiliation: Insurance
**Publication(s):**
*Shield, The*
Day Published: bi-m.
Lead Time: 2 mos.
Mtls Deadline: 2 mos. prior to pub. date
Spec. Requirements: 28-page; offset
  magazine; 84 x 11
Personnel: Bruce Meentemeyer, Managing
  Editor

*Contact*
Day Published: w.
Spec. Requirements: 8-pg.

### SHENANDOAH LIFE INSURANCE    5266
CO.
2301 Brambleton Ave., S.W.
Roanoke, VA 24015
Telephone: (703) 985-4400
FAX: (703) 985-4444
Mailing Address:
  P.O. Box 12847
  Roanoke, VA 24029
Industry Affiliation: Insurance
**Publication(s):**
*Shenandoah*
Day Published: bi-m.
Lead Time: 4 wks. prior to pub. date
Mtls Deadline: 4 wks. prior to pub. date
Contact: Donna Musselwhite
Spec. Requirements: 24 pg; letterpress
  magazine; offset; 8-1/2 x 11
Personnel: Donna Musselwhite, Editor

### SHERWIN, INC.    66427
5530 Borwick Ave.
South Gate, CA 90280
Telephone: (310) 861-6324
FAX: (310) 923-8370
Industry Affiliation: Chemicals, Plastics
**Publication(s):**
*Penetrant Progress*
Day Published: q.
Mtls Deadline: varies
Contact: Quality Control Dept.
Spec. Requirements: articles must relate to
  liquid penetrants
Personnel: Sam Robinson, Editor

### SHERWOOD MEDICAL CO.    3727
1915 Olive St.
St. Louis, MO 63103
Telephone: (314) 241-5700
Industry Affiliation: Drugs, Cosmetics,
  Pharmaceuticals
**Publication(s):**
*Sherwood Reporter*
Day Published: q.
Lead Time: 2 mos. prior to pub. date
Mtls Deadline: 2 mos. prior to pub. date
Spec. Requirements: 12-16 page; offset; 8
  1/2 x 11
Personnel: Rose Ann Collins, Editor

*News Beeps*
Day Published: bi-m.
Lead Time: 2 wks. prior to pub. date
Mtls Deadline: 2 wks. prior to pub. date
Personnel: Rose Ann Collins, Editor

### SIERRA PACIFIC POWER CO.    3824
6100 Neil Rd.
Reno, NV 89511
Telephone: (702) 689-4345
FAX: (702) 689-4988
Mailing Address:
  P.O. Box 10100
  Reno, NV 89520
Industry Affiliation: Utility: Related
**Publication(s):**
*This Week*
Day Published: w.
Lead Time: 1 wk. prior to pub. date
Mtls Deadline: 1 wk. prior to pub. date
Spec. Requirements: 6 pgs.; offset; 25 1/2
  x 11
Personnel: Robert Sagan, Editor

*Sierra Scene*
Day Published: m.
Lead Time: 2 wks. prior to pub. date
Mtls Deadline: 2 wks. prior to pub. date
Personnel: Bonnie Saviers, Editor

### SIGNET BANKING CORP.    5222
701 E. Franklin
Richmond, VA 23260
Telephone: (804) 771-7210
FAX: (804) 771-7311
Mailing Address:
  P.O. Box 25970
  Richmond, VA 23260
Industry Affiliation: Banks, Savings &
  Loans
**Publication(s):**
*Signal, The*
Day Published: m.
Lead Time: 1 mo.
Mtls Deadline: 1 mo. prior to pub. date
Contact: Public Relations
Spec. Requirements: 8 pg; offset tabloid;
  11 x 17
Personnel: Kyra Newman, Editor

*On Location*
Day Published: bi-m.
Lead Time: 1 mo prior to pub. date
Mtls Deadline: 1 mo. prior to pub. date
Spec. Requirements: 4-12 pg; 9 x 12
Personnel: Hamilton Holloway, Coordinator

### SIKORSKY AIRCRAFT    2452
N. Main St.
Bridgeport, CT 06601
Telephone: (203) 386-4000
FAX: (203) 386-7300
Industry Affiliation: Aircraft, Aerospace,
  Defense
**Publication(s):**
*Sikorsky News*
Day Published: m.
Lead Time: 1 mo.
Mtls Deadline: 1st of mo.
Spec. Requirements: 12-16 pgs.; offset
  newspaper; 11 x 14
Personnel: Dana Mullady, Editor
  Art Cooney

*Sikorsky Lifeline*
Day Published: s-a.
Lead Time: 1 mo.
Mtls Deadline: 1 mo.
Contact: Pub. Rels.
Personnel: William Tuttle, Editor

### SIMA-SURF INDUSTRY    68383
MANUFACTURERS ASSOCATION
P.O. Box 3447
Dana Point, CA 92629
Telephone: (714) 760-0784
FAX: (714) 760-0184
Industry Affiliation: Industry: Material
  Handling
**Publication(s):**
*Sima "wavelengths"*
Day Published: q.
Lead Time: 6-8 wks.
Mtls Deadline: 6-8 wks. prior

### SIMON WIESENTHAL CENTER    68366
9760 W. Pico Blvd.
Los Angeles, CA 90035
Telephone: (310) 553-9036
FAX: (310) 553-4521
Industry Affiliation: Associations: Trade,
  Fraternal

**Publication(s):**
*Response Magazine*
Day Published: q.
Personnel: Rabbi Abraham Cooper, Editor
  Emeritus
  Lydia Triantopoulus, Editor

### SISTERS OF PROVIDENCE    5324
HEALTH SYSTEM
520 Pike St., Ste. 2500
Seattle, WA 98101
Telephone: (206) 464-3355
Mailing Address:
  P.O. Box 11038
  Seattle, WA 98111
Industry Affiliation: Associations: Trade,
  Fraternal
**Publication(s):**
*The Good Work*
Day Published: q.
Lead Time: 2 mos. prior to pub. date
Mtls Deadline: 2 mos. prior to pub. date
Spec. Requirements: 8-page; offset; 11 x
  14 tabloid
Personnel: Susan Bronsitter, Editor

*In Brief*
Day Published: 5/yr.
Lead Time: 3 mos. prior to pub. date
Mtls Deadline: 3 mos. prior to pub. date

*Ceritas*
Day Published: 5/yr.
Lead Time: 3 mos. prior to pub. date
Mtls Deadline: 3 mos. prior to pub. date
Personnel: Julie Garner, Editor

### SIZZLER INTERNATIONAL, INC.    2105
12655 W. Jefferson Blvd.
Los Angeles, CA 90066
Industry Affiliation: Food, General
**Publication(s):**
*Collins Country*
Day Published: q.
Spec. Requirements: 24-page; offset; 8
  1/2 x 11
Personnel: Cheryl Russell, Editor

*Hotline*
Day Published: 8/yr.
Contact: Sizzler Family Steak Houses
Spec. Requirements: 16-24 page
Personnel: Cheryl Russell, Editor

### SMITH & NEPHEW RICHARDS INC.    4889
1450 E. Brooks Rd.
Memphis, TN 38116
Telephone: (901) 396-2121
FAX: (901) 348-6004
Industry Affiliation: Associations: Health
  Groups
**Publication(s):**
*Smith & Nephew Richards Reporter*
Day Published: m.
Spec. Requirements: 4-page; offset; tabloid
Personnel: Fran Taylor, Editor

### SMITHKLINE BEECHAM    4759
P.O. Box 7929
Philadelphia, PA 19101
Telephone: (215) 751-5000
FAX: (215) 751-3400
Industry Affiliation: Drugs, Cosmetics,
  Pharmaceuticals

**Materials Accepted/Included:** 01-Business news 02-By-line articles 03-Fashion news 04-Food news 05-Freelance copy 06-Letters to editor 07-Real estate news 08-Sports news 09-Travel news
10-Book rev. 11-Movie rev. 12-Music rev. 13-TV rev. 14-Theater rev. 15-Coming events 16-Obituaries 17-Question & answer 18-Social announcements 19-Artwork 20-Cartoons 21-Photos 22-TV listings
23-Audio rec. 24-Video rec. 25-Books 26-Films/film clips 27-Personnel news 28-Press releases 29-New product news/photos 30-Trade lit. 31-Contracts awarded 32-Display adv. 33-Classified adv.

11-79

**Publication(s):**
*S B News*
Day Published: 10/yr.
Spec. Requirements: 8-10 pgs.; offset newspaper; 11 1/2 x 12 1/2
Personnel: Deborah V. Keen, Editor

**SMITHKLINE BEECHAM ANIMAL** 3796
**HEALTH**
812 Springdale Dr.
Exton, PA 19341-2803
Telephone: (610) 363-3777
FAX: (610) 363-3783
Industry Affiliation: Drugs, Cosmetics, Pharmaceuticals
**Publication(s):**
*Topics In Veterinary Medicine*
Day Published: 3/yr.
Lead Time: 90 days
Mtls Deadline: 90 days prior to pub. date
Contact: Sales & Mktg. Communications
Spec. Requirements: 40-pg; offset mag; 8 3/8 x 11 3/4; 4 color pgs.
Personnel: Kathleen Etchison, Editor

**SMITHS INDUSTRIES AEROSPACE** 65157
**& DEFENSE SYSTEMS, INC.**
4141 Eastern Ave., S.E.
Grand Rapids, MI 49508
Telephone: (616) 241-7000
FAX: (616) 241-7533
Industry Affiliation: Aircraft, Aerospace, Defense
**Publication(s):**
*Interface*
Day Published: m.
Mtls Deadline: 1 mo. prior to pub. date
Spec. Requirements: 12 pg. letterpress newspaper; 81/2 x 11
Personnel: Jennifer Villarreal, Editor

**SNAP-ON TOOLS CORP.** 5441
2801 80TH St
Kenosha, WI 53143
Telephone: (414) 656-5200
Industry Affiliation: Industry: Light Tools, Equipment
**Publication(s):**
*Snap-On Dealer News:*
Day Published: q.
Lead Time: 3 mos.
Spec. Requirements: 16 pgs.; offset magazine; 8 1/2 x 11
Personnel: June Lemerand, Editor

*Snap-On Industrial News:*
Day Published: q.
Lead Time: 3 mos.
Spec. Requirements: 8 pgs.
Personnel: June Lemerand

**SOCIAL SECURITY** 3295
**ADMINISTRATION**
6401 Security Blvd.
Baltimore, MD 21235
Telephone: (800) 234-5772
Industry Affiliation: Associations: City, State, Federal
**Publication(s):**
*Oasis*
Day Published: m.
Spec. Requirements: 32-pgs.; offset; 81 x 107
Personnel: Robert N. Teeters, Editor

**SOCIETY CORP.** 4434
800 Superior Ave., 7th Fl.
Cleveland, OH 44114
Telephone: (216) 622-9000
Industry Affiliation: Advertising, Art, Public Relations

**Publication(s):**
*Soci Corporate Notes:*
Day Published: bi-w.
Spec. Requirements: 2-4-pg.; offset; 8 1/2 x 11
Personnel: Jackie M. Maslanka, Editor

**SOCIETY CORPORATION** 52474
127 Public Sq., 7th Fl.
Cleveland, OH 44114
Telephone: (216) 689-3000
FAX: (216) 689-5115
Industry Affiliation: Advertising, Art, Public Relations
**Publication(s):**
*Society Now*
Day Published: bi-m.
Personnel: Janet Gaydosh, Editor

**SOCIETY FOR HUMAN RESOURCE** 4470
**MANAGEMENT**
606 N. Washington St.
Alexandria, VA 22314
Telephone: (703) 548-3440
FAX: (703) 836-0367
Industry Affiliation: Associations: Trade, Fraternal
**Publication(s):**
*H R Magazine*
Day Published: m.
Lead Time: 3-4 mos.
Mtls Deadline: 15th; 2 mos. prior to pub. date
Spec. Requirements: 100 pg. min.
Personnel: Ceel Pasternak, Editor

**SOCIETY OF AUTOMOTIVE** 4760
**ENGINEERS INC.**
400 Commonwealth Dr.
Warrendale, PA 15096-0001
Telephone: (412) 776-4841
FAX: (412) 776-5760
Industry Affiliation: Associations: Trade, Fraternal
**Publication(s):**
*Sae Update*
Day Published: m.
Lead Time: 1 mo.
Materials: 10,16,27,28,29,30,32,33
Mtls Deadline: 15th of ea. mo.
Spec. Requirements: 4-8 pg; offset; 8 1/2 x 11
Personnel: Martha Swiss, Editor

*Automotive Engineer & Aerospace Engineer*
Lead Time: 1st of mo.
Materials: 32,33
Mtls Deadline: Ist of mo.
Personnel: Daniel J. Holt, Editor in Chief

**SOCIETY OF CHARTERED** 4761
**PROPERTY & CASUALTY**
**UNDERWRITERS**
P.O. Box 3009
Malvern, PA 19355-0709
Telephone: (215) 251-2728
FAX: (215) 251-2775
Industry Affiliation: Insurance
**Publication(s):**
*C P C U Journal*
Day Published: q.
Lead Time: 2 mos.
Mtls Deadline: 2 mos.
Spec. Requirements: 64-pg.; offset magazine; 8 1/2 x 11
Personnel: Deanne Sherman
　　　　Lisa Fittipaldi, Managing Editor
　　　　Sheila Todd, Marketing Ad Sales

*C P C U News*
Day Published: 10/yr.
Lead Time: 2 mos.
Mtls Deadline: 2 mos.
Spec. Requirements: 8-12 pgs.
Personnel: Lisa Fittipaldi, Editor
　　　　Rebecca Bodenner
　　　　Sharon Park, Editor

**SOCIETY OF WOMEN ENGINEERS** 52475
120 Wall St., 11th Fl.
New York, NY 10005
Telephone: (212) 509-9577
FAX: (212) 509-0224
Industry Affiliation: Associations: Trade, Fraternal
**Publication(s):**
*S W E*
Day Published: bi-m.
Lead Time: 5 mos.
Mtls Deadline: 5 mos. prior to pub. date
Spec. Requirements: double-spaced, typed articles
Personnel: Anne Perusek, Managing Editor

**SONAT, INC.** 2002
P.O. Box 2563
Birmingham, AL 35202
Telephone: (205) 325-3800
FAX: (205) 325-7358
Industry Affiliation: Petroleum, Gas
**Publication(s):**
*Sonat Tielines*
Day Published: q.
Spec. Requirements: 8 pg.; 8 1/2 x 11
Personnel: Sherrel Stewart, Editor

**SONOCO PRODUCTS CO.** 4837
N. Second St.
Hartsville, SC 29550
Telephone: (803) 383-7000
FAX: (803) 383-3378
Mailing Address:
　　P.O. Box 160
　　Hartsville, SC 29551-0160
Industry Affiliation: Petroleum, Gas
**Publication(s):**
*Sonoco World*
Day Published: q.
Lead Time: 1 mo.
Materials: 01,04,30
Mtls Deadline: last day of quarter
Spec. Requirements: 24 pg.; tabloid

**SOROPTIMIST INTERNATIONAL** 4800
**OF THE AMERICAS, INC.**
1616 Walnut St.
Philadelphia, PA 19103-5313
Telephone: (215) 732-0512
FAX: (215) 732-7508
Industry Affiliation: Associations: Trade, Fraternal
**Publication(s):**
*Soroptimist Of The Americas*
Day Published: bi-m.
Lead Time: 90 days
Materials: 05,06,10,21,28
Mtls Deadline: 90 days prior to pub. date
Spec. Requirements: 24 pg; 8 1/2 x 11
Personnel: Darlene Friedman, Editor

**SOUTH CAROLINA DEPARTMENT** 4843
**OF COMMERCE**
1201 Main St.
Columbia, SC 29201
Telephone: (803) 737-0400
Mailing Address:
　　P.O. Box 927
　　Columbia, SC 29202
Industry Affiliation: Associations: City, State, Federal

**Publication(s):**
*Economic Developments*
Day Published: q.
Lead Time: 45 days prior to pub. date
Materials: 01,02,05,28,29,30,31
Contact: Public Relations

**SOUTH CAROLINA ELECTRIC &** 4838
**GAS CO.**
1426 Main St.
Columbia, SC 29201
Telephone: (803) 748-3000
FAX: (803) 411-9000
Industry Affiliation: Utility: Electric
**Publication(s):**
*S C E & G News*
Day Published: fortn.
Lead Time: 2 wks.
Mtls Deadline: 4-6 wks. prior to pub. date
Spec. Requirements: 8-pgs.; offset; 11 1/2 x 16
Personnel: Wanda Hawkins, Editor
　　　　Mary G. Brown

**SOUTH CAROLINA STATE PORTS** 4844
**AUTHORITY**
176 Concord St.
Charleston, SC 29401
Telephone: (803) 723-8651
FAX: (803) 723-8710
Mailing Address:
　　P.O. Box 817
　　Charleston, SC 29402
Industry Affiliation: Shipping
**Publication(s):**
*South Carolina Port News*
Day Published: m.
Lead Time: 10th of previous mo.
Mtls Deadline: 10th of previous mo.
Spec. Requirements: 36-48 page; offset magazine; 8 1/2 x 11
Personnel: L. Marion Bull, Editor

**SOUTHEAST MICHIGAN, N.A.** 3438
3101 N. Woodward
Royal Oak, MI 48073
Telephone: (313) 280-8579
Industry Affiliation: Finance, Services
**Publication(s):**
*First Word, The*
Day Published: m.
Lead Time: 1 mo. prior to pub. date
Mtls Deadline: 1st of mo. prior to pub. date
Contact: Human Res.
Spec. Requirements: 4-8 pg.; offset; tabloid
Personnel: Sheila Darin, Editor

**SOUTHERN ARTS FEDERATION,** 2679
**INC.**
181 14th St., N.E., Ste. 400
Atlanta, GA 30309-7603
Telephone: (404) 874-7244
Industry Affiliation: Associations: Trade, Fraternal
**Publication(s):**
*Jazz South*
Day Published: q.
Lead Time: 6 wks.
Materials: 02,05,06,10,12,15,21
Mtls Deadline: q.
Spec. Requirements: 16-20 pgs.; offset; 8 1/2 x 11
Personnel: Tom Campbell, Editor

**Materials Accepted/Included:** 01-Business news 02-By-line articles 03-Fashion news 04-Food news 05-Freelance copy 06-Letters to editor 07-Real estate news 08-Sports news 09-Travel news 10-Book rev. 11-Movie rev. 12-Music rev. 13-TV rev. 14-Theater rev. 15-Coming events 16-Obituaries 17-Question & answer 18-Social announcements 19-Artwork 20-Cartoons 21-Photos 22-TV listings 23-Audio rec. 24-Video rec. 25-Books 26-Films/film clips 27-Personnel news 28-Press releases 29-New product news/photos 30-Trade lit. 31-Contracts awarded 32-Display adv. 33-Classified adv.

*Folk Arts Notes*
Day Published: s-a.
Personnel: Peggy Bulger, Editor

2680
## SOUTHERN ASSOCIATION OF COLLEGES & SCHOOLS
1866 Southern Ln.
Decatur, GA 30033-4097
Telephone: (404) 679-4500
Industry Affiliation: Colleges, Institutions, Science Research
**Publication(s):**
*Proceedings*
Day Published: bi-m.
Lead Time: 6 wks.
Materials: 21,28
Mtls Deadline: 6 wks. prior to pub. date
Spec. Requirements: 8-24 pgs.; offset; 8 1/2 x 11
Personnel: Teresa Greer, Editor

2681
## SOUTHERN BELL TELEPHONE CO.
2850 Campbellton Rd.
Atlanta, GA 30311
Telephone: (404) 529-8611
Industry Affiliation: Utility: Telephone
**Publication(s):**
*Information Edge*
Day Published: bi-m.
Spec. Requirements: 36 pg.; offset; 8 1/2 x 11

*Southern Bell Views*
Day Published: bi-m.

2250
## SOUTHERN CALIFORNIA WATER CO.
630 E. Foothill Blvd.
San Dimas, CA 91773
Telephone: (909) 394-3614
Industry Affiliation: Utility: Water
**Publication(s):**
*Connections*
Day Published: bi-m.
Personnel: Marilyn Florance, Editor

2682
## SOUTHERN COMPANY SERVICES, INC.
64 Perimeter Ctr., E.
Atlanta, GA 30346
Telephone: (404) 393-0650
FAX: (404) 668-2672
Industry Affiliation: Utility: Electric
**Publication(s):**
*Inside*
Day Published: m.
Spec. Requirements: 12 pg.; offset; 10 x 13 1/4
Personnel: David King, Editor

*Southern Highlights*
Day Published: m.
Spec. Requirements: 8-12 pg.
Personnel: Sam Heys, Editor

2453
## SOUTHERN CONNECTICUT GAS CO.
855 Main St.
Bridgeport, CT 06604
Telephone: (203) 382-8111
FAX: (203) 382-8120
Industry Affiliation: Utility: Gas
**Publication(s):**
*Pilot*
Day Published: bi-m.
Lead Time: 1 wk. prior to pub. date
Mtls Deadline: 1 wk. prior to pub. date
Spec. Requirements: 6 pg.; offset; 18 x 24
Personnel: Robert J. Brennan Jr., Editor

*News & Views*
Day Published: m.
Lead Time: 15th of mo. prior to pub. date
Mtls Deadline: 15th of mo. prior to pub. date
Personnel: Robert J. Brennan, Jr., Editor

3234
## SOUTHERN FOREST PRODUCTS ASSOCIATION
P.O. Box 641700
New Orleans, LA 70064
Telephone: (504) 443-4464
FAX: (504) 443-6612
Industry Affiliation: Lumber, Forestry, Building Materials
**Publication(s):**
*S F Newsletter*
Day Published: w.
Lead Time: 1 wk.
Materials: 01,10,25,28,29
Mtls Deadline: Mon. prior to pub. date
Spec. Requirements: 2 pg.; offset ; 8 1/2 x 11
Personnel: David Kellogg, Editor

3040
## SOUTHERN INDIANA GAS & ELECTRIC CO.
20 N.W. Fourth St.
Evansville, IN 47741
Telephone: (812) 464-4525
FAX: (812) 464-4554
Industry Affiliation: Utility: Electric
**Publication(s):**
*S I G E C O News*
Day Published: m.
Lead Time: 1 mo. prior to pub. date
Mtls Deadline: 1 mo. prior to pub. date
Contact: Public Information
Spec. Requirements: 8-16 pg.; offset; 8 1/2 x 11
Personnel: Mary Beth Reese, Editor
           Barbara Stahura

5079
## SOUTHERN METHODIST UNIVERSITY
6517 Hillcrest Ave., Ste. 204
Dallas, TX 75205
Telephone: (214) 987-7675
FAX: (214) 987-7663
Mailing Address:
   SMU Box 750174
   Dallas, TX 75275-0174
Industry Affiliation: Colleges, Institutions, Science Research
**Publication(s):**
*S M U Magazine*
Day Published: q.
Lead Time: 2 mos.
Mtls Deadline: Jul. 1, Oct. 1, Feb. 1, Apr. 1
Contact: Public Affairs
Spec. Requirements: film right reading, emulsion up
Personnel: Kathleen Tibbetts, Assistant Editor
           Susan White, Managing Editor
           Patricia Ann LaSalle, Editor in Chief

2454
## SOUTHERN NEW ENGLAND TELEPHONE CO.
227 Church St
New Haven, CT 06510
Telephone: (203) 771-5200
Industry Affiliation: Utility: Telephone
**Publication(s):**
*S N E Times*
Day Published: w.
Lead Time: 3 wks. prior to pub. date
Mtls Deadline: 3 wks. prior to pub. date
Spec. Requirements: 32-page; ; 8 1/2 x 11
Personnel: David Ohlsen, Editor

*S N E News*
Day Published: m.
Lead Time: 2 mos. prior to pub. date
Mtls Deadline: 2 mos. prior to pub. date
Contact: Information
Spec. Requirements: 4-page
Personnel: Karen George, Editor

2252
## SOUTHERN PACIFIC TRANSPORTATION CO.
One Market Plz., Rm. 950
San Francisco, CA 94105
Telephone: (415) 541-1000
Industry Affiliation: Utility: Telephone
**Publication(s):**
*Southern Pacific Bulletin*
Day Published: m.
Lead Time: 1 mo. prior to pub. date
Mtls Deadline: 1 mo. prior to pub. date
Spec. Requirements: 16 pg; offset magazine; 84 x 11
Personnel: Michael Brown, Editor

68387
## SOUTHERN STATES COOPERATIVE
P.O. Box 26234
Richmond, VA 23260
Telephone: (804) 281-1368
FAX: (804) 281-1141
Industry Affiliation: Agriculture, Services
**Publication(s):**
*Pacesetter*
Day Published: m.
Lead Time: 3 wks.
Mtls Deadline: last day of mo. prior to pub. date
Personnel: Shirley K. Sullivan, Editor

*Communique*
Day Published: m.
Lead Time: 2 wks.
Materials: 04,06
Mtls Deadline: 13th of mo. prior to pub. date
Personnel: Shirley K. Sullivan, Editor

*Cooperative Farmer*
Day Published: 9/yr.
Lead Time: 8 wks.
Materials: 04,06
Mtls Deadline: 90 days prior to pub. date
Personnel: Charles I. Batchelor, Editor
           Don R. Tindall, Publisher

*Statesman*
Day Published: 9/yr.
Contact: Corporate Communications
Personnel: Sylvia Hicks, Editor

5081
## SOUTHERN UNION CO.
504 Lavaca, Ste. 800
Austin, TX 78701
Telephone: (512) 370-8240
FAX: (512) 370-8236
Industry Affiliation: Utility: Gas
**Publication(s):**
*Southern Union Company Forum*
Day Published: m.
Contact: Pub. Rels.
Spec. Requirements: 8-12 pg. newsletter
Personnel: Tela Goodwin, Editor

4141
## SOUTHSIDE HOSPITAL
301 E. Main St.
Bay Shore, NY 11706
Telephone: (516) 968-3000
FAX: (516) 968-3315
Industry Affiliation: Hospitals
**Publication(s):**
*Southside Health*
Day Published: q.
Spec. Requirements: 8-pg.; offset; 11 x 17
Personnel: Karen J. Commander, Editor

*Southside Physician*
Day Published: q.
Personnel: Barbara Kreisler
           Karen J. Commander

5145
## SOUTHWESTERN BELL TELEPHONE CO.
308 S. Akard., Rm. 1104
Dallas, TX 75202
Telephone: (214) 464-4647
Mailing Address:
   P.O. Box 5521
   Dallas, TX 75202
Industry Affiliation: Utility: Telephone
**Publication(s):**
*Telephone Times*
Day Published: bi-w.
Spec. Requirements: 4 pgs.; offset newspaper; 11 1/2 x 15
Personnel: Jackie Mashburn, Editor

3235
## SOUTHWESTERN ELECTRIC POWER CO.
428 Travis
Shreveport, LA 71101
Telephone: (318) 673-3168
FAX: (318) 673-3169
Mailing Address:
   P.O. Box 21106
   Shreveport, LA 71156
Industry Affiliation: Utility: Electric
**Publication(s):**
*Southwestern*
Day Published: bi-m.
Lead Time: 6 wks.
Materials: 01,02,06,17,19,21,27,28,29
Mtls Deadline: 6 wks. prior to pub. date
Spec. Requirements: 12 page; offset magazine; 8 1/2 x 11
Personnel: Peter Main, Editor
           Traci George, Art Director

5167
## SOUTHWESTERN PUBLIC SERVICE CO.
600 S. Tyler St.
Amarillo, TX 79101
Telephone: (806) 378-2121
FAX: (806) 378-2995
Mailing Address:
   P.O. Box 1261
   Amarillo, TX 79170
Industry Affiliation: Utility: Electric
**Publication(s):**
*Southwesterner*
Day Published: bi-m.
Lead Time: 30 days days prior to pub. date
Mtls Deadline: 1st of Feb., Apr., June, Aug., Oct., Dec.
Spec. Requirements: 24-32 pg.; offset magazine; 8 1/2 x 11
Personnel: Laura Adams Dudley, Editor

*Grapevine*
Day Published: w.
Lead Time: 4 days prior to pub. date
Mtls Deadline: Wed. prior to pub. date
Personnel: Rhonda Cargill, Editor

4435
## SOUTHWEST GENERAL HOSPITAL
18697 Bagley Rd.
Cleveland, OH 44130
Telephone: (216) 826-8000
Industry Affiliation: Hospitals
**Publication(s):**
*Capsule*
Day Published: bi-m.
Spec. Requirements: 4-6 pgs.; offset; 12 x 16 1/2
Personnel: Debora Meskauskas
           Laura Munson
           Susan Garlando, Editor

**Materials Accepted/Included:** 01-Business news 02-By-line articles 03-Fashion news 04-Food news 05-Freelance copy 06-Letters to editor 07-Real estate news 08-Sports news 09-Travel news 10-Book rev. 11-Movie rev. 12-Music rev. 13-TV rev. 14-Theater rev. 15-Coming events 16-Obituaries 17-Question & answer 18-Social announcements 19-Artwork 20-Cartoons 21-Photos 22-TV listings 23-Audio rec. 24-Video rec. 25-Books 26-Films/film clips 27-Personnel news 28-Press releases 29-New product news/photos 30-Trade lit. 31-Contracts awarded 32-Display adv. 33-Classified adv.

11-81

*Southwest Today*
Day Published: 3/yr.
Personnel: Carol Jordan, Editor

**SOUTHWEST TEXAS METHODIST** 5085
**HOSPITAL**
7700 Floyd Curl Dr.
San Antonio, TX 78229
Telephone: (210) 692-4000
FAX: (210) 692-4982
Industry Affiliation: Hospitals
**Publication(s):**
*Images Of Southwest Texas Methodist Hospital*
Day Published: s-a.
Lead Time: 3 mos. prior to pub. date
Mtls Deadline: 3 mos. prior to pub. date
Spec. Requirements: 28 pg.; offset; 8 1/2 x 11
Personnel: Steve Finley, Editor

*Vital Signs*
Day Published: a.
Spec. Requirements: 28 pg.; 8 1/2 x 11
Personnel: Cyra Dumitru, Editor

**SPACE COAST DISABILITY** 68417
**RIGHTS ASSOCIATION**
331 Ramp Rd.
Coco Beach, FL 32931
Telephone: (407) 784-9008
FAX: (407) 784-3702
Industry Affiliation: Hospitals
**Publication(s):**
*Newsletter*
Day Published: q.
Personnel: Anne Roth

**SPARTAN STORES, INC.** 68440
850 76th St., S.W.
Grand Rapids, MI 49518
Telephone: (616) 878-2672
FAX: (616) 878-2775
Industry Affiliation: Retail Stores
**Publication(s):**
*Spartan News*
Day Published: s-w.
Personnel: Gary Evey, Editor

*Shield*
Day Published: bi-m.
Personnel: Tom Truesdale, Editor

**SPIEGEL, INC.** 2906
3500 Lacey Rd.
Downer Grove, IL 60515-5432
Telephone: (708) 986-7500
Industry Affiliation: Retail Stores
**Publication(s):**
*Focus Newsletter*
Day Published: m.
Lead Time: 1 mo.
Mtls Deadline: 1 mo. prior to pub. date
Spec. Requirements: 12 pg.; offset; 8 1/2 x 11
Personnel: Jianna Farago, Editor

**SPRINGS INDUSTRIES, INC.** 4840
205 N. White St.
Fort Mill, SC 29715
Telephone: (803) 547-3742
Industry Affiliation: Textiles, Apparel, Mills, Machinery

**Publication(s):**
*Springs Bulletin The*
Day Published: m.
Spec. Requirements: 12 page; offset; tabloid
Personnel: Ted S. Matthews, Editor

**SPRINT MID-ATLANTIC TELECOM** 4270
14111 Capital Blvd.
Wake Forest, NC 27587-5900
Telephone: (919) 554-7900
FAX: (919) 554-7474
Industry Affiliation: Utility: Telephone
**Publication(s):**
*Vision*
Day Published: m.
Lead Time: 1 mo.
Mtls Deadline: 15th of mo. prior to pub. date
Contact: Corporate Communications
Spec. Requirements: 24-28 page; offset; 8 1/2 x 11
Personnel: Tom Matthews, Editor
Tom Matthews, Editor in Chief
Roger Strange, Art Director

*Sprint Mid-Atlantic Telecom Today*
Day Published: bi-m.
Lead Time: 10 days
Mtls Deadline: 10 days prior to pub. date
Contact: Corporate Communications
Personnel: Sandy Pernell, Editor
Tom Matthews, Managing Editor

**STA-RITE INDUSTRIES** 66565
293 Wright St.
Delavan, WI 53115
Telephone: (414) 728-5551
Industry Affiliation: Hardware, Plumbing
**Publication(s):**
*Perspective*
Day Published: m.
Lead Time: 2 wks.
Mtls Deadline: 15th of Feb., May, Aug. & Nov.
Contact: Water Systems and Pool/Spa
Personnel: Rick Heine, Editor

*This Week*
Day Published: s-m.
Materials: 05,21,27,28,29
Mtls Deadline: 1st & 15th of ea. mo.
Contact: Water Systems
Personnel: Rick Heine, Editor

**ST. AGNES HOSPITAL** 3293
900 Caton Ave.
Baltimore, MD 21229
Telephone: (410) 368-2170
FAX: (410) 368-2947
Industry Affiliation: Hospitals
**Publication(s):**
*St. Agnes News*
Day Published: bi-m.
Lead Time: 1 mo. prior to pub. date
Mtls Deadline: 2nd Mon. of mo. prior to pub. date
Spec. Requirements: 8 page; offset; 11 1/2 x 17 1/2
Personnel: George J. Moniodis
Helen Becker, Editor

**STAINLESS FOUNDRY &** 5442
**ENGINEERING INC.**
5110 N. 35th St.
Milwaukee, WI 53209
Telephone: (414) 462-7400
FAX: (414) 462-7303
Industry Affiliation: Architects, Engineers, Business Service

**Publication(s):**
*Stainless Spirit*
Day Published: q.
Lead Time: 1-2 mos. prior to pub. date
Mtls Deadline: 1-2 mos. prior to pub. date
Spec. Requirements: 8 pg.; offset; 8 1/2 x 11
Personnel: Kathy Muszynski, Editor

**STANDARD OIL CO.** 52332
P.O. Box 5910-A
Chicago, IL 60680
Telephone: (312) 352-6111
Industry Affiliation: Petroleum, Gas
**Publication(s):**
*Span*
Day Published: q.
Personnel: R.L. Rahder, Editor

**STAR MARKET CO.** 3392
625 Mt. Auburn St.
Cambridge, MA 02138
Telephone: (617) 661-2209
FAX: (617) 661-2216
Industry Affiliation: Food, General
**Publication(s):**
*Star News*
Day Published: m.
Lead Time: 2 wks. prior to pub. date
Spec. Requirements: 8 pg.; tabloid; 11 x 17
Personnel: Polly McMahon, Editor

**STATE BAR OF TEXAS** 5088
1414 Colorado
Austin, TX 78701
Telephone: (512) 463-1436
Mailing Address:
P.O. Box 12487, Capitol Sta.
Austin, TX 78711
Industry Affiliation: Associations: Trade, Fraternal
**Publication(s):**
*Texas Bar Journal*
Day Published: m. except Aug.
Lead Time: 6 wks. prior to pub. date
Mtls Deadline: 10th of 2nd mo. prior to pub. date
Spec. Requirements: 100-pg.: offset; 74 x 106
Personnel: Karen R. Johnson, Editor in Chief
Kelley Jones, Managing Editor

**STATE CHEMICAL** 4439
**MANUFACTURING CO.**
3100 Hamilton Ave
Cleveland, OH 44114
Telephone: (216) 861-7114
FAX: (216) 861-5213
Industry Affiliation: Chemicals, Plastics
**Publication(s):**
*Communicator*
Day Published: w.
Materials: 01,17,19,20,21,27,29,30
Contact: Communications
Spec. Requirements: 4-pg.; 8 1/2 x 11
Personnel: Elizabeth Klomp, Managing Editor
Jackie Spector, Editor
Len Bergenstein, Art Director
Tom Slabe, Marketing Director

*Statement*
Day Published: q.
Materials: 01,17,19,20,21,27,29
Contact: Communications
Personnel: Elizabeth Klomp, Managing Editor
Ed Strainer, Production Manager
Len Bergenstein, Art Director
Tom Slabe, Marketing Director

**STATE COMPENSATION** 2254
**INSURANCE FUND**
1275 Market St.
San Francisco, CA 94103
Telephone: (415) 565-1065
Industry Affiliation: Insurance
**Publication(s):**
*Insight*
Day Published: m.
Lead Time: 2 wks.-1 mo.
Mtls Deadline: 1-2 wks. prior to pub. date
Spec. Requirements: 16-20 pg.; offset; 8 1/2 x 11
Personnel: Ron Christensen, Editor

*Retiree's Newsletter*
Day Published: q.
Lead Time: 2 wks.

**STATE DEPARTMENT OF** 3651
**EDUCATION**
550 High St., Walter Sillers Bldg., Ste. 502
Jackson, MS 39201
Telephone: (601) 359-3519
FAX: (601) 359-2326
Mailing Address:
P.O. Box 771
Jackson, MS 39205
Industry Affiliation: Associations: City, State, Federal
**Publication(s):**
*Mississippi Messages*
Day Published: q.
Lead Time: 6 wks.

*Briefly Stated*
Day Published: bi-m.
Lead Time: 2 wks.

**STATE FARM MUTUAL AUTO** 3620
**INSURANCE CO.**
1500 W. Hwy. 36
St. Paul, MN 55161
Telephone: (612) 631-4251
FAX: (612) 635-4691
Industry Affiliation: Insurance
**Publication(s):**
*Pine-Aire*
Day Published: m.
Lead Time: 1st of mo. prior to pub. date
Materials: 01,02,04,06,18,19,21
Mtls Deadline: 1 mo. prior to pub. date
Contact: (Editor) Public Affairs
Spec. Requirements: 24-30 pg.; offset; 8 1/2 x 11
Personnel: Karen Anderson, Editor

*Bellringer*
Day Published: m.
Lead Time: 15th of mo. prior to pub. mo.
Materials: 01,02,06,15,18,19
Mtls Deadline: 1 mo. prior to pub. date
Contact: (Editor) Public Affairs
Spec. Requirements: 32-40 pg; offset; 8 1/2 x 11
Personnel: Carolyn Sudduth, Editor

**Materials Accepted/Included:** 01-Business news 02-By-line articles 03-Fashion news 04-Food news 05-Freelance copy 06-Letters to editor 07-Real estate news 08-Sports news 09-Travel news 10-Book rev. 11-Movie rev. 12-Music rev. 13-TV rev. 14-Theater rev. 15-Coming events 16-Obituaries 17-Question & answer 18-Social announcements 19-Artwork 20-Cartoons 21-Photos 22-TV listings 23-Audio rec. 24-Video rec. 25-Books 26-Films/film clips 27-Personnel news 28-Press releases 29-New product news/photos 30-Trade lit. 31-Contracts awarded 32-Display adv. 33-Classified adv.

*North Central Manager*
Day Published: q.
Lead Time: 1 mo. prior to pub. date
Mtls Deadline: 1 mo. prior to pub. date
Contact: (Editor) Public Affairs
Spec. Requirements: 12-16 pg.
Personnel: Carolyn Sudduth, Editor

68624
## STATE FARM MUTUAL AUTO INSURANCE CO.
Michigan Regional Office, 410 East Dr.
Marshall, MI 49068
Telephone: (616) 781-4211
FAX: (616) 781-1247
Industry Affiliation: Insurance
**Publication(s):**
*Michigram, The*
Day Published: m.
Lead Time: 15th of mo. prior to pub. mo.
Mtls Deadline: 15th of mo. prior to pub. mo.
Spec. Requirements: 36 pg.; offset; 8 1/2 x 11
Personnel: Patty Loyer, Editor

3041
## STATE LIFE INSURANCE CO.
141 E. Washington St.
Indianapolis, IN 46204
Telephone: (317) 681-5300
FAX: (317) 681-5492
Mailing Address:
 P.O. Box 406
 Indianapolis, IN 46206
Industry Affiliation: Insurance
**Publication(s):**
*Bulletin*
Day Published: bi-m.
Lead Time: 1 mo. prior to pub. date
Mtls Deadline: 1st of mo. prior to pub. mo.
Spec. Requirements: 24-36 pg.; letterpress magazine; 8 1/2 x 11
Personnel: Cindy Duran, Editor

*141 Express*
Day Published: bi-m.
Lead Time: 1st of mo. prior to pub. mo.
Personnel: Susan Neher, Editor
 Cindy Lee Duran

3805
## STATE OF NEBRASKA
Lincoln Municipal Airport
Lincoln, NE 68524
Telephone: (402) 471-2371
Mailing Address:
 P.O. Box 82088
 Lincoln, NE 68501
Industry Affiliation: Aircraft, Aerospace, Defense
**Publication(s):**
*Pireps*
Day Published: m.
Lead Time: 1 mo.
Spec. Requirements: 6-page; offset; 8 1/2 x 11
Personnel: Ed Clark, Editor

3394
## STATE STREET BOSTON CORP.
225 Franklin St.
Boston, MA 02101
Telephone: (617) 654-4827
FAX: (617) 654-3386
Industry Affiliation: Finance, Services

**Publication(s):**
*State Street Now*
Day Published: 10/yr.
Spec. Requirements: 16 pg.; offset; 8 1/2 x 11
Personnel: Karen Mason, Editor

4148
## STATE UNIVERSITY OF N.Y. HEALTH SCIENCE CTR. AT SYRACUSE
750 E. Adams St.
Syracuse, NY 13210
Telephone: (315) 464-4836
Industry Affiliation: Colleges, Institutions, Science Research
**Publication(s):**
*H S C Today*
Day Published: m.
Lead Time: 3 wks. prior to pub. date
Mtls Deadline: 3 wks. prior to pub. date
Spec. Requirements: 8-12 pg.; tabloid; 11 1/2 x 17
Personnel: Leah Fleckenstein, Editor
 Doretta Settineri Royer

*H S C This Week*
Day Published: w.
Lead Time: 2 days prior to pub. date
Mtls Deadline: 1 day prior to pub. date
Personnel: Doretta Settineri Royer, Editor

5064
## ST. EDWARD'S UNIVERSITY
3001 S. Congress Ave.
Austin, TX 78704
Telephone: (512) 448-8400
Industry Affiliation: Colleges, Institutions, Science Research
**Publication(s):**
*Seu News*
Day Published: q.
Lead Time: 6 wks. prior to pub. date
Mtls Deadline: 6 wks prior to pub. date
Contact: University Relations
Spec. Requirements: 10-16 pg; offset; tabloid; alumni related
Personnel: Brenda Thompson, Editor

*Edwardian, The*
Day Published: bi-m.
Lead Time: 1 wk. prior prior to pub. date
Mtls Deadline: 2 wks. prior to pub. date
Contact: Student Publications
Personnel: Damian Morgan

*Tower, The*
Day Published: a.
Lead Time: 10 days prior to pub. date
Mtls Deadline: 10 days prior to pub. date
Contact: University Yearbook

*Hilltop Views*
Day Published: a.

2893
## ST. ELIZABETH MEDICAL CENTER
2100 Madison Ave
Granite City, IL 62040
Telephone: (618) 798-3000
Industry Affiliation: Hospitals
**Publication(s):**
*Healthtalk*
Day Published: bi-m.
Contact: Pub. Rels. Dept.
Spec. Requirements: 8 pg.; offset; tabloid
Personnel: Deborah Williams, Editor

4765
## STERLING DRUG, INC.
400 W. Stoever Ave.
Myerstown, PA 17067
Telephone: (717) 866-2141
FAX: (717) 866-3702
Industry Affiliation: Drugs, Cosmetics, Pharmaceuticals

**Publication(s):**
*Conveyor, The*
Day Published: q.
Lead Time: 20 days
Spec. Requirements: offset; 8 1/2 x 11, 8-12 pgs.
Personnel: John M. Seager, Editor

65911
## STEVENS PUBLISHING CORP.
225 N. New Rd.
P.O. Box 2604
Waco, TX 76702-2604
Telephone: (817) 776-9000
Industry Affiliation: Publishers, Books, Magazines
**Publication(s):**
*Hazmat News*
Day Published: s-m.
Lead Time: 1 mo. prior to pub. date
Mtls Deadline: 1 mo. prior to pub. date
Personnel: B. K. Morris, Editor
 Kurt Mahler
 Wallace Bennett

*Osha Week*
Day Published: w.
Lead Time: 2 wks. prior to pub. date
Mtls Deadline: 2 wks. prior to pub. date
Personnel: B. K. Morris, Editor
 Wallace Bennett

*Occupational Health & Safety News*
Day Published: s-m.
Lead Time: 2 mos. prior to pub. date
Mtls Deadline: 7 mos. prior to pub. date
Personnel: B. K. Morris, Editor
 Wallace Bennett

*Environmental Protection News*
Day Published: s-m.
Lead Time: 1 mo. prior to pub. date
Mtls Deadline: 1 mo. prior to pub. date
Personnel: B. K. Morris, Editor
 Wallace Bennett

2708
## ST. FRANCIS HOSPITAL
2230 Liliha St.
Honolulu, HI 96817
Telephone: (808) 547-6011
FAX: (808) 536-5421
Industry Affiliation: Hospitals
**Publication(s):**
*Ka Leo Reflections*
Day Published: q.
Spec. Requirements: 10-12 pg.; offset; 8-1/2 x 11
Personnel: Norma Kop, Editor

3036
## ST. FRANCIS HOSPITAL CENTER
1600 Albany St.
Beech Grove, IN 46107
Telephone: (317) 783-8300
Industry Affiliation: Hospitals
**Publication(s):**
*Intercom*
Day Published: m.
Mtls Deadline: 30-60 days prior to pub. date
Spec. Requirements: 16 pg.; offset; 8 1/2 x 11
Personnel: David Hofmann, Editor

*Spectrum*
Day Published: q.
Lead Time: 90 days prior to pub. date
Mtls Deadline: 30 days prior to pub. date
Personnel: Annette Miller, Editor

2497
## ST. FRANCIS HOSPITAL, INC.
Seventh & Clayton Sts.
Wilmington, DE 19805
Telephone: (302) 421-4100
FAX: (302) 575-8285
Industry Affiliation: Hospitals

**Publication(s):**
*St. Francis Capsule*
Day Published: m.
Lead Time: 1 mo. prior to pub. date
Mtls Deadline: 1 mo. prior to pub. date
Spec. Requirements: 16 pg.; offset; 8 1/2 x 11; 2 color
Personnel: Thomas J. Fanning, Editor
 Nancy Bahr, Writer

2234
## ST. JOHN'S HOSPITAL & HEALTH CENTER
1328 22nd St.
Santa Monica, CA 90404
Telephone: (310) 829-8016
FAX: (310) 829-8005
Industry Affiliation: Hospitals
**Publication(s):**
*Saint John's News*
Day Published: q.
Spec. Requirements: 12 page; 11 x 14
Personnel: Gary Morlano, Editor

4555
## ST. JOHN MEDICAL CENTER
1923 S. Utica
Tulsa, OK 74104
Telephone: (918) 744-2820
Industry Affiliation: Hospitals
**Publication(s):**
*Pager*
Day Published: m.
Lead Time: 15th of mo. prior to pub. date
Spec. Requirements: 8-12 pg.; offset; 84 x 11
Personnel: Renea Michalopulos, Editor

5353
## ST. JOSEPH'S HOSPITAL
19th & Murdoch Ave.
Parkersburg, WV 26101
Telephone: (304) 424-4111
FAX: (304) 424-4202
Mailing Address:
 P.O. Box 327
 Parkersburg, MD 26101
Industry Affiliation: Hospitals
**Publication(s):**
*St Joseph's News:*
Day Published: m.
Spec. Requirements: 4-6 pgs.; offset; 11 x 15 1/4
Personnel: Joe Webb, Editor

2023
## ST. JOSEPH'S HOSPITAL & MEDICAL CTR.
350 W. Thomas Rd.
Phoenix, AZ 85013
Telephone: (602) 285-3000
Mailing Address:
 P.O. Box 2071
 Phoenix, AZ 85001
Industry Affiliation: Hospitals
**Publication(s):**
*Vision*
Day Published: m.
Lead Time: 6 wks.
Mtls Deadline: 6 wks. prior to pub.
Spec. Requirements: 8-16 pgs.; 81/2 x 11
Personnel: Dorine Goss, Editor

*Barrow*
Day Published: q.
Contact: Mktg. Dept.
 St. Joseph's Hospital & Medical Ctr.
 P.O. Box 2071
 Phoenix, AZ 85001

3723
## ST. JOSEPH LIGHT & POWER CO.
520 Francis St.
St. Joseph, MO 64501
Telephone: (816) 233-8888

**Materials Accepted/Included:** 01-Business news 02-By-line articles 03-Fashion news 04-Food news 05-Freelance copy 06-Letters to editor 07-Real estate news 08-Sports news 09-Travel news 10-Book rev. 11-Movie rev. 12-Music rev. 13-TV rev. 14-Theater rev. 15-Coming events 16-Obituaries 17-Question & answer 18-Social announcements 19-Artwork 20-Cartoons 21-Photos 22-TV listings 23-Audio rec. 24-Video rec. 25-Books 26-Films/film clips 27-Personnel news 28-Press releases 29-New product news/photos 30-Trade lit. 31-Contracts awarded 32-Display adv. 33-Classified adv.

11-83

Mailing Address:
  P.O. Box 998
  St. Joseph, MO 64502
Industry Affiliation: Utility: Electric
**Publication(s):**
*Contact*
Day Published: 3/yr.
Lead Time: 30 days prior to pub.
Mtls Deadline: 30 days prior to pub. date
Spec. Requirements: 20-28-page; offset;
  84 x 106
Personnel: Barry Claywell, Editor

**ST. JOSEPH MEDICAL CENTER**          2235
501 S. Buena Vista St.
Burbank, CA 91505
Telephone: (818) 843-5111
Industry Affiliation: Hospitals
**Publication(s):**
*Guild At A Glance*
Day Published: 10/yr.
Lead Time: 2 wks. prior to pub. date
Mtls Deadline: 2 wks. prior to pub. date
Personnel: Melinda Stell, Editor

*Spotlight On Spirit*
Day Published: m.
Lead Time: 20th of mo., 1 mo. prior to
  pub. date
Mtls Deadline: 1 mo. prior to pub. date
Personnel: Melinda Stell, Editor

**ST. JOSEPH MEDICAL CENTER**          3037
700 Broadway
Fort Wayne, IN 46802
Telephone: (219) 425-3761
Industry Affiliation: Hospitals
**Publication(s):**
*Weekly, The*
Day Published: w.: Fri.
Lead Time: Mon.
Mtls Deadline: Mon.
Contact: Communications Dept.
Spec. Requirements: 2-4 pg.; offset; 8 1/2
  x 11
Personnel: Kathryn Schull

*S J Journal:*
Day Published: bi-m.
Lead Time: irreg.
Contact: Communications Dept.
Spec. Requirements: 16 pgs.
Personnel: Karen Horn, Editor

**ST. LOUIS AREA COUNCIL, B.S.A.**     68519
4568 W. Pine
St. Louis, MO 63108-2179
Telephone: (314) 361-0600
FAX: (314) 361-5165
Industry Affiliation: Associations: Trade,
  Fraternal
**Publication(s):**
*Duffel Bag*
Day Published: m.
Personnel: Paul Brockland, Editor

**ST. LOUIS COMMUNITY COLLEGE**        3724
  **AT FOREST PARK**
5600 Oakland
Saint Louis, MO 63110
Telephone: (314) 644-9744
FAX: (314) 644-9752
Industry Affiliation: Colleges, Institutions,
  Science Research

**Publication(s):**
*Dateline*
Day Published: w.: Thu.
Lead Time: Tue.
Mtls Deadline: Tue. prior to pub. date
Spec. Requirements: 10-20 pgs.; offset; 8
  1/2 x 11
Personnel: Marilyn E. Soete', Editor

**ST. LOUIS POLICE DEPARTMENT**        3758
1200 Clark Ave
St. Louis, MO 63103
Telephone: (314) 444-5603
Industry Affiliation: Associations: City,
  State, Federal
**Publication(s):**
*Police Journal*
Day Published: q.
Lead Time: 1 mo. prior to pub. date
Mtls Deadline: 10th of mo. prior to pub.
  date
Contact: Public Information Div.
Spec. Requirements: 16 pgs.; offset
  magazine; 8 1/2 x 11
Personnel: Candice Green, Editor

*Annual Report*
Day Published: a.
Lead Time: June prior to pub. date
Mtls Deadline: Aug. prior to mo. of pub.
  date
Personnel: Candice Green

**ST. LUKE'S-ROOSEVELT**               4126
  **HOSPITAL CENTER**
428 W. 59th St.
New York, NY 10019
Telephone: (212) 870-1887
Industry Affiliation: Hospitals
**Publication(s):**
*On Center*
Day Published: m.
Spec. Requirements: 4 pg.; offset; 8-1/2 x
  11
Personnel: Philip M. Doro, Editor
          Steven Barboza

**ST. MARY'S HEALTH CENTER**           3725
6420 Clayton Rd.
St. Louis, MO 63117
Telephone: (314) 768-8085
FAX: (314) 768-8011
Industry Affiliation: Hospitals
**Publication(s):**
*Voice*
Day Published: q.
Contact: Public Relations Department
Spec. Requirements: 12 pg; offset; 11 x 10
  1/4
Personnel: Karen Price, Editor

*Center Stat*
Day Published: bi-w.
Spec. Requirements: 12 pg.
Personnel: Kelly Pahl, Editor

**ST. MARYS HOSPITAL**                 3614
200 First St., S.W.
Rochester, MN 55905
Telephone: (507) 255-5123
FAX: (507) 284-8713
Industry Affiliation: Hospitals
**Publication(s):**
*Mayo Today*
Day Published: m.
Personnel: Christine Jensen, Editor

**STONE & WEBSTER**                    3395
  **ENGINEERING CORP.**
245 Summer St.
Boston, MA 02210
Telephone: (617) 589-8954

Mailing Address:
  P.O. Box 2325
  Boston, MA 02107
Industry Affiliation: Industry: Heavy
  Construction, Machinery
**Publication(s):**
*Triskelion, The*
Day Published: 9/yr.
Mtls Deadline: 1 mo.
Spec. Requirements: 8 pgs.; 8 1/2 x 11
Personnel: Donna Caturano, Editor

*Promotional Publications*
Contact: Corporate Communications
Personnel: Lee Jeffers Brami
          Jacquelyn M. Clermont

*Journal, The*
Day Published: q.
Contact: Corporate Communications
Personnel: Jacquelyn Clermont, Editor

*Stone & Webster Incorporate Newsletter*
Day Published: q.
Contact: Corporate Communications
Personnel: John Harris, Editor

**ST. PATRICK HOSPITAL**               70455
500 W. Broadway
St. Patrick Hospital
Missoula, MT 59806
Telephone: (406) 543-7271
Industry Affiliation: Hospitals
**Publication(s):**
*Messenger, The*
Day Published: m.
Contact: St. Patrick Hospital
          Telephone: (406) 543-7271
          500 W. Broadway
          Missoula, MT 59806
Personnel: Jeffrey Smith, Editor
          Lawrence I. White, Jr.,
          President

**ST. PAUL COMPANIES, INC., THE**      3615
385 Washington St.
Saint Paul, MN 55102
Telephone: (612) 221-7911
Industry Affiliation: Insurance
**Publication(s):**
*St. Paul News*
Day Published: m.
Lead Time: 3 wks.
Contact: Pub. Affrs.
Spec. Requirements: 12-16 pg.; magazine;
  8 1/2 x 11
Personnel: Beth Hammel, Manager

**ST. PAUL PIONEER PRESS**             3616
  **DISPATCH**
345 Cedar St.
Saint Paul, MN 55101
Telephone: (612) 222-5011
Mailing Address:
  345 Cedar St.
  Saint Paul, MN 55101
Industry Affiliation: Newspapers
**Publication(s):**
*On The Scene*
Day Published: q.
Lead Time: 3 wks. prior to pub. date
Mtls Deadline: 3 wks. prior to pub. date
Spec. Requirements: 12-16 pgs.; offset
  magazine; 8 x 10 3/4
Personnel: Pat Effenberger, Editor

**STRAWBRIDGE & CLOTHIER**             4766
801 Market St.
Philadelphia, PA 19107
Telephone: (215) 629-6000
Industry Affiliation: Retail Stores

**Publication(s):**
*Store Chat*
Day Published: bi-m.
Lead Time: 6 wks. prior to pub. date
Spec. Requirements: 24 pg.; offset; 8 1/2
  x 11
Personnel: Robert A. Juillet, Editor

**STRIDE RITE CORP.**                  3396
5 Cambridge Ctr.
Cambridge, MA 02142
Telephone: (617) 491-8800
Industry Affiliation: Shoes
**Publication(s):**
*Stride Riter*
Day Published: bi-m.
Lead Time: 1 mo. prior to pub. date
Mtls Deadline: 1 mo. prior to pub. date
Contact: Corp. Comm.
Spec. Requirements: 12 pg.; offset; 10 1/2
  x 17
Personnel: Lori Brackett, Editor

*Features*
Day Published: w.
Personnel: Melissa Brenton, Editor

**STUDEBAKER DRIVERS CLUB,**           2910
  **INC.**
P.O. Box 1040
Oswego, IL 60543
Telephone: (800) 527-3452
Industry Affiliation: Associations: Trade,
  Fraternal
**Publication(s):**
*Turning Wheels*
Day Published: m.
Lead Time: 6 wks. prior to pub. date
Mtls Deadline: 1st of mo. prior to pub. mo.
Personnel: Lawrence Swanson, Publication
          Director
          Linda Fox

**ST. VINCENT CHARITY HOSPITAL**       4430
  **& HEALTH CTR.**
2351 E. 22nd St.
Cleveland, OH 44115
Telephone: (216) 861-6200
FAX: (216) 363-2597
Industry Affiliation: Hospitals
**Publication(s):**
*Vital Signs*
Day Published: m.
Lead Time: 4 wks.
Spec. Requirements: 8-16 pg.; offset
  bulletin; 8 1/2 x 11

**ST. VINCENT HOSPITAL**               5436
835 S. Van Buren St.
Green Bay, WI 54301
Telephone: (414) 433-0111
Mailing Address:
  P.O. Box 13508
  Green Bay, WI 54301
Industry Affiliation: Hospitals
**Publication(s):**
*Health Review*
Day Published: bi-m.
Lead Time: 6 wks. prior to pub. date
Spec. Requirements: 16-24 pg.; offset; 8
  1/2 x 12
Personnel: Carol Kaufman, Editor

**SUBARU OF AMERICA, INC.**            52478
Subaru Plaza, Rte. 70, E.
Cherry Hill, NJ 08034
Telephone: (609) 488-8500
FAX: (609) 488-3274
Mailing Address:
  P.O. Box 6000
  Cherry Hill, NJ 08034
Industry Affiliation: Auto Suppliers

**Materials Accepted/Included:** 01-Business news 02-By-line articles 03-Fashion news 04-Food news 05-Freelance copy 06-Letters to editor 07-Real estate news 08-Sports news 09-Travel news 10-Book rev. 11-Movie rev. 12-Music rev. 13-TV rev. 14-Theater rev. 15-Coming events 16-Obituaries 17-Question & answer 18-Social announcements 19-Artwork 20-Cartoons 21-Photos 22-TV listings 23-Audio rec. 24-Video rec. 25-Books 26-Films/film clips 27-Personnel news 28-Press releases 29-New product news/photos 30-Trade lit. 31-Contracts 31-Contracts awarded 32-Display adv. 33-Classified adv.

**Publication(s):**
*Inside Track*
Day Published: m.
Lead Time: 6 wks.
Contact: Public Relations
Spec. Requirements: Target audience-
   Subaru Dealers across the US
Personnel: Paul A. Levey

4767

**SUN COMPANY INC.**
10 Penn Ctr., 1801 Market St.
Philadelphia, PA 19103
Telephone: (215) 977-3000
Industry Affiliation: Petroleum, Gas
**Publication(s):**
*Sun Magazine*
Day Published: 3/yr.
Spec. Requirements: 28 pg; offset
   magazine; 8 1/2 x 11
Personnel: B. Dotter, Editor

2255

**SUNKIST GROWERS, INC.**
14130 Riverside Dr.
Van Nuys, CA 91423
Telephone: (818) 986-4800
FAX: (818) 379-7511
Mailing Address:
   P.O. Box 7888
   Van Nuys, CA 91409
Industry Affiliation: Food, General
**Publication(s):**
*Slices*
Day Published: bi-m.
Lead Time: 10 days
Mtls Deadline: 1st of mo. prior to pub. date
Contact: Member & Public Relations
Spec. Requirements: 4-8 pg.; offset; 8 1/2
   x 11
Personnel: Dona Uhrig, Editor

*Sunkist Magazine*
Day Published: q.
Lead Time: 15 working days
Mtls Deadline: 1st of mo. prior to pub. date
Contact: Member & Public Relations
Spec. Requirements: 20-24 pg.; offset; 8
   1/2 x 11
Personnel: Clair Peters, Editor

5325

**SUPERINTENDENT OF PUBLIC
   INSTRUCTION**
Old Capitol Bldg.
603 S. Washington
Olympia, WA 98504
Telephone: (206) 753-6725
FAX: (206) 664-0756
Mailing Address:
   P.O. Box 47200
   Olympia, WA 98504-7200
Industry Affiliation: Associations: City,
   State, Federal
**Publication(s):**
*Washington Learning*
Day Published: m.
Lead Time: 4 wks.
Mtls Deadline: 4 wks.
Contact: Editorial Services
Spec. Requirements: 8 pg.; 11 3/8 x 17
   1/4
Personnel: Charlotte Manning, Editor

4989

**SUPERMARKETS, INC.**
1730 Montana Rd., N.W.
Albuquerque, NH 87107
Telephone: (505) 344-6525
FAX: (505) 344-0667
Mailing Address:
   P.O. Box 10267
   Albuquerque, NH 87184
Industry Affiliation: Retail Stores

**Publication(s):**
*Focal Point*
Day Published: q.
Lead Time: 2-3 wks. prior to pub. date
Mtls Deadline: 2 wks. prior to pub. date
Spec. Requirements: 2-4 pgs.; 8 1/2 x 11
Personnel: Becky Kenny, Editor

66421

**SUPERVALU, INC.**
11840 Valley View Rd.
Eden Prairie, MN 55344
Telephone: (612) 828-4000
Mailing Address:
   P.O. Box 990
   Minneapolis, MN 55440
Industry Affiliation: Retail Stores
**Publication(s):**
*Supervalu People*
Day Published: q.
Mtls Deadline: 1 mo. prior to pub. date
Personnel: Maria Murad, Editor

*Retail Update*
Day Published: m.
Personnel: Maria Murad, Editor

*Home Office News*
Day Published: m.
Personnel: Sara Reimers, Editor

2912

**SWEDISH AMERICAN HEALTH
   SYSTEM**
1400 Charles St.
Rockford, IL 61104
Telephone: (815) 968-4400
Industry Affiliation: Hospitals
**Publication(s):**
*Communicator*
Day Published: w.
Materials: 01,04,15,20,21,28
Mtls Deadline: Wed., 10:00 am
Spec. Requirements: 4-page; offset; 7 x 9
Personnel: Jan Hagenlocher, Editor

*Communicator Plus*
Day Published: m.
Spec. Requirements: 4 pg.; 11 1/2 x 17
Personnel: Angela Larson, Editor

4562

**SWEET ADELINES
   INTERNATIONAL**
5334 E. 46 St.
Tulsa, OK 74135-6603
Telephone: (918) 622-1444
FAX: (918) 665-0894
Mailing Address:
   P.O. Box 470168
   Tulsa, OK 74147-0168
Industry Affiliation: Music
**Publication(s):**
*Pitch Pipe, The*
Day Published: q.
Lead Time: 60 days
Materials: 06
Mtls Deadline: 60 days prior to pub. date
Spec. Requirements: 36 pg; offset; 8 3/8 x
   10 7/8
Personnel: Janet Weberling, Editor

4152

**SYRACUSE SAVINGS BANK**
One Clinton Sq.
Syracuse, NY 13202
Telephone: (315) 471-7101
Mailing Address:
   P.O. Box 4821
   Syracuse, NY 13221
Industry Affiliation: Banks, Savings &
   Loans

**Publication(s):**
*S S B News Letter*
Day Published: w.
Mtls Deadline: Tue. prior to pub. date
Contact: Mktg.
Spec. Requirements: 2-3 pg.; offset
   bulletin; 8 1/2 x 14
Personnel: George Hodge, Editor

5327

**TACOMA PUBLIC UTILITIES**
3628 S. 35th St.
Tacoma, WA 98409
Telephone: (206) 383-2471
FAX: (206) 520-8627
Mailing Address:
   P.O. Box 11007
   Tacoma, WA 98411
Industry Affiliation: Utility:  Water
**Publication(s):**
*Utilibits*
Day Published: m.
Lead Time: 60 days prior to pub. date
Mtls Deadline: 15th of mo. prior to pub.
   date
Spec. Requirements: 4 pg.; offset; 11 x 14
Personnel: Korte Brueckmann, Editor

66439

**TAMPA ELECTRIC CO.**
702 N. Franklin St.
Tampa, FL 33602
Telephone: (813) 228-4281
FAX: (813) 228-4259
Industry Affiliation: Utility:  Electric
**Publication(s):**
*Newsline*
Day Published: bi-w.
Lead Time: 10 days prior to pub. date
Mtls Deadline: 10 days prior to pub. date
Contact: Corporate Communication
Personnel: Mitch Lubitz, Student Writer

5095

**TANDYCRAFTS, INC.**
1400 Everman Pkwy.
Fort Worth, TX 76140
Telephone: (817) 551-9600
FAX: (817) 551-5763
Mailing Address:
   P.O. Box 1869
   Fort Worth, TX 76101
Industry Affiliation: Electrical, Electronic,
   Manufacturing
**Publication(s):**
*Communicator*
Day Published: m.
Lead Time: 1 mo. prior to pub. date
Mtls Deadline: 1 mo. prior to pub. date
Spec. Requirements: 12 pg.; offset; 8 1/2
   x 11
Personnel: Marilyn Laurence, Editor

5096

**TARRANT COUNTY HOSPITAL
   DISTRICT**
1500 S. Main St.
Fort Worth, TX 76104
Telephone: (817) 927-1365
FAX: (817) 927-1664
Industry Affiliation: Hospitals
**Publication(s):**
*Pacemaker*
Day Published: bi-w.
Lead Time: 1 wk. prior to pub. date
Mtls Deadline: Mon. prior to pub. date

3298

**TEACHERS ASSOCIATION OF
   BALTIMORE COUNTY MD., INC.**
305 E. Joppa Rd.
Baltimore, MD 21286
Telephone: (410) 828-6403
FAX: (410) 337-7081
Industry Affiliation: Associations: Trade,
   Fraternal

**Publication(s):**
*T A B C O Bulletin*
Day Published: m.
Lead Time: 1 wk. prior to pub. date
Mtls Deadline: 1 wk. prior to pub. date
Spec. Requirements: 4 pg. offset 11 x 17
Personnel: Carole C. Jeffries, Editor

*Bulletin Adjunct*
Day Published: m.
Lead Time: 1 wk. prior to pub. date
Mtls Deadline: 1 wk. prior to pub. date
Personnel: Carole C. Jeffries, Editor

4153

**TEACHERS INSURANCE &
   ANNUITY ASSOCIATION**
730 Third Ave.
New York, NY 10017
Telephone: (212) 490-9000
Industry Affiliation: Insurance
**Publication(s):**
*Topics*
Day Published: bi-m.
Spec. Requirements: 30 pg.; offset
   magazine; 8 1/2 x 11
Personnel: Sylvia Helm, Editor
   Gina Kucija, Art Director

4769

**TELEDYNE, INC.**
360 S. Church St.
Waynesboro, PA 49202
Telephone: (717) 762-3151
Industry Affiliation: Electrical, Electronic,
   Manufacturing
**Publication(s):**
*Landis Line*
Day Published: q.
Lead Time: 2 mos. prior to pub. date
Spec. Requirements: 8 pg.; offset tabloid;
   8 1/2 x 11
Personnel: W. H. Helfrick, Editor

*Thread Tips*
Day Published: q.
Spec. Requirements: 8 pg.
Personnel: W. H. Helfrick, Editor

4903

**TENNESSEE EDUCATION
   ASSOCIATION**
598 James Robertson Pkwy.
Nashville, TN 37219-1099
Telephone: (615) 242-8392
FAX: (615) 259-4581
Industry Affiliation: Associations:  Trade,
   Fraternal
**Publication(s):**
*Tennessee Teacher*
Day Published: 5/yr.
Mtls Deadline: 2 mos. prior to date of
   issue
Spec. Requirements: 32-40 pg.; offset
   magazine; 8 3/8 x 11
Personnel: Dawn Charles, Managing Editor
   Gene Bryant
   Etha Green

*T E A News*
Day Published: m.
Lead Time: 2 wks. prior to pub. date
Mtls Deadline: 2 wks. or 1st of mo. prior to
   pub. date
Contact: Communications
Spec. Requirements: 12 pg.
Personnel: Gene Bryant, Editor

4904

**TENNESSEE ELECTRIC COOP
   ASSOCIATION**
710 Spence Ln.
Nashville, TN 37217
Telephone: (615) 367-9284
Mailing Address:
   P.O. Box 100912
   Nashville, TN 37224
Industry Affiliation: Associations:  Trade,
   Fraternal

**Materials Accepted/Included:** 01-Business news 02-By-line articles 03-Fashion news 04-Food news 05-Freelance copy 06-Letters to editor 07-Real estate news 08-Sports news 09-Travel news
10-Book rev. 11-Movie rev. 12-Music rev. 13-TV rev. 14-Theater rev. 15-Coming events 16-Obituaries 17-Question & answer 18-Social announcements 19-Artwork 20-Cartoons 21-Photos 22-TV listings
23-Audio rec. 24-Video rec. 25-Books 26-Films/film clips 27-Personnel news 28-Press releases 29-New product news/photos 30-Trade lit. 31-Contracts awarded 32-Display adv. 33-Classified adv.

11-85

**Publication(s):**
*Tennessee Magazine, The*
Day Published: m.
Lead Time: 30 days prior to pub. date
Materials: 04,06,09,15,32,33
Spec. Requirements: 24-32 pgs.; offset magazine; 76 x 106
Personnel: Rodney Guge, Editor

*Leader's Letter*
Day Published: m.
Lead Time: 30 days prior to pub. date
Personnel: Rodney Guge, Editor

### TENNESSEE HOSPITAL ASSOCIATION
4905
500 Interstate Blvd., S.
Nashville, TN 37210-4634
Telephone: (615) 256-8240
Industry Affiliation: Hospitals
**Publication(s):**
*Tennessee Hospitals*
Day Published: m.
Lead Time: 3 wks. prior to pub. date
Mtls Deadline: 1 mo. prior to pub. date
Contact: Public Relations
Spec. Requirements: 4-8 pg.; 11 x 17
Personnel: Beth Atwood, Editor

*Senior Health News*
Day Published: bi-m.
Lead Time: 1 mo. prior to pub. date
Mtls Deadline: 1 mo. prior to pub. date
Spec. Requirements: 4 pg.; 8 1/2 x 11
Personnel: Beth Atwood, Editor

### TERRA CHEMICALS INT'L., INC.
3123
600 Fourth St.
Sioux City, IA 51102-6000
Telephone: (712) 277-1340
Mailing Address:
  P.O. Box 6000
  Sioux City, IA 51102
Industry Affiliation: Agriculture, Services
**Publication(s):**
*Terra Today*
Day Published: bi-m.
Spec. Requirements: 8 pg.; 8 1/2 x 11; 3-color
Personnel: Kim Mathers, Editor

### TEXACO, INC.
4154
2000 Westchester Ave.
White Plains, NY 10650
Telephone: (914) 253-4000
FAX: (914) 253-4655
Industry Affiliation: Petroleum, Gas
**Publication(s):**
*Texaco Marketer, The*
Day Published: q.
Spec. Requirements: 32-pg. color; offset; 8 1/2 x 11
Personnel: Terry Fisher, Editor

*Texaco Today*
Day Published: bi-m.
Spec. Requirements: 24-pg.
Personnel: Rosalie R. Jenkins, Editor

### TEXAS A & M UNIVERSITY SYSTEM
5148
Texas A & M Univ.
College Station, TX 77843
Telephone: (409) 845-2211
Mailing Address:
  229 Reed McDonald Bldg.
  College Station, TX 77843
Industry Affiliation: Colleges, Institutions, Science Research

**Publication(s):**
*Extension Today*
Day Published: q.
Lead Time: 1 mo.
Contact: Dept of Agricultural Communication
Spec. Requirements: 4-8 pgs.; offset; 17 x 12
Personnel: Edith Chenault, Editor

### TEXAS ASSOCIATION OF REALTORS
5172
8416 N. Interregional
Austin, TX 78753
Telephone: (512) 480-8200
Mailing Address:
  P.O. Box 2246
  Austin, TX 78761
Industry Affiliation: Associations: Trade, Fraternal
**Publication(s):**
*Texas Realtor*
Day Published: 10/yr.
Lead Time: 6 wks. prior to pub. date
Mtls Deadline: 6 wks. prior to pub. date
Spec. Requirements: 40 pg.; webb offset; 8 1/2 x 11 1/8
Personnel: Rachel Sarabee, Editor

### TEXAS AUTOMOBILE DEALERS ASSOCIATION
5173
1108 Lavaca St.
Austin, TX 78701
Telephone: (512) 476-2686
Mailing Address:
  P.O. Box 1028
  Austin, TX 78767
Industry Affiliation: Autos, Trucks
**Publication(s):**
*Dealers' Choice*
Day Published: q.
Lead Time: 2 mos. prior to pub. date
Materials: 01,15,17,21,24,25,29,30
Mtls Deadline: 3 mos. prior to pub. date
Spec. Requirements: 48 pg.; offset; 8-1/2 x 11
Personnel: John T. Devenport, Editor

### TEXAS COMMERCE BANCSHARES, INC.
5178
712 Main St.
Houston, TX 77002
Telephone: (713) 236-5009
FAX: (713) 236-5486
Mailing Address:
  P.O. Box 2558
  Houston, TX 77252
Industry Affiliation: Banks, Savings & Loans
**Publication(s):**
*Bankers' Hours*
Day Published: m.
Lead Time: 2 wks. prior to pub. date
Mtls Deadline: 2 wks. prior to pub. date
Spec. Requirements: 24 pg.; offset; 8 1/2 x 11
Personnel: David Byford, Editor

### TEXAS CONGRESS OF PARENTS & TEACHERS
5181
408 W. 11th
Austin, TX 78701
Telephone: (512) 476-6769
FAX: (512) 476-8152
Industry Affiliation: Associations: Trade, Fraternal

**Publication(s):**
*Texas P T A Communicator*
Day Published: 9/yr.
Lead Time: 1 mo. prior to pub. date
Mtls Deadline: 2 wks. prior to pub. date
Spec. Requirements: 16-24 pg.; offset; 8-1/2 x 11
Personnel: Rhonda Forbes, Editor

### TEXAS EASTMAN DIV., EASTMAN CHEMICAL CO.
5189
Kodak Blvd.
Longview, TX 75602
Telephone: (903) 237-5000
FAX: (903) 237-5371
Mailing Address:
  P.O. Box 7444
  Longview, TX 75607
Industry Affiliation: Chemicals, Plastics
**Publication(s):**
*Texas Eastman News*
Day Published: bi-w.
Lead Time: 2 wks. prior to pub. date
Mtls Deadline: 2 wks. prior to pub. date
Contact: Eastman Kodak Co.
        343 State St.
        Rochester, NY 14650
Spec. Requirements: 4-10 pg.; offset; 11 x 14 1/2
Personnel: L. Jan Taylor, Editor

### TEXAS ELECTRIC COOPS INC.
5193
8140 Burnet Rd., N.W. Sta.
Austin, TX 78758
Telephone: (512) 454-0311
Mailing Address:
  P.O. Box 9589
  Austin, TX 78766
Industry Affiliation: Associations: Trade, Fraternal
**Publication(s):**
*Texas Co-Op Power*
Day Published: m.
Lead Time: 30 days prior to pub. date
Mtls Deadline: 1st of mo. prior to pub. date
Spec. Requirements: 12-16 pg.; offset; 114 x 16
Personnel: George Macias, Editor
          Kurt E. Johnson, Editor

### TEXAS HIGH SCHOOL COACHES ASSOCIATION INC.
5099
1011 53 1/2 St.
Austin, TX 78751
Telephone: (512) 454-6709
FAX: (512) 454-3950
Mailing Address:
  P.O. Drawer 14627
  Austin, TX 78761
Industry Affiliation: Associations: City, State, Federal
**Publication(s):**
*Texas Coach*
Day Published: 9/yr.
Lead Time: 1 mo. prior the pub. date
Materials: 06,07,27,32
Mtls Deadline: 1 mo. prior the pub. date
Spec. Requirements: photo-glossy 5 x 7 or 8 x 10
Personnel: Sheryl Honeycutt, Editor
          Sheryl Honeycutt, Art Director
          Eddie Wolski, Marketing Director

### TEXAS INDEPENDENT PRODUCERS & ROYALTY OWNERS ASSOCIATIOIN
5100
1910 Interfirst Bank Tower
Austin, TX 78701
Telephone: (512) 477-4452
Industry Affiliation: Associations: Trade, Fraternal

**Publication(s):**
*T I P R O Reporter*
Day Published: a.
Mtls Deadline: 1 mo. prior to pub. date
Spec. Requirements: 100-116 pg.: 8 1/4 x 11 1/4 publ. trim
Personnel: Samantha Sipowicz, Editor
          Marilyn Kelso, Managing Editor

### TEXAS INSTRUMENTS, INC.
5150
7839 Churchill Way
Dallas, TX 75251
Telephone: (214) 917-3905
FAX: (214) 917-3850
Mailing Address:
  P.O. Box 650311, MS 3940
  Dallas, TX 75265
Industry Affiliation: Electrical, Electronic, Manufacturing
**Publication(s):**
*Dallasite*
Day Published: m.
Lead Time: 15 days prior to pub. date
Mtls Deadline: 1 mo. prior to pub. date

### TEXAS INSTRUMENTS INC.
66438
34 Forest St. MS 12-3
Attleboro, MA 02703
Telephone: (508) 699-1761
Industry Affiliation: Office Equipment, Services, Supplies
**Publication(s):**
*Attlegram*
Day Published: m.
Lead Time: 2 wks. prior to pub. date
Mtls Deadline: 1st Fri. prior to pub. date
Contact: Materials and Controls Group
Personnel: Linda Megathlin

### TEXAS MEDICAL ASSOCIATION
5151
401 W. 15th St.
Austin, TX 78701
Telephone: (512) 370-1300
FAX: (512) 370-1632
Industry Affiliation: Associations: Trade, Fraternal
**Publication(s):**
*Texas Medicine*
Day Published: m.
Lead Time: 60 days prior to pub. date
Mtls Deadline: 60 days prior to pub. date
Spec. Requirements: 100 pg.; offset; 8 3/8 x 10 7/8
Personnel: Rae Vajgert, Editor
          Kathy Trombatore

*Action*
Day Published: 10/yr.
Lead Time: 30 days prior to pub. date
Mtls Deadline: 1st of mo. prior to pub. date
Contact: Public Relations
Spec. Requirements: 4-page 8 1/2 X 11
Personnel: Tammy Wishard, Editor

### TEXAS NURSES ASSOCIATION
5153
7600 Burnet Rd., Ste. 440
Austin, TX 78757
Telephone: (512) 452-0645
FAX: (512) 452-0648
Industry Affiliation: Associations: Trade, Fraternal

---

Materials Accepted/Included: 01-Business news 02-By-line articles 03-Fashion news 04-Food news 05-Freelance copy 06-Letters to editor 07-Real estate news 08-Sports news 09-Travel news 10-Book rev. 11-Movie rev. 12-Music rev. 13-TV rev. 14-Theater rev. 15-Coming events 16-Obituaries 17-Question & answer 18-Social announcements 19-Artwork 20-Cartoons 21-Photos 22-TV listings 23-Audio rec. 24-Video rec. 25-Books 26-Films/film clips 27-Personnel news 28-Press releases 29-New product news/photos 30-Trade lit. 31-Contracts awarded 32-Display adv. 33-Classified adv.

**Publication(s):**
*Texas Nursing*
Day Published: 10/yr.
Lead Time: 10 days prior to pub. date
Materials: 32,33
Mtls Deadline: 10th of mo. prior to pub. mo.
Spec. Requirements: 16 pg.; offset; 8 x 11
Personnel: John Levis Brown, Editor

5175

**TEXAS PRESS ASSOCIATION**
718 W. Fifth St.
Austin, TX 78701
Telephone: (512) 477-6755
FAX: (512) 477-6759
Industry Affiliation: Associations: Trade, Fraternal
**Publication(s):**
*T P A Messenger*
Day Published: m.
Materials: 01,02,05,06,16,21,27,28,29,30
Mtls Deadline: 10th of mo. prior to pub. date
Spec. Requirements: 16 pg.; offset; tabloid
Personnel: Ed Sterling, Managing Editor

5176

**TEXAS PUBLIC EMPLOYEES ASSOCIATION**
512 E. 11th St.
Austin, TX 78701
Telephone: (512) 476-2691
FAX: (512) 476-1338
Mailing Address:
Box 12217
Austin, TX 78711
Industry Affiliation: Associations: Trade, Fraternal
**Publication(s):**
*Texas Public Employee*
Day Published: q.
Lead Time: 3 wks. prior to pub. date
Materials: 01,06,20,32
Mtls Deadline: 1st of Jan., Apr., Jul., Oct.
Contact: Bill Warren
Spec. Requirements: 12-32 pg.; offset tabloid; 10-1/4 x 14
Personnel: Lane A. Zivley, Editor

5186

**TEXAS SAFETY ASSOCIATION**
P.O. Box 9345
Austin, TX 78766-9345
Telephone: (512) 343-6525
FAX: (512) 343-0746
Industry Affiliation: Associations: City, State, Federal
**Publication(s):**
*Safety Talk*
Day Published: m.
Lead Time: 30 days
Materials: 20,21,34
Mtls Deadline: 18th of the mo. prior the pub. date
Spec. Requirements: 8 1/2 x 11
Personnel: Dyanne Fry Cortez, Editor

*Signal*
Day Published: q.
Lead Time: 30 days
Mtls Deadline: 1st of each mo.
Contact: Jim Johnson, Ed.
　　　　Telephone: (913) 551-6034
　　　　624 Scot St.
　　　　Kansas, KS 66105
Personnel: Jim Johnson, Editor

*Ddc Bulletin*
Day Published: bi-m.
Lead Time: 6 wks.
Personnel: Dyanne Fry Cortez, Editor

5188

**TEXAS SOCIETY CERTIFIED PUBLIC ACCOUNTANTS**
1421 W. Mockingbird, Ste. 100
Dallas, TX 75247-4957
Telephone: (214) 689-6000
FAX: (214) 689-6046
Industry Affiliation: Finance, Services
**Publication(s):**
*Today's C P A*
Day Published: bi-m.
Lead Time: 3 mos. prior to pub. date
Mtls Deadline: 3 mos.
Spec. Requirements: 48 pgs.; offset; 8 1/2 x 11
Personnel: Brux Austin, Editor

5190

**TEXAS SOCIETY OF ARCHITECTS**
1400 Norwood Tower
Austin, TX 78701
Telephone: (512) 478-7386
Industry Affiliation: Architects, Engineers, Business Service
**Publication(s):**
*Texas Architect*
Day Published: bi-m.
Lead Time: 2nd mo. prior to pub. date
Mtls Deadline: 1st of 2nd mo. prior to pub. date
Spec. Requirements: 72-100 pgs.; offset; 8 1/2 x 11
Personnel: Joel Barna, Editor
　　　　Charles Gallatin, Associate Editor

*Report*
Day Published: m.
Lead Time: 1 mo.
Mtls Deadline: 1st of mo. prior to pub. date
Personnel: David Brooks
　　　　Charles Gallatin

5191

**TEXAS SOCIETY OF PROFESSIONAL ENGINEERS**
P.O. Box 2145
Austin, TX 78768
Telephone: (512) 472-9286
Industry Affiliation: Architects, Engineers, Business Service
**Publication(s):**
*Texas Professional Engineer*
Day Published: bi-m.
Lead Time: 15th of mo.
Mtls Deadline: 15th of mo. prior to cover date
Spec. Requirements: 32-page; offset; 8 1/2 x 11
Personnel: Ed O'Donnell, Editor

5194

**TEXAS WESLEYAN UNIVERSITY**
1201 Wesleyan St.
Fort Worth, TX 76105
Telephone: (817) 531-4444
FAX: (817) 531-4425
Industry Affiliation: Colleges, Institutions, Science Research

**Publication(s):**
*Texas Wesleyan Today*
Day Published: q.
Lead Time: 6 wks. prior to pub. date
Mtls Deadline: 6 wks. prior to pub. date
Spec. Requirements: 40 pg.; offset; 84 x 11
Personnel: Dr. Gail Young, Editor
　　　　Brigitte Lueck

3400

**THERMO ELECTRON CORP.**
81 Wyman St.
Boston, MA 02254
Telephone: (617) 622-1000
FAX: (617) 622-1207
Mailing Address:
P.O. Box 9046
Waltham, MA 02254
Industry Affiliation: Electrical, Electronic, Manufacturing
**Publication(s):**
*Thermosphere*
Day Published: 3/yr.
Spec. Requirements: 16 pg; offset; 8 1/2 x 11
Personnel: Karen Kirkwood, Editor
　　　　Pat Cleary, Editor

3622

**THERMO KING CORP.**
314 W. 90th St
Minneapolis, MN 55420
Telephone: (612) 887-2200
Industry Affiliation: Cooling, Heating
**Publication(s):**
*Up Front*
Day Published: q.
Spec. Requirements: 8-12 pgs.; offset newspaper; 10 x 14
Personnel: Mike Komar, Editor

4770

**THIOKOL CORP.**
2475 Washington Blvd.
Ogden, UT 84401-2398
Telephone: (801) 629-2000
Industry Affiliation: Aircraft, Aerospace, Defense
**Publication(s):**
*Thiokol Magazine*
Day Published: m.
Personnel: Carole Lapine, Editor

3191

**THOMAS INDUSTRIES**
4360 Brownsboro Rd., Ste. 300
Louisville, KY 40207-1601
Telephone: (502) 893-4600
Mailing Address:
P.O. Box 35120
Louisville, KY 40232
Industry Affiliation: Electrical, Electronic, Manufacturing
**Publication(s):**
*T I Topics*
Day Published: bi-m.
Spec. Requirements: accepts intercompany news only.
Personnel: Laurie Lyons, Editor
　　　　Laurie Scanlan

5077

**THOMPSON INTERNATIONAL, INC.**
5880 Airline Rd.
Henderson, KY 42420
Telephone: (502) 826-3751
FAX: (502) 826-3881
Industry Affiliation: Industry: Heavy Construction, Machinery

**Publication(s):**
*Newsletter*
Day Published: m.
Spec. Requirements: 8-page; offset magazine; 6 x 9
Personnel: Jim Hunter, Editor

2615

**TIMES PUBLISHING CO.**
P.O. Box 1121
St. Petersburg, FL 33731-1121
Telephone: (813) 893-8111
Industry Affiliation: Newspapers
**Publication(s):**
*Times Talk*
Day Published: w.: Wed.
Lead Time: 1 wk. prior to pub. date
Spec. Requirements: 6 pg.; offset; 8 x 11
Personnel: Kerry Kriseman, Editor

66458

**T.L. JAMES & CO., INC.**
P.O. Box 1260
Ruston, LA 71273
Telephone: (318) 255-7912
Industry Affiliation: Associations: Trade, Fraternal
**Publication(s):**
*James Journal, The*
Day Published: q.
Lead Time: 30 days prior to pub. date
Mtls Deadline: 1st of Mar., Jun., Sep., Nov.
Personnel: James Frazier, Editor

4300

**TOLEDO BLADE CO.**
541 N. Superior St.
Toledo, OH 43660
Telephone: (419) 245-6280
FAX: (419) 245-6167
Industry Affiliation: Newspapers
**Publication(s):**
*Inside The Blade*
Lead Time: 1 mo.
Contact: Mktg.
Spec. Requirements: 18 pg.; offset magazine; 8 x 11

4443

**TOLEDO EDISON CO.**
300 Madison Ave.
Toledo, OH 43652
Telephone: (419) 249-5043
FAX: (419) 249-5165
Industry Affiliation: Utility: Electric
**Publication(s):**
*Monthly Communications*
Day Published: m.
Lead Time: 2 wks.
Spec. Requirements: 4-6 pg.; offset; 11 x 17
Personnel: Richard Wilkins, Editor

4771

**TOPFLIGHT CORP.**
160 E. Ninth Ave.
York, PA 17404
Telephone: (717) 843-9901
FAX: (717) 845-6087
Mailing Address:
P.O. Box 2847
York, PA 17404
Industry Affiliation: Associations: Trade, Fraternal
**Publication(s):**
*Topflight Today*
Day Published: q.
Lead Time: 2 mos. prior to pub. date
Mtls Deadline: 2 mos. prior to pub. date
Spec. Requirements: 4 pg.; offset bulletin; 84 x 11
Personnel: Jerry Dyer, Editor

4158

**TOWERS PERRIN**
245 Park Ave.
New York, NY 10167
Telephone: (212) 309-3400
Industry Affiliation: Associations: Trade, Fraternal

---

Materials Accepted/Included: 01-Business news 02-By-line articles 03-Fashion news 04-Food news 05-Freelance copy 06-Letters to editor 07-Real estate news 08-Sports news 09-Travel news 10-Book rev. 11-Movie rev. 12-Music rev. 13-TV rev. 14-Theater rev. 15-Coming events 16-Obituaries 17-Question & answer 18-Social announcements 19-Artwork 20-Cartoons 21-Photos 22-TV listings 23-Audio rec. 24-Video rec. 25-Books 26-Films/film clips 27-Personnel news 28-Press releases 29-New product news/photos 30-Trade lit. 31-Contracts awarded 32-Display adv. 33-Classified adv.

**Publication(s):**
*Contact*
Day Published: 26/yr.
Lead Time: 1 wk. prior to pub. date
Mtls Deadline: 1 wk. prior to pub. date
Contact: Andrew Lashley
      Telephone: (914) 745-4633
Spec. Requirements: 2-4-6 pg.; offset; 8-1/2 x 11
Personnel: Andrew Lashley, Editor

2265
**TOYOTA MOTOR SALES USA, INC.**
19001 S. Western Ave.
Torrance, CA 90501
Telephone: (310) 618-4000
Industry Affiliation: Auto Suppliers
**Publication(s):**
*Toyota Today*
Day Published: 10/yr.
Lead Time: 1 mo. prior to pub. date
Mtls Deadline: 1 mo. prior to pub. date
Spec. Requirements: 22-page; offset; 8 1/2 x 11
Personnel: Gloria Jahn, Public Affairs Director

52348
**TRANSACTION-PUBLISHERS**
Rutgers-The State Univ.
New Brunswick, NJ 08903
Telephone: (908) 932-2280
FAX: (908) 932-3138
Industry Affiliation: Advertising, Art, Public Relations
**Publication(s):**
*Society*
Day Published: bi-m.
Materials: 32
Mtls Deadline: adv.-6 wks. prior to pub. date
Contact: Marketing
Personnel: Irving Louis Horowitz

3267
**TRANSPORTATION COMMUNICATIONS INTERNATIONAL UNION**
3 Research Pl.
Rockville, MD 20850
Telephone: (301) 948-4910
FAX: (301) 948-1369
Industry Affiliation: Associations: Trade, Fraternal
**Publication(s):**
*Interchange*
Day Published: bi-m.
Lead Time: 1 mo.
Mtls Deadline: 30 days
Contact: D.S. Curry-Dir. of Pub.
    3 Research Pl.
    Rockville, MD 20850
Spec. Requirements: 16-56 pg.; offset; tabloid
Personnel: Robert A Scardelletti, Editor

*Telling It Like It Is*
Day Published: bi-m.
Personnel: Robert A. Scardelletti, Editor

4159
**TRANS WORLD AIRLINES INC.**
4080 Wedgeway Ct.
Hazelwood, MO 63045
Telephone: (314) 589-3000
Industry Affiliation: Airlines
**Publication(s):**
*Skyliner:*
Day Published: m.
Lead Time: 2 wks.
Spec. Requirements: 8-12 pgs.
Personnel: Pamela Blase, Editor

2461
**TRAVELERS INSURANCE CO.**
One Tower Sq.
Hartford, CT 06183
Telephone: (203) 277-0111
Industry Affiliation: Insurance

**Publication(s):**
*Protection*
Day Published: 3/yr.
Lead Time: 3 mos. prior to pub. date
Mtls Deadline: end of mo. prior to pub. date
Spec. Requirements: 32 pg. offset magazine; 8 1/2 x 11
Personnel: Keith Anderson, Editor

*Travelers Tribune*
Day Published: bi-m.
Lead Time: 1 mo. prior to pub. date
Mtls Deadline: end of mo. prior to pub. date
Personnel: Keith Anderson, Editor

5447
**TREES FOR TOMMORROW INC., NATURAL RESOURCES EDUCATION**
611 Sheridan St.
Eagle River, WI 54521
Telephone: (715) 479-6456
Mailing Address:
    P.O. Box 609
    Eagle River, WI 54521
Industry Affiliation: Lumber, Forestry, Building Materials
**Publication(s):**
*Northbound*
Day Published: q.
Lead Time: 6 wks. prior to pub. date
Mtls Deadline: 4 wks. prior to pub. date
Spec. Requirements: 1-2 pg.; offset; 8-1/2 x 11
Personnel: Martha Ehlinger, Editor

2267
**TRIANGLE DISTRIBUTING CO.**
12065 E. Pike St.
Santa Fe Springs, CA 90670
Telephone: (310) 699-3424
FAX: (310) 699-2318
Industry Affiliation: Associations: Trade, Fraternal
**Publication(s):**
*Triangle News*
Day Published: q.
Lead Time: 1 mo. prior to pub. date
Mtls Deadline: 1 mo. prior to pub. date
Spec. Requirements: 4 pg.; 9 x 12
Personnel: Jim Wood, Editor

3734
**TRINITY LUTHERAN HOSPITAL**
3030 Baltimore Ave.
Kansas City, MO 64108
Telephone: (816) 753-4600
FAX: (816) 751-4692
Industry Affiliation: Hospitals
**Publication(s):**
*Trinity Lutheran Today*
Day Published: bi-m.
Spec. Requirements: 8 pg.; offset; 8 x 10
Personnel: Shawn Arni, Editor

*Newsclips*
Day Published: w.
Contact: Communications Dept.
Spec. Requirements: 8 pg.; newsletter
Personnel: Shawn Arni, Editor
      Jay Hoffman

5106
**TRINITY UNIVERSAL INSURANCE CO.**
10000 N. Central Expy.
Dallas, TX 75231
Telephone: (214) 360-8000
FAX: (214) 360-8079
Mailing Address:
    P.O. Box 655028
    Dallas, TX 75265
Industry Affiliation: Insurance

**Publication(s):**
*Trinity Times*
Day Published: q.
Spec. Requirements: 16 pg.; offset; 84 x 11
Personnel: Valerie Cordes, Editor

4160
**TRI STATE INDUSTRIAL LAUNDRIES, INC.**
1634 Lincoln Ave., Box 4145
Utica, NY 13502
Telephone: (315) 732-4195
**Publication(s):**
*Coverall*
Day Published: q.
Spec. Requirements: 12-16 pg.; offset; 8 1/2 x 11
Personnel: Linda Daily, Editor

3639
**TRUSTMARK NATIONAL BANK**
148 S. Whitworth Ave.
Brookhaven, MS 39601
Telephone: (601) 833-4771
FAX: (601) 835-1815
Mailing Address:
    P.O. Box 539
    Brookhaven, MS 39601
Industry Affiliation: Banks, Savings & Loans
**Publication(s):**
*Golden Customer Newsletter*
Day Published: q.
Mtls Deadline: 1 mo. prior
Personnel: Maggie Baker
      Rebecca N. Vaughn

5159
**T.U. ELECTRIC**
1506 Commerce St., Ste. 1600
Dallas, TX 75201
Telephone: (214) 554-1414
Industry Affiliation: Utility: Electric
**Publication(s):**
*Synchronizer*
Day Published: m.
Contact: Communication Services
Spec. Requirements: 12 pgs.; offset; 11 x 17
Personnel: Linda L. Hawks, Editor

*Spotlight*
Day Published: bi-m.
Lead Time: 1 mo. prior to pub. date
Mtls Deadline: 1 mo prior to pub. date
Personnel: Mayfair Macauley, Editor

*Tesco Roundup*
Day Published: m.
Lead Time: 1-2 mos. prior to pub. date
Mtls Deadline: 1-2 mos. prior to pub. date
Contact: Steve Blankinship
    Bryan Tower
    2001 Bryan, Ste. 2100
    Dallas, TX 75201
Personnel: Steve Blankinship, Editor

5448
**TWIN DISC INC.**
1328 Racine St.
Racine, WI 53403
Telephone: (414) 634-1981
Industry Affiliation: Industry: Light Tools, Equipment
**Publication(s):**
*Twin Disc*
Day Published: bi-m.
Spec. Requirements: 8-12 pgs.; offset magazine; 8 1/2 x 11
Personnel: Joanne Klawinski, Editor

4778
**TYSON FOODS**
2210 Oakland Dr.
Springdale, AR 72765
Telephone: (501) 290-4000
FAX: (501) 290-4217
Industry Affiliation: Food, General

**Publication(s):**
*Tyson Update*
Day Published: bi-m.
Mtls Deadline: 15th of mo.
Spec. Requirements: 6-8 pgs.; offset; 8 1/2 x 11
Personnel: Steve Singleton, Editor

2030
**U-HAUL INTERNATIONAL, INC.**
2727 N. Central Ave.
Phoenix, AZ 85004
Telephone: (602) 263-6641
Industry Affiliation: Autos, Trucks
**Publication(s):**
*U-Haul International News*
Day Published: m.
Lead Time: 6 wks. prior to pub. date
Mtls Deadline: 1st of mo. prior to pub. date
Spec. Requirements: 16-24 pg.; offset; standard tabloid
Personnel: Jaci Kelchak, Managing Editor

*Front Line*
Day Published: m.
Lead Time: 6 wks. prior to pub. date
Mtls Deadline: 1st of mo. prior to pub. date
Spec. Requirements: 20 pg.
Personnel: Jaci Kelchak, Managing Editor

2918
**UARCO, INC.**
700 W. Main
Barrington, IL 60010
Telephone: (708) 381-7000
Industry Affiliation: Paper Products
**Publication(s):**
*Forum*
Day Published: m.
Spec. Requirements: 16 pg.; offset magazine; 8 1/2 x 11
Personnel: Steve Cornell, Editor

4773
**UGI CORP.**
P.O. Box 858
Valley Forge, PA 19482
Telephone: (215) 337-1000
FAX: (215) 992-3259
Industry Affiliation: Utility: Gas
**Publication(s):**
*U G I Horizons*
Day Published: q.
Lead Time: 30 days
Spec. Requirements: 8-pgs.; offset; 11 x 15 1/2
Personnel: Jocelyn Kelemen, Editor

2270
**UNION BANK**
350 California St.
San Francisco, CA 94120
Telephone: (714) 705-7393
Industry Affiliation: Banks, Savings & Loans
**Publication(s):**
*Unity*
Day Published: q.
Lead Time: 2 wks. prior to pub. date
Mtls Deadline: 2 wks. prior to pub. date
Contact: Public Relations Unit
Spec. Requirements: 12 pg.; offset magazine; 8-1/2 x 11
Personnel: Erika Vogler, Editor

5108
**UNION BANKERS INSURANCE CO.**
500 N. Akard
Dallas, TX 75201
Telephone: (214) 939-0821
FAX: (214) 954-7008
Industry Affiliation: Insurance

Materials Accepted/Included: 01-Business news 02-By-line articles 03-Fashion news 04-Food news 05-Freelance copy 06-Letters to editor 07-Real estate news 08-Sports news 09-Travel news 10-Book rev. 11-Movie rev. 12-Music rev. 13-TV rev. 14-Theater rev. 15-Coming events 16-Obituaries 17-Question & answer 18-Social announcements 19-Artwork 20-Cartoons 21-Photos 22-TV listings 23-Audio rec. 24-Video rec. 25-Books 26-Films/film clips 27-Personnel news 28-Press releases 29-New product news/photos 30-Trade lit. 31-Contracts awarded 32-Display adv. 33-Classified adv.

**Publication(s):**
*Chronicle, The*
Day Published: m.
Lead Time: 1 mo. prior to pub. date
Mtls Deadline: 1st of mo. prior to pub. date
Contact: Pub. Rels. & Comms.
Spec. Requirements: 12 pgs; offset; 8 1/2 x 11
Personnel: Cindy Voghpool, Editor
Marie Preston

68432
**UNION CAMP CORPORATION**
W. Lathrop Ave.
P.O. Box 570
Savannah, GA 31402
Telephone: (912) 238-7332
FAX: (912) 238-6410
Industry Affiliation: Paper Products
**Publication(s):**
*Digester, The*
Day Published: m.
Lead Time: 2 wks. prior to pub. date
Mtls Deadline: 10th of mo. prior to pub. date
Personnel: Sonia Showalter, Editor

*Savannah Mill Weekly*
Day Published: w.
Mtls Deadline: Mon. prior to pub. date
Personnel: Sonia Showalter, Editor

*In Touch With Safety*
Day Published: q.

68392
**UNION CENTRAL LIFE**
P.O. Box 179
Cincinnati, OH 45201
Telephone: (513) 595-2481
FAX: (513) 595-2661
Industry Affiliation: Insurance
**Publication(s):**
*Carillon Magazine*
Day Published: q.
Mtls Deadline: 3 wks. prior to pub. date
Personnel: Donna Casteel, Editor

*Marketing Minute*
Day Published: s-m.
Mtls Deadline: 1 wk. prior to pub. date
Personnel: Dianna Haverland, Editor

*Pep Talk*
Day Published: s-m.
Mtls Deadline: 2 wks. prior to pub. date
Spec. Requirements: tabloid
Personnel: Jennifer Ferrell, Editor

*Annual Report*
Day Published: a.
Mtls Deadline: Feb. prior to pub. date
Personnel: Donna Casteel, Editor

3735
**UNION ELECTRIC CO.**
P.O. Box 149
St. Louis, MO 63166-0149
Telephone: (314) 621-3222
Industry Affiliation: Utility: Electric
**Publication(s):**
*Union Electric News*
Day Published: m.
Lead Time: 2 mos. prior to pub. date
Spec. Requirements: 8-16 pg.; offset newspaper; 11 x 11
Personnel: Deborah J. Walther, Editor

2920
**UNION INSURANCE GROUP**
303 E. Washington St.
Bloomington, IL 61701
Telephone: (309) 829-1061
Industry Affiliation: Insurance

**Publication(s):**
*Pro-File*
Day Published: q.
Lead Time: 2 mos. prior to pub. date
Mtls Deadline: 2 mos. prior to pub. date
Spec. Requirements: 8-pg.; offset magazine; 8 1/2 x 11
Personnel: Ted Horn, Editor

3238
**UNION NATIONAL LIFE INSURANCE CO.**
8282 Goodwood Blvd.
Baton Rouge, LA 70806
Telephone: (504) 927-3430
FAX: (504) 231-7494
Mailing Address:
P.O. Box 2348
Baton Rouge, LA 70821
Industry Affiliation: Insurance
**Publication(s):**
*Record, The*
Day Published: w.
Lead Time: 1 wk. prior to pub. date
Mtls Deadline: Thu., 12:00 pm prior to pub. date
Spec. Requirements: 2-16 pg.; offset; 84 x 11
Personnel: Virginia McDonald, Editor

3706
**UNION PACIFIC RAILROAD**
1416 Dodge St.
Omaha, NE 68179
Telephone: (402) 271-4433
Industry Affiliation: Railroads
**Publication(s):**
*Info*
Day Published: bi-m.
Spec. Requirements: 8-pg.; offset newspaper; 114 x 164
Personnel: Anne Walsh, Editor

*Changes*
Day Published: bi-m
Personnel: Morris Gotschall, Editor

4941
**UNION PACIFIC RESOURCES CO.**
InterFirst Twr.
Ft. Worth, TX 76101
Telephone: (817) 877-7527
Mailing Address:
P.O. Box 7
Ft. Worth, TX 76101
Industry Affiliation: Petroleum, Gas
**Publication(s):**
*U P Resources*
Day Published: m.
Lead Time: 8th of mo. prior to pub. date
Mtls Deadline: 8th of mo. prior to pub. date
Contact: Govt. Rels. & Pub. Affrs.
Spec. Requirements: 28 pg.; offset; 8-1/2 x 11; color
Personnel: Candy Clinton, Editor

*U P Reporter*
Day Published: s-a.
Personnel: Victoria Guennewig, Editor

4896
**UNION PLANTERS**
P.O. Box 387
Memphis, TN 38147
Telephone: (901) 680-5500
Industry Affiliation: Agriculture, Services
**Publication(s):**
*Profile*
Day Published: bi-m.
Spec. Requirements: 12 pg.; offset; 8 1/2 x 11
Personnel: Dianne Higgs, Editor

4775
**UNION RAILROAD CO.**
135 Jamison Ln.
Monroeville, PA 15146

Mailing Address:
P.O. Box 68
Monroeville, PA 15146
Industry Affiliation: Railroads
**Publication(s):**
*U R R Employee Newsletter*
Day Published: m.
Lead Time: 3 wks prior to pub. date
Mtls Deadline: 1st of mo. prior to pub, date
Spec. Requirements: 2 sides-1 pg. typed/wrd. proc. prt.-hse 8 1/2 x 11
Personnel: Robert R. Firestone
Alice C. Saylor

3506
**UNISTRUT CORPORATION**
3971 S. Research Pk. Dr.
Ann Arbor, MI 48108-2217
Telephone: (313) 930-0030
FAX: (313) 930-0290
Industry Affiliation: Industry: Heavy Construction, Machinery
**Publication(s):**
*Uniworld*
Day Published: q.
Lead Time: 1 mo. prior to pub. date
Materials: 01,28,29,30,31
Mtls Deadline: 1 mo. prior to pub. date
Spec. Requirements: 4 pg.; offset tabloid; 11 X 17
Personnel: Denise Campbell

4144
**UNISYS**
Marcus Ave.
Great Neck, NY 11020
Industry Affiliation: Electrical, Electronic, Manufacturing
**Publication(s):**
*Long Island News*
Day Published: q.
Spec. Requirements: 8-16 pgs; offset newspaper; 84 x 11
Personnel: Steve Letzler, Editor

*Inside Information*
Day Published: w.
Spec. Requirements: 8-16 pgs.
Personnel: Steve Letzler, Editor

5110
**UNITED AMERICAN INSURANCE CO.**
2909 N. Buckner Blvd.
Dallas, TX 75228
Telephone: (214) 320-6718
FAX: (214) 320-6709
Mailing Address:
P.O. Box 810
Dallas, TX 75221
Industry Affiliation: Insurance
**Publication(s):**
*U A news*
Day Published: m.
Lead Time: 8 wks. prior to pub. date
Mtls Deadline: 1st of mo. prior to pub. date
Contact: Marketing
Spec. Requirements: 20 pg.; offset; 8 1/2 x 11
Personnel: Judy Hans, Editor

68419
**UNITED CEREBRAL PALSY ASSOCIATION OF NASSAU COUNTY, INC.**
380 Washington Ave.
Roosevelt, NY 11575
Telephone: (516) 378-2000
FAX: (516) 378-0357
Industry Affiliation: Associations: Health Groups

**Publication(s):**
*C P News*
Day Published: q.
Personnel: Hazel Stein

4449
**UNITED COMMERCIAL TRAVELERS OF AMERICA**
632 N Park St.
Columbus, OH 43215
Telephone: (614) 228-3276
FAX: (614) 228-1898
Mailing Address:
P.O. Box 159019
Columbus, OH 43215
Industry Affiliation: Associations: Trade, Fraternal
**Publication(s):**
*Sample Case*
Day Published: bi-m.
Lead Time: 2 mos.
Materials: 02,09,10,19,25,28,32
Contact: Editorial Dept.
Spec. Requirements: 32 pg.; offset; 82 x 106
Personnel: Megan Woitovich, Editor
Elizabeth M. Kowalski, Editorial Assistant
David Knapp, Art Director

2463
**UNITED ILLUMINATING CO.**
157 Church St.
New Haven, CT 06506
Telephone: (203) 499-2000
FAX: (203) 499-3626
Mailing Address:
P.O. Box 1564
New Haven, CT 06506
Industry Affiliation: Electrical, Electronic, Manufacturing
**Publication(s):**
*Powerlines*
Day Published: m.
Spec. Requirements: 36 pg.; offset magazine; 8 1/2 x 11
Personnel: Phil Vece, Editor

*Let's Talk*
Day Published: m.
Lead Time: 2 mos. prior to pub. date
Mtls Deadline: 2 mos. prior to pub. date
Personnel: Phil Vece, Editor

2923
**UNITED INSURANCE CO. OF AMERICA**
One E. Wacker Dr.
Chicago, IL 60601
Telephone: (312) 661-4500
Industry Affiliation: Insurance
**Publication(s):**
*Happenings*
Day Published: m.
Lead Time: 2 mos. prior to pub. date
Mtls Deadline: 2 mos. prior to pub. date
Contact: Corp. Comms.
Spec. Requirements: 10-24 pgs.; offset
Personnel: Jennifer R. McLarin, Editor
Ted Richardson

68583
**UNITED METHODIST COMMUNICATIONS**
810 12th Ave., S.
Nashville, TN 37203
Telephone: (615) 742-5428
FAX: (615) 742-5469
Industry Affiliation: Associations: Trade, Fraternal

**Materials Accepted/Included:** 01-Business news 02-By-line articles 03-Fashion news 04-Food news 05-Freelance copy 06-Letters to editor 07-Real estate news 08-Sports news 09-Travel news 10-Book rev. 11-Movie rev. 12-Music rev. 13-TV rev. 14-Theater rev. 15-Coming events 16-Obituaries 17-Question & answer 18-Social announcements 19-Artwork 20-Cartoons 21-Photos 22-TV listings 23-Audio rec. 24-Video rec. 25-Books 26-Films/film clips 27-Personnel news 28-Press releases 29-New product news/photos 30-Trade lit. 31-Contracts awarded 32-Display adv. 33-Classified adv.

11-89

**Publication(s):**
*U M Community*
Day Published: bi-m.
Spec. Requirements: 4 pg.; 8 1/2 x 11
Personnel: Helen Allen, Editor

### UNITED METHODIST PUBLISHING HOUSE, THE
4897

201 Eighth Ave., S.
Nashville, TN 37203
Telephone: (615) 749-6000
Mailing Address:
P.O. Box 801
Nashville, TN 37202
Industry Affiliation: Publishers, Books, Magazines
**Publication(s):**
*Our House*
Day Published: bi-m.
Lead Time: 2 mos.
Mtls Deadline: 1st wk. of 2 mos. prior
Contact: Emp. Comms.
Spec. Requirements: 12 pgs.; offset newsletter; 8 1/2 x 11
Personnel: Holly Hewitt, Editor

### UNITED PARCEL SERVICE
2465

55 Glen Lake Pkwy.
Atlanta, GA 30328
Telephone: (404) 913-6550
FAX: (404) 913-6971
Industry Affiliation: Trucking
**Publication(s):**
*The Big Idea*
Day Published: m.
Lead Time: 2 wks. prior to pub. date
Mtls Deadline: 2 wks. prior to pub. date
Spec. Requirements: 4-12 Page Plus 12-20 Page Of National Company News
Personnel: Nina Hall, Editor

### UNITED STATES ARMY
5271

9325 Gunston Rd., Ste. S108
Fort Belvoir, VA 22060-5581
Telephone: (703) 806-4486
FAX: (703) 806-4566
Industry Affiliation: Associations: City, State, Federal
**Publication(s):**
*Soldiers*
Day Published: m.
Lead Time: 4 mos.
Materials: 01,02,06,08,20
Mtls Deadline: 4 mos. prior to pub. date
Spec. Requirements: 56-page; offset; 84 x 10
Personnel: Eileen M. Bratz, Editor in Chief

### UNITED STATES JUNIOR CHAMBER OF COMMERCE, THE
4565

Four W. 21st St.
Tulsa, OK 74114-1116
Telephone: (918) 584-2481
FAX: (918) 584-4422
Mailing Address:
P.O. Box 7
Tulsa, OK 74102
Industry Affiliation: Associations: Trade, Fraternal

**Publication(s):**
*Jaycees Magazine*
Day Published: q.
Lead Time: 6 mos. prior to pub. date
Materials: 01,10,25,28
Mtls Deadline: 6 mos. prior to issue date
Spec. Requirements: 32 pg.; offset; 8-1/8 x 10-7/8
Personnel: Dave Nershi, Marketing Director
Shelley Spong, Editor in Chief
Christopher Beach, Editor
Shelley Spong, Associate Editor
Christopher Beach, Managing Editor
Bob Guest, Production Manager
Kurt Stenstrom, Art Director

### UNITED STATES PIPE & FOUNDRY CO.
2003

3300 1st Ave., N.
Birmingham, AL 35222
Telephone: (205) 254-7000
FAX: (205) 254-7494
Mailing Address:
P.O. Box 10406
Birmingham, AL 35202
Industry Affiliation: Steel, Iron
**Publication(s):**
*Us Piper*
Day Published: s-a.
Spec. Requirements: 20-page; offset magazine; 84 x 11
Personnel: George J. Bogs, Editor

### UNITED STATES SPORTS ACADEMY
69460

One Academy Dr.
Daphne, AL 36526
Telephone: (205) 626-3303
FAX: (205) 626-3874
Industry Affiliation: Associations: Trade, Fraternal
**Publication(s):**
*Sports Supplement*
Day Published: q.
Contact: Dir. of Pub. Rels.

### UNITED TELEPHONE CO. OF FLORIDA
2618

P.O. Box 165000
Altamonte Springs, FL 32715
Telephone: (407) 889-6000
Industry Affiliation: Utility: Telephone
**Publication(s):**
*Ambassador, The*
Day Published: bi-m.
Lead Time: 14 days prior to pub. date
Spec. Requirements: 4-6 pg.; tabloid
Personnel: Mildred Graham, Editor

### UNITED TELEPHONE CO. OF INDIANA, INC.
3045

U.S. 30, E.
Warsaw, IN 46580
Telephone: (419) 755-8011
Mailing Address:
P.O. Box 391
Warsaw, IN 46581
Industry Affiliation: Utility: Telephone
**Publication(s):**
*Annual Employee Report*
Day Published: a.: end of 1st qtr.
Personnel: Ron Kinley
Connie Horton
Dale Merkel, Editor
Kirby Sprouls

### UNITED TELEPHONE CO. OF OHIO
4450

665 Lexington Ave.
Mansfield, OH 44907
Telephone: (419) 755-8011
FAX: (419) 756-3111

Mailing Address:
P.O. Box 3555
Mansfield, OH 44907
Industry Affiliation: Utility: Telephone
**Publication(s):**
*Pathways*
Day Published: s-m.
Lead Time: 1st of mo. prior to pub. date
Contact: Pub. RelS.
Spec. Requirements: 8 pg.; offset; 11 1/2 x 17 1/2
Personnel: Dale Merkel, Editor

*Spirit, The*
Day Published: w.
Personnel: Bart Porter, Editor
William Whitmoyer

### UNITED UNIONS OF JOB CORPS
68418

1029 Vermont Ave., N.W., Ste. 1000
Washington, DC 20005
Telephone: (202) 347-2500
FAX: (202) 393-5364
Industry Affiliation: Industry: Heavy Construction, Machinery
**Publication(s):**
*Achiever, The*
Day Published: q.: fall, winter, spring, summer
Materials: 05,06,15,17,19,21,28,29,30
Mtls Deadline: 15th of Jan., Mar., June, Sep.
Contact: Achiever
Spec. Requirements: submit b & w photos; camera-ready artwork
Personnel: Gilbert A. Wolf, Editor in Chief
Madeline Coppola, Editor
Wenonah Cohen, Staff Writer

### UNITED WAY OF BUFFALO & ERIE COUNTY
68385

742 Delaware Ave.
Buffalo, NY 14209
Telephone: (716) 887-2626
FAX: (716) 882-0071
Industry Affiliation: Associations: Trade, Fraternal
**Publication(s):**
*Impact On Western New York*
Day Published: q.
Personnel: David Weissman, Editor

*United Way Annual Report*
Day Published: a.
Personnel: David Weissman, Editor

### UNITED WAY OF GREATER GREENSBORO
4265

P.O. Box 14998
Greensboro, NC 27415-4998
Telephone: (910) 378-6600
Industry Affiliation: Associations: Health Groups
**Publication(s):**
*Your Way*
Day Published: bi-m.
Lead Time: 1 mo.
Mtls Deadline: 1 mo. prior to pub. date
Spec. Requirements: 4-page; offset; 8 1/2 x 11
Personnel: Yvonne L. Amico, Editor

### UNITED WAY OF KING COUNTY
5333

107 Cherry St.
Seattle, WA 98104
Telephone: (206) 461-3740
FAX: (206) 461-8453
Industry Affiliation: Associations: City, State, Federal

**Publication(s):**
*By The Way*
Day Published: w.
Mtls Deadline: Wed.
Contact: Marketing
Personnel: Beatrice Fong, Editor

### UNITED WAY OF METROPOLITAN TARRANT COUNTY
5116

210 E. Ninth St.
Fort Worth, TX 76102
Telephone: (817) 878-0000
Industry Affiliation: Associations: City, State, Federal
**Publication(s):**
*Sharing*
Day Published: q.
Spec. Requirements: 4-8-page; offset; 11 x 17
Personnel: Lillian Perkins, Editor

### UNITED WAY OF ORANGE COUNTY
2276

18012 Mitchell
Irvine, CA 92714
Telephone: (714) 660-7600
Industry Affiliation: Associations: City, State, Federal
**Publication(s):**
*Together*
Day Published: q.
Lead Time: 6 wks. prior to pub. date
Mtls Deadline: 6 wks. prior to pub. date
Contact: Marketing
Spec. Requirements: 4 page, offset, 16 x 11 1/4
Personnel: Jeff Urbaniec, Editor

### UNITED WAY OF SUMMIT COUNTY
4454

90 N. Prospect St.
Akron, OH 44304
Telephone: (216) 762-7601
FAX: (216) 762-0317
Mailing Address:
P.O. Box 1260
Akron, OH 44309
Industry Affiliation: Associations: City, State, Federal
**Publication(s):**
*Common Ground*
Day Published: q.
Lead Time: 3 wks. prior to pub. date
Materials: 15,18,19,21,27,28
Mtls Deadline: 3 wks. (2nd wk. of mo. prior to pub. mo.)
Spec. Requirements: 2 pg.; offset; 8 1/2 x 14
Personnel: Kay Hehr Smith, Editor

### UNITED WAY OF THE GREATER DAYTON AREA
68422

184 Salem Ave.
Dayton, OH 45406
Telephone: (513) 225-3028
FAX: (513) 225-3074
Industry Affiliation: Associations: Health Groups
**Publication(s):**
*Spirit*
Day Published: bi-m.
Mtls Deadline: 15th of mo. prior to pub. date
Personnel: Rex D. Broome

### UNITED WAY OF THE NATIONAL CAPITAL AREA
2563

95 M St., S.W.
Washington, DC 20024
Telephone: (202) 488-2060
FAX: (202) 488-2060
Industry Affiliation: Associations: City, State, Federal

**Publication(s):**
*United Way Newsletter*
Day Published: 4-6/yr.
Spec. Requirements: 4-page; offset; 11 x 15
Personnel: Meredith Lewis, Editor

4455

## UNITED WAY SERVICES
3100 Euclid Ave.
Cleveland, OH 44115
Telephone: (216) 881-3170
Industry Affiliation: Associations: City, State, Federal
**Publication(s):**
*United Way Leader*
Day Published: q.
Lead Time: 1 mo.
Contact: Comms.
Spec. Requirements: 8 pgs.; letterpress newsletter; 8 1/2 x 11
Personnel: John David Sidley, Editor

4457

## UNIVERSITY CIRCLE INC.
10831 Magnolia Dr.
Cleveland, OH 44106
Telephone: (216) 791-3900
Industry Affiliation: Colleges, Institutions, Science Research
**Publication(s):**
*Newsletter*
Day Published: q.
Spec. Requirements: 6 pg.; offset; 84 x 11

4458

## UNIVERSITY OF CINCINNATI
Campus Services Bldg., Alumni Pub.
Cincinnati, OH 45221
Telephone: (513) 556-5217
FAX: (513) 556-3237
Mailing Address:
ML 141
Cincinnati, OH 45221
Industry Affiliation: Colleges, Institutions, Science Research
**Publication(s):**
*Cincinnati Horizons*
Day Published: 8/yr.
Lead Time: 2 mos. prior to pub. date
Spec. Requirements: 40 pgs.; offset; 8 1/2 x 11
Personnel: Jean M. Peck, Editor

4482

## UNIVERSITY OF DAYTON
300 College Park
Dayton, OH 45469
Telephone: (513) 229-3241
FAX: (513) 229-3063
Industry Affiliation: Colleges, Institutions, Science Research
**Publication(s):**
*University Of Dayton Campus Report, The*
Day Published: 18/yr.
Lead Time: 2 wks.
Mtls Deadline: 2 wks. prior to pub. date
Contact: Public Relations
Spec. Requirements: 8 page; offset; tabloid
Personnel: Kate Cassidy, Editor

*University Of Dayton Quarterly*
Day Published: q.
Lead Time: 2 mos.
Mtls Deadline: 2 mos. prior to pub. date
Contact: Public Relations
Spec. Requirements: 24 page; tabloid
Personnel: Thomas M. Columbus, Editor

3125

## UNIVERSITY OF IOWA HOSPITALS & CLINICS
200 Hawkins Dr.
Iowa City, IA 52242
Telephone: (319) 356-2731
FAX: (319) 356-3862
Industry Affiliation: Colleges, Institutions, Science Research

**Publication(s):**
*Pacemaker*
Day Published: m.
Lead Time: 2 mos.
Mtls Deadline: 3rd Mon. of mo.
Spec. Requirements: 12 pgs; offset; 8 1/2 x 11, 4 color
Personnel: Michael Sondergard, Editor

2619

## UNIVERSITY OF MIAMI
P.O. Box 248105
Coral Gables, FL 33124
Telephone: (305) 284-5500
FAX: (305) 284-2035
Industry Affiliation: Colleges, Institutions, Science Research
**Publication(s):**
*Veritas*
Day Published: m.
Contact: Office of Pub. Affairs
Spec. Requirements: 8-page; offset; 11 x 17
Personnel: Susan May, Senior Editor

3741

## UNIVERSITY OF MISSOURI
W1000 Engineering Bldg. E
Columbia, MO 65211
Telephone: (314) 882-3221
FAX: (314) 882-7584
Industry Affiliation: Colleges, Institutions, Science Research
**Publication(s):**
*Ingenuity*
Day Published: s-a.
Spec. Requirements: 24 pg.; 8 1/2 x 11
Personnel: Emily Jones Claassen, Editor

3761

## UNIVERSITY OF MONTANA SCHOOL OF JOURNALISM
University of Montana
Missoula, MT 59812
Telephone: (406) 243-0211
Industry Affiliation: Colleges, Institutions, Science Research
**Publication(s):**
*Montana Journalism Review*
Day Published: a.
Spec. Requirements: 60-page; offset; 11 x 8 1/2
Personnel: Warren J. Brier, Editor

3812

## UNIVERSITY OF NEBRASKA MEDICAL CENTER
600 S. 42nd St.
Omaha, NE 68198-5230
Telephone: (402) 559-4353
FAX: (402) 559-4103
Industry Affiliation: Colleges, Institutions, Science Research
**Publication(s):**
*Impact*
Day Published: s-a.
Lead Time: 2-3 mos. prior to pub. date
Mtls Deadline: Mon. prior to pub. date
Spec. Requirements: 4 pg.; offset bulletin; 7 x 94
Personnel: Sandy Goetzinger-Comer, Editor
Barbara Newcomer

*U N M C News*
Day Published: s-w.
Lead Time: 7-10 days prior to pub. date
Mtls Deadline: varies
Spec. Requirements: 24 pg.
Personnel: Barbara Newcomer, Editor

4169

## UNIVERSITY OF ROCHESTER
107 Administration Bldg. River Sta.
Rochester, NY 14627
Telephone: (716) 275-4124
Industry Affiliation: Colleges, Institutions, Science Research

**Publication(s):**
*University Of Rochester Currents*
Day Published: bi-w.
Lead Time: 1 wk.
Mtls Deadline: 1 wk.
Spec. Requirements: 4-page; offset; 17 1/2 x 11 1/4
Personnel: Kathy Quinn Thomas, Editor

*Research Review*
Day Published: q.
Lead Time: 3 mos.

5118

## UNIVERSITY OF ST. THOMAS
3812 Montrose Blvd
Houston, TX 77006
Telephone: (713) 522-7911
Industry Affiliation: Colleges, Institutions, Science Research
**Publication(s):**
*St. Thomas Magazine*
Day Published: s-a.
Lead Time: 2-4 mos. prior to pub. date
Mtls Deadline: 2-4 mos. prior to pub. date
Contact: Publications
Spec. Requirements: 16-20 pgs.; offset; 9 x 12 folded
Personnel: Patricia M. Winterstein, Editor

5212

## UNIVERSITY OF UTAH MEDICAL CENTER
50 N. Medical Dr.
Salt Lake City, UT 84132
Telephone: (801) 581-2121
Industry Affiliation: Colleges, Institutions, Science Research
**Publication(s):**
*Health Sciences Report*
Day Published: q.
Contact: Dept. of Development and Communication
Spec. Requirements: 8 page; offset; 11 x 14
Personnel: Susan Sample, Editor

5450

## UNIVERSITY OF WISCONSIN MADISON CENTER
Rm. 758, Warf Bldg.
Madison, WI 53706
Telephone: (608) 263-4163
FAX: (608) 263-6394
Industry Affiliation: Colleges, Institutions, Science Research
**Publication(s):**
*Center Lifelines*
Day Published: bi-m.
Spec. Requirements: 4 pg.; offset; 17 x 11 1/2
Personnel: Beth Fultz, Editor

5471

## UNIVERSITY OF WISCONSIN SYSTEM
1220 Linden Dr., 1848 Van Hise Hall
Madison, WI 53706
Telephone: (608) 263-3961
Industry Affiliation: Colleges, Institutions, Science Research
**Publication(s):**
*Wisconsin Ideas*
Day Published: 4-6/yr.
Lead Time: 45 days
Contact: System Adm.
Spec. Requirements: 16 pg.; 2 colors; 8 1/2 x 11
Personnel: Johnathan Henkes, Editor

2271

## UNOCAL CORP.
1201 W. Fifth St.
Los Angeles, CA 90017
Telephone: (213) 977-7600
Mailing Address:
P.O. Box 7600
Los Angeles, CA 90051
Industry Affiliation: Petroleum, Gas

**Publication(s):**
*Seventy Six*
Day Published: q.
Spec. Requirements: 26 pgs.; offset magazine; 86 X 116
Personnel: Mike Broadhurst, Editor

3257

## UNUM CORP.
2211 Congress St., P349
Portland, ME 04122
Telephone: (207) 770-4340
FAX: (207) 770-4510
Industry Affiliation: Insurance
**Publication(s):**
*Unum Today*
Day Published: bi-w.
Lead Time: every 2 wks.
Materials: 01
Mtls Deadline: 1 wk.
Contact: Corp. Staff
Spec. Requirements: 8-10 pgs.
Personnel: Eric Lake, Editor

4459

## URBAN APPALACHIAN COUNCIL
2115 W. Eighth
Cincinnati, OH 45204
Telephone: (513) 251-0202
Industry Affiliation: Agriculture, Services
**Publication(s):**
*Advocate, The*
Day Published: s-a.
Lead Time: 6-8 wks.
Mtls Deadline: 4 wks. prior to pub. date
Contact: Pub. Rels.
Spec. Requirements: 2 color typeset
Personnel: Larry J. Redden, Editor

*Urban Appalachian Voice*
Day Published: q.
Lead Time: 4 wks.
Contact: Pub. Rels.
Personnel: Jeanne Shanin

3258

## U.S. AIR FORCE
Office of Public Affairs
Loring AFB, ME 04751
Telephone: (207) 999-2170
FAX: (207) 999-2648
Industry Affiliation: Associations: City, State, Federal
**Publication(s):**
*Limelite*
Day Published: w.
Lead Time: 3 days
Materials: 02,06,15,19,20,21,27
Mtls Deadline: Fri.
Contact: Public Affairs Office
Spec. Requirements: 8 pgs. offset; tabloid
Personnel: Austin Carter, Editor

2504

## U.S. AIR GROUP, INC.
Crystal Pk., 4 Crystal Dr.
Arlington, VA 22227
Telephone: (703) 892-7000
Industry Affiliation: Airlines
**Publication(s):**
*Us Air News*
Day Published: bi-w.
Contact: Public Relations
Spec. Requirements: 4-8 page; offset; 11 1/2 x 14 1/2
Personnel: Ann C. Farley, Editor

4611

## U.S. BANCORP
P.O. Box 8837
Portland, OR 97208
Telephone: (503) 275-6111
Industry Affiliation: Banks, Savings & Loans

**Materials Accepted/Included:** 01-Business news 02-By-line articles 03-Fashion news 04-Food news 05-Freelance copy 06-Letters to editor 07-Real estate news 08-Sports news 09-Travel news 10-Book rev. 11-Movie rev. 12-Music rev. 13-TV rev. 14-Theater rev. 15-Coming events 16-Obituaries 17-Question & answer 18-Social announcements 19-Artwork 20-Cartoons 21-Photos 22-TV listings 23-Audio rec. 24-Video rec. 25-Books 26-Films/film clips 27-Personnel news 28-Press releases 29-New product news/photos 30-Trade lit. 31-Contracts awarded 32-Display adv. 33-Classified adv.

11-91

**Publication(s):**
*Focus On Us*
Day Published: m.
Lead Time: 1 mo. prior to pub. date
Mtls Deadline: 15th of mo. prior to pub. date
Contact: Personnel Dept.
Spec. Requirements: 4-8 pgs., magapaper, 9 x 12
Personnel: Mary L. Morris, Editor

**U.S. BORAX INC.** 2273
26877 Tourney Rd.
Valencia, CA 91355
Industry Affiliation: Chemicals, Plastics
**Publication(s):**
*Borax Pioneer*
Day Published: q.
Spec. Requirements: 24 pgs.; offset magazine; 84 x 11
Personnel: Tana Burrows, Editor

**U.S. DEPARTMENT OF AGRICULTURE** 2559
Office of Public Affairs
Administration Bldg., Rm. 213A
Washington, DC 20250
Telephone: (202) 720-8732
Industry Affiliation: Associations: City, State, Federal
**Publication(s):**
*U S D A Employee Newsletter*
Day Published: bi-w.
Lead Time: 4 wks. prior to pub. date
Mtls Deadline: 4 wks. prior to pub. date
Contact: Special Reports Division
Spec. Requirements: 4-pg.; bulletin; 8 1/2 x 11
Personnel: Ron Hall, Editor

**U.S. DEPARTMENT OF ENERGY** 2560
PA-5
Washington, DC 20585
Telephone: (202) 586-2050
Mailing Address:
    1000 Independence, S.W.
    Washington, DC 20585
Industry Affiliation: Associations: City, State, Federal
**Publication(s):**
*D O E This Month*
Day Published: m.
Lead Time: 2 wks. prior to pub. date
Mtls Deadline: 15th of mo. prior to pub. date
Contact: Public Affairs
Spec. Requirements: 16 pg.; 8 1/2 x 11
Personnel: Martin Moon, Editor

**U.S. DEPARTMENT OF ENERGY** 3924
P.O. Box 5400
Albuquerque, NM 87185-5400
Telephone: (505) 845-6202
Industry Affiliation: Associations: City, State, Federal
**Publication(s):**
*A L News*
Day Published: m.
Lead Time: 1st wk. of mo.
Mtls Deadline: 1st wk. of mo.
Spec. Requirements: 4-pg.; offset; 11 1/4 x 15 1/2
Personnel: Ben McCarty, Editor

**USF & A. INSURANCE** 3299
100 Light St.
Baltimore, MD 21202
Telephone: (301) 547-3000
Industry Affiliation: Insurance

**Publication(s):**
*Bulletin*
Day Published: 5/yr.
Lead Time: 3 mos.
Mtls Deadline: 3 mos. prior to pub. date
Contact: Pub. Dept.
Spec. Requirements: 32 pg.; offset; 84 x 106; full-color
Personnel: Stacy L. Mayhorne, Editor

**USG CORP.** 2924
125 S. Franklin St.
Chicago, IL 60606-4678
Telephone: (312) 606-4181
FAX: (312) 606-5566
Industry Affiliation: Lumber, Forestry, Building Materials
**Publication(s):**
*Form & Function*
Day Published: q.
Spec. Requirements: 16-page; offset magazine; 8 1/2 x 11
Personnel: William D. Leavitt, Editor

*Looking Ahead*
Day Published: bi-m.
Contact: Corporate Communications
Spec. Requirements: 8 pg.
Personnel: Heather Reicherts Jones, Editor
    Carolyn Hughes, Art Director

**U.S. INFORMATION AGENCY** 2570
301 Fourth St., S.W., Rm. 602
Washington, DC 20547-0001
Telephone: (202) 619-4355
Industry Affiliation: Associations: City, State, Federal
**Publication(s):**
*U S I A World*
Day Published: every 2 mos.
Lead Time: 2 mos. prior to pub. date
Mtls Deadline: 3 mos. prior to pub. date
Contact: Office Of Public Liasion
Spec. Requirements: 24 pgs.; offset magazine; 8 1/4 x 10 3/4
Personnel: Joan Zaffarano, Editor
    Karen Ceremsak

**U.S. POSTAL SERVICE, COMMUNICATIONS DEPT.** 5449
475 L'Enfant Plz. West, S.W.
Washington, DC 20260
Telephone: (202) 783-3238
Industry Affiliation: Associations: City, State, Federal
**Publication(s):**
*Postal Life*
Day Published: bi-m.
Contact: Supt. of Documents
    941 N. Capitol St., N.E.
    Washington, DC 20402-1571
Personnel: Michael A. Mahnke, Editor

**U.S. RAILROAD RETIREMENT BOARD** 68531
844 N. Rush St.
Chicago, IL 60611-2092
Telephone: (312) 751-4777
FAX: (312) 751-7154
Industry Affiliation: Railroads
**Publication(s):**
*All A-Board*
Day Published: 7/yr.
Personnel: William Poulos

**U.S. SAVINGS BONDS DIVISION** 2562
800 K. St. N.W., Ste. 800
Washington, DC 20226
Telephone: (202) 535-4569
Industry Affiliation: Advertising, Art, Public Relations

**Publication(s):**
*Bond Teller, The*
Day Published: q.
Lead Time: 6 wks.
Spec. Requirements: 4-6 pgs.; offset; 8 1/2 x 11 1/2
Personnel: Sheila Nelson, Editor

**US SMALL BUSINESS ADMINISTRATION** 2274
409 Third St., S.W.
Washington, DC 20416
Telephone: (800) 827-5722
Industry Affiliation: Finance, Services
**Publication(s):**
*Annual Report*
Day Published: a.
Spec. Requirements: 300-page; offset and letterpress; 7 1/2 x 10 1/4

**UTAH DEPARTMENT OF HUMAN SERVICES** 5213
120 N. 200 W.
Salt Lake City, UT 84103
Telephone: (801) 538-4001
Mailing Address:
    P.O. Box 45500
    Salt Lake City, UT 84145
Industry Affiliation: Associations: Health Groups
**Publication(s):**
*Clientell*
Day Published: m.
Lead Time: 1 mo. prior to pub. date
Mtls Deadline: 1st of mo. prior to pub. date
Spec. Requirements: public assistance recipients only.
Personnel: Donna Kramer, Editor

*Human Touch*
Day Published: m.
Lead Time: 2 wks. prior to pub. date
Mtls Deadline: 2 wks. prior to pub. date

**UTAH POWER, A DIVISION OF PACIFICORP, OREGON** 5214
201 S. Main
Salt Lake City, UT 84140-0022
Telephone: (801) 220-2592
FAX: (801) 220-3116
Mailing Address:
    1407 W. North Temple, Ste. 2200-OUC
    Salt Lake City, UT 84140-0022
Industry Affiliation: Utility: Related
**Publication(s):**
*Network*
Day Published: m.
Lead Time: 4 wks.
Mtls Deadline: 2 wks.
Contact: Employee Communications
Spec. Requirements: 8 page offset, tabloid

*Update*
Day Published: m.
Lead Time: 3 mos.
Mtls Deadline: 3 mos. prior to pub. date
Contact: Employee Communications
Personnel: Nancy Vourekamp
    Linda A. Anderson

*Newsbreak*
Day Published: w.
Lead Time: 1 wk.
Mtls Deadline: Thu. prior to pub. date
Contact: Employee Communications
Personnel: Margaret Oler-Kesler
    Marsha Cutler

**Safety Times**
Day Published: q.
Mtls Deadline: 1 mo. prior to pub. date
Contact: Employee Communications
Spec. Requirements: 8-12 pg.; 8 1/2 X 11

**UTAH STATE UNIVERSITY** 5215
Information Service
Logan, UT 84322-0500
Telephone: (801) 750-1355
Industry Affiliation: Colleges, Institutions, Science Research
**Publication(s):**
*Outlook*
Day Published: bi-m.
Spec. Requirements: 8-12 pg.; offset; 15 x 11 1/4
Personnel: Cliff Cahoon, Editor

**UTICA NATIONAL INSURANCE GROUP** 4170
180 Genesee St.
New Hartford, NY 13413
Telephone: (315) 734-2000
Mailing Address:
    P.O. Box 530
    Utica, NY 13503
Industry Affiliation: Insurance
**Publication(s):**
*You*
Day Published: q.
Lead Time: 1-3 mos. prior to pub. date
Mtls Deadline: Feb., Apr., July., Oct. prior to pub. date
Spec. Requirements: 24-32 pg.; offset; 8-1/2 x 11
Personnel: Marc Butler, Editor
    Michael Austin, Publisher

*Flash*
Day Published: bi-w.
Personnel: Marc Butler
    Michael Austin, Publisher

**VALENTINE, THE MUSEUM OF THE LIFE & HISTORY OF RICHMOND** 5272
1015 E. Clay St.
Richmond, VA 23219
Telephone: (804) 649-0711
FAX: (804) 643-3510
Industry Affiliation: Colleges, Institutions, Science Research
**Publication(s):**
*Valentine News*
Day Published: q.
Lead Time: 2 mos.
Mtls Deadline: 2 mos.
Spec. Requirements: 4 page; offset; 11 x 14
Personnel: Margaret J. Tinsley, Editor

**VALHI, INC.** 5197
5430 LBJ Fwy., Ste. 1700
Dallas, TX 75240
Telephone: (214) 233-1700
Industry Affiliation: Sugar
**Publication(s):**
*Sugarbeet*
Day Published: q.
Lead Time: 2 mos. prior to pub. date
Mtls Deadline: 2 mos. prior to pub. date
Spec. Requirements: 24 page; offset; 84 x 11
Personnel: Dale Hicks, Editor

**Materials Accepted/Included:** 01-Business news 02-By-line articles 03-Fashion news 04-Food news 05-Freelance copy 06-Letters to editor 07-Real estate news 08-Sports news 09-Travel news 10-Book rev. 11-Movie rev. 12-Music rev. 13-TV rev. 14-Theater rev. 15-Coming events 16-Obituaries 17-Question & answer 18-Social announcements 19-Artwork 20-Cartoons 21-Photos 22-TV listings 23-Audio rec. 24-Video rec. 25-Books 26-Films/film clips 27-Personnel news 28-Press releases 29-New product news/photos 30-Trade lit. 31-Contracts awarded 32-Display adv. 33-Classified adv.

*Sugar Scoop*
Day Published: m.
Lead Time: 3 wk. prior to pub. date
Mtls Deadline: 3 wks. prior to pub. date
Spec. Requirements: 6 page
Personnel: Dale Hicks, Editor

3906

**VALLEY HOSPITAL**
Linwood & N. Van Dien Ave.
Ridgewood, NJ 07450
Telephone: (201) 447-8011
FAX: (201) 447-8623
Industry Affiliation: Hospitals
**Publication(s):**
*Valley Reports*
Day Published: q. (one issue is Annual Report)
Spec. Requirements: 36-40 pgs.; offset; 8 x 8
Personnel: J. Lawrence Prendergast, Editor

2278

**VALLEY PRESBYTERIAN HOSPITAL**
15107 Vanowen St.
Van Nuys, CA 91405
Telephone: (818) 782-6600
FAX: (818) 902-5703
Mailing Address:
    P.O. Box 9102
    Van Nuys, CA 91409
Industry Affiliation: Hospitals
**Publication(s):**
*Health Watch*
Day Published: q.
Lead Time: 60 days
Mtls Deadline: 30-60 days
Spec. Requirements: 8 Page; 8 1/2 X 11
Personnel: Janna Wilson, Editor

3627

**VALSPAR CORP.**
1101 S. Third St.
Minneapolis, MN 55415
Telephone: (612) 332-7371
Industry Affiliation: Paint
**Publication(s):**
*Scope*
Day Published: m.
Spec. Requirements: 12 pgs.; offset; 84 x 11
Personnel: Gary Gardner, Vice President

3194

**VALVOLINE, INC.**
3499 Dabney Dr.
Lexington, KY 40509
Telephone: (606) 264-7777
FAX: (606) 264-7381
Mailing Address:
    P.O. Box 14000
    Lexington, KY 40512
Industry Affiliation: Petroleum, Gas
**Publication(s):**
*Valvoline World*
Day Published: s-a.
Lead Time: 4 mos.
Spec. Requirements: 16-20pg.; offset magazine; standard size
Personnel: Les Williams, Editor

5273

**VA., MD., & DE. ASSOCIATION OF ELECTRIC CO-OP.**
4201 Dominion Blvd., Ste. 101
Glen Allen, VA 23060
Telephone: (804) 346-3344
Industry Affiliation: Utility: Electric

**Publication(s):**
*Rural Living*
Day Published: m.
Lead Time: 60 days
Materials: 05,06,32,33
Mtls Deadline: 1st of mo.
Spec. Requirements: 32 page; offset magazine; 7 x 10
Personnel: Richard G. Johnstone, Jr., Editor
    Becky Potter, Production Manager
    John Bruce, Managing Editor

2279

**VARIAN ASSOCIATES, INC.**
3050 Hansen Way
Palo Alto, CA 94304
Telephone: (415) 493-4000
FAX: (415) 424-6082
Industry Affiliation: Electrical, Electronic, Manufacturing
**Publication(s):**
*Varian Associates Magazine*
Day Published: q.
Lead Time: 1 mo. prior to pub. date
Mtls Deadline: 1 mo. prior to pub. date
Contact: Eimac Division
    301 Industrial Way
    San Carlos, CA 94070
Personnel: Bill Bucy, Editor

3126

**VERNON CO.**
604 W. Fourth St., N.
Newton, IA 50208
Telephone: (515) 792-9000
FAX: (515) 791-7421
Industry Affiliation: Advertising, Art, Public Relations
**Publication(s):**
*Vernon Mirror*
Day Published: bi-m.
Lead Time: 2 wks.
Mtls Deadline: 1 wk. prior to pub. date
Contact: Mktg. Dept.
Spec. Requirements: 12 pg.; offset; 8 1/2 x 11
Personnel: Scott Newton, Editor

2280

**VETCO, INC.**
10777 N.W. Fwy., Ste. 110
Houston, TX 77092
Telephone: (713) 681-4685
Industry Affiliation: Photography
**Publication(s):**
*Direct Line*
Day Published: bi-m.
Spec. Requirements: 16-20 page; offset; 8 1/2 x 11
Personnel: Judith Etheredge, Editor

*Connections*
Day Published: q.
Personnel: Joanne Herrera

66437

**VIACOM INTERNATIONAL INC.**
1515 Broadway
New York, NY 10036
Telephone: (212) 258-6343
FAX: (212) 288-6354
Industry Affiliation: Radio, TV, Movies
**Publication(s):**
*Viacomments*
Day Published: q.
Personnel: Helen Steblecki, Editor

3504

**VICKERS, INC.**
5445 Corporate Dr.
Troy, MI 48007-0302
Telephone: (313) 641-4200
Mailing Address:
    P.O. Box 302
    Troy, MI 48007-0302
Industry Affiliation: Industry: Heavy Construction, Machinery

**Publication(s):**
*Vickers In Print*
Day Published: m.
Spec. Requirements: 4 pg.; offset newspapers; 114 x 17
Personnel: Joseph A. Peruzzi, Editor

*Distributor News*
Day Published: q.

3127

**VIKING PUMP, INC./A UNIT OF IDEX CORP.**
406 State St.
Cedar Falls, IA 50613
Telephone: (319) 266-1741
Industry Affiliation: Industry: Light Tools, Equipment
**Publication(s):**
*Pumpline*
Day Published: q.
Lead Time: 6 mos.
Mtls Deadline: 6 mos.
Contact: Mktg. Dept.
Spec. Requirements: 28 pg.; offset magazine; 5 1/2 x 8
Personnel: Anna Mae Hease, Editor

5452

**VILTER MANUFACTURING CORP.**
2217 S. First St.
Milwaukee, WI 53207
Telephone: (414) 744-0111
FAX: (414) 744-3483
Industry Affiliation: Cooling, Heating
**Publication(s):**
*Vilter Booster*
Day Published: s-a.
Spec. Requirements: 20-page; offset magazine; 8 1/2 x 11
Personnel: Mark A. Richfield, Editor

5277

**VIRGINIA ASSOCIATION OF PLUMBING HEATING COOLING CONTRACTORS**
2103 Lake Ave.
Richmond, VA 23230
Telephone: (804) 288-2080
FAX: (804) 282-1620
Industry Affiliation: Associations: Trade, Fraternal
**Publication(s):**
*Virginia P H C Image*
Day Published: m.
Mtls Deadline: 20th of mo. prior to issue date
Spec. Requirements: 24-72-pg.; offset; 7 5/16 x 9 3/4
Personnel: James B. Muncy, Editor

5278

**VIRGINIA BANKERS ASSOCIATION**
700 E. Main St., Ste. 1411
Richmond, VA 23219
Telephone: (804) 643-7469
FAX: (804) 643-6308
Mailing Address:
    P.O. Box 462
    Richmond, VA 23203
Industry Affiliation: Banks, Savings & Loans
**Publication(s):**
*Banking News*
Day Published: m.
Lead Time: 2-3 wks. prior to pub. date
Mtls Deadline: 6th of mo. prior to pub. date
Spec. Requirements: 8-16 pgs.; offset; 8 1/2 x 11
Personnel: Barbara A. Garrett, Editor

5280

**VIRGINIA CREDIT UNION LEAGUE**
3805 Cutshaw Ave.
Lynchburg, VA 23230
Telephone: (804) 237-9600
FAX: (804) 367-9025

Mailing Address:
    P.O. Box 11469
    Lynchburg, VA 24506-1469
Industry Affiliation: Finance, Services
**Publication(s):**
*Virginian*
Day Published: m.
Lead Time: 3 wks. prior to pub. date
Mtls Deadline: 3 wks. prior to pub. date
Spec. Requirements: 6 page; 84 x 11
Personnel: Nita Hoyt, Editor

5282

**VIRGINIA DEPARTMENT OF ALCOHOLIC BEVERAGE CONTROL**
2901 Hermitage Rd.
Richmond, VA 23220
Telephone: (804) 367-0649
FAX: (804) 367-2553
Mailing Address:
    P.O. Box 27491
    Richmond, VA 23261
Industry Affiliation: Associations: City, State, Federal
**Publication(s):**
*Inside Spirits*
Day Published: q.
Lead Time: 3 wks.
Materials: 05,06,15,19,20,21,27,28
Mtls Deadline: 10th working day of each quarter.
Contact: Pub. Affairs/Educational Svcs.
Spec. Requirements: 4-8-page; offset; 8 1/2 x 11
Personnel: Robert W. Chapman, Jr., Editor

5230

**VIRGINIA DEPARTMENT OF MENTAL HEALTH, RETARDATION-SUBSTANCE ABUSE SERVICES**
109 Governors St.
Richmond, VA 23219
Telephone: (804) 786-1530
Mailing Address:
    P.O. Box 1797
    Richmond, VA 23214
Industry Affiliation: Associations: Health Groups
**Publication(s):**
*Aware*
Day Published: bi-m.
Lead Time: 1 mo. prior to pub. date
Mtls Deadline: 1st wk. of 2nd mo. prior to pub. date
Spec. Requirements: 40 pgs. 8 1/2 X 11
Personnel: Harriet M. Russell, Director of Prevention

5283

**VIRGINIA DEPARTMENT OF TRANSPORTATION**
1401 E. Broad St.
Richmond, VA 23219
Telephone: (804) 786-2716
FAX: (804) 786-6250
Industry Affiliation: Associations: City, State, Federal
**Publication(s):**
*Bulletin*
Day Published: m.
Lead Time: 3 wks. prior to pub. date
Mtls Deadline: 1st of mo. prior to mo. of issue
Spec. Requirements: 44-48 pgs.; offset magazine; 6 x 9
Personnel: Charles Armstrong, Editor

5284

**VIRGINIA POWER CO.**
One James River Plz.
Richmond, VA 23219
Telephone: (804) 771-3000
FAX: (804) 771-3146

**Materials Accepted/Included:** 01-Business news 02-By-line articles 03-Fashion news 04-Food news 05-Freelance copy 06-Letters to editor 07-Real estate news 08-Sports news 09-Travel news 10-Book rev. 11-Movie rev. 12-Music rev. 13-TV rev. 14-Theater rev. 15-Coming events 16-Obituaries 17-Question & answer 18-Social announcements 19-Artwork 20-Cartoons 21-Photos 22-TV listings 23-Audio rec. 24-Video rec. 25-Books 26-Films/film clips 27-Personnel news 28-Press releases 29-New product news/photos 30-Trade lit. 31-Contracts awarded 32-Display adv. 33-Classified adv.

11-93

Mailing Address:
  P.O. Box 26666
  Richmond, VA 23261
Industry Affiliation: Utility: Electric
**Publication(s):**
*Vepco Currents*
Day Published: m.
Lead Time: 1 mo. prior to pub. date
Mtls Deadline: 10th of mo. prior to pub.
  date
Spec. Requirements: 6 page; offset; 14 x
  11
Personnel: Dan Genest, Editor

**WACHOVIA BANK OF GEORGIA**  2652
191 Peachtree St., N.E.
Atlanta, GA 30303
Telephone: (404) 332-5000
FAX: (404) 332-5294
Mailing Address:
  P.O. Box 4155
  Atlanta, GA 30303
Industry Affiliation: Banks, Savings &
  Loans
**Publication(s):**
*Wachovia News*
Day Published: m.
Lead Time: 1 mo.
Mtls Deadline: 1 mo.
Contact: Corp. Comm.
Spec. Requirements: 4 pge. newsletter; 8
  1/2 x 11
Personnel: Renee Lane, Editor

**WADDELL & REED INC.**  3742
6300 Lamar
Overland Park, KS 66201-9217
Telephone: (913) 236-1941
Mailing Address:
  P.O. Box 29217
  Shawnee Mission, KS 66202
Industry Affiliation: Finance, Services
**Publication(s):**
*W & R World*
Day Published: m.
Spec. Requirements: 16 page; offset;
  magazine
Personnel: Harriet Rose, Editor

**WAKE MEDICAL CENTER**  4266
3000 New Bern Ave.
Raleigh, NC 27610
Telephone: (919) 755-8120
Industry Affiliation: Hospitals
**Publication(s):**
*Scope*
Day Published: m.
Lead Time: 4 wks. prior to pub. date
Mtls Deadline: 4 wks. prior to pub. date
Contact: Public Relations Dept.
Spec. Requirements: 8 pg; offset; 11 x 14

*Microscope*
Day Published: w.
Lead Time: 2 wks. prior to pub. date
Mtls Deadline: 2 wks. prior to pub. date
Contact: Public Relations Dept.
Personnel: Linda Campora, Editor

**WALGREEN CO.**  2930
200 Wilmot
Deerfield, IL 60015
Telephone: (708) 940-2920
Industry Affiliation: Retail Stores

**Publication(s):**
*Walgreen World*
Day Published: bi-m.
Spec. Requirements: 24 pg.; offset; 8 1/2
  x 11
Personnel: Laurie L. Meyer, Editor

**WARD'S NATURAL SCIENCE**  68441
**ESTABLISHMENT, INC.**
5100 W. Henrietta Rd., P.O. Box 92912
Rochester, NY 14692-9012
Telephone: (800) 962-2660
FAX: (800) 635-8439
Industry Affiliation: Colleges, Institutions,
  Science Research
**Publication(s):**
*Ward's Bulletin*
Day Published: s-a.
Materials: 19,21,29
Mtls Deadline: varies
Personnel: Thomas Cassell, Editor

**WARNER ENTERPRISES**  66436
23 W. Holcroft Rd.
Rochester, NY 14612
Telephone: (716) 423-8290
FAX: (716) 422-9536
Industry Affiliation: Publishers, Books,
  Magazines
**Publication(s):**
*Freelance Editor-Writer*
Day Published: m. & s-m.
Lead Time: 1st Fri. ea. mo.
Materials: 01,04,08,09,10,11,12,14,25,26,
  28,29
Mtls Deadline: 1st Fri. ea. mo.
Personnel: David Warner, Editor

**WASHINGTON BUILDING**  2564
**CONGRESS, INC.**
3433 Connecticut Ave., N.W., Ste. 200
Washington, DC 20008
Telephone: (202) 244-6481
Industry Affiliation: Associations: Trade,
  Fraternal
**Publication(s):**
*Wbc Bulletin*
Day Published: m.
Spec. Requirements: 16 page; letterpress;
  8 1/2 x 11
Personnel: Robert E. Koehler, Editor

**WASHINGTON DEPARTMENT OF**  5335
**NATURAL RESOURCES**
Public Lands Bldg.
Olympia, WA 98504-7001
Telephone: (206) 902-1022
FAX: (206) 902-1776
Mailing Address:
  Communications Office
  Olympia, WA 98504
Industry Affiliation: Associations: City,
  State, Federal
**Publication(s):**
*Inside D N R*
Day Published: m.

*Forest Prescription*
Day Published: q.
Personnel: Julianne Crane, Editor

*Wellness News*
Day Published: bi-m.

**WASHINGTON GAS**  2565
1100 H St., N.W.
Washington, DC 20080
Telephone: (202) 624-6727
FAX: (202) 624-6010
Industry Affiliation: Utility: Gas

**Publication(s):**
*Inside Story*
Day Published: s-m.
Contact: Jim Ohido
         Telephone: (202) 624-6468
Spec. Requirements: 4-8 pg; offset
  newspaper; 11 x 15
Personnel: Jim Ohido, Editor

**WASHINGTON POST**  2566
1150 15th St., N.W.
Washington, DC 20071
Industry Affiliation: Newspapers
**Publication(s):**
*Shop Talk*
Day Published: s-m.
Lead Time: 2 wks. prior to pub. date
Mtls Deadline: 2 wks. prior to pub. date
Spec. Requirements: 4-8 pg; offset; 8 1/2
  x 11
Personnel: Christine Swerda, Editor

**WASHINGTON WATER POWER**  5340
**CO., THE**
E. 1411 Mission
Spokane, WA 99202
Telephone: (509) 482-4561
FAX: (509) 482-8725
Mailing Address:
  P.O. Box 3727
  Spokane, WA 99220-3727
Industry Affiliation: Utility: Related
**Publication(s):**
*Weekly*
Day Published: w.
Lead Time: 2 mos. prior to pub. date
Mtls Deadline: 2 wks. prior to pub. date
Spec. Requirements: 4 pg.; 8 1/2 x 11
Personnel: Jennifer Born, Editor
         Janet Hess, Art Director

**WATER EDUCATION FOUNDATION**  2290
717 K St., No. 517
Sacramento, CA 95814-3406
Telephone: (916) 448-7699
Industry Affiliation: Utility: Water
**Publication(s):**
*Western Water*
Day Published: bi-m.
Materials: 06
Spec. Requirements: 12-page; offset; 8
  1/2 x 11
Personnel: Rita Schmidt Sudman, Editor
         Sandra Bailey, Editorial
         Assistant

**WATKINS PRODUCTS INC.**  3628
150 Liberty St.
Winona, MN 55987
Telephone: (507) 457-3300
Industry Affiliation: Advertising, Art, Public
  Relations
**Publication(s):**
*Watkins World*
Day Published: m.
Lead Time: 2-3 mos.
Personnel: Bill Petrowiak, Editor

**WDCN CHANNEL 8**  4900
161 Rains Ave.
Nashville, TN 37203
Telephone: (615) 259-9325
FAX: (615) 248-6120
Mailing Address:
  P.O. Box 120609
  Nashville, TN 37212
Industry Affiliation: Radio, TV, Movies

**Publication(s):**
*Preview*
Day Published: m.
Lead Time: 2 mos. prior to pub. date
Materials: 21,22
Mtls Deadline: 8 wks. prior to pub. date
Spec. Requirements: 20 page; offset; 8
  1/2 x 11
Personnel: Sally Wood, Editor

**WELCH'S**  4901
100 Main St.
Concord, MA 01742
Telephone: (508) 371-1000
Industry Affiliation: Food, General
**Publication(s):**
*Welch's News*
Day Published: bi-m.
Spec. Requirements: 4-6 pgs.; offset; 10 x
  13
Personnel: James Weidman, III, Editor

**WEOKIE CREDIT UNION**  4566
8100 W. Reno Ave.
Oklahoma City, OK 73127
Telephone: (405) 235-3030
Mailing Address:
  P.O. Box 26090
  Oklahoma City, OK 73126
Industry Affiliation: Banks, Savings &
  Loans
**Publication(s):**
*Transmitter*
Day Published: m.
Lead Time: 2 wks.
Mtls Deadline: 2 wks.
Spec. Requirements: 4-pgs.; offset; 8 1/2 x
  11
Personnel: David Hutchings, Editor

**WEST BEND CO.**  5456
400 Washington St.
West Bend, WI 53095
Telephone: (414) 334-2311
Mailing Address:
  P.O. Box 278
  West Bend, WI 53095
Industry Affiliation: Home Appliances,
  Furnishings
**Publication(s):**
*Craftsman, The*
Day Published: bi-m.
Lead Time: 1 mo.
Mtls Deadline: 1 mo.
Spec. Requirements: 24 pgs.; offset; 8 1/2
  x 11
Personnel: Michelle Griswold, Editor

**WESTERN/SOUTHERN LIFE**  4463
**INSURANCE CO.**
400 Broadway
Cincinnati, OH 45202
Telephone: (513) 629-1800
Industry Affiliation: Insurance
**Publication(s):**
*Home Office News*
Day Published: m.
Spec. Requirements: 24-32 pgs.
Personnel: Sherrie O'Rear, Editor

**WESTERN RESOURCES, INC.**  3165
818 Kansas Ave.
Topeka, KS 66612
Telephone: (913) 575-6300
Mailing Address:
  P.O. Box 889
  Topeka, KS 66601
Industry Affiliation: Utility: Electric

---

**Materials Accepted/Included:** 01-Business news 02-By-line articles 03-Fashion news 04-Food news 05-Freelance copy 06-Letters to editor 07-Real estate news 08-Sports news 09-Travel news 10-Book rev. 11-Movie rev. 12-Music rev. 13-TV rev. 14-Theater rev. 15-Coming events 16-Obituaries 17-Question & answer 18-Social announcements 19-Artwork 20-Cartoons 21-Photos 22-TV listings 23-Audio rec. 24-Video rec. 25-Books 26-Films/film clips 27-Personnel news 28-Press releases 29-New product news/photos 30-Trade lit. 31-Contracts awarded 32-Display adv. 33-Classified adv.

**Publication(s):**
*Resource, The*
Day Published: m.
Lead Time: 6 wks.
Mtls Deadline: 1st of mo. prior to pub. date
Spec. Requirements: tabloid
Personnel: Marisa Daniels, Editor

**WESTERN STATE EQUIPMENT CO.** [2721]
P.O. Box 38
Boise, ID 83707
Telephone: (208) 888-2287
Industry Affiliation: Industry: Heavy
  Construction, Machinery
**Publication(s):**
*Westerner*
Day Published: q.
Lead Time: 3 wks. prior to pub. date
Spec. Requirements: 16 page; offset;
  tabloid
Personnel: Kevin Graveline, Editor

**WESTINGHOUSE ELECTRIC CORP.** [4782]
Westinghouse Bldg., Gateway Ctr.
Pittsburgh, PA 15222
Telephone: (412) 244-2000
FAX: (412) 642-2466
Industry Affiliation: Electrical, Electronic,
  Manufacturing
**Publication(s):**
*Westinghouse News*
Day Published: m.
Lead Time: 2 mos. prior to pub. date
Spec. Requirements: 8 pg; offset; 11 x 17
Personnel: R. Fayfich, Director

**WESTINGHOUSE HANFORD** [5316]
**COMPANY**
P.O. Box 1970
Richland, WA 99352
Telephone: (509) 376-7411
FAX: (509) 376-5560
Industry Affiliation: Advertising, Art, Public
  Relations
**Publication(s):**
*Hanford Reach*
Day Published: w.
Lead Time: 2 wks.
Materials: 01,02,05,06,09,15,17,18,20,21,
  27,31
Contact: Employee Communications
Spec. Requirements: 16 pg.; letterpress
  tabloid; 11 1/2 x 16
Personnel: T. Cozzens, Editor
         C. Stafford, Editor
         D. Cresswell, Editor

**WESTIN HOTEL** [5336]
2001 Sixth Ave.
Seattle, WA 98121
Telephone: (206) 443-5000
Mailing Address:
  P.O. Box 2028
  Seattle, WA 98111
Industry Affiliation: Hotels, Motels
**Publication(s):**
*Straight-Talk*
Day Published: m.
Mtls Deadline: 1st of mo. prior to pub. date
Contact: Corp. Comms.
  2000 Fifth Ave. Bldg.
  Seattle, WA 98121
Spec. Requirements: 8 pgs.; offset; 8 1/2
  x 11
Personnel: Lesley Liason, Editor

**WEST PENN POWER CO.** [4779]
800 Cabin Hill Dr.
Greensburg, PA 15601
Telephone: (412) 838-6000
FAX: (412) 830-5009
Industry Affiliation: Utility: Electric

**Publication(s):**
*West Penn News*
Day Published: m.
Lead Time: 1 mo.
Mtls Deadline: 1 mo.
Spec. Requirements: 24 pg; offset; 8 1/2 x
  11
Personnel: Sandra L. Kiebler, Editor

*Watt's New*
Day Published: s-a.
Spec. Requirements: 6 pg.
Personnel: Sandra L. Kiebler, Editor

**WEST TEXAS UTILITIES CO.** [5120]
P.O. Box 841
Abilene, TX 79604
Telephone: (915) 674-7617
FAX: (915) 674-7280
Industry Affiliation: Utility: Related
**Publication(s):**
*Electric Times*
Day Published: bi-m.
Spec. Requirements: 20 page; offset
  magazine; 84 x 11
Personnel: Stephen Williams, Editor

**WESTVACO CORP.** [3305]
299 Park Ave.
Covington, VA 24426
Telephone: (804) 233-9205
Industry Affiliation: Containers, Packages
**Publication(s):**
*News Letter*
Day Published: q.
Spec. Requirements: 8-14 page; offset
  magazine; 84 x 11
Personnel: Andy Dreszer, Editor

**W. H. BRADY CO.** [66435]
727 W. Glendale Ave.
Milwaukee, WI 53209
Telephone: (414) 332-8100
FAX: (414) 961-6059
Industry Affiliation: Industry: Light Tools,
  Equipment
**Publication(s):**
*Blue Streak Release*
Day Published: q.
Lead Time: 30 days
Mtls Deadline: 15th of mo.
Personnel: Laurie Bernardy, Editor

**WHIRLPOOL CORPORATION** [66422]
2000 M-63 N.
Benton Harbor, MI 49022
Telephone: (616) 923-5000
Industry Affiliation: Home Appliances,
  Furnishings
**Publication(s):**
*Whirlpool World*
Day Published: w.
Personnel: Greg Brooks, Editor

**WHIRLPOOL CORPORATION** [68406]
5401 Hwy. 41 N.
Evansville, IN 47711
Telephone: (812) 426-4474
FAX: (812) 426-4957
Industry Affiliation: Home Appliances,
  Furnishings
**Publication(s):**
*Advantage, The*
Day Published: d.
Lead Time: 1 wk.
Mtls Deadline: day prior to pub. date
Personnel: Janice Jillson, Editor

*Image, The*
Day Published: s-a.
Lead Time: 1 mo.
Mtls Deadline: varies
Personnel: Janice Jillson, Editor

**WHITING CORPORATION** [2935]
15700 Lathrop Ave.
Harvey, IL 60426
Telephone: (708) 331-4000
Industry Affiliation: Industry: Heavy
  Construction, Machinery
**Publication(s):**
*Whiting News*
Day Published: q.
Spec. Requirements: 8 pg.; offset
  magazine; 84 x 11
Personnel: Peter S. Hammond, Editor

**WHITTIER HOSPITAL MEDICAL** [2291]
**CENTER**
15151 Janine Dr.
Whittier, CA 90605
Telephone: (310) 945-3561
Industry Affiliation: Hospitals
**Publication(s):**
*Family Ties*
Day Published: bi-m.
Lead Time: 1 wk. prior to pub. date
Mtls Deadline: 1 wk. prior to pub. date
Spec. Requirements: 4-8 pg; offset; 8 1/2
  x 11
Personnel: Linda Schott, Editor

**WILKES-BARRE GENERAL** [4784]
**HOSPITAL**
N. River & Auburn Sts.
Wilkes Barre, PA 18764
Telephone: (717) 829-8111
Industry Affiliation: Hospitals
**Publication(s):**
*Horizons*
Day Published: s-a.
Lead Time: 2 mos.
Mtls Deadline: 1st of mo.
Spec. Requirements: 8 pgs.; 11 x 17
Personnel: James J. Schilling, Editor

**WILLIAM BEAUMONT HOSPITAL** [3424]
3601 W. 13 Mile Rd.
Royal Oak, MI 48073
Telephone: (313) 551-0740
Industry Affiliation: Hospitals
**Publication(s):**
*Beaumonitor*
Day Published: q.
Lead Time: 2 mos.
Spec. Requirements: 8-12 page; offset; 11
  x 17
Personnel: Lillian Lorenzi

**WILLIAMS CO., THE** [4568]
One Williams Ctr.
Tulsa, OK 74172
Telephone: (918) 588-2111
Industry Affiliation: Agriculture, Services
**Publication(s):**
*Line Marker*
Day Published: q.
Contact: Williams Pipe Line Co.
Spec. Requirements: 16-20 pgs.; offset
  magazine; 84 x 11
Personnel: Ceceilia Jacobs, Editor

*W N G Mainline*
Day Published: m.
Spec. Requirements: 4-6 pgs.
Personnel: Susie Hereden, Editor

*W F S Journal*
Day Published: m.
Spec. Requirements: 4-6 pgs.
Personnel: Doug Hicks, Editor

*W P L Pipeline*
Day Published: q.
Spec. Requirements: 2-4 pgs.
Personnel: Ceceilia Jacobs, Editor

*In Perspective*
Day Published: q.
Spec. Requirements: 30-40 pgs.

**WILMINGTON SAVINGS FUND** [2499]
**SOCIETY**
838 Market St.
Wilmington, DE 19899
Telephone: (302) 792-6000
FAX: (302) 571-7215
Mailing Address:
  P.O. Box 1889
  Wilmington, DE 19899
Industry Affiliation: Finance, Services
**Publication(s):**
*Insider*
Day Published: m.
Lead Time: 3 wks.
Mtls Deadline: 3 wks. prior to pub. date
Contact: Marketing/Communications
Spec. Requirements: 4 pg.
Personnel: Ginny Liss, Editor

**WIRE ROPE CORORATION OF** [3746]
**AMERICA, INC.**
609 N. Second St.
St. Joseph, MO 64501
Telephone: (816) 233-0287
FAX: (816) 233-2072
Mailing Address:
  P.O. Box 288
  St. Joseph, MO 64502
Industry Affiliation: Industry: Light Tools,
  Equipment
**Publication(s):**
*Rope Talk Magazine*
Day Published: a.
Spec. Requirements: 24 page; offset; 9 x
  11
Personnel: Mary Beth Valencia, Editor

*Reel People News*
Day Published: w.
Lead Time: 2 wks. prior to pub. date
Mtls Deadline: 2 wks. prior to pub. date
Personnel: Mary Beth Valencia, Editor

**WISCO INDUSTRIES INC.** [5472]
736 Janesville St.
Oregon, WI 53575
Telephone: (608) 835-3106
Industry Affiliation: Industry: Material
  Handling
**Publication(s):**
*Plaintalk*
Day Published: a.
Spec. Requirements: 4 pg.; offset; 8 1/2 x
  11
Personnel: Urban Johnson, Editor

**WISCONSIN ASSOCIATION OF** [5458]
**HOMES FOR THE AGING**
204 S. Hamilton St.
Madison, WI 53703
Telephone: (608) 255-2208
FAX: (608) 255-7064
Industry Affiliation: Associations: City,
  State, Federal

**Materials Accepted/Included:** 01-Business news 02-By-line articles 03-Fashion news 04-Food news 05-Freelance copy 06-Letters to editor 07-Real estate news 08-Sports news 09-Travel news 10-Book rev. 11-Movie rev. 12-Music rev. 13-TV rev. 14-Theater rev. 15-Coming events 16-Obituaries 17-Question & answer 18-Social announcements 19-Artwork 20-Cartoons 21-Photos 22-TV listings 23-Audio rec. 24-Video rec. 25-Books 26-Films/film clips 27-Personnel news 28-Press releases 29-New product news/photos 30-Trade lit. 31-Contracts awarded 32-Display adv. 33-Classified adv.

11-95

**Publication(s):**
*Communicator*
Day Published: bi-m.
Lead Time: 1 wk. prior to pub. date
Mtls Deadline: 1 wk. prior to pub. date
Contact: Member Services
Spec. Requirements: 20 pgs.; offset; 8 1/2 x 11
Personnel: John Sauer, Editor
     Janice Mashak, Member
     Services Director

**WISCONSIN BELL, INC.**    68377
722 N. Broadway, 13th Fl.
Milwaukee, WI 53202
Telephone: (414) 678-2691
FAX: (414) 678-2756
Industry Affiliation: Associations: City,
    State, Federal
**Publication(s):**
*Trend*
Day Published: m.
Mtls Deadline: 2 wks. prior to pub. date
Personnel: Lorna Sorenson, Editor

**WISCONSIN DAIRIES**    5459
   **COOPERATIVE**
P.O. Box 111
Baraboo, WI 53913
Telephone: (608) 356-8316
Industry Affiliation: Dairy Products
**Publication(s):**
*Dairy Express*
Day Published: m.
Spec. Requirements: 8 page; offset; 8 1/2 x 11
Personnel: Pamela Karg, Editor

**WISCONSIN DEPARTMENT OF**    5460
   **NATURAL RESOURCES**
101 S. Webster St.
Madison, WI 53707
Telephone: (608) 266-1510
FAX: (608) 264-6293
Mailing Address:
   P.O. Box 7921
   Madison, WI 53707-7921
Industry Affiliation: Associations: City,
    State, Federal
**Publication(s):**
*D N R Digest*
Day Published: m.
Lead Time: 1 mo.
Mtls Deadline: last wk. of mo.
Spec. Requirements: 16 pg; offset; 8 1/2 x 11
Personnel: Paul Holten, Editor in Chief
     Lisa Gaumnitz, Managing Editor

*Wisconsin Natural Resources Magazine*
Day Published: bi-m.; Feb., Apr., June,
   Aug., Oct., Dec.
Lead Time: 4 mos.
Materials: 05,21
Mtls Deadline: 4 mo. prior to pub. date
Spec. Requirements: 32 pg; offset; 8 1/2 x 11
Personnel: David L. Sperling, Editor in
     Chief
     Maureen Micozzi, Associate
     Editor
     Kathryn Kahler, Production
     Manager

**WISCONSIN ELECTRIC**    5474
   **COOPERATIVE ASSOCIATION**
P.O. Box 686
Madison, WI 53701
Telephone: (608) 273-0420
Industry Affiliation: Utility: Electric

**Publication(s):**
*Wisconsin Rec News*
Day Published: m.
Lead Time: 3 1/2 wks.
Mtls Deadline: 1st of mo. prior to pub. date
Spec. Requirements: 12 page; offset;
   tabloid
Personnel: Perry Baird, Editor

**WISCONSIN ELECTRIC POWER**    5478
   **CO.**
231 W. Michigan St.
Milwaukee, WI 53203
Industry Affiliation: Utility: Electric
**Publication(s):**
*Currently*
Day Published: w.
Materials: 01,27
Mtls Deadline: 10 days prior to pub. date
Contact: Anne Spaltholz
Spec. Requirements: 11 x 17 folded
Personnel: Anne Spaltholz, Managing
     Editor

*Synergy*
Day Published: m.
Materials: 01
Mtls Deadline: 6 wks. prior to pub. date
Contact: Robert Zahn
Personnel: Robert Zahn, Managing Editor

*Telenews*
Day Published: Mon-Fri.
Materials: 01,29
Contact: Anne Spaltholz, Mng. Ed.

**WISCONSIN FARM BUREAU**    5476
   **FEDERATION**
7010 Mineral Point Rd.
Madison, WI 53717
Telephone: (608) 833-8070
Mailing Address:
   P.O. Box 5550
   Madison, WI 53705
Industry Affiliation: Associations: Trade,
    Fraternal
**Publication(s):**
*Agventure*
Day Published: bi-m.
Lead Time: 30 days
Mtls Deadline: 2nd Mon. of mo. prior to
   pub. date
Spec. Requirements: magazine - 8 3/8 x
   10 7/8 in.
Personnel: Tom Thieding, Editor

**WISCONSIN NATURAL GAS CO.**    5479
233 Lake Ave.
Racine, WI 53407
Telephone: (414) 635-2177
FAX: (414) 632-0829
Industry Affiliation: Utility: Gas
**Publication(s):**
*Sendout*
Day Published: m.: 15th
Lead Time: 1st wk. of mo.
Mtls Deadline: 1st wk. of mo.
Spec. Requirements: 6 pg; offset; 8 1/2 x 11
Personnel: Dan Johnson, Editor

*Resource*
Day Published: bi-m.
Lead Time: 1 mo. prior
Mtls Deadline: 1 mo. prior
Spec. Requirements: 4 pg; offset; 8 1/2 x 11
Personnel: Jayne Herring, Editor

**WISCONSIN POWER & LIGHT CO.**    5480
222 W. Washington Ave.
Madison, WI 53703
Telephone: (608) 252-3182

Mailing Address:
   P.O. Box 192
   Madison, WI 53701
Industry Affiliation: Utility: Electric
**Publication(s):**
*Connections*
Day Published: m.
Lead Time: 2-3 mos.
Contact: Corp. Comm.
Spec. Requirements: 20-28 pgs.; offset
   magazine; 8 1/2 x 11
Personnel: Katie Dyke, Editor

**WLIW CHANNEL 21**    4175
P.O. Box 21
Plainview, NY 11803-0021
Telephone: (516) 367-2100
FAX: (516) 454-8924
Industry Affiliation: Radio, TV, Movies
**Publication(s):**
*Members Listing In Spotlight Magazine*
Day Published: m.
Lead Time: 8 wks.
Mtls Deadline: 1st of ea. mo.
Spec. Requirements: 12 pg; 8 1/2 x 11 4
   color
Personnel: Susan Avery Klein, Editor
     Holly Picard, Art Director

**WOLVERINE WORLD WIDE**    3511
9341 Courtland
Rockford, MI 49341
Telephone: (616) 866-5500
Industry Affiliation: Associations: City,
    State, Federal
**Publication(s):**
*Wolverine News*
Day Published: m.
Lead Time: 1 mo.
Spec. Requirements: 6 pg; offset
   magazine; 9 x 12
Personnel: James McCarty, Editor

**WOMEN'S INTERNATIONAL**    5462
   **BOWLING CONGRESS**
5301 S.76th St.
Greendale, WI 53129
Telephone: (414) 421-9000
FAX: (414) 421-3013
Industry Affiliation: Associations: Trade,
    Fraternal
**Publication(s):**
*Woman Bowler*
Day Published: 8/yr.
Lead Time: 6 wks.
Mtls Deadline: 6 wks. prior to pub. date.
Spec. Requirements: 48-64 pgs.; offset
   magazine; 82 x 107

*Record Guide*
Day Published: a.
Lead Time: 60 days
Mtls Deadline: 1st of year
Spec. Requirements: 48-80 pgs.; offset
   tournament program
Personnel: Karen Sytsma
     Renee Schlitz
     Marc Whitney

*Media Guide*
Day Published: a.
Lead Time: 8 wks.
Personnel: Marc Whitney

**WOMEN IN COMMUNICATIONS**    5123
   **INC.**
3717 Columbia Pike, Suite 310
Arlington, VA 22204-4255
Telephone: (703) 920-5555
FAX: (703) 920-5556
Industry Affiliation: Associations: Trade,
    Fraternal
**Publication(s):**
*Professional Communicatior, The*
Day Published: 5 times/yr.
Lead Time: 3 mos.
Materials: 01,02,05,06,10,21,25,27,28,29,
   30,32,33
Mtls Deadline: 6 wks.
Personnel: Leslie Sansom, Editor
     Larissa Kulczycky, Assistant
     Editor
     Lori Marie Sylvia, Editorial
     Assistant

*W I C I Membership & Resource Directory*
Day Published: a.
Personnel: Leslie Sansom, Editor

**WOODMAN OF THE WORLD LIFE**    3813
   **INSURANCE SOCIETY**
1700 Farnam St.
Omaha, NE 68102
Telephone: (402) 342-1890
FAX: (402) 271-7269
Industry Affiliation: Lumber, Forestry,
    Building Materials
**Publication(s):**
*Shavings*
Day Published: 11/yr.
Lead Time: 2 mos. prior to pub. date
Mtls Deadline: 2 mos. prior to pub. date
Contact: Communications Depatment
Spec. Requirements: 16 page
Personnel: Ernie May, Associate Editor

**WOODMEN ACCIDENT & LIFE CO.**    3808
1526 K Street
Lincoln, NE 68508
Telephone: (402) 476-6500
Mailing Address:
   P.O. Box 82288
   Lincoln, NE 68501
Industry Affiliation: Insurance
**Publication(s):**
*Excel*
Day Published: q.
Lead Time: 3 wks.
Mtls Deadline: 5th of mo. prior to pub. date
Contact: Marketing
Spec. Requirements: 24 page; offset
   magazine; 8 1/2 x 11
Personnel: Kathy Baugh, Editor

**WOODWARD & LATHROP, INC.**    2567
11th & G Sts., N.W.
Washington, DC 20013
Telephone: (202) 347-5300
Industry Affiliation: Associations: City,
    State, Federal
**Publication(s):**
*Woodlothian*
Day Published: m.
Spec. Requirements: 12 page; offset; 8
   1/2 x 10
Personnel: John F. Burgess, Editor

**WORLD'S FINEST CHOCOLATE,**    2939
   **INC.**
4801 S. Lawndale St.
Chicago, IL 60632
Telephone: (312) 847-4600
Industry Affiliation: Candy

**Materials Accepted/Included:** 01-Business news 02-By-line articles 03-Fashion news 04-Food news 05-Freelance copy 06-Letters to editor 07-Real estate news 08-Sports news 09-Travel news 10-Book rev. 11-Movie rev. 12-Music rev. 13-TV rev. 14-Theater rev. 15-Coming events 16-Obituaries 17-Question & answer 18-Social announcements 19-Artwork 20-Cartoons 21-Photos 22-TV listings 23-Audio rec. 24-Video rec. 25-Books 26-Films/film clips 27-Personnel news 28-Press releases 29-New product news/photos 30-Trade lit. 31-Contracts awarded 32-Display adv. 33-Classified adv.

11-96

**Publication(s):**
*Chocolate Shake*
Day Published: bi-w.
Lead Time: 1 wk. prior to pub. date
Materials: 01,02,04,06,08,09,11,15,17,19,
   20,21
Mtls Deadline: 2 wks. prior to pub. date
Contact: Graphic Services
Spec. Requirements: 4 pgs.; offset tabloid;
   11 x 8 1/2
Personnel: Nancy Tiffin, Editor

2569

**WORLD BANK**
1818 H. St., N.W.
Washington, DC 20006
Telephone: (202) 477-1234
Industry Affiliation: Banks, Savings &
   Loans
**Publication(s):**
*World Bank News*
Day Published: w.
Spec. Requirements: 12-page; offset;
   standard
Personnel: Chris Bright, Editor

2938

**WORLD BOOK, INC.**
1440 Kiewit Plz.
Omaha, NE 68131
Telephone: (312) 245-3456
Industry Affiliation: Publishers, Books,
   Magazines
**Publication(s):**
*World Booker, The*
Day Published: m.
Lead Time: 6 wks.
Personnel: John I. Prikupa
   William J. Burghardt

4035

**W.R. GRACE & CO.**
One Town Center Rd.
Boca Raton, FL 33486-1010
Telephone: (407) 362-2000
FAX: (407) 362-1342
Industry Affiliation: Chemicals, Plastics
**Publication(s):**
*Grace Insider Update*
Day Published: m.
Contact: Corporate Communications Div.
Personnel: Jane McGuiness, Editor

4176

**XEROX**
800 Long Ridge Rd.
Stanford, CT 06904
Telephone: (203) 329-8700
Industry Affiliation: Office Equipment,
   Services, Supplies

**Publication(s):**
*Xerox World*
Day Published: m.
Spec. Requirements: 8 pg.; offset; 8-1/2 x
   11
Personnel: Joseph Varilla, Editor

5463

**YOUNG RADIATOR CO.**
2825 Four Mile Rd.
Racine, WI 53404
Telephone: (414) 639-1010
FAX: (414) 639-1013
Industry Affiliation: Cooling, Heating
**Publication(s):**
*Young News & Views*
Day Published: q.
Lead Time: 1 mo.
Mtls Deadline: 1 mo. prior to issue date
Spec. Requirements: 4 pg; offset; 8 1/2 x
   11
Personnel: R.L. Slater, Editor

3128

**YOUNKERS, INC.**
Seventh & Walnut Sts.
Des Moines, IA 50397
Telephone: (515) 247-7194
Mailing Address:
   P.O. Box 1495
   Des Moines, IA 50397
Industry Affiliation: Retail Stores
**Publication(s):**
*Younkers Reporter*
Day Published: bi-m.
Lead Time: 1 mo.
Mtls Deadline: 1 mo. prior to pub. date
Spec. Requirements: 20-24 pg.; offset; 12
   x 18
Personnel: Amy Jo Reimer, Editor

5124

**ZALE CORP.**
901 W. Walnut Hill Ln.
Irving, TX 75038
Telephone: (214) 580-4000
Industry Affiliation: Associations: Trade,
   Fraternal
**Publication(s):**
*Around Zales*
Day Published: m.
Materials: 01,03,15,17,27
Mtls Deadline: varies
Contact: Corporate Communications
Spec. Requirements: 4-6 pg.
Personnel: Laura Moore, Editor
   Laura Jobe, Editor

*Cutting Edge*
Day Published: m.
Materials: 01,03,15,17,27,29,30
Mtls Deadline: varies
Contact: Corporate Communications
Personnel: Laura Moore, Editor
   Laura Jobe, Editor

*In The Large*
Day Published: q.
Materials: 01,03,15,17,21,27,29,30
Mtls Deadline: varies
Contact: Corporate Communications
Personnel: Laura Moore, Editor
   Laura Jobe, Editor

*Shrinkstoppers*
Day Published: m.
Materials: 21,27,29
Mtls Deadline: varies
Contact: Corporate Communications
Personnel: Laura Moore, Editor
   Laura Jobe, Editor

5464

**ZIMPRO ENVIRONMENTAL, INC.**
301 W. Military Rd.
Rothschild, WI 54474
Telephone: (715) 359-7211
Industry Affiliation: Associations: Trade,
   Fraternal
**Publication(s):**
*Reactor*
Day Published: 3/yr.
Lead Time: 4 mos. prior to pub. date
Materials: 01,02,05,19,20,21
Mtls Deadline: 4 mos. prior to pub. date
Spec. Requirements: 16 pg.; offset; 84 x
   11
Personnel: James M. Force, Editor

4788

**ZIPPO MANUFACTURING CO.**
33 Barbour St.
Bradford, PA 16701
Telephone: (814) 368-2700
FAX: (814) 362-2388
Industry Affiliation: Associations: Trade,
   Fraternal

**Publication(s):**
*Zip-A-Gram*
Day Published: bi-m.
Spec. Requirements: 4 pg.; offset
   magazine; 8 1/2 x 11
Personnel: Kelly Yohe, Editor

2962

**ZURICH-AMERICAN INSURANCE
GROUP**
1400 American Ln.
Schaumburg, IL 60196
Telephone: (708) 605-6000
FAX: (708) 605-3436
Industry Affiliation: Insurance
**Publication(s):**
*Pulse*
Day Published: m.
Lead Time: 1 mo. prior to pub. date
Mtls Deadline: 1 mo. prior to pub. date
Spec. Requirements: 4-8 pg.; offset; 11 x
   14
Personnel: Kathleen Savio, Editor

5418

**21ST CENTURY GENETICS
COOPERATIVE**
100 MBC Dr.
Shawano, WI 54166
Telephone: (715) 526-2141
Mailing Address:
   P.O. Box 469
   Shawano, WI 54166
Industry Affiliation: Agriculture, Services
**Publication(s):**
*Visions*
Day Published: m.
Lead Time: 2 wks.
Spec. Requirements: 8 page; offset; 11 x
   17
Personnel: Jim Leuenberger, Editor

**Materials Accepted/Included:** 01-Business news 02-By-line articles 03-Fashion news 04-Food news 05-Freelance copy 06-Letters to editor 07-Real estate news 08-Sports news 09-Travel news 10-Book rev. 11-Movie rev. 12-Music rev. 13-TV rev. 14-Theater rev. 15-Coming events 16-Obituaries 17-Question & answer 18-Social announcements 19-Artwork 20-Cartoons 21-Photos 22-TV listings 23-Audio rec. 24-Video rec. 25-Books 26-Films/film clips 27-Personnel news 28-Press releases 29-New product news/photos 30-Trade lit. 31-Contracts awarded 32-Display adv. 33-Classified adv.

11-97